IMPORTANT NOTICES

Martindale-Hubbell has used its best efforts in collecting and preparing material for inclusion in the Martindale-Hubbell® International Law Directory but cannot warrant that the information herein is complete or accurate, and does not assume, and hereby disclaims, any liability to any person for any loss or damage caused by errors or omissions in the Martindale-Hubbell® International Law Directory whether such errors or omissions result from negligence, accident or any other cause.

Lawyers providing information regarding themselves and their law firms for inclusion in the Martindale-Hubbell® International Law Directory are responsible for both the accuracy of the information submitted and compliance with local law and bar regulations.

The information contained in this Directory, including Martindale-Hubbell legal ratings, is intended primarily for the use of lawyers and law firms in the practice of their profession. It may not be used without acknowledgement in any advertisement or for any commercial, political or other purpose.

EXPLANATORY NOTES AND SYMBOLS

For All Listings:

For countries where we have no representation please contact us and we will endeavor to provide you with as much assistance as possible.

"*Practice Areas*" appearing at the end of a lawyer's professional biography indicates the area(s) of practice to which he or she devotes a significant portion of professional time. In each case, the information has been supplied by the attorney and constitutes a "representation" by the lawyer and does not imply approval of certification by any authority.

Professional Companies, Corporations or Associations: Chartered, Associated, P.C., P.A., S.C., Inc., Ltd., etc. following the name of an individual lawyer or law firm means that such office is operating as a Professional Company, Corporation or Association under the laws of that jurisdiction.

"IBA" denotes a member of the International Bar Association.

MARTINDALE-HUBBELL® INTERNATIONAL LAW DIRECTORY

— I —

EUROPE, ASIA
AUSTRALASIA
MIDDLE EAST, AFRICA
PROFESSIONAL BIOGRAPHIES

MARTINDALE-HUBBELL

WORLD HEADQUARTERS
121 Chanlon Road
New Providence, NJ 07974
U.S.A.
(908) 464-6800

INTERNATIONAL OFFICE
Halsbury House
35 Chancery Lane
London WC2A 1EL
England
(171) 400-2883

Published by Martindale-Hubbell®, a Reed Reference Publishing Company

Ira Siegel, President, CEO
Andrew W. Meyer, Executive Vice President
Peter E. Simon, Senior Vice President, Database Publishing
Stanley Walker, Senior Vice President, Marketing
Edward J. Roycroft, Senior Vice President, Sales

International Standard Book Number: 1-56160-110-1 (Set)

Printed and Bound in the United States of America
by R.R. Donnelley & Sons Company
Chicago, Illinois and Willard, Ohio

ISBN 1 - 56160 - 110 - 1

9 781561 601103

TABLE OF CONTENTS

Explanatory Notes and Symbols . . . . Facing Page Inside Front Cover

Important Notices . . . . Facing Title Page

Foreword . . . . Page   V

Martindale-Hubbell Legal Advisory Board . . . . Page   VII

User's Guide . . . . Page   IX

Index of Countries . . . . Page   XI

Index of Cities . . . . Page   XIII

International Bar Association (IBA) Overview . . . . Page   XIX

Directory of Law Firm Alliances, Networks,
    Clubs, Associations and other Affiliations . . . . Page XXIX

PROFESSIONAL BIOGRAPHIES SECTION (Volumes I & II only)
    Professional Listings of Law Offices

        Volume I: Europe, Asia, Australasia, Middle East & Africa (Eastern Hemisphere)
        Volume II: North America, The Caribbean, Central & South America (Western Hemisphere)

SERVICES, SUPPLIERS, CONSULTANTS SECTION (Volumes I & II only)
    Including Indexes and List of Categories

INDEXES (Volume III only)

    ALPHABETICAL
        Volume I: Europe, Asia, Australasia, Middle East & Africa (Eastern Hemisphere)
        Volume II: North America, The Caribbean, Central & South America (Western Hemisphere)

    AREAS OF PRACTICE
        Volume I: Europe, Asia, Australasia, Middle East & Africa (Eastern Hemisphere)
        Volume II: North America, The Caribbean, Central & South America (Western Hemisphere)

    INTERNATIONAL PATENTS - ALPHABETICAL

    INTERNATIONAL PATENTS - GEOGRAPHICAL

    INTERNATIONAL FIRMS AND ATTORNEYS RESIDENT IN
    ANOTHER COUNTRY

            Including:
                Practice Profiles Section — Canada Only
                Explanatory Notes and Symbols
                User's Guide
                Martindale-Hubbell Ratings
                List of Colleges, Universities and Law Schools
                Bar Roster

FOREWORD

Since 1867, Martindale-Hubbell's objective has been to provide information "to lawyers about lawyers". We began publishing international law firm listings 90 years ago as a service to American attorneys. Today, the *Martindale-Hubbell® Law Directory, International Edition* covers more than 130 countries on six continents and is consulted extensively throughout the world.

Due to our ongoing information "partnership" with the International Bar Association (IBA), we have been able to make the *International Edition* more comprehensive than ever before; this edition now encompasses more than 100,000 lawyers and 8,000 law firms. Within these pages users will note the assemblage of an unprecedented breadth and depth of international legal practice information; information that is invaluable and unavailable elsewhere. Together with the IBA, we are achieving our goal of providing a global network of legal contact information now increasingly specialized by areas of practice.

The three volumes of the *International Law Directory*, which contain profiles of lawyers and law firms, have been extensively revised and updated to give you convenient access to the latest-available information. This edition includes new sections for Bulgaria, Romania, and many other countries of the former Soviet Union.

The directory's first two volumes list countries alphabetically within regions such as Europe for ease of access. The North America section now includes more than 2,000 U.S. law offices with international interests and practice areas. These listings are also published on CD-ROM and distributed online via LEXIS®/NEXIS®. The directory's third volume - the Index - lists all attorneys alphabetically by name and directs you to full entries in the first two volumes.

When combined with the *International Law Digest* volume, these lawyer listings constitute the four-volume *Martindale-Hubbell International Edition*, an unparalleled international legal reference.

With the increasing levels of international business and the resulting cross-border legal practice, attorneys around the world are finding it more important than ever to have access to reliable and up-to-date information about their counterparts in other countries. The *Martindale-Hubbell Law Directory, International Edition*, is the most comprehensive and widely used resource of lawyers and law firms. I hope you feel that this 1995 edition meets your needs and I welcome your comments and suggestions for the future.

Ira Siegel
President, CEO

MARTINDALE-HUBBELL® LEGAL ADVISORY BOARD

The Martindale-Hubbell Legal Advisory Board was formed to insure that the Martindale-Hubbell Law Directory is responsive to the constantly changing needs of the legal profession.

The following lawyers selected from the private, corporate and International sectors of the profession, as well as the legal academic community, comprise the 1994-1995 Board.

USER'S GUIDE

The **Martindale-Hubbell®** **International Law Directory** now consists of:

- three numbered volumes of the **Martindale-Hubbell International Law Directory** (blue spine accent), containing listings for lawyers and firms in over 130 countries (including sections for Canada and U.S. lawyers with international interests)

- one Martindale-Hubbell International Law Digest (black spine accent)

Barristers Chambers in England appear in a separate sequence prior to the listings for Solicitors in each city.

Guam, Puerto Rico, U.S. Pacific Territories and the U.S. Virgin Islands can be found in the appropriate sections of the **Martindale-Hubbell International Law Directory** (see Countries Index).

SECTION DESCRIPTIONS

PROFESSIONAL BIOGRAPHIES (WHITE PAGES)

The Professional Biographies Section is arranged by region, country and then alphabetically by city or town, and name of attorney or law firm. It provides substantial biographical information on individual attorneys within law firms. Entries in this section include the firm name, contact information, statement of practice, firm profile, individual biographical information, representative clients, and references. A typical entry appears as follows:

Firm Name ——————→ *LETTERMAN & WOLFFE*

Year Established ————→ *Established in 1973*

Contact Information ——→ *126 AVENUE MAIN*
1040 BRUSSELS, BELGIUM
Telephone: 011 32-2 591 2237
Fax: 011 32-2 591 2238

Statement of Practice ——→ *European Community Law, International Banking and Business Law, General International Trade Law, Corporate, Competition and Administrative Law, Civil Litigation, Mergers and Acquisitions.*

Firm Profile ——————→ *FIRM PROFILE: The firm was established in 1973 and offers a full range of legal services. It is well known for its Commercial and European Community Law Practice. The client base is European and North American in scope. This 3 partner firm has a legal support staff of 12 consisting of paralegal personnel, CPAs and office administrators.*

MEMBERS OF FIRM

Individual Biographical Information ——→ **MITCHELL J. LETTERMAN,** born Brussels, Belgium, June 2, 1939; admitted 1967, Belgium. *Education:* University of Brussels (Dr. Jur., 1966); University of Chicago Post Graduate in International Studies, 1967. Lecturer in Law, University of Louvain, 1968-1971. Author: "The Legal Situation in the International Community," Brussels Institute of Economic Law, 1973. *Member:* Brussels Bar Association; International Law Association; International Bar Association.

Languages ——————→ **LANGUAGES:** French, English and German. ***PRACTICE AREAS:*** European

Percentage of Time ——→ Community Law, International Trade Law (55%, 175).

Number of Cases ———→ *JOHN WOLFFE* (1940-1993).

LEGAL SUPPORT PERSONNEL
PARALEGAL

Legal Support Personnel ——→ **LAUREN V. BERRY,** born Antwerp, Belgium, July 23, 1962. *Education:* University of Louvain (Graduated with Distinction, 1984), International Center for Paralegal Training. Certified Legal Assistant, Brussels, Belgium, 1985. *Member:* International Paralegal Association. Legal Research, Drafting, Legal Pleadings, Client Correspondence, Deposition Summaries and File Investigations. ***PRACTICE***

Practice Areas ————→ ***AREAS:*** Corporate Law.

Clients ——————→ REPRESENTATIVE CLIENTS: First Bank & Trust; Cooper International Management Co.; P.E. Emery Worldwide Shipping & Container Corporation; Clay & Curiale Property Management Co.; Amwell Properties, Ltd.

SERVICES, SUPPLIERS, CONSULTANTS (YELLOW PAGES)

This Section is arranged by region, alphabetically by country, by city or town, then by category of service provided, then by company name. Full listing information is given, and over 350 available categories provide easy access to needed support services utilized by lawyers and law firms.

USER AIDS

In the front matter, sections are provided to aid in the use of the Directory. "Explanatory Notes and Symbols", found on the page facing the inside front cover, provide a guide to the various symbols and notations which are utilized in the individual entries.

Page numbers in the 1995 Martindale-Hubbell International Law Directory are constructed in the format XXYYYZ, where XX is the province or international grouping, YYY is a consecutive page numbering, and Z is a code denoting section.

XX will be the region abbreviations as shown below:

EU	(Europe)	NA	(North America)
AS	(Asia)	CB	(The Caribbean)
AU	(Australasia)	CS	(Central & South America)
AF	(Middle East & Africa)		

Z may be one of the following:

B	for "Professional Biographies"	S	for "Services, Suppliers,
P	for "Practice Profiles"		Consultants"

For additional help or explanation, please call Martindale-Hubbell Customer Service, at (01) 908-464-6800 or in the United States and Canada (800)MARTIND(ALE).

COUNTRIES

Alphabetical Listing of Countries

Albania..See *EUROPE*
Algeria...See *MIDDLE EAST & AFRICA*
Anguilla...See *THE CARIBBEAN*
Antigua...See *THE CARIBBEAN*
Argentina.............................See *CENTRAL & SOUTH AMERICA*
Aruba..See *THE CARIBBEAN*
Australia...See *AUSTRALASIA*
Austria..See *EUROPE*

Bahamas..See *THE CARIBBEAN*
Bahrain...See *MIDDLE EAST & AFRICA*
Balearic Islands...(See Spain)
Bangladesh...See *ASIA*
Barbados...See *THE CARIBBEAN*
Republic of Belarus...See *EUROPE*
Belgium..See *EUROPE*
Belize.....................................See *CENTRAL & SOUTH AMERICA*
Bermuda...See *THE CARIBBEAN*
Bolivia...................................See *CENTRAL & SOUTH AMERICA*
Brazil.....................................See *CENTRAL & SOUTH AMERICA*
British Guiana...(See Guyana)
British Honduras..(See Belize)
British Virgin Islands.......................See *THE CARIBBEAN*
Brunei Darussalam...See *ASIA*
Bulgaria..See *EUROPE*
Burkina-Faso.......................See *MIDDLE EAST & AFRICA*
Burma..(See Myanmar)

Cambodia...See *ASIA*
Cameroon....................................See *MIDDLE EAST & AFRICA*
Canada...See *NORTH AMERICA*
Canary Islands..(See Spain)
Cayman Islands (British West Indies)...........See *THE CARIBBEAN*
Channel Islands..See *EUROPE*
Chile.......................................See *CENTRAL & SOUTH AMERICA*
People's Republic of China..................................See *ASIA*
Colombia.................................See *CENTRAL & SOUTH AMERICA*
Costa Rica...............................See *CENTRAL & SOUTH AMERICA*
Côte d' Ivoire.........................See *MIDDLE EAST & AFRICA*
Croatia..See *EUROPE*
Curacao................................(See Netherlands Antilles)
Cyprus..See *EUROPE*
Czechoslovakia.................(See Czech Republic and Slovakia)
Czech Republic...See *EUROPE*

Denmark..See *EUROPE*
Dominican Republic.......................See *THE CARIBBEAN*

Ecuador.................................See *CENTRAL & SOUTH AMERICA*
Egypt...See *MIDDLE EAST & AFRICA*
Eire...(See Ireland)
El Salvador.............................See *CENTRAL & SOUTH AMERICA*
England..See *EUROPE*
Estonia..See *EUROPE*
Ethiopia.......................................See *MIDDLE EAST & AFRICA*

Finland..See *EUROPE*
Formosa..(See Taiwan)
France..See *EUROPE*

Germany..See *EUROPE*
Ghana...See *MIDDLE EAST & AFRICA*
Gibraltar..See *EUROPE*
Greece..See *EUROPE*
Guam..See *ASIA*
Guatemala.............................See *CENTRAL & SOUTH AMERICA*
Guyana.................................See *CENTRAL & SOUTH AMERICA*

Haiti...See *THE CARIBBEAN*
Holland..(See The Netherlands)
Honduras.............................See *CENTRAL & SOUTH AMERICA*
Hong Kong..See *ASIA*
Hungary..See *EUROPE*

Iceland..See *EUROPE*
India..See *ASIA*
Indonesia...See *ASIA*
Iran...See *MIDDLE EAST & AFRICA*
Iraq...See *MIDDLE EAST & AFRICA*
Ireland..See *EUROPE*
Isle of Man..See *EUROPE*

Israel...See *MIDDLE EAST & AFRICA*
Italy..See *EUROPE*
Republic of Ivory Coast.......................(See Cote d' Ivoire)

Jamaica...See *THE CARIBBEAN*
Japan..See *ASIA*
Jersey..(See Channel Islands)
Jordan...See *MIDDLE EAST & AFRICA*

Kazakhstan...See *ASIA*
Kenya...See *MIDDLE EAST & AFRICA*
Korea..See *ASIA*
Kuwait...See *MIDDLE EAST & AFRICA*

Laos...See *ASIA*
Republic of Latvia..See *EUROPE*
Lebanon.......................................See *MIDDLE EAST & AFRICA*
Liechtenstein..See *EUROPE*
Lithuania..See *EUROPE*
Luxembourg..See *EUROPE*

Madeira..See *EUROPE*
Malaysia..See *ASIA*
Malta..See *EUROPE*
Mauritius.......................................See *MIDDLE EAST & AFRICA*
Mexico.......................................See *NORTH AMERICA*
Monaco..See *EUROPE*
Mongolia..See *ASIA*
Morocco.......................................See *MIDDLE EAST & AFRICA*
Myanmar..See *ASIA*

Negara Brunei Darussalam.................(See Brunei Darussalam)
Nepal..See *ASIA*
The Netherlands..See *EUROPE*
Netherlands Antilles.......................See *THE CARIBBEAN*
Netherlands East Indies.................(See Indonesia)
Netherlands Guiana.................................(See Surinam)
New Guinea...........................(See Papua New Guinea)
New Zealand...See *AUSTRALASIA*
Nicaragua.................................See *CENTRAL & SOUTH AMERICA*
Nigeria.......................................See *MIDDLE EAST & AFRICA*
Niue...See *AUSTRALASIA*
Northern Ireland..See *EUROPE*
Norway..See *EUROPE*

Oman...See *MIDDLE EAST & AFRICA*

Pakistan..See *ASIA*
Republic of Panama.......................See *CENTRAL & SOUTH AMERICA*
Papua New Guinea...See *AUSTRALASIA*
Paraguay.................................See *CENTRAL & SOUTH AMERICA*
Peru.......................................See *CENTRAL & SOUTH AMERICA*
Republic of The Philippines..................................See *ASIA*
Poland..See *EUROPE*
Portugal..See *EUROPE*
Puerto Rico.......................................See *THE CARIBBEAN*

Qatar...See *MIDDLE EAST & AFRICA*

Romania..See *EUROPE*
Russia..See *EUROPE*

St. Christopher (St. Kitts).......................See *THE CARIBBEAN*
Salvador..(See El Salvador)
Saudi Arabia.......................See *MIDDLE EAST & AFRICA*
Scotland..See *EUROPE*
Siam..(See Thailand)
Sierra Leone.......................See *MIDDLE EAST & AFRICA*
Singapore..See *ASIA*
Slovakia..See *EUROPE*
Slovenia..See *EUROPE*
South Africa.......................See *MIDDLE EAST & AFRICA*
Spain..See *EUROPE*
Sri Lanka..See *ASIA*
Sudan...See *MIDDLE EAST & AFRICA*
Surinam...................................See *CENTRAL & SOUTH AMERICA*
Sweden..See *EUROPE*
Switzerland..See *EUROPE*
Syria...See *MIDDLE EAST & AFRICA*

Taiwan ....See *ASIA*
Tanzania ....See *MIDDLE EAST & AFRICA*
Thailand ....See *ASIA*
Trinidad and Tobago ....See *THE CARIBBEAN*
Tunisia ....See *MIDDLE EAST & AFRICA*
Turkey...See *EUROPE*
Turks & Caicos Islands...........................See *THE CARIBBEAN*

Uganda...See *MIDDLE EAST & AFRICA*
Ukraine ....See *EUROPE*
United Arab Emirates.....................See *MIDDLE EAST & AFRICA*
United Arab Republic ....(See Egypt)
Uruguay.............................See *CENTRAL & SOUTH AMERICA*
U.S.A. ....See *NORTH AMERICA*
U.S. Pacific Territories.......................................See *ASIA*
U.S.S.R. ....(See Russia)
U.S. Virgin Islands................................See *THE CARIBBEAN*

Venezuela ....See *CENTRAL & SOUTH AMERICA*
Vietnam..See *ASIA*
Virgin Islands......................................(See British Virgin Islands)
(See U.S. Virgin Islands)

Wales ....(See England)
West Indies
(See Anguilla, Antigua, Bahamas, Barbados, Bermuda, British Virgin Islands,
Dominican Republic, Cayman Islands, Haiti, Jamaica, Netherlands Antilles,
St. Christopher (St. Kitts), Trinidad and Tobago, Turks and Caicos Islands,
U.S. Virgin Islands)

Yemen...See *MIDDLE EAST & AFRICA*
Yugoslavia..See *EUROPE*

Zimbabwe ....See *MIDDLE EAST & AFRICA*

CITIES

Alphabetical Listing of Cities

Aachen...Germany-Europe
Aalborg...Denmark-Europe
Aarau..Switzerland-Europe
Aarhus..Denmark-Europe
Aberdeen...Scotland-Europe
Abidjan........................Côte d' Ivoire-Middle East & Africa
Abu Dhabi...........United Arab Emirates-Middle East & Africa
Accra...............................Ghana-Middle East & Africa
Achern..Germany-Europe
Addis Ababa...................Ethiopia-Middle East & Africa
Adelaide, South Australia.................Australia-Australasia
Aden............................Yemen-Middle East & Africa
Agana..Guam-Asia
Aguadilla.............................Puerto Rico-The Caribbean
Ahmedabad...India-Asia
Aix-En-Provence....................................France-Europe
Ajax........................Ontario, Canada-North America
Akron, Ohio.................................U.S.A.-North America
Albany, New York..........................U.S.A.-North America
Albuquerque, New Mexico..................U.S.A.-North America
Alderney.............................Channel Islands-Europe
Alexandria...................Egypt-Middle East & Africa
Alexandria, Louisiana......................U.S.A.-North America
Alexandria, Virginia.......................U.S.A.-North America
Algiers...........................Algeria-Middle East & Africa
Alicante...Spain-Europe
Al-Khobar.................Saudi Arabia-Middle East & Africa
Allentown, Pennsylvania....................U.S.A.-North America
Almaty...Kazakhstan-Asia
Alofi...Niue-Australasia
Amman.............................Jordan-Middle East & Africa
Amsterdam.............................The Netherlands-Europe
Anaheim, California........................U.S.A.-North America
Anchorage, Alaska..........................U.S.A.-North America
Ankara..Turkey-Europe
Annapolis, Maryland........................U.S.A.-North America
Ann Arbor, Michigan........................U.S.A.-North America
Antwerp..Belgium-Europe
Apeldoorn............................The Netherlands-Europe
Arequipa........................Peru-Central & South America
Arezzo..Italy-Europe
Arlington, Virginia........................U.S.A.-North America
Arnhem................................The Netherlands-Europe
Asunción..................Paraguay-Central & South America
Athens..Greece-Europe
Atlanta, Georgia...........................U.S.A.-North America
Atlantic City, New Jersey..................U.S.A.-North America
Auckland............................New Zealand-Australasia
Augsburg...Germany-Europe
Augusta, Georgia...........................U.S.A.-North America
Aurora, Illinois...........................U.S.A.-North America
Austin, Texas..............................U.S.A.-North America

Bacolod City, Negros Occ............Republic of The Philippines-Asia
Baden...Austria-Europe
Baden-Baden..Germany-Europe
Bad Homburg vor der Höhe...........................Germany-Europe
Baghdad.............................Iraq-Middle East & Africa
Balingen...Germany-Europe
Baltimore, Maryland........................U.S.A.-North America
Banbury..England-Europe
Bandar Seri Begawan..................Brunei Darussalam-Asia
Bangalore...India-Asia
Bangkok..Thailand-Asia
Barcelona..Spain-Europe
Bari..Italy-Europe
Barnstaple...England-Europe
Barrie........................Ontario, Canada-North America
Barrington, Illinois.......................U.S.A.-North America
Basel...Switzerland-Europe
Basseterre..............St. Christopher (St. Kitts)-The Caribbean
Baton Rouge, Louisiana.....................U.S.A.-North America
Battle Creek, Michigan.....................U.S.A.-North America
Beijing (Peking)................People's Republic of China-Asia
Beirut............................Lebanon-Middle East & Africa
Belfast..Northern Ireland-Europe
Belgrade..Yugoslavia-Europe
Belize City.....................Belize (C.A.)-Central & South America
Belleville....................Ontario, Canada-North America
Belleville, Illinois.......................U.S.A.-North America
Bellevue, Washington.......................U.S.A.-North America
Belo Horizonte.................Brazil-Central & South America
Bemidji, Minnesota.........................U.S.A.-North America
Bensalem, Pennsylvania.....................U.S.A.-North America
Bergen..Norway-Europe
Berlin...Germany-Europe

Bern..Switzerland-Europe
Bethesda, Maryland.........................U.S.A.-North America
Bethlehem, Pennsylvania....................U.S.A.-North America
Beverly Hills, California..................U.S.A.-North America
Bielefeld..Germany-Europe
Bilbao..Spain-Europe
Biloxi, Mississippi........................U.S.A.-North America
Bingham Farms, Michigan....................U.S.A.-North America
Birmingham...England-Europe
Birmingham, Alabama........................U.S.A.-North America
Birmingham, Michigan.......................U.S.A.-North America
Black Mountain, North Carolina.............U.S.A.-North America
Blenheim......................Ontario, Canada-North America
Bloomfield Hills, Michigan.................U.S.A.-North America
Blue Bell, Pennsylvania....................U.S.A.-North America
Boca Raton, Florida........................U.S.A.-North America
Bochum...Germany-Europe
Bogotá................Colombia-Central & South America
Bologna...Italy-Europe
Bombay...India-Asia
Bonao...................Dominican Republic-The Caribbean
Bonn...Germany-Europe
Borås..Sweden-Europe
Boston, Massachusetts......................U.S.A.-North America
Boulder, Colorado..........................U.S.A.-North America
Bradford...England-Europe
Brampton......................Ontario, Canada-North America
Brandenburg..Germany-Europe
Brandon.......................Manitoba, Canada-North America
Brasília........................Brazil-Central & South America
Bratislava..Slovakia-Europe
Braunschweig.......................................Germany-Europe
Breckenridge, Colorado.....................U.S.A.-North America
Breda.................................The Netherlands-Europe
Bremen...Germany-Europe
Bridgetown........................Barbados-The Caribbean
Brisbane, Queensland.......................Australia-Australasia
Bristol..England-Europe
Brno..Czech Republic-Europe
Brooklyn, New York.........................U.S.A.-North America
Brownsville, Texas.........................U.S.A.-North America
Brussels...Belgium-Europe
Bucharest..Romania-Europe
Budapest...Hungary-Europe
Buenos Aires.............Argentina-Central & South America
Buffalo, New York..........................U.S.A.-North America
Bundall (Gold Coast), Queensland...........Australia-Australasia
Burgas...Bulgaria-Europe
Burlington, Vermont........................U.S.A.-North America

Cadereyta Jiménez..........................Mexico-North America
Cadiz..Spain-Europe
Cairns, Queensland.........................Australia-Australasia
Cairo.............................Egypt-Middle East & Africa
Calcutta...India-Asia
Calgary.......................Alberta, Canada-North America
Cali.................Colombia-Central & South America
Cambridge..England-Europe
Cambridge.....................Ontario, Canada-North America
Cambridge, Massachusetts...................U.S.A.-North America
Campinas........................Brazil-Central & South America
Canberra, Australian Capital Territory.....Australia-Australasia
Cancun, Quintana Roo.......................Mexico-North America
Cannes..France-Europe
Cape Town.................South Africa-Middle East & Africa
Caracas..................Venezuela-Central & South America
Cardiff..England-Europe
Carmel, Indiana............................U.S.A.-North America
Casablanca........................Morocco-Middle East & Africa
Charleroi..Belgium-Europe
Charleston, South Carolina.................U.S.A.-North America
Charlotte, North Carolina..................U.S.A.-North America
Charlotte Amalie, St. Thomas......U.S. Virgin Islands-The Caribbean
Charlottesville, Virginia..................U.S.A.-North America
Charlottetown.........Prince Edward Island, Canada-North America
Chartres..France-Europe
Chatham.......................Ontario, Canada-North America
Cheltenham...England-Europe
Chemnitz...Germany-Europe
Cherry Hill, New Jersey....................U.S.A.-North America
Chevy Chase, Maryland......................U.S.A.-North America
Chicago, Illinois..........................U.S.A.-North America
Chihuahua, Chihuahua.......................Mexico-North America
Christchurch...........................New Zealand-Australasia
Christiansted, St. Croix..........U.S. Virgin Islands-The Caribbean

XIII

Cincinnati, Ohio	U.S.A.-North America
Ciudad Juarez, Chihuahua	Mexico-North America
Clarksburg, West Virginia	U.S.A.-North America
Clarksdale, Mississippi	U.S.A.-North America
Clearwater, Florida	U.S.A.-North America
Cleveland, Ohio	U.S.A.-North America
Closter, New Jersey	U.S.A.-North America
Cold Spring, New York	U.S.A.-North America
Collingswood, New Jersey	U.S.A.-North America
Cologne	Germany-Europe
Colombo	Sri Lanka-Asia
Colón	Republic of Panama-Central & South America
Colorado Springs, Colorado	U.S.A.-North America
Columbia, South Carolina	U.S.A.-North America
Columbus, Ohio	U.S.A.-North America
Commugny	Switzerland-Europe
Concord, New Hampshire	U.S.A.-North America
Copenhagen	Denmark-Europe
Cork	Ireland-Europe
Corona Del Mar, California	U.S.A.-North America
Coronado, California	U.S.A.-North America
Costa Mesa, California	U.S.A.-North America
Covington, Kentucky	U.S.A.-North America
Cranford, New Jersey	U.S.A.-North America
Cruz Bay, St. John	U.S. Virgin Islands-The Caribbean
Dallas, Texas	U.S.A.-North America
Damascus	Syria-Middle East & Africa
Danvers, Massachusetts	U.S.A.-North America
Dar Es Salaam	Tanzania-Middle East & Africa
Dartmouth	Nova Scotia, Canada-North America
Dayton, Ohio	U.S.A.-North America
Decatur, Illinois	U.S.A.-North America
Denver, Colorado	U.S.A.-North America
Derby	England-Europe
Des Moines, Iowa	U.S.A.-North America
Dessau	Germany-Europe
Detmold	Germany-Europe
Detroit, Michigan	U.S.A.-North America
Dhaka	Bangladesh-Asia
Doha	Qatar-Middle East & Africa
Doncaster	England-Europe
Donostia-San Sebastian	Spain-Europe
Dordrecht	The Netherlands-Europe
Dornbirn	Austria-Europe
Dortmund	Germany-Europe
Dorval	Quebec, Canada-North America
Douala	Cameroon-Middle East & Africa
Douglas	Isle of Man-Europe
Dover, Delaware	U.S.A.-North America
Dresden	Germany-Europe
Dubai	United Arab Emirates-Middle East & Africa
Dublin	Ireland-Europe
Duisburg	Germany-Europe
Durban	South Africa-Middle East & Africa
Düsseldorf	Germany-Europe
Edinburgh	Scotland-Europe
Edmonds, Washington	U.S.A.-North America
Edmonton	Alberta, Canada-North America
Eindhoven	The Netherlands-Europe
Elbert, Colorado	U.S.A.-North America
El Paso, Texas	U.S.A.-North America
Erfurt	Germany-Europe
Erie, Pennsylvania	U.S.A.-North America
Esbjerg	Denmark-Europe
Essen	Germany-Europe
Essex, Connecticut	U.S.A.-North America
Evanston, Illinois	U.S.A.-North America
Exeter	England-Europe
Fairfax, Virginia	U.S.A.-North America
Falls Church, Virginia	U.S.A.-North America
Farmington Hills, Michigan	U.S.A.-North America
Faro	Portugal-Europe
Ferrara	Italy-Europe
Flemington, New Jersey	U.S.A.-North America
Florence	Italy-Europe
Fort Lauderdale, Florida	U.S.A.-North America
Fort Myers, Florida	U.S.A.-North America
Fort Wayne, Indiana	U.S.A.-North America
Fort Worth, Texas	U.S.A.-North America
Framingham, Massachusetts	U.S.A.-North America
Frankfurt/Main	Germany-Europe
Frederick, Maryland	U.S.A.-North America
Fredericton	New Brunswick, Canada-North America
Freeport	Bahamas-The Caribbean
Freetown	Sierra Leone-Middle East & Africa
Freiburg	Germany-Europe
Fresno, California	U.S.A.-North America
Fribourg	Switzerland-Europe
Frisco, Texas	U.S.A.-North America
Fuengirola	Spain-Europe
Fujairah	United Arab Emirates-Middle East & Africa
Funchal	Madeira-Europe
Funchal (Madeira)	Portugal-Europe
Gainesville, Florida	U.S.A.-North America
Gananoque	Ontario, Canada-North America
Garden City, New York	U.S.A.-North America
Gdańsk	Poland-Europe
Geneva	Switzerland-Europe
Genoa	Italy-Europe
Georgetown	Guyana-Central & South America
Georgetown, Delaware	U.S.A.-North America
Gerona	Spain-Europe
Ghent	Belgium-Europe
Gibraltar	Gibraltar-Europe
Glasgow	Scotland-Europe
Gmunden	Austria-Europe
Goes	The Netherlands-Europe
Görlitz	Germany-Europe
Gothenburg	Sweden-Europe
Granada	Spain-Europe
Gran Canaria	Spain-Europe
Grand Cayman	Cayman Islands (British West Indies)-The Caribbean
Grand Rapids, Michigan	U.S.A.-North America
Grand Turk	Turks & Caicos Islands-The Caribbean
Graz	Austria-Europe
Great Abaco	Bahamas-The Caribbean
Great Falls, Montana	U.S.A.-North America
Greensboro, North Carolina	U.S.A.-North America
Greensburg, Pennsylvania	U.S.A.-North America
Greenville, South Carolina	U.S.A.-North America
Greenwich, Connecticut	U.S.A.-North America
Grenoble	France-Europe
Groningen	The Netherlands-Europe
Guadalajara, Jalisco	Mexico-North America
Guangzhou (Canton), Guangzhou	People's Republic of China-Asia
Guatemala City	Guatemala (C.A.)-Central & South America
Guayaquil	Ecuador-Central & South America
Guaynabo	Puerto Rico-The Caribbean
Gulfport, Mississippi	U.S.A.-North America
Gütersloh	Germany-Europe
Hackensack, New Jersey	U.S.A.-North America
Haddonfield, New Jersey	U.S.A.-North America
The Hague	The Netherlands-Europe
Haifa	Israel-Middle East & Africa
Halifax	Nova Scotia, Canada-North America
Halle	Germany-Europe
Hamamatsu-Shi	Japan-Asia
Hamburg	Germany-Europe
Hamilton	Bermuda-The Caribbean
Hamilton	Ontario, Canada-North America
Hammond, Louisiana	U.S.A.-North America
Hannover	Germany-Europe
Hanoi	Vietnam-Asia
Harare	Zimbabwe-Middle East & Africa
Harrisburg, Illinois	U.S.A.-North America
Harrisburg, Pennsylvania	U.S.A.-North America
Hartford, Connecticut	U.S.A.-North America
Haverhill, Massachusetts	U.S.A.-North America
Heidelberg	Germany-Europe
Heilbronn	Germany-Europe
Helena, Montana	U.S.A.-North America
Helsingborg	Sweden-Europe
Helsinki	Finland-Europe
Hermeray	France-Europe
Hermosillo, Sonora	Mexico-North America
Herzilya	Israel-Middle East & Africa
Hightstown, New Jersey	U.S.A.-North America
Hildesheim	Germany-Europe
Ho Chi Minh City	Vietnam-Asia
Hof	Germany-Europe
Holland, Michigan	U.S.A.-North America
Hollywood, Florida	U.S.A.-North America
Hong Kong	Hong Kong -Asia
Honolulu, Hawaii	U.S.A.-North America
Houston, Texas	U.S.A.-North America
Hull	England-Europe
Huntsville, Alabama	U.S.A.-North America
Hyderabad	India-Asia
Ibiza	Spain-Europe
Indianapolis, Indiana	U.S.A.-North America
Innsbruck	Austria-Europe
Ipswich	England-Europe
Irvine, California	U.S.A.-North America
Islamabad	Pakistan-Asia
Istanbul	Turkey-Europe
Izmir	Turkey-Europe
Jackson, Mississippi	U.S.A.-North America
Jackson, Wyoming	U.S.A.-North America
Jacksonville, Florida	U.S.A.-North America
Jakarta	Indonesia-Asia
Jeddah	Saudi Arabia-Middle East & Africa
Jenkintown, Pennsylvania	U.S.A.-North America
Jericho, New York	U.S.A.-North America
Jersey City, New Jersey	U.S.A.-North America
Jerusalem	Israel-Middle East & Africa
Johannesburg	South Africa-Middle East & Africa
Joliet, Illinois	U.S.A.-North America

Jönköping	Sweden-Europe
Juneau, Alaska	U.S.A.-North America
Kaiserslautern	Germany-Europe
Kalamazoo, Michigan	U.S.A.-North America
Kalispell, Montana	U.S.A.-North America
Kampala	Uganda-Middle East & Africa
Kano	Nigeria-Middle East & Africa
Kansas City, Missouri	U.S.A.-North America
Kaohsiung	Taiwan-Asia
Karachi	Pakistan-Asia
Karlovy Vary	Czech Republic-Europe
Karlsruhe	Germany-Europe
Kassel	Germany-Europe
Kathmandu	Nepal-Asia
Kaunas	Lithuania-Europe
Kenai, Alaska	U.S.A.-North America
Kentville	Nova Scotia, Canada-North America
Khartoum	Sudan-Middle East & Africa
Kiel	Germany-Europe
Kiev	Ukraine-Europe
King Of Prussia, Pennsylvania	U.S.A.-North America
Kingston	Jamaica-The Caribbean
Kingston	Ontario, Canada-North America
Kitchener	Ontario, Canada-North America
Klosters	Switzerland-Europe
Knoxville, Tennessee	U.S.A.-North America
Kobe	Japan-Asia
Kolding	Denmark-Europe
Kolonia	U.S. Pacific Territories-Asia
Kralendijk, Bonaire	Netherlands Antilles-The Caribbean
Krefeld	Germany-Europe
Kristianstad	Sweden-Europe
Kuala Lumpur	Malaysia-Asia
Kuwait	Kuwait-Middle East & Africa
Lafayette, California	U.S.A.-North America
Lafayette, Louisiana	U.S.A.-North America
Lagos	Nigeria-Middle East & Africa
Lahore	Pakistan-Asia
La Jolla, California	U.S.A.-North America
Lake Charles, Louisiana	U.S.A.-North America
Lakewood, New Jersey	U.S.A.-North America
Lancaster, Pennsylvania	U.S.A.-North America
Lansdale, Pennsylvania	U.S.A.-North America
Lansing, Michigan	U.S.A.-North America
La Paz	Bolivia-Central & South America
Laramie, Wyoming	U.S.A.-North America
Laredo, Texas	U.S.A.-North America
Larnaca	Cyprus-Europe
Las Vegas, Nevada	U.S.A.-North America
Latrobe, Pennsylvania	U.S.A.-North America
Lausanne	Switzerland-Europe
Lawrenceville, Georgia	U.S.A.-North America
Lebanon, Ohio	U.S.A.-North America
Lebanon, Pennsylvania	U.S.A.-North America
Leeds	England-Europe
Leesburg, Virginia	U.S.A.-North America
Leghorn	Italy-Europe
Leiderdorp	The Netherlands-Europe
Leipzig	Germany-Europe
Lethbridge	Alberta, Canada-North America
Lexington, Kentucky	U.S.A.-North America
Lexington, North Carolina	U.S.A.-North America
Liege	Belgium-Europe
Lille	France-Europe
Lima	Peru-Central & South America
Limassol	Cyprus-Europe
Limerick	Ireland-Europe
Linköping	Sweden-Europe
Lisbon	Portugal-Europe
Liverpool	England-Europe
Livonia, Michigan	U.S.A.-North America
Ljubljana	Slovenia-Europe
Locarno	Switzerland-Europe
Lombard, Illinois	U.S.A.-North America
London	England-Europe
London	Ontario, Canada-North America
Londonderry, New Hampshire	U.S.A.-North America
Long Beach, California	U.S.A.-North America
Los Angeles, California	U.S.A.-North America
Louisville, Kentucky	U.S.A.-North America
Loulé	Portugal-Europe
Lowell, Massachusetts	U.S.A.-North America
Lübeck	Germany-Europe
Ludwigsburg	Germany-Europe
Ludwigshafen	Germany-Europe
Lugano	Switzerland-Europe
Lund	Sweden-Europe
Luxembourg	Luxembourg-Europe
Lynnfield, Massachusetts	U.S.A.-North America
Lyon	France-Europe
Macon, Georgia	U.S.A.-North America
Madison, Wisconsin	U.S.A.-North America
Madras	India-Asia
Madrid	Spain-Europe

Mainz	Germany-Europe
Málaga	Spain-Europe
Malmö	Sweden-Europe
Managua	Nicaragua (C.A.)-Central & South America
Manama	Bahrain-Middle East & Africa
Manchester	England-Europe
Manchester, New Hampshire	U.S.A.-North America
Manhasset, New York	U.S.A.-North America
Mannheim	Germany-Europe
Manuels	Northwest Territories, Canada-North America
Maplewood, New Jersey	U.S.A.-North America
Marbella	Spain-Europe
Mariehamn	Finland-Europe
Marietta, Georgia	U.S.A.-North America
Markham	Ontario, Canada-North America
Marseille	France-Europe
Mattighofen	Austria-Europe
Mattoon, Illinois	U.S.A.-North America
Mayaguez	Puerto Rico-The Caribbean
McAllen, Texas	U.S.A.-North America
McAllen, Virginia	U.S.A.-North America
McLean, Virginia	U.S.A.-North America
McMinnville, Oregon	U.S.A.-North America
Medellin	Colombia-Central & South America
Media, Pennsylvania	U.S.A.-North America
Melbourne, Victoria	Australia-Australasia
Memphis, Tennessee	U.S.A.-North America
Menlo Park, California	U.S.A.-North America
Mersin	Turkey-Europe
Messina (Sicily)	Italy-Europe
Metairie, Louisiana	U.S.A.-North America
Metro Manila	Republic of The Philippines-Asia
Mexicali, Baja California	Mexico-North America
Mexico, D.F.	Mexico-North America
Miami, Florida	U.S.A.-North America
Middelburg	The Netherlands-Europe
Middlesbrough	England-Europe
Milan	Italy-Europe
Millburn, New Jersey	U.S.A.-North America
Milwaukee, Wisconsin	U.S.A.-North America
Mineola, New York	U.S.A.-North America
Minneapolis, Minnesota	U.S.A.-North America
Minsk	Republic of Belarus-Europe
Mission Viejo, California	U.S.A.-North America
Mississauga	Ontario, Canada-North America
Mobile, Alabama	U.S.A.-North America
Modesto, California	U.S.A.-North America
Modling	Austria-Europe
Moenchengladbach	Germany-Europe
Moncton	New Brunswick, Canada-North America
Monroe, Michigan	U.S.A.-North America
Montclair, New Jersey	U.S.A.-North America
Monte Carlo	Monaco-Europe
Montego Bay	Jamaica-The Caribbean
Monterey, California	U.S.A.-North America
Monterrey, Nuevo León	Mexico-North America
Montevideo	Uruguay-Central & South America
Montreal	Quebec, Canada-North America
Morris Plains, New Jersey	U.S.A.-North America
Morristown, New Jersey	U.S.A.-North America
Moscow	Russia-Europe
Mount Clemens, Michigan	U.S.A.-North America
Mount Vernon, New York	U.S.A.-North America
Munich	Germany-Europe
Münster	Germany-Europe
Muscat	Oman-Middle East & Africa
Muskegon, Michigan	U.S.A.-North America
Myrtle Beach, South Carolina	U.S.A.-North America
Nagoya	Japan-Asia
Naha	Japan-Asia
Nairobi	Kenya-Middle East & Africa
Naples	Italy-Europe
Naples, Florida	U.S.A.-North America
Narberth, Pennsylvania	U.S.A.-North America
Nashville, Tennessee	U.S.A.-North America
Nassau	Bahamas-The Caribbean
Natal	Brazil-Central & South America
Natick, Massachusetts	U.S.A.-North America
Neuchâtel	Switzerland-Europe
Newark, New Jersey	U.S.A.-North America
New Brunswick, New Jersey	U.S.A.-North America
Newcastle-upon-Tyne	England-Europe
New Delhi	India-Asia
New Haven, Connecticut	U.S.A.-North America
New Orleans, Louisiana	U.S.A.-North America
Newport Beach, California	U.S.A.-North America
Newton, Massachusetts	U.S.A.-North America
New York, New York	U.S.A.-North America
Niagara Falls, New York	U.S.A.-North America
Nice	France-Europe
Nicosia	Cyprus-Europe
Nijmegen	The Netherlands-Europe
Nogales, Arizona	U.S.A.-North America
Norfolk, Virginia	U.S.A.-North America
Norristown, Pennsylvania	U.S.A.-North America
Northampton	England-Europe
North York	Ontario, Canada-North America
Norwalk, Connecticut	U.S.A.-North America

Norwich......England-Europe
Nottingham......England-Europe
Novo Hamburgo......Brazil-Central & South America
Novosibirsk......Russia-Europe
Nürnberg......Germany-Europe
Nyon......Switzerland-Europe

Oak Park, Illinois......U.S.A.-North America
Oakville......Ontario, Canada-North America
Oberhausen......Germany-Europe
Odense......Denmark-Europe
Offenbach am Main......Germany-Europe
Okemos, Michigan......U.S.A.-North America
Oklahoma City, Oklahoma......U.S.A.-North America
Oldenburg......Germany-Europe
Omaha, Nebraska......U.S.A.-North America
Orange, California......U.S.A.-North America
Orange, Connecticut......U.S.A.-North America
Oranjestad......Aruba-The Caribbean
Örebro......Sweden-Europe
Orlando, Florida......U.S.A.-North America
Osaka......Japan-Asia
Oshawa......Ontario, Canada-North America
Oslo......Norway-Europe
Osnabrück......Germany-Europe
Osterville, Massachusetts......U.S.A.-North America
Ottawa......Ontario, Canada-North America
Ouagadougou......Burkina-Faso-Middle East & Africa
Oviedo......Spain-Europe
Owensboro, Kentucky......U.S.A.-North America

Padua......Italy-Europe
Paignton, Devon......England-Europe
Palma De Mallorca......Spain-Europe
Palm Beach, Florida......U.S.A.-North America
Palm Springs, California......U.S.A.-North America
Palo Alto, California......U.S.A.-North America
Panamá......Republic of Panama-Central & South America
Paoli, Pennsylvania......U.S.A.-North America
Paramaribo......Surinam-Central & South America
Paramus, New Jersey......U.S.A.-North America
Paris......France-Europe
Parsippany, New Jersey......U.S.A.-North America
Pasadena, California......U.S.A.-North America
Pascagoula, Mississippi......U.S.A.-North America
Pensacola, Florida......U.S.A.-North America
Perth, Western Australia......Australia-Australasia
Perúgia......Italy-Europe
Pforzheim......Germany-Europe
Philadelphia, Pennsylvania......U.S.A.-North America
Philipsburg, St. Maarten......Netherlands Antilles-The Caribbean
Phnom Penh......Cambodia-Asia
Phoenix, Arizona......U.S.A.-North America
Pine Island, New York......U.S.A.-North America
Piraeus......Greece-Europe
Pittsburgh, Pennsylvania......U.S.A.-North America
Plauen......Germany-Europe
Plovdiv......Bulgaria-Europe
Plymouth......England-Europe
Plymouth Meeting, Pennsylvania......U.S.A.-North America
Ponce......Puerto Rico-The Caribbean
Pontiac, Michigan......U.S.A.-North America
Pordenone......Italy-Europe
Port-Au-Prince......Haiti-The Caribbean
Port Harcourt......Nigeria-Middle East & Africa
Port Huron, Michigan......U.S.A.-North America
Portland, Maine......U.S.A.-North America
Portland, Oregon......U.S.A.-North America
Port Louis......Mauritius-Middle East & Africa
Port Moresby......Papua New Guinea-Australasia
Porto......Portugal-Europe
Porto Alegre......Brazil-Central & South America
Port of Spain......Trinidad and Tobago-The Caribbean
Port Said......Egypt-Middle East & Africa
Portsmouth, New Hampshire......U.S.A.-North America
Potsdam......Germany-Europe
Poznań......Poland-Europe
Prague......Czech Republic-Europe
Pretoria......South Africa-Middle East & Africa
Princeton, New Jersey......U.S.A.-North America
Providence, Rhode Island......U.S.A.-North America
Providenciales......Turks & Caicos Islands-The Caribbean
Puerto Plata......Dominican Republic-The Caribbean
Pusan......Korea-Asia

Quebec......Quebec, Canada-North America
Queretaro......Mexico-North America
Quincy, Massachusetts......U.S.A.-North America
Quito......Ecuador-Central & South America

Raleigh, North Carolina......U.S.A.-North America
Ramsey, New Jersey......U.S.A.-North America
Rawalpindi......Pakistan-Asia
Reading......England-Europe
Reading, Pennsylvania......U.S.A.-North America
Red Bank, New Jersey......U.S.A.-North America

Redmond, Washington......U.S.A.-North America
Regina......Saskatchewan, Canada-North America
Remscheid......Germany-Europe
Reno, Nevada......U.S.A.-North America
Research Triangle Park, North Carolina......U.S.A.-North America
Resistencia, (Chaco)......Argentina-Central & South America
Reutlingen......Germany-Europe
Reykjavik......Iceland-Europe
Richmond, Virginia......U.S.A.-North America
Riga......Republic of Latvia-Europe
Rijeka......Croatia-Europe
Rijswijk......The Netherlands-Europe
Rio de Janeiro......Brazil-Central & South America
Riyadh......Saudi Arabia-Middle East & Africa
Road Town, Tortola......British Virgin Islands-The Caribbean
Roanoke, Virginia......U.S.A.-North America
Rockford, Illinois......U.S.A.-North America
Rock Island, Illinois......U.S.A.-North America
Rockville, Maryland......U.S.A.-North America
Rome......Italy-Europe
Roseland, New Jersey......U.S.A.-North America
Rostock......Germany-Europe
Rotterdam......The Netherlands-Europe
Rouen......France-Europe
Rugby......England-Europe
Ruwi......Oman-Middle East & Africa

Sacramento, California......U.S.A.-North America
Saddle Brook, New Jersey......U.S.A.-North America
Safat......Kuwait-Middle East & Africa
St. Catharines......Ontario, Canada-North America
St. George......New Brunswick, Canada-North America
St. Helier, Jersey......Channel Islands-Europe
Saint John......New Brunswick, Canada-North America
St. John's......Antigua-The Caribbean
St. John's......Northwest Territories, Canada-North America
St. Johnsbury, Vermont......U.S.A.-North America
St. Louis, Missouri......U.S.A.-North America
St. Paul, Minnesota......U.S.A.-North America
St. Peter, Jersey......Channel Islands-Europe
St. Peter Port, Guernsey......Channel Islands-Europe
St. Petersburg......Russia-Europe
St. Petersburg, Florida......U.S.A.-North America
Saipan......U.S. Pacific Territories-Asia
Salem, Massachusetts......U.S.A.-North America
Salerno......Italy-Europe
Salt Lake City, Utah......U.S.A.-North America
Salzburg......Austria-Europe
Sana'a......Yemen-Middle East & Africa
San Andrés......Colombia-Central & South America
San Antonio, Texas......U.S.A.-North America
San Diego, California......U.S.A.-North America
Sandton......South Africa-Middle East & Africa
San Fernando......Trinidad and Tobago-The Caribbean
San Francisco, California......U.S.A.-North America
San José......Costa Rica (C.A.)-Central & South America
San Jose, California......U.S.A.-North America
San Juan......Puerto Rico-The Caribbean
San Luis Potosí, S.L.P.......Mexico-North America
San Pedro Sula......Honduras (C.A.)-Central & South America
San Salvador......El Salvador (C.A.)-Central & South America
San Sebastian......Spain-Europe
Santa Ana, California......U.S.A.-North America
Santa Cruz......Bolivia-Central & South America
Santa Fe, New Mexico......U.S.A.-North America
Santa Monica, California......U.S.A.-North America
Santiago......Chile-Central & South America
Santiago de Compostela......Spain-Europe
Santiago de los Caballeros......Dominican Republic-The Caribbean
Santo Domingo......Dominican Republic-The Caribbean
São Paulo......Brazil-Central & South America
Sarasota, Florida......U.S.A.-North America
Saskatoon......Saskatchewan, Canada-North America
Sault Ste. Marie......Ontario, Canada-North America
Scarsdale, New York......U.S.A.-North America
Schwerin......Germany-Europe
Scottsdale, Arizona......U.S.A.-North America
Scranton, Pennsylvania......U.S.A.-North America
Seattle, Washington......U.S.A.-North America
Secaucus, New Jersey......U.S.A.-North America
Seminole, Florida......U.S.A.-North America
Seoul......Korea-Asia
Sergiev Posad......Russia-Europe
Seville......Spain-Europe
Shanghai......People's Republic of China-Asia
Sharjah......United Arab Emirates-Middle East & Africa
Shelby, North Carolina......U.S.A.-North America
Shenzhen......People's Republic of China-Asia
Sherbrooke......Quebec, Canada-North America
Sheridan, Wyoming......U.S.A.-North America
Simsbury, Connecticut......U.S.A.-North America
Singapore......Singapore-Asia
Sioux Falls, South Dakota......U.S.A.-North America
Sofia......Bulgaria-Europe
Sosua......Dominican Republic-The Caribbean
Southampton......England-Europe
Southfield, Michigan......U.S.A.-North America
Spartanburg, South Carolina......U.S.A.-North America

Springfield, Massachusetts	U.S.A.-North America
Springfield, Ohio	U.S.A.-North America
Stamford, Connecticut	U.S.A.-North America
Stavanger	Norway-Europe
Stockholm	Sweden-Europe
Stowe, Vermont	U.S.A.-North America
Strasbourg	France-Europe
Stroudsburg, Pennsylvania	U.S.A.-North America
Stuttgart	Germany-Europe
Sudbury	Ontario, Canada-North America
Summit, New Jersey	U.S.A.-North America
Surrey	British Columbia, Canada-North America
Sydney	Nova Scotia, Canada-North America
Sydney, New South Wales	Australia-Australasia
Syracuse, New York	U.S.A.-North America
Tacoma, Washington	U.S.A.-North America
Taipei	Taiwan-Asia
Tallahassee, Florida	U.S.A.-North America
Tallinn	Estonia-Europe
Tampa, Florida	U.S.A.-North America
Tampere	Finland-Europe
Ta'Xbiex	Malta-Europe
Tegucigalpa	Honduras (C.A.)-Central & South America
Tehran	Iran-Middle East & Africa
Tel Aviv	Israel-Middle East & Africa
Tenafly, New Jersey	U.S.A.-North America
Thessaloniki	Greece-Europe
Thunder Bay	Ontario, Canada-North America
Tijuana, Baja California	Mexico-North America
Timişoara	Romania-Europe
Tirana	Albania-Europe
Tokyo	Japan-Asia
Toledo, Ohio	U.S.A.-North America
Tonawanda, New York	U.S.A.-North America
Toronto	Ontario, Canada-North America
Toulouse	France-Europe
Towson, Maryland	U.S.A.-North America
Traunstein	Germany-Europe
Trenton, New Jersey	U.S.A.-North America
Trondheim	Norway-Europe
Troy, Michigan	U.S.A.-North America
Truro	Nova Scotia, Canada-North America
Tucson, Arizona	U.S.A.-North America
Tulsa, Oklahoma	U.S.A.-North America
Tunis	Tunisia-Middle East & Africa
Turin	Italy-Europe
Turku	Finland-Europe
Turnhout	Belgium-Europe
Ulaanbaatar	Mongolia-Asia
Ulm	Germany-Europe
Uniondale, New York	U.S.A.-North America
Upper Tumon	Guam-Asia
Uppsala	Sweden-Europe
Utrecht	The Netherlands-Europe
Vaasa	Finland-Europe
Vaduz	Liechtenstein-Europe
Valencia	Venezuela-Central & South America
Valencia	Spain-Europe
Valletta	Malta-Europe
The Valley	Anguilla-The Caribbean
Valley Forge, Pennsylvania	U.S.A.-North America
Valparaiso	Chile-Central & South America
Valparaiso, Indiana	U.S.A.-North America
Vancouver	British Columbia, Canada-North America
Vancouver, Washington	U.S.A.-North America
Venice	Italy-Europe
Ventura, California	U.S.A.-North America
Verona	Italy-Europe
Veurne	Belgium-Europe
Victoria	Hong Kong-Asia
Victoria	British Columbia, Canada-North America
Vienna	Austria-Europe
Vienna, Virginia	U.S.A.-North America
Vientiane	Laos-Asia
Vigo	Spain-Europe
Vilnius	Lithuania-Europe
Vineland, New Jersey	U.S.A.-North America
Vitória	Brazil-Central & South America
Vitoria	Spain-Europe
Wailuku, Hawaii	U.S.A.-North America
Walnut Creek, California	U.S.A.-North America
Waltham, Massachusetts	U.S.A.-North America
Warsaw	Poland-Europe
Warsaw, Indiana	U.S.A.-North America
Washington, D.C.	U.S.A.-North America
Wayne, Pennsylvania	U.S.A.-North America
Wellesley, Massachusetts	U.S.A.-North America
Wellington	New Zealand-Australasia
West Caldwell, New Jersey	U.S.A.-North America
West Chester, Pennsylvania	U.S.A.-North America
Westfield, New Jersey	U.S.A.-North America
West Hartford, Connecticut	U.S.A.-North America
Westmont, New Jersey	U.S.A.-North America
West Palm Beach, Florida	U.S.A.-North America
Westport, Connecticut	U.S.A.-North America
Westwood, New Jersey	U.S.A.-North America
Whitby	Ontario, Canada-North America
Whitehorse	Yukon Territory, Canada-North America
White Plains, New York	U.S.A.-North America
White River Junction, Vermont	U.S.A.-North America
Wichita, Kansas	U.S.A.-North America
Wiesbaden	Germany-Europe
Wilkes-Barre, Pennsylvania	U.S.A.-North America
Willemstad, Curaçao	Netherlands Antilles-The Caribbean
Wilmington, Delaware	U.S.A.-North America
Wilton, Connecticut	U.S.A.-North America
Windsor	Ontario, Canada-North America
Winnipeg	Manitoba, Canada-North America
Winston-Salem, North Carolina	U.S.A.-North America
Winter Park, Florida	U.S.A.-North America
Winterthur	Switzerland-Europe
Woodland Hills, California	U.S.A.-North America
Wuppertal	Germany-Europe
Xiamen	People's Republic of China-Asia
Yangon	Myanmar-Asia
Yarmouth	Nova Scotia, Canada-North America
Yellowknife	Northwest Territories, Canada-North America
York, Pennsylvania	U.S.A.-North America
Youngstown, Ohio	U.S.A.-North America
Zagreb	Croatia-Europe
Zaragoza	Spain-Europe
Zug	Switzerland-Europe
Zürich	Switzerland-Europe
Zweibrücken	Germany-Europe
Zwickau	Germany-Europe

INTERNATIONAL BAR ASSOCIATION
OVERVIEW

Formed in 1947 in New York State, the International Bar Association (IBA) is the world's largest international organisation of Law Societies, Bar Associations and individual lawyers engaged in transnational law. It is composed of over 16,000 individual lawyer members in 173 countries and 164 Law Societies and Bar Associations together representing more than 2.5 million lawyers.

The principal aims and objectives of the IBA are:

> To encourage the discussion of problems relating to professional organisation and status

> To promote an exchange of information between legal associations worldwide

> To support the independence of the judiciary and the right of lawyers to practise their profession without interference

> To keep abreast of developments in the law, and help in improving and making new laws

The IBA works towards these objectives through three main areas of activity:

> Support for the activities of Bar Associations and in particular developing bars;

> Support of human rights for lawyers worldwide;

> Services for its individual lawyer members through the three Sections and their specialist Committees.

IBA SECTIONS

Section on Business Law (SBL)

The Section on Business Law covers all the main subjects of interest to lawyers involved with the laws, practices and procedures affecting business, financial and commercial activities throughout the world.

It has 28 specialist Committees which deal with subjects of interest to a commercially oriented lawyer.

Meetings of all the Committees are held every year at IBA or Section Conferences, and Seminars on subjects of topical interest are held several times a year.

The Section publishes a journal, *International Business Lawyer,* which is circulated free to members eleven times a year.

SBL Committees

A   Maritime and Transport Law

B   Aeronautical Law

C   Antitrust and Trade Law

D   Procedures for Settling Disputes

E   Banking Law

F   Environmental Law

G   Business Organisations

H   Insurance

I   Investment Companies, Funds and Trusts

J   Insolvency and Creditors' Rights

K   Utility Law

L   Intellectual Property and Entertainment

M   International Sales and Related Commercial Transactions

N   Taxes

O   International Litigation

P   Employment and Industrial Relations Law

Q   Issues and Trading in Securities

R   International Computer and Technology Law

S   Products Liability, Advertising, Unfair Competition and Consumer Affairs

T   International Construction Projects

U   Savings and Mortgage Lending Institutions

W   Business Crime

X   International Franchising

Y   Tourism and Travel Law

Z   Outer Space

Co Corporate Counsel

Cm Communications Law

Section on General Practice (SGP)

The Section on General Practice offers the general practitioner assistance with the problems of everyday practice. It seeks to contribute to the developments of the profession and practice methods, and generally with the improvement of the standards of service which the profession offers the public.

It operates through 23 specialist Committees representing the different aspects of law covered by the general practitioner.

Regional meetings and Seminars throughout the year and annual meetings at IBA and Section Conferences, offer opportunities for personal contacts and exchanges of views.

The Section publishes its own journal, *International Legal Practitioner,* which is circulated free to members four times a year.

SGP Committees

1   Real Estate Law

2   Medicine and the Law

3   Indigenous Peoples and Development Law

4   Family Law

5   Estates and Trusts

6   Criminal Law

7   Administrative Law

8   Legal Education and Professional Development

9   Sports and Gaming Law

10   Practice Management and Technology

11   Discrimination and Gender Equality

12   Civil Litigation

13   Negligence and Damages

14   Migration and Nationality Law

16   Media Law

17   Access to Justice

18   Professional Conduct

19   Human Rights Law

20   Art and Cultural Property Law

21   Consumer Law

22   Closely Held and Growing Business Enterprises

23   Ombudsman

24   Working Group for Government Lawyers

Section on Energy & Natural Resources Law (SERL)

The Section on Energy and Natural Resources Law is open to lawyers in private practice, oil and mining companies, in government and academic circles and international organisations.

The Section operates through 6 Committees, which aim to advance the development and understanding of the law as it affects oil, gas, coal, electricity, nuclear and other mineral and energy resources, both nationally and internationally.

The main focus of its activities is a continuing education programme. Major seminars are held every other year bringing together specialists on energy and natural resources from all parts of the world. Specialist regional seminars are also held during the year.

The Section publishes a quarterly journal, the *Journal of Energy and Natural Resources Law,* which is circulated free to members.

SERL Committees

A   Oil Law

B   Mineral Law

C   Coal Law

D   Electricity Law

E   Nuclear Law

G   Gas Law

Fora

Eastern European Forum

The Eastern European Forum, established by the Section on Business Law, has as its aims and objectives:

- To assist lawyers in Eastern Europe in the development of their practice under radically changing legal systems;

- To provide lawyers from other countries with up-to-date information on legal developments in Central and Eastern Europe.

The main activities of the Forum are seminars, publications, a newsletter, discounts on other publisher's publications, and exchanges.

Judges' Forum

The Judges' Forum was set up in 1991 under the aegis of the Section on General Practice.

The Forum, representing judges worldwide, discusses topics of particular interest and concern to members of the judiciary such as the system of appointment to the judiciary, the length of service and remuneration levels.

Capital Markets Forum

The Section on Business Law's Capital Markets Forum is a private sector initiative established in order to monitor and assist in the orderly development of capital markets. As part of its activities, the Forum will be the focus of the IBA's participation in the International Capital Markets Group (which consists of the Fédération Internationale des Bourses de Valeurs and the International Federation of Accountants).

The Forum's activities include:

- The publication of occasional papers on matters of current importance

- The holding of seminars and discussion groups in various financial centres to discuss issues of concern to market participants

- The organisation of informative sessions and provision of material and speakers to address issues of concern for emerging markets

- Response to proposals facilitating international transactions in securities

Academics' Forum

The Academics' Forum was set up by the Section on Business Law, for all full and part-time, past and present law teachers who are members of the IBA.

Its objectives are:

- To exchange between members information and assistance, such as sabbatical exchanges and short term teaching "swaps", and provide help to visiting members with research materials, facilities and contacts

- To promote liaison between national Law Teachers' Associations and regional Associations such as the Commonwealth Law Teachers' Association

- To provide advice and, with the financial support of IBA's educational Trusts, teaching aids, materials and books to law teachers in developing countries

Asia Pacific Forum

The Asia Pacific Forum was established by the Section on Business Law (SBL) in 1992 at the International Bar Association's 24th Biennial Conference in Cannes.

Working alongside national Bars, it has as its aims and objectives:

- To provide a forum for lawyers involved in the region to establish contact and exchange information

- To provide the focus for the SBL's involvement throughout the region

- To disseminate information on all topics of relevance to the lawyers both practising in and with an interest in the region

Arab Region Forum

The Forum, working alongside national Bars in the region, has as its aims and objectives:

- To provide a forum for lawyers involved in the region to establish contact and exchange information

- to provide the focus for the SBL's interest in, and involvement throughout the region. A particular focus of interest is the continuing economic importance of the region, including the reconstruction and investment projects following current peace initiatives

- to disseminate information on all topics of relevance to lawyers both practising and with an interest in the area

IBA DIRECTORY

In conjunction with Martindale Hubbell, the IBA publishes an annual *Directory of Members* which is a unique work of reference, containing details of its 16,000 lawyer members worldwide and their specialities, and listing up to five main areas of practice.

Members' personal and professional details are available online through the LEXIS®/NEXIS® services as part of the Martindale-Hubbell library and membership notations are incorporated into the CD-ROM version of the Martindale-Hubbell database.

IBA CHARITABLE TRUSTS

The IBA Educational Trust and the IBA Foundation Inc are charitable trusts formed by the IBA which depend entirely on contributions of time, money, and expertise from the legal profession and others who support its objectives.

Their aims are:

To advance legal education throughout the world for the benefit of the public

To study and advance the administration of justice worldwide

To undertake research into common legal problems

International Bar Association, 2 Harewood Place, Hanover Square, London W1R 9HB, England. Tel: 44 (171) 629 1206 Fax: 44 (171) 409 0456.

LEXIS® and NEXIS® are registered trademarks of Reed Elsevier Properties Inc., used under license.

Geographical Listing of
IBA Member Organisations

ALGERIA
Mahmoud Khelili, President
Organisation Nationale des Avocats Algeriens
10 Rue Abane Ramdane
Palais de Justice
Algiers 1

ARGENTINA
Dr. Ernesto O'Farrell, President
Colegio de Abogados de la Ciudad de Buenos
  Aires
Montevideo 640
1019 Buenos Aires
Tel: (1) 325 3451 Tlx: 21545
Fax: (1) 325 0132
Languages: Eng

ARMENIA
Vladimir Darbinian, President
Armenian Lawyers Association
Khorudarani 8
Yerevan 10
Tel: 581 582
Fax: 582 449

AUSTRALIA
Stuart Fowler, President
Law Council of Australia
The National Council of Lawyers
18 Torrens Street
Braddon ACT 2601
Tel: (6) 247 3788 Tlx: 62406 ACSCI AA
Fax: (6) 248 0639

AUSTRIA
Dr. Klaus Hoffmann, President
Osterreichischer Rechtsanwaltskammertag
Rotenturmstrasse 13
1010 Vienna 1
Tel: 535 1275 Tlx: 111168 RAKA
Fax: 535 127513

BAHAMAS
J. Henry Bostwick, President
Bahamas Bar Association
Bostwick & Bostwick
50 George Street
PO Box N - 1605
Nassau
Tel: 322 2038
Fax: 328 2521

BAHRAIN
A.A. Alayobi, President
Bahrain Bar Society
PO Box 5025
Manama
Tel: 720566

BANGLADESH
K.M. Ahmed, President
National Bar Association of Bangladesh
Ibrahim Mansion
11 Purana Paltan
(2nd Floor) Dhaka 1000
Tel: (2) 502 448 Tlx: 642035 PCO BJ
Fax: (2) 263 957 Fax2: 866 979

BARBADOS
Beverley J. Walrond, President
Barbados Bar Association
Reece Chambers Mottley House
Coleridge Street Bridgetown
Tel: 436 6725
Fax: 429 3769

BELGIUM
Georges-Albert Dal Batonnier, President
Orde Francais des Avocate du Barreau de
  Bruxelles
Palais De Justice
1000 Brussels
Tel: (2) 508 6656
Fax: (2) 508 6453

Karel van Alsenoy, President
Nederlandse Ordre van Avocaten
Bij de Balie te Brussel
Palais de Justice Place Poelaert
B-1000 Brussels
Tel: (2) 508 6656 Tlx: 64869
Fax: (2) 514 1653

Jozef van den Heuvel Dean
Ordre National des Avocats de Belgique
Avenue de la Toison d'Or 65
1060 Brussels 6
Tel: (2) 534 6773
Fax: (2) 539 3920

BERMUDA
John H. Cooper, President
Bermuda Bar Association
P.O. Box 125
Hamilton HM AX
Tel: (809) 295 9393

BRAZIL
Jose Roberto Batochio, President
Federal Council of the OAB
Setor de Autarquias Sul
Quadra 5 Lote 2 Bloco N
70770 Brasilla DF
Tel: (61) 22608 12/0842 Tlx: 614675
Fax: (61) 2254947

Silvino J. Lopes Neto, President
Instituto dos Advogados do Rio Grande do Sul
Travessa Acylino de Carvalho
21-40, Bairro Centro
90.010 Porto Alegre RS
Tel: (512) 245788

BULGARIA
Todor Burilkov, President
Bulgarian Bar Association
1A Vitosha Blvd
1000, Sofia
Tel: (2) 875513
Fax: (2) 876514

CANADA
Thomas G. Heitzman, QC, President
The Canadian Bar Association
50 O'Connor Street Suite 902
Ottawa Ontario K1P 6L2
Tel: (613) 237 2925 Tlx: 61399
Fax: (613) 237 0185

CAYMAN ISLANDS
Michael Alberge, President
Cayman Islands Law Society
PO Box 309
George Town
Tel: (809) 949 8066 Tlx: (293) 4242
Fax: (809) 949 8080

CHILE
Sergio Urrejoia Monckeberg, President
Colegio de Abogados de Chile
Ahumada No. 341 Of 207 Piso 2o
Santiago
Tel: (2) 633 6720/639 6175
Fax: (2) 639 5072

CHINA
Ren Jisheng, President
All China Lawyers' Association
Room 3411 West Bldg. Guoyl Hotel
No. 1 Wenxing Dongzie
Beijing 100044
Tel: 8316886 Tlx: 22505 BOOTH CN
Fax: 0086 1 8313658

CYPRUS
Xenios I. Xenopoulos, President
Cyprus Bar Association
PO Box 1446
187 Ledra Street
Nicosia
Tel: 466156
Fax: 462135

CZECH REPUBLIC
Milan Skalnik, President
Czech Bar Association
110 Prague 1
Narodni 16 CFSR
Tel: 2491 3606-8
Fax: 24914386 Fax2: 2491 0162

DENMARK
Jan Erlund, President
Det Danske Advokatsamfund
Advokaternes Hus
Kronprinsessegade 28
1306 Copenhagen K
Tel: 33 96 97 98
Fax: 33 32 18 31

DOMINICA
Ronan A. David, President
Dominica Bar Association
Ronswan House
111 Bath Road
PO Box 194
Roseau
Tel: 448 2251
Fax: 448 7705

ECUADOR
Raul Izurieta Mora-Bowen, President
Federacion Nacional de Abogados del Ecuador
PO Box 638, Tarqui 809, Of 301
Quito
Tel: 562500 Tlx: 21040 RIMB
Fax: 564642

EGYPT
Ahmed Al Khawaga, President
Egyptian Bar Association
49 a Ramses Street
Cairo
Tel: (2) 451 360
Fax: (2) 747 488

ENGLAND
Charles Elly, President
The Law Society of England and Wales
113 Chancery Lane
London WC2A 1PL
Tel: (171) 242 1222 Tlx: 261203
Cbl: INTERPREY
Fax: (171) 405 9522

Peter H. Goldsmith, QC, Chairman
The General Council of the Bar
3 Bedford Row
London WC1R 4DB
Tel: (171) 242 0082
Fax: (171) 831 4778

REPUBLIC OF ESTONIA
Aare Terk, President
Estonia Bar Association
Viru Street 19
Tallinn 200 001
Tel: 419180
Fax: 440298

FIJI
Ram Krishna, President
Fiji Law Society
GPO Box 2588 Government Building
Suva
Tel: 303 508
Fax: 306 047

FINLAND
Pauli Alankoja, President
The Finnish Bar Association
Simonkatu 12 B 20
FIN-00100 Helsinki
Tel: (0) 694 2744
Fax: (0) 694 8237

FRANCE
Thiery Cahn, President
Confederation Nationale des Avocats
34 rue de Conde
75006 Paris
Tel: (1) 4354 6548
Fax: (1) 4354 7509

Jean Rene Farthouat, Batonnier
Batonnier
Barreau de Paris
Palais de Justice
Paris 75001
Tel: (1) 44 324848
Fax: (1) 4634 7765

GERMANY
Felix Busse, President
Deutscher AnwaltVerein EV
Adenaueralle 106
53113 Bonn
Tel: (228) 26 07 0 Tlx: 886969 1 DAV D
Fax: (228) 26 07 46 Fax(2): 228 2807 42

GHANA
Nutifafa Kuenyehia, President
Ghana Bar Association
PO Box 4150
Accra
Tel: 226 748

HONG KONG
Ronny F. Wong, QC, Chairman
Hong Kong Bar Association
The Supreme Court
38 Queensway, LG/2 Floor
Tel: (5) 869 0210
Fax: (5) 869 0189

Roderick B. Woo, President
The Law Society of Hong Kong
Room 1403 Swire House
11 Chater Road Central
Tel: 846 0500
Fax: 846 0387

HUNGARY
Janos Banati, President
Budapest Bar Association
Szalay u 7
1055 Budapest
Tel: 111 9800

Jeno Horvath, President
Hungarian Bar Association
Szemere Utca 8
1054 Budapest
Tel: (1) 1119 800

ICELAND
Ragnar Adalsteinsson, President
The Icelandic Bar Association
Alftamyri 9
108 Reykjavik
Tel: (1) 685 620
Fax: (1) 687 057

INDIA
Fali Nariman, President
Bar Association of India
93 Lawyers Chambers
Supreme Court of India
New Delhi 110001
Tel: (11) 385902 Tlx: 5465 BAR IN

The Chairman
Bar Council of India
21 Rouse Avenue
Institutional Area
New Delhi 110002
Tel: (11) 386845

INDONESIA
Harjono Tjitrosoebono, President
Ikadin (Indonesian Bar Association)
Jl Kali Besar Barat No 26
Jakarta 11230
Tel: (21) 673 290
Fax: (21) 690 1704

IRAN
G.E. Jahromi, Chairman
Barreau de Teheran
Conseil de C'ordre des Avocats
Kanoun Vokala Dadgostari
Palais de Justice
Teheran
Tel: 304 598

IRAQ
Darwood Al Aswad, Chairman
Iraqi Bar Association
Al Mansaar
Baghdad
Tel: 5375860 Tlx: 214176
Cbl: MOHAMOON

IRELAND
Patrick A. Glynn, President
Law Society of Ireland
Blackhall Place
Dublin 7
Tel: (1) 6710 711 Tlx: 31219
Fax: (1) 6710 136

Peter Shanley, SC Chairman
The Council of the Bar of Ireland
Law Library PO Box 2424
Four Courts
Dublin 7
Tel: (1) 735689
Fax: (1) 722254/720031

ISRAEL
Hoter-Ishai, President
Israel Bar Association
10 Daniel Frish Street
Tel Aviv 64731
Tel: (3) 691 8691
Fax: (3) 691 8696

ITALY
Manfredo Rossi, President
Ordine degli Avvocati e Procuratori di Roma
Palazzo di Giustizia
Plazza Cavour
00193 Rome
Tel: (6) 687 5294
Fax: (6) 686 4837

Michele Saponara, Chairman
Ordine degli Avvocati e Procuratori di Milano
Palazzo di Giustizia
20122 Milan
Tel: (2) 55 181 016
Fax: (2) 55 181 003

Giancarlo Zuccaccia
Ordine degli Avvocati e Procuratori di Perugia
Palazzo di Giustizia
Palazza Matteotti
06100 Perugia
Tel: (75)24254

JAMAICA
Lloyd Barnett, President
The Jamaican Bar Association
Chambers 15 Duke Street
Kingston
Tel: 922 3219/967 1528
Fax: 922 3728

JAPAN
Tsuneo Ouchil, President
Japan Bar Association
1-1-1 Kasumigaseki
Chiyoda-Ku Tokyo
Tel: (3) 3581 6867
Fax (3) 3506 8570

E. Fujbayashi, President
Japan Federation of Bar Associations
1-1 Kasumigaseki
1-Chome
Chiyoda-Ku Tokyo
Tel: (3) 3580 9841
Cbl: BAR FEDERATION
Fax: (3) 3580 2866

JORDAN
Kamal Nassar, President
Jordan Bar Association
PO Box 9024
Amman
Tel: 6658 18/9 Tlx: 22496 JO

KENYA
Willy Mutunga, Chairman
Law Society of Kenya
P.O. Box 72219
Parliament Road
Nairobi
Tel: (2) 25558/29915
Fax: (2) 223997

KOREA (SOUTH)
Lee-Sae Joong, President
Korean Bar Association
1553-1 Seocho-dong
Seocho-gu
Seoul
Tel: (2) 522 3761
Fax: (2) 522 3767

KUWAIT
Ahmad Alwohaib, President
Kuwait Bar Association
PO Box 13385
Kaifan

REPUBLIC OF LATVIA
Alvars Niedre, President
Latvia Bar Association
34 Brivibas Boulevard
225050 Riga
Tel: 282777
Fax: 283358

LESOTHO
W.C.M. Maqutu, President
Law Society of Lesotho
1st Floor Nohatho Centre
Kingsway
PO Box 478
Maseru 100
Tel: 313517 Tlx: 4220 LO
Fax: 310118

LIBYA
The President
Libyan Bar Association
PO Box 10441
Tripoli
Tel: 41955/46282

LIECHTENSTEIN
Dr. Walter Kieber, President
Liechtensteinische Rechtsanwaltskammer
Heiligkreuz 6
POB 822
Tel: (75) 235 8322
Fax: (75) 235 8282

REPUBLIC OF LITHUANIA
Kestutis Lipeika, Chairman
Lietuvos Respiblikos advokaturos prezidiumas
Jogalios Str 11
2600 Vlinius
Tel: (0122)624546
Fax: (0122) 221 859

LUXEMBOURG
The President
Ordre des Avocats du Barreau de Luxembourg
Barreau de Luxembourg
Palais de Justice
Boite Postale 361
Tel: 22 48 50
Fax: 46 10 08

MALAWI
Collins C.C. Chizumila, Chairman
Malawi Law Society
Box 1712
Blantyre
Tel: 620964
Fax: 652360

MALAYSIA
Encik Zainur Bin Zakaria, President
Malaysian Bar Council
No 5 Jalan Tun Perak
50050 Kuala Lumpur
Tel: (3) 2911 366
Fax: (3) 291 2439

MALTA
The President
Camera degli Avvocati
The Law Courts
Republic Street
Valletta
Tel: 23231

MAURITIUS
Anil Gayan, Chairman
Mauritius Bar Association
Chambers Cathedral Square
Port Louis
Tel: 208 5526
Fax: 208 5586

MEXICO
Octavio Igartua Araiza, President
Mexican Bar Association
Varsovia No 1
Esq con P de la Reforma
Colonia Juarez
06600 Mexico D.F.
Tel: 525 2485/525 2362 Tlx: 1763294
Fax: 525 2362

MONTSERRAT WEST INDIES
Kenneth C. Allen, President
Montserrat Bar Association
PO Box 1
Marine Drive
Plymouth
Tel: 491 2498/2848
Fax: 491 2943

MOROCCO
Abdellah Darmiche, Batonnier
Ordre des Avocats au Barreau de Casablanca
Tribunal de 1ere Instance de Casablanca
Casablanca
Tel: (2) 221172/262846
Fax: (2) 270274

NAMIBIA
G S Coetzee, SC President
Society of Advocates of Namibia
PO Box 1323
Windhoek
Tel: (61) 231151
Fax: 061 230 162

William Henry Dicks, President
Law Society of Namibia
PO Box 714
Windhoek
Tel: (61) 230 263
Fax: (61) 230 223

NEPAL
Radheshyam Adhikari, President
Nepal Bar Association
PO Box 2384
Kathmandu
Tel: (1) 212347 Tlx: 2435
Fax: (1) 226349

Kusum Shrestha, President
Nepal Law Society
Ramshah Path
PO Box 2384
Kathmandu
Tel: (1) 228 497
Fax: (1) 226 349

NETHERLANDS
Tom de Waard, Dean
Netherlandse Bar Association
PO Box 30851
2500 GW's - Gravenhage
Tel: (70) 328 8328
Fax: (70) 328 2787

NEW ZEALAND
Austin John Forbes, President
New Zealand Law Society
PO Box 5041
Wellington 1
Tel: (4) 4727837
Fax: (4) 4737909

NIGERIA
The President
Nigerian Bar Association
Ozumba Mbadiwe Street
Victoria Island
P M B 12610 Lagos
Tel: 610778, 610783, 617083

NORTHERN IRELAND
Aiden Canavan, President
The Law Society of Northern Ireland
Law Society House
98 Victoria Street
Belfast BT1 3JZ
Tel: (1232) 231 614
Fax: (1232) 232 606

Pat Coghlin, QC, Chairman
General Council of the Bar of Northern Ireland
Bar Library Royal Court of Justice
Chichester Street
Belfast BT1 3JP
Tel: (1232) 241 523
Fax: (1232) 231 850

NORWAY
Bjorg Ven, President
Norwegian Bar Association
Kristian Augusts Gate 9
N-0164 Oslo 1
Tel: 2203 5050
Fax: 2211 5325

PAKISTAN
Qazi Mohammed Jamil, Chairman
Pakistan Bar Council
Old Supreme Court Building
Peshawar Road
Rawalpindi
Tel: (51) 562539
Fax: (51) 563789

PANAMA
Jorge Hernan Rubio, President
Colegio Nacional de Abogados de Panama
Avenida Mexico Y Calle 38
Apartado 8643, Panama 5
Tel: 256371 Tlx: 2124
Fax: 250189

PAPUA NEW GUINEA
Loani Henao, President
Papua New Guinea Law Society
PO Box 1994
Boroko
Tel: 258 483
Fax: 256 609

PHILIPPINES
Avelino J Cruz Jr.
Philippine Bar Association
3/F Cityland Condominium IV
124 Valero Street Salcedo Village
Makati Metro Manila
Tel: (2) 815 3080 Tlx: 23045 SYQUIA PH
Cbl: SYLAW MANILA
Fax: (2) 815 3080

Mervyn G. Encanto
Integrated Bar of the Phillipines
Dona Julia Vargas Avenue
Ortigas Center
Pasig Metro Manila
Tel: (2) 634 4697
Fax: (2) 631 3014

Maurice C. Nubia, President
Philippine Lawyers Association
6th Floor, Fli-Am Resources Building
231 Juan Luna Street Binondo
Manila 1006
Tel: (2) 479 907
Fax: (2) 479 908

POLAND
Maciej Bednarkiewicz, President
Polish Bar Association
Swietojerska 16 Street
00-202 Warsaw
Tel: (2) 635 4062
Fax: (2) 635 2709

PORTUGAL
Julio Castro Caldas, President
Ordem dos Avogados
Conselho General
Largo De S Domingos 14-D
Lisbon 2
Tel: (1) 867 152/5 Tlx: 18404 LEXORD
Fax: (1) 862 403

ROMANIA
Victor Anagnoste, President
Romania Bar Association
Palatul Justitiei
Calea Rahovei 2-4, sector 4
Cod 70502, Bucharest
Tel: (1) 614 3368
Fax: (1) 312 1085

RUSSIAN FEDERATION
Georgy Voskresensky
President International Union
(Commonwealth) of Advocates
Uzhinskii per 1/14 Block 7
103 104 Moscow
Tel: 2912535/2914280
Fax: 2913426

SCOTLAND
Andrew R. Hardie, QC Dean
Faculty of Advocates
Advocates Library
Parliament House
Edinburgh EH1 1RF
Tel: (131) 226 5071
Fax: (131) 225 3642

Kenneth Ross, President
The Law Society of Scotland
26 Drumsheugh Gardens
Edinburgh EH3 7YR
Tel: (131) 226 7411 Tlx: 72436
Fax: (131) 225 2934

SIERRA LEONE
Francis A D Gabbidon, President
Sierra Leone Bar Association
84 Dundes Street
Freetown
Tel: (22) 224 702
Fax: (22) 224 439
Languages: Eng

SINGAPORE
Peter Cuthbert Low, President
The Law Society of Singapore
1 Colombo Court #08-29/30
Tel: 338-3165 Tlx: RS 42097 LAWSOC
Fax: 339-7358

SLOVAK REPUBLIC
Stefan Detvai, President
Slovak Bar Association
Oktobrove nam 13
Bratislava 813 42
Tel: (7) 315813/353471
Fax: (7) 315807/315873

SOUTH AFRICA
D. W. Venter, President
Association of Law Societies of the Republic of
   South Africa
PO Box 36626
Menlo Park 0102
Tel: (12) 324 3330/9
Fax: (12) 342 3305

Malcolm J D Wallis, SC Chairman
General Council of the Bar of South Africa
PO Box 2260
Johannesburg 2000
Tel: (11) 293 976
Fax: (11) 298 970

SPAIN
Eugeni Gay Montaivo, President
Consejo General de la Abogacia Espanola
Calle de Sarrano No 9
Madrid 28001
Tel: 522 7711 Tlx: 47312 MPAE
Fax: 431 9365

SRI LANKA
D W Abeyakoon, President
Bar Association of Sri Lanka
129 Hulftsdorp Street
Colombo 12
Tel: 547134
Fax: 448090

ST LUCIA WEST INDIES
Winston Francis Cenac, President
Saint Lucia Bar Association
7 High Street
PO Box 462
Castries
Tel: (45) 23891
Fax: (45) 27919
Areas of Practice: 14, 43, 50, 80

ST VINCENT WEST INDIES
Othniel R. Sylvester, QC, President
St. Vincent & The Grenadines Bar Association
   Chambers
Halifax Street, PO Box 951
Kingstown
Tel: 456 1523
Fax: 456 2622

SWAZILAND
Paul Shiubane, President
The Law Society of Swaziland
PO Box 512
Mbabane
Tel: 46085
Fax: 22986

SWEDEN
Sven Unger, President
Swedish Bar Association
Box 27321
102 54 Stockholm
Tel: (8) 245 870
Fax: (8) 660 0779

SWITZERLAND
Ulrich Hirt, President
Swiss Bar Association
Bollwerk 21
Postfach 8321
3001 Bern
Tel: (31) 312 2505
Fax: (31) 312 3103

SYRIA
Ahmad Ido, President
Ordre des Avocats Syriens
rue Mayssaloune
PO Box 7541
Damascus
Tel: (11) 222 864

TANZANIA
Evarist Hubert Mbuya, President
Tanganyika Law Society
PO Box 3003
Arusha
Tel: 057-3181 Tlx: 42082 EASATO

THAILAND
The President
The Thai Bar
Na Hub Puey Road
Bangkok 10200
Tel: 224 1552

TRINIDAD
Allan J. Alexander, President
Law Association of Trinidad & Tobago
c/o Chancery Chambers
55 Edward Street
Port of Spain
Tel: 623 4040
Fax: 625 1670

TUNISIA
Abdelwaheh El-Behi, Batonnier
Ordre National des Avocats de Tunisie
Palais de Justice
Tunis
Tel: (1) 560 315
Fax: (1) 568 923

TURKEY
Tuncay Alemdaroalu, President
Ankara Bar Association
Adliye Sarayl
Sihhiye
Ankara 06430
Tel: (312) 425 9877
Fax: (312) 309 2237

Ondar Sav, President
Union of Turkish Bars
Karanfil Sokak 5
62 Kizilay
Ankara
Tel: (312) 418 0512
Cbl: BAROBIRLIK
Fax: (312) 418 7857

UGANDA
Solomy Balungi Bossa, President
The Uganda Law Society
PO Box 426
Kampala
Tel: (41) 251 054
Fax: (41) 236 796

REPUBLIC OF UKRAINE
Victor V. Medvedchuk, President
The Union of Advocates of Ukraine
N74D 5/7 Shavchenko Avenue
Kiev 252002
Tel: (44) 229 0041
Fax: (44) 229 2812

USA
District of Columbia
Malcolm W. Monroe, President
The Federal Bar Association
1815 H Street NW Suite 408
Washington DC 20006
Tel: (202) 638 0252
Fax: (202) 775 0295

New York
Brian S. Goldstein, President
Customs & International Trade Bar
475 Park Avenue South
25th Floor
New York NY 10016
Tel: (212) 269 2330
Fax: (212) 269 5016

Barbara Paul Robinson, President
The Association of the Bar of the City of New
York
42 West 44th Street
New York NY 10036
Tel: (212) 386 6600
Fax: (212) 398 6634

Illinois
George Bushnell, President
American Bar Association
750 North Lake Shore Dirve
Chicago, Illinois 80811
Tel: (312) 988-5229 Tlx: 270593
Fax: (312) 988-5151 Fax2: (312) 988-4665

Faith F. Driscoll, President
National Association of Woman Lawyers
750 North Lake Shore Dirve
Chicago, Illinois 80811
Tel: (312) 988-6186
Fax: (312) 988-6281

VENEZUELA
Amparo Gonzalez de Jimenez, President
Federacion de Colegios de Abogados de
Venezuela
Av LaSalle, Torre Inpreabogado
Piso 11, Lee Caobos

ZAMBIA
Sakwiba Sirota, Chairman
Law Association of Zambia
1st Floor Wing 'L'
Permanent House Cairo Road
PO Box 35271 10101 Lusaka
Tel: (2) 615 824
Fax: (2) 615 824

ZIMBABWE
The President
Law Society of Zimbabwe
5th Floor Throgmorton House
51 Samora Machel Avenue
Harare
Tel: (4) 705041 Tlx: 24733
Fax: (4) 728 489

Geographical Listing of
IBA Sustaining Member Organisations

AUSTRALIA
Aust. Cap. Territory
R.P. Clynes, President
The Law Society of the Australian Capital
Territory
First Floor Law Society Building
11 London Circuit
Canberra, A C T
Tel: (6) 247-5700
Fax: (6) 247-3754

New South Wales
Maurie Stack, President
Law Society of New South Wales
170 Phillip Street
Sydney N S W 2000
Tel: (2) 220 0333 Tlx: 73065 LAW SOC AA
Fax: (2) 231 5809

Murray Tobias, QC, President
The New South Wales Bar Association
Selborne Chambers
174 Phillip Street
Sydney N S W 2000
Tel: (2) 232 4055
Fax: (2) 231 1904

Victoria
David J. Habersberger, QC, Chairman
Victorian Bar Council
Owen Dixon Chambers
205 William Street
Melbourne Victoria 3000
Tel: (3) 608 7111 Tlx: VIC BAR AA36782
Fax: (3) 670 2959

Roderick Smith, President
The Law Institute of Victoria
PO Box 263C
Melbourne Victoria 3001
Tel: (3) 607 9311 Tlx: 134873LAWINS AA
Fax: (3) 602 5270 Fax2: (3) 607 9558

AUSTRIA
Klaus Hoffman, President
Rechtsanwaltskammer Wien
Rotenturmstrasse 13
1010 Vienna
Tel: (1) 535 1275
Fax: (1) 535 127513

BELGIUM
Philippe Marchandise, President
Association Belge des Juristes d'Enterprise
36 rue Ravenstein (Bte 2)
1000 Brussels
Tel: (2) 512-7433
Fax: (2) 502-6570

BRAZIL
Clemencia B. Wolthers, President
Centro de Estudos das Sociedades de Advogados
Rua Libero Badaro, 293
250 andar
01009 Sao Paulo - SP
Tel: 37-9511
Fax: 37-2836

BULGARIA
Pavlina Todorova, President
Interadvocat Bar Association
PO Box 3 Sofia 1463
Tel: (2) 810152
Fax: (2) 814183

CANADA
Quebec
Louise Belanger, President
Chambre des Notaries du Quebec
630 Blvd Rene-Levesque Ouest
Montreal Quebec H3B 1T6
Tel: (514) 879-1793
Fax: (514) 879-1923

Phyllis A. L. Smith, QC President
Federation of Law Societies of Canada
445 Boul Saint-Laurent, Bureau 480
Montreal, Quebec
Tel: (514) 875-8350
Fax: (514) 875-6115

CHANNEL ISLANDS
Talmai Phillip Morgan, President
Guernsey International Legal Association
c/o PO Box 71 Arnold House
St. Julian's Avenue
St. Peter Port Guernsey
Tel: (1481) 726 541
Fax: (1481) 723 1100

ENGLAND
Christopher Clarke, QC, Chairman
The Commercial Bar Association
222-225 Strand Outer Temple
London WC2R 1ND
Tel: (71) 353 3502
Fax: (71) 353 3597

Richard Ferguson, QC, President
Criminal Bar Association
3 Gray's Inn Square
London WC1R 5AH
Tel: (171) 831 2311
Fax: (171) 404 4939

The Master
The City of London Solicitors Co
14 Charterhouse Square
London EC1M 6AX
Tel: (171) 251 0531
Fax: (171) 251 1642

FRANCE
Louis-Bernard Buchman, President
Association Francaise des Avocats Conseils
d'Entreprises
23-25 Avenue Mac-Mahon
75017 Paris
Tel: (1) 4766 3007
Fax: (1) 4763 3578

Pierre Charreton, President
Association Francaise des Juristes d'Entreprise
c/o Framatone
92084 Paris La Defense - Cedex 16

MALAYSIA
Maureen Lind, President
Sabah Law Association
3rd Floor 120 Gaya Street
Kota Kinabalu
Sabah
Tel: (88) 232 662
Fax: (88) 232 654

NETHERLANDS
J.W. Klinkenberg, President
Koninklijke Notariele Broederschap
PO Box 96827
2509 JE The Hague
Tel: (70) 330 7111
Fax: (70) 345 3226

E.H. Swaab, Dean
Amsterdam Bar Association
Parnassusweg 222 Kamet B 0.22
1076 AV Amsterdam
Tel: (20) 541 2068
Fax: (20) 541 2190

NORFOLK ISLAND
John Walsh
Norfolk Island Bar Association
c/o McIntyres International Law Practice
P.O. Box 223
Tel: (6723) 22123
Fax: (6723) 23602

PUERTO RICO, USA
Jose M. Sagardia-Perez, President
Puerto Rico Bar Association
PO Box 1900
San Juan 00902
Tel: (809) 721 3358
Fax: (809) 725 0330

ROMANIA
Niculae Cerveni, President
Bucharest Bar Association
Cod postal 70 621
Str Dr Riureanu nr 3 Sector 5
Bucharest
Tel: 154537
Fax: 121084

SCOTLAND
Alastair J. Campbell, Clerk
The Royal Faculty of Procurators in Glasgow
12 Nelson Mandela Place
Glasgow G2 1BT
Tel: (141) 552 3422
Fax: (141) 552 2935

T.H. Drysdale
The Deputy Keeper of H M Signet
Saltire Court
20 Castle Terrace
Edinburgh EH1 2ET
Tel: (131) 228 9900
Fax: (131) 228 1222

W. Seith B. Ireland, President
Glasgow Bar Association
c/o 28 St. Andrews Street
Glasgow G1 5PD
Tel: (141) 552 7363
Fax: (141) 553 2047

SOUTH AFRICA

Bophuthatswana
Edwin G. Harris President
The Law Society of Bophuthatswana
Private Bag X2184
Mafikeng 8670
Bophuthatswana
Tel: (140) 811075

Cape Province
C.F. Pohl, President
Law Society of the Cape of Good Hope
PO Box 4528
Cape Town 8000
Tel: (21) 24-8060 Tlx: 5-20043
Cbl: JURIDICAL
Fax: (21) 221355/8

Natal
Alan Brooke, President
The Law Society of Natal
Law Society Chambers
16 Change Lane
PO Box 1454
Pietermaritzburg 3200
Tel: (331) 51304 Tlx: 643586
Fax: (331) 949544

H. Mall, SC, Chairman
Society of Advocates of Natal
920 Salmon Grove Chambers
407 Smith Street
Durban 4001 Natal
Tel: (31) 3013099
Fax: (31) 3044415

Transvaal
D. G. Olivier, President
The Law Society of Transvaal
PO Box 1493
Pretoria
Tel: (12) 322 7294/9 Tlx: 3-21178 SA
Fax: (12) 322 0156

Stewart Cant, President
Association of Legal Advisors of South Africa
PO Box 95194
Grant Park 2051
Tel: (11) 483 3071

SPAIN
Eugeni Gay Montavo, President
Illustre Colegio d'Advocats de Barcelona
Mallorca 283
08037 Barcelona
Tel: (3) 487 2114 Tlx: 50533
Fax: (3) 487 1589

USA

Connecticut
Huston Putnam Lowry, Chairman
Section of International Law & World Peace of
  the Connecticut Bar Association
101 Corporate Place
Rocky Hill, Connecticut 06067
Languages: Eng Fr Ger Sp

Florida
The President
International Law Section of the Florida Bar
650 Apalachee Parkway
Tallahassee, Florida 32399-2300
Tel: (904) 561 5625
Fax: (904) 561 5825

Michigan
Timothy F. Stock
International Law Section
State Bar of Michigan
Room 649 Ford Motor Company
The American Road
Dearborn, Michigan 48121-1899
Tel: (313) 323 0240
Fax: (313) 845 5867

VENEZUELA
Roman Duque Corredor, President
Colegio de Abogados del Distrito Federal
Esquina de Pajaritos
Palacio de Justicia 5o
Caracas
Tel: 481 8602

DIRECTORY OF LAW FIRM ALLIANCES, NETWORKS, CLUBS, ASSOCIATIONS AND OTHER AFFILIATIONS

Small, low profile associations of law firms and clubs were first established in Europe and the United States in the 1960's to provide managing partners the opportunity to meet and discuss common issues. From this humble beginning, the concept of cooperation has evolved into sophisticated organizations to cost effectively assist members in better serving clients' changing needs.

While the objectives of these associations vary, they fall into two principal categories. One type is that which is formed for the joint practice of law, while the other is formed for various other purposes including the collection of information, publications and seminars, promotion of professionalism, referrals, etc.

The **Lex Mundi Directory** provides an overview of the scope and breadth of these alternative approaches to global expansion. The present list covers 180 associations, representing over 2,500 firms and more than 185,000 attorneys.

Stephen J. McGarry, Esq.
President — Lex Mundi

ACL INTERNATIONAL (Association of Commercial Lawyers)
Number of Firms: 29
Number of Attorneys: 550
Principal Region: International
Contact(s):
Mr. David R. Judah
Secretary/Treasurer
ACL Secretariat Office
Apollo House, 56 New Bond Street
London W1Y O5X
England
Tel: 44-171-499-7020
Fax: 44-171-499-2449

ACTIO (EEIG)
WESSING BERENBERG-GOSSLER ZIMMERMANN LANGE (Germany)
TRENITE VAN DOORNE (The Netherlands)
Number of Firms: 2
Number of Attorneys: 315
Principal Region: Europe
Contact(s):
Wolfgang von Meibom, Esq.
Wessing Berenberg-Gossler Zimmermann Lange
149, Avenue Louise
B-1050 Brussels
Belgium
Tel: 32-2-537-01-86
Fax: 32-2-534-25-31

ADVOCACY GROUP
PATTON BOGGS & BLOW
O'CONNOR & HANNAN
AKIN, GUMP, HAUER & FELD
Number of Firms: 13
Number of Attorneys: 1400
Principal Region: United States
Contact(s):
Mr. Timothy J. May
Patton Boggs & Blow
2550 M Street, N.W.
Washington, DC 20037
United States
Tel: 202-457-6000
Fax: 202-457-6315

ADVODAN (Nationwide Association of Danish Lawyers)
Number of Firms: 11
Number of Attorneys: 130
Principal Region: Denmark
Contact(s):
Mr. Nicolai R. Horten
Horten & Co.
Kongens Nytorv 22
DK-1050 Copenhagen K
Denmark
Tel: 45-33-14-32-36
Fax: 45-33-32-38-99

ADVOSELECT EEIG
Number of Firms: 51
Number of Attorneys: 217
Principal Region:
Contact(s):
Mr. Hellmut M. Damlachi
Hölderlinplatz 5
70193 Stuttgart
Germany
Tel: 49-711-2-23-73-12
Fax: 49-711-2-23-73-13

AKIN, GUMP, STRAUSS, HAUER & FELD (Dallas and Washington, D.C.)
DESMEDT & DASSESSE INTERNATIONAL (Brussels)
Number of Firms: 2
Number of Attorneys: 500
Principal Region: Europe
Contact(s):
Mr. Alan D. Feld
Akin, Gump, Strauss, Hauer & Feld
4100 First City Center
1700 Pacific Avenue
Dallas, TX 75201-4618
United States
Tel: 214-969-2800
Fax: 214-922-8043

ALLEN & OVERY (London)
LOEFF CLAEYS VERBEKE (Belgium, Luxembourg, Netherlands)
GIDE LOYRETTE NOUEL (France)
   Number of Firms: 3
   Number of Attorneys: 1256
   Principal Region: Europe
   Contact(s):
   Mr. Anthony J. Herbert
   Allen & Overy
   One Mew Change
   London EC4M 9QQ
   England
   Tel: 44-171-330-3000
   Fax: 44-171-330-9999

ALLENS ARTHUR ROBINSON GROUP
ALLEN ALLEN & HEMSLEY (Sydney, Canberra)
ARTHUR ROBINSON & HEDDERWICKS (Melbourne)
FEEZ RUTHNING (Brisbane, Gold Coast)
FINLAYSONS (Adelaide)
PARKER & PARKER (Perth)
Group and associated offices:
ALLENS ARTHUR ROBINSON (London, New York, Singapore, Port Moresby)
DUNSTAN STYLES & CO. (Hong Kong)
WIRIADINATA & WIDYAWAN (Jakarta, Indonesia)
AAR CHINA LIMITED (Shanghai)
   Number of Firms: 5
   Number of Attorneys: c. 600
   Principal Region: Australia/Asia/Pacific
   Contact(s):
   Mr. Timothy I. L'Estrange
   Allen Allen & Hemsley
   The Chifley Tower
   2 Chifley Square
   Sydney, New South Wales 2000
   Australia
   Tel: 61-2-230-4000
   Fax: 61-2-233-7022

   Mr. Andrew Guy
   Arthur Robinson & Hedderwicks
   Levels 27-34
   530 Collins Street
   Melbourne, Victoria 3000
   Australia
   Tel: 61-3-614-1011
   Fax: 61-3-614-4661

   Mr. Howard Stack
   Feez Ruthning
   Riverside Centre
   123 Eagle Street
   Brisbane, Queensland 4000
   Australia
   Tel: 61-7-833-3333
   Fax: 61-7-832-4233

   Mr. Alan McArthur
   Finlaysons
   81 Flinders Street
   Adelaide, South Australia 5000
   Australia
   Tel: 61-8-235-7400
   Fax: 61-8-232-2944

   Mr. John Chandler
   Parker & Parker
   AMP Building
   140 St. Georges Terrace
   Perth, Western Australia 6000
   Australia
   Tel: 61-9-322-0321
   Fax: 61-9-322-2243

ALLIANCE OF EUROPEAN LAWYERS (EEIG)
BODEN OPPENHOFF & RAEDLER (Germany)
DE BANDT, VAN HECKE & LAGAE (Belgium)
DE BRAUW BLACKSTONE WESTBROEK (The Netherlands)
JEANTET & ASSOCIÉS (France)
LAGERLÖF & LEMAN (Sweden)/URÍA & MENÉNDEZ (Spain)
   Number of Firms: 6
   Number of Attorneys: 960
   Principal Region: Europe
   Contact(s):
   Me. Gérard Mazet
   Jeantet & Associés
   87, Avenue Kléber
   75784 Paris Cédex 16
   France
   Tel: 33-1-45-05-80-08
   Fax: 33-1-47-04-20-41

   Thomas O. Verhoeven
   Oppenhoff & Raedler
   712 Fifth Ave. #30
   New York, NY 10019
   United States
   Tel: 212-801-3410
   Fax: 212-801-3415

AMERICAN LAW FIRM ASSOCIATION
   Number of Firms: 80
   Number of Attorneys: 4,000
   Principal Region: United States
   Contact(s):
   Mr. Melvin Katz
   Lester, Schwab, Katz & Dwryer
   120 Broadway
   New York, NY 10271
   United States
   Tel: 212-964-6611
   Fax: 212-267-5916

   Mr. Alvin Greene
   Chief Executive Officer
   11990 San Vicente Blvd.
   Suite 300
   Los Angeles, CA 90049
   United States
   Tel: 310-826-2532
   Fax: 310-826-6775

AMERICAN LAWYER'S CONSORTIUM
Number of Firms: 10
Number of Attorneys: 200
Principal Region: United States
Contact(s):
Mr. Otis McGee
Gee Lafayette Willis & Greene
1 Market Plaza
Spear Street Tower
Suite 3900
San Francisco, CA 94105-1123
United States
Tel: 415-495-4747
Fax: 415-495-5123

ARENT FOX KINTNER PLOTKIN & KAHN (Washington)
PRINCE SAAD AL FAISAL BIN ABDUL AZIZ (Saudi Arabia)
Number of Firms: 2
Number of Attorneys: 250
Principal Region: U.S./Saudi Arabia
Contact(s):
Steven R. Miles, Esq.
Arent Fox Kintner Plotkin & Kahn
1050 Connecticut Avenue, N.W.
Washington, DC 20036-5339
United States
Tel: 202-857-6000
Fax: 202-857-6395

ASSOCIATED BUSINESS LAWYERS IN EUROPE (ABLE)
LAWRENCE GRAHAM (United Kingdom)
ESCHE SCHÜMANN COMMICHAU (Germany)
LAFARGE, FLÉCHEUX, REVUZ (France)
GEATER & CO. (Belgium)/GEDDA & EKDAHL (Sweden)
PUELINCKX SCHILTZ LINDEN GROLIG (Belgium)
Number of Firms: 6
Number of Attorneys: 450
Principal Region: Europe
Contact(s):
Mr. Michael Richardson
Mr. Paul Kinsella
Mr. Robert Field
Mr. Bruce Manford
Lawrence Graham
190 Strand
London WC2R 1JN
England
Tel: 44-171-379-0000
Fax: 44-171-379-6854

Dr. Jürgen Brüggemann
Dr. Wolfgang Deuchler
Esche Schümann Commichau
Herrengraben 31
20459 Hamburg
Germany
Tel: 49-40-36-80-50
Fax: 49-40-36-28-96/7

THE ASSOCIATION OF EUROPEAN LAWYERS
Number of Firms: 34
Number of Attorneys: 500
Principal Region: Europe
Contact(s):
Mr. Julian Maitland-Walker
Charles Russell Solicitors
8-10 New Fetter Lane
London EC4R 1RS
England
Tel: 44-171-203-5000
Fax: 44-171-203-0200

AUSTRALIAN LEGAL NETWORK
Number of Firms: 6
Number of Attorneys: 33
Principal Region: Australia
Contact(s):
Sukhwant Singh, Esq.
Smith Williamson Singh
4th Floor, 19 Pier Street
Perth, Western Australia 6000
Australia
Tel: 61-09-325-7755
Fax: 61-09-325-4646

BAKER & McKENZIE
Number of Offices: 52
Number of Attorneys: 1,726
Principal Region: International
Contact(s):
Mr. John McGuigan
Baker & McKenzie
One Prudential Plaza, Suite 2500
130 East Randolph Drive
Chicago, IL 60601
United States
Tel: 312-861-8800
Fax: 312-861-8823

BERWIN LEIGHTON (London)
KATO NISHIDA & HASEGAWA (Tokyo)
Number of Firms: 2
Number of Attorneys: 190
Principal Region: Central and Eastern Europe
Contact(s):
S.J. Goodman, Esq.
Berwin Leighton
Adelaide House
London Bridge
London EC4R 9HA
England
Tel: 44-171-623-3144
Fax: 44-171-623-4416

BLAKE, CASSELS & GRAYDON
LAVERY, DE BILLY
Number of Firms: 2
Number of Attorneys: 450
Principal Region: Canada
Contact(s):
Mr. John Solursh
Blake, Cassels & Graydon
Box 25
Commerce Court West
Toronto, Ontario M5L 1A9
Canada
Tel: 416-863-2550
Fax: 416-863-2653

Mr. Andre Laurin
Lavery, de Billy
1 Place Ville Marie
Suite 4000
Montreal, Quebec H3B 4M4
Canada
Tel: 514-877-2987
Fax: 514-871-8977

BOEKEL DE NERÉE (The Netherlands)
HUYBRECHTS, ENGELS, CRAEN & PARTNERS (Antwerp, Belgium)
PLATTEEUW DE WITTE & GRISAR (Brussels, Belgium)
Number of Firms: 3
Number of Attorneys: 110
Principal Region: Europe
Contact(s):
Mr. M. de Haas
Boekel De Nerée
Postbus 2508
1000 CM Amsterdam
The Netherlands
Tel: 31-20-541-52-52
Fax: 31-20-644-69-48

BOMCHIL, CASTRO, GOODRICH, CLARO AND ASSOCIATES
Number of Firms: 17
Number of Attorneys: 400
Principal Region: International
Contact(s):
Mr. David Brill, Jr.
Goodrich Riquelme y Asociados
Paseo de la Reforma 355
06500 Mexico, D.F.
Mexico
Tel: 52-5-533-00-40
Fax: 52-5-525-12-27

BORDEN DUMOULIN HOWARD GERVAIS
HOWARD, MACKIE (Calgary)
BORDEN & ELLIOT (Toronto)
MACKENZIE GERVAIS (Montréal)
RUSSELL & DUMOULIN (Vancouver)
BORDEN DUMOULIN HOWARD GERVAIS (London)
Number of Firms: 4
Number of Attorneys: 421
Principal Region: Canada
Contact(s):
Mr. D'Arcy Brooks
Borden & Elliot
Scotia Plaza Building
40 King Street West
Toronto, Ontario M5H 3Y4
Canada
Tel: 416-367-6000
Fax: 416-367-6749

Mr. Michael A. Fitch
Russell & Dumoulin
1500-1075 West Georgia Street
Vancouver, B.C. V6E 3G2
Canada
Tel: 604-631-3131
Fax: 604-631-3232

Mr. Allan D. Nielsen
Howard, Mackie
1000 Canterra Tower
400 Third Avenue, S.W.
Calgary, Alberta T2P 4H2
Canada
Tel: 403-32-9500
Fax: 403-266-1395

Mr. Tass G. Grivakes
MacKenzie Gervais
Place Mercantile, 13th Floor
770 Sherbrooke Street West
Montréal, Québec H3Z 1G1
Canada
Tel: 514-842-9831
Fax: 514-288-7389

Mr. Alfred L.J. Page
Borden DuMoulin Howard Gervais
3/4 Royal Exchange Buildings, First Floor
London EC3V 3NL
England
Tel: 44-171-929-2099
Fax: 44-171-929-2044

BOUGHTON PETERSON YANG ANDERSON (Vancouver)
AIRD & BERLIS (Toronto)
Number of Firms: 2
Number of Attorneys: 200
Principal Region: Canada
Contact(s):
Mr. David S. Pedlow
Boughton Peterson Yang Anderson
25th Floor, 1055 Dunsmuir Street
P.O. Box 49200
Vancouver, British Columbia V7X 1S8
Canada
Tel: 604-687-6789
Fax: 604-683-5317

BROBECK HALE AND DORR INTERNATIONAL (Joint Venture in New York, London and Prague)
BROBECK, PHLEGER & HARRISON (San Francisco)
HALE AND DORR (Boston)
    Number of Firms: 2
    Number of Attorneys: 700
    Principal Region: Europe
    Contact(s):
    Mr. John W. Larson
    Brobeck Phleger & Harrison
    Spear Street Tower
    One Market Plaza
    San Francisco, CA 94105
    United States
    Tel: 415-442-0900
    Fax: 415-442-1010

    Mr. John D. Hamilton, Jr.
    Hale and Dorr
    660 State Street
    Boston, MA 02109
    United States
    Tel: 617-526-6000
    Fax: 617-526-5000

    Mr. Donald J. Guiney
    Brobeck Hale and Dorr International
    Veritas House
    125 Finsbury Pavement
    London EC2A INQ
    England
    Tel: 44-171-638-6688
    Fax: 44-171-638-5888
    Mr. David M. Ayres
    Brobeck Hale and Dorr International
    Brehova 1
    110 00 Prague 1
    The Czech Republic
    Tel: 42-2-232-49-91
    Fax: 42-2-232-84-44

BRYAN CAVE INTERNATIONAL GROUP
BAILEYS SHAW & GILLETT (England)
KADASAH LAW FIRM (Saudi Arabia)
ROSSBACH & PARTNER (Germany)
    Number of Firms: 3
    Number of Attorneys:
    Principal Region: International
    Contact(s):
    Mr. John V. Lonsberg
    Bryan Cave
    One Metropolitan Square
    Suite 3600
    211 North Broadway
    St. Louis, MO 63102
    United States
    Tel: 314-259-2251
    Fax: 314-259-2020

BUCHANAN INGERSOLL PROFESSIONAL CORPORATION
(Pittsburgh, Philadelphia, Harrisburg, Princeton, Lexington, Miami, Florida)
BOGNER, HENSEL, GERNS & SCHREIER (Berlin, Frankfurt)
CABINET VAN HAGEN (Paris)
DUMON, SABLON & VANHEESWIJCK (Brussels)
EDGE & ELLISON (Birmingham, London, Leicester)
VON WOBESER y SIERRA, S.C. (Mexico City)
WUDY HEUNG & CO. (Hong Kong)
    Number of Firms: 7
    Number of Attorneys: 500
    Principal Region: International
    Contact(s):
    A. Bruce Bowden, Esq.
    Buchanan Ingersoll Professional Corporation
    56th Floor
    600 Grant Street
    Pittsburgh, PA 15219
    United States
    Tel: 412-562-8844
    Fax: 412-562-1041

CHADBOURNE & PARKE (New York)
CHADBOURNE & PARKE ASSOCIATES (New Delhi)
THE ZANGER LAW FIRM (Kazakhstan)
BOROVTSOV & SALEI (Belarus)
UNION OF ADVOCATES (Moscow)
WATANABE, SUGIURA, NAKAMORI & NISHIDA (Japan)
    Number of Firms: 5
    Number of Attorneys: 280
    Principal Region: International
    Contact(s):
    Edward P. Smith, Esq.
    Chadbourne & Parke
    30 Rockefeller Plaza
    New York, NY 10112
    United States
    Tel: 212-408-5100
    Fax: 212-541-5369

    Gregory N. Ullman, Esq.
    Chadbourne & Parke Associates
    A16-B Anand Niketan
    New Delhi 110021
    India
    Tel: 91-11-301-7568
    Fax: 91-11-301-7351

    Mr. Maidan K. Suleimenov
    The Zanger Law Firm
    157 Abaya Street
    Suite 26
    27, 7th Floor
    Almaty
    Kazakhstan
    Tel: 7-3272-50-94-73
    Fax: 7-3272-50-94-74

    Mr. Valentin A. Borovtsov
    Borovtsov & Salei
    21 Chicherin Street
    Minsk 220029
    Republic of Belarus
    Tel: 7-0172-33-74-18
    Fax: 7-0172-33-74-22

Mr. Shunji Nakamori
Watanabe, Sugiura, Nakamori & Nishida
#1301 Aoyama Building 2-3
Kita-Aoyama, 1-Chome
Minato-Ku, Tokyo 107
Japan
Tel: 81-33-470-0271
Fax: 81-33-497-0621

CLUB DE ABOGADOS
Number of Firms: 34
Number of Attorneys: 603
Principal Region: International
Contact(s):
Mr. Antonio Alonso-Lasheras
J. & A. Garrigues
Antonio Maura, 16
Madrid 28014
Spain
Tel: 34-1-521-21-51
Fax: 34-1-531-70-16/521-39-73

COMMERCIAL LAW AFFILIATES (CLA)
Number of Firms: 157
Number of Attorneys: 4,000
Principal Region: International
Contact(s):
Mr. Leon I. Steinberg
Maslon Edelman Borman & Brand
330 Norwest Center
Minneapolis, MN 55402
United States
Tel: 612-672-8200
Fax: 612-672-8397

Ms. Wendy N. Lamphear, Executive Director
Commercial Law Affiliates
420 North Fifth Street
Suite 970
Minneapolis, MN 55401
United States
Tel: 612-339-8680
Fax: 612-337-5783

COMMONWEALTH LAW GROUP
Number of Firms: 12
Number of Attorneys: 200
Principal Region: Virginia
Contact(s):
Mr. James V. Meath
Williams, Mullen, Christian & Dobbins
Two James Center
Sixteenth Floor
1021 East Cary Street
Richmond, VA 23210-1320
United States
Tel: 804-643-1991
Fax: 804-783-6456

CORRESPONDENT LAW FIRMS OF PRICE WATERHOUSE (EEIG)
Number of Firms: 4
Number of Attorneys: 180
Principal Region: Europe
Contact(s):
Mr. Patrick Everard
Price Waterhouse
Southwark Tower
32 London Bridge Street
London SE1 9SY
England
Tel: 44-171-939-3000
Fax: 44-171-378-0647

DAVIES ARNOLD COOPER (London, Manchester, Lloyds)
RUIZ GALLARDON Y MUNIZ (Madrid, Spain)
PRICE BLANPAIN QUAGHEBEUR MAEYAERT (Brussels)
Number of Firms: 3
Number of Attorneys: 240
Principal Region: England and Continental Europe
Contact(s):
Mr. David Hertzell
Davies Arnold Cooper
6-8 Bouverie Street
London EC4Y 8DD
England
Tel: 44-171-936-2222
Fax: 44-171-936-2020

DEBEVOISE & PLIMPTON (New York)
KLEIN, HOLEC, DOSKOVA & PARTNERS (Prague)
BUSINESS AND LAW (Moscow)
Number of Firms: 3
Number of Attorneys: 350
Principal Region: Eastern Europe and CIS
Contact(s):
Mr. Barry R. Bryan
Debevoise & Plimpton
875 Third Avenue
New York, NY 10022
United States
Tel: 212-909-6000
Fax: 212-909-6836

DELTA EUROPEAN GROUP (EEIG) (Brussels, Germany, Netherlands, United Kingdom)
Number of Firms: 4
Number of Attorney: 64
Principal Region: Europe
Contact(s):
Mr. Patrick Sankey-Barker
Waltons & Morse
Plantation House
31-35 Fenchurch Street
London EC3M 3NN
England
Tel: 44-171-623-4255
Fax: 44-171-626-4153

DENTON INTERNATIONAL GROUP OF LAW FIRMS
DENTON HALL (Beijing, Brussels, Hong Kong, London, Los Angeles, Moscow, Singapore, Tokyo)
HEUKING KÜHN KUNZ WOJTEK (Berlin, Chemnitz, Düsseldorf, Frankfurt, Hamburg, Paris)
HOUTHOFF (Amsterdam, Rotterdam)
LAMBERT GROHMANN KERRES & DEISSENBERGER (Vienna - associated offices: Budapest, Prague, Ljubljana)
LIND & CADOVIUS (Copenhagen)
　Number of Firms: 5
　Number of Attorney: 600
　Principal Region: International
　Contact(s):
　Mr. Henry King
　Denton Hall
　Five Chancery Lane
　Clifford's Inn
　London EC4A 1BU
　England
　Tel: 44-171-242-1212
　Fax: 44-171-404-0087

　Dr. Wolfgang Kühn
　Heuking Kühn Kunz Wojtek
　Elisabethstrasse 16
　40217 Düsseldorf
　Germany
　Tel: 49-211-38-95-01
　Fax: 49-211-37-06-44

　Mr. Peter Hustinx
　Houthoff
　Parnassusweg 126
　1076 AT Amsterdam
　The Netherlands
　Tel: 31-20-570-02-00
　Fax: 31-20-570-02-80

　Mr. Christoph Kerres
　Lambert Grohmann Kerres & Deissenberger
　Laurenzerberg 2
　1010 Vienna
　Austria
　Tel: 43-1-51-550
　Fax: 43-1-51-550-50

　Mr. Frantz Palludan
　Lind & Cadovius
　Ostergade 38
　Postboks 2256
　1019 Copenhagen K
　Denmark
　Tel: 45-33-33-81-00
　Fax: 45-33-33-81-01

DEWEY BALLANTINE (New York)
THEODORE GODDARD (London)
KLEIN GODDARD (Paris)
　Number of Firms: 3
　Number of Attorneys: 600
　Principal Region: U.S./Europe
　(Joint offices: Warsaw/Prague/Budapest)
　Contact(s):
　Mr. Rupert Simpson
　Dewey Ballantine
　1301 Avenue of the Americas
　New York, NY 10019-6092
　United States
　Tel: 212-259-8000
　Fax: 212-259-6333

　Mr. Stuart May
　Theodore Goddard
　150 Aldersgate Street
　London EC1A 4EJ
　England
　Tel: 44-171-606-8855
　Fax: 44-171-606-4390

　Mr. John Sell
　Klein Goddard et Associés
　44, Avenue des Champs-Elysées
　75008 Paris
　France
　Tel: 33-1-495-20-00
　Fax: 33-1-495-30-97

DONOVAN LEISURE NEWTON & IRVINE (New York)
ALSOP WILKINSON (London)
　Number of Firms: 2
　Number of Attorney: 350
　Principal Region: U.S./U.K.
　Mr. J. Peter Coll, Jr.
　Donovan Leisure Newton & Irvine
　30 Rockefeller Plaza
　New York, NY 10112
　United States
　Tel: 212-632-3000
　Fax: 212-632-3315
　Mr. Roger Lane-Smith
　Alsop Wilkinson
　107-112 Leadenhall Street
　London EC3A 4AA
　England
　Tel: 44-171-248-4141
　Fax: 44-171-285-1060

DORSEY & WHITNEY (Minnesota)
AIKINS, MACAULAY & THORVALDSON (Manitoba)
　Number of Firms: 2
　Number of Attorneys:
　Principal Region: U.S./Canada
　Contact(s):
　Thomas O. Moe, Esq.
　Dorsey & Whitney
　220 South Sixth Street
　Minneapolis, MN 55402-1498
　United States
　Tel: 612-340-2600
　Fax: 612-340-2868

EAGLE INTERNATIONAL ASSOCIATES
Number of Firms: 78
Principal Region: International
Contact(s):
Mr. Frederick J. Pagnani, Chairman
707 Westchester Avenue
White Plains, NY 10604
United States
Tel: 914-949-9199
Fax: 914-949-8808

EAST EUROPE LAW, LTD. (Affiliate in Budapest)
BROWNSTEIN ZEIDMAN & LORE (Washington, D.C.)
RUDNICK & WOLFE (Chicago)
MARTIN MENDELSOHN, SOLICITOR (London)
Number of Firms: 3
Number of Attorneys: 392
Principal Region: Eastern Europe
Contact(s):
Mr. Philip F. Zeidman
Brownstein Zeidman & Lore
1401 New York Avenue, N.W.
Suite 900
Washington, DC 20005-2102
United States
Tel: 202-879-5700
Fax: 202-879-5773

ELF--EUROPEAN LAW FIRM (EEIG)
Number of Firms: 12
Number of Attorneys: 130
Principle Region: Europe
Contact(s):
Judith Brown, President of ELF
Lawrence Tucketts
Bush House
72 Prince Street
Bristol BS99 7JZ
England
Tel: 44-1272-29-5295
Fax: 44-1272-29-8313

Paul Wertenbroek
Poelmann Denneman Bruinsma
St. Antoniusstraat 9
Postbox 63
5600 AB Eindhoven
The Netherlands
Tel: 31-0-40-57-07-77
Fax: 31-0-40-57-08-09

EU-LEX INTERNATIONAL PRACTICE GROUP
Number of Firms: 58 - 39 Attorneys; 19 Accountants/Tax Advisors
Number of Attorneys; Accountants; Tax Advisors: 450
Principal Region: Europe
Contact(s):
Mr. Peter Spark
Eu-Lex Int'l Practice Group
Sea Containers House
Blackfriars Bridge
20 Upper Ground
London SE1 9LH
England
Tel: 44-171-620-1311
Fax: 44-171-401-3359

Ms. Ariel Lees-Jones
Eu-Lex Int'l Practice Group
Harvester House
37 Peter Street
Manchester M2 5GB
England
Tel: 44-161-839-9005
Fax: 44-161-839-9006

EURAVOCAT GROUP (EEIG)
Number of Firms: 10
Number of Attorneys:
Principal Region: Europe
Contact(s):
Mr. Chris Owen
Manches & Co.
Aldwych House
81 Aldwych
London WC2B 4RP
England
Tel: 44-171-404-4433
Fax: 44-171-430-1133

EUROADVOCATEN (EEIG)
Number of Firms: 16
Number of Attorneys: 210
Principal Region: Europe
Contact(s):
Mr. Christopher D. Dixon
Fox & Gibbons
2 Old Burlington Street
London W1X 2QA
England
Tel: 44-171-439-8271
Fax: 44-171-734-8843

EURO-AMERICAN LAWYERS GROUP
Number of Firms: 19
Number of Attorneys: 300
Principal Region: Europe/America
Contact(s):
Mr. John C.K. Elliott
Elliott & Company
Centurion House
Deansgate
Manchester M3 3WT
England
Tel: 44-161-834-9933
Fax: 44-161-832-3693

Mr. David C.H. Ross
Biggart Baillie & Gifford, W.S.
Dalmore House
310 St. Vincent Street
Glasgow G2 5QR
Scotland
Tel: 44-141-228-8000
Fax: 44-141-228-8310

EUROJURIS INTERNATIONAL

Number of Firms: 662
Number of Attorneys: 2,970
Principal Region: Europe
Contact(s):
Mr. Laurent Marlière
Avenue Molière, 248
1060 Brussels
Belgium
Tel: 32-2-344-42-76
Fax: 32-2-346-15-96

EURO-LINK FOR LAWYERS

Number of Firms: 97
Number of Attorneys: 2,500
Principal Region: Europe
Contact(s):
Mr. Ian Cooper
Euro-Link For Lawyers
Prospect House
32 Sovereign Street
Leeds LS1 4BJ
England
Tel: 44-1532-422-845
Fax: 44-1532-428-812

EUROPEAN ADVERTISING LAWYERS ASSOCIATION (EEIG)

Number of Firms: 14
Number of Attorneys: 14
Principal Region: International
Contact(s):
Mr. Steven Groom
Lewis Silkin
1 Butler Place
Buckingham Gate
London SW1H OPT
England
Tel: 44-171-222-8191
Fax: 44-171-222-4633

EUROPEAN IMMIGRATION LAWYERS GROUP

Number of Firms: 13
Number of Attorneys: 23
Principal Region: Europe
Contact(s):
Mr. Peter R.M. Wyatt
Gulbenkian Harris Andonian
181 Kensington High Street
Kensington
London W8 6SH
England
Tel: 44-171-937-1542
Fax: 44-171-938-2059

EUROPEAN LAW GROUP

Number of Firms: 10
Number of Attorneys:
Principal Region: Europe
Contact(s):
Mr. Roger Loveland
Penningtons
Royex House
5 Aldermanbury Square
London EC2V 7HD
England
Tel: 44-171-457-3000
Fax: 44-171-457-3240

FAMILY LAW NETWORK

Number of Firms: 400
Number of Attorneys:
Principal Region: National
Contact(s):
Richard Olson, Esq.
200 Spring Street
P.O. Box 1428
Eau Claire, WI 54702
United States
Tel: 1-800-647-8079/(in WI: 1-800-472-6930)
Fax: 715-836-0031

FASKEN MARTINEAU

FASKEN CAMPBELL GODFREY (Toronto)
MARTINEAU WALKER (Montréal and Québec City)
DAVIS & COMPANY (Vancouver - Affiliated)
Number of Firms: 3
Number of Attorneys: 500
Principal Region: Canada and International
Contact(s):
Robert B. Tuer, Q.C.
Fasken Campbell Godfrey
Toronto Dominion Centre
Toronto Dominion Bank Tower
P.O. Box 20
Toronto, Ontario M5K 1N6
Canada
Tel: 416-366-8381
Fax: 416-364-7813

FRASER & BEATTY McMASTER MEIGHEN

Number of Firms: 2
Number of Attorneys: 255
Principal Region: Canada
Contact(s):
Mr. Chris E. Pinnington
Fraser & Beatty
P.O. Box 100
1 First Canadian Place
Toronto, Ontario M5X 1B2
Canada
Tel: 416-863-4511
Fax: 416-863-4592

R. Jamie Plant, Esq.
McMaster Meighen
630 René-Lévesque Blvd. West
7th Floor
Montréal, Québec H3B 4H7
Canada
Tel: 514-879-1212
Fax: 514-878-0605

FRIED FRANK, HARRIS, SHRIVER & JACOBSON (New York)
BURAI-KOVACS, BUKI & PARTNER (Hungary)
  Number of Firms: 2
  Number of Attorneys: 350
  Principal Region: Eastern Europe
  Contact(s):
  Mr. David E. Birenbaum
  Fried Frank, Harris, Shriver & Jacobson
  1001 Pennsylvania Avenue, N.W.
  Suite 800
  Washington, DC 20004-2505
  United States
  Tel: 202-639-7050
  Fax: 202-639-7008

FULBRIGHT & JAWORSKI L.L.P. (Houston)
MILNER FENERTY (Calgary)
  Number of Firms: 2
  Number of Attorneys: 750
  Principal Region: North America
  Contact(s):
  Mr. A.T. Blackshear, Jr.
  Fulbright & Jaworski
  1301 McKinney, Suite 5100
  Houston, TX 77010-3095
  United States
  Tel: 713-651-5151
  Fax: 713-651-5246

GESICA
  Number of Firms: 209
  Number of Attorneys: 1,500
  Principal Region: International
  Contact(s):
  Mr. Richard Brown
  Laytons
  Saint Bartolomews
  Lewins Mead
  Bristol BS1 2NH
  England
  Tel: 44-1272-291-626
  Fax: 44-1272-293-369

GLOBALAW
  Number of Firms: 62
  Number of Attorneys: 1,600
  Principal Region: International
  Contact(s):
  Mr. Dennis Campbell
  Globalaw - The International Law Group
  Hans Sachs Gasse 13
  A-5020 Salzburg
  Austria
  Tel: 66-2-43-52-00
  Fax: 66-2-43-26-28

GLOBALEX
  Number of Firms: 5
  Number of Attorneys: 650
  Principal Region: United States, Europe, Far East
  Contact(s):
  Mr. Ralf Boer
  Foley Lardner
  Firstar Center
  777 East Wisconsin Avenue
  Milwaukee, WI 53202-5367
  United States
  Tel: 414-271-2400
  Fax: 414-289-3791

  Mr. Michael Johns
  Nicholson Graham & Jones
  25-31 Moorgate
  London EC2R 6AR
  England
  Tel: 44-171-628-9151
  Fax: 44-171-638-3102

GOODMAN LAPOINTE FERGUSON
GOODMAN AND CARR (Toronto)
LAPOINTE ROSENSTEIN (Montréal)
FERGUSON GIFFORD (Vancouver)
  Number of Firms: 3
  Number of Attorneys: 175
  Principal Region: Canada and International
  Contacts:
  Mr. Murray J. Perelman
  Goodman and Carr
  200 King Street West, Suite 2300
  Toronto, Ontario M5H 3W5
  Canada
  Tel: 416-595-2300
  Fax: 416-595-0567

  Alex S. Konigsberg, Q.C.
  Lapointe Rosenstein
  1010 Sherbrooke Street West
  Suite 1100
  Montréal, Québec H3A 2R7
  Canada
  Tel: 514-844-6392
  Fax: 514-288-7390

  Mr. Martin N. Gifford
  Ferguson Gifford
  666 Burrard Street
  Suite 500, Park Place
  Vancouver, British Columbia V6C 3H3
  Canada
  Tel: 604-687-3216
  Fax: 604-683-2780

GOODMAN PHILLIPS & VINEBERG (Canada)
PHILLIPS & VINEBERG (Montréal)
GOODMAN & GOODMAN (Toronto)
Number of Firms: 2
Number of Attorneys: 175
Principal Region: National and International
Contacts:
Mr. Charles J. Schwartz
Goodman & Goodman
Box 24, Suite 2400
250 Yonge Street
Toronto, Ontario M5B 2M6
Canada
Tel: 416-979-2211
Fax: 416-979-1234

Mr. Douglas C. Robertson
Phillips & Vineberg
5 Place Ville Marie, 17th Floor
Montréal, Québec H3B 2G2
Canada
Tel: 514-866-8541
Fax: 514-875-0344

GRAHAM & JAMES (California, Washington D.C.)
DEACONS (Hong Kong)
THE LAW FIRM OF SALAH AL-HEJAILAN (Saudi Arabia)
TAYLOR JOYNSON GARRETT (London)
HANAFIAH SOEHARTO PONGGAWA (Indonesia)
SLY & WEIGALL (Australia)
HAARMANN HEMMELRATH & PARTNER (Munich)
LAW OFFICES OF MISHARE M. AL-GHAZALI (Kuwait)
GALLASTEGUI Y LOZANO (Mexico City)
Number of Firms: 9
Number of Attorneys: 1,125
Principal Region: International
Contact(s):
Mr. J. Michael Cavanaugh
Graham & James
2000 M Street, N.W., Suite 700
Washington, D.C. 20036-3307
United States
Tel: 202-463-0800
Fax: 202-463-0823

GREAT LAKES LAW
WALTER & HAVERFIELD (Cleveland)
FOSTER, SWIFT, COLLINS & SMITH (Lansing, Detroit)
VON BRIESEN & PURTELL (Milwaukee)
WILSON & McILVAINE (Chicago)
MACKALL, CROUNSE & MOORE (Minneapolis)
SOMMER & BARNARD (Indianapolis)
NELLIGAN & POWER (Ottawa)
SHIBLEY RIGHTON (Toronto)
HARTER, SECREST & EMERY (Rochester, Syracuse, Albany)
TUCKER ARENSBERG (Pittsburgh)
DE GRANDPRÉ, GODIN (Montréal)
Number of Firms: 11
Number of Attorneys: 600
Principal Region: U.S./Canada
Contact(s):
Mr. Michael T. McMenamin
Walter & Haverfield
1300 Terminal Tower
Cleveland, OH 44113-2253
United States
Tel: 216-781-1212
Fax: 216-575-0911

Mr. William K. Fahey
Foster, Swift, Collins & Smith
313 South Washington Square
Lansing, MI 48933-2193
United States
Tel: 517-371-8100
Fax: 517-371-8200

Mr. Steven Campbell
Nelligan & Power
Suite 1900
66 Slater
Ottawa, Ontario K1P 5H1
Canada
Tel: 613-238-8080
Fax: 613-238-2098

GRUPO LEGAL PORTUGUES
SIMMONS & SIMMONS (London, Paris, Brussels, Lisbon,Milan, Abu Dhabi, Hong Kong, New York,)
J & A GARRIGUES (Spain)
PINHEIRO NETO & CO. (Brazil)
F. CASTELLO BRANCO, NOBRE GUEDES & P. REBELO DE SOUSA (Portugal)
Number of Firms: 4
Number of Attorneys: 724
Principal Region: Europe/Brazil
Contact(s):
Mr. P.A. de Chazal
Simmons & Simmons
21 Wilson Street
London EC2M 2TQ
England
Tel: 44-171-628-2020
Fax: 44-171-628-2070

HOLMAN DARVALL DURACK GROUP (Australia)
DARVALL McCUTCHEON (Melbourne)
HOLMAN WEBB (Sydney)
DWYER DURACK (Perth)
HOLMANS (Brisbane)
Number of Firms: 4
Number of Attorneys: 200
Principal Region: Australia
Contact(s):
Mr. Campbell Paine
Darvall McCutcheon
Level 32, Nauru House
80 Collins Street
Melbourne, Victoria 3000
Australia
Tel: 61-3-654-4466
Fax: 61-3-654-1793

IAG INTERNATIONAL (Integrated Advisory Group International)
Number of Firms: 46 (law, tax, audit & accounting)
Number of Professionals: 1,000
Principal Region: Europe, Scandinavia, North America
Contact(s):
<u>Chairman</u>:
Dr. Hans Rudolf Staiger
Staiger Schwald & Sauter
Postfach 7234
CH-8023 Zurich
Switzerland
Tel: 41-1-211-71-87
Fax: 41-1-221-18-62

Secretary:
Mr. Lance R. Blackstone
Blackstone Franks & Co.
Barbican House
26 Old Street
London EC1V 9HL
England
Tel: 44-171-250-3300
Fax: 44-171-250-1402

Ms. Catherine F. Wollaston
Wollastons
Brierly Place
New London Road
Chelmsford, Essex CM2 0AP
England
Tel: 44-1245-265-222
Fax: 44-1245-354-764

IGL (International Grouping of Lawyers)
Number of Firms: 50
Number of Attorneys: 390
Principal Region: Worldwide
Contact(s):
Secretary:
Mr. Pietro Cavasola
Studio Legale Cavasola - Assoc. Prof.
Via Depretis 86
00184 Rome
Italy
Tel: 39-6-488-15-16
Fax: 39-6-483-755

IMMLAW (National Consortium of Immigration Law Firms)
Number of Firms: 14
Number of Attorneys: 43
Principal Region: United States
Contact(s):
Mr. Allen E. Kaye, Esq.
Law Offices of Allen E. Kaye, P.C.
11 Park Place
New York, NY 10007
United States
Tel: 212-964-5858
Fax: 212-608-3734

James J. Orlow, Esq.
Orlow & Orlow, P.C.
1154 Public Ledger Building
600 Chestnut Street
Philadelphia, PA 19106
United States
Tel: 215-922-1183
Fax: 215-922-0516

INFORMATION CLUB
Number of Firms: 14
Number of Attorneys: 700
Principal Region: Europe
Contact(s):
Anthony Driessen, Esq.
Nauta Dutilh
Fellenoord 19
P.O. Box 6019
5600 HA Eindhoven
The Netherlands
Tel: 31-40-656-500
Fax: 31-10-461-375

INFORMATION TECHNOLOGY LAW GROUP/EUROPE
Number of Firms: 16
Principal Region: Europe
Contact(s):
Ranald Robertson, Esq.
Field Fisher Waterhouse
41 Vine Street
London EC3N 2AA
England
Tel: 441-171-481-4841
Fax: 441-171-488-0084

Dr. Jochen Pagenberg
Bardehle Pagenberg Dost Altenburg Frohwitter
Geissler & Partners
Galileiplatz I
8000 Munich 80
Germany
Tel: 49-89-92-80-50
Fax: 49-89-98-97-63

INSUROLAW
Number of Firms: 14
Number of Attorneys: 350+
Principal Region: Europe
Contact(s):
Mr. Christopher Blythe
Wansbroughs Willey Hargrave
Suite 670
One Lime Street
Lloyd's of London
London EC3M 7DQ
England
Tel: 44-171-497-3262
Fax: 44-171-497-1210

INTERACT EUROPE
Number of Firms: 9
Number of Attorneys:
Principal Region: Europe
Contact(s):
Mr. R.S. Aird
Pitmans
47 Castle Street
Reading, Berks RG1 7SR
England
Tel: 44-1734-580-224
Fax: 44-1734-585-097

INTERCOUNSEL

Number of Firms:
Number of Attorneys:
Principal Region:
Contact(s):
Peter A. Gelles, Esq.
Gelles & Lawrence
2049 Century Park East, S. 3350
Los Angeles, CA 90067
United States
Tel: 310-277-2222
Fax: 310-552-3269

INTERJURA CONSULTANCY SERVICES, LTD.

Number of Firms: 12
Number of Attorneys: 2,000
Principal Region: China
Contact(s):
Mr. Ronald E. Bornstein
Thelen, Marrin, Johnson & Bridges
Two Embarcadero Center
San Francisco, CA 94111-3995
United States
Tel: 415-392-6320
Fax: 415-421-1068

INTERLAW

Number of Firms: 46
Number of Attorneys: 2,500
Principal Region: International
Contact(s):
Americas
Mr. Jerry L. Metcalf, Chairman
Brown, Parker & Leahy, L.L.P.
1200 Smith Street, Suite 3600
Houston, TX 77002
United States
Tel: 713-654-8111
Fax: 713-654-1871

Asia/Pacific
Mr. Garry F.S. Boyce, Vice-Chairman
Hunt & Hunt
Gateway, Level 15
1 Macquarie Place
Sydney, New South Wales 2000
Australia
Tel: 61-2-391-3000
Fax: 61-2-391-3099

Europe
Mr. Peter Wahlin, Vice-Chairman
Advokatfirman Wahlin
Vastra Hamngatan 5
P.O. Box 2240
S-403 14 Goteborg
Sweden
Tel: 46-31-10-17-10
Fax: 46-31-11-11-23

INTERLEGES

Number of Firms: 19
Number of Attorneys: 130
Principal Region: Eastern & Western Europe, North America
Contact(s):
Mr. Philip D. Beck
Fryoman Beck King & Arad
750 Lexington
New York, NY 10022
United States
Tel: 212-319-0800
Fax: 212-750-0101

THE INTERLEX GROUP

Number of Firms: 29, 2 United States
Number of Attorneys: 2,500
Principal Region: International
Contact(s):
Mr. Philip Newhouse
Taylor Joynson Garrett
Carmelite
50 Victoria Embankment
Blackfriars
London EC4Y ODX
England
Tel: 44-171-353-1234
Fax: 44-171-936-2666

Mr. Lawrence B. Swibel
Hopkins & Sutter
Three First National Plaza
Chicago, IL 60602
United States
Tel: 312-558-6600
Fax: 312-558-6538

INTERNATIONAL ATTORNEYS CLUB

Number of Firms: 22
Number of Attorneys: 500
Principal Region: International
Contact(s):
Dr. Edgar von Schmidt-Pauli, Secretary
International Attorneys Club
Thiemestrasse 3
80802 Munich
Germany
Tel: 49-89-331-779
Fax: 49-89-341-322

INTERNATIONAL LAWYERS NETWORK

Number of Firms: 56
Number of Attorneys: 1000
Principal Region: Worldwide
Contact(s):
Number of Firms: 56
Number of Attorneys: 1000
Principal Region: Worldwide
Contact(s):
Mr. Lowell S. Lifschultz
Epstein Becker & Green
250 Park Avenue
New York, NY 10177
United States
Tel: 212-351-4500
Fax: 212-661-0989

THE INTERNATIONAL SOCIETY OF PRIMERUS LAW FIRMS
Number of Firms: 34
Number of Attorneys: 265
Principal Region: United States
Contact(s):
Mr. Scott Roland
600 Frey Building N.E.
Grand Rapids, MI 49503
United States
Tel: 1-800-968-2211
Fax: 616-458-0608

INTERNATIONAL WOMEN'S AVIATION LAWYERS GROUP
Number of Firms: 80
Number of Attorneys: 90
Principal Region: International
Contact(s):
Ms. Mia Wouters
Lafili & Van Crombrugghe
Vossendreef 6
Drève des Renards, 6
1180 Brussels
Belgium
Tel: 32-2-374-92-00
Fax: 32-2-375-45-25

INTERSERVE
Number of Firms: 10
Number of Professionals: 75
Principal Region: International
Contact(s):
Stephen E. Handel, Esq.
Attorney at Law
1021 Main Street, Suite 1100
Houston, TX 77002-6501
United States
Tel: 713-652-2828
Fax: 713-652-2424

JCS GROUP
EVERSHEDS (Birmingham, Bristol, Cardiff, Derby, Ipswich, London, Manchester, Middlesbrough, Newcastle-upon-Tyne, Norwich, Nottingham; Berlin, Brussels, Jersey)
CHAINTRIER CAILLARD & ASSOCIES (Paris)
SCHMIDT, VON DER OSTEN & HUBER (Essen, Berlin)
VAN WIJMEN & KOEDAM (Rotterdam, Breda)
Number of Firms: 4
Number of Attorneys: 1,000
Principal Region: Europe
Contact(s):
Mr. Peter Cole
Eversheds
Senator House
85 Queen Victoria Street
London EC4V 4JL
England
Tel: 44-171-919-4500
Fax: 44-171-919-4919

KAVER & MAILÄNDER (Stuttgart)
LEBOEUF, LAMB, GREENE & MCCRAE, L.L.P. (New York)
KUBIAK LUCOWICZ ZIELINSKI (Warsaw)
Number of Firms: 3
Number of Attorneys: 500
Principal Region: International
Contact(s):
Mr. Donald J. Greene
Leboeuf, Lamb, Greene & McCrae, L.L.P.
125 West 55th Street
New York, NY 10019
United States
Tel: 212-424-8000
Fax: 212-424-8500

LABNET (Labor Attorneys for Business Network)
BRITTAIN SLEDZ MORRIS & SLOVAK (Chicago)
BULLARD KORSHOJ SMITH & JERNSTEDT (Portland)
CLARK PAUL HOOVER & MALLARD (Atlanta)
COLEMAN COXSON PENELLO FOGLEMAN & COWEN (Washington)
CORBETT & KANE (San Francisco)
FOSTER HELLER & KILGORE (San Antonio)
McKNIGHT HUDSON LEWIS & HENDERSON (Memphis)
MILLISOR & NOBIL (Cleveland)
REXON FREEDMAN KLEPETAR & HAMBLETON (Los Angeles)
SKOLER ABBOTT & PRESSER, P.C. (Springfield)
STETTNER MILLER & COHN, P.C. (Denver)
Number of Firms: 11
Number of Attorneys: 136
Principal Region: United States
Contact(s):
Mr. Fletcher L. Hudson
Chairman - LABNET
6750 Poplar Avenue, Suite 301
P.O. Box 171375
Memphis, TN 38187-1375
United States
Tel: 901-756-1550
Fax: 901-756-1016

LAW EUROPE (EEIG)
Number of Firms: 12
Number of Attorneys: 150
Principal Region: Europe
Contact(s):
Mr. Yves Tavernier
Tavernier & Coppens
Lange Violettenstraat 293
9000 Ghent
Belgium
Tel: 32-9-225-52-17
Fax: 32-9-223-45-70

Mr. Quintin Barry
Donne Mileham & Haddock
42-46 Frederick Place
Brighton, East Sussex BN1 1AT
England
Tel: 44-1273-329-833
Fax: 44-1273-202-105

LAWLINK
Number of Firms: 17
Number of Attorneys: 250
Principal Region: New Zealand
Contact(s):
Ms. Lynda Hagen
Lawlink
P.O. Box 10-018
Level 1, 99 Boulcott Street
Wellington
New Zealand
Tel: 64-4-473-48-36
Fax: 64-4-473-46-84

LAWNET
Number of Firms: 78
Number of Attorneys: 1268
Principal Region: United Kingdom, Republic of Ireland, and the Channel Islands
Contact(s):
Mr. Simon Maddox
LawNet Europe
23 Jury Street
Warwick CV34 4EH
England
Tel: 44-1926-419-991
Fax: 44-1926-419-114

LAW OFFICES OF JAMES SOKOLOVE & AFFILATES
Number of Firms: 19
Number of Attorneys: 75
Principal Region: New England
Contact(s):
Ms. Fran Senner-Hurley
Law Offices of James Sokolove
One Boston Place, Suite 1260
Boston, MA 02108
United States
Tel: 617-742-0696
Fax: 617-742-5417

LAWRENCE GRAHAM (London)
ROSENMAN & COLIN (New York)
Number of Firms: 2
Number of Attorneys: 400
Principal Region: Europe and U.S.
Contact(s):
Mr. Michael Richardson
Lawrence Graham
190 Strand
London WC2R 1JN
England
Tel: 44-171-379-0000
Fax: 44-171-379-6854

Mr. Howard Rothman
Rosenman & Colin
575 Madison Avenue
New York, NY 10022-2585
United States
Tel: 212-940-8800
Fax: 212-940-8776

LAWROPE
Number of Firms: 9
Number of Attorneys: 100
Principal Region: Europe
Contact(s):
Ms. Isobel Evans
Harris Rosenblatt & Kramer
26-28 Bedford Row
London WC1R 4HE
England
Tel: 44-171-242-3254
Fax: 44-171-831-7475

LAW SOUTH
Number of Firms: 10
Number of Attorneys: 379
Principal Region: Southeast England
Contact(s):
Mrs. Christina Myers, Administrator
117B Guildford Street
Chertsey, Surrey KT16 9AF
England
Tel: 44-1932-560-902
Fax: 44-1932-571-250

LAWSPAN INTERNATIONAL (EEIG)
Number of Firms: 14
Number of Attorneys: 100
Principal Region: International
Contact(s):
Ms. Anna McKay
Roiter Zucker
5 Broadhurst Gardens
London NW6 3QX
England
Tel: 44-171-328-9111
Fax: 44-171-372-5858

LAWYERS ASSOCIATED WORLDWIDE (L.A.W.)
Number of Firms: 36
Number of Attorneys: 400
Principal Region: International
Contact(s):
Mr. James G. McPherson
Carson, Gross & McPherson
401 Bay Street, Suite 1400
Toronto, Ontario M5H 2Y4
Canada
Tel: 416-361-0900
Fax: 416-361-3459

LEGALINK
Number of Firms: 8
Number of Attorneys: 220
Principal Region: Europe
Contact(s):
Jorgen Hammarstrom, Esq.
Attorney's House
ANPR Stenback Street
Stenbackinkatu 26
00250 Helsinki
Finland
Tel: 358-0-04-74-21
Fax: 358-0-474-22-22

LEGALLIANCE (EEIG)
Number of Firms: 8
Number of Attorneys: 220
Principal Region: Europe
Contact(s):
Mr. Henri Ader
Ader, Jolibois & Associés
26, Boulevard Raspail
75007 Paris
France
Tel: 33-1-45-44-10-33
Fax: 33-1-45-48-80-27

LEGAL NETWORK INTERNATIONAL
Number of Firms: 34
Number of Attorneys: 2,600
Principal Region: International
Contact(s):
Marshall N. Margolis, Esq.
Steering Committee Chairman
Morris, Rose, Ledgett
BCE Place, Canada Trust Tower
161 Bay Street, Suite 2700
Toronto, Ontario M5J 2S1
Canada
Tel: 416-863-1600
Fax: 416-863-9500

Theodore Margolis, Esq.
Steering Committee - U.S.
Hannoch Weisman
4 Becker Farm Road
Roseland, New Jersey 07068-3788
United States
PO Box Address: P.O. Box 1040
Newark, New Jersey 07101-9819
United States
Tel: 201-535-5300
Fax: 201-994-7198

LEGAL RESOURCES GROUP
ALSOP WILKINSON (London, Liverpool, Manchester, Hong Kong)
DICKINSON DEES (Newcastle-Upon-Tyne)
McGRIGOR DONALD (Glasgow, Edinburgh, London)
OSBORNE CLARKE (Bristol, London, Paris, Copenhagen, Frankfurt)
PINSENT & COMPANY (Birmingham, London)
SIMPSON CURTIS (Leeds, London)
Number of Firms: 6
Number of Attorneys: 887
Principal Region: Europe
Contact(s):
Peter G. Condon, Esq.
Legal Resources Group
42 Bull Street
Birmingham B4 6AF
United Kingdom
Tel: 44-121-233-0151
Fax: 44-121-233-0048

LEWIS D'AMATO BRISBOIS & BISGAARD (California)
BUXBAUM AND CHOY (China)
Number of Firms: 2
Number of Attorneys: 275
Principal Region: International
Contact(s):
Mr. Christopher P. Bisgaard
Lewis D'Amato Brisbois & Bisgaard
Suite 1200
221 North Figueroa Street
Los Angeles, CA 90012
United States
Tel: 213-250-1800
Fax: 213-250-7900

LEX AFRICA
ARMSTRONGS (Botswana)
KAPLAN & STRATTON (Kenya)
WEBBER NEWDIGATE & CO. (Lesotho)
LORENTZ & BONE (Namibia)
WERKSMANS (South Africa)
ROBINSON BERTRAM & CO. (Swaziland)
SCANLEN & HOLDERNESS (Zimbabwe)
Number of Firms: 7
Number of Attorneys: 79
Principal Region: Africa
Contact(s):
Charles Butler, Esq.
Werksmans Attorneys
P.O. Box 927
Johannesburg 2000
Republic of South Africa
Tel: 27-11-488-0000
Fax: 27-11-484-3100/3200

LEX MUNDI
Number of Firms: 122
Number of Attorneys: 8,000+
Principal Region: Global
Nature of Association: Association of independent law firms who are not in a relationship for the joint practice of law.
Contact(s):
Mr. Stephen J. McGarry
1800 West Loop South
Suite 1880
Houston, TX 77027
United States
Tel: 713-626-9393
Fax: 713-666-4462

LIBRALEX
Number of Firms: 15
Number of Attorneys: 150
Principal Region: Europe
Contact(s):
Me. Bernard Cahen
Bernard Cahen & Associés
51, Avenue Raymond Poincaré
75116 Paris
France
Tel: 33-1-45-53-44-55
Fax: 33-1-45-53-58-23

Mr. Jean Bornet
Bornet & Associés
79, Avenue Winston Churchill
Laan B25
1180 Brussels
Belgium
Tel: 32-2-347-18-40
Fax: 32-2-347-10-92

LITOW, CUTLER , ZABLUDOWSKI & ALLEN (Miami)
ALAIN JAKUBOWICZ (Lyon)
Number of Firms: 2
Number of Attorneys: 30
Principal Region: U.S.
France
Contact(s):
Lawrence Litow, Esq.
Litow, Cutler, Zabludowski & Allen
One Biscayne Tower
Suite 3100
2 South Biscayne Boulevard
Miami, FL 33131
United States
Tel: 305-381-8400
Fax: 305-381-7910

LLR - European Tax Network
LOYENS - LEFEBVRE - RADLER
Number of Firms: 3
Number of Attorneys: 900
Principal Region: Belgium, France, Germany, Luxembourg, The Netherlands
Contact(s):
Mr. Wouter M. van Dalen
Loyens & Volkmaars
325 Weena
P.O. Box 2888
3000 CW Rotterdam
The Netherlands
Tel: 31-10-224-6224
Fax: 31-10-412-5839

Mr. Robert Baconnier
Bureau Francis Lefebvre
3, villa Emile Bergerat
92522 Neuilly-sur-Seine Cedex
France
Tel: 33-1-47-38-55-00
Fax: 33-1-47-38-55-55

Mr. A. Rädler
Oppenhoff, Rädler
Prinzeregentenplatz 10
8000 Munchen 80
Germany
Tel: 49-89-41-80-80
Fax: 49-89-41-80-81-00

LOEFF CLAEYS VERBEKE (Netherlands, Belgium, Luxembourg
BALANA Y EGUIA (Spain)
ALI BUDIARDJO, NUGROHO, REKSODIPUTRO (Indonesia)
Number of Firms: 3
Number of Attorneys: 350
Principal Region: International
Contact(s):
Mr. Jacques Steenbergen
Loeff Claeys Verbeke
Avenue de Tervueren, 268A
1150 Brussels
Belgium
Tel: 32-2-778-22-11
Fax: 32-2-762-68-89

LOGOS
Number of Firms: 13
Number of Attorneys: 215
Principal Region: Europe
Contact(s):
Mr. Hugh Johnson
Biddle & Co.
1 Gresham Street
London EC2V 7BU
England
Tel: 44-171-606-9301
Fax: 44-171-606-3305

MACINTYRE STRÄTER INTERNATIONAL LIMITED
Number of Firms: 24
Number of Attorneys: 329
Principal Region: International
Contact(s):
Mr. Guy A. Rigby/Mr. Charles J.B. Hornor
MacIntyre Sträter International
28 Ely Place
London EC1N 6RL
England
Tel: 44-171-242-0242
Fax: 44-171-405-4786

Mr. James M. Barton
Cummings & Lockwood
Ten Stamford Forum
P.O. Box 120
Stamford, CT 06904
United States
Tel: 203-351-4512
Fax: 203-351-4499

MACKRELL INTERNATIONAL
Number of Firms: 52
Number of Attorneys: 1,500+
Principal Region: International
Contact(s):
Mr. Michael Slorick
Mr. Paul Morgan
Ms. Caroline Smurthwaite
Mackrell International, Secretariat
Dukes Court, Duke Street
Woking, Surrey GU21 5BH
England
Tel: 44-1483-755-609
Fax: 44-1483-755-818

MALLESONS STEPHEN JAQUES (Australia)
KARTINI MULJADI S.H. & ASSOCIATES (Indonesia)
BATESON STARR (Hong Kong)
  Number of Firms: 4
  Number of Attorneys: 600
  Principal Region: Asia Pacific
  Contact(s):
  Mr. Tony D'Aloisio
  Mallesons Stephen Jaques
  Governor Phillip Tower
  1 Farrer Place
  Sydney, New South Wales 2000
  Australia
  Tel: 61-2-250-3000
  Fax: 61-2-250-3133

  Mallesons Stephen Jaques
  Rialto
  525 Collins Street
  Melbourne, Victoria 3000
  Australia
  Tel: 61-3-619-0619
  Fax: 61-3-614-1329

MARKS & MURASE INTERNATIONAL NETWORK
  Number of Firms: 30
  Number of Attorneys: 500
  Principal Region: International
  Contact(s):
  Mr. Martin J. Murphy
  Marks & Murase
  399 Park Avenue
  New York, NY 10022-4689
  United States
  Tel: 212-318-7700
  Fax: 212-752-5378

McCUTCHEN DOYLE BROWN & ENERSEN (California)
NOPADOL & KHAISRI (Bangkok)
  Number of Firms: 1
  Number of Attorneys: 240
  Principal Region: Pacific
  Contact(s):
  Mr. David R. Andrews
  McCutchen Doyle Brown & Enersen
  Three Embarcadero Center
  San Francisco, CA 94111
  United States
  Tel: 415-393-2000
  Fax: 415-393-2286

McDERMOTT, WILL & EMERY
ASSOCIATED (INDEPENDENT) OFFICES
BUFETE MULLERAT & ROCA (Barcelona, Lisbon, Madrid)
UETTWILLER GRELON LIPPENS DEKEYSER (Brussels)
UETWILLER GRELON GOUT CANAT & ASSOCIES (Paris)
PAISNER & CO. (London)
  Number of Firms: 7
  Number of Attorneys: 520
  Principal Region: International
  Contact(s):
  Mr. Lawrence Gerber
  McDermott, Will & Emery
  227 West Monroe Street
  Chicago, IL 60606-5096
  United States
  Tel: 312-372-2000
  Fax: 312-984-3679

McKENNA & CO. (London, Brussels, Budapest, Prague, Hong Kong, Tokyo)
MINTER ELLISON MORRIS FLETCHER (Australia)
SIGLE LOOSE SCHMIDT-DIEMITZ & PARTNERS (Germany)
  Number of Firms: 3
  Number of Attorneys:
  Principal Region: International
  Contact(s):
  Richard Taylor, Esq.
  McKenna & Co.
  Mitre House
  160 Aldersgate Street
  London EC1A 4DD
  England
  Tel: 44-171-606-9000
  Fax: 44-171-606-9100

  David Renton, Esq.
  Richard Earl, Esq.
  McKenna & Co.
  36th Floor Gloucester Tower
  11 Pedder Street
  Central
  Hong Kong
  Tel: 852-846-9100
  Fax: 852-845-3575

MINTER ELLISON MORRIS FLETCHER (Melbourne, Sydney, Brisbane, Gold Coast, Canberra, London, Hong Kong, Beijing)
MINTER ELLISON BAKER O'LOUGHLIN (Adelaide)
RUDD WATTS & STONE (New Zealand)
KHATTAR WONG & PARTNERS (Singapore)
MINTER ELLISON NORTHMORE HALE (Western Australia)
MAKARIM & TAIRA S (Indonesia)
  Number of Firms: 6
  Number of Attorneys: 800
  Principal Region: Pacific
  Contact(s):
  Mr. Robert J. Stewart
  Minter Ellison Morris Fletcher
  40 Market Street
  Melbourne, Victoria 3000
  Australia
  Tel: 61-3-617-4617
  Fax: 61-3-617-4666

MULTILAW
  Number of Firms: 30
  Number of Attorneys: 1500
  Principal Region: International
  Contact(s):
  Ms. Fiona Fairbairn
  Multilaw
  64 Queen Street
  London EC4R 1AD
  England
  Tel: 44-171-410-9269
  Fax: 44-171-410-9270

NATIONAL LAW NETWORK
Number of Firms: 90
Number of Attorneys: 9,528
Principal Region: United States
Contact(s):
Mr. F. Nicholas Imperato
National Law Network
112 Long Road
King of Prussia, PA 19406-3030
United States
Tel: 610-337-3880
Fax: 610-337-4614

NATIONAL NETWORK OF ESTATE PLANNING ATTORNEYS
Number of Firms: 400
Number of Attorneys: 600
Principal Region: National
Contact(s):
Mr. Edward M. (Ted) Lee
410 17th Street
Suite 1260
Denver, CO 80202
United States
Tel: 303-446-6100
       800-638-8681
Fax: 303-446-6060

NETWORK 92
Number of Firms: 14
Number of Attorneys:
Principal Region: Europe
Contact(s):
Mr. Jonathan Sheril
Saunders Sobell Leigh & Dobin
20 Red Lion Street
London WC1R 4AE
England
Tel: 44-171-242-2525
Fax: 44-171-405-4202

THE NETWORK
Number of Firms: 8
Number of Attorneys: 2,500
Principal Region: International
Contact(s):
Mr. Julian D. Nihill
Gardere & Wynne
1601 Elm Street, Suite 3000
Dallas, TX 75201
United States
Tel: 214-979-4500
Fax: 214-949-4967

NORTH SEA GROUP OF LAWYERS
Number of Firms: 9
Number of Attorneys:
Principal Region:
Contact(s):
Mr. John Winn
Birkett Westhorp & Long
20-32 Museum Street
Ipswich, Suffolk IP1 1HZ
England
Tel: 44-1473-232-300
Fax: 44-1473-230-524

NORTON ROSE
JOHNSON STOKES & MASTER
Number of Firms: 2
Number of Attorneys: 604
Principal Region: International
Contact(s):
Mr. Roger Birkby
Norton Rose
Kempson House
P.O. Box 570
Camomile Street
London EC3A 7AN
England
Tel: 44-171-283-6000
Fax: 44-171-283-6500

NORTON ROSE
LEE & LEE
Number of Firms: 2
Number of Attorneys: 526
Principal Region: International
Contact(s):
Mr. Roger Birkby
Norton Rose
Kempson House
P.O. Box 570
Camomile Street
London EC3A 7AN
England
Tel: 44-171-283-6000
Fax: 44-171-283-6500

NORTON ROSE M5 GROUP LIMITED
Number of Firms: 7
Number of Attorneys: 1,388
Principal Region: International
Contact(s):
Mr. Roger Birkby
Norton Rose
Kempson House
P.O. Box 570
Camomile Street
London EC3A 7AN
England
Tel: 44-171-283-6000
Fax: 44-171-283-6500

O'MELVENY & MYERS (Los Angeles, New York)
NORR, STIEFENHOFER & LUTZ (Germany, East Europe)
Number of Firms: 2
Number of Attorneys: 625
Principal Region: Europe
Contact(s):
Mr. C. Douglas Kranwinkle
Mr. Ko-Yung Tung
Mr. Ulrich Wagner
O'Melveny & Myers
Citicorp Center
153 East 53rd Street
New York, NY 10022-4611
United States
Tel: 212-326-2000
Fax: 212-326-2061

OMNI JURIS CONSULTANTS (EEIG)
Number of Firms: 31
Number of Attorneys: 125 Partners
Principal Region: Europe
Contact(s):
Bâtonnier Alain de la Bretesche
Omni Juris Consultants
10, rue de la Pépinière
75008 Paris
France
Tel: 33-1-42-93-12-31
Fax: 33-1-42-93-12-21

Mr. Simon Guest
Mrs. Janice H. Webster
Bell & Scott, W.S.
16 Hill Street
Edinburgh EH2 3LD
Scotland
Tel: 44-131-226-6703
Fax: 44-131-226-7602

OSLER RENAULT
OSLER, HOSKIN & HARCOURT (Toronto)
OGILVY RENAULT (Montréal)
Number of Firms: 2
Number of Attorneys: 366
Principal Region: International
Contact(s):
Mr. David W. Drinkwater
Osler Renault
20 Little Britain
London EC1A 7DH
England
Tel: 44-171-606-0777
Fax: 44-171-606-0222

PACIFIC RIM ADVISORY COUNCIL
Number of Firms: 24
Number of Attorneys: 3,000
Principal Region: Pacific
Contact(s):
Mr. Andres G. Gatmaitan
Chairman, Pacific Rim Advisory Council
SyCip Salazar Hernandez & Gatmaitan
105 Paseo de Roxas Makati
1200 Makati, Metro Manila
Phillipines
Tel: 63-2-817-9811
Fax: 63-2-818-7592

Mr. George H. Link
Former Chairman, Pacific Rim Advisory Council
Brobeck, Phleger & Harrison
550 South Hope Street
Los Angeles, CA 90071
United States
Tel: 213-489-4060
Fax: 213-745-3345

PALS (Private Association of Lawyers in Europe)
Number of Firms: 17
Number of Attorneys:
Principal Region: Europe
Contact(s):
Mr. Stuart M. Duncan
Stoneham Langton & Passmore
8 Bolton Street, Piccadilly
London W1Y 8AU
England
Tel: 44-171-499-8000
Fax: 44-171-629-4460

PANNONE LAW GROUP (EEIG)
PANNONE PRITCHARD ENGLEFIELD AND PANNONE & PARTNERS (England)
SPREAFICO MARSAGLIA (Italy)
CHANEY CONNOR LEMETAIS and GROUPE LEXEL (France)
BUFETE PINTO RUIZ and BUFETE HERNANDEZ GIL (Spain)
COELHO RIBEIRO E ASSOCIADOS (Portugal)
GUNNAR LINDS ADVOKATBYRA HB (Sweden)
MAS & GRAU (Andorra)
CABINET DANIEL TONDREAU (Brussels)
CANONICA CLOSTRE ET ASSOCIÉS (Geneva)
Number of Firms: 11
Number of Attorneys: 315
Principal Region: Europe
Contact(s):
Mr. Malcolm C. Keogh
Pannone Pritchard Englefield
14 New Street
London EC2M 4TR
England
Tel: 44-171-972-9720
Fax: 44-171-972-9723

THE PARLEX GROUP OF EUROPEAN LAWYERS
Number of Firms: 19
Number of Attorneys: 150
Principal Region: Europe
Contact(s):
Mr. John Trotter
Bates Wells & Braithwaite
61 Charterhouse Street
London EC1M 6HA
England
Tel: 44-171-251-1122
Fax: 44-171-251-2061

PERKINS COIE (USA, Hong Kong, London, Taipei)
RUSSELL & DUMOULIN (Canada)
Number of Firms: 2
Number of Attorneys: 450
Principal Region: International
Contact(s):
J. Shan Mullin, Esq.
Perkins Coie
1201 Third Avenue, 40th Floor
Seattle, WA 98101-3099
United States
Tel: 206-583-8561
Fax: 206-583-8500

Henri C. Alvarez, Esq.
Russell & DuMoulin
2100-1075 West Georgia Street
Vancouver, British Columbia V6E 3G2
Canada
Tel: 604-631-3129
Fax: 604-631-3232

PHILLIPS FOX
PHILLIPS FOX (Australia, New Zealand, Vietnam)
HENAOS (New Guinea)
  Number of Firms: 2
  Number of Attorneys: 400
  Principal Region: Australia, New Zealand
  Contact(s):
  Mr. Warwick Caisley
  Phillips Fox
  255 Elizabeth Street
  Sydney, New South Wales 2000
  Australia
  Tel: 61-2-286-8000
  Fax: 61-2-283-4144

  Mr. Campbell Paine
  Phillips Fox
  120 Collins Street
  Melbourne, Victoria 3000
  Australia
  Tel: 61-3-274-5000
  Fax: 61-3-274-5111

POPHAM HAIK SCHNOBRICH & KAUFMAN, LTD. (Denver, Miami, Minneapolis, Washington, D.C.)
KASPER KNACKE SCHUABLE WINTTERLIN & PARTNER
(Stuttgart and Leipzig, Germany)
POPHAM HAIK SCHNOBRICH & KAUFMAN, LTD. (Denver, Miami, Minneapolis, Washington, D.C.)
TIANPING LAW FIRM (China)
  Number of Firms: 3
  Number of Attorneys: 284
  Principal Region: United States
  International
  Contact(s):
  G. Marc Whitehead, Esq.
  Popham Haik Schnobrich & Kaufman, Ltd.
  3300 Piper Jaffray Tower
  Minneapolis, MN 55402
  United States
  Tel: 612-334-2517
  Fax: 612-334-8888

  Dr. Werner Wintterlin
  Kasper Knacke Schauble Wintterlin & Partner
  Schutzenstrasse 13
  D-7000 Stuttgart 1
  Germany
  Tel: 49-711-22-363
  Fax: 49-711-22-36410

  Xia Jun, Esq.
  Tianping Law Firm
  20 Wang Fujing Avenue
  Doncheng District
  Beijing 100006
  People's Republic of China
  Tel: 86-1-513-5261
  Fax: 86-1-513-5259

PÜNDER GROUP (Beijing, Brussels, Budapest, Moscow, New York, Warsaw)
BURUMA MARIS (The Netherlands)
CERHA, HEMPEL & SPIEGELFELD (Austria)
COPPENS, VAN OMMESLAGHE, HORSMANS & FAURES (Belgium)
DE PARDIEU - ACOURTE G.I.E. (France)
PÜNDER, VOLHARD, WEBER & AXSTER (Germany)
STOFFEL & PARTNER (Switzerland)
  Number of Firms: 6
  Number of Attorneys: 348
  Principal Region: International
  Contact(s):
  Mr. Thomas Gasteyer
  Mainzer Landstrasse 46
  60325 Frankfurt am Main
  Germany
  Tel: 49-69-71-99-01
  Fax: 49-69-71-99-4000

QLG (Quality Law Group)
  Number of Firms: 13
  Number of Attorneys: 450
  Principal Region: England and Scotland
  Contact(s):
  Miss Amanda Pugh
  QLG
  10 Bennetts Hill
  Birmingham B2 5RS
  England
  Tel: 44-121-643-7084
  Fax: 44-121-643-2257

REID & PRIEST L.L.P. (New York, Washington, D.C.)
CARREGAL & FUNES DE RIOJA (Argentina)
SINGHANIA & CO. (India)
  Number of Firms: 3
  Principal Region: International
  Contact(s):
  Richard M. Farmer, Esq. (for Carregal & Funes de Rioja)
  Reid & Priest L.L.P.
  40 West 57th Street
  New York, NY 10019
  United States
  Tel: 212-603-2240
  Fax: 212-603-2298

  Mark J. Riedy, Esq. (for Singhania & Co.)
  Reid & Priest L.L.P.
  Market Square
  701 Pennsylvania Avenue, N.W.
  Washington, D.C. 20004
  United States
  Tel: 202-508-4323
  Fax: 202-508-4321

THE RISK MANAGEMENT & INSURANCE COVERAGE COUNCIL
Number of Firms: 11
Number of Attorneys: 11
Principal Region: International
Contact (s):
Michael A. Rossi, Esq.
Hill Wynne Troop & Meisinger
10940 Wilshire Boulevard
Eighth Floor
Los Angeles, CA 90024-3902
United States
Tel: 310-443-7664
Fax: 310-443-7599
Internet Address: mrossin@reach.com

RUSSIN & VECCHI (Banghok, Ho Chi Minh City, Moscow, New York, Puerto Plata, San Francisco, Santo Domingo, Taipei, Washington, D.C.)
WALTER CONSTON, ALEXANDER AND GREEN (New York, Munich)
ADDUCI, MASTRIAMI, SCHAUMBERG & SCHILL (New York, Washington, D.C.)
Number of Firms: 3
Number of Attorneys: 155
Principal Region: International
Contact(s):
Mr. Jonathan Russin
Russin & Vecchi
1140 Connecticut Avenue, N.W.
Washington, D.C. 20036
United States
Tel: 202-223-4793
Fax: 202-223-4810

SCANDINAVIAN BUSINESS LAW GROUP
BERNING SCHLÜTER HALD (Copenhagen)
BÜTZOW & CO. (Helsinki)
VOGT & CO. (Olso)
TISELL & CO. (Stockholm)
(Joint Office: London, England; Representative Office: Talllin, Estonia)
Number of Firms: 4
Number of Attorneys: 85
Principal Region: Scandinavia
Contact(s):
Mr. Stig Bigaard
Berning Schlüter Hald
Bredgade 6
DK-1260 Copenhagen
Denmark
Tel: 45-33-14-33-33
Fax: 45-33-32-43-33

Mr. Henrik Hästö
Bützow & Co.
Pohjoisesplanadi 21 A
00100 Helsinki
Findland
Tel: 358-0-651-744
Fax: 358-0-665-417

Mr. Bjørn Kise
Voght & Co.
Roald Amundsensgt. 6
Postboks 1503 Vika
N-0117 Oslo
Norway
Tel: 47-22-41-01-90
Fax: 47-22-42-54-85

Mr. Per Winnberg
Tisell & Co. AB
Birger Jarlsgatan 32A
Box 7324
S-103 90 Stockholm
Sweden
Tel: 46-8-614-22-00
Fax: 46-8-611-22-55

SCANDINAVIAN LAW ALLIANCE
ADVOKATFIRMAN VINGE (Sweden)
KROMANN & MÜNTER (Denmark)
THOMMESSEN, KREFTING, GREVE & LUND (Norway)
Number of Firms: 3
Number of Attorneys: 320
Principal Region: Scandinavia
Contact(s):
Sven A. Olsson, Esq.
P.O. Box 1703
S-11187 Stockholm
Sweden
Tel: 46-8-614-30-00
Fax: 46-8-611-90-37

Carl Erik Krefting, Esq.
P.O. Boks 413 - Sentrum
N-0103 Oslo
Norway
Tel: 47-2-242-18-10
Fax: 47-2-242-35-57

Mogens Skipper-Pedersen, Esq.
Kromann & Münter
Rådhuspladsen 14
DK-1550 Copenhagen V
Denmark
Tel: 45-3-311-11-10
Fax: 45-3-311-80-28/315-01-57

SMITH LYONS
LANGLOIS ROBERT
BRYAN GONZALEZ VARGAS (Canada, Mexico, USA, Hong Kong, Kiev, Taipei)
Number of Firms: 3
Number of Attorneys:
Principal Region: International
Contact(s):
Mr. Gustavo Santillani
Bryan, Gonzalez Vargas y Gonzalez Baz
Torre Chapultepec
Ruben Dario No. 281, Piso 10
Bosque de Chapultepec
11580 Mexico, D.F.
Mexico
Tel: 52-5-282-11-55
Fax: 52-5-282-05-13

SMITH, LYONS, TORRANCE, STEVENSON & MAYER
(Vancouver)
FRED KAN & COMPANY (Hong Kong)
Number of Firms: 2
Number of Attorneys: 100
Principal Region: Pacific
Contact(s):
Mr. R. Stuart Angus
Smith, Lyons, Torrance, Stevenson & Mayer
World Trade Centre
550-999 Canada Place
Vancouver, British Colombia V6C 3C8
Canada
Tel: 604-662-8082
Fax: 604-685-8542

SOLON EUROPE
Number of Firms: 3
Number of Attorneys: 35
Principal Region: Europe
Contact(s):
Mr. J.C. Anderson
Gregory, Rowcliffe & Milners
No. 1 Bedford Row
London WC1R 4BZ
England
Tel: 44-171-242-0631
Fax: 44-171-242-6652

SOUTHEASTERN LAW FIRM ROUNDTABLE
Number of Firms: 10
Number of Attorneys:
Principal Region: Southeast United States
Contact(s):
Mr. Paul M. Talmadge, Jr.
Hurt, Richardson, Garner, Todd & Cadenhead
999 Peachtree Street, N.E.
Suite 1400
Atlanta, GA 30309-3999
Tel: 404-870-6000
Fax: 404-870-6020

STATE CAPITAL LAW FIRM GROUP
Number of Firms: 50
Number of Attorneys: 3,300
Principal Region: United States
Contact(s):
Mr. J. Phil Carlton
Chief Executive Officer
State Capital Law Firm Group
P.O. Box 12135
Raleigh, NC 27605
United States
Tel: 1-800-757-9701 or 919-781-7048
Fax: 919-787-3259

STEEL HECTOR & DAVIS
BENTATA HOET Y ASOCIADOS
Number of Firms: 2
Number of Attorneys: 217
Principal Region: South America
Contact(s):
Joseph P. Klock, Esq.
Steel Hector & Davis
200 S. Biscayne Blvd.
Miami, Florida 33131-2398
United States
Tel: 305-577-7000
Fax: 305-577-7001

Dr. Fernando Peláez-Pier
Bentata, Hoet & Asociados
Torre Europa, Pent House
Avenida Francisco de Miranda
Chacao, Caracas 1060
Venezuela
Tel: 58-2-951-20-67
Fax: 58-2-951-30-67

STUDIO AVV EUGENIO GRIPPO
SIMMONS & SIMMONS
STUDIO AVV EUGENIO GRIPPO (Milan, Rome)
SIMMONS & SIMMONS (London, Paris, Brussels, Abu Dhabi, Lisbon, Hong Kong, New York)
Number of Firms: 2
Number of Attorneys: 519
Principal Region: Italy
Contact(s):
Mr. P.A. de Chazal
Simmons & Simmons
21 Wilson Street
London EC2M 2TQ
England
Tel: 44-171-628-2020
Fax: 44-171-588-4129 or 588-9418

TECHLAW GROUP
Number of Firms: 14
Number of Attorneys: 3,300
Principal Region: International
Contact(s):
Dr. Lawrence Heller
TechLaw Group
225 West Swissvale Avenue
Pittsburgh, PA 15218-1632
United States
Tel: 412-244-0670
Fax: 412-244-9916

TELFA (Trans European Law Firms Association)
Number of Firms: 16
Number of Attorneys: 383
Principal Region: Europe
Contact(s):
President:
Mr. Andrew Baker
Wedlake Bell
16 Bedford Street
Covent Garden
London WC2E 9HF
England
Tel: 44-171-379-7266
Fax: 44-171-836-6117

Secretary-General:
Mr. Giancarlo Agace
TELFA
Bld. Brand Whitlock, 114-115
1200 Brussels
Belgium
Tel: 32-2-735-02-06
Fax: 32-2-735-37-13

TEN FIRM GROUP
CARLSMITH, BALL, WICHMAN, MURRAY, CASE, MUKAI & ICHIKI
(Honolulu)
CARLTON, FIELDS, WARD, EMMANUEL, SMITH & CUTLER (Tampa)
DAVIS, GRAHAM & STUBBS (Denver)
DAY, BERRY & HOWARD (Hartford)
GRAY, CARY, AMES & FRYE (San Diego)
LEWIS AND ROCA (Phoenix)
OPPENHEIMER WOLFF & DONNELLY (St. Paul)
SCHWABE, WILLIAMSON & WYATT (Portland)
SHOOK, HARDY & BACON (Kansas City)
  Number of Firms: 9
  Number of Attorneys: 1,800
  Principal Region: United States
  Contact(s):
  Mr. Gary Nelson
  Oppenheimer Wolff & Donnelly
  3400 Plaza VII
  Minneapolis, MN 55402
  United States
  Tel: 612-344-9300
  Fax: 612-344-9376

TERRALEX
  Number of Firms: 86
  Number of Attorneys: 4,200
  Principal Region: International
  Contact(s):
  Robert Paul, Esq.
  2050 Coral Way, Suite 302
  Miami, Florida 33145
  United States
  Tel: 305-858-8825
  Fax: 305-858-8986

THENETWORK OF TRIAL LAW FIRMS
  Number of Firms: 14
  Number of Attorneys:
  Principal Region: United States
  Contact(s):
  Ellis R. Mirsky, Esq.
  TheNetwork of Trial Law Firms
  120 White Plains Road, Suite 200
  Tarrytown, NY 10591
  United States
  Tel: 914-332-4400
  Fax: 914-332-1671

TOLEDO GROUP
  Number of Firms: 8
  Number of Attorneys: 1,000
  Principal Region: United States
  Contact(s):
  Mr. M. Jeffrey Burch
  Shumaker, Loop & Kendrick
  North Courthouse Square
  1000 Jackson
  Toledo, Ohio 43624-1573
  United States
  Tel: 419-241-9000
  Fax: 419-241-6894

TORY TORY DesLAURIERS & BINNINGTON (Toronto)
DESJARDINS DUCHARME STEIN MONAST (Montréal & Québec City)
LAWSON, LUNDELL, LAWSON & McINTOSH (Vancouver)
  Number of Firms: 3
  Number of Attorneys: 450
  Principal Region: National & International
  Contact(s):
  Mr. Jean-Maurice Saulnier, Esq.
  Desjardins Ducharme Stein Monast
  600 Rue de la Gauchetière Ouest
  Montréal, Québec H3B 4L8
  Canada
  Tel: 514-878-9411
  Fax: 514-878-9092

UNILAW - INTERNATIONAL
  Number of Firms: 22
  Number of Attorneys: 600
  Principal Region: International
  Contact(s):
  Mr. Jonathan W. Scott, Secretary
  Herbert Smith
  Exchange House
  Primrose Street
  London EC2A 2HS
  England
  Tel: 44-171-374-8000
  Fax: 44-171-496-0043

UNILAW - UNITED STATES
  Number of Firms: 10
  Number of Attorneys: 1,300
  Principal Region: United States
  Contact(s):
  Mr. C. Robert Monroe, UNILAW Chairman
  Lewis, Rice & Fingersh
  1010 Walnut, #500
  Kansas City, MI 64106
  United States
  Tel: 816-421-2500
  Fax: 816-474-6204

U.S. FORECLOSURE NETWORK
Number of Firms: 92
Number of Attorneys: 750
Principal Region: National
Contact(s):
Mr. David Nielsen
150 El Camino Real, Suite 120
Tostin, CA 92680
United States
Tel: 1-800-635-6128
Fax: 714-573-2650

WARSHAW BURSTEIN COHEN SCHLESINGER & KUH (New York)
EDGAR N. D'HOSE (Brussels)
Number of Firms: 2
Number of Attorneys: 51
Principal Region: United States
International
Contact(s):
Mr. Howard M. Cohen
Warshaw Burstein Cohen Schlesinger & Kuh
555 Fifth Avenue
New York, NY 10017
United States
Tel: 212-984-7700
Fax: 212-972-9150

WEBBER WENTZEL BOWENS
SHEPSTONE & WYLIE
FINDLAY & TAIT
Number of Firms: 3
Number of Attorneys: 100+
Principal Region: South Africa
Contact(s):
Brian King, Esq.
Webber Wentzel
60 Main Street
Johannesburg
South Africa
Tel: 27-11-832-2636
Fax: 27-11-834-6701/832-1623

WEIL, GOTSHAL & MANGES (New York)
NABARRO NATHANSON (London)
Number of Firms: 2
Number of Attorneys: 1000
Principal Region: International
Contact(s):
Mr. Stephen J. Dannhauser
Weil, Gotshal & Manges
767 Fifth Avenue
New York, NY 10153
United States
Tel: 212-310-8000
Fax: 212-310-8007

WINSTEAD SECHREST & MINICK P.C. (Austin, Dallas, Houston (TX), Washington, D.C., Mexico City)
TROWERS & HAMLINS (London, Dubai, Abu Dhabi (UAE), Oman, Singapore)
Number of Firms: 2
Number of Attorneys: 300
Principal Region: USA, U.K., Mexico and Middle East
Contact(s):
Mr. Timothy E. Young
Winstead Sechrest & Minick P.C.
Suite 800
100 Congress Avenue
Austin, TX 78701-4042
United States
Tel: 512-474-4330
Fax: 512-370-2850

Mr. Jonathan A. Pikoff
Winstead Sechrest & Minick, S.A. de C.V.
Galileo 20, Penthouse A
Col. Polanco
11560 Mexico, D.F.
Mexico
Tel: 52-5-280-67-66
Fax: 52-5-280-03-07

Mr. Donald L. Moorhouse
Trowers & Hamlins
10 Maltravers Street
London WC2R 3EF
England
Tel: 44-171-831-6292
Fax: 44-171-379-7269

Mr. William T. Johnson
Trowers & Hamlins
P.O. Box 23092
Mankhool Road
Dubai
United Arab Republic
Tel: 971-4-51-92-01
Fax: 971-4-51-92-05

WINTHROP, STIMSON, PUTNAM & ROBERTS (New York)
STANBROOK AND HOOPER (Brussels)
Number of Firms: 2
Number of Attorneys: 400
Principal Region: International
Contact(s):
Mr. William M. Evarts, Jr.
Winthrop, Stimson, Putnam & Roberts
One Battery Park Plaza
New York, NY 10004-1490
United States
Tel: 212-858-1000
Fax: 212-858-1500

WORLD LAW GROUP
  Number of Firms: 34
  Number of Attorneys: 6,000
  Principal Region: International
  Contact(s):
  Mr. Hans Wille
  von Erlach, Klainguti, Stettler Wille & Partners
  Dreikoenigsstrasse 7
  CH-8022 Zurich
  Switzerland
  Tel: 41-1-283-21-11
  Fax: 41-1-202-07-07

PROFESSIONAL BIOGRAPHIES SECTION

EUROPE, ASIA
AUSTRALASIA
MIDDLE EAST, AFRICA

The Professional Biographies Section presents information about lawyers and law firms that has proved to be most helpful in the selection of associate counsel or when data is desired for other reasons.

Most jurisdictions permit attorneys at law or counselors to associate in accordance with defined regulations of each Bar. The user of the International Volumes of the Directory should not necessarily infer that each firm presented is practicing as a partnership.

EUROPE	ASIA	AUSTRALASIA	MIDDLE EAST, AFRICA
Albania	Bangladesh	Australia	Algeria
Austria	Brunei Darussalam	New Zealand	Bahrain
Republic of Belarus	Cambodia	Niue	Burkina-Faso
Belgium	People's Republic of China	Papua New Guinea	Cameroon
Bulgaria	Guam		Cote d'Ivoire
Channel Islands	Hong Kong		Egypt
Croatia	India		Ethiopia
Cyprus	Indonesia		Ghana
Czech Republic	Japan		Iran
Denmark	Kazakhstan		Iraq
England	Korea		Israel
Estonia	Laos		Jordan
Finland	Malaysia		Kenya
France	Mongolia		Kuwait
Germany	Myanmar		Lebanon
Gibraltar	Nepal		Mauritius
Greece	Pakistan		Morocco
Hungary	Republic of the Philippines		Nigeria
Iceland	Singapore		Oman
Ireland	Sri Lanka		Qatar
Isle of Man	Taiwan		Saudi Arabia
Italy	Thailand		Sierra Leone
Republic of Latvia	U.S. Pacific Territories		South Africa
Liechtenstein	Vietnam		Sudan
Lithuania			Syria
Luxembourg			Tanzania
Madeira			Tunisia
Malta			United Arab Emirates
Monaco			Yemen
The Netherlands			Zimbabwe
Northern Ireland			
Norway			
Poland			
Portugal			
Romania			
Russia			
Scotland			
Slovakia			
Slovenia			
Spain			
Sweden			
Switzerland			
Turkey			
Ukraine			
Yugoslavia			

PROFESSIONAL BIOGRAPHIES SECTION

EUROPE

The Professional Biographies Section presents information about lawyers and law firms that has proved to be most helpful in the selection of associate counsel or when data is desired for other reasons.

Most jurisdictions permit attorneys at law or counselors to associate in accordance with defined regulations of each Bar. The user of the International Volumes of the Directory should not necessarily infer that each firm presented is practicing as a partnership.

Albania
Austria
Republic of Belarus
Belgium
Bulgaria
Channel Islands
Croatia
Cyprus
Czech Republic
Denmark
England
Estonia
Finland
France
Germany
Gibraltar
Greece
Hungary
Iceland
Ireland
Isle of Man
Italy
Republic of Latvia

Liechtenstein
Lithuania
Luxembourg
Madeira
Malta
Monaco
The Netherlands
Northern Ireland
Norway
Poland
Portugal
Romania
Russia
Scotland
Slovakia
Slovenia
Spain
Sweden
Switzerland
Turkey
Ukraine
Yugoslavia

EUROPE

This *Professional Biographies Section* contains some information about individuals and firms that have proved to be most helpful in the selection of resources...

No consideration, promise, or acknowledgement of any kind...

ALBANIA

ALBANIAN LEGAL ADVISORS LIMITED

VASO PASHA STREET, P.2, SH.2, AP. 7
TIRANA, ALBANIA
Telephone: +355 42 27 711
Fax: +355 42 23 838

Athens, Greece Office: Bahas, Gramatids & Associates: 9 Navarhou Nikodimou. Telephone: 3229325; 3229328; 3243271; 3243272. Telex: 223769 LGMB-GR. Telefax: 01 3229329.
London England Associated Office: Xemophon Protopapas, Queens House, 180/182 Tottenham Court Road, London WLP 9LE.

Violanda Theodori

SCHEELE, SCHWARTZ, ZIELCKE & PARTNER

P. MYZEQARI 31/18
TIRANA, ALBANIA
Telephone: 00355-42-22354
Fax: 00355-42-22354

Munich, Germany Office: Prinzregentenplatz 15, 81675. Telephone: 089/470 10 02. Fax: 089/470 10 06.

FIRM PROFILE: Scheele, Schwartz, Zielcke & Partner is an international law firm advising business clients and public institutions on all domestic and overseas corporate and commercial matters. The firm specializes in Eastern European and C.I.S. matters. Currently the firm is representing a broad range of clients in Europe, North America, South America, Asia and Africa.

(For biographical data and areas of practice see listing at Munich, Germany)

AUSTRIA

ECKERT & FRIES

ERZHERZOG RAINER RING 23
A-2500 BADEN/VIENNA, AUSTRIA
Telephone: 0043-2252/86351
Telex: 14463
Telefax: 0043-2252/86351/37

Austrian and International Company Law, Tax, Intellectual Property, Patent, Trademark, Design and Copyright Law, Commercial, General Contract, Industrial Property, Litigation, Banking, Bankruptcy, Product Liability, Environmental, Trade, Operating Licenses, Employment, Industrial Relations, Collection of Debt, Execution, Conveyancing and Commercial Register Law, Civil Law.

MEMBERS OF FIRM

PROF. DR. FRANZ ECKERT, born 1931; admitted, 1962, Austria.

DR. FRIEDRICH ECKERT, born 1933; admitted, 1964, Austria.

DR. RUDOLF FRIES, born 1958; admitted, 1985, Austria.

DDR. CHRISTA FRIES, born 1960; admitted, 1992, Austria.

ASSOCIATES

MAG. TAMARA HENDRICH, born 1966.

DR. MICHAEL TRÖTHANDL, born 1964.

SIMMA, BECHTOLD & BLUM

MARKTPLATZ 9
6850 DORNBIRN, AUSTRIA
Telephone: (5572) 25706
Telefax: (5572) 20933

General Civil Practice, Commercial, Corporation, Unfair Competition, International Business Transactions, International Trade, Conflict of Laws, EEC, Arbitration, Environmental, Trusts and Estates, Real Estate, Administrative, Constitutional, Tax, Divorce Law.

MEMBERS OF FIRM

DR. OTMAR SIMMA, born Bregenz, March 3, 1941; admitted, 1974, Austria. *Education:* University of Graz (Doctor of Jurisprudence, 1968). *Member:* Lawyers Association Vorarlberg. **PRACTICE AREAS:** General Civil Practice; Tax; Real Estate; Trusts and Estates; Divorce Law.

DR. ALFONS SIMMA, born Bregenz, February 25, 1949; admitted, 1977, Austria. *Education:* University of Innsbruck (Doctor of Jurisprudence, 1971). *Member:* Economic Association Vorarlberg. **LANGUAGES:** German and English. **PRACTICE AREAS:** Commercial; Corporation; Contract; Inheritance Law.

DR. EKKEHARD K. BECHTOLD, born Dornbirn, December 2, 1954; admitted, 1984, Austria. *Education:* University of Innsbruck (Doctor of Jurisprudence, 1977). *Member:* Lawyers Association of Vorarlberg (Commercial Court Vienna Board Member). **LANGUAGES:** German and English. **PRACTICE AREAS:** Commercial; Unfair Competition; Civil Litigation; Media Law.

DR. WOLFGANG BLUM, born October 18, 1961; admitted, 1992, Austria. *Education:* University of Innsbruck (Doctor of Jurisprudence, 1986). Author: "Security Forces and their ways of Proceeding," Springer, 1987. *Member:* Lawyers Association Vorarlberg. **LANGUAGES:** German and English. **PRACTICE AREAS:** Administrative; Constitutional; Environmental Law.

ASSOCIATES

DR. WILHELM O. KLAGIAN, born January 23, 1965. *Education:* University of Vienna (Doctor of Jurisprudence, 1991); University of Paris II. Assistant, Faculty of Law Vienna, 1985-1989. Author: "The Notion 'Legal Entity' within the Austrian Constitutional System," Springer, 1992. **LANGUAGES:** German, English and French. **PRACTICE AREAS:** General Civil Practice; Divorce; Landlord and Tenant Law.

Languages: German, English and French

MEINGAST & DALLAMASSL

Rechtsanwälte

MARKTPLATZ 14
A-4810 GMUNDEN, AUSTRIA
Telephone: +43-7612-34 21, 48 88, 48 89
Telefax: +43-7612-70 0 66

General Practice in Civil Law, Commercial Law and International Law.

FIRM PROFILE: Established in 1990 by the merger of the law firms Dr. Dallamassl (founded 1936) and Dr. Meingast (founded 1968).

MEMBERS OF FIRM

DR. KONRAD MEINGAST, born Gmunden, Austria, 1934; admitted, 1967, Austria. *Education:* University of Vienna (Doctor iuris, 1959). Judge, Supreme Disciplinary Commission for Austrian Lawyers. Honorary President, Association Internationale des Jeunes Avocats (President, 1975-1976). Co-President, AEA Commission for Human Rights. Vice-President, Association Européenne des Avocats-European Association of Lawyers, 1994—. Member, Permanent Senate of the Presidents' Conference of the European Lawyers' Organizations. *Member:* Austrian Bar Association; Association Européenne des Avocats - European Association of Lawyers; Union Internationale des Avocats; International Bar Association. **LANGUAGES:** German, English and French. **PRACTICE AREAS:** Civil Law; Commercial Law; Real Property; Administrative Law; Environmental Law; Probate Law; Bankruptcy Law; Debts Recovery; Private International Law.

DR. KURT DALLAMASSL, born Wels, Austria, 1944; admitted, 1979, Austria. *Education:* Universities of Innsbruck and Linz (Doctor iuris,
(This Listing Continued)

MEINGAST & DALLAMASSL, Gmunden—Continued

1973). *Member:* Austrian Bar Association. *LANGUAGES:* German and English. *PRACTICE AREAS:* Real Estate Law; Commercial Law; Mergers and Acquisitions; Arbitration; Litigation; Bankruptcy; Civil Law.

GRISS & PARTNER RECHTSANWÄLTE

Established in 1922

GLACISSTRASSE 67

A-8010 GRAZ, AUSTRIA

Telephone: 0316/830304 SERIE

Telex: 312492

Telecopier: 316-838117

Commercial, Corporate, Industrial Property (Patent and Trademarks, Licensing, Franchising), Unfair Competition, Product Liability, Accident and Insurance, Contract, Probate, Real Estate, Environmental, Banking and Trusts, International Transactions, Foreign Investment and Arbitration.

FIRM PROFILE: *Distinguished traditional law firm, established in 1922, offers a full range of legal services, with a strong international orientation.*

MEMBERS OF FIRM

DR. RUDOLF GRISS, born Graz, Austria, June 1, 1914; admitted, 1946, Austria. *Education:* Graz, Austria (Doctor of Law, 1937); Academy de Droit International de la Hague (1937). Honorary Consul of Brasil for Styria, 1968—. President of Red Cross Society of Styria, 1977—. Vice President of Red Cross Society of Austria, 1984—. President of Styrian Musical Society, 1983—. *LANGUAGES:* German, English Italian and French. *PRACTICE AREAS:* Contract; Probate; Real Estate; International.

DR. GUNTER R.J. GRISS, MCL, born Grôbming/Stmk, Austria, June 27, 1945; admitted, 1975, Austria. *Education:* University Graz (Dr. iur, 1967); University de Paris (Lic. 1969); University of Chicago (M.C.L., 1970). Off. Court Sworn Interpreter for English and French at District Court and Court of Appeals in Graz, 1974—. Hon. Consul of Republic of Brasil, 1988—. *Member:* Austrian Bar Association. *LANGUAGES:* German, English, French and Italian. *PRACTICE AREAS:* Commercial; Corporate; Competition; Industrial Property; International.

DR. GABRIELE KRENN, MAG.RER.SOC.OEC., born Graz, Austria, April 16, 1958; admitted, 1990, Austria. *Education:* University Graz (Dr.iur., 1981; MAG.RER.SOC.OEC., 1991). University Assistant and Lecturer, 1981-1985. *Member:* Austrian Bar Association. *LANGUAGES:* German, English and French. *PRACTICE AREAS:* Corporate Finance; Real Estate; Tax; Banking.

DR. EDWIN MÄCHLER, born Mödling, Austria, August 23, 1962; admitted, 1992, Austria. *Education:* University Graz (Mag.iur., 1985; Dr.iur., 1990). *Member:* Austrian Bar Association. *LANGUAGES:* German, English and French. *PRACTICE AREAS:* Administrative; Environmental; Contract; Litigation.

ASSOCIATE

MAG. WILHELM HOLLER. *LANGUAGES:* German, English and French. *PRACTICE AREAS:* Contract; Accident; Insurance; Litigation.

Languages: German, English, French and Italian.

RECHTSANWÄLTE HOFSTÄTTER & ISOLA KOMMANDIT-PARTNERSCHAFT

MARBURGERKAI 47

A-8010 GRAZ, AUSTRIA

Telephone: 43-316-815454

Fax: 43-316-815454-22

Banking, Bankruptcy, Commercial Law, Unfair Competition, Corporate, Litigation, Property and Real Estate, Inheritance, Debt Recovery, Reorganization of Corporations.

FIRM PROFILE: *Established in 1985, within a few years the firm has succeeded in having a reputation for offering a full range of quality legal services with concentration on Bankruptcy, Reorganization of Corporations and Commercial Law.*

(This Listing Continued)

MEMBERS OF FIRM

DR. HEIMO HOFSTÄTTER, born Graz, Austria, October 13, 1954; admitted, 1983, Austria. *Education:* University of Graz (Dr. iuris., 1978). Board Member, Austrian-Society against Cystic Fibroses. *LANGUAGES:* German and English. *PRACTICE AREAS:* Unfair Competition; Litigation; Property and Real Estate.

DR. ALEXANDER ISOLA, born Villach, Austria, July 24, 1957; admitted, 1986, Austria. *Education:* University of Graz (Dr. iuris., 1981); New York University (M.C.J., 1984). Board Member: Art-Society, Graz; Austrian Cancer Society, Syria. *Member:* EIPA European Insolvency Practitioners Association; AIJA International Association of Young Lawyers. *LANGUAGES:* German and English. *PRACTICE AREAS:* Bankruptcy; Reorganization of Corporations; Commercial Law.

ASSOCIATES

MAG. JOHANNES FRAISSLER, born 1963; admitted, 1993, Austria.

MAG. WALTER KRAUTGASSER, born 1964; admitted, 1993, Austria.

DR. JOSEF-MICHAEL DANLER

COLINGASSE 3/I

A-6020 INNSBRUCK, AUSTRIA

Telephone: 0512/580321

Fax: 0512/580322

Commercial Law (general), Companies, Trusts, Corporations, Banking, Insolvency, Tax Law, Debt Recovery, Property, Real Estate, Insurance Law and Law relating to road traffic, Sports Law, Family Law, Inheritance, Italian Commercial Law.

FIRM PROFILE: *Established in 1987; within a few years the firm has succeeded in having a reputation for offering a full range of quality legal services with concentration on civil law.*

DR. JOSEF-MICHAEL DANLER, born September 28, 1957; admitted, 1987, Austria. *Education:* University of Innsbruck (Dr. iur., 1981). *LANGUAGES:* German and English. *PRACTICE AREAS:* Commercial Law; Companies; Trusts; Corporations; Property; Real Estate; Torts; Sports Law.

ASSOCIATES

DR. SABINE DANLER-BRUNNER, born September 30, 1958. *Education:* University of Innsbruck (Dr. iur., 1981). *LANGUAGES:* German, English, Italian and French. *PRACTICE AREAS:* International Family Law; Separation and Divorce; Inheritance; Employment.

DR. GERNOT AMOSER, born January 10, 1963. *Education:* University of Innsbruck (Mag. iur., 1988; Dr. iur., 1992). *LANGUAGES:* German, English and French. *PRACTICE AREAS:* Banking Insolvency; Debt Recovery; Civil Liability; Administrative Law.

COUNSEL

AVV. DOTT. CESARE GEAT, born May 2, 1957; admitted, 1987, Italy (Not admitted in Austria). *Education:* University of Innsbruck (Dr. iur., 1982). *LANGUAGES:* Italian, German and English. *PRACTICE AREAS:* Italian Commercial Law; Companies; International Business Law; Partnerships; Trusts.

Languages: German, English, Italian, French and Spanish

LAW FIRM GREITER, PEGGER, KOFLER & PARTNER

Established in 1897

MARIA-THERESIEN-STRASSE 24

A-60213 INNSBRUCK 13, AUSTRIA

Telephone: 43-512-571811, 571812, 588646

Telefax: 43-512-58 4925, 571152

Administrative, Advertising, Antitrust, Aviation, Banking, Bankruptcy, Commercial, Competition, Corporate, Distributorship, Finance and Franchising, EEC, Foreign Investment, Immigration, Industrial Developments, Insurance, International Commercial Arbitration, International Contracts, International Private, Labor, Litigation, Product Liability, Property and Real Estate, Taxes, Trade Regulations and Transportation Law. Copyright, License Negotiations, Patents, Trademarks, Transfer of Technology, Intellectual Property. Capital Taxation, Corporate Taxation, Customs

(This Listing Continued)

Duties, Excise, Inheritance, Estate and Gift Taxation, International Taxation, Personal Income Taxation, Taxation of Foreign Nationals, Exchange Control.

FIRM PROFILE: The law firm was established by Dr. Josef Greiter in 1897, Dr. Franz Greiter entered in 1926 and Dr. Ivo Greiter entered in 1971.

MEMBERS OF FIRM

DR. IVO GREITER, born Innsbruck, Austria, November 7, 1940; admitted, 1971, Austria, Rechtsanwalt. *Education:* University of Innsbruck (Doctor of Jurisprudence, 1964). Internship with Oppenheimer, Wolff, Foster, Shepard and Donnelly in Brussels, 1977. Consultant, Booz, Allen & Hamilton, Management Consultants, London, Düsseldorf and New York, 1968. Author: "Collection of Supreme Court Judgements on Tourism, Concerning Ski Accidents, Ski Lift Accidents, Liability for the Security and Maintenance of the Ski Slopes, Liability for Accidents in Hotels and other Tourist and Leisure Facilities," 1979; "CMR-Gerichtsurteile, Entscheidungen zum Internationalen Transportrecht"; published and unpublished Decisions of the Supreme Court of Austria concerning Transport Law," 1985; "How to get your Money in Foreign Countries," A Survey of Court Costs and Lawyer's Fees in 151 Countries, Kluwer publishers, Netherlands, 1988; "How to get Compensation for Accidents in Austria," Transnational Lawyer, 1988. "Das Auskunftsrecht Des Aktionärs Und Des Partizipanten Gemäss §112 Aktiengesetz," öJZ, September, 1989; "Das Bankgeheimnis in der österr Judikatur," published and unpublished decisions of the Supreme Court, the Administrative Court and the Constitutional Court concerning the Austrian Banking Secrecy, 1990. Co-Author: Trade Handbook, *Austrian Chamber of Commerce in Vienna,* 1976; International Handbook, *Contracts of Employment,* Kluwer publishers, Netherlands, 1976; "International Estate Cases in International Academy of Estate and Trust Law," Edited by Judge Arthur K. Marshall, Los Angeles, 1979. Editor and Co-Author, Legal Section *Export-Import Handbook of the Austrian Chamber of Commerce in Vienna,* 1979-1983. *Member:* World Jurist Association, Washington (Austrian Chairman); American and International Bar Associations; International Law Association; Union Internationale des Avocats; International Chamber of Commerce; American Chamber of Commerce in Austria. *LANGUAGES:* German, English, French and Italian.

DR. FRANZ PEGGER, born Innsbruck, Austria, May 17, 1953; admitted, 1986, Austria, Rechtsanwalt. *Education:* University of Innsbruck (Magister Rerum Sociarum Oeconomiarumque; Master of Science of Business Management, 1974; Doctor of Jurisprudence, 1980). Legal Internship, Pestalozzi & Gmuer, Zürich, Switzerland, 1985 and Schürmann & Partners, Frankfurt, Germany, 1985. Teaching and Research Assistant, Institute of Auditing, Tax Consulting and Business Accounting, University of Innsbruck, 1978-1980. Teaching Assignment, Faculties of Business and Political Economics, concerning General Science of Business, Auditing and Accounting, University of Innsbruck, 1978—. *LANGUAGES:* German, English and French.

DR. STEFAN KOFLER, born Schwaz, Austria, March 2, 1958; admitted, 1987, Austria, Rechtsanwalt. *Education:* University of Innsbruck (Doctor of Jurisprudence, 1981). Practice with the High Court of Innsbruck, 1981-1982. Legal Internship, Studio Legale Avvocato Dr. Angelo Pesce e Associati, Milano, Italy, 1986 and Herbert Oppenheimer, Nathan & Vandyk, London, England, 1987. Author: "Agency and Distribution Agreements in Austria," International Agency and Distribution Agreements published by Butterworths, 1991; "Austrian Immigration and Nationality Law," International Immigration and Nationality Law published by The Center for International Legal Studies, Salzburg, Austria, 1993. Co-Author: "L'esecuzione delle sentenze austriache in Italia e delle sentenze italiane in Austria," 1993, about the enforceability of Austrian judgements in Italy and Italian judgements in Austria. *LANGUAGES:* German, English and Italian.

DR. CHRISTIAN ZANGERLE, born Silz, Austria, December 29, 1956; admitted, 1987, Austria, Rechtsanwalt. *Education:* University of Innsbruck (Doctor of Jurisprudence, 1981). Practice with High Court of Innsbruck. Admitted on the two-year course of the Government of Tyrol about Administration Law and Procedure. Co-author: "Summary of Doing Business in Austria," published in the European Manual for the Food Industry, 1992. *LANGUAGES:* German, English and Italian.

DR. NORBERT RINDERER, born Hohenems, Austria, April 11, 1960; admitted, 1992, Austria, Rechtsanwalt. *Education:* University of Innsbruck (Doctor of Jurisprudence, 1985). Practice with the High Court of Innsbruck. *LANGUAGES:* German, English.

(This Listing Continued)

OF COUNSEL

UTE GREITER - KNOOP, born Eutin, Germany, March 1, 1949; admitted, 1977, Germany (Not admitted in Austria). *Education:* University of Freiburg and Kiel (Jurisprudence); Courtship with High Court of Lübeck, Germany (1974). *LANGUAGES:* German, English and French.

Correspondence in: English, French, Italian and German.

HAUSKA & MATZUNSKI

Rechtsanwälte

Established in 1978

SALURNER STRAβE 16/I
A-6020 INNSBRUCK, AUSTRIA
Telephone: 0512/582716
Telefax: 0512/571467

Administrative, Banking, Bankruptcy, Commercial, Competition, Corporate, Contract, Debt Recovery, Distribution, Finance, Franchising, General Civil Practice, Insurance, Intellectual Property, Labor, Leasing, Litigation, Product Liability, Property and Real Estate, Torts, Trade, Tenancy, Transportation, Wills and Probate.

MEMBERS OF FIRM

DR. GERALD HAUSKA, born December 7, 1945; admitted, 1977, Rechtsanwalt, Austria. *Education:* University of Innsbruck (Dr. iur., 1972). *Member:* International Bar Association; UNILAW; Eurolink for Lawyers; German Chamber of Commerce in Austria; Italian Chamber of Commerce in Austria. *LANGUAGES:* German, English and Italian. *PRACTICE AREAS:* Banking; Commercial; Corporate; Contract; Distribution; Intellectual Property; Leasing; Real Estate; Trade; Tenancy.

DR. HERBERT MATZUNSKI, born September 2, 1959; admitted, 1989, Rechtsanwalt, Austria. *Education:* University of Innsbruck (Dr. iur., 1983). *Member:* UNILAW; Eurolink for Lawyers. *LANGUAGES:* German, English and French. *PRACTICE AREAS:* Bankruptcy; Debt Recovery; General Civil Practice; Insurance; Litigation; Torts.

DR. STEIDL & DR. BURMANN

MARIA-THERESIEN-STRASSE 29
A-6020 INNSBRUCK, AUSTRIA
Telephone: 43-512-583430; 43-512-584734
Telefax: 43-512-58473415

Administrative, Aviation, Banking, Bankruptcy, Commercial and Company Law, Competition, Criminal, Divorce, General Civil Practice, Industrial, Inheritance, Insurance, International Contracts, International Investments, Liability, Litigation, License Negotiations, Patents, Property and Real Estate, Tort Law, Trademarks.

FIRM PROFILE: The firm was established in 1962 and offers a full range of legal services.

MEMBERS OF FIRM

DIPLOM-DOLMETSCH DR. WILHELM STEIDL, born May 7, 1928; admitted, 1962, Austria. *Education:* University of Innsbruck (Doctor of Jurisprudence; Diploma for Interpreter for the English Language). Sworn Court Interpreter for the English Language. *LANGUAGES:* German, English, French and Italian.

DR. HARALD BURMANN, born October 22, 1948; admitted, 1977, Austria. *Education:* University of Innsbruck (Doctor of Jurisprudence). *LANGUAGES:* German, English and French.

DRS. UNGERINGER, ULLMANN

STADTPLATZ 20
A-5230 MATTIGHOFEN, AUSTRIA
Telephone: 43-7742-2267
Fax: 43-7742-4989

Administrative, Bankruptcy and Reconstruction, Commercial, Computer, Contract, Criminal, Immigration, Intellectual Property, Litigation, Personal Injury, Property and Real Estate, Telecommunication and Amateur Radio, Taxation, General Legal Practice.

(This Listing Continued)

DRS. UNGERINGER, ULLMANN, Mattighofen—
Continued

MEMBERS OF FIRM

DR. WERNER UNGERINGER, born November 3, 1939; admitted, 1973, Austria, Rechtsanwalt. *Education:* University of Vienna (Doctor of Jurisprudence, 1966). Co-Author: "Schmerzengeld und Verunstaltungsentschädigung," Vienna, 1986. DV-Rechtsprechung, Munich, 1991. *Member:* Austrian Bar Association. *LANGUAGES:* German and English.

DR. ANTON ULLMANN, born April 13, 1954; admitted, 1987, Austria, Rechtsanwalt. *Education:* University of Vienna; Technical University of Vienna; University of Salzburg (Magister Juris, 1981; Doctor of Jurisprudence, 1981). *Member:* Austrian Bar Association. *LANGUAGES:* German and English.

HÜGEL & PARTNER

Established in 1979

LERCHENGASSE 14
A-2340 MÖDLING BEI WIEN, AUSTRIA
Telephone: 43-2236-22390
Fax: 43-2236-43657

Commercial Law (general), Corporate Law, Mergers and Acquisitions, Tax Law, Real Estate, Distribution Law, Labor Law and Copyright.

FIRM PROFILE: The firm was established in 1979. It advises both foreign and domestic clients in respect of all matters arising in connection with the setting up and the running of businesses. The firm has developed particular expertise in structuring of business acquisitions, mergers and spin-offs. Another significant part of the firm's practice is the law of commercial agents and other distributors.

The firm presently consists of 4 partners and 4 associates. In 1992 it has opened an office in Vienna together with Univ. Prof. DDr. René Laurer, Attorney at Law and Dr. Armin Dallmann, LL.M., Attorney at Law. A partnership will be established shortly.

MEMBERS OF FIRM

HANNS HÜGEL, born Vienna, Austria, February 2, 1920; admitted, 1951, Austria. *Education:* University of Vienna (Dr.jur., 1948). *Member:* Lower Austria Bar Association; Wiener Juristische Gesellschaft. *LANGUAGES:* German and English. *PRACTICE AREAS:* Commercial Law; Real Estate Law.

HANNS F. HÜGEL, born Vienna, Austria, July 14, 1951; admitted, 1979, Austria. *Education:* University of Vienna (Dr.jur., 1974). Author: inter alia "Verschmelzung und Einbringung," Köln/Wien, Schmidt/Manz, 1993; "Umgründungssteuergesetz: Verschmelzung, Umwandlung," ecolex, 1991, 802, 875; ecolex, 1992, 44; "Rechtsscheinhaftung bei nicht offengelegter Haftungsbeschränkung im Rahmen einer ständigen Geschäftsverbindung," RdW, 1985, 34; "Aufsichtsratsveto und Entscheidungsbefugnis der Gesellschafterversammlung," GesRZ, 1982, 305. *Member:* Lower Austria Bar Association; International Bar Association. *LANGUAGES:* German and English. *PRACTICE AREAS:* Corporate Law; Mergers and Acquisitions; Tax Law; Copyright Law.

GÜNTHER VIEHBÖCK, born Gmunden, Austria, January 1, 1955; admitted, 1989, Austria. *Education:* Theresianische Militärakademie Wiener Neustadt (Lieutenant, 1978); University of Linz (Dr.jur., 1985). Author: "Der Ausgleichsanspruch nach dem neuen Handelsvertreterrecht," 1993. *Member:* Lower Austria Bar Association; Association Internationale des Jeunes Avocats; Anwaltsvereinigung Forum. *LANGUAGES:* German, Spanish and English. *PRACTICE AREAS:* Distribution Law; Commercial Law; Labor Law.

HERBERT SCHRITTESSER, born Metnitz, Klagenfurt, Austria, October 17, 1961; admitted, 1993, Austria. *Education:* University of Graz (Dr.jur., 1989). Thesis, "Product Liability of Importers and Dealers," 1988. *Member:* Lower Austria Bar Association. *LANGUAGES:* German, Italian and English. *PRACTICE AREAS:* Distribution Law; Real Estate Law; General Practice Law.

BERGER & AICHLREITER

Rechtsanwälte

Established in 1908

STERNECKSTRAßE 55
A-5020 SALZBURG, AUSTRIA
Telephone: +43/662/870836
Telefax: +43/662/879717
Telex: 6-33615
E-Mail-Address: berger@eunet.co.at

General Civil Practice, Company, Public Economic Law, Constitutional, Commercial, Unfair Competition, Contract, Administrative Law, Environment, Real Estate Law, EEC, Taxes, Public Procurement, Software, Licenses.

MEMBERS OF FIRM

DR. JULIUS BERGER (1876-1943).

DR. WOLFGANG BERGER (1912-1987).

DR. WOLFGANG BERGER, born 1950; admitted, 1978, Austria. *Education:* University of Salzburg (Dr. jur., 1972). Arbitrator, German-Austrian Chamber of Commerce. President, Austro-American Society, Salzburg, 1988—. *Member:* Salzburg Bar; IBA.

DR. JOSEF W. AICHLREITER, born 1947; admitted, 1988, Austria. *Education:* Universities of Vienna and Salzburg (Dr. jur., 1971). Professor, Economic Constitution and Administrative Law, University of Salzburg. Co-Editor: Wirtschaftsrechtliche Blätter. Author: "Österreichisches Verordnungsrecht." *Member:* Salzburg Bar; IBA.

Languages: German and English

DENNIS CAMPBELL AND ASSOCIATES

Established in 1978

HANS SACHS GASSE 13
A-5020 SALZBURG, AUSTRIA
Telephone: (662) 435200
Facsimile: (662) 432628

Practice is conducted outside Austria with emphasis on recognition and enforcement of foreign judgments throughout Europe and Asia, preparation of litigation against foreign defendants, and tracing of assets. Practice within Austria is limited to assistance of Austrian practitioners in questions relating to foreign law.

FIRM PROFILE: The practice was established as a consultancy with specialization in Eastern European transactions. In recent years, its focus has shifted to recognition and enforcement of judgements throughout Europe and Asia. The client base is primarily U.S. litigation firms. The firm has a staff of four associates and five administrative personnel.

DENNIS CAMPBELL, born Morris, Illinois, December 3, 1939; admitted, 1977, Iowa; 1990, New York (Not admitted in Austria). *Education:* California State University (B.A., 1967); University of the Pacific; McGeorge School of Law (J.D., 1973); Stockholm University (Graduate Diploma, Comparative Law, 1976). Fulbright Scholar. Fellow, Salzburg Seminar in American Studies. Editor: "Attacking Foreign Assets," Lloyds of London Press; "Recognition and Enforcement of Foreign Judgments," Sweet & Maxwell. Visiting Lecturer, Stockholm University, Warsaw University and Krakow University. Former Professor and Director, International Programs, McGeorge School of Law. Director, Center for International Legal Studies. *Member:* Iowa State Bar Association; New York State Bar Association; American Bar Association; International Bar Association. *LANGUAGES:* English and German. *PRACTICE AREAS:* Recognition and enforcement of foreign judgments.

CHRISTIAN CAMPBELL, admitted, 1992, New York (Not admitted in Austria). *Education:* Edinburgh University (LL.B.); University of the Pacific, McGeorge School of Law (LL.M.). *Member:* International Bar Association. *LANGUAGES:* German, Spanish and French.

SUSAN C.M. COTTER, Qualified, 1991, England and Wales. (Not Admitted in Austria). *Education:* University College, Cardiff (LL.B.); University of Wales (LL.M.).

Member of GLOBALAW (The International Law Group).

PFLANZL, HORVATITS & PFEIFER

Rechtsanwälte

GINZKEYPLATZ 10

A-5033 SALZBURG, AUSTRIA

Telephone: (43) 662-624848

Telefax: (43) 662-624848-22

Corporate, Commercial, Antitrust Law, Labour, Industrial Property, Unfair Competition Law, Foreign Investment, Product Liability, Intellectual Property and Taxation of Foreign Nationals.

DR. HERBERT PFLANZL, born July 29, 1940. *Education:* University of Salzburg (Dr.Jur.; Electronic Engineering). *LANGUAGES:* English.

DR. ÄGIDIUS HORVATITS, born June 11, 1950. *Education:* University of Salzburg (Dr.Jur.). Assistant to University Professor Dr. Max Kaser, Institute for Roman and Civil Law, University of Salzburg. *LANGUAGES:* English and Serbo-Croatian.

DR. HERBERT PFEIFER, born September 7, 1956. *Education:* University of Salzburg (Mag. Dr. Jur.). Assistant, University of Salzburg. Lecturer, Institute for Civil Law History, 1987-1990. *LANGUAGES:* English.

ASSOCIATES

Mag. Gerhild Scharzenberger
Dr. Andreas Reischl

SALPIUS & SCHUBECK

Established in 1981

WÄSCHERGASSE 15

A-5020 SALZBURG, AUSTRIA

Telephone: 662-(829389); (829390)

Fax: 662-(829388)

Los Angeles, California Office: 660 South Figueroa Street, Suite 1850, 90017. Telephone: 213-689-1200. Fax: 213-689-1222.

FIRM PROFILE: Business Law practice emphasizing in International Business, Trade, Debt Collection, Real Estate, Unfair Competition, Antitrust and Corporate Law, Taxation, Estates and Trusts, Litigation and Aviation Law.

DR. EUGEN SALPIUS, ACIArb, born April 12, 1946. *Education:* Rollins College, Florida, U.S.A.; University of Graz, Austria; University of Vienna, Austria (Dr. Jur.); Moscow State University, USSR (MGU); Hague Academy of International Law. Former Fellow Salzburg Seminar. Author: "Alien Acquisition of Real Property," Kluwer; "Transnational Legal Practice," Kluwer; "Legal Aspects of Doing Business in Western Europe," Kluwer; "The Liability of Contractors," Longman; "Basic Critical Issues in Major Construction Contracts," IBA. International Board of Advisors, McGeorge School of Law, University of the Pacific, European Program, University of Salzburg. *Member:* Austrian Bar Association; Chartered Institute of Arbitrators, London; International and American Bar Associations; Austrian Aero Club (Vice President). *LANGUAGES:* German, English, French, Russian, Polish and Italian. *PRACTICE AREAS:* International Business Transactions; Arbitration; Litigation; Aviation.

DR. CHRISTIAN SCHUBECK, born March 15, 1965. *Education:* University of Salzburg, Austria (Mag. Dr. Jur.); McGeorge School of Law, University of the Pacific (Diploma in Advanced International Legal Studies, 1990). *LANGUAGES:* German and English. *PRACTICE AREAS:* Litigation.

OF COUNSEL

KEVIN J. MOORE, born Pasadena, California, August 5, 1961; admitted, 1988, California. *Education:* San Diego State University (B.S., Accounting, 1984); Western State University (J.D., 1987); Downing College, Cambridge, England (International Law); McGeorge School of Law, University of the Pacific (LL.M. Taxation and Business—Transnational Legal Practice, 1989). *Member:* State Bar of California; American and International Bar Associations (Taxation Section, International Law and Practice Section, Subcommittee on European Tax Law, Real Estate, Probate and Trust Section); German American Chamber of Commerce; U.S. Tax Court; U.S. Court of International Trade. (Also Practicing Individually, Los Angeles, California). *LANGUAGES:* English and German. *PRACTICE AREAS:* Federal, State and International Tax; U.S. and Offshore Trusts.

GOTTFRIED WIESER

Established in 1985

BUROHAUS MIRABELL

FRANZ-JOSEF-STRASSE 33

A-5020 SALZBURG, AUSTRIA

Telephone: (0662) 88 24 88; 87 24 00

Cable Address: "iurconsult"

Telex: 632 066 iuris a

Telecopier: (0662) 87 66 23

Commercial, Corporate, Banking, Real Estate, Wills, Trusts and Estates, International.

DR. GOTTFRIED WIESER, born Austria, September 6, 1949; admitted, 1976, Austria; 1980, Principality of Liechtenstein. *Education:* University of Graz, Austria (Dr. iur., 1973). Legal Adviser to Private Trust Bank Corporation, Vaduz, Liechtenstein, 1983-1984. *Member:* Austrian Bar Association; International Bar Association. *LANGUAGES:* German, English and French.

ALLMAYER-BECK STOCKERT & SCHEUBA

Established in 1946

PARKRING 2

A-1011 VIENNA, AUSTRIA

Telephone: (1) 512-18-34

Telex: 134578 ablaw

Telecopier: (1) 513-37-49

Commercial, Corporate, Banking, Construction, Electronic Data Processing Law, EEC Law, Environmental Law, Foundation Law, Industrial Property and Copyright, Unfair Competition, Litigation and Arbitration, Media Law, Real Estate Transactions, Estate Law, Tax.

MEMBERS OF FIRM

DR. MAX JOSEF ALLMAYER-BECK, born Vienna, 1934; admitted, 1966, Austria. *Education:* University of Vienna Law School (Dr.iur., 1958); The John Hopkin's University-Bologna-Center, Bologna, Italy (1959-1960). *Member:* Viennese Bar; International Bar Association (IBA).

MAG.DR. JOHANNES STOCKERT, born Vienna, 1953; admitted, 1984, Austria. *Education:* University of Vienna Law School (Dr.iur., 1978); University of Economics Vienna (Mag. rer. soc. oec, 1978). *Member:* International Bar Association (IBA); Association Internationale des Jeunes Avocats (AIJA).

DR. ELISABETH SCHEUBA, born Vienna, 1961; admitted, 1990, Austria. *Education:* University of Vienna Law School (Dr. iur., 1984). Research Assistant to Prof. Dr. Rudolf Welser, Institute for Civil Law, University of Vienna Law School (1984-1986). *Member:* International Bar Association (IBA); Association Littéraire et Artistique (ALAI-Austria).

ASSOCIATES

Mag. Christian Tropsch   *Dr. Georg Kresbach*

Languages: German, English, French and Italian.

ANDRÉEWITCH & SIMON

STALLBURGGASSE 4

A-1010 VIENNA, AUSTRIA

Telephone: (1) 533-31-58

Telefax: (1) 533-20-91

Commercial and Corporate Law, Acquisitions and Joint Ventures, Unfair Competition Law, Litigation and Arbitration, Banking and Financing Transactions, Intellectual Property Rights, Real Estate Transactions, Estate Law, Computer, Product Liability and Telecommunications Law.

DR. MARKUS ANDRÉEWITCH, born Vienna, Austria, June 11, 1955; admitted, 1986, Austria. *Education:* University of Vienna (J.D., 1980). Author: "The Austrian Commercial Code," (Translation into English), Manz, Vienna, 1987; "Austrian Company Law" (co-author, 1994); numerous publications in legal periodicals on product liability, computer law, environmental law and business law. Foreign internships: Barnes, Richardson & Colburn, Washington, D.C., 1980; Cleary, Gottlieb, Steen & Hamilton, Brussels, 1981. *Member:* Vienna Bar Association; International Bar Association;

(This Listing Continued)

ANDRÉEWITCH & SIMON, Vienna—Continued

German Association on Computer Law. *LANGUAGES:* German, English and French.

DR. A. NICHOLAS SIMON, born Vienna, Austria, December 6, 1954; admitted, 1980, Massachusetts Supreme Judicial Court and United States District Court of Massachusetts; 1989, Austria. *Education:* Haverford College (B.A., 1977); Boston University School of Law (J.D., cum laude, 1980); University of Vienna School of Law (J.D., 1985). Associate: Craig & Macauley, Boston, 1980-1981; Cole & Corette, London Office, 1981-1983. Lecturer, Business Law, Webster University, Vienna Campus, 1985—; University of Economics and Business Administration, Vienna, 1991—. Recipient, Webster Excellency in Teaching Award, 1989. Author: "The Austrian Banking Act" (Translation into English, 1986); "Austrian Company Law" (co-author, 1994). *Member:* American Bar Association; Massachusetts Bar Association; Austrian Bar Association. *LANGUAGES:* German and English.

BICHLER & SPITZY

Established in 1980

WEYRGASSE 8
A-1030 VIENNA, AUSTRIA
Telephone: (0222) 712 66 94-0; 714 27 74-0
Telex: 13 17 27 bhs
Telefax: (0222) 712 64 82; 714 27 16

General Civil and International Practice. Commercial, Corporation, Transport, Property, Unfair Competition, Tax, Banking and Labor Law. No Criminal Law.

FIRM PROFILE: The firm was established in 1980 and offers a full range of legal services. It is especially well known for its Corporate and Business Law Practice. The client base is European, Japanese, North and South American in scope.

MEMBERS OF FIRM

Dr. Hans Bichler
Dr. Wolfgang Spitzy
Mag. Edgar Zrzavy
Dr. Esther Lenzinger

ASSOCIATES

Mag. Julia Unger
Mag. Laurenz Strebl
Mag. Christian Malburg
Mag. Bernd Widner
Sara Rodrigues-Toral

Languages: German, English, Spanish, Italian and French.

BINDER, GRÖSSWANG & PARTNERS

TUCHLAUBEN 7A
A-1010 VIENNA, AUSTRIA
Telephone: +43 (1) 533 44 63
Telecopier: +43 (1) 535 44 52

Brno, Czechoslovakia Office: Kounicova 67a, CS-65831. Telephone: +42 (5) 41 21 32 16. Fax: +42 (5) 41 21 15 28.

General Business Practice. Corporate, Banking, Securities, Commercial, Tax, Industrial Property, Patent, Unfair Competition, Copyright, Antitrust, Administrative, Food and Drug, Labor, Contract and Estate Law. International Transactions and Intercompany Relationships, Arbitration.

MEMBERS OF FIRM

DR. MARTIN BINDER, born Kufstein, May 7, 1924; admitted, 1953, Austria. *Education:* University of Vienna (Dr.jur., 1948). *LANGUAGES:* German, English and French.

DR. KLAUS GRÖSSWANG, born Vienna, March 6, 1940; admitted, 1970, Austria. *Education:* University of Vienna (Dr.jur., 1963). *LANGUAGES:* German and English.

DR. GEORG LEGAT, born Linz, June 29, 1950; admitted, 1981, Austria. *Education:* University of Vienna (Dr.jur., 1975). *LANGUAGES:* German and English.

(This Listing Continued)

DR. MICHAEL BINDER, born Vienna, September 4, 1955; admitted, 1985, Austria. *Education:* University of Vienna (Dr.jur., 1979); Yale (LL.M., 1982). *LANGUAGES:* German, English and French.

DR. MICHAEL KUTSCHERA, born Vienna, October 10, 1957; admitted, 1985, New York; 1987, Austria. *Education:* University of Vienna (Dr.jur., 1979); New York University (M.C.J., 1983). *LANGUAGES:* German, English and French.

ASSOCIATES

DR. CHRISTIAN KLAUSEGGER, born Vienna, October 18, 1962; admitted, 1992, Austria. *Education:* University of Vienna (Mag. rer. soc. oec., 1986; Dr.jur., 1987). *LANGUAGES:* German, English and French.

DR. TIBOR FABIAN, born Vienna, July 18, 1956; admitted, 1994, Austria. *Education:* University of Vienna (Dr.jur., 1980); University of Economics Vienna (Mag. rer. soc. oec., 1981). *LANGUAGES:* German, English and Croatian.

MAG. DAGMAR NEYER, born Vienna, Austria, April 20, 1968; (Not admitted in Austria). *Education:* University of Vienna Law School (Mag. jur., 1992). *LANGUAGES:* German and English.

MAG. STEPHAN MEUSBURGER, born Bregenz, Austria, June 28, 1967; (Not admitted in Austria). *Education:* University of Vienna Law School (Mag. jur., 1992). *LANGUAGES:* German, English and French.

DR. ALEXANDRA ZENZ, born Graz, Austria, November 18, 1965; (Not admitted in Austria). *Education:* University of Graz Law School (Mag.jur., 1990; Dr.jur., 1993). *LANGUAGES:* German, English and French.

Languages: German, English, French, Czech, Slovak and Croatian.

CERHA, HEMPEL & SPIEGELFELD

Established in 1921

PARKRING 2
A-1010 VIENNA, AUSTRIA
Telephone: (0222) (1) 514 35-0
Telefax: (0222) (1) 514 35 35

Joint Offices of Pünder Group:
Beijing, China Office: Suite C 603, Beijing Lufthansa Center, 50 Liangmaqiao Road, TJ-Beijing 100 016. Telephone: (86) (1) 465 15 68. Fax: (86) (1) 467 12 56.
Brussels, Belgium Office: Rue d'Arlon 92, B-1040 Brussels. Telephone: (32) (2) 230 90 11. Fax: (32) (2) 231 19 55.
Budapest, Hungary Office: Endrödy Sandor utca 48, H-1026 Budapest. Telephone: (36) 603 32 618. Fax: (36) 603 32 617.
Moscow, Russia Office: ul. Wolchonka, 18/2, RF-121 019, Moscow. Telephone: (7) (095) 202 64 90; (7) (543) 708 00 90 (from Germany); (49) (7545) 8 93 42 (from other countries). Fax (7) (095) 202 65 14; (7) (543) 708 00 99 (from Germany); (49) (7545) 8 93 43 (from other countries).
New York, New York Office: 152 West 57th Street, 10019. Telephone: (1) (212) 582 28 28. Fax: (1) (212) 582 24 24.
Warsaw, Poland Office: ul. Jasna 1, PL-00-013 Warsaw. Telephone: (48) (22) 27 15 26. Fax: (48) (22) 27 15 29.

Corporate, Commercial, Banking and Finance, Securities and Capital Markets, International Investments, Mergers and Acquisitions, (East-West) Joint Ventures, Taxation, EEC-Law, Arbitration, Franchising, Real Estate Transactions, Construction, Distributorship, Unfair Competition, Labour and Employment, Intellectual Property, Transportation, Maritime, Aviation, Estate and Inheritance Law.

DR. KARL HEMPEL, born Vienna, Austria, February 8, 1937; admitted, 1968, Austria. *Education:* University of Vienna (Dr.iur., 1959); Universities of Luxembourg and Strasbourg (Diplômes du Droit Comparé). President, Kuratorium, Ludwig Boltzmann, Institut fëGesetzgebungspraxis und Rechtsanwendung. Co-Author: "Österreichisches Wirtschafts-recht und das Recht der EG," 1990. Author: "Recent Developments in Central and Eastern Europe," 1991 and 1992; "Die rechtsberatenden Berufe in der EU," 1994. *Member:* Presidency of the Court of Arbitration of Austrian Federal Chamber of Commerce (1985—); IBA; UIA. *LANGUAGES:* German, English, French. *PRACTICE AREAS:* Banking; Arbitration; Tax; EEC-Law.

DR. DIETER CERHA, born Vienna, Austria, August 6, 1939; admitted, 1971, Austria. *Education:* University of Vienna (Dr.iur., 1964); London School of Economics. *Member:* Disciplinary Committee of Appeal of the

(This Listing Continued)

Viennese Bar. *LANGUAGES:* German, English. *PRACTICE AREAS:* Company and Commercial; Transport; Aviation; Estate and Inheritance.

DR. BENEDIKT SPIEGELFELD, born Linz, Austria, February 11, 1951; admitted, 1978, Austria. *Education:* University of Vienna (Dr.iur., 1974). *Member:* Austrian Franchising Association; IBA. *LANGUAGES:* German, English. *PRACTICE AREAS:* Cross Border Investment and Finance; Franchising; Real Estate Transactions and Development; Distributorship; Hungarian Law; Maritime Law; Arbitration.

DR. EDITH HLAWATI, born Vienna, Austria, June 8, 1957; admitted, 1986, Austria. *Education:* University of Vienna (Dr.iur., 1980); University of South Africa (Comparative Law). Practice with Theodore Goddard, London, 1982-1983. Author: Contributions in Law Journals on Austrian Banking Law. *Member:* IBA; British-German Jurists' Association. *LANGUAGES:* German, English, French. *PRACTICE AREAS:* Corporate Reorganization; Mergers and Acquisitions; Banking; Capital Markets; Employment.

DR. ALFRED NEMETSCHKE, born Vienna, Austria, July 8, 1960; admitted, 1990, Austria. *Education:* Universities of Vienna and Salzburg (Dr.iur., 1984); University of Cambridge (LL.M., 1986). *LANGUAGES:* German, English. *PRACTICE AREAS:* Real Estate Transactions; Construction; Trade Regulations; Joint Ventures (Eastern Countries).

DR. IRENE WELSER, born Vienna, Austria, April 2, 1964; admitted, 1992, Vienna. *Education:* University of Vienna (Dr.iur., 1988). Author: "Die Gewährleistung beim Werkvertrag," Manz, Vienna, 1989. Co-Author: "Schadenersatz statt Gewährleistung," Vienna, 1994. *LANGUAGES:* German, English and French. *PRACTICE AREAS:* Warranty; Liability for Damages and Product Liability; Unfair Competition; Intellectual Property.

ASSOCIATES

MAG. JULIAN FEICHTINGER, LL.M., born Linz, 1964. *Education:* University of Vienna (Mag. iur.); American University; Washington College of Law (LL.M.). *LANGUAGES:* German, English, French.

MAG. INGEBORG KONEGGER, born Spittal/Drau, 1969. *Education:* University of Vienna (Mag. iur.); Moscow State University, Law Faculty. *LANGUAGES:* German, English, Russian, Italian.

DR. THOMAS MAYER, LL.M., born St. Pölten, 1967, admitted 1994, New York (not admitted in Austria). *Education:* University of Vienna (Dr. iur.); New York University School of Law, New York (LL.M.). *Member:* American Bar Association; IBA. *LANGUAGES:* German, English.

DR. MICHAEL SEDLACEK, born Vienna, 1964. *Education:* University of Vienna (Mag. iur.); Center European Law; University of Innsbruck (Dr. iur.). Co-Author: "To Pay or Not to Pay, that is the Question?"; The Tax Journal, November, 1993; "More Than Anyone Bargained For," VAT-Planning No. 29, February, 1994. *LANGUAGES:* German, English.

DR. CLAUDINE VARTIAN, born Vienna, 1969. *Education:* University of Vienna (Dr. iur.). *LANGUAGES:* German, French, English.

DR. OSKAR WINKLER, born Vienna, 1959. *Education:* Vienna Business School (Mag. rer. soc. oec.); University of Vienna (Dr. iur.). *LANGUAGES:* German, English, French, Italian.

DR. ALFRED DALJEVEC

Established in 1968

MARIAHILFER STRAßE 23-25
A-1060 VIENNA, AUSTRIA
Telephone: 0222/587 41 07; 0222/586 21 06
Fax: 0222/586 21 06/17

Administrative Law, Business Law, Debt Recovery, Family Law, Labour Law, Professional Liability, Real Estate.

FIRM PROFILE: The firm has been established in 1968 under the former practice of Dr. Hanns Blaschke. The firm offers all legal services in the area of Business Law.

ALFRED DALJEVEC, born Vienna, September 4, 1936; admitted, 1968, Austria. *Education:* University of Vienna (Dr. jur., 1961). *Member:* Austrian Law Society. *LANGUAGES:* German and English.

DR. ARMIN DALLMANN

Established in 1992

GUSSHAUSSTRASSE 2
A-1040 VIENNA, AUSTRIA
Telephone: 43-1-504 41 42-0
Fax: 43-1-504 41 42 43

National and International Banking and Business Law, Mergers and Acquisitions, Corporate Law, General Commercial and International Trade Law.

FIRM PROFILE: The firm has been newly established in 1992. It works in close cooperation with Univ. Prof. DDr. René Laurer, Attorney at Law, and Hügel & Partner, Mödling. A partnership will be established shortly. The firm offers all legal services needed by its banking and commercial clients.

DR. ARMIN DALLMANN, born Salzburg, February 23, 1956; admitted, 1988, Austria. *Education:* University of Vienna (Dr. jur., 1980); Harvard Law School (International Tax Program, 1981; LL.M., 1982) Georgetown University, International Law Institute (Orientation in the United States Legal System, 1981). Foreign Associate, Shearman & Sterling, New York, 1983. *Member:* Vienna Bar Association; International Bar Association. *LANGUAGES:* English and German.

DORDA, BRUGGER & JORDIS

Rechtsanwälte - Partnerschaft

Established in 1976

DR KARL LUEGER-RING 12
A-1010 VIENNA, AUSTRIA
Telephone: 43-1-533 47 95-0
Telefax: 43-1-5 33 47 97

Representative offices in Prague and Bratislava

Commercial, Banking, Corporate, Mergers and Acquisitions, International Business Transactions, Conflict of Laws, Trusts and Estates, Unfair Competition, Product Liability, Trade, Labor, Landlord and Tenant, Real Estate, Civil Litigation.

FIRM PROFILE: Established in 1976 it merged in 1988 with the law firm of Dr. Jordis. It has steadily grown and is now, by Austrian standards, with its 12 lawyers and 2 paralegals one of the major Austrian law firms. It is well known for International Business Transactions, Banking, M & A, Corporate and General Commercial Law. Clients range from large U.S. based and international Corporations and their Austrian subsidiaries to big and medium size Austrian business entities (banks, industrial and commercial enterprises).

MEMBERS OF FIRM

DR. CHRISTIAN DORDA, born Vienna, 1947; admitted, 1976, Austria. *Education:* University of Vienna (Dr. jur., 1971). University lecturer (Hernstein International Management Institute) 1992—. Author: Regular contributions to Butterworths Journal of International Banking and Financial Law and for Euromoney publications. *LANGUAGES:* German, English and French. *PRACTICE AREAS:* Mergers and Acquisitions; Banking; International Law; Takeovers; Corporate.

DR. THERESA JORDIS, born Vienna, 1949; admitted, 1981, Austria. *Education:* University of Vienna (Dr. jur., 1971). Author: European Personnel Policies, Austrian Part (loose-leaf publication on European Labour Law and Practice). *LANGUAGES:* German, English and French. *PRACTICE AREAS:* Corporate; Trusts and Estates; Mergers and Acquisitions; Commercial; Labor.

DR. WALTER BRUGGER, born Vienna, 1954; admitted, 1983, Austria. *Education:* University of Vienna (Dr. jur., 1978). Author: Acquisition of Business Enterprises (Manz 1990); various publications in the fields of banking law and general business and corporate law; regular contributions to Butterworth's Journal of International Banking and Financial Law. *LANGUAGES:* German, English and Spanish. *PRACTICE AREAS:* Corporate; Banking; International Law; Unfair Competition; Construction.

DR. FLORIAN KREMSLEHNER, born Vienna, 1960; admitted, 1990, Austria. *Education:* University of Vienna (Dr. jur., 1985). *LANGUAGES:* German, English and Italian. *PRACTICE AREAS:* Trade Law; Anti-Trust; Civil Litigation; Environmental; Banking.

(This Listing Continued)

DORDA, BRUGGER & JORDIS, Vienna—Continued

MAG. THOMAS ANGERMAIR, born Vienna, 1964; admitted, 1992, Austria. *Education:* University of Vienna (Mag. jur., 1986). *LANGUAGES:* German and English. *PRACTICE AREAS:* Unfair Competition; Landlord and Tenant; Commercial; Real Estate; Corporate.

DR. PHILIPP MERAN, born Innsbruck, 1962; admitted, 1993, Austria. *Education:* University of Graz (Dr. jur., 1985). *LANGUAGES:* German and English. *PRACTICE AREAS:* Corporate; Commercial; Trademarks; Contracts; Litigation; International Law.

ASSOCIATES

DR. MARTIN BRODEY, LL.M. *LANGUAGES:* German, English and French. *PRACTICE AREAS:* Banking; Commercial; Anti-Trust; EC Law; International Law; Mergers and Acquisitions.

MAG. THOMAS CHRISTOPH. *LANGUAGES:* German and English. *PRACTICE AREAS:* Commercial; Real Estate; Administrative; Business Law; Civil Law.

DR. BERNHARD HÜTTLER. *LANGUAGES:* German and English. *PRACTICE AREAS:* Administrative Law; Commercial; Environmental; Mergers and Acquisitions; Litigation.

DR. ANDREAS ZAHRADNIK. *LANGUAGES:* German and English. *PRACTICE AREAS:* Corporate; Commercial; Business Law; Civil Law; Trade Law.

DDR. PETER LEWISCH. *LANGUAGES:* German and English. *PRACTICE AREAS:* Corporate; Commercial; Real Estate; Litigation; Administrative Law.

MAG. ALEXANDER WINTERSTEIN. *LANGUAGES:* German and English. *PRACTICE AREAS:* Litigation; Corporate; Commercial; Business Law.

MAG. NORBERT WIESINGER. *LANGUAGES:* German, French and English. *PRACTICE AREAS:* Corporate; Commercial; Labor; Litigation; Business Law.

LEGAL SUPPORT PERSONNEL

HELGA PILZ. PRACTICE AREAS: Investigations; Debt Collection; Client Correspondence.

Languages: German, English, French, Italian and Spanish.

DRAXLER & PARTNER

Rechtsanwälte

Established in 1975

REICHSRATSSTRAßE 11, 4TH FLOOR
1010 VIENNA, AUSTRIA
Telephone: (01) 408 35 44
Fax: (01) 408 35 44 30

Prague, Czech Republic Cooperation Office: JUDr. Jarmila Kolar. Na Prikope 12, Passage Cerna Ruze, CZ-19000 Prague 1. Telephone: 02/24 22 45 89. Fax: 02/24 22 45 89.

Commercial and Company, Mergers and Acquisitions, Real Estate, Landlord and Tenant, Complex Litigation, Debt Collection, EU Law, Property and Real Estate Law.

FIRM PROFILE: *The law firm of Draxler & Partner was established when a former staff member, Dr. Peter Stock, was taken into partnership with Dr.H.Peter Draxler, who had set up office in 1979 as the spiritual successor of his late father, Dr. Ludwig Draxler, a former Minister of Finance.*

Dr. H. Peter Draxler has many years of experience in advising industrial and commercial companies in all legal matters as well as in dealing with matters of particular complexity. Dr. Peter Sock is specialising in labour law and landlord and tenant law and is particularly experienced in litigation. They are also supported by qualified attorneys and associated with a team of specialists.

DR. H. PETER DRAXLER, admitted, 1975, Vienna.

DR. PETER STOCK, admitted, 1994, Vienna. *LANGUAGES:* German, English, Italian and Czech. *PRACTICE AREAS:* Mergers and Acquisi-

(This Listing Continued)

tions; Energy Law; Environmental law; Company Law; Labour Law; Real Property; Landlord and Tenant.

ASSOCIATES

Dr. Andreas Cwitkovits   Mag. Elisabeth Moser
Mag. Dr. Johannes Schramm

ECKERT & FRIES

VIENNA, AUSTRIA

(See Baden/Vienna, Austria)

Austrian and International Company Law, Tax, Intellectual Property, Patent, Trademark, Design and Copyright Law, Commercial, General Contract, Industrial Property, Litigation, Banking, Bankruptcy, Product Liability, Environmental, Trade, Operating Licenses, Employment, Industrial Relations, Collection of Debt, Execution, Conveyancing and Commercial Register Law, Civil Law.

EISELSBERG NATLACEN WALDERDORFF CANCOLA

Established in 1986

SCHWARZENBERGPLATZ 7
A-1030 VIENNA, AUSTRIA
Telephone: 1-715 55 95
Telefax: 1-715 55 99

General Business Practice, Administrative Law, Corporate, Banking, Industrial Property and Copyright, Unfair Competition, Antitrust, International Taxation and Tax Planning, Labour and Industrial Relations, EEC Law, Litigation and Arbitration.

FIRM PROFILE: *Partnership founded in 1986 by Dr. Maximilian Eiselberg (admitted, 1976) and Dr. Dieter Natlacen (admitted, 1983). In 1991 the firm merged with Rechtsanwälte Dr. Erich Schwinner, Dr. Georg Walderdorff (admitted, 1983), Vienna. All members of the firm are concentrating on Business-Law. Dr. Maximilian Eiselsberg is an author of several publications in the area of Corporate-Law (Kreditwesengesetz, Sparkassengesetz, Wertpapieremissionsgesetz, 1979; Firmenbuchgesetz, 1991; Spaltungsgesetz (Demerging-Act), 1993; Kartellgesetz (Antitrust Act), 1993; Stiftungsgesetz (Austrian Trust Act), 1993), speaker at conferences and seminars (specially on Umgründungsgesetz - Tax Reorganisation Act). Member of the Committee for Finance Policy of the Federation of Austrian Industrialists; extraordinary member of the Chamber of Chartered Accountants in the Committee for the Law on public companies and accounting; member of working groups on Trust Law within the Ministry of Justice and the Chamber of Notary Public and member of the supervisory board of several Austrian public companies; Dr. Dieter Natlacen is a University lector for Commercial Law at the Wirtschaftsuniversität Wien.*

The partners are members of IBA, UIA, AIJA, Associazione Internazionale Giuristi di Lingua Italiana and of Austrian Lawyers' Associations.

MEMBERS OF FIRM

DR. MAXIMILIAN EISELSBERG, born 1947. *LANGUAGES:* German, English and French. *PRACTICE AREAS:* Acquisitions and Sales; Restructuring and Demerging; Cartels and Antitrust; Corporate Finance; Tax Planning.

DR. DIETER NATLACEN, born 1954. *LANGUAGES:* German, English and Italian. *PRACTICE AREAS:* Industrial Property Rights; Computer Contracts; Agency and Distributorships; Product Liability; Food and Drug Regulation.

DR. GEORG WALDERDORFF, born 1953. *LANGUAGES:* German and English. *PRACTICE AREAS:* International Arbitration; Insolvency; Financial Services; Commercial Real Estate.

DR. RAIMUND CANCOLA, born 1960. *LANGUAGES:* German and English. *PRACTICE AREAS:* International Corporate and Finance; Reorganisation and Restructuring; Industrial Relations.

ASSOCIATES

Dr. Wolfgang Punz   Mag. Michael Steiner
Dr. Christian Baillou   Mag. Claudia Riedl
Dr. Andrea Pasquali

LAW OFFICES DR. G. FIALKA

Member-Office of the TASW-EWIV (Frankfurt/Main, Germany)

JOSEFSTÄDTER STRASSE 87
A-1080 VIENNA, AUSTRIA
Telephone: 43-1-408 78 380
Fax: 43-1-408 78 3822

General Practice, Litigation and Arbitration, (Int'l) Trade, Commercial, Corporate, Unfair Competition (Press, Media, Means of Communication), Administrative Law.

GEORG FIALKA, born 1951; admitted, 1979, Austria. *Education:* Vienna University of Economics and Business Administration, Doctor of Law, 1973, Master of Business Administration; Gustav Stresemann Institut Germany, EC Law, Edinburgh University/McGeorge School of Law (UK), Int'l Business Transactions. Author: Contribution on VAT, in: "Tax Consultant's Year-Book" (since 1978). Contribution to Rill (Edt.), Admin. Commercial Law, 1977. Lecturer: Vienna University of Economics and Business Administration (Commercial Law). *Member:* Vienna Bar Association; Vienna Law Society; American Lawyers Company Association; Int'l. Bar Association.

Languages: German, English, French and Spanish.

FIEBINGER & POLAK

Established in 1990

GRILLPARZERSTRASSE 7
1010 VIENNA, AUSTRIA
Telephone: (43) (1) 405 75 94
Telex: 116175 apkef a
Telefax: (43) (1) 408 81 77

Corporate, Commercial, Banking, Tax, Industrial Property, Patent Law, Unfair Competition, Media Law, Anti-Trust, Transportation Law, Real Estate Law, International Transactions, Arbitration, Contract Law.

MEMBERS OF FIRM

DR. RUDOLF K. FIEBINGER, born New York, July 26, 1956; admitted, 1986, Austria. *Education:* University of Vienna (Dr.iur., 1979). Lecturer, Dr. Richter course, 1976-1979. *Member:* Vienna Bar; Association Internationale de Jeunes Avocats (AIJA). **LANGUAGES:** German, Spanish, English and French. **PRACTICE AREAS:** Unfair Competition; Media Law; Industrial Property; Transportation Law; Arbitration; Corporate Law; Contract Law.

DR. PETER M. POLAK, born Vienna, Austria, May 25, 1960; admitted, 1986, California; 1989, Austria. *Education:* University of Vienna (Dr.iur., 1982); Boalt Hall School of Law, University of California, Berkeley (LL.M., 1984). Author: "Austrian Business Taxation," Co-authorship with Dr. Bernhard Gröhs, LL.M., Manz Publishing House, Vienna, 1990. Certified Court Interpreter for the English Language. Associate Professor, Webster University, St. Louis, Vienna Campus, 1989—. Associate, Gibson, Dunn & Crutcher, 1984-1985. *Member:* State Bar of California; Vienna Bar Association; International Bar Association (IBA); Association Internationale de Jeunes Avocats (AIJA); International Association of Boalt Hall Alumni Europe (President). **LANGUAGES:** German, English and French. **PRACTICE AREAS:** Banking; International Transactions; Arbitration; Anti-Trust; Corporate Law; Industrial Property; Copyright; Patent Law; Commercial Law.

ASSOCIATES

DR. IUR. MANUELA MAURER-KOLLENZ, born January 7, 1962; (Not admitted in Austria). *Education:* University of Graz, Law School (1984).

DR. JOHANNES JURANEK, born October 20, 1966; (Not admitted in Austria). *Education:* University of Vienna (Dr.iur., 1992). Assistant Professor, Institute for Public International Law, University of Vienna, School of Law, September 1989-June 1990. Author: "Die Richtlinien zur Harmonisierung der urheber-und leistungs-schutzrechtlichen Schutzfristen," Manz, 1994.

MAG. BERT ORTNER, born January 2, 1966; (Not admitted in Austria). *Education:* New York University (MCJ); University of Vienna (Mag.iur., 1989). Publications: Foreign Banking Secrecy Laws and US Discovery

(This Listing Continued)

or Grand Jury Proceedings - What Defenses can a Foreign Bank Raise?. **PRACTICE AREAS:** Banking Law; Corporate Law; Computer Law.

LEGAL SUPPORT PERSONNEL

JOHANNES WILLHEIM, born March 9, 1969. (Law Clerk).

Languages: German, English, French and Spanish

FOGLAR-DEINHARDSTEIN & BRANDSTAETTER

Established in 1922

PLANKENGASSE 7
A-1010 VIENNA, AUSTRIA
Telephone: (1) 512 15 71
Telefax: (1) 513 43 42
Telex: (0) 112947 legal

Administrative Law, Advertising and Marketing, Agency and Distributorships, Agricultural Law, Antitrust and Trade Regulation, Arbitration, Business Law, Chemicals and Chemistry, Civil Law, Commercial Law, Company Law, Contracts, Copyrights, Corporate Law, Environmental Law, European Community Law, Intellectual Property, Labor Law and Employment, Leases and Leasing, Litigation, Mergers and Acquisitions, Probate, Real Estate, Trademark, Trusts and Estates.

MEMBERS OF FIRM

DR. ANDREAS FOGLAR-DEINHARDSTEIN, born Vienna, December 11, 1951; admitted, 1980, Austria. *Education:* University of Vienna (Dr.jur., 1975). Assistant Professor, University of Vienna, School of Law, 1973-1976. Assistant Professor, Economic University of Vienna, 1983—. *Member:* International Bar Association (IBA). **LANGUAGES:** German and English. **PRACTICE AREAS:** Contracts; Commercial Acquisitions; Corporate Law.

DR. JUERGEN BRANDSTAETTER, born Vienna, April 9, 1956; admitted, 1985, Austria. *Education:* University of Vienna (Dr.jur., 1979). *Member:* International Bar Association (IBA); Legal Committee of Austrian Federation of Industrialists. **LANGUAGES:** German, English and French. **PRACTICE AREAS:** Arbitration; Chemicals; European Community Law; Industrial Property Rights; Unfair Competition.

ASSOCIATES

DR. PETER BRODNER, born Vienna, November 22, 1963; admitted, 1994, Austria. *Education:* University of Vienna (Dr.jur., 1991). **PRACTICE AREAS:** Food; Labor and Employment; Litigation.

MAG. CHRISTOPH GOTTESMANN, born Vienna, April 8, 1965; admitted, 1994, Austria. *Education:* University of Vienna (Mag.jur., 1989). **PRACTICE AREAS:** Agency and Distributorships; Commercial Leases and Leasing.

DR. KARIN SCHWARZER, born Vienna, August 18, 1960; admitted, 1991, Austria. *Education:* University of Vienna (Dr.jur., 1982). **PRACTICE AREAS:** Real Estate.

MAG. BEATE ABERHAM, born Neunkirchen, July 5, 1963; (Not admitted in Austria). *Education:* University of Vienna (Mag.jur., 1990). **PRACTICE AREAS:** Family Law.

MAG. AIMEE CSAKY, born Vienna, July 22, 1968; (Not admitted in Austria). *Education:* University of Vienna (Mag. jur., 1991). **PRACTICE AREAS:** Trademarks.

MAG. PAUL HOFFMANN, born Vienna, May 13, 1966; (Not admitted in Austria). *Education:* University of Vienna (Mag.jur., 1990). **PRACTICE AREAS:** Administrative Law; Cartels; Environmental Law.

MAG. KARL PICHLER, born Bad Hall, August 1, 1965. *Education:* University of Salzburg (Mag.jur., 1991). **PRACTICE AREAS:** Computers and Technology.

Languages: German, English and French.

FRIEDERS TASSUL & PARTNER

Established in 1955

STADIONGASSE 6 - 8
A-1010 VIENNA, AUSTRIA
Telephone: 0043 1 42 16 43
Cable Address: 11 15 79 lexco
Telecopier: 0043 1 408 6485

Corporate, Commercial, Banking, Securities, International Business Transactions, Mergers and Acquisitions, Joint Ventures, Industrial Property, Unfair Competition, Copyright, Tax, Administrative Law, Trade Regulations, Labour Law, Real Estate, Tenancy, Wills and Estates, Product Liability, Litigation and Arbitration, EU Law.

MEMBERS OF FIRM

DR. HANS FRIEDERS, born Weimar, December 1, 1921; admitted, 1953, Austria. *Education:* University of Vienna (Dr.Jur.). Examiner, Austrian Bar Exam, 1987—. *Member:* Vienna and International Bar Associations. *LANGUAGES:* German and English.

DR. CHRISTIAN TASSUL, born Vienna, Austria, July 4, 1956; admitted, 1984, Austria. *Education:* University of Vienna (Dr.Jur.). *Member:* Vienna Bar Association. *LANGUAGES:* German, English and French.

DR. GEORG FRIEDERS, born Vienna, Austria, February 17, 1956; admitted, 1985, Austria. *Education:* University of Vienna (Dr.Jur.); Boalt Hall School of Law, University of California, Berkeley (Master of Law). Author: "Products Liability - A Comparative View," Master's Thesis, 1982; "EFTA Legal Systems: An Introductory Guide," Butterworths, 1993. *Member:* Austrian Delegate to the Conseil des Barreaux de la Communauté Européenne (CCBE), 1991—; Vienna (Member, Executive Council) and International Bar Associations. *LANGUAGES:* German, English, French and Spanish.

DR. CHRISTOPH HORVATH, born Vienna, Austria, March 16, 1964; admitted, 1993, Austria. *Education:* University of Vienna (Dr. Jur.). Author: "Austrian Aliens Police Law - Theory and Practice," 1987; "EFTA Legal Systems: An Introductory Guide," Butterworths, 1993. *Member:* Vienna Bar Association. *LANGUAGES:* German, English and French.

ASSOCIATES

Mag. Wolf Anderluh
Mag. Michael Schubhart
Dr. Andreas Walter, LL.M. (University of Cambridge)
Mag. Joseph L. Steiner

Languages: German, English, French and Spanish

GABLER & GIBEL

Established in 1986

STALLBURGGASSE 4
A-1010 VIENNA, AUSTRIA
Telephone: (0043) 222 535 60 05
Telefax: (0043) 222 535 40 45

Commercial, Corporate, Tax, Banking, International Business Transactions (Mergers and Acquisitions), Unfair Competition, Real Estate Law, Intellectual Property, Labor Law, Trust and Estates, Civil Litigation.

FIRM PROFILE: Young and expanding firm offering services primarily in commercial, company and real estate law emphasizing personal contact to clients as the basis for successful cooperation.

MEMBERS OF FIRM

DR. MICHAEL GABLER, born Vienna, August 10, 1957; admitted, 1985, Austria. *Education:* University of Vienna (Dr. jur., 1980). Author: Specific Questions to §12 (3) MRG; "Purchase of a Business and it's Effect on Lease-Agreements," ImmZ 1991; "Erwerbsgesellschaftengesetz," ImmZ 1991. *Member:* Vienna Bar; International Bar Association (IBA); Association of Commercial Lawyers (ACL International). *LANGUAGES:* English and German. *PRACTICE AREAS:* Real Estate; Commercial Real Estate; Condominiums; Development and Syndications; Leases and Leasing; Unfair Competition.

MAG. DR. ERICH GIBEL, born Vienna, June 13, 1956; admitted, 1985, Austria. *Education:* University of Vienna (Dr. jur., 1979); University of Economics Vienna (Mag. rer. soc. oec., 1981). Author: "Land Transfer Tax," WBI; "Assignment for Security Purposes and Its Disclosure Requirements," Thesis, 1981; "Austria where East meets West," ACL-Networking,

(This Listing Continued)

1991. *Member:* Vienna Bar; International Bar Association (IBA); Association of Commercial Lawyers (ACL International). *LANGUAGES:* German, English and French. *PRACTICE AREAS:* Commercial Law; Company Law; Acquisitions and Sales; Contracts; Taxation; Trusts and Estates; Litigation.

LEGAL SUPPORT PERSONNEL

DR. CHRISTIAN BUTSCHEK, born Vienna, May 6, 1963. *Education:* University of Vienna (Mag.jur., 1986; Dr.jur., 1989). Author: "The Legal Position of the Beneficiary in Trust-Law," Thesis, 1989, same title revision of a supreme court judgement and adapted version, 364, JBI 1991. *LANGUAGES:* German, English and French.

DR. OTTO WÄCHTER, born Vienna, Austria, August 12, 1961. *Education:* University of Vienna (Dr.jur., 1987); University of Columbia (Summer Program). Co-Author: "Investing in Hungary," edited by Preslmayr & Partners and Auditor, 1991. *LANGUAGES:* German, English and French.

HANS-DIETER ORTNER, born Linz, Austria, December 25, 1959. *Education:* University of Vienna (Dr.iuris, 1985). *LANGUAGES:* German and English.

Languages: German, English and French

DR. FERDINAND R. GRAF

Established in 1966

OPPOLZERGASSE 6
1010 VIENNA, AUSTRIA
Telephone: 43-1-5330629; 43-1-5330620
Telefax: 43-1-533062018

Commercial and Civil Law, Contract Law, Torts, Arbitration, Banking and International Business Law, Company Law, Antitrust, Rent and Lease, Labour Law, Product Liability, Civil Litigation, Debt Collection, Enforcement of Claims, Unfair Competition.

FIRM PROFILE: The firm is one of the oldest in Vienna and was originally established in 1918 by Dr. Tafler who was later joined by Dr. Stölzle and by Dr. Graf in 1966. After the deaths of Dr. Tafler and Dr. Stölzle, Dr. Graf took over the firm and currently runs it.

MEMBERS OF FIRM

DR. FERDINAND R. GRAF, born 1936; admitted, 1966, Austria. *Education:* University of Vienna Law School (Dr.Juris, 1958). Member, Lawyers Club: Soupirium. *Member:* Austrian Bar Association (Member, Supreme Disciplinary Court in the Austrian Bar). *LANGUAGES:* German and English. *PRACTICE AREAS:* Arbitration; Secured Lending; Rent and Lease; Business Law; Common Market; Joint Ventures; Product Liability; Company Law.

ASSOCIATES

DR. ANNEMARIE GRAF, born 1936; admitted, 1966, Vienna. *Education:* University of Vienna Law School (Dr.Juris, 1958). *LANGUAGES:* German, English and French. *PRACTICE AREAS:* Business Law; Debt Collection; Civil Litigation.

COUNSEL

DR. GEORG GRAF, born 1962. *Education:* University of Vienna Law School (Dr.Juris, 1985); University of Chicago (M.A., 1986). Docent, Civil Law, University of Salzburg, 1988—. Numerous publications in Banking and Commercial Law. *LANGUAGES:* German and English. *PRACTICE AREAS:* Banking Law; Contract Law; Commercial Law; Consumer Law.

CAND. JUR. PHILIPP GRAF, born 1969. *Education:* University of Vienna Law School. Assistant, History of Law, University of Vienna Law School, 1991-1994. *LANGUAGES:* German, English and French. *PRACTICE AREAS:* Civil Law.

GRAF LIEBMANN MAXL PITKOWITZ

SCHREYVOGELGASSE 2
1010 VIENNA, AUSTRIA
Telephone: (43-1) 534-50
Telefax: (43-1) 534-50 50

General Commercial Practice, Corporate, Arbitration, Litigation, Transportation, Labor, Real Estate, Anti-Trust, Unfair Competition, Distribution, Tourism, Environmental, Banking, Aircraft Financing, Eastern Europe (Joint Ventures and Privatization), European Union.

(This Listing Continued)

PARTNERS

DR. NIKOLAUS PITKOWITZ, born Vienna, Austria, October 4, 1961; admitted, 1990, Austria. *Education:* University of Vienna (Juris Doctor, 1984); Georgetown University Law Center (Orientation in the U.S. Legal System, 1991). Co-Author: "Investing in Austria," Orac, 1994; "Investing in Hungary," Orac, 1st ed. 1990, 2nd ed 1991; "Investing in the Czech and Slovak Republic," Orac, 1st ed. 1990, 2nd ed. 1991, 3rd. ed. 1993. Author: "Wirkt der Rücktritt des Masseverwalters gemäß§ 21 KO ex tunc?" ÖJZ 677, 1990; "Large Scale Privatization in Czechoslovakia," ecolex 363, 1991; "Check-List Joint Ventures in Czechoslovakia," ecolex 370, 1991; "Security over Real Estate in the Czech and the Slovak Republic," BankArchiv, 519, 1993 and Všehrd 7 93; ; "The importance of Czech Investment Funds and Investment Companies in the View of Foreign Investors," Karlsbader Juristentage 1993; "The Greenfield Approach and the Role of Austria for Privatization in Eastern Europe," Columbia University, Privatization in Eastern Europe: Legal Economic and Social Aspects, 1994. University Lecturer, Hungarian, Czech and Slovak Law. *Member:* Austrian Bar; International Bar Association (IBA), DACH; American Foreign Lawyers Association (AFLA). *LANGUAGES:* German and English.

DR. MARTIN MAXL, born Bruck/Mur, Austria, March 19, 1961; admitted, 1994, Austria. *Education:* Universities of Graz, Paris (Centre Sevres) and Munich Schools of Arts; University of Graz (Juris Magister, 1988; Juris Doctor with honors, 1990; L, doctoral thesis, 1990-1992). Author: "Aspects of International Product Liability," (Thesis, 1990); "Product Liability, International Civil Procedure Law and International Private Law," JB1 156, 1992; "The Meaning of Silence in International Private Law," Iprax 398, 1989. "Bulgaria: New Investment Law," West-Ost-Journal 38, 1992. Assistant Professor and Lecturer in Law, University of Graz, Institute for Private Law, Private International Law and Comparative Law, 1988-1990. *Member:* Austrian Bar. *LANGUAGES:* German, English and French.

DR. HANNO LIEBMANN, born Graz, Austria, December 7, 1962; admitted, 1993, Austria. *Education:* University of Graz (Juris Magister 1987; doctoral thesis, 1990-1992); University of Vienna (Juris Doctor, with honors, 1992). Author: "Termination of Lease Agreements based on Personal Use," (Thesis, 1985); "Goodwill and Assessed Valuation," (Thesis, 1992); further publications on various issues, Handbook on Distribution Law (to be published 1995). *Member:* Austrian Bar. *LANGUAGES:* German, English and French.

DR. FERDINAND GRAF, born Vienna, Austria, February 12, 1965; admitted, 1993, New York; 1994, Austria. *Education:* University of Vienna (Juris Magister, 1989; Juris Doctor, with honors, 1990); New York University, School of Law (LL.M., 1991). Assistant Professor, University of Vienna, Institute for Private and Private International Law, 1988-1989. Internship at Arent, Fox, Kintner, Plotkin & Kahn, Washington, D.C., 1991. Author: "Legal Malpractice" (Textbook on legal malpractice) Orac 1991; "New Case Law related to Legal Malpractice," ecolex 1991, 305; "The Hypothetical Appeal, Aspects of Legal Malpractice in Austria," New York University Journal of International Law and Politics, 1651, 1992 "Novelty of a Model under the Austrian Act on the Protection of the Design of Models," ecolex 1/1995; "Lawyers' Liability," Austrian Part in Lloyd's of London Press (1995). *Member:* Austrian Bar; American Bar Association; Association of Austrian Fulbright Students; Center for International Legal Studies. *LANGUAGES:* German and English.

COUNSEL

DR. GABRIELA JÄGER, born Bratislava, Slovakia, 1952. *Education:* University of Bratislava School of Law (Magister Juris, 1976); University of Vienna School of Law (Doctor Juris, 1986). *LANGUAGES:* German, English, Czech, Slovakian, Russian; reading knowledge of: Bulgarian and Ukrainian.

MMAG. DR. MARKUS FELLNER, born Vienna, Austria, August 11, 1967. *Education:* University of Economics, Vienna (Magister Economics, 1989); University of Vienna School of Law (Juris Magister, 1992; Juris Doctor, with honors, 1994). Author: "Organisation of Independent Administrative Authorities," (doctoral thesis, 1994); "Valuation of Companies and Goodwill," (thesis, 1988). 1995 foreign lawyers program at Schulte, Roth & Zabel, New York. *LANGUAGES:* German, English and French.

MAG. PIA L. KUNZE, born Vienna, Austria, February 24, 1969. *Education:* University of Vienna (Juris Magister, 1993). *LANGUAGES:* German, English and French.

GROHS-HOFER-REINER

Established in 1925

FREYUNG 6/11 (SCHOTTENHOF)
A-1010 VIENNA, AUSTRIA
Telephone: 43-1-533 87 26 0
Fax: 43-1-533 87 28 34

General Business Practice, Banking, Company, Corporate, EEC-Law, Competition, Industrial Property, Estate and Probate Law, Environmental Law, Labour Law, International Transactions and Commercial Arbitration, Computer and Software Contracts.

MEMBERS OF FIRM

DR. ANDREAS GROHS, born Vienna, Austria, June 28, 1951; admitted, 1979, Austria. *Education:* University of Vienna (Dr. jur., 1975).

DR. WOLFGANG HOFER, born Scheibbs, Austria, January 24, 1953; admitted, 1980, Austria. *Education:* University of Vienna (Dr. jur., 1974).

DR. ANDREAS REINER, born Vienna, Austria, April 30, 1951; admitted, 1989, Austria. *Education:* University of Vienna (Dr. jur., 1973); University of Orléans, France (Master of Laws, 1979); Paris University (Post-Graduate Degree in European Community Law, 1980). Author: "ICC-Arbitration", Manz University Press, Vienna, 1989; Lecturer, University of Economics, Vienna. Counsel, ICC International Court of Arbitration, 1981-1985. Austrian Member, ICC International Court of Arbitration, 1991.

ASSOCIATES

DR. KARIN GELBENEGGER, born Salzburg, Austria, July 23, 1963. *Education:* University of Salzburg (Dr. jur., 1990).

DR. GEORGE HACKET, born Taunton, United Kingdom, May 27, 1966. *Education:* Universities of Innsbruck and Vienna (Dr. jur., 1992); McGill University of Montreal (LL.M., 1992). Author: "Space Debris and the corpus iuris spatialis", Paris 1994. Member of the International Institute of Space Law.

MAG. GERHARD SARIA, born Vienna, Austria, October 31, 1970. *Education:* University of Vienna (Mag. jur., 1993).

MAG. DR. HARALD SCHICHT, born Vienna, Austria, May 10, 1962. *Education:* University of Vienna (Dr.jur., 1985); University of Economics, Vienna (Mag. rer. oec. soc., 1990).

DR. URSULA SKREINER, born Graz, Austria, March 14, 1967. *Education:* Universities of Graz and Vienna (Dr. jur., 1994).

DR. ELISABETH STERN, born Vienna, Austria, March 20, 1963. *Education:* University of Vienna (Dr. jur., 1989). Lecturer, University of Economics, Vienna (1987). Author: "Statements under the UNCITRAL Sales Law", Manz University Press, Vienna, 1990; various articles including: "The 6th EC-Company Law directive", Doralt-Nowotny: Anpassungsbedarf, 1993; "Pensionsfunds", ÖBA, 1993; Take over bids, ÖBA, 1993.

Languages: German, English, French.

DR. WULF GORDIAN HAUSER, LL.M.

Established in 1986

DOMGASSE 4
A-1010 VIENNA, AUSTRIA
Telephone: (1) 513 77 40
Telefax: (1) 513 77 42

Mergers and Acquisitions, Commercial and Corporate Law, International Transactions, Foreign Investment in Austria and in former Eastern Block countries, Joint Ventures, Taxation, Probate Law, Construction and Banking Law, Transportation Law, Intellectual Property and Unfair Competition.

DR. WULF GORDIAN HAUSER, admitted, 1986, Austria; 1983, New York; 1984, District of Columbia. *Education:* University of Vienna (LL.M., and Ph.D., 1974); Georgetown University (LL.M., 1983). Phi Delta Phi. Fulbright Scholar. Author: "Taxation of legal services for foreign clients," Anw 1994, 659; "The confirmation of contested shareholders resolutions of AGs," Ecolex, 1990, 477; "Tax consequences of declaratory decrees under the Assets Liquidation Act (Vermögensabwicklungsgesetz)," Austrian Bar Journal, p. 118, 1989; "Austria - An Emerging International Tax Haven?" Tax Planning International Review, Vol. 16, No. 3, p. 28 (1989); "Austria - Tax Reform," Tax Planning International Review, Vol. 15, No. 7, p. 25

(This Listing Continued)

DR. WULF GORDIAN HAUSER, LL.M., *Vienna—*
Continued

(1988); "Legal and Tax Aspects of Joint Ventures in the United States," Austrian Journal of Corporate Law, p. 197, 1987 and p. 39, 1988; "Tax Reduction in the United States - An Example for Austria," Economic Policy Review, p. 596, 1986; "The American Income Taxation of Foreign Taxpayers," American Journal for Comparative Law, p. 252, 1986; "U.S. Taxation of Nonresidents," Austrian Tax Law Journal, p. 175, 1986; "Reagan's Tax Reform of 1981- Numbers-Facts-Analyses," Publication No. 148 of the Institute for Finance and Tax Law; "U.S. Air Traffic Accident Liability Law - What remains of the Warsaw Convention?" Austrian Journal for Comparative Law, pp. 161-223, 1984; Partner, 1986-1987 and Associate, 1980-1982, Dres. Cerha, Hempel & Spiegelfeld, Vienna. Associate: Wilkinson, Barker, Knauer & Quinn, Washington, D.C., 1983-1984; Cole & Corette, Washington, D.C., 1984-1985. *Member:* American and International Bar Associations; International Law Association; Arbitration Court of the Federal Economic Chamber, Vienna; Permanent Arbitration Court of the Chamber of Commerce, Vienna. *LANGUAGES:* German, English and French.

ASSOCIATES

DR. WINFRIED SCHWARZ. *Education:* University of Vienna (Mag.-jur., 1991; Dr.jur., 1992). *LANGUAGES:* German and English.

DR. WOLFGANG ZIEGLER. *Education:* University of Vienna (Mag. jur., 1990; Dr. jur., 1993). *LANGUAGES:* German, English and French.

MAG. ANGELIKA HEINZL. *Education:* University of Vienna (Mag. iur., 1992); studies in Johannesburg, South Africa and Louvain-La-Neuve, Belgium. Associates law offices, Dr. Summer, Dr. Schertler, 1993-1994; Scholarship for legal training at European Parliament and European Commission. *LANGUAGES:* German, English and French.

Languages: German, English and French.

HELLER, LÖBER, BAHN & PARTNERS

Established in 1970

SEILERGASSE 16

A-1010 VIENNA, AUSTRIA

Telephone: (431) 515 15 0

Fax: (431) 512 63 94

Telex: 114874 lawco a

Budapest, Hungary Office: János Zsigmond U. 7B, H-1121. Telephone: (361) 2093370. Fax: (361) 1868481.

Prague, Czech Republic Office: Italská 27, CZ-12000. Telephone: (422) 24231006. Fax: (422) 24218375.

Bratislava, Slovakia Office: Laurinská 12, SK-81101. Telephone: (427) 361439. Fax: (427) 361478.

Brussels, Belgium Office: Rue de la Loi 99/101 B-1040. Telephone: (322) 287 26 55. Fax: (322) 280 09 83.

Corporate, Commercial, Tax, Industrial Property, Unfair Competition, Antitrust, Banking, Contract and Estate Law. International Transactions and Arbitration.

FIRM PROFILE: Heller, Löber, Bahn & Partners are one of the largest law firms in Austria with their main office in Vienna and representative offices in Budapest, Pragu, Bratislava and Brussels.

MEMBERS OF FIRM

KURT HELLER, born Vienna, 1939; admitted, 1970, Austria. *Education:* University of Vienna Law School (Dr. iur.). Justice, Constitutional Court. Austrian Delegate, Commission of International Arbitration, International Chamber of Commerce. Board Member, International Arbitral Center, Federal Economic Chamber, Vienna. President-Elect, International Academy of Estate and Trust Law. *Member:* Vienna and International (Member, Business Law Section) Bar Associations; Austrian Association of Comparative Law (Member, Executive Council); Österreichischer Juristentag (Member, Executive Council). *LANGUAGES:* German and English. *PRACTICE AREAS:* Arbitration; International Contracts; Public Law.

HEINZ H. LÖBER, born Vienna, 1940; admitted, 1971, Austria. *Education:* University of Vienna Law School (Dr. iur.); New York University Law School (M.C.J.). *Member:* Vienna, Austrian (Member, Executive Council) and International (Member: IBA Council; Council of Business Law Section) Bar Associations; International Fiscal Association. *LAN-*

(This Listing Continued)

GUAGES: German and English. *PRACTICE AREAS:* Mergers and Acquisitions.

GEORG BAHN, born Vienna, Austria, 1943; admitted, 1973, Austria. *Education:* University of Vienna Law School (Dr. iur.) and Department of Political Sciences (Dr. rer.pol.); University of California, Santa Barbara, Department for Political Science. Member, Austrian Association on Foreign Policy and International Relations. *Member:* Vienna Bar Association; Association Internationale des Jeunes Avocats. *LANGUAGES:* German and English. *PRACTICE AREAS:* Real Estate.

WERNER HUBER, born Mistelbach, 1950; admitted, 1980, Austria. *Education:* University of Vienna Law School (Dr. iur.); College of Europe, Bruges, Belgium; Diplomatic Academy, Vienna. Member: Österreichischer Juristenverein; Vienna Bar Association; Union Internationale des Avocats. *LANGUAGES:* German, English and French. *PRACTICE AREAS:* Banking, Finance and Construction.

GÜNTHER J. HORVATH, born Salzburg, Austria, 1952; admitted, 1981, Austria. *Education:* University of Graz Law School (Dr. iur.); New York University Law School (M.C.J.). *Member:* Vienna and International (Chairman, SGP Committee 22) Bar Associations; Lex Mundi (Chairman-Elect). *LANGUAGES:* German and English. *PRACTICE AREAS:* Corporate Law; Arbitration.

WILLIBALD PLESSER, born Haide, Austria, 1955; admitted, 1986, Austria. *Education:* University of Vienna Law School (Dr. iur.) and Philosophical Faculty (Mag. phil.). *Member:* International League of Competition Law; Supervisory Council of AFS, Austria; Vienna Bar Association. *LANGUAGES:* German and English. *PRACTICE AREAS:* Mergers and Acquisitions; Contract.

MARIA TH. PFLÜGL, born Traunkirchen, 1956; admitted, 1989, Austria. *Education:* University of Vienna Law School (Dr. iur.) and Philosophical Faculty. *Member:* Vienna Bar Association; Union Internationale des Avocats; Association Internationale des Jeunes Avocats; International Fiscal Association. *LANGUAGES:* German, English and French. *PRACTICE AREAS:* Tax and Banking.

ULRIKE E. REIN, born Feldkirch, 1962; admitted, 1992, Austria. *Education:* University of Vienna Law School (Dr. iur.). *LANGUAGES:* German, English and French. *PRACTICE AREAS:* Administrative Law.

THOMAS ZOTTL, born Wörgl, 1961; admitted, 1992, Austria. *Education:* University of Innsbruck Law School (Dr. iur.); School of Economic and Social Sciences (Mag. rer. soc. oec.). *LANGUAGES:* German and English. *PRACTICE AREAS:* Tax and Contract Law.

CHRISTOF PÖCHHACKER, born Vienna, 1963; admitted, 1994, Austria. *Education:* University of Vienna Law School (Dr. iur.); University of Illinois at Urbana-Champaign, College of Law (M.C.L.). *LANGUAGES:* German and English. *PRACTICE AREAS:* Unfair Competition Law; Trademark Law.

FOREIGN COUNSEL

JENNY W.T. POWER, born Bombay, India, 1960; admitted, 1987, Florida (Not admitted in Austria). *Education:* University of Pennsylvania, Philadelphia, Pennsylvania; St. John's College, Annapolis, Maryland (B.A.); University of Miami School of Law (J.D., 1987). *Member:* The Florida Bar Association; American Bar Association. *LANGUAGES:* English and German. *PRACTICE AREAS:* Arbitration.

ASSOCIATES

PAUL S. LUIKI, born Pontiac, Michigan, USA, 1962; admitted, 1988, Ohio (Not admitted in Austria). *Education:* University of Vienna Law School (Mag. iur.); University of Iowa School of Law (J.D., 1988); University of Graz; University of Michigan (B.A.). *Member:* American Bar Association. *LANGUAGES:* English, German, French and Russian. *PRACTICE AREAS:* Environmental Law.

MARKUS STENDER, born Starnberg, 1965. *Education:* University of Graz Law School (Mag.iur.). *LANGUAGES:* German and English.

JOHANN PICHLER, born Wolfsberg, 1965. *Education:* University of Vienna Law School (MMag. iur.). *LANGUAGES:* German and English.

STEVEN GERALD ROBERTS, born Guernsey, Great Britain, 1962. *Education:* University of Vienna Law School (Mag. iur.). *LANGUAGES:* German and English.

ANNE GOSSET, born Uccle, Belgium, 1967; admitted, 1992, Brussels (Not admitted in Austria). *Education:* University of Brussels (U.L.B.) Law School (Lic.Jur., 1990); University of Exeter, U.K. (LL.M., 1991). *LANGUAGES:* French, English and German.

(This Listing Continued)

JAVIER ORTEGA DE LA PENA, born Vigo, Spain, 1965. *Education:* University of Vienna Law School (MMag.iur.). *LANGUAGES:* Spanish, German and English.

ANDREAS MAYR, born Linz, 1966; admitted, 1993, New York (Not admitted in Austria). *Education:* University of Salzburg Law School (Mag. iur.); Columbia University School of Law, New York (LL.M.); University of Essex School of Government, England. *LANGUAGES:* German and English.

ANDREAS WEILER, born Hall, 1961. *Education:* University of Innsbruck Law School (Dr. iur.). *LANGUAGES:* German, English, French and Italian.

FLORIAN GIBITZ, born Salzburg, 1963. *Education:* University of Salzburg Law School (Dr. iur.); University of Michigan Law School (LL.M.). *LANGUAGES:* German and English.

MANFRED WIENER, born Anger, 1966. *Education:* University of Graz Law School (Dr. iur.). *LANGUAGES:* German and English.

JENNIFER A. POWERS, born Connecticut, 1965; admitted, 1994, New York (Not admitted in Austria). *Education:* McGeorge School of Law (LL.M., 1992); University of Denver College of Law (J.D., 1991); Duke University (A.B., 1987). *Member:* American Bar Association. *LANGUAGES:* English, Spanish and German.

ELISABETH ALBRECHT, born Vienna, 1967; admitted, 1993, New York (Not admitted in Austria). *Education:* University of Vienna Law School (Mag. iur.); Cornell University (LL.M.). *LANGUAGES:* German, English and French.

FRANZ J. KOHLBACHER, born Graz, 1967. *Education:* University of Graz Law School (Mag.iur.). *LANGUAGES:* German and English.

PETER WAGESREITER, born Vienna, 1967. *Education:* University of Vienna Law School (Mag.iur.); University of Pennsylvania Law School (LL.M.). *LANGUAGES:* German and English.

RENÉ WALTER SCHNEIDER, born Graz, 1967. *Education:* University of Graz Law School (Mag. iur.); London School of Economics (LL.M.). *LANGUAGES:* German, English and French.

WILFRIED OPETNIK, born Eisenkappel, 1965. *Education:* University of Graz Law School (Mag. iur.); University of Leicester, GB (LL.M.). *LANGUAGES:* German, English and Spanish.

Languages: German, English and French.

DR. JOHANNES HOCK SEN.
DR. JOHANNES HOCK JUN.
DR. HERMANN GEISSLER

Established in 1894

STALLBURGGASSE 4
VIENNA 1, AUSTRIA
Telephone: 43 (1) 533 50 62
Facsimile: 43 (1) 533 09 89

General Business Practice, Corporate, Commercial, Unfair Competition, Tax, Construction Contracts and Litigation, Real Estate, Debt Collection, Wills, Probate, Administrative and Constitutional Law, Human Rights, Copyright and Trademark Law, Arbitration, Antitrust, Environmental Law.

DR. JOHANNES HOCK, SEN., born 1929; admitted, 1959, Austria. *Education:* University of Oregon (B.Sc.econ., 1951); University of Vienna (Dr. jur., 1952).

DR. JOHANNES HOCK, JUN., born 1958; admitted, 1987, Austria. *Education:* University of Vienna (Dr.jur., 1981); Columbia Summer Program Amsterdam (1983);. Assistant, University of Vienna (civil law, 1979-1981); Assistant, Supreme Constitutional Court (1981-1983); Member, Arbitral Centre of the Federal Economic Chamber, Vienna.

DR. HERMANN GEISSLER, born 1957; admitted, 1986, Austria. *Education:* University of Vienna (Dr.jur., 1980). Assistant Supreme Constitutional Court, 1981-1983.

Languages: German, English, French.

HULE & HEINKE

LILIENGASSE 1
A-1010 VIENNA, AUSTRIA
Telephone: (1) 512 84 67-0
Telefax: (1) 512 84 67-22

Complex Litigation and Arbitration, Construction, Commercial, Corporate, Unfair Competition, Real Estate, Insurance, Inheritance.

FIRM PROFILE: Dr. Hule is admitted in Austria. Dr. Heinke is admitted in Austria, and is a Canadian citizen.

MEMBERS OF FIRM

Dr. Michael Hule   **Dr. Eric Heinke**

ASSOCIATES

Mag. Marcus Bachmayr-Heyda **Mag. Berndt Pokorny**

Languages: German, English, and French.

JOHN & JOHN

TUCHLAUBEN 14
A-1010 VIENNA, AUSTRIA
Telephone: (1) 533 42 54
Telefax: (1) 532 07 79

General Civil Practice, Intellectual Property, Banking, Commercial, Company, Real Estate, Contract, Inheritance and Estate Law, International Contracts, Acquisitions Eastern Europe, Litigation, Tort Law, EC Law.

MEMBERS OF FIRM

DR. GÜNTHER R. JOHN, born May 2, 1954; admitted, 1991, Austria. *Education:* University of Vienna (Juris Doctor, 1976); University of California at Berkeley (LL.M., 1980). Research Fellow, Max-Planck-Institute for Foreign and International Patent, Copyright and Competition Law. *Member:* GRUR.

DR. BARBARA JOHN-RUMMELHARDT, born September 21, 1958; admitted, 1989, Austria. *Education:* University of Vienna (Juris Doctor, 1981); University of Philadelphia (LL.M., 1984).

Languages: German, English and French

DR. PETER KISLER
DDR. KARL PISTOTNIK

Established in 1957

BOERSEGASSE 12
A-1010 VIENNA, AUSTRIA
Telephone: 0043-222-5336285
Telex: 13-5644 PK LAW
Facsimile: 0043-222-5337185

Partnership, Corporations, Banking, Real Estate, Inheritance, Taxes.

DR. PETER KISLER, born 1927; admitted, 1957, Vienna. *LANGUAGES:* German, English, French and Italian.

DDR. KARL PISTOTNIK, born 1944; admitted, 1973, Vienna. *LANGUAGES:* German and English.

ASSOCIATE

DR. DIETHARD SCHIMMER, born 1960; admitted, 1988, Vienna. *LANGUAGES:* German and English.

KRAFT & WINTERNITZ

NIBELUNGENGASSE 11
1010 VIENNA, AUSTRIA
Telephone: +43 1 587 1660-0
Fax: +43 1 5863117

Corporate, Commercial, Antitrust and Trade Regulation, International Agency and Distributorships, Labor, Bankruptcy, Real Estate, Intellectual Property, Trademarks, Trusts and Estates, Civil and Commercial Litigation.

(This Listing Continued)

KRAFT & WINTERNITZ, Vienna—Continued

FIRM PROFILE: *The firm offers all legal services to clients in the business community with special expertise in Corporate and Commercial Law including Civil Litigation and Intellectual Property. In 1991 the firm has established a branch in Prague, Czech Republic.*

MEMBERS OF FIRM

RAINER MARIA KRAFT, born Vienna, 1955; admitted, 1987, Austria. *Education:* University of Vienna (Dr. iur., 1977); College of Europe, Bruges. Author: "The New Product Liability Act and its Consequences for German Producers", 1988; "The Product Liability in the CSFR", 1990; Numerous Publications on Commercial Agency and Distribution Agreements. *Member:* Austrian Bar Association; International Association of Young Lawyers (AIJA-National Vice President for Austria). *LANGUAGES:* German, English, Spanish and French. *PRACTICE AREAS:* Intellectual Property; Product Liability; Labor Law; International Agency and Distributorships; Trusts and Estates.

CHRISTIAN P. WINTERNITZ, born Vienna, 1954; admitted, 1985, Austria. *Education:* University of Vienna (Dr. iur., 1978); New York University (LL.M., 1987). *Member:* Austrian Bar Association; International Bar Association. *LANGUAGES:* German and English. *PRACTICE AREAS:* Corporate; Commercial; Antitrust and Trade Regulation; Bankruptcy; Real Estate.

WERNER J. LOIBL, born Vienna, 1958; admitted, 1988, Austria. *Education:* University of Vienna (Dr. iur., 1981); New York University (M.C.J., 1987). Author: "The Austrian Design Protection Act," Commentary, 1993. *Member:* Austrian Bar Association; International Association of Young Lawyers (AIJA). *LANGUAGES:* German and English. *PRACTICE AREAS:* International Business Law; Trademarks; Environmental; Civil and Commercial Litigation.

ASSOCIATES

WALTER SCHUHMANN, born Vienna, 1962. *Education:* University of Vienna (Dr. jur., 1993).

MIRJAM SORGO, born Salzburg, 1968. *Education:* University of Salzburg (Mag. jur., 1993).

HARTHUT R. SCHHIDTHAYR, born Vienna, 1963. *Education:* University of Vienna (Dr. iur., 1994).

CLAUS-DIETER KADITS, born Vienna, 1966. *Education:* University of Vienna (Mag.jur., 1993).

KUNZ SCHIMA WALLENTIN & PARTNER

PORZELLANGASSE 4-6
A-1090 VIENNA, AUSTRIA
Telephone: +43 1 313 74
Telefax: +43 1 313 74 80; 313 74 81

International Business Law, Corporate Law including cross-border Mergers and Acquisitions, Commercial Law and Administrative Law, Construction Law, Distribution Law, Environmental Law, Media and Entertainment Law, Tax Law, Labour Law, Intellectual Property Law, especially Copyright and Trademark Law, Unfair Competition Law, Real Estate Law, Insolvency Law, Reconstruction Law, Business Taxation, Antitrust Law - strong international clientele.

MEMBERS OF FIRM

DR. PETER KUNZ, born 1959; admitted, 1988, Austria. *Education:* University of Vienna, School of Law (Dr.iur., 1982). Internship, Pavia Ansaldo e Verusio, Milan, Italy, 1988. Author: Several publications in the field of corporate and commercial law. *LANGUAGES:* English and Italian. *PRACTICE AREAS:* International Business Law; Corporate Law; Commercial Law; Distribution Law; Environmental Law; Real Estate Law; Antitrust.

DR. GEORG SCHIMA, born 1960; admitted, 1991, Austria. *Education:* University of Vienna, School of Law (Dr.iur., 1983). Author: Numerous publications in the field of labour law, corporate law and commercial law. *LANGUAGES:* English and French. *PRACTICE AREAS:* (Collective) Labour Law; Corporate Law; Commercial Law; Distribution Law; Real Estate Law; Construction Law; Insurance Law.

DR. EBERHARD WALLENTIN, born 1955; admitted, 1986, Austria. *Education:* University of Salzburg, School of Law (Dr.iur., 1978); University of Vienna, Business School (Mag. rer. soc. oec., 1980). Author: Several

publications in the field of tax law. *LANGUAGES:* English. *PRACTICE AREAS:* Administrative Law; Corporate Law; Commercial Law; Insolvency Law; Reconstruction Law; Business Taxation; Trusts.

DR. THOMAS WALLENTIN, born 1957; admitted, 1988, Austria. *Education:* University of Vienna, School of Law (Dr.iur., 1979); University of Vienna, Business School (Mag. rer. soc. oec., 1981). Author: Several publications in the field of entertainment law. *LANGUAGES:* English and French. *PRACTICE AREAS:* International Media and Entertainment Law; Intellectual Property Law, especially Copyright and Trademark Law; Unfair Competition Law; Real Estate Law.

CONSULTANT

PROF. DR. FRANZ HELBICH, born 1924, Honorary Prof. for Tax Law at the University of Business Administration, Vienna; retired as lawyer, 1994. *Education:* University of Vienna, School of Law (Dr. jur., 1949). Author: Numerous publications in the field of Tax, Corporate Law and Trust and Foundation Law. *LANGUAGES:* English. *PRACTICE AREAS:* Tax Law; Corporate Law; Trust and Foundation Law.

LAMBERT GROHMANN KERRES & DEISSENBERGER

Established in 1983

LAURENZERBERG 2
A-1010 VIENNA, AUSTRIA
Telephone: (43-1) 515 50
Facsimile: (43-1) 515 50-50

Budapest, Hungary Office: CEWIT, Belgrad rkp 13-15, 1056. Telephone: (36-1) 266 5570.

Prague, Czechoslovakia Office: Bolzanova 1, 11503 Prague 1. Telephone: (42-2) 2422 8589; 2422 8018. Fax: (42-2) 2422 1843.

Business, Commercial, Corporate Law, Central Europe, Eastern Europe, Energy and Natural Resources Law, European Community Law, Joint Ventures, Mergers and Acquisitions, Franchising, Agency and Distributorships, Licensing, Banking, Forfeiting, International Arbitration, Mediation, Litigation, Trade, Countertrade, Unfair Competition, Intellectual Property, Computers, Trademarks, Real Estate, Property, Inheritance, Gift and Estate Tax.

MEMBERS OF FIRM

DR. PETER LAMBERT, LL.M., admitted, 1983, Austria. *Education:* University of Vienna (Dr.jur., 1979); McGeorge School of Law, California, U.S.A. (LL.M., 1983). Author: "Exchange Control Law in Austria," 1988; "Agency Law in Austria," American Bar Association, 1989. Lecturer, Austrian and Private International Law, McGeorge School of Law, 1986-1992. *LANGUAGES:* German, English and French. *PRACTICE AREAS:* Business; Banking; Litigation.

DR. ALEXANDER GROHMANN, admitted, 1984, Austria. *Education:* University of Vienna (Dr.jur., 1978). Author: "Joint Ventures in Czechoslovakia," ecolex, 1990; "Franchising," Manz, 1992. Lecturer, Franchising Law, Franchising Association. *LANGUAGES:* German and French. *PRACTICE AREAS:* Franchising; Real Estate; Inheritance and Estate Tax.

DR. CHRISTOPH KERRES, LL.M., admitted, 1988, Austria and New York. *Education:* University of Vienna (Mag. and Dr.jur., 1982); Georgetown University, Washington, D.C., U.S.A. (LL.M., 1987). Author: "Hungary - A New Market," CEWIT, 1989; "Countertrade," Kluwer, 1990; "Mergers & Acquisitions in the EC," Kluwer, 1991; various articles about legal developments in Central Europe, ecolex, 1990-1992. Lecturer: Eastern European Law, American Bar Association, 1989; Product Liability Law, International Bar Association, 1990. *LANGUAGES:* German, English, French and Spanish. *PRACTICE AREAS:* Corporate Law; Joint Ventures; Mergers and Acquisitions; Energy Law.

MAG. DR. ROLAND DEISSENBERGER, admitted, 1988, Austria. *Education:* University of Vienna (Dr.jur., 1981; Mag. rer. soc. oec., 1981). Publications about Computer Law. Lecturer, Austrian and Private International Law. *LANGUAGES:* German, English and French. *PRACTICE AREAS:* Intellectual Property; Computer Law; Licensing.

MAG. ALEXANDER STOLITZKA, admitted, 1993, Austria. *Education:* University of Vienna (Mag.jur., 1987). *Member:* Board, Austrian Regulation of Private Radio Station. *LANGUAGES:* German and English. *PRACTICE AREAS:* Trade; Countertrade; Central Europe.

(This Listing Continued)

(This Listing Continued)

DR. GEORG RÖHSNER, admitted, 1993, Austria. *Education:* University of Vienna (Dr.jur., 1984). *LANGUAGES:* German, English and French. *PRACTICE AREAS:* Media; Trademark; Arbitration.

DR. BRIGITTE VICTOR-GRANZER, admitted, 1991, Austria. *Education:* University of Vienna (Dr.jur., 1980); Mastère de Juriste d'Affaires Internationales de l'Ecole Supérieere de Commerce de Paris (M.S.J., 1991). *Member:* Austrian Bar Association. (Also Associate at Barsi Doumith Pavie et Associes, Paris, France). *LANGUAGES:* French, German and English. *PRACTICE AREAS:* European Community Law; Hungary, Czeck and Slovak Republics.

SENIOR ASSOCIATES

KATRINA WEINIG, admitted, 1986, Massachusetts (Not admitted in Austria). *Education:* Northwestern University Law School, Chicago, U.S.A. (J.D., 1985).

MAG. AURELIUS FREYTAG. *Education:* University of Vienna (Mag.-jur., 1984).

DR. CHRISTIAN WILLMANN. *Education:* University of Vienna (Mag.jur., 1984).

MAG. GERHARD M. EICHBERGER, LL.M.

MAG. MARTIN NEUWIRTH

Memberships of the Firm: Austrian, International, American (Country Coordinator) and New York State Bar Association (Chairman, Vienna Chapter); Union Internationale des Advocates; International Legal Materials (Corresponding Editor); Association of German Speaking Lawyers; American Society of International Law; Association of Franchising; CEWIT Center for East-West Information and Trade.

Languages: German, English, Spanish, French, Hungarian and Russian.

LATTENMAYER, LUKS & PARTNERS

Established in 1976

MAHLERSTRASSE 11
A-1010 VIENNA, AUSTRIA
Telephone: (431) 513-17-84
Telefax: (431) 513-75-94

Austrian Real Estate Law, Construction Law, Company Law, Corporate Law, Commercial Law, Banking, International Transactions, Intellectual Property, Mergers and Acquisitions, Employment, Litigation, Probate and Estate, Administrative Law, Criminal Law and Taxation.

FIRM PROFILE: The firm was established in 1976 and has grown to one of Vienna's leading real estate and commercial law firms. With 4 partners and 2 associates the firm serves the national and international clients' needs in areas such as corporate law, real estate law, mergers and acquisitions, building project contracts and more.

MEMBERS OF FIRM

DR. WALTER LATTENMAYER, born 1948; admitted, 1975, Austria. *Education:* University of Vienna Law School (Dr.jur., 1971). Lecturer, Department of Technology, University of Vienna. Author: "Wohnungseigentum," Einführung, Vertragsmuster, Schriftreihe Musterverträge, Orac. *Member:* Vienna Bar Association. *LANGUAGES:* German and English. *PRACTICE AREAS:* Corporate Law; Real Estate; Building Project Law; Commercial; Cross Border Contracts; Antitrust; Trade Regulation.

DR. ANDREAS LUKS, born 1950; admitted, 1987, Austria. *Education:* University of Vienna Law School (Dr.jur., 1982). *Member:* Vienna Bar Association. *LANGUAGES:* German and English. *PRACTICE AREAS:* General Civil Law; Criminal Law; Administrative Law; Adoption; Divorce; Wills; Probate Law; Litigation.

UNIV.-DOZ. DR. MICHAEL ENZINGER, born 1959; admitted, 1990, Austria. *Education:* University of Vienna Law School (Dr.jur., 1983); Corporate and Commercial Law (Ph.D.). Author: many publications in the Corporate and Commercial Law field as well as Intellectual Property. Assistant, Department of Commercial, Corporate and Negotiable Instruments Law, University of Vienna Law School, 1983-1991. Assistant Professor, University of Vienna Law School, since 1991. Member, Council of the Faculty of the University of Vienna, Law School. *Member:* Vienna Bar Association. *LANGUAGES:* German and English. *PRACTICE AREAS:* Commercial and Corporate Law; Landlords and Tenant Law; Company Formation; Antitrust and Trade Regulation; Trademarks.

DR. GEORG DIWOK, born 1962; admitted, 1992, Austria. *Education:* University of Vienna Law School (Dr.jur., 1986). Author: publications in

(This Listing Continued)

the Banking Law field. Assistant, Department of Commercial, Corporate and Negotiable Instruments Law, University of Vienna Law School, 1987-1992. *Member:* Vienna Bar Association. *LANGUAGES:* German and English. *PRACTICE AREAS:* Banking Law; Securities Law; Corporate Law; Labour Law; Litigation.

ASSOCIATES

DR. ANGELIKA NÖBAUER, born 1962; (Not admitted in Austria). *Education:* University of Vienna (Dr.jur., 1986). *LANGUAGES:* German and English. *PRACTICE AREAS:* General Civil Law; Building Law.

MAG. GERHARD RIEDER, born 1960; (Not admitted in Austria). *Education:* University of Graz (Mag.jur., 1990); University Course on Hospital Management (Dipl., Krankenhausmanager, 1994). *LANGUAGES:* German and English. *PRACTICE AREAS:* General Civil Law; Corporate Law; Health Care; Hospitals; Medical Malpractice.

Languages: German and English

DDR. RENÉ LAURER

Established in 1980

GUSSHAUSSTRASSE 2
A-1040 VIENNA, AUSTRIA
Telephone: 43-1-504 41 42-0
Telefax: 43-1-504 41 42 43

National and International Banking and Business Law, Insurance Law, Administrative Law, Environmental Law, General Commercial and International Trade Law.

FIRM PROFILE: The firm has been established in 1980. It works in close cooperation with Dr. Armin Dallmann, Attorney at Law and Hügel & Partner Mödling. A partnership will be established shortly. The firm offers all legal services needed by its banking and commercial clients.

DDR. RENÉ LAURER, Professor of Law, Vienna University of Economics, born Vienna, June 23, 1944; admitted, 1980, Austria. *Education:* University of Vienna (Dr. Jur., 1967; Dr. Rer. Pol., 1970). Professor of Law, International Law Institute, 1973. Author of several books and publications namely on Banking Law and Constitutional Law e.g. "Das Kreditwesengesetz," 1979 (co-author, re-edition, 1991); "Das Bankwesengesetz," 1993; "Das neue Banksteuergesetz"; "Zeitliche Aspekte der Aufhebung von Gesetzen und Verordnungen durch den Verfassungsgerlchtshof"; "Behördliche Auflagen im Wirtschaftsrecht." *Member:* Vienna Bar Association; Vereinigung deutscher Staatsrechtslehrer; Austrian Association of Administrative Sciences. *LANGUAGES:* French, English and German.

DRES. MASSER, GROSSMANN, KLINGSBIGL & LIRSCH

Established in 1960

SINGERSTRASSE 27/II
1010 VIENNA 1, AUSTRIA
Telephone: (43-1) 512-7555
Facsimile: (43-1) 513-7588
Telex: 135171 Causa

Corporate, Civil and Commercial Law, Competition Law, Intellectual Property, Media and Advertising Law, Insurance Law, Law of Freight and Forwarding, Aviation Law, Civil and Commercial Litigation, Real Estate Law, Management of Property and Trust, Transportation and Shipping Law.

FIRM PROFILE: Dr. Werner Masser founded his law firm in Vienna in 1960. The firm, currently known as Dres. Masser, Grossmann, Klingsbigl & Lirsch, has four partners and provides services to both national and international clients. The firm has numerous contacts and extensive experience in the former Eastern European bloc.

The firm is the Austrian Representative of TerraLex, a network of over 80 independent law firms specializing in international legal matters. The primary purpose of TerraLex is to enable individual member firms to better serve their clients' international interests through a worldwide support network of quality law firms.

(This Listing Continued)

**DRES. MASSER, GROSSMANN, KLINGSBIGL &
LIRSCH,** *Vienna—Continued*

MEMBERS OF FIRM

DR. WERNER MASSER, born Graz, Austria, May 2, 1929; admitted, 1960, Austria. *Education:* University of Graz (Dr. jur., 1951). Consul General of the Republic of Cyprus in the Republic of Austria and the Principality of Liechtenstein. Admissions Examiner, Austrian Bar Association. *LANGUAGES:* German and English.

DR. ERNST GROSSMANN, born Baden, Austria, November 18, 1940; admitted, 1969, Austria. *Education:* University of Vienna (Dr. jur., 1963). *LANGUAGES:* German and English.

DR. EDUARD KLINGSBIGL, born Vienna, Austria, May 12, 1950; admitted, 1978, Austria. *Education:* University of Vienna (Dr. jur., 1972). Disciplinary Committee, Viennese Bar Association. *LANGUAGES:* German and English.

DR. ROBERT LIRSCH, born Vienna, Austria, July 13, 1956; admitted, 1986, Austria. *Education:* University of Vienna (Dr. jur., 1980). *LANGUAGES:* German, English and Italian.

ASSOCIATES

DR. MARTIN DEURETSBACHER, born St. Poelten, Austria, November 5, 1963. *Education:* University of Vienna (Mag. jur., 1990; Dr. jur., 1993). *LANGUAGES:* English, Spanish and German.

MAG. RUDOLF FIDESSER, born Hollabrunn, Austria, September 5, 1962. *Education:* University of Vienna (Mag. jur., 1991). *LANGUAGES:* German and English.

MAG. FLORIAN MASSER, born Vienna, Austria, March 11, 1966. *Education:* University of Vienna (Mag. jur., 1992). *LANGUAGES:* German and English.

DR. THOMAS G. EUSTACCHIO, born Graz, Austria, May 18, 1969. *Education:* University of Graz (Mag.jur., 1991; Dr.jur., 1994); College of Europe, Bruges (Master of Arts in European Studies, 1993). *LANGUAGES:* German, English, French, Italian and Spanish.

All Members of the firm are members of the Viennese and Austrian Bar Associations.

DR. THOMAS MONDL

Established in 1988

TRATTNERHOF 2
(GRABEN 29A)
1010 VIENNA, AUSTRIA
Telephone: +43-1-535 57 44
Telefax: +43-1-535 06 49

Consulting Office: Frankfurt, Germany, at Boesebeck, Barz & Partner, Burnitzstrasse 40-42, P.O. Box 700126, 6000 Frankfurt/Main 70. Telephone: (069) 633 92-0. Cable Address: "Legal". Telex: 4 11 060 (legal d). Telefax: (069) 633 92/123). Teletex: 6999050.

Budapest at Dr. Peter Bardos, Szent István Park 16. Telephone: 361-1499-105. Fax: 361-1499-105.

The law firm of Dr. Mondl is in permanent cooperation with Boesebeck, Barz & Partner, Frankfurt, Berlin, Dresden, Warsaw, Vienna; Zagreb and with Dr. Peter Bardos, Budapest.

Commercial, Corporate, Contracting, General Civil and International Practice, Intellectual Property, Trade Mark and Patent, Product Liability, Unfair Competition, Property and Real Estate Law, Mergers and Acquisitions, Antitrust, Distributorship Agency and Franchising, Arbitration and Litigation, International Public and Private Law, Foreign Investment.

FIRM PROFILE: The firm was established in 1988 and offers a full range of legal services.

DR. THOMAS MONDL, born Vienna, Austria, August 26, 1959; admitted, 1988, Austria. *Education:* University of Vienna (Dr.jur., 1983). *LANGUAGES:* German and English.

ASSOCIATES

DR. ROLAND GARSTENAUER, born Salzburg, Austria, August 8, 1963; (Not admitted in Austria). *Education:* University of Salzburg, Austria (Dr. jur., 1992). *LANGUAGES:* German and English.

(This Listing Continued)

MAG. PETRA JANACZEK, born December 25, 1966; (Not admitted in Austria). *Education:* University of Vienna, Austria (1993). *LANGUAGES:* German, English and French.

Languages: German and English.

NEUDORFER GRIENSTEIDL HAHNKAMPER & STAPF

Established in 1988

ESSLINGGASSE 9
A-1010 VIENNA, AUSTRIA
Telephone: +43-1 533 43 44
Fax: 535 61 88; 533 43 44-12

General Business, Corporate, Banking, Contract, International Business Transactions, Mergers and Acquisitions, Joint Ventures, Foreign Investment in Austria, Central and Eastern Europe, Real Estate, Food and Drug, Labour, Environmental Law, Litigation and Arbitration.

MEMBERS OF FIRM

DR. HELMUT NEUDORFER, born 1939; admitted, 1970, Austria. *Education:* Vienna University Law School (Dr.iuris, 1961). *Member:* Austrian Bar (Member of the Supreme Disciplinary Court in the Austrian Bar); IBA (Section on Business Law); Lawyers Club (Iuventus). *LANGUAGES:* German and English.

DR. KLAUS GRIENSTEIDL, born 1939; admitted, 1970, Austria. *Education:* University of Vienna Law School (Dr.iuris, 1962). *Member:* Austrian Bar; Lawyers Club (Union). *LANGUAGES:* German.

DR. WOLFGANG HAHNKAMPER, born 1947; admitted, 1988, Austria. *Education:* Vienna University Law School (Dr.iuris, 1970). *Member:* Austrian Bar; IBA (Section on Business Law). *LANGUAGES:* German and English.

DR. CHRISTOF STAPF, born 1958; admitted, 1988, Austria. *Education:* Vienna University Law School (Dr.iuris, 1983). *Member:* Austrian Bar; International Association of Young Attorneys (AIJA). *LANGUAGES:* German and English.

Member of IAG International

Languages: German and English

RECHTSANWALTSKANZLEI ORTNER PÖCH FORAMITTI

Established in 1976

STRAUCHGASSE 1-3
1010 VIENNA, AUSTRIA
Telephone: (1) 535-37-21
Facsimile: (1) 533-15-55
Telex: 13 6953 eulex a
Cable Address: Eurolaw

Advertising Law, Aeronautical Law, Antitrust Law, Arbitration, Banking Law, Capital Market Law, Competition Law, Corporate Law, EU Law, Foreign Investments, International Contracts, Innovative Financing, International Private Law, Property and Real Estate Law including Restitution in Eastern Europe, Securities Law, Trade Regulations, General Legal Practice, Intellectual Property, Copyright Law, License Negotiation, Trademark Litigation and Transfer of Technology.

MEMBERS OF FIRM

DR. OTTO ORTNER, born 1936; admitted, 1970, Austria. *LANGUAGES:* German, English and French. *PRACTICE AREAS:* Banking Law; Capital Market Law; Corporate Law; Foreign Investments; International Contracts; Innovative Financing; Property and Real Estate including Restitution in Eastern Europe.

DR. PETER PÖCH, born 1940; admitted, 1972, Austria. *LANGUAGES:* German, English and French. *PRACTICE AREAS:* Banking Law; Securities Law; Capital Markets Law; Intellectual Property; Unfair Competition Law; Advertising Law; Antitrust Law; Arbitration; Corporate Law; EEC Law; Foreign Investments; International Contracts; International Private Law; Trade Regulations; Copyright Law; License Negotiation; Trademark Litigation.

(This Listing Continued)

DR. LOUIS FORAMITTI, born 1955; admitted, 1984, Austria. *LANGUAGES:* German and English. *PRACTICE AREAS:* Securities Law; Computer Law; Corporate Law; Venture Capital Finance; Aircraft Finance.

Languages: English, French and German.

PETSCH, FROSCH & PARTNER

Established in 1956

ESCHENBACHGASSE 11
A-1010 VIENNA, AUSTRIA
Telephone: (1) 586 21 80
Telefax: (1) 586 22 35

Milan, Italy Office: Via Falcone, 5, I-20123. Telephone: (2) 805 15 68. Telefax: (2) 805 15 70.

Administrative Law, Agency and Distributorships, Antitrust and Trade Regulation, Arbitration and Mediation, Banks and Banking, Business Law, Civil Law, Commercial Law, Company Law, Computers and Software, Construction Law, Consumer Law, Contracts, Copyrights, Corporate Law, Debtor and Creditor, Finance, Franchises and Franchising, Intellectual Property, International Law, Labour and Employment, Leases and Leasing, Litigation, Mergers, Acquisitions and Divestitures, Products Liability, Property, Real Estate, Taxation, Trademarks, Transportation, Trusts and Estates, Wills, Italian Law.

MEMBERS OF FIRM

DR. HELMUT PETSCH, born 1926; admitted, 1956, Vienna.

DR. GÜNTHER FROSCH, born 1944; admitted, 1973, Vienna.

DR. CHRISTOPH PETSCH, born 1957; admitted, 1986, Vienna.

DR. PETER KLEIN, born 1960.

ASSOCIATES

MAG. CHRISTOPH HACK, born 1964.

MAG. CRISTINA PENTIMALLI, born 1964.

Languages: German, English, Italian and French

PRESLMAYR & PARTNERS

DR. KARL LUEGER-RING 12
1010 VIENNA, AUSTRIA
Telephone: (+43 1) 533 16 95
Telefax: (+43 1) 535 56 86

Preslmayr & Partners is engaged in a broadly-based practice concentrating on a full range of civil legal services. The firm concentrates on Austrian commercial and corporate law, including EEC law, general civil law, and advises multinational corporations in European and Austrian activities. Further areas of particular expertise include the laws of industrial property, including copyright, unfair competition and antitrust, banking and finance, computer and software, food and drug, labour, bankruptcy, and further commercial litigation and arbitration. Although the firm is active in cooperating with international law firms, it has retained its independence from legal networks or similar affiliations.

MEMBERS OF FIRM

DR. KARL PRESLMAYR, born Vienna, Austria, February 5, 1936; admitted, 1965, Austria. *Education:* Humanistic Gymnasium (Latin and Ancient Greek, 1954); University of Vienna (Juris Doctor, 1958). Author: "Versicherung und Nachlaβ," JBl 402, 1961; Besprechung des Buches "Die Rechtsquelle der Kraftfahrzeug-Haftpflichtversicherung," JBl 568, 1961; "Besprechung der Sammlung der seit 1945 Ergangenen Höchstrichterlichen Entscheidungen in Versicherungssachen," Herausgegeben von Karl Wahle, JBl 620, 1962; "Zur Besteuerung der Freiwilligen Abfertigung nach der Einkommenssteuernovelle 1965," ÖStZ 223, 1965; Mein Erstes Buch, zugleich eine Besprechung des Buches "Unser Strafprozeβ," von Rudolf Zitta, Anw 532, 1984; "Schadenersatzpflicht im Fall unberechtigter Einwendungen Dritter im Verwaltungsverfahren," ÖJZ 654, 1984; "Vergleichende Werbung und Äuβerungsfreiheit gemäβ Artikel 10 EMRK," EuGRZ 221, 1985; "Unterliegt Scherz-Kaugummi der AntioxidantienVO?," ernährung 696, 1984; "Zur UWG-Novelle 1988," ÖJZ 617, 1988; "§1 UWG und Äuβerungsfreiheit gemäβ Art 10 Abs 2 MRK," Medien und Recht 151, 1988; Überblick über das österreichische Kosmetikrecht," Kosmetik International 162, 1990. Co-Author: "Zur Auslegung des § 2 (2) Amtshaftungsgesetz," JBl 307, 1963; "Die Exekution zur Erwirkung von Unterlassungen gemäβ 355 EO

(This Listing Continued)

bei mehrmaligem Zuwiderhandeln," ÖJZ 293, 1984; "Advertising Law in Europe and North America," published in German and English, Kluwer, 1991. "The European Economic Area (EEA)," 1992. Co-Author: "Investing in Austria," 1994, edited by Preslmayr & Partners and Auditor. Member, Committee of Bar Examiners, 1980—. Lecturer on Competition Law and Copyright Law, University of Vienna, 1988—. *Member:* Austrian Bar; DACH; International Arbitration Court of the Federal Economic Chamber, Vienna. *LANGUAGES:* German and English.

DR. FLORIAN GEHMACHER, born Seekirchen, Salzburg, Austria, July 21, 1946; admitted, 1974, Austria. *Education:* University of Vienna (Juris Doctor 1968). Permanent court appointed trustee in bankruptcy. *Member:* Austrian Bar. *LANGUAGES:* German and English.

DR. RAINER M. HERZIG, born Klosterneuburg, Austria, September 8, 1959; admitted, 1989, Austria. *Education:* University of Vienna (Juris Doctor, 1982); University of Lausanne (1983-1984). Author: "Rechtliche Probleme grenzüberschreitender Werbung," WB1 251, 1988; "Nochmals: Inländische Gerichtsbarkeit für Wettbewerbsverstösse aus dem Ausland? - Eine Replik zu RdW 1988, 285," RdW 415, 1988. Permanent court appointed trustee in bankruptcy. *Member:* Austrian Bar; International Association of Young Attorneys (AIJA). *LANGUAGES:* German, English and French.

ASSOCIATES

MAG. DIETER HAUCK, born Vienna, Austria, March 23, 1963. *Education:* University of Vienna (Juris Magister, 1989), Program for International Studies, University of Vienna (1990). Research Assistant, University of Vienna, Institute for International Law and Foreign Relations (1989-1991). Auditor, London School of Economics (Introduction to English Law, 1990). Co-Author: "The European Economic Area (EEA)," 1992 edited by Preslmayr & Partner. *LANGUAGES:* German and English.

DR. MARTIN PRESLMAYR, LL.M., (Exeter). *Born:* Vienna, Austria, May 4, 1965. *Education:* University of Vienna (Juris Magister, 1989; Juris Doctor, 1992); University of Exeter, England (Master of European Legal Studies, 1993). Assistant, University of Vienna, Institute of Private and Private International Law, 1989-1991. Lecturer, Richter Private Law School, Vienna. Research in EEC and International Law, University of Cambridge, England, Summer 1990 and 1991. Comparative Legal Research and Research in European Law, University of Oslo, Summer, 1993. Author: "Wirksamwerden des Vaterschaftsanerkenntnisses und neues Erbrecht," NZ 1990, 217; "Der Scheinhersteller im Produkthaftungsgesetz," ecolex 1991, 149; legal articles in the daily newspaper "Der Standard."; "Die Abgeltung von Leistungen in der Lebensgemeinschaft," in Harrer/Zitta (Hrsg), Familie und Recht, 1992; "Handbuch des Produkthaftungsgesetzes" (textbook on product liability law), Orac 1993; "Comparative Aspects on Special Problems within the European Product Liability Directive," University of Exeter, 1993. *LANGUAGES:* German and English.

DR. MATTHIAS SCHMIDT, born Vienna, Austria, December 2, 1963. *Education:* University of Vienna (Juris Magister, 1989; Juris Doctor, 1991). Assistant, University of Vienna, Institute for Private and Private International Law, 1990-1991. Program for foreign attorneys at the law firm of Walter, Conston, Alexander & Green, New York, 1992. *LANGUAGES:* German and English.

MAG. KURT WRATZFELD, born Bregenz, Austria, August 3, 1967. *Education:* University of Vienna (Juris Magister, 1991). *LANGUAGES:* German and English.

DR. STEFAN LANGER, born Vienna, Austria, December 14, 1968. *Education:* University of Vienna (Juris Magister, 1991; Juris Doctor, 1993); University of Cambridge, England (Summer School in English Legal Methods, 1992); University of California, Davis and Berkeley, USA (Orientation in U.S.A. Law Program, 1994). Junior Auditor, KPMG Alpen-Treuhand GmbH, Certified Accountants and Tax Counsels, Vienna, Austria, 1992-1993. Author: "Criminal Law Provisions In the Statutes On Stock Companies and Companies with Limited Liability," doctoral thesis, Orac, 1994. *LANGUAGES:* German, English and Norwegian.

MAG. PETER KONWITSCHKA, born Vienna, Austria, August 19, 1969. *Education:* University of Vienna (Juris Magister 1992). Research Assistant, University of Vienna, Institute for Commercial Law, 1992; Author: "Compensation of Rental Costs Incurred by the Lessee of a Motor Vehicle," JAP 1992, 116. *LANGUAGES:* German and English.

MAG. SUSANNE KOSESNIK-WEHRLE, LL.M. (Bruges), born Vienna, Austria, Mau 6, 1968. *Education:* University of Vienna (Juris Magister, 1991); College of Europe, Bruges (Master in European Community Law/Diplôme d'Etudes Européennes Approfondies, 1993) European Uni-

(This Listing Continued)

PRESLMAYR & PARTNERS, Vienna—Continued

versity Institute, Academy of European Law, Florence (Summer School in Human Rights and European Community Law, 1993). *LANGUAGES:* German, English, French and Italian.

MMAG. DR. MARKUS FELLNER, born Vienna, Austria, August 11, 1967. *Education:* University of Economics, Vienna (Magister Economics, 1989); University of Vienna School of Law (Juris Magister, 1992; Juris Doctor, with honors, 1994). Author: "Organisation of Independent Administrative Authorities" (doctoral thesis, 1994); "Valuation of Companies and Goodwill," (thesis, 1988). 1995 foreign lawyers program at Schulte, Roth & Zabel, New York. *LANGUAGES:* German, English and French.

Languages: German, English, French, Norwegian and Italian.

PRETTENHOFER & JANDL PARTNERSCHAFT

OPPOLZERGASSE 6
A-1010 VIENNA, AUSTRIA
Telephone: (1) 533 36 19
Telefax: (1) 533 36 19 24

Corporate, Commercial, Banking, Securities Industrial Property, Unfair Competition, Aviation, Antitrust, Tax, Food and Drug, Contract and Real Estate, Product Liability, International Transactions, Joint Ventures, Litigation and Arbitration.

MEMBERS OF FIRM

DR. PETER H. PRETTENHOFER, born 1937; admitted, 1967, Vienna.

DR. PETER JANDL, born 1943; admitted, 1976, Vienna.

Languages: German, English and French.

PRUNBAUER, PEYRER-HEIMSTÄTT & ROMIG

MAHLERSTRAßE 7
A-1010 VIENNA, AUSTRIA
Telephone: (1) 512 86 51
Telecopier: (1) 512 86 51/20

General Business, Corporate, Intellectual and Industrial Property, Unfair Competition, Antitrust, Trademark, Copyright, Patent Infringement, Administrative and Trade Regulation, International Transactions, Mergers, Acquisitions, Banking, Securities, Commodities, Taxation, Constitution, Contract, Estate, Labour, Environmental.

MEMBERS OF FIRM

DR. ANDREAS PEYRER-HEIMSTÄTT, born 1956; admitted, 1986, Austria. *Education:* University of Vienna (Dr. juris, 1979). University Assistant, Vienna University, 1980-1982.

DR. MARCELLA PRUNBAUER, M.C.J. (New York University), born 1957, admitted, 1987, Austria; 1983, New York. *Education:* University of Vienna (Dr. juris, 1980); New York University School of Law (M.C.J., 1982). Lecturer, University of Economics, 1992—. University Assistant, Vienna University, 1979-1981.

DR. LEONHARD ROMIG, born 1955; admitted, 1984, Austria. *Education:* University of Vienna (Dr. juris, 1976).

COUNSEL

DR. LUDWIG PFLEGER, born 1963; admitted, 1993, Austria. *Education:* University of Graz (Mag. juris, 1986, Dr. juris, 1990).

Languages: German, English and French.

PUSCHNER, POIGNER & SPERNBAUER

Established in 1988
SCHUBERTRING 8
A-1010 VIENNA, AUSTRIA
Telephone: 0222 513 80 91; 513 80 92; 513 80 93
International: +43 1 513 80 91 series
Telefax: +43 1 513 86 66
Telex: 75 211358 ewla a

Moscow, Russia Office: Starokonjushennyi Pereulok 1, SU-119 034. Telephone: +7 095 201 7308. Fax: +7 095 230 2687. Telex: 413399 ATORG SU.

Budapest, Hungary Office: Ferenczy Istvan Ut. 14, H-1053. Telephone: Ř137 84 08.

Banking, Corporate, Commercial, Taxation, Property, Contract and Real Estate Law, International Transactions and Arbitration.

FIRM PROFILE: The firm works for Austrian and international banks, insurance companies, industrial enterprises and trading firms. Based in Vienna, the firm offers legal services to domestic and international clients and is engaged in all areas of the law, in particular in business, corporate, banking and real estate law as well as arbitration. As a result of close ties to Eastern Europe services can also be offered in these countries, especially in Russia, Hungary, Poland, Bulgeria, Slovakia and the Czech Republic.

MEMBERS OF FIRM

DR. HAIMO PUSCHNER, born Vienna, Austria, April 3, 1935; admitted, 1968, Austria. *Education:* Commercial School, Vienna Chamber of Commerce; University of Vienna (Dr.Jur.). Examiner, Austrian Bar Exam, 1986—. Vice President, Austrian Gymnastics Association, 1965-1978. Member of the Board of INKU AG, 1970-1987. Member of the Board of Arab Bank (Austria) AG, 1987. Member of the Board of Allianz RAS Holding Aktiengesellschaft, Vienna (Holding Company of Allianz and Riunione Adriatica di Sicurtà insurance companies) since 1991-1993. Member of the Board of ITB Kapitalanlagegesellschaft m.b.H., Bank Vienna. *Member:* Austrian and International Bar Associations; Polish-Austrian Foundation in Partnership to the Polish Academy of Sciences (Polsko-Austriacka Fundacja Wspierania Gospodark Polskiej (Founding Member); East-West Lawyers Association (President, 1990—). *LANGUAGES:* German and English.

DR. JOHANN POIGNER, born Altmünster, Austria, September 26, 1953; admitted, 1990, Austria. *Education:* University of Vienna, Salzburg (Dr. jur, 1986). *Member:* East-West Lawyers Association. *LANGUAGES:* German, English and Russian.

MAG. MARTIN SPERNBAUER, born Linz, Austria, October 30, 1962; admitted, 1993, Austria. *Education:* University of Vienna (Mag. jur., 1988). *LANGUAGES:* German and English.

ASSOCIATES

MAG. NIKOLAUS ROSENAUER, born Vienna, Austria, November 25, 1967. *Education:* University of Vienna (Mag. jur., 1991). *LANGUAGES:* German and English.

Languages: German, English, Russian and Hungarian.

ROESSLER, PRITZ & PARTNER

Rechtsanwälte
SCHWEDENPLATZ 3-4
A-1010 VIENNA, AUSTRIA
Telephone: 0222/535 16 23-25; 0222/535 62 92
Facsimile: 222/533 42 48

Administrative, Antitrust, Arbitration, Business, Competition, Constitutional, Construction, Corporate, Distributorship, Agency and Franchise, Environmental, Labor, International, Litigation, Mergers, Real Estate, Rent and Lease, Trademarks.

MEMBERS OF FIRM

DR. DIETRICH ROESSLER, KTD., born Kommanditich, 1926; admitted, 1955, Austria; Austria Emer., 1994. *Education:* University of Vienna (Dr. jur.). Judge, Austrian Constitutional Court. *Member:* UIA: IFA: Vienna Bar Association.

DR. HANS PRITZ, born 1945; admitted, 1976, Austria. *Education:* University of Vienna (Dr. jur.). *Member:* AIJA; UIA (National Vice President); Vienna Bar Association. *LANGUAGES:* German, English and

(This Listing Continued)

French. *PRACTICE AREAS:* Administrative; Business; Competition; Construction; Labor Law.

DR. BIRGIT ROESSLER-THALER, born 1944; admitted, 1974, Austria. *Education:* University of Vienna (Dr. jur.). *Member:* AIJA; IFA; Vienna Bar Association. *LANGUAGES:* German, English and French. *PRACTICE AREAS:* Travel; Litigation; Real Estate.

Languages: English and French

RUSTLER, FROTZ & PARTNERS

MARIAHILFER STRASSE 196
A-1150 VIENNA, AUSTRIA
Telephone: (1) 89 129-0
Telefax: (1) 894 26 96

General Commercial and Civil Law, International Banking and Business Law, Corporate and Company Law, Mergers and Acquisitions, Tax Law, East-West Relations (Joint Ventures), Insurance Law, Real Estate Transactions and Construction Law, Rent and Lease, Unfair Competition, Antitrust, Copyright Law, Trademark Litigation, Industrial Models, Industrial Relations and Labor Law, Agency, Franchise and Distribution Law, Product Liability, Civil Litigation and Debt Collection.

FIRM PROFILE: Established in 1939, the firm offers a full range of services in the above fields of specialization. It is well known for Mergers and Acquisitions, Labor Law and Industrial Relations, Commercial Transactions, Real Estate Transactions and Rent and Lease. Clients range from medium sized and big Austrian Business Entities to International Corporations and their Austrian subsidiaries. The firm's six partners are supported by at least three associates and highly qualified staff.

MEMBERS OF FIRM

DR. HELFRIED RUSTLER, born Vienna, Austria, December 28, 1929; admitted, 1958, Austria. *Education:* University of Vienna (Dr. iur., 1951). *Member:* Austrian Bar Association; International Bar Association. *LANGUAGES:* German and English. *PRACTICE AREAS:* Real Estate Transactions and Construction; Rent and Lease; Product Liability; Civil Litigation.

DR. PETER RUSTLER, born Vienna, Austria, September 10, 1938; admitted, 1968, Austria. *Education:* University of Vienna (Dr. iur., 1961). *Member:* Austrian Bar Association; International Bar Association; Austrian Real Estate Broker Association (Director); Austrian Legal Experts' Committee on Landlord and Tenant Law. *LANGUAGES:* German and English. *PRACTICE AREAS:* Real Estate Transactions; Rent and Lease; Civil Litigation.

DR. STEPHAN FROTZ, born Wuppertal, Germany, May 21, 1957; admitted, 1987, Austria. *Education:* University of Vienna (Dr. iur., 1981). Research Scholar, Max Planck-Institute for Foreign and International Patent, Copyright and Competition Law. *Member:* Austrian Bar Association; International Bar Association; Austrian-German Chamber of Commerce; German-Scandinavian Lawyers' Association. *LANGUAGES:* German, English and French. *PRACTICE AREAS:* International Banking Law; Mergers and Acquisitions; Corporate and Tax Law.

DR. LOTHAR HOFMANN, born Waidhofen/Thaya, Austria, June 11, 1961; admitted, 1992, Austria; 1993, New York. *Education:* University of Vienna (Dr. iur., 1983); University of Chicago (LL.M., 1992). Research Scholar, Department for Commercial and Securities Law, University of Vienna. Fulbright Scholar, Practice with U.S. Law Firm in Chicago and Washington, D.C. Author: "Arbitration Clause and Proxy," 1991; "The Exclusion of Compensation in German and Austrian Agency Contracts," 1993. *Member:* Austrian Bar Association; International Bar Association; German-Scandinavian Lawyers' Association. *LANGUAGES:* German, English and Russian. *PRACTICE AREAS:* International Business and Finance; Intellectual Property Law; Competition Law; EEC Law.

DR. MANUELA M. PACHER, born Vienna, Austria, May 14, 1962; admitted, 1992, Austria. *Education:* University of Vienna (Dr. iur., 1985); University of Virginia (LL.M., 1987). *Member:* Austrian Bar Association; International Bar Association; German-Scandinavian Lawyers' Association. *LANGUAGES:* German, English and French. *PRACTICE AREAS:* Industrial Relations and Labor Law; Trademark Law and Litigation; Industrial Models; Civil Litigation.

DR. BRIGITTE WIENINGER, born Vienna, Austria, May 21, 1962; admitted, 1992, Austria. *Education:* University of Vienna (Dr. iur., 1986).

(This Listing Continued)

Member: Austrian Bar Association; International Bar Association. *LANGUAGES:* German, English and Greek. *PRACTICE AREAS:* Rent and Lease; Real Estate Transactions; East-West Relations.

SCHMIDT & KORNFELD

Established in 1973
MARIA HILFERSTRASSE 1D
A-1060 VIENNA, AUSTRIA
Telephone: 43 (1) 586 1521-23
Telecopier: 43 (1) 587 4206

Commercial, Corporate, Industrial and Intellectual Property, Patent, Trademark, Unfair Competition, Copyright, Computer, Product Liability, Food and Drug, Labor, Transport, Aviation, Travel and Tourism Law, International Transactions, Arbitration and Litigation, Advertising and Media Law.

FIRM PROFILE: Partners advise as special counsel in areas of respective concentration. Areas not mentioned above are covered by outside counsel in respective matters, employed on case to case basis. Clients based in Europe, North America, Australia and the Pacific Rim.

DR. HARALD SCHMIDT, born Vienna, Austria, 1944; admitted, 1973, Austria. *Education:* University of Vienna (J.D., 1966). Author: Austrian Patent-Law, 2nd Edition. *Member:* APLA, IBA/SBL (L.S.Y.), AIPPI, USTA, ECTA, GRUR, IFTTA. *LANGUAGES:* German, English and French. *PRACTICE AREAS:* Industrial and Intellectual Property; Advertising; Media Law.

DR. RAINER KORNFELD, born Vienna, Austria, 1953; admitted, 1983, Austria. *Education:* University of Vienna (J.D., 1977; Computer-Sciences and Software Engineering, 1974-1978). Chartered Accountant and Tax Adviser, 1977. *Member:* IBA/SBL (Vice-Chairman R), AIJA, CLA. *LANGUAGES:* German and English. *PRACTICE AREAS:* Computer; Transport; Corporate; Commercial Law.

ASSOCIATES

DR. MICHAEL WUKOSCHITZ, born Vienna, Austria, 1943; admitted, 1973, Austria. *Education:* University of Vienna (J.D., 1992). Assistant Director, Poly Tours Ltd., 1988—. *LANGUAGES:* German and English. *PRACTICE AREAS:* Transport; Travel and Tourism Law; International Sales.

Languages: German, English and French.

SCHNEIDER & SCHNEIDER

STEPHANSPLATZ 8A
JASOMIRGOTTSTRASSE 2
A-1010 VIENNA, AUSTRIA
Telephone: 533 51 01; 533 51 02
Cable Address: "Lawyer Wien"
Telex: 136845 law a
Telefax: 535 26 65

Corporate, Commercial, Tax, Industrial Property, Unfair Competition, Antitrust, Administrative, Contract and Estate Law. International Transactions. Arbitration.

MEMBERS OF FIRM

Dr. Franz Schneider   *Dr. Graham Schneider*

ASSOCIATE

Mag. Günther Loibner, LL.M.

Languages: German, English and French.

SCHÖNHERR BARFUSS TORGGLER & PARTNERS

Established in 1950
TUCHLAUBEN 13
A-1014 VIENNA, AUSTRIA
Telephone: (1) 534 37-0
Telefax: (1) 533 25 21

Brussels, Representative Office: 176 Avenue Louise, B-1050. Telephone: (322) 647 37 38. Telefax: (322) 647 65 39.

(This Listing Continued)

SCHÖNHERR BARFUSS TORGGLER & PARTNERS, Vienna—Continued

Corporate, Commercial, Banking, Securities, Industrial Property, Copyright, Unfair Competition, Antitrust, Tax, Administrative and Trade Regulations, Aviation, Food and Drug, Labor, Product Liability, Environmental Law, Real Estate Law, EEC Law, International Transactions, Joint Ventures, Litigation and Arbitration.

MEMBERS OF FIRM

DR. FRITZ SCHOENHERR (1920-1984).

DR.DR. WALTER BARFUSS, born 1937; admitted, 1967, Austria. *Education:* University of Vienna (Dr. iur. 1959; Dr. rer. pol. 1963). University Professor, Constitutional and Administrative Law, University of Vienna. Lecturer, Vienna University, 1969—. Co-editor: Oesterr. Lebensmittelrecht, 2nd ed, Manz, 1992; Kartellrecht, 4th ed., Manz, 1989. . President of the Vienna Law Association, 1988—. General Secretary of the Austrian Association on the Science of Administrative Law, 1988—. Vice President of the Austrian Association on Intellectual Property Law and Copyright Law, 1989—. Member: Codex-Commission (Food and Drug), Ministry of Health; Austrian Advisory Council on Advertising; Jury of the Austrian Advertising State Award; Ministry of Economics. *LANGUAGES:* German and English.

DR.DR. HELLWIG TORGGLER, born 1938; admitted, 1969, Austria. *Education:* Universities of Vienna, Graz, St. Gallen (Dr. iur. 1961; Dr. rer. pol. 1962); Southern Methodist University, Dallas (LL.M., 1963). Adjunct Professor, Commercial Law and Taxation, University of Graz, 1993—. Lecturer and Guest Professor, University of Economics, Vienna, 1984-1989. Co-Author of Straube (ed.), Commentary on the Austrian Commercial Code, vol 1, Manz, 1987 and vol 2, Manz, 1992. Editor: GmbHG, 5th Ed., Manz, 1994. Co-editor: Juristische Blätter. Arbitrator, Austrian Federal Chamber of Commerce. Member, Examining Board, Austrian Bar Exam. *LANGUAGES:* German, English, French and Italian.

DR. CHRISTIAN HAUER, born 1942; admitted, 1975, Austria. *Education:* University of Vienna (Dr. iur. 1967). Member, Examining Board for Judgeship. *LANGUAGES:* German, English and French.

MAG.DR. LOTHAR WILTSCHEK, born 1948; admitted, 1976, Austria. *Education:* University of Vienna (Dr. iur. 1971); University of Economics, Vienna (Mag. rer. soc. oec. 1978). Editor: UWG, 6th ed., Manz, 1994. *LANGUAGES:* German, English and French.

DR. GUIDO KUCSKO, born 1954; admitted, 1984, Austria. *Education:* University of Vienna (Dr. iur 1979). University Assistant at Vienna University, 1979-1980. Scholar at the Max Planck Institute for Foreign and International Patent, Copyright and Competition Law, Munich, 1979. Co-Author of Straube (ed.), Commentary on the Austrian Commercial Code, vol 1, Manz, 1987. Co-editor: Ecolex. *LANGUAGES:* German and English.

DR. CHRISTIAN SCHMELZ, born 1955; admitted, 1987, Austria. *Education:* University of Vienna (Dr. iur. 1979). University Assistant at Vienna University, 1980-1985. Lecturer, Vienna University, 1982—. Co-editor: Ecolex. *LANGUAGES:* German and English.

DR. HELMUT PREYER, born 1958; admitted, 1987, Austria. *Education:* University of Vienna (Dr. iur. 1981). Foreign Associate with London Law Firm, 1982-1983. National Liaison Member of London Court of International Arbitration, 1989—. *LANGUAGES:* German and English.

DR. CHRISTIAN HERBST, born 1959; admitted, 1988, Austria. *Education:* University of Salzburg (Dr. iur. 1982); School of Advanced International Studies JHU, Bologna (Diploma 1983); Harvard University (LL.M. 1984). Foreign Associate with New York City Law Firm, 1984. *LANGUAGES:* German and English.

MAG. DR. PETER MADL, born 1960; admitted, 1990, Austria. *Education:* University of Vienna (Dr. iur. 1983); University of Economics, Vienna (Mag. rer. soc. oec. 1987). University Assistant, Vienna University, 1983-1986. *LANGUAGES:* German and English.

DR. PETER FEYL, born 1961; admitted, 1990, Austria. *Education:* University of Vienna (Dr. iur 1984); University of Virginia (LL.M. 1986). *LANGUAGES:* German, English and French.

DR. CHRISTOPH LINDINGER, born 1962; admitted, 1991, Austria. *Education:* University of Salzburg (Dr. iur. 1984). *LANGUAGES:* German and English.

(This Listing Continued)

MAG. DR. THOMAS WENGER, born 1960; admitted, 1992, Austria. *Education:* University of Vienna (Dr. iur. 1983); University of Economics, Vienna (Mag. rer. soc. oec. 1987). *LANGUAGES:* German and English.

MAG. GEROLD ZEILER, born 1964; admitted, 1993, Austria. *Education:* University of Vienna (Mag. iur., 1988). *LANGUAGES:* German and English.

ASSOCIATES

Dr. Claudia Annacker
Dr. Helmut Engelbrecht
Dr. Christian Hausmaninger (LL.M.)
Dr. Christoph Herbst
Mag. Oliver Koch
Bernhard Mayr
Mag. Andreas Nadler

Mag. Andreas Natterer
Dr. Andreas Noedl
Dr. Charlotte Radaskiewicz
Dr. Rainer Tahedl
Mag. Thomas Talos (LL.M.)
Dr. Victor Turnherr
Mag. Stefan Warbeck
Mag. Gerold Wietrzyk

Dr. Hanno Wollmann (LL.M.)

Languages: German, English, French and Italian.

SCHUPPICH SPORN & WINISCHHOFER

FALKESTRASSE 6
A-1010 VIENNA, AUSTRIA
Telephone: (1) 5124799
Telecopier: (1) 5134064

MEMBERS OF FIRM

Dr. Walter Schuppich
Dr. Michael Winischhofer

Dr. Werner Sporn
Dr. Martin Schuppich

LAW OFFICES DR. F. SCHWANK

Established in 1986

STOCK EXCHANGE BUILDING
34 WIPPLINGERSTRASSE
A-1010 VIENNA, AUSTRIA
Telephone: +43-1-533 57 04
Telex: 136791 LEXEX A
Fax: +43-1-533 57 06

Brussels. Belgium Office: 6 Drève des Renards, 1180 Brussels, Belgium. Telephone: +32-2-376 92 00. Fax: +32-2-375 45 25. Contact: Francoise Carlier.

London, England Office: 3 Pump Court, Temple, London EC4Y 7AJ, UK. Telephone: +44-71-353 0711. Fax: +44-71-583 3391. Contact: Janette Gulleford M.A., chief executive.

Corporate/Commercial Law, Antitrust, Mergers and Acquisitions, Takeovers, Due Diligence, Corporate Reorganizsations, Joint Ventures, Computer Software Licensing, Franchising, Distribution Agreements, Foreign Investments, Financial, Banking, Finance, Securities, Equity and Bond Issues, EEC Law, EFTA Law, Trademarks and Patents, Taxation and Tax Planning, Insurance, Transport, Aviation, Environmental Law and Environmental Audits, Oil, Gas and Chemicals, Drug and Food Law.

FIRM PROFILE: The firm provides a broad range of commercial and financial legal services to well-known multinational corporations and financial institutions doing business in Austria, the CIS and Central Europe.

FRIEDRICH SCHWANK, Dr. iur. (University of Innsbruck 1972), FCIArb (London) Rechtsanwalt, Member: International Academy of Estate and Trust Law; Association Internationale pour la Protection de la Propriété Industrielle; Austrian National Committee of the International Chamber of Commerce and Senator of the Offshore Institute. *PRACTICE AREAS:* International Arbitration; Finance; Taxation; Aviation; Transportation; Mergers.

KORNELIA FRITSCH-VALLASTER, Dr.iur. (University of Innsbruck, 1981); LL.M. (London School of Economics, 1992), Rechtsanwältin. *PRACTICE AREAS:* EC; Corporate/Commercial; Environmental and Public International.

REGINE GORBACH, Dr. iur. (University of Innsbruck 1984). Rechtsanwaltsanwärterin. *PRACTICE AREAS:* Employment; Food Law; Franchise; Distributorships.

(This Listing Continued)

PRIYANTHI GUNASEKERA, LL.B. (University of Colombo 1978); LL.M. (New York University School of Law 1983); admitted in New York State and Sri Lanka (Not admitted in Austria). Member; American Bar Association. **PRACTICE AREAS:** Corporate; Securities; Licensing.

ANNE LEGROS, Maîtrise de droit (Université de Strasbourg III 1991); DJCE/DESS (Université de Aix-Marseille III 1992) (Not admitted in Austria). **PRACTICE AREAS:** EC/EEA; Tax Planning; Corporate.

MICKELA MOORE, Juris Doctor (Georgetown University Law Center 1985); admitted in New York State (Not admitted in Austria). Member: International Bar Association; Association Internationale des Jeunes Advocats (Executive Committee). **PRACTICE AREAS:** Corporate/Commercial; Finance; Intellectual Property; Arbitration.

OF COUNSEL

MERRAN LOEWENTHAL, LL.B. (University of Sydney 1973) Admitted to practice in England and Wales, New South Wales and Australia (Not admitted in Austria) Member: Solicitors' European Group of the Law Society of England and Wales; Law Society of New South Wales; Law Council of Australia (International Practice Section). **PRACTICE AREAS:** International Estates.

MAUREEN NOONAN, LL.B. (University of Sydney 1974) Diploma, Securities Industry of Australia, Admitted to practice in England and Wales and New South Wales (Not admitted in Austria). **PRACTICE AREAS:** Financial Services; Taxation; Trusts.

Languages: German, English, French, Spanish, Singhalese and Dutch

---

SIEMER - SIEGL - FÜREDER & PARTNER

Established in 1959

DOMINIKANERBASTEI 10
A-1010 VIENNA, AUSTRIA
Telephone: (43-1) 512 14 45
Telefax: (43-1) 513 79 84

Corporate, Commercial, Banking, International Law, Trademarks, EEC Law, International Arbitration, Litigation.

MEMBERS OF FIRM

DR. ROBERT SIEMER, born 1926. *Education:* University of Innsbruck.

DR. HEINRICH SIEGL, born 1940. *Education:* University of Vienna; University of Paris.

DR. HANNES FÜREDER, born 1956. *Education:* University of Vienna.

DR. MICHAEL BREITENFELD, born 1959. *Education:* University of Vienna.

Languages: German, English and French

SLADEK & MEYENBURG

NEUSTIFTGASSE 3
1070 VIENNA, AUSTRIA
Telephone: 0043/1/526 33 00
Telefax: 0043/1/526 33 21

Commercial, Company and Corporation, Unfair Competition, Bankruptcy, Labor and Real Estate Law, Foreign Investments in Austria and Central European Countries.

MEMBERS OF FIRM

DR. FRANZ CHRISTIAN SLADEK, born Klagenfurt, August 8, 1957. *Education:* University of Vienna (Doctor of Jurisprudence, 1980); Max-Planck-Institute for Foreign and International Patent and Copyright Law and Unfair Competition, Munich (1982). *LANGUAGES:* German and English. **PRACTICE AREAS:** Company Law; Commercial Law; Unfair Competition.

DR. MICHAEL MEYENBURG, born Graz, February 25, 1958. *Education:* University of Graz (Doctor of Jurisprudence, 1980); New York University School of Law (M.C.J., 1982). *LANGUAGES:* German, English and Italian. **PRACTICE AREAS:** Commercial Law; Unfair Competition; Labor Law.

COUNSEL

DR. ERNST GRUBECK (Retired, 1991).

DDR. STEINER - DR. WITT-DÖRRING

Established in 1988

NIBELUNGENGASSE 1-3/2/26
1010 VIENNA, AUSTRIA
Telephone: + 43 (1) 581 11 20; 581 11 21; 581 11 22
Telefax: + 43 (1) 581 11 25

General Business and Litigation Practice, Corporate, Trusts, Commercial, Labor Law, Real Estate Transactions and Financing, Foreign Investments, Mergers and Acquisitions, East-West Relations, Joint Ventures, Debt Collections, Industrial Property and Copyright, Distributorship, Agency and Franchising, Unfair Competition, Human Rights.

FIRM PROFILE: The firm is headed by DDr. Elizabeth Steiner and Dr. Daniela Witt-Dörring, supported by qualified attorneys and associated with a team of specialists. The firm provides Secretarial Services, also in Russian and Hebrew.

MEMBERS OF FIRM

DDR. ELISABETH STEINER, born Vienna, 1956; admitted, 1987, Austria. *Education:* University of Vienna Law School (Dr. jur., 1981); University of Economics, Vienna (Mag. rer. soc. oec., 1982; Dr. rer. soc. oec., 1984). *Member:* International Bar Association (IBA); Association Internationale des jeunes Avocats (AIJA); Vienna Bar Association. *LANGUAGES:* German, English and French. **PRACTICE AREAS:** General Business and Litigation Practice; Corporate; Labor Law; Debt Collection; Mergers and Acquisitions.

DR. DANIELA WITT-DÖRRING, born Vienna, 1958; admitted, 1988, Austria. *Education:* University of Vienna Law School (Dr. jur., 1981); University of Economics, Vienna (Mag. rer. soc. oec., 1983). *Member:* Vienna Bar Association. *LANGUAGES:* German, English and French. **PRACTICE AREAS:** Real Estate; Industrial Property; Distributorship; Unfair Competition; East-West Relations.

STROHAL & KRETSCHMER

WIESINGERSTRASSE 6
A-1010 VIENNA, AUSTRIA
Telephone: (43) (1) 513 19 11
Fax: 513191124
Telex: 135986 stlaw-a

Real Property, Joint Ventures, Company Law, Labour Law, Tax Law and Insolvency.

DR. THEODOR STROHAL, born Vienna, Austria, December 23, 1949; admitted, 1979, Austria. *Education:* University of Vienna (Dr.iuris, 1974). *Member:* AIJA. *LANGUAGES:* German, English, Spanish and Indonesian.

DR. WOLFGANG G. KRETSCHMER, born Vienna, Austria, March 16, 1957; admitted, 1987, Austria. *Education:* University of Vienna (Dr. iur., 1980); London School of Economics (LL.M., 1982). *Member:* IBA; Inter-Pacific Bar Association. *LANGUAGES:* German, English, French and Spanish.

STROMMER, REICH-ROHRWIG, KARASEK, HAINZ

Established in 1970

EBENDORFERSTRASSE 3
1010 VIENNA, AUSTRIA
Telephone: (43) (1) 40443.0
Fax: (43) (1) 4059200

Corporations, Contract and Commercial Law, Mergers and Acquisitions, Securities, Privatisations, Joint Ventures, Eastern Europe, Employment, Construction, Arbitration, Labour, Litigation, Tax, Finance, Hotels, Land Law, Landlord and Tenant Law, Antitrust, Aviation, Banking, Building, Business Crime, Competition, Trademarks.

PARTNERS

DR. ALFRED STROMMER, born Horn, Austria, June 20, 1936; admitted, 1970, Austria. *Education:* University of Vienna (Dr. iur., 1961; Faculté de droit, Paris). *Member:* Panel of Arbitrators of ICC (Paris); Board Member of the Association for Construction Law. *LANGUAGES:* German, English and French. **PRACTICE AREAS:** Corporate; Commercial

(This Listing Continued)

STROMMER, REICH-ROHRWIG, KARASEK, HAINZ,
Vienna—Continued

and Contractual Law; Construction Law; Hotels; Land Law; Tax; Mergers and Acquisitions; Arbitration; Project Finance.

DR. JOHANNES REICH-ROHRWIG, born Linz, Austria, November 4, 1954; admitted, 1983, Austria. *Education:* University of Vienna (Dr. iur., 1977). Member of Tax Committee of the Federal Chamber of Tax Advisers; Member of Committee of Corporate Law of the Federal Chamber of Tax Advisers. Lecturer at the University of Economics in Vienna. Examiner for judges. Author of the commentary on the Limited Liability Companies Act (GmbH-Gesetz), author of various articles on Corporate Law, Mergers and Acquisitions and Partnership Law. Co-editor of the commercial law journal "Ecolex". *LANGUAGES:* German and English. *PRACTICE AREAS:* Mergers and Acquisitions; Corporate Law; Securities and Capital Markets; Banking; Trademarks; Antitrust; Unfair Competition Law; Tax Law.

DR. GEORG KARASEK, born Vienna, Austria, July 2, 1953; admitted, 1985, Austria. *Education:* University of Vienna (Dr. iur., 1980). *Member:* Association for Construction Law of Austria. *LANGUAGES:* German, French and English. *PRACTICE AREAS:* Construction and Building Law; Trademarks; Antitrust; Unfair Competition Law; Aviation Law; Joint Ventures and Investments Eastern Europe.

DR. BERNHARD HAINZ, born Vienna, Austria, January 24, 1959; admitted, 1987, Austria. *Education:* University of Vienna (Dr. iur., 1981). Assistant at the Institute for Labour Law at the University of Vienna. Lecturer at the University of Vienna. Author of several articles on Labour Law. *LANGUAGES:* German and English. *PRACTICE AREAS:* Labour; Contract and Commercial Law; Unfair Competition; Landlord and Tenant Law; Administrative Law; EU Law.

DR. HORST EBHARDT, LL.M., born Graz, Austria, January 10, 1961; admitted, 1991, Austria. *Education:* Institut Catholique de Paris (1981); University of Paris Sorbonne (Haute Ecole de Sciences Politiques et Sociales, 1982-1983); University of Graz (Dr.iur., 1984); London School of Economics (LL.M., 1986). Associate: Dres. Fogler-Deinhardstein & Partner, Vienna, 1987-1990; Dr. Wulf Gordian Hauser, Vienna, 1990-1991; Brobeck Hale & Dorr International, Prague, 1991-1994. *Member:* Austrian Bar Association. *LANGUAGES:* German, English and French. *PRACTICE AREAS:* International Corporate; Cross Border Mergers and Acquisitions; Corporate Finance; Privatization (Czech Republic, Hungary, Romania); International Arbitration.

DR. EGON ENGIN-DENIZ, born Vienna, Austria, January 21, 1965; admitted, 1993, Austria. *Education:* University of Vienna (Dr.iur., 1990). Author of articles on Corporate Law. Lecturer, Camillo Sitte-Lehranstalt. *LANGUAGES:* German and English. *PRACTICE AREAS:* Construction Law; Landlord and Tenant Law; Unfair Competition; Copyright Law; Trademarks and Patents; Corporate Law.

OF COUNSEL

DR. WOLFGANG BRANDSTETTER, born Horn, Austria, October 7, 1957; admitted, 1986, Austria. *Education:* University of Vienna (Dr.iur., 1980). Author of several books and numerous articles on Criminal Law and Criminal Procedures. Assistant Professor, Institute for Criminal Law, University of Vienna. Lecturer, University of Vienna and Brno, Czech Republic. *LANGUAGES:* German and English. *PRACTICE AREAS:* Business Crime; Tax Crime; Criminal Procedure.

ASSOCIATES

DR. BERNT ELSNER, MBA, born Vienna, Austria, January 18, 1966. *Education:* University of Vienna (Dr.iur., 1991); University of Economics, Vienna (M.B.A., 1993). Legal Adviser, Austrian Constitutional Court, 1993-1994. *LANGUAGES:* German and English. *PRACTICE AREAS:* Tax Law; Constitutional Law; Commercial Law.

MAG. THOMAS FRAD, born Vienna, Austria, March 16, 1967. *Education:* University of Vienna (Mag.iur., 1994). President, National Union of Students, 1991-1993. Associate, Strommer Reich-Rohrwig & Partners, 1995—. *LANGUAGES:* German and English. *PRACTICE AREAS:* EU Law; Public Law; Civil Law.

DR. PETER HUBER, LL.M., born St. Johann/Tyrol, Austria, August 28, 1963. *Education:* University of Vienna (Dr.iur., 1987; M.B.A., 1987); Yale Law School (LL.M., 1988). Associate, Creditanstalt Investment Bank AG, Vienna, 1988-1989. Manager, Baring Brothers, Deutschland, GmbH, Frankfurt, 1990-1993. Associate, Strommer Reich-Rohrwig & Partners, 1993—. Author of various treatises and articles on Austrian Law. Lecturer,

(This Listing Continued)

Corporate and Business Law, University of Economics, Vienna. *LANGUAGES:* German and English. *PRACTICE AREAS:* Commercial; Corporate; Banking and Antitrust Law; Mergers and Acquisitions.

DR. URSULA ROBERTS-HOFFERT, born Berlin, Germany, May 11, 1966. *Education:* University of Vienna (Dr.iur., 1992). Associate, Strommer Reich-Rohrwig & Partners, February 1993—. Author of book on European Law and on National Environment Policy, 1994. *LANGUAGES:* German, English and French. *PRACTICE AREAS:* Employment; Labour Law; EU Law; Litigation; Environmental Law (in particular waste disposal); Unification of Law; Construction Law.

DR. FRIEDRICH SCHLEDERER, born Vienna, Austria, January 30, 1966. *Education:* University of Vienna (Dr.iur., 1991); University of Economics, Vienna (Since Oct. 1992). Associate, Strommer Reich-Rohrwig & Partners, 1992—. *LANGUAGES:* German, English and Czech. *PRACTICE AREAS:* Corporate; Construction; Litigation; Real Estate.

DR. OLIVER STURM, born Vienna, Austria, November 4, 1966. *Education:* University of Vienna (Dr.iur., 1995). Assistant, Institute of Civil Law, University of Vienna. Associate: Strommer Reich-Rohrwig & Partners, 1995—; Hofman & Maculan Bau AG Legal Dept., 1992-1994; Pullez & Boyer-Telmer, 1990-1992. *LANGUAGES:* German and English. *PRACTICE AREAS:* Construction and Building Law; Constitutional Law; Civil Law.

DR. NIKOLAUS WESELIK, born Vienna, Austria, February 4, 1966. *Education:* University of Vienna (Dr.iur., 1993); Bar examination (1994). Associate, Strommer Reich-Rohrwig & Partners, 1993—. *LANGUAGES:* German, English and French. *PRACTICE AREAS:* Construction and Building Law; EU Law; Contract and Commercial Law; Real Estate Law; Tabac Monopoly within the EU; Government Monopolies in connection with the EU.

Languages: German, English and French

DR. WERNER WALCH

BIBERSTRAβE 10

A-1010 VIENNA, AUSTRIA

Telephone: (0222) 512 57 10

Telefax: (0222) 513 80 74

Aviation, Transport, Corporation, Commercial, EEC Law, Insurance, Construction, Estate Law, Landlord and Tenant, Labour and Litigation.

DR. WERNER WALCH, admitted, 1979, Austria. *Education:* University of Vienna (Dr. jur.). *Member:* Austrian and International Bar Associations; European Air Law Association. *LANGUAGES:* German, English, French and Italian.

ASSOCIATES

Mag. Klaus Keider

MARKUS CHRISTIAN WEINL

KÄRNTNERRING 3/MAHLERSTRASSE 4

A-1010 VIENNA, AUSTRIA

Telephone: +43 1 512 68 83

Fax: +43 1 512 68 83-9

Commercial, Corporate, Mergers and Acquisitions, Securities, Real Estate, Trusts and Estates, Tax, Intellectual Property, International Law including EU Laws.

DR. MARKUS CHRISTIAN WEINL, born Austria, 1952; admitted, 1984, Austria; 1987, Principality of Liechtenstein; 1991, New York. *Education:* University of Innsbruck, Austria (Dr.jur., 1982; Masters, Business Management, 1984); The George Washington University, Washington, D.C. (LL.M., Comparative and International Law, 1992). *Member:* Austrian Bar Association; American Bar Association; International Bar Association. *LANGUAGES:* German, English and French.

WEISS-TESSBACH
RECHTSANWÄLTE OEG

Established in 1878

ROTENTURMSTRASSE 13
A-1010 VIENNA, AUSTRIA
Telephone: 0043 1 5331651
Telecopier: 0043 1 5335252

Budapest, Hungary Representative Office: Weiss-Tessbach, Vármegye u. 3-5, H-1052. Telephone: 0036 1 2674227; 2674228; 2674229. Telecopier: 0036 1 2674241.

Prague, Czech Republic Representative Office: Weiss-Tessbach, Celetna 11, 11000. Telephone: 0042 2 2318693; 2317237; 2319963. Telecopier: 0042 2 2317400.

Bratislava, Slovakia Representative Office: Weiss-Tessbach, Panska 31, 81102. Telephone: 0042 7 335769. Telecopier: 0042 7 331126.

Administrative Law, Advertising Law, Agricultural Law, Antitrust Law, Arbitration, Banking Law, Bankruptcy, Competition Law, Constitutional Law, Construction Law, Conveyancing, Corporate Law, Distributorship Agency and Franchise Law, EEC Law, Employer's Liability, Environmental Law, Foreign Investments, Immigration Law, Industrial Relations and Labor Law, Insurance Law, International Contracts, International Private Law, Litigation, Product Liability Law, Property and Real Estate Law, Rent and Lease, Trade Regulations, General Legal Practice, Copyright Law, Industrial Models, License Negotiation, Patent Litigation, Trademark Litigation, Trademark Prosecution, Transfer of Technology, General Intellectual Property Practice, Capital Taxation, Corporate Taxation, Indirect Taxation, Inheritance, Estate and Gift Taxation, International Taxation, Personal Income Taxation, Sales Turnover, Value Added Taxes, Taxation of Foreign Nationals, Exchange Control, East-West Relations (Countertrade, Joint Ventures), Hungarian Law, Czechoslovakia Law.

FIRM PROFILE: Founded in 1878, Weiss-Tessbach is the longest established and one of the largest Austrian law firms. It developed from an Austrian corporate, general commercial and competition law firm to the full range of Eastern European corporate legal services. The firm opened its Budapest office in 1990, its Prague office in 1992 and its Bratislava office in 1993. The firm is currently composed of seven partners, one U.S. attorney and 19 associates and expects to grow in Eastern Europe in particular.

MEMBERS OF FIRM

DR. KLAUS GALLE, born Vienna, May 1, 1932; admitted, 1964, Austria. *Education:* University of Vienna (Dr. iur., 1957). *LANGUAGES:* German, English and Italian. *PRACTICE AREAS:* Corporate Law; General Commercial Law; Industrial Relations and Labour Law; Banking; Finance and Insurance Law; Buildings Societies Law; Environmental Law; Litigation; Tax Law; Arbitration.

DR. GERHARD BENN-IBLER, born Vienna, August 21, 1940; admitted, 1970, Austria. *Education:* University of Vienna (Dr. iur., 1966). *LANGUAGES:* German and English. *PRACTICE AREAS:* Corporate Law; General Commercial Law; Computer Law; Antitrust; Unfair Competition; EEC Law; Intellectual Property Law; Property and Real Estate Law; Building Law; Environmental Law; Arbitration.

DR. RUDOLF KRILYSZYN, born Vienna, February 22, 1950; admitted, 1978, Austria. *Education:* University of Vienna (Dr. iur., 1973); McGeorge School of Law (European Prop., 1977). *LANGUAGES:* German and English. *PRACTICE AREAS:* Corporate Law; General Commercial Law; The Laws of Eastern European Countries; EEC Law; Industrial Relations and Labour Law; Banking Finance and Insurance Law; Immigration Law; Capital Markets; Data Protection; Telecommunication Arbitration.

DR. CHRISTIAN GASSAUER-FLEISSNER, born Vienna, July 3, 1957; admitted, 1985, Austria. *Education:* University of Vienna (Dr. iur., 1980). *LANGUAGES:* German, English and French. *PRACTICE AREAS:* Corporate Law; General Commercial Law; Antitrust; Unfair Competition; EEC Law; Intellectual Property Law; Entertainment Law; Arbitration.

DR. WIELAND SCHMID-SCHMIDSFELDEN, born St. Pölten, July 1, 1959; admitted, 1989, Austria. *Education:* University of Vienna (Dr. iur., 1984). *LANGUAGES:* German and English. *PRACTICE AREAS:* Corporate Law; General Commercial Law; The Laws of Eastern European Countries; EEC Law; Banking Finance and Insurance Law; Industrial Installations; Environmental Law; Telecommunication Arbitration.

(This Listing Continued)

MAG. DR. STEFAN EDER, born Vienna, April 4, 1962; admitted, 1992, Austria. *Education:* University of Vienna (Dr. iur., 1984; Mag. rer. soc. oec., 1987). *LANGUAGES:* German and English. *PRACTICE AREAS:* Corporate Law; General Commercial Law; Computer Law; The Laws of Eastern European Countries; Banking Finance and Insurance Law; Capital Markets; Data Protection; Arbitration.

MAG. IVO DESKOVIC, born Vienna, October 5, 1962; admitted, 1993, Vienna. *Education:* University of Vienna (Mag. iur., 1988). *LANGUAGES:* German and English. *PRACTICE AREAS:* Corporate Law; General Commercial Law; Property Law; Environmental Law.

ASSOCIATES

KOMAN ANGELIKA, born November 18, 1963, Eisenstadt, Mag.iur. *Education:* University of Vienna; University of Salzburg (Mag.iur., 1988); College of Europe Bruges (Diploma in European Administrative Affairs, 1990). *LANGUAGES:* German, English, French.

HANA BRDOVA, born March 21, 1968, Cadca (SR). Mag. iur. *Education:* University of Bratislava (Mag. iur., 1991). *LANGUAGES:* Slovak, German and Russian.

JOSEF CERNOHLÁVEK, born May 1, 1970; Ceske Budejovice. Mag. iur. *Education:* University of Prague (Mag. iur., 1993). *LANGUAGES:* Czechoslovakian, German and English.

DR. EVA DOBROHRUSKOVÁ, born Rychnow, Dr. iur., June 20, 1962; admitted, 1993, Czech Republic. *Education:* University of Prague (Dr.iur., 1987). *LANGUAGES:* Slovak and German.

SUSANNE FRUHSTORFER, born May 17, 1962; Gmunden. Dr. iur. *Education:* University of Salzburg (Dr. iur., 1985); University of Trier (Mag. iur., 1987). *LANGUAGES:* German, English and French.

DR. MONIKA HORVATH, born Budapest, October 26, 1966; admitted, 1992, Hungary. *Education:* University of Prague (Dr.iur.). *LANGUAGES:* Hungarian, English and German.

DR. TINSCHMIDTOVA IVETA, born Zilina, August 16, 1955; admitted, 1991, Slovak Republic. *Education:* University of Bratislava (Dr.iur). *LANGUAGES:* Slovak and German.

HEDY KRILYSZYN, born June 14, 1951; Vienna. Dr. iur. *Education:* University of Vienna (Dr. iur., 1973). *LANGUAGES:* German, English and French.

BARBARA KUCHAR, born August 1, 1966, Villach. Mag. iur. *Education:* University of Vienna (Mag. iur., 1991). *LANGUAGES:* German, English, Italian and French.

TIBOR KUZMIK, born February 20, 1968; Zuojmo (CR); Mag. iur. *Education:* University of Prague (Mag. iur., 1991). *LANGUAGES:* Czech, Russian, German and English.

JANA MARKECHOVÁ, born Fnina, Dr.iur., April 15, 1964; admitted, 1994, Slovak Rebuplik. *Education:* University of Bratislava (Dr.iur., 1986). *LANGUAGES:* Slovak, German, English.

ANDREA OLTI, born Budapest, January, 20, 1958; admitted, 1994, Hungary. *Education:* University of Budapest (Dr.iur.). *LANGUAGES:* Hungarian, English and German.

ANDRAS POSZTL, born September 19, 1970; Mor (Hungary). *Education:* University of Budapest. *LANGUAGES:* Hungarian and German.

RAINER RADLINGER, born January 3, 1966; Graz. Mag. iur. *Education:* University of Vienna (Mag. iur., 1991). *LANGUAGES:* German and English.

HANNO SCHATZMANN, born May 27, 1966; Vienna. Dr. iur., LL.M. *Education:* University of Vienna (Dr. iur., 1991); London School of Economics and Political Science (LL.M., 1991). *LANGUAGES:* German, English and French.

RUDOLF SCHWEIGHOFER, born Gloggnitz, Mag.iur., September 28, 1952. *Education:* University of Vienna (Mag.iur., 1990). *LANGUAGES:* German, English, French.

CHRISTIAN STREIT, born February 17, 1962, Vienna. Dr. iur. *Education:* University of Vienna (Mag. iur., 1987). *LANGUAGES:* German, English and French.

SABINE TEISCHL, born Vienna, Mag.iur., et rer.soc.oec., December 4, 1970. *Education:* University of Vienna (Mag.iur., 1994; Mag. rer. soc. oec., 1994). *LANGUAGES:* German, English, French, Italian.

(This Listing Continued)

WEISS-TESSBACH RECHTSANWÄLTE OEG, Vienna—
  Continued

RITA ZALAI, born November 13, 1967; Budapest. Dr. iur., LL.M. *Education:* University of Budapest; University of Hamburg (Dr. iur., 1992). *LANGUAGES:* Hungarian, German and Italian.

OF COUNSEL

MICHAEL MCFADDEN, born August 15, 1964; New York. Dr. iur.; admitted, 1990, New York (Not admitted in Austria). *Education:* George Washington University (B.A., 1989); Columbia University School of Law (Dr. iuris.). *LANGUAGES:* English and German.

Languages: German, English, French, Italian, Czech, Slovak, Hungarian, Russian and Serbo-Croatian

---

WILLHEIM, KLAUSER & PRÄNDL

Established in 1973

PLANKENGASSE 6/36
A-1010 VIENNA, AUSTRIA
Telephone: (1) 512 61 99
Telefax: (1) 512 68 51

Commercial, Corporate, European Community, Antitrust, Intellectual Property, Copyright, Entertainment and The Arts, Computers and Software, Mergers, Acquisitions and Divestitures, Agency and Distributorships, Administrative, Real Estate, Tenancy, Labor, Bankruptcy, Probate, Wills, Litigation, Arbitration.

MEMBERS OF FIRM

DR. FRIEDRICH WILLHEIM, born 1936; admitted, 1973, Austria. (Retired 1994).

DR. ALEXANDER KLAUSER, born 1959; admitted, 1990, Austria. *Education:* University of Vienna (Dr.iur., 1983). Internship, European Commission (DGIV), Brussels, 1989-1990. Lecturer, Private International Law, McGeorge School of Law, Salzburg, 1989—. Author: publications in the field of corporate acquisitions, insolvency, agency and competition law. *LANGUAGES:* German, English, French and Italian. *PRACTICE AREAS:* Civil Law; Commercial Law; Intellectual Property Law; Real Estate Law; Insolvency; Litigation.

DR. FELIX PRÄNDL, born 1959; admitted, 1992, Austria. *Education:* University of Vienna (Dr.iur., 1982); Tulane Law School (LL.M., 1984); Stanford Law School (J.S.M., 1986). Foreign Associate, San Francisco Law Firm, 1986, and Brussels EC Law Firm, 1992-1993. Author: several publications in the field of commercial law, EC law and arbitration. *LANGUAGES:* German and English. *PRACTICE AREAS:* Corporate Law; Commercial Law; European Community Law; Cross-Border Transactions; International Distribution; Computer Contracts; Labor Law.

WOLF, THEISS & PARTNERS

Established in 1957

SCHUBERTRING 8
A-1010 VIENNA, AUSTRIA
Telephone: (+43-1) 513 49 79-0
Fax: (+43-1) 513 49 79 25

General Commercial and Civil Law, EC Law, International Banking and Business Law, Law of Investment and Financial Markets, Insurance Law, Corporate and Company Law, Tax Law and International Tax Planning, Real Estate and Construction Law, Transportation Law, Labour and Industrial Relation Law, Agency and Distribution Law, Environmental Law, Civil Litigation and Debt Collection.

FIRM PROFILE: The firm was established in 1957 and offers a full range of legal services in the civil and commercial area. It is well known for its Banking, Insurance and Corporate Law practice. The client base is concentrated in Austria and Central and Western European countries.

MEMBERS OF FIRM

PETER KARL WOLF, born Vienna, Austria, 1928; admitted, 1957, Austria. *Education:* University of Vienna (Dr.jur. 1950). *Member:* Vienna Bar Association. *LANGUAGES:* German and English. *PRACTICE AREAS:* Banking and Business Law; Company and Tax Law; Transportation Law; Construction Law.

(This Listing Continued)

ANDREAS THEISS, born Vienna, Austria, 1946; admitted, 1977, Austria. *Education:* University of Vienna (Dr.jur. 1972). *Member:* Vienna Bar Association; International Bar Association. *LANGUAGES:* German and English. *PRACTICE AREAS:* Banking and Insurance Law; Real Estate and Leasing Law; Business Law; Civil Litigation.

ANDREAS SCHMID, born Vienna, Austria, 1962; admitted, 1991, Austria. *Education:* University of Vienna (Dr.jur. 1986); University of London, London School of Economics (LL.M. 1992). *Member:* Vienna Bar Association. *LANGUAGES:* German and English. *PRACTICE AREAS:* EC Law; Banking and Insurance Law; Real Estate Law; Commercial Arbitration and Civil Litigation.

CHRISTIAN HOENIG, born Vienna, Austria, 1962; admitted, 1991, Austria; 1992, New York. *Education:* University of Vienna (Dr.jur., 1984); University of Economics and Business Administration, Vienna (M.B.A., 1988); University of San Diego (M.C.L., magna cum laude, 1990). Author: co-contributor (Austria), E. Gaillard, "Insider Trading - the laws of Europe, the US and Japan," 1992; "Investing in Eastern Europe Through an Austrian Holding Company," The International Lawyer, vol. 26 (1992) 303. Co-Author: "Austria: New Tax Law on the Reorganization of Businesses," Tax Planning Int'l Review 1992, 8. *Member:* Vienna Bar Association; International Bar Association; International Fiscal Association; Union Internationale des Avocats. *LANGUAGES:* German, English and Spanish. *PRACTICE AREAS:* Corporate and Commercial Law; Banking Law; Distribution Law; International Tax Planning; Arbitration.

LOTHAR WACHTER, born Vienna, Austria, 1961; admitted, 1992, Austria. *Education:* University of Vienna (Dr.jur. 1985). *Member:* Vienna Bar Association. *LANGUAGES:* German and English. *PRACTICE AREAS:* Real Estate and Construction Law; General Civil and Commercial Law.

MARKUS THOMAS HEIDINGER, born Graz, Austria, 1963; admitted, 1993, Austria. *Education:* University of Graz (Mag.jur. 1987; Dr.jur., with distinction, 1989); University of London-King's College (LL.M., with merit, 1991). Author: "Duties and Liability of the Supervisory Board and the Advisory Board in Limited Liability Companies," 1989. Co-Author: "Corporate Structure after the Tax Reform 1989"; "Corporate Structure after the Tax Reform," 1994. *Member:* Vienna Bar Association; International Bar Association; Friends of the Institute of Advanced Legal Studies (London). *LANGUAGES:* German and English. *PRACTICE AREAS:* International Banking and Business Law; Financial Markets; Stock Exchange; Corporate Law.

STEFAN KOECK, born Vienna, Austria, 1963; admitted, 1993, Austria. *Education:* University of Vienna (Mag. jur., 1985; Dr. jur. with distinction, 1989); Northwestern University School of Law (LL.M., 1987). Academic Assistant, Institute of Labor Law, University of Vienna, 1985-1989. Lecturer in Law, University of Vienna, 1987-1990 and 1993—. *Member:* Vienna Bar Association; International Bar Association. *LANGUAGES:* German and English. *PRACTICE AREAS:* EC Law; Corporate Law; Antitrust; Labor Law; International Transactions.

RICHARD V. WOLF, born Paris, France, 1962; admitted, 1991, Austria. *Education:* University of Vienna (Dr. jur., 1985); Harvard Law School (LL.M., 1986). Chase Manhattan Bank, 1992-1993; Credit Lyonnais Bank, 1993-1994. *Member:* Vienna Bar Association. *LANGUAGES:* German, English and French. *PRACTICE AREAS:* Corporate and Business Law; Mergers and Acquisitions; Antitrust; EC Law; Intellectual Property.

ASSOCIATES

MAX BECKER, born Krems, Austria, 1964. *Education:* University of Vienna (Mag. jur., 1988); University of Economics and Business Administration, Vienna (M.B.A., 1991); University of San Diego (M.C.L., 1993). Academic Assistant, Institute of Criminal Law, University of Vienna, 1988-1990. *LANGUAGES:* German and English.

GERALD K. BRAUN, born Steyr, Austria, 1958. *Education:* University of Vienna (Dr. jur., 1982; Dr. phil., 1988); Institute of Advanced Studies, Vienna (Diploma in Political Sciences, 1985); University of Paris, National Foundation for Political Sciences (1985-1986); University of Chicago Law School (LL.M., 1994). Law Clerk, Austrian Constitutional Court, 1990-1993. *LANGUAGES:* German, English, French and Portuguese.

DANIELA EBERL, born Graz, Austria, 1963. *Education:* University of Vienna (Mag. jur., with distinction, 1990). Academic Assistant, Institute of Criminal Law, University of Vienna, 1986-1989. *LANGUAGES:* German and English.

BETTINA KNOETZL, born Neunkirchen, Austria, 1966. *Education:* University of Vienna (Mag. jur., 1988). Academic Assistant, Institute of

(This Listing Continued)

Civil Law, University of Vienna, 1989-1991. Bank Austria, Vienna, 1991-1993. *LANGUAGES:* German and English.

SUSI RATHAUSCHER, born Vienna, Austria, 1968. *Education:* University of Vienna (Mag. jur., 1993). *LANGUAGES:* German, English, French and Spanish.

EVA SPIEGEL, born Vienna, Austria, 1967. *Education:* University of Vienna (Mag. jur., 1992). *LANGUAGES:* German and English.

ZEINER & ZEINER

SCHELLINGGASSE 6
A-1010 VIENNA, AUSTRIA
Telephone: +43 1 512 23 64, +43 1 37 75
Telex: 115540 zein a
Facsimile: (Gr. II & III) +43 1 512 33 25

REVISER OF THE AUSTRIA LAW DIGEST FOR THIS DIRECTORY.

Prague, Czechoslovakia Office: Zeiner Golan Nir & Partners. Maiselova 15, 110 01 Prague 1. Telephone: +42 2 248 12 301. Facsimile: +42 2 248 12 307.

Corporate, Commercial, Antitrust, Tax, Labor, Industrial Property, Unfair Competition, Estate Law, Arbitration, Foreign Investments, International Transactions.

MEMBERS OF FIRM

Dr. Hans-Georg Zeiner   Dr. Martin J. Maxl
Dr. Brigitte Winzberger   Mag.jur. Petra Pacher, LL.M.

ASSOCIATES

Mag. jur. Ursula Nowak, LL.M.

Languages: German, English and French

REVISER OF THE AUSTRIA LAW DIGEST FOR THIS DIRECTORY.

BELGIUM

DE BANDT, VAN HECKE & LAGAE

MECHELSESTEENWEG 196
B-2018 ANTWERP, BELGIUM
Telephone: (32-3) 238.10.62
Telex: 71059 diurna b
Telecopier: (32-3) 216.47.17

REVISERS OF THE BELGIUM AND THE EUROPEAN COMMUNITIES LAW DIGESTS FOR THIS DIRECTORY.

Brussels, Belgium Office: rue Brederode 13, B-1000. Telephone: (32-2) 517.94.11. Telex: 25477 Lexlaw. Telecopier: (32-2) 517.94.94.
New York, N.Y. Office: 712 Fifth Avenue, New York, New York, 10019, U.S.A. Telephone: 212-801-3420. Telecopier: 212-801-3425.
London, England Office: Royex House, Aldermanbury Square, EC2V 7HR. Telephone: (44-171) 600.36.07. Telecopier: (44-171) 600.17.18.

Commercial, Maritime, Marine Insurance, Company and Private International Law. Industrial Relations.
Member of Alliance of European Lawyers (EEIG) which regroups six law firms from Continental Europe. The Alliance consists of De Bandt, van Hecke & Lagae at Brussels and Antwerp; De Brauw Blackstone Westbroek at The Hague, Amsterdam, Rotterdam and Eindhoven; Jeantet & Associés at Paris and Warsaw; Lagerlöf & Leman at Stockholm, Gothenburg and Malmö; Oppenhoff & Rädler at Berlin, Cologne, Frankfurt am Main, Leipzig and Münich; Uria & Menendez at Madrid and Barcelona.
The Alliance member firms have joint offices at Brussels, London, New York and Prague.

MEMBERS OF FIRM

WILFRED GORIS, born Antwerp, Belgium, November 2, 1943; admitted, 1966, Antwerp. *Education:* University of Louvain (Dr. Jur., 1966); University of Brussels (Lic. Econ. Law, 1971); University of Chicago Law School (M.C.L., 1973).

JAN THEUNIS, born Antwerp-Merksem, Belgium, July 17, 1950; admitted, 1974, Antwerp. *Education:* University of Louvain (Lic. Jur., 1974).

(This Listing Continued)

ASSOCIATES

DIRK SLAGMOLEN, born Duffel, Belgium, February 16, 1958; admitted, 1982, Antwerp. *Education:* University of Antwerp (Lic. Jur., 1981); University of Ghent (Vlerick School, Dipl. in Management, 1982); St. Aloysius School of Fiscal Sciences (Diploma, 1986).

ANN DEKKERS, born Antwerp, Belgium, February 28, 1963; admitted, 1987, Antwerp. *Education:* University of Louvain (Lic. Jur., 1987); University of Brussels (Lic. Maritime and Air Law, 1989).

LINDA DEDRIE, born Wilrijk, Belgium, April 25, 1954; admitted, 1990, Antwerp. *Education:* University of Antwerp (Lic. Jur., 1989).

EDOUARD SOUBRY, born Roeselare, Belgium, January 25, 1965; admitted, 1990, Brussels; 1994, Antwerp. *Education:* University of Louvain (Lic. Jur., 1988); University of Ghent (Vlerick School, Dipl. in Management, 1989); University of Cambridge (LL.B., 1990).

CHRISTIAAN HENDRICKX, born Mortsel, Belgium, August 24, 1964; admitted, 1989, Antwerp. *Education:* University of Louvain (Lic. Jur., 1988).

ANNICK DE KIMPE, born Alost, Belgium, May 28, 1966; admitted, 1991, Brussels; 1993, Antwerp. *Education:* University of Louvain (Lic. Jur., 1989); College of Europe, Bruges (Dipl. Eur. Studies, 1991).

ERIC DE BIE, born Ekeren, Belgium, January 3, 1967; admitted, 1993, Brussels. *Education:* University of Antwerp, Belgium (Lic.Jur., 1990); University of Louvain (Lic.Not., 1991); University of Michigan Law School (LL.M., 1992).

JEAN-FRANCOIS PETERS, born Antwerp, Belgium, May 18, 1964; admitted, 1992, Antwerp. *Education:* University of Louvain (Lic. Jur., 1990).

STEFAAN DECKMYN, born Bruges, Belgium, May 3, 1969; admitted, 1993, Antwerp. *Education:* University of Louvain (Lic. Ph., 1988; Lic. Jur., 1992); University of Chicago Law School (LL.M., 1993).

PHILIP RAEYMAKERS, born Ekeren, Belgium, September 25, 1965; admitted, 1993, Antwerp. *Education:* University of Antwerp (Lic. Jur., 1992).

MARC VAN DE PERRE, born Antwerp, Belgium, January 18, 1967; admitted, 1994, Antwerp. *Education:* University of Louvain (Lic. Jur., 1992); University of Chicago Law School (LL.M., 1993).

KURT VERHEGGEN, born St-Niklaas, Belgium, February 2, 1970; admitted, 1994, Antwerp. *Education:* University of Louvain (Lic. Jur., 1993); Tulane University Law School (LL.M., 1994).

REVISERS OF THE BELGIUM AND THE EUROPEAN COMMUNITIES LAW DIGESTS FOR THIS DIRECTORY.

DE CALUWE & DIERYCK

ANTWERP, BELGIUM

(See Dieryck, Van Looveren & Co.)

General Practice. Antitrust, Arbitration, Civil, Competition, Corporate, Criminal, EEC, Family, Food and Drug, Tax, Industrial Property, Insurance, Intellectual Property, Labor, Maritime, Transport Law, Public Contracts and Public Law.

DIERYCK, VAN LOOVEREN & CO.

KORTE LOZANASTRAAT, 20-26
B-2018 ANTWERP 1, BELGIUM
Telephone: 32 (3) 2387850; 2379896
Telefax: 32 (3) 2379899

Brussels, Belgium Office: De Caluwe, Putzeys, 'T Kint, Van Fraeyenhoven et Associes, 98 rue Saint-Bernard, B-1060. Telephone: 32 (2) 5365811. Telefax: 32 (2) 5365911.

General Commercial Practice, Antitrust, Arbitration, Civil, Competition, Corporate, Criminal, EEC, Family, Food and Drug, Tax, Industrial Property, Insurance, Intellectual Property, Labour, Maritime, Transport Law, Public Contracts and Public Law, Admiralty, Environmental Law.

(This Listing Continued)

DIERYCK, VAN LOOVEREN & CO., Antwerp—
Continued

PARTNERS

CHRISTIAN DIERYCK, born Antwerp, 1938; admitted, 1965, Antwerp. *Education:* University of Louvain (Dr. jur., 1961; Lic. econ., 1964). Professor, University of Louvain, 1993. *LANGUAGES:* Dutch, French, English, German. *PRACTICE AREAS:* Admiralty; Marine Insurance; Insurance; Banking.

WILFRIED VAN LOOVEREN, born Antwerp, 1942; admitted, 1971, Antwerp. *Education:* University of Louvain (Cand. Phil., 1963; Dr. jur., 1968). *LANGUAGES:* Dutch, French, English, German. *PRACTICE AREAS:* General Commercial Practice; Maritime; Customs Law; Corporate.

HUGO CALLENS, born Antwerp, 1949; admitted, 1974, Antwerp. *Education:* University of Louvain (Dr. jur., 1971). Co-Author: "European Civil Practice" (Belgian draft). *LANGUAGES:* Dutch, French, English, Swedish, German. *PRACTICE AREAS:* Real Estate; General Practice; Customs Law; Commercial; Corporate.

PAUL VERGUTS, born Wilrijk, 1949; admitted, 1977, Antwerp. *Education:* University of Louvain (Lic. jur., 1974); University of Ghent (M.A., 1983). Co-Author: "European Civil Practice" (Belgian draft). *LANGUAGES:* Dutch, French, English, German, Spanish. *PRACTICE AREAS:* Maritime; Transport Law; Commercial Litigation.

MARINA VAN DER AUWERAERT, born Antwerp, 1951; admitted, 1977, Antwerp. *Education:* University of Louvain (Lic. jur., 1974). *LANGUAGES:* Dutch, French, German, English. *PRACTICE AREAS:* Labour; Lease; Contracts.

WERNER VAN DER VEEKEN, born Antwerp, 1948; admitted, 1974, Antwerp. *Education:* University of Louvain (Dr. jur., 1970). *LANGUAGES:* Dutch, French, English, German. *PRACTICE AREAS:* General Practice; Environmental Law.

TRUDO MOTMANS, born Vilvoorde, 1956; admitted, 1985, Antwerp. *Education:* University of Antwerp (Cand. Phil., 1975); University of Louvain (Lic. jur., 1981). *LANGUAGES:* Dutch, French, English, German. *PRACTICE AREAS:* Corporate; Finance; Banking.

MARC GOOSSENS, born Antwerp, 1949; admitted, 1979, Antwerp. *Education:* University of Louvain (Lic. jur., 1974). *LANGUAGES:* Dutch, French and English. *PRACTICE AREAS:* Maritime; Intellectual Property; Competition.

Languages: Dutch, English, French, German, Italian, Spanish and Swedish.

ARTHUR FLIEGER
MECHELSESTEENWEG 82
2018 ANTWERP, BELGIUM
Telephone: (03) 238.77.66
Telefax: (03) 216.18.44

EEC Law, Commercial, Business, Domestic, Company, Partnership and Offshore Tax Law, Domestic, Transborder/Contract Law, Environmental Law, South American Law, Nafta, Mercosul.

ARTHUR FLIEGER, born Antwerp, Belgium, February 12, 1960; admitted, 1984, Antwerp. *Education:* Vrije Universiteit Brussel (Bachelor of Law, cum laude, 1980; Certificate International and European Law, 1984); Universitaire Instelling Antwerpen (Licencee, cum laude, 1983); Universitaire Faculteiten Sint Ignatius Antwerp (Certificate Maritime Law, 1983); Rijksuniversiteit Gent (Certificate Eastern European Studies, 1983; Certificate Portuary and Maritime Science, 1984). Author: "Le Commerce avec La Chine" EACL, 1987; "Some Legal Aspects of the Chinese Law Banking System ," EACL, 1987; "Some Aspects of Foreign Banking in China," EACL, 1988; "T.R.D. Maritime Law," Kluwer, 1988-1991. Regulations of the commission of the European Communities concerning the application of article 85 paragraph 3 of the EEC Treaty to certain categories of patent licence agreements, part 1 & 2, in The Big Idea, Inventors Association of St. Louis, 1990. Co-author with Prof. Dr. H. Matthys: "De Begrotingstelsels van de Instellingen van Openbaar Nut (I.De parastatalen,II. De niet parastatalen, III. De economische overheidsbedrijven, IV. De openbare kredietinstellingen). (i.e. the budget systems of the Belgian public institutions); Le système monétaire européen, SME, CRISP; Het Europees Monetair beleid, 1992, VUB. De Europese Interne Markt en de Ekonomische Monetaire

(This Listing Continued)

Unie (i.e. The Internal European Market and Economic European Union); De begrotingsstelsels en de strukturen in de instelligen van openbaar nut (i.e. The budget systems and structures in the public institutions); Management Pulieke sector (i.e. management of the administration); Inleiding tot de overheidsbegroting (i.e. Introduction to public budget), 1993; Ekonomische Monetaire Unie (E.M.U.) Europese Ekonomische Ruimte, 1994. Former Lecturer European University of Antwerp, 1987. Former Assistant attached at the Seminary for Commercial Law, Prof. Dr. Wymeersch, R.U.G. Commercial and Financial Law Department, Rijksuniversiteit Gent, 1987-1991. Assistant Professor with Prof. Dr. H. Matthys, European and public budget control, Vrije Universiteit Brussel Economics Political and Social Science Department and Department of Medicine and Pharmacology and Medical Science, Brussels. *Member:* Antwerp and Belgium Bar (can appear before all EC-Tribunals and Courts); American Bar Association; International Bar Association; European Association for Chinese Law, (Former Chairman, Standing Committee of the Banking, Foreign Exchange and Monetary Affairès, 1987); American Chamber of Commerce; American Belgian Association; Swiss Business Council; Associaçao Internacional de Estudos Juridicos e Economicos, São Paulo, Brazil (Co-Founder). *LANGUAGES:* Dutch, French, English, German, Spanish, Italian and Portuguese. *PRACTICE AREAS:* EEC Law; Commercial Law; International Business Law; Tax Law; Offshore Companies; Environmental Law; South American Law; Nafta; Mercosul.

LEGAL SUPPORT PERSONNEL

PROF. DR. H. MATTIJS, Vrije Universiteit, Brussels (Candidate Master & Doctorate, cum laude); Universitaire Instelling Antwerpen. Paralegal. *PRACTICE AREAS:* European and domestic budget control..

HUYBRECHTS, ENGELS, CRAEN & PARTNERS
A PROFESSIONAL CORPORATION
73 AMERIKALEI
B-2018 ANTWERP, BELGIUM
Telephone: 03/244.15.60
Telex: 71557 Casela B
Telecopier: 03/238.41.40

General and International Practice, Administrative Law, Civil Law, Criminal Law, Family Law, Insurance, Transport and Maritime Law, Commercial Law, Environmental Law, Contracts, Bank Law, Labor Law.

MARC A. HUYBRECHTS, born 1941; admitted, 1964, Antwerp. Dr. Iuris, LL.M., (Berkeley).

PETER ENGELS, born 1956; admitted, 1978, Antwerp. Lic. Iuris.

MARIE-CHRISTINE CRAEN, born 1957; admitted, 1980, Antwerp. Lic. Iuris.

ANNEMARIE COOX, born 1959; admitted, 1982, Antwerp. Lic. Iuris.

EDMOND J. BRONDEL, born 1958; admitted, 1982, Antwerp. Lic. Iuris.

DOMINIQUE NEIRYNCK, born 1951; admitted, 1973, Antwerp. Lic. Juris.

WOUTER DEN HAERYNCK, born 1962; admitted, 1985, Antwerp. Lic. Iuris, LL.M. in Admiralty (Tulane).

WILLEM SLOSSE, born 1965; admitted, 1988, Antwerp. Lic. Iuris.

Languages: English, French, German and Dutch.

LAFILI, VAN CROMBRUGGHE & PARTNERS
KARDINAAL MERCIERLEI 44, BERCHEM
B-2600 BERCHEM, ANTWERP, BELGIUM
Telephone: 03/281.11.20
Facsimile: 03/239.26.40

Brussels, Belgium Office: Vossendreef 6 Bus 1, B-1180. Telephone: 02/374.92.00. Facsimile: 02/375.45.25.

General Commercial Practice, International Contracts, Distributorship, Agency, Franchising, Belgian and EEC Competition, Corporate, Tax Foreign Investments, Arbitration, Litigation, Product Liability, Trade Regulations, Food and Drug Regulations, Banking, Environmental, Labor, Mari-

(This Listing Continued)

time, Administrative, Intellectual Property, Construction, Bankruptcy, Transport.

PARTNERS

ANN GHYSEBRECHTS, born 1962; admitted, 1985, Belgium.

JAN SWINNEN, born 1963; admitted, 1988, Belgium.

LAMBERTE NEVEN, born 1961; admitted, 1985, Belgium.

DIRK DELLAERT, born 1965; admitted, 1990, Belgium.

Languages: Dutch, French, English and German

LOEFF CLAEYS VERBEKE

"DE HERTOGHE", 8TH FLOOR
92 DESGUINLEI, B.8
B-2018 ANTWERP, BELGIUM
Telephone: 32-3-2385656
Telex: 72748 EURLAW B
Telecopier: 32-3-2387877

Amsterdam, The Netherlands Office: 15 Apollolaan, P.O. Box 75088, 1070 AB. Telephone: 31-20-5741200. Telex: 14292. Telecopier: 31-20-6718775.

Brussels, Belgium Office: 268 A Avenue de Tervueren, A-1150. Telephone: 02-778.22.11. Fax: 02-763.21.85.

Liège, Belgium Office: 13, Rue Simonon, (Place de Bronckart), B-4000. Telephone: 32-41-527722. Telecopier: 32-41-527511.

New York, New York Office: Swiss Bank Tower, 23rd Floor, 10 East 50th Street, 10022. Telephone: 212-759-9000. Fax: 212-759-9018.

Paris, France Office: 1, Avenue Franklin D. Roosevelt, 75008. Telephone: 33-1-49539125. Telecopier: 1-42891460.

Rotterdam, The Netherlands Office: 70 Weena, P.O. Box 74, 3000 AB. Telephone: 31-10-4034777. Telex: 23395 (LEX NL). Telecopier: 31-10-4149388.

Singapore Office: 20 Raffles Place, #08-03, Ocean Towers, Singapore 0104. Telephone: 65-5335332. Telecopier: 65-5330313.

Tokyo Office: NSE Building, 5th Floor, 1-7-1 Kanda Jinbo-cho, Chiyoda-ku, Tokyo 101, Japan. Telephone: 81-3-32599831. Fax: 81-3-32599888.

Barcelona, Spain Office: 550, 4° 1A, Av. Diagonal, 08021. Telephone: 34-3-2007117. Telecopier: 34-3-2023098.

Madrid, Spain Office: Balañá Eguía, Antonio Mauro 7, 5°, 28014. Telephone: 34-1-5312501. Telecopier: 34-1-5313530.

Jakarta, Indonesia Associated Office: Ali Budiardjo, Nugroho, Reksodiputro, Niaga Tower, 24th floor, Jalan Jenderal Sudirman Kav. 58, 12920. Telephone: 62.21.2505125/2505136. Telecopier: 62.21.2505121/2505001.

Luxembourg, Luxembourg Office: Zeyen Beghin Feider. 67, Rue Ermesinde, P.O. Box 5017, 1050. Telephone: 352.468946. Telex: 60736 (zflaw lu). Telecopier: 352.468947.

Belgian Attorneys may represent clients before all Belgian Courts, before the European Court of Justice and the Benelux Court of Justice, and are admitted to plead before all Courts of the Memberstates of the Common Market (EEC).

MEMBERS OF FIRM

WIM DEJONGHE, born 1961; admitted, 1989, Brussels; 1993, Antwerp. *Education:* University of Louvain (K.U. Leuven) (Lic. Jur, 1984).

LEO NEELS, born 1948; admitted, 1994, Antwerp. *Education:* University of Louvain (K.U. Leuven) (Lic. Jur., 1973; Dr. Jur., 1979). Professor, University of Louvain (K.U. Leuven) and University of Antwerp (UIA).

JOHN STOOP, born 1947; admitted, 1971, Antwerp. *Education:* University of Brussels (V.U.B.) (Dr. Jur., 1971).

ASSOCIATES

PHILIPPE HINNEKENS, born 1963; admitted, 1993, Brussels and Antwerp. *Education:* University of Louvain (K.U. Leuven) (Lic. Jur., 1986); University of Chicago, U.S.A. (LL.M., 1987). *Member:* International Fiscal Association.

HUGO KEULERS, born 1968; admitted, List of Stagiaires, 1991, Brussels; admitted, 1994, Antwerp. *Education:* University of Louvain (K.U. Leuven) (Lic. Jur., 1991).

(This Listing Continued)

SYLVIA KIERSZENBAUM, born 1965; admitted, 1992, Brussels; 1993, Antwerp. *Education:* University of Antwerp (U.F.S.I.A.) (Lic.Jur., 1988); Cornell University, U.S.A. (LL.M., 1989).

ERIK MAES, born 1963; admitted, List of Stagiaires, 1993, Antwerp. *Education:* University of Antwerp (U.I.A.) (Lic. Jur., 1988).

KARLIJN NIJS, born 1964; admitted, 1991, Brussels; 1993 Antwerp. *Education:* University of Louvain (K.U. Leuven) (Lic. Jur., 1987).

MICHAEL OLISLAEGERS, born 1967; admitted, List of Stagiaires, 1992, Brussels; 1993, Antwerp. *Education:* University of Antwerp (U.I.A.) (Lic. Jur., 1990); The London School of Economics (LL.M., 1991).

FILIP TILLEMAN, born 1962; admitted, 1992, Brussels; 1993, Antwerp. *Education:* University of Louvain (K.U. Leuven) (Lic. Jur., 1985); University of Brussels (U.L.B.) (Lic. Economic Law, 1987).

INGRID VAN CLEMEN, born 1961; admitted, 1986, Antwerp. *Education:* University of Antwerp (U.I.A.) (Lic. Jur., 1986).

PETER VAN DE VIJVER, born 1961; admitted, 1991, Antwerp. *Education:* University of Ghent (R.U.G.) (Lic. Jur., 1984); The Hopkins University, School of Advanced International Studies, Bologna and Washington, D.C. (M.A., International Relations, 1986).

RAYMOND VAN DE WEYER, born 1953; admitted, 1977, Antwerp. *Education:* University of Antwerp (U.I.A.) (Lic. Jur., 1977).

(For Personnel and other data, see Professional Biographies at Amsterdam, Barcelona, Brussels, Liège, New York, Paris, Rotterdam, Singapore and Tokyo)

KAREL MUL LAW OFFICES

Established in 1971

VLAAMSE KUNSTLAAN, 3
2020 ANTWERP, BELGIUM
Telephone: 32/(0)3/237.34.26
Facsimile: 32/(0)3/237.07.44

General Practice, Belgian and International Commercial Law, Debt Recovery, Enforcement of Foreign Legal Decisions.

FIRM PROFILE: The firm was established in 1971 and offers a full range of legal services. It is well know for its Commercial Law. The client base is European and North American.

KAREL MUL, born Antwerp, Belgium, June 19, 1948; admitted, 1971, Antwerp. *Education:* University of Ghent (Doctor Juris, 1971; Licenciaat Notary, 1971). Editor, Le Journal des Tribunaux, 1986—. Substitute Judge, Commercial Court, Antwerp, 1989—. *Member:* Antwerp Bar (President, Young Bar Association, 1983-1984; Member, Council of the Bar, 1984-1986); Arbitrator of the Chamber of Commerce of Antwerp. *Member:* ABA; IBA; AIJA. *LANGUAGES:* French, English, Dutch and German. *PRACTICE AREAS:* Commercial Law; Debt Recovery.

Languages: French, English, Dutch and German.

PUELINCKX, SCHILTZ, LINDEN, GROLIG

MEIR 24
2000 ANTWERP, BELGIUM
Telephone: 32-3-226.61.61
Fax: 32-3-226.92.98

Brussels, Belgian Office: Rue Royale 87-Koningstraat 87. Telephone: 02-218.80.70. Fax: 02-218.37.69.

MEMBERS OF ANTWERP FIRM

HUGO SCHILTZ, born October, 1927; admitted, 1953, Antwerp. *Education:* University of Leuven (Dr. Jur., Lic. Economics). Author: "An Introduction to Financial Law", 3rd ed., 1988. Vice Prime Minister and Minister of Budget, Belgium Government, 1988-1991. *Member:* Belgian Center for National and International Arbitration (Cepina). *LANGUAGES:* Dutch, French, English and German. *PRACTICE AREAS:* Public Affairs; Insurance Law; Arbitration and Litigation.

KOEN DE WINTER, born June, 1956; admitted, 1981, Antwerp. *Education:* University of Antwerp (Lic. Jur.); College of Europe Bruges (Advanced European Studies). *Member:* American Bar Association; International Bar Association; Arbitration Chamber of Commerce, Antwerp. *LANGUAGES:* Dutch, French, English and German. *PRACTICE*

(This Listing Continued)

PUELINCKX, SCHILTZ, LINDEN, GROLIG, Antwerp—
Continued

AREAS: Commercial Contracts; Intellectual Property; Unfair Trading Practices; Media Law.

JAN CERFONTAINE, born March, 1956; admitted, 1983, Antwerp. *Education:* University of Leuven (Lic. Jur.; Lic. phil.). Author: "Nederlandstalige Larcier," 1992 (Commercial Code with Case Law Annotation on Corporate Law, Banking and Finance). Assistant Professor, University of Ghent, 1987—. *Member:* Arbitration Chamber of Commerce, Antwerp. **LANGUAGES:** Dutch, French, English and German. **PRACTICE AREAS:** Company Law; Banking and Finance.

PASCAL MALLIEN, born December, 1958; admitted, 1982, Antwerp. *Education:* University of Leuven (Lic. Jur). **LANGUAGES:** Dutch, French, English and German. **PRACTICE AREAS:** Construction and Real Estate Law; Torts and Environmental Law.

MARC DE DECKER, born May, 1961; admitted, 1984, Antwerp. *Education:* University of Antwerp (Lic.Jur., Postgraduate Maritime Law). Author: "Inland Navigation". 1991. Assistant Professor, University of Antwerp, (UFSIA). **LANGUAGES:** Dutch, French and English. **PRACTICE AREAS:** Maritime Law; Transport Law.

ILSE RENAP, born April, 1967; admitted, 1991, Antwerp. *Education:* University of Leuven (Lic.Jur.); Tulane University (LL.M.). **LANGUAGES:** Dutch, French and English. **PRACTICE AREAS:** Intellectual Property Law; Media Law.

LUC VAN CANEGHEM, born October, 1965; admitted, 1989, Brussels; 1993, Antwerp. *Education:* University of Ghent (Lic. Jur.); University of Brussels (Lic. Spec. en Droit economique); King's College (LL.M.); University of London. **LANGUAGES:** Dutch, French and English. **PRACTICE AREAS:** Agency and Distribution Law; Consumer Protection Law.

ELS TRYPSTEEN, born December, 1967; admitted, 1992, Brussels; 1993, Antwerp. *Education:* University of Brussels (Lic. Jur.). **LANGUAGES:** Dutch, French and English. **PRACTICE AREAS:** Banking Law; Construction Law.

FRANK HENDRICKX, born March, 1969; admitted, 1992, Antwerp. *Education:* University of Leuven (KUL) (Lic. Jur.). **LANGUAGES:** Dutch, French and English. **PRACTICE AREAS:** Labor Law.

FIEN MADDENS, born April, 1969; admitted, 1993, Antwerp. *Education:* University of Leuven (Lic. Jur.). **LANGUAGES:** Dutch, French and English. **PRACTICE AREAS:** Environmental Law.

ABLE
(ASSOCIATED BUSINESS LAWYERS IN EUROPE)

BOULEVARD BRAND WHITLOCK 152
1200 BRUSSELS, BELGIUM
Telephone: (+32 2) 735 8272
Telefax: (+32 2) 732 01 43

Associated Business Lawyers in Europe consists of six law firms from Europe: Esche Schümann Commichau in Hamburg; Geater & Co. in Brussels (EU Law); Gedda & Ekdahl Advokatbyrå in Stockholm; Lafarge, Flécheux, Revuz in Paris; Lawrence Graham in London; and Puelinckx Schiltz Linden Grolig in Brussels.

(For details and lists of Partners and Counsel of the Member Firms of ABLE, see their respective listings).

AFSCHRIFT
RUE DU MONASTÈRE ● MUNSTERSTRAAT 10-12
B-1050 BRUSSELS, BELGIUM
Telephone: (32) 2-646.46.36; (32) 2-649.42.42
Fax: (32) 2-644.38.00

General and International Commercial Practice, Accounting Law, Administrative Law, Banking, Bankruptcy, Business Migration, Civil Law, Commercial Law, Competition, Corporate (including Mergers and Acquisitions), Finance, Gifts and Estates, Intellectual Property, International Contracts, Litigation, Real Estate, Rent and Lease, Tax, Torts, White Collar Crime.

(This Listing Continued)

THIERRY AFSCHRIFT. *Education:* University of Brussels (Lic. Jur., magna cum laude, 1976; Lic. Droit Economique, 1977; Lic. Droit Fiscal, 1978). Founder and President, Master in Tax Management, Solvay Business School. Chargé de Cours, Tax Law, Income Tax, V.A.T., Indirect Taxation, Real Estate Taxation, University of Brussels, Law Faculty and Solvay Business School, 1986. Author: *"L'évitement licite de l'impôt et la réalité juridique,"* Brussels, Larcier, 1994; *"La constitution d'une personne morale de droit étranger dans l'unique but d'éluder l'impôt belge"* in Mélanfes Vander Elst, pp. 27-42; *"Les fusions et scissions de sociét és e les impôts indirects,"* (in Ed. du Jeune Barreau, pp. 279-904); *"Les entreprises et la recherche des voies les moins imposées pour leurs dirigeants et leur personnel de cadre,"* (Ed. du Jeune Barreau, pp. 140-169). **PRACTICE AREAS:** Corporate; Mergers and Acquisitions; Commercial Law; Executive Compensation; Finance; Tax; Real Estate; White Collar Crime.

CORINNE BARTHOLME. *Education:* University of Brussels (Lic. Jur., cum laude, 1981). Lecturer, Solvay Business School, Master in Management, Registration Taxes. Member, Commission Administrative du Jeune Barreau, 1987-1989. Author: "Revue du notariat belge," Table décennale, 1986; *"La notion de cas spéciaux justifiant la surséance au recouvrement en cas de réclamation en matière d'impôts sur les revenus,"* (Rev. Liége, 1988, pp. 395-398); *"La conformitéde la régle du cumul des revenus des époux e la Convention de Sauvegarde des Droit de l'Homme et à la Constitution belge,"* (Rev. Not. b., 1984, pp. 454-462). **PRACTICE AREAS:** Civil Law; Commercial Contracts' Enforcement; Litigation; Inheritance Taxes; Registration Taxes; Gifts and Estates; Rent and Lease.

KATHY DEBOECK. *Education:* University of Brussels (Lic. Jur., cum laude, 1987; Lic. Droit Economique, 1988). Lecturer, Solvay Business School, Master in Tax Management, Income Tax. Author: Vade Mecum de la S.P.R.L., Brussels, Créadif, 1984, 4th. ed. (tax aspects); Vade Mecum des nouvelles sociétés coopératives, Brussels, Créadif, 1992 (tax aspects); Vade Mecurn de l'administrateur de la sociétéanonyme, Brussels, Créadif, 1992 (tax aspects); *"Fiscalité des artistes du spectacle et des sociétés d'artistes étrangères"* (H.O.R., 1993, pp. 53-66). **PRACTICE AREAS:** Commercial Contracts; Corporate; Mergers and Acquisitions; Tax; Intellectual Property; Accounting Law.

MARIELLE MORIS. *Education:* University of Brussels (Lic. Jur., summa cum laude, 1992); Prix Pierre de Harven (1992). Lecturer, Solvay Business School, Master in Tax Management, Income Tax. *Author:* "L'article 92, al. 3 du Code de la TVA est-il compatible avec les prinicipes généraux du droit" (J.L.M.B., 1992, pp. 343 ff.). **PRACTICE AREAS:** Income Tax; Local Taxes; Economical Criminal Law; General Principles of Law.

ANNE RAYET. *Education:* University of Brussels (Lic. Jur., magna cum laude, 1989). Assistant, University of Brussels, Real Property Rights and General Principles of Law. Author: *"Les impôts sur les revenus et la loi du 22 juillet 1992"* (J.T., 1992, pp. 805 ff.); *"La loi du 28 décembre 1992 portant des dispositions fiscales, financières et diverses"* (J.T., 1993, pp. 485 ff.); *"La loi du 22 juillet 1993 et l'évitement licite de l'impôt"* (J.T., 1993, pp. 833 ff.); *"L'allocation d'intér éts moratoires sur la restitution des sommes pauées indiument au trésor"* (J.L.M.B., 1992, pp. 326 ff.); *"Le pouvoir discrétionnaire de l'administration de l'enregistrement en matiére d'expertises de contrôle"* (J.L.M.B., 1992, pp. 337 ff.). **PRACTICE AREAS:** Administrative Law; Civil Law; Intellectual Property; Public Affairs; Real Estate; Gifts and Estates; Tax.

ANNEMIE ROMBOUTS. *Education:* University of Namur (Can. Jur., 1988); University of Leuven (Lic. Jur., magna cum laude, 1991). Assistant, Faculty of Law, Corporate Law, University of Leuven. Research Fellow, Faculty of Law, University of Leuven. Author: *"Het nieuwe artikel 41, §2 van de vennootschapswet. Wat met de geldigheid van aandelenopties?"* (T.R.V., 1992, pp. 142 ff.); *"La nouvelle loi sur le banchiment est-elle applicable aux infractions fiscales?"* (J.T., 1992, pp. 609 ff.); *"Les droits fondamentaux du contribuable"* (Ed. du Jeune Barreau, 1994); *"Wissel als witsel. De beteugeling van het witwassen van gelden via geldwissel in het Belgisch financieel en strafrecht"* (T.R.V., 1994, pp. 195 ff.). Co-Author: *"Requalification of transactions for tax purposes under section 344, §1 of the Belgian Income Tax Code - Potential application to Coordination Centers"* (Intertax, 1994, 381, ff.). **PRACTICE AREAS:** Corporate; Corporate Reorganizations; Finance; Securities; Tax; Torts.

PETER TERMOTE. *Education:* University of Brussels (Lic. Jur., summa cum laude, 1988; D.E.A. Droit Commerce Intern et D.I.P., 1989); Harvard Law School (1990); Solvay/U.L.B. (Certificate, Master in Tax Management, 1992). Fellowships: René-Marcq Award, 1988; French Government Award, 1989; ITT International Fellowship, 1990; BAEF Honorary Fellowship, 1990. Lecturer, Environmental Tax, Tax Administration

(This Listing Continued)

Program, Solvay Business School, University of Brussels. Author: *"Le régime fiscal des options"* (R.G.F., 1992, pp. 37-49). **PRACTICE AREAS:** Corporate; Tax; including Environmental Tax; Corporate Reorganizations; Commercial Law; Labor Law.

VINCIANE THOMISSE. *Education:* University of Brussels (Lic. Jur., 1986; Lic. Droit fiscal, 1990). Member, Commission Administrative du Jeunne Barreau de Bruxelles, 1993—. Chargée de Cours, Institut technique du bois, de la peinture et des industries graphiques, 1994. **PRACTICE AREAS:** General Practice; Debt Recovery; Income Tax; Insurance Law; Litigation.

MARTIN VAN BEIRS. *Education:* University of Brussels (Lic. Jur., magna cum laude, 1983); Solvay Business School (Postgraduate in Business Administration, 1989). Lecturer, Solvay Business School, Master in Tax Management, Corporate Tax, Special Topics. **PRACTICE AREAS:** Banking; Finance; Corporate; Mergers and Acquisitions; Securities; Tax.

PAUL VANDEPITTE. *Education:* University of Leuven (Lic. Jur., cum Laude, 1983); University of Brussels (Lic. Droit Economique, 1985). Co-Author: *"Les actions de concert, de contrôle et de contrôle conjoint dans le cadre de la loi du 2 mars 1989 tendant à assurer la transparence de l'actionnariat"* (R.P.S., 1990, pp. 81-115); *"Le champ d'appolication territoriale de la loi du 27 juillet 1967 sur les concessions de vente exclusives"* (J.T., 1990, pp. 725-729); *"De individuele controlebevoegdheld van de vennoot in kleine en middelgrote ondernemingen enkele beschouwingen"* (T.R.V., 1990, pp. 574-578). **PRACTICE AREAS:** Commercial Contracts; Agency and Distribution Law; Corporate; Mergers and Acquisitions; Unfair Trade Practices; Competition Law; Intellectual Property; Labor Law; Litigation.

SOPHIE VANHAELST. *Education:* University of Brussels (Lic. Jur., cum laude, 1989; Lic. Droit Economique, 1990). Lecturer, Solvay Business School, Master in Tax Management, Value Added Tax, Special Topics. **PRACTICE AREAS:** Consumer Protection; Commercial Contracts; Corporate; Corporate Reorganizations; Tax; Unfair Trade Practices.

INES WOUTERS. *Education:* University of Brussels (Lic. Jur., magna cum laude, 1984); Mac Gill University (Comparative Law, 1985). Lecturer, Solvay Business School, Master in Tax Management, Tax Procedure, Taxation of small and medium-sized enterprises. Co-Author: The employment contract in Belgian Law, Brussels, Créadif, 1989 (tax aspects); *"La validité d'une transaction en matiére fiscale"* (J.L.M.B., 1988, p. 1241). **PRACTICE AREAS:** Executive Compensation; International Taxation; International Commercial Contracts; Gifts and Estates; Taxation.

Authors: Le Code des impôts sur les revenus, Edition commentée du C.I.R. 1992, Brussels, Créadif, 1993.

Languages: French, Dutch, English, German and Spanish.

AKIN, GUMP, STRAUSS, HAUER, FELD & DASSESSE

(Brussels office of Akin, Gump, Strauss, Hauer & Feld, L.L.P.)

65 AVENUE LOUISE P.B.7
1050 BRUSSELS, BELGIUM
Telephone: 011-322-535-29-11
Telefax: (+32 2) 535 29 00
Telex: 20125 ECAKIN B

Dallas, Texas Office: Akin, Gump, Strauss, Hauer & Feld, L.L.P., 1700 Pacific Avenue, Suite 4100, 75201-4618. Telephone: 214-969-2800.

Austin, Texas Office: Akin, Gump, Strauss, Hauer & Feld, L.L.P., 2100 Franklin Plaza, 111 Congress Avenue, Suite 2100, 78701. Telephone: 512-499-6200.

Houston, Texas Office: Akin, Gump, Strauss, Hauer & Feld, L.L.P., 1900 Pennzoil Place-South Tower, 711 Louisiana Street, 77002. Telephone: 713-220-5800.

San Antonio, Texas Office: Akin, Gump, Strauss, Hauer & Feld, L.L.P., Nationsbank Plaza, 300 Convent Street, Suite 1500, 78205. Telephone: 210-270-0800.

New York, New York Office: Akin, Gump, Strauss, Hauer & Feld, L.L.P., 65 East 55th Street, 33rd Floor. Telephone: 212-872-1000. Fax: 212-872-1002.

Washington, D.C. Office: Akin, Gump, Strauss, Hauer & Feld, L.L.P., 1333 New Hampshire Avenue, N.W., Suite 400, 20036. Telephone: 202-887-4000.

(This Listing Continued)

Moscow, Russia Office: Akin, Gump, Strauss, Hauer & Feld, L.L.P., Bolshoi Sukharevsky Pereulok 26, 103051 Moscow, Russia. Telephone: 011-7095-974-2411 or (202) 887-4545. Fax: 011-7095-974-2412 or (202) 887-4544.

General EC and International Trade Law and Policy, Competition, Mergers and Acquisitions, Corporate, Labor, Tax, Banking, Insurance Law, Intellectual Property Law, Litigation.

PARTNERS

JAY D. ZEILER, born Leesburg, Virginia, June 6, 1943; admitted, 1973, District of Columbia and Virginia. *Education:* George Washington University (B.A., 1966); Washington & Lee University and George Washington University (J.D., with honors, 1972). Phi Delta Phi. Editor, Journal of International Law and Economics, 1971-1972. *Member:* The District of Columbia Bar; Virginia State Bar; American and International Bar Associations.

MARC DASSESSE, born Brussels, 1947; admitted, 1978, Belgium, Avocat. *Education:* University of Brussels (ULB) (Dr. Jur., 1969; Spec. Deg. in Economic Law, 1971); University of Cambridge (Diploma in Comparative Legal Studies, 1974). Co-author: "Banking and the Competition Law of the EEC" (with Mr S. Isaacs, Q.C.), Lloyds of London Press Ltd, 1978; "EEC Banking Law" (with Mr. S. Isaacs, Q.C.) Lloyds of London Press Ltd., 1985 (1st Edition); "EC Banking Law" (with Mr. S. Isaacs, Q.C. and Mr. G. Penn), 1994 (2nd edition); "Précis de Droit fiscal" (Belgian Tax Law) (with Mr. P. Minne), Bruylant, Brussels, 1990 (1st edition); 1991 (2nd Edition); 1994 (3rd Edition). Belgian and/or EC correspondent of: International Banking Law; Journal of International Banking Law; Butterworths Journal of International Banking Law; International Company and Commercial Law Review; Journal des Tribunaux - Droit Européen (Laucier, Brussels); Securities and Capital Markets Law Report; Bulletin for International Fiscal Documentation (International Fiscal Association); International Insurance Law Review; EC Tax Journal. Professor of Belgian Tax Law, Faculty of Law, Free University of Brussels (U.L.B.); Professor of EC Tax Law, Institute of European Studies of the Free University of Brussels (U.L.B.); Professor of EC Tax Law, Solvay Business School (Master of European Administration); Visiting Professor, Institut Universitaire International de Luxembourg (EC Banking and Financial Law Programme); Member, "Board of International Scholars", Banking and Financial Law Unit, Queen Mary & Westfield College, University of London. **LANGUAGES:** French, Dutch, English and German.

EDWIN VERMULST, born 's Hertogenbosch, Netherlands, 1958; admitted, Advokaat Utrecht. *Education:* Universiteit van Utrecht, Meester in de rechten (LL.M., 1983); University of Michigan Law School (LL.M., 1984; S.J.D., 1986). Author: Anti-Dumping Law and Practice in the United States and the European Communities (Elseviers 1989); Anti-Dumping Law and Practice: A Comparative Analysis (with John Jackson; Simon & Schuster 1990); Rules of Origin: A Comparative Study (University of Michigan Press 1994; with Paul Waer, Jacques Bourgeois). Guest Lecturer: Universities of Utrecht, Amsterdam, Antwerp; International Customs Academy, ROC. **LANGUAGES:** Dutch, English, German and French.

RICHARD M. GITTLEMAN, born Providence, Rhode Island, 1955; admitted, 1983, District of Columbia. *Education:* Brown University (A.B., 1977); American University (J.D., cum laude, 1982). Recipient, T. Morton McDonald Scholarship for outstanding legal research, 1982. Co-Author (with Patrick H. Mitchell) "The 1986 Zairian Investment Code: Analysis and Commentary," 2 ICSID Review Foreign Investment Law Journal 122 (1987). Author, "The Establishment and Operation of a Business Enterprise in the Republic of Zaire," 3 ICSID Review Foreign Investment Law Journal 263 (1988). *Member:* The District of Columbia Bar.

MARTINE DE WITTE, born Brussels, 1961; admitted, 1984, Belgium, Avocat. *Education:* University of Brussels (Lic. Jur., with honors, 1984; Special Degree in Tax Law, 1984). Fellowship, British Council University of London, Kings College, School of Law. Assistant Professor, University of Brussels School of Law, 1988. **LANGUAGES:** Dutch, English and French.

PETER VERHAEGHE, born Vilvoorde, Belgium, 1958. Advocate, admitted to the Brussels Bar, 1991. *Education:* Catholic University of Leuven (Lic. Jur., magna cum laude, 1981); Harvard Law School (LL.M., 1984). Member of the Legal and Taxation Committee of the American Chamber of Commerce in Brussels, Member of the International Fiscal Association, Member of the Board of Editors of "Fiscale Actualiteit" (Kluwer, CED-SAMSOM). Author: "Syllabus Inkomstenbelastingen", Vlaams Rechtsgenootschap, Leuven, p. 295, 1983; "Samenwonen, gezin en fiscus," Fiscale wegwijzer voor uw inkomens- en vermogensbeleid, Kluwer, Antwerpen, pp.

(This Listing Continued)

AKIN, GUMP, STRAUSS, HAUER, FELD & DASSESSE, Brussels—Continued

1-30, 1984; "Fiscale aspecten van het uitoefenen van het vrij beroep van arts," Handboek Artsenpraktijk, CED-SAMSOM, Brussel 1986; "Coordination Centers in Belgium: advertising, R&D, accounting and administrative activities - Preparatory and auxillary activities," Seminar binder Forum 187, Knokke, Federatie van Coördinatiecentra, Brussel, pp. 22, 1987; "Coordination Centers: joint ventures, mergers & acquisitions and corporate reorganizations," Seminar binder Forum 187, Federatie van Coördinatiecentra, Brussel, pp. 8, 1990; "Coordination centers and treasury management: investment funds - permissible dealings with affiliated institutions," Seminar binder Forum 187, Federatie van Coördinatiecentra, Brussel, pp. 7, 1991; "Where to place UCITS/investment funds in Europe for optimal tax treatment," Seminar binder Euromoney's first International Tax Planning Forum, Amsterdam, pp. 16, 1991; "Coordination centers make Belgium the market leader," International Tax Review, pp. 5-9, Supplement December 1991/January 1992, London; and various articles on different Belgian and international tax and corporate issues published in the newsletters "Artsenpraktijk", "Managing Europe", and "Fiscale Actualiteit" (1985—). Assistant Professor in Tax Law, Catholic University of Leuven, 1981-1983. *LANGUAGES:* French, English and German.

PAUL WAER, born Lier, Belgium, 1958; admitted, 1987, Brussels. *Education:* University of Antwerp (Lic. Jur., 1981); Osaka University of Foreign Studies (Special Degree in Japanese, 1982); Hitotsubashi University (Tokyo) Hogakush ushi (Certificate Foreign Research Fellow awarded, 1983; LL.M., 1985); Harvard University Law School (LL.M., 1987). Books: Rules of Origin in International Trade (University of Michigan Press; with Edwin Vermulst, Jacques Bourgeois). *LANGUAGES:* Dutch, English, Japanese, French and German.

SPECIAL COUNSEL

STEVEN E. BRUMMEL, born New York, 1952; admitted, 1977, New Jersey; 1979, District of Columbia. *Education:* University of Michigan (B.A., with honors in History, 1974); George Washington University Law School (J.D., 1977). European Editor, Computers and Law Magazine (U.K.).*Member:* New Jersey State Bar Association; The District of Columbia Bar. *LANGUAGES:* English and French.

ANNABELLE J. EWING, born Glasgow, Scotland, 1960; admitted, 1986, Solicitor. *Education:* University of Glasgow (LL.B. Honors Degree in EEC Law, 1981); The John Hopkins University, Bologna (Diploma in Advanced International Relations, 1982); Europa Institute, Amsterdam (Diploma in European Integration, 1983). Stagiaire, Fisheries Division of the European Commission (Legal Service), 1987; Co-EC correspondent : Securities and Capital Markets Law Report. *Member:* Law Society of Scotland. *LANGUAGES:* English, French and Italian.

OF COUNSEL

JAN VAN BESIEN, born Eeklo, Belgium, 1949; admitted, 1972, Brussels, Avocat. *Education:* University of Leuven (Lic. Jur. 1972); Fiscale Hogeschool, Brussels (Spec. Deg. in Fiscal Sciences, 1974). Author: "Indiening van een bezwaarschriftinzake inkomstenbelastingen," Fiscale Praktijkstudie nr. 8, 1988, Kluwer rechtswetenschappen, Antwerp; "De Inkomstenbelastingen/Procedures" in "De B.V.B.A. in de praktijk," since 1985, Kluwer rechtswetenschappen, Antwerp; "De inkomstenbelasting/Procedures" in "De N.V. in de praktijk," since 1985, Kluwer rechtswetenschappen, Antwerp; "Bedrijfsvoorheffing" in Aanwerven, Tewekstellen, Ontslaan, since 1988, Kluwer rechtswetenschappen, Antwerp. Board of Editors, "Tijdschrif voor Fiscaal Recht" Tax Law, Antwerp. *Member:* Brussels Bar. *LANGUAGES:* Dutch, French and English.

KENNETH E. NATALE, born Hammondsport, New York, 1952; admitted, 1977, Virginia; 1978, District of Columbia; 1986, New York. *Education:* University of Notre Dame (B.A., with high honors, 1974); George Washington University (J.D., 1977).

ASSOCIATES

ANN ROSE STOUTHUYSEN, born Turnhout, Belgium, 1960; admitted, 1983, Belgium, Avocat. *Education:* University of Leuven (Licenciaat in de Rechten, 1983). *LANGUAGES:* Dutch, English and French.

IAN ROXAN, born Toronto, 1956; admitted, 1981, Ontario, Barrister and Solicitor; 1994, England, Solicitor. *Education:* University of Toronto (B.A., 1976); Osgoode Hall Law School, Toronto (LL.B., with honors, 1979); University of Cambridge (M.Phil. in Economics, 1982; Ph.D. in Economics, 1991). Tax Policy Branch, Department of Finance Canada, 1983-1985. *Member:* Canadian Bar Association; International Fiscal Association;

(This Listing Continued)

Institute for Fiscal Studies, Canadian Tax Foundation. *LANGUAGES:* English and French.

STANLEY STEWART, born Gainesville, Florida, October 8, 1961; admitted, 1988, Texas. *Education:* Stanford University (B.A., 1984); Southern Methodist University (J.D., 1988). Leading Articles Editor, Southwestern Law Journal, 1987-1988. *Member:* Dallas and American Bar Associations; Dallas Association of Young Lawyers. *PRACTICE AREAS:* Financial Services Law.

CHRISTOPH ZEYEN, born Kiel, Germany, 1958; admitted, 1989, Hamburg, Rechtsanwalt. *Education:* Christian-Albrechts-Universitat (1980-1985). Research Assistant, Universitat des Saarlandes, 1986; Commission of the European Communities (DGIV), 1989. *Member:* German Bar Association. *LANGUAGES:* German, English and French.

DARREN S. TRIGONOPLOS, born Cumberland, Maryland, 1960; admitted, 1989, Virginia. *Education:* Washington & Lee University (B.A., cum laude, with honors in Journalism, 1982); Georgetown University (J.D., 1989). Omicron Delta Kappa.

FOLKERT GRAAFSMA, born Utrecht, The Netherlands, 1966; admitted, 1991, Belgium. *Education:* University of Nijmegen, The Netherlands (1989); University of Brussels (LL.M., 1990). *LANGUAGES:* Dutch, English, German and French.

ALAIN DE JONGE, born Sint-Niklass, Belgium, 1965; admitted, 1991, Brussels, Advokaat. *Education:* University of Brussels (V.U.B.) (Licentiaat in Law, 1988); Institute of European Studies (ULB), Brussels (Spec. Deg. European Law, grande distinction, 1988). 1st prize AEGEE European Moot Court, Florence, 1989. *LANGUAGES:* French, Dutch and English.

ELLEN L. MARX, born Bridgeport, Connecticut, 1961; admitted, 1992, New York. *Education:* Wake Forest University (B.A., 1983); University of Copenhagen, Denmark, Cand. Jur., 1990); Duke University School of Law (LL.M., 1991). *LANGUAGES:* English, French and Danish.

JOHN C. LEPORE, born Baltimore, Maryland, March 14, 1964; admitted, 1992, Maryland and Massachusetts; 1993, District of Columbia. *Education:* Boston College (A.B., magna cum laude, 1986); The Johns Hopkins University (M.P.H., 1991); Georgetown University (J.D., 1991). Phi Beta Kappa.

TOM NELSON, born Fort Worth, Texas, 1965; admitted, 1993, Texas. *Education:* University of Texas (B.B.A., 1987); Southern Methodist University School of Law (J.D., 1992).

PILAR DE LA CAL, born Madrid, Spain, 1965, admitted to practice law, 1988. admitted to Madrid Bar, 1994, Madrid, Avocat. *Education:* New York University School of Law (LL.M. Honors: Donald L. Brown Fellowship) 1994; College of Europe, Belgium (Diploma of Advanced European Studies : Honors - Spanish Foreign Affairs Ministry Scholarship 1990); Universidad Pontificia de Comillas (ICADE), Spain (Master's Degree in Law 1983 -1988); Master's Degree in Economics and Business Administration (1983-1989). Assistant Professor in European Community Law, Universidad Pontificia de Comillas (ICADE), Spain (Mergers & Acquisitions : The Process of Valuing a Company 1991 - 1993). *LANGUAGES:* Spanish, English, French, German and Italian.

BART DRIESSEN, born Rotterdam, The Netherlands, 1967; admitted 1994, Brussels, Advokaat. *Education:* Katholieke Universiteit Nijmegen (LL.M., 1989); University of Kent at Canterbury (M.A. in International Relations, 1991); Eötvös Loránd Tudomany Egyetem, Budapest (DR univ. Summa Cum Laude in International Law, 1993). Author, A Concept of Nation in International Law, T.M.C. Asser Institut, The Hague 1992. *LANGUAGES:* Dutch, English, Hungarian, German and French.

Languages: Danish, Dutch, English, French, German, Italian, Spanish.

(For biographical data of other personnel, see Professional Biographies at Austin, Dallas, Houston and San Antonio, Texas, New York, New York, Washington D.C. and Moscow, Russia)

ALLEN & OVERY

RUE DE LA LOI 99
BOX 8
1040 BRUSSELS, BELGIUM
Telephone: (32 2) 230 27 91
Facsimile: (32 2) 230 66 13

London, England Office: One New Change, EC4M 9QQ. Telephone: 0171 330 3000. Facsimile: 0171 330 9999.

(This Listing Continued)

Beijing, China Office: Suite 3204, Jing Guang Centre, Hu Jia Lou, Chaoyang District, 100020. Telephone: (86 1) 501 4681. Facsimile: (86 1) 501 4682.

Budapest, Hungary Office: Mádach Trade Center, Mádach Imre utca 13-14, H-1075. Telephone: (361) 268 1511. Facsimile: (361) 268 1515.

Dubai, United Arab Emirates Office: 501 Al Futtaim Tower,P.O. Box 3251, Deira. Telephone: (971 4) 282296. Facsimile: (971 4) 212860.

Frankfurt, Germany Office: Taunusanlage 11, 11th Floor, 60329. Telephone: (49 69) 242 6120. Facsimile: (49 69) 242 61220.

Hong Kong Office: 9th Floor, Three Exchange Square, 8 Connaught Place. Telephone: (852) 2840 1282. Telex: 68757. Facsimile: (852) 2840 0515.

Madrid, Spain Office: Antonio Maura 7, 6°, 28014. Telephone: (34 1) 521 2654. Facsimile: (34 1) 523 0458.

Moscow, Russia Office: 9 ul Tverskaya, Entrance No 5, 8th Floor, 103009. Telephone: (7 501) 940 4500. Facsimile: (7 501) 940 4501.

New York Office: Swiss Bank Tower, 10 East 50th Street, 10022. Telephone (1-212) 754 3340. Facsimile: (1-212) 754 7903.

Paris, France Office: 1 Avenue Franklin D. Roosevelt, 75008. Telephone (33-1) 49 53 06 37. Telex: 651079. Facsimile: (33-1) 49 53 91 52.

Prague, Czech Republic Office: Jindřišská 34, 110 00 Prague 1. Telephone: (42 2) 2410 3317. Facsimile: (42 2) 2410 3235.

Singapore Office: 20 Raffles Place #08-03, Ocean Towers, 0104. Telephone: (65) 533 0988. Facsimile: (65) 533 1322.

Tokyo, Japan Office: NSE Building, 5th Floor, 1-7-1 Kanda Jinbo-cho, Chiyoda-ku Tokyo 101. Telephone (81 3) 3259 9898. Facsimile (81 3) 3259 9888.

Warsaw, Poland Office: ul. Kopernika 17, IV Floor, 00-359. Telephone: (48 22) 262 226. Facsimile: (48 22) 262 360.

Firm engaged in EEC Law (including Antitrust and Dumping), International, Commercial and English Practice. Entitled to plead before the European Court of Justice and the European Commission.

RESIDENT PARTNERS

Michael J. Reynolds

RESIDENT CONSULTANTS

Colin Overbury

(For Complete List of Firm Personnel, see Professional Biographies at London, England).

ALLIANCE OF EUROPEAN LAWYERS (EEIG)

RUE BREDERODE, 13A
B-1000 BRUSSELS, BELGIUM
Telephone: (32-2) 505.02.11
Telecopier: (32-2) 502.26.44

The Alliance consists of De Bandt, van Hecke & Lagae at Brussels and Antwerp; De Brauw Blackstone Westbroek at The Hague, Amsterdam, Rotterdam and Eindhoven; Jeantet & Associés at Paris and Warsaw; Lagerlöf & Leman at Stockholm, Gothenburg and Malmö; Oppenhoff & Rädler at Berlin, Cologne, Frankfurt am Main, Leipzig and Münich; Uria & Menendez at Madrid and Barcelona.

(For details and lists of Partners and Counsel of the Member Firms of the Alliance of European Lawyers, see their respective listings of their offices in their home jurisdictions).

ARCHAMBEAU, AVOCAT

38, AVENUE MUTSAARD
1020 BRUSSELS, BELGIUM
Telephone: 32-2-268.57.16; 32-2-268.68.20
Telefax: 32-2-268.47.55
Lecture Room: 193 Avenue Louise, 1050 Brussels, Belgium

EEC, International and National Belgian Law Practice. Commercial, Corporation, Labour Contracts, Family Law and Litigation.
Firm authorized to appear before the European Commission and the European Court of Justice. Belgian firm authorized to appear before the Belgian Courts and other Courts in the EC.

(This Listing Continued)

GUY ARCHAMBEAU, born Liège, Belgium, November 1, 1947; admitted, 1973, Brussels. *Education:* University of Leuven (Dr. Juris, 1970; Special Degree in Labour and International Law, 1971; European Law, 1972). Supervisor of recently graduated law students of the University of Louvain.

S.G. ARCHIBALD

Established in 1962
RUE DE FACQZ, 63
1050 BRUSSELS, BELGIUM
Telephone: (02) 647.5394
Telecopier: (02) 648.6573

Paris, France Office: 10 Avenue de Messine, 75008. Telephone: (1) 44.13.28.00. Telex: 651873 ARCHI A. Telecopier: (1) 45.62.12.33. Cable Address: "Archibald-Paris".

Firm engaged in General International and European Practice.

LUCIE A. CARSWELL, born Elgin, Illinois, USA, March 26, 1955; admitted, 1986, District of Columbia (Not admitted in Belgium). *Education:* Northern Illinois University (B.A., 1980); George Washington University (J.D., 1985); University of Brussels, Institute for European Studies (Licence Spéciale en Droit Européen, 1987). *LANGUAGES:* English and French.

(For Biographical Information on other personnel, see Professional Biographies at Paris, France).

ASHURST MORRIS CRISP

AVENUE LOUISE 65
BRUSSELS 1050, BELGIUM
Telephone: (32-2) 537-6895
Fax: (32-2) 537 4353

London, England Office: Broadwalk House, 5 Appold Street, EC2A 2HA. Telephone: 0171-638-1111. Telex: 887067. Fax: 0171-972-7990.

Tokyo, Japan Office: Kioicho Building, 8th Floor, 3-12 Kioicho, Chiyoda-ku, 102. Telephone: (81-3) 5276 5900. Fax: (81-3) 5276 5922.

Paris, France Office: 8, rue Clément Marot, 75008. Telephone: (33-1) 47 20 0088. Fax: (33-1) 47 20 0093.

New Delhi, India Ofice: 6 Aurangzeb Road D-202. 110011. Telephone: (91 11) 301 4054. Facsimile: (91 11) 301 4089.

Firm engaged in English and International Practice. Brussels office involved in UK and EC Competition, Trade, Intellectual Property, Corporate and Commercial Law.

RESIDENT PARTNER

J.J. Ellison

BAKER & McKENZIE

40 BOULEVARD DU RÉGENT-REGENTLAAN 40
FIFTH FLOOR
1000 BRUSSELS, BELGIUM
Telephone: (02) 506-36-11
Intn'l. Dialing: (32-2) 506-36-11
Cable Address: ABOGADO
Telex: 23880
Answer Back: 23880 ABOGAD B
Facsimile: (32-2) 511-62-80

Associated Offices of Baker & McKenzie in: Almaty, Amsterdam, Bangkok, Barcelona, Beijing, Berlin, Bogotá, Brasília, Budapest, Buenos Aires, Cairo, Caracas, Chicago, Dallas, Frankfurt, Geneva, Hanoi, Ho Chi Minh City, Hong Kong, Juárez, Kiev, London, Madrid, Manila, Melbourne, México City, Miami, Milan, Monterrey, Moscow, New York, Palo Alto, Paris, Prague, Rio de Janeiro, Riyadh, Rome, St. Petersburg, San Diego, San Francisco, São Paulo, Singapore, Stockholm, Sydney, Taipei, Tijuana, Tokyo, Toronto, Valencia, Warsaw, Washington, D.C. and Zürich.
Correspondent Law Firm: Hadiputranto, Hadinoto & Partners, Jakarta.

General International, European and Belgian practice. Aviation, Banking and Finance, Bankruptcy, Insolvency and Reorganization, Corporate, EC Competition and Trade, Environmental Law, Intellectual Property, Labor and Employment Law, Litigation and Arbitration, Mergers and Acquisitions, Real Estate, Taxation, Telecommunications.

(This Listing Continued)

BAKER & McKENZIE, Brussels—Continued

Authorized to appear before courts.

Jacques H. J. Bourgeois	Anne Laurent
François Gabriel	Dominique Lechien
Jacques Ghysbrecht	Ignace Maes
Otto J. Grolig	Pierre Sculier
Paul G. Herten	Jozef Slootmans
Luc Hinnekens	Peter J. Sturtevant
Alain Huyghe	Koen Vanhaerents

Pierre Bové	Catherine I. Grisart
Mia Declercq	Arne K. E. Gutermann
Antoine D. R. M. De Raeve	Peter E. Leys
Yves J. J. M. de Voghel	Xavier Michel
Daniel D. Fesler	Jean-François Vandenberghe
Joanna R. Goyder (England)	Annick Van Hoorebeke
Johan L. Ysewyn	

BALON, BUYLE, MAINGAIN & PHILIPPE

Established in 1981

103 BOULEVARD AUGUSTE REYERS
1040 BRUSSELS, BELGIUM
Telephone: +32 2 732 16 10
Fax: +32 2 733 62 13

Commercial Law, Companies & Corporations, Banking, Securities & Finance, Social Law, Distribution and Franchising, European Community Law, Building & Construction, Tax Law, Mergers & Acquisitions, International Business and Trade Law, Arbitration, Torts and Civil Litigation.

FIRM PROFILE: The firm was founded in 1981 by Bernard Maingain and offers the complete range of legal services companies need. Its main clients are Belgian and European. The 5 partners have a legal support staff of 19 associates (This makes 24 lawyers), and an accountancy and secretarial staff of 11 people. All of its members are lawyers at the Brussels' Bar, but they can treat cases all over Belgium (no regional restriction). The firm is the Central Secretariat of the Integrated Advisory Group International (I.A.G. International), an association composed of independent and selected European high quality law, tax and accountancy firms (direct telephone +32 2 735 36 80, fax +32 2 733 62 13).

PARTNERS

FRANÇOISE BALON, born Elisabethville, Zaire, June 30, 1955; admitted, 1978, Belgium. *Education:* Université de Liège (Cand. Jur., 1975); Université Catholique de Louvain (Lic. Jur., 1978). Author: Various Publications on Building and Construction Law, e.g. book *La Mérule* . *Member:* Organization "La Mérule," Science Technique and Law. *LANGUAGES:* French and English. *PRACTICE AREAS:* Building and Construction Law.

JEAN-PIERRE BUYLE, born Ougrée, Belgium, January 14, 1955; admitted, 1979, Belgium. *Education:* Université Catholique de Louvain (Lic. Jur., 1977); Université Libre de Bruxelles (Special Degree in Economic Law, 1979). Prize of the Past Presidents-Jeune Barreau of Brussels. Teaching Assistant at Université Libre de Bruxelles, Commercial Law. Member, of the Bar Council. Lecturer at the French Brussels' Bar, Judicial Practice and Commercial Law. Author: Various Publications on Banking and Computer Law. Member, Various Legal Reviews. *Member:* European Society for Banking and Financial Law (President). *PRACTICE AREAS:* General Commercial Law; Companies & Corporations; Banking; Securities and Finance; Computer Law.

ANDRÉ LOMBART, born Brussels, Belgium, November 26, 1956; admitted, 1979, Belgium. *Education:* Université Catholique de Louvain (Lic. Jur., 1979). Author: Various Publications on Franchising. Co-Author of a Book on *Franchising in Europe Member:* The Eurofranchise Lawyers; International Bar Association; International Association of Young Lawyers (A.I.J.A.). *LANGUAGES:* French, English and Dutch. *PRACTICE AREAS:* Distribution Law; Franchising; Mergers and Acquisitions.

BERNARD MAINGAIN, born Brussels, Belgium, April 30, 1955; admitted, 1978, Belgium. *Education:* Université Catholique de Louvain (Lic. Jur., 1978). Prize of the Bar of Marseille (Concours international de plaidoirie de la francophonie); Prize of the secretaries of the "Conférence du stage," of the Bar of Paris. Teaching: Lecturer, at Inst. Tut Catholique De Hautes

(This Listing Continued)

Etudes Commerciales, (European Social Law), Facultés Universitaires Catholiques de Mons, European Social Law. Author: Various Publications on Social Law. *Member:* International Association Europe-Africa; Union Internationale de Avocats; Belgian Association of Social Law Practitioners. *LANGUAGES:* French, English and Dutch. *PRACTICE AREAS:* Mergers & Acquisitions; Labour Law; Social Security Law.

DENIS-MARIE PHILIPPE, born Charleroi, Belgium, February 20, 1955; admitted, 1977, Belgium. *Education:* Université Catholique de Louvain (Lic. Jur., 1976; Lic. Economics, 1979; Doctor Jur., 1983); Rijksuniversiteit Utrecht, The Netherlands (Special Degree in European Law, 1977). Author: Book on the "Comparative Law of Frustration"; Various Publications on Commercial Law, Obligations, Torts, European Law. Director, Belgian Review of Business Law. Teaching: Professor, Université Catholique de Louvain, Comparative Law and International Trade Law; Facultés Universitaires Catholiques de Mons, Business Law; Lecturer, University of Paris X, International Contracts *Member:* International Association of Young Lawyers (A.I.J.A.); International Bar Association. *LANGUAGES:* French, English, Dutch, German, Italian and Spanish. *PRACTICE AREAS:* General and International Commercial Law; Companies & Corporations; Torts; European Law; International Law.

ASSOCIATES

PATRICK D. CAROLUS, born Ath, Belgium, April 24, 1966; admitted, 1993, Belgium. *Education:* Facultés Universitaires St. Louis Bruxelles (Cand. Jur. 1990); Université Catholique de Louvain (Lic. Jur. 1993). *LANGUAGES:* French, English, Dutch. *PRACTICE AREAS:* Torts; Contracts; Commercial Law.

ERIC C. DE FORMANOIR, born Ghent, Belgium, April 5, 1968; admitted, 1993, Belgium. *Education:* Factultés Universitaires Notre Dame d la Paix Namur (Cand. Jur., 1989); Université Catholique de Louvain (Lic. Jur. 1992); University of Exeter, United Kingdom (LL.M. in European Legal Studies, 1993). *LANGUAGES:* Dutch, French, English. *PRACTICE AREAS:* European Law; Banking Law; Commercial Law; Real Estate Law.

IGNACIO DE LA SERNA, born Barcelona, Spain, December 22, 1964; admitted, 1987, Belgium. *Education:* Facultés Universitaires St. Louis Bruxelles (Cand. Jur., 1984); Université Catholique de Louvain (Lic. Jur., 1987); Rijksuniversiteit Utrecht, The Netherlands (Special Degree in European Law, 1990). Teaching: Assistant, Facultés Universitaires Catholiques de Mons, research on International Contracts. Author: Various Articles on Torts. *LANGUAGES:* French, English, Dutch and Spanish. *PRACTICE AREAS:* Commercial Law; European Law; International Contracts; Torts.

ANNE DEOME, born Brussels, Belgium, July 14, 1963; admitted, 1987, Belgium. *Education:* Université Catholique de Louvain (Lic. Jur., 1985). Author: Various Articles on Banking Law. *LANGUAGES:* French and Dutch. *PRACTICE AREAS:* Commercial Law; Banking Law.

ISABELLE C. DURANT, born Charleroi, Belgium, May 28, 1967; admitted, 1991, Belgium. *Education:* Facultés Universitaires Notre Dame de la Paix de Namur (Cand. Jur., 1987); Université Catholique de Louvain (Lic. Jur., 1990); Vrije Universiteit Brussel (Special Degree in Tax Law, 1991). Teaching: Assistant, Université Catholique de Louvain, Contracts. *LANGUAGES:* French, English and Dutch. *PRACTICE AREAS:* Contracts; Commercial Law; Franchising.

DAMIEN D'URSEL, born Ixelles, Belgium, May 9, 1964; admitted, 1994, Belgium. *Education:* Université Catholique de Louvain (Lic. Jur., 1987); Degree in Economics, 1993. *LANGUAGES:* French, Spanish, Dutch, English. *PRACTICE AREAS:* Banking Law; Commercial Law.

LAURENCE EVRARD, born Waremme, Belgium, May 24, 1969; admitted, 1994, Belgium. *Education:* Facultés Universitaires Notre Dame de la Paix Namur (Cand. Jur., 1989), Université Catholique de Louvain (Lic. Jur., 1989), Universitá degli Studi di Bologna (Erasmus Progamme, 1991); Rijks Universiteit Leiden (Cert ificate in International Law, 1993). *LANGUAGES:* French, Dutch, English, Italian. *PRACTICE AREAS:* Commerical Law; Franchising.

ERIC A. FELTEN, born Verviers, Belgium, April 27, 1964; admitted, 1988, Belgium. *Education:* Université Catholique de Louvain (Lic. Jur., 1988). Teaching: Assistant, Université Catholique de Louvain, Civil Law. Author: Various Articles on Civil Law. *LANGUAGES:* French and German. *PRACTICE AREAS:* Contracts; Torts; Intellectual Property; Criminal Law.

ISABELLE GERARD, born Anderlecht, Belgium, June 28, 1965; admitted, 1991, Belgium. *Education:* Université Libre de Bruxelles (Lic. Jur., 1989; Lic. Notariat, 1991). *LANGUAGES:* French, English, Dutch and

(This Listing Continued)

German. *PRACTICE AREAS:* Building and Construction Law; Obligations.

MARIE-PAULE GOMREE, born Charleroi, Belgium, September 15, 1960; admitted, 1985, Belgium. *Education:* Université de Liège (Lic. Jur., 1984). *LANGUAGES:* French and Dutch. *PRACTICE AREAS:* Labour Law; Social Security Law.

TOM HENS, born Turnhout, Belgium, September 15, 1967; admitted, 1990, Belgium. *Education:* Katholieke Universiteit Leuven (Lic. Jur., 1990). Teaching: Assistant, Katholieke Universiteit Leuven, Civil Law. Manager, I.A.G. International Central Secretariat. *LANGUAGES:* Dutch, English, French and German. *PRACTICE AREAS:* Contracts; Commercial Law; Transport Law.

PHILIP KEMPENEERS, born Wilrijk, Belgium, July 13, 1967; admitted, 1993, Belgium. *Education:* Universitaire Faculteiten Sint-Ignatius Antwerpen (Can. Jur. 1987), Katholieke Universiteit Leuven (Lic. Jur., 1990), Université Libre de Bruxelle s (License spéciale en Droit Social, 1991). *Member:* Belgische Vereniging voor Sportrecht. *LANGUAGES:* Dutch, French, English. *PRACTICE AREAS:* Labour Law.

FRANÇOIS G. LIBERT, born Charleroi, Belgium, June 30, 1961; admitted, 1985, Belgium. *Education:* Université Libre de Bruxelles (Lic. Jur., 1985; Lic. Notariat, 1986); Old College Edinburgh (European Young Lawyers Course, 1989). *Member:* International Young Lawyers Association (A.I.J.A.); Euro-Lawyers Association. *LANGUAGES:* French and English. *PRACTICE AREAS:* Building and Construction Law; European Law; Commercial Law.

CARLOS MOURATO, born Watermael-Boitsfort, Belgium, February 28, 1968; admitted, 1993, Belgium. *Education:* Facultés Universitaires St. Louis, Brussels (Can. Jur., 1988); Université Catholique de Louvain (Lic. Jur., 1991), Exeter University, England (LL.M. in European Legal Studies, 1992). Winner, European Law Moot Court Competition (Court of Justice of the European Communities, 91/92). *LANGUAGES:* French, English, Portuguese, Spanish. *PRACTICE AREAS:* Mergers and Acquisitions; Commercial Law; European Union Law; Private International Law.

ANNE NIVEAU, born Anderlecht, Belgium, August 18, 1964; admitted, 1988, Belgium. *Education:* Vrije Universiteit Brussel (Lic. Jur., 1987); Université Catholique de Louvain (Special Degree in Economic Law, 1988). *LANGUAGES:* Dutch, English and French. *PRACTICE AREAS:* Commercial Law; Franchising.

OLIVIER R. POELMANS, born Uccle, Belgium, December 3, 1964; admitted, 1988, Belgium. *Education:* Université Libre de Bruxelles (Lic. Jur., 1988). Author: Various Articles on Banking Law and Computer Law. *Member:* European Society for Banking and Financial Law, Belgium. *LANGUAGES:* French and English. *PRACTICE AREAS:* Banking Law; Computer Law; Commercial Law.

GENEVIÈVE M. RIGAUX, born Etterbeek, Belgium, April 21, 1957; admitted, 1980, Belgium. *Education:* Université Catholique de Louvain (Lic. Jur., 1980; Lic. Criminology, 1980). *LANGUAGES:* French. *PRACTICE AREAS:* Labour Law; Social Security Law.

CHRISTOPHE STEYAERT, born Washington, D.C., USA, September 25, 1962; admitted, 1985, Belgium. *Education:* Université Libre de Bruxelles (Lic. Jur., 1985; Special Degree in European Law, 1987). *Member:* European Society for Banking and Financial Law, Belgium (Secretary). *LANGUAGES:* French, English, Spanish and Italian. *PRACTICE AREAS:* European Law; Banking Law; Commercial Law.

BAPPERT, WITZ & SELBHERR
176, AVENUE LOUISE
B-1050 BRUSSELS, BELGIUM
Telephone: (0032) 2/6473300
Telecopier: (0032) 2/6476539

Freiburg, Germany Office: Leo-Wohleb-Strasse 6, D-79098. Telephone: (0049) 761/218080. Telecopier: (0049) 761/2180821.

Dresden, Germany Office: Berggartenstrasse 7, D-01309. Telephone: (0049) 351/4606131. Telecopier: (0049) 351/4655376.

German, EEC and International Practice. Not authorized to appear before the Belgian Courts.

(This Listing Continued)

PARTNERS IN CHARGE

GERHARD MANZ, born Stuttgart, Germany, April 23, 1952; admitted, 1978, Freiburg. *Education:* Universities of Berlin, Lausanne and Freiburg. *Member:* Freiburg, German and International Bar Associations; British-German Jurists' Association; Association Internationale des Jeunes Avocats. *LANGUAGES:* German, English, French and Italian.

ASSOCIATES

ANNE MCGREGOR, Solicitor, England and Wales.

(For complete biographical data see Professional Biographies at Freiburg, Germany)

BARENTS & KRANS
AVENUE DE LA TOISON D'OR 55, BTE 10-11
B-1060 BRUSSELS, BELGIUM
Telephone: +32 2 534 9739
Telefax: +32 2 534 9740

The Hague, Netherlands Office: Parkstraat 107, P.O. Box 30457, 2500 GL The Hague. Telephone: +31-70-376.06.06. Telecopier: +31-70-365.18.56.

Dutch attorneys may represent clients before all Dutch Courts, before the European Court of Justice and before the Benelux Court of Justice and are admitted to plead before all Courts of the Member States of the European Economic Community.

RESIDENT PARTNER

GERARD VAN DER WAL. *LANGUAGES:* English, French and German. *PRACTICE AREAS:* EC Law; Franchising and Distribution; Commercial Cooperation Agreements; Counterfeiting.

RESIDENT ASSOCIATE
Walter B.J. van Overbeek

BERLIOZ & CO.
Société d'Avocats
179 AVENUE LOUISE
1050 BRUSSELS, BELGIUM
Telephone: (32.2) 646.40.04
Telefax: (32.2) 644.14.88

Paris, France Office: 68, Boulevard de Courcelles, 75017 Paris. Telephone: (33.1) 44 01 44 01. Telefax: (33.1) 44 15 94 15; 42 67 04 43. Telex: 642 834.

Toulouse, France Office: 22 rue de la Dalbade, 31000 Toulouse. Telephone: (33) 61 25 06 97. Telefax: (33) 61 25 06 97.

Lyon, France Office: 48, rue du Président Edouard Herriot, 69002 Lyon. Telephone: (33) 78 38 12 79. Telefax: (33) 78 38 12 83.

Sophia Antipolis, France Office: Villantipolis n° 11, 473, route des Dolines, Sophia Antipolis, 06560. Telephone: (33) 93 65 42 50. Telefax: (33) 93 65 39 26.

London, England Office: 44-46 Kingsway, WC2B 6EN. Telephone: (44 171) 831-4022. Telex: 263 680 BERLAW. Telefax: (44 171) 831-8233.

New York, New York Office: 655 Madison Avenue, 10021. Telephone: 212-486-6302. Telex: 3717883. Telefax: 212-486-8668.

Vilnius, Kalvariju Office: g. 276-36, 2021 VILNIUS. Tlephone: (370.2) 62.46.04 - Contact: Valentinas MIKELENAS.

General French and International Law Practice, Advertising Law, Aeronautical Law, Arbitration, Banking and Financial Law, Commercial Leasing, Competition Law, Computer Law, Construction Law, Consumer Protection, Corporate Law, Criminal Law, Distributorship Law, Entertainment Law, Agency and Franchise Law, EC Law, Food and Drug Regulations, Foreign Investments, Industrial Relations and Labor Law, Insurance Law, International Private Law, Licensing, Litigation, Maritime and Transport Law, Financial Engineering, Public Contracts, State Enterprises, Taxation, Tax Planning, Mergers and Acquisitions Law, Product Liability, Property, Real Estate, Rent and Lease Law, Securities Law, Trade Regulations, Patent, Trademark and Copyright Law, Tax, East-West Trade, North-South Trade, Audio-visual Law, Telecommunications.

ANNE V. DELAUNAY, born 1967. *Education:* Université de Paris I (DEA de Droit Communautaire, 1990).

(This Listing Continued)

BERLIOZ & CO., Brussels—Continued

Languages: French, English, German, Italian, Spanish, Portuguese, Russian, Arabic, Malaysian

(For Biographical Data of the Paris Office, see Professional Biographies at France)

BERTOUILLE & ASSOCIÉS

RUE DE LA VALLÉE 51
1050 BRUSSELS, BELGIUM
Telephone: 02/647.97.00
Telecopier: 02/647.98.99

General Belgian, ECC and International Practice, Banking, Tax and Commercial Law, Trade and Finance Litigation, Industrial Property Law, Litigation.

PARTNERS

STÉPHANE BERTOUILLE, born Tournai, Belgium, October 1, 1950; admitted, 1975, Brussels. *Education:* University of Louvain (J.D., Licence en droit, 1973; Special Degree in Economics, Licence en Sciences Economiques, 1974); New York University Law School (LL.M., Corporate Law, 1975). Associate, Laing, Weldon, Courtois, Clarkson & Tetrault, Montreal, 1975. Partner, Puelinckx, Dillemans & De Scheemaecker, where he initiated his practice in 1976. Partner, De Scheemaecker, Laevens, Bertouille et Van Look, 1986. Founding Partner, Bertouille and Partners, 1990. Co-Author:"Branches and Subsidiaries in Europe, Corporate and Tax Aspects," Kluwer, 1976; "Foreign Investment in Real Estate in Europe," Kluwer, 1979. *LANGUAGES:* French, Dutch and English. *PRACTICE AREAS:* Business Law; Tax Law (Corporate, Personal and International Taxation); Corporate Law.

CATHERINE SBILLE, born Belgium, July 27, 1961; admitted, 1984, Brussels. *Education:* University of Louvain (Licence en Droit, 1984; Ecole Supérieure des Sciences Fiscales, 1989). *LANGUAGES:* French, English and Dutch. *PRACTICE AREAS:* Tax Law (Corporate, Personal and International Taxation); Corporate Law (Mergers and Acquisitions).

ASSOCIATES

VÉRONIQUE MARIEN, born Poole, United Kingdom, March 19, 1963; admitted, 1988, Brussels. *Education:* University of Brussels (Licence en Droit, 1986; Special degree in Business Law, V.U.B., 1987). Recipient, of BOELS award for Best Plea from the Bar Association, 1989. *PRACTICE AREAS:* Business and Corporate Law; Intellectual Property; Trademarks; Commercial Distribution Law; Transport Law; Arbitration.

BÉNÉDICTE TILMANT, born Mol, Belgium, July 9, 1966; admitted, 1989, Brussels. *Education:* University of Liège (Licence en Droit, 1988); Katholieke Universiteit Leuven (Licence spéciale, 1989). *LANGUAGES:* French, Dutch and English. *PRACTICE AREAS:* Labour Law and Social Security Regulation; Commercial Law; Bankruptcy and Insolvency.

JEAN-MARC TRIGAUX, born Uccle, Belgium, 1968; admitted, 1992, Brussels. *Education:* University of Louvain (Licence en Droit, 1990); Dickinson School of Law, Pennsylvania, USA (Master of Comparative Law, 1991). Assistant Professor, University of Louvain, 1992—. *LANGUAGES:* French, English and Dutch. *PRACTICE AREAS:* Business Law; Commercial Law and International Contracts; Commercial Distribution Law; Corporate Law; Belgian Antitrust Regulations.

ANNICK DE ZUTTER, born Assenede, Belgium, February 3, 1967; admitted, 1992, Brussels. *Education:* University of Ghent (Licence en Droit, 1991; European Law Degree, 1992). *LANGUAGES:* Dutch, French and English. *PRACTICE AREAS:* Commercial Law; Corporate Law.

CARL VANTOMME, born Waregem, Belgium, November 11, 1970; admitted, 1993, Brussels. *Education:* University of Leuven (Licence en Droit, 1993). *LANGUAGES:* Dutch, French and English. *PRACTICE AREAS:* Tax Law; Commercial Law.

ORTWIN CARRON, born Kortrijk, Belgium, 1969. *Education:* Katholieke Universiteit Leuven (1992; Special Degree in Tax Law, 1993). With, Coopers & Lybrand. *LANGUAGES:* Dutch, French and English. *PRACTICE AREAS:* Non-Resident Tax; Corporate Tax.

S J BERWIN & CO
Established in 1990

SQUARE DE MEEÛS 19, BTE 3
1040 BRUSSELS, BELGIUM
Telephone: 32 2 511 5340
Fax: 32 2 511 5917

London, England Office: 222 Grays Inn Road, WC1X 8HB. Telephone: 0171-837 2222. Fax: 0171-833 2860.

RESIDENT PARTNER

LEONARD HAWKES. LANGUAGES: French. *PRACTICE AREAS:* EU; Competition; Telecommunications; Mergers and Acquisitions; Financial Services and Banking; Anti-Dumping.

(For Biographical data on personnel at London, England, see Professional Biographies at those locations)

BILLIET & CO.

89 BOULEVARD DE WATERLOO
1000 BRUSSELS, BELGIUM
Telephone: 32-2 511 77 33; 32-2 514 53 78
Fax: 32-2 513 84 36

European Community Law, Banking, Securities, International Banking and Business Law, General International Trade Law, Corporate, Competition and Anti-Trust, Intellectual Property, Patent and Trademark Law, Arbitration and Litigation, Mergers and Acquisitions, Bankruptcy and Insolvency, Consumer and Trade Protection, Construction and Building Law, Distribution.

MEMBERS OF FIRM

JOHAN BILLIET, born Ghent, Belgium, January 25, 1954; admitted, 1977, Belgium. *Education:* University of Ghent (Jur. Lic., 1977; Criminology, 1977); University of Antwerp (Maritime Law, 1979). Alternate Judge (Brussels). Author: "The Belgian Distribution Law;" Pocket Memo About Subsidies;" Articles: about 30 articles in leading law reviews. Lecturer in Law, Ehsal (Brussels), 1985-1991. *Member:* Ligue Internationale Contre la Concurrence Deloyale, Association Internationale pour la Protection de la Propriété Industrielle.

GABRIEL-LUC BALLON, born Alost, Belgium, October 17, 1945; admitted, 1989, Belgium. *Education:* University of Louvain (Dr. Jur., 1968; Public Referendar, 1971 and Dr. Sc. iur., 1976). Author: "Punitive Damages," "The Invoice," "Pocket Memo about Artists;" Articles: about 170 articles in leading law reviews. Lecturer: Commercial Law, Commercial Contracts (Faculty of Economics, Antwerp and Louvain); Former scholar at the Max-Planck-Institut für auslandisches und internationales Patent, Urheber und Wettbewerbsrecht (Munich).

VALÉRIE CASTILLE, born Ghent, Belgium, February 8, 1967; admitted, 1992, Belgium. *Education:* University of Ghent (Lic. Jur., 1990; Lic. Communication, 1992). Assistant, University of Ghent.

MARK DE ZUTTER, born Louvain, Belgium, September 1, 1969; admitted, 1993, Belgium. *Education:* University of Louvain (Lic. Jur., Teaching degree (aggregate in law), certificate in mediation techniques, 1992); King's College, London (LL.M., European Competition Law, 1993).

Languages: French, English, German, Dutch and Russian

BIRD & BIRD

209A AVENUE LOUISE
1050 BRUSSELS, BELGIUM
Telephone: (32) 2 644 3616
Facsimile: (32) 2 644 2486

London, England Office: 90 Fetter Lane, London, EC4A 1JP. Telephone: (44) 171 242 6681. Facsimile: (44) 171 242 3643. Telex: 25581 Birds G.

EC/EEA Law involving Antitrust (Competition), Intellectual Property, Telecommunications, Information Technology, Pharmaceuticals.
(This Listing Continued)

RESIDENT LAWYERS

SIMON TOPPING, B.A. (Hons) (Oxford) Dip Law (PCL), Magister Iuris (German Law) (Trier), Licence Speciale En Droit European (Brussels), called to the bar, 1988, United Kingdom. *LANGUAGES:* English, French, German.

BRONA HEENAN, LL.B. (Hons) (Dublin, Ireland), admitted, 1994, Ireland.

BLOOM & KRETEN
RUE FRANS MERJAY, 21
B-1060 BRUSSELS (CHAUMONT-GISTOUX), BELGIUM
Telephone: 011-32-23-45-69-54

Towson, Maryland Office: 401 Washington Avenue. Telephone: 410-337-2295. Facsimile: 410-337-2296.

Sacramento, California Office: 77 Cadillac Drive. Telephone: 916-921-6181. Fax: 916-921-9213.

Hong Kong Office: 10/F Vogue Building, 67 Wyndham Street, Central Hong Kong.

Patent, Trademark and Copyright Law. Patent Litigation, Licensing and International Technology Transfers.

LEONARD BLOOM, born Wilmerding, Pennsylvania, March 2, 1929; admitted, 1957, Maryland and U.S. District Court, District of Maryland; 1981, U.S. Supreme Court; 1982, District of Columbia and U.S. Court of Appeals for the Federal Circuit; registered to practice before U.S. Patent and Trademark Office; registered to practice before Canadian Patent office (Not admitted in Belgium). *Education:* The Johns Hopkins University (B.E., 1951); University of Maryland (LL.B., 1957). Member, Order of the Coif. Member, Maryland Law Review, 1956-1957. Associate Professor, Law for Scientists and Engineers, Loyola College of Baltimore, 1980-1981. *Member:* District of Columbia Bar; Bar Association of the District of Columbia; Bar Association of Baltimore City; Baltimore County, Federal and American Bar Associations; American Intellectual Property Law Association; Licensing Executives Society; The Association of Corporate Patent Counsel; Maryland Patent Law Association; Institute of Electrical and Electronic Engineers; United States Trademark Association (Author, Maryland Section, State Trademark and Unfair Competition Law, 1988). [1st Lt., U.S. Air Force, 1951-1953]

BERNHARD KRETEN, born Elizabeth, New Jersey, December 9, 1946; admitted, 1989, California and U.S. District Court, Eastern District of California; 1990, U.S. Court of Appeals, Ninth and Federal Circuits; 1992, U.S. District Court, Central District of California. *Education:* University of Pennsylvania (B.S.M.E., 1970); McGeorge School of Law, University of the Pacific (J.D., cum laude, 1988). National Merit Scholar. Member, Traynor Honor Society, McGeorge School of Law, 1988. Author: Article on Intellectual Property Law, Docket, Sacramento County Bar Associations, April, 1991. *Member:* Sacramento County, Federal Circuit and American Bar Associations; State Bar of California. *LANGUAGES:* French and Latin.

(For complete biographical data on all personnel, see Professional Biographies at Towson, Maryland)

BOCCART BIGWOOD & ASSOCIES
RUE WASHINGTON 111-113
B-1050 BRUSSELS, BELGIUM
Telephone: +(32)-2-344.27.98
Fax: +(32)-2-344.15.90

FIRM PROFILE: Corporate Law, Labor Law, Civil Law, Commercial Law, Tax Law, Estate Law, Litigation and Arbitration, Family Law.

Member of European Lawyers Network (E.E.I.G.) which regroups five middle-sized law firms from Europe located in London, Amsterdam, Paris, Brussels, Koln and Berlin.

MEMBERS OF FIRM

JOHN BIGWOOD, born Uccle, Belgium, June 19, 1936; admitted, 1959, Belgium. *Education:* Universite Libre de Bruxelles (Law, 1959; School of Economics and Finance, 1961). *LANGUAGES:* French and English. *PRACTICE AREAS:* Corporate Law; Civil Law; Commercial Law; Estate Law; Litigation and Arbitration.

PIERRE CORVILAIN, born Saint-Gilles, Belgium, July 9, 1944; admitted, 1968, Belgium. *Education:* Universite Libre de Bruxelles (Law, 1968; *(This Listing Continued)*

Economic Law, 1969). *LANGUAGES:* French and English. *PRACTICE AREAS:* Social Law; Commercial Law; Estate Law; Civil Law; Arbitration.

JACQUES F. SIMONS, born Etterbeek, Belgium, August 28, 1945; admitted, 1970, Belgium. *Education:* Universite Catholique de Louvain (Law, 1970). *LANGUAGES:* French. *PRACTICE AREAS:* Labor Law; Social Security Law; Commercial Law; Civil Law.

JEAN-FRANÇOIS TERLINDEN, born Ixelles, Belgium, June 24, 1952; admitted, 1975, Belgium. *Education:* Universite Catholique de Louvain (Law, 1975). *LANGUAGES:* French and English. *PRACTICE AREAS:* Corporate Law; Civil Law; Commercial Law; Criminal Law; Insurance and Liability.

LUC VAN ROSSUM, born Uccle, Belgium, June 7, 1948; admitted, 1972, Belgium. *Education:* Universite Catholique de Louvain (Law, 1972). *LANGUAGES:* French. *PRACTICE AREAS:* Social Law; Town Planning Law; Civil Law; Commercial Law; Litigation and Arbitration.

THOMAS BRAUN, born Uccle, Belgium, May 30, 1959; admitted, 1982, Belgium. *Education:* Universite Catholique de Louvain (Law, 1982). *LANGUAGES:* French. *PRACTICE AREAS:* Civil Law; Commercial Law; Construction Law; Litigation and Arbitration.

BAUDOUIN PAQUOT, born Leuven, Belgium, June 16, 1960; admitted, 1983, Belgium. *Education:* Katholieke Universiteit Leuven (Law, 1983). *LANGUAGES:* French, Dutch and English. *PRACTICE AREAS:* Tax Law; Labor Law; Commercial Law.

MARION BOCCART, born Brussels, Belgium, August 4, 1960; admitted, 1983, Belgium. *Education:* Universite Catholique de Louvain (Law, 1983). *LANGUAGES:* French. *PRACTICE AREAS:* Labor Law; Family Law; Administrative Law.

ALAIN VANDEMEULEBROEKE, born Etterbeek, Belgium, January 11, 1957; admitted, 1982, Belgium. *Education:* Universite Libre de Bruxelles (Law, 1982). *LANGUAGES:* French. *PRACTICE AREAS:* Civil Law; Commercial Law.

ASSOCIATES

ANNE DE VRIENDT, born Berchem Sainte Agathe, Belgium, July 19, 1960; admitted, 1986, Belgium. *Education:* Universite Libre de Bruxelles (Germanic Languages, 1982; Law, 1986). *LANGUAGES:* French, Dutch, German and English. *PRACTICE AREAS:* Civil Law; Commercial Law; Corporate Law; Labor Law; Estate Law.

SYLVIE LACOMBE, born Kortrijk, Belgium, August 21, 1965; admitted, 1988, Belgium. *Education:* Universitaire Faculteiten Sint-Aloysius; Katholieke Universiteit Leuven (Law, 1988). *LANGUAGES:* French, Dutch and English. *PRACTICE AREAS:* Commercial Law; Civil Law; Labor Law; Family Law.

FRANÇOISE BOLLEN, born Etterbeek, Belgium, April 30, 1965; admitted, 1990, Belgium. *Education:* Universite Libre de Bruxelles (Law, 1989); Rijksuniversiteit Leyden (International Law, 1992). *LANGUAGES:* French and Dutch. *PRACTICE AREAS:* Corporate Law; Civil Law; Commercial Law; Estate Law.

JÉRÔME MATTHIEU DE WYNENDAELE, born Uccle, Belgium, June 15, 1966; admitted, 1993, Belgium. *Education:* Universite Catholique de Louvain (Law, 1991). *LANGUAGES:* French and English. *PRACTICE AREAS:* Civil Law; Corporate Law; Commercial Law.

BODEN DE BANDT DE BRAUW JEANTET
LAGERLÖF & URIA
RUE BREDERODE, 13A
B-1000 BRUSSELS, BELGIUM
Telephone: (32-2) 505.02.11
Telecopier: (32-2) 502.26.44

London, England Office: Royex House, Aldermanbury Square, EC2V 7HR. Telephone: (44-171) 796-2599. Telecopier: (44-171) 600-1718.

New York, N.Y., USA Office: 712 Fifth Avenue, 10019. Telephone: (1-212) 801-3400. Telecopier: (1-212) 801-3405.

Prague, Czech Republic Office: Jáchymova 2, Prague 1. Telephone: (42) 2-2325560; 2321130. Telefax: (42) 2-2324635; 2325336.

General European and International Practice.
Alliance of European Lawyers (EEIG) which regroups six law firms from Europe. The Alliance consists of De Bandt, van Hecke & Lagae at Brussels and Antwerp; De Brauw Blackstone Westbroek at The Hague, Amster- *(This Listing Continued)*

BODEN DE BANDT DE BRAUW JEANTET LAGERLÖF & URIA, Brussels—Continued

dam, Rotterdam and Eindhoven; Jeantet & Associés at Paris and Warsaw; Lagerlöf & Leman at Stockholm, Gothenburg and Malmö; Oppenhoff & Rädler at Berlin, Cologne, Frankfurt am Main, Leipzig and Münich; Uria & Menendez at Madrid and Barcelona.

PARTNERS

BERNARD VAN DE WALLE DE GHELCKE, born 1947; admitted, 1972, Brussels. *Education:* University of Louvain (Lic. Jur.; Lic. Eur. Law.); University of Brussels (Lic. Ec. Law). *LANGUAGES:* French, Dutch, English.

LOUIS H. VAN LENNEP, born 1948; admitted, 1973, The Hague (Not admitted in Belgium). *Education:* University of Leyden (Lic.Jur.). *LANGUAGES:* Dutch, English, French, German.

DIRK SCHROEDER, born 1953; admitted, 1981, Cologne (Not admitted in Belgium). *Education:* University of Cologne (Dr. jur.); Ecole Nationale d'Administration, Paris. *LANGUAGES:* German, English, French.

JAIME FOLGUERA CRESPO, born 1954; admitted, 1978, Madrid (Not admitted in Belgium). *Education:* University Autonoma of Madrid (Lic. Jur.); Instituto Nacional de Administracion Pública and Instituto de Empresa of Madrid. *LANGUAGES:* Spanish, English, French.

CHANTAL MOMEGE, born 1948; admitted, 1974, Lyons; 1984, Paris (Not admitted in Belgium). *Education:* University of Lyons (Lic. Jur.); Institut d'Etudes Politiques, Lyons (Section Financière); Institut d'Etudes Judiciaires, Lyons. *LANGUAGES:* French, English.

ERIK H. PIJNACKER HORDIJK, born 1958; admitted, 1983, Amsterdam (Not admitted in Belgium). *Education:* University of Utrecht (Lic. Jur.); College of Europe, Bruges (Adv. Eur. Studies). *LANGUAGES:* Dutch, English, French, German.

GERWIN VAN GERVEN, born 1960; admitted, 1985, Brussels. *Education:* University of Louvain (Lic. Jur.; Lic. Sc. Economics); Harvard Law School (LL.M.). *LANGUAGES:* Dutch, English, French.

JONAS BERGH, born 1955; admitted, 1988, Sweden (Not admitted in Belgium). *Education:* University of Uppsala (LL.M.). *LANGUAGES:* Swedish, English, French.

OF COUNSEL

BASTIAAN VAN DER ESCH, born 1922. *Education:* University of Leyden (Dr. Jur.); London School of Economics; University of Paris. *LANGUAGES:* Dutch, English, French, German.

ASSOCIATES

SARAH BEESTON, born 1966; admitted, 1993, England (Not admitted in Belgium). *Education:* Surrey University (B.Sc.). *LANGUAGES:* English, French, German.

NICO A.J. BEL, born 1963; admitted, 1990, Amsterdam (Not admitted in Belgium). *Education:* University of Leiden (Lic.Jur.); College of Europe, Bruges (Adv. Eur. Studies). *LANGUAGES:* Dutch, English, French.

SILKE BRAMMER, born 1961; admitted, 1993, Hamburg (Not admitted in Belgium). *Education:* Universities of Kiel and Lausanne; European University Institute, Florence (LL.M.). *LANGUAGES:* German, English, French, Italian.

FRANCESCA R. CROTTI, born 1966; admitted, 1990, Brussels. *Education:* University of Brussels (Lic. Jur.); London School of Economics (LL.M. Eur. Law). *LANGUAGES:* French, Italian, English, German, Chinese.

MARC G.A.M. CUSTERS, born 1965; admitted, 1993, The Hague (Not admitted in Belgium). *Education:* University of Nijmegen (Lic.Jur.). *LANGUAGES:* Dutch, English, French, Italian, German.

FREDERIC DEPOORTERE, born 1970; admitted, 1993, Brussels. *Education:* University of Louvain (Lic. Jur.). *LANGUAGES:* Dutch, French, English.

ANNE FEDERLE, born 1960; admitted, 1992, Cologne (Not admitted in Belgium). *Education:* Universities of Munich, Passau, Toulouse, Freiburg i. Br. and Louvain (LL.M.). *LANGUAGES:* German, English, French, Italian.

(This Listing Continued)

JAN HOLMBERG, born 1962; admitted, 1992, Sweden (Not admitted in Belgium). *Education:* University of Lund (LL.M.). *LANGUAGES:* Swedish, English.

VALÉRIE LANDES, born 1961; admitted, 1992, Paris (Not admitted in Belgium). *Education:* University of Paris XI (Maîtrise en Droit Privé); University of Paris I (D.E.A. English and US Law). *LANGUAGES:* French, English.

GUILLAUME LORIOT, born 1969; (Not admitted in Belgium). *Education:* University of Paris II (Maître en Droit Privé); University College London (LL.M.); College of Europe, Bruges (Adv. Eur. Studies). *LANGUAGES:* French, English, Spanish.

EDURNE NAVARRO-VARONA, born 1965; admitted, 1988, Barcelona (Not admitted in Belgium). *Education:* University of Barcelona (Lic. Jur., Dr. Jur.); University of Brussels (Lic. Eur. Law); University of Michigan (LL.M.). *LANGUAGES:* Spanish, French, English, German, Italian, Catalan.

KARL OLSSON, born 1963; (Not admitted in Belgium). *Education:* University of Lund (LL.M.); Europe Institute of the University of Amsterdam (Dipl.). *LANGUAGES:* Swedish, English.

ANNETJE T. OTTOW, born 1965; admitted, 1990, The Hague (Not admitted in Belgium). *Education:* University of Leyden (Lic. Jur.). *LANGUAGES:* Dutch, English, French.

KOEN PLATTEAU, born 1963; admitted, 1988, Brussels. *Education:* University of Ghent (Lic. Jur.); University of Brussels (Lic. Eur. Law) ; The American University (LL.M.). *LANGUAGES:* Dutch, English, French.

MONIQUE T.P.J. VAN OERS, born 1966; admitted, 1990, The Hague (Not admitted in Belgium). *Education:* University of Limburg, Maastricht (Lic. Jur.); University of Brussels (LL.M.). *LANGUAGES:* Dutch, English.

BRUNO VAN HEES, born 1967; admitted, 1994, Brussels. *Education:* University of Liège (Lic. Jur.; Maîtrise en Droit Européen); University of Essex (LL.M.). *LANGUAGES:* French, English, Dutch.

JOSE RAMÓN VIDAL PUIG, born 1964; admitted, 1989, Madrid (Not admitted in Belgium). *Education:* University of Valencia (Lic. Jur.); College of Europe, Bruges (Adv. Eur. Studies); University of Michigan (LL.M.). *LANGUAGES:* Spanish, English, French.

(For list of Partners and Counsel of the Member Firms of the Alliance of European Lawyers see Professional Biographies of: Oppenhoff & Rädler at Munich, Cologne, Frankfurt am Main, Berlin and Leipzig, Germany; De Bandt, van Hecke & Lagae, at Brussels and Antwerp, Belgium; De Brauw Blackstone Westbroek, at Amsterdam, The Hague, Rotterdam and Eindhoven, The Netherlands; Jeantet & Associés, at Paris, France and Warsaw, Poland; Lagerlöf & Leman at Stockholm, Gothenburg and Malmö, Sweden; Uria & Menendez, at Madrid and Barcelona, Spain).

BODEN OPPENHOFF RASOR RAUE

BRUSSELS, BELGIUM

(See Oppenhoff & Rädler)

BRICK COURT CHAMBERS

8 AVENUE DE LA JOYEUSE ENTREE
1040 BRUSSELS, BELGIUM
Telephone: + 32 2 230.31.61 (6 lines)
Fax: + 32 2 230.33.47

London, England Office: Brick Court Chambers, 15-19 Devereux Court, Temple, WC2R 3JJ. Telephone: (071) 583.0777. Telex: 892867 1Brick G. Fax: (071) 583.9401.

Barristers engaged in European and English Practice, in particular referral work from other Lawyers. Entitled to appear before the E.C. Commission and the European Court of Justice and before National Courts. Not practising before the Belgian Courts.
EEC, ECSC and Euratom Law including Competition, Dumping, Trade and Commercial Law, Agriculture, Customs, Banking, Insurance, Financial Services, Free Movement of Goods, Persons, Services and Capital, Internal Market, Intellectual Property, Employment, Public Procurement, Media, Transport (particularly sea and air), Consumer Protection and

(This Listing Continued)

Environment. International Trade and Commercial Litigation and Arbitration. European Human Rights (Commercial).

FIRM PROFILE: *Brick Court Chambers is one of the leading sets of commercial chambers in London and Brussels, with over 40 barristers including 15 Queen's Counsel. Members of chambers practice across the whole range of commercial law, but the undermentioned specialise in European Community law and appear regularly before the European Commission in Brussels and the European Court of Justice in Luxembourg, as well as in national courts.*

DAVID A.J. VAUGHAN, Q.C., called to the bar, 1963, England and Wales. Queen's Counsel, 1981.

NICHOLAS J. FORWOOD, Q.C., called to the Bar, 1970, England and Wales; 1981, Ireland. Queen's Counsel, 1987.

MARK CRAN, Q.C., called to the Bar, 1973, England and Wales. Queen's Counsel, 1988.

GERALD BARLING, Q.C., called to the Bar, 1972, England and Wales. Queen's Counsel, 1991.

DERRICK WYATT, Q.C., called to the Bar, 1972, England and Wales. Queen's Counsel, 1993.

RICHARD MACRORY, called to the Bar, 1973, England and Wales.

DAVID LLOYD JONES, called to the Bar, 1975, England and Wales.

MARK CLOUGH, called to the Bar, 1978, England and Wales.

JEAN-PIERRE SPITZER, called to the Bar, 1983, Paris, France.

NICHOLAS GREEN, called to the Bar, 1986, England and Wales.

DAVID ANDERSON, called to the Bar, 1985, England and Wales.

FERGUS RANDOLPH, called to the Bar, 1985, England and Wales.

SARAH LEE, called to the Bar, 1990, England and Wales.

HELEN DAVIES, called to the Bar, 1991, England and Wales.

PEDRO BROSA & ASOCIADOS

Established in 1965

165, AVENUE LOUISE, 9 ÈME ÉTAGE
1050 BRUSSELS, BELGIUM
Telephone: 32-2-644 16 09
Telefax: 32-2-644 30 25

Barcelona, Spain Office: Avda. Diagonal, 598, 1° 2ª , pral. 2ª y 5° 2ª , 08021. Telephone: 34-3-200 09 33. Telefax: 34-3-202 29 07.
Madrid, Spain Office: Alfonso XII, 18, 3° Izqda, 28014. Telephone: 34-1-522 82 02. Telefax: 34-1-522 39 89.
Bilbao, Spain Office: San Vicente, 8, Plta. 9° 48001. Telephone: 34-4-423 03 36. Telefax: 34-4-423 93 82.

European Economic Community Law, International Law.

MEMBERS OF FIRM

PEDRO BROSA, born Lérida, Spain, May 30, 1937; admitted, 1964, Barcelona (Not admitted in Belgium). *Education:* University of Barcelona (Licenciado en Derecho, 1959; Professor Mercantil, 1960). Lecturer, Taxation Law, University of Barcelona, 1962-1963. *Member:* Barcelona (Member Governing Body) and Madrid Bar Associations; Colegio de Titulares Mercantiles de Barcelona; Fomento del Trabajo Nacional (Member, Advisory Committee); English Chamber of Commerce in Spain. *LANGUAGES:* Spanish, English, French and Catalan. *PRACTICE AREAS:* General Practice; Commercial; Corporation; Banking and Financing; General Practice; Commercial; Corporation; Banking and Financing; Bankruptcy Law; General Business Consulting.

CARLOS SAHUQUILLO, born Barcelona, Spain, May 10, 1958; admitted, 1982, Barcelona (Not admitted in Belgium). *Education:* University of Barcelona (Licenciado en Ciencias Económicas y Empresariales, 1981; Licenciado en Derecho, 1982); Cátedra Durán y Bas (Diploma en Estudios de Derecho Civil Catalán, 1982). *Member:* Barcelona, American Bar Association; International Bar Association; Colegio de Economistas de Catalunya; Instituto de Censores Jurados de Cuentas de España; Asociación Española de Contabilidad y Administración de Empresas; Registro de Economistas Auditores; Registro Oficial de Auditores de Cuentas; International Tax Planning Association. *LANGUAGES:* Spanish, English, French and Catalan. *PRACTICE AREAS:* General Practice; Commercial; Corpora-

(This Listing Continued)

tion; Foreign Investments; Banking and Financing; General Business Consulting.

MARINA VALVERDE, born Madrid, Spain, October 1, 1967; admitted, 1994, Almería. *Education:* University of Madrid (Licenciada en Derecho, 1990). *LANGUAGES:* Spanish, French and English. *PRACTICE AREAS:* Community Law.

COUNSEL

MANUEL VICENS, born L'Ametlla del Vallés, Barcelona, Spain, October 20, 1937; admitted, 1987, Barcelona (Not admitted in Belgium). *Education:* University of Barcelona (Licenciado en Derecho, 1959). Author: "EL IVA y el Transporte," 1985; "Régimen del Transporte Multimodal," 1982; "Comentarios sobre el Estatuto de Autonomía de Cataluña," 1987. Lecturer, ESADE, Barcelona, 1982. Letrado Consistorial, 1987. Subsecretario General Adjunto del Gabinete Jurídico Central of the Generalitat de Cataluña, 1987. Counsel of the Spanish Delegation at the Diplomatic Conference at Geneva for the Adoption of an International Treaty Regarding International Multimodal Transportation of Merchandises, 1982. *Member:* Barcelona Bar Association; International Law Association; International Federation of Freight Forwarders Association. *LANGUAGES:* Spanish, English, French and Catalan. *PRACTICE AREAS:* Transportation; EEC and Constitutional Law.

Languages: Spanish, French, English and Catalan.

(For Biographical Data on Barcelona, Madrid and Bilbao, Spain Personnel, see Professional Biographies at Barcelona, Madrid and Bilbao, Spain).

BRUCKHAUS WESTRICK STEGEMANN

RUE DE LA LOI 99/101
B-1040 BRUSSELS, BELGIUM
Telephone: 32-2 2 87 26 11
Telefax: 32-2 2 30 39 03

Düsseldorf, Germany Office: Freiligrathstrasse 1, 40479 Düsseldorf. Telephone: (0211) 49 79-0. Telefax: (0211) 49 79-103. Telex: 858 7027 JUS D.
Frankfurt, Germany Office: Taunusanlage 11, 60329 Frankfurt am Main. Telephone: (069) 27308-0. Telefax: (069) 232664. Telex: 41 49 17 WEST C D.
Hamburg, Germany Office: Alsterarkaden 27, 20354 Hamburg. Telephone: (040) 36 90 60. Telefax:(040) 36 906-155. Telex: 212 522 EURO D.
Berlin, Germany Office: Friedrichstrasse 95 (IHZ), 10117 Berlin. Telephone: (030) 26 43-3303. Telefax: (030) 26 43-3366.
Leipzig Office: Grimmaische Strasse 25, 04109 Leipzig. Telephone: (0341) 127230. Telefax: (0341) 1272333.
Tokyo, Japan Office: Ark Mori Building, 22F, 12-32, Akasaka 1-chome, Minato-ku, Tokyo 107. Telephone: (81-3) 55610-236. Telefax: (81-3) 55610-238.
New York, New York Office: 767 Fifth Avenue, GM Building, New York 10153. Telephone: (212) 486-1100. Telefax: (212) 759-3151.
Moscow, Russia Office: Malyj Gnezdnikovskij per. 9 No. 2, 103099 Moscow. Telephone: (7-503) 9562300; (7-501) 9401200. Telefax: (7-503) 9562301; (7-501) 9401211.

Corporate Law, Commercial Law, Mergers, Acquisitions and Divestitures, Joint Ventures, Banks and Banking, Finance, Securities, Capital Markets, Leases and Leasing, Equipment Finance, Aircraft Finance and Leasing, Antitrust and Trade Regulation, German and EC Cartel Law, Competition, Unfair Trade, Intellectual Property (trademarks, patents, copyrights), Taxation, Property, Real Estate, Energy, Natural Resources, Environmental Law, Administrative Law, Computers and Software, Food and Drug, Biotechnology, Labour and Employment, Products Liability, Insurance, Litigation, Arbitration, Broadcasting, Telecommunications, Aviation, Subsidies and State Aids, Construction Law, Zoning, Planning and Land Use, Customs and Foreign Trade Law, European Community Law, German-French Investments, Russian and Post Soviet Commerce.
Members of the Brussels Office are not authorized to appear before the Belgian Courts.

MEMBERS OF FIRM

Dr. Cornelis Canenbley
Dr. Gerhard Wiedemann
Dr. Michael Schütte
(This Listing Continued)

BRUCKHAUS WESTRICK STEGEMANN, Brussels—Continued

COUNSEL

AUDREY STACEY WINTER, born Long Beach, California, 1956; admitted, 1980, Georgia; 1982, District of Columbia (Not admitted in Belgium). *Education:* University of Georgia (B.S., 1977; J.D., cum laude, 1980); Université Livre de Bruxelles (Licence Spéciale en droit européen, grande Distinction, 1981). Legal Trainee, Commission of the European Communities, 1981-1982. Attorney-Adviser, Office of the Assistant General Counsel for Import Administration, U.S. Department of Commerce, 1983-1984. *LANGUAGES:* English, German and French. *PRACTICE AREAS:* EC Law; EC Competition Law; International Trade; Antidumping.

(For complete biographical Data, see Professional Biographies at Düsseldorf and Hamburg, Germany)

BURLION, BOLLE, HOUBEN & CO.

RUE DU COMMERCE 34
B-1040 BRUSSELS, BELGIUM
Telephone: (32-2) 510 44 55
Cable Address: Attorney Brussels
Telecopier: (32-2) 510 44 88 (ITT Telefax Gr. 3, 3535)

Administrative law, Advertising and Marketing, Agency and Distributorships, Antitrust and Trade Regulation, Arbitration and Mediation, Aviation and Aerospace, Bankruptcy, Banks and Banking, Broadcasting, Business Law, Commercial law, Communications and Media, Company Law, Computers and Software, Construction Law, Consumer law, Contracts, Copyrights, Corporate Law, Debtor and Creditor, Environmental Law, Equipment Finance and Leasing, European Community Law, Finance, Franchises and Franchising, Intellectual Property, International law, Labour and Employment, Leases and Leasing, Litigation, Mergers and Acquisitions and Divestitures, Mortgages, Patents, Products Liability, Professional Liability, Property, Real Estate, Securities, Sports, Taxation, Telecommunications, Trade Regulation, Trademarks.

MEMBERS OF FIRM

ARLETTE BURLION, born Etterbeek, Belgium, April 26, 1936; admitted, 1959, Brussels. *Education:* Facultés Universitaires St. Louis, Brussels (Ph.B., 1956); University of Louvain (Dr. Jur., 1959). Author: "Revue Fiscale," 1960-1970. Co-author: "Trial Practice and Procedure Manual for Belgium," Litigation Section, American Bar Association, 1980.

MICHEL J. BOLLE, born Uccle, Belgium, June 10, 1945; admitted, 1968, Brussels. *Education:* Facultes Universitaires St. Louis, Brussels (Ph.B., 1965); University of Brussels (Dr. Jur., 1968); Postgraduate studies (Econ. Law, 1969; Tax Law, 1969).

MARCEL HOUBEN, born Houthalen, Belgium, June 15, 1949; admitted, 1977, Brussels. *Education:* University of Louvain (Ph.B., 1969; LL.B., 1972); Southern Methodist University, Dallas, Texas (LL.M., 1976). Author: "Severance Pay and Arbitration," (Awarded the American Arbitration Association Award) 1976; National Report for the IX International Congress held in Munich in 1978 of the International Society for Labor Law and Social Security, "Settlement of Labor Disputes in Belgium," 1978. Co-author: "Labor Relations in Belgium," 1976; "Comparative Labor Law," 1976. Assistant Professor of Labor Law, University of Louvain, 1972-1977.

WERNER VANDERHAEGHE, born Haaltert, Belgium, April 8, 1951; admitted, 1994, Brussels. *Education:* University of Ghent (Ph.B., 1971; LL.B., 1974); University of Texas at Austin School of Law, Austin, Texas (M.C.J., 1975). General Management Programme, Insead, Fontainebleu, France, 1993. Teaching and Research Assistant, University of Ghent, School of Law, 1975-1977. Associate, Cleary, Gottlieb, Steen & Hamilton, Brussels, 1978-1982. Assistant Counsel, Belgian Operations and EEC Affairs, Merck Sharp and Dohme, Europe, 1982. Counsel, Joint Ventures and Acquisitions, Sidmar N.V., 1983. Trainee, International Division, Generale Bank, 1984. Vice President, General Counsel Bekaert Group, 1985-1993. Visiting Professor, International Law, University of Louvain, 1988-1993.

ASSOCIATES

LUUS HILLEN, born Sint-Lambrechts-Woluwe, Belgium, May 26, 1962; admitted, 1987, Brussels. *Education:* Universitaire Faculteit St. Aloysius, Brussels (Ph.B., 1983); University of Louvain (LL.B., 1986).

(This Listing Continued)

DIRK CAESTECKER, born Brugge, Belgium, September 6, 1962; admitted, 1986, Brussels. *Education:* University of Louvain (Ph.B., Criminology, 1982; Ph.B., 1983; LL.B., 1986); Universitaire Faculteiten St. Aloysius, Fiskale Hogeschool, Brussels (Postgraduate Tax Studies, 1987).

YVES FEVRIER, born Brussels, Belgium, June 19, 1962; admitted, 1989, Brussels. *Education:* Université Libre de Bruxelles (LLB., 1986); Université de McGill, Montreal, Canada (LL.M., 1987).

CHRISTINE FLION, born Leuven, Belgium, February 20, 1963; admitted, 1987, Brussels. *Education:* Facultés Universitaires Saint Louis, Brussels (Ph.B., 1983); Université Catholique de Louvain (LL.B., 1986) Université Libre de Bruxelles (Postgraduate, Maritime and Air Law, 1987; International Law, 1988).

FILIP SAELENS, born Kinshasa, Zaire, October 10, 1966; admitted, 1990, Brussels. *Education:* Universitaire Faculteiten St. Aloysius Brussels (Ph.B., 1987); University of Louvain (LL.B., 1990). Erasmus Programme: social security in the European Community, Leuven (1990).

GOEDELE CLAUWERS, born Bree, Belgium, February 2, 1965; admitted, 1990, Brussels. *Education:* University of Louvain (LL.B., 1988); Institut Européen des Hautes Etudes Internationales, Nice, France (European Law, 1989); University of Ghent (Postgraduate Tax Law, 1990).

PASCALE TRUSSART, born February 8, 1963; admitted, 1994, Brussels. *Education:* Facultés Universitaires St. Louis, Brussels (Ph.B., 1983); Université Catholique de Louvain (LL.B., 1986).

GUY BREITENSTEIN, born Brussels, Belgium, June 12, 1965; admitted, 1991, Brussels. *Education:* University of Louvain (Ph.B., 1986; LL.B., 1989); Postgraduate Studies: University of Louvain and University of Liège (International and European Law, 1990).

BRUNO DE RADZITZKY D'OSTROWICK, born Milan, Italy, December 24, 1964; admitted, 1991, Brussels. *Education:* University of Louvain (Ph.B., 1987; LL.B., 1990); Postgraduate Studies: University of Brussels (International and European Law, 1991).

BENOIT MALVAUX, born Ixelles, Belgium, February 10, 1961; admitted, 1992, Brussels. *Education:* Facultés Université St. Louis (Ph.B., 1982); University of Louvain (LL.B., 1985; Postgraduate Studies (Tax Law, 1985).

KATHELIJNE WINDERICKX, born Brussels, Belgium, January 19, 1967; admitted, 1991, Brussels. *Education:* University of Ghent (LL.B., 1989); University of Brussels (Postgraduate European Law, 1990).

ILSE TACK, born Deinze, Belgium, April 2, 1969; admitted, 1992, Brussels. *Education:* University of Namur (Ph.B., 1989); University of Louvain (LL.B., 1992).

JAN ALEXANDER, born Roeselare, Belgium, July 1, 1969; admitted, 1993, Brussels. *Education:* University of Namur (Ph.B., 1989); University of Louvain (LL.B., 1992); University of Brussels (Postgraduate European Law, 1993).

ROBERT MARTENS, G.C.M., born Leuven, Belgium, June 11, 1968; admitted, 1991, Brussels. *Education:* Facultés Universitaires Notre Dame de la Paix, Namur (Ph.B., 1988); University of Leuven, (LL.B., 1991). Author: "Zure Regen: Internationale en Europeesrechtelijke aspecten," Die Keure, 1993; "Regionale Milieuheffingen," Kluwer Rechtswetenschappen, 1994. Lecturer, Environmental Law, University of Leuven, Institute of Environmental Law, 1993—.

ANNE-CATHERINE MASSAGÉ, born Asse, Belgium, May 10, 1968; admitted, 1993, Brussels. *Education:* Universitaire Faculteiten St. Aloysius (Ph. B., 1988); University of Louvain (LL.B., 1991); University of Louvain (Postgraduate Management, 1993).

SERGE RUYSSEVELDT, born Aaist, Belgium, June 22, 1964; admitted, 1994, Brussels. *Education:* University of Brussels (Ph.B., 1984; LL.B., 1987; Postgraduate Studies, Commercial and Economical Law, 1989). Legal Counsel, Arthur Andersen & Co., Brussels, 1989-1993.

ETIENNE LAHMANN, born Koersel, Belgium, January 14, 1966; admitted, 1990, Brussels. *Education:* University of Louvain (LL.B., 1989); University of Brussels (LL.B., Social Law, 1990); H.E.C., St. Louis (Grad., Fiscal Law, 1991).

BENEDIKTE JORION, born Roeselare, Belgium, February 21, 1968; admitted, 1992, Brussels. *Education:* University of Kortrijk (Ph.B., 1988); University of Leuven (LL.B., 1991); University of Athens-Thessaloniki (Erasmus, 1991). University of Leuven (Master, European and International Law; LL.M., 1992); Goethe-Institut, Freiburg (1994).

(This Listing Continued)

KOEN VAN MEENSEL, born Aarschot, Belgium, March 27, 1969; admitted, 1994, Brussels. *Education:* University of Leuven (Ph.B., 1989; LL.B., 1992); University of Stellenbosch, South Africa (LL.M., 1994).

Languages: English, Dutch, French and German

BYRNE, DE VRIES, FERON & WOUTERS

Sociét é civile d'avocats

SQUARE VERGOTE 39
B-1040 BRUSSELS, BELGIUM
Telephone: (32 2) 736 80 06
Fax: (32 2) 736 66 49

FIRM PROFILE: Byrne, de Vries, Feron & Wouters is a multi-national law firm whose members all have an academic background in foreign universities and have practiced in international law for several years.

Besides its general business law and litigation practice, the firm specializes in foreign investments (in Belgium and abroad), company law, mergers & acquisitions, joint ventures, subsidies and project financing, international tax law, financial and securities law, labour law, environment law, industrial and intellectual property law (including copyright law), arbitration as well as European Community law and international trade law (including customs, anti-dumping law and State aids).

PARTNERS

THIERRY DE VRIES, born Belgium, January 3, 1958; admitted, 1982, Brussels. *Education:* State University of Ghent, Belgium (J.D., 1981; Teaching Diploma, 1981); University of Toulouse, France (Postgraduate in International and European Law, 1982). British Council's European Young Lawyers Scholarship, Old College, Faculty of Law of Edinburgh, 1986. Secretary of the Royal Commission for the Revision of t he Penal Code, 1983-1987. *LANGUAGES:* Dutch, French, English. *PRACTICE AREAS:* Business Law; Real Estate Law; Intellectual Property Law; Environment Law.

MAURICE BYRNE, born Dublin, June 30, 1961; admitted, 1986 (Solicitor) Ireland (Not admitted in Belgium). *Education:* University College, Dublin (B.C.L., with honours, 1982; Diploma in European Law, 1985); University of Grenoble II, France (Diplome Superieur d'Études Francaises, 1979). Trainee, Legal Service of E.E.C. Commission Competition Team, February-July, 1986. *Member:* Dublin Solicitors Bar Association; Irish Belgian Business Association (Council Member); Brussels Association of Irish Lawyers (Founder Member). *LANGUAGES:* English, Irish and French. *PRACTICE AREAS:* European Community Law; Anti-dumping; Customs Law; Competition Law.

HAROLD WOUTERS, born Brussels, Belgium, August 3, 1961; admitted, 1985, Brussels. *Education:* University of Louvain (J.D., 1984); McGeorge School of Law, University of the Pacific (LL.M. in Business and Taxation and Transnational Practice, 1989); Solvay Business School, Brussels (Certificates in Specialized and International Taxation, 1990). Author: Les directives services d'investissement: Les relations avec les pays tiers, in J.T. Droit Eur., 1994, pp. 189 et. seq. (with B. Feron); La directive 93/22 concernant les services d'investissement dans le domaine des valeurs monlieves, in Revve Pratique des Sociétés, 1994 pp 209-262 (with B. Feron); Belgian Chapter of the *International Corporate Law Competition Yearbook,* 1994, Euromoney; Belgian Chapter of the *Guide to World Equity Markets 1994,* Euromoney Books, 1994, "Take-over bids under Belgian Law," in *Yearbook 1992 of the A.E.D.B.F.,* 1992, pp. 145 et. set. *LANGUAGES:* French, English. *PRACTICE AREAS:* Financial and Securities Law; Mergers and Acquisitions; Tax Law (International); Subsidies and Project Financing; International Trade Law; European Community Law.

BENOÎT FERON, born Leuven, Belgium, September 12, 1962; admitted, 1988, Brussels. *Education:* University of Louvain (J.D., 1985); Duke University School of Law (LL.M., 1987); State University of Ghent (Special Degree in European Law, 1988); University of Brussels, Solvay School of Commerce (Master in Tax Management, 1991). Assistant Professor of Law, University of Louvain. Author: Les directives services d'investissement: les relations avec les pays tiers, in J.T. Droit Eur., 1994, pp. 189 et seq. (with H. Wouters); La directive 93/22 concernant les services d'investissement dans le domaine des valeurs monlieves, in Revve Pratique des Sociétés, 1994, pp 209-262 (with H. Wouters); "Le timesharing: une nouvelle forme de propriété? Analyse en droit belge et en droit comparé", in *Annales de Droit de Louvain,* 1/1994, pp. 3-87 ; "La dualité d'intérêts des administrateurs d'une société anonyme," in *Revue Pratique des Sociétés* 1993, No. 6613, pp. 5-30 ; "Insider Trading in Belgium," in *The Laws of Europe, the US and Japan,* Insider Trading, Kluwer, 1992, p. 37 ; "Les conventions d'ac-

(This Listing Continued)

tionnairesune évolution inachevée", in *DAOR* 1991, No. 21 pp. 29-47 ; "L'exploitation abusive d'informations privilégiées, l'introduction en droit belge du délit d'initieé , in *Journal des Tribunaux,* 1989, pp. 573 et seg.; "Le référé-provision," note under Comm. Bxl. ref., 6 September 1988, in *DAOR,*1989, No. 10, pp. 112 et seg; "Actualités du référé commercial à travers les conditions d'intervention du President du Tribunal de commerce", in *Annales de droit de Louvain,* 1985, pp. 260 et seg. *LANGUAGES:* English, French and Dutch. *PRACTICE AREAS:* Company Law; Financial and Securities Law; Mergers and Acquisitions; International Contracts; Arbitration.

OF COUNSEL

GIOVANNELLA D'ANDREA, born Italy, April 22, 1966; admitted, 1992, Italy (Not admitted in Belgium). *Education:* University "La Sapienza", Rome Italy (Law Degree, 1990); IPSOA, Institute for Professional Education, Rome, Italy (April 1991); Hague Academy of International Law, The Hague, The Netherlands (July 1991); European Studies Institute, Free University of Brussels (Postgraduate Degree in European Law, June 1993). Author: "Advantages and disadvantages of the use of arbitral clauses in contracts," in *Consulenza,* Ed. Buffeti, No. 39, October 1989; "Competition rules on State aids in the EC Treaty," in *Europa Forum,* No. 2, February 1990; "BC-Net - a focus on Community actions to help businesses," in *Europa Forum,* No. 2, February 1992. *LANGUAGES:* Italian, French, English, Spanish. *PRACTICE AREAS:* European Community Law (including State aids and Competition Law); Foreign Investments; Funding and Project Finance; Environment Law; Energy Law.

ASSOCIATES

XAVIER CULOT, born Belgium, May 16, 1965; admitted, 1992, Brussels. *Education:* University of Louvain (J.D., 1988); Rijksuniversiteit van Lei den, The Netherlands (Diploma in International Law, 1989); Solvay Business School, Brussels (Certificate in International Taxation, 1993). *LANGUAGES:* French, Dutch, English. *PRACTICE AREAS:* Labour Law.

MAREE GALLAGHER, born Ireland, November 24, 1968; admitted, 1993, Ireland (Not admitted in Belgium). *Education:* University College, Dublin (Honours Bachelor of Arts Degree, 1991); College of Commerce (Diploma in Legal Studies, 1992); Sandymount Law School, Dublin (1992); The Incorporated Law Society of Ireland (1993). *Member:* Irish Belgian Business; Brussels Association of Irish Lawyers; SADSI (Dublin); SYS (Dublin); Former Auditor Rathmines Law Society. *LANGUAGES:* English, French. *PRACTICE AREAS:* European Community Law; International Trade.

English, French, Dutch, Italian and Spanish.

CANNART & ANDRÉ-DUMONT

Established in 1987

AVENUE DE LA RENAISSANCE 1
B-1040 BRUSSELS, BELGIUM
Telephone: (32-2) 732.18.81
Telefax: (32-2) 734.42.45

Legal Counseling, Litigation and Arbitration in Commercial and Contract Law, Company Law, Tax Law, Labour and Social Security Law, Intellectual and Industrial Property Law, Trade Practices Law, Competition Law, Real Estate and Construction Law, Banking and Finance Law, Computer and Telecommunications Law, Environmental Law.

MEMBERS OF FIRM

EMMANUEL DE CANNART D'HAMALE, born Brussels, Belgium, 1950; admitted, 1975, Brussels. *Education:* Université Catholique de Louvain (Bachelor in Philosophy, 1970; Licence en droit, 1973); Juristensonderprogramm des Deutschen Akademischen Austauschdienstes, Tübingen-Düsseldorf (1974-1975). Author: *Products Liability, a Manual of Practice in Selected Nations (Belgium),* New York, 1981-1987. Co-Author: *"Le Droit des Contrats Informatiques,"* Namur, 1983; *Les Contrats R.T.T. ou les rapports juridiques entre la Régie des télégraphes et des téléphones et les usagers"* J.T., 1983' *"Le devoir de conseil du fournisseur en informatique,"* R.D.C., 1989; "Die Kündigung von Vertragshändlerverträgen nach Belgischem Recht," Baden-Baden, 1993. Founder of the computer law reviews "Droit de l'Informatique et des Télécoms" (France) and "Computerrecht" (The Netherlands). *Member:* Belgisch-Deutsche Juristenvereinigung; Association belge du droit de l'informatique. *LANGUAGES:* French, English, German, Dutch. *PRACTICE AREAS:* Commercial and Contract Law; Company Law; Competition Law; Computer Law; Litigation and Arbitration.

(This Listing Continued)

CANNART & ANDRÉ-DUMONT, Brussels—Continued

HUBERT ANDRÉ-DUMONT, born Wilrijk, Antwerp, Belgium, 1956; admitted, 1982, Brussels. *Education:* Université Catholique de Louvain (Licence en Droit, 1982); University of Bristol, U.K. (LL.M., Commercial Law, 1985). Author: *Législation Zaïroise:* Code des Sociétés, Brussels, 1983; Contributor to the Chapter on Zaïre in "African Tax Systems," International Bureau for Fiscal Documentation, Amsterdam, 1984. Various articles on: International Construction Law (FIDIC, Project Management, Public Procurement). L'Entreprise et le Droit, Brussels, 1986, 1993 and International Construction Law Review, London, 1986, 1988, 1990 and 1991. Correspondent in Brussels for the International Construction Law Review, London, 1988. Lecturer in Business and Contract Law, EBS Brussels, 1989-1992. *Member:* International Bar Association. **LANGUAGES:** French, English, Dutch, German. **PRACTICE AREAS:** Company Law; Commercial and Contract Law; Real Estate and Construction Law; Banking and Finance.

SUZANNE DE CALLATAŸ, born Brussels, Belgium, 1941; admitted, 1975, Brussels. *Education:* Université Catholique de Louvain (Doctorat en Droit, 1968). Author: "Contrat de travail, droit du travail, élections sociales, Loi du 22 janvier 1985 et autres nouveautés," (J.T. 1985, 245-250 and 261-267); "L'utilisation de sociétés ou d'établissements à l'étranger. Les aspects européens et internationaux en matière de sécurité sociale," Orientations, 1988; "Elections sociales 1991. La protection occulte de candidats," Orientations, 1990. Co-Author: Chapter on Belgian Labour Law, International Bar Association's "International Handbook on Contracts of Employment." Professor, Labour Law, Ecole Pratiques des Hautes Etudes Commerciales (EPHEC), Brussels, 1976. *Member:* Association des juristes et praticiens de droit social. **LANGUAGES:** French, English. **PRACTICE AREAS:** Labour and Social Security Law.

CATHÉRINE ERKELENS, born Dendermonde, Belgium, 1962; admitted, 1984, Brussels. *Education:* University of Brussels (V.U.B.; Lic. Jur., 1984; Criminology, 1984). Recipient, IBM Belgium Prize 1985 (law and computers). Assistant, Faculty of Law, V.U.B., 1990. Author: Various articles on: Computer Law, Protection of Privacy, Trade Practices, Company Law (1985, 1992, 1993). *Member:* Association belge du droit de l'informatique (Director); Young Lawyers' International Association. **LANGUAGES:** Dutch, French, English, German. **PRACTICE AREAS:** Commercial and Contract Law; Trade Practices; Company Law; Computer and Telecommunications Law.

MICHEL GOETHALS, born Likasi, Zaïre, 1957; admitted, 1990, Brussels. *Education:* Université Catholique de Louvain (Licence en droit, 1980); Vrije Universiteit Brussel (Licenciaat in bedrijfsrecht, 1981). *Member:* International Fiscal Association; Young Lawyers' International Association. **LANGUAGES:** French, Dutch, English. **PRACTICE AREAS:** Tax Law.

ASSOCIATES

MANUEL CAMPOLINI, born Brussels, Belgium, 1955; admitted, 1989, Brussels. *Education:* Université de Liège (Licence en droit, 1980). Research Assistant, Université de Liège, 1982-1984. Author: "La télévision à haute définition européenne," Droit de l'Informatique et des Télécoms, 1993. *Member:* Association belge pour la protection du droit d'auteur (A.L.A.I.). **LANGUAGES:** French, Italian, English and German. **PRACTICE AREAS:** Intellectual and Industrial Property Law; Telecommunications Law.

GUIDO LAMAL, born Uccle, Belgium, 1965; admitted, 1991, Brussels. *Education:* Catholic University of Leuven (Lic. Jur., 1988); Juristensonderprogramm des Deutschen Akademischen Austauschdienstes, Tübingen-Düsseldorf (1988-1989). Research Assistant, Faculty of Law, K.U. Leuven, 1992. *Member:* Association des juristes et praticiens du droit social; Belgisch-Deutsche Juristenvereinigung. **LANGUAGES:** Dutch, French, German, English, Spanish. **PRACTICE AREAS:** Labour and Social Security Law.

THIERRY GEURTS, born Nioki, Zaïre, 1964; admitted, 1994, Brussels. *Education:* Université Catholique de Louvain (Licence en droit, 1988). **LANGUAGES:** French, Dutch and English. **PRACTICE AREAS:** Tax Law.

PATRICK BAETEN, born Ghent, Belgium, 1968; admitted, 1993, Brussels. *Education:* University of Ghent (Lic. Jur., 1991); Université Catholique de Louvain (Licence en droit international et en droit européen, 1992; Maîtrise en droit international et en droit européen, 1993). **LANGUAGES:** French, Dutch and English.

(This Listing Continued)

BERTRAND WITTAMER, born Uccle, Belgium, 1968; admitted, 1993, Brussels. *Education:* Université Catholique de Louvain (Licence en droit, 1991); College of Europe, Bruges (Master of European Legal Studies, 1992). **LANGUAGES:** French, English and Dutch.

STÉPHANIE DE GRUBEN, born Luxembourg (Grand-Duchy), 1964; admitted, 1989, Brussels. *Education:* Université Catholique de Louvain (Licence en droit, 1988). **LANGUAGES:** French, Dutch, German, English, Spanish.

CLAES & PARTNERS
REGENT BUILDING
BOULEVARD DU REGENTLAAN 58
B-1000 BRUSSELS, BELGIUM
Telephone: (32) 2-502.62.62
Fax: (32) 2-502.39.21

Corporate (including Mergers and Acquisitions), E.E.C., Business Migration, Labour Law (National/International), Environmental Law, Banking, Corporate Finance, Administrative Law, Commercial Law, Tax, Intellectual Property, Litigation, White Collar Crime.

MEMBERS OF FIRM

ETIENNE R. CLAES, born Beringen, Belgium, 1954; admitted, 1981, Brussels. *Education:* American Field Service Scholarship (Massachusetts, 1973); University of Leuven (Lic. Interpr., 1977; Lic. Jur., 1981); University of Brussels (LL.M., 1983). *Member:* American and International Bar Associations; British Institute International Comparative Law; Inter-Pacific Bar Association; English Immigration Law Practitioners' Association.

ERIC B. BODSON, born Mechelen, Belgium, 1957; admitted, 1983, Brussels. *Education:* University of Leuven (Lic. Jur., 1980; B.Ph., 1980); University of Louvain (U.C.L.-Lic. Droit Econ., 1981). Southwestern Legal Foundation, Texas (Am. and Internat. Law Certificate, 1981); EHSAL Management School, Brussels (Modern Fin. Management Certificate, 1988); Assistant, Faculty of Law, University of Louvain, 1981-1982.

JAN RAVELINGIEN, born Kortrijk, Belgium, 1962; admitted, 1986, Brussels. *Education:* University of Leuven (Lic. Jur., 1985); The Hague Institute of Social Studies (Postgraduate International Development, 1986). The Hague Asser Institute (International Commercial Arbitration Research Fellow, 1986); Assistant, Faculty of Law, University of Leuven, 1985-1989.

HERMAN CROUX, born Genk, Belgium, 1962; admitted, 1988, Brussels. *Education:* American Field Service Scholarship (Wisconsin, 1981); University of Leuven (B.Ph., 1983; Lic. Jur., 1986). Assistant, Faculty of Law, University of Leuven, 1986-1990; EHSAL Management School Brussels (Human Resources Management Certificate, 1992).

RAFAËL CLAES, born Geel, Belgium, May 29, 1965; admitted, 1989, Brussels. *Education:* University of Louvain (Lic.Jur., 1988); University of Brussels (Labor Law and Social Security Law Lic.Jur., 1989). Author: Freelance collaborator with "Lettres aux Employeurs.".

LUC NEEFS, born Turnhout, Belgium, 1965; admitted, 1990, Brussels. *Education:* University of Leuven (Lic. Jur., 1988). Assistant, Faculty of Law, University of Leuven, 1988—.

MATTHIAS NIYONZIMA, born Kirundo, Burundi, 1957; admitted, 1990, Brussels. *Education:* University of Bujumbura (Lic. Jur., 1983); University of Leuven (Doc. Jur., 1990). Recipient, Award, The Hague Academy of International Law, 1984. Lecturer: King's College London, 1986-1987; Faculty of Law, University of Leuven, 1987-1991. Research Fellow, Swiss Institute of Comparative Law, 1988. Assistant, Faculty of Law, 1983—.

L. PHILIP EYSKENS, born Turnhout, Belgium, 1968; admitted, 1991, Brussels. *Education:* University of Namur (Can. Jur., 1988); University of Galway (Erasmus, 1990); University of Leuven (Lic. Jur., 1991); Vlerick School of Management (M.B.A., 1992). British Council European Young Lawyers Programme London (1994). **LANGUAGES:** Kirundi and Kiswahili.

KATHLEEN LAMBRECHTS, born Herentals, Belgium, 1969; admitted, 1991, Brussels; 1994, New York. *Education:* University of Leuven (Lic. Jur., 1991). Fellow, Belgian-American Educational Foundation (1992).

CHRISTOPHE VANDERLINDEN, born Hasselt, Belgium, 1964; admitted, 1991, Brussels. *Education:* American Field Service Scholarship (Florida, 1983); University of Leuven (Lic. Jur., 1991); University of Brussels (Lic. Droit Soc., 1992).

(This Listing Continued)

TOM ARTS, born Genk, Belgium, 1966; admitted, 1992, Brussels. *Education:* University of Leuven (Lic. Jur., 1991); University of Nancy (D.E.S.E. Droit Eur., 1992; D.E.A. Droit CEE, 1992). Recipient, American Field Service Scholarship, Texas, 1985.

FRÉDÉRIC HENDRICKX, born Leuven, Belgium, 1969; admitted, 1993, Brussels. *Education:* Facultés Notre Dame de la Paix, Faculté de Droit, Namur (Can. Jur., 1988); University of Leuven (Lic. Jur., 1991); University of Copenhagen (Erasmus, 1991; Postgrad., Environmental Law, 1993).

MARLEEN DENEF, born Leuven, Belgium, 1968; admitted, 1993, Brussels. *Education:* American Field Service Scholarship (California, 1987); Faculté Notre Dame de la Paix, Fraculté de Droit, Namur (Can. Jur., 1989); University of Leuven (Lic. Jur., 1992); University of Granada (Erasmus, 1992); University of Louvain-la-Neuve (Lic. European and International Law, 1993).

HELGA STEVENS, born Sint-Truiden, Belgium, 1968; admitted, 1994, Brussels. *Education:* Rotary International Exchange Scholarship, Missouri, 1988; University of Leuven (Lic. Jur., 1993): University of Leeds (Erasmus, 1992); School of Law (Boalt Hall) Berkeley (LL.M., 1994).

PATRICK HEINRICH, born Wetzlar, Germany, 1970; admitted, 1994, Brussels. *Education:* University of Leuven (Lic. Jur., 1993); Duke University (LL.M., 1994).

JEROEN SMETS, born Ghent, Belgium, 1970; admitted, 1994, Brussels. *Education:* University of Leuven (Lic. Jur., 1993); University of Deusto, Bilbao (ERASMUS, 1992); University of Brussels (Postgraduate Business Law, 1995).

LI MA, born Jiangsu, China, 1969; admitted, 1992, Beijing; 1994, Brussels (Foreign Member). *Education:* Beijing University (Lic. Jur., 1991).

MIN LI, born Jiangxi, China, 1970; admitted, 1992, Beijing; 1994, Brussels (Foreign Member). *Education:* Beijing University (Lic. Jur., 1992).

CAROLINE DEN TANDT, born Leuven, Belgium, 1968; admitted, 1994, Brussels. *Education:* University of Leuven (Lic. Jur., 1992); University of Leuven (Lic, Econ., 1994).

Languages: English, Dutch, French, German, Italian, Spanish and Danish.

CLEARY, GOTTLIEB, STEEN & HAMILTON

Established in 1946

RUE DE LA LOI 23, BTE 5
1040 BRUSSELS, BELGIUM
Telephone: 32/2/287.20.00
Telex: 22635
Fax: 32/2/231.16.61

New York, New York Office: One Liberty Plaza, New York, N.Y. 10006. Telephone: 212-225-2000.

Washington, D.C. Office: 1752 N Street, N.W., Washington, D.C. 20036. Telephone: 202-728-2700.

Paris, France Office: 41, Avenue de Friedland, 75008 Paris, France. Telephone: 33-1-4074-6800.

London, England Office: City Place House, 55 Basinghall Street, London EC2V 5EH England. Telephone: 44-71-614-2200.

Hong Kong Office: 56th Floor, Bank of China Tower, One Garden Road, Hong Kong. Telephone: 852-521-4122.

Tokyo, Japan Office: Morgan Carroll Terai Gaikokuho Jimubengoshi Jimusho, 20th Floor, Shin Kasumigaseki Building, 3-2, Kasumigaseki 3-Chome, Chiyoda-Ku, Tokyo 100, Japan. Telephone: 81-3-3595-3911.

Frankfurt, Germany Office: Ulmenstrasse 37-39, 60325 Frankfurt am Main, Germany. Telephone: 49-69-971-03-0.

RESIDENT PARTNERS

WALTER W. OBERREIT, born Paterson, New Jersey, October 7, 1928; admitted, 1961, New York. *Education:* University of Michigan (A.B., 1951); Institut d'Etudes Politiques, Paris (Diplome, 1955); Yale University (LL.B., 1958). Resident at: New York Office, 1958-1962; Paris Office, 1962-1966; Brussels Office, 1966—.

MARIO SIRAGUSA, born Palermo, Italy, January 1, 1948; admitted, 1975, Rome, Italy. *Education:* University of Rome (Dr. Jur., 1970); College of Europe (Diploma, 1971); Harvard Law School (LL.M., 1972). Lecturer on EEC Law, College of Europe, Bruges, Belgium.

(This Listing Continued)

WOLFGANG KNAPP, born Ulm, West Germany, April 8, 1945; admitted, 1973, Germany; 1991, Brussels. *Education:* Universities of Tübingen, Paris, Hamburg, Bonn (Dr. Jur., 1973); University of Michigan (M.C.L., 1971); Louvain (Eq. Lic. en Droit, 1981). Resident at: New York Office, 1973-1974; Brussels Office, 1974-1983; Hong Kong Office, 1983-1986; at Brussels Office, 1986—.

JOHN S. MAGNEY, born Minneapolis, Minnesota, August 10, 1946; admitted, 1973, District of Columbia. *Education:* Marquette University (B.A., cum laude, 1968); Northwestern University (J.D., cum laude, 1972). Trial Attorney, Antitrust Division, U.S. Department of Justice, 1972-1975. *Member:* The District of Columbia Bar; American Bar Association.

GEORGE L. BUSTIN, born Perth Amboy, New Jersey, February 10, 1948; admitted, 1974, New York. *Education:* Princeton University (A.B., 1970); Harvard Law School (J.D. , 1973). Resident at: New York Office, 1973-1975; 1979-1984; Brussels Office, 1975-1979; 1984—. *Member:* New York State and American Bar Associations; Union Internationale des Avocats.

JEAN-LOUIS JORIS, born Wilrijk-Antwerp, Belgium, August 3, 1948; admitted, 1986, New York; 1991, Brussels. *Education:* Free University of Brussels (Lic. Jur., 1972); University of Michigan (M.C.L., 1975). Resident at New York Office, 1975-1976; at Brussels Office, 1976—.

DAVID G. SABEL, born Brooklyn, New York, May 4, 1950; admitted, 1978, New York. *Education:* Columbia University (B.A., 1972); Harvard Law School (J.D., 1976). Resident at New York Office, 1976-1990; at Brussels Office, 1991—.

JAN MEYERS, born Hasselt, Belgium, September 24, 1951; admitted, 1991, Brussels. *Education:* University of Louvain (Lic. Jur., summa cum laude, 1974); Harvard Law School (LL.M., 1975); Stanford Law School (J.S.D., 1982).

DIRK VANDERMEERSCH, born Ghent, Belgium, October 23, 1954; admitted, 1991, Brussels. *Education:* University of Ghent (Lic. Jur., magna cum laude, 1977; Lic. Criminology, 1977); Faculté Int. Droit Comparé, Strasbourg, France (Dipl., 1978); Harvard Law School (LL.M., 1979). Assistant, Faculty of Law, University of Ghent, 1977-1978. Resident at New York Office, 1979-1980; at Brussels Office, 1980—.

JACQUES REDING, born Luxembourg, September 1, 1954; admitted, 1991, Brussels. *Education:* Free University of Brussels (Lic. Jur., 1978; Lic. Spéciale Dr. Econ., 1979); University of Pennsylvania (LL.M., 1981). Also at New York Office, 1993—.

YOICHI SHIBASAKI, born Tokyo, Japan, June 1, 1951; admitted, 1976, Japan; 1985, New York. *Education:* Hitotsubashi University (LL.B., 1974); Legal Training & Research Institute, 1974-1976; University of California at Berkeley (LL.M., 1980). Lecturer and Professor, Catholic University of Leuven, 1987-1988 and 1990-1991.

ANTOINE WINCKLER, born Rome, Italy, October 12, 1955; admitted, 1992, Paris. *Education:* University of Paris Sorbonne, Ecole Normale Supérieure, Ecole Nationale d'Administration. Judge at the Tribunal Administratif de Nice, 1983-1984. Resident at: Brussels Office, 1985-1987, 1991—; Paris Office, 1987-1990.

MAURITS J.F.M. DOLMANS, born Arnhem, The Netherlands, January 1, 1960; admitted, 1986, New York; 1988, Rotterdam. *Education:* Rijks Universiteit Leiden (Master of Laws, 1984); Columbia University (LL.M., 1985). Resident at: New York Office, 1985; Brussels Office, 1986—.

RESIDENT ASSOCIATES

THIJS ALEXANDER, born Amsterdam, The Netherlands, April 22, 1963; admitted, 1991, New York. *Education:* University of Amsterdam (J.D., 1987); University of Michigan (LL.M., 1988).

BARBARA BRANDTNER, born Vienna, Austria, June 4, 1965. *Education:* University of Vienna (Mag.Iur., 1988); Collège of Europe (1990); University of Michigan (LL.M., 1992).

RANDALL COSTA, born Somerville, New Jersey, November 27, 1961; admitted, 1993, New York. *Education:* Yale University (B.A., 1985); Yale Law School (J.D., 1992).

ALINE DAUFRESNE, born Brussels, Belgium, January 26, 1966; admitted, 1993, Brussels, Belgium. *Education:* Free University of Brussels (Lic.Jur., 1989); Columbia Law School (LL.M., 1992).

LAURENT A. GARZANITI, born Liège, August 27, 1966. *Education:* Université de Liège (Lic.Jur., 1989); Cambridge University (LL.M., EEC Law, 1990); Columbia University (LL.M., 1991).

(This Listing Continued)

CLEARY, GOTTLIEB, STEEN & HAMILTON,
Brussels—Continued

MICHAEL A. GERSTENZANG, born Albany, New York, September 7, 1964; admitted, 1990, New York. Education: Georgetown University (B.S.F.S., 1986); Columbia Law School (J.D., 1989).

REINHARD HERMES, born Cologne, Germany, August 29, 1957; admitted, 1989, New York; 1990, Frankfurt. Education: Universities of Regensburg, Kiel and Hamburg (First State Examination, 1981; Second State Examination, 1986; Dr. jur., 1988); Harvard University, Kennedy School of Government (M.P.A., 1988). Assistant, Law of the Sea and Maritime Law Institute, University of Hamburg, 1983-1986. (Brussels, Belgium and Frankfurt, Germany Offices).

JAN W. HOEVERS, born Amersfoort, The Netherlands, July 22, 1965; admitted, 1991, New York; 1992, Brussels. Education: Leiden University (J.D., 1989); Harvard Law School (LL.M., 1990).

CAROLINE Y. LEVI, born Laeken, Belgium, November 24, 1966; admitted, 1991, Belgium. Education: ULB (Lic. Jur., 1989); College of Europe (Comp. Law, EEC Law, 1990); Columbia University (LL.M., 1991). Assistantship, Introduction to Law, Free University of Brussels, 1989-1990.

NICHOLAS LEVY, born London, United Kingdom, February 11, 1966; admitted, 1989, Inner Temple, London. Education: Worcester College, Oxford (B.A., 1987); The City University, London (Diploma in Law, 1988).

PATRICK J. MCDERMOTT, born Pensacola, Florida, August 27, 1952; admitted, 1989, Maryland; 1991, District of Columbia; 1993, Colorado. Education: University of Colorado (B.A., 1977; M.B.A., 1981); Georgetown University (J.D., cum laude, 1989). Member, Law and Policy in International Business, 1987-1989. Member: The District of Columbia Bar; Maryland State and American Bar Associations.

FILIP J. MOERMAN, born St. Amandsberg, Belgium, August 11, 1962; admitted, 1988, New York; 1991, Brussels. Education: University of Ghent (Lic. Jur., 1985); Columbia University School of Law (LL.M., 1987).

FRANCESCA M. MORETTI, born Venice, Italy, April 10, 1964; admitted, 1991, Brussels; 1992, Bologna, Italy. Education: University of Bologna (Lic. Jur., 1988); Harvard Law School (LL.M., 1990). (Brussels, Belgium and Frankfurt, Germany Offices).

TILL MÜLLER-IBOLD, born Hannover, Germany, December 31, 1958; admitted, 1988, Düsseldorf, Germany. Education: University of Hamburg, Germany (First State Exam, 1983; Dr. Jur., 1989); University of Madrid, Spain (1979-1980); University of Miami (LL.M., 1989). Assistant, University of Hamburg, Institute for EEC Law, 1983-1987.

CATHERINE NOIRFALISSE, born Liège, Belgium, August 2, 1965; admitted, 1993, Brussels. Education: University of Liège (Law Degree, 1988); Essex University (LL.M., in EC Law, 1992); University of Chicago Law School (LL.M., 1993).

MIGUEL ODRIOZOLA, born Berleberg, Germany, November 16, 1966; admitted, 1991, Madrid; 1993, New York. Education: Autonomous University of Madrid (LL.B., 1989); University of California at Los Angeles (LL.M., 1991); University of Chicago School of Law (LL.M., 1992; S.J.D., 1993).

STEPHEN E. POMPER, born Chicago, Illinois, August 23, 1965; admitted, 1994, New York (Not admitted in Belgium). Education: Harvard College (A.B., 1987); Yale Law School (J.D., 1993). Book Review Editor, Yale Journal of Regulation.

GIULIO CESARE RIZZA, born Siracusa, Italy, September 12, 1964; admitted, 1992, Siracusa, Italy. Education: L.U.I.S.S., Rome (J.D., 1988); University of California at Berkeley (LL.M., 1994).

GIUSEPPE SCASSELLATI-SFORZOLINI, born Bologna, Italy, February 12, 1960; admitted, 1986, Bologna, Italy; 1988, New York. Education: Harvard University, 1980; University of Bologna (Dr. Jur., 1984); University of Michigan (LL.M., 1987).

ANNETTE LUISE SCHILD, born Saarbrücken, Germany, January 9, 1961; admitted, 1992, Frankfurt. Education: Universität Tübingen; Tufts University; Flecher School of Law and Diplomacy (M.A.L.D., 1985). Instructor, Public International Law, UniversitäSaarbrücken, 1987-1990.

ROBBERT SNELDERS, born Hertogenbosch, Netherlands, April 20, 1968; admitted, 1993, New York. Education: University of Leiden, Netherlands (LL.M., 1990); College of Europe, Bruges, Belgium (Daels, 1991); Harvard Law School, Cambridge, Massachusetts (LL.M., 1992).

(This Listing Continued)

ROMANO FRANCESCO SUBIOTTO, born Geneva, May 15, 1961; Solicitor, admitted, 1988, England and Wales. Education: Universidad de Màlaga (Dipl. en Estudios Hispanicos, 1980); University of London, King's College (LL.B., 1984); University of Paris I, Panthéon-Sorbonne (Maítrise en Droit Privé, 1984); Harvard Law School (LL.M., 1986).

KAREN VANDEKERCKHOVE, born Leuven, Belgium, January 30, 1969; admitted, 1993, Belgium. Education: Facultes Notre Dame de la Paix, Namur (B.A., 1989); Katholieke Universiteit Leuven (LL.B., 1992); Harvard Law School (LL.M., 1993).

JAN VAN GYSEGEM, born Ghent, Belgium, July 20, 1966; admitted, 1991, Brussels and New York. Education: University of Ghent (Lic. Jur., 1989); New York University (LL.M., 1990).

AMARYLLIS VERHOEVEN, born Antwerp, Belgium, July 8, 1967. Education: Katholieke Universiteit Leuven (LL.B., summa cum laude, 1990); Faculteit St. Ignatius, Antwerp (B.A., summa cum laude, 1987); Harvard Law School (LL.M., 1991).

SABIEN VERMEULEN, born Ghent, Belgium, September 28, 1969; admitted, 1994, New York. Education: Facultes Notre Dame de la Paix, Namur (B.A., 1989); Katholieke Universiteit Leuven (LL.B., 1992); Harvard Law School (LL.M., 1993).

(For biographical data of the partners resident in the New York, Washington, Paris, London, Hong Kong, Tokyo and Frankfurt Offices, see Professional Biographies at New York, N.Y., Washington, D.C., Paris, France, London, England, Hong Kong, Tokyo, Japan and Frankfurt, Germany).

CLIFFORD CHANCE

Established in 1968

AVENUE LOUISE 65, BOX 2
1050 BRUSSELS, BELGIUM
Telephone: (32 2) 533 59 11
Fax: (32 2) 533 59 59

Amsterdam, The Netherlands Office: Apollolaan 171, 1077 AS, P.O. Box 7301, 1007 JH. Telephone: (31 20) 577 71 11. Fax: (31 20) 676 93 26.

Bahrain, Manama Associated Office: Law Office of Shaikh Isa bin Mohammed Al Khalifa. P.O. Box 20717. Telephone: (973) 531535; 531073. Fax: (973) 536272; 530608.

Barcelona, Spain Office: Pau Claris 102, 08009. Telephone: (34 3) 318 68 64. Fax: (34 3) 317 73 23.

Budapest, Hungary Office: Köves & Partners, Clifford Chance. Madách Trade Center, Madách Imre Út 14, 1075. Telephone: (36 1) 268 1600. Fax: (36 1) 268 1610.

Dubai, United Arab Emirates Office: 18th Floor, Dubai World Trade Centre, P.O. Box 9380. Telephone: (971 4) 314333. Fax: (971 4) 313990; 314565.

Frankfurt/Main, Germany Office: Friedrichstraβe 2-6, 60323. Telephone: (49 69) 971 4090. Fax: (49 69) 971 40977.

Hanoi, Vietnam Office: 52 Nguyen Binh Khiem. Telephone: (844) 229 182/3/4/5/6. Fax: (844) 229 190.

Hong Kong Office: 30th Floor, Jardine House, One Connaught Place. Telephone: (852) 2810 0229. Fax: (852) 2810 4708; 2810 4858; 2810 4743.

London, England Office: 200 Aldersgate Street, EC1A 4JJ. Telephone: (44 171) 600 1000. Fax: (44 171) 600 5555.

Madrid, Spain Office: Paseo de la Castellana 110, 28046. Telephone (341) 562 7674. Fax: (34 1) 562 49 93.

Milan, Italy Associated Office: Grimaldi e Clifford Chance. Via Gesú, 3, 20121. Telephone: (39 2) 7600 8040. Fax: (39 2) 7600 4950.

Moscow, Russia Office: Ul. Sadovaya - Samotechnaya 24/27, 2nd Floor, 103051. Telephone: (7 501) 258 50 50. Fax: (7 501) 258 50 51.

New York, New York Office: Swiss Bank Tower, 10 East 50th Street, 10022. Telephone: (1 212) 750 1440. Fax: (1 212) 758 6625.

Paris, France Office: 112 avenue Kléber, BP 163 Trocadéro, 75770 Paris Cedex 16. Telephone: (33 1) 44 05 52 52. Fax: (33 1) 44 05 52 00.

Riyadh, Saudi Arabia Associated Office: The Law Firm of Salah Al-Hejailan. P.O. Box 1454, 11431. Telephone: (966 1) 479 2200. Fax: (966 1) 479 1717.

Rome, Italy Associated Office: Grimaldi e Clifford Chance. Viale G. Rossini 7, 00198. Telephone: (39 6) 807 2251. Fax: (39 6) 807 8201.

Shanghai, People's Republic of China Office: Suite 898, Shanghai Centre, 1376 Nanjing Xi Lu, 200040. Telephone: (86 21) 279 8461. Fax: (86 21) 279 8462.

(This Listing Continued)

Singapore Office: 16 Collyer Quay #31-00, 0104. Telephone: (65) 535 1855. Fax: (65) 535 6855.

Tokyo, Japan Office: 6th Floor, South Hill Nagatacho Building, 11-30 Nagatacho 1-chome, Chiyoda-ku, 100. Telephone: (81 3) 3581 4311. Fax: (81 3) 3593 0651.

Warsaw, Poland Office: Warsaw Corporate Centre, ul. Emilii Plater 28, 00-688. Telephone: (48 2) 630 3344. Fax: (48 2) 630 3355.

EUROPEAN COMMUNITY LAW: International Trade/Commercial Policy of the European Community including GATT, Dumping, Origin, Safeguards, Customs and Voluntary Restraint Agreements, EC Financial Services, Intellectual Property, Company Law, Telecommunications, Public Procurement, Non-Tariff Barriers and Taxation; EC Anti-Trust/Competition Law and Merger Control, Representation of the interests of clients at Commission, Council, European Parliament and Member State level.

BELGIAN LAW: Banking and Financial Services, Corporate Law, Mergers and Acquisitions, International Joint Ventures, all aspects of Investment including Property, Loans and Mortgages, Tax, Employment, Administrative Law, Computer Law, Distribution Agreements, Communications, International Arbitration.

Firm engaged in Belgian, EC, English and General International Practice.

PARTNERS

ULICK G. BOURKE, Solicitor (England and Wales) 1970. **LANGUAGES:** English and French. **PRACTICE AREAS:** Transport; European Community Law; International Trade; EC Competition.

KEITH H. HENDRY, Advocate of the Supreme Court of South Africa, 1976. **LANGUAGES:** English and French. **PRACTICE AREAS:** Antitrust Law; European Community Law; Import and Export Law; Customs Law; International Business Law.

YVES HERINCKX, Avocat (Brussels) 1984; Solicitor (England and Wales) 1992. **LANGUAGES:** Dutch, English, French and Japanese. **PRACTICE AREAS:** Securities; Banking Law; Finance Law.

EDWARD B. PITT, Solicitor (England and Wales) 1976. **LANGUAGES:** English and French. **PRACTICE AREAS:** Intellectual Property; EC Competition Law; Antitrust and Trade Regulation; Mergers, Acquisitions and Divestitures; European Community.

LAWRANCE RANDALL, Solicitor (England and Wales) 1970. **LANGUAGES:** English and French. **PRACTICE AREAS:** Joint Ventures; Mergers and Acquisitions; Corporate Law; International Business Law; Property Law.

(For the names of Partners resident in other offices, see Professional Biographies for those offices).

COPPENS VAN OMMESLAGHE HORSMANS & FAURÈS

AVENUE LOUISE 81
1050 BRUSSELS, BELGIUM
Telephone: (32.2) 542.88.88
Facsimile: (32.2) 542.89.89

Firm Engaged in Belgian, European and International Law practice entitled to plead before the Belgian Courts, the European Commission and the European Court of Justice. Civil and Commercial, Corporations, Securities, Finance, Banking, Mergers and Acquisitions, Aviation and Transportation, Insurance, Taxation, International Transactions and Arbitration, Labour Law, Public and Administrative Law, E.C. Law, Construction Law, Building, Real Estate, Telecommunications, Distribution, Agency and Franchising, Intellectual Property, Bankruptcy and Insolvency, Torts, Environmental Law, Litigation including Supreme Court Cases.

FIRM PROFILE: Coppens, Van Ommeslaghe, Horsmans & Faurès is a leading Belgian firm, active in most areas of civil, commercial and business law. The firm is recognized for its strong academic ties. The firm, comprising more than 60 lawyers, was formed in 1994, when the long-established and well-known Belgian practices of Coppens, Horsmans & Partners and Van Ryn, Van Ommeslaghe Van Beirs Faurés & Flagey decided to join forces.

PARTNERS

PIERRE COPPENS, born 1920; admitted, 1946, Brussels. *Education:* University of Louvain (Dr.Jur., 1942); University of Paris (Special Commercial Law Doctorate, 1946); Political Sciences School of Paris (1947). Professor, University of Louvain Law School: Droit commercial comparé

(This Listing Continued)

(Comparative Commercial Law), 1948-1985; Droit commercial (Commercial Law), 1962-1985; Droit fiscal (Tax Law), 1962-1987.

PIERRE VAN OMMESLAGHE, born 1932; admitted, 1953, Brussels; 1980, Court of Cassation Bar. *Education:* University of Brussels (Dr. Jur., 1953; Licence en Sciences Economiques et Financières, 1955). Professor, University of Brussels Law School: Droit commercial comparé (Comparative Commercial Law), 1961-1970; Droit civil - Les obligations (Civil Law), 1969; Etudes approfondies de droit privé - Droit civil et commercial (Special topics of Civil and Commercial Law), 1968; Etudes approfondies de questions de droit commercial et de droit commercial comparé (special topics of Commercial Law and Comparative Commercial Law), 1970.

ANDRÉ FAURÈS, born 1933; admitted, 1956, Brussels. *Education:* University of Brussels (Dr. Jur., 1956; Licence en Sciences Economiques et Financières, 1955); Harvard School of Economics (Graduate School of Arts and Sciences, 1959-1960).

GUY HORSMANS, born 1935; admitted, 1954, Brussels. *Education:* University of Louvain (Dr.Jur., 1957; Lic., Political and Social Sciences). Professor, University of Louvain Law School; Droit commercial (Commercial Law); Droit commercial approfondi et comparé (Special Comparative Commercial Law); Intellectual Economic Law, 1969—. Director, Comparative Law Centre, Brussels.

FRANCIS GOFFIN, born 1949; admitted, 1973, Brussels. *Education:* University of Louvain (Lic.Jur., 1973).

JEANINE WINDEY, born 1950; admitted, 1973, Brussels. *Education:* University of Brussels (Lic. Jur., 1973). Assistant Professor, Secured Transactions, University of Brussels Law School, 1982.

ANDRE BAILLEUX, born 1948; admitted, 1982, Brussels. *Education:* University of Louvain (Lic. Jur., 1971); Ecole Supérieure des Sciences Fiscales, Brussels (Lic. Fisc., 1972). Professor, Tax Law, University of Mons (FUCAM).

JEAN-MARIE VERSCHUEREN, born 1948; admitted, 1973, Brussels. *Education:* University of Brussels (Lic. Jur., 1973).

ISABELLE HEENEN, born 1952; admitted, 1974, Brussels. *Education:* University of Brussels (Lic. Jur., 1974).

RENÉ GONNE, born 1956; admitted, 1979, Brussels. *Education:* University of Louvain (Lic.Jur., 1979).

JEAN-MICHEL DETRY, born 1950; admitted, 1974, Brussels. *Education:* University of Brussels (Lic. Jur., 1974); University of Michigan Law School (Master of Comparative Law, 1975).

GEOFFROY DE FOESTRAETS, born 1959; admitted, 1984, Brussels. *Education:* University of Louvain (Lic.Jur., 1981); University of Leyden (International Law, 1982).

ERIC DELTOUR, born 1957; admitted, 1983, Brussels. *Education:* University of Louvain (Lic.Jur., 1982).

VINCENT HORSMANS, born 1961; admitted, 1986, Brussels. *Education:* University of Louvain (Lic. Jur., 1985); Louisiana State University.

GHISLAINE GOES, born 1963; admitted, 1986, Brussels. *Education:* University of Louvain (Lic. Jur., 1986).

LOUIS PUTS, born 1961; admitted, 1986, Brussels. *Education:* University of Leuven (Lic. Jur., 1984); University of Brussels (Lic. Economic Law, 1986).

DOMINIQUE TORBEYNS, born 1951; admitted, 1973, Brussels. *Education:* University of Brussels (Lic.Jur., 1973).

MARTIN LEBBE, born 1955; admitted, 1979, Brussels. *Education:* University of Louvain (Lic.Jur., 1979).

VINCENT PIESSEVAUX, born 1961; admitted, 1984, Brussels. *Education:* University of Louvain (Lic.Jur., 1984 - Master in Economic Sciences, 1986).

ROBERT SACRE, born 1934; admitted, 1959, Brussels. *Education:* University of Louvain (Dr. Jur., 1957).

JOSIANE RONSSE, born 1955; admitted, 1978, Brussels. *Education:* University of Louvain (Lic. Jur., 1978).

Languages: French, Dutch, English, German and Spanish.

COUDERT BROTHERS

TOUR LOUISE
149 AVENUE LOUISE, BOX 8
B-1050 BRUSSELS, BELGIUM
Telephone: 542.18.11
Telecopier: (32) (2) 542.18.88; 539.28.88
Cable Address: "Treduoc"
Telex: 24284 "Couder B"

REVISERS OF THE FRANCE LAW DIGEST FOR THIS DIRECTORY

New York, New York 10036-7794: 1114 Avenue of Americas.
Washington, D.C.20006: 1627 I Street, N.W.
Los Angeles, California 90017: 1055 West Seventh Street, Twentieth Floor.
San Francisco, California 94111: 4 Embarcadero Center, Suite 3300.
San Jose, California 95113: Suite 1250, Ten Almaden Boulevard.
Paris 75008, France: Coudert Frères, 52, Avenue des Champs-Elysées, 75008.
London, EC4M 7JP England: 20 Old Bailey.
Beijing, People's Republic of China 100020: Suite 2708-09 Jing Guang Centre Hu Jia Lou, Chao Yang Qu.
Shanghai, People's Republic of China 200002: c/o Suite1804, Union Building, 100 Yanan Road East.
Hong Kong: 25th Floor, Nine Queen's Road Central.
Singapore, 0104: Tung Centre, 20 Collyer Quay.
Sydney N.S.W. 2000, Australia: Suite 2202, State Bank Centre, 52 Martin Place.
Tokyo 107, Japan: 1355 West Tower, Aoyama Twin Towers, 1-1-1 Minami-Aoyama, Minato-ku.
Moscow, Russia: Ulitsa Staraya Basmannaya 14.
01301 Sao Paulo, SP, Brazil: Machado, Meyer, Sendacz, e Opice, Advogados, Rua da Consolacao, 247, 8 Andar.
Bangkok 10500, Thailand: Bubhajit Building, 20 North Sathorn Road, 10th Floor.
Ho Chi Minh City, Vietnam: c/o Saigon Business Centre, 49-57 Dong Du Street, District 1.

European Communities Law, International Corporate and Trade Law. Firm engaged in General International Law Practice and authorized to appear before the Belgian Courts.

PARTNERS

JACQUES BUHART, born Mulhouse, France, July 11, 1950; admitted, 1977, Paris, France. *Education:* Ecole Sainte-Geneviève, Versailles; Ecole Supérieure de Commerce de Paris (1974); University of Paris, Faculty of Law (Licence en Droit des Affaires, 1975; Diplôme d'Etudes Supérieures Spécialisées, 1976); Institute of Comparative Law (1975); Academy of International Law, The Hague (1976). *Member:* International Bar Association (Vice-Chairman, Committee G, 1990—); International Competition Law Association. *LANGUAGES:* French and English.

STEPHEN O. SPINKS, born Auburn, Alabama, February 25, 1951; admitted, 1976, Georgia; 1986, New York. *Education:* Auburn University (B.A., cum laude, 1973); University of Georgia (J.D., 1976); Vrije Universiteit Brussel (LL.M., magna cum laude, 1977); Université Libre de Bruxelles (Equivalence de Licence en Droit, 1982). Trainee EEC Commission, Competition Directorate, 1979. *Member:* American Bar Association. *LANGUAGES:* English, French and Dutch.

PAULETTE VANDER SCHUEREN, born Etterbeek, Belgium, November 4, 1956; admitted, 1994, Brussels. *Education:* Universitaire Faculteiten Sint-Aloysius, Brussels; Katholieke Universiteit Leuven (Licenciaat in de Rechten, 1979); Collège d'Europe of Bruges (Certificat des Hautes Etudes Européennes, cum laude, 1980). Trainee, EEC Commission, Customs Union Service, 1980. *Member:* Association des Anciens du Collège d'Europe. *LANGUAGES:* Dutch, French, English and German.

ASSOCIATES

Peter Alexiadis	**Nathalie Gilson**
(Not admitted in Belgium)	**Roland P. Montfort**
Jean-Yves Art	**Dr. Karl H. Pilny**
Kent Karlsson	(Not admitted in Belgium)
David Chijner	**Olivier Prost**
Hervé F. Cogels	(Not admitted in Belgium)
Anthony Laurence Gardner	**Dirk Van Liedekerke**

(This Listing Continued)

SPECIAL CONSULTANT

PROF. VALENTINE KORAH, born London, England, February 11, 1928; admitted, 1952, England (Not admitted in Belgium). *Education:* Universit College, London (LL.B., 1949; LL.M., mark of distinction, 1951; Ph.D., 1966). Author: *Competition Law of Britain and the Common Market,* 3rd ed. 1982, Nijhoff; *EEC Competition Law and Practice,* 4th ed. 1990, ESC/Sweet & Maxwell; *Exclusive Dealing Agreements in the EEC:* Regulation 1983/83 and 1984/83, 1984, 2nd ed. with Warwick A. Rothnie, 1992, ELC at Sweet and Maxwell; *Patent Licensing and EEC Competition Rules:* Regulation 2349/84, 1985, ESC/Sweet & Maxwell; *R & D and the EEC Competition Rules - Regulation 418/85, 1986,* ESC/Sweet and Maxwell; *Franchising and the EEC Competition Rules, Regulation 4087/88,* ESC/Sweet and Maxwell, 1989; *Know-how Licensing and the EEC Competition Rules, Regulation 556/89,* ESC/Sweet and Maxwell, 1989. Contributor: U.K. Competition Law in Western Europe and the USA. Emeritus Professor of Competition Law, University College, London. Teaching dominant course on EEC Competition Law at the Collège d'Europe, Bruges, 1985—. Visiting Professor, University of Lusiada, Lisbon and Oporto, October 1989—; Visiting Professor, Universidad Carlos III, Madrid, 1992—; Visiting Professor, Fordham Law School for Spring Semester, 1991—; speaker and consultant for conferences on competition law. Member, Joint Bar/-Law Society Working Party on Competition Law Reform. Member, Foreign Advisory Board, the *Antitrust Bulletin, . Member:* American Bar Association (Member, Sections on: antitrust; International); Society of Public Teachers of Law.

REVISERS OF THE FRANCE LAW DIGEST FOR THIS DIRECTORY

(For biographical data of the Washington personnel, see Professional Biographies at Washington, D.C.).
(For biographical data of the New York personnel, see Professional Biographies at New York, N.Y.).
(For biographical data of the Los Angeles personnel, see Professional Biographies at Los Angeles, California).
(For biographical data of the San Francisco personnel, see Professional Biographies at San Francisco, California).
(For biographical data of the San Jose personnel, see Professional Biographies at San Jose California).
(For biographical data of the London personnel, see Professional Biographies at London, England).
(For biographical data of the Paris personnel, see Professional Biographies at Paris, France).
(For biographical data of the Hong Kong personnel, see Professional Biographies at Hong Kong).
(For biographical data on Beijing personnel, see Professional Biographies at Beijing, People's Republic of China).
(For biographical data of the Singapore personnel, see Professional Biographies at Singapore).
(For biographical data of the Tokyo personnel, see Professional Biographies at Tokyo, Japan).
(For biographical data of the Sao Paulo personnel, see Professional Biographies at Sao Paulo, Brazil).
(For biographical data of the Shanghai personnel, see Professional Biographies at Shanghai, People's Republic of China).
(For biographical data of the Sydney personnel, see Professional Biographies at Sydney, Australia).
(For biographical data of the Moscow personnel, see Professional Biographies at Moscow, U.S.S.R.).
(For biographical data of the Ho Chi Minh personnel, see Professional Biographies at Ho Chi Minh City, Vietnam).

COUTRELIS & ASSOCIES

235, RUE DE LA LOI
1040 BRUSSELS, BELGIUM
Telephone: 230.48.45
Fax: 230.82.06

Paris, France: 55 Avenue Marceau, 75116. Telephone: 44.43.91.30. Fax: 40.70.07.97.

Arbitration, Lobbying, Counseling and Litigation (both before National Courts and before the Court of Justice in Luxembourg) on Free Movement of Goods, Common Agricultural Policy, Antitrust, State Aids, Banking and Financial Law, Products Liability, Customs and Tariff Law, Food and Drug Regulations, Consumer Law, Environmental Law, Patents, Trademarks, Designs, Copyrights, Licensing, Distribution and Franchising Law.

FIRM PROFILE: The firm is well known for its expertise in European Community Law as it is applied within EC countries, as well as for its work regarding the likely effects of EC Law as it will be applied by EFTA

(This Listing Continued)

countries with the coming into force of the European Economic Area Agreement.

MEMBERS OF FIRM

ANDRÉ COUTRELIS, born Cairo, Egypt, April 15, 1944; admitted, 1982, Paris as Conseil Juridique; 1987, Paris, as Avocat (Not admitted in Belgium). *Education:* University of Paris (Licence en Droit, 1969; Certificat du Centre Universitaire d'Etudes des Communautés Européennes, 1969; DES Droit Public, 1971); University of California at Berkeley (LL.M., 1973). Lecturer in Law, Faculty of Law and Economic Sciences of Paris, 1969-1972. Banque Nationale de Paris, 1975-1976; Baker & McKenzie, Paris, 1976-1977. *Member:* International Bar Association; International Association of Boalt Alumni (IABA); Association des Juristes Européens; Association des Juristes de Banque. *LANGUAGES:* French, English, Greek and Arabic. *PRACTICE AREAS:* European Community Law.

NICOLE COUTRELIS, born Toulon, France, August 28, 1950; admitted, 1985, Paris as Avocat (Not admitted in Belgium). *Education:* University of Paris (Licence d'Histoire, 1970); University of Paris II (Licence en Droit, 1973). Office National Interprofessionnel des Céréales, 1972-1978; Représentation Permanente de la France auprès de la CEE, 1978-1982; Legal Service, Commission of the European Communities, 1982-1985. Lecturer, Seminars on EC Law, ENGREF (Ecole Nationale du Génie Rural, des Eaux et Forêts, Paris). *Member:* International Bar Association; Association des Juristes de Banque; Association des Juristes Européens; Association Française du Droit de l'Alimentation (AFDA); Secretary General of Association Internationale des Juristes pour le Droit de la Vigne et du Vin (AIDV) and of European Food Law Association (EFLA). *LANGUAGES:* French, English, Italian, Spanish and German. *PRACTICE AREAS:* European Community Law; Litigation; Food and Drug Regulation.

JOHN ANDREW JOHNSON, born Manchester, England, June 26, 1961; called to the Bar, 1983, Gray's Inn; (Not admitted in Belgium). *Education:* University of Newcastle-Upon-Tyne (LL.B., Hons., 1982); Inns of Court School of Law (1982-1983); University of Amsterdam, Amsterdam School of International Relations (LL.M., European Community Business Law, 1993). Pupillage, 2 Harcourt Buildings, Temple, 1985-1986; Prosecutor, Crown Prosecution Service, Leeds, 1986-1987; Legal Advisor HM Government, 1987-1991. *Member:* Bar European Group; Council of the Bar and Law Societies of the European Community. *LANGUAGES:* English, French, German and Dutch. *PRACTICE AREAS:* European Community Law.

RACHIDA SEMAIL, born Villacourt, France, July 22, 1964; admitted, 1994, Paris as Avocat. *Education:* Université des Sciences Sociales, Toulouse (Licence en Droit, 1986; Maîtrise en Droit Public, Relations Internationales, 1987; DEA Droit Économique International et Communautaire, 1988; Doctorat en Droit, 1992). Thesis: "la dénomination des produits agricoles et des denrées alimentaires en droit communautaire." Certificat d'aptitude à la profession d'Avocat, 1993. *LANGUAGES:* French, English and Arabic. *PRACTICE AREAS:* European Community Law; Food and Drug Regulation.

OF COUNSEL

JEAN-CLAUDE MASCLET, born Neuilly-sur-Seine, France, January 15, 1943. Professeur Agrégé des Facultés de Droit; Professor Paris I; Honorary Dean, Faculté de Droit Jean Monnet at Sceaux; Director, DESS "Enterprise et Droit Communautaire" at Faculté de Droit Jean Monnet; President, Commission pour l'étude des Communautés Européennes (CEDECE). Chevalier de la Légion d'Honneur; Chevalier des Palmes Académiques. Deputy-Mayor, Montmorency. Member, Editorial Boards of Revue Trimestrielle de Droit Européen and Revue Française de Droit Constitutionnel. *LANGUAGES:* French and English. *PRACTICE AREAS:* European Community Law; Constitutional Law; Administrative Law.

PIERRE-MARIE VINCENT, born Marseille, France, June 28, 1926. *Education:* Swiss Federal Institute of Technology, Zurich (M.Sc., Agronomy, 1953). Lecturer, Food Law, University Aix-Marseille III, 1988—. Director, Food Law, Educational Programme at CNAM, Paris, 1985—. Author: "La certification et la normalisation en France"; "Qualité de l'aliment. Législation et Réglementation"; "Industrial requirements in food safety"; "Sugars, Sweeteners and EC Regulations"; "Hemmnisse in grenzüberschreitenden Handel mit Lebensmitteln für eine besondere Ernährung". Manager, Plant Protection R & D, Pechiney-Progil, Lyons, 1954-1962; Monsanto Europe, Brussels, 1963-1972; Manager, Food Law Dept., Brooke Bond Liebig Continental Division, Schoten, Belgium, 1972-1977; Manager, Food Law Dept., Worldwide, Roquette Fréres, Lestrem, France, 1978-1990. Member: Chairman, French Food Law Association; Board Member, European Food Law Association; Board Member, Plant Protec-

(This Listing Continued)

tion and Environment Association; Board Member, Regional Center for Food Research, Innovation and Technology, Avignon; Chairman, Commission Générale des Méthodes d'Analyse. Member, Association Nationale des Industries Agroalimentaires. *LANGUAGES:* French, English, German, Italian and Spanish. *PRACTICE AREAS:* Food and Drug Regulation.

COVINGTON & BURLING

BRUSSELS, BELGIUM

(See Henriette A. Tielemans, Brussels, Belgium)

General Practice.

J. ET B. CREMADES ET ASSOCIÉS

AV. LOUISE, 391

1050 BRUSSELS, BELGIUM

Telephone: 648.9840

Telex: 62630 cormas b.

Fax: 647.8351

Madrid, Spain Office: J. y B. Cremades y Asociados, Goya 18, 2nd Floor, 28001. Telephone: 431.8354. Fax: 576.9794.
Paris, France Office: 51, Avenue Georges Mandel, 75116. Telephone: 45.53.55.50. Fax: 45.53.55.49.

General Practice. Commercial, Corporate, Foreign Investment, Licensing, Insurance, Banking and Finance, Oil and Gas, Real Estate and Patent Law, Aeronautical/Transporation, Commercial Arbitration, EEC, Competition Law, Customs Regulations, Environmental Law, Public Procurement.

PARTNERS

JUAN ANTONIO CREMADES, born Zaragoza, Spain, January 1, 1940; admitted, 1961, Zaragoza; 1966, Madrid; 1986, Paris. *Education:* University of Zaragoza (Law Degree, 1960); University of Paris (Law Degree, 1960; Ph.D., 1968); International Faculty of Comparative Law (1961). President, Union Internationale des Avocats, 1990-1991; Chairman, Committee of Regulation of Contracts of the International Chamber of Commerce, 1979-1980; International Maritime Arbitration Organization (CMI-ICC), 1979-1980. President, Spanish Chamber of Commerce in France since 1987. *Member:* Madrid Bar Association; Ordre des Avocats à la Cour de Paris; ICC International Court of Arbitration since 1969; Representative of the Paris Bar, 1992 and Brussels Bar (List B), 1986; Honorary member, Zaragoza, Mexico and Dominican Republic Bar Associations. (Also at Madrid, Spain and Paris, France Offices). *LANGUAGES:* Spanish, French and English.

BERNARDO M. CREMADES, born Zaragoza, Spain, July 20, 1943; admitted, 1969, Madrid; 1986, Paris, France. *Education:* University of Cologne (Ph.D., German Law, 1967); University of Seville (Ph.D., Spanish Law, 1968). Author of Litigating in Spain (Kluwer, 1989). Professor, Law Faculty, University of Madrid, 1975—. Arbitration in Spain (Butterworths, 1991) and Business Law in Spain (Butterworths, 1992). *Member:* Madrid Bar Association; International Council of Commercial Arbitration; International Bar Association; American Bar Association; Avocat à la Cour de Paris; Brussels Bar (List B), 1986. (Also at Madrid, Spain and Paris, France Offices). *LANGUAGES:* Spanish, French, German and English.

ASSOCIATES

FABIO NASARRE DE LETOSA, born Madrid, Spain, September 14, 1968; admitted, 1992, Zaragoza. *Education:* University of Zaragoza (Law Degree, 1991); University of Pau (Erasmus, 1991); College of Europe, Bruges (Diploma of High European Studies, 1992). *LANGUAGES:* Spanish, French and English. *PRACTICE AREAS:* European Community Law; Commercial Law.

(For complete biographical data on all personnel, see Professional Biographies at Madrid, Spain)

CRUMMY, DEL DEO, DOLAN, GRIFFINGER & VECCHIONE

AVENUE LOUISE 475, BTE. 8
B-1050 BRUSSELS, BELGIUM
Telephone: 011-322-646-0019
Telecopier: 011-322-646-0152

Newark, New Jersey Office: Crummy, Del Deo, Dolan, Griffinger & Vecchione, A Professional Corporation. One Riverfront Plaza, 07102. Telephone: 201-596-4500. Telecopier: 201-596-0545. Cable-Telex: 138154.

RESIDENT PARTNER

TERRY R. BRODERICK, born Chicago, Illinois, November 25, 1946; admitted, 1977, Pennsylvania; 1978, U.S. District Court, Eastern District of Pennsylvania; 1980, U.S. Court of Appeals, Third Circuit (Not admitted in Belgium). *Education:* Ripon College (A.B., 1968); Harvard Law School (J.D., 1971). Phi Beta Kappa. Author or Co-author: "The Maastricht Summit: Further Progress Toward European Union," International Business Lawyer 349, August, 1992; "Introduction To A New Europe: A Primer for 1992," International Business Lawyer 9, January, 1992; "New Biotechnology Legislation in the European Community and Federal Republic of Germany," International Business Lawyer 408, October, 1990; "Know How Licensing Agreements Under EC Group Exemption Regulation No. 556/89," International Business Lawyer 373, September, 1989; "Know-How-Lizenzvertrag nach der EG-Gruppenfreistellungsverordnung Nr. 556/89," Recht der Internationalen Wirtschaft 278, April 1989; "EEC Agreements for Exclusive Distribution and Purchasing," International Business Lawyer 162, May, 1986; "Forschungs-und Entwicklungsvertrag nach EG-Kartellrecht - Formularvertrag," Recht der Internationalen Wirschaft 5, January, 1986; "A Model EEC Research and Development Cooperation Agreement," International Business Lawyer 456, November, 1985; "EG-Patentlizenz-Formularvertrag," Recht der Internationalen Wirtschaft 349, May, 1985; "A Model EEC Patent Licensing Agreement," International Business Lawyer 161, April, 1985; "The EEC Commission's Group Exemption for Patent Licensing Agreements," International Business Lawyers 437, November, 1984; "Exclusive Licenses as Restraints of Trade Under U.S. and Common Market Antitrust Law," International Business Lawyer 345, September, 1984. Foreign Service Officer, U.S. Department of State, Washington, D.C., 1974-1977. *Member:* Pennsylvania and American (Member, Sections on: Antitrust; International Law) Bar Associations; International Bar Association (Member, Section on Business Law); American Society of International Law; Deutsch-Amerikanische Juristen Vereinigung. *LANGUAGES:* German.

REFERENCE: Bank Brussels Lambert; Branch: Brussels-Bois.

(For Biographical Data on all Personnel, see Professional Biographies at Newark, New Jersey)

CRUYPLANTS, ELOY, HUPIN & ASSOCIES

RUE DEFACQZ 78-80
1050 BRUSSELS, BELGIUM
Telephone: 32.2.534.20.20
Telefax: 32.2.534.30.18

Arbitration, Banking, Bankruptcy, Construction and Real Estate, Corporate, Environment, Industrial Property, Insurance, Labor Law, Medical Law, Mergers and Acquisitions, Competition and EEC Law, National and International Business, Public Contracts and Public Law, Taxation, Tourism, Transport.

MEMBERS OF FIRM

MAURICE ELOY, born Chatelet, Belgium, 1946; admitted, 1972, Brussels. *Education:* U.C.L. (Louvain, Lic. Dr. Jur., 1970). Professor of Tax Law, Facultés Universitaires of Mons, Ecole Supérieure des Sciences Fiscales of Brussels, HEC Saint-Louis of Brussels.

JEAN CRUYPLANTS, born Brussels, Belgium, 1949; admitted, 1975, Brussels. *Education:* U.C.L. (Louvain, Lic. Jur., 1974).

EMMANUEL HUPIN, born Leuven, Belgium, 1952; admitted, 1975, Brussels. *Education:* U.C.L. (Louvain, Lic. Jur., 1975).

ROBERT DE BAERDEMAEKER, born Boulogne-Billancourt, France, 1955; admitted, 1978, Brussels. *Education:* U.C.L. (Louvain, Lic. Jur.,

(This Listing Continued)

1978); University of Leiden, The Netherlands (Degree in International Public Law).

DIDIER CHAVAL, born Etterbeek, Belgium, 1960; admitted, 1984, Brussels. *Education:* U.C.L. (Louvain-La-Neuve, Lic. Jur., 1983).

BERNARD VANDENKERCKHOVE, born Etterbeek, Belgium, 1957; admitted, 1984, Brussels. *Education:* U.L.B. (Brussels, Lic. Jur., 1982).

ASSOCIATES

JACQUES BUEKENHOUDT, born Brussels, Belgium, 1951; admitted, 1974, Brussels. *Education:* U.L.B. (Brussels, Lic. Jur., 1974); University of Edinburgh (1983); University of Georgia (1992).

JEAN-PIERRE LERICHE, born Ath, Belgium, 1958; admitted, 1985, Brussels. *Education:* U.C.L. (Louvain-La-Neuve, Lic. Jur., 1981; Lic. Economic Law, 1983); U.L.B. (Brussels, Lic. Notariat, 1983).

OLIVIER DUGARDYN, born Brugge, Belgium, 1965; admitted, 1988, Brussels. *Education:* K.U.L. (Louvain, Lic. Jur., 1988).

EDGARD VAN DER STRAETEN, born Uccle, Belgium, 1963; admitted, 1988, Brussels. *Education:* U.L.B. (Brussels, Lic. Jur., 1987).

JEHAN DE THIER, born Louvain, Belgium, 1966; admitted, 1989, Brussels. *Education:* U.C.L. (Louvain, Lic. Jur., 1989).

VINCENT GEERAERT, born Genk, Belgium, 1965; admitted, 1988, Brussels. *Education:* K.U.L. (Leuven, Lic. Jur., 1988); U.C.L. (Louvain-La-Neuve, Lic. International and EEC Law, 1989).

PASCALE EVERAERT, born Brussels, Belgium, 1966; admitted, 1990, Brussels. *Education:* U.C.L. (Louvain-La-Neuve, Lic. Jur., 1990); Università degli Studi di Bologna (EEC Exchange Program, 1990).

OLIVIER LOUPPE, born Uccle, Belgium, 1966; admitted, 1991, Brussels. *Education:* U.L.B. (Brussels, Lic. Jur., 1989; Lic. EEC Law, 1990).

PIERRE BAUDIN, born Uccle, Belgium, 1963; admitted, 1992, Brussels. *Education:* U.C.L. (Louvain-La-Neuve, Lic. Jur., 1989).

BERNARD D'URSEL, born Ixelles, Belgium, 1961; admitted, 1986, Brussels. *Education:* U.C.L. (Louvain-La-Neuve, Lic. Jur., 1984); Ecole Supérieure des Sciences Fiscales, Brussels (Lic. Tax Law, 1989).

JOHANNES VAN LANGENDONCK, born Mortsel, Belgium, 1965; admitted, 1988, Brussels. *Education:* K.U.L. (Leuven, Lic. Jur., 1988); Ecole Supérieure des Sciences Fiscales, Brussels (Lic. Tax Law, 1993).

Languages: French, Dutch, English, Italian, German, Spanish and Danish.

BUFETE CUATRECASAS

78 AVENUE D'AUDERGHEM
1040 BRUSSELS, BELGIUM
Telephone: 735.06.43
Fax: 734.72.34

Barcelona, Spain Office: Balmes 76. Telephone: 290.55.00. Fax: 290.55.67.
Bilbao, Spain Office: Alameda de Mazarredo 5. Telephone 424.82.67. Fax: 424.82.34.
Madrid, Spain Office: Antonio Maura 10. Telephone: 521.94.47. Fax: 522.48.99.
Gerona, Spain Office: Ronda Ferrán Puig 4-6. Telephone: 22.71.02. Fax: 22.66.61.

Firm engaged in Spanish, EEC Law and General International Practice. Not authorized to appear before the Belgian Courts.

MEMBERS OF FIRM

EMILIO COCO, born Barcelona, Spain, January 27, 1954; admitted, 1978, Barcelona (Not admitted in Belgium). *Education:* University of Barcelona (Law Degree, 1978). Professor of Tax Law, ESADE. *Member:* Barcelona Bar Association. (Also at Barcelona Office). *LANGUAGES:* English and French.

ENRIC PICAÑOL, born Barcelona, Spain, October 2, 1952; admitted, 1976, Barcelona (Not admitted in Belgium). *Education:* University of Barcelona (Law Degree, 1976; Economics and Business Degree, 1977); University of London, LSE (Master of Laws, 1983); International Faculty of Comparative Law, Strasbourg (Diplomé 3ème cycle, 1976). Member, Editorial Board, Revista Juridica de Catalunya. *Member:* Barcelona Bar Association; IBA; ASIL; Law Society of England and Wales. (Also at Barcelona Office). *LANGUAGES:* English, French and German.

(This Listing Continued)

ANTONIO CREUS, born Barcelona, Spain, October 24, 1959; admitted, 1984, Spain (Not admitted in Belgium). *Education:* University of Barcelona (Law Degree, 1981); University College of London (Master of Laws). Average Adjuster. *Member:* Barcelona Bar Association. *LANGUAGES:* English, Portuguese, French and Italian.

RESIDENT ASSOCIATES

J. RAMÓN G. GALLARDO, born Burgos, Spain, January 5, 1965; admitted, 1988, Spain; 1990, Brussels. *Education:* University of Valladolid (Law Degree, 1988); University Pontificia of Salamanca (Master in European Communities, 1989); Université Libre de Bruxelles (Licence Spéciale en Droit Européen, 1990). *LANGUAGES:* French and English.

(For complete biographical data on personnel at Barcelona, Bilbao, Madrid and Gerona, Spain, see Professional Biographies at those locations)

DE BACKER & ASSOCIES
BOULEVARD BRAND WHITLOCK 30
1200 BRUSSELS, BELGIUM
Telephone: (32-2) 735.00.43
Telecopier: (32-2) 734.14.39

Commercial, Corporate, Mergers and Acquisitions, Banking, European Community Law, Tax, International Business Transactions, Antitrust, Real Estate, Construction, Town Planning, Litigation, Intellectual Property, Media and Audiovisual, Administrative Law.

PARTNERS

JEAN-MARIE DE BACKER, born Brussels, Belgium, 1945; admitted, 1971, Brussels. *Education:* University of Louvain (Dr.Jur., 1971). Author: "La responsabilité des administrateurs de société," Duculot.

GEORGES VANDERSANDEN, born Brussels, Belgium, 1942; admitted, 1976, Brussels. *Education:* University of Brussels (Doc. Jur., 1966; Lic. Eur. Law, 1967). Professor, Institute of European Studies, University of Brussels and College of Europe, Bruges, 1980-1990. Visiting Professor, Center of European Studies, University of Nancy, France, 1978-1990. Vice President, Belgian Association for European Law. Member, Board of Editors, "Yearbook of European Law"; "Cahiers de droit européen." Co-Editor, "Le droit de la CEE," 15 Vol., Brussels. Author: "Contentieux communautaire," with A. Barav, Brussels, 1977; "Settlement of disputes - Administrative Tribunals, Boards and Commissions in International Organisations," Encyclopedia of International Law, 1981.

OLIVIER RALET, born Brussels, Belgium, 1957; admitted, 1980, Brussels. *Education:* University of Brussels (Lic, Jur., 1980; Lic. Econ. Law, 1981). Author: "La responsabilité des administrateurs de société," Duculot. Assistant Professor, University of Brussels, 1983-1988.

JEAN-PAUL HORDIES, born Brussels, Belgium, 1955; admitted, 1980, Brussels. *Education:* University of Brussels (Lic.Jur., 1980; Lic.Eur.-Law, 1984). Lecturer, European Law, University of Lyon III, 1989—.

MARC VANDEMEULEBROEKE, born Brussels, Belgium, 1954; admitted, 1980, Brussels. *Education:* University of Brussels (Lic.Jur., 1980; Lic.Econ.Law, 1981). *Member:* Nihonjinkai; Belgian-Japan Association (Director, 1993—).

DOMINIQUE BUYSSCHAERT, born Kortrijk, Belgium, 1954; admitted, 1978, Brussels. *Education:* University of Leuven (Lic.Jur., 1978). *Member:* A.I.J.A.

GEERT BOGAERT, born Izegem, Belgium, July 20, 1953; admitted, 1977, Brussels. *Education:* University of Leuven (Lic. Jur., 1977); John Hopkins University, Bologna, Italy (1978). Editor, Distributierecht-Droit de la distribution, Kluwer, 1993. Member, Belgian-Italian Chamber of Commerce (Director).

PASCAL HOLLANDER, born Brussels, Belgium, 1961; admitted, 1984, Brussels. *Education:* University of Brussels (Lic.Jur., 1984); University of Pennsylvania Law School (LL.M., 1986).

ANNE DELFOSSE, born Brussels, Belgium, 1952; admitted, 1975, Brussels. *Education:* University of Brussels (Lic.Jur., 1975).

CATHERINE HOUSSA, born Huy, Belgium, 1958; admitted, 1981, Brussels; 1989, Paris. *Education:* University of Louvain (Lic.Jur., 1981).

AGNES MAQUA, born Brussels, Belgium, 1958; admitted, 1984, Brussels. *Education:* University of Louvain (Lic.Jur., 1983).

(This Listing Continued)

ASSOCIATES

KARIN WILLEMS, born Ghent, Belgium, 1961; admitted, 1984, Ghent; 1987, Brussels. *Education:* University of Ghent (Lic.Jur., 1984); University of Edinburgh (British Council Scholarship, 1987).

PASCALE DEBLIQUY, born Mons, Belgium, 1963; admitted, 1985, Brussels. *Education:* University of Louvain (Lic. Jur., 1985).

JEAN-FRANÇOIS GOFFIN, born Waremme, Belgium, 1962; admitted, 1988, Brussels. *Education:* University of Louvain (Lic.Jur., 1985); University of Leyden (Lic.Int.Law, 1986); Cornell University School of Law (LL.M., 1994).

JEAN VAN STEENWINCKEL, born Brussels, Belgium, 1962; admitted, 1989, Brussels. *Education:* University of Brussels (Lic.Jur., 1986; Lic. Tax Law, 1987).

FRANÇOIS DE MONTPELLIER, born Brussels, Belgium, 1963; admitted, 1989, Brussels. *Education:* University of Brussels (Lic.Jur., 1987; Lic.Econ.Law, 1988).

CARL LEERMAKERS, born Paris, France, 1966; admitted, 1990, Brussels. *Education:* University of Leuven (Lic.Jur., 1989; Lic. Notarial Law, 1990).

LAURE LEVI, born Brussels, Belgium, 1966; admitted, 1990, Brussels. *Education:* University of Brussels (Lic. Jur., 1989); College of Europe, Bruges (Lic. Eur. Studies, 1990).

BEATRICE TOUSSAINT, born Lausanne, Switzerland, 1965; admitted, 1991, Brussels. *Education:* University of Louvain (Lic. Jur., 1989); University of Brussels (Lic. Eur. Law., 1990); King's College, London (British Council Scholarship, 1993).

JOËL FRANTZEN, born Brussels, Belgium, 1967; admitted, 1991, Brussels. *Education:* University of Louvain (Lic. Jur., 1991).

YVES VAN COUTER, born Deinze, Belgium, February 9, 1967; admitted, 1991, Brussels. *Education:* University of Gent (Lic. Jur., 1990); University of Louvain (Lic. Int. and Eur. Law, 1991); Georgetown University (LL.M., 1994).

YVAN T'SERSTEVENS, born Elisabethville, Congo, 1965; admitted, 1992, Brussels. *Education:* University of Brussels (Lic. Jur., 1990; Lic. Econ. Law, 1991).

DOMINIQUE FELTEN, born Vielsalm, Belgium, 1967; admitted, 1992, Brussels. *Education:* University of Liège (Lic. Jur., 1990; Lic. Eur. Law, 1992).

ALESSANDRA D'ANGELO, born Liege, Belgium, 1967; admitted, 1993, Brussels. *Education:* University of Louvain (Lic. Jur., 1991); University of Ghent (Lic. Eur. Law, 1992).

BRIGITTE SCHWERS, born Brussels, Belgium, 1964; admitted, 1993, Brussels. *Education:* University of Brussels (Lic. Jur., 1989; Lic. Eur. Law, 1990).

NATASHA WAUTHION, born Seoul, South Korea, 1966; admitted, 1994, Brussels. *Education:* University of Brussels (Lic. Jur., 1988).

CAROLINE FRANCQ, born Charleroi, Belgium, 1968; admitted, 1993, Brussels. *Education:* University of Louvain (Lic. Jur., 1991; Degree in Philosophy, 1992); University of Paris II Assas (DEA, Intellectual Property, 1992).

MARIE ZURSTRASSEN, born Verviers, Belgium, 1966; admitted, 1994, Brussels. *Education:* University of Liège (Lic.Jur., 1991); University of Brussels (Lic.Econ.Law, 1993).

PHILIPPE GERARD, born Namur, Belgium, 1968; admitted, 1994, Brussels. *Education:* University of Louvain (Lic.Jur., 1991); University of Leyden (Lic.Int. and Eur.Law, 1992). Assistant Professor, University of Namur, 1992—.

MARIE-ANGE MARX, born Maastricht, The Netherlands, 1969; admitted, 1994, Brussels. *Education:* University of Brussels (Lic.Jur., 1993); College of Europe, Bruges (Lic.Eur.Studies, 1994).

Languages: French, Dutch, English, German, Spanish, Italian and Japanese.

DE BANDT, VAN HECKE & LAGAE

RUE BRÉDERODE 13
B-1000 BRUSSELS, BELGIUM
Telephone: (32-2) 517.94.11
Telex: 25477 Lexlaw
Telecopier: (32-2) 517.94.94

REVISERS OF THE BELGIUM AND THE EUROPEAN
COMMUNITIES LAW DIGESTS FOR THIS DIRECTORY.

Antwerp, Belgium Office: Mechelsesteenweg 196, B-2018. Telephone: (32-3) 238.10.62. Telex: 71059 diurna b. Telecopier: (32-3) 216.47.17.

New York, N.Y. Office: 712 Fifth Avenue, New York, New York, 10019, U.S.A. Telephone: 212-801-3420. Telecopier: 212-801-3425.

London, England Office: Royex House, Aldermanbury Square, EC2V 7HR. Telephone: (44-171) 600.36.07. Telecopier: (44-171) 600.17.18.

General European and International Practice.
General Civil and Commercial Law, EC Law, International Transactions, Companies, Mergers and Acquisitions, Tax, Employment, Banking, Finance, Aircraft Leasing and Financing, Real Estate, Estate Planning, Construction Law, Intellectual Property, Telecommunications, Computer, Insurance, Transport, Public and Administrative Law, Environment, Litigation (including Supreme Court of Belgium and EC Court of Justice), Arbitration.
Member of Alliance of European Lawyers (EEIG) which regroups six law firms from Continental Europe. The Alliance consists of De Bandt, van Hecke & Lagae at Brussels and Antwerp; De Brauw Blackstone Westbroek at The Hague, Amsterdam, Rotterdam and Eindhoven; Jeantet & Associés at Paris and Warsaw; Lagerlöf & Leman at Stockholm, Gothenburg and Malmö; Oppenhoff & Rädler at Barlin, Cologne, Frankfurt am Main, Leipzig and Münich; Uria & Menendez at Madrid and Barcelona.
The Alliance member firms have joint offices at Brussels, London, New York and Prague.

MEMBERS OF THE FIRM

JEAN-PIERRE DE BANDT, born Antwerp, Belgium, January 23, 1934; admitted, 1956, Antwerp; 1969, Brussels. *Education:* University of Louvain (Dr. Jur., 1956; Lic. Econ. Sc., 1959; Lic. Pol. & Sc., 1961); Harvard Law School (LL.M., 1960).

JEAN-PIERRE LAGAE, born Ghent, Belgium, November 27, 1932; admitted, 1956, Ghent; 1972, Brussels. *Education:* University of Ghent (Dr. Jur., Lic. Not., 1956); Harvard Law School (LL.M., 1958; S.J.D., 1962).

CARL BEVERNAGE, born Portstewart, U.K., June 22, 1943; admitted, 1970, Courtrai; 1971, Brussels. *Education:* University of Louvain (Dr. Jur., 1967); Tulane University Law School (LL.M., 1968).

JEAN-MARIE NELISSEN GRADE, born Diest, Belgium, September 28, 1945; admitted, 1969, Brussels; 1982, Supreme Court. *Education:* University of Louvain (Dr. Jur., 1967; Lic. Econ. Sc., 1968; Ph.D. Legal Education, 1976).

ROEL NIEUWDORP, born Rotterdam, The Netherlands, March 14, 1943; admitted, 1974, Brussels. *Education:* University of Louvain (Dr. Jur., 1966); University of Pennsylvania Law School (LL.M., 1969).

IVO ONKELINX, born Lincent, Belgium, May 12, 1944; admitted, 1974, Brussels. *Education:* University of Louvain (Dr. Jur., 1967); Johns Hopkins University, Bologna Center (1968); Northwestern University Law School (LL.M., 1969); St. Aloysius School of Fiscal Sciences, Brussels (1972).

PATRICK L. KELLEY, born Toronto, Ohio, U.S.A., December 28, 1941; admitted, 1968, New York; 1981, Brussels. *Education:* Princeton University (A.B., 1963); London School of Economics (1963-1964); Harvard Law School (J.D., 1967).

JOHAN VERBIST, born Halle, Belgium, December 12, 1950; admitted, 1974, Brussels; 1988, Supreme Court. *Education:* University of Louvain (Lic. Jur., 1974); New York University Law School (LL.M., 1976).

BERNARD VAN DE WALLE DE GHELCKE, born Bruges, Belgium, May 23, 1947; admitted, 1972, Brussels. *Education:* University of Louvain (Lic. Jur., 1970; Lic. Eur. Law., 1973); University of Brussels (Lic. Ec. Law, 1972).

EUGÈNE H.C. TCHEN, born Neuilly-sur-Seine, France, July 4, 1951; admitted, 1978, Brussels. *Education:* University of Brussels (Lic. Jur., 1974; Lic. Pol. and Dipl. Sc., 1976); University of Michigan Law School (M.C.L., 1977).

(This Listing Continued)

DIRK LEERMAKERS, born Duffel, Belgium, December 25, 1955; admitted, 1979, Brussels; 1987, New York. *Education:* University of Louvain (Lic. Jur., 1978); McGill University Law School (LL.M., 1980).

CHRISTIAN WILLEMS, born Brussels, Belgium, March 7, 1954; admitted, 1978, Brussels. *Education:* University of Brussels (Lic. Jur., 1977); University of Michigan Law School (M.C.L., 1982).

THIERRY DENAYER, born Overyse, Belgium, January 20, 1955; admitted, 1980, Brussels. *Education:* University of Louvain (Lic. Jur., 1978); European Taxation, Amsterdam (1979-1980).

JEAN-PIERRE BLUMBERG, born Antwerp, Belgium, May 3, 1957; admitted, 1982, Brussels. *Education:* University of Louvain (Lic. Jur., 1980); Cambridge University (LL.M., 1981).

FRANÇOIS DE BAUW, born Brussels, Belgium, May 14, 1957; admitted, 1979, Brussels. *Education:* University of Louvain-la-Neuve (Lic. Jur., 1979).

JACQUES PÉRILLEUX, born Liège, Belgium, April 27, 1951; admitted, 1979, Brussels. *Education:* University of Liège (Lic. Jur., 1974); F.N.R.S. (1974-1979); McGill University Law School (LL.M., 1977); Harvard Law School (LL.M., 1977; S.J.D., 1981); Dr. Jur., Belgium (1982).

CHRIS SUNT, born Lier, Belgium, February 5, 1955; admitted, 1980, Brussels. *Education:* University of Ghent (Lic. Jur., 1978); Harvard Law School (LL.M., 1980).

CARL DE MEYER, born Louvain, Belgium, August 19, 1958; admitted, 1981, Louvain; 1987, Brussels. *Education:* University of Louvain (Lic. Jur., 1981); Georgetown University Law School (LL.M., 1986).

GUIDO DE WIT, born Louvain, Belgium, September 21, 1957; admitted, 1984, Brussels. *Education:* University of Louvain (Lic. Jur., 1980); Harvard Law School (LL.M., 1982).

GODELIEVE SWARTENBROUX, born Brussels, Belgium, July 14, 1959; admitted, 1983, Brussels. *Education:* University of Louvain (Lic. Jur., 1982); D.A.A.D., Düsseldorf (1983).

LUC VANAVERBEKE, born Etterbeek, Belgium, February 7, 1958; admitted, 1982, Brussels. *Education:* University of Louvain (Lic. Jur., 1981); University of Illinois College of Law (M.C.L., 1982).

GERWIN VAN GERVEN, born Louvain, Belgium, February 23, 1960; admitted, 1985, Brussels. *Education:* University of Louvain (Lic. Jur., 1982; Lic. Econ. Sc., 1983); Harvard Law School (LL.M., 1984).

FRANÇOISE LEFEVRE, born Charleroi, Belgium, December 9, 1958; admitted, 1981, Brussels. *Education:* University of Brussels (Lic. Jur., 1981); Cambridge University (LL.M., 1985).

PATRICK PEETERS, born Antwerp, Belgium, August 5, 1956; admitted, 1988, Brussels. *Education:* University Faculty of Antwerp (Lic. Jur., 1979; Dr. Jur., 1988).

LUTGARDE SOMMERIJNS, born Louvain, Belgium, September 11, 1962; admitted, 1986, Brussels; 1991, New York. *Education:* University of Louvain (Lic. Jur., 1985); Boalt Hall Law School, University of California at Berkeley (LL.M., 1986).

OF COUNSEL

GEORGES VAN HECKE, born Cambridge, U.K., May 10, 1915; admitted, 1942, Brussels; 1964, Supreme Court. *Education:* University of Louvain (Dr. Jur., 1936; Lic. Pol. & Dipl. Sc., 1938).

RUSEN ERGEC, born Istanbul, Turkey, January 3, 1952; admitted, 1991, Brussels. *Education:* University of Brussels (Lic. Pol. Sc., 1975; Lic. Internat. Law, 1976; Lic. Jur., 1981; Dr. Jur., 1986).

ASSOCIATES

PETER JACOB, born Antwerp, Belgium, September 30, 1960; admitted, 1986, Brussels. *Education:* University of Antwerp (Lic. Jur., 1983); College of Europe, Bruges (Dipl. Eur. Studies, 1984).

ERIC POTTIER, born Liège, Belgium, May 1, 1962; admitted, 1985, Brussels. *Education:* University of Liège (Lic. Jur., 1985); Cambridge University (LL.M., 1992).

HENK VANHULLE, born Brugge, Belgium, November 5, 1962; admitted, 1986, Brussels. *Education:* University of Louvain (Lic. Jur., 1985); University of Illinois College of Law (LL.M., 1989).

LUCIE LAMBRECHT, born Torhout, Belgium, June 7, 1963; admitted, 1987, Brussels. *Education:* University of Louvain (Lic. Jur., 1986); London School of Economics (LL.M., 1987).

(This Listing Continued)

MARNIX VAN KEIRSBILCK, born Ostend, Belgium, May 3, 1960; admitted, 1988, California; 1991, Brussels. *Education:* University of Louvain (Lic. Jur., 1983; Lic. Econ. Sc., 1986); Harvard Law School (LL.M., 1986).

CATHARINA VAN SANTVLIET, born Lier, Belgium, July 28, 1963; admitted, 1987, Brussels. *Education:* University of Louvain (Lic. Jur., 1986); University of Aix-en-Provence (D.E.S.S., 1987); Harvard Law School (LL.M., 1989).

ELS KINDT, born Brugge, Belgium, May 31, 1964; admitted, 1989, Brussels. *Education:* University of Louvain (Lic. Jur., 1987); University of Georgia Law School (LL.M., 1988).

EDDY LIEVENS, born Ostend, Belgium, April 21, 1960; admitted, 1994, Brussels. *Education:* University of Brussels (Lic. Jur., 1983).

TANGUY VAN OVERSTRAETEN, born Braine-l'Alleud, Belgium, October 12, 1964; admitted, 1987, Brussels. *Education:* University of Brussels (Lic. Jur., 1987); University of Chicago Law School (LL.M., 1991).

LUC VERMEIRE, born Kortrijk, Belgium, November 7, 1963; admitted, 1987, Brussels. *Education:* University of Antwerp (Lic. Jur., 1986).

CAROLINE DOCCLO, born Ath, Belgium, June 8, 1962; admitted, 1987, Brussels. *Education:* University of Brussels (Lic. Jur., 1985); New York University Law School (LL.M., 1994).

KOEN PLATTEAU, born St-Agatha-Berchem, Belgium, August 25, 1963; admitted, 1988, Brussels. *Education:* University of Ghent (Lic. Jur., 1986); University of Brussels (Lic. Eur. Law, 1987); The American University, Washington, D.C. (LL.M., 1988).

GEERT LOWAGIE, born Varsenare, Belgium, January 29, 1964; admitted, 1988, Brussels. *Education:* University of Ghent (Lic. Jur., 1987); London School of Economics (LL.M., 1993).

MARTINE DE ROECK, born Wilrijk, Belgium, December 7, 1965; admitted, 1989, Brussels. *Education:* University of Antwerp (Lic. Jur., 1988); University of Chicago Law School (LL.M., 1989).

HENRI DELWAIDE, born Liége, Belgium, April 6, 1965; admitted, 1988, Brussels. *Education:* University of Liége (Lic. Jur., 1987); Harvard Law School (LL.M., 1992).

MARIEKE WYCKAERT, born Brussels, Belgium, September 25, 1961; admitted, 1985, Brussels. *Education:* University of Louvain (Lic. Jur., 1984); Boalt Hall Law School, University of California at Berkeley (LL.M., 1985).

JEAN-CHRISTOPHE TROUSSEL, born Ixelles, Belgium, July 19, 1965; admitted, 1988, Brussels. *Education:* University of Louvain-la-Neuve (Lic. Jur., 1988); University of Chicago Law School (LL.M., 1994).

DIDIER LECLERCQ, born Uccle, Belgium, April 6, 1965; admitted, 1989, Brussels. *Education:* University of Louvain-la-Neuve (Lic. Jur., 1988); University of Illinois College of Law (LL.M., 1989).

DOMINIQUE PIRET, born Charleroi, Belgium, January 13, 1964; admitted, 1989, Brussels. *Education:* University of Louvain-la-Neuve (Lic. Jur., 1989).

JAN VANDEMAELE, born Wevelgem, Belgium, January 19, 1966; admitted, 1989, Brussels. *Education:* University of Ghent (Lic. Jur., 1989); London School of Economics (LL.M., 1992).

VINCENT MACQ, born Uccle, Belgium, July 3, 1965; admitted, 1989, Brussels. *Education:* University of Louvain-la-Neuve (Lic. Jur., 1988); Georgetown University Law School (LL.M., 1991).

FRANCESCA ROMANA CROTTI, born Rome, Italy, June 12, 1966; admitted, 1990, Brussels. *Education:* University of Brussels (Lic. Jur., 1989); London School of Economics (LL.M., 1990).

OLIVIER VAN ERMENGEM, born Lier, Belgium, December 6, 1964; admitted, 1988, Brussels. *Education:* University of Louvain (Lic. Jur., 1988).

JOOST VERLINDEN, born Heist-op-den-Berg, October 9, 1965; admitted, 1991, Brussels. *Education:* University of Louvain (Lic. Jur., 1988); D.A.A.D., Düsseldorf (1991).

WIM BOSSENS, born Brussels, Belgium, December 24, 1962; admitted, 1991, Brussels. *Education:* University of Louvain (Lic. Jur., 1986).

JACQUES RICHELLE, born Uccle, Belgium, May 29, 1962; admitted, 1990, Brussels. *Education:* University of Brussels (Lic. Jur., 1988); Southern Methodist University Law School (LL.M., 1989).

(This Listing Continued)

ANNE-CLAIRE SCHEPENS, born Brussels, Belgium, June 19, 1963; admitted, 1988, Brussels. *Education:* University of Louvain-la-Neuve (Lic. Jur., 1986); Georgetown University Law School (LL.M., 1989).

FLIP PETILLION, born Ieper, Belgium, June 6, 1963; admitted, 1988, Brussels. *Education:* University of Louvain (Lic. Jur., 1987).

YVES MOREAU, born Liège, Belgium, August 6, 1965; admitted, 1990, Brussels. *Education:* University of Liège (Lic. Jur., 1988); University of Louvain (Lic. Not., 1989).

ANN MONSAERT, born Ghent, Belgium, October 9, 1966; admitted, 1990, Brussels. *Education:* University of Ghent (Lic. Jur., 1989); University of Nancy (D.E.S.E., 1990).

VINCENT DE DORLODOT, born Luxembourg, Grand-duchy of Luxembourg, March 23, 1965; admitted, 1990, Brussels. *Education:* University of Louvain-la-Neuve (Lic. Jur., 1988); Duke University Law School (LL.M., 1994).

JAN VAN LANCKER, born Ghent, Belgium, February 22, 1966; admitted, 1989, Brussels. *Education:* University of Ghent (Lic. Jur., 1989); University of Michigan Law School (LL.M., 1992).

CHRISTIAAN NYS, born Bonheiden, Belgium, May 24, 1967; admitted, 1990, Brussels. *Education:* University of Louvain (Lic. Jur., 1990).

BRIAN BAEL, born Brussels, Belgium, December 17, 1966; admitted, 1990, Brussels. *Education:* University of Brussels (Lic. Jur., 1989; Lic. Labour Law, 1990).

YVES BROSENS, born Hoogstraten, Belgium, December 16, 1965; admitted, 1990, Brussels. *Education:* University of Louvain (Lic. Jur., 1989); University of Louvain-la-Neuve (Lic. Econ. Law, 1990); University of Georgia Law School (LL.M., 1992).

VINCENT MIGNON, born Ixelles, Belgium, September 5, 1963; admitted, 1990, Brussels. *Education:* University of Louvain (Lic. Jur., 1989); University of Georgia Law School (LL.M., 1993).

DANIEL MISEUR, born Mechelen, Belgium, October 7, 1963; admitted, 1990, Brussels. *Education:* University of Brussels (Lic. Jur., 1989).

PHILIP VAN CAENEGEM, born Zottegem, Belgium, March 20, 1967; admitted, 1991, Brussels. *Education:* University of Louvain (Lic. Jur., 1989); University Laval, Quebec, Canada (LL.M., 1991).

SARAH WIJNS, born Tongeren, Belgium, September 3, 1965; admitted, 1991, Brussels. *Education:* University of Brussels (Lic. Jur., 1988); University of New Hampshire, Franklin Pierce Law Center (LL.M., 1990).

THIERRY LOHEST, born Ixelles, Belgium, October 17, 1966; admitted, 1991, Brussels. *Education:* University of Louvain-la-Neuve (Lic. Jur., 1989); Duke University Law School (LL.M., 1991).

GENEVIEVE MICHAUX, born Namur, Belgium, February 7, 1966; admitted, 1988, Brussels. *Education:* University of Brussels (Lic. Jur., 1988).

KAZUHIKO YAMAGISHI, born Tokyo, Japan, April 19, 1956; admitted, 1984, Tokyo (Not admitted in Belgium). *Education:* Chuo University (LL.B., 1979); University of Michigan Law School (LL.M., 1993).

ELS PONNET, born Zottegem, Belgium, June 28, 1965; admitted, 1992, Brussels. *Education:* University of Ghent (Lic. Jur., 1988); University of Brussels (Lic. Eur. Law, 1989).

ANTOINE HENRY DE FRAHAN, born Schaerbeek, Belgium, May 21, 1964; admitted, 1992, Brussels. *Education:* University of Brussels (Lic. Jur., 1990); Columbia University Law School (LL.M., 1992).

MICHEL MILDE, born Brussels, Belgium, June 5, 1965; admitted, 1991, Brussels. *Education:* University of Louvain-la-Neuve (Lic. Jur., 1989); University of Brussels (Lic. Labor Law, 1990).

ERIK CASSELMAN, born Louvain, Belgium, July 1, 1967; admitted, 1991, Brussels. *Education:* University of Louvain (Lic. Jur., 1990); D.A.A.D., Düsseldorf (1991).

JEAN-FRANCOIS WILLAME, born Berkeley, California, U.S.A., May 15, 1965; admitted, 1991, Brussels. *Education:* University of Louvain (Lic. Jur., 1988); University of Leiden (Cert. Int. Law, 1989); Duke University Law School (LL.M., 1992).

PATRICK A. DE RIDDER, born Leuven, Belgium, February 9, 1965; admitted, 1990, Brussels. *Education:* University of Leuven (Lic. Jur., 1990); University of Virginia (LL.M., 1992).

(This Listing Continued)

DE BANDT, VAN **HECKE & LAGAE,** Brussels—
Continued

JOSE-BENJAMIN LONGREE, born Verviers, Belgium, March 7, 1968; admitted, 1993, Brussels. *Education:* University of Liège (Lic. Jur., 1991); University of East Anglia (LL.M., 1992).

SERGEY MILANOV, born Karnobat, Bulgaria, April 23, 1961; admitted, 1993, New York (Not admitted in Belgium). *Education:* University of Sofia (Lic. Jur., 1988); Harvard Law School (LL.M., 1992).

KOEN VAN DE CASTEELE, born Kortrijk, Belgium, August 14, 1968; admitted, 1992, Brussels. *Education:* University of Louvain (Lic. Jur., 1991); College of Europe, Bruges (Adv. Eur. Studies, 1992).

BENEDICT GEERS, born Deinze, Belgium, February 15, 1968; admitted, 1992, Brussels. *Education:* University of Louvain (Lic. Jur., 1992); University of Illinois College of Law (LL.M., 1994).

HUGO DE MAERTELAERE, born St. Amandsberg, Belgium, April 26, 1968; admitted, 1992, Brussels. *Education:* University of Louvain (Lic. Jur., 1991); University of Ghent (Vlerick School, Dipl. in Management, 1992).

AN BEATRIJS VAN DAMME, born Ghent, Belgium, February 17, 1969; admitted, 1993, Brussels. *Education:* University of Louvain (Lic. Jur., 1992).

ERIK BOMANS, born Hasselt, Belgium, September 20, 1968; admitted, 1993, Brussels. *Education:* University of Louvain (Lic. Jur., 1991); Johns Hopkins University, Bologna Center (1992), Washington D.C. (M.A., 1993).

CHRISTIAAN FRANCK, born Louvain, Belgium, November 7, 1968; admitted, 1993, Brussels. *Education:* University of Louvain (Lic. Jur., 1991); D.A.A.D., Düsseldorf (1993).

PATRICK GEORTAY, born Etterbeek, Belgium, September 22, 1969; admitted, 1993, Brussels. *Education:* University of Liège (Lic. Jur., 1992); University of Leicester (LL.M., 1993).

BENOIT WALTREGNY, born Liège, Belgium, July 18, 1969; admitted, 1993, Brussels. *Education:* University of Liège (Lic. Jur., 1992); University of East Anglia (LL.M., 1993).

CHRISTIAN VAN DER STICHELE, born Luxembourg, Grand Duchy of Luxembourg, July 27, 1969; admitted, 1993, Brussels. *Education:* McGill University Law School (LL.B., 1992); University of Louvain (Lic. Jur., 1993).

FRANCIS VAN NUFFEL, born Wilrijk, Belgium, October 3, 1968; admitted, 1993, Brussels. *Education:* University of Antwerp (Lic. Jur., 1991).

INGE LAMBERTS, born Mortsel, Belgium, February 19, 1969; admitted, 1993, Brussels. *Education:* University of Louvain (Lic. Jur., 1992); University of Montpellier (D.E.A., 1993).

LAURENT RUZETTE, born Etterbeek, Belgium, September 23, 1969; admitted, 1993, Brussels. *Education:* University of Louvain-la-Neuve (Lic. Jur., 1992).

VALERIE MOORS, born Verviers, Belgium, October 2, 1970; admitted, 1993, Brussels. *Education:* University of Liège (Lic. Jur., 1993).

FREDERIC DEPOORTERE, born Ghent, Belgium, May 26, 1970; admitted, 1993, Brussels. *Education:* University of Louvain (Lic. Jur., 1993).

BRUNO VAN HEES, born Rocourt, Belgium, December 3, 1967; admitted, 1994, Brussels. *Education:* University of Liège (Lic. Jur., 1991); University of Essex (LL.M., 1993).

OLIVIER VAN CAUSENBROECK, born Gent, Belgium, April 4, 1970; admitted, 1994, Belgium. *Education:* University of Ghent (Lic. Jur., 1993); Harvard Law School (LL.M., 1994).

WERNER VAN LEMBERGEN, born Dendermonde, Belgium, April 10, 1967; admitted, 1994, Brussels. *Education:* University of Louvain (Lic.-Jur., 1991); Institute of International Studies, Geneva (D.E.S., 1993); University of Chicago Law School (LL.M., 1994).

DIDIER DEWYN, born Kortrijk, Belgium, January 15, 1969; admitted, 1993, Brussels. *Education:* University of Louvain (Lic. Jur., 1992).

(This Listing Continued)

XAVIER REUMONT, born Uccle, Belgium, October 14, 1970; admitted, 1994, Brussels. *Education:* University of Louvain (Lic. Jur., 1993); Harvard Law School (LL.M., 1994).

FREDERIC MEESSEN, born Verviers, Belgium, September 16, 1969; admitted, 1994, Brussels. *Education:* University of Liège (Lic. jur., 1992); University of Brussels (Lic. Econ. Law, 1994).

BASTIAAN BRUYNDONCKX, born Tervuren, Belgium, January 27, 1971; admitted, 1994, Brussels. *Education:* University of Louvain (Lic. Jur., 1994).

PHILIPPE DECHAMPS, born Verviers, Belgium, May 6, 1970; admitted, 1994, Brussels. *Education:* University of Louvain (Lic. Jur., 1993).

STEFAAN RAES, born Wilrijk, Belgium, April 9, 1957; admitted, 1981, Brussels. *Education:* University of Louvain (Lic. Jur., 1980); University of Chicago Law School (LL.M., 1981).

MARIE-CHRISTINE JANSSENS, born Deurne, Belgium, July 10, 1958; admitted, 1981, Brussels. *Education:* University of Louvain (Lic. Jur., 1981; Lic. History of Arts, 1981).

ANNE WALLEMACQ, born Charleroi, Belgium, June 23, 1966; admitted, 1990, Brussels. *Education:* University of Louvain-la-Neuve (Lic. Jur., 1989); University of Leiden (International and European Law, 1990).

LUC J. WINTGENS, born Schoten, Belgium, April 19, 1959; admitted, 1991, Brussels. *Education:* University of Louvain (Lic. Jur., 1982; Lic. Ph., 1985; Dr. Jur., 1990); Centre de Philosphie du Droit de Paris (Diploma, 1984); Yale Law School (LL.M., 1990).

GUIDO VAN LIMBERGHEN, born Asse, Belgium, February 15, 1961; admitted, 1991, Brussels. *Education:* University of Brussels (Lic. Jur., 1984; Lic. Not., 1985; Lic. Labor Law, 1986; Dr. Jur., 1989).

BEATRIX VANLERBERGHE, born Kortrijk, Belgium, May 10, 1967; admitted, 1991, Belgium. *Education:* University of Louvain (Lic. Jur., 1990); University of Essex (LL.M., 1991).

Languages: English, French, Dutch, German, Italian, Japanese

REVISERS OF THE BELGIUM AND THE EUROPEAN COMMUNITIES LAW DIGESTS FOR THIS DIRECTORY.

STUDIO LEGALE DE BERTI & JACCHIA

Established in 1990

AVENUE DU DIAMANT, 139
B-1040 BRUSSELS, BELGIUM
Telephone: 32-2-7353520
Facsimile: 32-2-7321985

Milan, Italy Office: Foro Buonaparte, 20, I-20121. Telephone: (39-2) 809486. Facsimile: (39-2) 8900391/864088. Telex: 310295 Dejalx I.

Rome, Italy Office: Lungotevere del Mellini, 10, I-00193. Telephone: (39-6) 3613489/3227419. Facsimile: (39-6) 3200824.

European Law, Italian and General International Practice.

RESIDENT ATTORNEYS

Massimo Moretto   **Francesco Torelli**

(For Complete List of Firm Personnel, see Professional Biographies at Milan, Italy).

DE BRAUW BLACKSTONE WESTBROEK

Attorneys and Civil Law Notaries

BREDERODESTRAAT 13A
B-1000 BRUSSELS, BELGIUM
Telephone: (2) 505 0211
Telecopier: (2) 502 2644

REVISERS OF THE NETHERLANDS LAW DIGEST FOR THIS DIRECTORY.

The Hague, The Netherlands Office: Zuid Hollandlaan 7, 2596 AL. Telephone: (70) 328 5 328. Telex: 32321. Telecopier: (70) 328 5 325.

Amsterdam, The Netherlands Office: Atrium - 7th Floor, Strawinskylaan 3115, 1077 ZX. Telephone: (20) 5 481 481. Telex: 10227. Telecopier: (20) 5 481 485.

(This Listing Continued)

Rotterdam, The Netherlands Office: 10th Floor, Coolsingel 139, 3012 AG. Telephone: (10) 401 88 99. Telex: 24676. Telecopier: (10) 411 35 48.

Eindhoven, The Netherlands Office: Parklaan 42a, 5613 BG. Telephone: (40)) 464442. Telecopier (40) 466288.

London, England Office: Royex House, Aldermanbury Square, EC2V 7HR. Telephone: (171) 600 1719. Fax: (171) 600 1718.

New York, New York Office: 712 Fifth Avenue, 30th Floor, 10019-4102. Telephone: (212) 801-3430. Fax: (212) 801-3435; (212) 801-3436.

Dutch Attorneys may represent clients before all Dutch Courts, before the European Court of Justice and the Benelux Court of Justice, and are admitted to plead before all Courts of the member states of the Common Market (EEC).

Member of Alliance of European Lawyers (EEIG) which regroups six law firms from Continental Europe. The Alliance consists of Oppenhoff & Rädler at Munich, Berlin, Cologne, Frankfurt am Main and Leipzig; De Bandt, van Hecke & Lagae at Brussels and Antwerp; DeBrauw Blackstone Westbroek at Amsterdam, The Hague, Rotterdam, Brussels, London and New York; Jeantet & Associés at Paris and Warsaw; Lagerlöf & Leman at Stockholm, Gothenburg and Malmö; Uria & Menendez at Madrid and Barcelona.

The Alliance member firms have joint offices at Brussels, London, New York and Prague.

ATTORNEY AT LAW
MEMBERS OF FIRM

LOUIS H. VAN LENNEP, born 1948; admitted, 1973, The Hague (Not admitted in Belgium). *Education:* Leyden University. Member, Board of Directors of Netherlands Institute of International Relations 'Clingendael'. *LANGUAGES:* English, French and German. *PRACTICE AREAS:* EC Law.

ERIK H. PIJNACKER HORDIJK, born 1958; admitted, 1983, Amsterdam (Not admitted in Belgium). *Education:* Utrecht University. *Member:* International Bar Association; Dutch Association for European Law. *LANGUAGES:* English, French and German. *PRACTICE AREAS:* EC Law.

ASSOCIATES

MONIQUE T.P.J. VAN OERS, born 1966; admitted, 1990, The Hague (Not admitted in Belgium). *Education:* Limburg University. *LANGUAGES:* English and French. *PRACTICE AREAS:* EC Law.

ANNETJE T. OTTOW, born 1965; admitted, 1990, The Hague (Not admitted in Belgium). *Education:* Leyden University. *LANGUAGES:* English, French and German. *PRACTICE AREAS:* EC Law.

NICO A.J. BEL, born 1963; admitted, 1990, Amsterdam. *Education:* Leyden University.

MARC G.A.M. CUSTERS, born 1965; admitted, 1993, The Hague. *Education:* Nijmegen University.

REVISERS OF THE NETHERLANDS LAW DIGEST FOR THIS DIRECTORY.

(For list of Partners and Counsel of the respective Member Firms see Professional Biographies at: Oppenhoff & Rädler at Munich, Cologne, Frankfurt am Main, Berlin and Leipzig, Germany; De Bandt van Hecke & Lagae at Brussels and Antwerp, Belgium; De Brauw Blackstone Westbroek at The Hague, Rotterdam and Amsterdam, Eindhoven, The Netherlands; Jeantet & Associés, at Paris, France and Warsaw, Poland; Lagerlöf & Leman at Stockholm, Gothenburg and Malmö, Sweden; Uria & Menendez at Madrid and Barcelona, Spain)

DE CALUWE & DIERYCK

BRUSSELS, BELGIUM

(See De Caluwe, Putzeys, 'T Kint, Van Fraeyenhoven et Associés)

General Practice. Antitrust, Arbitration, Civil, Competition, Corporate, Criminal, EEC, Family, Food and Drug, Tax, Industrial Property, Insurance, Intellectual Property, Labor, Maritime, Transport Law, Public Contracts and Public Law.

DE CALUWE, PUTZEYS, 'T KINT, VAN FRAEYENHOVEN
ET ASSOCIÉS

Established in 1957

98, RUE SAINT-BERNARD
B-1060 BRUSSELS, BELGIUM
Telephone: 32 (2) 5365811
Telefax: 32 (2) 5365911

Antwerp, Belgium Office: Dieryck, Van Looveren & Co. Korte Lozanastraat, 20-26, B-2018. Telephone: 32 (3) 2387850; 2379896. Telefax: 32 (3) 2379899.

General Commercial Practice (Belgian and International), Antitrust, Arbitration, Civil, Competition, Corporate, Criminal, EEC, Family, Food and Drug, Tax, Industrial Property, Insurance, Intellectual Property, Labor, Maritime, Transport Law, Public Contracts and Public Law, Banking.

PARTNERS

AIMÉ DE CALUWE, born Anderlecht, Belgium, 1920; admitted, 1944, Brussels. *Education:* University of Louvain (Dr. Jur., 1942). Author: "Le droit de la Concurrence: Les Pratiques du Commerce"; "Afbetalingsovereenkomsten". *LANGUAGES:* French, Dutch, English, German. *PRACTICE AREAS:* Antitrust; European Law; Competition; Industrial Property.

ANDRÉ DUMONT, born Antwerp, Belgium, 1926; admitted, 1954, Brussels. *Education:* University of Louvain (Dr. Jur., 1954). *LANGUAGES:* French, Dutch. *PRACTICE AREAS:* Criminal Law; Civil Law.

MICHEL GODIN, born Ixelles, Belgium, 1933; admitted, 1956, Brussels. *Education:* University of Brussels (Dr. Jur., 1956). Author: "Les Sociétés Coopératives". *LANGUAGES:* French, Dutch. *PRACTICE AREAS:* Labour Law; Civil Law.

JACQUES PUTZEYS, born Engis, Belgium, 1927; admitted, 1951, Brussels. *Education:* University of Louvain (Dr. Jur., 1951). Author: Revue "Administration Publique"; "Droit des Transports et Droit Maritime," 1984; ". Le Contrat de Transport Routier de Marchandises". Em. Professor, University of Louvain, 1969-1993. *LANGUAGES:* Dutch, French, English, German. *PRACTICE AREAS:* Public Law; Insurance; Transport and Maritime Law.

GEORGES CARLE, born Etterbeek, Belgium, 1937; admitted, 1961, Brussels. *Education:* University of Louvain (Dr. Jur., 1961). *LANGUAGES:* French, Dutch, English. *PRACTICE AREAS:* General Commercial Practice; Arbitration; Mergers and Acquisitions.

A. CLAUDE DELCORDE, born Etterbeek, Belgium, 1942; admitted, 1965, Brussels. *Education:* University of Louvain (Dr. Jur., 1965; Cert. Economic Sciences, 1966). Author: "Le Droit de la Concurrence: Les Pratiques du Commerce"; "Le droit de la concurrence: La loi belge sur les brevets". *LANGUAGES:* French, Dutch, English. *PRACTICE AREAS:* Industrial Property; Real Estate.

HENRI DEVOGELE, born Anderlecht, Belgium, 1935; admitted, 1958, Brussels. *Education:* University of Louvain (Dr. Jur., 1958). *LANGUAGES:* French, Dutch. *PRACTICE AREAS:* General Practice.

STÉPHANIE GEHLEN, born Luxembourg (G.D.L.), 1943; admitted, 1970, Brussels. *Education:* University of Louvain (Dr. Jur., 1966). *LANGUAGES:* French, Dutch, English. *PRACTICE AREAS:* Environmental Law; Public Law.

MICHEL GODHAIRD, born Etterbeek, Belgium, 1942; admitted, 1966, Brussels. *Education:* University of Louvain (Dr. Jur., 1966). Author: "Le Bail Commercial," (Répertoire Notarial). *LANGUAGES:* French, Dutch, English. *PRACTICE AREAS:* Civil Law; Corporate.

XAVIER LEURQUIN, born Uccle, Belgium, 1943; admitted, 1967, Brussels. *Education:* University of Louvain (Dr. Jur., 1967; Lic. EEC-Law, 1969). Author: "Le Droit de la Concurrence: Les Pratiques du Commerce". *LANGUAGES:* French, Dutch, English. *PRACTICE AREAS:* Public Contracts; Competition.

BERNARD DE CLIPPEL, born Antwerp, Belgium, 1948; admitted, 1970, Brussels. *Education:* University of Louvain (Dr. Jur., 1970). *LANGUAGES:* French, Dutch. *PRACTICE AREAS:* Tax Law.

ALBERT COOLEN, born Charleroi, Belgium, 1949; admitted, 1972, Brussels. *Education:* University of Louvain (Lic. Jur., 1972). Author: "Le Contrat de transport routier de marchandises". *LANGUAGES:* French, Dutch. *PRACTICE AREAS:* Transport LAW.

(This Listing Continued)

DE CALUWE, PUTZEYS, 'T KINT, VAN FRAEYENHOVEN ET ASSOCIÉS, Brussels—Continued

HERMAN LEMAIRE, born Leuven, Belgium, 1948; admitted, 1973, Brussels. *Education:* University of Louvain (Lic. jur., 1972). *LANGUAGES:* French, Dutch, English, German, Spanish. *PRACTICE AREAS:* General Commercial Practice; Mergers and Acquisitions; Banking.

BERNADETTE DE GRAEUWE D' AOUST, born Uccle, Belgium, 1950; admitted, 1974, Brussels. *Education:* University of Louvain (Lic.juris., 1974). *LANGUAGES:* French, Dutch, English. *PRACTICE AREAS:* Food and Drugs; Competition.

MARC MARLIERE, born Uccle, Belgium, 1956; admitted, 1979, Brussels. *Education:* University of Louvain (Lic.juris., 1979); Ecole Supérieure des Sciences Fiscales (Certificate, 1983). *LANGUAGES:* French, Dutch. *PRACTICE AREAS:* Tax Law.

Languages: Dutch, English, French, German, Italian and Spanish.

DECHERT PRICE & RHOADS

65 AVENUE LOUISE
1050 BRUSSELS, BELGIUM
Telephone: (02) 535-5411
Telefax: (02) 535-5400

Philadelphia, Pennsylvania: 4000 Bell Atlantic Tower, 1717 Arch Street, 19103-2793. Telephone: 215-994-4000.

New York, N.Y.: 477 Madison Avenue, 10022. Telephone: 212-326-3500.

Washington, D.C.: 1500 K Street, N.W., 20005. Telephone: 202-626-3300.

Harrisburg, Pennsylvania: Thirty North Third Street, 17101. Telephone: 717-237-2000.

Princeton, N.J.: Princeton Pike Corporate Center, P.O. Box 5218, 08543-5218. Telephone: 609-520-3200.

Boston, Massachusetts: Ten Post Office Square South, 02109. Telephone: 617-728-7100.

London, England: 2 Serjeants' Inn, EC4Y 1LT. Telephone: (0171) 583-5353. (Also see Titmuss Sainer Dechert).

Firm engaged in General and International Commercial Law Practice, European Communities Law, Belgian and U.S. Law.

RESIDENT PARTNERS

BERNARD E. AMORY, born Brussels, Belgium, 1958; admitted, 1984, Brussels. *Education:* University of Louvain (Licence en Droit, cum laude, 1981); University of Exeter (LL.M., 1983). Administrator, Competition Directorate, Commission of the European Communities, 1989-1991. Adjunct Professor, Law Faculty of the University of Namur, Belgium. *PRACTICE AREAS:* EC Law; Antitrust Law; Telecommunications Law.

RICHARD J. TEMKO, born Washington, D.C., 1949; admitted, 1975, New York; 1976, District of Columbia. *Education:* Williams College (B.A., 1972); Columbia University (J.D., 1974). *PRACTICE AREAS:* International Banking Law; Corporate Law; Taxation Law.

RESIDENT ASSOCIATES

PIERRE PHILIPPE BERTHE, born Washington, D.C., 1964; admitted, 1989, Brussels. *Education:* University of Brussels (Licence en Droit, 1989); University of Chicago Law School (LL.M., 1991).

STANISLAS DE PEUTER, born Turnhout, Belgium, 1961; admitted, 1987, Brussels. *Education:* Catholic University of Leuven (Licentie in de Rechten, 1984); Gemeentelijke Universiteit Amsterdam (LL.M., 1985).

JEAN-PIERRE LENAERTS, born Liege, Belgium, 1962; admitted, 1995, Brussels. *Education:* University of Liege (Licence en Droit, 1985; Licence Speciale en Droit Fiscal, 1989; Diplôme d'Economie et de Gestion, 1991).

ISABELLE MAHNAZ RAHMAN, born New York, N.Y., 1964; admitted, 1988, England. *Education:* University of Paris (License en Droit, 1985); University of Oxford (B.A., Jurisprudence, 1987).

URSULA SCHLIESSNER, born Giessen, Germany, 1961; admitted, 1989, Germany. *Education:* Ludwigs-Maximilians University, Munich (Referendar, 1986) (Assessor, 1989). With EC Commission DG XI, Directorate General Environment, Consumer Protection and Nuclear Safety, 1988-1989. Member, Advisory Board BNA-World Pharmaceuticals Report.

(This Listing Continued)

ALEXANDRE VERHEYDEN, born Beloeil, Belgium, 1967; admitted, 1990, Brussels. *Education:* University of Louvain (Licence en Droit, summa cum laude, 1990); University of Chicago Law School (LL.M., 1992). Assistant, Faculty of Law, University of Louvain.

Languages: French, Dutch, German and Portuguese.

(Members of the Firm, Counsel, Of Counsel, and Associates in Philadelphia and Harrisburg, Pennsylvania, New York, New York, Washington, D.C., Boston, Massachusetts, Princeton, New Jersey and London, England are listed in Biographical Section respectively)

DENTON HALL

A Member of the Denton International Group of Law Firms

RUE DU MARTEAU 15
1040 BRUSSELS, BELGIUM
Telephone: 32-2 223 0621
Telex: 69110
Fax: 32-2 223 0482

Other Offices: London, England; Milton Keynes, Buckinghamshire, England; Beijing, People's Republic of China; Hong Kong; Los Angeles, California; Singapore; Tokyo, Japan; Moscow, Russia.

Associated Offices: Amsterdam, Berlin, Chemnitz, Copenhagen, Dusseldorf, Frankfurt, Hamburg, Prague, Rotterdam and Vienna.

PARTNERS

ANDREW WATSON. LANGUAGES: French. *PRACTICE AREAS:* Competition and EC.

DAVID AITMAN (Also at London, England Office). *LANGUAGES:* French. *PRACTICE AREAS:* Competition and EC.

(For all Firm Personnel, see Professional Biographies at London, England).

DERINGER TESSIN HERRMANN & SEDEMUND

PLACE DES BARRICADES 13
B-1000 BRUSSELS, BELGIUM
Telephone: 32-2-219 82 50
Telefax: 32-2-219 88 32

Cologne, Germany Office: Heumarkt 14, D-50667 Cologne. Telephone: 49-221-205070. Telefax: 49-221-2050790. Telex: 8 881 356 ELAW D.

Frankfurt/Main Germany Office: Bockenheimer Landstraße 51-53, D-60325 Frankfurt a.M. Telephone 49-69-971090-0. Telefax: 49-69-971090-90.

Leipzig, Germany Office: Burgplatz 2, D-04109 Leipzig. Telephone: 49-341-711590. Telefax: 49-341-7115999.

Moscow, Russia Office: Ul. Bolschaja Ordynka 21, RF-113035 Moscow. Telephone: 7-095-2332450, 2315403. Telefax: 7-095-2334355.

General EC including Competition, Merger Control, Trade, Dumping, Foodstuffs, Environmental, Pharmaceutical, Agricultural and Subsidies Law. Belgian Corporate, Commercial, Industrial and Intellectual Property Rights Law. German Law Practice.

PARTNERS

DR. FRANK MONTAG, born Siegen, Germany, June 25, 1957; admitted, 1986, Cologne (Not admitted in Belgium). *Education:* United World College of the Atlantic, Wales (I.B., 1976); University of Bonn (Referendar, 1981; Dr. jur., 1984); University of Georgia, U.S.A. (LL.M., 1982). Author: "International Agreements with Preliminary Effects," Berlin, 1986; "International Organizations for the Research and Exploitation of Outer Space," Kaiser/v. Welck (eds.); "Outer Space and International Politics," Bonn, 1987; "The External Dimension of the Internal Market," EuZW, pp. 112-117,1990; "Basic Principles of EC-Merger Control," IWB, pp. 681-690, 1990; "Common Market Merger Control of Third-Country Enterprises," Comparative Law Yearbook of International Business, pp. 47-64, 1991; Periodical articles with J. Sedemund, "European Community Law," NJW, 1987-1991. Research Assistant, Institute for Public International and European Law, University of Bonn, 1982-1985. *Member:* German and International Bar Associations; German-American Lawyers Association; German Society for Foreign Affairs; European Air Law Association (Member, Management Committee); European Trade Law Association; Studien-

(This Listing Continued)

vereinigung Kartellrecht; Union des Avocats Européens (Member, Executive Committee). *LANGUAGES:* German, English and French.

DR. HANS-JOACHIM PRIEß, born Bremerhaven, Germany, February 19, 1958; admitted, 1988, Hamburg; 1991, Cologne (Not admitted in Belgium). *Education:* Kiel University (Dr. jur, 1988); Universities of Freiburg and Lausanne, Switzerland; Indiana University School of Law (LL.M., 1984); Harvard Law School. Author: "International Administrative Tribunal and Appeal Boards," Berlin, 1989; "The Development of the EC-Law Pertaining to Maritime Transport," Europarecht 1989, pp. 369-378; "The Protection of the External and Internal Trade of the European Communities Against Dumping and Subsidies," JuS 1991, pp. 629-634; "The European Community as a Member of a Customs Union," Europarecht 1991, pp. 187-195; "The obligation of the EC to render Administrative and Judicial Assistance," Europarecht 1991, pp. 342-355; "The Liability of EC-Member States arising from Violations of Community Law," NVwZ 1993, pp. 118-125; Contributor: Woefrum (ed.) Handbook United Nations, Munich 1991, pp. 635-640 (Civil Service International) and 1002-1007 (Administrative Tribunals International); "Combatting Fraud in the EC," EuZW 1994, pp. 297-304; "Public Procurement in the EU," Cologne et al., 1994. Research and Teaching Assistant, Institute for International Law at Kiel University, 1983. Lecturer in EC Law, College for Public Administration, Cologne, 1992. *Member:* German Bar Association; German-American Lawyers Association; Deutscher Juristentag E.V.; Customs Law Association; Association Internationale des Jeunes Avocats (A.I.J.A.). (Also at Frankfurt/Main Office). *LANGUAGES:* German, English and French.

DR. KLAUS HEINEMANN, born Aachen, Germany, March 31, 1959; admitted, 1991, Cologne (Not admitted in Belgium). *Education:* University of Cologne (Referendar, 1983; Dr. jur., 1988); McGill University, Montreal, Canada (LL.M., 1989). Author: "Burden of Proof in Case of Breach of Contract," Cologne, 1988; "Pre-Incorporation Transactions," Cologne, 1990; "Donation of Partnership Interests and its Revocation," DB 1990, 1649-1655 (Co-Author); "Shareholders Hanging by a Thread," ZHR 1991, 447-470; "EC Harmonization of Service Liability Rules," ZIP 1991, pp. 1193-1204; "The Case Law of European Merger Control," ZIP 1992, pp. 1367-1379 (Co-Author). Research Assistant, 1987-1988, and Assistant Professor, 1989-1991, Institute for Labour and Business Law, University of Cologne. *Member:* German Bar Association; Studienvereinigung Kartellrecht; German-French Lawyers Association; Canadian-German Lawyers Association. *LANGUAGES:* German, French and English.

GERALD SCHUBERT, born Hünfeld, October 26, 1953; admitted, 1981, Cologne (Not admitted in Belgium). *Education:* Universities of Würzburg, Geneva, London and Bonn (Referendar, 1978). *LANGUAGES:* German, French and English.

OF COUNSEL

DR. KARL-HEINZ NARJES, born Soltau, Germany, January 1, 1924; admitted, 1990, Cologne (Not admitted in Belgium). *Education:* University of Hamburg (degrees in law and economics, 1948; Dr. jur., 1953). Senior Civil Servant, Internal Revenue Service, Bremen, 1953. Career Officer, German Foreign Office, 1955. Member, Cabinet of the President of the EC Commission, Walter Hallstein, deputy head, 1958-1963, head, 1963-1967; Director-General of the EC Commission for Press and Information, 1968; Minister of Economic Affairs and Transport in the Land Schleswig-Hostein, 1969-1973; Member of the Bundestag and Member of the Steering Committee of the CDU/CSU parliamentary group, 1972-1981; Chairman of the Bundestag Committee of Economic Affairs, 1972-1976; CDU/CSU Spokesman for Energy and Economic Relations, Member of the Foreign Affairs Committee of the Bundestag, 1976-1980. Member, EC Commission for the Internal Market and Customs Union, Environment, Consumer Protection and Innovation, 1981-1985; Vice-President, EC Commission for Industry and Industrial Innovation, Science, Research and Development and Joined Research Centres, Telecommunication, 1985-1989. *Member:* German Bar Association; German Society for Foreign Affairs; Treteral Commission. *LANGUAGES:* German, English and French.

ASSOCIATES

DR. ANDRÉ R. FIEBIG, born Chicago, Illinois, August 29, 1964; admitted, 1989, Washington D.C. (Not admitted in Belgium). *Education:* University of Illinois (B.S., 1986); IIT Chicago-Kent College of Law (J.D., 1989); University of Tübingen (LL.M., 1991; Dr. jur., 1993). Author: "Europa-Abkommen: Etikettenschwindel oder Vorbereitung auf die EG-Vollmitgliedschaft," Integration, 1992, 47; "Die Bedeutung der konservativen Ära des US-Supreme Court," Demokratie und Recht 1992, 92; "The Recognition and Enforcement of Punitive Damage Awards in Germany," GJICL, 1992, 635. Clerk, United States District Court, Northern District

(This Listing Continued)

of Illinois, 1988-1989; Attorney, United States Department of Energy, 1989-1990. *LANGUAGES:* English, German and French.

LUC GOVAERT, born Ghent, Belgium, February 13, 1965; admitted, 1991, Brussels. *Education:* University of Antwerp (1985); University of Ghent (1988); University of Louvain-La-Neuve (DES, 1989); University of Heidelberg (LL.M., 1991). *Member:* Brussels Bar Association; Deutsch-Belgische Juristenvereinigung. *LANGUAGES:* Dutch, French, German and English.

(For complete biographical data on all personnel, see Professional Biographies at Cologne, Germany)

DSH DERKS • STAR BUSMANN

Attorneys at Law

391 AVENUE LOUISE, B 11
1050 BRUSSELS, BELGIUM
Telephone: 02-6403525
Telex: 64880 DSHBRU
Telefax: 02-6406904

Utrecht, Netherlands Office: 2 Pythagoraslaan, 3584 BB, P.O. Box 85250, 3508 AG. Telephone: 030-698698. Telefax: 030-698600.
Amersfoort, Netherlands Office: Office Building "De Runmolen", 98 Zonnehof, 7th and 8th Floor, 3811 ND, P.O. Box 506, 3800 AM. Telephone: 033-698698. Telefax: 033-698600.
Arnhem, Netherlands Office: Office Building "De Groenveste", 35-I Velperweg, 6824 BE, P.O. 3024, 6802 DA. Telephone: 085-511910. Telefax: 085-458169.
Hilversum, Netherlands Office: 37 Borneolaan, 1217 GX, P.O. Box 710, 1200 AS. Telephone: 035-218547. Telefax: 035-215039.
Hilversum, Netherlands Office: 4 Oude Enghweg, 1217 JC, P.O. Box 272, 1200 AG. Telephone: 035-244853. Telefax: 035-284216.
Berlin, Germany Office: 66, Bernadottestrasse, 14195 Berlin. Telephone: 30-8316300, 8324431, 8325715. Telefax: 30-8316528.

Firm engaged in EEC and General (International) Practice.

RESIDENT PARTNER

A. Robert Bosman (Not admitted in Belgium)

(For Complete biographical data on all Personnel see Professional Biographies at Utrecht, Netherlands).

D'HONDT & DE CARITAT

Established in 1975

PLACE GEORGES BRUGMANN 12
1060 BRUSSELS, BELGIUM
Telephone: (02) 345.19.92; (02) 345.07.44
Telefax: (02) 347.31.10

General Practice, Liability and Insurance, Banking and Commercial Law, Construction Law, Labour Law, Belgian and EEC Competition Law, Litigation.

PARTNERS

AMAND D'HONDT, born December 29, 1933; admitted, 1956, Brussels. *Education:* University of Louvain (Dr. jur., 1956). *LANGUAGES:* French, Dutch, English, German and Italian.

YVES DE CARITAT, born August 12, 1945; admitted, 1970, Brussels. *Education:* University of Brussels (Dr. jur., 1970). *LANGUAGES:* French and Dutch.

ASSOCIATES

PAUL DE MOORTEL, born September 4, 1950; admitted, 1975, Brussels. *Education:* University of Leuven (Lic. jur., 1975). *LANGUAGES:* Dutch, French, English and German.

THIERRY DE MOOR, born June 13, 1960; admitted, 1986, Brussels. *Education:* University of Louvain (Lic. jur., 1982). *LANGUAGES:* French, Dutch and English.

CHRISTOPHE VAN DEN HOVE, born March 17, 1960; admitted, 1985, Brussels. *Education:* University of Leuven (Lic. jur., 1984). *LANGUAGES:* French, Dutch, English and German.

ERIC JACQUES, born February 4, 1965; admitted, 1990, Brussels. *Education:* University of Louvain (Lic. jur., 1988). *LANGUAGES:* French, Dutch and English.

(This Listing Continued)

D'HONDT & DE CARITAT, Brussels—Continued

GEOFFROY CRUYSMANS, born September 12, 1968; admitted, 1992, Brussels. *Education:* University of Louvain (Lic. jur., 1991). *LAN-GUAGES:* French and Dutch.

JAN DECORTE, born November 22, 1968; admitted, 1991, Brussels. *Education:* University of Leuven (Lic. Jur., 1991). *LANGUAGES:* Dutch, French, English, Spanish and German.

CHARLES A. DILLEY

AVENUE EMILE DURAY, 64
1050 BRUSSELS, BELGIUM
Telephone: (322) 646-8800
Telefax: (322) 648-9734

General and International Law Practice. Firm authorized to appear before the Belgian Courts.

CHARLES A. DILLEY, born Cleveland, Ohio, June 6, 1938; admitted, 1965, New York; 1983, Brussels. *Education:* Yale University (B.A., M.cum laude, 1960); Institut des Sciences Politiques (Degree in political science, 1961); Harvard University (LL.B., 1964); Ecole Supérieure des Sciences Fiscales, Brussels (Degree in Taxation, 1968); University of Liège (LL.B., 1969; Dr. Jur., 1982). Phi Beta Kappa. Author: "Doing Business in Belgium," First Edition, 1969; "The Circular, an in-depth analysis of Belgium's special tax regime for foreign executives," 1979. *LANGUAGES:* English and French. *PRACTICE AREAS:* Mergers and Acquisitions; Real Estate Law; Fiscal Law; Corporate Law.

DOBSON & PINCI

AVENUE LOUISE, 216
1050 BRUSSELS, BELGIUM
Telephone: (32) (2) 647-0700
Telefax: (32) (2) 647-6440 E-Mail: 7242683@mcimail.com.

Milan, Italy Office: Via Santa Radegonda, 16, 20121. Telephone: (39) (2) 809816; 8056780. Telefax: (39) (2) 86464548; 86464601. E-Mail: 7232679@mcimail.com.

Rome, Italy Office: Via Panama 74, Int. 9, 00198. Telephone: (39) (6) 841-1611. Telefax: (39) (6) 841-1145. E-Mail: 7212680@mcimail.com.

Genoa, Italy Office: Via Garibaldi 7, 2nd Floor, 16124. Telephone: (39) (10) 206-851. Telefax: (39) (10) 202-738. E-Mail: 7222681@mcimail.com.

New York, New York Office: Manhattan Tower, 12th Floor, 600 Lexington Avenue, 10022-6018. Telephone: (212) 308-4440. Telefax: (212) 888-3839. E-Mail: 7262685@mcimail.com.

London, England Office: 1 Throgmorton Avenue, EC2N 2JJ. Telephone: (44) (171) 628-8163. Telefax: (44) (171) 920-0861. E-Mail: 7232682@mcimail.com.

Athens, Greece Office: 6 Yperidou Street, 105 58. Telephone: (30) (1) 324-3272. Telefax: (30) (1) 322-9329. E-Mail: 7252684@mcimail.com.

Atlanta, Georgia Office: 1776 Resurgens Plaza, 945 East Paces Ferry Road, N.E., 30326. Telephone: (404) 262-5680. Telefax: (404) 262-5699. E-Mail: 7272686@mcimail.com.

San Diego, California Office: 1629 Columbia Street, 92101. Telephone: (619) 236-1310. Telefax: (619) 239-1208. E-Mail: 7282687@mcimail.com.

Miami, Florida Office: 701 Brickell Avenue, Suite 2000, 33131. Telephone: (305) 579-0012. Telefax: (305) 375-8075; 579-4722. E-Mail: 7292688@mcimail.com.

Corporate, Banking and Securities Law with emphasis on Mergers and Acquisitions, Insurance, International Financial Transactions, Litigation, Arbitration, Employment Law, Debt Collection, Bankruptcy, Foreign Investments, Privatizations, Subsidiaries and Joint Ventures, Taxation, EU/Common Market Law, Antitrust, Environmental Law, Transportation, Shipping, Licensing, Fashion and Textiles, Franchising, Commercial Real Estate (Investment, Structuring, Development, Retail), Project Finance, Computer, Software and Telecommunications Law, Agency and Distribution, Energy (Production, Operations, and Transmission), Food and Drug, Commodities, Visa/Immigration, Wills and Estates, Sports Law, Broadcasting, Motion Picture, TV, Video, Intellectual Property and General Entertainment Law.

(This Listing Continued)

FIRM PROFILE: *Dobson & Pinci is an international law firm based in Europe and the United States that is staffed with both American and European attorneys. Of the small number of such firms, Dobson & Pinci holds a unique position because the firm's European offices are situated in Milan, Rome, Genoa, London, Brussels and Athens, thereby enabling the firm to serve clients conveniently and efficiently in both Northern and Southern Europe. The U.S. offices in New York, Atlanta, Miami and San Diego are placed in major U.S. cities to provide full support to the overall practice network. Each office is staffed by attorneys qualified to appear and litigate in the local courts.*

MEMBERS OF FIRM

MARCANTONIO PINCI, born Vicenza, Italy, October 27, 1963; admitted, 1990, Italy; 1990, New York. *Education:* University of Milan (J.D., 1988); Georgetown University Law Center (LL.M., 1989); Bocconi University, Milan (Master in Business Tax Law, Certificate, 1991). Author: "Milan Real Estate - Tax and Legal Aspects," Immobilier & Property, February, 1992; "Italy, Legal Tax and Financing Aspects of Italian Property Transactions for Foreign Investors and Developers," Sunbelt Conference on Real Estate Opportunities in Southern France, Northern Spain and Northern Italy, Cannes, December, 1991; "The Negotiating Phase - French Acquisitions in Italy," C&S Conference on Mergers and Acquisitions in Italy, Paris, November, 1991; "Acquisizione, Fusione e Partecipazione di Società Italiane ed Imprese Estere nel Quadro delle Direttive CEE in Materia di Imposizione Diretta," Seminar on International Tax Strategy, Turin, October, 1991; MIPIM 94 Conference: Italia: Nuove Opportunità per Investimenti Promozione e Finanziamenti Immobiliari - "Aspetti Legali e Fiscali degli Investimenti Immobiliari in Italia alla Luce dei Più Recenti Sviluppi Normativi," Cannes, March, 1994; "Enforcement of Judgments in Italy," Corporate Counsel's International Adviser, October, 1991; Seminar: "Enforcement of Judgments in Europe-Italy," New York State Bar Association, International Practice Section, New York, June 1991; "Dematerialization of Investment Securities," Georgetown University Law Center, 1989; "Insider Trading Regulations in the U.S., U.K., France and the E.E.C.: An Analysis from the Standpoint of the Italian Legal System," University of Milan, 1988; "Unico Azionista: Responsabilità ex Articolo 2362," University of Milan, 1986. Co-Author: "La Cooperazione Imprenditoriale Fra Italia e Stati Uniti: la Via Della Joint-Venture," Conference on Joint-Ventures, Milan, June 1992; "La Direttiva CEE 434/90 sul Regime delle Riorganizzazioni Societarie," Acquisizioni, April 1992; "Coal Gasification Projects in Italy," December 1994; "Il Nuovo Contratto d'Agenzia-D.L. 10.09.91 N° 303," published in France-Italie no. 6, November/December, 1993 and continued in same publication, no. 1, January/February, 1994; "Deregulation of Retail Licenses in Italy," April, 1994; "Structuring Italian Shopping Center, Investments for German Open-Ended Property Funds," September, 1994; Conference, Agenti di Commercio - "Lo Scioglimento del Rapporto di Agenzia nella Nuova Normative Italiana di Recepimento della Direttiva CEE 86/653," Milan, April 1993; "Incorporation of an Italian Company: An Overview of Italian Law," Corporate Counsel's International Adviser, February, 1993; "Legal Aspects of Property Investment in Europe," Corporate Real Estate Executive, International Association of Corporate Real Estate Executives (NACORE) July/August 1992; "Country Handbook on Italy," Italian American Business, 1992; "Italy, Financial Engineering and Tax Planning," C&S Conference: Property Investment in Italy, Paris, April 1991 and IBC Conference: European Commercial Property Development Opportunities, London, June 1991; "Acquisition and Management of Real Property in Italy by Non-Residents," Conference on "International Tax Strategy," Milan, November 1990. Advisor, Real Estate Masters Program (Shopping Center Development), Politecnico University of Turin, 1992—; Assistant to the General Counsel, Pirelli-Armstrong Tire Corp., New Haven, CT, 1990; Foreign Associate (Corporate Area), Foley, Hoag & Eliot, Boston, MA, 1989. *Member:* The Foreign Lawyers Forum of Washington, D.C.; International Bar Association. (Also at Milan Office).

ASSOCIATES

ANTHONY A. SISTILLI, born Steubenville, Ohio, May 19, 1966; admitted, 1992, Pennsylvania. *Education:* West Virginia University (B.A., magna cum laude, 1988); Temple University School of Law, International Studies, Rome (1990); West Virginia University College of Law (J.D., 1992); McGeorge School of Law, Sacramento, California (Diploma in Advanced International Legal Studies, Salzburg, Austria, 1992). Publications, Business Law Europe, European Law Press, European Correspondent, Rome (1993). Author: "New Rules on Domestic and International Arbitration," April 1994; "Protection of Computer Programs," English Edition 5/93, March 1993; "Mutual Fund Investments in Italy," English Edition 7/93, April 1993, "Security Interests in Receivables in Italy," English Edition 13/93, June 1993. Co-author: "Coal Gasification Projects in Italy,"

(This Listing Continued)

December 1994; "Franchising in Italy," Corporate Counsel's International Adviser, September 1994; "Progressing From National to European Structures," European Market Law Report, March 1994; "Taxation of Foreign Companies in Italy," Belle Cose, Summer 1994; Conference: "Cutting Through the Red Tape: U.S. Customs, F.D.A., U.S.D.A., and Other Legal Issues Facing Foreign Food and Beverage Manufacturers Entering the U.S. Market," New York, June, 1993. Approaching 2000 - The Corporation in Transition, "EEC Driven Changes in Italian Corporate Law," Salzburg, June 1993. *Member:* International Bar Association. (Also at Rome Office).

GIORGIO COGLIATI, born Rome, Italy, February 20, 1963. admitted to practice, 1992, Italy. *Education:* University of Milan (J.D., 1992); University of Paris (Certificate of EU Law, 1994). "Commercial Leases in Belgium," January 1993. *Member:* International Bar Association. (Also at Milan Office).

Languages: English, Italian, French, Greek, German, Spanish, Japanese and Russian

(For Complete Biographical Data on all Personnel and List of Representative Clients, see Professional Biographies at Milan, Italy)

DORSEY & WHITNEY

A Partnership including Professional Corporations

35 SQUARE DE MEEUS
B-1040 BRUSSELS, BELGIUM
Telephone: 011-32-2-504-4611
Facsimile: 011-32-2-504-4646

Minneapolis, Minnesota Office: 220 South 6th Street, 55402. Telephone: 612-340-2600. Cable Address: "Dorow". Telex: 290605. Answer-back: "Dorsey Law MPS".

New York, New York Office: 350 Park Avenue, 10022. Telephone: 212-415-9200.

Washington, D.C. Office: Suite 200, 1330 Connecticut Avenue, N.W., 20036. Telephone: 202-452-6900.

London, England Office: 3 Gracechurch Street, EC3V OAT. Telephone: 011-44-71-929-3334.

Rochester, Minnesota Office: 201 First Avenue, S.W., Suite 340. P.O. Box 848, 55902. Telephone: 507-288-3156.

Des Moines, Iowa Office: 801 Grand, Suite 3900, 50309. Telephone: 515-283-1000.

Billings, Montana Office: 1200 First Interstate Center, 401 North 31st Street, P.O. Box 7188, 59103. Telephone: 406-252-3800.

Great Falls, Montana Office: 507 Davidson Building, 8 Third Street, North, P.O. Box 1566, 59401. Telephone: 406-727-3632.

Missoula, Montana Office: 127 East Front Street, Suite 310, 59802. Telephone: 406-721-6025.

Denver, Colorado Office: 370 Seventeenth Street, Republic Plaza Building, Suite 4400, 80202-5644. Telephone: 303-629-3400.

Orange County, California Office: Center Tower, 650 Town Center Drive, Suite 1930, P.O. Box 5066, Costa Mesa, 92626. Telephone: 714-662-7300.

Fargo, North Dakota Office: Dakota Center, 51 North Broadway, Suite 201, P.O. Box 1344, 58107-1344. Telephone: 701-235-6000.

International Practice.

MEMBER OF FIRM

BARRY D. GLAZER, born 1948; admitted, 1973, Minnesota; Avocat in France (Not admitted in Belgium). *Education:* Miami University (A.B., 1970); University of Michigan (J.D., 1973). *PRACTICE AREAS:* International Law; Corporate Law; Commercial Law.

RESIDENT ASSOCIATE

BERND ULRICH GRAF, born 1963; admitted, 1990, Germany (Not admitted in Belgium). *Education:* University of Augsburg (J.D., 1987); University of Georgia (LL.M., 1988). *PRACTICE AREAS:* EC Law; International Trade Law; Commercial Law.

(For Complete Personnel and Biographical Data, see Professional Biographies at Minneapolis, Minnesota).

DROSTE

The Merged Firms of Droste, Pietzcker, Sprick, Ohlgart & Klosterfelde; Strobl, Killius & Vorbrugg; Triebel & Weil.

AVENUE DES GAULOIS 9
P.O. BOX 1040
B-1150 BRUSSELS, BELGIUM
Telephone: 02-7358945
Telefax: 02-7352251

Düsseldorf, Germany Office: Berliner Allee 48, 40212 Düsseldorf. Telephone: (0211) 13 680. Telecopier: (0211) 32 44 39.

Hamburg, Germany Office: Warburgstrasse 50, 20354 Hamburg. Telephone: (040) 4 1993-0. Telecopier: (040) 4 1993 200.

Munich, Germany Office: Marstallstrasse 8, 80539 Munich. Telephone: (089) 290120. Telecopier: (089) 29012 222. Telex: 524 973 skv.

Frankfurt/Main, Germany Office: Schaumainkai 91, 60596 Frankfurt/Main. Telephone: (069) 63 00 89-0. Telecopier: (069) 630089-99. .

Berlin, Germany Office: Kurfürstendamm 54-55, 10707 Berlin. Telephone: (030) 88 24 300. Telefax: (030) 88 24 393.

EU Law and Trade Law. Antitrust Law. EU Litigation. International Transactions. General German Practice. Firm not admitted to practice before the Belgian Courts.

FIRM PROFILE: Droste is one of the largest German firms. The firm is the result of the merger of Droste, Pietzcker, Sprick, Ohlgart & Klosterfelde in Hamburg (formed in 1887), Strobl, Killius & Vorbrugg in Munich (formed in 1961) and Triebel & Weil in Düsseldorf (formed in 1951). The firm's traditional areas of practice are: corporate law, including mergers and acquisitions; industrial including copyright, unfair competition and anti-trust law; trademark law; tax law, both domestic and international; real estate law. Further areas of particular expertise include banking and finance, computer and software law, environmental law, labour law, EU law and commercial litigation and arbitration.

RESIDENT PARTNER

DR. THOMAS JESTAEDT, born Belgrade, Yugoslavia, July 1, 1956; admitted, 1981, Germany (Not admitted in Belgium). *Education:* Universities of Bonn and Munich (Law Degree, 1979; Doctor of Laws, 1984); The University of Michigan Law School (LL.M., 1985). *Member:* European Lawyers' Union; German Association of Competition Lawyers; Licensing Executives Society; German-American Lawyers' Association. *LANGUAGES:* German, English, French, Dutch and Portuguese. *PRACTICE AREAS:* European Community Law; Antitrust and Trade Regulation; International Contracts; Trademarks.

COUNSEL

PROFESSOR DR. HERMANN-JOSEF BUNTE, born Papenburg, Germany, December 22, 1941; (Not admitted in Belgium). *Education:* Universities of Hamburg, Freiburg, Münster and Bielefeld (Law Degree, 1968; Second State Exam, 1972; Doctor of Laws, 1974. Qualification as university professor, 1983, Academic Advisory Committee to the Federal Cartel Office. Professor, Universities of Hagen and Münster and University of the German Federal Army in Hamburg. Formerly judge at the court of Appeals of Hamburg. *Member:* German Association of Private Law Professor; German Association of Competition Lawyers. *LANGUAGES:* German and English. *PRACTICE AREAS:* European Community Law; Antitrust and Trade Regulation; Contracts, in particular standard terms.

Languages: German, English, Franch, Spanish, Russian, Italian, Portuguese and Latvian.

(For list of personnel at Hamburg, Berlin, Düsseldorf, Frankfurt/Main and Munich, see Professional Biographies at those locations)

DUBARRY, LEVEQUE, LE DOUARIN & VEIL

Established in 1984

55, AVENUE DE TERVUEREN
B-1040 BRUSSELS, BELGIUM
Telephone: (32-2) 736.40.90
Telecopier: (32-2) 735.87.14

Paris, France Office: 9, rue Le Tasse, 75116. Telephone: (33-1) 45.27.39.00. Telecopier: (33-1) 45.27.31.20.

(This Listing Continued)

DUBARRY, LEVEQUE, LE DOUARIN & VEIL,
Brussels—Continued

Firm engaged in Belgian, French and General International Practice and admitted to appear before Belgian, French and European Economic Community Courts.
EEC law and European Court of Justice litigation. EEC antitrust laws, trade regulations, State subsidies, antidumping regulations. General Belgian and French Commercial and Corporate law and litigation.

JEAN-LOUIS LODOMEZ, born Kamina, Zaire, April 2, 1954; admitted, 1980, Brussels; 1990, Paris. Education: Institut pour Journalistes de Belgique (Graduate, 1975); Louvain University (Post-graduate degree in European Law, 1979). Lecturer in International Law FUCAM, Mons. LANGUAGES: French, English and Dutch.

(For complete biographical data on personnel at Paris, France Office, see Professional Biographies at that location).

CARTER WEAVER ELTZROTH

97 TOLLAAN
AVENUE DU PÉAGE 97
1932 ST.-STEVENS-WOLUWE
BRUSSELS, BELGIUM
Telephone: (32 2) 716 5482
(32 2) 688 0988
Telecopier: (32 2) 725 4478
(32 2) 688 0243

Engaged in American and International Law Practice, including before the institutions of the European Community, Media and Entertainment Law (Intellectual Property, Telecommunications). Commercial and Corporate Law. Not authorized to appear before the Belgian courts.

CARTER ELTZROTH, born 1952; admitted, 1982, New York; 1989, U.S. Supreme Court (Not admitted in Belgium). Education: College Stanislas, Paris (baccalauréat es lettres, 1971); University College, Oxford (B.A., 1977; M.A., 1980); Columbia University School of Law (J.D., 1980). General Counsel, Network Holdings S.A., 1994—. Chairman, Ad-hoc Group on Intellectual Property Rights of European Project-Digital Video Broadcasting, 1993—. Coordinator, Pay TV Working Group of Association of Commercial Television in Europe, 1993—. General Counsel, Benelux, Film Net International NV, 1992-1993. Law Clerk to Chief Judge Walter Cummings, U.S. Court of Appeals for the Seventh Circuit, 1980-1982. Member: American Bar Association; American Chamber of Commerce, Belgium; American Society for International Law; Association of the Bar of the City of New York; International Bar Association.

EUROLEGAL
G.E.I.E.

Joint Brussels Office of: Funck-Brentano & Associés, Graf von Westphalen & Modest, Winward Fearon & Co. and Kunodi & Raabe.

Established in 1990

AVENUE DE LA JOYEUSE ENTRÉE 1, BOÎTE 16
B-1040 BRUSSELS, BELGIUM
Telephone: 32.2.230.46.69
Telefax: 32.2.231.00.35

Hamburg, Germany Office: Graf von Westphalen & Modest. Poststrasse 9A, Postfach 30 36 10, D-20354 Hamburg. Telephone: (49) (40) 35 92 20. Telex: 211 729 mod. d. Teletex: 403 220-Modest. Telefax: (49) (40) 344573.
Cologne, Germany Office: Graf von Westphalen & Modest. Salierring 42, D-50517 Cologne. Telephone: (49) 221/208070. Telefax: (49) 221/239255.
Leipzig, Germany Office: Graf von Wesphalen & Modest. Katharinenstrasse 15, D(0)-7010 Leipzig. Telephone: (37) (41) 28 10 73.
Dresden, Germany Office: Graf von Westphalen & Modest. Winterbergerstrasse 2, D-8012 Dresden. Telephone: (49) 351/2349178. Telefax: (49) 351/2349172.
Paris, France Office: Funck-Brentano & Associés. 198, Avenue Victor Hugo, 75116 Paris. Telephone: (33) (1) 45 04 61 73. Telefax: (33) (1) 45 04 41 43.

(This Listing Continued)

London, England Office: Winward Fearon & Co. 35 Bow Street, London WC2E 7AU. Telephone: (44) 71/836 90 81. Telefax: (44) 71/836 83 82.
Vienna, Austria Office: Kunodi & Raabe. Hietzing, Am Platz 4, 1130 Vienna. Telephone: (43) 1/877 3 888. Telefax: (43) 1/877 3 999.

EEC Law, German, French, English, Austrian and International Law.

PROF. DR. P.S.R.F. MATHIJSEN, born Tilburg, Netherlands, March 7, 1924; (Not admitted in Belgium). Education: University of Minnesota (M.A. Economics, 1952); University of Leyden (M.A., 1951; Ph.D., 1957). Assistant Professor, Law School, University of Michigan, 1961-1962. Professor: Law Faculty, University of Nijmegen, Netherlands, 1967-1985; Law Faculty, University of Brussels, Belgium, 1986—. Attaché, ECSC Court of Justice, 1953-1958. Legal Adviser, EAEC Commission, 1958-1967. Director, DGIV Competition, EEC Commission, 1968-1977. Director General for Regional Policy, EC Commission, 1977-1986. Member of the Board, European Investment Bank, 1977-1986. Delegate General, CIAA, Brussels, Belgium, 1986-1989. Author: "A Guide to European Community Law," London/New York, 1972, 5. Edition, 1990. Member, Editorial Staff, "Encyclopedia of European Community Law," and "European Law Review," 1973—. (Also of Counsel: Radcliffes & Co., London, England). LANGUAGES: Dutch, French, English and German.

Member of Eurolegal

EVERSHEDS

65 RUE STEVIN
1040 BRUSSELS, BELGIUM
Telephone: (32) 2 230 8058
Fax: (32) 2 231 0677

London, England Office: Senator House, 85 Queen Victoria Street, London EC4V 4JL Telephone: (44) 171 919-4500. Fax: (44) 171 919-4919.
St. Helier, Jersey, Channel Islands Office: Suite 2, Seaton House, 17-19 Seaton Place. Telephone: (44) 1534 37321. Telex: 4192145 JAQUES G. Cable Address: "Quickness, Jersey". Fax: (44) 1534 38163.
Other Eversheds Offices:
Birmingham, Bristol, Cardiff, Derby, Ipswich, Leeds, Manchester, Middlesbrough, Newcastle-Upon-Tyne, Norwich, Nottingham, Berlin.

FIRM PROFILE: Member of the JCS Group. Other Group Members: Chaintrier, Caillard in Paris; Schmidt, von der Osten & Huber in Essen and Berlin; and Van Wijmen & Koedam in Rotterdam and Breda.

The JCS Group is an integrated group of law firms providing a comprehensive range of legal services to international clients.

English Solicitors and European Lawyers-European Community, International Commercial and Tax Planning Law.

PARTNER

DAVID CHURCH, born England, 1950; admitted, 1975, England. Education: University College, London (LL.B., 1971). Member: Law Society of England and Wales; American and International Bar Associations.

EUROPEAN COUNSEL

FRANK L. FINE, born Utica, New York, USA 1952; admitted, 1983, California; 1991, District of Columbia (Not admitted in Belgium). Education: Loyola University of Los Angeles (B.A., 1974); Loyola Law School, Los Angeles (J.D., 1982); Cambridge University (LL.M., 1986); The Hague Academy of International Law (Certificate, 1986). Member: Advisory Boards, North Western Journal of International Law and Business; New York International Law Review. Author: "Mergers and Joint Ventures in Europe: The Law and Policy of the EEC" (Graham and Trotman 2nd Edition, 1994). EEC Correspondent of ABA European Law Bulletin. Member: State Bar of California; American and International Bar Associations.

JILL C. HUGHES, B. Soc Sc; Solicitor; born 1942; admitted 1983. Member: Law Society of England and Wales; Solicitors Family Law Association.

JULIA A. CROSSLAND, LL.B.; Solicitor; born 1956; London University External, 1980; admitted England, 1980. Member: Law Society of England and Wales.

FASKEN MARTINEAU

Established in 1986

AVENUE FRANKLIN D. ROOSEVELT, 96 A
1050 BRUSSELS, BELGIUM
Telephone: 2-640-9796
Facsimile: 2-640-2779

Fasken Martineau is a national and international firm composed of the partners and associates of Martineau Walker (Montreal and Quebec City, Quebec) and Fasken Campbell Godfrey (Toronto, Ontario). Fasken Martineau also has an office in London, England.

Montreal, Quebec, Canada Office: Martineau Walker, Stock Exchange Tower, Suite 3400. P.O. Box 242, 800 Place-Victoria, H4Z 1E9. Telephone: 514-397-7400. Toll Free: 1-800-361-6266 (Ontario & Quebec). Facsimile: 514-397-7600. Telex: 05-24610 BUOY MTL.

Quebec City, Quebec, Canada Office: Martineau Walker, Immeuble Le Saint-Patrick, 140 rue Grande Allée est, bureau 800, G1R 5M8. Telephone: 418-640-2000. Toll Free: 1-800-463-2827 (Ontario & Quebec). Facsimile: 418-647-2455.

Toronto, Ontario, Canada: Fasken Campbell Godfrey, Toronto-Dominion Centre, Toronto Dominion Bank Tower, P.O. Box 20, M5K 1N6. Telephones: 416-366-8381. Toll Free: 1-800-268-8424 (Ontario & Quebec). Facsimile: 416-364-7813.

Vancouver (Affiliated): Davis & Company, 2800 Park Place, 666 Burrard Street, V6C 2Z7. Telephone: 604-687-9444. Fax: 604-687-1612.

London, England Office: Fasken Martineau, 10 Arthur Street, 5th Floor, EC4R 9AY. Telephone: 71-929-2894. Facsimile: 71-929-3634.

General Practice including Administrative, Admiralty, Appellate and Trial Advocacy in all Courts, Banking, Commercial Lending and Private Financing, Bankruptcy and Insolvency, Broadcasting, Combines and Antitrust, Communications and Entertainment, Computer and Technology Law, Corporate Finance, Corporate/Commercial, Corporate and Personal Taxation, Employment, Environmental, Estates and Estate Planning, Family, Foreign Investment, Franchising, Health Care, Intellectual Property, Insurance, Immigration, International Law, Labour Relations, Food and Drug, Licensing, Mining, Municipal, Partnership, Pension, Products Liability, Private Clients, Real Estate, Securities, Secured Transactions, Tax, Trademarks and Copyright, Transportation.

RESIDENT COUNSEL

LUCIEN LAMOUREUX, P.C., Q.C., born 1920; admitted, 1945, Ontario; 1987, Brussels (B. List). *Education:* University of Ottawa (B.A., B.Ph., L.Ph., M.A.); Osgoode Hall Law School (LL.B., 1945); Hon. LL.D. from Ottawa, Dalhousie, Guelph and Windsor Universities. Queen's Counsel, Member of Her Majesty's Privy Council Canada, 1974. Member and Speaker, House of Commons, 1965. Ambassador to Belgium and Grand Duchy of Luxembourg, 1974 and Portugal, 1980. Canadian Representative to Council of Europe, Strasbourg, Germany, 1974. (Resident) (Also Member, Hoffman & Jaspar, Brussels, Belgium). *PRACTICE AREAS:* European Community Law; Commercial; International.

(For complete biographical data on other personnel and offices, see professional biographies at Toronto, Ontario, Montreal and Quebec City, Quebec and London, England)

FEDDERSEN LAULE SCHERZBERG & OHLE HANSEN EWERWAHN

118, RUE D'ARLON
B-1040 BRUSSELS, BELGIUM
Telephone: 32 2 280 1544
Telefax: 32 2 280 0703

Frankfurt/Main, Germany Office: Stiftstraße 9-17, P.O. Box 100836, D-60313 Frankfurt am Main. Telephone: 49-69-29994-0. Telefax: 49-69-282615. Telex: 41 33 96 fls d.

Hamburg, Germany Office: Jungfernstieg 51 (Prien-Haus), D-20354 Hamburg. Telephone: 49-40-35 00 50. Telex: 21 27 99 99 lawt d. Telefax: 49-40-35 00 51 11.

Berlin, Germany Office: Kurfürstendamm 185, D-10707 Berlin. Telephone: 49-30-88 57 16 0. Telefax: 49-30-88 57 16 50.

Dresden, Germany Office: Königsbrücker Straße 17, D-01099 Dresden. Telephone: 49-03 51-567 02 77. Telefax: 49-03 51-567 02 79.

Prague, Czech Republic Office: Spanělská 2, CZ-120 00 Prague 2. Telephone: 42-2-268203; 268229. Telefax: 42-2-260310.

(This Listing Continued)

German, EC and General International Practice, but not Authorized to appear before the Belgian Courts.

FIRM PROFILE: The firm offers a full range of legal services. It is well known for its commercial, corporate, banking and tax law and its practice in the field of merger and acquisitions, real estate and environmental law. The firm has a broad national as well as international client base with a focus on Europe, the United States and Japan. The firm has 79 attorneys at law (8 of whom are notaries public) and 5 tax advisors.

MEMBERS OF FIRM

DR. GERRIT SCHOHE, born Göppingen, Germany, July 17, 1958; admitted, 1987, Germany; 1989, New York (Not admitted in Belgium). *Education:* Universities of Frankfurt, Lausanne and Freiburg (1976-1981); University of Michigan Law School (LL.M., 1986); University of Freiburg (Dr. jur., 1988). Author: "Die Haftung juristischer Personen für ihre Organe im internationalen Privatrecht," 1991. Co-Author with J. Schmeding: "Circumvention of Art. 177 EEC-Tready by Non-Admission of the Final Appeal?" Festchrift fuer Gaedertz, 1992. *Member:* German-American Lawyers' Association; German-French Lawyers' Association; European Lawyers' Union. *LANGUAGES:* German, French and English. *PRACTICE AREAS:* EC Law; International Trade; General International Practice including Corporate and Antitrust Law; Mergers and Acquisitions.

ASSOCIATES

STEFAN DINGEL, born Frankfurt/Main, Germany, June 2, 1962; admitted, 1992, Frankfurt/Main (Not admitted in Belgium). *Education:* University of Frankfurt/Main; Trainee Program in Berlin (2. State Examination, 1991); Duke University, Durham, North Carolina (Master of Laws, 1992). *Member:* DAJV (German American Lawyers Association). *LANGUAGES:* German, English and French. *PRACTICE AREAS:* Corporate Law; Partnership Law; EC Law; Antitrust Law; Mergers and Acquisitions.

FINNEGAN, HENDERSON, FARABOW, GARRETT & DUNNER

AVENUE LOUISE 326
BOX 37
BRUSSELS 1050, BELGIUM
Telephone: 011-322-646-0353
Facsimile: 011-322-646-2135

Washington, D.C. Office: Suite 700, 1300 I Street, N.W. Telephone: 202-408-4000. Cable Address: "Finderbow". Telex: 440275 ITT; 248740 RCA. Facsimile: 202-408-4400.

Tokyo, Japan Office: Richard V. Burgujian, Gaikokuho Jimu Bengoshi Jimusho, Toranomon No. 45 Mori Building, Third Floor, 1-5, Toranomon 5-chome Minato-Ku. Telephone: 0081-3-3431-6943. Facsimile: 0081-3-3431-6945.

General Practice.

RESIDENT PARTNER

THOMAS L. IRVING, born Salt Lake City, Utah, April 29, 1951; admitted, 1977, District of Columbia; 1982, U.S. Court of Appeals for the Federal Circuit; registered to practice before U.S. Patent and Trademark Office (Not admitted in Belgium). *Education:* University of Utah (B.A.-Chem., magna cum laude, 1974); Duke University School of Law (J.D., 1977). Phi Beta Kappa; Phi Kappa Phi. Recipient, American Jurisprudence Book Award in Evidence, Duke University School of Law, 1976. Author: "Preliminary Motions Under Rule 633," 67 JPOS 128, 1985; "The Federal Circuit and Chemical Practice, 1986-1987," Selected Legal Papers, Vol. V, No. 1, 1987; "Necessarily Non-Obvious? - Dillon and Pleuddemann," Selected Legal Papers, Vol. 9, No. 1, 1991, American Intellectual Property Law Association; "The Significant Federal Circuit Cases Interpreting Section 112," The American University Law Review, Vol. 41, No. 3, Spring 1992. Co-Author: "The Federal Circuit and Chemical Patent Practice, 1987-1988," Selected Legal Papers, Vol. VI, No. 1, 1988; "35 U.S.C. 112 and Chemical Practice," Basic Chemical and Biotechnology Practice, AIPLA, 1988, 1990; "The Federal Circuit and Chemical Patent Practice, 1988-1989," Selected Legal Papers, Vol. VII, No. 1, 1989; "Federal Circuit Patent Practice 1989-1990," Selected Legal Papers, Vol. VIII, Nos. 1 and 2, 1991; "Double Patenting: One Way, Whose Delay?" 1992; "Section 112, Paragraph Six: What Ends Are Justified by the Means?" 1992. Adjunct Professor of Patent Law, Washington College of Law, American University, 1988-1993. *Member:* American Bar Association (Member, Sections on: Patent, Trademark and Copyright Law); American Intellectual Property Law Association (Board of Directors, 1991-1994; Chairman, Chemical Practice Committee,

(This Listing Continued)

FINNEGAN, HENDERSON, FARABOW, GARRETT & DUNNER, Brussels—Continued

1989-1991; and Chairman, Chemical Practice Committee; Chemical Practice Committee Chair of Subcommittees on CAFC, District Court, 1985-1987 and CLE 1988-1989); American Chemical Society (Member, Division of Chemistry and the Law, 1983—; Program Chairman, 1985-1986; Chairman, 1987; Chairman, Nominations and Elections, 1988). *LANGUAGES:* Spanish, French.

(For Biographical data on all personnel, see Professional Biographies at Washington, D.C.)

FORRESTER NORALL & SUTTON

1 PLACE MADOU, BOX 34
1030 BRUSSELS, BELGIUM
Telephone: 219.16.20
Telecopier: 219.16.26
Telex: 23190 FORALX

EEC Law and International Practice.
Firm engaged in EEC and International Practice but not authorized to appear before the Belgian Courts.

FIRM PROFILE: *Forrester Norall & Sutton specializes in European Union law, public international law and the law of international trade. Its lawyers are drawn from several legal and linguistic backgrounds in the European Union and the United States, and the firm also maintains close relations with lawyers in national jurisdictions throughout Europe, North America and Asia. Advice is given to law firms all over the world, government departments, trade associations, corporations and private individuals, on legal matters falling within the firms area of specialization, notably EU trade and competition law and policy, areas covered by the community's "Internal Market" programme, GATT questions, public international law, air transport matters, EU/US/Japanese trade, industrial and investment issues, the legal and institutional evolution of relations between the EU and former state-trading countries in Eastern Europe, and the implications of the Maastricht Treaty. In addition to providing advice on substantive legal questions, the firm specializes in the legislative and other decision making procedures of the European Union. The firm represents clients in matters arising in the Commission, Council, Parliament, Economic and Social Committee, Court of Justice and Court of First Instance, as well as before national courts and arbitration tribunals in disputes involving EC law.*

MEMBERS OF FIRM

IAN S. FORRESTER, Q.C., born Glasgow, Scotland, January 13, 1945; admitted, Faculty of Advocates, Scotland, 1972; 1977, New York; appointed Queen's Counsel, 1988 (Not admitted in Belgium). *Education:* University of Glasgow (M.A., 1965; LL.B., 1967); Tulane University of Louisiana (M.C.L., 1969). Visiting Professor, European Law, Glasgow University. Author: "Distribution and Agency Agreements in EEC Competition Law," 1978 Swiss Review of International Antitrust Law; "EEC Customs Law: Rules of Origin and Preferential Duty Treatment," 1980 European Law Review; "Legal Professional Privilege: Limitations on the Commission's Powers of Inspection Following the AM&S Judgment," Common Market Law Review, 1983. Co-Author: ""The Laicization of Community Law," Common Market Law Review, 1984; "EEC Trade Law and the U.S.," Fordham Corporate Law Institute, 1987. "Annual Survey of EEC Competition Law," Oxford Yearbook of European Law, 1981—; "Software Licensing in the Light of Current EC Competition Law Considerations," European Competition Law Review, 1992. *Member:* American Bar Association; United Kingdom Association for European Law; British Institute of International and Comparative Law.

CHRISTOPHER NORALL, born Washington, D.C., June 17, 1946; admitted, 1971, New York (Not admitted in Belgium). *Education:* Christ's College, Cambridge University (B.A., Hons. 1967); University of Pennsylvania Law School (J.D., magna cum laude, 1970). Order of the Coif. Long Comment Editor, University of Pennsylvania Law Review, 1969-1970. Law Clerk, Hon. Edward Weinfeld, U.S. District Court, Southern District of New York, 1970-1971. Author: "Judicial Review of Anti-Dumping Measures," European Law Review, 1984; "New Trends in Anti-dumping Practice in Brussels," The World Economy, 1986. Co-Author: "The Laicization of Community Law," Common Market Law Review, 1984; "Annual Survey of EEC Competition Law," Oxford Yearbook of European Law, 1982—; "The New Amendments to the EC's Basic Anti-dumping Regulation," Common Market Law Review, 1989.

(This Listing Continued)

EU58B

ALASTAIR SUTTON, born Bristol, UK, January 6, 1945; admitted, as Barrister, 1972, Middle Temple (Not admitted in Belgium). *Education:* Aberdeen University (LL.B.); London University (LL.M.; Diploma in International and Comparative Air and Space Law). Author: "Trends in the Regulation of International Trade in Textiles," Yearbook of World Affairs, 1977; "Relations between the European Community and Japan in 1982 and 1983," Oxford Yearbook of European Law, 1983; "Financial Services and Competition Policy," Butterworths Competition Law, 1991. Consultant Editor: Butterworth's European Law Service, 1992; Commentary on EC Legal Development in 1992, Butterworth's Annual European Review, 1993. Lecturer in Public, International and European Community Law, University College London, 1967-1973. Directorate General for External Relations dealing with International Trade Policy Issues, 1973-1979, First Secretary in Charge of Trade, Industry and Investment Questions in the Delegation of the Commission in Tokyo, 1979-1984, Member of Cabinet of Lord Cockfield, Vice President of the Commission with Responsibility for the Internal Market, Financial Services, Customs and Taxation Issues, 1985-1988 and Head of Division for Insurance in the Directorate General for Financial Services and Company Law, 1989, Commission of the European Communities. Visiting Fellow: Centre for European Legal Studies, Faculty of Law, University of Cambridge, 1993; University of Sydney, Faculty of Law, Australia, 1994.

ALASDAIR R.M. BELL, born Glasgow, Scotland, August 2, 1963; admitted, as Solicitor, 1989, Scotland (Not admitted in Belgium). *Education:* University of Glasgow (LL.B. Hons., 1985; Diploma in Legal Practice, 1986); Europa Institute of the University of Amsterdam (Diploma, I.C.E.I., 1987). Author: "Anti-dumping Practice in the EEC: The Japanese Dimension," Legal Issues of European Integration, Vol. 2, 1987.

ARISTOTELIS KAPLANIDIS, born Thessaloniki, Greece, December 6, 1959; admitted, 1986, Thessaloniki (Not admitted in Belgium). *Education:* Aristotelian University, Thessaloniki (Diploma of Law, 1983); College of Europe, Bruges (Diploma of Advanced European Legal Studies, 1984).

JACQUELYN F. MACLENNAN, born Inverness, Scotland, June 24, 1961; admitted, as Solicitor in Scotland, 1986 (Not admitted in Belgium). *Education:* University of Edinburgh (LL.B., 1st Class Honours, 1983; Diploma in Legal Practice, 1984).

MADELEIN PERRICK, born The Hague, Netherlands, May 21, 1959; (Not admitted in Belgium). *Education:* University of Nijmegen (Meester in de Rechten, 1983); Europa Institute of the University of Amsterdam (Diploma, I.C.E.I., 1984).

MARK D. POWELL, born Birmingham, England, March 21, 1962; admitted, as Solicitor, 1989, Supreme Court of England and Wales (Not admitted in Belgium). *Education:* University of Lancaster (LL.B., Honours, 1983; Law Society Finals, 1985). Author: "Software Licensing and the Application of the EEC Competition Rules," 8 The Computer Lawyer, p. 13, July, 1991. Research Assistant, Directorate General for Competition, Commission of the European Communities, 1989-1990. *Member:* Law Society of England and Wales; Solicitors' European Group.

ISABELLE ROUDARD, born Ixelles, Belgium, March 12, 1962; (Not admitted in Belgium). *Education:* University of Paris I-Panthéon-Sorbonne (Maîtrise en droit, mention droit international et européen, 1983; Diplôme d' Etudes Supérieures Spécialisées (D.E.S.S.); droit du Marché Commun, 1984; Doctorat en Droit, mention très bien, 1984-1988); Max-Planck-Institute for Foreign and International Private Law (Hamburg) and Max-Planck-Institute for Foreign and International Patent, Copyright and Competition Law (Munich) (Research 1984-1988); Max-Planck-Institute for Foreign and International Patent, Copyright and Competition Law (Munich) (Research Fellow, 1988-1989). Author: "Compatibilité du règlement d' exemption par catégories des Licences de Brevet et du principe d' épuisement des droits: le problème des exportations directes en droit communautaire", La Semaine Juridique, ed. E., no. 10, 1989; "The French Legislation on Competition," European Competition Law Review, Vol. 10, 1989; "Droit européen des Licences exclusives de brevet (Droit communautaire, droit français, droit allemand)," Nouvelles Editions Fiduciaires, coll. Europe/Entreprise, 1989.

CHARLOTTE LUND THOMSEN, born Copenhagen, Denmark, October 13, 1963; (Not admitted in Belgium). *Education:* University of Copenhagen (Cand. jur., 1990). Stagiaire, Directorate General for Competition, Commission of the European Communities, 1990-1991.

ANNE NIELSEN, born Los Angeles, California, 1960; (Not admitted in Belgium). *Education:* University of Hawaii (B.A., High Honors; M.A.,

(This Listing Continued)

1982); Columbia University (J.D., 1985); College of Europe, Bruges (Diploma, Advanced European Legal Studies, 1991; Master of Advanced European Studies, 1992). Phi Beta Kappa. Clerk, Hon. Burton R. Lifland, Chief Bankruptcy Judge, Southern District of New York, 1986. Experience: Commission of the European Communities (Directorate General, Internal Market, 1992); Howard Rice, Nemerovski, Canady, Robertson & Falk, California; Murphy, Weir & Butler, California. *Member:* California and Hawaii Bar Associations.

TERESA COLAIANNI, born Bari, Italy, 1968; (Not admitted in Belgium). *Education:* University of Bari (Degree in Law, First Class Honours, 1991); Servizio Europa Umbria, Perugia (Diploma, Advanced Studies in European Community Law and Politics, 1992). Recipient, ESF Scholarship. School of Specialization in European Community Law, University of Bari, 1993. *Member:* Italian Lawyers' Association in Europe (AGAIE).

LENITA I. LINDSTRÖM, born Helsinki, Finland, 1966; (Not admitted in Belgium). *Education:* Faculty of Law, University of Helsinki (Jur. Kand., 1992). Experience: Loeff Claeys Verbeke, Brussels; Stagiaire, Directorate General for Competition, Commission of the European Communities, 1993. *Member:* Union of Finnish Lawyers.

COUNSEL

RICHARD OWEN PLENDER, Q.C., born Epsom, England, October 9, 1945; admitted, as Barrister, 1972, England and Wales (Berridale-Keith Prize), Appointed Queen's Counsel, 1989 (Not admitted in Belgium). *Education:* Cambridge University (M.A., 1970; LL.B., 1968), Rebecca Squire Prize, (LL.D., 1992); University of Illinois (LL.M., 1971; J.S.D., summa cum laude, 1972), College of Law Prize; Sheffield University (Ph.D., 1971). Honorary Senior Member, Robinson College, Cambridge. Specialist Legal Adviser to the States of Jersey, 1988—. Formerly Legal Adviser, United Nations High Commissioner for Refugees, 1976-1978. Legal Secretary to Advocates-General Warner and Slynn, Court of Justice of the European Communities, 1980-1983. Author: "International Migration Law," 2d. ed., 1988; "Basic Documents on International Migration Law," 1988; "Plender and Usher's Cases and Materials on the Law of the European Communities," 3rd ed., 1992; "Introduccion al Derecho Comunitario Europeo," with J. Perez Santos, 1985; "A Practical Introduction to European Community Law," 1980; "The European Contracts Convention: The Rome Convention on the Choice of Law for Contracts," 1991; articles in books and periodicals.

DANIEL BETHLEHEM, born London, England, 1960; admitted, 1988, England as Barrister, Middle Temple (Not admitted in Belgium). *Education:* University of the Witwatersrand (B.A., 1981); Bristol University (LL.B., Honours, 1985); Cambridge University (LL.M., 1989). Visiting Fellow, Research Centre for International Law, Cambridge University. Lector, EC and International Law, Trinity College, Cambridge. Author: "The Kuwait Crisis: Sanctions and their Economic Consequences," Grotius Publications Ltd., 1991. Co-Editor with E. Lauterpacht, C. Greenwood and M. Weller, "The Kuwait Crisis: Basic Documents," Grotius Publications Ltd., 1991.

Languages: English, French, Danish, Dutch, German, Greek, Italian, Portuguese and Japanese

FRESHFIELDS

RUE DE LA LOI 15
1040 BRUSSELS, BELGIUM
Telephone: (32 2) 230 08 20
Fax: (32 2) 230 17 30; 230 17 78

Other Offices in: Bangkok, Barcelona, Frankfurt, Hanoi, Hong Kong, London, Madrid, Moscow, New York, Paris, Singapore and Tokyo.

Firm Engaged in General and International Practice. Brussels Office Involved in all Aspects of EC Law and in English Corporate and Commercial Law and Litigation. Belgian Corporate, Commercial and Financial Law practised by Belgian Lawyers (admitted in Belgium).

RESIDENT PARTNERS

JOHN G. DAVIES, born Swansea, UK, 1956; admitted, 1980, as Solicitor England and Wales (Not admitted in Belgium). *Education:* Bristol University, UK (LL.B. Hons., 1977). Directorate General for Competition, EC Commission, 1981-1983. *Member:* Union des Avocats Europeens. *LANGUAGES:* English and French. *PRACTICE AREAS:* EC Law; Competition Law; International Transactions; Joint Ventures; Mergers and Acquisitions; Intellectual Property Law.

(This Listing Continued)

JON A. LAWRENCE, born England, 1961; admitted, 1986 as Solicitor England and Wales (Not admitted in Belgium). *Education:* Downing College, Cambridge (1983); MA Modern Languages with Law. *LANGUAGES:* English, French and German. *PRACTICE AREAS:* EC Law; Competition Law; Environmental Law; Commercial Litigation.

GUY SCHRANS, born 1937; admitted, 1967, Ghent; 1990, Brussels. *Education:* University of Ghent (Ph.D., 1966); Harvard University (LL.M., 1961). Professor, Commercial and Finance Law, University of Ghent. Arbiter, ICSID, Washington. *Member:* Belgian Conseil d'Etat. (Senior Belgian Avocat/Advocaat). *LANGUAGES:* English, Dutch, French and German.

FUNCK-BRENTANO & PARTNERS

AVENUE DE LA JOYEUSE ENTRÉE 1, BOÎTE 16
B-1040 BRUSSELS, BELGIUM
Telephone: (32) (2) 230.46.69
Telefax: (32) (2) 231.00.35

Paris, France Office: 198, Avenue Victor Hugo, 75116. Telephone: (33) (1) 45 04 61 73. Telefax: (33) (1) 45 04 41 43.

EEC Law, German, French and International Law.

PIERRE MATHIJSEN, born Tilburg, Netherlands, March 7, 1924; (Not admitted in Belgium). *Education:* University of Minnesota (M.A. Economics, 1952); University of Leyden (M.A., 1951; Ph.D., 1957). Assistant Professor, Law School, University of Michigan, 1961-1962. Professor: Law Faculty, University of Nijmegen, Netherlands, 1967-1985; Law Faculty, University of Brussels, Belgium, 1986—. Attaché, ECSC Court of Justice, 1953-1958. Legal Adviser, EAEC Commission, 1958-1967. Director, DG IV Competition, EEC Commission, 1968-1977. Director General for Regional Policy, EC Commission, 1977-1986. Member of the Board, European Investment Bank, 1977-1986. Delegate General, CIAA, Brussels, Belgium, 1986-1989. Author: "A Guide to European Community Law," London/New York, 1972, 6. Edition, 1993. Member, Editorial Staff, "Encyclopedia of European Community Law," and "European Law Review," 1973—. *LANGUAGES:* Dutch, French, English and German.

Member of Eurolegal

(For Biographical Data of the Paris Personnel, see Professional Biographies at Paris, France).

GAEDERTZ VIEREGGE QUACK KREILE

Rechtsanwälte

AVENUE DE TERVUREN 35
B-1040 BRUSSELS, BELGIUM
Telephone: (2) 736 07 97
Telefax: (2) 732 69 12

Berlin, Germany Office: Kurfürstendamm 157, D-10709 Berlin. Telephone: (30)890 05-0. Telefax: (30)892 26 06. Teletex: 30 88 15 qkp d. Telex: 17 30 88 15 qkp d.

Cologne, Germany Office: Theodor-Heuss-Ring 19-21, D-50668 Cologne. Telephone: (221)77 16-0. Telefax: (221)77 16-110. Teletex: 221 43 76 olga d. Telex: 88 85 143 olga d.

Frankfurt/Main, Germany Office: Airport Center, Hugo-Eckener-Ring, D-60549 Frankfurt/Main. Telephone: (69)69 48 52. Telex: 4032 145 zibr d.

Leipzig, Germany Office: August-Bebel-Str. 38, D-04275 Leipzig. Telephone: (341) 477 83 81/83. Telefax: (341) 477 83 88.

Munich, Germany Office: Widenmayerstrasse 32, D-80538 Munich. Telephone: (89)212147-0. Telefax: (89)228 55 62.

Wiesbaden, Germany Office: Kaiser-Friedrich-Ring 65, D-65185 Wiesbaden. Telephone: (611)88 05-0. Telefax: (611)81 03 09. Telex: 41 86 295 gaed d.

Prague, Czech Republic Office: Betlémska 1, CR-11000 Prague 1. Telephone: (2) 24 22 94 98. Telefax: (2) 232 12 29.

ECC Law Practice.
Firm engaged in the practice of European Communities Law. Not authorized to appear before the Belgian Courts.

FIRM PROFILE: The law firm Gaedertz Vieregge Quack Kreile is the result of a merger between 4 partnerships: Heydt Vieregge & Partner, Cologne; Gaedertz Henn & Partner, Wiesbaden; Quack Kühn & Partner, Berlin; Prof. Kreile & Partner, Munich.

(This Listing Continued)

GAEDERTZ VIEREGGE QUACK KREILE, Brussels—Continued

Gaedertz Vieregge Quack Kreile is one of the major German based law firms representing domestic and foreign clients in all fields of law that are relevant for national and international enterprises. An important part of the practice are the legal aspects of transnational transactions especially in EC. The firm advises not only German clients in international matters but also foreign enterprises about all implications of doing business in Germany. Thus many attorneys and also members of the support staff are fluent in English. Other languages such as French, Spanish, Portuguese, Italian, Russian, and Dutch are also spoken.

In addition, the offices in Cologne and Wiesbaden have the specialised capacity to administer large trademark portfolios worldwide including registration and litigation of trademarks and registered designs.

Clients of the firm include many well-known German and foreign companies active in a wide variety of businesses. Gaedertz Vieregge Quack Kreile also represents various trade associations as well as German federal, state and local governmental authorities.

In the Berlin, Wiesbaden and Frankfurt/Main offices, there are 10 attorneys qualified to act as "Notar," specially licensed to prepare and execute documents relating to incorporation of companies, real estate matters and other important commercial transactions where a special form of document is prescribed.

Gaedertz Vieregge Quack Kreile has more than 70 attorneys, including 42 partners, plus a support staff of approximately 150 people, working in the eight different offices.

The offices have for the most part city centre locations. The Frankfurt office is situated at the Airport-Centre of the Rhein-Main Airport.

MEMBERS OF FIRM

KARLHEINZ QUACK, born Berlin, Germany, 1926; admitted, 1954, Berlin. *Education:* University of Berlin. Co-author, Frankfurter Kommentar zum GWB (commentary on Law against restraints of competition). Various publications regarding Corporate and antitrust law. Lectureship at Freie Universitat Berlin (Free University of Berlin). *Member:* Berlin Bar Association; Lawyers Society Berlin; International Bar Association; German Association for Industrial Property Rights and Copyright. *LANGUAGES:* English, French. *PRACTICE AREAS:* Business Law; Corporate and German/EC Antitrust Law; Industrial Property Rights and Copyright; EC Law; Arbitration.

COUNSEL

GEORG ALBRECHTSKIRCHINGER, born Munich, 1930; admitted, 1959, Munich, subsequently Frankfurt/Main. *Education:* Harvard University, University of Munich. Co-Editor of European Journal of Business Law. Until 1991, Member of the Executive Board, General Council and European Coordinator of the Chemical Industry Association. *Member:* Board of the German Association for Industrial Property Rights and Copyright; German Group of the Association Internationale pour la Protection de la Propriété Intellectuelle; Licensing Executives Society. *LANGUAGES:* English, French. *PRACTICE AREAS:* EEC Law; Food and Drug Law; Commercial Law.

(For complete biographical data on personnel at Berlin, Cologne, Frankfurt/Main, Leipzig, Munich and Wiesbaden, Germany Offices as well as Prague, Czech Republic Office, see Professional Biographies at those locations).

J. & A. GARRIGUES

RUE D'ARLON, 118

1040 BRUSSELS, BELGIUM

Telephone: (322) 280-16-60
Facsimile: (322) 280-15-60

REVISERS OF THE SPAIN LAW DIGEST FOR THIS DIRECTORY.

Madrid, Spain Office: Antonio Maura, 16, 28014. Telephone: (34-1) 521-21-51. Facsimile: (34-1) 521-40-53; 531-70-16. Telex: 22153 Aboga.

Barcelona, Spain Office: Mallorca, 260-262, 4°, 2ª, 08008. Telephone: (34-3) 488-12-11. Facsimile: (34-3) 487-53-76; 487-99-26. Telex: 51285.

New York, New York Office: 115 East 57th Street, Suite 1230, 10022. Telephone: 1-212-751-9233. Facsimile: 1-212-355-3594. Telex: 14-9543.

Marbella, Spain Office: Avda. Ricardo Soriano, 65 - 5° 1. Telephone: (34-52) 86-22-11. Facsimile: (34-52) 82-68-84.

(This Listing Continued)

Oviedo, Spain Office: Marqués de Pidal, 6 - 3°C., 33004. Telephone: (34-8) 527-73-75. Facsimile: (34-8) 527-73-83.

Seville, Spain Office: Zaragoza, 50, 41001. Telephone: (34-5) 456-45-36. Facsimile: (34-5) 456-47-52.

Lisbon, Portugal Office: Grupo Legal Português (EEIG) in association with F. Castelo Branco, Nobre Guedes & P. Rebelo de Sousa, Simmons & Simmons and Pinheiro Neto & Co., Rua Castilho, n°32 - 9°/ 1200 Lisbon. Telephone: (351-1) 352-13-18. Facsimile: (351-1) 352-14-18.

Firm engaged in EC and International Practice but not authorized to appear before the Belgian Courts.

RESIDENT LAWYERS

STEPHEN PICKARD, born Canberra, Australia, 1954; admitted, 1979, Solicitor England and Wales; 1985, New York (Not admitted in Belgium). *Education:* Oxford Polytechnic (B.A., 1976, Law, Politics and Economist); Johns Hopkins University, Bologna (Graduate Diploma, 1980); Columbia University School of Law, New York (LL.M., 1983). Co-Author: "España y Portugal en las Comunidades Europeas," 1986; "1993 una guía para entender y actuar en el Mercado Unico," 1990. Author: "Iniciación a la Política de Competencia de la CEE," 1986. *Member:* American Bar Association. *LANGUAGES:* English, Spanish and French.

DIEGO MELLADO PASCUA, born Almeria, Spain, 1967; admitted, 1993, Spain (Not admitted in Belgium). *Education:* University of Granada (Law Degree, 1990); Institut d'Etudes Européenes, Brussels, Belgium (Master in European Community Law). *Member:* Madrid Bar Association. *LANGUAGES:* French, English and German.

REVISERS OF THE SPAIN LAW DIGEST FOR THIS DIRECTORY.

GERARD & ASSOCIES

Established in 1993

AVENUE LOUISE 523
B-1050 BRUSSELS, BELGIUM

Telephone: (32.2) 646.06.52
Telecopier: (32.2) 646.40.17

Civil and commercial law, company law, financial, banking and securities law, mergers and acquisitions, international contracts and transactions, insurance and reinsurance law, transport and maritime law, arbitration, public and administrative law, national and EC competition law, intellectual property, environmental law, litigation in general, including Supreme Courts.

FIRM PROFILE: The firm offers a full range of high quality legal services. Its clients are European, American, Asian and African. The firm has 9 partners and 10 associates and is established in Brussels. All of its partners are or have been linked to universities in Belgium and abroad as professor or assistant. It has working relations with major firms in most European countries and the U.S.A.

PARTNERS

PHILIPPE GERARD, born 1936; admitted, 1959, Brussels; 1984, Supreme Court Bar; proceedings before the Cour the cassation (supreme Court). *Education:* University of Brussels (Dr. Jur., 1959). Professor, University of Brussels - Business School Solvay: Droit commercial (commercial law), 1984—. *PRACTICE AREAS:* Proceedings before the Cour de cassation (supreme court); Constitutional and Administrative Law.

JEAN-LUC FAGNART, born 1942; admitted, 1964, Brussels. *Education:* University of Brussels (Dr. Jur., 1964; Licence en droit Économique, 1966). Professor, University of Brussels (ULB): Law School - Assurances de responsabilité (liability insurances), 1972—; Assurances de choses et réassurances (insurance and reinsurance), 1988—; Business School Solvay - Droit Commercial (commercial law), 1976-1984. *PRACTICE AREAS:* Insurance and Liability Law; Distribution Law; Consumer Law.

MICHEL MAHIEU, born 1943; admitted, 1965, Brussels. *Education:* University of Louvain (UCL) (Dr. Jur., 1965; Licence en notariat, 1965; Licence en droit et économie des assurances, 1968). Professor, University of Saint-Louis Law School, Brussels, Introduction to law and constitutional law. *PRACTICE AREAS:* Constitutional and Administrative Law; Civil Law; Insurance and Liability Law.

JACQUES LIBOUTON, born 1946; admitted, 1969, Brussels. *Education:* University of Brussels (Dr. Jur., 1969; Licenciaat in Verzekeringsrecht, 1970; Licence en droit Maritime et Aérien, 1971). Professor, University of

(This Listing Continued)

Brussels (ULB) - Law School: Affrêtement et transport en droit maritime et fluvial et transports terrestres et combinés (transportation law), 1982—. *PRACTICE AREAS:* Land; Maritime; River; Air Transportation; Insurance Law.

MICHEL FLAMEE, born 1952; admitted, 1976, Brussels. *Education:* University of Brussels (Lic. Jur., 1976; Dr. Jur., 1985). Professor, University of Brussels (VUB) - Law School: Handelsrecht (commercial law), 1986—; Economisch en financieel recht (business and financial law), 1986—; Bijzondere vraagstukken Europees institutioneel en materieel recht (special topics of EEC law), 1985—; International privaat handelsrecht (conflict of laws - commercial aspects), 1984—; Nijverheidswetgeving (industrial legislation), 1986—. *PRACTICE AREAS:* Competition Law; Financial Law; Company Law; Intellectual Property Law.

KATELIJNE RONSE, born 1954; admitted, 1981, Brussels. *Education:* University of Louvain (KUL) (Lic. Jur., 1977). Assistant Professor, University of Louvain Law School (KUL), Public and Insurance Law. *PRACTICE AREAS:* Administrative Law; Distribution Law; Liability and Insurance Law; Construction Law.

ROLAND FORESTINI, born 1961; admitted, 1985, Brussels. *Education:* University of Brussels (ULB) (Lic. Jur., 1985); Ecole Supérieure des Sciences Fiscales (ICHEC) (1988). Lecturer, Ecole Nationale de Fiscalité et des Finances (Ministry of Finance). Assistant Professor, University of Brussels (ULB), Tax Law. *PRACTICE AREAS:* Tax Law.

DIRK VAN GERVEN, born 1962; admitted, 1985, Brussels; 1989, New York. *Education:* University of Louvain (KUL) (Lic. Jur., 1985). Assistant Professor, University of Louvain Law School (KUL), Corporate Law, 1987—. *PRACTICE AREAS:* Company Law; Reorganizations; Labour Law; Financial Law; Competition Law.

FRANCOIS TULKENS, born 1963; admitted, 1986, Brussels. *Education:* University of Louvain (UCL) (Lic. Jur., 1986). Assistant Professor, University of Saint-Louis Law School, Brussels, Contract law, 1986—. *PRACTICE AREAS:* Constitutional and Administrative Law; Environmental Law; Insurance and Liability Law.

Languages: French, Dutch, English, German, Italian and Spanish

---

GEVERS PATENTS - BUREAU GEVERS

Established in 1898

BRUSSELS AIRPORT BUSINESS PARK
HOLIDAYSTRAAT 5
1831 DIEGEM
1831 BRUSSELS, BELGIUM
Telephone: 32-2-715 39 00
Fax: 32 2 720 50 70

Antwerp, Belgium Office: Rubenslei 2, B.8, B-2018 Antwerp. Telephone: 32-3-231 56 56. Telefax: 32-3-231 95 99. Telex: 26.407 Gevers B.

Patents, Trademarks, Designs, Copyright, Unfair Competition, License Agreements, Antitrust Matters.
Belgian Lawyers acting as Patent Agents are not Authorized to appear before the Belgian Courts as Avocats.

MEMBERS OF FIRM

JEAN-MARIE BURGRAEVE, *Education:* University of Louvain (Mechanical Civil Engineer, 1965).

JEAN CALLEWAERT, *Education:* University of Louvain (Chemical Engineer, 1961). Registered Belgian and European Patent Attorney. *Member:* Benelux Association of Trade Mark and Design Attorneys.

PIERRE CLAEYS, *Education:* University of Brussels (Cand. Biol. Sciences). Registered Belgian and European Patent Attorney.

JEAN-PAUL DEFFONTAINE, *Education:* University of Leuven (LL.B., 1991), University of Brussels (Master in Corporate Law, 1991).

CHRISTOPHE DE VROYE, *Education:* University of Leuven (LL.B., 1990); University of Brussels (Master in International Politics, 1993).

CHRISTINE FAURE DIDELLE, *Education:* University of Leuven (LL.B., 1990); University of Louvain-IAG (Master in Business Administration, 1991).

FLORENT GEVERS, *Education:* University of Louvain (Commercial Engineer, 1959); University of Strasbourg, France (Diplôme du C.E.I.P., 1968). Registered Belgian and European Patent Attorney. *Member:* Benelux Association of Trade Mark and Design Attorneys.

(This Listing Continued)

FRANCOIS GEVERS, Electromechanical Engineer (K.I.H. De Nayer, Mechelen, 1991).

GAELLE GEVERS, Master in Commercial and Financial Sciences (Brussels ICHEC, 1989).

JACQUES GEVERS, *Education:* University of Brussels (Commercial Engineer, 1964). Registered Belgian and European Patent Attorney. Registered to practice with the U.S. Patent Office. *Member:* Benelux Association of Trade Mark and Design Attorneys.

DOMINIQUE MARLOYE, *Education:* High School of Namur (Graduate in Legal Sciences, 1978). *Member:* Benelux Association of Trade Mark and Design Attorneys.

JACQUES PIERAERTS, Registered Belgian and European Patent Attorney.

JEAN-LÉON PIRE, *Member:* Benelux Association of Trade Mark and Design Attorneys.

ANDRIES QUATAERT, *Education:* University of Brussels (LL.B., 1986; Master in International and Comparative Law, 1987). *Member:* Benelux Association of Trade Mark and Design Attorneys.

CLAUDE QUINTELIER, *Education:* University of Nijmegen, The Netherlands (Bachelor in Physics, 1978). Registered Belgian, Dutch and European Patent Attorney.

YVES ROLAND, *Education:* University of Louvain (LL.B., 1974). *Member:* Benelux Association of Trade Mark and Design Attorneys.

YVON SCHMITZ, *Education:* University of Brussels (Bachelor in Chemical Sciences, 1965). Registered Belgian and European Patent Attorney.

GUY VAN DER STOCK, *Education:* University of Ghent (LL.D., 1963). Registered Belgian and European Patent Attorney. *Member:* Benelux Association of Trade Mark and Design Attorneys.

JEAN-PIERRE VAN DER STOCK, *Education:* University of Ghent (LL.D., 1955). Registered Belgian and European Patent Attorney. *Member:* Benelux Association of Trade Mark and Design Attorneys.

JOSEPH VAN REET, *Education:* University of Louvain (Bio Engineer, 1965). Registered Belgian Patent Attorney.

PHILIPPE VOSSWINKEL, *Education:* University of Mons (Candidate Civil Engineer, 1964). Registered Belgian Patent Attorney.

Languages: French, Dutch, English and German.

GIDE LOYRETTE NOUEL

RUE DE LA LOI 99.101
B-1040 BRUSSELS, BELGIUM
Telephone: (32.2) 231.11.40
Telecopier: (32.2) 231.11.77

Paris, France Office: 26 Cours Albert 1er, 75008. Telephone: (1) 40.75.60.00. Cable Address: "3 Avocagidva Paris 86." Telex: 651261F GILOY. Telecopier: (1) 43.59.37.79.

New York, New York Office: Swiss Bank Tower, 10 East 50th Street, 10022. Telephone: (1-212) 644-1201. Telex: 424353 GIDE. Telecopier: (1-212) 644-1205.

Warsaw, Poland Office: Ul. Kopernika 17, 00-359. Telephone: (48.22) 26.22.21. Telecopier: (48.22) 26.03.02.

Riyadh, Saudi Arabia Office: P.O. Box 4615, 11412. Telephone: (966.1) 476.60.39. Telex: 401677 NASHWA. Telecopier: (966.1) 476.18.96.

Tokyo, Japan Office: Homei Building 3F, 3-19 Akasaka 1-Chome, Minato-Ku, 107. Telephone: (81.3) 55.62.03.01. Telecopier: (81.3) 55.62.03.06.

Beijing, People's Republic of China Office: Suite 3309 A, Jing Guang Centre, Hu Jia Lou, Chaoyang District, 100020. Telephone: (86.1) 501 4511. Telecopier: (86.1) 501 4551.

Prague, Czech Republic Office: 34 Jindrisska, 11207. Telephone: (42.2) 24.21.34.65;24.21.36.50. Telecopier: (42.2) 24.21.09.12;24.22.58.53.

St. Petersburg, Russia Office: 34 Souvorovsky Prospect, App 45, P.O. Box 172, 193015. Telephone by satellite: (7.812) 850.16.85. Telecopier by satellite: (7.812) 850.16.86.

Moscow, Russia Office: 9, Ulitsa Tverskaya - App 66, 103009. Telephone by satellite: (7.501) 940.45.00. Telecopier by satellite: (7.501) 940.45.01.

(This Listing Continued)

GIDE LOYRETTE NOUEL, Brussels—Continued

Budapest VII, Hungary Office: EMKE Building, Rákóczi út 42, BP 409,
1072. Telephone: (36.1) 268.1236; 268.1237; 268.1238. Telecopier:
(36.1) 268.1239.

Madrid, Spain Office: Antonio Maura 7, 6°, 28014. Telephone: (34.1)
531.25.01. Telecopier: (34.1) 531.35.30.

Hanoi, Vietnam Office: Hanoi Business Centre, 51 Ly Thai To.
Telephone: (84.42) 66.122.3. Telecopier: (84.42) 66.030.1.

French, European Community and International Law.

RESIDENT PARTNER

OLIVIER D'ORMESSON, born Rabat, Morocco, September 26, 1953;
admitted, 1978, Paris; Licensed Legal Consultant, 1989, New York (Not
admitted in Belgium). *Education:* Ecole Supérieure de Commerce de Rouen
(Degree in Finance, Accountancy, 1976; D.E.C.S., 1977); University of
Paris (Maître en droit, 1977). Resident at Brussels Office, 1983-1986; Res-
ident at New York Office, 1990-1992; Resident at Brussels Office, 1993—.
Member: The Association of the Bar of the City of New York; New York
State and American Bar Associations; AIJA.

RESIDENT ASSOCIATES

Pierre Bourguignon
Jacques-Philippe Gunther
Anne Wachsmann
Laurent Caillaud
Olivier Assant

(For Biographical Data on Personnel, see Professional Biographies at
Paris, France).

HANS M. GILLIAMS

41, AVENUE DES ARTS, BOX 1
1040 BRUSSELS, BELGIUM
Telephone: (32-2) 505-0920
Fax: (32-2) 505-0997

*Practice focuses on European Community Law and Belgian Commercial
Law.*

HANS M. GILLIAMS, born Mortsel, Belgium, September 26, 1961;
admitted, 1987, New York; 1992, Brussels; also admitted to appear before
the Court of Justice of the European Communities and the Court of First
Instance of the European Communities. *Education:* University of Antwerp
(Cand. Juris, summa cum laude, 1981); University of Leuven (Lic. Juris,
summa cum laude, 1984); Harvard Law School (LL.M., 1985). Legal Secretary to the Hon. W. Van Gerven, Advocate-General at the Court of Justice
of the European Communities, Luxembourg, 1988-1992. *LANGUAGES:*
English, French, Dutch, German and Spanish. *PRACTICE AREAS:* Litigation involving European Community and Belgian Law; Antitrust Law;
State Aid; International Trade Law; Legal Issues relating to Privatization;
Public Procurement Law; Belgian Commercial Law.

GLEISS LUTZ HOOTZ HIRSCH & PARTNERS

Established in 1949

AVENUE LOUISE 475, BTE. 13
B-1050 BRUSSELS, BELGIUM
Telephone: (32) (2) 647 63 74
Telefax: (32) (2) 640 92 31
Telex: 65348 jura b

Stuttgart (Head Office), Germany Office: Maybachstrasse 6, D-70469
Stuttgart. Telephone: (49) (711) 89 97-0. Telefax: (49) (711) 85 50 96.
Telex: 722 439 jura d.

Frankfurt/Main, Germany Office: Eschersheimer Landstr. 19-21,
D-60322 Frankfurt/Main. Telephone: (49) (69) 955 14-0. Telefax: (49)
(69) 955 14 198; 955 14 199. Telex: 414 292glhcc d.

Berlin, Germany Office: Clara-Zetkin-Strasse 16, D-10117 Berlin.
Telephone: (49) (30) 2017 14-0. Telefax: (49) (30) 207 12 06.

Prague, Czech Republic Office: Jugoslávská 29, CR-120 00 Prague 2.
Telephone: (42) (2) 24007-510. Telefax: (42)(2) 24007-555.

*German, EC and International Practice, in particular Administrative, Anti-
Dumping, Anti-Trust, Arbitration, Banking, Capital Markets, Competition,
Commercial, Copyright, Corporate/Company, Corporate Finance, Environ-*

(This Listing Continued)

mental, Finance, Foreign Investment, Industrial Property Rights, Insurance, Labour, Litigation, Media, Mergers and Acquisitions, Real Property,
Regulated Industries, Securities, Tax, Telecommunications, Trade, Trademark, Unfair Competition, Zoning.
Not Authorized to Appear before the Belgian Courts.

FIRM PROFILE: The firm was established in 1949 in Stuttgart and developed from a German and later EC competition and anti-trust law boutique to a corporate practice with the full range of corporate legal services.
The firm opened its Brussels office in 1987, its Berlin and Frankfurt offices in 1990, and its Prague office in 1992. It employs in total 85 lawyers
and expects to grow in Central Europe in particular.

PARTNERS

DR. HANS-JÖRG NIEMEYER, born Siegen, 1956; admitted, 1985,
Germany; 1990, Registered as Foreign Attorney, Brussels. *Education:* Universities of Heidelberg, Munich and Münster (State Exams, 1981, 1985; Dr.
jur., 1989). Co-Author: "Hand- und Schulungsbuch der deutschen Rechts-
spraxis" (Manual on German Legal Practice), 1991. Author: "Die Europäische Fusionskontrollverordnung" (The European Merger Control Regulation), 1990; "Der sog. Jahrhundertvertrag nach deutschem Kartellrecht"
(Contract between the German Electricity Producers and the Coal Industry
in Accordance with German Antitrust Law), 1989. Lecturer on Law, University of Münster, 1985. With the Commission of the European Communities, 1986-1987. *Member:* German and International Bar Associations; Association for the Study of Antitrust Law; European Law Association; European Trade Law Association. *LANGUAGES:* German, English and
French. *PRACTICE AREAS:* EC State Aid; EC Trade Law; General EC
Law; German and EC Antitrust; German and EC Merger Control.

DR. WOLFGANG BOSCH (Resident Partner in the Stuttgart Office;
see CV and details listed under Stuttgart, Germany).

COUNSEL

PROF. DR. HANS JOACHIM GLAESNER, born Hildesheim, 1923;
admitted, 1987, Germany. *Education:* University of Göttingen (State Exams, 1950, 1954; Dr.jur., 1955). Author: "Das Recht als Gestaltungsmittel
der Politik der Europäischen Gemeinschaften" (The Role of Law as a Policy
Instrument in the European Communities), 1986. Co-author: "Der EWG-
Vertrag, Kommentar" (The EEC Treaty, a Commentary), 1960. Professor
of Law, University of Saarbrücken, 1987—. Visiting Professor of Law:
Fordham University of Law and Michigan Law School, 1988. Lecturer on
Law: University of Strasbourg/France, 1987-1989; University of Saar-
brücken, 1979-1989. Visiting Professor of Law, University of California,
Los Angeles and Berkeley, 1976. Director-General, Legal Services of the
Council of the EC, 1975-1986. Chef de Cabinet of Professors Dahrendort
and Brunner, Members of the Commission, 1973-1975. Director, Research
and Development Policy in the Commission of the EC, 1968-1973. Legal
Advisor to the Commission of the EC, 1960-1968. Counsellor, Federal
Ministry of Justice, Participation in Negotiating the EEC Treaties of Rome,
1956-1957. Judge, State of Lower Saxony, 1954-1956. *Member:* German
Society for Comparative Law; European and International Law Associa-
tions; International Bar Association; Society for International and Comparative Law. *LANGUAGES:* German, English and French. *PRACTICE
AREAS:* EC Institutions; EC State Aid; EC Trade Relations; General EC
Law; International Law.

GOMEZ-ACEBO & POMBO

RUE DE LA LOI, 99/101
1040 BRUSSELS, BELGIUM
Telephone: (322) 231-12-20
Fax: (322) 230-80-35

Madrid, Spain Office: Castellana, 164, 28046. Telephone: (341) 582 91
00. Fax: (341) 345 36 79; 582 91 14. Cable: Juristas. Telex: 23429
GAPO E.

Barcelona, Spain Office: Diagonal 442, 08037. Telephone: (343)
415-74-00. Fax: (343) 415-84-00.

Bilbao, Spain Office: Gran Vía, 31, 48009. Telephone: (344)
415-62-66/77. Fax: (344) 416-87-49.

Las Palmas (Canary Islands), Spain Office: Viera y Clavijo, 48, 35002.
Telephone: (342) 838-38-36. Fax: (342) 838-38-56.

Santiago de Compostela, Spain Office: Casas Reales, 4, 15704. Telephone:
(348) 157-33-46. Fax: (348) 157-35-46.

Seville, Spain Office: Av. de la Constitución, 40, 41001. Telephone: (345)
421-66-59; 422-18-93. Fax: (345) 421-08-14.

(This Listing Continued)

Valencia, Spain Office: Gran Vía Marqués del Turia, 49, 46005. Telephone: (346) 351-38-35. Fax: (346) 351-60-74.

Ricardo Garcia Vicente (Not admitted in Belgium)
Maria Luisa Tierno (Not admitted in Belgium)
Rosa Chover (Not admitted in Belgium)

(For Complete Biographical Data on all Personnel, see Professional Biographies at Madrid, Spain).

GOOVAERTS & ASSOCIES

116-118, AVENUE DES CERISIERS
1200 BRUSSELS, BELGIUM
Telephone: (02) 735.68.65 Intn'l Dialing: (32-2) 735.68.65
Facsimile: (32-2) 735.34.23

General and International Law Practice.

J. LEO GOOVAERTS, born 1940; admitted, 1965, Brussels. *Education:* University of Strasbourg (European Law, 1964-1965); University of Brussels (Doc. Jur., 1965); University of Louvain (First Lic. Economic Sciences, 1966); Harvard Law School (PIL, 1985). Author: "Legal Relationships between Spouses in Belgian and International Law," Dutch-French, 1982-1983; "Justified breach of Contract by the Employer in Belgian Labor Law," Dutch-French, 1987; "European Competition Law," French, 1987. Coauthor: "Effectiveness of Arbitration Clause in Distribution Agreements," Eng., 1987; "The Legal Status of Commercial Intermediaries in Belgium: Agency and Distribution Laws," Eng., 1988; "How to negotiate with power and respect," Dutch, 1992. *LANGUAGES:* French, Dutch and English. *PRACTICE AREAS:* International Distribution; Competition; Alternative Dispute Resolution; Liquidations; Tax; Arbitration and Mediation; Banking; Finance and Securities; Successions.

PAUL HERBINIAT, born 1957; admitted, 1980, Brussels. *Education:* University of Brussels (Lic.Jur., 1980). Author: "La Nature et l'Etendue des mesures Ordonnées sur Base de l'Art. 223 du Code Civil," J.J.P., 1984. Coauthor: "Relations Juridiques entre Epoux," 1982. *LANGUAGES:* French. *PRACTICE AREAS:* Separation and Divorce; International Family Law; Marital Property.

JEAN-PIERRE ARNOULD, born 1952; admitted, 1980, Brussels. *Education:* University of Brussels (Lic.Jur., 1978). *LANGUAGES:* French. *PRACTICE AREAS:* Public Law; Commercial Real Estate; Successions; Insurance; Torts.

JEAN-FRANÇOIS EYLENBOSCH, born 1959; admitted, 1984, Brussels. *Education:* University of Louvain (Lic.Jur., 1984). *LANGUAGES:* French, Dutch and English. *PRACTICE AREAS:* Company Law; Acquisitions and Sales; Liquidations; Bankruptcy; Legislative and Administrative Liability; Income Tax.

NOELLE KOZANECKI, born 1951; admitted, 1980, Brussels. *Education:* Catholic University of Louvain (Lic. Jur., 1974; Lic. Notarist, 1975). *LANGUAGES:* French, Dutch and English. *PRACTICE AREAS:* Commercial Real Estate; Inheritance; Successions.

CHRISTOPHE ROBBE, born 1963; admitted, 1988, Brussels. *Education:* University of Louvain (Lic. Jur., 1986); University of Brussels (Lic. Econ. Law, 1988). *LANGUAGES:* Dutch, French and English. *PRACTICE AREAS:* Finance and Securities; Competition; Trade Regulation; Products Liability; Consumer Protection; Distribution Agreements; Computer Contracts.

FREDERIC LAPOTRE, born 1965; admitted, 1990, Brussels. *Education:* University of Brussels (Lic. Jur., 1989). *LANGUAGES:* French and English. *PRACTICE AREAS:* Criminal Law; Construction Law; Separation and Divorce.

GOULDENS

GUIMARD CENTRE, RUE GUIMARD 6-8
B-1040 BRUSSELS, BELGIUM
Telephone: 32-2-230-3090
Facsimile: 32-2-230-3104

London, England Office: 22 Tudor Street, EC4Y 0JJ. Telephone: 0171-583-7777.Cable Address: "Toplaw London EC4". Telex: 21520 Toplaw G. Facsimile: 0171-583-3051.

(This Listing Continued)

St. Helier, Jersey, C.I. Office: P.O. Box 761, Ordnance House, 31 Pier Road, JE4 8ZZ. Telephone: 01534 66599. Facsimile: 01534 35195. Telex: 4192456 GDNJSY G.
Moscow, Russia Office: 20 Myasnitskaya St., 101851. Telephone: 7-095-921 7730. Fax: 7-095-921 3987.
Associated Offices in Paris and Hong Kong.

CONTACT PARTNER

J.J. DOYLE. LANGUAGES: French. *PRACTICE AREAS:* EC; Lobbying; International; Corporate.

GRAF VON WESTPHALEN & MODEST

AVENUE DE LA JOYEUSE ENTRÉE 1, BOITE 16
B-1040 BRUSSELS, BELGIUM
Telephone: (32) (2) 230.46.69
Telefax: (32) (2) 231.00.35

EEC Law, German, French and International Law.

P.S.R.F. MATHIJSEN, born Tilburg, Netherlands, March 7, 1924; (Not admitted in Belgium). *Education:* University of Minnesota (M.A., Economics, 1952); University of Leyden (M.A., 1951; Ph.D., 1957). Assistant Professor, Law School, University of Michigan, 1961-1962. Professor: Law Faculty, University of Nijmegen, Netherlands, 1967-1985; Law Faculty, University of Brussels, Belgium, 1986—. Attaché, ECSC Court of Justice, 1953-1958. Legal Adviser, EAEC Commission, 1958-1967. Director, DGIV Competition, EEC Commission, 1968-1977. Director General for Regional Policy, EC Commission, 1977-1986. Member of the Board, European Investment Bank, 1977-1986. Delegate General, CIAA, Brussels, Belgium, 1986-1989. Author: "A Guide to European Community Law," London/New York, 1972, 5. Edition, 1990. Member, Editorial Staff, "Encyclópedia of European Community Law," and "European Law Review," 1973—. *LANGUAGES:* Dutch, French, English and German.

(For biographical data of the personnel, see Professional Biographies at Paris, France; See also Eurolegal, Brussels, Belgium; Hamburg and Cologne personnel, see Hamburg and Cologne, Germany)

HAMMOND SUDDARDS

AVENUE LOUISE 250
1050 BRUSSELS, BELGIUM
Telephone: 00 32 2 627 7676
Fax: 00 32 2 627 7686

Leeds, England Office: 2 Park Lane. LS3 1ES. Telephone: 0113 234 3500. Fax: 0113 234 3600. Telex: 517201.
London, England Office: Moor House, 119 London Wall, London, EC2Y 5ET. Telephone: 0171 628 4767. Fax: 0171 628 6161.
Manchester, England Office: Trinity Court, 16 John Dalton Street, M60 8HS. Telephone: 0161 834 2222. Fax: 0161 834 2244.
Bradford, England Office: Pennine House, 39-45 Well Street. BD1 5NL. Telephone: 01274 734700. Fax: 01274 737547. Telex: 517201.

Corporate Finance including Acquisitions and Mergers, Corporate Finance, Commercial including Joint Ventures, Pensions, Banks and Building Societies, Intellectual Property, Commercial Litigation, Construction, Insolvency and Corporate Recovery, Debt Collection, Town and Country Planning, Environmental Law, Commercial Property, European Community Law, Information Technology Law, Employment, Utilities, Insurance Litigation, Media, Mortgage and Aviation Law.
Hammond Suddards has over 870 staff, including 58 partners, 100 Associates and 50 Legal Executives and Paralegals.

RESIDENT PARTNERS

KONSTANTINOS ADAMANTOPOULOS. PRACTICE AREAS: European Community Law.

STEPHEN TUPPER (Not admitted in Belgium). *PRACTICE AREAS:* European Community Law.

(For Lists of other Members, see Professional Biographies at Bradford, London, Manchester and Leeds, England)

HANOTIAU, BRUYNS et ASSOCIATES

391, AVENUE LOUISE (B.11)
B-1050 BRUSSELS, BELGIUM
Telephone: 32-2 640 3525
Fax: 32-2-648 5086

Paris, France Office: 14, Avenue Gourand, F-75017. Telephone: 33-1-44 156100. Fax: 33-1-44 151981.

General EEC, International and National Commercial Practice, Taxation, Corporate, Mergers and Acquisitions, Banking, Commercial Arbitration and Litigation, Competition, Computer Law, Trademarks, Patents and Copyright Law, Real Estate.

MEMBERS OF FIRM

BERNARD HANOTIAU, born Charleroi, Belgium, August 10, 1947; admitted, 1975, Brussels; 1988, Paris. *Education:* University of Louvain (Dr. Juris, 1970; Special Degree in Labour Law, 1972; Ph.D., Private International Law, 1979); Southern Methodist University Academy of American and International Law (1971); Columbia University School of Law (LL.M., 1973). Author: "Les Problèmes de Sécurité Sociale des Travailleurs Migrants," 1973, Le Droit International Privé Americain, 1979. Co-Author: "Le Droit des Contrats Informatiques," 1983. Professor of Law, Universities of Louvain-La-Neuve and Namur. *LANGUAGES:* English, French and Flemish. *PRACTICE AREAS:* Arbitration; International Commercial Law; Banking Law.

FRANÇOIS BRUYNS, born Ixelles, Belgium, July 10, 1952; admitted, 1976, Brussels. *Education:* University of Louvain (Dr. Jr., 1976). *LANGUAGES:* French and Flemish. *PRACTICE AREAS:* Leasing, Real Estate.

JEAN-PIERRE BRUSSELEERS, born Brasschaat, Belgium, April 15, 1954; admitted, 1980, Brussels. *Education:* University of Leuven (K.U.L., 1977); Universiteit van Amsterdam (Business Law, 1978); Tax Law, E.S.S.F., Brussels (1982). *LANGUAGES:* English, French and Flemish. *PRACTICE AREAS:* Taxation.

CEDRIC GUYOT, born Etterbeek, Belgium, February 11, 1958; admitted, 1986, Brussels. *Education:* University of Louvain, Louvain-la-Neuve (Dr. Jr., 1982; Special degree in E.E.C. Law, 1983); Temple University, Philadelphia (LL.M., 1985); University of Brussels, Solvay School of Commerce (Post Graduate degree in International Trade Law, 1989). *LANGUAGES:* English, French and Flemish. *PRACTICE AREAS:* Corporate, Financial and Securities Law.

STANISLAS VAN WASSENHOVE, born Leuven, Belgium, September, 1958; admitted, 1981, Brussels; 1990, Paris. *Education:* University of Louvain (Dr.Jr., 1981: Dr. Jr. in International public affairs, 1982). *LANGUAGES:* English, French and Flemish. *PRACTICE AREAS:* Labour and Social Security Law.

ASSOCIATES

PAUL LEFEBVRE, born Ghent, Belgium, December 21, 1960; admitted, 1985, Brussels. *Education:* State University of Ghent (Dr. Jr., 1983); University of Brussels (Special Degree in Economic Law, 1985; European Law, 1984); University of Cambridge, Magdalene College (LL.M., 1986). *LANGUAGES:* English, French and Flemish. *PRACTICE AREAS:* Corporate, Banking Law, Distributorship.

EVE-MARIE CLABOTS, born Huy, Belgium, December 26, 1961; admitted, 1988, Brussels. *Education:* University of Louvain, Louvain-la-Neuve (Dr. Jr., 1986; Degree in Law and Economics, 1988); Southern Methodist University, Academy of American and International Law, Dallas (1989). *LANGUAGES:* English and French. *PRACTICE AREAS:* Banking Law.

FRANÇOIS STEVENART MEEUS, born Uccle, Belgium, July 2, 1964; admitted, 1987, Brussels. *Education:* University of Louvain (Dr.Jr., 1987); State University of Utrecht (Special Degree in European Law, 1990); E.S.S.F. Brussels (Post Graduate Degree in Tax Law, 1992). *LANGUAGES:* French and Flemish. *PRACTICE AREAS:* Tax Law.

tGEERT GOETEYN, born Ghent, Belgium, December 12, 1966; admitted, 1990, Brussels. *Education:* University of Leuven (Dr. Jr., 1989); City University Business School, London (M.Sc., Shipping Trade and Finance, 1989-1990). *LANGUAGES:* English, Flemish and French.

SEBASTIEN RYELANDT, born Kinshasa, Zaire, March 23, 1966; admitted, 1991, Brussels. *Education:* University of Leuven (Dr.Jr., 1990); University of Brussels (Special Degree in Tax Law, 1991). *LANGUAGES:* English, Flemish and French.

(This Listing Continued)

NANCY LUYTEN, born Heist-op-den-Berg, Belgium, April 26, 1969; admitted, 1992, Belgium. *Education:* University of Leuven (Dr.Jr., 1992). *LANGUAGES:* English, Flemish and French.

HAVER & MAILAENDER

Established in 1965
AV. DE LA RENAISSANCE 1
B-1040 BRUSSELS, BELGIUM
Telephone: 02-7366375
Telecopier: 02-7360571

Stuttgart, Germany Office: Lenzhalde 83, D-70192. Telephone: (0711) 227440. Cable Address: "Intertax", Stuttgart. Telex: 721738 advo d. Telecopier: (0711) 2991935.

Dresden, Germany Office: Bautzner Strasse 23-25, D-01099. Telephone: 0351-51955. Telecopier: 0351-53538.

Frankfurt, Germany Office: Beethovenstrasse 4, D-60325. Telephone: 069-740190. Telecopier: 069-740247.

Commercial, Corporation, Banking and Financial Services, Mergers and Acquisitions, High Technology and Telecommunication, Transportation and Aviation, Construction and Engineering Contracts, Antitrust, EEC-Law, Licensing, Patent, Trademark, Copyright, Trade Law and Product Liability, International and Tax Law, Litigation and Arbitration.

Not authorized to appear before the Belgian Courts. Entitled to plead before the Court of Justice of the European Communities and before the EC-Commission.

FIRM PROFILE: The firm was established in Stuttgart in 1965 and opened its Brussels Office in 1987. The firm offers the full range of legal services for commercial matters. The Brussels Office concentrates on Community Law issues.

PARTNER IN CHARGE

DR. ROLF M. WINKLER, born Krakau, Poland, 1942; admitted, 1974, Stuttgart. *Education:* Universities of Berlin, Frankfurt and Tuebingen (Doctor of Law, 1970); University of California at Berkeley (Master of Laws, 1973). Author: "Die Rechtsnatur der Geldbusse im Wettbewerbsrecht der Europaeischen Wirtschaftsgemeinschaft," 1971, "The New Joint Venture Law of the European Community," 1994. Legal Assistant at the EEC Commission, Brussels, 1968-1969. Assistant at the University of Tubingen, 1969-1970. *Member:* German Bar Association; American Society of International Law; German-American Lawyers Association (Board Member); Canadian-German Lawyers Association (Board Member); International Bar Association (Member, Business Law Section). *LANGUAGES:* German, English and French. *PRACTICE AREAS:* European Community Law; International Law.

Languages: German, English, French and Italian

(For complete list of Partners, see Professional Biographies at Stuttgart and Frankfurt/Main, Germany)

HELLER, LÖBER, BAHN & PARTNERS

Established in 1994
RUE DE LA LOI 99/101
B-1040 BRUSSELS, BELGIUM
Telephone: (322) 287 2655
Fax: (322) 280 0983

Vienna, Austria Office: Seilergasse 16, A-1010. Telephone: (431) 515 15 0. Fax: (431) 512 63 94. Telex: 114874 lawco a.

Budapest, Hungary Office: János Zsigmond U. 7B, H-1121. Telephone: (361) 209 33 70. Fax: (361) 186 84 81.

Prague, Czech Republic Office: Italská 27, CZ-12000. Telephone: (422) 242 310 06. Fax: (422) 242 183 75.

Bratislava, Slovakia Office: Laurinská 12, SK-81101. Telephone: (427) 36 14 39. Fax: (427) 36 14 78.

Advice and Assistance in all areas of European Community Law and Austrian Law.

PARTNERS

MARIA TH. PFLÜGL, born Traunkirchen, 1956; admitted, 1989, Austria. *Education:* University of Vienna Law School (Dr. iur.) and Philosophical Faculty. *Member:* Vienna Bar Association; Union Internationale des Avocats; Association Internationale des Jeunes Avocats; International Fis-

(This Listing Continued)

cal Association. *LANGUAGES:* German, English and French. *PRACTICE AREAS:* Tax and Banking.

RESIDENT ASSOCIATES

AXEL REIDLINGER, born Vienna, Austria, 1967. *Education:* University of Vienna Law School (Mag.iur.); Vienna University of Economics and Business Administration (Mag.rer.soc.oec.); College of Europe, Bruges, Belgium (LL.M., in European Community Law). *LANGUAGES:* German, French and English.

HENGELER MUELLER WEITZEL WIRTZ

Rechtsanwälte

BOULEVARD DU RÈGENT 50, BTE. 6
B-1000 BRUSSELS, BELGIUM
Telephone: (2) 511 41 15
Telefax: (2) 514 02 12

Düsseldorf, Germany Office: Trinkausstrasse 7, D-40213 Düsseldorf. Telephone: (0211) 8304-0. Telefax: (02ll) 13 26 41 & 8 04 61. Telex: 85 87 300 whds d.

Frankfurt/Main, Germany Office: Bockenheimer Landstrasse 51, D-60325 Frankfurt/Main. Telephone: (069) 170 95-0. Telefax: (069) 72 57 73 & 7239 83. Telex: 41 45 95 jura d.

Berlin, Germany Office: Kurfürstendamm 54/55, D-10707 Berlin. Telephone: (030) 882 76 47. Telefax: (030) 882 7144.

Budapest, Hungary Office: Teréz krt. 38, H-1066. Telephone: (1) 1323121. Telefax: (1) 2690098.

New York Office: 712 Fifth Avenue, New York, New York, 10019. Telephone: (212) 586-4600. Telefax: (212) 586-4481.

German, EEC and International Law.

RESIDENT PARTNERS

DR. BERNHARD M. MAASSEN, born Munich, Germany, 1946; admitted, 1976, Frankfurt/Main. *Education:* Universities of Kiel, Freiburg and Bonn (Dr. jur.); University of California, Berkeley (LL.M.). (Also at Frankfurt/Main, Germany Office).

JOCHEN BURRICHTER, born Waltrop/Westfalen, Germany, 1941; admitted, 1973, Düsseldorf. *Education:* Universities of Münster and Freiburg. (Also at Düsseldorf, Germany Office).

DR. HORST SATZKY, born Baden-Baden, Germany, 1954; admitted, 1987, Frankfurt/Main. *Education:* Universities of Berlin and Kiel (Dr.jur.). Official Federal Cartel Office, Berlin, Federal Ministry of Economics, Bonn, 1985-1987. Foreign Associate, New York Law Firm, 1989-1990. (Also at Frankfurt/Main, Germany Office).

Languages: German, English and French

(For complete list of partners, see Professional Biographies at Düsseldorf, Frankfurt/Main and Berlin, Germany)

HERBERT SMITH

15, RUE GUIMARD
1040 BRUSSELS, BELGIUM
Telephone: 322-511 7450
Fax: 322-511 7772

London, England Office: Exchange House, Primrose Street, EC2A 2HS. Telephone: 0171-374-8000. Telex: 886633. Fax: 0171-496-0043.

Hong Kong Office: 17th Floor, Edinburgh Tower, 15 Queen's Road Central. Telephone: 852-8456639. Telex: 72266. Fax: 852-8459099.

Paris, France Office: 41 Avenue George V, 75008. Telephone: 3314-723-9124. Telex: 219602. Fax: 3314-720-9213.

RESIDENT PARTNERS

S. Kinsella

(For list of Partners see Professional Biographies at London, England)

HOGAN & HARTSON L.L.P.

AVENUE DES ARTS 41
1040 BRUSSELS, BELGIUM
Telephone: (32.2) 505.09.11
Fax: (32.2) 502.28.60

Washington, D.C. Office: Columbia Square, 555 13th Street, N.W. Telephone: 202-637-5600. Telex: 89-2757. Cable Address: "Hogander Washington". Fax: 202-637-5910.

London, England Office: Veritas House, 125 Finsbury Pavement, EC2A 1NQ. Telephone: (44 171) 638.9595. Fax: (44 171) 638.0884.

Moscow, Russia Office: 33/2 Usacheva Street, Building 3, 119048. Telephone: (7095) 245-5190. Fax: (7095) 245-5192.

Paris, France Office: Cabinet Wolfram, 14, rue Chauveau-Lagarde, 75008. Telephone: (33-1) 44.71.97.00. Fax: (33-1) 47.42.13.56.

Prague, Czech Republic Office: Opletalova 37, 110 00. Telephone: (42-2) 2422-9009. Fax: (42-2) 2421-5105.

Warsaw, Poland Office: Marszalkowska 6/6, 00-590. Telephone: (48 2) 628 0201; Int'l (48) 3912 1413. Fax: (48 2) 628 7787; Int'l (48) 3912 1511.

Baltimore, Maryland Office: 111 South Calvert Street, 16th Floor. Telephone: 410-659-2700. Fax: 410-539-6981.

Bethesda, Maryland Office: Two Democracy Center, Suite 720, 6903 Rockledge Drive. Telephone: 301-564-5000. Fax: 301-493-5169.

Colorado Springs, Colorado Office: 518 North Nevada Avenue, Suite 200. Telephone: 719-635-5900. Fax: 719-635-2847.

Denver, Colorado Office: One Tabor Center, Suite 1500, 1200 Seventeenth Street. Telephone: 303-899-7300. Fax: 303-899-7333.

McLean, Virginia Office: 8300 Greensboro Drive. Telephone: 703-848-2600. Fax: 703-448-7650.

General Practice. Firm engaged in the practice of European Union Law, United States Law and International Law. Not authorized to appear before the Belgian Courts.

RESIDENT PARTNERS

CLAUD V. S. ELEY, born Lexington, Virginia, May 31, 1957; admitted, 1982, Virginia (Not admitted in Belgium). *Education:* College of William & Mary (B.A., 1979); Emory University (J.D., 1982). *Member:* Virginia State Bar; Virginia, American and International Bar Associations. *PRACTICE AREAS:* International Commercial Transactions.

RANDY E. MILLER, born Manhattan, Kansas, October 24, 1953; admitted, 1982, District of Columbia (Not admitted in Belgium). *Education:* Yale University (B.A., cum laude, 1976); Georgetown University (J.D., cum laude, 1982). Policy Director to Senator Robert J. Dole, 1981-1983. *Member:* District of Columbia Bar; American and International Bar Associations; Court of International Trade Bar; ITC Trial Lawyers Bar Association. *PRACTICE AREAS:* European Regulatory and Business Law; International Trade Law.

RICHARD L.A. WEINER, born White Plains, New York, June 30, 1959; admitted, 1987, California; 1988, District of Columbia (Not admitted in Belgium). *Education:* Harvard University (A.B., magna cum laude, 1981); University of Cambridge (M.Phil., 1982); Columbia University (J.D., 1985). Expert Consultant, Commission of the European Communities, Directorate-General for External Relations, 1991-1992. *Member:* State Bar of California; District of Columbia Bar. *LANGUAGES:* English, French and Spanish. *PRACTICE AREAS:* European Communities Law; International Trade Law; Telecommunications Law.

RESIDENT COUNSEL

GERALD E. OBERST, JR., born Owensboro, Kentucky, November 16, 1954; admitted, 1981, District of Columbia (Not admitted in Belgium). *Education:* University of Kentucky (B.A., 1977); University of Virginia (J.D., 1981). Managing Editor, Virginia Journal of Natural Resources Law, 1980-1981. *Member:* District of Columbia Bar; Federal Communications Bar Association (Member, Section of International Law); Society of Satellite Professionals International. *LANGUAGES:* English and French. *PRACTICE AREAS:* Telecommunications Law; Satellite Technology Law.

PHILIPPA WATSON, born Dublin, Ireland, November 28, 1951; admitted as Barrister, 1973, King's Inn Dublin; 1988, Middle Temple, London; (Not admitted in Belgium). *Education:* Trinity College (M.A., 1973); University of Cambridge (LL.B., 1974; Ph.D., Law, 1977). Author: Social Security Law of the European Communities (English and Spanish versions). Contributor to: *Common Market Law of Competition,* Bellamy and Child, 1993; *Public Procurement,* Butterworth's London, 1992; *Substantive Law of the EEC,* Wyatt and Dashwood, Third Edition, 1993. Lecturer, "European

(This Listing Continued)

HOGAN & HARTSON L.L.P., Brussels—Continued

Communities Law," University of London, 1978-1979. Visiting Professor, "European Communities Law," Catholic University of Louvain, 1979-1980. Law Clerk to Judge A. O'Keeffe and Judge T.F. O'Higgins, European Court of Justice, Luxembourg, 1980-1985. Official, Commission of the European Communities, Directorate-General for Competition, 1985-1987. Founding Member and Secretary to the European Maritime Law Organization. *Member:* British Institute for International and Comparative Law. *LANGUAGES:* English and French. *PRACTICE AREAS:* European Communities Law.

OF COUNSEL

CLAYTON K. YEUTTER, born Eustis, Nebraska, December 10, 1930; admitted, 1963, Nebraska; 1977, District of Columbia (Not admitted in Belgium). *Education:* University of Nebraska (B.S., with high distinction, 1952; J.D., cum laude, 1963; Ph.D., 1966). Alpha Zeta; Gamma Sigma Delta; Phi Alpha Delta. Order of the Coif. Editor, Nebraska Law Review. Assistant Secretary for Marketing and Consumer Services, U.S.D.A., 1973-1974. Assistant Secretary (now Undersecretary) for International Affairs and Commodity Programs, U.S.D.A., 1974-1975. Deputy Special Trade Representative, Executive Office of the President, 1975-1977. U.S. Trade Representative, Executive Office of the President, 1985-1989. Secretary of Agriculture, 1989-1991. Counselor to the President, 1992. Director, University of Nebraska Mission to Colombia (South America), 1968-1970. Chairman, Republican National Committee, 1991-1992. President and CEO, Chicago Mercantile Exchange, 1978-1985. *Member:* Nebraska State Bar Association; District of Columbia Bar. *PRACTICE AREAS:* International Trade, Food and Agriculture.

(For complete biographical data on all personnel, see Professional Biographies at Washington, D.C.)

HUNTON & WILLIAMS

AVENUE LOUISE 106
1050 BRUSSELS, BELGIUM
Telephone: 011 (32-2)-646-0010
FAX: 011 (32-2)-646-0246

Warsaw, Poland Office: Ul. Bagatela 14, Vp., 00-585 Warsaw, Poland. Telephone: 011 (48-2) 625 21 07. Telecopier: 011 (48-2) 621 83 94.

Atlanta, Georgia Office: NationsBank Plaza, 600 Peachtree Street, N.E. Telephone: 404-888-4000. Fax: 404-888-4190.

New York, New York Office: 200 Park Avenue. Telephone: 212-309-1000. Cable Addresses: "Huntward, New York" and "Dialboard." Telex: 424 549 HUNT UI. Fax: 212-309-1100.

Washington, D.C. Office: 2000 Pennsylvania Avenue, N.W., P.O. Box 19230. Telephone: 202-955-1500. Telex: 350 362 H&W WASH UD. FAX: 202-778-2201 (Rapicom); 202-778-2202 (Ricoh230).

Richmond, Virginia Office: Riverfront Plaza, East Tower, 951 East Byrd Street. Telephone: 804-788-8200. Cable Address: "Huntward." Telex: 804-684-4251. Fax: 804-788-8218. TWX: 710-956-0061; Church Hill Office: 2300 East Marshall Street. Telephone: 804-775-2248.

Raleigh, North Carolina Office: One Hannover Square, P.O. Box 109. Telephone: 919-899-3000. FAX: 919-899-3096.

Knoxville, Tennessee Office: 2000 Riverview Tower, 900 South Gay Street. Telephone: 615-549-7700. FAX: 615-549-7704.

Fairfax, Virginia Office: 3050 Chain Bridge Road, P.O. Box 1147. Telephone: 703-352-2200. Fax: 703-273-6772.

Norfolk, Virginia Office: Crestar Bank Building, Suite 1000, 500 East Main Street. Telephone: 804-625-5501. Telex: 825 455 H&W NFK. FAX: 804-625-7720.

General and International Practice.
Office engaged in European Business Law and in European Communities Regulatory and Administrative practice, including Competition, Trade, Environmental, Energy, Health and Safety and Food and Drug Law.
Firm engaged in American Business Law, International Business Law and European Communities Law. Not Authorized to appear before the Belgian Courts.

PARTNERS

CHARLES A. BLANCHARD, born Richmond, Virginia, September 24, 1957; admitted, 1985, Virginia (Not admitted in Belgium). *Education:* University of Colorado at Boulder (B.A., 1980); Washington & Lee University (J.D., summa cum laude, 1985). Phi Beta Kappa. Order of the Coif. Member,

(This Listing Continued)

---

ber, Washington & Lee Law Review, 1983-1985. (Managing Partner) (Also, Warsaw, Poland Office). *LANGUAGES:* English and French.

RAY V. HARTWELL, III, born Anniston, Alabama, June 19, 1947; admitted, 1975, Virginia; 1980, District of Columbia (Not admitted in Belgium). *Education:* Washington & Lee University (B.A., 1969; J.D., summa cum laude, 1975). Omicron Delta Kappa; Order of the Coif; Delta Theta Phi. Winner, John W. Davis Prize, 1975. Editor-in-Chief, Washington & Lee Law Review, 1974-1975. Member, Editorial Advisory Boards, The Antitrust Bulletin and The Journal of Reprints for Antitrust Law and Economics, 1978—; Council Member, 1992—. Chair, Consumer Protection Committee, 1989-1992, Vice-Chair, Criminal Practice and Procedure Committee, 1987-1989, American Bar Association Section of Antitrust Law. Chairman, 1979-1980 and Member, Board of Governors, 1977-1981, Antitrust Franchising and Trade Regulation Section, Virginia State Bar. Member, International Bar Association; ABA Section of Science and Technology, Intellectual Property Law. [Lt.(j.g.), U.S. Navy, 1969-1972]. (Also, Richmond, Virginia, Washington, D.C. and Warsaw, Poland Offices). *LANGUAGES:* English and French.

TURNER T. SMITH, JR., born Washington, D.C., December 16, 1940; admitted, 1968, Virginia; 1977, District of Columbia (Not admitted in Belgium). *Education:* Princeton University (B.A., magna cum laude, 1962); Harvard Law School (LL.B., cum laude, 1968). Co-author, European Community Deskbook, 1992. Co-Editor, Understanding U.S. and European Environmental Law -- A Practitioner's Guide, 1989. Associate Editor, Oxford Journal of Environmental Law, 1989. Instructor: Environmental Law, William & Mary Law School, 1979-1980; Washington & Lee Law School, 1978. Chairman: Environmental Controls Committee, Corporation, Banking and Business Law Section, American Bar Association, 1973-1980; Chairman, Standing Committee on Environmental Law, American Bar Association, 1983-1986. Secretary/Treasurer, 1994, Member, Board of Directors, Environmental Law Institute, 1989. *Member:* International Bar Association. (Also, Washington, D.C. Office). *LANGUAGES:* English and French.

SPECIAL CONSULTANT

RICHARD MACRORY, born Headley, Surrey, England, March 30, 1950; admitted, 1974, London. *Education:* Oxford University (B.A., 1972; M.A., 1976); Barrister of Law, Grays Inn (1974). Editor-in-Chief, Journal of Environmental Law, Oxford University Press, 1988—. Denton Hall Professor of Environmental Law; Associate Director, ICCET. Co-Author: with B. Zaba: "Polluters Pay: The Control of Pollution Act," FOE Publications, London, 1974; with M. Lafontaine: "Public Inquiry & Enquete Publique - Forms of Public Participation in England & France," Institute for European Environmental Policy, London, 1982; with D. Gilbert: "Pesticide Related Law," British Crop Protection Council, Farnham, 1989. Author: "Nuisance," Oyez Longman, London, 1982; "Water Law: Principles & Practice," Oyez Longman, London, 1985; "The Water Act 1989," Sweet and Maxwell, London, Current Law Statutes Annotated Reprint, 1989. Member, Royal Commission on Environmental Pollution, 1991—. Council Member, UK Environmental Law Association, 1989-1992. Standing Counsel, Council for the Protection of Rural England, 1981-1992. Specialist Advisor, House of Commons Select Committee, 1989—. Member UK National Advisory Committee on Eco-Labelling, Chairman of Sub-Committee on Administration, 1990-1991. Member UK Vienna Centre East-West Committee Economic & Social Research Council, 1989-1991.

RESIDENT ASSOCIATES

LUCAS BERGKAMP, born Hertogenbosch, Netherlands, February 23, 1961; admitted, 1991, New York (Not admitted in Belgium). *Education:* University of Amsterdam Faculty of Law (J.D., 1985; Dr.Iur, 1988); University of Amsterdam Faculty of Medicine (M.D., 1988); Yale Law School (LL.M., 1989). Associate, Bryan, Cave, McPheeters & McRoberts, Washington, D.C., 1989-1990. Publications including: "An Overview of Recent Developments in EC Food Regulation and Consumer Protection," *World Food Regulation Review* (BNA), July 1993; "Dutch Environmental Law: An Overview of Recent Trends," *International Environment Reporter* (BNA) Vol 16, No. 4, February 1993; "Compensating Personal Injuries Caused by DES: 'No Causation Liability' In the Netherlands," *World Pharmaceuticals Report* (BNA), January 1993; "Eco-Labelling in Europe: New Market-Related Environmental Risks?," *International Environment Reporter* (BNA) Vol. 15, No. 19, September 1992; "Recent Developments in Environmental Liability in Europe," Integrated Environmental Management, 1992; "Mergers and Acquisitions in the New European Community," in: Transnational Joint Ventures, 1991; "Packaging Waste Developments in Europe," *International Environment Reporter* (BNA), 1991; "E.C. Food Regulation and Consumer Protection," *World Food Regulation Review* (BNA), 1991; "Regula-

(This Listing Continued)

tion of Drug Trials in the European Community," *World Pharmaceutical Standards Review* (BNA), 1991; "Opportunities in the EC for Generic Manufacturers: The Legal and Legislative Perspective," *World Pharmaceutical Standards Review* (BNA), 1991. National Reporter for the Netherlands, International Academy of Comparative Law, 1990. Editor-in-Chief, "Gids Jurisprudentie Gezondheidsrecht," (Cases in Health Law, Loose-leaf), 1990. Editorial Board, European Health Law Journal. Advisory Boards, World Pharmaceutical Standards Review (BNA) and World Food Regulation Review (BNA). *Member:* American Bar Association (Member, Sections on Business and International Law); Belgian Environmental Law Association; Netherlands Lawyers Association; Dutch Association for Health Law; Dutch Association for European Law; Dutch Environmental Law Association. *LANGUAGES:* English, Dutch, German and French.

ROSZELL D. HUNTER, born Gastonia, North Carolina, April 23, 1960; admitted, 1989, Virginia; 1991, District of Columbia (Not admitted in Belgium). *Education:* Hampden-Sydney College (B.A., 1982); University of Virginia (J.D., 1986). Notes Editor, Virginia Law Review, 1985-1986. Author: "Environmental Law in the European Economic Area," 16 Intl. Envir. Report (BNA) 504 (June 1993); "Standardization and the Environment," 16 Intl. Envir. Report (BNA) 185 (March 1993); "Proposed Waste Transfer System Within the EC," 14 Intl. Envir. Report (BNA) 695 (Dec. 1991); "The Extraterritorial Application of the Constitution--Unalienable Rights," 72 Virginia Law Review 649 (1986). Co-Author: "European Community Environmental Law Deskbook," ELI, 1992; "EC Environmental Legal System", 22 E.L.R. 10, 106 (1992); "The Revised European Community Civil Liability to Damage From Waste Proposal," 21 E.L.R. 10, 718 (1991); "Hazardous Wastes- The Knowing Endangerment Offence: United States v. Protex Inc.," 2 Journal of Environmental Law 262 (1990); Judicial Clerkships: Sir Anthony F. Mason, Chief Justice of the High Court of Australia, 1988; the Hon. Boyce F. Martin Jr., U. S. Court of Appeals for the 6th Circuit, 1986-1987. *LANGUAGES:* English, French and German.

HUYSMANS & PARTNERS

AVENUE DES GLOIRES NATIONALES 10
1080 BRUSSELS, BELGIUM
Telephone: 32 2 426.14.14
Fax: 32 2 426.20.30

FIRM PROFILE: *The firm was established in 1991 and offers a full range of legal services. The firm prides itself on combining the said services with a sound business judgment. The client base consists of a corporate clientele, a majority of which are European, African and North American corporations seeking to establish in Belgium. The firm has acquired a large experience in EEC, Corporate, Commercial, Banking and Tax Law and has successively assisted clients in tendering procedures and other procedures of an administrative nature.*

PARTNERS

FRANK HUYSMANS, born Deinze, June 25, 1949; admitted, 1988, Brussels. *Education:* University of Brussels (Lic.Jur., 1973); London Business School (Executive M.B.A., 1981). Secretary General and General Counsel, ITT Bell Telephone Manufacturing Company, 1975-1988. *LANGUAGES:* Dutch, French, English. *PRACTICE AREAS:* International Commercial and Trade Law; Intellectual Property Law; Mergers and Acquisitions; Licensing and Joint Ventures.

FERNAND COLPAERT, born Kortrijk, June 14, 1951; admitted, 1974, Brussels. *Education:* University of Brussels (Lic.Jur., 1974). *LANGUAGES:* Dutch, French. *PRACTICE AREAS:* Labour and Social Security Law.

JOHAN VANDEN EYNDE, born Brussels, March 23, 1952; admitted, 1982, Brussels. *Education:* University of Brussels (Lic.Jur., 1982). *LANGUAGES:* French, Dutch, English. *PRACTICE AREAS:* Company Law; Banking Law; Administrative Law.

CARINE VAN REGENMORTEL, born Antwerp, June 22, 1960; admitted, 1984, Brussels. *Education:* University of Antwerp (Lic.Jur., 1983); College of Europe, Bruges (Special Degree, European Law, 1984). Recipient, British Council Scholarship Award, 1988. *Member:* European Young Lawyers Programme, London. *LANGUAGES:* Dutch, French, English. *PRACTICE AREAS:* Commercial and Company Law; Competition Law; Mergers and Acquisitions.

JEAN-MARC WOLTER, born September 28, 1957; admitted, 1982, Brussels. *Education:* University of Brussels (Lic.Jur., 1981). *LANGUAGES:* French. *PRACTICE AREAS:* Property and Construction Law; Immigration Law; EEC Law; Non-EEC Nationals Law.

(This Listing Continued)

PHILIPPE JADOUL, born Antwerp, 1962; admitted, 1987, Brussels; 1994, solicitor of the Supreme Court of England and Wales. *Education:* University of Antwerp (Lic.Jur., 1985); European Young Lawyers Course (British Council) London, 1988; Course on American Law, Columbia University , New York, 1988. *LANGUAGES:* Dutch, French, English and German. *PRACTICE AREAS:* Corporate Law; Telecommunications; Commercial Law.

CHRISTOPHE RONSE, born Kortrijk, 1964; admitted, 1988, Brussels. *Education:* University of Louvain (Lic.Jur., 1987); University of Illinois (Master of Laws, 1988). *Education:* University of Louvain (Lic.Jur.); University of Illinois (Master of Laws). *LANGUAGES:* Dutch, French, English. *PRACTICE AREAS:* EC Law; Litigation; Intellectual Property Law.

SYLVIE DUBOIS, born Ghent, 1963; admitted, 1989, Brussels. *Education:* University of Ghent (Lic.Economics, 1985; Lic.Jur., 1989). *Education:* University of Ghent (Lic.Economics; Lic.Jur.). *LANGUAGES:* Dutch, French, English. *PRACTICE AREAS:* Environmental Law; Labour Law; Commercial Law.

BART VAN HYFTE, born Vilvoorde, 1965; admitted, 1989, Brussels. *Education:* University of Louvain (Lic.Jur., 1988). *LANGUAGES:* Dutch and French. *PRACTICE AREAS:* Commercial Law; Litigation; Civil.

SENIOR ASSOCIATES

KAREN STEVENS. *Education:* University of Louvain (Lic.Jur.). *LANGUAGES:* Dutch, French, English.

CHRISTEL VAN PETEGHEM. *Education:* University of Louvain (Lic.Jur.); Europa Institut, Saarbrücken. *LANGUAGES:* Dutch, French, English, German.

KRIS CROONEN. *Education:* University of Louvain (Lic.Jur.). *LANGUAGES:* Dutch, French, English.

AN LINGIER. *Education:* University of Brussels (Lic.Jur.). *LANGUAGES:* Dutch, French, English.

Languages: Dutch, French, English, German and Spanish.

JALLES ADVOGADOS

Established in 1986

RUE J-A DEMOT, 23
B-1040 BRUSSELS, BELGIUM
Telephone: 32-2-230.13.18
Telefax: 32-2-230.79.07

Lisbon, Portugal Office: Av. Álvares Cabral, 34 - 6°, P-1250 Lisbon. Telephone: 351-1-388.40.95. Telefax: 351-1-388.19.55.

Firm engaged in Portuguese, EC and International Practice.

(For a complete List of Members, see Professional Biographies at Lisbon, Portugal).

JANSON BAUGNIET

187, CHAUSSÉE DE LA HULPE
B-1170 BRUSSELS, BELGIUM
Telephone: (32.2) 675.30.30
Telecopier: (32.2) 675.30.31;
Telex: 26983 B JANBAU

General and International Law Practice,
Contracts, Commercial Transactions, Corporate Law, Real Estate, Torts and Insurances, Financial Laws, Labour Law, Banking Laws, Bankruptcy Laws, Aircraft Finance, Administrative and Constitutional Laws, Environmental Law, EU Law, Litigation, Arbitration, Trusts and Estates, Domestic Relations.
Total fee earners: 60.

MEMBERS OF THE FIRM

ROGER O. DALCQ, born 1928; admitted, 1951, Brussels. *Education:* University of Brussels (J.D., 1951; Lic., Economic Law, 1951; Lic., Insurance Law, 1954). Chief Editor: Journal des Tribunaux, Revue Générale des Assurances et des Responsabilités. Author: Traitéde la responsabilité civile (Vol. I Les causes de responsabilité, 1st ed.1959, 2nd ed.1967; Vol. II Le dommage et sa réparation, ed.1962). Professor emeritus of Law, Torts, Comparative Law and Insurance, University of Louvain.*Member:* Brussels Bar Association (Council Member and Secretary, 1967-1970); International Law Association (Hon. President, Belgian Section); Association In-

(This Listing Continued)

JANSON BAUGNIET, Brussels—Continued

ternationale des Jeunes Avocats and Société d' Etudes du Dommage Corpo-
rel; Belgian SectionAssociation Capitant (Vice President); Association Bel-
go-Zaïroise des Sciences Juridiques (President).

JACQUES DE GAVRE, born 1928; admitted, 1952, Brussels. *Education:* University of Brussels (J.D., 1952). Author: Le contrat de transaction
en droit civil et en droit judiciare privé(ed.1967). Professor of Law, Civil
and Family, University of Brussels. *Member:* Brussels Bar Association
(President, 1980-1982).

EDOUARD JAKHIAN, born 1935; admitted, 1958, Brussels. *Education:* University of Brussels (J.D., 1958). Vice-President, Union Internationale des Avocats, 1979-1988. *Member:* Brussels Bar Association (President,
1988-1990).

ANDRÉ JOSSART, born 1944; admitted, 1966, Brussels. *Education:*
University of Leuven (J.D., 1966).

JEAN-JACQUES VAN RAEMDONCK, born 1943; admitted, 1967,
Brussels. *Education:* University of Ghent (J.D., 1967). *Member:* Brussels
Bar Association (Council, 1983-1984).

FRANÇOIS GLANSDORFF, born 1944; admitted, 1968, Brussels. *Education:* University of Brussels (J.D., 1968; Lic. Economic Law, 1971). Professor of Law, Contracts, University of Brussels. *Member:* Brussels Bar Association (Vice-President, 1994—).

HENRI-PAUL LEMAITRE, born 1947; admitted, 1969, Brussels. *Education:* University of Brussels (J.D., 1969; Lic. Economic Law, 1974); Harvard University (LL.M., 1971); University of Michigan (Graduate student,
1972). Professor of Law, Business School (Business Law), University of
Brussels.

ALAIN D'IETEREN, born 1946; admitted, 1970, Brussels. *Education:*
University of Brussels (J.D., 1970; Lic. Economic Law, 1972). Assistant
Professor, Civil Law, University of Brussels, 1968-1980. President, Business
Law Commission, Association Internationale des jeunes Avocats, 1985-
1987.

ROSINE PÉRIER, born 1947; admitted, 1970, Brussels. *Education:*
University of Brussels (J.D., 1970).

MICHEL LEVY MORELLE, born 1950; admitted, 1973, Brussels.
Education: University of Brussels (J.D., 1973). *Member:* Brussels Bar Association (Council, 1990-1993).

PAUL-HENRY DELVAUX, born 1951; admitted, 1975, Brussels. *Education:* University of Louvain (J.D., 1974; Lic. Economic Law, 1975). Professor of Law, Torts and Insurance Law, University of Louvain.

MARTINE MUND, born 1951; admitted, 1974, Brussels. *Education:*
University of Brussels (J.D., 1974; Tax Law, 1978); University of Michigan
(M.C.L., 1976).

DOMINIQUE LAGASSE, born 1954; admitted, 1976, Brussels. *Education:* University of Louvain (J.D., 1976; Ph.D., 1985). Professor of Law,
Administrative Law, University of Brussels. Author: L'erreur manifeste
d'appréciation en droit administratif (ed. 1986).

GENEVIÈVE TASSIN, born 1957; admitted, 1981, Brussels. *Education:*
University of Louvain (J.D., 1980).

LUCAS VOGEL, born 1957; admitted, 1980, Brussels. *Education:* University of Brussels (J.D., 1980). Assistant Professor, Estate Law and Marriage Contracts, University of Brussels.

ALAIN GOLDSCHMIDT, born 1957; admitted, 1983, Brussels. *Education:* University of Brussels (J.D., 1981).

DANIEL DE CALLATAY, born 1960; admitted, 1983, Brussels. *Education:* University of Louvain (J.D., 1983). Assistant Professor, Civil Law
and Torts, University of Louvain, 1985-1991.

GRÉGOIRE JAKHIAN, born 1963; admitted, 1987, Brussels; 1989,
New York. *Education:* University of Brussels (J.D., 1986); New York University Law School (LL .M., 1987). Author: Le crédit hypothécaire
(ed.1994). Assistant Professor, Civil Law and Securities, University of Brussels, 1994—.

Languages: English, French, Dutch, German, Spanish, Italian

JEANTET & ASSOCIES
BRUSSELS, BELGIUM
(See Boden De Bandt De Brauw Jeantet Lagerlöf & Uria)

ROBERT LYMAN JILLSON
SQUARE DU VAL DE LA CAMBRE 10
B-1050 BRUSSELS, BELGIUM
Telephone: (32 2) 649.78.94
Fax: (32 2) 649.39.19

General International Practice.

ROBERT LYMAN JILLSON, born Detroit, Michigan, May 18, 1936;
admitted, 1962, Ohio; 1975, District of Columbia; 1982, New York. *Education:* University of Michigan (B.A., with High Honors in English, 1958;
J.D., 1961). Phi Beta Kappa. Articles Editor, Michigan Law Review, 1960-
1961. Stagiaire with F.C. Jeantet, Avocat a la Cour d'Appel de Paris, 1961-
1962. With, Squire, Sanders & Dempsey, 1962-1994. General Partner, 1971-
1994. Managing Partner, Brussels, 1982-1994. Partner in charge of Slovak
practice, 1992-1994. *Member:* Bar of the United States Supreme Court;
American Bar Association; The Association of the Bar of the City of New
York; International Bar Association; Order of the Coif; Chartered Institute
of Arbitrators, London (Associate). (Of Counsel to Csekes, Vilagi, Bratis-
lavia, Slovak Republic and Subrt & Havluj, Prague, Czech Republic).
LANGUAGES: English and French.

JONES, DAY, REAVIS & POGUE
AVENUE LOUISE 480, BTE 7
LOUIZALAAN 480, BUS 7
B-1050 BRUSSELS, BELGIUM
Telephone: 32-2-645-14-11
Telecopier: 32-2-645-14-45

In Atlanta, Georgia: 3500 One Peachtree Center, 303 Peachtree Street,
N.E. . Telephone: 404-521-3939. Cable Address: "Attorneys Atlanta".
Telex: 54-2711. Telecopier: 404-581-8330.
In Chicago, Illinois: 77 West Wacker. Telephone: 312-782-3939.
Telecopier: 312-782-8585.
In Cleveland, Ohio: North Point, 901 Lakeside Avenue. Telephone:
216-586-3939. Cable Address: "Attorneys Cleveland." Telex: 980389.
Telecopier: 216-579-0212.
In Columbus, Ohio: 1900 Huntington Center. Telephone: 614-469-3939.
Cable Address: "Attorneys Columbus." Telecopier: 614-461-4198.
In Dallas, Texas: 2300 Trammell Crow Center, 2001 Ross Avenue.
Telephone: 214-220-3939. Cable Address: "Attorneys Dallas." Telex:
730852. Telecopier: 214-969-5100.
In Frankfurt, Germany: Triton Haus, Bockenheimer Landstrasse 42,
60323 Frankfurt am Main. Telephone: 49-69-9726-3939. Telecopier:
49-69-9726-3993.
In Geneva, Switzerland: 20, rue de Candolle. Telephone: 41-22-320-2339.
Telecopier: 41-22-320-1232.
In Hong Kong: 1501 One Exchange Square, 8 Connaught Place.
Telephone: 852-2526-6895. Telecopier: 852-2810-5787.
In Irvine, California: 2603 Main Street, Suite 900. Telephone:
714-851-3939. Telex: 194911 Lawyers LSA. Telecopier: 714-553-7539.
In London, England: One Mount Street. Telephone: 44-71-493-9361.
Cable Address: "Surgoe London WI." Telecopier: 44-71-493-9666.
In Los Angeles, California: 555 West Fifth Street, Suite 4600. Telephone:
213-489-3939. Telex: 181439 UD. Telecopier: 213-243-2539.
In New York, New York: 599 Lexington Avenue. Telephone:
212-326-3939. Cable Address: "JONESDAY NEWYORK." Telex:
237013 JDRP UR. Telecopier: 212-755-7306.
In Paris, France: 62, rue du Faubourg Saint-Honore. Telephone:
33-1-44-71-3939. Cable Address: "Surgoe Paris." Telex: 290156 Surgoe.
Telecopier: 33-1-49-24-0471.
In Pittsburgh, Pennsylvania: 500 Grant Street, 31st Floor. Telephone:
412-391-3939. Cable Address: "Attorneys Pittsburgh". Telecopier:
412-394-7959.

(This Listing Continued)

In Riyadh, Saudi Arabia: Law Offices of Saud M.A. Shawwaf, P.O. Box 2700. Telephones: (966-1) 465-6543, (966-1) 464-8534 or (966-1) 464-8540. Telex: 401831 SAUCON SJ. Telecopier: (966-1) 464-8480.

In Taipei, Taiwan: 8th Floor, 2 Tun Hwa South Road, Section 2. Telephone: (886-2) 704-6808. Telecopier: (886-2) 704-6791.

In Tokyo, Japan: Toranomon MT Building, 4th Floor, 10-3, Toranomon 3-Chome, Minato-Ku, Tokyo 105, Japan. Telephone: 81-3-3433-3939. Telecopier: 81-3-5401-2725.

In Washington, D.C.: Metropolitan Square, 1450 G Street, N.W. Telephone: 202-879-3939. Cable Address: "Attorneys Washington." Telex: 89-2410 ATTORNEYS WASH. Telecopier: 202-737-2832.

General and International Practice. Firm Engaged in the Practice of International Business Law, European Communities Law and American Law. Not Authorized to Appear Before the Belgian Courts.

MEMBERS OF FIRM IN BRUSSELS

NORBERT KOCH, born Hamburg, Germany, May 25, 1927; admitted, 1990, Germany (Not admitted in Belgium). *Education:* Marburg and Hamburg Universities (Referendar, 1951; Dr. Jur., 1953). Hamburg Referendariat (Assessor, 1955). Leitender Reg. Direktor, Federal Cartel Office, 1958-1990. Legal Adviser, E.C. Commission, 1959-1990. Hilfsreferent, Ministry of Economics, Antitrust Division, 1957.

GHISLAIN JOSEPH, born Overijse, Belgium, June 26, 1950; (Not admitted in Belgium). *Education:* Free University of Brussels, Licentiaat Rechten (1973), Licentiaat Economisch Recht (1977); University of Michigan (LL. M., 1975); Ecole Superieure des Sciences Fiscales, Brussels, Belgium (Degree in Taxation, Certificat, 1981). Former Intern of the United Nations, 1976. Laureat of the Prize of the Belgian Minister of Foreign Trade, 1976. Member of the Belgian Institute of Accountants. Professor of International Tax Law and Director of the Post-Graduate Program "Master in Tax Management," Vlaamse Economische Hogeschool (VLEKHO), Brussels, Belgium.

LUC G. HOUBEN, born Hasselt, Belgium, August 28, 1953; admitted, 1982, New York (Not admitted in Belgium). *Education:* Katholieke Universiteit Leuven (Licenciaat in de Rechten, 1976; Licenciaat in het Notariaat, 1977); Centre Europeen Universitaire de Nancy, France (Certificat d'Etudes Europeennes, 1978) Columbia University, New York (LL.M., 1980). Internship, United Nations Institute for Training and Research, 1979. Trainee EEC Commission, Agriculture Directorate, 1978. Member: Association of Former Trainees of the E.E.C.; World Association of Former United Nations Interns and Fellows.

ASSOCIATES

JAMES E. THOMPSON, born Big Rapids, Michigan, August 30, 1960; admitted, 1987, Illinois; 1988, District of Columbia (Not admitted in Belgium). *Education:* University of Michigan (A.B., 1983; J.D., 1986). Clerkships: Clerk Stagiaire, Judge T. O'Higgins, European Court of Justice, Luxembourg; Stagiaire, External Relations Division, Legal Service of the European Communities, Brussels, Belgium, 1986-1987.

ANAND S. PATHAK, born Allahabad, India, April 18, 1963; admitted, 1989, Ohio (1986, Delhi) (Not admitted in Belgium). *Education:* University of Delhi (B.A., 1984); Clare College, Cambridge University (B.A., 1986; M.A., 1990); Yale University (LL.M., 1987; M.A., 1988). Clerkship: Stagiaire, Competition Division, Legal Service of the Commission of the European Communities, Brussels, Belgium, 1989-1990.

MARC N. BOMBEECK, born Brussels, Belgium, June 7, 1965; (Not admitted in Belgium). *Education:* University of Louvain (Lic. Jur., 1988); University of Antwerp (Lic. Maritime Sciences, 1989); Tulane University (LL.M., 1990).

BART A. SERVAES, born Leuven, Belgium, April 13, 1966; admitted, 1994, Belgium. *Education:* Katholieke Universiteit Leuven, Belgium (Licentiaat, 1989); Northwestern University (LL.M., 1990). Teaching Assistant, Corporate Law, Katholieke Universiteit Leuven, Belgium, 1991—.

Languages: Dutch, English, French, German, Hindi, Italian

CLAUDE KATZ

193 AVENUE BRUGMANN
1180 BRUSSELS, BELGIUM
Telephone: 32.2.345.91.83
Fax: 32.2.344.51.81

General International Practice, Commercial Law, Copyrights, Family Law, Trials Practice.

(This Listing Continued)

CLAUDE KATZ, born Brussels, Belgium, December 17, 1959; admitted, 1983, Belgium. *Education:* Paint Branch High School (1978); Universite Libre de Bruxelles, Brussels (1983, with grande distinction). University of Madison, Wisconsin, "US Law and Legal Structure", 1984. Recipient: Prix Janson, Brussels Young Bar Association, 1985; Prix La Vollée, Paris Young Bar Association, 1986. Member, Young Bar Association of Brussels, 1985-1987. *LANGUAGES:* French, English and Dutch.

KELLER AND HECKMAN

Established in 1962

BOULEVARD LOUIS SCHMIDT 87
B-1040 BRUSSELS, BELGIUM
Telephone: 32 (2) 732 52 80
Telecopier: 32 (2) 732 53 92

Washington, D.C. Office: Suite 500 West, 1001 G Street, N.W. Telephone: 202-434-4100. Cable Address: "Kelman" Telex: 49 95551. Telecopier: 202-434-4646.

ECC and International Practice. Office Engaged in European Business Law and European Communities Regulatory and Administrative Practice.

RESIDENT MEMBER

JEAN M. SAVIGNY, born Nogent-le-Rotrou, France, February 28, 1947; admitted, 1976, Paris (Not admitted in Belgium). *Education:* Faculté de Droit et des Sciences Economiques de Caen (Licence en Droit, 1969); Institut d'Etudes Politiques de Paris (Diplôme Section Economique et Financiére, 1971). Internship, Commission of the European Communities, Brussels, 1970; Associate, Clifford Turner, Paris, 1973-1976; Counsel France, John Deere, Orléans, 1976-1983; Section President, Labour Court, Orléans, 1982-1984; European Counsel, Corning Glass Works, Paris, London, 1984-1988; Partner Jeantet & Associés, 1988-1992. *Member:* International Bar Association. *LANGUAGES:* French, English, German. *PRACTICE AREAS:* European and International Practice.

RESIDENT ASSOCIATES

JEAN-PHILIPPE MONTFORT, born Brussels, Belgium, February 9, 1962; admitted, 1989, Brussels; 1994, Paris. *Education:* Université de Louvain (Licence en Droit, 1984; Diplôme en Administration des Entreprises, 1985); Georgetown University (LL.M., 1988). Associate, Jeantet & Associés, Brussels Office, 1988-1992. *LANGUAGES:* French, English. *PRACTICE AREAS:* European and International Practice.

LEGAL SUPPORT PERSONNEL

STAFF SCIENTIST

THOMAS C. BROWN, born Lancaster, Ohio, May 8, 1940. *Education:* Bowling Green State University (B.S., 1962).

(For complete biographical data on all personnel, see Professional Biographies at Washington, D.C.)

KELLEY DRYE & WARREN

A Partnership including Professional Associations

106 AVENUE LOUISE
1050 BRUSSELS, BELGIUM
Telephone: (2) 646-1110
Fax: (2) 640-0589

New York, N.Y. Office: 101 Park Avenue, 10178. Telephone: 212-808-7800. Telex: 12369. Fax: (212) 808-7897.

Los Angeles, California Office: 515 South Flower Street, 90071. Telephone: 213-689-1300. Fax: (213) 688-8150.

Stamford, Connecticut Office: Two Stamford Plaza, 281 Tresser Boulevard, 06901-3229. Telephone: 203-324-1400. Fax: (203) 327-2669; (203) 964-3188.

Washington, D.C. Office: 1200 19th Street, N.W., Suite 500, 20036. Telephone: 202-955-9600. Fax: (202) 955-9792.

Miami, Florida Office: 201 South Biscayne Boulevard, 2400 Miami Center, 33131. Telephone: 305-372-2400. Fax: (305) 372-2490.

Parsippany, New Jersey Office: 5 Sylvan Way, 07054. Telephone: 201-539-0099. Fax: (201) 539-3167.

Chicago, Illinois Office: Suite 1400, 303 West Madison Street, 60606. Telephone: 312-346-6350. Fax: (312) 346-8982.

(This Listing Continued)

KELLEY DRYE & WARREN, Brussels—Continued

Tokyo, Japan Office: Taniguchi Gaikokuho Jimu Bengoshi Jimusho
Kelley Drye Warren, Toranomon 37 Mori Building 5F 3-5-1,
Toranomon, Minato-ku Tokyo 105, Japan. Telephone: (3) 5472-6351.
Fax: (3) 5472-6431.

General and International Practice.
*Firm engaged in the Practice of International Business Law, European
Communities Law and U.S. Law. Not Authorized to appear before the
Belgian Courts.*

MEMBERS OF FIRM

BRIAN CHRISTALDI, born Passaic, N.J., 1940; admitted, 1967, N.Y.;
1966, D.C.; 1988, Calif. (Not admitted in Belgium). *Education:* Amherst
(B.A., 1962); Harvard (LL.B., 1965). *PRACTICE AREAS:* Banking Law;
Health, Health Care and Hospital Law; Securities.

ANDRÉ VAN LANDUYT, born Dendermonde, Belgium, 1953; admitted, 1976, Leuven, Belgium (not currently admitted in Belgium). *Education:*
Catholic University of Leuven (J.D., cum laude, 1976); University of Pennsylvania (LL.M., 1981).

(For Biographical data on all Personnel, see Professional Biographies at
New York, N.Y.).

KEMMLER, RAPP, BÖHLKE & CROSBY

9 ROND POINT SCHUMAN
B-1040 BRUSSELS, BELGIUM
Telephone: 230.90.75
Telecopier: 230 14 16

EC Law Practice.

*FIRM PROFILE: Firm established in the mid 1960's and engaged in the
practice of European Community Law. Not authorized to appear before the
Belgian Courts. Entitled to appear before the European Court of Justice.*

*Competition including State Aids and Merger Control, EC Litigation, En-
ergy (Coal and Electricity), Internal Market, Taxation (Indirect), Telecommunications and Air Transport, Environment.*

HANS G. KEMMLER, born Tübingen, Germany, July 18, 1932; admitted, 1967, Stuttgart; 1975, Frankfurt, Germany (Not admitted in Belgium).
Education: Universities of Tübingen, Munich and Paris.

BARBARA RAPP-JUNG, born Bautzen, Germany, March 11, 1940;
admitted, 1970, Stuttgart; 1975, Frankfurt, Germany (Not admitted in Belgium). *Education:* Universities of Tübingen, Munich, Saarbrücken and
Würzburg.

ALEXANDER BÖHLKE, born Pless, Germany, January 12, 1944; ad-
mitted, 1973, Frankfurt, Germany (Not admitted in Belgium). *Education:*
Universities of Berlin, Freiburg, Göttingen and Amsterdam (Diploma on
European Integration, 1972).

SCOTT CROSBY, born Aberdeen, Scotland, April 4, 1951; admitted,
1979, Scotland (Not admitted in Belgium). *Education:* Universities of St.
Andrews, Strasbourg and Edinburgh, College of Europe (Certificate of Advanced European Studies, 1977).

THOMAS RIORDAN, born Galway, Ireland, June 16, 1964; admitted,
1990, Dublin, Ireland (Not admitted in Belgium). *Education:* University
College Galway; Institute of European Studies, Brussels (Spec. Deg., European Law, 1993).

BERTRAND WÄGENBAUR, born Tübingen, Germany, July 16, 1959;
admitted, 1991, Aachen, Germany (Not admitted in Belgium). *Education:*
University of Bonn.

MARIA VICTORIA GIL CASADO, born Tudela, Spain, April 13,
1967; admitted, 1991, Bilbao, Spain (Not admitted in Belgium). *Education:*
Universities of Deusto, Bordeaux; Institute of European Studies, Brussels
(Spec. Deg., European Law, 1991).

Languages: English, French, German, Dutch, Italian and Spanish.

KILPATRICK & CODY

Established in 1874

AVENUE LOUISE 65, BTE 3
1050 BRUSSELS, BELGIUM
Telephone: (32) (2) 533-03-00
Telecopier: (32) (2) 534-86-38

Atlanta, Georgia Office: Suite 2800, 1100 Peachtree Street, 30309-4530.
Telephone: 404-815-6500. Telephone Copier: 404-815-6555. Telex:
54-2307.
Augusta, Georgia Office: Suite 1400, First Union Bank Building, P.O.
Box 2043, 30903. Telephone: 706-724-2622. Telecopier: 706-722-0219.
Washington, D.C. Office: Suite 800, 700 13th Street, N.W., 20005.
Telephone: 202-508-5800. Telephone Copier: 202-508-5858.
London, England Office: 68 Pall Mall, London SW1Y 5ES, England.
Telephone: (44) (71) 321 0477. Telecopier: (44) (71) 930 9733.

*United States and International Law. Firm engaged in American and In-
ternational Law Practice.*

MEMBERS OF FIRM

JEFFERSON DAVIS, JR., born Indianola, Mississippi, August 19,
1936; admitted, 1962, Georgia (Not admitted in Belgium). *Education:* Vanderbilt University (B.A., 1958); Emory University (LL.B., 1962). Phi Delta
Phi. *Member:* Atlanta, International and American Bar Associations; State
Bar of Georgia; Lawyers Club of Atlanta.

FREDERICK K. HELLER, JR., born Lynchburg, Virginia, June 9,
1947; admitted, 1973, Georgia (Not admitted in Belgium). *Education:* Yale
University (B.A., 1969; J.D., 1973). Editor, Yale Law Journal, 1972-1973.
Member: State Bar of Georgia; American and International Bar Associations; Lawyers Club of Atlanta.

ASSOCIATE

DAVID E. SATOLA, born Milwaukee, Wisconsin, June 27, 1960; admitted, 1986, Wisconsin; 1988, Georgia (Not admitted in Belgium). *Education:*
London School of Economics, London, England; Johns Hopkins University (B.A., 1982; M.A., 1984); University of Wisconsin (J.D., 1986). Member, Moot Court Board. Research and Articles Editor, Wisconsin International Law Journal, 1985-1986. Author: "Recent Developments in Edge Act
Corporations," 1985 Wisconsin International Law Journal 115, 1985. *Member:* State Bar of Georgia; State Bar of Wisconsin; American Bar Association; American Society of International Law; Union Internationale des
Avocats. *LANGUAGES:* French.

(For complete biographical data on all personnel, see Professional
Biographies at Atlanta, Georgia, Augusta, Georgia, Washington, D.C.
and London, England)

KRAMEYER, v. FALKENHAUSEN, HANKE & PARTNERS

Established in 1990

6. DREVE DES RENARDS
B-1180 BRUSSELS, BELGIUM
Telephone: 02/3749200
Telefax: 02/3754525

Essen, Germany Office: Gildehofstraße 1, P.O. Box 102031, D-45020
Essen. Telephone: 0201-820 15-0. Telefax: 0201-820 1510.
Halle, Germany Office: Hansering 4, D-06108 Halle. Telephone:
0345-28053. Telefax: 0345-21669.

*General Practice, Contracts, Company, Commercial, Construction and
Engineering, Corporation, Banking, Antitrust and Unfair Competition,
Labor, Patent and Trademark, Intellectual Property, Law of the former
GDR, Product Liability, Real Estate, Insurance, Family, Inheritance, En-
vironment, Energy and Natural Resources, Taxes, European Community,
Arbitration, Administration, Notaries.*

*FIRM PROFILE: The firm was established in 1952 in Essen and offers
the full range of legal services. It is well known for its practice in all fields
of Commercial Law. The client base in European and North American.
The firm has two branch offices in Halle (former GDR) and in Brussels
(Belgium).*

(This Listing Continued)

MEMBER OF FIRM

RAINER KLOTZBACH, born Masserberg, Germany, May 12, 1945; admitted, 1975, Essen; 1985, Notary Public; 1990, Brussels. *Education:* Universities of Munich and Muenster. *Member:* Essen and German Lawyers' Associations; Deutsche Vereinigung für Baurecht; Deutsche Vereinigung für gewerblichen Rechtschutz und Urheberrecht; Deutsch-deutsche Juristenveninigung. *LANGUAGES:* German, English and French. *PRACTICE AREAS:* General Practice; Company; Construction and Engineering; Antitrust and Unfair Competition; Product Liability; European Community.

LAFILI & VAN CROMBRUGGHE

VOSSENDREEF 6 BUS 1
B-1180 BRUSSELS, BELGIUM
Telephone: 02/374.92.00
Facsimile: 02/375.45.25

Antwerp, Belgium Office: Kardinaal Mercierlei 44, Berchem, B-2600. Telephone: 03/281.11.20. Facsimile: 03/329.26.40.

General Commercial Practice, International Contracts, Distributorship, Agency, Franchising, Belgian and EEC Competition, Corporate, Tax Foreign Investments, Arbitration, Litigation, Product Liability, Trade Regulations, Food and Drug Regulations, Banking, Environmental, Labor, Maritime, Administrative, Intellectual Property, Construction, Bankruptcy, Transport.

PARTNERS

LOUIS LAFILI, born 1947. adm. 1972, Belgium.

NICOLE VAN CROMBRUGGHE, born 1954. adm. 1977, Belgium.

DIRK SCHOENMAKERS, born 1955. adm. 1982, Belgium.

CHRISTOPH KOCKS, born 1958. adm., 1983, Belgium.

ASSOCIATES

MIA WOUTERS, born 1956. adm., 1984, Belgium.

SABINE SZULANSKI, born 1961. adm., 1985, Belgium.

KRISTOFFEL VERMEERSCH, born 1959. adm., 1985, Belgium.

NORA WOUTERS, born 1962. adm., 1986, Belgium.

LOUISE MA, born 1962. adm., 1986, Belgium.

NICOLE VAN RANST, born 1963. adm., 1986, Belgium.

PETER MARX, born 1962. adm., 1988, Belgium.

FRANCIS VANHOONACKER, born 1961. adm., 1988, Belgium.

DOMINIQUE BOGAERT, born 1960. adm., 1988, Belgium.

TAMARA LECLERCQ, born 1964. adm., 1988, Belgium.

JOOST VERBEEK, born 1963. adm., 1989, Belgium.

INGRID MEEUSSEN, born 1964. adm., 1990, Belgium.

CHRISTIANE CUNNINGHAM, born 1964. adm., 1990, Belgium.

NELL VAN RIET, born 1966. adm., 1990, Belgium.

FRANÇOISE CARLIER, born 1969. adm., 1992, Belgium.

FRÉDÉRIC CABAY, born 1967. adm., 1993, Belgium.

KOENRAAD JACOBS, born 1964; admitted, 1991, Belgium.

DAVID ENGELBOS, born 1969; admitted, 1992, Belgium.

DIDIER DENEUTER, born 1967; admitted, 1993, Belgium.

GEERTJE LEYSEN, born 1969; admitted, 1993, Belgium.

DAVID MACKARNESS (Solicitor, UK).

LEON VAN SCHALKWIJK (Advocate, South Africa).

Languages: French, Dutch, English, German, Italian, Chinese (Mandarin and Shangai) and Spanish

---

LAFLEUR BROWN

AV. LOUISE 386
1050 BRUSSELS, BELGIUM
Telephone: 011 322 647 1112; 647 7158
Telecopier: 011-322-648-7519

Montreal, Quebec Office: 1 Place Ville Marie, 37th Floor. Telephone: 514-878-9641. Telecopier: 514-878-1450. Cable Address: "Mankin". Telex: 05-25610.

Toronto, Ontario Office: Suite 920, 1 First Canadian Place. Telephone: 416-869-0994. Telecopier: 416-362-5818.

European Law, Telecommunication and Transport Law, Corporate and Commercial Law, International Cross-Border Financial Transactions, Securities Law, Licensing.

RESIDENT PARTNERS

HELENE DESLAURIERS, born Montreal, Quebec, April 13, 1949; admitted, 1972, Quebec. *Education:* University of Montreal (LL.L., 1971); University College, London (LL.M., 1973). *LANGUAGES:* French, Italian & Spanish. *PRACTICE AREAS:* Corporate and Commercial Law; E.C. Law; Telecommunications; Transport Law.

RICHARD LARUE, born Quebec City, Quebec, May 22, 1958; admitted, 1983, Quebec. *Education:* Petit Séminaire de Québec (D.E.C., 1977); Laval University (B.A.A., 1980; LL.B., 1982). Teaching and Research Assistant, Laval University, 1979-1982. *Member:* Montreal, Quebec and Canadian Bar Associations; Canadian Tax Foundation; Association Internationale des Jeunes Avocats; Montreal Junior Bar Association (Director, 1985 and Treasurer, 1986-1987); Corporation professionnelle des Administrateurs Agréés du Québec. *LANGUAGES:* French, German. *PRACTICE AREAS:* Corporate and Commercial Law; International Cross-Border Financial Transactions; Securities Law; Licensing.

(For Complete Biographical Data on all Personnel, see Professional Biographies at Montreal, Quebec)

LAGERLÖF & LEMAN

BRUSSELS, BELGIUM

(See Boden De Bandt De Brauw Jeantet Lagerlöf & Uria)

LA GIRAUDIERE, LARROZE ET ASSOCIÉS

AVENUE DES ARTS, 53
1040 BRUSSELS, BELGIUM
Telephone: (2) 511 44 66
Facsimile: (2) 514 56 62

Paris, France Office: 58, Rue de Monceau, 75008. Telephone: 33.1.44.95.25.25. Telex: 649622 F. Facsimile: 33.1.44.95.25.00.

Chicago, Illinois Associated Office: Clausen, Miller, Gorman, Caffrey and Witous. 10, South La Salle Street, 60603-1098. Telephone: (312) 855-1010. Facsimile: (312) 606-7777.

New York, New York Associated Office: Clausen, Miller, Gorman, Caffrey and Witous. 100 Maiden Lane, Suite 1600, 10038. Telephone: (212) 504-6020. Facsimile: (212) 504-6015.

General and International Practice, Corporations, EEC Regulations, Environment, Arbitration, Banking, Copyright, Insurance, Mergers and Acquisitions.

RESIDENT ASSOCIATES

VÉRONIQUE DESBROSSES, born Lyon, France, January 26, 1960; (Not admitted in Belgium). *Education:* College of Europe, Bruges (Diploma, 1984); University of Lyon (D.E.A., 1983). Consultant: International Labour Office (ILO), Geneva, 1985; Commission of the European Communities, 1986-1988. *LANGUAGES:* French, English and Spanish. *PRACTICE AREAS:* E.E.C. Law.

MARTINE REZZI, born Oran, Algeria, October 11, 1956; (Not admitted in Belgium). *Education:* College of Europe, Bruges (1984); University of Aix en Provence (Ph.D., 1984). Author: "Action de la Communauté dans le domaine de la recherche agricole," Agence Européenne d'Information, 1986; "Le sucre dans la CEE," Agence Européenne d'Information, 1987. Attachée de recherches, University of Aix en Provence, 1980-1982. Consultant, Com-

(This Listing Continued)

LA GIRAUDIERE, LARROZE ET ASSOCIÉS, Brussels—Continued

mission of the European Communities, 1983-1987. *LANGUAGES:* French, English and Italian. *PRACTICE AREAS:* E.E.C. Law.

(For complete biographical data on all personnel, see Professional Biographies at Paris, France)

LAWSPAN INTERNATIONAL
(E.E.I.G.)
RUE CAMILLE LEMONNIER, 68
1060 BRUSSELS, BELGIUM
Telephone: (32-2) 344.18.45
Telefax: (32-2) 347.21.23

FIRM PROFILE: *LAWSPAN INTERNATIONAL comprises 13 law firms throughout Europe. The grouping consists of:*

ASSOCIATION GREGOIRE at Brussels (Belgium), GROENBAEK & HANSEN at Randers (Denmark), ROITER ZUCKER at London (United Kingdom), TROY & ASSOCIES at Paris (France), Jean-Louis MICHEL-Paul-Jean VINCENCINI-Philippe VOULAND at Marseilles (France), ABRELL WENDLER NACKE & PARTNER at Düsseldorf, Frankfurt am Main, Munich and Dresden (Germany), TAKIS G. KOMMATAS LAW OFFICES at Athens (Greece), TEEKENS ADVOKATEN at Leiden and Leiderdorp (Holland), O'FLYNN EXHAMS & PARTNERS at Cork and Dublin (Ireland), SCHILTZ and SCHILTZ at Luxemburg (Luxemburg), ARTUR REIS E SOUSA at Lisbon (Portugal), CARRETERO ABOGADOS at Marbella (Spain), SÖDERLUND & PARTNERS at Stockholm (Sweden).

(For details and lists of Partners and Counsels of the Member Firms, contact Philippe DEHON at the registered office in Brussels).

LeBOEUF, LAMB, GREENE & MacRAE
L.L.P.

A Limited Liability Partnership including Professional Corporations

Formerly LeBoeuf, Lamb, Leiby & MacRae

14 RUE MONTOYER 5TH FLOOR
BRUSSELS 1040, BELGIUM
Telephone: 011-32-2-514-56 50
Facsimile: 011-32-2-514-50 48

Eastern United States:
New York, N.Y. Office: 125 West 55th Street. 10019-5389. Telephone: 212-424-8000. Facsimile: 212-424-8500. Telex: 1561363 or 423416.
Washington, D.C. Office: 1875 Connecticut Avenue, N.W., Suite 1200, 20036. Telephone: 202-986-8000. Facsimile: 202-986-8102. Telex: 440274.
Albany, New York Office: One Commerce Plaza, 99 Washington Avenue, Suite 2020, 12210. Telephone: 518-465-1500. Facsimile: 518-465-1585.
Boston, Massachusetts Office: 260 Franklin Street, 02110. Telephone: 617-439-9500. Facsimile: 617-439-0341; 439-0342.
Harrisburg, Pennsylvania Office: 320 Market Street, Suite E400, Strawberry Square. 17108. Telephone: 717-232-8199. Facsimile: 717-232-8720.
Pittsburgh, Pennsylvania Office: 601 Grant Street, 15219. Telephone: 412-594-2300. Facsimile: 412-594-5237.
Hartford, Connecticut Office: Goodwin Square, 225 Asylum Street, 13th Floor. Telephone: 203-293-3500. Facsimile: 203-293-3555.
Newark, New Jersey Office: The Legal Center, One Riverside Plaza. Telephone: 201-643-8000. Facsimile: 201-643-6111.
Western United States:
Los Angeles, California Office: 725 South Figueroa Street, Suite 3600, 90017-5422. Telephone: 213-955-7300. Facsimile: 213-955-7399. Telex: 678982.
Salt Lake City, Utah Office: 1000 Kearns Building, 136 South Main Street, 84101. Telephone: 801-320-6700. Facsimile: 801-359-8256.
San Francisco, California Office: One Embarcadero Center, Suite 400, 94111. Telephone: 415-951-1100. Facsimile: 415-951-1180; 951-1181. Telex: 470167.
Denver, Colorado Office: 633 17th Street, Suite 2800, 80202. Telephone: 303-291-2600. Facsimile: 303-297-0422.

(This Listing Continued)

Southern United States:
Jacksonville, Florida Office: 50 N. Laura Street, Suite 2800, 32202. Telephone: 904-354-8000. Facsimile: 904-353-1673.
European Community:
London, England Office: 2 Suffolk Lane, London EC4R OAT. Telephone: 011-44-171-626-3000. Facsimile: 011-44-171-626-2623. Modem: 011-44-171-626-2591.
Moscow, Russian Federation Office: Ulitsa Delegatskaya, 25 103473 Moscow, Russian Federation. Telephone: 011-7-503-956-3935. Facsimile: 011-7-503-956-3936.

General Practice, European Communities Law, Competition and Trade Law, Customs, Insurance and Financial Services, Environment, Public Procurement.
Firm Engaged in General International Practice and Authorized to Appear before E.C. Courts.

RESIDENT PARTNER

JAMES K. LOCKETT, born 1953; admitted, 1981, Washington; 1982, U.S. Court of International Trade (Not admitted in Belgium). *Education:* University of Washington (B.A., 1977); Gonzaga University (J.D., 1980); University of London, London, England (LL.M., 1983); Oxford University, England. Author: "EEC Anti-dumping Law and Trade Policy After Ball-bearing (II): Discretionary Decisions Masquerading as Legal Process?" Northwestern Journal of International Law and Business 365 (1987).

VISITING PARTNER

VERNON EDWARD VIG, born 1937; admitted, 1962, New York; 1979, France as Conseil Juridique; 1992, as Avocat. *Education:* Phillips Exeter; Carleton College (B.A., 1959); New York University (LL.B., 1962; LL.M., 1963). Faculté de Droit et des Sciences économiques, Paris, 1963-1964. Phi Beta Kappa; Phi Delta Phi. *Member:* New York State (Chair, Antitrust Section, 1987-1988), American and International Bar Associations; Union Internationale des Avocats. *LANGUAGES:* French.

RESIDENT OF COUNSEL

JOHN E. FERRY, born 1929; admitted, 1956, England, European Court of Justice (Not admitted in Belgium). *Education:* Oxford University (B.A., 1952) Gray's Inn. Author: "The Repose of Certainty and the Necessity of Uncertainty," International Antitrust, Barry Hawk, Ed., New York, 1979; "Procedure and Powers of the EEC Commission in Anti-trust Cases," European Industrial Property Review, May 1979; "Interim Relief Under the Rome Treaty," European Industrial Property Review, October 1980; "Selective Distribution and Other Post-Sales Restrictions," European Competition Law Review, Vol. 2, 1981; "How Do We Get There From Here?" in Antitrust and Trade Policies of the European Economic Community, Barry Hawk, Ed., New York, 1984. *Member:* International Bar Association; British Chamber of Commerce (Chairman of EEC Committee, 1989); Bar European Group. *LANGUAGES:* English, French, German.

LEIGH HANCHER, born 1958; (Not admitted in Belgium). *Education:* University of Glasgow, Scotland (First Class Honours in Public Law); European University Institute, Florence, Italy; University of Leiden, The Netherlands (Ph.D., cum laude, 1989). Lecturer, Commercial Law, Constitutional Law and European Community Law, University of Warwick, England, 1983-1987. Co-Author: with T.C. Daintith, "Energy Strategy in Europe, the Legal Framework," Berlin, 1986. Author: "EC Electricity Law," Chancery, London, 1992; "Regulating For Competition," Oxford, 1990; "EC State Aids," Chancery, 1993. Chair, Public Economic Law, Erasmus University, Rotterdam, The Netherlands. *LANGUAGES:* English, French, Italian, Dutch.

RESIDENT COUNSEL

JOHN DALTROP, born 1925; admitted, 1954, England (Not admitted in Belgium). *Education:* University College, London (LL.B., 1954). Head of Division, Commission of European Communities, 1973-1982. *LANGUAGES:* English, German, French.

RESIDENT ASSOCIATES

Beata I. Jostmeier (Not admitted in Belgium; Also at Moscow, Russia Office); *Guy Soussan* (Not admitted in Belgium); *Peter-Armin Trepte* (Not admitted in Belgium); *Wilko Van Weert.*

(This Listing Continued)

(Biographical data on all Members of the Firm, Counsel, Of Counsel, in Washington, D.C.; New York, New York; Albany, New York; Boston, Massachusetts; Harrisburg, Pennsylvania; Hartford, Connecticut; Newark, New Jersey; Los Angeles, California; Salt Lake City, Utah; San Francisco, California; Jacksonville, Florida; Pittsburgh, Pennsylvania; Denver, Colorado; London, England and Moscow, Russian, Federation are listed in the respective Biographical Sections)

LeBOEUF, LAMB, LEIBY & MacRAE

BRUSSELS, BELGIUM

(See LeBoeuf, Lamb, Greene & MacRae L.L.P.)

LEGALLIANCE (EEIG)

European Economic Interest Grouping of European Law Firms

RUE DE SUISSE, 29
B-1060 BRUSSELS, BELGIUM
Telephone: 322 534 1680
EEIG Register
Brussels No. 21

Brussels, Belgium Office: Willemart Avocats Associes. Rue de Suisse 29-35, B-1060. Telephone: 322-534-1680. Fax: 322-537-2741.

Tongeren, Belgium Office: P & R Stas, Avocats. Elisabethwal, 2, 3700. Telephone: (12) 23.12.44. Fax: (12) 23.03.64.

Namur, Belgium Office: Poncelet, Davreux & Bouillard, Avocats. Rue Lelievre 9, 5000. Telephone: (81) 22.21.81. Fax: (81) 22.06.22.

London, England Office: Baileys Shaw & Gillett. 17, Queen Square, GB, WC1N 3RH. Telephone: 44-71-8375455. Fax: 44-71-8370071. Telex: 51-28961.

Paris, France Office: Ader, Jolibois & Associes. 26, Boulevard Raspail, F-75007. Telephone: 33-1-45441033. Fax: 33-1-45488027. Telex: 42-201482.

Berlin, Germany Office: Gurland & Lambsdorff. Zimmerstraße 86-91, D-10117. Telephone: 30-2291018. Fax: 30-2385878.

Cologne, Germany Office: Gurland & Lambsdorff. Eugen-Langen-Str. 12, D-50968. Telephone: 221-9370710. Fax: 221-93707199.

Frankfurt, Germany Office: Gurland & Lambsdorff. Fürstenberger Str., 10-12, D-60322. Telephone: 69-9552340. Fax: 69-95523450.

Leipzig, Germany Office: Gurland & Lambsdorff. Hainstraße 17/19, D-04109. Telephone: 341-2114412. Fax: 341-2114617.

Milano, Italy Office: Scamoni E Associates. Via Mario Pagano 65, I-20145. Telephone: 39-2-48011171. Fax: 39-2-48012914.

Padova, Italy Office: Rizzieri E Associati. Passeggiata del Carmine 2, I-35100. Telephone: 39-49-8761913. Fax: 39-49-8752879.

Bologna, Italy Office: Fazio Francia Serafini Solazzi Trombetti. Via della Zecca 1, 40121. Telephone: 39-51-236991. Fax: 39-51-222486.

The Hague, Netherlands Office: Barents & Krans. Parkstraat 107, P.O. Box 30457, NL-2500 GL Den Haag. Telephone: 31-70-3760606. Fax: 31-70-3651856.

Brussels, Belgium Office: Barents & Krans. Avenue de la Toison d'Or 55, Bte 10-11, 1060. Telephone: 32-2-5349739. Fax: 32-2-5349740.

Barcelona, Spain Office: Sarda, Calomarde, Castelo y Asociados. Muntaner 407 1°, 2, E-08021. Telephone: 34-3-2016466. Fax: 34-3-2020096.

Madrid, Spain Office: Sarda, Calomarde, Castelo y Asociados. P° de la Castellana, 228, 3°, E-28046. Telephone: 34-1-3141934. Fax: 34-1-3141952.

Valencia, Spain Office: Sarda, Calomarde, Castelo y Asociados. Cronista Carreres, 13, 4° 8°, E-46003. Telephone: 346-352-9603. Fax: 346-394-2686.

Stockholm, Sweden Office: Advokatfirman Verum. Biblioteksgatan 11, P.O. Box 7149, S-10387. Telephone: 46-8-6117705. Fax: 46-8-6117190.

FIRM PROFILE: Legalliance EEIG, founded in 1990, is a grouping of European law firms. Its purpose is to enable a full and comprehensive legal service in European and international law and especially in the national law of the member states of the EU.

LETT, VILSTRUP & PARTNERS

99, RUE DE LA LOI
BTE. NO. 12
1040 BRUSSELS, BELGIUM
Telephone: (02) 231 11 85
Telex: 63017 jurist b
Facsimile: (02) 2 80 09 83

Copenhagen, Denmark Office: 3 Bredgade, 1260 Copenhagen K. Telephone: 33 15 48 00. Cable Address: "Lawhouse". Telex: 16080 LAWHS DK. Telefax: 45 33 15 59 95.

Firm engaged in EEC Law, Antitrust, International, Commercial and Danish Practice, Contract, Banking, Insurance, Admiralty, Taxation and Industrial Property Rights. Entitled to plead before the European Court of Justice and the European Commission.

RESIDENT LAWYER

ANNE RUBACH-LARSEN, born Randers, Denmark, December 9, 1962; admitted, 1989, Denmark and High Court of Denmark; 1993, England and Wales (Not admitted in Belgium). *Education:* University of Aarhus, Denmark (LL.B., 1986); London School of Economics (LL.M., 1991). *LANGUAGES:* Danish, Norwegian, Swedish, English, German and French.

(For Complete List of Firm Personnel, see Professional Biographies at Copenhagen, Denmark).

LIEDEKERKE WOLTERS WAELBROECK & KIRKPATRICK

341 AVENUE LOUISE - BOITE 8
B-1050 BRUSSELS, BELGIUM
Telephone: (322) 627.14.11
Telefax: (322) 627.15.00

Commercial, Corporation, Tax, International Business Transactions, Antitrust Law, Insurance Law, Real Estate, Successions, Litigation and Arbitration, Industrial Property and Trade Regulations, Computer Law, Cassation Procedure, European Community Law, Public Law, Environmental Law, Labor Law, Transport Law, City Planning, Construction Contracts, Law of Broadcasting.

FIRM PROFILE: Civil Cooperative Company

MEMBERS OF FIRM

JACQUES DE LIEDEKERKE, born 1928; admitted, 1950, Brussels. *Education:* D.Jur., Louvain. *LANGUAGES:* French, English, Dutch and Italian. *PRACTICE AREAS:* Securities Regulations; Mergers and Acquisitions; Industrial Property; Unfair Competition; Real Estate.

JOHN KIRKPATRICK, born 1934; admitted, 1957, Brussels; 1976, Supreme Court. *Education:* D.Jur., Brussels (ULB). Professor, Tax Law, Université libre de Bruxelles. *LANGUAGES:* French and English. *PRACTICE AREAS:* Taxation; Commercial Law; Cassation Procedure.

PHILIPPE DE CALLATAY, born 1933; admitted, 1956, Brussels. *Education:* D.Jur., Louvain. *LANGUAGES:* French and English. *PRACTICE AREAS:* Real Estate; Construction Contracts; Administrative Law.

LÉO STOOP, born 1938; admitted, 1966, Brussels. *Education:* D.Jur., Lic. Ec. Sc., Louvain. *LANGUAGES:* Dutch, French, English and German. *PRACTICE AREAS:* Commercial Law; Labor Law; Litigation.

MICHEL WAELBROECK, born 1932; admitted, 1956, Brussels. *Education:* D.Jur., Brussels (ULB); LL.M., New York University. Co-Author: Stein, Hay, Waelbroeck, "European Community Law and Institutions in Perspective," Bobbs - Merrill, 1976; Waelbroeck-Louis-Vignes-Dewost, "Droit de la Communauté Économique Européenne". Professor of European Community Law, Université libre de Bruxelles. Visiting Professor, Parker School of International and Comparative Law, Columbia University, 1980-1989. *Member:* Institute of International Law. *LANGUAGES:* French, English, Dutch, German, Italian, Spanish, Russian and Greek. *PRACTICE AREAS:* European Community Law; International Law.

CLAUDE A. GONTHIER, born 1946; admitted, 1970, Brussels. *Education:* D.Jur., Brussels (ULB); Post Graduate in Business Law. Former Assistant in Tax Law. *LANGUAGES:* French, English and Dutch. *PRACTICE AREAS:* Corporate Law; Mergers and Acquisitions; Taxation; Real Estate; Litigation; Arbitration.

(This Listing Continued)

*LIEDEKERKE WOLTERS WAELBROECK &
KIRKPATRICK, Brussels—Continued*

CLAUDE VERBRAEKEN, born 1947; admitted, 1970, Brussels. *Education:* D.Jur., Brussels (ULB); Post Graduate in Business Law. Former Assistant, Université libre de Bruxelles. *LANGUAGES:* French, English and Dutch. *PRACTICE AREAS:* Industrial Relations; Commercial Law; Litigation.

MARTINE DEMEUR, born 1949; admitted, 1972, Brussels. *Education:* Lic. Jur., Brussels (ULB). *LANGUAGES:* French, Dutch, English. *PRACTICE AREAS:* Industrial and Intellectual Property; Unfair Competition; Distribution; Contracts.

MARC VAN DER HAEGEN, born 1950; admitted, 1972, Brussels. *Education:* D.Jur., Brussels (ULB); Post Graduate in Business Law. Professor, Corporate Law, Brussels (Solvay Business School-Postgraduate Tax Program). *LANGUAGES:* French, English and Dutch. *PRACTICE AREAS:* Corporate Law; Banking Law; Mergers and Acquisitions; Issue and Trading Securities.

FRANCOISE COLINET, born 1951; admitted, 1973, Brussels. *Education:* Lic. Jur., Brussels (ULB). Former Assistant in Contract Law, Université libre de Bruxelles. *LANGUAGES:* French and English. *PRACTICE AREAS:* Real Estate; City Planning; Construction Contracts; Broadcasting.

MARC GODFROID, born 1949; admitted, 1972, Brussels. *Education:* Lic. Jur., Brussels (ULB). Former Assistant in Civil Law, Lecturer in Air Law, Université libre de Bruxelles. Co-author: Naveau and Godfroid: "Précis de droit aérien," Brussels, 1988. *LANGUAGES:* French, Dutch and English. *PRACTICE AREAS:* Transport Law; Insurance Law.

DIRK LINDEMANS, born 1950; admitted, 1974, Brussels. *Education:* Lic. Jur., Leuven; Post Graduate in Administrative Law, Brussels. Assistant in Administrative Law, Katholieke Universiteit Leuven. Author: "Kort Geding," 1985. *LANGUAGES:* Dutch, French, English. *PRACTICE AREAS:* Public Law; Environmental Law.

SIMONE NUDELHOLE, born 1953; admitted, 1977, Brussels. *Education:* Lic.Jur., Brussels (ULB). Lecturer in Civil Law, Université Libre de Bruxelles. *LANGUAGES:* French and English. *PRACTICE AREAS:* Estates and Charities; Conflicts of Law; Human Rights Law.

BERNARD BEYENS, born 1954; admitted, 1976, Brussels. *Education:* Lic.Jur., Brussels (ULB); Post Graduate in Business Law. *LANGUAGES:* French, English and Dutch. *PRACTICE AREAS:* Banking Law; Trade Regulations; Torts; Products Liability Law.

PHILIPPE MALHERBE, born 1955; admitted, 1978, Brussels. *Education:* Lic.Jur., Lic.Ec.Sc., Louvain; LL.M., University of California, Berkeley. Professor, Comparative International Taxation, Ecole supérieure des Sciences fiscales. *LANGUAGES:* French, English, Dutch and German. *PRACTICE AREAS:* Corporate Law; International Taxation; Securities Regulations.

ALEXANDRE VANDENCASTEELE, born 1950; admitted, 1977, Brussels. *Education:* Lic. Jur., Brussels (ULB); Post Graduate in Business Law, Post Graduate in European Law; M.C.J., New York University. Référendaire to Lord Mackenzie Stuart, Judge in the European Court of Justice, 1980-1982. *LANGUAGES:* French, English and Dutch. *PRACTICE AREAS:* European Community Law; Trade Regulations.

POL GLINEUR, born 1953; admitted, 1976, Brussels. *Education:* Université libre de Bruxelles (Lic. Jur., 1976). Author: "Droit et Ethique de l'Informatique," P.U.B., 1984. Lecturer: Tax Law, 1983; Commercial Law and Computer Law, 1983-1989, Université libre de Bruxelles. *LANGUAGES:* French. *PRACTICE AREAS:* Taxation; Insurance Law; Computer Law.

DENIS WAELBROECK, born 1955; admitted, 1979, Brussels. *Education:* Université libre de Bruxelles (Lic.Jur., 1979); Post Graduate in European Community Law, 1981. Référendaire to the President of the European Court of Justice, 1983-1985. Co-author: Schermers, Waelbroeck, "Judicial Protection in the European Communities", Kluwer, Fifth Edition. Lecturer in European Law, Université libre de Bruxelles, 1990. *LANGUAGES:* French, English, German and Danish. *PRACTICE AREAS:* European Community Law.

DANIEL GARABEDIAN, born 1959; admitted, 1982, Brussels. *Education:* Université libre de Bruxelles (Lic. Jur., 1982); Post Graduate in Tax Law, (1983); University of Michigan (LL.M., 1985). Assistant: Roman Law, 1980-1988, and Tax Law, 1985, Université libre de Bruxelles. *LAN-*

(This Listing Continued)

GUAGES: French and English. *PRACTICE AREAS:* Taxation; Corporate Law; Securities Regulations.

MAGDA VANDEBOTERMET, born 1962; admitted, 1985, Brussels. *Education:* Lic. Jur., Brussels (VUB). Former Assistant in Criminal Law and Procedure, Vrije Universiteit Brussel. *LANGUAGES:* Dutch, French, English and German. *PRACTICE AREAS:* Labor Law; Criminal Law; Criminal Procedure; Environmental Law; Litigation.

SABINE GEUBEL, born 1957; admitted, 1991, Brussels. *Education:* Université libre de Bruxelles (Lic. Jur.). Assistant in Tax Law, Université libre de Bruxelles. Lecturer in Master Tax Management, Solvay Business School, Brussels. *LANGUAGES:* French. *PRACTICE AREAS:* Taxation; Banking Law; Corporate Law.

Languages: French, English, Dutch, German, Italian, Spanish, Russian, Danish and Greek.

ADVOKATFIRMAN LINDAHL

33 BLVD DE LA CAMBRE 33, BTE 13
B-1050 BRUSSELS, BELGIUM
Telephone: 32-2-646 46 90
Fax: 32-2-646 45 80

Gothenburg, Sweden Office: Östra Hamngatan 36. Mailing Address: P.O. Box 11911, S-404 39 Göteborg. Telephone: 46-31 80 34 30. Telefax: 46-31 15 82 85.

Helsingborg, Sweden Office: Mariagatan 10. Mailing Address: P.O. Box 1214, S-251 12 Helsingborg. Telephone: 46-42 18 31 80. Telefax: 46-42 11 96 78 and 46-42 24 12 86. Telex: 72715 Counsel S.

Kristianstad, Sweden Office: Västra Vallgatan 26. Mailing Address: P.O. Box 167, S-291 22 Kristianstad. Telephone: 46-44 10 07 80. Telex: 32584 LUNDLAW S. Telefax: 46-44 11 85 14.

Malmö, Sweden Office: Hjälmaregatan 3, Scandinavian Center, S-211 18 Malmö. Telephone: 46-40 17 44 40. Telex: 32584 LUNDLAW S. Telefax: 46-40 11 13 54.

Stockholm, Sweden Office: Strandvägen 5 A. Mailing Address: P.O. Box 14240, S-104 40 Stockholm. Telephone: 46-8 670 5800. Telex: 19609 LINDAHL S. Telefax: 46-8 667 73 80.

Örebro, Sweden Office: Vasastrand 11-13. Mailing Address: P.O. Box 143, S-701 42 Örebro. Telephone: 46-19 10 48 00. Telefax: 46-19 10 44 45.

Corporate, Mergers and Acquisitions, Commercial Agreements, EC Law and Competition Law.

CARL NISSER, born Sweden, 1940; admitted, 1992, Sweden (Not admitted in Belgium). *Education:* University of Uppsala (LL.M., 1966); University of Strasbourg (D.E.S., 1967); Harvard Business School, Senior Management Program, 1981. District Court, 1967-1969; Court of Appeal, 1969-1971; Swedish Cartel Office, 1970-1971. Corporate Positions with Gränges Metallverken, Volvo and Goodyear, 1971-1989, in France, Belgium, the U.S. and Indonesia, 1989-1993. Resident Counsel with Advokatfirman Landahl, Brussels. Author: "Doing business in France," 1972; "Corporate Law and EC," 1973; "Practical guide to EC Law," 1991; "How to adopt to the new legal environment in the EC," 1993. *Member:* Swedish Bar Association; American Bar Association; International Bar Association. *LANGUAGES:* Swedish, English, French and German. *PRACTICE AREAS:* International Practice; Commercial and Corporate Law; European Community Law; Financial; Trade and Antitrust Law.

ASSOCIATE

PERNILLA BJURMAN, born Sweden, 1966; (Not admitted in Belgium). *Education:* University of Stockholm (LL.M., 1990); Certificat des droits de l'homme, Strasbourg, 1991; Master of Advanced European Legal Studies, College d'Europe, Bruges, 1992. Legal Assistant, Ashurst Morris Crisp, London, 1988. Associate Lawyer with Dr. Widmark, Stockholm, 1989-1990. Assistant Judge, Administrative County Court, Stockholm, 1990-1991. *LANGUAGES:* Swedish, English and French. *PRACTICE AREAS:* Business Law; Commercial Law; European Community Law.

LINKLATERS & PAINES

Established in 1973

RUE DU LUXEMBOURG 47-51
B-1040 BRUSSELS, BELGIUM
Telephone: (2) 513 78 00
Telex: 23207
Fax: (2) 513 25 83

London, England Office: Barrington House, 59-67 Gresham Street, EC2V 7JA. Telephone: 0171-606-7080. Cable Address: Linklaters, London, EC2V 7JA. Telegrams: Linklaters, London. Telex: 884349. Fax: 0171-606-5113.

English and Belgian Lawyers.
Firm engaged in EC, Belgian and English Law Practice.

RESIDENT PARTNERS

Alec Burnside
James Flynn

(For full list of offices see entry at London, England)

LOEFF CLAEYS VERBEKE

268 A AVENUE DE TERVUEREN
A-1150 BRUSSELS, BELGIUM
Telephone: 02-778.22.11.
Fax: 02-763.21.85.

Amsterdam, The Netherlands Office: 15 Apollolaan, P.O. Box 75088, 1070 AB. Telephone: 31-20-5741200. Telex: 14292 LEX NL. Telecopier: 31-20-6718775.

Antwerp, Belgium Office: "De Hertoghe," 8th Floor, 92 Desguinlei, B.8, B-2018. telephone: 32.3.2385656. Telex:72748 (EURLAWB). Telecopier: 32.3.2387877.

Liege, Belgium Office: 13, Rue Simonon, (Place de Bronckart), B-4000. Telephone: 32-41-527722. Telecopier: 32-41-527511.

New York, New York Office: Swiss Bank Tower, 23rd Floor, 10 East 50th Street, 10020. Telephone: 212-759-9000. Fax: 212-759-9018.

Paris, France Office: 1, Avenue Franklin D. Roosevelt, 75008. Telephone: 33-1-49539125. Telecopier: 33-1-42891460.

Rotterdam, The Netherlands Office: 70 Weena, P.O. Box 74, 3000 AB. Telephone: 31-10-4034777. Telex: 23395 (LEX NL). Telecopier: 31-10-4149388.

Singapore Office: 20 Raffles Place, #08-03, Ocean Towers, Singapore 0104. Telephone: 65-5335332. Fax: 65-5330313.

Tokyo Office: NSE Building, 5th Floor, 1-7-1 Kanda Jinbo-cho, Chiyoda-ku, Tokyo 101, Japan. Telephone: 81-3-32599831. Fax: 81-3-32599888.

Barcelona, Spain Office: 550, 4° 1A, Av. Diagonal, 08021. Telephone: 34-3-2007117. Telecopier: 34-3-2023098.

Madrid, Spain Office: Balañá Eguía, Antonio Mauro 7, 5°, 28014. Telephone: 34-1-5312501. Telecopier: 34-1-5313530.

Jakarta, Indonesia Associated Office: Ali Budiardjo, Nugroho, Reksodiputro, Niaga Tower, 24th floor, Jalan Jenderal Sudirman Kav. 58, 12920. Telephone: 62.21.2505125/2505136. Telecopier: 62.21.2505121/2505001.

Luxembourg, Luxembourg Office: Zeyen Beghin Feider. 67, Rue Ermesinde, P.O. Box 5017, 1050. Telephone: 352.468946. Telex: 60736 (zflaw lu). Telecopier: 352.468947.

Belgian attorneys may represent clients before all Belgian Courts, before the European Court of Justice and the Benelux Court of Justice, and are admitted to plead before all Courts of the Memberstates of the Common Market (EEC).

MEMBERS OF FIRM

PETER BIENENSTOCK, born 1954; admitted, 1982, New York (Not admitted in Belgium). *Education:* Georgetown University School of Languages and Linguistics (B.S., Russian, 1975); Columbia University (J.D., 1981). Contributor, Soviet-American Trade in the Belgium-USSR Investment Treaty (1989). *Member:* American Bar Association.

ANTOINE BRAUN, born 1924; admitted, 1950, Brussels. *Education:* University of Louvain (U.C.L.) (B.A., Philosophy, 1944; Dr.Jur., 1948; Lic. Political and Social Sciences, 1949).

ERIC CARLIER, born 1955; admitted, 1985, Brussels. *Education:* University of Louvain (U.C.L.) (Lic. Jur., 1980).

(This Listing Continued)

THIERRY CLAEYS, born 1946; admitted, 1972, Brussels. *Education:* University of Louvain (U.C.L.) (Dr. Jur., 1969; Lic. Notariat, 1970).

LUC DEMEYERE, born 1952; admitted, 1980, Brussels. *Education:* University of Louvain (K.U. Leuven) (Lic. Jur., 1976); University of Antwerp (UFSIA) (M.B.A., 1979). *Member:* Union Internationale des Avocats.

PIETER DE KOSTER, born 1958; admitted, 1990, Brussels. *Education:* University Faculties Sint Aloysius (U.F.S.A.L.) (B.A., Philosophy, 1977); University of Louvain (K.U. Leuven) (Lic. Jur, 1980); University of Louvain (U.C.L.) (Lic. European Law, 1981); Northwestern University, Chicago, USA (LL.M., 1982).

BRUNO DE DUVE, born 1950; admitted, 1988, Brussels. *Education:* University of Louvain (U.C.L.) (Lic. Jur., 1976). Professor at Ecole Supérieure des Sciences Fiscales (ICHEC), 1980—.

FERNAND DE VISSCHER, born 1952; admitted, 1979, Brussels. *Education:* University of Louvain (U.C.L.) (Lic. Philosophy, 1974; Lic.Jur., 1976). *Member:* Association Internationale pour la Protection de la Propriété Industrielle; Ligue Internationale du Droit de Concurrence; Association Littéraire et Artistique Internationale; Association Benelux des Conseils en Marques et Modèles.

PHILIP J. GHEKIERE, born 1960; admitted, 1987, New York; 1991, Brussels. *Education:* University of Louvain (K.U. Leuven) (Lic. Jur., 1983); New York University, U.S.A. (LL.M., 1986).

DANIEL GILLET, born 1960; admitted, 1990, Brussels. *Education:* University of Brussels (U.L.B.) (Lic. Jur., 1983; Lic. Fiscal Law, 1984); Sondernjuristenprogramme des Deutschen Akademischen Austauschdienstes, University of Tübingen, Düsseldorf, Germany (1985). Contributor, "Business Law in Europe".

GEERT GLAS, born 1961; admitted, 1987, Brussels. *Education:* University of Louvain (K.U. Leuven) (Lic. Jur., 1984); University of Illinois, USA (LL.M., 1985). Co-Author: "International Patent Litigation," (1989). Contributor/Member, Advisory Board: (i) "European Intellectual Property Review;" (ii) "World Intellectual Property Report.".

AXEL HAELTERMAN, born 1960; admitted, 1988, Brussels. *Education:* University of Louvain (K.U. Leuven) (Lic. Jur., 1983; Lic. Economics, 1984; Ph.D., 1992); Columbia University, New York, USA (LL.M., 1985). Professor, University of Louvain (K.U. Leuven), 1987—. *Member:* International Fiscal Association (Chairman, Belgian Branch); International Bar Association.

FRANCIS HERBERT, born 1946; admitted, 1981, Brussels. *Education:* University of Louvain (K.U. Leuven) (Dr. Jur., 1968); University of Amsterdam (Postgraduate International Course on European Integration, 1970). *Member:* Belgian Association for European Law; Union des Avocats Européens.

BENOÎT MICHAUX, born 1960; admitted, 1987, Brussels. *Education:* University of Louvain (U.C.L.) (B.A., Philosophy, 1982); University of Louvain (K.U. Leuven) (Lic. Jur., 1983). *Member:* Association Internationale pour la Protection de la Propriété Industrielle; Ligue Internationale du Droit de Concurrence.

TOM R. OTTERVANGER, born 1950; admitted, 1974, Rotterdam (Not admitted in Belgium). *Education:* Leyden University (1973). Professor, European Law, University of Brussels (V.U.B.). Visiting Professor, McGeorge School of Law, European Law Program, Salzburg, Austria, 1982—. *Member:* International Bar Association (Chairman, Subcommittee Distribution and Agency, 1987—); American Bar Association (Associate Member, Country Coordinator for The Netherlands, 1986—); Union Internationale des Avocats; Netherlands Association for Competition Law; Netherlands Association for European Law.

JEAN PIERRE RENARD, born 1950; admitted, 1977, Brussels. *Education:* University of Louvain (U.C.L.) (Lic. Jur., 1973; Lic. Economic Law, 1974). *Member:* Ligue Internationale du Droit de la Concurrence.

HENRI SCHEYVAERTS, born 1948; admitted, 1976, Brussels. *Education:* University of Louvain (U.C.L.) (Lic. Jur., 1972).

PIETER SMEDTS, born 1950; admitted, 1979, Brussels. *Education:* University of Louvain (K.U. Leuven) (Lic. Jur., 1973); University of Brussels (V.U.B) (Lic. Social Law, 1976).

RAYMOND SOREL, born 1921; admitted, 1947, Brussels. *Education:* University of Louvain (U.C.L.) (Dr. Jur., 1943).

JACQUES STEENBERGEN, born 1949; admitted, 1984, Brussels. *Education:* University of Antwerp (UFSIA) (B.A., Philosophy and Economics, 1969); University of Louvain (K.U. Leuven) (Lic. Jur., 1972;

(This Listing Continued)

LOEFF CLAEYS VERBEKE, Brussels—Continued

Ph.D., 1978). Professor of Competition Law, University of Louvain (K.U. Leuven), 1980—. Guest Professor Europa Institut, University of Amsterdam (Law of GATT in I.C.E.I., External Relations of E.E.C.) in Summer Course, 1980—. Member of Faculty International Law Institute, Washington, D.C., 1985—. *Member:* International Bar Association (Vice-Chairman, Subcommittee on Trade); Union Internationale des Avocats; Belgian Association for European Law. (Also at New York, N.Y.).

KOENRAAD VAN DEN BROECK, born 1961; admitted, 1987, Brussels. *Education:* University of Louvain (K.U. Leuven) (Lic. Jur., 1984).

HERMAN VAN HOOGENBEMT, born 1956; admitted, 1984, Brussels. *Education:* University of Ghent (R.U.G.) (Lic. Jur., 1979; Lic. Social Law, 1980). Assistant Professor, Social Law, University of Ghent, 1980—.

THIERRY VAN INNIS, born 1948; admitted, 1976, Brussels. *Education:* University of Louvain (K.U. Leuven) (Lic. Jur., 1972). Professor, Saint Aloysius School of Economics (EHSAL), 1984—.

LOUIS-H. VERBEKE, born 1947; admitted, 1982, Brussels. *Education:* University of Ghent (R.U.G.) (Dr. Jur., 1970; M.B.A., 1971); University of Virginia (LL.M., 1972). Co-Author: "Business Law in Europe". Guest Professor, Vlerick School of Management, 1983—. *Member:* International Bar Association; International Fiscal Association.

COUNSEL

TONY CLAEYS, born 1925; admitted, 1990, Brussels. *Education:* University of Ghent (R.U.G.) (Dr. Jur., 1949).

ASSOCIATES

BART ADRIAENS, born 1967; admitted, List of Stagiaires, 1992, Brussels. *Education:* University of Ghent (R.U.G.) (Lic. Jur., 1990); University of Brussels (U.L.B.) (special Lic. Social Law, 1991).

PIERRE APRAXINE, born 1966; admitted, List of Stagiaires, 1994. *Education:* University of Louvain (K.U. Leuven) (Lic. Jur., 1989); University of Brussels (U.L.B.); special licence in International Law, 1993.

PIETER BEVERNAGE, born 1968; admitted, List of Stagiaires, 1992, Brussels; 1994, New York. *Education:* University of Louvain (K.U. Leuven) (Lic. Jur., 1991); University of Chicago Law School, USA (LL.M., 1992).

CHANTAL BIERNAUX, born 1966; admitted, List of Stagiaires, 1994, Brussels. *Education:* University of Louvain (U.C.L.) (Lic. German Phil., 1988; Lic. Jur., 1994).

FABIENNE BOUQUELLE, born 1969; admitted, List of Stagiaires, 1992, Brussels. *Education:* University of Louvain (U.C.L.) (Lic. Jur., 1992).

NOËLLE BRIBOSIA, born 1948; admitted, 1981, Belgium. *Education:* Faculties St. Louis (B.A., Philosophy, 1968); University of Louvain (U.C.L.) (Lic. Jur., 1977).

PATRICIA CEYSENS, born 1965; admitted, 1991, Leuven. *Education:* University of Louvain (K.U. Leuven) (Lic.Jur., 1988).

LAURENT COLLON, born 1965; admitted List of Stagiaires, 1990, Brussels. *Education:* University of Brussels (U.L.B.) (Lic.Jur., 1989).

ALAIN CONSTANTINI, born 1969; admitted, List of Stagiaires, 1994, Brussels. *Education:* University of Louvain (U.C.L.) (Lic. Jur., 1992).

EMMANUEL CORNU, born 1967; Admitted, List of Stagiaires, 1990, Brussels. *Education:* University of Louvain (U.C.L.) Lic. Jur., 1990); Leyden University, The Netherlands (International and EC Law, 1991).

ERIC CUSAS, born 1962; admitted, 1993, Brussels. *Education:* University of Liège (U.L.G.) (Lic. Jur., 1988; degree in Business Administration, 1983).

LAURA DE BEER, born 1965; admitted, 1993, Brussels. *Education:* University of Brussels (U.L.B.) (Lic.Jur., 1988) (V.U.B.) (Lic. Social Law, 1989).

OLIVIER DEBRAY, born 1963; admitted, 1989, Brussels. *Education:* University of Louvain (K.U. Leuven) (Lic.Jur., 1986); University of Louvain (U.C.L.) (Degree in Economic Sciences, 1988).

TAYDE DE CALLATAY, born 1968; admitted, List of Stagiaires, 1991, Brussels. *Education:* University of Louvain (U.C.L.) (Lic. Jur., 1990); Leyden University, The Netherlands (International Law, 1991).

ERIC DE GRYSE, born 1970; admitted, List of Stagiaires, 1994, Brussels. *Education:* University of Louvain (K.U. Leuven) (Lic. Jur., 1993); University of Trier, Postgraduate (Magister Iuris, 1993).

(This Listing Continued)

STEFAN DE KEERSMAECKER, born 1970; admitted, List of Stagiaires, 1994, Brussels. *Education:* University of Louvain (K.U. Leuven) (Lic. Jur., 1992); University of Heidelberg, Germany (Erasmus Programme, 1993).

BERNARD DELTOUR, born 1965; admitted, List of Stagiaires, 1988, Brussels. *Education:* University of Louvain (K.U. Leuven) (Lic.Jur., 1988).

CARLOS DE WOLF, born 1961; admitted, 1992, Brussels. *Education:* University of Ghent (R.U.G.) (Lic. Jur., 1985); Vlerick School of Management (M.B.A., 1987).

THOMAS DENYS, born 1968; admitted, List of Stagiaries, 1992, Brussels. *Education:* University of Louvain (K.U.Leuven) (Lic. Jur., 1991); University of Salamanca, 1991 (Erasmus Programme); Deutscher Akademischer Austauschdienst 1992 (Tübingen / Düsseldorf, Germany).

ERIC DE PLAEN, born 1967; admitted, List of Stagiaires, 1992, Brussels. *Education:* University of Louvain (U.C.L.) (Lic. Jur., 1990).

LAURENT DU JARDIN, born 1965; admitted, List of Stagiaires, 1993, Brussels. *Education:* University of Louvain (U.C.L.) (Lic. Jur., 1988); Leyden University, The Netherlands (International Law, 1989).

JOOST EVERAERT, born 1962; admitted, 1993, Brussels. *Education:* University of Louvain (K.U. Leuven) (Lic.Jur., 1985); The Johns Hopkins University, School of Advanced International Studies, Washington, D.C. and Bologna (B.A. in International Relations, 1987).

PHILIPPE HAMER, born 1965; admitted, 1993, Brussels. *Education:* University of Louvain (U.C.L.) (Lic.Jur., 1988; Lic. Economics, 1988); University of Brussels (U.L.B.) (Lic. Business Law, 1990).

PAUL HERMANT, born 1965; admitted, 1992, Brussels. *Education:* University of Brussels (U.L.B.) (Lic. Jur., 1988) (Lic. Business Law, 1989); M.B.A., (Ecole de Commerce Solvay, U.L.B., 1992).

VÉRONIQUE HUYSMANS, born 1969; admitted, List of Stagiaires, 1994, Brussels. *Education:* University of Brussels (U.L.B.) (Lic. Jur., 1992); U.C.L.A. (USA) (LL.M., 1993).

FRANÇOISE JACQUES DE DIXMUDE, born 1967; admitted, List of Stagiaires, 1991, Brussels. *Education:* University of Louvain (U.C.L.); Lic. Jur., 1990); University of Louvain (K.U. Leuven) (Lic. Notariat, 1991); Leyden University (International Law, 1991).

DOMINIQUE KAESMACHER, born 1960; admitted, 1991, Brussels. *Education:* University of Liège (U.L.G.) (Lic. Jur., 1983).

BÉNÉDICTE LAGAE, born 1969; admitted, List of Stagiaires, 1992, Brussels. *Education:* University of Ghent (R.U.G.) (Lic. Jur., 1992).

PIETER LALEMAN, born 1968; admitted, List of Stagiaires, 1993, Brussels; 1994, New York. *Education:* University of Louvain (K.U. Leuven) (Lic. Jur., 1991); Heidelberg, Germany (Erasmus Programme, 1991): Vlerick School for Management (M.B.A., 1991).

ANN LAMBEETS, born 1961; admitted, 1989, Brussels. *Education:* University of Brussels (V.U.B.) (Lic.Jur., 1985).

HENRI-FRANÇOIS LENAERTS, born 1967; admitted, List of Stagiaires, 1991, Brussels. *Education:* University of Louvain (U.C.L.) (Lic. Jur., 1990); University of Ghent (R.U.G.) (Lic. Social and Economic Law, 1991).

PIERRE-OLIVIER MAHIEU, born 1966; admitted, 1992, Brussels. *Education:* University of Louvain (U.C.L.) (Lic.Jur., 1989); University of Madrid, 1989 (Erasmus Programme); University of Virginia, U.S.A. (LL.M., 1991). Assistant Professor, Faculties Sint-Louis.

DIRK MEEUS, born 1966; admitted, List of Stagiaires, 1991, Brussels; admitted, 1994, New York. *Education:* University of Louvain (K.U. Leuven) (Lic. Jur., 1990); University of Michigan, U.S.A. (LL.M., 1991).

GUIDO MÜLLER, born 1963; admitted, List of Stagiaires, 1993, Brussels; 1991, New York. *Education:* University of Louvain (U.C.L.) (Lic. Jur., 1986); Rheinische Friedrich-Wilhelms-Universität Bonn, Germany (Magister der Rechtsvergleichung, 1988); University of Ghent (Master of European Law, 1989); University of San Diego School of Law, USA (M.C.L., 1990).

LIESBET NOELS, born 1969; admitted, List of Stagiaires, 1994, Brussels. *Education:* University of Louvain (K.U. Leuven) (Lic. Jur., 1992); University of Salamanca (Erasmus Programme, 1993).

(This Listing Continued)

HAROLD NYSSENS, born 1969; admitted, List of Stagiaires, 1994, Brussels. *Education:* University of Louvain (K.U. Leuven) (Lic. Jur., 1992); European Institut, Saarbrücken, Germany (European Law, 1993).

MARC PITTIE, born 1969; admitted, List of Stagiaires, 1993, Brussels. *Education:* University of Louvain (U.C.L.) (Lic. Jur., 1992 and Lic. Applied Economic Sciences, 1993).

ANDRÉ RAPPE, born 1966; admitted, List of Stagiaires, 1993, Brussels. *Education:* University of Ghent (R.U.G.) (Lic. Jur., 1988); Vlerick School for Management (R.U.G.) (M.B.A., 1990).

KARIN RASSCHAERT, born 1968; admitted, List of Stagiaires, 1992, Brussels. *Education:* University of Ghent (R.U.G.) (Lic. Jur., 1991).

JAN SCHAMP, born 1966; admitted, List of Stagiaires, 1991, Brussels. *Education:* University of Louvain (K.U. Leuven) (Lic Jur., 1988); University of Georgia , USA (LL.M., 1989).

GUIDO SEPELIE, born 1962; admitted, List of Stagiaires, 1990, Brussels. *Education:* University of Louvain (K.U. Leuven) (Lic. Jur., 1986); University of Illinois, U.S.A. (LL.M., 1987).

THIERRY STIÉVENARD, born 1969; admitted, List of Stagiaires, 1991, Brussels. *Education:* University of Louvain (U.C.L.) (Lic. Jur., 1991). Assistant, University of Louvain (U.C.L.) (Public and Administrative Law).

NATALIE ULBURGHS, born 1966, admitted, List of Stagiaires, 1989, Brussels. *Education:* University of Louvain (K.U. Leuven) (Lic. Jur., 1989); Duke University, USA (LL.M., 1991); University of Poitiers, France (Erasmus Programme, 1989).

CHRISTEL VANASSCHE, born 1965; admitted, List of Stagiaires, 1991, Brussels. *Education:* University of Ghent (R.U.G.) (Lic. Jur., 1988); Centre Européen Universitaire de Nancy (degree in European Studies, 1989).

PASCAL VANDEN BORRE, born 1969; admitted, List of Stagiaires, 1992, Brussels. *Education:* University of Ghent (R.U.G.) (Lic. Jur., 1992; Special Licence in Economic Law, 1994).

BRUNO VANDERMEULEN, born 1964; admitted, List of Stagiaires, 1990, Brussels. *Education:* University of Louvain (K.U. Leuven) (Lic. Jur., 1988); University of Georgia , USA (LL.M., 1989).

INGE VANDERREKEN, born 1969; admitted, List of Stagiaires, 1993, Brussels. *Education:* University of Louvain (K.U. Leuven) (Lic. Jur., 1992); University of Brussels (U.L.B.); special Lic. social Law (1993).

PATRICIA VAN DE WIELE, born 1966; admitted, List of Stagiaires, 1991, Brussels. *Education:* University of Louvain (K.U. Leuven) (Lic. Jur., 1989); Europa-Institut Saarbrücken, Germany (European Integration, 1991).

MICHEL VAN DEN ABBEELE, born 1964; admitted, List of Stagiaires, 1991, Brussels. *Education:* University of Louvain (U.C.L.) (Lic. Jur., 1990).

ALEXANDER VANDENBERGEN, born 1968; admitted, List of Stagiaires, 1991, Brussels. *Education:* University of Louvain (K.U. Leuven) (Lic. Jur., 1991).

HANS VAN GOMPEL, born 1964; admitted, 1993, Brussels. *Education:* University of Louvain (K.U. Leuven) (Lic. Jur., 1987); D.E.S.S. Juriste d'Affaire International, University of Paris (1988).

FILIP VAN ELSEN, born 1963; admitted List of Stagiaires, 1990, Brussels. *Education:* University of Antwerp (U.I.A.) (Lic.Jur., 1987); University of Brussels (V.U.B.) (Master in International and Comparative Law, 1988).

OLIVIER VAN HERSTRAETEN, born 1963; admitted, List of Stagiaires, 1986, Brussels. *Education:* University of Louvain (U.C.L.) (Lic. Jur., 1986); Ecole Supérieure des Sciences Fiscales (ICHEC) (Lic. Fiscal Law, 1987); University of Brussels (U.L.B.) (Lic. Economics, 1988).

ANTHONY VAN LUCHEM, born 1966; admitted, List of Stagiaires, 1991, Brussels. *Education:* University of Louvain (K.U. Leuven) (Lic. Jur., 1989); University of Louvain (U.C.L.) (Lic. Business Law, 1990).

BART VANSCHOEBEKE, born 1969; admitted, List of Stagiaires, 1993, Brussels. *Education:* University of Louvain (K.U. leuven) (Lic. Jur., 1992); University of Brussels (U.L.B.); special Lic. Social Law (1993).

COLETTE VENDERICK, born 1964; admitted, List of Stagiaires, 1991, Brussels. *Education:* University of Liège (U.Lg) (Lic. Jur., 1987); University of Ghent (R.U.G.) (Lic. Social Law, 1988); Leyden University, The Netherlands (International Law, 1991).

(This Listing Continued)

FABIENNE VEYS, born 1965; admitted, List of Stagiaires, 1993, Brussels. *Education:* University of Ghent (R.U.G.) (Lic. Jur., 1991); Assistant University of Ghent (R.U.G.) (Labour Law).

PHILIP WALRAVENS, born 1963; admitted, 1992, Brussels. *Education:* University of Louvain (K.U. Leuven) (Lic. Jur., 1986).

ANN WITTERS, born 1968; admitted, List of Stagiaires, 1992, Brussels. *Education:* University of Ghent (R.U.G.) (Lic. Jur., 1991; Lic. Social and Business Law, 1992).

Languages: Dutch, French, English, German, Italian, Russian and Spanish.

(For Personnel and other data, see Professional Biographies at Amsterdam, Antwerp, Barcelona, Liège, New York, Paris, Rotterdam, Singapore and Tokyo)

LOVELL WHITE DURRANT

AVENUE LOUISE 523, BTE 24
1050 BRUSSELS, BELGIUM
Telephone: (2) 647 0660
Fax: (2) 647 1124

London, England Office: 65 Holborn Viaduct, EC1A 2DY. Telephone: 0171 236 0066. Fax: 0171 248 4212; 236 0084; 248 7273. Telex: 887122 LWD G.
New York, New York Office: 527 Madison Avenue, 10th Floor, 10022. Telephone: (212) 758 3773. Fax: (212) 486 0367.
Paris, France Office: 37 Avenue Pierre 1er de Serbie, 75008. Telephone: (1) 49 52 04 26. Fax: (1) 47 23 96 12.
Prague, Czech Republic Office: U Prasne brany 3, State Mesto, 1. Telephone: (2) 2481 1672. Fax: (2) 2481 1608.
Ho Chi Minh City, Vietnam Office: 141 Vo Van Tan Street, District 3. Telephone: (848) 298 787. Fax: (848) 392 868.
Hong Kong Office: 11th Floor, Peregrine Tower, Lippo Centre, Queensway. Telephone: 2810 4770. Fax: 2868 4051.
Beijing, Republic of China Office: Office 5D, CITIC Building, 19 Jianguomenwai Dajie, 100004. Telephone: (861) 506 3588. Fax: (861) 500 1972.
Tokyo, Japan Office: Shin-Kasumigaseki Building, 20th Floor, 3-3-2 Kasumigaseki, Chiyoda-ku, 100. Telephone: (3) 3503 2571. Fax: (3) 3503 0699.
Shanghai, People's Republic of China Associated Office: Room 1703, Shanghai International Trade Centre, 2200 Yan An Road (W). Telephone: (21) 219 4419. Fax: (21) 219 5462.

Firm engaged in English and General International Practice but not authorized to appear before the Belgian Courts.
English Lawyers.

RESIDENT PARTNERS

Simon W. Polito
John E. Pheasant
Nicholas M.G. Bromfield
Philip G.H. Collins

(For List of Partners see Professional Biographies at London, England).

LOYENS & VOLKMAARS

Tax Lawyers

Member of Loyens Lefebvre Rädler-European Tax Network

TERVURENLAAN 270/272, BOX 12
B-1150 BRUSSELS, BELGIUM
Telephone: 2-7720-510
Fax: 2-7723-217

Antwerp: Jan van Rijswijcklaan 128, B-2018. Telephone: 3-2370-822. Fax: 3-2379-636.

FIRM PROFILE: *Loyens & Volkmaars, a partnership of Netherlands, Netherlands Antilles and Belgian tax lawyers based in the Netherlands has, in the past seventy-five years, built up a leading position in the profession. The firm has specialized in tax law, a field to which it has deliberately restricted itself, offering a full range of services across the entire tax spectrum.*

Loyens & Volkmaars employs approximately 600 people. It works for a large variety of clients, including multinationals, large and medium-sized businesses, individuals, government agencies and institutional investors,

(This Listing Continued)

LOYENS & VOLKMAARS, Brussels—Continued

which are based in the Netherlands and elsewhere. To provide such a wide range of clients with the best possible service, Loyens & Volkmaars has offices in Europe, the U.S.A., the Caribbean and the Far East. Outside the Netherlands, the offices in Belgium, the Netherlands Antilles and Aruba have developed domestic tax law practices of high repute.

Loyens & Volkmaars, together with Bureau Francis Lefebvre and Oppenhoff Rädler forms Loyens Lefebvre Rädler-European Tax Network, combining the expertise of three firms whose tax law practices rank among the top of the profession in Europe.

MEMBERS OF FIRM

J.F.T. VAN HAAREN, born 1942.

E.J.O. PICAVET, born 1949.

M. VANDENDIJK, born 1958.

P.A.A. VANHAUTE, born 1954, Antwerp Office.

(For a full list of the Members of Firm, See Professional Biographies at Amsterdam, The Netherlands)

MACFARLANES
AVENUE LOUISE 106
1050 BRUSSELS, BELGIUM
Telephone: (02) 647 0650
Fax: (02) 646 4729
Telefax: 20317 OMSSA

London, England Office: 10 Norwich Street, EC4A 1BD. Telephone: (0171) 831 9222. Fax: (0171) 831 9607. Telex: 296361 MACFAR G.
Tokyo, Japan Office: Sanbancho KB-6 Building, 6 Sanbancho, Chiyoda-ku, 102. Telephone: (03) 3239 3661. Fax: (03) 3239 2884.

The office in Brussels is a joint office with O'Melveny & Myers (U.S. Lawyers) and Nörr, Stiefenhofer & Lutz (German Lawyers).
The office specializes in European Community Law, International Corporate and Commercial Matters and Trade Law but not authorized to appear before the Belgian Courts.

PARTNER

R. JANE WHITTAKER, born Lancashire, England, February 27, 1955; admitted, 1978, Solicitor, Supreme Court of England and Wales (Not admitted in Belgium). *Education:* University of Manchester (LL.B., Hons., 1975).

ASSOCIATE

GEOFFREY D. OLIVER, born Boston, Massachusetts, December 8, 1957; admitted, 1985, Massachusetts; 1988, District of Columbia (Not admitted in Belgium). *Education:* Harvard University (B.A., 1979); Cornell University (J.D., 1985). (Associate of O'Melveny & Myers).

Languages: English, French and German

(For Complete Biographical Data on other Personnel, See Professional Biographies at London, England)

MANNHEIMER SWARTLING
AVENUE DE TERVUEREN 13 A
B-1040 BRUSSELS, BELGIUM
Telephone: (32-2) 732 22 22
Telefax: (32-2) 736 96 52

Stockholm, Sweden Office: Vastra Tradgardsgatan 15, P.O. Box 1650, S-111 86. Telephone: +46-8 613 55 00. Telefax: +46-8 613 55 01. Telex: 13082.
Gothenburg, Sweden Office: Lilla Torget 1, P.O. Box 2235, S-403 14. Telephone: +46-31 10 96 00. Telefax: +46-31 10 96 01. Telex: 2591.
Malmö, Sweden Office: Stortorget 29, P.O. Box 4291, S-203 14. Telephone: +46-40 25 08 00. Telefax: +46-40 25 08 01. Telex: 32727.
Helsingborg, Sweden Office: Södra Storgatan 7, P.O. Box 1384, S-251 13. Telephone: +46-42 18 02 95. Telefax: +46-42 18 42 71.
New York, New York Office: 101 Park Avenue, 10178. Telephone: +1 212 682-0580. Telefax: +1 212 682-0982.
Frankfurt, Germany Office: Bockenheimer Landstrasse 97, D-60325. Telephone: +49-69 974 01 20. Telefax: +49-69 741 01 43.
Berlin, Germany Office: Haus der Schweiz, Friedrichstrasse 155-156, D-10117. Telephone: +49 30 202 20 10. Telefax: +49 30 202 20 110.

(This Listing Continued)

Moscow, Russia Office: Chistoprudny Bulvar 8, 101000 Moscow. Telephone: +7 (095) 929 90 05. Telefax: +7 (095) 929 90 06.

General Swedish and International Business Law Practice. Admiralty and Maritime Law. Antitrust, Marketing and Unfair Competition. Banking. Computer Law. Construction and Engineering Contracts and Disputes. Corporate Financing and Securities Law. Corporate Taxation. EC Law. Environmental Energy and Natural Resources Law. Industrial Property, Copyright and Trademarks. Labor Law. Mergers and Acquisitions. Real Estate Law. Reorganizations. Space Law. Litigation and Arbitration.

RESIDENT PARTNER

Tommy Pettersson

RESIDENT ASSOCIATES

Patrick Lindberg   **Nina Lindström**

(For biographical data on all personnel, see Professional Biographies at Stockholm, Sweden)

MARISSENS & PARTNERS
Established in 1980
AVENUE MOLIÈRE 183
1060 BRUSSELS, BELGIUM
Telephone: 02/343.95.32
Telecopier: 02/343.68.11

Firm engaged in Belgian, European and International law practice. Authorized to appear before the EC and Belgian Courts.
EC Internal and External Trade Regulation, EC Competition and Merger Control, Telecommunications, Air Law, Intellectual Property, Franchising, Licensing and Distribution, Mergers and Acquisitions, Taxation, Litigation.

FIRM PROFILE: Marissens & Partners provide legal assistance concentrated in the specialist areas mentioned above, with emphasis on EC legislative and regulatory advice. The firm has strong links with England and North America.

MEMBERS OF FIRM

EDUARD MARISSENS, born Vilvoorde, Belgium, December 6, 1949; admitted, 1972, Brussels. *Education:* University of Brussels (V.U.B.; Dr.Jur., 1972; Special Degree in Financial and Economic Law, 1973). *Member:* Brussels Bar Association; Scientific Committee of the Journal des Tribunaux-Droit Européen. *LANGUAGES:* English, French and Dutch. *PRACTICE AREAS:* EC Law; International Trade Law.

VÉRONIQUE GEBBINK, born Leuven, Belgium, October 4, 1963; admitted, 1986, Brussels. *Education:* University of Louvain-la-Neuve (Lic. Jur., 1986). *Member:* Brussels Bar Association. *LANGUAGES:* English, French and Dutch. *PRACTICE AREAS:* Litigation; Business Law.

ASSOCIATES

FRÉDÉRIQUE FAGES, born Montpellier, France, October 6, 1966; admitted, 1994, Paris. *Education:* University of Montpellier (D.E.A., 1990); College of Europe, Bruges, Belgium (1991). *LANGUAGES:* French, English and Spanish. *PRACTICE AREAS:* EC Law.

CARL DOTREMONT, born Leuven, Belgium, February 7, 1968; admitted, 1994, Brussels. *Education:* University of Leuven (Lic. jur., 1993); Universität Augsburg, Germany (Master of Law, 1994). *Member:* Brussels Bar Association. *LANGUAGES:* English, french, German and Dutch.

MATRAY, MATRAY ET HALLET
Established in 1990
AVENUE LOUISE, 500/9
1050 BRUSSELS, BELGIUM
Telephone: 32-2-647.79.80
Telecopier: 32-2-640.70.71

Cologne, Germany Office: Matray und Partner. Friesenplatz, 17a, D-50672. Telephone: (49) (221) 52 25 13. Telex: 888 5 332 heid. Telecopier: (49) (221) 52 52 60.
Liege, Belgium Office: 34/24, Boulevard Frère, Orban, 4000. Telephone: (32) (41) 52 70 68. Telex: MACOHA 42330. Telecopier: (32) (41) 52 08 57.

General and International Practice, Commercial Corporate, Tax, EEC, and Arbitration Law.

(This Listing Continued)

RESIDENT PARTNERS

MARIE-CLAIRE ERNOTTE, born June 8, 1963; admitted, 1990, Liege and Brussels. *Education:* University of Liege (Lic. Dr., 1986). *LANGUAGES:* French. *PRACTICE AREAS:* Contracts; Banking; Civil Law.

LUC BIHAIN, born January 24, 1966; admitted, 1989, Liège and Brussels. *Education:* University of Liège (Lic. Dr., 1989). *LANGUAGES:* French, English and Dutch. *PRACTICE AREAS:* Commercial Law; Criminal Law; Finance.

ASSOCIATES

FRANÇOISE VIDTS, born August 18, 1963; admitted, 1986, Brussels. *Education:* University of Brussels (Lic. Dr., 1986); New York University (LL.M., 1993). *LANGUAGES:* French, English and Turkish. *PRACTICE AREAS:* Contracts; Commercial Law.

MAYER, BROWN & PLATT

SQUARE DE MEEÛS 19/20, BTE. 4
1040 BRUSSELS, BELGIUM
Telephone: 011-32-2-512-9878
Fax: 011-32-2-511-3305
Telex: 20768 MBPBRU B

Chicago, Illinois Office: 190 South LaSalle Street, 60603-3441. Telephone: (312) 782-0600. Pitney Bowes: (312) 701-7711. Telex: 190404. Cable: LEMAY.

Washington, D.C. Office: 2000 Pennsylvania Avenue, N.W., 20006-1882. Telephone: (202) 463-2000. Pitney Bowes: (202) 861-0484, Pitney Bowes: (202) 861-0473. Telex: 892603. Cable: LEMAYDC.

New York, New York Office: 787 Seventh Avenue, Suite 2400, 10019-6018. Telephone: (212) 554-3000. Pitney Bowes: (212) 262-1910. Telex: 701842. Cable: LEMAYEN.

Houston, Texas Office: 700 Louisiana Street, Suite 3600, 77002-2730. Telephone: (713) 221-1651. Pitney Bowes: (713) 224-6410. Telex: 775809. Cable: LEMAYHOU.

Los Angeles, California Office: 350 South Grand Avenue, 25th Floor, 90071-1503. Telephone: (213) 229-9500. Pitney Bowes: (213) 625-0248. Telex: 188089. Cable: LEMAYLA.

London, England Office: 162 Queen Victoria Street, EC4V 4DB. Telephone: 011-44-71-248-1465. Fax: 011-44-71-329-4465. Telex: 8811095. Cable: LEMAYLDN.

Tokyo, Japan Office: (Kawachi Gaikokuho Jimu Bengoshi Jimusho). Urbannet Otemachi Building 13F 2-2, Otemachi 2-chome, Chiyoda-ku, Tokyo 100. Telephone: 011-81-3-5255-9700. Facsimile: 011-81-3-5255-9797.

Berlin, Germany Office: Spreeufer 5, 10178. Telephone: 011-49-30-240-7930. Facsimile: 011-49-30-240-79344.

Mexico City, Mexico, D.F., Mexico Correspondent: Jáuregui, Navarrete, Nader y Rojas, S.C. Abogados, Paseo de la Reforma 199, Pisos 15, 16 y 17, 06500. Telephone: 011-525-591-16-55. Facsimile: 011-525-535-80-62, 011-525-703-22-47. Cable: JANANE.

General Commercial Practice. Firm engaged in the Practice of International Corporate, Banking and Financial Law, European Communities Law and American Law. Not authorized to appear before the Belgian Courts.

PARTNERS

THIERRY G. F. BUYTAERT, born Gent, Belgium, October 7, 1951; admitted, 1974, Belgium. *Education:* St. Barbara College (A.B., 1969); Gent University (J.D., 1974). Member: Belgian Association of Corporate Lawyers, 1984-1990; European Banks International Company, Legal Committee, 1984-1990; Belgium Bankers Association Legal Committee, 1984-1990. *Member:* Belgian Association of Computer Law (Chairman, 1988-1990); ECU Banking Association (Chairman of the Legal Committee); Belgian Bankers Association; Belgian Research Center for Financial Affairs, (Member, L.C., 1986); Belgian German Lawyers Association; European Association for Banking and Financial Law (Director, 1988—); Belgian Institute for Financial Law (Member, Advisory Board, 1989—). *LANGUAGES:* Dutch, French, English, German.

(This Listing Continued)

S. ALAN HAMBURGER, born Greensboro, North Carolina, July 9, 1948; admitted, 1973, Georgia (Not admitted in Belgium). *Education:* University of Pennsylvania (B.A., B.A., 1970); Emory University (J.D., 1973).

ASSOCIATES

Susan J. Launi; Caroline Neyrinck.

McCANN FITZGERALD

RUE DE LA LOI 99 WETSTRAAT
B-1040 BRUSSELS, BELGIUM
Telephone: +32-2-230 3634
Fax: +32-2-230 2562

Dublin, Ireland Office: 2 Harbourmaster Place, Custom House Dock, Dublin, 1. Telephone: +353-1-829 0000/670 1111. Fax: +353-1-829 0010.

London, England Office: Imperial House, 15-19 Kingsway, London, WC2B 6UN. Telephone: +44-171-379 0914. Fax: +44-171-836 2759.

New York, New York Office: Thirtieth Floor, 399 Park Avenue, NY, 10022-4697. Telephone: +1-212-318 6700. Fax: +1-212-318 6710.

Corporate, Commercial, Banking and Financial Services, Foreign Investment, Mergers and Takeovers, Real Estate and Property Development, Litigation, Taxation, EU and Competition Law, Oil and Gas, Environmental Law, Aviation, Maritime and Shipping Law, Communications and Media, Insolvency, Labour Law, Pensions Law, Construction Contracts and Arbitration, Intellectual Property, Nationality, Probate, Trusts and General Practice.

DAMIAN COLLINS, born 1960; admitted, 1984, Ireland. *Education:* Trinity College, Dublin (B.A. Mod); European University Institute, Florence (LL.M.). *PRACTICE AREAS:* Anti-Trust and Trade Regulation; International Law.

All solicitors are members of the Incorporated Law Society of Ireland. All partners are members of the Dublin Solicitors Bar Association.

Languages: English, French, German and Spanish

McGUIRE, WOODS, BATTLE & BOOTHE

250 AVENUE LOUISE, BTE. 64
1050 BRUSSELS, BELGIUM
Telephone: (32 2) 629 42 11
Fax: (32 2) 629 42 22

REVISERS OF THE VIRGINIA LAW DIGEST FOR THIS DIRECTORY

Alexandria, Virginia Office: Transpotomac Plaza, Suite 1000, 1199 North Fairfax Street, 22314-1437. Telephone: 703-739-6200. Fax: 703-739-6270.

Baltimore, Maryland Office: The Blaustein Building, One North Charles Street, 21201-3793. Telephone: 410-659-4400. Fax: 410-659-4599.

Charlottesville, Virginia Office: Court Square Building, P.O. Box 1288, 22902-1288. Telephone: 804-977-2500. Fax: 804-980-2222.

Jacksonville, Florida Office: Barnett Center, Suite 2750, 50 North Laura Street, 32202-3635. Telephone: 904-798-3200. Fax: 904-798-3207.

McLean, (Tysons Corner) Virginia Office: 8280 Greensboro Drive, Suite 900, Tysons Corner, 22102-3892. Telephone: 703-712-5000. Fax: 703-712-5050.

Norfolk, Virginia Office: World Trade Center, Suite 9000, 101 West Main Street, 23510-1655. Telephone: 804-640-3700. Fax: 804-640-3701.

Richmond, Virginia Office: One James Center, 901 East Cary Street, 23219-4030. Telephone: 804-775-1000. Fax: 804-775-1061.

Washington, D.C. Office: The Army and Navy Club Building, 1627 Eye Street, N.W., 20006-4007. Telephone: 202-857-1700. Fax: 202-857-1713.

Zürich, Switzerland Office: P.O. Box 4930, Bahnhofstrasse 3, 8022. Telephone: (41-1) 225 20 00. Fax: (41-1) 225 20 20.

General Practice.

FIRM PROFILE: McGuire, Woods, Battle & Boothe is among the largest law firms in the United States, with over 400 attorneys practicing in ten cities. From modest local beginnings in the nineteenth century to a thriving national practice in the twentieth, McGuire, Woods balances the character of its history with the vitality of its growth. From its locations in Alexandria, Baltimore, Charlottesville, Jacksonville, Norfolk, Richmond, Tysons Corner, Washington, D.C., Brussels, Belgium, and Zurich, Switzerland, the firm serves the Mid-Atlantic region and other U.S. and foreign corporate

(This Listing Continued)

McGUIRE, WOODS, BATTLE & BOOTHE, Brussels—Continued

centers. This concentration of lawyers in one of the fastest growing, most populous areas of the nation, coupled with a long tradition of excellence and individual attention, distinguishes the firm from most others.

The firm is organized into business, litigation, real estate, and tax departments. Its strengths have long been recognized in public finance, securities, mergers and acquisitions, tax, product liability, litigation, retailing, real estate and land use, banking and financial services, and intellectual property. Specialization within the firm's nearly 50 areas of expertise often develops along with the particular needs of its clients and their industries. Among the industries represented by the firm are banking, computer equipment and software, real estate development, health care, insurance, telecommunications, manufacturing, distribution, and retailing. Its clients range from individuals to multinational corporations. Many client relationships have lasted for decades as fledgling businesses have evolved into Fortune 500 companies.

RESIDENT MEMBERS

DONALD E. KING, born Washington, D.C., January 22, 1951; admitted, 1976, Virginia (Not admitted in Belgium). *Education:* Loyola University at Chicago (A.B., cum laude, 1973); Harvard Law School (J.D., cum laude, 1976).

RESIDENT ASSOCIATES

JOANNE KATSANTONIS, born Cleveland, Ohio, November 16, 1964; admitted, 1989, Virginia (Not admitted in Belgium). *Education:* Virginia Polytechnic Institute and State University (B.S., 1986); University of Richmond, T.C. Williams School of Law (J.D., 1989).

CHRISTIANE ZUÑIGA, born New York, N.Y., April 10, 1966; admitted, 1992, New York (Not admitted in Belgium). *Education:* Georgetown University (B.A., magna cum laude, 1988); Yale University (J.D., 1991). Phi Beta Kappa.

REVISERS OF THE VIRGINIA LAW DIGEST FOR THIS DIRECTORY

(For Complete Biographical data on all Personnel, see Professional Biographies at Richmond, Virginia.)

McKENNA & CO
AVENUE DE CORTENBERG 66
BOX 10
B-1040 BRUSSELS, BELGIUM
Telephone: (32)(2)735.38.36
Telex: 27122
Fax: (32)(2)735.77.43

London, England Office: Mitre House, 160 Aldersgate Street, EC1A 4DD. Telephone: 0171-606-9000. Telex: 27251. Fax: 0171-606-9100. CDE Box 724. Telephone: 0171-929 1250. Fax: 0171-626 5749 DX Box 724.

London Lloyd's Office: 908 Lloyd's, One Lime Street, London EC3M 7DQ. Telephone: 071-929 1250. Fax: 071-626 5749 DX Box 724.

Budapest, Hungary Office: H-122. Maros utca 22, 1st Floor. Telephone: (36)(1) 202 6527; (36)(1) 202 6936; (36)(1) 201 9199; (36)(1) 156 5354. Fax: (36)(1) 156 5391.

Moscow, Russia Office: McKenna & Co, International, MosenkáPlaza, 24/27 Sadovaya-Samotyochnaya Street, Russian Federation, Moscow, 103051. Telephone: (7 501) 258 5000. Fax: (7 501)258 5100.

Prague, Czech Republic Office: Betlémský palác, First Floor, Husova 5, 110 00 Prague 1. Telephone: (42)(2) 2424 8518-22. Fax: 42(2) 2424 8524.

Warsaw, Poland Office: McKenna & Co Sp. zo.o., ul. Kopernika 30, Suite 213, 00-950, Warsaw. Telephone: (48) 22 26 69 88. Fax: (48) 22 26 41 93.

Hong Kong Office: 5th Floor, Lippo Tower, 89 Queensway, Hong Kong. Telephone: (852) 846 9100. Fax: (852) 845 3575.

Associated Firms:

Sigle Loose Schmidt-Diemitz and Partners: Stuttgart, Berlin, Leipzig, Frankfurt/Main, Chemnitz and Moscow. .

Minter Ellison: Sydney, Melbourne, Canberra, Brisbane and the Gold Coast.

(This Listing Continued)

Firm involved in all aspects of European Union Law and European Economic Area law (including competition, internal market, intellectual property and trade law matters) and English commercial law.

Entitled to appear before the European Commission and the European Court of Justice, but not admitted for Belgian practice.

RESIDENT PARTNER

RICHARD J. ECCLES, admitted, 1985.

ASSISTANT SOLICITOR

HELEN M K SMITH, admitted, 1994.

Languages: English, French and German

McKENNA & CUNEO
AVENUE LOUISE 287, BOX 7
B-1050 BRUSSELS, BELGIUM
Telephone: 011-32-2-646-4910
Telecopy: 011-32-2-646-0829

Washington, D.C. Office: 1575 Eye Street, N.W., 20005. Telephone: 202-789-7500.

Los Angleles, California Office: 444 South Flower Street, 90071. Telephone: 213-688-1000.

San Francisco, California Office: One Market, Steuart Street Tower, Twenty-Seventh Floor, 94105. Telephone: 415-267-4000.

Denver, Colorado Office: 370 Seventeenth Street, Suite 4800, 80203. Telephone: 303-634-4000.

San Diego, California Office: Symphony Towers, Suite 3200, 750 B Street, 92101. Telephone: 619-595-5400.

Dallas, Texas Office: 5700 Bank One Center, 1717 Main Street, 75201. Telephone: 214-746-5700.

Firm engaged in American, European and International Law Practice. Its Counsel, Willem Rycken, is authorized to appear before the Belgian and EC Courts.

MEMBERS OF FIRM

JOSEPH F. DENNIN, born New York, N.Y., June 9, 1943; admitted, 1969, California; 1970, New York; 1987, District of Columbia (Not admitted in Belgium). *Education:* Stanford University (A.B., with great distinction, 1965; J.D., 1968). Fulbright Scholar, University of Helsinki, 1968-1969. Associate, Simpson Thacher & Bartlett, 1969-1975. Counsel, Senate Select Committee on Intelligence, 1975-1976. Staff Assistant to the President, The White House, 1976-1978. Director of Operations, U.S. International Trade Commission, 1978-1979. Deputy Associate Attorney General, U.S. Department of Justice, 1979-1981. Deputy Assistant Secretary for Finance, Investments and Services, 1981-1982. Deputy Assistant Secretary for Africa, the Near East and South Asia, 1982-1984. Assistant Secretary for International Economic Policy, U.S. Department of Commerce, 1984-1986. Member, U.S.-Canada Binational Disputes Resolution Panel, 1989—. *Member:* The State Bar of California; The District of Columbia Bar (Member, Section on International Law); American Bar Association (Member, Sections on International Law and Litigation).

ROBERT D. SLOAN, born Chicago, Illinois, 1947; admitted, 1973, District of Columbia (Not admitted in Belgium). *Education:* University of Michigan (B.A., magna cum laude, 1969); Harvard Law School (J.D., with honors, 1972). Phi Beta Kappa. Adjunct Professor of European Community Law, Georgetown Law Center, 1990-1992. Vice President and Head of Sovereign Credit Management Division, The First National Bank of Chicago, 1984-1987. General Counsel, Multinational Force and Observers, Rome, Italy, 1982-1984. Office of the Legal Adviser, U.S. Department of State, 1977-1981. General Counsel to the Minority, Permanent Subcommittee on Investigations, U.S. Senate, 1973-1977. (Resident). *LANGUAGES:* French, German and Italian.

EUROPEAN OF COUNSEL

WILLEM RYCKEN, born Antwerp, Belgium, November 15, 1937; admitted, 1960, Antwerp; 1975, Brussels. *Education:* University of Leuven, Belgium (Ph.B., 1957; Dr. Jur., 1960; Sc.B., Econ., 1962); University College, Dublin, Ireland (1959); University of Texas Law School, U.S.A. (1963); Universitaire Faculteiten St. Aloysius, Fiskale Hogeschool, Brussels, Belgium (Corporate Tax Management, 1977). Visiting Professor of E.E.C. Law, Washington College of Law, The American University, Washington, D.C., 1984. Lecturer, Contract Law, University of Leuven, Belgium, 1985-1988. Trainee, EC Commission, Luxembourg, 1960. Associate, E.C. Law, Antwerp, 1960-1962; European Counsel, Brussels, 1963-1975;

(This Listing Continued)

Partner, 1975—. Treasurer of the Scholarship Committee, 1965-1975, National President, 1975-1976, Fulbright Alumni Association in Belgium and Luxembourg. Director and Secretary-General, Foundation for Scientific Research and Educational Exchange, 1979-1989. Vice Chairman of Competition Policy Subcommittee, 1980-1990, American Chamber of Commerce in Belgium. Membership Secretary, European Trade Law Association, 1989-1991. *LANGUAGES:* Dutch, English, French, German.

RESIDENT ASSOCIATES

PASCAL CARDONNEL, born Chamalieres, France, March 8, 1969; admitted, 1992, France; 1994, New York (Not admitted in Belgium). *Education:* Université Jean Moulin (Maîtrise en droit, 1990); Georgetown University Law Center (LL.M., 1990); Université Panthéon Sorbonne, Paris I (D.E.A., droit privé, 1991); C.F.P.P. (C.A.P.A., 1992). Assistant to Legal Attache, French Embassy, Washington, D.C., 1993-1994.

ANTOINETTE LONG, born Dublin, Ireland, March 2, 1966; admitted, 1990, Ireland (Not admitted in Belgium). *Education:* University College, Dublin (B.C.L., 1987); College of Europe, Bruges (Diploma, Adv. Eur. Studies, 1988); Kings Inn, Dublin (Barrister at Law, 1990). *LANGUAGES:* English, French, Italian.

KOEN VAN MALDEGEM, born Ghent, Belgium, July 7, 1964; admitted, 1991, Brussels. *Education:* State University of Ghent, Belgium (B.A., cum laude, 1984; J.D., cum laude, 1987); University of Leuven, Belgium (Sc.B., Econ., 1990). Legal Adviser of the Flemish Minister of Economics, 1990-1991. *LANGUAGES:* Dutch, French and English.

(For Complete Biographical Data on other Firm Personnel, see Professional Biographies at Washington, D.C., Los Angeles, San Francisco and San Diego, California, Denver, Colorado and Dallas, Texas)

MERTENS & DE COSTER

Established in 1980

AVENUE BRUGMANN, 12A BTE 15
1060 BRUSSELS, BELGIUM
Telephone: 32-2-343.63.01
Telefax: 32-2-343.47.33

E-Mail: CompuServe: 100336, 212 Internet: 100336, 212@compuserve.-com

Paris, France Office: 29, rue du Colonel Pierre Avia, 75508 Cedex 15. tel: 33-1-41.33.35.35 Fax: 33-1-41.33.35.36

Information Technology Law, Computer Law, EDI and Electronic Trading, Data Protection and Copyright, Commercial Law, Distribution, Corporate, Advertising Campaigns, Contracts, Litigation and Debt Collection, Construction Law.

FIRM PROFILE: Established in 1980, the firm offers a full range of legal services. The firm became well known in Computer Law after organized the first Belgian conferences on "Computer and the Law" in 1982. Corinne Mertens is the managing partner of an international network of law firms specialized in Information Technology Law called LegIT (International Specialists in Legal IT). It is also very active in Litigation and international debt collection. Staff: 2 partners, 3 associates.

MEMBERS OF FIRM

CORINNE MERTENS, born Brussels, Belgium, June 23, 1953; admitted, 1977, Brussels. *Education:* University of Brussels (Dr. Jur., Criminology, 1977); Solvay School (Business and Tax Management). Author: "Computer Law," 1982 and 1984. *Member:* Brussels Bar Association; British Chamber of Commerce (Chairman: Taxation and Legislation Committee; EC Committee); Italian Chamber of Commerce. *LANGUAGES:* French, English, Dutch and Italian. *PRACTICE AREAS:* Information Technology Law; Commercial Law; Construction Law.

PATRICK DE COSTER, born Brussels, Belgium, July 1, 1955; admitted, 1980, Brussels.

ASSOCIATES

ALBERT DENECKER, born 1965; admitted, 1987.

MARIE-THÉRÈSE KANZI, born 1957; admitted, 1993.

ANNEMIE LECOMPTE, born 1965; admitted, 1992.

MILLER & ASSOCIÉS

Law Offices

AVENUE LOUISE, 287
1050 BRUSSELS, BELGIUM
Telephone: 32-2-640.44.00
Facsimile: 32-2-648.99.95

Commercial, Corporate, Tax, Investments, International Business, Securities Law and Property.
Not authorized to appear before the Belgium Courts.

SHILOH MILLER, born 1948; admitted, 1975, Israel. *Education:* Tel-Aviv University (LL.B.). *Member:* The Israel Bar.

MENY BROID, born 1956; admitted, 1982, Israel; 1989, Pennsylvania. *Education:* Hebrew University of Jerusalem School of Law (LL.B.); Villanova University School of Law (1988-1989). *Member:* The Israel Bar; Pennsylvania Bar Association.

IRIT FAJWLEWICZ-FUCHS, born 1964; admitted, 1989, Israel. *Education:* Tel-Aviv University (LL.B.). *Member:* The Israel Bar.

MOQUET BORDE DIEUX GEENS & ASSOCIÉS

RUE DE LA BONTÉ 5-7
B-1050 BRUSSELS, BELGIUM
Telephone: (32-2) 538 68 69
Fax: (32-2) 538 68 67

Paris, France Office: 30 avenue de Messine, 75008. Telephone: (33-1) 42 99 04 50. Fax: (33-1) 45 63 91 49.
Lyon, France Office: 11 place Bellecour, 69002. Telephone: (33) 72 40 00 32. Fax: (33) 72 41 98 62.
Budapest, Hungary Office: Kossuth tér 16-17, III/2/a, H-1055 Budapest. 1245 Budapest, P.O. Box 1228. Telephone: (36-1) 1531 255. Fax: (36-1) 1531 229.
Tallinn, Estonia Office: 10 Pärnu str., EE 0001 Tallinn. Telephone: (372) 640 58 36. Fax: (372) 640 58 38.

Belgian (Dutch/French), EEC, French and International Law Practice.

RESIDENT MEMBERS OF FIRM

XAVIER DIEUX, born Haine-Saint-Paul, Belgium, 1955; admitted, 1978, Brussels. *Education:* Free University of Brussels (Licence en droit, 1978; Licence en droit, economique, 1979). Professor, Commercial Law and Comparative Commercial Law, Free University of Brussels - Law School. Partner, Van Ryn and Partners, 1986-1994. *LANGUAGES:* French, English and Dutch.

KOEN GEENS, born Antwerp, Belgium, 1958; admitted, 1989, Courtrai; 1994, Brussels. *Education:* Katholieke Universiteit Leuven (Licenciate of Law, 1980); Harvard University (LL.M., 1981). Professor, Katholieke Universiteit Leuven. Editor in Chief, Flemish Company Law Review (TRV). Member, Belgian High Council for Auditing and Accountancy, (President). *LANGUAGES:* Dutch, French, English and German.

ASSOCIATES

BERNARD GLANSDORFF, born Brussels, Belgium, 1941; admitted, 1967, Brussels. *Education:* Free University of Brussels (Doctorat en droit, 1964; Licence en droit economique, 1965). Professor, Commercial Law, Fundamentals of Private Law, Comparative Law, and Dean of the Law Faculty, 1988-1992, Free University of Brussels. *LANGUAGES:* Dutch, French and English.

JEAN-QUENTIN DE CUYPER, born Leuven, Belgium, 1965; admitted, 1993, Brussels. *Education:* Catholic University of Louvain (Licence en droit, 1988); University of Geneva (Master in International Law, 1990). *LANGUAGES:* French, English and Dutch.

DIDIER VILLERMAIN, born Brussels, Belgium, 1969; admitted, 1992, Brussels. *Education:* Free University of Brussels (Licence en droit, 1992); University of Amsterdam (1993). *LANGUAGES:* French, English and Dutch.

THIERRY LAMBERT, born Brussels, Belgium, 1967; admitted, 1994, Brussels. *Education:* Free University of Brussels (Licence en droit, 1992; Licence en droit economique, 1994). *LANGUAGES:* French, English and Dutch.

(This Listing Continued)

MOQUET BORDE DIEUX GEENS & ASSOCIÉS,
Brussels—Continued

BRUNO LAFORCE, born Antwerp, Belgium, 1969; admitted, 1992, Antwerp; 1994, Brussels. *Education:* Katholieke Universiteit Leuven (Licenciate of Law, 1992). **LANGUAGES:** Dutch, French, English, Spanish and German.

CONNY CROES, born Brussels, Belgium, 1971; admitted, 1994, Brussels. *Education:* Katholieke Universiteit Leuven (Licenciate of Law, 1993); Universite de Liége (Licence Spéciale en Droit Economique, 1994). **LANGUAGES:** Dutch, French and English.

MORGAN, LEWIS & BOCKIUS
RUE GUIRNARD 7
BRUSSELS B-1040, BELGIUM
Telephone: 32-2/512.55.01
Telecopy: 32-2/512.58.88

Philadelphia, Pennsylvania Office: 2000 One Logan Square, 19103-6993. Telephone: 215-963-5000.

Washington, D.C. Office: 1800 M Street, N.W., 20036. Telephone: 202-467-7000.

New York, New York Office: 101 Park Avenue, 10178. Telephone: 212-309-6000.

Los Angeles, California Office: 801 South Grand Avenue, 90017-3189. Telephone: 213-612-2500.

Miami, Florida Office: 5300 First Union Financial Center, 200 South Biscayne Boulevard, 33131-2339. Telephone: 305-579-0300.

Harrisburg, Pennsylvania Office: One Commerce Square, 417 Walnut Street, 17101-1904. Telephone: 717-237-4000.

Princeton, New Jersey Office: 100 Overlook Center, 08540. Telephone: 609-520-6600.

Newport Beach, California Office: 4675 MacArthur Court, Suite 740, 92660. Telephone: 714-851-6333.

London, England Office: 4 Carlton Gardens, Pall Mall. Telephone: 071-839-1677.

Frankfurt, Germany Office: Siesemayerstrasse 44, D-6000 Frankfurt/Main. Telephone: 069-72-3478.

Tokyo, Japan Office: CS Tower, 1-11-30 Akasaka, Minato-ku. Telephone: 81-3-587-2900.

Firm engaged in American and International Law Practice, but not authorized to appear before the Belgium Courts or to act as Belgium Lawyers.

FIRM PROFILE: Morgan, Lewis & Bockius is an international law firm with 750 lawyers and a diverse practice. Founded in 1873, the Firm was one of the first to develop an intergrated, multicity practice.

The Firm's practice areas include antitrust; arbitration and ADR proceedings; banking, thrift and consumer financial services; bankruptcy and reorganization; business and corporate; construction; customs; energy regulation; environmental; executive compensation and employee benefits; food, drug and cosmetics regulation; foreign direct investment in the United States; government contracts; government regulation; immigration; insurance and reinsurance; intellectual property and technology, including patent, trademark and copyright; international financings; international trade; labor and employment; legislation and government relations; leveraged lease and project financings; litigation; mergers and acquisitions; municipal finance; personal law; products liability; public utilities; real estate; securities; tax; and transportation law.

MEMBERS OF FIRM IN BRUSSELS

HOWARD M. LIEBMAN, born December 20, 1952; admitted, 1977, District of Columbia (Not admitted in Belgium). *Education:* Colgate University (A.B., 1974; A.M., 1975); Harvard Law School (J.D.,1977). Comments and Notes Editor, Harvard International Law Journal, 1976-1977. *Member:* American Bar Association (Chairman, European Tax Law Subcommittee, Section of International Law and Practice, 1988—); The District of Columbia Bar; International Fiscal Association.

ASSOCIATE IN BRUSSELS

ILSE VANDERVOORT, admitted, 1990, New York. *Education:* University of Antwerp (B.A., 1982); University of Louvain Law School (J.D., 1985); University of Brussels (LL.M, European Law, 1989); University of Bochum (LL.M., German Law, 1989).

JUNIA VAN OVERBEEK, admitted, 1985, Brazil (Not admitted in Belgium). *Education:* Pontificia Universidade Catolica de Minas Gerais,

(This Listing Continued)

Brazil (LL.B., 1985); Hull University (LL.M., 1989); University of Amsterdam, Holland (LL.M., 1991).

PHILLIPPE DEJONGHE, admitted, 1992, Belgium. *Education:* Catholic University of Louvain-le-Neuve (J.D., 1990).

LENA M. SANDBERG, (Not admitted in Belgium). *Education:* University of Copenhagen (LL.B., 1991); Free University of Brussels (LL.M., 1993).

Members of the Firm, Counsel, Of Counsel and Associates in Philadelphia and Harrisburg, Pennsylvania, Washington, D.C., New York, New York, Los Angeles and Newport Beach, California, Miami, Florida, Princeton, New Jersey, Frankfurt/Main, Germany and Tokyo, Japan are listed in the Biographical Section respectively.

THE MORRESI LAW OFFICE
Established in 1989

AVENUE DES NERVIENS 77
1040 BRUSSELS, BELGIUM
Telephone: (02) 7353410
Telefax: (02) 7354125

Bologna, Italy Office: Studio Legale Morresi. Via Dante 19. Telephone: (051) 399 822. Telefax: (051) 393 271.

FIRM PROFILE: Firm engaged in Practice in European Community Law and General International Trade Law. EEC Attorneys are entitled to plead before the Commission and the Court of Justice of the European Communities, in their National Courts and in the Courts of other Member States pursuant to EEC Council Directive 77/249.

AVV. RENZO MARIA MORRESI, born Modigliana (FO) Italy, January 25, 1952; admitted, 1981, Italy. *Education:* University of Bologna (J.D., summa cum laude, 1976); School of Advanced International Studies, The Johns Hopkins University (M.A., International Affairs, 1977). Former Counsel in Fiat Legal Services. Author of monographs on International Joint Ventures and on Franchising in the EEC. (Also at Bologna, Italy Office). **LANGUAGES:** English, French and Italian. **PRACTICE AREAS:** EEC Law; International Trade Law.

ALBERTO DAL FERRO, born Vicenza, Italy, March 9, 1955; admitted, 1984, Italy. *Education:* University of Padua (J.D., 1982; Doctor of Political Science, 1985). Formerly with, Research and Documentation Department, European Court of Justice, Luxembourg. (Resident Partner). **LANGUAGES:** English, French and Italian. **PRACTICE AREAS:** EEC Law.

GIUSEPPINA PO, born Modena, Italy, October 23, 1957; (Not admitted in Belgium). *Education:* University of Modena (J.D., 1981); College of Europe, Bruges (Belgium); Certificate of Advanced Studies in European Law (1981-1982).

PAOLA CRISCUOLO GAITO, born Portici (NA), Italy, June 16, 1967; admitted, 1994, Italy. *Education:* University of Naples (J.D., summa cum laude, 1991); Certificate of advanced studies in European Law by Europaforum (Italy 1992). Training: Legal Service of the Commission EC (1992); Directorate General of Internal Market and Financial Affairs of the Commission EC. **LANGUAGES:** English, French and Italian. **PRACTICE AREAS:** EEC Law.

REPRESENTATIVE CLIENTS: The Commission of the European Communities; Fiat; Montedison; Enron; Nesté; Ferrero.

MORRISON & FOERSTER
Established in 1883

AVENUE MOLIÈRE, 262
1060 BRUSSELS, BELGIUM
Telephone: 011-32-2-347-0400
Facsimile: 011-32-2-347-1824

Other offices located in: San Francisco, Los Angeles, New York, Washington, D.C., London, Hong Kong, Tokyo, Sacramento, Palo Alto, Walnut Creek, Orange County, Denver and Seattle.

Not Authorized to appear before the Belgian Courts.

FIRM PROFILE: Morrison & Foerster is one of the world's largest international law firms with 500 lawyers located in 14 offices worldwide. The firm's legal practice encompasses every major area of commercial law, including corporate finance, institutional lending, EC law, financial services, real estate, environmental and land use planning, mining and natural resources, agriculture, intellectual property, energy, telecommunications

(This Listing Continued)

and entertainment, insurance, alternative dispute resolution, products liability, bankruptcy and workouts, financial transactions, labor and employment, civil, criminal and securities litigation, antitrust, international trade and tax.

MEMBER OF FIRM

THOMAS C. VINJE, born February 14, 1954; admitted, 1983, Hawaii; 1986, California (Not admitted in Belgium). *Education:* University of Washington (B.A., summa cum laude, 1977); Columbia University School of Law (J.D., 1982). Phi Beta Kappa. James Kent Scholar. Note/Comment Editor, Columbia Journal of Transnational Law, 1980-1982. Law Clerk to Judge Martin Pence, United States District Court, District of Hawaii, 1982-1983 and to Judge Edmund Palmieri, United States District Court, Southern District of New York, 1983-1984. Co-Author: *European Software Law*, Oxford University Press, 1993; *World Antitrust Practice*, 1995. Chairman, U.S. Board of Editors, Droit de l'Informatique et des Télécoms. Member, Board of Editors, *Computer und Recht. Member:* Licensing Executives Society Benelux (Vice-Chairman, LES European Committee; Member, LES Copyright and ADR Committees). *LANGUAGES:* Norwegian and German. *PRACTICE AREAS:* Intellectual Property; Competition Law; International Arbitration; Licensing and Distribution.

OF COUNSEL

PETER I. B. GOLDSCHMIDT, born January 4, 1961; admitted, 1993, Denmark (Not admitted in Belgium). *Education:* Commercial College (Certificate, 1980); University of Copenhagen (LL.B., 1987). Official, European Commission, Directorate-General for Competition, 1989-1992. Head of Section, Danish Ministry of Business and Industry. *LANGUAGES:* Danish, French and German.

ASSOCIATES

KATHLEEN D. PAISLEY, born November 19, 1959; admitted, 1988, New York; 1989, District of Columbia (Not admitted in Belgium). *Education:* Florida State University (B.S., 1981); Florida Atlantic University (M.B.A., 1983); Yale Law School (J.D., 1986). Law Clerk to Honorable Gilbert S. Merritt, U.S. Court of Appeals, Sixth Circuit, 1986-1987. Legal Adviser to Judges Richard Allison, Charles Brower, Howard Holtzmann, American Arbitrators, Iran-United States Claims Tribunal, 1987-1991. *LANGUAGES:* Dutch.

LEGAL SUPPORT PERSONNEL

PENELOPE A. TURNER, born April 7, 1967; admitted, 1992, British Solicitor (not practicing). *Education:* Trinity College, Cambridge (2:1, 1988); Manchester Law School (1989). (Legal Analyst). *LANGUAGES:* French and German.

(For biographical data on San Francisco, Los Angeles, Sacramento, Walnut Creek, Palo Alto and Irvine, CA, New York, NY, Washington, DC, Denver, CO, Seattle, WA, London, England, Hong Kong and Tokyo, Japan see professional biographies at each of those cities).

NAUTA DUTILH

Attorneys, Civil Law Notaries, Tax Advisers

TERHULPSESTEENWEG 177/6
(CHAUSSÉE DE LA HULPE, 177/6)
B-1170 BRUSSELS, BELGIUM
Telephone: (32-2) 6730007
Telecopier: (32-2) 6722854

MEMBERS OF FIRM ATTORNEYS AT LAW

JEAN-J. EVRARD, born 1946; admitted, 1969, Belgium. *Education:* Louvain University.

PHILIPPE PETERS, born 1957; admitted, 1983, Belgium. *Education:* Louvain University.

PETER CALLENS, born 1959; admitted, 1982, Belgium. *Education:* Louvain University.

ASSOCIATES ATTORNEYS AT LAW

BENOIT STROWEL, born 1961; admitted, 1987, Belgium. *Education:* Louvain University.

RITA G. WEZENBEEK-GEUKE, born 1962; admitted, 1986, The Netherlands (Not admitted in Belgium). *Education:* Utrecht University.

(This Listing Continued)

THIERRY ONGENAE, born 1965; admitted, 1989, Belgium. *Education:* Louvain University.

(For Complete Biographical Data on all Personnel, see Professional Biographies at Rotterdam, The Netherlands)

NÖRR, STIEFENHOFER & LUTZ

Established in 1991
106 AVENUE LOUISE
1050 BRUSSELS, BELGIUM
Telephone: 32-2-6470650
Telecopier: 32-2-6464729

Munich, Germany (Head Office): Brienner Str. 28, 80333 Munich, Posfach 101121, 80085 Munich. Telephone: 49-89-280111. Telecopier: 49-89-280110.

Frankfurt/Main, Germany Office: Freiherr-vom-Stein-Straße 11, 60323 Frankfurt/Main. Telephone: 49-69-172917. Telecopier: 49-69-172916.

Berlin, Germany Office: Schlüterstraße 36, D-10629 Berlin. Telephone: 49-30-8836700. Telecopier: 49-30-8835052.

Dresden, Germany Office: Böhmertstraße 3, 01099 Dresden. Telephone: 49-351-5671188, 49-351-5671187. Telecopier: 49-351-5671186.

Prague, Czech Republic Office: Masarykovo nábřeži 30, 11000 Prague 1. Telephone: 42-2-24913396, 42-2-24913882. Telecopier: 42-2-24911836.

Budapest, Hungary Office: Becsí utca 5/I. 1-2, 1052 Budapest V. Telephone: 36-1-1174905; 36-1-1378293. Telecopier: 36-1-1184035.

Warsaw, Poland Office: Kancelaria Adwokacka Sp. Z o. o. UL. Nowogrodzka 50, 00950 Warsaw. Telephone: 48-2-6216232. Telecopier: 48-2-6251976.

Moscow, Russia Office: Ul. Levoberezhnaya, 32. 125475. Telephone: 7-095-4585822; 7-095-4585792. Telecopier: 7-095-4585782.

The office in Brussels is a joint office with Macfarlanes (City of London Solicitors). The office specializes in European Community Law, International Corporate and Commercial Matters and Trade Law but not authorized to appear before the Belgian Courts.

PARTNER IN CHARGE

DR. THOMAS SCHÜRRLE LL.M. (Not admitted in Belgium; For Complete Personnel and Biographical data, see Professional Biographies st Frankfurt, Germany).

RESIDENT FOREIGN LAWYERS

R. JANE WHITTAKER, born Lancashire, England, February 27, 1955; admitted, 1978, Solicitor, Supreme Court of England and Wales (Not admitted in Belgium). *Education:* University of Manchester (LL.B., Hons., 1975). (Partner of Macfarlanes). *LANGUAGES:* English. *PRACTICE AREAS:* European; Competition; Commercial; Intellectual Property Law.

Languages: German, English and French.

NORTON ROSE

40 RUE MONTOYER
1040 BRUSSELS, BELGIUM
Telephone: +2-237 6111
Fax: +2-237 6136

Other Offices: London, Bahrain, Hong Kong, Moscow, Paris, Piraeus, Prague and Singapore.

FIRM PROFILE: *Norton Rose is a leading City and International law firm with its principal office in the City of London. The firm provides a wide range of legal services primarily to the business and financial communities as well as to a number of sovereign governments and state organizations. We are known particularly for our corporate and debt finance, banking, company and commercial law, natural resources, insurance, property development, aerospace and maritime practices and wide-ranging expertise on tax matters. Norton Rose has a major litigation department handling all forms of commercial dispute resolution.*

In Brussels the firm specialises in competition and European Community law matters, in particular, in relation to the following areas: air transport; banking, insurance and financial services; energy; free movement of goods; freedom to establish in the European Union and provide services; health care and pharmaceuticals; intellectual property; merger control; public procurement; rail and road transport; shipping; State aids; telecommunications; trade issues, including dumping; treaties and agreements between the European Union and third countries.

(This Listing Continued)

NORTON ROSE, Brussels—Continued

RESIDENT PARTNERS

M.A. COLEMAN, admitted, 1977, England and Wales. *PRACTICE AREAS:* Competition; EC Law.

TREVOR I. SOAMES, admitted, 1984, Barrister; 1989, England and Wales. *PRACTICE AREAS:* Competition; EC Law.

Languages: English, French, Italian, Spanish, Portuguese, Dutch and German

(For Complete Biographical Data on all Personnel, see Professional Biographies at London, England).

OHLE HANSEN EWERWAHN

BRUSSELS, BELGIUM

(See Feddersen, Laule Scherzberg & Ohle Hansen Ewerwahn)

OPPENHEIMER WOLFF & DONNELLY

AVENUE LOUISE 250, BOX 31
1050 BRUSSELS, BELGIUM
Telephone: 32-2-647-4060
FAX: 32-2-648-6554

Chicago, Illinois Office: Two Prudential Plaza, 45th Floor, 183 North Stetson Avenue, 60601. Telephone: 312-616-1800. FAX: 312-616-5800.

Minneapolis, Minnesota Office: 3400 Plaza VII, 45 South Seventh Street, 55402. Telephone: 612-344-9300. FAX: 612-344-9376.

New York, N.Y. Office: Citicorp Center, 153 East 53rd Street, 10022. Telephone: 212-826-5000. FAX: 212-486-0708.

Paris, France Office: 53 Avenue Montaigne, 75008. Telephone: (33/1) 44 95 03 40. FAX:(33/1) 44 95 03 40.

St. Paul, Minnesota Office: 1700 First Bank Building, 55101. Telephone: 612-223-2500. FAX: 612-223-2596.

Washington, D.C. Office: 1020 Nineteenth Street, N.W., Suite 400, 20036. Telephone: 202-293-6300. FAX: 202-293-6200.

General and International Corporate and Tax Law, European Community Law, International Trade Law, International Commercial Arbitration, EC/U.S./Asia Trade Relations and Investments.

RESIDENT PARTNERS

JEAN RUSSOTTO, born April 3, 1940; (Not admitted in Belgium). *Education:* Cantonal Gymnasium, Lausanne, Switzerland (B.A., 1958); University of Lausanne (Doctorate of Laws, 1962); College of Europe, Bruges , Belgium; Harvard Law School (LL.M., 1965). *PRACTICE AREAS:* International Corporate Law; European Community Law.

ERIC OSTERWEIL, born January 11, 1935; admitted, 1960, New York. *Education:* Swarthmore College (B.A., 1956); Harvard Law School (J.D., 1959). *LANGUAGES:* English, French and Dutch. *PRACTICE AREAS:* International Tax and Structuring.

FREDERICK L. LUKOFF, born August 1, 1943; admitted, 1968, Idaho; 1976, District of Columbia (Not admitted in Belgium). *Education:* Pomona College (B.A., cum laude, 1964); Institut d'Etudes Politiques, Paris (C.E.P., 1965); Harvard Law School (J.D., 1968). *LANGUAGES:* English, French, Dutch and German. *PRACTICE AREAS:* International Corporate Law; European Community Law; Mergers and Acquisitions Law.

JAMES H. SEARLES, born May 23, 1952; admitted, 1979, Ohio (Not admitted in Belgium). *Education:* University of Wisconsin-Madison (B.A., with distinction, 1974); University of Toledo Law School (J.D., 1979). *PRACTICE AREAS:* European Community Law; International Trade Law.

DIDIER DE VLIEGHER, born October 4, 1959; admitted, 1983, Brussels. *Education:* University of Leuven (lic. jur., 1983); University of Brussels (lic. economic law, 1985). *PRACTICE AREAS:* Commercial Law.

(This Listing Continued)

RESIDENT ASSOCIATES

CEES VAN RIJ, born October 21, 1957; admitted, 1984, The Netherlands (Not admitted in Belgium). *Education:* College of Europe (Certificate of Advanced European Studies); Free University (Degree at Law). *LANGUAGES:* Dutch; French; English; German; Italian. *PRACTICE AREAS:* European Community Law; Dutch Labor and Commercial Law; Entertainment; Copyright Law.

FIONA CARLIN, born March 31, 1966; admitted, 1992, Belgium. *Education:* The College of Europe, Bruges, Belgium (1989); The Queen's University of Belfast (LL.B., 1988). *PRACTICE AREAS:* Competition Law; EC-Telecommunications.

JOSEPH A. JANES, born August 6, 1965; admitted, 1990, Ohio (Not admitted in Belgium). *Education:* Miami University-Oxford (B.A., 1987); American University, Washington College of Law (J.D., 1990). *LANGUAGES:* French.

SHEHNAZ R. SHEPHERD, born May 9, 1966; admitted, 1992, England (Not admitted in Belgium). *Education:* Middlesex University, England (LL.B., hons., 1988); Kings College University of London (LL.M., 1990). *LANGUAGES:* English and French. *PRACTICE AREAS:* Corporate/International Tax; Intellectual Property.

SOPHIE AUFORT, born August 19, 1968; admitted, 1995, Brussels. *Education:* Universite Paris - Assas (1991); Universite La Sorbonne (LL.M., cum laude, 1992); Universite Paris - Assas (J.D., cum laude, 1994). *LANGUAGES:* French, English, Swedish and Spanish. *PRACTICE AREAS:* International Corporate and Tax.

ANNE GABRIEL, born August 14, 1963; admitted, 1992, Brussels. *Education:* Universite Libre de Bruxelles (J.D., magna cum laude, 1989); University of Pennsylvania (LL.M., 1990). *LANGUAGES:* French, English and Dutch. *PRACTICE AREAS:* International Transactions, Corporate and Commercial.

RESIDENT OF COUNSEL

LINGCHON PU, born April 25, 1961; (Not admitted in Belgium). *Education:* University International Bus/Ecos (B.A., Economics, 1983); China University (Dipl., 1984); Free University Brussels (LL.M., 1988). *LANGUAGES:* English. *PRACTICE AREAS:* European Community Trade Law; European Community Policies; China Investment Law.

GRETTA GOLDENMAN, born August 19, 1944; admitted, 1992, California (Not admitted in Belgium). *Education:* Pacific Lutheran University (B.A., 1966); University of California, Graduate School of Public Policy (M.P.P., 1989); University of California, Boalt Hall School of Law (J.D., 1990). *PRACTICE AREAS:* Environmental.

PHILIPPE LOGELAIN, born January 30, 1946; admitted, 1983, Brussels. *Education:* University of Brussels (Ph.B., 1967; J.D., 1970). *PRACTICE AREAS:* Commercial and Tax Law.

OPPENHOFF & RÄDLER

RUE BREDERODE 13A
B-1000 BRUSSELS, BELGIUM
Telephone: (2) 5050211
Telecopier: (2) 5022644

Munich, Germany Office: Prinzregentenplatz 10, D-81675. Telephone: (089) 41808-0. Telecopier: (089) 41808-100.

Berlin, Germany Office: Meinekestr. 13, D-10719. Telephone: (030) 88471-0. Telecopier: (030) 88471-200.

Berlin, Germany Office: Rankestr. 21, D-10789. Telephone: (030) 21496-0. Telecopier: (030) 21496-100.

Cologne, Germany Office: Hohenstaufenring 62, D-50674. Telephone (0221) 2091-0. Telecopier: (0221) 2091-435. Telex: 8 882 294 bos. Teletex: 2627 221 4054BOS.

Frankfurt/Main, Germany Office: Bockenheimer Landstr. 51-53, D-60325. Telephone: (069) 170003-0. Telecopier: (069) 170003-33.

Frankfurt/Main, Germany Office: Myliusstr. 33-37, D-60323. Telephone: (069) 17093-0. Telecopier: (069) 17093-444.

Leipzig, Germany Office: Kommandant-Trufanow-Str. 14, D-04105. Telephone: (0341) 56649-0. Telecopier: (0341) 56649-99.

London, England Office: Royex House, Aldermanbury Square, GB-London EC2V 7HR. Telephone: (171) 600 3609. Telecopier: (171) 600 1718.

New York, New York Office: 712 Fifth Avenue, 30th Floor, 10019, USA. Telephone: (212) 801 3410. Telecopier: (212) 801 3415.

(This Listing Continued)

New York, New York Office: 712 Fifth Avenue, 29th Floor, New York 10019, USA. Telephone: (212) 397 7580/7546. Telecopier: (212) 397 4292.

Prague, Czech Republic Office: Alliance Prague, Jachymova 2, CZ-11000 Prague 1. Telephone: (2) 232 1130. Telecopier: (2) 232 6371.

FIRM PROFILE: *Oppenhoff & Rädler has been created by a merger of two large German firms, Boden Oppenhoff Rasor Raue and Rädler Raupach Bezzenberger. The firm at present has more than 90 partners and comprises together some 200 lawyers and tax advisers.*

Oppenhoff & Rädler acts for domestic and for international clients. The firm offers a comprehensive range of legal services, including: General Corporate and Commercial; Taxation; Banking, Finance and Securities; Mergers and Acquisitions; Real Estate; Litigation and Arbitration; Intellectual Property and Trademarks; Construction Law; Antitrust and European Community Law; Administrative and Environmental Law; Media, Communications and Entertainment Law; Technology and Computer Law; Food, Drug and Chemistry; Family Law; Wills.

Oppenhoff & Rädler is a member of the ALLIANCE OF EUROPEAN LAWYERS EEIG (members: Oppenhoff & Rädler, Germany; De Bandt, van Hecke & Lagae, Belgium; De Brauw Blackstone Westbroek, The Netherlands; Jeantet & Associés, France; Lagerlöf & Leman, Sweden; Uria & Menendez, Spain) and of the LLR EEIG (members: Loyens & Volkmaars, The Netherlands; Bureau Francis Lefebvre, France; Oppenhoff & Rädler, Germany).

RESIDENT PARTNERS

DR. DIRK SCHROEDER, born Darmstadt, Germany, November 21, 1953; admitted, 1981, Germany. *Education:* University of Cologne (Dr.jur.); Ecole Nationale d'Administration, Paris. *LANGUAGES:* German, English, French. *PRACTICE AREAS:* Antitrust and Trade Regulations; European Community Law.

(See Boden DeBandt DeBrauw Jeantet Lagerlöf & Uria)

PELTZER & RIESENKAMPFF

AVENUE DU DIAMANT 139
B-1040 BRUSSELS, BELGIUM
Telephone: 32-2-735 34 28
Telecopier: 32-2-735 26 78

Frankfurt/Main, Germany Office: Niedenau 68, 60325 Frankfurt/Main. Telephone: 49-69-71 73 66. Cable Address: "Peljus, Frankfurt" Telecopier: 49-69-7 24 10 63; 72 48 64. Telex: 416 307 pejus d. Teletex: 6997628 pejus.

Leipzig, Germany Office: Gottschedstrasse 44, 04109 Leipzig. Telephone: 341-2821 46; 341-28 21 68. Telecopier: 341-980 04 18.

EEC Law, German and General International Practice.
Not Authorized to appear before the Belgium Courts.

PARTNERS

Dr. Heinz-Joachim Freund   **Gudrun Hartung**

(For Complete Biographical Data, see Professional Biographies at Frankfurt, Germany)

PINSENT & CO.

79/81 AVENUE DE CORTENBERG
1040 BRUSSELS, BELGIUM
Telephone: 010-322 732 3600
Fax: 010-322 734 8793

Birmingham, England Office: 3 Colmore Circus, B4 6BH. Telephone: 0121-200 1050. Telex: 335101 PINSENT B'HAM. Cable Address: "Pinsent Birmingham Telex". Fax Direct Line: 0121-626 1040.

London, England Office: Royex House, Aldermanbury Square, EC2V 7HR. Telephone: 0171-600 4999. Fax: 0171-600 4947.

Agency and Distribution Agreements, Banking, Commercial Property, Computer Contracts, Conditions of Sale and Purchase, Construction Law, Contractual Disputes, Copyright, EC and Competition Law, Corporate and Financial Services Law, Employees' Share Schemes, Employment Law, Environmental Law, Flotations, Franchise and Licensing Agreements, Health and Safety at Work, Historic Houses, Insolvency, Insurance Litigation, Intellectual Property Litigation, International Carriage of Goods, Joint Ventures, Licensing, Management Buy-outs, Mergers and Acquisitions, Patent and Trade Mark Agreements, Product Liability, Professional

(This Listing Continued)

Indemnity, Property Development, Public Law, Share Valuation, Tax - Capital Taxes, Tax - Corporate Tax, Tax - Personal, Town and County Planning, Trade Mark Applications, Trusts and Settlements, Pensions.

RESIDENT MEMBER

Michael Renouf

Firm is member of the European Economic Interest Grouping

(For Complete Biographical data on all personnel, see Professional Biographies at Birmingham, England)

PRICE, BLANPAIN, QUAGHEBEUR & MAEYAERT

114 BLVD. BRAND WHITLOCK
B-1200 BRUSSELS, BELGIUM
Telephone: 32-2-735.45.11
Fax: 32-2-735.37.13

General Belgian, European Community and International Business Law. Authorized to Appear before the Belgian Courts, The European Court of Justice and Court of First Instance and The Benelux Court.

MEMBERS OF FIRM

CHARLES PRICE, born Sutton Coldfield, England, May 17, 1951; admitted, 1978, Brussels. *Education:* University of Sheffield, England (LL.B., Honours, 1972); Vrije Universiteit Brussels (Master in International and Comparative Law, 1973); Université Libre de Bruxelles (Lic. Droit, 1978).

BRUNO BLANPAIN, born Leuven, Belgium, July 15, 1960; admitted, 1984, Brussels. *Education:* Katholieke Universiteit Leuven (Lic. Rechten, 1983); University of Kentucky (Master of International Business Affairs, 1985). Alternate Judge, Brussels Labour Court.

MARC QUAGHEBEUR, born Kuurne, Belgium, December 22, 1961; admitted, 1984, Brussels. *Education:* Katholieke Universiteit Leuven (Lic. Rechten, 1983); Fiscale Hogeschool, Brussels (Postgraduate in Tax Law, 1985).

PAUL MAEYAERT, born Bruges, Belgium, December 28, 1959; admitted, 1986, Brussels. *Education:* Vrije Universiteit Brussels (Lic. Rechten, 1983; Bijz. Lic in het Bedrijfsrecht, 1986); College of Europe (Diploma of Advanced European Legal Studies, 1984).

FRANCOISE MOREAU, born Namur, Belgium, July 1, 1963; admitted, 1986, Brussels. *Education:* Université Catholique de Louvain (Lic. Droit, 1985).

ASSOCIATES

CLAUDINE DECKERS, born Gent, Belgium, October 17, 1965; admitted, 1990, Brussels. *Education:* Rijksuniversiteit Gent (Lic. Rechten, 1989); Université Libre de Bruxelles (Lic. spéciale en droit social, 1990).

LIEVE HOSTE, born Gent, Belgium, July 29, 1965; admitted, 1989, Brussels. *Education:* Rijksuniversiteit Gent (Lic. Rechten, 1988; Master in Corporate Law, 1993); Université Catholique de Louvain (Lic. spéciale en Droit Economique, 1989).

CAROLINE DAOUT, born Verviers, Belgium, February 2, 1967; admitted, 1991, Belgium. *Education:* Université Catholique de Louvain (Lic. Droit, 1991).

LUC VAN LITSENBORG, born Gent, Belgium, June 9, 1966; admitted, 1991, Belgium. *Education:* Katholieke Universiteit Leuven (Lic. Rechten, 1990); Rijksuniversiteit Gent (Bitz. Lic. in Fiscaliteit en Boekhoudkundig Onderzoek, 1991).

ANETTE HAUFF, born Konstanz, Germany, February 25, 1964; admitted, 1989, Brussels. *Education:* Université Catholique de Louvain (Lic. Droit., 1988).

LUC HERVE, born Liège, Belgium, December 27, 1966; admitted, 1989, Liège. *Education:* Université of Liège (Lic. Droit, 1989); Rijksuniversiteit (Lic. in de fiscaliteit en het boekhoudkundige, 1991).

THOMAS DE MEESE, born Antwerp, Belgium, December 4, 1969; admitted, 1993, Brussels. *Education:* Universiteit Antwerpen (Lic Rechten, 1992); College of Europe (Master of European Studies, 1993).

EMMANUEL PLAASCHAERT, born Malo-les-Bains, France, February 23, 1969; admitted, 1993, Brussels. *Education:* Université Notre Dame

(This Listing Continued)

PRICE, BLANPAIN, QUAGHEBEUR & MAEYAERT,
Brussels—Continued

de la Paix, Namur (Candidature en droit,1989); Katholieke Universiteit Leuven (Lic. Rechten, 1992); Universita degli Studi, Siena, Italy (Erasmus diploma, 1992).

Languages: English, Flemish, French, German and Italian

PRICE WATERHOUSE

Tax and Legal Consultants
PLACE SAINT-LAMBERT 14
1200 BRUSSELS, BELGIUM
Telephone: (32-2) 7731411
Fax: (32-2) 7623325

Local and International taxation and business law. Corporate and individual taxation; VAT, customs and excise duties, inheritance and gift tax; EC tax harmonization; international executive and assignment tax services. Trade business and contract law; company law; financial law; environmental law. Social security and labour law; foreigner's law. EC and Competition Law, including merger control and trade regulation.
Mergers; reorganizations, acquisitions and disposals; joint ventures.

FIRM PROFILE: The firm offers a full range of tax and legal services to both national and international clients. It cooperates with member firms of Correspondent Law Firms of Price Waterhouse EEIG and Price Waterhouse firms to render legal services throughout Europe, where appropriate, on a multidisciplinary basis. The Firm has 5 partners and 55 professionals of which 45 are Lawyers.

SENIOR TAX AND LEGAL PARTNER

JEAN-PAUL TIMMERMANS, born Meehelen, Belgium, September 27, 1938. *Education:* Doctor in Law, M.A. (Economics) and B.A. (Political and Social Sciences) at the Catholic University at Louvain; Certificate of Advanced European Studies, College of Europe, Bruges; Certificate of the School of Business Administration, S.M.U. Dallas, Texas, USA. Professor in Taxation at the Vlaamse Economische Hogeschool in Brussels and Lecturer at various other university institutions. *Member:* Institute if Registered Accountants. *LANGUAGES:* Dutch, English and French. *PRACTICE AREAS:* Corporate tax; Social Security; Immigration Law; Mergers and Acquisitions.

ASSOCIATES

LEO PEETERS, born Mortsel, Belgium, December 19, 1958. *Education:* Law degree at the University of Brussels (VUB), specialization in Business and Financial Law; MBA certificate at the Institut Solvay-CEPAC of the University of Brussels (ULB). *Member:* Belgian Professional Association of Company Lawyers. *LANGUAGES:* Dutch, English and French. *PRACTICE AREAS:* Business and Contract Law; Bank and Financial Law; Corporate Law; Privatization.

ALASTAIR GORRIE, born Blackburn, England, February 5, 1960. *Education:* City of London Polytechnic Solicitors Final Examination; Diploma of Advanced European Studies at the College of Europe, Bruges, Belgium; B.A. (Hons) Law at the Durham University, England. *Member:* Law Society of England and Wales. *LANGUAGES:* English and French. *PRACTICE AREAS:* EC law; Merger Control; Trade Regulations; Public Procurement.

PUELINCKX, SCHILTZ, LINDEN, GROLIG

Established in 1985
RUE ROYALE 87 - KONINGSSTRAAT 87
1000 BRUSSELS, BELGIUM
Telephone: 02-218.80.70
Fax: 02-218.37.69

Antwerp, Belgium Office: Meir 24, 2000. Telephone: 32-03/226.61.61.
Fax: 32-03/226.92.98.

MEMBERS OF BRUSSELS FIRM

ALPHONS PUELINCKX. *Education:* University of Leuven (Roman Philol., 1958; Philosophy, 1959; Dr. Jur., 1962); University of Köln (Wirtschaftsrecht, 1963); University of Chicago (M.C.L., 1965). Honorary Judge. *Member:* Belgian Center for National and International Arbitration (CEPINA) (Member, Panel of Arbitrators); International Chamber of

(This Listing Continued)

Commerce (ICC); Board of Visitors-University of Chicago Law School (1990-1992). *LANGUAGES:* Dutch, French, English and German. *PRACTICE AREAS:* International Litigation and Arbitration; Finance; Insurance; White Collar Crime.

ANDRE LINDEN. *Education:* University of Leuven (Dr. Jur., 1967). *LANGUAGES:* French, Dutch, English and German. *PRACTICE AREAS:* Intellectual Property; Construction and Real Estate Law; International Transactions.

LIEVE GROLIG-BULCKENS. *Education:* University of Leuven (Dr. Jur., 1965). *LANGUAGES:* Dutch, French and English. *PRACTICE AREAS:* Mergers and Acquisitions; Restructuring of Companies and Company Law; Tax Law.

JAN UYTTERSPROT. *Education:* University of Leuven (Dr. Jur., 1969; Lic. Not., 1969). *LANGUAGES:* Dutch, French and English. *PRACTICE AREAS:* Litigation and Arbitration.

GUIDO DEVILLE. *Education:* University of Leuven (Dr. Jur., 1979; Lic. Econ., 1980); Centre d'Etudes Européennes Nancy (Etudes supérieures en droit européen, 1981); Düsseldorf, Tübingen (Einfuehrungskurs in das Deutsche Recht, 1982 DAAD Fellowship). *LANGUAGES:* Dutch, French, German and English. *PRACTICE AREAS:* Labour and Social Security Law; European Competition Law.

JAN VINCENT LINDEMANS. *Education:* UFSAL University of Brussels (Cand. Jur., 1981); University of Leuven (Lic. Jur., 1984); University of London (European Young Lawyers Course, 1991). Legal Counsel at Kredietbank, 1987-1990. *LANGUAGES:* Dutch, French and English. *PRACTICE AREAS:* Banking and Securities Law; Insolvency.

ASSOCIATES

DOMINIQUE VAN BUNNEN. *Education:* University of Louvain (Lic. Jur., 1981); University of Brussels (Lic. en Droit Commercial, 1982). Associate, Van Cutsem, Wittamer, Piret, 1983-1987. *LANGUAGES:* French, Dutch and English. *PRACTICE AREAS:* Agency and Distribution Law; Leases; Intellectual Property Law; Unfair Trading Practices.

PASCALE HALIN. *Education:* University of Brussels (Lic. Jur., 1983; Lic. spéciale droit economique, 1984). *LANGUAGES:* French, Dutch and English. *PRACTICE AREAS:* Litigation and Arbitration.

CARLA CORBISIER. *Education:* University of Leuven (Lic. Jur. 1986). *LANGUAGES:* Dutch, French and English. *PRACTICE AREAS:* Environmental Law; Labour Law.

FABIENNE KUSTERS. *Education:* University of Leuven (Lic. Jur., 1986); London School of Economics and Political Science (LL.M., 1989). Assistant Professor, International and European Law, University of Leuven, 1986-1988. *LANGUAGES:* Dutch, French, English and German. *PRACTICE AREAS:* Construction and Real Estate Law.

BENOÎT KERVYN D'OUD MOOREGHEM. *Education:* University of Leuven (Lic. Jur., 1984). Associate, Stibbe & Simont, Brussels, 1987-1992. *LANGUAGES:* Dutch, French and English. *PRACTICE AREAS:* Labour Law.

MARIE VAN IN. *Education:* University of Leuven (Lic. Jur., 1986); Tübingen, Düsseldorf (Einführungskurs in das Deutsche Recht, 1987, DAAD Fellowship); University of Cambridge (LL.M., 1988). *LANGUAGES:* Dutch, French, English and German. *PRACTICE AREAS:* Mergers and Acquisitions; Company Law; Insurance Regulation.

JAN VREYS. *Education:* University of Leuven (Lic. Jur., 1987); University College London (LL.M., 1988). *LANGUAGES:* Dutch, French and English. *PRACTICE AREAS:* International Public Law; International Criminal Law.

KATRIEN BEULS. *Education:* University of Namur (Cand. Jur., 1988); University of Leuven (Lic. Jur., 1991); Ruprecht-Karls Universität, Heidelberg (1991). *LANGUAGES:* Dutch, French, English and German. *PRACTICE AREAS:* Company Law; Product Liability.

JOSEPH-EDOUARD SEPULCHRE. *Education:* University of Brussels (Lic. Jur., 1988). Associate: Oostvogels & Partners, 1988; Loeff Claeys Verbeke, 1989-1990; Ballon, Buyle, Lagasse, Maingain & Philippe, 1991. *LANGUAGES:* French, English and Dutch. *PRACTICE AREAS:* Distribution and Franchising Law; International Arbitration.

NICOLAS ANGELET. *Education:* University of Gent (Lic. Jur., 1987); University of Brussels (Lic. Speciale en Droit International, 1989; Lic. Speciale en Droit Europeen, 1990). Assistant Professor, International Law, University of Leuven. *LANGUAGES:* Dutch, French and English. *PRACTICE AREAS:* International Law.

(This Listing Continued)

MARIO DEKETELAERE. *Education:* University of Leuven (Lic. Jur., 1988; M.B.A., 1990); F.H.S., Brussels (Grad. Fiscal Sciences, 1991). Assistant Professor, University of Leuven. *LANGUAGES:* Dutch, French and English. *PRACTICE AREAS:* Environmental Law.

CHRISTEL VAN DEN EYNDEN. *Education:* University of Antwerp (Lic. Jur., 1987); Academy of International Law of The Hague (Certificate of International Law, 1987); Johns Hopkins University, School of Advanced International Studies, Bologna and Washington D.C. (Master of Arts in International Relations, 1987-1989). Legal Counsel, Washington Trade and Investment Group, 1989-1990. Associate, Wilmer, Cutler & Pickering, Brussels and Washington D.C., 1990-1993. *LANGUAGES:* Dutch, English, French, German and Italian. *PRACTICE AREAS:* E.C. and International Law.

NATHALIE BRYS. *Education:* FUSL Brussels (Cand. Jur., 1986); University of Leuven (Lif. Jur., 1989); ULB (Lic. en Droit Fiscal, 1990); University of London (LL.M., 1992). Legal Editor, EC and Competition Law, Sweet & Maxwell Ltd., London, 1993. *LANGUAGES:* Dutch, French, English and Spanish. *PRACTICE AREAS:* Banking and Insolvency Law.

PÜNDER, VOLHARD, WEBER & AXSTER

RUE D'ARLON 92
1040 BRUSSELS, BELGIUM
Telephone: (32)(2) 230 90 11
Fax: (32)(2) 231 19 55

Frankfurt/Main, Germany Office: Mainzer Landstrasse 46, 60325 Frankfurt/Main. Telephone: (49)(69) 71 99-01. Fax: (49)(69) 71 99-4000. Telex: 414 827.

Düsseldorf, Germany Office: Cecilienallee 6, 40474 Düsseldorf. Telephone: (49)(211) 43 55-0. Fax: (49)(211) 43 55-600.

Berlin, Germany Office: Katharina-Heinroth-Ufer, 10787 Berlin. Telephone: (49)(30) 254 6 5800. Fax: (49)(30) 2546 5900.

Leipzig, Germany Office: Burgplatz 7, 04109 Leipzig. Telephone: (49)(341) 21 49-0. Fax: (49)(341) 21 49-600.

Beijing, People's Republic of China Office: Suite C 603, Beijing Lufthansa Center, 50 Liangmaqiao Road, Beijing 100 016. Telephone: (86)(1) 465 15 68; (86)(1) 465 18 08; (86)(1) 465 13 45. Fax: (86)(1) 467 12 56.

Budapest, Hungary Office: Endrödy Sandor utca 48, 1026 Budapest. Telephone: (36) 60 33 26 18 international; (6) 60 33 26 18 national. Fax: (36) 60 33 26 17 international; (6) 60 33 26 17 national.

Moscow, Russia Office: ul. Wolchonka, 18/2, 121 019 Moskwa. Telephone: (7)(095) 202 64 90; (7)(095) 202 65 12; (7)(543) 708 00 900 from Germany; (49)(7545) 893 42 from other countries. Fax: (7)(095) 202 65 14; (7)(543) 708 00 990 from Germany; (49)(7545) 893 43 from other countries.

New York, New York Office: 152 West 57th Street, Carnegie Hall Tower, New York, N.Y. 10019. Telephone: (1)(212) 582 28 28. Fax: (1)(212) 582 24 24.

Warsaw, Poland Office: ul. Jasna 1, 00-013 Warszawa. Telephone: (48) 39 12 21 41. Fax: (48)(22) 27 15 29.

Administrative Law; Antitrust Law; Arbitration; Auditing and Valuations; Banking, Securities and Finance; Bankruptcy; Building Law; Chinese Law; Commercial Crime; Computer Law; Construction Law; Corporate Law; EU Law; Energy Law; Environmental Law; Franchising; Industrial Property Law; Insolvency; Intellectual Property Law; International and German Business Law; Labor and Employment Law; Litigation; Media Law; Mergers and Acquisitions; Pharmaceutical Law; Privatizations; Product Law; Public Law; Real Estate; Reorganizations; Russian Law; Tax Law; Telecommunications; Unfair Trade Law.

FIRM PROFILE: *Member of PÜNDER GROUP*

Members:

- *BURUMA MARIS, The Hague, Rotterdam*

- *CERHA, HEMPEL & SPIEGELFELD, Wien*

- *COPPENS, VAN OMMESLAGHE HORSMANS & FAURES, Bruxelles.*

- *DE PARDIEU-LACOURTE G.I.E., Paris.*

- *PÜNDER, VOLHARD, WEBER & AXSTER, Frankfurt/Main, Düsseldorf, Berlin, Leipzig*

- *STOFFEL & PARTNER, Zürich, Genève.*

Joint Offices of PÜNDER GROUP:

Beijing - Bruxelles - Budapest - Moskwa - New York - Warszawa

(This Listing Continued)

MEMBERS OF FIRM

OLIVER AXSTER, born Berlin, Germany, July 27, 1931; admitted, 1961, Düsseldorf (Not admitted in Belgium). *Education:* University of Texas, University of Chicago (J.D.); University of Bonn and University of Cologne. Author: Volume on Licensing Agreements of the "Gemeinschaftskommentar," (Text Book on German and EC Antitrust Laws). *Member:* Association for Antitrust Law Studies (Board Member); German and International Association for the Protection of Industrial Property and Copyright (Member, Board of German Association); International Bar Association; American Chamber of Commerce in Germany; L.E.S. Licensing Executive Society International (International President). *LANGUAGES:* German and English. *PRACTICE AREAS:* Antitrust Law; EU Law; Industrial Property Law.

HOLGER F. WISSEL, born Oldenburg, Germany, May 6, 1950; admitted, 1979, Düsseldorf (Not admitted in Belgium). *Education:* University of Münster. Assistant to the Law Faculty of the University of Münster, 1976-1978. Co-Author: Volume on Merger Control of the "Gemeinschaftskommentar;" "Vertikale Verträge - US-Guidelines 1985 and EG-Kartellrecht," 1986; "Environmental Liabilities and Regulation in Europe," 1993. Counsel to the Central Organization of the Advertising Industry, 1978-1981. Counsel to the Antitrust Department of the Federation of German Industry, 1981-1988. *Member:* German Association for the Protection of Industrial Property and Copyright; Association for Antitrust Law Studies; Federal Association of Pharmaceutical Manufacturers. *LANGUAGES:* German and English. *PRACTICE AREAS:* Antitrust Law; EU Law; Pharmaceutical Law; Environmental Law.

ASSOCIATE

KLAUS P. ROHARDT, born Koblenz, Germany, June 12, 1957; admitted, 1988, Cologne; 1994, Düsseldorf (Not admitted in Belgium). *Education:* Universities of Bonn, Geneva and Göttingen. Assistant, Max-Planck-Institute of Foreign and International Private Law, Hamburg, 1983-1986; Federation of German Industries, 1988-1994, responsible for EU Law. *Member:* German and International Bar Associations. *LANGUAGES:* German, English and French. *PRACTICE AREAS:* Antitrust Law; EU Law; Environmental Law.

(For complete biographical data on personnel at Frankfurt/Main, Düsseldorf, Berlin and Leipzig, Germany, Moscow, Russia, Warsaw, Poland, New York, New York and Beijing, People's Republic of China, see Professional Biographies at those locations)

RÄDLER RAUPACH BEZZENBERGER

BRUSSELS, BELGIUM

(See Oppenhoff & Rädler)

RICHARDS BUTLER

AVENUE DE LA RENAISSANCE 1
BTE 11
1040 BRUSSELS, BELGIUM
Telephone: 2-732 20 55
Fax: 2-735 46 91

London, England Office: Beaufort House, 15 St Botolph Street, EC3A 7EE. Telephone: 0171-247 6555. Telex: 949494 RBLAW G. Fax: 0171-247 5091.

Abu Dhabi, United Arab Emirates Office: Al-Sayegh Richards Butler. P.O. Box 46904, Saif Bin Ghobash Building, Zayed the Second Street. Telephone: 2-725561. Telex: 22261 RBLAW EM. Fax: 2-778630.

Hong Kong Office: Alexandra House, Twentieth Floor, 16-20 Chater Road. Telephone: 810 8008. Telex: 62554 RBLAWHX. Fax: 810 0664.

Paris, France Office: 134 rue du Faubourg Saint Honoré, 75008. Telephone: 1-44 13 63 53. Fax: 1-42 89 20 60.

RESIDENT CONTACT

Katharine C. Baragona

(For Complete List of Partners, see Professional Biographies at London, England)

CLAUDE L. ROSENFELD

Established in 1975

AVENUE DE LA RENAISSANCE 1 BTE 3
B-1040 BRUSSELS, BELGIUM
Telephone: 02/736.59.24; 732.79.75
Fax: 02/736.95.82

Tax and Commercial Law.

FIRM PROFILE: *The firm was established in 1975 an offers a full range of legal services concerning commercial, contracts, civil, taxation and labor law. Belgian Member of European Commercial Law Circle (ECLC).*

CLAUDE L. ROSENFELD, born Brussels, Belgium, May 18, 1946; admitted, 1975, Belgium. *Education:* Université Catholique de Louvain-la-Neuve (M.B.A., 1986); Ecole Supérieure de Sciences Fiscales (Master, 1991); Université Libre d e Bruxelles (Ph.D., 1970). Lecturer on Law, Chambre de Commerce de Bruxelles. *Member:* Bar of Brussels and Düsseldorf; Belgisch-Deutsche Juristenvereinigung; I.A.G. Alumni; Société Belgo-Allemande; IBA. *LANGUAGES:* French, Dutch, German and English. **PRACTICE AREAS:** Commercial; Contracts; Taxation Law.

LAW OFFICES OF
ROBERT J. SAVOYE

142 AVENUE LOUISE
1050 BRUSSELS, BELGIUM
Telephone: 32.2.644.20.70
Fax: 32.2.644.20.75

General Areas of International Law Practice, Corporate Law, Labor Law, Real Estate Law, Nationality and Immigration Law. Firm authorized to appear before Belgian courts.

ROBERT J. SAVOYE, born Cambridge, U.K., December 6, 1943; admitted, 1993, Belgium. *Education:* Cathedral College, New York, N.Y.; Marist College, Poughkeepsie, N.Y. (B.A., 1966); University of Brussels (Doctor of Law, 1969). Author, "Exporting to Belgium - Legal Aspects of Selling," Chapter 9, *Doing Business in Belgium - 1993* , American Chamber of Commerce in Belgium. Faculty, Marketing through Distributors, Management Center Europe, American Management Association, 1992-1994. Internship, Legal Department General Motors Continental, Antwerp, Belgium, 1969. Management Trainee, Irving Trust Co., 1969-1970. International Counsel, Belgian American Mercantile Corporation, New York, N.Y., 1970-1972. Legal Counsel, 3M Belgium and Luxemburg, 1972-1989. Chairman: Work's Council, 3M Belgium 1976-1981; Legal Committee, DETIC, (Trade Association of Glue Manufactures) 1984-1990. Member: Legal Committee of CEFIC (European Trade Association of Chemical Manufactures) 1986-1991; Legal Committee, AGIM, (Trade Association of the Pharmaceutical Industry) 1983-1989; Belgian Trade Association of Chemical Manufacturers, 1982-1994. Chairman, Sub-Committee of Trade and Investment Committee, American Chamber of Commerce in Belgium, 1990—. Associate, Paul D. Sher & Associates, Brussels, Belgium, 1990-1994. *Member:* ABJE, Belgian Company Lawyer's Association (Statutory Auditor, 1986-1993). *LANGUAGES:* English, French and Dutch. **PRACTICE AREAS:** Corporate Law; International Business Law; International Distribution Agreements; Computer Software Contracts; Mergers and Acquisitions.

SCHÖN NOLTE FINKELNBURG & CLEMM

RUE PÈRE DE DEKEN 33
B-1040 BRUSSELS, BELGIUM
Telephone: (2) 732 2680
Telecopier: (2) 735 96 04

Other Offices: Hamburg, Berlin and Dresden, Germany.

Firm engaged in EC Law, German and General International Practice, not admitted to the Belgium Bar.

PARTNERS IN CHARGE

PROF. DR. HANS-JÜRGEN RABE, born Hamburg, Germany, 1935; admitted, 1964, Hamburg (Not admitted in Belgium). *Education:* Universities of Heidelberg, Berlin and Hamburg (Dr. jur., 1962). Editor, "Europarecht," (Periodical on European Law). Co-Editor, Neue Juristische Wo-

(This Listing Continued)

chenschrift (NJW). Professor of EEC Law, University of Hamburg, 1992—. *Member:* German Bar Association (Member, Executive Committee, 1971; President, 1978-1983); International Bar Association (Member, Council, 1975-1993); State of Hamburg Constitutional Court; Deutscher Juristentag (President, 1993); Association of Food Law (Member, Council, 1978—); Association of the Bar of the City of New York; American Bar Association. *LANGUAGES:* German, English and French. **PRACTICE AREAS:** Antitrust and Trade Regulation; European Community Law; Food and Drug Regulation; International Arbitration.

DR. GEORG M. BERRISCH, LL.M., born Düsseldorf, Germany, 1960; admitted, 1991, Hamburg (Not admitted in Belgium). *Education:* McGill University, Montreal, Canada (LL.M., 1990); University of Passau (Dr.jur., 1991). *LANGUAGES:* German, English and French. **PRACTICE AREAS:** European Community Law; International Law; Environmental Law; Antitrust and Trade Regulation; Antidumping; Customs.

SEYFARTH, SHAW, FAIRWEATHER & GERALDSON

Established in 1991

AVENUE LOUISE 500, BOX 8
1050 BRUSSELS, BELGIUM
Telephone: (32) (2) 647.60.25
Fax: (32) (2) 640.70.71

Chicago, Illinois Office: Mid Continental Plaza, 55 E. Monroe Street. Telephone: 312-346-8000.

Washington, D.C. Office: 815 Connecticut Avenue, N.W. Telephone: 202-463-2400.

Los Angeles, California Office: 2029 Century Park East. Telephone: 310-277-7200.

New York, N.Y. Office: 900 Third Avenue, 16th Floor. Telephone: 212-715-9000.

San Francisco, California Office: Suite 2900, 101 California Street. Telephone: 415-397-2823.

Sacramento, California Office: 400 Capitol Mall, Suite 2350. Telephone: 916-558-4828.

Matray, Matray et Hallet, 34/24, Boulevard Frère-Orban, 4000, Liege, Belgium. Telephone: (32) (41) 52 70 68. Telex: macoha 42330. Telecopier: (32) (41) 52 08 57.

Joint venture law firm: Seyfarth, Shaw & Wong, 80 Raffles Place, #58-01 UOB Plaza, Singapore 0104. Telephone: (65) 532 4588. Facsimile: (65) 532 5711; (65) 532 5722.

International Commercial and Government Contracting. Corporate and Transactional Work. Trade and Economic Regulatory Matters. International Construction Contract Claims.

MEMBERS OF FIRM

MARTIN J. GOLUB, born New Bedford, Massachusetts, December 31, 1947; admitted, 1977, Massachusetts; 1980, District of Columbia and U.S. Claims Court; 1981, U.S. Supreme Court; 1991, Brussels, Belgium as a foreign lawyer by the Ordre francais des Avocats du Barreau de Bruxelles; not admitted to practice before the Belgian Courts. *Education:* Princeton University (A.B., cum laude, 1969); Boston College (J.D., cum laude, 1977). Co-Author: "Les Marchés publics aux Etats-Unis," 8 Droit et Pratique du Commerce International 573, 1982; "La Rupture du Contrat de Vente de Marchandises aux Etats-Unis," Revue de Droit des Affaires Internationales, No. 4, p.407, 1986; "U.S. Government Procurement: Opportunities and Obstacles Faced by Foreign Contractors," 20 Geo. Wash. J. Int'l L. & Econ. 567, 1987. Author: "Libya and Fiat: Protectionist Politics and Defense Procurement," 15 Defense & Foreign Affairs, No. 12, p. 40, 1987; "Dirigeant d'Entreprise et Droit Pénal Etranger: Peut-on se préserver des surprises?" Commission Droit et Vie des Affaires, 1991. *Member:* The District of Columbia Bar; Boston, Massachusetts and American (Vice Chairman, International Procurement Committee, ABA Section of Public Contract Law, 1989—) Bar Associations. [LTJG, U.S. Coast Guard, 1971-1974; LT, U.S. Coast Guard Reserve, 1974-1978]. (Also at Washington, D.C. Office). *LANGUAGES:* English, French. **PRACTICE AREAS:** Government Contracts Law; International Commercial Transactions; International Arbitration and Litigation.

(For complete biographical data on all personnel, see Professional Biographies at Chicago, Illinois)

PAUL D. SHER & ASSOCIATES

471 AVENUE LOUISE
1050 BRUSSELS, BELGIUM
Telephone: (32-2) 646.54.10
Fax: (32-2) 640.69.21; Internet ID: 707-6466 @ MCIMAIL. COM

FIRM PROFILE: A law firm which includes U.S. and Belgian trained attorneys whose principal areas of practice are: the establishment and maintenance of European subsidiaries and branches of foreign-based companies and trade federations and their personnel, European and U.S. agency, distribution, and licensing agreements, and the administrative and regulatory aspects of trade throughout the EC. Member of EFLAW (EEIG) which regroups ten European law firms specializing in franchising, distribution, and licensing.

PAUL D. SHER, born Chicago, Illinois, August 20, 1950; admitted, 1978, Tennessee; 1987, Belgium (Brussels Bar - Foreign Member). *Education:* Indiana University (B.A., 1972); Vanderbilt University (J.D., 1976); Vrije Universiteit, Brussels, Belgium (LL.M., cum laude, 1977). Internship, Commission of the European Communities (E.C.), Antitrust Directorate, 1977-1978. Associate Editor, Vanderbilt Journal of Transnational Law, 1975-1976. Associate, Dechert Price & Rhoads, Brussels, Belgium, 1980-1987. Member, Board of Directors and Chairman, Trade and Investment Committee, American Chamber of Commerce in Belgium. Faculty: Management Center Europe (American Management Association), "Marketing through Distributors" and "The Franchising Alternative: Tools for Survival and Expansion." Academic Advisor and Administrator for Belgium, Philip C. Jessup International Law Moot Court Competition, 1978-1988. Editor, "Doing Business in Belgium - 1993," published by the American Chamber of Commerce in Belgium. Author, Chapter 10: "Exporting to Belgium through an Intermediary." Member, Commission des Membres de Barreaux Etrangers Etablis à Bruxelles (Barreau de Bruxelles - Ordre Francais des Avocats), since 1992. *Member:* Tennessee, American and International Bar Associations; Barreau de Bruxelles - Ordre Francais des Avocats (Foreign Member). *LANGUAGES:* English, French, Dutch and Italian. *PRACTICE AREAS:* European Company Law; European Agency; Distribution, Franchising and Licensing; European Trade Law; U.S. Business Immigration.

ANNE V. SCHOLLEN, born Brussels, Belgium, October 21, 1966; admitted, 1993, Belgium. *Education:* Université Libre de Bruxelles, Brussels, Belgium (Lic. Jur., 1991); Duke Summer Institute in Transnational Law, Brussels, Belgium (1991); Duke University Law School (LL.M., 1992). Legal Counsel, Bonn & Schmitt, Luxembourg, 1992-1993. First Prize, Prix de l'Eloquence, extemporaneous speaking competition, Brussels, Belgium, 1990. *Member:* Association Internationale des Jeunes Avocats. *LANGUAGES:* French, English and Dutch. *PRACTICE AREAS:* Commercial Law; Corporate Law; Banking Law.

COUNSEL

MARC MATTHYS, born Brussels, Belgium, October 6, 1958; admitted, 1981, Belgium. *Education:* Université Libre de Bruxelles (Lic. Jur., cum laude, 1981); Military School of Administration (summa cum laude, 1982). Author: "Le contrat d'agence en Belgique: le projet de loi," Echo de la Bourse, September, 1993; "Représentation, agence et distribution en France," Echo de la Bourse, October 1988; "Etablir une société aux U.S.A.," Echo de la Bourse, September 1988; "L' opposabilitié des conditions générales contractuelles," Echo de la Bourse, August 1988; "La Gèrance libre, contrat pour une distribution integrée," Echo de la Bourse, July 1988; "Le contrat de Franchise," Echo de la Bourse, June 1988; "Contracts de concession et d' agence en Belgique," Echo de la Bourse, May 1988; "La prescription de l' article 2273 de code civil est-elle ou non fondée sur une présomption de paiement?," Journal des Juges de Paix, 1986; "Baux commerciaux-indemnités d' eviction, conséquence de la perte du fonds de commerce et non du droit au bail," Journal de Juges de Paix, 1985. Legal Assistant: Dechert Price & Rhoads, Brussels, Belgium, 1980-1981; White & Case, Brussels, Belgium, 1979-1980. *Member:* Barreau de Bruxelles; Conference du Jeune Barreau; International Bar Association. *LANGUAGES:* French, Dutch and English. *PRACTICE AREAS:* Commercial Distribution; Agency, Franchising and Company Law.

SIMÉON & ASSOCIÉS

AVENUE DE TERVUREN 13
B-1040 BRUSSELS, BELGIUM
Telephone: (2) 732 69 69
Fax: (2) 732 70 71

Paris, France Office: 5, Avenue Percier, 75008. Telephone: (1) 40 75 08 08. Fax: (1) 40 75 04 50.
Warsaw, Poland Office: Siméon Karniol Malecki, Aleje Jerozolimskie 30. 00024. Telephone: (48) 22 27 04 64. Fax: (48) 22 27 48 08; 39 12 32 01.
Hanoi, Vietnam Office: 13 Tran Hung Dao. Telephone: (84 4) 251 588; (84 4) 244 345. Fax: (84 4) 251 514.
Ho Chi Minh Ville, Vietnam Office: IBC Centre. 1A Me Linh Square. Telephone: (84) 8 294 890. Fax: (84) 4 294 876.

The office specializes in European Community Law, International Corporate and Commercial Matters and Trade Law.

PARTNER

ERIC MORGAN DE RIVERY, born Tours, France, August 18, 1952; admitted, 1978, Paris (Not admitted in Belgium). *Education:* University of Tours (Licencié en Droit, 1973); University of Paris (DES Droit des Affaires, 1974); Harvard Law School (LL.M., 1977). *LANGUAGES:* French and English.

ASSOCIATES

MONICA CUNNINGHAM, born Cambridge, United Kingdom, March 21, 1969; admitted, 1995, Brussels (Not admitted in Belgium). *Education:* King's College, University of London (LL.B., English and French Law, 1991); University of Paris I (Maître en Droit Privé, 1991); College of Europe, Bruges (LL.M., European Law, 1994). *LANGUAGES:* English, French and Dutch.

JACQUES DERENNE, born Marche-en-Famenne, Belgium, April 16, 1964; admitted, 1991, Brussels; 1994, Paris. *Education:* University of Liege (Licence en Droit, 1987) and College of Europe (Diploma in Advanced European Legal Studies, 1988). *LANGUAGES:* French and English.

GAËLLE LE BRETON, born Boulogne Billancourt, France, July 25, 1968; admitted, 1995, Paris. *Education:* University of Paris I (D.E.A. de Droit Privé, 1990); Collège d'Euro pe, Bruges (Diplôme de Hautes Etudes Juridiques Européennes, 1992); Institut Universitaire Européen, Florence (Diplôme d'Etudes Juridiques Comparatives, Internationales et Européennes (LL.M.), 1993). *LANGUAGES:* French, English, Italian and German.

(For Complete Biographical Data on all Personnel, see Professional Biographies at Paris, France).

SIMMONS & SIMMONS

Established in 1962

RUE D'ARLON 118
1040 BRUSSELS, BELGIUM
Telephone: 32-2-280 16 70
Telecopier: 32-2-280 04 84

London, England Office: 21 Wilson Street, EC2M 2TQ. Telephone: 44-171-628 2020; 44-171-528 9292. Facsimile: 44-171-628-2070. Telex: 888562SIMMON G.
Paris, France Office: 2, Avenue Bugeaud, 75116. Telephone: 33-1-45016767. Telecopier: 33-1-45012232. Telex: TRANSAV 649381F.
Lisbon, Portugal Office: Rua Castilho, n° 32-9°, 1250. Telephone: 351-1-352 1318. Fax: 351-1-352 1418.
Milan, Italy Office in joint practice with Studio Avv. Eugenio Grippo: Via Dei Boschetti 1, 20121. Telephone: 39-2-76003012. Telecopier: 39-2-782770.
Abu Dhabi Office: The Blue Tower, Khalifa Street, P.O. Box 5931. Telephone: 971 2 347882. Telecopier: 971 2 347832.
Hong Kong Office: 24th Floor, Jardine House, One Connaught Place, Central. Telephone: 852-28681131. Telecopier: 852-28105040. Telex: 75888 SANDS HX.
New York, New York Office: 115 East 57th Street, 10022. Telephone: 1-212-688-6620. Telecopier: 1-212-355-3594.

EC, English and International Law Practice but not authorized to appear before the Belgian Courts.

(This Listing Continued)

SIMMONS & SIMMONS, Brussels—Continued

RESIDENT PARTNERS

ANTHONY J.W. ORR, born Calcutta, India, March 5, 1951; admitted, 1975, England and Wales (Not admitted in Belgium). *Education:* St. Johns College, Oxford (M.A.). *Member:* Law Society; International Bar Association. *LANGUAGES:* English, French, Dutch and German. *PRACTICE AREAS:* International Business Law; European Community Law.

SEBASTIAN C.A.D. FARR, born Hong Kong, January 25, 1959; called to the Bar (England and Wales) 1981; admitted, 1991, England and Wales. *Education:* Kingston University (LL.B.). Contributor, Division on State Aids, Butterworths "Competition Law." Author: "Harmonisation of Technical Standards in the EC," 1992. *Member:* International Bar Association. *LANGUAGES:* English and French. *PRACTICE AREAS:* EC Competition Law; Trade Law; Mergers; Anti-Dumping Law; Customs Law; EC Environmental Law.

(For List of other Partners, see Professional Biographies at London, England).

SIMONT & SIMONT

BRUSSELS, BELGIUM

(See Stibbe Simont Monahan Duhot)

SKADDEN, ARPS, SLATE, MEAGHER & FLOM

523 AVENUE LOUISE
BOX 30
1050 BRUSSELS, BELGIUM
Telephone: 011-32-2-648-7666
Fax: 011-32-2-640-3032

New York, New York Office: 919 Third Avenue, 10022. Telephone: 212-735-3000. Fax: 212-735-2000; 212-735-2001. Telex: 645899 Skarslaw.

Boston, Massachusetts Office: One Beacon Street, 02108. Telephone: 617-573-4800. Fax: 617-573-4822.

Washington, D.C. Office: 1440 New York Avenue, N.W., 20005. Telephone: 202-371-7000. Fax: 202-393-5760.

Wilmington, Delaware Office: One Rodney Square, 19899. Telephone: 302-651-3000. Fax: 302-651-3001.

Los Angeles, California Office: 300 South Grand Avenue, 90071. Telephone: 213-687-5000. Fax: 213-687-5600.

Chicago, Illinois Office: 333 West Wacker Drive, 60606. Telephone: 312-407-0700. Fax: 312-407-0411.

San Francisco, California Office: Four Embarcadero Center, 94111. Telephone: 415-984-6400. Fax: 415-984-2698.

Houston, Texas Office: 1600 Smith Street, Suite 4460, 77002. Telephone: 713-655-5100. Fax: 713-655-5181.

Newark, New Jersey Office: One Riverfront Plaza, 07102. Telephone: 201-596-4440. Fax: 201-596-4444.

Tokyo, Japan Office: 12th Floor, The Fukoku Seimei Building, 2-2-2, Uchisaiwaicho, Chiyoda-ku, 100. Telephone: 011-81-3-3595-3850. Fax: 011-81-3-3504-2780.

London, England Office: 25 Bucklersbury EC4N 8DA. Telephone: 011-44-71-248-9929. Fax: 011-44-71-489-8533.

Hong Kong Office: 30/F Peregrine Tower, Lippo Centre, 89 Queensway, Central. Telephone: 011-852-820-0700. Fax: 011-852-820-0727.

Sydney, New South Wales, Australia Office: Level 26-State Bank Centre, 52 Martin Place, 2000. Telephone: 011-61-2-224-6000. Fax: 011-61-2-224-6044.

Toronto, Ontario Office: Suite 1820, North Tower, P.O. Box 189, Royal Bank Plaza, M5J 2J4. Telephone: 416-777-4700. Fax: 416-777-4747.

Paris, France Office: 105 rue du Faubourg Saint-Honoré, 75008. Telephone: 011-33-1-40-75-44-44. Fax: 011-33-1-49-53-09-99.

Frankfurt, Germany Office: MesseTurm, 27th Floor, 60308. Telephone: 011-49-69-9757-3000. Fax: 011-49-69-9757-3050.

(This Listing Continued)

Beijing, China Office: 1605 Capital Mansion Tower, No. 6 Xin Yuan Nan Road, Chao Yang District, 100004. Telephone: 011-86-1-466-8800. Fax: 011-86-1-466-8822.

Budapest, Hungary Office: Mahart Building, H-1052 Apáczai Csere János u.11, Vl.em. Telephone: 011-36-1-266-2145. Fax:011-36-1-266-4033.

Prague, Czech Republic Office: Revolucni 16, 110 00. Telephone: 011-42-2-231-75-18. Fax: 011-42-2-231-47-33.

Moscow, Russia Office: Pleteshkovsky Pereulok 1, 107005. Telephone: 011-7-501-940-2304. Fax: 011-7-501-940-2511.

Firm engaged in American, International and European Economic Community Law practice, and the practice of the laws of other jurisdictions in which its lawyers are admitted.

PARTNERS

PATRICK J. FOYE, born New York, N.Y., 1957; admitted, 1982, New York (Not admitted in Belgium). *Education:* Fordham College (B.A., cum laude, 1978; J.D., 1981). Associate Editor, Fordham Law Review, 1980-1981. (Also at New York, New York and Budapest, Hungary Offices).

COUNSEL

FERNAND KEULENEER, born Geel, Belgium, 1957; admitted, 1982, Brussels. *Education:* University of Louvain (Lic. Jur., 1980; Lic. Sc. Ec., 1981); Yale Law School (LL.M., 1982).

HENRY L. HUSER, born Prairie du Chien, Wis., 1958; admitted, 1984, Wisconsin (Not admitted in Belgium). *Education:* University of Wisconsin-Madison (B.A., 1981; J.D., cum laude, 1984).

HENDRIK J. CORNELIS, born Rijswijk, NL, 1959; admitted, 1985, Netherlands; 1988, Amsterdam (Not admitted in Belgium). *Education:* Leiden University Law School (Meester in de Rechten, 1984); Harvard Law School (LL.M., 1985).

(For Biographical data on other Personnel, see New York, New York Professional Biographies).

SLAUGHTER AND MAY

RUE D'ARLON 69/71
1040 BRUSSELS, BELGIUM
Telephone: (2) 230 5631
Fax: (2) 230 7699

London, England Office: 35 Basinghall Street, EC2V 5DB. Telephone: (0171) 600 1200. Telex: 883486; 888926. Fax: (0171) 726 0038; (0171) 600 0289; (0171) 600 1455 (G-4).

Paris, France Office: 112 Avenue Kléber, 75116. Telephone: (1) 44.05.60.00. Telex: 642514. Fax: (1) 44.05.60.60; (1) 44 05 60 99 (G-4).

Frankfurt am Main, Germany Office: Westend-Carree Grüneburgweg 16, D-60322 Frankfurt am Main. Telephone: (69) 9551370. Fax: (69) 5964126.

Hong Kong Office: 27th Floor, Two Exchange Square. Telephone: (852) 521 0551. Telex: HX 86230. Fax: (852) 845 2125; (852) 845 9079.

Tokyo, Japan Office: Mitsui Asahi Building, 1-1 Kanda Sudacho, Chiyoda-ku, 101. Telephone: (3) 3258 5700. Telex: 2227208. Fax: (3) 3258 5708.

New York, New York Office: 126 East 56th Street, 10022-3613. Telephone: (212) 888-1112. Fax: (212) 888-1170; (212) 832-2021; (212) 832-0075 (G-4).

Firm engaged in all aspects of EC Law and in English Corporate and Commercial Law.

RESIDENT PARTNERS

P.P. Chappatte
W.J. Sibree

SQUIRE, SANDERS & DEMPSEY

AVENUE LOUISE, 165, BOX 15
1050 BRUSSELS, BELGIUM
Telephone: 011-32-2-648-1717
Cable Address: "Coxsquire"
TLX: 61961 Brussels Squire B
Fax: 011-32-2-648-1064

Cleveland, Ohio Office: 4900 Society Center, 127 Public Square, Cleveland, Ohio 44114-1304. Telephone: 216-479-8500. Fax's: 216-479-8780, 216-479-8781, 216-479-8787, 216-479-8795, 216-479-8793, 216-479-8776, 216-479-8788.

Columbus, Ohio Offices: 1300 Huntington Center, 41 South High Street, Columbus, Ohio 43215. Telephone: 614-365-2700. Fax: 614-365-2499.

Jacksonville, Florida Office: One Enterprise Center, Suite 2100, 225 Water Street, Jacksonville, Florida 32202. Telephone: 904-353-1264. Fax: 904-356-2986.

Miami, Florida Office: 201 South Biscayne Boulevard, Suite 2900 Miami Center, Miami, Florida 33131. Telephone: 305-577-8700. Fax: 305-358-1425.

New York, New York Office: 520 Madison Avenue, 32nd Floor, New York, New York 10022. Telephone: 212-872-9800. Fax: 212-872-9814.

Phoenix, Arizona Office: Two Renaissance Square, 40 North Central Avenue, Suite 2700, Phoenix, Arizona 85004-4441. Telephone: 602-528-4000. Fax: 602-253-8129.

Washington, D.C. Office: 1201 Pennsylvania Avenue, N.W., P.O. Box 407, Washington, D.C. 20044. Telephone: 202-626-6600. Fax: 202-626-6780.

London, England Office: 1 Gunpowder Square, Printer Street, London EC4A 3DE. Telephone: 011-44-71-830-0055. Fax: 011-44-71-830-0056.

Prague Office: Adria Palace, Jungmannova 31/36, 11000 Prague 1, Czech Republic. Telephone: 011-42-2-231-5661. Fax: 011-42-2-231-5482.

Bratislava Office: Mudronova 37, 811 01 Bratislava, Slovak Republic. Telephone: 011-42-7-313-362; 011-42-7-315-370. Fax: 011-42-7-313-918.

Budapest, Hungary Office: Deak Ferenc Ut. 10, Office 304, H-1052 Budapest V., Hungary. Telephone: 011-36-1-266-2024. Fax: 011-36-1-226-2025.

Kiev, Ukraine Office: vul. Prorizna 9, Suite 20, Kiev 252035, Ukraine. Telephones: 011-7-044-244-3452, 011-7-044-244-3453, 011-7-044-228-8687. Fax: 011-7-044-228-4938.

General and International Practice.
Firm engaged in American and General International Practice but not authorized to appear before the Belgian Courts.

RESIDENT PARTNERS

THOMAS J. RAMSEY, born Akron, Ohio, November 22, 1945; admitted, 1973, Ohio; 1988, District of Columbia (Not admitted in Belgium). *Education:* Miami University (B.A., 1967); The Ohio State University (J.D., 1972); University of Amsterdam, Europa Institute-Netherlands (Diploma, in European Communities Law, 1974). Office of the Attorney General of Ohio, 1973-1974. Attorney Adviser, Office of the Legal Adviser, U.S. Department of State, 1975-1984. U.S. Deputy Coordinator and Deputy Director of the Bureau for International Policy, Communications & Information, U.S. Department of State, 1985-1988. *Member:* The District of Columbia Bar; Ohio State Bar Association; American Bar Association (Co-Chairman, Communications Law Division, Science and Technology Section, 1987; Chairman, Telecommunications Law Committee, Science and Technology Section, 1986-1988). *PRACTICE AREAS:* Telecommunication.

BRIAN HARTNETT, born Dublin, Ireland, 1957; admitted, 1982, Ireland (Not admitted in Belgium). *Education:* Trinity College, Dublin (LL.B., 1981); University of Amsterdam (Diploma in European Law, 1982); Kings Inn, Dublin (Barrister at Law, 1982). *LANGUAGES:* English, French, Spanish. *PRACTICE AREAS:* International.

RESIDENT OF COUNSEL

GUY J. PEVTCHIN, born Brussels, Belgium, 1920. *Education:* University of Brussels (Doctor of Laws, 1951). Lecturer on E.E.C. law, University of Paris (Paris X), 1981—. E.E.C. Counsel for Union Carbide Europe, 1953-1983. *Member:* American Bar Association; Association Belge pour le Droit Européen; Belgian Arbitration Association. *Honorary Member:* Belgian Association of Company Lawyers (Chairman, 1974-1976); Law Society (England). *LANGUAGES:* French, English, Dutch and German. *PRACTICE AREAS:* International.

(This Listing Continued)

RESIDENT ASSOCIATES

REBECCA O'DONNELL, born Dublin, Ireland, 1970. *Education:* University College Dublin (B.C.L., 1991); Kings Inn, Dublin (Barrister at Law, 1993). *LANGUAGES:* English, French, German, Irish.

PETER ALEXIADAS, born Sydney, Australia, 1959; admitted, 1983, New South Wales, Australia. *Education:* University of Sydney (B.A., 1982; LL.B., 1983; LL.M. (Hons), 1987); London School of Economics (LL.M., 1988); Institute of Public International Law & International Relations, University of Thessaloniki, Greece (Certificate in Public International Law, cum laude, 1983). EC Correspondent, European Intellectual Property Review, since January 1990; EC Correspondent, International Company & Commercial Law Review, since January 1991; General Editor, European Competition Law Yearbook, since 1995; Co-Editor, "Intellectual & Industrial Property," European Union Law Reporter (CCH). Visiting Instructor, Institute of Public International Law & International Relations, University of Thessaloniki. *Member:* International Bar Association; Brussels Telecommunications Forum; International Law Association. *LANGUAGES:* English, Greek, French. *PRACTICE AREAS:* Competition; Telecommunications; Intellectual Property.

HARTMUT SEIBEL, born Kassel, Germany, 1960; admitted, 1989, Germany; 1992, Brussels. *Education:* Georg-August-University, Gottingen, Germany (1.jur. State Exam, 1986; 2.jur State Exam ("Assessor"), 1989). Trainee, Internal Market and Industrial Policy Directorate, Commission of the European Communities, 1990. *LANGUAGES:* German (native), English, French. *PRACTICE AREAS:* European Community; Telecommunications; German Law.

(For Biographical Data on Cleveland and Columbus, Ohio, Miami and Jacksonville, Florida, New York, New York, Phoenix, Arizona, Washington, D.C., London, England, Prague, Czech Republic, Bratislava, Slovak Republic, Budapest, Hungary and Kiev, Ukraine Personnel, see Professional Biographies at those Points Respectively).

STANBROOK AND HOOPER

Established in 1977

42, RUE DU TACITURNE
1040 BRUSSELS, BELGIUM
Telephone: (02) 230 50 59
Telex: 61975 STALAW B
Telecopier: (02) 230 57 13

General, International and EEC Law Practice, EEC Anti-Dumping, Customs, Public Procurement and Competition (Antitrust) Law, Aviation Law, Consumer and Environmental Law, EEC-US/Asia Trade Relations, GATT Law, International Trade, International Taxation and Exchange Control, Licensing and Extradition Law, U.K. Corporate and Commercial Law, Greek and Spanish Law.

MEMBERS OF FIRM

CLIVE STANBROOK, O.B.E., QC, born April 10, 1948; admitted, 1972, England and Wales; 1986, Turks and Caicos Islands; 1988, New York; 1989, Queen's Counsel (Not admitted in Belgium). *Education:* University College London (LL.B., Hons.). Author: "Dumping," (A Manual on EEC Anti-Dumping Law Procedures), 1980. "Dumping and Subsidies," (Community Law and Procedures), 1983. Co-Author: "Common Commercial Policy of the EEC," for Halsbury's Laws of England, 4th Edition, Vol. 51, Butterworths, 1991. Co-Editor: "International Trade - Law and Practice," Euromoney, 1990. *PRACTICE AREAS:* EC Trade and Competition Law; EC Litigation.

PHILIP BENTLEY, QC, born December 5, 1948; admitted, 1970, England and Wales; 1991, Queen's Counsel (Not admitted in Belgium). *Education:* St. Catharine's College Cambridge (B.A. Hons.); Faculté de Droit d'Aix en Provence (1972-1973). Author: "State and Community Aids for European Industry," 1983. Co-Editor of "A World Guide to Foreign Exchange Regulations," 1990. Country Correspondent to the "Journal of International Banking Law," 1986. *PRACTICE AREAS:* EC Trade; Public Procurement and Financial Services Law; EC Litigation.

JOHN RATLIFF, born January 13, 1957; admitted, 1980, Middle Temple, England and Wales (Not admitted in Belgium). *Education:* University College, Oxford (B.A. Hons., 1979); European Commission Internship (1981, Hon. Sir Peter Bristow Award Holder); Young Lawyers' Programme to Germany (1981-1982); Europa Institute, University of Amsterdam (Diploma in European Integration Law, 1983). Editor Competitor, Section of Sweet & Maxwell Encyclopedia of Community Law. *Member:* International Bar Association; British-German Lawyers Association. *PRACTICE*

(This Listing Continued)

STANBROOK AND HOOPER, Brussels—Continued

AREAS: EC Competition Law; Merger Control; EC Agricultural Law; EC Litigation.

BERNARD O'CONNOR, born April 18, 1954; admitted, 1980, Ireland (Not admitted in Belgium). *Education:* Trinity College Dublin (B.A., Hons., Legal Science, 1977); Incorporated Law Society of Ireland (Solicitor); University of Amsterdam (Diploma in European Integration Law, 1985); European University Institute, Florence (LL.M., 1986). Editor: "Business Guide to European Community Legislation," 1993. *Member:* International Bar Association, Energy Section. *PRACTICE AREAS:* EC Trade; Agro-Food and Environmental Law.

JOSE RIVAS DE ANDRES, born November 21, 1961; admitted, 1986, Saragossa, Spain (Not admitted in Belgium). *Education:* University of Saragossa (Licenciatura en Derecho); College of Europe, Bruges (Diploma of Advanced European Studies, 1987). Recipient, Manuel Lasala Llanas Award, Prize for International Law. Author: of the Spanish Section of "The Guide to Foreign Exchange Regulations," Euromoney. *PRACTICE AREAS:* EC Competition and Media Law.

ASSOCIATES

DAVID K.H. CANTOR, born New York, N.Y., 1948; admitted, 1981, California; 1989, New Jersey (Not admitted in Belgium). *Education:* Wesleyan University (B.A., 1970); Brandeis University (M.A., 1974); Institute on International and Comparative Law, University of San Diego School of Law, Paris, France (Diplôme, 1978); Boalt Hall School of Law, University of California, Berkeley (J.D., 1980). Fellow, American Film Institute Center for Advanced Film Studies, 1976-1977. *PRACTICE AREAS:* EC Telecommunications and Media Law; Environmental Law.

GEORGE METAXAS-MARANGHIDIS, born December 9, 1957; admitted, 1984, Athens, Greece (Not admitted in Belgium). *Education:* University of Athens (Law Degree, 1980); University of Munich (1987). Legal Adviser, European Patent Office, 1987-1989. *Member:* German-Greek Lawyers Association. (Also at Athens, Greece Office). *PRACTICE AREAS:* EC Intellectual Property; Media and Telecommunications Law.

ELISABETHANN WRIGHT, born October 18, 1961; admitted, 1989, Ireland (Not admitted in Belgium). *Education:* Queen's University of Belfast (LL.B., 1984); Institute of Professional Legal Studies, Belfast, N. Ireland (Certificate of Professional Legal Studies, 1985); College of Europe, Bruges (1986). *Member:* The Inn of Court of Northern Ireland; Association Internationale des Jeunes Avocats. *PRACTICE AREAS:* EC Pharmaceutical; Agro-Food and Public Procurement Law.

ADRIAN J.R. GARNER, born April 6, 1962; admitted, 1985, England; 1989, Jersey (Not admitted in Belgium). *Education:* University of Aix-Marseille (Diplôme d'études juridiques); University of Lille, France; University of Buckingham (LL.B. Hons, 1984); Inns of Court School of Law, Gray's Inn, London (1985). *PRACTICE AREAS:* EC Financial Services Law.

MARINA C. WHEELER, born December 5, 1964; admitted, 1987, England (Not admitted in Belgium). *Education:* Cambridge University; Fitzwilliam College (B.A., Hons., 1986); Inns of Court School of Law, Gray's Inn, London (1987); Université Libre de Bruxelles (Licence Speciale en Droit Européen, 1990). *Member:* United Kingdom Environmental Law Association. *PRACTICE AREAS:* EC Environmental and State Aids Law.

CATRIONA HATTON, born February 13, 1963; admitted, 1989, Ireland (Not admitted in Belgium). *Education:* Trinity College, Dublin (B.A. Hons, Legal Science, 1985); Incorporated Law Society of Ireland (Solicitor); Vrije Universiteit Brussel (Masters in International and European Law). *PRACTICE AREAS:* EC Competition; Financial Services Law.

CARLOS BERMEJO ACOSTA, born December 18, 1968; admitted, 1993, Salamanca, Spain (Not admitted in Belgium). *Education:* University of Salamanca (Licenciado en Derecho); University of Louvain-la-Neuve (Licence Spécial en Droit-Economique, 1992); College of Europe, Bruges (Master's Degree, European Law, 1993). *PRACTICE AREAS:* EC Trade; EC Litigation.

OF COUNSEL

IVOR STANBROOK, born London, England, 1924; admitted, 1960, Barrister, England. *Education:* Universities of London, Oxford and East Anglia. British Colonial Service, Nigeria. Member, British Parliament, 1970-1992. *PRACTICE AREAS:* Extradition Law.

LORD COCKFIELD, admitted, 1942, England. *Education:* London School of Economics (Honours Degree, Law and Economics). Inland Revenue Commissioner, United Kingdom Government. Managing Director, International Chemical and Pharmaceutical Service. Advisor, Chancellor of the Exchequer, 1970-1973. Life Peer (Member, British House of Lords), 1978. Secretary of State for Trade, British Cabinet, 1982. Chancellor, Duchy of Lancaster and Privy Counsellor. Vice-President, Commission of the European Communities, 1985-1988. Program Planner, Single EU Market, 1992.

ANTHONY HOOPER, Q.C., born Redhill, United Kingdom, September 16, 1937; admitted, 1965, England and Wales; 1967, British Colombia; 1987, Queens Counsel (Not admitted in Belgium). *Education:* University of Cambridge (B.A., Hons., LL.B.). Professor of Law, Osgoode Hall Law School, York University, Ontario, 1972-1974 and University of British Columbia, 1965-1968. Assistant Recorder of Crown Courts. *LANGUAGES:* English and French.

Languages: English, French, German, Dutch, Spanish, Italian and Greek

---

STEPHENSON HARWOOD

Established in 1990

AVENUE DU DIAMANT 139
1040 BRUSSELS, BELGIUM
Telephone: (322) 735 9190
Fax: (322) 732 2237

London, England Office: One St. Paul's Churchyard, EC4M 8SH. Telephone: (44) 0171 329 4422. Telex: 886789 SHSPC G. Fax: (44) 0171 606 0822.

Guangzhou, People's Republic of China Associated Office: Stephenson Harwood & Lo, Room 516, China Hotel, Liu Hua Lu, 510015. Telephone: (8620) 669 3490. Telex: 44888 CHLGZ CN. Fax: (8620) 669 3479.

Hong Kong Associated Office: Stephenson Harwood & Lo, 18th Floor, Edinburgh Tower, The Landmark, 15 Queen's Road Central. Telephone: 852-2868 0789. Telex: 66278 SHL HX. Fax: 852-2868 1504.

Kuwait Associated Office: Al Sarraf, Al Ruwayeh & Stephenson Harwood, Salhiya Complex, Gate 1 3rd Floor, P.O. Box 1448, Safat 13015. Telephone: 965 240 0061/2/3. Fax: 965 240 0064.

Madrid, Spain Office: Fernando El Santo 15-3°, 28010. Telephone: (341) 319 1212. Fax: (341) 319 1940.

Stephenson Harwood's European Community Law Group, with members in the Brussels and London offices, deals with a wide variety of Community law matters, including competition law, trade law and agricultural law, as well as the law relating to the completion of the internal market. The Group supports the activities of specialists in the firm dealing with matters such as commercial contracts, employment, intellectual property, banking, insurance, company law, taxation, environmental protection, the arts, broadcasting, leisure and transportation.

CONTACT PARTNERS

Antony Mair

(For Complete List of Stephenson Harwood's Overseas Offices, Please see London, England Office)

STIBBE SIMONT MONAHAN DUHOT

RUE WAFELAERTS 47-51 (BOX 1)
1060 BRUSSELS, BELGIUM
Telephone: 533.52.11
Telex: 24.519
Telefax: 533.52.12

Amsterdam, Netherlands Office: Strawinskylaan 2001, 1077 ZZ Amsterdam, P.O. Box 75640, 1070 AP. Telephone: 020 5460606. Fax: 020 5460123.

Paris, France Office: 154 Rue de l'Université, 75007 Paris. Telephone: (1) 40 62 20 00. Fax: (1) 40 62 20 62.

London, United Kingdom Office: 66 Gresham Street, London EC2V 7NH. Telephone: 44.71.600.4400. Fax: 44.71.600.4411.

New York, New York Office: 335 Madison Avenue, 10017. Telephone: 1-212-972-4000. Telex: 277253 (Stib UR). Telecopier: 1-212-972-4929.

Commercial Law, Corporations, Mergers and Acquisitions, Banking, Securities and Finance, Bankruptcy and Insolvency, EC Law, Competition, Anti-trust, Contracts, Building and Construction, Trademarks, Intellectual

(This Listing Continued)

Property, Arbitration and Litigation, Tax Law, Public and Administrative Law.

PARTNERS
AVOCATS À LA COUR DE CASSATION

LUCIEN SIMONT, born 1932; admitted, 1955, Brussels; 1975, Supreme Court. *Education:* University of Brussels (1955). President, Supreme Court Bar, 1988-1990. Professor, Commercial Law, University of Brussels. *LANGUAGES:* French, Dutch and English.

LUDOVIC DE GRYSE, born 1940; admitted, 1964, Brussels; 1975, Supreme Court. *Education:* University of Louvain (1964). Teaching Fellow and Instructor, University of Chicago, 1966-1967. Professor, University of Antwerp. President, Supreme Court Bar, 1990-1992. *LANGUAGES:* Dutch, French and English.

AVOCATS

MICHEL VAN DOOSSELAERE, born 1927; admitted, 1952, Brussels. *Education:* University of Brussels (1952). Representative for Belgium, Conference Interntionale des barreaux de tradition juridique commune. President, Brussels Bar, 1984-1986. Council Member, Brussels Bar, 1980-1983. *Member:* C.C.B.E. (Belgian Delegation to the Council); I.B.A. (Council and Management Committee). *LANGUAGES:* French, Dutch and English.

ETIENNE HEILPORN, born 1939; admitted, 1961, Brussels. *Education:* University of Brussels (1961). Professor, University of Brussels. Council Member, Brussels Bar, 1981-1984. *LANGUAGES:* French and English.

ANNE-MARIE STRANART, born 1937; admitted, 1960, Brussels. *Education:* University of Brussels (1960). Professor, Proceedings and Securities, University of Brussels. Council Member, Brussels Bar, 1984-1986. *LANGUAGES:* French and English.

JACQUES MALHERBE, born 1940; admitted, 1962, Brussels. *Education:* University of Louvain (1962; Economic Sciences, 1965); Harvard University Law School (LL.M., 1964). Professor of tax law and accounting, University of Louvain; Professor of international tax law, Ecole Supérieure des Sciences Fiscales; Guest Professor of international tax law, Universities of Paris I and Paris XII; Member of Council of Brussels Bar, 1981-1983. *LANGUAGES:* French, Dutch, English, German, Spanish, Italian and Russian.

ANDRÉ BRUYNEEL, born 1941; admitted, 1974, Brussels. *Education:* University of Brussels (1964; Economic Law, 1965; European Law, 1966); Harvard Law School (LL.M., 1967). Professor, Financial Law and Contracts, University of Brussels. Council Member, Brussels Bar, 1991-1994. *LANGUAGES:* French and English.

MICHÈLE BORGERS, born 1940; admitted, 1967, Brussels. *Education:* University of Brussels (1963). *LANGUAGES:* French and English.

MARC WAGEMANS, born 1947; admitted, 1969, Brussels. *Education:* University of Brussels (1969; Economic Law, 1970; Maritime and Air Law, 1972); Harvard University Law School (LL.M., 1971). Council Member, Brussels Bar, 1986-1989. *LANGUAGES:* French and English.

FRANCE MAUSSION, born 1949; admitted, 1972, Brussels. *Education:* University of Brussels (1972). Professor, University of Brussels. *LANGUAGES:* French and English.

PAUL ALAIN FORIERS, born 1952; admitted, 1973, Brussels. *Education:* University of Brussels (1974; Economic Law, 1975). Professor, Contracts, University of Brussels. *LANGUAGES:* French and English.

HANS VAN HOUTTE, born 1947; admitted, 1972, Brussels. *Education:* University of Louvain (1969; European Law, 1970; Ph.D. Legal Education, 1977); Harvard University Law School (LL.M., 1971); Hague Academy of International Law (1977). Professor, Conflicts of Law, Arbitration Law and International Business Law, University of Louvain. Administrator Cepani. *Member:* International Law Association (Secretary General, Belgian Branch); Institute International Trade Law and Practice (Corresponding Member). *LANGUAGES:* Dutch, French, English and German.

JEAN-PIERRE FIERENS, born 1948; admitted, 1973, Brussels. *Education:* University of Louvain (1972); University of Louvain-la-Neuve (Economic Law, 1973); ICHEC Brussels School of Fiscal Sciences (1976); Columbia University (LL.M., 1980). Member of Council, Brussels Bar, 1992—. *LANGUAGES:* French, Dutch and English.

VERA VAN HOUTTE, born 1947; admitted, 1979, Brussels. *Education:* University of Louvain (1969); Harvard University Law School (LL.M., 1971). *LANGUAGES:* Dutch, French and English.

(This Listing Continued)

LUDO CORNELIS, born 1951; admitted, 1980, Brussels. *Education:* University of Brussels (1974; Economic Law, 1976; J.D., 1981). Professor, Torts, Contracts and Financial Law, University of Brussels. *LANGUAGES:* Dutch, French and English.

CHRISTIAN VAN BUGGENHOUT, born 1949; admitted, 1971, Brussels. *Education:* University of Brussels (1971). *LANGUAGES:* Dutch, French and English.

BRIGITTE DAUWE, born 1952; admitted, 1975, Brussels. *Education:* University of Brussels (1975; Commercial Law, 1976). *LANGUAGES:* French, Dutch and English.

ONNO BROUWER, born 1954; admitted, 1980, Amsterdam; 1989, Brussels. *Education:* University of Amsterdam (Doctoraat Nederlands Recht); London School of Economics (Summer Program in English Law, 1978). Legal Secretary, Court of Justice of the European Communities, 1985-1989. *LANGUAGES:* Dutch, French, English, German and Italian.

PATRICK VAN LEYNSEELE, born 1955; admitted, 1979, Brussels. *Education:* University of Brussels (1978); University of Miami (M.C.L., 1979). *LANGUAGES:* French, Dutch, English and Spanish.

HERMAN CRAENINCKX, born 1955; admitted, 1981, Brussels. *Education:* University of Ghent (1978); Post Universitaire Management School (1979). *LANGUAGES:* Dutch, French and English.

NICOLE CAHEN, born 1948; admitted, 1973, Brussels. *Education:* University of Brussels (1972; Administrative Law, 1974). Assistant Professor, University of Brussels. *LANGUAGES:* French.

JOHN PARAMORE, born 1954; admitted, 1980, Brussels. *Education:* University of Brussels (1980; Tax law, 1981). *LANGUAGES:* French and English.

SANDRINE HIRSCH, born 1958; admitted, 1983, Brussels. *Education:* University of Brussels (1982); University of Michigan Law School (LL.M., 1983). *LANGUAGES:* French and English.

RAPHAEL VERSTRAETEN, born 1960; admitted, 1983, Brussels. *Education:* University of Louvain (1983); University of Paris II (Criminal Law, 1985). Professor, University of Louvain. *LANGUAGES:* Dutch, French and English.

RUDY NAUWELAERTS, born 1961; admitted, 1984, Brussels. *Education:* University of Brussels (1984). *LANGUAGES:* Dutch, French and English.

MONIQUE KESTEMONT-SOUMERYN, born 1948; admitted, 1985, Brussels. *Education:* University of Brussels (1970; Administrative Law, 1974). Assistant Professor, Administrative Law, University of Brussels. *LANGUAGES:* French.

ASSOCIATES
AVOCATS

JACQUES AUTENNE, born 1942; admitted, 1991, Brussels. *Education:* University of Louvain (1967). Professor, Tax Law, University of Louvain. *LANGUAGES:* French and English.

INGEBORG DE HERDT, born 1956; admitted, 1979, Brussels. *Education:* University of Brussels (1979). Assistant Professor, University of Brussels. *LANGUAGES:* Dutch and French.

BÉATRICE THIEFFRY, born 1957; admitted, 1984, Brussels. *Education:* University of Brussels (1980). *LANGUAGES:* French.

ILSE VERHELST, born 1960; admitted, 1983, Brussels. *Education:* University of Brussels (1983). *LANGUAGES:* Dutch and French.

MYRIAM VAN VARENBERGH, born 1960; admitted, 1983, Brussels. *Education:* University of Louvain (1983; Agreg., 1983); Tax School of Brussels (Tax Management, 1985); University of Wisconsin Law School (Summer Program in U.S. Law, 1988). *LANGUAGES:* Dutch and French.

PAUL VAN DER PUTTEN, born 1958; admitted, 1982, Brussels. *Education:* University of Brussels (1982). *LANGUAGES:* Dutch, French and English.

KRISTIEN VAN LINT, born 1960; admitted, 1983, Brussels. *Education:* University of Ghent (1983); University of Strasbourg (Intellectual Property, 1984). *LANGUAGES:* Dutch and French.

DENIS VAN OMMESLAGHE, born 1960; admitted, 1982, Brussels. *Education:* University of Brussels (1982; Economic Law, 1983). *LANGUAGES:* French.

(This Listing Continued)

STIBBE SIMONT MONAHAN DUHOT, Brussels— Continued

MICHÈLE GREGOIRE, born 1960; admitted, 1983, Brussels. *Education:* University of Brussels (1983; J.D., 1992); University of Geneva (D.E.S., 1987). Assistant Professor, University of Brussels and University of Geneva, 1988-1989. *LANGUAGES:* French.

AUDRY STEVENART, born 1961; admitted, 1985, Brussels. *Education:* University of Brussels (1985). *LANGUAGES:* French.

ANNICK BAUDRI, born 1963; admitted, 1986, Brussels. *Education:* University of Brussels (1986; Tax law, 1987). *LANGUAGES:* Dutch, French and Italian.

DAVID D'HOOGHE, born 1962; admitted, 1985, Brussels. *Education:* University of Louvain (1985); Northwestern University, Chicago (LL.M., 1986). *LANGUAGES:* Dutch and French.

JACQUES SIMONET, born 1963; admitted, 1986, Brussels. *Education:* University of Brussels (1986). *LANGUAGES:* French.

BENOÎT NIBELLE, born 1963; admitted, 1987, Brussels. *Education:* University of Louvain (1986); University of Brussels (Tax law, 1987). *LANGUAGES:* French.

MARIANA VAN CAUTER, born 1962; admitted, 1986, Brussels. *Education:* University of Louvain (1985); Sorbonne University (1986, D.E.S.S., Foreign Trade); Fiscale Hogeschool Brussels (Tax law, 1988). *LANGUAGES:* Dutch and French.

AXEL MILLER, born 1965; admitted, 1987, Brussels. *Education:* University of Brussels (1987). *LANGUAGES:* French and English.

JAN PEETERS, born 1963; admitted, 1987, Brussels. *Education:* University of Antwerp (1986); University of California at Berkeley (LL.M., 1987). *LANGUAGES:* Dutch, French and English.

ROSITA GEELEN, born 1961; admitted, 1987, Brussels. *Education:* University of Brussels (1987). Assistant Professor, University of Brussels. *LANGUAGES:* Dutch and French.

SOPHIE GREGOIRE, born 1963; admitted, 1987, Brussels. *Education:* University of Brussels (1987). *LANGUAGES:* French.

GUY BLOCK, born 1959; admitted, 1987, Brussels. *Education:* University of Liège (1985); University of Antwerp (Maritime Law, 1986); University of Tulane Law School (LL.M., 1987). Assistant Professor, University of Liège. *LANGUAGES:* French and English.

ANNICK MOTTET, born 1964; admitted, 1987, Brussels. *Education:* University of Liège (1987); European College of Bruges (Advanced European Legal studies, 1988). *LANGUAGES:* French and Dutch.

KOEH DEMAEYER, born 1961; admitted, 1988, Brussels. *Education:* University of Louvain (1988). *LANGUAGES:* Dutch, French, English, German and Spanish.

MARC FYON, born 1964; admitted, 1989, Brussels. *Education:* University of Louvain (1987; Economics, 1988); University of California at Los Angeles (LL.M., 1989). *LANGUAGES:* French, Dutch and English.

Languages: French, Dutch, English, German, Italian, Spanish

(For a List of other Partners and Associates, see Professional Biographies at Amsterdam, The Netherlands, Paris, France, London, United Kingdom, and New York, New York)

TAYLOR JOYNSON GARRETT

Established in 1989

14 RUE MONTOYER
1040 BRUSSELS, BELGIUM
Telephone: (32) 2 514 0402
Facsimile: (32) 2 514 0088

London, England Office: Carmelite, 50 Victoria Embankment, Blackfriars, EC4Y 0DX. Telephone: (44) 171 353 1234. Facsimile: (44) 171 936 2666.

Bucharest, Romania Office: Bd. Nicolae Titulescu Nr. 1, Bloc A7, Scara 3, Etaj 9, Apart. 88, Sector 1. Telephone: (401) 211 88 98. Facsimile: (401) 211 75 89.

(This Listing Continued)

Affiliated firms and offices:
Graham & James in San Francisco, Los Angeles, Newport Beach, Sacramento, Palo Alto, Washington DC, New York, Raleigh, Milan. Joint Offices in Bangkok, Guangzhou, Hanoi, Taipei, Beijing. Graham & James affiliated offices in Riyadh, Jeddah, Jakarta, Mexico City, Tokyo, Kuwait, Bahrain, Sydney, Melbourne, Brisbane, Perth, Canberra.
Deacons, Hong Kong.
Haarmann, Hemmelrath & Partner in Dusseldorf, Berlin, Munich, Frankfurt, Leipzig, Prague.

RESIDENT PARTNER

Martin Baker

Languages: French and English

THEODORE GODDARD

79 AVENUE DE CORTENBERG/KORTENBERGLAAN 79
1040 BRUSSELS, BELGIUM
Telephone: 732 27 00
Fax: 735 23 52

London, England Office: 150 Aldersgate Street, EC1A 4EJ. Telephone: (44) (171) 606 8855. Telex: 884678. Fax: (44) (171) 606 4390.

St. Helier, Jersey, Channel Islands Office: Theodore Goddard Jersey, P.O. Box 344, Osprey House, 5 Old Street, St. Helier, Jersey JE4 8UZ. Telephone: (44) (534) 76085. Telex: 4192289. Fax: (44) (534) 35227.

Paris, France Office: Klein Goddard, 44 Avenue des Champs Elysées, 75008, Paris, France. Telephone: (33) (1) 44 95 20 00. Fax: (33) (1) 49 53 03 97.

Warsaw, Poland Office: Dewey Ballantine Theodore Goddard Sp.z o.o, ul. Klonowa 8, 00-591, Warsaw, Poland. Telephone: (48) (22) 49 32 88. Fax: (48) (22) 49 80 23. Satellite: (48) (39) 12 21 85.

Prague, Czech Republic Office: Dewey Ballantine Theodore Goddard, 6th Floor, Revolucni 13, 110 15 Prague 1. Telephone: (42) (2) 24810283. Fax: (42) (2) 231 0983.

Budapest, Hungary Office: Dewey Ballantine Theodore Goddard, Vadasz utca 31, H-1054 Budapest, Hungary. Telephone: (36) (1) 111 9620. Fax: (36) (1) 112 2272.

Associated offices in London, England: c/o Dewey Ballantine, 150 Aldersgate Street, London EC1A 4EJ. Telephone: (44) (171) 606 6121. Fax: (44) (171) 600 2754; New York, USA: c/o Dewey Ballantine, 1301 Avenue of the Americas, New York, NY 10019-6092. Telephone: (1) (212) 259 8000. Fax: (1) (212) 259 6333; Washington, USA: c/o Dewey Ballantine, 1775 Pennsylvania Avenue, N.W., Washington D.C., 20006-4605. Telephone: (1) (202) 862 1000. Fax: (1) (202) 862 1093; Los Angeles, USA: c/o Dewey Ballantine, 333 South Hope Street, Los Angeles, California, 90071. Telephone: (1) (213) 626 3399. Fax: (1) (213) 625 0562.

PARTNER RESIDENT IN BRUSSELS

Philip Woolfson

THIEFFRY ET ASSOCIÉS

Established in 1977

100 AVENUE DE TERVUEREN
BRUSSELS 1040, BELGIUM
Telephone: (2) 733.97.15
Telefax: (2) 733.97.16

Paris, France Office: 23 avenue Hoche, 75008. Telephone: (1) 45.62.45.54. Telex: "THIEFRY 640 689 F". Telefax: (1) 42.25.80.07.

New York, N.Y. Office: 780 Third Avenue, 10017. Telephone: 212-750-0080. Telefax: 212-750-0054.

Hong Kong Office: Bank of China Tower, 21st Floor, 1 Garden Road. Telephone: (852) 25 23 4833. Telefax: (852) 25 24 6438.

Shanghai, People's Republic of China Office: Room 1406 Ruijin Building, 205 Maoming Nan Lu, 200020. Telephone: (86-21) 472 79 93; 472 70 96. Fax: (86-21) 472 43 92.

Associated Offices: Shenzhen, People's Republic of China; Beirut, Lebanon; Cairo, Egypt; Jeddah, Saudi Arabia.

VALERIE DELORGE, born August 3, 1966; admitted, 1991, Brussels. *Education:* Université Libre de Bruxelles (Licence en Droit, 1989); College

(This Listing Continued)

d'Europe, Bruges (Diplôme de Hautes Etudes Européenes, 1990); King's College, London (LL.M., European Competition Law, 1993). *LANGUAGES:* French, English, Italian and Dutch.

THOMMESSEN KREFTING GREVE LUND

AVENUE LOUISE 475/B 12
BRUSSELS 1050, BELGIUM
Telephone: 32 2 646 3620
Fax: 32 2 646 4049

In Alliance With: Vinge, Sweden and Kromann & Münter, Denmark.
Oslo, Norway Office; Tollbodgaten 27, P.O. Box 413 Sentrum, 0103. Telephone: 47 22 42 18 10. Telefax: 47 22 42 35 57.
London, England Office: 44/45 Chancery Lane, WC2A 1JB. Telephone: 44 71 404 4825. Fax: 44 71 404 1471.
Bergen, Norway Office: Valkendorfsgate 1A, P.O. Box 349, 5000. Telephone: 47 55 31 13 50. Fax: 47 55 31 74 75.
Paris, France Representation Office: 21, Rue Jean Goujon, 75008. Telephone: 331 40.75.37.37. Fax: 331 45.63.05.49.
Hong Kong Representation Office: 2003 Hutchison House, 10 Harcourt Road Central. Telephone: 852 523 6149. Fax: 852 810 5343.

General Business Law. Tax, Corporation, Commercial, Industrial, Shipping, Banking and Government Relations.

RESIDENT PARTNER

FINN E. ENGZELIUS, born Røros, Norway, September 10, 1943; admitted, 1973, Norway; 1981, Supreme Court of Norway. *Education:* University of Oslo (Candidate in Jurisprudence, 1971). External Examiner, Legal Faculty University of Oslo. Associate Judge, Hadeland, 1971-1973. Sulzburg Seminar, American Law & Legal Institutions, 1977. Member, Oslo Tax Assessment Board, 1983-1987. Magistrate, Oslo Superior Tax Assessment Board, 1987—. *Member:* Norwegian Bar Association; International Fiscal Association, International Bar Association. *LANGUAGES:* Scandinavian Languages, English and French. *PRACTICE AREAS:* International Arbitration; Bankruptcy; European Union; Petroleum; Tax Law.

RESIDENT ASSOCIATE

KJERSTIN M. BULL-BERG, born Bergen, Norway, January 31, 1958; admitted, 1989, Norway (Not admitted in Belgium). *Education:* University of Bergen (Candidate of Jurisprudence, 1984). Legal Adviser in the Banking, Insurance and Security Commission, 1984-1990. *Member:* Norwegian Bar Association. *LANGUAGES:* Scandinavian Languages and English. *PRACTICE AREAS:* Finance; Business; Inside Trading Law.

(For biographical data on all personnel, see Professional Biographies at Oslo, Norway)

THOMPSON, HINE AND FLORY

RUE DES CHEVALIERS RIDDERSTRAAT 14 - B.10
B-1050 BRUSSELS, BELGIUM
Telephone: 011(32-2) 511-9326
Fax: 011(32-2) 513-9206

Akron, Ohio Office: 50 S. Main Street, Suite 502, 44308-1828. Telephone: 216-376-8090. Fax: 216-376-8386.
Cincinnati, Ohio Office: 312 Walnut Street, 14th Floor, 45202-4029. Telephone: 513-352-6700. Fax: 513-241-4771. Telex: 938003.
Cleveland, Ohio Office: 1100 National City Bank Building, 629 Euclid Avenue, 44114-3070. Telephone: 216-566-5500. Fax: 216-556-5583. Telex: 980217. Cable Address "Thomflor".
Columbus, Ohio Office: One Columbus, 10 West Broad Street, 43215-3435. Telephone: 614-469-3200. Fax: 614-469-3361.
Dayton, Ohio Office: 2000 Courthouse Plaza, 45402-1706. Telephone: 513-443-6600. Fax: 513-443-6637; 443-6635.
Palm Beach, Florida Office: 125 Worth Avenue, 33480-4466. Telephone: 407-833-5900. Fax: 407-833-5951.
Washington, D.C. Office: 1920 N Street, N.W., 20036-1601. Telephone: 202-331-8800. Fax: 202-331-8330. Telex: 904173. Cable Address: "Caglaw".

General and International Practice.

FIRM PROFILE: Thompson, Hine and Flory was established in Cleveland in 1911. Today it is among the nation's largest law firms with approximately 330 attorneys. Our lawyers serve as advisors to a full spectrum of clients ranging from individuals and sole proprietorships to multinational

(This Listing Continued)

corporations, financial institutions, governments and nonprofit organizations.

RESIDENT COUNSEL

LUDO DEKLERCK, born Diksmuide, Belgium, February 3, 1960; admitted, 1986, Belgium. *Education:* University of Kortrijk (KULAK), Kortrijk, Belgium (Ph.B., 1980); University of Brussels (V.U.B.) (1984-1985) University of Leuven (KUL), Leuven, Belgium (LL.B., 1984). Member: Belgian Institute of Standardization; International League of Competition Law; American Chamber of Commerce in Belgium. *LANGUAGES:* English, French, Dutch and German. *PRACTICE AREAS:* General and International Practice; Belgian Law; International Trade Law.

(For biographical data on all Lawyers in all Offices, see Professional Biographies at Cleveland, Ohio)

THÜMMEL, SCHÜTZE & PARTNER

Established in 1981

AVENUE DES ARTS, 41
B-1040 BRUSSELS, BELGIUM
Telephone: (0032) 2-512 7846
Telefax: (0032) 2-512 7023

Stuttgart, Germany Office: Landhausstraße 90, 70190 Stuttgart. Telephone: (0711) 1667-0, Telefax: (0711) 286 44 66, 2 62 69 10.
Paris, France Office: 46, Rue de Bassano, F-75008 Paris. Telephone: (0033) 1-53 67 50 00. Telefax: (0033) 1-47 20 78 76.
Dresden, Germany Office: Friedrichstraße 33, 01067 Dresden. Telephone: (0351) 496 5302. Telefax: (0351) 496 5346.
Berlin, Germany Office: Lützowstraße 33/36, 10785 Berlin. Telephone: (030) 2 61 11 31. Telefax: (030) 2 61 90 49. Telex: 3 01304.
Frankfurt, Germany Office: Eschersheimer Laudshraße 10 60322 Frankfurt. Telephone: (069) 9591350. Telefax: (069) 95913530.
Singapore Office: 9, Battery Road, #16-01 Straits Trading Building, Singapore 0104. Telephone: (00 65) 53 53 112. Telefax: (00 65) 53 43 100.

Firm engaged in International Law Practice, but not authorized to appear before the Belgium Courts or to act as Belgium Advocates and Solicitors.

DR. JUR. DANIEL EWERT, born Nassau, Germany, August 19, 1960; admitted, 1991, Germany. *Education:* Universities of Mainz, Dijon; Referendar (1985); Université libre de Bruxelles (Licence Spéciale Droit Européen, 1986). Assistant at the Institute for International law at Marburg University, 1987. Assessor, 1990. Doctor of Jurisprudence, 1990. *Member:* Deutsche Gesellschaft für Rechtsvergleichung; Union International des Avocats. *LANGUAGES:* German, English and French.

(For Complete Biographical Data on all Personnel, see Professional Biographies at Stuttgart, Germany).

HENRIETTE A. TIELEMANS

44 BTE 8 AVENUE DES ARTS
1040 BRUSSELS, BELGIUM
Telephone: 011-32-2-512.98.90
Fax: 011-32-2-502.15.98

Correspondent Office of Covington & Burling: 1201 Pennsylvania Avenue, N.W., Washington D.C. Telephone: 202-662-6000. Fax: 202-662-6291.

General Practice.

RESIDENT MEMBERS OF FIRM

DAVID L. HARFST, born Oak Park, Illinois, February 14, 1950; admitted, 1983, District of Columbia (Not admitted in Belgium). *Education:* Wesleyan University (B.A., 1972); Yale University (J.D., 1982). Recipient, 1991, Sixth Annual Award for Scholarship Administrative Law Section, ABA. Co-author with J. Mashaw: "The Struggle for Auto Safety," Harvard U. Press, 1990. Visiting Lecturer, Food and Drug Law and Automobile Safety Regulation, Yale Law School, 1984-1991. (Resident, Brussels, Belgium Correspondent Office).

HENRIETTE A. TIELEMANS, born Antwerp, Belgium, May 6, 1953; admitted, 1980, Brussels. *Education:* University of Antwerp (Lic. Jur., 1976); Harvard University (LL.M., 1978). Visiting Professor, National University of Rwanda, 1979. Assistant Professor, Law Faculty, University of Antwerp, 1976-1977, 1979-1980.

(This Listing Continued)

HENRIETTE A. TIELEMANS, Brussels—Continued

RESIDENT ASSOCIATES

HERMAN I. DE BAUW, born Heist-op-den-Berg, Belgium, December 10, 1958; admitted, 1984, Brussels. *Education:* University of Louvain (Lic. Jur., 1981; Graduate Degree in American Studies, 1982); University of Virginia (LL.M., 1983).

PETER W. L. BOGAERT, born Lubumbashi, Zaire, May 1, 1959; admitted, 1984, Brussels. *Education:* Catholic University of Leuven (B.Phil., 1979; Lic.Jur., cum laude, 1982); Oxford University (B.A., magna cum laude, 1984).

KATLEEN HENDRIX, born Lokeren, Belgium, September 2, 1968; admitted, 1993, Brussels. *Education:* University of Louvain (Lic. Jur., 1991); College of Europe, Bruges (Adv. Eur. Studies, 1992); DAAD German Law Program for Foreign Lawyers (1993).

PHILIPP TAMUSSINO, born New York, N.Y., January 11, 1964; admitted, 1991, New York (Not admitted in Belgium). *Education:* Karl-Franzens-Universitat Graz, Austria (Maj. iur., 1987; Dr. iur., 1989); New York University (LL.M., 1990).

DIRK P. TIREZ, born Ghent, Belgium, June 4, 1964; admitted, 1990, New York; 1991, Brussels. *Education:* College of Europe, Bruges (Adv. Eur. Studies, 1988); University of Michigan (LL.M., 1989).

TOURNICOURT & VANISTENDAEL

Established in 1985

TERKAMERENLAAN 33
BOULEVARD DE LA CAMBRE 33
1050 BRUSSELS, BELGIUM
Telephone: 32.2.648.53.20
Fax: 32.2.646.03.43

Affiliated Office: Lievens & Dursin. President Kennedypark 37, 8500 Kortrijk, Belgium. Telephone: 056-22 97 20. Fax: 056-22 62 23.

Income Tax, Corporate Tax, V.A.T., Indirect Tax, Custom Duties and Criminal Tax Law, International Taxation, Corporate Law.

MEMBERS

REINHOLD TOURNICOURT, born 1946; admitted, 1974, Brussels. *Education:* University of Louvain (Dr. Juris, 1970); Southern Methodist University, Dallas, Texas (M.C.L., 1971). *Member:* Brussels Bar; National Bar Association (Member, Tax Committee).

FRANS VANISTENDAEL, born 1942; admitted, 1975, Brussels. *Education:* University of Louvain (Dr.Iur., 1965; Ph.D. Law, 1977); Yale Law School (LL.M., 1969). Professor of Taxation and Jurisprudence, Faculty of Law, Katholieke Universiteit Leuven, Belgium, 1972—. Royal Commissioner for Tax Reform, 1986-1987. President, Supervisory Board of the Auditing Profession, 1985—. *Member:* Brussels Bar; National Union of Tax Consultants, Belgium (Honorary Member).

MICHELINE VAN DE WIELE, born 1949; admitted, 1973, Brussels. *Education:* University of Louvain (Dr.Iur., 1971); Inst. Sup. Comm., St. Louis (1976); Lic. Economics and Tax Sciences, St. Aloysius, Brussels (1984). *Member:* I.F.A.

LUC DE BROE, born 1959; admitted, 1982, Brussels. *Education:* University of Louvain (Lic. Jur., 1982); Ecole Supérieure Sciences Fiscales, Brussels (Lic. Fisc., 1985); Northwestern University (LL.M., 1986). Recipient, International Fiscal Association-Mitchell B. Caroll Price Award for Taxation of Crossborder Leasing, 1988.

ASSOCIATES

FRANÇOISE MAHIEU, born 1949; admitted, 1971, Brussels. *Education:* University of Louvain (Dr. Juris., 1971).

HILDE VAN DEN KEYBUS, born 1964; admitted, 1987, Brussels. *Education:* University of Louvain, K.U. Leuven (Lic.Iur., 1987); St. Aloysius School of Fiscal Sciences, Brussels (1988); Juristenprogramm des DAAD, Tübingen-Dusseldorf (1989-1990).

MARTINE EULAERTS, born 1965; admitted, 1988, Brussels. *Education:* University of Louvain, K.U. Leuven (Lic.Iur., 1988); Ecole Supérieure Sciences Fiscales, Brussels (Dipl. Fisc., 1990).

LUK VANDENBERGHE, born 1965; admitted, 1988, Antwerp; 1990, Brussels. *Education:* University of Louvain, K.U. Leuven (Lic.Iur., 1988);

(This Listing Continued)

St. Aloysius School of Fiscal Sciences, Brussels (1989); Diplôme d'Etudes Approfondies, University of Nancy-France (1991-1992).

CAROLINE VANDERKERKEN, born 1968; admitted, 1991, Brussels. *Education:* University of Louvain, K.U. Leuven (Lic. Iur., 1991); St. Aloysius School of Fiscal Sciences, Brussels (1992).

CHRISTIAAN BARBIER, born 1968; admitted, 1991, Brussels. *Education:* University of Louvain, K.U. Leuven (Lic. Iur., 1991); St. Aloysius School of Fiscal Sciences, Brussels (1992).

PHILIP KERFS, born 1969; admitted, 1992, Brussels. *Education:* University of Louvain, K.U. Leuven (Lic. Iur., 1992).

GÉRY LAUWERS, born 1968; admitted, 1993, Brussels. *Education:* University of Louvain, U.C.L. (Lic. Iur., 1991); University of Brussels, U.L.B. (Lic. Tax Law, 1992).

Languages: Dutch, French, English and German

TRANS EUROPEAN LAW FIRMS ASSOCIATION (TELFA)

Established in 1990

114/8 BOULEVARD BRAND WHITLOCK
B-1200 BRUSSELS, BELGIUM
Telephone: +32.2.735.02.06
Facsimile: +32.2.735.37.13

Telfa is an International Association established under Belgian law whose members are independent law firms with the common objectives of servicing legal requirements throughout the EU, providing direct and immediate access to the institutions of the Communities and coordinating services provided from its Central Office in Brussels.

Telfa members are located in Austria, Belgium, Denmark, France, Germany, Greece, Hungary, Italy, Luxembourg, the Netherlands, Portugal, Spain, Switzerland and the United Kingdom; in addition associate members are located in the Channel Islands and Ireland.

All the members provide comprehensive advice to the business world in their own jurisdictions, a positive approach to solving legal problems utilizing back-up available to members which provides clients with assistance throughout the EU, and experience in negotiating with Communities institutions and dealing with Community legal procedures.

For further details contact: Giancarlo Agace, Secretary General

---

TRENITÉ VAN DOORNE

AVENUE LOUISE 149
1050 BRUSSELS, BELGIUM
Telephone: 32-2-537 5159
Telefax: 32-2-537 6961

Amsterdam, Netherlands Office: De Lairessestraat 133. Mailing Address: P.O. Box 75265, 1070 AG AMSTERDAM. Telephone: 31 (0) 20-6879 123. Telex: 16144 tvda nl. Telefax: 31 (0) 20-6789 589.

Rotterdam, Netherlands Office: Weena 666. Mailing Address: P.O. Box 190, 3000 AD ROTTERDAM. Telephone: 31 (0) 20-404 2111. Telefax: 31 (0) 10-404 2333.

Rijswijk, Netherlands Office: Haagweg 175. Mailing Address: P.O. Box 1073, 2280 CB RIJSWIJK. Telephone: 31 (0) 70-390 10 15. Telefax: 31 (0) 70-399 68 44.

The Hague, Netherlands Office: Churchillplein 5. Mailing Address: P.O. Box 17207, 2502 CE THE HAGUE. Telephone: 31 (0) 70-338 3131. Telefax: 31 (0) 70-358 4798.

Willemstad, Curaçao, Netherlands Antilles Office: Promes, Trenité Van Doorne. Julianaplein 22, P.O. Box 504. Telephone: 599-9-613400. Telefax: 599-9-612023.

Tokyo, Japan Office: Akasaka Wing Building 5 F, 6-6-15 Akasaka, Minato-ku, 107. Telephone: 813-5563-2911. Telefax: 813-5563-2912.

(This Listing Continued)

Firm engaged in practice of Law of the European Communities, GATT Law, Public International Law, International Transactions and Arbitrations.

MEMBERS OF FIRM

PIERRE V.F. BOS, born 1949; admitted, 1977, Amsterdam, 1987, Rotterdam, The Netherlands and before the Court of Justice and the Courts of First Instance of the European Communities in Luxembourg (Not admitted in Belgium). *Education:* University of Leiden (1975). *LANGUAGES:* English, French and German. *PRACTICE AREAS:* Law of the European Communities.

MARCO C.E.J. BRONCKERS, born 1956; admitted, 1982, The Hague; 1987, Rotterdam, The Netherlands and before the Court of Justice and the Courts of First Instance of the European Communities in Luxembourg (Not admitted in Belgium). *Education:* University of Amsterdam (J.D., 1979; S.J.D., 1985); University of Michigan (LL.M., 1980). Lecturer, International Trade Law, Europa College, Bruges, Belgium, 1986-1993. *LANGUAGES:* English, French and German. *PRACTICE AREAS:* Law of the European Communities; GATT Law.

ASSOCIATES
ATTORNEY AT LAW

ALEXANDRA H.C. KAMERLING, born 1968; admitted, 1993, as Solicitor of the Supreme Court of England and Wales (Not admitted in Belgium). *Education:* Cambridge University (1989); College of Law, Guildford (1990). *LANGUAGES:* Dutch, English, French and Spanish. *PRACTICE AREAS:* EC Competition.

OF COUNSEL

PROF. DR. RICHARD H. LAUWAARS, born 1940; (Not admitted in Belgium). *Education:* University of Leiden (1963; S.J.D., cum laude, 1970). Professor, Law of European Organizations, Vrije Universiteit, Amsterdam, 1972-1980. Visiting Professor, Law of the European Communities, International Human Rights and International Trade, University of Michigan Law School, 1979-1980. Professor, Law of International Organizations, University of Amsterdam, 1981—. Guest Lecturer, University of Minnesota, 1988. Doctor of Law Honoris Causa, Shenandoah University (Winchester, U.S.A.), 1992. Director, Europe Institute, Amsterdam, 1981—. *LANGUAGES:* English, French and German. *PRACTICE AREAS:* Law of the European Communities; Public International Law.

Trenité Van Doorne forms together with Wessing Berenberg-Gossler Zimmermann a European Economic interest grouping. Wessing has offices in Berlin, Brussels, Düsseldorf, Hamburg, Leipzig and Munich. Trenité Van Doorne is a member of Lex Mundi.

Languages: Dutch, English, French, German

TURNER KENNETH BROWN

19 AVENUE DES ARTS
1040 BRUSSELS, BELGIUM
Telephone: 010 322 218 2188; 010 322 218 3322
Fax: 010 322 217 4895

London, England Offices: 100 Fetter Lane, EC4A 1DD. Telephone: 071-242 6006 (National); 44 71 242 6006 (International). Telex: 297696 TKBLAW G. Fax: 071-242 3003 Groups 2 & 3.
Reading, England Office: Abbot's House, Abbey Street RG1 3BD. Telephone: 0734-504700.

MEMBERS OF FIRM

Robert Jackson (Non-Resident)   **Robert Bell** (Non-Resident)

(For Complete List of Firm Personnel, see Professional Biographies in London, England)

U G L D

(UETTWILLER, GRELON, LIPPENS, DEKEYSER & ASSOCIES)

Société Civile Professionnelle

73, AVENUE VANDENDRIESSCHE
1150 BRUSSELS, BELGIUM
Telephone: (32.2) 772.87.50
Fax: (32.2) 772.87.52

Paris, France Office: U G G C (Uettwiller, Grelon, Gout, Canat & Associés) 68, boulevard de Courcelles, 75017. Telephone: 48.88.89.00. Telefax: 48.88.05.50.

(This Listing Continued)

Litigation/Arbitration, Corporate, Commercial Law, Distribution Law, Computer Law, Construction Law, Food and Drug Regulations, Banking and Finance, Tax, EC Law, Representation of Public Bodies, Environmental Law, Cultural Property Law, Intellectual Property, Contract Law (domestic and international), Labour Law, Employee Benefits, Health Law, Real Estate, Transportation Law, Bankruptcy Law, Teaching Duties, Foreign Law: Belgium, Eastern Europe, French speaking African Countries, Italy, Spain, USA.

FIRM PROFILE: Uettwiller, Grelon, Gout, Canat et Associes (Paris), in association with Paul Lippens de Cerf and Manoël Dekeyser have decided to open a Belgian office. This firm will offer all the legal services needed for business and in particular, EEC regulations and a Belgian practice.

PARTNERS

MANOËL DEKEYSER, born 1960; admitted, 1986, Brussels. *Education:* University of Louvain (Law Degree, 1984); University of Brussels (Special Degree in Tax Law, 1985); University of Brussels, Notary School (1989). Author: "Legal and Tax Aspects of Belgian Mergers"; "Legal Form of Investment in Belgium" (Les Cahiers Juridiques et Fiscaux de l'Exportation).

PAUL LIPPENS DE CERF, born 1960; admitted, 1986, Brussels. *Education:* University of Louvain (LL.B. and Special Degree in European Studies, 1983); Georgetown University, Washington D.C. (Masters of Law, 1985). Lecturer, International Satellite Telecommunications and EEC Law, Colloquium on the Law of Outer Space, Brighton, 1987. Author: "European Economic Space," Revue des Affaires Européennes, 1992; "Normalization of Telecommunications in Europe," Revue des Affaires Européennes, 1991. *Member:* European Center of Space Law (ESA); International Bar Association (Antitrust & Trade and Telecommunications Committees).

ASSOCIATES

MARIA-ISABEL JIMENEZ ROJAS, born 1956; admitted, 1984, Brussels. *Education:* University of Madrid (Law Degree, 1980); Brussels Free University (Law Degree, 1983). Co-Author: "Treaty on Competition Law in Europe.".

PHILIP VAN DOORN, born 1959; admitted, 1986, Brussels; 1992 Paris. *Education:* University of Brussels (Law Degree in Private and Public Law, 1983); University of Nancy (Masters Degree in European Law); Centre Européen Universitaire.

Languages: French, English and Spanish

URÍA & MENÉNDEZ

BRUSSELS, BELGIUM

(See Boden De Bandt De Brauw Jeantet Lagerlöf & Uría)

VAN BAEL & BELLIS

AVENUE LOUISE, 165
B-1050 BRUSSELS, BELGIUM
Telephone: (02) 647 73 50
Fax: (02) 640 64 99
Telex: 20583 FORUM B

Firm engaged in European Communities, International Business and Belgian Law Practice.

PARTNERS

IVO VAN BAEL, born Antwerp, Belgium, February 15, 1939; admitted, 1971, Brussels. *Education:* University of Louvain (Ph.B., 1958; Dr. Jur.; Lic. Not., 1961); University of Bologna Law School (1960); Johns Hopkins University, Bologna Center (1962); University of Michigan Law School (M.C.L., 1963). Co-Author: "Anti-Dumping and Other Trade Protection Laws of the EEC," CCH, 3rd. ed. 1995; "EEC Competition Law," CCH, 3rd ed. 1993. Professor on EEC Antitrust and Anti-Dumping Procedure, College of Europe, Bruges, 1983—; Visiting Professor on Trade Law at the University of Amsterdam, Postgraduate Program in European Law, 1987—. Adjunct Professor on EEC Antitrust Law at the University of Tokyo, 1993-1994. *Member:* Center for International Commercial Arbitration, Los Angeles, 1987—; American Bar Association (European Coordinator for the European Law Committee, 1986—; Chairman of the Special Task

(This Listing Continued)

VAN BAEL & BELLIS, Brussels—Continued

Force on EC 1992, 1990-1992, Chairman, Task Force on European Community, 1992-1993, Section of International Law and Practice); International Bar Association (Council Member, 1982-1987 and Chairman, Antitrust and Trade Law Committee, 1987-1989, Section on Business Law; Chairman, Committee on Liaison with International Organizations, 1982-1987).

JEAN-FRANÇOIS BELLIS, born Waha, Belgium, June 7, 1949; admitted, 1972, Brussels. *Education:* University of Brussels (Lic. Jur., 1972); University of Michigan Law School (LL.M., 1974). Professor on EC Trade Law, University of Liège; Institute of European Studies, University of Brussels. Co-Author: "Anti-Dumping and Other Trade Protection Laws of the EEC," CCH, 3rd. ed., 1995; "EEC Competition Law," CCH, 3rd. ed., 1993. Legal Secretary to Lord Mackenzie Stuart, Court of Justice of the European Communities, 1979-1980. *Member:* European Trade Law Association (Founding Member); Union des Avocats Européens (Founding Member).

PHILIPPE DE BAERE, born Bruges, Belgium, June 5, 1961; admitted, 1988, Brussels. *Education:* University of Antwerp (Cand. Jur., 1981); University of Louvain (Lic. Jur., 1984; Cand. Pol. Sc., 1984). Fellow, University of Louvain, 1984-1986.

DAVID W. HULL, born Atlanta, Georgia, U.S.A., May 9, 1957; admitted, 1983, Georgia (Not admitted in Belgium). *Education:* Davidson College (B.A., 1979); University of Georgia (J.D., 1983); University of Brussels (Lic. Sp. European Law, 1984).

ANDRZEJ WINCENTY JOHN KMIECIK, born London, England, June 2, 1963; admitted, 1989, Solicitor, England and Wales (Not admitted in Belgium). *Education:* Merton College, Oxford (B.A., 1985); College of Law, London (1985-1987); College of Europe (Diploma of Advanced European Legal Studies, 1990).

PETER L'ECLUSE, born Roeselare, Belgium, May 16, 1963; admitted, 1987, Brussels. *Education:* University of Louvain (Ph.B., 1985; Lic. Jur., 1986); George Washington University (M.C.L., 1987). Teaching Assistant, EC Law, University of Louvain, 1990—.

OF COUNSEL

THE BARONESS DIANA ELLES, born 1922; Barrister-at-Law, Lincolns Inn, 1956. Member, House of Lords, 1972—; U.K. delegate to United Nations, 1972. U.K. delegate to European Parliament, 1973-1975. Member, European Parliament, 1979-1989, Vice-President, European Parliament, 1982-1987. Chairman, Legal Affairs Committee, European Parliament, 1987-1989. Chairman, Conservative Party International Office, 1973-1978. Opposition Spokesman on Foreign and European Affairs, 1975-1979. *Member:* Royal Institute of International Affairs (1974; Council Member, 1977-1986). Chairman, Institute of Directors' Advisory Council; Governor, Reading University; Governor, British Institute Florence; President, British Conservative Association in France; Trustee, Industry and Parliament Trust; Vice-President, United Kingdom Association of European Lawyers; Member, International Law Association.

ASSOCIATES

RAINER MICHAEL BIERWAGEN, born Weinheim, Germany, April 23, 1957; admitted, 1989, Germany (Not admitted in Belgium). *Education:* Universities of Heidelberg, Geneva and Freiburg; First State Examination, 1981; Legal Internship (Referendarzeit) 1984-1987; Second State Examination 1987; Research Fellow, University of Konstanz 1986-1989; Dr. Jur., 1989. Author: " GATT Article VI and the Protectionist Bias in Anti-Dumping Laws," Kluwer, 1990.

FABRIZIO DI GIANNI, born Naples, Italy, June 9, 1964; admitted, 1990, Rome (Not admitted in Belgium). *Education:* University of Naples (Lic. Jur., 1987); College of Europe (Diploma of Advanced European Legal Studies, 1989).

PASCAL FAES, born Wilrijk, Belgium, September 8, 1960; admitted, 1991, Belgium. *Education:* University of Gent (Lic. Jur., 1984); Special degree of Economics, University of Brussels; Diploma of tax management, University of Brussels. Lecturer in Tax Management at Vlekho, Brussels and at European Business School.

ROLAND MAYER, born Winterthur, Switzerland, February 25, 1964; (Not admitted in Belgium). *Education:* University of Neuchâtel, Switzerland (Lic. Jur., 1987); College of Europe (Diploma of Advanced European Legal Studies, 1989). Assistant of Legal Studies, College of Europe, 1989-1990.

(This Listing Continued)

RICHARD LUFF, born Barcelona, Spain, June 20, 1963; admitted, 1986, Brussels. *Education:* University of Brussels (Lic. Jur., 1986; Postgraduate degree in Economic Law, 1987; License spéciale en droit européen, 1989); London School of Economics (LL.M. in International Business and Finance Law, 1990).

CATHERINE LONGEVAL, born Sint Niklaas, Belgium, June 20, 1964; admitted, 1992, Belgium. *Education:* University of Louvain (Lic. Jur., 1987); Institute of European Studies, Brussels (LL.M., European Law, 1989).

DANIEL G. LAWTON, born Royal Oak, Michigan, U.S.A., June 18, 1963; admitted, 1988, Illinois (Not admitted in Belgium). *Education:* University of Michigan (A.B., 1985); Harvard University (J.D., 1988).

JOHANNES CHRISTIAN BONER, born Chur, Switzerland, October 6, 1963; (Not admitted in Belgium). *Education:* Fribourg University, Switzerland (Lic. Jur., 1988); Exeter University (1985); College of Europe (Diploma of Advanced European Legal Studies, 1989).

JEAN-MICHEL COUMES, born Toulouse, France, January 15, 1964; (Not admitted in Belgium). *Education:* University of Toulouse (Maîtrise, 1985; D.E.S.S. International Trade Law, 1986-1987); College of Europe (Diploma of Advanced European Legal Studies, 1989).

JAMES F.M. FLETT, born London, England, October 27, 1964; admitted, 1990, Solicitor, England and Wales (Not admitted in Belgium). *Education:* London School of Economics (LL.B., Law, 1987); College of Law, London (1987-1988); College of Europe (Diploma of Advanced European Legal Studies, 1991).

LAURENT L. GEELHAND DE MERXEM, born Paris, France, March 6, 1965; admitted, 1991, Brussels. *Education:* University of Brussels (Lic. Jur., 1988; LL.M., 1989); University of Washington School of Law (LL.M., 1990).

BENOIT SERVAIS, born Rocourt, Belgium, May 29, 1966; admitted, 1990, Brussels. *Education:* University of Liège (Lic. Jur., 1989); College of Europe (Diploma of Advanced European Legal Studies, 1990).

GUY EVANS, born Hillingdon, England, February 15, 1966; admitted, 1990, Barrister-at-Law (Not admitted in Belgium). *Education:* University of Kent (B.A., Hons., English/French Law, 1989); University of Bordeaux (Certificate of French Law, 1988); College of Europe (Diploma of Advanced European Legal Studies, 1991).

MARIA VILAR BADIA, born Barcelona, Spain, December 17, 1967; (Not admitted in Belgium). *Education:* University of Barcelona (Bachelor degree in Law, 1990); University of Exeter (LL.M., 1991). Intern with Directorate-General IV of the Commission of the European Communities, 1992.

CIARAN KEANEY, born Dublin, Ireland, July 29, 1965; admitted, 1991, Solicitor, Ireland (Not admitted in Belgium). *Education:* Trinity College Dublin (LL.B., 1987); University College Dublin (Diploma in European Law, 1989); Trinity College Dublin (M.A., 1990).

CECILE NEUVENS, born Namur, Belgium, June 26, 1965; admitted, 1990, Belgium. *Education:* University of Louvain-la-Neuve (Lic. Jur., 1988); College of Europe (Diploma of Advanced European Legal Studies, 1990); Duke University School of Law (LL.M., 1993).

SOPHIE DELODDERE, born Ronse, Belgium, April 12, 1966; admitted, 1992, Brussels. *Education:* University of Gent (Lic. Jur., 1989); University of Virginia (LL.M., 1992).

KRIS VAN HOVE, born Leuven, Belgium, December 30, 1965; admitted, 1992, Brussels. *Education:* University of Leuven (Lic. Jur., 1989); University of Paris (DSU, European Law, 1990); University of Duke (LL.M., 1992).

ERIK HELLNERS, born Göteborg, Sweden, March 2, 1965; (Not admitted in Belgium). *Education:* University of Uppsala (Jur. Kand., LL.M., 1991). Intern with the Swedish Delegation to the EC, 1992.

MARKUS WELLINGER, born Nyon, Switzerland, September 7, 1966; admitted, 1993, Brussels. *Education:* University of Brussels (Lic. Jur., 1989); Institute of European Studies, Brussels (M.A., European Law, 1991); University of Keele (M.A., Diplomatic Studies, 1992).

ISABELLE SEROIN, born Orange, France, November 28, 1968; admitted, 1992, Paris (Not admitted in Belgium). *Education:* University of Paris (Lic. Dr., 1990; Maîtrise, 1991; D.E.S.S., 1992); College of Europe (Diploma of Advanced European Legal Studies, 1993).

(This Listing Continued)

STEVEN DE SCHRIJVER, born Wilrijk, Belgium, May 10, 1969; admitted, 1993, Brussels. *Education:* University of Antwerp (Lic. Jur., 1992); University of Virginia (LL.M., 1993).

VANDERELST WIJCKMANS EVERAERT & WITTERS

FOUNTAIN PLAZA
BELGICASTRAAT 7
1930 ZAVENTEM (BRUSSELS), BELGIUM
Telephone: 32 2 725 60 63
Fax: 32 2 725 70 38

General Business and EC Law Practice.
Mergers and Acquisitions, Antitrust and Unfair Trade Practices Law, Distribution, Agency and Franchising, Labor Law, Food and Drug Law, Real Estate and Construction Law, Immigration Law, Litigation and Arbitration.

ALAIN VANDERELST, born Berchem (Antwerpen), Belgium, November 30, 1959; admitted, 1983, Brussels. *Education:* University of Antwerp (Lic. Jur., 1982); Georgetown University Law Center (LL.M., 1983). *Member:* Brussels Bar Association. **LANGUAGES:** Dutch, French and English. **PRACTICE AREAS:** Mergers and Acquisitions; Antitrust and Unfair Trade Practices Law; Distribution, Agency and Franchising.

FRANK WIJCKMANS, born Wilrijk (Antwerpen), Belgium, April 11, 1962; admitted, 1986, Brussels. *Education:* University of Antwerp (Lic. Jur., 1985); University of Virginia (LL.M., 1986). *Member:* Brussels Bar Association. **LANGUAGES:** Dutch, French and English. **PRACTICE AREAS:** Mergers and Acquisitions; Antitrust and Unfair Trade Practices Law; Litigation and Arbitration.

PIET EVERAERT, born Usumbura, Burundi, March 28, 1961; admitted, 1986, Brussels. *Education:* University of Louvain (Lic. Jur., 1984); College of Europe (Diploma in Advanced European Legal Studies, 1985). *Member:* Brussels Bar Association. **LANGUAGES:** Dutch, French and English. **PRACTICE AREAS:** Labor Law; Real Estate and Construction Law; Food and Drug Law; Immigration Law.

ANNE-MARIE WITTERS, born Hasselt, Belgium, June 26, 1963; admitted, 1988, Brussels. *Education:* University of Louvain (Lic. Jur., 1986); University of Georgia (LL.M., 1987). *Member:* Brussels Bar Association. **LANGUAGES:** Dutch, French and English. **PRACTICE AREAS:** Distribution, Agency and Franchising; Food and Drug Law; Litigation and Arbitration.

ADVOKATFIRMAN VINGE

AVENUE LOUISE 475/B12
B-1050 BRUSSELS, BELGIUM
Telephone: +32-2-646 36 20
Telefax: +32-2-646 41 46

Stockholm, Sweden Office: Smalandsgatan 20, P.O. Box 1703, S-111 87. Telephone: 08-614 30 00. Telex: 11150 VINGE S. Telefax: 08-611 90 37.

Gothenburg, Sweden Office: Nils Ericsonsgatan 17, P.O. Box 11025, S-404 21. Telephone: 031-80 51 00. Telex: 21119 VINGE S. Telefax: 031-15 88 11.

Malmö, Sweden Office: Östergatan 30, P.O. Box 4255, S-203 13. Telephone: 040-748 40. Telex: 8305122 VINGE S. Telefax: 040-97 27 72.

Helsingborg, Sweden Office: Kullagatan 60, P.O. Box 1064, S-251 10. Telephone: 042-18 33 70. Telefax: 042-18 23 04.

London, England Office: 44/45 Chancery Lane, WC2A 1JB. Telephone: +44-71 404 4825. Telex: 25585 VINGE G. Telefax: +44-71-831 6860.

Paris, France Office: 21 Rue Jean Goujon, F-75008. Telephone: +33 1 407 53 737. Telefax: +33 1 456 305 49.

Hong Kong Office: 2003 Hutchison House, 10 Harcourt Road, Central. Telephone: +852-5236 149. Telefax: +852-810 5343.

EC-Law, Swedish and International Law Practice, Contracts, Corporate, Transport, Foreign Investments in Scandinavia, Arbitration.

(This Listing Continued)

RESIDENT PARTNERS

CARL WETTER, born January 29, 1949. *Education:* University of Uppsala (filosofie kandidat, B.A., 1974; juris kandidat, LL.M.,1977). Swedish Ministry for Foreign Affairs, 1976-1977. Associated with the firm since 1977. *Member:* Swedish Bar Association (1983).

BJÖRN NICOLAI, born October 1, 1957. *Education:* University of Uppsala (juris kandidat, LL.M., 1985). Associated with the firm since 1985. *Member:* Swedish Bar Association (1991).

RESIDENT ASSOCIATES

RIKARD AZELIUS, born October 14, 1961. *Education:* University of Lund (juris kandidat, LL.M., 1987, civilekonom, M.B.A., 1987). Service in Swedish Courts, 1987-1989. Associate with Mannheimer Swartling Advokatbyrå, 1990-1994. Associated with the firm since 1994. *Member:* Swedish Bar Association (1993).

JESSICA KARLBERG LAGRELIUS, born July 12, 1964. *Education:* University of Uppsala (juris kandidat, LL.M., 1988). Service at the Swedish Competition Authority, 1988-1994. Associated with the firm since 1994.

VOGEL & VOGEL

AVENUE DU DIAMANT, 139
B-1040 BRUSSELS, BELGIUM
Telephone: (32) 2.735.34.28
Fax: (32) 2.735.49.30

Paris, France Office: 6, Avenue Pierre 1 er de Serbie, 75116. Telephone: (33.1) 53.67.76.20. Fax: (33.1) 53.67.76.75.

Frankfurt/Main, Germany Office: Kettenhofweg 29, D-60325. Telephone: (49) 69.7103616. Fax: (49) 69.722726.

Antitrust Law, European Community Law, International Business Law, International Investment Law, Mergers and Acquisitions, Product Distribution Law, Products Liability Law, Unfair Competition Law.

FIRM PROFILE: The firm offers a full range of legal services especially in the fields of Frendi and EEC, Antitrust Law, Distribution and General Business Law.

LOUIS VOGEL, born Saarbrücken, Germany, October 22, 1954; admitted, 1981, Paris; 1990, New York (Not admitted in Belgium). *Education:* Institut d'Etudes Politiques de Paris (Diplômé, 1976); Yale Law School (LL.M., 1982); University of Paris I (Panthéon-Sorbonne) and Paris II Law School (Panthéon-Assas), Doctor of Law (1985); Agrégé des Facultés de Droit (1989). Author: "Droit commercial européen," with B. Goldman and A. Lyon-Caem, 835p., Dalloz, 1994; "Le droit européen des affaires," Dalloz, 128 p., 2nd ed., 1994; "Droit de la concurrence et concentration économique," 427 p., Economica, 1988; "Chronique du droit de la concurrence," Revue du Marché Commun, 1991—; "Chronique Concurrence," Revue Contrats Concurrence Consommation, 1991—; "Chronique de jurisprudence communautaire," Semaine juridique, 1990—; "French Merger Law," Fordham Corporate Law Institute, 1990. Professor of Law, University of Paris Law School. Director, Juris Classeurs de droit international et de droit comparé. Director, Encyclopédie Dalloz de Droit Commercial. *Member:* American Bar Association; Comité Français de Droit International Privé; International Law Association; Société de Législation Comparée; Union des Avocats Européens; Association des juristes franco-allemands, Deutscher Anwaltverein. (Also at Paris, France Office). **LANGUAGES:** French, English and German. **PRACTICE AREAS:** Antitrust Law; European Community Law; International Business Law.

(For Biographical Data on all Personnel, see Professional Biographies at Paris, France)

WEIL, GOTSHAL & MANGES

A Partnership including Professional Corporations

1 PLACE MADOU, BOX 34
1030 BRUSSELS, BELGIUM
Telephone: 011-32-2-217-4003
Telecopier: 011-32-2-217-0215

New York, N.Y. Office: 767 Fifth Avenue. Telephone: 212-310-8000. Cable Address: "Wegoma". Telex: 424281; 423144. Telecopier: 212-310-8007.

Dallas, Texas Office: 100 Crescent Court, Suite 1300. Telephone: 214-746-7700. Fax: 214-746-7777.

(This Listing Continued)

WEIL, GOTSHAL & MANGES, Brussels—Continued

Houston, Texas Office: Suite 1600, 700 Louisiana Street. Telephone: 713-546-5000. Telecopier: 713-224-9511.

Menlo Park, California Office: 2882 Sand Hill Road, Suite 280. Telephone: 415-926-6200. Telecopier: 415-854-3713.

Miami, Florida Office: Suite 2100, 701 Brickell Avenue. Telephone: 305-577-3100. Telecopier: 305-374-7159.

Washington, D.C. Office: Suite 700, 1615 L Street, N.W. Telephone: 202-682-7000. Telecopier: 202-857-0939; 857-0940. Telex: 440045.

Budapest, Hungary Office: H-1065 Budapest, Revay Utca 10. Telephone: 011-361-269-1144. Fax: 011-361-269-1233.

Prague, Czechoslovakia Office: Charles Bridge Center, Krizovnicke nam. 1, 110 00 Prague 1, Czech Republic. Telephone: 011-42-2-24-09-73-00. Telecopier: 011-42-2-24-09-73-10.

Warsaw, Poland Office: ul Senatorska 12 00-082 Warsaw. Telephone: 011-48-22-27-61-44. Telecopier: 011-48-22-27-48-38.

General Practice.

RESIDENT PARTNER

RANDOLPH W. TRITELL, born Floral Park, New York, April 18, 1953; admitted, 1978, New York and District of Columbia (Not admitted in Belgium). *Education:* State University of New York at Stony Brook (B.A., 1974); University of Pennsylvania (J.D., 1977). Phi Beta Kappa. Editor, University of Pennsylvania Law Review. Adjunct Professor, Federal Trade Commission Law, New York University School of Law, 1989. Member, 1978-1986 and Executive Assistant to the Chairman, 1985-1986, Federal Trade Commission. *Member:* New York State (Member, Executive Committee, Section of Antitrust Law, 1990-1993; Chairman, Antitrust Exemptions Committee, 1990-1992), Federal (Chair, International Committee, Antitrust and Trade Regulation Section; Member, Editorial Board, Antitrust Law Developments) and American (Member, Sections on: Antitrust Law; International Law and Practice) Bar Associations.

(For complete biographical data on New York, New York, Dallas, Texas, Houston, Texas, Menlo Park, California, Miami, Florida, Washington, D.C., Budapest, Hungary, London, England, Prague, Czech Republic and Warsaw, Poland, see Professional Biographies at those locations)

WESSING BERENBERG-GOSSLER ZIMMERMANN LANGE

149 AVENUE LOUISE, BOX 42
B-1050 BRUSSELS, BELGIUM
Telephone: +32 (2) 537 01 86
Telefax: +32 (2) 534 25 31

Munich, Germany Office: Vilshofener Str. 8, D-81679 Munich, P.O. Box 86 08 67, D-81635 Munich. Telephone: 49-89-98 28 021. Telefax: 49-89-98 12 14.

Düsseldorf, Germany Office: Königsallee 92 A, D-40212 Düsseldorf, P.O. Box 10 53 61, D-40044 Düsseldorf. Telephone: 49-211-83 87-0. Telex: 858 19 14 wess d. Cable Address: "Wegolex". Telefax: 49-211-32 36 16.

Hamburg, Germany Office: Neuer Wall 46, D-20354 Hamburg. Telephone: 49-40-36 80 30. Cable Address: "Unilaw". Telex: 2-14111 Jura d. Teletex: 40 32 91 Unilaw. Telefax: 49-40-36 80 32 80.

Frankfurt, Germany Office: Freiherr-Vom-Stein-Strasse 24-26, D-60323 Frankfurt. Telephone: 49-69-971300. Telefax: 49-69-97130100.

Berlin, Germany Office: Spreeufer 5, D-10178 Berlin. Telephone: 49-30-238 45 45. Telefax: 49-30-238 45 34.

Leipzig, Germany Office: Ferdinand-Rhode-Strasse 16, D-04107 Leipzig. Telephone: 49-341-213 13 80. Fax: 49-341-213 13 88.

Dresden, Germany Office: Heinrichstrasse 16, D-01097 Dresden. Telephone: 49-351-567 12 12. Telefax: 49-351-567 12 13.

General Practice. Commercial, Corporation, International, Tax, Economic Criminality, Antitrust, Unfair Competition, Patent, Press, Copyright and Trademark Law. Foreign Investments in Brazil, Portugal and Mexico. Estate, EEC-Law, Bank Law, International Arbitration Proceedings.

WOLFGANG VON MEIBOM, born 1944; admitted, 1973, Germany (Not admitted in Belgium). *Education:* Universities of Bonn, Berlin, Fairfield University, Connecticut, 1966. *Member:* International Bar Association; Association for the Protection of Industrial Property and Copyright. *LANGUAGES:* English and French. *PRACTICE AREAS:* EC Law; Trade

(This Listing Continued)

Regulation; Antitrust; Intellectual Property; Patent; Trademark; Copyright; Competition; Licensing.

KLAUS-JÜRGEN MICHAELI, born 1943; admitted, 1973, Germany (Not admitted in Belgium). *Education:* University of Giessen; Georgetown Law School, Washington, D.C. Assistant at University of Giessen, 1971-1973. Prof. L.c. (BG). *Member:* International Bar Association; Association for the Protection of Industrial Property (Chairman of the Board, Section West); German-Italian Lawyers Association. *LANGUAGES:* English. *PRACTICE AREAS:* EC Law; Intellectual Property; Patent; Trade Mark; Copyright; Food and Drug; Trade Regulation; EC Law.

DR. WOLFGANG GAEBELEIN, born 1925; admitted, 1955, Germany (Not admitted in Belgium). *Education:* Universities of Jena and Frankfurt-/Main. Author: "Die Grenzen der Abänderbarkeit von Entscheidungen nach § 18 FGG," 1951. *Member:* Federal Association of German Industry, BDI (Chairman, Legal Committee, 1978). *LANGUAGES:* English and Portuguese. *PRACTICE AREAS:* Corporate; Trade Regulation; EC Law.

UTE ZINSMEISTER, born 1962; admitted, 1992, Düsseldorf and before the Court of Justice and the Court of First Instance of the European Communities in Luxembourg (Not admitted in Belgium). *Education:* University of Munich. *Member:* Belgian-German Association of Jurists; European Association of Lawyers. *LANGUAGES:* English and French. *PRACTICE AREAS:* EC Law.

WHITE & CASE

AVENUE LOUISE 306-310
B-1050 BRUSSELS, BELGIUM
Telephone: (32-2) 647-05-89
Facsimile: (32-2) 647-16-75

New York, New York: Telephone: 212-819-8200. Facsimile: 212-354-8113.

Washington, D.C.: Telephone: 202-872-0013. Facsimile: 202-872-0210.

Los Angeles, California: Telephone: 213-620-7700. Facsimile: 213-687-0758; 213-617-2205.

Miami, Florida: Telephone: 305-371-2700. Facsimile: 305-358-5744.

Mexico City, Mexico: Telephone: (52-5) 207-9717. Facsimile: (52-5) 208-3628.

Tokyo, Japan: Telephone: (81-3) 3239-4300. Facsimile: (81-3) 3239-4330.

Hong Kong: Telephone: (852) 2822-8700. Facsimile: (852) 2845-9070; Grice & Co., Solicitors, Telephone: (852) 2826-0333. Facsimile: (852) 2526-7166.

Singapore, Republic of Singapore: Telephone: (65) 225-6000. Facsimile: (65) 225-6009.

Bangkok, Thailand: Pacific Legal Group Ltd., In Association With White & Case, Telephone: (662) 236-6154/7. Facsimile: (662) 237-6771.

Hanoi, Viet Nam: Representative Office, Telephone: (84-4) 227-575/6/7. Facsimile: (84-4) 227-297.

Bombay, India: Telephone: (91-22) 282-6300. Facsimile: (91-22) 282-6305.

London, England: Telephone: (44-171) 726-6361. Facsimile: (44-171) 726-4314; (44-171) 726-8558.

Paris, France: Telephone: (33-1) 42-60-34-05. Facsimile: (33-1) 42-60-82-46.

Stockholm, Sweden: Telephone: (46-8) 679-80-30. Facsimile: (46-8) 611-21-22.

Helsinki, Finland: Telephone: (358-0) 631-100. Facsimile: (358-0) 179-477.

Moscow, Russia: Telephone: (7-095) 201-9292/3/4/5. Facsimile: (7-095) 201-9284.

Budapest, Hungary: Telephone: (36-1) 269-0550; (36-1) 131-0933. Facsimile: (36-1) 269-1199.

Prague, Czech Republic: Telephone: (42-2) 2481-1796. Facsimile: (42-2) 232-5522.

Warsaw, Poland: Telephone/Facsimile: (48-22) 26-80-53; (48-22) 27-84-86. International Telephone/Facsimile: (48-39) 12-19-06.

Istanbul, Turkey: Telephone: (90-212) 275-68-98; (90-212) 275-75-33. Facsimile: (90-212) 275-75-43.

Ankara, Turkey: Telephone: (90-312) 446-2180. Facsimile: (90-312) 437-9677.

Jeddah, Saudi Arabia: Law Office of Hassan Mahassni, Telephone: (966-2) 651-3535. Facsimile: (966-2) 651-3636.

Riyadh, Saudi Arabia: Law Office of Hassan Mahassni, Telephone: (966-1) 476-7099. Facsimile: (966-1) 479-0110.

Almaty, Kazakhstan: Telephone: (7-3272) 50-7491/2. Facsimile: (7-3272) 61-0842.

(This Listing Continued)

General International Practice but not authorized to appear before Belgian Courts.

RESIDENT ASSOCIATES

PONTUS LINDFELT, born Sollefteå, Sweden, February 23, 1961; (Not admitted in Belgium). *Education:* University of Lund (juris kandidat LL.B., LL.M., 1988).

MARGARET G. WACHENFELD, born Orange, New Jersey, March 19, 1961; admitted, 1990, New York (Not admitted in Belgium). *Education:* Wellesley College (B.A., 1983); Duke University (LL.M.; J.D., 1989); University of Copenhagen, Ph.D., 1992).

(For biographical data as to other locations, see Professional Biographies at New York, New York; Washington, D.C.; Los Angeles, California; Miami, Florida; Mexico City, Mexico; Tokyo, Japan; Hong Kong; Singapore, Republic of Singapore; Bangkok, Thailand; Hanoi, Viet Nam; Bombay, India; London, England; Paris, France; Stockholm, Sweden; Helsinki, Finland; Moscow, Russia; Budapest, Hungary; Prague, Czech Republic; Warsaw, Poland; Istanbul and Ankara, Turkey; Jeddah and Riyadh, Saudi Arabia; Almaty, Kazakhstan).

WILDE SAPTE

27 AVENUE DES ARTS
1040 BRUSSELS, BELGIUM
Telephone: (32-2) 280 1404
Facsimile: (32-2) 280 1764

London, England Office: 1, Fleet Place, EC4M 7WS. Telephone: 0171-246 7000. Facsimile: 0171-246 7777. Telex: 887793 lde/cde 145.

Hong Kong Office: 31st Floor, One Exchange Square. Telephone: (852) 2810 5081. Facsimile: (852) 2810 1295.

New York, New York Office: 19th Floor, 450 Lexington Avenue, 10017. Telephone: (212) 867 4530. Facsimile: (212) 557 4451.

Paris, France Office: 217 rue du Faubourg St. Honoré, 75008. Telephone: (33-1) 44 95 02 70. Facsimile: (33-1) 42 89 62 25.

Tokyo, Japan Office: 2nd Floor, AIG Building, 1-1-3 Marunouchi, Chiyoda-ku 100. Telephone: (81-3) 3215 3801. Facsimile: (81-3) 3215 3868.

Lloyd's Office: 40 Lime Street, London, EC3M 5DG. Telephone: 0171 246 7000. Fax: 0171 246 7722.

Banking, Corporate Lending, Acquisition Finance, Aviation, Shipping, Leasing, Work-outs, Trade Finance, Structured Finance, Project Finance, Insolvency, Property, Insurance, Employment, Charities, EC Law and Company and Commercial.

FIRM PROFILE: Wilde Sapte's European Group, with members in the Brussels, Paris and London offices, deals with a wide variety of Community law matters. The Brussels office handles the interests of client in the European forum, offering specific advice on Community law matters and providing a centre for pan-European transactions. Wilde Sapte has a general commercial practice and is particularly active in the fields of banking and finance, competition, transport and aviation, mergers and acquisitions, information technology and environmental law.

CONTACT PARTNERS

Steven Blakeley

(For complete list of all personnel, see Professional Biographies at London, England)

WILMER, CUTLER & PICKERING

RUE DE LA LOI 15 WETSTRAAT
B-1040 BRUSSELS, BELGIUM
Telephone: (32 2) 231-0903
Facsimile: (32 2) 230-4322

Washington, D.C. Office: 2445 M Street, N.W., 20037-1420. Telephone: 202-663-6000. Facsimile: 202-663-6363. Internet: Law@Wilmer.Com.

London, England Office: 4 Carlton Gardens, London, SW1Y 5AA. Telephone: (44 71) 839-4466. Facsimile: (44 71) 839-3537.

Berlin, Germany Office: Friedrichstrasse 95, D-10117. Telephone: (49 30) 2643-3601. Facsimile: (49 30) 2643-3630.

General Practice.
Firm engaged in European, American, and International Law Practice, but not authorized to appear before the Belgian Courts.

(This Listing Continued)

RESIDENT PARTNERS AND COUNSEL

W. SCOTT BLACKMER, born November 7, 1952; admitted, 1983, District of Columbia (Not admitted in Belgium). *Education:* Brigham Young University; University of Grenoble; University of Nevada (B.A., 1975); University of California at Berkeley (J.D., 1981). Editor-in-Chief, California Law Review. Clerk to Judge Marc Poché, California Court of Appeals; Judge William Schwarzer, N.D. California. Editorial Board, The Computer Lawyer (Contributing Editor on Telecommunications and EC Developments).

PAUL A. VON HEHN, born January 16, 1950; admitted, 1981, Germany (Not admitted in Belgium). *Education:* University of Tübingen. First State Examination, (1978); Second State Examination, (1981). Columbia University (LL.M., 1983); University of East Asia, Macau (Diploma in Chinese Law, 1989).

JAMES S. VENIT, born February 14, 1946; admitted, 1980, New York (Not admitted in Belgium). *Education:* Yale University (B.A., 1967); Columbia University (M.A., 1971; Ph.D., 1976); New York University (J.D., 1979). Editor, New York University Law Review. Author, *Oedipus Rex: Recent Developments in the Structural Approach to Joint Ventures Under EEC Competition Law,* 14 Journal of World Competition Law 5 (1991); *The Evaluation of Concentrations Under the Merger Control Regulation: The Nature of the Beast,* 14 Fordham International Law Journal 412 (1990-1991).

DR. ANDREAS WEITBRECHT, born November 14, 1947; admitted, 1986, Germany (Not admitted in Belgium). *Education:* University of Bonn. First State Examination (1974); Second State Examination (1979). University of California at Berkeley (LL.M., 1984); University of Augsburg (Dr. Jur., 1986). Assistant Professor (European Community Law, International Competition Law, and Administrative Regulation of Business), Augsburg University, 1980-1985.

MARC C. HANSEN, born January 2, 1960; admitted, 1985, New York; 1990, Denmark (Not admitted in Belgium) (Not admitted in Belgium). *Education:* University of Nice (Faculty of Law, 1978-1979); University of Copenhagen (Cand. Jur., 1983); University of Michigan (LL.M., 1984). Co-author, *Collective Dominance Under the EC Merger Regulation,* 30 Common Market Law Review 787 (1993); *The GATT Protocol of Provisional Application: A Dying Grandfather?* 27 Columbia Journal of Transnational Law 263 (1989).

ASSOCIATES

CHRISTIAN L. DUVERNOY, born October 3, 1962; admitted, 1989, New York; 1990, District of Columbia. *Education:* Harvard University (A.B., 1984); Free University of Berlin; University of Michigan (J.D., 1988). Author, *European Community Rules of Origin,* 2 ABA International Trade Committee Newsletter 7 (Summer 1989). Stagiaire, Court of Justice of the European Communities.

DR. CONSTANTIN VON ALVENSLEBEN, born May 16, 1962; admitted, 1992, Germany. *Education:* University of Bonn; Free University of Berlin; First State Examination (1988). University of Bonn (Dr. jur. 1991). Second State Examination (1992). Author, Die Rechte der Arbeitnehmer bei Betriebsübergangen im EG-Recht (1992).

SARAH WAYWELL, born April 12, 1965; admitted as Solicitor, 1990, England and Wales (Not admitted in District of Columbia). *Education:* Universities of Leicester and Strasbourg (LL.B., Hons., Diplôme d'Etudes Juridiques, Françaises, 1987).

(For Complete Biographical Data on all Personnel, see Professional Biographies at Washington, D.C.)

WINTHROP, STIMSON, PUTNAM & ROBERTS

RUE DU TACITURNE 42
BRUSSELS B-1040, BELGIUM
Telephone: 011-322-230-1392
Telefax: 011-322-230-9288

New York Main Office: One Battery Park Plaza. New York, N.Y., 10004-1490. Telephone: 212-858-1000.

Stamford, Connecticut Office: Financial Centre, 695 East Main Street, P.O. Box 6760, 06904-6760. Telephone: 203-348-2300.

Washington, D.C. Office: 1133 Connecticut Avenue, N.W., 20036. Telephone: 202-775-9800.

(This Listing Continued)

WINTHROP, STIMSON, PUTNAM & ROBERTS,
Brussels—Continued

Palm Beach, Florida Office: 125 Worth Avenue, 33480. Telephone: 407-655-7297.

London Office: 2 Throgmorton Avenue, London EC2N 2AP, England. Telephone: 011-4471-628-4931.

Toyko, Japan Office: 608 Atagoyama Bengoshi Building 6-7, Atago 1-chome, Minato-ku, Tokyo 105 Japan. Telephone: 011-813-3437-9740.

Hong Kong Office: 2505 Asia Pacific Finance Tower, Citibank Plaza, 3 Garden Road Central. Telephone: 011-852-530-3400.

Firm engaged in American and International Law Practice, but not authorized to appear before the Belgium Courts.

MEMBER OF FIRM

RAYMOND S. CALAMARO, born Cairo, Egypt, May 28, 1944; admitted, 1970, New York; 1975, U.S. Supreme Court; 1976, District of Columbia (Not admitted in Belgium). Education: Cornell University (A.B., 1966); New York University (J.D., 1969). Associate Editor, New York University Journal of International Law and Politics, 1968-1969. Legislative Director for U.S. Senator Gaylord Nelson, 1973-1975. Deputy Assistant U.S. Attorney General, 1976-1979. Clinton-Gore Transition Team Leader, 1992-1993. Member: Association of the Bar of the City of New York; The District of Columbia Bar.

RESIDENT ASSOCIATES

JON G. FILIPEK, born Alexandria, Virginia, March 15, 1961; admitted, 1988, Virginia; 1989, District of Columbia; 1993, New York (Not admitted in Belgium). Education: University of Virginia (B.A., 1983); Harvard University (J.D., 1988). Phi Beta Kappa. Author: "Agriculture in the Uruguay Round," 30 Harvard Int'l L.J. 123, 1989. Member: The District of Columbia Bar; Virginia State Bar; American Bar Association (Member, International Law Section). LANGUAGES: Spanish.

RITA RIQUE-PEARSON, born Los Angeles, California, December 19, 1964. Education: Yale College (B.A., 1987); Harvard University (J.D., 1991). Legal Advisor to Member of the European Parliament, Brussels, 1991-1993. LANGUAGES: Spanish, French.

BERNARD SPINOIT

Correspondent Office Stewart and Stewart, Washington, D.C.

BOULEVARD DEWANDRE 13
B-6000 CHARLEROI, BELGIUM
Telephone: (071) 32-51-31
Telex: 51769
Telefax: (0) 71.32.35.26

General and International Practice. Customs and International Trade Law, Antidumping and Countervailing Duty Law.

MEMBERS OF FIRM

BERNARD SPINOIT, born Louvain, Belgium, February 8, 1954; admitted, 1979, Charleroi. Education: Université Catholique de Louvain (Ph.B., 1976; J.D., 1979; B.A. cum laude, Economics, 1980; M.A., cum laude, Economics, 1981); Georgetown University (LL.M., 1982); George Washington University (M.B.A., 1982). Phi Alpha Delta. Fulbright Scholar. Co-Author: with Alexis Jacquemin, "Economic and Legal Aspects of Cooperative Research: A European View," CEPS Working Document No. 16 (Economic), Brussels, Centre for European Policy Studies, November 1985. Collaborated with Alexis Jacquemin, Compétition Européenne et Coopération entre Entreprises en Matière de Recherche-Development, Luxembourg, Office des publications Officielles des Communautés Européennes, 1986, 124. Member: American Bar Association; International Bar Association; American Society of International Law. (Also of Counsel to Stewart & Stewart, Washington, D.C.). LANGUAGES: English, French, Dutch and German.

ANNE WESE, born Vilvoorde, Belgium, December 5, 1952; admitted, 1980, Charleroi. Education: University of Louvain (J.D., 1977, licence en notariat, 1978).

Languages: French, English, Dutch and German.

ADVOCATENKANTOOR CALLANT & SEGHERS
VOLDERSSTRAAT 42-44
9000 GHENT, BELGIUM
Telephone: 32-9-2241226
Fax: 32-9-2330237

EEC Law, Private International Law, Commercial Law, Debt Collection, Insurance Law, Litigation and General Practice.

MEMBERS OF FIRM

Marc Callant
Jan Seghers
Dominique Morel de Westgaver
Luc De Muynck

Wolfgang Winter
Gerhard Frank
Jean-Pierre Durieux
Christophe Desurmont

Member of Eurojuris, International Network of Lawyers

Languages: Dutch, French, Italian, English and German

D. VAN DE GEHUCHTE & PARTNERS
Established in 1975
HOOGSTRAAT 35
B 9000 GHENT, BELGIUM
Telephone: (0) 9.225.71.57; (0) 9.225.76.31; (0) 9.225.78.05
Telefax: (0) 9.224.18.70

Member of Branson EEIG with offices in: Goes, Netherlands; Paris, Lyon and Montpellier, France; Madrid, Spain; Bergen, Norway.

Social Law, Mergers and Acquisitions, Products Liability, Corporate Law, European Community Law, Finance, Administrative Law, Constitutional Law, Insurance, Commercial Law, Transportation, Company Law, Contracts, Social Security Law, Construction Law, Family Law, Fiscal Law, Motor Vehicle Insurance, Criminal Law, Civil Law, Maritime Law and Air Transport, International Private Law, Law of Arbitration, Tax Law, Czechoslovak Law.

FIRM PROFILE: The office offers a general practice oriented towards commercial, industrial and financial clients. The lawyers/attorneys may represent clients for all Belgian courts, before the European court of justice and the Benelux court of justice and are admitted to plead before all courts of the member states of the common market.

MEMBERS OF FIRM

DIRK VAN DE GEHUCHTE, born Ghent, Belgium, January 17, 1953; admitted, 1975, Ghent. Education: University of Ghent (distinction, 1975). Author: "De Competitie Tussen Openbare en Private Instellingen in de Kredietsector," Kluwer, 1976; "Product Liability," LVZ, 1989; CED-SAMSON, 1990. Co-Author: "Acquisition and Stopping of a Business"; "Czechoslovakia a new way paved with a new legislation," Kluwer, 1990; "The New Law on Product Liability," Kluwer, 1991. Co-Author: with Dany Cornelis: "Environmental Liabilities: the Obligation to Disclose," Kluwer Int., 1993. Member: Flemish Bar Conference; Association of Fellows and Legal Scholars of the Center of International Legal Studies, Salzburg, Austria (Honorary Member); International Bar Association. LANGUAGES: Dutch, French and English. PRACTICE AREAS: Social Law; Mergers and Acquisitions Law; Product Liability Law; Corporate Law.

ASSOCIATES

PHILIPPE JANSSEN, born Waregem, Belgium, February 28, 1962; admitted, 1986, Ghent. Education: State University Ghent (Licentiaat, 1986). LANGUAGES: Dutch, English and French. PRACTICE AREAS: Motor Vehicle Insurance Law; Criminal Law; Contracts; Civil Liability Law; Family Law.

PETER DE PELSEMAEKER, born Ghent, Belgium, September 12, 1958; admitted, 1983, Ghent. Education: University of Ghent (1983). LANGUAGES: Dutch, French and English. PRACTICE AREAS: Commercial Law; Company Law; Law of Contracts; Social Security Law; Finance.

LINDA DE CONINCK, born Ghent, Belgium, March 7, 1965; admitted, 1990, Ghent. Education: Rijksuniversiteit Ghent (1990). LANGUAGES: Dutch, French and English. PRACTICE AREAS: Social Law; Company Law; Family Law; Contracts.

MYRIAM GHYSELEN, born Dendermonde, Belgium, April 23, 1967; admitted, 1990, Ghent. Education: Rijksuniversiteit Ghent (great distinction, 1990). Assistant, University of Ghent. LANGUAGES: Dutch,

(This Listing Continued)

French, English and German. *PRACTICE AREAS:* Tax Law; Commercial Law.

COLLABORATORS

LUC BUYST, born Ghent, Belgium, August 15, 1968; admitted, 1991, Ghent. *Education:* Rijksuniversiteit Ghent (1991). *LANGUAGES:* Dutch, French and English. *PRACTICE AREAS:* Commercial Law; Family Law; Contracts.

DANY CORNELIS, born Dendermonde, Belgium, February 4, 1967; admitted, 1991, Ghent. *Education:* Katholieke Universiteit Leuven (1990); Baccalaureaat Bedrijfseconomie Leuven (1991). Co-Author: with Dirk Van de Gehuchte: "Environmental Liabilities: the Obligation to Disclose," Kluwer Int., 1993. *LANGUAGES:* Dutch, French and English. *PRACTICE AREAS:* Commercial Law; Social Law; Company Law.

PASCALE ROOSE, born Oostende, Belgium, June 19, 1967; admitted, 1992, Ghent. *Education:* Rijksuniversiteit Gent (Licentiaat in de Rechtsgeleerdheid, 1991); Vlerick School voor Management (Licentiaat in de fiscaliteit en het boekhoudkundig onderzoek). *LANGUAGES:* Dutch, French and English. *PRACTICE AREAS:* Fiscal Law; Commercial Law; Economical Law.

JOHAN MATTHIEU, born Aalst, Belgium, February 5, 1968; admitted, 1993, Ghent. *Education:* Rijksuniversiteit Gent (Licentiaat in de Rechtsgeleerdheid, 1992); Vrije Universiteit Brussel (Licentiaat in de Fiscaliteit). *LANGUAGES:* Dutch, French and English. *PRACTICE AREAS:* Fiscal Law; Commercial Law; Economical Law.

Languages: Dutch, French, English and German

LOEFF CLAEYS VERBEKE

13 RUE SIMONON
(PLACE DE BRONCKART)
4000 LIÈGE, BELGIUM
Telephone: 32-41-527722
Telecopier: 32-41-527511

Amsterdam, The Netherlands Office: 15 Apollolaan, P.O. Box 75088, 1070 AB. Telephone: 31-20-5741200. Telex: 14292. Telecopier: 31-20-6718775.

Brussels, Belgium Office: 268 A Avenue de Tervueren, A-1150. Telephone: 02-778.22.11. Fax: 02-763.21.85.

Antwerp, Belgium Office: "De Hertoghe", 8th Floor, 92 Desguinlei, B.8, B-2018. Telephone: 32.3.2385656. Telex: 72748 (EURLAWB). Telecopier: 32.3.2387877.

New York, New York Office: Swiss Bank Tower, 23rd Floor, 10 East 50th Street, 10022. Telephone: 212-759-9000. Fax: 212-759-9018.

Paris, France Office: 1, Avenue Franklin D. Roosevelt, 75008. Telephone: 33-1-49539125. Telecopier: 33-1-42891460.

Rotterdam, The Netherlands Office: 70 Weena, P.O. Box 74, 3000 AB. Telephone: 31-10-4034777. Telex: 23395 (LEX NL). Telecopier: 31-10-4149388.

Singapore Office: 20 Raffles Place, #08-03, Ocean Towers, Singapore 0104. Telephone: 65-5335332. Telecopier: 65-5330313.

Tokyo Office: NSE Building, 5th Floor, 1-7-1 Kanda Jinbo-cho, Chiyoda-ku, Tokyo 101, Japan. Telephone: 81-3-32599831. Fax: 81-3-32599888.

Barcelona, Spain Office: 550, 4° 1A, Av. Diagonal, 08021. Telephone: 34-3-2007117. Telecopier: 34-3-2023098.

Madrid, Spain Office: Balañá Eguía, Antonio Mauro 7, 5°, 28014. Telephone: 34-1-5312501. Telecopier: 34-1-5313530.

Jakarta, Indonesia Associated Office: Ali Budiardjo, Nugroho, Reksodiputro, Niaga Tower, 24th floor, Jalan Jenderal Sudirman Kav. 58, 12920. Telephone: 62.21.2505125/2505136. Telecopier: 62.21.2505121/2505001.

Luxembourg, Luxembourg Office: Zeyen Beghin Feider. 67, Rue Ermesinde, P.O. Box 5017, 1050. Telephone: 352.468946. Telex: 60736 (zflaw lu). Telecopier: 352.468947.

Belgian Attorneys may represent clients before all Belgian Courts, before the European Court of Justice and the Benelux Court of Justice, and are admitted to plead before all Courts of the Memberstates of the Common Market (EEC).

(This Listing Continued)

MEMBERS OF FIRM

JEAN-PIERRE BOURS, born 1945; admitted, 1972, Liège. *Education:* University of Liège (U.Lg.) (Dr. Jur., 1968) degree Fiscal Sciences, 1969). Professor Ecole des Hautes Etudes Commerciales de Liège. *Member:* International Fiscal Association.

ASSOCIATES

VINCENT BERNARD, born 1964; admitted, 1993, Liège. *Education:* University of Liège (U.Lg.) (Lic. Jur., 1987); Collège d'Europe (Bruges) (degree European Studies, 1988).

MARIE-PAULE HANSENNE, born 1954; admitted, 1986, Liège. *Education:* University of Liège (U.Lg.) (Lic. Jur., 1978).

JEAN-PAUL LACOMBLE, born 1966; admitted, 1992, Liège. *Education:* University of Liège (Lic. Jur., 1989).

ALBERT DOMINIQUE LEJEUNE, born 1961; admitted, 1994, Liège. *Education:* University of Liège (U.Lg.) (Lic. Jur., 1989).

JOËLLE MICHA, born 1969; admitted, List of Stagiaires 1993, Liège. *Education:* University of Louvain (U.C.L.) (Lic. Jur., 1993).

NATHALIE PIROTTE, born 1967; admitted, List of Stagiaires 1991 Liège. *Education:* University of Liège (U.Lg.) (Lic. Jur., 1991).

(For Personnel and other data, see Professional Biographies at Amsterdam, Antwerp, Barcelona, Brussels, New York, Paris, Rotterdam, Singapore and Tokyo)

MATRAY, MATRAY ET HALLET

Société Civile d'Avocats à Forme Coopérative

Established in 1944

34/24, BOULEVARD FRÈRE-ORBAN
4000 LIEGE, BELGIUM
Telephone: (32) (41) 52 70 68
Telex: macoha 42330
Telecopier: (32) (41) 52 08 57

Cologne, Germany Office: Matray und Partner. Friesenplatz, 17a, D-50672 Cologne. Telephone: (49) (221) 52 25 13. Telex: 888 5 332 heid. Telecopier: (49) (221) 52 52 60.

Brussels, Belgium Office: Matray, Matray & Hallet. Avenue Louise, 500/9, 1050. Telephone: 32-2-647.79.80. Telecopier: 32-2-640.70.71.

General and International Practice, Commercial, Corporation, Labor Law, Tax, EEC, International Arbitration.

MEMBERS OF FIRM

LAMBERT MATRAY, born Liege, Belgium, June 6, 1921; admitted, 1944, Liege. *Education:* University of Liege (Dr. Jur., 1944). *LANGUAGES:* French, German and Dutch. *PRACTICE AREAS:* Commercial Law; Company Law; Commercial Arbitration.

DIDIER MATRAY, born Liege, Belgium, June 5, 1951; admitted, 1973, Liege. *Education:* University of Liege (Lic. Dr., 1973). *LANGUAGES:* French, German, English and Italian. *PRACTICE AREAS:* Commercial Law; Finance; Banking; Mergers and Acquisitions; Corporate Law; Commercial Arbitration.

PHILIPPE HALLET, born Liege, Belgium, September 9, 1950; admitted, 1973, Liege. *Education:* University of Liege (Lic. Dr., 1973). *LANGUAGES:* French. *PRACTICE AREAS:* Labour and Employment; Social Law.

CHARLY HANOT, born St-Josse, Belgium, July 12, 1946; admitted, 1970, Liege. *Education:* University of Liege (Dr. Jur., 1969). *LANGUAGES:* French. *PRACTICE AREAS:* Civil Law; Contracts; Debtor and Creditor; Family Law; Property.

PIERRE LEJEUNE, born November 13, 1957; admitted, 1981, Liege. *Education:* University of Louvain, U.C.L. (Lic. Dr., 1981). *LANGUAGES:* French. *PRACTICE AREAS:* Administrative Law; Banking; Environmental Law.

BRUNO LHOEST, born August 1, 1959; admitted, 1986, Liege. *Education:* University of Liege (Lic. Dr., 1985). *LANGUAGES:* French and English. *PRACTICE AREAS:* Family Law; Insurance; Leases and Leasing.

ANDREA TILGENKAMP, born September 1, 1966; admitted, 1989, Liège. *Education:* University of Louvain (Lic. Dr., 1989).

(This Listing Continued)

MATRAY, MATRAY ET HALLET, Liege—Continued

ASSOCIATES

WANDA VOGEL, born December 8, 1956; admitted, 1980, Liége. *Education:* University of Liége (Lic. Dr., 1980). Legal Secretary, Court of Justice EC, 1985-1990. *LANGUAGES:* French, German, English and Dutch. *PRACTICE AREAS:* Belgian and EC Competition Law; Mergers and Acquisitions; General EC Practice.

EBERHARD DALLUGE, born October 2, 1947; admitted, 1983, Bonn (Not admitted in Belgium). *Education:* University of Bonn. *LANGUAGES:* German, French and English. *PRACTICE AREAS:* Civil Law; Debtor and Creditor; Insurance.

GENEVIÈVE TUTS, born July 26, 1966; admitted, 1990, Liège. *Education:* University of Liège (Lic. Dr., 1989); University of Brussels (Lic in European Law, 1990). *LANGUAGES:* French and English. *PRACTICE AREAS:* Labor Law; Social Law.

ISABELLE HOCK, born March 1, 1969; admitted, 1991, Liége. *Education:* University of Liége (Lic. Dr., 1991). *LANGUAGES:* French and German. *PRACTICE AREAS:* Civil Law; Commercial Law; Human Rights.

CHRISTINE BRÜLS, born October 17, 1968; admitted, 1992, Liége. *Education:* University of Louvain (Lic. Dr., 1992); Magister Legum WWU, 1992. *LANGUAGES:* German, French, English and Dutch. *PRACTICE AREAS:* General Practice.

GWENDOLINE PARTSCH, born July 28, 1970; admitted, 1992, Liège. *Education:* University of Liège (Lic. Dr., 1992). *LANGUAGES:* French, English, German and Dutch. *PRACTICE AREAS:* Administrative Law.

SIMON-PIERRE CARDON, born January 30, 1970; admitted, 1993, Liège. *Education:* University of Louvain (Lic. Dr., 1993). *LANGUAGES:* French and Dutch. *PRACTICE AREAS:* General Practice.

OLIVIER KELLENS, born April 29, 1970; admitted, 1994, Liège. *Education:* University of Liège (Lic. Dr., 1993). *LANGUAGES:* French, Dutch and English. *PRACTICE AREAS:* General Practice.

NICOLAS THIRION, born July 15, 1971; admitted, 1994, Liège. *Education:* University of Liège (Lic. Dr., 1994). *LANGUAGES:* French, Dutch and English. *PRACTICE AREAS:* General Practice.

SCHUERMANS & SCHUERMANS

Established in 1931

DE MERODELEI 112
B-2300 TURNHOUT, BELGIUM
Telephone: (32) 14-437718
Telefax: (32) 14-424059

General National and International Practice. Commercial, Insurance and Intellectual Property Law.

RAYMOND SCHUERMANS (1906-1994).

LUC SCHUERMANS, born 1940; admitted, 1963, Belgium. *Education:* University of Louvain (Dr. Jur., Lic. Not., 1963); Facolta di Giurisprudenza, Roma (Research Fellow, National Science Foundation, 1964-1965); Harvard University Law School (LL.M., 1966). Professor of Law, University of Antwerp, 1974—.

JOZEF A. KEUSTERMANS, born 1961; admitted, 1986, New York; 1988, Belgium. *Education:* University of Louvain (Lic. Jur., 1984); University of California at Los Angeles, School of Law (LL.M., 1985). Researcher, Center for Intellectual Property Rights, Leuven, Brussels, 1989—.

EMIEL KERSEMANS, born 1945; admitted, 1971, Belgium. *Education:* University of Louvain (Dr. Jur., 1969; Lic. Not., 1970); University of Amsterdam (Post Graduate Degree on European Integration, 1970).

INGRID M. ARCKENS, born 1961; admitted, 1986, Belgium. *Education:* University of Louvain (Lic. Jur., 1984); New York University School of Law (LL.M., 1986).

KATRIEN VAN MIERLO, born 1964; admitted, 1988, Belgium. *Education:* University of Ghent (Lic. Jur., 1988).

JAN SURMONT, born 1967; admitted, 1991, Belgium. *Education:* University of Poitiers (Erasmus) and Louvain (Lic. Jur., 1990); Université de Louvain (Licencié de droit économique, 1991).

VERA HUYSMANS, born 1968; admitted, 1991, Belgium. *Education:* University of Saarbrücken (Erasmus) and Antwerp (Lic. Jur., 1991).

(This Listing Continued)

PAUL VAN ROMPAEY, born 1965; admitted, 1992, Belgium. *Education:* University of Louvain (Lic. Jur., 1988; Lic. Not., 1989); Illinois Institute of Technology, Chicago-Kent School of Law (LL.M., M.A.L.S., 1990).

PETER TEERLINCK, born 1968; admitted, 1992, Belgium. *Education:* University of Namur, Siena (Erasmus) and Louvain (Lic. Jur., 1991); University of Brussels (Licencié de droit européen, 1992).

BART CLAESSENS, born 1970; admitted, 1993, Belgium. *Education:* University of Ghent (Lic. Jur., 1992); Mc Gill University (1993).

Languages: Dutch, French, English, Italian and German.

GEVAERT PLC

13-14 SASSTRAAT
VEURNE 8630, BELGIUM
Telephone: 58-31.13.51
Telecopier: 58-31.44.17

Commercial Law, Computer Law.

HUGO M.I. GEVAERT, born De Panne, Belgium, February 29, 1936; admitted, 1960, Belgium. *Education:* College Veurne (Latin-Greek Studies, 1954); University Gent (Law Degree, 1959). Author: *Legal Prevention in Computercontracts,* Edited by die Keure, Bruges, Belgium, 1982; *Computer & Insurance,* Ced-Samsom, 1986; "Checklist Computer," Ced-Samsom, 1987; Checklist Computercontracts (Flemish and French, second edition). Professor, Vlerick School of Management, a.o. Member, Editorial Board, Silex Law Journal, 1985-1986. Columnist, 1983— and General Counsel, 1983—, Datanews, Computermagazine. Lecturer: I.P.O., Institute for Post University Studies, University U.F.S.I.A., Antwerp, 1981— and E.M.S.A. EHSAL Brussels, 1981—; Computable Information Seminars, Holland, 1986—. Foreign Contributor, Rutgers Computer & Technology Law Journal, USA, 1986—. Member, International Editorial Advisory Board of Software Protection, Law & Technology Press, USA, 1986—. President, Flemish Association Technology and Law, 1984—. Secretary General, Belgian Telecom Users Association, 1983-1988. Chairman, Bar Counsel, 1982-1984 and 1986-1988. *Member:* Belgian Association for Computers and the Law; Dutch Association of Copyright. [Major Reserve Air Force]. *LANGUAGES:* Flemish, Dutch, French, English and German.

BULGARIA

IVO BAEV
ATTORNEY AT LAW

Established in 1989

29 FERDINANDOVA STREET
BURGAS 8000, BULGARIA
Telephone: 359-56-47010
Fax: 359-56-42491

Business Law, Taxes, Company Law, Commercial Law, Criminal Law, Inheritance Law, Real Estate and Litigation, Foreign Investment, Privatisation.

IVO BAEV, born Burgas, Bulgaria, August 22, 1957; admitted, 1984, Bulgaria as Barrister. *Education:* Sofia University (Law Degree, 1982). *Member:* Burgas Bar Association; Union of Bulgarian Lawyers; International Bar Association. *LANGUAGES:* Bulgarian, English, Russian and French (Correspondence Only).

APOSTOLOV & ASSOCIATES

Law Office

36, P. KARAVELOV STR.
4000 PLOVDIV, BULGARIA
Telephone: (+359 32) 222 119; (+359 799) 34 863
Telecopier: (+359 32) 223 288

FIRM PROFILE: Established in 1991. The Firm has 2 partners and 2 associates. The Firm's Practice Areas are Foreign Investment, Privatization, Business and Tax Law, Bankruptcy, Litigation, Criminal Law, Real Estate, Administrative Law, Intellectual Property.

(This Listing Continued)

SVETOSLAV L. APOSTOLOV, born Plovdiv, Bulgaria, March 11, 1955. *Education:* St. Kliment Ochridsky, State University in Sofia, (J.D., 1979). Junior Judge, Plovdiv County Court (1979-1981); Participated as visiting fellow, in The American Bar Association's, Central and East European Internship Program - CEELI (Washington, D.C., May-September, 1992). *Member:* Plovdiv Bar Association; International Bar Association. (Senior Partner). *LANGUAGES:* English and Russian.

BORISLAV BOYANOV

Attorneys at Law

Established in 1980

24 PATRIARCH EVTIMII BOULEVARD
SOFIA 1000, BULGARIA
Telephone: (359 2) 877028; (359 2) 814426
Fax: (359 2) 807813

Plovdiv, Bulgaria Office: 36A Petko Karavelov St. Telephone: (359 32) 222119. Fax: (359 32) 223288.

Stara Zagora, Bulgaria Office: 35A Metodi Kusev St. Telephone: (359 42) 55625. Fax: (359 42) 40083.

Bourgas, Bulgaria Office: 34 Ivan Shishman St. Telephone/Fax: (359 56) 11783.

FIRM PROFILE: *The firm consisting of four partners, four associates and one administrator in Sofia, one partner and two associates in Plovdiv, two partners and three associates in Stara Zagora and one partner in Bourgas offers a full range of legal services with concentration in Foreign Investments, Business and Tax Law, Arbitration and Litigation, Banking, Finance, Intellectual Property.*

SOFIA OFFICE
SENIOR PARTNER

BORISLAV T. BOYANOV, admitted, 1984, Sofia, Bulgaria. *Education:* Sofia University (1982); Academy of American and International Law, Dallas (1990). Publications: Victimology, Critical Review on Practice of the Supreme Court of Bulgaria, Business Organizations in Bulgaria, Foreign Investments, Transfer of Technologies, Aircraft Finance, Joint Ventures, Equipment, Leasing, Environmental Law, Commercial Agencies and Distributorships, Taxes in Bulgaria. Lecturer, Civil Law, University of Economy, 1986-1987. Junior Judge, Sofia City Court, 1983-1984. *Member:* Sofia Bar Association (Specialized Bureau for Business Law, Vice-President, 1988-1990); International Bar Association (Member, Counsel of the Eastern European Forum); Center for International Legal Studies; British Bulgarian Legal Association.

PLOVDIV OFFICE
MANAGING PARTNER

SVETOSLAV APOSTOLOV, admitted, 1981, Plovdiv, Bulgaria. *Education:* Sofia University (1979). *Member:* Plovdiv Bar Association; International Bar Association.

STARA ZAGORA OFFICE
MANAGING PARTNER

ALEXANDER KOMSIISKI, admitted, 1984, Stara Zagora, Bulgaria. *Education:* Sofia University (1980). *Member:* Stara Zagora Bar Association (Deputy Chairman, 1990—).

BOURGAS OFFICE
MANAGING PARTNER

EVGENI ATANASOV, admitted, 1993, Bourgas, Bulgaria. *Education:* Sofia University (1980). *Merber:* Bourgas Bar Association.

Languages: English, French, Turkish and Russian.

REPRESENTATIVE CLIENTS: Philip Morris; The Coca Cola Company; Sony Corporation; American Standard Inc.; Westinghouse; Maxus Energy Corporation; American Cyanamid Company; McDonald's; Bulgarian-American Enterprise Fund; United Technologies; Semi-Tech (Global) Corporation; Motorola GmbH; Loctire; Ansett; International Aero Engines AG; Interbrew; Socotab Leaf Tobacco Co.; Radio Free Europe/Radio Liberty; Curtis Instruments Inc.; Metromedia Company; Herbalife; Dow Chemical; Sun Chemical; Reebok International; Rexon Inc.; Storck International; Total S.A.; Northern Telecom; Balkan Bulgarian Airlines; Daewoo Corporation; Bank Advisory Committee for Bulgarian Foreign Trade Bank (financial institutional creditors-London Club).

DR. COELER & PARTNER, RECHTSANWÄLTE

4A BENKORSKI STR.
BG-1000 SOFIA, BULGARIA
Telephone: +0359 2-818866 or 897024 or 806432
Fax: +0359 2-881727

Hamburg, Germany Office: Alsterterrasse 2, D-20354 Hamburg. Telephone: (+49 40) 41 46 45 -0 . Fax: (+49 40) 41 46 45 44.

International Trade, Business, Commercial and Corporate Law, Investment, Privatization, Restitution, Real Estate, Patent Law, Banking, General Practice, Litigation and Arbitration.

FIRM PROFILE: *The firm offers a full range of legal services and is well known for its international practice. The firm is a member of EUROLINK for Lawyers, network of Independent legal practices in Europe.*

Marin D. Arsov

Languages: Bulgarian, English, German, Russian, Japanese and French

DJINGOV, STOIMENOVA & PARTNERS

Attorneys at Law

Established in 1994

12 TUNJA ST.
SOFIA 1606, BULGARIA
Telephone: (359-2) 525 606
Fax: (359-2) 520 568

Foreign Investment, Corporate Law, Securities, Taxation, Real Estate, Franchise, Banking, Bankruptcy and Reorganization, Labor Law, Privatization, Negotiations, Intellectual Property, Litigation and Representation before Governmental Institutions.

ASSEN DJINGOV, born Sofia, 1965; admitted, 1993. *Education:* Sofia University (J.D., 1992); Academy of American and International Law, Dallas, Texas (1993). Law Clerk, Commercial Department, Sofia City Court, 1992. Legal Aide, Minister of Justice, 1992-1993. Principal Drafter, Law on Concessions on Exploration of Natural Resources. Internship, Gibson, Dunn & Crutcher, Washington, D.C., 1993.

VANIA STOIMENOVA, born Sofia, 1965; admitted, 1990. *Education:* Sofia University (J.D., 1990); Central European University; Budapest College (1992-1993). Recipient, scholarship, University of California at Berkeley, School of Law, 1993. Law Clerk, Civil Law Department, Sofia City Court, 1990. Practising Individually, 1990—.

MARIUS VELICHKOV, born Vratsa, 1965; (admission pending). *Education:* Sofia University (J.D., 1992). Law Clerk, Commercial Department, Sofia City Court, 1992. Commercial and Joint Venture Specialist, U.S. Embassy Sofia, 1993-1994.

GEORGI GOUGINSKI, born Sofia, 1966; admitted, 1994. *Education:* Sofia University (J.D., 1992); American University, College of Law, Washington, D.C. (LL.M., International Trade and Banking Law, 1994). Law Clerk, Commercial Department, Sofia City Court, 1991. Associate, Lilia Kasabova Law Firm (member of Supreme Judicial Council), Business Law and Litigation areas of practice, 1991-1992. Legal Consultant, C.I.G., Inc., Washington, D.C., 1993-1994. *Member:* American Society of International Law.

Languages: English, Spanish and Russian.

REPRESENTATIVE CLIENTS: CARE Small Business Assistance Corporation /Bulgaria; Les Moines Ltd.; Buro Market S.A.; Bulgarian Association of Writers; Literaturen Forum Ltd.; Alma Tour Ltd; Peace Corps; Bulgarian-American Enterprise Fund; First Data Corp.

FRICK & FRICK

Representation Sofia

BOULEVARD WITOSCHA 25
P.O. BOX 475
BG-1000 SOFIA, BULGARIA
Telephone: +359-2/81.33.88
Telefax: +359-2/81.33.85

Zurich, Switzerland Office: Uraniastrasse 12, P.O. Box 996, CH-8021. Telephone: +41-1/211.29.11. Telefax: +41-1/211.29.30.

(This Listing Continued)

FRICK & FRICK, Sofia—Continued

Zug, Switzerland Office: Unter Altstadt 28, P.O. Box 234, CH-6301. Telephone: +41-42/22.66.30. Telefax: +41-42/22.66.36.

Prague, Czech Republic Office: Office 422a, 4th Floor, Národni trida 10, CZ-11319 Prague 1. Telephone: +42-2/24.91.30.44. Telefax: +42-2/24.91.34.35.

In Association with Law Offices in China: Beijing - Qingdao - Shanghai.

General Commercial Practice, Privatization Projects, Corporate Law, International Contracts, Joint Venture Contracts, International Arbitration, Mergers and Acquisitions, Intellectual Property, Inheritance Law, Litigation and Real Estate Law.

RESIDENT MEMBER

STOYAN GUGLEV, born Provadia, Bulgaria, July 24, 1952. *Education:* Charles University Law Faculty, Prague (1978). *LANGUAGES:* English, Bulgarian, Russian and Czech.

The Firm is a Member of CONSULEGIS EEIG Attorneys at Law, a European-Wide grouping of Law Firms.

(For Complete Biographical Data on all Personnel, see Zurich, Switzerland)

GOLEMINOV & GOLEMINOV

Established in 1992

36 A ANRI BARBUS STREET
SOFIA 1113, BULGARIA
Telephone: (359-2) 700-081
Fax: (359-2) 706-203; (359-2) 463-341

International Business and Banking Law, Foreign Investment Law, Commercial Law, Banking Law, Company Law, Taxation Law, Intellectual Property Law, Civil Law, International Arbitration and Litigation.

FIRM PROFILE: Although "Goleminov and Goleminov" was established in 1992, because of previous restrictions, concerning the legal practice in Bulgaria, most of its members are very experienced and distinguished lawyers, with long term practice. The firm offers a full range of legal services, mainly in Business- related Law and Litigation. The firm represents both national and international clients. Most of the staff are fluent in foreign languages. The firm has two partners, nine lawyers and associated offices in Sofia, Plovdiv, Stara Zagora, Varna, Bourgas and Russe.

PARTNERS

TCHOUDOMIR C. GOLEMINOV, born Plovdiv, Bulgaria, March 10, 1930; admitted, 1992, Bulgaria. *Education:* Sofia University, Faculty of Law (LL.B., 1956); Comparative Law Institute, Strassburg, France; Comparative Law Institute, Turin, Italy (Doctor of Civil and Commercial Law); University of Birmingham, Institute of European Studies, UK. Author: "Producer's Liability for Poor Quality"; "Unjustified Enrichment According to Bulgarian Contract Law"; "Legal Guaranties in Sale and Delivery Contracts of Industrial Goods Contracts". Professor, Civil and Commercial Law, Sofia University, 1975—; Plovdiv University, 1992—. Associate Member, Bulgarian Academy of Sciences. *Member:* Bulgarian Bar Association; International Bar Association; Bulgarian Comparative Law Association (Chairman); Bulgarian-Swiss Law Society; Bulgarian-French Law Society; International Comparative Law Association, Paris, France. *LANGUAGES:* French, Russian and Italian. *PRACTICE AREAS:* International Business Law; International Banking Law; Commercial Law; Company Law; Civil Law; Intellectual Property Law; International Arbitration; International Litigation.

IORDAN T. GOLEMINOV, born Sofia, Bulgaria, March 13, 1963; admitted, 1990, Bulgaria. *Education:* Sofia University, Faculty of Law (LL.B., 1990); Franklin Pierce Law Center, Concord, New Hampshire, U.S.A. (1993). Professor, Intellectual Property Law, Plovdiv University, School of Law. *Member:* Bulgarian Bar Association; International Bar Association; Bulgarian Comparative Law Association; Bulgarian-Swiss Law Society; International Association for the Advancement of Teaching and Research in Intellectual Property. *LANGUAGES:* English and Russian. *PRACTICE AREAS:* International Business Law; International Banking Law; Company Law; Intellectual Property Law; Litigation.

Languages: English, Russian, French, German and Italian

INTERADVOCAT LAW OFFICE

1 JURI VENELIN STR.
SOFIA 1000, BULGARIA
Telephone: (359+2) 810 052
Fax: (359+2) 814 163

Prague, Czech Republic Office: Velisar Haritonov, Ph.D. Telephone: 2779229.

Budapest, Hungary Office: Dr. Nadash Gabor. Telephone/Fax: +1223591.

Maryland, USA Office: Metodi Tilev, LL.M. Fax: 301 +689-5268.

Litigation, Commercial Law, Corporations, Civil Law, Real Estate, Law of Contract, Corporate Tax, Insolvency, Foreign Investment, Privatization, Arbitration, Criminal Law.

FIRM PROFILE: Registered in 1990 as a response to the newly established post totalitarian Professional structures. All of its highly educated members, acting as independent private practitioners by the National Bar, speak foreign languages and are completely capable of offering an entire range of legal services.

MEMBERS OF BOARD

Pavlina Todorova	Rumjna Radkova
Maja Peeva	Vladislav Kantutis
Svetozar Zafirov	

MEMBERS OF FIRM

A. Diankov	N. Boteva
D. Shopova	P. Todorova
E. Encheva	R. Pehlivanov
G. Antonova	R. Dimitrova
G. Vikiov	R. Mutafova
H. Trandev	R. Radkova
J. Djambazova	St. Tonchev
J. Spasov	Sv. Zafirov
K. Lazarova	T. Nenov
K. Vikjova	Z. Spasova
M. Maleev	V. Novkerishki
M. Boyadjieva	V. Kadunkov
M. Kadankova	V. Kantutis
M. Peeva	V. Stoikova
M. Boumbarov	Vl. Penev

ASSOCIATES

A. Ivanov; K. Handjiev; Sn. Maleeva; L. Josifova; Kr. Terzieva.

PETYA KOLCHEVA LAW OFFICE

26 "GURKO" STREET
SOFIA 1000, BULGARIA
Telephone: (359-2) 897078; (359-2) 650397
Facsimile: (359-2) 650380

Corporate, Business, Finance and Banking, Financial Leasing, Tax Law, Real Estate Transactions.

MEMBERS OF FIRM

PETYA STANIMIROVA KOLCHEVA, born Plovdiv, Bulgaria, March 4, 1964; admitted, 1991, Bulgaria. *Education:* Sofia University Law School (Graduate, 1988). *Member:* Sofia Bar Association. *LANGUAGES:* English, Russian and Bulgarian.

ASSOCIATES

MITKO DIMITROV, born 1970; admitted, 1993, Bulgaria.

REPRESENTATIVE CLIENTS: Popular Bank, Inc.; Financial Brokerage House Elana; Leasing Company Doverie; Chrysler Car, Inc.; Soros Foundation in Bulgaria; New Bulgarian University; Pension Fund Doverie.

KRISTIAN KRASTEV
LAW OFFICE

WORLD TRADE CENTER
36 B DRAGAN TZANKOV BLVD.
OFFICE 513
1040 SOFIA, BULGARIA
Telephone: +359-2/73 15 41
Fax: +359-2/738 551
Telex: 23424

FIRM PROFILE: The law firm Kristian Krastev is the first private law office established in Bulgaria following independence from socialism. The firm has pursued a speciality in providing legal counsel on Commercial and Corporate Law, International Trade and Foreign Investment, European Community Law, International Banking and Business Law, Acquisitions, Administrative Law, Litigation and International Arbitration, International Banking and Finance Law. The firm is entitled to plead before the European Commission.

KRISTIAN KRASTEV, born Sofia, Bulgaria, May 16, 1953; admitted, 1990, Bulgaria. *Education:* Law Faculty, University Kliment Ohridski, Sofia (Graduate, 1979). Legal Adviser: Trade Commission, State Department of USA for Bulgaria; Bulgarian Chamber of Commerce, 1989. Deputy, National Council of the European Movement, Bulgaria. Author: "Eastern European Trade & Law - CCI," Chicago; "Country Handbook on Bulgaria," Kluwer, Netherlands, 1992. President, Control Committee, Bulgaria-Italy Society. Member, Managing Committees, Academic Forum. Honorary Member, Union of Lawyers, Ukraine. *Member:* International Bar Association; Arbitration Suisse Association; Ukraine Bar Association; Interadvocate Bar Association, Bulgaria (President).

Languages: English, Russian, German, French and Italian.

CHRISTO T. MARINOV

Attorney at Law

Established in 1989

20 PROF. ASEN ZLATAROV STR.
1504 SOFIA, BULGARIA
Telephone: (359 2) 44-11-88
Fax: (359 2) 44-11-88

General Corporate, Commercial and Civil Practice, Foreign Investment, Property Law, Taxation.

CHRISTO T. MARINOV, born August, 1928. *Education:* Sofia University, Faculty of Law. General Counsel: Balkantrans; Transimpex; IKQ Consultancy Complex, 1968-1989. Chairman of Board of Directors, First Private Bank, 1989-1992.

Languages: Bulgarian, English and German.

REPRESENTATIVE CLIENTS: Delegation of the Commission of the EC; ICL; HILTI; ICI; Abbott; Voest Alpine; Schenker; DHL; Rohm & Haas; Noack; Hoffmann La Roche; EQE; CA Leasing.

NENOV ASSOCIATES

Established in 1992

37 SOLUNSKA STREET
1000 SOFIA, BULGARIA
Telephone: 359 2 898525
Fax: 359 2 805869

Business Law Agency, Distributorship, Franchising, Entertainment and Publishing, Copyrights, Corporate Law, Privatization, Civil Law, Civil Litigation, Arbitration and Mediation.

FIRM PROFILE: NENOV ASSOCIATES' practice covers all the aspects of the commercial relations: from the initial trade negotiations or establishing of a new company in Bulgaria through contract concluding and execution up to solving of the emerged disputes by a mediation talks or in the court, including debt collection and insolvency procedure. The firm has two partners and three associates, all of them young but experienced in different law areas. For specific matters the firm uses the expertise of some of the most distinguished Bulgarian jurists as outer consultants.

(This Listing Continued)

MEMBERS OF FIRM

TODOR NENOV, born Sofia, Bulgaria, October 16, 1962; admitted, 1992, Bulgaria. *Education:* Sofia University, Faculty of Law (1986). Judge, Sofia City Court and Sofia District Court, 1988-1992. *Member:* Bulgarian Bar Association; International Bar Association (Section, Business Law Committee L); INTERADVOKAT Bar Association, Sofia. *LANGUAGES:* English and Russian. *PRACTICE AREAS:* Commercial and Contract Law; Intellectual Property Law; Copyrights; Agency and Distributorship; Bankruptcy; Civil Litigation.

MARIA MITREVA, born Burgas, Bulgaria, December 12, 1964; admitted, 1992, Bulgaria. *Education:* Sofia University, Faculty of Law (1986). *Member:* Bulgarian Bar Association. *LANGUAGES:* Russian and English. *PRACTICE AREAS:* Civil Law; Property; Insurance; Family Law; Corporate Law; Securities.

Languages: English, Russian and Spanish

PETROV & BRESKOVSKI

MLADOST, BL. 98-V-A-1
1156 SOFIA, BULGARIA
Telephone: (359-2) 70-48-14
Telecopier: (359-2) 831-758

REVISERS OF THE BULGARIAN LAW DIGEST FOR THIS DIRECTORY

New York, New York Representative Office: Telephone: (212) 864-3891. Telecopier: (212) 864-3891.

Florence, Italy Representative Office: Via Fagiuoli 29, I-50135 Firenze, Italy. Telephone: (39-55) 676-002. Telecopier: (39-55) 4685-200.

Foreign Investment and Joint Ventures, Commercial Transactions, Privatization, Intellectual Property, Customs, Taxation, Real Estate, Project Finance, Foreign Trade and related matters.

RESIDENT PARTNERS

VLADIMIR PETROV, born Sofia, Bulgaria, October 26, 1945. *Education:* Sofia University (Master of Laws, 1970; Ph.D., 1987); Columbia University Law School, New York (Fulbright Scholar, 1993-1994). Author: two books and more than 70 law review articles on Bulgarian and International Business Law. Professor, Civil Law, Sofia University, 1989—. Vice Dean, Law Faculty, Sofia University, 1990—. Visiting Scholar, Tokyo University, 1991. *LANGUAGES:* Bulgarian, English and Russian.

VASSIL BRESKOVSKI, born Sofia, Bulgaria, June 11, 1965. *Education:* Sofia University (Master of Laws, 1990); University of Michigan Law School (LL.M., 1993); European University Institute, Academy of European Law, Florence, Italy (Certificate in European Law, Summer, 1993); London School of Economics (Certificate in Economics, Summer, 1991). Research Fellow, European University Institute, Department of Law, Florence, Italy, 1994—. Arnold & Porter, Washington, D.C., 1994. Consultant, United Nations Secretariat, New York, New York, July-August 1994. Clerk, Sofia City Court, 1990-1991. Associate Editor, Survey of East European Law, 1994—. Author: "Corporate Directors' Duty of Care in Eastern Europe," 29 International Lawyer (Spring 1995); "Comparative Analysis of Insider Trading Regulation in the United States and the European Community; Models for Eastern Europe?," 1 Parker School, Columbia Journal on East European Law (No.2, 1994); "Bulgaria and the GATT - A Case Study for Accession," 17 World Competition, Law and Economics Review (December 1993); "Bulgarian Industrial Property: Report on the New Law on Patents," 16 European Intellectual Property Review (May 1994); A number of notes and reviews published in BNA's Eastern Europe Reporter, European Intellectual Property Review and Survey of East European Law. *LANGUAGES:* Bulgarian, English, Russian, German and Italian.

REVISERS OF THE BULGARIAN LAW DIGEST FOR THIS DIRECTORY

IVAN TODOROV & CO.

Established in 1991

24 NIKOLA KOFARDJIEV STR.
SOFIA 1606, BULGARIA
Telephone: +359 2 521 880; 543 005; 518 616; 542 908
Telefax: +359 2 521 880
Telex: 24 611

Moscow, Russia Office: 63 Shabolovka Str., 3rd floor.

(This Listing Continued)

IVAN TODOROV & CO., Sofia—Continued

FIRM PROFILE: *Ivan Todorov & Co. was established in 1991 and its areas of practice include Commercial and Business Law, Foreign Investments Law, Corporate Law, Real Estate, Agency, Banking, Administrative Law, Social Security, Taxation, Intellectual Property and Company Law. Among its clients are Ernst & Young, Reuters, Harlequin Publishing, Apple Computers, Boston Consulting Group, Petroconsultants Ltd., Lego Trading, Arthur Andersen & Co., European Bank for Reconstruction and Development, London, Intracom, Salini, Fiat, Daewoo, The Ministry of Industry of Bulgaria, Oxford Centre, Papastratos International etc. The firm has 3 partners, 7 lawyers and a legal support staff of 5 people.*

MEMBERS OF FIRM

IVAN TODOROV, PH.D.. *Education:* Sofia University, Faculty of Law (1983); The Institute of State and Law Sciences (Ph.D., thesis); South Carolina University (Programme, October/November, 1990). Junior Judge, Sofia City Court. National Reporter: "Administrative Modernization of Central and Eastern Europe," United Nations Project, 1991. Consultant, European Bank for Reconstruction and Development. *LANGUAGES:* Bulgarian, English and Russian. *PRACTICE AREAS:* Business Law; Administrative Law.

TRIFON STANEV. *Education:* Sofia University, Faculty of Law (1980); Institute of State and Law Sciences (1983-1986). Judge, Sofia City Court. Consultant and Arbitrator, Supreme State Arbitration Court. Department Chief, Ministry of Justice. Secretary, Council on Legislature, Ministry of Justice. Member, National Commission on Competition. *LANGUAGES:* Bulgarian, English and Russian. *PRACTICE AREAS:* Commercial Law; Contract Law; Civil Procedure Law.

VALENTIN GEORGIEV, PH.D.. *Education:* Sofia University, Faculty of Law (1982). Head of the Law Department, Bourgas University. *LANGUAGES:* Bulgarian, English and Russian. *PRACTICE AREAS:* Corporate Law; Commercial Law.

Languages: English, German, French and Russian.

LAWYERS HOUSE TONCHEV & STOIKOVA

Established in 1992

44, SOLUNSKA STR.

OFFICE ADDRESS: *27, NEOFIT RILSKI STR.*

SOFIA 1000, BULGARIA

Telephone: *+359 2 891 245; +359 2 898 665*

Telefax: *+359 2 279 798*

FIRM PROFILE: *Lawyers House "Tonchev & Stoikova" is a civil partnership which was established in 1992. Its areas of practice includes Commercial and Business Law, Privatization Law, Foreign Investment Law, Corporate Law, Real Estate, Banking and Taxation Law and Litigation. The partnership includes two partners who are fully admitted lawyers.*

MEMBERS OF FIRM

STEFAN J. TONCHEV, born Sofia, Bulgaria, December 23, 1956; admitted, 1980, Bulgaria. *Education:* Sofia University, Faculty of Law (LL.B., 1980); Moscow University, Faculty of Law (LL.D., 1987). Assistant Professor, International Law, Sofia University, 1987-1988. *LANGUAGES:* Russian and English. *PRACTICE AREAS:* Company Law; Commercial Law; Real Estate; Privatization Law; Litigation; Civil Law.

VESSELA S. STOIKOVA, born Sofia, Bulgaria, January 9, 1956; admitted, 1981, Bulgaria. *Education:* Sofia University, Faculty of Law (LL.B., *(This Listing Continued)*

(This Listing Continued)

1981). *LANGUAGES:* English and Russian. *PRACTICE AREAS:* Company Law; Commercial Law; Foreign Investment Law; Banking and Taxation Law; Litigation; Civil Law.

CHANNEL ISLANDS

CALDER & COMPANY

Attorneys and Solicitors

Cayman Islands, Turks & Caicos Islands

Anguilla, British Virgin Islands

ONE ROYAL CONNAUGHT SQUARE

P.O. BOX 70

ALDERNEY GY9 3BU, CHANNEL ISLANDS

Telephone: *(+44) (0) 1 481 822 795*

Facsimile: *(+44) (0) 1 481 823 491*

FIRM PROFILE: *Advice on the Laws of the Cayman Islands, the Turks & Caicos Islands, Anguilla and the British Virgin Islands particularly transactions involving Corporations and Trusts in all four jurisdictions and other low tax jurisdictions.*

DOUGLAS CALDER, born Plymouth, England, June 6, 1939; admitted, 1967, as Solicitor, England; 1969, as Attorney at Law, Cayman Islands; Notary Public, Cayman Islands; 1972, as Attorney, Turks & Caicos Islands; 1994, as Solicitor, Anguilla; 1994, as Solicitor, British Virgin Islands. *Education:* St. Paul's School, London; St. Catharine's and Magdalene Colleges, Cambridge University, England (M.A. and LL.M., Cantab). Co-author: "The Cayman Islands," for Spitz "Tax Havens Encyclopaedia," published by Butterworths, London. Formerly Senior Partner of Maples and Calder, Attorneys at Law, Cayman Islands. Legal Secretary to The Church of England in the Cayman Islands. Chairman of the Board, Guinness Flight and Calder, S.a.r.l., P.O. Box 250, St. Peter Port, Guernsey, Channel Islands. *Member:* Cayman Islands Law Society (President, 1974-1975); International Tax Planning Association. *PRACTICE AREAS:* International Business Law; Corporations and Trusts.

BAILHACHE LABESSE

14-16 HILL STREET

P.O. BOX 207

ST. HELIER, JERSEY JE1 1BD, CHANNEL ISLANDS

Telephone: *+44 1534 888777*

Fax: *+44 1534 888778*

FIRM PROFILE: *Formed in 1994 by the merger of the two long established practices, Bailhache Labesse is one of the largest legal practices in Jersey. It consists of eight partners, all of whom have either been called to the Jersey Bar as Advocates of the Royal Court or been admitted as Jersey Solicitors, together with some 65 members of staff. The practice is involved in the provision of a wide range of legal services, with particular expertise in commercial litigation, banking and securities work. In addition, trust and corporate work is undertaken and advice can be provided on all aspects of Jersey taxation.*

MEMBERS

JACQUES LABESSE, born Jersey, Channel Islands, 1932; admitted, 1957, England and Wales (Inner Temple); Jersey Bar. *Education:* Jesus College, Oxford (M.A., 1954). *Member:* Jersey Law Society (Former President). *LANGUAGES:* French. *PRACTICE AREAS:* Trust and Company; Private Clients.

WILLIAM BAILHACHE, born Jersey, Channel Islands, 1953; admitted, 1975, England and Wales (Middle Temple); 1976, Jersey Bar. *Education:* Merton College, Oxford (M.A., 1978). Appointed Crown Advocate, 1989. Former Secretary, Jersey Law Society. *Member:* Jersey Law Society; Government of Jersey Audit Commission. *PRACTICE AREAS:* Litigation; Property; Banking and Securities.

GRAHAM BOXALL, born Paignton, England, 1945; admitted, 1975, England and Wales (Grays Inn); 1975, Jersey Bar. *Education:* Edinburgh University (M.A., 1968). *Member:* Jersey Law Society. *PRACTICE AREAS:* Trusts; Commercial; Banking and Securities.

STEVEN SLATER, born Leeds, England, 1954; admitted, 1978, England and Wales (Inner Temple); 1985, Jersey Bar. *Education:* City University-

(This Listing Continued)

sity, London (B.Sc., Hons., 1975). *PRACTICE AREAS:* Trusts; Commercial; Banking and Securities; Private Clients.

JOHN BISSON, born Jersey, Channel Islands, 1952; admitted, 1987, Ecrivain (Jersey Solicitor). *Member:* Jersey Law Society; Society of Trust and Estate Practitioners. *PRACTICE AREAS:* Property; Commercial; Banking and Securities.

MICHAEL O'CONNELL, born Newry, Northern Island, 1962; admitted, Ecrivain (Jersey Solicitor); 1987, Jersey Bar. *Education:* Birmingham Polytechnic (B.A., Hons., 1984). *Member:* Jersey Law Society. *PRACTICE AREAS:* Litigation; Property; Banking and Securities.

LINDA WILLIAMS, born Liverpool, England, 1942; admitted, 1973, English Solicitor; 1988, Ecrivain (Jersey Solicitor). *Education:* King's College, London (LL.B. Hons. 1964). President, Association of Solicitors, Supreme Court of England and Wales, Practising in Jersey. *Member:* Jersey Law Society; Society of Trust and Estate Practitioners. *PRACTICE AREAS:* Trust and Company; Private Clients.

DEBORAH LANG, born North Walsham, England, 1961; admitted, 1989, Ecrivain (Jersey Solicitor); 1989, Jersey Bar. *Education:* Nottingham University (LL.B., Hons., 1984). *Member:* Jersey Law Society. *PRACTICE AREAS:* Matrimonial; Employment; Property; Private Clients.

CONSULTANT

MICHAEL GOULD, born Swanage, England, 1931; admitted, 1953, Jersey Bar. *Education:* London University (LL.B., Hons., 1952). Former Batonnier (Chairman) of the Jersey Bar. Chairman, Jersey Criminal Injuries Compensation Board. *Member:* Jersey Law Society. *LANGUAGES:* French. *PRACTICE AREAS:* General Practice.

PRACTICE DIRECTOR

EDMUND BENDELOW, born Preston, England, 1950. *Education:* University of Wales (B.Sc., Hons., 1976); University of Exeter (M.B.A., 1994). Chairman, European Branch of the Offshore Institute. Managing Director, Bailhache Labesse Trustees Limited, the Firm's In-House Trust Company.

BEDELL & CRISTIN

Advocates & Notaries Public

Established in 1939

NORMANDY HOUSE
GRENVILLE STREET
P.O. BOX 75
ST. HELIER, JERSEY JE4 8PP, CHANNEL ISLANDS
Telephone: 44-534-72949
Fax: 44-534-78754

The practice pioneered international finance business in Jersey and continues to play a leading role in the continued development and enhancement of financial services. Full range of legal services including banking and finance, collective investment funds, insolvency, trust and company formation, administration and advice, commercial and private conveyancing, commercial and private litigation, probate, family law, criminal law. Nine partners - one assistant advocate - thirty-seven other fee earners - twenty-six support staff. Member of Interlex.

PARTNERS

ANITA REGAL. LANGUAGES: English. *PRACTICE AREAS:* Conveyancing; Probate; Trust and Company Formation and Advice.

SUSAN PEARMAIN. LANGUAGES: English. *PRACTICE AREAS:* Family Law; Criminal Law; Notarials.

ANTHONY DESSAIN. LANGUAGES: English. *PRACTICE AREAS:* Banking and Finance; Insolvency; Trust and Company Formation; Trust and Company Administration and Advice; Notarials.

ALAN DART. LANGUAGES: English. *PRACTICE AREAS:* Banking and Finance; Trust and Company Formation; Trust and Company Administration and Advice.

MICHAEL RICHARDSON. LANGUAGES: English. *PRACTICE AREAS:* Banking and Finance; Collective Investment Funds; Trust and Company Formation; Trust and Company Administration and Advice.

SIMON HOWARD. LANGUAGES: English. *PRACTICE AREAS:* Banking and Finance; Collective Investment Funds; Trust and Company Formation; Trust and Company Administration and Advice.

(This Listing Continued)

ZILLAH HOWARD. LANGUAGES: English. *PRACTICE AREAS:* Banking and Finance; Trust and Company Administration and Advice.

RICHARD GERWAT. LANGUAGES: English. *PRACTICE AREAS:* Banking and Finance; Collective Investment Funds; Trust and Company Formation; Trust and Company Administration and Advice.

CONSULTANT

LAURENCE WHEELER. LANGUAGES: English and French.

ANDREW BEGG & CO.

Established in 1986

20 BRITANNIA PLACE, BATH STREET
ST. HELIER, JERSEY JE2 4HN, CHANNEL ISLANDS
Telephone: +44 534 34234
Facsimile: +44 534 27272

Advocates qualified to advise on all aspects of Jersey Law, to appear in the Royal Court of Jersey and provide Company and Trust formation and administration Services.

ANDREW P. BEGG, born Jersey, Channel Islands, July 21, 1957; admitted, 1980, England and Wales; 1985, Jersey. *Education:* Exeter University (LL.B.); Inns of Court School of Law (Degree of Utter Barrister). *LANGUAGES:* English, French and Spanish.

ASSOCIATE

SIMON R. WAKEFIELD, born Oswestry, England, December 9, 1944; admitted, 1971, England and Wales. *Education:* College of Law, Lancaster Gate, London, England (Solicitors' Professional Examination). *Member:* Law Society of England and Wales. *LANGUAGES:* English and French.

DAVID CAPPS & CO.

Established in 1977

SIR WALTER RALEIGH HOUSE
48-50 THE ESPLANADE
ST. HELIER, JERSEY, CHANNEL ISLANDS
Telephone: 01534 89123
Fax: 01534 80522
Telex: 4192148 Capco G

Douglas, Isle of Man Office: Capco House, 31/37 North Quay. Telephone: 01624 662977. Fax: 01624 662988. Telex: 626109 Capco G.

Associated Trust Company: Capco Trust (Nevis) Limited, Springates Building, Government Road, Charlestown. Telephone: 0101 809 469 1558. Fax: 0101 809 469 1559. Telex: 397680 Capco KC.

International Company and Trust Formation and Management, Shipping, General Trading, Commercial and Property, Investment and Corporate Finance.

FIRM PROFILE: After completing Articles with a leading City of London Shipping Law firm David Capps came to Jersey in 1974 where he subsequently established David Capps & Co. which now employs a total of twenty five people including one qualified lawyer and six paralegals. The firm specializes in the formation and administration of companies and trusts in the world's leading jurisdictions. While all types of commercial transactions are handled the firm is a well known specialist on all matters relating to shipping. The firm works with a worldwide network of professional contacts and prides itself on its speed of service. Through its offices in Douglas, Isle of Man and Nevis, West Indies, the firm operates wholly offshore. It is a member of the following groups: European Maritime Law Organisation; British Nordic Lawyers Association; British Maritime Law Association; Lawyers Associated Worldwide (LAW). The partners are members of the International Bar Association.

DAVID J. CAPPS, admitted, 1974, English Solicitor; 1985, Barrister and Solicitor of the Supreme Court of Victoria, Australia; 1988, Solicitor of the Supreme Court of Hong Kong. *Education:* University of Birmingham (LL.B.); College of Law, Guildford (Distinctions in Company Law and Partnership and Accounts). *Member:* The Law Society, International Bar Association. *LANGUAGES:* English and French. *PRACTICE AREAS:* Shipping; International Commercial and Trading; Companies and Trusts; Property; Investment and Financial Matters; Tax.

CRILLS

Established in 1961

P.O. BOX 72

44 ESPLANADE

ST. HELIER, JERSEY JE4 8PZ, CHANNEL ISLANDS

Telephone: + 44 534 73521

Fax: + 44 534 66455

FIRM PROFILE: Crills has its roots in the old and well established partnership of Crill, Cubitt Sowden and Tomes, formed by the amalgamation in 1961 of three well-known practices (Crill & Benest, Lyndon Rive & Tomes and T. Cubitt Sowden). The firm has been known simply as Crills since 1984. The main areas of practice are:

International Business Law: company and trust law, commercial law and the law and regulation of banking, captive insurance and reinsurance business. Generally, this department advises on all aspects of law and regulation relating to offshore planning and the affairs of the firm's commercial clients, including banks. This work includes advice on the new uses continually being found for Jersey trusts. Contacts: Antony R. Hillman and Peter R. Cushen.

Litigation: a significant amount of litigation of an international nature is undertaken in addition to purely local matters. The firm handles all forms of major civil and criminal disputes before the Jersey courts and gives evidence as to matters of law for presentation to the courts of other jurisdictions. Contacts: Richard J. Michel and Julian C. Gollop.

General Local Law: generally, this department advises on all matters of Jersey law and in relation to all aspects of both business and domestic activities, including matters relating to family law and succession. Some facets of this work have an international connection, such as obtaining grants of probate following the decease of foreign domiciled persons leaving assets situated in Jersey. Contacts: Richard J. Michel and Peter R. Cushen.

MEMBERS

RICHARD JOHN MICHEL, born London, England, January 9, 1943; admitted, 1967, London, England; 1968, Jersey, Channel Islands. *Education:* Victoria College, St. Helier, Jersey (1957-1959). *Member:* The Honourable Society of the Middle Temple; The Jersey Law Society; The Institute of Arbitrators, Channel Islands Branch (Chairman, 1987-1990). *LANGUAGES:* English and French. *PRACTICE AREAS:* Litigation (International and Domestic).

PETER ROY CUSHEN, born London, England, December 31, 1958; admitted, 1981, London, England; 1984, Jersey, Channel Islands. *Education:* Southampton University (LL.B., 1980). *Member:* The Honourable Society of the Inner Temple; The Jersey Law Society. *LANGUAGES:* English. *PRACTICE AREAS:* Trust Law.

JEREMY JOHN NOTLEY CAPLAN, born South India, October 9, 1941; admitted, 1967, London, England. *Education:* Magdalene College, Cambridge University (M.A., 1963); College of Law, Guildford (1965). *Member:* Law Society of England and Wales. *LANGUAGES:* English. *PRACTICE AREAS:* Property.

ANTONY ROYSTON HILLMAN, born Torquay, England, October 9, 1956; admitted, 1982, London, England. *Education:* Balliol College, Oxford University (M.A., 1978); College of Law, Guildford (1979). *Member:* Law Society of England and Wales. *LANGUAGES:* English. *PRACTICE AREAS:* Banking; Insurance.

JULIAN CLIVE GOLLOP, born Somerset, England, January 14, 1960; admitted, 1983, England; 1990, Channel Islands. *Education:* Kingston Polytechnic (B.A., Hons., 1982). *Member:* The Honourable Society of Gray's Inn; The Jersey Law Society. *LANGUAGES:* English. *PRACTICE AREAS:* Litigation.

EVERSHEDS

SUITE 2, SEATON HOUSE

17-19 SEATON PLACE

ST. HELIER, JERSEY, CHANNEL ISLANDS

Telephone: (44) 1534-37321

Telex: 4192145 JAQUES G

Cable Address: "Quickness, Jersey"

Fax: (44) 1534-38163

London, England Office: Senator House, 85 Queen Victoria Street, London EC4V 4JL. Telephone: (44) 171 919-4500. Fax: (44) 171 919-4919.

Brussels, Belgium Office: 65 Rue Stevin, 1040. Telephone: (32) 2 230 8058. Fax: (32) 2 231 0677.

Other Eversheds Offices:

Birmingham, Bristol, Cardiff, Derby, Ipswich, Leeds, Manchester, Middlesbrough, Newcastle-Upon-Tyne, Norwich, Nottingham, Berlin, Jersey.

Company, Commercial, Trusts, Tax, General International, Banking, Financial Transactions, Wills.

RESIDENT PARTNERS

M.J.T. Chamberlayne   **R. Harman**

(For Complete List of other Personnel, see London, England, and Brussels, Belgium).

GALSWORTHY & STONES

English Solicitors

P.O. BOX 145 PIERMONT HOUSE

33-35 PIER ROAD

ST. HELIER, JERSEY JE4 8QP, CHANNEL ISLANDS

Telephone: 01534-31471

Fax: 01534-33536

Banking and Finance, Company, Commercial, Conveyancing (English), Shipping, Taxation, Trusts, Wills and Probate.

MEMBERS OF FIRM

P.E. Milner   N.T. Bentley

J.J.R. Johnson   M.E. Powell

CONSULTANT

J.S. Stones

GOULDENS

P.O. BOX 761, ORDNANCE HOUSE

31 PIER ROAD

ST. HELIER, JERSEY JE4 8ZZ, CHANNEL ISLANDS

Telephone: 01534 66599

Facsimile: 01534 35195

Telex: 4192456 GDNJSY G

London, England Office: 22 Tudor Street, EC4Y 0JJ. Telephone: 0171-583-7777. Cable Address: "Toplaw London EC4". Telex: 21520 Toplaw G. Facsimile: 0171-583-3051.

Brussels, Belgium Office: Guimard Centre, Rue Guimard 6-8, B-1040. Telephone: 32-2-230-3090. Facsimile: 32-2-230-3104.

Moscow, Russia Office: 10 Myasnitskaya St., 101851. Telephone: 7-095-921 7730. Fax: 7-095-921 3987.

Associated Offices in Paris and Hong Kong.

MEMBERS OF FIRM

P. MATTHAMS (Resident Partner). *LANGUAGES:* French and German. *PRACTICE AREAS:* Offshore Trusts; International Tax Planning.

D.P.H. BURGESS. *LANGUAGES:* French. *PRACTICE AREAS:* Corporate; Company Commercial.

JENNET A. DAVIES. *LANGUAGES:* Italian. *PRACTICE AREAS:* Trust; Private Client.

DAVID MORGAN WHITEHEAD & CO.

English Solicitors
WESTAWAY CHAMBERS
39 DON STREET
P.O. BOX 302
ST. HELIER, JERSEY, CHANNEL ISLANDS
Telephone: (534) 72766
Telex: 4192019 CILAW G
Fax: (534) 33979; 58308

Company/Commercial Law, Taxation, Foreign Investments, Trusts, Offshore Companies, English Conveyancing and Offshore Funds.

PARTNERS

David St. Clair Morgan   Nicholas St. Clair Morgan, LL.B.

CONSULTANT

Conrad Winston Whitehead, LL.B.

ENGLISH BARRISTERS

Francine Webster, LL.B.

ASSOCIATE ADVOCATES

P.A. Hooper Valpy   Philip Sinel
Julie Melia

Trust and Company Services are provided by the C.I. Law Trust Group of Companies, a Jersey Trust Company wholly owned, controlled and managed by the partners of David Morgan Whitehead & Co.

Languages: French, German, Spanish, English and Italian

MOURANT DU FEU & JEUNE

Advocates, Solicitors & Notaries Public
Established in 1947
18 GRENVILLE STREET
P.O. BOX 87
ST. HELIER, JERSEY JE4 8PX, CHANNEL ISLANDS
Telephone: International Direct Dialing 44-534 609000
Facsimile: 44-534 609333

Commercial, Banking & Corporate Law, Company Formation, Trust Advice, Trust Formation, Litigation, Debt Recovery, Family Law, Conveyancing, Probate, Company & Trust Administration.

FIRM PROFILE: *Founded on 1st January 1947, Mourant du Feu & Jeune is the largest legal practice in Jersey having a total of 160 staff together with 12 equity partners, 4 associates and 2 consultants. In keeping with the growth and strength of the financial sector in Jersey, commercial and banking law is a speciality.*

Trust and company administration services are provided by Mourant & Co. Limited, a Jersey company wholly owned, controlled and managed by the partners of Mourant du Feu & Jeune.

MEMBERS OF THE FIRM

D.O. MOON, (PARTNER) SOLICITOR & NOTARY PUBLIC, born 1940; admitted, 1966, as Jersey Solicitor. *Member:* International Bar Association (Honorary Vice-Consul for Finland). *LANGUAGES:* English and French. *PRACTICE AREAS:* Company and Commercial Law; Collective Investment Funds.

P. DE C. MOURANT, (PARTNER) ADVOCATE, born 1943; admitted, 1965 to English Bar (Middle Temple); 1967, to Jersey Bar. *LANGUAGES:* English and French. *PRACTICE AREAS:* Litigation; Construction Law; Family Law.

K.S. BAKER, (PARTNER) ADVOCATE, born 1930; admitted, 1952 to English Bar (Gray's Inn); 1971, to Jersey Bar. *Education:* King's College, London University (1948-1951). *Member:* International Academy of Estate & Trust Law; International Bar Association. *LANGUAGES:* English and French. *PRACTICE AREAS:* Trust Law.

R.F.V. JEUNE, (PARTNER) ADVOCATE & NOTARY PUBLIC, born 1949; admitted, 1972 to English Bar (Middle Temple); 1975 to Jersey Bar. *Member:* Honorary Consul for the Netherlands. *LANGUAGES:* English and French. *PRACTICE AREAS:* Company & Trust Administration

(This Listing Continued)

Services; Trustees of Pension Schemes and E.S.O.P.'s & other Employee Benefits; Offshore Asset Administration.

C.E. COUTANCHE, (PARTNER) SOLICITOR, born 1946; admitted, 1979, as Jersey Solicitor. *Member:* Jersey Chamber of Commerce Council. *LANGUAGES:* English. *PRACTICE AREAS:* Conveyancing; Probate; Private Client.

I.C. JAMES, (PARTNER) SOLICITOR, born 1950; admitted, 1976 as English Solicitor; 1985 as Jersey Solicitor. *Education:* The Queen's College, Oxford University (1969-1973). *Member:* International Bar Association. *LANGUAGES:* English. *PRACTICE AREAS:* Corporate & Banking Law.

A.R. BINNINGTON, (PARTNER) ADVOCATE, born 1958; admitted, 1981 to English Bar (Middle Temple); 1984, to Jersey Bar. *Education:* St. Catharine's College, Cambridge University (1977-1980). *Member:* Jersey Law Society Committee; International Litigation Practitioners Forum (Honorary Consul for Belgium); International Bar Association. *LANGUAGES:* English and French. *PRACTICE AREAS:* Commercial & Banking Litigation.

J.D.P. CRILL, (PARTNER) SOLICITOR, born 1954; admitted, 1985 as Jersey Solicitor. *Member:* International Bar Association. *LANGUAGES:* English. *PRACTICE AREAS:* Company & Trust Administration Services; Corporate and Financial Structuring; Employee Benefits.

T.J. HERBERT, (PARTNER) ADVOCATE, born 1959; admitted, 1982 to English Bar (Middle Temple); 1985 to Jersey Bar. *Education:* Trinity College, Oxford University (1978-1981). *Member:* International Bar Association. *LANGUAGES:* English and French. *PRACTICE AREAS:* Corporate & Commercial Law.

J.A. RICHOMME, (PARTNER) SOLICITOR, born 1957; admitted, 1982 as English Solicitor; 1988 as Jersey Solicitor. *Education:* Durham University (1976-1979). *Member:* International Bar Association. *LANGUAGES:* English and French. *PRACTICE AREAS:* Corporate & Commercial Law.

E.A. BREEN, (PARTNER) SOLICITOR, born 1953; admitted, 1986 as Jersey Solicitor. *Education:* Southampton University (1976-1979). *LANGUAGES:* English and French. *PRACTICE AREAS:* Conveyancing; Probate; Private Client.

C.L.I. DAVIES, (PARTNER) ADVOCATE, born 1965; admitted, 1987 to English Bar (Middle Temple); 1989 to Jersey Bar. *Education:* University College, Oxford University (1983-1986). *LANGUAGES:* English. *PRACTICE AREAS:* Corporate & Commercial Law.

P.C. HARRIS, (ASSOCIATE) ADVOCATE, born 1957; admitted, 1987 to English Bar (Middle Temple); 1990 to Jersey Bar. *Education:* University of Kingston (1981-1984). *LANGUAGES:* English. *PRACTICE AREAS:* Civil Litigation; Family & Criminal Law.

N.M. HAMEL, (ASSOCIATE) SOLICITOR, born 1959; admitted, 1990 as Jersey Solicitor. *LANGUAGES:* English. *PRACTICE AREAS:* Trust Law.

N.C. DAVIES, (ASSOCIATE) ADVOCATE, born 1967; admitted, 1989 to English Bar (Middle Temple); 1991 to Jersey Bar. *Education:* St. Hilda's College; Oxford University (1985-1988). *LANGUAGES:* English. *PRACTICE AREAS:* Corporate and Commercial Law.

A.J.R. SYVRET, (ASSOCIATE) SOLICITOR, born 1968; admitted, 1992 as Jersey Solicitor. *Education:* Exeter University (1986-1989). *LANGUAGES:* English. *PRACTICE AREAS:* Corporate and Commercial Law.

OGIER & LE CORNU

Established in 1927
P.O. BOX 404
PIROUET HOUSE
UNION STREET
ST. HELIER, JERSEY JE4 8WZ, CHANNEL ISLANDS
Telephone: 011 44 1534 504000
Telex: 4192144 Facsimilie: 011 44 1534 35328

International Business Law, Commercial Law, Company and Trust Law, Litigation and General Local Law.

FIRM PROFILE: *The Firm was founded in 1927 and offers a full range of legal services to serve an International practice embracing Institutional and Personal Clients in many geographical areas, including Europe, North America and Africa. The Firm has representative offices in London, Paris,*

(This Listing Continued)

OGIER & LE CORNU, St. Helier, Jersey—Continued

Amsterdam and Geneva and its Lawyers travel extensively to meet clients needs. This nine partner Firm has a legal support staff of approximately 50.

MEMBERS OF FIRM

MALCOLM LESLIE SINEL, born Jersey, Channel Islands, January 31, 1933; admitted, 1970, England; 1971, Channel Islands. *Education:* RAF College, Cranwell; Victoria College, Jersey (1947-1951). *Member:* The Honourable Society of the Middle Temple; The Jersey Law Society. *LANGUAGES:* English and French. *PRACTICE AREAS:* Banking Law; Trust Law; Offshore Funds Law; Company and General Commercial Matters.

JULIAN ANTHONY CLYDE-SMITH, MA (CANTAB), born Jersey, Channel Islands, September 23, 1950; admitted, 1971, England; 1974, Channel Islands. *Education:* Christ College, Cambridge (1968-1970). Notary Public. Crown Advocate. *Member:* The Honourable Society of the Middle Temple; The Jersey Law Society. *LANGUAGES:* English and French. *PRACTICE AREAS:* Local Law; Litigation; Banking Law; Trust Law; Company and General Commercial Matters.

JONATHAN GREVILLE WHITE, LLB (BRISTOL POLYTECHNIC), born Knowle Warwickshire, England, September 28, 1955; admitted, 1981, Solicitor of the Supreme Court of England and Wales; 1986, Channel Islands. *Education:* Polytechnic of Bristol (1974-1977). *Member:* The Law Society of England and Wales; The Jersey Law Society. *LANGUAGES:* English and French. *PRACTICE AREAS:* General Commercial Matters; Litigation; Trust Law; Banks and Banking; Property.

MARC SILVANUS DOREY YATES, BA HONS. (BUCKINGHAM), born Jersey, Channel Islands, February 5, 1960; admitted, 1982, England; 1985, Channel Islands. *Education:* Victoria College, Jersey (1971-1978); University College at Buckingham (1979-1980). *Member:* Gray's Inn; Jersey Law Society. *LANGUAGES:* English and French. *PRACTICE AREAS:* Banking Law; Trust Law; Leases and Leasing; Company Law and General Commercial Matters.

STEPHEN ALEXANDER MEIKLEJOHN, BA HONS. (MANCHESTER POLYTECHNIC), born Jersey, Channel Islands, November 24, 1959; admitted, 1982, England; 1985, Channel Islands. *Education:* De la Salle College (1965-1978); Manchester Polytechnic (1978-1981). *Member:* Gray's Inn; The Jersey Law Society. *LANGUAGES:* English. *PRACTICE AREAS:* Local Litigation; Criminal Law; Family Law; Personal Injury; Wills and Estates.

RICHARD WILKINSON THOMAS, MA (OXON), born Bolton, England, April 2, 1950; admitted, 1976, Solicitor of the Supreme Court of England and Wales; 1988, Channel Islands. *Education:* St. John's College, Oxford (1969-1973). *Member:* Law Society of England and Wales; The Jersey Law Society. *LANGUAGES:* English and French. *PRACTICE AREAS:* Offshore Funds Law; Banking Law; Trust Law; Company and General Commercial Matters.

SARAH ELIZABETH FITZ, BA THEO. (CNNA), born Chertsey, England, September 24, 1961; admitted, 1986, England; 1989, Channel Islands. *Education:* Polytechnic of Central London (1985-1986). *Member:* The Honourable Society of the Middle Temple; The Jersey Law Society. *LANGUAGES:* English. *PRACTICE AREAS:* Local Litigation; Family Law; Criminal Law; Drugs and Narcotics; Children.

TIMOTHY JOHN LE COCQ, BA HONS. (KEELE), born Jersey, Channel Islands, December 9, 1956; admitted, 1981, England; 1985, Channel Islands. *Education:* De la Salle College, Jersey (1961-1974); University of Keele (1974-1977). Graduate Member, British Psychological Society. *Member:* The Honourable Society of the Inner Temple; The Jersey Law Society. *LANGUAGES:* English and French. *PRACTICE AREAS:* Litigation; Intellectual Property Law; Computers and Software; Libel and Defamation; Torts.

COUNSEL

COMMERCIAL DEPARTMENT

CLIVE A.C. CHAPLIN, English and Jersey Solicitor.

MICHAEL FRANCIS LOMBARDI, Scottish Solicitor, admitted in Hong Kong, Bermuda and England.

PAUL BIRKBY SUGDEN, English Barrister.

NICHOLAS JOHN KERSHAW, English Barrister.

HEIDI JAN WILSON, English Solicitor.

(This Listing Continued)

CHRISTOPHER BYRNE, English Solicitor.

NICHOLAS CROCKER, English Solicitor.

LITIGATION DEPARTMENT

PIERRE STANLEY LANDICK, English Barrister and Jersey Advocate.

NICHOLAS JULIAN DOWRA CHAPMAN, English Solicitor.

MATTHEW JOHN THOMPSON, English Solicitor.

CARL LESLIE THOMAS ASHCROFT-NOWICKI, English Barrister.

CATHERINE ANN BELL, English Solicitor.

EMMA REBECCA DE STE CROIX, English Barrister.

PRIVATE CLIENTS AND LOCAL LITIGATION DEPARTMENT

RUI TREMOCERIO, Portuguese Law Degree. English Law Degree.

DAVID W. ROBERTS

Established in 1977

QUEEN'S HOUSE
DON ROAD
P.O. BOX 173
ST. HELIER, JERSEY, CHANNEL ISLANDS
Telephone: (44) 534 35111
Fax: (44) 534 36206

Offshore Company and Trust Formation and Administration, General Commercial, Corporate and Property Law.

FIRM PROFILE: *The firm provides offshore legal advice principally in relation to the formation and subsequent administration of offshore companies and trusts, together with related property and commercial advice. The firm's client base is international but principally from Europe, Middle and Far East and Africa.*

DAVID W. ROBERTS, admitted, 1973, Solicitor of Supreme Court of England and Wales. *Education:* LL.B. *LANGUAGES:* English.

MICHAEL J. KEARNS, admitted, 1983, Solicitor of Supreme Court of England and Wales. *Education:* LL.B. *LANGUAGES:* English and Swahili.

NICOLA C. FARTHING, admitted, 1993, Solicitor of Supreme Court of England and Wales. *Education:* LL.B. *LANGUAGES:* English.

THEODORE GODDARD JERSEY

OSPREY HOUSE
5 OLD STREET
P.O. BOX 344
ST. HELIER, JERSEY JE4 8UZ, CHANNEL ISLANDS
Telephone: (44) (534) 76085
Telex: 4192289
Fax: (44) (534) 35227

London, England Office: 150 Aldersgate Street, EC1A 4EJ. Telephone: (44) (171) 606 8855. Telex: 884678. Fax: (44) (171) 606 4390.

Brussels, Belgium Office: 79 avenue de Cortenberg/Kortenberglaan 79, B-1040 Brussels. Telephone: (32) (2) 732 2700. Fax: (32) (2) 735 23 52.

Paris, France Office: Klein Goddard, 44 Avenue des Champs Elysées, 75008, Paris, France. Telephone: (33) (1) 44 95 20 00. Fax: (33) (1) 49 53 03 97.

Warsaw, Poland Office: Dewey Ballantine Theodore Goddard Sp.z. c/o, ul. Klonowa 8, 00-591, Warsaw, Poland. Telephone: (48) (22) 49 32 88. Fax: (48) (22) 49 80 23. Satellite: (48) (39) 12 21 85.

Prague, Czech Republic Office: Dewey Ballantine Theodore Goddard, 6th Floor, Revolucni 13, 110 15 Prague 1. Telephone: (42) (2) 24810283. Fax: (42) (2) 231 0983.

Budapest, Hungary Office: Dewey Ballantine Theodore Goddard, Vadasz utca 31, H-1054 Budapest, Hungary. Telephone: (36) (1) 111 9620. Fax: (36) (1) 112 2272.

(This Listing Continued)

Associated offices in London, England: c/o Dewey Ballantine, 150 Aldersgate Street, London EC1A 4EJ. Telephone: (44) (171) 606 6121. Fax: (44) (171) 600 2754; New York, USA: c/o Dewey Ballantine, 1301 Avenue of the Americas, New York, NY 10019-6092. Telephone: (1) (212) 259 8000. Fax: (1) (212) 259 6333; Washington, USA: c/o Dewey Ballantine, 1775 Pennsylvania Avenue, N.W., Washington D.C., 20006-4605. Telephone: (1) (202) 862 1000. Fax: (1) (202) 862 1093; Los Angeles, USA: c/o Dewey Ballantine, 333 South Hope Street, Los Angeles, California, 90071. Telephone: (1) (213) 626 3399. Fax: (1) (213) 625 0562.

PARTNERS RESIDENT IN ST. HELIER, JERSEY

Christopher E. Lloyd   *Robert A. Clifford*

MICHAEL VOISIN & CO.

TEMPLAR HOUSE, DON ROAD
P.O. BOX 31
ST. HELIER, JERSEY JE4 8NU, CHANNEL ISLANDS
Telephone: 44-534 500300
Telex: 4192235 Volaw G
Fax: 44-534 500350

General Legal Practice, including banking law, bankruptcy, commercial law, mutual funds, unit trusts, corporate law, international private law, real estate law, commercial litigation.

PARTNERS

MICHAEL M.G. VOISIN, (Advocate of the Royal Court).

JOHN G.P. WHEELER, (Advocate of the Royal Court).

IAN W.S. STRANG, (Solicitor of the Royal Court).

JOHN P. KENDALL, (Solicitor of the Royal Court).

ASHLEY D. HOY, (Advocate of the Royal Court).

DAVID J. PETIT, (Advocate of the Royal Court).

ASSOCIATE

ROBIN G. MORRIS, (Advocate of the Royal Court).

NIGEL HARRIS & PARTNERS

Established in 1960

OAK WALK
ST. PETER, JERSEY, CHANNEL ISLANDS
Telephone: (0534) 44291
Telex: 4192302 Global G Lex
Fax: (0534) 42703

Geneva, Switzerland Associated Office: Biner Bradley Nigel Harris & Partners. 6 Avenue de Frontenex, Place des Eaux-Vives, Case Postale 34, 1211 Geneva 3. Telephone: (41-22) 786-8640. Facsimile: (41-22) 786-8311.

International Tax Planning, Company and Commercial Law, Trust, EEC and Securities Law.

MEMBERS OF FIRM

EDWARD JOHN NIGEL HARRIS, born Alderley Edge, England, November 14, 1914; admitted, 1939, England and Wales. *Education:* Lees School, Cambridge, Trinity College, Cambridge (B.A., Cantab honors in Law, 1939); Fellow of the Ins. of Taxation. *LANGUAGES:* English and French. *PRACTICE AREAS:* International Tax Planning; Offshore Structures; Trust Law.

PAUL EGERTON-VERNON, born Chester, England, March 22, 1945; admitted, 1971, England and Wales. *Education:* University of Durham (Bachelor of Arts, honors French, 1967); College of Law, Lancaster Gate (Solicitors Examination, 1971). International Editor, Law Society Gazette, London, 1973— . *Member:* Law Society of England and Wales. (Also Member, Rakisons, London, England). *LANGUAGES:* English, French and Spanish. *PRACTICE AREAS:* Company and Commercial Law; European Community Law; Tax Law.

ROBERT DAVID JOHNSON, born Southport, England, March 31, 1946; admitted, 1970, England and Wales. *Education:* College of Law, Lancaster Gate (1966); Liverpool College of Commerce (1969). *Member:* The Law Society of England and Wales. *LANGUAGES:* English. *PRACTICE AREAS:* Company and Commercial Law; Trust and Tax Law.

(This Listing Continued)

CHRISTOPHER PIERS MARTIN HARRIS, born Preston, England, August 3, 1953; admitted, 1979, London, England and Wales. *Education:* Trinity College Cambridge (1st class Hons., 1974); College of Law Chester (Part I Law Qualifying, 1976; Part II Law Qualifying, 1977). *Member:* The Law Society of England and Wales. Solicitors European Group (Jersey Branch). *LANGUAGES:* English. *PRACTICE AREAS:* Trust Law; International Tax Planning; Captive Insurance; Offshore Structures.

NICOLA KIRSTINE ADAMSON, born Bridge of Allen, Scotland, March 28, 1959; admitted, 1984, Scotland; 1989, England and Wales. *Education:* University of Edinburgh (LL.B. Hons., 1981; Dip. L.P., 1982). Tutor in Commercial and Mercantile Law, Department of Scots Law, University of Edinburgh, 1982-1984. *Member:* Law Society of Scotland; Law Society of England and Wales; Writer to the Signet. *LANGUAGES:* English. *PRACTICE AREAS:* Company and Commercial Law; Offshore Structures.

ST. JOHN A. ROBILLIARD, born Guernsey, Channel Islands, September 17, 1953; admitted, 1985, Barrister, Grays Inn. *Education:* Emmanuel College, Cambridge (M.A., 1975; LL.B., 1976). Former Lecturer in Law, Manchester University. Editor, "The Use of Offshore Jurisdictions.". *LANGUAGES:* English and French. *PRACTICE AREAS:* Trust Law; International Tax Planning.

KIRAN C. PATEL, born Uganda, November 23, 1964; admitted, 1990, England and Wales. *Education:* Trent Polytechnic (LL.B., 1987). *LANGUAGES:* English. *PRACTICE AREAS:* Company and Commercial Law; Offshore Structures.

ANITA M. LOVELL, born Great Yarmouth, England, July 8, 1951; admitted, 1979, England and Wales. *Education:* College of Law, Chester (Part I Law Qualifying, 1974; Part II Law Qualifying, 1977). *Member:* Law Society of England and Wales; Association of Solicitors of the Supreme Court of England and Wales Practising in Jersey. *LANGUAGES:* English. *PRACTICE AREAS:* Company and Commercial Law; Offshore Structures; Trust and Tax Law.

BABBÉ LE POIDEVIN ALLEZ

Advocates of the Royal Court of Guernsey

Established in 1989

HIRZEL COURT
P.O. BOX 612
ST. PETER PORT, GUERNSEY, CHANNEL ISLANDS
Telephone: (1481) 710585
Fax: (1481) 712245

International, Commercial and Domestic Practice in Guernsey, Alderney and Sark including Litigation, Probate and Trust Administration, Client Support, Cross-Border Insolvency and Fund Tracing, Agency Work.

PARTNERS

RICHARD BABBÉ, Advocate, Barrister Inner Temple.

NICHOLAS LE POIDEVIN, Advocate, Barrister Gray's Inn.

GEOFFREY ALLEZ, Advocate, Barrister Gray's Inn.

ANDREW LAWS, Advocate, Barrister Gray's Inn.

CLERK

Joseph Le Cheminant

CAREY LANGLOIS & CO.

Established in 1898

7 NEW STREET
P.O. BOX 98
ST. PETER PORT, GUERNSEY GY1 4BZ, CHANNEL ISLANDS
Telephone: 44-481-727272
Fax: 44-481-711052

Commercial, Banking, Insurance, Shipping, Investment Vehicles, Company and Trust Formation and Administration, International Tax Structures, Estates, Litigation, Conveyancing and Matrimonial.

FIRM PROFILE: The firm is one of the oldest and largest in Guernsey.

(This Listing Continued)

CAREY LANGLOIS & CO., St. Peter Port, Guernsey—Continued

PARTNERS

JOHN EMILE LANGLOIS, born Leicester, England, October 31, 1942; called to English Bar by Gray's Inn, 1970; called to Guernsey Bar, 1971 (Advocate of the Royal Court of Guernsey). *Education:* University of London (LL.B., Honors, 1970). Deputy (Member) of the States of Guernsey, 1984—. President, States Housing Authority. President, States Island Development Committee. *Member:* International Bar Association; Fellow of the Chartered Institute of Arbitrators of the United Kingdom. Contributing Author: Guidelines for Guernsey Directors (Institute of Directors) (1992); Jordan's International Corporate Procedures (updated annually); The Trident Practical Guide to Offshore Trusts (1991). *LANGUAGES:* English and French. *PRACTICE AREAS:* Trust Law; Commercial Law.

NIGEL THOMAS CAREY, born Guernsey, May 29, 1948; admitted, 1974, English Solicitor; called to the Guernsey bar, 1975. *Education:* Elizabeth College, Guernsey; Southampton University (LL.B., 1970). Ordinary Member of the Guernsey Financial Services Commission. *LANGUAGES:* English and French. *PRACTICE AREAS:* Mutual Funds; Company and Commercial Banking.

ROSALYN LE COUTEUR BRELSFORD, called to English Bar by Gray's Inn, 1969; called to Guernsey Bar, 1973 (Advocate of the Royal Court of Guernsey, Notary Public). *Education:* University of London (B.A., Hons., 1960; Dip. Ed., 1961). *LANGUAGES:* English and French. *PRACTICE AREAS:* Probate and Testamentary Matters; Family Law.

MICHAEL JOHN SEYMOUR EADES, born Rostrop, West Germany, January 7, 1957; admitted, 1980, Barrister-at-Law; 1981, Guernsey. Advocate of the Royal Court, Guernsey. Contributor to Longman's Capital Taxes and Estate Planning in Europe. *Member:* Guernsey Bar Council. *LANGUAGES:* English and French. *PRACTICE AREAS:* Trust Law; Commercial Law.

IAN HALDEN BEATTIE, born Egypt, September 24, 1952; admitted, 1980, Solicitor Supreme Court; 1984, Guernsey. *Education:* London University (Law Degree). *LANGUAGES:* English and French. *PRACTICE AREAS:* Land Law; Conveyancing.

JOHN P. GREENFIELD, born Boston, England, August 21, 1950; admitted, 1975, Solicitor of the Supreme Court of England and Wales; 1986, Advocate of the Royal Court, Guernsey; Notary Public. *Education:* University of Hull (LL.B., Hons., 1972); Guildford College of Law (1973). *LANGUAGES:* English. *PRACTICE AREAS:* Civil and Commercial Litigation; Personal Injury Claims; Advocacy.

COLLAS, DAY & ROWLAND

MANOR PLACE
P.O. BOX 140
ST. PETER PORT, GUERNSEY, CHANNEL ISLANDS
Telephone: (481) 723191
Fax: (481) 711880; 711881 (Grps 2 & 3)

Banking, Company & Commercial, Conveyancing, Debt Recovery, Litigation, Matrimonial, Probate & Wills, Trusts.

MEMBERS OF FIRM

PETER ATKINSON, Solicitor and Notary Public. *LANGUAGES:* English and French. *PRACTICE AREAS:* Company; Commercial; Commercial Litigation.

RICHARD COLLAS, Barrister and Notary Public. *LANGUAGES:* English and French. *PRACTICE AREAS:* Litigation.

NICHOLAS OZANNE, Barrister and Notary Public. *LANGUAGES:* English and French. *PRACTICE AREAS:* Conveyancing; Wills; Leases.

RICHARD OGIER, Solicitor. *LANGUAGES:* English and French. *PRACTICE AREAS:* Conveyancing.

CHRISTOPHER BOUND, Solicitor. *LANGUAGES:* English and French. *PRACTICE AREAS:* Company; Commercial; Commercial Litigation; Company Formations.

MARK FERBRACHE, Barrister. *LANGUAGES:* English and French. *PRACTICE AREAS:* Litigation.

PAULINE ALLEN, Barrister. *LANGUAGES:* English and French. *PRACTICE AREAS:* Trusts; Pensions.

(This Listing Continued)

IAIN HARRIS, Barrister. *LANGUAGES:* English and French. *PRACTICE AREAS:* Litigation.

SEAN CHEONG, English Solicitor. *LANGUAGES:* English, Malay and Cantonese. *PRACTICE AREAS:* Company; Commercial.

IAN KIRK, Solicitor. *PRACTICE AREAS:* Company; Commercial.

Languages: English and French

CONYERS, DILL & PEARMAN

Established in 1982
SUITE 6, TOWER HILL HOUSE
LE BORDAGE
P.O. BOX 265
ST. PETER PORT, GUERNSEY GY1 3QU, CHANNEL ISLANDS
Telephone: (44) 1481 727429
Facsimile: (44) 1481 711 750

Hamilton, Bermuda Office: Clarendon House, 2 Church Street, P.O. Box HM 666, HM CX. Telephone: (809) 295-1422. Telex: 3213 CODAN BA. Facsimile: (809) 292-4720.

Hong Kong Office: Suite 401, Three Exchange Square, 8 Connaught Place, Central. Telephone: (852) 2524-7106. Facsimile: (852) 2845-9268.

British Virgin Islands Office: Todman Building No. 1, Main Street, P.O. Box 3140, Road Town, Tortola. Telephone: (809) 494-2065/6. Facsimile: (809) 494-4929.

Firm engaged in Bermuda and General International Law Practice, but not authorized to appear before the Guernsey Courts or to act as Guernsey Advocates.

FIRM PROFILE: Companies & Trusts particularly transactions involving Bermuda companies. Advice on & arrangement for the incorporation of companies in other low tax jurisdictions and for the administration of such companies.

RESIDENT ASSOCIATE

ALISDAIR N. SCOTT, born England, April 1, 1941; admitted, 1976, England and Wales as Solicitor; 1982, Hong Kong; 1985, Victoria, Australia. Resident Associate, Guernsey, Channel Island Office (Not admitted in Channel Islands). *LANGUAGES:* English. *PRACTICE AREAS:* Company Law; Shipping.

(For Complete Biographical Data on all Personnel, see Professional Biographies at Hamilton, Bermuda).

FERBRACHE & CO.

Barristers, Advocates of the Royal Court of Guernsey, Notaries Public
HADSLEY HOUSE
LEFEBVRE STREET
P.O. BOX 212
ST. PETER PORT, GUERNSEY GY1 4JE, CHANNEL ISLANDS
Telephone: (+44 1481) 712277
Fax: (+44 1481) 710900

Company Formation and Management Services, Trust Creation and Administration, Collective Investment Schemes, Captive Insurance, Asset Protection, Banking, Estate Planning, Property Matters, Matrimonial, Probate and Litigation.

In association with The Bank of Best Asia Limited, the firm is a joint venture partner in East Asia Mentor Limited (formerly The Mentor Group). This Company specialises in Corporate, Trust and Nominee services for corporate or private clients working either directly or in association with their professional advisors-brochure ava8ilaboe upon request.

MEMBERS OF FIRM

MARY FERBRACHE, born 1950, Barrister, Notary Public, Admitted Inner Temple, 1985. *LANGUAGES:* English and French. *PRACTICE AREAS:* Conveyancing; Probate; Matrimonial and Family Law; Contract Law.

ROGER DADD, born 1943, Barrister, Admitted Inner Temple, 1987. *LANGUAGES:* English and French. *PRACTICE AREAS:* Companies and Trusts; Collective Investment Schemes; Captive Insurance; Aeronautical and Marine.

(This Listing Continued)

SADIE MORGAN, born 1946, Barrister, Admitted Inner Temple, 1986. **LANGUAGES:** English and French. **PRACTICE AREAS:** Tort; Matrimonial and Family Law; Conveyancing; Contract Law.

JASON MORGAN, born 1966, Barrister, Admitted Inner Temple, 1989. **LANGUAGES:** English, German and French. **PRACTICE AREAS:** Companies and Trusts; Litigation; Civil and Criminal Law.

OZANNE VAN LEUVEN PERROT & EVANS

Advocates and Notaries Public

1, LE MARCHANT STREET
ST. PETER PORT, GUERNSEY, CHANNEL ISLANDS
Telephone: +44 481 723466
Fax: +44 481 727935

Banking, Securities and Finance, Commercial Law, Tax, Mergers and Acquisitions, Company and Trust Law, Arbitration and Litigation, Trademarks and Intellectual Property, General Practice.

FIRM PROFILE: *The firm was established in 1945, and offers a full range of legal services. Of the seven partners, six qualified as English Barristers before taking the necessary qualifications in Guernsey and in France, to be called to the Guernsey Bar, whilst the seventh partner is an English Solicitor. The firm can also call upon the expertise of three associate Advocates and three English Barristers, one of whom is also a Hong Kong "silk".*

The firm specializes in offshore commercial and corporate work peculiar to Guernsey, and in particular, work in connection with mutual funds and company and trust law. To assist International clients who wish to take advantage of Guernsey as a financial centre, six of the partners established and control "The Legis Group," a group of companies which provide a range of company and trust formation and administration services. A brochure on the services provided by The Legis Group is available on request.

MEMBERS OF FIRM

J.N. VAN LEUVEN, SENIOR PARTNER, NOTARY PUBLIC, born 1947; admitted, 1970, England (Inner Temple); 1971, Guernsey, Channel Islands. *Education:* Cambridge University (1966-1970); Caen University (1971). Associate, Chartered Institute of Arbitrators. **LANGUAGES:** English and French. **PRACTICE AREAS:** Banking; Trust and Commercial Law.

R.A. PERROT, MANAGING PARTNER, NOTARY PUBLIC, born 1946; admitted, 1974, England (Inner Temple); 1975, Guernsey, Channel Islands. *Education:* Royal Military College of Science, Shrivenham (B.Sc., Physics); Caen University (1975). Member, States of Deliberation, 1982-1988. President, States Electricity Board and States Post Office Board, 1985-1988. **LANGUAGES:** English and French. **PRACTICE AREAS:** Commercial Law.

R.A.R. EVANS, born 1938; admitted, 1962, England (Lincoln's Inn); 1981, Guernsey, Channel Islands. *Education:* Oxford University (1956-1959); Caen University (1978). **LANGUAGES:** English and French. **PRACTICE AREAS:** Establishment and Operation of Collective Investment Schemes; Company and Trust Law.

G.T.A. BAINBRIDGE, NOTARY PUBLIC, born 1954; admitted, 1978, England (Gray's Inn); 1980, Guernsey, Channel Islands. *Education:* Brunel University (1973-1977); College of Law (1978); Caen University (1979). Associate, Chartered Institute of Arbitrators. **LANGUAGES:** English and French. **PRACTICE AREAS:** Conveyancing; Family; Probate; Tort; Contract Law.

P.T.R. FERBRACHE, NOTARY PUBLIC, born 1951; admitted, 1972, England (Gray's Inn); 1981, Guernsey, Channel Islands. *Education:* University of London and Inns of Court School of Law (1968-1972); Caen University (1980). **LANGUAGES:** English and French. **PRACTICE AREAS:** Litigation; Family; Conveyancing; Probate; Tort; Contract Law.

P.A. HARWOOD, NOTARY PUBLIC, born 1947; admitted, 1972, Solicitor of the Supreme Court of England; 1982, Guernsey, Channel Islands. *Education:* Southampton University (1966-1969); College of Law, Guilford (1969); Caen University (1981). Corporate Finance Executive, Hill Samuel & Co., London, 1977-1980. Chairman, TSB Bank Channel Islands Limited, 1991. **LANGUAGES:** English and French. **PRACTICE AREAS:** Establishment and Operation of Collective Investment Schemes; Banking; Company and Trust Law.

(This Listing Continued)

E.A.G. PRENTICE, NOTARY PUBLIC, born 1949; admitted, 1983, England (Inner Temple); 1984, Guernsey, Channel Islands. *Education:* University of London (1979-1982); Caen University (1984). **LANGUAGES:** English and French. **PRACTICE AREAS:** Litigation; Family; Conveyancing; Probate; Tort; Contract Law.

CROATIA

LAW OFFICES MIROLJUB MAĆESIĆ

Advocates, Lawyers

POD KASTELOM 4
P.O. BOX 366
51000 RIJEKA, CROATIA
Telephone: +(385 51) 213 118; 215 010
Telex: 24382 LEGIS RH; 24704 NAVIS RH
Fax: +(385 51) 215 030

Arbitration, Commercial, Shipping, Construction, Banking Law, Company Law, Insurance, Marine and Aviation, Joint Venture Capital, Private Client.

MIROLJUB MAĆESIĆ, admitted, 1984, Croatia. *Education:* B.A.; LL.B. *Member:* Croatian Bar Association.

OF COUNSEL

GEORGE IVKOVIĆ, admitted, 1970, Croatia. *Education:* B.A.; LL.B. *Member:* Croatian Bar Association.

Languages: English and Italian

REPRESENTATIVE CLIENTS: Liverpool & London P & I Ass. Ltd., Liverpool; Through Transport Mutual Insurance Ass. Ltd.; The Standard Steamship Owners' P & I Ass. (Bermuda) Ltd.; Newcastle P & I Ass.; UK P & I Club; British Marine Mutual Insurance Ass. Ltd.; NE P & I Assurance Foremingen Skuld; The Swedish Club; Unitas; The Steamship Mutual Underwriting Ass. Ltd.; Verein Hamburger Assecuradeure; Assurance Foremingen Gard; Verein Bremer Seeversicherer; The Dutch P & I Club.

BOESEBECK, BARZ & PARTNER

Established in 1993

TRG BANA J. JELACICA 3
41000 ZAGREB, CROATIA
Telephone: (385) (41) 42 71 16
Telecopier: (385) (41) 42 87 99

REVISERS OF THE GERMAN LAW DIGEST FOR THIS DIRECTORY.

Frankfurt am Main, Germany Office: Darmstaedter Landstrasse 125, 60598 Frankfurt am Main. Telephone: (49) (69) 96 236-0. Telefax: (49) (69) 96 236-100.
Berlin, Germany Office: Schlueterstrasse 37, 10629 Berlin. Telephone: (49) (30) 8857 45-0. Telecopier: (49) (30) 8857 45-99.
Dresden, Germany Office: Heideparkstrasse 4, 01099, DRESDEN. Telephone: (49) (351) 56 70 550. Telecopier: (49) (351) 50 23 476.
Vienna, Austria Office (Sprechstelle): Graben 29A, 1010 Vienna. Telephone: (43) (1) 53 55 744. Telecopier: (43) (1) 5350 649.
Warsaw, Poland Office: ul. Wspólna 25, 00519 Warsaw. Telephone: (48) (2) 62 83 029. Telecopier: (48) (22) 29 41 05.

Commercial, Corporation, Contracts, Mergers and Acquisitions, Banking, Antitrust, Distributorship Agency and Franchising, Computer Law (EDP Law), Patents and Trademarks, Capital Market, Financial Services, Product Liability, Property and Real Estate. Foreign Investment, Administrative, Environmental, Trade Regulations, Food and Drug Regulations.

MIRKO BOGDANOVIC, born Osijek Croatia, November 15, 1956; admitted, 1991, in Germany as Legal Consultant in Croatian Law. *Education:* University of Split. **LANGUAGES:** Croatian, English, German. **PRACTICE AREAS:** Croation Civil and Commercial Law; Foreign Investments; Litigation.

MLADEN BELE, born Zagreb, Croatia September 20, 1956. *Education:* University of Zagreb (Dipl pravn). **LANGUAGES:** Croatian, English, Ger-

(This Listing Continued)

BOESEBECK, BARZ & PARTNER, Zagreb—Continued

man. *PRACTICE AREAS:* Croation Civil and Commercial Law; Foreign Investments; Litigation.

REVISERS OF THE GERMAN LAW DIGEST FOR THIS DIRECTORY.

SCHEELE, SCHWARTZ, ZIELCKE & PARTNER

DORDICEVA 6

41001 ZAGREB, CROATIA

Telephone: 00385-41-421 106

Fax: 00385-41-428 350

Munich, Germany Office: Prinzregentenplatz 15, 81675. Telephone: 089/470 10 02. Fax: 089/470 10 06.

FIRM PROFILE: Scheele, Schwartz, Zielcke & Partner is an international law firm advising business clients and public institutions on all domestic and overseas corporate and commercial matters. The firm specializes in Eastern European and C.I.S. matters. Currently the firm is representing a broad range of clients in Europe, North America, South America, Asia and Africa.

(For biographical data and areas of practice see listing at Munich, Germany)

VUKMIR

GORNJE PREKRIŽJE 51

41000 ZAGREB, CROATIA

Telephone: (+385-41) 273 933

Facsimile: (+385-41) 273 933

Telex: 21239 c ingr rh

Intellectual Property Law, Transfer of Technology Contracts, Commercial Law, Corporate and Business Law, and Arbitration.

MLADEN VUKMIR, born Zagreb, Croatia, September 15, 1960; admitted, 1991, Croatia. *Education:* Law Faculty University of Zagreb (Dipl.iur., 1985); Franklin Pierce Law Center, Concord, NH, USA (MIP, 1990). Author: Green Paper of the EEC on Copyright Law and Challenge of Technologies; Recent Developments in the Intellectual Property Law in the U.S.A.; The Roots of Anglo-American Intellectual Property Law in Roman Law, etc. *Member:* International Bar Association. *LANGUAGES:* Croatian, English, Italian, German and French. *PRACTICE AREAS:* Intellectual Property Law; Technology Transfer; Commercial Law.

OF COUNSEL

DR. BRANKO VUKMIR, born Zagreb, Croatia, April 30, 1927; admitted, 1959, Zagreb, Croatia. *Education:* Law Faculty University of Zagreb (Dipl.iur., 1950; S.J.D., 1957); Harvard Law School, Cambridge, MA, USA (LL.M., 1953). Author: Engineering Contracts; World Bank (books); over 200 articles in various legal journals. Professor, Faculty for Foreign Trade, University of Zagreb, 1983-1985. Senior Legal Advisor, UNCTC, New

(This Listing Continued)

York, 1989-1991. Danish Honorary Consul General in Zagreb. *LANGUAGES:* Croatian, English, French and German. *PRACTICE AREAS:* Corporate; Business Law; Contract Law; Arbitration.

CYPRUS

LAW OFFICES OF CHRISTODOULOS G. PELAGHIAS

ACROPOLIS BLDG., SUITE 14

27, GREGORY AFXENTIOU AVE.

P.O. BOX 672

LARNACA, CYPRUS

Telephone: + 357-4-654900, + 357-4-658380

Telex: 4047 ACROPOLE CY

Facsimile: + 357-4-620319, + 357-4-654972

Corporate, International Tax, Maritime and Admiralty, Foreign Investment, Shipping and Offshore Companies, Banking, Litigation, General Practice.

FIRM PROFILE: The firm specializes in international tax planning, shipping and offshore companies and foreign investment in Central/Eastern Europe and the former Soviet Union. The firm is successor to the law practice of the late George Chr. Pelaghias established in 1952. Ambassador Pelaghias (dec. 1988), served in several senior diplomatic posts including that of Director General of the Ministry of Foreign Affairs of the Republic of Cyprus.

MEMBERS OF FIRM

CHRISTODOULOS G. PELAGHIAS, born Larnaca, Cyprus, May 10, 1953; admitted, 1985, New York; 1990, Cyprus. *Education:* Columbia University (M.A., Intl. Affairs, 1979; M. Phil., Pol. Sci., 1982; J.D., 1982). Reviser, Digest of Commercial Laws of the World-Cyprus, Oceana, Dobbs Ferry, New York 1995. *Member:* American Bar Association; New York State Bar Association (International Law and Practice Section; Chairperson, Cyprus Chapter); Association of the Bar of the City of New York; Maritime Law Association of the United States; International Tax Planning Association; Cyprus Bar Association. *LANGUAGES:* Greek, English and French.

SHERLE R. SCHWENNINGER, born Elwood, Nebraska, U.S.A., February 19, 1951; admitted, 1978, District of Columbia. *Education:* National Law Center, George Washington University (J.D., 1977). Author: "Revitalizing the World Economy," World Policy Journal, 1992; "American Priorities in a New World Era," World Policy Journal, 1989; "The Democrats and a New Grand Strategy-U.S. Foreign Policy in the Post Cold War World," World Policy Journal, 1986-1987. Founding Editor, World Policy Journal. Director, World Policy Institute. Consultant: New York State Commission on Trade and Competitiveness; The Andy Warhol Foundation. *Member:* District of Columbia Bar. *LANGUAGES:* English and German. *PRACTICE AREAS:* International Trade and Finance; Foreign Investment in Central/Eastern Europe & successor states of former Soviet Union.

Languages: Greek, English, French and German.

REPRESENTATIVE CLIENTS: Barclays Bank PLC; Eagle Star International Services (Cyprus) Ltd; Svenska Orient Linien AB (Sweden); Billspedition AB (Sweden); Rederiaktiebolaget Transatlantic (Sweden); Safe Service AB (Sweden); Bylock & Nordsjofrakt AB (Sweden); Prentice Hall (U.S.A.); Elsag Bailey, Inc. (USA); Finmeccanica S.p.A. (Italy).
REFERENCES: Barclays Bank PLC.

DR. ANDREAS P. POETIS & CO.

41 - 43 ARTEMIS AVENUE, POETIS TOWER

P.O. BOX 362

LARNACA, CYPRUS

Telephone: 357 4 65 27 28; 357 4 65 57 77; 357 4 62 60 07; 357 4 62 68 76

Telex: 3353 DRPOETIS

Telefax: 00 357 4 651277

Famagusta, Cyprus Office: 36, Syngletikes Street. Telephone: 65313.

Shipping, Companies, Patent, Trademark. General Practice.

(This Listing Continued)

DR. ANDREAS P. POETIS, born Larnaca, Cyprus, November 30, 1943; admitted, 1968, Cyprus. *Education:* Faculty of Law, University of Athens (LL.B., excellent; Dr. jur.). Author: "The Transfer of the Share of a Partner in a Partnership, according to the Law of England, Cyprus and Greece," 1975; "The Law 9/75," 1975; "The Retrospective Effect of Article 26 of the Law 36/75," 1975; "The res iudicata in England and European Legal System," 1974; "Bills of Exchange," 1986; "Joint Accounts," 1987; "The Law of Life Insurance"; "The Inability to Claim of an Unregistered Partnership Under Section 62 of the Partnership Act". *Member:* Famagusta Bar Association. *LANGUAGES:* Greek, English and French.

SYLVIA A. POETIS, born Famagusta, Cyprus, July 27, 1951; admitted, 1975, Cyprus. *Education:* Faculty of Law, University of Athens (LL.B.). *Member:* Famagusta Bar Association. *LANGUAGES:* Greek, English and French.

YIOTA KALLI, born Famagusta, Cyprus, July 24, 1955; admitted, 1983, Cyprus. *Education:* Faculty of Law, University of Athens (LL.B.). *Member:* Famagusta Bar Association. *LANGUAGES:* Greek, English and French.

HELEN CONSTANTINOU, born Famagusta, Cyprus, March 29, 1957; admitted, 1985, Cyprus. *Education:* Faculty of Law, University of Thessaloniki (LL.B.). *Member:* Famagusta Bar Association. *LANGUAGES:* Greek and English.

JENNIFER E. SAVVOPOULOS, born Worcester, England, January 31, 1971; admitted, 1994, Cyprus. *Education:* School of Law, Staffordshire University, U.K. (LL.B., hons). Author: "Marine Pollution in Cyprus". *Member:* Larnaca Bar Association. *LANGUAGES:* English, Greek and French.

CLAUDIUS A. ANTONIADES, born Nicosia, Cyprus, May 4, 1933; admitted, 1960, Cyprus. *Education:* Middle Temple U.K. (Barrister-at-Law). Experience: Barrister, 9 years; Attorney General, 20 years; President, Family Court, 3 years. *Member:* Famagusta Bar Association. *LANGUAGES:* Greek, English, French and German.

ANDREAS NEOCLEOUS & CO.

Advocates and Legal Consultants

NEOCLEOUS HOUSE
199, MAKARIOS III AVENUE
P.O. BOX 613
LIMASSOL, CYPRUS
Telephone: 357 5 362818
Telefax: 357 5 359262
Telex: 2948 NEOLAW CY

Company and Commercial Matters, Banking and Insurance, Patent Copyright and Trade Marks Law, Litigation, Maritime Admiralty and Arbitration Law, International Tax Law, Tax Planning Advice, Foreign Investment and Overseas Property Advice, Private Client Work, Matrimonial and Family Law, Conveyancing, Probate and Trusts.

FIRM PROFILE: ANDREAS NEOCLEOUS & CO., was founded by Andreas Neocleous in 1965 and is based in Limassol, Cyprus. Though small in comparison with its European counterparts, it is amongst the large firms on the Island with 11 qualified lawyers, 2 Consultants, 5 legal executives and 3 qualified accountants. The firm has established close bonds with International Fiscal Services Group and the Euro-American Lawyers Association. It has an extensive international network of corresponding and associate offices including permanent representation arrangements in London, New York, Paris, Rotterdam, Zurich and Athens. The firm has established an office in Moscow and in Budapest, Hungary.

The firm's main characteristic is the allotment of work in different departments, which ensures a trend of specialization in the provision of services.

Its main areas of practice is General Commercial Law and all aspects of Litigation inherent to it. Apart from a strong presence in the area of Insurance and Banking Law the firm is well known for its corporate department which not only registers and manages legal entities, but also advises and assists clients on all matters involving International Corporate and Tax Law as well as Cross Border Transactions.

The role of the corporate department has recently been significantly broadened by the firm's specialist position in assisting Western Corporations to expand in Eastern Europe or Eastern European Corporations to expand in

(This Listing Continued)

other areas of the world. The newly established Moscow and Budapest offices play a key role in this respect.

Shipping is another main area of practice. All types of Maritime Work are undertaken such as: Registration of Shipping Companies and Ships, Ship Mortgages and Finance Agreements, Freight and Marine Insurance claims.

MEMBERS OF FIRM

ANDREAS NEOCLEOUS, born 1939; admitted, 1965, Cyprus. *Education:* Athens University. Founder and Managing Partner, Law Firm of Andreas Neocleous & Co. Author: "Cyprus International Tax Planning," Longman, 2nd Edition, 1991; "Franchising in Cyprus," Matthew Bender, 1993 and numerous contributions to law journals and periodicals such as the Tax Planning International Review and The International Business Lawyer. Former member, Cyprus Parliament; Cyprus Bar Council. *Member:* Cyprus Bar Association; International Bar Association; Mediterranean Maritime Arbitration Association; American Bar Association (Associate). *LANGUAGES:* Greek and English. *PRACTICE AREAS:* Commercial Law; Tax Law; Corporate Law; Banking Law; Insurance Law; Arbitration Law; Maritime Law.

TAKIS CHRISTOFOROU, born Limassol, Cyprus, 1947; admitted, 1972, Cyprus. *Education:* Athens University, 1971. Former Member, Cyprus Bar Council. *Member:* Cyprus Bar Association. *LANGUAGES:* Greek and English. *PRACTICE AREAS:* Litigation Law; Insurance Law; Accident Claims.

SOTERIS PITTAS, born Nicosia, Cyprus, 1960; admitted, 1988, Cyprus. *Education:* Athens University; London School of Economics (LL.M.). *Member:* Cyprus Bar Association. *LANGUAGES:* Greek and English. *PRACTICE AREAS:* Admiralty; Company Law; Marine Insurance; International Trade Law; Banking Law.

LEFKIOS TSIKKINIS, born Limassol, Cyprus, 1942; admitted, 1968, Cyprus. *Education:* Athens University. *Member:* Cyprus Bar Association. *LANGUAGES:* Greek and English. *PRACTICE AREAS:* Wills, Successions and Probates; Foreign Investment; International Taxation; Contract Law; Commercial Practice; Civil Practice.

ANDREAS CHARALAMBOUS, born Limassol, Cyprus, 1960; admitted, 1989, Cyprus. *Education:* Athens University. *Member:* Cyprus Bar Association. *LANGUAGES:* Greek and English. *PRACTICE AREAS:* Banking Law; Insurance Law; Accident Claims; Commercial Practice; Civil Practice.

PANICOS CLEOVOULOU, born Paphos, Cyprus, 1960; admitted, 1987, Cyprus. *Education:* Salonica University. *Member:* Cyprus Bar Association. *LANGUAGES:* Greek and English. *PRACTICE AREAS:* Commercial Practice; Civil Practice.

CHARA COLOTA, born Limassol, Cyprus, 1965; admitted, 1992, Cyprus. *Education:* University of Heidelberg; Bristol University (LL.M.). Author, "International Conventions," 1992. *Member:* Cyprus Bar Association. *LANGUAGES:* Greek, English and German. *PRACTICE AREAS:* Company Law; Conveyancing; Intellectual Property.

ELIAS NEOCLEOUS, born Limassol, Cyprus, 1968; admitted, 1992, Cyprus. *Education:* Oxford University (B.A., Jurisprudence); Barrister of the Inner Temple. Author: "Increasing Tax Opportunities for Treaty-Heavens," 1992; "Structuring Foreign Investment in China," 1993; "Asset Protection Planning and Cyprus International Trusts," 1994; "Ship Registration and Mortgages in Cyprus," 1994. *Member:* Cyprus Bar Association; International Bar Association; International Tax Planning Association. *LANGUAGES:* Greek, English and Italian. *PRACTICE AREAS:* Tax Law; Corporate Law; Trusts Estate Planning; Maritime and Admiralty Law; International Trade and Finance Law.

IPHIGENIA AYIOMAMITOU, born Famagusta, Cyprus, 1968; admitted, 1993, Cyprus. *Education:* Cambridge University; University College of London (LL.M.); Barrister of the Inner Temple. Author: "Franchising in Cyprus," Mathew Bender, 1993. *Member:* Cyprus Bar Association; International Bar Association. *LANGUAGES:* Greek, English and French. *PRACTICE AREAS:* Admiralty; Company Litigation; Commercial Litigation; Administrative Law.

ANTONIS GLYKIS, born Paphos, Cyprus, 1967; admitted, 1993, Cyprus. *Education:* Salonica University. *Member:* Cyprus Bar Association. *LANGUAGES:* Greek and English. *PRACTICE AREAS:* Commercial Practice; Civil Practice; Criminal Law.

ANNA PANAYIOTIDOU, born Limassol, Cyprus, 1965; admitted, 1993, Cyprus. *Education:* Salonica University (1992). *Member:* Cyprus Bar

(This Listing Continued)

ANDREAS NEOCLEOUS & CO., Limassol—Continued

Association. *LANGUAGES:* Greek and English. *PRACTICE AREAS:* Family Law; Divorce Law; Banking Law; Insolvency Law.

Member of Cyprus Bar Association; International Bar Association; Cyprus Association for Insurance Law; Mediterranean Maritime Arbitration Association; Eastern European Forum, the Euro-American Lawyers Group and GLOBALAW the International Law Group.

Languages: Greek, English, German, French, Italian, Hungarian and Russian

---

PATRIKIOS PAVLOU & CO.

Established in 1963

OMEGA COURT, 3RD FLOOR
4, R. FEREOS STREET
P.O. BOX 4543
LIMASSOL, CYPRUS
Telephone: +357 5 364738; 344271
Fax: +357 5 344548
Telex: 6269 PATRAD

Cyprus and International Law Practice. General Practice, Commercial Law, Company Law, Administration of Companies, Banking, Insurance, Property Law and Conveyancing, Personal Injuries, Civil & Criminal Litigation.

MEMBERS OF FIRM

PATRIKIOS PAVLOU, born Limassol, Cyprus, March 10, 1939; admitted, 1963, Cyprus. *Education:* Gray's Inn (Barrister at Law, 1962). *Member:* Limassol Bar Association; Cyprus Bar Association. *LANGUAGES:* Greek and English.

STAVROS PAVLOU, born London, UK, July 17, 1960; admitted, 1986, Cyprus. *Education:* London School of Economics (B.Sc., Economics); City University (Dipl. Law); Gray's Inn (Barrister at Law, 1985). *Member:* Limassol Bar Association; Cyprus Bar Association. *LANGUAGES:* Greek and English.

REA LIMNATITOU, born Limassol, Cyprus, July 6, 1959; admitted, 1983, Cyprus. *Education:* Athens University (Law Degree). *Member:* Limassol Bar Association; Cyprus Bar Association. *LANGUAGES:* Greek and English.

CHRYSOSTOMOS NICOLAOU, born Famagusta, Cyprus, November 14, 1967; admitted, 1993, Cyprus. *Education:* Athens University (Law Degree). *Member:* Limassol Bar Association; Cyprus Bar Association. *LANGUAGES:* Greek and English.

STELLA LOUCA PAVLOU, born Famagusta, Cyprus, November 29, 1964; admitted, 1994, Cyprus. *Education:* Athens University (Law Degree). *Member:* Limassol Bar Association; Cyprus Bar. *LANGUAGES:* Greek and English.

GEORGE THEOCHARIDES, born Limassol, Cyprus, July 7, 1969; admitted, 1994, Cyprus. *Education:* University of Wales, Aberystwyth (LL.B., Honors). *Member:* Limassol Bar Association; Cyprus Bar Association. *LANGUAGES:* Greek and English.

REPRESENTATIVE CLIENTS AND REFERENCES: Bank of Cyprus Ltd.; Cyprus Popular Bank Ltd.; Lombard Natwest Bank Ltd.; Royal Insurance PLC (local representative); Coopers & Lybrands; Limassol Hoteliers Association.

GEORGE L. SAVVIDES & CO.

(incorporating Marcos S. Kyprianou & Co)

Advocates - Legal Consultants

Established in 1984

OMEGA COURT, 1ST, 2ND AND 4TH FLOORS
4 RIGAS FEREOS STREET
P.O. BOX 4098
3720 LIMASSOL, CYPRUS
Telephone: 357-5-376886
Fax: 357-5-374930, 374557
Telex: 4970 Juris CY

Nicosia Office: 1 Glafkos Street, 1085. Telephone: 357-2-422355. Fax: 357-2-421819.

(This Listing Continued)

Litigation, Banks and Banking, Corporate Law, Company Law (including Offshore company formation and administration), Commercial Law, Admiralty and Maritime Law (including ship and mortgage registration), Arbitration, Taxation, Personal Injury, Insurance, Sale of Land, Criminal, Property, Debtor and Creditor, Contracts, Wills, Probate, Trusts and Estates, Trademarks, General Practice.

MEMBERS OF FIRM

GEORGE L. SAVVIDES, born Nicosia, Cyprus, September 22, 1959; admitted, 1983, Cyprus. *Education:* University of Exeter (LL.B. Hons.), Middle Temple, Barrister-at-Law, Cyprus Bar Examinations. Author: "Cyprus-Legal Aspects of Ship Finance and Mortgages"; "Cyprus-Offshore Companies and Ship Registration". *Member:* Honourable Society of the Middle Temple; Famagusta Bar Association; Cyprus Bar Association; Associate of the Chartered Institute of Arbitrators; Overseas Member, Institute of Trade Mark Agents; International Bar Association; Mediterranean Maritime Arbitration Association. *LANGUAGES:* Greek and English. *PRACTICE AREAS:* Admiralty Law; Maritime Law; Corporate Law; Company Law; Banks and Banking Law; Litigation; Taxation Law; Commercial Law; Arbitration; Insurance Law; Trademark Law.

MARKOS S. KYPRIANOU, born Limassol, Cyprus, January 22, 1960; admitted, 1985, Cyprus. *Education:* Athens University, (Law Degree); Cambridge University (LL.M.); Harvard Law School (LL.M.). Member, House of Representatives, Republic of Cyprus, 1991—. *Member:* Nicosia, Cyprus and American Bar Associations. *LANGUAGES:* Greek, English and French. *PRACTICE AREAS:* Corporate Law; Admirality and Maritime Law; Company Formation; Administration and Litigation; Taxation; Banks and Banking; Contracts.

ELECTRA G. SAVVIDES, born Limassol, Cyprus, August 2, 1959; admitted, 1984, Cyprus. *Education:* Athens University (Law Degree); LL.M. (Lond.), Cyprus Bar Examinations. *Member:* Limassol Bar Association; Cyprus Bar Association. *LANGUAGES:* Greek and English. *PRACTICE AREAS:* Banks and Banking Law; Corporate Law; Company Law; Personal Injury Law; Insurance Law; Probate Law; Wills; Trust Law; Estates; Trademark Law.

CHRISTAKIS K. MELIDES, born Nicosia, Cyprus, January 25, 1954; admitted, 1981, Cyprus. *Education:* Athens University (Law Degree), Cyprus Bar Examinations. *Member:* Limassol Bar Association; Cyprus Bar Association. *LANGUAGES:* Greek and English. *PRACTICE AREAS:* Litigation; Personal Injury; Insurance; Banks and Banking; Copyright Law; Debtor and Creditor; Commercial Law; Family Law; Criminal Law.

LIA E. MARKOU, born Larnaca, Cyprus, October 16, 1965; admitted, 1990, Cyprus. *Education:* University of Kent (B.A. Hons); LL.M. (Lond.); LL.M. (Cantab.), Cyprus Bar Examinations. *Member:* Limassol Bar Association; Cyprus Bar Association. *LANGUAGES:* Greek and English. *PRACTICE AREAS:* Contract Law; Admiralty Law; Maritime Law; Sale of Land; Property Law; Wills; Probate Law; Commercial Law.

ASSOCIATES

ANTHONY N. KONIS, born Famagusta, Cyprus, May 25, 1964; admitted, 1990, Cyprus. *Education:* Athens University (Law Degree); Cyprus Bar Examination. *Member:* Famagusta Bar Association; Cyprus Bar Association. *LANGUAGES:* Greek and English. *PRACTICE AREAS:* Litigation; Personal Injury Law; Debtor Creditor Law; Criminal Law.

PANAYIOTA PITTA, born Nicosia, Cyprus, February 10, 1967; admitted, 1992, Cyprus. *Education:* University of Hull (LL.B., Honours) of Gray's Inn, Barrister. Member, Honourable Society of Gray's Inn. *Member:* Nicosia and Cyprus Bar Associations. *LANGUAGES:* Greek, English and French. *PRACTICE AREAS:* Corporate Law; Conveyancing; Property Law; Litigation.

MANDO PAPAGEORGHIOU, born Nicosia, Cyprus, August 11, 1969; admitted, 1992, Cyprus. *Education:* University of East Anglia, Norwich (LL.B., Hons.); Gray's Inn, Barrister; Cyprus Bar Examinations. *Member:* Nicosia Bar Association; Cyprus Bar Association. *LANGUAGES:* Greek, English and French. *PRACTICE AREAS:* Admiralty Law; Maritime Law; Corporate Law; Insurance; Commercial Law.

KALIA N. GEORGHIOU, born Limassol, Cyprus, August 23, 1968; admitted, 1993, Cyprus. *Education:* Athens University (Law Degree); University of Bristol (LL.M.), Cyprus Bar Examinations. *Member:* Limassol Bar Association; Cyprus Bar Association. *LANGUAGES:* Greek and English. *PRACTICE AREAS:* Litigation; Criminal Law; Personal Injury Law; Debtor Creditor Law; Trademark Law; Family Law.

(This Listing Continued)

OLGA SOPHOCLEOUS, born Limassol, Cyprus, November 27, 1970; admitted, 1993, Cyprus. *Education:* University of Kent, Canterbury (B.A., Hons.); Middle Temple (Barrister-at-Law); Cyprus Bar Examinations. *Member:* Honourable Society of the Middle Temple; Limassol Bar Association; Cyprus Bar Association. *LANGUAGES:* Greek and English. *PRACTICE AREAS:* Litigation; Personal Injury Law; Debtor Creditor Law; Commercial Law; Banks and Banking Law; Insurance Law.

MARKELLA ONISIFOROU, born Cardiff, Wales, May 13, 1972; admitted, 1994, Cyprus. *Education:* University of Keele (B.A., Hons.). *Member:* Limassol Bar Association. *LANGUAGES:* Greek and English. *PRACTICE AREAS:* Banks and Banking; Corporate Law; Company Law; Personal Injury; Insurance; Probate; Wills; Trusts and Estates; Trademarks.

CONSULTANTS

LOUKIS G. SAVVIDES, born Limassol, Cyprus, April 3, 1923; admitted, 1949, Cyprus. *Education:* London University (LL.B. Hons.), Middle Temple, Barrister-at-Law. District Judge 1961-1971. President, District Court, 1971-1978. Judge, Supreme Court of Cyprus, 1978-1991. *Member:* Honourable Society of the Middle Temple; Fellow, Chartered Institute of Arbitrators; Famagusta Bar Association; Cyprus Bar Association; Committee of legal cooperation of the Council of Europe (Former Vice Chairman); Committee of Experts on Family Law of the Council of Europe (Former Chairman); Law Reform Committee on Family Law Republic of Cyprus (Former Chairman). *LANGUAGES:* Greek and English. *PRACTICE AREAS:* Arbitration; Taxation Law; Admiralty Law; Maritime Law; Trust Law; Estates; Wills; Personal Injury Law.

CORINA L. DEMETRIOU, born Nicosia, Cyprus, November 8, 1964. *Education:* University of Keele (B.A., Hons.); University of Hull (LL.M., International Law). *LANGUAGES:* Greek and English. *PRACTICE AREAS:* Contracts; Conveyancing; Property Law; Commercial Law.

Languages: Greek and English.

REPRESENTATIVE CLIENTS AND REFERENCES: Bank of Cyprus, Ltd.; Bank of Cyprus (Finance) Ltd; Cyprus Popular Bank Ltd.; Lombard Natwest Ltd.; Hellenic Bank (Finance) Ltd.; Municipal Corporation of Limassol; Minerva Insurance Co. Ltd.; Minerva Finance & Investment Co. Ltd.; Paneuropean Insurance Co. Ltd.; Royal Insurance (Int.) Ltd.; General Insurance of Cyprus, Ltd.; Metropolitan Insurance Co. Ltd.; Black Sea Shipping Company; Blasco Ship Management Ltd.; Dobson Fleet Management Ltd.; Ingersoll-Rand (U.S.A.); Hempel's Marine Paints A/S (Denmark); Dupol-Rubbermaid GmbH (Germany); KPMG Peat Marwick; Pannell Kerr Forster; Ernst & Young; Airtours PLC; Clerical Medical Group of Companies; Bristol-Myers; Owners Abroad; Olympic Holidays Ltd.

BAUDEL GELINAS & PARTNERS

CAPITAL CENTER
MAKARIOS AVENUE
NICOSIA, CYPRUS
Telephone: (357-2) 45 07 90
Telefax: (357-2) 45 06 20

Paris, France Office: Baudel Gelinas Delclaux, Landon & Benech. 69, Avenue Victor Hugo, 75783 Paris Cedex 16, France. Telephone: (33-1) 44 17 36 60. Telefax: (33-1) 40 67 91 40.

International Business Law, International Commercial Arbitration. International Taxation.
Firm Engaged in General International Practice. Admitted to Practice in Cyprus.

MEMBERS OF FIRM

JULES-MARC BAUDEL (Not Member of the Cyprus Bar; Also at Paris, France Office).

PAUL-A. GÉLINAS (Not Member of the Cyprus Bar; Also at Paris, France Office).

ANTIS A. TRIANTAFYLLIDES, born Nicosia, Cyprus, October 12, 1933; admitted, 1954, England; 1955, Cyprus. *Education:* Inns of Court, Gray's Inn London (Barrister-at-Law). Member, Court of Arbitration of the International Chamber of Commerce, 1982—. *Member:* English Bar; Cyprus Bar. (Also Member of Antis Triantafyllides and Sons, Nicosia, Cyprus). *LANGUAGES:* Greek and English.

STELIOS A. TRIANTAFYLLIDES, born Nicosia, Cyprus, June 20, 1960; admitted, 1984, Cyprus. *Education:* Oxford University, Worcester College (B.A., Jurisprudence); University of California at Berkeley (LL.M.). Author: "Duties of Majority Shareholders to the Minority under English and American Corporate Law," 1983; "Offshore Operations in Cyprus: a New Opportunity for International Business," 1984. *Member:* Cyprus Bar.

(This Listing Continued)

(Also Member of Antis Triantafyllides and Sons, Nicosia, Cyprus). *LANGUAGES:* Greek and English.

(For Biographical Data on Paris, France Personnel, see Professional Biographies at Paris France).

DR. K. CHRYSOSTOMIDES & CO.

29, STASIKRATES STREET, SUITE 101, 1ST FLOOR
P.O. BOX 2119
NICOSIA, CYPRUS
Telephone: (02) 448278, 448908, 448562
Cable Address: "Chryslaw, Nicosia"
Telex: 2863 JURA CY
Telecopier: (02) 451391

Limassol, Cyprus Office: John Kennedy Av., Kanika Enaerios Complex, Ires Tower, 7th Floor, P.O. Box 3083. Telephone: (05) 366767.
Larnaca, Cyprus Office: Stylianos Lenas Street, Academia Centre, Block 2B, 3rd Floor. Telephone: (04) 626533.

General Practice, Litigation, Corporate, Foreign Investments, Taxation, International and Private International Law, Shipping and Admiralty Law, Aviation Law, Banking, Insurance, Trademarks and Patent Law.

MEMBERS OF FIRM

DR. KYPROS CHRYSOSTOMIDES, born Cyprus, July 11, 1942; admitted, 1973, Cyprus. *Education:* Athens Law School (LL.B, 1964); University of Luxemburg (Diplome de Droit Compare); University of Bonn, West Germany (Doctor of Laws, 1967). Author: "Doing Business in Cyprus," 1980; "The Legal and Tax Aspects of Foreign Investments in Cyprus," 1977; "Die Aufbringung des anfänglichen Kapitals der GmbH und der Private Company," 1964; "Travel Contracts and Hotel-keepers Liability," Article, 1972; "Competence and Incompatibility in the European Convention on Human Rights," Article, 1973; "Taxation of Companies in Cyprus" in "Taxation of Companies in Europe" of the Bureau of Fiscal Documentation; "Cyprus - An Excellent Base for Off-shore Captive Insurance Companies," Article, 1982; "Cyprus - New Off-shore Bank Center," Article, 1982; "The Network of Tax Treaties Between Cyprus and Eastern European Countries," Article, 1992. *Member:* Cyprus Bar Association; Gesellschaft für Rechtsvergleichung; UNIDROIT (Correspondent); Association of Attenders and Alumni of the Hague Academy of International Law; International Fiscal Association; International Tax Planning Association; Cyprus Bar Council (Treasurer, 1975-1978); International Bar Association; Mediterranean and Middle East Institute of Arbitration (Treasurer, 1989—). *LANGUAGES:* Greek, English, German and French. *PRACTICE AREAS:* Corporate Law; Taxation Law; Banking Law.

ELENI K. CHRYSOSTOMIDES, born Cyprus, December 16, 1951; admitted, 1974, Cyprus. *Education:* University College London, Gray's Inn (LL.B., Hons; Barrister at Law, 1973). Author: "Infringement of Trade Mark under Cyprus Law," 1990. *Member:* Cyprus Bar Association; The Senate of the Inns of Court and the Bar; Institute of Trade Mark Agents (Overseas Member). *LANGUAGES:* Greek, English and French. *PRACTICE AREAS:* Contract Law; Sale of Goods Law; Passing Off and Trademarks Law.

CHRYSTALLA S. PITSILLI, born Cyprus, October 22, 1962. Called to the Bar: 1985, Middle Temple, England; admitted, 1986, Cyprus. *Education:* University of Kent at Canterbury (B.A., Hons., Law); The City University, London (M.A. in Law and Practice), Council of Legal Education (Barrister). *Member:* Cyprus Bar Association; The Senate of the Inns of Court and the Bar; Young Lawyers' International Association. *LANGUAGES:* Greek and English. *PRACTICE AREAS:* Corporate Law; Shipping Law; Admiralty Law; Trusts Law; General Practice.

ALEXANDROS H. TALIADOROS, born Cyprus, June 7, 1957; admitted, 1985, Cyprus. *Education:* University of Salonica, Law School. *Member:* Cyprus Bar Association. *LANGUAGES:* Greek and English. *PRACTICE AREAS:* Litigation; Insurance Law; Trademarks Law; Patent Law.

IACOVIDOU ANDRI, born Cyprus, January 4, 1964; admitted, 1987, Cyprus. *Education:* University of Athens, Law School. *Member:* Cyprus Bar Association. *LANGUAGES:* Greek and English. *PRACTICE AREAS:* Corporate Law; General Practice.

MARIA LAZARI, born Cyprus, April 1, 1961; admitted, 1985, Cyprus. *Education:* University of Athens, Law School. *Member:* Cyprus Bar Association. *LANGUAGES:* Greek and English. *PRACTICE AREAS:* General Practice.

(This Listing Continued)

DR. K. CHRYSOSTOMIDES & CO., Nicosia—Continued

YIANNAKIS ECONOMIDES, born Cyprus, August 4, 1955; admitted, 1982, Cyprus. *Education:* University of Athens, Law School; University College, London (LL.M.). *Member:* Cyprus Bar Association. *LANGUAGES:* Greek and English. *PRACTICE AREAS:* Shipping Law; Insurance Law; General Practice.

ELENI KEKKOU, born Cyprus, April 4, 1958; admitted, 1985, Cyprus. *Education:* Law School of Athens University (Law Degree, 1982). *LANGUAGES:* Greek and English. *PRACTICE AREAS:* General Civil Practice; General Insurance Law; Personal Injury Law; Negligence Law; Commercial Law.

MARIA CHRISTODOULOU, born Cyprus, May 13, 1969; admitted, 1993, Cyprus. *Education:* Law School of Athens University (Law Degree, 1992). *Member:* Cyprus Bar Association. *LANGUAGES:* Greek and English. *PRACTICE AREAS:* General Practice; Debt Collection; Banking Law.

MARY ANN MARCOU, born Cyprus, August 27, 1971; admitted, 1994, Cyprus. *Education:* Sheffield University (LL.B., 1991); Cambridge University, Trinity Hall (LL.M., 1992); Gray's Inn (Barrister, 1993). *Member:* Cyprus Bar Association. *LANGUAGES:* Greek, English and French. *PRACTICE AREAS:* General Practice; Corporate Law.

Languages: Greek, English, German and French.

REPRESENTATIVE CLIENTS: S.C. Johnson Company Ltd (Johnson Wax); Compagnie Nationale Air France; Societé Générale (Cyprus) Ltd (OBU); BCI; Teledirect Services (M.E.) Ltd.; Barclays Bank Plc (OBU); Chanel S.A.; F.W. Woolworth & Co. (Cyprus) Ltd.; Raychem Technologies Ltd; Hellenic Bank Ltd.; YKK Zipper Middle East S.A.L.; Alfa-Laval (Cyprus) Ltd; IATA Bank Settlement Plan-Cyprus; Swarovski (Cyprus) Ltd.; Canadian Fracmaster Offshore (Cyprus) Ltd.; Befrachtungskontor Schoening GmbH and Co.; BHF Bank; Pancanadian Petroleum Offshore (Cyprus) Ltd.

LELLOS P. DEMETRIADES LAW OFFICE

9TH FLOOR, THE CHANTECLAIR HOUSE
2 SOPHOULIS STREET
P.O. BOX 1646
NICOSIA 136, CYPRUS
Telephone: 357-2-444391
Cable Address: HELENUS-NICOSIA CYPRUS
Telex: 3111 HELENUS CY
Facsimile: 357-2-451620

Commercial, Corporations (Off-Shore Companies), Tax, Insurance, Intellectual Property, Trusts, International Trade, Admiralty, Arbitration, Trademarks and Human Rights.

MEMBERS OF FIRM

LELLOS P. DEMETRIADES, born Nicosia, Cyprus, February 3, 1933; admitted, 1955, Cyprus and called to the English bar. *Education:* Barrister Gray's Inn, London (1955). *Member:* Cyprus Bar Association. *LANGUAGES:* Greek and English. *PRACTICE AREAS:* Company Law; Tax Law; Trusts; Insurance Law; Commercial Law.

JOANNA J. LOIZIDOU, born Nicosia, Cyprus, June 30, 1944; called to the English bar, 1965; admitted, 1966, Cyprus. *Education:* Grenoble University, France (French Language, 1963); Strasbourg University, France (French Language, 1964); Barrister of Gray's Inn, London (1965). *Member;* Cyprus Bar Association. *LANGUAGES:* Greek, English and French. *PRACTICE AREAS:* Insurance Law; Litigation; Competition Law; Commercial Law; Arbitration.

ACHILLEAS L. DEMETRIADES, born Nicosia, Cyprus, September 6, 1961; called to the English bar, 1985; admitted, 1988, Cyprus. *Education:* Southampton University, Southampton, England (LL.B., 1984); Barrister of Gray's Inn, London (1985); Georgetown University, Washington D.C. (LL.M., Intern. Law, 1987). *Member:* Cyprus Bar Association; International Bar Association, International Association Young Lawyers. *LANGUAGES:* Greek, English and French. *PRACTICE AREAS:* Copyright Law; Trademarks Law; Intellectual Property Law; Commercial Law; International Trade; Admiralty; Human Rights.

VICKY LOIZIDES, born Nicosia, Cyprus, May 12, 1971; 1993, called to the English Bar; admitted, 1994, Cyprus. *Education:* Diavox Lausanne, Switzerland (1989); Bristol University, Bristol, England (LL.B. Hons, 1992). Barrister of Gray's Inn, London (1993). *LANGUAGES:* Greek, English and French. *PRACTICE AREAS:* Insurance Law; Tax Law; Commercial Law; Litigation; Trademark Law.

(This Listing Continued)

EU120B

CONSTANTINOS DEMETRIADES, born Nicosia, Cyprus, July 5, 1967; admitted, 1993, Pupil Advocate, Cyprus. *Education:* Keele University, Staffordshire, England (B.A., Law and Sociology); University of North London (Postgraduate Diploma in Purchasing & Selling). *LANGUAGES:* Greek, English and French. *PRACTICE AREAS:* Commercial Law; Company Law.

EVRIPIDOU, GEORGIADES & CO.

EAGLE HOUSE, AYIOI OMOLOYITES
16 KYRIAKOS MATSIS AVENUE
P.O. BOX 1451
1082 NICOSIA, CYPRUS
Telephone: 357-2-315939
Telex: 4954 EVRIPID CY
Facsimile: 357-2-315553

Corporate, Banking and Finance Law, Shipping, Insurance, Commercial, Building Contracts, Intellectual Property Law and General Civil Litigation.

FIRM PROFILE: *E. Evripidou, Georgiades & Co. is a new partnership established on 1st January, 1991 to meet the needs of sophisticated international clients. Evros I. Evripidou worked for two years in London as head of the Chartered Ships Section of the P & O Shipping Group and Marcos Georgiades for 3 years with Slaughter and May in London. Our firm offers a unique combination of skills acquired by the diverse professional training and work experience of our partners in the City of London and in Cyprus.*

MEMBERS OF FIRM

EVROS I. EVRIPIDOU, born Cyprus, June 18, 1951; admitted, 1974, England; 1979, Cyprus. *Education:* Middle Temple (Barrister-at-Law, 1974): University of London, University College (LL.B., 1975, DIP. Shipping Law, 1976, LL.M., 1977). *Member:* Honourable Society of the Middle Temple; Convocation of University of London; Cyprus Bar Association; Council of Nicosia Bar Association (Vice-President Committee for Restoration of Human Rights). *LANGUAGES:* Greek and English. *PRACTICE AREAS:* Shipping Law; Insurance Law; Corporate Law.

NICOS A. GEORGIADES, born Famagusta, Cyprus, June 6, 1963; admitted, 1987, England; 1988, Cyprus. *Education:* University of London, Queen Mary College (LL.B., 1986); Middle Temple (Barrister-at-Law, 1987). *Member:* Honourable Society of the Middle Temple; Cyprus Bar Association; Executive Committee of the Young Professionals' Association of the Conservative Democratic Rally Party. *LANGUAGES:* Greek and English. *PRACTICE AREAS:* Commercial Law; Building Contracts Law; Corporate Law; General Civil Litigation.

MARCOS A. GEORGIADES, born London, England, January 26, 1962; admitted, 1988, England; 1990, Cyprus. *Education:* University of London, Queen Mary College (LL.B., 1984); Oxford University; Worcester College (B.C.L., 1985). Solicitor of the Supreme Court of Judicature of England and Wales, 1988. *Member:* The Law Society of England; Cyprus Bar Association; Council of the Cyprus Institute of International and European Law. *LANGUAGES:* English and Greek. *PRACTICE AREAS:* Corporate Law; Banking Law; Finance Law; Intellectual Property Law.

GEORGE A. LIASIDES, born Cyprus, March 26, 1963; admitted, 1993, England; 1994, Cyprus. *Education:* Kingston University (LL.B., 1988). Solicitor of the Supreme Court of Judicature of England and Wales, 1993. *Member:* The Law Society of England; Cyprus Bar Association. *LANGUAGES:* English and Greek. *PRACTICE AREAS:* Civil Litigation; Family Law.

LEGAL SUPPORT PERSONNEL

ANDREAS ANTONIOU, born Palekythro, Cyprus, June 15, 1941. Registered Advocates' Clerk, Legal Research, all work associated with Registrar of Companies and Registrar of Ships. (Paralegal).

NEOPHYTOS EVRIPIDOU, born Limassol, Cyprus. Ex Senior Registrar of Nicosia District Court. Member of Panel of Rent Control Court, Probate and Administration of Estates, Legal Research and Registration of Trademarks. (Paralegal).

REPRESENTATIVE CLIENTS: Reebok Cyprus Ltd., Reebok, Greece; Guinness Flight (Cyprus) Ltd.; Barclays Bank PLC; Bank DD Sarajevo; Philiki Insurance Co., Ltd.; Worldwide Ocean Chartering, S.A.; Teleprint International S.A.S.; Imperial Stockbrokers, Ltd.

EMILIOS CH. LEMONARIS LAW OFFICES

Established in 1969

AYIA ELENI TOWER, 3RD FLOOR, OFFICE NO. 34
6 AYIAS ELENIS STREET
P.O. BOX 2095
NICOSIA, CYPRUS
Telephone: 2-454-725
Fax: 2-451-987

EMILIOS LEMONARIS, born September 2, 1936; admitted, 1967, Barrister at Law, Honourable Society of Lincoln's Inn, London; 1969, Cyprus. *LANGUAGES:* English and Greek. *PRACTICE AREAS:* Admiralty and Maritime Law; Agency and Distribution; Banks and Banking; Business Law; Civil Law; Commercial Law; Company Law; Finance; Intellectual Property; International Law; Litigation; Patents and Trademarks; Probate; Taxation; International Trusts.

TASSOS PAPADOPOULOS & CO.

Established in 1971

CHANTECLAIR BUILDING, 2ND FLOOR
2, SOFOULI STREET
NICOSIA, CYPRUS
Telephone: (02) 442999, 442994, 442997
Telex: 3990 TASLAW
Facsimile: (02) 459090

Corporate and Company Law including Offshore Companies, Commercial, Shipping including Litigation on Shipping Law, Maritime, Banking, Insurance, Administration of Estates, Wills and Succession, International Transactions, Building and Engineering Contracts, Trade Marks and Patent, Private International, Administrative, Taxation and Arbitration, Civil and Criminal Litigation, General Practice.

FIRM PROFILE: Tassos Papadopoulos and Co. was founded in 1971 as a two partner firm and now has a total staff of 25 (4 partners, 7 associate lawyers and 14 legal support personnel) and also has offices in all the towns of Cyprus.

Apart from the full range of legal services we offer, our firm has a specialized corporate, commercial shipping, Trade Marks-Patents and Offshore Company Department which is capable of catering to all the needs of the corporate client and businessman.

Many of the staff are holders of more than one degree and are fluent in foreign languages.

MEMBERS OF FIRM

TASSOS N. PAPADOPOULOS, born Nicosia, January 7, 1934; admitted, 1955, Nicosia, Cyprus. *Education:* Gray's Inn, Inns of Court, London, England (Barrister, 1955). Advocate, Nicosia, 1955-1959. Member, Cyprus Constitutional Commission, drafting Constitution of the Republic of Cyprus, 1959-1960. Minister of Interior, 1959-1960, Minister of Finance, 1960-1961, Minister of Labour and Social Insurance, 1960-1970, contemporaneously, Minister of Health, 1964-1967, Minister of Agriculture, 1967-1969, Cyprus Republic. Member of Parliament, 1970-1976. President, House of Representatives, 1976. Representative, Greek Cypriot-Turkish Cypriot Intercommunal Talks, 1976-1978; Member of Parliament as of May 1991 and Parliamentary Leader of Democratic Party. *Member:* Cyprus Bar Association. *LANGUAGES:* Greek, English and French. *PRACTICE AREAS:* Corporate Law; Building and Engineering Law; International Trade Contracts; Taxation.

PAMBOS C. IOANNIDES, born Nicosia, October 12, 1947; admitted, 1971, Cyprus. *Education:* National University of Athens, Law Faculty (LL.B., 1971); University College London (LL.M., 1982). *Member:* Cyprus Bar Association. *LANGUAGES:* Greek and English. *PRACTICE AREAS:* Shipping Law; Maritime Litigation; Company; Banking; Insurance.

NICOS G. PAPAEFSTATHIOU, born Paphos, September 25, 1955; admitted, 1979, Cyprus. *Education:* University of Salonica, Law Faculty (LL.B., 1978); Queen Mary College London (LL.M. in Commercial and Corporate Law, 1989). *Member:* Cyprus Bar Association. *LANGUAGES:* Greek and English. *PRACTICE AREAS:* Civil Litigation; Criminal Litigation; Insurance; Accidents; Arbitration; Commercial Law; Corporate Law.

MARINA G. MARANGOS, born Nicosia, August 24, 1957; admitted, 1979, Cyprus; 1980, England. *Education:* Cambridge University (B.A.

(This Listing Continued)

Hons., 1978; M.A. Hons., 1982); Gray's Inn London (Barrister, 1979). *Member:* English Bar Association; Cyprus Bar Association. *LANGUAGES:* Greek, English and French.

ASSOCIATES

NAIRY DER ARAKELIAN - MERHEJE, born Nicosia, September 10, 1958; admitted, 1983, Cyprus. *Education:* University of Reading (LL.B., Hons., 1979); The Law Society (Solicitors' Final Qualification Examination, London, 1980). *Member:* Cyprus Bar Association. *LANGUAGES:* Greek, English, French and Armenian. *PRACTICE AREAS:* Corporate; Commercial; Offshore Enterprises; Trademarks and Service Marks.

MARIOS G. ELIADES, born Nicosia, May 11, 1963; admitted, 1990, Cyprus. *Education:* University of Kent (B.A. Hons. in Law, 1986); University of London, King's College (LL.M., 1987). *Member:* Cyprus Bar Association. *LANGUAGES:* Greek, English and French. *PRACTICE AREAS:* Civil Litigation; Criminal Litigation; Industrial Disputes; Trademarks; Admiralty.

ALEXANDRA K. ALEXANDROU, born Nicosia, April 12, 1966; admitted, 1990, Cyprus. *Education:* National University of Athens, Law Faculty (LL.B., 1989); Leicester University (LL.M., 1992). *Member:* Cyprus Bar Association. *LANGUAGES:* Greek, English and French. *PRACTICE AREAS:* Administrative Law; Civil Litigation.

CONSTANTINOS G. LYCOURGOS, born Nicosia, February 10, 1964; admitted, 1993, Cyprus. *Education:* University of Paris II (Licence en Droit, 1985; Maitrise en Droit Public, 1986; DEA de Droit Communautaire, 1987; Doctorat en Droit, 1991). Lecturer, European Community Law, University of Paris II, 1988-1989. *Member:* Cyprus Bar Association. *LANGUAGES:* Greek, French and English. *PRACTICE AREAS:* Corporate Law; Offshore Enterprises; Civil Litigation.

ANGELOS P. DAVID, born Nicosia, September 15, 1967; admitted, 1993, Cyprus. *Education:* Salonica University (LL.B., 1991). *Member:* Cyprus Bar Association. *LANGUAGES:* Greek and English. *PRACTICE AREAS:* Civil Litigation; Criminal Litigation; Banking; Family Law; Industrial Disputes.

KYRIAKOS N. THEODORIDES, born Nicosia, May 18, 1968; admitted, 1993, Cyprus. *Education:* University of Wales (LL.B., 1991); University of Bristol (LL.M., 1992). *Member:* Cyprus Bar Association. *LANGUAGES:* Greek and English. *PRACTICE AREAS:* Civil Litigation; Criminal Litigation; Administration of Estates; Banking.

LOUCIA ASTREOU, born Nicosia, November 30, 1966; admitted, 1993, Cyprus; 1993, Solicitor of the Supreme Court, London. *Education:* University of Keele (B.A., Hons., Law and Psychology, 1989); The College of Law, Guildford (1990). *Member:* Cyprus Bar Association; The Law Society, London. *LANGUAGES:* Greek and English. *PRACTICE AREAS:* Civil Litigation; Criminal Litigation; Personal Injury; Insurance.

REPRESENTATIVE CLIENTS: Cyprus Popular Bank Ltd.; Wardley Cyprus Ltd. (wholly owned subsidiary of Hong-Kong Bank); Byblos Bank Ltd.; Beogradska Banka; Cyprus Ports Authority; Cyprus Hotel Association; Evergreen Shipping Lines; Eurotrade Ltd.; NKS Shacolas Group of Companies (Insurance, International Commerce, Shipping, Woolworths Cyprus); R. Christofidou Ltd. (agents of Eurosure Insurance, Continental Insurance, L'Union Nationale); J. & P. Construction Ltd.; Lefkaritis Bros. Ltd. (oil refinery, imports retail sales); Cyems Ltd. (electrical mechanical supplies and installation company); Yugo Arab Co. Ltd.; Louis Group of Companies (biggest chain of Hotels in Cyprus, Tourist and Travel Office and Agents of Alitalia, TWA, Singapore Airlines); Saba & Co. Auditors; Saba (T.M.P.) Co.; (Trade Marks and Patent Registration); Sedigep Ltd. (Cyprus Agricultural Exports Co-operative Society); Louis Berger (Engineering Consultants); Tobacco Institute.

GEORGE L. SAVVIDES & CO.

(incorporating Marcos S. Kyprianou & Co)

Advocates - Legal Consultants

Established in 1984

1 GLAFKOS STREET
1085 NICOSIA, CYPRUS
Telephone: (357) 2 422355
Fax: (357) 2 421819
Telex: 4970 Juris CY

Limassol Office: Omega Court, 1st, 2nd and 4th Floor, 4 Regas Fereos Street, P.O. Box 4098, 3720. Telephone: 357-5-376886. Fax: 357-5-374930, 374557. Telex: 4970 Juris CY.

(This Listing Continued)

GEORGE L. SAVVIDES & CO., Nicosia—Continued

Litigation, Banks and Banking, Corporate Law, Company Law (including Offshore company formation and administration), Commercial Law, Admiralty and Maritime Law (including ship and mortgage registration), Arbitration, Taxation, Personal Injury, Insurance, Sale of Land, Criminal, Property, Debtor and Creditor, Contracts, Wills, Probate, Trusts and Estates, Trademarks, General Practice.

REPRESENTATIVE CLIENTS AND REFERENCES: Bank of Cyprus, Ltd.; Bank of Cyprus (Finance) Ltd; Cyprus Popular Bank Ltd.; Lombard Natwest Ltd.; Hellenic Bank (Finance) Ltd.; Municipal Corporation of Limassol; Minerva Insurance Co. Ltd.; Minerva Finance & Investment Co. Ltd.; Paneuropean Insurance Co. Ltd.; Royal Insurance (Int.) Ltd.; General Insurance of Cyprus, Ltd.; Metropolitan Insurance Co. Ltd.; Black Sea Shipping Company; Blasco Ship Management Ltd.; Dobson Fleet Management Ltd.; Ingersoll-Rand (U.S.A.); Hempel's Marine Paints A/S (Denmark); Dupol-Rubbermaid GmbH (Germany); KPMG Peat Marwick; Pannell Kerr Forster; Ernst & Young; Airtours PLC; Clerical Medical Group of Companies; Bristol-Myers; Owners Abroad; Olympic Holidays Ltd.

(For Complete Biographical Information on all Personnel, See Professional Biographies at Limassol)

ANTIS TRIANTAFYLLIDES AND SONS

Established in 1955

TRIANTAFYLLIDES BUILDING
CAPITAL CENTER 9TH FLOOR
P.O. BOX 1255
NICOSIA, CYPRUS
Telephone: (02) 462925
Cable Address: "Trianta" Nicosia
Telex: 3828 TRIANTA CY
Telefax: (02) 450620

Paris, France Office: 167 BIS, Avenue Victor Hugo, 75116. Telephone: (33-1) 45 53 38 38. Telefax: 45 53 63 48.

Corporate, Banking, Tax, Foreign Investments, Investments in Eastern Europe and the C.I.S., International Trusts, International Arbitration, Maritime and Admiralty Law, Trademarks and Patents, General Commercial and Civil Practice.

FIRM PROFILE: The Law Firm Antis Triantafyllides and Sons was established in 1955 and it is one of the oldest firms on the island with a highly international practice providing services in all areas of law. Mr. Antis Triantafyllides is the Cyprus Member of the Court of Arbitration of the International Chamber of Commerce.

MEMBERS OF FIRM

ANTIS A. TRIANTAFYLLIDES, born Nicosia, Cyprus, October 12, 1933; admitted, 1954, England; 1955, Cyprus. Education: Inns of Court, Gray's Inn London (Barrister-at-Law). Author: "Cyprus-The New Location for International Commercial Arbitration," 1988. Member, Court of Arbitration of the International Chamber of Commerce, 1982—. Member: Cyprus Bar. (Also Member of Derains-Gelinas and Co., Nicosia, Cyprus). LANGUAGES: Greek and English. PRACTICE AREAS: Banking; International Arbitration; General Commercial and Civil Practice.

GEORGE A. TRIANTAFYLLIDES, born Nicosia, Cyprus, July 29, 1956; admitted, 1981, Cyprus. Education: Oxford University, Worcester College (M.A. (Jurisprudence); B.C.L.). Member: Cyprus Bar. LANGUAGES: Greek and English. PRACTICE AREAS: Tax; Maritime and 'Admiralty Law; General Commercial and Civil Practice.

STELIOS A. TRIANTAFYLLIDES, born Nicosia, Cyprus, June 20, 1960; admitted, 1984, Cyprus. Education: Oxford University, Worcester College (M.A. (Jurisprudence); University of California at Berkeley (LL.M.). Author: "Duties of Majority Shareholders to the Minority under English and American Corporate Law," 1983; "Offshore Operations in Cyprus: a New Opportunity for International Business," 1984. Member, Committee on Offshore Business of the Cyprus Bar Council, 1988—. Member: Cyprus Bar. (Also Member of Derains-Gelinas and Co., Nicosia, Cyprus). LANGUAGES: Greek and English. PRACTICE AREAS: Corporate; Foreign Investments in Eastern Europe and the C.I.S.; Trademarks and Patents.

MICHAEL CLEOPAS, born Famagusta, Cyprus, November 4, 1948; admitted, 1977, Cyprus. Education: Athens University, Law School (B.A.). Member, Cyprus Bar Disciplinary Council. Member: Cyprus Bar. LANGUAGES: Greek and English. PRACTICE AREAS: General Commercial and Civil Practice.

(This Listing Continued)

DESPO KYRIALLI, born Nicosia, Cyprus, August 13, 1961; admitted, 1984, Cyprus. Education: University of Newcastle (LL.B.); Inns of Court, Gray's Inn London (Barrister-at-Law). Member: Cyprus Bar. LANGUAGES: Greek and English. PRACTICE AREAS: General Commercial and Civil Practice.

STELLA CHRISTODOULIDOU, born Nicosia, Cyprus, June 1, 1970; admitted, 1992, Cyprus. Education: University of Leicester (LL.B Hons.), Inns of Court; Gray's Inn, London (Barrister-at-Law). Member: Cyprus Bar. LANGUAGES: Greek and English. PRACTICE AREAS: General Commercial and Civil Practice.

DORINA PAPADOPOULOU, born Nicosia, Cyprus, January 3, 1969; admitted, 1992, Cyprus. Education: University of Leicester (LL.B Hons). Member: Cyprus Bar. LANGUAGES: Greek and English. PRACTICE AREAS: General Commercial and Civil Practice.

Languages: Greek, English and French.

REPRESENTATIVE CLIENTS: R.J. Reynolds Tobacco International S.A.; Pepsico Inc.; Merck Sharp & Dohme (Middle East) Limited; Bristol-Myers Squibb (U.S.A.); Newmont Mining Corp. (USA); Toshiba International (Japan); F. Hoffmann La Roche AG (Switzerland); Henkel K.G a.A. (W. Germany); Schering A.G. (W. Germany); Cable and Wireless plc (U.K.); Eagle Star Life Assurance Company Limited (U.K.); Inchcape Middle East Limited; Gallaher International Ltd. (U.K.); Banque Nationale De Paris plc; West of England Protection and Indemnity Association (U.K.); National Bank of Greece; Hellenic Bank; Coopers & Lybrand; University of Cyprus; Cyprus Chamber of Commerce and Industry.
REFERENCES: Bank of Cyprus Ltd.

CHRISTODOULOS G. VASSILIADES & CO.

EL GRECO HOUSE, OFFICE 104
20 QUEEN FREDERICA STREET
P.O. BOX 1343
NICOSIA, CYPRUS
Telephone: 357 2 473688
Fax: 357 2 455259
Telex: 2055 JAMESCY

Formation and Maintenance of Offshore Companies, Corporate, Banking and Finance Law, Shipping, Tax, Investments in Eastern Europe, Trade Marks.

CHRISTODOULOS G. VASSILIADES, born March 31, 1957; admitted, 1984, Cyprus.

LOUISA CHR. MASSONIDOU, born September 12, 1968; admitted, 1993, Cyprus.

CZECH REPUBLIC

BINDER, GRÖSSWANG & PARTNERS

KOUNICOVA 67A
CS-65831 BRNO, CZECH REPUBLIC
Telephone: +42 (5) 41 21 32 16
Fax: +42 (5) 41 21 15 28

Vienna, Austria Office: Tuchlauben 7a, A-1010. Telephone: +43 (1) 533 44 63. Fax: +43 (1) 535 44 52.

Advice and Assistance in respect of foreign investments in Czechoslovakia, in particular the establishment of Czechoslovakia companies with foreign participation, including Joint-Venture Companies.

Kocián, Šolc, Touška a spol.

KARLOVY VARY, CZECH REPUBLIC

(See Prague, Czech Republic)

Corporate and Commercial Law, Mergers and Acquisitions, Privatization, Joint Ventures, Real Estate, Banking and Finance, Securities, Bankruptcy, Competition Law, Commercial Litigation.

ADVOKÁTNÍ KANCELÁŘ

V JÁMĚ 12
110 00 PRAGUE 1, CZECH REPUBLIC
Telephone: +42 (2) 26 02 93; 26 90 29; 24 22 84 51
Telefax: +42 (2) 26 02 93; 26 90 29; 24 22 84 51

Practice in local law in all aspects of doing business.

DR. RENATA SCHOLZOVÁ, born Prague, Czech Republic; admitted, 1984, Czech Republic. *Education:* Charles University, Faculty of Law. *Member:* Czech Bar Association; International Bar Association. *LANGUAGES:* Czech, English, Russian and Slovac. *PRACTICE AREAS:* Company Law; Commercial Law; Litigation.

ALLEN & OVERY

JINDŘIŠSKÁ 34
110 00 PRAGUE 1, CZECH REPUBLIC
Telephone: (42 2) 2410 3317
Facsimile: (42 2) 2410 3235

London, England Office: One New Change, EC4M 9QQ. Telephone: 0171 330 3000. Facsimile: 0171 330 9999.

Beijing, China Office: Suite 3204, Jing Guang Centre, Hu Jia Lou, Chaoyang District, 100020. Telephone: (86 1) 501 4681. Facsimile: (86 1) 501 4682.

Brussels, Belgium Office: Rue de la Loi 99, Box 8, 1040. Telephone: (32 2) 230 27 91. Facsimile (32 2) 230 66 13.

Budapest, Hungary Office: Mádach Trade Center, Mádach Imre utca 13-14, H-1075. Telephone: (361) 268 1511. Facsimile: (361) 268 1515.

Dubai, United Arab Emirates Office: 501 Al Futtaim Tower,P.O. Box 3251, Deira. Telephone: (971 4) 282296. Facsimile: (971 4) 212860.

Frankfurt, Germany Office: Taunusanlage 11, 11th Floor, 60329. Telephone: (49 69) 242 6120. Facsimile: (49 69) 242 61220.

Hong Kong Office: 9th Floor, Three Exchange Square, 8 Connaught Place. Telephone: (852) 2840 1282. Telex: 68757. Facsimile: (852) 2840 0515.

Madrid, Spain Office: Antonio Maura 7, 6°, 28014. Telephone: (34 1) 521 2654. Facsimile: (34 1) 523 0458.

Moscow, Russia Office: 9 ul Tverskaya, Entrance No 5, 8th Floor, 103009. Telephone: (7 501) 940 4500. Facsimile: (7 501) 940 4501.

New York Office: Swiss Bank Tower, 10 East 50th Street, 10022. Telephone (1-212) 754 3340. Facsimile: (1-212) 754 7903.

Paris, France Office: 1 Avenue Franklin D. Roosevelt, 75008. Telephone (33-1) 49 53 06 37. Telex: 651079. Facsimile: (33-1) 49 53 91 52.

Singapore Office: 20 Raffles Place #08-03, Ocean Towers, 0104. Telephone: (65) 533 0988. Facsimile: (65) 533 1322.

Tokyo, Japan Office: NSE Building, 5th Floor, 1-7-1 Kanda Jinbo-cho, Chiyoda-ku Tokyo 101. Telephone (81 3) 3259 9898. Facsimile (81 3) 3259 9888.

Warsaw, Poland Office: ul. Kopernika 17, IV Floor, 00-359. Telephone: (48 22) 262 226. Facsimile: (48 22) 262 360.

Firm engaged in advising on all legal aspects of doing business in the Czech & Slovak Republics with an international practice and advice on local law provided by qualified local lawyers.

CONTACT PARTNERS

Alison M. Beardsley (Also at London, England)

RESIDENT ASSOCIATES

Trevor Brown   **Charles Worth**

(For Complete Biographical Data on all Personnel, see Professional Biographies at London, England)

ALLIANCE PRAGUE

JÁCHYMOVA 2
110 00 PRAGUE 1, CZECH REPUBLIC
Telephone: (42) 2 232 11 30; 232 55 60; 232 80 94
Fax: (42) 2 232 63 71; 232 29 04; 301 73 54

Foreign investment in the Czech Republic, Privatizations, Corporate Law, Banking and Securities Law, Mergers and Acquisitions, Joint Ventures, Intellectual Property Law, Real Estate Law, Tax Law, Commercial Law, Administrative Law, Litigation.

(This Listing Continued)

FIRM PROFILE: The firm was established as a joint office by the "Alliance of European Lawyers" and Czech lawyers. Thanks to the close cooperation between Czech lawyers and continental European lawyers the firm can offer high quality legal services coupled with a true understanding of the Czech legal and business environment. The client base comprises leading European, North American and Japanese corporations and major Czech companies. The firm provides its services in the Czech, Slovak, English, French, German, Dutch, Italian, Spanish, Hungarian and Russian language.

MEMBER FIRMS "ALLIANCE OF EUROPEAN LAWYERS"

DE BANDT, VAN HECKE & LAGAE at Brussels and Antwerp, Belgium

DE BRAUW BLACKSTONE WESTBROEK at Amsterdam, The Hague, Rotterdam and Eindhoven, The Netherlands

JEANTET & ASSOCIES at Paris, France and Warsaw, Poland

LAGERLÖF & LEMAN at Stockholm, Gothenburg and Malmö, Sweden

OPPENHOFF & RÄDLER at Berlin, Frankfurt am Main, Cologne, Leipzig and Munich, Germany

URÍA & MENÉNDEZ at Madrid and Barcelona, Spain

The member firms have joint offices at Brussels, London and New York.

CZECH LAWYERS

PETR SRAMEK, born 1950. *Education:* Charles University (JUDr., 1973); School of Economics (1980). Foreign legal practice, Canada, 1991. *Member:* Chamber of Commercial Lawyers; Fraternity of Central European Lawyers; German-Czech Lawyers Association.

JUDR. GABRIEL BRENKA, born 1951. *Education:* Comenius University, Bratislava (1974). Civil Judge, 1976-1979; Ministry of Foreign Affairs, 1979-1984; 1989-1992; Czechoslovak Counsel at USA, 1984-1989; Attorney at Law, 1992. *Member:* Czech Bar Association. (Also practicing individually).

JUDR. MARTIN ŠEBEK, born 1961. *Education:* Charles University, Prague (1984). Foreign legal practice, France, 1990; Canada, 1991. *Member:* Czech Bar Association; Masaryk Czech-French Association (President); Junior Lawyers Association (Vice Chairman).

VACLAV VALVODA, born 1965. *Education:* Charles University (JUDr., 1988). Foreign legal practice, Belgium, 1990-1992. *Member:* Chamber of Commercial Lawyers.

JUDR. GABRIEL POTHE, born 1964. *Education:* Comenius University, Bratislava (1986); Vienna University (1990); Central European University (1994). *Member:* Czech Chamber of Commercial Lawyers.

ALEXANDR CESAR, born 1965. *Education:* Charles University (JUDr., 1988).

HANA HEROLDOVA, born 1964. *Education:* Charles University (JUDr., 1988).

IVAN ŘEZNIČEK, born 1965. *Education:* Charles University (Mgr., 1988).

ALEŠ MUSIL, born 1966. *Education:* Charles University, Prague (1992); College of Europe, Brugge (1994).

VÁCLAV ROVENSKÝ, born 1969. *Education:* Charles University, Prague (1991). Foreign legal practice, USA, 1990-1991.

DANIEL VLČEK, born 1969. *Education:* Charles University, Prague (1990).

LUDĚK VRÁNA, born 1969. *Education:* Charles University, Prague (1992); Institut des Hautes Etudes Européennes, Strasbourg (1993). Foreign legal practice, Belgium (1994).

DAGMAR SYNKOVÁ, born 1966. *Education:* Charles University, Prague (1994).

MIROSLAV DUBOVSKÝ, born 1970. *Education:* Charles University, Prague (1993).

HANA RECHZIEGELOVÁ, born 1969. *Education:* Charles University, Prague (1994).

PAVEL GÉCI, born 1969. *Education:* Charles University, Prague (1993).

RESIDENT FOREIGN LAWYERS

JAAP DE KEIJZER, born 1962. *Education:* University of Utrecht (LL.M., 1989; M.Sc., 1989). *Member:* IBA (SERL).

(This Listing Continued)

ALLIANCE PRAGUE, Prague—Continued

RAINER FRANK, born 1962. *Education:* University of Tübingen (first and second state examination resp. 1986 and 1991). *Member:* German-Czech Lawyers Association.

ANTHONY LACOUDRE, born 1968. *Education:* Université de Paris II-Assas (Maitrise de Droit, 1990); Université de Sceaux/HEC (Dess, 1991).

GABRIELLE PRINSEN, born 1965. *Education:* University of Leiden (LL.M., 1991).

OF COUNSEL

JAN DĚDIČ, born 1951. *Education:* Charles University, Prague (1974). Associate Professor and Head of Department of Law, Prague School of Economics. Member, Legislative Council of the Czech Government. *Member:* Chamber of Commercial Lawyers.

ALTHEIMER & GRAY

PLATNERSKA 4
110 00 PRAGUE 1, CZECH REPUBLIC
Telephone: 42-2 2481-2782
Fax: 42-2-2481-0125 or 232-9595
REVISERS OF THE POLAND LAW DIGEST FOR THIS DIRECTORY.

Chicago, Illinois Office: 10 South Wacker Drive, 60606. Telephone: 312-715-4000. Fax: 312-715-4800. Telex: RCA 297102 A G UR.
Warsaw, Poland Office: ul. Nowogrodzka 50, 00-950. Telephones: 011-48-22-298-357; 011-48-39-12-1338. Fax: 011-48-2-628-3640.
Kiev, Ukraine Office: Kontraktova Ploscha 4, Building 3, Room 304, 254145. Telephone: 011-7-044-230-2534. Fax: 011-7-044-230-2535.
Bratislava, Slovakia Office: Nam. SNP 15, 811 06. Telephone: 011-42-7-362-736. Fax: 011-42-7-367-960.
Istanbul, Turkey Office: Tesvikiye Cad. 107, Tesvikiye Palas 7, Tesvikiye 80200 Istanbul, Turkey. Telephone: 011-90-212-227-6750. Fax: 011-90-212-227-6759.

Privatizations and Acquisitions, Joint Ventures and Foreign Investment, Government Affairs, Real Estate Development, Architecture, Engineering and Construction, Banking and Finance, Bankruptcy, Licensing and Distribution, Insurance, Telecommunications, Securities, Taxation and Customs.

EUROPEAN COUNSEL

PETR KOTAB, born Prague, Czechoslovakia, June 1, 1963; admitted, 1990, Czechoslovakia. *Education:* Charles University School of Law (Master of Law, summa cum laude, 1985; Doctor of Law, 1985); postgraduate studies specializing in financial law 1986-1989. Member of the faculty, Charles University School of Law, 1986—. Former Member: Expert Commission for Financial Legislation of the Legislative Council of the Government of the Czech Republic, 1990-1992; Branch Commission for Privatization and De-etatization of the Ministry of Industry of the Czech Republic, 1990-1992. Author: "Legal Forms and Techniques of Privatization in Czechoslovakia," Materials of the XXIst Colloquy on European Law, Council of Europe, 1991; "Capitalization of Receivables (Debt-Equity Swaps) in the Czech Legal Environment," In: Pravo a podnikani 7/1993, Prague. Co-Author: "Foreign Investment in Central and Eastern Europe," The Parker School of Foreign and Comparative Law, Columbia University, 1993; "Introduction into Studies of Financial Science and Czech Financial Law," Society of Czechoslovak Lawyers USEHRD, 1994. Member, Chamber of Commercial Lawyers of the Czech Republic. *LANGUAGES:* Czech, English and Russian. *PRACTICE AREAS:* Corporate Law; Financial Law; Taxation; Mergers and Acquisitions; Law of Joint Ventures and Foreign Investment; Securities Law.

ALENA BANYAIOVA, born Most, Czechoslovakia, May 2, 1949; admitted, 1992, Czechoslovakia. *Education:* Charles University School of Law (Master of Law, 1972; Doctor of Law, 1973, Candidate of Sciences, Ph.D., 1988); St. Louis University School of Law (Visiting Attorney program sponsored by the American Bar Association and the International Academy of Trial Lawyers), 1991-1992. Research Scholar, Czechoslovak Institute of State and Law, Academy of Sciences, 1988-1990. Arbitrator and Judge, Commercial Division, Czechoslovak State Arbitration Agency, 1972-1988, 1990-1992. Intern, Armstrong, Teasdale, Schlafly & Davis, St. Louis, Missouri (Visiting Attorney program sponsored by the American Bar Association and the International Academy of Trial Lawyers), 1991-

(This Listing Continued)

1992. *Member:* Chamber of Attorneys of the Czech Republic. *LANGUAGES:* Czech, English, Russian.

ASSOCIATES

IVO BARTA, born February 14, 1967. *Education:* Comenius University School of Law, Bratislava (Doctor of Law, summa cum laude); Catholic University of Leuven School of Law (LL.M., magna cum laude, with specialization in the Law of the European Communities, 1992); University of Michigan School of Law (LL.M., in U.S. Business and Financial Law, 1993). Scholar at the Centre for Advanced Legal Studies of the Catholic University of Leuven School of Law. Fulbright Scholar (John Marshall) University of Michigan School of Law. Member, Faculty of Law of Comenius University. *LANGUAGES:* Slovak, English, Czech, Russian and German.

DAVID FALADA, born Prague, Czechoslovakia, September 26, 1966; admitted, 1994, Czech Republic. *Education:* Charles University School of Law, Prague (Doctor of Law, 1988); The John Hopkins University; Paul H. Nitze School of Advanced International Studies, Bologna, Italy (Bologna Center Diploma in International Studies, May, 1991). Instructor, Charles University School of Law. *Member:* Chamber of Commercial Lawyers of the Czech Republic. *LANGUAGES:* Czech, English, Italian, German. *PRACTICE AREAS:* Corporate; Labor; Civil and Administrative.

BRADLEY J. HASKINS, born Battle Creek, Michigan, July 7, 1959; admitted, 1985, Texas; 1987, New York (Not admitted in Czech Republic). *Education:* University of Michigan, Honors College (A.B., cum laude, 1982); University of Michigan (J.D., cum laude, 1985). Phi Delta Phi. Member: International Law Society, Appellate Law Program; Christian Law Students. Project Chairman, Jaycees project expanding Michigan's international trading opportunities with East Europe, Michigan to East Europe, 1991-1992. (Also at Kiev Office). *PRACTICE AREAS:* Corporate; Banking; International.

JAN MYSKA, born Prague, Czechoslovakia, April 9, 1969; (Not admitted in Czech Republic). *Education:* Charles University School of Law (Master of Law, summa cum laude, 1993); Charles University School of Law postgraduate studies specializing in corporate and civil law. *LANGUAGES:* Czech, English and Russian. *PRACTICE AREAS:* Corporate; Civil and Administrative Law.

MAREK NOSEK, born Ceske Budejovice, Czechoslovakia, June 19, 1963. *Education:* Charles University School of Law (Master of Law, 1985; Doctor of Law, 1985). Ceskoslovenska Obchodni Banka, A.S., Prague, 1985-1991. Author: "Legal Aspects of Documentary Credits and Documentary Collections," Bankovni a komercni informace, 1987; "Debt-Equity Swaps as a Method of Reducing Foreign Debts," Bankovni a komercni informace, 1988; "Emerging Capital Markets," Bankovni a komercni informace, 1989. Member of the Faculty, Charles University School of Law, 1991-1992. *LANGUAGES:* Czech, English and Russian. *PRACTICE AREAS:* Financial Law; Corporate Law.

SUSAN TIETJEN, born Suffern, New York, January 28, 1958; admitted, 1988, New York; 1989, District of Columbia (Not admitted in Czech Republic). *Education:* Wesleyan University, Middletown, Connecticut (B.A., History and German, 1980); Philipps-Universitat, Marburg, Germany (graduate study in German literature and language, 1981-1982); Universitat Hamburg, Hamburg, Germany (graduate study in law, 1985-1986); University of Michigan Law School (J.D., 1985). Recipient, William W. Bishop Award for International Law, 1984. Member, Board of Directors of American Chamber of Commerce in the Czech Republic. *Member:* New York State, American and International Bar Associations. *LANGUAGES:* English and German. *PRACTICE AREAS:* Corporate; Financing; Mergers and Acquisitions; International.

GABRIELA VENDLOVA, born Kolin, Czechoslovakia, September 5, 1968; (Not admitted in Czech Republic). *Education:* Charles University School of Law, Prague (Master of Law, summa cum laude, 1992). Wrote thesis on Aspects of Protectionism and Anti-Dumping Policy on the World Market. Legislative Assistant, Federal Assembly of the Czech and Slovak Federal Republic, 1990-1992. Fellow, Office of Congressman James P. Moran, U.S. Congress, 1992-1993. *LANGUAGES:* Czech, Slovak, Russian and English.

PARTNERS

JAMES E. CARROLL, born Evanston, Illinois, July 31, 1956; admitted, 1982, Illinois (Not admitted in Czech Republic). *Education:* Loras College (B.A., maxima cum laude, 1978); Cambridge University (LL.M. in International Law, 1980); Northwestern University (J.D., 1982). Delta Epsilon Sigma; Phi Alpha Theta. Member, Northwestern Journal of Interna-

(This Listing Continued)

tional Law and Business, 1981-1982. Author: "Of Icebergs, Oil Wells and Treaties: Hydrocarbon Exploitation Offshore Antarctica," 19 Stanford Journal of International Law, 1983. Co-author: "Recent Developments in Polish Insurance Law," De Paul Business Law Journal, Spring/Summer 1991. *Member:* Chicago, Illinois State, American and International Bar Associations. (Also at Chicago, Warsaw, Bratislava, Istanbul and Kiev Offices). *PRACTICE AREAS:* International Law; Finance Law; Mergers and Acquisitions.

LOUIS B. GOLDMAN, born Chicago, Illinois, April 11, 1948; admitted, 1975, California; 1976, New York; 1991, Illinois (Not admitted in Czech Republic). *Education:* University of California at Berkeley (A.B., magna cum laude, 1970); University of Chicago (J.D., cum laude, 1974). Phi Beta Kappa; Order of the Coif. Member, University of Chicago Law Review, 1972-1973. Co-Author: "Repossessing the Spirit of St. Louis: Expanding The Protection of Sections 1110 and 1168 of The Bankruptcy Code," The Business Lawyer, Vol. 41, No. 1, 1985. Co-Author: "Recent Developments in Polish Insurance Law," De Paul Business Law Journal, Spring/Summer 1991. Law Clerk to Judge Charles B. Renfrew, U.S. District Court, Northern District of California, 1974-1975. Member, Chicago-Prague Sister Cities Committee of the City of Chicago. *Member:* State Bar of California; Association of the Bar of the City of New York; Chicago, New York State (Member, Committee on International Banking, Securities and Financial Transactions, Committee on International Investment and Development), American (Member, Sections on: Corporation, Banking and Business Law; Taxation; International Law and Practice) and International Bar Associations; New York County Lawyers Association (Member, Special Committee on the Peoples Republic of China). (Also at Chicago, Warsaw, Bratislava and Istanbul Offices). *PRACTICE AREAS:* Securities Law; Mergers and Acquisitions Law; International Law.

JEFFREY NORMAN SMITH, born Milwaukee, Wisconsin, May 5, 1960; admitted, 1985, Illinois (Not admitted in Czech Republic). *Education:* University of Michigan (B.B.A., with high distinction, 1982); Northwestern University (J.D., cum laude, 1985). Phi Beta Kappa; Beta Gamma Sigma. *Member:* Chicago, Illinois State and American Bar Associations. (Also at Chicago, Warsaw and Bratislava Offices). *PRACTICE AREAS:* Mergers and Acquisitions; Joint Ventures; Privatizations; Finance Law; International Law.

REVISERS OF THE POLAND LAW DIGEST FOR THIS DIRECTORY.

(For complete biographical data on personnel at Chicago, Illinois, Warsaw, Poland, Kiev, Ukraine, Bratislava, Slovakia and Istanbul, Turkey, see Professional Biographies at those locations)

BAKER & McKENZIE

ČELAKOVSKÉHO SADY, NO. 4
110 00 PRAGUE 1, CZECH REPUBLIC
Telephone: (02) 24 22 7330; 24 22 5687; 265 492; 268 536;
262 792; 262 391
Int'l Dialing: (42-2) 24 22 7330; 24 22 5687; 265 492; 268 536;
262 792; 262 391
Facsimile: (42-2) 24 22 2124; 26 75 26

Associated Offices of Baker & McKenzie in: Almaty, Amsterdam, Bangkok, Barcelona, Beijing, Berlin, Bogotá, Brasília, Brussels, Budapest, Buenos Aires, Cairo, Caracas, Chicago, Dallas, Frankfurt, Geneva, Hanoi, Ho Chi Minh City, Hong Kong, Juárez, Kiev, London, Madrid, Manila, Melbourne, México City, Miami, Milan, Monterrey, Moscow, New York, Palo Alto, Paris, Rio de Janeiro, Riyadh, Rome, St. Petersburg, San Diego, San Francisco, São Paulo, Singapore, Stockholm, Sydney, Taipei, Tijuana, Tokyo, Toronto, Valencia, Warsaw, Washington, D.C. and Zürich.
Correspondent Law Firm: Hadiputranto, Hadinoto & Partners, Jakarta.

Corporate, Corporate Financing, Banking, Tax, Privatization, Commercial, Real Estate, Litigation.

PARTNERS

DR. MARTIN RADVAN, born Prague, Czechoslovakia, June 21, 1948; admitted, 1971, Czech Republic; 1982, New York, U.S.A. *Education:* Charles University, Prague (J.D., 1971; JUDr/JSD., 1973); New York University (LL.M., 1984). *Member:* New York State and American Bar Associations; Association of Czech Lawyers; Czech Bar Chamber. *LANGUAGES:* Czech, Slovak, Russian and English.

(This Listing Continued)

ASSOCIATES

DR. ANDREA BEDNAŘÍKOVÁ, born Prague, Czech Republic, May 14, 1967; admitted, 1994, Czech Republic. *Education:* Law Faculty of Charles University (Iuris Doctoris, 1990); Faculty of Law of the University of Cambridge (Diploma in legal studies, 1993). Judge of the District Court, Prague 10, 1991-1994. *Member:* Czech Lawyers Association. *LANGUAGES:* English and Russian.

EDMUND J. GEMMELL, born Reading, England, June 3, 1967; admitted, 1992, England and Wales (Not admitted in Czech Republic). *Education:* Kent University (1989); Birmingham Polytechnic (1991). *Member:* Law Society of England and Wales; Sports Lawyers Association; British Association for Sport and the Law. *LANGUAGES:* English and French.

ROMAIN NACU, born Prague, Czechoslovakia, January 10, 1970; admitted, 1993, Czech Republic. *Education:* Charles University (Mgr., 1993). *LANGUAGES:* Czech, French, Slovak, German, Russian.

DR. FRANTIŠEK SCHULMANN, born Brocket Hall, Welwyn, Herts GB, March 5, 1947; admitted, 1978, Czech Republic. *Education:* Charles University, Prague (J.D., 1974; Doctor of Law, 1980). *Member:* Czech Bar Association. *LANGUAGES:* Czech, English and Slovak.

MAREK J. SVOBODA, born České Budějovice, Czech Republic, May 9, 1962; admitted, 1986, England and Wales (Not admitted in Czech Republic). *Education:* Cambridge University (B.A., 1984; M.A., 1986); Inns of Court School of Law (Bar Dip., 1985). *Member:* Bar of England and Wales; Lincoln's Inn. *LANGUAGES:* English, Czech, French and German.

BAKEŠ & PARTNERS

NA PRIKOPE 27
113 49 PRAGUE 1, CZECH REPUBLIC
Telephone: 011-42-2-268426
Fax: 011-42-2-268334

Commercial Law, Civil Law, Financial and Banking Law, Taxes, Securities and Real Estate Law.

FIRM PROFILE: The firm was established in March 1991. The firm has extensive experience in the field of financial and banking law. Clients of the firm are major Czech and foreign banks, investment and saving companies.

PARTNERS

PROF. DR. SC. MILAN BAKEŠ, born Žamberk, Czechoslovakia, October 11, 1930. *Education:* Charles University, Prague (1961; Dr. Sc. Law, 1981). *Member:* International Bar Association; International Fiscal Association; International Bureau of Fiscal Documentation. *LANGUAGES:* English and Russian. *PRACTICE AREAS:* Tax; Banking and Administrative Law.

JUDR. BARBORA DUNOVSKA, born Prague, Czechoslovakia, March 15, 1963. *Education:* Charles University, Prague (Master of Law, 1985; Doctor of Law, 1986). Graduate Fellow - Department of Civil Law, Faculty of Law, 1987. *Member:* International Fiscal Association. *LANGUAGES:* English, German and Russian. *PRACTICE AREAS:* Financial Law; Commercial Law; Securities Law.

ASSOCIATES

Dr. Eva Blechova *Mgr. Miloš Fiedler*
Mgr. František Bouček *Dr. Miroslav Zámiška*

BECKER & POLIAKOFF, P.A.

Established in 1972
ZASTOUPENI V CR
APOLINARSKA 06
128 00 PRAGUE 2, CZECH REPUBLIC
Telephone: 011 42 2 298005
Fax: 011 42 2 296807

Miami, Florida Office: 6161 Blue Lagoon Drive, Suite 250. Telephone: 305-262-4433.
West Palm Beach, Florida Office: 500 Australian Avenue, 9th Floor. Telephone: 407-655-5444.
Sarasota, Florida Office: 630 South Orange Avenue. Telephone: 813-366-8826.
Clearwater, Florida Office: The Clearwater Tower, 33 North Garden Avenue, Suite 960. Telephone: 813-443-3781.

(This Listing Continued)

BECKER & POLIAKOFF, P.A., Prague—Continued

Fort Myers, Florida Office: 13515 Bell Tower Dr., Suite 101. Telephone: 813-433-7707.

Tampa, Florida Office: One North Dale Mabry, Suite 820. Telephone: 813-874-7550.

Orlando, Florida Office: Maitland Center, 901 North Lake Destiny Drive, Suite 145, Maitland, Florida. Telephone: 407-875-0955.

St. Petersburg, Florida Office: 5999 Central Ave., Suite 104. Telephone: 813-345-3420.

Guanzhou (Canton), People's Republic of China Office: A-1 Unit, Room 1506, 371-375 Huan Shi Dong Road. Telephone: 86-20-778-1663. Fax: 86-20-777-9738.

Advice and Assistance with foreign investments in Czechoslovakia in particular the establishment of Czechoslovakia companies with foreign participation, including Joint-Venture Companies.

Gary A. Poliakoff (Not admitted in Czech Republic)

Alan S. Becker (Not admitted in Czech Republic)

(For complete Biographical data on all Personnel see Professional Biographies at Fort Lauderdale, Florida)

BEITEN BURKHARDT MITTL & WEGENER

Rechtsanwälte

NA BOJIŠTI 24

120 00 PRAGUE 2, CZECH REPUBLIC

Telephone: (2) 24 91 5808

Telefax: (2) 24 91 5804

Munich, Germany Office: Leopoldstrasse 236, D-80807. Telephone: (089) 35065-00. Telefax: (089) 35065-123.

Berlin, Germany Office: Kurfürstenstrasse 72-74, D-10787 Berlin. Telephone: (0 30) 264 71-0. Telefax: (0 30) 264 71-123.

Frankfurt/Main, Germany Office: Arndtstrasse 28, D-60325 Frankfurt/Main. Telephone: (0 69) 75 60 95-0. Telefax: (0 69) 75 60 95-12.

Nürnberg, Germany Office: Obere Turnstrasse 8, D-90429 Nürnberg. Telephone: (09 11) 2 79 71-0. Telefax: (09 11) 2 79 71-99.

Leipzig, Germany Office: Käthe-Kollwitz-Strasse 54, D-04109 Leipzig. Telephone: (03 41) 4 77 25 97. Telefax: (03 41) 4 77 25 99.

Potsdam, Germany Office: Heinrich-Mann-Allee 105 B, D-14473 Potsdam. Telephone: (0331) 33 43 06. Telefax: (0331) 33 43 29.

Hof, Germany Office: Oberer Torplatz 1, D-95028 Hof. Telephone: (09281) 80 23. Telefax: (09281) 1 65 69.

Plauen, Germany Office: Lindenstrasse 5, D-08523 Plauen. Telephone: (03741) 22 35 11; 22 49 62. Telefax: (03741) 22 49 62.

New York, New York Office: 215 East 73rd Street, New York, NY 10021. Telephone: (212) 570-2141. Telefax: (212) 734-7011.

London, England Office: Swedenborg House, 21 Bloomsbury Way, London, WC1A 2TH. Telephone: (0171) 2 42 44 66. Telefax: (0171) 2 42 44 67.

Moscow, Russia Office: Ul. Alekseja Tolstovo D.30/1, 103001 Moscow. Telephone and Telefax: (095) 202 37 60; 290 05 56.

Budapest, Hungary Office: József Nádor Tér 9, H-1051 Budapest. Telephone: (1) 2 66 18 10. Telefax: (1) 2 66 18 11.

Hong Kong Office: 605 B, Sixth Floor, Peregrine Tower, Lippo Centre, 89 Queensway. Telephone: (852) 2524 6468. Telefax: (852) 2524 7028.

Beijing, People's Republic of China Office: Unit 10, 29th Floor, Jing Guang Centre, Hu Jia Lou, Chao Yang Qu, 100020. Telephone: (86-1) 501 4569; 501 3388 Ext. 2910. Telefax: (86-1) 501 3034.

Commercial Law, Company Law, M & A, Joint Ventures, Finance, Banking, Leasing, Domestic and International Tax, Antitrust, EC Law, Real Property and Private Construction, Electronic Data Processing (Protection and Licensing), Media, Publishing, Unfair Competition, Trademarks, Copyright, Labour, General and Special Administrative Law Particularly Public Construction and Planning Regulations and Public International Law, Environmental Law, Agricultural Law, Privatization and Restitution (former GDR), Probate, Family and Estate Planning, Insolvency and Sports, Insurance, Automobile Accidents and Injuries.

(This Listing Continued)

FIRM PROFILE: BEITEN BURKHARDT MITTL & WEGENER is a nation-wide and international law firm with 108 lawyers. The firm's head office is in Munich. All the firm's offices provide a comprehensive range of services in the main areas of civil and commercial law.

GERHARD SCHMIDT, born Lauf an der Pegnitz, 1957; admitted, 1986, Germany. *Education:* Universities of Erlangen-Nürnberg, Lausanne and Strasbourg (law degree, 1982; Dr.jur., 1984); Institut Européen d'Administration des Affaires, INSEAD (Business Administration Studies); Fontainebleau, France (M.B.A., 1984). Licensed as Steuerberater (Tax Advisor), 1988. Professor, University ("Fachhochschule") Mainz II. Publications on Public Law. Member of the Supervisory Board: Sappi Europe AG; Hannoversche Papierfabriken Alfeld-Gronau AG. *Member:* German-Czech Jurists' Association (Vice President). *LANGUAGES:* German, English and French. *PRACTICE AREAS:* Company Law; Acquisitions and Sales; Restructuring; Tax Planning; Financial Services.

HEINER DRÜKE, born Soest, 1958; admitted, 1990, Germany (Not admitted in Czech Republic). *Education:* Universities of Bonn and Berkeley, California (law degree, 1984; Dr.jur., 1989). Publications on Public Law. Legislative Aide to Member of the German Parliament, 1986-1988. *LANGUAGES:* German and English. *PRACTICE AREAS:* Company Law; Acquisitions and Sales; Restructuring; Financial Services.

VÁCLAV JERMAN, born Prague, Czech Republic, 1944; admitted, 1993, Czech Republic. *Education:* University of Agriculture, Prague (degree, 1967); Charles University, Prague (law degree, 1974; Dr.jur., 1975). South West Legal Foundation Scholarship in Dallas, USA, 1993; International Development Law Institute, Rome, Italy, 1994. Member, Executive Committee of the Fund of National Property of the Czech Republic, 1993-1994. *LANGUAGES:* Czech, English and Russian. *PRACTICE AREAS:* Company Law; Acquisition and Sales; Restructuring Cartels; Public, Administrative and Environmental Law; Ecclesiastical Law; Zoning, Planning and Land Use.

MARTIN NEUPERT, born Nuremberg, 1962; admitted, 1994, Germany. *Education:* University of Erlangen-Nürnberg (law degree, 1989). Contributor to, "Wirtschaft und Recht in Osteuropa," monthly review. *Member:* German-Czech Jurists' Association. *LANGUAGES:* German and English. *PRACTICE AREAS:* Company Law; Acquisition and Sales; Restructuring; European Community Law.

LAW OFFICE
JUDR. PAVEL BLANICKÝ

BOLZANOVA 1

115 03 PRAGUE 1, CZECH REPUBLIC

Telephone: (0042-2) 2421 0446

Fax: (0042-2) 2422 9215

Business, Real Estate, Corporate, Commercial, and Copyright Law.

JUDR. PAVEL BLANICKÝ, born Prague, Czech Republic, February 26, 1943; admitted, 1970, Czech Republic. *Education:* Charles University (1970, JUDr., 1971). *Member:* Czech Bar Association. *LANGUAGES:* Czech, English and Russian.

GABRIEL BRENKA
LAW OFFICES

JÁCHYMOVA 2

110 00 PRAGUE 1, CZECH REPUBLIC

Telephone: (0042-2) 2 232 11 30; 2 232 55 60; 232 80 94

Fax: (0042-2) 232 63 71; 232 29 04; 301 73 54

Private and Public International Law, Czech and Slovak Civil and Commercial Law.

JUDR. GABRIEL BRENKA, born Nove Zamky, Czechoslovakia, 1951. *Education:* University of Comenius, Bratislava (1974). Civil Judge, District Court, Levice and Slovakia, 1976-1979. Attorney-at-Law, Czechoslovak Ministry of Foreign Affairs, 1979-1984. Czechoslovak Consul, Embassy, Washington, D.C., 1984-1989. Legal Adviser, Czechoslovak Ministry of Foreign Affairs, 1989-1992. Member, Legislative Council of the Czechoslovak Government, 1991-1992. (Also with Alliance, Prague).

Languages: Slovak, Czech, English, Hungarian and Russian

BROBECK HALE AND DORR INTERNATIONAL

(A joint venture founded by the independent law firms of Brobeck, Phleger & Harrison and Hale and Dorr)

BREHOVA 1
110 00 PRAHA 1
PRAGUE, CZECH REPUBLIC
Telephone: 422 232-8461
Facsimile: 422 232-8444

London, England Office: Veritas House, 125 Finsbury Pavement, London EC2A 1NQ. Telephone: 44 071 638 6688. Facsimile: 44 071 638 5888.

Offices of the Founding Firms: San Francisco, Los Angeles, Palo Alto, San Diego and Newport Beach, California; New York, New York; Denver, Colorado; Austin, Texas; Boston, Massachusetts; Washington, D.C; Manchester, New Hampshire.

General International Practice, including Mergers and Acquisitions. Joint Ventures, Securities, Licensing and Distribution, Privatization, Real Estate and other Project Development. International Arbitration. General Austrian Law Practice.

MEMBERS OF FIRM

DAVID M. AYRES, born Worcester, Massachusetts, October 26, 1956; admitted, 1982, Massachusetts (Not admitted in Czech Republic). *Education:* Middlebury College (B.A., magna cum laude, 1978); Columbia University (J.D., 1982). Phi Beta Kappa. **LANGUAGES:** Russian and French. **PRACTICE AREAS:** International; Corporate; Securities.

DONALD J. GUINEY (Not admitted in Czech Republic; Resident, London, England Office).

RESIDENT ASSOCIATES

LYNNE D. HOULE, born Pomeroy, Ohio, April 10, 1964; admitted, 1995, Massachusetts (Not admitted in Czech Republic). *Education:* Ohio University (B.S., summa cum laude, 1986); Stanford University (J.D., 1992). Editor, Czechoslovakian Business Law, Kluwer Law and Taxation Publishers, 1992. **PRACTICE AREAS:** International; Corporate.

PAUL J. SESTAK, born Czechoslovakia, July 19, 1962; admitted, 1990, New York (Not admitted in Czech Republic). *Education:* College of Education, Ceske Budejovice, Czechoslovakia, 1980-1984; University of Zurich (Cand. Jur., 1987); University of Wisconsin (J.D., cum laude, 1989). **LANGUAGES:** Czech, Slovak, Russian, French and German. **PRACTICE AREAS:** International; Corporate.

(For Complete Biographical Data on all Personnel, see Professional Biographies at London, England).

BUBNÍK & MYSLIL

Established in 1990

NÁRODNÍ 32
110 00 PRAGUE, CZECH REPUBLIC
Telephone: 011-42-2 2423 0507; 2421 3050
Fax: 011-42-2 2421 3047

International Business and Trade Law, Corporate and Company Law, International Joint-Ventures, Mergers and Acquisitions, International Commercial Arbitration.

FIRM PROFILE: Established in 1990 by Partners of the former Law Offices No. 1. Specialized exclusively in international legal matters. Represents a number of well-known multinational groups of companies.

MEMBERS OF FIRM

GERHARDT BUBNÍK, born Prague, Czech Republic, July 23, 1935; admitted, 1963, Czechoslovakia. *Education:* Charles University (Dr.jur., 1967); Harvard Law School (LL.M., 1969). Arbitrator, Prague, Vienna and Paris. *Member:* Czech Bar Association; International Association for the Protection of Industrial Property; Czech Society of International Law; International Tax Planning Association. **LANGUAGES:** Czech, English and German.

STANISLAV MYSLIL, born May 7, 1930; admitted, 1970, Czechoslovakia. *Education:* Charles University (Post-Graduate studies, partly Lon-

(This Listing Continued)

don University). Former Chief of Division, Legal Department, Ministry for Foreign Affairs. United Nations Legal Officer. *LANGUAGES:* Czech, English and German.

ČERMÁK, HOŘEJŠ, VRBA

Established in 1990

NÁRODNÍ 32
110 00 PRAGUE 1, CZECH REPUBLIC
Telephone: 0 422 242 11 678
Telex: 122 991 APPC
Telefax: 0 422 242 14 187

Intellectual, Industrial and Property Law, Commercial, Company and Corporation Law, Real Estate Law, Arbitration.

FIRM PROFILE: The firm was established in 1990, but for over 40 years some partners of the firm have specialized in the fields of industrial and intellectual property law. The firm's distinguished legal staff also provides traditional legal services in the areas of commercial, investment and business matters.

The firm employs a considerable number of outside consultants from various fields of law and technology who do specialized work for the firm. The firm also has in-house patent attorneys and an administrative staff of about 25 employees.

MEMBERS OF FIRM

DR. KAREL ČERMÁK, born Prague, September 13, 1934; admitted, 1960, Prague. *Education:* Charles University (Doctor of Jurisprudence, 1965). Arbitrator: International Arbitration Court, Vienna; Czech Chamber of Commerce and Industry, Prague. *Member:* Czech Bar Association (Vice President); International League of Competition Law. **LANGUAGES:** Czech, English, German, French and Russian. **PRACTICE AREAS:** Intellectual, Industrial and Property Law; Arbitration.

DR. ING. MILAN HOŘEJŠ, born Užhorod, September 12, 1924; admitted, 1955, Prague. *Education:* Charles University (Doctor of Jurisprudence, 1949); Czech Technical University (Agricultural Engineer, 1962). *Member:* Czech Bar Association; International League of Competition Law; Czech Group of the International Association for the Protection of Industrial Property (President). **LANGUAGES:** Czech, German, Hungarian, English and French. **PRACTICE AREAS:** Intellectual, Industrial and Property Law.

DR. VLADISLAV VRBA, born Zálužany, January 7, 1931; admitted, 1959, Prague. *Education:* Charles University (Doctor of Jurisprudence, 1954). Arbitrator, Czech Chamber of Commerce and Industry, Prague. *Member:* Czech Bar Association. **LANGUAGES:** Czech, German, Spanish, French and Russian. **PRACTICE AREAS:** Commercial Law; Corporate Law; Arbitration.

DR. JAN MATĚJKA, born Prague, October 25, 1946; admitted, 1973, Prague. *Education:* Charles University (Doctor of Jurisprudence, 1972). *Member:* Czech Bar Association. **LANGUAGES:** Czech, English, German and Russian. **PRACTICE AREAS:** Commercial Law; Corporate Law; Real Estate Law; Arbitration.

ING. KAREL JUZL, born Prague, July 10, 1941. *Education:* Faculty of Chemistry, Czech Technical University (Chemical Engineer, 1963). *Member:* Czech Chamber of Patent Attorneys. **LANGUAGES:** Czech, English, German and Russian. **PRACTICE AREAS:** Patent Applications and Searches.

ING. ZDENĚK SADOVSKÝ, born Přerov, March 4, 1946. *Education:* Faculty of Mechanical Engineering, Czech Technical University (Mechanical Engineer, 1969). *Member:* Czech Chamber of Patent Attorneys. **LANGUAGES:** Czech, English, German and Russian. **PRACTICE AREAS:** Patent Applications and Searches.

CILÍNKOVÁ, CILÍNEK & SEMERÁKOVÁ

Established in 1969

BOLZANOVA 1
115 11 PRAGUE 1, CZECH REPUBLIC
Telephone: (42) 2 268 304
Fax: (42) 2 242 27 299

Associated Law Office: Hamburger, Weinschenk and Molnar, 36 West 44th Street, New York, New York 10036. Telephone: (212) 719-5930. Facsimile: (212) 840-0825.

(This Listing Continued)

CILÍNKOVÁ, CILÍNEK & SEMERÁKOVÁ, Prague—
Continued

Civil, Commercial and Criminal Law. Insurance and Compensation for Damages Law. Real Estate Law.

MEMBERS OF FIRM

JUDR. MARIE CILÍNKOVÁ, born Slavkov, Czechoslovakia, March 2, 1943; admitted, 1968, Czechoslovakia. *Education:* Charles University (Doctor of Law, 1980). *Member:* Czech Bar Association; British-Czech Bar Association. *LANGUAGES:* Czech, Slovak, English and Russian. *PRACTICE AREAS:* Civil Law; Commercial Law; Compensation for Damages Law.

JUDR. VLADISLAV CILÍNEK, born Orlová, Czechoslovakia, October 27, 1938; admitted, 1965, Czechoslovakia. *Education:* Charles University (Doctor of Law, 1975). *LANGUAGES:* Czech, Slovak and Russian. *PRACTICE AREAS:* Civil Law; Criminal Law; Commercial Law; Real Estate Law.

JUDR. ING. ALENA SEMERÁKOVÁ, born Náchod, Czechoslovakia, December 21, 1950; admitted, 1992, Czechoslovakia. *Education:* Charles University (Doctor of Law, 1987). *LANGUAGES:* Czech, Slovak, English, German and Russian. *PRACTICE AREAS:* Civil Law; Insurance Law; Compensation for Damages Law.

DEWEY BALLANTINE THEODORE GODDARD

REVOLUCNI 13
110 00 PRAGUE 1, CZECH REPUBLIC
Telephone: (42-2) 2481-0283
Fax: (42-2) 231-0983

Dewey Ballantine Offices:

New York, New York Office: 1301 Avenue of the Americas, 10019-6092. Telephone: 212-259-8000. Fax: 212-259-6333.

Washington, D.C. Office: 1775 Pennsylvania Avenue, N.W., 20006-4605. Telephone: 202-862-1000. Fax: 202-862-1093.

Los Angeles, California Office: 333 South Hope Street, 90071-1406. Telephone: 213-626-3399. Fax: 213-625-0562.

London, England Office: 150 Aldersgate Street, London EC1A 4EJ, England. Telephone: (44-71) 606-6121. Fax: (44-71) 600-3754.

Hong Kong Office: Asia Pacific Finance Tower, Suite 3907, Citibank Plaza, 3 Garden Road, Central, Hong Kong. Telephone: 852-2509-7000. Fax: 852-2509-7088.

Theodore Goddard Offices:

London, England Office: 150 Aldersgate Street, EC1A 4EJ. Telephone: (44-71) 606-8855. Fax: (44-71) 606-4390.

Paris, France Office: Klein Goddard, 44 Avenue des Champs Elysées, 75008. Telephone: (33-1) 4495-2000. Fax: 011 (33-1) 4953-0397.

Brussels, Belgium Office: 79 avenue de Cortenberg/Kortenberglaan 79, B-1040. Telephone: (32-2) 732-2700. Fax: (32-2) 735-2352.

Other Dewey Ballantine Theodore Goddard Offices:

Budapest, Hungary Office: Vadasz utca 31. H-1054. Telephone: (36-1) 111-9620. Fax: (36-1) 112-2272.

Warsaw, Poland Office: ul. Klonowa 8, 00-591. Telephone: 011-48-22-49-32-88. Fax: 011-48-22-49-80-23.

Kraków, Poland Office: Pl. Axentowicza 6. 30-034 Kraków Poland. Telephone: 48-12-340-339. Fax: 48-12-333-624.

General Corporate and Commercial Practice.

FIRM PROFILE: *Dewey Ballantine Theodore Goddard is a joint venture between the U.S.-based international law firm of Dewey Ballantine and the British-based international law firm of Theodore Goddard. Dewey Ballantine Theodore Goddard also has offices in Warsaw and Budapest*

MANAGING LAWYER

OLOF N. A. CLAUSSON, born Frändefors, Sweden, 1957; admitted, 1985, New York (Not admitted in Czech Republic). *Education:* University of Stockholm School of Law (LL.B., 1981); University of Pennsylvania (LL.M., 1984). Clerkship, Sollentuna District Court, Sweden, 1981-1983.

(This Listing Continued)

RESIDENT ASSOCIATES

LUBOS BORIK, born Komarno, Slovakla, 1968. *Education:* University of Komensky, Bratislava, Faculty of Law (1986-1987); Charles University, Prague, Faculty of Law (Master of Law, 1991); Vrije Universiteit Brussel (LL.M., 1992). *LANGUAGES:* Czech, English, Russian.

PAVLINA DRTINOVA, born Usti nad Labem, Czech Republic, 1967. *Education:* Charles University, Prague, Faculty of Law (Master of Law, 1991). *LANGUAGES:* Czech, English, Russian.

JUDR. PETR KOTRLIK, born Hradec Kralove, Czech Republic, 1960; admitted, 1991, Czech Republic. *Education:* Charles University, Prague, Faculty of Law (Master of Law, 1987; Doctor of Law, 1989). Judge, Prague Court, 1989-1991. *Member:* Czech Bar Association. *LANGUAGES:* Czech, English, Russian.

COUNSEL

JUDR. TOMAS POHL, born Prague, Czech Republic, 1952; admitted, 1991, Czech Republic. *Education:* Charles University, Prague, Faculty of Law (Master of Law, 1976; Doctor of Law, 1979). Arbitrator and Judge, State Arbitration Agency (Appellate Division), 1980-1991; State Arbitration Agency (Prague), 1976-1980. Author: The Business Articles (Sagit, 1992); Specimens of Business Contracts (Sagit, 1992); Bankruptcy, Bankruptcy, Bankruptcy (Sagit, 1993). *Member:* Czech Bar Association; The Czech Society for the Building Laws. *LANGUAGES:* Czech, English, Russian.

FEDDERSEN LAULE SCHERZBERG & OHLE HANSEN EWERWAHN

SPANĚLSKÁ 2
CZ-120 00 PRAGUE 2, CZECH REPUBLIC
Telephone: 42-2-268203; 268229
Telefax: 42-2-260310

Frankfurt/Main, Germany Office: Stiftstraße 9-17, P.O. Box 100836, D-60313 Frankfurt am Main. Telephone: 49-69-29994-0. Telefax: 49-69-282615. Telex: 41 33 96 fls d.

Hamburg, Germany Office: Jungfernstieg 51 (Prien-Haus), D-20354 Hamburg. Telephone: 49-40-35 00 50. Telex: 21 27 99 99 lawt d. Telefax: 49-40-35 00 51 11.

Berlin, Germany Office: Kurfürstendamm 185, D-10707 Berlin. Telephone: 49-30-88 57 16 0. Telefax: 49-30-88 57 16 50.

Dresden, Germany Office: Königsbrücker Straße 17, D-01099 Dresden. Telephone: 49-03 51-567 02 77. Telefax: 49-03 51-567 02 79.

Brussels, Belgium Office: 118, Rue d'Arlon, B-1040 Brussels. Telephone: 32-2-280-1544. Telefax: 32-2-280-0703.

General Practice, Administrative Law, Admiralty, Antitrust, Arbitration, Aviation, Banking, Commercial and Corporate Law, Environmental Law, Insurance, Labor Law, License, Merger and Acquisition, Patent, Trade Mark and Copyright, Real Estate, Securities Law, Tax, Transportation, Unfair Competition, Litigation.

FIRM PROFILE: *The firm offers a full range of legal services. It is well known for its commercial, corporate, banking and tax law and its practice in the field of merger and acquisitions, real estate and environmental law. The firm has a broad national and international client base with a focus on Europe, the United States and Japan. The firm has 79 attorneys at law (8 of whom are notaries public) and 5 tax advisors.*

MEMBERS OF FIRM

MARKUS HAUPTMANN, born Leverkusen, Germany, January 11, 1959; admitted, 1991, Germany. *Education:* University of Cologne (1. State Exam, 1985); Summer Program London School of Economics 1983; Legal Internship Program in Cologne and Phoenix, AZ (2. State Exam, 1990). Assistant to Professor Dr. Wiedemann, University of Cologne, 1985-1989 and 1990. *Member:* German-American Lawyers Association. *LANGUAGES:* German, English. *PRACTICE AREAS:* Corporate Law; Banking Law; Law of the New Laender (former GDR).

ASSOCIATES

DR. OLGA HUMLOVÁ-UELTZHÖFFER, born Prague, Czech Republic, October 18, 1967; admitted, 1994, Czech Republic. *Education:* Charles University, Prague, Czech Republic (Dr.jur., 1991); Ruprecht-Karls-University, Heidelberg, Germany (LL.M., 1992). Author: "Das neue Recht der Wertpapierbörse in der CSFR," (New Stock Exchange Law in the CSFR), WIRO 1992; "Das tschechoslowakische Gesetz über Kapitalanlagegesellschaften," (Czechoslowak Investment Company Law), WIRO

(This Listing Continued)

1992; "Das neue tschechische Wertpapierrecht," (New Law of the Czech Security Law), WIRO 1993; "Das tschechische Konkurs-und Vergleichsgesetz," (Czech Insolvency Law), WIRO 1993; "Comparison of German Jurisdiction and Czech Law Practice," Právni Rozhledy, 1993. *LANGUAGES:* Czech, Slovak, German, English and Russian. *PRACTICE AREAS:* Corporate Czech and German Law; Commercial Czech and German Law; Banking; Stock Exchange and Securities; Joint Venture; Mergers and Acquisitions.

FIALA, PROFOUS, MAISNER & SPOL.

Established in 1990

Formerly Balaštík, Fiala, Profous & Spol. (1990-1992)

SÁZAVSKÁ 32,
PRAGUE 2, VINOHRADY, CZECH REPUBLIC
Telephone: (42-2) 256 857; 256 865; 257 238; 258 462
Fax: 256 912

Corporate Law, Privatization, Real Estate, Joint Ventures, Contract Law, Banking, Bankruptcy, Commercial Litigation.

PARTNERS

JUDR. KAREL FIALA, born Prague, Czechoslovakia, May 21, 1958; admitted, 1982, Czechoslovakia. *Education:* Law School of Charles University, Prague (1982; Doctor of Law, 1983); Southwestern Legal Foundation, University of Dallas (1991). Professional Experience: Pragoexport Trade Corporation Association of Advocates; Balaštík, Fiala, Profous & spol.; Fiala, Profous, Maisner & spol. *Member:* Czech Bar Association; American Chamber of Commerce in Czech Republic. *LANGUAGES:* Czech, German and English. *PRACTICE AREAS:* Commercial Law; Privatisation; Corporate Practice; Commercial Litigation.

JUDR. MILOŠ PROFOUS, born Czechoslovakia, January 3, 1963; admitted, 1989, Czechoslovakia. *Education:* Law School of Charles University, Prague (Doctor of Law, 1985). Professional Experience: Association of Advocates; Balaštík, Fiala, Profous & spol.; Fiala, Profous, Maisner & spol. *Member:* Czech Bar Association (Civil Law Section); Union of Czech Lawyers; American Chamber of Commerce in Czech Republic. *LANGUAGES:* Czech, English and Russian. *PRACTICE AREAS:* Corporate Practice; Privatisation; Real Estate Law.

JUDR. MARTIN MAISNER, born Prague, Czechoslovakia, January 9, 1959; admitted, 1982, Czechoslovakia. *Education:* Law School of Charles University, Prague (1982; Doctor of Law, 1984). Professional Experience: District Administration, Foreign Technical Assistance Staff, North Africa (Adviser-Interpreter), SSŽ Highway and Railway Building Comp.; Balaštík, Fiala, Profous & spol.; Fiala, Profous, Maisner & spol. *Member:* Czech Bar Association; Union of Czech Lawyers; American Chamber of Commerce in Czech Republic. *LANGUAGES:* Czech, Slovak, English and Russian. *PRACTICE AREAS:* Commercial Law; Privatisation; Contract Law; Bankruptcy Law.

ASSOCIATES

MGR. TOMÁŠ MACHUREK. *LANGUAGES:* Czech, English and Russian. *PRACTICE AREAS:* Corporate Practice; Commercial Litigation; Real Estate Law.

MGR. BLANKA CHMELÍKOVÁ. *LANGUAGES:* Czech and German. *PRACTICE AREAS:* Corporate Practice; Commercial Litigation; Bankruptcy Law.

MGR. NORBERT OSTRČIL. *LANGUAGES:* Czech and German. *PRACTICE AREAS:* Corporate Practice; Commercial Litigation; Bankruptcy Law.

MGR. PAVOL GÉCI. *LANGUAGES:* Czech, Slovak and German. *PRACTICE AREAS:* Corporate Practice; Litigation; Administration Law.

MGR. EVA HERRMANNOVA. *LANGUAGES:* Czech, English, Polish and Russian. *PRACTICE AREAS:* Corporate Practice.

DENISA TICHÁ. *LANGUAGES:* Czech and German. *PRACTICE AREAS:* Corporate Practice; Commercial Litigation.

PAVLA NOVÁ. *LANGUAGES:* Czech and English. *PRACTICE AREAS:* Corporate Practice; International Law.

(This Listing Continued)

SPECIAL COUNSEL

FRANK A. ORBAN, III, ESQ., admitted, District of Columbia; Pennsylvania; U.S. Supreme Court. *Education:* Harvard University (B.A., 1966); University of Pennsylvania (J.D., 1968). *LANGUAGES:* English, German, French, Latin and Russian. *PRACTICE AREAS:* International Trade and Investment.

FRICK & FRICK

OFFICE 422A, 4TH FLOOR
NARODNI TRIDA 10
CZ-11319 PRAGUE 1, CZECH REPUBLIC
Telephone: +42-2/24.91.30.44
Fax: +42-2/24.91.34.35

Zurich, Switzerland Office: Uraniastrasse 12, P.O. Box 996, CH-8021.
Telephone: +41-1/211.29.11. Telefax: +41-1/211.29.30.
Zug, Switzerland Office: Unter Altstadt 28, P.O. Box 234, CH-6301.
Telephone: +41-42/22.66.30. Telefax: +41-42/22.66.36.
Sofia, Bulgaria Office: Blvd. Witoscha 25, P.O. Box 475, BG-1000.
Telephone: +359-2/81.33.88. Telefax: +359-2/81.33.85.
In Association with Law Offices in China: Beijing - Qingda o - Shanghai.

General Commercial Practice, Privatization Projects, Corporate Law, International Contracts, Joint Venture Contracts, National and International Arbitration, Mergers and Acquisitions, Intellectual Property, Construction, Tax Law, Inheritance Law, Litigation and Real Estate Law.

RESIDENT MEMBERS

DR. MAGDA PISTOROVA, born Brno, Czech Republic, October 10, 1958. *Education:* Faculty of Law, Brno (1983). *LANGUAGES:* English, German, Czech and Russian. *PRACTICE AREAS:* Privatization Law; Company Law; Taxation Law; Labour Law; Arbitration.

DR. JANA STEPANKOVA, born Prague, Czech Republic, June 23, 1961. *Education:* Faculty of Law, Prague (1986). *LANGUAGES:* German, Czech and Russian. *PRACTICE AREAS:* Company Law; Contract Law; Property Law; Arbitration.

The Firm is a Member of CONSULEGIS EEIG Attorneys at Law, a European-Wide grouping of Law Firms.

(For Complete Biographical Data on all Personnel, see Zurich, Switzerland)

GAEDERTZ VIEREGGE QUACK KREILE

Rechtsanwälte
BETLÉMSKA 1
CR-11000 PRAGUE 1, CZECH REPUBLIC
Telephone: (2) 24 22 94 98
Telefax: (2) 232 12 29

Berlin, Germany Office: Kurfürstendamm 157, D-10709 Berlin.
Telephone: (30)890 05-0. Telefax: (30)892 26 06. Teletex: 30 88 15 qkp d. Telex: 17 30 88 15 qkp d.
Cologne, Germany Office: Theodor-Heuss-Ring 19-21, D-50668 Cologne.
Telephone: (221)77 16-0. Telefax: (221)77 16-110. Teletex: 221 43 76 olga d. Telex: 88 85 143 olga d.
Frankfurt/Main, Germany Office: Airport Center, Hugo-Eckener-Ring, D-60549 Frankfurt/Main. Telephone: (69)69 48 52. Telefax: (69)69 48 60. Telex: 4032 145 zibr d.
Leipzig, Germany Office: August-Bebel-Str. 38, D-04275 Leipzig.
Telephone: (341) 477 83 81/83. Telefax: (341) 477 83 88.
Munich, Germany Office: Widenmayerstrasse 32, D-80538 Munich.
Telephone: (89)212147-0. Telefax: (89)228 55 62.
Wiesbaden, Germany Office: Kaiser-Friedrich-Ring 65, D-65185 Wiesbaden. Telephone: (611)88 05-0. Telefax: (611)81 03 09. Telex: 41 86 295 gaed d.
Brussels, Belgium Office: Avenue de Tervuren 35, B-1040 Brussels.
Telephone: (2) 736 07 97. Telefax: (2) 732 69 12.

FIRM PROFILE: The law firm Gaedertz Vieregge Quack Kreile is the result of a merger between 4 partnerships: Heydt Vieregge & Partner, Cologne; Gaedertz Henn & Partner, Wiesbaden; Quack Kühn & Partner, Berlin; Prof. Kreile & Partner, Munich.

Gaedertz Vieregge Quack Kreile is one of the major German based law firms representing domestic and foreign clients in all fields of law that are relevant for national and international enterprises. An important part of the practice are the legal aspects of transnational transactions especially in

(This Listing Continued)

GAEDERTZ VIEREGGE QUACK KREILE, Prague—Continued

EC. The firm advises not only German clients in international matters but also foreign enterprises about all implications of doing business in Germany. Thus many attorneys and also members of the support staff are fluent in English. Other languages such as French, Spanish, Portuguese, Italian, Russian, and Dutch are also spoken.

In addition, the offices in Cologne and Wiesbaden have the specialized capacity to administer large trademark portfolios worldwide including registration and litigation of trademarks and registered designs.

Clients of the firm include many well-known German and foreign companies active in a wide variety of businesses. Gaedertz Vieregge Quack Kreile also represents various trade associations as well as German federal, state and local governmental authorities.

In the Berlin, Wiesbaden and Frankfurt/Main offices, there are 10 attorneys qualified to act as "Notar," specially licensed to prepare and execute documents relating to incorporation of companies, real estate matters and other important commercial transactions where a special form of document is prescribed.

Gaedertz Vieregge Quack Kreile has more than 70 attorneys, including 42 partners, plus a support staff of approximately 150 people, working in the eight different offices.

The offices have for the most part city centre locations. The Frankfurt office is situated at the Airport-Centre of the Rhein-Main Airport.

MEMBERS OF FIRM

DR. ALBRECHT PILTZ, born Poessneck, 1948; admitted, 1976, Cologne. *Education:* University of Bonn (Dr. jur.). Co-Editor and Author: "Handbuch Wirtschaft und Recht in Osteuropa," (Handbook Business and Law in Eastern Europe). *Member:* Cologne Bar Association; German Association for Industrial Property Rights and Copyright; German-Czech-Slovakian Jurists Association; German-Polish Jurists Association; German-Bulgarian Jurists Association. **LANGUAGES:** English. **PRACTICE AREAS:** Business Law, in particular Intellectual Property; Labour Law; Copyright and Publishing Law; Mergers and Acquisitions.

ASSOCIATES

DR. ARSÈNE VERNY, (M.E.S.), born Aussig Elbe, Czech Republic, 1956; admitted, 1993, Cologne. *Education:* Universities of Mainz, Cologne, RWTH-Aachen and Budapest (University of Economic Sciences). Co-Editor and Author: "Handbuch Wirtschaft und Recht in Osteuropa," "Zur Umsetzung von EG-Recht." *Member:* Association for the Study of Cartel Law; German-Czech-Slovakian Economy Association; German-Polish Jurists Association; German-Bulgarian Jurists Association. **LANGUAGES:** Czech, Slovaki, English, German and Russian.

PROF. DR. STANISLAV STUNA, born Prague, 1925; admitted, 1990, Prague. *Education:* Charles University, Prague. Assistant Lecturer at Karls-University and "Kandidatur" of Economics, 1954. Head of the Faculty of Law at the Academy of Economics, Prague 1954-1968. Assistant Professor, 1956, Professor, 1966, Dean of Academy of Economics, 1968, Corporate Counsel, 1969-1989 and Head of the Faculty of Law at the Academy of Economics, 1989. Member, Legislative Committee on Economics of the Federal Parliament and Head of the Legislative Commission for the Adoption of the New Commercial Code of the Federal Parliament of the Czech and Slovakian Federal Republic. Author: "Manual of Business Law," head of authors of "Commentary on the Commercial Code," Co-Author of "Handbook of Business and Law in Eastern Europe". Author: Various other publications in the Fields of the New Business Law of the Czech Republic. **LANGUAGES:** Czech, Slovaki, German.

DR. ANNA SLECHTOVA, born Prague, 1953; admitted, 1991, Prague. *Education:* Charles University (Doctorate, 1977). Member, International Department of Czech Foreign Ministry, 1993-1994. **LANGUAGES:** Czech, German, English, French and Russian. **PRACTICE AREAS:** Transportation Law; Construction Law; Business Law; Labour Law.

DR. VALLAV SPLICHAL, born Kutná Hova, 1936. *Education:* Charles University (Doctorate, 1959). Lawyer in the govermental tobacco monopoly until 1984. Leading state official in Kutná Hova, 1991-1992. Company Lawyer, July 1992-September, 1994. **LANGUAGES:** Czech, Slovak, German, English, French and Russian.

(For complete biographical data on personnel at Berlin, Cologne, Frankfurt/Main, Leipzig, Munich and Wiesbaden, Germany Offices as well as Brussels, Belguim Office, see Professional Biographies at those locations).

GIDE LOYRETTE NOUEL

34 JINDRISSKA

11207 PRAGUE, CZECH REPUBLIC

Telephone: (42.2) 24.21.34.65; 24.21.36.50
Telecopier: (42.2) 24.21.09.12; 24.22.58.53

Paris, France Office: 26 Cours Albert 1er, 75008. Telephone: (1) 40.75.60.00. Cable Address: "3 Avocagidva Paris 86." Telex: 651261F GILOY. Telecopier: (1) 43.59.37.79.

New York, New York Office: Swiss Bank Tower, 10 East 50th Street, 10022. Telephone: (1-212) 644-1201. Telex: 424353 GIDE. Telecopier: (1-212) 644-1205.

Brussels, Belgium Office: Rue de la Loi 99.101, B-1040. Telephone: (32.2) 231.11.40. Telecopier: (32.2) 231.11.77.

Warsaw, Poland Office: Ul. Kopernika 17, 00-359. Telephone: (48.22) 26.22.21. Telecopier: (48.22) 26.03.02.

Riyadh, Saudi Arabia Office: P.O. Box 4615, 11412. Telephone: (966.1) 476.60.39. Telex: 401677 NASHWA. Telecopier: (966.1) 476.18.96.

Tokyo, Japan Office: Homei Building 3F, 3-19 Akasaka 1-Chome, Minato-Ku, 107. Telephone: (81.3) 55.62.03.01. Telecopier: (81.3) 55.62.03.06.

Beijing, People's Republic of China Office: Suite 3309 A, Jing Guang Centre, Hu Jia Lou, Chaoyang District, 100020. Telephone: (86.1) 501 4511. Telecopier: (86.1) 501 4551.

St. Petersburg, Russia Office: 34 Souvorovsky Prospect, App 45, P.O. Box 172, 193015. Telephone by satellite: (7.812) 850.16.85. Telecopier by satellite: (7.812) 850.16.86.

Moscow, Russia Office: 9, Ulitsa Tverskaya - App 66, 103009. Telephone by satellite: (7.501) 940.45.00. Telecopier by satellite: (7.501) 940.45.01.

Budapest VII, Hungary Office: EMKE Building, Rákóczi út 42, BP 409, 1072. Telephone: (36.1) 268.1236; 268.1237; 268.1238. Telecopier: (36.1) 268.1239.

Madrid, Spain Office: Antonio Maura 7, 6°, 28014. Telephone: (34.1) 531.25.01. Telecopier: (34.1) 531.35.30.

Hanoi, Vietnam Office: Hanoi Business Centre, 51 Ly Thai To. Telephone: (84.42) 66.122.3. Telecopier: (84.42) 66.030.1.

French and International Law.

RESIDENT ASSOCIATES

Daniel Azan
Michaëla Mozerova
Eliska Barthelemy
Anne-Laure Fantova
Nicolas de la Taste

(For Biographical Data on Personnel, see Professional Biographies at Paris, France).

GLATZOVÁ & CO

BETLÉMSKÝ PALÁC

HUSOVA 5

110 00 PRAGUE 1, CZECH REPUBLIC

Telephone: +42-2 2440 1440
Fax: +42-2 2424 8701

General Corporate and Commercial Law, Mergers and Acquisitions, Securities, Construction Law.

MEMBERS OF FIRM

DR. VLADIMÍRA GLATZOVÁ, born Prague, Czech Republic; admitted, 1988, Czech Republic; Slovak Republic. *Education:* Charles University, Prague (Doctor of Law); University of London, Queen Mary and Westfield College, London. *Member:* Czech Bar Association; International Bar Association. **LANGUAGES:** Czech, English, German, French and Russian.

ASSOCIATES

DR. VÍT HORÁCEK, born Kladno, Czech Republic; admitted, 1991, Czech Republic; Slovak Republic. *Education:* Charles University, Prague (Doctor of Law); University of Birmingham, Birmingham. *Member:* Czech Bar Association; AIJA; Czech Society for International Law. **LANGUAGES:** Czech, English, German, French and Russian.

KATHLEEN HELEN LEVEY, born Newark, New Jersey; admitted, 1992, New Jersey (Not admitted in Czech Republic). *Education:* Temple

(This Listing Continued)

University, Philadelphia, Pennsylvania (J.D.); Brown University, Providence, Rhode Island; Smith College, Northampton, Massachusetts. *Member:* New Jersey State and American Bar Associations. *LANGUAGES:* English.

TOMÁS RUŽIČKA, born Prague, Czech Republic; admitted, 1991, Czech Republic; Slovak Republic. *Education:* Charles University, Prague (Magister of Law). *Member:* Czech Bar Association. *LANGUAGES:* Czech, English, Spanish, German and Russian.

DR. JIŘÍ SMOLAŘ, born Prague, Czech Republic; admitted, 1977, Czech Republic; Slovak Republic. *Education:* Charles University, Prague (Doctor of Law). *Member:* Czech Bar Associations. *LANGUAGES:* Czech, English and German.

GLEISS LUTZ HOOTZ HIRSCH & PARTNERS

Established in 1949

JUGOSLÁVSKÁ 29

CR-120 00 PRAGUE 2, CZECH REPUBLIC

Telephone: (42) (2) 24007-510

Telefax: (42) (2) 24007-555

Stuttgart (Head Office), Germany Office: Maybachstrasse 6, D-70469 Stuttgart. Telephone: (49) (711) 89 97-0. Telefax: (49) (711) 85 50 96. Telex: 722 439 jura d.

Frankfurt/Main, Germany Office: Eschersheimer Landstr. 19-21, D-60322 Frankfurt/Main. Telephone: (49) (69) 955 14-0. Telefax: (49) (69) 955 14-198; 955 14-199. Telex: 414 292glhcc d.

Berlin, Germany Office: Clara-Zetkin-Strasse 16, D-10117 Berlin. Telephone: (49) (30) 20 17 14-0. Telefax: (49) (30) 207 12 06.

Brussels, Belgium Office: Avenue Louise 475, Bte. 13, B-1050 Brussels. Telephone: (32) (2) 647 63 74. Telefax: (32) (2) 640 92 31. Telex: 65348 jura b.

German, EC and International Practice, in particular Administrative, Anti-Dumping, Anti-Trust, Arbitration, Banking, Capital Markets, Competition, Commercial, Copyright, Corporate/Company, Corporate Finance, Environmental, Finance, Foreign Investment, Industrial Property Rights, Insurance, Labour, Litigation, Media, Mergers and Acquisitions, Real Property, Regulated Industries, Securities, Tax, Telecommunications, Trade, Trademark, Unfair Competition, Zoning.

FIRM PROFILE: *The firm was established in 1949 in Stuttgart and developed from a German and later EC competition and anti-trust law boutique to a corporate practice with the full range of corporate legal services. The firm opened its Brussels office in 1987, its Berlin and Frankfurt offices in 1990, and its Prague office in 1992. It employs in total 85 lawyers and expects to grow in Central Europe in particular.*

PARTNERS

DR. RALF THAETER, born Emden, 1961; admitted, 1991, Germany (Not admitted in Czech Republic). *Education:* University of Passau (State Exams 1987, 1990; Dr. jur., 1991); American University - Washington College of Law/USA (LL.M., 1992; Fulbright Scholar). Co-author with Dr. Scheifele: "Unternehmenskauf, Joint Venture und Firmengründung in der Tschechischen Republik" (Acquisitions, Joint Ventures and Forming Companies in the Czech Republic), 1993. Author: "Sowjetisches Unternehmenssteuerrecht und seine Prinzipien" (Soviet Enterprise Taxation and its Principles), 1991. *Member:* German and American Bar Associations. *LANGUAGES:* German, English and Russian. *PRACTICE AREAS:* Banking; Corporations; International Law; Mergers and Acquisitions; Privatizations.

COUNSEL

JUDR. TOMÁŠ LINHART, born Prague, 1955; admitted, 1984, Czechoslovakia. *Education:* University of Berlin/Germany, Charles University Prague/Czechoslovakia (State Exams, 1979; JUDr., 1981). *LANGUAGES:* Czech, German, Russian, Slovak and English. *PRACTICE AREAS:* Corporations; Czech and Slovak Institutions and Laws; International Law; Joint Ventures; Privatizations.

DR. IVO NESROVNAL, born Bratislava, 1964; admitted, 1992, Czech Republic. *Education:* Comenius University of Bratislava/Czechoslovakia (State Exams, 1986; Dr. jur., 1986); George Washington University, National Law Center/USA (LL.M., 1992). Author: "Protection of Citizens' Rights in Civil Procedure," 1986. *Member:* Czech Bar Association. *LANGUAGES:* Czech, Slovak, German, English and Russian. *PRACTICE*

(This Listing Continued)

AREAS: Banking; Corporations; Czech and Slovak Institutions and Laws; Mergers and Acquisitions; Privatizations.

DR. MARTIN KUBÁNEK, born Prague, 1962; admitted, 1991, Czech Republic. *Education:* Charles University, Prague/Czechoslovakia (State Exams, 1984; Doctor of Laws, 1985). Author: "Legal Aspects of the New International Economic Order of UNO," 1984 (original in Czech). *Member:* Czech Bar Association. *LANGUAGES:* Czech, German, English and Russian. *PRACTICE AREAS:* Banking; Corporations; Mergers and Acquisitions; Privatizations.

GRÜN & PARTNER

Established in 1989

LINDAVSKÁ 785/20

181 00 PRAGUE 8, CZECH REPUBLIC

Telephone: +42-2/8552871

Fax: +42-2/8552871

International, Czech and Slovak Domestic Practice, Representation before Czech Judicial and Administrative Bodies, Commercial Law, International Contracts, Company and Corporation, Arbitration.

JUDR. IVAN GRÜN, born Czechoslovakia, March 24, 1946. *Education:* Law School of the Charles University, Prague (Doctor of Law, 1978). *Member:* International Bar Association, London; Eastern European Forum; British-Czechoslovak Law Association. *LANGUAGES:* Czech, Slovak, Russian, Spanish, Bulgarian, German and English.

IVAN GRÜN, born Czechoslovakia, August 7, 1967. *Education:* Law School of Kl. Ochridski University, Sofia (Lic. Jur., 1992). *LANGUAGES:* Czech, Slovak, Russian, and Bulgarian.

HAARMANN, HEMMELRATH & PARTNER

CERMÁKOVA 7

CZ-1200 00 PRAGUE 2, CZECH REPUBLIC

Telephone: (42-2) 24 23 90 36

Telefax: (42-2) 24 23 88 42

Munich Office: Effnerstrasse 38, D-81925 München. Telephone: (089) 924 00-0. Telefax: (089) 92400-133. Telex: 523900 HUP D.

Düsseldorf Office: Martin-Luther-Platz 26, D-40212 Düsseldorf. Telephone: (0211) 8399-0. Telefax (0211) 8399-1333.

Berlin Office: Budapester Strasse 40a, D-10787 Berlin. Telephone: (030) 264 73-0. Telefax: (030) 264 73-133.

Frankfurt/Main Office: Neue Mainzer Strasse 75, D-60311 Frankfurt/Main. Telephone: (069) 920 59-0. Telefax: (069) 920 59-133.

Leipzig Office: Neumarkt 24, D-04109 Leipzig. Telephone: (0341) 1263-0. Telefax: (0341) 1263-133.

Tokyo Office: Shiroyama JT Mori Building, 8F, 3-1 Toranomon, 4-chome, Minato-ku, Tokyo 105. Telephone: 81-3-34 59 54 85. Telefax: 81-3-35 78 89 56.

Corporate and Business Law, International and National Tax Law, Accounting Services, all Areas of Mergers and Acquisitions, Financial Transactions, Foundation and Liquidation of Companies, Structuring of Funds, Venture Capital, Management and Leveraged Buy-outs, National and Cross-border Leasing Transactions, Banking, International Law, Antitrust Law, Unfair Competition and Intellectual Property Rights Law, EEC Law, Real Estate Transactions.

FIRM PROFILE: *The firm, established in 1987, has strongly developed as a multi-disciplinary firm in Germany with seven offices. The firm is affiliated with Graham & James (US, Italy, Japan and China), Taylor Joynson Garrett (UK) and Deacons (Hong Kong and Southeast Asia) and is a member of the international tax and audit network RSM International.*

RESIDENT MEMBERS OF FIRM

MICHAEL PETERSEN-GYÖGYÖSI, born Salzburg, Austria, August 25, 1956; admitted, 1986. *Education:* Universities of Geneva and Munich (J.D., 1981); Duke University School of Law (LL.M., 1986). *LANGUAGES:* German, English, French and Mandarin. *PRACTICE AREAS:* Corporate; Arbitration; Trademarks.

PAVEL HRDINA, born Sumperk, Czechoslovakia, September 24, 1950; admitted, 1991. *Education:* Universities of Prague and Tübingen (J.D., 1974). *LANGUAGES:* Czech, Slovakian, German and Russian. *PRACTICE AREAS:* Commercial and Corporate; Real Estate; Tax; Labour.

(This Listing Continued)

HAARMANN, HEMMELRATH & PARTNER, Prague— Continued

DIPL.-ING. JANA KOCMÁNKOVÁ, born Teplice, Czechoslovakia, July14, 1965; admitted, 1993, danovy poradce (Certified Rax Advisor); auditor (Certified Public Accountant). *Education:* University of Prague. *LANGUAGES:* Czec, German, English, Spanish and Russian. *PRACTICE AREAS:* National and International Tax Law; Audit; National and International Leasing Transactions; Accounting Services.

Languages: German, English, French, Japanese, Mandarin, Czech, Russian, Slovakian, Dutch, Spanish and Italian.

(For Biographical Data on other Members of Firm, See Professional Biographies at Munich, Düsseldorf, Berlin, Frankfurt and Leipzig, Germany and Tokyo, Japan).

DR. SVETOZAR HANAK

V. JAME 1
11000 PRAGUE, CZECH REPUBLIC
Telephone: 02/722 8380
Fax: 02/742 28970

International Commercial Arbitration, Joint Ventures, Company Contracts, Admiralty and Maritime.

SVETOZAR HANAK, born Prague, January 28, 1922; admitted, 1990, Czech Republic. *Education:* Masaryk University, Brno (JUDR, 1948). President, Arbitration Court of Prague, 1985—. Co-President, Gdynia Court for Marine and Inland Navigation. *Member:* ICCA; Prague Bar Association. *LANGUAGES:* Czeck, English, German and French (Spoken only: Polish, Serbo-Croatian, Spanish and Italian). *PRACTICE AREAS:* Commercial Law; Business Law; Contracts; Admiralty; Maritime.

HELLER, LÖBER, BAHN & PARTNERS

Established in 1990

ITALSKÁ 27
CZ-12000 PRAGUE, CZECH REPUBLIC
Telephone: (422) 242 31006
Fax: (422) 242 18375

Vienna, Austria Office: Seilergasse 16, A-1010. Telephone: (431) 515 15 0. Fax: (431) 512 63 94. Telex: 114874 lawco a.
Budapest, Hungary Office: János Zsigmond U. 7B, H-1121. Telephone: (361) 2093370. Fax: (361) 1868481.
Bratislava, Slovakia Office: Laurinská 12, SK-81101. Telephone: (427) 361439. Fax: (427) 361478. Brussels, Belgium Office: Rue de La Loi 99/101, B-1040. Telephone: (322) 287 26 55. Fax: (322) 280 09 83.

Advice and assistance in the preparation, negotiation and conclusion of Foreign Trade Contracts, including advice and assistance in the establishment of Czech Joint-Venture Companies with foreign participation, including Tax Advice.

PARTNERS

GÜNTHER J. HORVATH, born Salzburg, Austria, 1952; admitted, 1981, Austria. *Education:* University of Graz Law School (Dr. iur.); New York University Law School (M.C.J.). *Member:* Vienna and International (Chairman, SGP Committee 22) Bar Associations; Lex Mundi (Chairman-Elect). *LANGUAGES:* German and English. *PRACTICE AREAS:* Corporate Law; Arbitration.

WILLIBALD PLESSER, born Haide, Austria, 1955; admitted, 1986, Austria. *Education:* University of Vienna Law School (Dr. iur.) and Philosophical Faculty (Mag. phil.). *Member:* International League of Competition Law; Supervisory Council of AFS, Austria; Vienna Bar Association. *LANGUAGES:* German and English. *PRACTICE AREAS:* Mergers and Acquisitions; Contract.

RESIDENT COUNSELS

JOSEF VEJMELKA, born Prague, Czech Republic, 1955; admitted, 1990, Czech Republic. *Education:* Charles University of Prague Law School (Dr. iur.); Post Graduate Studies at Charles University of Prague; State Bar Examination in Civil Law, Economic Law, Administrative Law and Criminal Law. *LANGUAGES:* Czech, Slovak, Russian, German and English.

PETR WÜNSCH, born Prague, Czech Republic, 1953; admitted, 1991, Czech Republic. *Education:* Charles University of Prague Law School (Dr.

(This Listing Continued)

iur.). State Bar Examination in Civil Law, Economic Law, Administrative Law and Criminal Law. *LANGUAGES:* Czech, Slovak, German, Swedish, Russian and English.

ASSOCIATES

DANA KOPŘIVOVÁ, born Prague, Czech Republic, 1962; admitted, 1994. *Education:* Charles University of Prague Law School (Dr. iur.). *LANGUAGES:* Czech, Slovak, Russian, Serbocroatian and English.

MONIKA PEČENKOVÁ, born Prague, Czech Republic, 1968. *Education:* Charles University of Prague Law School (Mag. iur.). *LANGUAGES:* Czech, Russian, German and English.

JAN CERNY, born Tanvald, Czech Republic, 1952. *Education:* Masaryk University of Brno Law School (Mag. iur.). *LANGUAGES:* Czech and German.

HOGAN & HARTSON L.L.P.

OPLETALOVA 37
110 00 1 PRAGUE, CZECH REPUBLIC
Telephone: (42-2) 2422-9009
Fax: (42-2) 2421-5105

Washington, D.C. Office: Columbia Square, 555 13th Street, N.W. Fax: 202-637-5600. Telex: 89-2757. Cable Address: "Hogander Washington". Fax: 202-637-5910.
Brussels, Belgium Office: Avenue des Arts 41, 1040. Telephone: (32.2) 505.09.11. Fax: (32.2) 502.28.60.
London, England Office: Veritas House, 125 Finsbury Pavement, EC2A 1NQ. Telephone: (44 171) 638.9595. Fax: (44 171) 638.0884.
Moscow, Russia Office: 33/2 Usacheva Street, Building 3, 119048. Telephone: (7095) 245-5190. Fax: (7095) 245-5192.
Paris, France Office: Cabinet Wolfram, 14, rue Chauveau-Lagarde, 75008. Telephone: (33-1) 44.71.97.00. Fax: (33-1) 47.42.13.56.
Warsaw, Poland Office: Marszalkowska 6/6, 00-590. Telephone: (48 2) 628 0201; Int'l (48) 3912 1413. Fax: (48 2) 628 7787; Int'l (48) 3912 1511.
Baltimore, Maryland Office: 111 South Calvert Street, 16th Floor. Telephone: 410-659-2700. Fax: 410-539-6981.
Bethesda, Maryland Office: Two Democracy Center, Suite 720, 6903 Rockledge Drive. Telephone: 301-564-5000. Fax: 301-493-5169.
Colorado Springs, Colorado Office: 518 North Nevada Avenue, Suite 200. Telephone: 719-635-5900. Fax: 719-635-2847.
Denver, Colorado Office: One Tabor Center, Suite 1500, 1200 Seventeenth Street. Telephone: 303-899-7300. Fax: 303-899-7333.
McLean, Virginia Office: 8300 Greensboro Drive. Telephone: 703-848-2600. Fax: 703-448-7650.

Advising multinational firms and Czech and Slovak enterprises on Czech and Slovak privatization, corporate finance, joint ventures, licensing and distribution agreements, international transactions and project development, with particular emphasis upon energy project finance. General civil practice.

PARTNER

RAYMOND J. BATLA, JR., born Cameron, Texas, September 1, 1947; admitted, 1973, Texas and District of Columbia (Not admitted in Czech Republic). *Education:* Texas Tech University and University of Texas (B.S.C.E., with highest honors, 1970); University of Texas (J.D., with honors, 1973). Tau Beta Pi; Chi Epsilon; Phi Delta Phi; Order of the Coif. Research Scholar, Texas Law Review, 1972-1973. Member, International Observer Delegation to Czechoslovak National Elections, 1990. Litigation Columnist and Editorial Advisory Board, "Natural Gas," The Journal for Producers, Pipelines, Distributors and End Users, 1984-1991; Secretary, Council on Alternate Fuels, Washington, D.C., 1987—. *Member:* District of Columbia Bar; Bar Association of the District of Columbia; Federal, American (Member, Sections on: International Law; Corporation, Banking and Business Law; Member, Special Committee for Energy Finance, 1989—), Federal Energy (Chairman, Committee on International Energy Transactions, 1993-1994) and International Bar Associations; State Bar of Texas; Natural Gas Roundtable; Central and Eastern Europe Law Institute. *LANGUAGES:* English, Czech. *PRACTICE AREAS:* Energy Finance; International Law; Corporate Law.

(This Listing Continued)

COUNSEL

PAVEL BRADAC, born Marienbad, Czechoslovakia, May 19, 1948; admitted, 1973, Czechoslovakia. *Education:* Charles University Law School in Prague (J.D., 1973; LL.D., 1981); American University (LL.M., 1987). Guest Lecturer, Central European Legal Systems, U.S. Department of State, Foreign Service Institute, 1986-1988. Chief Attorney, District Construction Company, Opava, Czechoslovakia, 1977-1982. Prosecuting Attorney, Chief of Civil Division, District Attorney's Office, Opava, Czechoslovakia, 1973-1977. *Member:* Czech Bar Association. *LANGUAGES:* Czech, English, Russian, German. *PRACTICE AREAS:* Commercial Law; Litigation; Arbitration.

COLIN W. CRAIK, born Hopewell, Virginia, March 17, 1956; admitted, 1981, Solicitor, England and Wales; 1989, New York (Not admitted in Czech Republic). *Education:* Bristol University, Bristol, England (LL.B., 1977); King's College, University of London, England (LL.M., 1981). *Member:* New York State (Member, Sections on: Business Law; International Law) and American (Member, Sections on: Business Law; International Law; Member, Committee on Central and Eastern European Law, International Law Section) Bar Associations; Law Society of England. *PRACTICE AREAS:* Corporate/Commercial Law.

JAN TANZER, born Czechoslovakia, March 19, 1950; admitted, 1981, Czech Republic. *Education:* Prague School of Economics (B.S., 1973); Charles University School of Law School in Prague (J.D., 1981). Deputy General, International Finance and Foreign Exchange Department, Federal Ministry of Finance, CSFR, 1990-1992. Co-Author: with V. Petrus, "Foreign Exchange Act," Czech Chamber of Commerce and Industry, 1992. *LANGUAGES:* Czech, English, German, Russian. *PRACTICE AREAS:* Commercial Law; Taxation.

ASSOCIATES

JANA HRSTKOVÁ, (Not admitted in Czech Republic). *Education:* Charles University (M.G.R., 1994). *Member:* Elsa Law Society; European Law Students Association; Rotaract Club. *LANGUAGES:* Czech, Russian, English. *PRACTICE AREAS:* Corporate Law; Finance Law.

MILAN LOVÍŠEK, born Povazska Bystrica, Czechoslovakia, August 11, 1963; admitted, 1993, Czech Republic. *Education:* Comenius Law School, Bratislava, Czechoslovakia (J.D., 1986); George Washington Law School (LL.M., 1992). Author: Human Rights (Bratislava, Czechoslovakia, 1991). Assistant Professor, Comenius Law School, Czechoslovakia, 1990-1991. *Member:* Czech Bar Association. *LANGUAGES:* Czech, Slovak, English, Russian, Polish. *PRACTICE AREAS:* Commercial; Intellectual Property.

(For complete biographical data on all personnel, see Professional Biographies at Washington, D.C.)

HOLAS & PARTNERS

PARÍZSKÁ 28
11000 PRAGUE 1, CZECH REPUBLIC
Telephone: (42-2) 2310591-2; 2313786
Fax: 24810561

FIRM PROFILE: *The firm was established in 1990 with the accent of following fields of law: privatisation, property, business law, as well as, civil, criminal, family law.*

The firm employs a considerable number of outside consultants from various fields of law and technology, who do the specialized work for the firm including some members of the staff of Charles University, and cooperates with Mrs. Brigita Moews - a member of BRD Rechtsanwaltskam., and Mr. Thomas Hruby, who is also a member of C.B.A.

MEMBERS OF FIRM

JUDR. TOMÁŠ HOLAS, born Prague, August 6, 1946. *Education:* Charles University, 1973 (Doctor of Jurisprudence, 1974). Publications in Jewish Periodicals. *Member:* Czech Bar Association, since 1977. *LANGUAGES:* Czech, Slovak, German and French.

JUDR. OLGA LÖBLOVÁ, born Prague, January 25, 1956. *Education:* Charles University, 1979 (Doctor of Jurisprudence, 1981). *Member:* Czech Bar Association, since 1982. *LANGUAGES:* Czech, Slovak, Russian and English.

MGR. FILIP MARCO, born Prague, September 11, 1967. *Education:* Charles University, 1991. Engaged with the firm since 1992. *LANGUAGES:* Czech, Slovak, Russian and English.

(This Listing Continued)

MGR. IVAN CHYTIL, born Prague, May 20, 1965. *Education:* Charles University, 1991. Engaged with the firm since 1992. *LANGUAGES:* Czech, Slovak and Russian.

MGR. KRYSTOF MANN, born Prague, August 28, 1969. *Education:* Charles University, 1993. Engaged with the firm since 1993. *LANGUAGES:* Czech, Slovak, Russian, Spanish and English.

JUDR. RUDOLF VOKOUN, CSC., born Kladno, December 28, 1954. *Education:* Charles University 1978 (Doctor of Jurisprudence 1979, CSc. 1987). Also Assisting Professor of Charles University. Specialization: criminal law. Author of many scientific publications. *LANGUAGES:* Czech, Slovak, Russian and English.

MGR. JANA NACHTIGALLOVÁ, born Prague, March 15, 1941. *Education:* Charles University, 1978. *LANGUAGES:* Czech and Slovak.

HORÁK CHVOSTA VÍCH

Established in 1991

NOSTITZ PALACE
MALTÉZSKÉ NÁM. 1
118 00 PRAGUE 1, CZECH REPUBLIC
Telephone: (422) 245 10 452
Telefax: (422) 532 152

Commercial, Corporate, Privatizations, Mergers and Acquisitions, General and International Litigation and Arbitration, Restructuring and Bankruptcy, Banking and Financial, Foreign Investments, Taxes, Intellectual Property, Patents and Advertising, Labor Law.

MEMBERS OF FIRM

DR. JIŘÍ HORÁK, born Prague, Czech Republic, March 8, 1954; admitted, 1978, Czech Republic. *Education:* Charles-University, Law Faculty, Prague. *Member:* Czech Bar Association. *LANGUAGES:* English, German, Russian, Czech, Slovak and Spanish. *PRACTICE AREAS:* Commercial; Corporate and Labor Law; Litigation and Arbitration; Privatization; Mergers and Acquisitions.

DR. LUDĚK CHVOSTA, born Tábor, Czech Republic, September 21, 1956; admitted, 1979, Czech Republic. *Education:* Charles University, Law Faculty, Prague (Post Graduate, International Trade Law, 1985). *Member:* Czech Bar Association. *LANGUAGES:* English, German, Russian, Czech, Slovak and Spanish. *PRACTICE AREAS:* Commercial and Corporate Law; International Trade Law; Mergers and Acquisitions; Privatizations; Securities; Tax Law; Finance Law.

DR. MICHAEL VÍCH, born Prague, Czech Republic, September 3, 1964; admitted, 1987, Czech Republic. *Education:* Charles University, Law Faculty, Prague. *Member:* Czech Bar Association. *LANGUAGES:* English, German, Russian, Czech, Slovak and Spanish. *PRACTICE AREAS:* Commercial and Corporate Law; Labor Law; Privatizations; General and International Litigation and Arbitration.

ASSOCIATE

MGR. BARBORA EHRLICHOVÁ, born Prague, Czech Republic, February 7, 1969; admitted, 1992, Czech Republic. *Education:* Charles University, Law Faculty, Prague. *LANGUAGES:* English, Russian, Slovak and Czech. *PRACTICE AREAS:* Commercial and Corporate Law; Labor Law; Privatizations.

HRÁSKÝ, HRÁSKÁ & PARTNERS

OSTROVSKÉHO 911/30
150 00 PRAGUE 5, CZECH REPUBLIC
Telephone: (02) 54 71 38
Fax: (02) 54 71 38

International and Czech Domestic Practice, Corporate and Commercial Law, Real Estate, Foreign Investment, Representation before all Czech Judicial and Administrative Bodies.

JUDR. MICHAL HRÁSKÝ, born Prague, Czechoslovakia, January 16, 1957; admitted, 1984, Czechoslovakia. *Education:* Charles University, Prague (Doctor of Law, 1981); Queen Mary College, London (Course in Banking and Commercial Law, 1990). Attorney Examination with Distinction. *Member:* Czech Bar Association; British-Czech Legal Association. *LANGUAGES:* Czech, English and Russian. *PRACTICE AREAS:* Commercial Law; International Transactions; Real Estate.

(This Listing Continued)

HRÁSKÝ, HRÁSKÁ & PARTNERS, Prague—Continued

JUDR. ALEXANDRA HRÁSKÁ, born Prague, Czechoslovakia, September 15, 1951; admitted, 1978, Czechoslovakia. *Education:* Charles University, Prague (Doctor of Law, 1975). Attorney Examination with Distinction. *Member:* Czech Bar Association; British-Czech Legal Association. *LANGUAGES:* Czech and English. *PRACTICE AREAS:* Civil and Commercial Law; Environmental Law; International Relations.

HRUŠKA KLOUČEK KRATOCHVÍL SLÁDEK & TOPINKA

Established in 1991

MALÁTOVA 17

150 00 PRAGUE 5, CZECH REPUBLIC

Telephone: (42 2) 530 143; (42 2) 536 614

Fax: (42 2) 530 143; (42 2) 536 614

General Practice.

FIRM PROFILE: One of the largest law practices in Czech Republic (former CONIUNCTIM, LAW FIRM) providing a wide range of legal assistance in various branches of law, including advice and assistance to foreigners doing business in Czech Republic.

Contact persons: JUDr. Martin Sládek; JUDr. Petr Topinka.

PARTNERS

JUDR. PAVEL HRUŠKA, born Czechoslovakia, June 4, 1951; admitted, 1974, Czechoslovakia. *Education:* Charles University, Prague, Faculty of Law (1974). The State Arbitrary of the Czech Republic, 1974-1977. The Office of the Czech Government, Legislative Law Department, 1978-1990. Legal Advisor to the Czech Prime Minister, 1990-1991. Member, Legislative Council, Czech Government. *Member:* Czech Law Society (Chamber of Commercial Lawyers). *LANGUAGES:* Czech and Slovak. *PRACTICE AREAS:* Company Commercial; Bankruptcy; Privatization.

JUDR. ZDENĚK KLOUČEK, born Czechoslovakia, May 5, 1947; admitted, 1973, Czechoslovakia. *Education:* Charles University, Prague, Faculty of Law (1973). Member, Experts Committee of Legislative Council of the Czech Government for Criminal, Civil and Business Law. *Member:* Czech Bar Association (Member, Specialists Group for Criminal Law). *LANGUAGES:* Czech, Slovak and German. *PRACTICE AREAS:* Criminal Law; Business Law; Civil Law.

JUDR. JIŘÍ KRATOCHVÍL, born Czechoslovakia, January 19, 1959; admitted, 1983, Czechoslovakia. *Education:* Charles University, Prague, Faculty of Law (1983). The Office of Head Architect, 1987-1990. *Member:* Czech Bar Association. *LANGUAGES:* Czech and Slovak. *PRACTICE AREAS:* Real Estate; Administrative Law; Civil Law; Conveyancing, Construction, Leases and Real Estate Litigation.

JUDR. MARTIN SLÁDEK, born Czechoslovakia, March 10, 1959; admitted, 1982, Czechoslovakia. *Education:* Charles University, Prague, Faculty of Law (1982). In-house Lawyer, Skoda Praha, 1989-1990. Participant, UKCELS program, London, 1992. *Member:* Czech Bar Association. *LANGUAGES:* Czech, Slovak, English and Russian. *PRACTICE AREAS:* Company Law; Commercial Law.

JUDR. PETR TOPINKA, born Czechoslovakia, December 28, 1957; admitted, 1982, Czechoslovakia. *Education:* Charles University, Prague, Faculty of Law (1982). Lawyer of the Committee of Human Rights, 1989. Head of the Office of the Czech Deputy Prime Minister, 1990. *Member:* Czech Bar Association. *LANGUAGES:* Czech, Slovak, English and Russian. *PRACTICE AREAS:* Administrative Law; Civil Law; Family Law; Human Rights.

ASSOCIATES

Mgr. Martin Balik   JUDr. Lena Džmuráňová

KOCIÁN, ŠOLC, TOUŠKA a spol.

JINDŘIŠSKÁ 34

110 00 PRAGUE 1, CZECH REPUBLIC

Telephone: (42-2) 24103316

Fax: (42-2) 24103234

Karlovy Vary Office: U Imperialu 31, 360 21, Karlovy Vary, Czech Republic. Telephone: (42-17) 32 25 996. Fax: (42-17) 32 27 781.

(This Listing Continued)

Corporate and Commercial Law, Mergers and Acquisitions, Privatization, Joint Ventures, Real Estate, Banking and Finance, Securities, Bankruptcy, Competition Law, Commercial Litigation.

FIRM PROFILE: Established in 1990, the firm has offices in Karlovy Vary and Prague with nine partners and 11 other lawyers. The firm cooperates closely, but not exclusively, with law firms in the United Kingdom, the Slovak Republic, Germany, France, Canada, Belgium and the Netherlands.

PARTNERS

JIŘÍ BALAŠTÍK, born Brno, Czech Republic, May 31, 1951; admitted, 1978, Czech Republic. *Education:* Masaryk University Law School, Brno (1974; Doctor of Law, 1975). Legislative Council, Czechoslovak Government, 1989-1992; Deputy Minister of Justice, Czech Republic, 1990. *Member:* Czech Bar Association (Member of the Management Board, 1990-1993). *LANGUAGES:* Czech and English. *PRACTICE AREAS:* Corporate; International Chamber of Commerce, Corresponding Member and Commercial Law; Privatisation; Real Estate; Banking; Joint Ventures; Competition Law.

PAVLA HENZLOVÁ, born Teplice, Czech Republic, October 15, 1955; admitted, 1993, Czech Republic. *Education:* Charles University Law School, Prague (1980; Doctor of Law, 1980). *Member:* Czech Bar Association. *LANGUAGES:* Czech and English. *PRACTICE AREAS:* General Commercial Law; Civil Law; Labour Law.

ALEXANDR KOCIÁN, born Prague, Czech Republic, March 7, 1946; admitted, 1975, Czech Republic. *Education:* Charles University Law School, Prague (1973; Doctor of Law, 1979). *Member:* Czech Bar Association (Member of the Disciplinary Board, 1990-1993). *LANGUAGES:* Czech and German. *PRACTICE AREAS:* Lease Contracts; General Corporate; Taxation; Real Estate; Commercial Litigation; Bankruptcy.

BOŽENA KRŠKOVÁ, born Dubicko, Czech Republic, April 8, 1934; admitted, 1970, Czech Republic. *Education:* Charles University Law School, Prague (1958; Doctor of Law, 1967). *Member:* Czech Bar Association (Member of the Disciplinary Board, 1994). *LANGUAGES:* Czech. *PRACTICE AREAS:* Civil Law; Litigation; Labour Law; Criminal Law.

JIŘÍ KURUC, born Hradec Králové, Czech Republic, January 5, 1958; admitted, 1994, Czech Republic. *Education:* Charles University Law School, Prague (1990; Doctor of Law, 1991). *Member:* Czech Bar Association. *LANGUAGES:* Czech. *PRACTICE AREAS:* Construction Law; Legal Due Diligence; General Corporate.

PETR PEŠEK, born Frankfurt am Main, Germany, May 23, 1956; admitted, 1994, Czech Republic. *Education:* Charles University Law School, Prague (1988; Doctor of Law, 1988). *Member:* Czech Bar Association. *LANGUAGES:* Czech, English and Russian. *PRACTICE AREAS:* Corporate and Commercial Law; Privatisation; Taxation.

MARTIN ŠOLC, born Ostrava, Czech Republic, May 28, 1953; admitted, 1982, Czech Republic. *Education:* Charles University Law School, Prague (1976; Doctor of Law, 1982). *Member:* Czech Bar Association (Vice-President, 1990-1993; President, 1994); International Bar Association. *LANGUAGES:* Czech, English and German. *PRACTICE AREAS:* Mergers and Acquisitions; Privatisation; Securities; General Commercial Law.

MIKULÁŠ TOUŠKA, born Prague, Czech Republic, December 6, 1963; admitted, 1989, Czech Republic. *Education:* Charles University Law School, Prague (1986; Doctor of Law, 1987). *Member:* Czech Bar Association. *LANGUAGES:* Czech and English. *PRACTICE AREAS:* Corporate Law; Privatisation; Banking; Finance; Securities.

VLADIMÍR ZEITHAML, born Hradec Králové, Czech Republic, November 30, 1955; admitted, 1980, Czech Republic. *Education:* Charles University Law School, Prague (1979; Doctor of Law, 1981). *Member:* Czech Bar Association (Member of the Disciplinary Board, 1990-1993). *LANGUAGES:* Czech, English and Russian. *PRACTICE AREAS:* Intellectual Property; General Commercial Law; Privatisation.

KRÁL, KRÁL & PARTNERS

NAD SVAHEM 8

140 00 PRAGUE 4, CZECH REPUBLIC

Telephone: (422) 692 84 37

Fax: (422) 692 84 37

Law of joint Ventures and Foreign Investment in Czech Republic, Real Estate Law, Business Law, Law of Czech association to EC.

(This Listing Continued)

JUDR. RICHARD KRÁL, CSC., born Prague, Czechoslovakia, April 9, 1935; admitted, 1993, Czech Republic. *Education:* Charles University Faculty of Law (Doctor of Law, 1958; CSc. - Phd in International Law, 1974). Former Head of Legal Service of Foreign Ministry, on behalf of Czechoslovakia negotiated number of International Agreements e.g.; Agreements on Settlement of Claims from Nationalisation and other Property Right Claims. Ambassador to Indonesia, Australia and Singapore, 1984-1989. *LANGUAGES:* Czech, English, Russian and German.

JUDR. RICHARD KRÁL, LLM, born Prague, Czechoslovakia, December, 1963; admitted, 1991, Czechoslovakia. *Education:* Charles University Faculty of Law (Doctor of Law, 1986); University of Amsterdam (LL.M. in EC Law, 1991). Assistant Professor, Charles University Faculty of Law, 1986. *LANGUAGES:* Czech, English, Russian and German.

LOVELL WHITE DURRANT

U PRASNE BRANY 3, STARE MESTO
PRAGUE 1, CZECH REPUBLIC
Telephone: (2) 2481 1672
Fax: (2) 2481 1608

London, England Office: 65 Holborn Viaduct, EC1A 2DY. Telephone: 0171 236 0066. Fax: 0171 248 4212; 236 0084; 248 7273. Telex: 887122 LWD G.

New York, New York Office: 527 Madison Avenue, 10th Floor, 10022. Telephone: (212) 758 3773. Fax: (212) 486 0367.

Paris, France Office: 37 Avenue Pierre 1er de Serbie, 75008. Telephone: (1) 49 52 04 26. Fax: (1) 47 23 96 12.

Brussels, Belgium Office: Avenue Louise 523, Bte 24, 1050. Telephone: (2) 647 0660. Fax: (2) 647 1124.

Ho Chi Minh City, Vietnam Office: 141 Vo Van Tan Street, District 3. Telephone: (848) 298 787. Fax: (848) 392 868.

Hong Kong Office: 11th Floor, Peregrine Tower, Lippo Centre, Queensway. Telephone: 2810 4770. Fax: 2868 4051.

Beijing, Republic of China Office: Office 5D, CITIC Building, 19 Jianguomenwai Dajie, 100004. Telephone: (861) 506 3588. Fax: (861) 500 1972.

Tokyo, Japan Office: Shin-Kasumigaseki Building, 20th Floor, 3-3-2 Kasumigaseki, Chiyoda-ku, 100. Telephone: (3) 3503 2571. Fax: (3) 3503 0699.

Shanghai, People's Republic of China Associated Office: Room 1703, Shanghai International Trade Centre, 2200 Yan An Road (W). Telephone: (21) 219 4419. Fax: (21) 219 5462.

Joint Ventures, Project Finance, Manufacturing and Technology Transfer Agreements, Property and Banking Transactions.

RESIDENT PARTNER

Christopher H.D. Smith

(For List of Partners see Professional Biographies at London, England)

McKENNA & CO

BETLÉMSKÝ PALÁC, FIRST FLOOR
HUSOVA 5
110 00 PRAGUE 1, CZECH REPUBLIC
Telephone: (42)(2) 2424 8518-22
Fax: (42)(2) 2424 8524

London, England Office: Mitre House, 160 Aldersgate Street, EC1A 4DD. Telephone: 071 606 9000. Telex: 27251. Fax: 071-606-9100. CDE Box 724.

London Lloyd's Office: 908 Lloyd's, One Lime Street, London EC3M 7DQ. Telephone: 0171-929 1250. Fax: 0171-626 5749 DX Box 724.

Brussels, Belgium Office: Avenue de Cortenberg 66, Box 10, B-1040. Telephone: (32)(2)735.38.36. Telex: 27122. Fax: (32)(2)735.77.43.

Budapest, Hungary Office: H-1122. Maros utca 22, 1st Floor. Telephone: (36)(1) 202 6527; (36)(1) 202 6936; (36)(1) 201 9199; (36)(1) 156 5354. Fax: (36)(1) 156 5391.

Moscow, Russia Office: McKenna & Co, International, MosenkáPlaza, 24/27 Sadovaya-Samotyochnaya Street, Russian Federation, Moscow, 103051. Telephone: (7 501) 258 5000. Fax: (7 501)258 5100.

Prague, Czech Republic Office: Betlémský palác, First Floor, Husova 5, 110 00 Prague 1. Telephone: (42)(2) 2424 8518-22. Fax: 42(2) 2424 8524.

(This Listing Continued)

Warsaw, Poland Office: McKenna & Co Sp. zo.o., ul. Kopernika 30, Suite 213, 00-950, Warsaw. Telephone: (48) 22 26 69 88. Fax: (48) 22 26 41 93.

Hong Kong Office: 5th Floor, Lippo Tower, 89 Queensway, Hong Kong. Telephone: (852) 846 9100. Fax: (852) 845 3575.

Associated Firms:

Sigle Loose Schmidt-Diemitz and Partners: Stuttgart, Berlin, Leipzig, Frankfurt/Main, Chemnitz and Moscow. .

Minter Ellison: Sydney, Melbourne, Canberra, Brisbane and the Gold Coast.

Firm involved in advising in international transactions relating to the Czech Republic and Slovakia, including privatisations, mergers and acquisitions, joint ventures, banking, property, insurance, information technology, pensions and establishing a business presence in the Czech Republic and Slovakia.

RESIDENT SOLICITORS

DUNCAN WESTON, admitted 1990. (B.A., Keele); LL.M. (LSE).

Languages: English, Czech, German, Russian

NÖRR, STIEFENHOFER & LUTZ

Established in 1990

MASARYKOVO NÁBŘEŽI 30
11000 PRAGUE 1, CZECH REPUBLIC
Telephone: 42-2-24913396, 42-2-24913882
Telecopier: 42-2-24911836

Munich, Germany Office: Brienner Str. 28, 80033 Munich, Postfach 101121, 80085 Munich. Telephone: 49-89-280111. Telecopier: 49-89-280110.

Frankfurt/Main, Germany Office: Freiherr-vom-Stein-Straße 11, 60323 Frankfurt/Main. Telephone: 49-69-172917. Telecopier: 49-69-172916.

Berlin, Germany Office: Schlüterstraße 36, D-10629 Berlin. Telephone: 49-30-8836700. Telecopier: 49-30-8835052.

Dresden, Germany Office: Böhmertstraße 3, 01099 Dresden. Telephone: 49-351-5671188, 49-351-5671187. Telecopier: 49-351-5671186.

Budapest, Hungary Office: Becsí utca 5/I. 1-2, 1052 Budapest V. Telephone: 36-1-1174905; 36-1-1378293. Telecopier: 36-1-1184035.

Warsaw, Poland Office: Kancelaria Adwokacka Sp. Z o. o. UL. Nowogrodzka 50, 00950 Warsaw. Telephone: 48-2-6216232. Telecopier: 48-2-6251976.

Brussels, Belgium EEC Office: 106 Avenue Louise, 1050 Brussels. Telephone: 32-2-6470650. Telecopier: 32-2-6464729.

Moscow, Russia Office: Ul. Levoberezhnaya, 32. 125475. Telephone: 7-095-4585822; 7-095-4585792. Telecopier: 7-095-4585782.

General and International Practice, Privatization, Mergers and Acquisitions, Joint Ventures, Tax, Labor Law, Antitrust Law, Trademark Law.

PARTNERS IN CHARGE

DR. HANS-PETER ZIER, born Stuttgart, Germany, February 26, 1950; admitted, 1976, Germany (Not admitted in Czech Republic). *Education:* Universities of Geneva, Munich and London (King's College). With Linklaters & Paines, London, 1977-1978. *Member:* International Bar Association; British-German Jurists' Association; German-American Lawyers' Association. *LANGUAGES:* German, English, French and Italian. *PRACTICE AREAS:* Commercial Law; Privatization; Mergers and Acquisitions.

GEORG A. JAHN, born Mannheim, Germany, September 12, 1950; admitted, 1980, Germany; 1984, New York (Not admitted in Czech Republic). *Education:* Universities of Munich, Geneva, Freiburg and Bonn; University of Virginia, School of Law, Charlottesville (M.C.L., 1977). With Winthrop, Stimson, Putnam & Roberts, New York, 1981-1983. *Member:* German Society for the Protection of Industrial Property and Copyright Law; AIPPI. *LANGUAGES:* German and English. *PRACTICE AREAS:* Advertising/Unfair Competition Law; Copyright Law; Trademark Law; License Law; Joint Ventures.

ASSOCIATES

MGR. JAROSLAV MELZER, born Vitkov, former Czechoslovakia, November 8, 1957; admitted, 1988, Germany; 1993, Czech Republic. *Education:* University of Heidelberg. *LANGUAGES:* German, Czech and English. *PRACTICE AREAS:* Commercial; Banking; Joint Ventures; Tax; Mergers and Acquisitions Law.

DR. JIŘÍ ČERNÝ, born Sudkov, former Czechoslovakia, February 16, 1928; admitted, 1950, former Czechoslovakia. *Education:* Masaryk Univer-

(This Listing Continued)

NÖRR, STIEFENHOFER & LUTZ, Prague—Continued

sity Brno. Lecturer, Commercial Law, 1980-1990. *Member:* Chamber of Commercial Lawyers, Prague. *LANGUAGES:* Czech, German, English and Russian. *PRACTICE AREAS:* Czech Commercial Law; Corporate Law; Administrative Law.

DR. JAROSLAV VEČERÁ, born Prague, former Czechoslovakia, November 1, 1949; admitted, 1974, former Czechoslovakia. *Education:* Charles University, Prague. *LANGUAGES:* Czech, German and Russian. *PRACTICE AREAS:* Commercial Law; Corporate Law; Administrative Law; Trademark Law.

SILVIA SPARFELD, born Weidenhausen, Germany, March 21, 1962; admitted, 1992, Germany (Not admitted in Czech Republic). *Education:* Universities of Giessen, M.A. (slavic languages). *LANGUAGES:* German, English, Russian, French, Spanish, Czech. *PRACTICE AREAS:* Czech Commercial Law; Antitrust; Tax; Joint Ventures.

ELISABETH HUBER, born Munich, Germany, 1966; admitted, 1994, Germany (Not admitted in Czech Republic). *Education:* Universities of Bonn, Lausaane, Munich. *LANGUAGES:* German, English, French, Spanish, Czech. *PRACTICE AREAS:* Czech Commercial; Privatization Law.

ANGELIKA WEISS, born Kötzting, Germany, April 28, 1964; admitted, 1994, Germany (Not admitted in Czech Republic). *Education:* University of Passau, Germany; Charles University, Prague. *LANGUAGES:* German, Czech, English and Russian. *PRACTICE AREAS:* Czech Commercial Law; Civil Law; Tax Law.

Languages: Czech, Slovak, Russian, German, English, French, Italian, Spanish, Polish.

NORTON ROSE

INTERNATIONAL BUSINESS CENTRE
PROBŘEŽNÍ 3
186 00 PRAGUE 8, CZECH REPUBLIC
Telephone: +42 2 232 7501
Fax: +42 2 232 7604

Other Offices: London, Bahrain, Brussels, Hong Kong, Moscow, Paris, Piraeus and Singapore.

FIRM PROFILE: Norton Rose is a leading City and International law firm with its principal office in the City of London. The firm provides a wide range of legal services primarily to the business and financial communities as well as to a number of sovereign governments and state organizations. We are known particularly for our corporate and debt finance, banking, company and commercial law, natural resources, insurance, property development, aerospace and maritime practices and wide-ranging expertise on tax matters. Norton Rose has a major litigation department handling all forms of commercial dispute resolution.

In Prague the firm specialises in acquisitions; banking; energy and natural resources; corporate; joint ventures; privatisation; project finance.

RESIDENT LAWYERS

DAVID G. LACEY, admitted, 1987, Australia; 1991, England and Wales.

CONSULTANTS

JENNIE S. MILLS, admitted, 1980, England and Wales.

Languages: English, French and German

(For Complete Biographical Data on all Personnel, see Professional Biographies at London, England).

DR. RÖDL spol. s.r.o.

PLATNÉRSKÁ 4
110 00 PRAGUE 1, CZECH REPUBLIC
Telephone: 42/2/2 31 15 13
Telefax: 2 32 70 50

Associated Offices of Dr. Bernd Rödl & Partner: Nurnberg, Munich, Bayreuth, Hof, Plauen, Chemnitz, Radebeul and Jena.

General Practice, Corporations, Commercial, Unfair Competition, Labor, Employment, Probate, Mergers & Acquisitions, Family Law, Litigation, Arbitration, Antitrust, Tax Law, International Tax, International Arbitration, Computer Law, EC, EC Competition Law, Trademark, Banking,

(This Listing Continued)

Building and Planning, Licensing, Legal Education, Environmental Law, Joint Ventures, Eastern German Law, Treuhand Matters.

PROF. DR. SC. MILAN BAKEŠ, born Žamberk, Czechoslovakia, October 11, 1939; admitted, 1990, Czechoslovakia. *Education:* Karls University, Prague (1961; Dr. SC., Law, 1981). Author: "Rechtliche Regelung von Devisenbezichungen," 1964. Professor, Karls University, Prague, 1984—; Dozent, 1972-1983; Visiting Professor, UCLA, Los Angeles, California, 1988. *Member:* Czech Bar Association. *LANGUAGES:* English and Russian.

SCHEELE, SCHWARTZ, ZIELCKE & PARTNER

WENZELSPLATZ 56
110 00 PRAGUE 1, CZECH REPUBLIC
Telephone: 0042-2-24230523
Fax: 0042-2-24230523

Munich, Germany Office: Prinzregentenplatz 15, 81675. Telephone: 089/470 10 02. Fax: 089/470 10 06.

FIRM PROFILE: Scheele, Schwartz, Zielcke & Partner is an international law firm advising business clients and public institutions on all domestic and overseas corporate and commercial matters. The firm specializes in Eastern European and C.I.S. matters. Currently the firm is representing a broad range of clients in Europe, North America, South America, Asia and Africa.

(For biographical data and areas of practice see listing at Munich, Germany)

SKADDEN, ARPS, SLATE, MEAGHER & FLOM

REVOLUCNI 16
110 00 PRAGUE 1, CZECH REPUBLIC
Telephone: 011-42-2-231-75-18
Fax: 011-42-2-231-93-41

New York, New York Office: 919 Third Avenue, 10022. Telephone: 212-735-3000. Fax: 212-735-2000; 212-735-2001. Telex: 645899 Skarslaw.

Boston, Massachusetts Office: One Beacon Street, 02108. Telephone: 617-573-4800. Fax: 617-573-4822.

Washington, D.C. Office: 1440 New York Avenue, N.W., 20005. Telephone: 202-371-7000. Fax: 202-393-5760.

Wilmington, Delaware Office: One Rodney Square, 19899. Telephone: 302-651-3000. Fax: 302-651-3001.

Los Angeles, California Office: 300 South Grand Avenue, 90071. Telephone: 213-687-5000. Fax: 213-687-5600.

Chicago, Illinois Office: 333 West Wacker Drive, 60606. Telephone: 312-407-0700. Fax: 312-407-0411.

San Francisco, California Office: Four Embarcadero Center, 94111. Telephone: 415-984-6400. Fax: 415-984-2698.

Houston, Texas Office: 1600 Smith Street, Suite 4460. Telephone: 713-665-5100. Fax: 713-655-5181.

Newark, New Jersey Office: One Riverfront Plaza, 07102. Telephone: 201-596-4440. Fax: 201-596-4444.

Tokyo, Japan Office: 12th Floor, The Fukoku Seimei Building, 2-2-2, Uchisaiwaicho, Chiyoda-ku, 100. Telephone: 011-81-3-3595-3850. Fax: 011-81-3-3504-2780.

London, England Office: 25 Bucklersbury EC4N 8DA. Telephone: 011-44-71-248-9929. Fax: 011-44-71-489-8533.

Hong Kong Office: 30/F Peregrine Tower, Lippo Centre, 89 Queensway, Central. Telephone: 011-852-820-0700. Fax: 011-852-820-0727.

Sydney, New South Wales, Australia Office: Level 26-State Bank Centre, 52 Martin Place, 2000. Telephone: 011-61-2-224-6000. Fax: 011-61-2-224-6044.

Toronto, Ontario Office: Suite 1820, North Tower, P.O. Box 189, Royal Bank Plaza, M5J 2J4. Telephone: 416-777-4700. Fax: 416-777-4747.

Paris, France Office: 105 rue du Faubourg Saint-Honoré, 75008. Telephone: 011-33-1-40-75-44-44. Fax: 011-33-1-49-53-09-99.

Brussels, Belgium Office: 523 avenue Louise, Box 30, 1050. Telephone: 011-32-2-648-7666. Fax: 011-32-2-640-3032.

Frankfurt, Germany Office: MesseTurm, 27th Floor, 60308. Telephone: 011-49-69-9757-3000. Fax: 011-49-69-9757-3050.

(This Listing Continued)

Beijing, China Office: 1605 Capital Mansion Tower, No. 6 Xin Yuan Nan Road, Chao Yang District, 100004. Telephone: 011-86-1-466-8800. Fax: 011-86-1-466-8822.

Budapest, Hungary Office: Mahart Building, H-1052 Apáczai Csere János u.11, Vl.em. Telephone: 011-36-1-266-2145. Fax: 011-36-1-266-4033.

Moscow, Russia Office: Pleteshkovsky Pereulok 1, 107005. Telephone: 011-7-501-940-2304. Fax: 011-7-501-940-2511.

Firm engaged in general American and International law practice, but not authorized to appear before the Czech Courts.

COUNSEL

MARC R. PACKER, born New York, N.Y., 1959; admitted, 1985, New York (Not admitted in Czech Republic). *Education:* The Wharton School, University of Pennsylvania (B.S., 1981); Columbia Law School (J.D., 1984).

(For Biographical data on other Personnel, see Professional Biographies at New York, New York).

SQUIRE, SANDERS & DEMPSEY

ADRIA PALACE
JUNGMANNOVA 31/36
110 00 PRAGUE 1, CZECH REPUBLIC
Telephone: 011-42-2-231-5661; 011-42-2-231-5678; 011-42-2-231-5698
Fax: 011-42-2-231-5482

Cleveland, Ohio Office: 4900 Society Center, 127 Public Square, Cleveland, Ohio 44114-1304. Telephone: 216-479-8500. Fax's: 216-479-8780, 216-479-8781, 216-479-8787, 216-479-8795, 216-479-8777, 216-479-8793, 216-479-8776, 216-479-8788.

Columbus, Ohio Offices: 1300 Huntington Center, 41 South High Street, Columbus, Ohio 43215. Telephone: 614-365-2700. Fax: 614-365-2499.

Jacksonville, Florida Office: One Enterprise Center, Suite 2100, 225 Water Street, Jacksonville, Florida 32202. Telephone: 904-353-1264. Fax: 904-356-2986.

Miami, Florida Office: 201 South Biscayne Boulevard, Suite 2900 Miami Center, Miami, Florida 33131. Telephone: 305-577-8700. Fax: 305-358-1425.

New York, New York Office: 520 Madison Avenue, 32nd Floor, New York, New York 10022. Telephone: 212-715-4990. Fax: 212-715-4915.

Phoenix, Arizona Office: Two Renaissance Square, 40 North Central Avenue, Suite 2700, Phoenix, Arizona 85004-4441. Telephone: 602-528-4000. Fax: 602-253-8129.

Washington, D.C. Office: 1201 Pennsylvania Avenue, N.W., P.O. Box 407, Washington, D.C. 20044. Telephone: 202-626-6600. Fax: 202-626-6780.

London, England Office: 1 Gunpowder Square, Printer Street, London EC4A 3DE. Telephone: 011-44-71-830-0055. Fax: 011-44-71-830-0056.

Brussels, Belgium Office: Avenue Louise, 165-Box 15, 1050 Brussels, Belgium. Telephone: 011-32-2-648-1717. Fax: 011-32-2-648-1064.

Bratislava Office: Mudronova 37, 811 01 Bratislava, Slovak Republic. Telephone: 011-42-7-313-362; 011-42-7-315-370. Fax: 011-42-7-313-918.

Budapest, Hungary Office: Deak Ferenc Ut. 10, Office 304, H-1052 Budapest V., Hungary. Telephones: 011-36-1-266-2024. Fax: 011-36-1-226-2025.

Kiev, Ukraine Office: vul. Prorizna 9, Suite 20, Kiev 252035, Ukraine. Telephones: 011-7-044-244-3452, 011-7-044-244-3453, 011-7-044-228-8687. Fax: 011-7-044-228-4938.

General and International Practice.
Firm engaged in American and General International Practice but not authorized to appear before the Courts of the Czech Republic.

PARTNERS

JAMES F. ALLEN, born Wadsworth, Ohio, 1940; admitted, 1978, Ohio (Not admitted in Czech Republic). *Education:* University of Michigan (B.S.E., 1963); The Ohio State University (M.A., 1972); University of Toledo (J.D., magna cum laude, 1978). *Member:* Columbus and Ohio State Bar Associations. *LANGUAGES:* Russian, Czech, German. *PRACTICE AREAS:* Environmental; Energy.

JAN MATEJCEK, born Prague, Czechoslovakia, 1954; admitted, 1981, Ontario (Not admitted in Czech Republic). *Education:* University of Toronto, Ontario, Canada (B.A., 1976); University of Windsor, Ontario, Canada (LL.B., 1980). Phi Alpha Delta International Law Fraternity. *Member:* Canada-Czech and Slovak Chamber of Commerce (Director and Vice President); Canadian-German Chamber of Industry and Commerce. *LAN-*

GUAGES: English, Czech, German. *PRACTICE AREAS:* International Mergers and Acquisitions; Securities; Energy.

RICHARD S. SURREY, born Washington, D.C., 1950; admitted, 1978, District of Columbia (Not admitted in Czech Republic). *Education:* Dartmouth College (B.A., 1972), Member, Casque & Gauntlet; Fletcher School of Law & Diplomacy (1974); University of Miami (J.D., 1978). Articles and Comments Editor, University of Miami Law Review. Jessup International Moot Court Competition Team. General Counsel, National Security Agency, 1989-1992. Senior Councillor, Atlantic Council of the United States. *Member:* International Committee, National Planning Association; District of Columbia Bar Association; American Bar Association, International Section. *PRACTICE AREAS:* International Corporate and Financing.

CAROL M. WELU, born Dubuque, Iowa, 1951; admitted, 1979, District of Columbia (Not admitted in Czech Republic). *Education:* University of Dayton (B.A., summa cum laude, 1974); University of Miami (J.D., cum laude, 1979). Articles and Comments Editor, Law Review. *Member:* American Bar Association. *PRACTICE AREAS:* International Corporate Transactions; Arbitration.

OF COUNSEL

JOHN M. CLAPP, born Cambridge, United Kingdom, 1958; admitted, 1984, England; 1988, New York (Not admitted in Czech Republic). *Education:* Cambridge University (B.A., 1981; M.A., 1985); The College of Law, Lancaster Gate, London (Solicitors' Final Examination, 1982). *Member:* American Bar Association; Law Society. *LANGUAGES:* German, French. *PRACTICE AREAS:* Securities; Banking; Equipment Financing.

JULIAN JUHASZ, born Kosice, Czechoslovakia, 1954; admitted, 1994, Law Society of Upper Canada (Not admitted in Czech Republic). *Education:* Comenius University, Bratislava (LL.M., 1978); Osgoode Hall Law School, York University (LL.B., 1992). *Member:* Slovak Canadian Chamber of Commerce (Director). *LANGUAGES:* Slovak (native), English, Czech, Russian. *PRACTICE AREAS:* Commercial; Corporate Law.

JAROMIR RUZICKA, born Prague, Czechoslovakia, 1925; admitted, 1991, Czechoslovakia. *Education:* Charles University, Prague, 1949. Director of the Legal Department of the Ministry of Foreign Trade, 1971-1989. Legal Advisor to the Minister of Foreign Trade and Chief of the Cabinet of the Ministry of Foreign Trade, 1989-1990. *LANGUAGES:* Czech (native), English, German, Russian, Spanish.

COUNSEL

IVAN CESTR, born Kolin, Czechoslovakia, 1959; admitted, 1993, Czech Republic. *Education:* Charles University (LL.D., 1978). *Member:* Czech Advocacy Bar. *LANGUAGES:* Czech (native), English, Russian. *PRACTICE AREAS:* Civil; Commercial; Administrative; Labor and Environmental Law.

RUDOLF KOZUSNÍK, born Syria, Damascus, 1956; admitted, 1992, Czech Republic. *Education:* Charles University, Prague, 1982. *LANGUAGES:* Czech (native), English. *PRACTICE AREAS:* Commercial and Civil Law; Real Estate; Labor; Customs Law.

LUBOS TICHY, born Czechoslovakia, 1948; admitted, 1976, Prague, Czechoslovakia. *Education:* Charles University (JUDr., 1973); Charles University (CSc., 1984) (equivalent to U.S. Ph.D.). Chairman of the Department of European Community Law, Charles University, Prague (1990—). *Member:* Board of Directors of Czech Advocacy Bar; editorial boards of Pravo a Zakonnost, Bulletin Advokacie, Vsehrd (Czech legal publications). *LANGUAGES:* Czech (native), English, German, Russian.

RESIDENT ASSOCIATES

JOHN G. LOUGHREY, born Argentia Newfoundland, Canada, 1961; admitted, 1986, Arizona and U.S. District Court, District of Arizona; 1987, U.S. Court of Appeals, Ninth Circuit; 1989, U.S. District Court, Northern District of Texas (Not admitted in Czech Republic). *Education:* Butler University (B.A., cum laude, 1983); Indiana University (J.D., magna cum laude, 1986). Order of the Coif. *Member:* State Bar of Arizona (Member, International Law Section); American Bar Association (Member, Litigation Dispute Resolution and International Law Sections); International Bar Association (Member, Business Law Section, Eastern European Forum). *PRACTICE AREAS:* International Corporate and Financing; Joint Ventures and Privatization; Dispute Resolution.

KEVIN T. CONNOR, born Waterbury, Connecticut, 1959; admitted, 1989, Ohio (Not admitted in Czech Republic). *Education:* Central Connecticut State University (B.A., magna cum laude, 1981); Ohio State University (J.D., with honors, 1989). Order of the Coif. *Member:* International (East-

(This Listing Continued)

SQUIRE, SANDERS & DEMPSEY, Prague—Continued

ern European Forum), American and Ohio State Bar Associations. *LANGUAGES:* Spanish, Czech. *PRACTICE AREAS:* International Corporate and Financing.

ROLAND J. BEHM, born Lexington, Missouri, 1960; admitted, 1987, District of Columbia (Not admitted in Czech Republic). *Education:* Southern Methodist University (B.A., 1982); University of Georgia (J.D., 1987). *PRACTICE AREAS:* International Corporate; Joint Ventures and Privatization; Project Finance.

OLIVER C. BRAHMST, born Hamburg, Germany, 1960; admitted, 1990, Ontario (Not admitted in Czech Republic). *Education:* University of Toronto (B.A., 1985); University of Ottawa (LL.B., cum laude, 1988); Osgoode Hall Law School (LL.M., magna cum laude, 1994). *Member:* Canadian-German Lawyers Association; German-Canadian Chamber of Commerce; Canadian Tax Foundation. *LANGUAGES:* German. *PRACTICE AREAS:* International Corporate and Financing; Taxation; Joint Ventures and Privatization.

EVAN Z. LAZAR, born Washington, D.C., 1963; admitted, 1987, Pennsylvania (Not admitted in Czech Republic). *Education:* Temple University (B.S., 1984; J.D., cum laude, 1987). Staff Member, Temple Law Review, 1985-1987. *Member:* Philadelphia, Pennsylvania, International and American Bar Associations. *LANGUAGES:* Hebrew, Czech. *PRACTICE AREAS:* International, Finance, Real Property, Corporate and Business Law.

HEIDI PEMBERTON, born Schenectady, New York, 1960; admitted, 1987, Massachusetts (Not admitted in Czech Republic). *Education:* Bryn Mawr College (A.B., 1982); University of Pennsylvania (J.D., 1987). *LANGUAGES:* French.

JANET LEVINE NAHIRNY, born Atlanta, Georgia, 1966; admitted, 1992, Georgia (Not admitted in Czech Republic). *Education:* Yale University (B.A., cum laude, 1988); Columbia University (J.D., with honors, 1992). Member, Columbia Law Review, 1991-1992. Law Clerk to Judge Mark L. Wolf, U.S. District Court, District of Massachusetts, 1992-1993. *Member:* State Bar of Georgia. *LANGUAGES:* French. *PRACTICE AREAS:* International Corporate and Real Estate Law.

SASHA S. STEPAN, born Melbourne, Australia, 1968; admitted, 1993, Supreme Court of Victoria and High Court of Australia (Not admitted in Czech Republic). *Education:* Monash University, Melbourne (B.Ec. (Hons), 1990; LL.B., 1992). *Member:* Law Institute of Victoria; International Bar Association. *LANGUAGES:* Czech, German. *PRACTICE AREAS:* Corporate and Commercial Law; Finance; Privatization.

(For Biographical Data on Cleveland and Columbus, Ohio, Miami and Jacksonville, Florida, New York, New York, Phoenix, Arizona, Washington, D.C., London, England, Brussels, Belgium, Prague, Czech Republic, Bratislava, Slovak Republic, Budapest, Hungary and Kiev, Ukraine Personnel, see Professional Biographies at those Points Respectively).

TUREK, MUCHA, KOSTOHRYZ

Established in 1990

NÁRODNÍ 32

CS-110 00 PRAGUE 1, CZECH REPUBLIC

Telephone: 0042-2-242 25650; 0042-2-242 12440; 0042-2-242 25686
Fax: 0042-2-242 12946

General Practice of Law, Estates, Probate.

FIRM PROFILE: *The firm was established in 1990, after the privatization of the Czechoslovak Bar, by members of the former Law Offices No. 1 in Prague. It is well known for its specialization in Estates, Probate and connected Genealogical Research and Selected General Practice.*

PARTNERS

JUDR. OTAKAR TUREK, born Nový Jičín, Czechoslovakia, September 21, 1934; admitted, 1971, Czechoslovakia. *Education:* Law School of Charles University, Prague (1958). Diplomatic Service, 1960-1970. *LANGUAGES:* Czech, English, German and Spanish. *PRACTICE AREAS:* Estates; Probate; Genealogical Research; General Practice.

JUDR. JIŘÍ MUCHA, born Hradec Králové, Czechoslovakia, May 11, 1946; admitted, 1973, Czechoslovakia. *Education:* Law School of Charles University, Prague (1969); Intl. Faculty of Comparative Law, Montreal (1968) and Strasbourg (1969). *LANGUAGES:* Czech, English, German

(This Listing Continued)

and French. *PRACTICE AREAS:* Estates; Probate; Genealogical Research.

JUDR. MILAN KOSTOHRYZ, born Prague, Czechoslovakia, March 10, 1953; admitted, 1984, Czechoslovakia. *Education:* Law School of Charles University, Prague (1977). Foreign Exchange Service, 1978-1982. *LANGUAGES:* Czech, English, German and French. *PRACTICE AREAS:* Estates; Probate; Genealogical Research; General Practice.

Languages: Czech, English, German and French.

WEIL, GOTSHAL & MANGES

A Partnership including Professional Corporations

CHARLES BRIDGE CENTER

KRIZOVNICKE NAM. 1

110 00 PRAGUE 1, CZECH REPUBLIC

Telephone: 011-42-2-24-09-73-00
Telecopier: 011-42-2-24-09-73-10

New York, N.Y. Office: 767 Fifth Avenue. Telephone: 213-310-8000. Cable Address: "Wegoma". Telex: 424281; 423144. Telecopier: 213-310-8007.

Dallas, Texas Office: 100 Crescent Court, Suite 1300. Telephone: 214-746-7700. Fax: 214-746-7777.

Houston, Texas Office: Suite 1600, 700 Louisiana Street. Telephone: 713-546-5000. Telecopier: 713-224-9511.

Menlo Park, California Office: 2882 Sand Hill Road, Suite 280. Telephone: 415-926-6200. Telecopier: 415-854-3713.

Miami, Florida Office: Suite 2100, 701 Brickell Avenue. Telephone: 305-577-3100. Telecopier: 305-374-7159.

Washington, D.C. Office: Suite 700, 1615 L Street, N.W. Telephone: 202-682-7000. Telecopier: 202-857-0939; 857-0940. Telex: 440045.

Brussels, Belgium Office: 1 Place Madou, Box 34, 1030 Brussels. Telephone: 011-32-2-217-4003. Telecopier: 011-32-2-217-0215.

Budapest, Hungary Office: H-1065 Budapest, Revay Utca 10. Telephone: 011-361-269-1144. Fax: 011-361-269-1233.

Warsaw, Poland Office: ul Senatorska 12 00-082 Warsaw. Telephone: 011-48-22-27-61-44. Telecopier: 011-48-22-27-48-38.

General Practice.

RESIDENT PARTNERS

JOSEPH C. TORTORICI, born New York, N.Y., June 6, 1959; admitted, 1985, New York (Not admitted in Czech Republic). *Education:* Columbia College (B.A., cum laude, 1981); Columbia University School of Law (J.D., 1984). Editor, Columbia Journal of Environmental Law, 1983-1984. Member, Board of Directors, American Chamber of Commerce in the Czech Republic. *PRACTICE AREAS:* Corporate Law.

RESIDENT ASSOCIATES

SANFORD G. HAUSNER, born Abington, Pennsylvania, December 1, 1960; admitted, 1986, Texas, New York and New Jersey (Not admitted in Czech Republic). *Education:* New York University (B.S., 1982); Brooklyn Law School (J.D., 1985); New York University School of Law (LL.M. in Taxation, 1987).

KENNETH E. SCHIFF, born January 29, 1963; admitted, 1987, New Jersey; 1988, New York (Not admitted in Czech Republic). *Education:* New York University (B.S., 1984); Brooklyn Law School (J.D., 1987). *Member:* American Bar Association.

KAREL MUZIKAR, JR., (Not admitted in Czech Republic). *Education:* Charles University (J.D., 1986; Ph.D., 1988); New York University (M.A., 1991). *LANGUAGES:* English, French, German, French, Russian and Armenian.

KAROLINA HORAKOVA, (Not admitted in Czech Republic). *Education:* Pace University (B.A., Economics, 1990); Charles University (J.D., 1991). *LANGUAGES:* Czech, Russian, English, French.

(For complete biographical data on New York, New York, Dallas, Texas, Houston, Texas, Menlo Park, California, Miami, Florida, Washington, D.C., Brussels, Belgium, Budapest, Hungary, London, England and Warsaw, Poland, see Professional Biographies at those locations)

WEISS & HASCHE

A Merger of the law firms Hasche Albrecht Fischer, Hamburg, Ott Weiss Eschenlohr & Partner, Munich and Rosenberg, Berlin.

DĚLNICKÁ 30
170 00 PRAGUE 7, CZECH REPUBLIC
Telephone: (2) 683 40 23
Telefax: (2) 683 40 23

Hamburg, Germany Office: Valentinskamp 88, 20355 Hamburg. Telephone: (040) 35 00 20. Cable Address: "Lawyers" Telex: 215461 LAWY D. Teletex: 402276 LAWY D. Telefax: (040) 35 00 21 52.

Munich, Germany Office: Brienner Strasse 11/V (Luitpoldblock). 80333 Munich. Telephone: (089) 23 80 70. Cable Address: "Interlaw" Munich. Telex: 5 22957 Law. Telefax: (089) 23 80 71 10.

Leipzig, Germany Office: Karl-Tauchnitz-Strasse 10 B, 04107 Leipzig. Telephone: (0341) 216 720. Telefax: (0341) 216 72 33.

Berlin, Germany Office: Meinekestrasse 13, 10719 Berlin. Telephone: (030) 881 97 83. Telefax: (030) 882 34 79.

Commercial, International Trade, Maritime, Transport, Forwarding, Shipbuilding, Shipfinancing, Tax, Banking, Corporation, Mergers and Acquisitions, Antitrust, Unfair Competition, Industrial Property, Real Estate, Environment, Common Market, Insurance, Aviation, Arbitration, Media, Administrative, Labor, Computer, German Reunification, Litigation.

ASSOCIATE
(PRAGUE OFFICE)

DR. PETR ZIMA, born Prague, Czechoslovakia, January 23, 1953; admitted, 1992, Czech Republic. *Education:* University of Prague (Dr.jur., 1976). Judge, Civil Court, Prague, 1977-1980. In-house Counsel, Intrans, 1980-1988. Deputy Director, Legal Department, Czech Federal Railway Authority, 1989-1992. *Member:* Czech Bar Association. **LANGUAGES:** Czech, German, English, French and Russian.

Languages: Czech, German, Russian, French and English

WEISS-TESSBACH

spol s.r.o.

Established in 1992

CELETNA 11
11000 PRAGUE, CZECH REPUBLIC
Telephone: 0042 2 2318693; 2317237; 2319963
Telecopier: 0042 2 2317400

Vienna, Austria Office: Weiss-Tessbach Rechtsanwälte OEG, Rotenturmstrasse 13, A-1010. Telephone: 0043 1 5331651. Telecopier: 0043 1 5335252.

Budapest, Hungary Representative Office: Weiss-Tessbach Kft., Vármegye u.3-5, H-1052. Telephone: 0036 1 2674227; 2674228; 2674229. Telecopier: 0036 1 2674241.

Bratislava, Slovakia Representative Office: Weiss-Tessbach spol s.r.o., Panska 31, 81102. Telephone: 0042 7 335769. Telecopier: 0042 7 331126.

Administrative Law, Advertising Law, Agricultural Law, Antitrust Law, Arbitration, Banking Law, Bankruptcy, Competition Law, Constitutional Law, Construction Law, Conveyancing, Corporate Law, Distributorship Agency and Franchise Law, EEC Law, Employer's Liability, Environmental Law, Foreign Investments, Immigration Law, Industrial Relations and Labor Law, Insurance Law, International Contracts, International Private Law, Litigation, Product Liability Law, Property and Real Estate Law, Rent and Lease, Trade Regulations, General Legal Practice, Copyright Law, Industrial Models, License Negotiation, Patent Litigation, Trademark Litigation, Trademark Prosecution, Transfer of Technology, General Intellectual Property Practice, Capital Taxation, Corporate Taxation, Indirect Taxation, Inheritance, Estate and Gift Taxation, International Taxation, Personal Income Taxation, Sales Turnover, Value Added Taxes, Taxation of Foreign Nationals, Exchange Control, East-West Relations (Countertrade, Joint Ventures), Hungarian Law, Czechoslovakian Law.

FIRM PROFILE: Founded in 1878, Weiss-Tessbach offers the full range of Eastern European corporate legal services. The firm opened its Prague office in 1992 and is currently composed of seven partners, one U.S. attorney and 23 associates and expects to grow in Eastern Europe in particular.

(This Listing Continued)

PARTNERS IN CHARGE

DR. WIELAND SCHMID-SCHMIDSFELDEN, born St. Pölten, July 1, 1959; admitted, 1989, Austria. (Not admitted in Czech Republic). **LANGUAGES:** German and English. **PRACTICE AREAS:** Corporate Law; General Commercial Law; The Laws of Eastern European Countries; EEC Law; Banking Finance and Insurance Law; Industrial Installations; Environmental Law; Telecommunication Arbitration.

MAG. DR. STEFAN EDER, born Vienna, April 4, 1962; admitted, 1992, Austria. (Not admitted in Czech Republic). **LANGUAGES:** German and English. **PRACTICE AREAS:** Corporate Law; General Commercial Law; Computer Law; The Laws of Eastern European Countries; Banking Finance and Insurance Law; Capital Markets; Data Protection; Arbitration.

RESIDENT ASSOCIATES

DR. EVA DOBROHRUSKOVÁ, born Rychnow, Czech Republic, June 20, 1962; admitted, 1993, Czech Republic. **LANGUAGES:** Slovak and German.

WHITE & CASE

STAROMESTSKE NAMESTI 15
110 00 1 PRAGUE, CZECH REPUBLIC
Telephone: (42-2) 2481-1796
Facsimile: (42-2) 5522; (42-2) 232-5585

New York, New York: Telephone: 212-819-8200. Facsimile: 212-354-8113.

Washington, D.C.: Telephone: 202-872-0013. Facsimile: 202-872-0210.

Los Angeles, California: Telephone: 213-620-7700. Facsimile: 213-687-0758; 213-617-2205.

Miami, Florida: Telephone: 305-371-2700. Facsimile: 305-358-5744.

Mexico City, Mexico: Telephone: (52-5) 207-9717. Facsimile: (52-5) 208-3628.

Tokyo, Japan: Telephone: (81-3) 3239-4300. Facsimile: (81-3) 3239-4330.

Hong Kong: Telephone: (852) 2822-8700. Facsimile: (852) 2845-9070; Grice & Co., Solicitors, Telephone: (852) 2826-0333. Facsimile: (852) 2526-7166.

Singapore, Republic of Singapore: Telephone: (65) 225-6000. Facsimile: (65) 225-6009.

Bangkok, Thailand: Pacific Legal Group Ltd., In Association With White & Case, Telephone: (662) 236-6154/7. Facsimile: (662) 237-6771.

Hanoi, Viet Nam: Representative Office, Telephone: (84-4) 227-575/6/7. Facsimile: (84-4) 227-297.

Bombay, India: Telephone: (91-22) 282-6300. Facsimile: (91-22) 282-6305.

London, England: Telephone: (44-171) 726-6361. Facsimile: (44-171) 726-4314; (44-171) 726-8558.

Paris, France: Telephone: (33-1) 42-60-34-05. Facsimile: (33-1) 42-60-82-46.

Brussels, Belgium: Telephone: (32-2) 647-05-89. Facsimile: (32-2) 647-16-75.

Stockholm, Sweden: Telephone: (46-8) 679-80-30. Facsimile: (46-8) 611-21-22.

Helsinki, Finland: Telephone: (358-0) 631-100. Facsimile: (358-0) 179-477.

Moscow, Russia: Telephone: (7-095) 201-9292/3/4/5. Facsimile: (7-095) 201-9284.

Budapest, Hungary: Telephone: (36-1) 269-0550; (36-1) 131-0933. Facsimile: (36-1) 269-1199.

Warsaw, Poland: Telephone/Facsimile: (48-22) 26-80-53; (48-22) 27-84-86. International Telephone/Facsimile: (48-39) 12-19-06.

Istanbul, Turkey: Telephone: (90-212) 275-68-98; (90-212) 275-75-33. Facsimile: (90-212) 275-75-43.

Ankara, Turkey: Telephone: (90-312) 446-2180. Facsimile: (90-312) 437-9677.

Jeddah, Saudi Arabia: Law Office of Hassan Mahassni, Telephone: (966-2) 651-3535. Facsimile: (966-2) 651-3636.

Riyadh, Saudi Arabia: Law Office of Hassan Mahassni, Telephone: (966-1) 476-7099. Facsimile: (966-1) 479-0110.

Almaty, Kazakhstan: Telephone: (7-3272) 50-7491/2. Facsimile: (7-3272) 61-0842.

General International Practice.

(This Listing Continued)

WHITE & CASE, Prague—Continued

RESIDENT PARTNERS

CARL H. AMON III, born Boston, Massachusetts, June 13, 1943; admitted, 1969, New York (Not admitted in Czech Republic). *Education:* Dartmouth College (A.B., 1965); University of Michigan (J.D., 1968).

DANIEL J. ARBESS, born Montreal, Canada, January 23, 1961; admitted, 1986, New York (Not admitted in Czech Republic). *Education:* Osgoode Hall Law School (LL.B.; 1984); Harvard University (LL.M., 1987). *Member:* The Association of the Bar of the City of New York; American Bar Association.

RESIDENT ASSOCIATES

JAMES R. COWAN, born Sacramento, California, September 20, 1964; admitted, 1992, California (Not admitted in Czech Republic). *Education:* Harvard University (A.B., 1986); Oxford University (M.S., 1988); University of California, Los Angeles (J.D., 1992).

ROBERT B. IRVING, born Miami, Florida, April 7, 1964; admitted, 1992, New York (Not admitted in Czech Republic). *Education:* Yale University (B.A., 1985); Ecole Superior de Commerce de Paris (C.I.A.M., 1987); University of Miami (J.D., 1990).

CARLO L. KOSTKA, born New York, N.Y., October 1, 1960; admitted, 1991, New York (Not admitted in Czech Republic). *Education:* Columbia University (B.A., 1982; M.A., 1984); Harvard University (J.D., 1990).

MONIKA B. KRIZEK, born Prague, Czech Republic, April 11, 1962; admitted, 1990, New York; 1991, District of Columbia (Not admitted in Czech Republic). *Education:* Barnard College (A.B., 1983); Boston University (J.D., 1988).

RADAN KUBR, born Prague, Czech Republic, August 8, 1966; admitted, 1990, Geneva, Switzerland; 1994, Czech Republic. *Education:* Geneva Law School (J.D., 1988); College of Europe (LL.M., 1993).

JOHN C. LEARY, born Los Angeles, California, October 27, 1965; admitted, 1993, California (Not admitted in Czech Republic). *Education:* Georgetown University (B.S.F.S., 1987); Hastings College of the Law, University of California (J.D., 1992).

EMIL NEMEC, born Bratislava, Slovak Republic, March 15, 1967; admitted, 1994, Czech Republic. *Education:* Comenius University (J.D., 1989); George Washington University (LL.M., 1992).

MONIKA RUTLAND, born Prerov, Czechoslovakia, August 20, 1958; admitted, 1989, Connecticut; 1994, Czech Republic. *Education:* Charles University (J.D., 1982); University of Texas (M.C.J., 1988).

(For biographical data as to other locations, see Professional Biographies at New York, New York; Washington, D.C.; Los Angeles, California; Miami, Florida; Mexico City, Mexico; Tokyo, Japan; Hong Kong; Singapore, Republic of Singapore; Bangkok, Thailand; Hanoi, Viet Nam; Bombay, India; London, England; Paris, France; Brussels, Belgium; Stockholm, Sweden; Helsinki, Finland; Moscow, Russia; Budapest, Hungary; Warsaw, Poland; Istanbul and Ankara, Turkey; Jeddah and Riyadh, Saudi Arabia; Almaty, Kazakhstan.)

ZEINER GOLAN NIR & PARTNERS

MAISELOVA 15
110 00 PRAGUE 1, CZECH REPUBLIC
Telephone: +42 2-248 12 301; 231 0928; 231 1833
Facsimile: +42 2-248 12 307

REVISERS OF THE CZECH REPUBLIC LAW DIGEST FOR THIS DIRECTORY

Vienna, Austria Office: Zeiner & Zeiner, Attorneys at Law, Schellinggasse 6, A-1010. Telephone: (43) (1) 5122364; 5123775. Telefax: (43) (1) 5123325.

Ramat-Gan, Israel Office: Golan, Nir & Partners, Attorneys at Law, 3, Habonim Street. Telephone: (972) (3) 5751411; 5751431. Telefax: (972) (3) 5751511.

Corporate, Commercial, Antitrust, Tax, Labor, Industrial Property, Unfair Competition, Estate Law, Arbitration, Foreign Investments, International Transactions.

(This Listing Continued)

PARTNERS

JUDR. MILAN KYJOVSKÝ, admitted, 1990, Czechoslovakia. *Education:* Masaryk University Faculty of Law (Student Assistant, Department of International Law, 1985-1987; Juris Doctor, 1987). Legal Internship, law office, Brno, specializing in International Law, 1987-1990. Independent legal practice in Brno, 1990-1991. Visiting Attorney, Jolidon, Krneta, Gullotti & Hirt, Bern, Switzerland, 1991. *Member:* Czech Chamber of Advocates; AIPPI (Czech Section). *LANGUAGES:* Czech, English, German and Russian.

THOMAS E. MUDD, J.D., admitted, 1988, U.S. District Court, Southern District of Mississippi; 1990, Florida (Not admitted in Czech Republic). *Education:* University of Wyoming (Bachelor of Science, Industrial Relations, 1984); Mississippi College (Juris Doctor, 1987); University of the Pacific in conjunction with University of Salzburg (Diploma, Comparative Law, 1988). Legal Internship in Austria, 1987-1988. Legal practice in United States, 1988-1991. *Member:* International Bar Association; American Bar Association; Florida Bar; Mississippi Bar. *LANGUAGES:* English and German.

JUDR. JAN KOTÍK, admitted, 1992, Czech Republic. *Education:* Charles University (JUDr., 1985). Lecturer, University of Copenhagen, Denmark, Czech Law, 1990-1991. *Member:* Czech Bar Association; INTA. *LANGUAGES:* Czech, Danish, English, French, German and Russian.

ASSOCIATES

MAGISTR PAVLINA KOPPOVA. *Education:* Charles University Faculty of Law (Magistr Juris, 1989). *LANGUAGES:* Czech and English.

OF COUNSEL

PROF. JUDR. ZDENĚK KUČERA, DRSC., admitted, 1951, Czechoslovakia. *Education:* Charles University Faculty of Law (Juris Doctor, 1951; Doctor of Legal Science, 1984). Legal practice in Prague, 1951-1955. Legal Adviser: foreign trade firm in Prague, 1959-1964; Ministry of Foreign Trade, 1964-1966. Professor, Private International Law, Charles University, 1967—. Czechoslovak delegate, sessions of the Hague Conference on Private International Law. Deputy Chairman, Arbitration Court of the Czechoslovak Chamber of Commerce and Industry. *LANGUAGES:* Czech, English and German.

REVISERS OF THE CZECH REPUBLIC LAW DIGEST FOR THIS DIRECTORY

DENMARK

INTER-LEX LAWYERS

Established in 1986

BADEHUSVEJ 16
9000 AALBORG, DENMARK
Telephone: 98 13 17 11
Fax: 98 13 18 11

Esbjerg, Denmark Office: Strandbygade 65, 6701. Telephone: 75 45 46 00; 75 21 21 21. Fax: 75 13 83 14.

Aarhus, Denmark Office: Strandvejen 94, 8100. Telephone: 86 12 12 00. Fax: 86 11 00 00.

Odense, Denmark Office: Fisketorvet 3, 5100 Odense C. Telephone: 66 14 22 22. Fax: 66 13 56 04.

Mergers and Acquisitions, Taxation and International Tax Planning, Insolvency including Liquidations and Receiverships, Civil Litigation, Corporate and Competition Law.

FIRM PROFILE: The Inter-Lex Lawyers was formed in 1986 as a cooperation between 4 independent law firms in the 4 major Danish cities outside Copenhagen. The cooperation has 17 partners and 11 associates.

ANDERS HJULMAND, born Aalborg, Denmark, 1951; admitted, 1979, Denmark and Supreme Court of Denmark. *Education:* University of Aarhus (Law Degree, 1976). Lecturer on Law, University of Aalborg. *Member:* Aalborg and Danish Law Associations. *LANGUAGES:* English and German. *PRACTICE AREAS:* International Contracting; Disposal of Business; Transport Law.

(This Listing Continued)

ASSOCIATES

BIRTHE ØSTERGAARD, born Horsens, Denmark, 1946; admitted, 1973, Denmark and High Court of Denmark. *Education:* University of Aarhus (Law Degree, 1970). *Member:* Aalborg and Danish Law Associations. *LANGUAGES:* English and German. *PRACTICE AREAS:* Insolvency Law; Company Law; Banking Law.

LIS SØRENSEN, born Aalborg, Denmark, 1956; admitted, 1985, Denmark and High Court of Denmark. *Education:* University of Aarhus (Law Degree, 1982). *Member:* Aalborg and Danish Law Associations. *LANGUAGES:* English and German. *PRACTICE AREAS:* Law of Succession; Estate of Deceased Persons; Law of Domestic Relations; Matrimonial Legislation; Bankruptcy; Suspension of Payment; Composition.

ANDERS HEDETOFT, born Vejle, Denmark, 1963; admitted, 1990, Denmark and High Court of Denmark. *Education:* University of Copenhagen (Law Degree, 1987). Tutor in Contraction Law, University of Copenhagen, 1987-1993 and University of Aalborg, 1993—. *Member:* Aalborg and Danish Law Associations. *LANGUAGES:* English and German. *PRACTICE AREAS:* Contraction Law; Transport Law; Tenancy Law; Turnkey Law.

PER CHRISTENSEN, born Randers, Denmark, 1967; admitted, 1994, Denmark. *Education:* University of Aarhus (Law Degree, 1991); School of Economics & Business Administration, Aarhus (B.A., Financial Accounting, 1992). Tutor, Contraction and Company Law, University of Aalborg, 1994. *Member:* Aalborg and Danish Law Associations. *LANGUAGES:* English. *PRACTICE AREAS:* Taxation Law; Company Law; Contraction Law.

AROS ADVOKATER

Established in 1994

FRUE KIRKEPLADS 4

P.O. BOX 312

DK-8100 AARHUS C, DENMARK

Telephone: 45 89 31 00 00

Telefax: 45 89 31 01 01

Copenhagen Branch Office: Kongens Nytorv 22, DK-1050 Copenhagen K, Denmark. Telephone: 45 33 14 32 36. Telefax: 45 33 13 09 04.

Contract Law, EU Law, Company Law, Mergers and Acquisitions, Bankruptcy and Insolvency Law, Financing and Banking Law, Insurance Law, Intellectual Property Law, Competition Law, Construction Law, Public Law, Labour Law, Tax Law, Arbitration and Litigation.
The firm is predominantly a commercial law practice offering legal advice in the areas of Danish, EU and International law.

FIRM PROFILE: *Established in 1994 by a merger among 3 renowned law firms to give clients the benefit of their combined resources. With almost 100 employees, of whom 37 are lawyers, it is the largest law firm outside Copenhagen. The firm has a broadly based practice and is distinguished by offering a full range of high-quality legal services.*

MEMBERS OF FIRM

EJLER MUNCH ANDERSEN, born Denmark, May 12, 1929; admitted, 1957, Danish High Court; 1971, Danish Supreme Court. *Education:* University of Aarhus. *Member:* Danish Bar Association (Member, Steering Committee, 1973-1983; Vice Chairman, 1977-1981); Chairman of the Committee for Trade and Industry, 1981-1984, of the Committee for Education, 1985-1986 and of the Committee for Information and Education, 1985— under the Danish Bar Association; Bankruptcy and Insolvency Law Committee, 1981 and 1986—; International Bar Association. *LANGUAGES:* Danish, English and German. *PRACTICE AREAS:* Mergers and Acquisitions; Company Law; Insolvency Law; Company Reconstructions and Reorganizations.

LIDA HULGAARD, born Denmark, August 12, 1939; admitted, 1969, Danish High Court; 1978, Danish Supreme Court. *Education:* University of Aarhus. External Lecturer, Law Faculty University of Aarhus, 1970-1976. Co-Author: "Laerebog om indkomstskat," (Textbook on Danish Income Tax); Articles on Danish Income Tax. Board Member of Giro Bank A/S, Difko Holding A/S, PFA A/S. *Member:* Danish Bar Association; International Fiscal Association. *LANGUAGES:* Danish and English. *PRACTICE AREAS:* Tax Law; Commercial Law; Company Law.

CLAUS SØGAARD-CHRISTENSEN, born Denmark, March 7, 1950; admitted, 1978, Danish High Court; 1983, Danish Supreme Court. *Education:* University of Aarhus. External Lecturer, Law Faculty University of

(This Listing Continued)

Aarhus, 1972-1986. *Member:* Danish Bar Association; Association International Jeunes Avocats (Member, Business Section); International Bar Association. *LANGUAGES:* Danish and English. *PRACTICE AREAS:* General Business Law; International Corporate Law.

JØRN CHRISTENSEN, born Denmark, June 4, 1939; admitted, 1969, Danish High Court. *Education:* University of Aarhus. *Member:* Danish Bar Association. *LANGUAGES:* Danish and English. *PRACTICE AREAS:* Real Estate; Administration of Estates of Deceased; Family Law.

K.O. PEDERSEN, born Denmark, April 15, 1939; admitted, 1969, Danish High Court; 1974, Danish Supreme Court. *Education:* University of Aarhus. *Member:* Danish Bar Association. *LANGUAGES:* Danish and English. *PRACTICE AREAS:* Construction Law; Real Estate; Building and Housing Societies; Company Reconstructions and Reorganizations; Civil Law; Criminal Law.

JØRGEN HOLST, born Denmark, April 11, 1949; admitted, 1975, Danish High Court; 1980, Danish Supreme Court. *Education:* University of Aarhus. *Member:* Danish Bar Association. *LANGUAGES:* Danish and English. *PRACTICE AREAS:* Construction Law; Energy Supply Law; Banking Law; Litigation and Arbitration.

NIELS ULRICH MADSEN, born Denmark, January 24, 1950; admitted, 1978, Danish High Court; 1983, Danish Supreme Court. *Education:* University of Aarhus. External Lecturer in Tax Law, Law Faculty University of Aarhus, 1975-1984. *Member:* Danish Bar Association; International Bar Association. *LANGUAGES:* Danish, English and German. *PRACTICE AREAS:* Tax Law; Tax Planning; Company Law; Mortgages and Real Estate.

LARS SVENNING ANDERSEN, born Denmark, February 11, 1949; admitted, 1979, Danish High Court; 1984, Danish Supreme Court. *Education:* University of Aarhus (Ph.D., 1994). Author: "Lømodtageres retsstilling ved Virksomhedsoverdragelse" (Employees' Rights in the Event of Transfers of Businesses or Undertakings) (1990); "Funktionaerret" (Salaried Employees Law) (1994). *Member:* Danish Bar Association. *LANGUAGES:* Danish and English. *PRACTICE AREAS:* Labour Law; Arbitration and Litigation.

STEFFEN EBDRUP, born Denmark, July 22, 1954; admitted, 1982, Danish High Court; 1987, Danish Supreme Court. *Education:* University of Aarhus. *Member:* Danish Bar Association. *LANGUAGES:* Danish and English. *PRACTICE AREAS:* Commercial and Company Law; Litigation; Mortgages; Real Estate; Advice on Projects and Financing Law.

JENS JERSLEV, born Denmark, January 3, 1954; admitted, 1981, Danish High Court; 1986, Danish Supreme Court. *Education:* University of Aarhus; College d'Europe, Brugge, Belgium (1982-1983). *Member:* Danish Bar Association; Union International des Avocats. *LANGUAGES:* Danish and English. *PRACTICE AREAS:* Commercial and Company Law; Insolvency Law; Company Reconstructions and Reorganizations; Maritime and Transport Law; EU Law.

JENS ANDERSEN-MØLLER, born Denmark, November 22, 1952; admitted, 1982, Danish High Court; 1987, Danish Supreme Court. *Education:* University of Aarhus. External Lecturer, Law Faculty University of Aarhus, 1984. *Member:* Danish Bar Association. *LANGUAGES:* Danish and English. *PRACTICE AREAS:* Danish Public Law; Construction Law; Law of Tort; Environmental Law; Litigation.

KAREN-MARGRETHE SCHEBYE, born Denmark, October 14, 1959; admitted, 1986, Danish High Court; 1991, Danish Supreme Court. *Education:* University of Aarhus. *Member:* Danish Bar Association. *LANGUAGES:* Danish, German and English. *PRACTICE AREAS:* Labour Law.

PER HEMMER, born Denmark, July 31, 1957; admitted, 1988, Danish High Court; 1993, Danish Supreme Court. *Education:* University of Aarhus; University of Miami (M.C.L., 1987). External Lecturer, Law Faculty University of Aarhus, 1984-1986. *Member:* Danish Bar Association; Association International Jeunes Avocats. *LANGUAGES:* Danish, English and German. *PRACTICE AREAS:* Copyright; Trademark; Unfair Marketing Practices; Agency and Distributorship; Licensing.

POUL LAUGE JENSEN, born Denmark, July 25, 1946; admitted, 1988, Danish High Court; 1994, Danish Supreme Court. *Education:* University of Aarhus. *Member:* Danish Bar Association. *LANGUAGES:* Danish and English. *PRACTICE AREAS:* Real Estate; Civil Law; Compulsory Sales of Real Estate.

TORBEN BRØGGER, born Denmark, June 14, 1960; admitted, 1989, Danish High Court. *Education:* University of Aarhus; Vrije University of

(This Listing Continued)

AROS ADVOKATER, Aarhus—Continued

Brussels (LL.M., 1991). External Lecturer in EU Law, Law Faculty University of Aarhus. *Member:* Danish Bar Association. *LANGUAGES:* Danish and English. *PRACTICE AREAS:* European Community Law; International Contract Law; Competition Law; Danish Public Law.

ULLA JACOBSEN, born Denmark, January 28, 1958; admitted, 1986, Danish High Court; 1991, Danish Supreme Court. *Education:* University of Aarhus. *Member:* Danish Bar Association. *LANGUAGES:* Danish, English and German. *PRACTICE AREAS:* Labour Law.

POUL VIGGO BARTELS PETERSEN, born Denmark, July 18, 1959; admitted, 1988, Danish High Court; 1993, Danish Supreme Court. *Education:* University of Aarhus. External Lecturer, Law Faculty University of Aarhus and Aarhus School of Business. *Member:* Danish Bar Association; European Lawyers Association. *LANGUAGES:* Danish and English. *PRACTICE AREAS:* Company Law; International Distributorship and Agency; Commercial Law; Mergers and Acquisitions.

HENRIK STEEN JENSEN, born Denmark, November 17, 1963; admitted, 1992, Danish High Court. *Education:* University of Aarhus. *Member:* Danish Bar Association; Aarhus Advokatforening. *LANGUAGES:* Danish and English. *PRACTICE AREAS:* Tax Law; Building and Housing Societies; Insolvency Law; Administration of Estates.

ASSOCIATES

MOGENS HEINSEN, born Denmark, February 8, 1963; admitted, 1990, Danish High Court. *Education:* University of Aarhus; University of Heidelberg (LL.M., 1992). External Lecturer in Law, Law Faculty University of Aarhus, 1988-1991. *Member:* Danish Bar Association; Internationsl Association of Young Lawyers; Deutsch-Nordische Juristenvereinigung. *LANGUAGES:* Danish, German and English. *PRACTICE AREAS:* Company Law; International Business Law (Particularly German).

JAKOB B. SØRENSEN, born Denmark, February 28, 1963; admitted, 1991, Danish High Court. *Education:* University of Aarhus; University of London, King's College (E.Y.L.C., 1990). External Lecturer in Contract Law, Law Faculty University of Aarhus, 1992—. *Member:* Danish Bar Association; European Lawyers Association. *LANGUAGES:* Danish, English and German. *PRACTICE AREAS:* Company Law; Mergers and Acquisitions; Competition Law; International Business Law.

TORBEN BALLE, born Denmark, April 26, 1959; admitted, 1987, Danish High Court. *Education:* University of Aarhus; King's College, London (LL.M., 1993). External Lecturer in Commercial Law, University of Aalborg, 1987. *Member:* Danish Bar Association. *LANGUAGES:* Danish, English and German. *PRACTICE AREAS:* European Community Law; Insurance Law; Bankruptcy Law.

INTER-LEX LAWYERS

Established in 1986

STRANDVEJEN 94

8100 AARHUS, DENMARK

Telephone: 86 12 12 00

Fax: 86 11 00 00

Esbjerg, Denmark Office: Strandbygade 65, 6701. Telephone: 75 45 46 00; 75 21 21 21. Fax: 75 13 83 14.

Odense, Denmark Office: Fisketorvet 3, 5100 Odense C. Telephone: 66 14 22 22. Fax: 66 13 56 04.

Aalborg, Denmark Office: Badehusvej 16, 9000. Telephone: 98 13 17 11. Fax: 98 13 18 11.

Mergers and Acquisitions. Tax. Insolvency including Liquidations and Receiverships. Civil Litigation. Corporate and Competition Law.

FIRM PROFILE: *The Inter-Lex Lawyers was formed in 1986 as a cooperation between 4 independent law firms in the 4 major Danish cities outside Copenhagen. The cooperation has 17 partners and 11 associates.*

OLE HOLMGAARD KRISTENSEN, born 1941; admitted, 1970, Denmark. *LANGUAGES:* Scandinavian and English. *PRACTICE AREAS:* Insolvency Law; Real Estate; Estate Law; Environmental Law.

MOGENS SKOUENBORG, born 1943; admitted, 1973, Denmark. *LANGUAGES:* Scandinavian and English. *PRACTICE AREAS:* Acquisitions and Disposals; Contracting Law; Business.

OLE RAVNSBO, born 1945; admitted, 1973, Denmark. *LANGUAGES:* English, Scandinavian and German. *PRACTICE AREAS:*

(This Listing Continued)

Mergers and Acquisitions; Civil Litigation; Corporate Law; Competition Law.

KNUD O. CHRISTENSEN, born 1944; admitted, 1977, Denmark. *LANGUAGES:* Scandinavian and English. *PRACTICE AREAS:* Company Law; Acquisitions; Insolvency Law; Agent and Sole Distributorship Agreements.

JØRGEN KJæR, born 1944; admitted, 1975, Denmark. *LANGUAGES:* Scandinavian and English. *PRACTICE AREAS:* Leasehold; Litigation; Acquisitions.

SØREN PEDERSEN, born 1960; admitted, 1988, Denmark. *LANGUAGES:* Scandinavian, English and German. *PRACTICE AREAS:* Agent and Sole Distributorship Agreements; Insolvency; Liquidations and Receiverships; Public Law; Lawsuits; Contract Law.

STORM MORTENSEN

AARHUS, DENMARK

(See Kromann & Münter, Copenhagen, Denmark)

ADVODAN

Nationwide Association of Danish Lawyers

Established in 1988

KONGENS NYTORV 22

DK-1050 COPENHAGEN K, DENMARK

Telephone: +45 33 14 32 36

Telefax: +45 33 32 38 99; +45 33 91 02 22

Advodan Aalborg: Voss & Wagner, Algade 54, Box 1109, 9100 Aalborg. Telephone: 45 98123200. Fax: 45 98131050.

Advodan Aarhus: Villumsen & Naeser, Søndergade 4, DK-8100 Aarhus C, Denmark. Telephone: +45 86129400. Fax: +45 86129922.

Advodan Copenhagen: Horten & Co., Kongens Nytorv 22, DK-1050, Copenhagen K, Denmark. Telephone: +45 33143236. Fax: +45 33323899; +45 33910222.

Advodan Faaborg: Jørgensen, Klausen & Rasmussen, Østergade 14 A, DK-5600 Faaborg, Denmark. Telephone: +45 62610465. Fax: +45 62610424.

Advodan Fredericia: Advokaterne i Fredericiagaarden Danmarksgade 11, DK-7000, Fredericia, Denmark. Telephone: +45 75929333. Fax: +45 75922963. Haderslev: Ditlevsen,Berg & Partners, Nørregade 39, DK-6100, Haderslev, Denmark. Telephone: +45 74523500. Fax: +45 74533574.

Advodan Kolding: Advokaterne Nøhr, Gråbrødregade 14, DK-6000 Kolding, Denmark. Telephone: +45 75542111. Fax: +45 75542419.

Advodan Løgumkloster: Lüth, Gram-Hansen & Jan Hansen. Østergrade 6A. DK-6240 Løgumkloster, Denmark. Telephone: +4574743111. Fax: +45 74743430.

Advodan Roskilde: Jørgen Hindhede, Skomagergade 1, DK-4000 Roskilde, Denmark. Telephone: +45 42351660. Fax: +45 46320885.

Advodan Svendborg: Advokaterne Bertel Rasmussen, Kreyers Pakhus, Kroyers Strade 3°, DK 5700 Svendborg. Telephone: 45 62212124. Fax: 4562220966.

Advodan Sønderborg: Boserup, Højer & Christensen, Sundsmarkvej 20, DK-6400 Sønderborg, Denmark. Telephone: +45 74423605. Fax: +45 74434442.

Advodan Tingley: Advokaterne i Tinglev. Hovedgaden 45, DK-6360, Tingley, Denmark. Telephone: +4574643313. Fax: +4574643906.

Advodan Tønder: Kiilerich-Hansen & Dreyer. Vestergade 14, DK-6270. Tønder, Denmark. Telephone: +4574721010. Fax: +4574725931.

Advodan Vojens: Ditlevsen, Berg & Partners, Rådhuscentret 21, DK-6500 Vojens, Denmark. Telephone: +45 74542156. Fax: +45 74590524.

Advodan Vordingborg: Advokat Hedin, Københavnsvej 28, DK-4760 Vordingborg, Denmark. Telephone: +45 53770044. Fax: +45 53770644.

Advodan Haderslev: Kitlevsen, Berg & Partnere, Nørregade 39 C, 6100 Haderslev, Denmark. Telephone: 4574523500. Fax: 4574533574.

Advodan Horsens: Advokaterne Nørretorv, Nørretorv 2, 8700 Horsens, Denmark. Telephone: 4575615022. Fax: 4575621698.

(This Listing Continued)

Advodan Skanderborg: Advokaterne Mygind, Vermeij, Vermeij, 8660 Skanderborg, Denmark. Adelgrade 102 A. Telephone: 45 86525677. Fax: 45 86525579.

Advodan Skagen: Advokatfirmaet Axel S. Pallesen, Smøgen 9, 9990 Skagen, Denmark. Telephone: 4598444000. Fax: 4598445179.

Advodan Store Heddinge: Advokaterne på Trianglen, 4660 Store Heddinge, Denmark. Telephone: 4553702900. Fax: 4553704061.

Advodan Præstø: Advokat Jørn Hedin, Adelgade 71, 4720 PrÆstø. Telephone: 4555993944. Fax: 4553770644.

Agency and Exclusive Distribution. Anti-trust and Competition. Aviation , Bankruptcy and Probate. Book, Film and Music Publishing. Commercial Arbitration and Litigation. Corporate Mergers and Acquisitions. EEC Law. Employment and Dismissal. Energy and Water Supply. Environmental Protection. Fishery. Industrial Property Rights and Licensing. Insurance Coverage. International Borrowing and Lending. Labor Protection. Local Government Relations. Planning and Building Permits. Real Estate. Ships and Shipping. Taxation. Tenancy. Turn-key and Construction Projects.

MEMBERS

Niels-Peter Andreasen	Nicolai R. Horten
Jakob S. Arrevad	Bjarne Becher Jensen
Erik Berg	Elo Jensen
Hans Boserup	Børge Jørgensen
Erling Christensen	Ch Lundegaard
Kield Christensen	Nicolai Mallet
Bjarne L. Ditlevsen	Henrik Nøhr
Erik Dreyer	Karsten Nøhr
Jens Gehl	Ulrik Næser
K. Gram-Hansen	Axel S. Pallesen
Troels Grundstrup	J. Bertel Rasmussen
Jan Hansen	Holger Rendtorff
Johs. Hansen	Fritz Reuther
Jørn K. Hedin	Finn Schwarz
Jørgen Hindhede	Erik Vermeij
Carsten Højer	Helle Mygind Vermeij
Hans R. Horten	Karl Villumsen

ASSOCIATES

Peder Agger	Henrik Moeller
Karen Bang	Lars Nauheimer
Jens Jacob Bugge	Charlotte Neubert
Lars Carstens	Ole Graesbøll Olesen
Lemmy Fialin	Jørn Petersen
Thorkild Glavind	Birgitte Randrup
Michael GoeskjÆr	Søren Rasmussen
Lorens E. Hansen	Susanne Rasmussen
Stefan Poul Hansen	Henriette Soeltoft
Ove Henningsen	Michael Sønderskov
Gert Drews Jensen	Anette Moll Sørensen
Paul C. Jeppesen	Annette W. Sørensen
Lars Jespersen	Bente Koudal Sørensen
Lars CMR. Keaergaard	Kai Schmüchker Steen Andersen
Kjeld Klausen	Peter Ulrik Urskov
Charlis Vogelbein	

Languages: Danish, English, German, Portuguese, Dutch, Scandinavian. Correspondents throughout Europe and USA. Special relations to Holland, Poland and Portugal.

Member of European Law Group: Denmark, Belgium, England, France, Germany, Holland, Italy, Spain and Switzerland.

PETER ALSTED

Established in 1964

90, VESTER VOLDGADE
DK-1552 COPENHAGEN V, DENMARK
Telephone: +45 33 15 15 63
Fax: +45 33 13 07 07

General International Practice, Commercial and Corporate.

PETER ALSTED, born Hellerup, Denmark, January 13, 1934; admitted, 1962, Denmark; 1968, Supreme Court of Denmark. *Education:* University of Copenhagen (graduate in Law, 1958). Author, Articles i.a. on: "Taxation of Dividends," Skattepolitisk Oversight (Danish Publication), 1978; "Danish Company Law," Internationale Wirtschafts Briefe (German Language), 1992; "Employment Law in Denmark", "Agency and Distribution in Denmark," The European Handbook, 1993 (English Publication); "Danish

(This Listing Continued)

Company Law." Co-Author: EG Handbuch für Gesellschaftsrecht (German Language), 1995. *Member:* Danish Society of Counsels; Union Internationale des Avocats (Corresponding Member). *LANGUAGES:* English, French, German and The Scandinavian Languages.

ADVOKATERNE AMALIEGADE NO. 42

Established in 1947

AMALIEGADE 42
DK-1256 COPENHAGEN K, DENMARK
Telephone: 45 33 11 33 99
Telex: 27 223 amalex dk
Telefax: 45 33 32 46 25

Paris, France Office: 36, rue Tronchet, F-75009. Telephone: 1-42661449. Telex: 660877 Carler F. Telefax: 1-42665945.

Admiralty Law, Arbitration, Aviation Law, Bankruptcy, Banking and Finance, Commercial Agency and Distribution, Commercial Law, Construction Law, Copyright and trademarks, Corporate Law, EEC Law, Environment Law, Insurance Law, Labour Law, Mergers and Acquisitions, Sale, Purchase and Administration of Real Estate, Restrictive Trade Practice and Monopolies, Tax Law, Transport Law, Travel and Tourism Law, Trusts.

FIRM PROFILE: *Advokaterne Amaliegade 42, is a medium sized law firm concentrating on and cross- frontier legal advice. We believe that the client shall decide what problems are important and our ambition is to offer solutions whether the problems concern his private life or that of his business. We consider that efficient advice cannot be given without a full understanding of the business of the client and his cultural background.*

MEMBERS OF FIRM

T. INGEMANN HANSEN, born Copenhagen, December 7, 1936; admitted, 1967, Denmark; 1971, High Court; 1976, Supreme Court. *Education:* Copenhagen University (Graduate at Law, 1961). Officer of the Crown (Ministry of Education and Ministry of Finance), 1961-1967. City Counsellor of Frederiksberg, 1985-1989. Lay Judge, Housing Tribunal, Copenhagen, 1978. Member, Public Rent Control Board, Frederiksberg, 1974. *Member:* Danish Bar Association; I.B.A.; Rotary International, Underwriting Member Lloyds, London. *LANGUAGES:* Danish, English, German, French and Scandinavian. *PRACTICE AREAS:* Banking; Finance; Trusts.

P.R. MEURS-GERKEN, born Copenhagen, April 2, 1941; admitted, 1971, Denmark; 1974, High Court; 1979, Supreme Court. *Education:* Copenhagen University (Graduate at Law, 1968); Universities of Bonn, Cambridge, Barcelona (1961-1963). Lecturer on Real Estate Law at Copenhagen University, 1969-1972. President, A.I.J.A., 1981. Vice-President, Alliance Française, Denmark, 1978. Member of Court of Arbitration of the International Chamber of Commerce, 1979. Board Member of Danish Committee of International Arbitrators, 1984. General Secretary of Chambre de Commerce Franco-Danoise, 1983. *Member:* Danish Bar Association (Member of the Committee of International Relations); I.B.A.; A.I.J.A.; U.I.A.; E.A.L.; F.I.D.E. *LANGUAGES:* Danish, English, French, German, Dutch, Portuguese, Spanish, Italian and Scandinavian. *PRACTICE AREAS:* Arbitration; Commercial Law; Corporate Law; Travel and Tourism Law.

MOGENS TRYGVE LIED FLAGSTAD, born Frederiksberg, February 15, 1946; admitted, 1976, Denmark and High Court; 1981, Supreme Court. *Education:* Copenhagen University (Graduate at Law, 1973); Aix-en-Provence University (Diplomé d'Etudes Supérieurs d'Université de Droit). Lecturer on Tax Law, Copenhagen University, 1976-1983. Trainee Supervisor at the Danish Bar Association, 1977-1984. General Manager and Legal Counselor, Tjaereborg Sterling Group, 1985-1987. *Member:* Danish Bar Association; I.B.A. *LANGUAGES:* Danish, English, French, German and Scandinavian. *PRACTICE AREAS:* Aviation Law; Banking; Finance; Construction Law; Tax Law; Travel and Tourism Law.

PATRICE CARON, born Rouen, France, August 11, 1951. *Education:* University of Rouen (Licence droit privé, 1973); University of Copenhagen (1974); University of Paris I (Certificate CUECE and DES Droit des Communautés Européennes, 1975). Admitted as advocate at the Bars in Paris and in Denmark. *Member:* A.I.J.A.; Paris Bar; Danish Bar Association. (Resident, Paris, France Office). *LANGUAGES:* French, Danish and English. *PRACTICE AREAS:* Banking; Finance; Corporate Law; EEC Law; Mergers and Acquisitions; Tax Law.

SUZANNE FLAGSTAD, born Copenhagen, April 4, 1954; admitted, 1984, Denmark. *Education:* Copenhagen University (Graduate at Law,

(This Listing Continued)

ADVOKATERNE AMALIEGADE NO. 42, Copenhagen—Continued

1981). Company Secretary to Fjerde Soforsikring A/S (Sum Alliance Group), 1984-1987. *Member:* Danish Bar Association. **LANGUAGES:** Danish, English and Scandinavian. **PRACTICE AREAS:** Bankruptcy; Corporate Law; Insurance Law; Purchase and Administration of Real Estate.

JAN THOR KROYER, born Elsinore, May 11, 1950; admitted, 1978, Denmark, High Court and Supreme Court. *Education:* Copenhagen University (Graduate at Law, 1975). Practicing Lawyer in Greenland, 1984-1987; A.P. Moller Group (Maersk Drilling), 1988-1989. *Member:* Danish Bar Association; A.I.J.A. (National Vice President, 1979-1982). **LANGUAGES:** Danish, English, French, German and Scandinavian. **PRACTICE AREAS:** Admiralty Law; Bankruptcy; Banking; Finance; Construction Law; Tax Law; Transport Law.

ASSOCIATES

HENRIK AMAND HANSEN, born Frederiksberg, February 20, 1965; admitted, 1993, Denmark. *Education:* Copenhagen University (Graduate at Law, 1990). **LANGUAGES:** Danish, English and Scandinavian. **PRACTICE AREAS:** Corporate Law; Contracts; Bankruptcy.

FEDERICO MANILI, born Rieti, September 20, 1963. *Education:* Rome University (Graduate at Law, 1989). *Member:* AIJA. **LANGUAGES:** Italian, Danish, French and English. **PRACTICE AREAS:** Italian Civil Law; International Private Law; International Commercial Law; EEC Law.

JOSE BARNILS, born Barcelona, April 7, 1964. *Education:* Barcelona University (Graduate at Law, 1987); London School of Economics (LL.M., 1984); McGill University (Dip. in Air and Space Law, 1990). **LANGUAGES:** Spanish, Catalan, English, Italian and Danish. **PRACTICE AREAS:** Transport Law; Commercial Law.

IB CHRISTIAN PEDERSEN, born Odense, October 6, 1967. *Education:* Copenhagen University (Graduate at Law, 1992); University Robert Schumann Strasbour (1991). **LANGUAGES:** Danish, English, French and German. **PRACTICE AREAS:** Commercial Law; Tax Law; Labour Law; Family Law.

REPRESENTATIVE CLIENTS: Air France S.A.; Automobiles Citroön A/S; Baltica A/S; Benetton S.p.A., Carli Gry International A/S; COFACE; Den Danske Bank A/S; Duba Mobelindustri A/S; Uniroyal Englebert Dak A/S; Euorpaeisko A/S; GEC Alsthom; Glaverbel A/S; J&B Byggeproduktion A/S; Realkredit Danmark A/S (The Danish Mortgage Credit Association); Meadox Medicals Inc.; Maerssk Drilling (A.P. Moller Group); NKT A/S/; Planbyg A/S; Régie Nationale des Usines Renault; Scantech A/S; Stormax International A/S; Transworld Airlines.
REFERENCES: Belgian, French, Italian, Portuguese, Spanish, Swiss, U.S., Australian and Brazilian Embassies.

SOREN BECH

NY OSTERGADE 3, 5
1101 COPENHAGEN K, DENMARK
Telephone: 33 1334 01
Fax: 33 9134 01

Bankruptcy, Business and Transport Law.

SOREN BECH, born October 29, 1955; admitted, 1986, Denmark; 1994, Publicly Appointed Defense Counsel, Copenhagen District Court, The High Court and The Supreme Court including The Maritime and Commercial Court. *Education:* University of Copenhagen (1982). Associate Professor, Procedural Law and Bankruptcy Law, 1986-1989; Associate Professor, Business Law, 1989-1994, University of Copenhagen; Associate Professor, Transport Law, Copenhagen Business School, 1994. Lecturer, Danish Federation of Industries, Transport and Maritime Law, International Trade, Insurance Export Financing and Export Know How, 1985-1992. Lecturer for HK Freight Forwarding Department, Transport Law, Liability of the Freight Forwarder and Insurance Relations, 1985-1990. Author: Articles, International Law, The Division of the Sea and The Legal Position of Ships in Open Sea (Denmarks Skibsfart 1984). Member of Board of Directors of Danish and Overseas Companies. **LANGUAGES:** Danish, English, German, French, Swedish and Norwegian.

BECH-BRUUN & TROLLE

NR. FARIMAGSGADE 3
1364 COPENHAGEN K, DENMARK
Telephone: +45 33 12 12 33
Telefax: +45 33 15 25 55
Telex: 16110 BBTLAW

General Corporate and Commercial Law, Agency and Distributorship, Aviation, Entertainment Law, Banking, Capital Markets, Computer Law, EC Law and EC Competition Law, Finance, Stock Exchange Regulations, Insolvency, Inheritance, Media Law, Telecommunications, Management, Merchandising, Insurance, Antitrust, Intellectual Property, Trade Practices, Taxation, VAT, Duties, International Contracts, International Arbitration, Labour and Employment Law, Mergers and Acquisitions, Private Associations, Litigation, Construction, Oil and Mineral Resources, Maritime Law, Local Governments, Real Estate, Environmental Law, Bankruptcy, Suspension of Payments, Debt Rescheduling.

FIRM PROFILE: Bech-Bruun & Trolle dates back to 1888. Bech-Bruun & Trolle employs 140 people, 55 of whom are lawyers. The firm renders a full range of legal services, nationally and internationally, to financial, commercial and industrial clients. The objective of the firm is to provide high-quality cost-effective legal assistance, meeting our clients' needs. Bech-Bruun & Trolle conducts business in the Scandinavian languages as well as in English, German, French, Dutch and Italian.

MEMBERS OF FIRM

ESKIL TROLLE, born Copenhagen, Denmark, March 17, 1938; admitted, 1965, Denmark; 1967, High Court of Denmark; 1973, Supreme Court of Denmark; 1985, appointed by the Ministry of Justice to plead public cases in the Supreme Court of Denmark. *Education:* University of Copenhagen (Law Degree, 1961); London (English Maritime Law, 1961). The Ministry of Justice, 1961-1965; Assistant Judge, 1963-1964. Author: "Branches and Subsidiaries in the Common Market," London, 1976; "Business Law in Europe," London, 1982. *Member:* Copenhagen and Danish Bar Associations; International Bar Association; International Chamber of Commerce. **LANGUAGES:** Danish, Swedish, Norwegian and English. **PRACTICE AREAS:** Company Law; Stock Exchange Regulations; Local Governments.

ARNE BIERFREUND, born Copenhagen, Denmark, March 10, 1942; admitted, 1970, Denmark; 1971, High Court of Denmark; 1976, Supreme Court of Denmark. *Education:* University of Copenhagen (Law Degree, 1967). Norton Rose, London, 1973-1974. *Member:* Copenhagen Bar Association; Danish Bar Association; International Bar Association. **LANGUAGES:** Danish, Swedish, Norwegian, English and German. **PRACTICE AREAS:** Litigation; Construction Law; International Contracts.

HENRIK ANDERSEN, born Copenhagen, Denmark, June 16, 1942; admitted, 1971, Denmark and High Court of Denmark; 1977, Supreme Court of Denmark. *Education:* University of Copenhagen (Law Degree, 1968). Trustee, Maritime and Commercial Court of Copenhagen. *Member:* Copenhagen Bar Association; Danish Bar Association; International Bar Association; International Fiscal Association. **LANGUAGES:** Danish, English and French. **PRACTICE AREAS:** Insolvency; Reconstructions; VAT; Duties; Maritime Law.

SVEND PALUDAN-MÜLLER, born Copenhagen, Denmark, January 1, 1943; admitted, 1972, Denmark; 1973, High Court of Denmark; 1978, Supreme Court of Denmark. *Education:* University of Copenhagen (Law Degree, 1968). Trustee, Maritime and Commercial Court of Copenhagen. *Member:* Copenhagen Bar Association; Danish Bar Association; Danish Insurance Law Association. **LANGUAGES:** Danish, English and German. **PRACTICE AREAS:** Insurance Law; Environmental Law; Administrative Law; Insolvency.

LEIF LUND-ANDERSEN, born Copenhagen, Denmark, December 28, 1943; admitted, 1973, Denmark; 1974, High Court of Denmark; 1980, Supreme Court of Denmark. *Education:* University of Copenhagen (Law Degree, 1968); The Danish Ministry of Commerce. *Member:* Danish Bar Association; Copenhagen Bar Association (Member of Board, 1978-1983); Bar Council of Copenhagen (Member of Board, 1978-1987); International Bar Association. **LANGUAGES:** Danish and English. **PRACTICE AREAS:** Company Law; Insolvency; Management.

SVEN KROGSTRUP, born Aarhus, Denmark, September 10, 1943; admitted, 1973, Denmark and High Court of Denmark. *Education:* University of Copenhagen (Law Degree, 1970); Université de Grenoble. Practice in Jeddah, Saudi Arabia, 1978-1980. **LANGUAGES:** Danish and English. **PRACTICE AREAS:** Aviation; Company Law; Mergers and Acquisitions.

(This Listing Continued)

STEEN HALMIND, born Fredericia, Denmark, May 11, 1944; admitted, 1974, Denmark and High Court of Denmark. *Education:* University of Aarhus (Law Degree, 1971). *Member:* Danish Bar Association. *LANGUAGES:* Danish and English. *PRACTICE AREAS:* Finance; Company Law; Insolvency; Computer Law.

SØREN MEISLING, born Frederiksberg, Denmark, October 17, 1947; admitted, 1975, Denmark; 1976, High Court of Denmark; 1981, Supreme Court of Denmark. *Education:* University of Copenhagen (Law Degree, 1972). *Member:* Danish Bar Association; International Bar Association. *LANGUAGES:* Danish, Swedish, Norwegian, English and German. *PRACTICE AREAS:* Mergers and Acquisitions; Company Law; Natural Resources.

OLE DAMSBO, born Copenhagen, Denmark, November 13, 1947; admitted, 1977, Denmark; 1978, High Court of Denmark; 1983, Supreme Court of Denmark. *Education:* Niels Brock Business School (1967); University of Copenhagen (Law Degree, 1973). Tutor at the University of Copenhagen, 1973-1978. Examiner and Special Lecturer, Intellectual Property Law, University of Copenhagen, 1991—. Author: "Investment in China," Copenhagen, 1987; "Investment in Vietnam," Copenhagen, 1994; Author of sundry law review articles. *Member:* Danish Bar Association; Copenhagen Bar Association (Member of Board, 1983-1988); International Bar Association; Danish Society on Intellectual Property; AIPPI. *LANGUAGES:* Danish, Swedish, Norwegian, English, German and French. *PRACTICE AREAS:* Intellectual Property; Industrial Property; Trade Practices; Antitrust.

JANNE GLAESEL, born Copenhagen, Denmark, April 26, 1953; admitted, 1980, Denmark and High Court of Denmark; 1990, Supreme Court of Denmark. *Education:* University of Copenhagen (Law Degree, 1978). Co-Author: "Research and Development Contracts," Copenhagen, 1992. *Member:* Danish Bar Association; Copenhagen Bar Association; Danish Society on Intellectual Property. *LANGUAGES:* Danish, Swedish, Norwegian, English and German. *PRACTICE AREAS:* Intellectual Property; Trade Practices; EC Competition Law; Mergers and Acquisitions; International Contracts; Inheritance; Estate Planning.

MARIANN NORRBOM, born Copenhagen, Denmark, September 11, 1949; admitted, 1981, Denmark; 1982, High Court of Denmark; 1987, Supreme Court of Denmark. *Education:* University of Copenhagen (Law Degree, 1977). *Member:* Copenhagen and Danish Bar Associations; Danish Society for Labour Law (Member of the Board and Secretary); International Society for Labour Law and Social Security (Member, Executive Committee). *LANGUAGES:* Danish and English. *PRACTICE AREAS:* Labour Law; Employment Law; Administrative Law; Pension Schemes.

JAN SCHANS CHRISTENSEN, born Bennekom, The Netherlands, August 15, 1957; admitted, 1984, Denmark; 1986, High Court of Denmark. *Education:* University of Copenhagen (Law Degree, 1981); Columbia University School of Law, New York (Research Assistant, 1987-1988; LL.M., 1988); University of Copenhagen (Dr. jur., 1991). Associate Editor, Columbia Business Law Review, 1987-1988. Author: "Hostile Takeovers in the USA," Copenhagen, 1989; "Contested Takeovers in Danish Law: A Comparative Analysis based on a Law and Economics Approach," Copenhagen, 1991; "Management and shareholders," Copenhagen, 1992. Lecturer of Advanced Corporate Law, University of Copenhagen. Debevoise & Plimpton, New York, 1988-1989. *Member:* Danish Bar Association; Copenhagen Bar Association; International Bar Association; Danish Corporate Law Association (Co-Founder). *LANGUAGES:* Danish, Swedish, Norwegian, English, German and Dutch. *PRACTICE AREAS:* Company Law; Mergers and Acquisitions; Natural Resources; Energy Law.

JACOB HJORTSHØJ, born Copenhagen, Denmark, January 4, 1959; admitted, 1985, Denmark and High Court of Denmark; 1990, Supreme Court of Denmark. *Education:* University of Copenhagen (Law Degree, 1982). Lecturer in Company Law, University of Copenhagen. *Member:* Danish Bar Association; Copenhagen Bar Association; International Bar Association; Danish and International Fiscal Association. *LANGUAGES:* Danish, Swedish, Norwegian and English. *PRACTICE AREAS:* Company Law; Taxation; Mergers and Acquisitions.

JØRGEN REIMER JENSEN, born Copenhagen, Denmark, January 17, 1958; admitted, 1985, Denmark and High Court of Denmark; 1990, Supreme Court of Denmark. *Education:* University of Copenhagen (Law Degree, 1982); University of Michigan Law School (LL.M., 1986). Sullivan & Cromwell, New York, 1986-1987. *Member:* Danish Bar Association; Copenhagen Bar Association; International Bar Association. *LANGUAGES:* Danish and English. *PRACTICE AREAS:* Capital Markets; Company Law; Mergers and Acquisitions; International Contracts.

POUL HVILSTED, born Silkeborg, Denmark, April 19, 1956; admitted, 1985, Denmark and High Court of Denmark; 1991, Supreme Court of Denmark. *Education:* University of Aarhus (Law Degree, 1982). *Member:* Danish Bar Association; Copenhagen Bar Association; Danish Environmental Law Association (Board Member); European Environmental Law Association (Board Member). *LANGUAGES:* Danish and English. *PRACTICE AREAS:* Company Law; Environmental Law; Litigation.

BJARKE VEJBY, born Kaduna, Nigeria, July 17, 1957; admitted, 1985, Denmark and High Court of Denmark; 1990, Supreme Court of Denmark. *Education:* University of Copenhagen (Law Degree, 1982). *Member:* Danish Bar Association; Copenhagen Bar Association; Danish Society for Labour Law. *LANGUAGES:* Danish and English. *PRACTICE AREAS:* Labour Law; Employment Law; Media Law; Litigation; Telecommunications.

JON DYHRE HANSEN, born Odense, Denmark, March 18, 1959; admitted, 1987, Denmark; 1993, High Court of Denmark. *Education:* University of Aarhus (Law Degree, 1984). *Member:* Danish Bar Association; Copenhagen Bar Association. *LANGUAGES:* Danish and English. *PRACTICE AREAS:* Real Estate; Environmental Law; Company Law.

ASSOCIATES

MORTEN ULRICH, born Holbaek, Denmark, September 21, 1957; admitted, 1984, Denmark and High Court of Denmark; 1994, Supreme Court of Denmark. *Education:* University of Copenhagen (Law Degree, 1981). *Member:* Danish Bar Association. *LANGUAGES:* Danish and English. *PRACTICE AREAS:* Labour Law; Employment Law; Litigation.

KARIN ARNSTEDT, born Copenhagen, Denmark, February 5, 1957; admitted, 1985, Denmark and High Court of Denmark. *Education:* University of Copenhagen (Law Degree, 1982). *Member:* Danish Bar Association. *LANGUAGES:* Danish, English and French. *PRACTICE AREAS:* Agency and Distributorship; Litigation; Trade Practices.

MICHAEL SERRING, born Frederiksberg, Denmark, April 13, 1960; admitted, 1987, Denmark and High Court of Denmark; 1992, Supreme Court of Denmark. *Education:* University of Copenhagen (Law Degree, 1984). Lecturer, Contract Law, University of Copenhagen, 1985-1988. *Member:* Danish Bar Association. *LANGUAGES:* Danish, Swedish, Norwegian and English. *PRACTICE AREAS:* Insolvency; Bankruptcy; Litigation.

MORTEN KOFMANN CHRISTENSEN, born Copenhagen, Denmark, October 10, 1962; admitted, 1989, Denmark and High Court of Denmark. *Education:* University of Copenhagen (Law Degree, 1986); London School of Economics and Political Science (LL.M., 1990). Contributing Editor, The European Law Digest, 1990. The Commission of the European Communities, Directorate General for Competition, 1990-1991. Lecturer: EC Law, Copenhagen Business School, 1991-1993; Competition Law, University of Copenhagen, 1992—. *Member:* Danish Bar Association; Copenhagen Bar Association; International Bar Association; International League of Competition Law; The Law Society's Solicitors' European Group; The Institute of European Law. *LANGUAGES:* Danish, Swedish, Norwegian and English. *PRACTICE AREAS:* EC Competition Law; EC Law; International Contracts.

MIKKEL BAARING LERCHE, born Copenhagen, Denmark, January 31, 1963; admitted, 1989, Denmark; 1992, High Court of Denmark. *Education:* University of Copenhagen (Law Degree, 1986). Author: (with Jan Schans Christensen): Chapter on Danish Law in the Butterworth Treatise on International Agency and Distribution Agreements, 1991; (with Ole Damsbo): Investments in Vietnam, Copenhagen, 1994. *Member:* Danish Bar Association; Copenhagen Bar Association; International Bar Association. *LANGUAGES:* Danish, English, Swedish, Norwegian and German. *PRACTICE AREAS:* Company Law; Mergers and Acquisitions; International Contracts.

CARSTEN PEDERSEN, born Copenhagen, Denmark, December 30, 1961; admitted, 1989, Denmark and High Court of Denmark; 1994, Supreme Court of Denmark. *Education:* University of Copenhagen (Law Degree, 1986). Lecturer, University of Copenhagen, 1987-1989. *Member:* Danish Bar Association; Copenhagen Bar Association; International Bar Association. *LANGUAGES:* Danish, English and French. *PRACTICE AREAS:* Litigation; Construction Law; International Contracts.

ESTHER SCHMITH, born Dronninglund, Denmark, August 10, 1943; admitted, 1990, Denmark. *Education:* University of Copenhagen (Law Degree, 1972). The Ministry of Inland Revenue, Head of Section, 1972-1980. Secretary to the Minister, 1977-1980. Head of Tax Department, Revisor Centret (now Ernst & Young), Chartered Accountants, 1980-1988. Lecturer, Danish School of Administration, 1978-1980. *Member:* Committee

(This Listing Continued)   *(This Listing Continued)*

BECH-BRUUN & TROLLE, Copenhagen—Continued

on taxation of spouses, appointed by the Minister of Inland Revenue (1983-1984); The Danish Branch of The International Fiscal Association (Member of Council, 1985—; Executive Committee, Treasurer and Secretary, 1986—; Tax Committee of the Bar Council, 1991—); Danish Bar Association. *LANGUAGES:* Danish and English. *PRACTICE AREAS:* Taxation; Company Law; Mergers and Acquisitions.

BIRGITTE FJELDHOFF, born Svendborg, Denmark, July 22, 1962; admitted, 1989, Denmark; 1990, High Court of Denmark. *Education:* University of Copenhagen (Law Degree, 1986). *Member:* Danish Bar Association. *LANGUAGES:* Danish and English. *PRACTICE AREAS:* Bankruptcy; Suspension of Payments; Debt Rescheduling.

JØRGEN OVESEN, born Viborg, Denmark, April 18, 1960; admitted, 1990, Denmark and High Court of Denmark. *Education:* University of Copenhagen (Law Degree, 1987); London School of Economics and Political Science (LL.M., 1992). *Member:* Danish Bar Association. *LANGUAGES:* Danish and English. *PRACTICE AREAS:* Labour Law; Employment Law; Private Associations.

LARS SKANVIG BRAMHELFT, born Copenhagen, Denmark, October 24, 1964; admitted, 1991, Denmark and High Court of Denmark. *Education:* University of Aarhus and Copenhagen (Law Degree, 1988); Duke University, School of Law, North Carolina (LL.M., 1993). *Member:* Danish Bar Association; Association International des Jeunes Avocats (AIJA). *LANGUAGES:* Danish, Swedish, Norwegian and English. *PRACTICE AREAS:* Insolvency; Reconstructions; Litigation.

HELLE JØRGSHOLM, born Copenhagen, Denmark, April 10, 1962; admitted, 1991, Denmark; 1993, High Court of Denmark. *Education:* University of Copenhagen (Law Degree, 1988). *Member:* Danish Bar Association; Copenhagen Bar Association; Danish Society on Intellectual Property. *LANGUAGES:* Danish and English. *PRACTICE AREAS:* Intellectual Property; Mergers and Acquisitions; International Contracts.

MORTEN LAU SMITH, born Copenhagen, Denmark, March 13, 1964; admitted, 1992, Denmark and High Court of Denmark. *Education:* University of Copenhagen (Law Degree, 1989); University of Southampton (LL.M., 1989). Co-Author: with Mette Dithmar, chapter on Danish Law, "Remedies for International Sellers of Goods," 1993. *Member:* Danish Bar Association. *LANGUAGES:* Danish and English. *PRACTICE AREAS:* Litigation; International Contracts.

CHARLOTTE FLACH, born Aarhus, Denmark, August 17, 1960; admitted, 1992, Denmark. *Education:* University of Copenhagen (Law Degree, 1989). *Member:* Danish Bar Association. *LANGUAGES:* Danish and English. *PRACTICE AREAS:* Labour Law; Employment Law; Litigation.

JESPER FABRICIUS, born Grenaa, Denmark, June 17, 1964; admitted, 1992, Denmark. *Education:* University of Copenhagen (Law Degree, 1989); College of Europe, Belgium (LL.M., 1993). Lecturer, University of Copenhagen, 1990-1992. *Member:* Danish Bar Association. *LANGUAGES:* Danish, Swedish, Norwegian, English, German and French. *PRACTICE AREAS:* Mergers and Acquisitions; Company Law; EC Law; International Contracts.

JAKOB DORNONVILLE DE LA COUR, born Copenhagen, Denmark, September 20, 1963; admitted, 1993, Denmark. *Education:* University of Copenhagen (Law Degree, 1990). *Member:* Danish Bar Association. *LANGUAGES:* Danish, English and French. *PRACTICE AREAS:* Intellectual Property; Insolvency.

MORTEN LANGER, born Copenhagen, Denmark, March 6, 1964; admitted, 1993, Denmark and High Court of Denmark. *Education:* University of Copenhagen (Law Degree, 1990). Lecturer, Copenhagen School of Economics and Business Administration, 1990. *Member:* Danish Bar Association; Danish Society for Labour Law. *LANGUAGES:* Danish and English. *PRACTICE AREAS:* Labour Law; Employment Law; Litigation.

HENRIK GROOS, born August 23, 1965; admitted, 1993, Denmark and High Court of Denmark. *Education:* University of Copenhagen (Law Degree, 1989); Scholar, Free University of Berlin, Germany, 1989-1990. *Member:* Danish Bar Association. *LANGUAGES:* Danish, German and English. *PRACTICE AREAS:* Real Property; Litigation; Company Law.

HENRIETTE SOJA, born Virum, Denmark, August 4, 1963; admitted, 1993, Denmark. *Education:* University of Copenhagen (Law Degree, 1988). Lecturer, The Danish School of Administration, 1989-1991. Co-Author: with Poul Hvilsted, chapter on Danish Law, "Environmental liabilities and regulation in Europe," 1993. The Ministry of Environment, 1988-1991.

(This Listing Continued)

Member: Danish Bar Association. *LANGUAGES:* Danish, German and English. *PRACTICE AREAS:* Environmental Law; Administrative Law.

TOM BORK PETERSEN, born Aarhus, Denmark, December 22, 1962; admitted, 1990, New York; 1993, Denmark. *Education:* University of Aarhus (Law Degree, 1987); University of Michigan Law School (1988-1989; LL.M., 1989); European University Institute, Florence, Italy (Ph.D. Scholar, 1987-1988 and 1989-1990). *Member:* New York State Bar Association; Danish Bar Association. *LANGUAGES:* Danish, English, French and Italian. *PRACTICE AREAS:* EC Law; Intellectual Property; Antitrust; Licensing/Franchising.

LISE WEIDNER, born London, England, June 9, 1966; admitted, 1994, Denmark. *Education:* University of Copenhagen (Law Degree, 1991). *Member:* Copenhagen and Danish Bar Associations. *LANGUAGES:* Danish, English and Spanish. *PRACTICE AREAS:* Employment Law; Company Law; Mergers and Acquisitions.

ANNEMETTE SELMER, born Slagelse, Denmark, July 31, 1966; admitted, 1994, Denmark. *Education:* University of Copenhagen (Law Degree, 1990); University of Chicago, The Law School (LL.M., 1993). *Member:* Danish Bar Association. *LANGUAGES:* Danish and English. *PRACTICE AREAS:* Intellectual Property; Competition Law; Trade Practices.

KRISTIN JONASSON, born Hillerød, Denmark, October 3, 1967; admitted, 1994, Denmark. *Education:* University of Copenhagen (Law Degree, 1991). *Member:* Danish Bar Association. *LANGUAGES:* Danish, Icelandic and English. *PRACTICE AREAS:* Insolvency; Real Estate.

STRANGE BECK, born Astrup, Denmark, May 25, 1952; admitted, 1994, Denmark. *Education:* University of Aarhus (Law Degree, 1975; Political Sciences, 1975-1976). Assistant Professor, Faculty of Law, University of Aarhus, 1976-1987. Head of Department of Legal and Commercial Affairs and Member of Management, TV2/DANMARK, 1987-1992. Member, Ministry of Cultural Affairs Expert Committee on the Audiovisual Eureka. *Member:* Danish Bar Association; International Bar Association (Section on Business Law); Danish Association of Entertainment Lawyers (Board Member). *LANGUAGES:* Danish, Swedish, Norwegian, English, German and French. *PRACTICE AREAS:* Media Law; Intellectual Property; Licensing; Competition Law; International Contracts.

ADVOKATFIRMAET BERNING SCHLÜTER HALD

Member of SLG

(Scandinavian Business Law Group)

Copenhagen: Berning Schlüter Hald

Helsinki: Bützow & Co.

Oslo: Vogt & Co.

Stockholm: Tisell & Co. AB

6 BREDGADE
DK-1260 COPENHAGEN K, DENMARK
Telephone: +45 33 14 33 33
Telex: 16413 Juris dk
Telefax: +45 33 32 43 33

London, England Office: Scandinavian Business Law Group. 2 Suffolk Lane, EC4R OAT. Telephone: 44 171 623 3121. Telefax: 44 171 936 2545.

General Danish and International Business Law Practice. National and International Contracts, Company, Commercial, Finance, Real Estate, Taxation, Mergers and Acquisitions, Intellectual Property Law, Construction Law, Oil and Gas Law, Insolvency Law and Restructuring, Marketing and Unfair Competition, Telecommunications, Computer Law, Arbitration and Litigation.

FIRM PROFILE: *The firm was established by a merger in 1989. It provides a full range of services to national and international corporate clients.*

MEMBERS OF FIRM

OLE HALD, born Sønderborg, Denmark, April 8, 1939; admitted, 1968, Denmark; 1975, Supreme Court of Denmark. *Education:* University of Copenhagen (Candidatus Juris, 1963). Lecturer, Law of Contracts, Property and Torts, University of Copenhagen, 1967-1971. Correspondent to Lloyds' of London, The International Construction Law Review, 1983—. *Member:* Copenhagen Bar Association; Danish Law Society; IBA; International Fis-

(This Listing Continued)

LANGUAGES: Scandinavian and English. PRACTICE AREAS: General Commercial Law; Corporate Law; Employment Law; Real Estate Law.

ELLEN SKODBORGGAARD, born Denmark, November 14, 1961; admitted, 1990, Denmark; 1992, High Court of Denmark. Education: University of Copenhagen (Candidata Juris, 1987). Tutor, Property Law, University of Copenhagen, 1990-1991. Member: Danish Bar Association. LANGUAGES: Scandinavian and English. PRACTICE AREAS: Commercial Law; Real Estate Law; Environmental Law.

OLAF KOKTVEDGAARD, born Denmark, April 23, 1966; admitted, 1994, Denmark. Education: University of Copenhagen (Candidatus Juris, 1989); Harvard Law School (LL.M., 1992). The Danish Ministry of Justice, Head of Section and Assistant District Attorney for the City of Copenhagen both, 1989-1991. Tutor, Contract Law, Torts and Property Law, University of Copenhagen, 1992-1994. Member: Danish Bar Association. LANGUAGES: Scandinavian and English. PRACTICE AREAS: General Commercial Law; Antitrust and Competition Law; Copyright; Computer Law.

KARSTEN LILJEGREN, born Denmark, September 1, 1959. Education: University of Copenhagen (Candidatus Juris, 1991). Tax consultant, BDO ScanRevision 1986-1992. Member: Danish Bar Association. LANGUAGES: Scandinavian and English.

PERNILLE PETERSEN, born Denmark, February 1, 1966. Education: University of Copenhagen (Candidata Juris, 1990); London School of Economics, University of London (LL.M., 1991). Assistant Attorney, The Danish Ministry of Foreign Affairs, 1991-1992. Member: Danish Bar Association. LANGUAGES: Scandinavian, English and French.

LARS WILLE JENSEN, born Denmark, June 23, 1966. Education: University of Copenhagen (Candidatus Juris, 1994). Member: Danish Bar Association. LANGUAGES: Scandinavian, English, German and French.

PETER THØNNINGS, born Denmark, May 16, 1968. Education: University of Aarhus (Candidatus Juris, 1994). Member: Danish Bar Association. LANGUAGES: Scandinavian and English.

Languages: Scandinavian, English, German and French

DRAGSTED

Law Firm

Established in 1982

29, TOLDBODGADE

DK-1253 COPENHAGEN K, DENMARK

Telephone: 33 33 88 88

Telex: 21425 trust dk

Fax: 33 13 40 44

Paris, France Branch Office: Dragsted Cabinet Scandinave, 29, Avenue Hoche, 75008. Telephone: 7824 8384. Telefax: 7275 9219.

Lyon, France Branch Office: Dragsted, Cabinet Scandinave, 10 Quai du Général Sarrail, 69006. Telephone: 7824 8384. Telefax: 7275 9219.

General Practice. Admiralty, Aeronautical, Banking, Commercial, Compensation, Construction, Corporation, EEC, Finance, Insurance, Intellectual Property, Litigation, Natural Resources, Taxation, Transportation, Real Estate, Insolvency, Reconstruction.

MEMBERS OF FIRM

MOGENS BACH, born Svendborg, Denmark, July 16, 1942; admitted, 1973. Education: University of Copenhagen (Law Degree, 1969). Member: Copenhagen and International Bar Associations; Danish Bar and Law Society (Board Member, First Circuit). PRACTICE AREAS: Admiralty; Transportation; Insurance Law; Aeronautical Law.

JAN MARTENS, born Copenhagen, Denmark, June 14, 1946; admitted, 1977. Education: University of Copenhagen (Law Degree, 1974). Member: Copenhagen and International Bar Associations; Danish Bar and Law Society.

GABRIEL ROHDE, born Copenhagen, Denmark, March 15, 1947; admitted, 1977. Education: University of Copenhagen (Law Degree, 1974). Lecturer, University of Copenhagen, Faculty of Law, 1978-1982. Member: Copenhagen and International Bar Associations; Danish Bar and Law Society.

JES ANKER MIKKELSEN, born Nakskov, Denmark, March 3, 1951; admitted, 1979. Education: University of Copenhagen (Law Degree, 1976). Member: Copenhagen and International Bar Associations; Comité Maritime International; Maritime Association of Gothenburg; European Maritime Lawyers Organization; International Association for Insurance Law;

Danish Bar and Law Society. PRACTICE AREAS: Admiralty; Transportation; Insurance Law; Aeronautical Law.

CHRISTIAN HARBOE WISSUM, born Frederiksberg, Denmark, November 26, 1954; admitted, 1986. Education: University of Copenhagen (Law Degree, 1979); City University Business School, London (1983). Member: Copenhagen and International Bar Associations; Danish Bar and Law Society; Association Internationale des Jeunes Avocats. PRACTICE AREAS: Finance Law.

OLE ERLICH-ERIKSEN, born Copenhagen, Denmark, August 13, 1951; admitted, 1980. Education: University of Copenhagen (Law Degree, 1977). Member: Danish Bar and Law Society; Nordic Legal Society; Society of Legal Aid to the Maritime and Commercial Court of Copenhagen. PRACTICE AREAS: Bankruptcy; Insolvency Law.

HENRIK VALDORF-HANSEN, born Copenhagen, Denmark, October 28, 1955; admitted, 1983. Education: University of Copenhagen (Law Degree, 1980). Member: International Bar Association; Danish Bar and Law Society; CMI. PRACTICE AREAS: Admiralty; Transportation; Insurance Law.

JØRGEN E. FRANDSEN, born Copenhagen, Denmark, February 3, 1956; admitted, 1984. Education: University of Copenhagen (Law Degree, 1981). Member: International Bar Association; Danish Bar and Law Society.

DAVID RUBIN, born Copenhagen, Denmark, July 3, 1958; admitted, 1987. Education: Shipping, A.P. Møller (1979); University of Copenhagen (Law Degree, 1984). Lecturer on Law, International and EEC Law, University of Copenhagen, 1984-1986. Member: International Bar Association; Danish Bar and Law Society. PRACTICE AREAS: Admiralty; Transportation; Insurance Law; Aeronautical Law.

JESPER MÜLLER, born Copenhagen, Denmark, December 13, 1956; admitted, 1986. Education: University of Copenhagen (Law Degree, 1983). Tutor on the Law of Contracts and Torts, University of Copenhagen, 1984—. Member: Danish Bar and Law Society. PRACTICE AREAS: Media; Intellectual Property.

ROBERT MIKELSONS, born Copenhagen, Denmark, September 1, 1960; admitted, 1988. Education: University of Copenhagen (Law Degree, 1984). Member: Danish Association of Tax Advisers; International Fiscal Association. PRACTICE AREAS: Taxation.

ASSOCIATES

HENRIK HALDBO, born Copenhagen, Denmark, September 11, 1964; admitted, 1991. Education: University of Copenhagen (Law Degree, 1989). Member: Danish Bar and Law Society.

TROELS ASKERUD, born Copenhagen, Denmark, April 4, 1964; admitted, 1991. Education: University of Copenhagen (Law Degree, 1987); Nordic Institute of Maritime Law (1987). Member: Danish Bar and Law Society.

CLAUS ABILDSTRØM, born Copenhagen, Denmark, January 30, 1964; admitted, 1992. Education: University of Copenhagen (Law Degree, 1989). Member: Danish Bar and Law Society.

ULLA FABRICIUS, born Virum, Denmark, November 7, 1962; admitted, 1992. Education: University of Copenhagen (Law Degree, 1988); Nordic Institute of Maritime Law (1987). Ministry of Energy, 1988-1989. Member: Danish Bar and Law Society; CMI; Wista.

ULRIK ANDERSEN, born Copenhagen, Denmark, October 1, 1963; admitted, 1992. Education: University of Copenhagen (Law Degree, 1988); University of Bristol (LL.M., 1988). Member: Danish Bar and Law Society; European Maritime Lawyers Organization; CMI; European Air Law Association.

MARIANNE THORSEN, born Copenhagen, Denmark, September 5, 1962; admitted, 1993. Education: University of Copenhagen (Law Degree, 1990). Member: Danish Bar and Law Society.

JENS HOEJER LARSEN, born Copenhagen, Denmark, July 1, 1965; admitted, 1993. Education: University of Copenhagen (Law Degree, 1990). Member: Danish Bar and Law Society; CMI; AIDA.

LISBETH BORK, born Viborg, Denmark, October 18, 1965; admitted, 1993. Education: University of Aarhus (Law Degree, 1990). Member: Danish Bar and Law Society; CMI; AIDA.

RIKKE DALSGAARD, born Haslev, Denmark, March 16, 1962; admitted, 1993. Education: University of Copenhagen (Bachelor of Arts, 1985; Law Degree, 1990); UN Geneva International Law Trainee Program

(This Listing Continued)

(This Listing Continued)

DRAGSTED, Copenhagen—Continued

(1990). *Member:* Danish Bar and Law Society; CMI; International Law Association (Committee Member, International Civil and Commercial Litigation); Lawyers Association for Tax Law; The Danish Association for European Law; The Committee of Foreign Affairs.

Languages: Scandinavian, English, French, German and Italian

FALBE-HANSEN, BRUUN & BRUUN

34 SVANEMÖLLEVEJ
DK 2100 COPENHAGEN Ö , DENMARK
Telephone: +45 31 296322
Cable Address: "Nafalius"-Copenhagen
Telefax: +45 31 291088

REVISERS OF THE DENMARK LAW DIGEST FOR THIS DIRECTORY.

General Practice. Commercial, Corporation and Probate Law. Foreign Investments, Monopolies and Restrictive Trade Practices. Taxation, Real Estate Law and Admiralty.

MEMBERS OF FIRM

ROBERT GELVAN, born Copenhagen, Denmark, November 16, 1928; admitted, 1958, Denmark; 1967, Supreme Court of Denmark. *Education:* University of Copenhagen (Law Degree, 1953); Yeshiva University, New York, Ford Foundation Fellowship, 1953-1954. Permanent Assistant to several Probate and Surrogate Courts, Appointed 1970. *Member:* Copenhagen and Danish Bar Associations. *LANGUAGES:* Danish, English, French, German, Norwegian and Swedish.

MICHAEL RØNN, born Copenhagen, Denmark, August 22, 1950; admitted, 1978, Denmark; 1981, Greenland; 1985, High Court of Denmark. *Education:* General Danish State College (Certificate in Modern Languages); Faculty of Law, Copenhagen (Bachelor of Laws). Tutor in Business Law and Conditions, Copenhagen School of Economics and Business Administration, 1980-1986. Permanent Assistant to several probate and surrogate courts, appointed 1989. *LANGUAGES:* Danish, Swedish, English and German.

OLE RATHJE, born Copenhagen, Denmark, March 4, 1944; admitted, 1974, Denmark; 1977, High Court of Denmark 1982, Supreme Court of Denmark. *Education:* University of Copenhagen (cand.jur., 1971). *Member:* Copenhagen and Danish Bar Associations. *LANGUAGES:* Danish, English and French.

GEORG PETERSEN, born Denmark, September 10, 1942; admitted, 1973, Denmark; 1974, High Court of Denmark; 1979, Supreme Court of Denmark. *Education:* University of Copenhagen (cand.jur., 1970). *Member:* Copenhagen Bar Association. *LANGUAGES:* Scandinavian and English.

GITTE SEEBERG, born Copenhagen, Denmark, June, 1960; admitted, 1989, Denmark; 1990, High Court of Denmark. *Education:* University of Copenhagen (Candidatus Juris, 1986). *Member:* Copenhagen Bar Association. *LANGUAGES:* Scandinavian, English.

REPRESENTATIVE CLIENTS: Beatrice International Food (Europe); Black & Decker, Ltd., London; Chrysler Corp. U.S.A. Inc.; Time Warner, U.S.A., Warner Bros. International Corp.; DEB Group Ltd., U.K.; E.C.G.D. (Export Credit Guarantee Department), U.K.; Eurosoft AB, Sweden and Norway; The Goodyear Tire & Rubber Co. U.S.A.; Kleinwort Benson Ltd., U.K.; Merrill Lynch, Holland, U.K. and U.S.A.; Minnesota Mining and Manufacturing Co. (3M), U.S.A.; Sears Holdings Ltd., U.K.; Sika Group, Switzerland; Sterling Winthrop Inc., U.S.A.; TLC Beatrice International Holdings, U.S.A.

REVISERS OF THE DENMARK LAW DIGEST FOR THIS DIRECTORY.

J.P. GALMOND

Established in 1983

H.C. ANDERSENS BOULEVARD 51, 4.TV.
1553 COPENHAGEN V, DENMARK
Telephone: +45 33 13 45 30
Fax: +45 33 93 55 30

Hamburg, Germany Office: Bollmann, Kiesselbach & Partner, Neuer Wall 42, 20354 Hamburg. Telephone: +49 40 36 22 41. Fax: +49 40 36 69 30.

St. Petersburg, Russia Office: Millionnaya 27, 191186 St. Petersburg. Telephone: +7 812 315 4860. Fax: +7 812 315 8734.

(This Listing Continued)

Firm engaged in Danish, German, Russian, and International Law Practice. Entitled to plead before the European Commission, Danish and Russian Courts.

European Community Law, Russian Law, International Banking and Business Law, General International Trade Law, Commercial Law and Litigation and International Arbitration.

FIRM PROFILE: Established in 1983. The firm has a broadly-based practice with a reputation of offering a full range of quality legal services. The client base is mainly European and Russian. The firm has one owner and 5 (6) assistants practicing in Denmark and Russia. In addition the firm has a close association with the Hamburg-based office, Bollmann, Kiesselbach & Partner in Germany.

MEMBERS OF FIRM

JEFFREY PETER GALMOND, born Frederiksberg, Denmark, June 1, 1950; admitted, 1975, Denmark. *Education:* University of Copenhagen (Master of Law, 1975). *LANGUAGES:* Danish, English and German.

SUNE SKADEGAARD THORSEN, born Hellerup, Denmark, October 14, 1961; admitted, 1990, Denmark. *Education:* University of Copenhagen (Master of Law, 1986). *LANGUAGES:* Danish, English and German.

LINE HELL HANSEN, born Gentofte, Denmark, December 20, 1966; admitted, 1992, Denmark. *Education:* University of Copenhagen (Master of Law, 1992). *LANGUAGES:* Danish, English and German.

LARS BRUHN, born Korsør, Denmark, June 12, 1960; admitted, 1994, Denmark. *Education:* University of Copenhagen (Master of Law, 1986). *LANGUAGES:* Danish, English and German.

VLADISLAV ZABRODIN, born St. Petersburg, Russia, January 13, 1967; admitted, 1991, Russia (Not admitted in Denmark). *Education:* University of St. Petersburg (Master of Law, 1991). *LANGUAGES:* Russian and English.

IGOR MISHIN, born St. Petersburg, Russia, September 23, 1967; admitted, 1991, Russia (Not admitted in Denmark). *Education:* University of St. Petersburg (Master of Law, 1991). *LANGUAGES:* Russian and English.

GORRISSEN & FEDERSPIEL

12, H.C. ANDERSENS BOULEVARD
DK-1553 COPENHAGEN V, DENMARK
Telephone: +45 33 15 75 33
Telex: 15 598 gfjus
Fax: +45 33 15 77 33

General Practice. Commercial and Corporate Law, Admiralty, Ship and Aircraft Financing, Banking, Securities, Environmental Law, Construction Law, Oil and Gas Law, Insurance, Taxation and Administrative and EC Law.

MEMBERS OF FIRM

JØRGEN GORRISSEN, born Copenhagen, Denmark, August, 19, 1925; admitted, 1953, Denmark; 1959, Supreme Court of Denmark. *Education:* University of Copenhagen (Law Degree, 1950). *Member:* Danish Bar Association.

THOMAS FEDERSPIEL, born Copenhagen, Denmark, October 25, 1935; admitted, 1964, Denmark; 1969, the Supreme Court of Denmark. *Education:* Rungsted Statsskole and University of Copenhagen (law), graduated 1960 (Candidatus Juris). With Slaughter & May, London and Davis, Polk & Wardwell, New York, 1966-1967. Member of the Board of Queen Margrethe's and Prince Henrik's Foundation, 1970—. Honorary Legal Adviser to the British Embassy in Copenhagen, 1977—. *Member:* Danish Bar Association (Chairman, Standing Committee on Private International Law, 1971-1981); Association of Advocates of Copenhagen (Member, Board, 1971-1976); Bar Council of Copenhagen (Member, 1974-1980); Association of Lawyers (Member Board 1990—); Danish Law Society; American Bar Association (Honorary Member 1981). International Bar Association (Member, Council, 1971-1984; President, 1980-1982; Honorary Member, 1982). *LANGUAGES:* English, French and German.

HENRIK CHRISTRUP, born Copenhagen, Denmark, April 8, 1936; admitted, 1965, Denmark; 1971, Supreme Court of Denmark. *Education:* University of Copenhagen (Law Degree, 1959). With Ministry of Justice, 1959-1965. *Member:* Danish Bar Association.

JAN ERLUND, born Copenhagen, Denmark, March 18, 1939; admitted, 1968, Denmark; 1976, Supreme Court of Denmark. *Education:* Univer-

(This Listing Continued)

sity of Aarhus (Law Degree, 1964); Scandinavian Institute for Maritime Law, Norway, 1964-1965. Lecturer on Law, Copenhagen School of Economics and Business Administration, 1967-1971. *Member:* Danish Bar Association (President 1991—); International Bar Association; Comité Maritime International. *LANGUAGES:* English.

HERMAN D. FEDERSPIEL, born Copenhagen, Denmark, December 7, 1939; admitted, 1970, Denmark; 1986, The Supreme Court of Denmark. *Education:* Rungsted Statsskole and University of Copenhagen (law), graduated 1966 (Candidatus Juris); University of Paris, School of Jurisprudence. Assistant Lecturer in Public International Law at University of Copenhagen, 1967-1968. With Debevoise & Plimpton, New York, 1972-1973. Member of Committee on Competition and Intellectual Property of Commission Consultative des Barreaux de la Communauté Européenne and of Danish Ministry of Justice's Committee on Commercial Agents. *Member:* Danish Bar Association; Danish Law Society; International Bar Association. *LANGUAGES:* English, French and German.

TROELS ANDERSEN, born Copenhagen, Denmark, June 30, 1943; admitted, 1974, Denmark; 1981, Supreme Court of Denmark. *Education:* University of Copenhagen (Law Degree, 1969). *Member:* Danish Bar Association. *LANGUAGES:* English and German.

HENRIK LIND, born Holbaek, Denmark, September 19, 1947; admitted, 1975, Denmark; 1984, Supreme Court of Denmark. *Education:* University of Copenhagen (Law Degree, 1972); European Economic Commission, Brussels, (1973) and New York University (Master of Comparative Jurisprudence, 1978). *Member:* Danish Bar Association; International Bar Association. *LANGUAGES:* English.

JAN-ERIK SVENSSON, born Copenhagen, Denmark, October 17, 1949; admitted, 1977, Denmark; 1982, Supreme Court of Denmark. *Education:* Bagsvaerd Gymnasium; University of Copenhagen (law) graduated 1974 (Candidatus Juris). With Arnold & Porter in Washington, D.C., 1982-1983. *Member:* Danish Bar Association; Danish Law Society; International Bar Association. *LANGUAGES:* English.

KLAUS VILSTRUP, born Elsenore, Denmark, March 5, 1951; admitted, 1979, Denmark; 1985, Supreme Court of Denmark. *Education:* University of Copenhagen (Law Degree, 1976); Scandinavian Institute of Maritime Law, Oslo (1975); Loyola Law School, Los Angeles (1981). Lecturer: Business School of Copenhagen, 1976-1980; A.P. Moeller Shipping School, 1977-1986. *Member:* Danish Bar Association; C.M.I (Danish Branch). *LANGUAGES:* English.

KLAUS SOEGAARD, born Aalborg, Denmark, October 17, 1955; admitted, 1983, Denmark; 1988, Supreme Court of Denmark. *Education:* University of Aarhus (Law Degree, 1980); University of the Pacific, California (LL.M., 1985). *Member:* Danish Bar Association; International Bar Association. *LANGUAGES:* English.

NIELS T. HEERING, born Copenhagen, Denmark, February 7, 1955; admitted, 1984, Denmark and High Court of Denmark. *Education:* Lyngby Statsskole; University of Copenhagen (law) graduated 1981 (Candidatus Juris). With Davis, Polk & Wardwell, New York, 1984-1985. *Member:* Danish Bar Association; Danish Law Society; International Bar Association; International Fiscal Association. *LANGUAGES:* English.

MICHAEL STEEN JENSEN, born Copenhagen, Denmark, February 7, 1958; admitted, 1987, Denmark; 1988, High Court of Denmark. *Education:* University of Copenhagen (Candidatus Juris, 1984). With Linklaters & Paines, London, 1990-1991. *Member:* Danish Bar Association; Danish Law Society. *LANGUAGES:* English.

ALEX LAUDRUP, born Copenhagen, Denmark, August 31, 1946; admitted, 1975, Denmark; 1985, Supreme Court of Denmark. *Education:* University of Copenhagen (Law, 1972). Author: "INCO Terms 1990," G.E.C. Gad, 1990. Lecturer, BIMCO and Danish Bar Association. Member, C.M.I. *Member:* I.B.A.; Shipowners' Council of Copenhagen (General Manager). *LANGUAGES:* English, German and French.

PETER APPEL, born Karup, Denmark, July 3, 1961; admitted, 1988, Denmark and High Court of Denmark. *Education:* University of Copenhagen (Law Degree, 1985); Scandinavian Institute for Maritime Law, Oslow University (1985); London School of Economics, London University (LL.M., 1990). Lecturer: A.P. Moeller Shipping School, 1986-1989; Copenhagen Business School, 1993-1994. *Member:* Danish Bar Association. *LANGUAGES:* English.

(This Listing Continued)

OF COUNSEL

ERIK STRØJER, born Odense, Denmark, September 19, 1919; admitted, 1948, Denmark; 1956, Supreme Court of Denmark. *Education:* University of Copenhagen (Law Degree, 1945). Assistant Professor, Civil Law, 1951-1961. *Member:* Danish Bar Association; Copenhagen Bar Association (Chairman, 1973-1977).

Languages: Danish, Swedish, Norwegian, English, French and German.

HJEJLE, GERSTED & MOGENSEN

Established in 1878

24, AMAGERTORV

DK-1160 COPENHAGEN, DENMARK

Telephone: 45 33 134262
Cable Address: "Shawlaw"
Telex: 15428 Shalaw
Telefax: 45 33 111250

General Practice. Corporation, Commercial Tax, Contract, Arbitration. Monopolies and Restrictive Trade Practices.

MEMBERS OF FIRM

GUNNAR GERSTED, born Vejen, Denmark, November 29, 1906; admitted, 1937, Denmark; 1948, Supreme Court of Denmark. *Education:* University of Copenhagen. Author: *Liquidation of Insolvent Companies,* 1959. *Member:* Danish Bar Association (Member of the Board, 1963-1965). *LANGUAGES:* Danish, English, German, Swedish and Norwegian.

KRISTIAN MOGENSEN, born Roskilde, Denmark, February 24, 1926; admitted, 1957, Denmark; 1962, Supreme Court of Denmark. *Education:* University of Copenhagen. *Member:* Danish (Member of the Board, 1969-1977) and Copenhagen (Vice Chairman, 1962-1964) Bar Associations; Nordic Union of Lawyers (Chairman, 1986—). *LANGUAGES:* Danish, English, German, Swedish and Norwegian.

AAGE SPANG-HANSSEN, born Copenhagen, Denmark, November 11, 1930; admitted, 1957, Denmark; 1963, Supreme Court of Denmark. *Education:* University of Copenhagen. Lecturer on Law, University of Copenhagen, 1955-1960. Member of the Executive Committee of Fiscal Association, 1972-1979. Judge in the Danish Labour Court, 1992—. *Member:* Danish (Member of the Board, 1977-1984) and Copenhagen (Member of the Board, 1965-1969; 1975-1980; Chairman, 1986-1991) Bar Associations. *LANGUAGES:* Danish, English, German, Swedish and Norwegian.

HENRIK WEDELL-WEDELLSBORG, born Copenhagen, Denmark, November 3, 1942; admitted, 1972, Denmark; 1977, Supreme Court of Denmark. *Education:* University of Copenhagen. Stage at Law firm of Gide, Loyrette, Nouel, Paris, France, 1974. *Member:* Danish (Chairman, Standing Committee on the Professions of Lawyers, 1979-1981), Copenhagen (Member of the Board, 1977-1982) and International Bar Associations; Danish Law Society. *LANGUAGES:* Danish, English, French, German, Swedish and Norwegian.

STEFFEN JUUL, born Copenhagen, Denmark, October 7, 1941; admitted, 1973, Denmark; 1981, Supreme Court of Denmark. *Education:* University of Copenhagen; Institute Europeen Universite de Nancy, France (1987-1988). Lecturer on Law, University of Copenhagen, 1974-1981. *Member:* Danish (Member of the Board, 1989—), Copenhagen (Member of the Board, 1985-1991) Bar Associations; Danish delegation to CCBE (1991—) International Bar Associations. *LANGUAGES:* Danish, English, French, Swedish and Norwegian.

OLUF ENGELL, born Copenhagen, Denmark, July 30, 1945; admitted, 1973, Denmark; 1982, Supreme Court of Denmark. *Education:* University of Copenhagen. *Member:* Danish, Copenhagen (Member of the Board, 1987—; Chairman, 1992—) and International Bar Associations; London Court of International Arbitration; European Users Council. *LANGUAGES:* Danish, English, German, Swedish and Norwegian.

KARSTEN HAVKROG PEDERSEN, born Middelfart, Denmark, September 30, 1949; admitted, 1978, Denmark; 1983, Supreme Court of Denmark. *Education:* University of Aarhus. Adjunkt, University of Aarhus, 1974-1975. *Member:* Danish Bar Association. *LANGUAGES:* Danish, English, Swedish and Norwegian.

FLEMMING HEEGAARD, born Copenhagen, Denmark, March 15, 1954; admitted, 1981, Denmark; 1987, Supreme Court of Denmark. *Education:* University of Copenhagen. *Member:* Danish (Member, Tax Committee, 1989—) and Copenhagen (Member of the Board, 1992—) Bar Associa-

(This Listing Continued)

HJEJLE, GERSTED & MOGENSEN, Copenhagen— Continued

tions; International Fiscal Association. *LANGUAGES:* Danish, English, German, Swedish and Norwegian.

MICHAEL SVANHOLM, born Copenhagen, Denmark, September 28, 1959; admitted, 1986, Denmark; 1991, Supreme Court of Denmark. *Education:* University of Copenhagen. *Member:* Danish and Copenhagen Bar Associations. *LANGUAGES:* Danish, English, German, Swedish and Norwegian.

TOVE H. DAHL, born Frederiksberg, Denmark, January 6, 1952; admitted, 1987, Denmark. *Education:* University of Copenhagen. *Member:* Danish and Copenhagen Bar Associations. *LANGUAGES:* Danish, Swedish, English, German and Norwegian.

CHRISTIAN SCHOW MADSEN, born Fjerritslev, Denmark, January 22, 1963; admitted, 1989, Denmark; 1994, Supreme Court of Denmark. *Education:* University of Aarhus. *Member:* Danish and Copenhagen Bar Associations. *LANGUAGES:* Danish, English, Swedish and Norwegian.

HORTEN & CO.

Established in 1963

KONGENS NYTORV 22

DK-1050 COPENHAGEN K, DENMARK

Telephone: +45 33143236

Telefax: +45 33323899; +45 33910222

Agency and Exclusive Distribution. Anti-trust and Competition. Aviation, Bankruptcy and Probate. Book, Film and Music Publishing. Commercial Arbitration and Litigation. Corporate Mergers and Acquisitions. EEC Law. Employment and Dismissal. Energy and Water Supply. Environmental Protection. Fishery. Industrial Property Rights and Licensing. Insurance Coverage. International Borrowing and Lending. Labor Protection. Local Government Relations. Planning and Building Permits. Real Estate. Ships and Shipping. Taxation. Tenancy. Turn-key and Construction Projects.

PARTNERS

HANS R. HORTEN, born Copenhagen, Denmark, July 27, 1918; admitted, 1952, Denmark; 1959, Supreme Court of Denmark. *Education:* University of Copenhagen (1943), Ministry of Finances and Taxation, High Court of Taxation, Public Trustee's Office. Defending Counsel at High Court, 1959-1973. *Member:* Danish Bar Association; Danish Law Society. *LANGUAGES:* English and Scandinavian. *PRACTICE AREAS:* Litigation; Local Government Relations and Public Law (Town Renovation, Slum Clearance and Valuation); Rental Law.

HOLGER RENDTORFF, born Copenhagen, Denmark, January 27, 1941; admitted, 1968, Denmark; 1976, Supreme Court of Denmark. *Education:* University of Copenhagen (1964); New York University, School of Law, Master of Comparative Jurisprudence, 1971. Lecturer on Law: University of Copenhagen, 1964-1969; School of Public Administration, 1965-1969. *Member:* Danish Bar Association; Danish Law Society. *LANGUAGES:* English and Scandinavian. *PRACTICE AREAS:* Public Administrative Law; Expropriation - Supply-Company Law; Arbitration - Litigation.

BJARNE BECHER JENSEN, born Koege, Denmark, February 9, 1949; admitted, 1976, Denmark; 1981, Supreme Court of Denmark. *Education:* University of Copenhagen (1973). *Member:* Danish Bar Association; Danish Law Society. *LANGUAGES:* English and Scandinavian. *PRACTICE AREAS:* Company Law; Mergers and Acquisitions; Establishing and Transfer of Business; Intellectual Property Law; Town Planning and other Planning Law; Litigation.

NICOLAI R. HORTEN, born Copenhagen, Denmark, April 1, 1947; admitted, 1980, Denmark; 1983, High Courts of Denmark. *Education:* Canadian Air Force Flight Academy (1967); Royal Danish Air Force Flight Academy (1969); University of Copenhagen (1980). Post-graduate Teacher, Danish Law Society, 1984—. *Member:* Danish Bar Association; Danish Law Society. *LANGUAGES:* English and Scandinavian. *PRACTICE AREAS:* Contracting and Real Estate Law; Commercial Rental Law; Corporate Law; Administration of Real Estate; Litigation.

FRITZ REUTHER, born Copenhagen, Denmark, September 10, 1930; admitted, 1955, Denmark; 1967, Supreme Court of Denmark. *Education:* University of Copenhagen (1955). Tax-authorities, 1956-1958, Ministerium of Finance, Customs Department, 1959-1961. *Member:* Danish Bar Associ-

(This Listing Continued)

ation. *PRACTICE AREAS:* Taxation; Transport and Customs Laws; Real Estate; Trading with Restaurants; Civil and Criminal Cases.

JAKOB S. ARREVAD, born June 5, 1949; admitted, 1973, Denmark; 1982, Supreme Court of Denmark. *Education:* University of Copenhagen (1973). Assistant Law Professor, University of Copenhagen, 1973-1978. *Member:* Danish and International Bar Associations; Danish Law Society; International Association of Entertainment Lawyers. *LANGUAGES:* English and Scandinavian. *PRACTICE AREAS:* Intellectual and Industrial Property Rights and Licensing; Agency and Exclusive Distribution Law; International Taxation; Criminal Law; Commercial Arbitration and Litigation; Mediation.

FINN SCHWARZ, born Copenhagen, Denmark, May 29, 1958; admitted, 1984, Denmark; 1994, Supreme Court of Denmark. *Education:* University of Copenhagen (1981). *Member:* Danish Bar Association; Danish Law Society. *LANGUAGES:* English and Scandinavian. *PRACTICE AREAS:* Corporate Law; Employment Law; Local Government Relation and Public Law; Environmental Law; Indemnity Law; Medical Law; Criminal Law; Litigation.

NICOLAI MALLET, born Hamburg, Germany, May 17, 1960; admitted, 1988. *Education:* University of Copenhagen (Law Degree, 1985); Christian-Albrechts-Universität zu Kiel, Freie Universität; Humboldt Universität, Berlin (LL.M., 1990-1992). *Member:* Danish Bar and Law Society. *LANGUAGES:* German, English and Scandinavian.

JENS GEHL, born Roskilde, Denmark, August 8, 1945; admitted, 1979, Denmark; 1990, Supreme Court of Denmark. *Education:* University of Copenhagen, 1972. *Member:* International Bar Association; Danish Law Society. *LANGUAGES:* English and Scandinavian. *PRACTICE AREAS:* Contracting and Real Estate Law; International Business; Corporate Law.

ASSOCIATES

LARS BECHER CARSTENS, born Copenhagen, Denmark, November 24, 1958; admitted, 1983, Denmark; 1992, Supreme Court of Denmark. *Education:* University of Copenhagen (1983). *Member:* Danish Bar Association; Copenhagen Bar Association; Danish Law Society. *LANGUAGES:* English, German and Scandinavian. *PRACTICE AREAS:* Litigation; Local Government Relations and Public Law (Town renovation, Slum Clearance and Valuation); Rental Law; Family Law; Wills and Successions.

ANETTE MOLL SØRENSEN, born Kolding, Denmark, August 12, 1963; admitted, 1988, Denmark; 1992, High Court of Denmark. *Education:* University of Copenhagen (1988). *Member:* Danish Bar Association; Danish Law Society. *LANGUAGES:* English and Scandinavian. *PRACTICE AREAS:* Litigation; Rental Law; Real Estate (Real Estate Associations); Mortgage; Local Government Relations and Public Law (Town Renovation, Slum Clearance and Valuation); Indemnity Law.

BIRGITTE RANDRUP, born Copenhagen, Denmark, May 27, 1961; admitted, 1989, Denmark. *Education:* University of Copenhagen (1986). Lecturer of Law, University of Copenhagen 1987-1989. Associated at the Danish Ombudsmand, 1991-1993. *LANGUAGES:* English and Scandinavian. *PRACTICE AREAS:* Public Law; Public Administrative Law; General Practice; Litigation.

OLE GRAESBØLL OLESEN, born Grenå, Denmark, October 28, 1959; admitted, 1994. *Education:* University of Århus (1985). 1985-1994 Ministry of Foreign Affairs, Ministry of Commerce and Trade, Ministry of Justice. *Member:* Danish Bar and Law Society. *LANGUAGES:* English and Scandinavian. *PRACTICE AREAS:* Public Administrative Law; General Practice; Litigation; Criminal Law; Consumer Protection Law.

MICHAEL GOESKJÆR, born Sorø, Denmark, August 18, 1960; admitted, 1986, Denmark; 1989, High Court of Denmark. *Education:* University of Copenhagen (1986). *Member:* Danish Bar Association; Danish Law Society; The ELSA Lawyers Society. *LANGUAGES:* English, German and Scandinavian. *PRACTICE AREAS:* Business Law; Civil Court Cases; International Dealers and Agent Contracts; Corporate Law; Trademark.

JENS JAKOB BUGGE, born Copenhagen, Denmark, March 7, 1964; admitted, 1992, Denmark. *Education:* University of Copenhagen (1990). Lecturer of Law, University of Copenhagen, 1991-1992. *LANGUAGES:* English and Scandinavian. *PRACTICE AREAS:* General Practice; Litigation; Contracting; Intellectual Property (Patents, Utility Model, Trademarks, Designs & EU-Intell. Prop. Law).

HENRIETTE SØLTOFT, born Copenhagen, Denmark, August 11, 1967; admitted, 1992, Denmark. *Education:* University of Copenhagen (1992). *LANGUAGES:* English, French and Scandinavian. *PRACTICE*

(This Listing Continued)

AREAS: General Practice; Public Procurement; Public Law; Business Entities; European Community Law; Litigation.

Languages: Danish, English, German and Scandinavian. Correspondents throughout Europe and USA. Member of European Law Group.

REPRESENTATIVE CLIENTS: The City of Copenhagen; EL AL Scandinavia; The Jewish Community in Denmark; K.L.M., Denmark; Cray Research, Inc.; Buschman Company Europe; Rhône-Poulenc Rorer, Denmark; Stenlose Council.

JARDING & KYED

Established in 1945

2, FREDERIKSBERGGADE
P.O. BOX 1008
DK 1006 COPENHAGEN, DENMARK
Telephone: Int. + (45) 33 145 145
Telefax: Int. + (45) 33 112 741

General Practice, Litigation, EEC, Corporate and Commercial Law, Banking, Financing, Investments, Labour Law, Real Estate, Taxation, Mergers and Acquisitions, Administrative Law, Environment, Insurance, Succession and Probate Law, Bankruptcy and Insolvency Law, Indemnity Law. Hotel and Catering Trade.

MEMBERS OF FIRM

NIELS OLUF KYED, born Øster Starup, Denmark, May 13, 1937; admitted, 1966, Denmark; 1978, Supreme Court of Denmark. *Education:* University of Copenhagen; New York University; Institute of Comparative Law (M.C.J.). *Member:* Danish Bar Association. **LANGUAGES:** Danish, Scandinavian, English and German. **PRACTICE AREAS:** Corporate Law; Banking; Financing; Investments; Mergers and Acquisitions; Hotel and Catering Trade.

MARIANNE HARTLING, born Copenhagen, Denmark, July 16, 1944; admitted, 1980, Denmark; 1989, Supreme Court of Denmark. *Education:* University of Copenhagen. *Member:* Danish Bar Association. **LANGUAGES:** Danish, Scandinavian, and English. **PRACTICE AREAS:** Litigation; Labour Law; Succession and Probate Law.

FINN OVERGAARD, born Frederiksberg, Denmark, November 6, 1958; admitted, 1987, Denmark; 1993, Supreme Court of Denmark. *Education:* University of Copenhagen. Lecturer on Law, University of Copenhagen, 1986—. Copenhagen Handelsbank, legal department, 1982-1985. *Member:* Danish Bar Association. **LANGUAGES:** Danish, Scandinavian and English. **PRACTICE AREAS:** Corporate and Commercial Law; Mergers and Acquisitions; Litigation; Bankruptcy and Insolvency Law; Indemnity Law; Insurance Law.

KURT SØGAARD NIELSEN, born Furendal, Denmark, February 25, 1950; admitted, 1986, Denmark. *Education:* University of Copenhagen. *Member:* Danish Bar Association. **LANGUAGES:** Danish, Scandinavian and English. **PRACTICE AREAS:** Real Estate; Environment; Insurance Law.

DORTHE FOGELSTRØM, born Copenhagen, Denmark, August 18, 1962; admitted, 1991, Denmark. *Education:* University of Copenhagen. *Member:* Danish Bar Association. **LANGUAGES:** Danish, Scandinavian, English, French and German. **PRACTICE AREAS:** EEC Law; Administrative Law.

OF COUNSEL

BO ANDERSEN, born Copenhagen, Denmark, July 12, 1933; admitted, 1966, Denmark. *Education:* University of Copenhagen. *Member:* Danish Bar Association. **LANGUAGES:** Danish, Scandinavian, English, French and German. **PRACTICE AREAS:** Taxation; Commercial Law.

Languages: Scandinavian, English, French and German

KAHLKE • VANDBORG

2, FREDERIKSBERGGADE
DK 1459 COPENHAGEN K, DENMARK
Telephone: +45 33 12 38 80
Fax: +45 33 32 91 19

General Practice. Commercial and Corporate Law, Taxation, International Contracts, Media Law, EU Law, Insolvency Law, Reconstructions and Inheritance of Control, Property Management and Administration, Trade

(This Listing Continued)

Associations, Leasing, EDP Law, Environmental Law, Litigation and Arbitration, Entertainment.

MEMBERS OF FIRM

MORTEN W. VANDBORG, born 1951; admitted, 1979, Denmark; 1986, Supreme Court of Denmark. *Education:* University of Copenhagen (1975). *Member:* Danish Bar Association; Union International des Avocats. **LANGUAGES:** English.

JOHN KAHLKE, born 1954; admitted, 1981, Denmark; 1986, Supreme Court of Denmark. *Education:* University of Copenhagen (1977); Universities Paris and Edinburg (Post Graduate Studies). *Member:* Danish Bar Association; AIJA (International Association of Young Lawyers). **LANGUAGES:** English, French, German, Spanish and Italian.

TOVE MEURS-GERKEN, born 1958; admitted, 1990, Denmark and High Court. *Education:* University of Copenhagen (1986). *Member:* Danish Bar Association; AIJA (International Association of Young Lawyers). **LANGUAGES:** English, French and German.

HENRIK BONNE, born 1965; admitted, 1993, Denmark; 1994, High Court. *Education:* University of Copenhagen (1989). *Member:* Danish Bar Association; AIJA (International Association of Young Lawyers). **LANGUAGES:** English and French.

SIGURD KAHLKE, born 1925; admitted, 1953, Denmark; 1961, Supreme Court of Denmark. *Education:* University of Copenhagen (1948). *Member:* Danish Bar Association. **LANGUAGES:** English and German.

KIERKEGAARD & MALBY

AMALIEGADE 4
P.O. BOX 3004
DK-1021 COPENHAGEN K, DENMARK
Telephone: (45) 33 14 35 15
Fax: (45) 33 13 19 25

Mergers and Acquisitions, Corporate and Commercial Law, Tax Law, Monopolies and Restrictive Trade Practices, Patent Law, Bankruptcy and Insolvency Law, Litigation and Arbitration, International Financial Law, Exchange Control, European Community Law, Bank and Investment Law, Real Estate.

MEMBERS OF FIRM

AXEL KIERKEGAARD, born Naestved, Denmark, July 4, 1940; admitted, 1966, Denmark; 1968, High Court; 1973, Supreme Court of Appeal. *Education:* University of Copenhagen (Candidatus Juris). Lecturer on Law, University of Copenhagen, 1965-1976. Member, The National Committee for Revision of Act on Registration of Real Estate. Chairman of Liberal Professions of Denmark, 1981-1994. *Member:* Danish Bar Association; International Bar Association. **LANGUAGES:** Scandinavian, English, German and French.

CARSTEN MALBY, born Randers, Denmark, December 21, 1950; admitted, 1975, Denmark; 1979, High Court; 1984, Supreme Court of Appeal. *Education:* University of Copenhagen (Candidatus Juris, 1975). Lecturer on Law, University of Copenhagen, 1984—. *Member:* Danish Bar Association. **LANGUAGES:** Scandinavian, English and German.

ANNE BIRGITTE GAMMELJORD, born Copenhagen, Denmark, June 12, 1956; admitted, 1983, Denmark and High Court; 1989, Supreme Court of Appeal. *Education:* University of Copenhagen (Candidatus Juris). *Member:* Danish Bar Association. **LANGUAGES:** Scandinavian, German and English.

ASSOCIATES

STEEN PETERSEN, born Copenhagen, Denmark, April 6, 1951; admitted, 1982, Denmark; 1984, High Court; 1989, Supreme Court of Appeal. *Education:* University of Copenhagen (Candidatus Juris, 1979). Danish Ministry of Justice. *Member:* Danish Bar Association; Danish Association on EEC Law; Danish Environmental Law Association; International Law Association; International Association on Insurance. **LANGUAGES:** Scandinavian, English and German.

ALLAN LUND CHRISTENSEN, born Copenhagen, Denmark, March 9, 1950; admitted, 1984, Denmark; 1985, High Court; 1990, Supreme Court of Appeal. *Education:* University of Copenhagen (Candidatus Juris). *Member:* Danish Bar Association. **LANGUAGES:** Scandinavian, English, German and Russian.

HENRIK OSCAR HORNSLETH, born Washington, U.S.A., August 16, 1960; admitted, 1990, Denmark; High Court 1991. *Education:* Univer-

(This Listing Continued)

KIERKEGAARD & MALBY, Copenhagen—Continued

sity of Copenhagen (Candidatus Juris, 1987). *Member:* Danish Bar Association; Club International Du Droit De La Distribution; Danish Association on Protection of Industrial Property; Danish Copyright Society. *LANGUAGES:* Scandinavian, English and German.

SØREN FOGH, born Copenhagen, Denmark, May 26, 1964; admitted, 1992, Denmark. *Education:* University of Copenhagen (Candidatus Juris, 1989); King's College, London (LL.M., Commercial and Corporate Law, Merit, 1993). *Member:* Danish Bar Association. *LANGUAGES:* Scandinavian and English.

UFFE BØGELUND JENSEN, born Aarhus, Denmark, April 30, 1963; admitted, 1992, Denmark; 1994, High Court. *Education:* University of Aarhus (Candidatus Juris, 1989). *Member:* Danish Bar Association. *LANGUAGES:* Scandinavian and English.

CHRISTA JØRGENSEN, born Copenhagen, Denmark, December 7, 1962; admitted, 1994, Denmark. *Education:* University of Copenhagen (Candidata Juris, 1991). *Member:* Danish Bar Association. *LANGUAGES:* Scandinavian and English.

Languages: Scandinavian, English, German, Russian and French

KOCH-NIELSEN & GRØNBORG

Established in 1946

APPLEBY'S HOUSE
APPLEBYS PLADS 1
POSTBOKS 19
DK-1001 COPENHAGEN K, DENMARK
Telephone: 45 32 96 08 08
Telex: 19288 kglaw dk
Telefax: 45 32 96 07 07

Tax Law, Vat and Duty Law, Customs and Excise Law, International Banking and Financing, Investments and Securities, Contract Law, Construction Law, Insolvency Law and Reconstruction, International Leasing, Corporate and Commercial Law, Mergers and Acquisitions, Real Estate, European Community Law, Competition Law, Product Liability Law, Distribution and Agency Contracts, International Sales, Insurance Law, Consumer Protection Law, Environmental Law and Planning, Maritime and Admiralty Law, Leisure, Holiday and Travel, Food and Drug Regulation, Labor Law, Energy and Mining Law, International Private Law, Probate and Administration of Estates, Wills and Settlements, Aviation Law, Litigation and Arbitration.

FIRM PROFILE: The firm provides a full range of legal services to Danish and International clients.

MEMBERS OF FIRM

ROBERT KOCH-NIELSEN, born Nexø, Denmark, August 12, 1934; admitted, 1962, Denmark; 1968, Supreme Court of Denmark. *Education:* University of Copenhagen (Faculty of Law); New York University, Institute of Comparative Law (M.C.J.). Author: "Income Tax," 1970. Lecturer, University of Copenhagen, Faculty of Law, Private Law and Tax Law, 1964-1972. *Member:* Danish Bar Association (General Council, 1981-1987); International Fiscal Association (Member, Executive Committee, 1981-1987; President, Danish Branch, 1980—); Association of Copenhagen Lawyers. *LANGUAGES:* Danish, English, German, Swedish and Norwegian. *PRACTICE AREAS:* Tax Law; Mergers and Acquisitions.

JØRGEN GRØNBORG, born Aarhus, Denmark, March 5, 1936; admitted, 1963, Denmark; 1968, Supreme Court of Denmark. *Education:* University of Aarhus (Faculty of Law). Lecturer, University of Copenhagen, Faculty of Law, Contracts, Torts, Civil Law, 1961-1972. Delegate, 1979-1986 and President, 1987, the Council of Bars and Law Societies of the European Community. *Member:* Danish Bar Association (Member of Board, Copenhagen Section, 1969-1977; General Council, 1977-1985); Association of Copenhagen Lawyers (Member of Board, 1966-1971 and 1980-1985); The Danish Institute of Arbitration (Copenhagen Arbitration, Vice Chairman, 1981—); International Bar Association. *LANGUAGES:* Danish, English, French, German, Swedish and Norwegian. *PRACTICE AREAS:* Contract Law; International Banking and Financing; Construction Law; Litigation and Arbitration; Energy and Mining Law.

ERIK OVERGAARD, born Hadsund, Denmark, November 3, 1936; admitted, 1963, Denmark; 1976, Supreme Court of Denmark. *Education:* University of Aarhus (Faculty of Law). Contributing Editor, EC Tax Review. Inland Revenue Department, 1963-1965. *Member:* Danish Bar Asso-

(This Listing Continued)

ciation; Association of Copenhagen Lawyers; Tax Bill Preparation Committees and The Permanent Advisory Board to the Minister of Taxation; International Fiscal Association; International Bar Association. *LANGUAGES:* Danish, English, German, Swedish and Norwegian. *PRACTICE AREAS:* Tax Law; Mergers and Acquisitions; Corporate and Commercial Law.

CLAUS KAARE PEDERSEN, born Copenhagen, Denmark, October 4, 1946; admitted, 1974, Denmark; 1980, Supreme Court of Denmark. *Education:* University of Copenhagen (Faculty of Law). Author: "International Arbitration in Denmark," Case Western Reserve Journal of International Law, 1982. *Member:* Danish Bar Association; Association of Young Lawyers in Denmark (Chairman, 1974); Association of Copenhagen Lawyers (Member of Board, 1985-1990); International Bar Association. *LANGUAGES:* Danish, English, Swedish and Norwegian. *PRACTICE AREAS:* Construction Law; Litigation and Arbitration; Corporate Law; Commercial Law; Contract Law; Insurance Law.

ERIK MALBERG, born Frederiksberg, Denmark, October 28, 1946; admitted, 1976, Denmark; 1982, Supreme Court of Denmark. *Education:* University of Copenhagen (Faculty of Law). *Member:* Danish Bar Association; Association of Copenhagen Lawyers; International Bar Association. *LANGUAGES:* Danish, English, Swedish and Norwegian. *PRACTICE AREAS:* Insolvency Law and Reconstruction; Investments and Securities; Litigation and Arbitration; Corporate and Commercial Law; Contract Law.

CHRISTIAN MOLDE, born Sorø, Denmark, September 9, 1946; admitted, 1973, Denmark; 1986, Supreme Court of Denmark. *Education:* University of Copenhagen (Faculty of Law). Lecturer, University of Copenhagen, Faculty of Law, Private Law, 1973-1980. *Member:* Danish Bar Association; Association of Copenhagen Lawyers. *LANGUAGES:* Danish, English, Swedish and Norwegian. *PRACTICE AREAS:* Real Estate; Environmental Law and Planning; Corporate and Commercial Law; Insolvency Law and Reconstruction; International Leasing.

HANS SEVERIN HANSEN, born Copenhagen, Denmark, October 1, 1950; admitted, 1979, Denmark; 1984, Supreme Court of Denmark. *Education:* University of Copenhagen (Faculty of Law). Lecturer, University of Copenhagen, Faculty of Law, Private Law, 1976-1978. *Member:* Danish Bar Association; Association of Copenhagen Lawyers; International Fiscal Association. *LANGUAGES:* Danish, English, Swedish and Norwegian. *PRACTICE AREAS:* Tax Law; Corporate and Commercial Law; Mergers and Acquisitions; Litigation and Arbitration; Contract Law.

JENS HENNING ELMERKJAER, born Glostrup, Denmark, February 2, 1952; admitted, 1979, Denmark; 1985, Supreme Court of Denmark. *Education:* University of Copenhagen (Faculty of Law); College of Europe, Belgium (DHEE); University of Nancy, France (D.E.A.). Lecturer, University of Copenhagen, Faculty of Law, Private Law, 1973-1975 and 1979-1982; The Copenhagen School of Economics and Business Administration, Business Economy, Tax Law and Commercial Law, 1979—. *Member:* Danish Bar Association; Association of Copenhagen Lawyers; Union Internationale des Avocats. *LANGUAGES:* Danish, English, German, French, Swedish and Norwegian. *PRACTICE AREAS:* Real Estate; Insolvency Law and Reconstruction; Corporate and Commercial Law; Wills and Settlements; European Community Law.

CHRISTIAN EMMELUTH, born Kolding, Denmark, March 1, 1953; admitted, 1980, Denmark; 1988, Supreme Court of Denmark. *Education:* University of Copenhagen (Faculty of Law); New York University, Institute of Comparative Law (M.C.J.). Lecturer, University of Copenhagen, Faculty of Law, Private Law, 1978-1980 and 1981-1987. *Member:* Danish Bar Association; Association of Copenhagen Lawyers; International Bar Association. *LANGUAGES:* Danish, English, German, Swedish and Norwegian. *PRACTICE AREAS:* Tax Law; Vat and Duty Law; European Community Law; Corporate and Commercial Law; International Leasing.

FINN J. LERNØ, born Copenhagen, Denmark, April 27, 1953; admitted, 1982, Denmark; 1987, Supreme Court of Denmark. *Education:* University of Copenhagen (Faculty of Law); California State University, Northridge. Co-Author: "The Commentaries to the Stamp Duty Act," 1985; Supplement, 1988; 2nd edition, 1994. National Correspondent to international publication on distributorships and agencies and to Committee S of IBA/SBL. *Member:* Danish Bar Association; Association of Copenhagen Lawyers; International Bar Association. *LANGUAGES:* Danish, English, Swedish and Norwegian. *PRACTICE AREAS:* Distribution and Agency Contracts; Mergers and Acquisitions; Food and Drug Regulation; Advertising Law; Competition Law.

SVEND ERIK HOLM, born Aulum, Denmark, July 25, 1954; admitted, 1983, Denmark; 1989, Supreme Court of Denmark. *Education:* University

(This Listing Continued)

of Aarhus (Faculty of Law). *Member:* Danish Bar Association; Association of Copenhagen Lawyers. *LANGUAGES:* Danish, English, Swedish and Norwegian. *PRACTICE AREAS:* Tax Law; Real Estate.

MICHAEL REKLING, born Copenhagen, Denmark, February 18, 1958; admitted, 1986, Denmark; 1989, Supreme Court of Denmark. *Education:* University of Copenhagen (Faculty of Law). Ministry of Justice, 1981-1988. Lecturer, University of Copenhagen, Faculty of Law, Contracts, Torts, Civil Law, 1985-1989. *Member:* Danish Bar Association; Association of Copenhagen Lawyers; International Bar Association. *LANGUAGES:* Danish, English, Swedish and Norwegian. *PRACTICE AREAS:* International Banking and Financing; International Sales; Contract Law; Product Liability Law; Consumer Affairs.

PETER FOGH, born Copenhagen, Denmark, March 31, 1957; admitted, 1985, Denmark; 1990, Supreme Court of Denmark. *Education:* University of Copenhagen (Faculty of Law); London School of Economics and Political Science (LL.M.). Co-Author: "The Commentary on Ships' Registration in Basic Legal Documentation," 1989. *Member:* Danish Bar Association; Association of Copenhagen Lawyers; International Bar Association. *LANGUAGES:* Danish, English, Swedish and Norwegian. *PRACTICE AREAS:* International Banking and Financing; International Private Law; International Leasing; Maritime and Admiralty Law; Insurance Law; Litigation and Arbitration.

CASPER MÜNTER, born Copenhagen, Denmark, December 27, 1958; admitted, 1985, Denmark; 1994, Supreme Court of Denmark. *Education:* University of Copenhagen (Faculty of Law); New York University, Institute of Comparative Law (M.C.J.). *Member:* Danish Bar Association; Association of Copenhagen Lawyers; International Bar Association. *LANGUAGES:* Danish, English, Swedish and Norwegian. *PRACTICE AREAS:* Aviation Law; Investments and Securities; Mergers and Acquisitions; Corporate and Commercial Law; Franchising.

ASSOCIATES

CARL NIELSEN, born Odense, Denmark, July 2, 1933; admitted, 1961, Denmark; 1977, Supreme Court of Denmark. *Education:* University of Aarhus (Faculty of Law). *Member:* Danish Bar Association; Association of Copenhagen Lawyers. *LANGUAGES:* Danish, English, German, Swedish and Norwegian. *PRACTICE AREAS:* Probate and Administration of Estates; Wills and Settlements; Real Estate; Litigation and Arbitration.

MOGENS MOE, born Copenhagen, Denmark, March 13, 1944. *Education:* University of Copenhagen (Faculty of Law), PhD. 1974. Lecturer, University of Copenhagen, Faculty of Law, Construction Law, 1976-1980, Administrative Law 1980-1983 and 1983-1990, Environmental law, 1990—. Head of Division, Danish Environment Protection Agency, Division of Law and Inspection, 1985-1994. *Member:* Danish Society for Environmental Law (Member of Board, 1994—). *LANGUAGES:* Danish, English, French, Swedish and Norwegian. *PRACTICE AREAS:* Environmental Law and Planning; Administrative Law.

PIYA MUKHERJEE, born Calcutta, India, October 16, 1962; admitted, 1990, Denmark and Court of Appeal of Denmark. *Education:* University of Copenhagen (Faculty of Law); King's College, London (LL.M.). *Member:* Danish Bar Association; Association of Copenhagen Lawyers. *LANGUAGES:* Danish, English, Swedish and Norwegian. *PRACTICE AREAS:* Insolvency Law and Reconstruction.

BJØRN WITTRUP, born Tved, Denmark, October 4, 1961; admitted, 1990, Denmark; 1991, Court of Appeal of Denmark. *Education:* University of Aarhus (Faculty of Law). *Member:* Danish Bar Association; Association of Copenhagen Lawyers. *LANGUAGES:* Danish, English, Swedish and Norwegian. *PRACTICE AREAS:* Insolvency Law and Reconstruction; Tax Law; Litigation and Arbitration.

FRANTS DALGAARD-KNUDSEN, born Ringkjøbing, Denmark, September 15, 1960; admitted, 1990, Denmark; 1991, Court of Appeal of Denmark. *Education:* Universities of Aarhus, Waterloo, Frankfurt, Oslo and Firenze. Research Fellow at European University Institute, 1984-1987 (1991: PhD.) and Nordic Institute for Maritime Law, 1987. National expert to Corte Suprema di Cassazione, CED, Roma and the EEC-Commission, Enlex, 1986-1988. Lecturer, University of Copenhagen, Faculty of Law, Legal Informatics, 1988—. National Research Council Fellow, 1990. Author: "Mineral Concessions and Law in Greenland," 1991; "Exploitation Concessions: Contracts or Permits?," 1987. Co-Author: "European Environmental Yearbook." *Member:* Danish Bar Association; International Bar Association; American Society of International Law. *LANGUAGES:* Danish, English, Italian, German, French, Swedish and Norwegian. *PRACTICE AREAS:* European Community Law; Energy and Mining Law; Real Estate; Mergers and Acquisitions.

(This Listing Continued)

HENNING BIIL, born Svendborg, Denmark, July 24, 1963; admitted, 1991, Denmark and Court of Appeal of Denmark. *Education:* University of Copenhagen (Faculty of Law). *Member:* Danish Bar Association; German Nordic Lawyers' Association. *LANGUAGES:* Danish, English, German, Swedish and Norwegian. *PRACTICE AREAS:* Corporate and Commercial Law; Litigation and Arbitration; International Private Law; Insurance Law; Construction Law.

NETE WEBER, born Copenhagen, Denmark, September 25, 1962; admitted, 1991, Denmark; 1993, Court of Appeal of Denmark. *Education:* University of Copenhagen (Faculty of Law). *Member:* Danish Bar Association; Association of Copenhagen Lawyers. *LANGUAGES:* Danish, English, Swedish and Norwegian. *PRACTICE AREAS:* Insolvency Law and Reconstruction.

PIA ELISABETH VOSS, born Halling, Denmark, April 15, 1964; admitted, 1991, Denmark; 1992, Court of Appeal of Denmark. *Education:* University of Copenhagen (Faculty of Law). *Member:* Danish Bar Association; Association of Copenhagen Lawyers; The Danish Association of Labour Law. *LANGUAGES:* Danish, English, Swedish and Norwegian. *PRACTICE AREAS:* Labor Law; Litigation and Arbitration; Contract Law; Insolvency Law and Reconstruction.

THOMAS STAMPE, born Odder, Denmark, April 12, 1965; admitted, 1991, Denmark and Court of Appeal of Denmark. *Education:* University of Copenhagen (Faculty of Law). *Member:* Danish Bar Association. *LANGUAGES:* Danish, English, Swedish and Norwegian. *PRACTICE AREAS:* Construction Law; Litigation; Arbitration.

JENS KROGH PETERSEN, born Roskilde, Denmark, May 12, 1967; admitted, 1994, Denmark. *Education:* University of Copenhagen (Faculty of Law). *Member:* Danish Bar Association. *LANGUAGES:* Danish, English, Swedish and Norwegian. *PRACTICE AREAS:* Insolvency Law; Reconstruction Law.

MARTIN SIMONSEN, born Copenhagen, Denmark, May 19, 1966; admitted, 1994, Denmark. *Education:* University of Copenhagen (Faculty of Law). *Member:* Danish Bar Association.; Association of Copenhagen Lawyers. *LANGUAGES:* Danish, English, Swedish and Norwegian. *PRACTICE AREAS:* Corporate and Commercial Law; Mergers and Acquisitions; Competition Law; Contract Law; Food and Drug Regulation.

EVA THEISEN SANVIG, born Aarhus, Denmark, October 13, 1962; admitted, 1994, Denmark. *Education:* University of Aarhus (Faculty of Law). *Member:* Danish Bar Association. *LANGUAGES:* Danish, German, English, Swedish and Norwegian. *PRACTICE AREAS:* Insolvency Law; Reconstruction; Employment and Labor Law; Litigation and Arbitration.

KROMANN & MÜNTER

Established in 1989

RAADHUSPLADSEN 14
DK-1550 COPENHAGEN V, DENMARK
Telephone: 45 33 11 11 10
Cable Address: "Danadvocate"
Telex: 19514 danadv dk
Telefax: 45 33 11 80 28; 45 33 15 01 57

Aarhus, Denmark Office: Raadhuspladsen 3, 8100 Aarhus C, Denmark. Telephone: +45 86 12 71 11. Telefax: +45 86 18 41 55.
London, England Office: 44/45 Chancery Lane, London WC2A 1JB, England. Telephone: +44 171 404 4825. Telefax: +44 171 404 1471.
Brussels, Belgium Office: Avenue Louise 475/B12, B-1050 Brussels, Belgium. Telephone: +32 2 646 3620. Telefax: +32 2 646 4049.
Paris, France Office: 21, rue Jean Goujon, 75008 Paris, France. Telephone: +33 1 4075 3737. Telefax: +33 1 4563 0549.
Hong Kong Office: 2003 Hutchison House, 10 Harcourt Road Central, Hong Kong. Telephone: +852 2523 6149. Telefax: +852 2810 5343.

Company Law, Finance Law, Intellectual Property and Media Law, EC Legislation and Competition Law, Property and Environmental Law, Tax Law, Insolvency, Technology Law, Energy Law, Maritime Law.

FIRM PROFILE: Kromann & Münter was founded in 1989 by the merger of the two law firms Kromann, Nørregaard & Friis and Münter & Partners, founded in 1889 and 1956 respectively. In 1992 Kromann & Münter merged with the law firm Storm Mortensen, Aarhus.

(This Listing Continued)

KROMANN & MÜNTER, Copenhagen—Continued

COPENHAGEN, DENMARK OFFICE
PARTNERS

OLE NØRREGAARD, born Copenhagen, Denmark, February 27, 1930; admitted, 1959, Denmark; 1965, Supreme Court of Denmark. *Education:* University of Copenhagen (Law Degree, 1955). *Member:* Danish Bar Association; Association of Copenhagen Lawyers; International Bar Association. *LANGUAGES:* Scandinavian, English and German. *PRACTICE AREAS:* Corporate and Commercial Law.

PETER FRIIS, born Århus, Denmark, June 24, 1930; admitted, 1964, Denmark and High Court of Denmark. *Education:* University of Århus (Law Degree, 1956); New York University Institute of Comparative Law; Boalt Hall School of Law, University of California, 1959-1960. Ministry of Justice, 1957-1964. Lecturer on Law, Copenhagen School of Economies and Business Administration, 1963-1970. With Legal Department, Carlsberg Breweries, 1964-1967. *Member:* Association of Copenhagen Lawyers; Danish Bar Association; International Bar Association. *LANGUAGES:* Scandinavian, English and German. *PRACTICE AREAS:* Corporate and Commercial Law; Company Law.

VILLY LAURIDSEN, born Ribe, Denmark, February 14, 1935; admitted, 1971, Denmark; 1980, Supreme Court of Denmark. *Education:* University of Copenhagen (Law Degree, 1967). *Member:* Association of Copenhagen Lawyers; Danish Bar Association; International Bar Association. *LANGUAGES:* Scandinavian, English and German. *PRACTICE AREAS:* Corporate and Commercial Law; Real Property; Environmental Law.

KURT SKOVLUND, born Vordingborg, Denmark, May 8, 1938; admitted, 1966, Denmark; 1976, Supreme Court of Denmark. *Education:* Copenhagen University (Law Degree, 1963). *Member:* Association of Copenhagen Lawyers; Danish Bar Association; International Bar Association. *LANGUAGES:* Scandinavian and English. *PRACTICE AREAS:* Corporate and Commercial Law; Insolvency.

FINN RØNNE, born Rønne, Denmark, April 23, 1940; admitted, 1970, Denmark; 1977, Supreme Court of Denmark. *Education:* Copenhagen University (Law Degree, 1966). Danish Ministry of Justice, 1966-1970. *Member:* Association of Copenhagen Lawyers; Danish Bar Association; International Bar Association. *LANGUAGES:* Scandinavian and English. *PRACTICE AREAS:* Corporate and Commercial Law; Real Property; Environmental Law.

ERIK MOHR MERSING, born Svendborg, Denmark, October 19, 1939; admitted, 1969, Denmark; 1978, Supreme Court of Denmark. *Education:* Copenhagen University (Law Degree, 1965). Lecturer on Law, Copenhagen University, 1966-1973. Member of the National Committee for Revision of the Copyright Act, 1976-1990. *Member:* Association of Copenhagen Lawyers (Board Member, 1975-1980); Danish Bar Association (Chairman, Standing Committee on Competition and Intellectual Property Law, 1986-1989); International Bar Association. *LANGUAGES:* Scandinavian and English. *PRACTICE AREAS:* Corporate and Commercial Law; Intellectual Property; Media; EU Legislation; Competition; Technology Law.

MOGENS SKIPPER-PEDERSEN, born Lee, Denmark, January 15, 1940; admitted, 1971, Denmark; 1979, Supreme Court of Denmark. *Education:* Aarhus University (Law Degree, 1966); New York University (M.C.J., 1968). Danish Ministry of Justice, 1966-1971. *Member:* Danish Bar Council, 1984-1989; International Bar Association (Council Member, 1985—); Association of Copenhagen Lawyers (Board Member, 1980-1984); Danish Bar Association (Chairman, Standing Committee on Corporate Law, 1989-1992); Company Law Panel of the Ministry of Industry, 1991—. *LANGUAGES:* Scandinavian and English. *PRACTICE AREAS:* Corporate and Commercial Law; Company Law.

HENRIK STENBJERRE, born Nr. Sundby, Denmark, February 14, 1940; admitted, 1975, Denmark; 1983, Supreme Court of Denmark. *Education:* University of Copenhagen (Law Degree, 1965); Harvard Business School, 1977. *Member:* Association of Copenhagen Lawyers; Danish Bar Association; International Bar Association. *LANGUAGES:* Scandinavian, English and German. *PRACTICE AREAS:* Corporate and Commercial Law; Finance Law.

JØRGEN BOE, born Frederiksberg, Denmark, March 24, 1946; admitted, 1974, Denmark; 1980, Supreme Court of Denmark. *Education:* University of Copenhagen (Law Degree, 1971). Lecturer on Law: University of Copenhagen, 1972-1975; Copenhagen School of Economics and Business Administration, 1976-1989. Author: "The Senior Executive's Agreement." *Member:* Danish Bar Association; International Bar Association. *LAN-*

(This Listing Continued)

GUAGES: Scandinavian and English. *PRACTICE AREAS:* Corporate and Commercial Law; Company Law.

ERLING BORCHER, born Frederiksberg, Denmark, May 21, 1944; admitted, 1974, Denmark; 1982, Supreme Court of Denmark. *Education:* University of Copenhagen (Law Degree, 1971). *Member:* Association of Copenhagen Lawyers; Danish Bar Association; International Bar Association. *LANGUAGES:* Scandinavian, English, French and German. *PRACTICE AREAS:* Corporate and Commercial Law; Intellectual Property; Media; EU Legislation; Competition; Technology Law.

JOHN JAKOBSEN, born Lyngby Jutland, Denmark, January 2, 1942; admitted, 1974, Denmark; 1979, Supreme Court of Denmark. *Education:* University of Copenhagen (Law Degree, 1971). Lecturer on Law, Faculty of Law, University of Copenhagen, 1971-1974. *Member:* Association of Copenhagen Lawyers; Danish Bar Association; International Bar Association. *LANGUAGES:* Scandinavian and English. *PRACTICE AREAS:* Corporate and Commercial Law; Insolvency.

JESPER LUNDGREN, born Copenhagen, Denmark, October 10, 1945; admitted, 1975, Denmark and High Court of Denmark. *Education:* University of Copenhagen (Law Degree, 1972). *Member:* Association of Copenhagen Lawyers; Danish Bar Association; International Bar Association. *LANGUAGES:* Scandinavian, English and German. *PRACTICE AREAS:* Corporate and Commercial Law.

FLEMMING ANDERSEN, born Copenhagen, Denmark, June 28, 1947; admitted, 1976, Denmark; 1982, Supreme Court of Denmark. *Education:* Copenhagen University (Law Degree, 1972). *Member:* Association of Copenhagen Lawyers; Danish Bar Association; International Bar Association; Danish Branch of International Fiscal Association. *LANGUAGES:* Scandinavian and English. *PRACTICE AREAS:* Corporate and Commercial Law; Tax Law.

VAGN THORUP, born Ribe, Denmark, March 22, 1950; admitted, 1978, Denmark; 1979, High Court of Denmark. *Education:* University of Copenhagen (Law Degree, 1975). *Member:* Association of Copenhagen Lawyers; Danish Bar Association; International Bar Association. *LANGUAGES:* Scandinavian, English and German. *PRACTICE AREAS:* Corporate and Commercial Law; Intellectual Property; Media; EC Legislation; Competition; Technology Law.

MICHAEL KELDSEN, born Copenhagen, Denmark, October 2, 1950; admitted, 1979, Denmark; 1985, Supreme Court of Denmark. *Education:* Copenhagen University (Law Degree, 1976). *Member:* Association of Copenhagen Lawyers; Danish Bar Association. *LANGUAGES:* Scandinavian, English and German. *PRACTICE AREAS:* Corporate and Commercial; Maritime; Energy Law.

MICHAEL BUDTZ, born Copenhagen, Denmark, May 7, 1952; admitted, 1979, Denmark; 1989, Supreme Court of Denmark. *Education:* University of Copenhagen (Law Degree, 1976); University of California, Los Angeles (LL.M., 1982). *Member:* Association of Copenhagen Lawyers; Danish Bar Association; American Bar Association; International Bar Association. *LANGUAGES:* Scandinavian, English and German. *PRACTICE AREAS:* Corporate and Commercial Law; Maritime; Energy Law.

NIELS WALTHER-RASMUSSEN, born Hellerup, Denmark, July 25, 1952; admitted, 1981, Denmark; 1985, New York; 1987, Supreme Court of Denmark. *Education:* Copenhagen University School of Law (Law Degree, 1978); New York University (M.C.J., 1985). With Paul, Weiss, Rifkind, Wharton & Garrison, New York, 1985-1986. *Member:* Association of Copenhagen Lawyers; Danish Bar Association; American Bar Association; International Bar Association. *LANGUAGES:* Scandinavian and English. *PRACTICE AREAS:* Corporate and Commercial Law; Finance Law.

NIELS BALSLEV, born Frederiksberg, Denmark, May 26, 1950; admitted, 1984, Denmark and High Court of Denmark. *Education:* University of Copenhagen (Law Degree, 1981). Lecturer on Law, Copenhagen School of Economics and Business Administration, 1982-1984. *Member:* Danish Bar Association. *LANGUAGES:* Scandinavian and English. *PRACTICE AREAS:* Corporate and Commercial Law; Real Property; Environmental Law.

JØRGEN KJERGAARD MADSEN, born Denmark, January 20, 1956; admitted, 1987, Denmark and High Court of Denmark; 1989, New York. *Education:* The Aarhus School of Economics and Business Administration (Business Finance, 1980); Aarhus University, Denmark (Law Degree, 1984); New York University (M.C.J., 1988). Lecturer, Business Law, Copenhagen School of Economics and Business Administration, 1986-1987. With Lillick, McHose & Charles, Los Angeles, 1988-1989. *Member:* Association of Copenhagen Lawyers; Danish Bar Association; American Bar

(This Listing Continued)

Association and International Bar Association. *LANGUAGES:* Scandinavian and English. *PRACTICE AREAS:* Corporate and Commercial Law; Finance Law.

HENRIK PEYTZ, born Denmark, November 3, 1959; admitted, 1986, Denmark; 1987, High Court of Denmark. *Education:* Copenhagen University (Law Degree, 1983). Lecturer on Law, Copenhagen University, 1983-1984. Ministry of Justice, 1983-1984. With Clifford Chance, Brussels, 1990. Insead, Fontainebleau (MBA, 1991). *Member:* Danish Bar Association; Association of Copenhagen Lawyers. *LANGUAGES:* Scandinavian, English, French and German. *PRACTICE AREAS:* Corporate and Commercial Law; EU Law; Tax Law.

HENRIK MØGELMOSE, born Kerteminde, Denmark, March 13, 1958; admitted, 1986, Denmark; 1988, High Court of Denmark; 1992, New York. *Education:* Aarhus University (Law Degree, 1983); University of Chicago Law School (LL.M., 1991). Lecturer, Business Law, Copenhagen School of Economics and Business Administration, 1986-1990. With the Law Firm Skadden, Arps, Slate, Meagher and Flom, New York, 1991-1992. *Member:* Danish Bar Association; Association of Copenhagen Lawyers; American Bar Association (Business Law Section); The Association of the Bar of the City of New York; International Bar Association (Member; Business Law Section; Capital Markets Forum). *LANGUAGES:* Scandinavian and English. *PRACTICE AREAS:* Corporate and Commerical Law; Finance Law.

ANDERS LAVESEN, born Copenhagen, Denmark, August 31, 1961; admitted, 1989, Denmark; 1991, High Court of Denmark. *Education:* University of Copenhagen (Law Degree, 1986); London School of Economics and Political Science (LL.M., 1990). With the Law Firm Denton, Hall, Burgin and Warrens, London, 1990. *Member:* Danish Bar Association. *LANGUAGES:* Scandinavian and English. *PRACTICE AREAS:* Corporate; Commercial Law; Company Law.

AARHUS, DENMARK OFFICE
PARTNERS

JØRGEN B. JEPSEN, born April 25, 1945; admitted, 1973, Denmark; 1978, Supreme Court of Denmark. *Education:* University of Aarhus (Law Degree, 1970). *Member:* Danish Bar Association (Chairman, Committee on Legal Procedure and Public Law, 1985-1991; Member, Danish Rules Committee Board of Inquiry concerning arrest of property and injunction, 1986-1992; Member, Committee on Danish attorneys' recognition as specialists, 1989-1992; Vice-Chairman, Environmental Committee, 1991—; Committee Member, Danish Committee on Environmental Law, 1991—). *LANGUAGES:* Scandinavian and English. *PRACTICE AREAS:* Corporate and Commercial Law; Real Property; Environmental Law; Litigation.

CARSTEN FODE, born Randers, Denmark, March 2, 1949; admitted, 1977, Denmark; 1982, Supreme Court of Denmark. *Education:* University of Aarhus (Law Degree, 1973); Harvard Law School (LL.M., 1976). Lecturer, Company Law, University of Aarhus, 1976-1983. Officially Appointed Examiner, Law Faculty, University of Aarhus, 1988—. *Member:* Danish Bar Association; International Bar Association. *LANGUAGES:* Scandinavian and English. *PRACTICE AREAS:* Corporate and Commercial Law; Finance Law.

BENT MÜLLER, born July 14, 1947; admitted, 1978, Denmark; 1983, Supreme Court of Denmark. *Education:* University of Aarhus (Law Degree, 1975). *Member:* Danish Bar Association; International Bar Association. *LANGUAGES:* Scandinavian and English. *PRACTICE AREAS:* Corporate and Commercial Law; Real Property; Environmental Law.

JAN BØRJESSON, born Odense, Denmark, November 15, 1955; admitted, 1983, Denmark; 1989, Supreme Court of Denmark. *Education:* University of Aarhus (Law Degree, 1980). Instructor, Part Time, University of Aarhus, 1979-1983. Instructor, Part Time, Company Law, Aarhus School of Business Administration and Economics, 1983-1989. External Lecturer, Mergers and Acquisitions, University of Aarhus, 1990—. *Member:* Danish Bar Association; International Fiscal Association. *LANGUAGES:* Scandinavian, English and German. *PRACTICE AREAS:* Corporate and Commercial Law; Company; Tax Law.

SVEND OLE ESPENSEN, born Holsted, Denmark, June 20, 1946; admitted, 1979, Denmark and High Court of Denmark; 1987, Frankfurt, West Germany. *Education:* University of Aarhus (Law Degree, 1976). Secretary, Ministry of Foreign Affairs, 1968-1969. External Lecturer: Commercial Law, Aarhus School of Business Administration and Economics, 1979-1980; EU Law, University of Aarhus, 1991; International Law, Aarhus School of Business Administration and Economics, 1987—. *Member:* Danish, German and International Bar Associations; Frankfurt Law Society; Young Lawyers International Association. *LANGUAGES:* Scandinavian,

(This Listing Continued)

English, German and French. *PRACTICE AREAS:* Corporate and Commercial Law; Intellectual Property; Media; EC Legislation; Competition; Technology Law.

HANS-JØRN ANDERSEN, born Herning, Denmark, May 5, 1955; admitted, 1983, Denmark; 1984, High Court of Denmark; 1987, Frankfurt, West Germany. *Education:* University of Copenhagen (Law Degree, 1980). *Member:* Danish and German Bar Associations; Aarhus and Frankfurt Law Societies; Young Lawyers International Association. *LANGUAGES:* Scandinavian, English and German. *PRACTICE AREAS:* Corporate and Commercial Law; Insolvency.

JØRN VESTERGAARD-JENSEN, born Herning, Denmark, June 11, 1955; admitted, 1989, Denmark; 1992, High Court of Denmark. *Education:* The Aarhus School of Business Administration and Economics (B.Sc. Economics, 1979; M.Sc. Economics, 1982; Ph.D. Economics, 1985); University of Aarhus (Law Degree, 1986); UOP McGeorge School of Law (LL.M., 1990). Author: "Joint Ventures i Østeuropa," Copenhagen, 1986. Research Assistant, Institute of Foreign Trade, Aarhus School of Business Administration and Economics, 1982-1986. Instructor in Law, Industrial Property Rights, 1992—. *Member:* Danish Bar Association; Deutsch-Nordische Juristenverein e.V.; International Law Association; Comité Maritime International (Danish Branch); Deutsch-Amerikanische Juristenvereingung e.V.; International Bar Association; Danish Association for the Protection of Industrial Property; Inter-Pacific Bar Association. *LANGUAGES:* Scandinavian, English and German. *PRACTICE AREAS:* Corporate and Commercial Law; Intellectual Property; Media; EC Legislation; Competition; Technology Law.

COPENHAGEN ASSOCIATES

METTE VALENTIN, born Give, Denmark, March 27, 1963; admitted, 1989, Denmark; 1992, High Court of Denmark. *Education:* University of Copenhagen (Law Degree, 1986); Harvard Law School (LL.M., 1990). *Member:* Danish Bar Association. *LANGUAGES:* Scandinavian and English. *PRACTICE AREAS:* Intellectual Property and Media Law.

METTE PORSKAER WINTHER, born Denmark, March 22, 1964; admitted, 1990, Denmark and High Court of Denmark. *Education:* University of Copenhagen (Law Degree, 1987). *Member:* Danish Bar Association. *LANGUAGES:* Scandinavian and English. *PRACTICE AREAS:* Insolvency.

KIRSTEN KRISTENSEN, born Sandved, Denmark, January 30, 1954; admitted, 1990, Denmark; 1991, High Court of Denmark. *Education:* University of Copenhagen (Law Degree, 1987). *Member:* Danish Bar Association. *LANGUAGES:* Scandinavian and English. *PRACTICE AREAS:* Insolvency; Estate Administration; Business Successions.

MICHAEL SEIFFERT, born Denmark, October 19, 1964; admitted, 1991, Denmark; 1992, High Court of Denmark. *Education:* University of Copenhagen (Law Degree, 1988). *Member:* Danish Bar Association. *LANGUAGES:* Scandinavian, English and German. *PRACTICE AREAS:* Intellectual Property Law.

METTE LOMHOLT FOGT, born Roskilde, February 27, 1963; admitted, 1991, Denmark. *Education:* University of Copenhagen (Law Degree, 1988). *Member:* Danish Bar Association. *LANGUAGES:* Scandinavian and English. *PRACTICE AREAS:* Technology Law.

BENTE MØLL PEDERSEN, born Dorf Kirkeby, Denmark, November 5, 1954; admitted, 1992, Denmark; 1993, High Court of Denmark. *Education:* University of Copenhagen (Law Degree, 1989). Lecturer, Law of Property, 1990-1992; Tax Law, 1992—, University of Copenhagen. *Member:* Association of Copenhagen Lawyers; Danish Bar Association; Danish Branch of International Fiscal Association; International Association of Young Lawyers. *LANGUAGES:* Scandinavian and English. *PRACTICE AREAS:* Tax Law.

CLAUS JUEL HANSEN, born Frederiksberg, Denmark, October 5, 1965; admitted, 1992, Denmark. *Education:* University of Copenhagen (Law Degree, 1989). Lecturer, University of Copenhagen, 1990-1994. *Member:* Danish Bar Association. (Resident Associate, London Office). *LANGUAGES:* Scandinavian and English. *PRACTICE AREAS:* Corporate and Commercial Law.

JESPER LAU HANSEN, born Copenhagen, Denmark, October 29, 1965; admitted, 1992, Denmark and High Court of Denmark. *Education:* University of Copenhagen (Law Degree, 1989); University of Cambridge, England (LL.M., 1993). *Member:* Danish Bar Association. *LANGUAGES:* Scandinavian and English. *PRACTICE AREAS:* Company Law; Mergers and Acquisitions; Securities Regulations.

(This Listing Continued)

KROMANN & MÜNTER, Copenhagen—Continued

KIM HÅKONSSON, born Copenhagen, Denmark, December 15, 1963; admitted, 1992, Denmark; 1994, High Court of Denmark. *Education:* University of Copenhagen (Law Degree, 1989). *Member:* Danish Bar Association. *LANGUAGES:* Scandinavian and English. *PRACTICE AREAS:* Intellectual Property Law.

PETER KETELSEN, born Gentofte, Denmark, January 12, 1964; admitted, 1992, Denmark. *Education:* University of Copenhagen (Law Degree, 1989). *Member:* Danish Bar Association. *LANGUAGES:* Scandinavian and English. *PRACTICE AREAS:* Company Law.

KRISTIAN ELVANG-GØRANSSON, born Naestved, Denmark, May 7, 1966; admitted, 1993, Denmark; 1994, High Court of Denmark. *Education:* University of Copenhagen (Law Degree, 1990). *Member:* Danish Bar Association. *LANGUAGES:* Scandinavian and English. *PRACTICE AREAS:* Technology Law.

ERIK BERTELSEN, born Aarhus, Denmark, September 16, 1964; admitted, 1993, Denmark. *Education:* University of Aarhus (Law Degree, 1989); Free University of Brussels (LL.M., 1992). *Member:* Danish Bar Association. (Resident Associate, Brussels Office). *LANGUAGES:* Scandinavian, English and German. *PRACTICE AREAS:* EU Law and Competition Law.

MERETE LARSEN, born Frederiksberg, Denmark, November 29, 1966; admitted, 1993, Denmark. *Education:* University of Copenhagen (Law Degree, 1990). *Member:* Danish Bar Association. *LANGUAGES:* Scandinavian, English and Spanish. *PRACTICE AREAS:* Property Law; Finance Law.

JENS MUNK PLUM, born Sønderborg, Denmark, March 28, 1965; admitted, 1993, Denmark. *Education:* University of Copenhagen (Law Degree, 1990); Vrije Universiteit, Brussels (LL.M., 1994). *Member:* Danish Bar Association. *LANGUAGES:* Scandinavian and English.

PETER VILSØE, born Denmark, March 5, 1968; admitted, 1993, Denmark. *Education:* University of Copenhagen (Law Degree, 1990). *Member:* Danish Bar Association. *LANGUAGES:* Scandinavian and English.

ANDERS STUBBE ARNDAL, born Ribe, Denmark, April 14, 1966; admitted, 1994, Denmark and High Court of Denmark. *Education:* University of Aarhus (Law Degree, 1991). *Member:* Danish Bar Association. *LANGUAGES:* Scandinavian and English.

ERIK RYKIND-ERIKSEN, born Copenhagen, Denmark, November 21, 1965; admitted, 1993, Denmark. *Education:* University of Copenhagen (Law Degree, 1991); Copenhagen School of Business Administration and Economics (Bachelor of Commerce, 1993). *Member:* Danish Bar Association. *LANGUAGES:* Scandinavian and English. *PRACTICE AREAS:* Company Law; Technology Law.

PETER BANG, born Copenhagen, Denmark, September 30, 1964; admitted, 1994, Denmark. *Education:* University of Copenhagen (Law Degree, 1991). *Member:* Danish Bar Association. *LANGUAGES:* Scandinavian, English and French.

METTE HEDELUND FRANDSEN, born Copenhagen, Denmark, May 8, 1967; admitted, 1994, Denmark. *Education:* University of Copenhagen (Law Degree, 1991). *Member:* Danish Bar Association. *LANGUAGES:* Scandinavian and English.

LAU NORMANN JØRGENSEN, born Bro, Denmark, March 11, 1966; admitted, 1994, Denmark. *Education:* University of Copenhagen (Law Degree, 1991); University of Brussels (LL.M. cum laude, 1991). Lecturer on EU Law, University of Copenhagen, 1993—. *Member:* Danish Bar Association. *LANGUAGES:* Scandinavian, English, German and French. *PRACTICE AREAS:* EU Law; Technology Law.

CHRISTIAN KLEDAL, born Charlottenlund, Denmark, December 31, 1966; admitted, 1994, Denmark. *Education:* University of Copenhagen (Law Degree, 1991). *Member:* Danish Bar Association. *LANGUAGES:* Scandinavian and English.

NIELS PETERSEN, born Charlottenlund, Denmark, February 16, 1967; admitted, 1994, Denmark. *Education:* University of Copenhagen (Law Degree, 1991). *Member:* Danish Bar Association. *LANGUAGES:* Scandinavian and English.

(This Listing Continued)

EU158B

AARHUS ASSOCIATES

ULRIK FLEISCHER-MICHAELSEN, born Usserød, Denmark, December 18, 1961; admitted, 1989, Denmark and High Court of Denmark. *Education:* Copenhagen School of Business Administration and Economics (Bachelor of Commerce, 1989); University of Aarhus (Law Degree, 1986). *Member:* Danish Bar Association; International Fiscal Association. *LANGUAGES:* Scandinavian, English and German. *PRACTICE AREAS:* Tax Law.

JESPER RASMUSSEN, born Denmark, September 26, 1962; admitted, 1990, Denmark; 1991, High Court of Denmark. *Education:* University of Aarhus (Law Degree, 1987); University of London, King's College, School of Law (LL.M., 1993). *Member:* Danish Bar Association. *LANGUAGES:* Scandinavian and English.

BRIAN SØRENSEN, born August 13, 1964; admitted, 1992, Denmark; 1994, High Court of Denmark. *Education:* University of Aarhus (Law Degree, 1988). *Member:* Danish Bar Association. *LANGUAGES:* Scandinavian and English. *PRACTICE AREAS:* Construction Law.

HELENE AMSINCK BOIE, born Copenhagen, May 5, 1964; admitted, 1992, Denmark; 1993, High Court of Denmark. *Education:* University of Aarhus (Law Degree, 1989). *Member:* Danish Bar Association. *LANGUAGES:* Scandinavian, English, German and French. *PRACTICE AREAS:* Insolvency.

TORBEN HØHOLT JENSEN, born Taars, Denmark, September 21, 1964; admitted, 1992, Denmark; 1993, High Court of Denmark. *Education:* University of Aarhus (Law Degree, 1989). *Member:* Danish Bar Association. *LANGUAGES:* Scandinavian and English.

HANS CHRISTIAN PAPE, born August 10, 1965; admitted, 1993, Denmark. *Education:* University of Aarhus (Law Degree, 1990). *Member:* Danish Bar Association. *LANGUAGES:* Scandinavian and English. *PRACTICE AREAS:* Real Property; Tenancy Law.

KIRSTEN NOTHLEVSEN HOLVAD, born Denmark, June 26, 1966; admitted, 1994, Denmark. *Education:* University of Aarhus (Law Degree, 1991). *Member:* Danish Bar Association. *LANGUAGES:* Scandinavian and English.

Member of the Scandinavian Law Alliance: VINGE KROMANN THOMMESSEN with offices in London, Brussels, Paris and Hong Kong.

Languages: English, French, German and Scandinavian.

LASSEN & RICARD

Established in 1985

NYBROGADE 12

1203 DK COPENHAGEN K, DENMARK

Telephone: 45 1 33322012

Telex: 21344 LRLAW

Telecopier: 45 1 33322474

General Practice, Antitrust and Trade Regulations, Banking, Bankruptcy, Business Law, EU Antitrust and Competition, Copyright, Corporate, Entertainment. Environmental, Litigation, Oil and Concessions, Communications and Media, Real Estate, Securities, Tax and Trademark Law. The firm is admitted to all Danish courts and the EEC court.

FIRM PROFILE: Lassen & Ricard advise a large number of Danish and foreign clients, primarily regarding commercial law and with a special emphasis on cases related to countries outside of Denmark.

We attach importance to the personal contact between our client and the lawyer or team of lawyers in order to secure the trust we feel is extremely important between client and attorney. The firm is co-author of the book "Directors' duties and responsibilities in the European communities," published by the London Chamber of Commerce and Industry.

Lassen & Ricard conducts business in the Danish, English, French, German, Swedish and Norwegian languages.

MEMBERS OF FIRM

LENNART RICARD, born Copenhagen, Denmark, May 4, 1943; admitted, 1970, Denmark; 1980, Supreme Court of Denmark. *Education:* University of Delaware and University of Copenhagen (Law Degree, 1970). Lecturer on Business Law, Business School of Copenhagen, 1975. *Member:* Danish Bar Association (Member of Board, 1983—); Bar Council of Copenhagen; International Bar Association. *LANGUAGES:* Danish, English, French, German, Swedish and Norwegian. *PRACTICE AREAS:* Banks and Banking; Environmental Law; International Law.

(This Listing Continued)

STEEN LASSEN, born Copenhagen, Denmark, October 30, 1944; admitted, 1971, Supreme Court of Denmark. *Education:* City of London College, University of Copenhagen (Law Degree, 1971); Harvard Law School (LL.M. in Business Law and Law of the Sea, 1977). Associate, Sullivan & Cromwell, New York, 1977-1978. Author: "Passage Through Straits," The Scandinavian International Law Journal, 1979. Lecturer on Corporate Law, Danish Bar Association's Postgraduate Education, 1979. *Member:* Danish and International Bar Associations; Danish Copyright Society. *LANGUAGES:* Danish, English, German, Swedish and Norwegian. *PRACTICE AREAS:* Broadcasting; Company Law; Intellectual Property.

PETER M. LAMBERT, born Copenhagen, Denmark, February 11, 1961; admitted, 1987, Court of Appeal of Denmark. *Education:* University of Copenhagen (Law Degree, 1987). Lecturer on Property, University of Copenhagen. *LANGUAGES:* Danish, English, German, Swedish and Norwegian. *PRACTICE AREAS:* Arbitration and Mediation; Construction Law; Property Law.

ASSOCIATES

NINA HENNINGSEN, born Copenhagen, Denmark, March 27, 1965; admitted, 1991, Denmark. *Education:* Duke University (summer course, 1990); University of Copenhagen (Law Degree, 1991). *LANGUAGES:* Danish, English, Swedish and Norwegian. *PRACTICE AREAS:* Antitrust and Trade Regulation; Communications and Media; Trademarks.

MARTIN GORMSEN, born Copenhagen, Denmark, March 16, 1968; admitted, 1993, Denmark. *Education:* University of Copenhagen (Law Degree, 1993). Author: "The Justicia," 1992; "Incorporation of the European Convention on Human Rights into Danish Law.". *LANGUAGES:* Danish, English, Swedish and Norwegian. *PRACTICE AREAS:* Agency and Distributorships; Computers and Software; Labour and Employment.

MARCUS RUBIN, born Copenhagen, Denmark, 1970; admitted, 1994, Denmark. *Education:* Duke University/ULB Summer School in Transnational Law Bruxelles 1992; London University (LL.M. International Business Law, 1992-1993); stagiaire at the EU-Commission in Competition Law (1993-1994) and University of Copenhagen (Law degree, 1994). *LANGUAGES:* Danish, English, Swedish and Norwegian. *PRACTICE AREAS:* EU; Antitrust; Competition Law.

REPRESENTATIVE CLIENTS: Agfa; British Broadcasting Corp.; CNN; Dainippon Screen; Danish Radio and Television; Eurosport; The Federation of Investment Funds in Denmark; Le Point; Matsushita; Nord-Deutscher Rundfunk; Norwegian Radio and Television; Rai Uno; Recognition; Seiko; Sony Music Entertainment; Zweites Deutsches Fernsehen; Remy Martin; The Union of Broadcasting Organizations regarding Cable Distribution in Denmark.

LETT & CO.
BORGERGADE 111
1300 COPENHAGEN K, DENMARK
Telephone: 45 33 12 00 66
Telefax: 45 33 12 12 66

General Practice. Corporation, Commercial, Antitrust, EEC, Contract, Mergers and Acquisitions, Insurance, Banking, Admiralty, Tax Law, Real Estate, Employment, Intellectual Law, Administrative Law, Litigation and Construction and Engineering Disputes.

MEMBERS OF FIRM

ERIK STEGLICH-PETERSEN, born Copenhagen, Denmark, November 13, 1922; admitted, 1960, Denmark; 1968, Supreme Court of Denmark. *Education:* University of Copenhagen. *Member:* Danish Bar Association. *LANGUAGES:* Danish, Norwegian, Swedish, English and German.

JESPER LETT, born Copenhagen, Denmark, November 22, 1941; admitted, 1972, Denmark; 1977, Supreme Court of Denmark. *Education:* University of Copenhagen. Trainee with S.C.A.C., Nantes, France, 1966-1967. Ministry of Justice, 1967-1968. Co-Author: "Mergers in the EEC," 1988. Lecturer on Law, The Copenhagen School of Economics and Business Administration, 1972-1980. Officially appointed examiner, 1980—. *Member:* Danish Bar Association; International Bar Association. *LANGUAGES:* Danish, Norwegian, Swedish, English and French. *PRACTICE AREAS:* Corporation; Contract; Mergers and Acquisitions; Tax Law; Administrative Law; Litigation; Construction and Engineering Disputes.

GEORG LETT, born Copenhagen, Denmark, September 25, 1946; admitted, 1976, Denmark; 1981, Supreme Court of Denmark. *Education:* University of Copenhagen. Author: "Act on Product Liability", an extensive commentary 2nd ed., 1991; "Environmental Impairment Liability Insurance," 1992; "Product Liability and Insurance," 1992; "The General and Product Liability Insurance," 1993. Trainee with the ECC Commission,

Brussels, 1974. *Member:* International Bar Association; Danish Bar Association; "AIDA"; Union Internationale des Avocats. *LANGUAGES:* Danish, Norwegian, Swedish, English, German and French. *PRACTICE AREAS:* Mergers and Acquisitions; Liability; Insurance and EEC.

JOHN PETERSEN, born Copenhagen, Denmark, February 11, 1947; admitted, 1979, Denmark; 1990, Supreme Court of Denmark. *Education:* University of Copenhagen. Lecturer on Law, University of Copenhagen, 1977-1989. Assistant District Attorney, Copenhagen, 1979-1983 and 1988—. Prosecutor of the Impeachment, 1993—. *Member:* Danish Bar Association. *LANGUAGES:* Danish Norwegian, Swedish, German and English. *PRACTICE AREAS:* Arbitration; Litigation; Real Estate and Criminal Law.

BJARNE JOHANNESEN, born Copenhagen, Denmark, November 18, 1944; admitted, 1983, Denmark; 1988, Supreme Court of Denmark. *Education:* University of Copenhagen. *Member:* Danish Bar Association. *LANGUAGES:* Danish and English. *PRACTICE AREAS:* Real Estate; Construction and Engineering Disputes; Arbitration.

MORTEN SAMUELSSON, born Copenhagen, Denmark, January 27, 1960; admitted, 1988, Denmark, 1993, Supreme Court of Denmark. *Education:* University of Copenhagen (Ph.D., 1990). Author: "Real Estate Broker Liability", 1990; "Liability for Professional Advisors," 1993. Trainee with the European Parliament, Luxembourg, 1984 and Haight Gardner, N.Y.C., 1992. Lecturer on Product Liability, Insurance Employee's School. Assistant District Attorney, Copenhagen, 1994—. *Member:* International Bar Association and Danish Bar Association. *LANGUAGES:* Danish, German, French and English. *PRACTICE AREAS:* Corporation; Insurance; Torts and Litigation.

MICHAEL GRØNBECH, born Copenhagen, Denmark, March 19, 1946; admitted, 1974, Denmark; 1980, Supreme Court of Denmark. *Education:* University of Copenhagen. *Member:* Danish and International Bar Associations. *LANGUAGES:* Danish, Swedish, Norwegian and English. *PRACTICE AREAS:* Transport and CMR.

TORBEN BYSKOV PETERSEN, born Lemvig, Denmark, May 29, 1957; admitted, 1987, Denmark and High Court of Denmark. *Education:* University of Aarhus, Denmark (1984). *Member:* Danish Bar Association. *LANGUAGES:* Danish, Swedish, Norwegian, English and German. *PRACTICE AREAS:* Corporation; Contract; Litigation; Mergers and Acquisitions.

ESBEN BIGAARD, born Copenhagen, Denmark, April 4, 1947; admitted, 1980, Denmark and High Court of Denmark. *Education:* University of Copenhagen (1974). Assistant to the Probate Court of Copenhagen, 1985—. *Member:* Danish Bar Association. *LANGUAGES:* Danish, Norwegian, Swedish, German and English. *PRACTICE AREAS:* Commercial Law and Probate Advice and Succession.

CHRISTINA NEUGEBAUER, born Copenhagen, Denmark, June 30, 1964; admitted, 1990, Denmark and High Court of Denmark. *Education:* University of Copenhagen. Lecturer on Liability and Insurance Law, Insurance School, 1988—. *Member:* Danish Bar Association. *LANGUAGES:* Danish, Swedish, Norwegian, German, French and English. *PRACTICE AREAS:* Insurance; Torts and Litigation.

ASSOCIATES

PERNILLE SØLLING, born Copenhagen, Denmark, August 1, 1960; admitted, 1990, Denmark and High Court of Denmark. *Education:* University of Copenhagen. Lecturer on Business and Insurance Law, Insurance School, 1990. *Member:* Danish Bar Association. *LANGUAGES:* Danish, Swedish, Norwegian and English. *PRACTICE AREAS:* Liability; Insurance; Intellectual Law; Litigation.

CLAUS ULRIK HOLBERG, born Copenhagen, Denmark, March 10, 1963; admitted, 1992, Denmark; 1993, High Court of Denmark. *Education:* University of Copenhagen (1989). *Member:* Danish Bar Association. *LANGUAGES:* Danish and English. *PRACTICE AREAS:* Liability; Tax and Corporation.

ULRIK CHRISTRUP, born Copenhagen, Denmark, June 13, 1967; admitted, 1993, Denmark and High Court of Denmark. *Education:* University of Copenhagen (1990). *Member:* Danish Bar Association. *LANGUAGES:* Danish, English, Swedish and Norwegian. *PRACTICE AREAS:* Liability,; Insurance; Business; Corporation and Tax Law.

JUNIOR ASSOCIATES

ANNE HASLØV, born August 13, 1964. *Education:* University of Copenhagen (1992).

(This Listing Continued)
(This Listing Continued)

LETT & CO., Copenhagen—Continued

METTE TANG HOMANN, born October 31, 1953. *Education:* University of Copenhagen (1989).

MALENE STAMPE, born March 28, 1967. *Education:* University of Copenhagen (1993).

JACOB RASMUSSEN, born May 18, 1970. *Education:* University of Copenhagen (1993).

JANE JUUL KJAER, born October 19, 1964. *Education:* University of Copenhagen (1988).

HANS HENRIK TAUSEN, born March 18, 1960. *Education:* University of Copenhagen (1993).

KRISTIAN HÖLGE, born December 2, 1968. *Education:* University of Copenhagen (1994).

MORTEN JOACHIM CHRISTENSEN, born March 31, 1965. *Education:* University of Copenhagen (1994).

MARK KANT DOVEY, born May 12, 1963. *Education:* University of Copenhagen (1994).

LETT, VILSTRUP & PARTNERS

3, BREDGADE
1260 COPENHAGEN K, DENMARK
Telephone: 33 15 48 00
Cable Address: "Lawhouse"
Telex: 16080 LAWHS DK
Telefax: 45 33 15 59 95

Brussels, Belgium Office: 99, Rue de la Loi, Bte. No. 12, 1040. Telephone: (2) 231 11 85. Telex: 63017 jurist b. Facsimile: (02) 2 80 09 83.

General Practice. Corporation, Commercial, Antitrust, EEC, Contract, Insurance, Banking, Admiralty, Tax Law and Industrial Property Rights.

MEMBERS OF FIRM

FRANZ BÜLOW, born Copenhagen, Denmark, July 31, 1910; admitted, 1931, Denmark; 1949, Supreme Court of Denmark. *Education:* University of Copenhagen. *Member:* Danish Bar Association. *LANGUAGES:* Danish, Norwegian, Swedish, English and German.

ULRIK LETT, born Copenhagen, Denmark, March 24, 1938; admitted, 1967, Denmark; 1978, Supreme Court of Denmark. *Education:* University of Copenhagen. *Member:* Danish Bar Association. *LANGUAGES:* Danish, Norwegian, Swedish, English and German. *PRACTICE AREAS:* M & A; Banking; Securities and Finance.

BO VILSTRUP, born Copenhagen, Denmark, December 1, 1942; admitted, 1970, Denmark; 1985, Supreme Court of Denmark. *Education:* University of Copenhagen; Stanford University, California. *Member:* Danish Bar Association. *LANGUAGES:* Danish, Norwegian, Swedish and English. *PRACTICE AREAS:* Banking; Securities and Finance; Companies; Corporation.

ULF ANDERSEN, born Esbjerg, Denmark, November 28 1942; admitted, 1972, Denmark; 1979, Supreme Court of Denmark. *Education:* University of Copenhagen. *Member:* Danish Bar Association. *LANGUAGES:* Danish, Norwegian, Swedish and English. *PRACTICE AREAS:* Tax Law; Construction Law.

SØREN JENSTRUP, born Copenhagen, Denmark, June 9, 1952; admitted, 1979, Denmark; 1984, Supreme Court of Denmark. *Education:* University of Copenhagen; City of London Polytechnic (1973). *Member:* Danish Bar Association. *LANGUAGES:* Danish, Norwegian, Swedish, English and German. *PRACTICE AREAS:* Arbitration; Litigation.

PER SCHMIDT, born Copenhagen, Denmark, December 6, 1930; admitted, 1958, Denmark. *Education:* University of Copenhagen (Law Degree, 1955). *Member:* Copenhagen Bar Association (Member of Board, 1974; Chairman, 1980-1983); Danish Bar and Law Society (Council Member, 1983-1989). *LANGUAGES:* Danish, Norwegian, Swedish, English and German. *PRACTICE AREAS:* Contract; Corporation; Arbitration.

JAN HOLGERSEN, born Copenhagen, Denmark, August 14, 1956; admitted, 1984, Denmark; 1990 Supreme Court of Denmark. *Education:* University of Copenhagen. *Member:* Danish Bar Association. *LANGUAGES:* Danish, Norwegian, Swedish, English and French. *PRACTICE AREAS:* EC-Law; Litigation; Real Property Law.

(This Listing Continued)

SUSANNE MARK, born Aars, Denmark, July 4, 1957; admitted, 1988, Denmark; 1989, High Court of Denmark. *Education:* University of Copenhagen; University of New York (M.C.J., 1989). *Member:* Danish Bar Association. *LANGUAGES:* Danish, Norwegian, Swedish and English. *PRACTICE AREAS:* Computer; Communication and Information Law; Intellectual Property Law.

VIVI BRUHN KNUDSEN, born Copenhagen, Denmark, June 2, 1957; admitted, 1990, Denmark and High Court of Denmark. *Education:* University of Copenhagen. *Member:* Danish Bar Association. *LANGUAGES:* Danish, Norwegian, Swedish and English. *PRACTICE AREAS:* Environmental Law.

THOMAS BANG, born Copenhagen, Denmark, August 5, 1956; admitted, 1989, Denmark; 1992, High Court of Copenhagen, Department of Justice. *Member:* Danish Bar Association. *LANGUAGES:* Danish, Norwegian, Swedish and English.

ASSOCIATES

MARIANNE JYBAEK, born Stavning, Denmark, February 21, 1958; admitted, 1987, Denmark; 1988, High Court of Denmark. *Education:* University of Aarhus; University of London (LL.M., 1989). *Member:* Danish Bar Association. *LANGUAGES:* Danish, Norwegian, Swedish and English. *PRACTICE AREAS:* Commercial Law; EC-Law.

STIG LYNGHØJ NIELSEN, born Hørsholm, Denmark, February 2, 1951; admitted, 1980, Denmark; 1994, Supreme Court of Denmark. *Education:* University of Copenhagen. *Member:* Danish Bar Association. *LANGUAGES:* Danish, Norwegian, Swedish and English. *PRACTICE AREAS:* Real Property Law; Construction Law.

BO BERNER HANSEN, born Charlottenlund, Denmark, September 12, 1962; admitted, 1991, Denmark; 1992, High Court of Denmark. *Education:* University of Copenhagen. *Member:* Danish Bar Association. *LANGUAGES:* Danish, Norwegian, Swedish and English.

ARTUR BUGSGANG, born Ringe, Denmark, July 6, 1957; admitted, 1992, Denmark; 1993, High Court of Denmark. *Education:* University of Copenhagen. *Member:* Danish Bar Association. *LANGUAGES:* Danish, Norwegian, Swedish, English and German. *PRACTICE AREAS:* Tax Law.

PHILIP RENDTORFF, born Gentofte, Denmark, March 27, 1964; admitted, 1993, Denmark and City Court of Denmark; 1994, High Court of Denmark. *Education:* University of Copenhagen. *Member:* Danish Bar Association. *LANGUAGES:* Danish, Norwegian, Swedish and English.

MIRIAM HOLM-NIELSEN, born Copenhagen, Denmark, October 27, 1964; admitted, 1993, Denmark and City Court of Denmark. *Education:* University of Copenhagen. *Member:* Danish Bar Association. *LANGUAGES:* Danish, Norwegian, Swedish, English and French.

METTE LARSEN, born Frederiksvaerk, Denmark, August 1, 1962; admitted, 1993, Denmark and City Court of Denmark. *Education:* University of Copenhagen. *Member:* Danish Bar Association. *LANGUAGES:* Danish, Norwegian, Swedish, English and Russian.

ESBEN KJAER, born Gentofte, Denmark, September 16, 1967; admitted, 1994, Denmark and City Court of Denmark. *Education:* University of Copenhagen. *Member:* Danish Bar Association. *LANGUAGES:* Danish, Norwegian, Swedish and English.

CHARLOTTE BERG, born Kalundborg, Denmark, May 31, 1964; admitted, 1994, Denmark and City Court of Denmark. *Education:* University of Copenhagen. *Member:* Danish Bar Association. *LANGUAGES:* Danish, Norwegian, Swedish, English and German.

LIND & CADOVIUS

38, ØSTERGADE
DK-1100 COPENHAGEN K, DENMARK
Telephone: 45 33 33 81 00
Cable Address: "Cophjur"
Telex: 21016 cphlaw
Fax: 45 33 33 81 01

General Practice. Corporation, Contract, Constructing, Financing, Computer, Insurance, Banking, Energy, Labor, Maritime and Tax Law, Business Transfers, Trust and Estates, Succession and Family Law, Litigation.

FIRM PROFILE: The firm was established provides a full range of services to national and international corporate clients and is one of the largest Danish law firms specializing in Commercial law. The firm is associ-

(This Listing Continued)

ated with the Denton Hall Group, England; Heuking Kühn & Partners, Germany; Houthoff, The Netherlands; and Lambert Grohmann Kerres & Deisenberger, Austria.

MEMBERS OF FIRM

POVL HOLM-JØRGENSEN, born Gentofte, Denmark, April 29, 1932; admitted, 1961, Denmark; 1967, Supreme Court of Denmark. *Education:* University of Copenhagen. *Member:* Danish Bar Association. *LANGUAGES:* Danish, English, Norwegian and Swedish. *PRACTICE AREAS:* Succession and Family Law; Litigation.

JØRGEN CADOVIUS, born Copenhagen, Denmark, March 20, 1945; admitted, 1974, Denmark; 1979, Supreme Court of Denmark. *Education:* University of Copenhagen. *Member:* Danish Bar Association. *LANGUAGES:* Danish, English, Norwegian and Swedish. *PRACTICE AREAS:* Company Law; Mergers and Acquisitions; Insolvency.

C.K. KNUDSEN, born Tømmerup, Denmark, May 23, 1945; admitted, 1973, Denmark; 1979, Supreme Court of Denmark. *Education:* University of Copenhagen. *Member:* Danish Bar Association. *LANGUAGES:* Danish, English, Norwegian and Swedish. *PRACTICE AREAS:* Real Estate; Mergers and Acquisitions; Construction Law.

NICOLAI WESTERGAARD, born Copenhagen, Denmark, August 30, 1946; admitted, 1976, Denmark; 1983, Supreme Court of Denmark. *Education:* University of Aarhus; University of Copenhagen. Lecturer, University of Copenhagen, 1972-1973 and 1975-1982. Judge, Labor Court, 1985. *Member:* Danish Bar Association. *LANGUAGES:* Danish, English, German, Norwegian and Swedish. *PRACTICE AREAS:* Labour Law; Insurance Law; Litigation.

JON STOKHOLM, born Copenhagen, Denmark, April 23, 1951; admitted, 1978, Denmark; 1983, Supreme Court of Denmark. *Education:* University of Copenhagen. Trainee, Haight, Gardner, Poor & Havens, New York, 1980-1981. Stanford Business School, 1991. Chairman, Advisory Committee on Tax Matters, Danish Bar Association, 1989. Member of the Bar Council of the Danish Bar Association, 1990. *Member:* Danish Bar Association; International Bar Association, CMI (Danish Branch); International Association for Insurance Law (Danish Branch). *LANGUAGES:* Danish, English, German, Norwegian and Swedish. *PRACTICE AREAS:* Contract Law; Energy Law; Tax Law.

FRANTZ PALLUDAN, born Gentofte, Denmark, April 4, 1953; admitted, 1981, Denmark; 1986, Supreme Court of Denmark. *Education:* University of Copenhagen. *Member:* Danish Bar Association. International Bar Association. *LANGUAGES:* Danish, English, Norwegian and Swedish. *PRACTICE AREAS:* Banking and Financing; Mergers and Acquisitions; Company Law.

BIRGITTE HORN, born Aalborg, Denmark, April 16, 1958; admitted, 1985, Denmark; 1990, Supreme Court of Denmark. *Education:* University of Copenhagen. *Member:* Danish Bar Association. *LANGUAGES:* Danish, English, Norwegian and Swedish. *PRACTICE AREAS:* Tax Law; Labour Law; Insolvency.

MADS BERENDT, born Copenhagen, Denmark, April 7, 1954; admitted, 1982, Denmark; 1989, Supreme Court of Denmark. *Education:* University of Copenhagen. *Member:* Danish Bar Association. *LANGUAGES:* Danish, English, Norwegian, Swedish and German. *PRACTICE AREAS:* Real Estate; Intellectual Property Rights; Labour Law.

HANS MADSEN, born Copenhagen, Denmark, September 16, 1959; admitted, 1986, Denmark. *Education:* University of Copenhagen; New York University (LL.M., 1990). Trainee, Haight, Gardner, Poor & Havens, New York, 1987-1988. Associate, Skadden, Arps, Slate, Meagher & Flom, 1990-1991. *Member:* Danish Bar Association; American Bar Association. Danish Petroleum Law Society. *LANGUAGES:* Danish, English, Norwegian and Swedish. *PRACTICE AREAS:* Contract Law; Mergers and Acquisitions; Competition Law.

ASSOCIATES

DORTHE SØRUP, born Hjørring, Denmark, December 1, 1957; admitted, 1985, Denmark; 1994, Supreme Court of Denmark. *Education:* University of Aarhus. *Member:* Danish Bar Association. *LANGUAGES:* Danish, English, German, Norwegian and Swedish. *PRACTICE AREAS:* Succession and Family Law; Litigation.

NIELS SCHIERSING, born Copenhagen, Denmark, November 15, 1960; admitted, 1988, Denmark; 1990, High Court of Denmark. *Education:* University of Copenhagen (Law Degree, 1985). *Member:* International Fiscal Association; Danish Bar Association. *LANGUAGES:* Danish, English,

(This Listing Continued)

Norwegian and Swedish. *PRACTICE AREAS:* Tax Law; Corporate Law; Arbitration; Litigation.

CARSTEN CEUTZ, born Copenhagen, Denmark, August 19, 1961; admitted, 1990, Denmark; 1992, High Court of Denmark. *Education:* University of Copenhagen; Trainee, ECC, 1985-1986. *Member:* Danish Bar Association. *LANGUAGES:* Danish, Swedish, English, French and Norwegian. *PRACTICE AREAS:* Intellectual Property Rights; Insolvency; Litigation.

MAX KRASNIK, born Copenhagen, Denmark, August 29, 1963; admitted, 1991, Denmark. *Education:* University of Copenhagen. Trainee, Denton Hall, London, 1994. *Member:* Danish Bar Association; International Bar Association. *LANGUAGES:* Danish, English, French, German, Norwegian and Swedish. *PRACTICE AREAS:* Contract Law; EEC Law; Intellectual Property Rights.

MARIANNE FRIEDLÆNDER, born Copenhagen, Denmark, June 16, 1963; admitted, 1991, Denmark. *Education:* University of Copenhagen; University of Michigan Law School (LL.M., 1993). *Member:* Danish Bar Association. *LANGUAGES:* Danish, English, Norwegian and Swedish. *PRACTICE AREAS:* Corporate Law; Mergers and Acquisitions; Securities Law.

ANDERS AAGAARD, born Copenhagen, Denmark, April 29, 1959; admitted, 1991, Denmark. *Education:* University of Copenhagen; University of Oslo. Trainee: Heuking Kühn Kunz Wojtek, Frankfurt, 1992. *Member:* Danish Bar Association; International Bar Association; CMI, Danish Petroleum Law Society. *LANGUAGES:* Danish, English, French, German, Norwegian and Swedish. *PRACTICE AREAS:* Contract Law; Energy Law; Maritime Law.

LOTTE HUMMELSHØJ, born Aarhus, Denmark, April 2, 1963; admitted, 1992, Denmark and High Court of Denmark. *Education:* University of Copenhagen. *Member:* Danish Bar Association. *LANGUAGES:* Danish, English, French, Norwegian and Swedish. *PRACTICE AREAS:* EEC Law; Corporate Law; Commercial Law.

CHRISTIAN HERSKIND, born Fredericia, Denmark, October 19, 1961; admitted, 1992, Denmark. *Education:* University of Copenhagen; University of Glasgow; University of London (LL.M.). *Member:* Danish Bar Association; International Bar Association. *LANGUAGES:* Danish, English, German, Norwegian and Swedish. *PRACTICE AREAS:* Corporate Law; Tax Law; Commercial Law.

JESS THIERSEN, born Copenhagen, Denmark, February 6, 1965; admitted, 1992, Denmark. *Education:* University of Copenhagen. *Member:* Danish Bar Association. *LANGUAGES:* Danish, English, Norwegian and Swedish. *PRACTICE AREAS:* Litigation; Tax Law; Commercial Law.

METTE BOJE-LARSEN, born Copenhagen, Denmark, August 10, 1966; admitted, 1995, Denmark. *Education:* University of Copenhagen, University of Kent at Canterbury (LL.M.). *Member:* Danish Bar Association. *LANGUAGES:* Danish, English, Norwegian and Swedish. *PRACTICE AREAS:* Commercial Law; Intellectual Property Rights; Insolvency.

LEGAL SUPPORT PERSONNEL

MARTIN LAVESEN

SØREN ZINCK

MAZANTI-ANDERSEN, KORSØ JENSEN & PARTNERE

Established in 1856

69, ST. KONGENSGADE
1264 COPENHAGEN, DENMARK
Telephone: 45-33-143536
FAX: 45-33-111073

Commercial and Corporate Law, Tax Law, Litigation, Arbitration, Mergers, Acquisitions, Property, Financing, Investments, Insurance Law, Product Liability, Construction Law, Offshore Law, Transport Law, Antitrust, EU Law, Bankruptcy, Reconstruction of Companies.

EGON HØGH, born Jutland, Denmark, December 23, 1922; admitted, 1955, Denmark; 1965, Supreme Court of Denmark. *Education:* University of Copenhagen (Master of Law, 1951). *Member:* Danish Bar Association. *LANGUAGES:* Scandinavian and English. *PRACTICE AREAS:* Commercial Law; Cooperative Law; Company Law; Contract Law.

(This Listing Continued)

MAZANTI-ANDERSEN, KORSØ JENSEN & PARTNERE, Copenhagen—Continued

HANS HENRIK GAMBORG, born Copenhagen, Denmark, July 31, 1934; admitted, 1961, Denmark; 1970, Supreme Court of Denmark. *Education:* University of Copenhagen (Master of Law, 1958). *Member:* Danish Bar Association; Society of Defense Lawyers Assigned by the Ministry of Justice. *LANGUAGES:* Scandinavian and English. *PRACTICE AREAS:* Civil Law; Criminal Litigation; Administration of Property Law.

FLEMMING OTZEN, born Elsinore, Denmark, November 16, 1939; admitted, 1972, Denmark; 1975, High Courts of Denmark. *Education:* Copenhagen School of Economics and Business Administration (B.B.A., 1961); University of Copenhagen (Master of Law, 1969). *Member:* Danish Bar Association; International Fiscal Association. *LANGUAGES:* Scandinavian, English and German. *PRACTICE AREAS:* Tax Law; Corporation Law; Commercial Law.

ANDERS COLD, born Copenhagen, Denmark, March 19, 1943; admitted, 1974, Denmark; 1984, Supreme Court of Denmark. *Education:* University of Copenhagen (Master of Law, 1971). Associate Professor, University of Copenhagen, 1971-1977. *Member:* Danish and International Fiscal Associations and International Fiscal Association. *LANGUAGES:* Scandinavian and English. *PRACTICE AREAS:* Mergers and Acquisitions; Commercial Law; Company Law; Tax Law.

J. KORSØ JENSEN, born Odense, Denmark, November 23, 1946; admitted, 1972, Denmark; 1981, Supreme Court of Denmark. *Education:* University of Copenhagen (Master of Law, 1969). Associate Professor, Bankruptcy and Procedural Law, University of Copenhagen, 1970-1983. Assistant to the Maritime and Commercial Court, Bankruptcy Department, 1980. Board of Advisors, University of the Pacific, McGeorge School of Law, European Law Internship Program. *Member:* Copenhagen and Danish (Council Member, 1991—) Bar Associations; International Bar Association (Business Section). *LANGUAGES:* Scandinavian, English and German. *PRACTICE AREAS:* Mergers and Acquisitions; Commercial Law; Bankruptcy Law.

GEORG DEDICHEN, born Copenhagen, Denmark, September 11, 1944; admitted, 1977, Denmark; 1984, Supreme Court of Denmark. *Education:* University of Copenhagen (Master of Law, 1972). Trainee, Joachim Grieg & Co., Oslo, Shipbrokers, 1980-1992. Lecturer on General Law of Transport of Goods, Copenhagen Business College, Niels Brock. *Member:* Danish Bar Association. *LANGUAGES:* Scandinavian, English and French. *PRACTICE AREAS:* Mergers and Acquisitions; Insurance Law; Transport Law; Computer Law.

HANNE MAGNUSSEN, born Copenhagen, Denmark, July 23, 1948; admitted, 1977, Denmark; 1984, Supreme Court of Denmark. *Education:* University of Copenhagen (Master of Law, 1974). Associate Professor, University of Copenhagen, 1974-1977. Legal Aid of Copenhagen, 1971-1986. *Member:* Copenhagen and Danish Bar Associations; Danish Marketing Society. *LANGUAGES:* Scandinavian, English and Italian. *PRACTICE AREAS:* Tax Law; Customs and Excise Law; Agents and Distribution.

JAKOB LUND POULSEN, born Copenhagen, Denmark, June 16, 1955; admitted, 1984, Denmark; 1989, Supreme Court of Denmark. *Education:* University of Copenhagen (Master of Law, 1981). Associate Professor: Procedural Law, University of Copenhagen, 1983—. *Member:* Danish Bar Association; Society of Defense Lawyers Assigned by the Ministry of Justice. *LANGUAGES:* Scandinavian and English. *PRACTICE AREAS:* Industrial Property Rights Law; Company Law; Criminal Litigation.

LISE HØGH, born Copenhagen, Denmark, July 30, 1958; admitted, 1986, Denmark; 1992, Supreme Court of Denmark. *Education:* University of Copenhagen (Master of Law, 1982); College of Europe EEC Law (1983). Lecturer on The Copenhagen School of Economics and Business Administration. *Member:* Danish and International Bar Associations; International Fiscal Association. *LANGUAGES:* Scandinavian, English, French and German. *PRACTICE AREAS:* Company Law; Cooperative Law; EU Law; Mergers and Acquisitions.

MARIANNE JUSTESEN, born Copenhagen, Denmark, May 10, 1959; admitted, 1987, High Courts of Denmark. *Education:* University of Copenhagen (Master of Law, 1984). Lecturer, Copenhagen Commercial School, 1985. Member, AIJA, 1987. *Member:* Danish Bar Association. *LANGUAGES:* Scandinavian, English and German. *PRACTICE AREAS:* Bankruptcy Law; Employment Law.

HELLE HEDEMAN, born Copenhagen, Denmark, November 14, 1963; admitted, 1990, High Courts of Denmark. *Education:* University of

(This Listing Continued)

Copenhagen (Master of Law, 1987); London School of Economics and Political Sciences (LL.M., 1991). *Member:* Danish Bar Association. *LANGUAGES:* Scandinavian and English. *PRACTICE AREAS:* Banking; EU Law; Competition Law.

ROLF USSING, born Copenhagen, Denmark, August 6, 1964; admitted, 1991, Denmark; 1992, High Courts of Denmark. *Education:* University of Copenhagen (Master of Law, 1988). Lecturer, Danish Bar Association, Contract Law, Company Take-overs. *Member:* Danish Bar Association. *LANGUAGES:* Scandinavian and English. *PRACTICE AREAS:* Bankruptcy Law; Litigation.

HENRIK B. SANDERS, born Esslingen, Germany, December 24, 1965; admitted, 1994, Denmark. *Education:* University of Copenhagen (Master of Law, 1991). Lecturer, Niels Brock, Copenhagen Business College, General Law of Transport of Goods. *Member:* Danish Bar Association. *LANGUAGES:* Scandinavian, English and German. *PRACTICE AREAS:* Bankruptcy Law; Transport Law.

MICHAEL JACOBSEN, born Copenhagen, Denmark, March 31, 1967; admitted, 1994, Denmark. *Education:* University of Copenhagen (Master of Law, 1991). *LANGUAGES:* Scandinavian and English. *PRACTICE AREAS:* Commercial Law; Contract Law; Lease Law.

Languages: Danish, English, German, Scandinavian, French and Italian

---

MOLTKE-LETH ADVOKATER

Lawyers Associated Worldwide

(LAW)

AMALIEGADE 12
DK-1256 COPENHAGEN, DENMARK
Telephone: 45.33.11.65.11
Facsimile: 45.33.11.49.11

Association Law, Banking Law, Bankruptcy Law, Civil Law, Commercial Law, Computer Law, Conveyance of Companies Law, Corporate Law, EEC Law, Employment Law, Environmental Law, Inheritance of Control Law, Intangible Law, Law of Succession, Litigation, Penal Law, Real Estate Law, Rent and Lease Law, Tax Law.

MEMBERS OF FIRM

TORBEN MOLTKE-LETH, born Copenhagen, Denmark, March 9, 1940; admitted, 1969, Denmark and High Court of Denmark. *Education:* University of Copenhagen (Master of Law, 1966). *Member:* Copenhagen and Danish Bar Association; International Bar Association; International Fiscal Association. *LANGUAGES:* Scandinavian and English. *PRACTICE AREAS:* Corporate Law; Commercial Law; Tax Law; Real Estate Law.

TORBEN SVEJSTRUP, born Copenhagen, Denmark, March 19, 1943; admitted, 1974, Denmark; 1980, Supreme Court of Denmark. *Education:* University of Copenhagen (Master of Law, 1969). *Member:* Copenhagen and Danish Bar Association. *LANGUAGES:* Scandinavian and English. *PRACTICE AREAS:* Association Law; Intangible Law; Marketing Law.

JØRGEN LANGE, born Copenhagen, Denmark, March 27, 1947; admitted, 1978, Denmark; 1984, Supreme Court of Denmark. *Education:* University of Copenhagen (Master of Law, 1975). Lecturer on Property Law, Danish Bar Association, 1988—. *Member:* Copenhagen and Danish Bar Association. *LANGUAGES:* Scandinavian, English and German. *PRACTICE AREAS:* Property Law; Commercial Law; Bankruptcy Law.

MIKAEL BERNHOFT, born Copenhagen, Denmark, January 22, 1948; admitted, 1977, Denmark; 1982, Supreme Court of Denmark. *Education:* University of Copenhagen (Master of Law, 1973). Associate Professor, University of Copenhagen, 1977-1982. *Member:* Copenhagen and Danish Bar Association. *LANGUAGES:* Scandinavian and English. *PRACTICE AREAS:* Commercial Law; Banking Law; Criminal Litigation.

GRETHE JØRGENSEN, born Copenhagen, Denmark, September 20, 1956; admitted, 1984, Denmark. *Education:* University of Copenhagen (Master of Law, 1981); London School of Economics and Political Sciences (LL.M., 1986). *Member:* Copenhagen and Danish Bar Association; International Fiscal Association; International Association of Young Lawyers; European Lawyers' Union. *LANGUAGES:* Scandinavian and English. *PRACTICE AREAS:* Commercial Law; EEC Law; Corporate Law.

(This Listing Continued)

ASSOCIATES

ANNETT RYE ENGEL, born Copenhagen, Denmark, November 8, 1946; admitted, 1988, Denmark and High Court of Denmark. *Education:* University of Copenhagen (Master of Law, 1985). *Member:* Copenhagen and Danish Bar Association; Danish Association of Housing Law; International Fiscal Association; Danish Association of Young Lawyers; The Foreign Politics Association. *LANGUAGES:* Scandinavian, English and German. *PRACTICE AREAS:* Commercial Law; Corporate Law; Real Estate Law.

BIRGITTE SKJØDT, born Copenhagen, Denmark, September 10, 1956; admitted, 1987, Denmark; 1991, High Court of Denmark. *Education:* University of Copenhagen (Master of Law, 1984). *Member:* Copenhagen and Danish Bar Association; International Fiscal Association. *LANGUAGES:* Scandinavian and English. *PRACTICE AREAS:* Commercial Law; Bankruptcy Law; Employment Law.

ADVOKATFIRMAET B. HELMER NIELSEN

RÅDHUSPLADSEN 4
COPENHAGEN 1550, DENMARK
Telephone: 45 33 14 66 66
Facsimile: 45 33 14 66 67

Brussels, Belgium Office: Avenue Louise 303, B-1050. Telephone: 32 2 644 2862. Telefax: 32 2 640 5231.

Banking, Commercial Matters, Competition, Construction, Corporate, Dumping, Energy and Natural Resources, EEC Practice, Environment, Financing, Industrial Property Rights, Insolvency, International Transactions, Investments, Litigation, Mergers and Acquisitions, Taxation, Real Property and Venture Capital Transactions.

MEMBERS OF FIRM

ERIK CHRINTZ-HANSEN, born Odense, Denmark, March 6, 1927; admitted, 1956, Denmark; 1969, Supreme Court of Denmark. *Education:* University of Copenhagen. *Member:* Copenhagen and Danish Bar Associations. *LANGUAGES:* Scandinavian and English.

KNUD ANKER-MØLLER, born Roskilde, Denmark, January 13, 1931; admitted, 1960, Denmark; 1975, Supreme Court of Denmark. *Education:* University of Copenhagen. *Member:* Copenhagen and Danish Bar Associations. *LANGUAGES:* Scandinavian and English. *PRACTICE AREAS:* Construction Law; Environment Law.

ANDREAS FISCHER, born Copenhagen, Denmark, July 2, 1932; admitted, 1963, Denmark; 1970, Supreme Court of Denmark. *Education:* University of Copenhagen. Co-author, "Karnov's Lovsamling" (annotated edition of Danish statutes). *Member:* Copenhagen, Danish and International Fiscal Associations. *LANGUAGES:* Scandinavian, German and English.

KARL STEPHENSEN, born Copenhagen, Denmark, October 12, 1941; admitted, 1972, Denmark and Supreme Court of Denmark. *Education:* University of Copenhagen. *Member:* Danish Bar Association; Association of Lawyers Appointed by the Maritime and Commercial Court in Copenhagen. *LANGUAGES:* Scandinavian and English. *PRACTICE AREAS:* Insolvency; Corporate Reconstruction.

STEEN HELMER NIELSEN, born Copenhagen, Denmark, March 19, 1944; admitted, 1971, Denmark; 1990, Supreme Court of Denmark. *Education:* University of Copenhagen. *Member:* Danish Bar Association. *LANGUAGES:* Scandinavian and English.

NIELS ERIK NIELSEN, born Copenhagen, Denmark, March 14, 1948; admitted, 1975, Denmark; 1980, Supreme Court of Denmark. *Education:* University of Copenhagen. Author and Lecturer, take-overs, MBO Taxation and venture capital. Member, Copenhagen Court of International Arbitration. *Member:* Copenhagen and Danish Bar Associations. *LANGUAGES:* Scandinavian and English.

TROELS HELMER NIELSEN, born Copenhagen, Denmark, September 6, 1945; admitted, 1976, Denmark; 1988, Supreme Court of Denmark. *Education:* University of Copenhagen. *Member:* Copenhagen and Danish Bar Associations; Danish Association for the Protection of Industrial Property; Danish Association for Copyright Protection; Danish Computer Law Association. *LANGUAGES:* Scandinavian and English.

CHRISTIAN KRUSE MADSEN, born Copenhagen, Denmark, November 11, 1952; admitted, 1979, Supreme Court of Denmark. *Education:*

(This Listing Continued)

University of Copenhagen. *Member:* Copenhagen and Danish Bar Associations. *LANGUAGES:* Scandinavian and English.

OLE ESKE BRUUN, born Copenhagen, Denmark, November 16, 1950; admitted, 1980, Denmark; 1988, Supreme Court of Denmark. *Education:* University of Copenhagen. *Member:* Copenhagen and Danish Bar Associations; Danish Society for Construction. *LANGUAGES:* Scandinavian and English. *PRACTICE AREAS:* Construction Law; Real Estate Law; Company Law; Bankruptcy Law.

JENS AUKEN, born Copenhagen, Denmark, April 15, 1949; admitted, 1982, Denmark; 1987, Supreme Court of Denmark. *Education:* University of Copenhagen. *Member:* Danish Bar Association. *LANGUAGES:* Scandinavian, English and German.

JETTE HASSING RONØE, born Løvel, Denmark, October 24, 1949; admitted, 1986, High Courts of Denmark. *Education:* University of Copenhagen (M.A., French and Italian, 1978; LL.B., 1980); University of Paris, Sorbonne; University of Rome. External Assistant Professor, The Copenhagen School of Economics and Business Administration, French Law and Language. *Member:* Copenhagen and Danish Bar Associations; UIA, Danish Association of European Law and ICC. *LANGUAGES:* Scandinavian, French, English, Italian and German.

ERIK JUSTESEN, born Copenhagen, Denmark, December 28, 1955; admitted, 1985, New York; 1987, Denmark and High Court of Denmark. *Education:* University of Copenhagen; New York University School of Law (Master of Comparative Jurisprudence (MJC) 1983); Boston University - Brussels (Master of Science of Management (MSM) 1984). *Member:* Copenhagen, Danish and New York State Bar Associations; AIJA/IBA. *LANGUAGES:* Scandinavian, English, French and German.

NIELS KORNERUP, born Copenhagen, Denmark, September 3, 1960; admitted, 1987, Denmark; 1989, High Court of Denmark. *Education:* University of Copenhagen; University of Cambridge. Lecturer, University of Copenhagen, Law of Contracts and Torts, 1987—. Lecturer, The Copenhagen School of Economics and Administration, Law on Transport and Commercial Law, 1985-1990. *Member:* Copenhagen and Danish Bar Associations. *LANGUAGES:* Scandinavian and English.

JENS CHR. HESSE RASMUSSEN, born Copenhagen, Denmark, August 27, 1960; admitted, 1990, High Court of Denmark. *Education:* AFS-Scholarship, Los Angeles, USA; University of Copenhagen. *Member:* Copenhagen and Danish Bar Associations. *LANGUAGES:* Scandinavian and English.

ASSOCIATES

JØRGEN HOFFMEYER, born Slangerup, Denmark, November 1, 1918; admitted, 1947, Supreme Court of Denmark. *Education:* University of Copenhagen. *Member:* Copenhagen and Danish Bar Associations; IBA. *LANGUAGES:* Scandinavian, German and English.

SØREN LARSEN, born Copenhagen, Denmark, September 3, 1950; admitted, 1982, Denmark; 1984, High Courts of Denmark. *Education:* University of Copenhagen. *Member:* Danish Bar Association. *LANGUAGES:* Scandinavian and English.

ANNEMARIE KRUSE MADSEN, born Copenhagen, Denmark, February 1, 1952; admitted, 1983, Supreme Court of Denmark. *Education:* University of Copenhagen. *Member:* Copenhagen and Danish Bar Associations. *LANGUAGES:* Scandinavian and English.

CARSTEN PALS, born Copenhagen, Denmark, March 21, 1954; admitted, 1985, Supreme Court of Denmark. *Education:* University of Copenhagen. *Member:* Copenhagen and Danish Bar Association; Danish Lawyers' Fiscal Association. *LANGUAGES:* Scandinavian and English.

NIELS HELLESEN, born Copenhagen, Denmark, August 18, 1960; admitted, 1987, Supreme Court of Denmark. *Education:* University of Copenhagen. *Member:* Copenhagen and Danish Bar Associations. *LANGUAGES:* Scandinavian and English.

TROELS TUXEN, born Copenhagen, Denmark, February 5, 1961; admitted, 1989, High Court of Denmark. *Education:* University of Copenhagen. *Member:* Copenhagen and Danish Bar Associations. *LANGUAGES:* Scandinavian and English. *PRACTICE AREAS:* Insolvency; Corporate Reconstruction.

MICHAEL VINTHER, born Horsens, Denmark, August 8, 1963; admitted, 1990, High Court of Denmark. *Education:* University of Copenhagen. *Member:* Copenhagen and Danish Bar Associations. *LANGUAGES:* Scandinavian, English and German.

(This Listing Continued)

ADVOKATFIRMAET B. HELMER NIELSEN,
Copenhagen—Continued

OLE NORGAARD, born Copenhagen, Denmark, April 22, 1965; admitted, 1991, High Court of Denmark. *Education:* University of Copenhagen; University of Heidelberg, Germany (LL.M.). *Member:* Copenhagen and Danish Bar Associations; AIJA; German-Danish Chamber of Commerce; Danish-German Committee for Trade and Industry. *LANGUAGES:* Scandinavian, German and English.

ANDERS MARTIN HANSEN, born Copenhagen, Denmark, January 3, 1962; admitted, 1991, High Court of Denmark. *Education:* University of Copenhagen. *Member:* Copenhagen and Danish Bar Associations; AIJA. *LANGUAGES:* Scandinavian and English.

MARTIN PETER NAESBY, born Esbjerg, Denmark, April 11, 1961; admitted, 1991, High Court of Denmark. *Education:* University of Copenhagen; University of Bonn, Germany. *Member:* Copenhagen and Danish Bar Associations. *LANGUAGES:* Scandinavian, German and English.

HANS HENRIK CHROIS CHRISTENSEN, born Nr. Snede, Denmark, May 14, 1965; admitted, 1993, Denmark. *Education:* University of Copenhagen. *Member:* Copenhagen and Danish Bar Associations; Danish-German Committee for Trade and Industry. *LANGUAGES:* Scandinavian, English, German and French.

PHILIP RISBJØRN, born Frederiksberg, Denmark, July 11, 1965; admitted, 1994, Denmark and High Court of Denmark. *Education:* University of Copenhagen. *Member:* Copenhagen and Danish Bar Associations. *LANGUAGES:* Scandinavian, English and French. *PRACTICE AREAS:* Construction Law; Insolvency Law.

PIA JUUL NIELSEN, born Copenhagen, Denmark, June 8, 1966; admitted, 1994, Denmark. *Education:* University of Copenhagen. *Member:* Copenhagen and Danish Bar Associations. *LANGUAGES:* Scandinavian and English. *PRACTICE AREAS:* Insolvency Law; Company Law.

FLORENCE ICHON, born Mexico, November 17, 1965; admitted, 1992, Cour d'Appel de Paris. *Education:* University of Aix-Marseille, France (Magistère, D.E.S.S., D.J.C.E.). *LANGUAGES:* French, English, Spanish and Danish. *PRACTICE AREAS:* Mergers and Acquisitions; Commercial Agreements; Banking Law.

STEEN JENSEN, born Frederiksberg, Denmark, April 14, 1966; admitted, 1994, Denmark. *Education:* University of Copenhagen (Master of Laws); University of London. *Member:* Copenhagen and Danish Bar Associations; The British Nordic Lawyers Association. *LANGUAGES:* Scandinavian and English. *PRACTICE AREAS:* Company Law; Contract Law; Mergers and Acquisitions.

NIELSEN & NØRAGER

Law Offices

Established in 1983

FREDERIKSBERGGADE 16
DK-1459 COPENHAGEN K, DENMARK
Telephone: +45 33 11 45 45

Cable Address: Metrolaw
Telefax: +45 33 11 80 81

General Practice, Business Law, Mergers and Acquisitions, Banking and Financing Law, Computer Law, Intellectual Property, Copyright, Patent, Trademark and Entertainment Law, Insurance Law, EEC and International Law, Litigation in the High and Supreme Courts of Denmark.

MEMBERS OF FIRM

OLE FINN NIELSEN, born Copenhagen, Denmark, April 29, 1942; admitted, 1971, Denmark; 1977, Supreme Court of Denmark. *Education:* University of Copenhagen. Lecturer, University of Copenhagen, 1969-1970. *Member:* Copenhagen, Danish and International Bar Associations; Association for the Protection of Industrial Property. *LANGUAGES:* Danish, English and German. *PRACTICE AREAS:* International Contracts; Mergers and Acquisitions; Entertainment Law.

JACOB NØRAGER-NIELSEN, born Nørresundby, Denmark, December 24, 1941; admitted, 1973, Denmark; 1978, Supreme Court of Denmark. *Education:* University of Copenhagen. Author: "Commentary on the Sale of Goods Act," 1979 and 1993; "Purchase on Credit," 1983; "Computer Contracts," 1987. Associate Professor, University of Copenhagen, 1972-1987. *Member:* Copenhagen, Danish and International Bar Associations; Associ-

(This Listing Continued)

ation for the Protection of Industrial Property. *LANGUAGES:* Danish, Swedish, Norwegian and English. *PRACTICE AREAS:* Contract and Business Law; Computer Law; Litigation; Insurance Law.

JØRGEN KJAELDGAARD, born Copenhagen, Denmark, June 20, 1952; admitted, 1981, Denmark; 1992, Supreme Court of Denmark. *Education:* University of Copenhagen. *Member:* Copenhagen, Danish and International Bar Associations; Association Internationale des Jeunes Avocats. *LANGUAGES:* Danish, English, German and French. *PRACTICE AREAS:* Financing and Banking Law; Mergers and Acquisitions; Company and Corporate Law.

ARNE GERLYNG-HANSEN, born Copenhagen, Denmark, March 4, 1956; admitted, 1984, Denmark; 1990, Supreme Court of Denmark. *Education:* University of Copenhagen. Associate Professor, University of Copenhagen, 1987-1991. *Member:* Copenhagen and Danish Bar Associations. *LANGUAGES:* Danish and English. *PRACTICE AREAS:* Insurance Law; Financing Law; Contract Law.

MORTEN ELDRUP-JØRGENSEN, born Aarhus, Denmark, January 26, 1962; admitted, 1988, Denmark. *Education:* University of Copenhagen (Law Degree, 1985); INSEAD, France (M.B.A., 1988). *Member:* Copenhagen and Danish Bar Associations. *LANGUAGES:* Danish, English, French and German. *PRACTICE AREAS:* Mergers and Acquisitions; Company Law; International Contracts.

ASSOCIATES

ERIK BROCKENHUUS-SCHACK, born Halsted, Denmark, May 20, 1946; admitted, 1979, Denmark; 1987, Supreme Court of Denmark. *Education:* University of Aarhus; University of Copenhagen. *Member:* Copenhagen and Danish Bar Associations. *LANGUAGES:* Danish and English. *PRACTICE AREAS:* Commercial Arbitration; Litigation.

JENS RAVNKILDE, born Copenhagen, Denmark, June 17, 1947; admitted, 1989, Denmark. *Education:* University of Copenhagen (Dr. Phil.); Oxford University (B. Phil.); University of California at Berkeley. Former Associate Professor, University of Copenhagen, 1986-1989. *Member:* Copenhagen and Danish Bar Associations. *LANGUAGES:* Danish, English and German. *PRACTICE AREAS:* Insurance Law; Tort; Intellectual Property.

PER NEUMANN, born Copenhagen, Denmark, May 7, 1957; admitted, 1987, Denmark; 1992, High Court of Denmark. *Education:* University of California, San Diego (1976); University of Copenhagen (1982). Producer, National Film School of Denmark, 1987. *Member:* Copenhagen and Danish Bar Associations; International Association of Entertainment Lawyers; Danish Association of Entertainment and Media Law (Chairman). *LANGUAGES:* Danish and English. *PRACTICE AREAS:* Media and Entertainment Law; Motion Picture Finance.

HENRIK NEDERGAARD THOMSEN, born Roskilde, Denmark, January 10, 1965; admitted, 1993, Denmark; 1993, High Court of Denmark. *Education:* University of Copenhagen. *Member:* Copenhagen and Danish Bar Associations; Danish and International Associations for Insurance Law; Danish Association of Environmental Law; Danish Association of European Law. *LANGUAGES:* Danish, Swedish, Norwegian, English and German. *PRACTICE AREAS:* Company and Corporate Law; Financing Law; Insurance Law; Construction Law.

MALENE R. EHLERS, born Copenhagen, Denmark, April 2, 1964; admitted, 1992, New York; 1993, Denmark. *Education:* University of Copenhagen; Duke University School of Law (LL.M.). *Member:* Danish Bar Association; New York Bar Association. *LANGUAGES:* Danish and English. *PRACTICE AREAS:* Media and Entertainment Law; International Contracts.

Languages: Danish, Swedish, Norwegian, English, German and French

---

ADVOKATERNE NIKOLAJ PLADS 25

Established in 1988

NIKOLAJ PLADS 25
1067 COPENHAGEN, DENMARK
Telephone: +45 33 32 26 26
Cable Address: "Parlexden"
Telex: 16600 Fotex dk, att. Parlexden
Telefax: +45 33 32 39 41

General Practice. Taxation, Company, Commercial, Real Estate and Tenancy Law.

(This Listing Continued)

MEMBERS OF FIRM

PETER DYHR, born Hellerup, Denmark, June 25, 1940; admitted, 1971, Denmark; 1978, Supreme Court of Denmark. *Education:* University of Copenhagen (Candidatus Juris, 1963); University of Illinois (Master of Comparative Law, 1964). Author: "Taxation of Stockholders in Foreign Corporations," 1964; "The Definition of Capital Gains," 1976; Regular Correspondent to "Taxation of Companies in Europe"; "Annotated Edition of the Capital Gains Tax Code" (with Bent Colding), 1966; "Taxation of Multinational Corporations in Denmark," 1979. Lecturer, Danish Administrative School, 1966-1970. Member, Danish Ministry of Taxes, International Taxation Division, 1964-1970. Founder and Member of the Parlex Group of European Lawyers, 1971—. *Member:* Copenhagen and Danish (Member, Committee on Taxation, 1984-1991) Bar Associations; World Association of Lawyers; International Fiscal Association. *LANGUAGES:* Scandinavian, English, French and German. *PRACTICE AREAS:* Taxation Company Law; International Trade Law.

STEEN CHRISTENSEN, born Copenhagen, Denmark, February 20, 1944; admitted, 1970, Denmark; 1976, Supreme Court of Denmark. *Education:* University of Copenhagen (Candidatus Juris, 1967). *Member:* Copenhagen and Danish (Member, Committee on Tenancy Law, 1982-1985) Bar Associations. *LANGUAGES:* Scandinavian, English, German and French. *PRACTICE AREAS:* Litigation; Commercial Law; Real Estate.

ANNE LOUISE HUSEN, born Kongens Lyngby, Denmark, March 6, 1954; admitted, 1983, Denmark. *Education:* University of Copenhagen (Candidata Juris, 1979). Lecturer: Danish Bar Association, 1985—and Tenancy Law, University of Copenhagen, 1988—. *Member:* Copenhagen and Danish Bar Associations. *LANGUAGES:* Scandinavian, English and German. *PRACTICE AREAS:* Tenancy Law; Administration of Real Estate; Family Law.

HANS HENRIK LESCHLY, born Randers, Denmark, June 14, 1939; admitted, 1983, Denmark. *Education:* University of Copenhagen (candidatus juris, 1965); University of Wisconsin (1960-1961); IMEDE (1970-1971). *Member:* Copenhagen and Danish Bar Associations. *LANGUAGES:* Scandinavian, English, German and French. *PRACTICE AREAS:* Commercial Law; Real Estate; Employment Law.

PETER TOMMERUP, born Slagelse, Denmark, January 28, 1951; admitted, 1985, Denmark. *Education:* University of Copenhagen (Candidatus Juris, 1977). *LANGUAGES:* Scandinavian, English and German. *PRACTICE AREAS:* Building Law; Condominiums.

ASSOCIATE

CHARLOTTE FOX MAULE ARUP, born June 15, 1965; admitted, 1994, Denmark. *Education:* University of Copenhagen (candidata juris, 1989). *Member:* Copenhagen and Danish Bar Associations. *LANGUAGES:* Scandinavian, English and German. *PRACTICE AREAS:* Litigation; Taxation; Decedent's Estates.

Languages: Scandinavian, English, French and German.

REPRESENTATIVE CLIENTS: Buhrmann-Tetterode N.V.; Electrolux, Denmark; Braun Electric, Denmark, A/S.
REFERENCE: Mr. Murray I. Litmans, Pittsburgh, Pa.

NORSKER & JACOBY

(Incorporating Marstrand's Law Offices)

Established in 1900

3 KVAESTHUSGADE

1251 COPENHAGEN K, DENMARK

Telephone: 33 11 08 85
Telefax: 33 93 75 30

International Business Law, Industrial Property, Intellectual Property, Copyrights, Patents, Trademarks, Insurance, Corporate and Competition Law, Mergers and Acquisitions, Computer and Media Law, Civil Litigation, Corporate Rescue, Probate, Family Law and General Practice.

FIRM PROFILE: *The firm was established in 1900 and offers a full range of legal service. It is well known for its industrial property and commercial law. The client base is European and North Central American. This 7 Partner firm has a legal support staff of 11 lawyers and 21 office administrators.*

(This Listing Continued)

MEMBERS OF FIRM

M. MARSTRAND-JØRGENSEN, born Copenhagen, Denmark, December 12, 1947; admitted, 1972, Denmark. *Education:* University of Copenhagen (LL.M., 1972). Assistant Professor, University of Copenhagen, 1972-1988. Author: "Company Law in Europe," Kluwer, 1981; "IP-Yearbook," 1994. *Member:* Danish Bar Association; Danish Law Society; International Bar Association; AIPPI; ECTA (Committee Member); INTA. *LANGUAGES:* Scandinavian, English, German, French and Spanish. *PRACTICE AREAS:* Intellectual Property; Copyrights; Patents; Trademarks; Insurance; Professional Indemnity.

NILS-ERIK NORSKER, born Copenhagen, Denmark, February 4, 1943; admitted, 1968, Denmark. *Education:* University of Denmark (LL.M., 1968). *Member:* AIJA, Danish Bar Association and Danish Law Society; International Bar Association. *LANGUAGES:* Scandinavian and English. *PRACTICE AREAS:* Arbitration; Litigation.

ERIK HOVGAARD, born Aalborg, Denmark, February 26, 1951; admitted, 1977, Denmark. *Education:* University of Aarhus (LL.M., 1977). *Member:* Danish Bar Association; Danish Law Society. *LANGUAGES:* Scandinavian and English. *PRACTICE AREAS:* Construction Law; Company Law; Real Estate; Taxation.

FLEMMING KRAGH HANSEN, born Nakskov, Denmark, December 31, 1951; admitted, 1977, Denmark. *Education:* University of Denmark (LL.M., 1977). Assistant Professor, University of Copenhagen, 1985. *Member:* IBA, Danish Bar Association and Danish Law Society. *LANGUAGES:* Scandinavian and English. *PRACTICE AREAS:* Banks and Banking; Securities; Commercial Law; Environmental Law.

SYS ROVSING KOCH, born Aarhus, Denmark, May 19, 1953; admitted, 1977, Denmark. *Education:* University of Denmark (LL.M, 1977). Assistant Professor, University of Copenhagen, 1977-1982. Appointed Advocate at the Probate Court of Copenhagen, 1990. *Member:* Danish Bar Association, Danish Law Society; Association of Danish Family Lawyers (Member of the Board, 1990); Law Society Commission (Member on Family, Inheritance and Probate Law, 1991). *LANGUAGES:* Scandinavian, English and German. *PRACTICE AREAS:* Family Law; Probate; Trusts and Estates.

PETER TAUBY SØRENSEN, born Copenhagen, Denmark, June 1, 1951; admitted, 1977, Denmark. *Education:* University of Copenhagen (LL.M., 1977). *Member:* Danish Bar Association; Danish Law Society. *LANGUAGES:* Scandinavian and English. *PRACTICE AREAS:* Transportation; Insolvency; Unfair Competition.

SVEN-ERIK POULSEN, born Frederiksvaerk, Denmark, February 25, 1944; admitted, 1972, Denmark. *Education:* University of Copenhagen (LL.M., 1972). Trustee, Maritime and Commercial Court of Copenhagen. *Member:* Danish Bar Association; Danish Law Society. *LANGUAGES:* English, German and Scandinavian. *PRACTICE AREAS:* Criminal Law; Bankruptcy.

ASSOCIATES

JOHN SKJØTH, born Vejle, Denmark, October 30, 1946; admitted, 1980, Denmark. *Education:* University of Aarhus (LL.M., 1977). *Member:* Danish Bar Association; Danish Law Society. *LANGUAGES:* Scandinavian and English. *PRACTICE AREAS:* Arbitration; Litigation; Labour; Employment.

PREBEN STOKKENDAL, born Copenhagen, Denmark, December 18, 1955; admitted, 1984, Denmark. *Education:* University of Copenhagen (LL.M., 1984). *Member:* Danish Bar Association; Danish Law Society. *LANGUAGES:* Scandinavian and English. *PRACTICE AREAS:* Corporate Law; Products Liability.

CARSTEN TOLDERLUND, born Aarhus, Denmark, August 8, 1959; admitted, 1987, Denmark. *Education:* University of Copenhagen (Master of Law, 1983); University of London (LL.M., 1984). *Member:* Danish Bar Association; Danish Law Society; The Law Society of England. *LANGUAGES:* Scandinavian, English, French, German and Spanish. *PRACTICE AREAS:* Mergers & Acquisitions; International Law; Admiralty; Maritime Law.

FINN TRÄFF, born Copenhagen, Denmark, November 14, 1962; admitted, 1987, Denmark. *Education:* University of Copenhagen (LL.M., 1987). *Member:* AIJA, Danish Bar Association; Danish Law Society. *LANGUAGES:* Scandinavian, English, German and Italian. *PRACTICE AREAS:* European Community Law; Property.

JESPER TROMMER VOLF, born Copenhagen, Denmark, October 16, 1962; admitted, 1988, Denmark. *Education:* University of Copenhagen

(This Listing Continued)

NORSKER & JACOBY, Copenhagen—Continued

(LL.M., 1988). *Member:* Danish Bar Association; Danish Law Society. *LANGUAGES:* English, German, French, Russian and Scandinavian. *PRACTICE AREAS:* Finance; Reorganisation; Business Law.

PETER SCHÄFER, born Copenhagen, Denmark, November 26, 1967; admitted, 1991, Denmark. *Education:* University of Copenhagen (LL.M., 1991). *Member:* Danish Bar Association; Danish Law Society. *LANGUAGES:* Scandinavian, English and German. *PRACTICE AREAS:* Energy; Computers; Entertainment and the Arts.

HENRIK SJØRSLEV, born Nykøbing Mors, Denmark, June 2, 1966; admitted, 1991, Denmark. *Education:* University of Copenhagen (LL.M., 1991). *Member:* Danish Bar Association; Danish Law Society. *LANGUAGES:* English, French, German and Scandinavian. *PRACTICE AREAS:* White Collar Crime; Bankruptcy; Torts.

PETER FREDERIKSEN, born Vesleby, Denmark, July 25, 1964; admitted, 1989, Denmark. *Education:* Frederikssund (1983); University of Copenhagen (Cand.jur., 1989). *LANGUAGES:* English and Scandinavian. *PRACTICE AREAS:* Bankruptcy; Banking.

LONE BRANDENBORG, born Copenhagen, Denmark, May 21, 1968; admitted, 1994, Denmark. *Education:* University of Copenhagen (LL.M., 1994). *LANGUAGES:* English, German and Scandinavian. *PRACTICE AREAS:* Family Law; Estates; Banking.

LISBET ANDERSEN, born Copenhagen, Denmark, January 6, 1963; admitted, 1994, Denmark. *Education:* University of Copenhagen (LL.M., 1994); Copenhagen School of Commerce (MBA, 1990). *LANGUAGES:* English, German, French and Scandinavian. *PRACTICE AREAS:* Intellectual Property; Litigation.

OF COUNSEL

KNUD NORSKER, born Copenhagen, Denmark, January 19, 1917; admitted, 1942, Denmark. *Education:* University of Copenhagen (LL.M., 1942). *Member:* Danish Bar Association; Danish Law Society.

NYBORG & RØRDAM

Established in 1983

ST. KONGENSGADE 77
1264 COPENHAGEN K, DENMARK
Telephone: +45 33 12 45 40
Telefax: +45 33 93 45 40

Litigation in the Courts of Denmark. Company Law, Mergers and Acquisitions, National and International Contracts and Business Law. Banking and Finance, Administrative Law, Bankruptcy Law, Intellectual Property, Copyright, Patent, Trademark and Entertainment Law, Competition Law, EEC and International Law. National and International Tax Law.

MEMBERS OF FIRM

JOHN HAVE, born December 15, 1951; admitted, 1979, Denmark; 1986, Supreme Court of Denmark. *Education:* University of Copenhagen (1976). *Member:* Copenhagen and Danish Bar Associations; The Association of Liquidators (associated to the Maritime and Commercial Court, Probate Division). *LANGUAGES:* Scandinavian and English. *PRACTICE AREAS:* Bankruptcy; Insolvency; Reconstruction Law.

ERIK NYBORG, born February 4, 1948; admitted, 1983, Denmark; 1989, Supreme Court of Denmark. *Education:* University of Copenhagen. Member, Board of Directors, Danish Film Authors. *Member:* Copenhagen, Danish and International Bar Associations; Danish Association of Intellectual Property Law; Association of Entertainment and Media Law. *LANGUAGES:* Scandinavian and English. *PRACTICE AREAS:* Business Law; Copyright Law; Entertainment Law.

THOMAS RØRDAM, born October 17, 1952; admitted, 1983, Denmark; 1991, Supreme Court of Denmark. *Education:* University of Århus; University of California at Berkeley (LL.M.). Author: Textbook, "Property Law and Articles on Property Law and Criminal Law," Danish Law Reviews. Associate Professor, University of Copenhagen, 1984-1992. *Member:* Copenhagen and Danish Bar Associations (Chairman, Committees of: Human Rights and Criminal Law; Member, General Council); Association For Labour Law; Association for Criminal Law; Association of Entertainment and Media Law. *LANGUAGES:* Scandinavian and English. *PRACTICE AREAS:* Litigation; Criminal Law; Labour Law; Entertainment Law.

(This Listing Continued)

LARS KJELDSEN, born June 8, 1955; admitted, 1985, Denmark; 1991, Supreme Court of Denmark. *Education:* University of Copenhagen; Nordic Institute of Maritime Law, Oslo. *Member:* Copenhagen and Danish Bar Associations; Danish Tax Scientific Association. *LANGUAGES:* Scandinavian and English. *PRACTICE AREAS:* Litigation; National and International Tax Law; Business Law.

LARS LOKDAM, born March 13, 1961; admitted, 1990, Denmark; 1994, High Court of Denmark. *Education:* University of Århus. *Member:* Copenhagen and Danish Bar Associations; Danish Company Lawyers Association; The European Corporate Lawyers Association; Danish Association of European Law. *LANGUAGES:* Scandinavian and English. *PRACTICE AREAS:* Business Law; Company Law; Mergers and Acquisitions; Competition Law.

HANS ABILDSTRØM, born May 2, 1962; admitted, 1992, Denmark. *Education:* University of Copenhagen. *Member:* Copenhagen and Danish Bar Associations; Association of Entertainment and Media Law. *LANGUAGES:* Scandinavian and English. *PRACTICE AREAS:* Intellectual Property; Entertainment Law; Business Law; Bankruptcy Law.

BIRGITTE BRØBECH, born December 16, 1957; admitted, 1993, Denmark. *Education:* University of Copenhagen. *Member:* Copenhagen and Danish Bar Associations. *LANGUAGES:* Scandinavian and English.

OPPENHEJM, LUND & PARTNERE

Established in 1877

6, ESPLANADEN
DK-1263 COPENHAGEN K, DENMARK
Telephone: 45-33-123537; 45-33-143537
Cable Address: "Opraol"
Telex: 16 119 DANLEX DK
Telefax: 45-33-320609

FIRM PROFILE: Oppenhejm, Lund & Partners is an association between originally 5 law firms of which the oldest was established on May 24, 1877 by the grandfather of the current senior partner. The association has 11 partners each doing general business practices and each specializing in specific areas. The association offers a full range of legal services and puts great emphasis on the personal contact between the individual lawyer and the client. The association is a member of P.A.L.S., a legal club with representatives in 17 European countries.

SV. OPPENHEJM, born Copenhagen, Denmark, 1920; admitted, 1948, Denmark; 1958, Supreme Court. *Education:* University of Copenhagen. *LANGUAGES:* English, German, French, Swedish, Norwegian and Italian. *PRACTICE AREAS:* International Commercial Relations; International Tax Law; Legal Affairs regarding Italy.

PAUL LUND, born Kolding, Denmark, January 16, 1929; admitted, 1960, Denmark; 1968, Supreme Court. *Education:* University of Copenhagen. *LANGUAGES:* English, German and Scandinavian. *PRACTICE AREAS:* Corporate and Environmental Law.

HANS SCHULTZER, born Copenhagen, Denmark, 1928; admitted, 1958, Denmark; 1964, Supreme Court. *Education:* University of Copenhagen. *LANGUAGES:* English, French, Swedish and Norwegian. *PRACTICE AREAS:* Licenses and other Business Contracts.

PALLE HAARGAARD, born Frederiksberg, Denmark, January 18, 1939; admitted, 1963, Denmark; 1971, High Court; 1976, Supreme Court. *Education:* University of Copenhagen. *LANGUAGES:* English, German, Norwegian and Swedish. *PRACTICE AREAS:* General Business Practice.

MADS GIERDING, born Copenhagen, Denmark, October 14, 1952; admitted, 1979, Denmark; 1989, Supreme Court. *Education:* University of Copenhagen. *LANGUAGES:* English, German and Scandinavian. *PRACTICE AREAS:* Finance, Leasing and Banking Law.

CARSTEN BRINK, born Copenhagen, Denmark, July 29, 1953; admitted, 1977, Denmark; 1986, Supreme Court. *Education:* University of Copenhagen. *LANGUAGES:* English, German, Italian and Scandinavian. *PRACTICE AREAS:* Insolvency Law; Mergers and Acquisitions; Labor Law; Marketing Law.

KELD PARSBERG, born Frederiksberg, Denmark, October 26, 1953; admitted, 1977, Denmark; 1986, Supreme Court. *Education:* University of Copenhagen. *LANGUAGES:* English, German, French, Italian, Norwegian and Swedish. *PRACTICE AREAS:* Transportation; Maritime Law.

(This Listing Continued)

STEFFEN SCHLEIMANN, born Copenhagen, Denmark, April 8, 1955; admitted, 1982, Denmark; 1987, High Court. *Education:* University of Copenhagen. *LANGUAGES:* English and Scandinavian. *PRACTICE AREAS:* Tax and VAT Law.

KJELD JØRGENSEN, born May 29, 1956; admitted, 1981, Denmark; 1992, Supreme Court. *Education:* University of Copenhagen. *LANGUAGES:* English, German and Scandinavian. *PRACTICE AREAS:* Construction Law; Property and Real Estate; Distributorship.

KENT B. BRIXTOFTE, born Køge, Denmark, December 16, 1958; admitted, 1984, Denmark. *Education:* University of Copenhagen. *LANGUAGES:* English, German and Scandinavian. *PRACTICE AREAS:* Real Estate.

SØREN NORINGRIIS, born Aalborg, Denmark, May 7, 1965; admitted, 1994, Denmark. *Education:* University of Copenhagen and Aarhus. Lecturer, University of Copenhagen. *LANGUAGES:* English and Scandinavian. *PRACTICE AREAS:* Insolvency Law.

PEDERSEN & JANTZEN

NYROPSGADE 45

COPENHAGEN V 1602, DENMARK

Telephone: 33 12 95 12

Telex: 19261 LEXACT DK

Facsimile: 33 12 95 15

General Practice and Arbitration, Banking, Bankruptcy, Commercial Law, Common Market Law, Construction, Contract Law, Corporate Law, Electronic Data Processing, Environment Law, Investments, Monopolies, Real Estate, Restrictive Trade Practices, Taxation, Trademarks.
The law firm is admitted to all Danish Courts.

MEMBERS OF FIRM

JØRGEN PEDERSEN, born Rødovre, Denmark, May 1, 1919; admitted, 1946, Denmark; 1947, High Court; 1956, Supreme Court. *Education:* University of Copenhagen (candidatus juris, 1943). Lecturer on Law, Commercial College, Copenhagen, 1950-1962. Manager, Tax Department, 1945-1951. Business Manager, The Danish Association for Author's Rights, 1960-1964. Member of the Register Selection of the Danish Ministry of Justice, 1970. *Member:* Copenhagen Bar Association (Member of Board, 1961-1964); Danish Bar Association (Chairman, 1973-1977). *LANGUAGES:* Scandinavian, English and German.

KRISTIAN LUND KRISTENSEN, born Ribe, Denmark, November 29, 1933; admitted, 1961, Denmark; 1963, High Court; 1971, Supreme Court. *Education:* University of Aarhus, Denmark (Candidatus Juris, 1961). Lecturer, University of Aarhus, 1958-1959. *Member:* Danish Bar Association (Member, Contact Group with the Danish Commerce and Companies Agency); International Bar Association; Danish Association of Company Law. *LANGUAGES:* Scandinavian, English and German.

POUL JOHANNESSEN, born Hjørring, Denmark, March 23, 1937; admitted, 1965, Denmark; 1967, High Court; 1972, Supreme Court. *Education:* University of Aarhus, Denmark (Candidatus Juris, 1962). Lecturer, Administrative Law: University of Aarhus, 1962; University of Copenhagen, 1963-1966. *Member:* Danish Bar Association (Chairman, permanent council on Administrative Law, 1980—). *LANGUAGES:* Scandinavian, English and German.

LEIF VILHELM ARNESEN, born Slagelse, Denmark, July 10, 1941; admitted, 1970, Denmark; 1971, High Court. *Education:* University of Wisconsin (International Law, 1962-1963); University of Copenhagen (Candidatus Juris, 1967); Columbia University (M.B.A., 1972). Partner, A.P. Møller Shipping, 1981-1989. *Member:* Danish Bar Association; International Bar Association. *LANGUAGES:* Scandinavian and English.

PER CARSTEN PEDERSEN, born Frederiksberg, Denmark, May 3, 1943; admitted, 1970, Denmark; 1972, High Court; 1980, Supreme Court. *Education:* University of Copenhagen (Candidatus Juris, 1967). *Member:* Danish Bar Association; Danish Association of Company Law. *LANGUAGES:* Scandinavian and English.

KLAUS FIALA, born Frederiksberg, Denmark, February 8, 1945; admitted, 1974, Denmark and High Court; 1984, Supreme Court. *Education:* University of Copenhagen (Candidatus Juris, 1969). Author: "Corporations Law," Håndbog i Selskabsret, Danish Federation of Crafts and Small Industries, 1973. Trustee, Maritime and Commercial Court of Copenhagen. *Member:* Danish Bar Association. *LANGUAGES:* Scandinavian, English and German.

(This Listing Continued)

OSCAR MOSGAARD, born Esbjerg, Denmark, December 7, 1956; admitted, 1984, Denmark; 1983, High Court. *Education:* State University of New York, Buffalo (1979); University of Aarhus (Candidatus Juris, 1981); University of London, Kings College (Postgraduate, 1982); McGeorge School of Law, Salzburg (Postgraduate, 1987). Co-Editor: "European Economic Interest Groupings" and "Business Law in Europe," both Kluwer. Lecturer on Law: Commercial College, Esbjerg, 1981; Commercial College, Copenhagen, 1983-1985; University of Copenhagen, 1983-1985; University of Copenhagen, Company Law, 1988-1993; Lecturer on Company Law, Danish Bar Association, 1987; Lecturer on Corporate Law, Danish Association of Chartered Accountants, 1993. Stage at Lebuhn & Puchta, Hamburg, Germany, 1989; Stage at Roche Hardcastles (now Osborne, Clark Roche), London, 1982. *Member:* Copenhagen and Danish Bar Association; Nordic Union of Lawyers; International Bar Association; E.L.A.; AIJA; L'Association Européenne Juridique et Fiscal (Danish Chairman); German-Nordic Law Association; Danish Association of Company Law. *LANGUAGES:* Scandinavian, English and German.

KARSTEN KIELLAND, born Copenhagen, Denmark, August 17, 1955; admitted, 1984, Denmark and High Court. *Education:* University of Copenhagen (Candidatus Juris, 1981). Lecturer, Company Law, Danish Bar Association. *Member:* Copenhagen and Danish Bar Associations; Danish Association for the Protection of Industrial Property; International Association of Young Lawyers (AIJA); Danish Computer Law Association; Danish Association for Copyright Protection; Danish Association of Company Law. *LANGUAGES:* Danish, Norwegian and English.

CARSTEN MATHIESEN, born Sønderborg, Denmark, April 7, 1958; admitted, 1985, Denmark; 1988, High Court. *Education:* Aarhus University (Candidatus Juris, 1982). *Member:* Danish Bar Association; Association of Copenhagen Lawyers; German-Nordic Law Association. *LANGUAGES:* Scandinavian, German and English.

JAKOB STILLING, born Copenhagen, Denmark, May 23, 1961; admitted, 1987, Denmark; 1989, High Court. *Education:* University of Copenhagen (Candidatus Juris, 1984). Trainee, EEC, Economic and Social Committee, Brussels, 1982. *Member:* Danish Bar Association. *LANGUAGES:* Scandinavian, German and English.

DAN TERKILDSEN, born Copenhagen, Denmark, May 10, 1963; admitted, 1991, Denmark. *Education:* University of Copenhagen (Candidatus Juris, 1987). Lecturer, Commercial Law, University of Copenhagen. *Member:* Danish Bar Association. *LANGUAGES:* Danish, English and German.

KAMILLA KREBS, born Virum, Denmark, October 4, 1963; admitted, 1989, Denmark; 1993, High Court. *Education:* University of Copenhagen (Candidatus Juris, 1989). *Member:* Danish Bar Association. *LANGUAGES:* Scandinavian and English.

HÁKUN DJURHUUS, born Fanø, Denmark, October 12, 1963; admitted, 1992, Denmark; 1993, High Court. *Education:* University of Aarhus (Candidatus Juris, 1989). *Member:* Copenhagen and Danish Bar Association; AIJA; Danish Society of Construction Law; Danish Society of Environmental Law; Danish Association of Company Law. *LANGUAGES:* Scandinavian and English.

CHRISTIAN LUNDGREN, born Virum, Denmark, September 16, 1966; admitted, 1994, Denmark. *Education:* University of Copenhagen. Teacher, Commercial Law, University of Copenhagen. *Member:* Danish Bar Association; International Bar Association (Section on Business Law; Committee C, Antitrust and Trade Law; Committee X, International Franchising); AIJA; Danish Association of Company Law. *LANGUAGES:* Scandinavian, English and French.

PLESNER & LUNOE

34, ESPLANADEN

DK 1263 COPENHAGEN, DENMARK

Telephone: +45 33 121133

Telefax: +45 33 120014

Telex: 27467 Lunoe dk

Brussels, Belgium Office: Rue de la Loi 23, B-1040. Telephone: 2-287-2000. Telefax: 2-231-1661.

General Practice, Corporation, EC Law, International Contracts, Litigation and Arbitration, Patents, Trademarks and Copyright, Computer Law, Telecommunication, Media, Antitrust and Trade Practices, Tax, Real Estate, Trust and Estates, Banking, Construction and Insurance Law, Insolvency, Energy and Products Liability.

(This Listing Continued)

PLESNER & LUNOE, Copenhagen—Continued

MEMBERS OF FIRM

SVEND LUNOE, born Copenhagen, Denmark, October 22, 1901; admitted, 1935, Denmark; 1962, Supreme Court of Denmark. *Education:* University of Copenhagen (Master of Law). *Member:* Danish Bar Association. *LANGUAGES:* Danish, Swedish, Norwegian, English and German.

MOGENS PLESNER, born Copenhagen, Denmark, January 22, 1920; admitted, 1948, Denmark; 1958, Supreme Court of Denmark. *Education:* University of Copenhagen (Master of Law). *Member:* Danish and International Bar Associations; Danish Association for the Protection of Industrial Property (President, 1980—); International Association for the Protection of Industrial Property (President, Danish Group, 1980—); Danish Lawyers' Association (Chairman, Disciplinary Board, 1981-83); LES; ECTA. *LANGUAGES:* Danish, Swedish, Norwegian, English and German.

JØRGEN BALLHAUSEN, born Gentofte, Denmark, February 23, 1929; admitted, 1956, Denmark; 1969, Supreme Court of Denmark. *Education:* University of Copenhagen (Master of Law). *Member:* Danish Bar Association. *LANGUAGES:* Danish, Swedish, Norwegian, English and German.

CARSTEN TVEDE-MØLLER, born Copenhagen, Denmark, May 30, 1935; admitted, 1963, Denmark; 1970, Supreme Court of Denmark. *Education:* Bowdoin College, Maine and University of Copenhagen. Lecturer on Corporate Law, University of Copenhagen, 1971-1973. *Member:* Danish Bar Association; Copenhagen Society of Advocates (Member of Board, 1970-1975). *LANGUAGES:* Danish, Swedish, Norwegian, English and German.

HENRIK HOLM-NIELSEN, born Copenhagen, Denmark, February 14, 1938; admitted, 1965, Denmark; 1967, High Court of Denmark; 1971, Supreme Court of Denmark. *Education:* University of Copenhagen (Master of Law). Assistant Professor, Civil Law, University of Copenhagen, 1967-1986. Lecturer on Industrial Property, 1968-1986. Assistant to the District Attorney of the High Court, 1972—. *Member:* Danish and International Bar Associations; Danish Law Society (Board Member, 1985—); Danish Copyright Association; Danish Association for the Protection of Industrial Property; International Association for the Protection of Industrial Property; LES. *LANGUAGES:* Danish, Swedish, Norwegian, English and German.

KAREN DYEKJAER-HANSEN, born Denmark, February 21, 1940; admitted, 1972, Denmark; 1973, High Court of Denmark; 1979, Supreme Court of Denmark. *Education:* University of Copenhagen (Master of Law, 1964); New York University (LL.M., 1968; M.C.J., 1968). Department of Justice, Denmark, 1964-1966. Associate, Cleary, Gottlieb, Steen & Hamilton, New York, 1968-1969 and 1974-1975. Assistant Judge, Court of Hørsholm, Denmark, 1969-1970. Assistant Professor, University of Copenhagen, 1969-1987. Appointed Member, Permanent Governmental Board on Rules of Procedure for Litigation, 1987—. *Member:* Danish and International Bar Associations; Danish Association of European Law; Danish Association for the Protection of Industrial Property; Union Avocats European (Regional Delegate); ECTA; LIDA. *LANGUAGES:* Danish, Swedish, Norwegian, English, German and French.

CHRISTIAN BOJSEN-MØLLER, born Vejle, Denmark, March 17, 1944; admitted, 1974, Denmark; 1981, Supreme Court of Denmark. *Education:* University of Copenhagen (Master of Law, 1971). *Member:* Danish Bar Association; International Bar Association. *LANGUAGES:* Danish, Swedish, Norwegian and English.

PETER-ULRIK PLESNER, born Copenhagen, Denmark, July 20, 1946; admitted, 1974, Denmark; 1976, High Court of Denmark; 1981, Supreme Court of Denmark. *Education:* University of Copenhagen (Master of Law, 1971). *Member:* Danish Bar Association; International Association for the Protection of Industrial Property. *LANGUAGES:* Danish, Swedish, Norwegian, English and German.

JENS JORDAHN, born Aalborg, Denmark, May 8, 1944; admitted, 1974, Denmark; 1979, Supreme Court of Denmark. *Education:* University of Copenhagen. *Member:* Danish Bar Association; International Bar Association; Danish Society of Construction and Consulting Law. *LANGUAGES:* Danish, Swedish, Norwegian, English, French and German.

STEEN E. CHRISTENSEN, born Copenhagen, Denmark, April 2, 1947; admitted, 1975, Denmark; 1985, Supreme Court of Denmark. *Education:* University of Copenhagen (Master of Law). *Member:* Danish Bar Association; International Bar Association. *LANGUAGES:* Danish, Swedish, Norwegian, English and German.

(This Listing Continued)

MIKAEL ROSENMEJER, born Aabenraa, Denmark, May 15, 1947; admitted, 1977, Denmark; 1986, Supreme Court of Denmark. *Education:* University of Copenhagen. Lecturer on Law, University of Copenhagen, 1974-1979. *Member:* Danish Bar Association; International Bar Association; Danish Insurance Law Association (President, 1988—); AIDA (Deputy Secretary General, 1988—); AIDA Working Parties on Products Liability and on Pollution and Insurance; President of AIDA's VIII World Congress, 1990. Danish Society of Consulting and Construction Law; Danish Society of Computer Law. *LANGUAGES:* Danish, Swedish, Norwegian, English and German.

PER HAAKON SCHMIDT, born Frederiksberg, Denmark, February 22, 1953; admitted, 1981, Denmark; 1986, High Court of Denmark; 1986, Supreme Court. *Education:* University of Copenhagen (Master of Law, 1978; Dr. Juris. [LL.D.], 1989); Duke University, North Carolina (LL.M., 1983). Assistant Professor, University of Copenhagen, 1980-1982. Assistant District Attorney, 1984—. Trainee, Haight, Gardner, Poor & Havens, 1983-1984 *Member:* Danish Bar Association; International Association for the Protection of Industrial Property; Danish Copyright Association. *LANGUAGES:* Danish, Swedish, Norwegian, English and German.

PETER WENGLER-JØRGENSEN, born New York, New York, May 16, 1955; admitted, 1983, Denmark and High Court of Denmark; 1989, Supreme Court of Denmark. *Education:* University of Copenhagen (Master of Law, 1980); New York University (M.J.C., 1984). Assistant Professor, Commercial Law, University of Copenhagen, 1984-1986. *Member:* Danish Bar Association; International Bar Association. *LANGUAGES:* Danish, Swedish, Norwegian, English and German.

JENS ZILSTORFF, born Copenhagen, Denmark, May 31, 1955; admitted, 1984, Denmark. *Education:* University of Copenhagen (Master of Law). *Member:* Danish Bar Association; Copenhagen Society of Advocates. *LANGUAGES:* Danish, Swedish, Norwegian, English, German and French.

ZYGMUNT S. AUSTER, born Stettin, Poland, August 5, 1956; admitted, 1984, High Court of Denmark; 1989, Supreme Court of Denmark. *Education:* University of Copenhagen (Master of Law, 1981); Copenhagen School of Economics and Business Administration (Economical Degree, 1979). *Member:* Danish Law Society; Danish Bar Association; Danish Association for the Protection of Industrial Property. *LANGUAGES:* Danish, Swedish, Norwegian, English, German and Polish.

CHRISTIAN TH. KJØLBYE, born Copenhagen, Denmark, August 22, 1957; admitted, 1985, Denmark and High Court of Denmark; 1991, Supreme Court of Denmark. *Education:* University of Copenhagen (Master of Law, 1982); New York University (LL.M., 1987). Assistant Professor, University of Copenhagen, 1987-1988. *Member:* Danish and International Bar Associations; International Association for the Protection of Industrial Property; Young Lawyers International Association (AIJA). *LANGUAGES:* Danish, Swedish, Norwegian, English, French and German.

ANNE WORM-PETERSEN, born Copenhagen, January 4, 1960; admitted, 1986, Denmark. *Education:* University of Copenhagen (Master of Law). *Member:* Danish Bar Association. *LANGUAGES:* Danish, Swedish, Norwegian, English and German.

TORBEN BONDROP, born Frederiksberg, Denmark, January 27, 1958; admitted, 1987, Denmark and High Court of Denmark. *Education:* University of Copenhagen (Master of Law). *Member:* Danish Bar Association; International Association for Insurance Law; AIDA (Danish Section, Secretary to the Board, 1989); Young Lawyers' International Association (AIJA); International Association for the Protection of Industrial Property. *LANGUAGES:* Danish, Swedish, Norwegian, English and German.

SENIOR ASSOCIATES

TINA REISSMANN, born Esbjerg, Denmark, May 26, 1960; admitted, 1990, Denmark and High Court of Denmark. *Education:* University of Copenhagen (Master of Law, 1987). *LANGUAGES:* Danish, Swedish, Norwegian, English and German.

PEER MEISNER, born Copenhagen, Denmark, March 9, 1964; admitted, 1991, Denmark and High Court of Denmark. *Education:* University of Copenhagen (Master of Law, 1988). *LANGUAGES:* Danish, Swedish, Norwegian and English.

TINA CLAUSEN, born Copenhagen, Denmark, May 16, 1963; admitted, 1991, Denmark and High Court of Denmark. *Education:* University of Copenhagen (Master of Law, 1988). *LANGUAGES:* Danish, Swedish, Norwegian, English and German.

(This Listing Continued)

CHARLOTTE BERTELSEN, born Copenhagen, Denmark, August 18, 1962; admitted, 1993, Denmark and High Court of Denmark. *Education:* University of Copenhagen (Master of Law 1987). *LANGUAGES:* Danish, Swedish, Norwegian, English and French.

PETER BJERREGAARD, born Greenwich, Connecticut, USA, September 2, 1960; admitted, 1993, Denmark and High Court of Denmark. *Education:* University of Copenhagen (Master of Law, 1990). *LANGUAGES:* Danish, Swedish, Norwegian, English, German and French.

MERETHE ECKHARDT-HANSEN, born Copenhagen, Denmark, January 29, 1964; admitted, 1993, Denmark and High Court of Denmark. *Education:* University of Copenhagen (Master of Law, 1990). Lecturer on Competition Law and Intellectual Property Law, University of Copenhagen, 1993. *LANGUAGES:* Danish, Swedish, Norwegian, English, German and French.

SØREN STENDERUP JENSEN, born Sønderborg, Denmark, March 8, 1961; admitted, 1993, Denmark. *Education:* University of Copenhagen (Master of Law, 1987); European University Institute, Florence, Italy (Doctor of Laws, 1991). Assistant Professor, University of Copenhagen. *LANGUAGES:* Danish, Swedish, Norwegian, English, German and Italian.

JACOB CHRISTENSEN, born Aarhus, Denmark, November 7, 1967; admitted, 1994, Denmark and High Court of Denmark. *Education:* University of Copenhagen (Master of Law, 1991). *LANGUAGES:* Danish, Swedish, Norwegian, English, German and French.

PONTOPPIDAN, PHILIP & PARTNERS

VOGNMAGERGADE 7
DK-1120 COPENHAGEN K, DENMARK
Telephone: 45 33 13 11 12
Cable Address: LAWOFFICE
Telex: 15211 Lawoff dk
Telefax: 45 33 32 80 45

General Tax Practice, General Legal Practice, Administrative, Advertising, Agricultural, Antitrust, Arbitration, Banking, Bankruptcy, Commercial, Competition, Construction, Corporate, Distributorship, Agency and Franchise, EEC, Entertainment, Food and Drug Regulations, Foreign Investments, Health, Hospital and Malpractice, Insurance, International Contracts, International Private, Maritime and Admiralty, Oil and Mining, Product Liability, Property, Real Estate and Transportation Law, Litigation. Mergers and Acquisitions.

MEMBERS OF FIRM

ALLAN PHILIP, born Copenhagen, Denmark, August 30, 1927; admitted, 1957, Supreme Court of Denmark. *Education:* Universities of Copenhagen, Dijon, Cambridge, Chicago, Berkeley (Candidatus Juris, Doctor Juris, Diploma in Comparative Legal Studies, Docteur en Droit HC - Clermont-Ferrand). Lecturer of Law, 1953-1963 and Professor of Law, 1963-1975, University of Copenhagen. President, Comité Maritime International. *Member:* Danish Bar Association; Institut de Droit International; Maritime Law Association of the United States (Honorary Member). *LANGUAGES:* Danish, English, French, German, Swedish and Norwegian.

MOGENS GAARDEN, born Copenhagen, Denmark, July 20, 1946; admitted, 1974, Supreme Court of Denmark. *Education:* University of Copenhagen. *Member:* Danish Bar Association; Danish Society of Advocates. *LANGUAGES:* Danish, English, Norwegian and Swedish.

HENNING HANSEN, born Copenhagen, Denmark, December 10, 1949; admitted, 1983, Supreme Court of Denmark. *Education:* University of Copenhagen; The Copenhagen School of Economics and Business Administration. *Member:* Danish Bar Association; Danish Society of Advocates. *LANGUAGES:* Danish, English, German, Norwegian and Swedish.

JESPER ROTHE, born Copenhagen, Denmark, September 26, 1955; admitted, 1984, Supreme Court of Denmark. *Education:* University of Copenhagen. *Member:* Danish Bar Association; Danish Society of Advocates. *LANGUAGES:* Danish, English, French, German, Swedish and Norwegian.

COUNSEL

HJALTE RASMUSSEN, born Copenhagen, Denmark, 1940. *Education:* Universities of Copenhagen, Aarhus and Michigan (Candidatus Juris, PhD, Doctor Juris). Professor of European Community Law, The Copenhagen School of Economics and Business Administration, The European Institute for Public Administration (Maastricht) and the College of Europe

(This Listing Continued)

(Burges). Chairman of the Dutch Society for European Studies. President, European Community Studies Association. Member, Conseil Universitaire (Jean Monnet programme). *LANGUAGES:* Danish, English, French, German, Swedish and Norwegian..

OLE JØRGEN PONTOPPIDAN, born Copenhagen, Denmark, April 4, 1919; admitted, 1949, Supreme Court of Denmark. *Education:* University of Copenhagen (Candidatus Juris). *Member:* Danish Bar Association. *LANGUAGES:* Danish, English, German, Swedish and Norwegian.

ASSOCIATES

TROELS THORSEN, born Sakskøbing, June 7, 1957; admitted, 1984, Denmark; 1985, High Court of Denmark. *Education:* Universities of Copenhagen and Illinois; Southern Denmark Business School. *Member:* Danish Bar Association; Danish Society of Advocates. *LANGUAGES:* Danish, English, German, Norwegian and Swedish.

PEER B. PETERSEN, born Magleby, Denmark, July 8, 1960; admitted, 1991, High Court of Copenhagen. *Education:* University of Copenhagen. *Member:* Danish Bar Association. *LANGUAGES:* English, German, Norwegian, Swedish and Danish.

JENS HJORTSKOV, born Hareskov, Denmark, December 19, 1963; admitted, 1991, High Court of Denmark. *Education:* University of Copenhagen; King's College London; Scandinavian Institute of Maritime Law (Oslo). *LANGUAGES:* English, German, Norwegian, Swedish and Danish.

KENNETH HEDEGAARD, born Odense, Denmark, June 15, 1965. *Education:* University of Copenhagen. *LANGUAGES:* English, German, Norwegian, Swedish and Danish.

THORBJØRN SWANSTRØM, born Odense, Denmark, September 5, 1968. *Education:* University of Copenhagen. *LANGUAGES:* Scandinavian, English, German and French.

BO SMITH, born Kalundborg, Denmark, November 13, 1964. *Education:* University of Copenhagen; University of Kiel, Germany (LL.M.); College of Europe, Bruges, Belgium (M.A.E.S.). *LANGUAGES:* Danish, English, French, German and Swedish.

HELLE MEINECHE, born Hornsyld, Denmark, June 10, 1964. *Education:* University of Copenhagen. *LANGUAGES:* Danish, English and French.

Languages: Danish, English, German, French, Norwegian and Swedish.

QVIST, DAHL & PARTNERS, ADVOKATAKTIESELSKAB

PILESTRAEDE 58, 4.
1112 COPENHAGEN K, DENMARK
Telephone: +45 33 12 45 22
Fax: +45 33 93 60 23

Associated Brussels, Belgium Office: Stanbrook and Hooper S.C., European Community Lawyers, Rue du Taciturne 42, 1040. Telephone: (32 2) 230 50 59. Telex: 61975 Stalaw b. Telecopier: (32 2) 230 57 13.

Associated Hamburg, Germany Office: Curschmann, Rollenhagen & Partner, Baumwall 7, P.O. Box 113111, 20421. Telephone: (49 4) 0 36 95 90. Telex: 211 630 JUS D. Telecopier: (49 40) 36 95 936.

Associated Lisbon, Portugal Office: Noronha E. Andrade, Cardoso Alves E. Associados, Rua das Amoreiras 23-2, 1200. Telephone: (351 1) 3875948/69. Telecopier: (3511) 387 980.

Associated London, England Office: Stanbrook & Henderson, 2 Harcourt Buildings, Temple EC4Y 9DB. Telephone: (44 71) 353 01 01. Telecopier: (44 71) 404 52 58.

Associated Paris, France Office: Cabinet Leva & Associes, 109 Avenue Henri-Martin, 75116. Telephone: (33 1) 45 04 51 00. Telecopier: (33 1) 45 04 22 79.

Areas of Commercial Law, such as e.g. Corporation, Mergers and Acquisition, Contract, Construction, Real Estate, Financing, Competition, Intellectual Property Law, Environment, Bankruptcy, Agency and Distribution, Employment, Insurance, Tax, International Private Law, Telecommunications, Transport as well as Litigation and Arbitration.

FIRM PROFILE: Qvist, Dahl & Partners is the Danish partner of the European firm of Stanbrook & Partners. Apart from the Danish clientele Qvist, Dahl & Partners advices a large number of international clients , and over the last half century, the firm has built up a particular strong

(This Listing Continued)

QVIST, DAHL & PARTNERS, ADVOKATAKTIESELSKAB, Copenhagen—Continued

practice within Franco-Danish, Hispano-Danish and German-Danish commercial relations.

MEMBERS

FRANTZ DAHL, born 1929; admitted, 1962, Denmark. *Education:* University of Aarhus Law School (Master of Law, 1952). Representative, Danish Bar and Law Society in the governing board of the UIA. Chairman, Danish Section of the ICJ. Chairman, Human Rights Commission of the Danish Bar and Law Society. Vice President, The Copenhagen Society of Jurists. Secretary General, Hispano-Danish Business Counsel. *LANGUAGES:* English, German, French, Spanish and the Scandinavian languages.

MIKAEL FRYDLUND, born 1946; admitted, 1975, Denmark. *Education:* University of Copenhagen Law School (Master of Law, 1972). Board Member of Danish Companies. *LANGUAGES:* English and the Scandinavian languages.

PREBEN GAMST, born 1957; admitted, 1986, Denmark. *Education:* University of Copenhagen Law School (Master of Law, 1983). Lecturer, Education of Accountants. Board Member of Danish Companies. *LANGUAGES:* English and the Scandinavian languages.

BERTIL JACOBI, born 1939; admitted, 1969, Denmark. *Education:* University of Copenhagen Law School (Master of Law, 1963). Delegate, Danish Bar and Law Society of Union Internationale des Avocats (UIA). Board Member of Danish Companies. *LANGUAGES:* English, French, German and the Scandinavian languages.

TOM PALUDAN, born 1935; admitted, 1963, Denmark. *Education:* University of Copenhagen Law School (Master of Law, 1960). Board Member of Danish Companies. *LANGUAGES:* English, German and the Scandinavian languages.

BIRGIT PHILIPP, born 1943; admitted, 1989, Denmark. *Education:* University of Copenhagen Law School (Master of Law, 1986). Secretary General, Danish Section of ICJ. Board Member of the Hispano-Danish Business Counsil and the Business Club of Portugal in Denmark. *LANGUAGES:* Spanish, Portuguese, English, French, German and the Scandinavian languages.

IB QVIST, born 1927; admitted, 1959, Denmark. *Education:* University of Aarhus Law School (Master of Law, 1952). Board Member of Danish Companies, Financial Institutions and Foundations. *LANGUAGES:* English and the Scandinavian languages.

BJARNE RASMUSSEN, born 1954; admitted, 1982, Denmark. *Education:* University of Copenhagen Law School (Master of Law, 1979). Publicly Elected Member, Assessment Committee, Municipality of Gladsaxe, 1978-1985. Deputy Mayor, City Counsil in Gladsaxe. Board Member of Danish Companies. *LANGUAGES:* English and the Scandinavian languages.

MICHAEL SVENDSEN, born 1949; admitted, 1977, Denmark. *Education:* University of Copenhagen Law School (Master of Law, 1989). Lecturer, Comparative Law, The Copenhagen Business School. Head of the Legal Department, Association of Commercial Agents of Denmark. Member, Legal Counsel of the Danish Chamber of Commerce. Member, Commission on International Commercial Practice "ICC-Denmark". *LANGUAGES:* English, German and the Scandinavian languages.

HENRIK TEIDE, born 1945; admitted, 1975, Denmark. *Education:* University of Copenhagen Law School (Master of Law, 1972). Lecturer, Property and Financing Law, University of Copenhagen, 1972-1989. Board Member of Danish Companies. *LANGUAGES:* English and the Scandinavian languages.

ANDERS TORBØL, born 1946; admitted, 1986, Denmark. *Education:* University of Copenhagen Law School (Master of Law, 1972). Lecturer, Community Law, Denmark's International Study Programme (Business Section, University of Copenhagen. Visiting Professor, EEC-law, Nebraska State University, 1987. Member, Board of Franco-Danish Chamber of Commerce. Member, Danish Council for European Politics. *LANGUAGES:* French, English, German and the Scandinavian languages.

ANDERS WORSØE, born 1958; admitted, 1992, Denmark. *Education:* University of Copenhagen Law School (Master of Law, 1989). Author: Articles for International Publications. Lecturer, EC-law, University of Copenhagen, 1991-1993. Admitted as Danish Counsel in Hamburg. *LAN-*

(This Listing Continued)

GUAGES: English, German, Spanish, French and the Scandinavian languages.

ASSOCIATES

JESPER ANDERSSON, born 1966; admitted, 1993, Denmark. *Education:* University of Copenhagen Law School (Master of Law, 1990). Lecturer, Commercial Law, University of Copenhagen, 1993—. *LANGUAGES:* English, German and the Scandinavian languages.

HANS U.V. PEDERSEN, born 1964; admitted, 1990, Denmark. *Education:* University of Copenhagen Law School (Master of Law, 1988). *LANGUAGES:* English, German and the Scandinavian languages.

ERIK LARSSON, born 1951; admitted, 1982, Denmark. *Education:* Efterslaegten (1971);University of Copenhagen Law School (Master of Law, 1979). Author: Articles in Various Publications. Lecturer, Financial Law, University of Copenhagen. Board Member, of Danish Companies and Public Bodies. *LANGUAGES:* English, German and the Scandinavian languages.

QVISTE & PARTNERS
22 AMALIEGADE
DK-1256 COPENHAGEN, DENMARK
Telephone: +45 33 91 33 00
Telex: 16750 QLAW
Telefax: +45 33 91 33 63

International Tax Planning, Taxation, Wills and International Inheritance Planning, Commercial, Corporation, Contracts, Mergers and Acquisitions, Banking, Securities, Trust, Forestry and Agriculture, Litigation.

MEMBERS OF FIRM

JØRN QVISTE, born Copenhagen, Denmark, February 15, 1943; admitted, 1975 Denmark; 1991, Supreme Court of Denmark. *Education:* University of Copenhagen (Law Degree, 1972). *Member:* Danish Bar Association; International Bar Association; International Fiscal Association; The International Academy of Estate and Trust Law. *LANGUAGES:* Scandinavian and English. *PRACTICE AREAS:* National and International Tax; International Succession; Corporations.

KLAVS VON LOWZOW, born Denmark, September 29, 1958; admitted, 1986, Denmark and High Court Denmark. *Education:* University of Aarhus (Law Degree, 1983). *Member:* Copenhagen and Danish Bar Associations. *LANGUAGES:* Scandinavian, English and German. *PRACTICE AREAS:* Corporations; International Contracts; Agriculture and Forestry.

ASSOCIATES

JACOB MONBERG, born Copenhagen, Denmark, August 27, 1963; admitted, 1991, Denmark; 1994, High Court of Denmark. *Education:* University of Copenhagen (Law Degree, 1988). *Member:* Danish Bar Association,. *LANGUAGES:* Scandinavian and English. *PRACTICE AREAS:* Taxation; Trusts and Foundations; Inheritance.

OLE THYREGOD, born Copenhagen, Denmark, October 29, 1964; admitted, 1992, Denmark. *Education:* University of Copenhagen (Law Degree, 1989). *LANGUAGES:* Scandinavian and English. *PRACTICE AREAS:* Taxation; Inheritance; Corporations.

MICHAEL GORM MADSEN, born Copenhagen, Denmark, February 16, 1966; admitted, 1993, Denmark. *Education:* University of Copenhagen (Law Degree, 1990). *LANGUAGES:* Scandinavian and English. *PRACTICE AREAS:* Corporation; Taxation.

REUMERT & PARTNERS
BREDGADE 26
DK-1260 COPENHAGEN K, DENMARK
Telephone: +45 33 93 39 60
Cable Address: "MARITIMELAW"
Telex: 16339 mtlaw dk
Telefax: +45 33 93 39 50

London, England Office: One Knightrider Court, EC4V 5JP. Telephone: +44 71 236 4406. Telex: 915952. Telefax: +44 71 236 4599.

General Business Practice, Corporate, Tax, Banking and Finance, Bankruptcy, EEC, Intellectual Property, Construction, Insurance, Litigation and International Arbitration, Real Estate, Ship Building and Financing, Aviation, Shipping and Maritime, Energy and Offshore and Transportation Law.

(This Listing Continued)

MEMBERS OF FIRM

FINN HJALSTED, born Copenhagen, Denmark, January 2, 1928; admitted, 1958, Denmark; 1966, Supreme Court of Denmark. *Education:* University of Copenhagen (Law Degree, 1953); University of Paris; McGill University, Quebec, Canada (LL.M., in International Aviation Law, 1960). External Lecturer on Aviation Law, University of Copenhagen, 1962-1968. Chairman of the Board of Directors of Danish War Insurance for Ships and the Danish War Insurance for Cargo. *Member:* Danish Bar Association; International Bar Association; Comité Maritime International; Union International des Avocats; Institute Iberoamericano de Derecho Aeronautico y del Especio de la Aviaction Commercial; Royal Aeronautical Society. *LANGUAGES:* Danish, English, French and Scandinavian. *PRACTICE AREAS:* Maritime Law; Aviation Law; Transportation Law; Insurance Law; International Arbitration Law.

OLAF ESKILDSEN, born Copenhagen, Denmark, May 24, 1934; admitted, 1964, Denmark; 1969, Supreme Court of Denmark. *Education:* University of Copenhagen (Law Degree, 1961). *Member:* Danish Bar Association; Copenhagen Bar Association; AIPPI; Ecta; International Trade Mark Association (INTA) and The Danish Copyright Society. *LANGUAGES:* Danish, English and Scandinavian. *PRACTICE AREAS:* Industrial Property Rights Law; Unfair Competition Law; Commercial Law.

BENT NIELSEN, born Randers, Denmark, June 17, 1939; admitted, 1965, Denmark; 1971, Supreme Court of Denmark. *Education:* University of Aarhus (Law Degree, 1961); Scandinavian Institute of Maritime Law, Oslo, Norway. Author: "CMI's Report to IMO on draft salvage convention", (1989). *Member:* Danish Bar Association; International Bar Association; Comité Maritime International (Titular Member). *LANGUAGES:* Danish, English and Scandinavian. *PRACTICE AREAS:* Maritime Law; Insurance Law.

PETER PREIS, born Slinfold, England, June 18, 1944; admitted, 1972, Denmark; 1979, Supreme Court of Denmark. *Education:* University of Copenhagen (Law Degree, 1969); Scandinavian Institute of Maritime Law, Oslo, Norway. Lecturer on Law, University of Copenhagen, 1969-1973, *Member:* Danish Bar Association; Copenhagen Bar Association; Danish Insurance Association. *LANGUAGES:* Danish, English and Scandinavian. *PRACTICE AREAS:* Corporate Law; Commercial and Banking Law; Finance Law; Mergers and Acquisitions Law; Stock Market Flotations Law; Construction Law.

SVEN ROSENMEYER PAULSEN, born Aabenraa, Denmark, January 23, 1947; admitted, 1975, Denmark; 1982, Supreme Court of Denmark. *Education:* University of Copenhagen (Law Degree, 1971); Scandinavian Institute of Maritime Law, Oslo, Norway (1972). *Member:* Danish Bar Association; International Bar Association; Comité Maritime International. *LANGUAGES:* Danish, English, German, Dutch and Scandinavian. *PRACTICE AREAS:* Project Financing Law; Leasing Law; Maritime Law.

ULRIK JACOBSEN, born Copenhagen, Denmark, May 30, 1948; admitted, 1978, Denmark; 1985, Supreme Court of Denmark. *Education:* University of Copenhagen (Law Degree, 1975). *Member:* Danish Bar Association; International Bar Association; Danish Energy Law Society. *LANGUAGES:* Danish, English, German and Scandinavian. *PRACTICE AREAS:* Banking and Finance Law; Corporate Law; Mergers and Acquisitions Law; Energy Law; Natural Resources Law.

MARIANNE PHILIP, born Copenhagen, Denmark, July 14, 1957; admitted, 1983, Denmark; 1989, Supreme Court of Denmark. *Education:* University of Copenhagen (Law Degree, 1980); Duke University, North Carolina, USA (LL.M., 1983). *Member:* Danish Bar Association; Comité Maritime International. *LANGUAGES:* Danish, English, German and Scandinavian. *PRACTICE AREAS:* Corporate Law; Banking and Finance Law; Bankruptcy Law; Mergers and Acquisitions Law; Commercial Law.

DORTE WAHL, born Frederiksberg, Denmark, June 21, 1956; admitted, 1983, Denmark; 1992, Supreme Court of Denmark. *Education:* University of Copenhagen (Law Degree, 1980). *Member:* Danish Bar Association; Copenhagen Bar Association; AIPPI; Ecta; PTMG; International Trade Mark Association (INTA); The Danish Copyright Society. *LANGUAGES:* Danish, English and Scandinavian. *PRACTICE AREAS:* Industrial Property Rights Law; Unfair Competition Law; Commercial Law.

CHRISTIAN HENNINGS, born Odense, Denmark, February 9, 1954; admitted, 1984, Denmark; 1991, Supreme Court of Denmark. *Education:* University of Copenhagen (Law Degree, 1981). Lecturer on Law at the Copenhagen Business School, 1990-1991. *Member:* Danish Bar Association; Copenhagen Bar Association; Danish Insurance Association; International Bar Association; Comité Maritime International. *LANGUAGES:* Danish,

(This Listing Continued)

English, German, Dutch and Scandinavian. *PRACTICE AREAS:* Maritime and Transport Law; Project and Ship Financing Law; Insurance Law.

CARSTEN RAASTEEN, born Roskilde, Denmark, July 4, 1958; admitted, 1985, Denmark; 1990, Supreme Court of Denmark. *Education:* University of Copenhagen (Law Degree, 1982). Lecturer on Law: University of Copenhagen, 1986-1988; Copenhagen Business School, 1990-1991. *Member:* Danish Bar Association; International Bar Association. *LANGUAGES:* Danish, English and Scandinavian. *PRACTICE AREAS:* Banking Law; Commercial Contracts Law; Business Organization Law.

HENRIK THAL JANTZEN, born Copenhagen, Denmark, April 13, 1959; admitted, 1986, Denmark; 1991, Supreme Court of Denmark. *Education:* University of Copenhagen (Law Degree, 1983). *Member:* Danish Bar Association, Copenhagen Bar Association; Comité Maritime International; International Bar Association and Danish Insurance Association. *LANGUAGES:* Danish, English and Scandinavian. *PRACTICE AREAS:* Maritime and Insurance Law; Shipping and Transportation Law.

JENS ROSTOCK-JENSEN, born Portland, Oregon, USA, June 26, 1957; admitted, 1986, Denmark; 1991, Supreme Court of Denmark. *Education:* University of Oregon ; University of Copenhagen (Law Degree, 1983). *Member:* Danish Bar Association; Copenhagen Bar Association; Comité Maritime International; International Association for Insurance Law; Danish Energy Law Society; Nordic Society for Aviation Law (Member of Board, 1991—). *LANGUAGES:* Danish, English, German and Scandinavian. *PRACTICE AREAS:* Maritime Law; Insurance Law; Product Liability Law; Aviation Law.

PER ZERMAN, born Copenhagen, Denmark, September 8, 1958; admitted, 1985, Denmark; 1986, Danish High Court. *Education:* University of Copenhagen (Law Degree, 1982); The London School of Economics and Political Science (LL.M., 1987). Author: "Service of Writs Abroad", Danish Law Society's Gazette ("Advokaten") 1981; "Taking of Evidence Abroad", Danish Law Society's Gazette (Advokaten"), 1982; "Investment in the People's Republic of China," 1987; *Member:* Danish Bar Association; Copenhagen Bar Association; The Danish Law Society's Working Group on Information on the EC Single Market (1992). *LANGUAGES:* Danish, English and Scandinavian. *PRACTICE AREAS:* Banking and Finance Law; Mergers and Acquisitions Law; Commercial Law.

ASSOCIATES

SUZANNE HELSTEEN, born Copenhagen, Denmark, March 17, 1949; admitted, 1976, Denmark; 1986, Supreme Court of Denmark. *Education:* University of Copenhagen (Law Degree, 1973); Sorbonne, Paris (Certificat du Centre Universitaire d'Etudes des Communautés Européennes, 1977). *Member:* Danish Bar Association; Copenhagen Bar Association. *LANGUAGES:* Danish, English, French and Scandinavian. *PRACTICE AREAS:* Construction Law; Real Property Law; Environment Law; Energy Law; General Corporate and Commercial Law.

HANS HENRIK SKJØDT, born Frederikshavn, Denmark, March 21, 1952; admitted, 1980, Denmark; 1986, Supreme Court of Denmark. *Education:* University of Copenhagen, (Law Degree, 1977). *Member:* Danish Bar Association; International Fiscal Association (IFA); AIPPI, The Danish Copyright Society. *LANGUAGES:* Danish, English and Scandinavian. *PRACTICE AREAS:* Tax Law; Industrial Property Rights Law; Company Law.

KIM RASMUSSEN, born Denmark, January 18, 1963; admitted, 1989, Denmark and Danish High Court; 1991, New York. *Education:* University of Copenhagen (Law Degree, 1986); New York University School of Law (LL.M., 1990). Foreign Legal Intern, Watson, Farley & Williams, New York, 1990-1991. *Member:* Danish Bar Association; Danish Association of European Law. *LANGUAGES:* Danish, English and Scandinavian. *PRACTICE AREAS:* Corporate Law; Commercial Law; Banking and Finance Law.

NIELS GRAM-HANSSEN, born Copenhagen, Denmark, January 15, 1960; admitted, 1990, Denmark; 1993, Danish High Court. *Education:* University of Copenhagen (Law Degree, 1987). *Member:* Danish Bar Association; Copenhagen Bar Association. *LANGUAGES:* Danish, English and Scandinavian. *PRACTICE AREAS:* Corporate Law; Construction Law; Real Estate Law.

HANS KRISTIAN VAD HANSEN, born Skjern, Denmark, May 17, 1963; admitted, 1994, Denmark. *Education:* University of Copenhagen (Law Degree, 1987); University of Exeter, Great Britain (LL.M., 1988). *Member:* Danish Bar Association; Copenhagen Bar Association. *LANGUAGES:* Danish, English, French and Scandinavian. *PRACTICE*

(This Listing Continued)

REUMERT & PARTNERS, Copenhagen—Continued

AREAS: EEC Law; Company and Corporate Law; Financing Law; Competition Law; Real Estate Law.

SØREN JOHANSEN, born Copenhagen, Denmark, January 16, 1965; admitted, 1992, Denmark and Danish High Court. *Education:* University of Wisconsin; University of Copenhagen (Law Degree, 1989). *Member:* The Danish Bar Association. *LANGUAGES:* Danish, English, German and Scandinavian. *PRACTICE AREAS:* Financing Law; Corporate Law; Bankruptcy and Insolvency Law; General Business Law.

NICOLAI LINDGREEN, born Copenhagen, Denmark, March 20, 1967; admitted, 1993, Denmark; 1994, Danish High Court. *Education:* University of Copenhagen (Law Degree, 1990). *Member:* Danish Bar Association; The Danish Copyright Society. *LANGUAGES:* Danish, English and Scandinavian. *PRACTICE AREAS:* Industrial Property Rights Law; Competition Law; EC Law.

MORTEN PIHL-ANDERSEN, born Copenhagen, Denmark, December 22, 1966; admitted, 1993, Denmark. *Education:* University of Copenhagen (Law Degree, 1990). Lecturer on Law, University of Copenhagen, 1992—. *Member:* Danish Bar Association. *LANGUAGES:* Danish, English and Scandinavian. *PRACTICE AREAS:* Company and Corporate Law; Commercial Law; Real Estate Law.

SØREN TRUELSEN, born Copenhagen, Denmark, December 27, 1965; admitted, 1994, Denmark and Danish High Court. *Education:* University of Copenhagen (Law Degree, 1991). *Member:* Danish Bar Association. *LANGUAGES:* Danish, English, German and Scandinavian. *PRACTICE AREAS:* Maritime and Insurance Law; Transportation Law; Finance Law.

FLEMMING HORN-ANDERSEN, born Copenhagen, Denmark, April 28, 1965; admitted, 1994, Denmark and Danish High Court. *Education:* University of Copenhagen (Law Degree, 1991). *Member:* Danish Bar Association. *LANGUAGES:* Danish, English and Scandinavian. *PRACTICE AREAS:* Insolvency Law; Real Property Law; General Corporate and Commercial Law.

CONSULTANT

SØREN THORSEN, born Copenhagen, Denmark, May 16, 1923; admitted, 1951, Denmark; 1958, Supreme Court of Denmark. *Education:* University of Copenhagen (Law Degree, 1948). *Member:* Danish Bar Association; ComitéMaritime International (Titular Member); The Danish Petroleum Law Society and The Danish Association of European Law. *LANGUAGES:* Danish, English, German, French and Scandinavian. *PRACTICE AREAS:* Corporate Law; Landlord and Tenancy Law; International Contracts Law; Litigation Law; Offshore Law; Insurance Law; Commercial Law.

VAGN VICTOR HANSEN, born Copenhagen, Denmark, February 2, 1924; admitted, 1951, Denmark; 1959, Supreme Court of Denmark. *Education:* University of Copenhagen (Law Degree, 1948). *Member:* Danish Bar Association; Comité Maritime International; International Bar Association. *LANGUAGES:* Danish, English, German, French and Scandinavian. *PRACTICE AREAS:* Maritime Law; Corporate Law; Finance Law; Shipping Law; Aircraft Law.

POUL SCHMITH

47 VIMMELSKAFTET
1161 COPENHAGEN K., DENMARK
Telephone: 33-15 20 10
Telex: 16010 CHPLAW DK
Telefax: (Int. 45) 33 15 61 15
Cable Address: "Copenlaw"

General Practice. Corporation, Real Estate, Company, Commercial, Contract, Litigation, Arbitration, Common Market, Admiralty and Insurance Law.

MEMBERS OF FIRM

MICHAEL GREGERS LARSEN, born Frederiksberg, DK, November 6, 1944; admitted, 1974, Denmark; 1979, Supreme Court of Denmark. *Education:* University of Copenhagen. Lecturer on Law, University of Copenhagen, 1971-1979. Counsel to the Danish Government (Department and Government Agencies, 1992—). *Member:* Danish Bar Association; Danish Petroleum Law Association. *LANGUAGES:* Danish, English, French, German, Swedish and Norwegian. *PRACTICE AREAS:* Contract Law; Litigation; EU-Law.

(This Listing Continued)

M. ELKIAER ANDERSEN, born Copenhagen, DK, October 17, 1945; admitted, 1975, Denmark; 1980, Supreme Court of Denmark. *Education:* University of Copenhagen; Trainee with Haight, Gardner, Poor & Havens, N.Y., N.Y., 1977-1978. *Member:* Danish Bar Association; Comité Maritime Internationale, Danish Branch; American Bar Association (Associate); Asia-Pacific Lawyers Association; International Bar Association; Danish Petroleum Law Association; Danish Society for Construction and Consulting Law; Danish Society for Environmental Law. *LANGUAGES:* Danish, English, Swedish and Norwegian. *PRACTICE AREAS:* Admiralty Law; Arbitration Law; Commercial Law; Contract; Bankruptcy.

N.V. FALLING OLSEN, born Copenhagen, DK, November 19, 1946; admitted, 1977, Denmark; 1982, Supreme Court of Denmark. *Education:* University of Copenhagen. *Member:* Danish Bar Association. *LANGUAGES:* Danish, English, Swedish and Norwegian. *PRACTICE AREAS:* Corporate Law; Commercial Law; Real Estate Law.

FINN MEJNERTSEN, born Roskilde, DK, July 10, 1950; admitted, 1978, Denmark; 1983, Supreme Court of Denmark. *Education:* University of Copenhagen. *Member:* Danish Bar Association; International Fiscal Association. *LANGUAGES:* Danish, English, Swedish and Norwegian. *PRACTICE AREAS:* Litigation; Commercial Law; Bankruptcy Law.

HANS CHR. VINTEN, born Soenderborg, DK, May 8, 1945; admitted, 1981, Denmark; 1986, Supreme Court of Denmark. *Education:* University of Aarhus, 1973. Danish Tax Department, 1973-1980. *Member:* Danish Bar Association; International Fiscal Association. *LANGUAGES:* English, German, Swedish and Norwegian. *PRACTICE AREAS:* Litigation; Tax Law; Insurance Law.

KARSTEN HAGEL-SØRENSEN, born 1950; admitted, 1991, Denmark. *Education:* University of Copenhagen. Asst. Professor in International Law, University of Copenhagen, 1978-1988. Deputy Permanent Secretary, Ministry of Justice, 1989-1991. *Member:* Danish Bar Association; Danish Society for European Law; Danish Petroleum Law Association; Danish Society for Environmental Law. *LANGUAGES:* Danish, English, French, German, Swedish and Norwegian. *PRACTICE AREAS:* EU-Law; Constitutional and Administrative Law; Human Rights Law.

KURT BARDELEBEN, born 1957; admitted, 1986, Denmark; 1991, Supreme Court of Denmark. *Education:* University of Copenhagen. *Member:* Danish Bar Association; Danish Society for Construction and Consulting Law; Danish Society for Environmental Law. *LANGUAGES:* Danish, English, German Swedish and Norwegian. *PRACTICE AREAS:* Land Development and Planning Law; Environmental Law; Construction Law.

HANS JUHLER, born 1957; admitted, 1989, Denmark. *Education:* University of Copenhagen. *Member:* Danish Bar Association. *LANGUAGES:* Danish, English, German, Swedish and Norwegian. *PRACTICE AREAS:* Labour Law; Litigation and Arbitration.

SUNE FUGLEHOLM SVENDSEN, born Menziken, Switzerland, 1963; admitted, 1989, Denmark. *Education:* University of Copenhagen; University of Michigan (LL.M.). Lecturer, EU-Law, University of Copenhagen. Trainee, Height, Gardner, Poor and Havens, New York, N.Y., 1991-1992. *Member:* Danish Bar Association; Danish Society for European Law. *LANGUAGES:* Danish, English, Swedish and Norwegian. *PRACTICE AREAS:* EU-Law; Constitutional Law; Administrative Law; Litigation; Tort Law.

ASSOCIATES

JUNIOR PARTNERS

Henrik Berg; Lars Apostoli; Steffen Svaerke.

Birgitte Kjærulff Vognsen; Kirsten Kemp; Anders Vangsø Mortensen; Morten Kroon; John Adamsen; Hanne Krag Ingvardsen; Lise Høy Falsner; Christian Gorrisen; René Offersen; Jesper Svenningsen; Niels Henrik Nielsen; Kristian Lind Jensen; Lars Merrild Hareskov; Jesper S. Perregaard; Henrik Hauge Andersen; David Auken.

Member of LOGOS--a network of law firms in the European Union.

Languages: Danish, English, German, Swedish, Norwegian, Spanish, Portuguese and French

I.A. STROBEL

Established in 1955

37 H.C. ANDERSENS BOULEVARD
1553 COPENHAGEN V, DENMARK
Telephone: 45 33 91 02 03
Telecopier: 45 33 32 82 02

Taxation, Corporation and General Practice.

I.A. STROBEL, born Copenhagen, Denmark, November 1, 1925; admitted, 1955, Denmark and Superior Courts of Denmark; 1961, Supreme Court of Denmark. *Education:* University of Copenhagen. Member of General Council, International Fiscal Association and National Reporter to the XXVIII Congress. *Member:* Danish Bar Association.

Languages: Scandinavian, English, German and French

ADVOKATFIRMAET O. BONDO SVANE

Established in 1933
TRONDHJEMS PLADS 3
DK-2100 COPENHAGEN, DENMARK
Telephone: (Int'l +45) 35 27 95 95
Telex: 19310 COMLAW DK
Telefax: (Int'l +45) 31 38 13 38

International Practice, including Company, Corporate Law, Mergers and Acquisitions, Banking, Financing, Foreign Investment and Overseas Property, Shipping, Offshore Investments, Bankruptcy and Insolvency, Recovery, International Private Law, Contracts, Arbitration, Property and Tenancy, Conveyancing, Commercial and Intellectual Property, Copyrights, Patents, Design, Licensing, Employment, Industrial Injury and Compensation, Pension Schemes, Computer Law, Franchise, Insurance, Family Law, Wills, Probate and Trusts, Taxation, Investments.

MEMBERS OF FIRM

HELGE HASSEL, born 1928; admitted, 1958, Denmark; 1963, Supreme Court of Denmark. *Education:* University of Copenhagen (Cand.Jur.). Member of Board: Copenhagen Society of Advocates, 1967-1972; Copenhagen Bar Association, 1969-1974. *Member:* Danish Bar Association; IBA; UIA. *PRACTICE AREAS:* Corporate; Recovery; Mergers and Acquisitions.

FINN ILLUM, born 1927; admitted, 1962, Denmark; 1969, High Court of Denmark. *Education:* University of Copenhagen (Cand.Jur.). *PRACTICE AREAS:* Banking and Financing; Maritime and Ship Building.

STEEN OLE LARSEN, born 1946; admitted, 1974, Denmark; 1981, Supreme Court of Denmark. *Education:* University of Copenhagen (Cand.Jur.). *Member:* IBA. *PRACTICE AREAS:* Competition; Intellectual Property; Bankruptcy.

POUL FLEMMING HANSEN, born 1947; admitted, 1979, Denmark; 1993, Supreme Court of Denmark. *Education:* University of Copenhagen (Cand.Jur., 1974). Teacher, Administrative Law, University of Copenhagen, 1976-1981. Secretary, Ministry of Justice, 1974-1976. *PRACTICE AREAS:* Taxation; Banking; Financing and Litigation.

POUL M. MIKKELSEN, born 1952; admitted, 1980, Denmark; 1982, High Court of Denmark. *Education:* University of Aarhus/University of Copenhagen (Cand.Jur., 1977). *Member:* Danish Bar Association.

H.P. DRISDAL HANSEN, born 1944; admitted, 1975, Denmark; 1981, Supreme Court of Denmark. *Education:* University of Copenhagen (Cand.Jur.). Examiner, Copenhagen Business University, 1988—. *PRACTICE AREAS:* Construction.

LEIF V. DJURHUUS, born 1953; admitted, 1983, Denmark; 1990, Supreme Court of Denmark. *Education:* University of Copenhagen (Cand.Jur., 1979). *PRACTICE AREAS:* Construction; Tenancy and Property; Litigation and Arbitration.

ERIC KORRE HORTEN, born 1953; admitted, 1982, Denmark; 1990, Supreme Court of Denmark. *Education:* University of Copenhagen (Cand.Jur., 1977); University of Natal, Durban, South Africa (1977); Copenhagen Business University (H.D., 1984). Assistant Professor, Copenhagen Business University, 1985-1990. Lecturer, University of Copenhagen, 1979-1982. *Member:* Danish Bar Association; IBA; UAE. *PRACTICE AREAS:* Mergers and Acquisitions; Information Technology; Contract; Arbitration.

MS. PERNILLE BIGAARD, born 1953; admitted, 1980, Denmark; 1988, Supreme Court of Denmark. *Education:* University of Copenhagen

(This Listing Continued)

(Cand.Jur., 1977). *PRACTICE AREAS:* Bankruptcy and Corporate Recovery; Company and Commercial.

JØRGEN G. PERMIN, born 1956; admitted, 1986, Denmark; 1991, High Court of Denmark. *Education:* University of Copenhagen (Cand.Jur., 1983). *Member:* Danish Bar Association; IBA. *PRACTICE AREAS:* Banking and Financing; Company and Commercial.

JACOB BIER, born 1961; admitted, 1989, Denmark; 1992, High Court of Denmark. *Education:* University of Copenhagen (Cand.Jur., 1986). Lecturer, Contract Law, University of Copenhagen, 1987-1990. *PRACTICE AREAS:* Company and Commercial; Mergers and Acquisitions; Banking.

ASSOCIATES

BENT BRAMSEN, born 1946; admitted, 1975, Denmark; 1977, High Court of Denmark. *Education:* University of Copenhagen (Cand.Jur., 1972). *PRACTICE AREAS:* Competition; Insurance.

MS. ANNE KATHRINE SCHOEN, born 1959; admitted, 1988, Denmark; 1991, High Court of Denmark. *Education:* University of Copenhagen (Cand.Jur., 1985). *PRACTICE AREAS:* Employment; Maritime and Transport; Litigation.

MS. METTE BRUYANT-LANGER, born 1960; admitted, 1989, Denmark; 1990, High Court of Denmark. *Education:* University of Copenhagen (Cand.Jur., 1986). *PRACTICE AREAS:* Company and Commercial.

HANS HEDEGAARD, born 1963; admitted, 1993, High Court of Denmark. *Education:* University of Copenhagen (Cand.Jur., 1989). *PRACTICE AREAS:* Company; Bankruptcy and Corporate Recovery.

THOMAS WEINCKE, born 1963; admitted, 1993, Denmark; 1994, High Court of Denmark. *Education:* University of Copenhagen (Cand.Jur., 1990). *PRACTICE AREAS:* Competition; Intellectual Property and Information Technology Contracts.

MS. MARIANNE BRUHN ANDERSEN, born 1956; admitted, 1993, Denmark. *Education:* University of Copenhagen (Cand.Jur., 1990). *PRACTICE AREAS:* Commercial and Intellectual Property; Bankruptcy and Insolvency.

TOMMY PAULSEN, born 1963; admitted, 1993, Denmark; 1994, High Court of Denmark. *Education:* University of Copenhagen (Cand.Jur., 1990). *PRACTICE AREAS:* Construction; Tenancy and Property; Litigation and Arbitration.

TORBEN MAURITZEN, born 1964; admitted, 1994, Denmark. *Education:* University of Copenhagen (Cand.Jur., 1991); University of Oslo, Norway. *PRACTICE AREAS:* Transport Law; Bankruptcy; Insurance.

SØREN THOR JENSEN, born 1964; admitted, 1993, Denmark. *Education:* University of Copenhagen (Cand.Jur., 1989). *PRACTICE AREAS:* Banking and Financing; Real Estate.

JUNIOR ASSOCIATES

EIVIND EINERSEN, born 1969. *Education:* University of Copenhagen, 1992. *PRACTICE AREAS:* Commercial Law; Information Technology; Real Property.

MS. MICHALA ROEPSTORFT, born 1965; admitted, 1990, Denmark. *Education:* University of Copenhagen (Cand.Jur., 1990). *PRACTICE AREAS:* Bankruptcy; Corporate Recovery.

CATHERINE MARIANNE KENDAL, born Denmark, 1968. *Education:* Royal Holloway and Bedford New College, London, 1986; University of Copenhagen (Cand. Jur., 1987); Trinity Hall, Cambridge University, United Kingdom (LL.M., 1992). *LANGUAGES:* Danish, English, French. *PRACTICE AREAS:* EU Law; Information Technology; Intellectual Property.

Languages: Danish and other Scandinavian Languages, English, French and German

VISTISEN & RYBERG

Law Firm

KØBMAGERGADE 3

P.O. BOX 72

DK-1003 COPENHAGEN K, DENMARK

Telephone: +45 33 33 71 73

Telefax: +45 33 33 71 74

FIRM PROFILE: *The object of the firm is to run a modern and service-minded law office where the newest technology is applied in a way that secures the clients a rapid and efficient assistance.*

The firm's primary field of activity is business law. The clientele comprises Danish enterprises, international groups, foundations, federations of employers, municipalities and embassies. The firm has built up a well functioning international network of law firms.

TORBEN VISTISEN, born Copenhagen, Denmark, 1947; admitted, 1978, Denmark. *Education:* University of Copenhagen (1972). *LANGUAGES:* English, Italian, German and French. *PRACTICE AREAS:* International Law; Company Law; Association Law; Contract Law.

BJØRN RYBERG, born Bjerringbro, Denmark, 1960; admitted, 1988, Denmark. *Education:* University of Copenhagen (1983). Assistant Professor, Intellectual Property Law, Copenhagen School of Economics and Business Administration. Lecturer, Copenhagen Science Park Symbion, the Technical University of Denmark. *LANGUAGES:* English. *PRACTICE AREAS:* Computer Law; EEC Competition Law; Intellectual Property Law; Patent Law.

WATSON, FARLEY & WILLIAMS

LILLE KONGENSGADE 20

DK-1074 COPENHAGEN K, DENMARK

Telephone: (45 33) 91 33 03

Fax: (45 33) 91 49 12

New York, New York Office: 380 Madison Avenue, 10017. Telephone: 212-922-2200. Telex: 6790626 WFW NY. Fax: 212-922-1512.

London, England Office: 15 Appold Street, London EC2A 2HB. Telephone: (44 71) 814 8000. Telex: 8955707 WFW LON G. Fax: (44 71) 814 8141.

Paris, France Office: 19 rue de Marignan, 75008 Paris. Telephone: (33 1) 45 63 15 15. Telex: WFW PAR 651096 F. Fax: (33 1) 45 61 09 01.

Oslo, Norway Office: Beddingen 8, Aker Brygge, 0250 Oslo. Telephone: (47 22) 83 83 08. Telex: 79209 WFW N. Fax: (47 22) 83 83 13.

Athens, Greece Office: Alassia Building, Defteras Merarchias 13, 185-35 Piraeus. Telephone: (30 1) 422 3660. Telex: 24 1311 WFW GR. Fax: (30 1) 422 3664.

Moscow, Russia Office: 36 Myaskovskovo Street, Moscow 121019. Telephone: (7 502) 224 1700 (international only); (7 095) 291 8046/5968. Fax: (7 502) 224 1701 (international only); (7 095) 202 9027.

Firm engaged in General International Practice, Corporate, Commercial and Financing, Shipping, Aviation, Banking, Taxation, Commercial Litigation and Arbitration and European Community Law. Not qualified to advise on Danish law.

RESIDENT SOLICITOR

CHRISTOPHER LOWE, Admitted as Solicitor, 1987. Author, Articles for Lloyds List, Financial Times and Insolvency Practitioner. *Education:* University of Wales, Aberystwyth (LL.B.) *Member:* Committee Maritime Internationale (CMI). *PRACTICE AREAS:* Banking; Cross Border Leasing; Asset Finance; Ship Finance.

(For Biographical Data on additional partners, see Professional Biographies at London, England, Paris, France, Oslo, Norway, Piraeus, Greece and Moscow, Russia)

INTER-LEX LAWYERS

Established in 1986

STRANDBYGADE 65

6701 ESBJERG, DENMARK

Telephone: 75 45 46 00 and 75 21 21 21

Fax: 75 13 83 14

Aarhus, Denmark Office: Strandvejen 94, 8100. Telephone: 86 12 12 00. Fax: 86 11 00 00.

Aalborg, Denmark Office: Badehusvej 16, 9000. Telephone: 98 13 17 11. Fax: 98 13 18 11.

Odense, Denmark Office: Fisketorvet 3, 5100 Odense C. Telephone: 66 14 22 22. Fax: 66 13 56 04.

Mergers and Acquisitions, Taxation and International Tax Planning, Insolvency including Liquidations and Receiverships, Civil Litigation, Corporate and Competition Law.

FIRM PROFILE: *The Inter-Lex Lawyers was formed in 1986 as a cooperation between 4 independent law firms in the 4 major Danish cities outside Copenhagen. The cooperation has 17 partners and 11 associates.*

SVEN KOCH, born Aalborg, Denmark, March 11, 1926; admitted, 1954, Denmark. *Education:* University of Copenhagen (Law Degree, 1951). *Member:* Esbjerg and Danish Law Associations. *LANGUAGES:* English and German. *PRACTICE AREAS:* General Practice; Criminal Litigation.

VIGGO DRESING, born Copenhagen, Denmark, September 8, 1938; admitted, 1969, Denmark. *Education:* University of Copenhagen (Law Degree, 1966). *Member:* Esbjerg and Danish Law Associations; International Bar Association. *LANGUAGES:* English and German. *PRACTICE AREAS:* Corporate Law; Environment Law.

STEEN FALSNER, born Hellerup, Denmark, March 6, 1948; admitted, 1978, Denmark. *Education:* University of Copenhagen (Law Degree, 1975). *Member:* Esbjerg and Danish Law Associations. *LANGUAGES:* English, German and French. *PRACTICE AREAS:* Commercial Leasing; Financing; Construction Law.

DAN B. LARSEN, born Aalborg, Denmark, September 22, 1954; admitted, 1981, Denmark. *Education:* University of Aarhus (Law Degree, 1978). *Member:* Esbjerg and Danish Law Associations; International Bar Association. *LANGUAGES:* English and German. *PRACTICE AREAS:* Insolvency; Competition Law.

KLAUS K. KJAER, born Esbjerg, Denmark, August 4, 1960; admitted, 1988, Denmark. *Education:* University of Aarhus (Law Degree, 1985). Lecturer on Law, 1988—, Esbjerg School of Business Administration. *Member:* Esbjerg and Danish Law Associations. *LANGUAGES:* English and German. *PRACTICE AREAS:* Insurance Law; Civil Litigation; Commercial Law.

ASSOCIATES

LARS SØRENSEN, born Varde, Denmark, March 27, 1963; admitted, 1992, Denmark. *Education:* University of Aarhus (Law Degree, 1989). *Member:* Esbjerg and Danish Law Associations. *LANGUAGES:* English and German. *PRACTICE AREAS:* General Practice.

KJELD KLASTRUP, born Ravnkilde, Denmark, May 22, 1946; admitted, 1976, Denmark. *Education:* University of Aarhus (Law Degree, 1972). *Member:* Esbjerg and Danish Law Associations. *LANGUAGES:* English and German. *PRACTICE AREAS:* Insurance Law; Insolvency; Civil Litigation.

AAGE FLEBO, born Esbjerg, Denmark, June 8, 1961; admitted, 1994, Denmark. *Education:* University of Aarhus (Law Degree, 1991). *Member:* Esbjerg and Danish Law Associations. *LANGUAGES:* English and German. *PRACTICE AREAS:* General Practice.

OLE NIELSEN & PARTNERE ADVOKATER A/S

Established in 1975

JERNBANEGADE 29

P.O. BOX 830

DK-6000 KOLDING, DENMARK

Telephone: 45-75504000

Telefax: 45-75541050

Warsaw, Poland Subsidiary: Ole Nielsen & Partners Law Offices sp. z o.o., Ul. Langiewicza 15, PL-02-071 Warsaw. Telephone: +48 22 25 53 81-82. Telefax: +48 22 25 03 44.

Kiel, Germany Office: Ole Nielsen & Partner, Danische Advokaten, Eggerstedtstrasse 13, D-24103 Kiel. Telephone: +49 431 97 406 17. Telefax: +49 431 97 406 30.

Vejle, Denmark Office: Ole Nielsen & Partnere Advokater A/S, Enghavevej 11, Enghavecentret, DK-7000 Vejle. Telephone: +45 75 72 22 22. Telefax: +45 75 72 24 22.

Business Law including Company, Tax, International Tax, Litigation, Arbitration, International Construction, Distribution, Agency and Licensing Contracts, Foreign Investment, Real Estate, Bankruptcy, Insurance, Transportation, Privatization, EC Law, Mergers and Acquisitions, Foreign Investment in Eastern Europe, Joint Ventures, Project Financing, Bank Guarantees, Product Liability, Public and Administrative Law, Industrial Property Rights, Labour Law, Computer Law, Leasing, Banking.

FIRM PROFILE: *The firm was founded in 1975 and now the groupemploys a total staff of 43 (7 partners, 7 associate lawyers and 29 support staff members comprising a general manager, sworn translators, foreign correspondents, paralegal assistants, lawyers' secretaries and office administrators).*

The newly established office in Vejle employs 2 lawyers and 3 support staff members, whereas the Polish Subsidiary which was established in 1990, employs 8 Polish employees (4 Polish lawyers, one sworn translator, two foreign correspondents and one administrator).

The German office was opened in 1992 and is ad-hoc staffed.

MEMBERS OF FIRM

OLE NIELSEN, born December 28, 1927; admitted, 1956, Denmark; 1957, High Court of Denmark. Executive Vice President of LEGO A/S, 1961-1974. *Member:* Danish Bar Association; International Bar Association (Member, Business Law Section Committee of Antitrust Law and Monopolies and Committee of Taxes); Member of the Board of "Deutsch-Nordische Juristenvereinigung". *LANGUAGES:* Scandinavian Languages, English, German and French. *PRACTICE AREAS:* Company Law; National and International Tax Law; Mergers and Acquisitions; Arbitration Law; EC Law.

NIELS BO ANDERSEN, born November 9, 1954; admitted, 1982, Denmark and High Court of Denmark; 1987, Supreme Court of Denmark. *Education:* University of Copenhagen (1979). *Member:* Danish Bar Association; International Bar Association (Member, Business Law Section, Committee of Procedures for Settling Disputes, Committee of Taxes and Committee of International Franchising). *LANGUAGES:* Scandinavian Languages, English and German. *PRACTICE AREAS:* Tax Law; Litigation; Bankruptcy; Company Law; Arbitration Law.

PETER TAERØ NIELSEN, born January 18, 1954; admitted, 1983, Denmark. *Education:* University of Aarhus (1980); University of Oslo, Norway (Maritime Law, 1979). *Member:* Danish Bar Association; International Bar Association (Member, Council of Eastern European Forum and of Business Law Section, Committee of International Construction Contracts); Danish Society for Construction and Consulting Law. *LANGUAGES:* Scandinavian Languages, English and German. *PRACTICE AREAS:* Mergers and Acquisitions; Foreign Investment in Eastern Europe; Privatisation; Joint Ventures; Licensing; Construction Law; Project Financing; Bank Guarantees.

JENS LAURSEN, born August 31, 1946; admitted, 1975, Denmark; 1978, High Court of Denmark; 1983, Supreme Court of Denmark. *Education:* University of Aarhus (1972). *Member:* Danish Bar Association; International Bar Association (Member, Business Law Section, Committee of Intellectual Property). *LANGUAGES:* Scandinavian Languages, English and German. *PRACTICE AREAS:* Company Law; Litigation; Product Liability; Industrial Property Rights; Public and Administrative Law.

(This Listing Continued)

NIELS DE WOLFF, born September 25, 1958; admitted, 1988, Denmark; 1991, High Court of Denmark. *Education:* University of Aarhus (1985). *Member:* Danish Bar Association; International Union of Lawyers (UIA); Union des Avocats Europeens (UAE); Danish Society for Construction and Consulting Law. *LANGUAGES:* Scandinavian Languages, English and German. *PRACTICE AREAS:* Company Law; Transportation; Labour Law; Litigation; Bankruptcy; Computer Law; Construction Law.

JESPER KNUDSEN, born May 9, 1957; admitted, 1985, Denmark; 1989, High Court of Denmark. *Education:* University of Aarhus (1981). *Member:* Danish Bar Association; International Union of Lawyers, UIA. *LANGUAGES:* Scandinavian Languages, English and German. *PRACTICE AREAS:* Company Law; Litigation; Bankruptcy; Real Estate; Leasing.

TORBEN OXBØLL, born January 2, 1954; admitted, 1983, Denmark; 1983, High Court of Denmark; 1988, Supreme Court of Denmark. *Education:* University of Copenhagen (1979). *Member:* Danish Bar Association. (Resident, Vejle, Denmark Office). *LANGUAGES:* Scandinavian Languages, English and German. *PRACTICE AREAS:* Tax Law; Litigation; Foreign Investment in Eastern Europe; Criminal Law.

ASSOCIATES

ØJVIND HULGAARD, born May 23, 1965; admitted, 1993, Denmark. *Education:* University of Aarhus (1990). *LANGUAGES:* Scandinavian Languages, English.

PIA SØGAARD-NIELSEN, born July 17, 1962; admitted, 1993, Denmark. *Education:* University of Aarhus (1990); The Bilingual Commercial Correspondent Examination in Spanish and English, Southern Denmark Business School (1983). *LANGUAGES:* Scandinavian Languages, English, German and Spanish.

MICHAEL ROSCHMANN SKOVGAARD, born May 4, 1965; admitted, 1994, Denmark. *Education:* University of Aarhus (1991). *LANGUAGES:* Scandinavian Languages, English and German.

VIBEKE ESMANN, born January 6, 1960; admitted, 1988, Denmark. *Education:* State University of New York, Binghamton, New York (1979); University of Aarhus (1985); Duke University, Durham, North Carolina (1994). (Resident, Vejle, Denmark Office). *LANGUAGES:* Scandinavian Languages, English.

ANNE-LYKKE MAU JACOBSEN, born August 3, 1968. *Education:* University of Aarhus (1992); Institute in Transnational Law at Duke University of North Carolina (Summer Course in American and International Law). *LANGUAGES:* Scandinavian Languages, English, German and French.

PHILIP SØREN THORSEN, born March 21, 1966. *Education:* International Baccalaureate Atlantic College (1984); University of Aarhus (1992). *LANGUAGES:* Scandinavian Languages, English and French.

ADVOKATFIRMAET LARS CHRISTENSEN

Established in 1862

JERNBANEGADE 4

DK 5100 ODENSE C, DENMARK

Telephone: (45) 66 11 78 11

Cable Address: "Kenoklaw"

Telefax: 45 66 14 43 28

Hamburg, Germany Office: Dänische Advokaten, 2 Hamburg 1, An der Alster 71. Telephone: 40-24 91 92. Cable Address: "Scanlaw Hamburg". Telefax: 040 24 0409.

General Practice. Corporation, Commercial, Real Estate, Tax, Insurance and Probate Law.

MEMBERS OF FIRM

LARS CHRISTENSEN, born Ørslev, Denmark, May 12, 1918; admitted, 1945, Denmark. *Education:* University of Copenhagen. *Member:* Danish Bar Association (Member of the Board, 1973-1979). *LANGUAGES:* Scandinavian, English and German.

HANS FOLKMAR, born Odense, Denmark, October 14, 1923; admitted, 1953, Denmark. *Education:* University of Copenhagen. *Member:* Danish Bar Association. *LANGUAGES:* Scandinavian, English and German.

POUL MØLLER ANDERSEN, born Skanderborg, Denmark, September 25, 1940; admitted, 1969, Denmark. *Education:* University of Aarhus. *Member:* Danish Bar Association. *LANGUAGES:* Scandinavian, English and German.

(This Listing Continued)

ADVOKATFIRMAET LARS CHRISTENSEN, Odense—Continued

HOLGER SVANBERG, born Marstal, Denmark, January 3, 1944; admitted, 1976, Denmark. *Education:* University of Aarhus. *Member:* Danish Bar Association. *LANGUAGES:* Scandinavian and English.

KNUD KASPER DAMSGAARD, born Svendborg, Denmark, December 9, 1950; admitted, 1979, Denmark. *Education:* University of Copenhagen. *Member:* Danish Bar Association. *LANGUAGES:* Scandinavian, English and German.

JENS PETER HENRIKSEN, born Haderslev, Denmark, August 9, 1949; admitted, 1977, Denmark. *Education:* University of Copenhagen. *Member:* Danish Bar Association. *LANGUAGES:* Scandinavian, English and German.

HANS VESTERGAARD, born Gråsten, Denmark, January 17, 1950; admitted, 1978, Denmark. *Education:* University of Aarhus. *Member:* Danish Bar Association. *LANGUAGES:* Scandinavian, English and German.

LARS RASMUSSEN, born Hammel, Denmark, April 26, 1963; admitted, 1990, Denmark. *Education:* University of Aarhus. *Member:* Danish Bar Association. *LANGUAGES:* Scandinavian, English and German.

HENRIK POPP HANSEN, born Haderslev, Denmark, September 23, 1961; admitted, 1990, Denmark. *Education:* University of Aarhus. *Member:* Danish Bar Association. *LANGUAGES:* Scandinavian, English and German.

OTTO FREDERIK SPLIID, born Bogense, Denmark, August 1, 1961; admitted, 1991, Denmark. *Education:* University of Aarhus. *Member:* Danish Bar Association. *LANGUAGES:* Scandinavian, English and German.

PETER RINGSTED, born Odense, Denmark, June 11, 1956; admitted, 1986, Denmark. *Education:* University of Aarhus; London School of Economics. Lecturer, Maritime Law. *Member:* Danish Bar Association. *LANGUAGES:* Scandinavian, English and German.

Languages: Scandinavian, English and German

REFERENCES: Den Danske Bank af 1871 A/S; Unibank A/S; Sparekassen Bikuben.

INTER-LEX LAWYERS

Established in 1986

FISKETORVET 3

5100 ODENSE C, DENMARK

Telephone: 66 14 22 22

Fax: 66 13 56 04

Esbjerg, Denmark Office: Strandbygade 65, 6701. Telephone: 75 45 46 00; 75 21 21 21. Fax: 75 13 83 14.

Aarhus, Denmark Office: Strandvejen 94, 8100. Telephone: 86 12 12 00. Fax: 86 11 00 00.

Aalborg, Denmark Office: Badehusvej 16, 9000. Telephone: 98 13 17 11. Fax: 98 13 18 11.

Mergers and Acquisitions, Taxation and International Tax Planning, Insolvency including Liquidations and Receiverships, Civil Litigation, Corporate and Competition Law.

FIRM PROFILE: The Inter-Lex Lawyers was formed in 1986 as a cooperation between 4 independent law firms in the 4 major Danish cities outside Copenhagen. The cooperation has 17 partners and 11 associates.

FLEMMING JOHNSEN, born Skive, Denmark, November 26, 1943; admitted, 1975, Denmark. *Education:* University of Aarhus (Law Degree, 1971). *Member:* Odense and Danish Law Associations; Danish Board of Counsels. *LANGUAGES:* English and German. *PRACTICE AREAS:* Tax Law; Company Law; Business Advisory Services; Acquisitions; Disposal of Business.

LARS PILGARD, born Aalborg, Denmark September 27, 1947; admitted, 1978, Denmark. *Education:* University of Aarhus (Law Degree, 1975). *Member:* Odense and Danish Law Associations. *LANGUAGES:* German and English. *PRACTICE AREAS:* Contracting Law; Insolvency Law; Company Law; Arbitration.

UWE TEICHERT, born Ansund, Denmark, June 16, 1949; admitted, 1978, Denmark. *Education:* University of Copenhagen (Law Degree, 1974). *Member:* Odense and Danish Law Associations. *LANGUAGES:* German

(This Listing Continued)

and English. *PRACTICE AREAS:* Acquisition/Disposal of Business; Leasehold; Competition Law; Environmental Law.

IB THRANE, born Esbjerg, Denmark, August 7, 1954; admitted, 1981, Denmark. *Education:* University of Aarhus (Law Degree, 1978). *Member:* Odense and Danish Law Associations. *LANGUAGES:* English and German. *PRACTICE AREAS:* Company Law; Acquisitions/Disposal of Business; Financing.

MICHAEL CLEMMENSEN, born Vojens, Denmark, March 20, 1960; admitted, 1988, Denmark. *Education:* University of Copenhagen (Law Degree, 1985). *Member:* Odense and Danish Law Associations. *LANGUAGES:* English, German and French. *PRACTICE AREAS:* EEC Law; Agent and Sole Distribution Agreements; Intangible and Incorporeal Law.

JESPER HAUSCHILDT, born Skagen, Denmark, March 21, 1962; admitted, 1991, Denmark. *Education:* University of Aarhus (Law Degree, 1988). *Member:* Odense and Danish Law Associations. *LANGUAGES:* English and German. *PRACTICE AREAS:* Contracting Law; Leasehold; Indemnity Law; Civil Litigation.

HANS HENRIK BANKE, born Broby, Denmark, February 17, 1960; admitted, 1987, Denmark. *Education:* University of Aarhus (Law Degree, 1984). *Member:* Odense and Danish Law Associations. *LANGUAGES:* English. *PRACTICE AREAS:* Company Law; Civil Litigation; Acquisitions/Disposal of Business.

ASSOCIATES

ERIK SCHAFFALITZKY DE MUCKADELL, born Hellerup, Denmark, January 16, 1952; admitted, 1980, Denmark. *Education:* University of Copenhagen (Law Degree, 1977). *Member:* Odense and Danish Law Associations. *LANGUAGES:* English and German. *PRACTICE AREAS:* Law of Succession; Estate of Deceased Persons; Probate; Compulsory Sales.

HANS HAAGES, born Copenhagen, Denmark, February 18, 1950; admitted, 1989, Denmark. *Education:* University of Copenhagen (Law Degree, 1986). *Member:* Odense and Danish Law Associations. *LANGUAGES:* English and German. *PRACTICE AREAS:* Employment Law; Personal and Family Law; Land Law.

JAN I. KRISTENSEN, born Kolding, Denmark, July 2, 1962; admitted, 1992, Denmark. *Education:* University of Aarhus (Law Degree, 1989). *Member:* Odense and Danish Law Associations. *LANGUAGES:* English and German. *PRACTICE AREAS:* International Law; Company Law; Tax Law; Insolvency Law; Agent and Sole Distribution Agreements; Civil Litigation.

LAW OFFICES
VALENTIN MADSEN & SCHMIDT

Established in 1984

8 MAGELOES

5000 ODENSE C, DENMARK

Telephone: 45 66 12 26 26

Fax: 45 66 12 23 37

International Business Law including Contracts, Corporate and Commercial Law, European Community Law, Advertising, Marketing and Competition Law, Industrial and Intellectual Property Law, Mergers and Acquisitions, Agencies and Distributorships, Franchising and Licensing, Computer and Media Law, Banking, Financing, Securities, Maritime Law, Shipping and Transportation Law, Litigation and Arbitration.

FIRM PROFILE: Small firm offering highly specialized legal services to directors and management of companies with international activities, in particular in Europe, the US and Canada and the Far East. A qualified, legal, paralegal and administrative staff is supported by an international network of well reputed law firms specializing in Business Law, including members of International Bar Association and of IAG International, Integrated Advisory Group, with offices in all major European communities.

MEMBERS OF FIRM

JOHN VALENTIN MADSEN, born Aarhus, Denmark, June 8, 1931; admitted, 1982, Denmark; 1985, High Court of Denmark; 1991, Supreme Court of Denmark. *Education:* Yale University 1950; Princeton University 1950-1951; Aarhus University (LL.M., 1951-1957); Harvard Graduate School of Business Administration (A.M.P., 1980). Legal Counsel, Danish Employers' Confederation, 1957-1961. General Counsel, LEGO Group, 1961-1968. General Counsel and Vice-President, Burmeister & Wain Engineers and Shipbuilders A/S, 1968-1972. President: Vingaarden A/S and its

(This Listing Continued)

associated companies, 1972-1978; Skandinavisk Henkel A/S, 1978-1980. Private law practice, 1981—. Vice-Consul for Portugal, 1974-1982. *Member:* Danish Bar Association; International Bar Association (Section on Business Law); Danish Society for the Protection of Industrial Property; International Association for the Protection of Industrial Property; International Chamber of Commerce; Danish Management Association; Licensing Executives' Society; IAG International; Integrated Advisory Group. *LAN-GUAGES:* Scandinavian, English, German and French. *PRACTICE AREAS:* International Contracts and Corporate Law.

FLEMMING SCHMIDT, born Copenhagen, Denmark, February 25, 1952; admitted, 1986, Denmark. *Education:* Copenhagen University, 1972-1979; Scandinavian Institute for Maritime Law, Norway, 1978-1979. Lecturer, Maersk Shipping School, 1984-1986. With Den Danske Bank, Foreign Department, 1979-1980. General Counsel, A.P. Møller Group, 1980-1986. Private law practice, 1986—. *Member:* Danish Bar Association; International Bar Association. *LANGUAGES:* Scandinavian, English, German and French. *PRACTICE AREAS:* Banking; Financing; Securities; Maritime Law.

ENGLAND

SHOOSMITHS & HARRISON

Established in 1845

52-54 THE GREEN
BANBURY OX16 9AB, ENGLAND
Telephone: 0295 267971
Fax: 0295 265620

(For full details, see entry for Northampton)

EDGE & ELLISON

Established in 1870

RUTLAND HOUSE, 148 EDMUND STREET
BIRMINGHAM B3 2JR, ENGLAND
Telephone: (44) 121 200 2001
Fascimile: (44) 121 200 1991

London, England Office: 18-19 Southampton Place. Telephone: (44) 171 404 4701. Facsimile: (44) 171 831 9152.
Leicester Office: Regent Court, Regent Street. Telephone: (44) 0116 2470123. Facsimile: (44) 0116 2470030.
Associated Office: Dumon, Sablon & Vanheeswijck, Brussels, Belgium.
Associated Office: Buchanan Ingersoll, Pittsburgh, Harrisburg, Philadelphia and Miami, U.S.A.

Corporate & Commercial, Commercial Property, Litigation, Banking & Insolvency. Specializations include Licensing, Pensions, Computer Agreements, Employment, International Business Services, Environment, Pensions, Building & Construction, Planning, Insurance & Personal Injury, Entertainment Media & Leisure, Anti-Trust, Tax Planning, Intellectual Property and Debt Collection.

FIRM PROFILE: Edge & Ellison is a large, national, commercial practice whose primary objective is to focus its diverse skills and broad experience for the benefit of its clients. The firm comprises some 61 Partners, 240 lawyers and a total staff of 530, and has offices in Birmingham, London and Leicester and longstanding relationships with law firms in the United States and Europe.

BIRMINGHAM OFFICE
RESIDENT PARTNERS

JOHN A. J. AUCOTT, admitted, 1969, England and Wales. (Senior Partner). *LANGUAGES:* French. *PRACTICE AREAS:* Commercial Litigation; Defamation; Fraud; Insurance Litigation; Alternative Dispute Resolution; Judicial Review; Personal Injury (Defendant).

DIGBY M. JONES, admitted, 1980, England and Wales. *Education:* LL.B. (Hons) University College London. (Deputy Senior Partner); (Head of Corporate and Commercial Department). *LANGUAGES:* French. *PRACTICE AREAS:* Corporate Finance Law; Mergers & Acquisitions; Leveraged & Management Buyouts; Corporate Restructuring; Venture Capital; Financial Restructuring; International Transactions.

GIL D. M. HAYWARD, admitted, 1970, England and Wales. *Education:* LL.B. (Hons) Liverpool University. (Managing Partner). *PRACTICE*

(This Listing Continued)

AREAS: Commercial Property Law; Property Development &/or Syndication Law; Property Law; Landlord & Tenant Law; Conveyancing.

CHRISTIAN T. L. FORGAARD, admitted, 1965, England and Wales. *Education:* LL.B. Birmingham University. *PRACTICE AREAS:* Corporate Finance Law; Corporate Law; Financial Restructuring; Venture Capital; Mergers & Acquisitions; Leveraged & Management Buyouts.

DAVID L. GOLDSMITH, admitted, 1967, England and Wales. *Education:* LL.B. (Hons) Manchester University. (Head of Commercial Property Department). *PRACTICE AREAS:* Commercial Property Law; Property Development &/or Syndication Law; Landlord & Tenant Law; Conveyancing.

ROBERT O. DAUNCEY, admitted, 1969, England and Wales. *PRACTICE AREAS:* Corporate Law; Commercial Law; Mergers & Acquisitions; Commercial Property Law.

DAVID M. OWEN, admitted, 1973, England and Wales. *PRACTICE AREAS:* Corporate Law; Mergers & Acquisitions; Directors & Officers Liabilities; Company Secretarial; Corporate Restructuring Law; European Community Law.

GRAHAM D. G. SMITH, admitted, 1971, England and Wales. *Education:* Guildford College of Law, Surrey. *PRACTICE AREAS:* Commercial Property Law; Residential Property Law; Landlord & Tenant Law; Conveyancing.

ANDREW J. POTTS, admitted, 1971, England and Wales. *Education:* Bristol University. *LANGUAGES:* French. *PRACTICE AREAS:* Licensing Law; Employment Law; Commercial Litigation; Criminal Law; Fraud.

JOHN B. HINCHLIFFE, admitted, 1975, England and Wales. *Education:* LL.B. (Hons) Birmingham University. *PRACTICE AREAS:* Commercial Property Law; Property Law; Property Development &/or Syndication Law; Building; Construction.

IAN C. REAVES, admitted, 1973, England and Wales. *Education:* B.A. (Hons) Nottingham University. (Head of Banking Department). *PRACTICE AREAS:* Banking Law; Retail Banking; Building Societies; Franchise Law; Property Finance; Asset Finance.

RICHARD A. ALDERSON, admitted, 1976, England and Wales. *Education:* LL.B. Bristol University. *Member:* Institute of European Law. *PRACTICE AREAS:* Commercial Law; Agency & Distribution; Sports Law.

DIGBY H. ROSE, admitted, 1975, England and Wales. *Education:* M.A. Cambridge University. (Head of Litigation Department). *PRACTICE AREAS:* Commercial Litigation; Tort Law; Intellectual Property Law; Professional Indemnity; Partnership Law.

ANNE M. O'MEARA, admitted, 1980, England and Wales. *Education:* Bachelor of Law (LL.B.) Birmingham University. *PRACTICE AREAS:* Commercial Property Law; Property Development &/or Syndication Law; Residential Property Law; Conveyancing; Landlord & Tenant Law; Land Use Law.

JOHN C. P. SULLIVAN, admitted, 1980, England and Wales. *Education:* B.A. (Jurisprudence) Oxford University. Licensed Insolvency Practitioner. *Member:* Society of Practitioners of Insolvency; Insolvency Lawyers Association. (Head of Insolvency Department). *LANGUAGES:* French, German. *PRACTICE AREAS:* Insolvency Law; Banking Law; Bankruptcy; Commercial Litigation; Corporate Law.

SIMON RAMSHAW, admitted, 1981, England and Wales. *Education:* LL.B. (Hons) Newcastle-upon-Tyne University. *PRACTICE AREAS:* Employee Benefit Law; Pension & Profit Sharing Law.

FRANCES M. KIRKHAM, admitted, 1978, England and Wales. *Education:* B.A. (Hons) London University. *Member:* Chartered Institute of Arbitrators (Fellow and Council Member). *LANGUAGES:* French, Spanish, German. *PRACTICE AREAS:* Building and Construction; Building Contracts; Commercial Law; Contract Law.

JAMES K. RETALLACK, admitted, 1981, England and Wales. *Education:* LL.B. Manchester University. *Member:* Employment Lawyers Association. *PRACTICE AREAS:* Employment Law; Employer/Employee Relations; Employment Discrimination; Employee Benefit Law; Immigration; European Community Law.

MICHAEL J. O'SULLIVAN, admitted, 1977, England and Wales. *Education:* LL.B. (Hons) Warwick University. *PRACTICE AREAS:* Commercial Property Law; Property Finance; Securitisation; Property Development &/or Syndication Law; Landlord & Tenant Law.

(This Listing Continued)

EDGE & ELLISON, Birmingham—Continued

TIM C. WINN, admitted, 1984, England and Wales. *Education:* B.A. (Hons) Chelmer Institute. *LANGUAGES:* French, German. *PRACTICE AREAS:* Corporate Finance Law; Venture Capital; Securities Offerings; Mergers & Acquisitions; Securities Law; International Capital Markets.

ROGER D. BIRCHALL, admitted, 1985, England and Wales. *Education:* LL.B. (Hons) Hull University. *PRACTICE AREAS:* Corporate Finance Law; Mergers & Acquisitions; Leveraged & Management Buyouts; Venture Capital.

ANGELA C. DAVIS, admitted, 1982, England and Wales. *Education:* LL.B. Durham University. *Member:* Institute of Arbitrators. *PRACTICE AREAS:* Commercial Litigation; Defamation; Fraud; Trading Standards/Office of Fair Trading; Equipment Leasing; Commercial Leasing.

STEVE J. EDMONDS, admitted, 1978, England and Wales. *Education:* LL.B. (Hons) (Law) Warwick University. *PRACTICE AREAS:* Criminal Law; Fraud; Environmental Insurance Litigation; Environmental & Industrial Disease Law; Computer Law; Data Protection.

CAROLINE H. EGAN, admitted, 1982, England and Wales. *Education:* St. Anne's College, Oxford University. *Member:* Society for Computers & Law; Association of Women Solicitors. *PRACTICE AREAS:* Intellectual Property Law; Computer Agreements; Television Law; Commercial Law; Sports Law; Biotechnology.

DAVID J. HULL, admitted, 1986, England and Wales. *Education:* LL.B. (Hons) Sheffield University. *Member:* Birmingham Law Society. *PRACTICE AREAS:* Entertainment Law; Mergers & Acquisitions; Securities Offerings; Corporate Restructuring; Financial Restructuring.

ROBIN H. HUMPHREYS, admitted, 1981, England and Wales; 1986, Hong Kong. *Education:* LL.B. (Hons) Southampton University. *LANGUAGES:* French. *PRACTICE AREAS:* Insurance Litigation; Personal Injury (Defendant & Plaintiff); Medical Negligence (Plaintiff); Road Traffic Accidents; Environmental & Industrial Disease Law; Industrial Accidents Law; Mass Torts.

SHELAGH Y. MASON, admitted, 1984, England and Wales. *Education:* LL.B. Kings College University of London. *Member:* Association of Women Solicitors; Women in Business - West Midlands (Chairman); Women in Property (West Midlands-Secretary). *PRACTICE AREAS:* Commercial Property Law; Property Development &/or Syndication Law; Landlord & Tenant Law; Conveyancing.

CHRIS D. RAWSTRON, admitted, 1986, England and Wales. *Education:* LL.B. (Hons) Birmingham University. *Member:* Birmingham Company and Commercial Law Committee. *PRACTICE AREAS:* Entertainment Industry Transactions; Corporate Finance Law; Directors & Officers Liabilities; Venture Capital; Finance Restructuring; Joint Ventures.

GWYN E. WILLIAMS, admitted, 1970, England and Wales. *Education:* Liverpool University. *LANGUAGES:* Welsh. *PRACTICE AREAS:* Environmental Law; Contamination Law; Mining & Mineral Law; European Community Law; Public Sector Competitive Tendering; Public EC Procurement.

CHRISTOPHER C. WILLIAMS, admitted, 1970, England and Wales. *LANGUAGES:* French. *PRACTICE AREAS:* Commercial Property Law; Property Finance; Property Development &/or Syndication Law; Landlord & Tenant Law.

IAN S. WITHERS, admitted, 1970, England and Wales. *PRACTICE AREAS:* Commercial Property Law; Property Law; Landlord & Tenant Law; Conveyancing.

GORDON I. SCOTT, admitted, 1976, England and Wales. *Education:* Oxford University. *LANGUAGES:* French, German. *PRACTICE AREAS:* Property Litigation; Mortgage Enforcements; Commercial Litigation; Professional Indemnity; Intellectual Property Law.

DAVID I. L. LLOYD JONES, admitted, 1979, England and Wales. *Education:* University of Kent. *Member:* Chartered Institute of Arbitrators. *PRACTICE AREAS:* Building & Construction; Building Contracts; Property Litigation; Alternative Dispute Resolution; Arbitration Law.

JAYNE B. WILLETTS, admitted, 1982, England and Wales. *Education:* LL.B. (Hons) University College of London. *PRACTICE AREAS:* Commercial Litigation; Professional Indemnity; Intellectual Property Law; Defamation; Lloyds Litigation.

(This Listing Continued)

MARTIN DAMMS, admitted, 1976, England and Wales. *Education:* LL.B. Birmingham University. *PRACTICE AREAS:* Planning; Land Use Law; Local Authorities; Environmental Law; Contamination Law.

VERONICA DEAN, admitted, 1984, England and Wales. *Education:* LL.B. University of Wales, Cardiff. *PRACTICE AREAS:* Employment and Employee Benefits; Employment Law; Employer/Employee Relations; Employment Discrimination.

ANDREW MADDEN, admitted, 1981, England and Wales. *Education:* LL.B. Birmingham University. *PRACTICE AREAS:* Corporate Law; Mergers and Acquisitions; Securities Offerings; Corporate Restructuring; Corporate Finance Law; Privatisations; Directors and Officers Liabilities; Venture Capital; Company Secretarial; Financial Restructuring; Commercial; Commercial Law; Contract Law; Joint Ventures.

ANGELA HARDMAN, admitted, 1984, England. *Education:* University of Cardiff (LL.B.). *LANGUAGES:* German and Czechoslovakian. *PRACTICE AREAS:* Commercial Litigation; General Litigation; Litigation Defence; Securities Litigation; Mortgage Reinforcements; Debt Recovery; Banking Law; Debt Recovery; Bankruptcy.

DANIEL LUNN, admitted, 1987, England and Wales. *PRACTICE AREAS:* Corporate; Personal Insolvency.

RUSSELL ORME, admitted, 1989, England and Wales. *PRACTICE AREAS:* Corporate Finance; Management Buy-Outs and Buy-Ins; Acquisitions and Reconstructions; Receivership Sales.

NEIL PEARSON, admitted, 1987, England and Wales. *LANGUAGES:* Dutch, French. *PRACTICE AREAS:* Mergers and Acquisitions; Cross-Border Mergers and Acquisitions; EC Competition; Flotations.

SARAH WATSON, admitted, 1987, England and Wales. *LANGUAGES:* French. *PRACTICE AREAS:* Litigation; Breach of Contract; Negligence; Warranties; Professional Indemnity.

STEVE GARRETT, admitted, 1973, England and Wales. *PRACTICE AREAS:* Insurance; Medical Negligence; Personal Injury; Road Traffic Accidents; Employer Liability.

LEICESTER OFFICE
RESIDENT PARTNERS

HENRY T. DOYLE, admitted, 1979, England and Wales. *Member:* The Society of English and American Lawyers. *LANGUAGES:* German, Spanish. *PRACTICE AREAS:* Residential Property Law; Conveyancing; Landlord & Tenant Law; Wills; Probate Law.

MICHAEL A. PARK, admitted, 1980, England and Wales. *Education:* Sheffield University. *LANGUAGES:* German. *PRACTICE AREAS:* Commercial Property Law; Property Development &/or Syndication Law; Building Contracts; Conveyancing; Landlord & Tenant Law.

MARK I. NEWCOMBE, admitted, 1984, England and Wales. *Education:* LL.B. Manchester University. *PRACTICE AREAS:* Commercial Property Law; Property Finance; Residential Property Law; Building Contracts; Land Use Law; Conveyancing; Planning; Landlord & Tenant Law.

HELEN A. READETT, admitted, 1982, England and Wales. *Education:* B.A. (Hons) Birmingham University. *Member:* Insolvency Practitioners Association. *PRACTICE AREAS:* Insolvency; Bankruptcy; Banking Law; Finance Law.

DAVID E. WEST, admitted, 1977, England and Wales. *Education:* Birmingham University. *LANGUAGES:* French, German. *PRACTICE AREAS:* Commercial Law; Corporate Finance Law; Mergers & Acquisitions.

CHARLES DARBY, admitted, 1986, England and Wales. *Education:* LL.B. University College London. *LANGUAGES:* French. *PRACTICE AREAS:* Commercial Litigation; Fraud; White Collar Fraud; Securities Litigation; Mortgage Reinforcement; Professional Indemnity; Corporate; Insolvency Law; Corporate Restructuring; Debt Recovery; Directors and Officers Liability; Financial Restructuring; Bankruptcy; Commercial; Commercial Law; Consumer Law; Competition Law; Contract Law.

BRENDAN WALSH, admitted, 1986, England and Wales. *PRACTICE AREAS:* Property; Commercial Property Development; Commercial Property Finance; Retail Property; Property Investment; Property Joint Ventures.

(For Biographical data on partners in London, see Professional biographies at London, England)

EVERSHEDS

10 NEWHALL STREET
BIRMINGHAM B3 3LX, ENGLAND
Telephone: (44) 121 233 2001
Fax: (44) 121 236 1583

Other Eversheds Offices:
Bristol, Cardiff, Derby, Ipswich, Leeds, London, Manchester,
Middlesbrough, Newcastle-upon-Tyne, Norwich, Nottingham, Berlin,
Brussels, Jersey.

Acquisitions and Mergers, Agency/Distribution, Agriculture, Banking, Commercial Property, Company Law, Competition Law, Construction, Corporate Finance, Corporate Tax, EC Law, Employment, Environment, Entertainment, Information Technology, Franchising, Insolvency, Intellectual Property, Litigation, Management Buy-Outs, Pensions and Employee Benefits, Personal Tax & Financial Planning, Property Development, Shipping, Trading Contracts.
Partners within Eversheds: 273.

REGIONAL MANAGING PARTNERS

Ian Jollie

BIRMINGHAM PARTNERS

David S. Haggett	John M. Jennings
Michael R. Arnold	Pat A. Johnstone
Peter G. Battye	W. Ian Jollie
Adrian D. Bland	Peter R.F. Manford
David Blyth	Peter J. McHugh
Peter R. Bromage	Martin N. McKenna
Jeff R. Drew	Sarah McKenna
Stephen L. Duffield	Milton N. Psyllides
Harry O. Forrester	Jim E. Rowley
Chris J. Garnett	Michael R. Seabrook
Anne E. Harris	Brian R. Shaw
Philip J. Harrison	Sarah A. Shilcof
Meg E.M. Heppel	Malcolm Titcomb
Martin W. Hopkins	Nigel G. Watkins
David J. Hubball	H. Stephen Williams
Andrew D.G. Inglis	C. Piers Wolf
	David A. Young

MARTINEAU JOHNSON

Established in 1828

ST PHILIPS HOUSE
ST PHILIPS PLACE
BIRMINGHAM B3 2PP, ENGLAND
Telephone: 0121-200 3300 (National); 44-121-200-3300 (International)
Fax: 0121-200 3330 (National); 44-121-200-3330 (International)

Banking, Corporate and Corporate Finance, Commercial Agreements, Commercial Disputes, Copyright, Employment, Environmental Law, European Law, Intellectual Property, Landlord and Tenant, Liquidations and Receiverships, Property and Development.

PARTNERS

MICHAEL D.H. SHEPHERD, admitted, 1966. *Education:* Oxon (M.A.). (Senior Partner). **PRACTICE AREAS:** Company Commercial; Commercial Property; Real Estate; Real Property; Taxation.

JAMES M.G. FEA, admitted, 1964. *Education:* Winchester. **PRACTICE AREAS:** Charities; Trusts and Estates; Wills; Probate; Taxation.

MICHAEL R. WINWOOD, admitted, 1966. *Education:* Bradfield. **PRACTICE AREAS:** Corporate Finance; Merger and Acquisition Takeovers; Stock Exchange; Flotations; Investments; Mergers; Acquisitions and Divestitures.

HUGH B. CARSLAKE, admitted, 1973. *Education:* Trinity (B.A.; LL.B.). **PRACTICE AREAS:** Ecclesiastical Law; Charitable Organisations; Notarial Services; Religious Institutions; Taxation.

IAN MARSHALL, admitted, 1974. *Education:* Cambridge (B.A.). **PRACTICE AREAS:** Employment; Business Law; Collective Bargaining; Industrial Relations; Labour.

DAVID J. GWYTHER, admitted, 1975, England. *Education:* LL.B. (Sheff). (Deputy Senior Partner). **PRACTICE AREAS:** Debt Collection; Litigation Commercial; Contracts; Negligence; Professional Liability.

(This Listing Continued)

EDWARD I. COX, admitted, 1977. *Education:* Bristol (B.A.). **PRACTICE AREAS:** Commercial Property; Housing; Real Estate; Real Property; Tenancy.

DAVID F. ALLISON, admitted, 1978. *Education:* Oxford (M.A.). (Managing Partner). **PRACTICE AREAS:** Company and Commercial (General); Competition Law; Agency and Distributorships; Common Market; Franchises and Franchising.

ANDREW N. SPOONER, admitted, 1978. *Education:* (LL.B.). **PRACTICE AREAS:** Banking; Alternative Dispute Resolution; Alcoholic Beverages; Family Law; Licensing.

BRIAN M. PARLOUR, admitted, 1979. **PRACTICE AREAS:** Banks and Banking; Construction - Contentious Landlord and Tenant; Partnerships; Personal Injury.

JEREMY J. MARTINEAU, admitted, 1981. *Education:* Cambridge (B.A.). **PRACTICE AREAS:** Company and Commercial (General); Corporate Finance; Employee Benefits; Joint Ventures; Mergers.

ANDREW J. STILTON, admitted, 1981. *Education:* Cambridge (B.A.; M.A.). **PRACTICE AREAS:** Corporate Finance; Insolvency and Corporate Reconstruction; Bankruptcy; Company Law; Flotations.

SIMON M.J. ARROWSMITH, admitted, 1984. *Education:* Cambridge (B.A.; Ph.D.). **PRACTICE AREAS:** Education; Health Care; Hospitals.

IAN P. BAKER, admitted, 1983. *Education:* Oxford (B.A.; LL.B.). **PRACTICE AREAS:** Banks and Banking; Corporate Finance; Company and Commercial (General); European Community Law; Investments.

JOANNA LAWSON-KING, admitted, 1982. *Education:* Kings College (LL.B.). **PRACTICE AREAS:** Property - Commercial Property; Finance; Leases and Leasing; Real Estate; Real Property.

BRIAN W. AIKMAN, admitted, 1982. *Education:* Birmingham (LL.B.). **PRACTICE AREAS:** Environment; Litigation; Insurance; Bankruptcy; Entertainment and the Arts; Reinsurance.

BARRY K. SANKEY, admitted, 1983. *Education:* Oxford (B.A., Oxon; M.A., Oxon). **PRACTICE AREAS:** Environment; Hazardous Materials; Land Use; Science and Technology; Planning and Land Use.

ROGER W. BLEARS, admitted, 1984. *Education:* Nottingham (LL.B.). **PRACTICE AREAS:** Banking; Corporate Finance; Government Contracts; Investments; Leveraged and Management Buy-outs and Buy-Ins; Mergers; Acquisitions and Divestitures; Venture Capital.

QUENTIN H. BUTLER, admitted, 1982. *Education:* Oxford. **PRACTICE AREAS:** Agricultural; Property - Commercial Property; Real Estate; Real Property.

WILLIAM T. BARKER, admitted, 1986. *Education:* Keele (B.Sc.). **PRACTICE AREAS:** Computers and Software; Intellectual Property; Copyright; Software; Trademarks.

DAVID M. COOPER, admitted, 1987. *Education:* Oxford (B.A.). **PRACTICE AREAS:** Libel and Defamation; Employment; Litigation-Commercial; Communications and Media; Discrimination.

NICOLAS E. EAST, admitted, 1982. *Education:* Nottingham (LL.B.). **PRACTICE AREAS:** Property - Commercial Property; Real Estate; Real Property.

MATTHEW S. HANSELL, admitted, 1985. *Education:* Wales (LL.B.). **PRACTICE AREAS:** Probate; Charities; Tax; Trusts and Estates; Wills.

ANDREW R. WHITEHEAD, admitted, 1988. *Education:* Birmingham (LL.B.). **PRACTICE AREAS:** Corporate Law; Energy; Power; Public Utilities; Utilities.

All our lawyers are members of the Law Society of England and Wales

Languages: English, French, Spanish, Italian and German

PINSENT & CO.

3 COLMORE CIRCUS
BIRMINGHAM B4 6BH, ENGLAND
Telephone: 0121-200 1050
Telex: 335101 PINSENT B'HAM
Cable Address: "Pinsent Birmingham Telex"
Fax: Direct Line 0121-626 1040

London, England Office: Royex House, Aldermanbury Square, EC2V 7HR. Telephone: 0171-600 4999. Fax: 0171-600 4947.

(This Listing Continued)

PINSENT & CO., Birmingham—Continued

Brussels, Belgium Office: Avenue de Cortenberg 79/81, 1040. Telephone: 010-322 732 3600. Fax: 010-322 734 8793.

Agency and Distribution Agreements, Banking, Commercial Property, Computer Contracts, Conditions of Sale and Purchase, Construction Law, Contractual Disputes, Copyright, EC and Competition Law, Corporate and Financial Services Law, Employees' Share Schemes, Employment Law, Environmental Law, Flotations, Franchise and Licensing Agreements, Health and Safety at Work, Historic Houses, Insolvency, Insurance Litigation, Intellectual Property Litigation, International Carriage of Goods, Joint Ventures, Licensing, Management Buy-outs, Mergers and Acquisitions, Patent and Trade Mark Agreements, Product Liability, Professional Indemnity, Property Development, Public Law, Share Valuation, Tax - Capital Taxes, Tax - Corporate Tax, Tax - Personal, Town and County Planning, Trade Mark Applications, Trusts and Settlements, Pensions.

MEMBERS OF FIRM

DAVID C. COOKE, admitted, 1961. *Education:* Manchester (LL.B.). Senior Partner.

JULIAN M. J. TONKS, admitted, 1982. *Education:* Oxon (M.A.). *PRACTICE AREAS:* Trusts and Settlements Law; Tax - Capital Law; Corporate and Personal Law.

MICHAEL J. O'DRISCOLL, admitted, 1961. *Education:* Oxon (B.A.). *PRACTICE AREAS:* Pension Schemes Law.

CHARLES R. KING-FARLOW, admitted, 1965. *Education:* Oxon (M.A.; LL.B.). *PRACTICE AREAS:* Historic Houses; Tax - Capital and Corporate Law; Trusts and Settlements Law.

JOHN C. J. ORCHARD, admitted, 1967. *Education:* Cantab (M.A.; LL.B.). *PRACTICE AREAS:* Commercial Property Law; Property Development Law; Capital Taxes Law.

PATRICK J. GREEN, admitted, 1966. *Education:* Cantab (M.A.; LL.B.). *PRACTICE AREAS:* Agency and Distribution Agreements Law; EC and Competition Law; Joint Ventures Law; Mergers and Acquisitions Law.

NEIL M. MAYBURY, admitted, 1966. *Education:* B'Ham (LL.B.). *PRACTICE AREAS:* Computer Contracts Law; Copyright Law; Intellectual Property Law; Patent and Trade Mark Agreements Law.

J. BRIAN HOPKINSON, admitted, 1973. *Education:* Oxon (B.A.). *PRACTICE AREAS:* Agency and Distribution Agreements Law; Conditions of Sale and Purchase Law; Health and Safety at Work Law; International Carriage of Goods.

PAUL N. DOWNING, admitted, 1974. *Education:* Essex (B.A.). (Resident Member, London Office). *PRACTICE AREAS:* Contractual Disputes Law; Insurance Litigation.

BARRY G. K. BRICE, admitted, 1975. *Education:* Oxon (M.A.). *PRACTICE AREAS:* Commercial Property Law; Property Development.

DAVID J. COOKE, admitted, 1981. *Education:* Cantab (M.A.). *PRACTICE AREAS:* Flotations; Insolvency Law; Management Buy-outs; Mergers and Acquisitions Law; Venture Capital Law.

DAVID J. PETT, admitted, 1980. *Education:* Oxon (M.A.). *PRACTICE AREAS:* Employee's Share Schemes; Corporate Tax Law; Personal Tax Law.

ANDREW K. EASTGATE, admitted, 1980. *Education:* Oxon (B.A.). *PRACTICE AREAS:* Flotations; Management Buy-outs; Mergers and Acquisitions Law; Venture Capital Law.

ANDREW J. PATON, admitted, 1981. *Education:* Exeter (LL.B.). *PRACTICE AREAS:* Product Liability Law; Professional Indemnity Law.

DAVID J. HUGHES, admitted, 1980. *Education:* Oxon (M.A.). *PRACTICE AREAS:* Banking Law; Flotations; Joint Ventures; Mergers and Acquisitions.

MARTIN J. WHITE, admitted, 1979. *Education:* Cantab (M.A.). *PRACTICE AREAS:* Environmental Law; Public Law; Town and Country Planning Law.

COLIN J. GOODIER, admitted, 1972. *Education:* Cantab (M.A.). *PRACTICE AREAS:* Contractual Disputes Law; Employment Law; Franchise and Licensing Agreements; Products Liability Law.

(This Listing Continued)

A. DAVID W. ROBINSON, admitted, 1979. *Education:* London (LL.B.). (Resident, London, England Office). *PRACTICE AREAS:* Professional Indemnity Law.

JOHN HAMILTON PRATT, admitted, 1976. *Education:* Oxford University (M.A.); University d'Aix-Marseille, Aix-en-Provence, France (Diploma, Comparative Law). *PRACTICE AREAS:* Franchising; Competition Law; International Trade; Corporate Finance.

H. ANSON GAME, admitted, 1978. *Education:* Dunhelm (B.A., Hons.). (Resident, London, England Office). *PRACTICE AREAS:* Insurance Litigation; Professional Indemnity Law.

ANDREW P. LONG, admitted, 1980. *Education:* Oxon (B.A.). *PRACTICE AREAS:* Professional Indemnity Law.

G. PATRICK A.S. TWIST, admitted, 1981. *Education:* Keele (B.A.). *PRACTICE AREAS:* Banking Law; Insolvency Law; Corporate and Commercial Law.

STEPHEN V. BROWN, admitted, 1982. *Education:* Cantab (B.A.). *PRACTICE AREAS:* Commercial Property Law; Property Development Law.

ASHLEIGH M. BRADFORD, admitted, 1979. *PRACTICE AREAS:* Professional Indemnity Law.

R. JON P. AUSTIN, admitted, 1981. *Education:* Bristol (B.A., Hons.). *PRACTICE AREAS:* Commercial Property Law; Property Development Law.

DAVID J. PHILPOT, admitted, 1987. *Education:* Bristol (LL.B.). *PRACTICE AREAS:* Commercial Property Law; Property Development Law.

ANDREW J. STACEY, admitted, 1974. *Education:* Bristol (LL.B.). *PRACTICE AREAS:* Environmental Law; Health and Safety at Work; Licensing Law; Public Law; Town and County Planning Law.

CARL P. GARVIE, admitted, 1986. *Education:* Cantab (M.A.). *PRACTICE AREAS:* Banking Law; Insolvency Law; Commercial Litigation.

SIMON D. V. GRONOW, admitted, 1986. *Education:* Cantab (M.A.). *PRACTICE AREAS:* Mergers and Acquisitions Law; Corporate and Financial Services Law.

GREGORY J. LOWSON, admitted, 1984. *Education:* Liverpool (B.A.). *PRACTICE AREAS:* Banking Law; Insolvency Law; Commercial Litigation.

ALAN C. FARKAS, admitted, 1984. *Education:* Sussex (B.A.). *PRACTICE AREAS:* Corporate Finance Law; Mergers and Acquisitions.

ANDREW G. WALSH, admitted, 1979. *Education:* Oxon (M.A.); Cantab (LL.B.). (Resident Member, London Office). *PRACTICE AREAS:* Corporate Law; Management Buy-outs; Privatisations.

STEVEN CLIFFORD, admitted, 1978. *Education:* Leicester (LL.B.). *PRACTICE AREAS:* Building Society.

AMANDA JANE PERRY ALLEN, admitted, 1986. *Education:* Birmingham (LL.B.). *PRACTICE AREAS:* Corporate Finance.

ELEANOR MARY DEADY, admitted, 1981. *Education:* Kings, London (LL.B.). *PRACTICE AREAS:* Commercial Property.

HEATHER LYNNS MARGARET JONES, admitted, 1978. *Education:* Birmingham (LL.B., Hons.). *PRACTICE AREAS:* Environment; Public Sector.

DAVID PATRICK RYAN, admitted, 1985. *Education:* Oxon (B.A.). *PRACTICE AREAS:* Corporate and Personal Tax.

ELIZABETH MARY SHELLEY, admitted, 1980. *Education:* Leicester (LL.B.). *PRACTICE AREAS:* Professional Indemnity.

KARL PETER WERNHAM, admitted, 1985. *Education:* Cantab (B.A.). *PRACTICE AREAS:* Contractual Disputes Law.

JEREMY PAUL PHILLIPS, admitted, 1984. *Education:* Birmingham (LL.B.). (Resident Member, London Office). *PRACTICE AREAS:* Corporate Finance.

KEVIN JOHN PERRY, admitted, 1985. *Education:* Queen Mary, London (LL.B.). (Resident Member, London Office). *PRACTICE AREAS:* Construction; Contractual Disputes Law.

NIGEL S. BURNELL, admitted, 1977. *Education:* Keble College (M.A., 1974). *PRACTICE AREAS:* Corporate Pensions; Pension Schemes Law.

(This Listing Continued)

MARTIN E. CHITTY, admitted, 1986. *Education:* Dunhelm (B.A., Hons). *PRACTICE AREAS:* Employment Law.

FIONA HEYES, admitted, 1987. *Education:* Sheffield (LL.B.). (Resident Member, London Office). *PRACTICE AREAS:* Professional Indemnity Law.

KATE J. TAYLOR, admitted, 1988. *Education:* Exeter (LL.B., Hons.). *PRACTICE AREAS:* EC Law.

SHEILA WILSON, admitted, 1987. *Education:* Lancaster (LL.B., Hons.). (Resident Member, London Office). *PRACTICE AREAS:* Professional Indemnity Law.

CAMERON A. WOODROW, admitted, 1986. *Education:* Oxon (B.A., Hons.). *PRACTICE AREAS:* Company and Commercial.

ALISON BOND, admitted, 1988. *Education:* Cantab (B.A.). *PRACTICE AREAS:* Corporate.

LEON D. FLAVELL, admitted, 1987. *Education:* University College London (LL.B.). (Resident Member, London Office). *PRACTICE AREAS:* Venture Capital; Management Buy-Outs.

ALAN E. GREENOUGH, admitted, 1974. *Education:* Bristol (LL.B.,). *PRACTICE AREAS:* Corporate Finance.

JILL MARIE TOMASIN, admitted, 1984. *Education:* B'Ham (LL.B., Hons). *PRACTICE AREAS:* Intellectual Property.

CONSULTANTS

GRAHAM J. HEARNE, CBE

CHRISTOPHER H. HARMER

ANDREW M. LEFEVER

Firm is member of the Legal Resources Group.

WANSBROUGHS WILLEY HARGRAVE

BIRMINGHAM, ENGLAND

(See London, England)

WRAGGE & CO.

Established in 1834

55 COLMORE ROW
BIRMINGHAM B3 2AS, ENGLAND
Telephone: 0121 233 1000 (National);
44 121 233 1000 (International)
Telecopier: 0121 214 1099 (National);
44 121 214 1099 (International)

Company, Commercial, Banking, Corporate Finance, Corporate Rescue, Corporate Taxation, Bankruptcy and Insolvency, Financial Services, Joint Ventures, Management Buyouts and Buyins, Venture Capital, Commercial Contracts, Competition Anti-Trust, Computer Contracts, Defamation, Entertainment, European Communities, Government Relations, Franchising, Media, Intellectual Property, Arbitration, Building and Construction, Procurement, Employment, Labor Law, Mergers and Acquisitions, Environment, Immigration, Insurance Litigation, Landlord and Tenant, Licensing, Planning Zoning, Professional Negligence Malpractice, Commercial Property Real Estate, Property Development, Property Finance, Charities, Pensions, Public Authorities, Personal Tax, Probate, Trusts, National Health Services Trusts.

PARTNERS

JOHN R. A. CRABTREE, admitted, 1973, England. *Education:* University of Birmingham (LL.B., 1970). (Senior Partner). *LANGUAGES:* English. *PRACTICE AREAS:* Mergers and Acquisitions; Corporate Finance.

CHRISTOPHER W. HUGHES, admitted, 1966, England. *Education:* University College, London (LL.B., 1963). Notary Public. *Member:* Law Society; Society of Notaries; Solicitors' European Group; Birmingham Law Society (President, 1989-1990). (Managing Partner). *LANGUAGES:* French, Spanish and English. *PRACTICE AREAS:* Corporate Law; Commercial Law; Professional Standards.

(This Listing Continued)

R. M. GILBERT, admitted, 1972, England. *Education:* University College, London (LL.B., 1969). Licensed Insolvency Practitioner. *Member:* Law Society; Insolvency Lawyers Association; Institute of Directors. (Deputy Senior Partner). *LANGUAGES:* English. *PRACTICE AREAS:* Mergers and Acquisitions; Insolvency; Joint Ventures.

PETER M. WALL, admitted, 1972, England. *Education:* University of Bristol (BA.). Birmingham Law Society's Gold Medal, 1972. Commissioner of Taxes, 1980-1989. *Member:* Law Society. (Deputy Senior Partner). *LANGUAGES:* English. *PRACTICE AREAS:* Management and Finance.

DAVID J. ASKIN, admitted, 1970, England. *Education:* St. Catherine's College, Cambridge (MA., 1967; LL.M., 1968). Scholar, St. Catherine's College. *Member:* Law Society. *LANGUAGES:* English and French. *PRACTICE AREAS:* Commercial Property; Landlord and Tenant; Property Development; Property Finance.

DAVID M. BIRCH, admitted, 1974, England. *Education:* University College, London (LL.B., 1971). Chair, Norton Rose M5 Americas Group. Former President, Canada U.K. Chamber of Commerce. *Member:* Law Society; British Insurance Law Association; International Bar Association (Chair: International Committee). *LANGUAGES:* English. *PRACTICE AREAS:* Commercial and Insurance Litigation; Professional Negligence.

STEPHEN J. BRAITHWAITE, admitted, 1973, England. *Education:* Queens' College, Cambridge (MA., 1972). *Member:* Law Society. *LANGUAGES:* English and French. *PRACTICE AREAS:* Corporate Finance; Joint Ventures; Management Buy-outs; Mergers and Acquisitions; Venture Capital.

ROBERT J. CADDICK, admitted, 1975, England. *Education:* Emmanuel College, Cambridge (MA., 1974). *Member:* Law Society. *LANGUAGES:* English and French. *PRACTICE AREAS:* Commercial Property; Property Development; Property Finance.

VIVIEN COCKERILL, admitted, 1987, England. *Education:* University of Birmingham (LL.B., 1984) and Limoges, France. *Member:* Association of Pension Lawyers; Law Society. *LANGUAGES:* English and French. *PRACTICE AREAS:* Financial Services; Pensions.

ANDREW MANNING COX, admitted, 1980, England. *Education:* Selwyn College, Cambridge (MA., 1979). Scholar, University of Cambridge. *Member:* Law Society; Society of Notaries. *LANGUAGES:* English and French. *PRACTICE AREAS:* Commercial Litigation; Construction Litigation; Employment.

MARK DAKEYNE, admitted, 1983, England. *Education:* Magdalene College, Cambridge (MA., 1982). *Member:* Law Society. *LANGUAGES:* English. *PRACTICE AREAS:* Commercial Property; Landlord and Tenant; Property Development; Property Finance; Environmental Law.

SUSAN J. DEARDEN, admitted, 1986, England. *Education:* Birmingham University (LL.B., Hons., 1983). *Member:* Law Society; BIIBA Liabilities Association (West Midlands Region); Birmingham Medico Legal Society. *LANGUAGES:* English. *PRACTICE AREAS:* Insurance Litigation; Personal Injury; Medical Negligence.

JOHN H. DUNCOMBE, admitted, 1966, England. *Education:* University of Nottingham (LL.B., 1962). *Member:* Law Society. *LANGUAGES:* English. *PRACTICE AREAS:* Commercial Property; Joint Ventures; Property Development; Property Finance.

MAURICE J. DWYER, admitted, 1983, England. *Education:* University of Warwick (LL.B., 1980). *Member:* Law Society. *LANGUAGES:* English and French. *PRACTICE AREAS:* Banking; Corporate Law; Joint Ventures; Venture Capital.

IFOR H. EDWARDS, admitted, 1966, England. *Education:* Corpus Christi, Oxford (MA., 1965). Deputy District Judge, 1983-1988. *Member:* Chartered Institute of Arbitrators (West Midlands Committee); Law Society. *LANGUAGES:* English, French and Welsh. *PRACTICE AREAS:* Construction Litigation; Employment Litigation.

RICHARD J. ELLISON, admitted, 1982, England. *Education:* Mansfield College, Oxford (MA., 1979). *LANGUAGES:* English. *PRACTICE AREAS:* Banking and Finance Litigation and Recovery; Construction Litigation.

ANDREW GALLA, admitted, 1980, England. *Education:* Birmingham University (LL.B., 1977). *Member:* Law Society. *LANGUAGES:* English. *PRACTICE AREAS:* Property Development; Commercial Property; Landlord and Tenant.

(This Listing Continued)

WRAGGE & CO., Birmingham—Continued

JOHN H. HALL, admitted, 1964, England. *Member:* Law Society. *LANGUAGES:* English. *PRACTICE AREAS:* Corporate Law; Joint Ventures; Education.

DAVID W. HAMLETT, admitted, 1980, England. *Education:* Downing College, Cambridge (MA., 1979). *Member:* Law Society. *LANGUAGES:* English. *PRACTICE AREAS:* Institutional and Venture Capital; EC Law; Competition Law; Commercial Agreements; Licensing; Intellectual Property.

GORDON D. HARRIS, admitted, 1984, England. *Education:* University College, London (LL.B., 1981). *Member:* Chartered Institute of Patent Agents; Institute of Trade Mark Agents; United States Trade Mark Association. *LANGUAGES:* English and German. *PRACTICE AREAS:* Defamation; Litigation; Entertainment; Franchising; Intellectual Property.

RICHARD HAYWOOD, admitted, 1980, England. *Education:* University of Birmingham (LL.B., 1977). Licensed Insolvency Practitioner. *Member:* Law Society; Insolvency Lawyers Association (Education and Training Committee); Insolvency Practitioners Association; Society of Practitioners of Insolvency. *LANGUAGES:* English. *PRACTICE AREAS:* Corporate Finance; Corporate Restructuring Workouts; Banking; Insolvency.

MARK D. HICK, called to the Bar, 1979; admitted, 1985, England. *Education:* University of Leeds (LL.B., 1978). *Member:* British Insurance Law Association; Chartered Insurance Institute; Law Society. *LANGUAGES:* English. *PRACTICE AREAS:* Insurance Litigation; Personal Injury; Products and Professional Indemnity Claims.

GERALD B.G. HINGLEY, admitted, 1970, England. *Education:* University of Nottingham (BA., 1966). *Member:* Association of Pension Lawyers (Head of Pensions and Trusts Department). *LANGUAGES:* English. *PRACTICE AREAS:* Pensions.

DANIEL M. HEMMING, admitted, 1979, England. *Education:* Birmingham Polytechnic (B.A., Hons., 1975). *Member:* Law Society. *LANGUAGES:* English. *PRACTICE AREAS:* Planning Law; Compulsory Purchase and Compensation; Highways.

LUCY C. HOWCROFT, admitted, 1986, England. *Education:* University of Birmingham (LL.B. Law with French, 1983). *Member:* Law Society. *LANGUAGES:* French and English. *PRACTICE AREAS:* Banking and Insolvency (Non-contentious).

JACK J. JACOVOU, admitted, 1983, England. *Education:* Coventry Polytechnic (BA., 1979). *Member:* Law Society. *LANGUAGES:* English and Greek. *PRACTICE AREAS:* Commercial Property; Landlord and Tenant; Property Finance.

W.H. JONES, admitted, 1984, England. *Education:* University of Newcastle (BA., 1968); University of Lancaster (MA., 1969); University of Liverpool (PhD., 1975). *Member:* Chartered Institute of Patent Agents; Institute of Trade Mark Agents; British Computer Society; Society for Computers and Law. *LANGUAGES:* French and English. *PRACTICE AREAS:* Intellectual Property; Computer and Information Technology Law; Defamation; Litigation; Licensing.

SUZANNE LLOYD HOLT, admitted, 1974, England. *Education:* Royal Holloway College, London (BA., 1966). *Member:* British-Italian Law Association; Chartered Institute of Arbitrators; Franco-British Lawyers Association; Associazione Giuristi di Lingua Italiana; International Bar Association; Law Society; Solicitors European Group. *LANGUAGES:* French, Italian, German, Spanish and English. *PRACTICE AREAS:* Construction Litigation; Landlord and Tenant Litigation; Property Litigation.

IAN R. METCALFE, admitted, 1983, England. *Education:* St. Catherine's College, Oxford (MA., 1980). General Committee: Lords Taverners (West Midlands Region); Warwickshire County Cricket Club. *Member:* Law Society. *LANGUAGES:* English. *PRACTICE AREAS:* Corporate Finance; Management Buyouts; Mergers and Acquisitions; Company Law; Venture Capital.

JEREMY S. MILLINGTON, admitted, 1988, England. *Education:* Nottingham University (LL.B.). *LANGUAGES:* English. *PRACTICE AREAS:* Corporate Finance; Mergers and Acquisitions.

NICOLA J. MUMFORD, admitted, 1986, England. *Education:* Trent Polytechnic, Nottingham (B.A., 1983). *Member:* Law Society. *LANGUAGES:* English. *PRACTICE AREAS:* Commercial Litigation; Insolvency; Immigration.

(This Listing Continued)

JULIAN C. PALLETT, admitted, 1983, England. *Education:* Wadham College, Oxford (MA., 1983). *Member:* Law Society. *LANGUAGES:* English. *PRACTICE AREAS:* Banking; Insolvency.

DAVID E. PETTINGALE, admitted, 1982, England. *Education:* Gonville & Caius, Cambridge (MA., 1982). *Member:* Law Society. *LANGUAGES:* English. *PRACTICE AREAS:* Commercial Property; Building Societies; Insolvency.

ASHLEY R. PIGOTT, admitted, 1986, England. *Education:* St. Edmund Hall, Oxford University. *Member:* Chartered Institute of Arbitrators (Associate). *LANGUAGES:* French. *PRACTICE AREAS:* Construction; Litigation; Arbitration.

QUENTIN S. POOLE, admitted, 1981, England. *Education:* University of Warwick (LL.B., 1976). Licensed Insolvency Practitioner. *Member:* Law Society; Insolvency Lawyers Association. *LANGUAGES:* English. *PRACTICE AREAS:* Banking; Commercial and Insolvency Litigation.

KEVIN J. POOLE, admitted, 1983, England. *Education:* Jesus College, Cambridge (MA., 1982). *Member:* Law Society. *LANGUAGES:* English and French. *PRACTICE AREAS:* Mergers and Acquisitions; Corporate Finance; Financial Services; Taxation.

PETER W. SMITH, admitted, 1978, England. *Education:* Jesus College, Oxford (MA., 1977). *Member:* Law Society. *LANGUAGES:* English and French. *PRACTICE AREAS:* Corporate Tax; Mergers and Acquisitions; Corporate Finance; Financial Services; Local Authority Waste Disposal Schemes.

PETER D. THORNE, admitted, 1984, England. *Education:* Polytechnic of Central London (BA., 1981). *Member:* Law Society. *LANGUAGES:* English. *PRACTICE AREAS:* Commercial Property; Landlord and Tenant; Property Development; Property Finance.

JOHN R. TURNER, admitted, 1980, England. *Education:* Christ's College, Cambridge (MA., 1979). *Member:* Law Society; United Kingdom Environmental Law Association. *LANGUAGES:* English. *PRACTICE AREAS:* Environmental Law.

DAVID VAUGHAN, admitted, 1987, England. *Education:* University of Edinburgh (MA., 1983). *Member:* Law Society. *LANGUAGES:* English. *PRACTICE AREAS:* Mergers and Acquisitions; Corporate Finance.

MICHAEL WHITEHOUSE, admitted, 1977, England. *Education:* University of Liverpool (LL.B., 1974). *Member:* Law Society. *LANGUAGES:* English. *PRACTICE AREAS:* Company Commercial; Corporate Finance; Management Buy-Outs; Mergers and Acquisitions; Venture Capital; Joint Ventures.

LOUISE S. WOODHEAD, admitted, 1985, England. *Education:* University of Nottingham (LL.B., 1982). *Member:* Association of Charity Lawyers; Law Society. *LANGUAGES:* English. *PRACTICE AREAS:* Taxation; Trusts and Probate; Charities.

Languages: English, French, German, Italian, Spanish, Chinese (Cantonese, Mandarin)

HAMMOND SUDDARDS

PENNINE HOUSE
39-45 WELL STREET
BRADFORD BD1 5NL, ENGLAND
Telephone: 01274 734700
Fax: 01274 737547
Telex: 517201

Leeds, England Office: 2 Park Lane. LS3 1ES. Telephone: 0113 234 3500. Fax: 0113 234 3600. Telex: 517201.

Brussels, Belgium Office: Avenue Louise 250, 1050. Telephone: 00 32 2 627 7676. Fax: 00 32 2 627 7686.

London, England Office: Moor House, 119 London Wall, London, EC2Y 5ET. Telephone: 0171 628 4767. Fax: 0171 628 6161.

Manchester, England Office: Trinity Court, 16 John Dalton Street, M60 8HS. Telephone: 0161 834 2222. Fax: 0161 834 2244.

Corporate Finance including Acquisitions and Mergers, Corporate Finance, Commercial including Acquisitions and Mergers, Corporate Tax, Commercial including Joint Ventures, Pensions, Banks and Building Societies, Intellectual Property, Commercial Litigation, Construction, Insolvency and Corporate Recovery, Debt Collection, Town and Country Planning, Environmental Law, Commercial Property, European Community Law, Information Technology Law, Employment, Utilities, Insurance Litigation, Media, Mortgage and Aviation Law.

(This Listing Continued)

Hammond Suddards has over 870 staff, including 58 Partners, 100 Associates and 50 Legal Executives and Paralegals.

RESIDENT PARTNERS

MICHAEL E. GREGSON. PRACTICE AREAS: Commercial Property.

SIMON R.B. STELL. PRACTICE AREAS: Commercial Litigation.

Languages: Arabic, Dutch, French, German, Hebrew, Italian, Portuguese, Russian, Spanish, Ukrainian, Urdu, Greek, Czech, Serbo-Croatian, Lithuanian, Malay and Punjabi.

(For lists of other Members see Professional Biographies at Leeds, London and Manchester, England and Brussels, Belgium)

BEVAN ASHFORD

Solicitors

35 COLSTON AVENUE
BRISTOL BS1 4TT, ENGLAND
Telephone: 01179 230111 (National) 44 1179 230111 (International)
Fax: 01179 291865

Also offices at: Cardiff, Exeter, London, Plymouth, Taunton and Tiverton.

FIRM PROFILE: *The firm is one of the largest regional firms in the country, and was responsible for founding ADVOC, a network of similar independent legal firms extending across Europe. Major commercial work is concentrated in the Bristol, Cardiff and Exeter offices, with particular expertise in corporate transactions, property development and finance, employment law, commercial litigation, intellectual property and media law. Bristol is also well known for its national practice for the National Health Service and consequently has a strong medical litigation department.*

PARTNERS

RICHARD H. ANNANDALE, admitted, 1977, England. *LANGUAGES:* English and French. *PRACTICE AREAS:* Medical Negligence; Risk Management in Health Service; Personal Injury.

PAUL H. BARBER, admitted, 1976, England. *LANGUAGES:* English, French and German. *PRACTICE AREAS:* Medical Negligence; Mental Health; Personal Injury - Defendant.

JILL F. H. BROADHEAD, admitted, 1978, England. *LANGUAGES:* English. *PRACTICE AREAS:* Defendant medical negligence; Associated hospital litigation; Registered nursing home litigation.

PAUL A. COOPER, admitted, 1977, England. *LANGUAGES:* English and French. *PRACTICE AREAS:* Corporate Finance; Mergers and Acquisitions; Disposals of Companies/Businesses; General Company Work; Taxation; Stock Exchange.

J.G. (IAIN) FAIRBAIRN, admitted, 1979, England. *LANGUAGES:* English and French. *PRACTICE AREAS:* NHS Matters, establishment of NHS Trusts and general and constitutional advice; Property Development, major receiverships.

STEPHEN D. HUGHES, admitted, 1987, England. *LANGUAGES:* English and Italian. *PRACTICE AREAS:* Commercial Property; Non-contentious Construction Law.

NICOLAS C. JARRETT-KERR, admitted, 1972, England. *LANGUAGES:* English. *PRACTICE AREAS:* Inheritance and Capital Taxes Planning; Trusts; Agriculture.

D. GARETH JONES, admitted, 1980, Wales. *PRACTICE AREAS:* Intellectual Property; Technology; Transfer Exploitation; Insolvency; Computer Law.

ROBERT C. LEE, admitted, 1977, England. *LANGUAGES:* English. *PRACTICE AREAS:* Commercial Property Development; Landlord and Tenant.

GREGORY W. LOVETT, admitted, 1984, England. *LANGUAGES:* English. *PRACTICE AREAS:* VAT and Property; Development; Property Advise to the Public Sector, primarily NHS bodies.

CHARLES A.J. METHERELL, admitted, 1985, England. *LANGUAGES:* English. *PRACTICE AREAS:* Contentious Construction; Commercial Litigation.

DAVID J. OWENS, admitted, 1984, England. *LANGUAGES:* English. *PRACTICE AREAS:* Employment; Insolvency; General Commercial Litigation.

(This Listing Continued)

PETER J. SCOTT, admitted, 1972, England. *LANGUAGES:* English. *PRACTICE AREAS:* Commercial Property and Development Work; Joint Ventures with the NHS.

MICHAEL C. STRATHDEE, admitted, 1979, England. *LANGUAGES:* English. *PRACTICE AREAS:* General Company/Commercial; Franchising; Minority Shareholder; Advice on Acquisitions; Professional Partnerships.

SUSAN J. THOMPSON, admitted, 1985, England. *LANGUAGES:* English. *PRACTICE AREAS:* Medical Negligence; Mental Health/Child Protection; Registered Nursing Homes.

JOE F. C. WAKEFORD, admitted, 1987, England. *LANGUAGES:* English. *PRACTICE AREAS:* Insurance: Professional Indemnity; Personal Injury; Healthcare: Medical Negligence; Libel and Defamation.

ANDREW T. E. WHITEFIELD, admitted, 1968, England. *LANGUAGES:* England and French. *PRACTICE AREAS:* NHS Litigation; Construction Law Litigation.

DAVID G. WIDDOWSON, admitted, 1985, England. *LANGUAGES:* English. *PRACTICE AREAS:* Employment and Industrial Relations Law; General Commercial Litigation; Commercial Arbitration.

DAVID R. WOOD, admitted, 1969, England. *LANGUAGES:* English. *PRACTICE AREAS:* Environment; Local Government; Property; Town Planning.

ASSOCIATES

MICHAEL D. DRAPER, admitted, 1987, England. *LANGUAGES:* English. *PRACTICE AREAS:* Conveyancing; Landlord and Tenant; Property; Real Estate.

KEN A. MCKAY MORTIMER, admitted, 1974, England. *LANGUAGES:* English. *PRACTICE AREAS:* Commercial Property and Development.

ELIZABETH R. OATEN, admitted, 1987, England. *LANGUAGES:* English. *PRACTICE AREAS:* Medical Malpractice; Civil Litigation; Personal Injury; Licensing; Gaming and Liquor.

JEAN SAPETA, admitted, 1989, England. *LANGUAGES:* English. *PRACTICE AREAS:* Employment, Discrimination; Medical Malpractice; Personal Injury.

PAUL G. SILCOCKS, admitted, 1977, England. *LANGUAGES:* English. *PRACTICE AREAS:* Commercial Property.

JOHN TOWNSEND, admitted, 1984, England. *LANGUAGES:* English. *PRACTICE AREAS:* Company Commercial; Insolvency.

KATHARINE M. TUCKEY, admitted, 1989, England. *LANGUAGES:* English. *PRACTICE AREAS:* Family and Children's Law.

CATHRYN J. VICKERS, admitted, 1989, England. *LANGUAGES:* English. *PRACTICE AREAS:* Property Development; Property Advice to the Public Sector, NHS Bodies.

CHERYL A. WILD, admitted, 1990, England. *LANGUAGES:* English. *PRACTICE AREAS:* Property; Landlord and Tenant; Conveyancing.

RINA YOUNG, admitted, 1982, England. *LANGUAGES:* English. *PRACTICE AREAS:* Planning; Environmental.

CONSULTANTS

ROBERT BIRKETT, admitted, 1948, England. *LANGUAGES:* English and French. *PRACTICE AREAS:* Registered Homes Act.

GERARD T. GENT, admitted, 1978, England. *LANGUAGES:* English, Dutch, French and German. *PRACTICE AREAS:* Banking; Competition Law; International Trade.

DEREK H. G. PARSONS, admitted, 1979, England. *LANGUAGES:* English and French. *PRACTICE AREAS:* Construction Law and ADR.

TIM M. W. YOUNG, admitted, 1968, England. *LANGUAGES:* English. *PRACTICE AREAS:* Advising Health Authorities and NHS Trusts on Commercial and Constitutional Issues.

BURGES SALMON

Established in 1841

NARROW QUAY HOUSE
PRINCE STREET
BRISTOL BS1 4AH, ENGLAND
Telephone: 0117 927 6567; (National) 44 117 927 6567; (International)
Fax: 0117 929 4705

Agriculture, Asset Protection, Banking, Building Societies, Commercial and Residential Property, Construction and Building, Company and Commercial Law, Commercial Finance and Tax, Charities, Debt Collection, Employment, Insolvency, International Law, Landlord & Tenant, Licensing, Litigation, Matrimonial and Family, Pensions, Tax and Estate Planning, Planning and Environment, Professional Negligence, Foreign Property, Intellectual Property, Offshore & Unit Trusts, Wills and Probate.

FIRM PROFILE: Founded in 1841, Burges Salmon is one of the leading law firms outside London with over 250 lawyers and support staff. Burges Salmon has strong international links and has access to international offices through its membership of the Norton Rose M5 Group of independent law firms.

PARTNERS

H. ANDREW C. DENSHAM, admitted, 1965, England. *Education:* LL.B. *Member:* Law Society. (Senior Partner). *LANGUAGES:* English. *PRACTICE AREAS:* Agricultural Law; European Community Law; Property Litigation.

PETER D. LAWS, admitted, 1967, England. *Member:* Law Society. *LANGUAGES:* English and French. *PRACTICE AREAS:* Property Law; Property Development; Syndication Law; Conveyancing.

DAVID J. MARSH, admitted, 1968, England. *Education:* M.A. (Oxford). *Member:* Law Society. (Managing Partner). *LANGUAGES:* English. *PRACTICE AREAS:* Corporate Law; Securities Offerings; International Law; Investment Law; Securities Law.

ROBIN S. BATTERSBY, admitted, 1968, England. *Member:* Law Society. *LANGUAGES:* English. *PRACTICE AREAS:* Property Law; Commercial Property Law; Land Use Law; Property Development; Syndication Law.

GEORGE M. DYSON, admitted, 1972, England. *Education:* B.A. Hons Jurisprudence (Oxford). *Member:* Law Society. Fellow, Chartered Institute of Arbitrators. *LANGUAGES:* English and French. *PRACTICE AREAS:* Employment Law; Contract Law; Employer/Employee Relations; Employment Discrimination; Arbitration Law.

J. NEIL PORTER, admitted, 1960, England. *Education:* M.A. MEd (Oxford) Sheffield Prize. *Member:* Law Society. *LANGUAGES:* English. *PRACTICE AREAS:* Individual Tax Planning; Agricultural Law; Trust Law; Wills; Administration of Estates.

HARRY W. WIGGIN, admitted, 1965, England. *Education:* M.A. (Cambridge). *Member:* Law Society; Institute of Taxation (Member, Council and of Technical Committee); International Fiscal Association (Member, British Branch Committee); International Bar Association; Institute for Fiscal Studies. *LANGUAGES:* English. *PRACTICE AREAS:* International Transactions; International Tax; International Practice; International Law; Tax Shelters Law.

RICHARD T. WYNN-JONES, admitted, 1973, England. *Education:* B.A. (Oxford). *Member:* Law Society; Institute of Directors. *LANGUAGES:* English and French. *PRACTICE AREAS:* Commercial Law; Joint Ventures; Agency & Distribution; Partnership Law; International Trade.

A. W. MARTIN MITCHELL, admitted, 1976, England. *Education:* M.A. (Oxford). *Member:* Law Society. *LANGUAGES:* English. *PRACTICE AREAS:* Estate Planning; Individual Tax Planning; Tax Shelters Law; Trust Law; Probate Law.

JAMES A. F. BUXTON, admitted, 1984, England. *Education:* M.A. (Cambridge). *Member:* Law Society. *LANGUAGES:* English. *PRACTICE AREAS:* Agricultural Law; Property Litigation; European Community Law; Landlord & Tenant.

ADRIAN LLEWELYN EVANS, admitted, 1979, England. *Education:* B.A. (Hons.) Durham. *Member:* Law Society. *LANGUAGES:* English. *PRACTICE AREAS:* Commercial Litigation; Tort Law; Securities Litigation; International Law; Arbitration Law.

(This Listing Continued)

GUY W. STOBART, admitted, 1980, England. *Member:* Law Society; Licensed Insolvency Practitioner. *LANGUAGES:* English, German and French. *PRACTICE AREAS:* Banking Law; Asset Based Lending; Insolvency Law; Financial Restructuring Law; Bankruptcy.

ROBERT J. SMYTH, admitted, 1978, England. *Education:* B.Sc. Economics (Wales). *Member:* Law Society. *LANGUAGES:* English. *PRACTICE AREAS:* Commercial Property Law; Landlord & Tenant Law; Conveyancing; Environmental Law.

PETER R. WILLIAMS, admitted, 1982, England. *Education:* B.A. *Member:* Law Society; Society of Labour Lawyers. *LANGUAGES:* English. *PRACTICE AREAS:* Property Litigation; Agricultural Law; Commercial Property Law; Landlord & Tenant Law; Residential Property Law.

STEPHEN J. MCNULTY, admitted, 1981, England. *Education:* M.A. (Oxford). *Member:* Law Society; British Italian Law Association. *LANGUAGES:* English, French, German and Italian. *PRACTICE AREAS:* Commercial Property Law; Landlord & Tenant Law; Residential Property Law; European Law.

R. ALAN BARR, admitted, 1982, England. *Education:* LL.B. (Wales). Recipient, Calcott Memorial Essay and Sweet & Maxwell Law Price. *Member:* Law Society; International Bar Association. *LANGUAGES:* English. *PRACTICE AREAS:* Mergers & Acquisitions; Leveraged & management buyouts; Securities Offerings; Corporate Restructuring; International Law.

CHARLES J. C. WYLD, admitted, 1982, England. *Education:* M.A. (Oxford). *Member:* Law Society. *LANGUAGES:* English, French and Spanish. *PRACTICE AREAS:* Charitable Trusts & Foundations; Agricultural Law; Estate Planning; Trust Law; International Law.

WILLIAM J. W. NEVILLE, admitted, 1987, England. *LANGUAGES:* English and German. *PRACTICE AREAS:* Agricultural Law; European Community Law; Competition Law.

STUART A. KING, admitted, 1984, England. *Education:* LL.B. (London). *Member:* Law Society. *LANGUAGES:* English. *PRACTICE AREAS:* Property Law; Commercial Property Law; Landlord & Tenant Law; Commercial Leasing; Insolvency Law.

JOHN B. DUNN, admitted, 1977, England. *Member:* Law Society. *LANGUAGES:* English. *PRACTICE AREAS:* Commercial Property Law; Landlord & Tenant Law; Property Development & Syndication Law; Conveyancing; Insolvency Law.

CATHERINE M. HALLAM, admitted, 1984, England. *Education:* B.A. (Oxford). *Member:* International Academy of Matrimonial Lawyers; Solicitors Family Law Association. *LANGUAGES:* English. *PRACTICE AREAS:* Matrimonial Law; Family Law; Divorce Law; Child Custody.

ROGER G. HAWES, admitted, 1985, England. *Education:* LL.B. *Member:* Law Society; Bristol Junior Chamber of Commerce. *LANGUAGES:* English. *PRACTICE AREAS:* Corporate Finance Law; Banking Law; Building Societies; Corporate Law; Insolvency Law.

TIMOTHY M. ILLSTON, admitted, 1986, England. *Member:* Law Society; Association of Pension Lawyers. *LANGUAGES:* English. *PRACTICE AREAS:* Corporate Tax Planning; International Tax; Pension & Profit Sharing; Employee Stock Ownership Plans (ESOPS); Employee Benefit Law.

CHRISTOPHER M. J. GODFREY, admitted, 1986, England. *Education:* M.A. (Oxford). *Member:* Law Society. *LANGUAGES:* English and French. *PRACTICE AREAS:* Corporate Law; Unit Trusts; Mergers & Acquisitions; Leveraged & Management Buyouts; Securities Offerings.

MARCUS R. HARLING, admitted, 1985, England. *Education:* LL.B. *Member:* Law Society. *LANGUAGES:* English. *PRACTICE AREAS:* Commercial Litigation; Alternative Dispute Resolution; Arbitration Law; Building Contracts; International Construction Contracts.

PAUL S. N. HAGGETT, admitted, 1985, England. *Education:* B.A. (Cambridge). *Member:* Law Society. *LANGUAGES:* English, French & German. *PRACTICE AREAS:* Commercial Litigation; Banking Law; Insolvency Law; Fraud; White Collar Fraud.

RICHARD J. BEDFORD, admitted, 1986, England. *Education:* LL.B. *Member:* Law Society. *LANGUAGES:* English. *PRACTICE AREAS:* Property Litigation; Securities Litigation; Mortgage Reinforcements; Commercial Property Law; Landlord & Tenant Law.

SIMON A. COPPEN, admitted, 1987, England. *Education:* B.A. Law (Oxford). *Member:* Law Society; Licensing Executives Society. *LANGUAGES:* English and French. *PRACTICE AREAS:* Commercial Law;

(This Listing Continued)

Intellectual Property Law; Computer Law; Competition Law; International Trade.

LINDA S. DALBY, admitted, 1977, England. *Education:* LL.B. (London). *Member:* Bristol Law Society. *LANGUAGES:* English. *PRACTICE AREAS:* Property Law; Commercial Leasing; Commercial Property Law; Landlord & Tenant; Conveyancing.

CATHERINE G. L. ELLIOTT, admitted, 1980, England. *Education:* B.A. Hons English and European Studies (Sussex). *Member:* Law Society. *LANGUAGES:* English, French, German and Spanish. *PRACTICE AREAS:* Commercial Property Law; Property Finance; Conveyancing; Landlord & Tenant Law; Secured Lending.

EVERSHEDS
11-12 QUEEN SQUARE
BRISTOL BS1 4NT, ENGLAND
Telephone: (44) 1179 299555
Fax: (44) 1179 292766

(For full details, see entry for Eversheds, Cardiff)

OSBORNE CLARKE
30 QUEEN CHARLOTTE STREET
BRISTOL BS99 7QQ, ENGLAND
Telephone: 0117-230220
Fax: 0117-279209

London, England Office: 6-9 Middle Street, EC1A 7JA. Telephone: 0171 600 0155. Fax: 0171 726 2772.
Brussels, Belgium Office: Avenue de Cortenburg 79/81, 1040. Telephone: 010 32 2 732 36 00. Fax: 010 32 2 734 87 93.
Copenhagen, Denmark Office: H.C. Andersens Boulevard 37, DK-1553 Copenhagen V. Telephone: 010 45 33-11 46 00. Fax: 010 45 33-93 03 06.
Paris, France Office: OJFI, 374 Rue Saint Honore, 75001. Telephone: 010 33 (1) 42 86 57 57. Fax: 010 33 (1) 42 86 57 58.
Lyon, France Office: Espace Republique, 10 Rue Stella BP 2099, 69226 Lyon, Cedex 02. Telephone: 010 33 72 41 16 16. Fax: 010 33 72 41 16 06.
Frankfurt/Main, Germany Office: Westendstrasse 24. Telephone: 010 49 069 174348. Fax: 010 49 069 174937.

General and Commercial Practice. Notaries Public.

MEMBERS OF FIRM

R.W. SMERDON (Senior Partner). *PRACTICE AREAS:* Corporate.

L.C. PERRIN (Managing Partner). *PRACTICE AREAS:* Litigation.

C.J. CURLING. PRACTICE AREAS: Corporate.

D.A. ARCHER. PRACTICE AREAS: Corporate.

R.I. JOHNSON. PRACTICE AREAS: Litigation; Banking.

W.A. TACEY. PRACTICE AREAS: Property.

R.S. WHITING. PRACTICE AREAS: Pensions.

A.R.G. JAMES. PRACTICE AREAS: Property.

C.B. EVANS. PRACTICE AREAS: Property.

M.S. JOHNSON. PRACTICE AREAS: Property.

J.W. SHARPE. PRACTICE AREAS: Tax and Trust.

D.K. TICEHURST. PRACTICE AREAS: Media; Employment.

A.P. WOOD. PRACTICE AREAS: Intellectual Property.

R.J. LAMBERT. PRACTICE AREAS: Corporate.

C.R. WATTS. PRACTICE AREAS: Corporate.

J.G. ORME. PRACTICE AREAS: Litigation.

J.P. SIMON. PRACTICE AREAS: Corporate.

J.P. MASSY-COLLIER. PRACTICE AREAS: Corporate.

P.D. COOK. PRACTICE AREAS: Insolvency; Corporate Recovery.

S.J. SPEIRS. PRACTICE AREAS: Property.

SANDRA BROWN. PRACTICE AREAS: Tax and Trust.

P.G.S. MOSS. PRACTICE AREAS: Corporate Tax.

(This Listing Continued)

A.R. JOHN. PRACTICE AREAS: Corporate; Environment.

R.N.F. DREWETT. PRACTICE AREAS: Property; Agriculture.

T.D. BIRT. PRACTICE AREAS: Corporate.

R.E. BAINES. PRACTICE AREAS: Corporate Recovery; Insolvency.

CLARE L. ROBINSON. PRACTICE AREAS: Litigation.

W. PAUL SUTTON. PRACTICE AREAS: Litigation.

S.A. BESWICK. PRACTICE AREAS: Corporate.

P.N.S. MAY. PRACTICE AREAS: Litigation.

B.O. ROXBURGH. PRACTICE AREAS: Corporate.

JANE A. GRIFFITHS. PRACTICE AREAS: Property.

JANICE A. COLLINO. PRACTICE AREAS: Commercial; EC.

RICHARD J. BRETTON. PRACTICE AREAS: Litigation.

MARGARET E. CHILDS. PRACTICE AREAS: Corporate Banking.

ASSOCIATES

M.J. DORE. PRACTICE AREAS: Property.

J.M. HADDRELL. PRACTICE AREAS: Property.

C.C. LUKER. PRACTICE AREAS: Pensions.

C.T.W. ANDERSON. PRACTICE AREAS: Property.

SANDRA C. GODDEN. PRACTICE AREAS: Litigation.

F.W. RILEY. PRACTICE AREAS: Corporate.

JANE M. ROGERS. PRACTICE AREAS: Litigation.

JULIA L. COCKELL. PRACTICE AREAS: Property.

H.A. MCPHERSON. PRACTICE AREAS: Property.

M.J. O'HAIRE. PRACTICE AREAS: Property.

CAROLINE A. SALISSE. PRACTICE AREAS: Employment.

JANE A. LOUGHER. PRACTICE AREAS: Property.

KATHRYN L. GATES. PRACTICE AREAS: Property.

M. BRADY. PRACTICE AREAS: Corporate.

JANET JOULE. PRACTICE AREAS: Litigation.

STUART MILLER. PRACTICE AREAS: Litigation; German.

STEPHANIE MATTHEWS. PRACTICE AREAS: Tax and Trust; French.

TRACEY MERRETT. PRACTICE AREAS: Planning.

KATE F. ANTONY-WILKINSON. PRACTICE AREAS: Corporate.

JANIS LAW. PRACTICE AREAS: Corporate.

PAULA H. NASH. PRACTICE AREAS: Litigation.

MARIANNE V. NANKERVIS. PRACTICE AREAS: Litigation.

CONSULTANTS

C.N. Clarke	D.C.E. Pockney
Lord Manners	S.J.D. Awdry
	T.R. Urquhart

CHIEF EXECUTIVE

D.N.T. Jones, F C A

WANSBROUGHS WILLEY HARGRAVE
BRISTOL, ENGLAND

(See London, England)

MILLS & REEVE

Established in 1789

FRANCIS HOUSE
112 HILLS ROAD
CAMBRIDGE CB2 1PH, ENGLAND
Telephone: +44 (0) 1223 64422
Fax: +44 (0) 1223 355848

Norwich, England Office: Francis House 3/7 Redwell Street, NR2 4TJ.
Telephone: +44 (0) 1603 660155. Fax: +44 (0) 1603 633027.

Agriculture, Banking and Building Societies, Bloodstock, Building and Engineering, Charities and Legacies, Commercial Property, Commercial Litigation, Commercial Tax, Company, Corporate Finance, Debt Collection, Ecclesiastical Law, Education, Employment, Entertainment, European, Investment Services, Health and Public Authorities, Insolvency, Insurance, Landlord and Tenant, Licensing, Matrimonial and Family, Medical Litigation, Pensions, Personal Accident and Injury, Personal Tax and Estate Planning, Planning and Environment, Professional Negligence, Residential and Foreign Property, Trademarks, Copyright and Patents, Wills and Probate.

FIRM PROFILE: Founded in 1789, Mills & Reeve is one of the largest law firms outside London with over 100 lawyers and a total staff of around 400. Mills & Reeve has strong international links and has access to international offices throughout its membership of the Norton Rose M5 Group of independent legal practices.

PARTNERS

MICHAEL ORR, born 1938; admitted, 1965, England. *Education:* M.A. (Oxon). *Member:* Law Society. (Senior Partner). *LANGUAGES:* English. *PRACTICE AREAS:* Contract Law; Commercial Property.

WILLIAM BARR, born 1949; admitted, 1973, England. *Education:* LL.B. (Sheffield). Co-Author: Agricultural Tenancies. *Member:* Law Society; Agricultural Law Association. (Managing Partner). *LANGUAGES:* English. *PRACTICE AREAS:* Agricultural Law; Estate Planning; Individual Tax Planning.

CHRISTOPHER JACKSON, born 1934; admitted, 1959, England. *Education:* LL.B. (London). *Member:* Law Society. *LANGUAGES:* English and French. *PRACTICE AREAS:* Institutional and Residential Conveyancing; Charities.

TIM PEARCE HIGGINS, born 1938; admitted, 1965, England. *Education:* M.A. (Cantab). *Member:* Law Society. *LANGUAGES:* English and French. *PRACTICE AREAS:* Trust Law; Wills; Probate Law; Successions.

TONY COWPER, born 1948; admitted, 1972, England. *Member:* Law Society. *LANGUAGES:* English. *PRACTICE AREAS:* Commercial Property Law; Property Finance.

MICHAEL BARLEY, born 1944; admitted, 1976, England. *Education:* B.A. (Oxon). *Member:* Law Society; British-German Jurists Association; Solicitors European Group. *LANGUAGES:* English and German. *PRACTICE AREAS:* Corporate Law; Corporate Finance Law; Venture Capital; Corporate Restructuring; Leveraged and Management Buyouts; Bloodstock.

DUNCAN OGILVY, born 1952; admitted, 1976, England. *Member:* Law Society. *LANGUAGES:* English. *PRACTICE AREAS:* Commercial Property; Property Development; NHS/Healthcare; Educational Institutions.

PETER HALLINAN, born 1957; admitted, 1981, England. *Education:* B.A. (Trent Polytechnic). *Member:* Law Society. *LANGUAGES:* English. *PRACTICE AREAS:* Property Law; Commercial Property Law; Property Development.

GRAEME MENZIES, born 1954; admitted, 1980, England. *Education:* B.A. (Cantab). *Member:* Law Society; ACIA. *LANGUAGES:* English. *PRACTICE AREAS:* Commercial Litigation; Intellectual Property Litigation.

BRIAN MARSHALL, born 1954; admitted, 1984, England. *Education:* B.A. (London); M.Phil. (Cantab). *Member:* Law Society. *LANGUAGES:* English. *PRACTICE AREAS:* Corporate Law; Competition Law; Partnerships.

ROGER BAMBER, born 1955; admitted, 1981, England. *Education:* M.A. (Cantab). *Member:* Law Society; Solicitors Family Law Association. *LANGUAGES:* English. *PRACTICE AREAS:* Matrimonial Law; Family Law; Child Custody; Divorce Law.

(This Listing Continued)

JOHN LAPRAIK, born 1958; admitted, 1983, England. *Education:* LL.B. (Reading). *Member:* Law Society. *LANGUAGES:* English and French. *PRACTICE AREAS:* Professional Negligence; Commercial Litigation; Banking Law.

PENELOPE ELLIOTT, born 1955; admitted, 1985, England. *Education:* M.A. (Cantab). *Member:* Law Society; Agricultural Law Association. *LANGUAGES:* English, French and Italian. *PRACTICE AREAS:* Agricultural Law; Estate Planning.

BEVERLEY FIRTH, born 1957; admitted, 1981, England. *Education:* LL.B. (Newcastle University). *Member:* Law Society. *LANGUAGES:* English. *PRACTICE AREAS:* Environmental Law; Contamination Law; Planning.

GLYNNE STANFIELD, born 1961; admitted, 1985, England. *Education:* M.A. (Oxon). *Member:* Law Society. *LANGUAGES:* English. *PRACTICE AREAS:* Corporate Law; Intellectual Property; Computer Software; High-Technology.

HOWARD WESTON, born 1943; admitted, 1966, England. *Education:* M.A. (Cantab). *Member:* Law Society. *LANGUAGES:* English. *PRACTICE AREAS:* Medical Negligence.

GUY HINCHLEY, born 1960; admitted, 1985, England. *Education:* LL.B. (London). *Member:* Law Society. *LANGUAGES:* English. *PRACTICE AREAS:* Commercial Property Law; Conveyancing.

RONALD PLASCOW, born 1956; admitted, 1981, England. *Education:* LL.B. (Sheffield University). *Member:* Law Society; Official Referees Solicitors Association; Society of Construction Law; Associate of Chartered Institute of Arbitrators; Arbitration Club. *LANGUAGES:* English. *PRACTICE AREAS:* Building and Engineering Contracts; Building and Engineering Litigation; Arbitration; Alternative Dispute Resolution Techniques.

JAMIESON WHEATLEY, born 1961; admitted, 1987, England. *Education:* LL.B. (Southampton University). *LANGUAGES:* English. *PRACTICE AREAS:* Commercial Litigation; Insolvency.

WANDA BARRY, born 1964; admitted, 1988, England. *Education:* LL.B. Huddersfield Polytechnic. *Member:* Law Society. *LANGUAGES:* English. *PRACTICE AREAS:* Professional Negligence.

RAITH PICKUP, born 1963; admitted, 1987, England. *Education:* B.A. (Oxon). *Member:* Law Society; Society of Construction Law. *LANGUAGES:* English. *PRACTICE AREAS:* Building and Engineering Contracts; Arbitration and Litigation.

EVERSHEDS

FITZALAN HOUSE
FITZALAN ROAD
CARDIFF CF2 1XZ, WALES
Telephone: (44) 1222 471147
Fax: (44) 1222 464347

Bristol, England: 11-12 Queen Square, BS1 4NT. Telephone: (44) 1179 299555. Fax: (44) 1179 292766.

Other Eversheds Offices:
Birmingham, Derby, Ipswich, Leeds, London, Manchester, Middlesbrough, Newcastle-upon-Tyne, Norwich, Nottingham, Berlin, Brussels, Jersey.

Acquisitions and Mergers, Agency/Distribution, Agriculture, Banking, Commercial Property, Company Law, Competition Law, Construction, Corporate Finance, Corporate Tax, EC Law, Employment, Environment, Entertainment, Information Technology, Franchising, Insolvency, Intellectual Property, Litigation, Management Buy-Outs, Pensions and Employee Benefits, Personal Tax & Financial Planning, Property Development, Shipping, Trading Contracts.
Partners within Eversheds: 273.

REGIONAL MANAGING PARTNER

David B. Vokes

CARDIFF AND BRISTOL PARTNERS

C. Belcher	*C.F. Janzen*
W. Benjamin	*C. Jenkins*
R.A.S. Butler	*P.J.W. Jones*
N. Cannar	*W. Juckes*
I. Davies	*P. Lowe*

(This Listing Continued)

P.M. Dennett	A.D. Meredith
K.J. Doolan	H. Molyneux
V.J. Du-Feu	P.H.A. Morris
E. Evans	R.J. Moseley
P. Fisher-Jones	J. Phillips
A. Hayward	J. Richards
J.D. Holt	R.G. Thomas
W.C. Hopkins	P.D. Vaughan
B. Hughes	D.B. Vokes
E. Hughes	M.H. Warren
L. James	D.A. Whiteley
D.K.M. James	A.M. Williams
	D. Woodward

WIGGIN AND CO.

Established in 1973

4TH FLOOR, THE QUADRANGLE
IMPERIAL SQUARE
CHELTENHAM GL50 1YX, ENGLAND
Telephone: 0242 224114 (National)
44 242 224114 (International)
Cable Address: "Wigginco Cheltenham UK"
Fax: 0242 224223

Los Angeles, California Office: Fox Plaza, Suite 1730, 2121 Avenue of the Stars, 90067. Telephone: 310-556-7878. Telex: 698218. Fax: 310-556-7882.

London, England Office: 3 Albany Courtyard, Piccadilly W1V 9RA. Telephone: 0171 287 8833. Fax: 0171 287 8628.

International Taxation, Domestic and Offshore Trust Law, Company and Commercial Law, Commercial Property and Entertainment Law.
A Member of The Wiggin Group of European Lawyers and Tax Advisors with Associated Firms in Munich and Utrecht.

MEMBERS OF FIRM

J. NICHOLAS STONES, born 1946; admitted, 1970, England.

MICHAEL R. FULLERLOVE, born 1948; admitted, 1974, England; Birmingham University (LL.B.), Oxford University (B.C.L.).

TIMOTHY W. OSBORNE, born 1951; admitted, 1976, England; London University (LL.B.).

C. RODERICK J. MARLOW, born 1949; admitted, 1977, England; Cambridge University (M.A.; LL.B.).

DENIS C. MOORE, born 1953; admitted, 1978, England; Oxford University (M.A.).

DAVID C.W. TOVEY, born 1953; admitted, 1979, England; Oxford University (M.A.).

PAUL M. WILSON, born 1956; admitted, 1981, England; Cardiff University (LL.B.).

MICHAEL W. TURNER, born 1960; admitted, 1984, England; Reading University (LL.B.). (Resident Lawyer, Los Angeles Office).

PAUL D. HUNSTON, born 1960; admitted, 1985, England; Birmingham University (LL.B.).

EVERSHEDS

11 ST. JAMES COURT
FRIAR GATE
DERBY DE1 1BT, ENGLAND
Telephone: (44) 1332 360992
Fax: (44) 1332 371469

(For full details see entry for Eversheds, Nottingham).

GOODGER AUDEN

Solicitors & Notaries Public

Established in 1852

10 GOWER STREET
DERBY DE1 1RW, ENGLAND
Telephone: (1332) 349843
Facsimile: (1332) 363039

Secretariat address of LAW (Lawyers Associated Worldwide) with LAW Offices throughout Europe, the Middle East, Australasia and the Americas. Acquisitions and Mergers, Agency/Distribution, Company Law, Competition Law, Computer Law, Debt Recovery, Labor Law, Personal Injury, Matrimonial Law, Immigration Law, Intellectual Property Law, Environmental Law, Real Estate, Litigation and Arbitration.

PARTNERS

Peter W. Scragg, (Notary)	Margaret J. Nickson
Richard T. Cundy	Robert T. J. Bond, (Notary)
Michael F. Nickson	Anthony C. Russell
Richard C. Crowe	William H. D. Auden
Barry J. Challender	Ellen P. Sellors
	Andrew D. Levey

CONSULTANTS

Robin A. Russian, (Notary)

ASSOCIATES

Ian D. Choyce	Julie Nicklin
Colin J. Rutter	Fiona Brooks

Languages: English, French, German, Spanish, Gujarati, Hindi and Urdu.

NABARRO NATHANSON

THE LODGE
SOUTH PARADE
DONCASTER DN1 2DQ, ENGLAND
Telephone: 01302-344455
Fax: 01302-738408

London, England Office: 50 Stratton Street, London W1X 5FL, England. Telephone: 0171-493-9933. Telex: 8813144 NABARO G. Fax: 0171-629-7900.

Hull, England Office: 12 Marina Court, Castle Street, Hull HU1 1TJ, England. Telephone: 01482-219111. Fax: 01482-218444.

Budapest, Hungary Office: Istanhegyi ut 9/b, Budapest 1126, Hungary.

Warsaw, Poland Office: ul. Senatorska 12, 00-082 Warsaw, Poland. Telephone: 48-2-227 6144/7901/9227. Fax: 48-2-227 4838.

Deira, Dubai, United Arab Emirates Office: P.O. Box 13779. Telephone: (9714) 287157. Fax: (0974) 287086.

General Practice.

PARTNERS

S. MCKENNA. PRACTICE AREAS: Commercial Property.

J. BLACKWELL. PRACTICE AREAS: Planning; Mineral Law.

S. DAYKIN. PRACTICE AREAS: Commercial Litigation; Personal Injury.

N. LOGAN. PRACTICE AREAS: Commercial Property.

R. WILLIAMS. PRACTICE AREAS: Employment; Industrial Relations.

I. MACPHERSON. PRACTICE AREAS: Commercial Litigation.

K. PUGH. PRACTICE AREAS: Employment.

M. RENGER. PRACTICE AREAS: Environment.

G. WATKINS. PRACTICE AREAS: Commercial Litigation; Health and Safety.

N. POINTON. PRACTICE AREAS: Commercial Property.

K. HUTCHESON. PRACTICE AREAS: Commercial Property.

T. SHAW. PRACTICE AREAS: Commercial Property.

(This Listing Continued)

NABARRO NATHANSON, Doncaster—Continued

R. HOLT. PRACTICE AREAS: Company/Commercial.

P. LISTER. PRACTICE AREAS: Commercial Property.

(For Personnel and Biographical Data, see Professional Biographies at London, England).

BEVAN ASHFORD

Solicitors

CURZON HOUSE, SOUTHERNHAY WEST
EXETER EX4 3LY, ENGLAND
Telephone: 01392 411111 (National) 44 1392 411111 (International)
Fax: 01392 50764

Also offices at: Bristol, Cardiff, London, Plymouth, Taunton and Tiverton.

FIRM PROFILE: *The firm is one of the largest regional firms in the country, and was responsible for founding ADVOC, a network of similar independent commercial legal firms extending across Europe. Major commercial work is concentrated in the Exeter, Plymouth, Bristol and Cardiff offices, with particular expertise in corporate transactions, property development and finance, employment law, commercial litigation, intellectual property and media law. Bristol is also well known for its national practice for the National Health Service and consequently has a strong medical litigation department.*

PARTNERS

DAVID BEADEL, admitted, 1974, England. **LANGUAGES:** English. **PRACTICE AREAS:** Professional Malpractice; Personal Injury; Media Law.

GERVASE CHANNER, admitted, 1974, England. **LANGUAGES:** English. **PRACTICE AREAS:** Agricultural Property.

JOHN S. EVANS, admitted, 1984, England. **LANGUAGES:** English, German and French. **PRACTICE AREAS:** Labour and Employment; Commercial Litigation.

MALCOLM L. ILEY, admitted, 1976, England. **LANGUAGES:** English. **PRACTICE AREAS:** Town Planning; Compulsory Purchase; Contamination Law; Municipal Law.

CHRISTOPHER J.C. PALMER, admitted, 1971, England. **LANGUAGES:** English. **PRACTICE AREAS:** Matrimonial Law; Civil Litigation.

JAMES E. PETTIT, admitted, 1973, England. **LANGUAGES:** English. **PRACTICE AREAS:** Personal Taxation; Trusts; Notary Public.

ANDREW C. ROTHWELL, admitted, 1980, England. **LANGUAGES:** English. **PRACTICE AREAS:** Commercial Leases; Mining and Minerals; Property Development.

SIMON ROUS, admitted, 1985, England. **LANGUAGES:** English and French. **PRACTICE AREAS:** Mergers, Acquisitions and Divestitures; Business Organization.

MARTIN THORNTON, admitted, 1974, England. **LANGUAGES:** English and French. **PRACTICE AREAS:** Trademarks; Intellectual Property; Protection; Construction Contracts; Waste Management; Advertising and Labelling; Construction Litigation.

NABARRO NATHANSON

12 MARINA COURT
CASTLE STREET
HULL HU1 1TJ, ENGLAND
Telephone: 01482-219111
Fax: 01482-218444

London, England Office: 50 Stratton Street, London W1X 5FL, England. Telephone: 0171-493-9933. Telex: 8813144 NABARO G. Fax: 0171-629-7900.
Doncaster, England Office: The Lodge, South Parade, Doncaster DN1 2DQ, England. Telephone: 01302-344455. Fax: 01302-738408.
Budapest, Hungary Office: Istanhegyi ut 9/b, Budapest 1126, Hungary.
Warsaw, Poland Office: Ul. Senatorska 12, 00-082 Warsaw, Poland. Telephone: 48-2-227 6144/7901/9227. Fax: 48-2-227 4838.

(This Listing Continued)

Deira, Dubai, United Arab Emirates Office: P.O. Box 13779. Telephone: (9714) 287157. Fax: (0974) 287086.

General Practice.

PARTNERS

B. RAPER. PRACTICE AREAS: Company Law; Commercial Law.

J. LAUBSCHER. PRACTICE AREAS: Company Law; Commercial Law.

(For Personnel and Biographical Data, see Professional Biographies at London, England).

EVERSHEDS

CHURCHGATES HOUSE
CUTLER STREET
IPSWICH IP1 1UR, ENGLAND
Telephone: (44) 1473 233433
Fax: (44) 1473 233666

(For full details see entry for Eversheds, Norwich).

BOOTH & CO.

Established in 1775

SOVEREIGN HOUSE
SOUTH PARADE
LEEDS LS1 1HQ, ENGLAND
Telephone: 0113-832000
Telex: 557439 - Booth G.
Cable Address: WAFER LEEDS
Facsimile: 0113-832060

Company and Commercial, Corporate Finance, Banking & Building Society Law, Pensions, Corporate Tax, European Community Law, UK and EC Anti-Trust Law, Asset Finance, Commercial & Civil Litigation, Employment, Insolvency, Credit Management, Personal Injury, Intellectual Property, Patents & Trade Marks, Commercial Property, Planning, Environment, Construction, Agriculture, Residential Property, Wills & Trusts, Personal Taxation, Family.

FIRM PROFILE: *Founded in 1775, Booth & Co. is one of the foremost commercial practices in the North. The firm provides a full range of legal services to commercial and private clients. A member of the Norton Rose M5 Group of independent legal practices.*

PARTNERS

ROGER IBBOTSON, born Leeds, January 2, 1943; admitted, 1966, England. *Education:* Manchester University (LL.B., 1963); College of Law, Guildford (Solicitor's Final Examination, 2nd Class Honours). *Member:* Leeds Law Society (Chairman, Civil Litigation Sub-Committee). **PRACTICE AREAS:** Litigation; Professional Negligence; Personal Injury.

DAVID H. SIMPSON, born West Linton, Peebles Scotland, February 17, 1941; admitted, 1967, England and Wales. *Education:* Lincoln College, Oxford (B.A. Law, 1962). **PRACTICE AREAS:** Property Work; Institutional Clients.

JOHN A. BRADBURY, born Sheffield; admitted, 1970, England. *Education:* Leeds University (LL.B.). (Notary). **PRACTICE AREAS:** Commercial Property; Secured Lending.

MAURICE C. COWEN, born London, England, January 29, 1946; admitted, 1970, England. *Education:* Sheffield University (LL.B., 1967). (Senior Partner). **PRACTICE AREAS:** Corporate Finance.

W. LENNOX TOWERS, born Lennoxtown, Scotland, September 24, 1946; admitted, 1971, England. *Education:* Exeter University (LL.B., Hons., 1968). (Notary). **PRACTICE AREAS:** Commercial Law; Commercial Taxation; Asset Finance.

STEPHEN J. ROSENVINGE, born Harrogate, England, October 12, 1946; admitted, 1970, England. *Education:* Ampleforth College, York. **PRACTICE AREAS:** Commercial Property Development; Leases.

JOHN C. PRIESTLEY, born Leeds, England, January 22, 1947; admitted, 1971, England. *Education:* Kings College, England (LL.B., AKC, 1968). *Member:* Society of Practitioners of Insolvency. (Senior Partner). **PRACTICE AREAS:** Commercial Litigation; Banking Litigation; Insolvency.

(This Listing Continued)

JOHN D. PIKE, born Beckenham, Kent, October 4, 1947; admitted, 1972, England. *Education:* Jesus College, Cambridge (B.A., 1969; M.A., 1972). *Member:* Law Society Solicitors Benevolent Association. (Notary). *LANGUAGES:* French. *PRACTICE AREAS:* Commercial Property; Environmental.

DAVID A. SALTER, born Sheffield, England, August 27, 1948; admitted, 1972, England. *Education:* Pembroke College, Cambridge. General Editor, Longman Litigation Practice. Co-author: Humphrey's Matrimonial Causes (Longman); Family Courts: Emergency Remedies and Procedures (Jordans). Author, Matrimonial Consent Orders and Agreements (Longman). *Member:* Law Society's Family Law Committee; Solicitor's Family Law Association Procedure Working Party (Chairman); Family Law Sub-Committee of the Supreme Court Procedure Committee; Solicitor's Family Law Association Main Committee. (Notary). *PRACTICE AREAS:* Family law.

RICHARD COCKRAM, born United Kingdom, November 4, 1947; admitted, 1973, England; 1984, Hong Kong. *Education:* Pembroke College, Cambridge (B.A., 1970); College of Law Guildford Law Society Final (1971). Associate, Institute of Arbitrators, Society of Construction Lawyers. *PRACTICE AREAS:* Construction Law.

ANTHONY P. RUANE, born Leeds, England, 1950; admitted, 1975, England. *Education:* St. Michael's College, Leeds; Leeds University (LL.B., 1969); Leeds Polytechnic - Professional Examinations College of Law, Chester (Accounts). *Member:* Leeds Law Society (Member, Non-Contentious Sub-Committee). *PRACTICE AREAS:* Residential Property.

PETER J. CHERRY, born Seascale, Cumbria, August 14, 1954; admitted, 1978, England. *Education:* B.A. *PRACTICE AREAS:* Commercial Litigation.

D. MARK JONES, born August 1, 1954; admitted, 1979, England. *Education:* Cambridge University (B.A., Law, 1976). (Managing Partner). *PRACTICE AREAS:* Litigation; Intellectual Property.

TIMOTHY P. TONKIN, born Redruth, Cornwall, February 14, 1951; admitted, 1977, England. *Education:* Exeter College, Oxford (M.A., Hons., 1973). *LANGUAGES:* French. *PRACTICE AREAS:* Commercial Property; Property Development.

MARK A. CHIDLEY, born Beckenham, Kent, March 24, 1955; admitted, 1979, England. *Education:* University of Southampton (LL.B., 1979). *Member:* International Bar Association. *PRACTICE AREAS:* Banking Law; Venture Capital.

PAUL D. GROOBEY, born Sheffield, England, May 21, 1954; admitted, 1982, England. *Education:* Leeds Polytechnic (B.A.). *PRACTICE AREAS:* Commercial Property.

JAMES F. STONE, born July 9, 1957; admitted, 1981, England. *Education:* Exeter University (LL.B., 1978). *PRACTICE AREAS:* Commercial Property; Agriculture.

MICHAEL A. REEVEY, born Harrogate, England, November 23, 1957; admitted, 1982, England. *Education:* Mansfield College, Oxford (M.A., Oxon); Leeds Polytechnic - Law Society Finals. *PRACTICE AREAS:* Property Development; Property Finance.

IAN W. McINTOSH, born St. Albans, Herts, May 28, 1959; admitted, 1983, England. *Education:* Bristol University (LL.B., Hons, 1980). *PRACTICE AREAS:* Corporate Finance; Venture Capital.

A. JOHN LEAKE, born York, England, April 28, 1957; admitted, 1982, England. *Education:* Hull University (LL.B., 1979). *PRACTICE AREAS:* Property Development; Joint Ventures.

TIMOTHY J. WHELDON, born Hull, England, January 29, 1959; admitted, 1983, England. *Education:* Hymers College, Hull; Manchester Polytechnic (B.A., Hons.). *LANGUAGES:* French. *PRACTICE AREAS:* Corporate Law; Commercial Law.

WILLIAM F. CHARNLEY, born Wigan, England, August 21, 1960; admitted, 1987, England. *Education:* Lancaster University (LL.B., ACIS). *PRACTICE AREAS:* Corporate Finance.

G.H. NEVILLE PEEL, born May 27, 1940; admitted, 1967, England. *Education:* Manchester University (B.A. Honours History II I). Co-author, "Pensions and Insurance on Family Breakdown," Jordans, Family Law, 1992. Member, Council of the University of Sheffield. *PRACTICE AREAS:* Pensions.

PAUL J. HOWELL, born Liverpool, England, August 22, 1953; admitted, 1977, England. *Education:* Liverpool University (LL.B., 1974). *PRACTICE AREAS:* Trusts and Personal Tax Planning.

(This Listing Continued)

G. ADAM BENNETT, born Sheffield, England, December 10, 1961; admitted, 1985, England. *Education:* Christ's College, Cambridge (M.A., Cantab, 1982); College of Law, Guildford. Editor, Halsbury's Laws of England on Building Societies, 1992. *PRACTICE AREAS:* Building Societies.

GILLIAN E. HOLDING, born Chester, England, March 4, 1959; admitted, 1984, England. *Education:* Birmingham University (LL.B., Law with French, Hons., 1981); University of Limoges, France (Diplôme D'Etudes Juridiques Francaises, 1980); City of London Polytechnic (M.A., Business Law, 1985). *Member:* Law Society; Solicitors European Group; Association International Des Jeunes Avocats. *LANGUAGES:* French, German. *PRACTICE AREAS:* EEC; Anti-Trust Law; Competition Law.

IAN C. SAMPSON, born Dartford, Kent, October 13, 1960; admitted, 1987, England. *Education:* University of Kent at Canterbury (B.A.). *LANGUAGES:* French. *PRACTICE AREAS:* EEC; Competition Law; Computer Law; Intellectual Property.

RICHARD A. KEMPNER, born London, England, July 30, 1962; admitted, 1987, Solicitor England. *Education:* Durham University (B.A, 1st Class, Hons., Law, 1984); Lancaster Gate College of Law (1985). Author, "Chapter in Longman's Work - Joint Venture - 'Technology Joint Venture', 1991. Lecturer: ESC Panel on IP, 1990 Onwards; European Panel on IP & Computers, 1992. *Member:* Law Society; International Bar Association; Franco British Business Club; International Committee VISTA; LES. *LANGUAGES:* French. *PRACTICE AREAS:* Intellectual Property.

WILLIAM BALLMANN, born Wiesbaden, Germany, 1955; admitted, 1983, England. *Education:* Leeds University (LL.B.); Guildford College of Law. *PRACTICE AREAS:* Insolvency Law.

SANDRA A. HUMPHREY, born Lyndhurst, Hants; admitted, 1983, England. *Education:* Bristol University (LL.B., 1980); College of Law Guildford (Solicitors Final Examination, 1981). *Member:* Law Society; AWS (Yorkshire). *PRACTICE AREAS:* Corporate Finance; Mergers and Acquisitions; Joint Ventures.

THOMAS DAVID FLANAGAN, born Middlesbrough, England, January 16, 1954; admitted, 1980, England. *Education:* University College of London (LL.B., 1976); College of Law, Lancaster Gate (Part 2, 1977). Author: "Transfer of Undertakings", "Variation of Contract" and "Employment or Self-Employment", Tolleys Employment Law. *Member:* Law Society; The City of London Law Society; The London Solicitors; Litigation Association. *PRACTICE AREAS:* Employment Law.

GRAHAM M. BRIGGS, born Bradford, England, August 19, 1959; admitted, 1984, England. *Education:* Leicester University, College of Law, Chester. *PRACTICE AREAS:* Insolvency Law.

RICHARD F. DINNING, born Newcastle upon Tyne, England, October 4, 1952; admitted, 1978, England. *Education:* Manchester Polytechnic (B.A., Hons., Law). *PRACTICE AREAS:* Property Finance.

RICHARD P.E. BERRY, born Huddersfield, England, June 6, 1962; admitted, 1986, England. *Education:* Queen's College, Oxford (LL.B., 1983). *PRACTICE AREAS:* Banking Law; Acquisition Finance; Debt Rescheduling.

IAN A.W. HASTINGS, born Sunderland, England, August 6, 1960; admitted, 1985, England. *Education:* University of Newcastle upon Tyne (LL.B., 1982). *PRACTICE AREAS:* Banking and Financial Litigation.

RICHARD A. WHEELDON, born Shipley, England, November 21, 1961; admitted, 1985, England. *Education:* Manchester University (LL.B., 1982). *LANGUAGES:* German. *PRACTICE AREAS:* Town and Country Planning; Property Development.

Languages: English, Welsh, French, German, Spanish, Russian, Portuguese, Dutch and Italian.

EVERSHEDS

CLOTH HALL COURT
INFIRMARY STREET
LEEDS LS1 2JB, ENGLAND
Telephone: (44) 1132 430391
Fax: (44) 1132 456188

Other Eversheds Offices:
Birmingham, Bristol, Cardiff, Derby, Ipswich, London, Manchester, Middlesbrough, Newcastle-upon-Tyne, Norwich, Nottingham, Berlin, Brussels, Jersey.

(This Listing Continued)

EVERSHEDS, Leeds—Continued

Acquisitions and Mergers, Agency/Distribution, Agriculture, Banking, Commercial Property, Company Law, Competition Law, Construction, Corporate Finance, Corporate Tax, EC Law, Employment, Environment, Entertainment, Information Technology, Franchising, Insolvency, Intellectual Property, Litigation, Management Buy-Outs, Pensions and Employee Benefits, Personal Tax & Financial Planning, Property Development, Shipping, Trading Contracts.
Partners within Eversheds: 273.

MANAGING PARTNER

David Ansbro

LEEDS PARTNERS

R.M. Ainscoe	J.A. Hodgson
D.A. Ansbro	S.M. Hopkins
F.B. Atkinson	B.J. Horrocks
A.N. Brown	R.K. Hutchinson
J.H. Bryan	R.S. Johnson
P.R.P. Chadwick	A.W. Latchmore
R. Chapman	J.P. Margerison
S.D. Cirell	S.D. Palmer
N.D. Crocker	R.M. Potterton
D. Davis	I.A. Richardson
R.C. Davis	P.H. Scrivener
J.H. Finnigan	J.M. Sinclair
J.M. Foster	P.A. Smith
D.J. Gray	A.J. Staniforth
J.R. Guest	D.M. Strachan
M.W. Harrison	J.J.O. Sutcliffe
J.R. Heaps	P.J.S. Thompson
	P.E.A. Winter

HAMMOND SUDDARDS

2 PARK LANE
LEEDS LS3 1ES, ENGLAND
Telephone: 0113 234 3500
Fax: 0113 234 3600
Telex: 517201

Brussels, Belgium Office: Avenue Louise 250, 1050. Telephone: 00 32 2 627 7676. Fax: 00 32 2 627 7686.
London, England Office: Moor House, 119 London Wall, London, EC2Y 5ET. Telephone: 0171 628 4767. Fax: 0171 628 6161.
Manchester, England Office: Trinity Court, 16 John Dalton Street, M60 8HS. Telephone: 0161 834 2222. Fax: 0161 834 2244.
Bradford, England Office: Pennine House, 39-45 Well Street. BD1 5NL. Telephone: 01274 734700. Fax: 01274 737547. Telex: 517201.

Corporate Finance including Acquisitions and Mergers, Corporate Finance, Commercial including Acquisitions and Mergers, Corporate Tax, Commercial including Joint Ventures, Pensions, Banks and Building Societies, Intellectual Property, Commercial Litigation, Construction, Insolvency and Corporate Recovery, Debt Collection, Town and Country Planning, Environmental Law, Commercial Property, European Community Law, Information Technology Law, Employment, Utilities, Insurance Litigation, Media, Mortgage and Aviation Law.
Hammond Suddards has over 870 staff, including 58 partners, 100 Associates and 50 Legal Executives and Paralegals.

RESIDENT PARTNERS

ALAN I. BOTTOMLEY (Senior Partner).

J. RICHARD ARCHER. PRACTICE AREAS: Pensions.

DAVID W.K. ARMITAGE. PRACTICE AREAS: Corporate Law.

JOHN G. BECKETT. PRACTICE AREAS: Commercial Property.

EDWARD COULSON. PRACTICE AREAS: Defendant Insurance Litigation.

PETER CROSSLEY. PRACTICE AREAS: Commercial Litigation.

LUCCI DAMMONE. PRACTICE AREAS: Commercial Litigation.

JOHN D. DE MAIN. PRACTICE AREAS: Commercial Property.

DAVID GOODMAN. PRACTICE AREAS: Planning.

(This Listing Continued)

IAN GREENFIELD. PRACTICE AREAS: Corporate Law.

PHILIP W. HARLING. PRACTICE AREAS: Commercial Property.

JOHN H.G. HELLER. PRACTICE AREAS: Commercial Litigation.

MICHAEL S. HENLEY. PRACTICE AREAS: Commercial Litigation.

MARK W. HILTON. PRACTICE AREAS: Commercial Litigation.

C. NOEL HUTTON. PRACTICE AREAS: Corporate Law.

SIMON R. INMAN. PRACTICE AREAS: Corporate Law.

CHRISTOPHER W. JONES. PRACTICE AREAS: Insolvency.

ANDREW R. JORDAN. PRACTICE AREAS: Corporate Law.

HELEN F. KAVANAGH. PRACTICE AREAS: Insolvency.

CHRISTOPHER MARKS. PRACTICE AREAS: Commercial Property.

ROSAMOND J. MARSHALL SMITH. PRACTICE AREAS: Tax.

ANDREW H. MCDOUGALL. PRACTICE AREAS: Commercial Litigation.

PETER METCALF. PRACTICE AREAS: Commercial Litigation.

J. PATRICK MITCHELL. PRACTICE AREAS: Corporate Law.

TIMOTHY J. RUSSELL. PRACTICE AREAS: Employment Law.

IAN R. SHUTTLEWORTH. PRACTICE AREAS: Commercial Property.

DAVID J. WILLIAMS. PRACTICE AREAS: Commercial Litigation.

(For Lists of other Members, see Professional Biographies at Bradford, London and Manchester, England and Brussels, Belgium)

WALKER MORRIS

KING'S COURT
12 KING STREET
LEEDS LS1 2HL, ENGLAND
Telephone: (0113) 283 2500
Fax: (0113) 245 9412

Corporate Finance, Mergers, Acquisitions and Divestitures, Flotations, Pensions, Management Buy Outs/Ins and General Commercial. Banking, Insolvency, Corporate Tax, Intellectual Property, Building Society and Housing Association Law.
Commercial Property and Planning Law, Acquisition of Sites for Development, Environmental Law, Investments, Joint Ventures.
Commercial Litigation, Domestic and International Construction Law, Employment, Insurance, Property Litigation, Commercial Fraud, Intellectual Property, Banking and Secured Lending, Corporate Debt Recovery.
FIRM PROFILE: Walker Morris has a staff of 300, including 26 partners and 147 lawyers.

PARTNERS

CHRISTOPHER S. CAISLEY, born 1951; admitted, 1978, England. Education: Grange Grammar School, Bradford. Vice Consul to the Netherlands, West & North Yorkshire. Member: Law Society. **PRACTICE AREAS:** Commercial Litigation; Sports Law.

PATRICK CANTRILL, born 1958; admitted, 1984, England and Wales; 1986, Hong Kong. Education: University College, London University. Member: Leeds Law Society (Chairman of European Sub-Committee and Council Member); Licensing Executive Society International; European Communities Trade Marks Association; British-German Jurists' Association; Association Internationale des Jeunes Avocats. **PRACTICE AREAS:** Intellectual Property; Competition Law; Trade Mark; Filing and Searching Services.

IAN GILBERT, born 1957; admitted, 1981, England. Education: Sheffield University. Member: Law Society. **PRACTICE AREAS:** Venture Capital; Corporate Finance; Takeovers; Mergers; Management Buy Out/Ins.

ROGER LIMBERT, born 1946; admitted, 1971, England. Education: Leeds University, Guildford College of Law. Member: Law Society; Building Societies Association (Panel of Legal Advisors to small societies). **PRACTICE AREAS:** Building Society Law; Compliance Law; Professional Negligence; Fraud; Insurance Litigation; Commercial Litigation.

(This Listing Continued)

PHILIP MUDD, born 1959; admitted, 1983, England. *Education:* Bristol University. *Member:* Law Society; SPI and the Insolvency Lawyers' Association, Licensed Insolvency Practitioner. **PRACTICE AREAS:** Banking Law; Insolvency Law; Debt Restructuring; Corporate Rescue; Lending; Realisation Work.

DAVID DUCKWORTH, born 1945; admitted, 1968, England. *Education:* Darwen Grammar School. *Member:* Law Society. **PRACTICE AREAS:** Property Development; Secured Property Lending; Commercial Property; Building Societies.

PETER SMART, born 1950; admitted, 1979, England. *Education:* Alleynes School, Leeds Metropolitan University. *Member:* Law Society. **PRACTICE AREAS:** Corporate Finance; Mergers and Acquisitions.

WANSBROUGHS WILLEY HARGRAVE

LEEDS, ENGLAND

(See London, England)

ALSOP WILKINSON

INDIA BUILDINGS
LIVERPOOL L2 ONH, ENGLAND
Telephone: 0151-227 3060
Telex: 627369
Fax: 0151-236 9208

London, England Office: 6 Dowgate Hill, EC4R 2SS. Telephone 0171-248 4141. Telex: 885593. Fax: 0171-623 8286.

Manchester, England Office: 11 St. James's Square, M2 6DR. Telephone: 0161-834 7760. Telex: 667965. Fax: 0161-831 7515.

Hong Kong Office: 4010 Jardine House, 1 Connaught Place, Central. Telephone: 852-524 2003. Fax: 852-810 1345.

New York, New York Office: 230 Park Avenue, Suite 1150, New York, New York, 10169. Telephone: (212) 499-7500. Fax: (212) 499-7505.

Brussels, Belgium Office: Avenue de Cortenberg, 79-81, 1040. Telephone: 2-732-36-00. Fax: 2-734-87-93.

Key Practice Areas: Banking, Commercial Litigation and Arbitration, Commercial Property, Commodities, Construction, Corporate and Commercial, Corporate Fraud and Investigations, Corporate Taxation, Employee Benefits, Employment, Environment and Planning, Insolvency, Insurance and Reinsurance, Intellectual Property and Computer Law, Marine, Pensions, Private Client.

FIRM PROFILE: *One of the largest commercial law practices in the U.K. Established 1821 and offering a full service to corporate and mercantile clients.*

RESIDENT PARTNERS

D.H. Morris	N.W. Jones
D.D. Mason	M.J. Prince
D. Edmundson	C.J. Pinsent
(Managing Partner)	M. Beardwood
D.H. Mawdsley	M.G. Hill
R.J. Phillips	R.I. Campbell
W.M.C. Pinfold	D. Cadwallader
R.J. Paton	B.E. Harris
D.R. Jacks	Kate Ive
P.J. Rooney	Keith Lewin
	Joanne Bibby

CONSULTANT

S. Christie

ASSOCIATES

Ian Ferguson-Smith	W.D. Wright

Member of The Legal Resources Group

(For the Names of Partners Resident in Other Offices, see Listings for Those Offices)

LEES LLOYD WHITLEY

Established in 1820
CASTLE CHAMBERS
CASTLE STREET
LIVERPOOL L2 9TJ, ENGLAND
Telephone: 0151-227 3541
International: +44 151 227 3541
Fax: 0151-227 2460
International: +44 151 227 2460

London, England Office: 34 Ely Place, Holborn Circus, EC1N 6TD. Telephone: 0171-404 6663. International: +44 171 404 6663. Fax: 0171-404 6665. International: +44 171 404 6665.

FIRM PROFILE: *The firm provides a comprehensive service to business and private clients regionally, nationally and internationally.*

PARTNERS

TERENCE D. HARVEY. PRACTICE AREAS: Construction Disputes; Insolvency.

WILLIAM E. TWIDALE. PRACTICE AREAS: Property.

DAVID THOMAS. PRACTICE AREAS: Company; Commercial.

JOHN M.B. WILEY. PRACTICE AREAS: Insolvency; Employment Law.

ANTHONY J. MARRIOTT. PRACTICE AREAS: Insolvency; Commercial Litigation.

DEREK C. KENDALL. PRACTICE AREAS: Property.

DAVID A. SEWELL. PRACTICE AREAS: Commercial Property.

FRANK J. ROGERS. PRACTICE AREAS: Medical Negligence; Personal Injury.

PAUL J. ARMSTRONG. PRACTICE AREAS: Property; Probate; Trusts.

MARTIN V. WALKER. PRACTICE AREAS: Company; Commercial.

JOHN M. HUGMAN. PRACTICE AREAS: Family Law.

MARCUS P. BEMROSE. PRACTICE AREAS: Property.

GRAHAM P. SMITH. PRACTICE AREAS: Debt Recovery.

ANN V. CUTTING. PRACTICE AREAS: Employment Law.

BARRISTERS—LONDON, ENGLAND

The legal profession in England and Wales is divided into two branches: solicitors and barristers. To reflect that division, Professional Biographical listings are now divided into two separate sequences. Barrister listings precede those of solicitors.

Solicitors provide the bulk of first line legal advice, undertaking detailed investigative work and dealing with substantial amounts of paperwork on behalf of their clients. Barristers are a smaller group, providing a specialist service in advocacy and advice, and are experts in particular areas of law.

Barristers are permitted to accept instructions directly from overseas lawyers, including in-house counsel acting on behalf of their employer, and also, in certain cases, from clients themselves. The only exception to this rule is where litigation has already been initiated by or against the client in the English courts. Barristers are also permitted to appear or to advise in foreign jurisdictions, subject to local rules.

Barristers are organized into sets of chambers and are self-employed; they are not partners. They may share expenses such as premises, facilities, and the services of chambers' Clerks, but they are

(This Listing Continued)

individual practitioners. This complete independence may result, for example, in members of the same chambers being retained by opposing sides in the same case.

A set of chambers is comprised of barristers of differing seniority and frequently different specializations. When a barrister is instructed to provide advice or to act as an advocate, he or she does so personally. As sole practitioners providing a specialist service, barristers do not provide major administrative legal services such as the organization of witnesses and their evidence.

1 ATKIN BUILDING
CHAMBERS OF I.N. DUNCAN WALLACE, Q.C.

1 ATKIN BUILDING
GRAY'S INN
LONDON WC1R 5BQ, ENGLAND
Telephone: 44/0171/404/0102
Fax: 44/0171/405/7456

I.N. DUNCAN WALLACE, Q.C., Barrister, Consultant and Arbitrator specializing in Construction Law. Visiting Professor: King's College, London; Centre of Construction Law and Management, 1988—. Visitor, UC Berkeley (Boalt Hall), 1978—. Editor (Author), Hudson on Building Contracts (principal Commonwealth text-book) 8th, 9th and 10th and 11th (1994) Editions. Author: Construction Contracts: Principles and Policies (1987); The FIDIC International Civil Engineering Contract 2nd and 3rd Editions (1979); The Fifth Edition ICE Conditions (1978); Building and Civil Engineering Standard Forms (1969; 1973); Further Building and Civil Engineering Standard Forms (1973). Editorial Board, Construction Law Review. Draftsman, Singapore SIA Private Sector Contract, 1980, 1987, 1993—. **LANGUAGES:** French. **PRACTICE AREAS:** Construction Law; Arbitration.

BRICK COURT CHAMBERS

15-19 DEVEREUX COURT
LONDON WC2R 3JJ, ENGLAND
Telephone: 0171-583-0777
Facsimile: 0171-583-9401

CHAMBERS PROFILE: *Brick Court Chambers is an established commercial set of Chambers in the Temple. It presently has forty four members including eighteen QC's. The core of Chambers' work consists of all aspects of international trade, finance and commerce with particular emphasis on banking, insurance and shipping.*

Christopher Clarke, QC	Charles Hollander
Philip Owen, QC	Mark Clough
Sir Nicholas Lyell, QC	Mark Howard
Sydney Kentridge, QC	William Wood
David Vaughan, QC	Andrew Popplewell
Nicholas Chambers, QC	Richard Lord
Richard Aikens, QC	George Leggatt
Jonathan Sumption, QC	Catharine Otton-Goulder
Hilary Heilbron, QC	Mark Brealey
Nicholas Forwood, QC	David Anderson
Mark Cran, QC	Michael Swainston
Jonathan Hirst, QC	Fergus Randolph
Julian Malins, QC	David Garland
Gerald Barling, QC	Nicholas Green
Peregrine Simon, QC	Richard Slade
Timothy Charlton, QC	Harry Matovu
Derrick Wyatt, QC	Cyril Kinsky
Mark Hapgood, QC	Paul Wright
Peter Irvin	Sarah Lee
Peter Brunner	Helen Davies
David Lloyd Jones	Tom Adam
Stephen Ruttle	Alan Roxburgh

CHAMBERS OF MARTIN BURR

Established in 1993

ELDON CHAMBERS
30-32 FLEET STREET
LONDON EC4Y 1AA, ENGLAND
Telephone: 0171-353-4636; 0171-353-4637
Fax: 0171-353-4637

CHAMBERS PROFILE: *General Practice, Tax, Chancery, Ecclesiastical, Common Law, Planning and Local Government.*

Chambers consists of 22 members.

MARTIN BURR. LANGUAGES: German. **PRACTICE AREAS:** Tax; Chancery; Ecclesiastical.

BARRISTERS CHAMBERS OF MICHAEL CRYSTAL, Q.C.

3/4 SOUTH SQUARE, GRAY'S INN
LONDON WC1R 5HP, ENGLAND
Telephone: 0171-696 9900
Fax: 0171-696 9911
Dx: LDE 338 (Chancery Lane)

All fields of Commercial Law: Corporate & International Insolvency, Company Law, Banking, Commercial Agreements, International Trade, Financial Services, Professional Negligence, Personal Insolvency, Pre-trial Remedies & Enforcement of Judgments.

CHAMBERS PROFILE: *Members of these Chambers practise in business and financial law and have a well known expertise in insolvency law. They advise (in writing, in conference or on the telephone) on matters, whether contentious or not, concerning the areas of law listed above.*

As well as their work in the English Courts, several members of Chambers have conducted litigation or acted as expert witnesses on English law in foreign courts. Members of Chambers accept instructions from overseas lawyers direct as well as from English solicitors and members of the professional bodies authorized by the General Council of the Bar to instruct Council without the intervention of a Solicitor.

MEMBERS OF CHAMBERS

Michael Crystal, Q.C.	Susan Prevezer
Muir Hunter, Q.C.	Mark Phillips
Christopher Brougham, Q.C.	Robin Dicker
Gabriel Moss, Q.C.	David Alexander
Simon Mortimore, Q.C.	Antony Zacaroli
John Higham, Q.C.	Mark Arnold
Marion Simmons, Q.C.	Lexa Hilliard
Clive Cohen, S.C.	Stephen Atherton
John Briggs	Sandra Bristoll
David Marks	Adam Goodison
Richard Hacker	Hilary Stonefrost
Martin Pascoe	Lloyd Tamlyn
Richard Sheldon	Glen Davis
Richard Adkins	Andreas Gledhill
Robin Knowles	Fidelis Oditah
William Trower	Roxanne Ismail

LEGAL SUPPORT PERSONNEL

David Hatchard (Chief Executive)	Michael Killick (Clerk)
	Lynne Isaacs (Administrator)
Neil Atkin (Clerk)	Jason Pithers (Clerk)
James Costa (Clerk)	

BARRISTERS CHAMBERS OF MR. PETER CURRY, Q.C.

4 STONE BUILDINGS
LINCOLN'S INN
LONDON WC2A 3XT, ENGLAND
Telephone: 0171-242 5524
Fax: 0171-831 7907
DX: 385

Company and related Commercial Litigation and Advice, Chancery (particularly Trusts), Litigation and Advice, Insolvency and Financial Services, Professional Negligence.

MEMBERS OF CHAMBERS

THOMAS PETER ELLISON CURRY, Q.C., called, 1973, England and Queen's Counsel. *Education:* M.A. (Oxon). *PRACTICE AREAS:* Chancery, Equity; Corporate Law.

PHILIP LINNELL HESLOP, Q.C., called, 1970, England; 1985, Queen's Counsel. *Education:* B.A.; LL.B. (Cantab). *PRACTICE AREAS:* Business Law; Commodities; Corporate Law.

EDWARD ALAN DAVIDSON, Q.C., called, 1966, England. *Education:* M.A.; LL.B. (Cantab). *PRACTICE AREAS:* Chancery, Equity; Trusts and Estates; Professional Negligence.

STEPHEN HUNT, called, 1968, England. *Education:* B.A. (Oxon). *PRACTICE AREAS:* Chancery, Equity; Trusts and Estates.

JOHN MARTIN BERTIN, called, 1972, England. *Education:* M.A. (Cantab). *PRACTICE AREAS:* Business Law; Chancery; Corporate Law.

ANTHONY GEORGE BOMPAS, Q.C., called, 1975, England. *Education:* B.A. (Oxon). *PRACTICE AREAS:* Corporate Law; Business Law; Professional Negligence.

ROBERT HENRY THOROTON HILDYARD, Q.C., called, 1977, England. *Education:* B.A. (Oxon). *PRACTICE AREAS:* Corporate Law; Natural Resources; Mergers and Acquisitions.

PETER ROBERT GRIFFITHS, called, 1977, England. *Education:* B.A. (Cantab). *PRACTICE AREAS:* Bankruptcy; Business Law; Corporate Law.

JOHN CONSTANT SHANNON MCBURNEY BRISBY, called, 1978, England. *Education:* M.A. (Oxon). *PRACTICE AREAS:* Business Law; Commodities; Corporate Law.

JONATHAN RUPERT CROW, called, 1981, England. *Education:* B.A. (Oxon). *PRACTICE AREAS:* Corporate Law; Entertainment and The Arts; Mergers and Acquisitions.

MALCOLM DAVIS-WHITE, called, 1984, England. *Education:* B.A. (Oxon) B.C.L. *PRACTICE AREAS:* Business Law; Corporate Law; Bankruptcy.

ROBERT JOHN MILES, called, 1987, England. *Education:* B.A. (Oxon) B.C.L. *PRACTICE AREAS:* Business Law; Commodities; Corporate Law.

ROSALIND VERONICA NICHOLSON, called, 1987, England. *Education:* B.A. (Oxon). *PRACTICE AREAS:* Bankruptcy; Commodities; Corporate Law.

SARAH JANE HARMAN, called, 1987, England. *Education:* B.A. (Oxon). *PRACTICE AREAS:* Bankruptcy; Commodities; Corporate Law.

CHRISTOPHER HARRISON, called, 1988, England. *Education:* B.A. (Oxon). *PRACTICE AREAS:* Bankruptcy; Commodities; Corporate Law.

JONATHAN SAMUEL BRETTLER, called, 1988, England. *Education:* LL.B (LSE); B.C.L. (Oxon). *PRACTICE AREAS:* Bankruptcy; Commodities; Corporate Law.

PAUL JEROME GREENWOOD, called, 1991, England. *Education:* B.A.; B.C.L. (Oxon). *PRACTICE AREAS:* Bankruptcy; Corporate Law; Business Law.

ANDREW MAURICE GRAY CLUTTERBUCK, called, 1992, England. *Education:* B.A. (Oxon). *PRACTICE AREAS:* Bankruptcy; Commodities; Corporate Law.

NICHOLAS IVAN COX, called, 1992, England. *Education:* B.A. (Oxon) M.B.A. *PRACTICE AREAS:* Bankruptcy; Commodities; Corporate Law.

(This Listing Continued)

RICHARD GEOFFREY HILL, called, 1992, England. *Education:* B.A. (Cantab).

LEGAL SUPPORT PERSONNEL

DAVID GODDARD (Clerk).

Languages: French and Spanish

BARRISTERS CHAMBERS DOUGHTY STREET CHAMBERS

11 DOUGHTY STREET
LONDON WC1N 2PG, ENGLAND
Telephone: 0171 404 1313
Fax: 0171 404 2283

CHAMBERS PROFILE: Members of Chambers frequently appear in international and foreign courts and in appeals from Commonwealth Courts to Privy Council. Several have argued cases before the European Court of Human Rights in Strasbourg. Senior Counsel in Chambers are practising members of several Commonwealth Bars, and have been admitted to practise in other Commonwealth jurisdictions for particular cases.

40 Members of Chambers specializing in the following areas: Contract and Equity, Criminal Law, Discrimination, Employment, European, International and Commonwealth Law, Housing, Landlord and Tenant, Immigration, Inquests, Media Law and Defamation, Medical Negligence, Mental Health, Personal Injury, Prisoners' Rights, Proceedings Against the Police, Professional Negligence, Public and Administrative Law.

GEOFFREY ROBERTSON, Q.C.. PRACTICE AREAS: International Criminal Law; European, International and Commonwealth Law; Extradition; Private and Public Law; International Human Rights; Communications and Media Law.

SIR LOUIS BLOM-COOPER, Q.C. PRACTICE AREAS: International Criminal Law; European, International and Commonwealth Law; Extradition; Private and Public Law; International Inquiries.

RICHARD MAXWELL, Q.C.. PRACTICE AREAS: Personal Injury; Commercial Litigation; Criminal Law; Public Inquiries; Planning; Judicial Review.

HELENA KENNEDY, Q.C.. PRACTICE AREAS: Criminal Law; Judicial Review; Public Inquiries; Sex Discrimination Work.

PETER THORNTON, Q.C.. LANGUAGES: English, French and German. *PRACTICE AREAS:* International Criminal Law; European, International and Commonwealth Law; Extradition; International Human Rights; Prisoners' Rights.

CHRISTOPHER SALLON, Q.C. *LANGUAGES:* English and French. *PRACTICE AREAS:* International Criminal Law; Fraud & Drug Trafficking.

LEGAL SUPPORT PERSONNEL

CHRISTINE KINGS (Practice Manager).

MICHELLE SIMPSON (Senior Clerk).

Languages: French, German, Italian, Greek, Spanish and Sinhale

ERSKINE CHAMBERS

30 LINCOLN'S INN FIELDS
LONDON WC2A 3PF, ENGLAND
Telephone: (44) 171-242 5532
Fax: (44) 171-831 0125
Lix: Lon 033
DX: LDE 308

Company Law, Corporate Insolvency, Financial Services and related Commercial fields, Comprehensive range of services are provided including advice, Litigation and the drafting of documentation both in the United Kingdom and in other jurisdictions, particularly in Commonwealth countries.

(This Listing Continued)

ERSKINE CHAMBERS, London—Continued

Erskine Chambers is also able to provide barristers qualified to give expert evidence on questions of English Company Law.

MEMBERS OF CHAMBERS

Richard Sykes, Q.C.	David Mabb
R.A.K. Wright, Q.C.	Martin Moore
W.F. Stubbs, Q.C.	David Chivers
Oilver Weaver, Q.C.	Ceri Bryant
Sir Thomas Stockdale	Richard Snowden
Robin Potts, Q.C.	Catherine Roberts
David Richards, Q.C.	Philip Gillyon
John Cone	Mary Stokes
Leslie Kosmin, Q.C.	Andrew Thompson
Michael Todd	Prof. Dan Prentice

LEGAL SUPPORT PERSONNEL

Michael Hannibal (Senior Clerk)
Mark Swallow (Clerk)
Christopher Reade (Clerk)

Languages: English, French and German.

ESSEX COURT CHAMBERS

(FORMERLY FOUR ESSEX COURT)

24 LINCOLN'S INN FIELDS
LONDON WC2A 3ED, ENGLAND
Telephone: 0171 813 8000
Telex: 888465 COMCAS G
Fax: 0171 813 8080
DX: 320 London Chancery Lane WC2

For round the clock information and assistance, telephone information on 0171 813 8000. International 44 171 813 8000 (Voice Mail).

CHAMBERS PROFILE: *Types of work undertaken: Barristers at Essex Court Chambers advise across the whole spectrum of international and commercial law and act as advocates in all categories of litigation and commercial arbitration worldwide.*

At Essex Court Chambers the principal fields of work are arbitration, aviation, banking and financial services, commercial agreements, commodity transactions, competition law, corporate affairs, european law, insurance and reinsurance, international commercial fraud, international trade and transport, maritime law and professional negligence.

Additional specializations: Within chambers individual barristers also practice in a variety of other areas including administrative law and judicial review, construction and engineering, competition law, computer law, employment law, entertainment law, EC law, French law, human rights, immigration law, industrial relations, insolvency, intellectual property, Irish law, oil and gas, public international law, tribunals and inquiries and VAT law.

Jean-Yves de Cara, Professeur Agrégé des facultés de droit can be instructed on his own or with other members of Chambers on questions of EC and French law.

MEMBERS OF CHAMBERS

Gordon Pollock, QC	David Joseph
Ian Hunter, QC	Richard Millett
Stewart Boyd, QC	Huw Davies
John Thomas, QC	Joe Smouha
V.V. Veeder, QC	Martin Griffiths
Prof. Rosalyn Higgins, QC	Karen Troy-Davies
Michael Collins, QC	John Lockey
Richard Siberry, QC	Peter Duffy
Jonathan Gilman, QC	Simon Bryan
Bernard Eder, QC	David Foxton
Roderick Cordara, QC	Phillipa Watson
Anthony Dicks	Professor Malcolm Shaw
Anthony Bessemar-Clark	Sara Cockerill
Jack Beatson	John Snider
Simon Crookenden	Vernon Flynn
Andrew Hochhauser	Brian Dye
Richard Jacobs	Nigel Eaton
David Mildon	Claire Blanchard

(This Listing Continued)

Victor Lyon	Perdita Cargill-Thompson
Mark Smith	Vaughan Lowe
Geraldine Andrews	Toby Landau
Graham Dunning	Paul Stanley
Mark Templeman	Martin Hunter
Steven Berry	James O'Reilly

Professor Jean-Yves de Cara

SENIOR CLERK

David Grief

CLERKS

Joe Ferrigno
Nigel Jones
Richard Branchflower
Mathew Kesbey

Languages: French, German, Italian and Spanish

FOUNTAIN COURT CHAMBERS

FOUNTAIN COURT, TEMPLE
LONDON EC4Y 9DH, ENGLAND
Telephone: 0171-583-3335
Out of Hours: 0831-465305
Telex: 8813408 FONLEG G
Fax: 0171-353-0329; 0171-353-1794
LIXNo: LONO35

CHAMBERS PROFILE: *A large and long established set of Chambers, practising primarily in the commercial field but with a wide range of other specialties. Much of the work is international in character. The size of Chambers enables it to supply teams of Counsel at all levels of seniority, to deal with large-scale litigation. Areas include in particular: arbitration, sale of goods, international trade, banking and financial services, shipping, aviation (including air transport licensing), "City" regulatory work (including Lloyd's disciplinary tribunals), professional negligence, insurance and reinsurance, takeovers and mergers, oil and gas contracts. EEC law is an aspect of much of this work. Other specialities include: administrative law and judicial review, building disputes, employment law (including industrial disputes and sex discrimination), media and entertainment law, medical and pharmaceutical law (including medical negligence), Parliamentary bills, personal injury (including disaster litigation).*

CONRAD DEHN, QC, M.A. (Oxon), called, 1952; 1968, QC.

THE HON. CHRISTOPHER BATHURST, QC, called, 1959; 1978, QC.

PETER SCOTT, QC, M.A. (Oxon), called, 1960; 1978, QC.

BRUCE COLES, QC, LL.B. (Melb.) B.C.L., called, 1963; 1984, QC.

GORDON LANGLEY, QC, B.A., B.C.L. (Oxon), called, 1966; 1983, QC.

CHARLES GIBSON, M.A. (Oxon), called, 1966.

MICHAEL BAKER, QC, B.A. (Oxon), called, 1966; 1990, QC.

TIMOTHY WALKER, QC, B.C.L., M.A. (Oxon), called, 1968; 1985, QC.

ANTHONY BOSWOOD, QC, B.A., B.C.L., called, 1970; 1986, QC.

PETER GOLDSMITH, QC, M.A. (Cantab), LL.M. (Lond), called, 1972; 1987, QC.

TREVOR PHILIPSON, QC, B.A., B.C.L. (Oxon), called, 1972; 1989, QC.

MICHAEL LEREGO, M.A., B.C.L., called, 1972.

ANDREW SMITH, QC, B.A. (Oxon), called, 1974; 1990, QC.

CHARLES FALCONER, QC, B.A. (Cantab), called, 1974; 1991, QC.

MICHAEL BRINDLE, B.A. (Oxon), LL.B. (Manch), called, 1975.

NICHOLAS UNDERHILL, B.A. (Oxon), called, 1976.

NICHOLAS STADLEN, QC, B.A. (Cantab), called, 1976; 1991, QC.

TIMOTHY WORMINGTON, B.A., B.C.L. (Oxon), called, 1977.

DAVID RAILTON, B.A. (Oxon), called, 1979.

BRIAN DOCTOR, B.C.L., B.A., LL.B. (South Africa), called, 1991.

(This Listing Continued)

MRS. GILLIAN KEENE, B.A. (Oxon), called, 1980.

THE HON. MICHAEL MCLAREN, B.A. (Cantab), called, 1981.

SIMON BROWNE WILKINSON, B.A. (Cantab), called, 1981.

PHILIP BROOK SMITH, B.Sc., M.Sc., called, 1982.

RAYMOND COX, B.A. (Oxon), called, 1982.

THOMAS KEITH, called, 1984.

MURRAY SHANKS, M.A. (Cantab), called, 1984.

MRS. DAPHNE LOEBL, B.A. (Hons) (Cantab), called, 1985.

GUY PHILIPPS, B.A. (Oxon) Dip. Law, called, 1986.

STEPHEN MORIARTY, B.A. (Oxon), called, 1986.

CRAIG ORR, M.A. (Cantab) B.C.L., called, 1986.

TIMOTHY HOWE, B.A. (Oxon), called, 1987.

BANKIM THANKI, M.A. (Oxon), called, 1988.

PATRICIA ROBERTSON, B.A. (Oxon), called, 1988.

JEFFREY CHAPMAN, B.A. (Sussex), LL.M. (Cantab), called, 1989.

BRIAN NAPIER, M.A. (Edin), M.A. Ph.D. (Cantab), called, 1990.

DERRICK DALE, B.A. (Cantab), LL.M. (Harvard), called, 1990.

MARCUS SMITH, B.A. (Hons) Oxon B.C.L., called, 1991.

PAUL GOTT, B.A. (Cantab), B.C.L. (Oxon), called, 1991.

VERONIQUE BUEHRLEN, M.A. (St. Andrew's) Dip. Law, called, 1991.

ANDREW MITCHELL, B.C.L. (Oxon), LL.B. (Cantab), called, 1992.

RICHARD N. HANDYSIDE, LL.B. (Hons) (Bris), called, L 1993.

JOHN C. TAYLOR, B.A. (Hons) (Cantab), called, M 1993.

RICHARD J.L. COLEMAN, B.A. (Hons) (Cantab), LL.M., called, L 1994.

ACADEMIC ASSOCIATES

PETER CARTER, QC, M.A. (Oxon) B.C.L., called, 1947; 1990, QC.

RICHARD HOOLEY, M.A. (Cantab), called, 1984.

ANDREW BURROWS, M.A. (Oxon), called, 1985.

EXECUTIVE MANAGER/SENIOR CLERK

Barry Down

Languages: French, German and Italian

BARRISTERS CHAMBERS OF MR. MILTON GRUNDY

U.K. Tax Specialists

Established in 1965

GRAY'S INN CHAMBERS
GRAY'S INN
LONDON WC1R 5JA, ENGLAND
Telephone: 0171-242 2642
Fax: 0171-831 9017 (Grps. 2 & 3); 0171-405 4078 (Grp. 4)
DX: 352 London

Revenue Law.

MEMBERS OF CHAMBERS

MILTON GRUNDY, M.A. (Cantab), called, 1954, England. **LANGUAGES:** French. **PRACTICE AREAS:** Taxation.

ANDREW PARK, Q.C., B.A. (Hons.), called, 1964, England. **PRACTICE AREAS:** Taxation.

MICHAEL FLESCH, Q.C., LL.B., called, 1963, England. **PRACTICE AREAS:** Taxation.

DAVID GOLDBERG, Q.C., LL.B., called, 1971, England. **PRACTICE AREAS:** Taxation.

(This Listing Continued)

DAVID GOY, Q.C., LL.M., called, 1973, England. **PRACTICE AREAS:** Taxation.

HILDA WILSON, B.A. (Hons.), called, 1953, England. **PRACTICE AREAS:** Taxation.

JOHN WALTERS, M.A., called, 1977, England. **LANGUAGES:** French and German. **PRACTICE AREAS:** Taxation.

FELICITY CULLEN, LL.B., called, 1985, England. **LANGUAGES:** French. **PRACTICE AREAS:** Taxation.

PHILIP BAKER, M.A. (Cantab), B.C.L. (Oxon), Ph.D. (Lond), called, 1979, England. **LANGUAGES:** French and Chinese (Mandarin and Cantonese). **PRACTICE AREAS:** Taxation.

HUGH MCKAY, LL.B., LL.M., called, 1990, England. **PRACTICE AREAS:** Taxation.

LEGAL SUPPORT PERSONNEL

JOHN REGAN (Clerk).

BARRISTERS CHAMBERS 2 HARE COURT

Established in 1894

2 HARE COURT, TEMPLE
LONDON EC4Y 7BH, ENGLAND
Telephone: 0171-583 1770 Voicebank: (0426) 910242
Fax: 0171-583 9269 Dx: 281 LDE

CHAMBERS PROFILE: *In the field of commercial law work specialization includes International Trade, Banking, Insurance, Shipping, Financial Services and Intellectual Property and many other areas of commercial, financial and business law and employment law. Specialist advice is available together with representation before courts and tribunals in England, Europe and the Commonwealth.*

In the field of public law our members have extensive experience in litigation for and against central and local government, governmental agencies and regulatory authorities in English, European and Commonwealth courts and tribunals and in related advisory work.

Two Hare Court have several noted practitioners of public international law of whom one was formerly Legal Advisers to the Foreign and Commonwealth Office and two hold chairs of international law. Two senior members are based in Brussels and practice exclusively in European Community Law.

COLIN WILLIAM G. ROSS-MUNRO, Q.C., called, 1951, England; 1972, Silk. *Education:* B.A.

STANLEY ERIC BRODIE, Q.C., called, 1954, England; 1975, Silk. *Education:* M.A.

ANTHONY PAUL LESTER, Q.C., (Lord Lester of Herne Hill Q.C.) called, 1963, England; 1975, Silk. *Education:* B.A.; LL.M.

SIR IAN MACTAGGART SINCLAIR, Q.C., called, 1952, England; 1979, Silk. *Education:* B.A.; LL.M.

IAN BROWNLIE, Q.C., called, 1958, England; 1979, Silk. *Education:* B.A.; D.C.L.

DAVID TORRANCE DONALDSON, Q.C., called, 1968, England; 1984, Silk. *Education:* M.A.; Dr.Jur.

ROBERT MICHAEL ENGLEHART, Q.C., called, 1969, England; 1986, Silk. *Education:* M.A.; LL.M.

DAVID HUNT, Q.C., called, 1969, England; 1987, Silk. *Education:* M.A. (Cantab).

MISS BARBARA DOHMANN, Q.C., called, 1971, England. *Education:* Mainz and Paris.

ANDREW CARTWRIGHT PUGH, Q.C., called, 1961, England. *Education:* M.A.

IAN STEWART FORRESTER, Q.C., called, 1972, Scotland; 1989, Silk. *Education:* M.A.; LL.B.

ROYSTON MILES GOODE, Q.C., called, 1988, England; 1990, Silk. *Education:* LL.B.; LL.D.

GERALD LEVY, called, 1964, England. *Education:* M.A.

(This Listing Continued)

BARRISTERS CHAMBERS 2 HARE COURT, London—
Continued

PROF. JEFFREY LIONEL JOWELL, Q.C. (HON), called, 1965, England; 1993, Silk. *Education:* B.A.; LL.B.

PROF. MAURICE HARVEY MENDELSON, Q.C., called, 1965, England; 1992, Silk. *Education:* M.A.; D.Phil.

STEPHEN ANDREW NATHAN, Q.C., called, 1969, England; 1993, Silk. *Education:* M.A.

JONATHAN HARVIE, Q.C., called, 1973, England; 1992, Silk. *Education:* M.A. (Oxon).

MISS PRESILEY LAMORNA BAXENDALE, Q.C., called, 1974, England; 1992, Silk. *Education:* M.A.

DAWN OLIVER, called, 1965, England. *Education:* M.A., Ph.D.

ALASTAIR SUTTON, called, 1974, England. *Education:* LL.B., LL.M.

CHARLES JOHN R. FLINT, called, 1975, England. *Education:* M.A.

HUGO ARTHUR MICKLEM PAGE, called, 1977, England. *Education:* M.A.

BEVERLEY ANN MACNAUGHTON LANG, called, 1978, England. *Education:* B.A. (Oxon).

MISS JUDITH HELEN BEALE, called, 1978, England. *Education:* B.A.; M.Phil.

THOMAS ALAN GEORGE BEAZLEY, called, 1979, England. *Education:* B.A.; LL.B.

DAVID PHILIP PANNICK, Q.C., called, 1979, England; 1992, Silk. *Education:* M.A.; B.C.L.

IAN ALEXANDER MILL, called, 1981, England. *Education:* M.A.

PAUL ANTHONY GOULDING, called, 1984, England. *Education:* M.A.; B.C.L.

ANTHONY NICHOLAS GEORGE PETO, called, 1985. *Education:* B.A.; B.C.L.

MISS MONICA GUNNEL CONSTANCE CARSS-FRISK, called, 1985, England. *Education:* LL.B.; B.C.L.

GERARD JOSEPH PATRICK CLARKE, called, 1986, England. *Education:* B.A.

ADAM VALENTINE SHERVEY LEWIS, called, 1985, England. *Education:* M.A.

MARK RICHARD SHAW, called, 1987, England. *Education:* B.A.; LL.M.

ANDREW JAMES DOMINIC GREEN, called, 1988, England. *Education:* LL.B.

ROBERT PAUL THOMPSON HOWE, called, 1988, England. *Education:* M.A.; B.C.L.

ADRIAN BRIGGS, called, 1989, England. *Education:* B.C.L.; M.A.

MS. DINAH GWEN LISON ROSE, called, 1989, England. *Education:* B.A.

MICHAEL FORDHAM, called, 1990, England. *Education:* B.A. (Hons), B.C.L., LL.M. (Virginia).

PUSHPINDER SAINI, called, 1991, England. *Education:* M.A., B.C.L.

THOMAS HENRY CROXFORD, called, 1992, England. *Education:* B.A.

JAVAN WILLIAM HERBERG, called, 1992, England. *Education:* LL.B., B.C.L.

JOANNA KATE POLLARD, called, 1993, England. *Education:* B.A.

ANDREW MICHAEL HUNTER, called, 1993, England. *Education:* B.A., B.C.L.

LEGAL SUPPORT PERSONNEL

JULIA HORNOR (Practice Manager).

MARTIN SMITH (Senior Clerk).

Languages: French, German, Dutch, Italian, Spanish, Japanese, Swedish, Finnish, Norwegian, Danish, Hindi, Urdu and Punjabi.

BARRISTERS CHAMBERS OF LORD IRVINE, Q.C.

11 KING'S BENCH WALK, TEMPLE
LONDON EC4Y 7EQ, ENGLAND
Telephone: 0171-583 0610
Fax: 0171-583 9123/3690 (Grps 2 & 3)
DX: 368 London

Employment Law, Commercial Law, Public Law and Administrative Law.

CHAMBERS PROFILE: *These Chambers specialise in advisory work, arbitration and litigation in three main areas: Commercial Law, including insurance, banking, carriage of goods, sale of goods, competition law, private international law and professional negligence, Public (Administrative) Law, including judicial review, public bodies' contracts, and most aspects of the law relating to local government and Employment (Labour) Law, including both individual and collective disputes. We deal with issues of European Community law in all three of these areas.*

Members of Chambers regularly appear in overseas jurisdictions, and will accept instructions to appear or to advise either directly from overseas lawyers or through English solicitors. We are also available to give expert evidence of English law. Languages spoken, other than English, include Afrikaans, Bengali, French, German, Irish, Italian and Spanish, A full Chambers brochure is available on request from the Senior Clerk (Philip Monham).

MEMBERS OF CHAMBERS

Lord Irvine of Lairg	Siobhan Ward
Eldred Tabachnik	Philip Sales
James Goudie	John Cavanagh
Richard Field	Nigel Giffin
Patrick Elias	Charles Béar
Michael Supperstone	Peter Wallington
Elizabeth Slade	Jonathan Swift
Alan Wilkie	Timothy Pitt-Payne
Alistair J. McGregor	Peter Oldham
Anthony Blair	Sean Jones
Elisabeth Laing	Akhlaq Choudhury
Christopher Jeans	Paul Nicholls
Adrian Lynch	Daniel Stilitz

LEGAL SUPPORT PERSONNEL

Philip Monham (Clerk)

Languages: Afrikaans, French, German, Irish, Italian and Spanish.

KEATING CHAMBERS
BARRISTERS CHAMBERS OF JOHN FRANCIS UFF, Q.C.

10 ESSEX STREET, OUTER TEMPLE
LONDON WC2R 3AA, ENGLAND
Telephone: 0171-240-6981
Fax: 0171-240-7722 (Grps 2 & 3)
Telex: 8955650
DX: 1045 London/Chancery Lane

Paris, France Office: Centre d'Affaires Messine, 19 Avenue de Messine, 75008. Telephone: (331) 40 76 63 00. Fax: (331) 42 89 51 85.

Construction Law and International Arbitration Specialists. Building and Engineering contracts, Litigation and Arbitration (Including ICC arbitration). Contracts, disputes relating to civil, mechanical and electrical engineering projects, process plant, the oil & gas industry and dredging; Contracts and disputes relating to computers and other aspects of information technology; Environmental law; European Community law, particularly procurement law and competition law.

CHAMBERS PROFILE: *Chambers work has for many years been centered primarily on the construction industry and allied fields including property and high technology industries. Senior members of Chambers sit as Arbitrators and legal assessors in international and domestic arbitrations, and as mediators or conciliators in Alternative Dispute Resolution.*

The steadily increasing involvement by Members of Chambers in advising and acting in ICC Arbitrations has led to the opening of an office in Paris.

(This Listing Continued)

MEMBERS

JOHN FRANCIS UFF, Q.C., called, 1970, England; 1983, Queen's Counsel; Assistant Recorder. *Education:* Ph.D., B.Sc. (King's Coll. London); F.I.C.E., C. Eng., ACIArb., Nash Professor of Engineering Law and Director of the Centre for Construction Law at Kings College London. *PRACTICE AREAS:* Construction Law; Professional Negligence; Commercial Arbitration.

DONALD NORMAN KEATING, Q.C., called, 1950, England; 1972, Queen's Counsel; Recorder. *Education:* B.A. (King's Coll. London), ACIArb. *LANGUAGES:* English. *PRACTICE AREAS:* Construction Law; Professional Negligence; Commercial Arbitration.

RICHARD FERNYHOUGH, Q.C., called, 1970, England; 1986, Queen's Counsel; Recorder. *Education:* LL.B. (Univ. Coll. London), FCIArb. *LANGUAGES:* English, French and German. *PRACTICE AREAS:* Construction Law; Professional Negligence; Commercial Arbitration.

JOHN MARTIN COLLINS, Q.C., called, 1952, England; 1972, Queen's Counsel; Judge of the Jersey and Guernsey Court of Appeal. *Education:* LL.B. Manchester). *LANGUAGES:* English and French. *PRACTICE AREAS:* Construction Law; Professional Negligence; Commercial Arbitration.

CHRISTOPHER SYDNEY THOMAS, Q.C., called, 1973, England; 1989, Queen's Counsel. *Education:* B.A. (Kent), Dip de Droit Comparé. *LANGUAGES:* English and French. *PRACTICE AREAS:* Construction Law; Professional Negligence; Commercial Arbitration.

JOHN WHEELER MARRIN, Q.C., called, 1974, England; 1990, Queen's Counsel. *Education:* M.A. (Cantab). *LANGUAGES:* English and French. *PRACTICE AREAS:* Construction Law; Professional Negligence; Commercial Arbitration.

STEPHEN ANDREW FURST, Q.C., called, 1975, England; 1991, Queen's Counsel; Assistant Recorder. *Education:* B.A. (Oxon), LL.B. (Leeds). *LANGUAGES:* English and French. *PRACTICE AREAS:* Construction Law; Professional Negligence; Commercial Arbitration; Landlord and Tenant; Information Technology.

TIMOTHY STANLEY ELLIOTT, Q.C., called, 1975, England; 1992, Queen's Counsel. *Education:* M.A. (Oxon). *LANGUAGES:* English. *PRACTICE AREAS:* Construction Law; Professional Negligence; Commercial Arbitration.

VIVIAN ARTHUR RAMSEY, Q.C., called, 1979, England; 1992, Queen's Counsel. *Education:* M.A. (Oxon), C.Eng., M.I.C.E., Special Professor department of Civil Engineering, Nottingham University. *LANGUAGES:* English and French. *PRACTICE AREAS:* Construction Law; Professional Negligence; Commercial Arbitration.

ALAN CHARLES STEYNOR, called, 1975, England; Assistant Recorder. *Education:* M.A. (Cantab), ACIArb. *LANGUAGES:* English and French. *PRACTICE AREAS:* Construction Law; Professional Negligence; Commercial Arbitration; Landlord and Tenant.

ROBERT GAITSKELL, Q.C., called, 1978, England. *Education:* B.Sc. (Eng.), C. Eng, F.I.E.E., ACIArb. *LANGUAGES:* English. *PRACTICE AREAS:* Construction Law; Professional Negligence; Commercial Arbitration; Information Technology.

PHILIP VINCENT BOULDING, called, 1979, England. *Education:* B.A., LL.B. (Cantab). *LANGUAGES:* English and French. *PRACTICE AREAS:* Construction Law; Professional Negligence; Commercial Arbitration; Landlord and Tenant.

ROSEMARY ELIZABETH JACKSON, called, 1981, England. *Education:* LL.B. (Lond), AKC (King's Coll. Lond). *LANGUAGES:* English. *PRACTICE AREAS:* Construction Law; Professional Negligence; Party Wall; Arbitration.

MARCUS LOUIS TAVERNER, called, 1981, England. *Education:* LL.B. (Leicester), LL.M. (Lond), ACIArb. *LANGUAGES:* English. *PRACTICE AREAS:* Construction Law; Professional Negligence; Arbitration.

PETER WILLIAM COULSON, called, 1982, England. *Education:* B.A. (Keele), ACIArb. *LANGUAGES:* English and French. *PRACTICE AREAS:* Construction Law; Professional Negligence; Arbitration.

IAN PENNICOTT, called, 1982, England. *Education:* B.A., LL.M. (Cantab), Member of the Hong Kong Bar. *LANGUAGES:* English. *PRACTICE AREAS:* Construction Law; Professional Negligence; Arbitration.

(This Listing Continued)

PAUL ANTHONY DARLING, called, 1983, England. *Education:* B.A., B.C.L. (Oxon). *LANGUAGES:* English. *PRACTICE AREAS:* Construction Law; Professional Negligence; Arbitration; Bloodstock and Horse Racing.

FINOLA MARY O'FARRELL, called, 1983, England. *Education:* B.A. (Dunlem). *LANGUAGES:* English. *PRACTICE AREAS:* Construction Law; Professional Negligence; Arbitration; Landlord and Tenant.

ADRIAN JOHN WILLIAMSON, called, 1983, England. *Education:* M.A. (Cantab). *LANGUAGES:* English and French. *PRACTICE AREAS:* Construction Law; Professional Negligence; Arbitration.

ALEXANDER DAVID NISSEN, called, 1985, England. *Education:* LL.B. (Hons.) (Manchester). *LANGUAGES:* English. *PRACTICE AREAS:* Construction Law; Professional Negligence; Arbitration.

MICHAEL FREDERICK THOMAS BOWSHER, called, 1985, England. *Education:* B.A. (Oxon) ACIArb., Cleary, Gottlieb, Steen & Hamilton, Brussels Office, 1989-1992. *LANGUAGES:* English, French and German. *PRACTICE AREAS:* Construction Law; Arbitration; European Community Law; Competition and Procurement Law; Local Authority Contracts; Information Technology.

NERYS ANGHARAD JEFFORD, called, 1986, England. *Education:* M.A. (Oxon), LL.M. (Virginia). *LANGUAGES:* English, French and German. *PRACTICE AREAS:* Construction Law; Professional Negligence; Arbitration; European Community Law.

LOUISE ELIZABETH RANDALL, called, 1988, England. *Education* B.A. (Hons) (Keele). *LANGUAGES:* English. *PRACTICE AREAS:* Construction Law; Professional Negligence; Arbitration; Landlord and Tenant.

ROBERT JONATHAN EVANS, called, 1989, England. *Education:* M.A. (Cantab), LL.B. (Lond.), C.Eng, MICE, ACIArb. *LANGUAGES:* English and French. *PRACTICE AREAS:* Construction Law; Professional Negligence; Arbitration.

SARAH JANE HANNAFORD, called, 1989, England. *Education:* B.A. (Oxon). *LANGUAGES:* English, French and Spanish. *PRACTICE AREAS:* Construction Law; Professional Negligence; Arbitration.

SIMON JOHN HARGREAVES, called, 1991, England. *Education:* B.A. (Oxon). *LANGUAGES:* English. *PRACTICE AREAS:* Construction Law; Professional Negligence; Arbitration.

RICHARD ANTHONY HARDING, called, 1992, England. *Education:* B.A. *LANGUAGES:* English, German, Spanish, Arabic, French and Persian. *PRACTICE AREAS:* Construction Law; Professional Negligence; Arbitration.

JANE KATHERINE LEMON, Q.C., Called, 1993, England. *Education:* B. A. (Hons., Oxon). *LANGUAGES:* English. *PRACTICE AREAS:* Construction Law; Professional Negligence; Arbitration.

PIERS A. STANSFIELD, Called, 1993, England. *Education:* LL.B. Hons (Bristol). *LANGUAGES:* English. *PRACTICE AREAS:* Construction Law; Professional Negligence; Arbitration.

LEGAL SUPPORT PERSONNEL

BARRY BRIDGMAN (Senior Clerk). *LANGUAGES:* English.

PHIL GOLDSMITH (First Junior Clerk). *LANGUAGES:* English.

JOHN MUNTON (Second Junior Clerk). *LANGUAGES:* English.

---

5 KING'S BENCH WALK
CHAMBERS OF DAVID COCKS Q.C.

5 KING'S BENCH WALK, TEMPLE
LONDON EC4Y 7DN, ENGLAND
Telephone: 0171 797 7600
Fax: 0171 797 7648 DX: 478 London Chancery Lane WC2

CHAMBERS PROFILE: The set has always specialized in a wide variety of criminal and common law work. There are eleven silks and 30 juniors, which has added to the increasingly specialist service that chambers is able to offer.

The criminal work undertaken is divided between prosecution and defence and all members of chambers do a mixture of both. There is particularly strong expertise within the fields of commercial fraud, Inland Revenue and VAT offences, drugs and the problems arising from the Drug Trafficking

(This Listing Continued)

5 KING'S BENCH WALK CHAMBERS OF DAVID COCKS Q.C., London—Continued

Offences Act, extradition, child abuse, obscene publications, road traffic, licensing and offences requiring forensic experts.

The strengths within the common law areas of work include commercial law, personal injury work, family law and judicial review work. Representation is provided at a wide variety of disciplinary tribunals and inquiries. Pro bono work in the Privy Council is undertaken by silks and work for the Free Representation Unit by juniors.

Chambers has corporate membership of the British Institute of Human Rights.

Individual members have also developed areas of practice in which they have a special expertise and several members have written or collaborated on authoritative legal works in their specialized areas.

For urgent business outside office hours the answerphone will give duty number to contact any member.

David Cocks, QC	Jonathan Fischer
Sir Derek Spencer, QC	John Ryder
Anthony Arlidge, QC	Linda Dobbs
Henry Green, QC	Ian Leist
James Stewart, QC	Alexander Milne
Linda Stern, QC	Richard Kovalevsky
Peter Rook, QC	Rupert Overbury
David Radcliffe	Janine Sheff
David Lederman, QC	Mark Lucraft
Austen Issard-Davies	Angela Morris
Richard Sutton, QC	Brendan Morris
Christopher Ball, QC	Robert Boyle
Peter Carter	David Marshall
Rosamund Horwood-Smart	Jane Bewsey
John Black	Shane Collery
Nigel Peters	Francis Feehan
Nicholas Fooks	David Williams
David Etherington	John Anderson
David Green	Allison Clarke
Stephen Harvey	Paul Hardy
Patricia Lynch	Sara Lawson

LEGAL SUPPORT PERSONNEL

K.J. Darvill (Clerk)	M.S. Bennett (Clerk)

Languages: French, German, Italian, Portuguese, Russian and Spanish

4 PUMP COURT, CHAMBERS OF BRUCE MAULEVERER, Q.C.

4 PUMP COURT, MIDDLE TEMPLE
LONDON EC4Y 7AN, ENGLAND
Telephone: 0171 353 2656
Telecopier: 0171 583 2036

CHAMBERS PROFILE: The main emphasis of Chambers' work covers a broad range of commercial litigation and advisory work. Members specialize in such areas as banking, financial services and Stock Exchange work; disciplinary tribunals; domestic and international arbitration; insurance and reinsurance; consumer credit; international trade and transport (including carriage and sale of goods). Members also have considerable expertise in all aspects of construction work; professional negligence; gaming and licensing; property (including landlord and tenant); employment law; and personal injury. In addition, individual barristers have developed areas of special interest such as matrimonial finance, entertainment law and judicial review work. Direct professional access work is welcomed by all members.

MEMBERS OF CHAMBERS

Bruce Mauleverer, Q.C.	Nigel Tozzi
John Beveridge, Q.C.	Andrew Fletcher
Anthony Temple, Q.C.	Lindsay Boswell
David Friedman, Q.C.	Peter Hamilton
David Blunt, Q.C.	Alexander Charlton
Christopher Moger, Q.C.	David Sears
Jeremy Storey, Q.C.	James Cross
Michael Douglas	Duncan McCall

(This Listing Continued)

Jonathan Marks	Aidan Christie
Laurence Marsh	Andrew Neish
Allen Dyer	Kirsten Houghton
Jeremy Nicholson	Dominic McCahill
Jonathan Acton Davis	Phyllida Cheyne
John Rowland	Simon Henderson
Oliver Ticciati	Michael Davie

BARRISTERS CHAMBERS OF ROBERT REID, Q.C.

9 OLD SQUARE, LINCOLN'S INN
LONDON WC2A 3SR, ENGLAND
Telephone: 0171-405 4682
Fax: 0171-831 7107 (Grps 2 & 3)
DX: 305 London/Chancery Lane

MEMBERS

ROBERT REID, called, 1965, England and Queen's Counsel. *Education:* M.A. (Oxon).

MICHAEL DRISCOLL, called, 1970, England and Queen's Counsel. *Education:* B.A., LL.B. (Cantab).

NICHOLAS PATTEN, called, 1974, England and Queen's Counsel. *Education:* M.A. (Oxon) B.C.L.

JUDITH JACKSON, called, 1975, England and Queen's Counsel. *Education:* LL.M., LL.B.

SIMON BERRY, called, 1977, England and Queen's Counsel. *Education:* LL.B.

DAVID HODGE, called, 1979, England. *Education:* B.A., B.C.L. (Oxon).

DANIEL HOCHBERG, called, 1982, England. *Education:* M.A. (Oxon).

JOHN DAGNALL, called, 1983, England. *Education:* B.A. (Oxon) B.C.L.

JOHN MCGHEE, called, 1984, England. *Education:* M.A. (Oxon).

TIMOTHY HARRY, called, 1983, England. *Education:* M.A. (Oxon).

EDWIN JOHNSON, called, 1987, England. *Education:* B.A. (Oxon).

THOMAS LEECH, called, 1988, England. *Education:* B.A. (Oxon) B.C.L.

KATHARINE HOLLAND, called, 1989, England. *Education:* B.A. (Oxon) B.C.L.

CHRISTOPHER STONER, called, 1991, England. *Education:* LL.B.

ANDREW P.D. WALKER, called, 1991, England. *Education:* B.A. (Cantab).

SIMON BURRELL, called, 1988, England. *Education:* B.A. (Oxon).

MICHAEL PRYOR, called, 1992, England. *Education:* LL.B. (Hons.).

LEGAL SUPPORT PERSONNEL

Martin Poulter (Clerk)

BARRISTERS CHAMBERS OF PATRICK C. SOARES

8 GRAY'S INN SQUARE, GRAY'S INN
LONDON WC1R 5AZ, ENGLAND
Telephone: 0171-242 3529
Fax: 0171-404 0395
DX: 411 Lond/Chancery Lane

Revenue Law, Trusts and Estates Law (with particular emphasis on International Estates, Trusts and Tax Planning).

MEMBERS OF CHAMBERS

PATRICK C. SOARES, LL.B. (Lond), LL.M. (Lond) FTII, called, 1983, England; formerly a Solicitor. Head of Chambers.

BARRY MCCUTCHEON, B.A. (Trinity USA), LL.M. (Lond) FTII, called, 1975, England.

(This Listing Continued)

DAVID BROWNBILL, LL.B. (Nottingham), called, 1989, England; formerly a Solicitor.

IAN FERRIER, M.A. (Oxon), called, 1976, England.

RT. HON. DENZIL DAVIES, B.A., P.C., called, 1965, England.

CLIFFORD JOSEPH, M.A. (Oxon), LMRTPI, called, 1975, England; 1991, California; formerly a Solicitor.

IZZET SINAN, M.A. (Cantab), LL.M. (Cantab), M.A. (Brussels) EEC Law, called, 1981, England.

LEGAL SUPPORT PERSONNEL

MARIE BURKE (Clerk).

LISA TAYLOR (Clerk).

CHAMBERS OF ROBERT WEBB Q.C.

5 BELL YARD

LONDON WC2A 2JR, ENGLAND
Telephone: 0171 333 8811
Fax: 0171 333 8831
Dx: LDE 400

5 Bell Yard, is a set barristers chambers practising in most areas of civil and commercial law. In particular, expertise is offered in: *Aviation Law:* Liability, passenger and cargo, leasing, regulatory, C.A.A. and European, insurance.
Commercial Law: Banking, carriage of goods, commercial contracts, company and insolvency, insurance and reinsurance.
Civil Law: Building and engineering, landlord and tenant, personal injury, professional and medical negligence, product and environmental liability, mass disasters.
Public and Employment Law: Judicial review, mental health, National Health Service, pharmaceutical, coroners, town and country planning, individual and collective employment, trade union, disciplinary tribunals, public inquiries.

BARRISTERS

Robert Webb, Q.C.

Robin Mathew, Q.C.	Michael Crane, Q.C.
Edward Bailey	Andrew Hillier
Dennis Matthews	Kenneth Munro
Gordon Bennett	Philip Shepherd
Angus Macpherson	Michael Soole
Anthony Radevsky	Andrew Lydiard
Paul Dean	Charlotte Jones
Michael Sullivan	Giles Kavanagh
David Fisher	Philip Reed
Matthew Reeve	Stephen Schaw-Miller
Raymond Ng	Robert Lawson
Akhil Shah	Hannah Brown
William Hansen	John Russell

LEGAL SUPPORT PERSONNEL

KEVIN MOORE (Clerk and Administration).

ADRIAN HAWES (Clerk and Administration).

ALEXANDERS EASTON KINCH

Established in 1992
203 TEMPLE CHAMBERS
TEMPLE AVENUE

LONDON EC4Y ODB, ENGLAND
Telephone: 0171-353 6221
Fax: 0171-583 0662 (Gps 2 and 3)
DX: LDE 264 London/Chancery Lane

Taxation, Private Client, Property (Commercial, High Class Residential, Agricultural and Landed Estates), Litigation (Commercial and Private), Probate and Trust, Company and Commercial.

FIRM PROFILE: The firm was established in 1992 following the merger of ALEXANDERS with the London practice of EASTON KINCH & BAILEY. ALEXANDERS EASTON KINCH is a City of London private client firm whose suite of offices are in close proximity to the Inns of Court, the Royal Courts of Justice as well as to the major financial institutions in the City of London. Unlike many firms in the City, this firm is through choice small in the conviction that greater size does not necessarily lead to greater efficiency and can tend to depersonalize the relationship between solicitor and client. As a result of this policy, there is always close partner/client contact throughout the relationship.

MEMBERS OF FIRM

ANTHONY R. MELLOWS, T.D., Ph.D., LL.D.; admitted, 1960. Professor of Law, University of London. **PRACTICE AREAS:** Taxation; Trusts; Private Clients.

JAMES A. JOHNSON, admitted, 1958. **PRACTICE AREAS:** Wills; Probate; Trusts.

(MRS.) ELISABETH A. JUPP, LL.B. (London); admitted, 1969. **PRACTICE AREAS:** Property; Commercial; Residential; Agricultural; Landed Estate.

MARTYN J. DALDORPH, M.A. (Cantab) admitted, 1971. **PRACTICE AREAS:** Litigation; Company; Commercial.

RICHARD D. O'HALLORAN, LL.B. (London); admitted, 1973. **PRACTICE AREAS:** Litigation; Commercial; Private.

GRAHAM D. OGILVIE, M.A. (Cantab); admitted, 1976. **PRACTICE AREAS:** Wills; Probate; Trusts.

MARK BUZZONI, LL.B., (Hons) (Bris); admitted, 1980. **PRACTICE AREAS:** Taxation; Probate; Trusts; Settlements.

(MISS) SUSAN J. GREENWOOD, B.A. (London) admitted, 1981. **PRACTICE AREAS:** Litigation; Private; Family.

(MRS.) JENNIFER M. WAKEFIELD, M.A. (Cantab) admitted, 1978. **PRACTICE AREAS:** Wills; Probate; Trusts.

ALLEN & OVERY

Established in 1930

ONE NEW CHANGE

LONDON EC4M 9QQ, ENGLAND

Telephone: (44) 0171 330 3000

Cable Address: "Allove, London-EC2"

Telex: 881 2801

Facsimile: (44) 0171 330 9999

Beijing, China Office: Suite 3204, Jing Guang Centre, Hu Jia Lou, Chaoyang District, 100020. Telephone: (86 1) 501 4681. Facsimile: (86 1) 501 4682.

Brussels, Belgium Office: Rue de la Loi 99, Box 8, 1040. Telephone: (32 2) 230 27 91. Facsimile (32 2) 230 66 13.

Budapest, Hungary Office: Mádach Trade Center, Mádach Imre utca 13-14, H-1075. Telephone: (361) 268 1511. Facsimile: (361) 268 1515.

Dubai, United Arab Emirates Office: 501 Al Futtaim Tower,P.O. Box 3251, Deira. Telephone: (971 4) 282296. Facsimile: (971 4) 212860.

Frankfurt, Germany Office: Taunusanlage 11, 11th Floor, 60329. Telephone: (49 69) 242 6120. Facsimile: (49 69) 242 61220.

Hong Kong Office: 9th Floor, Three Exchange Square, 8 Connaught Place. Telephone: (852) 2840 1282. Telex: 68757. Facsimile: (852) 2840 0515.

Madrid, Spain Office: Antonio Maura 7, 6°, 28014. Telephone: (34 1) 521 2654. Facsimile: (34 1) 523 0458.

Moscow, Russia Office: 9 ul Tverskaya, Entrance No 5, 8th Floor, 103009. Telephone: (7 501) 940 4500. Facsimile: (7 501) 940 4501.

New York Office: Swiss Bank Tower, 10 East 50th Street, 10022. Telephone (1-212) 754 3340. Facsimile: (1-212) 754 7903.

Paris, France Office: 1 Avenue Franklin D. Roosevelt, 75008. Telephone (33-1) 49 53 06 37. Telex: 651079. Facsimile: (33-1) 49 53 91 52.

Prague, Czech Republic Office: Jindřišská 34, 110 00 Prague 1. Telephone: (42 2) 2410 3317. Facsimile: (42 2) 2410 3235.

Singapore Office: 20 Raffles Place #08-03, Ocean Towers, 0104. Telephone: (65) 533 0988. Facsimile: (65) 533 1322.

Tokyo, Japan Office: NSE, Building 5th Floor, 1-7-1 Kanda Jinbo-cho, Chiyoda-ku Tokyo 101. Telephone (81 3) 3259 9898. Facsimile (81 3) 3259 9888.

Warsaw, Poland Office: ul. Kopernika 17, IV Floor, 00-359. Telephone: (48 22) 262 226. Facsimile: (48 22) 262 360.

FIRM PROFILE: *Established as a two-partner firm in 1930, Allen & Overy is now one of the largest firms in the country with 123 partners and some 1200 staff (including over 500 lawyers). Primarily a commercial practice with a substantial international element, the main areas of work are Company and Commercial (divided into corporate finance and M & A, international and domestic banking, international capital markets and insolvency). Litigation, Property, Private Client, EC and Competition Law, Environmental Law and Corporate Taxation. Other areas include Pensions, Share Incentives, Employee Benefits, Intellectual Property, Information Technology, Energy, Project Finance and Construction.*

PARTNERS

IAN A. ANNETTS, admitted, 1987, England. *Education:* Oxon (B.A.).

ALISTAIR H. ASHER, admitted, 1981, England. *Education:* Soton (LLB).

ANNE E. BALDOCK, admitted, 1984, England. *Education:* (LL.B.).

ANDREW M.H. BALLHEIMER, admitted, 1987, England. *Education:* Cantab (M.A.). (Resident Partner in Tokyo, Japan).

ALISON M. BEARDSLEY, admitted, 1983, England. *Education:* Oxon (B.A.). (Also at Prague, Czech Republic).

PAUL H. D. BEDFORD, admitted, 1982, England. *Education:* Warwick (LL.B.).

GUY G. BERINGER, admitted, 1980, England. *Education:* Cantab (M.A.).

NICHOLAS M. H. BIRD, admitted, 1975, England.

PETER E. M. BORROWDALE, admitted, 1977, England. *Education:* Manch (LL.B.). Recipient, Industrial Law Prize.

JONATHAN L. F. BRAYNE, admitted, 1980, England. *Education:* Cantab (M.A.). (Resident Partner in Hong Kong).

ANDREW T. BRODIE, admitted, 1983, England. *Education:* Cantab (M.A.).

(This Listing Continued)

RODERICK M. BROWN, admitted, 1975, England. *Education:* Oxon (B.A.).

KATHERINE A. BUCKLEY, admitted, 1983, England. *Education:* Oxon (B.A.).

KENNETH CHAN (Resident Partner in Hong Kong).

STEPHEN P. CHATER, admitted, 1981, England. *Education:* Oxon (M.A.).

PAUL CHEDGY, admitted, 1968, England. *Education:* Oxon (B.A.).

ANDREW J. C. CLARK, admitted, 1981, England. *Education:* Cantab (M.A.).

ADAM A. CLEAL, admitted, 1982, England. *Education:* Leeds (LL.B.).

MICHAEL A. CONLON, admitted, 1992, England. *Education:* Cantab (M.A.).

RICHARD W. L. CRANFIELD, admitted, 1980, England. *Education:* Cantab (M.A.).

PAUL CROOK, admitted, 1978, England. *Education:* Cantab (LL.B.). (Resident Partner in Paris, France).

ROGER G. DAVIES, admitted, 1972, England. *Education:* Cantab (M.A.). Recipient, Harry Strouts Prize.

STEPHEN R. N. DENYER, admitted, 1980, England. *Education:* Dunelm (B.A.). (Resident Partner in Warsaw, Poland).

MICHAEL G. DUNCAN, admitted, 1981, England. *Education:* Cantab (B.A.).

IAN F. ELDER, admitted, 1984, England. *Education:* St. Andrews (M.A.); Edin. (LL.B.). (Also at Budapest, Hungary).

IAN J.A. FERGUSON, admitted, 1985, England. *Education:* Soton (LL.B.).

MARK W. FRIEND, admitted, 1982, England. *Education:* Cantab (M.A.).

GEOFFREY W. FULLER, admitted, 1986, England. *Education:* Oxon (M.A.).

CERIS M. GARDNER, admitted, 1988, England. *Education:* London (B.A.).

MARK G.P. GEARING, admitted, 1985, England. *Education:* Oxon (M.A.).

JUDITH A.E. GILL, admitted, 1985, England. *Education:* Oxon (M.A.).

KEITH G. GODFREY, admitted, 1976, England. *Education:* London (LL.B.).

JEFFREY B. GOLDEN, admitted, 1978, New Jersey; 1979, New York. *Education:* Columbia University School of Law, New York.

JONATHAN M. W. GOODWIN, admitted, 1980, England. *Education:* Cantab (M.A.).

JONATHAN GOULD, admitted, 1976, England. *Education:* (LL.B.). (Resident Partner in Hong Kong).

SIMON A. HADDOCK, admitted, 1986, England. *Education:* Leeds (LL.B.). (Resident Partner in Hong Kong).

BRIAN W. HARRISON, admitted, 1985, England. *Education:* Auckland (B.A.).

HELEN M. HARRISON-HALL, admitted, 1984, England. *Education:* Oxon (M.A.).

GUY HENDERSON, admitted, 1982, England. *Education:* Cantab (B.A.). (Resident Partner in Hong Kong).

ANTHONY J. HERBERT, admitted, 1965, England. *Education:* Cantab (M.A.). Recipient, Alfred Syrett Prize.

PETER B. HOCKLESS, admitted, 1981, England. *Education:* Cantab (M.A.).

GILLIAN A. HOLGATE, admitted, 1987, England. *Education:* Manchester (LL.B.).

PETER R. J. HOLLAND, admitted, 1968, England. *Education:* Oxon (M.A.).

(This Listing Continued)

JONATHAN HORSFALL TURNER, admitted, 1970, England. *Education:* Cantab (M.A.). Recipient, Charles Steele Prize.

RICHARD HORSFALL TURNER, admitted, 1966, England. *Education:* Oxon (B.A.). (Resident Partner in Deira, Dubai).

TIMOTHY J. HOUSE, admitted, 1986, England. *Education:* London, (LL.B.).

SUSAN D. HOWARD, admitted, 1987, England. *Education:* Oxon (B.A.).

GIDEON D. HUDSON, admitted, 1969, England. *Education:* Oxon (M.A.).

DAVID C. HUGHES, admitted, 1979, England. *Education:* London (LL.B.). (Resident Partner in Hong Kong).

ANTHONY R. HUMPHREY, admitted, 1975, England. *Education:* Dunelm (B.A.).

ROBERT J. HUNTER, admitted, 1984, England. *Education:* (M.A., LL.M.).

NIGEL D. JOHNSON, admitted, 1978, England. *Education:* Oxon (M.A.).

RUPERT J. L. JONES, admitted, 1978, England. *Education:* Birmingham (LL.B.).

ERNEST W. JOWETT, admitted, 1978, England.

ANTHONY C. KEAL, admitted, 1976, England. *Education:* Oxon (B.A.).

COLLEEN A. KECK, admitted, 1987, England. *Education:* Saskatchewan (B.A.).

G. JOHN KENDALL, admitted, 1976, England. *Education:* Oxon (M.A.).

DAVID S. KRISCHER, admitted, 1992, England. *Education:* Oxon (B.A.); Northwestern U.S.A. (J.D.); Oberlin, U.S.A. (B.A.).

DAVID E. LEWIS, admitted, 1976, England. *Education:* Exeter (LL.B.).

MICHAEL LUI (Resident Partner in Hong Kong).

DONALD M. MCGOWN, admitted, 1983, England. *Education:* Soton (LL.B.).

CHARLES MCKENNA, admitted, 1978, England. *Education:* Dunelm (B.A.).

DAVID L. MACKIE, admitted, 1971, England. *Education:* Oxon (M.A.).

MARK J. MANSELL, admitted, 1985, England. *Education:* London (LL.B.).

CLARE M. MAURICE, admitted, 1978, England. *Education:* Birmingham (LL.B.).

PATRICK M. MEARS, admitted, 1982, England. *Education:* London (LL.B.).

JONATHAN S.T. MELLOR, admitted, 1986, England. *Education:* Leicester (LL.B.). (Resident Partner in Hong Kong).

PETER H. T. MIMPRISS, admitted, 1967, England.

PAUL N. MONK, admitted, 1974, England. *Education:* Oxon (M.A.).

CHARLES P. MORGAN, admitted, 1978, England. *Education:* Cantab (M.A.).

DAVID H. MORLEY, admitted, 1982, England. *Education:* Cantab (M.A.).

J. ANDREW MORTON, admitted, 1968, England. *Education:* Oxon (B.A.).

DAVID T.J. MURRAY, admitted, 1983, England. *Education:* Cantab (M.A.).

EDWARD H. MURRAY, admitted, 1986, New York; 1992, England. *Education:* B.A., J.D.

SIDNEY A. MYERS, admitted, 1984, England. *Education:* Oxon (B.A.). (Resident Partner in Hong Kong).

JUDITH P. NAYLOR, admitted, 1986, England. *Education:* Oxon (B.A.).

(This Listing Continued)

WILLIAM V. W. NORRIS, admitted, 1959, England. Recipient, Mellersh Prize.

PHILIP A. OWEN, admitted, 1968, England.

G. MERVYN PARRY, admitted, 1975, England. *Education:* Cantab (M.A.).

ALAN D. PAUL, admitted, 1980, England. *Education:* Oxon (B.A.; M.A.).

ALEXANDER M. PEASE, admitted, 1981, England. *Education:* Oxon (M.A.). (Resident Partner in Tokyo, Japan).

PAUL M. PHILLIPS, admitted, 1988, England. *Education:* Cantab (B.A.).

STEPHEN POLLARD, admitted, 1986, England. *Education:* Oxon (B.A.).

MICHAEL W. PORTER, admitted, 1972, England. *Education:* Cantab (M.A.).

ALAN F. RAE SMITH, admitted, 1986, England. *Education:* Cantab (M.A.).

DAVID REID, admitted, 1976, England. *Education:* (B.A.). (Resident Partner in New York, U.S.A.).

MICHAEL J. REYNOLDS, admitted, 1977, England. *Education:* (B.A.). (Resident Partner in Brussels, Belgium).

JOHN S. RINK, admitted, 1972, England. *Education:* (LL.B.). (Managing Partner).

CHRISTOPHER K. ROBERTS, admitted, 1980, England. *Education:* Cantab (M.A.). (Resident Partner in Hong Kong).

RICHARD A. P. ROWLAND, admitted, 1969, England. *Education:* Cantab (M.A.; LL.B.).

CHRISTOPHER L. RUSHTON, admitted, 1991, England. *Education:* Australian BL. (Resident Partner in Hong Kong).

KEVIN M. T. RYAN, admitted, 1965, England.

JULIA A. SALT, admitted, 1980, England. *Education:* Oxon (B.A.).

MICHAEL P. SCARGILL, admitted, 1980, England. *Education:* Oxon (B.A.).

PETER F. SCHULZ, admitted, 1983, England. *Education:* Cantab (M.A.). (Also at Madrid, Spain).

JOHN A. SCRIVEN, admitted, 1979, England. *Education:* Cantab (B.A.).

NICHOLAS A. SEGAL, admitted, 1979, England. *Education:* Oxon (M.A.). Recipient, Carl Albert Prize.

CARL SHELDON, admitted, 1985, England. *Education:* Cantab (M.A.). (Resident Partner in Frankfurt am Main, Germany).

DEREK S. SLOAN, admitted, 1973, England. *Education:* Oxon (B.A.).

CATRIONA M. SMITH, admitted, 1982, England. *Education:* St. Andrews (M.A.).

IAN G. STANLEY, admitted, 1984, England. *Education:* Cantab (B.A.).

GORDON C. STEWART, admitted, 1980, England. *Education:* Oxon (M.A.).

ROBERT P.B. STRIVENS, admitted, 1985, England. *Education:* Cantab (B.A.).

DAVID ST.J. SUTTON, admitted, 1966, England. *Education:* (B.A.). (Resident Partner in Paris, France).

RICHARD H. SYKES, admitted, 1969, England. *Education:* Oxon (M.A.).

JEREMY D. THOMAS, admitted, 1982, England. *Education:* Cantab (M.A.).

PETER G. TOTTY, admitted, 1965, England. *Education:* Oxon (M.A.).

ANDREW TRAHAIR, admitted, 1987, England. *Education:* University of New South Wales, Australia (LL.B.).

H. JOHN TREMBATH, admitted, 1966, England. *Education:* Oxon (B.A.).

WILLIAM TUDOR JOHN, admitted, 1969, England. *Education:* Cantab (M.A.). (Senior Partner).

(This Listing Continued)

ALLEN & OVERY, London—Continued

JOSEPH TSE (Resident Partner in Hong Kong).

RICHARD W. C. TURNOR, admitted, 1980, England. *Education:* Oxon (B.A.).

GRAHAM D. VINTER, admitted, 1983, England. *Education:* Oxon (B.A.).

CHRISTOPHER R. WALFORD, admitted, 1962, England. *Education:* Oxon (M.A.).

PETER M. WATSON, admitted, 1981, England. *Education:* Oxon (B.A.).

MARK R. WELLING, admitted, 1981, England. *Education:* Cantab (M.A.).

BOYAN S. WELLS, admitted, 1981, England. *Education:* Oxon (M.A.).

DAVID L. WILLIAMS, admitted, 1977, England. *Education:* (B.Sc.).

ANDREW WILSON, admitted, 1984, England. *Education:* Bristol (LL.B.). (Resident Partner in Paris, France).

GUY N. WILSON, admitted, 1966, England. *Education:* Cantab (B.A.). (Also at Beijing, People's Republic of China).

PHILIP R. WOOD, admitted, 1970, England. *Education:* Oxon (B.A.). Recipient, Clements Inn, Sheffield & Edmund Thomas Child Prizes.

DAVID H. WOOTTON, admitted, 1975, England. *Education:* Cantab (B.A.).

JOHN P. WOTTON, admitted, 1978, England. *Education:* Cantab (M.A.).

ALLENS ARTHUR ROBINSON

LEVEL 5
BUCKLERSBURY HOUSE
3 QUEEN VICTORIA STREET
LONDON EC4N 8EL, ENGLAND
Telephone: (171) 248 6130
Rapifax: (171) 248 6334

Allens Arthur Robinson is an international network of group and associated offices representing the Allens Arthur Robinson group in Australia. The firm is engaged in Australian and International Law Practice, but not practising as English solicitors.

Group and Associated Offices:

New York, NY: Allens Arthur Robinson, 280 Park Avenue, 10017. Telephone: (1 212) 867 1555. Rapifax: (1 212) 867 7979.

Singapore: Allens Arthur Robinson, 65 Chulia Street #42-05, OCBC Centre, 0104. Telephone: (65) 535 6622. Rapifax: (65) 535 4855.

Hong Kong: Dunstan Styles & Co., Suite 1504, One Exchange Square, 8 Connaught Place, Central. Telephone: (852) 2840 1202. Rapifax: (852) 2840 0686.

Jakarta, Indonesia: Wiriadinata & Widyawan, Niaga Tower, 26th Floor, Jl. Jend. Sudirman, Kav 58, 12190. Telephone: (62 21) 250 5175. Rapifax: (62 21) 250 5185.

Port Moresby, Papua New Guinea: Allens Arthur Robinson, Level 11, Pacific Place, Cnr Musgrave Street & Champion Parade. Telephone: (675) 202 000. Rapifax: (675) 200 588.

Shanghai, People's Republic of China: AAR China Limited, Fuxing Xi Lu 37 Long 6 Hao. 200031. Telephone: (86 21) 437 7582. Rapifax: (86 21) 473 7819.

Allens Arthur Robinson's international network of offices represents:

Sydney, New South Wales, Australia: Allen Allen & Hemsley, The Chifley Tower, 2 Chifley Square, 2000. Telephone: (61 2) 230 4000. Rapifax: (61 2) 233 7022.

Canberra, Australian Capital Territory, Australia: Allen Allen & Hemsley, 3rd Floor, 16 Moore Street, 2601. Telephone: (61 6) 247 5800. Rapifax: (61 6) 257 1369.

Melbourne, Victoria, Australia: Arthur Robinson & Hedderwicks, Levels 27-34, 530 Collins Street, 3000. Telephone: (61 3) 614 1011. Rapifax: (61 3) 614 4661.

Brisbane, Queensland, Australia: Feez Ruthning, Riverside Centre, 123 Eagle Street, 4000. Telephone: (61 7) 833 3333. Rapifax: (61 7) 832 4233.

(This Listing Continued)

Surfers Paradise, Queensland, Australia: Feez Ruthning, Level 14, 50 Cavill Avenue, 4217. Telephone: (61 75) 70 0200. Rapifax: (61 75) 92 2285.

Perth, Western Australia, Australia: Parker & Parker, AMP Building, 140 St George's Terrace, 6000. Telephone: (61 9) 322 0321. Rapifax: (61 9) 322 2243.

Adelaide, South Australia, Australia: Finlaysons, 81 Flinders Street, 5000. Telephone: (61 8) 235 7400. Rapifax: (61 8) 232 2944.

FIRM PROFILE: *Allens Arthur Robinson in London provides Australian legal advice on investment, banking (particularly capital markets), corporate transactions, mergers and acquisitions and privatisations related to Australia. It is also involved with the firm's Asian network of offices in corporate investment and privatisation transactions in Asia. The firm is engaged in Australian and International law practice, but not practising as English Solicitors.*

RESIDENT PARTNER

JIM DUNSTAN, admitted, 1972, New South Wales; 1987, Hong Kong. **LANGUAGES:** English. **PRACTICE AREAS:** Banking Law; Foreign Investment; Privatisations.

(For complete personnel and biographical data, see Professional Biographies at Sydney, Australia.)

ALLIANCE OF EUROPEAN LAWYERS (EEIG)

ROYEX HOUSE
ALDERMANBURY SQUARE
LONDON EC2V 7HR, ENGLAND
Telephone: (44-171) 796-2599
Telefax: (44-171) 600-1718

The Alliance consists of *De Bandt, van Hecke & Lagae* at Brussels and Antwerp; *De Brauw Blackstone Westbroek* at The Hague, Amsterdam, Rotterdam and Eindhoven; *Jeantet & Associés* at Paris and Warsaw; *Lagerlöf & Leman* at Stockholm, Gothenburg and Malmö; *Oppenhoff & Rädler* at Berlin, Cologne, Frankfurt am Main, Leipzig and Münich; *Uria & Menendez* at Madrid and Barcelona.

(For details and lists of Partners and Counsel of the Member Firms of the Alliance of European Lawyers, see their respective listings of their offices in their home jurisdictions).

ALLISON & HUMPHREYS

Established in 1967

EAST INDIA HOUSE
109-117 MIDDLESEX STREET
LONDON E1 7JF, ENGLAND
Telephone: 0171 570 6000
Fax: 0171 570 6060 DX: 870 City EC3

Company and Commercial Law, Corporate Finance, Taxation, Information Technology, European Community Law, Competition Law, Entertainment, Telecommunications, Intellectual Property, Litigation including Professional Negligence and Judicial Review, Property and Conveyancing, Pensions, Employment and Immigration, Private Client.

FIRM PROFILE: *Allison & Humphreys is a growing city firm with a general commercial and private practice and a number of areas of particular expertise. Film and television, tax, pension and private client work are traditional areas of the firm's work. In recent years it has developed a leading reputation in cable and satellite broadcasting including domestic and international regulation. It has a growing reputation also in judicial review and major professional negligence litigation. The firm expects continued growth especially in company/commercial matters, litigation and European Community law and quickly developing areas such as telecommunications and information technology. There are at present 14 partners and 37 other fee earners engaged.*

Language capability of firm: English, Afrikaans, German, French, Spanish, Italian and Dutch.

PARTNERS

CHARLES W. HUMPHREYS, born 1938; admitted, 1962, England. *Education:* Oxford University (B.A.). **LANGUAGES:** English and French. **PRACTICE AREAS:** Accounts Liability; Business Law; Partnerships; Company and Commercial; Computers and Software; Corporate Law; Pro-

(This Listing Continued)

fessional Liability; Professional Negligence; Taxation; Trade Marks.

J. ANTHONY BALLARD, born 1945; admitted, 1974, England. *Education:* Cambridge University (M.A.). *LANGUAGES:* English and French. *PRACTICE AREAS:* Antitrust and Trade Regulation; Broadcasting; Communications; Media and Entertainment; Video; Copyright; Film; Publishing; TV Production and Distribution; Theatre; European Community Law; Libel and Defamation; Regulated Industries; Telecommunications; Satellites.

RONALD G. THOM, born 1950; admitted, 1974, England. *Education:* Southampton University (LL.B.). *LANGUAGES:* English. *PRACTICE AREAS:* Pensions.

ELLEN M. FLEMING, born 1948; admitted, 1977, England. *Education:* Cambridge University (M.A.). *LANGUAGES:* English and French. *PRACTICE AREAS:* Antitrust and Trade Regulation; Broadcasting; Company and Commercial Law; Computers and Software; Corporate Law; European Community Law; Telecommunications; Business Law; Joint Ventures.

MICHAEL A. CROFT BAKER, born 1936; admitted, 1960, England. *Education:* King's College, London University (LL.B.). *LANGUAGES:* English. *PRACTICE AREAS:* Antitrust and Trade Regulation; Chancery and Equity; Charitable Organisations; Immigration and Naturalisation; Work Permits; Pensions and Profit Sharing; Probate; Taxation and Estates.

CHARLES F. SANDS, born 1938; admitted, 1966, England. *Education:* Oxford University (M.A.). *LANGUAGES:* English and French. *PRACTICE AREAS:* Banks and Banking; Asset Based Finance; International Banking; Business Law; Buying and Selling; Company and Commercial Law; Corporate Law; International Corporate and Finance; Mergers, Acquisitions and Divestitures; Securities.

STEPHEN N. GIBBS, born 1955; admitted, 1979, England. *Education:* Cambridge University (M.A.). *LANGUAGES:* English. *PRACTICE AREAS:* Appellate Practice; Civil Law; Computers and Software; Partnerships; Recovery; Debtor and Creditor; Libel and Defamation; Professional Indemnity; Reinsurance; Litigation; Negligence; Professional Liability (Accountants, Directors and Officers); Malpractice; Professional Negligence; Torts.

E. ANN HUNT, born 1941; admitted, 1981, England. *Education:* King's College, London University (B.A.). *LANGUAGES:* English, French and German. *PRACTICE AREAS:* Communications; Media and Entertainment; Publishing; Video; Film; TV Production and Distribution; Theatre; Libel and Defamation; Labour and Employment.

EDWARD P.O. MERCER, born 1956; admitted, 1980, England. *Education:* Cambridge University (M.A.). *LANGUAGES:* English. *PRACTICE AREAS:* Antitrust and Trade Regulation; Unfair Competition; Broadcasting; Cable Communications; Privatisation; Consumer Law; European Community Law Legislative and Administrative; Municipal; Regulated Industries; Telecommunications (Contracts, Information Technology, Regulation).

ROGER G.C. WESSON, born 1958; admitted, 1983, England. *Education:* Oxford University (M.A.). *LANGUAGES:* English. *PRACTICE AREAS:* Company and Commercial Law; Business Law; Computers and Software; Consumer Law; Corporate Law; Entertainment; Film; Motion Pictures and Television; Music; Labour and Employment; Mergers, Acquisitions and Divestitures.

ROWENA C. LORD, born 1958; admitted, 1983, England. *Education:* Oxford University (M.A., B.C.L.). *LANGUAGES:* English. *PRACTICE AREAS:* Broadcasting; Communications and Media; Entertainment and the Arts; Reinsurance; Litigation; Telecommunications; Professional Negligence.

MARK A. LEWIS, born 1960; admitted, 1986, England. *Education:* Oxford University (B.A.). *LANGUAGES:* English. *PRACTICE AREAS:* Appellate Practice; Bankruptcy; Torts; Civil Law; Computers and Software; Copyrights; Recovery; Debtor and Creditor; Professional Indemnity; Libel and Defamation; Mortgages; Negligence; Professional Liability; Professional Negligence; Litigation.

ANDREW M. BLANKFIELD, born 1962; admitted, 1987, England. *Education:* Cambridge University (M.A.). *LANGUAGES:* English and French. *PRACTICE AREAS:* Bankruptcy; Business Law; Company and Commercial Law; Consumer Law; Corporate Law; Insolvency; Finance; Labour and Employment; Mergers, Acquisitions and Divestitures; Securities.

(This Listing Continued)

MOIRA A.C. GILMOUR, born 1956; admitted, 1981, Scotland; 1987, England. *Education:* Glasgow University (M.A., LL.B.). *LANGUAGES:* English, French and German. *PRACTICE AREAS:* Commercial Property Investment and Development; Commercial Mortgages; Landlord and Tenant; Planning; Environmental.

ALSOP WILKINSON

6 DOWGATE HILL
LONDON EC4R 2SS, ENGLAND
Telephone: 0171-248 4141
Telex: 885593
Fax: 0171-623 8286

Liverpool, England Office: India Buildings, L2 ONH. Telephone: 0151-227 3060. Telex: 627369. Fax: 0151-236 9208.

Manchester, England Office: 11 St. James's Square, M2 6DR. Telephone: 0161-834 7760. Telex: 667965. Fax: 0161-831 7515.

Hong Kong Office: 4010 Jardine House, 1 Connaught Place, Central. Telephone: 852-524 2003. Fax: 852-810 1345.

New York, New York Office: 230 Park Avenue, Suite 1150, New York, New York, 10169. Telephone: (212) 499 7500. Fax: (212) 499 7505.

Brussels, Belgium Office: Avenue de Cortenberg, 79-81, 1040. Telephone: 2-732-36-00. Fax: 2-734-87-93.

Key Practice Areas: Banking, Commercial Litigation and Arbitration, Commercial Property, Commodities, Construction, Corporate and Commercial, Corporate Fraud and Investigations, Corporate Taxation, Employee Benefits, Employment, Environment and Planning, Insolvency, Insurance and Reinsurance, Intellectual Property and Computer Law, Marine, Pensions, Private Client.

FIRM PROFILE: One of the largest commercial law practices in the U.K. Established 1821 and offering a full service to corporate and mercantile clients.

RESIDENT PARTNERS

R. Lane-Smith, Chairman	**J.M. Landale**
D.M. Cooke, Managing Partner	**E.C. Walters**
G.W. Godar	**H.A. Ryan**
P.B. Wayte	**M.A. Stubbs**
P.D. Gordon-Saker	**M.S.J. Sims**
S.R. Wethered	**N.F.W. Sanderson**
M.J. Clarke	**D.G. Hughes**
G.C. Day	**P.R. Greenwood**
S.A. Blair	**M. Collins**
S.M. Haller	**N.L. Ellis**
M.H. Vickers	**P.V. Thomas**
W.H. Dalzell	**J. Legrand**
A.T. Leek	**T.B. O'Regan**
R.J.I. Parker	**J.G. Fenton**
A.J. Gowman	**G.C. Hurstfield**
P.L. Webster	**A.H. Young**
P.J. Boursnell	**N.J. Pike**
S.V. Croxon	**R.J. Curl**

CONSULTANTS

R.A. Albert (admitted only in the   **B.D.S. Lock**
State of New York)

Member of The Legal Resources Group

(For the Names of Partners Resident in Other Offices, see Listings for Those Offices)

AMHURST BROWN COLOMBOTTI

2 DUKE STREET, ST. JAMES'S
LONDON SW1Y 6BJ, ENGLAND
Telephone: (0171) 930-2366
Telex: 261857 AMBRON
Fax: (0171) 930-2250

Warsaw, Poland Office: ul. Koszykowa 59 m.6, 00-660. Telephone: 48 (22) 29 16 84; 48 (2) 625 30 51; 48 (2) 625 31 25. Satellite: 48 (39) 12 06 02. Fax: 48 (2) 6213289. Telex: 816370 AMPOL.

Milan, Italy Office: Via Settembrini 17, 20124. Telephone: (02) 6698 4270. Fax: (02) 6698 4252.

Madrid, Spain Office: Paseo del General Martinez Campos 41 8-B, 28010. Telephone: (91) 410 72 24. Fax: (91) 410 55 92.

(This Listing Continued)

AMHURST BROWN COLOMBOTTI, London— Continued

Corporate and Commercial Law, Property, Banking, Trust, Employment, Immigration, Litigation, International Arbitration, Intellectual Property, Family Law.

PARTNERS

P.D. Smithson	M.A. Akhtar
M.S. Duval (Also at Warsaw, Poland Office)	L.R. Barrero
	R.E.W. Brine
A.F.L. Amhurst	M.R.C. Minnitt
(Also at Milan, Italy Office)	N.B. Forsyth
V.L. Brown	A.J.R. Hamilton
C.E.P. Colombotti	S.N. Morris
(Also at Milan, Italy Office)	A.G. Facey
D.J. Eldridge (Also at Warsaw,	(Also at Milan, Italy Office)
Poland Office)	S.M. Chapman
R.G. Newman	J.R. Coomber
C.R. Langford	H.P. Gibbons
P.F.G. Amandini	F. Bingham

DR. ANVARI & ASSOCIATES LAW OFFICE

SUITE ONE
120, GLOUCESTER TERRACE
LONDON W2 6HP, ENGLAND
Telephone: (0171) 724 9073
Fax: (0171) 706 3602

Consultant on the Laws of Iran.
Iranian lawyer practicing in London, registered with the Law Society of England since 1982.

DR. A.K. ANVARI, admitted, 1958, Iran. *Education:* Tehran University (Doctor of Law; Faculty of Law); University of Tehran (LL.B., 1955; First Rank Licenciate and Winner of First Grade Scientific Medal). President, 1972-1973 and Professor and Lecturer in Business Law, Isfahan Management College. Member, Board of Directors, 1972 and Vice-President of the Iranian Bar Association, 1976-1981. Examiner of the Iranian Bar Examinations, 1970-1981. Councillor of Iran and Vice-President, 1975-1979, The Law Association for Asia and the Western Pacific. Councillor, International Bar Association; A.C.I. Arb. *LANGUAGES:* Persian and English. *PRACTICE AREAS:* International Trade; Construction; Contracts; Disputes; Banking; Finance; Investment; Oil and Gas; Arbitration; Commercial Litigation.

ARIAS, FABREGA & FABREGA

Established in 1911

3RD FLOOR, KINGSLAND HOUSE
122-124 REGENT STREET
LONDON W1R SFE, ENGLAND
Telephone: (171) 287 3277
Fax: (171) 287 3177

Panamá, Republic of Panama Office: 16th Floor, Plaza Bancomer Building, 50th Street, 5. Telephone: 63-9200. Cable Address: "Arifa". Telex: TRT 2120 ARIFA PA; 2251 ARIFA PA; INTEL 2574 ARIFA PG; 3543 ARIFA PG. Telecopier: Groups 1, 2 & 3: 63-8919/64-0710.

Affiliated Offices: Arias, Fabrega & Fabrega Trust Co. BVI Limited. P.O. Box 3150, Wickham's Cay, Road Town, Tortola, British Virgin Islands. Telephones: (809) 494-4977/4978. Telex: 7939 ARTITRUST VB, Fax: (809) 494-4980.

Arias Fabrega & Fabrega Company Services HK Limited. Suite 710, New World Tower, 18 Queen's Road, Central Hong Kong. Telephone: 5-253-903/5-254-088. Telex: 68483 ARIFA HX. Fax: 5-845-0048.

Firm engaged in Panamanian and International Law Practice, but not authorized to appear before the English Courts or to act as Solicitors.

FIRM PROFILE: The firm was established in 1911 and offers a full range of commercial, corporate and international legal services. Its client base includes financial, commercial and industrial institutions in Panama and in North and South America, Europe and Asia. The firm has offices

(This Listing Continued)

---

in London as well as affiliated service companies in the British Virgin Islands and Hong Kong. At present the firm has ten partners, twelve associate lawyers, one of counsel, twelve paralegals, and approximately eighty support and clerical staff.

(For Complete Biographical Data on all Personnel, see Professional Biographies at Panama, Republic of Panama)

AROSEMENA, NORIEGA & CONTRERAS

Established in 1975

GROSVENOR GARDENS HOUSE
35-37 GROSVENOR GARDENS
LONDON SW1W OBS, ENGLAND
Telephone: 0171-828-6313
Cable Address: "Arolon" Facsimile Transceiver: 0171-828-3917 GI/GII/GIII

Panamá, Republic of Panama Office: Edificio Banco do Brazil, Calle Elvira Mendez No. 10. Telephones: 64-3411; 64-3773. Cable Address: "Arolex Panama" Telex: 3158 PG. Facsimile Transceivers: CCITT GI/GII/GIII, Nos. 64-4569; 63-8539.

Firm engaged in Panamanian Law Practice, but not authorized to appear before the English Courts or to act as Solicitors.

FIRM PROFILE: The London Office renders services and provides opinions relating to Panama law, as well as serving as a promotional outlet in Europe for the Panama Office.

(For Complete Biographical Data on all Personnel, see Professional Biographies at Panama, Panama).

ASHURST MORRIS CRISP

Established in 1821

BROADWALK HOUSE
5 APPOLD STREET
LONDON EC2A 2HA, ENGLAND
Telephone: 0171 638 1111
Telex: 887067
Fax: 0171 972 7990

Brussels, Belgium Office: Avenue Louise 65, 1050. Telephone: (32-2) 537 6895. Fax: (32-2) 537 4353.

Paris, France Office: 8, rue Clément Marot, 75008. Telephone: (33-1) 47 20 0088. Fax: (33-1) 47 20 0093.

Tokyo, Japan Office: Kioicho Building, 8th Floor, 3-12 Kioicho, Chiyoda-ku, 102. Telephone: (81-3) 5276 5900. Fax: (81-3) 5276 5922.

New Delhi, India Office: 6 Aurangzeb Road D-202. Telephone: (91 11) 301 4054. Facsimile: (91 11) 301 4089.

FIRM PROFILE: Established in 1821, Ashursts is a leading London commercial practice, with 62 partners and total staff of over 600. It acts for clients in respect of their commercial interests in a national and international context. Many members of staff are fluent in foreign languages. The firm's main areas of work are Acquisitions and Mergers, Banking and Finance, Company and Commercial, Competition, Construction, EC, Employment, Energy, Environment, Insolvency, Insurance, Intellectual Property, Litigation, Major Projects, Multi-Media, Pensions, Planning, Property and Tax.

MEMBERS OF FIRM

A.J. Soundy	D.R. Kershaw
R.B. James	A.W.N. Kitchin
L.D. Rutman	(Resident, Tokyo Office)
C.D. Crosthwaite	J.A. Sultoon
(Resident, Paris Office)	M.D. Cunliffe
I.R. Scott	S.J. Machin
M.A.F. Macpherson	I.B. Nisse
J.N. May	J.N. Sheldon
D.J. Macfarlane	I.C. Starr
D.E.P. Albert	J.C. Evans
G.S. Green	W. Innes
C.J. Amos	J.A. Nimmo
M.C. Johns	C. Vigrass
D.R. Perks	R.B. Walsom
E.C.A.S. Sparrow	S.R.P. Mostyn-Williams
R.J. Finbow	R.S. Gubbins
C.J. Ashworth	C.J. Leach

(This Listing Continued)

MEMBERS OF FIRMMEMBERSnued)

J.G. Watson	N.T. Ward
G.S. Wheatcroft	T. Forschbach
A.S. Clark	(Resident, Paris Office)
A.A. Dear	G.P. Webb
J.J. Ellison	S.L. Crawford
(Resident, Brussels Office)	M.P. Elsey
M.A. Wippell	M.C. Elvy
C. Atkins	P.A.D. Hurst
S.D. White	R. Kendall
S.T. Cookson	R.C. King
C.S.H. Geffen	A.N. Parr
E.A. Morris	G. Picton-Tubervill
I.J. Webb	(Resident, New Delhi Office)
I. Johnson	M.G. Robins
J.G. Hill	J. Sanders
A.G. Knight	A. Ghee
S.E. Roy	M.J.A. Thum (Consultant)

BAKER & McKENZIE

Solicitors

100 NEW BRIDGE STREET
LONDON EC4V 6JA, ENGLAND
Telephone: (0171) 919-1000
Intn'l. Dialing: (44-171) 919-1000
Cable Address: ABOGADO
Telex: 25660
Answer Back: 25660 ABOGA G
Facsimile: (44-71) 919-1999

Associated Offices of Baker & McKenzie in: Almaty, Amsterdam, Bangkok, Barcelona, Beijing, Berlin, Bogotá, Brasília, Brussels, Budapest, Buenos Aires, Cairo, Caracas, Chicago, Dallas, Frankfurt, Geneva, Hanoi, Ho Chi Minh City, Hong Kong, Juárez, Kiev, Madrid, Manila, Melbourne, México City, Miami, Milan, Monterrey, Moscow, New York, Palo Alto, Paris, Prague, Rio de Janeiro, Riyadh, Rome, St. Petersburg, San Diego, San Francisco, São Paulo, Singapore, Stockholm, Sydney, Taipei, Tijuana, Tokyo, Toronto, Valencia, Warsaw, Washington, D.C. and Zürich.
Correspondent Law Firm: Hadiputranto, Hadinoto & Partners, Jakarta.

Commercial. Corporate. Corporate Tax. Banking and Finance. European Community and Competition Law. Intellectual Property and Technology Law. Telecommunications and Broadcasting. Litigation and Arbitration. Insolvency. Insurance. Shipping. Employment. Immigration. Pensions and Employee Benefits. Private Clients. Property. Construction and Engineering. Environment. Central and Eastern Europe. Japanese Investment.

MEMBERS OF FIRM

Christopher M. Bown	Geoffrey A. Kay
Michael D. Caro	Peter J. Knight
Nigel M. Carrington	Russell M. E. Lewin
Gerald C. M. Cooke	James E. macLachlan
Richard J. Davidson	Lynda M. Martin Alegi
Anthony P. Davies	Nicholas P. Pearson
Robert L. Drake	Robert D. A. Pick
Gabriel Fisher	Bruce S. Porter
Alison J. M. Flood	James W. B. Rider
David A. Fraser	Gary Senior
Timothy E. D. Gee	Harry Small
B. Robert H. Hall	Michael D. Smith
Thomas J. Handler	Timothy R. Steadman
Andrew Hart	Hugh Stewart
Michael L. Hart	Peter W. Strivens
Michael J. E. Herington	W. Jeremy Sykes
Michael D. Ingle	Robert J. West
Donald G. Jerrard	David Winter
Andrew Joanes	Jeremy B. Winter

Fraser R. Younson

(This Listing Continued)

CONSULTANTS
ON THE LAWS OF THE UNITED STATES

Schuyler K. Henderson	**Thomas L. Philipp**
(Not admitted in England)	(Not admitted in England)

LOCAL PARTNERS

Andrew Keltie	**Beatriz Helen Pessoa de Araujo**
Alison Midgley	**Peter Richards-Carpenter**
Nigel A. Moss	**Paul E. Stibbard**
Helen L. Stroud	

BARLOW LYDE & GILBERT

Established in 1841

BEAUFORT HOUSE
15 ST. BOTOLPH STREET
LONDON EC3A 7NJ, ENGLAND
Telephone: 0171-247 2277
Telex: 913281
Fax: 0171-782 8500

Other London, England Office: Suite 893, Lloyd's, One Lime Street, London EC3M 7DQ. Telephone: 0171-782 8051. Fax: 0171-782 8053.
Hong Kong Office: 4001 Gloucester Tower, The Landmark, Central, Hong Kong. Telephone: 526 4202. Telex: 82205. Fax: 810 5994.

Insurance, Reinsurance, Arbitration/Litigation, Professional Indemnity, Insolvency, Aerospace, Construction, Company, Commercial, Consumer, Directors' and Officers Liability, Defamation, EC Law, Employment, Environmental Liability, Financial Risks, Financial Services, Medico-Legal, Product Liability, Public Liability, Property, Insurance Regulation, Shipping, Tax.

IAN D. P. JENKINS, (Senior Partner), LL.B., admitted, 1972, England. Associate: Corporation of Lloyd's; City of London Solicitors' Company; Union Internationale des Avocats. **LANGUAGES:** English. **PRACTICE AREAS:** Litigation; Professional Indemnity; Directors' and Officers Liability; Insurance.

DAVID MASSA, M.A. (Oxon), admitted, 1962, England. **LANGUAGES:** English. **PRACTICE AREAS:** Arbitration; Litigation; Professional Indemnity; Defamation; Insurance.

IAN AWFORD, LL.B., F.R.Ae.S admitted, 1967, England, Solicitor; 1988, Hong Kong. *Member:* American Bar Association (International Associate); City of London Solicitors' Company; Corporation of Lloyd's (Associate); International Bar Association; International Chamber of Commerce; Inter Pacific Bar Association (Aerospace Law Committee); International Institute of Space Law of the International Astronautics Federation; Fellow of the Royal Aeronautical Society. **LANGUAGES:** English. **PRACTICE AREAS:** Arbitration; Litigation; Aerospace; Insurance.

EDWARD W. HATHAWAY, B.A., LL.B., admitted, 1976, England. *Member:* Institute of Chartered Secretaries & Administrators; Chartered Institute of Arbitrators; International Bar Association; City of London Solicitors' Company. **LANGUAGES:** English. **PRACTICE AREAS:** Arbitration; Commercial Litigation; A.D.R.; Professional Indemnity.

COLIN V. CROLY, B.Com.; LL.B.; LL.M. admitted, 1980, England. *Member:* Association Internationale du Droit des Assurances (Secretary General); International Bar Association, United Kingdom Environmental Law Association. **LANGUAGES:** English. **PRACTICE AREAS:** Reinsurance; Arbitration; Litigation; Environmental Liability.

STUART A. M. MACKINNON, admitted, 1980, England, Solicitor; 1968, South Africa. **LANGUAGES:** English. **PRACTICE AREAS:** Arbitration; Litigation; Professional Indemnity; Insurance.

RICHARD H. J. DEDMAN, M.A., (Cantab.) admitted, 1978, England. *Member:* Association Internationale pour Law Protection de La Propriete Industrielle. **LANGUAGES:** English. **PRACTICE AREAS:** Commercial Litigation; Arbitration; Construction; Intellectual Property; Information Technology; Professional Indemnity; Insurance.

CHARLES D. HOPKINS, admitted, 1975, England. **LANGUAGES:** English. **PRACTICE AREAS:** Property.

ANTHONY ROSE, admitted, 1970, England. *Member:* International Bar Association; British Venture Capital Association. **LANGUAGES:** English. **PRACTICE AREAS:** Company and Commercial; Insurance Regulation.

(This Listing Continued)

BARLOW LYDE & GILBERT, London—Continued

JOHN F. MORRELL, LL.B., Warw. admitted, 1977, England. *LANGUAGES:* English. *PRACTICE AREAS:* Litigation; Public Liability; Insurance.

JOHN W. GRIFFIN, B.Sc.; LL.B. admitted, 1980, England. *Member:* City of London Solicitors' Company. *LANGUAGES:* English. *PRACTICE AREAS:* Litigation; Professional Indemnity; Insurance.

DAVID A. D. ARTHUR, B.A., Kent. admitted, 1978, England. *LANGUAGES:* English. *PRACTICE AREAS:* Arbitration; Litigation; Professional Indemnity; Insurance.

NICHOLAS M. L. HUGHES, B.A. (Law) M.R. A.S. admitted, 1981, England. *Member:* Association of Insurance & Risk Managers in Industry & Commerce (Honorary Secretary, Director); Liveryman: City of London Solicitors' Company; Royal Aeronautical Society; United Kingdom Environmental Law Association; British Insurance Law Association. *LANGUAGES:* English. *PRACTICE AREAS:* Aerospace; Product Liability; Environmental Liability; Insurance.

ANDREW H. C. CORDELL, M.A., (Oxon.) admitted, 1981, England. *LANGUAGES:* English and French. *PRACTICE AREAS:* Arbitration; Litigation; Professional Indemnity; Insurance.

JOHN C. LACKINGTON, M.A., (Cantab.) admitted, 1972, England. *LANGUAGES:* English. *PRACTICE AREAS:* Litigation; Professional Indemnity; Insurance; Personal Injury.

JAMES B. MITCHELL, B.Sc.; A.R.C.S.; LL.B., Lond. admitted, 1980, England. *LANGUAGES:* English. *PRACTICE AREAS:* Property.

STUART HALL, M.A., (Cantab.) admitted, 1975, England; 1986, Hong Kong. *LANGUAGES:* English. *PRACTICE AREAS:* Arbitration; Litigation; Professional Indemnity; Insurance.

KENNAN D. MICHEL, (Managing Partner) LL.B.; ACA. admitted, 1977, England, Solicitor. Associate, Institute of Chartered Accountants in England and Wales, 1982. *LANGUAGES:* English. *PRACTICE AREAS:* Company and Commercial; Tax.

PATTI BRINLEY-CODD, LL.B., Lond., admitted, 1983, England. *Member:* Food Law Group. *LANGUAGES:* English. *PRACTICE AREAS:* Commercial; Litigation; Consumer; Employment; Defamation; Medico-Legal; Product Liability; Professional Indemnity.

CHRISTOPHER S.K. SHARROCK, (Resident, Hong Kong Office) M.A., (Cantab.) admitted, 1981, England; 1987, Hong Kong. *Member:* The Law Society of Hong Kong. *LANGUAGES:* English. *PRACTICE AREAS:* Arbitration; Litigation; Professional Indemnity; Insurance.

HELEN W. CORMACK, LL.B. admitted, 1982, England. *LANGUAGES:* English and French. *PRACTICE AREAS:* Arbitration; Litigation; Professional Indemnity; Insurance.

JOHN HANSON, M.A., (Oxon.) admitted, 1977, England, Barrister & Solicitor, N.T. & Western Australia. *Member:* United Kingdom Environmental Law Association. *LANGUAGES:* English. *PRACTICE AREAS:* Arbitration; Litigation; Reinsurance; Brokers Errors and Omissions; All Risks Property and Casualty Insurance.

TIM HARDY, M.A., (Oxon.) admitted, 1982, England. *Member:* British Insurance Law Association. *LANGUAGES:* English. *PRACTICE AREAS:* Arbitration; Litigation; Reinsurance.

OLIVER J. LEONARD, B.A. admitted, 1978, England. *Member:* International Bar Association; Northern Ireland Law Society; Republic of Ireland Law Society. *LANGUAGES:* English. *PRACTICE AREAS:* Arbitration; Litigation; Insolvency; Professional Indemnity; Insurance.

DOUGLAS HOWIE, M.A., (Cantab.) admitted, 1980, England; 1984, Hong Kong. *Member:* British Venture Capital Association. *LANGUAGES:* English. *PRACTICE AREAS:* Company and Commercial; Insolvency; Financial Services.

MICHAEL E. JONES, B.A., (Hons), Law and German admitted, 1981, England. *Member:* British Venture Capital Association; British German Jurists Association; German Chamber of Industry and Commerce. *LANGUAGES:* English and German. *PRACTICE AREAS:* Company and Commercial; Insolvency; Insurance.

NIGEL C.C. BAMPING, LL.B., (Lond.); AKC. admitted, 1978, England. *Member:* Ecclesiastical Law Society; City of London Solicitors' Company. *LANGUAGES:* English. *PRACTICE AREAS:* Arbitration; Litigation; Professional Indemnity; Insurance.

(This Listing Continued)

CLIVE P. O'CONNELL, LL.B., (Lond.) admitted, 1982, England. *LANGUAGES:* English. *PRACTICE AREAS:* Reinsurance; Litigation; Arbitration; Environmental Liability.

GILES ADAMS, M.A., (Cantab.) admitted, 1983, England. *LANGUAGES:* English. *PRACTICE AREAS:* Litigation; Professional Indemnity; Insurance.

ANDREW SCOTT, B.A.; LL.M. admitted, 1985, England. *Member:* City of London Solicitors' Company. *LANGUAGES:* English. *PRACTICE AREAS:* Arbitration; Litigation; Professional Indemnity; Insurance.

RICHARD M.C. HARRIS, B.A. admitted, 1985, England. *LANGUAGES:* English. *PRACTICE AREAS:* Litigation; Public Liability; Insurance.

RAYMOND MEAD, LL.B. admitted, 1979, England. *Member:* London Maritime Arbitrators Association; International Chamber of Commerce. *LANGUAGES:* English. *PRACTICE AREAS:* Shipping; Arbitration; Litigation; Insurance.

MICHAEL S. MENDELOWITZ, B.A.; LL.B. (Witwatersrand); B.C.L., (Oxon.) admitted, 1989, England (Formerly a barrister, called 1980); Advocate of the Supreme Court of South Africa (called 1977). *Member:* Association Internationale du Droit des Assurances (Assistant Secretary General); United Kingdom Environmental Law Association. *LANGUAGES:* English and Afrikaans. *PRACTICE AREAS:* Reinsurance and Insurance; Environmental Liability; Litigation and Arbitration.

ELIZABETH PYGOTT, B.A.; M.A., (Lond.) admitted, 1977, England. *Member:* British Insurance Law Association; Medico-Legal Society (Honorary Secretary); City of London Solicitors' Company; Chartered Institute of Arbitrators. *LANGUAGES:* English and Russian. *PRACTICE AREAS:* Litigation; Professional Indemnity; Medico-Legal; Insurance.

MALCOLM ROGERSON, M.A., (Cantab.) admitted, 1981, England. *LANGUAGES:* English. *PRACTICE AREAS:* Property.

PAUL HOWICK, B.A., Hull. admitted, 1982, England. *LANGUAGES:* English. *PRACTICE AREAS:* Arbitration; Litigation; Reinsurance; Insurance.

LEONORA WILSON, B.A.; LL.B. admitted, 1987, England, Solicitor, New South Wales. *Member:* International Bar Association. *LANGUAGES:* English. *PRACTICE AREAS:* Aerospace; Arbitration; Litigation; Insurance.

ROBERT J. WILKINSON, B.A. admitted, 1983, England. *LANGUAGES:* English. *PRACTICE AREAS:* Aerospace; Arbitration; Litigation; Insurance.

DAVID SMYTH, B.A. admitted, 1985, England. *LANGUAGES:* English. *PRACTICE AREAS:* Litigation; Professional Indemnity; Insurance.

FRANCIS J. KEAN, LL.B. admitted, 1985, England. *LANGUAGES:* English and French. *PRACTICE AREAS:* Litigation; Directors' and Officers' Liability; Professional Indemnity; Financial Risks; Insurance.

NIGEL WAGLAND, LL.B. admitted, 1980, England. *Member:* London Maritime Arbitrators Association. *LANGUAGES:* English. *PRACTICE AREAS:* Shipping; Arbitration; Litigation; Insurance.

SARAH CLOVER NEE PINDER, LL.B. admitted, 1983, England. *LANGUAGES:* English and French. *PRACTICE AREAS:* Arbitration; Litigation; Professional Indemnity; Insurance.

CLARE CANNING, M.A., (Cantab.) admitted, 1986, England. *LANGUAGES:* English and French. *PRACTICE AREAS:* Arbitration; Litigation; Reinsurance; Insurance; Professional Indemnity; Political Risks.

RODERICK WHITE, (Resident, Hong Kong Office) LL.B.Y (Oxon) admitted, 1984, England; 1987, Hong Kong. *Member:* International Bar Association. *LANGUAGES:* English. *PRACTICE AREAS:* Shipping; Arbitration; Litigation; Commodities; Insurance; Aerospace; International Trade.

PETER MILLS, (Resident, Hong Kong Office) LL.B. admitted, 1979, New Zealand; 1984, England; 1990, Hong Kong. *LANGUAGES:* English. *PRACTICE AREAS:* Shipping; Arbitration; Litigation; Commodities; Insurance.

JULIAN RANDALL, (Resident, Hong Kong) M.A. (Oxon) admitted, 1986, England; 1990, Hong Kong. *LANGUAGES:* English. *PRACTICE AREAS:* Arbitration; Litigation; Professional Indemnity; Insurance; Defamation.

(This Listing Continued)

MICHAEL GRAHAM, LL.B. admitted, 1975, England. *Member:* British Insurance Law Association. *LANGUAGES:* English. *PRACTICE AREAS:* Commercial Litigation; Arbitration; Insurance; Reinsurance; Professional Indemnity (Insurance Brokers).

ROBERT OAKES, LL.B. (Cantab) admitted 1978, England. *LANGUAGES:* English. *PRACTICE AREAS:* Arbitration; Litigation; Construction; Insurance.

CHRISTOPHER L. BELL, LL.B., Lond. admitted, 1990, England. Formerly a Barrister. *LANGUAGES:* English. *PRACTICE AREAS:* Arbitration; Litigation; Reinsurance; Insurance.

ANDREW CROUCHMAN, M.A. (Cantab) admitted, 1991, England. *LANGUAGES:* English. *PRACTICE AREAS:* Insurance; Reinsurance.

JANET LAMBERT, LL.B. admitted, 1980, England. *LANGUAGES:* English. *PRACTICE AREAS:* Commercial Litigation; Arbitration; Reinsurance; Insurance.

LUCIAN SIMMONS, LL.B. (Lond) admitted, 1991, England. Formerly a Barrister. *LANGUAGES:* English. *PRACTICE AREAS:* Litigation; Professional Indemnity; Insurance; Election Law.

COLIN PORTER, B.A. (Law and French) admitted, 1984, England. *LANGUAGES:* English and French. *PRACTICE AREAS:* Arbitration; Litigation; Reinsurance; Insurance; Directors' and Officers Liability; Professional Indemnity.

DAVID KIRKPATRICK, LL.B. admitted, 1985, England. *LANGUAGES:* English. *PRACTICE AREAS:* Commercial Litigation; Professional Indemnity.

GARY J. FREER, M.A. (Cantab) admitted 1986, England. *Member:* Employment Lawyers Association. *LANGUAGES:* English and French. *PRACTICE AREAS:* Commercial; Litigation; Professional Indemnity; Employment Law; Food Safety Law.

OSCAR HARRISON-HALL, B.Sc., admitted, 1984, England. *LANGUAGES:* English. *PRACTICE AREAS:* Commercial Litigation.

DAVID R. W. KNAPP, LL.B., admitted, 1986, England. *LANGUAGES:* English. *PRACTICE AREAS:* Litigation; Public; Employers and Motor Liability; Insurance.

KEVIN BITMEAD, B.A., Business Law, admitted, 1984, England. *LANGUAGES:* English. *PRACTICE AREAS:* Personal Injury; Employers Liability; Public Liability; Motor; Health and Safety Law.

SIMON CHUMAS, LL.B., admitted, 1980, England. *LANGUAGES:* English. *PRACTICE AREAS:* Shipping Arbitration; Litigation; Insurance.

ROGER GREGORY, LL.B., admitted, 1984, England. *Member:* British Venture Capital Association; Institute of Directors; Freeman of the City of London. *LANGUAGES:* English. *PRACTICE AREAS:* Company and Commercial.

CONSULTANTS

SIR DENIS MARSHALL, admitted, 1937, England. Ex-President of the Law Society. *LANGUAGES:* English. *PRACTICE AREAS:* Insurance; Reinsurance; Professional Indemnity.

JOHN BUTLER, Non Solicitor. *LANGUAGES:* English. *PRACTICE AREAS:* Arbitration; Insurance; Reinsurance.

DAVID ANTON, Chartered Accountant and Non Solicitor. *PRACTICE AREAS:* Professional Negligence; Commercial Litigation; Corporate Finance; Share Valuation.

BATES, WELLS & BRAITHWAITE

Established in 1970

61 CHARTERHOUSE STREET
LONDON EC1M 6HA, ENGLAND
Telephone: 0171 251 1122
Fax: 0171 251 2061

Associated Offices: Sudbury, Ipswich, Suffolk, England.

FIRM PROFILE: *A Member of the Parlex Group of European Lawyers, European Economic Interest Groupings Number 0001 with members in Belgium, Denmark, France, Germany, Greece, Ireland, Italy, Luxembourg, Netherlands, Scotland and Spain and associate members in Austria, Finland, Iceland, Norway, Sweden and Switzerland.*

Bates Wells & Braithwaite has a distinctive philosophy being committed to
(This Listing Continued)

not only working for company commercial clients, but also acting for a wide range of professional and voluntary organizations. It is probably best known for its work in the charity sector where it is one of the leading firms. It acts for many of the larger charities in the United Kingdom. In addition, it also has a strong company commercial base doing work for smaller and medium sized businesses. Its family law department is well known in the City of London and its immigration and nationality law department is also highly respected. The firm also does commercial and domestic conveyancing.

ANDREW PHILLIPS, (Senior Partner) Author: "Charitable Status a Practical Guide.". Senior Partner. *PRACTICE AREAS:* Commercial and Charity Law.

HUGH CRAIG. *PRACTICE AREAS:* Company and Commercial Law.

JOHN TROTTER. *PRACTICE AREAS:* Litigation especially Judicial Review.

STEPHEN LLOYD, Author: "The Barclays Guide to Law for the Small Business." Co-Author: "Charities the New Law.". *LANGUAGES:* French. *PRACTICE AREAS:* Commercial and Charity Law.

FRANCES HUGHES. *PRACTICE AREAS:* Family Law.

FIONA MIDDLETON, Co-Author: "Charities the New Law"; "Charity Investment: Law and Practice.". *PRACTICE AREAS:* Charity Law.

WILLIAM GARNETT. *PRACTICE AREAS:* Litigation.

PAULINE FOWLER. *PRACTICE AREAS:* Family Law.

JENNIFER WARREN. *PRACTICE AREAS:* Commercial Property.

PHILIP TROTT. *LANGUAGES:* French. *PRACTICE AREAS:* Immigration and Employment Law.

BEACHCROFT STANLEYS

Established in 1762
20 FURNIVAL STREET
LONDON EC4A 1BN, ENGLAND
Telephone: 0171 242 1011
Fax: 0171 831 6630
DX: 45 London

Paris, France Associated Office: 24 Place du General Catroux. 75017. Telephone: 010 331 47 63 88 97. Fax: 010 331 42 27 42 26.
Brussels, Belgium Office: 85 rue de Prince Royal. 1050. Telephone: 010 32 2 511 64 25. Fax: 010 32 2 511 95 25.

FIRM PROFILE: *Beachcroft Stanleys is a long-established City of London practice offering all round company and commercial expertise, with an emphasis on litigation particularly in the areas of Insurance and Health Care Services.*

The firm's policy of maintaining client satisfaction is consistently met by establishing close links with its' clients, through the client partner relationship, understanding the nature of the client's business and delivering quality services that meet the client's needs in each case.

MEMBERS OF FIRM

ELIZABETH ADAMS, born April 15, 1955; admitted, 1980. *LANGUAGES:* English. *PRACTICE AREAS:* Employment; Employer/Employee Relations.

MALCOLM AUSTWICK, born June 17, 1959; admitted, 1983. *LANGUAGES:* English. *PRACTICE AREAS:* Commercial Property.

JAMES BESHOFF, born November 1, 1962; admitted, 1986. *LANGUAGES:* English and German. *PRACTICE AREAS:* Corporate Restructuring; Mergers and Acquisitions; Joint Ventures.

TREVOR BLYTHE, born October 4, 1947; admitted, 1974. *LANGUAGES:* English. *PRACTICE AREAS:* Commercial Litigation; Property Litigation.

PETER BRAZEL, born December 11, 1960; admitted, 1985. *LANGUAGES:* English, French and German. *PRACTICE AREAS:* Mergers and Acquisitions; Joint Ventures; Corporate Finance.

MARISA BROADHURST, born June 8, 1946; admitted, 1970. *LANGUAGES:* English and Spanish. *PRACTICE AREAS:* Public and Administrative Law; Commercial Property.

(This Listing Continued)

BEACHCROFT STANLEYS, London—Continued

ANTHONY CHERRY, born November 2, 1955; admitted, 1979. *LANGUAGES:* English. *PRACTICE AREAS:* Insurance; Product and Employer's Liability.

RICHARD EVANS, born June 28, 1952; admitted, 1976. *LANGUAGES:* English and Italian. *PRACTICE AREAS:* Litigation; Insurance; Reinsurance.

BARRY FRANCIS, born March 14, 1953; admitted, 1977. *LANGUAGES:* English. *PRACTICE AREAS:* Advertising; Health; Joint Ventures.

GEORGE FRANCIS, born March 15, 1947; admitted, 1975. *LANGUAGES:* English and Norwegian. *PRACTICE AREAS:* Offshore Trusts; Tax Shelters; Asset Protection.

JULIAN GIZZI, born February 13, 1957; admitted, 1981. *LANGUAGES:* English. *PRACTICE AREAS:* Commercial and Administrative Law.

NICHOLAS HALL, born July 18, 1947; admitted, 1971. *LANGUAGES:* English. *PRACTICE AREAS:* Mergers and Acquisitions; Employment; Occupational Pension Schemes.

SIMON HODSON, born May 9, 1956; admitted, 1981. *LANGUAGES:* English and French. *PRACTICE AREAS:* Corporate; Finance; International.

JOHN HOLMES, born May 6, 1960; admitted, 1984. *LANGUAGES:* English. *PRACTICE AREAS:* Medical Litigation; Healthcare.

DAVID HUNT, born May 21, 1952; admitted, 1968. Member of Parliament. *LANGUAGES:* English.

JOHN HURDLEY, born January 15, 1941; admitted, 1966. *LANGUAGES:* English. *PRACTICE AREAS:* Corporate Law; Merger and Acquisitions; Commercial Law.

PETER ILLION, born October 27, 1935. *LANGUAGES:* English. *PRACTICE AREAS:* Company Law.

ANDREW KENNEDY, born May 20, 1943; admitted, 1967. *LANGUAGES:* English and French. *PRACTICE AREAS:* Insurance; Water; Corporate.

JULIAN KORN, born November 14, 1945; admitted, 1971. *LANGUAGES:* English and French. *PRACTICE AREAS:* Wills; Trusts; Tax.

PETER KRAUS, born September 7, 1932; admitted, 1961. *LANGUAGES:* English, French, German and Hebrew. *PRACTICE AREAS:* Commercial Litigation.

IVAN KREMER, born September 28, 1946; admitted, 1970. *LANGUAGES:* English. *PRACTICE AREAS:* Commercial Property; NHS Estates; Care in the Community.

PHILIP LAWRENCE, born October 31, 1955; admitted, 1982. *LANGUAGES:* English. *PRACTICE AREAS:* Commercial Litigation; Construction Litigation; Environmental Law.

LAURENCE MARKHAM, born September 13, 1957; admitted, 1981. *LANGUAGES:* English. *PRACTICE AREAS:* Corporate Law; Mergers and Acquisitions; Insolvency.

BRENDAN MCCARTHY, born May 20, 1962; admitted, 1987, Ireland; 1991, England and Wales. *LANGUAGES:* English and Irish. *PRACTICE AREAS:* Insurance Litigation; Construction Litigation; Policy Coverage.

STEVEN MITCHELL, born November 14, 1951; admitted, 1976. *LANGUAGES:* English and German. *PRACTICE AREAS:* Insurance Litigation.

PHILIP MURPHY, born March 10, 1946; admitted, 1970. *LANGUAGES:* English. *PRACTICE AREAS:* Commercial Property.

RICHARD PAIN, born September 23, 1942; admitted, 1967. *LANGUAGES:* English. *PRACTICE AREAS:* Commercial Property; Property Development; Landlord/Tenant.

JOHN PHELPS, born May 25, 1954; admitted, 1978. *LANGUAGES:* English and French. *PRACTICE AREAS:* Commercial Property; VAT.

BRUCE RALSTON, born March 22, 1959; admitted, 1983. *LANGUAGES:* English. *PRACTICE AREAS:* Insurance Litigation.

(This Listing Continued)

JEAN RICHARDS, born January 31, 1951; admitted, 1975. *LANGUAGES:* English and French. *PRACTICE AREAS:* Commercial Property; Health Service.

KENNETH RIDEHALGH, born 1939. *LANGUAGES:* English. *PRACTICE AREAS:* Food; Marine; Offshore Trusts.

PAUL SOLON, born April 26, 1949; admitted, 1973. *LANGUAGES:* English. *PRACTICE AREAS:* Trusts; Tax; Estate Planning.

REBECCA WHITING, born May 24, 1962; admitted, 1987. *LANGUAGES:* English. *PRACTICE AREAS:* Commercial Litigation.

GAY WILDER, born March 7, 1959; admitted, 1982. *LANGUAGES:* English. *PRACTICE AREAS:* Medical Negligence Litigation.

CHRISTOPHER WILKES, born November 14, 1955; admitted, 1980. *LANGUAGES:* English. *PRACTICE AREAS:* Commercial Litigation; Insurance.

Member of Legal Network International

BEAUMONT AND SON

Established in 1836

LLOYDS CHAMBERS
1 PORTSOKEN STREET
LONDON E1 8AW, ENGLAND
Telephone: 0171-481 3100
Telex: 889018 BOSUN G
Fax: 0171-481 3353

Rio de Janeiro, Brazil Office: Rua Anfilófio de Carvalho, 29/518, CEP 20015-900. Telephone: (5521) 532 1445. Fax: (5521) 240 8541.

Singapore Office: 101 Thomson Road, #29-02 United Square, Singapore 1130. Telephone: (65) 352 2363. Fax: (65) 352.4282.

Paris, France Associated Office: Cabinet Garnault, 17 Avenue de Lamballe, 75016. Telephone: (1) 44.14.53.70. Telex: 645.858 ALORM PARIS. Fax: (1) 44.14.53.99.

Aviation Insurance and Liability Claims, Air and Space Law, Commercial Aviation, Aircraft Purchases, Sales and Financing. Insurance and Reinsurance Litigation. Marine and Road Transport. Liability Claims. Foreign and Kingdom Litigation. Real Property. Conveyancing. Company and Commercial, Corporate Banking, Finance and Equipment Leasing. Employment Law. Libel, Common Law, Tax, EC Law.

MEMBERS

TIMOTHY STUART BROOKE UNMACK, born Taunton, U.K., August 5, 1937; admitted, 1965, England. *Education:* Christ Church, Oxford School of Jurisprudence (M.A. Hon); Qualified as Solicitor of the Supreme Court. *Member:* International Law Association; Law Society; Royal Aeronautical Society. *LANGUAGES:* French, German, Italian, Spanish and Russian. *PRACTICE AREAS:* Aviation; Aerospace; Insurance; Reinsurance; Litigation.

PHILIP GUY COBBAN SANDERS, born Clevedon, U.K., September 18, 1945; admitted, 1969, Law Society of England and Wales. *Education:* College of Law, Lancaster Gate, London; Law Society (Qualifying Exam). Examiner in Air Law, Chartered Insurance Institute, 1981-1985. *Member:* Law Society; International Bar Association; Asia-Pacific Lawyers Association; International Association of Defence Counsel. *LANGUAGES:* Spanish. *PRACTICE AREAS:* Aviation; Aerospace; Litigation; Insurance; Reinsurance.

SEAN SPENCER JAMES GATES, born Bogner Regis, Sussex, U.K., February 4, 1949; admitted, 1972, England and Wales. *Education:* British Institute of International and Comparative Law (German Law Diploma, 1974); College of Law, Guildford, U.K. (Solicitors Qualifying Exams, 1972). *Member:* Law Society; Royal Aeronautical Society; Insurance Institute of London; International Bar Association; International Association of Defence Council. *LANGUAGES:* German. *PRACTICE AREAS:* Aviation; Aerospace; Personal Injury; Litigation; Insurance.

NEIL R. MCGILCHRIST, born London, England, December 8, 1946; admitted, 1969, Barrister Middle Temple. *Education:* Wadham College, Oxford (M.A. Law); Inns of Court School of Law. President, Oxford University Law Society, 1966. *LANGUAGES:* French. *PRACTICE AREAS:* Aviation; Aerospace; Litigation; Insurance; Banking.

DENNIS ANTHONY KILBRIDE, born Ruislip, Middlesex, U.K., July 29, 1948; admitted, 1979, England and Wales. *Education:* Brunel University, London, U.K (LL.B. Honors, 1976); College of Law, Lancaster Gate,

(This Listing Continued)

London (Law Society Finals, 1979). Past Examiner in Air Law, Chartered Insurance Institute, London, 1985-1987. *Member:* Law Society of England and Wales; International Bar Association; Asia-Pacific Law Association. *LANGUAGES:* French. *PRACTICE AREAS:* Aviation; Aerospace; Litigation; Insurance; Transport.

ALAN JOHN GIBBS, born Weston-Super-Mare, England, June 28, 1950; admitted, 1973, England and Wales. *Education:* College of Law (Part 1 Qualifying Exam, 1970; Part 2 Qualifying Exam, 1973). *Member:* Law Society; City of London Solicitor's Company. *PRACTICE AREAS:* Property; Commercial; Conveyancing.

PHILIP M. BASS, born Wegberg, Germany, October 12, 1956; admitted, 1981, England and Wales. *Education:* Exeter University (LL.B. Hons., 1978); College of Law (Solicitors Qualifying Examinations, 1979); University College London (Diploma in Air Space Law). *Member:* International Bar Association; Royal Aeronautical Society; Guild of Pilots and Air Navigators; West London Aero Club. (Resident, Singapore Office). *LANGUAGES:* French and Spanish. *PRACTICE AREAS:* Aviation; Aerospace; Personal Injury.

DAVID JOHN WILLCOX, born Epsom, Surrey, U.K., March 25, 1957; admitted, 1981, England and Wales. *Education:* Sheffield University (Upper Second Class Degree in Law, Honors). *Member:* Law Society. *PRACTICE AREAS:* Aviation; Aerospace; Litigation; Commercial; Insurance.

JAMES ANDREW MARSHALL EDMUNDS, born England, May 19, 1945; admitted, 1971, England and Wales. *Education:* University of London (Bachelor of Laws, 1968); College of Law (Solicitors Qualifying Examination, 1969). *LANGUAGES:* French. *PRACTICE AREAS:* Banking; Aviation; Finance.

JOSEPH SIMON GOODRIDGE, born Banbury, U.K., February 17, 1958; admitted, 1984, England and Wales. *Education:* School of Modern History, Mansfield College, Oxford (Honors Degree, 1979); College of Law, Guildford (Solicitors Finals, 1981; Common Professional Examination, 1980). *LANGUAGES:* French. *PRACTICE AREAS:* Immigration; Liability; Aviation Claims; Competition Law; Re-Insurance.

DAVID N. CLARK, born London, England, March 8, 1952; admitted, 1980, England and Wales. *Education:* Southampton University (LL.B. Law Degree); College of Law (Solicitor Qualifying Examination, 1977). *Member:* Law Society. *LANGUAGES:* French and Portuguese. *PRACTICE AREAS:* Aviation; Aerospace; Litigation; Insurance; Personal Injury.

P. ROSS WILLIAMS, born Chippenham, England, September 4, 1957; admitted, 1984, London and Wales; 1990, New York. *Education:* Birmingham Polytechnic (B.A. Hons. Law, 1979); Exeter University (LL.M., 1985). *LANGUAGES:* Spanish. *PRACTICE AREAS:* Construction; Litigation; Insurance; Shipping.

DAVID BRUCE JOHNSTON, born Cuckfield, Sussex, England, September 4, 1957; admitted, 1988, England. *Education:* University of Kent (B.A. Hons. Law and South East Asia Studies). *Member:* Law Society of England and Wales. *LANGUAGES:* French, German and Spanish. *PRACTICE AREAS:* Personal Injury; Aviation; Aerospace; Litigation; Insurance.

CATHERINE D. WEST, born Pulborough, West Sussex, July 7, 1960; admitted, 1989, England and Wales. *Education:* Manchester University (American Studies, B.A. Hons., 1984); Chester College of Law (Common Professional Examinations, 1986); Law Society (Final Examinations, 1987). *Member:* Law Society. *LANGUAGES:* Spanish and French. *PRACTICE AREAS:* Aviation; Aerospace; Litigation; Insurance.

MARTYN PETER PLASKETT, born London, December 7, 1962; admitted, 1989, England and Wales. *Education:* University College, University of Durham (Engineering, BSC Hons., 1984); College of Law, Guildford (Common Professional Examination, 1985 and Law Society Solicitors' Finals Examination, 1986). *Member:* Law Society of Great Britain. (Resident, Brazil Office). *LANGUAGES:* English and Portuguese. *PRACTICE AREAS:* Aviation; Aerospace; Litigation; Insurance.

NIGEL JONATHON DAVID WRIGHT, born London, England, March 27, 1965; admitted, 1990, England and Wales. *Education:* Nottingham University (LL.B., 1986); Lancaster Gate (1988). *Member:* Law Society of England and Wales. *LANGUAGES:* French. *PRACTICE AREAS:* Aviation; Insurance; Litigation; Commercial.

PATRICIA A. BARNES, born England, February 26, 1945; admitted, 1979, England as Barrister; 1990, England as Solicitor. *Education:* Man-

(This Listing Continued)

chester University (1966); Polytechnic of Central London (Bar Finals, 1979). *LANGUAGES:* French and Spanish.

LINDSAY MILLAR, born Melbourne, Australia, October 9, 1960; admitted, 1988, England and Wales. *Education:* Wadham College (B.A., Hons., 1983); College of Law, Guildford. *PRACTICE AREAS:* Tax.

LUCIA AINSWORTH, born Huddersfield, England, January 18, 1966; admitted, 1993, England. *Education:* Brunel University (LL.B., upper second class honours, 1989); Chester, College of Law (LSF, second class honours, 1990). *LANGUAGES:* Italian. *PRACTICE AREAS:* Commercial.

RAVI SHANKAR, born Malaysia, April 18, 1965; admitted, 1991, England; 1989, Malaysia as Advocate and Solicitor; 1987, England as Barrister-at Law. *Education:* Lancashire Polytechnic (LL.B., 1986); Council of Legal Education (Barrister-at-Law, 1987). *LANGUAGES:* French and Malay.

PENELOPE TERNDRUP, born Lydney, Great Britain, January 4, 1969; admitted, 1994, London, England. *Education:* University of Wales College Cardiff (B.A., 1991); College of Law, Chester (1992). *LANGUAGES:* Italian. *PRACTICE AREAS:* Company; Commercial; Aviation; Leasing.

JONATHAN PETER ST. JOHN HARDING, born Lincoln, Lincolnshire, September 29, 1968; admitted, 1994, England and Wales. *Education:* Maqoalene College, Cambridge (M.A., Law, 1990); College of Law, York (1992). Law Society Finals. *Member:* Law Society of England and Wales. *LANGUAGES:* French. *PRACTICE AREAS:* Aviation Law.

DANIEL S. SOFFIN, born Richmond, Virginia, September 30, 1959; admitted, 1992, Pennsylvania; 1994, England and Wales; Solicitor of the Supreme Court of England and Wales. *Education:* Emory University, Atlanta, Georgia (B.A., 1980); Georgia State University (M.B.A., 1984: M.H.A., 1985); Temple University Law School, Philadelphia, Pennsylvania (J.D., 1991). *Member:* Law Society, of England and Wales; American Bar Association. *LANGUAGES:* French and English. *PRACTICE AREAS:* Aviation; Insurance; Commercial.

PATRICK E. SLOMSKI, born August 12, 1967; admitted, 1994, United Kingdom. *Education:* Downing College (B.A., hons., 1988); Cambridge University (Diploma, 1986); Poly of West London (C.P.E., 1991). *Member:* Law Society of England and Wales. *PRACTICE AREAS:* Litigation, Aviation; Insurance; Re-Insurance.

AUSTIN BARHAM, born Pembury, England, March 10, 1967; admitted, 1994, England. *Education:* Loughborough University (B.S., Hons., 1989); College of Law (Law Society Finals, 1991). *Member:* Law Society of England and Wales. *PRACTICE AREAS:* Aviation; Personal Injury; Tour Operating.

JOHN W. FLETCHER, born Vanderbijlpark, South Africa, January 26, 1958; admitted, 1984, South Africa as Attorney; 1992, England and Wales. *Education:* University of the Witwatersand, Johannesburg (B.A., 1980; LL.B., 1984); Cambridge University (M.Phil., 1987); Common Professional Examination (1989); Law Society Finals (1991). *Member:* Law Society of England and Wales. *PRACTICE AREAS:* Commercial.

BECKMAN & BECKMAN

20 BALCOMBE STREET
DORSET SQUARE
LONDON NW1 6NB, ENGLAND
Telephone: (0171) 724 1435
Fax: (0171) 724 7017
DX: 41717 Marylebone 2

Corporate and Commercial Law, Civil Litigation, Taxation, Insolvency and Receivership, Trademark and Copyright, Personal Injury, Leasing, Property, Landlord and Tenant, Wills, Trusts, Estates and Probate, Matrimonial and Family Law, International Child Abduction and all proceedings relating to Children.

FIRM PROFILE: *Beckman & Beckman is an established firm based in Central London. Legal Aid work is undertaken. It is a five partner firm with a large body of associates and support staff.*

NORMAN BECKMAN, born November 16, 1930; admitted, 1956, England. *PRACTICE AREAS:* Corporate Contracts; Commercial Contracts; Employment Law; Commercial Advice; Commercial Trouble Shooting.

PHILIP BECKMAN, born March 27, 1933; admitted, 1959, England. Awarded, Prizes: John Mackrell; Cliffords Inn; Maurice Norden. *Member:*

(This Listing Continued)

BECKMAN & BECKMAN, London—Continued

Law Society of England and Wales. *PRACTICE AREAS:* Corporate Law; Commercial Law; Property Law; Landlord and Tenant Law.

BRIAN BECKMAN, born March 14, 1941; admitted, 1985, England. *Member:* Law Society of England and Wales. *PRACTICE AREAS:* Wills, Trusts, Estate and Probate Law; Property Law; Landlord and Tenant Law; Corporate Law; Commercial Law.

STEPHEN BRIGGS, born May 9, 1952; admitted, 1983, England. *Member:* Law Society of England and Wales. *PRACTICE AREAS:* Civil Litigation; Commercial Landlord and Tenant Law; Building Disputes.

ANNE-MARIE HUTCHINSON, born August 1, 1957; admitted, 1985, England. Chair of Reunite, National Council for Abducted Children. Member, Lord Chancellor's Panel on Child Abduction. *Member:* Law Society of England and Wales; Family Law Association. *PRACTICE AREAS:* Children; Adoptions; Child Abduction; Child Care; Child Custody; Family Law; Divorce; International Family Law; Matrimonial Law.

BEITEN BURKHARDT MITTL & WEGENER

Rechtsanwälte

SWEDENBORG HOUSE
21 BLOOMSBURY WAY
LONDON WC1A 2TH, ENGLAND
Telephone: (0171) 2 42 44 66
Telefax: (0171) 2 42 44 67

Munich, Germany Office: Leopoldstrasse 236, D-80807. Telephone: (089) 35065-00. Telefax: (089) 35065-123.

Berlin, Germany Office: Kurfürstenstrasse 72-74, D-10787 Berlin. Telephone: (0 30) 264 71-0. Telefax: (0 30) 264 71-123.

Frankfurt/Main, Germany Office: Arndtstrasse 28, D-60325 Frankfurt/Main. Telephone: (0 69) 75 60 95-0. Telefax: (0 69) 75 60 95-12.

Nürnberg, Germany Office: Obere Turnstrasse 8, D-90429 Nürnberg. Telephone: (09 11) 2 79 71-0. Telefax: (09 11) 2 79 71-99.

Leipzig, Germany Office: Käthe-Kollwitz-Strasse 54, D-04109 Leipzig. Telephone: (03 41) 4 77 25 97. Telefax: (03 41) 4 77 25 99.

Potsdam, Germany Office: Heinrich-Mann-Allee 105 B, D-14473 Potsdam. Telephone: (0331) 33 43 06. Telefax: (0331) 33 43 29.

Hof, Germany Office: Oberer Torplatz 1, D-95028 Hof. Telephone: (09281) 80 23. Telefax: (09281) 1 65 69.

Plauen, Germany Office: Lindenstrasse 5, D-08523 Plauen. Telephone: (03741) 22 35 11; 22 49 62. Telefax: (03741) 22 49 62.

New York, New York Office: 215 East 73rd Street, New York, NY 10021. Telephone: (212) 570-2141. Telefax: (212) 734-7011.

Moscow, Russia Office: Ul. Alekseja Tolstovo D.30/1, 103001 Moscow. Telephone and Telefax: (095) 202 37 60; 290 05 56.

Prague, Czech Republic Office: Na Bojišti 24, 120 00 Prague 2. Telephone: (2) 24 91 5808. Telefax: (2) 24 91 5804.

Budapest, Hungary Office: József Nádor Tér 9, H-1051 Budapest. Telephone: (1) 2 66 18 10. Telefax: (1) 2 66 18 11.

Hong Kong Office: 605 B, Sixth Floor, Peregrine Tower, Lippo Centre, 89 Queensway. Telephone: (852) 2524 6468. Telefax: (852) 2524 7028.

Beijing, People's Republic of China Office: Unit 10, 29th Floor, Jing Guang Centre, Hu Jia Lou, Chao Yang Qu, 100020. Telephone: (86-1) 501 4569; 501 3388 Ext. 2910. Telefax: (86-1) 501 3034.

Commercial Law, Company Law, M & A, Joint Ventures, Finance, Banking, Leasing, Domestic and International Tax, Antitrust, EC Law, Real Property and Private Construction, Electronic Data Processing (Protection and Licensing), Media, Publishing, Unfair Competition, Trademarks, Copyright, Labour, General and Special Administrative Law Particularly Public Construction and Planning Regulations and Public International Law, Environmental Law, Agricultural Law, Privatization and Restitution (former GDR), Probate, Family and Estate Planning, Insolvency and Sports, Insurance, Automobile Accidents and Injuries.

FIRM PROFILE: BEITEN BURKHARDT MITTL & WEGENER is a nation-wide and international law firm with 108 lawyers. The firm's head office is in Munich. All the firm's offices provide a comprehensive range of services in the main areas of civil and commercial law.

GUNTER ZIMMER, born Mainz, 1961; admitted, 1990, Germany; 1993, as Solicitor in England and Wales. *Education:* Universities of Stutt-

(This Listing Continued)

gart-Hohenheim (Agriculture), Mainz (law degree, 1987); King's College, London. *Member:* German-British Jurists' Association; European Young Lawyers Association. *LANGUAGES:* German and English. *PRACTICE AREAS:* Company Law; Acquisitions and Sales; Restructuring; Tax Planning; Pensions; Financial Services.

(For Complete Biographical Data on all Personnel, see Munich, Germany Professional Biographies)

MARGARET BENNETT

Solicitors

Established in 1990

CHARLTON HOUSE
5A BLOOMSBURY SQUARE
LONDON WC1A 2LX, ENGLAND
Telephone: 0171-404 6465
Fax: 0171-240 5492

Practitioners in Matrimonial Law with Divorce Counselling Service. Specialist Family Law practice for international cases with connections with Family Law practices worldwide.

M.H. BENNETT, admitted, 1972, England and Wales; 1983, Hong Kong. Founding Fellow of International Academy of Matrimonial Lawyers. Chairman, Family Law Committee, International Bar Association, 1994—. Speaker at First World Congress on Family Law and Children's Rights, 1993.

ASSOCIATES

CAROLINE GORDON-SMITH, Qualified 1986.

DAVID STERRETT, Qualified 1990.

EMMA WOOD, Qualified 1989.

JOHN DARNTON, Qualified 1985.

CONSULTANT

LADY PATRICIA HARRIS, Consultant Counsellor.

Languages: French, Italian and German.

BERLIOZ & CO.

Société d'Avocats

44-46 KINGSWAY
LONDON WC2B 6EN, ENGLAND
Telephone: (44 171) 831 4022
Telefax: (44 171) 831 8233

Paris, France Office: 68, Boulevard de Courcelles, 75017 Paris. Telephone: (33.1) 44 01 44 01. Telefax: (33.1) 44 15 94 15; 42 67 04 43.

Lyon, France Office: 48, rue du Président Edouard Herriot, 69002 Lyon. Telephone: (33) 78 38 12 79. Telefax: (33) 78 38 12 83.

Toulouse, France Office: 22, rue de la Dalbade, 3100 Toulouse. Telephone: (33) 61 25 06 97. Telefax: (33) 61 25 06 57.

Sophia Antipolis, France Office: Villantipolis n° 11, 473, route des Dolines, Sophia Antipolis, 06560. Telephone: (33) 93 65 42 50. Telefax: (33) 93 65 39 26.

Brussels, Belgium Office: 179 avenue Louise, 1050. Telephone: (32.2) 646.40.04. Telefax: (32.2) 644.14.88.

New York, New York Office: 655 Madison Avenue, 10021. Telephone: 212-486-6302. Telex: 3717883. Telefax: 212-486-8668.

Vilnius, Kalvariju Office: g. 276-36, 2021 VILNIUS. Telephone: (370.2)62.46.04. Contact: Valentinas MIKELENAS.

General French and International Law Practice, Advertising Law, Aeronautical Law, Arbitration, Banking and Financial Law, Commercial Leasing, Competition Law, Computer Law, Construction Law, Consumer Protection, Corporate Law, Criminal Law, Distributorship Law, Entertainment Law, Agency and Franchise Law, EC Law, Food and Drug Regulations, Foreign Investments, Industrial Relations and Labor Law, Insurance Law, International Private Law, Licensing, Litigation, Maritime and Transport Law, Financial Engineering, Public Contracts, State Enterprises, Taxation, Tax Planning, Mergers and Acquisitions Law, Product Liability, Property, Real Estate, Rent and Lease Law, Securities Law, Trade Regulations, Patent, Trademark and Copyright Law, Tax, East-West Trade, North-South Trade, Audio-visual Law, Telecommunications.

(This Listing Continued)

MICHEL CARDIN, born 1945; admitted, 1988, Paris. *Education:* Université de Paris (Doctorat d'Etat en Droit International Privé, 1973). In house lawyer for: TOTAL, 1972-1985; THOMSON, 1985-1987.

Languages: French, English, German, Italian, Spanish, Portuguese, Russian, Arabic, Malaysian

(For Biographical Data of the Paris Office, see Professional Biographies at Paris, France)

BERRYMANS

Established in 1900

SALISBURY HOUSE
LONDON WALL
LONDON EC2M 5QN, ENGLAND
Telephone: 010 44 171 638 2811
Local: 0171 638 2811
Fax: 0171 920 0361
Telex: 892070 Berryman G

Southampton, England Office: The White House, Grosvenor Square, SO1 2BE. Telephone: 01703 236464. Fax: 01703 236117.

Birmingham, England Office: 21 Bennetts Hill, B2 5QP. Telephone: 0121 643 8777. Fax: 0121 643 4909.

Paris, France Associated Office: Bertagna Gruia Berrymans. 59 Avenue Marceau, 75116. Telephone: (1) 47 230590. Fax: (1) 47 230409.

Other Associated Offices: Abu Dhabi, Dubai, Brussels, Düsseldorf, Madrid and Singapore.

Firm engaged Nationally and Internationally in all aspects of Insurance Litigation, Commercial Litigation, Non-Contentious Company and Commercial, Commercial Property, Private Client.
Mergers and Acquisitions, Joint Ventures, General Company and Commercial, Commercial Property, Construction, Personal Injury, Professional Indemnity, Insurance and Reinsurance, Recovery, Medical Law Service, Environmental Law, Private Client.

FIRM PROFILE: Berrymans is a leading City of London Litigation and Commercial Law Practice with strong connections throughout the London insurance market.

The firm is known for its expertise in Litigation and Dispute Resolution of all types in the UK and abroad and has an increasing involvement with International Arbitration (also specialising in leading cases involving Environmental Claims and Disputes) expanding Non-Contentious Company/-Commercial Practice.

With a total staff in excess of 150, Berrymans has built on its expertise to provide a modern, positive international service. The Berrymans Europe EEIG, a European grouping of like minded lawyers is continuing to expand to cover the European Community Countries.

The firms agency service covers representation in the London courts, including a full report of proceeding within 24 hours.

MEMBERS OF FIRM

PAUL TAYLOR, born London, England, 1946; admitted, 1969, England. *Education:* Kings College; London University (LL.B., Hons., 1966-1967); College of Law, London. Joint Editor, Berryman's Building Claim Cases. Editor, Binghams and Berrymans' Motor Claim Cases. *Member:* Law Society of England and Wales; International Association of Defense Counsel; FIDIC-(Professional Liability Committee); ADR (Task Committee); Association des Juristes Franco Britanniques; Official Referees Solicitors Association. *LANGUAGES:* French. *PRACTICE AREAS:* Construction; Professional Negligence.

DIANA HOLTHAM, born London, England, 1956; admitted, 1980, England. *Education:* Exeter University (LL.B., Hons., 1977). Joint Editor, Berrymans Building Claim Cases. *Member:* Law Society of England and Wales; Society of Construction Law; Official Referees Solicitors Association. *PRACTICE AREAS:* Construction Law; Professional Negligence.

MICHAEL SWAN, born London, England, 1947; admitted, 1973, England. *Member:* Law Society. *LANGUAGES:* French. *PRACTICE AREAS:* Personal Injury.

MARTIN BRUFFELL, born England, 1955; admitted, 1981, England. *Education:* University of Leeds (LL.B., Hons., 1978); Lancaster Gate Law School (1979). *Member:* Law Society of England and Wales; City of London Solicitors. *LANGUAGES:* French. *PRACTICE AREAS:* Personal Injury; Health and Safety.

(This Listing Continued)

DAVID WILKINSON, born England, 1956; admitted, 1979, England; 1984, Hong Kong. *Education:* Guildford College of Law (1978). *Member:* Law Society of England and Wales; British Insurance Law Association. *LANGUAGES:* French. *PRACTICE AREAS:* Insurance/Reinsurance; Professional Negligence.

CHARLOTTE CAPSTICK, born Wales, 1958; admitted, 1984, England. *Education:* Oxford University (B.A., Jurisprudence, 1980). *Member:* Law Society of England and Wales. *LANGUAGES:* French. *PRACTICE AREAS:* Professional Negligence; Insurance Litigation.

ADRIAN FOTHERGILL, born England, 1950; admitted, 1975, England. *Education:* External London University (LL.B., Hons.); College of Law, Lancaster Gate (1973). *Member:* Law Society of England and Wales; City of London Solicitors Company. *LANGUAGES:* French. *PRACTICE AREAS:* Commercial Property.

CATHERINE HAWKINS, born England, 1961; admitted, 1985, England. *Education:* Manchester University (LL.B., 1982). *Member:* Official Referees Solicitors Association. *PRACTICE AREAS:* Insurance Law; Commercial Litigation; Recovery Actions.

SARAH SHEMMINGS, born England, 1956; admitted, 1982, England. *Member:* Law Society of England and Wales; UK ELA (Environmental Law Association). *PRACTICE AREAS:* Environmental Law.

CHERYL BLUNDELL, born England, 1960; admitted, 1985, England. *Education:* Exeter University (LL.B., 1982); College of Law, Guildford (1983). *Member:* Institute of Risk Management; Health Sector Special Interest Groups; Law Society. *LANGUAGES:* French. *PRACTICE AREAS:* Medical Law.

PETER BOHM, born England, 1952; admitted, 1976, England. *Education:* Queens' College, Cambridge (M.A., Law, 1973). *Member:* Law Society; British-German Jurists' Association; British-Nordic Lawyers' Association. *PRACTICE AREAS:* Company and Business Acquisitions and Sales; Company Law; Commercial Law; Employment Law.

TERRY RENOUF, born Jersey, Channel Islands, 1960; admitted, 1987, England. *Education:* Durham University. *Member:* Law Society of England and Wales. *PRACTICE AREAS:* Personal Injury; Industrial Diseases; Employers Liability; Public Liability.

IAN LATIMER, born Oldham, England, 1957; admitted, 1982, England. *Education:* Kingston University (B.A., Law). *Member:* Law Society of England and Wales. *LANGUAGES:* German. *PRACTICE AREAS:* Personal Injury; Medical Negligence.

RICHARD BEATY, born Cambridge, England, 1959; admitted, 1990, England. *Education:* University of Essex. *Member:* Chartered Institute of Arbitration. *PRACTICE AREAS:* Professional Indemnity.

TIMOTHY OLIVER, born Reading, England, 1961; admitted, 1986, England. *Education:* Exeter University. *Member:* Law Society of England and Wales. *PRACTICE AREAS:* Liability Insurance.

JEREMY BENFIELD, born England, 1961; admitted, 1986, England. Contributor: Binghams and Berrymans Motor Claims, Insurance Chapter. *LANGUAGES:* French. *PRACTICE AREAS:* Insurance and Reinsurance; Professional Negligence.

CHRIS WIGGIN, born Bloxwich, England, 1954; admitted, 1983, England. *Education:* University of Keele. *Member:* Law Society; Birmingham Law Society. *PRACTICE AREAS:* Personal Injury; Professional Negligence; Employers Liability; Public Liability; Construction Law.

NEIL ASHFORD, born Ilfracombe, England, 1959; admitted, 1985, England. *Education:* University of East Anglia. *PRACTICE AREAS:* Insurance; Commercial Litigation; Personal Injury.

BERWIN LEIGHTON

ADELAIDE HOUSE
LONDON BRIDGE
LONDON EC4R 9HA, ENGLAND
Telephone: 0171-623-3144
Telecopier: (Groups 2 & 3) 0171-623-4416
Cable Address: "BerwincoLondon EC4"
Telex: 886420 BLGHTN

New York, N.Y. Firm: 135 East 57th Street, 11th Floor, 10022. Telephone: 212-754-5400. Fax: (Groups 2 & 3) 212-754-5401. Telex: 426986 BLGHTN.

(This Listing Continued)

BERWIN LEIGHTON, London—Continued

Brussels, Belgium Office: 13 B Avenue de Tervuren, Tervurenlaan, 1040. Telephone: (2) 732 3144. Fax: (2) 732 3979.

PARTNERS

N. SINCLAIR. LANGUAGES: English. **PRACTICE AREAS:** Corporate Finance; Financial Services.

L. HELLER. LANGUAGES: English and French. **PRACTICE AREAS:** Commercial Property; Property Taxation; Planning.

E. SIBLEY. LANGUAGES: English. **PRACTICE AREAS:** International Accountancy Litigation; Aviation Re-Insurance; Direct Selling; Franchising; Libel Matters.

T.S. LYON. LANGUAGES: English, French and German. **PRACTICE AREAS:** Asset Finance and Leasing.

B.J. BARTLETT. LANGUAGES: English. **PRACTICE AREAS:** Corporate and Commercial Law; Corporate Rescues and Reconstructions.

D.B. RHODES. LANGUAGES: English. **PRACTICE AREAS:** Commercial Property; Public Sector Property Law.

R.M. BUCK. LANGUAGES: English. **PRACTICE AREAS:** Property Development; Joint Ventures.

D.A. SEGAL. LANGUAGES: English. **PRACTICE AREAS:** Corporate Finance; Mergers and Acquisitions; Takeovers; Share Planning.

L.H.A. HOMAN. LANGUAGES: English and French. **PRACTICE AREAS:** Asset Finance; Tax-based Leasing and Securitisation; Company Acquisitions and Sales.

M.H. BRUMMER. LANGUAGES: English. **PRACTICE AREAS:** Property Financing.

M. GOLDMEIER. LANGUAGES: English. **PRACTICE AREAS:** Construction Litigation.

M.G. WILSON. LANGUAGES: English. **PRACTICE AREAS:** Banking Litigation; Financial Services Litigation; Insurance Litigation.

P.D. RUDOLF. LANGUAGES: English. **PRACTICE AREAS:** Property Development and Investment.

L.H. EVANS. LANGUAGES: English and French. **PRACTICE AREAS:** Entertainment and Communications Law; EEC Competition Law; Eastern Bloc Joint Ventures; Computers; Intellectual Property.

R.E. DOWNHILL. LANGUAGES: English. **PRACTICE AREAS:** Commercial Taxation.

R.J. JONES. LANGUAGES: English. **PRACTICE AREAS:** Company Rescues and Re-Structuring; Mergers and Acquisitions; Flotations and New Issues; Venture Capital; MBO's.

P.F. STONE. LANGUAGES: English, French and Spanish. **PRACTICE AREAS:** Entertainment; Intellectual Property; UK and EEC Competition Law; Anti-Trust.

J.H. OVERS. LANGUAGES: English. **PRACTICE AREAS:** Commercial Taxation (including VAT).

E.J. ROTHWELL. LANGUAGES: English. **PRACTICE AREAS:** General Commercial Litigation.

W.N. TAYLOR. LANGUAGES: English and French. **PRACTICE AREAS:** Planning; Highways and Infrastructure; Environment Law.

P.J. BRETHERTON. LANGUAGES: English. **PRACTICE AREAS:** Commercial Property; Property Development.

P.F. ROBINSON. LANGUAGES: English and Afrikaans. **PRACTICE AREAS:** Mergers and Acquisitions; Corporate Finance; New Issues; Joint Ventures.

E.M. PALLEY. LANGUAGES: English. **PRACTICE AREAS:** Banking.

I.C. LOWE. LANGUAGES: English and French. **PRACTICE AREAS:** Corporate and Commercial Litigation; Computers; Information Technology and Intellectual Property Litigation.

J.P. KELLETT. LANGUAGES: English. **PRACTICE AREAS:** Shipping and Aviation Finance; Leasing; Sale/Purchase; Joint Ventures.

J.M. POWELL. LANGUAGES: English. **PRACTICE AREAS:** Corporate and Personal Taxation.

(This Listing Continued)

R. HAWKINS. LANGUAGES: English. **PRACTICE AREAS:** Property Financing and Insolvency.

C.R.E. LATTER. LANGUAGES: English, French and German. **PRACTICE AREAS:** Mergers and Acquisitions; Corporate Finance; New Issues; Joint Ventures.

V.A. METTER. LANGUAGES: English and Afrikaans. **PRACTICE AREAS:** Commercial Property.

A.J. ROSE. LANGUAGES: English. **PRACTICE AREAS:** Banking Litigation; Financial Institutions Litigation; Insurance Litigation.

N.J. DAVIES. LANGUAGES: English and French. **PRACTICE AREAS:** Shipping and Aviation Finance; Sale/Purchase; Leasing; Joint Ventures.

J.E. BENNETT. LANGUAGES: English. **PRACTICE AREAS:** Mergers and Acquisitions; Equity Financing; Joint Ventures; Share Schemes; Re-Constructions.

S.L. ALLAN. LANGUAGES: English, French, Italian and Spanish. **PRACTICE AREAS:** Commercial Property.

P.W. STELEY. LANGUAGES: English. **PRACTICE AREAS:** Retail Property Development.

M.R. GIBSON. LANGUAGES: English. **PRACTICE AREAS:** Construction Law.

T.J. FLEET. LANGUAGES: English. **PRACTICE AREAS:** Construction Law.

S.J. KILDAHL. LANGUAGES: English. **PRACTICE AREAS:** Property Financing and Insolvency.

D.G. HALLIDAY. LANGUAGES: English. **PRACTICE AREAS:** Banking.

J.M.C. BLACKBURNE. LANGUAGES: English. **PRACTICE AREAS:** Shipping; Insurance; Re-Insurance; Professional Indemnity; Construction Litigation.

C.D.M. CANN. LANGUAGES: English. **PRACTICE AREAS:** Commercial Property; Institutional Property; Portfolio Management.

R.D. COHEN. LANGUAGES: English. **PRACTICE AREAS:** Property, Rating and Construction Litigation; Arbitration.

C.L. MILTON. LANGUAGES: English. **PRACTICE AREAS:** Property Development.

C.A. MCCORMACK. LANGUAGES: English. **PRACTICE AREAS:** Commercial Property; Retail Property Development; Local Government Property Work.

S.J. GOODMAN. LANGUAGES: English. **PRACTICE AREAS:** Eastern Europe; International Company Law; Mergers and Acquisitions; Corporate Finance; Japanese Investment in UK; Joint Ventures.

T.J. PUGH. LANGUAGES: English. **PRACTICE AREAS:** Planning; Highways; Infrastructure; Water; Environment Law.

D.A. ROBINS. LANGUAGES: English. **PRACTICE AREAS:** Insolvency; Stockbroking and Cross-Border Finance; Re-Constructions and Re-Organisations.

P.H. OLMER. LANGUAGES: English, French and Hebrew. **PRACTICE AREAS:** Commercial Property; Acquisitions; Disposals; Leasing; Development; Portfolio Transactions.

M.E. DALEY. LANGUAGES: English. **PRACTICE AREAS:** Banking.

D.P. ROSENBERG. LANGUAGES: English, German and Hebrew. **PRACTICE AREAS:** Mergers and Acquisitions; Corporate Finance; New Issues; Reconstructions; Joint Ventures.

L.D.H. HASSETT. LANGUAGES: English, French and German. **PRACTICE AREAS:** Banking Litigation; Financial Institutions Litigation; Insurance Litigation.

I.W. LYNCH. LANGUAGES: English. **PRACTICE AREAS:** Property Development; General Commercial Conveyancing.

F.A.G. CARPANINI. LANGUAGES: English and Italian. **PRACTICE AREAS:** Venture Capital; Joint Ventures; Acquisitions and Mergers.

SENIOR ASSOCIATES

A. BUNKER. LANGUAGES: English and French. **PRACTICE AREAS:** Commercial Taxation; Tax Investigations; Taxation Litigation.

(This Listing Continued)

S.A. NUNES. *LANGUAGES:* English and Swahili. *PRACTICE AREAS:* Pensions; Immigration.

G.S. CRIGHTON. *LANGUAGES:* English. *PRACTICE AREAS:* Planning and Environment Law; Retail Development Planning.

D.P. TAYLOR. *LANGUAGES:* English. *PRACTICE AREAS:* Commercial Property; Public Sector Property Law.

I.R. TREHEARNE. *LANGUAGES:* English, French and German. *PRACTICE AREAS:* Planning and Environment Law; Development Planning.

S J BERWIN & CO

Established in 1982

222 GRAYS INN ROAD
LONDON WC1X 8HB, ENGLAND
Telephone: 0171-837 2222
Fax: 0171-833 2860 DX 255 London

Brussels, Belgium Office: Square de Meeûs 19, Bte 3, 1040. Telephone: 32 2 511 5340. Fax: 32 2 511 5917.

Agency & Distribution, Anti-trust & Trade Regulation, Arbitration, Banking, Civil Law, Commercial Law, Commercial Litigation, Commercial Property, Communications and Media, Company Law, Computers & Software, Construction, Copyright, Corporate Finance, Development/Project Finance, Employee Benefits, Entertainment & Media, Environmental, EU & Competition, Franchising, Immigration, Insolvency, Intellectual Property, International Law, Investments, Employment, Mergers & Acquisitions, Patents, Planning, Securities, Taxation (Corporate, Personal, International), Telecommunications, Trademarks, Trusts & Estates, Venture Capital.

SENIOR PARTNER

DAVID T.D. HARREL, admitted, 1975, England. *Education:* LL.B. (Hons). (Head, Litigation Department). *PRACTICE AREAS:* Commercial/International Litigation.

PARTNERS

STEPHEN P. WILLSON, admitted, 1971, England. (Head, Property Department). *PRACTICE AREAS:* Commercial Property/Planning.

PHILIP GOLDENBERG, admitted, 1972, England. *Education:* MA (Oxon). *PRACTICE AREAS:* Corporate Finance; Employee Share Ownership; Environmental Law.

STEPHEN D. KON, admitted, 1980, England. *Education:* B.A. (Hons). (Head, Commercial Department). *LANGUAGES:* French. *PRACTICE AREAS:* EU/Competition Law.

JONATHAN A. METLISS, admitted, 1973, England. *Education:* LL.B. (Hons). (Head, Insolvency Group). *PRACTICE AREAS:* Corporate Finance; Reconstructions (Reorganizations); Insolvency.

JONATHAN E. BLAKE, admitted, 1979, England. *Education:* M.A. LL.M. (Cantab) ATII. (Head, Venture Capital Group). *LANGUAGES:* French. *PRACTICE AREAS:* Venture Capital.

JOHN D. ELDRIDGE, admitted, 1979, England. *Education:* B.A. (Hons). *LANGUAGES:* French. *PRACTICE AREAS:* Commercial Property.

ROBERT P. BURROW, admitted, 1975, England. *Education:* M.A. (Cantab). (Head, Corporate Finance). *LANGUAGES:* French, Spanish. *PRACTICE AREAS:* Corporate Finance; Mergers and Acquisitions.

MRS. GILLIAN S. SMITH, admitted, 1977, England. *Education:* M.A. (Oxon); LL.B. (Cantab). *LANGUAGES:* French. *PRACTICE AREAS:* Banking.

JOHN F.G. WILLIAMS, admitted, 1966, England. *Education:* M.A. (Oxon); LL.B. (Cantab). *PRACTICE AREAS:* Corporate Finance.

CHARLES ABRAMS, admitted, 1976, England. *Education:* B.A. (Cantab). (Head, Securities Regulation Group). *PRACTICE AREAS:* Securities Law.

JEFFREY S. SMITH, admitted, 1978, England. *Education:* B.Sc. (Hons). *PRACTICE AREAS:* Commercial Property.

MICHAEL A. TRASK, admitted, 1983, England. *Education:* M.A. (Oxon). *PRACTICE AREAS:* International/Corporate Tax; Trusts and Estates.

(This Listing Continued)

PETER W. ANDERSON, admitted, 1978, England. *Education:* M.A. (Cantab). *PRACTICE AREAS:* Corporate Finance; Takeovers and Acquisitions; Insolvency.

BRUCE GARDNER, admitted, 1981, England. *Education:* LL.B.; LL.M. *PRACTICE AREAS:* Securities Law.

MISS NICOLA S. WALKER, admitted, 1980, England. *Education:* LL.B. (Hons). *PRACTICE AREAS:* Commercial Litigation/Employment.

PETER J. DAVIS, admitted, 1978, England. *Education:* M.A. (Cantab). *LANGUAGES:* German. *PRACTICE AREAS:* Commercial Property.

MICHAEL ROSE, admitted, 1954, England. *Education:* B.A. (Hons). *LANGUAGES:* French, Italian, German, Spanish. *PRACTICE AREAS:* International Commercial Law; Environmental Law.

IAN A.E. INSLEY, admitted, 1981, England. *Education:* LL.B.; LL.M. *LANGUAGES:* French. *PRACTICE AREAS:* Commercial Litigation; Construction Law; Environmental Law.

TIMOTHY H.C. TAYLOR, admitted, 1980, England. *Education:* B.A. (Oxon). *LANGUAGES:* French. *PRACTICE AREAS:* International/Commercial Litigation.

MRS. JOSYANE R. GOLD, admitted, 1981, England. *Education:* LL.B. *LANGUAGES:* French. *PRACTICE AREAS:* Venture Capital.

MISS PATRICIA E. THOMAS, admitted, 1974, England. *Education:* M.A. (Oxon). *PRACTICE AREAS:* Planning and Environmental Law.

DAVID S. RYLAND, admitted, 1981, England. *Education:* B.A. (Oxon). *LANGUAGES:* Latin/Greek. *PRACTICE AREAS:* Commercial Property; Development Finance; Insolvency.

JOHN M. OSLER, admitted, 1964, England. *Education:* M.A. (Oxon). *LANGUAGES:* French. *PRACTICE AREAS:* Corporate Finance; Mergers and Acquisitions.

BRYAN J. PICKUP, admitted, 1964, England. *Education:* M.A. (Cantab). *LANGUAGES:* French. *PRACTICE AREAS:* Commercial Property; Licensing.

NIGEL S. PALMER, admitted, 1979, England. *Education:* M.A. (Oxon). *LANGUAGES:* French, Italian, German. *PRACTICE AREAS:* Entertainment and Media; Trademarks and Copyright.

MARTIN J. BOWEN, admitted, 1983, England. *Education:* B.A. (Hons). *PRACTICE AREAS:* Venture Capital.

NICHOLAS SHATTOCK, admitted, 1984, England. *Education:* B.A. (Hons). *LANGUAGES:* French. *PRACTICE AREAS:* Commercial Property.

MISS RHONDA BAKER, admitted, 1987, England. *Education:* M.A. (Cantab). *LANGUAGES:* French. *PRACTICE AREAS:* Entertainment and Media; Trademarks and Copyright.

PETER B.G. MCINERNEY, admitted, 1982, England. *Education:* LL.B. *PRACTICE AREAS:* Entertainment and Media.

MARTIN C. WRIGHT, admitted, 1979, England. *Education:* B.A. (Hons). *PRACTICE AREAS:* Commercial Property.

GRAEME D. LEVY, admitted, 1985, England. *Education:* M.A. (Cantab). *PRACTICE AREAS:* Corporate Finance; Takeovers and Acquisitions; Insolvency.

RICHARD M. SLOWE, admitted, 1970, England; Barrister. *PRACTICE AREAS:* Commercial Litigation/Advocacy.

RAY D. BLACK, admitted, 1976, England; 1977, Hong Kong; 1983, Victoria, Australia; 1989, New York. *Education:* LL.B. *LANGUAGES:* French, Hebrew. *PRACTICE AREAS:* Intellectual Property; Commercial Litigation.

DAVID L. HINDS, admitted, 1976, England; 1981, New Zealand; 1988, New South Wales, Australia. *Education:* M.A. (Cantab); LL.M. Tax. *LANGUAGES:* French, German, Spanish. *PRACTICE AREAS:* Corporate/International Tax.

MICHAEL N. METLISS, admitted, 1984, England. *Education:* B.A. (Hons). *PRACTICE AREAS:* Commercial Litigation; Insolvency.

SIMON N. MCLEOD, admitted, 1982, England. *Education:* LL.B. *PRACTICE AREAS:* Corporate Finance; Mergers and Acquisitions; MBO's.

RALPH J. COHEN, admitted, 1983, England. *Education:* LL.B. *LANGUAGES:* French. *PRACTICE AREAS:* EU/Trade/Commercial.

(This Listing Continued)

S J BERWIN & CO, London—Continued

ELEANOR E. PAUL, admitted, 1982, Scotland; 1990, England. *Education:* LL.B. (Hons.). *PRACTICE AREAS:* Commercial; Intellectual Property; Telecommunications; Franchising.

MATTHEW D.J. HUDSON, admitted, 1987, England. *Education:* LL.B. *LANGUAGES:* French. *PRACTICE AREAS:* Corporate Finance; MBO's.

JOHN R. OLSEN, *Member:* New York State Bar Association; State Bar of California. *LANGUAGES:* French, German, Spanish. *PRACTICE AREAS:* Trademarks.

RHODRI DAVIES, admitted, 1987, England. *Education:* University College, London (LL.B.). *LANGUAGES:* Welsh. *PRACTICE AREAS:* Banking.

GEOFFREY N. HALEY, admitted, 1971, England. *Education:* LL.B., M.B.A., MCIM. *PRACTICE AREAS:* Construction; Project Finance; Energy; Transportation; Urban Renewal.

NICK WILLIAMS, admitted, 1984, England. *Education:* M.A. (Cantab). *PRACTICE AREAS:* Corporate Finance; Take-overs; Mergers and Acquisitions.

KAY B. BUTLER, admitted, 1987, England. *Education:* LL.B. (Hons); LL.M. Tax. *LANGUAGES:* French. *PRACTICE AREAS:* Corporate Taxation; VAT.

MAURICE FIREMAN, admitted, 1966, England. *Education:* B.A. Hons., M.A. (Cantab). *LANGUAGES:* French. *PRACTICE AREAS:* Commercial Property.

SIMON E. HOLMES, admitted, 1983, England. *Education:* M.A. (Cantab); Li.Sp.Dr.Eur. (Brussels University). *LANGUAGES:* French. *PRACTICE AREAS:* EU/Trade.

JEREMY R. SCHRIRE, admitted, 1986, England. *Education:* B.A. Hons. (University of Cape Town); LL.B. (London School of Economics). *LANGUAGES:* Afrikaans. *PRACTICE AREAS:* Commercial.

DOMINIC P. ADAMS, admitted, 1987, England. *Education:* LL.B. (Hons). *PRACTICE AREAS:* Taxation.

STEVEN DAVIS, admitted, 1989, England. *Education:* LL.B. (Hons). *LANGUAGES:* French. *PRACTICE AREAS:* Venture Capital.

CONSULTANTS

JONATHAN M.L. STONE, admitted, 1969, England. *Education:* M.A. (Oxon). *LANGUAGES:* French, Italian, German.

LORD CLINTON-DAVIS, admitted, 1953, England. *Education:* LL.B. Member of the Commission of the European Communities responsible for Transport, Environmental and Nuclear Safety, 1985-1989. *LANGUAGES:* French. *PRACTICE AREAS:* Environmental Law.

SIDNEY PREVEZER, admitted, 1956, England. *Education:* M.A. (Cantab); LL.M. (Harvard). *LANGUAGES:* French and German. *PRACTICE AREAS:* Commercial/Litigation.

BIDDLE & CO.

1 GRESHAM STREET
LONDON EC2V 7BU, ENGLAND
Telephone: 0171-606 9301
Telex: 888197 BIDDLE G
Facsimile: 0171-606 3305

Company and Commercial Law, Taxation, Intellectual Property, Commercial Property, Defamation and Media Law, Litigation, Employment, Pensions Law, Personal Finance, Trusts, Probate and Wills.

PARTNERS

Hugh Johnson	David Hooper
Martin Sharman	Martin Webster
Christopher Winder	Jonathan Reardon
Peter Watson	Kim Walker
David Biddle	Mark Cawthron
Charles Rossetti	Belinda Benney
Charles Mathiesen	Christopher Mullen
Ian Clark	Julia Busby

(This Listing Continued)

Patrick Walsh	Roger Fink
Martin Winter	William Dixon
Hugh Arthur	Julian Harris
Desmond O'Connell	Martin Lane
Geoffrey Tyler	David Lancaster
	James Wolsey

Member of Logos: A Group of Law Firms with offices throughout the European Community.

BIGHAM ENGLAR JONES & HOUSTON

LLOYDS SUITE 699
1 LIME STREET
LONDON EC3M 7DQ, ENGLAND
Telephone: 71-283-9541
Cable: "Kedge"
Telex: 893323 BEJH G
Telefax: 016262382 GR I II III

New York, N.Y. Office: 14 Wall Street, 10005-2140. Telephone: 212-732-4646. Cable: "Kedge." Telex: RCA 235332 BEJHUR. Telefax: 2126190781 GR I II III; 2122279491 GR I II III.
Newark, New Jersey Office: One Gateway Center, 07102-5311. Telephone: 201-643-1303. Telecopier: 201-643-1124.

Firm engaged in American and International Law Practice, but not authorized to appear before the English Courts or to act as Solicitors.

(For Biographical data on all Partners, see Professional Biographies at New York, New York)

BINGHAM, DANA & GOULD

39 VICTORIA STREET
LONDON SWIH 0EE, ENGLAND
Telephone: 011-44-171-799-2646
Telecopy: 011-44-171-799-2654

Boston, Massachusetts Office: 150 Federal Street. Telephone: 617-951-8000. Telecopy: 617-951-8736.
Hartford, Connecticut Office: 100 Pearl Street. Telephone: 203-244-3770. Telefax: 203-527-5188.
Washington, D.C. Office: 1550 M Street, N.W. Telephone: 202-822-9320. Telecopy: 202-833-1506.

General Business Practice, International Finance, Cross-Border Acquisitions, Joint Ventures, Equity Investments, Debt Restructuring, International Tax Planning, International Licenses.
Firm engaged in American and International Law Practice, but not authorized to appear before the English Courts or to act as Solicitors.

RESIDENT PARTNERS

JAY S. ZIMMERMAN, born 1954; admitted, 1981, New York; 1982, Massachusetts (Not admitted in England). *Education:* Harvard University (A.B., magna cum laude, 1976; J.D., cum laude, 1980).

MARK A. ANDREW, born 1959; admitted, 1985, Massachusetts (Not admitted in England). *Education:* Northwestern University (B.A., 1981; J.D., magna cum laude, 1985). Order of the Coif. Member, Northwestern Law Review, 1984-1985. Author: "United States v. Welden: The Constitutionality of the Victim and Witness Protection Act of 1982," 79 N.W.U.L. Rev. 566, 1984.

RESIDENT ASSOCIATES

T. MALCOLM SANDILANDS, born 1965; admitted, 1990, Massachusetts (Not admitted in England). *Education:* New College, Oxford University (B.A., 1986); University of Michigan (J.D., cum laude, 1989).

LORAINE DE JONG, born 1963; admitted, 1990, California; 1991, District of Columbia (Not admitted in England). *Education:* Boston University, College of Communication (B.S., magna cum laude, 1985); London School of Economics and Political Science; Rutgers University (J.D., with high honors, 1989). Member, 1987-1989 and Notes and Comments Editor, 1988-1989, Rutgers Law Journal.

SUSAN SPRING, born 1967; admitted, 1991, England. *Education:* Bristol University (LL.B., with honors, 1987); Guildford College of Law (Law Society Finals, 1988). *LANGUAGES:* French.

(For Complete Biographical Data on all Personnel, see Professional Biographies at Boston, Massachusetts)

BIRD & BIRD
90 FETTER LANE
LONDON EC4A 1JP, ENGLAND
Telephone: (44) 171 242 6681
Telex: 25581 BIRDS G
Facsimile: (44) 171-242 3643

Brussels, Belgium Office: 209A Avenue Louise, 1050. Telephone: (32) 2 644 3616. Fax: (32) 2 644 2486.

Arbitration, Banking, Biotechnology, Charities, Company Law, Commercial Law, Commercial Litigation, Competition, EC Law, Employment, Environmental Law, Corporate Finance, Health Care and Hospital Law, Intellectual Property, Medical Negligence, Media and Entertainment Law, Multimedia, Property, Planning Law, Public Sector Law, Shipping, Sports Law, International Trade, Information Technology, Technology Transfer, Telecommunications, Taxation.

PARTNERS

DAVID HARRISS, MA (Cambridge), admitted, 1977. *PRACTICE AREAS:* Intellectual Property Law; Copyright, Trademark & Patent Law; Trade Secrets; Brands Law; Technology Law.

GRAHAM E. CAMPS, admitted, 1970. *PRACTICE AREAS:* Individual Tax Planning; Administration of Estates; Trust Law; Wills; Probate; Successions; Heritage Law.

JOHN R. PARKER, LL.B. (Southampton) admitted, 1972. *PRACTICE AREAS:* Commercial Litigation; Personal Injury Law; Medical Negligence; Health (Health Care) & Hospital Law; Property Litigation.

DR. MILES GAYTHWAITE, BSc. (Glasgow) PHD (Cambridge), admitted, 1978. *PRACTICE AREAS:* Intellectual Property Law; Copyright, Trademark & Patent Law; Technology Transfer; Technology Law; Biotechnology; Pharmaceuticals.

TREVOR M. COOK, BSc. (Southampton), admitted, 1977. *PRACTICE AREAS:* Intellectual Property Law; Copyright, Trademark & Patent Law; Pharmaceuticals; Publishing Law; Information Technology; Biotechnology; European Community Law.

ROBERT N. SCOTT, LL.B. (Bristol), admitted, 1974. *PRACTICE AREAS:* Commercial Property Law; Environmental Law; Property Finance; Land Use Law.

PENELOPE J. CHRISTIE, MA (Cambridge), admitted, 1977. *PRACTICE AREAS:* Commercial Litigation; Property Litigation; Personal Injury; Professional Indemnity; Employment Law.

PAULINE SMITH, LL.B (Sheffield), admitted, 1974. *PRACTICE AREAS:* Charitable Trusts & Foundations; Heritage Law; Estate Tax Planning; Administration of Estates; Trust Administration; Successions.

DAVID W. BYAM-COOK, BA Hons (Kent), admitted, 1976. *PRACTICE AREAS:* Corporate Finance Law; Mergers & Acquisitions; Leveraged & Management Buyouts; Project Finance; Partnership Law; Employment Law.

GRAHAM J.H. SMITH, LL.B (Bristol), admitted, 1978. *PRACTICE AREAS:* Commercial Litigation; Intellectual Property Law; Computer Law; Products Liability Law; Telecommunications Law.

C. PAUL HICKSON, MA (Cambridge), admitted, 1983. *PRACTICE AREAS:* Commercial Property; Building & Construction; Landlord & Tenant; Conveyancing.

JUSTIN R.C. WALKEY, BA Hons, admitted, 1984. *PRACTICE AREAS:* Commercial Law; Media Law; Entertainment Law; Sports Law.

M. DAVID KERR, MA (Cambridge), admitted, 1985. *PRACTICE AREAS:* Commercial Law; Information Technology; Facilities Management; Telecommunications Law; European Community Law.

MORAG MACDONALD, BA, Hons (Cambridge), admitted, 1988. *PRACTICE AREAS:* Intellectual Property Law; Brands Law; Copyright, Trademarks & Patent; Information Technology; European Community Law; Media Law.

DAVID M.C. STONE, MA (Cambridge), admitted, 1983. *PRACTICE AREAS:* Commercial Litigation; Personal Injury; Medical Negligence; Professional Negligence; Health Law; Defamation; Mortgage Enforcement.

CHRISTOPHER W. REES, MA (Cambridge), admitted, 1979. *PRACTICE AREAS:* Corporate Law; Commercial Law; Computer Law; Intellec-

(This Listing Continued)

tual Property Licensing; Technology Transfer; Multimedia; Facilities Management.

ROBERT S.W. BARRY, B Pharm Dip Law (London), admitted, 1989. *PRACTICE AREAS:* Intellectual Property Law; Copyright, Trademark & Patent Law; Pharmaceuticals; Technology Law.

STEPHEN J. HUBNER, MA (Cambridge), admitted, 1988. *PRACTICE AREAS:* Commercial Property Law; Environmental Law; Landlord & Tenant; Conveyancing.

P. DUNCAN QUINAN, LL.B (Southampton), admitted, 1981. *PRACTICE AREAS:* Commercial Litigation; Alternative Dispute Resolution; Maritime Law; International Trade; Transportation Law.

PHILLIP J. DANN, M.A., LL.M. (Cambridge), admitted, 1991. *PRACTICE AREAS:* Commercial Law; Telecommunications Law; Satellite Law; Computer Law; Media Law; Facilities Management.

MARK R.L. LEWIS, B.A. (Oxford), admitted 1978. *PRACTICE AREAS:* Corporate Finance Law; Mergers & Acquisitions; Leveraged & Management Buyouts; Securities Offerings; Corporate Restructuring.

HAMISH R. SANDISON, M.A. (Cambridge), LL.M. (Berkeley), admitted, 1980, District of Columbia; 1991, England and Wales. *PRACTICE AREAS:* Intellectual Property Law; Information Technology; Media Law; Public Sector Competitive Tendering; EC Public Procurement; Data Protection; Copyright.

DAVID H. AYERS, B.A. (Durham), admitted, 1987. *PRACTICE AREAS:* Commercial Law; Company Law; Mergers and Acquisitions; Telecommunications; Sponsorship; Sports Law.

RICHARD J. WARD, B.A. (Oxford), admitted, 1985. *PRACTICE AREAS:* Corporate Finance; Commercial Taxation; VAT.

SALLY A. NICOLSON, admitted, 1986. *PRACTICE AREAS:* Trademarks; Brands Law; Intellectual Property Law; Copyright.

GRAHAM S. MCGOWAN, admitted, 1965. *PRACTICE AREAS:* Local Government; Commercial Property; Planning.

RODERICK R. GRAHAM, M.A. (Cambridge), admitted, 1990. *PRACTICE AREAS:* Facilities Management; Telecommunications; Information Technology; Commercial Law.

CHARLES M. CROSTHWAITE, B.A. (York), admitted, 1977. *PRACTICE AREAS:* Corporate Finance; Mergers and Acquisitions; Securities Offerings; Leveraged and Management Buyouts.

ASSOCIATES

MADELINE J. BALL, LL.B Hons, admitted, 1989.

DAVID R. BARRON, LL.B Hons (Birmingham), admitted, 1989.

ROGER M BICKERSTAFF, M.A., M.L.Phil (Cambridge), admitted, 1990.

CAROLINE A. BODLEY, LL.B (Bristol), admitted, 1988.

LORNA C. BRAZELL, B.Sc. (Hons) (Edinburgh), admitted, 1994.

THOMAS P. BROADHURST, BSc, Ph.D. (Cambridge), admitted, 1990.

PETER R. BROWNLOW, LL.B (Leeds), admitted, 1991.

A. GAYNOR CLEMENTS, B.A. (Hons) (Aberystwyth, Wales), admitted, 1990.

DOMINIC C. J. COOK, LL.B, admitted, 1992.

ROBERT K. COOPER, LL.B Hons (Leicester), admitted, 1994.

ANTHONY G. COYNE, LL.B Hons (Brunel), admitted, 1988.

PAUL M. DILLON, LL.B Hons (Liverpool), admitted, 1990.

ALEXANDRA V.L. DRAKE, B.A. Hons Law (Durham), admitted, 1988.

FIONA H.S. FORSYTH, B.A. Joint Honours (Bangor, North Wales), admitted, 1994.

JULIAN M. GYNGELL, LL.B. (Sydney), admitted, 1986, Australia; 1991, England and Wales.

NEIL T. JENKINS, B.Sc. (Bristol), admitted, 1988.

CATHERINE M. MELIA, B.A. Law (Sussex), admitted, 1989.

DAVID R. MORGAN, M.A. (Oxford), admitted, 1966.

(This Listing Continued)

BIRD & BIRD, London—Continued

JANE M. MUTIMEAR, LL.B Hons (Sheffield), admitted, 1990.

ANNE-MARIE O'BRIEN, B.A. Hons, LL.B. (Otago, New Zealand), admitted 1991, New Zealand.

RORY G. O'CONNOR, LL.B (Bristol), admitted, 1988.

SUSAN L. PIKE, B.A. (Oxford), admitted, 1989.

GRANT POWELL, LL.B (Bristol), admitted, 1990.

FREDERICK H. PRICE, M.A. (Edinburgh), admitted, 1991.

FELICITY A. REEVE, B.A. (Hons) (Oxford), admitted, 1993.

DAVID G. REUBEN, LL.B (London), admitted, 1993.

JOHN J. REYNOLDS, B.A. (Oxon) admitted, 1991.

PAULINE R. RILEY, LL.B Hons (London), admitted, 1981.

JOANNA O. SIMS, LL.B Hons (Leicester), admitted, 1987.

JOANNE STANNARD, LL.B. (Hons) (London), admitted, 1990.

KATHARINE J. STEPHENS, M.Eng (Bristol), admitted, 1990.

ANDREW J. WHITE, B.A., (Cambridge) LL.M., (London) admitted, 1990.

ROBERT G. WILLIAMS, B.Sc. (Hons) (Exeter), admitted, 1994.

SOPHIE A. WILLIAMS, B.A. Hons. (Oxford) admitted, 1992.

DAVID L. WILSON, B.Sc Hons (London), called to the Bar, 1993.

STUDIO LEGALE BISCONTI

1 COLLEGE HILL
LONDON EC4R 4RA, ENGLAND
Telephone: (44-0171) 4899924
Telex: 893544 BRACTO G
Fax: (44-0171) 4898740

Rome, Italy Office: Via Bissolati, 76, 00187. Telephone: (39-6) 479881. Telex: 610409 BRACTO I. Fax: (39-6) 487-2070.

Milan, Italy Office: Via Santo Spirito, 14, 20121. Telephone: (39-2) 782641. Telex: 335009 BRACTO I. Fax: (39-2) 781188.

New York, New York Office: 730 Fifth Avenue, 10019. Telephone: (212) 956-9400. Telex: 225120 BRACTON UR. Fax: (212) 956-9405.

Corporate Practice, Mergers and Acquisitions, Securities, International Finance and Banking, International Law, Domestic and International Taxation, EEC Law, Corporate Law, Labor, Bankruptcy, Environmental Law, Energy, Antitrust, Unfair Compensation, Telecommunications. Patent, Trademarks, Alternative Dispute Resolution. Counselling in International Commercial Transactions.

GIUSEPPE BARRECA, born Rome, Italy, March 22, 1960; admitted to practice, 1984; admitted, 1986, Italy (Not admitted in England). *Education:* Italy, University of Rome (Doctor of Jurisprudence, maxima cum laude, 1984). Academy of American and International Law, Southwestern Legal Foundation, Dallas, 1988; L.U.I.S.S. Libera Universita' Internazionale degli Studi Sociali, Rome (Professorial Assistant, 1985-1987). *Member:* Italian Bar Association (Rome); International Bar Association. **LANGUAGES:** Italian and English.

BLAKE, CASSELS & GRAYDON

Established in 1857
27 AUSTIN FRIARS
LONDON EC2N 2QQ, ENGLAND
Telephone: 0171-374-2334
Facsimile: 0171-638-3342

Toronto, Ontario Office: Box 25, Commerce Court West, M5L 1A9. Telephone: 416-863-2400. Facsimile: 416-863-2653. Telex: 06-219687. Internet: toronto@blakes.ca.

Ottawa, Ontario Office: World Exchange Plaza, 20th Floor, 45 O'Connor Street, K1P 1A4. Telephone: 613-788-2200. Facsimile: 613-594-3965. Internet: ottawa@blakes.ca.

Calgary, Alberta Office: Bankers Hall East, Suite 3500, 855-2nd Street S.W., T2P 4J8. Telephone: 403-260-9600. Facsimile: 403-263-9895. Internet: calgary@blakes.ca.

(This Listing Continued)

Vancouver, British Columbia Office: 1700-1030 West Georgia Street, V6E 2Y3. Telephone: 604-631-3300. Telecopier: 604-631-3309 - 16th Floor; 604-631-3305 - 17th Floor. Internet: vancouvr@blakes.ca.

Firm engaged in Canadian and International Law Practice, but not authorized to appear before the English Courts or to act as Solicitors.

FIRM PROFILE: *Blake, Cassels & Graydon is one of Canada's leading national law firms, with over 350 lawyers, serving its national and international clients through five offices across Canada and in Europe.*

PARTNERS

DAVID G. GLENNIE, born Toronto, Ontario, 1954; admitted, 1982, Ontario (Not admitted in England). *Education:* University of Toronto (B.A., 1976; M.A., 1977; LL.B., 1980). Selected publications: "Canada," Mergers and Acquisitions (IFR, loose-leaf text); "Regulation S: the Canadian Response," International Financial Law Review, 01-89; "Placements of Canadian Securities in Europe" (Conference), 06-89; "Competition Law in Canada," International Financial Law Review, 07-89; "New Investments and Acquisitions in Canada," AIJA Annual Congress, 09-89; "Canada's Competition Tribunal Under Attack," International Financial Law Review, 06-90; "Regulation S and Tefra - Implications for International Offerings," Securities and Corporate Regulation Review, 09-90; "Canada/U.S. Securities Laws - New Proposals," Journal of International Banking Law, 05-91; "Merger Enforcement Guidelines," Butterworths Journal of International Banking and Financial Law, 06-91; "Canada/U.S. Reciprocal Disclosure System for Securities," Butterworth's Journal of International Banking and Financial Law, 09-91; "International Securities Law Aspects of Privatizations," American Bar Association, Section of Business Law, 04-92. Co-Chairman, International Offerings of Debt and Equity Securities, AIJA Annual Congress, 09-91. Secretary, Banking and Finance Commission, AIJA, 1991—. *Member:* Canadian Bar Association; International Bar Association; Union Internationale des Avocats; AIJA. **PRACTICE AREAS:** Business; Securities.

ASSOCIATES

JEFFREY R. LLOYD, born 1964; admitted, 1991, Ontario (Not admitted in England). *Education:* University of Alberta (B.Comm., 1986); University of Toronto (LL.B., 1989). *Member:* Canadian and International Bar Associations; AIJA. **PRACTICE AREAS:** Business; Securities.

(For biographical data on other personnel, see Professional Biographies at Toronto and Ottawa, Ontario, Calgary, Alberta and Vancouver, British Columbia)

BLAKE DAWSON WALDRON

LEVEL 5
66 GRESHAM STREET
LONDON EC2V 7BB, ENGLAND
Telephone: (0171) 600 3030
Facsimile: (0171) 600 3392

Sydney, New South Wales, Australia Office: Grosvenor Place 225 George Street 2000. Telephone: (02) 2586000. Facsimile: (02) 2586999. Telex: AA22867DWN.

Melbourne, Victoria, Australia Office: 101 Collins Street, 3000. Telephone: (03) 679 3000. Facsimile: (03) 679 3111. Telex: AA31033.

Brisbane, Queensland, Australia Office: Riverside Centre, 123 Eagle Street, 4000. Telephone: (07) 259 7000. Facsimile: (07) 259 7111. Telex: AA22867DWN.

Perth, Western Australia, Australia Office: Forrest Centre, 221 St. George's Terrace, 6000. Telephone: (09) 366 8000. Facsimile: (09) 366 8111. Telex: AA22867DWN.

Canberra, Australian Capital Territory, Australia Office: 12 Moore Street, 2601. Telephone: (06) 234 4000. Facsimile: (06) 234 4111. Telex: AA22867DWN.

Port Moresby, Papua New Guinea Office: Mogoru Moto Building, Champion Parade. Telephone: (675) 21 1977. Facsimile: (675) 212630. Telex: NE 22223.

Jakarta, Indonesia Associated Office: Soebagjo, Roosdiono, Jatim & Djarot. Chase Plaza, Jalan Jendral Sudirman Kav 21, 12910. Telephone: (6221) 570 6436. Fax: (6221) 570 6437. Telex: 62 941 SRJDIA.

Port Vila, Vanuatu Associated Office: Hudson & Co. Lo Lam House, Kumul Highway. Telephone: (678) 22166. Fax: (678) 24260.

FIRM PROFILE: *One of Australia's largest national law firms providing legal services in all areas required by commerce, finance and government. The firm has offices in all the major Australian commercial centres. Our*

(This Listing Continued)

practice also has international offices in London, Port Moresby and associated offices in Jakarta and Port Vila.

LONDON RESIDENT PARTNER

JUSTIN SHMITH. *PRACTICE AREAS:* Banking; Finance.

LONDON SENIOR ASSOCIATE

AMANDA BARNETT. *PRACTICE AREAS:* Corporate and Commercial Law.

(For complete personnel and biographical data, see professional biographies at Sydney, Australia)

BODEN OPPENHOFF RASOR RAUE

LONDON, ENGLAND

(See Oppenhoff & Rädler)

BOMCHIL CASTRO GOODRICH CLARO AROSEMENA & ASSOCIATES

Established in 1971

3RD FLOOR, GLOBE HOUSE
4 TEMPLE PLACE
LONDON WC2R 3HP, ENGLAND
Telephone: (44 171) 240 1755
Fax: (44 171) 240 1808

European Representative Offices:
Paris, France Office: 15, rue Greuze, 75116. Telephone: 47270310. Fax: 47 27 37 81.
Lisbon, Portugal Office: Av. Infante Santo, 17, 8 Esq. Telephone: 397 3490. Telex: 65986 INTLAW. Fax: 397 3155.
Associated Offices:
Buenos Aires, Argentina Office: M. & M. Bomchil.
La Paz, Bolivia Office: C. R. & F. Rojas Estudio de Abogados.
São Paulo, Brazil Office: Castro, Barros, Sobral e Xavier Advogados.
Rio de Janeiro, Brazil Office: Castro, Barros, Sobral e Xavier Advogados.
London, England Office: Castro, Barros, Sobral e Xavier Advogados.
Santiago, Chile Office: Claro y Cia.
Bogotá, Colombia Office: Brigard & Urrutia.
Quito, Ecuador Office: Bustamante & Bustamante.
San Salvador, El Salvador Office: Romero Pineda & Asociados.
Guatemala, Guatemala Office: Mayora & Mayora.
San Pedro Sula, Honduras Office: Mejía y Asociados.
Mexico, D.F., Mexico Office: Goodrich, Riquelme y Asociados.
Tijuana, Baja California, Mexico Office: Goodrich, Riquelme y Asociados.
Paris, France Office: Goodrich, Riquelme y Asociados.
Managua, Nicaragua Office: Alvarado y Asociados.
Panama, Republic of Panama Office: Arosemena, Noriega & Contreras.
London, England Office: Arosemena, Noriega & Contreras.
Asuncion, Paraguay Office: Estudio Mersan Abogados.
San Juan (Hato Rey), Puerto Rico Office: Fidler, Gonzalez & Rodriguez.
Montevideo, Uruguay Office: Bado, Kuster, Zerbino & Rachetti.
Caracas, Venezuela Office: Bentata, Hoet & Asociados.

FIRM PROFILE: *Association of Latin American Law Firms not authorized to appear before the English courts or to act as Solicitors.*

EXECUTIVE SECRETARY

David H. Brill, Jr.

(Mr. Brill may be reached at the following address: Paseo de la Reforma 355 2° piso, 06500 México, D.F. Telephone: (525) 5 33 00 40. Fax: (525) 5 25 12 27.)

(For address and complete information on each associated firm, see appropriate country)

BOODLE HATFIELD

Established in 1730
43 BROOK STREET
LONDON W1Y 2BL, ENGLAND
Telephone: 0171 629 7411
Fax: 0171 629 2621

Southampton, England Office: Town Quay House, 7 Town Quay, SO1 0XN. Telephone: 01703 332001. Fax: 01703 222480.
Oxford, England Office: 6 Worcester Street, Oxford OX1 2BX. Telephone: 01865 790744. Fax: 01865 798764.
Madrid, Spain Associated Office: Villanueva 29, 28001. Telephone: 577 5502. Fax: 431 0413. Telex: 48564.
Bonn, Germany Associated Office: Oxfordstrasse 24, 53111 Bonn. Telephone: 0228/726250. Fax: 0228/650479.
Paris, France Associated Office: 250 bis Boulevard Saint Germain, Paris, 75007. Telephone: 4 9 54 90 00. Fax: 49 54 90 01.

Commercial and Residential Property, Planning, Environment, Construction, Corporate and Commercial, Employment, Commercial Litigation, Intellectual Property, Insolvency, UK and International Tax and Financial Planning, Trusts, EC Competition Law, Services in Spain, Germany and France.

PARTNERS

P.E.W. SCOBLE, admitted, 1962, London. ***PRACTICE AREAS:*** Landlord and Tenant; Residential Property; Leasehold Reform.

B.A.J. RADCLIFFE, admitted, 1963, London. ***LANGUAGES:*** Italian. ***PRACTICE AREAS:*** Commercial and Residential Property; Development; Planning.

N.S. HASSALL, admitted, 1962, London. ***PRACTICE AREAS:*** Trusts and Tax; Pensions; Charities.

M.B. WOOD, admitted, 1967, London. ***PRACTICE AREAS:*** Commercial Property; Town Centre and Industrial Developments.

D.A. D'ARCY HUGHES, admitted, 1969, Southampton. ***PRACTICE AREAS:*** Commercial and Residential Property.

R.M. MOYSE, admitted, 1970, London. ***PRACTICE AREAS:*** Tax; Trusts; International Financial Planning.

S. RALPH, admitted, 1975, London. Licensed Insolvency Practitioner. ***LANGUAGES:*** French. ***PRACTICE AREAS:*** Commercial Litigation; Insolvency; Partnership Disputes.

J.H. GRICE, admitted, 1970, Southampton. ***PRACTICE AREAS:*** Commercial and Residential Property.

M.G. TULLOCH, admitted, 1970, London. ***LANGUAGES:*** French and German. ***PRACTICE AREAS:*** Property Litigation; Family and Matrimonial Law.

T.J.C. MANNING, admitted, 1973, London. ***PRACTICE AREAS:*** Commercial Property; Development; Joint Ventures; Funding.

A.N. DRAKE, admitted, 1976, London. ***PRACTICE AREAS:*** Acquisitions and Disposals; Employment; Distributorship Agreements.

SUE LAING, admitted, 1978, Oxford. ***PRACTICE AREAS:*** Tax; Trusts; UK and International Financial Planning.

V.R. COCKRELL, admitted, 1975, Southampton. ***PRACTICE AREAS:*** Residential Property.

KATE HOWE, admitted, 1982, London. ***PRACTICE AREAS:*** Tax; VAT; UK and International Financial Planning.

T.E.F. SUTHERLAND, admitted, 1972, London. ***PRACTICE AREAS:*** Commercial Property; Environmental Law.

LUCY A. SLATER, admitted, 1984, London. ***PRACTICE AREAS:*** Commercial Property; Planning.

K.J.B. TURTON, admitted, 1985, London. ***LANGUAGES:*** German. ***PRACTICE AREAS:*** Commercial Property; Development; Construction.

A. IRASTORZA, admitted, 1977, Madrid; 1985, London. ***LANGUAGES:*** Spanish and French. ***PRACTICE AREAS:*** Anglo-Spanish Service; English and Spanish Corporate Law; Anglo-French Service.

M.C.L. MACPHERSON, admitted, 1985, Southampton. ***PRACTICE AREAS:*** Acquisitions and Disposals; Joint Ventures; MBO's; Insolvency.

P.S. GARRY, admitted, 1981, London. ***PRACTICE AREAS:*** Commercial Litigation; Insolvency; Fraud.

(This Listing Continued)

BOODLE HATFIELD, London—Continued

J.C.K. HAMBLIN, admitted, 1987, Southampton. **LANGUAGES:** French and Spanish. **PRACTICE AREAS:** Commercial Litigation; Construction.

S.F. JONES, admitted, 1991, London. Chartered Patent Agent. **PRACTICE AREAS:** Intellectual Property; Patent, Trade Mark and Design Law; Pharmaceuticals.

C.J. WHITEHOUSE, admitted, 1993, London. **PRACTICE AREAS:** Tax and Financial Planning; Trusts.

D.L. SHERMAN, admitted, 1968, New York; 1972, Arizona. (Not admitted in England). **LANGUAGES:** French and German. **PRACTICE AREAS:** International Corporate Law.

N.J. PAGE, admitted, 1981, Southampton. **PRACTICE AREAS:** M and A; Joint Ventures; Company and Commercial.

P.J. PENNAL, admitted, 1989, London. **PRACTICE AREAS:** Commercial Litigation; Environment.

N.P. STONE, admitted, 1985, London. **PRACTICE AREAS:** M and A; Banking; Company and Commercial.

S.A. RENTON, admitted, 1976, London. **LANGUAGES:** Russian and Czech. **PRACTICE AREAS:** M and A; Joint Ventures; Company and Commercial.

C.H. PUTT, admitted, 1984, London. **LANGUAGES:** German. **PRACTICE AREAS:** M and A; Equity Finance; Anglo-German Service.

KRISTIEN GEEURICKX, admitted, 1981, Belgium (Not admitted in England). **LANGUAGES:** Dutch and French. **PRACTICE AREAS:** European Law; Competition Law.

BOWMAN GILFILLAN HAYMAN GODFREY

36 JOHN STREET
LONDON WC1N 2AT, ENGLAND
Telephone: (0171) 430-0888
Fax: (0171) 430-2030

Johannesburg, South Africa Office: Bowman Gilfillan Hayman Godfrey Inc., JCI House, 12th Floor, 28 Harrison Street, P.O. Box 2439, 2001. Telephone: 27-11-836-2811. Telefax: 27-11-836-6909.

South African Corporate and Commercial Law, Income Tax, Property Law, Mining Law, Litigation, Labor Law, Estate Planning and Administration.
Members of the Law Society of the Transvaal, South Africa.

DAVID PETER ANDERSON, admitted, 1988, Supreme Court of South Africa; 1991, Solicitor of the Supreme Court of England and Wales. *Education:* B.A. (Rand); LL.B. (Rand).

BRACEWELL & PATTERSON, L.L.P.

A Registered Limited Liability Partnership

Established in 1945

43 BROOK STREET
LONDON W1Y 2BL, ENGLAND
Telephone: 011-44-171-355-3330
Telex: 261414
Cable Address: "Bookin London W 1"
Fax: 011-44-171-629-2621

Houston, Texas Office: South Tower Pennzoil Place, 711 Louisiana Street, Suite 2900, 77002-2781. Telephone: 713-223-2900. Telex: 76-2141. Cable Address: "Bracepat-Houston". Fax: 713-221-1212.
Austin, Texas Office: 100 Congress Avenue, Suite 1900, 78701-4042. Telephone: 512-472-7800. Fax: 512-472-9123.
Dallas, Texas Office: Lincoln Plaza, 500 N. Akard Street, Suite 4000, 75201-3387. Telephone: 214-740-4000. Fax: 214-740-4010.
Washington, D.C. Office: 2000 K Street, N.W., Suite 500, 20006-1809. Telephone: 202-828-5800. Telex: 89-2573. Cable Address: "Bracepat WSH". Fax: 202-223-1225.

(This Listing Continued)

General International Law.
Firm engaged in American and International Law Practice, but not authorized to appear before the English Courts or to act as Solicitors.

PARTNERS

KEVIN J. ALEXANDER, born London, England, December 26, 1953; admitted, 1979, England, Solicitor of the Supreme Court of England and Wales; 1985, New York. *Education:* St. John's College, Cambridge, England (B.A., Hons, 1976); College of Law, Guildford, England. *Member:* Law Society of England and Wales; American Bar Association. **PRACTICE AREAS:** Corporate.

(For Data on all Firm Personnel see Professional Biographies at Houston, Dallas and Austin, Texas and Washington, D.C.).

BRECHER & CO.

Established in 1953

78 BROOK STREET, GROSVENOR SQUARE
LONDON W1Y 2AD, ENGLAND
Telephone: 0171 493 5141
Fax: 0171 493 6255
Telex: 263486 Brelaw G

Associated Offices: Paris, Berlin, Munich, Frankfurt.

Banking and Asset Finance, Company and Commercial, Commercial Litigation, Commercial Property and Private Client. Within these departments, specialist teams provide expert advice in the areas of Alternative Dispute Resolution, Aviation, Computing, Construction Law, Corporate Taxation, Employment Law, Family, Franchising, Insolvency, Intellectual Property, Planning and Environmental Law and Professional Indemnity, Shipping.

FIRM PROFILE: Brecher & Co. was founded in the mid 1950's and has developed rapidly and broadly into the leading London commercial law practice that it is today. The firm provides a full range of legal services for both domestic and international clients. In Europe, the firm has particular experience representing French, German and Swiss clients in their English legal affairs. There are also long-standing links with North America.

TREVOR ASSERSON, born London, November 26, 1956; admitted, 1982, England; 1992, Israel. *Education:* Oxford University; Lancaster Gate College of Law. **LANGUAGES:** French and Hebrew. **PRACTICE AREAS:** Commercial Litigation.

ANDREW BESSER, born London, September 17, 1962; admitted, 1987, England. *Education:* London School of Economics, University of London (LL.B., Hons.); Chancery Lane College of Law. **LANGUAGES:** French, Hebrew. **PRACTICE AREAS:** Banking and Asset Finance; Insolvency; Corporate Law.

GILLIAN BISHOP, born Farnborough, Kent, September 25, 1958; admitted, 1982, England. *Education:* Queen Mary College; University of London (LL.B.); Chancery Lane College of Law. **PRACTICE AREAS:** Commercial Litigation; Family and Employment Law.

DAVID BRECHER, born London, May 4, 1927; admitted, 1952, England. *Education:* Cambridge (Cantab, M.A.); Law Society School of Law. (Senior Partner). **PRACTICE AREAS:** General Commercial Practice; Property.

HENRY BRECHER, born April 11, 1932; admitted, 1954, England. *Education:* London School of Economics, University of London; Law Society School of Law (Solicitors Final Examinations, Hons.). **PRACTICE AREAS:** Commercial Property; Trusteeship.

VALERIE BRECHER, born London, January, 1955; admitted, 1979, England. *Education:* City of London School of Business Studies; Lancaster Gate College of Law. **PRACTICE AREAS:** Commercial Property; Landlord & Tenant; Property Development.

MICHAEL BROUGHTON, admitted, 1978, England. *Education:* Bristol University (B.A., English & Philosophy); University of the West of England; Guildford College of Law. **PRACTICE AREAS:** Town and Country Planning; Environmental Law; Highway Law; Compulsory Purchase; Local Government; Grant related work.

MELANIE CURTIS, born London, April 11, 1957; admitted, 1982, England. *Education:* Queen Mary College, University of London (LL.B.); Chancery Lane College of Law. **LANGUAGES:** French. **PRACTICE AREAS:** Commercial Property; Property Development.

NICHOLAS DOFFMAN, born London, November 27, 1961; admitted, 1987, England. *Education:* Middlesex University (LL.B.); Lancaster Gate

(This Listing Continued)

College of Law. *PRACTICE AREAS:* Commercial and Residential Property.

SUSAN FREEMAN, born London; admitted, 1977, England. *Education:* Leicester University (LL.B.); Lancaster Gate College of Law. *LANGUAGES:* French. *PRACTICE AREAS:* Commercial Property.

IAN GREEN, born London, September 10, 1951; admitted, 1975, England. *Education:* Bristol University (LL.B., Hons.); Lancaster Gate College of Law (Hons.). *PRACTICE AREAS:* Corporate and Commercial Law.

KEVIN GREENE, born London, July 13, 1960; admitted, 1984, England. *Education:* London School of Economics, University of London (LL.B., Hons.); Lancaster Gate College of Law. *LANGUAGES:* French. *PRACTICE AREAS:* Construction Law; International Arbitration; Environmental Law.

AUSTEN HALL, born Winchester, England, September 23, 1960; admitted, 1986, England. *Education:* University of Southampton (LL.B. and LL.M.); Chancery Lane College of Law. *LANGUAGES:* German. *PRACTICE AREAS:* Banking; Aviation and Shipping; Trade Finance; Leasing; Corporate and Commercial.

GEOFFREY HERMAN, born High Wycombe, Bucks, February 5, 1944; admitted, 1966, England. *Education:* Lancaster Gate College of Law. *PRACTICE AREAS:* Commercial Property.

LYNNE HUGHES, born Cheshire, October 7, 1959; admitted, 1985, England. *Education:* Newcastle upon Tyne University (LL.B. Hons); Chester College of Law. *PRACTICE AREAS:* Commercial Property.

NICKY HYAMS, born Manchester, October 13, 1962; admitted, 1988, England. *Education:* London School of Economics. *PRACTICE AREAS:* Commercial Property; Secured Lending.

HOWARD KLEIMAN, born Wallasey, Merseyside, September 13, 1960; admitted, 1985, England. *Education:* Leicester University (LL.B. Hons); Chester College of Law. *PRACTICE AREAS:* Corporate and Commercial; Share Sales; Business Acquisitions.

ALAN LANGLEBEN, born London, April 13, 1947; admitted, 1970, England. *Education:* Sheffield (LL.B., Hons.); Lancaster Gate College of Law. *LANGUAGES:* French. *PRACTICE AREAS:* Litigation; General Practice; Commercial; Property; Employment; Professional Indemnity; Alternative Dispute Resolution.

CLIVE NEWNHAM, born Wimbledon, London, September 23, 1959; admitted, 1984, England. *Education:* Downing College, Cambridge (Cantab M.A.); Guildford College of Law. *PRACTICE AREAS:* Commercial Property; Landlord & Tenant; Secured Lending; Receivership; Environmental Law.

PAUL SALSBURY, born Kingston, Surrey, February 1, 1959; admitted, 1982, England. *Education:* London School of Economics, University of London (LL.B.); Guildford College of Law. *PRACTICE AREAS:* Banking & Asset Finance; Secured Lending; Corporate; Commercial; Insolvency; Environmental Law.

MAURICE SILVERMAN, born London, July 18, 1933; admitted, 1955, England. *PRACTICE AREAS:* Commercial Property.

NORMA SIMON, born New York City, U.S.A.; admitted, 1980, England. *Education:* London School of Economics, University of London (LL.B.); Lancaster Gate College of Law. *LANGUAGES:* Spanish. *PRACTICE AREAS:* Private and Charitable Trusts (U.K. and International); Taxation of Trusts; Charity Law; Estate Planning; Wills; Inheritance Tax.

SHEILA STEWART, born St. Andrews, Scotland, January 30, 1957; admitted, 1981. *Education:* Kings College, University of London (LL.B.); Lancaster Gate College of Law. *PRACTICE AREAS:* Commercial Property; Landlord & Tenant; Secured Lending.

HENRY TEPER, born London, September 19, 1930; admitted, 1954, England. *Education:* Lancaster Gate College of Law. *PRACTICE AREAS:* Commercial Property.

ALAN WISEMAN, born Stockport, Cheshire, February 17, 1934; admitted, 1960, England. *Education:* St. Catharine's College, Cambridge (Economics and Law). *LANGUAGES:* French, Spanish. *PRACTICE AREAS:* Commercial Property; Secured Lending; Property Development.

(This Listing Continued)

CONSULTANT

LEON STERLING, born London, 1933; admitted, 1956, England (Consultant). *PRACTICE AREAS:* Commercial Property; Property Investment and Development; Secured Lending.

BRIGER & ASSOCIATES
25 DOVER STREET
LONDON W1X 3PA, ENGLAND
Telephone: (171) 499-4822
Telecopier: (171) 491-8087
Cable Address: "Briger, London W1."

New York, N. Y. Office: 300 Park Avenue, 24th Floor 10022-7402. Telephone: 212-758-4000. Cable Address: "Brigren". Telecopier: 888-7587.

Rio de Janeiro, Brazil Office: Briger e Associados, Edificio Centro Candido Mendes, Rua da Assembleia, 10-GR, 2720, 20119-900 Rio de Janeiro, Brazil. Telephone: (021) 531-1213. Telecopier: (021) 531-1447.

Firm engaged in General International Practice but not authorized to practice before English Courts.

PETER L. BRIGER, born New York, N.Y., May 30, 1934; admitted, 1960, New York; 1964, U.S. Claims Court; 1965, U.S. Tax Court; 1970, U.S. Supreme Court; 1983, U.S. District Court, Southern District of New York (Not admitted in England). *Education:* Princeton University (A.B., magna cum laude, 1956); Columbia University (LL.B., 1959). With Office of Chief Counsel, U.S. Treasury Department, 1962-1963. Attorney-Advisor, U.S. Tax Court, 1963-1964. *Member:* The Association of the Bar of the City of New York; New York State and American Bar Associations. *PRACTICE AREAS:* Taxation Law; International Law; Corporate Law.

ASSOCIATE

ANDREW W. SHELDRICK, born Huddersfield, England, December 16, 1954; admitted, 1979, England; 1981, New York, U.S. Tax Court, U.S. Claims Court and U.S. District Court, Southern and Eastern Districts of New York. *Education:* Jesus College, Cambridge University, Cambridge, England (M.A., 1976); Inns of Court School of Law, London, England; National Law Center, George Washington University (M.C.L., 1979). *Member:* The Association of the Bar of the City of New York; New York State and American (Member, Section of International Law and Practice) Bar Associations. *PRACTICE AREAS:* Taxation Law; International Law; Corporate Law.

(For Complete Biographical Data on all Personnel see Professional Biographies at New York, N.Y.)

BRISTOWS COOKE & CARPMAEL
Established in 1837

10 LINCOLN'S INN FIELDS
LONDON WC2A 3BP, ENGLAND
Telephone: (0171) 400 8000
Fax: (0171) 400 8050

Intellectual property and technology litigation and licensing, including patents, brands, trade marks, trade secrets, copyright, registered design, design right, antitrust, and unfair competition, EC Law, computer and information technology law, including construction law, corporate law, commercial litigation, partnership law, insolvency law, real estate, environmental law and arbitration.

MEMBERS OF THE FIRM

SIMON H. COOKE, born London, England, April 16, 1932; admitted, 1957, England. *Education:* Gonville & Caius College, Cambridge (Natural Sciences and Law - B.A., 1954; M.A., 1958) College of Law. *Member:* Law Society of England and Wales; Chartered Institute of Patent Agents, AIPPI (Associate Member). *PRACTICE AREAS:* Intellectual Property; Commercial Law.

EDWARD F. WILLIAMS, born London, England, March 7, 1937; admitted, 1962, England. *Education:* University College of Wales, Aberystwyth (Law - LL.B., 1959), College of Law. *Member:* City of London Solicitors Company; Law Society of England and Wales. *PRACTICE AREAS:* Commercial Property; Charter and Bye-law work for chartered or established bodies; Charities.

(This Listing Continued)

BRISTOWS COOKE & CARPMAEL, London—Continued

IAN M. JUDGE, born Radlett, England, December 4, 1941; admitted, 1967, England. *Education:* Trinity Hall, Cambridge University (Natural Sciences and Law, 1963) College of Law. *Member:* Law Society of England and Wales; Chartered Institute of Patent Agents (Associate Member); AIPPI. *PRACTICE AREAS:* Intellectual Property Litigation; Licensing.

DAN W. GRAHAM, born Washington, D.C. USA, May 6, 1942; admitted, 1967, England. *Education:* Gonville & Caius College, Cambridge (Economics and Law, 1964) College of Law. *Member:* Law Society of England and Wales; International Bar Association (Business Law Section, Committee C, Anti-Trust). *PRACTICE AREAS:* Commercial Law; Competition Law; Electrical and Mechanical Engineering.

DAVID J.C. BROWN, born Edinburgh, Scotland, May 8, 1942; admitted, 1973, England. *Education:* Royal Naval College, Greenwich Naval Architure (1965) College of Law. *Member:* Law Society of England and Wales. *PRACTICE AREAS:* Intellectual Property Litigation; Arbitration.

Q.G. PAUL COOKE, born Gestingthorpe, England, April 18, 1948; admitted, 1972, England. *Education:* College of Law, London, 1972. City of London Solicitors Company prize winner for commercial law. *Member:* Law Society of England and Wales. *PRACTICE AREAS:* Corporate Transactions (mergers, acquisitions, reconstructions); High Tech Venture Capital.

MICHAEL J. ROWLES, born Cheltenham, England, October 4, 1948; admitted, 1974, England. *Education:* Selwyn College, Cambridge (Law, 1970); College of Law, Guildford. *Member:* Law Society of England and Wales; Association of Charity Lawyers. *PRACTICE AREAS:* Commercial Property; Chartered and Charitable Bodies.

JOHN D. LACE, born Bristol, England, September 11, 1947; admitted, 1973, England. *Education:* Bristol Polytechnic, 1969; College of Law, Guildford. *Member:* Law Society of England and Wales. *PRACTICE AREAS:* Corporate Law; Commercial Law; Competition Law; Partnership Law; Insolvency Law.

RICHARD DE STE. CROIX, born Jersey, July 15, 1947; admitted, 1974, England. *Education:* Pembroke College, Oxford University (Law - B.A., 1969); College of Law, Guildford. *Member:* Employment Lawyers' Association; UK Environmental Law Association; International Bar Association. *PRACTICE AREAS:* Commercial Litigation (employment, civil fraud and environmental claims).

JOHN P.M. ALLCOCK, born Hertfordshire, England, July 8, 1941; admitted, 1977, England. *Education:* Kings College University of London (Engineering, 1963), Faculté Polytechnique de Mons, Belgium (High Voltage Engineering, 1964). *Member:* Law Society of England and Wales; Chartered Institute of Patent Agents (Fellow); European Patent Attorney; Registered Trade Mark Agent; Institution of Electrical Engineers, MIEE, CEng. *PRACTICE AREAS:* Intellectual Property Litigation; Licensing; Information Technology Law.

JAMES J.S. HUDSON, born London, England, May 13, 1949; admitted, 1977, England. *Education:* University of London (Law, 1971), College of Law. *Member:* Law Society of England and Wales; Official Referees Solicitors Association (Secretary, 1990—); Society of Construction Lawyers. *PRACTICE AREAS:* Construction; Engineering Litigation; Arbitration.

PHILIP G. WESTMACOTT, born Northumberland, England, April 15, 1954; admitted, 1978, England. *Education:* Trinity College, Cambridge University (Engineering and Law, 1975), College of Law. *Member:* Law Society of England and Wales; Holborn Law Society; London Computer Law Group. *PRACTICE AREAS:* Intellectual Property Litigation; Licensing; Information Technology Law.

EDWARD J. NODDER, born Lewes, England, June 29, 1956; admitted, 1980, England. *Education:* Christs College, Cambridge University (Natural Sciences and Law, 1977), College of Law. *Member:* Law Society of England and Wales; Chartered Institute of Patent Agents (Associate). *PRACTICE AREAS:* Intellectual Property Litigation; Licensing; Information Technology Law; EC Law.

SALLY A. FIELD, born Rotherham, England, May 16, 1957; admitted, 1981, England. *Education:* Durham University (Law, 1978), College of Law. *Member:* Law Society of England and Wales; Chartered Institute of Patent Agents (Associate Member). *PRACTICE AREAS:* Intellectual Property Litigation; Licensing; Information Technology Law.

NIGEL R. CORNWELL, born Chelmsford, England, November 7, 1954; admitted, 1982, England. *Education:* Bristol University (Modern

(This Listing Continued)

Languages, 1977), College of Law. *Member:* Law Society of England and Wales; Construction Law Society; City of London Solicitors Company. *PRACTICE AREAS:* Construction Law; Engineering Law.

PAUL A. WALSH, born London, England, December 21, 1956; admitted, 1982, England. *Education:* Hertford College, Oxford University (Law, 1979). *Member:* Licensing Executives Society. *PRACTICE AREAS:* Intellectual Property Litigation; Licensing.

KEVIN E. APPLETON, born Kent, England, April 18, 1956; admitted, 1983, England. *Education:* College of Law, London (1983). *Member:* Law Society of England and Wales. *PRACTICE AREAS:* Commercial and Intellectual Property Litigation; Arbitration.

ALAN JOHNSON, born Newcastle, England, June 23, 1959; admitted, 1983, England. *Education:* St. Edmund Hall, Oxford University (Law - B.A., 1980). *Member:* Law Society of England and Wales; Chartered Institute of Patent Agents (Associate Member). *PRACTICE AREAS:* Intellectual Property.

ALEXANDRA R.G. LETHBRIDGE, born Chelmsford, England, June 25, 1960; admitted, 1984, England. *Education:* Durham University (Law and Politics - B.A., 1981). *Member:* Law Society of England and Wales. *PRACTICE AREAS:* Real Estate; Landlord and Tenant; Environmental Law; Planning Law.

LINDA A. KENT, born Guildford, England, October 10, 1961; admitted, 1986, England. *Education:* Southampton University (Law, LL.B., 1982). *Member:* Law Society of England and Wales; Official Referees Solicitors Association; International Bar Association; Society of Construction Lawyers. *PRACTICE AREAS:* Construction and Engineering Litigation; Arbitration; ADR; Competition Law.

AVRIL C.B. MARTINDALE, born Stirling, Scotland, June 1, 1961; admitted, 1985, Scotland; 1992, England. *Education:* Glasgow University (Law, 1982). *Member:* Licensing Executives Society. *PRACTICE AREAS:* Commercial Intellectual Property; Competition Law; EC Law.

MARK CLINTON, born Woking, England, April 15, 1959; admitted, 1984, England. *Education:* University of Kent (Law, 1980). *Member:* Law Society of England and Wales; Official Referees Association; Society of Construction Law. *PRACTICE AREAS:* Construction and Engineering Litigation; Arbitration; ADR.

WILLIAM B.R. SAUNDERS, born February 16, 1953; admitted, 1986, England. *Education:* Oxford University (Classics, 1976). *Member:* Law Society of England and Wales. *PRACTICE AREAS:* Corporate Finance; Company Law.

BROBECK HALE AND DORR INTERNATIONAL

(A joint venture founded by the independent law firms of Brobeck,

Phleger & Harrison and Hale and Dorr)

VERITAS HOUSE
125 FINSBURY PAVEMENT
LONDON EC2A 1NQ, ENGLAND
Telephone: (0171) 638 6688
Facsimile: (0171) 638 5888

Prague, Czech Republic Office: Brehova 1, 110 00 Praha 1. Telephone: 422 232-8461. Facsimile: 422 232-8444.

Offices of the Founding Firms: San Francisco, Los Angeles, Palo Alto, San Diego and Newport Beach, California; New York, New York; Denver, Colorado, Austin, Texas; Boston, Massachusetts; Washington DC; Manchester, New Hampshire.

General Corporate and Tax Practice, with particular emphasis on High Technology, Biotechnology, Securities and International Business Transactions.

MEMBERS OF FIRM

DAVID M. AYRES (Not admitted in England; Resident, Prague, Czech Republic Office).

DONALD J. GUINEY, born Boston, Massachusetts, September 22, 1956; admitted, 1985, Massachusetts (Not admitted in England). *Education:* Harvard College (A.B., magna cum laude, 1978); Columbia University (J.D., 1984). Harlan Fiske Stone Scholar. Head Articles Editor, Columbia Journal of Transnational Law, 1983-1984. *Member:* Boston, Massachusetts, American (Member, Sections on: Corporate; International; Tax) and Inter-

(This Listing Continued)

national Bar Associations. *PRACTICE AREAS:* Corporate; Mergers and Acquisitions; Securities; Venture Capital; International Tax Law.

RESIDENT ASSOCIATES

ALLISON B. BENNINGTON, born Los Angeles, California, September 19, 1963; admitted, 1990, California (Not admitted in England). *Education:* University of California at Berkeley (B.A., 1985); Hastings College of the Law, University of California (J.D., 1990). *Member:* Bar Association of San Francisco (Member, Sections on International Law and Practice, Corporate, Business, Intellectual Property, Tax); American Bar Association (Member, Sections on International Law and Practice, Corporate, Business, Intellectual Property, International Tax); State Bar of California (Member, Sections on Corporate, Business, Intellectual Property, Tax). *PRACTICE AREAS:* International Business Transactions; Corporate Finance; Mergers and Acquisitions; International Corporate Taxation; Intellectual Property; General Corporate Representation.

CHRISTOPHER A. GREW, born New York, New York, November 14, 1962; admitted, 1988, England and Wales; 1991, New York. *Education:* University of Michigan (B.A., 1984); Inns of Court School of Law (1987); Cambridge University (B.A., with honors, 1986; M.A., 1990). *Member:* New York State Bar Association; American Bar Association; Honorable Society of Middle Temple. *PRACTICE AREAS:* International Transactions; Securities; Privatizations; High Technology and Biotechnology Matters.

CHARLOTTE H. VON CLEMM, born London, England, August 15, 1965; admitted, 1993, Massachusetts (Not admitted in England). *Education:* Harvard College (B.A., magna cum laude, 1987); Harvard Law School (J.D., cum laude, 1992). *Member:* Massachusetts and American Bar Associations. *PRACTICE AREAS:* General Corporate; International Corporate; Securities.

(For Complete Biographical Data on all Personnel, see Professional Biographies at Prague, Czech Republic).

BROWN & WOOD

BLACKWELL HOUSE
GUILDHALL YARD
LONDON EC2V 5AB, ENGLAND
Telephone: 0171-606-1888
Telecopier: 0171-796-1807

New York, New York Office: One World Trade Center, 10048-0557. *Telephone:* 212-839-5300.
San Francisco, California Office: 555 California Street, 94104-1715. *Telephone:* 415-772-1200.
Washington, D.C. Office: 815 Connecticut Avenue, N.W., Suite 701, 20006-4004. *Telephone:* 202-973-0600.
Los Angeles, California Office: 10900 Wilshire Boulevard, 90024-3959. *Telephone:* 310-443-0200.
Trenton, New Jersey Office: 172 West State Street, 08608-1104. *Telephone:* 609-393-0303.
Tokyo, Japan Office: Shiroyama JT Mori Building, 3-1 Toranomon 4-chome, Minato-ku. *Telephone:* 011-813-5472-5360.
Hong Kong Office: Suite 2606, Asia Pacific Finance Tower, Citibank Plaza, 3 Garden Road, Central. Telephone: 011-852-2509-7888.

General Practice.
Firm engaged in American and International Law Practice.

RESIDENT PARTNERS

RICHARD A. CASSELL, born London, England, July 30, 1955; admitted, 1981, England; 1984, District of Columbia. *Education:* University College, London, England (B.A., 1976); University of Pennsylvania (LL.M., 1984).

ROBERT T. JONES, born Los Angeles, California, May 23, 1938; admitted, 1964, California; 1975, District of Columbia (Not admitted in England). *Education:* Stanford University (B.A., 1960); Harvard University (LL.B., 1963).

WILSON C. MCLEOD, born Hamilton, Ontario, Canada, August 25, 1938; admitted, 1969, Massachusetts; 1975, England. *Education:* McMaster University (B.A., 1960); Harvard University (LL.B., 1963).

(This Listing Continued)

CHRISTOPHER B. MEAD, born New Rochelle, New York, February 26, 1952; admitted, 1979, New York (Not admitted in England). *Education:* Middlebury College (B.A., 1974); Fordham University (J.D., 1978).

RESIDENT ASSOCIATES

DYKE M. DAVIES, born Dade City, Florida, March 14, 1963; admitted, 1989, Massachusetts (Not admitted in England). *Education:* University of Arkansas (B.A., 1984); Harvard University (J.D., 1988).

SUSAN M. GIRARD, born Darby, Pennsylvania, May 22, 1962; admitted, 1992, Delaware, New Jersey and Pennsylvania (Not admitted in England). *Education:* Villanova University (B.S., 1984; J.D., 1991).

WILLIAM S. MARTIN, born Mexico City, Mexico, September 24, 1965; admitted, 1994, New York (Not admitted in England). *Education:* University of California, Los Angeles (B.A., 1989); Harvard University (J.D., 1992).

DREW D. SALVEST, born Perth Amboy, New Jersey, September 29, 1957; admitted, 1988, New York (Not admitted in England). *Education:* Amherst College (B.A., 1978); New York University (J.D., 1987).

(For Complete Biographical Data on all Partners and Associates, see Professional Biographies at New York, New York)

BRYAN CAVE

A Partnership including a Professional Corporation

Established in 1873

29 QUEEN ANNE'S GATE
LONDON SW1H 9BU, ENGLAND
Telephone: 011-44-171-222-0511
Facsimile: 011-44-171-222-1240

St. Louis, Missouri Office: One Metropolitan Square, 211 North Broadway, Suite 3600, 63102-2750. Telephone: (314) 259-2000. Facsimile: (314) 259-2020.
Washington, D.C. Office: 700 Thirteenth Street, N.W., 20005-3960. Telephone: (202) 508-6000. Facsimile: (202) 508-6200.
New York, N.Y. Office: 245 Park Avenue, 10167-0034. Telephone: (212) 692-1800. Facsimile: (212) 692-1900 and Other New York, N.Y. Office: 575 Lexington Avenue, 10022. Telephone: (212) 371-1660. Facsimile: (212) 593-0243.
Kansas City, Missouri Office: 3300 One Kansas City Place, 1200 Main Street, 64141-6914. Telephone: (816) 374-3200. Facsimile: (816) 374-3300.
Overland Park, Kansas Office: 7500 College Boulevard, Suite 1100, 66210-4035. Telephone: (913) 338-7700. Facsimile: (913) 338-7777.
Phoenix, Arizona Office: 2800 North Central Avenue, Twenty-First Floor, 85004-1098. Telephone: (602) 230-7000. Facsimile: (602) 266-5938.
Los Angeles, California Office: 777 South Figueroa Street, Suite 2700, 90017-5418. Telephone: (213) 243-4300. Facsimile: (213) 243-4343.
Santa Monica, California Office: 120 Broadway, Suite 500, 90401-2305. Telephone: (310) 576-2100. Facsimile: (310) 576-2200.
Irvine, California Office: 18881 Von Karman, Suite 250, 92715-1500. Telephone: (714) 757-8100. Facsimile: (714) 757-8106.
Frankfurt, Federal Republic of Germany Office: In Cooperation with Rossbach & Partner, Stresemannallee 33, D-60596 Frankfurt am Main. Telephone: 011-49-69-631 50 24. Facsimile: 011-49-69-631 31 64.
Riyadh 11465 Saudi Arabia Office: In Cooperation with Kadasah Law Firm, P.O. Box 20883. Telephones: 011-966-1-465-1371 and 1165. Facsimile: 011-966-1-464-3789.
Dubai, U.A.E. Office: Al-Mehairi-Bryan Cave, Holiday Centre, Commercial Tower, Suite 1103, P.O. Box 13677, UAE. Telephone: 011-971-4-314-123. Facsimile: 011-971-4-318-287.
Hong Kong Office: Suite 2106, Lippo Tower, 21/F, Lippo Centre, 89 Queensway. Telephone: 011-852-2522-2821. Facsimile: 011-852-2522-3820.

General and International Law Practice. Business, Corporate Financing, Import and Export, Intellectual Property, Tax and Trusts and Estates Law.
Firm engaged in American and International Law Practice, but not authorized to appear before the English courts or to act as Solicitors.

(This Listing Continued)

BRYAN CAVE, London—Continued

PARTNERS

CURT M. DOMBEK, born Missouri, 1958; admitted, 1983, Missouri; 1984, California. *Education:* Harvard University (A.B., magna cum laude with highest honors in Statistics, 1980; J.D., magna cum laude, 1983). Edwards Whitaker Scholar. Editor-in-Chief, Harvard Journal of Law and Public Policy, 1982-1983. Author: "Harmonizing Allocations of Risk for Commercial Space Activities," Inter-Pacific Bar Association, April 1991. (Also at Washington, D.C. Office). *LANGUAGES:* German.

JOSEPH A. FIELD, III, born California, 1946; admitted, 1974, California; 1976, District of Columbia (Not admitted in England). *Education:* Princeton University (A.B., 1969); Columbia University (J.D., 1972). *LANGUAGES:* French.

PAUL E. HAUSER, born New Jersey, 1954; admitted, 1981, New York (Not admitted in England). *Education:* Aberdeen University (M.A. Hons, 1977); Harvard University (J.D., cum laude, 1980). Author: "Residence and the Consultative Document: The U.S. Experience," British Tax Review, 29-40, 1989. (Resident Manager).

CATHY B. HORTON, born Ohio, 1962; admitted, 1986, Ohio and U.S. District Court, Northern District of Ohio; 1987, U.S. Court of Appeals, Sixth Circuit (Not admitted in England). *Education:* University of Michigan (B.A., with distinction, 1983); Ohio State University College of Law (J.D., 1986).

WILLIAM D. MORRISON, born Pennsylvania, 1940; admitted, 1966, New York; 1975, California (Not admitted in England). *Education:* Princeton University (B.A., 1962); Yale University (LL.B., 1965). Author: "Working Within the Saudi Legal System," Saudi Arabia: Keys to Business Success, McGraw Hill, 1981. *Member:* The Association of the Bar of the City of New York (Member, Committee on Foreign and Comparative Law, 1971-1974). (Resident).

RESIDENT ASSOCIATES

DEBORAH A. CHAPNICK, born Connecticut, 1965; admitted, 1993, New York (Not admitted in England). *Education:* Yale College (B.A., cum laude, 1987); University of Virginia (J.D., 1992); London University (LL.M., 1994). *LANGUAGES:* French.

CAROLE A. COLLEY, born Ohio, 1953; admitted, 1989, Missouri (Not admitted in England). *Education:* Randolph-Macon Woman's College (A.B., cum laude, 1975); Simmons College (M.S., 1980); Harvard Law School (J.D., 1989).

PETER T. MASSARO, born Connecticut, 1963; admitted, 1991, Ohio (Not admitted in England). *Education:* The Catholic University of America (B.A., Classical Studies, highest honors, 1985; M.A., Classical Studies, 1986); The University of Michigan Law School (J.D., cum laude, 1991). Phi Beta Kappa. *PRACTICE AREAS:* Trusts and Estates.

(For a complete list of representative clients, see St. Louis, Missouri listing)

CAMERON MARKBY HEWITT

SCEPTRE COURT
40 TOWER HILL
LONDON EC3N 4BB, ENGLAND
Telephone: 0171-702-2345
Telex: 925779 CAMLAW G
Facsimile: 0171-702-2303

Other London, England Office: Lloyd's, Room 639, 6th Floor, 1 Lime Street, London, EC3M 7DQ. Telephone: 0171-623-7100 (Exts. 4412/4437) Fax: 0171-929-4700.

Aberdeen, Scotland Office: Migvie House, North Silver Street, Aberdeen, AB1 1RJ. Telephone: 01224-622002. Fax: 01224-622066.

Bristol, England Office: 3rd Floor, 21 Prince Street, Bristol, Avon BS1 4PH. Telephone: 01179-272080. Fax: 01179-272426.

Brussels, Belgium Office: 66 Avenue Louise-B.16, B-1050, Brussels, Belgium. Telephone: (02) 511 39 39. Fax: (02) 511 29 17.

Advertising, Asset Finance and Leasing, Aviation, Banking (UK) and Corporate Reconstruction, Banking (International) and Trade Finance, Banking Litigation, Banking Regulation & Securitization, Building and Engineering, Building Societies, Commercial Litigation and Dispute Management, Company Law, Corporate Finance, EC and Competition Law, Employment and Employee Relations, Environment, Financial Services Regu-

(This Listing Continued)

---

lation & Compliance, Fraud and White Collar Crime, Insolvency, Insurance Litigation, Insurance (Corporate/Commercial), Intellectual Property, Information Technology, Management Buy-Outs, Media and Entertainment, Mergers and Acquisitions, Oil and Gas, Pensions, Planning, Professional Negligence, Real Estate Development, Real Estate Finance, Real Estate Investment, Reinsurance, Shipping, Taxation, United Kingdom Immigration and Nationality, Venture and Development Capital.

FIRM PROFILE: Cameron Markby Hewitt is one of the leading City firms providing a full range of legal services to the financial, commercial, insurance and industrial sectors both in the United Kingdom and overseas.

PARTNERS

W.T.C. Shelford	Penelope A. Bruce
J.J. White	S.K. Tester
J.A.E. Young	M.E.M. Elborne
M.H. Wadsworth	P.D. Aldred
M.R. Galaud	S.J. Morris
S.A.K. Boome	G.A. Williamson
A. Jones	J.E. Hall
R.D. Lambourne	C. St. John Smith
A.G.G. Lewis	A.J. Crawford
A.J. Bryce	M. Aspery
P.L. Hewes	P. Maguire
G.R.T. Smyth	K.V. Gregory
N.A. Johnson	A.J. Hobkinson
C.D.A. Romney	Amanda J.M. Chumas
C. Larlham	F. Dufficy
A.C.G. Brown	J.S. Armstrong
B.J. Burnett-Hitchcock	D.J. Kidd
J.L.T. Newbegin	T.R. Brymer
R.E. Parsons	Julia Onslow-Cole
N.R. James	S.J. Foster
M.F. Baker	Fiona M. O'Neill
R.A. Goodman	S.C. Hegarty
A.D. Morris	V.A. Wheatley
G. Brafman	R.W. Meredith
B.R. Westbrook	S.P. Charge
R.G. Martin	M. Jones
M.J.J. Freeman	P. Richardson
N.S.D. Agar	H. R. Morrison
R.E. Topley	A.L. Walker
A.L.R. Fincham	R. Curd
G.S. Barrett	A.J. Sheach
N.W. Paul	Penelope Warne
R. Griggs	Louise M. Anderson
B.A. Schofield	T.J. Fox
A. McKnight	H.A. Kaye
J.R.E. Shaw	E.C. Benzecry
Sara Lovick	D. Hamilton
Margaret J.L. Wailen	A.J. Dyson
S.H. Hallam	B.H. Hearndon

CONSULTANTS

John E. Cama	R. Denoon Duncan

Languages: Afrikaans, Danish, Dutch, English, Finnish, French, German, Gujerati, Hindi, Indonesian, Italian, Malay, Polish, Portuguese, Russian, Serbo-Croat, Spanish and Turkish.

CAMPBELL HOOPER

Established in 1754

35 OLD QUEEN STREET
LONDON SW1H 9JD, ENGLAND
Telephone: 0171 222 9070
Telex: 23518 Chaw G
Fax: 0171-222-5591
DX 2365 Victoria

FIRM PROFILE: Founded in 1754, Campbell Hooper is a well established medium sized firm based in Westminster. Its range of expertise and experience allows it to compete with the larger city firms, but it manages to retain a close client/solicitor relationship. Legal services offered are: private client, corporate client, conveyancing (commercial and domestic), intellectual property, taxation and finance, EEC, civil litigation, entertainment and employment. The firm has an international client base ranging from established corporations to private individuals.

(This Listing Continued)

MEMBERS OF FIRM

R. S. LEVY, born London, England, June 3, 1933; admitted, 1960, England. *Education:* Oxford (Brasenose College (M.A., 1957); Gibson and Weldon, Law Society (Honours, 1960). *Member:* City of Westminster Law Society. *PRACTICE AREAS:* Domestic Conveyancing.

D. M. WILLS, born London, England, February 7, 1942; admitted, 1967, England. *Education:* University of Bristol (LL.B., 1964); College of Law, Guildford. *LANGUAGES:* French, German. *PRACTICE AREAS:* Entertainment/Commercial/Divorce.

J. S. SIDDALL, born Sheffield, England, September 4, 1942; admitted, 1968, England. *Education:* University of Manchester (LL.B., 1964); Guildford College of Law, 1965. *Member:* Law Society. *LANGUAGES:* French. *PRACTICE AREAS:* Commercial Property.

MICHAEL OLIVER, born London, England, March 15, 1930; admitted, 1953, England. *Education:* Law Society School of Law, London, 1948-1953; Private Legal Education, Los Angeles, California, 1982-1983. *Member:* Beverly Hills, Los Angeles County and American Bar Associations; State Bar of California; International Bar Association; The Law Society of England and Wales; British Academy of Film and Television Arts, Los Angeles; National Youth Theatre of Great Britain (Member of Council); London Academy of Music and Dramatic Art (Governor); Royal National Theatre (Member of the Board). *LANGUAGES:* French. *PRACTICE AREAS:* Entertainment Industry; Motion Pictures; Television; Theatre; Media.

PHILIP MCNAIR, born Beaconsfield, England, July 9, 1929; admitted, 1954, England. *Education:* Eton College; School of Law, Lancaster Gate, 1952-1953. *PRACTICE AREAS:* Copyright; Entertainment; Intellectual Property.

J. M. RHODES, born Wellington, England, December 8, 1948; admitted, 1974, England and Wales as Solicitor. *Education:* College of Law; Law Society's Qualifying Examination, 1972. *Member:* The Law Society; London Solicitors; Litigation Solicitors; Solicitors Family Law Association. *PRACTICE AREAS:* Civil Litigation; Family Law.

D. A. SALMON, born Kings Lynn, England, October 12, 1956; admitted, 1981, England. *Education:* Exeter University (Law, 1978); Guildford, Surrey (1979). *PRACTICE AREAS:* Construction; Entertainment.

CAROLYN S. JENNINGS, born London, England, April 12, 1952; admitted, 1982, England. *Education:* Birmingham University (B.Soc.Sc. Joint Honours Geography/Political Science, 1974; London School of Economics, University of London (International Politics) (M.Sc., 1975); College of Law (Lancaster Gate) 1981. *Member:* Immigration Law Practitioners Association; The Royal Television Society; Women in Film and Television. *PRACTICE AREAS:* Entertainment; Immigration.

M. J. WRIGHT, born London, England, May 20, 1957; admitted, 1981, England. *Education:* Guildford College of Law, 1979. *Member:* The Law Society. *PRACTICE AREAS:* Company/Commercial.

S. ALDRICH, born Durham, England, January 8, 1962; admitted, 1987, England. *Education:* University of Keele Staffordshire (B.Soc.Sci., Hons, 1983); College of Law, Chester Law Society Final Exam, 1985. *Member:* The Law Society, Chancery Lane, London. *PRACTICE AREAS:* Commercial Property.

SARAH THERESE ANTICONI, born London, England, July 6, 1963; admitted, 1988, England and Wales. *Education:* Manchester Polytechnic (LL.B., Hons., 1984); College of Law, Lancaster Gate, London (1985). *Member:* Law Society; Solicitors Family Law Association; Immigration Law Practitioners Association. *PRACTICE AREAS:* Civil Litigation; Family Law; Immigration.

NEVILLE ROSS, born Prestwich, November 25, 1944; admitted, 1980, England. *Education:* Pembroke College, Cambridge (M.A.). *Member:* Law Society. *PRACTICE AREAS:* Tax; Commercial Law.

ANDREW RAJAN, born Belfast, Northern Ireland, November 13, 1961; admitted, 1987, England and Wales. *Education:* Boys Model School, Belfast; University of Leicester (Second Honours, 1984); College of Law, Chester (1985). *Member:* Law Society of England and Wales. *PRACTICE AREAS:* Commercial.

ALEXANDER GEORGE CUPPAGE, born London, England, June 23, 1949; admitted, 1973, England. *Education:* Law College, Guildford, Surrey (1970-1971). *Member:* The Law Society. *LANGUAGES:* English and French. *PRACTICE AREAS:* Private Client; Tax and Trust; Agricultural Law; Charities.

(This Listing Continued)

JONATHAN WRIGHT WHITEHEAD, born London, England, November 25, 1959; admitted, 1985, England. *Education:* University of East Anglia (LL.B., 1981); Guildford College of Law (Solicitors Final Exam, 1982). *Member:* Young Solicitors Group.

HELEN PATRICIA MEYLER, born England; admitted, 1980, England. *Education:* Exeter University (1977); Guildford College of Law (Law Society Exams, 1978). *Member:* Law Society.

CONOR MAGILL, born Sheffield, Yorks, June 3, 1951; admitted, 1978, England and Wales as Solicitor. *Education:* University of Dublin (B.A. Hons., 1973); College of Law (Second Class Honours, 1974). *LANGUAGES:* French.

ANITA GILL, born Kampala, Uganda, April 26, 1960; admitted, 1988, England and Wales. *Education:* University of Central England, Birmingham (1982). *LANGUAGES:* Gujrati. *PRACTICE AREAS:* Domestic Conveyancing.

CONSULTANTS

B. J. JACKSON. *PRACTICE AREAS:* Commercial.

P. L. CUDBIRD. *PRACTICE AREAS:* Commercial.

A. P. COLEMAN. *PRACTICE AREAS:* Commercial.

N. DURBRIDGE. *PRACTICE AREAS:* Intellectual Property.

J. I. WILLIAMS. *PRACTICE AREAS:* Commercial Property.

J. A. WRIGHT, born England, June 8, 1929; admitted, 1952, England. *Education:* London (LL.B., 1951). *Member:* Law Society. *PRACTICE AREAS:* Tax and Trust Specialist.

ASSISTANT SOLICITORS

CLAIRE GREENWELL. *PRACTICE AREAS:* Commercial Property.

GAYNOR JACKSON. *PRACTICE AREAS:* Probate.

JOANNA LAWSON. *PRACTICE AREAS:* Commercial.

ALISON WILLIAMS. *PRACTICE AREAS:* Civil Litigation.

DAVID ASHLEY. *PRACTICE AREAS:* Commercial Property.

WILLIAM GRANGER. *PRACTICE AREAS:* Civil Litigation; Construction.

CARNELUTTI

FIRST FLOOR, 76 SHOE LANE
LONDON EC4A 3JB, ENGLAND
Telephone: 0171-242 2268
Telefax: 0171-353 3352

Milan, Italy Office: Studio Carnelutti. Corso Matteotti 10, 20121. Telephone: 02-7600.2042. Cable Address: "Unilaw Milano". Telex: 321094 UNILAW I. Telefax: 02-78.47.79.

New York, New York Office: Werbel, Mc Millin and Carnelutti. 711 Fifth Avenue, 10022. Telephone: 212-832-8300. Telefax: 212-832-3353.

Firm engaged in Italian and International Law Practice, but not authorized to appear before the English Courts or to act as Solicitors.

FIRM PROFILE: Founded in the late 19th Century, Carnelutti is now a leading Italian Law Firm with twelve Partners and over twenty associates. The firm specialises in National, EU, International and Commercial Law.

FRANCESCO SEASSARO. *LANGUAGES:* Italian, English and French. *PRACTICE AREAS:* Commercial; Corporate; Banking; Tax.

(For Biographical Data and Complete Personnel of Milan Office, see Professional Biographies at Milan, Italy)

ROBERT D. CARROW

BARRISTERS' CHAMBERS
33 BEDFORD ROW
LONDON WC1, ENGLAND
Telephone: 171 242-6476
Telecopier: 171 831-6065

San Francisco, California Office: One Embarcadero Center, Suite 880, 94111. Telephone: 415-981-1691. Telecopier: 415-492-8419. Telex: 470562 LAW UI. Cable Address: "Juris".

Business Litigation and Arbitration. Torts, Plaintiff and Defense. Crime. Expert Testimony and Consultation on American Law.

(This Listing Continued)

ROBERT D. CARROW, London—Continued

ROBERT D. CARROW, born Marshall, Minnesota, February 5, 1934; admitted, 1959, California; 1978, U.S. Supreme Court; 1981, Bar of England and Wales; 1983, New York. *Education:* University of Colorado; University of Minnesota (B.A., 1956); Stanford University (J.D., 1958). Phi Delta Phi. Member, Board of Editors, Minnesota Law Review, 1956-1957. Judge Pro Tem, Superior Court of California (San Francisco), 1992—. *Member:* Bar Association of San Francisco; Los Angeles, New York State, American and International Bar Associations; Midland-Oxford Circuit (England); The Association of Trial Lawyers of America; Honourable Society of the Middle Temple (London); The Inns of Court Society in California (Executive Cmty., 1982-1985). (Also Of Counsel to Goldstein & Phillips, A Professional Corporation, San Francisco, California).

CHADBOURNE & PARKE

86 JERMYN STREET
SW1 6JD LONDON, ENGLAND
Telephone: 44-171-925-7400
Facsimile: 44-171-839-3393

New York, N.Y. Office: 30 Rockefeller Plaza, 10112. Telephone: 212-408-5100. Telecopier: 212-541-5369.

Washington, D.C. Office: Suite 900, 1101 Vermont Avenue, N.W., 20005. Telephone: 202-289-3000. Telecopier: 202-289-3002.

Los Angeles, California Office: 601 South Figueroa Street, 90017. Telephone: 213-892-1000. Telecopier: 213-622-9865.

Moscow, Russia Office: 38 Maxim Gorky Naberezhnaya, 113035. Telephone: 7095-974-2424. Telecopier: 7095-974-2425, International satellite lines via U.S.: Telephone: 212-408-1190. Telecopier: 212-408-1199.

Hong Kong Office: Suite 3704, Peregrine Tower, Lippo Centre, 89 Queensway. Telephone: (852) 2842-5400. Telecopier: (852) 2521-7527.

New Delhi, India Office: Chadbourne & Parke Associates, A16-B Anand Niketan, 110 021. Telephone: 91-11-301-7568/7581/7582. Telecopier: 91-11-301-7351.

General Practice.

RESIDENT PARTNER

PAUL A. RANDOUR, born Bakersfield, California, August 15, 1935; admitted, 1961, California (Inactive); 1962, New York (Not admitted in England). *Education:* Stanford University (A.B., 1957; LL.B., 1960); Leiden University, Leiden, The Netherlands (Jur. Drs., 1961). Phi Beta Kappa. Order of The Coif. Senior Vice President and General Counsel, American Brands, Inc., 1986-1991. *Member:* The Association of the Bar of the City of New York; International Bar Association.

RESIDENT COUNSEL

PETER K. ECK, born Washington, D.C., December 12, 1945; admitted, 1981, New Jersey and U.S. District Court, District of New Jersey; 1982, New York and U.S. District Court, Southern District of New York (Not admitted in England). *Education:* Northwestern University (B.A., 1967); Pennsylvania State University (M.A., 1970); Fordham University (J.D., 1980). Instructor, Business Law I, Dominican College 1984. *Member:* Association of the Bar of the City of New York; New Jersey State, New York State and American Bar Associations.

(For Biographical Data of other Personnel, see Professional Biographies at New York, N.Y., Washington, D.C., Los Angeles, California, Moscow, Russia, Hong Kong and New Delhi, India)

CHARLES RUSSELL

Solicitors

Established in 1760

HALE COURT, LINCOLN'S INN
LONDON WC2A 3UL, ENGLAND
Telephone: 0171-242-1031
Fax: 0171-831-0872
DX: 19 London Chancery Lane

Other London, England Office: 1095 Lloyd's, One Lime Street, EC3M 7DQ. Telephone: 0171-626-3038. Fax: 0171-929-0044.

(This Listing Continued)

Cheltenham, England Office: Killowen House, Bayshill Road, GL50 3AW. Telephone: 0242-221122. Fax: 0242-584700. DX: 7442 Cheltenham.

Swindon, England Office: One Sanford Street, SN1 1QQ. Telephone: 0793-617444. Fax: 0793-617436. DX: 38606 Swindon 2.

Guildford, England Office: The Old Magistrates' Court, 71 North Street. Telephone: 0483 302525. Fax: 0483 302567. DX: 83165 Guildford 2.

Company/Commercial-Computer, Media and Telecommunications, European Community, Employment and Employee Benefits, Environmental, Intellectual Property, Insolvency, Property Finance and Development Planning, Shipping, Agricultural Law, Litigation and Arbitration, Insurance and Re-insurance, Matrimonial, Private Client, Tax, Wills and Trusts.

PARTNERS

JOHN E. DAVIS, born 1937; admitted, 1963, England. *Education:* Cambridge University M.A. (Senior Partner). *PRACTICE AREAS:* Property Law; Building Contracts; Property Development/Syndication Law; Conveyancing.

PETER GEORGE, born 1935; admitted, 1962, England. *PRACTICE AREAS:* Family Law; Divorce Law; Children's Law; Matrimonial Law; Child Custody; Juvenile Law; Child Dependency Proceedings.

RICHARD G. CROUCH, born 1939; admitted, 1964, England. *Education:* Nottingham University LL.B. (Hons). *PRACTICE AREAS:* Property Law; Commercial Property Law; Landlord & Tenant Law; Conveyancing.

JOHN C.B. SOUTH, born 1937; admitted, 1961, England. *LANGUAGES:* French. *PRACTICE AREAS:* General Practice; Joint Ventures; Securities Offerings; Financial Restructuring.

IAN S. LOCKHART, born 1940; admitted, 1967, England. *Education:* Cambridge University M.A. *PRACTICE AREAS:* Charitable Trusts & Foundations; Trust Law; Wills; Administration of Estates.

MICHAEL T.J. PETERS, born 1941; admitted, 1965, England. *PRACTICE AREAS:* Residential Property Law; Conveyancing; Landlord & Tenant; Wills.

COLIN RUSSELL, admitted, 1970, England. *Education:* Oxford University M.A. *PRACTICE AREAS:* Estate Planning; Trust Law; Wills; Heritage Law; Charitable Trusts & Foundations.

DAVID LONG, born 1946; admitted, 1973, England. *Education:* Oxford University M.A. *LANGUAGES:* French, Italian and German. *PRACTICE AREAS:* Wills; Administration of Estates; Probate Law; Charitable Trusts & Foundations.

LAURENCE WATT, born 1946; admitted, 1970, England. *LANGUAGES:* French. *PRACTICE AREAS:* Commercial Litigation; Tort Law; General Litigation; Defamation; Maritime Law.

W.PAUL HARRIMAN, born 1946; admitted, 1973, England. *Education:* University of Dublin B.A. (Hons). *LANGUAGES:* French. *PRACTICE AREAS:* Estate Planning; Trust Law; Administration of Estates; Trust Administration.

MICHAEL P. BENNETT, born 1950; admitted, 1974, England; LL.B. *PRACTICE AREAS:* Property Law; Commercial Property Law; Property Development; Property Finance.

RICHARD A. CLARK, born 1947; admitted, 1973, England. *PRACTICE AREAS:* Corporate Law; Mergers & Acquisitions; Partnership Law; Venture Capital.

ADRIAN A.V. CHRISTIAN, born 1948; admitted, 1972, England; (Hons). *LANGUAGES:* French. *PRACTICE AREAS:* Property Law; Commercial Property Law; Conveyancing; Landlord & Tenant.

FRANCIS R.S. RUNDALL, born 1951; admitted, 1975, England. *Education:* Durham University B.A. (Hons) Law. *PRACTICE AREAS:* Agency & Distribution; Joint Ventures; Mergers & Acquisitions; Corporate Finance Law; Venture Capital.

PATRICK RUSSELL, born 1952; admitted, 1979, England. *Education:* Oxford University B.A. *PRACTICE AREAS:* Sports Law; Reinsurance Law; Judicial Review; Commercial Litigation; Building Contracts.

KEITH M. POWELL, born 1945; admitted, 1978, England. *PRACTICE AREAS:* Property Law; Commercial Property Law; Landlord & Tenant Law; Residential Property Work; Conveyancing.

JEREMY WALTERS, born 1946; admitted, 1973, England. *Education:* Oxford University M.A. *PRACTICE AREAS:* Agricultural Property; Property Law; Commercial Property.

(This Listing Continued)

MICHAEL SCOTT, born 1952; admitted, 1978, England; 1979, Hong Kong. *Education:* Oxford University M.A. *PRACTICE AREAS:* Commercial Law; International Transactions; Asian-Pacific; Media Law; Charitable Trusts & Foundations.

MARK A.C. MONCREIFFE, born 1953; admitted, 1978, England. *Education:* Cambridge University M.A.; Lic. En Dr. Eur. *LANGUAGES:* French. *PRACTICE AREAS:* Cable T.V.; Cable Franchising; Satellite Law; Telecommunications Law; Telecommunications Contracts; Satellite.

GEOFFREY JORDAN, born 1949; admitted, 1975, England. *Education:* B.A. (Hons); LL.B. *LANGUAGES:* French. *PRACTICE AREAS:* Commercial Property Law; Landlord & Tenant; Property Development-/Syndication Law; Planning; Conveyancing.

DAVID H. REISSNER, born 1954; admitted, 1978, England. *Education:* LL.B. (Hons). *LANGUAGES:* French. *PRACTICE AREAS:* General Litigation; Tort Law; Property Litigation; Personal Injury; Medical Negligence (Defendant).

ROGER T.W. PIERCE, born 1954; admitted, 1979, England. *Education:* LL.B. (Hons). *PRACTICE AREAS:* Property Law; Commercial Property Law; Landlord & Tenant; Conveyancing.

JAMES D. HOLDER, born 1954; admitted, 1978, England. *Education:* Cambridge University M.A. *LANGUAGES:* French. *PRACTICE AREAS:* Corporate Law; Mergers & Acquisitions; Leveraged Management Buyouts; Insolvency Law; Corporate Finance Law.

PETER SCANDRETT, born 1952; admitted, 1977, England. *Education:* Cambridge University M.A. Law. *PRACTICE AREAS:* Employment Law; Intellectual Property Law; Commercial Litigation; Defamation.

AMANDA L. CROWE, born 1953; admitted, 1978, England. *Education:* Southampton University LL.B. (Hons). *PRACTICE AREAS:* Commercial Property Work-Investment Purchase and Management Work.

HILARY BROWNE-WILKINSON, born 1941; admitted, 1986, England. *Education:* LL.B (Hons) London. *PRACTICE AREAS:* Employment Law.

NORMAN H. STARRITT, born 1948; admitted, 1972, England. *Education:* LL.B. (Hons). *PRACTICE AREAS:* Banking Law; Commercial Law; Corporate Law; Environmental Law; Education Law; Health & Hospital Law.

DAVID J. HORNER, born 1949; admitted, 1975, England. *Education:* Sheffield University LL.B. (Hons). *LANGUAGES:* French. *PRACTICE AREAS:* Landlord & Tenant Law; Building & Construction; Property Finance; Planning; Environmental Law.

PAUL CLARK, born 1957; admitted, 1982, England. *Education:* Oxford University B.A. (Jurisprudence). Co-Author: "Practical Trust Precedents," Longman, 1986; "Practical Will Precedents," Longman, 1987; Inheritance Tax on Lifetime Gifts," Sweet & Maxwell, 1987. *PRACTICE AREAS:* Estate Planning; Individual Tax Planning; Tax Shelters Law; Trust Law; Wills.

DAVID M. DAVIDSON, born 1947; admitted, 1972, England. *PRACTICE AREAS:* Family Law; Child Abduction; Child Custody.

JEREMY M. HOLT, born 1956; admitted, 1980, England. *Education:* Oxford University M.A. *LANGUAGES:* French. *PRACTICE AREAS:* Commercial Law; Information Technology; Facilities Management; Computer Law; Computer Software.

JULIAN MAITLAND-WALKER, born 1949; admitted, 1974, England. Editor: The Competition Law Review; The European Business Lawyer. *LANGUAGES:* French. *PRACTICE AREAS:* Commercial Law; European Community Law; Competition Law; Antitrust Law; Licensing Law.

STEPHEN L. CARTER, born 1955; admitted, 1980, England. *Education:* Durham University B.A. (Hons) Law. *PRACTICE AREAS:* Insurance Law; Reinsurance Law; Commercial Litigation.

RICHARD NORTON, born 1959; admitted, 1985, England. *Education:* LL.B. (Hons). *LANGUAGES:* French and German. *PRACTICE AREAS:* Mergers & Acquisitions; Leveraged & Management Buyouts; Securities Offerings; Corporate Finance Law; Venture Capital.

DAVID GREEN, born 1953; admitted, 1978, England. *Education:* LL.B. *PRACTICE AREAS:* Employment Law; Employee Stock Ownership; Employer/Employee Relations; Employment Discrimination.

SIMON GILBERT, born 1957; admitted, 1983, England. *Education:* Oxford University M.A. *PRACTICE AREAS:* Mergers & Acquisitions; Corporate Restructuring; Corporate Finance Law; Securities Offerings.

(This Listing Continued)

GRANT HOWELL, born 1956; admitted, 1977, England. *Education:* Birmingham University LL.B. (Hons). Author: "Family Breakdown and Insolvency," Butterworths, 1993. *PRACTICE AREAS:* Family Law; Divorce Law; Children's Law; Matrimonial Law; Child Custody.

NEIL D. SCONCE, born 1940; admitted, 1968, England. *LANGUAGES:* German. *PRACTICE AREAS:* Property Law; Landlord & Tenant; Conveyancing.

JUNE J. MARRIOTT, born 1946; admitted, 1971, England. *LANGUAGES:* French. *PRACTICE AREAS:* Property Law; Landlord & Tenant; Property Finance; Residential Property Law; Conveyancing.

GEORGE L. DUNCAN, born 1955; admitted, 1984, England. *Education:* Oxford University M.A.; London University Ph.D. *Member:* Associate Institute of Taxation. *PRACTICE AREAS:* Pension & Profit Sharing; VAT & Customs Law; Estate Planning; Individual Tax Planning; Trust Law.

NIGEL MORTON, born 1958; admitted, 1983, England. *Education:* B.A. (Hons) Law. *PRACTICE AREAS:* Property Law; Commercial Property Law; Landlord & Tenant Law; Property Finance.

DAVID H. BERRY, born 1960; admitted, 1985, England. *Education:* Manchester University LL.B. (Hons). *LANGUAGES:* French. *PRACTICE AREAS:* Commercial Law; Cable TV; Satellite Law.

WILLIAM LONGRIGG, born 1960; admitted, 1987, England. *Education:* Warwick University B.A. (Hons). *LANGUAGES:* Italian, French and German. *PRACTICE AREAS:* Family Law; Divorce Law; Children's Law; Matrimonial Law; Child Custody.

MICHAEL WOOD, born 1950; admitted, 1976, England. *LANGUAGES:* French and Arabic. *PRACTICE AREAS:* Shipping/Insurance Litigation; Insolvency.

GRAHAM CHRYSTIE, born 1947; admitted, 1973, Scotland. *PRACTICE AREAS:* Employee Benefits; Pensions; Life Assurance.

RICHARD MACDONALD BRIDGE, born 1948; admitted, 1977, England. *Education:* Nottingham University (B.Sc., Mech. Eng., B.A., Law). *PRACTICE AREAS:* Entertainment; Copyright; Communications and Media; Computers and Software.

MARYLY LA FOLLETTE, born 1942; admitted, 1987. *Education:* San Francisco State University and University of California (Berkeley) (B.A., Hons., M.A.). *LANGUAGES:* German. *PRACTICE AREAS:* Family Law; Child Abduction; Child Custody.

CONSULTANTS

Colin Chapman
David I. Bressloff
Margaret Windridge

CLEARY, GOTTLIEB, STEEN & HAMILTON

Established in 1946

CITY PLACE HOUSE
55 BASINGHALL STREET
LONDON EC2V 5EH, ENGLAND
Telephone: 44-171-614-2200
Cable Address: "Cleargolaw London"
Telex: 887659.
Facsimile: Gps. 3 44-171-600-1698; 44-171-588-5163

New York, New York Office: One Liberty Plaza, New York, N.Y. 10006. Telephone: 212-225-2000.

Washington, D.C. Office: 1752 N Street, N.W., Washington, D.C. 20036. Telephone: 202-728-2700.

Paris, France Office: 41, Avenue de Friedland, 75008 Paris, France. Telephone: 33-1-4074-6800.

Brussels, Belgium Office: Rue de la Loi 23, Bte 5, 1040 Brussels, Belgium. Telephone: 32-2-287-2000.

Hong Kong Office: 56th Floor, Bank of China Tower, One Garden Road, Hong Kong. Telephone: 852-521-4122.

Tokyo, Japan Office: Morgan Carroll Terai Gaikokuho Jimubengoshi Jimusho, 20th Floor, Shin Kasumigaseki Building, 3-2, Kasumigaseki 3-Chome, Chiyoda-Ku, Tokyo 100, Japan. Telephone: 81-3-3595-3911.

Frankfurt, Germany Office: Ulmenstrasse 37-39, 60325 Frankfurt am Main, Germany. Telephone: 49-69-971-03-0.

(This Listing Continued)

CLEARY, GOTTLIEB, STEEN & HAMILTON, London—Continued

Firm engaged in American and International Law Practice, but not authorized to appear before the English Courts or to act as Solicitors.

RESIDENT PARTNERS

MANLEY O. HUDSON, JR., born Boston, Massachusetts, June 25, 1932; admitted, 1964, New York (Not admitted in England). *Education:* Harvard University (A.B., 1953); Harvard Law School (LL.B., magna cum laude, 1956). Law Clerk to Mr. Justice Stanley Reed, The Supreme Court of the United States, 1956-1957. Resident at: Paris Office, 1958-1963, 1982-1983; New York Office, 1963-1967, 1967-1971, 1980-1982; Brussels Office, 1967. *Member:* Association of the Bar of the City of New York; New York County Lawyers' Association; New York State and American Bar Associations; American Society of International Law.

EDWARD F. GREENE, born New York, N.Y., October 18, 1941; admitted, 1969, New York; 1983, District of Columbia; 1987, Japan as Gaikokuho-Jimu-Bengoshi (Not admitted in England). *Education:* Amherst College (B.A., 1963); Harvard University (LL.B., cum laude, 1966). Author: "A Reappraisal of Current Regulation of Mergers and Acquisitions," 132 University of Pennsylvania Law Review, 1984; "Problems of Enforcement in the Multinational Securities Market," 9 University of Pennsylvania Journal of International Business Law, 1987. Co-Author: "U.S. Regulation of the International Securities Markets," Prentice-Hall Law and Business, 1992. Teaching Fellow, Boston College of Law, 1966-1967. Assistant Professor, Corporation and Commercial Law, Wayne State Law School, 1967-1968. Adjunct Professor, Georgetown University Law School, 1979-1984. Adjunct Professor, University of Pennsylvania Law School, 1984-1987. Appointed as Professor to the Nomura Chair of International Securities Regulation, University of Tokyo, 1989. Deputy Director, Division of Corporation, Finance, Securities and Exchange Commission, 1978-1979. Director, 1979-1981, General Counsel, 1981-1982, Securities and Exchange Commission. Resident at: Tokyo Office, 1987-1990; London Office, 1991—. Member, Financial Accounting Standards Advisory Council, 1986-1987. Member, Legal Advisory Committee of the New York Stock Exchange and the National Association of Securities Dealers. *Member:* The Association of the Bar of the City of New York; District of Columbia Bar; American Bar Association; American Law Institute.

JAMES A. DUNCAN, born New York, N.Y., September 22, 1953; admitted, 1980, New York (Not admitted in England). *Education:* Yale University (B.A., 1975); Harvard Law School (J.D., magna cum laude, 1979); New York University (LL.M., Taxation, 1984). Resident at: New York, 1979-1991; London, 1992—. *Member:* Association of the Bar of the City of New York; New York State Bar Association; International Fiscal Association.

DANIEL A. BRAVERMAN, born Landstuhl, Germany, January 10, 1958; admitted, 1986, New York (Not admitted in England). *Education:* Harvard College (B.A., 1980); Yale Law School (J.D., 1985). Phi Beta Kappa. Resident at: London Office, 1987-1992; New York Office, 1992-1994. Publications: "U.S. Legal Considerations Affecting Global Offerings of Shares in Foreign Companies," Norton and Auerback, *International Finance in the 1990s:* Challenges and Opportunities, Blackwell Publishers (1993); "U.S. Registration Requirements and International Exchange Offers: Current Problems and Proposed Solutions," *Insights,* Vol. 6, No. 7, July 1992 (with Edward F. Greene); "Regulation S and Other New Measures affecting the International Capital Markets," *The Review of Securities & Commodities Regulation,* Vol. 23, No. 18, October 17, 1990 (with Leslie N. Silverman); "New SEC and IRS Euro-documentation after U.S. initiatives," *International Financial Law Review,* June and July 1990 (with Albert S. Pergam); "Registration Requirements for Securities Offered Abroad," *Review of Securities & Commodities Regulation,* Vol. 21, No. 22, December 21, 1988 (with Leslie N. Silverman).

GLEN M. SCARCLIFFE, born Lincoln, England, June 29, 1957; admitted, 1980, England and Wales; 1987, New York. *Education:* Cambridge University (B.A., 1978; M.A., 1983); University of Pennsylvania (J.D., magna cum laude, 1985). *Member:* New York State and American Bar Associations; Honourable Society of the Middle Temple.

ASSOCIATES

SEBASTIAN R. SPERBER, born Astoria, New York, September 24, 1964; admitted, 1989, New York (Not admitted in England). *Education:* Columbia University (B.A., 1985; J.D., 1988). Harlan Fiske Stone Scholar. Editor-in-Chief, Columbia Journal of Transnational Law, 1987-1988. Au-

(This Listing Continued)

thor: "Debt-Equity Swapping: Reconsidering Accounting Guidelines," 26 Columbia Journal of Transnational Law 377 (1988).

ANN K. LAEMMLE, born Austin, Texas, April 27, 1956; admitted, 1990, New York (Not admitted in England). *Education:* University of Texas (B.S., 1979; J.D., 1989).

JENNIFER M. SCHNECK, born New York, N.Y., November 24, 1961; admitted, 1990, New York (Not admitted in England). *Education:* Swarthmore College (B.A., 1983); New York University School of Law (J.D., 1989). Executive Editor, New York University Law Review, 1988-1989. Author: "Recent Problems Arising Under Regulation S," *Insights,* Vol. 8, No. 8, August 1994 (with Edward F. Greene); Note, "Closing the Book on the Public Lending Right," 63 New York University Law Review, 878 (1988). Law Clerk to Honorable Amalya L. Kearse, United States Court of Appeals, 1989-1990.

PHOEBE B. MCKINNELL, born Boston, Massachusetts, July 21, 1964; admitted, 1991, New York and Massachusetts (Not admitted in England). *Education:* University of Chicago (B.A., 1986); Columbia Law School (J.D., 1990). Harlan Fiske Stone Scholar.

CHRISTOPHER J. WALTON, born Richmond, Virginia, April 12, 1965; admitted, 1991, New York (Not admitted in England). *Education:* College of William and Mary (B.A., 1987); Harvard Law School (J.D., cum laude, 1990). Articles and Comments Editor, International Law Journal. Author: "Recent Developments-United States-Canada Free Trade Agreement," 29 Harvard International Law Journal 572 (Spring 1988).

ROBERT T. BRADFORD, born Bellefonte, Pennsylvania, October 12, 1965; admitted, 1990, Maryland; 1991, District of Columbia (Not admitted in England). *Education:* Princeton University (A.B., 1987); New York University (J.D., 1990). *Member:* The District of Columbia Bar; Maryland State Bar Association.

ASHAR QURESHI, born Lahore, Pakistan, January 21, 1965; admitted, 1991, New York (Not admitted in England). *Education:* Harvard College (B.A., 1987); Harvard Law School (J.D., 1990).

CLINTON H. ELLIOTT, born Boston, Massachusetts, October 11, 1961; admitted, 1992, Massachusetts; 1993, New York (Not admitted in England). *Education:* Williams College (B.A., 1983); University of Michigan Law School (J.D., 1991). Ford Fellowship, 1991-1992. *Member:* Boston and New York State Bar Associations; American Society of International Law.

ELENA L. DALY, born Moscow, Russia, December 27, 1961; admitted, 1986, U.S.S.R. (Not admitted in England). *Education:* Moscow State University (J.D., summa cum laude, 1986); Moscow State University (post graduate academic program, 1989); University of California, Boalt Hall School of Law (LL.M., 1991). Author: "Recent Developments in US Soviet Studies (politics and law)," Collection of Scholars' Essays of Moscow State University, 1990; "The Views of Western Sovietologists on the Communist Influence on the Soviet Legal System," Sovetskoe Gosudarstvo i Pravo (Soviet State and Law, Journal of the Soviet Academy of Sciences), 1988.

MICHAEL T. PRIOR, born Brooklyn, New York, October 3, 1964; admitted, 1993, New York (Not admitted in England). *Education:* Vassar College (B.A., 1986); Brooklyn Law School (J.D., summa cum laude, 1992). Articles Editor, Brooklyn Journal of International Law. Member, Board of Trustees, Brooklyn Law School. *Member:* New York State Bar Association.

JACQUELINE DUVAL-MAJOR, born Princeton, New Jersey, April 28, 1966; admitted, 1993, New York (Not admitted in England). *Education:* Syracuse University (B.A., 1987) Phi Beta Kappa; Cornell Law School (J.D., magna cum laude, 1992). Order of the Coif. Note Editor, Cornell Law Review. Author: " One-Way Ticket Home: The Federal Doctrine of Forum Non Conveniens and the International Plaintiff," 77 Cornell Law Review 650, 1992. *Member:* New York State Bar Association.

JOHN L. FARRY, born St. Cloud, Minnesota, May 27, 1965; admitted, 1993, New York; 1994, District of Columbia (Not admitted in England). *Education:* Georgetown University (B.A., 1987; J.D., cum laude, 1992). *Member:* New York State Bar Association; The District of Columbia Bar.

DAVID A. CHRISTMAN, born New York, N.Y., January 1, 1959; admitted, 1994, New York (Not admitted in England). *Education:* New York University (B.A., 1986); New York University School of Law (J.D., magna cum laude, 1993). Order of the Coif. Note and Comment Editor, New York University Law Review.

(This Listing Continued)

(For biographical data of the partners resident in the New York, Washington, Brussels, Paris, Hong Kong, Tokyo, and Frankfurt Offices, see Professional Biographies at New York, N.Y., Washington, D.C., Brussels, Belgium, Paris, France, Hong Kong, Tokyo, Japan and Frankfurt, Germany)

CLIFFORD CHANCE

200 ALDERSGATE STREET
LONDON EC1A 4JJ, ENGLAND
Telephone: (44 171) 600 1000
Fax: (44 171) 600 5555

Amsterdam, The Netherlands Office: Apollolaan 171, 1077 AS, P.O. Box 7301, 1007 JH. Telephone: (31 20) 577 71 11. Fax: (31 20) 676 93 26.

Bahrain, Manama Associated Office: Law Office of Shaikh Isa bin Mohammed Al Khalifa. P.O. Box 20717. Telephone: (973) 531535; 531073. Fax: (973) 536272; 530608.

Barcelona, Spain Office: Pau Claris 102, 08009. Telephone: (34 3) 318 68 64. Fax: (34 3) 317 73 23.

Brussels, Belgium Office: Avenue Louise 65, Box 2, 1050. Telephone: (32 2) 533 59 11. Fax: (32 2) 533 59 59.

Budapest, Hungary Office: Köves & Partners, Clifford Chance. Madách Trade Center, Madách Imre Út 14, 1075. Telephone: (36 1) 268 1600. Fax: (36 1) 268 1610.

Dubai, United Arab Emirates Office: 18th Floor, Dubai World Trade Centre, P.O. Box 9380. Telephone: (971 4) 314333. Fax: (971 4) 313990; 314565.

Frankfurt/Main, Germany Office: Friedrichstraße 2-6, 60323. Telephone: (49 69) 971 4090. Fax: (49 69) 971 40977.

Hanoi, Vietnam Office: 52 Nguyen Binh Khiem. Telephone: (844) 229 182/3/4/5/6. Fax: (844) 229 190.

Hong Kong Office: 30th Floor, Jardine House, One Connaught Place. Telephone: (852) 2810 0229. Fax: (852) 2810 4708; 2810 4858; 2810 4743.

Madrid, Spain Office: Paseo de la Castellana 110, 28046. Telephone (34 1) 562 7674. Fax: (34 1) 562 49 93.

Milan, Italy Associated Office: Grimaldi e Clifford Chance. Via Gesú, 3, 20121. Telephone: (39 2) 7600 8040. Fax: (39 2) 7600 4950.

Moscow, Russia Office: Ul. Sadovaya - Samotechnaya 24/27, 2nd Floor, 103051. Telephone: (7 501) 258 50 50. Fax: (7 501) 258 50 51.

New York, New York Office: Swiss Bank Tower, 10 East 50th Street, 10022. Telephone: (1 212) 750 1440. Fax: (1 212) 758 6625.

Paris, France Office: 112 avenue Kléber, BP 163 Trocadéro, 75770 Paris Cedex 16. Telephone: (33 1) 44 05 52 52. Fax: (33 1) 44 05 52 00.

Riyadh, Saudi Arabia Associated Office: The Law Firm of Salah Al-Hejailan. P.O. Box 1454, 11431. Telephone: (966 1) 479 2200. Fax: (966 1) 479 1717.

Rome, Italy Associated Office: Grimaldi e Clifford Chance. Viale G. Rossini 7, 00198. Telephone: (39 6) 807 2251. Fax: (39 6) 807 8201.

Shanghai, People's Republic of China Office: Suite 898, Shanghai Centre, 1376 Nanjing Xi Lu, 200040. Telephone: (86 21) 279 8461. Fax: (86 21) 279 8462.

Singapore Office: 16 Collyer Quay #31-00, 0104. Telephone: (65) 535 1855. Fax: (65) 535 6855.

Tokyo, Japan Office: 6th Floor, South Hill Nagatacho Building, 11-30 Nagatacho 1-chome, Chiyoda-ku, 100. Telephone: (81 3) 3581 4311. Fax: (81 3) 3593 0651.

Warsaw, Poland Office: Warsaw Corporate Centre, ul. Emilii Plater 28, 00-688. Telephone: (48 2) 630 3344. Fax: (48 2) 630 3355.

FIRM PROFILE: Firm provides a comprehensive range of legal services for domestic and international clients including: International and domestic Banking and Finance, Mergers and Acquisitions, General Corporate and Commercial Work, Environmental and European Community Law, Litigation, Intellectual Property, Shipping and International Trade, Aviation, Securities Regulation, Insurance, Natural Resources, Property, Taxation and Public Policy.

PARTNERS RESIDENT IN LONDON

SENIOR PARTNER

Keith Clark

PARTNERS

GABRIELLE M. ABBOTT. LANGUAGES: German. **PRACTICE AREAS:** Real Estate - Property Law; Real Estate - Commercial Law; Real Estate - Dev./Syndications Law.

(This Listing Continued)

NEIL F. ADDISON. PRACTICE AREAS: Corporate Finance; Corporate Law; Mergers, Acquisitions and Divestitures.

ROGER M.B. BAGGALLAY. PRACTICE AREAS: Banking Litigation; Bank Fraud.

JAMES BAIRD. PRACTICE AREAS: Venture Capital; Corporate Law; Mergers, Acquisitions and Divestitures; Leveraged and Management Buyouts.

ANTHONY H.M. BANKES-JONES. PRACTICE AREAS: Structured Finance; Project Finance; Securitisation; Asset Based Lending.

JAMES M. BARLOW. PRACTICE AREAS: Investments Law; Broker-Dealer Regulation; Securities; Offshore Corporations.

JOHN BASSINDALE. PRACTICE AREAS: Ship Mortgage Reinforcement; Maritime; Oil and Gas; Admiralty; Commodities Law.

CHRISTOPHER BATES. PRACTICE AREAS: International Investments Law; Investment Banking; Corporate Law; Mergers, Acquisitions and Divestitures; Securities.

JONATHAN BEASTALL. PRACTICE AREAS: Corporate Law; Takeovers; Corporate Finance; Mergers, Acquisitions and Divestitures.

JOHN BEECHEY. PRACTICE AREAS: Construction Law; Complex Litigation; International Commercial Arbitration; Alternative Dispute Resolution.

PETER M.W. BLAKE. PRACTICE AREAS: Project Finance; Nuclear Power Law; Technology Transfer; Power Project Development.

ASHLEY R.B. BOOKER. LANGUAGES: French. **PRACTICE AREAS:** Insolvency Law; Banking Law; Complex Litigation; Bankruptcy.

LEON BOSHOFF. PRACTICE AREAS: Fraud and Deceit; Insurance Defense; Reinsurance; Insurance Coverage; Insurance.

TEDDY BOURNE. LANGUAGES: French and Italian. **PRACTICE AREAS:** International Real Estate; Commercial Real Estate; Retail Property; Commercial Property Development; Commercial Property Investment.

EDWARD L. BRADLEY. PRACTICE AREAS: Corporate Law; Finance and Securities; Mergers and Acquisitions.

ANTHONY M. BRIAM. LANGUAGES: German. **PRACTICE AREAS:** Real Estate Dev./Syndications Law; Real Estate - Property Law; Real Estate - Commercial Law.

PETER M. BROOKS. LANGUAGES: French. **PRACTICE AREAS:** Corporate Finance; Mergers, Acquisitions and Divestitures; Corporate Law; Takeovers.

MICHAEL D. BROWN. PRACTICE AREAS: Environmental Law; Complex Litigation; Alternative Dispute Resolution; Enforcement of Judgements.

JEREMY T. BROWNLOW. PRACTICE AREAS: Takeovers; Mergers, Acquisitions and Divestitures; Corporate Finance; Corporate Law.

KAZ BRUNICKI. LANGUAGES: Polish. **PRACTICE AREAS:** Asset Based Lending; Banking Law; Project Finance.

ALAN D. BRYSON. PRACTICE AREAS: Patent, Trademark and Copyright; Arbitration; Industrial/Intellectual Property.

SIMON G.F. BURGESS. LANGUAGES: French. **PRACTICE AREAS:** Corporate Law; Mergers, Acquisitions and Divestitures; Takeovers; Corporate Finance.

ROBIN H. BURLEIGH. PRACTICE AREAS: Takeovers; Corporate Finance; Corporate Law; Mergers, Acquisitions and Divestitures.

JANE A. BUSH. PRACTICE AREAS: Property Finance; Leveraged Buyouts; Banking Law; ESOPS; Securitisation.

MARK CAMPBELL. PRACTICE AREAS: Asset Based Lending; Restructuring; Derivatives; Banking Law.

CLIVE CARPENTER. PRACTICE AREAS: Corporate Finance; Aviation Finance; Banking; Asset Based Finance.

JANE E. CARVER. LANGUAGES: French. **PRACTICE AREAS:** Real Estate; Insolvency; Secured Finance; Bank Loan Workouts.

JEREMY P. CARVER. LANGUAGES: French. **PRACTICE AREAS:** Oil and Gas; Arbitration; Boundary Disputes; International Law.

(This Listing Continued)

CLIFFORD CHANCE, London—Continued

ARMEL C. CATES. LANGUAGES: French. **PRACTICE AREAS:** Project Finance; Building Societies; International Finance and Securities; Securities Trusteeship; Corporate Banking.

BOB CHARLTON. PRACTICE AREAS: Asset Based Lending; Banking Law; Equipment Leasing; Project Finance.

PETER J. CHARLTON. PRACTICE AREAS: Mergers, Acquisitions and Divestitures; Corporate Law; Corporate Finance; Financial Restructuring.

DAVID R. CHILDS. PRACTICE AREAS: Corporate Finance; Securities; Privatisations; Mergers, Acquisitions and Divestitures.

KEITH CLARK. LANGUAGES: French. **PRACTICE AREAS:** Banking Law; Banking Regulation; Finance Law; Restructuring.

JULIA CLARKE. PRACTICE AREAS: Leveraged and Management Buyouts; Venture Capital; Mergers, Acquisitions and Divestitures; Corporate Law.

KATHERINE A. COATES. PRACTICE AREAS: Corporate Law; Insurance Law; Investment Fund Law; Securities.

JEANNE CONSTABLE. PRACTICE AREAS: Banking Law.

HELEN M. COX. PRACTICE AREAS: Pensions; Employee Benefits; Retirement Benefits.

MICHAEL CUTHBERT. PRACTICE AREAS: Securities Offerings; Mergers and Acquisitions; North America; Oil and Gas; Energy.

RODNEY C. DAVIS. PRACTICE AREAS: Zoning and Planning; Real Estate Dev./Syndications Law; Land Use; Estate - Property Law.

SIMON DAVIS. PRACTICE AREAS: Company Law; Breach of Contract; Commercial Dispute Resolution; Commercial Litigation; Business Torts.

DAVID DUNNIGAN. PRACTICE AREAS: Finance Law; International Capital Markets; Securities; Securities Banking Regulation; Eurobonds.

ANDREW N.L. EDGAR. LANGUAGES: Italian. **PRACTICE AREAS:** Food and Drug Regulation; Product Safety; Litigation; Products Liability.

MICHAEL J. EDWARDS. PRACTICE AREAS: Real Estate - Property Law; Real Estate - Commercial Law; Real Estate Dev./Syndications Law.

PETER EDWARDS. PRACTICE AREAS: International Finance; Banking Law; Asset Based Lending; Structured Finance.

MICHAEL J. EHRLICH. LANGUAGES: French. **PRACTICE AREAS:** Taxation; Tax on Individuals and Businesses.

ALAN ELIAS. PRACTICE AREAS: Privatisations; Construction Contracts; Real Estate Development; Real Estate Finance; Construction Law.

PETER J. ELLIOTT. PRACTICE AREAS: Tax on Individuals and Businesses; International Tax; Corporate Tax Planning; Tax Controversies; Taxation.

JONATHAN ELMAN. PRACTICE AREAS: Taxation.

CHRISTOPHER FIELD. LANGUAGES: French. **PRACTICE AREAS:** Restructuring; Securitisation and other Structured Finance; Leveraged Buyouts; Financial Products.

MICHAEL S. FRANCIES. PRACTICE AREAS: Media Law; Corporate Law; Mergers, Acquisitions and Divestitures; Corporate Finance.

DOUGLAS FRENCH. PRACTICE AREAS: Taxation and Tax Planning; Corporate and Commercial Tax; Taxation of Mergers and Acquisitions.

KATE GIBBONS. PRACTICE AREAS: Structured Finance; Restructuring; Finance Law; Asset Based Lending.

CLIFFORD GODFREY. PRACTICE AREAS: Banking Law; Restructuring; Project Finance; Loan Workouts.

MARGARET GOSSLING. PRACTICE AREAS: International Finance; Secured Finance; Project Finance.

LYNNE GRAINGER. PRACTICE AREAS: Privatisations; Mergers, Acquisitions and Divestitures; Corporate Finance; Corporate Law.

(This Listing Continued)

ROBIN R.E. GRIFFITH. PRACTICE AREAS: Customs Law; European Community Law; Environmental Law; Antitrust and Trade Regulation.

DAVID H. GRIFFITHS. PRACTICE AREAS: Computer Regulation; High Technology; Computer Software; Computer Law.

ROBERT M.J. HALDANE. PRACTICE AREAS: Corporate Law; Mergers, Acquisitions and Divestitures; Corporate Finance.

BRIAN HALL. PRACTICE AREAS: Land Use; Zoning and Planning; Environmental Law; Administration Law.

MARK D. HARDING. LANGUAGES: French and German. **PRACTICE AREAS:** Banking Regulation; Commodities Futures Law; Securities Regulation; Financial Services Regulation; Broker-Dealer Regulation.

NEIL H. HARVEY. LANGUAGES: French and Spanish. **PRACTICE AREAS:** Corporate Law; Mergers, Acquisitions and Divestitures; Takeovers; Corporate Finance.

THOMAS M. HAWES. PRACTICE AREAS: Tax Shelters; Tax Treaties; Taxation; Tax Planning.

BEN HAWKES. PRACTICE AREAS: Offshore Corporations; International Investments Law; Insurance Law; Securities.

TIMOTHY J. HERRINGTON. PRACTICE AREAS: Broker-Dealer Regulation; Securities; International Investments Law; Mutual Funds.

ELIZABETH M. HIESTER. LANGUAGES: Spanish. **PRACTICE AREAS:** Entertainment Industry Transactions; Technology Law; Cable TV; Telecommunications Law.

RUPERT C.S. HILL. PRACTICE AREAS: Real Estate Dev./Syndications Law; Real Estate - Commercial Law; Real Estate - Property Law; Land Use.

PATRICK HOLMES. PRACTICE AREAS: Project Finance; Structured Finance; Secured Lending; Asset Based Finance.

JOHN R. HORNBY. LANGUAGES: French. **PRACTICE AREAS:** Patent, Trademark and Copyright; Chemicals and Chemistry; Litigation; Biotechnology.

JULIAN HOW. PRACTICE AREAS: Marine Insurance; Transportation Law; Offshore Pollution; Maritime; Arbitration; Ship Financing.

GEOFFREY M.T. HOWE. PRACTICE AREAS: Insolvency; Acquisitions, Divestitures, Mergers; Corporate Law.

MICHAEL J. HOWELL. LANGUAGES: French. **PRACTICE AREAS:** Joint Ventures; Antitrust Law; Commercial Law; Technology Transfer.

KATHARINE A. HOWLES. LANGUAGES: French and German. **PRACTICE AREAS:** Mergers, Acquisitions and Divestitures; Corporate Law; Cross-Border Transactions; Privatisations.

MARTIN C.A. HUGHES. PRACTICE AREAS: Restructuring; Sovereign Debt; Banking Law.

MARK HYDE. PRACTICE AREAS: Debtor and Creditor; Workouts; Insolvency; Litigation.

ALAN J. INGLIS. PRACTICE AREAS: MBO/MBIs; Asset Based Lending; Structured Finance; Restructuring.

IAN C. JACKSON. PRACTICE AREAS: Banking Law; Securities; Securities Banking Regulation.

PAUL G. JACOBS. PRACTICE AREAS: Real Estate - Property Law; Real Estate Dev./Syndications Law; Real Estate - Commercial Law; Land Use.

SIMON T. JAMES. PRACTICE AREAS: Banking Litigation; Securities Litigation; Litigation; Alternative Dispute Resolution.

CHRISTOPHER JOHNSON. PRACTICE AREAS: Pension and Profit Sharing Law; Employment Law; Employee Benefit Law; Employer-Employee Relationships; Pensions.

ALAN M. JONES. PRACTICE AREAS: Energy; Project Finance and Infrastructure; Natural Resources; Joint Ventures; Privatisations.

DAVID JONES-PARRY. PRACTICE AREAS: Litigation; Complex Litigation; Enforcement of Judgments; Arbitration; Securities Litigation.

NICHOLAS R.V. JORDAN. PRACTICE AREAS: Insurance Law; Building Societies; Financial Regulations; Securities.

(This Listing Continued)

ANTHONY J. KING. PRACTICE AREAS: Real Estate - Commercial Law; Real Estate - Property Law; Real Estate Dev./Syndications Law.

ELISABETH J. KNOX. PRACTICE AREAS: Asset Based Lending; Banking Law; Project Finance.

DANIEL J. KOSSOFF. PRACTICE AREAS: Corporate Finance; Corporate Law; Mergers, Acquisitions and Divestitures; Financial Restructuring.

MATTHEW R. LAYTON. PRACTICE AREAS: Corporate Law; Venture Capital; Mergers, Acquisitions and Divestitures; Leveraged and Management Buyouts.

STEPHEN M. LEWIS. LANGUAGES: French, German and Spanish. **PRACTICE AREAS:** Insurance Law; Litigation; Reinsurance/Reinsurance Contracts; Reinsurance Law; Arbitration.

ROBERT M.R. MACGREGOR. PRACTICE AREAS: Real Estate Dev./Syndications Law; Real Estate - Commercial Law; Real Estate - Property Law.

ROBERT MACVICAR. PRACTICE AREAS: Capital Markets; Structured Finance.

VANESSA G. MARSLAND. PRACTICE AREAS: Litigation; Computers and Software; Intellectual Property.

NICHOLAS MARTIN-SMITH. LANGUAGES: French. **PRACTICE AREAS:** Aviation Finance and Securitisation; Asset Based Finance; Project Finance.

MICHAEL R. MATHEWS. PRACTICE AREAS: Project Financing; Equipment Leasing; Banking Law.

DAVID W. MAYHEW. PRACTICE AREAS: Complex Litigation; Regulatory Law.

CHRISTOPHER MCGONIGAL. PRACTICE AREAS: Oil and Gas; International Business Law; Complex Litigation; Arbitration.

RICHARD MCILWEE. PRACTICE AREAS: Taxation.

CHRISTOPHER J. MILLARD. PRACTICE AREAS: Data Protection; Computer Law; Telecommunications; Information Technology; Intellectual Property.

WENDY MILLER. PRACTICE AREAS: Real Estate - Property Law; Litigation; Securities Enforcement.

ROGER W. MOORE. PRACTICE AREAS: Corporate Law; Corporate Finance; Mergers, Acquisitions and Divestitures.

IAIN C.S. MORPETH. PRACTICE AREAS: Real Estate - International; Leases and Leasing - Commercial; Real Estate - Finance; Real Estate Dev./Syndications Law.

MARK MORRISON. PRACTICE AREAS: Marine Insurance; Oil and Gas; Charter Parties; Arbitration and Mediation.

HABIB N. MOTANI. PRACTICE AREAS: Finance and Securities; Securities Banking Regulation; Acquisitions, Divestitures, Mergers; Financial Products.

CHRISTOPHER L. NAPIER. PRACTICE AREAS: Litigation; Arbitration and Mediation; Environmental Law; Environmental Insurance.

ROBIN C.R. NEILL. PRACTICE AREAS: Commercial Law - International Arbitration; International Arbitration; Arbitration and Mediation; Commercial Law - Arbitration and Mediation.

MURRAY NORTH. PRACTICE AREAS: Family Business; Estate Planning; Taxation; Trust Law.

ALEXANDRE R.M. NOURRY. PRACTICE AREAS: Antitrust Law; Commercial Law; European Community Law; Utilities; Rail Transport.

PATRICK S. O'CONNOR. PRACTICE AREAS: Banking Law; Financial Institutions Law.

DERHAM C. O'NEILL. PRACTICE AREAS: Venture Capital; Corporate Law; Scandinavia; Leveraged and Management Buyouts.

TERRY O'NEILL. LANGUAGES: French. **PRACTICE AREAS:** Insurance Law; Reinsurance Law; Commodities Law.

CHRISTOPHER H.A. OAKLEY. PRACTICE AREAS: Securitisation; Structured Finance; Finance Law; Banking Law; Asset Based Finance.

JOHN W. OSBORNE. PRACTICE AREAS: Antitrust Law; International Business Law; European Community Law.

(This Listing Continued)

CHRISTOPHER C. OSMAN. PRACTICE AREAS: Employment Discrimination; Employment Law; Litigation.

ROBERT PALACHE. PRACTICE AREAS: Securitisation; Structured Finance.

RAJIV PARKASH. LANGUAGES: French and German. **PRACTICE AREAS:** Business Acquisitions; Antitrust Law; Commercial Law; Joint Ventures.

EDWIN G. PATTON. PRACTICE AREAS: Oil and Gas; Commodities Law; Maritime; Arbitration.

DAVID C.L. PERKINS. PRACTICE AREAS: Patent, Trademark and Copyright; Competition/Antitrust Law; Pharmaceuticals; Biotechnology; Industrial/Intellectual Property.

CHRISTOPHER C. PERRIN. PRACTICE AREAS: Admiralty; Maritime; Transportation Law; Maritime Negligence.

RICHARD J. PETTIT. LANGUAGES: French and German. **PRACTICE AREAS:** Banking Law; International Banking; Asset Based Lending; Project Finance.

TIM PLEWS. PRACTICE AREAS: Commodities Futures; Broker-Dealer Regulation; Financial Services; Securities Regulation; Stock Exchange Regulation.

GARTH POLLARD. PRACTICE AREAS: Family Business; Partnerships; Taxation; Estate Planning.

STUART G. POPHAM. LANGUAGES: French. **PRACTICE AREAS:** Retail Banking; Restructuring; Banking Law; Loan Workouts.

JOHN S. POTTS. PRACTICE AREAS: Hostile Takeover; Securities Litigation; Litigation; Regulatory Law.

MARK REES-JONES. PRACTICE AREAS: Insolvency; Real Estate - Property Law; Asset Based Lending; Real Estate Dev./Syndications Law.

DAVID E. REID. LANGUAGES: French. **PRACTICE AREAS:** Tax on Individuals and Businesses; Taxation; ESOPS; Family Business.

STEPHEN C. REISBACH. PRACTICE AREAS: Taxation; Value Added Tax.

MARTIN E. RICHARDS. PRACTICE AREAS: Mergers, Acquisitions and Divestitures; Corporate Finance; Takeovers; Corporate Law.

STEPHEN J. ROITH. LANGUAGES: French. **PRACTICE AREAS:** Project Finance; Finance Law; Securities.

ANDREW J. ROLFE. PRACTICE AREAS: Commercial Real Estate; Real Estate Finance; Real Estate; Real Estate Investment; Real Estate Syndication.

HOWARD D. ROSS. PRACTICE AREAS: Tax Controversies; Commercial Tax; Oil and Gas Taxation; Taxation; International Tax Planning.

IAIN D. ROXBOROUGH. PRACTICE AREAS: Computer Law; Securities Litigation; Arbitration; Enforcement of Judgments.

EDWARD SADLER. PRACTICE AREAS: Restructuring; Cross Border Leasing; Equipment Leasing; Corporate Taxation; Tax of Individuals and Businesses.

JEREMY V. SANDELSON. LANGUAGES: French. **PRACTICE AREAS:** Litigation; Complex Litigation; Securities Litigation.

PAUL SEVERS. PRACTICE AREAS: Securisation; Commercial Mortgages; Structured Finance; Real Estate Finance; Asset Based Finance.

SANDY SHANDRO. PRACTICE AREAS: Litigation; Bankruptcy; International Insolvency.

DAVID W. SHASHA. PRACTICE AREAS: Mergers, Acquisitions and Divestitures; Central and Eastern European Investment; Joint Ventures; Corporate Law.

STEPHEN E. SHEA. LANGUAGES: French. **PRACTICE AREAS:** Taxation.

AUDLEY SHEPPARD. PRACTICE AREAS: International Commercial Arbitration.

NICK SHERWIN. PRACTICE AREAS: Taxation; Pensions and Profit Sharing - Superannuation; Trusts; Life Insurance.

RODNEY H.T. SHORT. LANGUAGES: French. **PRACTICE AREAS:** Bank Loan Workouts; Finance Law; Asset Based Lending; Project Finance.

ADAM SIGNY. PRACTICE AREAS: Takeovers; Mergers, Acquisitions and Divestitures; Corporate Law; Corporate Finance.

(This Listing Continued)

CLIFFORD CHANCE, London—Continued

PAUL SIMPSON. PRACTICE AREAS: Mining and Minerals; Power Projects; Energy Project Development; Transportation; Project Finance.

PEREGRINE A.L. SIMSON. LANGUAGES: French. **PRACTICE AREAS:** Securities Litigation; Complex Litigation; Corporate Law; Mergers and Acquisitions.

GRAHAM SMITH. PRACTICE AREAS: Commercial Law; Computer Law; European Community Law; Antitrust Law.

ROBERT E. SMITH. PRACTICE AREAS: Asset Based Lending; Banking Law; Municipal Finance Law; Project Finance.

MICHAEL T. SMYTH. PRACTICE AREAS: Libel; Defamation; Complex Litigation; Public Law; Media Law; Litigation.

DAVID STEINBERG. PRACTICE AREAS: Reinsurance; Civil Litigation; Insurance; Insolvency; Bankruptcy.

MARK R.O. STEWART. PRACTICE AREAS: Leveraged Buyouts; Restructuring; Banking Law; Asset Based Lending; Loan Workouts.

DAVID C. STONE. PRACTICE AREAS: Real Estate Dev./Syndications Law; Asset Based Lending; Banking Law; Project Finance.

RICHARD G. SUTTON-MATTOCKS. PRACTICE AREAS: Mergers, Acquisitions and Divestitures; Corporate Finance; Takeovers; Corporate Law.

MALCOLM J. SWEETING. PRACTICE AREAS: Finance Law; Banking Law.

PETER C. TAYLOR. PRACTICE AREAS: Asset Based Finance; Corporate Banking; Project Financing.

PETER D. TAYLOR. PRACTICE AREAS: Industrial/Intellectual Property; Patent, Trademark and Copyright; Copyright Law; Litigation.

BARRY M. THOMAS. PRACTICE AREAS: Corporate Law; Mergers, Acquisitions and Divestitures; Shareholder Agreements; Joint Ventures.

MARIAN R. THOMAS. PRACTICE AREAS: Taxation; Tax Controversies; Tax on Individuals and Businesses.

ROBIN T. TREMAINE. PRACTICE AREAS: Taxation; Pension and Profit Sharing Law; Tax of Individuals and Businesses; ESOPS.

ANTHONY A. VLASTO. LANGUAGES: French and German. **PRACTICE AREAS:** Marine Insurance; Marine Disasters; Carriage of Goods by Sea; Marine Salvage Rights; Admiralty and Maritime Law.

ANTHONY J. WARD. PRACTICE AREAS: Government; Property; Real Estate; Zoning, Planning and Land Use.

JAMES B. WHEATON. PRACTICE AREAS: Government Procurement; Joint Ventures; European Community Law; Antitrust Law.

GEOFFREY M. WHITE. PRACTICE AREAS: Equipment Leasing; Banking Law; Asset Based Lending; Aviation Finance; Aircraft Leasing; Aerospace Law.

ANDREW J.O. WILKINSON. PRACTICE AREAS: Insurance Law; Corporate Insolvency; Company Law; Corporate Restructuring.

ANTHONY N. WILLIAMS. PRACTICE AREAS: Mergers, Acquisitions and Divestitures; Central and Eastern European Investment; Joint Ventures; Corporate Law.

ANNE H. WILLIAMSON. LANGUAGES: French. **PRACTICE AREAS:** Asset Based Lending; Aircraft Finance and Leasing.

ANTHONY M.D. WILLIS. PRACTICE AREAS: Arbitration and Mediation; International Civil Litigation; Fraud and Deceit; Litigation; Complex Litigation.

TIMOTHY WOODALL. PRACTICE AREAS: Litigation; Enforcement of Judgments; Defamation; Complex Litigation.

JOHN D. WOODHALL. PRACTICE AREAS: Secured Transactions; Securitisation; Secured Finance; Securities; Secured Lending.

CHRISTOPHER WYMAN. PRACTICE AREAS: Energy and Natural Resources Projects; Power Projects; Project Finance; Infrastructure Projects.

ANDREW YIANNI. PRACTICE AREAS: Secured Lending; Sovereign Debt Rescheduling; International Banking; Asset Based Finance.

ELIZABETH J. YOUNG. PRACTICE AREAS: Commercial Property.

(This Listing Continued)

Languages: Arabic, Czech, Danish, Dutch, English, Finnish, Flemish, French, German, Greek, Hungarian, Italian, Japanese, Mandarin, Norwegian, Polish, Portuguese, Russian, Spanish and Swedish

(For the names of Partners resident in other offices, see Professional Biographies for those offices)

CLYDE & CO.

51 EASTCHEAP
LONDON EC3M 1JP, ENGLAND
Telephone: (44) 171 623 1244
Telex: 884886 CLYDE G
Facsimile: (44) 171 623 5427

Guildford, England Office: Beaufort House, Chertsey Street, Guildford GU1 4HA. Telephone: (44) 1483 31161. Telex: 859477 CLYDE G. Fax: (44) 1483 67330.

Cardiff, Wales Office: Crown Buildings, Cathays Park, Cardiff CF1 3PX. Telephone: (44) 1222 824569/824407. Telex: 497006 Clyd CF G Fax: (44) 1222 824200.

Hong Kong Office: 15th Floor, Asia Pacific Finance Tower, Citibank Plaza, 3 Garden Road, Hong Kong. Telephone: (852) 878 8600. Telex: 61972 Clyde HX. Fax: (852) 522 5907.

South East Asia Office: 10 Collyer Quay #13-06, Ocean Building, Singapore 0104. Telephone: (65) 538 7696. Fax: (65) 538 7661.

Middle East Regional Office: City Tower 2, 3rd Floor, Sheikh Zymed Road, Dubai, United Arab Emirates. Telephone: (971) 4-311102. Telex: 46644 Clyde EM. Fax: (971) 4-319920.

Latin American Regional Office: Clyde & Co. Consultores, SC Ltda. Avenida Paulista, 1274, 01310, Sao Paulo-SP Brazil. Telephone: (55) 11 285-4677. Facsimile: (55) 11 251 2997.

Latin American Regional Office: Clyde & Co. Consultores SA Ltda., Centro Comercial El Parque, (Antes Parque Canaima), Avenida Francisco de Miranda, Piso 8 - Los Palos Grandes, Caracas, Venezuela. Telephone: (58) 2 285-5411. Facsimile: (58) 2 285-5098.

Associate Offices: Paris and St. Petersburg.

Contact Names:
Admiralty and Maritime: . . . . Anthony Thomas
Insurance Litigation (non-marine and general): . . . . Michael Payton
Insurance (non-contentious): . . . . Verner Southey
Reinsurance: . . . . Bryan Young
Company/Commercial: . . . . Verner Southey
Commercial and Corporate Litigation: . . . . Jonathan Wood
Asset Based Finance: . . . . Simon Poland/Andrew Wells
Energy: . . . . Peter Felter
Employment: . . . . Paul Newdick
European Community Law: . . . . Patrick Devine
Aviation: . . . . Colin Franke
Transportation: . . . . Michael Parker

PARTNERS

Michael Payton	Christopher Gooding
Robert Chapman	Robert Pilcher
Martin Heath	Nigel Brook
Peter Morgan	David Best
David Hall	John Whittaker
Michael Harrisson	Stephen Tricks
Ralph Evers	David Page
Howard Townson	Simon Jones
Simon Fletcher	Jonathan Wood
Peter Farthing	**Peter Felter
John Dunt	Andrew Bickley
Verner Southey	Robert Wilson
Stuart Macdonald	Brian Nash
Richard Glencross	Nicholas Graydon
Colin Franke	David Silver
Peter Shelford	Richard Tanner
Anthony Rooth	Paul Newdick
Aidan Heathcote	David Salt
Robert Heanley	Judith Fruin-Ball
Jane Andrewartha	Benjamin Macfarlane
Anthony Thomas	Christopher Duffy
Alec Emmerson	Christopher Jones
Clive Thorp	Bryan Young
John Blacker	Jack Newman
Derek Hodgson	Christopher Harris
Jonathan Silver	Conrad Walker

(This Listing Continued)

Paul Bugden	John Mitchell
Roderick Smith	Angela Maxwell
Nigel Chapman	Simon Baker
Patrick Heffernan	Patrick Devine
Julian Gray	Colin Masters
Ian Ross	Yvonne Jefferies
Corinna Cresswell	John Fisher
Nicholas Greensmith	Diane Rickard
Margaret Kelly	Kathleen Cooper
Andrew Wells	Neil Fleeson
Michael Parker	***Kenneth Basch
Simon Poland	Anthony Garrod
Jon Rayman	Ruth Naylor
Benjamin Browne	Raymond Bell
Sheila Simison	Michael Roderick
David Reynolds	Philip Hooley

CONSULTANTS

Gordon Blacker	Michael Wilford
	Jane Martineau

SENIOR ASSOCIATES

*Jerry Wheatley	*Barry Turner
*Michael Bassett	Russell Rawlings
*Stephen Pink	*Martin Hall

*Not admitted as solicitors
**Advokat (Denmark)
***Attorney (Illinois)

A multinational partnership of solicitors and registered foreign lawyers.
All partners are solicitors except where otherwise shown.
Authorized by the Law Society under the Financial Services Act 1986.

Languages: Afrikaans, Bahasa, Cantonese, Danish, English, Finnish, French, German, Greek, Gujarati, Hebrew, Hokkien, Indonesian, Italian, Japanese, Norwegian, Portuguese, Punjabi, Russian, Spanish, Swedish, Urdu.

COLLYER-BRISTOW

Established in 1760

4 BEDFORD ROW
LONDON WC1R 4DF, ENGLAND
Telephone: 0171-242 7363
Telex: 21615
Fax: 0171-405 0555

Corporate and Commercial Advice. Commercial Property Advice including Major Shopping Centre Developments, Office Development Schemes, Planning, Agricultural, and Building Advice. Litigation including Commercial and Contract Disputes, Employment and Property Disputes, Intellectual Property, Professional Disciplinary and Negligence Advice, Sport and Arts, sponsorship and related advice, Personal Litigation including Personal Injury, Medical Negligence, Defamation, Inheritance Disputes. Family Law including Divorce, Separation and Financial Matters, Child Custody, Wardship and Abduction, International Forum Shopping Advice, Cohabitation Law, and Emergency Applications. Private Client Advice including Tax Planning, Wills, Trusts, Financial and Investment Advice. Charities. European Legal Advice.

MEMBERS OF FIRM

ALAN RUTHVEN BURDON-COOPER, born Stanmore, Middlesex, June 27, 1942; admitted, 1968, England. *Education:* Emmanuel College; Cambridge University (M.A., 1963; LL.B., 1966).

GILES MARTIN THORMAN, born Calcutta, May 23, 1943; admitted, 1968, England. *Education:* St. John's College; Cambridge University (M.A., 1965; LL.M., 1966).

IAN ROGER WOOLFE, born Nottingham, England, May 16, 1946; admitted, 1970, England. *Education:* Gonville and Caius College, Cambridge University (M.A., 1974; LL.M., 1978).

JEREMY IAN LEVISON, born Ryde, Isle of Wight, February 3, 1952; admitted, 1976, England. *Education:* University, Kent (1973); International Academy of Family Lawyers.

JOHN DONALDSON SANER, born North Ferriby, East Yorkshire, September 14, 1950; admitted, 1979, England. *Education:* Oxford University (B.A., 1972).

(This Listing Continued)

MICHAEL JOHN DRAKE, born London, England, August 14, 1947; admitted, 1971, England. *Education:* Selwyn College, Cambridge University (B.A., 1968; M.A., 1971); International Litigation Practitioners Forum.

MATTHEW WILLIAM BROOKER MARSH, born London, England, June 6, 1953; admitted, 1977, England. *Education:* Kingston Polytechnic (B.A. Hons., 1975); International Litigation Practitioners Forum. Fellow of Chartered Institute of Arbitrators.

CLAIRE MELTZER, born London, England, September 18, 1926; admitted, 1979, London. *Education:* Kings College, London University (B.A. Hons., 1947).

SIMON CHARLES PIGOTT, born London, England, October 29, 1956; admitted, 1983, England and Wales. *Education:* University of Southampton (B.Sc. Hons., 1977).

PAUL JEREMY SILLIS, born London, England, May 3, 1956; admitted, 1980, England and Wales; 1983, Hong Kong and Victoria, Australia. *Education:* Magdalene College; Cambridge University (M.A., 1977).

REINA MARIA MAY, born Amsterdam, The Netherlands, January 1, 1950; admitted, 1978, England. *Education:* Amsterdam University (LL.B., 1973); London School of Economics.

RAYMOND KEITH ALEXANDER, born London, England, April 8, 1950; admitted, 1974, England and Wales. *Education:* University College, London University (LL.B., 1971).

JOANNA PATRICIA KENNEDY, born St. Andrews, Scotland, July 12, 1950; admitted, 1976, England and Wales. *Education:* Trinity College, Dublin (M.A., 1972).

ANNA JULIA WILSON, born Essex, England, May 4, 1960; admitted, 1985, England. *Education:* Nottingham University (LL.B., 1982).

ASSOCIATES

Lucy K. Elgood	Janet C. Armstrong-Fox
Cathy Nickson	Philip J.H. Stinson

The Firm is a member of Eurolink an International Network of Law Firms within Europe and has Associated firms in Belgium, France, Germany, Italy, Luxembourg and The Netherlands.

Languages: English, French, German, Dutch and Italian

CONSTANT & CONSTANT

Solicitors

Established in 1911

SEA CONTAINERS HOUSE
20 UPPER GROUND BLACKFRIARS BRIDGE
CDE BOX NO. 1067
LONDON SE1 9QT, ENGLAND
Telephone: 0171-261 0006 (IDD: 44 71)
24 Hour Service: 0171-638 3535
Fax: 0171-401 2161; 0171-401 2731 Groups 2/3
Telex: 927766 TWOCTS G

Paris, France Office: 190 boulevard Haussmann, 75008. Telephone: (1) 42 89 08 89. Fax: (1) 42 89 21 00.

Shipping, Corporate and Commercial, Banking and Finance, Property and Private Client.

JOHN FREDERICK SMITH, born London, England, April 15, 1937; admitted, 1963, England. *Education:* Lancaster Gate College of Law. *LANGUAGES:* English. *PRACTICE AREAS:* Company; Commercial; Litigation; Shipping Law; Banking.

JONATHAN WILLIAM ECCLESTONE, born Charmouth, Dorset, England, August 8, 1943; admitted, 1966, England. *Education:* College of Law, London. *LANGUAGES:* English. *PRACTICE AREAS:* Marine; Corporate; Banking; International Trade.

ANTHONY RUSSELL MILLER, born Plymouth, England, January 11, 1942; admitted, 1965, England. *Education:* College of Law Lancaster Gate; College of Law Guildford. *LANGUAGES:* English and French. *PRACTICE AREAS:* Insurance; Admiralty; Salvage and Towage; Marine Casualties.

BRIAN GILLOTT, born England, July 26, 1946; admitted, 1972, England. *Education:* University of Hull (LL.B.); Guildford College of Law. *Member:* Law Society; City of London Solicitors Company; Freeman of the

(This Listing Continued)

CONSTANT & CONSTANT, London—Continued

City of London. *LANGUAGES:* English. *PRACTICE AREAS:* Maritime; Company; Commercial.

PETER JOHN RUDD, born London, England, January 6, 1945; admitted, 1971, England. *Education:* Guildford College of Law. *LANGUAGES:* English. *PRACTICE AREAS:* Maritime; Insurance; Commercial.

ANDRÉ CHARLES HARRIES, admitted, 1972, England. *Education:* William & Mary College, Williamsburg, VA (B.A., Hons, 1964); University College, London University, London, England (LL.B., 1969). *LANGUAGES:* English and French. *PRACTICE AREAS:* Commercial Agreements; Banking; Shipping.

TIMOTHY JAMES LLEWELLYN, born Bath, England, July 13, 1938; admitted, 1977, England. *Education:* University of London (LL.B., 1973). Senior Lecturer, Maritime Studies, City of London Polytechnic, 1968-1974. *Member:* Law Society (1975—). *LANGUAGES:* English. *PRACTICE AREAS:* Maritime Law; Insurance Law; Commercial Litigation.

RICHARD THOMAS HENRY WILSON, born Preston, England, December 7, 1948; admitted, 1973, England. *Education:* St. John's College Oxford (M.A. Law, 1971); Liverpool College of Law (1972). *LANGUAGES:* English. *PRACTICE AREAS:* Commercial/Residential Property; Private Client; Personal Tax.

GRAHAM MICHAEL CRANE, born Leicester, England, May 31, 1949; admitted, 1975, England. *Education:* City of London Polytechnic (B.A. Law (Hons), 1970). *Member:* French Maritime Law Association. *LANGUAGES:* English and French. *PRACTICE AREAS:* Commercial Litigation.

MICHAEL JOHN BREWSTER, born London, England, November 1, 1950; admitted, 1977, England. *Education:* College of Law London (1976-1977). *LANGUAGES:* English. *PRACTICE AREAS:* Maritime; Company; Commercial.

ANTHONY JOHN WOODWELL BURTON, born Northampton, England, January 2, 1947; admitted, 1974, England. *Education:* Lancaster Gate College of Law. *LANGUAGES:* English and Greek. *PRACTICE AREAS:* Marine; Private Client.

NIGEL STUART WILLSON, born Rotherham, Yorkshire, England, February 9, 1950; admitted, 1977, England. *Education:* University of London (LL.B., 1972); Lancaster Gate College of Law. *LANGUAGES:* English. *PRACTICE AREAS:* Shipping; Commercial; Insurance; Litigation.

JOHN WILLIAM DICKINSON, born Loughborough, England, April 19, 1951; admitted, 1975, England. *Education:* College of Law, Guildford, Surrey (1973-1974). *Member:* Law Society; London Maritime Arbitrators Association (Supporting Member). *LANGUAGES:* English. *PRACTICE AREAS:* Commercial Litigation; General Litigation.

ALISON MARY LEWZEY, born London, England, August 12, 1952; admitted, 1976, England. *Education:* University of Exeter (LL.B., 1973); Guildford College of Law (1974). *Member:* The Law Society. *LANGUAGES:* English. *PRACTICE AREAS:* Shipping; Finance; Banking; Company; Commercial.

JEREMY JOHN THOMAS, born Hampshire, England, March 8, 1946; admitted, 1972, England; 1975, India. *Education:* Guildford College of Law. *Member:* Law Society. *LANGUAGES:* English and French. *PRACTICE AREAS:* Commercial Litigation; Oil; Commodities; Charterparty; Bill of Lading; EC Law.

JOHN ALBERT PRICE, born London, England, 1950; admitted, 1981, England. *Member:* Law Society. *LANGUAGES:* English. *PRACTICE AREAS:* Shipping; Commercial Litigation.

NIGEL EMERSON, born England, December 21, 1956; admitted, 1981, England and Wales. *Education:* Corpus Christi College, Cambridge (M.A., 1982). *LANGUAGES:* English and German. *PRACTICE AREAS:* Banking; Company; Commercial; Shipping finance; Joint Ventures.

GRAHAM PILKINGTON, born Australia, April 18, 1956; admitted, 1979, Australia; 1984, England. *Education:* Melbourne University (LL.B., 1977); City of London Polytechnic (LL.M., 1983). *LANGUAGES:* English. *PRACTICE AREAS:* Commercial Litigation; Shipping Litigation.

ANDREW ALISTAIR MAXWELL, born Birkenhead, Cheshire, England, December 1, 1954; admitted, 1984, England. *Education:* Bristol Polytechnic (1979-1982). *Member:* Law Society. *LANGUAGES:* English. *PRACTICE AREAS:* Admiralty; Commercial Litigation; Aviation Claims.

(This Listing Continued)

EU232B

ANDREW HOWARD CHARLIER, born Redhill, England, November 30, 1962; admitted, 1988, England and Wales; 1994, France. *Education:* University of Birmingham; Universite de Limoges (1985); College of Law, Guildford. *Member:* Law Society of England and Wales. (Resident, Paris, France Office). *LANGUAGES:* English and French. *PRACTICE AREAS:* Shipping; Company; Commercial; Banking.

IAN MICHAEL TAYLORSON, born Derby, England, May 20, 1949; admitted, 1975, England. *Education:* City of London Polytechnic (B.A. Law (Hons.), 1970). *LANGUAGES:* English. *PRACTICE AREAS:* Company; Commercial.

THOMAS ERNEST BEESLEY, born High Wycombe, England, July 13, 1946; admitted, 1976, England. *Education:* College of Law, London. *LANGUAGES:* English. *PRACTICE AREAS:* Company; Commercial; Property; Private Client.

PHILIPPA SHERRATT, born Rinteln, Germany, September 9, 1959; admitted, 1985, England. *Education:* College of Law, Guildford and Leeds (LL.B.). *LANGUAGES:* English. *PRACTICE AREAS:* Property; General Litigation.

TANYA ROSANNE RICKARD, born 1961; admitted, 1987, England. *Education:* King's College, London University (LL.B.; LL.M.; AKC). *LANGUAGES:* English. *PRACTICE AREAS:* Shipping; Contracts; Commercial.

DENIS JOHN DOWLING, born 1962; admitted, 1988, England. *Education:* Stafforsdshire University (B.A., 1984). *LANGUAGES:* English. *PRACTICE AREAS:* Commercial and Residential Property; Banking; Private Client.

ANDREW CHARLES TERRY, born 1957; admitted, 1984, England. *Education:* Sheffield University (B.A., 1978; M.A., 1979). *LANGUAGES:* English. *PRACTICE AREAS:* International Corporate Taxation; Personal Taxation.

Languages: Danish, English, French, German, Greek, Hungarian and Serbo-Croat.

CORRS CHAMBERS WESTGARTH

2ND FLOOR
103 CANNON STREET
LONDON EC4N 5AD, ENGLAND
Telephone: (171) 929 4955
International: +44171 929 4955
Fax: (171) 929 4164

Melbourne, Victoria, Australia Office: 600 Bourke Street, Vic. 3000. Telephone: (03) 672 3000. International: +613 672 3000. Fax: (03) 602 5544.

Sydney, New South Wales, Australia Office: Level 32, Governor Phillip Tower, 1 Farrer Place, 2001. International: (02) 210 6500. Fax: (02) 210 6611.

Brisbane, Australia Office: Comalco Place. 12 Creek Street, QLD, 4000. Telephone: (07) 228 9333. International: +617 228 9333. Fax: (07) 229 2844.

Gold Coast, Queensland, Australia: Level 4, Corporate Centre One, 2 Corporate Court, Bundall, QDL, 4217. International Telephone: (075) 77 7777. Fax: (075) 74 0478.

Canberra, Australia Office: Level 5, Advance Bank Centre, 60 Marcus Clarke Street, ACT, 2601. Telephone: (06) 257 7566. International: +616 257 7566. Fax: (06)257 7563.

Perth, Western Australia Office: Commonwealth Bank Building. 150 St. George's Terrace, W.A. 6000. Telephone: (09) 321 8531. International: +619 321 8531. Fax: (09) 322 6953.

Commercial and Corporate Law including:
Banking & Finance, Computer & Communications, Corporate Reconstruction & Insolvency, Corporatisation, Customs & International Trade, Energy & Resources, Family Law, Franchising, Funds Management, Industrial Relations, Insurance & Product Liability, Intellectual Property, International Law, Joint Ventures, Litigation in all areas of practice, Mergers & Acquisitions, Planning, Pollution & Environment Law, Privatization, Professional Liability, Property Development & Construction, Securitisation, Stamp Duty, Superannuation, Taxation, Telecommunications.

PARTNERS

Tim Brookes (Not admitted in England;
(This Listing Continued)

Marcus E. Fletcher (Not admitted in England)

(For list of Personnel at Brisbane, Canberra, Bundall, Melbourne, Perth and Sydney, Australia see Professional Biographies at those locations).

COUDERT BROTHERS

A Partnership of English Solicitors
and Registered Foreign Lawyers
20 OLD BAILEY
LONDON EC4M 7JP, ENGLAND
Telephone: (44) (71) 248-3000
Telex: 887071 Couder G
Cable Address: "Treduoc" London
Telecopier: (44) (71) 248-3001, 248-3002

REVISERS OF THE FRANCE LAW DIGEST FOR THIS DIRECTORY

New York, New York 10036-7794: 1114 Avenue of the Americas.

Washington, D.C. 20006: 1627 I Street, N.W.

Los Angeles, California 90017: 1055 West Seventh Street, Twentieth Floor.

San Francisco, California 94111: 4 Embarcadero Center, Suite 3330.

San Jose, California 95113: Suite 1250, Ten Almaden Boulevard.

Paris 75008, France: Coudert Frères, 52 Avenue des Champs-Elysées.

Brussels B-1050, Belgium: Tour Louise. 149 Avenue Louise-Box 8.

Beijing, People's Republic of China 100020: Suite 2708-09 Jing Guang Centre Hu Jia Lou, Chao Yang Qu.

Shanghai, People's Republic of China 200002: c/o Suite 1804, Union Building, 100 Yanan Road East.

Hong Kong: 25th Floor, Nine Queen's Road Central.

Singapore 0104: Tung Centre, 20 Collyer Quay.

Sydney N.S.W. 2000, Australia: Suite 2202, State Bank Centre, 52 Martin Place.

Tokyo 107, Japan: 1355 West Tower, Aoyama Twin Towers, 1-1-1 Minami-Aoyama, Minato-ku.

Moscow, Russia: Ulitsa Staraya Basmannaya 14.

01301 Sao Paulo, SP, Brazil: Machado, Meyer, Sendacz, e Opice, Advogados, Rua da Consolacao, 247, 8 Andar.

Bangkok 10500, Thailand: Bubhajit Building, 20 North Sathorn Road, 10th Floor. Ho Chi Minh City, Vietnam: c/o Saigon Business Centre, 49-57 Dong Du Street, District 1.

General English and International Law Practice. Corporation, Tax and Estate Law.

RESIDENT PARTNERS

BARRY METZGER, born Newark, New Jersey, June 11, 1945; admitted, 1970, District of Columbia (Not admitted in England). *Education:* Princeton University (A.B., 1966); Harvard Law School (J.D., cum laude, 1969). Member, 1967-1969 and President, 1968-1969, Harvard Legal Aid Bureau. Assistant to the Principal, Ceylon Law College, Colombo, Ceylon, 1969-1971. Director of Asian Programs, International Legal Center, New York, 1971-1974. Vice President, International Legal Aid Association, 1972-1980. Resident Partner, Coudert Brothers, Hong Kong, 1979-1984. Resident Partner, Coudert Brothers, Sydney, 1984-1989. Member, Committee on Asian Law, Association for Asian Studies, 1973-1976. Member, New South Wales Attorney General's Committee on Commercial Resolution, 1986-1987. Arbitrator, I.C.C. Court of Arbitration. *Member:* American and International Bar Associations.

STEVEN R. BEHARRELL, born December 22, 1944; admitted, 1969, England. *Education:* British Institute and Sorbonne University, Paris; College of Law, London. Author: "Special Legal considerations for BOT (Build Own Transfer) and other Non-Recourse Finance," Second International Construction Projects Conference, London 1989; "Privatization of Energy Projects - The Legal Techniques and Consequences," LAWASIA Conference 1988. "The Electricity Pool in England and Wales: The Generator's Perspective," published in Journal of Energy and Natural Resources Law. *Member:* International Bar Association (Member, Oil Committee, 1989—). *LANGUAGES:* French.

PHILIP ANTHONY BURROUGHS, born London, England, October 2, 1955; admitted, 1980, England. *Education:* University of Bristol (LL.B.,

(This Listing Continued)

---

honors, 1977); College of Law, Lancaster Gate. *Member:* Law Society of England and Wales; City of London Law Society; British Council of Shopping Centres; The City of London Property Association. *PRACTICE AREAS:* Real Estate.

HUGH E. THOMPSON, born Lytham, September 29, 1944; admitted, 1970, England (as a Solicitor). *Education:* Christ Church, Oxford University (B.A., Hons., 1966; M.A., 1969). *Member:* Law Society of England and Wales; International Bar Association.

JULIAN D.M. LEW, born Johannesburg, South Africa, February 3, 1948; admitted, 1970, England; 1981, English Solicitor; 1985, New York. *Education:* University of London (LL.B. (Hons.), 1969); University of Louvain, Louvain, Belgium (LL.M., 1971; Ph.D., 1977). Author: *Applicable Law in International Commercial Arbitration,* Oceana, Dobbs Ferry, New York, 1978; Co-Editor, *International Trade, Law & Practice,* Euromoney, 1982; Editor, *Contemporary Problems in International Commercial Arbitration,* Centre for Commercial Law Studies and Kuwer, 1986; Editor, *The Immunity of Arbitrators,* School of International Arbitration and Lloyds of London Press, 1990. Research Fellow, City of London Polytechnic, 1976-1979. Associate Professor, University of Namur, Beljium, 1985—; Hoad School of International Arbitration, Centre of Commercial Law Studies, Queen Mary and Westfield College, University of London. (Resident). *LANGUAGES:* English and French.

COLIN D. LONG, born June 4, 1946; admitted, 1970, England. *Education:* Bristol University (LL.B., honors, 1967). Member, Editorial Panel: 'Computer Law & Security Report;' 'Telecomms Regulation Review'. Author: "Telecommunications Law and Practice," 1988. Vice Chairman, International Bar Association Communications Law Committee. Founder of UK Communication Lawyers Association. Council Member of Society for Computers and Law. *Member:* UK Parliamentary Information Technology Committee.

JEREMY MCCALLUM, born April 7, 1956; admitted, 1983, England. *Education:* Pembroke College, Cambridge University (MA); City University, London ; College of Law, Lancaster Gate, London. Member, Tax Committee, American Chamber of Commerce. *Member:* Law Society of England and Wales.

PETER F. SIMPSON, born Berkhamsted, United Kingdom, June 23, 1948; admitted, 1973, England. *Education:* Oriel College (M.A., 1970).

RESIDENT ASSOCIATES

Stuart Blythe	Richard Kennedy Guelff
Sara Bond	(Not admitted in England)
Jonathan Bor	Julian E. James
Michael P. Chissick	Dean Poster
Samantha Crowfoot	Julian Stait
Kim Hoa To	

REVISERS OF THE FRANCE LAW DIGEST FOR THIS DIRECTORY

(For biographical data of the Washington personnel, see Professional Biographies at Washington, D.C.).
(For biographical data of the Los Angeles personnel, see Professional Biographies at Los Angeles, California).
(For biographical data of the San Francisco personnel, see Professional Biographies at San Francisco, California).
(For Biographical data of the San Jose personnel, see Professional Biographies at San Jose, California).
(For biographical data of the New York personnel, see Professional Biographies at New York, N.Y.).
(For biographical data of the Brussels personnel, see Professional Biographies at Brussels, Belgium).
(For biographical data of the Paris personnel, see Professional Biographies at Paris, France).
(For biographical data of the Tokyo personnel, see Professional Biographies at Tokyo, Japan).
(For biographical data of the Beijing personnel, see Professional Biographies at Beijing, People's Republic of China).
(For biographical data of the Hong Kong personnel, see Professional Biographies at Hong Kong).
(For biographical data of the Singapore personnel, see Professional Biographies at Singapore).
(For biographical data of the Sao Paulo personnel, see Professional Biographies at Sao Paulo, Brazil).
(For biographical data of the Shanghai personnel, see Professional Biographies at Shanghai, People's Republic of China).
(For biographical data of the Sydney personnel, see Professional Biographies at Sydney, Australia).

(This Listing Continued)

COUDERT BROTHERS, *London—Continued*

(For biographical data of the Moscow personnel, see Professional Biographies at Moscow, U.S.S.R.).
(For biographical data of the Ho Chi Minh City personnel, see Professional Biographies at Ho Chi Minh City, Vietnam).

COVINGTON & BURLING

LECONFIELD HOUSE
CURZON STREET
LONDON W1Y 8A5, ENGLAND
Telephone: 011-44-171-495-5655
Fax: 011-44-171-495-3101

Washington, D.C. Office: 1201 Pennsylvania Avenue, N.W., 20044. Telephone: 202-662-6000.
Brussels, Belgium: Correspondent Office of Covington & Burling, 44 Avenue des Arts (Bte. 8), 1040. Telephone: 011-32-2-512-9890. Fax: 011-32-2-502-1598.

General Practice.

RESIDENT MEMBERS OF FIRM

CHARLES E. LISTER, born Columbus, Indiana, June 18, 1938; admitted, 1966, District of Columbia (Not admitted in England). *Education:* Harvard University (A.B., 1960); Oxford University, England (B.A., 1962; B.C.L., 1963; M.A., 1965); George Washington University (M.C.L., 1965). Law Clerk to Justice John M. Harlan, U.S. Supreme Court, 1966-1968. Associate Professor, Yale Law School, 1968-1970. (Also at Brussels, Belgium).

RICHARD F. KINGHAM, born Lafayette, Indiana, August 2, 1946; admitted, 1973, District of Columbia (Not admitted in England). *Education:* George Washington University (B.A., 1968); University of Virginia (J.D., 1973). Order of the Coif. Articles Editor, Virginia Law Review, 1972-1973. Lecturer, University of Virginia School of Law, 1977—. Author: "Das US-Amerikanische Zulassungsverfahren fur Arzneimittel: Verfahren fur Zweitanmeldungen und Vorschlage zur Verlangerung der Patentlaufzeit," Pharma - Recht, 1985; "Proposed Revisions of FDA's New Drug Regulations," Food Drug Cosm. L.J., 1983; "The Effects of U.S. Regulatory Requirements on International Pharmaceutical Marketing and Research," Proceedings of the 73rd Annual Meeting of the American Society of International Law, 1979; "Proposed Drug Regulation Reform Act of 1978," Food Drug Cosm. L.J., 1978. Member, Committee on Issues and Priorities for New Vaccine Development, Institute of Medicine, National Academy of Sciences, 1983-1986; National Advisory Allergy and Infectious Diseases Council, National Institutes of Health, 1988—.

BRADFORD L. SMITH, born Milwaukee, Wisconsin, January 17, 1959; admitted, 1986, New York; 1987, District of Columbia (Not admitted in England). *Education:* Princeton University (A.B., 1981); University of Geneva Graduate Institute of International Studies (Diplôme Program, 1984); Columbia University (J.D., 1985).

BRUCE S. WILSON, born Battle Creek, Michigan, March 24, 1959; admitted, 1988, Virginia (Inactive); 1989, District of Columbia (Not admitted in England). *Education:* University of Virginia (B.A., 1981; J.D., 1986).

RESIDENT OF COUNSEL

ROBERT B. STEVENS, born Leicester, England, June 8, 1933; admitted, 1956, England. *Education:* Oxford University (B.A., 1955; B.C.L., 1956; M.A., 1959; D.C.L., 1984); Yale University (LL.M., 1958). Barrister, Commercial Bar, London, 1960-1991. Assistant Professor, 1959-1961, Associate Professor, 1961-1965 and Professor of Law, 1965-1976, Yale University. Provost, Tulane University, 1976-1978. President, Haverford College, 1978-1987. Chancellor, University of California, Santa Cruz, 1987-1991. Master, Pembroke College (Oxford), 1993—.

RESIDENT ASSOCIATES

EVAN R. COX, born New York, N.Y., October 14, 1960; admitted, 1988, California and District of Columbia (Not admitted in England). *Education:* Michigan State University (B.A., 1982); University of California, Berkeley (J.D., 1987).

ALLEN DIXON, born Washington, D.C., October 5, 1955; admitted, 1984, District of Columbia; 1990, California (Not admitted in England). *Education:* University of Maryland (B.S., 1977); American University (J.D., 1983).

(This Listing Continued)

PAMELA S. EDDY, born Waynesburg, Pennsylvania, January 19, 1956; admitted, 1981, District of Columbia (Not admitted in England). *Education:* University of Pittsburgh (B.A., with highest honors, 1978); George Washington University (J.D., with honors, 1981). Member, George Washington Law Review, 1979-1981.

AMY GLICKMAN, born New York, N.Y., May 5, 1963; admitted, 1988, New York; 1989, District of Columbia (Not admitted in England). *Education:* Harvard College (B.A., 1971); Yale Law School (J.D., 1988).

MARY FAITH HIGGINS, born New Haven, Connecticut, January 1, 1950; admitted, 1974, California (Not admitted in England). *Education:* Connecticut College (A.B., 1971); Harvard University (J.D., 1974).

CAROLYN MITCHELL, born New York, N.Y., December 21, 1958; admitted, 1986, New York (Not admitted in England). *Education:* Yale University (B.A., 1980); Columbia University (J.D., 1989).

HILARY PRESCOTT, born Cardiff, United Kingdom, January 11, 1960; admitted, 1985, United Kingdom. *Education:* University of Sussex (B.A., 1982); Guildford University (1985).

TERRY TONG, born Hong Kong, October 15, 1963; admitted, 1987, United Kingdom and Hong Kong. *Education:* Queen Mary College, University of London (LL.B., 1984); Queen Mary and Westerfield College, University of London (LL.M., 1991).

(For complete biographical data on all personnel, see Professional Biographies at Washington, D.C. and Brussels, Belgium)

CRAVATH, SWAINE & MOORE

33 KING WILLIAM STREET, 10TH FLOOR
LONDON EC4R 9DU, ENGLAND
Telephone: 0171-606-1421
Facsimile: 0171-860-1150

New York City Office: Worldwide Plaza, 825 Eighth Avenue, 10019. Telephone: 212-474-1000. Facsimile: 212-474-3700. Cable Address: "Cravath, New York". Telex: 1-25547.
Hong Kong Office: Suite 2609, Asia Pacific Finance Tower, Citibank Plaza, 3 Garden Road, Central, Hong Kong. Telephone: 852-509-7200. Facsimile: 852-509-8282.

General Practice.
Firm engaged in American and International Law Practice, but not authorized to appear before the English courts or to act as Solicitors.

RESIDENT PARTNER

JOHN E. YOUNG, born Tulsa, Oklahoma, July 11, 1935; admitted, 1961, New York (Not admitted in England). *Education:* California Institute of Technology (B.S., 1956); Harvard University (LL.B., 1959). *Member:* The Association of the Bar of the City of New York; New York State and American Bar Associations.

EUROPEAN COUNSEL

SARAH C. MURPHY, born Evanston, Illinois, June 26, 1955; admitted, 1984, New York (Not admitted in England). *Education:* Williams College (B.A., 1977); Fordham University (J.D., 1983). *Member:* New York State and American Bar Associations.

(For biographical data of all Resident Partner and European Counsel, see Professional Biographies at New York, New York)

NICHOLAS CRITELLI ASSOCIATES, P.C.

Established in 1967

11 STONE BUILDINGS
LINCOLN'S INN
LONDON, ENGLAND
Telephone: 011-44-171-404-5055
FAX: 011-44-171-405-1551

Des Moines, Iowa Office: Suite 500, 317 Sixth Avenue, 50309-4128. Telephone: 515-243-3122. Telecopier (Fax): 515-243-3121.

Commercial Litigation, International, Insurance, Intellectual Property, Negligence and Products Liability.

FIRM PROFILE: Nicholas Critelli Associates, P.C. was established in 1967 as a specialty trial law firm. In the United States, the firm limits its practice to advocacy in the state and federal courts in matters concerning commercial litigation, intellectual property, fraud, antitrust, negligence,

(This Listing Continued)

malpractice and business and commercial related crime. In England and Wales, Mr. Critelli practices in the areas of international civil litigation and commercial matters and business crime.

NICK CRITELLI, JR., born Des Moines, Iowa, February 15, 1944; admitted, 1967, Iowa; 1971, U.S. Supreme Court; 1990, New York; 1991, England and Wales (Barrister Middle Temple, Non-practicing). *Education:* Drake University (B.A., 1966; J.D., 1967). Adjunct Professor of Trial Law and Practice, Drake University Law School, 1980-1989. Member, Iowa Supreme Court Advisory Committee on Rules of Evidence, 1982—, Chairman, 1983-1989. Member, Civil Justice Reform Act Committee, U.S. District Court, 1990—. Chairman, Iowa State Bar Association Professionalism Committee, 1989—. Chairman, Iowa State Bar Association Special Committee on Foreign Practice, 1989—. Chairman, Iowa State Bar Association Litigation Legislation Committee, 1988-1990. Governor, 1981—, Iowa Academy of Trial Lawyers, President, 1986-1987. Barrister, Honourable Society of Middle Temple Inn of Court (London, England). President and Master of the Bench, Honorable Society of Blackstone Inn of Court, Des Moines, Iowa. *Member:* Iowa State (Member, Litigation Section), New York State (Member, Litigation and International Law Sections), American (Member, Litigation, Torts and Insurance and International Law Sections) and International Bar Associations; American Board of Trial Advocates (Diplomat). Fellow: American College of Trial Lawyers; International Society of Barristers. (Certified as Civil Trial Advocate by the National Board of Trial Advocacy).

REFERENCES: Boatmen's Bank of Des Moines, N.A.; Iowa State Bar Association.

CROCKERS

10 GOUGH SQUARE
LONDON EC4A 3NJ, ENGLAND
Telephone: 071-353 0311
Cable Address: "Wilcro", London E.C.4
Telex: 93121 33171 CR G
Fax: 0171-583 1417
REVISERS OF THE ENGLAND LAW DIGEST FOR THIS DIRECTORY.

FIRM PROFILE: *The firm was founded by Sir William Charles Crocker before the First World War. The foundation of the practice was built on the handling of compensation claims on behalf of Insurance Companies and Lloyd's Underwriting Syndicates. During the two decades between the wars, Sir William expanded the firm's field of operation into company and commercial work, conveyancing and probate.*

Crockers provides a service in all branches of the law, including Company and Commercial Work, Domestic and Commercial Conveyancing, Tax Planning, Wills and Probate and Litigation; Commercial Litigation still forms a major part of the firm's business, in particular Libel, Copyright, Personal Injury and Commercial Disputes.

The firm has eight partners and eleven other fee earners. Mr. Richard Hudson is the senior partner.

The firm's clients include leading Lloyd's brokers and underwriting agents, property developers, insurance companies, charities and a broad range of private companies. Litigation work for the major insurers is principally, but by no means limited to, libel and copyright actions and personal injury claims. The firm also has a substantial private client base on whose behalf all varieties of work are undertaken.

RICHARD DAVID HUDSON, M.A., LL.B. (Cantab), admitted 1958, England (as Solicitor with honors). *PRACTICE AREAS:* Company and Commercial Law.

SIMON THOMAS KINGSTON, admitted 1973, England. *PRACTICE AREAS:* Commercial Property.

ALAN GORDON ARCHIBALD MACFADYEN, M.A. (Oxon), admitted 1965, England. *PRACTICE AREAS:* Probate; Wills; Trusts and Estates.

DAVID COLIN BELLCHAMBER, LL.B. (London), admitted 1975, England. *PRACTICE AREAS:* General Litigation.

RUPERT CHRISTOPHER GREY, LL.B. (London), admitted 1975, England. *PRACTICE AREAS:* Libel and Defamation; Intellectual Property Law.

MADHUMITA MOGFORD, LL.B. (Bris), admitted 1986, England. *PRACTICE AREAS:* Libel; Media Litigation.

(This Listing Continued)

PETER LESLIE EDGAR NORMAN, B.A., admitted 1984, England. *PRACTICE AREAS:* Motoring Litigation.

KATY A. JONES, LL.B. (Bris), admitted 1988, England. *PRACTICE AREAS:* Company and Commercial Law.

CONSULTANT

JAMES WILLIAM TAILBY CROCKER, M.A. (Cantab), admitted 1952, England.

REFERENCE: National Westminster Bank PLC., London.
REVISERS OF THE ENGLAND LAW DIGEST FOR THIS DIRECTORY.

CROSSMAN BLOCK

Solicitors
Established in 1765
ALDWYCH HOUSE
ALDWYCH
LONDON WC2B 4DB, ENGLAND
Telephone: 0171-836-2000
Facsimile: 0171-240-2648

Corporate and Commercial work, Banking Intellectual Property, Employment and Pensions, Bankruptcy, Competition Law, Distributorship Agency and Franchise Law, Immigration, Product Liability, Commercial Litigation and Arbitration, General Property Law, Property Development, Environmental Planning, International Tax Planning and Asset Protection, Charities.

FIRM PROFILE: *Crossman Block is a commercial firm providing a wide range of advice both to UK and international companies, business institutions and charities. It also advises individuals on financial planning, inheritance and trusts. All client work receives the personal attention of a partner and it is the firm's policy to provide not only the best technical advice but also practical, imaginative and commercial solutions to clients' problems.*

PARTNERS

SIMON ANTHONY ALLEN BLOCK, born 1935; admitted, 1960, England. *Education:* Cambridge University. *LANGUAGES:* English. *PRACTICE AREAS:* Company and Commercial Work; Employee Share Schemes; Pension Matters.

ANTHONY BROUGHAM, born 1950; admitted, 1976, England. *Education:* Oxford University. *LANGUAGES:* English. *PRACTICE AREAS:* Property Development; Property Finance; Banking.

PAUL MICHAEL CLEMENTS, born 1954; admitted, 1977, England. *Education:* Birmingham University. *LANGUAGES:* English. *PRACTICE AREAS:* Commercial Litigation; Insurance Law; Environmental Law; Employment Law; Arbitration; International Disputes; Personal Injuries.

MARTIN GRAHAM EMMISON, born 1947; admitted, 1971, England. *Education:* Cambridge University. *LANGUAGES:* English. *PRACTICE AREAS:* Corporate Affairs especially U.S. related matters.

CHARLES ANTHONY FARRER, born 1950; admitted, 1974, England. *Education:* Cambridge University. *LANGUAGES:* English. *PRACTICE AREAS:* Property; Development; Property Finance.

COLIN ANGUS FERGUSSON, born 1949; admitted, 1973, England. *Education:* Cambridge University. *LANGUAGES:* English. *PRACTICE AREAS:* Company and Commercial; Banking; Corporate Finance.

RUPERT THOMAS HARWOOD LESCHER, born 1945; admitted, 1976, England. *Education:* Dublin University. *LANGUAGES:* English, French and Spanish. *PRACTICE AREAS:* Company and Commercial; Corporate Finance; Banking.

STEPHEN RICHARD LEWIN, born 1952; admitted, 1977, England. *Education:* Birmingham University. *LANGUAGES:* English. *PRACTICE AREAS:* Estate Planning; Inheritance and Capital Gains Tax; Charities.

MICHAEL JOHN LUCKMAN, born 1960; admitted, 1985, England. *Education:* Exeter University. *LANGUAGES:* English. *PRACTICE AREAS:* Intellectual Property; Computers; Sponsorship.

PHILIP JAMES MADDOCK, born 1962; admitted, 1987, England. *Education:* Cambridge University. *LANGUAGES:* English and Danish. *PRACTICE AREAS:* Company and Commercial; Telecommunications; Broadcasting; Insurance.

(This Listing Continued)

CROSSMAN BLOCK, London—Continued

ROBERT VINCENT O'DONOVAN, born 1951; admitted, 1976, England. *Education:* Cambridge University. **LANGUAGES:** English, Dutch and German. **PRACTICE AREAS:** Company and Commercial Law.

PHILIP JOHN PEACOCK, born 1943; admitted, 1968, England. *Education:* London University. **LANGUAGES:** English. **PRACTICE AREAS:** Company and Commercial; Middle Eastern Law.

URSULA SUSAN TAYLOR, born 1958; admitted, 1985, England. *Education:* Cambridge University. **LANGUAGES:** English and German. **PRACTICE AREAS:** Conveyancing.

MICHAEL DENIS THOMAS, born 1962; admitted, 1987, England. *Education:* University of Essex. **LANGUAGES:** English. **PRACTICE AREAS:** Company Litigation.

PAUL MARCUS GEORGE VOLLER, born 1955; admitted, 1981, England. *Education:* University of Keele. **LANGUAGES:** English and French. **PRACTICE AREAS:** Company and Commercial; Banking; Charities.

RAYMOND M. J. WERBICKI, born September 17, 1949; admitted, 1976, Ontario; 1988, England. *Education:* University of Toronto; University of Western Ontario; University of London. **LANGUAGES:** English. **PRACTICE AREAS:** Commercial; Banking and Finance Litigation; Arbitration.

CROWELL & MORING

Established in 1979

DENNING HOUSE
90 CHANCERY LANE
LONDON WC2A 1ED, ENGLAND
Telephone: 011-44-171-413-0011
Fax: 011-44-171-413-0333

REVISERS OF THE DISTRICT OF COLUMBIA LAW DIGEST FOR THIS DIRECTORY

Washington, D.C. Office: 1001 Pennsylvania Avenue, N.W., 20004-2595. Telephone: 202-624-2500. Telex: W.U.I. (International) 64344; W.U. (Domestic) 89-2448. Cable Address: "Cromor." Fax: (202) 628-5116.
Irvine, California Office: 2010 Main Street, Suite 1200, 92714-7217. Telephone: 714-263-8400. Fax: 714-263-8414.

General Practice.

OF COUNSEL

ANTHONY J. COLEBY, born Winchester, Hampshire, England, April 10, 1957; admitted, 1983, Solicitor, Supreme Court of England and Wales. *Education:* Exeter College, Oxford (M.A., 1979); Guilford University (1981). **PRACTICE AREAS:** Banks and Banking; Securities; Finance; Business; Corporate.

PETER A. D. TEARE, born Berlin, West Germany, July 10, 1959; admitted, 1983, Solicitor, Supreme Court of England and Wales; 1986, Colorado. *Education:* Leeds University, England (LL.B., 1980). **PRACTICE AREAS:** International Business; Litigation; Commercial Law.

ASSOCIATES

SUSAN E. McLAUGHLIN, born Widnes, England, May 15, 1960; admitted, 1984, England and Wales. *Education:* Leeds University, England (LL.B., 1981); Osgood Hall Law School, Canada (LL.M., 1984). Barrister, Member of Lincoln's Inn.

SARAH E. LAMBIE, born Perth, Scotland, January 20, 1968; admitted, 1993, Solicitor, Supreme Court of England and Wales. *Education:* University of Kent at Canterbury, England (B.A., 1989).

REVISERS OF THE DISTRICT OF COLUMBIA LAW DIGEST FOR THIS DIRECTORY

(For complete biographical data on personnel at Washington D.C. and Irvine, California, see Professional Biographies at those locations)

CURTIS, MALLET-PREVOST, COLT & MOSLE

Established in 1830

TWO THROGMORTON AVENUE
LONDON EC2N 2DL, ENGLAND
Telephone: 171-638-7957
Telecopier: 171-638-5512

REVISERS OF THE ARGENTINA, BOLIVIA, BRAZIL, CHILE, COLOMBIA, COSTA RICA, DOMINICAN REPUBLIC, ECUADOR, EL SALVADOR, GUATEMALA, HONDURAS, MEXICO, NICARAGUA, PERU, URUGUAY AND VENEZUELA LAW DIGESTS FOR THIS DIRECTORY.

New York, New York Office: 101 Park Avenue, 10178-0061. Telephone: 212-696-6000. Telecopier: 212-697-1559. Cable Address: "Migniard New York". Telex: 12-6811 Migniard; ITT 422127 MGND.
Newark, New Jersey Office: One Gateway Center, Suite 403. Telephone: 201-622-0605. Telecopier: 201-622-5646.
Washington, D.C. 20006 Office: Suite 1205L, 1801 K Street, N.W. Telephone: 202-452-7373. Telecopier: 202-452-7333. Telex: ITT 440379 CMPUI.
Houston, Texas Office: 2 Houston Center, 909 Fannin Street, Suite 3725. Telephone: 713-759-9555. Telecopier: 713-759-0712.
Mexico City, D.F., Mexico Office: Torre Chapultepec, Ruben Dario 281, Col. Bosques de Chapultepec, 11530 Mexico, D.F. Telephone: 525-282-0444. Telecopier: 525-282-0637.
Paris, France Office: 8 Avenue Victor Hugo, 75116 Paris. Telephone: 45-00-99-68. Telecopier: 45-00-84-06.
Frankfurt am Main 1 Office: Staufenstrasse 42. Telephone: 069-971-4420. Telecopier: 69-17 33 99.

General and International Law Practice.
Firm engaged in American and International Practice but not authorized to appear before the English courts or to act as Solicitors.

RESIDENT PARTNER

BRUCE B. PALMER, born Brooklyn, New York, October 4, 1948; admitted to bar, 1974, Illinois; 1978, District of Columbia; (Not admitted in England). *Education:* Baldwin-Wallace College (B.A., 1970); DePaul University (J.D., 1973); New York University (LL.M., 1974).

RESIDENT ASSOCIATES

ROBERT N. DAWBARN, born London, England, December 8, 1968; admitted, 1994, England and Wales. *Education:* University of Wales College Cardiff (LL.B., Hons., 1989). Member of the Law Society.

ROBERT E. STEMMONS, born Springfield, Missouri, April 4, 1960; admitted, 1986, Missouri; 1987, New York; 1988, Massachusetts (Not admitted in England). *Education:* Harvard University (A.B., cum laude, 1982); University of Missouri (J.D., 1986). Author: "The Adoption and Confusion of Microeconomic Theory and Policy in Antitrust Law," Missouri Law Review, Winter, 1986. *Member:* American Bar Association. **REPORTED CASES:** State v. Clevenger, 733 S.W.2d 782 (Mo.App.1987).

REVISERS OF THE ARGENTINA, BOLIVIA, BRAZIL, CHILE, COLOMBIA, COSTA RICA, DOMINICAN REPUBLIC, ECUADOR, EL SALVADOR, GUATEMALA, HONDURAS, MEXICO, NICARAGUA, PERU, URUGUAY AND VENEZUELA LAW DIGESTS FOR THIS DIRECTORY.

(For complete biographical data on all personnel, see Professional Biographies at New York, New York)

DAVENPORT LYONS

1 OLD BURLINGTON STREET
LONDON W1X 1LA, ENGLAND
Telephone: 0171-287 5353
Fax: 0171-437 8216
Telex: 267097 Lonsol G

Commercial and Corporate Law, International and Local Copyright and Media Law, Entertainment Law, Property Law and Litigation.

FIRM PROFILE: The firm was founded over 50 years ago and has an emphasis on commercial and corporate matters, particularly those with an international element. The firm is very well known in the fields of media and entertainment law. The firm has an active commercial property department and effective litigation department. The firm's private client de-

(This Listing Continued)

partment has considerable experience in trust and tax matters both within the UK and overseas.

PARTNERS

LEON MORGAN, admitted, 1964, England. *Education:* Law Society, London; College of Law, London. (Senior Partner). *LANGUAGES:* French. *PRACTICE AREAS:* General Company/Commercial; Broadcasting, Television, Film and Music Publishing.

DAVID ROCKBERGER, admitted, 1971, England. *Education:* Cambridge University College of Law (M.A., 1967; LL.M., 1968). *LANGUAGES:* French. *PRACTICE AREAS:* General Company/Commercial; Music Publishing, Film and Television.

GRAHAM ATKINS, admitted, 1972, England. *Education:* Oxford University; College of Law, Lancaster Gate (M.A., Oxon, 1969). *LANGUAGES:* French. *PRACTICE AREAS:* Commercial Property.

JAMES WARE, admitted, 1972, England. *Education:* Oxford University College of Law, Guildford (B.A. Oxon, 1968). *LANGUAGES:* French and German. *PRACTICE AREAS:* General Company/Commercial; Copyright, Music, Entertainment and Media Law; Computer Law.

ANTHONY FIDUCIA, admitted, 1978, England. *Education:* Bristol University, College of Law, Lancaster Gate (B.A., Bristol, 1973). *LANGUAGES:* French and Italian. *PRACTICE AREAS:* General Company/-Commercial; Corporate Acquisitions and Disposals; Franchising; Television, Film and Video.

JAMES MACKIE, admitted, 1980, England. *Education:* Southampton University (LL.B., Hons. 1974); College of Law, Chester. *LANGUAGES:* French. *PRACTICE AREAS:* Commercial Litigation; Copyright; Entertainment and Media; Building and Construction.

MICHAEL HATCHWELL, admitted, 1988, England. *Education:* Nottingham Trent University (B.A., Hons., 1984); College of Law, Guildford. *LANGUAGES:* French and Danish. *PRACTICE AREAS:* General Company/Commercial; EC and Competition Law.

DAVID GORE, admitted, 1979, England. *Education:* Leicester University (B.A., Hons., 1972); College of Law, Lancaster Gate. *LANGUAGES:* French. *PRACTICE AREAS:* Commercial Litigation; Copyright; Defamation.

CONSULTANTS

DANTE CAMPAILLA, admitted, 1953, England. *Education:* Cambridge University; Gibson & Weldon College, London (B.A. Cantab, 1950; M.A., Cantab, 1953). *LANGUAGES:* French, Italian and Spanish. *PRACTICE AREAS:* Commercial & Domestic Business & Property Transactions.

OSCAR BEUSELINCK, admitted, 1951, England. *LANGUAGES:* Flemish, French and German. *PRACTICE AREAS:* Defamation, Entertainment, Media and Film Litigation Law.

DAVIES ARNOLD COOPER

6-8 BOUVERIE STREET
LONDON EC4Y 8DD, ENGLAND
Telephone: 171-936 2222
Telex: 262894
Facsimile: 171-936 2020

Other London, England Office: Room 991 Lloyd's Building, 1 Lime Street. Telephone: 171-283 8658. Facsimile: 171-283 8063.

Manchester, England Office: 60 Fountain Street. Telephone: 161-839 8396. Facsimile: 161-839 8309.

Madrid, Spain Office: Serrano Anguita, 10-5 DCHA. Telephone: 1-446 3566. Facsimile: 1-445 1600.

Corporate, Commercial, Banking, Taxation, Insolvency, Competition, Entertainment Law, Computer Law, Intellectual Property, Employment, Commercial Property and Funding, Town Planning and Environmental Law, Construction, Commercial Litigation, Marine and Aviation, Insurance and Reinsurance, Product Liability, Personal Injury, Professional Indemnity, Crisis Management, Disaster Litigation.

PARTNERS

DAVID A. MCINTOSH, born 1944; admitted, 1968, England and Wales. Co-Author: "Personal Injury Awards in EC Countries" and "Civil Procedures in EC Countries," Lloyds of London Press. Active in Debates on the Lord Chancellor's Civil Justice Review for improving personal in-

(This Listing Continued)

jury compensation law and reforming of the legal profession including the Corporate Accountability Bill (DAC). *Member:* Law Society of England and Wales; International Bar Association (Vice Chairman, Committee on Consumer Affairs, Advertising, Unfair Competition and Products Liability; Secretary, Product Liability Committee); American Bar Association; Defence Research and Trial Lawyers Association of America; Chartered Institute of Arbitrators (Associate Member); International Association of Defense Counsel; Professional Liability Underwriters Association. *PRACTICE AREAS:* Insurance and Commercial Litigation; Products Liability Law; Pharmaceutical Law.

JOHN PARKER, born 1940; admitted, 1965, England. *Education:* Corpus Christi College, Oxford. *Member:* Law Society of England and Wales. *PRACTICE AREAS:* Professional Liability; Insurance; Product Liability; Litigation.

DAVID ROGERS, born 1947; admitted, 1975, England. *Education:* College of Law. Author: "Defence Strategy for Serious Personal Injuries." *Member:* Law Society of England and Wales; BMLA (Committee on Passenger Liability). *PRACTICE AREAS:* Litigation; Personal Injury.

MICHAEL DOBIAS, born 1950; admitted, 1975, England. *Education:* University of Birmingham (LL.B.). Author: articles for "IADC Defense Council Journal and Products Liability International." *Member:* Law Society of England and Wales; International Bar Association; London Solicitors Litigation Association; British Insurance Law Association; International Association of Defense Counsel. *PRACTICE AREAS:* Insurance; Litigation.

SIMON PEARL, born 1953; admitted, 1977, England. *Education:* Horace Mann School, New York; University of Birmingham (LL.B., Hons.). Author: "How to defend a major multi-party pharmaceutical claim," Health and Law Letter, June, 1990; "The Product Liability Directive Revisited with Pharmaceuticals: latest developments in Europe," King's College Publication, January, 1991; Chapter on, "Product Liability and Insurance Law," Lloyd's of London Press, 1994. Co-Author: "Aids - an overview of the legal implications," Law Society Gazette, May, 1989. *Member:* Law Society of England and Wales; Medico/Legal Society; International Bar Association; American Bar Association (Associate Member). *PRACTICE AREAS:* Medical Malpractice; Drugs and Narcotics; Litigation.

JOHN COATON, born 1951; admitted, 1976, England. *Education:* Nottingham University; College of Law. *Member:* Law Society of England and Wales. *PRACTICE AREAS:* Property; Real Estate.

JOHN SMITH, born 1947; admitted, 1976, England. *Education:* Alleyns School, Dulwich; College of Law, Lancaster Gate. *Member:* Law Society of England and Wales. *PRACTICE AREAS:* Insurance; Litigation; Professional Liability; Personal Injury.

NICHOLAS ROCHEZ, born 1954; admitted, 1980, England. *Education:* Middlesex and the City of London University; College of Law, Lancaster Gate. Member of Academic Board, B.P.P. Law School. *Member:* Law Society of England and Wales; City of London Law Society. *PRACTICE AREAS:* Insurance; Litigation; Professional Liability; Employment Law.

MARK BEATTIE, born 1952; admitted, 1979, England. *Education:* Trinity College, Cambridge; College of Law, Lancaster Gate. Co-Author: "Directors & Officers Liability - How to minimize your risk." *Member:* Law Society of England and Wales. *PRACTICE AREAS:* Company Law; Intellectual Property; Business Law; Corporate Law.

KENNETH MCKENZIE, born 1953; admitted, 1978, England. *Education:* Exeter University. Author: "Lloyds: Why Blame the Victim." Co-Author: "Directors and Officers Liability: How to minimize your risk"; Syndicate 2000 "Guide to Corporate Capital at Lloyd's"; Syndicate 2001 "Corporate Capital Vehicles" "British Insurance Law Association," Gazette Contributor. *Member:* Law Society of England and Wales. *PRACTICE AREAS:* Insurance; Litigation; Professional Liability.

ALAN FISHER, born 1951; admitted, 1978, England. Visiting Lecturer, MSc degree course dealing with the transportation of dangerous substances, the CIMAH regulations and risk management, University of Hertfordshire. *Member:* Law Society of England and Wales; Chartered Insurance Institute. *PRACTICE AREAS:* Insurance; Energy; Litigation.

ANNE WARE, born 1954; admitted, 1980, England. *Member:* Law Society of England and Wales. *PRACTICE AREAS:* Pharmaceutical Product Liability; Medical Malpractice; Drugs and Narcotics; Medico-Legal Litigation.

(This Listing Continued)

DAVIES ARNOLD COOPER, London—Continued

DANIEL GOWAN, born 1951; admitted, 1976, New Zealand; 1983, England. *Education:* St. Kentigern College, Auckland; University of Otago, New Zealand. *Member:* Law Society of England and Wales; Chartered Institute of Arbitrators (Committee Member, London Branch). *PRACTICE AREAS:* Construction Law; Litigation.

ANDREW HIGGS, born 1953; admitted, 1980, England. *Education:* Grey College; Durham University; Chester College of Law. Author: "Waybills - A Case of Common Law Laissez-faire in European Commerce," The Journal of Business Law, September, 1992; "An Overview of the Implications of the Carriage of Goods by Sea Act 1992," The Journal of Business Law, September, 1993; "Litigation of Oil and Gas Insurance - Why is it Rare in Practice?" Kluwer Publishers, 1993. *Member:* Law Society of England and Wales; London Maritime Arbitrators Association (Associate Member); Chartered Institute of Arbitrators; Institute of Petroleum; International Bar Association; Inter-Pacific Bar Association. *PRACTICE AREAS:* Marine; Litigation; Insurance; Commercial Law; Energy.

GERALD O'MAHONEY, born 1953; admitted, 1984, England. *Member:* Law Society of England and Wales. *PRACTICE AREAS:* Insurance; Re-insurance; Commercial Litigation.

MICHAEL FLETCHER, born 1942; admitted, 1967, England. *Education:* Kings College, University of London; College of Law, Lancaster Gate. Co-Author: Contributor, to Volume 10 Encyclopaedia of Forms and Precedents, Fifth Edition, Butterworths. *Member:* Law Society of England and Wales; City of London Club. *PRACTICE AREAS:* Pensions Law; Company Law; Business Law; Commercial Law; Finance.

DAVID ROBERTS, born 1948; admitted, 1973, England. *Education:* Exeter University; College of Law, Lancaster Gate. *Member:* Law Society of England and Wales. *PRACTICE AREAS:* Property; Real Estate.

DAVID HERTZELL, born 1955; admitted, 1983, England. *Education:* Brasenose College; Oxford and Guildford College of Law. *Member:* Law Society of England and Wales. (Managing Partner). *PRACTICE AREAS:* Professional Indemnity; Insurance; Litigation.

ROBERT LEE, born 1959; admitted, 1984, England. *Education:* University College, Cardiff. *Member:* Law Society of England and Wales. *PRACTICE AREAS:* Property; Real Estate.

MICHAEL COVER, born 1950; admitted, 1973, as Barrister; 1988, England. *Education:* Southampton University. Chairperson, Dictionary of Listings Committee. *Member:* Law Society of England and Wales; International Trademark Association. (Resident, Manchester Office). *PRACTICE AREAS:* Intellectual Property; Litigation; Environmental Law; Drugs and Narcotics.

NICHOLAS SINFIELD, born 1959; admitted, 1984, England. *Education:* University College, London. Member, Arson Prevention Bureau Working Party on Fraudulent Arson. *Member:* Law Society of England and Wales. (Resident, Lloyds Office). *PRACTICE AREAS:* Insurance; Litigation; Fraud.

LAURENCE MESSER, born 1949; admitted, 1974, England. *Education:* Durham University; Guildford College of Law. *Member:* Law Society of England and Wales; London Young Solicitors Group (Chairman, 1982); Royal Town Planning Institute (Council Member, 1987-1991); Law Society Planning and Environmental Law Committee, 1982-1992; Planning Panel (1992). *PRACTICE AREAS:* Property; Real Estate; Environmental.

NIGEL MONTGOMERY, born 1956; admitted, 1981, England. *Education:* Cambridge University. *Member:* Law Society of England and Wales; Society of Insurance Receivers; Society of Practitioners of Insolvency and Insolvency Lawyers Association. *PRACTICE AREAS:* Finance; Insolvency; Banking.

JOHN JACKSON, born 1953; admitted, 1980, England. *Member:* Law Society of England and Wales. (Resident, Manchester Office). *PRACTICE AREAS:* Finance; Business Law; Company Law; Commercial Law.

BETH WILKINS, born 1981. *Education:* University College, London. Trustee, Manchester Charity Service; Member, Manchester Family Court Services Committee. *Member:* Law Society of England and Wales; North West S.F.L.A. (Founder; Good Practice Committee); Manchester Law Society (Council Member). (Resident, Manchester Office). *PRACTICE AREAS:* Family Law.

MARJORIE HOLMES, born 1956; called to the Bar, 1980; admitted, 1988, England. *Education:* London School of Economics; Cambridge University. Author: "Third Party Rights Against Insurers Act," P&I International

(This Listing Continued)

tional. Co-Author: "Civil Procedures in EC Countries," published by Lloyd's of London Press. *Member:* Law Society of England and Wales; Institute of Arbitrators (Associate Member); International Bar Association. *PRACTICE AREAS:* Marine; Litigation; Commercial Law.

CHARLES WANDER, born 1954; admitted, 1979, England. *Education:* Wolverhampton Polytechnic. *Member:* Law Society of England and Wales. *PRACTICE AREAS:* Corporate Law; Commercial Law; Mergers and Acquisitions; Joint Ventures; Banking and Finance.

JOHN BOLTON, born 1943; admitted, 1989, England. *Education:* United States Naval Academy; State University of New York at Buffalo (BSc.; MSc., Engineering, 1965); Canisius College (M.B.A., 1972); University of South West England (L.S.F., 1985). Author: "Delay and Disruption Claims, Design and Build and Fast Track Construction." *Member:* Law Society of England and Wales; Official Referees Solicitor Association; Chartered Institute of Arbitrators (Fellow); International Bar Association. *PRACTICE AREAS:* Construction Law; Litigation.

NICHOLAS RUDGARD, born 1954; admitted, 1980, England. *Education:* St. John's College, Oxford. Author: "Product Liability - the wording." *Member:* Law Society of England and Wales. *PRACTICE AREAS:* Litigation; Insurance; Personal Injury; Product Liability.

MARK SCOGGINS, born 1957; admitted, 1993, England and Wales. *Education:* Cambridge University, Fitzwilliam College (B.A., 1980; M.A., 1984); Inns of Court School of Law. Author: "Occupational Stress Liabilities"; "Corporate Accountability Bill Review." Co-Author: "Privilege and the Photocopier," 1992. Visiting Lecturer: Police Staff College, Bramshill; Emergency Planning College, Easingwold; Chartered Insurance Institute College of Insurance, London; Centre of Advanced Litigation, Nottingham Trent University. *Member:* Law Society of England and Wales; Joint Working Party of the Law Society and the Bar on the Civil Courts (Co-opted Assistant, 1992-1993); Society for Computers and the Law; Selden Society. *PRACTICE AREAS:* Litigation; Insurance; Professional Liability.

TANIA SLESS, born 1961; admitted, 1985, Ireland; 1991, England and Wales. *Education:* Trinity College, Dublin. Co-Author: "Personal Injury Awards in EU and EFTA Countries," Lloyds of London Press. *Member:* Law Society of England and Wales. *PRACTICE AREAS:* Litigation; Personal Injury; Insurance.

ANDREW WILLCOCK, born 1945; admitted, 1972, England. *Member:* Law Society of England and Wales; Official Referees Solicitors Association; Society for Computers and Law. (Resident, Manchester Office). *PRACTICE AREAS:* Construction Law; Litigation; Insurance.

HILARY NICHOLLS, born 1953; admitted, 1981, England. *Education:* University of Wales. *Member:* Law Society of England and Wales; O.R.S.A. (Sub-Committee on Information Technology). *PRACTICE AREAS:* Construction Law; Litigation.

ROBERT VINEY, born 1951; admitted, 1987, England. *Education:* Sussex University. *Member:* Law Society of England and Wales. *PRACTICE AREAS:* Insurance; Litigation; Professional Liability.

NICHOLAS BRADLEY, born 1960; admitted, 1986, England. *Education:* Nottingham University; Guildford College of Law. Member, Freeman-Citizen & Glover of London. *Member:* Law Society of England and Wales; Chartered Insurance Institute. *PRACTICE AREAS:* Litigation; Insurance; Intellectual Property.

ADRIAN HARRIS, born 1956; admitted, 1986, England. Co-Author: "New Problems for Fixed Charge Receiverships"; "Controlling Legal Costs in a Receivership." *Member:* Law Society of England and Wales. *PRACTICE AREAS:* Insolvency Law; Banking Law; Mergers and Acquisitions.

CHRISTOPHER REES, born 1955; admitted, 1979, England. *Education:* Newcastle University. *Member:* Law Society of England and Wales. *PRACTICE AREAS:* Strategic Planning; Housing and Local Government Law.

JOHN NELMES, born 1957; admitted, 1983, England. *Education:* Christies College, Cambridge. *Member:* Law Society of England and Wales. *PRACTICE AREAS:* Banking; Property Finance; Insolvency.

JEREMY WOOD, born 1959; admitted, 1984, England. *Education:* Cardiff University. Author: "Construction Insurance and UK Construction Contracts;" "Syndicate 2001: Corporate Capital in Lloyds." *Member:* Law Society of England and Wales; Chartered Insurance Institute; British Insurance Law Association; Life Insurance Legal Society (Chairman). *PRACTICE AREAS:* Insurance; Commercial Law; Company Law.

(This Listing Continued)

JOHN WEBSTER, born 1959; admitted, 1993, England. Author: "Post Accident Management," "EUROS-European Flag". Contributor to and Co-Creator of the Maritime Helpline in the "International Maritime Journal". **PRACTICE AREAS:** Personal Injury; Professional Indemnity; Insurance Recovery.

PAUL LOCKETT, born 1962; admitted, 1987, England. *Education:* Manchester University. Member: Law Society of England and Wales. **PRACTICE AREAS:** Company Law; Corporate Finance; Employment Law.

CONSULTANTS

Anthony Harris   Clive Boxer

DAVIS POLK & WARDWELL

1 FREDERICK'S PLACE
LONDON EC2R 8AB, ENGLAND
Telephone: 011-44-171-418-1300
Telex: 888238
Telecopier: 011-44-171-418-1400

New York, N.Y. Office: 450 Lexington Avenue, 10017. Telephone: 212-450-4000. Cable Address: "Davispolk New York". Telex: ITT-421341; ITT-423356. Telecopier: 212-450-4800.

Washington, D.C. Office: 1300 I Street, N.W., 20005. Telephone: 202-962-7000. Telecopier: 202-962-7111.

Paris, France Office: 4, Place de la Concorde, 75008. Telephone: 011-331-4017-3600. Telecopier: 011-331-42.65.22.34. Cable Address: "Davispolk Paris".

Tokyo, Japan Office: In Tokyo practicing as Reid Gaikokuho-Jimu-Bengoshi Jimusho. Tokio Kaijo Building Annex, 2-1, Marunouchi 1-Chome, Chiyoda-Ku, Tokyo 100, Japan. Telephone: 011-81-3-201-8421. Telecopier: 011-81-3-201-8444. Telex: 2224472 DPWTOK.

Frankfurt, Germany Office: MesseTurm, 60308 Frankfurt am Main, Federal Republic of Germany. Telephone: 011-49-69-97-57-03-0. Telecopier: 011-49-69-74-77-44.

Hong Kong Office: The Hong Kong Club Building, 3A Chater Road. Telephone: 852 533 3300. Fax: 852 533 3388.

American and General International Practice.
Firm engaged in American and International Law Practice, but not authorized to appear before the English courts or to act as Solicitors.

SENIOR COUNSEL

JOSEPH CHUBB, born New York, N.Y., October 23, 1940; admitted, 1966, New York (Not admitted in England). *Education:* Yale University (B.A., 1962; LL.B., 1966). *Member:* The Association of the Bar of the City of New York; International and American Bar Associations; Federal Bar Council.

RESIDENT PARTNERS

PAUL KUMLEBEN, born Bloemfontein, South Africa, August 15, 1954; admitted, 1983, New York. *Education:* University of Cape Town, South Africa (B.A., 1976); University of Natal, South Africa (LL.B., 1978); Oxford University (Rhodes Scholar), England (B.A., 1981); Chicago-Kent College of Law (J.D., 1982). *Member:* The Association of the Bar of the City of New York.

DAVID M. WELLS, born Wilmington, Delaware, October 21, 1946; admitted, 1976, New York (Not admitted in England). *Education:* Harvard University (A.B., 1968); Georgetown University (J.D., 1974). *Member:* The Association of the Bar of the City of New York; New York State and American Bar Associations.

COUNSEL

JOHN D. PATON, born Morrinsville, New Zealand, November 7, 1958; admitted, 1982, New Zealand; 1985, New York; 1986, U.S. Tax Court. *Education:* Queen Charlotte College; University of Auckland (BCOM LL.B., 1982); Cornell University (LL.M., 1984).

SENIOR ATTORNEY

JEFFREY M. OAKES, born Philadelphia, Pennsylvania, December 30, 1952; admitted, 1980, New York (Not admitted in England). *Education:* Princeton University (B.A., 1975); University of Miami (J.D., 1979). *Member:* American Bar Association.

(This Listing Continued)

ASSOCIATES

Julia K. Cowles (Not admitted in England); **Lisa F. Firenze** (Not admitted in England); **Miriam Haber** (Not admitted in England); **Marcelle R. Joseph** (Not admitted in England); **Stowell R. R. Kelner** (Not admitted in England); **Deanna L. Kirkpatrick** (Not admitted in England); **Reinhard B. Koester** (Not admitted in England); **Nicholas Adams Kronfeld** (Not admitted in England); **Michael T. Mollerus** (Not admitted in England).

(For Complete Biographical Data on all Personnel see Professional Biographies at New York City)

DE BANDT, VAN HECKE & LAGAE

ROYEX HOUSE
ALDERMANBURY SQUARE
LONDON EC2V 7HR, ENGLAND
Telephone: (44-171) 600.36.07
Telecopier: (44-171) 600.17.18

REVISERS OF THE BELGIUM AND THE EUROPEAN COMMUNITIES LAW DIGESTS FOR THIS DIRECTORY.

Brussels, Belgium Office: rue Brederode 13, B-1000. Telephone: (32-2) 517.94.11. Telex: 25477 Lexlaw. Telecopier: (32-2) 517.94.94.
Antwerp, Belgium Office: Mechelsesteenweg 196, B-2018. Telephone: (32-3) 238.10.62. Telex: 71059 diurna b. Telecopier: (32-3) 216.47.17.
New York, N.Y. Office: 712 Fifth Avenue, New York, New York, 10019, U.S.A. Telephone: 212-801-3420. Telecopier: 212-801-3425.

Belgium, European and International Practice.
Member of Alliance of European Lawyers (EEIG) which regroups six law firms from Continental Europe. The Alliance consists of De Bandt, van Hecke & Lagae at Brussels and Antwerp; De Brauw Blackstone Westbroek at The Hague, Amsterdam, Rotterdam and Eindhoven; Jeantet & Associés at Paris and Warsaw; Lagerlöf & Leman at Stockholm, Gothenburg and Malmö; Oppenhoff & Rädler at Berlin, Colone, Frankfurt am Main, Leipzig and München; Uria & Menendez at Madrid and Barcelona.
The Alliance member firms have joint offices at Brussels, London, New York and Prague.

RESIDENT ATTORNEY

JOHAN DE BRUYCKER, born Gent, Belgium, August 26, 1962; admitted, 1988, Brussels. *Education:* University of Ghent (Lic. Jur., 1987); University of Paris (D.S.U., 1988); University of Georgia Law School (LL.M., 1990).

REVISERS OF THE BELGIUM AND THE EUROPEAN COMMUNITIES LAW DIGESTS FOR THIS DIRECTORY.

DEBEVOISE & PLIMPTON

Established in 1931

1 CREED COURT
5 LUDGATE HILL
LONDON EC4M 7AA, ENGLAND
Telephone: (44-171) 329-0779
Telecopier: (44-171) 329-0860

New York Office: 875 Third Avenue, 10022. Telephone: 212-909-6000. Telex: (Domestic) 148377 DEBSTEVE NYK. Telecopier: (212) 909-6836.

Washington, D.C. Office: 555 13th Street, N.W., 20004. Telephone: 202-383-8000. Telex: 405586 DPDC WUUD. Telecopier: (202) 383-8118.

Los Angeles, California Office: 601 South Figueroa Street, Suite 3700, 90017. Telephone: 213-680-8000. Telecopier: 213-680-8100.

Paris, France Office: 21 Avenue George V, 75008. Telephone: (33-1) 40 73 12 12. Telecopier: (33-1) 47 2050 82. Telex: 648141F DPPAR.

Budapest, Hungary Office: 1065 Budapest, Révay Köz 2.III/2. Telephone: (36-1) 112-8067. Telecopier: (36-1) 132-7995.

Hong Kong Office: 13/F Entertainment Building, 30 Queen's Road Central. Telephone: (852) 2810-7918. Fax: (852) 2810-9828.

Firm engaged in American and International Practice but not authorized to appear before the English Courts or act as Solicitor.

FIRM PROFILE: OFFICE PROFILE: Opened in 1989, the London office of Devevoise & Plimpton has a diverse international practice, including work in global and other equity offerings; privatizations; mergers and acquisitions; debt financings, including cross-border and project financings;

(This Listing Continued)

DEBEVOISE & PLIMPTON, London—Continued

telecommunication matters; joint ventures and other Central and Eastern European transactions; international tax planning; financial services; general corporate, tax and commercial law advice in connection with the formation and ongoing operations of subsidiaries and joint ventures; and licensing, distribution and other international commercial contracts. The London office works closely with a network of local counsel and tax advisers, as well as with our offices in Paris, Budapest and Hong Kong, our attorneys and affiliates based in Prague and Moscow, and our U.S. offices.

RESIDENT PARTNERS

GEORGE B. ADAMS, born September 16, 1930; admitted, 1957, N.Y.; 1965, U.S. District Court, Southern District of New York; 1973, U.S. Court of Appeals, 2nd Circuit (Not admitted in England). *Education:* Yale (B.A., 1952); Harvard (LL.B., cum laude, 1957). Member, National Panel of Arbitrators, American Arbitration Association. *Member:* The Association of the Bar of the City of New York; New York State, American and International Bar Associations. Affiliate Member, The Law Society. Fellow, American Bar Foundation. *PRACTICE AREAS:* Corporate Law; International Finance and Corporate Finance Law; International Business Law.

HUGH ROWLAND, JR., born October 7, 1941; admitted, 1968, N.Y. (Not admitted in England). *Education:* Yale (B.A., 1963; LL.B., 1967); University of Strasbourg, France (Diplôme, 1965). Order of the Coif. Chairman, Moot Court Board, 1966-1967. *Member:* The Association of the Bar of the City of New York. *PRACTICE AREAS:* Taxation Law; International Business Law; Corporate Law.

ROBERT R. BRUCE, born March 8, 1944; admitted, 1972, District of Columbia; 1980, U.S. Supreme Court (Not admitted in England). *Education:* Harvard (B.A., 1966); John F. Kennedy School of Government, Harvard (M.P.A., 1970); Harvard (J.D., 1970). Director, Communications Planning, Public Broadcasting Service, 1970-1972. General Counsel, Federal Communications Commission, 1977-1981. *Member:* The District of Columbia Bar. *PRACTICE AREAS:* Communications; Intellectual Property; Administrative and Technology Law.

RESIDENT COUNSEL

RAYMOND G. WELLS, born July 22, 1953; admitted, N.Y., 1979 (Not admitted in England). *Education:* Yale (B.A., 1975); Columbia (J.D., 1978). Member, Columbia Journal of Transnational Law, 1976-1978. *Member:* American College of Investment Counsel. *PRACTICE AREAS:* Corporate Law; Corporate Financing Law; Secured Transactions Law.

RESIDENT ASSOCIATES

KATHERINE ASHTON, born September 23, 1960; admitted, 1986, New York (Not admitted in England). *Education:* Harvard (A.B., 1981; J.D., 1985). *Member:* The Association of the Bar of the City of New York (Member, Foreign and Comparative Law Committee); American and International Bar Associations. *PRACTICE AREAS:* Corporate Finance Law; Privatizations; Mergers and Acquisitions; Joint Ventures.

DAVID BREWSTER, born September 19, 1963; admitted, 1988, New South Wales, Australia (Not admitted in England). *Education:* Sydney (B.Ec., 1984; LL.B., 1987); New South Wales (1989-1990); Columbia (LL.M., 1992). *Member:* Law Society of New South Wales. *PRACTICE AREAS:* Mergers and Acquisitions; Corporate Law; Securities Law.

EDMUND H. PRICE, born February 20, 1965; admitted, 1992, New York and District of Columbia (Not admitted in England). *Education:* Colgate (B.A., cum laude, 1987); George Washington (J.D., with high honors, 1991). *Member:* Bar Association of the District of Columbia. *PRACTICE AREAS:* Commodities Futures Law; Corporate Law; Investment Law; Securities Regulation Law.

CHRISTINE A. WORRELL, born September 9, 1968; admitted, 1993, New York (Not admitted in England). *Education:* Brown University (A.B., 1989); Harvard University (J.D., 1992). *PRACTICE AREAS:* Corporate Law; Securities Law; Mergers and Acquisitions.

(For Biographical Data of other Partners, see Professional Biographies at New York, N.Y.)

DE BRAUW BLACKSTONE WESTBROEK

Attorneys and Civil Law Notaries

ROYEX HOUSE
ALDERMANBURY SQUARE
LONDON EC2V 7HR, ENGLAND
Telephone: (171) 600 1719
Telecopier: (171) 600 1718

REVISERS OF THE NETHERLANDS LAW DIGEST FOR THIS DIRECTORY.

The Hague, The Netherlands Office: Zuid Hollandlaan 7, 2596 AL. Telephone: (70) 328 5 328. Telex: 32321. Telecopier: (70) 328 5 325.

Amsterdam, The Netherlands Office: Atrium - 7th Floor, Strawinskylaan 3115, 1077 ZX. Telephone: (20) 5 481 481. Telex: 10227. Telecopier: (20) 5 481 485.

Rotterdam, The Netherlands Office: 10th Floor, Coolsingel 139, 3012 AG. Telephone: (10) 401 88 99. Telex: 24676. Telecopier: (10) 411 35 48.

Eindhovenn, The Netherlands Office: Parklaan 42a, 5613 BG. Telephone: (40) 464442. Telecopier (40) 466288.

Brussels, Belgium Office: Brederodestraat 13A, B-1000. Telephone: (2) 505 0211. Telecopier: (2) 502 2644.

New York, New York Office: 712 Fifth Avenue, 30th Floor, 10019-4102. Telephone: (212) 801-3430. Fax: (212) 801-3435; (212) 801-3436.

Dutch Attorneys may represent clients before all Dutch Courts, before the European Court of Justice and the Benelux Court of Justice, and are admitted to plead before all Courts of the member states of the Common Market (EEC).

Member of Alliance of European Lawyers (EEIG) which regroups six law firms from Continental Europe. The Alliance consists of Oppenhoff & Rädler at Munich, Berlin, Cologne, Frankfurt am Main and Leipzig; De Bandt, van Hecke & Lagae at Brussels and Antwerp; DeBrauw Blackstone Westbroek at Amsterdam, The Hague, Rotterdam, Brussels, London and New York; Jeantet & Associés at Paris and Warsaw; Lagerlöf & Leman at Stockholm, Gothenburg and Malmö; Uria & Menendez at Madrid and Barcelona.

The Alliance member firms have joint offices at Brussels, London, New York and Prague.

ATTORNEY AT LAW
MEMBER OF FIRM

LODEWIJK J. HIJMANS VAN DEN BERGH, born 1963; admitted, 1988, The Hague (Not admitted in England). *Education:* Utrecht University. *LANGUAGES:* English. *PRACTICE AREAS:* Corporate Law; Financial Law; Securities Law.

ASSOCIATES

BERNARD W. ROELVINK, born 1962; admitted, 1989, Rotterdam. *Education:* Leyden University. *LANGUAGES:* English and German. *PRACTICE AREAS:* Corporate Law.

REMMINE A. DUDOK VAN HEEL, born 1965; admitted, 1989, Amsterdam (Not admitted in England). *Education:* Utrecht University. *LANGUAGES:* English and French. *PRACTICE AREAS:* Corporate Law; Labour Law.

N. BERNARD SPOOR, born 1963; admitted, 1991, Amsterdam (Not admitted in England). *Education:* Groningen University.

REVISERS OF THE NETHERLANDS LAW DIGEST FOR THIS DIRECTORY.

(For list of Partners and Counsel of the respective Member Firms see Professional Biographies at: Oppenhoff & Rädler at Munich, Cologne, Frankfurt am Main, Berlin and Leipzig, Germany; De Bandt van Hecke & Lagae at Brussels and Antwerp, Belgium; De Brauw Blackstone Westbroek at The Hague, Rotterdam and Amsterdam, Eindhoven, The Netherlands; Jeantet & Associés, at Paris, France and Warsaw, Poland; Lagerlöf & Leman at Stockholm, Gothenburg and Malmö, Sweden; Uria & Menendez at Madrid and Barcelona, Spain)

DECHERT PRICE & RHOADS

(also see Titmuss Sainer Dechert)

2 SERJEANTS' INN

LONDON EC4Y 1LT, ENGLAND

Telephone: (0171) 583-5353

Telefax: (0171) 353-3683

Philadelphia, Pennsylvania: 4000 Bell Atlantic Tower, 1717 Arch Street, 19103-2793. Telephone: 215-994-4000. Telefax: 215-994-2222.

New York, N.Y.: 477 Madison Avenue, 10022. Telephone: 212-326-3500.

Washington, D.C.: 1500 K Street, N.W., 20005. Telephone: 202-626-3300.

Harrisburg, Pennsylvania: Thirty North Third Street, 17101. Telephone: 717-237-2000.

Princeton, New Jersey: Princeton Pike Corporate Center, P.O. Box 5218, 08543-5218. Telephone: 609-520-3200.

Boston, Massachusetts: Ten Post Office Square South, 02109. Telephone: 617-728-7100.

Brussels, Belgium: 65 Avenue Louise, 1050. Telephone: (02) 535-5411.

General Practice.

FIRM PROFILE: *Dechert Price & Rhoads, one of the largest U.S. law firms, has recently joined forces with the leading City of London law firm Titmuss Sainer & Webb. The combined U.K. practice is now known as Titmuss Sainer Dechert and together the two firms have over 450 lawyers in eight offices.*

RESIDENT PARTNERS

EDWARD L. KLING, born Cincinnati, Ohio, 1947; admitted, 1974, California (Not admitted in England). *Education:* Babson College (B.S., 1968); Oxford University, Oxford, England (B.A., 1971; B.A., Jurisprudence, 1973; M.A., 1974). Co-Editor and Contributing Author: *Obtaining Discovery Abroad,* 1990 ABA and *Joint Ventures in Europe,* 1991 Butterworths.

PETER DRAPER, born Lancashire, England, 1952; admitted, 1976, England (as Solicitor). *Education:* Warwick University (LL.B. with honors, 1973).

(Members of the Firm, Counsel, Of Counsel, and Associates in Philadelphia and Harrisburg, Pennsylvania, New York, New York, Washington, D.C., Boston, Massachusetts, Princeton, New Jersey and Brussels, Belgium are listed in the Biographical Section respectively)

DENTON HALL

A Member of the Denton International Group of Law Firms

FIVE CHANCERY LANE

CLIFFORD'S INN

LDE BOX 242

LONDON EC4A 1BU, ENGLAND

Telephone: 0171-242 1212

Telex: 263567 BURGIN G

Fax: 0171-404 0087

Milton Keynes, Buckinghamshire, England Office: Regency Court, 206/208 Upper Fifth Street, MK9 2HR. Telephone: 01908-690260. Fax: 01908-668535.

Beijing, People's Republic of China Office: 3325 China World Tower, China World Trade Centre, 1 Jianguomenwai Avenue, 100004. Telephone: 86-1 505 4891/2. Fax: 86-1 505 4893.

Brussels, Belgium Office: Rue du Marteau 15, 1040. Telephone: 32-2 223 0621. Telex: 69110. Fax: 32-2 223 0482.

Hong Kong Office: 10/F Hutchison House, 10 Harcourt Road Central. Telephone: 852-820 6272. Telex: 65750 DHB HX. Fax: 852-810 6434.

Los Angeles, California Office: 22nd Floor Fox Plaza, 2121 Avenue of the Stars, 90067. Telephone: 1-310 282 8888. Fax: 1-310 282 8900.

Singapore Office: 152 Beach Road, #08-05 Gateway East, 0718. Telephone: 65-2911219. Cable Address: "Burginhal Singapore". Telex: 22803 DHBW. Fax: 65-2938102.

Tokyo, Japan Office: 2nd Floor, Ichibancho 27 Building, 27 Ichibancho, Chiyoda-Ku, 102. Telephone: 81-3 3222 5977. Fax: 81-3 3222 5980.

Moscow, Russia Office: Aerostar, Third Floor, Leningradski Prospect, Korpus 9. Telephone 7-502 224 1494; Fax 7-502 224 1495.

Associated Offices: Amsterdam, Berlin, Chemnitz, Copenhagen, Dusseldorf, Frankfurt, Hamburg, Rotterdam and Vienna.

(This Listing Continued)

Banking and Financial Markets, Commercial Property, Company and Commercial, Competition/EC, Construction, Corporate Finance, Development, Employment and Immigration, Environmental Law, Energy and Natural Resources, Media/Entertainment, Infrastructure Projects and Privatization, Insolvency, Insurance, Intellectual Property, Leisure, Litigation and Arbitration, Pensions, Planning, Private Clients, Retail, Tax, Telecommunications.

MEMBERS OF FIRM

DAVID AITMAN (Also at Brussels, Belgium Office). *LANGUAGES:* French. *PRACTICE AREAS:* Competition and EC.

ANTHONY ALEXANDER. *LANGUAGES:* French, German. *PRACTICE AREAS:* Banking and Financial Markets; Corporate Finance.

ROBERT ALLAN. *LANGUAGES:* French. *PRACTICE AREAS:* Entertainment; Music; Video.

BILL ANDERSON. *PRACTICE AREAS:* Entertainment; Defamation; Commercial Litigation.

ADRIAN BARR-SMITH. *PRACTICE AREAS:* Media and Communications; Entertainment; Sports.

MONICA BLAKE. *PRACTICE AREAS:* Property; Retail.

NEIL BOGLE. *PRACTICE AREAS:* Energy and Natural Resources.

ANTHONY BONSOR. *LANGUAGES:* French, Spanish. *PRACTICE AREAS:* Banking and Financial Markets.

GILL BRIANT. *LANGUAGES:* French. *PRACTICE AREAS:* Property; Development.

ANDREW BRITTON. *PRACTICE AREAS:* Corporate Finance; Corporate Law.

SIMON BROWN. *LANGUAGES:* French. *PRACTICE AREAS:* Corporate Finance; Corporate Law.

MYLES CAVE-BROWNE-CAVE. *PRACTICE AREAS:* Energy and Natural Resources.

HELEN CHARLTON. *LANGUAGES:* French. *PRACTICE AREAS:* Competition and EC.

DIANA COURTNEY. *PRACTICE AREAS:* Property; Property Finance.

DAVID COURTNEY-HATCHER. *PRACTICE AREAS:* Construction; Construction Litigation.

STEPHANIE DALE. *PRACTICE AREAS:* Employment; Immigration.

JAMES DALLAS. *PRACTICE AREAS:* Energy and Natural Resources; Privatisation.

DAVID DANSKIN (At Milton Keynes, England Office). *PRACTICE AREAS:* Property; Local Government.

PENNY DAVIES. *PRACTICE AREAS:* Property; Retail.

ANDREW DAWS. *PRACTICE AREAS:* Corporate Finance; Corporate Law.

CHRIS DENNY (At Milton Keynes, England Office). *PRACTICE AREAS:* Property; Retail.

KEN DEARSLEY (Also at Los Angeles, California Office). *PRACTICE AREAS:* Media; Entertainment; Film; TV Finance; TV Production and Distribution.

PETA DOLLAR. *LANGUAGES:* French. *PRACTICE AREAS:* Property; Development.

JANE DOUGLAS. *PRACTICE AREAS:* Corporate Tax.

ROBERT FINNEY. *PRACTICE AREAS:* Banking and Financial Markets.

ROGER FLYNN. *PRACTICE AREAS:* Property; Development.

JOHN GARNER (At Milton Keynes, England Office). *PRACTICE AREAS:* Property.

ELLEN GATES. *PRACTICE AREAS:* Energy; Natural Resources; Project Finance.

VIRGINIA GLASTONBURY. *PRACTICE AREAS:* Banking; Property; Property Finance.

PETER GODDARD. *PRACTICE AREAS:* Property; Property Finance.

(This Listing Continued)

DENTON HALL, London—Continued

ROBERT GOLDSPINK. LANGUAGES: French. **PRACTICE AREAS:** Commercial Litigation; Fraud.

PHILIP GOODWIN. LANGUAGES: Afrikaans. **PRACTICE AREAS:** Corporate Finance; Corporate Law.

ANTONY GRANT. PRACTICE AREAS: Commercial; Corporate Finance; Banking.

CHARLES GREEN. PRACTICE AREAS: Corporate Finance; Corporate Law.

PAUL GRIFFIN. PRACTICE AREAS: Energy and Natural Resources.

MALCOLM GROOM. PRACTICE AREAS: Energy and Natural Resources.

GILLA HARRIS. PRACTICE AREAS: Commercial Litigation.

NICHOLAS HIGHAM. PRACTICE AREAS: Intellectual Property; Information Technology; Communications.

IAN HODGSON. PRACTICE AREAS: Banking; Property; Property Finance.

JOHN HOUGHTON. PRACTICE AREAS: Property; Planning.

JAMES IRVINE. PRACTICE AREAS: Commercial Litigation; Intellectual Property.

CLIVE JENKINS. PRACTICE AREAS: Property; Retail.

JERRY KATZMAN. PRACTICE AREAS: International Corporate and Commercial.

HENRY KING. PRACTICE AREAS: Commercial; Corporate Finance; International Tax.

CINDY LESLIE. PRACTICE AREAS: Commercial Litigation; Insolvency.

STEVE LEWIS. PRACTICE AREAS: Corporate Finance; Corporate Law.

ED MARLOW. PRACTICE AREAS: Banking and Financial Markets; Project Finance.

RICHARD METCALF (ALso at Moscow, Russia Office). **LANGUAGES:** French, German. **PRACTICE AREAS:** Energy and Natural Resources.

DAVID MILES. PRACTICE AREAS: Corporate Law; Corporate Finance; Property.

JOHN MILES. PRACTICE AREAS: Commercial Litigation; Energy Litigation.

DAVID MORONEY. PRACTICE AREAS: Energy and Natural Resources.

HOWARD MORRIS. PRACTICE AREAS: Insolvency.

HILARY NEWISS. PRACTICE AREAS: Litigation; Biotechnology.

HELEN NORRIS. LANGUAGES: French. **PRACTICE AREAS:** Property; Planning.

JENNIFER PALMER. PRACTICE AREAS: Private Clients.

CAROLE PEET (At Milton Keynes, England Office). **PRACTICE AREAS:** Property Litigation.

JULIAN POPE. PRACTICE AREAS: Construction; Construction Litigation.

JUDITH PORTRAIT. PRACTICE AREAS: Private Clients.

MARTIN QUICKE. PRACTICE AREAS: Property.

MICHAEL RIDLEY. PRACTICE AREAS: Media; Entertainment; TV Production.

JOHN ROSENHEIM. LANGUAGES: German, French. **PRACTICE AREAS:** Commercial Litigation.

KEVIN RYAN. PRACTICE AREAS: Commercial Litigation; Arbitration; Insurance.

DREW SCOTT. PRACTICE AREAS: Corporate Tax.

MICHAEL STEINER. LANGUAGES: Czech, Russian. **PRACTICE AREAS:** Commercial Litigation; Insolvency.

(This Listing Continued)

EU242B

NICK STRAW. PRACTICE AREAS: Property; Property Finance.

ROGER SUTCLIFFE. PRACTICE AREAS: Property; Development.

JONATHAN TATTEN. PRACTICE AREAS: Commercial Litigation; Insurance; Marine.

PETER TAYLOR. PRACTICE AREAS: Property Litigation.

ROBERT THOMSON. PRACTICE AREAS: Commercial Litigation; Insurance.

CLIVE THORNE. LANGUAGES: French. **PRACTICE AREAS:** Intellectual Property Litigation; Commercial Litigation.

GERALD TISDALL. PRACTICE AREAS: Property Litigation.

LIZ TOUT. PRACTICE AREAS: Commercial Litigation; Arbitration.

MARK TURNER. PRACTICE AREAS: Intellectual Property; Commercial; Information Technology; Biotechnology.

NICHOLAS WEST. PRACTICE AREAS: Media; Entertainment.

ALAN WILLIAMS. PRACTICE AREAS: Media; Entertainment; Copyright; Defamation; Publishing.

THOMAS WINSOR. PRACTICE AREAS: Energy and Natural Resources; Project Finance; Regulatory.

CHARLES WOOD. LANGUAGES: French. **PRACTICE AREAS:** Energy and Natural Resources; Project Finance; Privatisation; Regulatory.

CONSULTANTS

MICHAEL BROTHWOOD. LANGUAGES: French. **PRACTICE AREAS:** Energy and Natural Resources.

PATRICK BURGIN. LANGUAGES: French. **PRACTICE AREAS:** Energy; Corporate Finance.

MICHAEL CATHERALL. PRACTICE AREAS: Private Clients.

MICHAEL FLINT. LANGUAGES: French. **PRACTICE AREAS:** Media; Communications; Entertainment; Copyright.

CHRISTOPHER HOPKINSON (At Milton Keynes, England Office). **LANGUAGES:** French. **PRACTICE AREAS:** Property; Commercial Litigation; Local Government.

BRIAN MCGEOUGH. PRACTICE AREAS: Property; Charity Law.

IKO MESHOULAM. LANGUAGES: French, Hebrew. **PRACTICE AREAS:** Intellectual Property; Commercial.

JOHN SALTER. LANGUAGES: French. **PRACTICE AREAS:** Environmental Law; Planning; Property; Energy.

TOM TAYLOR. PRACTICE AREAS: Property.

DEWEY BALLANTINE

150 ALDERSGATE STREET
LONDON EC1A 4EJ, ENGLAND
Telephone: 011-44-171-606-6121
Telefax: 011-44-171-600-3754

New York, New York Office: 1301 Avenue of the Americas, 10019-6092. Telephone: 212-259-8000. Fax: 212-659-6333.

Washington, D.C. Office: 1775 Pennsylvania Avenue, N.W., 20006-4605. Telephone: 202-862-1000. Fax: 202-862-1093.

Los Angeles, California Office: 333 South Hope Street. Telephone: 213-626-3399. Fax: 213-625-0562.

Hong Kong Office: Asia Pacific Finance Tower, Suite 3907, Citibank Plaza, 3 Garden Road, Central, Hong Kong. Telephone: 852-2509-7000. Fax: 852-2509-7088.

Budapest, Hungary Office: Dewey Ballantine Theodore Goddard, Vadasz utca 31, H-1054 Budapest Hungary. Telephone: (36-1) 111-9620. Fax: (36-1) 112-2272.

Prague, Czech Republic Office: Dewey Ballantine Theodore Goddard, Revolucni 13, 110 00 Prague 1, Czech Republic. Telephone: (42-2) 2481-0283. Fax: (42-2) 231-0983.

Warsaw, Poland Office: Dewey Ballantine Theodore Goddard, ul. Klonowa 8, 00-591 Warsaw, Poland. Telephone: 48-22-493-288. Fax: 48-22-498-023.

Kraków, Poland Office: Dewey Ballantine Theodore Goddard, Pl. Axentowicza 6. 30-034 Kraków Poland. Telephone: 48-12-340-339. Fax: 48-12-333-624.

General Practice.
(This Listing Continued)

RESIDENT PARTNERS

FRED R. GANDER, born Cambridge, Ohio, October 1, 1958; admitted, 1986, Virginia (Not admitted in England). *Education:* Georgetown University (B.S.B.A., magna cum laude, 1981; J.D., magna cum laude, 1986). Editor-in-Chief, The Tax Lawyer, 1985-1986. Certified Public Accountant, Virginia, 1985. *Member:* Virginia State Bar; American Bar Association. *PRACTICE AREAS:* Tax.

BRIAN J. MORRIS, born Miami, Florida, November 5, 1954; admitted, 1980, New York. *Education:* Marist College (B.A., 1976); University of London, England; Fordham University (J.D., 1979). *Member:* The Association of the Bar of the City of New York; New York State and American Bar Associations. *PRACTICE AREAS:* Corporate.

(For Biographical data of all Partners, see Professional Biographies at New York, N.Y.)

DIAZ-BASTIEN & TRUAN ABOGADOS

(Spanish Law Firm)

Established in 1978

111 PARK STREET
LONDON W1Y 3FB, ENGLAND
Telephone: (171) 409.20.18; 491.33.08
Facsimile: (171) 629.29.02

Madrid, Spain Office: Hermosilla 21 2° Izda, 28001. Telephone: (91) 577.36.60; 577.36.61; 577.36.62. Facsimile: (91) 575.54.68.
Marbella, Málaga Office: Sierra Blanca 2, 3° A, 29600 Marbella. Telephone: (5) 277.63.62; 277.63.03. Facsimile: (5) 282.54.52.

Administrative, Anti-Trust, Arbitration. Aviation, Banking and Finance, Bankruptcy/Insolvency, Civil Litigation, Commercial, Commercial Property, Company, Competition, Constitutional, Construction, Debt Recovery, Distribution, Employment, Entertainment, European Community, Franchising, House Purchase/Conveyancing, Import/Export, Insolvency, Insurance, Intellectual Property, International, Investment and Financial Services, Media, Mergers and Acquisitions, Mortgages/Hypothecs, Partnerships, Pharmaceutical, Planning, Real Estate Purchase, Shipping/Admiralty, Tax-Company, Tax-International, Tax-Offshore, Transport, Wills and Probate.

RESIDENT MEMBER

Rafael Truan

DIBB LUPTON BROOMHEAD

Solicitors

125 LONDON WALL
LONDON EC2Y 5AE, ENGLAND
Telephone: 0171 600 0202
Fax: 0171 600 1650

Leeds, England Office: 117 The Headrow. Leeds LS1 5JX. Telephone: 0113 243 9301. Fax: 0113 245 2632.
Manchester, England Office: Carlton House, 18 Albert Square, Manchester M2 5PE. Telephone: 0161 839 2266. Fax: 0161 839 4469.
Birmingham, England Office: Windsor House, Temple Row, Birmingham B2 5LF. Telephone: 0121 200 1188. Fax: 0121 236 9228.
Sheffield, England Office: Fountain Precinct, Balm Green, Sheffield S1 1RZ. Telephone: 0114 272-0202. Fax: 0114 270 0568.

FIRM PROFILE: Dibb Lupton Broomhead was founded over 200 years ago. It is one of the ten largest law firms in the UK and is the largest commercial practice not based exclusively in the City of London. The firm has substantial Commercial, litigation, property and corporate recovery departments. It has a national reputation for intellectual property, information technology law, insolvency work and debt collection, and it is also firmly established in banking, property development, franchising, environmental law, employment, construction and EC law.

PARTNERS

ROBIN SMITH (Senior Partner).

PAUL RHODES (Managing Partner).

JOHN ALDERTON. *PRACTICE AREAS:* Corporate Recovery.

(This Listing Continued)

JILL ANDREW. *PRACTICE AREAS:* Employment.

PETER ANSON. *PRACTICE AREAS:* Insurance Litigation.

SUSAN ARCHER. *PRACTICE AREAS:* Litigation.

DAVID BARRETT. *PRACTICE AREAS:* Information Technology.

KEIR BARRIE. *PRACTICE AREAS:* Commercial.

PETER BARTON. *PRACTICE AREAS:* Commercial.

SPENCER BATISTE, M.P.. PRACTICE AREAS: Commercial.

ANDREW BENNETT. *PRACTICE AREAS:* Litigation.

STUART BENSON. *PRACTICE AREAS:* Litigation.

BRUCE BENTLEY. *PRACTICE AREAS:* Litigation.

JULIA BOLER. *PRACTICE AREAS:* Trusts.

JOHN BOOTH. *PRACTICE AREAS:* Property.

JEREMY BOWDEN. *PRACTICE AREAS:* Corporate Recovery.

DAVID BRADLEY. *PRACTICE AREAS:* Employment.

MICHAEL BROOM. *PRACTICE AREAS:* Insurance Litigation.

TONY BUGG. *PRACTICE AREAS:* Corporate Recovery.

MICHAEL BURTON. *PRACTICE AREAS:* Banking.

JANE BUSH. *PRACTICE AREAS:* Litigation.

NICK BUTLER. *PRACTICE AREAS:* Commercial.

COLIN CADMAN. *PRACTICE AREAS:* Litigation.

ANDREW CALLAGHAN. *PRACTICE AREAS:* Property Litigation.

ANN CARRINGTON. *PRACTICE AREAS:* Banking.

ANDREW CHAMBERLAIN. *PRACTICE AREAS:* Employment.

ANDREW CHAPPELL. *PRACTICE AREAS:* Litigation.

MARTIN COWELL. *PRACTICE AREAS:* Litigation.

TINA COWEN. *PRACTICE AREAS:* Commercial.

MARGARET COX. *PRACTICE AREAS:* Pensions.

PETER CRANSTON. *PRACTICE AREAS:* Corporate Recovery.

JONATHAN CROOKES. *PRACTICE AREAS:* Insurance Litigation.

ANDREW DARWIN. *PRACTICE AREAS:* Commercial.

RUSSELL DAVIDSON. *PRACTICE AREAS:* Property.

PETER DAVIS. *PRACTICE AREAS:* Property.

NIGEL DICKSON. *PRACTICE AREAS:* Corporate Recovery.

ANN DUCHART. *PRACTICE AREAS:* Trusts.

PAUL EARDLEY. *PRACTICE AREAS:* Commercial.

HUGH EVANS. *PRACTICE AREAS:* Banking.

IAN FALSHAW. *PRACTICE AREAS:* Property.

MICHAEL FINNEY. *PRACTICE AREAS:* Corporate Recovery.

PAUL FIRTH. *PRACTICE AREAS:* Property.

NICHOLAS FISHER. *PRACTICE AREAS:* Banking.

KAREN FRIEBE. *PRACTICE AREAS:* Property.

DAVID GLOVER. *PRACTICE AREAS:* Commercial.

JEREMY GOLDRING. *PRACTICE AREAS:* Corporate Recovery.

NICHOLAS GOODMAN. *PRACTICE AREAS:* Corporate Recovery.

MARTIN GRABINER. *PRACTICE AREAS:* Property.

DAVID GRAY. *PRACTICE AREAS:* Litigation.

MARTIN HALLAM. *PRACTICE AREAS:* Property.

JANE HAMPSON. *PRACTICE AREAS:* Insurance Litigation.

CHRIS HARLOWE. *PRACTICE AREAS:* Corporate Recovery.

JONATHAN HAWKSWELL. *PRACTICE AREAS:* Litigation.

DAVID HAYES. *PRACTICE AREAS:* Property.

DAVID HICKMAN. *PRACTICE AREAS:* Litigation.

DAVID HILL. *PRACTICE AREAS:* Employment.

(This Listing Continued)

DIBB LUPTON BROOMHEAD, London—Continued

PHILIP HOLDEN. PRACTICE AREAS: Corporate Recovery.

ANDREW HOLT. PRACTICE AREAS: Commercial.

WILL HOLT. PRACTICE AREAS: Commercial.

ALEX HOLTUM. PRACTICE AREAS: Intellectual Property.

STEPHEN HORNSBY. PRACTICE AREAS: Commercial.

PAUL HOUGHTON. PRACTICE AREAS: Litigation.

PAUL HOWARD. PRACTICE AREAS: Litigation.

JOHN HUGHES. PRACTICE AREAS: Banking.

MARK JACKSON. PRACTICE AREAS: Corporate Recovery.

ALAN JACOBS. PRACTICE AREAS: Insurance Litigation.

ALAN JONES. PRACTICE AREAS: Employment.

ANDREW KERR. PRACTICE AREAS: Commercial.

GERARD KHOSHNAW. PRACTICE AREAS: Litigation.

DAVID KILVINGTON. PRACTICE AREAS: Litigation.

TIM KNIGHT. PRACTICE AREAS: Pensions.

NIGEL KNOWLES. PRACTICE AREAS: Commercial.

MARTIN LEE. PRACTICE AREAS: Pensions.

IAN LENNOX. PRACTICE AREAS: Property.

ROGER MASON. PRACTICE AREAS: Property.

RICHARD MCGRANE. PRACTICE AREAS: Property.

NEIL MCLEAN. PRACTICE AREAS: Property.

KEVIN MCLOUGHLIN. PRACTICE AREAS: Insurance Litigation.

PETER MICHAU. PRACTICE AREAS: Commercial.

NEIL MICKLETHWAITE. PRACTICE AREAS: Corporate Fraud.

ANDREW MORRIS. PRACTICE AREAS: Commercial.

DUNCAN MOSLEY. PRACTICE AREAS: Corporate Recovery.

SIMON NEILSON-CLARKE. PRACTICE AREAS: Corporate Recovery.

PAUL NICHOLLS. PRACTICE AREAS: Employment.

RICHARD OLLIS. PRACTICE AREAS: Intellectual Property.

MICHAEL ORLIK. PRACTICE AREAS: Property.

PAUL PATTINSON. PRACTICE AREAS: Intellectual Property.

PHILIP PERRY. PRACTICE AREAS: Property.

TIM POPE. PRACTICE AREAS: Corporate Recovery.

ANDREW PRICE. PRACTICE AREAS: Commercial.

LAWRENCE RADLEY. PRACTICE AREAS: Property.

TONY RANDLE. PRACTICE AREAS: Commercial.

TIM REED. PRACTICE AREAS: Commercial.

JEREMY ROPER. PRACTICE AREAS: Intellectual Property.

JOHN ROWLANDS. PRACTICE AREAS: Property.

KEVIN ROYLE. PRACTICE AREAS: Corporate Recovery.

COLIN RUSS. PRACTICE AREAS: Litigation.

NICK SEDDON. PRACTICE AREAS: Commercial.

ANDREW SHERRATT. PRACTICE AREAS: Commercial.

DAVID SIMON. PRACTICE AREAS: Professional Indemnity.

NEIL SLATER. PRACTICE AREAS: Property.

GODFREY SMALLMAN. PRACTICE AREAS: Professional Indemnity.

ROBERT SMART. PRACTICE AREAS: Litigation.

MARK SMITH. PRACTICE AREAS: Banking.

DAVID SMYLLIE. PRACTICE AREAS: Corporate Recovery.

CLIVE STATON. PRACTICE AREAS: Insurance Litigation.

(This Listing Continued)

EU244B

PAUL STONE. PRACTICE AREAS: Litigation.

RICHARD SUTTON. PRACTICE AREAS: Intellectual Property.

MARK SWINDELL. PRACTICE AREAS: Commercial.

NEIL THOMPSON. PRACTICE AREAS: Commercial.

CHRIS TRIPPETT. PRACTICE AREAS: Commercial.

CHRIS TULLEY. PRACTICE AREAS: Intellectual Property.

DAVID TURNEY. PRACTICE AREAS: Litigation.

CATHERINE USHER. PRACTICE AREAS: Property.

GRAEME WEBBER. PRACTICE AREAS: Environmental.

TOM WHITESIDE. PRACTICE AREAS: Banking.

ROGER WHITTAKER. PRACTICE AREAS: Banking.

GRAHAM WILKINSON. PRACTICE AREAS: Corporate Recovery.

JOHN WINKWORTH-SMITH. PRACTICE AREAS: Litigation.

JULIA WOOD. PRACTICE AREAS: Commercial.

RICHARD WRIGHT. PRACTICE AREAS: Corporate Recovery.

MATTHEW WRIGLEY. PRACTICE AREAS: Tax and Trusts.

REPRESENTATIVE CLIENTS: Aerostructures Hamble Holdings; Bailey (Ben) Construction; Betterware; Bridon; British Mohair Holdings; Brooke Tool Engineering (Holdings); Carclo Engineering Group; CentreGold; Charles Sidney; Compco Holdings; Elliott (B), Foster (John) & Son; Freeport Leisure; Gent (S R); Greenway Holdings; Hartons Group; Hay (Norman); Headway; Hewitt Group; Hopkinsons Group; JBA Holdings; Johnson & Firth Brown; Kembrey; Leeds Group; Lister & Co.; Lynx Holdings; On Demand Information; Proteus International; Raine; Sanderson Electronics; Stagecoach; Stylo; Suter; TT Group; Watmoughs (Holdings); Yorkshire-Tyne Tees Television (Holdings).

DOBSON & PINCI

1 THROGMORTON AVENUE
LONDON EC2N 2JJ, ENGLAND
Telephone: (44) (171) 628-8163
Telefax: (44) (171) 920-0861 E-Mail: 7232682@mcimail.com.

Milan, Italy Office: Via Santa Radegonda, 16, 20121. Telephone: (39) (2) 809816; 8056780. Telefax: (39) (2) 86464548; 86464601. E-Mail: 7232679@mcimail.com.

Rome, Italy Office: Via Panama 74, Int. 9, 00198. Telephone: (39) (6) 841-1611. Telefax: (39) (6) 841-1145. E-Mail: 7212680@mcimail.com.

Genoa, Italy Office: Via Garibaldi 7, 2nd Floor, 16124. Telephone: (39) (10) 206-851. Telefax: (39) (10) 202-738. E-Mail: 7222681@mcimail.com.

New York, New York Office: Manhattan Tower, 12th Floor, 600 Lexington Avenue, 10022-6018. Telephone: (212) 308-4440. Telefax: (212) 888-3839. E-Mail: 7262685@mcimail.com.

Brussels, Belgium Office: Avenue Louise, 216, 1050. Telephone: (32) (2) 647-0700. Telefax: (32) (2) 647-6440. E-Mail: 7242683@mcimail.com.

Athens, Greece Office: 6 Yperidou Street, 105 58. Telephone: (30) (1) 324-3272. Telefax: (30) (1) 322-9329. E-Mail: 7252684@mcimail.com.

Atlanta, Georgia Office: 1776 Resurgens Plaza, 945 East Paces Ferry Road, N.E., 30326. Telephone: (404) 262-5680. Telefax: (404) 262-5699. E-Mail: 7272686@mcimail.com.

San Diego, California Office: 1629 Columbia Street, 92101. Telephone: (619) 236-1310. Telefax: (619) 239-1208. E-Mail: 7282687@mcimail.com.

Miami, Florida Office: 701 Brickell Avenue, Suite 2000, 33131. Telephone: (305) 579-0012. Telefax: (305) 375-8075; 579-4722. E-Mail: 7292688@mcimail.com.

Corporate, Banking and Securities Law with emphasis on Mergers and Acquisitions, Insurance, International Financial Transactions, Litigation, Arbitration, Employment Law, Debt Collection, Bankruptcy, Foreign Investments, Privatizations, Subsidiaries and Joint Ventures, Taxation, EU/-Common Market Law, Antitrust, Environmental Law, Transportation, Shipping, Licensing, Fashion and Textiles, Franchising, Commercial Real Estate (Investment, Structuring, Development, Retail), Project Finance, Computer, Software and Telecommunications Law, Agency and Distribution, Energy (Production, Operations, and Transmission), Food and Drug, Commodities, Visa/Immigration, Wills and Estates, Sports Law, Broadcasting, Motion Picture, TV, Video, Intellectual Property and General Entertainment Law.

(This Listing Continued)

FIRM PROFILE: Dobson & Pinci is an international law firm based in Europe and the United States that is staffed with both American and European attorneys. Of the small number of such firms, Dobson & Pinci holds a unique position because the firm's European offices are situated in Milan, Rome, Genoa, London, Brussels and Athens, thereby enabling the firm to serve clients conveniently and efficiently in both Northern and Southern Europe. The U.S. offices in New York, Atlanta, Miami and San Diego are placed in major U.S. cities to provide full support to the overall practice network. Each office is staffed by attorneys qualified to appear and litigate in the local courts.

MEMBERS OF FIRM

MARCANTONIO PINCI, born Vicenza, Italy, October 27, 1963; admitted, 1990, Italy; 1990, New York. *Education:* University of Milan (J.D., 1988); Georgetown University Law Center (LL.M., 1989); Bocconi University, Milan (Master in Business Tax Law, Certificate, 1991). Author: "Milan Real Estate - Tax and Legal Aspects," Immobilier & Property, February, 1992; "Italy, Legal Tax and Financing Aspects of Italian Property Transactions for Foreign Investors and Developers," Sunbelt Conference on Real Estate Opportunities in Southern France, Northern Spain and Northern Italy, Cannes, December, 1991; "The Negotiating Phase - French Acquisitions in Italy," C&S Conference on Mergers and Acquisitions in Italy, Paris, November, 1991; "Acquisizione, Fusione e Partecipazione di Società Italiane ed Imprese Estere nel Quadro delle Direttive CEE in Materia di Imposizione Diretta," Seminar on International Tax Strategy, Turin, October, 1991; MIPIM 94 Conference: Italia: Nuove Opportunità per Investimenti Promozione e Finanziamenti Immobiliari - "Aspetti Legali e Fiscali degli Investimenti Immobiliari in Italia alla Luce dei Più Recenti Sviluppi Normativi," Cannes, March, 1994; "Enforcement of Judgments in Italy," Corporate Counsel's International Adviser, October, 1991; Seminar: "Enforcement of Judgments in Europe-Italy," New York State Bar Association, International Practice Section, New York, June 1991; "Dematerialization of Investment Securities," Georgetown University Law Center, 1989; "Insider Trading Regulations in the U.S., U.K., France and the E.E.C.: An Analysis from the Standpoint of the Italian Legal System," University of Milan, 1988; "Unico Azionista: Responsabilità ex Articolo 2362," University of Milan, 1986. Co-Author: "La Cooperazione Imprenditoriale Fra Italia e Stati Uniti: la Via Della Joint-Venture," Conference on Joint-Ventures, Milan, June 1992; "La Direttiva CEE 434/90 sul Regime delle Riorganizzazioni Societarie," Acquisizioni, April 1992; "Coal Gasification Projects in Italy," December 1994; "Il Nuovo Contratto d'Agenzia-D.L. 10.09.91 N° 303," published in France-Italie no. 6, November/December, 1993 and continued in same publication, no. 1, January/February, 1994; "Deregulation of Retail Licenses in Italy," April, 1994; "Structuring Italian Shopping Center, Investments for German Open-Ended Property Funds," September, 1994; Conference, Agenti di Commercio - "Lo Scioglimento del Rapporto di Agenzia nella Nuova Normativa Italiana di Recepimento della Direttiva CEE 86/653," Milan, April 1993; "Incorporation of an Italian Company: An Overview of Italian Law," Corporate Counsel's International Adviser, February, 1993; "Legal Aspects of Property Investment in Europe," Corporate Real Estate Executive, International Association of Corporate Real Estate Executives (NACORE) July/August 1992; "Country Handbook on Italy," Italian American Business, 1992; "Italy, Financial Engineering and Tax Planning," C&S Conference: Property Investment in Italy, Paris, April 1991 and IBC Conference: European Commercial Property Development Opportunities, London, June 1991; "Acquisition and Management of Real Property in Italy by Non-Residents," Conference on "International Tax Strategy," Milan, November 1990. Advisor, Real Estate Masters Program (Shopping Center Development), Politecnico University of Turin, 1992—; Assistant to the General Counsel, Pirelli-Armstrong Tire Corp., New Haven, CT, 1990; Foreign Associate (Corporate Area), Foley, Hoag & Eliot, Boston, MA, 1989. *Member:* The Foreign Lawyers Forum of Washington, D.C.; International Bar Association. (Also at Milan Office).

GIOVANNI LOMBARDO, born Rome, Italy, March 7, 1962; admitted, 1990, Italy. *Education:* La Sapienza University, Rome (J.D., 1985). Author: "A Practical Guide to Italian Rates - The New ICI," Belle Cose, Summer 1993; "Pension Reform in Italy," Belle Cose, June, 1993; "A New Cut in the VAT Rates on Maintenance Work in Italy," Belle Cose, Autumn 1994; "First Time Buyers in Italy," Belle Cose, Spring 1994; "Taxation of Foreign Companies in Italy," Belle Cose, Summer 1994. Conferences: State Bar of Georgia, "Doing Business in Southern Europe," Atlanta, May 1994; "Italy and Europe: The Economic Situation In the Current Political and Regulatory Climate," London, September 1994; "Italian Water Privatisation and the Galli Law," Birmingham, U.K., November 1994. *Member:* International Bar Association; Association of Personal Injury Lawyers. (Also at Athens Office).

(This Listing Continued)

ASSOCIATES

ANDREA VOGHERA, born Alba, Italy, February 23, 1969. admitted to practice, 1993, Italy. *Education:* Catholic University, Milan (J.D., 1993); Schiller International University of London. Seminars: "European Community Law: An Introduction for Lawyers," Otzenhausen, Germany, 1994. *Member:* International Bar Association.

ROGER O'BRIEN, born Yorkshire, England, August 1, 1964. *Education:* College of Law, Chancery Lane (B.A., Law, 1988); Manchester University (B.A., Hons., 1985).

FLAVIA UBERTI, born Milan, Italy, November 15, 1971. admitted to practice, 1994, Italy. *Education:* State University of Milan (J.D., 1994). Author: "The Interpretation of Conventions of Uniform Law: the Geneva Convention of June 7, 1930," Milan, 1994.

GIUSEPPE AMATO, born Catania, Italy, August 9, 1968. admitted to practice, 1994, Italy. *Education:* University of Pavia (J.D., 1994). Author: "Enforcement Policy in the E.E.C. and in the U.S.A.," Ireland, 1994; "Franchising e concorrenza nell'ordinamento comunitario e in quello interno," Pavia, 1994.

COUNSEL

ANDREW DUNCAN ROBSON COLVIN, born Berlin, Germany, July 13, 1948; admitted, 1972, London; 1987, Paris. *Education:* University of Kent (B.A., 1970), Inns of Court School of Law; Institut d'Etudes Europeennes, Université Libre de Bruxelles, Fondazione Giorgio Cini, Venice, Italy; University of Siena, Italy. Author: "Italian Competition Law," Corporate Lawyer, 1991; "The Control of Broadcasting in Italy: A Commentary on the New MAMMI Law," World Competition, December, 1990. Co-Author: "Round-up of New Laws in Italy," April, 1994; "Privatisation in Italy," Corporate Counsel's International Advisor, May, 1993. "Pension Reform in Italy," Belle Cose, June, 1993; "Agency and Distribution Agreements in Italy," Corporate Counsel's International Advisor, June, 1993; Legal Advisor and Company Secretary, Monsanto Oil Company of the U.K., Inc., 1982-1985; Fluor Corporation Subsidiaries, 1977-1982. (Also at Milan Office).

Languages: English, Italian, French, Greek, German, Spanish, Japanese and Russian

(For Complete Biographical Data on all Personnel and List of Representative Clients, see Biographical card at Milan, Italy)

DORSEY & WHITNEY

A Partnership including Professional Corporations

3 GRACECHURCH STREET
LONDON EC3V 0AT, ENGLAND
Telephone: 011-44-171-929-3334
Facsimile: 011-44-171-929-3111

Minneapolis, Minnesota Office: 220 South 6th Street, 55402. Telephone: 612-340-2600. Cable Address: "Dorow". Telex: 290605. Answer-back: "Dorsey Law MPS".

New York, New York Office: 350 Park Avenue, 10022. Telephone: 212-415-9200.

Washington, D.C. Office: Suite 200, 1330 Connecticut Avenue, N.W., 20036. Telephone: 202-452-6900.

Brussels, Belgium Office: 35 Square De Meeûs, B-1040. Telephone: 011-32-2-504-4611.

Rochester, Minnesota Office: 201 First Avenue, S.W., Suite 340. P.O. Box 848, 55902. Telephone: 507-288-3156.

Des Moines, Iowa Office: 801 Grand, Suite 3900, 50309. Telephone: 515-283-1000.

Billings, Montana Office: 1200 First Interstate Center, 401 North 31st Street, P.O. Box 7188, 59103. Telephone: 406-252-3800.

Great Falls, Montana Office: 507 Davidson Building, 8 Third Street, North, P.O. Box 1566, 59401. Telephone: 406-727-3632.

Missoula, Montana Office: 127 East Front Street, Suite 310, 59802. Telephone: 406-721-6025.

Denver, Colorado Office: 370 Seventeenth Street, Republic Plaza Building, Suite 4400, 80202-5644. Telephone: 303-629-3400.

Orange County, California Office: Center Tower, 650 Town Center Drive, Suite 1930, P.O. Box 5066, Costa Mesa, 92626. Telephone: 714-662-7300.

Fargo, North Dakota Office: Dakota Center, 51 North Broadway, Suite 201, P.O. Box 1344, 58107-1344. Telephone: 701-235-6000.

(This Listing Continued)

DORSEY & WHITNEY, London—Continued

General and International Law.
Firm engaged in American and International Law Practice, but not autho-
rized to appear before the English courts or to act as Solicitors.

MEMBERS OF FIRM

PETER E. KOHL, born 1958; admitted, 1983, Minnesota (Not admitted
in England). *Education:* Harvard College (A.B., 1980); Georgetown University (J.D., 1983). *PRACTICE AREAS:* International Corporate Law.

STEVEN E. CARLSON, born 1952; admitted, 1978, New York; 1985,
Minnesota. *Education:* Yale University (B.A., 1973); Columbia University
(J.D., 1977). *PRACTICE AREAS:* Banking Law; International Law.

ASSOCIATE

AJAY SUD, born New Delhi, India, January 16, 1958; admitted, 1991,
New York. *Education:* Columbia College (A.B., 1979); Columbia University (J.D., 1990). Harlan Fiske Stone Scholar. *PRACTICE AREAS:* General Corporate; Securities.

(For Complete Personnel and Biographical Data, see Professional
Biographies at Minneapolis, Minnesota).

DAVID DU PRÉ & CO.

90/92 PARKWAY, REGENTS PARK
LONDON NW1 7AN, ENGLAND
Telephone: (0171) 284-3040
Fax: (0171) 485-1145

Divorce, Family Law, International and Domestic Matrimonial Finance,
Child Custody (including kidnapping and wardship cases), Mediation of
Marital Disputes.

FIRM PROFILE: *Close to the centre of London, the firm specialises ex-*
clusively in Family and Divorce Law, especially financial disputes.

DAVID R.K. DU PRÉ, born London, England, September 24, 1950;
admitted, 1973, Lincoln's Inn; 1974, Barrister, England; 1980, Solicitor,
England. *Education:* Kingston Polytechnic; London University (LL.B.).
Trained and Qualified as a Family Mediator, 1992. *Member:* Law Society,
England; Solicitors Family Law Association; International Society of Fam-
ily Law; Family Mediators Association. *PRACTICE AREAS:* Family Law;
Divorce Law; Matrimonial Law; Child Custody; Child Abduction.

EDGE & ELLISON

Established in 1870

18 - 19 SOUTHAMPTON PLACE
LONDON WC1A 2AJ, ENGLAND
Telephone: (44) 171 404 4701
Fascimile: (44) 171 831 9152

Birmingham, England Office: Rutland House, 148 Edmund Street.
Telephone: (44) 121 200 2001. Facsimile: (44) 121 200 1991.
Leicester Office: Regent Court, Regent Street. Telephone: (44) 0116
470123. Facsimile: (44) 0116 470030.
Associated Office: Dumon, Sablon & Vanheeswijck, Brussels, Belgium.
Associated Office: Buchanan Ingersoll, Pittsburgh, Harrisburg,
Philadelphia, Miami, U.S.A.

KEITH AINSWORTH, admitted, 1982, England and Wales. *Education:*
LL.B. (Hons) Birmingham University. *PRACTICE AREAS:* Banking and
Finance; Banking Law; Banking Regulation; Project Finance; Corporate
Finance Law; Financial Restructuring Law; Corporate Law; Venture Capi-
tal; Financial Services and Securities.

NICHOLAS P. ALLEN, admitted, 1985, England and Wales. *Education:* B.A. (Hons) University of East Anglia. *Member:* Anglo-Czech Lawyers Association. *PRACTICE AREAS:* Advertising Law; Commercial
Law; Joint Ventures; International Transactions; Pharmaceuticals; Corporate Law; Corporate Finance Law.

JANE COOPER, admitted, 1980, England and Wales. *Education:* M.A.
Dundee University. *PRACTICE AREAS:* Commercial Property Law;
Property Law; Landlord & Tenant Law; Conveyancing.

SIMON M. GORDON, admitted, 1983, England and Wales. *Education:*
Cambridge University. *Member:* Worshipful Company of Plumbers. *LAN-*

(This Listing Continued)

GUAGES: French. *PRACTICE AREAS:* Corporate Law; Commercial
Law; Mergers & Acquisitions; Securities Offerings; Employment Law.

DAVID MANDELL, admitted, 1984, England and Wales. *Education:*
B.A. (Hons) (Jurisprudence) Oxford University. *PRACTICE AREAS:*
Mergers & Acquisitions; Corporate Finance Law; Securities Offerings; Leveraged & Management Buyouts; Venture Capital; Corporate Restructuring.

NICHOLAS P. MASON, admitted, 1987, England and Wales. *Education:* Birmingham University. *PRACTICE AREAS:* Commercial Litigation; Intellectual Property Law; Employment Law.

CHARLES MIDDLETON-SMITH, admitted, 1978, England and
Wales. *LANGUAGES:* French, German. *PRACTICE AREAS:* Commercial Litigation; Tort Law; Property Law; Mortgage Enforcements.

BARRY SAMUELS, admitted, 1992, England and Wales. *Education:*
LL.B. Manchester. *PRACTICE AREAS:* Litigation; Commercial Litigation; Tort Law; Fraud; Property Litigation; Securities Litigation.

SUSAN WOODMAN, admitted, 1981, England and Wales. *Education:*
University of Reading. *Member:* The City of London Solicitors Company.
LANGUAGES: French. *PRACTICE AREAS:* Advertising Law; Agency &
Distribution; Commercial Law; Corporate Law; Corporate Finance Law;
Venture Capital; Employer/Employee Relations.

(For biographical data on partners in Birmingham and Leicester, see
Professional Biographies at Birmingham, England)

EVERSHEDS

SENATOR HOUSE
85 QUEEN VICTORIA STREET
LONDON EC4V 4JL, ENGLAND
Telephone: (44) 171 919 4500
Fax: (44) 171 919 4919

St. Helier, Jersey, Channel Islands Office: Suite 2, Seaton House, 17-19
Seaton Place. Telephone: (44) 1534 37321. Telex: 4192145. Jaques G.
Cable Address: "Quickness, Jersey." Fax: (44) 1534 38163.
Brussels, Belgium Office: 65 Rue Stevin, 1040. Telephone: (32) 2230
8058. Fax: (32) 2231 0677.
Other Eversheds Offices:
Birmingham, Bristol, Cardiff, Derby, Ipswich, Leeds, Manchester,
Middlesbrough, Newcastle-upon-Tyne, Norwich, Nottingham, Berlin,
Brussels, Jersey.

Acquisitions and Mergers, Agency/Distribution, Agriculture, Banking,
Commercial Property, Company Law, Competition Law, Construction,
Corporate Finance, Corporate Tax, EC Law, Employment, Energy, Envi-
ronment, Entertainment, Information Technology, Franchising, Immigra-
tion, Insolvency, Intellectual Property, Litigation, Management Buy-Outs,
Pensions and Employee Benefits, Personal Tax & Estate Planning, Prop-
erty Development, Property Litigation.
Partners within Eversheds: 273.

FIRM PROFILE: *Member of the JCS Group. Other Group Members:*
Chaintrier, Caillard in Paris; Schmidt, von der Osten & Huber in Essen
and Berlin; and Van Wijmen & Koedam in Rotterdam and Breda.

The JCS Group is an integrated group of law firms providing a compre-
hensive range of legal services to international clients.

REGIONAL MANAGING PARTNERS

Peter Scott

LONDON PARTNERS

Elaine Aarons	**Paul Heatherington**
Rod Ainsworth	**Bernard Hollingsworth**
Adrian Biggs	**Martin Issitt**
Helga Breen	**Rosalind Kellaway**
Douglas Brown	**Charles Lambrick**
George Butler	**Harold Lewis**
John Butler	**Roger Lewis**
Roger Button	**Tim Maloney**
Robin Bynoe	**Martin Mendelsohn**
David Church	**Neil Morris**
Ann Churchill	**John Northam**
Peter Coles	**Geoff Prevett**
Tom Daltry	**Jeremy Raisman**
Isabel Davies	**Jon Roper**

(This Listing Continued)

Jon Denman
Sheila Dobson
David Fowell
John Glasson
Aleen Gulvanessian
John Hall
Brenda Harris
Linda Harrison
Christopher Heaps

John Sabel
Peter Scott
Christopher Sly
Richard Stephens
Margaret Wakelin-Saint
Andrew Wallis
Richard Ward
Felicity Wooldridge
Tony Yablon

FAEGRE & BENSON

Professional Limited Liability Partnership

Established in 1985

10 EASTCHEAP
LONDON EC3M 1ET, ENGLAND
Telephone: 44-171-623-6163
Facsimile: 44-171-623-3227

REVISERS OF THE MINNESOTA LAW DIGEST FOR THIS DIRECTORY.

Minneapolis, Minnesota Office: 2200 Norwest Center, 90 South Seventh Street, 55402-3901. Telephone: 612-336-3000. Facsimile: 612-336-3026.
Denver, Colorado Office: 2500 Republic Plaza, 370 Seventeenth Street, 80202-4004. Telephone: 303-592-5900. Facsimile: 303-592-5693.
Des Moines: Iowa Office: 400 Capital Square, 400 Locust Street, 50309-2335. Telephone: 55-248-9000. Facsimile: 515-248-9010.
Washington, D. C. Office: The Homer Building, Suite 450 North, 601 Thirteenth Street, N.W. Telephone: 202-783-3880. Facsimile: 202-783-3899.
Frankfurt, Germany Office: Westendstrasse 24, 6000 Frankfurt am Main 1. Telephone: 49-69-1743 43. Facsimile: 49-69-1743 49.

General Practice.
Firm Engaged in American and International Law Practice, but not authorized to appear before the English courts or to act as Solicitors.

RESIDENT MEMBERS

THOMAS E. JOHNSON, born La Bolt, South Dakota, 1936; admitted, 1964, Minnesota; 1966, New York (Not admitted in England). *Education:* Macalester College (A.B., 1958); Harvard University (J.D., 1964). Contributing Editor, Tax Planning International Review, 1977—. Editor, U.S. Expatriate Taxation, 1978—. *Member:* New York State, American and International Bar Associations; International Fiscal Association.

SCOTT M. JAMES, born Buffalo, New York, 1950; admitted, 1976, Maryland; 1977, District of Columbia (Not admitted in England). *Education:* Swarthmore College (B.A., 1972); Catholic University of America (J.D., 1976). *Member:* District of Columbia Bar; American and International Bar Associations; The Association of Trial Lawyers of America.

RESIDENT ASSOCIATE

TRACEY CHIPPENDALE-HOLMES, born London, England, 1965; admitted, 1993, England. *Education:* University of Surrey, England (B.S.C., 1990); The College of Law, Lancaster Gate, London (L.S.F., 1991); University College, England (LL.M., 1994). *Member:* Law Society of England and Wales.

EUROPEAN COMMUNITY COUNSEL

PAUL EGERTON-VERNON, born Chester, England, 1945; admitted, 1971, Solicitor of Supreme Court of England and Wales. *Education:* Durham University, England (B.A. (Honours), 1967); The College of Law, Lancaster Gate, London (1971). *Member:* Law Society of England and Wales.

REVISERS OF THE MINNESOTA LAW DIGEST FOR THIS DIRECTORY.

(For complete Biographical Data on all personnel, see Professional Biographies at Minneapolis, Minnesota)

FARRER & CO.

Established in 1701

66 LINCOLN'S INN FIELDS
LONDON WC2A 3LH, ENGLAND
Telephone: 0171-242 2022
Fax: 0171-831 9748
Telex: 24318 FARRER G
DX 32

FIRM PROFILE: *Farrer & Co. has been practising in Lincoln's Inn Fields for 200 years. The firm has a broadly based practice with a reputation for combining expertise with a high standard of personal service. It advises an extremely varied cross section of notable companies, institutions and private individuals. The firm emphasises the client-partner relationship and is run through the following four departments:*

COMMERCIAL.

Acquisitions and formations, company mergers and reorganizations, dissolutions and winding up. Employment, pensions and immigration. Partnerships, joint ventures and shareholders agreements. Intellectual property and media law. Merchandising, sponsorship and licensing agreements. Stock Exchange listings, Yellow Book and Take-Over Code. Banking, Financial Services Act and Consumer Credit. Administrative law, constitutions, rules and disciplinary procedures.

LITIGATION.

Media related work including pre-publication advice, defamation, copyright and other intellectual property claims. Property work including all aspects of building contract claims and landlord and tenant matters. Family law including all financial and child related issues. High Court litigation both in the Chancery Division (e.g. partnership disputes) and Queen's Bench Division for all aspects of national and international commercial litigation and arbitration.

PRIVATE CLIENT.

All personal legal work, settlements and trust administration, capital tax planning, offshore tax planning for UK and non-UK residents, charities, heritage planning, family work in conjunction with the matrimonial section of the Litigation Department, the personal aspects of private company and intellectual property work in association with the Commercial Department, the personal aspects of property and planning work - domestic, agricultural and commercial - in association with the Property Department, Wills and probate/administration of estates.

PROPERTY.

Commercial, agricultural, institutional and domestic property work of all types. Development schemes, planning and environmental law. Conveyance, landlord and tenant, joint ventures. Property security work. Farming and European Community agricultural law and practice, quotas.

PARTNERS

Richard A. Griffiths
(Senior Partner)
A. Mark Farrer
M. Henry Boyd-Carpenter
Charles F. Woodhouse
Donald A. Lockhart
W. Jeremy de Souza
Miss Mary E. Falk
John H. Evans
Nigel S.D. Bulmer
Raymond D. Cooper
Christopher R. Jessel
Geoffrey W. Richards
Robert G. Clinton
Ivor J. Dicker
Colin F. Riseam
Richard W. J. Parry
John Morcom

John H. Owen
James Thorne
The Hon. Mark T. Bridges
W. James Furber
Mrs. Fiona S. Shackleton
Mrs. Judith L. Hill
Michael J. Chantler
Miss Elizabeth J. Potter
R. Stephen Blair
Miss Anne E. Yardley
Peter J. Downy
Adrian C. Parkhouse
Charles R.A. Anderson
Robert E. Foster
Jonathan M. Bayliss
Francis Nation-Dixon
Miss Sian Blore

(This Listing Continued)

FARRER & CO., London—Continued

Simon J. Bruce

CONSULTANTS

Sir Matthew Farrer, K.C.V.O.   Shelton V. Perera

ASSOCIATES

Miss Susan F.M. Stuart   Mrs. A. Margaret Smithson
               Miss Julia L. Brown

Languages: French and German.

FASKEN MARTINEAU

Established in 1986

10 ARTHUR STREET, 5TH FLOOR
LONDON EC4R 9AY, ENGLAND
Telephone: 171-929-2894
Facsimile: 171-929-3634

Fasken Martineau is a national and international firm composed of the
partners and associates of Fasken Campbell Godfrey (Toronto,
Ontario) and Martineau Walker (Montreal and Quebec City, Quebec).
Fasken Martineau also has an office in Brussels and Belgium.

Toronto, Ontario, Canada Office: Fasken Campbell Godfrey,
Toronto-Dominion Bank Tower, Toronto-Dominion Centre, P.O. Box
20, M5K 1N6. Telephones: 416- 366-8381. Toll Free: 1-800-268-8424
(Ontario & Quebec) Facsimile: 416-364-7813.

Montreal, Quebec, Canada Office: Martineau Walker, Stock Exchange
Tower, Suite 3400. P.O. Box 242, 800 Place-Victoria, H4Z 1E9.
Telephone: 514-397-7400. Toll Free: 1-800-361-6266 (Ontario &
Quebec). Facsimile: 514-397-7600. Telex: 05-24610 BUOY MTL.

Quebec City, Quebec, Canada Office: Martineau Walker, Immeuble Le
Saint-Patrick, 140, rue Grande Allée est, bureau 800 G1R 5M8.
Telephone: 418-640-2000. Toll Free: 1-800-463-2827 (Ontario &
Quebec) Facsimile: 418-647-2455.

Vancouver (Affiliated): Davis & Company, 2800 Park Place, 666 Burrard
Street, V6C 2Z7. Telephone: 604-687-9444. Fax: 604-687-1612.

Brussels, Belgium Office: Fasken Martineau, Avenue Franklin D.
Roosevelt, 96 A, 1050 Brussels, Belgium. Telephone: 2-640-9796.
Facsimile: 2-640-2779.

*General Practice including Administrative, Admiralty, Appellate and Trial
Advocacy in all Courts, Banking, Commercial Lending and Private Fi-
nancing, Bankruptcy and Insolvency, Broadcasting, Combines and Anti-
trust, Communications and Entertainment, Computer and Technology
Law, Corporate Finance, Corporate/Commercial, Corporate and Personal
Taxation, Employment, Environmental, Estates and Estate Planning,
Family, Foreign Investment, Franchising, Health Care, Intellectual Prop-
erty, Insurance, Immigration, International Law, Labour Relations, Food
and Drug, Licensing, Mining, Municipal, Partnership, Pension, Products
Liability, Private Clients, Real Estate, Securities, Secured Transactions,
Tax, Trademarks and Copyright, Transportation.*

RESIDENT PARTNERS

JOHN S. M. TURNER, born Peterborough, Canada, 1961; admitted,
1989, Ontario (Not admitted in England). *Education:* Queen's University
(B.Sc., honors, 1983; LL.B., 1986); Cambridge University, Cambridge, England (LL.M., 1987). Author: "Solicitors Liability in Negligent Misrepresentations in Offer Documents," The Company Lawyer (U.K.), 1989. *Member:* County of York Law Association. (Resident). *PRACTICE AREAS:*
Corporate Law; Commercial Law; Securities Law.

MARK D. WALKER, born Montreal, Quebec, March 9, 1954; admitted,
1981, Quebec; 1987, Ontario (Not admitted in England). *Education:* McGill
University (B.Sc., 1975; LL.B., 1979; B.C.L., 1980). *Member:* Montreal,
Quebec and Canadian Bar Associations. (Resident).

(For complete biographical data on other personnel and offices, see
Professional Biographies at Toronto, Ontario, Montreal and Quebec
City, Quebec and Brussels, Belgium)

LAW OFFICES OF
GARY M. FERMAN

Established in 1981

19/20 GROSVENOR STREET
LONDON W1X 9FD, ENGLAND
Telephone: (0171)-499-5702
Fax: (0171)-236 2533

*General and International Practice. Commercial, Corporate, Licensing,
Tax, International Estate Administration and Immigration Law.
Firm engaged in American and International Law Practice, but not autho-
rized to appear before the English courts or to act as Solicitors.*

GARY M. FERMAN, admitted, 1973, New York. *Education:* University
of California at Berkeley (A.B., with great Distinction, 1968); University of
Sussex, Brighton, England (M.A., 1970); Harvard University (J.D., 1972).
Phi Beta Kappa. Author: "Acquisition Strategy: Legal Aspects in Corporate
Investment and Acquisitions by Foreign Companies in the U.S.A.," Gra-
ham & Trotman Ltd., 1979. Adjunct Associate Professor, University of
Notre Dame, London Law Centre, 1982. Adjunct Lecturer in Business
Law, U.S. Int. University-Europe, 1988. *Member:* American Bar Associa-
tion; American Immigration Lawyers' Association. *LANGUAGES:* En-
glish and French.

PAUL W. FERRELL

Attorney and Counselor at Law

Established in 1983

19/20 GROSVENOR STREET
LONDON W1X 9FD, ENGLAND
Telephone: 0171-493 1595; 0171-493 7915
Fax: 0171-236 2533

*Firm engaged in Immigration and Nationality Law. Not Authorized to
appear before the English Courts.*

PAUL W. FERRELL, born Pittsburgh, Pennsylvania, November 9,
1950; admitted, 1976, Florida (Not admitted in England). *Education:* Eck-
erd College (B.A., 1972); Stetson University College of Law (J.D., 1976).
Author: "The Corporate Alien and Treaty Visa Nationality," 7 Georgetown
Immigration Law Journal, pg. 283, 1993. *Member:* American Bar Association; American Immigration Lawyers Association; Immigration Law Practitioners Association and Society of English and American Lawyers (Executive Committee, 1987-1993).

REPRESENTATIVE CLIENTS: Balfour Beatty Limited; James Capel & Co.,
Knight-Ridder Business Information Services, Logica plc.; Ove Arup Partner-
ship, Quality Family Entertainment, Inc.; Rentokil plc; Smith New Court plc.;
Vickers plc

FIELD FISHER WATERHOUSE

41 VINE STREET
LONDON EC3N 2AA, ENGLAND
Telephone: 0171-481 4841
Fax: 0171-488 0084
Telex: 262613 ADDIDEM G

Brussels, Belgium Office: 40 Avenue Lambeau, 1200. Telephone: 010 322
736 6360. Fax: 010 322 736 0931.

*Company/Commercial, Corporate Finance, EC/Competition, Banking/Fi-
nance, Taxation, Employment/Immigration, Licensing, Franchising, Intellectual Property, Commercial Property, Litigation, Private Client, Travel
and Tourism, IT/Computer Law, Heavy involvement with Japan, Korea,
China, the EC, Scandinavia and the US.*

PARTNERS

D. G. Rawlins	T. J. Davies
A.P.P. Honigmann	P. J. Stewart
J. A. Nelson-Jones	A T.B. Rider
D. K. Birley	P.M. Abell
J.A. Wilson	M. C. MacKenzie
J.R. Facer	N.P. Rose
P.B. Hayes	G. J. Nuttall
C. McArthur	A.M. MacLaren
J.R.S. Price	A.G. Little
P.G. Glazebrook	P.A. Sykes

(This Listing Continued)

S. G. Gibbs
A. M. Fisher
M.N. Tod
J.K. Fife
F.H. Coffell
C. M. Bond
P.E. Scanlon
R. S. Bagehot
D. M. Lowe
R. M. Nelson-Jones
M.J. Wright
C. Richmond
R.M. Wills
N. R. Noble

G.V. Davis
D.R.C. Robertson
R.P. Webber
C.E. Pinfold
I.S. Barnard
M.L.L. Tompkins
C.S. McGuinness
S. Lorber
N.C. Beecham
A.D. Janik
J.M. Barrett
N.P. Thompsell
P. McNeil
S.T. Chamberlain

Languages: Danish, English, French, German, Japanese, Mandarin, Polish, Spanish and Swedish.

FINERS

Solicitors

Established in 1935

179 GREAT PORTLAND STREET
LONDON W1N 6LS, ENGLAND
Telephone: 44-171-323-4000
Telecopier: 44-171-580-7069

National and International Commercial Law, Corporations, Banking, Intellectual Property, Contracts and Insolvency, Property, Planning and Environmental Law, Corporate, Personal and Estate Taxation, Litigation, Arbitration and Alternative Dispute Resolution, Immigration, Employment and Licensing, Sports and Entertainment Law.

FIRM PROFILE: Finers is a rapidly expanding London commercial firm with a wide range of national and international clients. We are accustomed to working with Law Firms from overseas and dealing with clients from all parts of the World. We are members of the International Lawyers Group and specialize in cross-border transactions.

PARTNERS

DAVID SWEDE, admitted, 1970. (Managing Partner).

PETER JAY, B.Comm.; admitted, 1971. *PRACTICE AREAS:* Company/Commercial.

SAMUEL CHARKHAM, B.A.; admitted 1977. *PRACTICE AREAS:* Property.

MICHAEL BIBRING, LL.B.; admitted, 1979. *PRACTICE AREAS:* Property.

MICHAEL SIMMONS, M.A.; LL.M.; admitted 1958. *PRACTICE AREAS:* Company/Commercial.

LEON MARKS, M.A.; admitted 1964. *PRACTICE AREAS:* Litigation/Insolvency.

MELVYN ORTON, LL.B.; admitted, 1970. *PRACTICE AREAS:* Property.

STEPHEN ARTHUR, LL.B.; admitted, 1974. *PRACTICE AREAS:* Tax.

PAUL SHEETER, admitted, 1983. *PRACTICE AREAS:* Property.

RICHARD GERSTEIN, B.A.; admitted, 1982. *PRACTICE AREAS:* Litigation.

MICHAEL PINNER, M.A.; LL.B.; admitted, 1962. *PRACTICE AREAS:* Property.

PHILIP RUBENS, LL.B.; admitted, 1986. *PRACTICE AREAS:* Litigation.

RICHARD CURTIN, LL.B.; admitted, 1986. *PRACTICE AREAS:* Litigation.

KATHERINE MILLER, LL.B.; admitted, 1988. *PRACTICE AREAS:* Property.

JOHN D'ARDENNE, M.A.; admitted, 1978. *PRACTICE AREAS:* Company/Commercial; Immigration.

JOHN HEWITT, admitted, 1979. *PRACTICE AREAS:* Litigation.

JEFFREY COHEN, LL.B.; admitted, 1986. *PRACTICE AREAS:* Wills/Trusts/Probate.

(This Listing Continued)

PAUL CUNNINGHAM, LL.B.; admitted 1980. *PRACTICE AREAS:* Property.

ANTHONY BARLING, LL.B.; admitted, 1974. *PRACTICE AREAS:* Company/Commercial/Employment.

CHRISTOPHER BUTLER, LL.B.; admitted, 1982. *PRACTICE AREAS:* Litigation/Matrimonial.

VIVIEN PRIESTLEY, LL.B.; admitted, 1989. *PRACTICE AREAS:* Property.

GENN ROWELL, LL.B. (QUB); LL.M (Lond); Admitted, 1991. *PRACTICE AREAS:* Company Litigation.

ASSOCIATES

IAN GERRARD, LL.B.; admitted, 1988. *PRACTICE AREAS:* Litigation.

STEPHEN MESSIAS, B.Sc.; admitted, 1989. *PRACTICE AREAS:* Property.

LAWRENCE KELLY, LL.B.; admitted, 1990. *PRACTICE AREAS:* Litigation.

STEVEN BERNSTEIN, LL.B.; admitted, 1990. *PRACTICE AREAS:* Company/Commercial.

MARK FENTON, LL.B.; admitted, 1990. *PRACTICE AREAS:* Litigation.

YVONNE BAKER, LL.B.,; admitted, 1984. *PRACTICE AREAS:* Property.

JANE HOLLINSHEAD, LL.B.; admitted, 1993. *PRACTICE AREAS:* Property.

ANDREW SHUFFLEBOTHAM, LL.B.; admitted, 1988. *PRACTICE AREAS:* Property.

MICHAEL BABCOCK, B.A.; M.Sc.; LL.M.; admitted, 1994. *PRACTICE AREAS:* Company/Commercial.

DANIEL MARKS, LL.B.; admitted, 1992. *PRACTICE AREAS:* Litigation.

MARK BROWN, LL.B.; Admitted, 1995. *PRACTICE AREAS:* Litigation.

JONATHAN DICKINS, B.A. (Oxford); Admitted, 1990. *PRACTICE AREAS:* Property.

CONSULTANTS

ALFRED YOUNG, LL.B.; admitted, 1955. *PRACTICE AREAS:* Property.

MICHAEL GREEN, LL.B.; admitted, 1956. *PRACTICE AREAS:* Property.

MELVYN STEIN, LL.B.; admitted, 1969. *PRACTICE AREAS:* Commercial/Sports Law.

DERRICK BRETHERTON, admitted, 1948. *PRACTICE AREAS:* Property.

ARNOLD A. FINER, admitted, 1935.

FLADGATE FIELDER

HERON PLACE
3 GEORGE STREET
LONDON W1H 6AD, ENGLAND
Telephone: 011-44-171-486-9231
Facsimile: 011-44-171-935-7358

Basingstoke, England Office: Walgate House, 25 Church Street, RG21 1QQ. Telephone: 011-44-01256-463-044. Facsimile: 011-44-01256-471-600.

English, European particularly in the German speaking countries and US General Law Practice.
Primarily a Corporate practice with a substantial International element, including advising on German law. The main areas of work are Corporate, Corporate Finance, Banking and Financial Services, Intellectual Property, Venture Capital, MBO's and Litigation (including Professional Negligence), Real Estate, Taxation, Insolvency, Environmental, EC and Competition, Immigration, Pensions, Employment and Employee Benefits, Trusts and Estates, and Private Client.

(This Listing Continued)

FLADGATE FIELDER, London—Continued

PARTNERS

HOWARD KEEN, admitted, 1957. *Education:* LL.B. University of London (1st Class Honors). Awarded, Scholarship in Law, London University, 1954. *PRACTICE AREAS:* Commercial Leases; Commercial Property Purchases/Disposals; Property Finance including Secured Lending; Insolvency; Business Planning; Corporate Recovery & Asset Realization.

ANTHONY BAKER, admitted, 1958. *Education:* M.A., LL.M. Cambridge University. Awarded, John MacKrell Prize. *Member:* Society of Trusts & Estate Practitioners; Association of Charity Lawyers. *PRACTICE AREAS:* Partnership; Tax; Wills; Trusts; Probate; Charities.

BRIAN LEVY, admitted, 1963. *Education:* LL.B. University of London. *LANGUAGES:* French. *PRACTICE AREAS:* Property Development/Construction; Property Management; Commercial Leases; Commercial Property; Timeshare.

BRYAN DOWLER, admitted, 1961. *Education:* College of Law, Lancaster Gate. *LANGUAGES:* Thai. *PRACTICE AREAS:* Institutional Investment Property; Banking; Tax (Overseas Tax Planning).

FRED FISHBURN, admitted, 1958. *Education:* M.A. Oxford University. *LANGUAGES:* French and German. *PRACTICE AREAS:* Property Development; Landlord & Tenant; Conveyancing; Joint Ventures.

MARTIN LANE, admitted, 1965. *Education:* Stowe. *PRACTICE AREAS:* Residential Conveyancing.

JOHN BATES, admitted, 1966. *Education:* LL.B. University of London; College of Law, Lancaster Gate. *LANGUAGES:* French and German. *PRACTICE AREAS:* Real Property; Banking; Construction; Secured Lending.

RICHARD STANTON, admitted, 1967. *Education:* Marlborough. *Member:* Society of Trusts & Estate Practitioners. *PRACTICE AREAS:* Domestic Property Purchases; Wills and Probate; Trusts; Taxation.

CHARLES BOUNDY, admitted, 1970. *Education:* M.A. Cambridge University. *LANGUAGES:* French and German. *PRACTICE AREAS:* Mergers & Acquisitions; Business Purchases; Company; Employment; Commercial; Competition; Joint Venture; Partnership.

STUART TILLING, admitted, 1970. *Education:* College of Law. *PRACTICE AREAS:* Banking; Insolvency; Professional Negligence; Landlord & Tenant; Intellectual Property.

PAUL LEESE, admitted, 1973. *Education:* LL.B., Sheffield University; London Law School. *PRACTICE AREAS:* Professional Negligence; General Commercial Litigation; Corporate Recovery & Asset Realization.

HARVEY ROLLINSON, admitted, 1981. *Education:* B.A., Hons., Law. *PRACTICE AREAS:* Commercial Property; Property and Site Development; Property Investment; Landlord & Tenant; Secured Lending.

ANDREW MCKENZIE, admitted, 1971. *Education:* Trinity College, Cambridge Law; College of Law, Guildford. *Member:* Society of Trust & Estate Practitioners. *PRACTICE AREAS:* Tax and Trust Law and VAT; Offshore Corporate and Trust.

ALLEN COHEN, admitted, 1979. *Education:* B.A., University College, London. *Member:* Israel Bar Association. *LANGUAGES:* Hebrew and Yiddish. *PRACTICE AREAS:* Conveyancing; Landlord & Tenant; Secured Lending; Housing Associations.

ROGER LOOSLEY, admitted, 1971. *Education:* College of Law, Guildford. *Member:* Society for Computer & the Law; Computer Law Association (USA); British Computer Association. *PRACTICE AREAS:* Mergers & Acquisitions; Company; Commercial Contracts; Intellectual Property; Copyright; Business Planning; Partnership.

ASHLEY WILKIN, admitted, 1975. *Education:* LL.B. Birmingham. *Member:* The Society of Trust & Estate Practitioners. *PRACTICE AREAS:* Tax; Wills; Enduring Powers of Attorney; Trusts; Probate; Financial Planning.

PHILIP BARTH, admitted, 1982. *Education:* B.A., Cambridge University. *Member:* Immigration Law Practitioners' Association; The Russian Law Society. *PRACTICE AREAS:* Corporate; Share Issues; Financial Services; Immigration.

BARBARA EILON, admitted, 1985. *Education:* B.A., University of East Anglia, College of Law. *LANGUAGES:* French. *PRACTICE AREAS:* Housing Association Law; Secured Lending; Property Finance;

(This Listing Continued)

Commercial Property; Acquisition & Disposals; Property Management; Commercial Leases.

JANET KEELEY, admitted, 1984. *Education:* LL.B., Bristol University. *Member:* International Litigation Practitioners Forum. *LANGUAGES:* French and German. *PRACTICE AREAS:* Property Litigation; Landlord & Tenant; Insolvency; General Commercial Litigation; Corporate Recovery & Asset Realization; Debt Collection.

MARK BUCKLEY, admitted, 1985. *Education:* B.A., Northumberland University. *Member:* International Bar Association. *PRACTICE AREAS:* Commercial Litigation; Banking; Insolvency; Intellectual Property; Injunctions.

LYNN POVEY, admitted, 1985. *Education:* LL.B. University of Nottingham. *PRACTICE AREAS:* Property Management; Commercial Leases; Commercial Property Purchases/Disposals; Domestic Property Purchases; Property Finance including Secured Lending; Property Development/Construction.

STEPHEN THAIR, admitted, 1973 as Solicitor; 1976 as Barrister and Solicitor (Papua New Guinea). *Education:* LL.B.; U.C.W., Aberystwyth; College of Law, Guildford. *Member:* UK Environmental Law Association. *PRACTICE AREAS:* Property Management; Commercial Leases; Commercial Property Purchases/Disposals; Property Development/Construction; Environmental Law; Town & Country Planning.

SIMON EKINS, admitted, 1987. *Education:* B.Sc., York University; College of Law, London. *LANGUAGES:* French. *PRACTICE AREAS:* Commercial Litigation; Banking Litigation; Commercial Contracts; Intellectual Property; Copyright; Professional Negligence; Defamation; Corporate Recovery & Asset Realization.

BARRIE BARKER, admitted, 1965. *Education:* College of Law. *PRACTICE AREAS:* Insurance Litigation; Personal Injury Litigation; Construction Litigation; Professional Indemnity; General Commercial Litigation; Defamation; Town and Country Planning.

AVRAM KELMAN, admitted, 1987, Israel; 1988, New York; 1991, New Zealand; 1993, England and Wales. *Education:* B.A., LL.B. The Hebrew University, Jerusalem, Israel; M.A. University of London. *Member:* Israel Bar Association; New York State Bar Association; The American Bar Association. *LANGUAGES:* Hebrew. *PRACTICE AREAS:* Mergers & Acquisitions; International Commerce; Secured Lending; Company; Commercial Contracts; Business Planning; Corporate Recovery & Asset Realisation.

DANIEL R. SHIER, admitted, 1983, New York; 1993, England and Wales. *Education:* Columbia College; Columbia University School of International Affairs; Emory Law School. Consultant; United Nations High Commissioner for Refugees. *LANGUAGES:* French. *PRACTICE AREAS:* International Business Transactions and Securities Offerings; Offshore Corporate and Trust.

ANDREW KAUFMAN, admitted, 1971, England and Wales; 1988, Hong Kong. *Education:* M.A., St. John's College, Oxford, 1968. *Member:* International Bar Association. *LANGUAGES:* German and French. *PRACTICE AREAS:* International Commerce; Company; Employment.

NICOLAS GREENSTONE, admitted, 1972. *Education:* B.A., University College, Oxford University, Hons., 1963-1966; Jurisprudence College of Europe, Bruges, Belgium (Diploma of Advanced European Studies Specialized in EC anti-trust law). *LANGUAGES:* French. *PRACTICE AREAS:* Corporate Finance; Flotations; Mergers & Acquisitions; Management Buy-Outs; Venture Capital.

JULIUSZ WODZIANSKI, admitted, 1984. *Education:* LL.B., Leeds. *PRACTICE AREAS:* Property Development and Construction; Institutional Investment; Property Acquisition and Rules; Landlord and Tenant.

The firm has lawyers admitted in Germany, New York, Israel and New Zealand.

Languages: German, French, Hebrew, Danish, Italian, Norwegian, Spanish and Thai.

FORT & SCHLEFER

Established in 1945

(Formerly Kominers, Fort & Schlefer)

FIRST FLOOR, 9 GRAYS INN SQUARE
LONDON WC1R 5JF, ENGLAND
Telephone: 0171-404-1300
Fax: 0171-404-1301

Washington, D.C., Office: 1401 New York Avenue, N.W., 20005. Telephone: 202-467-5900. Telecopier: 202-783-6898. Cable Address: "Marlaw".

Firm engaged in American and General International Law Practice in the areas of Maritime, U.S. Federal Procurement, Financing, Corporate, Environmental, Antitrust, Aviation, Legislative Affairs, Health Care, Banking, and International Trade and Export Controls, but not authorized to appear before English Courts or to act as Solicitors.

FIRM PROFILE: Fort & Schlefer, founded in 1945, is a firm of 19 attorneys practicing primarily in matters that involve federal law. With a national and international clientele, Fort & Schlefer combines the sophisticated practice of large firms with the efficiency and direct partner involvement of small, specialty firms. Lines of communication are short, informal and efficient with all matters under the control of an experienced partner.

Fort & Schlefer has experience in general and project financing, complex litigation before federal and state courts and agencies, government regulation of business, government procurement, commercial contracts, and the advocacy of proposed legislation in the United States Congress. Fort & Schlefer also has special qualifications in the fields of federal procurement law, government regulations and support of transportation with particular emphasis in all facets of the maritime and aviation industries, antitrust law, health law, environmental law, banking and transnational law, federal jurisdiction and procedure, and laws relating to charitable organizations.

MEMBERS OF FIRM

ALICE N. GRAN, born New York, N.Y., 1949; admitted, 1973, District of Columbia. *Education:* University of Rochester (B.A., with high honors, 1970); George Washington University (J.D., with honors, 1973; LL.M., in Taxation, with highest honors, 1987). *Member:* The District of Columbia Bar; American and International Bar Associations. (Resident Partner). **LANGUAGES:** German and French. **PRACTICE AREAS:** Corporate Finance Law; Maritime and Shipping Regulation Law; U.S. Taxation.

FOX & GIBBONS

Established in 1962

2 OLD BURLINGTON STREET
LONDON W1X 2QA, ENGLAND
Telephone: (44-171) 439 8271
Telex: 267108
Telefax: (44-171) 734 8843

Dubai, United Arab Emirates Office: P.O. Box 1756. Telephone: (9714) 310220. Fax: (9714) 310201. Telex: 45614 GBLAW EM.

Abu Dhabi, United Arab Emirates Office: Kudsi Fox & Gibbons Office: P.O. Box 46010. Telephone: (9712) 322858. Fax: (9712) 331586.

Cairo, Egypt Office: 126 Mohei El Din Abul Ezz Street, 9th Floor, Mohandiseen, Giza, Cairo, Egypt. Telephone: (202) 3485955. Fax: (202) 3492210.

Ruwi, Oman Office: P.O. Box 3552, Postal Code 112. Telephone: (968) 564346. Fax: (968) 564395. Telex: 5630 GIBLAW ON.

Gibraltar Office: P.O. Box 246. Telephone: (350) 77750. Fax: (350) 77800.

Fujairah, United Arab Emirates Office: P.O. Box 701. Telephone: (971 9) 229390. Fax: (971 9) 226470.

Kuwait Associated Office: P.O. Box 26473, Safat, 13125 Safat. Telephone: (965) 2462323/2462525/2462929. Fax: (965) 242 5830. Telex: 30844 ZINA KT.

Yemen Associated Office: P.O. Box 148, Crater, Aden. Telephone: (9672) 255305/253824. FAX: (9672) 255305/255117.

Lebanon Associated Office: Saba K. Zreik Law Offices. Autostrade Dora Cite, Dora 3 Building, 10TH Floor, P.O. Box 90-710, Beirut, Lebanon. Telephone: (961 1) 881322. Fax: (961 1] 881387; Telex: 42949 MANAL LE

(This Listing Continued)

Company and Commercial, Litigation, Arbitration, Construction, Property, Offshore Investment, Trust and Tax Planning, Intellectual Property, Employment. Shipping including Collision, Salvage, Pollution, Towage and Offshore Support Activities, Charter Party Disputes, Bills of Lading, Cargo Claims, Marine Insurance, Ship Sales and Purchases and Ship Financing, Banking: including Trade Finance, Letters of Credit, Bills of Exchange, Syndicated Loans, Sub Participations, Asset Financing, Project Financing, Swaps, Secured and Unsecured Lending, Establishment of Bank Branches and Subsidiaries and Islamic Financing.

LONDON OFFICE PARTNERS

Robert Gibbons (Senior Partner)   **Paul Sheridan**
Richard Dunn   **Rachel Harrap**
Christopher Dixon   **John Lord**
Paul Gibbs   **Richard de Belder**
Robert Sprawson   **Nigel Frudd**
            Madeleine Smallwood

CONSULTANTS

Desmond Parte (Tax Executive)
Michael Reddy

(For a list of other Personnel, see Biographical Cards at Dubai and Abu Dhabi, United Arab Emirates, Cairo, Egypt, Ruwi, Sultanate of Oman, Gibraltar, Kuwait, Fujairah, United Arab Emirates, Lebanon and Yemen)

FOX WILLIAMS

CITY GATE HOUSE
39-45 FINSBURY SQUARE
LONDON EC2A 1UU, ENGLAND
Telephone: 0171-628 2000
Fax: 0171-628 2100

International Law Practice including Corporate, Corporate Finance, Venture Capital, Commercial, Anti-trust, Product Liability, Joint Venture, Banking and Financial Services, Labor and Labor Incentive Schemes, Commercial Real Estate, Commercial Litigation and Arbitration.

PARTNERS

RONALD DAVID FOX, M.A. (Oxon.), admitted, 1972, England.

CHRISTINE JOY WILLIAMS, M.A. (Oxon.), admitted, 1977, England.

PAUL LAWRENCE OSBORNE, LL.B. (Warw.), admitted, 1983, England.

NIGEL MILLER, LL.B. (Man.), admitted, 1983, England.

STEPHEN LEE SIDKIN, LL.B. (Lond.); M.A. (Bus. Law), admitted, 1981, England.

MARK ANDREW WATSON, M.A. (Cantab.), admitted, 1981, England.

BRYAN JEREMY EMDEN, B.A., admitted, 1981, England.

LINDSAY JAMES HILL, B.Soc.Sc. (Keele), admitted, 1983, England.

ROBIN TUTTY, LL.B. (L'Pool), admitted, 1975, England.

ELIZABETH MAYER, M.A. (Oxon.), admitted, 1987, England.

JANE ELIZABETH MANN, M.A. (Cantab), admitted 1981, England.

ASSOCIATES

GAVIN FOGGO, B.A. (Dunelm), admitted, 1992, England.

SALLY ANNE GRIFFITHS, LL.B. (Law with French) (Leics.), D.E.J.F. (Strasbourg), admitted, 1991, England.

IAN DALZELL HUNTER, B.A. (Bristol), admitted, 1989, England.

DIANE AMANDA PITTEM, LL.B., LL.M. (Cantab), admitted, 1990, England.

SIMON JOSEPH TAYLOR, LL.B. (Hons) (Hull), admitted, 1988, England.

ADAM JAMES EPSTEIN, B.A. (Cantab), admitted, 1991, England.

VISHVAS CHHOTALAL KANJI, LL.B. (Lond.), admitted, 1987, England.

PHILIPPA JANE ALDRICH, B.A. (Oxon), admitted, 1989, England.

(This Listing Continued)

FOX WILLIAMS, London—Continued

LISA CLARE BOOTH, B.A. (Oxon), admitted, 1993, England.

SAMANTHA KATE BOOTH DUGAN, B.A. (Warw.), admitted, 1993, England.

MARK GEDAY, M.A. (Oxon), admitted, 1993, England.

FREEHILL HOLLINGDALE & PAGE

Established in 1852

BIRCHIN COURT
20 BIRCHIN LANE
LONDON EC3V 9DJ, ENGLAND
Telephone: International: (44 171) 283 9006
Fax: (44 171) 454 9650

Sydney, New South Wales, Australia Office: Level 38, MLC Centre, 19-29 Martin Place, 2000. Telephone: (02) 225 5000. International: +(612) 225 5000. Telex AA 121885. Fax: (02) 322 4000.

Canberra City, Australian Capital Territory, Australia Office: London Court, 13 London Circuit, 2601. Telephone:(06) 240 6100. International: +(616) 240 6100. Telex: AA121885. Fax: (06) 240 6222.

Melbourne, Victoria, Australia Office: 101 Collins Street, 3000. Telephone: (03) 288 1234. International: +(613) 288 1234. Telex: AA33004. Fax: (03) 288 1567.

Perth, Western Australia Office: Australia Place, 15-17 William Street, 6000. Telephone: (09) 327 5777. International: +(619) 327 5777. Telex: AA92937. Fax: (09) 322 5954.

Brisbane, Queensland, Australia Office: Central Plaza II, 66 Eagle Street, 4000. Telephone: (07) 258 6666. International: +(617) 258 6666. Fax: (07) 258 6444.

Singapore Office: 6 Battery Road, #31-01, 0104. Telephone: (65) 225 1288. Telex: (RS) 42674. Fax: (65) 225 3314.

Hanoi, Vietnam Office: 34A Quang Trung Street. Telephone: (844) 227 839. Fax: (844) 227 909.

Ho Chi Minh City, Vietnam Office: 203 Dong Khoi Street, #3-05. Telephone: (848) 242 630; (848) 242 733. Fax: (848) 242 736.

MEMBERS OF FIRM IN LONDON

MARTIN MOULE HUDSON, admitted, 1970. *Education:* Monash University, Melbourne (B.Jurs.; LL.B.). *PRACTICE AREAS:* Corporate; Joint Ventures; Partnerships; Intellectual Property; Mergers and Acquisitions; Privatisation; Infrastructure; Trade Practices.

KEVIN ALAN LEWIS, admitted, 1981. *Education:* Harvard University (SJD); University of Western Australia (B.Juris., Hons.; LL.B., Hons.); University of Sydney (M.B.A.). *PRACTICE AREAS:* Capital Markets; Corporate; Fund Raisings; Mergers and Acquisitions; Privatisation; Infrastructure.

(For Biographical data on all other Personnel, see Professional Biographies at Brisbane, Canberra, Perth and Sydney, Australia and Singapore)

DJ FREEMAN

Established in 1952

43 FETTER LANE
LONDON EC4A 1NA, ENGLAND
Telephone: 44 171-583-4055
Fax: 44 171-353-7377 (Groups 2 - 3)
DX: 103 London

Hamburg, Germany Associated Office: Westphal & Voges, Esplanade 41, D-2000 Hamburg 36. Telephone: 49 40 35 17 96. Fax: 49 40 35 17 90.

Berlin, Germany Associated Office: Westphal & Voges, Chausseestraße 22, 1040. Telephone: 372 282 9886. Fax: 49161 2411 446.

The Firm which was founded in 1952, now has 48 partners and a total staff of 282. It represents a diverse range of corporate interests at both national and international level. Many members of staff are fluent in foreign languages.

Acquisitions and Mergers, Banking and Finance, Commercial Litigation, Computer Law, Construction, Corporate Finance, Corporate Tax, EEC and Competition Law, Employment, Media and Entertainment, Insolvency, Insurance, Intellectual Property, Management Buy-Outs, Pension

(This Listing Continued)

Schemes, Planning and Environmental, Project Finance, Real Estate, Shipping, Taxation.

PARTNERS

David J. Solomon	David J. Coupe
Jonathan Morris Lewis	Timothy H. Daniel
Colin S. Joseph	J.C. Christopher Comyn
N. Anthony Leifer	David R. Kendall
Godfrey M. Bruce-Radcliffe	James M. Innes
Helen M. Pallot	E. Howard Oakley
W. Michael Wharton	Alan Perry
Stephen D. Koehne	S.J. Gniadkowski
Graham A. Ceadel	Barbara R. Naftalin
Toby J. Greenbury	David L. Johnson
Edward B. Totman	Peter G. Taylor
Charles A. Crick	Susan E. Lewis
Marcus W.R. Rutherford	Andrew W. Sanders
Paul E. Clark	Moira A. Fraser
Richard J. Spiller	Christine N. Derrett
Vivien M. Tyrell	Sally L. Hine
Alan M. Magnus	Susan Aslan
Susan L. Hall	Dorothy Cory Wright
Anthony A. Edwards	Clive Davies
John M. Summers	Simon Corke
Antony M. Gostyn	Dr. David Tiplady
Elizabeth B. Hartley	Jane Moorman
Christopher Hancock	Richard Hopley
Antoinette M. Jucker	Henry Clinton Davis

FRERE CHOLMELEY BISCHOFF

Solicitors

Established in 1750

4 JOHN CARPENTER STREET
LONDON EC4Y 0NH, ENGLAND
Telephone: 0171-615 8000
Fax: 0171-615 8080
Telex: 27623
LDE: DX 140

Paris, France Office: 42 Avenue du Président Wilson, 75116. Telephone: (33) (1) 44 34 71 00. Fax: (33) (1) 44 34 71 11.

Rome, Italy Office: and Studio Legale Associato, 47, Viale Bruno Buozzi, 00197. Telephone: (39) (6) 808 0133. Fax: (39) (6) 808-0134.

Milan, Italy Office: and Studio Legale Associato, Piazza Castello 24, 20121 Milan. Telephone: (39) (2) 720 03 457. Fax: (39) (2) 720 03 469.

Monte Carlo,Monaco Office: "Est Ouest", 24 Boulevard Princesse Charlotte, MC 98000. Telephone: (33) (93) 50 85 70. Fax: (33) (93) 50 22 10.

Berlin, Germany Office: Im Internationalen Handelszentrum, Friedrichsstrasse 95, 10117. Telephone: (49) (30) 26 43 2000. Telex: 305996 Kbihzd. Fax: (49) (30) 26 43 1900.

Moscow, Russia Office: ul. Sadovaya Samotyochnaya 24/27, 103051 Moscow. Telephone: (7) 095 258 5058. Fax: (7) 095 258 5060. Telex: 412348 ALM SU.

Dubai, United Arab Emirates Office: Suite 802, EBIL Building, PO Box 2510, Deira, Dubai. Telephone: (9714) 267085/268336. Fax: (9714) 260206. Telex: 45493 LAWMC EM.

FIRM PROFILE: Frere Cholmeley Bischoff is a major City law firm with a strong European presence and offers a full range of commercial services from its network of offices. The firm is dedicated to supplying effective representation and sophisticated advice of the highest standards to corporate, government and private clients throughout the world. Specializations include Mergers and Acquisitions, Corporate Finance, Cross-Border Transactions, Unit Trusts, Banking and Financial Law, Taxation, Real Estate, Litigation and Arbitration, Environmental Law, European Community Law, Competition and Anti-Trust Law, Aviation Law, Media, Communications and Entertainment, Labour Law. Private Client, Family Law.

MEMBERS OF FIRM

FRANK G. PRESLAND, born 1944; admitted, 1973. *Education:* LSE, London (B.Sc; Econ, Hons.). Partner, 1976. Chairman, 1992. Litigation Department. *PRACTICE AREAS:* International Commercial Litigation and Arbitration.

(This Listing Continued)

J. RICHARD MILLAR, born Hove, 1940; admitted, 1963. *Education:* Wellington College, College of Law, 1962-1963. Partner, 1969; Joint Chairman, 1993. Company and Commercial Department. Member: Law Society's Company Law Committee, Chairman sub-committee on Collective Investment Schemes. *PRACTICE AREAS:* Company Law; Financial Services Law.

STEVEN C. SUGAR, born York, 1949; admitted, 1978. *Education:* Peterhouse, Cambridge (B.A.); LSE (M.Sc). Partner, 1981. Managing Partner, 1993. Company and Commercial Department. *PRACTICE AREAS:* Corporate Law; Regulatory Matters in Accounting and Broadcasting.

ANTHONY J. BLACKBURN, born Newcastle Upon Tyne, 1939; admitted, 1963. *Education:* Durham University; University College, London (LL.B., LL.M.). Partner, 1968. Property Department. *PRACTICE AREAS:* Commercial and Residential Property.

WILLIAM S. GIBBS, born 1939; admitted, 1965. *Education:* Cambridge (M.A.). Partner, 1972. Property Department. *PRACTICE AREAS:* Property Law; General Commercial Conveyancing.

W. JAMES B. JOWITT, born Harrogate, 1941; admitted, 1968. *Education:* Trinity College, Cambridge (M.A.). Partner, 1972. Company and Commercial and Private Clients Departments. *PRACTICE AREAS:* Tax and Estate Planning; Heritage Property; General Corporate; Banking.

E. TIMOTHY RAZZALL, CBE, born London, 1943; admitted, 1969, London. *Education:* Worcester College, Oxford (B.A.). Teaching Associate, Northwestern University, Chicago, 1965-1966. Partner, 1973. Company and Commercial Department. *PRACTICE AREAS:* Corporate Finance.

JULIAN F.J. WALTON, born Hunstanton, 1946; admitted, 1970. *Education:* Downside School. Partner, 1974. Head of Company and Commercial Department. *PRACTICE AREAS:* Corporate Finance; Mergers and Acquisitions; Telecommunications and General Corporate.

JOHN PEDDER, born Newcastle-Upon-Tyne, 1943; admitted, 1969. *Education:* Peterhouse, Cambridge (M.A.). Partner, 1974. Property Department. *PRACTICE AREAS:* Commercial Conveyancing, including Portfolio Acquisitions and Management; Profit Sharing Leases; Mortgage Funding; Securities Work.

JOHN L. DREWITT, born 1937; admitted, 1962. Partner, 1975. Private Client Department. *PRACTICE AREAS:* Estate Planning; Capital Taxation; Charities; Family Law.

DR. MICHAEL H. CARL, born Karlsruhe, Germany, 1942; admitted, 1974 as Rechtsanwalt (Karlsruhe, since 1979 Dusseldorf), 1979 as solicitor. *Education:* Universities of Freiburg, Br., Lausanne, Berlin. 1977 Prize of the European Communities. Partner 1987. Head of Anglo-German Group. *PRACTICE AREAS:* Anglo-German Commercial Law including EC-law; Corporate Commercial including International Commercial Litigation.

DAVID C. WILLIS, born Oxford, England, 1945; admitted, 1975. *Education:* Oxford University (M.A., Hons., Jurisprudence). Initially qualified and practised as a Barrister. Partner, 1978. Private Client Department. *PRACTICE AREAS:* Estate Planning; Trusts Capital Taxation; Matrimonial Work and Family Law.

D. JASPER G. HUNT, born London, 1948; admitted, 1972. *Education:* Trinity College, Oxford (M.A.). Partner, 1975. Property Department. *PRACTICE AREAS:* General Commercial Conveyancing, including Investment Funding; Shopping Centre Developments.

CHRISTOPHER H. DIGBY-BELL, born 1948; admitted, 1972. *Education:* Marlborough College; College of Law, London. Partner, 1989. Property Department. Business Development Partner Since, 1992. *PRACTICE AREAS:* Property Law including Investment, Development, Financing.

IAN R. GIBSON, born Bridlington, 1948; admitted, 1972. *Education:* The Queen's College, Oxford (B.A.). Partner, 1978. Company and Commercial Department. *PRACTICE AREAS:* Company Law; Corporate Taxation.

ANTONY H. THOMLINSON, born London, 1950; admitted, 1975. *Education:* Keble College, Oxford (B.A., M.A.). Partner, 1979. Company and Commercial Department. *PRACTICE AREAS:* Banking; Company and Financial Services Law.

ANTHONY J. PATTERSON, born Bolton, 1951; admitted, 1975. *Education:* University College, London (LL.B.). Partner, 1980. Head of Property Department. *PRACTICE AREAS:* Commercial Property, particularly Development Work; Landlord and Tenant.

(This Listing Continued)

J. HOWARD COOKE, born Exeter, 1952; admitted, 1976. *Education:* Queen Mary College, London (LL.B.). Partner, 1980. Company and Commercial Department. *PRACTICE AREAS:* Banking/Finance.

ROGER C. STEEL, born Scarborough, 1952; admitted, 1976. *Education:* University College, London (LL.B., Hons.). Partner, 1982. Litigation Department. Head of Employment Law Group. *PRACTICE AREAS:* Employment Law Issues.

ALAN D. JENKINS, born Weymouth, 1952; admitted, 1977. *Education:* New College, Oxford (B.A.). Partner, 1983. Head of Litigation Department. *PRACTICE AREAS:* International Commercial Litigation; Fraud; Professional Negligence, financially related litigation.

SUSAN M. TAYLOR, born N. Humberside, 1951; admitted, 1978. *Education:* Exeter (LL.B.); St. Anne's College, Oxford (BCL). Partner, 1985. Company and Commercial Department. *PRACTICE AREAS:* Taxation.

NICHOLAS E. VALNER, born Guildford, 1953; admitted, 1979. *Education:* Oxford University (B.A.). Partner, 1985. Litigation Department. *PRACTICE AREAS:* Litigation; Arbitration; Civil Litigation.

SOPHIE C. HAMILTON, born London, 1955; admitted, 1979. *Education:* Clare College, Cambridge (B.A.). Partner, 1985. Property Department and Environmental Law Group. *PRACTICE AREAS:* Commercial Property and Development Work; Environmental Law.

NORMAN A. CHAPMAN, born 1950; admitted, 1980. *Education:* Leeds University (LL.B.). Partner, 1986. Litigation Department. *PRACTICE AREAS:* Litigation.

RONALD G. PATERSON, born Edinburgh, 1956; admitted, 1980. *Education:* Trinity College, Cambridge (M.A.). Partner, 1980. Company and Commercial Department. *PRACTICE AREAS:* Corporate Finance; General Corporate; Regulatory.

JOHN M. BALFOUR, born Calcutta, India, 1952; admitted, 1979. *Education:* Oxford University (B.A., 1975; M.A., 1979). Partner 1986. Head of Aviation Department, Partner in Charge of Brussels Office. *Member:* Law Society's Solicitors European Group; Royal Aeronautical Society (and Vice Chairman of its Air Law Group Committee); European Air Law Association (Treasurer); Union Internationale Des Advocates. Publications: Contributor, Shawcross and Beaumont: Air Law; Contributing Editor, Forms and Precedents: Carriage by Air; Contributor, Air Transport and the European Community; Joint Editor and Contributor, Proceedings of the Second Annual Conference of the European Air Law Association; Author, Air Law and the European Community. *PRACTICE AREAS:* Air Law and in Particular EC Air Law.

SIMON N. J. PULLEN, born London, 1954; admitted, 1980. *Education:* Magdelen College, Oxford (B.A., Hons., Jurisprudence). Partner, 1986. Company and Commercial. *PRACTICE AREAS:* Banking and Finance.

CRAIG F. EADIE, born 1955; admitted, 1980. *Education:* Worcester College, Oxford (B.A., 1973-1976); Universite d'Aix, Marseilles, France (1977-1978). Partner, 1986. Company and Commercial Department. *PRACTICE AREAS:* Media and Communications.

PETER M. HOWARD, born Twickenham, 1951; admitted, 1976. *Education:* Fitzwilliam College, Cambridge (B.A., Hons.; M.A.); The College of Law, Guilford. Partner, 1987. Property Department. *PRACTICE AREAS:* Commercial Property Investment; Development and Funding; Landlord and Tenant.

A. MAXWELL HUDSON, born London, 1955; admitted, 1980. *Education:* New College, Oxford (B.A.). Partner, 1987. Company and Commercial Department. *PRACTICE AREAS:* Corporate Finance; Financial Services.

PAMELA M. THOMPSON, born 1956; admitted, 1982. *Education:* St. Hilda's College, Oxford (M.A.). Partner, 1986. Company and Commercial Department. *PRACTICE AREAS:* Company Law; Financial Services including Unit Trusts and Offshore Funds.

JAYNE C. ELKINS, born London, 1959; admitted, 1983. *Education:* King's College, London (LL.B., AKC). Partner, 1987. Property Department. *PRACTICE AREAS:* Commercial Property.

ALASTAIR R. TULLOCH, born Johannesburg, South Africa, 1955; admitted, 1980. *Education:* Magdelen College, Oxford (M.A.). Partner, 1988. Company and Commercial Department. *PRACTICE AREAS:* Share Sales; Asset Sales; Joint Ventures; Technology Transfers; UK and EEC Competition Law; Russian Law.

(This Listing Continued)

FRERE CHOLMELEY BISCHOFF, London—Continued

PAUL A. ROBERTS, born Coventry, 1957; admitted, 1981. *Education:* Jesus College, Oxford (M.A., Law). Partner, 1988. Property Department. *PRACTICE AREAS:* Commercial Property with Special Interest in Central and Local Government Work; Landlord and Tenant.

SHEILA FYFE, born Halifax, 1950; admitted, 1984. *Education:* Nottingham (B.A.); Manchester (M.A.). Partner, 1989. Company and Commercial Department. *PRACTICE AREAS:* Company Law.

DAVID J. R. ROBINSON, born 1955; admitted, 1981. *Education:* Cambridge (M.A.). Partner, 1989. Head of Private Client Department. *PRACTICE AREAS:* Estate Planning; Capital Taxation; Heritage Property.

JANE C. RICHARDS, born 1956; admitted, 1982. *Education:* St. Hugh's College, Oxford (M.A.). Partner, 1989. Litigation Department. *PRACTICE AREAS:* Employment Law; General Commercial Litigation.

IAN V. GASCOIGNE, born 1957; admitted, 1982. *Education:* St. John's College, Oxford (B.A.). Partner, 1989. Litigation Department. *PRACTICE AREAS:* High Court Commercial Litigation, International Element.

PATRICK H. ISHERWOOD, born 1947; admitted, 1977. *Education:* Birmingham University (B.A); Birmingham and Kansas (Ph.d). Partner, 1989. Litigation Department. *PRACTICE AREAS:* Intellectual Property; Entertainment/Media Work.

ROBERT P. COOKE, born 1958; admitted, 1985. *Education:* University College, Oxford (M.A.). Partner, 1988. Company and Commercial Department. *PRACTICE AREAS:* Property Financing; Banking.

SYLVIA GOULDING, born Folkstone, Kent; admitted, 1983. *Education:* University of Exeter (LL.B., Hons.). Partner, 1989. Property Department. *PRACTICE AREAS:* Commercial Property; Planning Law.

BRUCE G. J. GRIPTON, born 1959; admitted, 1984. *Education:* Exeter College, Oxford (M.A.). Partner, 1990. Company and Commercial Department. *PRACTICE AREAS:* Company Law; Mergers and Acquisitions.

DAVID M. HODSON, born 1953; admitted, 1978. *Education:* Leicester University (LL.B., Hons.). Law Society part II Distinction in Accounts 1976. Partner 1991. Private Client Department. Head of Family Law Group. Member; Law Society Solicitors Family Law Association. Lecturer and Writer on Family Law. *PRACTICE AREAS:* All Aspects of Family Law and Family Law Taxation.

FRANCES A. SPENCER, born 1957; admitted, 1983. *Education:* Hertford College, Oxford (B.A.); Universite d'Aix-Marseilles, France. Partner, 1991. Company and Commercial Department. *PRACTICE AREAS:* Company Law; Pensions and Employment.

SMITA EDWARDS, born Nairobi, Kenya 1961; admitted, 1986. *Education:* University of East Anglia (LL.B., Hons.). Partner, 1992. Property Department. *PRACTICE AREAS:* Commercial Property and Planning; Planning Law.

RUSSELL L. BOWYER, born 1961; admitted, 1986. *Education:* Grey College, Durham (B.A., Hons., Law). Partner, 1992. Company and Commercial Department. *PRACTICE AREAS:* Commercial Contracts; Information Technology; Intellectual Property; Competition Law.

MARK B. FRANKLIN, born Lincoln, 1959; admitted, 1984. *Education:* Southampton University (LL.B., Hons.). Partner, 1993. Company and Commercial Department. Member: Royal Aeronautical Society (MRAes). Publications: Contributing Editor, Volumes 6 and 7 of Butterworth's Encyclopedia of Forms and Precedents re: Carriage of Air; re Civil Aviation. *PRACTICE AREAS:* Air Law.

CAROLINE A. BASSETT, born 1961; admitted, 1985. *Education:* Jesus College, Oxford (M.A.). Partner, 1993. Litigation Department. *PRACTICE AREAS:* Intellectual Property; Entertainment Law; Commercial Litigation.

STEPHEN J. HERMER, born Cardiff, 1961; admitted, 1988. *Education:* Peterhouse, Cambridge (B.A.). Partner, 1993. Company and Commercial Department. *PRACTICE AREAS:* Corporate Law; Mergers and Acquisitions.

CHRISTOPHER M. LAKE, born Nantwich, 1961; admitted, 1986. *Education:* Durham University (B.A.). Partner, 1993. Litigation Department. *PRACTICE AREAS:* Commercial Litigation; Arbitration; Professional Negligence.

(This Listing Continued)

RUAIRIDH M. ROSS, born 1960; admitted, 1986. *Education:* Bristol University (LL.B., Hons.). Partner, 1994. Company and Commercial Department. *PRACTICE AREAS:* Corporate Finance.

HILARY A. RODGERS, born 1962; admitted, 1987. *Education:* Southampton University (LL.B., Hons.). Partner, 1994. Private Client Department. *PRACTICE AREAS:* Family Law.

SIMON D. MORGAN, admitted, 1987. *Education:* Cantab (B.A.). Partner, 1994. Company and Commercial Department. *PRACTICE AREAS:* Company Commercial.

Languages: English, German, French, Italian, Spanish, Russian and Arabic

---

FRESHFIELDS

65 FLEET STREET
LONDON EC4Y 1HS, ENGLAND
Telephone: (44 171) 936-4000
Telex: 889292
Cable Address: "Freshfields, London, EC4Y 1HS".
Telegram Address: "Freshfields, London"
Fax: 0171-832-7001
ISDN G4 Fax: 0171 936 3960

Brussels, Belgium Office: Rue de la Loi 15, 1040. Telephone: (32 2) 230 08 20. Fax: (32 2) 230 17 30; 230 17 78.
Paris, France Office: 69 Boulevard Haussmann, 75008. Telephone: (33 1) 44 56 44 56. Fax: (33 1) 44 56 44 00. ISDN G4 Fax: (1) 44 51 18 88.
Frankfurt/Main, Germany Office: MesseTurm, Friedrich-Ebert-Anlage 49, 60327 Frankfurt am Main. Telephone: (49 69) 975 70101. Fax: (49 69) 748917/748918.
Madrid, Spain Office: Fortuny, 6-3°, 28010. Telephone: (34 1) 319 1024. Fax: (34 1) 308 4636.
Hong Kong Office: 24th Floor, One Exchange Square. Telephone: (852) 846 3400. Fax: (852) 810 6192. G4 Fax: 8525022009.
Tokyo, Japan Office: Ark Mori Building, 8F, 1-12-32 Akasaka, Minato-ku, 107. Telephone: (813) 3583 3483. Fax: (813) 3583 1561/1571.
New York, New York Office: Suite 2750, 45 Rockefeller Plaza, 10111. Telephone: (212) 765-8685. Fax: (212) 397-7713.
Singapore Office: 16 Collyer Quay #33-01, Hitachi Tower, 0104. Telephone: (65) 5356211. Fax: (65) 5335007/5338007/5339007.
Bangkok, Thailand Office: Sathorn City Tower, 11th Floor, 175 South Sathorn Road, Khet Sathorn, 10120. Telephone: (662) 679 6123. Fax: (662) 679 6133/6134.
Moscow, Russia Office: Bolshaya Polyanka ul., 24/2, 109180. Telephone: (7 502) 222 1098. Fax: (7 502) 222 1099.
Barcelona, Spain Office: Diputació 246 - 2°, 08007. Telephone: (34 3) 301 9758. Fax: (34 3) 301 4234.
Hanoi, Vietnam Office: 50 Ly Thoung Kiet. Telephone: (84 4) 247 422/3/4. Fax: (84 4) 268 300.

RESIDENT PARTNERS IN LONDON

RICHARD M. BALLARD, born England, 1953; admitted, 1978, England. *Education:* Queens' College, Cambridge. Contributor: Tolley's Company Law; Tolley's Tax Planning. UK Member, Editorial Board, Euromoney's International Tax Review. *Member:* Law Society. *LANGUAGES:* English. *PRACTICE AREAS:* Corporate Tax; Corporate Tax Planning.

ROGER F. BERNER, born England, 1952; admitted, 1976, England. Contributor; Tolley's Company Law. *Member:* Law Society; International Bar Association. *LANGUAGES:* English. *PRACTICE AREAS:* Corporate Tax; Corporate Tax Planning; International Tax; Tax Controversies.

LUCIENNE BLEASDALE, born 1956; admitted, 1984. *Education:* York College for Girls, Leeds; Metropolitan University; Christ's College, Cambridge. *LANGUAGES:* French. *PRACTICE AREAS:* Banking; Corporate Rescues; Insolvency.

PETER J. R. BLOXHAM, born England, 1952; admitted, 1977, England. *Education:* St. John's College, Cambridge. *Member:* Law Society. *LANGUAGES:* French and English. *PRACTICE AREAS:* Insolvency; International Finance; Project Finance; Ship Finance; International Banking; Financial Restructuring Law.

PAUL BOWDEN, born England, 1955; admitted, 1981, England. *Education:* Bristol University. Editor and Author: "Tolley's Environmental Handbook." Member of the Editorial Board of "The Litigator" (Sweet & Maxwell). *Member:* Law Society (Advisory Board, Centre of Advanced

(This Listing Continued)

Litigation); Joint Bar-Law Society Working Party on the Civil Courts, 1992-1993; UK Environmental Law Association Practice and Procedure Working Party. *LANGUAGES:* French and English. *PRACTICE AREAS:* Pollution Litigation; Environmental and Industrial Disease Law; Hazardous Materials Law; Mass Torts.

RACHEL C. BRANDENBURGER, born England, 1954; admitted, 1979, England. *Education:* St. Hilda's College, Oxford. Co-Author: "Encyclopedia of Competition Law," Mergers Chapter, Butterworths. *Member:* Law Society; Solicitors European Group; Union des Avocates Europeens. Competition Law Sub-Committee of City of London Law Society. *LANGUAGES:* French, German and English. *PRACTICE AREAS:* EC and UK Anti-Trust Law; Regulatory Law; Telecommunications.

NICHOLAS A. CARTER, born 1958; admitted, 1984. *Education:* Magdalen College, Oxford (Physiological Sciences). *PRACTICE AREAS:* Contentious and Non-Contentious Intellectual Property; Litigation and Arbitration; Trade Mark Protection; Enforcement and Anti-Counterfeiting; Pharmaceuticals and Biotechnology; Patents; Copyrights; Designs.

TIMOTHY CAVE, born 1960; admitted, 1986. *Education:* Bristol University. *PRACTICE AREAS:* Commercial and Property Litigation.

RICHARD H.C. CHALK, born 1961; admitted, 1987, Solicitor, Hong Kong; 1990, Australian Capital Territory. *Education:* Downing College, Cambridge. *PRACTICE AREAS:* Commercial Litigation; Fraud; Asset Recovery; Banking; Litigation; Insolvency.

RICHARD A. CHAMBERLIN, born England, 1951; admitted, 1975, England. *Education:* Jesus College, Cambridge. *Member:* Law Society; International Academy of Estate and Trust Law. *LANGUAGES:* French, Spanish, Greek and English. *PRACTICE AREAS:* International Banking; Securitisation; International Capital Markets; Trust Law; Charitable Trusts and Foundations.

ANTHONY L. CHAPMAN, born England, 1946; admitted, 1975, England. *Education:* London University. Author: "Chapman's Inheritance Tax." *Member:* Law Society. Fellow, Institute of Taxation. *LANGUAGES:* English. *PRACTICE AREAS:* Corporate Tax Planning; International Tax.

MURRAY J. CLAYSON, born England, 1961; admitted, 1985, England. *Education:* Sidney Sussex College, Cambridge (M.A., LL.M.). *Member:* Law Society; Institute of Taxation (Fellow, 1991) (FTII). *LANGUAGES:* English. *PRACTICE AREAS:* Corporate Tax; Corporate Tax Planning; Tax Shelters; International Tax; Tax Controversies; Revenue Law.

MICHAEL L. H. CLODE, born Scotland, 1943; admitted, 1970, England. *Education:* Lancaster Gate Law School, London; College of Law, Guildford. *Member:* Law Society; International Bar Association; British-Middle East Law Council. *LANGUAGES:* English. *PRACTICE AREAS:* Corporate Law; Insolvency Law; Project and Ship Finance; Energy Law; Oil and Gas Law.

JENNY K.A. CONNOLLY, born 1956; admitted, 1992, Solicitor. *Education:* Swarthmore College, Swarthmore, Pennsylvania; University of Chicago Law School, Chicago, Illinois. *Member:* Illinois Bar Association (1982). *PRACTICE AREAS:* Company and Commercial Law; Privatisations; Private Mergers and Acquisitions.

HARRIET L. CREAMER, born England, 1959; admitted, 1983, England. *Education:* Girton College, Cambridge. Author: "Regulation of Securities in the UK," IFR, 1987; "Hybrid Instruments of Corporate Finance," Sweet & Maxwell, 1984. *Member:* Law Society; City of London Solicitors' Company. *LANGUAGES:* French and English. *PRACTICE AREAS:* Securities Law; Securities Offerings.

PHILIP M. CROALL, born England, 1959; admitted, 1985, England. *Education:* Emmanuel College, Cambridge. *Member:* Law Society; Chartered Institute of Arbitrators (Associate). *LANGUAGES:* English. *PRACTICE AREAS:* Commercial Litigation; Litigation Defence; Securities Litigation; Professional Indemnity; Alternative Dispute Resolution; Arbitration.

GAVIN L. B. DARLINGTON, born England, 1949; admitted, 1974, England. *Education:* Downing College, Cambridge. Chairman, Sub-Committee G2 and Vice Chairman, Committee G, Business Law Section, International Bar Association. Council Member, Eastern European Forum, Business Law Section. *Member:* Law Society; International Bar Association. *LANGUAGES:* English. *PRACTICE AREAS:* Commercial Law; Joint Ventures; Mergers and Acquisitions; Hostile Takeover; Securities Offerings; International Finance.

(This Listing Continued)

JAMES P. L. DAVIS, born England, 1946; admitted, 1972, England. *Education:* Balliol College, Oxford. *Member:* Law Society. *LANGUAGES:* English. *PRACTICE AREAS:* Corporate Law; Mergers and Acquisitions; Corporate Finance Law.

KENNETH N. DIERDEN, born England, 1952; admitted, 1977, England. *Education:* Southampton University. Contributor to 'Tolley's Company Law' and "Tolley's Directors' Handbook.". *LANGUAGES:* English. *PRACTICE AREAS:* Employment Law; Pension and Profit Sharing; Employee Benefit Law.

TIM EMMERSON, born 1954; admitted, 1987. *Education:* University of Sussex; College of Europe (Bruges). *LANGUAGES:* French. *PRACTICE AREAS:* General Corporate; Corporate Finance; Financial Services; Lloyd's Insurance.

F. ROGER ENOCK, born England, 1957; admitted, 1984, England. *Education:* Lancaster University; City of London Polytechnic. *Member:* Law Society. *LANGUAGES:* English. *PRACTICE AREAS:* Insurance Litigation; Reinsurance Litigation; Insolvency.

DAVID P. EREIRA, born England, 1956; admitted, 1981, England. *Education:* Manchester University. *Member:* Law Society; International Bar Association (Section on Business Law, Sub-Committees on Aviation and Banking); Justice. *LANGUAGES:* Italian and English. *PRACTICE AREAS:* International Banking; Property Finance; Asset Finance; Aviation Finance; Project Finance; Insolvency Law; Financial Restructuring Law.

EDWARD T. H. EVANS, born England, 1954; admitted, 1980, England. *Education:* Trinity College, Cambridge. *Member:* Law Society; International Bar Association (Member, Energy and Natural Resources Law Section). *LANGUAGES:* English. *PRACTICE AREAS:* International Banking; International Finance; Project Finance; Energy Law; Oil and Gas Law.

SIMON J.M. EVANS, born Wales, 1957; admitted, 1984, England. *Education:* Sidney Sussex College, Cambridge. *Member:* Law Society; Share Scheme Lawyers Group. *LANGUAGES:* English. *PRACTICE AREAS:* Employee Stock Ownership Plans (ESOPs); Pension and Profit Sharing; Employee Benefit Law; Employment Law; Immigration.

IAN M. FALCONER, born England, 1957; admitted, 1983, England. *Education:* Mansfield College, Oxford. *Member:* Law Society. *LANGUAGES:* German and English. *PRACTICE AREAS:* Banking Law; Securitisation; International Capital Markets; Building Societies; Financial Restructuring Law.

NEIL A. FALCONER, born Hong Kong, 1962; admitted, 1988, England. *Education:* King's College, London. *LANGUAGES:* English. *PRACTICE AREAS:* Aviation Finance; Aircraft Leasing; International Finance; Asset Finance; Asset Based Lending; Project Finance.

SARAH V. FALK, born 1962; admitted, 1986. *Education:* Sidney Sussex College, Cambridge. *PRACTICE AREAS:* Corporate Tax; Corporate Tax Planning; Corporate Finance.

IAN M. FISHER, born England, 1947; admitted, 1971, England. *Education:* Liverpool University. *Member:* Law Society; City of London Law Society; City of London Land Law Sub-Committee. *LANGUAGES:* English. *PRACTICE AREAS:* Commercial Property Law; Property Law; Landlord and Tenant Law; Conveyancing.

J. CHRISTOPHER T. FOSTER, born Melbourne, Australia, 1939; admitted, 1972, England. *Education:* University of Melbourne. *Member:* Law Society. *LANGUAGES:* English. *PRACTICE AREAS:* Commercial Litigation.

JULIAN FRANCIS, born Leybourne, England, December 1, 1954; admitted as solicitor 1980. *Education:* Trinity College, Cambridge (B.A., 1977; M.A., 1981). *LANGUAGES:* German, English and French.

J. M. PENELOPE FREER, born England, 1950; admitted, 1973, England. *Education:* Lady Margaret College, Oxford. *Member:* Law Society; City of London Law Society. *LANGUAGES:* English. *PRACTICE AREAS:* Commercial Property Law; Property Law; Property Finance; Land Use Law; Landlord and Tenant Law.

JAMES P. GEORGE, born England, 1952; admitted, 1984, England. *Education:* Reading University. *Member:* Law Society; City of London Law Society; Berks, Bucks and Oxon Law Society. *LANGUAGES:* English. *PRACTICE AREAS:* Commercial Property Law; Property Finance; Power Project Development; Privatisations; Securitisation.

JOHN P.A. GODDARD, born England, 1955; admitted, 1980, England. *Education:* Magdalene College, Cambridge. *Member:* Law Society. *LAN-*

(This Listing Continued)

FRESHFIELDS, London—Continued

GUAGES: English. **PRACTICE AREAS:** Commercial and Banking Litigation.

DAVID GRAHAM, born England, 1958; admitted, 1984, England. *Education:* Lincoln College, Oxford. *Member:* Law Society; City of London Solicitors' Company. **LANGUAGES:** English. **PRACTICE AREAS:** Corporate Law; Corporate Finance Law; Mergers and Acquisitions; Hostile Takeover; Securities Offerings.

JOHN K. GRIEVES, born England, 1935; admitted, 1961, England. *Education:* Keble College, Oxford; Harvard Business School (Advanced Management Program). *Member:* Law Society. (Senior Partner). **LANGUAGES:** English.

SIMON A. D. HALL, born England, 1955; admitted, 1979, England. *Education:* St. Catharine's College, Cambridge. *Member:* Law Society; City of London Solicitors' Company; American Bar Association. **LANGUAGES:** English. **PRACTICE AREAS:** International Banking; International Finance; Asset Finance; Project Finance; Aviation Finance; Ship Finance; Insolvency Law; Financial Restructuring Law; Power Project Development.

RICHARD W. HARRIS, born England, 1941; admitted, 1966, England. *Education:* Peterhouse, Cambridge. *Member:* Law Society. **LANGUAGES:** English. **PRACTICE AREAS:** Corporate Law.

THOMAS W. R. HEAD, born India, 1950; admitted, 1976, England. *Education:* Merton College, Oxford. *Member:* Law Society. **LANGUAGES:** English. **PRACTICE AREAS:** Corporate Law; Mergers and Acquisitions; Securities Offerings; Corporate Restructuring; Joint Ventures.

IAN L. HEWITT, born England, 1947; admitted, 1972, England. *Education:* St. Edmund Hall, Oxford; University College, London. *Member:* Law Society; International Bar Association. **LANGUAGES:** English. **PRACTICE AREAS:** Joint Ventures; International Transactions; Commercial Law; Energy Law.

STEPHEN L. HOYLE, born England, 1955; admitted, 1981, England. *Education:* St. Catharine's College, Oxford; Gonville and Caius College, Cambridge; Northwestern Law School, Chicago. Editor, International Tax Review. *Member:* Law Society. **LANGUAGES:** German and English. **PRACTICE AREAS:** International Tax; Corporate Tax Planning; Tax Shelters.

PETER J. JEFFCOTE, born England, 1948; admitted, 1980, England. *Education:* Wimbledon College. *Member:* Law Society. **LANGUAGES:** English. **PRACTICE AREAS:** Revenue Law; Pensions and Employment Law.

RAJAT K. JINDAL, born 1961; admitted, 1985, London; 1987, Hong Kong. **LANGUAGES:** French and Hindi. **PRACTICE AREAS:** Commercial Litigation.

MARK A. KALDERON, born England, 1957; admitted, 1983, England. *Education:* Balliol College, Oxford. *Member:* Law Society. **LANGUAGES:** German and English. **PRACTICE AREAS:** Banking Law; Finance Law; Securitisation; International Capital Markets; Aircraft Leasing.

VANESSA J. KNAPP, born England, 1956; admitted, 1981, England. *Education:* Exeter University. *Member:* Law Society. **LANGUAGES:** French and English. **PRACTICE AREAS:** Corporate Law; Mergers and Acquisitions; Securities Offerings; Corporate Finance Law.

WILLIAM P.L. LAWES, born 1964; admitted, 1986, Barrister and Solicitor, New Zealand; 1990, Solicitor, England. *Education:* Victoria University of Wellington, New Zealand; Gonville & Caius College, Cambridge. **PRACTICE AREAS:** Corporate Finance; General Corporate Matters.

PAUL M. LEONARD, born England, 1942; admitted, 1966, England. *Education:* Sheffield University. *Member:* Law Society; International Bar Association. **LANGUAGES:** English and French. **PRACTICE AREAS:** Commercial Litigation; Arbitration Law; Insurance Law; Reinsurance Law.

GEOFFREY LE PARD, born England, 1956; admitted, 1981, England. *Education:* Bristol University. *Member:* Law Society. **LANGUAGES:** English. **PRACTICE AREAS:** Commercial Property Law; Property Law; Property Development; Syndication Law; Landlord and Tenant Law.

ROBERT LEWIS, born England, 1951; admitted, 1977, England. *Education:* St. John's College, Oxford. Editor, Tolley's Environment Handbook. Co-Author: "Environmental Liability," 1990. Chairman, Air Pollution Working Party, UK Environmental Law Association. Member of the

(This Listing Continued)

Editorial Board, Environmental Law and Management. *Member:* Law Society. **LANGUAGES:** English. **PRACTICE AREAS:** Environmental Law; Environmental Liability; Water and Power; Water Quality Law; Contamination Law; Hazardous Waste Law; Offshore Pollution.

TIMOTHY A. LING, born England, 1948; admitted, 1973, England. *Education:* Queen's College, Oxford. *Member:* Law Society. **LANGUAGES:** English. **PRACTICE AREAS:** Corporate Tax.

TIMOTHY M. R. LINTOTT, born England, 1952; admitted, 1978, England; 1984, Hong Kong; 1985, Victoria, Australia. *Education:* Christ's College, Cambridge. *Member:* Law Society; Hong Kong Law Society. **LANGUAGES:** English. **PRACTICE AREAS:** International Finance; Aviation Finance; Aircraft Leasing Asset Finance; Asset Based Lending; Ship Finance; Transportation Law; Project Finance.

ANDREW LITTLEJOHNS, born England, 1956; admitted, 1980, England. *Education:* Lincoln College, Oxford. *Member:* Law Society. **LANGUAGES:** French and English. **PRACTICE AREAS:** International Banking; International Finance; Aviation Finance; Aircraft Leasing.

N. PAUL LOMAS, born England, 1958; admitted, 1984, England. *Education:* Emmanuel College, Cambridge; Insead M.B.A., 1987. *Member:* Law Society. **LANGUAGES:** French and English. **PRACTICE AREAS:** Commercial Litigation; Securities Litigation; European Community Law; Competition Law.

MICHAEL M. MACCABE, born England, 1944; admitted, 1969, England. *Education:* Lincoln College, Oxford (1963-1964). *Member:* Law Society. **LANGUAGES:** French, German and English. **PRACTICE AREAS:** International Banking; Corporate Restructuring Law; Insolvency Law; International Transactions; Joint Ventures.

PETER R. MACKLIN, born England, 1946; admitted, 1971, England. *Education:* Durham University. Council Member, The British Property Federation. *Member:* Law Society. **LANGUAGES:** English. **PRACTICE AREAS:** Commercial Property Law; Property Finance; Property Development and/or Syndication; Landlord and Tenant Law.

RUTH MARKLAND, born England, 1953; admitted, 1977, England. *Education:* Southampton University. *Member:* Law Society. **LANGUAGES:** English. **PRACTICE AREAS:** Corporate Law; Leveraged and Management Buyouts; Venture Capital; Corporate Restructuring Law.

LINDSAY G.D. MARR, born England, 1955; admitted, 1981, England. *Education:* Gonville and Caius College, Cambridge. *Member:* Law Society; City of London Solicitors' Company; International Bar Association. **LANGUAGES:** English. **PRACTICE AREAS:** Commercial Litigation; Arbitration; International Construction Contracts.

ROGER S. MCCORMICK, born England, 1951; admitted, 1975, England. *Education:* Wadham College, Oxford. *Member:* International Bar Association; Law Society. **LANGUAGES:** French and English. **PRACTICE AREAS:** International Banking; International Finance; Project Finance; Commercial Law; Joint Ventures; Oil and Gas Law; Power Project Development.

LAURIE GLENN MCFADDEN, born Canada, 1957; admitted, 1981, Canada; 1989, England. *Education:* University of Alberta, Canada; Magdalene College, Cambridge. *Member:* Law Society; City of London Solicitors' Company; Canada Club. **LANGUAGES:** English. **PRACTICE AREAS:** Corporate Law; Mergers and Acquisitions; Hostile Takeover; Securities Offerings.

STEPHEN MCGAIRL, born England, 1951; admitted, 1976, England; 1992, Avocat, Paris. *Education:* Worcester College, Oxford. *Member:* Law Society; Société Française de Droit Aérien et Spatial. **LANGUAGES:** French, English and Russian. **PRACTICE AREAS:** International Financing; Asset and Project Finance; Investment and Finance in Russia and the CIS.

ANTHONY S. MCWHIRTER, born England, 1954; admitted, 1979, England. *Education:* Downing College, Cambridge. **LANGUAGES:** English. **PRACTICE AREAS:** Tax and Regulatory Planning for Mutual Funds; Corporate Tax; International Tax; Corporate Tax Planning; Tax Controversies; Tax Shelters.

LOIS M. MOORE, born Pennsylvania, 1952; admitted, 1981, England. *Education:* The College of Wooster, Wooster, Ohio; University of Aberdeen, Scotland (B.A., 1973). *Member:* Law Society. **LANGUAGES:** English. **PRACTICE AREAS:** Corporate Law; Mergers and Acquisitions; Leveraged and Management Buyouts; Securities Offerings; Telecommunications.

(This Listing Continued)

TREVOR A. MOORE, born England, 1957; admitted, 1981, England. *Education:* St. Catharine's College, Cambridge. *Member:* Law Society. *LANGUAGES:* French, German and English. *PRACTICE AREAS:* Commercial Property Law; Property Law; Property Finance; Property Development.

CHRISTOPHER A. MORRIS, born England, 1960; admitted, 1984, England. *Education:* Lincoln College, Oxford. *Member:* Law Society; The City of London Solicitors' Company. *LANGUAGES:* Italian and English. *PRACTICE AREAS:* Commercial Property Law; Securitisation; Property Finance; Insolvency Law.

GUY W. MORTON, born England, 1952; admitted, 1979, England. *Education:* Corpus Christi College, Oxford. *Member:* Law Society; City of London Solicitors' Company. *LANGUAGES:* English. *PRACTICE AREAS:* International Investment Law; Broker-Dealer Regulation; Financial Institutions Law; Securities Law.

ALAN M. NEWTON, born England, 1957; admitted, 1982, England. *Education:* Exeter College, Oxford. *Member:* Law Society; The City of London Solicitors' Company. *LANGUAGES:* English. *PRACTICE AREAS:* International Capital Markets; Finance Law; Securitisation; Securities Law.

GEOFFREY NICHOLAS, born 1962; admitted, 1987, Solicitor. *Education:* Sheffield University. *PRACTICE AREAS:* Commercial Litigation; Lloyd's Insurance; Banking; City Fraud; International Arbitration.

GRAHAM B. NICHOLSON, born England, 1949; admitted, 1974, England. *Education:* Trinity Hall, Cambridge. *Member:* Law Society. *LANGUAGES:* English. *PRACTICE AREAS:* Corporate Law.

BARRY J. O'BRIEN, born Wales, 1952; admitted, 1978, England. *Education:* University College London. *Member:* Law Society; City of London Law Society. *LANGUAGES:* English. *PRACTICE AREAS:* Corporate Law; Mergers and Acquisitions; Privatisations; Hostile Takeovers; Securities Offerings.

RAJ D. PARKER, born India, 1960; admitted, 1988, England. *Education:* Southampton University. *LANGUAGES:* French and English. *PRACTICE AREAS:* Commercial Litigation; Insurance and Reinsurance Litigation; Lloyd's Litigation; General Litigation; Judicial Review; Environmental Insurance Litigation; Commercial Sports Law.

WILLIAM N. PARKER, born England, 1941; admitted, 1966, England. *Education:* Sheffield University. *Member:* Law Society. *LANGUAGES:* English and French. *PRACTICE AREAS:* Corporate Law; International Finance.

JOHN PART, born England, 1939; admitted, 1969, England. *Education:* Trinity College, Dublin. *Member:* Law Society. *LANGUAGES:* English, French and Spanish. *PRACTICE AREAS:* Commercial Law; Antitrust Law; Unfair Competition Law; Competition Law.

ALAN C. W. PECK, born England, 1949; admitted, 1974, England. *Education:* University College, Oxford. (Managing Partner). *LANGUAGES:* English.

RICHARD A.R. PHILLIPS, born England, 1955; admitted, 1981, England. *Education:* Balliol College, Oxford. *Member:* Law Society. *LANGUAGES:* English. *PRACTICE AREAS:* Project Finance; Banking Regulation; Commercial Law; Corporate Law; Mergers and Acquisitions.

JEREMY A.E. PITKIN, born England, 1955; admitted, 1980, England. *Education:* King's College, London (LL.B.). *Member:* Law Society. *LANGUAGES:* English. *PRACTICE AREAS:* International Finance; Securitisation; Securities Offerings; Corporate Finance Law; Securities Law; International Capital Markets.

DAVID N. POLLARD, born England, 1956; admitted, 1980, England; 1986, Hong Kong. *Education:* St. John's College, Cambridge. Author: "Employment and Pension Rights in Corporate Insolvency," Tolley 1994. Contributor, "A Practitioner's Guide to Corporate Insolvency and Corporate Rescues," Westminster Management Consultants, 1991; "Tolley's Employment Law"; Journal of Business Law; British Pension Lawyer; Pensions World; Butterworths Journal of International Banking and Financial Law; Business Law Review. *Member:* Law Society; Association of Pension Lawyers; Industrial Law Society; Employment Lawyers Association. *LANGUAGES:* English. *PRACTICE AREAS:* Employment Law; Pension and Profit Sharing; Employee Benefit Law; Employee Stock Ownership Plans (ESOP).

SUSAN M. PORTER, born England, 1959; admitted, 1984, England. *Education:* Trinity College, Cambridge. Author: "Trading in the UK," Tol-

(This Listing Continued)

ley's Tax Planning. *Member:* Law Society. *LANGUAGES:* English. *PRACTICE AREAS:* Corporate Tax; Corporate Tax Planning.

GRAHAM N. PRENTICE, born England, 1955; admitted, 1980, England. *Education:* Churchill College, Cambridge. *Member:* Law Society. *LANGUAGES:* English. *PRACTICE AREAS:* Commercial Property Law; Property Law; Building and Construction; Property Development and/or Syndication Law Planning.

CHRISTOPHER R. PUGH, born England, 1957; admitted, 1983, England. *Education:* University College London. *Member:* Law Society. *LANGUAGES:* French and English. *PRACTICE AREAS:* Commercial Litigation; Fraud; Insolvency.

NIGEL K. RAWDING, born England, 1958; admitted, 1984, England. *Education:* Sidney Sussex College, Cambridge. Co-Author: "The Freshfields Guide to Arbitration and ADR-Clauses in International Contracts," Kluwer, 1993. *Member:* Law Society; Chartered Institute of Arbitrators. *LANGUAGES:* English. *PRACTICE AREAS:* Commercial Litigation; International Arbitration; Alternative Dispute Resolution.

MARK S. RAWLINSON, born England, 1957; admitted, 1984, England. *Education:* Sidney Sussex College, Cambridge. *Member:* Law Society; Cambridge University Hawks Club. *LANGUAGES:* English. *PRACTICE AREAS:* Corporate Law; Mergers and Acquisitions; Hostile Takeovers; Securities Offerings.

D. ALAN REDFERN, born England, 1932; admitted, 1958, England. *Education:* Sidney Sussex College, Cambridge (Exhibitioner). Co-Author: "Law and Practice of International Commercial Arbitration;" "The Freshfields Guide to Arbitration and ADR." *Member:* ICC Commission in International Arbitration; Swiss Arbitration Association; Law Society; Middle East Association. Fellow, Chartered Institute of Arbitrators. *LANGUAGES:* English and French. *PRACTICE AREAS:* Arbitration; Building and Construction; International Trade; Oil and Gas Law; Commercial Litigation; Alternative Dispute Resolution; Sovereignty Law.

JONATHAN H. REES, born England, 1960; admitted, 1984, England. *Education:* Wadham College, Oxford. *Member:* Law Society. *LANGUAGES:* English. *PRACTICE AREAS:* Corporate Law; Corporate Finance Law; Mergers and Acquisitions; Corporate Restructuring.

STEPHEN M. REVELL, born England, 1956; admitted, 1981, England. *Education:* Christ's College, Cambridge. Co-Author: "Securities Regulations in the UK," IFR, 1987; "Bond Market Compliance-Regulations of London's Euromarkets," IFR, 1992. Editor: "Capital Markets Forum Yearbook," 1993. *Member:* Law Society; International Bar Association; Capital Markets Forum. *LANGUAGES:* English. *PRACTICE AREAS:* Finance Law; Securitisation; Securities Law; Securities Offerings; Derivatives Law; International Capital Markets; Building Societies.

A. PHILIP RICHARDS, born England, 1956; admitted, 1980, England. *Education:* Lincoln College, Oxford. *Member:* Law Society. *LANGUAGES:* English. *PRACTICE AREAS:* Mergers and Acquisitions; Hostile Takeover; Securities Offerings; Corporate Finance Law; Life Insurance Law; Insurance Regulations.

JOSANNE P. J. RICKARD, born England, 1949; admitted, 1973, England. *Education:* King's College, London. *LANGUAGES:* English. *PRACTICE AREAS:* Commercial Litigation; Insolvency; Securities Litigation.

SALLY J. ROE, born England, 1956; admitted, 1981, England. *Education:* St. Hilda's College, Oxford. *Member:* Law Society. *LANGUAGES:* French and English. *PRACTICE AREAS:* Building and Construction; Building Contracts; International Construction Contracts; Property Litigation; EC Law; Public Procurement.

CLIVE W. ROUGH, born England, 1956; admitted, 1980, England. *Education:* Jesus College, Cambridge. *Member:* Law Society. *LANGUAGES:* English. *PRACTICE AREAS:* International Banking; International Finance; International Capital Markets; Project Finance.

ANTHONY M. V. SALZ, born England, 1950; admitted, 1974, England. *Education:* Exeter University. Editorial Committee, Practical Law for Companies (PLC). Contributor: "Mergers and Acquisitions," (Gee & Co.). *Member:* Law Society; City of London Solicitors' Company. *LANGUAGES:* English. *PRACTICE AREAS:* Corporate Law; Mergers and Acquisitions; Privatisations; Hostile Takeover; Securities Offerings.

FRANCIS G. SANDISON, born Scotland, 1949; admitted, 1974, England. *Education:* Magdalen College, Oxford. Co-Author: "Whiteman on Income Tax," 3rd Edition, 1988. Author: "Tolley's Profit Sharing," 1978. Co-Author: "Business Operations in the United Kingdom". Contributor:

(This Listing Continued)

FRESHFIELDS, London—Continued

"Simon's Taxes"; "Tolleys Tax Planning," (until 1988); "The Tax Journal". Chairman, City of London Law Society's Revenue Law Sub-Committee. The Law Society's Corporation Tax Sub-Committee. *Member:* Law Society; The Addington Society. *LANGUAGES:* English. *PRACTICE AREAS:* Corporate Tax; International Tax; Corporate Tax Planning; Tax Controversies.

D. CHARLES AP SIMON, born England, 1947; admitted, 1977, England. *Education:* Christ's College, Cambridge. *Member:* Law Society; City of London Solicitors' Company. *LANGUAGES:* English. *PRACTICE AREAS:* Corporate Law; Mergers and Acquisitions; Securities Offerings; Corporate Finance Law.

D. NICHOLAS SPEARING, born England, 1954; admitted, 1978, England. *Education:* Hertford College, Oxford. Co-Author: Mergers section in Butterworth's 'Competition Law'. Contributor, "Agency" title, Encyclopedia of Forms and Precedents. Past Chairman, Law Society's Solicitors' European Group. *Member:* Joint Bar-Law Society Working Party on Competition Law. *LANGUAGES:* English. *PRACTICE AREAS:* Competition Law; Commercial Law; Agency and Distribution; Joint Ventures.

JAMES T. STARKY, born England, 1958; admitted, 1983, England. *Education:* New College, Oxford. *Member:* Law Society. *LANGUAGES:* English. *PRACTICE AREAS:* International Finance; Securitisation; Securities Offerings; International Capital Markets.

BEN STAVELEY, born England, 1956; admitted, 1981, England. *Education:* Magdalene College, Cambridge. *Member:* Law Society; UK Institute of Taxation (Associate). *LANGUAGES:* English. *PRACTICE AREAS:* Corporate Tax; Corporate Tax Planning.

SIMON B. STEBBINGS, born England, 1958; admitted, 1983, England; 1986, Solicitor of the Supreme Court, Hong Kong. *Education:* Worcester College, Oxford. *Member:* Law Society; Singapore Institute of Arbitrators. *LANGUAGES:* English. *PRACTICE AREAS:* International Arbitration; International Construction; Contracts; Commercial Litigation.

PETER S. STREATFEILD, born England, 1954; admitted, 1979, England. *Education:* Pembroke College, Cambridge. *Member:* Law Society. *LANGUAGES:* English. *PRACTICE AREAS:* Corporate Law; Privatisations; Leveraged and Management Buyouts; Commercial Law; Venture Capital.

HUGH W. J. STUBBS, born England, 1946; admitted, 1972, England; 1985, Hong Kong. *Education:* Exeter University. Joint Author: "Arbitrate or Litigate." Author: "So You Want to Sue the Auditor." International Legal Practitioner. *Member:* Law Society; International Bar Association (Secretary, General Practice Section; Chairman, Civil Litigation Committee, 1988-1992). *LANGUAGES:* English. *PRACTICE AREAS:* Commercial Litigation; Intellectual Property.

DAVID N. TAYLOR, born England, 1959; admitted, 1984, England. *Education:* Jesus College, Cambridge. *Member:* Law Society. *LANGUAGES:* English. *PRACTICE AREAS:* Corporate Tax; Corporate Tax Planning; Tax Shelters; Revenue Law.

IAN TAYLOR, born England, 1951; admitted, 1976, England. *Education:* Gonville and Caius College, Cambridge. *Member:* Law Society. *LANGUAGES:* French, German, Portuguese and English. *PRACTICE AREAS:* Commercial Litigation.

PAUL G. TAYLOR, born 1956; admitted, 1984. *PRACTICE AREAS:* Non-Contentious Intellectual Property; Computer Law; Information Technology; Telecommunications Law.

IAN K. TERRY, born England, 1955; admitted, 1980, England. *Education:* Keble College, Oxford. *Member:* Law Society. *LANGUAGES:* English. *PRACTICE AREAS:* Commercial Litigation; Fraud; Lloyd's Litigation; International Law.

MICHAEL THOMPSON, born England, 1954; admitted, 1979, England. *Education:* Trinity College, Cambridge. Co-Author: Tax Implications of Securitization in the United Kingdom (part of "Asset Securitization" published by Euromoney). *Member:* Law Society; City of London Solicitors' Company. *LANGUAGES:* English. *PRACTICE AREAS:* Corporate Tax; Corporate Tax Planning; Tax Controversies; Revenue Law.

PATRICK F. WALLACE, born England, 1959; admitted, 1986, England. *Education:* King's College, London University; University of Paris 1 (Pantheon Sorbonne); Harvard Law School. Harkness Fellow, 1982. *Mem-*

(This Listing Continued)

ber: Law Society; City of London Solicitors' Company. *LANGUAGES:* French, German and English. *PRACTICE AREAS:* Commercial Law; Antitrust Law; Contract Law; Privatisations; Energy Law; Project Finance.

FRIED, FRANK, HARRIS, SHRIVER & JACOBSON

4 CHISWELL STREET
LONDON EC1Y 4UP, ENGLAND
Telephone: 011-44-171-972-9600
Fax: 011-44-171-972-9602
Telex: 011-44-171-972-9602

New York, New York Office: One New York Plaza, 10004. Telephone: 212-859-8000. Cable Address: "Steric New York." W.U. Int. Telex: 620223. W.U. Int. Telex: 662119. W.U. Domestic: 128173. Telecopier: 212-859-4000 (Dex 6200).

Washington, D.C. Office: Suite 800, 1001 Pennsylvania Avenue, N.W., 20004-2505. Telephone: 202-639-7000.

Los Angeles, California Office: 725 South Figueroa Street, 90017. Telephone: 213-689-5800.

Paris, France Office: 7, Rue Royale, 75008. Telephone: (+331) 40 17 04 04. Fax: (+331) 40 17 08 30.

Firm engaged in American and International Law Practice, but not authorized to appear before the English Courts or to act as Solicitors.

PARTNERS

JERRY L. SMITH, born Tulsa, Oklahoma, October 18, 1938; admitted, 1964, New York (Not admitted in England). *Education:* Oklahoma University (B.A., 1960); Cornell University (LL.B., 1963); Université d'Aix-en Provence-Marseilles (1963-1964). Phi Beta Kappa; Order of the Coif. *Member:* The Association of the Bar of the City of New York; American Bar Association (Member, Sections on: Corporation, Banking and Business Law; International Law and Practice; Antitrust Law); American Society of International Law.

ROBERT P. MOLLEN, born Aberdeen, Maryland, June 1, 1955; admitted, 1979, District of Columbia; 1991, New York (Not admitted in England). *Education:* Georgetown University (B.S.F.S., summa cum laude, 1975); Harvard University (J.D., magna cum laude, 1979). Author: "Regulation of Foreign Investment Managers with U.S. Clients," International Financial Law Review, Dec., 1982 and April, 1983; "Investment Advisers Caught in SEC Net," International Financial Law Review, Sept. 1992. *Member:* The District of Columbia Bar; International Bar Association. (Also at Washington, D.C. Office).

RESIDENT ASSOCIATES

LOUIS CAMMAROSANO, born Mt. Vernon, New York, September 7, 1961; admitted, 1991, New York (Not admitted in England). *Education:* Fordham University (B.A., 1983; J.D., 1990).

AMORY B. SCHWARTZ, born Munich, West Germany, March 7, 1962; admitted, 1989, New York (Not admitted in England). *Education:* Princeton University (A.B., magna cum laude, 1985); University of London, England (M.A., 1986); Columbia University (J.D., 1989).

(For Biographical Data of New York, New York, Personnel, see Professional Biographies at New York, New York).
(For Biographical Data of Washington, D.C. Personnel, see Professional Biographies at Washington, D.C.).
(For Biographical Data of Los Angeles, California Personnel, see Professional Biographies at Los Angeles, California).
(For Biographical Data of Paris Personnel, see Professional Biographies at Paris, France).

FRORIEP RENGGLI

Swiss Lawyers

1 KNIGHTRIDER COURT
LONDON EC4V 5JP, ENGLAND
Telephone: (+44)171 236 60 00
Fax: (+44)171 248 02 09

Zurich, Switzerland Office: Bellerivestrasse 201, 8034. Telephone: (+41)1 386 60 00. Telecopier: (+41)1 383 60 50 (Address until April 30, 1995: General Wille-Strasse 10, 8027. Telephone: (+41) 12017420. Telex: 815596 frp ch. Telecopier: (+41) 12023666).

(This Listing Continued)

Geneva, Switzerland Office: 4, Rue Charles-Bonnet, 1206. Telephone: (+41)-22 347 18 18. Telex: 423651 frob ch. Telecopier: (+41)-22 347 71 59.

Zug, Switzerland Office: Baarerstrasse 75, 6300. Telephone: (+41)-42 21 33 71. Telecopier: (+41)-42 23 07 15.

Fuerth (Nürnberg), Germany Office: Friedrichstrasse 6, 90762. Telephone: (+49)-911 77 39 82. Telecopier: (+49)-911 749 84 51.

Swiss and International Commercial, Corporate and Civil Practice, Commercial Litigation and Arbitration, Private and Public International Law, Banking, Taxation, Immigration, International Judicial Assistance, Estate, Real Property.

Firm engaged in Swiss and International Practice, but not authorized to appear before the English Courts or to act as Solicitors.

FIRM PROFILE: Established in 1966, Froriep Renggli has grown to be one of the leading and largest Swiss law firms with principal offices in Zurich, Geneva and Zug. The firm is engaged in a broad range of Swiss and International practice. Froriep Renggli currently has a total of thirty-two lawyers, twelve of whom are partners. Two of the associates are qualified German lawyers, four lawyers are also admitted in New York and one is an English solicitor. Most of the lawyers have had, in addition to their Swiss training, legal education in England or the United States and/or have practice as foreign consultants with law firms there or elsewhere abroad. The firm has a three lawyers strong London office, an office in Fürth/Nürnberg, Germany, and an associated office in Bratislava, Slovakia. These, combined with an extensive network of correspondent lawyers, enhance the firm's international advisory, transactional and litigation capabilities.

RESIDENT PARTNERS

BRUNO W. BOESCH, born Stockholm, Sweden, April 5, 1949; admitted, 1972, Geneva, Zurich and Zug (Not admitted in England). *Education:* University of Geneva (Lic. iur., 1972); New York University Institute of Comparative Law (M.C.J., 1975). *LANGUAGES:* French, English, German and Swedish. *PRACTICE AREAS:* International Contract Law; Finance; Banks and Banking; Cross-Border Transactions; Joint-Ventures; International Arbitration; Litigation; Acquisitions and Financing; International Mergers and Acquisitions; Hotels and Resorts; International Trade and Estates; White Collar Crime.

JEAN-LUC HERBEZ, born Geneva, Switzerland, March 27, 1945; admitted, 1976, Switzerland (Not admitted in England). *Education:* University of Geneva (Lic. oec., 1970; Lic. iur., 1976); University of Pennsylvania Law School, Center for Study of Financial Institutions, Philadelphia (LL.M., 1981). Languages; French, German, English and Italian. *PRACTICE AREAS:* Commercial Law; Corporate Law; Contract Law; Taxation; Finance; Banking; Finance and Securities.

RESIDENT ASSOCIATES

JÉRÔME DE MONTMOLLIN, born Geneva, Switzerland, March 14, 1958; admitted, 1983, Switzerland (Not admitted in England). *Education:* University of Neuchâtel (Lic. iur., 1980). *LANGUAGES:* French, Italian, German and English. *PRACTICE AREAS:* Corporate Law; Contract Law; Company Law; Business Law; Bankruptcy; Securities.

BRUNO HEYNEN, born Solothurn, Switzerland, March 29, 1960; admitted, 1989, Switzerland. *Education:* University of St. Gallen (Lic. iur., 1987). *LANGUAGES:* German, English and French. *PRACTICE AREAS:* Corporate Law; Commercial Law; Banking; Family Law and Estates.

(For Biographical Data on all Members, see Professional Biographies at Zurich, Switzerland).

FULBRIGHT & JAWORSKI L.L.P.

Established in 1919

2 ST. JAMES'S PLACE

LONDON SW1A 1NP, ENGLAND

Telephone: 011-44171-629-1207

Telecopier: 011-4471-493-8259

Houston, Texas Office: 1301 McKinney, Suite 5100, 77010-3095. Telephone: 713-651-5151. Cable Address: "Fulbright." Telecopier: 713-651-5246. Telex: 76-2829.

Washington, D.C. Office: Market Square, 801 Pennsylvania Avenue, N.W., 20004-2604. Telephone: 202-662-0200. Telecopier: 202-662-4643. Telex: 19-7471.

(This Listing Continued)

Austin, Texas Office: 600 Congress Avenue, Suite 2400, 78701. Telephone: 512-474-5201. Telecopier: 512-320-4599.

San Antonio, Texas Office: 300 Convent Street, Suite 2200, 78205. Telephone: 210-224-5575. Telecopier: 210-223-6459.

Dallas, Texas Office: 2200 Ross Avenue, Suite 2800, 75201. Telephone: 214-855-8000. Telecopier: 214-855-8200.

New York, New York Office: 666 Fifth Avenue, 10103. Telephone: 212-486-9500. Telecopier: 212-318-3000. Telex: TWX 710-581-3676.

Los Angeles, California Office: 865 South Figueroa Street, 29th Floor, 90017-2571. Telephone: 213-892-9200. Telecopier: 213-680-4518. Telex: 69-1208.

Hong Kong Office: 2901 Central Plaza, 18 Harbour Road, Wanchai. Telephone: 011-852-511-5100. Fax: 011-852-511-9515.

General International Practice. United States law practice relating to Energy, Commercial and Corporate, International Trade Transactions, Taxation, Arbitration of Commercial Disputes.

Firm engaged in American and International Law Practice, but not authorized to appear before the English Courts or to act as Solicitors.

RESIDENT PARTNER

STEPHEN F. VOGEL, born Enterprise, Alabama, August 7, 1953; admitted, 1978, Louisiana; 1979, Ohio; 1982, District of Columbia (Not admitted in England). *Education:* University of Kentucky (B.A., 1975); Ohio State University (J.D., 1978); New York University (LL.M., 1983). Phi Beta Kappa. *Member:* Ohio and American Bar Associations; The District of Columbia Bar; State Bar of Louisiana. *PRACTICE AREAS:* International Tax Law.

PARTICIPATING ASSOCIATE

NANCY B. TURCK, born Teaneck, New Jersey, September 7, 1947; admitted, 1980, New York; U.S. Court of International Trade (Not admitted in England). *Education:* Pembroke College (B.A., 1968); Brown University (M.A., 1968); Georgetown University (J.D., 1978). *Member:* New York State, American and International Bar Associations. *PRACTICE AREAS:* Corporation Law; International Transactions.

(For Biographies of Houston, Texas Members, see Houston, Texas Professional Biographies).

(For Biographies of Washington, D.C. Members, see Washington, D.C. Professional Biographies).

(For Biographies of Austin, Texas Members, see Austin, Texas Professional Biographies).

(For Biographies of San Antonio, Texas Members, see San Antonio, Texas Professional Biographies).

(For Biographies of Dallas, Texas Members, see Dallas, Texas Professional Biographies).

(For Biographies of Los Angeles, California Personnel, see Los Angeles, California Professional Biographies).

(For Biographies of New York, New York Personnel, see New York, New York, Professional Biographies).

(For Biographies of Hong Kong Personnel, see Hong Kong Professional Biographies).

LAW OFFICE DIANE GELON

8 COLDBATH SQUARE

LONDON EC1R 5HL, ENGLAND

Telephone: 0171-833-3121

Telefax: 0171-833-2550

Tax, Commercial, Immigration, Entertainment and Arts Law.

DIANE GELON, born Los Angeles, California, August 17, 1948; admitted, 1986, New York (Not admitted in England). *Education:* University of California, Los Angeles (A.B., 1971); Yeshiva University, Cardozo School of Law (J.D., 1984); University of London, London School of Economics (LL.M., 1986). *Member:* Immigration Law Practitioners' Association. *PRACTICE AREAS:* Entertainment; Arts; Tax.

GIBSON, DUNN & CRUTCHER

Established in 1890

30/35 PALL MALL
LONDON SW1Y 5LP, ENGLAND
Telephone: 011-44-171-925-0440
Telex: 27731 GIBTRK G; 916176 GIBTRK G
Telecopier: 011-44-171-925-2465
Cable Address: GIBTRASK LONDON W1

Los Angeles, California Office: 333 South Grand Avenue, 90071-3197. Telephone: 213-229-7000. Telex: 188171 GIBTRASK LSA (TRT), 674930 GIBTRASK LSA (WUT). Telecopier: 213-229-7520. Cable Address: GIBTRASK LOS ANGELES.

General Corporate and International Law Practice.
Firm engaged in American and International Practice, but not authorized to appear before the English Courts or to act as Solicitors.

FIRM PROFILE: Gibson, Dunn & Crutcher, originating in Los Angeles, has been providing legal services to clients since 1890. Today, the firm has grown to one of the largest law firms in the world with approximately 650 attorneys in 17 offices situated in most of the world's important business centers. The firm has experts in virtually every area of the law, particularly those which relate to commercial transactions and disputes, and has more effective geographical coverage in the United States than any other major firm. The firm's lawyers and staff are dedicated to providing quality service on a timely and cost effective basis.

Our London office is positioned to serve our U.S. clients throughout the growing European market and to serve our European clients throughout the U.S. Indeed, our London office is now among the largest offices of all U.S.-based law firms in the United Kingdom. This office provides both U.S. and non-U.S. clients with a full range of legal services in connection with a variety of corporate operations and transactions, including transnational mergers, acquisitions, and joint ventures, international financings, restructurings and bankruptcies, and international commercial transactions—from licensing and distribution to trade dispute matters. In addition to providing significant corporate and tax planning advice required for such transactions, this office also has a well-developed practice advising individuals and families on complex income and estate planning and corporate and investment matters. This office also has substantial expertise in advising clients on the developing law of the European Economic Community and the new free market systems emerging in Central and Eastern Europe.

PARTNERS

ANTHONY BONANNO, born December 13, 1946; admitted, 1975, District of Columbia (Not admitted in England). *Education:* Dickinson College (B.A., 1968); George Washington University (J.D., 1974); Georgetown University (LL.M., 1977). IRS James E. Markham, Jr., Memorial Award, 1978. Adjunct Professor of Tax Law, Georgetown Law School, 1980, 1981, 1982; Notre Dame Law School, London, 1984. Member, Chief Counsel's Office, Internal Revenue Service, 1974-1978. *PRACTICE AREAS:* International Tax Law.

MITRI J. NAJJAR, born August 7, 1956; admitted, 1981, District of Columbia; 1991, New York (Not admitted in England). *Education:* University of Michigan (B.A., with highest honors and high distinction, 1978; J.D., cum laude, 1981). Phi Beta Kappa. *LANGUAGES:* Arabic and French. *PRACTICE AREAS:* International; Corporate.

PAUL R. HARTER, born October 11, 1957; admitted, 1984, New York and California (Not admitted in England). *Education:* Yale University (B.A., summa cum laude, 1979); Harvard University (J.D., cum laude, 1983). Phi Beta Kappa. *LANGUAGES:* French, Russian. *PRACTICE AREAS:* International; Securities; Banking; General Corporate.

WENDY M. SINGER, born February 5, 1950; admitted, 1975, New York; 1981, Avocat, Paris; 1994, England and Wales (Not Practicing as a Solicitor). *Education:* Harvard University (A.B., magna cum laude 1970; J.D., cum laude, 1974). Phi Beta Kappa. (London, England and Paris, France Offices). *LANGUAGES:* English, French. *PRACTICE AREAS:* Taxation; International Law.

ASSOCIATES

GREGORY L. SURMAN, born October 15, 1962; admitted, 1987, California (Not admitted in England). *Education:* University of California, Los Angeles (B.A., 1984); Boalt Hall School of Law, University of California, Berkeley (J.D., 1987). Managing Editor, Industrial Relations Law Journal, 1986-1987. *PRACTICE AREAS:* Corporations; International.

(This Listing Continued)

HENRY A. THOMPSON, born November 16, 1951; admitted, 1989, Pennsylvania; 1992, District of Columbia (Not admitted in England). *Education:* Georgetown University (B.S., 1974); Georgetown University Law Center (J.D., cum laude, 1989).

DARA L. FREEDMAN, born October 17, 1966; admitted, 1992, California; 1993, District of Columbia (Not admitted in England). *Education:* Rice University (B.A., 1988); Emory University (J.D., 1991). Order of the Coif. Articles Editor, Emory Law Journal, 1991. Law Clerk to Senior Judge Kenneth R. Harkins, U.S. Claims Court, 1991-1992. *LANGUAGES:* Spanish. *PRACTICE AREAS:* Taxation.

ARTHUR M. ROGERS, III, born May 27, 1967; admitted, 1993, Virginia (Not admitted in England). *Education:* Hamilton College (B.A., 1989); Emory School of Law (J.D., with distinction, 1992). Notes and Comments Editor, Emory Law Journal.

(For information on firm personnel, address and telephone information regarding the firm's offices located in Century City, Irvine, San Diego, Menlo Park and San Francisco, California; Denver, Colorado; Washington, D.C.; New York, N.Y.; Dallas, Texas; Seattle, Washington; Paris, France; Hong Kong; Tokyo, Japan and Jeddah and Riyadh, Saudi Arabia (Affiliated Offices), see professional biographies at Los Angeles, California)

GILES & ASSOCIATES

BLAKE LODGE
BRIDGE LANE
LONDON SW11 3AD, ENGLAND
Telephone: (44 171) 223 2765
Facsimile: (44 171) 350 0156

General International Commercial Law, Mergers and Acquisitions, Joint Ventures, European Community Law, Computer Software Distribution and Licensing, Intellectual Property, Project Finance, Sports and Leisure and International Bankruptcy and Reorganizations.

FIRM PROFILE: The firm was established in 1991 and offers a range of services relating to international commercial transactions. The client base is European and North American in scope. The firm is comprised of two American attorneys, an English solicitor and company secretary.

Mr. A.P. Giles is Counsel to four regional American law firms: MERSHON, SAWYER, JOHNSTON, DUNWODY & COLE, Miami, Naples, West Palm Beach and Key West Florida; NOSSAMAN, GUTHNER, KNOX & ELLIOTT, San Francisco, Los Angeles, Irvine, Sacramento, California and Washington, D.C.; WILLIAMS, MULLEN, CHRISTIAN & DOBBINS, Richmond, Virginia and Washington, D.C.; WISE & MARSAC, Detroit, Ann Arbor, Birmingham, Michigan.

A. PATRICK GILES, born Minneapolis, Minnesota, March 18, 1940; admitted, 1969, Michigan. *Education:* Dartmouth College (A.B., 1962); Amos Tuck School of Business (M.B.A., 1963) ; University of Michigan Law School (J.D., 1968); International Law Seminar, International Court of Justice (Diploma, 1969). *Member:* International Bar Association; American Bar Association; State Bar of Michigan; Law Society of England and Wales (Honorary Member). (Also Of Counsel, Mershon Sawyer Johnston Dunwody & Cole, Miami, Florida and London, England). *LANGUAGES:* English. *PRACTICE AREAS:* Mergers and Acquisitions; International Bankruptcy and Reorganizations; Project Finance; Sports and Leisure.

MICKELA MOORE, born Chicago, Illinois, June 1, 1959; admitted, 1987, New York (Not admitted in England). *Education:* Bradley University (B.A., 1981); University of Madrid (Certificate, 1980); Georgetown University Law Center (J.D., 1985). *Member:* International Bar Association; American Bar Association; New York State Bar Association; Association International des Jeunes Advocates (Executive Committee). *LANGUAGES:* English, French and Spanish. *PRACTICE AREAS:* European Community Law; International Commercial Agreements; Intellectual Property.

ELINOR MILLARD, born Bangor, Wales, December 30, 1947; admitted, 1970, Solicitor, England and Wales. *Education:* College of Law (1968). *Member:* Law Society of England and Wales. *LANGUAGES:* English and Welsh. *PRACTICE AREAS:* Wills and Trusts; Property; Intellectual Property.

GILL JENNINGS & EVERY

Patent Attorneys and Trademark Agents

Established in 1912

BROADGATE HOUSE
7 ELDON STREET
LONDON EC2M 7LH, ENGLAND
Telephone: (0171) 377 1377
Cables: Gillpateco London
Telex: 22765 GILPAT G
Fax: (0171) 377 1310

Cambridge, England Office: 122 Cambridge Science Park, Milton Road, Cambridge CB4 4FZ. Telephone: (01223) 423617.

Munich, Germany Office: Isartorplatz 5, D-80331 Munchen 2. Telephone: (089) 22 43 53.

Intellectual property litigation including advocacy and representation in the Patents County Court. Identifying, protecting and evaluating patent, design and trademark rights throughout the world and especially in the European Patent Office on all technologies including computer software, electronics, optics, engineering, automation, polymers, chemistry, pharmaceuticals, cosmetics, biotechnology and genetic engineering. Advocacy and representation in the Boards of Appeal and Opposition Divisions of the European Patent Office.

PARTNERS

Peter Jackson, MA, CPA, EPA	Robin Lawrence, BSc, CPA, EPA
Stephen Rackham, BSc, CPA, EPA	Michael Brunner, BSc, CPA, EPA
Robert Perry, MA, CPA, EPA	
Alan Blum, BSc, CPA, EPA, MITMA	Robert Skone James, MA, CPA, EPA

Helen Jones, MA, CPA, EPA

ASSOCIATES

Alan Laird, MA, PhD, CPA, EPA	David Wells, BSc, CPA, EPA
Philip Harris, LL.B., MITMA	Wendy Peet, BSc, CPA, EPA
Rowena Bercow, BA, MITMA	Janice Payne, BEng, CPA, EPA
Adam Flint, MA, CPA, EPA	Charlotte Curwen, MA, CPA, EPA
Martyn Draper, BEng, CPA	Peter Finnie, BSc
Stephen Haley, BEng	Nicola Hope, BSc, MITMA
Steven Howe, BSc	Bill Illingworth-Law, BSc, MSc
Jim Ribeiro, BSc	Lucy Samuels, BA
Michael Gordon, BSc, CPA, EPA	Richard Carter, BSc
	Alasdair MacQuarrie, LL.B.

LAW OFFICES OF
RICHARD S. GOLDSTEIN

50 STRATTON STREET, SUITE 432
LONDON W1X 5FL, ENGLAND
Telephone: 0171-491-6675
Fax: 0171-629-7900

New York, N.Y. Office: 145 West 57th Street. Telephone: 121-956-0502.

San Francisco, California Office: Law Offices of Goldstein and Fanning, Bank of America, Suite 2950, 555 California Street. 94104-1605. Telephone: 415-981-7000. Facsimile: 415-981-8579.

Practice limited to U.S. Immigration, Nationality Law and Consular Law.

RICHARD S. GOLDSTEIN, born Brooklyn, New York, January 2, 1945; admitted, 1974, New York, U.S. District Court, Southern and Eastern Districts of New York and U.S. Court of Appeals, Second Circuit; 1978, U.S. Supreme Court. *Education:* Brooklyn College (B.A., 1966); Brooklyn Law School (LL.B., 1973). Editor-in-Chief, The Transnational Immigration Law Reporter, 1981-1983. Invited to Lecture in Japan on U.S. Business Visas and U.S. Immigration Law as Guest of Government of Japan, October 1980, 1981, 1982, 1985, 1986, 1987, 1990 and April 1992 and as Guest of Keidanren (Federation of Economic Organizations) in Japan, November 1984, June 1988, March 1989, February 1990, April 1991, April 1992 and April 1993. Member, Advisory Board for Immigration and Nationality Law, The International Common Law Exchange Society and its Journal, The Common Law Lawyer, 1981—. Chairman, Immigration Law Seminars, World Trade Institute, New York, Miami, Houston, San Francisco and Chicago, 1981-1984. *Member:* Brooklyn (Chairman, Committee

(This Listing Continued)

on Immigration, 1981-1983; Federal (Chairman: Committee on Immigration and Naturalization, 1981-1989, and Invited Lecturer at Annual Conferences, 1981-1990; Immigration Seminars, Washington, June 1980, Boston, March 1981, New York, December, 1984 and Washington, March 1982, 1983, 1985, 1986, 1987 and 1988) and International (Chairman, Comparative Immigration Law Seminar, London, England, 1979, Washington, D.C., 1982, and Rome Italy, May, 1983; Immigration Law Conference Chairman for Confederation of British Industries (CBI) in London in 1988, 1989 and 1990; Immigration Law Conference Chairman for American Chamber of Commerce in England in 1990, 1991 and November, 1993 and British American Chamber of Commerce in June 1992; Guest Lecturer at Department of Trade and Industry Conference in June 1990 in London and Manchester; American Immigration Lawyers Association (President, New York Chapter, 1981-1982; Member, Board of Governors, 1982-1985); Consular Law Society (Assistant Secretary, 1981-1985); American Foreign Law Association; Inter-Pacific Bar Association (Chairman, Immigration and Nationality Law Committee, 1991—; Chairman, Comparative Immigration Law Seminars: Sydney 1992, Taipei 1993 and Singapore 1994).

(For complete biographical data on all personnel, see Professional Biographies at New York, N.Y.)

A & L GOODBODY

PINNACLE HOUSE
23-26 ST. DUNSTAN'S HILL
LONDON EC3R 8HL, ENGLAND
Telephone: 0171-929-2425
Fax: 0171-489-9677

Dublin, Ireland Office: 1 Earlsfort Centre, Hatch Street, 2. Telephone: (01) 6613311. Telex: 30569 and 93296. Fax: (01) 6613278.

New York, New York Office: 1 Rockefeller Plaza, Suite 1421, 10020. Telephone: 212-582-4499. Fax: 212-333-5126.

Brussels, Belgium Office: Rue des Deux Eglises 7, Boite 8, 1040. Telephone: 02-230-7512. Fax: 02-230-6422.

General Corporate and Business practice, Mergers and Acquisitions, Securities, Banking, Aircraft and Shipping Finance, Financial Services, Fund Management, Intellectual Property, European Union Law, Competition Law, Pensions, Litigation, Arbitration, Labour Law, Taxation, Property, Development and Building Contracts, Environmental Law, Private Client Services.

FIRM PROFILE: Founded more than one hundred years ago A & L Goodbody is one of the largest and most progressive Firms in Ireland. The Firm has experience and expertise in both international and domestic legal practice in company and commercial law, litigation, property, taxation and private client matters. The Firm has branch offices in London, Brussels and New York. These offices advise on Irish and EU legal issues.

RESIDENT MEMBER OF FIRM

JAMES G. GRENNAN, born Limerick, Ireland, November 14, 1962; admitted, 1988, Ireland.

RESIDENT ASSOCIATE

TIM SCANLON, born Dublin, Ireland, October 26, 1965; admitted, 1991, Ireland. (Not admitted in England).

Languages: English, French, German and Spanish.

(For Complete Biographical Data on all Firm Personnel, see Professional Biographies at Dublin, Ireland).

GOTTESMAN JONES & PARTNERS

Established in 1970

ALDWYCH HOUSE, ALDWYCH
LONDON WC2B 4HN, ENGLAND
Telephone: 0171-242 8953
Telefax: 0171-405 3190; 0171-405 0527

General and International Law Practice. Corporate, Financial, Securities and Tax Law.
Firm engaged in United States and International Law Practice, but not authorized to appear before the English Courts or to act as Solicitors.

A. EDWARD GOTTESMAN, born Hillside, New Jersey, July 29, 1937; admitted, 1959, New York (Not admitted in England). *Education:* The College of the University of Chicago (A.B., 1954); Yale Law School (LL.B., 1957). Fellow, The Association of the Bar of the City of New York, 1957-

(This Listing Continued)

GOTTESMAN JONES & PARTNERS, *London—*
Continued

1959. President, American Chamber of Commerce (United Kingdom), 1979-1981. *Member:* The Association of the Bar of the City of New York (Secretary, Special Committee to Study Commitment Procedures, 1960-1965); American Bar Association (Member, International Business Law Committee); American Society of International Law; American Foreign Law Association (Secretary, 1959-1963). Chairman, Derby International Corporation, Exeter International Corporation. *LANGUAGES:* French. *PRACTICE AREAS:* International Business; International Finance.

GRANT L. JONES, born Chicago, Illinois, August 22, 1942; admitted, 1967, Florida; 1977, District of Columbia (Not admitted in England). *Education:* University of Florida (B.S.B.A., cum laude, 1964; J.D., 1967). Board Member, University of Florida Law Review, 1966. Author: "Reporting Exports and Imports of Monetary Instruments," U.S. Taxation of International Operations, Prentice-Hall, 1973; " Foreign Investors and U.S. Tax Laws," Venture Capital Journal, August, 1993. Research Aide, Florida Second District Court of Appeal, 1967-1968. Legal Officer, United Nations High Commissioner for Refugees, 1968-1969. Lecturer, University of Notre Dame Law School, London, 1976-1977. *Member:* The Florida Bar; District of Columbia Bar; American Bar Association (Member, Sections on: Taxation; and Corporations, Banking and Business Law); International Bar Association (Member, Business Law Section); International Fiscal Association. *PRACTICE AREAS:* International Business; International Business Taxation; International Joint Ventures; Limited Partnerships; Company Acquisitions and Sales; Company Formation; Offshore Companies; International Contracts; Corporate Finance; Corporate Taxation; International Corporate Finance; International Corporate Law; International Corporate Taxation; Offshore Corporations; International Finance; Cross Border Investment; Foreign Investment; Offshore Investment; International Taxation; International Trusts.

JOSEPH A. CONSOLO, born Oak Park, Illinois, June 29, 1951; admitted, 1978, New York (Not admitted in England). *Education:* University of Notre Dame (A.B., magna cum laude, 1973); Columbia University (J.D., 1977). *Member:* New York State and American Bar Associations. *LANGUAGES:* Japanese. *PRACTICE AREAS:* Securities Offerings; Securities Regulations; Offshore Corporations; Cross Border Mergers and Acquisitions; International Joint Ventures.

LAURA L. COX, born October 18, 1964; admitted, 1990, Pennsylvania (Not admitted in England). *Education:* Ohio State University (B.A., 1987); University of Cincinnati (J.D., 1990). Phi Alpha Delta. Recipient, Helmer Prize. Lead Articles Editor, Cincinnati Law Review, 1990. Author: "Political Accountability and the Independent Counsel: A Sheep in Wolf's Clothing?, Morrison v. Olson, 108 S. Ct. 2567, 1988," 57 U. Cin. L. Rev. 1471, 1989; "Poison Pills: Recent Developments in Delaware Law," 58 U. Cin. L. Rev. 611, 1989. *Member:* Pennsylvania Bar Association; American Bar Association (Business Law Section). *PRACTICE AREAS:* Business and Corporate Law; Securities; Mergers; Acquisitions and Divestitures; Banking Regulations.

Languages: English, French and Japanese.

GOULDENS

22 TUDOR STREET
LONDON EC4Y 0JJ, ENGLAND
Telephone: 0171-583-7777
Cable Address: "Toplaw London EC4"
Telex: 21520 Toplaw G
Facsimile: 0171-583-3051

Brussels, Belgium Office: Guimard Centre, Rue Guimard 6-8, B-1040. Telephone: 32-2-230-3090. Facsimile: 32-2-230-3104.
St. Helier, Jersey, C.I. Office: P.O. Box 761, Ordnance House, 31 Pier Road, JE4 8ZZ. Telephone: 01534 66599. Facsimile: 01534 35195. Telex: 4192456 GDNJSY G.
Moscow, Russia Office: 20 Myasnitskaya St., 101851. Telephone: 7-095-921 7730. Fax: 7-095-921 3987.
Associated Offices in Paris and Hong Kong.

MEMBERS OF FIRM

C.H.C. SCOTT. PRACTICE AREAS: Property.

D. COOPER. PRACTICE AREAS: Planning.

(This Listing Continued)

D.P.H. BURGESS. LANGUAGES: French. **PRACTICE AREAS:** Corporate; Company Commercial.

C.J. MACDONALD-BROWN. PRACTICE AREAS: Litigation; Intellectual Property.

J.C.S. NIEBOER. PRACTICE AREAS: Corporate; Company Commercial.

J.J. DOYLE. LANGUAGES: French. **PRACTICE AREAS:** EC; Lobbying; International; Corporate.

P.W.R. WESTLEY. PRACTICE AREAS: Property.

CLAIRE M. EDELEANU. PRACTICE AREAS: Corporate; Company Commercial.

CLARE H. DEANESLY. PRACTICE AREAS: Property; Environment.

M.B. THORNEYCROFT. PRACTICE AREAS: Corporate; Company Commercial.

M.J. PIERS. PRACTICE AREAS: Insurance; Insolvency; Banking.

JENNET A. DAVIES. LANGUAGES: Italian. **PRACTICE AREAS:** Trusts; Private Client.

S.N. SEATON. PRACTICE AREAS: Corporate; Company Commercial.

C.D. BERRY. PRACTICE AREAS: Banking; Insolvency.

A.C. GREAVES. PRACTICE AREAS: Corporate; Company Commercial.

ANGELA TURNER. PRACTICE AREAS: Planning.

DIANA D. SPOUDEAS. LANGUAGES: Greek and French. **PRACTICE AREAS:** Corporate; Company Commercial.

R.T. CARMEDY. PRACTICE AREAS: Corporate; Banking.

T.M. BUDD. PRACTICE AREAS: Corporate; Banking.

FIONA E. RUSSELL. PRACTICE AREAS: Litigation; Intellectual Property.

KAY BALAAM. PRACTICE AREAS: Property.

J.D. CAMPBELL. PRACTICE AREAS: Corporate; Banking.

I.F. LUPSON. PRACTICE AREAS: Insurance; Litigation.

C.J. PARKINSON. PRACTICE AREAS: Corporate; Media.

LEILA PORTER. PRACTICE AREAS: Corporate; Company Commercial.

B.S. DONNELLY. PRACTICE AREAS: Litigation; Insolvency; Banking.

A.J. HENDERSON. PRACTICE AREAS: Litigation; Employment.

P.L. NIELD. PRACTICE AREAS: Corporate; Company Commercial.

H. WINTER. PRACTICE AREAS: Corporate; Company Commercial.

A.T. GUMPERT. PRACTICE AREAS: Commercial Property.

J.J. PAPADAKIS. PRACTICE AREAS: Corporate; Company Commercial.

J.R. PHILLIPS. PRACTICE AREAS: Corporate; Company Commercial.

Languages: Spanish, German, Japanese, Hebrew, Punjabi, Malay, Tamil, Italian, French, Cantonese, Russian, Romanian, Gaelic.

GRAHAM & JAMES

CARMELITE
50 VICTORIA EMBANKMENT
BLACKFRIARS
LONDON EC4Y 0DX, ENGLAND
Telephone: 0171-353-1840
Telecopier: 0171-353-1841

Other offices located in: San Francisco, Los Angeles, Newport Beach, Palo Alto, Sacramento and Fresno, California; Washington, D.C.; New York, New York; Milan, Italy; Beijing, China; Tokyo, Japan; Dusseldorf, Germany; Taipei, Taiwan.

(This Listing Continued)

Associated Offices: Deacons in Association with Graham & James, Hong Kong; Sly and Weigall, Sydney, Melbourne, Brisbane, Perth and Canberra, Australia.

Affiliated Offices: Graham & James in Affiliation with Taylor Joynson Garrett, London, England, Bucharest, Romania and Brussels, Belgium; Hanafiah Soeharto Ponggawa, Jakarta, Indonesia; Deacons and Graham & James, Bangkok, Thailand; Haarmann, Hemmelrath & Partner, Berlin, Munich, Leipzig, Frankfurt and Dusseldorf, Germany; Mishare M. Al-Ghazali & Partners, Kuwait; Sly & Weigall Deacons in Association with Graham & James, Hanoi, Vietnam and Guangzhou, China; Gallastegui y Lozano, S.C., Mexico City, Mexico; Law Firm of Salah Al-Hejailan, Jeddah and Riyadh, Saudi Arabia.

Firm engaged in American and International Law Practice but not authorized to appear before English Courts or to act as Solicitors.

RESIDENT PARTNER

DAVID M. FINDLAY, born Buckie, Scotland, 1957; admitted, 1982, California (Not admitted in England). *Education:* Epsom College (G.C.E.'s, 1974); London School of Economics (LL.B., with honors, 1979); Inns of Court School of Law (called to the Bar of England and Wales, 1980). Struben Prize Winner from The Honourable Society of the Inner Temple. Author: "Setoff Under International Loan Agreements: Danger Spots and Detours," 99 Banking Law Journal 447, May, 1982. (Also Consultant to Taylor Joynson Garrett). *PRACTICE AREAS:* Corporate Law; Financial Restructuring.

LAW OFFICE EDWARD S. GUDEON

Established in 1978

17 BULSTRODE STREET

LONDON W1M 5FQ, ENGLAND

Telephone: (0171) 486-0813

Fax: (0171) 224-2337

Practice limited to U.S. Immigration and Nationality Law. Not authorized to appear before the English Courts or to act as Solicitor.

EDWARD S. GUDEON, born New York, N.Y., February 23, 1940; admitted, 1965, New York (Not admitted in England). *Education:* Bucknell University (B.A., 1962); Fordham University (LL.B., 1965). *Member:* American Immigration Lawyers Association. *PRACTICE AREAS:* U.S. Immigration and Nationality law only; consular practice, visas and work permits and citizenship matters.

GULBENKIAN HARRIS ANDONIAN

181 KENSINGTON HIGH STREET

LONDON W8 6SH, ENGLAND

Telephone: 0171-937 1542

Fax: 0171-938 2059

A practice specializing virtually exclusively in UK Business Immigration Law. The sole UK Member of The European Immigration Lawyers Group. Multi-national and company work permits business and immigration visas.

PARTNERS

PAUL GULBENKIAN, admitted, 1965, England. Senior Partner. Part-time Immigration Adjudicator. Joint Editor, Immigration Law and Business In Europe, 1993. *PRACTICE AREAS:* Immigration.

LIONEL HARRIS. PRACTICE AREAS: Immigration.

BERNARD ANDONIAN. PRACTICE AREAS: Immigration.

PETER WYATT. PRACTICE AREAS: Immigration.

D. SCHAFFER

D. BUCKOKE

R. SMITH

H. RICHARDS

ASSOCIATE

D. BENAIM. PRACTICE AREAS: Immigration.

HAMMOND SUDDARDS

MOOR HOUSE

119 LONDON WALL

LONDON EC2Y 5ET, ENGLAND

Telephone: 0171 628 4767

Fax: 0171 628 6161

Leeds, England Office: 2 Park Lane. LS3 1ES. Telephone: 0113 234 3500. Fax: 0113 234 3600. Telex: 517201.

Brussels, Belgium Office: Avenue Louise 250, 1050. Telephone: 00 32 2 627 7676. Fax: 00 32 2 627 7686.

Manchester, England Office: Trinity Court, 16 John Dalton Street, M60 8HS. Telephone: 0161 834 2222. Fax: 0161 834 2244.

Bradford, England Offic: Pennine House, 39-45 Well Street. BDL 5NL. Telephone: 01274 734700. Fax: 01274 737547. Telex: 517201.

Corporate finance including Acquisitions and Mergers, Corporate Finance, Commercial including Acquisitions and Mergers, Corporate Tax, Commercial including Joint Ventures, Pensions, Banks and Building Societies, Intellectual Property, Commercial Litigation, Construction, Insolvency and Corporate Recovery, Debt Collection, Town and Country Planning, Environmental Law, Commercial Property, European Community Law, Information Technology Law, Employment, Utilities, Insurance Litigation, Media, Mortgage and Aviation.

Hammond Suddards has over 870 staff including 58 partners 100 Associates and 50 Legal Executives and Paralegals.

RESIDENT PARTNERS

CHRISTOPHER J. ARNHEIM. PRACTICE AREAS: Corporate Law.

LAURENCE COHEN. PRACTICE AREAS: Intellectual Property.

ROBIN COLE. PRACTICE AREAS: Commercial Property.

BRIAN EAGLES. PRACTICE AREAS: Media Law.

STEPHEN GALE. PRACTICE AREAS: Insolvency.

CHRISTOPHER F. HAAN. PRACTICE AREAS: International Tax.

DAVID JONES. PRACTICE AREAS: Construction Litigation.

RICHARD H. KEMP. PRACTICE AREAS: Information Technology.

ANDREW KNIGHT. PRACTICE AREAS: Banking.

JANE MARGARET MARSHALL. PRACTICE AREAS: Pensions.

ANDREW MALCOLM POWELL. PRACTICE AREAS: Pensions.

IAN SEARLE. PRACTICE AREAS: Insolvency.

PETER SILKE. PRACTICE AREAS: Pensions.

PETER SIMPSON. PRACTICE AREAS: Corporate Law.

GARY WATSON. PRACTICE AREAS: Commercial Property.

STEPHEN D. YORK. PRACTICE AREAS: Commercial Litigation.

(For lists of other Members, see Professional Biographies at Bradford, Manchester, Leeds and Brussels, Belgium)

HANCOCK, ROTHERT & BUNSHOFT

FORUM HOUSE

15/18 LIME STREET, SIXTH FLOOR

LONDON EC3M 7AP, ENGLAND

Telephone: 0171-220-7567

Telecopy: 0171-220-7609

San Francisco, California Office: 10th Floor Four Embarcadero Center, 94111-4168. Telephone: 415-981-5550. Telecopy: 415-955-2599.

Los Angeles, California Office: Suite 1230, 515 South Figueroa Street, 90071-3339. Telephone: 213-623-7777. Telecopy: 213-623-5405.

Tahoe City, California Office: Lighthouse Center, 850 North Lake Boulevard, Suite 15, P.O. Box 7199, 95730-7199. Telephone: 916-583-7767. Telecopy: 916-581-3215.

Associated Office: Staiger, Schwald & Sauter. Genferstrasse 24, 8002 Zurich, Switzerland. Telephone: 01-282-8686. Telecopy: 01-283-8787. Telex: 813-273-GND.

General Civil and Trial Practice in all State and Federal Courts. Corporation, Business, Insurance, Admiralty, Probate, Tax and International Law.

(This Listing Continued)

HANCOCK, ROTHERT & BUNSHOFT, London—
Continued

Firm engaged in American and International Law Practice, but not authorized to appear before the English Courts or to act as Solicitors.

(For complete biographical data, see professional biographies at San Francisco, California).

HARBOTTLE & LEWIS

Established in 1955

HANOVER HOUSE
14 HANOVER SQUARE
LONDON W1R 0BE, ENGLAND
Telephone: 0171-629 7633
Fax: 0171-493 0451
Dx: 44617

FIRM PROFILE: *"Established in 1955, a leading entertainment law firm with a broad practice incorporating: Company and Commercial matters including Takeovers, Mergers, Restructurings, Insolvency, Employment Law, Flotations, Joint Ventures, Banking and Finance; Aviation Law, Regulation, Finance and Leasing; Competition/Antitrust Law; European Community Law; Tax; Trust & Probate; Immigration; Charity Law; all matters relating to Entertainment, Media, Intellectual Property, Trademarks and Copyright including Advertising, Computer Games, Film, Television, Theatre, Opera, Book and Periodical Publishing, Music and Video; Recording, Publishing, Merchandising, Management and Distribution Agreements; Commercial Litigation; Residential and Commercial Property Development, Investment, Acquisitions, Disposals and Town and Country Planning and Sports Law."*

SENIOR PARTNER

MICHAEL H.D. BOWLER, born 1939; admitted, 1965, England. *PRACTICE AREAS:* Commercial Litigation; Intellectual Property Law; Defamation; Tort Law; Entertainment Law.

MANAGING PARTNER

COLIN M. HOWES, born 1956; admitted, 1981, England. *Education:* M.A. (Oxford). *LANGUAGES:* French. *PRACTICE AREAS:* Aviation Law; Commercial Law; Corporate Law; European Community Law; Contract Law.

PARTNERS

ALAN J. PATTEN, born 1943; admitted, 1969, England. *Education:* LL.B. (Manchester). *LANGUAGES:* French and German. *PRACTICE AREAS:* Property Law; Commercial Property Law; Property Development and Syndication Law; Landlord and Tenant Law; Property Finance.

ROBERT A. STORER, born 1947; admitted, 1971, England. *Education:* LL.B. (London). *PRACTICE AREAS:* Entertainment Industry Transactions; Media Law; Motion Picture Finance; Television Law; Motion Picture Contracts.

GERRARD TYRRELL, born 1957; admitted, 1981, England. *Education:* LL.B. (Bristol). *PRACTICE AREAS:* Commercial Litigation; Intellectual Property Law; Defamation; Entertainment Law; Publishing Law.

ANDREW R. STINSON, born 1957; admitted, 1981, England. *Education:* LL.B. (Wales). *PRACTICE AREAS:* Music Recording Law; Music Publishing Law; Entertainment Industry Transactions; Copyright Law; Advertising Law.

JUSTIN C.M. DUNLOP, born 1956; admitted, 1981, England. *Education:* M.A. (Cambridge). *PRACTICE AREAS:* Property Law; Commercial Property Law; Landlord and Tenant Law; Conveyancing; Property Development and Syndication Law.

MARIAN A. DERHAM, born 1960; admitted, 1984, England. *Education:* LL.B. (London). *PRACTICE AREAS:* Commercial Law; Contract Law; Corporate Law; Mergers and Acquisitions; Entertainment Industry Transactions; Communications and Media.

ROBERT K. REILLY, born 1958; admitted, 1985, England. *Education:* LL.B. (Bristol). *PRACTICE AREAS:* Conveyancing; Commercial Property Law; Property Law; Planning; Residential Property Law.

MARK D. PHILLIPS, born 1961; admitted, 1986, England. *Education:* LL.B. (London). *LANGUAGES:* French. *PRACTICE AREAS:* Commer-

(This Listing Continued)

cial Law; Computer Software Law; Copyright Law; Corporate Law; Agency and Distribution Law.

ANN HARRISON, born 1958; admitted, 1983, England. *Education:* B.Sc. (Surrey). *Member:* Society of Women Solicitors. *LANGUAGES:* German and French. *PRACTICE AREAS:* Entertainment Industry Transactions; Copyright Law; Music Recording Law; Music Publishing Law; Video Law.

FRANCES BUTLER-SLOSS, born 1959; admitted, 1982, England and Wales; 1989, New York. *Education:* LL.B. (Bristol); Inns of Court School of Law (1982). *PRACTICE AREAS:* Aircraft Leasing; Route Licensing; Airline Competition; Commercial Aviation Law; Charities; Commercial Law.

MEDWYN JONES, born 1955; admitted, 1980, England and Wales. *Education:* LL.B. (Sheffield); Chester Law School (Solicitors Exams, 1978). *Member:* Law Society. *PRACTICE AREAS:* Television Production and Distribution; Television Finance; Entertainment Law.

CONSULTANTS

G. LAURENCE HARBOTTLE, born 1924; admitted, 1952, England. *Education:* M.A. (Cambridge). *PRACTICE AREAS:* Theater Law; Charitable Trusts and Foundations; Publishing Law; Wills; Administration of Estates.

JOHN B. STUTTER, born 1930; admitted, 1956, England. *Education:* M.A., LL.M. (Cambridge). *PRACTICE AREAS:* Commercial Law; Contract Law; Insolvency Law; Corporate Tax; Mergers and Acquisitions; Employment Law.

CHARLES J. LEVISON, born 1941; admitted, 1967, England. *Education:* LL.M. (Cambridge). *Member:* Law Society. *LANGUAGES:* English and French. *PRACTICE AREAS:* Entertainment Law; Broadcasting Law; Telecommunications Law; Copyright Law; Commercial Law.

HARTWIG PC

Solicitors / Rechtsanwälte

15 WILLIAM MEWS, KNIGHTSBRIDGE
LONDON SWIX 9HF, ENGLAND
Telephone: (US) 011 44 171-235 1504
(UK) 0181 681 2893
Fax: (US) 1 800 654 1023
(UK) 0181 681 8183

New York, N.Y. Office: Suite 7912, 350 Fifth Avenue. 10118.
Other Offices located in Croydon, Hamburg, Frankfurt, Düsseldorf and Saarbrücken.

English / US / German / EC Corporate and Commercial, Intellectual Property, Insurance, Customs Law, Real Property, Probate, Litigation, Arbitration, Private Client. Licensed Insolvency Practitioners. Tax Practitioners. European Notaries, Bilingual Documentation.

HANS J. HARTWIG, LL.B., ATII; Solicitor, England and Wales, 1960; New York, 1976 (§ 53 Judiciary Law), Germany, 1978. Secretary, Society of English and American Lawyers. Cornell Law Association. Past Chairman, Legal Committee, British Chambers of Commerce.

Nicola von Tersch, LL.B., *Solicitor*	**Janet Aspden, LL.B.,** *Solicitor*
Horst Johlke, Rechtsanwalt	**Manfred Kuhn, LL.M.,** *Rechtsanwalt and Solicitor*

HASELTINE LAKE & CO.

(Chartered Patent Agents, European Patent Attorneys and Trademark
Agents. Not Solicitors)

Established in 1860

HAZLITT HOUSE
28 SOUTHAMPTON BUILDINGS
CHANCERY LANE

LONDON WC2A 1AT, ENGLAND
Telephone: +44 (0) 171 405 6093
Cables: SCOPO LONDON WC2
Telex: 21995 SCOPO
Fax: +44 (0) 171 405 0965

Bristol (England) Office: Temple Gate House, Temple Gate, BS1 6PT.
Telephone: +44 (0) 117 926 0197. Cables: SCOPO BRISTOL. Telex:
449559 LAKES. Fax: +44 (0) 929 0387.

Leeds (England) Office: Park House, Park Square, LS1 2PS. Telephone:
+44 (0) 113 244 616. Cables: SCOPO LEEDS. Telex: 557723
HASEL. Fax: +44 (0) 113 244 4511.

Associated Practice in Munich, Germany:

*Haseltine Lake Partners, Motorama Haus 502, Rosenheimer Strasse 30,
D-81669 München. Telephone:* (089) 448 89 89. *Cables:* SCOPO
MUENCHEN. *Telex:* 522936 HASMU. *Fax:* (089) 48 56 86.

Associated British Practice specializing in Trademarks and Service Marks:

*Haseltine Lake Trademarks, Hazlitt House, 28 Southampton Buildings,
Chancery Lane, London WCA 1AT, England. Telephone:* +44 (0) 171
242 4176. *Cables:* SCOPO LONDON WC2. *Telex:* 21995 SCOPO.
Fax: +44 (0) 171 405 0965 *also available at Bristol and Leeds offices
listed above.*

Patents, Trademarks, Service Marks, Registered Designs, Advice on Unregistered Design Rights, Copyright and Licensing.

*Registered as British Chartered Patent Agents and European Patent Attorneys, and Admitted to Practice under the Patent Cooperation Treaty and
before the British Patent Office, the British Patent Court, the British Patents County Court and the European Patent Office.*

PARTNERS

(HASELTINE LAKE & CO., HASELTINE LAKE TRADEMARKS)

Michael A. Bull	**Warren Silverman**
Christopher R. K. Fanc	**Michael J. Abrams**
(Partnership Chairman)	**John R.A.M. Cheyne**
John K. Godsill	(Managing Partner)
Richard D. Overbury	**James H. Sunderland**
Ian R. Muir	(Resident, Munich)
Michael R. Jones	**David A. Nash**
Guy S. Bedggood	**Timothy C. Stebbing**
	(Resident, Munich)

ADDITIONAL PARTNERS OF HASELTINE LAKE & CO.

Christine L. Fenlon	**David C. O'Connell**
Christopher C. Gibbs	

ADDITIONAL PARTNERS OF HASELTINE LAKE TRADEMARKS:

Christopher J. Leadbeater	**Jane More O'Ferrall**

ASSOCIATES

HASELTINE LAKE & CO.

Lawrence E. Billington	**Mary E. Yeadon**
Bentley G. Bond	

HASELTINE LAKE TRADEMARKS

M.H. Krause

WILLIAM HEATH & CO.

Established in 1969

16 SALE PLACE
LONDON W2 1PX, ENGLAND
Telephone: 0171-402 3151
Facsimile: 0171 402 0373

Skelly & Company, 87 E Northcote Road, SW11 6PL. Telephone: 071-350
1068. Fax: 071-228 5178.

*Law for the individual and smaller corporations. Immigration, House Purchase, Landlord and Tenant, Wills, Family, Litigation. Since our first
entry, we have helped many individuals from overseas.*

WILLIAM HEATH, born, 1939. admitted, 1963, England. Member of
Council, Law Society of England and Wales.

EDWIN R. LEE, Born, 1949. admitted, 1973, England.

DAVID M. FLEMING, born, 1958. admitted, 1982, England.

BAKUL C. JOSHI, born, 1960. admitted, 1984, England.

HARBINDER SANGHA, born, 1962. admitted, 1989, England.

SEAN PATRICK SKELLY, born 1938; admitted, 1961, England.

ASSOCIATE

DAWN DIXON, born, 1966. admitted, 1990, England.

This Firm is regulated by The Law Society in the conduct of investment
business.

HEDLEYS

Solicitors

15 ST HELEN'S PLACE
BISHOPSGATE
LONDON EC3A 6DJ, ENGLAND
Telephone: (0171) 638 1001
Fax: (0171) 588 7547
DX: 598 CITY

Surrey, England Office: 6 Bishopsmead Parade, East Horsley, KT24
6SR. Telephone: 0483 284567. Fax: 0483 284817. DX: 46106
COBHAM.

Commercial, Property, Trust and Estate, Litigation, Leisure.

FIRM PROFILE: *The firm specializes in cross-frontier matters, providing
a service to clients who reside in one country and who own assets or have
legal opportunities or problems in another country. The approach is to seek
fast, practical and cost-effective solutions to clients' problems. Founder
Member of the EU-LEX International Practice Group.*

PARTNERS

COLIN CHARLES JENKINS, LL.B. (LONDON), admitted, 1955,
England. **LANGUAGES:** English, French, Portuguese and Spanish (reading). **PRACTICE AREAS:** Business Law; Charitable Organizations; Commercial Law; Company Law; Real Estate; Resorts and Leisure; Timeshare;
Taxation; Trusts and Estates; Cross Frontier Law.

ROGER SEWELL TAYLOR, admitted, 1970, England. **LANGUAGES:** English. **PRACTICE AREAS:** Business Affairs; Commercial
Property; Wills and Succession.

DAVID GLYNNE HENSHALL, LL.B. (SOUTHAMPTON), admitted, 1983, England. **LANGUAGES:** English, German and French (reading). **PRACTICE AREAS:** Agency and Distributorships; Business Law;
Commercial Law; Debtor and Creditor; Litigation.

JUDITH AMANDA JANE GLEESON, M.A. (OXFORD), admitted,
1981, England. **LANGUAGES:** English and French. **PRACTICE AREAS:**
Litigation; Employment; Business Affairs; Immigration and Nationality.

SOLICITORS

CLAIRE CORINNE JACKSON, LL.B. (BRISTOL), admitted, 1976,
England. **LANGUAGES:** English and French. **PRACTICE AREAS:** Succession; Wills; Tax; Trusts and Estates.

RICA JEPSEN, LL.B. (LONDON), admitted, 1986, England. **LANGUAGES:** English, French, Spanish and Cantonese. **PRACTICE AREAS:**
Conveyancing; Landlord and Tenant; Company and Commercial.

(This Listing Continued)

HEDLEYS, London—Continued

PAUL VINCENT BURKE, LL.B. (SHEFFIELD), admitted, 1990, England. *LANGUAGES:* English and French. *PRACTICE AREAS:* Litigation; Business Law.

SAMANTHA STEER, LL.B. (READING), admitted, 1990, England. *LANGUAGES:* English and French. *PRACTICE AREAS:* Litigation; Family; Landlord and Tenant.

BARBARA M. TAYLOR, LL.B. (LONDON); admitted, 1988, England. *LANGUAGES:* English, Polish, Russian and Italian. *PRACTICE AREAS:* Business Affairs; Employment; Commercial Law.

CONSULTANTS

DR. FRANK GERRARD HOLLAND, LL.M. (London), Dr. Jur. (Heidelberg), Dip. de Sciences Politiques (Paris), Rechtsanwalt (Berlin), P.P. Arb; admitted, 1946, England. *LANGUAGES:* English, German, French and Spanish.

HERBERT SMITH

Established in 1882

EXCHANGE HOUSE
PRIMROSE STREET
LONDON EC2A 2HS, ENGLAND

Telephone: 0171-374-8000
Telex: 886633
Fax: 0171-496-0043

Paris, France Office: 41 Avenue George V., 75008. Telephone: 3314-723-9124. Telex: 219602. Fax: 3314-720-9213.

Hong Kong Office: 17th Floor, Edinburgh Tower, 15 Queen's Road Central. Telephone: 852-8456639. Telex: 72266. Fax: 852-8459099.

Brussels, Belgium Office: 15, Rue Guimard, 1040. Telephone: 322-511 7450. Fax: 322-511 7772.

A City-based firm since its foundation in 1882, Herbert Smith is one of the country's largest and best known firms of solicitors with a substantial international practice in commercial and corporate law. It has offices in Brussels, Hong Kong and Paris and is about to open an office in Shanghai, People's Republic of China.

Operating from modern purpose-designed offices in London, Herbert Smith has developed highly efficient working systems and know-how databases to support its traditional emphasis on the quality of its service and relationships with its clients.

Principal Areas of Work:

Company Department: (Contact: Richard Bond). The Department handles corporate finance; Stock Exchange matters; takeovers, mergers and divestments; company law and practice; project and asset finance; banking and international finance; securities and financial services regulation; venture capital and management buyouts; taxation; insolvency; EC and competition law; investment and pension funds; employment; employee benefits; immigration; commercial trusts; energy; utilities.

Litigation Department: (Contact: Charles Plant). Herbert Smith is widely acknowledged for its range of experience in commercial litigation. The department has specialist teams covering commercial disputes; insurance and reinsurance; banking and finance; EC and competition law; construction; corporate fraud; intellectual property; computer law and information technology; international arbitration; defamation; shipping; professional negligence; employment; insolvency and commercial property.

Property Department: (Contact: Garry Hart). The firm deals with all aspects of legal work involving commercial land and buildings in England and Wales. Main areas of activity include institutional and other property investments; development projects; leases; funding and other refinancings; rent reviews; environmental law; town planning; compensation and investigating and reporting property portfolios.

Nature of Clientele: The firm's clients include banks and other financial institutions, sovereign states and government agencies and public and private companies.

Foreign Connections: The firm has offices in Brussels, Hong Kong and Paris, which are an integral part of the firm. The offices are staffed both by solicitors from the London office and by lawyers familiar with the local language and business customs.

The firm's Hong Kong and Paris offices offer the same range of expertise as that described above. The principal contacts in these offices are: Company - Tim Bellis (Hong Kong); Neil Brimson (Paris); Litigation - Tim Parkes (Hong Kong); Alastair Morley (Paris); Property - Nigel Bacon

(This Listing Continued)

(Hong Kong); Ian Gosling (Paris). The firm's Brussels office concentrates on EC and competition law (Contact: Craig Pouncey). The firm's China practice will be headed by Jack Young (Hong Kong and Shanghai).

PARTNERS

E.I. Walker-Arnott	P.T. Bellis
C.P. Tootal	I.T. Gault
D.P. Natali	C.E. Chamberlain
G.R.R. Hart	I.A. Rothnie
L.A. Collins	J.W. Scott
R.J. Wellings	M.L. Allen
D.M. Bolton	D.M.J. Brock
T.B.H. Phillips	J.C. Barnes
C.W. Plant	Rosamund Sparrow
R.D. Bond	M. Newbery
C.H. Harrison	P.M. Carrington
A.D. Preece	Lucy Hutchinson
H.R.A. Anderson	T.H. Birch Reynardson
D.E.A. Higgins	D.C. Reston
A.J.T. Willoughby	E.P. Greeno
S.J. Barton	D.A. Willis
B.M.A. Curwen	C.D. Barnard
M.R. Munden	J.M. Wilson
G.D. Bland	A.J. Calderwood
Dorothy K. Livingston	Heather Gething
R.J.H. Fleck	Sonya Leydecker
G.F. Kinmonth	G.R. More
R.D.A. Fraser	Roxane Eban
C.D. Tavener	Brenda Coleman
J.R. Farr	D.N. Francis
J.R. Wood	D.C.G. Foster
S.G. Barnard	Shelagh McKibbin
A.D. Macaulay	P.W. Long
D.L. Gold	G.J. Roberts
Margaret Mountford	S. Kinsella
C.G.C.H. Baker	C.A. McLachlan
R.M. Neill	J. O'Shea
Marian P. Pell	N.P. Tott
N.J. Brimson	Patricia Shih
J.N. Robinson	M.D. Johnson
W.J. Moodie	C.J.H. Parsons
R.A. Jowett	J.S. Ogilvie
M.E. Davis	J.C. Young
A.R. Morley	P.J. Frost
N.K. Bacon	T.M. Mehigan
D. Martin	Helene Kydd
E.P.G. Robinson	A.I. Alder
S.C. Hancock	A. Tortoishell
I.F.B. Gosling	T.J. Steadman
P.M.C. Trosset	Irene Dallas
D.M.B. Clarke	N. Warriner
T.W. Turtle	N.J. Farr
M.I. Kingston	J.S. Reynolds
T.C. Parkes	J.J. Fox
M.J. Bakes	Elizabeth McKnight
Caroline Goodall	N.J. Gardner
J.D. Sissons	A.D.R. Dempster
J.R.N. Leyland	J.E. Palmer
D.S. Paterson	

CONSULTANTS

H.W. Higginson,	N.R.A. Baker
C.B.E., M.C., M.A., LL.B.	

HILL TAYLOR DICKINSON

IRONGATE HOUSE
22-30 DUKE'S PLACE
LONDON EC3A 7LP, ENGLAND
Telephone: 0171 283-9033; 071 895-0888
Telex: 888470 HILTAD G
Fax: 0171 283-1144

Hong Kong Associated Office: Hampton, Winter and Glynn. 38th Floor, Asia Pacific Finance Tower, Citibank Plaza, 3, Garden Road Central.
Piraeus, Greece Office: K. Paleologou 5, 18535 Piraeus. Telephone: (30) 1 4220330. Fax: (30) 1 4225458.

Shipping, Air and General Transport, Insurance and Reinsurance, Commercial Litigation, Property, Building and Construction Law and Planning, Pensions, Company and Commercial, Leasing, Franchising, Industrial Relations and Defendant Employment and Injury, Insolvency.

MEMBERS OF FIRM

Peter Albertini	Michael McCarthy
Nigel John Binnersley	Nicholas Moore
Rhys Clift	Paul Oughton
Stephen Cropper	Maria Pittordis
Chris Darke	John Pople
Malcolm Entwistle	Tim Railton
John Evans	Adam Ridley
Jeff Isaacs	Kevin Sach
Andrew Johnson	Malcolm Taylor
Sunil Kakkad	Richard Taylor
Nicholas Mallard	Tim Taylor
Michael Mallin	Robert Wallis

ASSOCIATES

Michael Cox	Peter MacDonald-Eggers
Patrick Foss	Trevor Marshall
Antony Griffiths	Ralph Nathan
Ian Hempseed	Hilary Vernon
Andrew Waldron	

ASSISTANT SOLICITORS

Graeme Baird	Richard Jowett
Mark Bethell	Danielle Kingdon
Alan Burcombe	Benjamin Larkin
A.John Caddies	Eleanor Maxwell
Andrew Colyer	Edward Newitt
Rula Dajani	Dominic Ogden
Lucy Edwards	Roderick Palmer
Nicola Hogg	Sally Rich
David Hoyes	Mark Tilley
Euros Jones	Daniel Wilde
Gavin Jones	Christopher Zavos

CONSULTANTS

Derek Kirby Johnson

HOBSON AUDLEY

Established in 1983

7 PILGRIM STREET
LONDON EC4V 6DR, ENGLAND
Telephone: 0171 248 2299; 0171 956 9175
Facsimile: 0171 248 0672

Company Commercial, Financial and Marketing Services, Energy, Natural Resources, Publishing, Banking, Venture Capital, Manufacturing Industries. Commercial Litigation including Banking, Building Disputes, Employment and Industrial Relations, Intellectual Property Law, Landlord and Tenant, Air Transport Licensing, Computer Litigation, Arbitrations, Commercial Disputes. Commercial Property Department - Sales and Acquisitions, Industrial and Commercial Property, including Shopping Centers, Securing Commercial Mortgages, Planning Law Representing Clients.

MEMBERS OF FIRM

MICHAEL BERNSTEIN, admitted, 1960, England. *Education:* London School of Economics; University of London (LL.B., 1957). *PRACTICE AREAS:* Commercial Property.

(This Listing Continued)

GERALD A. HOBSON, admitted, 1971, England. *Member:* International Bar Association; The City of London Solicitors Company; London Solicitors Litigation Association. *PRACTICE AREAS:* Commercial Litigation; Employment Law.

MAXWELL C. AUDLEY, admitted, 1980, England. *Education:* University of Bonn; University of Bradford (B.A., 1976). *Member:* International Bar Association. *LANGUAGES:* French and German. *PRACTICE AREAS:* Corporate/Company Commercial.

ANDREW L. JOYCE, admitted, 1978, England. *Education:* Cambridge University (B.A., 1975). *PRACTICE AREAS:* Commercial Litigation.

RUPERT M. A. CONNELL, admitted, 1978, England. *PRACTICE AREAS:* Corporate Insolvency; Banking; Company Commercial.

LANCE J. FEAVER, admitted, 1981, England. *Education:* Bristol University (LL.B., 1978). *PRACTICE AREAS:* Corporate/Company Commercial Law.

CAROLINE L. WHITELEY, admitted, 1983, England. *Education:* University of Birmingham (LL.B., 1980). *PRACTICE AREAS:* Commercial Litigation; Employment Law.

DAVID A. WALTER, admitted, 1984, England. *Education:* University of Sussex (B.A. Hons., 1977). *PRACTICE AREAS:* Corporate/Company Commercial Law.

MALCOLM PETER ROBSON, admitted, 1981, England. *Education:* Birmingham University (LL.B., Hons., 1978). *PRACTICE AREAS:* Commercial Litigation.

ANTHONY L. BROCKBANK, admitted, 1986, England. *Education:* Oxford University (M.A. (Oxon), 1982). *PRACTICE AREAS:* Corporate/-Company Commercial Law.

HOGAN & HARTSON L.L.P.

VERITAS HOUSE
125 FINSBURY PAVEMENT
LONDON, EC2A 1NQ, ENGLAND
Telephone: (44 171) 638.9595
Fax: (44 171) 638.0884

Washington, D.C. Office: Columbia Square, 555 13th Street, N.W. Telephone: 202-637-5600. Telex: 89-2757. Cable Address: "Hogander Washington". Fax: 202-637-5910.
Brussels, Belgium Office: Avenue des Arts 41, 1040. Telephone: (32.2) 505.09.11. Fax: (32.2) 502.28.60.
Moscow, Russia Office: 33/2 Usacheva Street, Building 3, 119048. Telephone: (7095) 245-5190. Fax: (7095) 245-5192.
Paris, France Office: Cabinet Wolfram, 14, rue Chauveau-Lagarde, 75008. Telephone: (33-1) 44.71.97.00. Fax: (33-1) 47.42.13.56.
Prague, Czech Republic Office: Opletalova 37, 110 00. Telephone: (42-2) 2422-9009. Fax: (42-2) 2421-5105.
Warsaw, Poland Office: Marszalkowska 6/6, 00-590. Telephone: (48 2) 628 0201; Int'l (48) 3912 1413. Fax: (48 2) 628 7787; Int'l (48) 3912 1511.
Baltimore, Maryland Office: 111 South Calvert Street, 16th Floor. Telephone: 410-659-2700. Fax: 410-539-6981.
Bethesda, Maryland Office: Two Democracy Center, Suite 720, 6903 Rockledge Drive. Telephone: 301-564-5000. Fax: 301-493-5169.
Colorado Springs, Colorado Office: 518 North Nevada Avenue, Suite 200. Telephone: 719-635-5900. Fax: 719-635-2847.
Denver, Colorado Office: One Tabor Center, Suite 1500, 1200 Seventeenth Street. Telephone: 303-899-7300. Fax: 303-899-7333.
McLean, Virginia Office: 8300 Greensboro Drive. Telephone: 703-848-2600. Fax: 703-448-7650.

General Practice. Firm engaged in American and International Law Practice but not authorized to appear before English courts or to act as Solicitors.

PARTNERS

RAYMOND J. BATLA, JR., born Cameron, Texas, September 1, 1947; admitted, 1973, Texas and District of Columbia (Not admitted in England). *Education:* Texas Tech University and University of Texas (B.S.C.E., with highest honors, 1970); University of Texas (J.D., with honors, 1973). Tau Beta Pi; Chi Epsilon; Phi Delta Phi; Order of the Coif. Research Scholar, Texas Law Review, 1972-1973. Member, International Observer Delegation to Czechoslovak National Elections, 1990. Litigation Columnist and Editorial Advisory Board, "Natural Gas," The Journal for Producers, Pipelines,

(This Listing Continued)

HOGAN & HARTSON L.L.P., London—Continued

Distributors and End Users, 1984-1991; Secretary, Council on Alternate Fuels, Washington, D.C., 1987—. *Member:* District of Columbia Bar; Bar Association of the District of Columbia; Federal, American (Member, Sections on: International Law; Corporation, Banking and Business Law; Member, Special Committee for Energy Finance, 1989—), Federal Energy (Chairman, Committee on International Energy Transactions, 1993-1994) and International Bar Associations; State Bar of Texas; Natural Gas Roundtable; Central and Eastern Europe Law Institute. *LANGUAGES:* English, Czech. *PRACTICE AREAS:* Energy Finance; International Law; Corporate Law.

DANIEL H. MACCOBY, born Manhattan, Kansas, November 22, 1953; admitted, 1981, District of Columbia (Not admitted in England). *Education:* Harvard University (A.B., magna cum laude, 1975); Georgetown University (J.D., cum laude, 1981). Editor, Georgetown Law Journal, 1979-1981. *Member:* District of Columbia Bar; American (Member, Business Law and International Law Sections) and International Bar Associations. *PRACTICE AREAS:* International Commercial Law; Corporate and Securities Law; Privatization.

(For complete biographical data on all personnel, see Professional Biographies at Washington, D.C.)

HOLMAN, FENWICK & WILLAN

Solicitors

&

Registered Foreign Lawyers

MARLOW HOUSE
LLOYDS AVENUE
LONDON EC3N 3AL, ENGLAND
Telephone: 0171-488-2300
Telex: 8812247 HFWLON
Telefax: 0171-481-0316

Paris, France Office: 3 Rue la Boëtie, 75008. Telephone: 44-94-40-50. Telex: 281699F HFWPA A. Telefax: 42-65-46-25.
Hong Kong Office: 1418 Two Pacific Place, 88 Queensway, Hong Kong. Telephone: 2522 3006. Telex: 63536 HFWHK HX. Telefax: 2887 8110.
Singapore Office: 10 Collyer Quay, #08-02, Ocean Building, Singapore, 0104. Telephone: 534-0195. Telex: HFWSIN RS 26188. Telefax: 534-5864.
Piraeus, Greece Office: 6th Floor, 86 Filonos Street. Telephone: 429-3978. Telefax: 429-3118.
Rouen, France Office: 47 Avenue Gustave Flaubert, 76000. Telephone: 32.08.18.60. Telefax: 35.89.90.54.

A major shipping, maritime and commercial law firm providing legal advice on Admiralty, all aspects of Maritime Law and International Trade, Oil, Gas and Energy, Commodities, Transportation, Insurance and Reinsurance, Corporate Litigation and Insolvency, Ship Finance, Company and Commercial Matters, European Competition Law, Commercial Property, Aviation and Professional Negligence.

PARTNERS

W. ARCHIE BISHOP (Senior Partner). *PRACTICE AREAS:* Admiralty Law; Marine Salvage Rights; Casualties; Offshore Pollution; Marine Disasters.

J. COLIN SHEPPARD. *PRACTICE AREAS:* P and I Clubs; Charter Parties and Bills of Lading; Marine Insurance Law; Casualties; Marine Disasters.

BRIAN G. ROBINSON. *PRACTICE AREAS:* Maritime Law; Ship Finance; Ship Registration; Finance, Commercial Finance.

TOM P. BUTLER. *PRACTICE AREAS:* Marine Insurance Law; P and I Clubs; Commodities; International Trade; Admiralty and Maritime Law, Shipping.

GRAHAM E.T. HOGG. *PRACTICE AREAS:* P and I Clubs; Offshore Pollution; Charter Parties and Bills of Lading; Marine Insurance Law; Marine Disasters.

J. RODERIC M. O'SULLIVAN. *PRACTICE AREAS:* Natural Resources; Oil and Gas; Admiralty and Maritime Law, Maritime Finance; Admiralty and Maritime Law, Vessel Finance; Corporate Law.

(This Listing Continued)

LOUIS A. BELL. *PRACTICE AREAS:* P and I Clubs; Maritime Law; Charter Parties and Bills of Lading; Marine Insurance Law; International Trade.

CHARLES R. LOWE. *PRACTICE AREAS:* Casualties; Marine Salvage Rights; Marine Disasters; Marine Insurance Law; Offshore Pollution.

KEITH MICHEL. *PRACTICE AREAS:* International Trade; P and I Clubs; Maritime Law; Marine Insurance Law; Charter Parties and Bills of Lading.

PETER B. SCRASE. *PRACTICE AREAS:* Admiralty and Maritime Law; Commercial Law; Intellectual Property; Labor (Labour) and Employment; Insurance.

PETER REES SMITH (Resident, Hong Kong Office).

ROBERT G. WILSON. *PRACTICE AREAS:* P and I Clubs; Maritime Law; Charter Parties and Bills of Lading; Admiralty Law; Marine Insurance Law.

MICHAEL T. STEVENS (Resident, Hong Kong Office).

HUGH M. BROWN. *PRACTICE AREAS:* Admiralty Law; Marine Salvage Rights; Casualties; Offshore Pollution; Marine Disasters.

JONATHAN M. FINE. *PRACTICE AREAS:* International Trade; P and I Clubs; Casualties; Maritime Law; Charter Parties and Bills of Lading.

THE LORD BYRON. *PRACTICE AREAS:* Charter Parties and Bills of Lading; Marine Insurance Law; International Trade; Admiralty and Maritime Law; Commodities.

ALAN P.R. WALLS. *PRACTICE AREAS:* Admiralty and Maritime Law, Marine Disasters; Personal Injury.

STEPHEN P. DRURY. *PRACTICE AREAS:* Company Law, Acquisitions and Sales; Corporate Law, Banking; Aviation and Aerospace Finance; Finance, Commercial Finance; Admiralty and Maritime Law, Maritime Finance.

GREGORY Q. GRAY. *PRACTICE AREAS:* Arbitration and Mediation; Charter Parties and Bills of Lading; International Trade; Admiralty and Maritime Law; Construction Law, Arbitration.

HUGH J. LIVINGSTONE. *PRACTICE AREAS:* Commercial Law; P and I Clubs; Maritime Law; Charter Parties and Bills of Lading; Marine Insurance Law.

DAVID V.G. DE PASS. *PRACTICE AREAS:* Probate, Taxation, Trusts and Estates; Wills.

STEVEN J. PAULL. *PRACTICE AREAS:* Admiralty and Maritime Law, Shipping; International Trade; Construction Law; Corporate Law, Insolvency; Litigation.

JOHN N. KRZYWKOWSKI (Resident, Piraeus, Greece Office).

DAN P. TINDALL. *PRACTICE AREAS:* International Trade; Ship Mortgage Reinforcement; Maritime Law; Ship Finance; Ship Registration.

PAUL T. ASTON (Resident, Singapore Office).

RICHARD W. CRUMP. *PRACTICE AREAS:* Admiralty and Maritime Law, Charter Parties; Admiralty and Maritime Law, Maritime Insurance; Admiralty and Maritime Law, Marine Casualty; Admiralty and Maritime Law, Maritime Negligence; Admiralty and Maritime Law, Shipping.

JOHN P.J. DUFF. *PRACTICE AREAS:* Insurance.

GUILLAUME BRAJEUX (Resident, Paris, France Office).

JEAN-JACQUES OLLU (Resident, Paris, France Office).

MICHAEL G. DONITHORN. *PRACTICE AREAS:* Charter Parties and Bills of Lading; Casualties; Marine Insurance; International Trade; P and I Clubs.

ROBIN G.G. OSBORNE. *PRACTICE AREAS:* Corporate Law, International Finance; Corporate Law, Banking; Admiralty and Maritime Law, Maritime Finance; International Trade; Ship Mortgage Reinforcement.

JAMES C. GOSLING. *PRACTICE AREAS:* Admiralty Law; Marine Salvage Rights; Casualties; Offshore Pollution; Marine Disasters.

OTTILIE M. SEFTON. *PRACTICE AREAS:* International Trade; P and I Clubs; Maritime Law; Marine Insurance Law; Charter Parties and Bills of Lading.

SIMON K. BLOWS. *PRACTICE AREAS:* International Trade; P and I Clubs; Maritime Law; Charter Parties and Bills of Lading.

(This Listing Continued)

TIMOTHY P. CLEMENS-JONES (Resident, Paris, France Office).

GEORGE M.T. EDDINGS. PRACTICE AREAS: Arbitration and Mediation; International Arbitration; International Trade; Charter Parties; Bills of Landing.

JULIAN C. PIERCE. PRACTICE AREAS: International Trade; P and I Clubs; Maritime Law; Charter Parties and Bills of Lading; Marine Insurance Law.

GLENN S. MOORE. PRACTICE AREAS: Admiralty and Maritime Law; Aviation and Aerospace; Commercial Law; Professional Liability; Transportation.

PHILIP W.Y. MO (Resident, Hong Kong Office).

VIVIENNE PITROFF. PRACTICE AREAS: Admiralty and Maritime Law; Antitrust and Trade Regulations, Restrictive Trade; Commercial Law, Sale of Goods; Commodities; Entertainment and The Arts, Music.

R. NICHOLAS HUTTON. PRACTICE AREAS: Company Law, Acquisitions and Sales; Company Law, Commercial; Company Law, Contracts; Company Law, Restructuring; Corporate Law, Insolvency.

GUY V.J. HARDAKER (Resident, Hong Kong Office).

BRIDGET H.R. WHEELER. PRACTICE AREAS: International Trade; Commodities; Insurance; Maritime Law; Banks and Banking, Bank Fraud.

ANTHONY J. JEX (Resident, Hong Kong Office).

SIMON W. CONGDON. PRACTICE AREAS: Admiralty and Maritime Law; Bankruptcy; Commercial Law; Corporate Law; Litigation.

OLIVER M. PURCELL (Resident, Paris, France Office).

JAY A. TOOKER. PRACTICE AREAS: Banks and Banking; Company Law; International Trade; Ship Finance; Ship Registration.

PETER G. BENNETT. PRACTICE AREAS: Bankruptcy; Environmental Law; International Trade; Charter Parties and Bills of Lading; Marine Insurance Law.

PATRICIA M. FRANCIES. PRACTICE AREAS: Commodities; International Law, Sales; P and I Clubs; Marine Insurance Law; Charter Parties and Bills of Lading.

ANDREW A. BANDURKA. PRACTICE AREAS: Arbitration and Mediation; Insurance, Professional Indemnity; Insurance, Reinsurance; Insurance Defense; Litigation.

MARCUS R. BOWMAN. PRACTICE AREAS: Admiralty Law; P and I Clubs; Maritime Law; Marine Insurance Law; Charter Parties and Bills of Lading.

PAUL A.J. SUPRAMANIAM (Resident, Singapore Office).

PAUL J. HATZER (Resident, Hong Kong Office).

PHILIP A. WAREHAM. PRACTICE AREAS: Agency and Distributorships; Antitrust and Trade Regulation; European Community Law; Intellectual Property; Franchises and Franchising.

SIMON S. DAVIDSON (Resident, Hong Kong Office).

HENRY W. DUNLOP. PRACTICE AREAS: Admiralty and Maritime Law, Arbitration; International Law, Conflict of Laws; Transportation, Carriage of Goods; Transportation, Insurance; Transportation, Shipping.

PAUL R. WORDLEY. PRACTICE AREAS: Environmental Law; Insurance; Litigation; Professional Liability; Reinsurance.

SENIOR MANAGERS

TIM J. BODEN. PRACTICE AREAS: Admiralty Law; Marine Salvage Rights; Casualties; Marine Disasters.

DOUGLAS W. GRANT. PRACTICE AREAS: Insurance Coverage; Insurance, General Liability; Insurance, Indemnity; Insurance, Professional Indemnity; Insurance, Reinsurance.

CONSULTANTS

CHRISTOPHER A. HALES

IAN M. MCLACHLAN

Languages: English, Danish, French, German, Greek, Italian, Serbo Croat, Spanish, Hungarian and Swedish

HOLME ROBERTS & OWEN LLC

U.S. Counsellors at Law

Established in 1898

4TH FLOOR, MELLIER HOUSE
26A ALBEMARLE STREET
LONDON W1X 3FA, ENGLAND
Telephone: 44-171-499-8776
Telecopier: 44-171-499-7769

REVISERS OF THE COLORADO LAW DIGEST FOR THIS DIRECTORY

Denver, Colorado Office: Suite 4100, 1700 Lincoln, 80203. Telephone: 303-861-7000. Telex: 45-4460. Telecopier: 303-866-0200.
Boulder, Colorado Office: Suite 400, 1401 Pearl Street, 80302. Telephone: 303-444-5955. Telecopier: 303-444-1063.
Colorado Springs, Colorado Office: Suite 1300, 90 South Cascade Avenue, 80903. Telephone: 719-473-3800. Telecopier: 719-633-1518.
Salt Lake City, Utah Office: Suite 1100, 111 East Broadway, 84111. Telephone: 801-521-5800. Telecopier: 801-521-9639.
Moscow, Russia Office: 14 Krivokolenny Pr., Suite 30, 101000. Telephone: 095-925-7816. Telecopier: 095-923-2726.

Firm engaged in U.S. and International Law Practice, International Business and International Tax, but not authorized to appear before the English Courts or to act as Solicitors.

MEMBERS OF FIRM

BRUCE R. KOHLER, born Springfield, Massachusetts, April 15, 1943; admitted, 1970, New York; 1973, Colorado (Not admitted in England). *Education:* Harvard University (A.B., magna cum laude, 1965; J.D., cum laude, 1969). Phi Beta Kappa. Chairman, Colorado Italy Council, 1989. U.K. Representative of the Colorado International Trade Office. *Member:* International Bar Association. (Co-Chair, International Practice). (Managing Resident Member; Co-Director, Moscow Office). *LANGUAGES:* English, Italian, Danish. *PRACTICE AREAS:* International Business Law; Corporate Law; Real Estate Lending Law.

JUDITH L. L. ROBERTS, born Seattle, Washington, December 27, 1939; admitted, 1979, Colorado (Not admitted in England). *Education:* University of Michigan (A.B., magna cum laude, 1962); University of Tübingen, Germany, Fulbright Scholar; University of Wisconsin (M.A., 1964); University of Denver (J.D., 1979). Phi Beta Kappa. Woodrow Wilson Fellow. Order of St. Ives. Staff, Denver Law Journal, 1977-1979. Member, Colorado Governor's Soviet Advisory Council; Chairman of Board, Denver World Trade Center, 1991-1992; Director, Colorado-Taiwan Trade and Investment Office, 1988-1991; Resident Lawyer, London, 1981-1982. *Member:* Denver, Colorado and International Bar Associations. (Co-Chair, International Practice). (Co-Director, Moscow Office; London Office). *PRACTICE AREAS:* International Business Law.

SPECIAL COUNSEL

LAWRENCE A. LEPORTE, born Wisconsin, May 19, 1961; admitted, 1986, Virginia; 1989, Illinois (Not admitted in England). *Education:* Lawrence University (B.A., magna cum laude, 1983); Northwestern University (J.D., 1986). *PRACTICE AREAS:* International Transactions; Corporate.

DAVID K. SCHOLLENBERGER, born Akron, Ohio, September 14, 1955; admitted, 1982, Colorado; 1985, Massachusetts (Not admitted in England). *Education:* Colorado College (B.A., 1977); University of Denver (J.D., 1982). Author: "Technology Licensing in the European Community," Chapter 11 in Book, European Community Law After 1992: An Overview for Lawyers Outside the Community, Kluwer, 1992; "International Commercial Arbitration in Europe," Chapter 19 in 1988 Revision of Book, The Law of Transnational Business Transactions, Clark Boardman, 1982. *Member:* Denver, Colorado, American and International Bar Associations; Society of Computers and Law. *LANGUAGES:* German and French. *PRACTICE AREAS:* International; Intellectual Property; Commercial; Corporate.

ASSOCIATES

PAUL G. THOMPSON, born Des Moines, Iowa, November 17, 1963; admitted, 1989, Colorado; 1990, District of Columbia (Not admitted in England). *Education:* University of Iowa (B.B.A., with highest distinction, 1985); University of Michigan (J.D., 1989). Contributing Author: "Business Ventures in Eastern Europe and the Soviet Union: The Emerging Legal Framework for Foreign Investment," Prentice Hall Law & Business, 1991. Co-Author: "Securities Regulation in Central Europe: Hungary and

(This Listing Continued)

HOLME ROBERTS & OWEN LLC, London—Continued

Czechoslovakia," Denv. J. Intl. L. & Pol'y, 1992; "Roll-Up Transactions," Clark Boardman, 1992; "Securities Regulations in Central Europe: Poland, Hungary and Czech and Slovak Federal Republics," Clark Boardman, 1993. *Member:* Denver, Colorado and American Bar Associations; District of Columbia Bar. (Also at Denver, Colorado and Moscow, Russia Offices). *PRACTICE AREAS:* International Law; Corporate Law; Securities Law.

REVISERS OF THE COLORADO LAW DIGEST FOR THIS DIRECTORY

(For Complete Biographical Data on all Personnel, see Professional Biographies at Denver, Colorado)

HOPKINS & WOOD

Established in 1982

2/3 CURSITOR STREET
LONDON EC4A 1NE, ENGLAND
Telephone: 0171-404-0475
Fax: 0171-430-2358

Commercial Litigation, Corporate and Commercial, Venture Capital and Development Capital, Management Buy-Outs, Management Buy-Ins and Investment Capital Work, Mergers and Acquisitions, Banking, Intellectual Property including Patent Copyright Designs and Trade Marks, Competition, EC, Computers and Telecommunications, Franchising, Insurance, Real Property and Planning, Environmental Law, Offshore and Domestic Trusts and Tax.

FIRM PROFILE: *The firm has a strong reputation for litigation (where it has been involved in many major cases), for intellectual property and high technology work, particularly involving computers and telecommunications, and for corporate finance and all types of investment capital work.*

MEMBERS OF FIRM

ROGER C. B. HOPKINS, born 1947; Barrister 1969; admitted, 1976, England. *Education:* Oxford University (M.A.). *Member:* International Bar Association; City of London Solicitors Company; American Bar Association. *LANGUAGES:* French and German. *PRACTICE AREAS:* Commercial Litigation.

IAN C. WOOD, born 1950; admitted, 1977, England. *Education:* Durham University (B.Sc.; M.Sc.). *Member:* Union of European Practitioners in Industrial Property. Associate: The Chartered Institute of Patent Agents; Institute of Trade Mark Agents. *PRACTICE AREAS:* Intellectual Property.

SIMON J. J. SMITH, born 1954; admitted, 1980, England. *Education:* Warwick University (B.A.). *Member:* City of London Solicitors Company. *PRACTICE AREAS:* Property Law.

BERRY G. C. HOLDING-PARSONS, born 1948; Barrister 1975; admitted, 1981, England. *Education:* Cambridge University (B.A.). *Member:* French Chamber of Commerce, London (Council Member); British Insurance Law Association; International Bar Association. *LANGUAGES:* French (fluent) and German. *PRACTICE AREAS:* Commercial Litigation.

JANE A. JALES, born 1957; admitted, 1981, England. *Education:* Bristol University (LL.B.). *Member:* City of London Solicitors Company. *PRACTICE AREAS:* Commercial Litigation.

SIMON RENDELL, born 1962; Barrister, 1986; admitted, 1991, England. *Education:* Cambridge University (B.A.). *Member:* Fast Legal Advisory Group; Competition Law Association; Public Network Operators Interest Group. *PRACTICE AREAS:* Commercial; Computer Law; Telecommunications.

ANDREW J. SAUL, born 1962; admitted, 1986, England. *Education:* Oxford University (B.A.). *Member:* Institute of Directors. *PRACTICE AREAS:* Corporate Finance; Venture Capital; Mergers and Acquisitions; Joint Ventures and Strategic Alliances; Banking.

ADRIAN M. LIFELY, born 1959; admitted, 1986, England. *Education:* University College, Cardiff (L.L.B.). *PRACTICE AREAS:* Commercial Litigation.

CHRISTOPHER R.B. HOYLE, born 1959; admitted, 1983, Barrister and Solicitor, New Zealand; 1987, England. *Education:* Canterbury University, Christchurch, New Zealand (LL.B., Hons); Cambridge University (LL.M., Hons); University of London (Dip I.P.L.). *Member:* British Com-

(This Listing Continued)

---

puter Society (Affiliate). *PRACTICE AREAS:* Commercial Law; Computer Law; Telecommunications.

BEVERLEY MYERS, born 1963; Barrister, 1987; admitted, 1992, England. *Education:* Cambridge University; Chemical and Biological Science/Law (M.A.). *Member:* Union of European Practitioners in Industrial Property. Associate: The Chartered Institute of Patent Agents. *PRACTICE AREAS:* Intellectual Property.

CONSULTANTS

ROGER D. CORAL, born 1957; admitted, 1982, England. *Education:* London School of Economics (LL.B.). *PRACTICE AREAS:* Property.

PAUL B. J. MATTHEWS, born 1955; Barrister 1981; admitted, 1987, England. *Education:* London University (LL.B.); Oxford University (B.C.L.). Co-Author: "Discovery" Visiting Senior Lecturer, King's College, London University. *Member:* British Institute of International and Comparative Law; City of London Solicitors Company. *LANGUAGES:* French and Italian. *PRACTICE AREAS:* Commercial Litigation; Trusts.

BRENDAN PATTERSON, born 1957; admitted, 1981, England. *Education:* University College, Cardiff (LL.B.). *PRACTICE AREAS:* Property Law.

HOWARD KENNEDY

Established in 1936

HARCOURT HOUSE
19 CAVENDISH SQUARE
LONDON W1A 2AW, ENGLAND
Telephone: 0171 636 1616
Fax: 0171 499 6871

Incorporating Slingsby Farmiloe & Greenfield and Anthony Feldman & Co.

Padua, Italy Associated Office: Camilotti, Ceccon, Polettini, 35137 Padua, Via S. Fermo 26. Telephone: (049) 651.355. Telex: 828641 LEXFOR 1. Fax: (049) 666 086.

Hong Kong Associated Office: Slao Wen and Leung, 15th Floor, Hang Seng Building, 77 Des Voeux Road, C. Telephone: 852 810 4113. Fax: 852 869 7060.

Members of Intercounsel, Juridique Européen, and Transnational Taxation Network and Morison International.

Banking, Business Law, Enterprise Investment Schemes, Corporate Law and Listed Companies, Mergers and Acquisitions, Corporate Finance, Charity Law, Employment Law and all forms of International Trust and Corporate Structures, Intellectual Property, Environmental Law, European Community Law, Computer Contracts, Take-Overs, Family Law, Financial Services, Venture Capital, Corporate Tax, Hotels, Restaurants, Tourism and Travel, Trusts, Shipping Finance, Off-Shore Companies, Immigration, Licensing, Litigation (Commercial, Personal and Insolvency), Personal Tax Planning and Probate, Private International Law, Real Estate, Planning and Financing, Commercial and Residential Conveyancing, Securities and Secured Transactions, Partnership and Joint Ventures.

FIRM PROFILE: *A medium size commercial practice covering property law, company, commercial and corporate finance law, banking, litigation, trusts, tax planning, wills and probate and international and domestic transactions for overseas clients. The practice aims to combine the benefits of size and expertise with a high degree of personal care and attention.*

PARTNERS

A.L. BANES. LANGUAGES: English and French. *PRACTICE AREAS:* Charity Law; Corporate Law; Commercial Law; Mergers and Acquisitions; Corporate Finance; Venture Capital; Taxation; Securities Transactions; Joint Ventures.

D.J.A. BLAKEMAN. LANGUAGES: English. *PRACTICE AREAS:* Commercial and Residential Conveyancing; Landlord and Tenant.

EILEEN CARROLL. LANGUAGES: English. *PRACTICE AREAS:* Alternative Dispute Resolution; Arbitration; International Arbitration; Mediation; First and Third Party Liability; General Liability; Insurance Coverage; Professional Indemnity; Reinsurance; Litigation.

G.H. CRAIG. LANGUAGES: English and French. *PRACTICE AREAS:* Real Estate; Charities; Commercial Law; Property Developments and Investments.

(This Listing Continued)

M.E. DOBRIN. LANGUAGES: English, German and French. **PRACTICE AREAS:** Commercial Property; Restaurant and Hotels; Liquor Licensing.

C.A. EMDEN. LANGUAGES: English. **PRACTICE AREAS:** Commercial and Property Litigation; Insolvency; Immigration.

A.D.J. FARMILOE. LANGUAGES: English and French. **PRACTICE AREAS:** Private International Law; Corporate Law; Taxation; Industrial Relations; Labour Law; Bankruptcy; Immigration; General Intellectual Property Practice; Copyright.

A.S. FELDMAN. LANGUAGES: English and French. **PRACTICE AREAS:** Distribution Agreements; International Art Law; Aircraft Finance and Leasing; Bankruptcy; Banking Litigation; Business Law; Chancery and Equity; Intellectual Property Rights; Leases and Leasing; Litigation; Construction Disputes; Military Law; Negligence; Professional Negligence; Property; Resorts and Leisure; Wills.

A.V.W. GREENFIELD. LANGUAGES: English, French, Spanish, German, Dutch, Russian and Italian. **PRACTICE AREAS:** Private International Law; Corporate Law; Taxation; Property; Real Estate; Industrial Relations and Labour Law; Bankruptcy; Immigration; General Intellectual Property Practice; Copyright.

M.L. HARRIS. LANGUAGES: English. **PRACTICE AREAS:** Corporate Finance; Venture Capital; Securities Transactions; Mergers and Acquisitions; Commercial Law.

R.A. KOHN. LANGUAGES: English and Hebrew. **PRACTICE AREAS:** Commercial Litigation; Property Litigation; Breaches of Contract.

K. LASSMAN. LANGUAGES: English. **PRACTICE AREAS:** Corporate Finance; Corporate Law; Venture Capital; Mergers and Acquisitions; Commercial Law.

A.S. LEVENE. LANGUAGES: English. **PRACTICE AREAS:** Personal Tax Planning; Probate; Commercial Property; Secured Lending.

T.J.A. NEWEY. LANGUAGES: English. **PRACTICE AREAS:** Breaches of Contract; Commercial Disputes.

M.P. PHILLIPS. LANGUAGES: English and Dutch. **PRACTICE AREAS:** Corporate Finance; Venture Capital; Securities Transactions; Mergers and Acquisitions; Commercial Law; Intellectual Property.

D.R. SEATON. LANGUAGES: English. **PRACTICE AREAS:** Estate Planning; Business; Commercial; Company; Employment; Taxation.

C.A. SLINGSBY. LANGUAGES: English, French and Italian. **PRACTICE AREAS:** Private International Law; Corporate law; Taxation; Property Real Estate; Industrial Relations and Labour Law; Bankruptcy; Immigration; General Intellectual Property Practice; Copyright; Inheritance and Probate.

P. SPRINGALL. LANGUAGES: English and Russian. **PRACTICE AREAS:** Secured Lending; Corporate Real Estate; Environmental Liability; Hazardous Materials; Hazardous Waste; Leases and Leasing; Mortgages; Property; Real Estate; Sports and Leisure; Value Added Tax.

SUSAN P. TAYLOR. LANGUAGES: English and French. **PRACTICE AREAS:** Commercial and Residential Conveyancing; Landlord and Tenant.

JANE TYSON. LANGUAGES: English. **PRACTICE AREAS:** Commercial Property; Secured Lending; Banking; Insolvency.

J.M. WEIDER. LANGUAGES: English. **PRACTICE AREAS:** Commercial Litigation; Breach of Contract; Entertainment Disputes; Debt Recovery and Negligence; Domestic and International Arbitration; Defamation; Landlord and Tenant; Matrimonial.

P. WELBURN. LANGUAGES: English, German and Italian. **PRACTICE AREAS:** Secured Lending; International Business; International Joint Ventures; Construction Law; Corporate Real Estate; Trade Law; Leases and Leasing; Mortgages; Product Safety; Property.

CONSULTANTS

R.H. GLICK. LANGUAGES: English, French and Spanish. **PRACTICE AREAS:** International Tax and Corporate Structures; Personal Tax Planning Trusts and Probate.

(This Listing Continued)

M. PHILIPS. LANGUAGES: English. **PRACTICE AREAS:** Real Estate; Finance; Joint Ventures.

HON. P. PRICE MEP. LANGUAGES: English and French. **PRACTICE AREAS:** European Public Affairs; European Community Law.

HYLTON-POTTS
7 CHEVAL PLACE, KNIGHTSBRIDGE
LONDON SW7 1EW, ENGLAND
Telephone: 0171 225 1881
Fax: 0171 584 3751; 0171 589 4008

Litigation, Intellectual Property, Business Law and Immigration.

FIRM PROFILE: *The firm offers a full range of legal services. Rodney Hylton-Potts is a member of the International Bar Association, American Bar Association and New York Bar Association.*

SOLICITORS

RODNEY HYLTON-POTTS. PRACTICE AREAS: Litigation; Intellectual Property; Business Law; Immigration.

JOHN C. WRIGHT. PRACTICE AREAS: Property Work.

JAQUES & LEWIS
LONDON, ENGLAND

(See Eversheds)

JEANTET & ASSOCIES
ROYEX HOUSE, ALDERMANBURY SQUARE
LONDON EC2V 7HR, ENGLAND
Telephone: (44) 171 600 36 08
Fax: (44) 171 600 17 18

Paris, France Office: 87, avenue Kléber, 75116. Telephone: (33) 1 45 05 80 08. Fax: (33) 1 47 04 20 41; (33) 1 47 55 95 10.

Brussels, Belgium Office: Rue Brederode 13 A, B, 1000. Telephone: (32) 2505 02 11. Fax: (32) 2502 26 44.

New York, New York Office: 712 Fifth Avenue, 10019. Telephone: (212) 801 3440. Fax: (212) 801 3445.

Prague, Czech Republic Office: Blanicka 28, 12000. Telephone: (42) 2 256 251. Fax: (42) 2 254 233.

Budapest, Hungary Office: Szemere Utca 17.IV./1, 1054. Telephone: (36) 2 203 40759. Fax: (36) 2 201 63 79.

Bucarest, Romania Office: Strada Docentilor 7, Sector 1. Telephone: (40) 1 312 99 36. Fax: (40) 1 312 97 56.

Warsaw, Poland Office: Ul. Wiejska 12a, PL 00-490. Telephone: (48) 2/628 24 12. Fax: (48) 2/628 24 11.

Moscow, Russia Correspondent Office: Krasnopresnenskaya NAB, 12, International Trade Center, Office 2009, CEI - 123610. Telephone: (7) 502 253 00 41. Fax: (7) 502 253 20 42.

General Practice in French, EEC and International Business Law (i.e. inter alia Corporate, Tax, Mergers and Acquisitions, Securities, Banking, Patent and Trademarks, Labor, Finance, Litigation, International Estates, Arbitration, Computer Law, French and European Economic Community Antitrust, Insurance and Product Liability Law, Distribution, Consumer, Transportation Law).

Member of Alliance of European Lawyers (EEIG) which regroups six law firms from Continental Europe. The Alliance consists of De Bandt, van Hecke & Lagae at Brussels and Antwerp; De Brauw Blackstone Westbroek at The Hague, Amsterdam, Rotterdam and Eindhoven; Jeantet & Associés at Paris and Warsaw; Lagerlöf & Leman at Stockholm, Gothenburg and Malmö; Oppenhoff & Rädler at Berlin, Cologne, Frankfurt am Main, Leipzig and Münich; Uria & Menendez at Madrid and Barcelona.

PHILIPPE SARRAILHE, born Dakar, Senegal, September 29, 1949; admitted, 1972, Paris (Not admitted in England). *Education:* Law Schools of Paris X (Licence en Droit and Diplôme Institut d'Etudes Judiciaires, 1972); Paris I (D.E.S.S. Commerce International, 1976); Paris X (D.E.A. Droit des Affaires, 1980); University of Pennsylvania (LL.M., 1978). Author: "Contracts and Investments in Venezuela", "Product Liability

(This Listing Continued)

JEANTET & ASSOCIES, London—Continued

(France)," Oceana. Panelist: Mergers and Acquisitions, Joint Ventures, Banking, EEC Law. Assistant Lecturer, EEC Law and International Trade Law, University of Paris II Law School, 1982-1985. *Member:* ABA; IBA; NYSBA; Association of the Bar of the City of New York; American Foreign Law Association (Vice-President). (Also at Paris, France). *LANGUAGES:* French, English, Spanish, Italian and Portuguese.

(For a list of Partners and Counsel of the respective Member Alliance Firms see Professional Biographies at: Oppenhoff & Rädler at Munich, Cologne, Frankfurt/Main and Berlin, Germany; De Bandt van Hecke & Lagae at Brussels, Belgium; De Brauw Blackstone Westbroek at The Hague, Rotterdam and Amsterdam, The Netherlands; Jeantet & Associés, at Paris, France; Uria & Menendez at Madrid and Barcelona, Spain, Brussels and New York).

JEFFREY GREEN RUSSELL

Established in 1972

56 NEW BOND STREET
LONDON W1Y 9DG, ENGLAND
Telephone: 0171 499 7020
Telex: 298408 Jeflex G
Facsimile: 0171 499 2449

Corporate and Commercial Law, Mergers, Flotations, Corporate Finance, Banking, Commercial Property, Property Development, Property Finance, Commercial Litigation, Defamation, Intellectual Property, Liquor and Gaming Licensing, Franchising, Employment, Debt-Collection and Insurance Litigation, Fraud Investigations Law.
Jeffrey Green Russell is the founding member of ACL International, an association of commercial lawyers with members in Europe, Scandinavia, the United States, Canada, Asia, Africa and the Middle East.

PARTNERS

PHILIP GRAHAM COHEN, born London, England, April 11, 1952; admitted to the Roll, 1979, England. *Education:* Peterhouse, Cambridge (M.A., Senior Scholar, 1975); Lancaster Gate College of Law. Author: "Privacy and Parliament Survey of Computer Copyright Law," The European Systems Journal. *Member:* Law Society. *LANGUAGES:* English, French, German, Spanish and Catalan. *PRACTICE AREAS:* Commercial Litigation; Intellectual Property Law.

ANTHONY RICHARD COLES, born Witney, England, 1944; admitted to the Roll, 1969, England. *Education:* Lancaster Gate College of Law. Winner of City of London Solicitors Company Grotius Prize. *Member:* Law Society. *LANGUAGES:* English and French. *PRACTICE AREAS:* Company Law; Commercial Law.

DAVID ALAN CONNICK, born London, England, August 22, 1956; Admitted to the Roll, 1982, England. *Education:* Clifton College, Bristol; Guildford College of Law. *Member:* Law Society. *LANGUAGES:* English. *PRACTICE AREAS:* Commercial Property.

JANET LAURA ENGELS, born London, England, December 2, 1955; admitted to the Roll, 1980, England. *Education:* London Guildhall University (B.A., 1977); London Guildhall University College of Law. *Member:* Law Society; Solicitors' Benevolent Association. *LANGUAGES:* English and French. *PRACTICE AREAS:* Commercial Property Law.

TILLY HALLIWELL, born The Wirral, Cheshire, England, July 3, 1945; Admitted to the Roll, 1971, England. *Education:* University of Manchester (LL.B., Hons., 1967); Guildford College of Law. *Member:* Law Society. *LANGUAGES:* English and French. *PRACTICE AREAS:* Company Law; Commercial Law; Liquor and Entertainment; Licensing Law.

PHILIP NORMAN HARRIS, born London, England, January 26, 1943; admitted to the Roll, 1970, England. *Education:* Queens University, Belfast (LL.B., 1966); Guildford College of Law. International Lecturer on the use of Trusts in Civil Law countries. *Member:* Law Society. *LANGUAGES:* English. *PRACTICE AREAS:* Personal Finance Law; International Tax Law.

PETER WILLIAM JOHNSON, born Durham, England, July 20, 1952; admitted to the Roll, 1978, England. *Education:* University of Aston, Birmingham (B.Sc. 1973); Chester and Lancaster Gate Colleges of Law. *Member:* Law Society. *LANGUAGES:* English. *PRACTICE AREAS:* Commercial Property Development; Construction Law; Planning Law; Landlord & Tenant.

(This Listing Continued)

DAVID RAYMOND JUDAH, born London, England, February 19, 1956; admitted to the Roll, 1981, England. *Education:* Queen Mary College, University of London (LL.B., 1978); Lancaster Gate College of Law. *Member:* Law Society; Association of Commercial Lawyers, International (Secretary and Treasurer). *LANGUAGES:* English and French. *PRACTICE AREAS:* Company Law; Commercial Law.

ROGER BRYAN LINCOLN, born London, England, November 24, 1938; admitted to the Roll, 1962, England. *Education:* Balliol College, Oxford (M.A., 1959); Chancery Lane College of Law. *Member:* Law Society; British Insurance Law Association (ex-treasurer, 1983-1989); Liveryman, Worshipful Company of Plaisterers; Chairman of Queenhithe Ward Club; London Solicitors Litigation Association; Freeman of the City of London. *LANGUAGES:* English. *PRACTICE AREAS:* Insurance Law and Litigation.

DAVID JOSEPH ELLISON PLATT, born, Hull, England, 1958; Admitted to the Roll, 1982, England. *Education:* University of Oxford (M.A., 1979); Guildford College of Law. *Member:* Law Society. *LANGUAGES:* English and French. *PRACTICE AREAS:* Property Development Law; Planning Law; Environmental Law.

FRANKLIN RICHARD PRICE, born London, England, August 7, 1959; admitted to the Roll, 1984, England. *Education:* London Guildhall University (LL.B., 1981); Chancery Lane College of Law. *Member:* Law Society. *LANGUAGES:* English and French. *PRACTICE AREAS:* Litigation esp. Property; Construction; Landlord & Tenant.

SIMON CHRISTOPHER REES-HOWELL, born London, England, May 2, 1952; admitted to the Roll, 1978, England. *Education:* Highgate School (Head Boy); Lancaster Gate College of Law. *Member:* Law Society. *LANGUAGES:* English. *PRACTICE AREAS:* Defamation and Intellectual Property Litigation.

JULIAN MORGAN SKEENS, born Dovercourt, England, December 26, 1951; admitted to the Roll, 1980, England. Legal Editor: "Disco Club & Leisure International". *Member:* Law Society. *LANGUAGES:* English and French. *PRACTICE AREAS:* Liquor and Gaming Licensing.

PENELOPE ANNE SPENCER, born Ipswich, Suffolk, England, October 19, 1957; admitted to the Roll, 1983, England. *Education:* University of Keele (B.A. (Hons) 1980); Guildford College of Law. *Member:* Law Society. *LANGUAGES:* English and French. *PRACTICE AREAS:* Property Development Law; Planning Law; Environmental Law.

MARK ROBERT SPRAGG, born Leicester, England, April 6, 1957; admitted to the Roll, 1982, England. *Education:* Nottingham Trent University (B.A., 1979); Guildford College of Law. Freeman of the City of London Solicitors Company. *Member:* Law Society; London Solicitors Litigation Association. *LANGUAGES:* English. *PRACTICE AREAS:* Commercial Litigation; Fraud Investigations Law.

PETER STEVENS, born 1948; admitted, 1973, England. *Education:* University of Manchester (LL.B., 1970). Planning Expert, Educational Videos, Television Education Network. *Member:* Law Society; United Kingdom Environmental Law Association. *PRACTICE AREAS:* Town Planning; Corporate Law; Retail; Health; Highways; Purchase; Compensation.

RAMESH KANJI VALA, born Nairobi, Kenya, June 23, 1953; admitted to the Roll, 1979, England. *Education:* London School of Economics (LL.B., 1976); Lancaster Gate College of Law. *Member:* Law Society. *LANGUAGES:* English, French, Gujarati and Swahili. *PRACTICE AREAS:* Commercial Property Law; Property Finance Law; Banking Law.

ANTHONY SCOTLAND GRASSICK WALKER, born Plymouth, England, May 17, 1957; admitted to the Roll, 1985, England. *Education:* Bournemouth University (B.A., 1980); Guilford College of Law. *Member:* Law Society; Union Internationale des Avocats; London Solicitors Litigation Association. *LANGUAGES:* English and French. *PRACTICE AREAS:* Civil Litigation; Company/Commercial; Insolvency.

CLIVE WHITFIELD-JONES, born Denbigh, Wales, December 10, 1949; admitted to the Roll, 1975, England. *Education:* University of Keele (B.A., 1972); Lancaster Gate College of Law. *Member:* Law Society; Royal Automobile Club. (Senior Partner). *LANGUAGES:* English. *PRACTICE AREAS:* Commercial Property Law; Property Finance Law; Banking Law.

CONSULTANT

JEFFREY ISAAC GREEN, born Manchester, England, December 24, 1933; admitted to the Roll, 1958, England. *Education:* London School of Economics (LL.B., 1955). General Editor, "Practical Commercial Precedents"; Contributor, Tolley's "International Tax Planning". *Member:* Law

(This Listing Continued)

Society; International Fiscal Association; International Tax Planning Association. *LANGUAGES:* English, French and German. *PRACTICE AREAS:* Company/Commercial Law; International Tax Structuring Law.

ASSISTANT SOLICITORS

CHARLES BAYNE-JARDINE. *LANGUAGES:* English. *PRACTICE AREAS:* Property Law.

GEORGE BAYNTON. *LANGUAGES:* English. *PRACTICE AREAS:* Property Law.

STELIOS SIMON COUTSAVLIS. *LANGUAGES:* English. *PRACTICE AREAS:* Property Law.

STEPHEN JOHN DANIELS. *LANGUAGES:* English. *PRACTICE AREAS:* Property Law.

JONATHAN METCALF FELL. *LANGUAGES:* English. *PRACTICE AREAS:* Company Law/Commercial Law.

DOMINIQUE S. GARLAND. *LANGUAGES:* English. *PRACTICE AREAS:* Insurance Litigation.

STEVEN WILLIAM GIFFORD. *LANGUAGES:* English. *PRACTICE AREAS:* Leisure Licensing.

ANDREW MCCALLUM. *LANGUAGES:* English. *PRACTICE AREAS:* Commercial Litigation.

ALASTAIR MCCLEAN. *LANGUAGES:* English. *PRACTICE AREAS:* Property Law.

MARK FALCON MILLAR. *LANGUAGES:* English. *PRACTICE AREAS:* Company Law; Commercial Law.

SARAH JANE MITCHELL. *LANGUAGES:* English. *PRACTICE AREAS:* Insurance Litigation.

ANDREW CHRISTOPHER MOORE. *LANGUAGES:* English. *PRACTICE AREAS:* Insurance Litigation.

JOHN RICHARD O'CONNELL. *LANGUAGES:* English and French. *PRACTICE AREAS:* Company; Commercial; Employment.

JANE PARKER. *LANGUAGES:* English. *PRACTICE AREAS:* Commercial Property.

JAMES IAN RICHARDSON. *LANGUAGES:* English. *PRACTICE AREAS:* Insurance Litigation.

KATE WILSON. *LANGUAGES:* English. *PRACTICE AREAS:* Commercial Litigation.

KENNETH WILSON. *LANGUAGES:* English. *PRACTICE AREAS:* Property Law.

LEGAL EXECUTIVES

ANTHONY JOHN BOWN, F.Inst.L.Ex. *LANGUAGES:* English. *PRACTICE AREAS:* Commercial Litigation.

KEVIN CHINNERY. *LANGUAGES:* English. *PRACTICE AREAS:* Commercial Litigation.

NIGEL FROST. *LANGUAGES:* English. *PRACTICE AREAS:* Commercial Litigation.

JONATHAN HEWSTON. *LANGUAGES:* English. *PRACTICE AREAS:* Commercial Litigation.

JAMES HUTTON. *LANGUAGES:* English. *PRACTICE AREAS:* Insurance Litigation.

FLORA MACKINNON. *LANGUAGES:* English. *PRACTICE AREAS:* Private Client, Wills and Trusts.

EILEEN MCMAHON. *LANGUAGES:* English. *PRACTICE AREAS:* Insurance Litigation.

DAVID NEWBY. *LANGUAGES:* English. *PRACTICE AREAS:* Insurance; Litigation.

GRAHAM SCOTT. *LANGUAGES:* English. *PRACTICE AREAS:* Commercial Litigation.

CHRISTOPHER GEORGE TURNER, F.Inst.L.Ex. *LANGUAGES:* English. *PRACTICE AREAS:* Commercial Litigation; Matrimonial; Employment; Insurance Litigation.

JONES, DAY, REAVIS & POGUE

ONE MOUNT STREET
LONDON WIY 5AA, ENGLAND
Telephone: 44-171-493-9361
Cable Address: "Surgoe London W1"
Telecopier: 44-171-493-9666

In Atlanta, Georgia: 3500 One Peachtree Center, 303 Peachtree Street, N.E. Telephone: 404-521-3939. Cable Address: "Attorneys Atlanta". Telex: 54-2711. Telecopier: 404-581-8330.

In Brussels, Belgium: Avenue Louise 480, 7th Floor. B-1050 Brussels. Telephone: 32-2-645-14-11. Telecopier: 32-2-645-14-45.

In Chicago, Illinois: 77 West Wacker. Telephone: 312-782-3939. Telecopier: 312-782-8585.

In Cleveland, Ohio: North Point, 901 Lakeside Avenue. Telephone: 216-586-3939. Cable Address: "Attorneys Cleveland." Telex: 980389. Telecopier: 216-579-0212.

In Columbus, Ohio: 1900 Huntington Center. Telephone: 614-469-3939. Cable Address: "Attorneys Columbus." Telecopier: 614-461-4198.

In Dallas, Texas: 2300 Trammell Crow Center, 2001 Ross Avenue. Telephone: 214-220-3939. Cable Address: "Attorneys Dallas." Telex: 730852. Telecopier: 214-969-5100.

In Frankfurt, Germany: Triton Haus, Bockenheimer Landstrasse 42, 60323 Frankfurt am Main. Telephone: 49-69-9726-3939. Telecopier: 49-69-9726-3993.

In Geneva, Switzerland: 20, rue de Candolle. Telephone: 41-22-320-2339. Telecopier: 41-22-320-1232.

In Hong Kong: 1501 One Exchange Square, 8 Connaught Place. Telephone: 852-2526-6895. Telecopier: 852-2810-5787.

In Irvine, California: 2603 Main Street, Suite 900. Telephone: 714-851-3939. Telex: 194911 Lawyers LSA. Telecopier: 714-553-7539.

In Los Angeles, California: 555 West Fifth Street, Suite 4600. Telephone: 213-489-3939. Telex: 181439 UD. Telecopier: 213-243-2539.

In New York, New York: 599 Lexington Avenue. Telephone: 212-326-3939. Cable Address: "JONESDAY NEWYORK." Telex: 237013 JDRP UR. Telecopier: 212-755-7306.

In Paris, France: 62, rue du Faubourg Saint-Honore. Telephone: 33-1-44-71-3939. Cable Address: "Surgoe Paris." Telex: 290156 Surgoe. Telecopier: 33-1-49-24-0471.

In Pittsburgh, Pennsylvania: 500 Grant Street, 31st Floor. Telephone: 412-391-3939. Cable Address: "Attorneys Pittsburgh". Telecopier: 412-394-7959.

In Riyadh, Saudi Arabia: Law Offices of Saud M.A. Shawwaf, P.O. Box 2700. Telephones: (966-1) 465-6543, (966-1) 464-8534 or (966-1) 464-8540. Telex: 401831 SAUCON SJ. Telecopier: (966-1) 464-8480.

In Taipei, Taiwan: 8th Floor, 2 Tun Hwa South Road, Section 2. Telephone: (886-2) 704-6808. Telecopier: (886-2) 704-6791.

In Tokyo, Japan: Toranomon MT Building, 4th Floor, 10-3, Toranomon 3-Chome, Minato-Ku, Tokyo 105, Japan. Telephone: 81-3-3433-3939. Telecopier: 81-3-5401-2725.

In Washington, D.C.: Metropolitan Square, 1450 G Street, N.W. Telephone: 202-879-3939. Cable Address: "Attorneys Washington." Telex: 89-2410 ATTORNEYS WASH. Telecopier: 202-737-2832.

General and Administrative Practice including International, Corporate, Taxation, Securities, Litigation, Commercial, Arbitration, Creditors' Rights, Bankruptcy, Real Estate, Banking, Estate and Trust Planning.
Firm engaged in American and International Law Practice but not authorized to appear before English Courts or to act as Solicitors.

MEMBERS OF FIRM IN LONDON

HUGH W. CHAPMAN, born Edinburgh, Scotland, May 27, 1945; admitted, 1970, England; 1978, District of Columbia. *Education:* Oxford University, England (B.A., 1967; M.A., 1976); George Washington University (LL.M., 1978).

JERE ROGERS THOMSON, born Somerville, New Jersey, August 9, 1943; admitted, 1970, Pennsylvania; 1977, Ohio; 1981, District of Columbia (Not admitted in England). *Education:* Williams College (A.B., 1965); University of Pennsylvania (J.D., 1968). Order of the Coif. Law Clerk to Judge Weigel, U.S. District Court, Northern District of California, 1968-1969.

STEPHEN E. FIAMMA, born New York, New York, November 23, 1953; admitted, 1979, New York (Not admitted in England). *Education:* Princeton University (A.B., 1975); New York University (J.D., 1978; LL.M., 1982).

JAI S. PATHAK, born Allahabad, India, January 14, 1959; admitted, 1984, Delhi, India; 1985, Ohio (Not admitted in England). *Education:* Delhi

(This Listing Continued)

JONES, DAY, REAVIS & POGUE, London—Continued

University (B.A., 1978); Jawaharlal Nehru University (M.A., 1980); Oxford University (B.A., 1984; M.A., 1989); University of Virginia (LL.M., 1985).

ASSOCIATES

DAVID P. CURTIN, born Buffalo, New York, January 8, 1958; admitted, 1985, Massachusetts; 1989, New York (Not admitted in England). *Education:* Princeton University (A.B., 1980); Boston College (J.D., 1985). Order of the Coif.

ELIZABETH A. OBERLE-ROBERTSON, born New York, New York, March 9, 1963; admitted, 1989, New York (Not admitted in England). *Education:* Johns Hopkins University (B.A., 1984); Oxford University, England (B.A., 1986; M.A., 1990); Yale University (J.D., 1988). Phi Beta Kappa.

JANE D. WESSEL, born Portsmouth, England, July 18, 1957; admitted, 1991, Illinois (Not admitted in England). *Education:* University of Exeter, England (B.A., 1980); Loyola University, Chicago (J.D., 1991).

Languages: English, French, Hindi, Italian.

KENNEDYS

(Solicitors, Registered Foreign Lawyers, Privy Council and International

Law Agents)

LONGBOW HOUSE

14-20 CHISWELL STREET

LONDON EC1Y 4TY, ENGLAND

Telephone: 0171-638-3688

Telex: 886120 Kenedy G

Fax: 0171-638-2212

Associated Offices: Paris, New York, San Francisco, Karachi and Hong Kong

Arbitration, Banking and Finance, Commercial, Company, Construction, Consumer Credit and Debt Recovery, Insurance and Reinsurance, International Trade, Medical Negligence, Personal Injury, Professional Liability and Indemnity, Property, Shipping and Transportation.

PARTNERS

Stephen M. Cantle	Janet Sayers
Richard S. Harris	John D. Yates
David T. Scrutton	*Jennifer M. Hennah
*Nicholas P. G. Thomas	Roderick A.M. Campbell
Ivan N. de C. McCracken	**Gary D. Wadsworth
(Contact Partner)	Michael F.J. Walker
*C. Eric Sumner	Christopher J. Stenning
James Shaw	Andrew S. Coates
Nicholas D. Williams	Gina C. Watson
Iain A.G. Morrison	***Juergen W. Schulze
Timothy J. Wilson	Felicity K. Reynolds
Shane Sayers	Seán T. Craig
Simon J. Gibson	Manoj Vaghela

CONSULTANTS

Sandra Harris
****Jean-Claude Gofard

*Also Admitted in Hong Kong
**Also Admitted in New Zealand
***Also Admitted in Hamburg, Germany
****Avocat (France) and Abogado (Spain)

Corresponds in: English, German, French and Spanish.

KEVORKIAN & PARTNERS

38 HERTFORD STREET
LONDON W1Y 7TG, ENGLAND
Telephone: 0171 355 2051
Fax: 0171 355 4975

Paris, France Office: 46, Avenue d'Iéna, 75116. Telephone: 40.69.50.00. Telecopier: 47.20.54.64.
New York, New York Office: 135 E. 57th Street, 10022. Telephone: (212) 838 5600. Telecopier: (212) 753 6971. Telex: 238725.

(This Listing Continued)

United States and International Law.
Firm engaged in American and International Law Practice, but not authorized to appear before the English Courts or to act as Solicitors.

RESIDENT PARTNER

JAMES A. LOUGHRAN, born 1931; admitted, 1959, New York; 1960, Connecticut (Not admitted in England). *Education:* Fordham University (A.B., 1953); University of Pennsylvania (LL.B., 1958); Columbia University (M.I.A., 1959). Fulbright Scholar, Argentina, 1963. Author: "Some Reflections on the Argentine Problem," Journal of Inter-American Economic Affairs, 1964; "Britain-Banking Capital of the World," 1980. Vice Chairman, National Constructors Association, 1977-1978. *Member:* Law Society of England and Wales as Overseas Lawyer; American Bar Association; Chartered Institute of Arbitrators, London (Associate Member). [1st Lieut., U.S. Marine Corps, 1953-1955]. *LANGUAGES:* Spanish, French and Italian.

ASSOCIATE

KRIS GLEDHILL, born York, England, February 5, 1964; admitted, 1985, Virginia (Not admitted in England). *Education:* University College, Oxford (B.A. Jurisprudence, 1984); University of Virginia (LL.M., 1985).

CONSULTANT

ANTHONY STOKOE, admitted, 1981, England. *Education:* London PCL (B.A., Law, Hons).

KILPATRICK & CODY

Established in 1874

68 PALL MALL
LONDON SW1Y 5ES, ENGLAND
Telephone: (44) (171) 321 0477
Telecopier: (44) (171) 930 9733

Atlanta, Georgia Office: Suite 2800, 1100 Peachtree Street. Telephone: 404-815-6500. Telephone Copier: 404-815-6555. Telex: 54-2307.
Augusta, Georgia Office: Suite 1400, First Union Bank Building, P.O. Box 2043, 30903. Telephone: 706-724-2622. Telecopier: 706-722-0219.
Washington, D.C. Office: Suite 800, 700 13th Street, N.W., 20005. Telephone: 202-508-5800. Telephone Copier: 202-508-5858.
Brussels, Belgium Office: Avenue Louise 65, BTE 3, 1050 Brussels. Telephone: (32) (2) 533-03-00. Telecopier: (32) (2) 534-86-38.

United States and International Law.
Firm engaged in American and International Law Practice.

MEMBERS OF FIRM

KEITH T. OTT, born Atlanta, Georgia, May 16, 1958; admitted, 1983, Georgia (Not admitted in England). *Education:* University of Florida (B.A., with high honors, 1980); Georgetown University (J.D., cum laude, 1983). Phi Beta Kappa; Omicron Delta Kappa; Florida Blue Key. Member, Law and Policy in International Business Journal, 1981-1983. Author: "The Economic Recovery Tax Act, Section 223," 14 Law and Policy in International Business 885, Fall, 1982. *Member:* International Bar Association; Law Society of England and Wales (Overseas Lawyer).

RICHARD PAUL KECK, born London, England, January 19, 1960; admitted, 1985, Georgia (Not admitted in England). *Education:* Emory University (B.S., 1982); Harvard Law School (J.D., cum laude, 1985). Phi Beta Kappa. *Member:* Atlanta and American Bar Associations; State Bar of Georgia.

(For complete biographical data on all personnel, see Professional Biographies at Atlanta, Georgia, Augusta, Georgia, Washington, D.C. and Brussels, Belgium)

KINGSLEY NAPLEY

Solicitors

Established in 1938

KNIGHTS QUARTER
14 ST. JOHN'S LANE
LONDON EC1M 4AJ, ENGLAND
Telephone: 0171 814 1200
Facsimile: 0171 490 2288

Bankruptcy and Insolvency, Business Affairs, Company Law and Shareholders, Company Formation and Acquisition, Crime "White Collar" Fraud, Corruption, General Crime and Motoring, Employment, Entertain-

(This Listing Continued)

ment Artists and Performers, Family, Child Care General, Matrimonial and Wardship, Medical Negligence, Immigration and Nationality, Libel, Slander and Defamation, Liquor, Betting and Gambling, Litigation, Civil and Commercial, Military and Admiralty, Partnerships, Property, Building and Construction, Conveyancing, Housing, Landlord and Tenant, Land Tribunals and Planning, Race and Sex Discrimination, Taxation, Business, Personal, Wills, Trusts and Probate, Regulatory.

FIRM PROFILE: Although internationally known for its work in major cases many of which have media attention, Kingsley Napley remains a widely based general practice devoted to providing quality service over the extensive range of legal work for both individual and corporate clients.

PARTNERS

JOHN CLITHEROE, admitted, 1959. PRACTICE AREAS: Criminal.

FRANCIS WEAVER, admitted, 1968. PRACTICE AREAS: Property.

DAVID SPEKER, admitted, 1969. PRACTICE AREAS: Litigation.

ANTONY SACKER, admitted, 1963. PRACTICE AREAS: Company and Commercial.

CHRISTOPHER MURRAY, admitted, 1972. PRACTICE AREAS: Criminal.

MICHAEL CAPLAN, admitted, 1977. PRACTICE AREAS: Criminal.

PAUL TERZEON, admitted, 1978. PRACTICE AREAS: Litigation.

PAMELA COLLIS, admitted, 1981. PRACTICE AREAS: Family.

STEPHEN POLLARD, admitted, 1985. PRACTICE AREAS: Criminal.

RICHARD OSBORN, admitted, 1980. PRACTICE AREAS: Litigation.

PAUL TILLEY, admitted, 1965. PRACTICE AREAS: Property.

MARC SELBY, admitted, 1979. PRACTICE AREAS: Property.

ADRIAN WHITE, admitted, 1981. PRACTICE AREAS: Property.

RICHARD FOX, admitted, 1986. PRACTICE AREAS: Litigation.

VALERIE KLEANTHOUS, admitted, 1979. PRACTICE AREAS: Family.

JANE KEIR, admitted, 1987. PRACTICE AREAS: Family.

CHRISTINE MARSH, admitted, 1986. PRACTICE AREAS: Medical Negligence.

DEBORAH GEHM, admitted, 1986. PRACTICE AREAS: Regulatory.

KEITH LAWS, admitted, 1975. PRACTICE AREAS: Property.

DAVID SMYTHE, admitted, 1988. PRACTICE AREAS: Litigation.

JOHN HARDING, admitted, 1988. PRACTICE AREAS: Commercial.

JULIA CAHILL, admitted, 1982. PRACTICE AREAS: Medical Negligence.

CLIFFORD KING, admitted, 1972. PRACTICE AREAS: Property.

ASSOCIATES

Camilla Baldwin	Cythia Hunt
Sandra Brown	Jane Ivinson
Lvay Childs	Katherine Reid
Nicholas Greenfield	Michael Statham-Fletcher
Nicholas Hart	Julia Winstone
	Linda Woolley

CONSULTANTS

John Sandler

Languages: French, German and Spanish

KIRKLAND & ELLIS

A Partnership including Professional Corporations

199 BISHOPSGATE

LONDON EC2M 3TY, ENGLAND

Telephone: 171 814 6682

Facsimile: 171 814 6622

Los Angeles, California Office: 300 South Grand Avenue. Telephone: 213-680-8400. Facsimile: (213) 626-0010.

(This Listing Continued)

Denver, Colorado Office: 1999 Broadway. Telephone: 303-292-3000. Facsimile: (303) 291-3300.

Washington, D.C. Office: 655 Fifteenth Street, N.W. Telephone: 202-879-5000. Facsimile: (202) 879-5200.

Chicago, Illinois: 200 East Randolph Drive. Telephone: 312-861-2000. Facsimile: 312-861-2200. Telex: 25-4361.

New York, New York Office: Citicorp Center, 153 East 33rd Street. Telephone: 212-446-4800. Facsimile: 212-446-4900.

General Practice.

RESIDENT PARTNERS

SAMUEL A. HAUBOLD, (P.C.), born Watertown, South Dakota, July 29, 1938; admitted, 1966, Illinois; 1991, New York (Not admitted in England). Education: Northwestern University (J.D., 1960); Harvard Law School (LL.B., 1966). Member: Illinois State, American and International Bar Associations. PRACTICE AREAS: Insurance Coverage; Commercial Litigation.

STUART L. MILLS, born Jackson, Michigan, December 5, 1961; admitted, 1988, Illinois (Not admitted in England). Education: University of Michigan (B.B.A., 1985; M.S.T., Accounting, 1985); University of Chicago (J.D., 1988). PRACTICE AREAS: Corporate; Mergers and Acquisitions; Venture Capital; Securities.

(For Biographical Data on Chicago, Illinois, Washington, D.C., New York, N.Y., Denver, Colorado and Los Angeles, California, see Professional Biographies at those points Respectively).

LADAS & PARRY

HIGH HOLBORN HOUSE

52-54 HIGH HOLBORN

LONDON WCIV 6RR, ENGLAND

Telephone: 44-171-242-5566

Telex: 264255

Telecopy: 44-171-405-1908 (Groups 2 & 3)

Cable Address: "Lawlan London W.C.1"

New York, N.Y. Office: 26 West 61st Street, 10023. Telephone: 212-708-1800. Telex: 233288. Telecopy: 212-246-8959. Cable Address: "Lawlan New York".

Chicago, Illinois Office: 224 South Michigan Avenue, 60604. Telephone: 312-427-1300. Telex: 203649. Telecopy: 312-427-6663; 312-427-6668. Cable Address: "Lawlan Chicago".

Los Angeles, California Office: 5670 Wilshire Boulevard, 90036. Telephone: 213-934-2300. Telex: 240423. Telecopier: 213-934-0202. Cable Address: "LAWLAN LSA".

Munich, Germany Office: Altheimer Eck 2, D-80331 Munich. Telephone: (089) 269077. Fax: (089) 269040. Telex: 5-28474 Lawlan D. Cable Address: "Lawlan Munich".

Patents, Trademarks, Copyright, Licensing, Franchising and Related Practice.

Firm engaged in American and International Law Practice, but not authorized to appear before the English Courts except the Patent County Court, or to act as Solicitors.

Admission to English Patents County Court enables representation in all patent related causes including invalidation and infringement.

PARTNER IN ATTENDANCE

IAIN C. BAILLIE, born Kenmore, Perthshire, Scotland, July 14, 1931; admitted, 1966, New York. Admitted to practice before United Kingdom Patent Office (Not admitted in England except for Patents County Court). Education: Glasgow University (B.Sc., 1953); Fordham University (J.D., 1965).

ASSOCIATES

ANTHONY R. MARTINO, born Foggia, Italy, May 18, 1959; called to the Bar of The Honourable Society of the Inner Temple, 1982. Education: Nottingham University (B.A., 1980); City of London Polytechnic (M.A., 1987).

HUGH R. WOTHERSPOON, born Portsmouth, England, February 19, 1958; admitted, 1985, Solicitor of the Supreme Court of England and Wales. Education: Exeter University (B.Sc., 1981; B.A., 1982); College of Law (Guildford) 1983.

UNITED KINGDOM PATENT AND TRADEMARK AGENTS

(This Listing Continued)

LADAS & PARRY, London—Continued

(OTHER THAN PATENTS COUNTY COURT, NOT ADMITTED TO ENGLISH COURTS)

MARTYN M. MOLYNEAUX, born Chelmsford, Essex, England, August 25, 1944. Admitted to practice before the United Kingdom Patent Office, United Kingdom Trade Marks Registry and European Patent Office. *Education:* Fellow of the Institution of Electrical Engineers, Chelmer Institute (H.N.C. Radio Engineering 1966).

JOHN L. PEARSON, born Hillingdon, Middlesex, England, April 17, 1930. Admitted to practice before the United Kingdom Patent Office, United Kingdom Trade Marks Registry and before European Patent Office. *Education:* University College London (B.Sc. Chemistry (Special) 1953).

CHRISTINE A. SHOLL, born Hillingdon, England. UK Trade Mark Agent; Affiliate Member of the Institute of Trade Mark Agents; Member of the European Communities Trade Mark Practitioners Association.

(For biographical data of the New York personnel, see Professional Biographies at New York, New York)
(For biographical data of the Chicago personnel, see Professional Biographies at Chicago, Illinois)
(For biographical data of the Los Angeles personnel, see Professional Biographies at Los Angeles, California)
(For biographical data of the Munich personnel, see Professional Biographies at Munich, Germany)

LAGERLÖF & LEMAN

ROYEX HOUSE
ALDERMANBURY SQUARE
LONDON EC2V 7HR, ENGLAND
Telephone: Int. 44-171-606 1715
Telefax: Int. 44-171-600 1718

Stockholm, Sweden Office: Strandvägen 7A, P.O. Box 5402, S-114 84, Stockholm. Telephone: Int. 46-8-665 66 00. Telefax: Int. 46-8-667 68 83. Telex: 17715 Laglaw S.
Gothenburg, Sweden Office: Västra Hamngatan 24, P.O. Box 2252, S-403 14, Gothenburg. Telephone: Int. 46-31-17 10 00. Telefax: Int. 46-31-13 56 62. Telefax Maritime department: Int. 46-31-11 65 37.
Malmö, Sweden Office: Stortorget 8, S-211 34, Malmö. Telephone: Int. 46-40-704 50. Telefax: Int. 46-40-97 19 17.
Berlin, Germany Office: Meinekestrasse 13, D-10719 Berlin. Telephone: Int. 49-30-884 710. Telefax: Int. 49-30-882 4852.
Paris, France Office: 87 Avenue Kléber, F-75116 Paris. Telephone: 33-1-45 05 1208. Telefax: 33-1-47 55 0975.
New York, N.Y. Office: 712 Fifth Avenue, 30th Floor, New York, N.Y. 10019-4102 U.S.A. Telephone: Int. 1-212-801-3450. Telefax: Int. 1-212-801-3455.

Corporate and Commercial law, including Tax, Banking, Financing, Insurance, Real Estate, Computer, Patent, Trademark, Copyright, Labor, Trade Regulation and Antitrust Law. International Legal Transactions. Arbitration and Litigation in Civil Matters. EC Law. International Private Law. Maritime and Admiralty Law.
Member of Alliance of European Lawyers (EEIG).

PARTNERS

PER RUNELAND, born Kalmar, Sweden, 1942. *Education:* Wharton School, University of Pennsylvania, USA (B.S. in Economics, 1963); University of Uppsala (filosofie kandidat, M.A., 1969; juris kandidat, LL.M., 1969). *Author:* Chapter for Sweden in "Legal Aspects of Doing Business in Europe," Kluwer. *Member:* Swedish and International Bar Associations. *LANGUAGES:* Swedish, English, German, French and Russian. *PRACTICE AREAS:* General Commercial Law (including East-West Trade); International Arbitration; Litigation.

BERTIL OLGÅRD, born Hörby, Sweden, 1947. *Education:* University of Lund (juris kandidat, LL.M., 1974). Service with Swedish Courts; Judgeship Court of Appeal, 1977-1978. *Member:* Swedish and International Bar Associations. *LANGUAGES:* Swedish and English. *PRACTICE AREAS:* General Commercial Law; Corporate Law; Banking and Finance.

ASSOCIATES

EVA-LOTTA NILSSON, born Södertälje, Sweden, 1961. *Education:* University of Uppsala (LL.M., 1986). *Member:* Swedish Bar Association. *LANGUAGES:* Swedish, English and French. *PRACTICE AREAS:* General Commercial Law; Intellectual Property Law; Corporate Law.

(This Listing Continued)

JARL MATTSSON, born Lund, Sweden, 1962. *Education:* Kingston University (Diploma in English Law, 1988); University of Lund (juris kandidat, LL.M., 1988); Columbia University (Diploma in American Law, 1989); Vrije Universiteit, Brussels (Master of International and Comparative Law, LL.M., 1990); ICRC (Diploma in International and Humanitarian Law, 1991). Service with Swedish Courts. Legal Affairs, European Free Trade Association, Geneva, 1990-1991; Legal and Constitutional Affairs, Commonwealth Secretariat, London, 1993. *LANGUAGES:* Swedish, English and French. *PRACTICE AREAS:* General Commercial Law; Common Market Law; International Trade.

LANE & MITTENDORF

Established in 1952

24 QUEEN ANNE'S GATE
LONDON SW1H 9AA, ENGLAND
Telephone: 0171 233-1849
Telecopier: 0171 233-1850

New York, New York Office: 99 Park Avenue. Telephone: 212-972-3000. Cable Address: "Calamit", New York. Telecopier: 212-972-5647; 972-5663.
Washington, D.C. Office: 919 18th Street, N.W. Telephone: 202-785-4949. Cable Address: "Calamit" Telecopiers: 202-785-5351; 466-5289. Telex: 440087.
West Palm Beach, Florida Office: 811 North Olive Avenue. Telephone: 407-832-6966.
Edison, New Jersey Office: 499 Thornall Street. Telephones: 908-494-5100; 212-984-5600. Telecopier: 908-494-7271.

General Practice.

MEMBERS OF FIRM

THOMAS A. HARNETT, born New York, N.Y., March 22, 1924; admitted, 1949, New York (Not admitted in England). *Education:* Fordham University (LL.B., 1949). Superintendent of Insurance of State of New York, 1975-1977. Regent, University of Hartford, 1980-1983. *Member:* New York State (Chairman, Insurance Negligence Law Section, 1974-1975; Member, House of Delegates, 1974-1975) and American (Member of Council, 1969-1976 and Chairman, 1975-1976, Insurance, Negligence and Compensation Law Section) Bar Associations; International Association of Defense Counsel (Vice President, 1982-1984); Federation of Insurance and Corporate Counsel. Fellow: International Academy of Trial Lawyers; American Bar Foundation; New York State Bar Foundation. (Also in New York, N.Y. Office).

JOHN W. MCGRATH, born Brooklyn, New York, July 25, 1932; admitted, 1960, New York; 1974, District of Columbia (Not admitted in England). *Education:* Williams College (A.B., 1954); New York Law School (J.D., 1959). Research Counsel, New York State Constitutional Convention, 1967-1968. Advisor to members, 1969 U.S. Presidential Mission for the Western Hemisphere headed by Nelson A. Rockefeller. *Member:* The District of Columbia Bar; The Association of the Bar of the City of New York; New York State Bar Association. (Also in New York, N. Y. Office).

DAVID ORLIN, born Albany, New York, November 16, 1926; admitted, 1950, New York (Not admitted in England). *Education:* Syracuse University (A.B., 1947); Harvard University (LL.B., 1950). Phi Beta Kappa. *Member:* The Association of the Bar of the City of New York; New York State and American Bar Associations. (Also in New York, N. Y. Office).

(For biographical data on other personnel, see Professional Biographies at New York, New York, Edison, New Jersey, Washington, D.C. and West Palm Beach, Florida)

LANE & PARTNERS

46/47 BLOOMSBURY SQUARE
LONDON WC1A 2RU, ENGLAND
Telephone: 0171-242-2626
Telefax: 0171-242-0387
Telex: 8812495 LANLAW G

New York, New York: Marks & Murase, 399 Park Avenue, 10022-4689. Telephone: (212) 318-7700.
Washington, D.C.: Marks & Murase, Suite 750, 2001 L Street, N.W., 20036-4910. Telephone: (202) 955-4900.
Los Angeles, California: Marks & Murase, Wells Fargo Center, Suite 1570, 333 South Grand Avenue, 90071. Telephone: (213) 620-9690.

(This Listing Continued)

Brussels, Belgium: Vandemeulebroeke, Marc F., De Backer & Associes, Boulevard Brand Whitlock 30, 1200. Telephone: 32 (2) 735.00.43.

Düsseldorf, Germany: Bellstedt & Partner, Ross-Str, 130, D-476 Düsseldorf, Telephone: 49 (211) 4709001. Fax: 49 (211) 4543102.

Hamburg, Germany: Kreye & Kreye, Fontenay-Allee 12, 20354. Telephone: 49 (40) 44 73 95/96.

Mexico City, Mexico: De Villafranca Y De Villafranca, A.C., Avenida de la Paz, 23, San Angel-Villa Obregon, 01000 Mexico D.F. Telephone: 52 (5) 550-7611.

Milan, Italy: Studio Legale Gilioli, Piazzale Principessa Clotilde, 8, 20121. Telephone: 39 (2) 2900 2932.

Oslo, Norway: Stabell Tellman Strom Elde, Advotkatfirma DA MNA, Haakon VII's gate 2, P.O. Box 1364 Vika N-0114. Telephone: 47 (22) 838360.

Paris, France: Salans Hertzfeld & Heilbronn, 9, Rue Boissy d'Anglas, 75008. Telephone: 33 (1) 42.68.48.00.

Seoul, Korea: Min, Sohn & Kim, 723-2, Yoksam 2-dong, Kangnam-ku, Seoul 135-082. Telephone: 82 (2) 564-3320/6.

Stockholm, Sweden: Advokatfirman Landahl, Cardellgatan 1, P.O. Box 5209, S-102 45. Telephone: 46 (8) 666 67 00.

Tokyo, Japan: Asahi Law Offices (Masuda & Ejiri - Tokyo Yaesu) 7th (Reception) and 8th Floors, New ATT Bldg. 11-7, Akasaka 2-Chome, Minato-ku, Tokyo 107. Telephone: 81 (3) 3505-0003.

Toronto, Ontario, Canada: Fasken Campbell Godfrey, Toronto Dominion Bank Tower, P.O. Box 20, Toronto Dominion Centre, M5K 1N6. Telephone: (416) 366-8381. Lahore, Pakistan: Cornelius Lane and Hujbi, Nawa-I-Waqt House 4 Fabina Jinnah Road, Lahore 5400 Pakistan. Telephone: 010 92 62 6360868 or 6306301. Fax: 010 92 42 6303301.

FIRM PROFILE: Lane & Partners forms part of an international association consisting of lawyers from each of the firms listed above. This international association enables the firm to provide a broadly based international service to its corporate clients.

Our lawyers are well versed in international business practices and are skilled in working with clients of different cultures, customs and languages.

PARTNERS

TERENCE M. LANE, born Mussooree, India, October 5, 1918; admitted 1953, (Solicitor Honours, 1953) Solicitor of Supreme Court of England and Wales. *Education:* University of London (B.A., 1940); University of Indiana; Law Society's School of Law Formerly District Judge, Tanganyika Territory (Tanzania). *Member:* Law Society of England and Wales; International Bar Association; British Institute of International and Comparative Law; International Fiscal Association; Institute of Trade Mark Agents. Fellow of the Chartered Institute of Arbitrators. *PRACTICE AREAS:* International Arbitration; Construction Law.

RICHARD E. HARDMAN, admitted 1964, Solicitor of the Supreme Court of England and Wales (Solicitor Honours, 1963) *Education:* Oxford University (B.A., 1960; M.A., 1962); The College of Law. *Member:* Law Society of England and Wales. *PRACTICE AREAS:* Property Law.

KEITH S. GALLON, admitted, 1970, Solicitor of the Supreme Court of England and Wales. *Education:* Leeds University (B.A., 1966); The College of Law. *Member:* Law Society of England and Wales. *PRACTICE AREAS:* Company Law; Commercial Law.

WILLIAM S. MORTON, admitted 1973, Solicitor of the Supreme Court of England and Wales. *Education:* Oxford University (B.A., 1970); The College of Law. *Member:* Law Society of England and Wales. *PRACTICE AREAS:* Company Law; Commercial Law.

MICHAEL VARVILL, admitted 1974, Solicitor of the Supreme Court of England and Wales. *Education:* London University (LL.B., 1976); The College of Law. *Member:* Law Society of England and Wales; Institute of Trade Mark Agents; Chartered Institute of Arbitrators (Associate). *PRACTICE AREAS:* Litigation; Intellectual Property; Competition Law.

RICHARD W. VENABLES, admitted, 1971, Solicitor of Supreme Court of England and Wales. *Education:* Oxford University (B.A., 1968); The College of Law. *Member:* Law Society of England and Wales; Chartered Institute of Transport; Royal Aeronautical Society (Associate). *PRACTICE AREAS:* Aviation Law; Travel Law.

LUDOVIC A.P. DE WALDEN, admitted 1978, Solicitor of Supreme Court of England and Wales. *Education:* Durham University (B.A., 1973); Johns Hopkins University School of Advanced International Studies (Fellowship 1973/74). The College of Law. *Member:* Law Society of England

(This Listing Continued)

and Wales; Chartered Institute of Arbitrators (Associate) ; Solicitors European Group. *LANGUAGES:* French, Italian and Polish. *PRACTICE AREAS:* International Litigation; Arbitration.

MARK P. BARBER, admitted, 1975, Solicitor of the Supreme Court of England and Wales. *Education:* University of Warwick (LL.B., Hons.). *Member:* Law Society of England and Wales. *PRACTICE AREAS:* Property Law.

Q.M. PIERS LANE, admitted 1982, Solicitor of the Supreme Court of England and Wales. *Education:* Dundee University (M.A., 1975); The College of Law. *Member:* Law Society of England and Wales. *PRACTICE AREAS:* Commercial Litigation.

COLIN M.S. HALL, admitted, 1982, Solicitor of the Supreme Court of England and Wales. *Education:* University of Southampton (LL.B., Hons., 1978); The College of Law. *Member:* Law Society of England and Wales. *PRACTICE AREAS:* Construction Law; Litigation; Arbitration.

NICHOLAS LIGHTBODY, admitted, 1987, Solicitor of the Supreme Court of England and Wales. *Education:* University of Sussex (B.A., Honours, 1976); College of Law (C.P.E. and Solicitors Finals, 1985). Member: Law Society of England and Wales, 1983; United Kingdom Environmental L aw Association, 1992. Fellow, Royal Society for the Encouragement of Arts (RSA), 1994. *Member:* Law Society Yacht Club (Treasurer, 1990—). *PRACTICE AREAS:* Commercial Property Law; Insolvency; Environmental Law.

ASSOCIATES

MARTIN R.C. MOYES, born London, England, May 10, 1930; admitted 1979, Solicitor of the Supreme Court of England and Wales. *Education:* Eton College; City of London Polytechnic (M.A., 1982). *Member:* Law Society of England and Wales; The Competition Law Association; European Food Law Association; The Industrial Law Society. *LANGUAGES:* French. *PRACTICE AREAS:* EEC Law; Labor Law.

ROBIN J. SPRINGTHORPE, admitted, 1989, Solicitor of the Supreme Court of England and Wales. *Education:* University of Oxford (B.A., Oxon); The College of Law. *Member:* The Law Society. *PRACTICE AREAS:* International Litigation; Arbitration.

NIGEL MARTIN EDWARDS, admitted, 1991, Solicitor of the Supreme Court of England and Wales. *Education:* University of Manchester (LL.B., Hons.); The College of Law. *Member:* The Law Society of England and Wales. *PRACTICE AREAS:* Company Law; Commercial Law.

SANDRA ANNETTE BOOYSEN, Admitted, 1994, Solicitor of the Supreme Court of England and Wales. Education: Rhodes University, South Africa (B.A., 1986); University of de Witwatersrand, South Africa (LL.B., with distinction, 1988); The College of Law. *Member:* La w Society of England and Wales. *PRACTICE AREAS:* Commercial Litigation.

R. COLIN KEEL, admitted, 1989, Pennsylvania (Not admitted in England). *Education:* Commonwealth of Pennsylvania (J.D., 1989); Muhlenberg College (B.A., summa cum laude, Phi Beta Kappa, 1986). *Member:* American Bar Association. *LANGUAGES:* Spanish. *PRACTICE AREAS:* Aviation and Travel Law; Litigation.

LANE POWELL SPEARS LUBERSKY

A Partnership including Professional Corporations

MITRE HOUSE
12-14 MITRE STREET
LONDON EC 3A 5BU, ENGLAND
Telephone: 0171-621-9054
Telecopier: 0171-623-8720

Anchorage, Alaska Office: Suite 1650, 550 West Seventh Avenue. Telephone: 907-277-9511. Telecopier: 907-276-2631. Cable Address: "Arctic Law".

Mount Vernon, Washington Office: 325 Pine Street Plaza, Suite B. Telephone: 206-336-9595. Telecopier: 206-336-5845.

Olympia, Washington Office: Evergreen Plaza Building, 711 Capitol Way. Telephone: 206-754-6001. Telecopier: 206- 754-1605.

Seattle, Washington Office: 1420 Fifth Avenue, Suite 4100. Telephone: 206-223-7000. Cable Address: "Embre". Telex: 32-8808. Telecopier: 206- 223-7107.

(This Listing Continued)

LANE POWELL SPEARS LUBERSKY, London—
Continued

Portland, Oregon Office: 520 S.W. Yamhill Street, Suite 800. Telephone: 503-226-6151. Telecopier: 503- 224-0388.
Los Angeles, California Office: 333 South Hope Street, Suite 2400. Telephone: 213-680-1010. Telecopier: 213- 680-1784.
San Francisco, California Office: 2 Embarcadero Center, Suite 2330, 94111. Telephone: 415-421-8624. Telecopier: 415-421-8625.

General Practice and Litigation in Federal and State Courts and before Federal and State Administrative Tribunals. Admiralty and Maritime, Alternative Dispute Resolution, Antitrust, Appellate Practice, Aviation, Banking and Financial Institutions, Bankruptcy and Reorganizations, Communications and Media Law, Construction and Engineering, Corporate and Corporate Finance, Emerging Companies, Employee Benefits, Environmental, Forest Products and Natural Resources, Hospital and Healthcare, Immigration, Insurance, Intellectual Property and Computer Law, International Transactions, Labor Relations and Employment Law, Municipal Law and Municipal Finance, Public Utility and Energy Law, Real Estate and Land Use, Retailing, Securities, Taxation, Toxic Torts, Transportation, Trusts and Estates, Venture Capital, White Collar Criminal Law.

(For complete biographical data on personnel at Anchorage, Alaska, Los Angeles and San Francisco, California, Portland, Oregon, Mt. Vernon, Olympia and Seattle, Washington, see Professional Biographies at those locations)

LATHAM & WATKINS

ONE ANGEL COURT
LONDON EC2R 7HJ, ENGLAND
Telephone: +-44-171-374 4444
Telecopier: +-44-171-374 4460

Los Angeles, California Office: 633 West Fifth Street, Suite 4000, 90071. Telephone: 213-485-1234. Telecopier: 213-891-8763.
Costa Mesa, California Office: Suite 2000, 650 Town Center Drive, 92626-1918. Telephone: 714-540-1235. Telecopier: 714-755-8290.
San Diego, California Office: Suite 2100, 701 B Street, 92101-8197. Telephone: 619-238-1234. Telecopier: 619-238-2895.
San Francisco, California Office: 505 Montgomery Street, Suite 1900, 94111. Telephone: 415-391-0600. Fax: 415-395-8095.
Washington, D.C. Office: Suite 1300, 1001 Pennsylvania Avenue, N.W., 20004. Telephone: 202-637-2200. Telecopier: 202-637-2201.
Chicago, Illinois Office: Suite 5800 Sears Tower, 60606. Telephone: 312-876-7700. Telecopier: 312-993-9767.
Newark, New Jersey Office: One Newark Center. Telephone: 201-639-1234. Fax: 201-639-7298.
New York, N.Y. Office: Suite 1000, 885 Third Avenue, 10022-4802. Telephone: 212-906-1200. Telecopier: 212-751-4864.
Moscow, Russia Office: Suite C200, 113/1 Leninsky Prospeckt, 117198. Telephone: +-7 503 956-5555. Fax: +-7 503 956-5556.
Warsaw, Poland Office: St. Szpitalna 1, Suite 49, 9th Floor, 00-018. Telephone: +-48-2-227-9610. Telecopier: +-48-2-227-9610. Hong Kong Office: 11th Floor Central Building, Number One Pedder Street, Central Hong Kong. Telephone: 011-852-841-7779. Fax: 011-852-841-7749.

RESIDENT PARTNERS

WILLIAM A. LONG, born Cincinnati, Ohio, May 27, 1937; admitted, 1967, California; 1978, District of Columbia (Not admitted in England). *Education:* Xavier University (A.B., magna cum laude, 1959); University of Pennsylvania (M.B.A., 1961); Boston College (J.D., magna cum laude, 1967). Order of the Coif. Member, Board of Editors, Boston College Law Review, 1966-1967. Deputy Under Secretary of Defense (Acquisition Management), 1981-1983. *Member:* Los Angeles County (Member, Public Contracts Section), Federal and American Bar Associations; District of Columbia Bar; State Bar of California. (Also at Warsaw, Poland Office).

JOSEPH BLUM, born Philadelphia, Pennsylvania, May 5, 1957; admitted, 1982, District of Columbia (Not admitted in England). *Education:* Wesleyan University (B.A., magna cum laude, 1979); University of Michigan (J.D., cum laude, 1982). Phi Beta Kappa; Order of the Coif. Senior Editor, Michigan Yearbook of International Legal Studies, 1981-1982. Special Assistant, Hon. William H. Webster, Director, Federal Bureau of Investigation, 1983-1985. Fellow, Robert Bosch Foundation, Germany, 1985-1986. *Member:* District of Columbia Bar; German-American Legal Association.

(This Listing Continued)

DENNIS B. NORDSTROM, born Camp LeJune, North Carolina, February 14, 1961; admitted, 1986, California (Not admitted in England). *Education:* College of William & Mary (B.B.A., 1983); Pepperdine University; University of Virginia (J.D., 1986). *Member:* State Bar of California; American Bar Association. (Also at Warsaw, Poland Office).

ASSOCIATES

SHEILA M. HOPKINS, born Utica, New York, June 24, 1959; admitted, 1987, New York; 1988, District of Columbia (Not admitted in England). *Education:* Harvard University (A.B., magna cum laude, 1981); University of Cape Town, South Africa (M.A., cum laude, 1983); University of Pennsylvania (J.D., 1985). Phi Beta Kappa. Author: "An Analysis of U.S.-South African Relations in the 1980's: Has Engagement Been Constructive?" 7 Journal of Comparative Business and Capital Market Law 89-115, 1985. Law Clerk to the Honorable Richard J. Cardamone, Second Circuit Court of Appeals, 1985-1986. *Member:* New York State and American Bar Associations; The District of Columbia Bar; Bar Association of the District of Columbia. (Resident).

KAREN A. CONNOLLY, born New York, N.Y., March 5, 1961; admitted, 1986, California (Not admitted in England). *Education:* University of Delaware (B.S., magna cum laude, 1983); University of California, Hastings College of the Law (J.D., cum laude, 1986). *Member:* Los Angeles County and American Bar Associations; State Bar of California. (Resident).

GEORGE VAN KULA III, born Bainbridge, Maryland, August 28, 1963; admitted, 1988, California (Not admitted in England). *Education:* University of Notre Dame (B.A., cum laude, 1985); University of Michigan (J.D., cum laude, 1988). *Member:* Los Angeles County and American Bar Associations; State Bar of California. (Resident).

KENNETH A. SCHUHMACHER, born Trenton, New Jersey, September 3, 1965; admitted, 1992, California; 1994, District of Columbia (Not admitted in England). *Education:* Dartmouth College (A.B., summa cum laude, 1987); University of Michigan (J.D., cum laude, 1990); Cambridge University (LL.M., with high honors, 1991). Phi Beta Kappa. *Member:* State Bar of California; District of Columbia Bar. (Also at Washington, D.C. Office).

(For biographical data on Los Angeles, California, Costa Mesa, California, San Diego, California, San Francisco, California, Washington, D.C., Chicago, Illinois, New York, New York, Moscow, Russia, Warsaw, Poland and Hong Kong personnel, see Professional Biographies at each of those cities)

LAWRENCE GRAHAM

Established in 1730

190, STRAND
LONDON WC2R 1JN, ENGLAND
Telephone: (0171) 379 0000
Fax: (0171) 379 6854
Tlx: 22673 LAWGRA G

Other London, England Office: 1, Seething Lane, EC3N 4AX. Telephone: (0171) 481 8361. Fax: (0171) 480 5156. Tlx: 887133 JURIST G.
New York, N.Y. Office: 575 Madison Avenue, 10022-2585. Telephone: (212) 940 6500.
New York Associated Office: Rosenman & Colin.
Hamburg Associated Office: Esche Schümann Commichau.
Antwerp Associated Office: Puelinckx Schiltz Linden Grolig.
Brussels Associated Office: Geater & Co.; Puelinckx Schiltz Linden Grolig.
Stockholm Associated Office: Gedda & Ekdahl.
Paris Associated Office: Lafarge Flécheux Revuz.

Lawrence Graham is a major London based commercial practice, established in 1730, with approximately 180 Lawyers. It operates through six departments - Company and Commercial, Commercial Real Estate, Litigation, Tax, Shipping and Private Client. It is well known for its commercial expertise, insurance and financially related work. It has a well established client base both in the UK and in North America. Also it has specializations in European Community law and experience in conducting business in Eastern Europe and Russia. It is a founding member of ABLE (Associated Business Lawyers in Europe). The firm is recognized for its ability in UK stock exchange and Investment Trust work.

PARTNERS

GAVIN PURSER, admitted, 1963. (Senior Partner and Head of Shipping Department). **PRACTICE AREAS:** Shipping; Litigation.

(This Listing Continued)

MICHAEL RICHARDSON, admitted, 1957. (Head of Corporate Department). *PRACTICE AREAS:* Corporate; International.

CHARLES WILKINSON, admitted, 1969. *PRACTICE AREAS:* Corporate; Stock Exchange.

HUGH HAMILTON, admitted, 1963. (Head of Private Client Department). *PRACTICE AREAS:* Private Client; Probate.

SIMON RANDALL, C.B.E., admitted, 1968. *PRACTICE AREAS:* Local Government.

MARTYN GOWAR, admitted, 1970. (Head of Tax Department). *PRACTICE AREAS:* Taxation.

CHARLES OUIN, admitted, 1973. *PRACTICE AREAS:* Corporate; Commercial.

MICHAEL EDWARDS, admitted, 1971. (Head of Litigation Department). *PRACTICE AREAS:* Insurance; Reinsurance; Personal Injury; Litigation.

PAUL KINSELLA, admitted, 1974. *PRACTICE AREAS:* Commercial Real Estate.

GEOFFREY PICKERILL, admitted, 1973. *PRACTICE AREAS:* Corporate; Venture Capital; MBO's.

ALASDAIR NICHOLSON, admitted, 1963. *PRACTICE AREAS:* Private Client; Conveyancing.

JOHN CRAIG, admitted, 1973. *PRACTICE AREAS:* Real Estate; Environmental.

MICHAEL DUFFY, admitted, 1977. (Head of Commercial Real Estate Department). *PRACTICE AREAS:* Real Estate.

MICHAEL LAX, admitted, 1977. *PRACTICE AREAS:* Shipping; Litigation.

ROBERT SMITH, admitted, 1977. *PRACTICE AREAS:* Corporate; Pensions.

ROGER COOPER, admitted, 1981. *PRACTICE AREAS:* Shipping; Litigation.

PAUL WALKER, admitted, 1976. *PRACTICE AREAS:* Corporate; Banking.

CHRISTOPHER CREAGH BROWN, admitted, 1971. *PRACTICE AREAS:* Litigation; Matrimonial.

TIM THORNTON JONES, admitted, 1974. *PRACTICE AREAS:* Taxation.

RICHARD WOOD, admitted, 1974. *PRACTICE AREAS:* Private Client; Capital Taxes.

BILL RICHARDS, admitted, 1976. *PRACTICE AREAS:* Commercial Litigation.

CLIVE INCE, admitted, 1980. *PRACTICE AREAS:* Litigation; Insurance.

MICHAEL SMYTH, admitted, 1979. *PRACTICE AREAS:* Corporate; Commercial.

ROGER BENSON, admitted, 1981. *PRACTICE AREAS:* Commercial Real Estate.

JOHN VERRILL, admitted, 1981. *PRACTICE AREAS:* Corporate Insolvency; Mergers and Acquisitions.

MICHAEL STORAR, admitted, 1980. *PRACTICE AREAS:* Corporate; Stock Exchange.

ANDREW DOBSON, admitted, 1980. *PRACTICE AREAS:* Commercial Litigation.

NICHOLAS NARRAWAY, admitted, 1982. *PRACTICE AREAS:* Corporate.

BRUCE MANFORD, admitted, 1981. *PRACTICE AREAS:* Corporate; Stock Exchange.

JOHN GRAHAM, admitted, 1980. *PRACTICE AREAS:* Litigation; Insurance; Personal Injury.

CATHERINE PERCY, admitted, 1983. *PRACTICE AREAS:* Litigation; Insurance; Construction.

ROBERT FIELD, admitted, 1981. *PRACTICE AREAS:* Taxation; Corporate; VAT.

(This Listing Continued)

TONY ELLIOTT, admitted, 1976. *PRACTICE AREAS:* Real Estate; Development Planning; Environmental.

DAVID BARNES, admitted, 1977. *PRACTICE AREAS:* Real Estate.

DAVID HAYWARD, admitted, 1978. *PRACTICE AREAS:* Real Estate.

ANDREW HORT, admitted, 1980. *PRACTICE AREAS:* Litigation; Insurance.

IMOGEN RUMBOLD, admitted, 1988. *PRACTICE AREAS:* Shipping; Litigation.

NICK HEATHER, admitted, 1985. *PRACTICE AREAS:* Corporate; Stock Exchange.

PAM ISAACS, admitted, 1982. *PRACTICE AREAS:* Commercial Litigation.

VICKI JORDAN, admitted, 1984. *PRACTICE AREAS:* Insurance Litigation.

PENNY FRANCIS, admitted, 1984. *PRACTICE AREAS:* Property Litigation.

ELIZABETH CARR, admitted, 1955. *PRACTICE AREAS:* Insurance Litigation.

ROBERT CLIFFORD HOLMES, admitted, 1980. *PRACTICE AREAS:* Real Estate.

RICHARD ELPHICK, admitted, 1984. *PRACTICE AREAS:* Corporate; Banking.

ANDREW WADE, admitted, 1984. *PRACTICE AREAS:* Real Estate.

TREVOR BLANEY, admitted, 1977. *PRACTICE AREAS:* Real Estate; Planning; Environmental.

STEPHEN TURNER, admitted, 1982. *PRACTICE AREAS:* Commercial Real Estate; Environmental.

NEIL EVERATT, admitted, 1983. *PRACTICE AREAS:* Shipping; Litigation.

ANTHONY THOMPSON, admitted, 1985. *PRACTICE AREAS:* Taxation.

JONATHAN RILEY, admitted, 1985. *PRACTICE AREAS:* Media; Energy Law; Facilities Management; Commercial Contracts.

ALAN HART, admitted, 1981. *PRACTICE AREAS:* Construction; Litigation.

JEFFREY G. ELWAY, admitted, 1985. *PRACTICE AREAS:* Corporate; Stock Exchange.

ROBERT WALKER, admitted, 1981. *PRACTICE AREAS:* Shipping Litigation; Finance.

CONSULTANTS

COLIN PRESTIGE. PRACTICE AREAS: Private Client; Trust.

MICHAEL ORR. PRACTICE AREAS: Insurance Litigation; Personal Injury.

PAUL QUESTIER. PRACTICE AREAS: Real Estate.

JOHN WALL, C.B.E. *PRACTICE AREAS:* Litigation.

JAMES MACKINTOSH. PRACTICE AREAS: Investment Trust.

EMILE KANAAN (Middle East Consultant).

Languages: French, German, Spanish, Italian, Dutch, Russian, Arabic/Hebrew, Chinese, Hindi, Latin, Polish, Punjabi and Malay

LAWRENCE JONES

Established in 1905

SEA CONTAINERS HOUSE
20 UPPER GROUND
BLACKFRIARS BRIDGE
LONDON SE1 9LH, ENGLAND
Telephone: 0171-620-1311
Telex: 886804 Lawrence G
Fax: 0171-620-0860

Property, Banking, Company and Commercial, Transport, Litigation, International Finance and Trade, Intellectual Property, Entertainment Law, Aviation, Sports Law.

MEMBERS OF FIRM

MICHAEL R. WAUGH. PRACTICE AREAS: Commercial Property; Sports Law.

MICHAEL KEMLO. PRACTICE AREAS: Commercial Law; Transport; Litigation.

JOHN MASTERS. PRACTICE AREAS: Company/Property; Commercial Law.

MICHAEL J. OFFER. LANGUAGES: French and German. **PRACTICE AREAS:** Company/Commercial; Aviation.

MICHAEL C. E. CONAGHAN. PRACTICE AREAS: Banking; Commercial Property; Insolvency.

LYNDSAY R. BROWN. PRACTICE AREAS: Banking; Property; Trust; Probate.

DAVID N. SMETS. PRACTICE AREAS: Litigation.

COLIN D. CLARK. PRACTICE AREAS: Commercial Property.

NICOLA A. FINCHAM. PRACTICE AREAS: Company/Commercial; Financial Instruments; Securities.

PETER B. SPARK. LANGUAGES: French. **PRACTICE AREAS:** Company/Commercial; Employment; Intellectual Property; European Community Law.

NEIL R. MEAKIN. PRACTICE AREAS: Banking/Litigation.

RICHARD V. HOWARD. PRACTICE AREAS: Company/Commercial; Entertainment Law; Intellectual Property.

ASSOCIATES

SUSAN B. FLETCHER. LANGUAGES: French. **PRACTICE AREAS:** Litigation.

MOHINDER K. CHIMA. LANGUAGES: Punjabi and Hindi. **PRACTICE AREAS:** Banking; Property; Trust; Probate.

JEREMY C.D. BURKE. PRACTICE AREAS: Commercial Property.

ANNETTE M. NEWPORT. LANGUAGES: German. **PRACTICE AREAS:** Company/Commercial; Aviation.

NEIL G. GORDON. PRACTICE AREAS: Property.

ANDREW S. GOLDSMITH. PRACTICE AREAS: Litigation; Banking.

LAYTONS

Solicitors and Privy Council Agents

CARMELITE
50 VICTORIA EMBANKMENT
BLACKFRIARS
LONDON EC4Y 0LS, ENGLAND
Telephone: 0171-842 8000
Fax: 0171-842 8080
LIX: LON140
DX: 253 Chancery Lane

Principal Offices:
Bristol, England Office: Saint Bartholomew's, Lewins Mead, Bristol BS1 2NH. Telephone: 0117 929 1626. Fax: 0117 929 3369.
Manchester, England Office: Sunlight House, Quay Street, Manchester M3 3LD. Telephone: 0161 834 2100. Fax: 0161 834 6862.
Surrey, England Office: 76 Bridge Road, Hampton Court, East Molesey, Surrey KT8 9HF. Telephone: 0181 941 0622. Fax: 0181 783 0967.

(This Listing Continued)

Commercial and General Practice including Company Law, Commercial, Insolvency, Employment, Intellectual Property, E.C. Law, Commercial and Civil Litigation, Construction, Real Property, Environmental, Charities, Trusts, Wills and Probate, Matrimonial and Tax.

PARTNERS

John H. Crowther	Simon C.N. Day
David M. Hillyer	David R. Mears
Richard J. Kennett	John E. Godwin
Anthony Harris	Anne E. Dixon
David C. Pollock	William F.R. Brydon
Christopher R.B. Taylor	Michael J. Thornton
John V. Redmond	Ann M. Newby
Patrick R.N. Kelly	W. Nicholas Guppy
Richard G. Brown	Ian A. Burman
John V. Gavan	Eric R. Quirk
Cameron B. Sunter	Christine E. Barker
David L. Courtier-Dutton	Neale A. Andrews
Gordon E. Bon	

LeBOEUF, LAMB, GREENE & MacRAE L.L.P.

A Limited Liability Partnership including Professional Corporations

Formerly LeBoeuf, Lamb, Leiby & MacRae

2 SUFFOLK LANE
LONDON EC4R 0AT, ENGLAND
Telephone: 011-44-171-626-3000
Facsimile: 011-44-171-626-2623 Modem: 011-44-171-626-2591

Eastern United States:
New York, N.Y. Office: 125 West 55th Street, 10019-5389. Telephone: 212-424-8000. Facsimile: 212-424-8500. Telex: 1561363 or 423416.
Washington, D.C. Office: 1875 Connecticut Avenue, N.W., Suite 1200, 20009. Telephone: 202-986-8000. Facsimile: 202-986-8102. Telex: 440274.
Albany, New York Office: One Commerce Plaza, 99 Washington Avenue, Suite 2020, 12210. Telephone: 518-465-1500. Facsimile: 518-465-1585.
Boston, Massachusetts Office: 260 Franklin Street, 02110. Telephone: 617-439-9500. Facsimile: 617-439-0341; 439-0342.
Harrisburg, Pennsylvania Office: 320 Market Street, Suite E400 Strawberry Square, 17108. Telephone: 717-232-8199. Facsimile: 717-232-8720.
Pittsburgh, Pennsylvania Office: 601 Grant Street, 15219. Telephone: 412-594-2300. Facsimile: 412-594-5237.
Hartford, Connecticut Office: Goodwin Square, 225 Asylum Street, 13th Floor. Telephone: 203-293-3500. Facsimile: 203-293-3555.
Newark, New Jersey Office: The Legal Center, One Riverfront Plaza, 07102. Telephone: 201-643-8000. Facsimile: 201-643-6111.
Western United States:
Los Angeles, California Office: 725 South Figueroa Street, Suite 3600, 90017-5422. Telephone: 213-955-7300. Facsimile: 213-955-7399. Telex: 678982.
Salt Lake City, Utah Office: 1000 Kearns Building, 136 South Main Street, 84101. Telephone: 801-320-6700. Facsimile: 801-359-8256.
San Francisco, California Office: One Embarcadero Center, Suite 400, 94111. Telephone: 415-951-1100. Facsimile: 415-951-1180; 951-1181. Telex: 470167.
Denver, Colorado Office: 633 17th Street, Suite 2800, 80202. Telephone: 303-291-2600. Facsimile: 303-297-0422.
Southern United States:
Jacksonville, Florida Office: 50 N. Laura Street, Suite 2800, 32202. Telephone: 904-354-8000. Facsimile: 904-353-1673.
European Community:
Brussels, Belgium Office: 14 rue Montoyer 5th Floor. 1040 Brussels. Telephone: 011-32-2-514-56 50. Facsimile: 011-32-2-514-50 48.
Moscow, Russian Federation Office: Ulitsa Delegatskaya, 25 103473 Moscow, Russian Federation. Telephone: 011-7-503-956-3935. Facsimile: 011-7-503-956-3936.

General Practice. Firm engaged in American and International Law Practice, but not authorized to appear before the English Courts or to act as Solicitors.

(This Listing Continued)

RESIDENT PARTNER

THOMAS E. BURKE, (P.C.), born 1932; admitted, 1958, New York (Not admitted in England). *Education:* Niagara University (A.B., cum laude, 1953); Columbia University (J.D., 1958).

ASSOCIATES

Kathryn A. Howell (Not admitted in England); **Myra Rogers Anderson** (Not admitted in England).

(Biographical data on all Members of the Firm, Counsel, Of Counsel, in Washington, D.C.; New York, New York; Albany, New York; Boston, Massachusetts; Harrisburg, Pennsylvania; Hartford, Connecticut; Newark, New Jersey; Los Angeles, California; Salt Lake City, Utah; San Francisco, California; Jacksonville, Florida; Pittsburgh, Pennsylvania; Denver, Colorado; Brussels, Belgium and Moscow, Russian Federation are listed in the respective Biographical Sections)

LEBOEUF, LAMB, LEIBY & MACRAE

LONDON, ENGLAND

(See LeBoeuf, Lamb, Greene & MacRae L.L.P.)

LEWIS SILKIN
SOLICITORS

1 BUTLER PLACE
BUCKINGHAM GATE
LONDON SW1H 0PT, ENGLAND
Telephone: 44 171 222 8191
FAX: 44 171 222 4633

Corporate Commercial Practice.

PARTNERS

John Fraser, M.P.	Fergus Payne
Roger Alexander	Clare Grayston
Andrew Thomas	Richard Waller
Andrew Stone	Trevor Watkins
Thomas Coates	Gareth Edwards
John Levy	Patricia Negus-Fancey
Ronald Farrants	Jonathan Reuben
Philip Foster	Michael Burd
Stephen Groom	Tim Bailey
Patrick Rees	Jonathan Collins
Gillian Bastow	Donald Stewart
Leonard Goodrich	Dennis Wilkins

REPRESENTATIVE CLIENTS: Abbott Mead Vickers PLC; Gold Greenlees Trott PLC; The RTZ Corporation PLC, Hewlett-Packard Limited; Arco British Limited; Credit Agricole Personal Finance PLC; Mobins Management Systems, Inc.; Liz Claiborne, Inc.; Saatchi & Saatchi Plc.
REFERENCES: Maurice Nessen, Kramer Levin Naptalis Nessen Kamin & Frankel; Walter Epstein; Rubin Baum Levin Constant and Friedman.

LINKLATERS & PAINES

Established in 1920

BARRINGTON HOUSE
59-67 GRESHAM STREET
LONDON EC2V 7JA, ENGLAND
Telephone: 0171-606-7080
Cable Address: Linklaters, London, EC2V 7JA
Telegrams: Linklaters, London
Telex: 884349
Fax: 0171-606 5113

Brussels, Belgium Office: Rue du Luxembourg 47-51, B-1040. Telephone: (2) 513 78 00. Telex: 23207. Fax: (2) 513 25 83.
Frankfurt/Main, Germany Office: Grüneburgweg 14, D-60322 Frankfurt/Main. Telephone: (69) 59 01 25. Fax: (69) 597 45 02.
Hong Kong Office: 14th Floor, Alexandra House, Chater Road. Telephone: (852) 2842 4888. Telex: 83695. Fax: (852) 2810 8133; 852 2810 1695.

New York, USA Office: 885 Third Avenue, Suite 2600, 10022. Telephone: (212) 751 1000. Telex: 127812. Fax: (212) 751 9335.
Paris, France Office: 21, boulevard de la Madeleine, 75001. Telephone: 44 55 54 54. Telex: 214042. Fax: 42 96 00 99.
Singapore Office: 6 Battery Road, #36-01, 0104. Telephone: (65) 221 1110. Telex: 33320. Fax: (65) 221 3334.
Tokyo, Japan Office: Mitsui Asahi Building 3F, 1-1 Kanda Suda-cho, Chiyoda-ku, 101. Telephone: (3) 3258 3691. Telex: 2227236. Fax: (3) 3258 3692.

Corporate Finance: Mergers and Acquisitions, EEC and Anti-trust, Employment and Employee Benefits, European Transactions Unit, Financial Services, Insolvency, International Finance and Banking, Investment Funds, Projects and Assets, Commercial Property, Investment and Development, Planning and Environment, Construction and Engineering, Intellectual Property, Technology and Communications, Litigation, Tax, Trusts.

FIRM PROFILE: Linklaters & Paines is one of the world's largest law firms with a strongly international practice operating from the UK and major financial centres around the world.

The firm: Linklaters' development has been in response to the commercial needs of its clients - major corporations, banks and financial institutions. Since its formation over 150 years ago, Linklaters has had offices in the heart of the City of London. With the growth in global financial markets and cross-border transactions, Linklaters developed internationally - opening branch offices in Brussels, Frankfurt, Hong Kong, Moscow, New York, Paris, Singapore and Tokyo. More recently, the firm has opened a representative office in Washington.

The firm aims to acheive pre-eminence in its chosen areas of practice through the excellence, practicality, innovation and helpfulness of its people. Its goal is to meet and, where possible, exceed the expectations of its clients by delivering a first-class service and by continuing to invest in its people, and the training, know-how and technology to support them.

PARTNERS

J.J.B. Skinner	Anthony T. Thurnham
Charles M. Allen-Jones	A.G. Hickinbotham (Resident, Frankfurt/Main Office)
H.R.J. Human	
David G. Lloyd	Julia E. Maynard
W. Ralph Aldwinckle	Anthony L. Angel
John N. Phipson	Beverley A. Adam
William Grant	David H. Weber
James A.D. Wyness	Anthony L. Morris
L.T. Berkowitz	Elizabeth A. Bennett
C.N. Gorman	John S. Kilner
Donald L. Williams	David Barnes
Richard F. Wheen	Steven M. Turnbull
Keith P. Benham	S.R.R. Edlmann
D.L. Egerton-Smith	Christopher J.D. Style
David A. Greenhalgh	Graeme R. Brister
Robert G. Finch	Martin J.H. Elliott
John Edwards	Jean-Marc Lefèvre (Resident, Paris Office)
Robert Z. Swift	
Paul I. Harris	Alan V. Barker
David F. Hall	Keith J. Thomson
Malcolm G.W. Campbell	S. D. Boughton (Resident, Hong Kong Office)
Brinsley R.I. Nicholson	
Jeremy P. Marriage	T.O.G. Wethered
J.W. Anthony Cann	Raymond J. Jeffers
Peter S. Farren	A.J. Grundy
J. Terence Kyle	Michael W. Canby (Resident, Paris Office)
Haydn Puleston Jones	
D.M. Barnard (Resident, New York Office)	C.I. Johnson-Gilbert
	Malcolm J. Gammie
David W. Cheyne	J.M. Croock
Jeffrey Bailey	N.W. Reid
Andrew J.F. Nichols	Alan M. Stevens (Resident, Hong Kong Office)
G.T.H. de C. Clarke	
William Allan	Guy C.H. Brannan
A. Lachlan Burn	Paul M. Nelson
Jane F. Murphy	W. Alan Walls
Richard H. Tapsfield	Stephen J.H. Cromie
Jeremy R.C. Brown	A.J. Carmichael
Andrew M. Peck	Peter N. Cornell
Alan W. Black	Raymond K. Jackson
Christopher B. Coombe	Timothy J.M. Shipton
John F. Ellard	Maeve N.M. Feeny

(This Listing Continued)

(This Listing Continued)

LINKLATERS & PAINES, London—Continued

PARTNERS (Continued)

Andrew C. Brackfield
Stephen R. Williams
Simon H.T. Clark
Caird Forbes-Cockell
(Resident, New York Office)
David C. Mullarkey
(Resident, Hong Kong Office)
Diana F. Good
Nikhil V. Mehta
Gilles R.L. Endreo
(Resident, Paris Office)
B. Christopher Cooke
Peter S. Gray
(Resident, Tokyo Office)
R.G. Whaite
Ronald W. Gibbs
Richard W. Godden
James J. Rice
Charles E.M. Clark
Derek N. McMenamin
Richard C.T. Holden
Marshall F. Levine
John W. Turnbull
Nicholas W. Eastwell
Christopher W. McFadzean
(Resident, Singapore Office)
Thomas A. Scott
M.S. Middleditch
Andrew R. Legg
Hilary M. Lord
Peter D.S. King
Alexandra L. Marks
Geoffrey N. Russell
Eryl M. Besse
(Resident, Paris Office)
Shane G. Griffin
Robyn M.B. Durie
John C. Tucker
Dorothée Bontoux
(Resident, Paris Office)
Janet Cooper
Robert Elliott
Michael J. Firth
(Resident, Hong Kong Office)
Mike Hardwick
Tom Hope
(Resident, Hong Kong Office)

Conor Hurley
Clare Moulder
Andrew Roberts
(Resident, Tokyo Office)
Christopher Walker
Giles White
(Resident, Hong Kong Office)
Pauline Ashall
Christopher Bright
Jane Brown
Raymond M. Cohen
(Resident, Hong Kong Office)
Ruth Goldman
Clive B. Ransome
(Resident, Hong Kong Office)
Stuart Salt
Bertrand Andriani
(Resident, Paris Office)
Ian Arstall
(Resident, Singapore Office)
Alec Burnside
(Resident, Brussels Office)
Oliver Frankel
Mark Humphries
Andrew Malcolm
(Resident, Hong Kong Office)
Anne Marshall
Nia Morris
Lee Parker
(Resident, New York Office)
Jeremy G. Parr
(Resident, Hong Kong Office)
Stephen Bull
Simon Burch
Julian Davies
Charles Hellier
Andrew Henshaw
Jonathan Inman
Guy Lewin-Smith
Patrick Plant
Nicholas Rees
Terence Sheat
Mark Stamp
Jeremy Stokeld
Michael Sullivan

All of these partners are solicitors except for Jean-Marc Lèfevre, Gilles Endréo, Dorothée Bontoux and Bertrand Andriani, all of whom are Avocats à la Cour de Paris.

LLOYD & CO.

Established in 1985

FOURTH FLOOR, SWEDEN HOUSE
14 TRINITY SQUARE
LONDON EC3N 4AA, ENGLAND
Telephone: 0171-816 0681
Fax: 0171-816 0682/3/4
Telex: 290567 Lloyd G

A firm specializing in all aspects of maritime, transport, insurance and international trade law with a City office and a worldwide network of legal correspondents.
LITIGATION: Disputes involving charter parties and other contracts of sea and land carriage; insurance and general average; ship building and container construction; sale and purchase of second hand tonnage; commodities; ship finance; crew; salvage; collision; oil pollution and wreck removal.
COMMERCIAL: Drafting of ship building and sale and purchase contracts; ship registration (offshore and U.K. Mainland); drafting of loan agreements and security documentation for ship acquisition and registration; drafting of contracts of affreightment including charter parties and

(This Listing Continued)

---

bills of lading. Advice in relation to marine insurance and general average. Advising in relation to combined transport and freight forwarder's liability.

MEMBERS OF FIRM

MICHAEL W.A. LLOYD, born 1948; admitted, 1972, England as Solicitor. Education: Southampton University. PRACTICE AREAS: ITF Disputes; Ship Finance and Registration; Flagging and Major Commercial and Arbitral Disputes; Ship Sale and Purchase.

CHRISTOPHER D.K. EDWARDS, born 1953. Education: Cambridge University (Master's Degree). LANGUAGES: French. PRACTICE AREAS: Ship Sale and Purchase; Ship Finance; Charterparty and Bill of Lading Disputes; Insurance Claims; Ship Arrests.

SUSAN J. HAYDON, born 1956; admitted, 1983, England as Solicitor. Education: Manchester University (Degree in Politics, History and Sociology). Partner, Lloyd & Co., 1989—. PRACTICE AREAS: Litigation; Formation and Management of Corporate Bodies; Property Law.

LOVELL WHITE DURRANT

65 HOLBORN VIADUCT
LONDON EC1A 2DY, ENGLAND
Telephone: 0171 236 0066
Fax: 0171 248 4212; 236 0084; 248 7273
Telex: 887122 LWD G

New York, New York Office: 527 Madison Avenue, 10th Floor, 10022. Telephone: (212) 758 3773. Fax: (212) 486 0367.
Paris, France Office: 37 Avenue Pierre 1er de Serbie, 75008. Telephone: (1) 49 52 04 26. Fax: (1) 47 23 96 12.
Brussels, Belgium Office: Avenue Louise 523, Bte 24, 1050. Telephone: (2) 647 0660. Fax: (2) 647 1124.
Prague, Czech Republic Office: U Prasne brany 3, State Mesto, 1. Telephone: (2) 2481 1672. Fax: (2) 2481 1608.
Ho Chi Minh City, Vietnam Office: 141 Vo Van Tan Street, District 3. Telephone: (848) 298 787. Fax: (848) 392 868.
Hong Kong Office: 11th Floor, Peregrine Tower, Lippo Centre, Queensway. Telephone: 2810 4770. Fax: 2868 4051.
Beijing, Republic of China Office: Office 5D, CITIC Building, 19 Jianguomenwai Dajie, 100004. Telephone: (861) 506 3588. Fax: (861) 500 1972.
Tokyo, Japan Office: Shin-Kasumigaseki Building, 20th Floor, 3-3-2 Kasumigaseki, Chiyoda-ku, 100. Telephone: (3) 3503 2571. Fax: (3) 3503 0699.
Shanghai, People's Republic of China Associated Office: Room 1703, Shanghai International Trade Centre, 2200 Yan An Road (W). Telephone: (21) 219 4419. Fax: (21) 219 5462.

Arbitration, Aviation, Banking, Building and Engineering, China, Collective Investment Schemes, Commercial, Commodities, Competition and Trade Regulation, Computers, Construction, Corporate Finance, Corporate Law, East-West Trade, EEC, Employment, Energy, Environmental Law, Financial Services, Fraud and Asset Recovery, Insolvency, Insurance, Intellectual Property, Litigation, Management Buy-Outs and Venture Capital, Media Law, Mergers and Acquisitions, Pensions, Planning, Product Liability, Property, Rating, Shipping, Taxation, Trusts and Estate Planning.

PARTNERS

CAVAN TAYLOR, born 1935; admitted, 1961. Education: M.A., LL.M. (Cantab). Member: Law Society; City of London Solicitors' Company; International Bar Association; UK Energy Lawyers' Group. (Senior Partner). LANGUAGES: English and French. PRACTICE AREAS: Company and Commercial Work.

WILLIAM G. WATKINS, born 1933; admitted, 1960. Education: M.A. (Oxon). Member: Law Society; City of London Solicitors' Company; International Bar Association. LANGUAGES: English. PRACTICE AREAS: Corporate Finance; Capital Markets; Corporate Banking.

MICHAEL P. ARSCOTT, born 1935; admitted, 1961. Education: B.A. (Cantab). Member: Law Society; City of London Solicitors' Company. LANGUAGES: English. PRACTICE AREAS: Property.

ANTHONY PUGH-THOMAS, born 1939; admitted, 1965. Education: M.A., LL.M. (Cantab). Past President, London Solicitors' Litigation Association. Council Member and Treasurer of Justice. Honorary Solicitor, Georgian Group. Governor, Bute House, Girls Preparatory School. Member: City of London Solicitors' Company (Freeman); London Law Society (Member: Commercial Court Users' Committee; Court Appeal Users' Committee); Joint Bar/Law Society (Member, Working party on Banking

(This Listing Continued)

Law); International Bar Association. *LANGUAGES:* English. *PRACTICE AREAS:* Commercial Litigation; Banking; City related Litigation.

HUGH N. HENSHAW, admitted, 1961. *Member:* Law Society; City of London Solicitors' Company. *LANGUAGES:* English. *PRACTICE AREAS:* Estate Planning; Taxation; Trusts.

GORDON K. TOLAND, born 1939; admitted, 1965. *Education:* B.A., LL.B. (Cantab). *Member:* Law Society; City of London Solicitors' Company; International Fiscal Association. *LANGUAGES:* English. *PRACTICE AREAS:* Corporate; Financial; Corporate Tax.

R. NICHOLAS H. GOULD, born 1942; admitted, 1967. *Education:* B.A. (Cantab). *Member:* Law Society; City of London Solicitors' Company; International Bar Association (Co-Chairman, Committee T, International Construction Contracts). Fellow, Chartered Institute of Arbitrators. *LANGUAGES:* English and Swedish. *PRACTICE AREAS:* Construction and Engineering Law.

MICHAEL B. MAUNSELL, born 1942; admitted, 1967. *Education:* B.A., LL.B., M.A. (Cantab). *Member:* Law Society; City of London Solicitors' Company; City of London Law Society (Former Chairman, Recruitment and Training Sub-Committee); International Bar Association. (Joint Managing Partner). *LANGUAGES:* English. *PRACTICE AREAS:* Corporate and Commercial Law.

PATRICK R. PHILLIPPS, born 1940; admitted, 1964. *Education:* French Lit (Grenoble). *Member:* Law Society; City of London Solicitors' Company. *LANGUAGES:* English and French. *PRACTICE AREAS:* Corporate and Commercial Law.

M.DAVID SHANKLAND, born 1939; admitted, 1967. *Education:* B.A. (Cantab). Solicitor to The Honorable Society of Lincoln's Inn. *Member:* Law Society; City of London Solicitors' Company; Land Law Sub-Committee, London Law Society. *LANGUAGES:* English, French and German. *PRACTICE AREAS:* Commercial Property.

CHRISTOPHER J. HANSON, born 1940; admitted, 1965. *Education:* M.A. (Oxon). Licensed Insolvency Practitioner. *Member:* Law Society (Member, Insolvency Sub-Committee); City of London Solicitors' Company (Member, Insolvency Sub-Committee); City of London Law Society (Chairman). *LANGUAGES:* English. *PRACTICE AREAS:* Corporate Insolvency; Banking.

TIM F.M. OLSEN, born 1942; admitted, 1967. *Education:* B.A. (Leeds). Licensed Insolvency Practitioner. *Member:* Law Society; City of London Solicitors' Company (Liveryman); Society of Practitioners of Insolvency; Association of European Insolvency Practitioners. *LANGUAGES:* English. *PRACTICE AREAS:* Corporate Insolvency; Bank Security Documentation.

DAVID S. BAKER, born 1942; admitted, 1967. *Education:* LL.B. (Leeds). *Member:* Law Society; City of London Solicitors' Company; International Bar Association; The Chartered Institute of Arbitrators. (Partner, Tokyo Office). *LANGUAGES:* English, French, German and Japanese. *PRACTICE AREAS:* General Commercial; International Dispute Resolution; Construction and Engineering; Insurance and Reinsurance; Banking and Securities; Insolvency.

J. BRYAN GORDON, born 1942; admitted, 1971. *Education:* LL.B., Hons. (London). *Member:* Law Society; City of London Solicitors' Company. *LANGUAGES:* English. *PRACTICE AREAS:* General Commercial Property.

W.IAN R. WARD, born 1936; admitted, 1962, Barrister; 1976. *Education:* Inn's Court, School of Law. *Member:* Law Society; City of London Solicitors' Company. Fellow, Institute of Arbitrators. *LANGUAGES:* English. *PRACTICE AREAS:* Shipping; Marine Insurance.

PETER G. HORROCKS, born 1944; admitted, 1968. Licensed Insolvency Practitioner and Legal Consultant under the laws of the State of New York. *Member:* Law Society; Commercial Law League of America; City of London Solicitors' Company (Liveryman); Commercial Law League; Joint Committee of Law Society and Bar on Insolvency Matters; Insolvency Lawyers' Association Limited (Council Member); Society of Practitioners of Insolvency (Chairman, Constitutional Committee); City of London Law Society (Member, Insolvency Sub-Committee). *LANGUAGES:* English. *PRACTICE AREAS:* Commercial and Corporate Law; Insolvency; Liquidations; Receiverships; Administration and Commercial Matters.

RUSSELL A. STRACHAN, admitted, 1970. *Education:* B.A. (Oxon). *Member:* Law Society; City of London Solicitors' Company. *LANGUAGES:* English. *PRACTICE AREAS:* Pensions; Employee Benefits.

(This Listing Continued)

ANDREW D. WALKER, born 1945; admitted, 1970. *Education:* B.A., M.A. (Oxon). *Member:* Law Society; City of London Solicitors' Company (Member, Litigation Sub-Committee, 1977-1981). (Litigation Partner; Former Managing Partner; Previously, Senior Partner in Hong Kong). *LANGUAGES:* English and French. *PRACTICE AREAS:* Litigation; Arbitration and Alternative Dispute Resolution.

ANDREW R. CURRAN, born 1947; admitted, 1971. *Education:* M.A. (Oxon). *Member:* Law Society; City of London Solicitors' Company. *LANGUAGES:* English. *PRACTICE AREAS:* Corporate Finance; Tax.

JOHN R.H. KITCHING, born 1946; admitted, 1971. *Education:* B.A., M.A. (Cantab). *Member:* Law Society; City of London Solicitors' Company; City Law Club. *LANGUAGES:* English and French. *PRACTICE AREAS:* Corporate Finance; Venture Capital; MBOs.

DAN C. MACE, born 1946; admitted, 1970. *Education:* LL.B. Hons. (Bristol). *Member:* Law Society (Member, Company Law Committee); City of London Solicitors' Company (Member, Law Sub-Committee; Chairman, 1993); IBA (Member, Committee Q). *LANGUAGES:* English. *PRACTICE AREAS:* Corporate Finance; Company Law; Securities.

NEIL J. FAGAN, born 1947; admitted, 1971. *Education:* LL.B., Hons. (Southampton). *Member:* Law Society; City of London Solicitors' Company; International Association of Gaming Attorneys; International Bar Association; Royal Lymington Yacht Club. *LANGUAGES:* English and French. *PRACTICE AREAS:* Commercial Litigation.

ROBERT J. ANDERSON, born 1946; admitted, 1972. *Education:* B.Sc. (Edinburgh). *Member:* Law Society; City of London Solicitors' Company. *LANGUAGES:* English. *PRACTICE AREAS:* Intellectual Property.

PHILIP G.H. COLLINS, born 1948; admitted, 1973. *Education:* LL.B. (Exeter); B.C.L. (Oxon). *Member:* Law Society; City of London Solicitors' Company (Member, EC Sub-Committee); International Bar Association (Antitrust and Trade Law Committee); American Bar Association (Associate: Antitrust Law Section). (Partner, Brussels Office). *LANGUAGES:* English and French. *PRACTICE AREAS:* UK and EC Competition Law.

CHRIS I. MAJOR, born 1948; admitted, 1973. *Education:* B.A., M.A. (Oxon). *Member:* Law Society; City of London Solicitors' Company; British American Chamber of Commerce; International Bar Association (Member: UK Committee; Committee on Taxation). *LANGUAGES:* English, French and Russian. *PRACTICE AREAS:* Corporate Tax.

D. BARRY D. MOODY, born 1949; admitted, 1973. *Education:* LL.B., Hons. (Nottingham). *Member:* Law Society; City of London Solicitors' Company. *LANGUAGES:* German and French. *PRACTICE AREAS:* Commercial Property; Development Work; Landlord and Tenant.

CHARLES P. RENTOUL, born 1943; admitted, 1973. *Education:* B.A., Hons., M.A. (Oxon). *Member:* Law Society; City of London Solicitors' Company. *LANGUAGES:* English. *PRACTICE AREAS:* Commercial Property.

DAVID SPARKS, born 1941; admitted, 1975. *Education:* (B.Sc., Econ). *Member:* Law Society; City of London Solicitors' Company. *LANGUAGES:* English. *PRACTICE AREAS:* Banking.

C. HARRIET DAWES, O.B.E., born 1943; admitted, 1978. *Education:* B.A., M.A. (Oxon). *Member:* Law Society; City of London Solicitors' Company; Association of Pension Lawyers (Member, Barber Committee); Occupational Pensions Board; Occupational Pensions Advisory Service. *LANGUAGES:* English and French. *PRACTICE AREAS:* Pensions Law.

DAVID FARRINGTON, born 1945; admitted, 1969, England; 1983, Hong Kong. *Education:* LL.B. (London). *Member:* Law Society; City of London Solicitors' Company; London Maritime Arbitrators Association; Average Adjusters Association; International Chamber of Commerce (Member, Committee on Arbitration); International Bar Association. *LANGUAGES:* English and French. *PRACTICE AREAS:* Cross Border Dispute Resolution; Arbitration; Dry Marine.

RUSSELL H.P. SLEIGH, born 1949; admitted, 1973. *Education:* B.A., M.A. (Oxon). *Member:* Law Society; City of London Solicitors' Company; Union Internationale des Avocats; Association des Juristes Franco-Britanniques. *LANGUAGES:* English and French. *PRACTICE AREAS:* Commercial Litigation.

ADRIAN D. LICKORISH, born 1948; admitted, 1974. *Education:* LL.B., LL.M. (London). *Member:* Law Society; City of London Solicitors' Company. *LANGUAGES:* English. *PRACTICE AREAS:* Banking.

PETER L. WARNOCK, born 1949; admitted, 1975. *Education:* LL.B. (Leeds). Associate Member, AEPPC. *Member:* Law Society; City of Lon-

(This Listing Continued)

LOVELL WHITE DURRANT, London—Continued

don Solicitors' Company. *LANGUAGES:* English. *PRACTICE AREAS:* Property; Secured Lending; Insolvency.

LESLEY A. MACDONAGH, born 1952; admitted, 1976. *Member:* Law Society (Member: Council; Planning Law Committee; Lands Tribunal Consultative Committee); City of London Solicitors' Company. *LANGUAGES:* English. *PRACTICE AREAS:* Planning; Local Government; Environmental Law.

CHARLES P. DODSON, born 1949; admitted, 1972. *Education:* M.A. (Oxon) Jurisprudence. Director, European Dispute Resolution Ltd. (CEDR). *Member:* Law Society; City of London Solicitors' Company. (Joint Managing Partner). *LANGUAGES:* English. *PRACTICE AREAS:* Litigation.

CHRISTOPHER K. GRIERSON, born 1951; admitted, 1976. *Education:* B.A., Hons. (Durham). *Member:* New York State, American and International Bar Associations; Law Society; American Bankruptcy Institute; European Association of Insolvency Practitioners; London Solicitors' Litigation Association; City of London Solicitors' Company. *LANGUAGES:* English and French. *PRACTICE AREAS:* Litigation; Insolvency; Insurance Law.

MICHAEL B. HUTCHINGS, born 1948; admitted, 1973. *Education:* B.A. (College of William & Mary). UK Contributor, European Competition Law Review. *Member:* Law Society (Member, International Committee); City of London Solicitors' Company; London Young Solicitors' Group (Chairman, 1980); Solicitors' European Group (Chairman, 1990); British Institute of International and Comparative Law (Member, Executive Committee). *LANGUAGES:* English, French and German. *PRACTICE AREAS:* European Community Law.

A. SHAUN LAMPLOUGH, born 1948; admitted, 1973. *Member:* Law Society; City of London Solicitors' Company. *LANGUAGES:* English. *PRACTICE AREAS:* Commercial Property.

IAN D. SMITH, born 1948; admitted, 1976. *Education:* B.A., Law (Cantab). *Member:* Law Society; City of London Solicitors' Company; International Bar Association. *LANGUAGES:* English. *PRACTICE AREAS:* Building and Engineering Law; Energy Law.

ANDREW P.F. WILLIAMSON, born 1942; admitted, 1980. *Education:* B.A., LL.B. (S. Africa). *Member:* Law Society; City of London Solicitors' Company; London Law Society (Chairman, Employment Law Sub-Committee). *LANGUAGES:* Afrikaans and English. *PRACTICE AREAS:* Employment; Labour Law.

ANDREW W. FOYLE, born 1949; admitted, 1974. *Education:* M.A. (Cantab). *Member:* Law Society; City of London Solicitors' Company; Chartered Institute of Arbitrators; IBA. (Partner, Hong Kong Office). *LANGUAGES:* English. *PRACTICE AREAS:* Commercial Litigation; Arbitration.

ANDREW GAMBLE, admitted, 1978. *Education:* B.A. *Member:* Law Society; City of London Solicitors' Company. *LANGUAGES:* English. *PRACTICE AREAS:* Banking.

DAVID MACFARLANE, born 1950; admitted, 1976. *Education:* B.A., Hons (Kent); LL.M. (London). *Member:* Law Society; City of London Solicitors' Company (Member, Committee on Shipping and Aviation Law); Institute of Petroleum. Supporting Member, London Maritime Arbitration Association. *LANGUAGES:* English. *PRACTICE AREAS:* International Trade and Finance.

SIMON W. POLITO, born 1949; admitted, 1976. *Education:* LL.B. (Liverpool); called to the Bar, 1972; Law Society (1974 Harry Strout prize). *Member:* Law Society; City of London Solicitors' Company; Joint Working Party on Competitive Laws of UK and Irish Bars and Law Societies. (Partner, Brussels Office). *LANGUAGES:* English and French. *PRACTICE AREAS:* EC and UK Competition Laws.

MICHAEL J. SEYMOUR, born 1949; admitted, 1974. *Education:* LL.B. (Exeter). Vice President, London Solicitors' Litigation Association. Director, LSLA Limited. *Member:* Law Society; City of London Solicitors' Company; Chartered Institute of Arbitrators. *LANGUAGES:* English. *PRACTICE AREAS:* Commercial Litigation; International Litigation; Arbitration; Property.

MICHAEL F. STANCOMBE, born 1953; admitted, 1979. *Education:* LL.B., Hons., Law Society Finals (London). *Member:* Law Society; City of London Solicitors' Company; British Council for Offices; City Property Owners Association; Development Property Forum. *LANGUAGES:* En-

(This Listing Continued)

glish. *PRACTICE AREAS:* Property Investment; Development; Portfolio Management.

NICHOLAS P. FROME, born 1953; admitted, 1979. *Education:* LL.B. (London). Licensed Insolvency Practitioner. *Member:* Law Society; City of London Solicitors' Company; International Bar Association. *LANGUAGES:* English. *PRACTICE AREAS:* Corporate Banking; Insolvency.

MATTHEW O.F. HILL, born 1953; admitted, 1978. *Education:* B.A., M.A. (Cantab). *Member:* Law Society; City of London Solicitors' Company. *LANGUAGES:* English. *PRACTICE AREAS:* Corporate; Commercial; Employee Share Schemes.

CHARLES L. PIKE, born 1949; admitted, 1974. *Education:* M.A. (Cantab). *Member:* Law Society; City of London Solicitors' Company. *LANGUAGES:* English. *PRACTICE AREAS:* Estate Planning; Taxation; Trusts.

JOHN G. TROTTER, born 1951; admitted, 1977. *Education:* B.A. (Oxon). *Member:* Law Society; City of London Solicitors' Company; British Insurance Law Association; London Solicitors' Litigation Association; Media Society; International Bar Association. *LANGUAGES:* English. *PRACTICE AREAS:* Insurance; Reinsurance; Professional Indemnity; Media Litigation.

CHARLES V.S. MANDUCA, born 1954; admitted, 1979. *Education:* LL.B. (London); Solicitors' Examinations Part II. *Member:* Law Society; City of London Solicitors' Company; London Solicitors' Litigation Association; Freeman Worshipful Company of Solicitors. *LANGUAGES:* English. *PRACTICE AREAS:* Commercial Litigation.

GEOFFREY B.B. YEOWART, born 1949; admitted, 1975, England and Wales; 1981, Hong Kong. *Education:* LL.B. (S'hampton); LL.M. (London). *Member:* Law Society; City of London Solicitors' Company. *LANGUAGES:* English. *PRACTICE AREAS:* Banking.

ROBERT J. KIDBY, born 1951; admitted, 1977. *Education:* LL.B. Hons. (London). *Member:* Law Society; City of London Solicitors' Company. *LANGUAGES:* English. *PRACTICE AREAS:* Commercial Property.

DEREK SIMLER, born 1940; admitted, 1978. *Education:* B.A., LL.B. (S. Africa); South African Law Society Exams; UK Law Society, I and II). *Member:* Law Society; City of London Solicitors' Company. *LANGUAGES:* English. *PRACTICE AREAS:* Pensions; Pensions Law; Pension Litigation; Pension Insolvency.

NOEL D. CAMPBELL, born 1951; admitted, 1976. *Education:* LL.B., Hons. (Liverpool). Licensed Insolvency Practitioner. Associate, Chartered Institute of Arbitrators. *Member:* Law Society; City of London Solicitors' Company; International Bar Association (Member, Committees J and O). *LANGUAGES:* English. *PRACTICE AREAS:* Insolvency; Asset Tracing; Commercial Fraud.

JOHN F. POWELL, born 1944; admitted, 1970. *Education:* M.A. (Cantab). *Member:* Law Society; City of London Solicitors' Company. *LANGUAGES:* English. *PRACTICE AREAS:* Reinsurance; Insurance; Dispute Resolution.

JOHN COOPER, born 1955; admitted, 1979; 1992, Paris. *Education:* M.A. (Cantab). *Member:* Law Society; City of London Solicitors' Company. (Partner, Paris Office). *LANGUAGES:* English, French and Latin. *PRACTICE AREAS:* Mergers and Acquisitions; Company Law; Restructurings; Commercial Contracts; Set-Ups; Joint Ventures; Tax.

SIMON M.P. MACDONAGH, born 1953; admitted, 1979. *Education:* Law Society, Parts I and II. *Member:* Law Society; City of London Solicitors' Company; Anglo American Real Property Institute; British Council for Offices; Westminster City Council. *LANGUAGES:* English. *PRACTICE AREAS:* Commercial Property; Property Financing; Property Joint Ventures.

NICHOLAS R. MACFARLANE, born 1952; admitted, 1977. *Education:* B.A. (Lancaster). *Member:* Law Society; City of London Solicitors' Company; Patent Solicitors' Association (Founder Member, 1983; Committee Member, 1985); City of London Club. *LANGUAGES:* English. *PRACTICE AREAS:* Intellectual Property; Litigation.

GAVIN J. MCQUATER, born 1954; admitted, 1979, England and Wales; 1990, Hong Kong; 1991, Barrister and Solicitor, Australian Capital Territory. *Education:* M.A., Hons., B.A., Hons. (Cantab). *Member:* Law Society; City of London Solicitors' Company. (Partner, Hong Kong Office). *LANGUAGES:* English. *PRACTICE AREAS:* Corporate; Financial; Commercial.

(This Listing Continued)

R. HUGH NINEHAM, born 1953; admitted, 1978. *Education:* M.A. (Cantab). *Member:* Law Society; City of London Solicitors' Company; Securities Institute. *LANGUAGES:* English. *PRACTICE AREAS:* General Corporate Law; Transactional Work.

A. JOHN A. PENSON, born 1955; admitted, 1980. *Education:* B.A., 1st class Hons. (Oxon). *Member:* Law Society; City of London Solicitors' Company. *LANGUAGES:* English. *PRACTICE AREAS:* Corporate Banking; Financing and Structuring; Acquisitions and Bids; Buy-outs; Buy-Ins; Trade and Commodity Finance; Property Finance.

JOHN E. PHEASANT, born 1953; admitted, 1979. *Education:* Oxon (Modern Languages). Recipient, John Mackrell Law Society Prize. Co-Author: "Competition Law," Butterworth. *Member:* Law Society; City of London Solicitors' Company; EC Committee of Licensing Executive Committee; Advisory Board of the Regulatory Policy Research Centre and Regulatory Policy Institute, Oxford. (Partner, Brussels Office). *LANGUAGES:* English, French and German. *PRACTICE AREAS:* EC Competition; Trade Regulation.

PATRICK P. SHERRINGTON, born 1951; admitted, 1980. *Education:* LL.B. (Exeter): LL.M. (Illinois). *Member:* Law Society; City of London Solicitors' Company; Solicitors European Group; Committee Member, Chartered Institute of Arbitrators, Hong Kong Branch; Law Society of Hong Kong (Vice President and Council Member; Member: Policy and Resources Committee; Future of Legal Profession Committee; Staff Committee; Insolvency Law Committee; Foreign Lawyers Committee); Chairman, External Affairs Committee and Editorial Board, Hong Kong Lawyer; Hong Kong Bar and Law Society (Member Joint Committee on: Grey Areas and Touting and Commission Taking); Hong Kong Law Reports (Editorial Board); Hong Kong Advocacy Institute (Member, Board of Governors and Board of Studies); Inter-Pacific Bar Association (Council Member); Law Asia (Council Member); International Bar Association; Financial Executives Institute (HK) Limited; Insolvency Group of Hong Kong Society of Accountants. Fellow, Chartered Institute of Arbitrators. (Partner, Hong Kong Office). *LANGUAGES:* English. *PRACTICE AREAS:* Commercial Litigation.

J.RODNEY SMYTH, born 1953; admitted, 1980. *Education:* M.A. (Cantab). *Member:* Law Society; City of London Solicitors' Company. *LANGUAGES:* English. *PRACTICE AREAS:* Corporate; Securities; Financial Services; Market Law and Regulation; Asset Management; Custody.

DAVID A. COX, born 1956; admitted, 1979. *Education:* LL.B. (Exeter). *Member:* Law Society; City of London Solicitors' Company. *LANGUAGES:* English and French. *PRACTICE AREAS:* Property Litigation.

ANTHONY C.R. DAVIS, born 1956; admitted, 1981. *Education:* M.A. (Oxon); M.A. (London); ATII; FTII. *Member:* Law Society (Member: Revenue Law Committee and VAT Sub-Committee); City of London Solicitors' Company; VAT Practitioners Group. Fellow, The Institute of Taxation. *LANGUAGES:* English. *PRACTICE AREAS:* Business Taxation.

KEITH GAINES, born 1956; admitted, 1981. *Education:* LL.B., Hons. (Birmingham). *Member:* Law Society; City of London Solicitors' Company; International Bar Association. *LANGUAGES:* English. *PRACTICE AREAS:* Insolvency; Asset Tracing; Commercial Fraud.

DAVID A. HARPER, born 1954; admitted, 1978. *Education:* B.A. (Oxon). *Member:* Law Society; City of London Solicitors' Company; Employment Lawyers Association. *LANGUAGES:* English. *PRACTICE AREAS:* Employment Law; Employee Benefits.

DAVID A. HARRIS, born 1954; admitted, 1979. *Education:* LL.B., Hons. (London). *Member:* Law Society; City of London Solicitors' Company; The Securities Institute. *LANGUAGES:* English. *PRACTICE AREAS:* Corporate Finance; Capital Markets.

DON C. KELLY, born 1956; admitted, 1980. *Education:* B.A., M.A. (Cantab). *Member:* Law Society; City of London Solicitors' Company. *LANGUAGES:* English. *PRACTICE AREAS:* Corporate Tax.

ALLAN G. MURRAY-JONES, born 1952; admitted, 1980. *Education:* B.E.C., LL.B. *Member:* Law Society; City of London Solicitors' Company. *LANGUAGES:* English. *PRACTICE AREAS:* Corporate Finance; Capital Markets.

JANE S. RIGLER, born 1952; admitted, 1976. *Education:* LL.B., Hons. (London). *Member:* Law Society; City of London Solicitors' Company. *LANGUAGES:* English. *PRACTICE AREAS:* Property.

MICHAEL A. STANGER, born 1953; admitted, 1981. *Education:* B.Sc. Eng., ACGI (London). *Member:* Law Society; City of London Solicitors'

(This Listing Continued)

Company; Society of Construction Law; UK Oil Lawyers Group; International Bar Association (Section on Energy and Natural Resources Group); Institute of Petroleum; London Chamber of Commerce and Industry. *LANGUAGES:* English. *PRACTICE AREAS:* Building and Engineering.

E.CHRISTIAN J. WELLS, born 1955; admitted, 1980. *Education:* B.A., Hons. (Kingston). *Member:* Law Society (Member, Multi-National Practices Working Party); City of London Solicitors' Company; City of London Law Society (Member, Insurance Sub-Committee); International Chamber of Commerce (Member, Insurance Sub-Committee). *LANGUAGES:* English, French and German. *PRACTICE AREAS:* Insurance; Reinsurance.

RICHARD T. WHITEHOUSE, born 1952; admitted, 1979. *Education:* M.A. (Cantab). *Member:* Law Society; City of London Solicitors' Company. *LANGUAGES:* English. *PRACTICE AREAS:* Corporate Finance; General Corporate Law.

H. JOHN H. PEARSON, born 1947; admitted, 1971. *Education:* LL.B. (London). *Member:* Law Society; City of London Solicitors' Company; Association of Pension Lawyers (Member, International Sub-committee); International Pension and Employee Benefits Association. *LANGUAGES:* English, French and Norwegian. *PRACTICE AREAS:* Pensions Law and Documentation; Purchases and Insolvencies; Pension Litigation.

QUENTIN D.R. ARCHER, born 1955; admitted, 1981. *Education:* M.A., LL.M. (Cantab). *Member:* Law Society (Working Party on relations with lawyers in Central and Eastern Europe and ICC East-West Committee); City of London Solicitors' Company; British-Czech and Slovak Law Association (Treasurer); US Computer Law Association; International Bar Association; British-Russian Law Association. *LANGUAGES:* English, French and Russian. *PRACTICE AREAS:* Computers and Telecommunications; Intellectual Property.

PAUL A. OLDMAN, born 1952; admitted, 1982. *Education:* LL.B. (Manchester). *Member:* Law Society; City of London Solicitors' Company. (Partner, Hong Kong Office). *LANGUAGES:* English. *PRACTICE AREAS:* Banking; Transactional Finance; Corporate Acquisitions; Project Finance; Aircraft Finance.

RICHARD A. SHEAN, born 1951; admitted, 1975. *Education:* LL.B., Hons. (London). Licensed Insolvency Practitioner. *Member:* Law Society; City of London Solicitors' Company; Society of Practitioners of Insolvency; Insolvency Practitioners Association; AEPPC. *LANGUAGES:* English. *PRACTICE AREAS:* Corporate Insolvency; Voluntary Arrangements; Receiverships; Administrations and Liquidations.

RICHARD J.L. STONES, born 1948; admitted, 1980. *Education:* B.A., M.A. (Oxon). Member, Securities Institute, 1993. *Member:* Law Society; City of London Solicitors' Company (Member, Whittington Company, 1989-1991). *LANGUAGES:* English and French. *PRACTICE AREAS:* Corporate; Securities; Financial Services; Market Law and Regulation; Asset Management; Custody.

JOHN T. YOUNG, born 1957; admitted, 1981. *Education:* B.A., M.A. (Cantab). *Member:* Law Society; City of London Solicitors' Company; Society of Scottish Lawyers in London. *LANGUAGES:* English. *PRACTICE AREAS:* UK and EC Insurance Law; Regulation; Transactions.

LESLEY M. AINSWORTH, born 1957; admitted, 1981. *Education:* M.A. (Oxon); St. Hilda's College. *Member:* Law Society; City of London Solicitors' Company. *LANGUAGES:* English and French. *PRACTICE AREAS:* UK and EC Competition Law.

CATHERINE M. ALLINSON, admitted, 1977. *Education:* B.Sc. (London). *Member:* Law Society; City of London Solicitors' Company. *LANGUAGES:* English. *PRACTICE AREAS:* Banking.

ANGELA M. DIMSDALE GILL. *Education:* Bristol, Oxford, University of Pennsylvania. *Member:* Law Society; City of London Solicitors' Company. *LANGUAGES:* English, French and Spanish. *PRACTICE AREAS:* Litigation; Professional Negligence; Construction; Fraud; Pension Funds; General Contractual Disputes.

PETER J. FISHER, born 1958; admitted, 1982. *Education:* B.A., M.A. (Cantab). *Member:* Law Society; City of London Solicitors' Company; City of London Law Society Revenue Law Committee. *LANGUAGES:* English. *PRACTICE AREAS:* Corporate Tax; Property Tax; Hong Kong Tax.

MICHAEL GALLIMORE, born 1958; admitted, 1983. *Education:* M.A., Hons. (Cantab). *Member:* Law Society (Member, Planning and Environmental Sub-committee); City of London Solicitors' Company. *LANGUAGES:* English. *PRACTICE AREAS:* Planning; Local Government; Environmental Law.

(This Listing Continued)

LOVELL WHITE DURRANT, London—Continued

FRANCIS P.A. GIACON, born 1958; admitted, 1982. *Education:* LL.B. (London). *Member:* Law Society; City of London Solicitors' Company; British-Italian Law Association. *LANGUAGES:* English, French and Italian. *PRACTICE AREAS:* Commercial Property.

MICHAEL S. GOLDING, born 1956; admitted, 1980. *Education:* B.A. (Oxon). *Member:* Law Society; City of London Solicitors' Company; Solicitors' European Group; ECTA; AIPPI; INTA; ACG. *LANGUAGES:* English. *PRACTICE AREAS:* Intellectual Property.

DAVID A. LATHAM, born 1954; admitted, 1980. *Education:* M.A., LL.B. (Cantab). *Member:* Law Society; City of London Solicitors' Company (Member, Intellectual Property Committee); Competition Law Association, English Group of the Ligue International du Droit de la Concurrence (Treasurer); International Committee with special interest in anti-counterfeiting; International Trade Mark Association. Associate Member: Chartered Institute of Patent Agents; Institute Trade Mark Agents. *LANGUAGES:* English and French. *PRACTICE AREAS:* Intellectual Property.

RODDY H.R. MCKEAN, born 1956; admitted, 1987. *Education:* LL.B., Hons. (Edinburgh). *Member:* Law Society; City of London Solicitors' Company. *LANGUAGES:* English. *PRACTICE AREAS:* Corporate Finance; Company Law.

DAVID J. MOSS, born 1956; admitted, 1981, England; 1983, Hong Kong. *Education:* M.A. (Cantab). *Member:* Law Society; City of London Solicitors' Company; Inter-Pacific Bar Association. *LANGUAGES:* English. *PRACTICE AREAS:* Banking; International Trade; Energy Work.

HEATHER ROWE, born 1957; admitted, 1981. *Education:* LL.B., Hons. (Manchester). Recipient; Law Society Finals Hons; John Mackrell Prize. Editor, Newsletter, Committee R International Bar Association. Chairman, UK Editorial Board, Droit de L'Informatique et des Telecoms. Consultant Editor, IT Law Today. Correspondent Panelist, The Computer Law and Security Review. *Member:* Law Society; City of London Solicitors' Company; International Chamber of Commerce (Chairman, International Working Party on Data Protection and Privacy); Chartered Institute of Arbitrators. *LANGUAGES:* English and French. *PRACTICE AREAS:* Banking; Computer and Telecommunications; IT Law.

NICHOLAS M.G. BROMFIELD, born 1958; admitted, 1983. *Education:* B.A. (Oxon). *Member:* Law Society; City of London Solicitors' Company; European Trade Law Associations; Solicitors' European Group. (Partner, Brussels Office). *LANGUAGES:* English and French. *PRACTICE AREAS:* EC Competition; Trade Regulation; Anti-dumping; GATT and Eastern Europe.

DEBORAH A. GREGORY, born 1959; admitted, 1984. *Education:* LL.B., Hons. (Man); Law Society Part II. *Member:* Law Society; City of London Solicitors' Company; Insolvency Practitioners' Association; Insolvency Lawyers Association; Society of Practitioners in Insolvency; AEPPC. *LANGUAGES:* English. *PRACTICE AREAS:* Insolvency Law.

GRAHAM N.C. LIVINGSTON, born 1955; admitted, 1981. *Education:* M.A. (Oxon). *Member:* Law Society; City of London Solicitors' Company; London Solicitors' Litigation Association. *LANGUAGES:* English, French and German. *PRACTICE AREAS:* Commercial Litigation.

MICHAEL S. MATHEOU, born 1957; admitted, 1982, England and Wales; 1983, Hong Kong; 1991, Australian Capital Territory. *Education:* LL.B., Hons. (Nottingham); Solicitors' Final. *Member:* Law Society; City of London Solicitors' Company. *LANGUAGES:* English. *PRACTICE AREAS:* Construction Law; Commercial Dispute Resolution.

JENNIFER MCDERMOTT, born 1957; admitted, 1981. *Education:* LL.B. (London). *Member:* Law Society; City of London Solicitors' Company; British Insurance Law Association; Chartered Insurance Institute; London Solicitors Litigation Association. *LANGUAGES:* English and French. *PRACTICE AREAS:* Commercial Litigation; Insurance and Reinsurance; Litigation and Arbitration; Judicial Reviews.

JAMES H. REEVES, born 1955; admitted, 1980. *Education:* Law Tripos (Parts I and II) (Cantab). *Member:* Law Society; City of London Solicitors' Company. *LANGUAGES:* English. *PRACTICE AREAS:* Corporate Finance; Company Law.

LINDSAY WILNER, admitted, 1977. *Education:* B.A., Hons. (Reading). *Member:* Law Society; City of London Solicitors' Company. *LANGUAGES:* English and French. *PRACTICE AREAS:* General Property Practice.

(This Listing Continued)

CHRISTOPHER H.D. SMITH, born 1946; admitted, 1973. *Education:* LL.B., English and Scottish Law (St. Andrews). *Member:* Law Society; City of London Solicitors' Company. (Head of Prague Office). *LANGUAGES:* English, French and Spanish. *PRACTICE AREAS:* East-West Trade Group.

PHILIP D. GERSHUNY, born 1958; admitted, 1985. *Education:* B.A., Hons. (Sussex). *Member:* Law Society; City of London Solicitors' Company; ICC UK Taxation Committee. *LANGUAGES:* English. *PRACTICE AREAS:* Corporate Tax; Property Tax; Insurance Tax; Charity Tax; Inland Revenue Investigations.

DAVID J. HUNTER, born 1952; admitted, 1978. *Education:* LL.B., Hons. (Leeds). *Member:* Law Society; City of London Solicitors' Company. *LANGUAGES:* English. *PRACTICE AREAS:* Property; Local Planning; Parliamentary Planning; Rating.

DAVID LANE, born 1959; admitted, 1983. *Education:* M.A., Hons. (Cantab). *Member:* Law Society; City of London Solicitors' Company. *LANGUAGES:* English. *PRACTICE AREAS:* Commercial Property; Secured Lending; Insolvency.

MARK C. MCGAW, born 1957; admitted, 1982, Ontario; 1987, England and Wales; 1994, Hong Kong. *Education:* LL.B. (Toronto); LL.M. (Cantab). *Member:* Law Society; City of London Solicitors' Company; Law Society of Upper Canada; International Bar Association. (Partner, Hong Kong Office). *LANGUAGES:* English. *PRACTICE AREAS:* Building Law; Engineering Law.

CHARLES D.STJ. PENNEY, born 1960; admitted, 1984. *Education:* B.A., M.A., Law 1st class Hons. (Cantab). Secretary, UK Takeover Panel, 1992-1994. *Member:* Law Society; City of London Solicitors' Company. *LANGUAGES:* English and French. *PRACTICE AREAS:* Corporate Finance.

ELIZABETH T. SLATTERY, born 1958; admitted, 1983. *Education:* LL.B., Hons. (Leeds). *Member:* Law Society; City of London Solicitors' Company; Employment Lawyers Association. *LANGUAGES:* English. *PRACTICE AREAS:* Employment Law.

DAVID G.T. HUDD, born 1958; admitted, 1983. *Education:* M.A. (Oxon) Jurisprudence. *LANGUAGES:* English. *PRACTICE AREAS:* Capital Markets; Structured Finance; Securitisation.

JULIE M. BRADSHAW, born 1960; admitted, 1985. *Education:* M.A. (Oxon). *Member:* Law Society; City of London Solicitors' Company. *LANGUAGES:* English. *PRACTICE AREAS:* Corporate Finance; Company Law.

LAURENCE A. CROWLEY, born 1958; admitted, 1983. *Education:* B.A. (Oxon). Licensed Insolvency Practitioner. *Member:* Law Society; City of London Solicitors' Company. *LANGUAGES:* English and French. *PRACTICE AREAS:* Corporate Insolvency; Commercial Law; USM Company Work.

JOHN DAVIDSON, born 1959; admitted, 1985. *Education:* M.A., B.C.L. (Oxon). Partner in New York Office. *Member:* New York State and American Bar Associations; Law Society; City of London Solicitors' Company; New York County Lawyers Association. (Partner, New York Office). *LANGUAGES:* English and French. *PRACTICE AREAS:* Securities; Corporate Law; Commercial Law; Insurance Regulation and Transactions; Venture Capital; Banking.

LEAH R. DUNLOP, born 1959; admitted, 1985. *Education:* LL.B. (Southampton). *Member:* Law Society; City of London Solicitors' Company; British Venture Capital Association. *LANGUAGES:* English and Italian. *PRACTICE AREAS:* Corporate Law; Venture Capital; Lloyd's Market.

R. MARK HULEATT-JAMES, born 1950; admitted, 1976. *Education:* B.A. (Rhodes University, South Africa); Lancaster Gate College of Law. *Member:* Law Society; City of London Solicitors' Company; Chartered Institute of Arbitrators (ACIArb). (Partner, Paris, France Office). *LANGUAGES:* English and French. *PRACTICE AREAS:* Commercial Litigation; Arbitration.

JANE M. SAMSWORTH, born 1951; admitted, 1978. *Education:* B.A., Hons. (Sussex); Law Society Finals I an II (Lancaster Gate); APMI. Associate, Institute of Pensions Management. *Member:* Law Society; City of London Solicitors' Company; Association Of Pension Lawyers; OPAS Limited (Council). *LANGUAGES:* English. *PRACTICE AREAS:* Pensions; Pension Litigation.

(This Listing Continued)

KEVIN S. ASHMAN, born 1957; admitted, 1983. *Education:* B.A., B.C.L., M.A. (Oxon). *Member:* Law Society; City of London Solicitors' Company. *LANGUAGES:* English. *PRACTICE AREAS:* Corporate Tax.

JEREMY N. COLE, born 1958; admitted, 1985. *Education:* LL.B., Hons. (Exeter). *Member:* Law Society; City of London Solicitors' Company; Association Eurpreene des Practiciens des Prosedures Collectives (AEPPC); Society of English and American Lawyers; British-American Chamber of Commerce. *LANGUAGES:* English. *PRACTICE AREAS:* Insolvency; Asset Tracing; Commercial Fraud.

LAURENCE M. GARSIDE, born 1959; admitted, 1984. *Education:* LL.B., 1st class Hons. (Bristol). *Member:* Law Society; City of London Solicitors' Company. *LANGUAGES:* English. *PRACTICE AREAS:* Corporate Finance.

RUTH M. GRANT, born 1957; admitted, 1983. *Education:* LL.B., 1st class Hons. (Bristol). *Member:* Law Society; City of London Solicitors' Company. *LANGUAGES:* English and French. *PRACTICE AREAS:* Insurance Litigation.

DAVID F. HARLOCK, born 1960; admitted, 1985. *Education:* LL.B., Hons. (Southampton). *Member:* Law Society; City of London Solicitors' Company. *LANGUAGES:* English. *PRACTICE AREAS:* Commercial Property.

ANTHONY R. MARSHALL, born 1956; admitted, 1984. *Education:* M.A. (Cantab). (Partner, Hong Kong Office). *LANGUAGES:* English, French and German. *PRACTICE AREAS:* Construction Work, including drafting of contract conditions.

N. PHILIP QUENBY, born 1961; admitted, 1986. *Education:* B.A., Hons, M.A. (Cantab). *Member:* Law Society; City of London Solicitors Company. *LANGUAGES:* English, French and German. *PRACTICE AREAS:* International Trade; Commodities; Trade Finance.

PETER L. TAYLOR, born 1956; admitted, 1979, Barrister; 1988, Solicitor. *Education:* M.A., Law (Cantab). Editorial Advisor, International Insurance Law Review. *Member:* Law Society; City of London Solicitors' Company; Chambre de Commerce, Francaise de Grande Bretagne (Member, Tax and Law Committee); UK Environmental Law Association; International Bar Association. *LANGUAGES:* English, French and German. *PRACTICE AREAS:* Insurance; Reinsurance; Shipping.

D.S. CHEUNG, born 1962; admitted, 1988. *Education:* LL.M., LL.B. (London). *Member:* Law Societies of Hong Kong, England and Wales; City of London Solicitors' Company. (Head, China Practice, Hong Kong). *LANGUAGES:* Chinese (Mandarin, Fujian, Cantonese and Shanghainese) and English. *PRACTICE AREAS:* Banking and Finance; Corporate Finance; Insolvency.

MARCO COMPAGNONI, born 1962; admitted, 1987. *Education:* LL.B. (Newcastle upon Tyne). *Member:* Law Society; City of London Solicitors' Company; British Italian Law Association. *LANGUAGES:* English and Italian. *PRACTICE AREAS:* Company Law; Insurance Law; Acquisitions and Disposals; Joint Ventures; Venture Capital.

MATTHEW J. COTTIS, born 1962; admitted, 1987. *Education:* B.A. (Oxon). *Member:* Law Society; City of London Solicitors' Company. *LANGUAGES:* English. *PRACTICE AREAS:* Banking.

ROBERT P. FOLLIE, born 1951; admitted, 1987. *Education:* Law Degree (Law Faculty of Rouen); Diploma from Institut d'Etudes Politiques de Paris. *Member:* IBA; UIA; European Lawyers Association. (Partner, Paris Office). *LANGUAGES:* French and English. *PRACTICE AREAS:* Corporate; Banking; Competition Law; Petroleum and Mining.

GRAHAM P.K. HUNTLEY, born 1960; admitted, 1986. *Education:* B.A., Hons. (Durham). *Member:* Law Society; City of London Solicitors' Company; London Solicitors' Litigation Association. *LANGUAGES:* English. *PRACTICE AREAS:* Commercial Litigation; Investigations.

GREG J. SINFIELD, born 1958; admitted, 1989. *Education:* B.A., Hons. (Cantab). *Member:* Law Society; City of London Solicitors' Company; VAT Practitioners Group. *LANGUAGES:* English. *PRACTICE AREAS:* Value Added Tax; Customs Duty.

JOHN GILBERT, born 1950; admitted, 1987. *Education:* M.A. (Oxon). *Member:* Law Society; City of London Solicitors' Company. *LANGUAGES:* English and French. *PRACTICE AREAS:* Banking; Secured Lending; Trade and Structured Finance.

CARY KOCHBERG, born 1959; admitted, 1986, Ontario; 1992, England. *Education:* B.A., Hons. (University of Toronto); LL.B. (1st) Osgoode Law School. *Member:* Law Society of England and Wales; City of

(This Listing Continued)

London Solicitors' Company; Law Society of Upper Canada. *LANGUAGES:* English. *PRACTICE AREAS:* Insolvency; Asset Tracing; Commercial Fraud.

ROBIN G.N. SPENCER, born 1958; admitted, 1991. *Education:* M.A. (Cantab). *Member:* Law Society; City of London Solicitors' Company. *LANGUAGES:* English. *PRACTICE AREAS:* Insolvency; Insurance.

PETER G. VOISEY, born 1960; admitted, 1987. *Education:* M.A., Hons. (Cantab). *Member:* Law Society; City of London Solicitors' Company. *LANGUAGES:* English, French and German. *PRACTICE AREAS:* Capital Markets; Corporate Finance; Stock Exchange.

CONSULTANTS

G.J.B. Hutchings
R.S. Reston

All Partners in the Firm are Solicitors except R. Follie.
J. Cooper and R. Follie are Avocats au Barreau de Paris.

MACFARLANES

10 NORWICH STREET
LONDON EC4A 1BD, ENGLAND
Telephone: 0171-831 9222
Telex: 296381 MACFAR G
Fax: 0171 831 9607

Brussels, Belgium Office: Avenue Louise 106, 1050. Telephone: (02) 647 06 50. Fax: (2) 646 4729. Telefax: 20317 OMSSA.

Tokyo, Japan Office: Sanbancho KB-6 Building, 6 Sanbancho, Chiyoda-ku, 102. Telephone: (03) 3239 3661. Fax: (03) 3239 2884.

Corporate, Commercial and Banking, Litigation, Property, Tax and Financial Planning.

PARTNERS

V.E. Treves	J.H. Hornby
R.M. Formby	J.H.R. Manners
D. Hayes	B.C. Barker
J.J. Dilger	P.J. Busby
C.H.W. Parish	N.J.L. Doran
G.S.H. Smeed	R.M.E. Reuben
M.A. Hayes	C.P. Phippen
P.H. Turnbull	K.D. Tuffnell
J.G. Rhodes	R.J. Whittaker
W.L. King	C.D.Z. Martin
J.E. Moore	A.L. Millmore
D.J.C. Wyld	S.N. Hillson
A.D. Evans	J.F. Howard
C.M. Field	C. Lampard
N.A. Thomas	D.J. Courtenay-Stamp
A.G.W. Jackson	S.R. Martin
J.E. Rees	C.H. Meek
C.J. Road	D.R. Shugar
R.H. Sutton	J.S. Walters
J.M. Skelton	M.D. Pintus
B.G.O. Clutton	M.A. Furman
J.S. Macfarlane	P.D. Hubbard
A.G. Thompson	T.J. Lewis
	T.D. Steele

ASSOCIATE

M.H. Leth

CONSULTANT

S.J.M. Buckley

MACLAY MURRAY & SPENS

Established in Scotland in 1871

10 FOSTER LANE
LONDON EC2V 6HH, ENGLAND
Telephone: 0171-606-6130
Fax: 0171-600-0992; 0171-600-0993

Edinburgh, Scotland Office: 3 Glenfinlas Street, EH3 6AQ. Telephone: 0131-226-5196. Telex: 727238 Vindex. Fax: 0131-226-3174; 0131-225-9610.

(This Listing Continued)

MACLAY MURRAY & SPENS, London—Continued

Glasgow, Scotland Office: 151 St. Vincent Street, G2 5NJ. Telephone: 0141-248-5011. Telex: 77474 Vindex. Fax: 0141-221-2968; 0141-248-5819.

Brussels, Belgium Office: Scotland Europa Centre, 35 Square De Meeus, B-1040. Telephone: 322 927 2001. Fax: 322 927 2401.

RESIDENT PARTNERS

ANDREW H. PRIMROSE, admitted, 1964, Scotland. *Education:* B.A. (Oxon); LL.B. Notary Public. *Member:* Royal Faculty of Procurators in Glasgow; International Bar Association; UK Environmental Law Association; Law Society of Scotland. *LANGUAGES:* English. *PRACTICE AREAS:* Commercial Property Development and Finance; Environmental; Construction Law; Timeshare.

J. ANTHONY S. MURRAY, admitted, 1972, Scotland; 1992, England and Wales. *Education:* B.A. (Cantab); LL.B. *Member:* Royal Faculty of Procurators in Glasgow; British Institute of International and Corporate Law; Law Society of Scotland. *LANGUAGES:* English and French. *PRACTICE AREAS:* Securities; Corporate Law; Company Law.

HILARY A. KANE, admitted, 1986, Scotland. *Education:* LL.B. Notary Public. *Member:* Law Society of Scotland. *LANGUAGES:* English. *PRACTICE AREAS:* Corporate Law; Mergers Acquisitions and Divestitures; Banks and Banking.

(For Complete Personnel and Biographical Data, see Professional Biographies at Glasgow, Scotland)

MALLESONS STEPHEN JAQUES

2ND FLOOR ALDERMARY HOUSE
10-15 QUEEN STREET
LONDON EC4N 1TX, ENGLAND
Telephone: (44-171) 982 0982
Fax: (44-171) 982 9820

Sydney, Australia Office: Level 60, Governor Phillip Tower, 1 Farrer Place, 2000. Telephone: (612) 250 3000. Fax: (612) 250 3133.

Melbourne, Australia Office: Level 28, Rialto, 525 Collins Street, 3000. Telephone: (613) 619 0619. Fax: (613) 614 1329.

Perth, Australia Office: Ground Floor, St. Georges Square, 225 St. George's Terrace, 6000. Telephone: (619) 324 8333. Fax: (619) 3211017.

Brisbane, Australia Office: Level 30, Waterfront Place, 1 Eagle Street, 4000. Telephone: (617) 231 7500. Fax: (617) 221 1211.

Canberra, Australia Office: Level 10, Advance Bank Centre, 60 Marcus Clarke Street, 2601. Telephone: (616) 268 3900. Fax: (616) 257 3100.

Hong Kong Office: Bateson Starr in association with Mallesons Stephen Jaques, Suite 801, Asia Pacific Finance Tower, Citibank Plaza, 3 Garden Road, Central Hong Kong. Telephone: (852) 848 4600. Fax: (852) 868-0124.

Beijing, The Peoples Republic of China Office: Suite 701, Scite Tower, 22 Jianguomenwai Street, 100004. Telephone: (861) 512 3565 ext 701. Fax: (861) 523 2018.

Taipei, Taiwan Office: 14th Floor, Mallesons Stephen Jaques, 138 Min Sheng East Road, Sec 3. Telephone: (886-2) 712 5808. Fax: (886-2) 712 9080.

Jakarta, Indonesia Associated Office: Law Firm Kartini Muljadi S.H. & Associates, in association with Mallesons Stephen Jaques, Level 5, Bina Mulia I Building, J1 H.R. Rasuna Said Kav 10, 12950. Telephone: (6221) 525 6968. Fax: (6221) 525 5561.

Port Moresby, Papua New Guinea Office: Beresford Love, agents for Mallesons Stephen Jaques, Level 3, Hunter Building, Hunter Street. Telephone: (675) 211 942. Fax: (675) 211 586.

Singapore Office: Level 36, Hong Leong Building, 16 Raffles Quay 0104. Telephone: (65) 321 8930. Fax: (65) 225 9060.

New York, New York, U.S.A. Office: 9th floor, Suite 911, 609 Fifth Avenue, 10017-1021. Telephone: (1-212) 319-9500. Fax: (1-212) 319-9506.

Firm engaged in Australian and International Law Practice, but not admitted as Solicitors in England.

RESIDENT PARTNER

Rick Ladbury

(For complete biographical data on all Personnel, see Professional Biographies at Sydney, Australia).

LAW OFFICES OF
JOHN J. MALLOY

28 GROSVENOR STREET
LONDON WIX 9FE, ENGLAND
Telephone: 0171-917-9640
Telecopier: 0171-917-6002
Telex: 849348 HQFROG

Danbury, Connecticut Office: 40 Old Ridgebury Road, 06810. Telephone: 203-791-0262. Telecopier: 203-791-0402.

New York, New York Office: 300 Park Avenue, Seventeenth Floor, 10022. Telephone: 212-572-6295. Telecopier: 212-572-6499.

International Corporate Transactions, Taxation, Real Estate, Wills, Trusts, Probate, Mergers and Acquisitions, Contracts, Trademarks, Joint Ventures, Incorporations, General Corporate Matters, Immigration.

FIRM PROFILE: Firm engaged in American and International Law Practice but not authorized to appear before the English Courts or to act as Solicitors.

JOHN J. MALLOY, born Fountain Hill, Pennsylvania, May 25, 1948; admitted, 1973, Illinois; 1974, U.S. Tax Court; 1986, Connecticut; 1989, U.S. District Court, District of Connecticut; 1993, New York. *Education:* Moravian College (B.A., cum laude with distinction in Political Science, 1970); University of Notre Dame (J.D., 1973). Certificate of Completion, University of Notre Dame London Centre for Legal Studies. Adjunct Professor, Business Law, Ancell School of Business, Western Connecticut State University, 1988-1990. Chief Legal Officer, Eveready Battery Company, Inc., 1986-1987. International Area Attorney, Union Carbide Corporation, 1977-1986. Attorney, International Operations, Schering-Plough Corporation, 1974-1977. *Member:* Illinois State, Connecticut and New York State Bar Associations; The Corporate Bar Association of Westchester and Fairfield.

REPRESENTATIVE CORPORATE CLIENTS: Eveready Battery Company, Inc.; Ralston Purina Overseas Battery Company; High Performance Appliances, Inc.; International Alloy Services, Inc.; Bennet & Company, Inc.

MANCHES & CO.

Established in 1937

ALDWYCH HOUSE
81 ALDWYCH
LONDON WC2B 4RP, ENGLAND
Telephone: 0171-404-4433
Fax: 0171-430-1133
Telex: 266174 LDE

Oxford, England Office: 3 Worcester Street, OX1 2PZ. Telephone: 01865-722106.

Company and Commercial Law, Property, Litigation, Trusts and Probate and Family Law.

FIRM PROFILE: We are committed to achieving the objectives of our clients by finding solutions to their problems in a professional courteous and efficient manner. We believe in an imaginative and energetic approach to the practice of law, placing particular emphasis on personal service, speed of response, value for money, accessibility and the highest standards of professional excellence.

PARTNERS

Alasdair Simpson, Senior Partner
Alun G. Lamerton, Chief Executive

COMPANY COMMERCIAL

Simon Smith	Melvin Pedro
Peter Angel	Peter Stevens
Patrick Baddeley	Alistair Wilson
Robert Jonckheer	Stephen Goldstraw
David Tighe	Ian Yonge
Chris Shelley	Chris Owen

(This Listing Continued)

Simon Walker

COMMERCIAL PROPERTY

Louis Manches	Brian Hilditch
Bob Rowan	Richard Shaw
Derek Collinson	Nick Brent
Richard Frost	Giles Village
Nigel Brown	Caroline Greenbourne
	Linda Convery

COMMERCIAL LITIGATION

James Foster	Bernard Nyman
Charles Gordon	Nicholas Pryor
Julie Bond	Peter Shaw
John Rubinstein	Richard Cook
John Roebuck	Christopher Jones
	Steven Maier

FAMILY LAW

Jane Simpson	Helen Ward
Richard Sax	Jane Craig

TAX, WILLS & TRUSTS

Julian Hayden

CONSULTANTS

Sydney Gale
Michael Fowler
Timothy Robertson

MASONS

Established in 1947

30 AYLESBURY STREET

LONDON EC1R 0ER, ENGLAND

Telephone: 0171 490 4000
Telecopier: 0171 490 2545
Telex: 811117
DX: 53313 Clerkenwell

Hong Kong Office: 1301-05, One Pacific Place, 88 Queensway. Telephone: 852-2521 5621. DX: 9103. Fax: 852-2845 2956. Telex: 78000.

Guangzhou, People's Republic of China Office: Room S1804 18th Floor, South Tower, Guangzhou World Trade Centre, 371-375 Huanshi Dong Lu, 510060. Telephone: 86 20 766 0000. Fax: 86 20 777 1718.

Brussels, Belgium Office: Avenue Louise 391-Bte 1, B-1050. Telephone: (32) 2-646 0260. Fax: (32) 2-646 7323.

Cairo, Egypt Associated Office: Dr. Hatem Gabr. 5 Salah Salem Road, Heliopolis. Telephone: 2-669988/2-668245.

Bristol, England Office: Broad Street House, 5-8 Broad Street, BS1 2HW. Telephone: 0117-922 6622.Fax: 0117-922 6105. DX: 78154 Bristol.

Manchester, England Office: World Trade Centre, Exchange Quay, Manchester. M5 3EJ. Telephone: 0161-877 377. Fax: 0161-877 6869. DX: 25769 Old Trafford.

Leeds, England Office: Minerva House, 29 East Parade, LS1 5TN. Telephone: 0113 233 8905. Fax: 0113 245 4285. DX: 706955 Leeds Park Square.

FIRM PROFILE: Masons has offices in London, Bristol, Manchester, Leeds, Brussels, Hong Kong and Guangzhou and associated offices in the USA, across Scandinavia and in Cairo. The firm works regularly in continental Europe, the Middle East, the Pacific Rim, Africa and the Indian subcontinent.

Masons provides a broad range of legal services and is well known for advising the construction, engineering and computer industries. While the firm's main specialities include large-scale (often international) dispute
(This Listing Continued)

resolution and advice on major projects generally, Masons also offers a full range of commercial, legal risk management and private client services.

SENIOR PARTNER

John Bishop

MANAGING PARTNER

Anthony Bunch

PARTNERS

John Bishop
Adrian Watney
Neil Biggs
Barrie Lloyd
Peter Instone
Martin Harman
Peter Stockdale
Chris Williams
Anthony Bunch
Iain Monaghan
Robert McCallough
Phillip Capper
Martin Roberts
Iain Black (Resident, Hong Kong Office)
Guy Jordan
Mark Collingwood
Laurence Fryer
Mark Roe
Peter Wood
Steven Bond
Frances Alderson
Keith Hartley
Richard Davis
Mark Lane
Russell Booker
Adam Harris
Edward Davies
Anne Molyneux
Andrew Hibbert
Jonathan Cheung (Resident, Hong Kong Office)
Dean Lewis (Resident, Hong Kong Office)
Robert Lewington (Resident, Hong Kong Office)
John Moritz
Christopher Dering
Bonnie Martin
Peter Cassidy
Arun Singh
Ian Radford
Lawrence Davies
Dudley Solan
Richard Laudy
Clive Seddon
Mark Richards
Timothy Hill (Resident, Hong Kong Office)
Siobhan Cross
Ann Kilvington
Colin Rowe
Stephen Aldred
Steven Janes
Nigel Weiss
Luan Kane
Mark Catchpoole
Richard Williams
Rachel Burnett
Kate Gordon
Nicholas Berry
Shelagh Gaskill
Beverley Pike

Languages: English, French, German, Spanish, Italian, Mandarin, Cantonese, Hindi, Urdu, Punjabi, Malay and Turkish

MATHESON ORMSBY PRENTICE

1 PEMBERTON ROW
FETTER LANE
LONDON EC4A 3BA, ENGLAND
Telephone: +44 171 404 0998
Fax: +44 171 583 5644

Dublin, Ireland Office: 3 Burlington Road. Telephone: +353-1-6760981. Telex: 500-93310 MOP EI. Cable Address: "Matsack" Dublin. Fax: Group 3/Group +353-1-6760501.

Corporate and Commercial Law, Mergers and Acquisitions, Joint Ventures, Banking and Financial Services, Investment Fund Management, Aircraft and Ship Financing, Structured Finance, Corporate Insolvency and Rescues, Taxation, Intellectual Property and Information Technology Law, European Community Law, Competition Law, Trade Law, Pensions and Employment Law, Insurance and Reinsurance, Environmental Law, Real Estate, Construction Law, Commercial Litigation and Arbitration, Telecommunications, Oil and Gas and Mineral Exploration, Food and Drug Law, Consumer Law, Entertainment Law, Sports Law, Debt Recovery, Immigration Law and Probate, Trusts and Estate Planning.

FIRM PROFILE: Matheson Ormsby Prentice was founded in 1825 and is one of Ireland's largest and leading law firms with a substantial domestic and international practice specializing in Corporate and Commercial Law, Mergers and Acquisitions, Banking and Financial Services, Corporate and Structural Finance, Investment Fund Management, European Community Law, Intellectual Property and Information Technology Law, Competition Law, Taxation and Environmental Law.

MEMBERS OF FIRM

STANLEY G. WATSON, born 1962; admitted, 1988, Ireland and England and Wales. *Education:* University College, Dublin (B.C.L., 1985); Incorporated Law Society of Ireland (Solicitor, 1988). *PRACTICE AREAS:* Corporate; Commercial Law.

All Partners are Members of the Incorporated Law Society of Ireland and Dublin Solicitors Bar Association.

Languages: English, French, German and Italian

REFERENCES: Citibank N.A., Dublin; Allied Irish Banks, Dublin; Bank of Ireland, Dublin.

MAXWELL BATLEY

27 CHANCERY LANE
LONDON WC2A 1PA, ENGLAND
Telephone: 0171 405 7888; International Telephone: 44 171 405 7888
Fax: 0171 242 7133; International Fax: 44 171 242 7133

Banking, Company/Commercial, Corporate Finance, Litigation, Trust, Pensions, Tax & Estates, Commercial and Residential Property.

FIRM PROFILE: The firm aims to provide practical, commercially-oriented and sometimes innovative advice, promptly and cost effectively. It attaches particular importance to direct partner involvement.

PARTNERS

MICHAEL JOHN CASSIDY. PRACTICE AREAS: International Investment; Commercial Property.

MARTIN SHEETER. PRACTICE AREAS: Commercial Property.

PETER RADFORD. PRACTICE AREAS: Commercial Property.

RAYMOND LEVINE. PRACTICE AREAS: Commercial Property Development; Commercial Property Finance.

FRASER MCCOLL. PRACTICE AREAS: Banking, Company and Commercial.

FRANK O'SHEA. PRACTICE AREAS: Trust; Pensions; Tax; Estates.

PHILIP KNIGHTS. PRACTICE AREAS: Property Litigation; Commercial Litigation; Employment.

IAN MCINTYRE, *Member:* International Bar Association. *PRACTICE AREAS:* Company and Commercial; Venture Capital; Information Technology.

NIGEL WILSON. PRACTICE AREAS: Commercial Property.

PHILIP ADAMS. PRACTICE AREAS: Property Litigation; Commercial Litigation.

(This Listing Continued)

EU290B

TIMOTHY HARRIS. PRACTICE AREAS: Commercial Property.

JEREMY FIELDHOUSE. PRACTICE AREAS: Commercial Property.

CHRISTOPHER NORTH. PRACTICE AREAS: Corporate Finance.

CANDICE M. BLACKWOOD, *Member:* Law Society of Scotland. *PRACTICE AREAS:* Commercial Property.

JONATHAN ASHBRIDGE. PRACTICE AREAS: Company and Commercial.

Languages: French, German, Italian and Spanish.

MAYCOCK'S

Solicitors

BROADGATE HOUSE
7 ELDON STREET
LONDON EC2M 7LS, ENGLAND
Telephone: 0171 375 0586
Fax: 0171 375 0587

Intellectual Property Matters, Patent and Trademarks Law.

FIRM PROFILE: The Firm specializes in all aspects of contentious and non-contentious intellectual property matters, including European law relating to Intellectual Property and in the management of Litigation in other European jurisdictions.

PARTNER

JOHN D'AUVERGNE MAYCOCK, MA LLM (Cantab) MITMA; Solicitor, admitted 1971, England; Registered Trade Mark Agent. *LANGUAGES:* French. *PRACTICE AREAS:* Patents; Trade Marks; Copyright; Designs; Licensing; Litigation; Anti-counterfeiting.

CONSULTANT

OLIVER MALAND, BA, Dip Law, Barrister 1981, Gray's Inn, England. *PRACTICE AREAS:* Patents; Trade Marks; Copyright; Designs; Licensing; Litigation; Anti-counterfeiting; Information Technology; Computer Contracts.

MAYER, BROWN & PLATT

(Mayer, Friedlich, Spiess, Tierney, Brown & Platt)

162 QUEEN VICTORIA STREET
LONDON EC4V 4DB, ENGLAND
Telephone: 011-44-171-248-1465
Fax: 011-44-171-329-4465
Telex: 8811095
Cable: LEMAYLDN

Chicago, Illinois Office: 190 South LaSalle Street, 60603-3441. Telephone: (312) 782-0600. Pitney Bowes: (312) 701-7711. Telex: 190404. Cable: LEMAY.

Washington, D.C. Office: 2000 Pennsylvania Avenue, N.W., 20006-1882. Telephone: (202) 463-2000. Pitney Bowes: (202) 861-0484, Pitney Bowes: (202) 861-0473. Telex: 892603. Cable: LEMAYDC.

New York, New York Office: 787 Seventh Avenue, Suite 2400, 10019-6018. Telephone: (212) 554-3000. Pitney Bowes: (212) 262-1910. Telex: 701842. Cable: LEMAYEN.

Houston, Texas Office: 700 Louisiana Street, Suite 3600, 77002-2730. Telephone: (713) 221-1651. Pitney Bowes: (713) 224-6410. Telex: 775809. Cable: LEMAYHOU.

Los Angeles, California Office: 350 South Grand Avenue, 25th Floor, 90071-1503. Telephone: (213) 229-9500. Pitney Bowes: (213) 625-0248. Telex: 188089. Cable: LEMAYLA.

Tokyo, Japan Office: (Kawachi Gaikokuho Jimu Bengoshi Jimusho). Urbannet Otemachi Building 13F 2-2, Otemachi 2-chome, Chiyoda-ku, Tokyo 100. Telephone: 011-81-3-5255-9700. Facsimile: 011-81-3-5255-9797.

Berlin, Germany Office: Spreeifer 5, 10178. Telephone: 011-49-30-240-7930. Facsimile: 011-49-30-240-79344.

Brussels, Belgium Office: Square de Meeûs 19/20, Bte. 4, 1040. Telephone: 011-32-2-512-9878. Fax: 011-32-2-511-3305. Telex: 20768 MBPBRU B.

(This Listing Continued)

Mexico City, Mexico, D.F., Mexico Correspondent: Jáuregui, Navarrete, Nader y Rojas, S.C., Abogados, Paseo de la Reforma 199, Pisos 15, 16 y 17, 06500. Telephone: 011-525-591-16-55. Fax: 011-525-535-80-62; 011-525-703-22-47. Cable: JANANE.

General Practice.

Firm engaged in American and General International Practice but not authorized to appear before the English Courts or to act as Solicitors.

PARTNERS

RICHARD A. COLE, born Syracuse, New York, February 21, 1951; admitted, 1976, Illinois and U.S. District Court, Northern District of Illinois (Not admitted in England). *Education:* Brown University (A.B., magna cum laude, 1973); Cornell University (J.D., magna cum laude, 1976). Phi Beta Kappa; Order of the Coif. Member, Board of Editors, Cornell Law Review, 1975-1976. Co-Author: *International Banking Centres,* Euromoney Publications, 1982; "Commercial Paper - The Bankers Trust Case," Journal of International Banking Law, Vol. 1, Issue 1, 1986; "The College Retirement Equities Fund No-Action Letter," Butterworths Journal of International Banking and Financial Law, Vol. 2, No. 1, 1987; "Securities Act Arbitration," International Financial Law Review, Vol. VI, No. 9, 1987; "Multi-Currency Global Medium Term Notes," International Financial Law Review, Vol. VI, No. 11, 1987; "Preliminary Merger Talks May Require Disclosure," Butterworths Journal of International Banking and Financial Law, Vol. III, No. 3, 1988; "Securities Exchange Act Arbitration," International Financial Law Review, Vol. VIII, No. 7 (1989); "MTN Programmes and Regulations S," International Law Review, Vol. 1X, No. 10 (1990); "Rule 144A: Outside Issuers and the U.S. Market," Global Investment Management, Volume 1, No. 3 (1991); "American Depositary Receipts," Journal of International Banking Law, Volume 6, issue 12 (1991).

IAN R. COLES, born Mexborough, England, September 12, 1956; admitted, 1979, England; 1983, New York. *Education:* Cambridge University, England (B.A., 1978); Harvard University (LL.M., 1981). Churchill Scholar (Cambridge University). Walter Wigglesworth & Hardwick Scholar. Megarry Student (Lincoln's Inn). Co-author: with Jason H.P. Kravitt and C. Mark Nicolaides, "Cross-Border Securitization in Europe," International Financial Law Review, November, 1991. Author: "Remittances," 1979 British Tax Review 233. Lecturer-in-Law, City of London Polytechnic, 1978-1980. Contributing Author: *A Guide to the Capital Markets Activities of Banks and Bank Holding Companies,* Michael G. Capatides. *Member:* New York State Bar Association; Bar Association of Commerce, Finance and Industry; International Bar Association (Member, Section on Business Law).

PETER M. GAINES, born New York, N.Y., March 5, 1951; admitted, 1975, Illinois; 1988, New York (Not admitted in England). *Education:* University of Wisconsin (B.A., 1972; J.D., 1975). Order of the Coif. Note and Comment Editor, Wisconsin Law Review, 1974-1975.

DOUGLAS M. RUTHERFORD, born Dallas, Texas, April 1, 1959; admitted, 1983, Illinois and U.S. District Court, Northern District of Illinois; 1988, District of Columbia (Not admitted in England). *Education:* Carleton College (B.A., magna cum laude, 1980); New York University (J.D., 1983). Phi Beta Kappa. Research Editor, Moot Court Board, 1982-1983. Moot Court Advocacy Award Winner. Author: "Chapter 6, Uniform Commercial Code," Securitization of Financial Assets (Prentice Hall Law and Business, 1991). *Member:* American Bar Association (Member, Secured Transactions Subcommittee, UCC Committee, Business Law Section).

ASSOCIATES

Marwan Al-Turki; Catherine M. Collins (Not admitted in England); **Manzer Ijaz; Nabil L. Khodadad** (Not admitted in England); **Stefan H. Sarles** (Not admitted in England); **Mark R. Uhrynuk** (Not admitted in England); **Thomas C. Wexler** (Not admitted in England); **Nigel A. Wright; Karen L. Young** (Not admitted in England).

Attorneys in London Office listing speak the following languages: Arabic, Chinese (Mandarin), Farsi, French, German, Italian, Japanese, Spanish.

McCANN FITZGERALD
IMPERIAL HOUSE, 15-19 KINGSWAY
LONDON WC2B 6UN, ENGLAND
Telephone: +44-171-379 0914
Fax: +44-171-836 2759

Dublin, Ireland Office: 2 Harbourmaster Place, Custom House Dock, Dublin, 1. Telephone: +353-1-829 0000/670 1111. Fax: +353-1-829 0010.
Brussels, Belgium Office: Rue de la Loi 99 Wetstraat, Brussels B-1040. Telephone: +32-2-230 3634. Fax: +32-2-230 2562.
New York, New York Office: Thirtieth Floor, 399 Park Avenue, NY, 10022-4697. Telephone: +1-212-318 6700. Fax: +1-212-318 6710.

Corporate, Commercial, Banking and Financial Services, Foreign Investment, Mergers and Takeovers, Real Estate and Property Development, Litigation, Taxation, EU and Competition Law, Oil and Gas, Environmental Law, Aviation, Maritime and Shipping Law, Communications and Media, Insolvency, Labour Law, Pensions Law, Construction Contracts and Arbitration, Intellectual Property, Nationality, Probate, Trusts and General Practice.

JOHN A. CRONIN, born 1959; admitted, 1984, Ireland; 1991, England and Wales. *Education:* Trinity College, Dublin (B.A., Mod. Legal Science). **PRACTICE AREAS:** Banks and Banking; Assets Finance; Financial Services.

BARBARA JUDGE, born 1961; admitted, 1986, Ireland. *Education:* Trinity College, Dublin (B.A. Mod.). **PRACTICE AREAS:** Asset Finance; Banks and Banking; Corporate Law.

All solicitors are members of the Incorporated Law Society of Ireland. All partners are members of the Dublin Solicitors Bar Association.

Languages: English, French, German and Spanish

McCARTHY TÉTRAULT
1 PEMBERTON ROW
FETTER LANE
LONDON EC4A 3BA, ENGLAND
Telephone: 011-44-171-353-2355
Facsimile: 011-44-171-583-5644

Vancouver, British Columbia Office: Suite 1300, 777 Dunsmuir Street, P.O. Box 10424, Vancouver, British Columbia V7Y 1K2. Telephone: 604-643-7100. Facsimile: 604-643-7900.
Surrey, British Columbia Office: Suite 1300, Station Tower, Gateway 13401-108th Avenue, Surrey, British Columbia V3T 5T3. Telephone: 604-583-9100. Fax: 604-583-9150.
Calgary, Alberta Office: Suite 3200, 421-7 Avenue, S.W., Calgary, Alberta T2P 4K9. Telephone: 403-260-3500. Facsimile: 403-260-3501.
London, Ontario Office: Suite 2000, One London Place, 255 Queens Avenue, London, Ontario N6A 5R8. Telephone: 519-660-3587. Facsimile: 519-660-3599.
Toronto, Ontario Office: Suite 4700, Toronto Dominion Bank Tower, Toronto-Dominion Centre, Toronto, Ontario M5K 1E6. Telephone: 416-362-1812. Facsimile: 416-868-0673.
Ottawa, Ontario Office: Suite 1000, 275 Spark Street, Ottawa, Ontario K1R 7X9. Telephone: 613-238-2000. Facsimile: 613-563-9386.
Montréal, Québec Office: "le Windsor" 1170 rue Peel, Montréal, Québec H3B 4S8. Telephone: 514-397-4100. Facsimile: 514-875-6246.
Québec, Québec Office: Le Complexe St-Amable 1150, rue Claire Fontaine 7e Étage, Québec, Québec G1R 5G4. Telephone: 418-521-3000. Facsimile: 418-521-3099.

FIRM PROFILE: McCarthy Tétrault, Canada's national law firm, is a partnership of more than 534 lawyers across Canada. The firm's history pre-dates that of Canadian confederation: McCarthy & McCarthy was founded in Toronto in 1855 and Clarkson, Tétrault was founded in Montréal in 1885. The McCarthy Tétrault partnership was created on February 1, 1990.

McCarthy Tétrault is also Canada's largest law firm and maintains offices in Surrey, Vancouver, Calgary, London (Ontario), Toronto, Ottawa, Montréal, and Québec. In 1987, the firm also opened an office in London, England to provide services to continental Europe. The firm's patent and trade-mark agents can provide legal services in English, French, German, and Spanish.

Our mission is to provide our clients with the highest quality legal services in a timely and cost-effective way. We provide legal services through rela-

(This Listing Continued)

McCARTHY TÉTRAULT, London—Continued

tionships built on trust and confidence while drawing on the specialized knowledge and experience of lawyers throughout the firm.

The firm provides clients with legal expertise and advice in 13 different practice areas including: banking and insolvency; business; corporate finance and securities; communications and entertainment; constitutional-/administrative/regulatory law; estate, wills and trusts; intellectual property and technology; labour and employment; litigation; natural resources; pensions and retirement income planning; real estate/municipal/environmental law; and taxation.

OLIVER J. BORGERS, born Toronto, Ontario, 1960; admitted, 1988, Ontario (Not admitted in England). *Education:* University of Toronto (B.A. (Hons.), 1983; LL.M., 1988); University of Ottawa (LL.B., 1986). *PRACTICE AREAS:* Competition and Antitrust; Corporate Reorganizations; Foreign Investment; Mergers and Acquisitions; Securities.

HARRY W. MACDONELL, Q.C., born July 19, 1929; admitted, 1956, Ontario (Not admitted in England). *Education:* Carleton University (B.Comm., 1952); Osgoode Hall Law School (LL.B., 1956). (Also at Toronto, Ontario Office). *PRACTICE AREAS:* Corporate Reorganization and Energy.

(For biographical data on Vancouver, British Columbia; Surrey, British Columbia; Calgary, Alberta; London, Ontario; Toronto, Ontario; Ottawa, Ontario; Montréal and Québec; Québec, Québec personnel, see professional Biographies at each of those cities)

McCLURE NAISMITH ANDERSON & GARDINER

Established in 1826

12 MASONS AVENUE
LONDON EC2V 5BT, ENGLAND
Telephone: 0171-600-5408
Facsimile: 0171-600-5409

Commercial and Company Law, Banking, Commercial Property, Intellectual Property, Civil Litigation, Environmental Law.

FIRM PROFILE: *Established in 1826 in Glasgow, the firm is now one of Scotland's leading commercial law firms. The London office of the firm was opened in May, 1991.*

RESIDENT PARTNER

ROBIN T. SHANNAN, born Wanlockhead, Scotland, January 26, 1952; admitted, 1977, Scotland (Not admitted in England). *Education:* University of Dundee (M.A., 1973; LL.B., 1975). *Member:* Law Society of Scotland (Working Party of the Law Society on Banking Law, 1987-1989); International Bar Association. *LANGUAGES:* English. *PRACTICE AREAS:* Corporate Acquisition and Disposals; Banking.

CONSULTANT

ANDREW PAGE, born London, England, November 29, 1935; admitted, 1963, England. *Education:* Oxford University (M.A., Jurisprudence, 1959). *Member:* The Law Society; International Bar Association; The Industrial Law Society; The Employment Lawyers Association; The Association of Personal Injury Lawyers. *LANGUAGES:* English. *PRACTICE AREAS:* Employment Law; Personal Injury; Professional Indemnity Litigation.

G. PAUL GILKS, born Nottingham, England, May 12, 1954; admitted, 1979, England. *Education:* London University (LL.B., 1976). Recipient, Andrews Prizeman Award, London University. *Member:* The Law Society; Solicitors European Group. *LANGUAGES:* English and French. *PRACTICE AREAS:* Corporate Finance; Banking.

McGRIGOR DONALD

63 QUEEN VICTORIA STREET
LONDON EC4N 4ST, ENGLAND
Telephone: 44 171 329 3299
Fax: 44 171 329 4000

Glasgow, Scotland Office: Pacific House, 70 Wellington Street, G2 6SB. Telephone: 44 41 248 6677. Facsimile: 44 41 204 1351/221 1390.
Edinburgh, Scotland Office: Erskine House, 68-73 Queen Street, EH2 4NF. Telephone: 44 31 226 7777. Fax: 44 31 226 7700.

(This Listing Continued)

English Affiliated Firm: Morrison Skirrow, Solicitors.

Scottish and International Law.

MANAGING PARTNER

ROBERT M. GLENNIE, born Scotland, April 4, 1951; admitted, 1977, Scotland. *Education:* Strathclyde University (LL.B., 1975).

(For Complete Biographical Data on all Personnel, see Professional Biographies at Glasgow, Scotland).

McKENNA & CO

Established in 1882

MITRE HOUSE
160 ALDERSGATE STREET
LONDON EC1A 4DD, ENGLAND
Telephone: 0171-606 9000
Telex: 27251
Fax: 0171-606 9100 CDE: Box 724

London Lloyd's Office: 908 Lloyd's, One Lime Street, London EC3M 7DQ. Telephone: 0171-929 1250. Fax: 0171-626 5749 DX Box 724.
Brussels, Belgium Office: Avenue de Cortenberg 66, Box 10, B-1040. Telephone: (32)(2)735.38.36. Telex: 27122. Fax: (32)(2)735.77.43.
Budapest, Hungary Office: H-1122. Maros utca 22, 1st Floor. Telephone: (36)(1) 202 6527; (36)(1) 202 6936; (36)(1) 201 9199; (36)(1) 156 5354. Fax: (36)(1) 156 5391.
Moscow, Russia Office: McKenna & Co, International, MosenkáPlaza, 24/27 Sadovaya-Samotyochnaya Street, Russian Federation, Moscow, 103051. Telephone: (7 501) 258 5000. Fax: (7 501)258 5100.
Prague, Czech Republic Office: Betlémský palác, First Floor, Husova 5, 110 00 Prague 1. Telephone: (42)(2) 2424 8518-22. Fax: 42(2) 2424 8524.
Warsaw, Poland Office: McKenna & Co Sp. zo.o., ul. Kopernika 30, Suite 213, 00-950, Warsaw. Telephone: (48) 22 26 69 88. Fax: (48) 22 26 41 93.
Hong Kong Office: 5th Floor, Lippo Tower, 89 Queensway, Hong Kong. Telephone: (852) 846 9100. Fax: (852) 845 3575.
Associated Firms:
Sigle Loose Schmidt-Diemitz and Partners: Stuttgart, Berlin, Leipzig, Frankfurt/Main, Chemnitz and Moscow. .
Minter Ellison: Sydney, Melbourne, Canberra, Brisbane and the Gold Coast.

FIRM PROFILE: *McKenna & Co. is a major London-based UK and international law firm. The firm's practice is directed primarily towards industrial and commercial corporate clients, financial institutions and governments, covering the legal areas of corporate finance, financial services, banking, project and asset finance, tax mergers and acquisitions, company and commercial law; property (real estate) ownership, acquisition, finance and development; dispute resolution, litigation and arbitration; and including related topics such as anti-trust, employment and pensions, planning and environmental law, and intellectual property.*

The range of advice spans corporate and property matters, commercial transactions, infrastructure projects (notably relating to transport and energy) and privatizations. It includes expertise in specialized subjects such as construction, healthcare and pharmaceuticals, energy, insurance, utilities and waste management, information technology and biotechnology, coupled with a high degree of industry knowledge of these areas.

The firm's clients are largely European (a substantial part of the practice consisting of representing European subsidiaries of US corporations), but also significant are Japanese and other Asia-Pacific based companies.

The firm's partners and staff include people with qualifications in subjects other than law which are relevant to their area of expertise (such as medicine in the healthcare practice) and languages spoken include most of the major European languages, Chinese and Japanese.

PARTNERS

CHRISTOPHER B. POWELL-SMITH, TD Clements Inn & Travers Smith Prizes, admitted 1959. (Senior Partner). *PRACTICE AREAS:* Corporate Law; Corporate Finance; Securities.

PAUL R. ELLINGTON, admitted 1963. *PRACTICE AREAS:* Corporate Law; Corporate Finance.

RICHARD J. J. TAYLOR, M.A. (Oxon), admitted 1969. *PRACTICE AREAS:* European Community; Anti-trust Law; Trade Regulation; Investment in Europe.

(This Listing Continued)

JOHN B. DRIFFIELD, LL.B. (Leeds), admitted 1960. *PRACTICE AREAS:* Property; Commercial Property.

ROBERT J. WINDMILL, admitted 1964. *PRACTICE AREAS:* Corporate Law; Investment in Eastern Europe.

IAN C. GATENBY, M.A. (Oxon), admitted 1968. *PRACTICE AREAS:* Zoning, Planning and Land Use.

GUY BILLINGTON, M.A. (Cantab), admitted 1971. *PRACTICE AREAS:* Corporate Law; Corporate Finance; Securities.

MICHAEL W. RICH, M.A. (Cantab), admitted 1971. *PRACTICE AREAS:* Mergers, Acquisitions and Divestitures.

STEPHEN K. WHYBROW, M.A.; LL.B. (Cantab), admitted 1971. *PRACTICE AREAS:* Intellectual Property.

ROBERT J. PHILLIPS, admitted 1971. *PRACTICE AREAS:* Project Finance; Energy; Project Development; Transport Projects.

ROBIN J.A. WILLIAMS, M.A. (Oxon), admitted 1973. *PRACTICE AREAS:* Insurance.

SEAN M. WATSON, LL.B. (Man.), admitted 1972. *PRACTICE AREAS:* Corporate Law; Corporate Finance; Securities.

NICHOLAS A. BROWN, B.A. (Bristol), admitted 1974. *PRACTICE AREAS:* Property; Commercial Property.

C. FIONA WOOLF, B.A. (Keele), admitted 1973. *PRACTICE AREAS:* Energy; Electricity; Energy Regulations; Power Projects.

B. ANTHONY R. CONCANON, F.C.A., admitted 1976. *PRACTICE AREAS:* Corporate Law; Corporate Taxation.

JULIAN A. OGLEY, B.A. (Oxon), admitted 1973. *PRACTICE AREAS:* Corporate Law; Corporate Finance; Securities.

ANTHONY L. MARKS, LL.B. (Bristol), Admitted 1975. *PRACTICE AREAS:* Litigation; Alternative Dispute Resolution.

IAN C. DODDS-SMITH, M.A. (Cantab), admitted 1976. *PRACTICE AREAS:* Healthcare; Products Liability.

PETER J. LONG, B.A. (Oxon), admitted 1978. *PRACTICE AREAS:* Construction.

JOHN M. CUNLIFFE, LL.B. (Liverpool) B.C.L. (Oxon) Timprom Martin, Edmund Thos Child, John Marshall and Cliffords Inn Prizes, admitted 1959. *PRACTICE AREAS:* Employee Benefits; Pensions.

RICHARD S. PRICE, B.A., LL.B. (Leeds), admitted 1977. *PRACTICE AREAS:* Company Law; Waste Management; Utilities; Rail.

ROBERT S. DERRY-EVANS, M.A. (Oxon), admitted 1977. (Managing Partner).

R. CHARLES C. GAIT, M.A. (Cantab), admitted 1980. *PRACTICE AREAS:* Property; Commercial Property.

E. ANN MINOGUE, M.A. (Cantab), admitted 1980. *PRACTICE AREAS:* Construction.

NEIL C. AITKEN, admitted 1977. *PRACTICE AREAS:* Litigation; Alternative Dispute Resolution.

HENRY C. SHERMAN, B.A. (Oxon), admitted 1978. *PRACTICE AREAS:* Construction.

JULIAN P. THURSTON, M.A. (Oxon), admitted 1979. *PRACTICE AREAS:* Computer and Software; Biotechnology; Commercial Law.

GARY R. HICKINBOTTOM, M.A. (Oxon), admitted 1981. *PRACTICE AREAS:* Healthcare; Litigation.

JUSTIN EDE, LL.B. (Wales), admitted 1978. *PRACTICE AREAS:* Litigation; Alternative Dispute Resolution.

PETER N. SMITH, LL.B. (Bris), admitted 1980. *PRACTICE AREAS:* Corporate Law; Investments; Corporate Finance.

ANDREW S. IVISON, M.A. (Cantab), admitted 1980. *PRACTICE AREAS:* Banks and Banking; Finance.

JOHN T. UWINS, M.A. (Cantab); B.A. (Cantab), admitted 1981. *PRACTICE AREAS:* Construction.

MICHAEL C. LANGDON, M.A. (Oxon), admitted 1981. *PRACTICE AREAS:* Property; Property Litigation.

E. KATE KELLEHER, M.A. (Oxon), admitted 1980. *PRACTICE AREAS:* Corporate Law; Corporate Taxation.

(This Listing Continued)

TIMOTHY P. F. HARDY, admitted 1977. *PRACTICE AREAS:* Litigation; Alternative Dispute Resolution.

ANTHONY F. LORING, B.A. (London), admitted 1979. *PRACTICE AREAS:* Corporate Law; Corporate Insolvency; Corporate Recovery.

SIMON B. JEFFREYS, M.A. (Cantab), admitted 1982. *PRACTICE AREAS:* Labour Law; Employment Law; Immigration Law; Naturalization Law.

DAVID R. MARKS, LL.B. (Liverpool); LL.M. (Oxon), admitted 1983. *PRACTICE AREAS:* European Community; Anti-trust Law; Trade Regulations.

STEPHEN J. FORSTER, M.A. (Cantab), admitted 1979. (Resident in Budapest). *PRACTICE AREAS:* Mergers, Acquisitions and Divestitures; Investment in Central and Eastern Europe.

NICHOLAS M. HADLEY, LL.B., Ph.D. (Law) (Birmingham), admitted 1979. *PRACTICE AREAS:* Property; Commercial Property.

TIMOTHY J. BURTON, LL.B. (Soton), admitted 1982. *PRACTICE AREAS:* Insurance.

DAVID H. RENTON, B.A. (Sussex) J.D. (Berkeley, California), admitted 1976, California. (Resident in Hong Kong). *PRACTICE AREAS:* Finance; Project Finance; Corporate Law; Corporate Finance.

JONATHAN M. VIVIAN, M.A., LL.B. (Cantab), admitted 1980. *PRACTICE AREAS:* Property; Commercial Property.

CHRISTOPHER J.S. HODGES, M.A. (Oxon), admitted 1979. *PRACTICE AREAS:* Healthcare; Products Liability.

ANTHONY B. KITSON, LL.B. (Warwick), admitted 1975. *PRACTICE AREAS:* Zoning, Planning and Land Use.

ROBERT C. LANE, LL.B. (London), admitted 1982. *PRACTICE AREAS:* Energy; Electricity; Energy Regulation.

MARTIN C. MENDELSSOHN, LL.B. (Bristol), admitted 1982. *PRACTICE AREAS:* Mergers, Acquisitions and Divestitures; Investment in Europe.

JONATHAN P. BECKITT, LL.B. (Bristol), admitted 1984. *PRACTICE AREAS:* Property Law.

ROBERT H. PORTER, admitted 1984. *PRACTICE AREAS:* Property; Commercial Property.

MARK V. HENRICK, LL.B. (Reading), admitted 1981. *PRACTICE AREAS:* Corporate Law; Corporate Finance; Utilities; Investments.

JAMES S. RICHARDS, M.A. (Oxford), admitted 1984. *PRACTICE AREAS:* Banks and Banking; Finance.

JOHN R. NACCARATO, LL.B. (Soton), admitted 1984. *PRACTICE AREAS:* Banks and Banking; Finance.

RICHARD H. TYLER, M.A. (Cantab), admitted 1985. *PRACTICE AREAS:* Corporate Law; Corporate Finance; Securities.

MARK L. TYLER, M.A. (Oxon); LL.M. (Lond), admitted 1979. *PRACTICE AREAS:* Labour and Employment; Occupational Health and Safety; Health Care.

TREVOR BUTCHER, LL.B. (Leics.), admitted 1986. (Resident in Hong Kong). *PRACTICE AREAS:* Construction.

ELENA KIRILLOVA, LL.B. (N.S.W. Australia), admitted 1991. *PRACTICE AREAS:* Commercial Law; Natural Resources; Investment in the CIS.

SUSAN C. BARTY, LL.B. (Bristol), admitted 1985. *PRACTICE AREAS:* Litigation.

PAMELA M. CASTLE, B.Sc. (London), admitted 1988. *PRACTICE AREAS:* Environmental Law.

RAFIQUE A. KHAN, LL.B. (Leeds), admitted 1986. *PRACTICE AREAS:* Energy and Natural Resources.

NIGEL C. MOORE, LL.B. (Warks); M.A. (London), admitted 1986. *PRACTICE AREAS:* Pensions and Employee Benefits.

MARK B. NICHOLS, LL.B. (London), admitted 1990. *PRACTICE AREAS:* Corporate Tax.

MICHAEL G. DRAPER, admitted, 1984. *Education:* (Can Tab). *PRACTICE AREAS:* Corporate; Finance; Securities.

(This Listing Continued)

McKENNA & CO, London—Continued

CONSULTANTS

RICHARD H. MALTHOUSE, John Mackrell Prize, M.A. (Cantab) admitted 1957. (Former Senior Partner).

RICHARD F. PORTER, M.A.; LL.B. (Cambridge), admitted 1958. **PRACTICE AREAS:** Property.

DR. H. ELIZABETH DRIVER, B.S.c.; MBBS. Diptox MRC PATH (London). **PRACTICE AREAS:** Healthcare.

EDWARD J. SWAN, admitted, 1976. *Education:* (B.A.); Juris Doctor (New York).

MEMERY CRYSTAL

31 SOUTHAMPTON ROW
LONDON WC1B 5HT, ENGLAND
Telephone: 0171-242 5905
Telex: 298957 MEMLAW G
Fax: 0171-242 2058

General Practice, Corporate, Commercial, International, Property, Trust, Probate, Litigation, Tax, Immigration, Intellectual Property.

PARTNERS

Peter M. Crystal	Douglas L. Robertson
D. Harvey Rands	Lesley A. Gregory
Jonathan P. Davies	Bernard D.F. Clarke
Andrew G. St J. Newman	

CONSULTANT

W.V. John Memery

MERSHON, SAWYER, JOHNSTON, DUNWODY & COLE

A Partnership including Professional Associations
Established in 1920

BLAKE LODGE
BRIDGE LANE
LONDON SW11 3AD, ENGLAND
Telephone: 44-171-978-7748
44-171-350-0156

REVISERS OF THE FLORIDA LAW DIGEST FOR THIS DIRECTORY.

Miami, Florida Office: Suite 4500 First Union Financial Center, 200 South Biscayne Boulevard. Telephone: 305-358-5100. Cable Address: "Mercole." Telex: 515705. Fax: 305-376-8654.

Naples, Florida Office: Pelican Bay Corporate Centre, Suite 501, 5551 Ridgewood Drive. Telephone: 813-598-1055. Fax: 813-598-1868.

West Palm Beach, Florida Office: 777 South Flagler Drive, Suite 900. Telephone: 407-659-5990. Fax: 407-659-6313.

Key West, Florida Office: 3132 North Side Drive, Suite 102. Telephone: 305-296-1774. Fax: 305-29 6-1715.

General Civil Trial and Appellate Practice in all Courts and Administrative Agencies, Admiralty, Antitrust, Banking, Bankruptcy, Construction, Corporation, Environmental Law, Estate Planning, Finance, Health Care, Intellectual Property, International, Labor and Employment Relations, Land Use Law, Probate, Products Liability, Real Property, Securities and Federal, State and Local Tax Law.

MEMBER OF FIRM

BARRY G. CRAIG, (P.A.), born Hartford, Connecticut, October 31, 1941; admitted, 1968, Florida and District of Columbia. *Education:* Wesleyan University (B.A., with high honors and distinction, 1963); Yale Law School (LL.B., 1967). Phi Beta Kappa. Editor and Business Manager, Yale Law Journal, 1965-1967. Chairman of the Board, St. Francis Hospital, Miami Beach, Florida, 1982-1984. Member, Board of Directors, Florida Association of Hospital Attorneys, 1983-1991. Director and Secretary, 1983-1986, Director and Vice President, 1986-1988, President, 1988-1990, Director and Member of the Executive Committee of the International Bank of Miami, N.A., 1984-1992. Director, Saztec International, Inc., Trustee Per-

(This Listing Continued)

forming Arts Center Trust. *Member:* The District of Columbia Bar; The Florida Bar; American Bar Association. **PRACTICE AREAS:** International Law; Business Law; Banking Law; Tax Exempt Financing Law.

OF COUNSEL

A. PATRICK GILES, born Minneapolis, Minnesota, March 18, 1940; admitted, 1969, Michigan. *Education:* Dartmouth College (A.B., 1962); Amos Tuck School of Business (M.B.A., 1963) ; University of Michigan Law School (J.D., 1968); International Law Seminar, International Court of Justice (Diploma, 1969). *Member:* State Bar of Michigan; American and International Bar Associations; Law Society of England and Wales (Honorary Member). (Also Member, Giles & Associates, London, England). **PRACTICE AREAS:** Mergers and Acquisitions; International Bankruptcy and Reorganizations; Project Finance; Sports and Leisure.

REVISERS OF THE FLORIDA LAW DIGEST FOR THIS DIRECTORY.

MILBANK, TWEED, HADLEY & McCLOY

ROPEMAKER PLACE
25 ROPEMAKER STREET
LONDON EC2Y 9AS, ENGLAND
Telephone: 44-171-374-0423
Cable Address: "MILTUK G"
Fax: 44-171-374-0912

Offices of an Affiliated Partnership:

New York, New York Office: 1 Chase Manhattan Plaza, 10005. Telephone: 212-530-5000. Cable Address: "Miltweed NYK" ITT: 422962; 423893. Fax: 212- 530-5219. ABA/net: Milbank NY. MCI Mail: Milbank Tweed.

Midtown Office: 50 Rockefeller Plaza, 10020. Telephone: 212-530-5800. Fax: 212-530-0158.

Los Angeles, California Office: 601 South Figueroa Street, 30th Floor, 90017. Telephone: 213-892-4000. Fax: 213-629-5063. Telex: 678754. ABA Net: Milbank LA.

Washington, D.C. Office: Suite 1100, 1825 Eye Street, N.W., 20006. Telephone: 202-835-7500. Cable Address: "Miltweed Wsh". ITT 440667. Fax: 202-835-7586. ABA/net: Milbank DC.

Tokyo, Japan Office: Nippon Press Center Building, 2-1, Uchisaiwai-cho 2-chome, Chiyoda-ku, Tokyo 100. Telephone: 81-3-3504-1050. Fax: 81-3-3595-2790; 81-3-3502-5192.

Hong Kong Office: 3007 Alexandra House, 16 Chater Road. Telephone: 852-2526-5281. Fax: 852-2840-0792; 852-2845-9046. ABA/net: Milbank HK.

Singapore Office: 14-02 Caltex House, 30Raffles Place, 0104. Telephone: 65-534-1700. Fax: 65-534-2733.

Moscow, Russia Office: 24/27 Sadovaya-Samotyochnaya, Moscow, 103051. Telephone: 7-502-258-5015. Fax: 7-502-258-5014.

Jakarta, Indonesia Correspondent Office: Makarim & Taira S., 17th Floor, Summitmas Tower, Jl, Jend. Sudirman 61, Jakarta. Telephone: 62-21252-1272 or 2460. Fax: 62-21-252-2750 or 2751.

Firm includes registered foreign Lawyers and Solicitors.

RESIDENT PARTNERS

NICHOLAS BUCKWORTH, born Glasgow, Scotland, 1961; admitted, 1986, England. *Education:* Dollar Academy; Dundee University ((lB. (Hons), 1983); Chester College of Law.

PHILLIP D. FLETCHER, born Bridgetown, Barbados, 1957; admitted, 1983, District of Columbia; 1984, California; 1991, New York (Not admitted in England). *Education:* Georgetown University School of Foreign Service (B.S.F.S., 1979); Fletcher School of Law and Diplomacy (M.A., 1983); University of California at Berkeley (Boalt Hall) (J.D., 1983). *Member:* The District of Columbia Bar; State Bar of California; New York State and American Bar Associations; Council on Foreign Relations. **LANGUAGES:** French.

KENNETH MACRITCHIE, born Glasgow, Scotland, 1956; admitted, 1978, Scotland; 1990, England. *Education:* University of Glasgow (LL.B., 1976). *Member:* Law Society of Scotland; Law Society of England. **PRACTICE AREAS:** Banking Law; Project Financing; Power Project Development.

RESIDENT ASSOCIATES

JOHN DEWAR, born 1965; admitted, 1991, England and Wales. *Education:* Sidney Sussex College (B.A., 1988; M.A., 1992); Guildford Law College (1989).

(This Listing Continued)

EDMUND GLENTWORTH, born London, England, 1963; admitted, 1987, England. *Education:* New College (M.A. (Hons), 1985); The City University (Dip. Law, 1986); Inns of Court School of Law (Barrister, 1987); Ecolé Nationale D'Administration (Diplome, 1989). Her Majesty Diplomatic Service, Serving in Foreign and Commonwealth Office, London, Paris and Amman, 1987-1992. *LANGUAGES:* French, Russian.

DOMINIC J.F. GREGORY, born Bath, England,; admitted, 1994, England. *Education:* Queen Mary & Westfield College (1990); Guildford College of Law (1992).

DAVID M. HUDANISH, born Perth Amboy, New Jersey, May 8, 1965; admitted, 1991, New Jersey; 1992, New York and District of Columbia (Not admitted in England). *Education:* Georgetown University (B.A., magna cum laude, 1987; J.D., cum laude, 1991). Phi Beta Kappa. *Member:* The District of Columbia Bar; New York State and American Bar Associations.

HELFRIED J. SCHWARZ, born Vienna, Austria, 1960; admitted, 1988, Connecticut; 1989, New York (Not admitted in England). *Education:* University of Vienna (Dr. jur., 1982); New York University School of Law (M.C.J., 1988). Law Clerk, Court of Appeals Vienna, 1982-1983. *Member:* American and International Bar Associations; International Fiscal Association. *LANGUAGES:* German, English and French.

NIGEL THOMPSON, born Northampton, England, 1967; admitted, 1992, England. *Education:* Trinity College, Oxford (1989); College of Law (1990).

MINTER ELLISON

Australian Solicitors

20 LINCOLN'S INN FIELDS
LONDON WC2A 3ED, ENGLAND
Telephone: 0171-831 7871
Fax: 0171-404 6722

Melbourne, Victoria, Australia, Office: 40 Market Street, 3000. Telephone: 617 4617. Fax: 617 4666.

Sydney, New South Wales, Australia Office: 44 Martin Place, 2000. Telephone: (02) 210 4444. Fax: (02) 235 2711.

Brisbane, Queensland, Australia Office: Waterfront Place, 1 Eagle Street, 4000. Telephone: (07) 226 6333. Fax: (07) 229 1066.

Gold Coast, Queensland, Australia Office: Surfers Paradise, Level 7, 50 Cavill Avenue, 4217. Telephone: (07) 708 444. Fax: (075) 922 640.

Canberra, Australian Capital Territory, Australia Office: 8-10 Hobart Place, 2600. Telephone: (06) 248 7533. Fax: (06) 249 8208.

Adelaide, Australia Associated Office: Minter Ellison Baker O'Loughlin. 1 King William Street, 5000. Telephone: (08) 233 5555. Fax: (08) 212 7518.

Auckland, New Zealand Associated Office: Rudd Watts & Stone. BNZ Tower, 125 Queen Street, P.O. Box 3798. Telephone: (09) 309 4863. Fax: NZ (09) 379 3326.

Wellington, New Zealand Associated Office: Rudd Watts & Stone. Trust Bank Centre, 125 The Terrace, 1. Telephone: (04) 472 4899. Fax: (04) 473 8232.

Singapore Associated Office: Khattar Wong & Partners. 80 Raffles Place, #25-01 UOB Plaza, 0104. Telephone: 535 6844. Fax: 534 4892.

Jakarta, Indonesia Associated Office: Makarim & Taira S., Level 17, Summitmas Tower, Jl. Jend. Sudirman 61-62, 12069. Telephone: +62 21 252 1272. Fax: +62 21 252 2750.

Beijing, People's Republic of China Associated Office: Oxford Associates Inc., 205 International Club, 21 Jianguomenwai Dajie, 100020. Telephone: +86 1 501 4681. Fax: +86 1 501 4682.

Perth, Western Australia, Australia Associated Office: Minter Ellison Northmore Hale. 152-158 St. George's Tce, 6000. Telephone: (09) 429 7444. Fax: (09) 429 7666.

Hong Kong Associated Office: McKenna & Co. in association with Minter Ellison. Lippo Tower, 5th Floor, 89 Queensway. Telephone: 2846 9100. Fax: 2845 3575.

International law firm practising in all areas of commercial and corporate law. The firm is organized into specialist practice groups: Alternative Dispute Resolution, Banking and Finance, Commercial Litigation, Corporate, Insolvency, Insurance, International Business and Trade Law, Labour Law, Major Projects and Construction, Media Law, Planning and Environment, Property, Government and Public Administration, Resources, Securities, Industry, Superannuation, Taxation and Revenue, Technology and Trade Protection.

(This Listing Continued)

RESIDENT PARTNER

MICHAEL D. WHALLEY, B. Comm. LL.B. (Hons.). *PRACTICE AREAS:* Banking and Finance; Commercial Law; International Business and Trade Law.

(For List of Partners in Melbourne, Sydney, Brisbane and Canberra Offices, see Professional Biographies at those locations)

MISHCON DE REYA

21 SOUTHAMPTON ROW
LONDON WC1B 5HA, ENGLAND
Telephone: 0171 405 3711
Fax: 0171 404 5982
Telex: 21455 Mislex G
DX: 37954 Kingsway

Corporate and Commercial Law, Competition and Restrictive Trade Practices (Antitrust), Corporate Finance, Banking, Taxation, Insolvency and Receivership, International Transactions and Financings, Immigration, Stock Exchange and Security, Computers and Technology, Trademarks, Copyright, Entertainment and Media, Satellite and Cable, Labour Relations and Employment, Civil Litigation, Criminal Litigation, Products Liability, Libel and Slander, Leasing, Real Property and Construction, Environment, Wills, Trusts and Estates, Family and Child Abduction.

CHAIRMAN

JOHN JACKSON, born Membury, Devon, England, May 26, 1929. *Education:* Queens' College, Cambridge (B.A., 1952; LL.B., 1953); London, Inner Temple (Barrister at Law, 1954). Non-Solicitor, Chairman of Firm. (Barrister).

MEMBERS OF FIRM

MICHAEL CHRISTOPHER KINKEAD ALLEN, born Huntingdon, England, January 7, 1940; admitted, 1966, England. *Education:* Oxford University (M.A.). *Member:* Law Society of England and Wales. *LANGUAGES:* French. *PRACTICE AREAS:* Taxation Law; Estates and Succession Law; Probate Law; Private Clients; Charities.

MARY ANDERSON, born London, England, August 6, 1960; admitted, 1984, England. *Member:* Law Society of England and Wales. *PRACTICE AREAS:* Real Estate Law; Secured Lending; Environmental Law.

PETER M. ARMSTRONG, born Ndola, Zambia, August 4, 1949; admitted, 1982, England and Wales. Author: "Common Law Defence of Qualified Privilege and the Media: Should Other Jurisdictions Follow US Approach?," International Bar Association, 1988. *Member:* Law Society of England and Wales; International Bar Association (Vice Chairman, Intellectual Property and Entertainment Law Committee, 1992—; Chairman, Copyright Law Sub-committee, 1991—); Solicitors' European Group. *PRACTICE AREAS:* Entertainment Law; Media Law.

JONATHAN BERGER, born London, England, January 7, 1962; admitted, 1986, England. *Member:* Law Society of England and Wales; International Bar Association. *PRACTICE AREAS:* Entertainment Law; Media Law.

JONATHAN CAMERON, born Glasgow, Scotland, November 11, 1953; admitted, 1981, England. *Education:* Edinburgh University (B.A., 1975); Oxford University (J.D., 1978). *LANGUAGES:* Italian and French. *PRACTICE AREAS:* Television Law; Copyright Law; Multi Media Law.

SANDRA S. DAVIS, born London, England, July 3, 1956; admitted, 1981, England. Author: "International Child Abduction," Sweet and Maxwell, 1993. Member, Lord Chancellor's Child Abduction Panel. *Member:* Law Society of England and Wales; Solicitors Family Law Association. *LANGUAGES:* French and German. *PRACTICE AREAS:* Divorce Law; Family Law; Child Abduction Law.

STEPHEN DAVIS, born August 8, 1956; admitted, 1981, England. *Member:* The Law Society of England and Wales. *PRACTICE AREAS:* Commercial Litigation; Banking Law.

PHILIP FREEDMAN, born London, England, November 29, 1947; admitted, 1972, England. Author: "Checklist For Commercial Lettings," H.S. Publications, 1983, 1984, 1986; "Valuation and Investment Appraisal," Chapter 11, Estates Gazette, 1983; "Service Charges Law and Practice," H.S. Publications, 1985. Co-Author: The Accountant Manual I.C.A.; "Handbook of Dilapidations," Sweet & Maxwell, 1992. *Member:* Law Society of England and Wales (Member, Land Law and Succession Committee, 1987—). *PRACTICE AREAS:* Real Estate Law; Planning Law.

(This Listing Continued)

MISHCON DE REYA, London—Continued

SIMON GALLANT, born London, England, January 18, 1960; admitted, 1985, England. Lecturer in Law, University of Bristol, 1985-1986. *Member:* Law Society of England and Wales; International Bar Association (Vice Chairman, Defamation and Media Section); Association Internationale des Jeunes Avocats, A.I.J.A. *PRACTICE AREAS:* Defamation and Media Law; Intellectual Property Litigation; Commercial Litigation.

DAVID HARVEY, born June 24, 1954; admitted, 1979, England and Wales. *Member:* Law Society of England and Wales. *PRACTICE AREAS:* Banking Law.

BRIAN J. HEPWORTH, born Salford, England, November 14, 1950; admitted, 1981, England and Wales. *Member:* Law Society of England and Wales. *PRACTICE AREAS:* Defamation Law; Intellectual Property Litigation; Contempt of Court Law.

RONALD J. HOOBERMAN, born June 11, 1943; admitted, 1970, England. *Member:* Law Society of England and Wales. *LANGUAGES:* French. *PRACTICE AREAS:* Commercial Property.

NEF S. JANDU, born Uganda, June 13, 1955; admitted, 1981, England. *Education:* Kingston University (B.A., Hons., 1978). *Member:* Law Society of England and Wales; Society of Asian Lawyers. *LANGUAGES:* Punjabi. *PRACTICE AREAS:* Real Estate Law.

ANTHONY JULIUS, born London, England, July 16, 1956; admitted, 1981, England. Author: "Criminal Injuries Compensation Board," Hemstel Press, 1985; "Prison Board of Visitors," Oyez, 1985. *Member:* Law Society of England and Wales; International Bar Association (IL/A). *PRACTICE AREAS:* Commercial Law; International Litigation; Administrative Law; Regulatory Law; Libel and Contempt.

JULIE KILLIP, born Manchester, England, November 28, 1958; admitted, 1984, England. Co-Author: The Accountant Manual I.C.A. Insolvency Section. *Member:* Law Society of England and Wales. *PRACTICE AREAS:* Commercial Litigation; Banking Law; Insolvency Law.

JANET LEE, born April 22, 1957; admitted, 1983, England. *Member:* Law Society of England and Wales. *LANGUAGES:* Dutch and Italian. *PRACTICE AREAS:* Property Litigation.

GARY MILLER, born London, England, March 4, 1954; admitted, 1977, England and Hong Kong; 1983, Australia; 1985, New York. Author: "Fraudulent Documents and Bank Liability: A Hong Kong Perspective," "Agency in Hong Kong." *Member:* Law Society of England and Wales; Law Society of Hong Kong; New York State Bar Association. *LANGUAGES:* Cantonese. *PRACTICE AREAS:* Banking; Commercial and Fraud Litigation; Insurance Claims.

PAUL M. MILLETT, born London, England, May 19, 1961; admitted, 1986, England. *Member:* Law Society of England and Wales. *PRACTICE AREAS:* Mergers and Acquisitions Law; Corporate Finance Law; Joint Ventures.

MICHAEL R. MITZMAN, born London, England, January 24, 1933; admitted, 1957, England. *Member:* Law Society of England and Wales; Solicitors European Group. *LANGUAGES:* French, Italian, German and Hebrew. *PRACTICE AREAS:* Real Estate Law; Planning Law.

ANTHONY MORTON-HOOPER, born Kent, England, August 18, 1954. *Member:* Law Society of England and Wales; Freeman City of London Solicitors Company; Young Solicitors Group of England and Wales (Chairman, 1989-1990); The Law Society (Member, International Committee, 1989-1991). *PRACTICE AREAS:* Commercial Litigation.

MARGARET ANNE RAE, born St. Albans, England, September 20, 1949; admitted, 1977, England. *Education:* Warwick University (LL.B., 1971); Inn's of Court, School of Law (1973). Author: "Children and the Law, Women and the Law," Longmans, 1986; "Child Care Law," Toneys, 1992. *LANGUAGES:* French. *PRACTICE AREAS:* Divorce Law; Adoption Law; Children's Law.

STEPHEN READING, born London, England, May 25, 1957; admitted, 1984, England. *Member:* Law Society of England and Wales. *PRACTICE AREAS:* Civil Litigation; Criminal Litigation; Labour Relations Law; Employment Law; Commercial Credits Law; Finance Law.

PAUL B. SALMON, born London, England, December 6, 1956; admitted, 1982, England. *Member:* Law Society of England and Wales. *PRACTICE AREAS:* Corporate Finance Law; Merger Law; Acquisitions Law; Insolvency Law; Joint Ventures Law.

(This Listing Continued)

KAREN SANIG, born England, November 14, 1963; admitted, 1989, England and Wales. *Member:* Law Society of England and Wales. *PRACTICE AREAS:* Defamation Law; Media Law.

ALAN Z. SPIERS, born London, England, October 11, 1960; admitted, 1986, England and Wales. *Education:* Queen Mary's College; University of London (LL.B., Hons.), Law Society's Final Examinations, 1984. *PRACTICE AREAS:* Real Estate Law.

JULIE SCOTT-BAYFIELD, born England; admitted, 1965, England. Member, Freeman City of London Solicitors Company. *Member:* Law Society of England and Wales; Holborn Law Society. *PRACTICE AREAS:* Defamation Law; Copyright Law; Publishing Agreements Law; General Advice Newspapers Law; Publishers Law.

TIMOTHY R. SOUTHERN, born London, England, August 4, 1955; admitted, 1980, England and Wales. *Member:* Law Society of England and Wales. *PRACTICE AREAS:* Real Estate Law.

KEVIN JAMES STEELE, born Hammersmith, London, England, June 9, 1960; admitted, 1989, England. *Education:* University of Oxford; Lancaster Gate College of Law. *Member:* Law Society of England and Wales. *PRACTICE AREAS:* Litigation; Property Law; Construction Law.

GRAHAM STEDMAN, born Kent, England, May 10, 1956; admitted, 1980, England and Wales. Author, "Takeovers." Co-Author: "Shareholders' Agreements;" and "Computer Contracts." *Member:* Law Society of England and Wales. *PRACTICE AREAS:* Corporate Finance Law; Mergers and Acquisitions Law; Joint Ventures Law; Information Technology Law.

CHARLES R. WHIDDINGTON, born Warrington, England, June 29, 1957; admitted, 1982, England; 1984, New York. Co-Author: The Accountant Manual, I.C.A., 1990. *Member:* Law Society of England and Wales; New York State and American Bar Associations; International Bar Association (Member, International Business Section, Antitrust Committee). *PRACTICE AREAS:* Corporate Law; Antitrust Law; Trademarks Law.

CONSULTANTS

LORD MISHCON, born London, England, August 14, 1915; admitted, 1937, England. Appointed, Honorary Queen's Counsel, 1992. Member, National Theatre Board (Government Appointed). Formerly Principal Opposition Spokesman in the House of Lords on Legal Affairs. *Member:* Law Society of England and Wales. *PRACTICE AREAS:* Commercial Negotiations; Litigation; General Law; Private Clients.

R. GEORGE ANTICONI, born London, England, October 29, 1933; admitted, 1959, England. *Member:* Law Society of England and Wales. *LANGUAGES:* French. *PRACTICE AREAS:* Copyright Law; Entertainment Law; Media Law.

GEORGE BARACS, born Budapest, Hungary, January 13, 1914; admitted, 1945, Hungary; 1963, England. Contributor, Commercial and Consumer Law (Clarendon Press, Oxford, 1993). Treasurer, British-Hungarian Law Association. *Member:* Law Society of England and Wales; International Bar Association and its East European Forum. *LANGUAGES:* German and Hungarian. *PRACTICE AREAS:* British-Hungarian Company Matters.

CLAUDE E. FIELDING, born Hamburg, Germany, June 29, 1926; admitted, 1950, London. *Member:* Law Society of England and Wales; International Bar Association; Liveryman and Freeman of the City of London Solicitors Company. *LANGUAGES:* German, French and Italian. *PRACTICE AREAS:* Copyright Law; Entertainment Law; Media Law.

DAVID K. WINSOR, born Vienna, Austria, December 7, 1924; admitted, 1954, England. *Member:* Law Society of England and Wales. *LANGUAGES:* German. *PRACTICE AREAS:* Planning Law; Taxation Law.

GEORGE C. J. MOORE

10 KING'S BENCH WALK, TEMPLE
LONDON EC4 7EB, ENGLAND
Telephone: 01-353-2501

Florida Office: Suite 812, 105 S. Narcissus Avenue, West Palm Beach, 33401. Telephone: 407-833-9000. Telefax: 407-833-9990.

West Indies Office: P.O. Box 163, Grand Turk. Telephone: 809-946-2089.

International, U.S. and Foreign Law. Laws of England, British Commonwealth and West Indies. General and Trial Practice including International Business Transactions, Trade Corporations, Foreign Investment, Immigration and Investor Visas, Banking, Real Property, Estates, Litigation.

(This Listing Continued)

GEORGE C. J. MOORE, born Tennessee, 1942; admitted, 1970, England and Wales (Barrister, Inner Temple); 1971, Jamaica; 1972, Florida; 1974, Turks & Caicos Islands; 1976, U.S. Supreme Court; 1977, Supreme Court of the West Indies Associated States, Antigua, British Virgin Islands, Grenada, Montserrat and St. Lucia. *Education:* University of Florida (B.A., 1963); St. Andrew's University, Scotland (B. Phil., 1966); Cambridge University (B.A. honors, M.A. in English Law, 1968; LL. B. in International Law, 1969). Editor, *Florida Bar Journal* special issues on "Immigration Reform," and "Florida's New Internationalism". Legislative Assistant to U.S. Senator Charles McC. Mathias, Jr., Washington, D.C., 1970-1972. Chairman, Florida Economic Growth and International Development Commission, 1989-1990. Chairman, 1983-1984, Florida Council of International Development; Chairman Emeritus, 1990—. Vice Chairman, Florida District Export Council, U.S. Department of Commerce, 1982-1991; Chairman, 1991-1992. *Member:* American Bar Association (Member: International Law Section, Editorial Advisory Board, *The International Lawyer,* 1978-1984); The Florida Bar (Chairman, International Law Section, 1994-1995); American Society of International Law.

MORGAN, LEWIS & BOCKIUS

4 CARLTON GARDENS, PALL MALL
LONDON SW1Y 5AA, ENGLAND
Telephone: 0171-839-1677 International +44171-839-1677
Telex: 884267
Cable Address: "Morlebock"
Fax: 0171-839-3650/0171-930-8456 International
+44171-839-3650/+44171-930-8456

Philadelphia, Pennsylvania Office: 2000 One Logan Square, 19103-6993. Telephone: 215-963-5000. Fax: 215-963-5299.

Washington, D.C. Office: 1800 M Street, N.W., 20036-5869. Telephone: 202-467-7000. Fax: 202-467-7176.

New York, New York Office: 101 Park Avenue, 10178-0060. Telephone: 212-309-6000. Fax: 212-309-6273.

Los Angeles, California Office: 801 South Grand Avenue, 90017-4615. Telephone: 213-612-2500. Fax: 213-612-2554.

Miami, Florida Office: 5300 First Union Financial Center, 200 South Biscayne Boulevard, 33131-2339. Telephone: 305-579-0300. Fax: 305-574-0321.

Harrisburg, Pennsylvania Office: One Commerce Square, 417 Walnut Street, 17101-1904. Telephone: 717-237-4000. Fax: 717-237-4004.

Princeton, New Jersey Office: 100 Overlook Center, 08540. Telephone: 609-520-6600. Fax: 609-520-6639.

Newport Beach, California Office: 4675 MacArthur Court, Suite 740, 92660. Telephone: 714-851-6333.

Brussels, Belgium Office: Rue Guimard 7, B-1040. Telephone: 32-2/512.55.01. Telecopy: 32-2/512.58.88.

Frankfurt/Main Germany Office: Siesemayerstrasse 44 Telephone: +49-069-72-3478. Fax: 4969-726781.

Tokyo, Japan Office: CS Tower, 1-11-30 Akasaka, Minato-Ku. Telephone: 81-3-587-2900.

The London office is a multi-national practice of registered Foreign Lawyers and Solicitors and is engaged in American, English and International Law Practice. Areas of law covered include: Corporate and Commercial Law, International Tax Planning, Mergers and Acquisitions, Joint Venturers, Management Buy-outs and Buy-ins, Corporate Finance and Security Work, and Secured Lending, Statutory and Regulatory advice, E.C. Law, Insolvency, Commercial Property Work, Commercial and International Litigation, Employment Law and Insurance Law. Languages spoken include French and German.

MEMBERS OF FIRM IN LONDON

CHARLES G. LUBAR, born May 20, 1941; admitted, 1966, Maryland; 1967, District of Columbia (Not admitted in England). *Education:* Yale University (B.A., 1963); Harvard Law School (J.D., 1966); Georgetown University (LL.M. in Taxation, 1967). Contributing Editor: *International Tax Report,* 1974-1988; *European and Middle East Tax Report,* 1974-1978. Tax Editor: *The Overseas American,* 1974-1978; *Tax Thriller,* Tax Planning International Review, October 1987. Lecturer in Law, University College, Nairobi, Kenya, 1970. Attorney-Advisor, Interpretive Division, Chief Counsel's Office, Internal Revenue Service, 1967-1969. Legal Advisor, East African Development Bank, Kampala, Uganda, 1970. Associate Member, The Law Society. President, Yale Club of London.

THOMAS J. BENZ, born October 29, 1948; admitted, 1976, New York (Not admitted in England). *Education:* Georgetown University (B.S.F.S.,

(This Listing Continued)

1970; M.S.F.S., 1973); Cornell University (J.D., 1975). Editor-in-Chief, Cornell International Law Journal, 1974-1975. Member, Editorial Board, Global Law & Business, 1990—. Associate Member, The Law Society.

ROBERT BRIAN RAKISON, born September 19, 1947; admitted, 1974, England. LL.B. (Hons.) University of London. 1989-1994 Secretary/-Vice-chairman, IAG International. *Member:* The Law Society-Solicitors European Group; International Bar Association (Section on Business & Eastern European Forum); British Institute of International Comparative Law Association of Estonia, Latvia and Lithuania; Union International de Avocats.

STEVEN F. LOBLE, born January 4, 1958; admitted, 1984, England. MA (Cantab.). *Member:* Association Internationale des Jeunes Avocats; American Bar Association; City of London Solicitors Company; City of Westminster Law Society; Society of English and American Lawyers.

OF COUNSEL IN LONDON

JILL B. DEAL, admitted, 1979, District of Columbia (Not admitted in England). *Education:* University of California at Berkeley (A.B., 1964); Catholic University of America (J.D., 1979).

JOAN BAILEY INGRAM, admitted, 1973, Pennsylvania (Not admitted in England). *Education:* Swarthmore College (B.A., 1968); University of Pennsylvania (J.D., 1972).

ASSOCIATES IN LONDON

ZOË J. ASHCROFT, admitted, 1989, England; 1990, Hong Kong. *Education:* Bristol University (LL.B., 1986).

MICHAEL A. CASHMAN, admitted, 1985, New South Wales; 1991, England. *Education:* Macquarie University (BEC/LL.B., 1985).

RACHEL MARKS, admitted, 1974, England. *Education:* Cambridge University (M.A., 1973).

STEVEN A. NAVARRO, admitted, 1987, New Jersey; 1988, New York (Not admitted in England). *Education:* State University of New York at Albany (B.A., 1984); Georgetown University (J.D., 1987).

ASTRID BIGBIE OWEN, admitted, 1983, New York (Not admitted in England). *Education:* London School of Economics, England (LL.B., 1978); Harvard University (LL.M., 1982).

JOHN H. WILLIAMSON, admitted, 1990, Texas; 1991, District of Columbia (Not admitted in England). *Education:* Princeton University (A.B., 1987); University of Texas (J.D., 1990).

Members of the Firm, Counsel, Of Counsel and Associates in Philadelphia and Harrisburg, Pennsylvania, Washington, D.C., New York, New York, Los Angeles and Newport Beach, California, Miami, Florida, Princeton, New Jersey, Brussels, Belgium, Frankfurt/Main, Germany and Tokyo, Japan are listed in the Biographical Section respectively.

MORGAN & MORGAN

11 BRUTON STREET, BERKELEY SQUARE
LONDON W1X 7AG, ENGLAND
Telephone: 44-171-493-1978
Telex: 297157 MORGAN G
Fax: 44-171-493-1979

Offices:

Panama, Republic of Panama: Torre Swiss Bank Building, 16th Floor. 53E Street. P.O. Box 1824. Telephone: 507-63-8822. Fax: 507-63-9918/64-8317.

Madrid, Spain: General Yague 5, Esc. Dcha. 2nd A. Telephone: 34-1-555-7736. Fax: 34-1-556-3689.

Subsidiary Offices:

Morgan & Morgan Corporation Services, S.A.: 63, Rue de Lausanne, P.O. Box 2565, 1211, Geneva, Switzerland. Telephone: 41-22-7380630. Fax: 41-22-7387321. Telex: 412693 PCMO CH.

Morgan & Morgan Trust Corporation, Ltd.: Corzo Elvezia 25, Ch-6900 Lugano, Switzerland. Telephone: 4191-23-4040/23-4044. Fax: 4191-23-9346.

Panazur, Inc.: Loewenstrasse 40, Ch-8023 Zurich 1, Switzerland. Telephone: 41-1-225-1414. Fax: 41-1-225-1400.

Morgan & Morgan Trust Corporation, Ltd.: Pasea Estate, P.O. Box 3149, Road Town, Tortola, British Virgin Islands. Telephone: 1-809-49-42011. Fax: 1-809-49-42015.

Morgan & Morgan Corporation Services (Portugal), Lda.: Alameda D. Alfonso Henriquez #39 7o. Dto. Lisboa, 1000 Portugal. Telephone: 351-1-8475418. Fax: 3510-1-8475418.

(This Listing Continued)

MORGAN & MORGAN, London—Continued

Morymor Trust Corporation Ltd.: 50 Shirley Street, 2nd Floor. P.O. Box N-341, Nassau, Bahamas. Telephone: 1-809-3265859. Fax: 1-809-3225567.

Morgan & Morgan Trust Corporation (Belize) Ltd.: 35 A Regent Street. P.O. Box 1777, Belize City, Belize. Telephone: 501-276688. Fax: 501-276689.

Morgan & Morgan (Hong Kong) Ltd.: 8th Floor, Heng Shan Centre, 145 Queen's Road East Wanchai, Hong Kong. Telephone: 852-8661686. Fax: 852-8660686.

Morgan & Morgan Corporate Services Pte. Ltd.: 45 Cantonment Road, Singapore 0208. Telephone: (65) 323-4366. Fax: 65-224-2866.

Affiliated Offices:

Panama Shipping Consultants (Hong Kong), Transacciones Maritimas, Ltd. (Piraeus), Welborn Corporation (Tokyo), Panama Corporate Agency (Lugano).

General Practice, Litigation, Admiralty, Banking, Administrative, Taxation, International, Contracts, Business, Commercial, Corporate, Company, Trusts, Immigration, Labor, Mining, International Patent and Trademark Law.

FIRM PROFILE: Morgan & Morgan is one of the leading and oldest law firms in Panama with 16 partners and 10 associates. The supporting staff in Panama numbered 127 in 1993 and includes other specialized professionals. The firm also has offices in David, Chiriqui province which is the most important agricultural center in Panama.

Morgan & Morgan is very proud of its extensive general practice in Panama where its team of well trained attorneys specialize in practically all fields of the law, with a strong emphasis in litigation. The Firm is greatly involved in Administrative Law in areas such as Government Contracts and Practice before Governmental Departments and Administrative Agencies. In addition, the firm places high value on the international training and experience which its partners and associates have attained especially with regard to formation and administration of corporations in the various jurisdictions where the Law Firm has subsidiary offices.

Morgan & Morgan considers itself the leader in the commercialization of Panama open registry for ships which has now grown to be one of the largest in the world. Their Maritime Department took on added importance in 1982 when Panama became an accredited international maritime litigation forum. Lawyers in this department specialize in representation in all manner of claims before the Maritime Court of Panama including arrest of ships and claims before the Panama Canal Claims Commission.

RESIDENT PARTNER

CARLOS DOMINGO DE PUY, born 1952; admitted, 1975, Republic of Panama. Education: University of Panama (LL.B., 1975); University of London (LL.M., 1976); University of Cambridge (M.Litt., 1977). Author: "El Derecho Aéreo Internacional y la Contratación Bilateral Panameña," 1975; "De la Jurisdicción de Almirantazgo en la República de Panamá," 1977; "Special Drawing Rights; A Legal Aspect," 1978. Member: National Bar Association of Panama; Inter-American Bar Association; International Bar Association. LANGUAGES: Spanish, English and French. PRACTICE AREAS: Ship Registration and Finance; Corporate Law; Company Law; Taxation.

REPRESENTATIVE CLIENTS: Banco Central Hispano ; Banque Indosuez; Banque Paribas; Pictet et Cie.; Societe Generale; Bank Hapoalim, B.M.; Sakura Bank; The Industrial Bank of Japan; The Long Term Credit Bank of Japan; The Mitsubishi Trust & Banking Corp.; Republic National Bank of New York; Bank of China; Banco Provincial S.A.I.C.A. (Venezuela); Sea Land Corp.; Evergreen International; Norton Lilly Inc.; Baxter Travenol Laboratories, Inc.; Aoki Corp.; Toshiba Corp.; Sohio Natural Resources; Skanska A.B.; Mitsubishi Warehouse Transportation Co., Ltd.; The Mitsui Warehouse Co., Ltd.; Aramco Services, Inc.; Federal Deposit Insurance Corp.; Hyundai Corp.; Bot Lease Co., Ltd.; Mansion House Group; Corporación de Inversión y Desarrollo Bespa, S.A.; Sociedad Financiera Finalven, S.A. (Caracas).

For complete biographical data on all Personnel, see professional biographies at Panama, Republic of Panama.

MORRIS, RATHNAU & DE LA ROSA

LINCOLN'S INN
10 OLD SQUARE
LONDON WC2A 3SU, ENGLAND
Telephone: 0171-4050758
Fax: 0171-8318237

Chicago, Illinois Office: 100 West Monroe Street, Suite 1600, 60603. Telephone: 312-606-0876. Fax: 312-606-0879.

General Practice.

(For Complete Biographical Data on all personnel, see Professional Biographies at Chicago, Illinois)

MORRISON & FOERSTER

Established in 1883

21-26 GARLICK HILL
LONDON EC4V 2AU, ENGLAND
Telephone: 011-44-171-815-1150
Facsimile: 011-44-171-815-1159

Other offices located in: San Francisco, Los Angeles, New York, Washington, D.C., Brussels, Hong Kong, Tokyo, Sacramento, Palo Alto, Walnut Creek, Orange County, Denver and Seattle.

General International Financial and Commercial Practice, including Foreign Investment in the United States. Banking, Corporation, Real Estate, Securities, Tax, Energy, Environmental and Intellectual Property Law. Firm engaged in American and International Law Practice, but not authorized to appear before the English Courts or to act as Solicitors.

FIRM PROFILE: Morrison & Foerster is one of the world's largest international law firms with 500 lawyers located in 14 offices worldwide. The firm's legal practice encompasses every major area of commercial law, including corporate finance, institutional lending, financial services, real estate, environmental and land use planning, mining and natural resources, agriculture, intellectual property, energy, telecommunications and entertainment, insurance, alternative dispute resolution, products liability, bankruptcy and workouts, financial transactions, labor and employment, civil, criminal and securities litigation, antitrust, international trade and tax.

MEMBERS OF FIRM

BRADFORD S. GENTRY, born June 21, 1955; admitted, 1982, Massachusetts (Not admitted in England). Education: Swarthmore College (B.A. in Biology, 1977, Phi Beta Kappa); Harvard Law School (J.D., magna cum laude, 1981). Member: American Bar Association (Co-Chair, Business Section Subcommittee on International Environmental Law).

GARY M. RINCK, born February 28, 1952; admitted, 1977, California; 1990, New York and Japan (Gaikokuho-Jimu-Bengoshi) (Not admitted in England). Education: Yale University (B.A., 1974); Harvard Law School (J.D., 1977); Oxford University (D.L., 1980). Senior Editor, Harvard Journal on Legislation, 1976-1977. Law Clerk to Judge William P. Gray, U.S. District Court, Central District, California, 1978-1979. Member: International Bar Association; American Intellectual Property Association; Lawyers' Executive Society.

(For biographical data on San Francisco, Los Angeles, Sacramento, Walnut Creek, Palo Alto and Irvine, CA, New York, NY, Washington, DC, Denver, CO, Seattle, WA, Brussels, Belgium, Hong Kong and Tokyo, Japan see professional biographies at each of those cities).

MORRISON, MAHONEY & MILLER

MARLON HOUSE
71/74 MARK LANE
LONDON EC3N 3AX, ENGLAND
Telephone: 01-488-0984
Telex: 8811764

Boston, Massachusetts Office: 250 Summer Street. Telephone: 617-439-7500. Cable Address: "Inscounsel". Telecopier: 617-439-7590.

Raynham, Massachusetts Office: Raynham Woods Executive Building, 175 Paramount Drive. Telephone: 508-880-6200. Fax: 508-880-6351.

Springfield, Massachusetts Office: Baybank Tower, 1500 Main Street. Telephone: 413-737-4373.

Worcester, Massachusetts Office: Mechanics Bank Office Tower, 100 Front Street, Suite 1025. Telephone: 508-757-7777.

(This Listing Continued)

Yarmouth Port, Massachusetts Office: 86 Willow Street. Telephone: 508-362-5595.

Providence, Rhode Island Office: 56 Exchange Terrace, Fourth Floor. Telephone: 401-331-4660.

Hartford, Connecticut Office: 100 Pearl Street. Telephone: 203-293-4144.

Grand Rapids, Michigan Office: 5800 Foremost Drive, S.E. Telephone: 616-949-6252. Facsimile: 616-949-0311.

Southfield, Michigan Office: 25800 Northwestern Highway. Telephone: 810-353-9500. Facsimile: 810-353-9524.

New York, New York Office: 100 Maiden Lane, Suite 1600A. Telephone: 212-825-1212. Facsimile: 212-825-1313.

San Francisco, California Office: 650 California Street, Suite 2650. Telephone: 415-989-1772. Facsimile: 415-989-1784.

Insurance Law including Property and Liability Insurance Coverage Claims and Issues, Reinsurance, Environmental and Pollution Defense and Coverage, Arson, Insurance Fraud, Professional Liability including Medical, Legal, Accounting, Directors and Officers, Architects and Engineers, Subrogation, Regulatory, Company Business Law, Mergers and Acquisitions, General and Corporate Representation of Insurers, Agents and Brokers, Life, Accident, Health, Sports, Products Liability including Pharmaceutical and Medical Devices, General Liability, Construction, Marine and Inland Marine, Aviation, Workers Compensation for Insurers and Self-Insureds. General Litigation in all State and Federal Courts.

(For Complete Personnel and Biographical Data, see Professional Biographies at Boston, Massachusetts)

MORSE & MOWBRAY

A PROFESSIONAL CORPORATION

Established in 1970

LAMB BUILDING TEMPLE
LONDON EC4Y 7AS, ENGLAND
Telephone: 0171-353-6701
Telex: 261551 Jurist G
Fax: (Groups 2 & 3) 01-353-4686

Las Vegas, Nevada Office: Suite 1400 Bank of America Plaza, 300 South Fourth Street, 89101. Telephone: 702-384-6340. Telecopier: 702-384-4596.

General Civil and Trial Practice in all State and Federal Courts. Corporation, Tax, Real Property, Probate, Insurance, Negligence, Labor and Family Law.

HAROLD M. MORSE, born San Francisco, California, March 22, 1947; admitted, 1974, California and Nevada (Not admitted in England). Education: University of Southern California (B.S., 1970); Creighton University (J.D., 1973); University of Cambridge (LL.M., 1988). Phi Alpha Delta. Master, American Inns of Court. Co-Author: Article, "Judgments," Nevada Civil Practice Manual, 1988; Chairman, 1979-1981 and Member, 1985-1990, Southern Nevada Medical-Legal Screening Panel, 1979-1981; Treasurer, 1989-1990, Nevada Defense Trial Lawyers Association. Member: Clark County Bar Association; State Bar of California; State Bar of Nevada; American Board of Trial Advocates; Nevada Trial Lawyers Association; Nevada Defense Trial Lawyers Association; The Association of Trial Lawyers of American.

(For complete biographical data on all personnel, see Professional Biographies at Las Vegas, Nevada)

ETUDE DE MAITRES MUDRY & IGLEHART

20 OLD BAILEY, 5TH FLOOR
LONDON EC4M 7JP, ENGLAND
Telephone: (0171) 248-8006
Telefax: (0171) 248-3001

Geneva, Switzerland Office: 4, Rue Charles Bonnet, Case 269, 1211 Geneva 12. Telephone: 41 +22 +347 40.66. Telex: 429356 LMM CH. Facsimile: 41 +22 +346.04.11.

Contracts, Corporate Law (Swiss and International), Swiss Taxation (Individuals and Companies), U.S. Taxation (Individuals), Treaty Taxation, Banking Law, Administrative Law and Procedure, Labor Law, Interna-

(This Listing Continued)

tional Commercial Arbitration, International Business Transactions, Estate Law, Real Property Law, Trusts.

MEMBERS OF FIRM

Louis Marc Mudry   **John Hawes Iglehart**

ASSISTANT

John D. Hilton

Languages: French, English and German

(For complete biographical data on all personnel, see Professional Biographies at Geneva, Switzerland)

NABARRO NATHANSON

50 STRATTON STREET
LONDON W1X 5FL, ENGLAND
Telephone: 0171-493-9933
Telex: 8813144 NABARO G
Fax: 0171-629-7900

Doncaster, England Office: The Lodge, South Parade, Doncaster DN1 2DQ, England. Telephone: 01302-344455. Fax: 01302-738408.

Hull, England Office: 12Marina Court, Castle Street, Hull HU1 1TJ, England. Telephone: 01482-219111. Fax: 01482-218444.

Budapest, Hungary Office: Istanhegyi ut 9/b, Budapest 1126, Hungary.

Warsaw, Poland Office: ul. Senatorska 12, 00-082 Warsaw, Poland. Telephone: 48-2-227 6144/7901/9227. Fax: 48-2-227 4838.

Deira, Dubai, United Arab Emirates Office: P.O. Box 13779. Telephone: (9714) 287157. Fax: (0974) 287086.

General Practice.

FIRM PROFILE: Nabarro Nathanson was founded in 1958 and its origin dates back to the beginning of this century. Today Nabarro Nathanson is one of the UK's leading law firms. With about 100 partners leading more than 700 legal and support staff, the firm has offices in London, South Yorkshire, Humberside, Budapest (Hungary), Warsaw (Poland) and Dubai (United Arab Emirates).

The firm provides a wide range of legal services covering international trade, company law, commercial property, construction law, taxation, EC and competition law, intellectual property, banking and finance, insurance, mergers and acquisitions, international litigation, pensions and employee benefits, employment law and trade disputes, mining and mineral rights, insolvency, environmental law, energy, and the public sector and planning.

Clients include banks, financial and City institutions, nationalized industries, public and private companies, central, local and overseas governments, professional practices and public bodies.

PARTNERS

J. GREENWOOD (Senior Partner). **PRACTICE AREAS:** Commercial Real Estate.

D. BRAMSON (Commercial Real Estate Department Head; Senior Partner Elect). **PRACTICE AREAS:** Commercial Real Estate.

L. ZIMAN (Banking Law Department Head). **PRACTICE AREAS:** Company Law; Commercial Law; Banking Law.

G. FREER. PRACTICE AREAS: Commercial Real Estate.

P. GORTY. PRACTICE AREAS: Company Law; Commercial Law.

J. SAMSON. PRACTICE AREAS: Commercial Real Estate.

B. LAND. PRACTICE AREAS: Company Law; Commercial Law; Corporate Finance.

D. HAWKINS. PRACTICE AREAS: Property; Planning.

C. BODDINGTON. PRACTICE AREAS: Company Law; Commercial Law; International Trade.

D. ABRAM. PRACTICE AREAS: Commercial Property; Public Law.

M. WELCH. PRACTICE AREAS: Company Law; Commercial Law.

J. QUARRELL. PRACTICE AREAS: Pensions.

W. MARTIN. PRACTICE AREAS: Company Law; Commercial Law.

P. SIGLER. PRACTICE AREAS: Commercial Litigation; Insolvency.

P. SUMMERFIELD. LANGUAGES: German and Spanish. **PRACTICE AREAS:** Commercial Litigation; International Litigation.

(This Listing Continued)

NABARRO NATHANSON, London—Continued

G. LANDER. PRACTICE AREAS: Commercial Property.

G. LUST. PRACTICE AREAS: Commercial Property.

I. TRAVERS. PRACTICE AREAS: Property Litigation.

R. EVANS. PRACTICE AREAS: Commercial Property.

C. DAVEY (Managing Partner). *LANGUAGES:* Italian.

J. HELLER. LANGUAGES: French and German. *PRACTICE AREAS:* Company Law; Commerical Law.

M. PRIOR. PRACTICE AREAS: Insolvency.

D. SENDROVE. LANGUAGES: Polish. *PRACTICE AREAS:* Commercial Property.

C. HOPKINS. PRACTICE AREAS: Public Law.

V. YEEND. PRACTICE AREAS: Commercial Property.

K. HUTCHESON. PRACTICE AREAS: Commercial Property.

P. FITZMAURICE. PRACTICE AREAS: Pensions.

M. KEMP. PRACTICE AREAS: Commercial Property.

M. BRIDGEWATER. PRACTICE AREAS: Construction Law.

J. ROSSHANDLER. PRACTICE AREAS: Construction Law.

L. ELKS. PRACTICE AREAS: Commercial Law; EC/Competition Law.

K. STIMPSON. PRACTICE AREAS: Commercial Property.

R. HOLT. PRACTICE AREAS: Company Law; Commercial Law; Employment.

C. COX. PRACTICE AREAS: Corporate Taxation.

G. BENWELL. PRACTICE AREAS: Taxation.

P. MOON. LANGUAGES: French. *PRACTICE AREAS:* Taxation; Employment.

T. SYMES. PRACTICE AREAS: Environment.

P. KENDALL. PRACTICE AREAS: Commercial Property.

P. DENLEY. PRACTICE AREAS: Commercial Property.

J. MURRAY. PRACTICE AREAS: Pensions.

G. JONES. LANGUAGES: German. *PRACTICE AREAS:* Company Law; Common Law; Energy Law.

T. HERBERT-SMITH. PRACTICE AREAS: Commercial Property.

P. KEMPSTER. PRACTICE AREAS: Corporate Tax.

A. ALI. PRACTICE AREAS: Construction Law.

R. WAKEFIELD. PRACTICE AREAS: Construction Law.

P. LISTER. PRACTICE AREAS: Commercial Property.

J. BLACKWELL. PRACTICE AREAS: Planning Law; Mineral Law.

L. MCCAW. PRACTICE AREAS: Corporate Finance.

E. HIDE. PRACTICE AREAS: Commercial Litigation; Employment.

S. SHONE. PRACTICE AREAS: Commercial Property.

C. LUCK. PRACTICE AREAS: Company Law; Commercial Law.

R. GERSHUNY. PRACTICE AREAS: Commercial Litigation.

M. DAVIES. LANGUAGES: German, French and Polish. *PRACTICE AREAS:* Company Law; Commercial Law.

S. MCKENNA. PRACTICE AREAS: Commercial Property.

B. RAPER. PRACTICE AREAS: Company Law; Commercial Law.

P. RIDOUT. PRACTICE AREAS: Health Care.

J. BELTON. PRACTICE AREAS: Banking.

J. RICKARD. PRACTICE AREAS: Property Litigation.

A. WRIGHT. PRACTICE AREAS: Commercial Property.

N. HUGHES. PRACTICE AREAS: Planning.

M. MENDELBLAT. PRACTICE AREAS: Construction Law.

M. JOSCELYNE. PRACTICE AREAS: Tax.

(This Listing Continued)

N. PARADISE. PRACTICE AREAS: Litigation.

S. JOHNSTON. PRACTICE AREAS: Company Law; Commercial Law; Banking.

D. PARRY. PRACTICE AREAS: Commercial Property.

M. SAUNDERS. LANGUAGES: French. *PRACTICE AREAS:* Energy Law.

C. WAKEFORD. PRACTICE AREAS: Property Litigation.

R. WILLIAMS. PRACTICE AREAS: Employment; Industrial Relations.

S. DAYKIN. PRACTICE AREAS: Litigation; Personal Injury.

I. MACPHERSON. PRACTICE AREAS: Litigation.

A. PENNINGTON. PRACTICE AREAS: Commercial Law.

M. RENGER. PRACTICE AREAS: Environment.

G. WATKINS. PRACTICE AREAS: Litigation; Health & Safety.

K. PUGH. PRACTICE AREAS: Employment.

N. LOGAN. PRACTICE AREAS: Commercial Property.

N. CHEFFINGS. PRACTICE AREAS: Property Litigation.

J. BYRNE. PRACTICE AREAS: Company Law; Commercial Law; Energy Law.

A. INGLIS. PRACTICE AREAS: Intellectual Property.

D. STRINGER. PRACTICE AREAS: Commercial Property.

E. COHEN. PRACTICE AREAS: Tax and Trusts.

P. GODFREY. LANGUAGES: German. *PRACTICE AREAS:* Commercial Litigation.

E. CRAWFORD. PRACTICE AREAS: Commercial Litigation; Employment.

N. DOWNING. PRACTICE AREAS: Construction Law.

G. GRAVES. PRACTICE AREAS: Planning.

J. LAUBSCHER. PRACTICE AREAS: Company Law; Commercial Law.

A. PENNEY. PRACTICE AREAS: Private Tax.

N. POINTON. PRACTICE AREAS: Commercial Property.

R. MCDAID. PRACTICE AREAS: Banking.

D. LLOYD. PRACTICE AREAS: Commercial Property.

J. MENDELOW. PRACTICE AREAS: Company Law; Commercial Law.

MICHAEL PARTRIDGE. PRACTICE AREAS: Construction Law.

CYRUS MEHTA. PRACTICE AREAS: European/Competition Law.

PETER FORD. PRACTICE AREAS: Pensions Law.

MARK BOARDMAN. PRACTICE AREAS: Construction Law.

JENNIFER DONOHUE. PRACTICE AREAS: Financial Services/Regulations.

TIM SHAW. PRACTICE AREAS: Commercial Real Estate.

NIGEL HEILPERN. PRACTICE AREAS: Commercial Real Estate.

GLYN TAYLOR. PRACTICE AREAS: Company/Commercial Law.

JONATHAN WARNE. PRACTICE AREAS: Commercial Litigation.

CONSULTANTS

Ronald Gulliver, FCA
Howard Rogg
Sir John Boynton, MC
Ray Ambrose

NADER MIDEAST LAW LTD.

41, REDCLIFFE CLOSE
276, OLD BROMPTON ROAD
LONDON SW5 9HY, ENGLAND
Telephone: 0171 373 0975
Fax: 0171 835 2251

Jeddah, Saudi Arabia, Head Office: 19 Abo Zinadah Street, Off. Madina Road, Mushrefa Dist., P.O. Box 3595, Jeddah 21481. Telephone: 02-665 2067. Telex: 603285 Jaber SJ.

Riyadh, Saudi Arabia Office: Villa No. 481, Farazdak Street, Al-Dhobbat Quarters, Al-Malaz District, P.O. Box 89704, Riyadh 11692. Telephone: 01-479 3733. Fax: 01-479 2311.

Company, Commercial, Maritime, Foreign Investment, Insurance, Aviation, Labour, Contracts, Sharia (Islamic Law), Civil, Litigation and Arbitration and International Law.

FIRM PROFILE: *The firm offers legal advice in all lines of law and Shariah in Saudi Arabia and in the Middle East. The firm can also facilitate business contacts and promotions through associate firms in Saudi Arabia. The Firm is not licensed to practice Law in the UK. Meeting with Dr. M.M.J. Nader or other lawyers by appointment.*

FIRM ADMINISTRATOR
MRS. GULALAI BAGI
(For Biographical data on other Members see Professional Biographies at Jeddah and Riyadh, Saudi Arabia).

NICHOLSON GRAHAM & JONES

Established in 1858

25-31 MOORGATE
LONDON EC2R 6AR, ENGLAND
Telephone: 0171-628-9151
Fax: 0171-638-3102

Advertising Law, Antitrust Law, Arbitration, Banking Law, Bankruptcy, Company Law, Competition Finance Law, Construction Law, Consumer Protection Law, Conveyancing, Corporate Law, Customs and Excise Law, Distributorship, Agency and Franchise Law, EEC Law, Employer's Liability, Entertainment Law, Environmental Law, Foreign Investments, Immigration Law, Industrial Relations and Labour Law, Insurance Law, Insolvency, International Contracts, International Private Law, Litigation, Negligence Law, Pension Law, Personal Injury Law, Product Liability Law, Property and Real Estate Law, Rent and Lease, Stock Exchange Matters, Take-overs, Trade Regulations, General Legal Practice. Copyright Law, Licensing Negotiation, Trademark Litigation, Transfer of Technology. Capital Taxation, Corporate Taxation, Customs Duties, Deferred Taxation, Indirect Taxation, Inheritance, Estate and Gift Taxation, International Taxation, Personal Income Taxation, Sales, Turnover, Value Added Taxes, Taxation of Foreign Nationals, Exchange Control, General Tax Practice. Trust Law. Travel and Tourism.

FIRM PROFILE: *Founded in 1858 and based in the heart of the City of London, the firm now comprises 35 partners, 40 other lawyers and a total staff of 170. We act for a wide range of clients including listed and privately owned companies, public and private sector institutions, local government and private individuals. The firm's primary offices are in London and Brussels and we are founder members of GlobaLex, and international alliance of independent law firms with offices in the USA, Europe, the Far East. We provide a full service, international legal service offering cost effective, responsive commercial advice.*

PARTNERS

PHILIP LOUIS MORGENSTERN (Senior Partner). **PRACTICE AREAS:** Corporate Finance.

ANTHONY WALKER. PRACTICE AREAS: Commercial Litigation.

P. STEPHEN O. ROBERTS. PRACTICE AREAS: Corporate Finance.

MICHAEL S.M. JOHNS (Managing Partner). **PRACTICE AREAS:** Corporate Finance.

MICHAEL E.H. JACOBS. PRACTICE AREAS: Domestic and International Tax.

TIMOTHY S.H. ROBINSON. PRACTICE AREAS: Travel and Tourism; Litigation.

(This Listing Continued)

ELIZA G. MELLOR. PRACTICE AREAS: Domestic and International Tax; Trusts.

IAN M. PITTAWAY. PRACTICE AREAS: Pensions.

RICHARD J.E. SMITH. PRACTICE AREAS: Commercial Property.

RICHARD G.W. HERBERT. PRACTICE AREAS: Corporate; Commercial.

DAVID W. RACE. PRACTICE AREAS: Commercial; Construction.

JOHN N. ELGAR. PRACTICE AREAS: Corporate; Commercial.

RICHARD J. TALBOT. PRACTICE AREAS: Banking.

NADINE R.G. STRAHL. PRACTICE AREAS: Commercial Property.

CHRISTOPHER E.R. SELSBY. PRACTICE AREAS: Commercial Property.

J. PIERS W. COLEMAN. PRACTICE AREAS: Commercial Property; Election Law.

JOHN GARBUTT. PRACTICE AREAS: Planning; Environmental.

PAUL J. HOWCROFT. PRACTICE AREAS: Banking; Commercial Litigation.

PETER R. ALLEN. PRACTICE AREAS: Corporate; Commercial.

PETER J. DOCKING. PRACTICE AREAS: Pensions.

SARAH J. TIER. PRACTICE AREAS: Pensions.

ROBERT V. HADLEY. PRACTICE AREAS: Commercial Litigation.

LISA J. WEIL. PRACTICE AREAS: Corporate; Commercial.

JOHN D. MAGNIN. PRACTICE AREAS: Commercial Litigation.

GAIL A. HARCUS. PRACTICE AREAS: Wills and Probate.

CYNTHIA M. BARBOR. PRACTICE AREAS: Travel and Tourism; Commercial Litigation.

V. JANE HARTE-LOVELACE. PRACTICE AREAS: Banking; Commercial Litigation.

ANNE T. MCCARTHY. PRACTICE AREAS: Banking; Commercial Litigation.

SHASHI H. RAJANI. PRACTICE AREAS: Insolvency.

JENNIFER H. COTTRELL. PRACTICE AREAS: Domestic and International Tax.

STEVEN J. SCATES. PRACTICE AREAS: Planning; Commercial Property.

DANIELLE HARRIS. PRACTICE AREAS: Corporate; Commercial.

RICHARD I. GLYNN. PRACTICE AREAS: Sport; Corporate; Commercial.

EDWARD C. HAYES. PRACTICE AREAS: Pensions.

JULIAN ST. J. HEMMING. PRACTICE AREAS: Employment; Litigation.

(All Partners and Solicitors in the firm are Members of The Law Society of England and Wales)

Languages: English, French, German, Italian, Spanish, Dutch and Hebrew.

ROBERT L. NORGREN

Established in 1973

HEREDITABLE HOUSE
28 DOVER STREET
LONDON W1X 3PA, ENGLAND
Telephone: 171-495 5512
Fax: 171-495 5913

European and U.S. Commercial Law and International Petroleum Law.

ROBERT L. NORGREN, born Chicago, Illinois, August 22, 1930; admitted, 1958, Illinois; 1960, New York (Not admitted in England). *Education:* Brown University; Beloit College (B.A., 1952); Northwestern University (J.D., 1958); University of Bern, Switzerland; University of Chicago (M.C.L., 1960); Harvard University Graduate School of Business Administration, 1970. Visiting Lecturer, London Graduate School of Business Studies, 1969 and 1971. Lecturer, The College of Petroleum Studies, Oxford,

(This Listing Continued)

ROBERT L. NORGREN, London—Continued

1985—. Director and General Attorney, Conoco Europe Ltd., London, 1970-1972. Private practitioner in London since 1973. *Member:* International Bar Association; Law Society of England and Wales (Honorary); Institute of Petroleum. *LANGUAGES:* German, French, Spanish, Italian and Portuguese.

NORONHA-ADVOGADOS

4TH FLOOR, 193/195 BROMPTON ROAD
LONDON SW3 1NE, ENGLAND
Telephone: (0171) 581.5040
Telex: 849323
Facsimile: (0171) 581.8002

São Paulo, Brazil Office: Av. Brigadeiro Faria Lima, 2100, 3rd Floor, 01452-919. Telephone: (011) 816.6609. Telex: (011) 32677 NMSA BR. Facsimile: (011) 212.2495 (Gps II & III).

Brasília, D.F., Brazil Office: SCS - Q 3, Edifício Planalto - Entrada 40 - s/310, 70300-500. Telephone: (061) 223-8315. Telex: (061) 3888 NMSA BR. Facsimile: (061) 223.8031.

Miami, Florida Office: 1221 Brickell Avenue, Suite 1040, 33131. Telephone: (305) 372.0844. Telex: ITT 441219 NWE. Facsimile: (305) 372.1792 (Gps II & III).

Lisbon, Portugal Office: Praça Marquês de Pombal, 16A - 5° Piso, 1200. Telephone: (01) 355-7435/7650. Facsimile: (01) 355-7854.

Practice Limited to Brazilian; Portuguese; European Community and International Law.

PARTNER

ELIANA MARIA FILIPPOZZI, born São Paulo, S.P., Brazil, January 31, 1961; admitted, 1984, São Paulo; 1991, Portugal (Not admitted in England). *Education:* University of São Paulo Law School; Queen Mary College, University of London. *Member:* Brazilian Bar Association; Portuguese Bar Association; International Bar Association; International Association of Young Lawyers; E.C. Lawyers Association. *LANGUAGES:* Portuguese, English and Italian.

ASSOCIATES

ROBERT WILLIAMS, born London, England; admitted, 1986, London. Chartered Accountant.

MARK GOODFELLOW, admitted, 1992, London. *Member:* Law Society of England and Wales.

Languages: Portuguese, English, Italian, French and Spanish.

References will be furnished upon request.

NORTON ROSE

Established in 1794

KEMPSON HOUSE
P.O. BOX 570
CAMOMILE STREET
LONDON EC3A 7AN, ENGLAND
Telephone: 0171-283 6000
Cable Address: "Norose"
Telex: 883652 NOROSE G
Fax: 0171-283 6500; 0171-623 2030 (Group 4)

Manama, Bahrain Office: Unitag House, Government Avenue, P.O. Box 20437. Telephone: +973 232224. Cable Address: "Norbah Bahrain" Telex: 9276 NORBAH BN Fax: +973 259810.

Brussels, Belgium Office: 40 Rue Montoyer, 1040. Telephone: +32 2 237 6111. Fax: +32 2 237 6136.

Hong Kong Office: 17th Floor, Prince's Building, 10 Chater Road. Telephone: +852 2843 2211. Telex: NOJON HX 75107. Fax: +852 2845 9121.

Moscow, Russia Office: Bolshoi Sukharevsky Pereulok 26, 103051. Telephone: +7 095 244 3639; (Satellite)** +7 502 220 4211. Fax: +7 095 244 3968; (Satellite)** +7 502 220 4212. **International calls only.

Paris, France Office: 35, rue La Boétie, 75008. Telephone: +33 1 40 76 03 06. Fax: +33 1 40 76 03 18.

(This Listing Continued)

Piraeus, Greece Associated Office: Norton Rose Consultants O.E. 126 Kolokotroni Street, 185 35. Telephone: +1 428 0202; +1 428 2429; +1 452 5360. Telex: 213851 JUST GR. Fax: +1 428 2427; +1 428 2428.

Prague, Czech Republic Office: International Business Center, Probřežní 3, 186 00 Prague 8. Telephone: +42 2 232 7501. Fax: +42 2 232 7604.

Singapore Office: 5 Shenton Way, #33-08, UIC Building, 33rd Floor, 0106. Telephone: +65 223 7311. Telex: NOPURA RS 28880. Fax: +65 224 5758.

FIRM PROFILE: *Norton Rose is a leading City and International law firm with its principal office in the City of London. The firm provides a wide range of legal services primarily to the business and financial communities as well as to a number of sovereign governments and state organizations. We are known particularly for our corporate and debt finance, banking, company and commercial law, natural resources, insurance, property development, aerospace and maritime practices and wide-ranging expertise on tax matters. Norton Rose has a major litigation department handling all forms of commercial dispute resolution.*

In addition to our principal office in London, we have offices in Bahrain, Brussels, Hong Kong, Moscow, Paris, Piraeus, Prague and Singapore. In England, the firm is a member of the Norton Rose M5 Group, seven independent legal practices which work together regularly on a co-operative basis. The services of the Group are therefore available in the major financial, commercial and industrial centres in England.

PARTNERS RESIDENT IN LONDON

SENIOR PARTNERS

T. TONY KAY, admitted, 1961, New Zealand; 1969, England and Wales. *PRACTICE AREAS:* Insolvency and Restructuring; Corporate Rescue.

PARTNERS

DAVID A. ASHWORTH, admitted, 1970. *PRACTICE AREAS:* Secured Lending, Refinancing, Restructuring and Insolvency; Commercial Property; Property Aspects of Share and Asset; Acquisitions and Sales; Flotations; MBOs and MBIs; Investment Portfolio Sales and Purchases.

JAMES BAGGE, admitted, 1979, Barrister; 1993. *PRACTICE AREAS:* Business Crime; Statutory and Regulatory Investigations; Disciplinary Tribunals; Banking and Financial Services Litigation.

ANDREW W.J. BAMBER, admitted, 1984. *PRACTICE AREAS:* Banking; Acquisition Finance; Factoring; Insolvency and Restructuring.

MARK A.L. BANKES, admitted, 1986. *PRACTICE AREAS:* Corporate Finance.

RICHARD W. BARRATT, admitted, 1984. *PRACTICE AREAS:* Intellectual Property; Technology; Telecommunications.

ROGER BIRKBY, admitted, 1971. (Managing Partner). *PRACTICE AREAS:* Banking; Capital Markets; Project Financing.

ROBIN G. BROOKS, admitted, 1982. *PRACTICE AREAS:* Corporate Finance; Mergers and Acquisitions; Privatisation; Capital Markets.

DAVID S. BURNAND, admitted, 1966. *PRACTICE AREAS:* Corporate Finance; Joint Ventures; Mergers and Acquisitions; Debenture Stocks.

PETER M.G. BURROWS, admitted, 1977. *PRACTICE AREAS:* Secured Lending, Refinancing, Restructuring and Insolvency; Commercial Property; Property Aspects of Share and Assets Acquisitions and Sales; Flotations; MBOs and MBIs; Investment Portfolio Sales and Purchases.

RICHARD BUTLER, admitted, 1985. *PRACTICE AREAS:* Property Litigation; Construction Litigation; Mortgage Enforcement; Rent Review Arbitration; Landlord and Tenant Advice.

RICHARD J. CALNAN, admitted, 1977. *PRACTICE AREAS:* Insolvency; Corporate Rescue; Banking.

JOHN CHALLONER, admitted, 1977. *PRACTICE AREAS:* Commercial Tax.

DOUGLAS J. COLLIVER, admitted, 1971. *PRACTICE AREAS:* Banking; Capital Markets; Acquisition Finance; Debt Restructuring.

MARGARET A. COLTMAN, admitted, 1980. *PRACTICE AREAS:* Corporate Finance; Capital Markets; Venture Capital; Mergers and Acquisitions.

C. JOHN COOK, admitted, 1975, Barrister; 1990. *PRACTICE AREAS:* Competition; EC Law; Government; Regulation.

(This Listing Continued)

SIMON F.T. COX, admitted, 1980. *PRACTICE AREAS:* Collective Investment Media; Financial Services; Corporate Finance.

DAVID R. CRANE, admitted, 1975. *PRACTICE AREAS:* Equipment Leasing; Project Finance; Public Sector Finance; Computer Law; Private Company; Corporate.

ALAN M. CROOKES, admitted, 1981. *PRACTICE AREAS:* Equipment Leasing; Private Company; Corporate; Privatisation; Venture Capital; Joint Ventures; Transport Law.

VALERIE E.M. DAVIES, admitted, 1979. *PRACTICE AREAS:* Commercial Litigation; Insolvency Litigation; Intellectual Property; Banking, Insolvency and Financial Services Litigation.

NICHOLAS P. EDGELL, admitted, 1978. *PRACTICE AREAS:* Sale and Carriage of Goods; Charterparties; Insurance; Shipbuilding, Rigs and Engineering; Shippping Insolvency.

JONATHAN H. ELLIS, admitted, 1985. *PRACTICE AREAS:* Project Finance; Banking.

ROB P. FALKNER, admitted, 1982, Barrister and Solicitor, New Zealand High Court; 1989, Solicitor of Supreme Court of England and Wales. *PRACTICE AREAS:* Financial Services Litigation; Banking Securities; Insurance; Competition; EC Law.

PATRICK FARRELL, admitted, 1983. *PRACTICE AREAS:* Aviation and Aerospace Regulation; Litigation; Insurance; Sale and Carriage of Goods; Space Law; Travel and Tourism; Gaming and Liquor Licensing.

PETER FERGUSSON, admitted, 1968. *PRACTICE AREAS:* Inward Investment; Executive Immigration; Private Company; Corporate; Employment Law.

MICHAEL V. FOWKE, admitted, 1968. *PRACTICE AREAS:* Commercial Property Investment; Development and Funding; Secured Lending, Refinancing, Restructuring and Insolvency; Local Government.

PAUL A. GILES, admitted, 1973. *PRACTICE AREAS:* Aerospace Finance.

PETER L. GRAHAM, admitted, 1971. *PRACTICE AREAS:* Company Law; Partnership Law; Insurance Company Law; Joint Ventures; Mergers, Acquisitions and Reconstructions.

A. COLIN GRAVES, admitted, 1965. *PRACTICE AREAS:* Commercial Property.

BRIAN J. GREENWOOD, admitted, 1976. *PRACTICE AREAS:* Town and Country Planning; Environmental Law; Local Government Law; Rating; Compulsory Purchase; National Heritage.

GORDON C.C. HALL, admitted, 1980. *PRACTICE AREAS:* Aerospace Finance; Ship Finance.

PETER M. HALL, admitted, 1987. *PRACTICE AREAS:* Construction; Engineering; Project Finance.

PETER A. HARDY, admitted, 1983. *PRACTICE AREAS:* Non-Marine Insurance.

H. ROGER HEWARD, admitted, 1972, New Zealand; 1977, England and Wales. *PRACTICE AREAS:* Shipping Litigation; Marine Insurance; Shipping Insolvency.

LOUISE HIGGINBOTTOM, admitted, 1983. *PRACTICE AREAS:* Commercial Tax; Employee Benefits.

MICHAEL D. INGS, admitted, 1985. *PRACTICE AREAS:* Banking; Acquisition Finance; Project Finance.

HUGH R. JACKSON, admitted, 1971. *PRACTICE AREAS:* Residential Property.

MICHAEL J.A. LEE, admitted, 1966. *PRACTICE AREAS:* International Arbitration; Alternative Dispute Resolution; Licensing; Commercial Litigation; Statutory and Regulatory Investigations; Disciplinary Tribunals; Defamation; Banking and Financial Services Litigation.

DAVID T.R. LEWIS, admitted, 1972. *PRACTICE AREAS:* Corporate Finance; Mergers and Acquisitions.

STUART R. LIPPIATT, admitted, 1982. *PRACTICE AREAS:* Pensions.

MARK J. LLOYD WILLIAMS, admitted, 1987, Barrister; 1993. *PRACTICE AREAS:* Corporate Finance; Joint Ventures; Financial Services.

(This Listing Continued)

MICHAEL R. MACFADYEN, admitted, 1966. *PRACTICE AREAS:* Charities; Court of Protection; National Heritage; Personal Tax; Private Client; Wills and Probate; Domestic and International Trusts.

FRANCIS O. MACKIE, admitted, 1976. *PRACTICE AREAS:* Insurance; Reinsurance.

TIMOTHY J. MARSDEN, admitted, 1986. *PRACTICE AREAS:* Collective Investment Media; Financial Services; Corporate Finance.

PETER M. MARTYR, admitted, 1979. *PRACTICE AREAS:* Insurance; Oil and Commodity Contracts; Sale and Carriage of Goods; Ship Management.

MAURO MATTIUZZO, admitted, 1982. *PRACTICE AREAS:* Energy and Natural Resources; Inward Investment; Private Company; International Corporate.

ROBIN H. MITCHELL, admitted, 1980. *PRACTICE AREAS:* Commercial Property Investment; Development and Funding; Construction Contracts; Tax Based Property Schemes; Finance Leasing; Enterprise Zone Trusts.

LINDSAY B. MORGAN, admitted, 1982. *PRACTICE AREAS:* Commercial Property Investment, Development and Funding; Hospitals.

E. CHRISTOPHER D. NORFOLK, admitted, 1972. *PRACTICE AREAS:* Commercial Tax.

JONATHAN W. ODY, admitted, 1965. *PRACTICE AREAS:* Commercial Property Investment, Development and Funding; Collective Investment Media.

STEPHEN W. PARISH, admitted, 1976. *PRACTICE AREAS:* Banking and Capital Markets; Project Finance; Sovereign Debt.

CHRISTOPHER C. PEARSON, admitted, 1984. *PRACTICE AREAS:* Corporate Finance; Mergers and Acquisitions.

ANDREW G. PHILLIPS, admitted, 1984. *PRACTICE AREAS:* Corporate Finance; Mergers and Acquisitions.

TIMOTHY POLGLASE, admitted, 1986. *PRACTICE AREAS:* Banking and Debt Finance; Banking Regulation; Acquisition Finance.

DOUGLAS POTTER, admitted, 1979. *PRACTICE AREAS:* Shipping Casualties; Shipping Insolvency.

R. ANDREW POWELL, admitted, 1970. *PRACTICE AREAS:* Shipping Casualties; Shipbuilding, Rigs and Engineering; Marine Insurance; Shipping Insolvency.

SANDY R.G. PRATT, admitted, 1978. *PRACTICE AREAS:* Insolvency; Corporate Rescue.

CHARLES L. PROCTOR, admitted, 1980. *PRACTICE AREAS:* Banking and Capital Markets; Venture Capital; Corporate Finance.

PETER J. REES, admitted, 1981. *PRACTICE AREAS:* Construction and Engineering; Arbitration; Alternative Dispute Resolution; Insurance and Reinsurance; Commercial Litigation.

CHRISTOPHER P. ROBINSON, admitted, 1967. *PRACTICE AREAS:* Corporate; Employment Law; Partnership Law; Sale and Purchase of Goods.

CHRISTOPHER J.L. RYAN, admitted, 1971. *PRACTICE AREAS:* Intellectual Property; Computer Law; Commercial Litigation; Banking Litigation.

SIMON L. SACKMAN, admitted, 1977. *PRACTICE AREAS:* Corporate Finance; Mergers and Acquisitions; Corporate.

PAUL SHADAREVIAN, admitted, 1990. *PRACTICE AREAS:* Town and Country Planning; Local Government Law; Compulsory Purchase.

JOHN H. SHELTON, admitted, 1981. *PRACTICE AREAS:* Ship Finance.

ISLA M. SMITH, admitted, 1980. *PRACTICE AREAS:* Commercial Tax.

BARBARA STEPHENSON, admitted, 1982. *PRACTICE AREAS:* Corporate Finance; Mergers and Acquisitions; Private Company; Corporate; Venture Capital.

FRANCIS I. SUMNER, admitted, 1966. *PRACTICE AREAS:* Corporate Finance; Mergers and Acquisitions; Corporate; Partnership.

GUY C. SUTTON, admitted, 1965. *PRACTICE AREAS:* Commercial Litigation; Employment Law; Trade Unions; Disciplinary Tribunals.

(This Listing Continued)

NORTON ROSE, London—Continued

IAN M.S. SWABEY, admitted, 1969. **PRACTICE AREAS:** Collective Investment Media; Financial Services; Corporate Finance; Banking.

CHRISTOPHER L. SWIFT, admitted, 1986. **PRACTICE AREAS:** Corporate Finance; MBO, Venture and Development Capital; Banking and Capital Markets; Acquisition Finance.

MICHAEL P.G. TAYLOR, admitted, 1972. **PRACTICE AREAS:** Construction; Energy and Natural Resources; Project Finance.

THEOCHARIS P. THEOCHARI, admitted, 1985. **PRACTICE AREAS:** Ship Finance.

PETER G. THORNE, admitted, 1971. **PRACTICE AREAS:** Aerospace Finance; Aerospace Regulation and Litigation; Space Law.

PHILIP T. VALLANCE, admitted, 1981, Australia; 1988, England and Wales. **PRACTICE AREAS:** Aerospace Finance.

TIMOTHY J.T. WALKER, admitted, 1981. **PRACTICE AREAS:** Ship Finance.

LYNN WEST, admitted, 1983. **PRACTICE AREAS:** Commercial Litigation; Disasters; Health and Safety; Hospitals; Personal Injury; Product Liability; Banking and Financial Services Litigation.

PHILLIP J. WHALE, admitted, 1980, New Zealand; 1992, England and Wales. **PRACTICE AREAS:** Banking; Acquisition Finance; Project Finance.

PAUL L. WILLIAMS, admitted, 1982. **PRACTICE AREAS:** Personal Injury; Shipping Casualties; Charterparties; Marine Insurance.

CYNTHIA J. WITCOMBE, admitted, 1983. **PRACTICE AREAS:** Sovereign Debt; Project Finance; Banking; Capital Markets; Trade Finance.

SUSAN A. WRIGHT, admitted, 1981. **PRACTICE AREAS:** Ship Finance; Aerospace Finance.

CONSULTANTS

NICHOLAS D.F. BOHM, admitted, 1968.

W.A. JAMES LEAVER, admitted, 1956.

JAMES R. LINGARD, admitted, 1959.

PAT WATSON, admitted, 1980.

Languages: Afrikaans, Arabic, Bahasa Malay, Cantonese, Chinese, Czech, Danish, Dutch, French, German, Greek, Gujarati, Hebrew, Hindi, Irish (Erse), Italian, Japanese, Malay, Maltese, Norwegian, Omani, Parhiguese, Polish, Russian, Shona, Spanish, Swahili, Swedish, Welsh.

O'MELVENY & MYERS

Established in 1885

10 FINSBURY SQUARE
LONDON EC2A 1LA, ENGLAND
Telephone: 011-44-171-256-8451
Facsimile: 011-44-171-638-8205

Los Angeles, California Office: 400 South Hope Street. Telephone: 213-669-6000. Cable Address: "Moms." Facsimile: 213-669-6407.

Century City, California Office: 1999 Avenue of the Stars, 7th Floor, 90067-6035. Telephone: 310-553-6700. Facsimile: 310-246-6779.

Newport Beach, California Office: 610 Newport Center Drive, Suite 1700. Telephone: 714-760-9600. Cable Address: "Moms." Facsimile: 714-669-6994.

San Francisco, California Office: Three Embarcadero Center West Tower, 275 Battery Street, Suite 2600. Telephone: 415-984-8700. Facsimile: 415-984-8701.

New York, N.Y. Office: Citicorp Center. 153 East 53rd Street, 54th Floor. Telephone: 212-326-2000. Facsimile: 212-326-2061.

Washington, D.C. Office: 555 13th Street, N.W., Suite 500 West. Telephone: 202-383-5300. Cable Address: "Moms." Facsimile: 202-383-5414.

Newark, New Jersey Office: One Gateway Center, 7th Floor, 07102. Telephone: 201-639-8600. Facsimile: 201-639-8630.

Tokyo, Japan Office: Sanbancho KB-6 Building, 6 Sanbancho, Chiyoda-ku, Tokyo 102, Japan. Telephone: 011-81-3-3239-2800. Facsimile: 011-81-3-3239-2432.

(This Listing Continued)

Hong Kong Office: 1104 Lippo Tower, Lippo Centre, 89 Queensway, Central Hong Kong. Telephone: 011-852-523-8266. Facsimile: 011-852-522-1760.

General American and International Practice but not authorized to appear before the English courts or act as Solicitors.

RESIDENT PARTNER

CHRISTOPHER D. HALL, born Watford, Hertfordshire, England, August 28, 1954; admitted, 1977, District of Columbia; 1979, New York. *Education:* Oxford University, Oxford, England (B.A., first class honours, in Jurisprudence, 1976); George Washington University (M.C.L., 1977). Member, Editorial Board, International Banking Law, London, England, 1983-1990. *Member:* The Association of the Bar of the City of New York; The District of Columbia Bar; New York State Bar Association. **LANGUAGES:** French and Spanish.

SPECIAL COUNSEL

CHRISTOPHER N. KANDEL, born Baltimore, Maryland, May 11, 1960; admitted, 1985, California; 1986, Maryland; 1987, District of Columbia (Not admitted in England). *Education:* Yale University (B.A., magna cum laude); Cornell Law School (J.D., cum laude, 1985). Member, Cornell International Law Journal, 1983-1985. Co-Author: "Fraudulent Conveyance Concerns in Leveraged Buyout Lending," The Business lawyer, Vol. 43, No. 1, November, 1987.

MARY MOLYNEUX, born Walgett, Australia, October 18, 1955; admitted, 1984, New South Wales, Australia; 1985, Victoria, Australia, High Court of Australia, California and U.S. District Court, Central District of California. *Education:* University of Sydney, Australia (LL.B., 1980); University of Oxford, England (B.C.L., 1982). Member, Editorial Committee, 1978-1979 and Editor-in-Chief, 1979, Sydney Law Review. Law Clerk for Justice Brennan, High Court of Australia, 1983. Tutor in Law, University of Sydney, 1980, 1985.

(For Complete Personnel and Biographical Data see Professional Biographies at Los Angeles, California).

OPPENHOFF & RÄDLER

ROYEX HOUSE
ALDERMANBURY SQUARE
GB LONDON EC2V 7HR, ENGLAND
Telephone: (171) 600 3609
Telecopier: (171) 600 1718

Munich, Germany Office: Prinzregentenplatz 10, D-81675. Telephone: (089) 41808-0. Telecopier: (089) 41808-100.

Berlin, Germany Office: Meinekestr. 13, D-10719. Telephone: (030) 88471-0. Telecopier: (030) 88471-200.

Berlin, Germany Office: Rankestr. 21, D-10789. Telephone: (030) 21496-0. Telecopier: (030) 21496-100.

Cologne, Germany Office: Hohenstaufenring 62, D-50674. Telephone (0221) 2091-0. Telecopier: (0221) 2091-435. Telex: 8 882 294 bos. Teletex: 2627 221 4054BOS.

Frankfurt/Main, Germany Office: Bockenheimer Landstr. 51-53, D-60325. Telephone: (069) 170003-0. Telecopier: (069) 170003-33.

Frankfurt/Main, Germany Office: Myliusstr. 33-37, D-60323. Telephone: (069) 17093-0. Telecopier: (069) 17093-444.

Leipzig, Germany Office: Kommandant-Trufanow-Str. 14, D-04105. Telephone: (0341) 56649-0. Telecopier: (0341) 56649-99.

Brussels, Belgium Office: Rue Brederode 13A, B-1000. Telephone: (2) 5050211. Telecopier: (2) 5022644.

New York, New York Office: 712 Fifth Avenue, 30th Floor, 10019, USA. Telephone: (212) 801 3410. Telecopier: (212) 801 3415.

New York, New York Office: 712 Fifth Avenue, 29th Floor, New York 10019, USA. Telephone: (212) 397 7580/7546. Telecopier: (212) 397 4292.

Prague, Czech Republic Office: Alliance Prague, Jachymova 2, CZ-11000 Prague 1. Telephone: (2) 232 1130. Telecopier: (2) 232 6371.

FIRM PROFILE: *Oppenhoff & Rädler has been created by a merger of two large German firms, Boden Oppenhoff Rasor Raue and Rädler Raupach Bezzenberger. The firm at present has more than 90 partners and comprises together some 200 lawyers and tax advisers.*

Oppenhoff & Rädler acts for domestic and for international clients. The firm offers a comprehensive range of legal services, including: General Corporate and Commercial; Taxation; Banking, Finance and Securities; Mergers and Acquisitions; Real Estate; Litigation and Arbitration; Intellectual

(This Listing Continued)

Property and Trademarks; Construction Law; Antitrust and European Community Law; Administrative and Environmental Law; Media, Communications and Entertainment Law; Technology and Computer Law; Food, Drug and Chemistry; Family Law; Wills.

Oppenhoff & Rädler is a member of the ALLIANCE OF EUROPEAN LAWYERS EEIG (members: Oppenhoff & Rädler, Germany; De Bandt, van Hecke & Lagae, Belgium; De Brauw Blackstone Westbroek, The Netherlands; Jeantet & Associés, France; Lagerlöf & Leman, Sweden; Uria & Menendez, Spain) and of the LLR EEIG (members: Loyens & Volkmaars, The Netherlands; Bureau Francis Lefebvre, France; Oppenhoff & Rädler, Germany).

RESIDENT PARTNER

DR. MICHAEL LAPPE, born Bochum, Germany, August 17, 1957; admitted, 1987, Germany (Not admitted in England). *Education:* University of Bochum (Dr.jur.); University of Münster. *LANGUAGES:* German, English. *PRACTICE AREAS:* Company Law; Corporate Law; Finance; Mergers, Acquisitions and Divestitures; Securities.

OSBORNE CLARKE

6-9 MIDDLE STREET
LONDON EC1A 7JA, ENGLAND
Telephone: 0171 600 0155
Fax: 0171 726 2772

Bristol, England Office: 30 Queen Charlotte Street, BS99 7QQ. Telephone: 0272 230220. Fax: 0272 279209.

Brussels, Belgium Office: Avenue De Cortenburg 79/81, 1040. Telephone: 010 32 2 732 36 00. Fax: 010 32 2 734 87 93.

Copenhagen, Denmark Office: H.C. Andersens Boulevard 37, DK-1553 Copehagen V. Telephone: 010 45 33-11 46 00. Fax: 010 45 33-93 03 06.

Paris, France Office: OJFI, 374 Rue Saint Honore, 75001. Telephone: 010 33 (1) 42 86 57 57. Fax: 010 33 (1) 42 86 57 58.

Lyon, France Office: Espace Rebuplique 10 Rue Stella BP 2099, 69226 Lyon, Cedex 02. Telephone: 010 33 72 41 16 16. Fax: 010 33 72 41 16 06.

Frankfurt/Main, Germany Office: Westendstrasse 24. Telephone: 010 49 069 174348. Fax: 010 49 069 174937.

General and Commercial Practice. Notaries Public.

(For complete biographical data on all personnel, see Professional Biographies at Bristol, England)

OSLER RENAULT

Canadian Barristers and Solicitors

20 LITTLE BRITAIN
LONDON EC1A 7DH, ENGLAND
Telephone: 0171-606-0777
Fax: 0171-606-0222

Paris, France Office: 4, rue Bayard, 75008. Telephone: 1.42.89.00.54. Fax: 1.42.89.51.60.

New York, N.Y. Office: 200 Park Avenue, Suite 3217, 10166-0193. Telephone: 212-867-5800. Fax: 212-867-5802.

Hong Kong Office: Suite 1708, One Pacific Place, 88 Queensway. Telephone: 011-852-2877-3933. Fax: 011-852-2877-0866.

Singapore Office: 65 Chulia Street, #40-05 OCBC Centre, Singapore 0104. Telephone: (65) 538-2077. Fax: (65) 538-2977.

Osler Renault is an international partnership of Osler, Hoskin & Harcourt and Ogilvy Renault.

Osler, Hoskin & Harcourt has offices at: P.O. Box 50, 1 First Canadian Place, Toronto, Ontario, Canada M5X 1B8. Telephone: 416-362-2111. Fax: 416-862-6666 and 50 O'Connor Street, Suite 1500, Ottawa, Ontario, Canada K1P 6L2. Telephone: 613-235-7234. Fax: 613-235-2867.

Ogilvy Renault has offices at: 1981 McGill College Avenue, Suite 1100, Montreal, Quebec, Canada H3A 3C1. Telephone: 514-847-4747. Fax: 514-286-5474 and Suite 1600, 45 O'Connor Street, Ottawa, Ontario, Canada K1P 1A4. Telephone: 613-780-8661; 613-230-5459 and 500 Grande-Allée Est, Suite 520, Quebec, Quebec, G1R 2J7. Telephone: 418-640-5000. Fax: 418-640-1500.

General Canadian and International Practice but not authorized to appear before the English courts or act as Solicitors in the United Kingdom.

(This Listing Continued)

RESIDENT IN LONDON

DAVID W. DRINKWATER, born Toronto, Ontario, 1948; admitted, 1976, Ontario; 1989, Solicitor, Supreme Court of England and Wales. *Education:* University of Western Ontario (B.A., Honours, 1970); Dalhousie University (LL.B., 1973); London School of Economics (LL.M., 1974).

MICHAEL M. FORTIER, born Ste-Foy, Quebec, 1962; admitted, 1985, Quebec. *Education:* Laval University (LL.B., 1984).

CLARA M. GONZÁLEZ-MARTIN, born Peterborough, Ontario, 1965; admitted, 1992, Ontario (Not admitted in England). *Education:* University of Toronto (B.A., 1988; LL.B., 1990).

OSWALD HICKSON COLLIER

Established in 1903

1 PEMBERTON ROW
FETTER LANE
LONDON EC4A 3EX, ENGLAND
Telephone: (0171) 583-5333
Fax: (0171) 353-0743
DX 200 London

Associated Law Firm: Norman MacLeod, Suite 200, 381 Bush Street, San Francisco, California, 94104. Telephone: 415-362-4090.

Media Law, Insurance, Property, Trust, Probate, Taxation and Marine.

MEMBERS OF FIRM

Paul Davies	Richard A. Shillito
Timothy J. L. Cox	Richard Osborne
Michael Hudson	Nicholas G. Alway
Miles Tomkins	Jane Anderson
Diana H. Cornforth	Keith Mathieson

PAISNER & CO

Established in 1932

BOUVERIE HOUSE
154 FLEET STREET
LONDON EC4A 2DQ, ENGLAND
Telephone: 0171 353 0299
Telex: 263189
Fax: 0171 583 8621

Brussels, Belgium Office: 73 Avenue Roger Vandendriessche, 1150. Telephone: 2772 47 49. Fax: 2772 30 45.

Associated Independent Firms: McDermott, Will & Emery (Boston, Chicago, Los Angeles, Miami, Newport Beach, New York, Washington D.C., St. Petersburg, Russia, Tallinn, Estonia, Vilnius, Lithuania).

UGCC Paisner EEIG - Uettwiller Grelon Gout Canat & Associés (Paris, France); Uettwiller Grelon Lippens Dekeyser & Associés (Brussels, Belgium).

FIRM PROFILE: Paisner & Co is a commercial firm with six major practice areas - Company and Commercial, Corporate and International Tax, Commercial Litigation, Commercial Property, Employment and Pensions and Estate Planning and Trusts.

The firm also has a number of specialist areas including asset finance and leasing, corporate finance and mergers and acquisitions, environment, insolvency, insurance/reinsurance, intellectual property, property litigation, employee/executive share incentives and charities.

The firm's clients are found across a broad range of industry sectors including banking, catering, insurance and reinsurance, leisure, mail order, manufacturing, media, property development and investment, publishing, retail and wholesale.

PARTNERS

H.M. Paisner	S.E. Levinson
M.D. Paisner	D.A. Parkin
J. Briggs	S.M. Rosefield
B.C.S. Bean	N.M. Russell
G.J. Hayhurst	S.S. Lazarus
M.S. Polonsky	D.H.J. Cohen
K.G. Stella	J.J. Sacher
A.B. Shellim	C.J. Adams
D.N. Levy	J.R. Kropman

(This Listing Continued)

PAISNER & CO, London—Continued

PARTNERS (Continued)

S.J. Nelson	S.R. Marshall
S.J. Simler	M. Tofalides
J.W. Thomas	S.N.P. Phelps
H. Frydenson	J.S. Schwarz
C.A. Fisher	L. Fazzani
J. Auckland	D.U. Leibowitz
R.J. Wilkinson	C.A. Baylis
C.Y. Mulcahy	A.M. Piper
H.J.H. Nicholls	A.C. Magnus

J.T.C. Handoll (Brussels)

CONSULTANT PARTNER

Lady Morris of Kenwood

CONSULTANTS

S.F. Robin   G.F.L. Proctor

Languages: French, German, Italian, Spanish, Portuguese, Dutch, Hungarian, Russian, Flemish, Hindi, Gujarati, Greek, Hebrew and Afrikaans.

PANNONE & PARTNERS

The merged law firm of Pritchard Englefield and Tobin and

Pannone March Pearson

14 NEW STREET
LONDON EC2M 4TR, ENGLAND
Telephone: 0171-972-9720
Fax: 0171-972-9722

Part of the Pannone Law Group EEIG with Offices in Manchester, London, Paris, Lyon, Brussels, Milan, Barcelona, Madrid, Lisbon, Andorra, Stockholm and Geneva.

Manchester, England Offices: 123 Deansgate, Manchester, M3 2BU. Telephone: 0161-832 3000. Facsimile: 0161-834 2067 and 41 Spring Gardens, Manchester, M2 2BB. Telephone: 0161-832 3000. Facsimile: 0161-832 2655.

Frankfurt, Germany Office: Pritchard Englefield & Tobin, a member of Pannone & Partners, Wiesenau 51, D-60323 Frankfurt. Telephone: (69) 710 1824. Facsimile: (69) 710 3022.

Rome, Italy Office: Pritchard Englefield & Tobin, a member of Pannone & Partners, Via Ofanto 18, 00198. Telephone: 85 303005. Facsimile: 85 303007.

Hong Kong, Office: Pritchard Englefield & Wang, in association with Pannone & Partners, 9 Queen's Road Central, Hong Kong. Telephone: 843 7333. Facsimile: 845 5566.

Guernsey, Channel Islands Office: Pritchard Englefield & Tobin, in association with Pannone & Partners, Commerce House, St. Peter Port, Guernsey, GY1 3NJ, C.I. Telephone: 0481 728 206. Facsimile: 0481 727 747.

Pannone & Partners was formed in September 1992 through the merger of London lawyers Pritchard Englefield & Tobin and Manchester-based Pannone March Pearson. Its constituent firms were the first firm of solicitors to be awarded British Standard 5750, the first English solicitors to open offices in Germany and the first law firm to establish a European Economic Interest Grouping. As a firm committed to Europe it can field considerable numbers of lawyers fluent in German, French, Italian, Spanish, Swedish and Danish as well as English, able to provide wide ranging advice covering Corporate and Commercial law both in Great Britain and in Europe, Commercial Litigation, Personal Injury, Wills, Probate and Trusts, Family law, Medical Negligence, Advocacy, Fraud, Criminal Investigations, Buying and Selling Property both in Great Britain and abroad, Construction, Employment and Environment law.

PARTNERS

RODGER J. PANNONE, (Senior Partner) President of the Law Society of England and Wales, 1993-1994. *LANGUAGES:* English. *PRACTICE AREAS:* Disaster Law; International Labour Law; Complex Litigation.

JULIAN J. TOBIN, O.B.E. *LANGUAGES:* English. *PRACTICE AREAS:* Commercial Conveyancing; Town Planning; Environment; Local Government; General Commercial.

(This Listing Continued)

HANS H. MARCUS. *LANGUAGES:* English, German and Italian. *PRACTICE AREAS:* International Transactions; Commercial Law.

MICHAEL L. COHN. *LANGUAGES:* English. *PRACTICE AREAS:* Commercial Litigation; Construction; Landlord and Tenant; Professional Negligence.

DAVID R. LEVENE. *LANGUAGES:* English and French. *PRACTICE AREAS:* Commercial Property including Property Investment; Secured Lending; Property Development; Landlord and Tenant.

DAVID KING-FARLOW. *LANGUAGES:* English and French. *PRACTICE AREAS:* Personal and Inheritance Tax Planning; Offshore Tax Planning; Wills, Probate and Trusts; Charities; Pensions; Court of Protection.

JOHN E. RHODES, (Honorary Secretary, British-German Jurists Association). *LANGUAGES:* English, German and French. *PRACTICE AREAS:* Agency and Distribution; Commercial Law; International Transactions; International Joint Ventures; Immigration; Copyright and Trade Marks; Computer Contracts; Media Law.

DAVID S. GLASS. *LANGUAGES:* English and French. *PRACTICE AREAS:* Mergers and Acquisitions; Corporate Finance; Joint Ventures; Corporate Mortgage and Security Law; Banking Law.

ANTONY COLMAN. *LANGUAGES:* English, German and Hebrew. *PRACTICE AREAS:* Commercial Litigation; Transport Law; Product Liability; Private International Law.

ANTHONY H. HARRIS. *LANGUAGES:* English. *PRACTICE AREAS:* Banking Law; Public Company Mergers and Acquisitions; Corporate Finance; Joint Ventures.

STUART C. MCINNES. *LANGUAGES:* English and French. *PRACTICE AREAS:* Commercial Litigation; Personal Injury Litigation.

DAVID M. RATCLIFFE. *LANGUAGES:* English and German. *PRACTICE AREAS:* Mergers and Acquisitions; Joint Ventures; General Company and Commercial; Employment.

MALCOLM C. KEOGH (Notary Public). *LANGUAGES:* English and French. *PRACTICE AREAS:* European Community Law; Transport Law; Petroleum Retailing; Overseas Property Acquisitions.

DR. RUDOLF GRAUPNER (German Attorney and English Solicitor). *LANGUAGES:* English, German and French. *PRACTICE AREAS:* European Community Law; International Law (including Procedure and The Human Rights Convention).

COLIN W. DUNSTON. *LANGUAGES:* English, German and French. *PRACTICE AREAS:* Wills; Probate; Personal Tax Planning; Trusts; Charities.

BELINDA M. AVERY. *LANGUAGES:* English, German and French. *PRACTICE AREAS:* Employment Law; Commercial Litigation.

DOMENIC PINI, (Chairman British-Italian Law Association). *LANGUAGES:* English and Italian. *PRACTICE AREAS:* Banking Law; International Transactions; Commercial Law.

ROSALIND S. ASHBY. *LANGUAGES:* English and German. *PRACTICE AREAS:* Commercial Litigation; Personal Injury Litigation (including skiing accidents); Contested Trust and Probate.

MARIAN J. W. JOSEPH. *LANGUAGES:* English and German. *PRACTICE AREAS:* Family Law; Matrimonial; Commercial Litigation; Civil Litigation.

DIANA L. WRIGHT. *LANGUAGES:* English, German and French. *PRACTICE AREAS:* Commercial Litigation.

DR. KARSTEN KUEHNE (Not admitted in England; German Rechtsanwalt). *LANGUAGES:* English and German. *PRACTICE AREAS:* German Law; Commercial Law; International Transactions.

GRAINNE M. BARTON. *LANGUAGES:* English. *PRACTICE AREAS:* Medical Negligence.

MICHAEL DALTON. *LANGUAGES:* English. *PRACTICE AREAS:* Commercial Litigation; International Transactions.

STEPHEN P. GREEN (Honorary Consul for the Netherlands). *LANGUAGES:* English. *PRACTICE AREAS:* Commercial Property; Intellectual Property; Environmental Law.

LESLIE HYMAN. *LANGUAGES:* English. *PRACTICE AREAS:* Corporate; Local Authorities; Finance.

(This Listing Continued)

C. SØREN R. TATTAM (Honorary Consul for Sweden in Manchester). *LANGUAGES:* English, Danish and Swedish. *PRACTICE AREAS:* Mergers and Acquisitions; Corporate Finance; Joint Ventures; Banking and Corporate Mortgage and Security Law; Technology Licensing.

TIMOTHY WELLS. *LANGUAGES:* English. *PRACTICE AREAS:* Corporate; Mergers and Acquisitions; Joint Ventures; Partnerships; Community Law; Commercial and Intellectual Property.

ROBERT G. PAYNE. *LANGUAGES:* English. *PRACTICE AREAS:* Conveyancing; Wills; Trusts; Charities; Probate.

MICHAEL S. JONES. *LANGUAGES:* English and French. *PRACTICE AREAS:* Commercial Mortgages; Property Development.

VINCENT B. O'FARRELL (Notary Public). *LANGUAGES:* English. *PRACTICE AREAS:* Defamation; Chancery; Contract; General Tort (other than PI).

ANDREW G. SIMPKIN. *LANGUAGES:* English. *PRACTICE AREAS:* Commercial Property; Finance; Taxation.

PETER M. LAKIN. *LANGUAGES:* English. *PRACTICE AREAS:* Commercial Fraud; Criminal Law; Advocacy in Crown Court and Higher Criminal Courts.

JOHN M. KITCHINGMAN. *LANGUAGES:* English and Spanish. *PRACTICE AREAS:* Medical Negligence; Family Law; Financial Claims following Divorce.

C. ROBIN F. FOZARD. *LANGUAGES:* English. *PRACTICE AREAS:* Mergers and Acquisitions; Corporate Finance; Joint Ventures; Corporate Insolvency.

HUGH A.S. JONES. *LANGUAGES:* English. *PRACTICE AREAS:* Estate Planning; Wills; Trusts; Personal Tax Planning; Charities; Pensions; Mentally Handicapped; Court of Protection.

JOY M. KINGSLEY. *LANGUAGES:* English. *PRACTICE AREAS:* Residential Conveyancing; Specialized Service to Banks and Building Societies; Lending and Repossession Work; Relocations.

CHRISTINE A. BRADLEY. *LANGUAGES:* English. *PRACTICE AREAS:* Contentious and Non-contentious Employment Law.

STEVEN R. GRANT. *LANGUAGES:* English. *PRACTICE AREAS:* Company Law; Administrative Law; Mergers and Acquisitions; Local Government; Joint Ventures; Corporate Finance; Corporate Privatisation.

S. WILLIAM LISTER. *LANGUAGES:* English. *PRACTICE AREAS:* Commercial Litigation; Intellectual Property Litigation.

ROBERT C.M. ASHWORTH. *LANGUAGES:* English. *PRACTICE AREAS:* Property Development; Oil Industry Retail and Transport Facilities; Town and Country Planning; Commercial Mortgages; Landlord and Tenant; VAT on Property.

CATHERINE E. JONES. *LANGUAGES:* English. *PRACTICE AREAS:* Divorce, Separation and Financial Claims; Children Disputes and Adoption; Family Matters.

D. NEIL GERRARD. *LANGUAGES:* English. *PRACTICE AREAS:* Corporate Fraud; Directors Criminal Liabilities; I.R. and VAT Investigations; Product Liability; Health and Safety; Sports Law.

ANNE CLARKE. *LANGUAGES:* English. *PRACTICE AREAS:* Probate; Wills; Trust Administration; Income Tax.

GARETH O. JESSOP. *LANGUAGES:* English. *PRACTICE AREAS:* Construction and Engineering and Technical Contracts; Professional and Consulting Contracts; Professional Negligence.

FRANK P. PATTERSON. *LANGUAGES:* English. *PRACTICE AREAS:* Injury Litigation; Product Liability Litigation; Aviation Accident Litigation; USA/International Accident Litigation; Immigration Law; Industrial Accident; Industrial Disease Litigation.

CATHERINE J.B. LEECH. *LANGUAGES:* English and French. *PRACTICE AREAS:* Personal Injury Litigation; Aviation Accident Litigation; Product Liability.

GRAEME D. SMITH. *LANGUAGES:* English. *PRACTICE AREAS:* Commercial Litigation; Property Litigation.

MICHAEL J. HOWLETT. *LANGUAGES:* English. *PRACTICE AREAS:* Corporate Finance; Public Company Work.

STEPHEN L. JONES. *LANGUAGES:* English, French and Russian. *PRACTICE AREAS:* Mental Health; Medical Negligence.

(This Listing Continued)

UDO G. POPE. *LANGUAGES:* English and German. *PRACTICE AREAS:* Local Government; Corporate; Charities.

SALLY A. MARSDEN. *LANGUAGES:* English. *PRACTICE AREAS:* Contentious and Non-contentious Construction and Technical Contracts; Engineering.

CONSULTANTS

SUSAN EMPRINGHAM. *LANGUAGES:* English and German. *PRACTICE AREAS:* Private International Law.

MARK MILDRED. *LANGUAGES:* English and French. *PRACTICE AREAS:* Personal Injury; Housing Association Law; Landlord and Tenant; Defamation.

ANTHONY V. ELISIO. *LANGUAGES:* English and Italian. *PRACTICE AREAS:* Private International Law; Italian Law.

JAMES H. OGDEN. *LANGUAGES:* English. *PRACTICE AREAS:* Trusts.

HON. MICHAEL L.W. FLOWER. *LANGUAGES:* English. *PRACTICE AREAS:* Personal Taxation; Trusts; Inheritance Tax Planning; Wills.

DAVID S. GANDY, C.B., O.B.E.. *LANGUAGES:* English and French. *PRACTICE AREAS:* Criminal.

LEGAL SUPPORT PERSONNEL

DR. ANDREAS A. LINTL (Austrian Lawyer). *LANGUAGES:* English and German. *PRACTICE AREAS:* Company; Transport; Personal Injury in Austria.

DR. SYBILLE STEINER (German Lawyer). *LANGUAGES:* English, German and French. *PRACTICE AREAS:* East German Restitution Claims; Private International Law; Family Law; German Law generally Litigation.

ROCCO FRANCO (Italian Lawyer and English Solicitor). *LANGUAGES:* English, Italian and Spanish. *PRACTICE AREAS:* International Transactions; Italian and English Commercial Law; International Trade and Arbitration.

PATTON, MORENO & ASVAT

4TH FLOOR, VICTORY HOUSE
99-101 REGENT STREET
LONDON W1R 7HB, ENGLAND
Telephone: (171) 434-2024
Telex: 92 56 82 PMALON G
Fax: (171) 321 2003

Panama, Republic of Panama Office: Hong Kong Bank Building, 6th Floor, Samuel Lewis Avenue, P.O. Box 6-4298 El Dorado. Telephone: (507) 64-8044; (507) 64-8359. Telex: 6452 PAMALAW. Fax Nbrs (507) 63-7887; (507) 63-7038.

Road Town, Tortola British Virgin Islands Office: Patton, Moreno & Asvat (BVI) Limited. P.O. Box 3174. Telephone: (809) 494 4694. Fax: (809) 494 4695.

Nassau, Bahamas Affiliated Office: Patton, Moreno & Asvat (Bahamas) Ltd. 27 Cumberland Street, Cumberland House.

General Practice. Admiralty, Banking, Corporation, Privatization, Taxation, Patent and Trademark Law.

FIRM PROFILE: The international law firm Patton, Moreno & Asvat was established in Panama on May 6, 1981 by the partners who today give their names to the firm.

Head office of the practice is situated at the heart of the business centre in Panama City, while the European office, which was opened in 1986, is in the St. James's area of London's West End.

In 1988 an affiliated office was established in Tortola in the British Virgin Islands under the company name of Patton, Moreno & Asvat (BVI) Limited and in June 1994 another affiliated office was opened in Nassau, Bahamas under the name of Patton, Moreno & Asvat (Bahamas) Ltd.

The practice, which employs some forty attorneys and staff, is engaged in general civil and commercial law mainly in the areas of banking, contracts, corporations, ship finance and maritime related work, patents and trademarks, immigration, taxation and trusts.

The firm enjoys a close professional relationship with leading law firms in the major financial centers of the world.

(This Listing Continued)

PATTON, MORENO & ASVAT, London—Continued

Whilst the firm is primarily engaged in a general commercial practice, lawyers are encouraged to engage in pro bono activities in their spare time.

RESIDENT PARTNERS

BRETT R. PATTON P., born Los Angeles, California, February 19, 1951; admitted, 1976, Louisiana; 1977, Canal Zone; 1981, Republic of Panama (Not admitted in England). *Education:* Loyola University (B.B.A. in Economics); Tulane University (J.D.). Blue Key; Phi Alpha Delta. Practiced as a Foreign Law Consultant in London, England (Law Society-Foreign Lawyers' Section), 1977-1980; 1986—. Author: "Law of Trusts, Panama," Barry Spitz Theasurus of World Tax Data, Volume II, Isle of Man (February 1988); "Registration, Security and Enforcement of Aircrafts in Panama," Richard Hames and Graham McBain, Aircraft Finance, Kluwer Academic Publishers, London (1988); "Section on Panama," Shipping Finance, Euromoney Publications PLC, London (1991). Lecturer, Business Law, Florida State University, Panama Branch, 1980—. Delegate United Nations Conference on Conditions for Registration of Ships, 1985. Ambassador of the Republic of Panama on Special Mission to Europe, 1990. *Member:* Colegio Nacional de Abogados de Panamá; Louisiana State, American and International Bar Associations; Maritime Law Association of Panama (President, 1983-1985); Maritime Law Association of the United States; Latin American Institute for Advanced Studies (Founding Member). *LANGUAGES:* Spanish and English. *PRACTICE AREAS:* Corporate Law; Shipping Law.

ENRIQUE R. JELENSZKY C., born Panama, Republic of Panama, May 27, 1965; admitted, 1988, Panama; 1989, New York (Not admitted in England). *Education:* Universidad Santa Maria La Antigua, School of Law (Licenciate of Law and Political Sciences, summa cum laude); Duke University Law School (LL.M.). Author: "Income Tax on Remittances," Thesis, 1987. *Member:* Colegio Nacional de Abogados; Maritime Law Association of Panama. *LANGUAGES:* Spanish and English. *PRACTICE AREAS:* Corporate Law; Taxation Law.

PAYNE HICKS BEACH

Solicitors

Established in 1730

10 NEW SQUARE

LINCOLN'S INN

LONDON WC2A 3QG, ENGLAND

Telephone: 0171-465-4300

Fax: 0171-465-4429

Telecom Gold/Dialcom Mailbox 87: PHI001

Agricultural Law, Bankruptcy and Insolvency, Business Law, Charitable Organizations, Company and Commercial Law, Commercial Property, Consumer Law, Family and Matrimonial Law, General Conveyancing, Litigation, Private Client, Trusts and Estates, Wills.

FIRM PROFILE: As one of London's oldest established firms, Payne Hicks Beach has continued to build on its strong reputation as a Family and Private Client firm, but looks as much to the future as to the past, with thriving work in the Company and Commercial, Litigation and General and Commercial Property fields.

PARTNERS

G.S. Brown	J.H.W. Hamilton
D.J. Leverton	R.L. Butcher
D.J. FitzGerald	C.M. Jarman
A.H. Crawford	A.C. Murdie
G.W. Green	A.P. Berry
J.T.H. Thomas	I.F. Airey
P.L. Stockwell	A.H. Palmer
	M.R.T. Kinross

CONSULTANTS

A.B.V. Hughes
R.E. MacWatt
P. Temple-Morris, MP

TRUST AND TAX MANAGER

A.L. Walker, ATII

PENNINGTONS

Established in 1791

ROYEX HOUSE

5 ALDERMANBURY SQUARE

LONDON EC2V 7HD, ENGLAND

Telephone: 0171-457 3000

Fax: 0171-457 3240

Telex: 951567 Penshp G

Paris, France Office: 140 avenue Victor Hugo, 75116. Telephone: (1) 47 27 57 55. Fax: (1) 47 27 36 05.

Basingstoke, England Office: Clifton House, Bunnian Place, Basingstoke, Hampshire RG21 1QY. Telephone: 01256.469091. Fax: 01256.479425.

Bournemouth, England Office: 70 Richmond Hill, Bournemouth Dorset BH2 6JA. Telephone: 01202.551991. Fax: 01202.295403.

Godalming, England Office: Highfield, Brighton Road, Godalming, Surrey GU7 1NS. Telephone: 01483.423003. Fax: 01483.424177.

Newbury, England Office: Phoenix House, 9 London Road, Newbury, Berkshire RG13 1JL. Telephone: 01635.523344. Fax: 01635.523444.

Corporate and Commercial Law, Stock Market Flotations, Commercial Property, Corporate Reconstruction, Intellectual Property, European Community Law, Employment and Employee Relations, National and International Litigation, Insurance and Reinsurance, Environment and Planning, Personal Financial Planning and Taxation, Matrimonial Law, Shipping, Natural Resources, Project Finance, Counter Trade (Eastern Europe), Software, Computer and Telecommunication Licensing.

PARTNERS

D.H. Kemp	J.R. Wharton
R.G. Stubblefield	S.T. Lovenbury
L.C. Fynn	J.A. Calnan
D.G. Stedman	J.G. Dickins
(Managing Partner)	J.P. Ewens
D.A. Peck	Julia C. Palmer
R.A. Loveland	D.J. Raine
T.M. Simon	D.A. Thomas
A.P. Bussy	M.J. O'Donoghue
M.B. Fellingham	Sarah Taylor
P.G. Eaton	M. R. Telfer
W.H. Frankel	J. M. Hamilton Barns
R.J. Allsopp	S. C. Nightingale
J.R.E. Mathé	(Notary Public)
Lesley J. Lintott	H.D. Bryant
P. Hadow	Tracy D. Gane
Sarah E. Panizzo	M.P. Byatt
Catriona H. Smith	Michelle A. Dunne
D.A.P. Giacon	P.A. Milton
A.J. Arnold	N.P.S. Mills
J. Cohen	S.R.T. Freeman
M.P. Felce	P.D. Doyle
M. Nathanson	G. Walkley
A.R. Templeman	K.R.J. Corkan
A. John	V.J. Hawrych
A.G. Irvine	Catherine H. Gordon
N.A. McMichael	C.P. Mather
Susan Dixon	Helen M. Goss
C.M. Brooks (Avocat à la Cour)	C.C. Hay
T.W. Rossiter	M.A. Rowlands
J.W.M. Chadwick	R.J. Duncan
Susan Philipps	R.L.H. Wright
J.M. Rouse	H.C.M. Page (Avocat à la Cour;
G.F. Bosi	Resident Partner, Paris, France Office)

CONSULTANTS

C.R. Benzecry	T.J.P. Miles
I.R. Ponsford	V.P. Philip (Barrister)
A.J. Bonar	P.B. Allan, (Senior
H.J. Brown	Manager-Marine)
S.A. Cracknell	R. Gurland
Sandra D. Graham	(American Law Consultant)
C.R. Poncia	F.C. Cheung (Hong Kong)

(This Listing Continued)

ASSOCIATES

R.M. Cracknell

P.J. Matthison

J.V.H. Murray

D.G. Lambert

Victoria A. Hopgood

Susan A. Kavanagh

G.A. Gillingham

C.J.O. Chidley

G.R. Gover

P.D.P. McElligott

H.R.J. Gardner

Helen M. Whitlock

C.C. Andrea

Susan A. Leslie

S. Malik, (Barrister)

A. Di Castri
  (Italian Procuratore Legale)

R. Bullworthy, (Planning
  Consultant)

A.J. Dolbear (F. Inst. L. Ex.)

WILLIAM F. PEPPER

VERITAS HOUSE
125 FINSBURY PAVEMENT
LONDON EC2A 1PA, ENGLAND
Telephone: 0171-638-1190
Telecopier: 0171-417-9706

International Law, International Commercial Law, Cross Border Transactions, Joint Ventures, Property Development, Banking and Finance and Financial Services Regulation.

DR. WILLIAM F. PEPPER, born New York, N.Y., August 16, 1937; admitted, 1977, Rhode Island; 1988, U.S. Court of Appeals, First and Sixth Circuits and U.S. Supreme Court; 1991, England as Barrister. *Education:* Columbia College (B.A., 1959); Columbia University (M.A., 1960); London School of Economics and Political Science, University of London, England (Certificate, 1961); University of Massachusetts (Ed.D., 1973); Boston College (J.D., cum laude, 1975). Associate Chartered Institute of Arbitrators. Order of the Coif. Co-Author with Florynce Kennedy: *Sexual Discrimination in Employment Before & After Title VII,* Michie-Bobbs Merrill, Pub. 1981. Author: *The Self-Managed Child,* Harper & Row, 1973; *The Effects of War,* Ramparts, 1968 (subsequently Look Magazine, 1967); *Vietnam and Nuremberg Considerations,* Columbia University Forum, 1967; *Foreign Capital Investment in Member States of the Gulf Cooperation Council,* The Arab Law Quarterly, Autumn, 1991; *Crimes of States Against Individuals Resulting From Iraq's Aggression and The Protection of Jus Cogens Norms, By the Application of Universal Jurisdiction under United States Law,* Brooklyn Journal of International Law, Summer, 1992. *Member:* American Bar Association (Member, Sections on: International Law and Practice; Business Law; Individual Rights and Responsibilities); International Bar Association (Member, Committees on: Business Law: Procedures for Settling Disputes; Banking Law; International Sales and Related Commerical Transactions; International Franchising; International Litigation; Issues and Trading in Securities; General Practice: Civil Litigation; Administration of Justice; Defamation/Media Law; Human Rights; Administrative Law). *LANGUAGES:* Spanish and French.

PEPPER, HAMILTON & SCHEETZ

Established in 1890

CITY TOWER
40 BASINGHALL STREET
LONDON EC2V 5DE, ENGLAND
Telephone: (44) 171-628-1122
Telecopy: (44) 171-628-6010

Philadelphia, Pennsylvania Office: 3000 Two Logan Square, Eighteenth and Arch Streets, 19103-2799. Telephone: 215-981-4000. Fax: 215-981-4750.

Washington, D.C. Office: 1300 Nineteenth Street, N.W., 20036-1685. Telephone: 202-828-1200. Fax: 202-828-1665.

Detroit, Michigan Office: 100 Renaissance Center, 36th Floor, 48243-1157. Telephone: 313-259-7110. Fax: 313-259-7926.

Harrisburg, Pennsylvania Office: 200 One Keystone Plaza, North Front and Market Streets, P.O. Box 1181, 17108-1181. Telephone: 717-255-1155. Fax: 717-238-0575.

Berwyn, Pennsylvania Office: 1235 Westlakes Drive, Suite 400, 19312-2401. Telephone: 610-640-7800. Fax: 610-640-7835.

(This Listing Continued)

New York, New York Office: 450 Lexington Avenue, Suite 1600, 10017-3904. Telephone: 212-878-3800. Fax: 212-878-3835.

Wilmington, Delaware Office: 1201 Market Street, Suite 1401, P.O. Box 1709, 19899-1709. Telephone: 302-571-6555. Fax: 302-656-8865.

Westmont, New Jersey Office: Sentry Office Plaza, Suite 321, 216 Haddon Avenue, 08108-2811. Telephone: 609-869-9555. Fax: 609-869-9595.

Moscow, Russia Office: 19-27 Grokholsky Pereulok, 129010. Telephone: 011-7-095-280-4493. Fax: 011-7-095-280-5518.

General Practice.
Firm engaged in American and International Law Practice, but not authorized to appear before the English Courts or to act as Solicitors.

PARTNERS

JOHN H. MCFADDEN, born New York, NY, 1947; admitted, 1979, New York (Not admitted in England). *Education:* Harvard University (B.A., with honors, 1970); Columbia University (M.B.A., 1973); Fordham University (J.D., 1978). (Managing Partner). *LANGUAGES:* French. *PRACTICE AREAS:* International Law.

OF COUNSEL

SALLY J. MARCH, born Algoma, WI, 1955; admitted, 1980, California; 1982, Wisconsin (Not admitted in England). *Education:* Lawrence University (B.A., cum laude, 1977); University of California, Hastings (J.D., with honors, 1980); University of London (LL.M., 1987). Author: "Protecting Computer Software: Creative Solutions to Creative Problems," Patent World, July 1987. Co-author: "Joint Ventures in the USSR," World Wide Information, Inc., 1989. *Member:* International Bar Association. (Also at Moscow, Russia Office). *LANGUAGES:* Russian. *PRACTICE AREAS:* International Law.

ASSOCIATE

KATHERINE E. WARD, born Ann Arbor, MI, 1953; admitted, 1977, Michigan (Not admitted in England). *Education:* University of California at Santa Barbara (B.A., with high honors, 1972); University of Michigan (J.D., with honors, 1977). Phi Alpha Delta. Director, Writing and Advocacy Program, University of Michigan Law School, 1984-1986. *PRACTICE AREAS:* International Commercial Transactions.

PERKINS COIE

36/38 CORNHILL
LONDON EC3V 3ND, ENGLAND
Telephone: 0171-369-9966
Facsimile: 0171-369-9968

REVISERS OF THE WASHINGTON LAW DIGEST FOR THIS DIRECTORY

Hong Kong Office: 23rd Floor Asia Pacific Finance Tower, Citibank Plaza, 3 Garden Road. Telephone: (852) 2878-1177. Facsimile: (852) 2524-9988 DC-9230-IC.

Taipei, Taiwan Office: 8/F, TFIT Tower, 85 Jen Ai Road, Section 4, Taipei 106, Taiwan, R.O.C. Telephone: 886-2-778-1177. Facsimile: 886-2-777-9898.

Seattle, Washington Office: 1201 Third Avenue, 40th Floor. Telephone: 1-(206)-583-8888. Facsimile: 1-(206)-583-8500.

Anchorage, Alaska Office: 1029 West Third Avenue, Suite 300. Telephone: 1-(907) 279-8561. Facsimile: 1-(907) 276-3108.

Bellevue, Washington Office: Suite 1800, One Bellevue Center, 411 - 108th Avenue, N.E. 98804. Telephone: 1-(206) 453-6980. Facsimile: 1-(206) 453-7350. Telex: 32-0319.

Los Angeles, California Office: 1999 Avenue of the Stars, Ninth Floor. 90024. Telephone: 310-788-9900. Facsimile: 310-788-3399.

Olympia, Washington Office: 1110 Capitol Way South, Suite 405. 98501. Telephone: 1-(206) 956-3300. Facsimile: 1-(206) 956-1208.

Portland, Oregon Office: U.S. Bancorp Tower, Suite 2500, 111 S.W. Fifth Avenue. Telephone: 503-295-4400. Facsimile: 503-295-6793.

Spokane, Washington Office: North 221 Wall Street, Suite 600. Telephone: 509-624-2212. Facsimile: 509-458-3399.

Washington, D.C. Office: 607 Fourteenth Street, N.W. 20005-2011. Telephone: 1-(202) 628-6600. Facsimile: 1-(202) 434-1690.

General Practice emphasizing International Project Finance, Aircraft Finance, Banking, Corporate Finance and Privatization.
Firm engaged in American and International Law Practice, but not authorized to appear before the English Courts or to act as Solicitors.

(This Listing Continued)

PERKINS COIE, London—Continued

FIRM PROFILE: *Perkins Coie's London office was established in January 1994. With offices in Hong Kong, Taipei, and seven cities in the United States, Perkins Coie's London office rounds out the firm's coverage of international commercial transactions for a diverse group of clients in finance and industry.*

Founded in the Pacific Northwest, Perkins Coie has more than 340 lawyers, many with significant international expertise in cross-border financial transactions, particularly project finance, aircraft finance, banking, corporate finance and privitization. The firm is also well known for its work in telecommunications, high-technology---intellectual property, antitrust, trade regulation, tax, environmental and natural resources matters.

ANDREW BOR, born Prague, Czechoslovakia, April 25, 1953; admitted, 1981, New York; 1983, Washington (Not admitted in England). *Education:* Harvard College (A.B., cum laude, 1975); University of Washington (B.S., 1977); Vanderbilt University (J.D., 1980). Executive Articles Editor, Vanderbilt Law Review, 1979-1980. *Member:* Washington State, American and International Bar Associations.

H. KENT ROWEY, born Craig, Colorado, 1959; admitted, 1988, California (Not admitted in England). *Education:* University of California at Los Angeles (B.A., magna cum laude, 1983); New York University School of Law (J.D., 1987). *Member:* Los Angeles County and American Bar Associations; State Bar of California.

PETER S. O'DRISCOLL, born Los Angeles, California, 1962; admitted, 1988, New York (Not admitted in England). *Education:* Oral Roberts University (B.A., summa cum laude, 1984); Northwestern University (J.D., 1987). *Member:* The Association of the Bar of the City of New York; New York State, American and International Bar Associations.

ASSOCIATE

ALEXANDRA D. JAIN, born New York, N.Y., August 23, 1966; admitted, 1994, New York (Not admitted in England). *Education:* Princeton University (A.B., 1988); Fordham University (J.D., 1992). Staff Member, Fordham University Law Journal, 1991-1992. *LANGUAGES:* French, Spanish. *PRACTICE AREAS:* Finance.

REVISERS OF THE WASHINGTON LAW DIGEST FOR THIS DIRECTORY

(For biographical data on personnel resident in other offices of Perkins Coie, see Professional Biographies at Hong Kong, Taipei, Taiwan, Bellevue, Seattle and Spokane, Washington, Los Angeles, California, Portland, Oregon and Washington, D.C.)

PETERS & PETERS

2 HAREWOOD PLACE
HANOVER SQUARE
LONDON W1R 9HB, ENGLAND
Telephone: (0171) 629 7991 *International:* (+44-171) 629 7991
Fax: (0171) 499 6792 *International:* (+44-171) 499 6792 DX: 44625

Civil and Commercial Litigation, White Collar Crime, International Business Law, Intellectual Property, Law of the European Union.

FIRM PROFILE: *Established over 50 years ago, Peter & Peter is known worldwide as a law firm offering a wide range of specialist legal services to corporate and individual clients. The firm is particularly well known and highly regarded for work (frequently international in character) in the civil and criminal contentious areas, as well as for providing specialist services in a number of non-contentious areas. Members of the firm continue to receive frequent requests to deliver papers and make presentations to national and international conferences from many Governmental and inter-Governmental Agencies. In addition, members of the firm, from time to time, have been called upon to act as consultants both to Government and inter-Governmental Bodies.*

PARTNERS

RAYMOND CANNON, admitted, 1955, England. Contributing Author: "The Complete Guide & Franchising in Canada" and "Franchises." *Member:* The Law Society; International Franchise Association; Advisory Council to Council of Franchise Suppoiers; International Affairs Committee; Legal Committee and Affiliate of British Franchise Association; Legal Committee of European Franchise Federation; American Bar Association; International Bar Association. *PRACTICE AREAS:* International Business and Commerce; Agency; Distribution; Franchising; Licensing; Intellectual Property.

MONTY RAPHAEL, admitted, 1962, England. *Education:* LL.B. (Hons.). Chairman, White Collar Criminal Unit, John Moores University of Liverpool. Former Deputy Stipendiary Magistrate. Former Assistant Recorder of the Crown Court. *Member:* The Law Society; The City of Westminster Law Society; British Academy of Forensic Science; International Bar Association (Founder, Business Crime Committee); International Association of Penal Law; British-German Jurists Association; London Criminal Courts Solicitors' Association (President, 1982-1984). *PRACTICE AREAS:* White Collar Crime; Tax Delinquency; Civil and Commercial Litigation.

KEITH E. OLIVER, admitted, 1980, England. *Education:* B.A. *Member:* The Law Society; International Bar Association; Association International des Jeunes Avocats (AIJA); British Italian Lawyers Association; London Criminal Courts Solicitors Association. *LANGUAGES:* French. *PRACTICE AREAS:* White Collar Crime; Civil and Commercial Litigation; Tax Delinquency.

JULIA BALFOUR-LYNN, admitted, 1984, England. *Education:* B.A. (Hons.). *Member:* The Law Society; The City of Westminster Law Society; International Bar Association; Association Internationale des Jeunes Avocats (AIJA). *LANGUAGES:* French. *PRACTICE AREAS:* Civil Litigation; White Collar Crime.

LOUISE DELAHUNTY, admitted, 1984, England. *Education:* LL.B. (Hons). *Member:* The Law Society; The City of Westminster Law Society; International Bar Association; Hong Kong Law Society; London Criminal Courts Solicitors' Association. *LANGUAGES:* French. *PRACTICE AREAS:* Civil and Commercial Litigation; White Collar Crime; Labour Law.

JOANNE RICKARDS, admitted, 1989, England. *Education:* LL.B. (Hons.). *Member:* The Law Society; The City of Westminster Law Society; International Bar Association. *PRACTICE AREAS:* White Collar Crime; Tax Delinquency; Customs Infractions.

KATHRYN GARBETT, admitted, 1988, England. *Education:* LL.B. (Hons.). *Member:* The Law Society; The City of Westminster Law Society; International Bar Association. *PRACTICE AREAS:* Civil and Commercial Litigation; Defamation; Labour Law.

PHELPS DUNBAR, L.L.P.

Established in 1853

SUITE 976, LEVEL 9, LLOYD'S
1 LIME STREET
London EC3M 7DQ
Telephone: 011-44-171-929-4765
Telecopier: 011-44-171-929-0046
Telex: 987321

REVISERS OF THE LOUISIANA LAW DIGEST FOR THIS DIRECTORY

New Orleans, Louisiana Office: Texaco Center, 400 Poydras Street. Telephone 504-566-1311. Telecopier: 504-568-9130, 504-568-9007. Cable Address: "Howspencer." Telex: 584125 WU. Telex: 6821155 WUI.

Baton Rouge, Louisiana Office: Suite 701, City National Bank Building, P.O. Box 4412. Telephone: 504-346-0285. Telecopier: 504-381-9197.

Jackson, Mississippi Office: Suite 500, Security Centré North, 200 South Lamar Street, P.O. Box 23066. Telephone: 601-352-2300. Telecopier: 601-360-9777.

Tupelo, Mississippi Office: Seventh Floor, One Mississippi Plaza, P.O. Box 1220. Telephone: 601-842-7907. Telecopier: 601-842-3873.

Houston, Texas Office: Suite 501, 4 Houston Center, 1331 Lamar Street. Telephone: 713-659-1386. Telecopier: 713-659-1388.

FIRM PROFILE: *Phelps Dunbar is a law firm of approximately 200 attorneys, 80 of whom are partners. The firm was established in 1853. In addition to its office in London, England, the firm has offices in New Orleans, Louisiana; Baton Rouge, Louisiana; Jackson, Mississippi; Tupelo, Mississippi; and Houston, Texas. The firm is organized into various groups reflecting the firm's areas of practice.*

We are proud of the legal abilities and the personal qualities of our attorneys. Among past and present members, we count a United States Ambassador, a Chief of Protocol of the United States, an Associate Justice of the Mississippi Supreme Court, three Justices of the Louisiana Supreme Court,

(This Listing Continued)

two Judges of the United States District Court, a United States Attorney, a City Attorney, a President of the American Bar Association, two Presidents of the Maritime Law Association of the United States, four Presidents of the Louisiana State Bar Association, a President of the Mississippi State Bar and three university board Presidents.

The firm's areas of practice include admiralty; antitrust; aviation; bankruptcy and creditors' rights; commercial litigation; construction; corporate and securities; employee benefits; energy/mineral law; environmental; estate planning; fidelity and surety; financial institutions; gaming; health care; insurance coverage; labor/civil rights; life, health and accident insurance; municipal finance; professional indemnity/risk and contract review; public service commission; real estate, equipment and secured transactions; tax; and tort and insurance.

MEMBERS OF FIRM

HARRY S. REDMON, JR., born New Orleans, Louisiana, March 24, 1934; admitted, 1959, Louisiana (Not admitted in England). *Education:* Tulane University; Louisiana State University (B.S., 1957; J.D., 1959). Phi Delta Phi. *Member:* New Orleans, Louisiana State and American Bar Associations; Lawyer-Pilots Bar Association; Maritime Law Association of the United States; International Association of Defense Counsel (Chairman, Excess and Reinsurance Committee, 1984-1986); New Orleans Association of Defense Counsel; Louisiana Association of Defense Counsel; International Association of Gaming Attorneys. Fellow: Louisiana Bar Foundation; American Bar Foundation; American College of Trial Lawyers. (Also at New Orleans, Louisiana Office).

JAMES H. ROUSSEL, born New Orleans, Louisiana, December 28, 1939; admitted, 1964, Louisiana (Not admitted in England). *Education:* Dartmouth College (A.B., 1961); Tulane University (J.D., 1964). Phi Delta Phi. *Member:* New Orleans, Louisiana State and American Bar Associations; Maritime Law Association of the United States (Member, Committees on: Maritime Legislation, 1975—; Maritime Financing, 1980—); Southeastern Admiralty Law Institute; Louisiana State Law Institute. (Also at New Orleans, Louisiana Office). *PRACTICE AREAS:* Admiralty Law; Marine Insurance Law; Diving and Offshore Personal Injury Law.

RICHARD N. DICHARRY, born New Orleans, Louisiana, September 12, 1951; admitted, 1975, Louisiana (Not admitted in England). *Education:* Loyola University (B.A., magna cum laude, 1972; J.D., 1975); Boston University (LL.M., 1978). Blue Key. Member, Loyola Moot Court Board, 1974-1975. *Member:* Louisiana State and American Bar Associations. (Also at New Orleans, Louisiana Office).

REPRESENTATIVE CLIENTS: Acadian Gas Pipeline System; American Steamship Owners Mutual P & I Assn.; Amoco Production Company; Bank of Mississippi; Beech Aircraft Corp.; The Boeing Co.; The Britannia Steamship Insurance Assn., Ltd.; Citibank, N.A.; City National Bank of Baton Rouge; CNG Transmission Corp.; Connecticut General Life Insurance Co.; E. F. Hutton Co.; Energy Development Corporation; Fidelity and Deposit Co. of Maryland; Freeport-McMoRan Inc.; GATX Corp.; General Electric Company and Subsidiaries; Halliburton Company; Hibernia National Bank; Hilton Hotels Corp.; Howard Weil Financial Corp.; Institute of London Underwriters; International Business Machines Corp.; John E. Chance & Associates, Inc.; Louisiana Gas Service Co., Inc.; Missouri Pacific Railroad Co.; Morgan Guaranty Trust Company of New York; North Mississippi Medical Center; The Peoples Water Service Company, Inc.; Phibro Energy USA, Inc.; Rubicon Inc.; Santa Fe International Corp.; The Southern Farm Bureau Companies; Southern Marine & Aviation Underwriters, Inc.; Standard Steamship Owners P&I Association; Steamship Mutual Underwriters Assn., Ltd.; Texas Commerce Bank, National Association; The Times-Picayune Publishing Corp.; Transco Exploration Company; Underwriters at Lloyd's, London.

REVISERS OF THE LOUISIANA LAW DIGEST FOR THIS DIRECTORY

(For Complete Biographical Data on all Personnel, see Professional Biographies at New Orleans, Louisiana)

PICKERING KENYON

Established in 1560

23/24 GREAT JAMES STREET
LONDON WC1N 3EL, ENGLAND
Telephone: 0171-404-5522
Fax: 0171-404-0070

International Law Practice dealing with all aspects of business, specializations including Corporate, Corporate Finance, Stock Exchange, Commercial, Secured and Unsecured Lending, Financial Services Completion, European Community Law, Intellectual Property Law, Insurance and Reinsurance, Insolvency, International Asset Recovery, International Contracts, International Private Law, Entertainment Law, Commercial Property/Real

(This Listing Continued)

Estate, National and International Commercial Litigation and Arbitration, Inheritance, Taxation, Immigration, Matrimonial.

FIRM PROFILE: Pickering Kenyon is a firm of about 20 lawyers. It has a high calibre commercial practice involving both corporations and individuals as clients and provides a personalized, specialist service. This frequently involves expert teams of lawyers of different expertise, as well as teamwork with professionals in other fields. The firm has strong links with other British professionals and lawyers in other jurisdictions.

PARTNERS

WILLIAM J. PERRY, M.A. (Oxon), admitted, 1977. Associate, Chartered Institute of Arbitrators. Member, City of London Solicitors Company. Fellow, Royal Society for Arts Manufacturers and Commerce. *Member:* British Institute of Management. *PRACTICE AREAS:* Litigation; Insurance/Reinsurance.

PETER D. WOOTTON, LL.B. (London), admitted 1976. *PRACTICE AREAS:* Corporate Law; Commercial Law.

IAN R. HORNER, LL.B., admitted, 1972. *PRACTICE AREAS:* Corporate and Property Finance.

CHRISTOPHER R. OAKLEY, B.A., admitted, 1974. *PRACTICE AREAS:* Litigation.

MARIE-GARRARD NEWTON, LL.B., admitted, 1971. *PRACTICE AREAS:* Property Law.

RICHARD J. HOMEWOOD, M.A., admitted, 1983. *PRACTICE AREAS:* Insolvency/Entertainment.

CHRISTOPHER B. RODDA, B.A., admitted, 1987. *PRACTICE AREAS:* Litigation.

Languages: English, French, German, Punjabi, Hindi and Swahili.

PINHEIRO NETO - ADVOGADOS

76 SHOE LANE
LONDON EC4A 3JB, ENGLAND
Telephone: (0171) 583-5055
Fax: (0171) 242-4190

São Paulo, Brazil, Main Office: Rua Boa Vista 254. Telephone: (011) 232-5022. Fax: (011) 232-9161.
Rio de Janeiro, Brazil Office: Avenida Rio Branco, 131. Telephone: (021) 221-5877. Fax: (021) 242-3292.
Brasília, Brazil Office: SCS-Q1 B1 Ed. Central, Brasília, DF. Telephone: (061) 223-2347. Fax: (061) 226-0676.
Lisbon, Portugal Office: Rua Castilho, 32-9°. 1200 Lisbon, Portugal. Telephone: (01) 352-1318. Fax: (01) 352-1418.
Brussels, Belgium Office: Rue D'Arlon, 118, 1040 Brussels, Belgium. Telephone: (2) 280-1660. Fax: (2) 280-1560.

Corporation and Commercial Law. Taxation, Contracts, Banking and Financial Law, International Financial Transactions, Labor Law, Wills and Estates, Mining and Litigation.
Firm engaged in Brazilian and International Law Practice, but not authorized to appear before the English Courts or to act as Solicitors.

RESIDENT PARTNER

J. ANTHONY CLARE, born London, England; admitted, to the Roll of Solicitors of the Supreme Court, England (1963). *Education:* Charter House School (1951-1959); Christ Church College, Oxford (1956-1959).

(For Biographical Data of the Brazilian Members of Firm, see Professional Biographies at São Paulo, Brazil).

PINSENT & CO.

ROYEX HOUSE
ALDERMANBURY SQUARE
LONDON EC2V 7HR, ENGLAND
Telephone: 0171-600 4999
Fax: 0171-600 4947

Birmingham, England Office: 3 Colmore Circus, B4 6BH. Telephone: 0121-200 1050. Telex: 335101 PINSENT B'HAM. Cable Address: "Pinsent Birmingham Telex". Fax Direct Line: 0121-626 1040.
Brussels, Belgium Office: Avenue de Cortenberg 79/81, 1040. Telephone: 010-322 732 3600. Fax: 010-322 734 8793.

(This Listing Continued)

PINSENT & CO., London—Continued

Agency and Distribution Agreements, Banking, Commercial Property, Computer Contracts, Conditions of Sale and Purchase, Construction Law, Contractual Disputes, Copyright, EC and Competition Law, Corporate and Financial Services Law, Employees' Share Schemes, Employment Law, Environmental Law, Flotations, Franchise and Licensing Agreements, Health and Safety at Work, Historic Houses, Insolvency, Insurance Litigation, Intellectual Property Litigation, International Carriage of Goods, Joint Ventures, Licensing, Management Buy-outs, Mergers and Acquisitions, Patent and Trade Mark Agreements, Product Liability, Professional Indemnity, Property Development, Public Law, Share Valuation, Tax - Capital Taxes, Tax - Corporate Tax, Tax - Personal, Town and County Planning, Trade Mark Applications, Trusts and Settlements, Pensions.

RESIDENT MEMBERS

Paul N. Downing	Jeremy Paul Phillips
A. David W. Robinson	Kevin John Perry
H. Anson Game	Fiona Heyes
Andrew G. Walsh	Sheila Wilson
	Leon D. Flavell

(For Complete Biographical data on all personnel, see Professional Biographies at Birmingham, England)

PIPER & MARBURY

14 AUSTIN FRIARS
LONDON EC2N 2HE, ENGLAND
Telephone: 0171-638-3833
FAX: 0171-638-1208

Baltimore, Maryland Office: Charles Center South, 36 South Charles Street, 21201-3010. Telephone: 410-539-2530. FAX: 410-539-0489.

Washington, D.C. Office: 1200 Nineteenth Street, N.W., 20036-2430. Telephone: 202-861-3900. FAX: 202-223-2085.

Easton, Maryland Office: 117 Bay Street, 21601-2703. Telephone: 410-820-4460. FAX: 410-820-4463.

Garrison, New York, Office: Garrison Landing. Telephone: 914-424-3711. Fax: 914-424-3045.

New York, N.Y. Office: 31 West 52nd Street, 10019-6118. Telephone: 212-261-2000. FAX: 212-261-2001.

Philadelphia, Pennsylvania Office: Suite 1500, 2 Penn Center Plaza, 19102-1715. Telephone: 215-656-3300. FAX: 215-656-3301.

General Practice.

MEMBER OF FIRM

GEORGE P. STAMAS, born Baltimore, Maryland, January 13, 1951; admitted, 1976, Maryland and District of Columbia (Not admitted in England). *Education:* The Wharton School of Finance, University of Pennsylvania (B.S., in Economics, 1973); University of Maryland (J.D., 1976). Attorney, Division of Enforcement, Securities and Exchange Commission, 1977-1979. (Also at Baltimore, Maryland, Washington, D.C. and New York, NY). **PRACTICE AREAS:** Corporation Law; Securities Regulation Law; Mergers and Acquisitions Law.

ASSOCIATES

SIMONE BRYCH, born Dortmund, Germany, April 28, 1961; admitted, 1988, Germany. *Education:* Ludwig-Maximilian University, Munich (First State Examination, 1986); University of San Diego (M.C.L., cum laude, 1989).

PRITCHARD ENGLEFIELD & TOBIN

LONDON, ENGLAND

(See Pannone & Partners)

PROCOPÉ & HORNBORG

BURNE HOUSE
88/89 HIGH HOLBORN
LONDON WC1V 6LS, ENGLAND
Telephone: 44-171-831 0292
Telefax: 44-171-831 9074

Helsinki, Finland Office: Mannerheimintie 20 B, 00100. Telephone: 358-0-694 4466. Telefax: 358-0-694 8651.

Tampere, Finland Office: Hämeenkatu 12 A, 33100. Telephone: 358-31-2145 800. Telefax: 358-31-2148 078.

Firm engaged in Finnish and International Law Practice, but not authorized to appear before the English Courts or to act as Solicitors.

RESIDENT PARTNER

OLLI HAPPONEN, born Tuusniemi, Finland, March 7, 1953; admitted, 1990, Finland (Not admitted in England). *Education:* Helsinki School of Economics (B.Sc. Econ., 1974); University of Helsinki (LL.M., 1980). *Member:* Finnish Bar Association; Union of Finnish Lawyers. **LANGUAGES:** Finnish, English, Swedish and German.

(For Biographical Data on all Personnel, see Professional Biographies at Helsinki, Finland.)

RADCLIFFES & CO.

Established in 1844

5 GREAT COLLEGE STREET
WESTMINSTER
LONDON SW1P 3SJ, ENGLAND
Telephone: 0171-222 7040
Telex: 919302
Fax: 0171-222 6208
LDE 113

Banking and Financial Institutions, Company and Commercial, Charities, Employment, Entertainment and Media, European Community Law, Health, Information Technology, Insolvency, Judicial Review, Landlord and Tenant, Litigation, Family and Matrimonial, Parliamentary Petitioning, Private Clients, Property, Public Affairs and Government Relations, Tax.

FIRM PROFILE: Radcliffes & Co. is a thriving company and commercial, property and litigation firm with an established reputation for private client work. It has a strong reputation for matrimonial work and a fast developing niche in the field of public affairs and government relations (helped by the firm's location close to the Houses of Parliament). The aim of the firm is to help all clients achieve their objectives both quickly and cost-effectively.

The firm has strong links with lawyers worldwide. In particular, it is the sole English firm for Commercial Law Affiliates, a US based association of law firms comprising over 4000 commercial lawyers linked worldwide. It has close links with a trust company in Geneva, Radcliffes Trustee Company SA which it established in 1974 and close working relationships with Anthony Hancock in France (Belley) and Studio Legale Barberi and Studio Aletti in Italy (Milan).

MEMBERS OF FIRM

ANGUS GRAHAM FERGUSON YOUNG, B.A., admitted, 1960.

CECIL LYDDON SIMON, B.A., LL.B., admitted, 1963.

DAVID WEBSTER ANDREWS, LL.B., (Hons), admitted, 1965.

ROBERT ROSS VALLINGS, admitted, 1969.

THOMAS HENRY RAYMOND CRAWLEY, admitted, 1965.

GUY RICHARD GREENHOUS, admitted, 1972.

ANTHONY CHARLES HAND, admitted, 1973.

MICHAEL JAMES ELKS, M.A., admitted, 1974.

ROLAND CHARLES GRAEME GILLOTT, admitted, 1972.

ROGER BAWTREE COBDEN-RAMSAY, LL.B., admitted, 1975.

RICHARD PETER JEREMY PRICE, LL.B., (Hons), admitted, 1972.

ROBIN MICHAEL BARON, admitted, 1973.

MARTYN RODNEY THURSTON, LL.B., admitted, 1971.

PETER DONALD RICHARDSON BROWN, LL.B., admitted, 1965.

(This Listing Continued)

YANNO PATRINOS, M.A., admitted, 1965.

CHRISTOPHER JOHN JACKSON, LL.B., admitted, 1975.

SIR GERRARD ANTHONY NEALE, admitted, 1966.

IRVINE ROBERT CUSSINS BIEBER, admitted, 1965.

ROGER PETER JACKSON, B.A. (Hons), admitted, 1976.

ROBERT PETER HIGHMORE, M.A., admitted, 1982.

MICHAEL JOHN HIGGINSON, M.A., admitted, 1983.

MARTIN VINCENT WALSH, B.A., admitted, 1984.

RAYMOND MERVYN AUERBACK, LL.B., admitted, 1972.

GEOFFREY EDWARD WOOLHOUSE, admitted, 1979.

ROBERT PHILIP SEAR, B.A., admitted, 1978.

KAREN SUSAN MAYNE, LL.B., admitted, 1984.

OENONE MARGARET WRIGHT, B.A. (Hons), admitted, 1983.

ROBERT CAIRD WILSON, LL.B., admitted, 1981.

CAROL LEIGHTON DAVIS, LL.B., admitted, 1969.

TIMOTHY MARTIN NEWSOME, B.Comm., LL.B., admitted, 1991.

ANDREW ERNEST PARSONS, LL.B., (Hons.), admitted, 1987.

RAKISONS

Solicitors

Established in 1979

27 CHANCERY LANE

LONDON WC2A 1NF, ENGLAND

Telephone: 0171-404 5212 International: +44171-404 5212

Telex: 295751 COMLAW G

Fax: 0171-831 1926 International: +44171-831 1926

Brussels, Belgium Office: Bld Auguste Reyers 103, 1040. Telephone: +322-735 3680. Fax: +322-733 6213.

Jersey, Channel Islands Associate Office: Nigel Harris & Partners, Oak Walk, St. Peter. Telephone: +441534-44291. Telex: 4192302 Global GLex. Fax: +441534-42703.

Geneva, Switzerland Associate Office: Biner Bradley Nigel Harris & Partners, 6 Avenue De Frontenex, Place Des Eaux-Vives, 1207. Telephone: +4122-786 8640. Fax: +4122-786 8311.

London Associate Office: Grundberg Mocatta, Gate House, 29 Abingdon Road, Kensington, W8 6AH. Telephone: 0171-938 4966. International: +44171-938 4966. Telex: 23405 Grndbr G. Fax: 0171-938 5307. International: +44171-938 5307.

Corporate and Commercial Law, Mergers and Acquisitions, Joint Ventures, Management Buy-outs & Buy-ins, Corporate Finance and Security Work, Statutory and Regulatory Advice, International/E.C. Law, Insolvency, International Tax Planning, Commercial Property Work, Commercial Litigation, Employment Law and Gaming/Licensing.

MEMBERS

ANTHONY STEPHEN WOLLENBERG, born 1949; admitted, 1977, England. LL.B. (Hons.) London. *Member:* The Law Society; International Bar Association (Section on Business Law-Business Crime); International Association of Gaming Attorneys. *LANGUAGES:* French and German. *PRACTICE AREAS:* Commercial Litigation; Company Commercial; Gaming and Licensing; Underwriting Recoveries; Securities and Futures.

JULIUS JOEL ADLER, admitted, 1978, Israel; 1983, England. LL.B. (Hons.) Tel Aviv; LL.M. London. *Member:* The Law Society; International Bar Association (Section on Business Law-Banking); British Venture Capital Association; British-Czechoslovak Law Association. *LANGUAGES:* German and Hebrew. *PRACTICE AREAS:* Company Commercial; Banking; International; Trading; Mergers and Acquisitions.

MICHAEL PAUL EGERTON-VERNON, born 1945; admitted, 1971, England. B.A. (Hons.) Durham. International Editor, "Law Society Gazette". Joint Editor, "Use of Offshore Jurisdictions," 1991. *Member:* The Law Society (Competition Law Committee); Association of Solicitors of the Supreme Court of England and Wales Practising in Jersey (President); The Addington Society. (Also Member, Nigel Harris & Partners, St. Peter, Jersey, Channel Islands). *LANGUAGES:* French and Spanish. *PRACTICE AREAS:* Company Commercial; EC.

(This Listing Continued)

SUSAN ANN LAWS, born 1956; admitted, 1980, England. LL.B. (Hons.) Southampton. *Member:* Society for Computers & Law; British Italian Law Association. *LANGUAGES:* French and Italian. *PRACTICE AREAS:* Company Commercial; Motor Industry; Distribution.

PAUL HOWARD MANNING, born 1953; admitted, 1978, England. LL.B. (Hons.) London. *Member:* The Law Society; International Bar Association (Section on Business Law-International & EC Environmental); European Environmental Lawyers Association; Holborn Law Society Environmental Committee; United Kingdom Environmental Law Association. *LANGUAGES:* French. *PRACTICE AREAS:* Commercial Property; Environmental Law; Town and Country Planning Law.

ROBIN JOHN STAAL, born 1957; admitted, 1982, England. B.A. (Hons.) Leeds. *Member:* The Law Society. *PRACTICE AREAS:* Commercial Property; Secured Lending.

ALEXANDER MARIAN GEISLER, born 1956; admitted, 1984, England. LL.B. (Hons.) City of London. *Member:* The Law Society. *PRACTICE AREAS:* Commercial Litigation; Motor Industry.

JANET FRANCES LONG, born 1954; admitted, 1987, England. *Member:* The Law Society; Insolvency Practitioners' Association; Insolvency Lawyers Association. *PRACTICE AREAS:* Commercial Litigation; Insolvency.

SIMON PAUL RICHARD VIVIAN, born Oxford, England, July 22, 1962; admitted, 1987, England. *Education:* Nottingham University (LL.B., 1985). *Member:* The Law Society. *PRACTICE AREAS:* Corporate; Commercial; Banking; Regulatory.

ASSOCIATES

JEAN ROSEMARIE BEVAN, born 1963; admitted, 1985, Barrister; 1990, Solicitor, England. LL.B. (Hons.) Liverpool. *Member:* The Law Society. *PRACTICE AREAS:* Company Commercial.

MARIANNE FRANCES WHEATLEY, born 1962; admitted, 1989, England. B.A. (Hons.) Leicester. *Member:* The Law Society. *LANGUAGES:* French. *PRACTICE AREAS:* Litigation; Employment.

JONATHAN THOMAS BROWN, born 1966; admitted, 1990, England. LL.B. (Hons.) Manchester; Diploma in EC Law, London. *LANGUAGES:* French. *PRACTICE AREAS:* Company Commercial.

MARK KENRICH, born 1961; admitted, 1985, England. B.A. (Hons.) Durham. *Member:* The Law Society. *LANGUAGES:* French. *PRACTICE AREAS:* Commercial Property; Investment.

RICHARD HINCHLIFFE, admitted, 1994, England. LL.B. (Hons.) Leicester Strasbourg. *LANGUAGES:* French. *PRACTICE AREAS:* Company; Commercial; Corporate.

NIGEL MARK INCLEDON KIDWELL, born 1965; admitted, 1990, England. LL.B. (Hons.) Nottingham. *Member:* The Law Society. *LANGUAGES:* French and German. *PRACTICE AREAS:* Litigation.

DAWN SHERIDAN TUCKER, born 1963; admitted, 1992, England. LL.B. (Hons.) Westminster. *Member:* The Law Society. *LANGUAGES:* French. *PRACTICE AREAS:* Commercial Property.

HANNAH ELIZABETH MARSHALL, born 1966; admitted, 1992, England. M.A. Cambridge. *Member:* The Law Society. *PRACTICE AREAS:* Commercial Property.

JUSTIN PETER FLETCHER, born Liverpool, England, September 16, 1964; admitted, 1992, England. *Education:* Brunel University (LL.B., Hons., 1988); Bristol. Author: "American Society of International Law." *Member:* The Law Society. *PRACTICE AREAS:* Contract; Commercial; Employment.

OF COUNSEL

ANDERS GRUNDBERG, born 1942; admitted, 1968, Barrister; 1977, England. *Member:* The Law Society; Swedish Chamber of Commerce in the United Kingdom (Council Member); Finnish-British Trade Guild; Association of Overseas Swedes. *LANGUAGES:* Swedish, Danish and Norwegian. *PRACTICE AREAS:* Company Commercial; International.

Member of IAG INTERNATIONAL - an Integrated Advisory Group of 46 Independent Professional Firms in 54 Cities in Austria, Belgium, Cyprus, Czechoslovakia, Denmark, England, Estonia, Finland, France, Germany, Holland, Hungary, Isle of Man, Italy, Jersey, Liechtenstein, Luxembourg, Monaco, Norway, Portugal, Russia, Scotland, Spain, Sweden and Switzerland.

REDEKER SCHÖN DAHS & SELLNER

Established in 1929

43 BROOK STREET
LONDON W1Y 2BL, ENGLAND
Telephone: (0171) 3225823
Telefax: (0171) 6292621

Bonn, Germany Office: Oxfordstrasse 24, 53111 Bonn. Telephone: (0228) 72625-0. Telefax: (0228) 650479.

Cologne, Germany Office: Kaiser-Wilhelm-Ring 22, 50672 Cologne. Telephone: (0221) 912 8680. Telefax: (0221) 912 86838.

Hamburg, Germany Office: Büschstrasse 12, 20354 Hamburg. Telephone: (040) 342737/8. Telefax: (040) 352144.

Leipzig, Germany Office: Mozartstr. 1, 04107 Leipzig. Telephone: (0341) 213780. Telefax: (0341) 2137830.

German Law, General International Law, Firm engaged in German and International Law Practice, but not authorized to appear before the English Courts or to act as Solicitors.

PARTNER

DR. PETER-ANDREAS BRAND, born Hanover, April 2, 1958; admitted, 1986, Hanover; 1988, Bonn; registered as foreign lawyer in Eng land and Wales. *Education:* University of Göttingen (Dr. jur., 1984). Author: "Der Rechtsanwalt und der Anwaltsnotar in der DDR," (1985). *Member:* German Chamber of Industry and Commerce, London; British Chamber of Commerce, Cologne; German-German Lawyers' Association; Solicitors European Group; Association of German speaking Lawyers in Great Britain; German-Israeli Lawyer's Association; German-British Jurists' Association. *LANGUAGES:* German and English.

(For data on all firm personnel see Professional Biographies at Bonn)

REUMERT & PARTNERS

Established in 1988

ONE KNIGHTRIDER COURT
LONDON EC4V 5JP, ENGLAND
Telephone: +44 171 236 4406
Telex: 915952
Telefax: +44 171 236 4599

Copenhagen, Denmark Office: Bredgade 26, DK-1260 Copenhagen K. Telephone: +45 33 93 39 60. Cable Address: "MARITIMELAW". Telex: 16339 mtlaw dk. Telefax: +44 33 93 39 50.

General Business Practice, Corporate, Tax, Banking and Finance, Bankruptcy, EEC, Intellectual Property, Construction, Insurance, Litigation and International Arbitration, Real Estate, Ship Building and Financing, Aviation, Shipping and Maritime, Energy and Offshore and Transportation Law.

FIRM PROFILE: Firm engaged in Danish and International Law Practice, but not authorized to appear before the English Courts or to act as Solicitors.

ASSOCIATES

SØREN JOHANSEN, born Copenhagen, Denmark, January 16, 1965; admitted, 1992, Denmark and Danish High Court (Not admitted in England). *Education:* University of Wisconsin; University of Copenhagen (Law Degree, 1989). *Member:* The Danish Bar Association. *LANGUAGES:* Danish, English, German and Scandinavian. *PRACTICE AREAS:* Financing Law; Corporate Law; Bankruptcy and Insolvency Law; General Business Law.

(For Biographical Data on all Personnel, see Professional Biographies at Copenhagen, Denmark)

REYNOLDS PORTER CHAMBERLAIN

CHICHESTER HOUSE
278-282 HIGH HOLBORN
LONDON WC1V 7HA, ENGLAND
Telephone: (0171) 242-2877
Telex: 265092 REPORTG
Fax: (0171) 242-1431
British Document Exchange: LDE No. 81, London

Other London, England Office: Suite 681, Lloyd's, 1 Lime Street, EC3M 7DQ.

(This Listing Continued)

Arbitration, Commercial and Corporate, Construction, Consumer Protection, Corporation Law, Education, Employment, Family Law, General Liability Litigation, Immigration, Insolvency, Insurance and Re-Insurance, Intellectual Property, Mergers and Acquisitions, Personal Injury, Professional Indemnity, Property, Tax, Trusts.

FIRM PROFILE: Reynolds Porter Chamberlain is a London firm which offers clients modern expertise combined with traditional personal service. Clients range from internationally known businesses to private individuals. The firm is the founding member and UK member of TerraLex, an international legal network.

Reynolds Porter Chamberlain has a substantial base in commercial, litigation and personal work and is particularly well known for insurance and professional indemnity work. Specific areas of law include: corporate finance, insolvency, banking, tax, commercial litigation, company commercial, intellectual property, employment, education, immigration, personal injury, commercial property, construction, trusts and family law.

CONTACT PARTNER

Stephen D. Mayer

PARTNERS

Alan K. Toulson, Senior Partner	**Geraldine R. Elliott**
Paul D. Nicholas	**Stephen G. Kirby**
Charles E.C. Gardner	**Timothy R.B. Anderson**
Stephen D. Mayer	**Jonathan M. Davies**
Barney Micklem	**Clare Jaycock**
Edward N. Meerloo	**Colin J. Russell**
David G. Haywood	**A. Carolynn Usher**
Jeffrey L. Freeman	**J. Richard Forrest**
Ronald B. Norman	**Duncan G. Harman-Wilson**
W. Robert J. Hogarth	**Rosemary Gare**
Caroline Byram	**Alexander N. Hamer**
Hon. A. Julian Aylmer	**Karen Y. Pollock**
Alexander M.J. Ulm	**Rhiannon Williams**
Tim C. Brown	**Andrew G.F. Hobson**
Neil E. Le Roux	**Mark T. Johnstone**
Oenone M. Grant-Duprez	**Charles F.E. Suchett-Kaye**
Simon K.P.T. Greenley	**Susan C. Maunsell**

Languages: English, French, German, Italian and Spanish

RICE FOWLER

SUITE 692, LEVEL 6 LLOYD'S
1 LIME STREET
LONDON EC3M 7DQ, ENGLAND
Telephone: 0171-327-4222
Telecopier: 0171-929-0043

New Orleans, Louisiana Office: 36th Floor, Place St. Charles, 201 St. Charles Avenue, 70130. Telephone: 504-523-2600. Telecopier: 504-523-2705. Telex: 9102507910. ELN: 62548910.

San Francisco, California Office: Embarcadero Center West, 275 Battery Street, 27th Floor, 94111. Telephone: 415-399-9191. Telecopier: 415-399-9192. Telex: 451981.

San Diego, California Office: Emerald-Shapery Center, 402 W. Broadway, Suite 850, 92101. Telephone: 619-230-0030. Telecopier: 619-230-1350.

Beijing, China Office: Beijing International Convention Centre, Suite 7024, No. 8 Beichendong Road, Chaoyang District, 100101, P.R.C. Telephone: (861) 493-4250. Telecopier: (861) 493-4251.

Bogota, Colombia Office: Avenida Jimenez #4-03 Oficina 10-05, Bogota, Colombia. Telephone: (571) 342-1062. Telecopier: (571) 342-1062.

WINSTON EDWARD RICE, born Shreveport, Louisiana, February 22, 1946; admitted, 1971, Louisiana; 1990, Colorado; 1992, Texas (Not admitted in England). *Education:* Louisiana State University (J.D., 1971). Phi Kappa Phi; Phi Eta Sigma; Phi Delta Phi; Order of the Coif. Member, Board of Editors, 1969-1970 and Associate Editor, 1970-1971, Louisiana Law Review. *Member:* New Orleans, Louisiana State, Colorado and American (Vice-Chairman, Committee on Maritime Insurance Law, Section of Tort and Insurance Practice, 1979-1983) Bar Associations; State Bar of Texas; Maritime Law Association of the United States (Member: Executive Committee, 1991—; Chairman, Committee on International Law of the Sea, 1991—; Chairman, Subcommittee on Offshore Exploration and Development, 1985-1988; Vice-Chairman, Committee on International Law of the Sea, 1989-1991); New Orleans Association of Defense Counsel; Louisi-

(This Listing Continued)

ana Association of Defense Counsel; Southeastern Admiralty Law Institute; Average Adjusters Association of the United States; Average Adjusters Association (U.K.); Defense Research Institute; Federation of Insurance and Corporate Counsel. (Also at New Orleans, Louisiana Office). *PRACTICE AREAS:* Maritime Law; Energy Law; Insurance Law.

FORREST BOOTH, born Evanston, Illinois, October 31, 1946; admitted, 1976, District of Columbia; 1977, California (Not admitted in England). *Education:* Amherst College (B.A., cum laude, 1968); Harvard University (J.D., 1971 [75]). Author: "Bad Faith - Legal Trends in Suits Against Insurers," 4 U.S.F. Maritime Law Journal 1. *Member:* Bar Association of San Francisco; The State Bar of California; The District of Columbia Bar; American Bar Association; Barristers Club of California; Maritime Law Association of the United States (Committee on Marine Insurance); Pacific Admiralty Seminar Steering Committee; Asian-Pacific Lawyers Association; Average Adjusters Association (U.K.); San Francisco Board of Marine Underwriters; U.S.F. Maritime Law Journal Board of Advisors. [Lieut., U.S. Navy, 1969-1972]. (Also at San Francisco, California Office). *PRACTICE AREAS:* Maritime Law; Appeals; Insurance Law.

ANTONIO J. RODRIGUEZ, born New Orleans, Louisiana, December 7, 1944; admitted, 1973, Louisiana. *Education:* United States Naval Academy (B.S., with merit, 1966); Loyola University of the South (J.D., cum laude, 1973). Alpha Sigma Nu; Phi Alpha Delta. Associate Editor, Loyola Law Review, 1971-1973. Professor of Maritime Law, (The Law of Collision, Limitation of Liability, and Oil Pollution), Tulane University School of Law, 1981—. Chairman, Navigation Safety Advisory Council, U.S. Department of Transportation, 1990-1994. Member, Rules of the Road Advisory Council, U.S. Department of Transportation, 1987-1990. U.S. Department of Transportation (U.S. Coast Guard) - "Distinguished Public Service Award" (1993). Author of Article: "How to Minimize Your Exposure: Practical Strategies in the Defense of Marine Pollution Claims," *Environmental Claims Journal (1993). Co-Author:* "The Oil Pollution Act of 1990," 15 *Tulane Maritime Law Journal 1,* 1990; "Overview of U.S. Law of Shipowners' Limitation of Liability," Maritime Law Association Reports (1991) (Reprinted, *Il Diritto Marittimo,* Genoa, Italy (1992). *Member:* New Orleans, Louisiana State, Federal and American (Member, Committee on Admiralty and Maritime Litigation and Natural Resources, Energy and Environmental Law and Sub-Committees on Collision and Litigation and Limitation of Liability) Bar Associations; Louisiana State Law Institute; Maritime Law Association of the United States (Member: Committees on Navigation and Coast Guard Matters, and Limitation of Liability); Southeastern Admiralty Law Institute; Average Adjusters Association of the United States; Average Adjusters Association (U.K.); U.S. Court of International Trade. Fellow, Louisiana Bar Foundation. [With USN, 1966-1970; Captain, United States Naval Reserve]. (Also at New Orleans, Louisiana Office). *PRACTICE AREAS:* Maritime Law; Environmental Law; Insurance Law.

WILLIAM L. BANNING, born Los Angeles, California, November 24, 1951; admitted, 1977, California; U.S. District Court, Southern and Central Districts of California; U.S. Court of Appeals, Ninth Circuit. *Education:* University of California at Santa Barbara (B.A., 1973); University of Southern California (J.D., with honors, 1977). Recipient, U.S.C. Law School Legion Lex Alumni Association Scholarship. Member, Industrial Relation Law Journal, 1976-1977. Speaker, American Trial Lawyers Association Annual Convention, 1993, "Maritime Personal Injury Claims - Defense Perspective." Best Lawyers in America. *Member:* San Diego County and American Bar Associations; The State Bar of California; Maritime Law Association of the United States; Association of Average Adjusters of the United States; Pacific Law Corporation; America's Leading Lawyers. (Also at San Diego, California Office).

(For Biographical Data on Other Personnel, see Professional Biographies at New Orleans, Louisiana and San Francisco, California).

RICHARDS BUTLER

Established in 1920

BEAUFORT HOUSE
15 ST BOTOLPH STREET
LONDON EC3A 7EE, ENGLAND
Telephone: 0171-247 6555
Telex: 949494 RBLAW G
Fax: 0171-247 5091

Abu Dhabi, United Arab Emirates Office: Al-Sayegh Richards Butler. P.O. Box 46904, Saif Bin Ghobash Building, Zayed the Second Street. Telephone: 2-725561. Telex: 22261 RBLAW EM. Fax: 2-778630.

(This Listing Continued)

Hong Kong Office: Alexandra House, Twentieth Floor, 16-20 Chater Road. Telephone: 810 8008. Telex: 62554 RBLAW HX. Fax: 810 0664.
Brussels, Belgium Office: Avenue de la Renaissance 1, Bte 11, 1040. Telephone: 2-732 20 55. Fax: 2-735 46 91.
Paris, France Office: 134 rue du Faubourg Saint Honoré, 75008. Telephone: 1-44 13 63 53. Fax: 1-42 89 20 60.

Admiralty, Aviation and Aircraft Finance, Commercial and EC, Commercial Litigation, Computers, Construction, Corporate, Eastern Europe, Employment, Environmental Law, Finance and Banking, Hospitals and Health, Insolvency, Insurance and Re-Insurance, Intellectual Property, International Trade and Commodities, Leisure, Litigation, Local Government, Media and Entertainment, Pensions, Real Estate, Regulation and Compliance, Shipping, Ship Finance and Tax.

PARTNERS

ALEXANDER T.C. ANDREWS, admitted, 1985. *Education:* Keble College, Oxford (M.A. Oxon). *PRACTICE AREAS:* Maritime Law; Charter Parties and Bills of Lading; P&I Clubs; Maritime Negligence Law; Marine Insurance Law; Marine Disasters.

TIMOTHY J. ARCHER, admitted, 1969. *Education:* Merton College, Oxford (M.A. Oxon - 2nd class). *Member:* Law Society; Royal Aeronautical Society; International Bar Association. *PRACTICE AREAS:* Commercial Litigation; Employment Law; Employer/Employee Relations; Employment Discrimination.

E. GEORGE ARGHYRAKIS, (admission pending). *Education:* University of Bristol (B.A.). *LANGUAGES:* Greek, Spanish and French. *PRACTICE AREAS:* Maritime Law.

JOHN S. AUSTIN, admitted, 1980. *Education:* Fitzwilliam, Cambridge (M.A. Law). *Member:* Law Society. *PRACTICE AREAS:* Commercial Property Law; Property Finance; Property Development and/or Syndication Law; Land Use Law; Landlord and Tenant Law; Conveyancing; Local Authorities; Health and Hospital Law.

JOHN M. AYLWIN, admitted, 1967. *Education:* Emmanuel College, Cambridge (M.A. Law). *Member:* Law Society; City of London Solicitors Co.; International Bar Association. *PRACTICE AREAS:* Property Law; Environmental Law; Environmental Liability; Contamination Law.

COLIN BAMFORD, admitted, 1974. *Education:* Trinity Hall Cambridge (M.A.). *Member:* International Bar Association. *PRACTICE AREAS:* Banking Law; International Banking; Banking Regulation; Broker-Dealer Regulation; Project Finance.

STUART N. BEARE, admitted, 1964. *Education:* Clare College, Cambridge (M.A., LL.B.). *Member:* City of London Solicitors' Company Court of Assistants; Baltic Exchange; Maritime International (Titular Member of Comité); London Maritime Arbitrators' Association (Supporting Member). *PRACTICE AREAS:* Maritime Law; Charter Parties and Bills of Lading; Marine Insurance Law; Offshore Pollution.

ANDREW P. BIGGS, admitted, 1975, England and Wales; 1977, Hong Kong. *Education:* College of Law. *Member:* Law Society; Hong Kong Law Society; Notary Public, Hong Kong. (Resident, Hong Kong Office). *PRACTICE AREAS:* International Banking; Corporate Finance Law; Mergers and Acquisitions; Securities Offerings; Eurobonds.

ROGER W. BILLIS, admitted, 1978. *Education:* Brasenose College, Oxford (M.A.). *Member:* Law Society; Baltic Exchange; London Maritime Arbitrators' Association. *PRACTICE AREAS:* Ship Finance; Ship Registration; Aviation Finance; Aircraft Leasing; International Finance.

MICHAEL D. BLOOMFIELD, admitted, 1980. *Education:* University of Wales (B.Sc.). *LANGUAGES:* Spanish. *PRACTICE AREAS:* Admiralty Law.

KAY BOOTH, admitted, 1987. *Education:* Brunel University (LL.B.). *PRACTICE AREAS:* Banking Law.

DAVID J. BOUTCHER, admitted, 1981. *Education:* University of Kent (B.A. Honours, Economics and Law). *Member:* Law Society. *PRACTICE AREAS:* Corporate Law; Corporate Finance Law; Mergers and Acquisitions; Corporate Restructuring.

GRAEME J. BOWTLE, admitted, 1966. *Education:* New College, Oxford (M.A.). *Member:* British Maritime Law Association; Law Society. *PRACTICE AREAS:* Ship Finance; Asset Finance; Maritime Law; Ship Mortgage Reinforcement; Ship Registration.

CHARLES A. BROWN, admitted, 1983. *PRACTICE AREAS:* Maritime Law.

(This Listing Continued)

RICHARDS BUTLER, London—Continued

MARGARET CAMPBELL, admitted, 1981. *Education:* Wadham College Oxford (M.A. Jurisprudence). *Member:* Law Society. **PRACTICE AREAS:** Insurance Law; Re-insurance Law; Marine Insurance; Arbitration Law; Charter Parties and Bills of Lading; P&I Clubs.

LISTA M. CANNON, admitted, 1974, England and Wales; 1976, New York. *Education:* University of London (LL.B. Hons). **PRACTICE AREAS:** Commercial Litigation; Insurance Litigation; Insurance Regulation; Securities Litigation; Environmental Law.

MARK F. CONNOLEY, admitted, 1980. *Education:* St. Edmund Hall, Oxford (Jurisprudence). **PRACTICE AREAS:** Insurance Law; Marine Insurance; Maritime Law.

DAVID J. COOGANS, admitted, 1987. *Education:* Anglia University (B.A., Hons., Law). **PRACTICE AREAS:** Shipping Law.

FRANK J. DONAGH, admitted, 1961. *Education:* Bristol (LL.B). *Member:* Law Society. (Corporate Finance). **PRACTICE AREAS:** Corporate Law.

LINDSAY T. EAST, admitted, 1973. *Education:* Worcester College, Oxford (M.A.). **PRACTICE AREAS:** Maritime Law; Charter Parties and Bills of Lading; P&I Clubs; Marine Insurance Law; Marine Disasters; Casualties.

HUGH R. EDWARDS, admitted, 1966. *Education:* University College, London (LL.B). *Member:* Law Society. **PRACTICE AREAS:** Commercial Property Law; Planning.

STEPHEN EDWARDS, admitted, 1976. *Education:* Witwatersrand University, Johannesberg, SA (B.A. WITS); Cambridge, Trinity Hall (M.A. Cantab). *Member:* Law Society; International Bar Association. **PRACTICE AREAS:** Intellectual Property Law; Copyright Law; Broadcasting Law; Television Law; Entertainment Industry Transactions.

JOHN F. EMMOTT, admitted, 1978. *Education:* University of Sydney (B.A.; LL.B). *Member:* Law Society, City of London Solicitors' Co. **PRACTICE AREAS:** Maritime Law; Charter Parties and Bills of Lading; International Trade; Transportation Law.

DIANA FABER, admitted, 1983. *Education:* University College, London. *Member:* Law Society. **PRACTICE AREAS:** Maritime Law; Charter Parties and Bills of Lading; P&I Clubs; Maritime Negligence Law; Through Transport; Debt Recovery.

IAN M. FLETCHER, admitted, 1971, Scotland; 1978, England and Wales. *Education:* University of Glasgow (LL.B. LTCL; LRAM; ARCO; WS; MIPA). *Member:* The Law Society of Scotland; The Law Society; The Scottish Law Agents Society; The Institute of Directors; The Society of Practitioners of Insolvency; The Insolvency Lawyers Association, Ltd.; The Insolvency Practitioners Association; International Bar Association; City of London Solicitors; The WS Society. **PRACTICE AREAS:** Banking Law; Insolvency Law; Corporate Restructuring Law.

DUNCAN FRANCIES, admitted, 1968. *Member:* Law Society. **PRACTICE AREAS:** Admiralty Law; Maritime Law; Maritime Negligence Law; Maritime Title Law; Offshore Pollution.

ELIZABETH HARDY, admitted, 1986. *Education:* St. Edmund Hall, Oxford (Jurisprudence). (Resident, Hong Kong). **PRACTICE AREAS:** Corporate Law; Corporate Finance Law; Mergers and Acquisitions; Hostile Takeovers; Securities Takeovers.

GRAHAM D. HARRIS, admitted, 1981. *Education:* Oriel College, Oxford (M.A. Jurisprudence). **PRACTICE AREAS:** Maritime Law; Marine Insurance Law; Ship Mortgage Reinforcement; Transportation Law; Roald Haulage.

RICHARD H.J.P. HARVEY, admitted, 1980. *Education:* Christ Church, Oxford (M.A., English Language, Literature). **PRACTICE AREAS:** Admiralty Law; Lloyds Litigation; P&I Clubs; Marine Insurance Law; Marine Salvage Rights; Marine Disasters; Offshore Pollution.

KATHERINE M. HOLMES, 1973, admitted as Barrister; 1990, admitted as Solicitor, England and Wales. Vice Chairman, ICC Commission on Law Practices Related to Competition. *Member:* Solicitors European Group; UIA (EC Section); Law Society; Bar European Group; BACFI. **PRACTICE AREAS:** European Community Law; Competition Law; International Trade; Customs and Excise Law; Products Liability Law.

(This Listing Continued)

STELLA HOLT, admitted, 1984. *Education:* Exeter (LL.B. Hons). **PRACTICE AREAS:** Commercial Litigation; Tort Law; Intellectual Property Law; Copyright Law; Computer Law.

CHRISTOPHER G. HOWSE, admitted, 1978. *Education:* University of Geneva; University of Bristol. *Member:* Law Society; Hong Kong Law Society. (Resident, Hong Kong Office). **PRACTICE AREAS:** Insurance Law; Marine Insurance; Commercial Litigation; Arbitration Law.

ANDREW S. HUGHES, admitted, 1982. (Resident, Hong Kong Office). **PRACTICE AREAS:** Maritime Law.

PAUL F. JOHNSTON, admitted, 1982. *Education:* Birmingham (LL.B.). **PRACTICE AREAS:** Commercial Property Law; Property Finance; Property Development and/or Syndication; Landlord and Tenant Law.

JAMES A. KELIHER, admitted, 1988. *Education:* Liverpool University (LL.B.). **PRACTICE AREAS:** Corporate Law.

MICHAEL A. MACKENZIE-SMITH, admitted, 1979. *Education:* Queen's College, Oxford (French and Modern History). *Member:* Law Society; Paris Bar Association (Avocat à la Cour). (Resident, Paris Office). **PRACTICE AREAS:** Commercial Law; International Trade; International Practice; Commercial Litigation; Arbitration Law.

DAVID L. MARCHESE, admitted, 1976. *Education:* New College, Oxford (B.A.; M.A.). *Member:* Law Society; Licensing Executives Society. **PRACTICE AREAS:** Commercial Law.

JOHN D. MCGUINNESS, admitted, 1980. *Education:* Birmingham University (LL.B. Hons). (Resident, Hong Kong Office). **PRACTICE AREAS:** Banking Law.

ROBERT MCNALLY, admitted, 1982. *Education:* University College, London (LL.B., Hons.). **PRACTICE AREAS:** Commercial Property Law.

PETER G. MICHELMORE, admitted, 1976. *Education:* University of Bristol (LL.B.). *Member:* Law Society; International Bar Association; UIA. **PRACTICE AREAS:** Corporate Law; Corporate Finance Law; Mergers and Acquisitions; Securities Offerings; Venture Capital.

ADAM R.M. MORGAN, admitted, 1978. *Education:* Christ's College, Cambridge. *Member:* Law Society; Hong Kong Law Society; International Business Association. **PRACTICE AREAS:** Asset Finance; Aviation Finance; Ship Finance; Asset Based Lending; Financial Restructuring Law.

A. DAVID MORRISON, admitted, 1984, Scotland; 1985, Hong Kong; 1992, England and Wales. *Education:* University of Aberdeen (LL.B.; Dip. L.P.). *Member:* Law Society of Scotland; Law Society of Hong Kong; Law Society of England. (Resident, Hong Kong). **PRACTICE AREAS:** Commercial Litigation; Securities Litigation; Fraud; International Trade.

ROBIN C. NICHOLSON, admitted, 1980, England and Wales; 1982, Hong Kong. *Education:* University of Kent (B.A., Law). (Resident, Hong Kong Office). **PRACTICE AREAS:** Corporate Finance Law; Mergers and Acquisitions; Securities Offerings; Corporate Restructuring; Venture Capital.

RICHARD C. NICOLL, admitted, 1974. *Education:* King's College, London (LL.B.). *Member:* Law Society. **PRACTICE AREAS:** Commercial Property Law; Property Development and/or Syndication Law; Planning; Property Finance; Property Litigation.

DAVID M. NORMAN, admitted, 1981, England and Wales; 1984, Hong Kong. *Education:* Balliol College, Oxford (B.A.). *Member:* Law Society. (Resident, Hong Kong Office). **PRACTICE AREAS:** Corporate Finance Law; International Banking; Mergers and Acquisitions; Securities Offerings; Corporate Restructuring; Joint Ventures.

KEN G. OLLERTON, admitted, 1973. *Education:* University College, London. **PRACTICE AREAS:** Commercial Litigation; Computer Law.

ROGER J. PARKER. PRACTICE AREAS: Commercial Litigation; Professional Indemnity; Property Litigation; Insurance Law; Building and Construction.

RICHARD P.S. PHILIPPS, admitted, 1978. *Education:* Queens' College, Cambridge (M.A.). *Member:* BAFTA. **PRACTICE AREAS:** Media Law; Entertainment Law; Motion Picture Finance; Motion Picture Contracts.

TIMOTHY D. PIGOTT, admitted, 1973. *Education:* Magdalene College, Cambridge (M.A.). *Member:* Law Society; Association of Pension Lawyers. **PRACTICE AREAS:** Pension and Profit Sharing Law; Employee Benefit Law.

(This Listing Continued)

JON R. PIKE, admitted, 1983. *Education:* Sheffield University (LL.B. Hons). *Member:* Law Society. **PRACTICE AREAS:** Commercial Property Law; Property Finance; Property Development and/or Syndication Law; Landlord and Tenant Law.

LESLIE J. POWELL, admitted, 1972. **PRACTICE AREAS:** Corporate Tax; International Tax; Corporate Tax Planning; Tax Shelters.

DAVID M. PULLEN, admitted, 1967. *Education:* Oxford (Jurisprudence). Instructor, University of Pennsylvania Law School, 1963-1964. *Member:* London Maritime Arbitrators Association. **PRACTICE AREAS:** International Trade; Commodities Law; Customs and Excise Law; Import and Export Law; European Community Law.

LAURENCE G. REES, admitted, 1976. **PRACTICE AREAS:** Employment Law.

STEPHEN T. SAYER, admitted, 1969. *Member:* Law Society; Society of Anglo-American Lawyers; Lawyers Club. **PRACTICE AREAS:** Commercial Law; Competition Law.

JEFF F. SHERWOOD, admitted, 1976. *Member:* International Bar Association; Royal Aeronautical Society; Law Society; SBA; City of London Solicitors Co.; European Air Law Association. **PRACTICE AREAS:** Aviation Law; Aviation Finance; Aircraft Leasing; Aviation Licensing.

S.P. MICHAEL SKREIN, admitted, 1973. **PRACTICE AREAS:** Aviation Law; Commercial Litigation; Litigation Defense; Defamation; Intellectual Property Law; Judicial Review; Media Law.

BARRY H. SMITH, admitted, 1974. *Education:* Queen Mary College, University of London (LL.B. Hons). *Member:* Copinger Society. **PRACTICE AREAS:** Media Law; Television Law; Entertainment Law.

ELIZABETH M. SOUTHORN, admitted, 1974. *Education:* St. Anne's College, Oxford (M.A.). **PRACTICE AREAS:** English Licensing Law including betting, gaming and liquor licensing; Advocacy.

DAVID A. STOKES, admitted, 1984, England and Wales; 1986, Hong Kong. *Education:* Exeter University (LL.B.). (Resident, Hong Kong). **PRACTICE AREAS:** Admiralty Law; International Trade; Charter Parties and Bills of Lading; P&I Clubs.

C. HOWARD K. SWINDALL, admitted, 1980. *Education:* College of Law, Guilford. *Member; Law Society.* **PRACTICE AREAS:** Commercial Property.

ANDREW D. TAYLOR, admitted, 1980. *Education:* Lincoln College, Oxford (M.A.). **PRACTICE AREAS:** Maritime Law; International Trade; P&I Clubs; Marine Insurance Law; Marine Disasters.

ANTHONY L.G. TREW, admitted, 1968. *Education:* College of Law, Lancaster Gate, London. *Member:* Law Society; International Bar Association. (Resident, Abu Dhabi Office). **PRACTICE AREAS:** Aviation Law; Banking Law; Corporate Law; International Law; Commercial Litigation; Maritime Law; Transportation Law.

ANTHONY J.B. VERNON, admitted, 1977. *Member:* International Bar Association. **PRACTICE AREAS:** Commercial Litigation; Business Crimes; White Collar Fraud; Professional Indemnity; International Law.

KEITH WALLACE, admitted, 1971. *Member:* Law Society; Holborn Law Society; City of London Solicitors Association Pension Lawyers (Founding Committee Member); Life Associate Legal Society (Past President); International Foundation Employee Benefit Plans (European Committee Member); International Pension and Employee Benefit Lawyers Association; Unit Trust Association; Occupational Pensions Advisory Service (Council Member); National Association of Pension Funds (Chairman, Law and Accounts Sub-Committee); Forum of Professional Independent Trustees (Honorary Secretary). **PRACTICE AREAS:** Employment Law; Employee Benefit Law; Unit Trusts; Investment Law; Class Actions; Charitable Trusts and Foundations.

DAVID G. WARNE, admitted, 1972. **PRACTICE AREAS:** Commercial Litigation; Insolvency.

TIMOTHY E. WATTS, admitted, 1978. **PRACTICE AREAS:** Corporate Law; Corporate Finance Law; Mergers and Acquisitions; Privatisations; Securities Offerings; Corporate Restructuring.

CHRISTOPHER J. WILLIAMS, admitted, 1986. *Education:* University of Reading. **PRACTICE AREAS:** Corporate Finance; Company/Commercial Law.

(This Listing Continued)

JON YORKE, admitted, 1986. *Education:* University of Essex. *Member:* IPA; SPI; ILA; Law Society. **PRACTICE AREAS:** Insolvency Law; Bankruptcy; Corporate Restructuring Law; Financial Restructuring Law.

CONSULTANTS

R.E. Towner	*D.Li Morgan*
J. Rainford	*M.L.B. Robinson*

M.W. RIDLEY & CO.

Solicitors and Attorneys-at-Law

Established in 1982

26 WILFRED STREET
BUCKINGHAM GATE
LONDON SW1E 6PL, ENGLAND
Telephone: 44 (0) 171 828 7656
Fax: 44 (0) 171 630 9256

FIRM PROFILE: *M.W. Ridley & Co. is a broadly based business law practice with particular emphasis on North American and other overseas companies setting up and operating in the United Kingdom.*

The firm's clients include manufacturing and service companies, in particular computer software and other companies in high technology fields.

Central to the firm's service philosophy is personal contact and close case management. This results in realistic fee levels, practical advice and the ability to meet deadlines.

Established in 1982, the firm practices from offices in central London close to Buckingham Palace. The two partners, both originally with major City of London firms, are supported by qualified and experienced support staff.

PARTNERS

MARK W. RIDLEY, born 1951; admitted, 1976. *Education:* Lancing College and Guildford Law School. *Member:* Law Society; American Chamber of Commerce (UK); British Computer Society; Royal Ocean Racing Yatch Club. *LANGUAGES:* English. **PRACTICE AREAS:** Company and Commercial Law; Formations, Acquisitions and Sales; Computer Software Contracts; Agency, Distributorship and Commercial Agreements; Securities Law; Employment Law; Work Permits.

PAUL S. SAMUEL, born 1951; admitted, 1976. *Education:* London University (LL.B., Hons.). *Member:* Bar of California; Institute of Directors; American Chamber of Commerce (UK). *LANGUAGES:* English. **PRACTICE AREAS:** Commercial Litigation and Arbitration; General Company and Commercial Law; Computer Software Contracts.

ASSOCIATES

CHARLES F. GLANVILLE, born 1956; admitted, 1984. *Education:* Exeter University and College of Law, Lancaster Gate. *Member:* Law Society; Royal Corinthian Yacht Club. *LANGUAGES:* English. **PRACTICE AREAS:** Commercial Property Law; Acquisitions and Disposals; Lease Renewals; Planning Law; Secured Lending; Residential Conveyancing.

ROGERS & WELLS

58 COLEMAN STREET
LONDON EC2R 5BE, ENGLAND
Telephone: 44-171-628-0101
Facsimile: 44-171-638-2008
Telex: 884964 USLAW G

REVISERS OF THE NEW YORK LAW DIGEST FOR THIS DIRECTORY.

New York, New York Office: Two Hundred Park Avenue, New York, N.Y., 10166-0153. Telephone: 212-878-8000. Facsimile: 212-878-8375. Telex: 234493 RKWUR.

Washington, D.C. Office: 607 Fourteenth Street, N.W., Washington, D.C. 20005-2011. Telephone: 202-434-0700. Facsimile: 202-434-0800.

Los Angeles, California Office: 444 South Flower Street, Los Angeles, California 90071-2901. Telephone: 213-689-2999. Facsimile: 213-689-2900.

Paris, France Office: 47, Avenue Hoche, 75008-Paris, France. Telephone: 33-1-44-09-46-00. Facsimile: 33-1-42-67-50-81. Telex: 651617.

Frankfurt, Germany Office: Lindenstrasse 37, 60325 Frankfurt/Main, Federal Republic of Germany. Telephone 49-69-97-57-11-0. Facsimile: 49-69-97-57-11-33.

(This Listing Continued)

ROGERS & WELLS, London—Continued

General Practice.
Firm engaged in American and International Law Practice, but not authorized to appear before the English Courts or to act as Solicitors.

PARTNERS

ERIC C. BETTELHEIM, born Chicago, Illinois, 1952; admitted, 1976, California and U.S. District Court, Northern District of California; 1979, England and Wales; 1984, New York. *Education:* University of Rochester (A.B., with honors, 1972); Oxford University, England (B.A., with honors, 1975; M.A., 1980); University of Chicago (J.D., 1976). "Policing the U.K. Commodity Markets," Euromoney Nov., 1984; "Obstacles to Transnational Futures Training," International Financial Law Review, Feb., 1986; "The Financial Services Bill—A Legal Perspective," The International Commodities Clearing House Quarterly Review, Spring, 1986; "An Investors Guide to the Commodity Futures Markets," Butterworths, March, 1986; "Regulating Foreign Options Internationally," International Financial Law Review, Sept., 1986; "Regulation of Options," The Chicago Board Options Exchange, Autumn, 1987; "Institutional Use of Traded Options Regulation and Taxation," London Traded Options Market, Dec., 1987; "Regulating Lookalikes," International Financial Law Review, Feb., 1988; "Futures Fund Regulation and Distribution," Futures Fund Management, TASS Asset Management Ltd., Autumn 1991; "Regulation in Perspective," Chapter for Financial Futures by Desmond Fitzgerald, 1993; Review of "The Transformation of Threadneedle Street," by James J. Fishman, Northwestern Journal of International Law & Business, July 1993; "The Regulation of OTC Derivative Products," Chapter for Futures Trading Law & Regulation, edited by Helen Parry, Eric Bettelheim & William Rees, Longmans, 1993; "Futures Funds - Regulation and Distribution," Chapter for 1994 edition of Futures Fund Management; "A Brief Guide to Regulation for Managed Future Funds in the US and Japan," Chapter for Financial Times Report European Managed Futures, by Beverly Chandler, March 1994. Co-Author, with: Arthur Andersen, "A Guide to International Regulation, Tax and Accounting," Futures and Options World, Nov., 1986, Dec., 1986 and Jan., 1987; Robert C. Creighton, "Regulation of Futures Funds," Futures and Options World, June, 1989, Edward B. Black, "Reconstruction and Regulation since October 19, 1987," Financial Futures and Options IFR Publishing, 1989; Jerry W. Markham, "The Transnor Decision and its Aftermath ("Futures Shock")," Oil & Gas Law and Taxation Review, Washington, May 1990; Jerry W. Markham, "More on Transnor," Oil & Gas Law and Taxation Review, Washington, June 1990; Edward Black, "Sorting Through UK Funds to Find A Fund Audience," Futures Magazine, London, October 1991; Kenneth Raisler, "Legal Aspects of Commodity Derivatives for Commodity Linked Finance," Euromoney, 1992; Edward Black, "CTA Registration in Europe," The MFA Reporter, April 1993; Edward Black, "Regulation by the Revenue," Securities & Investment Review, May 1994; Johannes Gäbel, "Derivatives in Germany," Managed Derivatives, October 1994. *Member:* New York State and American Bar Associations; State Bar of California; Maritime Law Association of the United States; Futures Industry Association; Inner Temple. *PRACTICE AREAS:* Banking Law; Securities Law; Commodities Law.

DANIEL BUSHNER, born Independence, Missouri, 1952; admitted, 1984, New York (Not admitted in England). *Education:* Princeton University (B.A., magna cum laude, 1975); Oxford University, England (M.A., 1977); Georgetown University (J.D., 1983). Editor, Georgetown Law Journal, 1981-1983. Author: "U.S. Regulatory Relaxation Continues," *Corporate Finance*, August 1994; "SEC Package Paves the Way for Foreign Issuers," *Corporate Finance*, March 1994; "L'introduzione sui mercati USA dei titoli di Societa non stantunitensi tramite l'utilizzo di ADRs," *Assoziazione Italiana Degli Analisti Finanziari*, October 1993; "Easy access to US securities markets," *Corporate Finance*, November 1992; "Why Offshore Funds?" *Global Investor*, September 1992; "Listing and offerings of securities in the US," *Corporate Finance*, February 1992; "US Open to Euro-Insurers - How the SEC Lifted the Burden," Corporate Finance, November, 1991; "SEC Set to Ease Crossborder Deals," Corporate Finance, July 1991. Co-Author: "Rule 12g3-2(b) Backdoor or Trapdoor?" International Financial Law Review, April 1991; "Levelling the Playing Field or Moving the Goal Posts?" Corporate Finance, 1990; "ADRS: A Defensive Role in International Takeovers," International Financial Law Review, September, 1989. *Member:* New York State and American (Member, Section on International Law and Practice) Bar Associations. *LANGUAGES:* Russian. *PRACTICE AREAS:* Securities Law; Structured Finance; General Corporate.

SIDNEY CHARLES KURTH, born Billings, Montana, January 6, 1955; admitted, 1983, New York; 1986, District of Columbia (Not admitted in England). *Education:* Hampshire College (B.A., 1979); Columbia University

(This Listing Continued)

sity (J.D., 1982). Harlan Fiske Stone Scholar. Managing Editor, Columbia Journal of Environmental Law, 1981-1982. *Member:* The Association of the Bar of the City of New York; American and International Bar Associations; The Institute of Directors; The Securities Institute; The Reform Club.

CONSULTANT

HUGH DYKES, born Burnham, Somerset, U.K., May 17, 1939. *Education:* Pembroke College, Cambridge University, Cambridge, U.K. (M.A., Economic, 1963). Author: "Invest 100," Westropp's, 1964; "Start Your Own Business," Westropp's, 1965. Parliamentary Private Secretary: Ministry of Defence, 1970-1972; Cabinet Office, 1972-1974. Council, Wider Share Ownership Counsel, 1971. Member, Board of Governors, Royal National Orthopaedic Hospital, 1975—. Vice-Chairman, Conservative Friends of Israel. Treasurer, Anglo-Israel Parliamentary Group, 1975-1980. Chairman Coningsby Club, 1969-1970. Member, European Parliament, 1974-1977. Secretary, 1975-1978 and Chairman, 1980-1981, Conservative Parliamentary European Affairs Committee. Chairman, Conservative Group for Europe, 1978-1981. Joint Honourary Secretary, European Movement, 1980-1986. Chairman: All-Party Europe Group of MP's, 1988; European Movement, 1990 and 1992. (Adviser on E. C. and Legislative Affairs). *LANGUAGES:* French, German, Spanish, Italian and Russian. *PRACTICE AREAS:* E.C. and Legislative matters.

ASSOCIATES

EDWARD B. BLACK, born Coventry, England, June 11, 1956; admitted, 1980, England and Wales as Solicitor of the Supreme Court of Judicature of England and Wales; 1983, New York. *Education:* Oriel College, Oxford University, England (B.A., with honours, 1977; M.A., 1982). Co-Author: "Reconstruction and Regulation since October 19, 1987," Financial Futures and Options-Recent Developments, IFR Publishing, 1989; "Sorting Through UK Rules to Find a Fund Audience," Futures, October 1991; "Legal Aspects of Commodity Derivatives in the United Kingdom," Commodity-Linked Finance, Euromoney, 1992; "Derivative Products - Their Use And Regulation," Global Investor International Investment Fund Management Supplement, September 1992; "UK Authorized and Unauthorized Funds," Global Investor International Investment Fund Management Supplement, September 1992; "Securities Lending in the UK," International Securities Lending Legal Guide, 1993; "Regulation by the Revenue: The UK Tax Regime for Securities Lending," Securities & Investment Review, May 1994; "Financial Futures and Options," Chapter of *United Kingdom Securities and Investments Regulation Handbook*, Graham & Trotman, 1995; "Clearing and Settlement: Futures and Options Markets," Chapter of *United Kingdom Securities and Investments Regulation Handbook*, Graham & Trotman, 1995. *Member:* New York State Bar Association (Member, Section of International Law); Law Society of England and Wales. *LANGUAGES:* French.

ROSSANO Y. MANSOORI-DARA, born Leeds, England, February 23, 1963; admitted, 1988, New York (Not admitted in England). *Education:* Downing College (Law, 1985); Inns of Court (Law, 1986). Recipient: Greystone Law Scholarship to Cambridge; Inner Temple Major Scholarship. *Member:* Bar of England and Wales; New York State Bar Association. *LANGUAGES:* Italian.

Languages: Greek, German, French and English.

REVISERS OF THE NEW YORK LAW DIGEST FOR THIS DIRECTORY.

(For biographical data of all partners, see Professional Biographies at New York, New York)

ROSCHIER-HOLMBERG & WASELIUS

36/38 CORNHILL

LONDON EC3V 9DR, ENGLAND

Telephone: 44-171-9290 966

Fax: 44-171-9290 933

Helsinki, Finland Office: Keskuskatu 7 A, 00100. Telephone: (0) 3580-228 551. Telex: 12 2310 ADVOX. Cable Address: "Cognitor." Telefax: (0) 664 303; (0) 175 451. Teletex: 1000901.

Vaasa, Finland Office: Alatori, 65100.

General Practice. International Financing, Commercial Banking, Industrial Property Rights, Trade and Market, Maritime, Aviation, Corporate, Establishing, Taxation and Real Estate Law, Litigation, EC Law.

(This Listing Continued)

ASSOCIATES

LAURI PELTOLA, born Längelmäki, Finland, May 24, 1950; admitted, 1978, Finland. *Education:* University of Helsinki (LL.B., 1974). *Member:* Finnish Bar Association. *LANGUAGES:* Finnish, Swedish, English, German and French.

ROSLING KING

2/3 HIND COURT
FLEET STREET
LONDON EC4A 3DL, ENGLAND
Telephone: 0171-353 2353
Telex: 8813671 ROSKIN G
Facsimile: 0171-583 2035

MEMBERS OF FIRM

MALCOLM D. MACFARLANE, born 1950; admitted, 1975, England and Wales.

OWEN T. RAFFERTY, born 1949; admitted, 1976, England and Wales.

GEORGINA N. SQUIRE, born 1958; admitted, 1983, England and Wales.

GRAHAM J.A. CLARK, born 1945; admitted, 1973, England and Wales.

ANDREW T. HARDMAN, born 1962; admitted, 1986, England and Wales.

ANNABEL J. CRUMLEY, born 1963; admitted, 1988, England and Wales.

RICHARD A.G. ANSTEY, born 1942; admitted, 1970, England and Wales.

ASSOCIATES

HELEN F. BRIGHT, born 1958; admitted, 1985, England and Wales.

SIMON W. COLLEDGE, born 1963; admitted, 1989, Scotland; 1992, England and Wales.

MICHAEL J. GREEN, born 1966; admitted, 1991, England and Wales.

GERALDINE A. KEAVNEY, born 1964; admitted, 1991, England and Wales.

KEITH THOMAS, born 1965; admitted, 1990, England and Wales.

OTHER LAWYERS

SARA BARTOLOZZI, born 1968; admitted, 1993, England and Wales.

THOMAS J. BRAMALL, born 1965; admitted, 1991, England and Wales.

PHILIP BREMER, born 1966; admitted, 1990, New Zealand.

DUNCAN M. CAMPBELL, born 1964; admitted, 1987, Australia.

ANDREW DAVIDSON, born 1961; admitted, 1990, New Zealand.

RACHEL FELSTEAD, born 1965; admitted, 1993, England and Wales.

FREDDIE N. GRIVE, born 1966; admitted, 1992, England and Wales.

KATHY M. HALLILEY, born 1962; admitted, 1990, Australia.

JACQUELINE A. KNAGGS, born 1966; admitted, 1991, England and Wales.

JESSICA KNIGHT, born 1968; admitted, 1993, England and Wales.

PAUL LOWE, born 1968; admitted, 1992, England and Wales.

ANDREW T. LYON, born 1966; admitted, 1993, England and Wales.

ANDREW J. MASON, born 1966; admitted, 1990, Australia.

JANE T. PERRY, born 1965; admitted, 1991, England and Wales.

FRANCES STAPLEFORD, born 1967; admitted, 1991, England and Wales.

ROWE & MAW

20 BLACK FRIARS LANE
LONDON EC4V 6HD, ENGLAND
Telephone: 0171.248.4282
Fax: 0171.248.2009

Lloyd's, London Office: One Lime Street, Suite 894, London EC4M 7DQ. Telephone: 0171.327.4144. FAX: 0171.623.7965.
Brussels Office: 35, Square DeMeeus, Brussels 1040, Belgium. Telephone: 322.502.5517. Fax: 322.502.5421.

FIRM PROFILE: Rowe & Maw is a leading English practice providing business solutions to a broad range of commercial clients, both in the United Kingdom and overseas. In addition to our Brussels office, we have close working relationships with other law firms throughout Europe and the United States enabling us to provide our clients with a quality service, wherever they may be doing business.

PARTNERS

DUDLEY WILLIAM MALCOLM COUPER, born 1935; admitted, 1961, England. *Education:* Oxford University. *PRACTICE AREAS:* Commercial Property Law.

JOHN KEITH OLDALE, born 1937; admitted, 1962, England. *Education:* London University. *PRACTICE AREAS:* Commercial Law; Advertising Law.

FRANCIS GOODWIN MARKHAM, born 1937; admitted, 1965, England. *Education:* Cambridge University. *PRACTICE AREAS:* Property Law.

MICHAEL JOHN BOYD WEBSTER, born 1942; admitted, 1968, England. *Education:* Bristol University. *PRACTICE AREAS:* Information Technology Law; Corporate Finance Law; Company Law.

ANTHONY JOHN MORTON BLACKLER, born 1941; admitted, 1967, England. *Education:* Cambridge University. *Member:* International Bar Association. *PRACTICE AREAS:* Construction Law; Litigation; A.D.R..

STUART CAMPBELL JAMES, born 1944; admitted, 1967.

RICHARD ANDREW POWLES, born 1945; admitted, 1971, England. *Education:* Oxford University. *PRACTICE AREAS:* Private Client Law.

JOHN WILLIAM TOOMEY, born 1946; admitted, 1971, England. *Education:* London University. *PRACTICE AREAS:* Commercial Property Law.

RICHARD DUNCAN LINSELL, born 1947; admitted, 1973, England. *Education:* Cambridge University. *Member:* International Bar Association. *PRACTICE AREAS:* Commercial Law; International Law; Corporate Finance Law; Company Law.

JANE HEATH, born 1935; admitted, 1959, England. *Education:* Law Society School of Law. *Member:* Association of Pension Lawyers. *PRACTICE AREAS:* Pensions Law.

ANDREW GEORGE WHITE, born 1950; admitted, 1974, England. *Education:* Oxford University. *Member:* Association of Pension Lawyers. *PRACTICE AREAS:* Pension Law; Life Insurance Law; Financial Services Law.

JAMES MITCHELL DENKER, born 1947; admitted, 1976, England. *Education:* University of Pennsylvania, U.S.A.; Cambridge University, England. *Member:* International Academy of Estate and Trust Law; International Bar Association. *LANGUAGES:* French. *PRACTICE AREAS:* International Estate Planning and Probate Law.

CHARLES PATRICK ASHCROFT, born 1951; admitted, 1977, England. *Education:* Oxford University. *Member:* International Bar Association. *PRACTICE AREAS:* Corporate Law; Securities Law; Financial Services Law; Mergers and Acquisitions Law.

STEPHEN DAVID GARE, born 1950; admitted, 1976, England. *Education:* Cambridge University. *Member:* City of London Solicitors Company Intellectual Property Sub-Committee; U.K. Law Monitoring Group of Anti-Counterfeiting Group; Solicitors' European Group. *PRACTICE AREAS:* Intellectual Property Law; Information Technology Law; Litigation.

DAVID GUY GIDNEY, born 1952; admitted, 1977, England. *Education:* Oxford University. *PRACTICE AREAS:* Commercial Property Law; Development Law; Investment Law.

(This Listing Continued)

ROWE & MAW, London—Continued

JOHN RUSHTON, born 1950; admitted, 1975, England. *Education:* Cambridge University. *PRACTICE AREAS:* Construction Law; Commercial Litigation; Arbitration Law.

IAN CHRISTIE, born 1951; admitted, 1978, England. *Education:* Leeds University. *PRACTICE AREAS:* Commercial Property Law; Retail Law; Landlord and Tenant Law.

RICHARD ERIC CHAMPION JONES, born 1954; admitted, 1975, England. *Education:* Oxford University. *Member:* Chartered Institute of Arbitrators (Associate Member); Society of Construction Law. *PRACTICE AREAS:* Litigation; Construction Law.

MICHELE-ANNE MARY FREYNE, born 1950; admitted, 1978, England. *Education:* Trinity College, Dublin. *PRACTICE AREAS:* Property Litigation Law; Matrimonial Law.

ANDREW JAMES CARRUTHERS, born 1949; admitted, 1975, England. *Education:* Oxford University. *Member:* Company of City of London Solicitors International Litigation Practitioners Forum; Association of Pension Lawyers; London Solicitors Litigation Association; UIA. *PRACTICE AREAS:* Commercial and Corporate Litigation; Arbitration; Pension Law.

KARELYN MANDY WARNFORD-DAVIS, born 1954; admitted, 1979, England. *Education:* Oxford University. *PRACTICE AREAS:* Corporate Finance Law; Mergers and Acquisitions Law; Venture Capital Law.

MICHAEL REGAN, born 1955; admitted, 1980, England. *Education:* Oxford University. (Partner in change of Lloyd's Office). *PRACTICE AREAS:* Construction/Engineering Law; Insurance Law; Litigation.

ARUNDEL MCDOUGALL, born 1953; admitted, 1978, England. *Education:* Oxford University. *LANGUAGES:* French. *PRACTICE AREAS:* Commercial Litigation; Products Liability Law; Sale of Goods; Pension Law; Pharmaceutical Law.

MICHAEL NOTT, born 1936; admitted, 1971, England. *Education:* Exeter University. *PRACTICE AREAS:* Aviation Law; Commercial Law; EEC; Travel Law.

DAVID IVE, born 1950; admitted, 1974, England. *Education:* Birmingham University. *Member:* British Branch of the International Fiscal Association. *PRACTICE AREAS:* Tax Law.

MARK ADAM PRINSLEY, born 1956; admitted, 1981, England. *Education:* Oxford University. *Member:* Institute of Trade Mark Agents (Associate Member). *PRACTICE AREAS:* Intellectual Property Law; Information Technology Law.

RICHARD DEREK COLLINGWOOD MAUGHAN, born 1949; admitted, 1975, England and Wales. *Education:* University of London. *PRACTICE AREAS:* Commercial Property Law.

HUGH DEVAS, born 1950; admitted, 1975, England. *Education:* Oxford University. *PRACTICE AREAS:* Environmental Law; Commercial Law.

SPENCER HOWARD KERVEN WILLIAMS, born 1946; admitted, 1971, England. *PRACTICE AREAS:* Commercial Property Law.

JULIAN WENTWORTH ROSKILL, born 1950; admitted, 1974, England. *Education:* College of Law, London. *Member:* City of London Solicitors Company. *LANGUAGES:* French. *PRACTICE AREAS:* Contentious and Non-Contentious Employment Relations Law; Industrial Relations Law.

STEPHEN JOHN BOTTOMLEY, born 1954; admitted, 1980, England. *Education:* University of East Anglia. *PRACTICE AREAS:* Corporate Finance Law; Venture Capital Law.

BERND RATZKE, born 1956; admitted, 1982, England. *Education:* University of Durham. *LANGUAGES:* German. *PRACTICE AREAS:* Corporate Law; Corporate Finance Law; Insolvency Law.

GILLIAN MARY BIRKBY, born 1948; admitted, 1981, England. *Education:* Dundee University. *Member:* Institute of Arbitrators (Associate Member); Society of Construction Law. *LANGUAGES:* French and Spanish. *PRACTICE AREAS:* Construction Law; Litigation; Arbitration.

EDMUND MARK SAUTTER, born 1958; admitted, 1983, England. *Education:* Cambridge University. *PRACTICE AREAS:* Commercial Litigation.

SEAN MICHAEL CONNOLLY, born 1960; admitted, 1984, England. *Education:* University of London. *Member:* International Bar Association.

(This Listing Continued)

PRACTICE AREAS: Insurance Law; Reinsurance Law; International Litigation; Arbitration Law.

JAMES ARTHUR BLACK, born 1953; admitted, 1977, England. *Education:* College of Law, London. *PRACTICE AREAS:* Commercial Property Law; Property Development Funding Law; Agricultural Property Law.

JEREMY CLAY, born 1961; admitted, 1985, England. *Education:* Oxford University. *PRACTICE AREAS:* Commercial Property Law; Property Finance Law.

ROSEMARY ELISABETH SCUDAMORE MARTIN, born 1960; admitted, 1985, England. *Education:* Sussex University. *PRACTICE AREAS:* Company Law; Corporate Finance Law; Corporate Acquisitions and Disposals Law.

ANNA KELLY, born 1961; admitted, 1985, England. *Education:* Oxford University. *Member:* Association of Pension Lawyers. *LANGUAGES:* French, German and Italian. *PRACTICE AREAS:* Pensions Law.

STEPHEN JOSEPH WALSH, born 1958; admitted, 1985, England. *Education:* Oxford University. *PRACTICE AREAS:* Banking Law; Property Finance Law; Consumer Credit Law.

JULIE MELLINDA DICKINS, born 1958; admitted, 1982, England. *Education:* Bristol University. *LANGUAGES:* French, German and Russian. *PRACTICE AREAS:* Property Litigation Law.

CHRISTOPHER PETER LANGFORD, born 1961; admitted, 1985, England. *Education:* Oxford University. *PRACTICE AREAS:* Insurance Law; Commercial Litigation.

TREVOR ANTHONY NICHOLLS, born 1950; admitted, 1985, Solicitor, England. *Education:* Polytechnic of Central London. Qualified as a Civil Engineer, 1973. *PRACTICE AREAS:* Construction Law.

DAVID MARTIN ALLEN, born 1959; admitted, 1984, England. *Education:* Bristol University. Licensed Insolvency Practitioner. *Member:* Insolvency Lawyers Association. *PRACTICE AREAS:* Insolvency Law.

STEPHANIE BATES, born 1960; admitted, 1985, England. *Education:* Southampton University. *PRACTICE AREAS:* Corporate Finance Law; Mergers and Acquisitions Law; General Corporate Law.

PETER ALAN STEINER, born 1950; admitted, 1988, England. *Education:* Cambridge University. *LANGUAGES:* German. *PRACTICE AREAS:* Tax Law.

PAUL JOSEPH MAHER, born 1959; admitted, 1984, England. *Education:* Bristol University. *PRACTICE AREAS:* Corporate Law; Mergers and Acquisitions Law.

ERIC MICHAEL GUMMERS, born 1961; admitted, 1985, England. *Education:* Cambridge University. *LANGUAGES:* French and German. *PRACTICE AREAS:* Commercial Law.

SIMON BAXTER, born 1961; admitted, 1987, England. *Education:* Sussex University. *LANGUAGES:* French and German. *PRACTICE AREAS:* EC Law; Corporate Law.

ANDREW SHARPLES, born 1959; admitted, 1985, England. *Education:* Durham University. *PRACTICE AREAS:* Corporate Finance Law; Company Law.

KAREN HEATHER KENDALL ABBOTT, born 1963; admitted, 1987, England. *Education:* Bristol University. *PRACTICE AREAS:* Insurance Law; Reinsurance Law; Commercial Litigation.

ANDREW KENNETH STEWART, born 1962; admitted, 1986, England. *Education:* Bristol University. *PRACTICE AREAS:* Corporate Law; Company Law.

PENELOPE JANE CHAPMAN, born 1960; admitted, 1986, England. *Education:* Oxford University. *PRACTICE AREAS:* Private Client Law; Charities Law.

PHILIPPA SUSAN JAMES, born 1956; admitted, 1980, England. *Education:* University of Wales. *PRACTICE AREAS:* Pensions Law.

MICHAEL WAINWRIGHT, born 1958; admitted, 1983, England. *Education:* Oxford University. *PRACTICE AREAS:* Corporate Finance Law; Financial Services Law; Corporate Law.

(This Listing Continued)

OF COUNSEL

NIGEL NAWTON GRAHAM MAW, born 1933; admitted, 1961, England. *Education:* Cambridge University. Lecturer, Institute of Directors. *Member:* Associate Institute of Taxation Incorporated. (Senior Partner). *LANGUAGES:* French and German. *PRACTICE AREAS:* Corporate Law; Mergers and Acquisitions Law; Taxation Law; International Joint Ventures; Licensing Law.

GEORGE EDWARD STRINGER, born 1937; admitted, 1961, England. *Education:* Manchester University. *LANGUAGES:* French. *PRACTICE AREAS:* Construction Law; International Arbitration Law.

GEORGE VERRINDER MASON, born 1930; admitted, 1953, England. *Education:* Law Society School of Law. *PRACTICE AREAS:* Property Law.

TACO VAN TIJN, born 1924; admitted, 1957, England; 1977, Solicitor of the Supreme Court of England and Wales. Barrister Inner Temple, England and Wales. *LANGUAGES:* Dutch, French and German. *PRACTICE AREAS:* Conflicts of Law; International Law.

Languages: Dutch, French, German, Italian, Spanish and Russian

---

SABI & ASSOCIATES

SCEPTRE HOUSE
169/173 REGENT STREET
LONDON W1R 7FB, ENGLAND
Telephone: 0171 734 4104
Fax: 0171 287 0986
Telex: 25532 PROFNL G

Consultants in Iranian Law, International Arbitration, Iran-U.S. Claims Tribunal, Expert Evidence on Iranian Law, International Commercial Contracts, Oil, Gas, Constructions, Banking, Finance.
Not authorized to appear before the English Courts. Founded 1939 by late Musa Sabi (translated all major Iranian codifications into English). The clientele includes major oil companies, multinational corporations; state agencies and governments.

HAMID SABI, admitted, 1974, Iran (Not admitted in England). *Education:* Tehran University (B.A., 1970); Dundee University (LL.B., 1974). *LANGUAGES:* Persian and English.

FARKHONDEH SABI, admitted, 1975, Iran (Not admitted in England). *Education:* Tehran University (LL.B., 1967); Universite de Paris (DEA, 1983). *LANGUAGES:* Persian, English and French.

SALANS HERTZFELD & HEILBRONN

103 MOUNT STREET
LONDON W1Y 5HE, ENGLAND
Telephone: 44.171.491.3735
Fax: 44.171.408.0843

Paris, France, Office: 9, Rue Boissy D'Anglas, 75008. Telephone: 42.68.48.00. Telex: 280990 PARILEX. Fax: 42.68.15.45; 42.68.15.46; 42.68.15.47.
New York, N.Y. Office: 750 Lexington Avenue, 10022. Telephone: 212.644.0800. Fax: 212.644.1003.
Moscow, Russia Office: Gazetnyi Pereulok, 17/9, (Ex. UL. Ogareva). 103009. Telephone: 7.501.940.2944. Fax: 7.501.940.2806.
Warsaw, Poland Office: ul. Podwale 7, 00-252. Telephone: 48.22 31.96.88; 31.25.72; 31.29.20. Fax: 48.22 31.39.32; 31.15.65.
St. Petersburg, Russia Office: Dom Zhurnalistov, 70 Nevskii Prospekt. 191 025. Telephone: 7.812.272.4572; 273.6844. Fax: 7.812.273.6844.
Other St. Petersburg, Russia Office: 6 Inzhenernaya Ulitsa, 191011. Telephone: 7.812.850.1504; 210.4040; 210. 4447; 210.4008; 210.4032; 210.4005; 210.4348; 210.4812. Fax: 7.812.850.1505; 210.4114. Office Move planned for March 15, 1995.
Kiev, Ukraine Office: Ukrainskii Dim, Vul. Kreshchatik 2 (4th Floor), 252601. Telephone: 7.044.228.5451. Fax: 7.044.228.6398.
Almaty, Kazakhstan Office: 10A Abaya Prospect, Corner "Furmanova," 11th Floor, Suite 5, 480013. Telephone: 7 3272 634 053; 634 049.
Other Almaty, Kazakhstan Office: 86 Gogol Street, 5th Floor, 480091. Office move planned for April 1, 1995.

International business law, East-West joint ventures and privatizations, corporate restructuring, banking, corporate finance, project finance, construction, media, taxation and arbitration. Firm engaged in American and

(This Listing Continued)

International Law Practice, but not authorized to appear before the English Courts or to act as Solicitors.

MEMBERS OF FIRM

BRIAN D. FIX, born Rochester, New York, May 31, 1944; admitted, 1968, New York; 1969, District of Columbia; 1992, Avocat, Paris, France. *Education:* Columbia University (B.A., 1965; LL.B., 1968). *LANGUAGES:* English, French. *PRACTICE AREAS:* Finance; Corporate; Eastern European Commerce.

GEORGE P. MACDONALD, born Janesville, Wisconsin, March 15, 1945; admitted, 1971, Michigan and District of Columbia. *Education:* University of Notre Dame (A.B., 1967); University of Michigan (J.D., 1970); University of London (M.A., 1971; Diploma, Intellectual Property Law, 1987). Editor-in-Chief, Michigan Journal of Law Reform. *LANGUAGES:* English, French and Russian. *PRACTICE AREAS:* Finance; Intellectual Property; Corporate; Eastern European Commerce.

ROBERT I. STARR, born Philadelphia, Pennsylvania, November 19, 1937; admitted, 1962, Illinois; 1972, U.S. Supreme Court; 1976, District of Columbia. *Education:* Northwestern University (B.A., 1958); University of Chicago Law School (J.D., 1962; Master of Comparative Law, 1964); Université d'Aix Marseille, France (M Comp L, 1964). Co-Editor of *Butterworth's Central and East European Business Law Bulletin.* Author: *Practical Aspects of Trading with the USSR,* 1990; *Joint Ventures in the USSR,* 1989. Chairman, Committee on East-West Trade and Investment of the American Chamber of Commerce (UK). *LANGUAGES:* English, French, Russian. *PRACTICE AREAS:* Eastern European Commerce.

ASSOCIATES

ETHAN S. BURGER, born New York, N.Y., February 11, 1959; admitted, 1989, District of Columbia. *Education:* Harvard University (A.B., 1981); Georgetown University Law Center (J.D., 1989). *LANGUAGES:* English and Russian. *PRACTICE AREAS:* Eastern European Commerce.

NATASHA SIVAKOFF, born Middlebury, Connecticut, January 15, 1965; admitted, 1992, Connecticut. *Education:* Smith College (B.A., 1987); University of Wisconsin (M.A., 1988); University of Connecticut (J.D., 1992). *LANGUAGES:* English, French and Russian. *PRACTICE AREAS:* Eastern European Commerce.

CONSULTANT

DAVID SURATGAR, born London, England, October 23, 1938. *Education:* Oxford University (B.A., Jurisprudence, 1959; M.A., 1960); Hague Academy of International Law (Certificate, 1960); Columbia University (Master of International Affairs, International Law & Economics, 1961; Ph.D., written and oral requirements, International & Comparative Law, 1965); Parker School for Foreign and Comparative Law for Practicing Lawyers (Certificate, 1961); Harvard Business School (Corporate Finance Course, 1969). Editor: Columbia Journal of Transnational Law, 1963-1965; Journal of Maritime Law and Commerce, 1966-1973; Default and Rescheduling. Author: Handbook on International Debt Rescheduling. Co-Author: International Financial Law and Debt Equity Conversions. Adjunct Professor, International Finance Law, Georgetown University Law School, 1969-1973. Lecturer: New York University School of Law, 1965; Hague Academy of International Law, 1969; Dundee University Law Faculty-Centre for Energy Law, 1991. Legal Counsel: World Bank, 1965-1973; Bank of England; UK National Water, 1973—(responsible for project finance and international advisory services). Group Director, 1988— and Deputy Chairman, 1992—, Morgan Grenfell International. Member of the Board: SIFIDA S.A.; Egyptian Tourism Investment Co., 1992 and Major Projects Association. Member of Council: Royal Institute of International Affairs, 1993 and Federal Trust, 1991. *Member:* Gray's Inn, London; International Bar Association. *LANGUAGES:* English, French and Persian.

(For complete biographical data on all personnel, see Professional Biographies at Paris, France)

SAMIR SALEH AND ASSOCIATES

Established in 1977

6 BRISTOL HOUSE
80A SOUTHAMPTON ROW
LONDON WC 1, ENGLAND
Telephone: (0171) 430 2102; (0171) 831 0941
Telex: 262433 Ref. 3617
Telecopier: (0171) 430 18 99

Beirut, Lebanon Office: Anis Saleh Law Offices, Dakdouk Building,
Tabaris Square, P.O. Box 8069. Telephone: 335580.

Banking, Arbitration, Commercial and Civil Law, Opinions and Assistance in the Laws of Contracts of the Arab Middle East.
Lawyer Practicing in London, admitted in England as Law Consultant (Islamic and Middle Eastern Law) but not authorized to appear before the English Courts nor to act as a Solicitor.

SAMIR SALEH, born Lebanon; admitted, 1954, Lebanese Bar (Not admitted in England). *Education:* Universite St. Joseph (Baccalaureat), Lyon and Beirut Law Faculties (Licence en Droit); McGill University, Montreal, Canada (LL.M.). Author: "Collision Between Aircraft (in French)," McGill University Law Faculty; Air Law (in Arabic); Analysis of the Law of Commercial Agencies in Lebanon (in French); Commercial Arbitration in the Arab Middle East (Graham and Trotman, London, 1984); "Commercial Agency and Distributorship in the Arab Middle East," (Graham and Trotman, London, 1989). Lecturer, Law Faculty of the Lebanese University, 1959-1969. Legal Adviser to his Majesty the Sultan of Oman, 1971-1976. Granted overseas lawyer status by the Law Society of London. Vice-Chairman of the Court of Arbitration, International Chamber of Commerce, Paris, 1982-1988. *Member:* Lebanese Bar; Associate, Chartered Institute of Arbitrators, England (1980-1990). *LANGUAGES:* Arabic, French, English and Russian. *PRACTICE AREAS:* Arab Middle East Law.

SAUNDERS SOBELL LEIGH & DOBIN

Established in 1913

20 RED LION STREET
LONDON WC1R 4AE, ENGLAND
Telephone: 0171-242 2525
Fax: 0171-405 4202
LIX LONOG3

Saunders Sobell is a central London Commercial Law Firm of 19 partners and approximately 100 staff. The firm has four main areas of focus commercial property; corporate and financial affairs; business communications and insurance. In Response to the increasing business opportunities created by the single European Market, we are members of Network 92 and International Association of Law firms.

MEMBERS OF FIRM

BRIAN L. SOBELL, born August 31, 1937; admitted, 1959, England. *LANGUAGES:* English. *PRACTICE AREAS:* Commercial Property.

JOHN D. STAPLEY, born January 31, 1942; admitted, 1964, England. *LANGUAGES:* English. *PRACTICE AREAS:* Commercial Property.

HOWARD K. ZETTER, born October 10, 1946; admitted, 1971, England. *LANGUAGES:* English. *PRACTICE AREAS:* Commercial Litigation.

DAVID P. MARGO, born May 14, 1951; admitted, 1975, England. *LANGUAGES:* English. *PRACTICE AREAS:* Commercial Property.

CLIVE A. SHARPLES, born September 1, 1947; admitted, 1974, England. *LANGUAGES:* English. *PRACTICE AREAS:* Residential Development.

LAURENCE M. KAYE, born September 1, 1949; admitted, 1975, England. *LANGUAGES:* French and English. *PRACTICE AREAS:* Company Law; Commercial Law; Intellectual Property.

MICHAEL N. ROBIN, born December 13, 1954; admitted, 1979, England. *LANGUAGES:* English. *PRACTICE AREAS:* Litigation; Insurance.

JOHN D. LEAN, born October 22, 1947; admitted, 1974, England. *LANGUAGES:* English. *PRACTICE AREAS:* Commercial Property.

KENNETH W. LEIGH, born July 2, 1938; admitted, 1959, England. *LANGUAGES:* English. *PRACTICE AREAS:* Private Client Work.

(This Listing Continued)

JOHN C.L. BAILEY, born January 7, 1956; admitted, 1982, England. *LANGUAGES:* English. *PRACTICE AREAS:* Company Law; Commercial Law.

STEPHEN R. STEPHENS, born April 24, 1955; admitted, 1985, England. *LANGUAGES:* English. *PRACTICE AREAS:* Commercial Property; Shopping Centre Developments.

HILLARY R. COHEN, born May 12, 1954; admitted, 1980, England. *LANGUAGES:* English. *PRACTICE AREAS:* Construction; Litigation.

DENNIS R. ROSENTHAL, born August 18, 1944; admitted, 1977, England. *LANGUAGES:* German and English. *PRACTICE AREAS:* Company Law; Commercial Law.

JEFFREY A. TYRRELL, born December 12, 1951; admitted, 1979, England. *LANGUAGES:* English. *PRACTICE AREAS:* Construction; Litigation.

JONATHAN M.H. ROSS, born July 23, 1957; admitted, 1983, England. *LANGUAGES:* English. *PRACTICE AREAS:* Commercial Litigation.

RICHARD LAUGHARNE, born September 22, 1949; admitted, 1980, England. *LANGUAGES:* English. *PRACTICE AREAS:* Residential Development.

HAROLD R. SHUPAK, born April 5, 1948; admitted, 1973, England. *LANGUAGES:* English. *PRACTICE AREAS:* Company Law; Commercial Law.

DAVID TOMKINS, born October 20, 1943; admitted, 1974, England. *LANGUAGES:* English. *PRACTICE AREAS:* Commercial Property.

JACQUELINE HARVEY, born December 2, 1961; admitted, 1988, England. *LANGUAGES:* English. *PRACTICE AREAS:* Commercial Litigation.

ALON DOMB, born June 2, 1962; admitted, 1988, England. *LANGUAGES:* Hebrew and English. *PRACTICE AREAS:* Company Law; Commercial Law.

DEBORAH MILLS, born November 3, 1963; admitted, 1989, England. *LANGUAGES:* English. *PRACTICE AREAS:* Commercial Property.

ROSALIND JOSEPH, born February 25, 1947; admitted, 1984, England. *LANGUAGES:* English. *PRACTICE AREAS:* Commercial Property.

NATALIE KONTARSKY, born June 12, 1961; admitted, 1986, England. *LANGUAGES:* English. *PRACTICE AREAS:* Commercial Litigation.

VIVIEN SINGLETON GREEN, born December 29, 1951; admitted, 1988, New York; 1991, England. *LANGUAGES:* French and English. *PRACTICE AREAS:* Commercial Litigation.

STEPHEN BISHOP, born June 25, 1968; admitted, 1992, England. *LANGUAGES:* English. *PRACTICE AREAS:* Commercial Property.

DECLAN TIERNEY, born September 1, 1965; admitted, 1992, England. *LANGUAGES:* English. *PRACTICE AREAS:* Commercial Litigation.

IAN WELLAND, born April 30, 1965; admitted, 1990, England. *LANGUAGES:* English. *PRACTICE AREAS:* Commercial Litigation.

NIGEL STAMP, born July 3, 1954; admitted, 1990, England. *LANGUAGES:* English. *PRACTICE AREAS:* Intellectual Property.

DAVID STEVENS, born February 2, 1965; admitted, 1990, England. *LANGUAGES:* English. *PRACTICE AREAS:* Commercial Litigation.

PAUL MARTIN, born September 11, 1962; admitted, 1991, England. *LANGUAGES:* English. *PRACTICE AREAS:* Litigation; Insurance.

SCANDINAVIAN BUSINESS LAW GROUP

2 SUFFOLK LANE
LONDON EC4R OAT, ENGLAND
Telephone: 44 171 623 3121
Telefax: 44 171 936 2545

Copenhagen, Denmark Office: Berning Schluter Hald. 6, Bredgade, DK-1260 Copenhagen K. Telephone: +45 33 14 33 33. Telefax: +45 33 32 43 33. Telex: 16413 JURIS DK.

(This Listing Continued)

Member of the Law Society with Foreign Status. Danish and International Law.

RESIDENT PARTNER

KLAUS EWALD MADSEN, born Copenhagen, Denmark, August 10, 1962; admitted, 1994, Supreme Court of Denmark. *Education:* University of Copenhagen (Candidatus Juris, 1986). *Member:* Copenhagen Bar Association; Danish Law Society; IBA. *LANGUAGES:* English and Scandinavian. *PRACTICE AREAS:* Corporate Law; Tax Law; Intellectual Property Law; Environmental Law.

(For biographical data on all Personnel, see Professional Biographies at Copenhagen, Denmark).

SCHNEIDER & CO

9 STAPLE INN, HOLBORN
LONDON WC1V 7QH, ENGLAND
Telephone: 0171-242-1711; International: (+44-171)-242-1711
Facsimile: 0171-242-1311; International: (+44-171)-242-1311

Industrial and Intellectual Property, Computer and Information Technology, EU and Competition Law, Commercial and Corporate Transactions, Commercial Litigation.

FIRM PROFILE: an imaginative international practice, representing an interesting alternative to the large London firms, whose lawyers have all trained and been with prestigious and substantial firms. Schneider & Co. is small, but highly efficient (e.g: fully computerised) and does not employ "assistant" or "associate" lawyers, the experienced lawyers handle the work themselves.

The firm or one or more of its lawyers are members of the following organisations: Law Society of England and Wales, Intellectual Property Lawyers' Association, Chartered Institute of Patent Agents, Institute of Trade Mark Agents, International Trade Mark Association, Society for Computers and Law, Deutsche Vereinigung für gewerblichen Rechtsschutz und Urheberrecht (GRUR), Competition Law Association, Union Internationale des Avocats.

MEMBERS OF FIRM

ERNEST SCHNEIDER, born Lancaster, England, 1958; admitted, 1986, England and Wales. *Education:* Lycée Classique d'Echternach, Luxembourg; University of Lancaster (joint B.A., hons; Economics and Social Sciences); Leeds Business School, Metropolitan University (postgraduate EU Law).

SIMON PAGE, born London, England, 1962; admitted, 1988, England and Wales. *Education:* St. Paul's School, London; Exeter University (B.Sc., hons; B.A., hons; Chemistry and Law).

GLENDA CAMPBELL, (Consultant). born Florence, Italy, 1954; admitted, 1990, England and Wales. Head of Commercial Litigation, College of Law Guildford, 1994. *Education:* International School, Geneva, Switzerland; Edinburgh University (LL.B., hons).

Languages: English, French, German, Italian, Spanish, Hungarian and Letzebuergesch.

SECRETAN TROYANOV & PARTNERS

Established in 1987

7/9 BREAM'S BUILDINGS, CHANCERY LANE
LONDON EC4A 1DY, ENGLAND
Telephone: (+44 171)-404-1199
Telefax: (+44 171)-405-0240

Geneva, Switzerland Office: 2, Rue Charles-Bonnet, P.O. Box 189, 1211 Geneva 12. Telephone: (+4122) 789.7000. Cable Address: "Intercounsel". Telex: 427 475 Setr CH. Telefax: (+4122) 789.7070.

Moscow, Russia Office: Ulitsa Usacheva 35, Suite 222, Moscow 119048. Telephone: (+7095) 245.5203. Telefax: (+7095) 244.1663. Telephone/Telefax by satellite from outside Russia: 007.502.220.3137/8.

Swiss and General International Practice. Firm engaged in Swiss and International Practice, including Russian Law, but not authorized to appear before the English Courts or to act as Solicitors.

(This Listing Continued)

PARTNER IN CHARGE

HORACE GAUTIER, born Geneva, Switzerland, 1956; admitted, 1980, Switzerland; Authorized to practice before the Geneva and Zurich Courts. *Education:* University of Geneva (Licence en droit, 1979). *Member:* Geneva Bar Association; Geneva Law Society; Swiss Bar Association; Geneva Association of Business Law; Holborn Law Society; International Bar Association; International Litigation Practitioners Forum; British-Swiss Chamber of Commerce; British Institute of International and Comparative Law.

RESIDENT ASSOCIATE

MICHEL NUSSBAUMER, born Fribourg, Switzerland, 1963; admitted, 1988, Switzerland. *Education:* University of Fribourg (Licence en droit, 1986); University of California at Berkeley (LL.M., 1990); Moscow State University (1991). *Member:* Geneva Bar Association; Swiss Bar Association.

Languages: French, English, Russian (Official Translator, Geneva Chancellery), German, Italian, Spanish and Hungarian.

(For Complete Biographical Data on all Firm Personnel, see Professional Biographies at Geneva, Switzerland).

SEDGWICK, DETERT, MORAN & ARNOLD

A Multi-National Partnership
LLOYDS AVENUE HOUSE
6 LLOYDS AVENUE
LONDON EC3N 3AX, ENGLAND
Telephone: 0171-929-1829
Fax: 0171-929-1808

San Francisco, California Office: 16th Floor, One Embarcadero Center. Telephone: 415-781-7900. Cable Address: "Sedma". Fax: 415-781-2635.

Los Angeles, California Office: 9th Floor, Wilshire Colonnade, 3701 Wilshire Boulevard. Telephone: 213-386-2833. Fax: 213-487-5456. Telex: 356455.

Irvine, California Office: 3 Park Plaza, 17th Floor. Telephone: 714-852-8200. Fax: 714-852-8282.

Chicago, Illinois Office: The Rookery Building, Seventh Floor, 209 South La Salle Street. Telephone: 312-641-9050. Fax: 312-641-9530.

New York, New York Office: 41st Floor, 59 Maiden Lane. Telephone: 212-422-0202. Fax: 212-422-0925.

Zurich, Switzerland Office: Spluegenstrasse 3, CH-8002. Telephone: 011-411-201-1730. Fax: 011-411-201-4404.

General Civil Litigation and Trial Practice. Aviation, Business, Construction, Directors and Officers Liability, Employment and Labor, Entertainment, Environmental, Fidelity and Surety, General Liability, Health Care, Insurance and Reinsurance, Intellectual Property, Products Liability and Professional Malpractice.

MEMBERS OF FIRM

ADAM C. BARKER, born Windsor, England, August 31, 1955; admitted, 1978, England as Barrister; 1982, New York and U.S. District Court, Southern and Eastern Districts of New York; 1990, U.S. Court of Appeals, Fourth Circuit; 1991, District of Columbia; 1992, England as Solicitor. *Education:* Queens College, Cambridge, England (B.A., 1977; M.A., 1977). Member, Editorial Board, *International Insurance Law Review,* 1993—. Member, Middle Temple, London, England, 1976-1992. Member, General Council of the Bar, London, 1978-1992. *Member:* New York State Bar Association (Member, Young Lawyers Committee, 1985); The District of Columbia Bar; American Bar Association; Law Society.

DAVID E. BORDON, born Los Angeles, California, December 29, 1943; admitted, 1969, California (Not admitted in England). *Education:* University of California at Berkeley (A.B., 1965); Boalt Hall School of Law, University of California (J.D., 1968). Phi Delta Phi. Mayor, City of Belvedere, California, 1974. Registered Foreign Lawyer. *Member:* Bar Association of San Francisco; American Bar Association (Member, Committee on Fidelity and Surety, Section of Tort and Insurance Practice, 1973—; Vice Chairman, 1976—).

ROBERT B. BUDELMAN, JR., born New York, N.Y., 1937; admitted, 1963, New Jersey; 1966, New York. Registered Foreign Lawyer (Not admitted in England). *Education:* Fairleigh Dickinson University (B.A., 1959); Catholic University (LL.B., 1962); Institute of Comparative Law, National University of Mexico. Editor, "The Legal Issue," Catholic University Law School Paper, 1961-1962. Co-Editor and Co-Author: "Your Future and the Law," American Law Student Association Publication, 1962.

(This Listing Continued)

SEDGWICK, DETERT, MORAN & ARNOLD, London—
Continued

Co-Author: "Three Ways to Minimize Liability for Computer or EDT Failure," Banking Law Report, Vol. 1, No. 11, 1985; "Safe Deposit Boxes - Dealing with Losses," Gibbs-Hartly Cooper, 1981. Author: "Lloyd's Financial Institution Policy - A Comparison of Coverage," published privately, 1983. Advisory Board Member, The Banking Law Institute, 1984. Township Committeeman, Police Commissioner and Deputy Mayor, Township of Washington, Bergen County, New Jersey, 1967-1969. Director and Counsel, Bergen Republic Development Council, 1964-1967. President, Alumni Association, 1964 and Member, Board of Trustees, 1985-1991, Fairleigh Dickinson University. *Member:* New Jersey State, New York State and American Bar Associations; English Law Society (Overseas Member). [With National Guard and U.S. Army Ready Reserve, 1954-1962]

    ERIK J. STENBERG, born Montreal, Canada, July 10, 1957; admitted, 1983, California and U.S. District Court, Northern District of California; 1984, U.S. District Court, Eastern District of California (Not admitted in England). *Education:* University of Cincinnati (B.M., 1979); Hastings College of the Law, University of California (J.D., 1983). Articles Editor, Hastings International and Comparative Law Review, 1982-1983. *Member:* State Bar of California; American Bar Association (Member: Section on Tort and Insurance Practice); Defense Research Institute. (Also at Zurich, Switzerland Office). *LANGUAGES:* German.

CONSULTANT

    JOLYON K.A. GREY, born Enigu, Nigeria, June 4, 1946; admitted, 1968, England as Barrister. *Education:* Pembroke College, Cambridge, England (B.A., 1967; M.A., 1971). Immigration Appeals Adjudicator, 1992—. *Member:* Inner Temple; General Council of the Bar (England and Wales). *LANGUAGES:* French.

ASSOCIATE

    ROSALIND MILNER, born Manchester, England, March 7, 1968; admitted, 1993, England. *Education:* Kebler College (B.A., 1989); Guildford College of Law (Law Society Finalist, 1991).

(For complete biographical data on all personnel at Los Angeles, San Francisco and Irvine, California, Chicago, Illinois, New York, New York and Zurich, Switzerland, see Professional Biographies at those locations).

SHAW AND CROFT

115 HOUNDSDITCH
LONDON EC3A 7BU, ENGLAND
Telephone: 0171-283 6293
Telex: 8956444 ASHORE GB
Fax: 0171-626 3639

Admiralty, Arbitration, Commodities, Commercial Litigation, Commercial Property, Corporate, Employment, Insurance, Re-Insurance, Personal Injury, Ship Finance, Shipping Litigation.

FIRM PROFILE: *Shaw and Croft is a firm of about 20 lawyers providing specialist legal services to the shipping, trading, banking, insurance industries and other commercial clients throughout the World.*

PARTNERS

    ROGER A. CROFT, born 1946; admitted, 1978, England. *Member:* International Bar Association. *PRACTICE AREAS:* Collisions; Salvage; Marine Insurance; Wreck Removal; Environmental Claims.

    NICHOLAS V. TAYLOR, born 1939; admitted, 1976, England. *Education:* LL.B. (Lond). [Former Merchant Navy Officer]. *PRACTICE AREAS:* Marine Litigation; Arbitration; Cargo and Ship Damage; Total Loss; Marine Insurance.

    RICHARD A. SHAW, born 1940; admitted, 1966, England. *Education:* M.A. (Oxon). Consulting Editor, Kennedy's Law of Salvage. *PRACTICE AREAS:* Collision; Salvage; Marine Insurance; Contracts of Carriage; Limitation of Liability.

    ROBERT A. MCCUNN, born 1948; admitted, 1986, England. *Education:* LL.B. (Lond). *PRACTICE AREAS:* Oil Trade; Commodity Trade; Shipping Litigation; Commercial Litigation; Arbitration; Money Laundering Claims; Asset Tracing.

    RICHARD M.F. COLES, born 1947; admitted, 1972, England. *Education:* LL.B. (Hull). *Member:* Chartered Institute of Transport. *PRACTICE*

(This Listing Continued)

AREAS: Ship Finance; Ship Sale and Purchase; Ship Management; Corporate Law; Employment Law.

    GILES AD DE BERTODANO, born 1950; admitted, 1984, England. *Education:* LL.B. (Buckingham). [Former Merchant Navy Officer]. *PRACTICE AREAS:* Admiralty Litigation; Shipping Litigation.

    J.P. HAMISH EDGAR, born 1953; admitted, 1979, England. *Education:* B.A. (Lond). *PRACTICE AREAS:* Marine Insurance; Charter Parties; Bills of Lading; Salvage Collision; Personal Injury; General Commercial Litigation.

    JONANTHON R. KENYON, born 1954; admitted, 1980, England. *Education:* LL.B. (Liverpool). *PRACTICE AREAS:* Admiralty Litigation; Shipping Litigation; Marine Insurance; Pollution Claims.

    JOHN M. MASKELL, born 1942; admitted, 1966, England. *Education:* M.A., LL.B. (Cantab). *Member:* International Bar Association (Arbitrator). *PRACTICE AREAS:* Shipping Litigation; Commercial Litigation; Arbitration; Ship Sale and Purchase.

All Partners are members of the Baltic Exchange.

SHEARMAN & STERLING

199 BISHOPSGATE
LONDON EC2M 3TY, ENGLAND
Telephone: (44-171) 920-9000
Fax: (44-171) 920-9020

New York, N.Y. Office: 599 Lexington Avenue, New York, New York 10022-6069 and Citicorp Center, 153 East 53rd Street, New York, New York 10022-4676. Telephone: (212) 848-4000. Telex: 667290 Num Lau. Fax: 599 Lexington Avenue: (212) 848-7179. Citicorp Center: (212) 848-5252.

Abu Dhabi, United Arab Emirates Office: P.O. Box 2948. Telephone: (971-2) 324477. Fax: (971-2) 774533.

Beijing, People's Republic of China Office: Suite #2205, Capital Mansion, No. 6, Xin Yuan Nan Road. Chao Yang District Beijing, 100004. Telephone: (861) 465-4574. Fax: (861) 465-4578.

Budapest, Hungary Office: Szerb utca 17-19, 1056 Budapest. Telephone: (36-1) 266-3522. Fax: (36-1) 266-3523.

Düsseldorf, Federal Republic of Germany Office: Königsallee 46, D-40212 Düsseldorf. Telephone: (49-211) 13 62 80. Telex: 8 588 294 NYLO. Fax: (49-211) 13 33 09.

Frankfurt, Federal Republic of Germany Office: Bockenheimer Landstrasse 55, D-60325 Frankfurt am Main. Telephone: (49-69) 97-10-70. Fax: (49-69) 97-10-71-00.

Hong Kong, Hong Kong Office: Standard Chartered Bank Building, 4 Des Voeux Road Central, Hong Kong. Telephone: (852) 2978-8000. Fax: (852) 2978-8099.

Los Angeles, California Office: 725 South Figueroa Street, 21st Floor, 90017-5421. Telephone: (213) 239-0300. Fax: (213) 239-0381, 614-0936.

Paris, France Office: 12 rue d'Astorg, 75008. Telephone: (33-1) 44-71-17-17. Telex: 282964 Royale. Fax: (33-1) 44-71-01-01.

San Francisco, California Office: 555 California Street, 94104-1522. Telephone: (415) 616-1100. Fax: (415) 616-1199.

Taipei, Taiwan Office: 7th Floor, Hung Kuo Building, 167 Tun Hwa North Road. Telephone: (886-2) 545-3300. Fax: (866-2) 545-3322.

Tokyo, Japan Office: Shearman & Sterling (Thomas Wilner Gaikokuho-Jimu-Bengoshi Jimusho), Fukoku Seimei Building, 5th Fl. 2-2-2, Uchisaiwaicho, Chiyoda-ku, Tokyo 100, Japan. Telephone: (81 3) 5251-1601. Fax: (81 3) 5251-1602.

Toronto, Ontario, Canada Office: Commerce Court West, Suite 4405, P.O. Box 247, M5L 1E8. Telephone: (416) 360-8484. Fax: (416) 360-2958.

Washington, D.C. Office: 801 Pennsylvania Avenue, N.W., Suite 900, 20004-2604. Telephone: (202) 508-8000. Fax: (202) 508-8100.

General Practice.
Firm engaged in American and General International Law Practice but not authorized to appear before the English courts or to act as Solicitors.

FIRM PROFILE: *Shearman & Sterling, founded in 1873, has more than 500 lawyers in 15 offices throughout the world. The firm's practice encompasses most major areas of business law, including: Antitrust and Trade Regulation; Banking; Bankruptcy and Corporate Reorganization; Compensation and Benefits; Environmental; Finance (including Corporate Finance, Domestic Private Finance, Financial Institutions, International Private Finance and Project Finance); Individual Clients, Trusts and Estates; In-*

(This Listing Continued)

surance; *International Trade and Government Relations; Litigation and Arbitration; Mergers and Acquisitions; Oil and Gas; Privatizations; Real Estate; and Tax. The Firm is also engaged in the practice of French, German and Hungarian law through its offices in France, Germany and Hungary.*

RESIDENT PARTNERS

THOMAS JOYCE, born St. Paul, Minnesota, 1939; admitted, 1964, New York (Not admitted in England). *Education:* St. John's University, Collegeville, Minnesota (B.A., 1960); University of Notre Dame (LL.B., 1963). (Managing Partner).

JOHN A. MARZULLI, JR., born Montclair, New Jersey, 1953; admitted, 1978, New Jersey; 1979, New York (Not admitted in England). *Education:* Middlebury College (B.A., 1975); New York University (J.D., 1978). Law Clerk to Hon. George H. Barlow, Hon. Clarkson S. Fisher, and Hon. Anne E. Thompson, U.S. District Court, District of New Jersey, 1978-1980.

EUROPEAN COUNSEL

JAMES M. BARTOS, born New York, N.Y., 1952; admitted, 1979, New York (Not admitted in England). *Education:* Yale University (B.A., 1975); Columbia University (J.D., 1978).

INTERNATIONAL FINANCIAL COUNSEL

JOHN G. STEWART, born Washington, D.C., 1954; admitted, 1982, New York (Not admitted in England). *Education:* Princeton University (A.B., 1977); University of Virginia Law School (J.D., 1981).

RESIDENT ASSOCIATES

D. Max Aaron
(Not admitted in England)
Thomas D. Abbondante
(Not admitted in England)
Aaron M. Brown
(Not admitted in England)
Andrew J. Foley
(Not admitted in England)

Kenneth A.K. Martin
(Not admitted in England)
Mark W. Mancinelli
(Not admitted in England)
Laura S. Miller
(Not admitted in England)
Kenneth Schneider
(Not admitted in England)

(For Biographical data of all partners, see Professional Biographies at New York, N.Y.)

SHOOK, HARDY & BACON

MANNING HOUSE
22 CARLISLE PLACE
LONDON SW1P 1JA, ENGLAND
Telephone: 011-44-171 821 5595
FAX: 011-44-171 834 5918

Kansas City, Missouri, Shook, Hardy & Bacon P.C. Office: 1200 Main, One Kansas City Place.
Overland Park, Kansas, Shook, Hardy & Bacon P.C. Office: 40 Corporate Woods.
Zurich, Switzerland Office: Bahnhofstrassee 20, CH-8800 Thalwil. Telephone: 011-41-1-721-0038. Facsimile: 011-41-1-721-2384.
Milan, Italy, Shook, Hardy & Bacon Italia S.R.I. Office: Via Meravigli 3, 3rd Floor, 20123. Telephone: 011-392-723-371. Fax: 011-392-7200-3637.

Practice in all major areas of U.S. and International Commercial Practice. Product Liability, Litigation and Arbitration. Firm Not Authorized to Appear Before the English Courts or Act as Solicitors.

LAUREL J. HARBOUR, born Anthon, IA., 1947; admitted, 1975, Missouri (Not admitted in England). *Education:* University of Iowa (B.A., with highest distinction, 1969; M.A., 1971; J.D., magna cum laude, 1974). Phi Beta Kappa; Order of the Coif. *Member:* International Bar Association; Defense Research Institute. *PRACTICE AREAS:* Products Liability.

EUGENE S. PECK, born Kansas City, KS., 1946; admitted, 1983, Oklahoma; 1984, Missouri (Not admitted in England). *Education:* University of Kansas (B.A., 1968; M.A., 1970; J.D., 1983). Staff Member, 1981-1982 and Note and Comment Editor, 1982-1983, Kansas Law Review. *Member:* Oklahoma Bar Association. *PRACTICE AREAS:* Products Liability.

RANDALL E. PRATT, born Independence, MO., 1963; admitted, 1988, Missouri; 1990, Kansas, U.S. Court of International Trade and U.S. Court of Appeals for the Federal Circuit (Not admitted in England). *Education:* Graceland College; University of Missouri (B.S.B., 1986; J.D., 1988). Mem-

(This Listing Continued)

ber, Missouri Journal of Dispute Resolution, 1987, Missouri Law Review, 1988. *Member:* International Bar Association. *PRACTICE AREAS:* Corporate Law; Mergers and Acquisitions.

T. ANDREW RAGUSIN, born Trieste, Italy, 1957; admitted, 1984, California; 1988, New York (Not admitted in England). *Education:* Free University of Brussels, Belgium (LL.B., 1980); Southern Methodist University (M.C.L., 1981; J.D., 1983). Author: "Brother-Sister Corporate Guaranties: Increased Legal Acknowledgement of Business World Realities," Journal of Corporation Law, 1986. Co-Author: "Belgium: defensive tricks under attack," International Financial Law Review, October, 1991; "Accor's Takeover of Wagons-Lits: an abrupt end to the honeymoon," International Financial Law Review, June, 1992. *Member:* Union Internationale Des Avocats; Belgian-Italian Chamber of Commerce; Luxembourg Italian Chamber of Commerce; U.S. Chamber of Commerce in Brussels. *LANGUAGES:* French, Italian, German. *PRACTICE AREAS:* International Law.

LISA J. MIGLIC, born Melbourne Victoria, Australia, 1960; admitted, 1986, Victoria, Australia; 1994, England. *Education:* University of Adelaide, South Australia (LL.B., 1984). *PRACTICE AREAS:* Products Liability.

DENNIS R. NEUTZE, born Baltimore, MD., 1943; admitted, 1970, Maryland; 1980, District of Columbia (Not admitted in England). *Education:* United States Naval Academy (B.S., 1965); University of Maryland (J.D., 1970); Boston University (M.A., 1974); George Washington University (LL.M., 1979); London School of Economics (LL.M., 1985). Order of the Coif. Notes and Comments Editor, University of Maryland Law Review, 1969-1970. [JAGC, U.S. Navy, 1970-1972]. *PRACTICE AREAS:* Products Liability.

(For complete biographical data on all personnel and list of Representative Clients, see Professional Biographies at Kansas City, Missouri)

SHOOSMITHS & HARRISON

Established in 1845

3 JOHN STREET
LONDON WC1N 2ES, ENGLAND
Telephone: 0171 242 3333
Fax: 0171 405 6462

(For full details, see entry for Northampton)

SHUTTS & BOWEN

A Partnership including Professional Associations

Established in 1910

48 MOUNT STREET
LONDON W1Y 5RE, ENGLAND
Telephone: 44171493-4840
Telefax: 44171493-4299

Miami, Florida Office: 1500 Miami Centre, 201 South Biscayne Boulevard. Telephone: 305-358-6300. Cable Address: "Shuttsbo". Telefax: 305-381-9982.
Key Largo, Florida Office: Suite A206, 31 Ocean Reef Drive. Telephone: 305-367-2881.
Orlando, Florida Office: 20 North Orange Avenue, Suite 1000. Telephone: 407-423-3200. Fax: 407-425-8316.
West Palm Beach, Florida Office: One Clearlake Centre, 250 Australian Avenue, Suite 500. Telephone: 407-835-8500. Fax: 407-650-8530.
Amsterdam, The Netherlands Office: Shutts & Bowen, B.V., Europa Boulevard 59, 1083 AD, Amsterdam. Telephone: (31 20) 661-0969. Fax: (31 20) 642-1475.

General Civil Practice in all Courts. Corporation, Probate, Trusts, Real Estate, Insurance, Banking and Admiralty Law. Federal, State and Local Taxation. Securities, International, Labor Relations and Collective Bargaining (Management), Equal Employment Opportunity, Wage-Hour, Occupational Safety and Health and Bankruptcy Law.

(This Listing Continued)

SHUTTS & BOWEN, London—Continued

RESIDENT OF COUNSEL

STEPHEN J. GRAY, born September 13, 1950; admitted, 1975, Virginia; 1978, District of Columbia. *Education:* Johns Hopkins University (B.A., 1972); American University (J.D., cum laude, 1975); Georgetown University (LL.M., Tax, 1989). *PRACTICE AREAS:* International and U.S. Tax Law.

MARSHALL J. LANGER, (P.A.), born New York, N.Y., May 30, 1928; admitted, 1951, Florida. *Education:* Wharton School, University of Pennsylvania (B.S., 1948); University of Miami (J.D., summa cum laude, 1951). Author: "Practical International Tax Planning," Practising Law Institute, 3rd Edition, 1985—. Co-author: "Income Taxation of Foreign Related Transactions," Matthew Bender, 1980—. Adjunct Professor of Law, University of Miami, 1965-1974 and 1978—. President, Greater Miami Tax Institute, 1967. Vice President, U.S.A. Branch, International Fiscal Association, 1978-1984. *Member:* Dade County, American, International and Inter-American Bar Associations; The Florida Bar; American Foreign Law Association (President, Miami Chapter, 1955). *PRACTICE AREAS:* International Law; Taxation Law.

REPRESENTATIVE CLIENTS: Aerolinas Argentinas; ABN Amero Bank N.V.; American Airlines; American Express International Banking Corp.; Bank Hapoalim B. M.; BankAmerica International, Bank of America NT&SA; Banque Sudameris; Bell Atlantic-Tricon Leasing Corp.; Burger King Corp.; Chryser Corp.; CitiBank (Florida), N.A.; CPC International Inc; Crown Life Insurance Company of Canada; First Nationwide Bank; First Union National Bank of Florida; General Electric Co.; Georgia Pacific Corp.; Great Western Bank; Guardian Life Insurance Company of America; Hamburg International Reinsurance Co.; Intercontinental Bank; International Recovery Corp.; J. P. Morgan Florida Federal Savings Bank; Lincoln National Life Insurance Co.; Louis Dreyfus Property Group; Manufacturers Life Insurance Co.; Merrill Lynch Bank & Trust Co. Ltd.; Miami Children's Hospital; Mutual Life Insurance Company of New York; New England Mutual Life Insurance Co.; New York Life Insurance Co.; Provident Life and Accident Insurance Co.; Sir Robert McAlpine & Sons (Bahamas) Ltd.; Sony Corp.; Southern Bell Telephone & Telegraph Co.; Spec's Music, Inc.; SunBank Miami, N.A.; Tele-communications Inc. (TCI); The Bank of Tokyo, Ltd. Miami Agency; The Equitable Life Assurance Society of the United States; The Fuji Bank Ltd.; The Prudential Insurance Company of America; The Travelers Companies; Trustmark Insurance Co.; UNUM Life Insurance Co.; Universal City Florida Partners; William Penn Life Insurance Co.; The Whiting Turner Contracting Co.

SIDLEY & AUSTIN

A Partnership including Professional Corporations

Established in 1866

BROADWALK HOUSE
5 APPOLD STREET
LONDON EC2A 2AA, ENGLAND
Telephone: 011-44-171-621-1616
Telecopier: 011-44-171-626-7937

Chicago, Illinois Office: One First National Plaza, 60603. Telephone: 312-853-7000. Telecopier: 312-853-7036.

Los Angeles, California Office: 555 W. Fifth Street, 40th Flr., 90013-1010. Telephone: 213-896-6000. Telecopier: 213-896-6600.

New York, New York Office: 875 Third Avenue, 10022. Telephone: 212-906-2000. Telecopier: 212-906-2021.

Washington, D.C. Office: 1722 Eye Street, N.W., 20006. Telephone: 202-736-8000. Telecopier: 202-736-8711.

Tokyo, Japan Office: Taisho Seimei Hibiya Building, 7th Floor, 9-1, Yurakucho, 1 Chome, Chiyoda-ku, 100. Telephone: 011-81-3-3218-5900. Facsimile: 011-81-3-3218-5922.

Singapore Office: 36 Robinson Road, #18-01 City House, Singapore 0106. Telephone: 011-65-224-5000. Telecopier: 011-65-224-0530.

General Practice.
Firm engaged in American and International Law Practice but not authorized to appear before the English courts or to act as Solicitors.

RESIDENT PARTNER

MARK A. ANGELSON, born Jersey City, New Jersey, February 14, 1951; admitted, 1976, New York and U.S. District Court, Southern and Eastern Districts of New York; 1980, U.S. Supreme Court (Not admitted in England). *Education:* Rutgers University (A..B., magna cum laude, 1972; J.D., 1975). Phi Beta Kappa. Resident in London, 1977-1979 and 1989—, New York, 1975-1977, 1979-1982 and 1986-1989, Singapore, 1982-1985.

(This Listing Continued)

JEAN A.Y. DU PONT, born New York, New York, October 6, 1960; admitted, 1988, District of Columbia (Not admitted in England). *Education:* Princeton University (A.B., cum laude, 1982); Edmond A. Walsh School of Foreign Service; Georgetown University (M.S.F.S.; J.D., magna cum laude, 1988). Notes and Comments Editor, Georgetown Law Journal. Assistant Editor, International Decisions, American Journal of International Law, 1988-1989. Co-author: "When the Home Office is Liable for Foreign Branch Deposits," Banking Law Review, Vol. 2, No. 3. Winter, 1990. *LANGUAGES:* French, Spanish. *PRACTICE AREAS:* International Trade and Financial Regulation.

ROBERT M. PLEHN, born New York, N.Y., April 23, 1962; admitted, 1989, New York (Not admitted in England). *Education:* Vassar College (A.B., 1984); Harvard University (J.D., 1988). Phi Beta Kappa. Author: "Securitization of Third World Debt," The International Lawyer, Spring, 1989. *LANGUAGES:* French, Spanish. *PRACTICE AREAS:* Corporate, Banking and International Law.

ROBERT L. SIGMON

Established in 1963

2, PLOWDEN BUILDINGS
MIDDLE TEMPLE
LONDON EC4Y 9AS, ENGLAND
Telephone: 0171-583-4851
International: +44-171-583-4851
Cable Address: "Interjuris" London
Fax: 0171-583-4852
International: +44-171-583-4852

General and International Law Practice. Corporation, Tax and Probate Law. International Commercial Transactions and Administration of Estates.

ROBERT L. SIGMON, born Roanoke, Virginia, April 3, 1929; admitted, 1953, Virginia; 1962, District of Columbia, U.S. Court of Appeals, 2nd Circuit and U.S. Supreme Court (Not admitted in England). *Education:* University of Virginia (B.A., 1951; LL.B., 1954); London School of Economics. *Member:* British Institute of International and Comparative Law (Member, Council of Management); Selden Society. *LANGUAGES:* French and Spanish.

ASSOCIATE

JOHN HIRD WILLIAMS, born London, England; admitted, 1952, England (as Solicitor of the Supreme Court of Judicature). *Education:* King's College, University of London (LL.B., 1951). *Member:* The Law Society.

OF COUNSEL

DAVID H. FROMKIN, born Milwaukee, Wisconsin, August 27, 1932; admitted, 1953, Illinois; 1954, U.S. Court of Military Appeals; 1959, New York; 1963, U.S. Supreme Court (Not admitted in England). *Education:* University of Chicago (B.A., 1950; J.D., 1953); University of London (A.P.D. in Law, 1958). *Member:* The Association of the Bar of the City of New York; Illinois State and American Bar Associations; American Judicature Society; American Society of International Law; Selden Society. (New York, N.Y. 10022 Office: 20 Beekman Place. Telephone: 838 6333; Cable Address: "Interjuris Newyork").

THE SIMKINS PARTNERSHIP

Established in 1963

45-51 WHITFIELD STREET
LONDON W1P 5RJ, ENGLAND
Telephone: +44 171 631 1050
Fax: +44 171 436 2744

Media and Entertainment Law, Intellectual Property, International Trade, Company and Commercial, Litigation, Arbitration, European Community Law, Property Law, Immigration, Family Law, Trusts, Wills and Probate.

FIRM PROFILE: The Simkins Partnership is a leading firm in a number of specialist industry fields including film, television, theatre, music, advertising, photography and leisure. With 20 partners and 23 other fee earners, it also provides a full range of commercial and private client services. The firm is the UK member of an international network of advertising lawyers,

(This Listing Continued)

Advertising Law International, and a member of MacIntyre Strater International a network of law and accountancy firms.

MEMBERS OF FIRM

CHARLES ARTLEY, born 1950; admitted, 1976, England. *Education:* Cambridge University. *PRACTICE AREAS:* Commercial Litigation.

NIGEL BENNETT, born 1945; admitted, 1971, England. *Education:* Cambridge University. *Member:* International Bar Association; American Bar Association. *LANGUAGES:* English and French. *PRACTICE AREAS:* Media Law; Sports Law.

IAN BURLINGHAM, born 1942; admitted, 1968, England. *Education:* Bristol University. *Member:* International Bar Association; American Film Marketing Panel of Arbitrators. *PRACTICE AREAS:* Entertainment Law (Film and Television); Arbitration.

DAVID CAMPBELL, born 1945; admitted, 1970, England. *Education:* Southampton University. *PRACTICE AREAS:* Commercial Property Law.

TIM CURTIS, born 1960; admitted, 1985, England. *Education:* Cambridge University. *PRACTICE AREAS:* Entertainment Law (Film, Television, Advertising and Theatre).

CYRUS FATEMI, born 1952; admitted, 1977, England. *Education:* Leeds University. *LANGUAGES:* English and Farsi. *PRACTICE AREAS:* Commercial Property Law.

DAVID FRANKS, born 1949; admitted, 1973, England. *PRACTICE AREAS:* Entertainment Law (Music and Theatre).

DOMINIC FREE, born 1956; admitted, 1985, England. *Education:* University of Auckland, N.Z.; Cornell University, U.S.A. *PRACTICE AREAS:* Commercial Litigation; Arbitration; International Trade and Maritime Law.

LEE GOLDSMITH, born 1956; admitted, 1981, England. *Education:* Leeds University. *PRACTICE AREAS:* Commercial Litigation.

LAWRENCE HARRISON, born 1961; called to the bar, 1985; admitted, 1989, England. *Education:* University College, London; Cambridge University. *PRACTICE AREAS:* Entertainment Law (Music and Theatre).

SIMON LONG, born 1957; admitted, 1981, England. *Education:* City of London Polytechnic. Co-Author: "The T and C Music Guide.". *PRACTICE AREAS:* Entertainment Law (Music).

ADRIAN NELSON, born 1958; admitted, 1983, England. *Education:* King's College, London. *PRACTICE AREAS:* Property Law; Private Client Law.

TONY QUICK, born 1948; admitted, 1973, England. *Education:* Cambridge University. *LANGUAGES:* English and Spanish. *PRACTICE AREAS:* Company and Commercial Law.

SARA ROBINSON, born 1955; admitted, 1981, England. *Education:* Leeds University. Contributor, Solicitors Family Law Association Guide to Family Law in Europe. Press Officer, Solicitors Family Law Association. *Member:* Family Mediators Association (Solicitor Mediator). *LANGUAGES:* English and French. *PRACTICE AREAS:* Family Law.

BOB RUTTEMAN, born 1944; admitted, 1969, England. *Education:* Bristol University. *PRACTICE AREAS:* Commercial Property Law; Landlord and Tenant Law.

MICHAEL SIMKINS, born 1934; admitted, 1958, England. *Education:* King's College, London. *PRACTICE AREAS:* Entertainment Law (Film, Television and Theatre).

CHARLES SWAN, born 1956; admitted, 1983, England. *Education:* Cambridge University. General Secretary, Advertising Law International. Consulting Editor, Butterworths Encyclopedia of Forms and Precedents (Advertising). Co-Author: "The Photographers' Guide to the 1988 Copyright Act". *LANGUAGES:* English, Portuguese and French. *PRACTICE AREAS:* Advertising Law; Copyright Law.

RICHARD TAYLOR, born 1948; admitted, 1975, England. *Education:* Bristol University. *Member:* International Association of Entertainment Lawyers; Society for Computers and Law. *LANGUAGES:* English and French. *PRACTICE AREAS:* Entertainment Law (Music and Interactive Media).

JULIAN TURTON, born 1952; admitted, 1980, England. *Education:* Bristol University. Treasurer, International Association of Entertainment Lawyers. Editor, "Neighbouring Rights, Artists, Producers and their Col-

(This Listing Continued)

lection Societies". *LANGUAGES:* English and German. *PRACTICE AREAS:* Entertainment Law; Advertising Law.

PAUL WALKER, born 1950; admitted, 1974, England. *Education:* London University. *Member:* City of London Solicitors Company. *PRACTICE AREAS:* Company and Commercial Law.

SIMMONS & SIMMONS

Established in 1896

21 WILSON STREET
LONDON EC2M 2TQ, ENGLAND
Telephone: 44-171-628 2020; 44-171-528 9292
Facsimile: 44-171-628 2070
Telex: 888562 SIMMON G

Paris, France Office: 2, Avenue Bugeaud, 75116. Telephone: 33-1-45016767. Telecopier: 33-1-45012232. Telex: TRANSAV 649381F.

Brussels, Belgium Office: Rue d'Arlon 118, 1040. Telephone: 32-2-280-16 70. Telecopier: 32-2-280 04 84.

Lisbon, Portugal Office: Rua Castilho, n° 32-9°, 1250. Telephone: 351-1-352 1318. Fax: 351-1-352-1418.

Milan, Italy Office in joint practice with Studio Avv. Eugenio Grippo: Via Dei Boschetti 1, 20121. Telephone: 39-2-76003012. Telecopier: 39-2-782770.

Abu Dhabi Office: The Blue Tower, Khalifa Street. P.O. Box 5931. Telephone: 971 2 347882. Telecopier: 971 2 347832.

Hong Kong Office: 24th Floor, Jardine House, One Connaught Place, Central. Telephone: 852-28681131. Telecopier: 852-28105040. Telex: 75888 SANDS HX.

New York, New York Office: 115 East 57th Street, 10022. Telephone: 1-212-688-6620. Telecopier: 1-212-355-3594.

Simmons & Simmons is one of the largest firms of solicitors in the City of London with more than 100 partners and a total staff of over 1000. Since the firm's foundation in 1896 the firm has grown to be a full service international law firm and types of work done include Corporate Law, Mergers and Acquisitions, Banking and Capital Markets, Financial Services, Insolvency, Commercial and Trade Law, Insurance, Litigation, Arbitration, Real Estate/Property, Environmental, Construction, Intellectual Property, Computer, Competition Law, EC Law, Business and Personal Taxation, Employment, Immigration, Pensions.

PARTNERS

ALAN M. CARR, born London, England, September 1, 1936; admitted, 1961, England and Wales. *Education:* Kings College, Cambridge. (Senior Partner). *LANGUAGES:* English and French. *PRACTICE AREAS:* Mergers and Acquisitions; Corporate Finance.

ALASDAIR P. NEIL, MANAGING PARTNER, born Shrewsbury, England, January 14, 1939; admitted, 1965, England and Wales. *Education:* Worcester College, Oxford (B.A.). *Member:* Law Society; International Bar Association; Society of English and American Lawyers. (Managing Partner). *LANGUAGES:* English and French. *PRACTICE AREAS:* Corporate Finance; Company and Commercial Law.

JOHN M. BRADSHAW, born Surrey, England, October 22, 1938; admitted, 1966, England and Wales. *Education:* Corpus Christi College, Cambridge (M.A.). *LANGUAGES:* English and French. *PRACTICE AREAS:* Commercial Litigation.

PAUL A. DE CHAZAL, born Funchal, Madeira, September 25, 1942; admitted, 1967, England and Wales; 1981, Hong Kong. *Education:* Sidney Sussex College, Cambridge (B.A.). *Member:* Law Society; International Bar Association; City of London Solicitors' Company; Association Internationale pour la Protection de la Propriété Industrielle; American Bar Association; Anglo-Portuguese Society (Executive Committee Member, 1986-1989); Belgian-Luxembourg Chamber of Commerce (Honorary General Secretary); French Chamber of Commerce; Portuguese Chamber of Commerce; American Chamber of Commerce; Japan Society; Union Internationale des Avocats; Inter-Pacific Bar Association; L'Association des Juristes Franco-Britanniques. *LANGUAGES:* English, French, Spanish and Portuguese. *PRACTICE AREAS:* Commercial Law; European Community Law; Intellectual Property; Insurance Law.

ANTHONY C. DOVE, born Manchester, England, July 22, 1945; admitted, 1969, England and Wales. *Education:* Cambridge University (M.A.). *Member:* Law Society. *LANGUAGES:* English and French. *PRACTICE AREAS:* Company Law.

(This Listing Continued)

SIMMONS & SIMMONS, London—Continued

WILLIAM J.L. KNIGHT, born England, September 11, 1945; admitted, 1969, England and Wales; 1979, Hong Kong. *Education:* Bristol University (LL.B.). Author: "Acquisition of Private Companies," 6th Edition. *Member:* Law Society (Past Chairman, Company Law Committee); International Bar Association; C.C.B.E. *LANGUAGES:* English. *PRACTICE AREAS:* Corporate Finance; Company Law.

CHARLES D. SCANLAN, born December 23, 1944; admitted, 1970, England and Wales. *Education:* Balliol College, Oxford. *Member:* Law Society. *LANGUAGES:* English. *PRACTICE AREAS:* Pensions; Life Insurance.

PATRICK D. DANIELS, born Croydon, England, April 20, 1940; admitted, 1965, England and Wales. *Education:* Durham University (LL.B., Hons.). Contributor: Tolley's Company Law; Management of Currency Risk; Management of Interest Rate Risk. *Member:* Law Society; The British Institute of International and Comparative Law; The British-German Jurists Association; The City of London Solicitors' Company. *LANGUAGES:* English and German. *PRACTICE AREAS:* Financial Services; Mutual Funds; Futures Trading; Taxation.

KEVIN M. MOONEY, born London, England, November 14, 1945; admitted, 1971, England and Wales. *Education:* Bristol University (LL.B.). *Member:* City of London Solicitors; Association; Patent Solicitors Association; Association Internationale pour la Protection de la Propriété Industrielle; American International Property Law Association; International Trademark Association; American Bar Association. *LANGUAGES:* English and French. *PRACTICE AREAS:* Intellectual Property; Product Liability.

OLIVER J.R. KINSEY, born Bath, England, July 17, 1945; admitted, 1970, England and Wales. *Education:* Queens' College, Cambridge (M.A.). *Member:* Law Society; International Bar Association; Worshipful Company of Scriveners (Court Assistant); Freeman of the City of London. (Managing Partner, Litigation Department). *LANGUAGES:* English, French and Spanish. *PRACTICE AREAS:* Insurance and Reinsurance Litigation; General Commercial Litigation and Arbitration.

W. EDWIN M. GODFREY, born Sheffield, England, October 20, 1947; admitted, 1971, England and Wales. *Education:* Queens' College, Cambridge (M.A.). Editor, "Joint Ventures," Butterworths Encyclopaedia of Forms and Precedents, 5th Edition, 1990. Author: "Coping with Conflict" in Der Schweizer Anwalt No 142, January 1993. *Member:* International Bar Association (Chairman, Sub-Committee on Structure and Ethics of Business Law Practice, 1990—; Vice-Chairman, 1988-1990; Standing Committee on Professional Ethics, 1990; Vice Chairman, Committee on Anti-Trust Law, 1981-1986); Law Society; Solicitors European Group; City of London Law Society and Solicitors' Company (Secretary of Commercial Law Sub-Committee); Freeman of the City of London; United Kingdom Environmental Law Association; British-Italian Law Association; British-Russian Law Association (Secretary); International and Comparative Law Center of the Southwestern Legal Foundation, Dallas, Texas (Member, Advisory Board); Hertford Citizens Advice Bureau (Honorary Legal Adviser). *LANGUAGES:* English, German, French, Dutch and Italian. *PRACTICE AREAS:* International Commercial Law.

NICHOLAS F.B. HEALD, born Newton Abbot, England, November 12, 1947; admitted, 1972, England and Wales. *Member:* Law Society; City of London Solicitors Company; Solicitors Benevolent Fund. *LANGUAGES:* English. *PRACTICE AREAS:* Commercial Property.

ALAN J. BUTLER, born London, England, April 26, 1947; admitted, 1973, England and Wales. *Education:* St. Edmund Hall, Oxford (B.A.). *Member:* Law Society; City of London Solicitors Company. *LANGUAGES:* English. *PRACTICE AREAS:* Commercial Property.

JERRY C. WALTER, born England, August 22, 1948; admitted, 1973, England and Wales. *Education:* Sidney Sussex College, Cambridge (M.A., LL.B.). *Member:* Law Society (Insurance Law Committee); International Bar Association (East-West Forum, Business Law Section); American Bar Association (International Commercial Transactions Committee); Securities Institute; International Chamber of Commerce (Financial Services Commission); British-Polish Legal Association; British Hungarian Legal Association; British Privatization Export Council. *LANGUAGES:* English. *PRACTICE AREAS:* Corporate Law; International Transactions.

JANET GAYMER, born Nuneaton, England, July 11, 1947; admitted, 1973, England and Wales. *Education:* St. Hilda's College, Oxford (M.A.); London University (LL.M.). *Member:* Law Society; International Bar Association; Union Internationale des Avocats. *LANGUAGES:* English and French. *PRACTICE AREAS:* Employment Law.

PETER J. FREEMAN, born Portsmouth, England, October 2, 1948; admitted, 1977, England and Wales. *Education:* Trinity College, Cambridge (M.A.); Université Libre de Bruxelles. Joint General Editor (with Richard Whish), "Butterworths Competition Law." Member, Advisory Council, "context" legal databases. *Member:* Regulatory Policy Institute, Oxford (Vice Chairman); Union Internationale des Avocats; City of London Solicitors Company; Law Society; Solicitors European Group; International Bar Association; Competition Law Association; Bar Law Society Joint Working Party on Competition Law. *LANGUAGES:* English, French and German. *PRACTICE AREAS:* European Community Law; Competition Law.

STEPHEN R. ELVIDGE, born Sheffield, England, September 11, 1949; admitted, 1974, England and Wales. *Education:* Fitzwilliam College, Cambridge (M.A.). *Member:* Law Society; City of London Solicitors' Company. *LANGUAGES:* English. *PRACTICE AREAS:* Commercial Property.

GEOFFREY A.A. DURELL, born England, April 24, 1943; admitted, 1973, England and Wales. *LANGUAGES:* English. *PRACTICE AREAS:* Commercial Property Law.

STEPHEN SCHOFIELD, born Prestwich, England, May 22, 1951; admitted, 1977, England and Wales; 1983, Hong Kong. *Education:* Liverpool University (LL.B.). *Member:* International Trade Mark Association; Inter Pacific Bar Association; Law Society of Hong Kong. *LANGUAGES:* English. *PRACTICE AREAS:* Commercial Law; Trade Law; Intellectual Property Law.

STUART J. EVANS, born December 31, 1947; admitted, 1972, England and Wales. *Education:* Leeds University (LL.B.). Author: Chapter on Acquisitions and Disposals, Takeovers and Mergers, "A Practitioner's Guide to the Stock Exchange Yellow Book," 5th Edition. *LANGUAGES:* English. *PRACTICE AREAS:* Corporate Finance; Takeover Bids; Mergers; Flotations.

GRAHAM W.H. ROWBOTHAM, born England, June 25, 1948; admitted, 1973, England and Wales. *Education:* St. John's College, Oxford (B.A., M.A.). Member, Editorial Advisory Board, International Financial Law Review. *Member:* Law Society; City of London Solicitors' Company; International Bar Association (Banking, Securities and Computer Law Committees). *LANGUAGES:* English and French. *PRACTICE AREAS:* Banking Law; Finance; Law of Electronic Systems serving Banking and Financial Markets.

RICHARD E.H. SLATER, born Bolton, England, November 9, 1950; admitted, 1977, England and Wales. *Education:* City University (B.Sc., Chemistry); Cambridge University (B.A., Law). *LANGUAGES:* English. *PRACTICE AREAS:* Company Law; Financial Services.

ANDREW M. CAMPBELL, born England, June 3, 1950; admitted, 1975, England and Wales. *Education:* St. John's College, Oxford (M.A.). *LANGUAGES:* English. *PRACTICE AREAS:* Commercial Litigation.

ANTHONY J.W. ORR, born Calcutta, India, March 5, 1951; admitted, 1975, England and Wales. *Education:* St. John's College, Oxford (M.A.). *Member:* Law Society; International Bar Association. *LANGUAGES:* English, French, Dutch and German. *PRACTICE AREAS:* International Business Law; European Community Law.

GEORGE R. KENNEDY, born Grappenhall, England, November 1, 1944; admitted, 1969, England. *Education:* London University (LL.B.). *Member:* Law Society; Association Européenne des Practiciens des Procédures Collectives; Insolvency Lawyers' Association; Society of Practitioners of Insolvency. *LANGUAGES:* English and French. *PRACTICE AREAS:* Insolvency; Company Law; Commercial Law.

WILLIAM F.P. NOAD, born London, England, October 2, 1950; admitted, 1976, England and Wales. *Education:* Guildford College of Law. *Member:* Law Society. *LANGUAGES:* English. *PRACTICE AREAS:* Commercial Property.

R. CHARLES S. POLLOCK, born Hong Kong, February 6, 1951; admitted, 1976, England and Wales. *Education:* Trinity College, Cambridge (M.A.). *LANGUAGES:* English and French. *PRACTICE AREAS:* Property.

PETER M.W. NIAS, born Oxford, England, November 24, 1953; admitted, 1979, England and Wales. *Education:* Manchester University (LL.B., Hons.). *Member:* Law Society (Revenue Law International Tax Sub-Committee); International Chamber of Commerce (U.K. Taxation Committee). *LANGUAGES:* English, Swedish, French and German. *PRACTICE AREAS:* Corporate Commercial Taxation.

(This Listing Continued)

DAVID B. BARKER, born Cheltenham, England, November 24, 1951; admitted, 1978, England and Wales; 1991, Hong Kong. *Education:* Hertford College, Oxford (B.A.). *Member:* Law Society of Hong Kong. *LANGUAGES:* English. *PRACTICE AREAS:* Commercial Property Law.

KENNETH J. WOFFENDEN, born Stockport, England, October 22, 1954; admitted, 1979, England and Wales; 1986, Hong Kong. *Education:* Pembroke College, Cambridge (M.A.). *Member:* Law Society; International Bar Association. *LANGUAGES:* English, French and Russian. *PRACTICE AREAS:* Corporate Finance; Company.

JEREMY D. SIVYER, born Romford, England, May 13, 1955; admitted, 1979, England and Wales. *Education:* University of Sheffield (LL.B.). *Member:* Law Society; International Bar Association. *LANGUAGES:* English, French and Spanish. *PRACTICE AREAS:* Commercial Law.

J. EDWARD A. TROUP, born England, January 26, 1955; admitted, 1981, England and Wales. *Education:* Corpus Christi College, Oxford (M.A., M.Sc.). *Member:* Law Society; Institute of Taxation; Institute for Fiscal Studies; International Fiscal Association. *LANGUAGES:* English. *PRACTICE AREAS:* Corporate Tax.

JOHN L. STEPHENS, born England, July 23, 1951; admitted, 1977, England and Wales. *Education:* Coventry University (B.A.). *LANGUAGES:* English and French. *PRACTICE AREAS:* Commercial Property.

CHARLES P. GOODALL, born West Yorkshire, England, July 14, 1950; admitted, 1976, England and Wales. *Education:* Sherborne School, St. Catharine's College, Cambridge (M.A., LL.M.). *Member:* Law Society,. *LANGUAGES:* English. *PRACTICE AREAS:* Banking; Capital Markets.

JOHN F. MITCHELL, born Belfast, Ireland, September 26, 1952; called to Bar, 1975; admitted, 1979, England and Wales. *Education:* Pembroke College, Cambridge (M.A.). *LANGUAGES:* English. *PRACTICE AREAS:* Town and Country Planning; Compulsory Purchase and Rating.

PHILIP J. VAUGHAN, born May 1, 1955; admitted, 1979, England and Wales; 1986, Hong Kong. *Education:* Jesus College, Cambridge (M.A.). *Member:* Law Society; American Bar Association. *LANGUAGES:* English. *PRACTICE AREAS:* Private International Law; Contract and Tort Litigation; Professional Negligence; Product Liability; Insurance.

G.S. PAUL MITCHARD, HEAD OF LITIGATION, born Paulton, England, January 2, 1952; admitted, 1977, England and Wales; 1984, Hong Kong. *Education:* Lincoln College, Oxford (M.A.). Practising Arbitrator, Accredited CEDR Mediator and on CPR's International Panel of Distinguished Neutrals. *Member:* International Bar Association; American Bar Association; Law Society; Fellow of the Chartered Institute of Arbitrators. *LANGUAGES:* English and French. *PRACTICE AREAS:* Litigation; International Arbitration; Mediation.

GORDON STEWART, born England, April 18, 1953; admitted, 1978, England and Wales. *Education:* Durham University (B.A., Hons.). *Member:* Law Society. *LANGUAGES:* English. *PRACTICE AREAS:* Banking.

CHRISTOPHER WILKINSON, born May 11, 1954; admitted, 1978, England and Wales. *Education:* University College, London (LL.B.). Contributor, "Butterworths Encyclopedia of Forms and Precedents.". *LANGUAGES:* English. *PRACTICE AREAS:* Corporate Law.

C. DAVID THOMPSON, born England, November 2, 1954; admitted, 1979, England and Wales. *Education:* Fitzwilliam College, Cambridge (B.A.). *Member:* Law Society. *LANGUAGES:* English. *PRACTICE AREAS:* Commercial Property; Acquisition; Exploitation and Disposal.

HELEN NEWMAN, born England, October 18, 1956; admitted, 1980, England and Wales. *Education:* King's College, London (LL.B.). *Member:* Association Internationale pour la Protection de la Propriété Industrielle; International Trademark Association; MARQUES; Anti Counterfeiting Group; European Communities Trade Mark Association. *LANGUAGES:* English and French. *PRACTICE AREAS:* Intellectual Property.

GEORGE G. LITTLER, born Oslo, Norway, May 1, 1950; admitted, 1978, England and Wales. *Member:* Law Society. *LANGUAGES:* English. *PRACTICE AREAS:* Property Law.

SIMON R. MORGAN, born Wales, June 16, 1955; admitted, 1980, England and Wales; 1988, Hong Kong. *Education:* Liverpool University (LL.B.). *Member:* Law Society of Hong Kong; Law Society of England and Wales; Fellow Chartered Institute of Arbitrators. *LANGUAGES:* English. *PRACTICE AREAS:* Litigation; Insolvency; Arbitration.

W. IAIN CULLEN, born Woking, England, May 13, 1953; admitted, 1980, England and Wales. *Education:* Sussex University (B.A., Hons.).

(This Listing Continued)

Member: Law Society; International Bar Association; American Bar Association. *LANGUAGES:* English, French and German. *PRACTICE AREAS:* Financial Services.

MARTIN R. SMITH, born August 27, 1955; admitted, 1981, England and Wales. *Education:* St. Catharine's College, Cambridge (M.A.); University of Pennsylvania (LL.M.). Contributor, "Butterworths Competition Law," 1990. *Member:* International Bar Association; American Bar Association; Law Society; Solicitors' European Group. *LANGUAGES:* English, French and Dutch. *PRACTICE AREAS:* Competition Law; EC Law.

MICHAEL J. WYMAN, admitted, 1976, England and Wales. *Member:* Association of Pensions Lawyers. *LANGUAGES:* English. *PRACTICE AREAS:* Pensions.

HARVEY CHALMERS, born Glasgow, Scotland, February 18, 1947; admitted, 1974, Scotland; 1978, England and Wales. *Education:* University of Glasgow (LL.B., Hons.); Magdalene College, Cambridge (Ph.D.). *Member:* Law Society; Law Society of Scotland. *LANGUAGES:* English and French. *PRACTICE AREAS:* Banking.

CAROL HEWSON, born Birmingham, England, October 8, 1955; admitted, 1980, England and Wales. *Education:* Kings College, London (LL.B.). *Member:* Law Society; City of London Solicitors' Company. *LANGUAGES:* English, French and German. *PRACTICE AREAS:* Insolvency; General Commercial and Property Litigation.

WILLIAM S. DAWSON, born Corbridge, England, September 10, 1955; admitted, 1980, England and Wales. *Education:* Selwyn College, Cambridge (M.A.). Contributor, Tolley's Practical Guide to Company Acquisitions. *Member:* Law Society. *LANGUAGES:* English. *PRACTICE AREAS:* Employment Law; Commercial Litigation.

ALISTAIR F. BIRD, born England, December 10, 1955; admitted, 1980, England and Wales. *Education:* University of London (LL.B.). Co-Author: "European Corporate Finance Law.". *LANGUAGES:* English. *PRACTICE AREAS:* Corporate Law.

PETER D. KENNERLEY, born England, June 9, 1956; admitted, 1981, England and Wales. *Education:* Sidney Sussex College, Cambridge (M.A.). *Member:* Law Society. *LANGUAGES:* English. *PRACTICE AREAS:* Corporate law; Mergers and Acquisitions; Joint Ventures.

HOWARD S.G. MATHER, born Preston, England, July 10, 1957; admitted, 1982, England and Wales. *Education:* New College, Oxford (B.A.). *LANGUAGES:* English. *PRACTICE AREAS:* Corporate Finance; Company Law.

COLIN E. LEAVER, born Cuckfield, England, May 25, 1958; admitted, 1982, England and Wales; 1990, Hong Kong. *Education:* Lincoln College, Oxford (M.A.). *Member:* Law Society of Hong Kong. *LANGUAGES:* English. *PRACTICE AREAS:* Corporate Finance; Company Law.

PHILIP T. NUNN, born England, November 3, 1949; admitted, 1974, England and Wales; 1981, Hong Kong. *Education:* Nottingham University (LL.B.). *Member:* Hong Kong Housing Authority Building Committee; Co-Chairman Buildings Appeal Committee; Associate of the Chartered Institute of Arbitrators. *LANGUAGES:* English. *PRACTICE AREAS:* Construction Law; Project Finance; Development Law.

ROBERT BRYAN, born March 6, 1955; admitted, 1981, England and Wales. *Education:* Chelmsford CIFE (B.A.). *Member:* Law Society; Society of Construction Law; Official Referees' Solicitors Association. *LANGUAGES:* English and French. *PRACTICE AREAS:* Construction Law.

RICHARD A. ARMITAGE, born Ely, England, April 26, 1957; admitted, 1982, England and Wales. *Education:* University of Sussex (B.A.). *Member:* Law Society; Union Internationale des Avocats; American Bar Association; International Bar Association. *LANGUAGES:* English, French and German. *PRACTICE AREAS:* Competition and Regulatory Law; European Community Law; Commercial Contracts.

RICHARD A. J. ALLNUTT, born Chichester, England, July 15, 1952; admitted, 1976, England and Wales. *Education:* Jesus College, Oxford (M.A.). *Member:* Law Society; City of London Solicitors' Company. *LANGUAGES:* English. *PRACTICE AREAS:* Company Law; Commercial Law.

MICHAEL H. PROSSER, born Wolverhampton, England, May 24, 1949; admitted, 1972, South Africa; 1978, England and Wales; 1992, New York State as Foreign Legal Consultant. *Education:* University of the Orange Free State, South Africa (LL.B.). *Member:* Law Society; City of London Solicitors' Company; American Bar Association; International Bar

(This Listing Continued)

SIMMONS & SIMMONS, London—Continued

Association. **PRACTICE AREAS:** Corporate/Securities Law; Commercial Law; Mergers and Acquisitions.

JOHN R. QUALTROUGH, born April 30, 1953; admitted, 1978, England and Wales. *Education:* City of London Polytechnic (B.A.). *Member:* City of London Law Society's Planning Law Sub-Committee. **LANGUAGES:** English. **PRACTICE AREAS:** Planning and Local Government.

ROGER H. BUTTERWORTH, born England, March 1, 1955; admitted, 1979, England and Wales. *Education:* Trinity Hall, Cambridge (M.A.). *Member:* Law Society. **LANGUAGES:** English. **PRACTICE AREAS:** Corporate Finance; Mergers and Acquisitions; Privatisations.

ROBERT L. SCHON, born London, England, December 27, 1953; admitted, 1980, England and Wales. *Education:* Southampton University (LL.B.); Boston University (LL.M., Taxation). Author: "Encyclopedia of Forms and Precedents, Tax and Joint Ventures." *Member:* Law Society; Confederation of British Industry. **LANGUAGES:** English, German and French. **PRACTICE AREAS:** Corporate Tax Law; Joint Ventures; Tax and Property Transactions.

DAVID J. SANDY, born England, January 3, 1955; admitted, 1981, England and Wales. *Education:* Keble College, Oxford. **LANGUAGES:** English. **PRACTICE AREAS:** Commercial Litigation.

ROWAN C.B. FREELAND, born Colchester, England, December 13, 1956; admitted, 1982, England and Wales. *Education:* St. Catherine's College, Oxford (B.A.). *Member:* Patent Solicitors' Association; Licensing Executives Society; Computer Law Association. **LANGUAGES:** English. **PRACTICE AREAS:** Intellectual Property; Computer Law.

DAVID R. DICKINSON, born England, December 13, 1950; admitted, 1974, England and Wales. *Member:* Law Society; Inter Pacific Bar Association; Securities Institute. **LANGUAGES:** English. **PRACTICE AREAS:** International Capital Markets; Structured Finance; Corporate Trust.

DAVID J. WAY, born Bournemouth, England, July 1952; admitted, 1977, England and Wales. *Education:* St. Catharine's College, Cambridge (M.A.). *Member:* Law Society; International Bar Association; Confederation of British Industry; Society of Trust and Estate Practitioners (International Committee); Land Trust Association (Committee). **LANGUAGES:** English. **PRACTICE AREAS:** International Tax; Private Clients; Trusts and Estates.

TIMOTHY J.W. BARNARD, born Beckenham, England, March 27, 1953; admitted, 1978, England and Wales. *Education:* Magdalene College, Cambridge (M.A.). *Member:* Law Society. **LANGUAGES:** English. **PRACTICE AREAS:** Commercial Property.

ALAN J. KARTER, born Glasgow, Scotland, January 12, 1955; admitted, 1979, Scotland; 1984, England and Wales. *Education:* Edinburgh University (LL.B.). Author: "Investment Advertisements," A Practitioner's Guide to Corporate Finance and the Financial Services Act 1986, Chapter 3. *Member:* Law Society; Law Society of Scotland. **LANGUAGES:** English and French. **PRACTICE AREAS:** Corporate Law; Corporate Finance; Banking and Securitisation.

GARETH J. DAVIES, born London, England, July 5, 1955; admitted, 1979, England and Wales. *Education:* Sheffield University (LL.B.); City of London Polytechnic (M.A.). Author: "Butterworths Encyclopedia of Forms & Precedents: (1) Sale of Goods, (2) Joint Ventures." *Member:* Law Society. **LANGUAGES:** English and French. **PRACTICE AREAS:** Intellectual Property; Food Law; Commercial Law; Privatisation.

GAVIN G.D. BACON, born Redhill, England, March 29, 1957; admitted, 1982, England and Wales. *Education:* Bristol University (LL.B., Hons.). *Member:* International Bar Association; American Bar Association; Law Society of England and Wales. **LANGUAGES:** English. **PRACTICE AREAS:** Commercial Litigation; Defamation; Financial Services Litigation.

SIMON J. WATSON, born Hastings, England, May 13, 1958; admitted, 1983, England and Wales. *Education:* St. Catherine's College, Oxford (M.A.). *Member:* Law Society. **LANGUAGES:** English, French and German. **PRACTICE AREAS:** Labour Law.

JAMES H.D. ROOME, born London, England, October 7, 1958; admitted, 1984, England and Wales. *Education:* Southampton University (LL.B.). *Member:* Society of Practitioners of Insolvency; Insolvency Lawyers Association; Association Européenne des Practiciens des Procédures Collectives. **LANGUAGES:** English. **PRACTICE AREAS:** Corporate Law; Contentious and Non-Contentious Insolvency.

(This Listing Continued)

JOHN SIRS, born Hartlepool, England, October 25, 1950; admitted, 1979, England and Wales. *Education:* Kent University (B.A.). *Member:* The Chartered Insurance Institute. **LANGUAGES:** English. **PRACTICE AREAS:** Commercial Leases; Development Agreements.

JOHN W. DAVIES, born London, England, December 30, 1955; admitted, 1980, England and Wales. *Education:* Merton College, Oxford (M.A.). *Member:* Law Society. **LANGUAGES:** English. **PRACTICE AREAS:** Banking; Capital Markets.

WILLIAM M. RODGER, born Colchester, England, July 2, 1955; admitted, 1980, England and Wales; 1984, Cayman Islands. *Education:* University of Reading (LL.B.). *Member:* Law Society; British Insurance Law Association. **LANGUAGES:** English and French. **PRACTICE AREAS:** Insurance and Reinsurance Litigation; Commercial Litigation; Environmental Litigation.

JANE MCKEE, born London, England, February 14, 1955; admitted, 1980, England and Wales. *Education:* Leicester University (LL.B.). *Member:* Law Society. **LANGUAGES:** English and French. **PRACTICE AREAS:** Commercial Property.

JANE BORROWS, born Liverpool, England, October 26, 1955; admitted, 1981, England and Wales. *Education:* Queen Mary College, London (LL.B.). *Member:* Law Society; International Bar Association; City of London Solicitors' Company. **LANGUAGES:** English, French and Spanish. **PRACTICE AREAS:** Securitisation; Capital Markets; Banking.

MARK T. HODGSON, born Bishop Auckland, County Durham, December 2, 1957; admitted, 1983, England and Wales. *Education:* Emmanuel College, Cambridge (M.A.). **LANGUAGES:** English. **PRACTICE AREAS:** Intellectual Property; Pharmaceutical Law.

CHRISTOPHER I. WATSON, AVOCAT À LA COUR, SOLICITOR, born Swansea, Wales, 1957; admitted, 1983, England and Wales; 1993, Paris. *Education:* New College, Oxford (M.A.). **LANGUAGES:** English, French, German and Italian. **PRACTICE AREAS:** Company Law; Commercial Law; Competition; (all French and English Law) and European Community Law.

CATHERINE WHITEHEAD, born Manchester, England, May 25, 1959; admitted, 1983, England and Wales. *Education:* Kings College, London (LL.B., Hons.). *Member:* Law Society. **LANGUAGES:** English. **PRACTICE AREAS:** Commercial Property.

ROY R. MONTAGUE-JONES, born Aldershot, England, July 21, 1958; admitted, 1983, England and Wales. *Education:* Gonville & Caius College, Cambridge (M.A.). Co-Author, "Mergers & Acquisitions in Europe." Contributor: The Acquisition of Private Companies (6th Ed., 1992). *Member:* Law Society; International Bar Association. **LANGUAGES:** English. **PRACTICE AREAS:** Company Law; Corporate Finance.

HEATHER SAVAGE, born Bolton, England, May 2, 1959; admitted, 1984, England and Wales. *Education:* Girton College, Cambridge (M.A.). Contributor, "Tax Advice for Corporate Transactions." *Member:* Share Scheme Lawyers Group; International Pensions and Employee Benefit Lawyers Association; The Esop Centre; The Association of Women Solicitors; Law Society; London Young Solicitor's Group. **LANGUAGES:** English. **PRACTICE AREAS:** Employee Incentives; Corporate Tax.

SIMON J. PITHERS, born Scotland, February 10, 1959; admitted, 1984, England and Wales. *Education:* Bristol University (LL.B., Hons.). **LANGUAGES:** English. **PRACTICE AREAS:** Corporate, Corporate Finance and International Trade.

PHILIP J. ORANGE, born England, October 10, 1950; admitted, 1981, England and Wales. *Education:* Trinity College, Cambridge (B.A.). *Member:* Law Society; Association of Pension Lawyers; British Italian Law Association. **LANGUAGES:** English, Italian and French. **PRACTICE AREAS:** Tax Law; Life Insurance; Pensions.

QUENTIN D.F. BARGATE, born December 27, 1955; admitted, 1981, England and Wales. *Education:* Middlesex Polytechnic (B.A.); University of Wales, Cardiff (M.Sc.). *Member:* Law Society; City of London Solicitors' Company; London Maritime Arbitrators Association (L.M.A.A.); Companion, The Nautical Institute; Associate of the Chartered Institute of Arbitrators. **LANGUAGES:** English. **PRACTICE AREAS:** Maritime Law; Commercial Litigation; Arbitration.

JEFFREY C. KEEY, born Meriden, England, September 25, 1956; admitted, 1982, England and Wales; 1985, Hong Kong. *Education:* St. Edmund Hall, Oxford (B.A.). *Member:* Law Society. **LANGUAGES:** English. **PRACTICE AREAS:** Company Law; Corporate Finance.

(This Listing Continued)

MARK D. AUSTIN, born London, England, November 11, 1958; admitted, 1984, England and Wales. *Education:* Warwick University (LL.B.). *LANGUAGES:* English, French and German. *PRACTICE AREAS:* Town and Country Planning; General Commercial Property.

CHRISTOPHER M. BRAITHWAITE, born November 30, 1958; admitted, 1984, England and Wales. *Education:* University of Kent, Canterbury. Co-Chair of International/London Insurance Sub-Committee of the American Bar Association Litigation Section. *LANGUAGES:* English. *PRACTICE AREAS:* Commercial Litigation; Insurance; Commodities; Banking.

COLIN J. PASSMORE, born England, January 25, 1959; admitted, 1984, England and Wales; 1986, Hong Kong. *Education:* Southampton University (LL.B.). *Member:* Law Society. *LANGUAGES:* English. *PRACTICE AREAS:* Commercial Litigation.

MARK P. DAWKINS, born London, England, May 2, 1960; admitted, 1985, England and Wales. *Education:* Exeter University (LL.B.). *LANGUAGES:* English and French. *PRACTICE AREAS:* Commercial Litigation; Financial Services; Regulatory Investigations.

PAUL D. HALE, born London, England, August 1, 1959; admitted, 1985, England and Wales. *Education:* Worcester College, Oxford (M.A.). *Member:* Law Society, City of London Solicitors' Company; VAT Practitioners Group. *LANGUAGES:* English. *PRACTICE AREAS:* Taxation.

STEPHEN R. TROMANS, born England, February 2, 1957; admitted, 1981, England and Wales. *Education:* Selwyn College, Cambridge (M.A.). Fellow, Royal Society of Arts. Author: "Best Practicable Environmental Option - A New Jerusalem?" 1987; "Commercial Leases," 1987; "The Environmental Protection Act 1990 - Text and Commentary," 1991. Joint Editor "Encyclopedia of Environmental Law," 1993. Co-Author: "Planning Law - Practice and Precedents," 1991; "Contaminated Land," 1994. Special Advisor to House of Lords European Communities Committee. *Member:* UK Environmental Law Association (Chairman); Law Society (Member, Planning Committee; Chairman, Environmental Law Sub Committee). *LANGUAGES:* English. *PRACTICE AREAS:* Environmental Law.

ANNA KENNEDY, born Redhill, England, April 23, 1959; admitted, 1983, England and Wales. *Education:* University of Wales, Cardiff (LL.B., Hons.). *Member:* Law Society. *LANGUAGES:* English. *PRACTICE AREAS:* Property Litigation; Insolvency; Utilities Regulation; Joint Ventures.

TONY J. WOODGATE, born Melbourne, Australia, May 11, 1960; admitted, 1984, Australia; 1989, England and Wales. *Education:* Monash University (LL.B., Hons.; B.Sc.); Gonville & Caius, College, Cambridge, (LL.M.); Birkbeck College; University of London (P.C. Econ). *Member:* Law Society; Solicitors European Group. *LANGUAGES:* English and French. *PRACTICE AREAS:* EC Law; Competition Law; International Trade Law; UK Competition Law; Commercial Law.

JONATHAN MELROSE, born Liverpool, England, April 21, 1959; admitted, 1985, England and Wales. *Education:* Exeter College, Oxford (M.A.). *Member:* Law Society; International Bar Association; Union Internationale des Avocats; The Securities Institute; Commodities Committee of the Futures and Options Association. *LANGUAGES:* English, French and German. *PRACTICE AREAS:* Financial Services (including investment funds); Commodities and Derivatives.

CLARE POTTER, born Ipswich, England, September 16, 1960; admitted, 1986, England and Wales. *Education:* Somerville College, Oxford (M.A.). *Member:* Law Society; International Bar Association; Solicitors' European Group. *LANGUAGES:* English and French. *PRACTICE AREAS:* UK and EC Competition Law; International Trade Law; EC Law; Commercial Law; Utilities Regulation.

STEPHEN D. COLECLOUGH, born West Bromwich, England, April 6, 1962; admitted, 1986, England and Wales. *Education:* Sheffield University (LL.B., Hons.). Tax Consultant, Butterworths Company Law Service. Associate, Institute of Taxation (A.T.I.I.). Contributor, Butterworths Encyclopedia of Forms and Precedents. *Member:* Law Society (VAT Sub-Committee; Revenue Law Committee); VAT Practitioners' Group; Institute of Taxation Technical Committee Indirect Taxes Sub Committee; International Bar Association. *LANGUAGES:* English, French, German and Spanish. *PRACTICE AREAS:* Corporate Tax Law; VAT; Customs Duties; International Tax; National Insurance.

JANE NEWMAN, born England, November 7, 1960; admitted, 1987, England and Wales. *Education:* Birmingham University (LL.B., Hons.); Lincoln College, Oxford (B.C.L.). *LANGUAGES:* English, French and

(This Listing Continued)

German. *PRACTICE AREAS:* Company Law; Commercial Law; Corporate Finance; Insurance.

ANTONY J.R. SMITH, born London, England, March 25, 1952; admitted, 1978, England and Wales. *Education:* Gonville & Caius College, Cambridge (M.A.). *Member:* Law Society. *LANGUAGES:* English, Spanish, French and Portuguese. *PRACTICE AREAS:* Banking Law; Capital Markets; Structured Finance.

ANDREW PIKE, born Neath, Glamorgan, July 24, 1946; admitted, 1970, England and Wales. *Education:* Birmingham University (LL.B., Hons.). Author: "Engineering Tenders, Sales and Contracts," 1982; "I.Mech. E/I.E.E. Conditions of Contract," 1984; "Practical Building Forms and Agreements," 1993. *Member:* Law Society; International Bar Association; Society of Construction Law. *LANGUAGES:* English. *PRACTICE AREAS:* Construction Law.

COLIN N. DODD, born Clwyd, Wales, January 17, 1955; admitted, 1983, England and Wales; 1984, Hong Kong. *Education:* Kings College, London (LL.B.). *Member:* Chartered Institute of Arbitrators (ACIArb); Official Referees Solicitors Association; Society of Construction Law. *LANGUAGES:* English. *PRACTICE AREAS:* Construction; International Trade and Commercial Dispute Resolution.

NICHOLAS WILLIAMS, AVOCAT À LA COUR, SOLICITOR, born London, England, June 4, 1957; admitted, 1985, England and Wales; 1993, Paris. *Education:* University of Warwick (B.A., Hons). *LANGUAGES:* English, French and Spanish. *PRACTICE AREAS:* International Commercial Law; Employment Law; Insolvency.

ANDREW N.B. WINGFIELD, born London, England, July 30, 1959; admitted, 1985, England and Wales; 1986, Hong Kong. *Education:* University of Bristol (B.Sc.). *Member:* Law Society of England and Wales; Law Society of Hong Kong; Hong Kong Society of Accountants (Legal Committee). *LANGUAGES:* English. *PRACTICE AREAS:* General Corporate Law; Banking and Securities.

JAMES H. BRESSLAW, born London, England, January 7, 1961; admitted, 1986, England and Wales. *Education:* Pembroke College, Cambridge (M.A.). *Member:* Law Society. *LANGUAGES:* English. *PRACTICE AREAS:* Banking; International Finance; Securitisation.

THOMAS S. KEEVIL, born Somerset, England, December 20, 1960; admitted, 1986, England and Wales. *Education:* Southampton University (LL.B.). *Member:* Law Society; City of London Solicitors Company; The London Solicitors Litigation Association; American Bar Association; International Bar Association. *LANGUAGES:* English. *PRACTICE AREAS:* Commercial and Trade Litigation.

GERALD S. KAMSTRA, born England, May 13, 1954; admitted, 1986, England and Wales. *Education:* Keble College, Oxford (M.A.); Leicester University (Ph.D.). *Member:* Chartered Institute of Patent Agents (Associate Member); Association Internationale pour la Protection de la Propriété Industrielle (British Branch). *LANGUAGES:* English, Spanish and French. *PRACTICE AREAS:* Intellectual Property.

ANDREW C. WARD, born Watford, England, September 24, 1961; admitted, 1986, England and Wales. *Education:* Christ Church, Oxford (M.A.). Secretary, British Law Association for Estonia, Latvia and Lithuania. *Member:* Law Society (Member, Working Party on Relations in Central and Eastern Europe). *LANGUAGES:* English. *PRACTICE AREAS:* Corporate Finance; Company Law.

MILES A. ALEXANDER, born London, England, February 6, 1956; admitted, 1989, England and Wales. *Education:* University of Wales (LL.B.). *Member:* Law Society; London Solicitors Litigation Association; American Bar Association. *LANGUAGES:* English. *PRACTICE AREAS:* Product Liability; Insurance and Reinsurance Litigation; Commercial Litigation.

SEBASTIAN C.A.D. FARR, born Hong Kong, January 25, 1959; called to the bar (England and Wales) 1981; admitted, 1991. *Education:* Kingston University (LL.B.). Contributor, Division on State Aids, Butterworths "Competition Law." Author: "Harmonization of Technical Standards in the EC," 1992. *Member:* International Bar Association. *LANGUAGES:* English and French. *PRACTICE AREAS:* EC Competition Law; Trade Law; Mergers; Anti-Dumping Law; Customs Law; EC Environmental Law.

AUDREY C. CAMPBELL, born Kettering, England, November 13, 1959; admitted, 1984, England and Wales. *Education:* Leicester University (LL.B., Hons). *Member:* The Law Society; City of London Solicitors' Company. *LANGUAGES:* English and German. *PRACTICE AREAS:* Corporate Finance; Mergers and Acquisitions; Corporate and Commercial.

(This Listing Continued)

SIMMONS & SIMMONS, London—Continued

JULIAN Z. BERGER, born London, England, January 5, 1960; admitted, 1984, England and Wales. *Education:* Sheffield University (LL.B., Hons). *Member:* The Law Society; International Bar Association. (Resident, Milan Office). *LANGUAGES:* English and Italian. *PRACTICE AREAS:* Business and Corporate Matters; Venture Capital; Joint Ventures; International Business Transactions.

CHARLES J. MAYO, born London, England, April 17, 1960; admitted, 1985, England and Wales. *Education:* Downing College, Cambridge. *Member:* Law Society; International Bar Association. *LANGUAGES:* English. *PRACTICE AREAS:* Corporate Finance; Venture Capital.

MICHELLE PAVER, born Malawi, Africa, September 7, 1960; admitted, 1987, England and Wales. *Education:* Lady Margaret Hall, Oxford (M.A.). *Member:* Chartered Institute of Patent Agents (Associate Member). *LANGUAGES:* English. *PRACTICE AREAS:* Intellectual Property.

HILARY BELCHAK, born London, England, March 17, 1949; admitted, 1984, England and Wales. *Education:* London LL.B., LL.M. *Member:* International Bar Association; Inter-Pacific Bar Association; Immigration Law Practitioners Association; American Immigration Lawyers Association. *LANGUAGES:* English. *PRACTICE AREAS:* UK Immigration and Nationality Law.

MARK CARROLL, born Coventry, England, July 24, 1962; admitted, 1986, England and Wales. *Education:* King's College, London (LL.B.). *LANGUAGES:* English and French. *PRACTICE AREAS:* Corporate and Corporate Finance.

MELANIE FARQUHARSON, born Woodford Green, England, September 15, 1963; admitted, 1988, England and Wales. *Education:* Cambridge (St. Catharine's College). *Member:* International Bar Association; Competition Law Association; Solicitors' European Group. *LANGUAGES:* English, French and German. *PRACTICE AREAS:* EC and Competition Law.

JOHN HOUGHTON, born Eastleigh, Hampshire, England, February 20, 1962; admitted, 1986, Barrister, England and Wales; 1988, Solicitor, England and Wales. *Education:* Brunel University (LL.B., Hons.); University College, London (LL.M.). *Member:* Society of Practitioners of Insolvency; Law Society. *LANGUAGES:* English. *PRACTICE AREAS:* Insolvency; Banking; Reconstructions and Corporate.

KATHY MYLREA, born Montreal, Canada, November 6, 1958; admitted, 1986, Upper Canada; 1992, England and Wales. *Education:* Brown University, Providence, Rhode Island, U.S.A.); University of Toronto, Canada (LL.B.). Fellow, Royal Society of Arts. *Member:* International Bar Association; United Kingdom Environmental Law Association. *LANGUAGES:* English. *PRACTICE AREAS:* Environmental Law.

SIMPSON THACHER & BARTLETT

A Partnership which includes Professional Corporations

100 NEW BRIDGE STREET
LONDON EC4V 6JE, ENGLAND
Telephone: 0171 246 8000
Telecopier: 0171 329 3883

New York, NY Office: 425 Lexington Avenue, 10017-3954. Telephone: 212-455-2000. Telecopier: 212-455-2502. ESL 62928462.

Columbus, Ohio Office: One Riverside Plaza, 43215. Telephone: 614-461-7799. Telecopier: 614-461-0040.

Tokyo Office: Ark Mori Building, 29th Floor, 12-32, Akasaka 1-Chome, Minato-Ku, Tokyo 107, Japan. Telephone: 81-3-5562-8601. Telecopier: 81-3-5562-8606. ESL 62765846.

Hong Kong Office: Asia Pacific Finance Tower - 32nd Floor, 3 Garden Road, Central, Hong Kong. Telephone: 852-2514-7600. Telecopier: 852-2869-7694.

General Practice.
Firm engaged in American and International Law Practice, but not authorized to appear before the English Courts or to act as Solicitors.

RESIDENT PARTNERS

D. RHETT BRANDON, born Burlington, North Carolina, March 20, 1954; admitted, 1980, New York (Not admitted in England). *Education:* Duke University (B.A., magna cum laude, 1976; J.D., 1979). *Member:* The Association of the Bar of the City of New York; New York State and American Bar Associations; International Bar Association.

(This Listing Continued)

ALAN M. KLEIN, born Midland, Michigan, December 31, 1960; admitted, 1986, New York (Not admitted in England). *Education:* Haverford College (B.A., History, with honors, 1981); Harvard University (J.D., cum laude, 1984). Phi Beta Kappa. *Member:* Association of the Bar of the City of New York; New York State and American Bar Associations.

JOHN D. LOBRANO, born Norwalk, Connecticut, February 18, 1957; admitted, 1984, New York (Not admitted in England). *Education:* Amherst College (B.A., magna cum laude, 1979); New York University (J.D., 1983). Articles Editor, Annual Survey of American Law, 1982-1983. *Member:* The Association of the Bar of the City of New York; New York State and American Bar Associations.

RESIDENT ASSOCIATES

A. Danzey Burnham (Not admitted in England)	**Gregory J. Ruffa** (Not admitted in England)
Gordon R. Caplan (Not admitted in England)	**Christina Lynn Scobey** (Not admitted in England)
James T. Duncan, Jr. (Not admitted in England)	**Ryerson Symons** (Not admitted in England)
Michael J. Nooney (Not admitted in England)	

(For biographical data of the New York, N.Y. partners, see Professional Biographies at New York, N.Y.).

SINCLAIR ROCHE & TEMPERLEY

Established in 1934

BROADWALK HOUSE
5 APPOLD STREET
LONDON EC2A 2NN, ENGLAND
Telephone: 0171 638 9044
Fax: 0171-638 0350/0351/0354
Telex: 889281 Sinord G

Hong Kong Office: 42nd Floor, Bank of China Tower, No. 1 Garden Road, Central Hong Kong. Telephone: (852)-28200200. Telex: 63646 Snclrhx. Fax: (852)-28459244.

Singapore Office: 16 Collyer Quay, #12-02, Singapore 0104. Telephone: (65) 533 1181. Fax: (65) 532 5454. Telex: 20433 Snclr.

Shanghai, People's Republic of China Office: 25th Floor, JF News Tower, 300 Han Kou Road. Telephone: (8621)-3512312. Fax: (8621)-3512056.

Hanoi, Vietnam Office: 16 Nguyen Truong To , Ba Dinh District. Telephone: (84 42)-50002. Fax: (84 42)-60770.

Bucharest, Romania Office: Splaiul Independentei 7, Block 101, Apt. 57, Sector 5. Telephone: (401) 312 0411. Fax: (401) 312 0412.

International commercial practice.

FIRM PROFILE: Founded in the City of London in 1934, Sinclair Roche & Temperley is a leading international firm of solicitors offering a wide range of services encompassing project, ship and aircraft finance, banking, commercial and shipping litigation and arbitration, company/commercial, privatisation, taxation, oil and gas and commercial property. The firm also has offices in Hong Kong, Singapore, Shanghai, Vietnam, a representative office in Bucharest and a presence in Oslo, Norway.

PARTNERS

John Morris	**Patrick Knox**
Harvey Williams	**Peter Murray** (Resident, Hong Kong Office)
George Hodgkinson	
Robert Gaisford	**David Beaves** (Resident, Hong Kong Office)
Jonathan Hunt	
Gregory O'Neill	**Michael Stockwood**
Ben Leach	**Jeffrey Morgan**
Gavin le Fleming Shepherd	**Simon Tatham**
Struan Robertson	**Mark Russell**
Bernard Glicksman	**Richard Thomas**
Ian Gaunt (Resident, Hong Kong Office)	**Michael Brooks** (Resident, Hong Kong Office)
Nigel Taylor	**Richard Lovell** (Resident, Singapore Office)
Simon Taylor	
Robin Slade	**Alan Bercow**
Stuart Fitzpatrick	**Roderick Cowper**
Kevin Dean	**Simon Cox**
Stephen Fordham (Resident, Singapore Office)	**Guy Liddle**
	Helen Boyle

(This Listing Continued)

Robin Hallam	Stuart Beadnall
David Relf	Stuart Mannering
Anthony Hurndall	Campbell Steedman

CONSULTANTS

Frank Rehder, C.V.O.	Joyce Pratt

Languages Spoken: Cantonese, Dutch, English, French, German, Hungarian, Italian, Mandarin, Norwegian, Polish, Romanian, Russian, Spanish, Swedish, Vietnamese.

SKADDEN, ARPS, SLATE, MEAGHER & FLOM

25 BUCKLERSBURY
LONDON EC4N 8DA, ENGLAND
Telephone: 011-44-171-248-9929
Fax: 011-44-171-489-8533

New York, New York Office: 919 Third Avenue, 10022. Telephone: 212-735-3000. Fax: 212-735-2000; 212-735-2001. Telex: 645899 Skarslaw.

Boston, Massachusetts Office: One Beacon Street, 02108. Telephone: 617-573-4800. Fax: 617-573-4822.

Washington, D.C. Office: 1440 New York Avenue, N.W., 20005. Telephone: 202-371-7000. Fax: 202-393-5760.

Wilmington, Delaware Office: One Rodney Square, 19899. Telephone: 302-651-3000. Fax: 302-651-3001.

Los Angeles, California Office: 300 South Grand Avenue, 90071. Telephone: 213-687-5000. Fax: 213-687-5600.

Chicago, Illinois Office: 333 West Wacker Drive, 60606. Telephone: 312-407-0700. Fax: 312-407-0411.

San Francisco, California Office: Four Embarcadero Center, 94111. Telephone: 415-984-6400. Fax: 415-984-2698.

Houston, Texas Office: 1600 Smith Street, Suite 4460, 77002. Telephone: 713-655-5100. Fax: 713-655-5181.

Newark, New Jersey Office: One Riverfront Plaza, 07102. Telephone: 201-596-4440. Fax: 201-596-4444.

Tokyo, Japan Office: 12th Floor, The Fukoku Seimei Building, 2-2-2, Uchisaiwaicho, Chiyoda-ku, 100. Telephone: 011-81-3-3595-3850. Fax: 011-81-3-3504-2780.

Hong Kong Office: 30/F Peregrine Tower, Lippo Centre, 89 Queensway, Central. Telephone: 011-852-820-0700. Fax: 011-852-820-0727.

Sydney, New South Wales, Australia Office: Level 26-State Bank Centre, 52 Martin Place, 2000. Telephone: 011-61-2-224-6000. Fax: 011-61-2-224-6044.

Toronto, Ontario Office: Suite 1820, North Tower, P.O. Box 189, Royal Bank Plaza, M5J 2J4. Telephone: 416-777-4700. Fax: 416-777-4747.

Paris, France Office: 105 rue du Faubourg Saint-Honoré, 75008. Telephone: 011-33-1-40-75-44-44. Fax: 011-33-1-49-53-09-99.

Brussels, Belgium Office: 523 avenue Louise, Box 30, 1050. Telephone: 011-32-2-648-7666. Fax: 011-32-2-640-3032.

Frankfurt, Germany Office: MesseTurm, 27th Floor, 60308. Telephone: 011-49-69-9757-3000. Fax: 011-49-69-9757-3050.

Beijing, China Office: 1605 Capital Mansion Tower, No. 6 Xin Yuan Nan Road, Chao Yang District, 100004. Telephone: 011-86-1-466-8800. Fax: 011-86-1-466-8822.

Budapest, Hungary Office: Mahart Building, H-1052 Apázcai Csere János u.11, Vl.em. Telephone: 011-36-1-266-2145. Fax: 011-36-1-266-4033.

Prague, Czech Republic Office: Revolucni 16, 110 00. Telephone: 011-42-2-231-75-18. Fax: 011-42-2-231-47-33.

Moscow, Russia Office: Pleteshkovsky Pereulok 1, 107005. Telephone: 011-7-501-940-2304. Fax: 011-7-501-940-2511.

General Practice. Firm Engaged in American and International law practice, but not authorized to appear before the English Courts or to act as Solicitors.

BRUCE M. BUCK, born New York, N.Y., 1946; admitted, 1971, New York (Not admitted in England). *Education:* Colgate University (A.B., 1967); Columbia University (J.D., 1970).

DOUGLAS E. NORDLINGER, born Freeport, N.Y., 1956; admitted, 1981, District of Columbia (Not admitted in England). *Education:* Duke University (A.B., summa cum laude, 1978); Harvard University (J.D., cum laude, 1981). Phi Beta Kappa; Pi Sigma Alpha; Phi Eta Sigma. (Also at Washington, D.C. Office.)

(This Listing Continued)

SCOTT V. SIMPSON, born Los Angeles, Cal., 1956; admitted, 1983, New York (Not admitted in England). *Education:* George Washington University (B.A., with honors, 1978); Fordham University (J.D., 1982); New York School of Business (M.B.A., 1983). Editor-in-Chief, Fordham Urban Law Journal, 1981-1982.

RICHARD L. MUGLIA, born Plainfield, N.J., 1951; admitted, 1983, New York; 1985, California (Not admitted in England). *Education:* Williams College (B.A., cum laude, 1973); Yale University (M.P.H., 1976); Columbia University (J.D., 1982).

(For Biographical data on other Personnel, see New York, New York Professional Biographies).

SLAUGHTER AND MAY

Established in 1889

35 BASINGHALL STREET
LONDON EC2V 5DB, ENGLAND
Telephone: (0171) 600 1200
Telex: 883486; 888926
Fax: (0171) 726 0038; (0171) 600 0289; (0171) 600 1455 (G-4)

Paris, France Office: 112 Avenue Kléber, 75116. Telephone: (1) 44.05.60.00. Telex: 642514. Fax: (1) 44.05.60.60; (1) 44 05 60 99 (G-4).

Brussels, Belgium Office: Rue D'Arlon 69/71, 1040. Telephone: (2) 230 5631. Fax: (2) 230 7699.

Frankfurt am Main, Germany Office: Westend-Carree Grüneburgweg 16, D-60322 Frankfurt am Main. Telephone: (69) 9551370. Fax: (69) 5964126.

Hong Kong Office: 27th Floor, Two Exchange Square. Telephone: (852) 521 0551. Telex: HX 86230. Fax: (852) 845 2125; (852) 845 9079.

Tokyo, Japan Office: Mitsui Asahi Building, 1-1 Kanda Sudacho, Chiyoda-ku, 101. Telephone: (3) 3258 5700. Telex: 2227208. Fax: (3) 3258 5708.

New York, New York Office: 126 East 56th Street, 10022-3613. Telephone: (212) 888-1112. Fax: (212) 888-1170; (212) 832-2021; (212) 832 0075 (G-4).

PARTNERS

G.I. Henderson	R.J. Thornhill
G.F. Renwick	(Resident, Hong Kong Office)
M. Read	G.J. Airs
F.W. Neate	R.N.S. Grandison
T.J.B. Pallister	C.R. Smith
(Resident, New York Office)	G.P. White
G.P. Balfour	N.J. Archer
R.R.S. Beaumont	A.G. Balfour
P.J. Langley	C.M. Horton
R.D.B. Cooper	(Resident, Hong Kong Office)
M.J.D. Roberts	E.A. Barrett
T.G. Freshwater	P.P. Chappatte
H.M. Nowlan	(Resident, Brussels Office)
G.D. Child (Resident, Frankfurt	R.J.N. Cripps
am Main Office)	P. Jolliffe
C.F. FitzGerald	C.D. Randell
G.P.J. Finn	W.S.M. Robinson
J.S. Haw	R.V. Carson
M. Pescod	J.S. Edge
C. Hall	S.L. Edwards
G.M. Ridley	J.M. Featherby
P.A.S. Grindrod	F. Murphy
(Resident, Tokyo Office)	P.M. Olney
P.T. Jennings	(Resident, Hong Kong Office)
J.H. Macaskill	P.H. Stacey
R. Slater	C.W.Y. Underhill
P.J.L. Kett	O.A. Wareham
(Resident, Paris Office)	R.J. Clark
T.A. Kinnersley	S.J. Cooke
R.A.M. Welsford	P.L.R. Deckers
D.J. Beales	(Resident, Paris Office)
J.E.F. Rushworth	F. Ferguson
M.G.C. Nicholson	D.L. Finkler
S.M. Edge	C.W. Harvey-Kelly
N.P.G. Boardman	(Resident, Hong Kong Office)
J. Hine	A.A. Maggiar
T.N. Clark	(Resident, Paris Office)

(This Listing Continued)

SLAUGHTER AND MAY, London—Continued

I.W. Goldie	S.J. Phillips
M. Hughes	J.D. Rice
G.W. James	M.A. Whelton
E.A. Codrington	M.D. Bennett
R.M.G. Goulding	R.D. de Carle
A.R.F. Hall	S.P. Hall
C.J. Hickson	W.J. Sibree
A.J.R. Newhouse	(Resident, Brussels Office)
G.E.S. Seligman	R.C. Stern
J.H. Savory	J.R. Triggs
P.F.J. Bennett	E.G.L. Wylde
St. J.A. Flaherty	A. Beare
(Resident, Hong Kong Office)	J.D. Boyce
R.M. Fox	M.E.M. Hattrell
D.T. Frank	K.I. Hodgson
H.R. Jacobs	N. Kheraj
C.F.I. Saul	L.M. Mc Roberts
C.J. Saunders	N.J. Swycher

SONNENSCHEIN NATH & ROSENTHAL

ROYEX HOUSE
ALDERMANBURY SQUARE
LONDON EC2V 7HR, ENGLAND
Telephone: 0171-600-2222
Facsimile: 0171-600-2221

New York, N.Y. Office: 1221 Avenue of the Americas, 24th Floor. Telephone: 212-768-6700. Facsimile: 212-391-1247.

Washington, D.C. Office: 1301 K Street, N.W., Suite 600 East Tower. Telephone: 202-408-6400. Fax: 202-408-6399.

San Francisco, California Office: 685 Market Street, 10th Floor. Telephone: 415-882-5000. Facsimile: 415-543-5472; 882-5038.

Los Angeles, California Office: 601 South Figueroa Street, Suite 1500. Telephone: 213-623-9300. Facsimile: 213-623-9924.

St. Louis, Missouri Office: One Metropolitan Square, Suite 3000. Telephone: 314-241-1800. Facsimile: 314-259-5959.

Kansas City, Missouri Office: One Kansas City Place, Suite 3850, 1200 Main Street, 64105. Telephone: 816-421-4400. Facsimile: 816-421-5107.

Regulatory and Commercial Litigation, Labor, Corporate, Property and Insurance Litigation and Regulation.

DOUGLAS DAVID HACKING, admitted, 1975, New York; 1977, England and Wales. *Education:* Charterhouse School; Clare College, Cambridge; The Middle Temple. Harmsworth Major Enrrance Exhibitioner of the Middle Temple. Asbury Scholar. Fellow: Charrered Institute of Arbitrators, 1979. Member, House of Lords since 1971, Member, Committee on the Law and Institutions of the European Communities, Former Member, Joint Committee of the House of Commons and Lords on Consolidation Bills. Chairman, Steering Committee for the London International Arbitration Trust. (Managing Partner). *PRACTICE AREAS:* Commercial Litigation.

DIANE M. MELLETT, born London, England, September 9, 1960; admitted, 1986, England and Wales; 1992, Illinois. *Education:* University of Birmingham, England (LL.B., Hons., 1983); College of Law, Chancery Lane, London, England (Solicitors Finals Examination, 1984); IIT-Kent College of Law (J.D., 1991). *Member:* Law Society of England and Wales. *PRACTICE AREAS:* Litigation; Labor and Employment Law; International.

CHRISTOPHER MARTIN, born July 30, 1962; admitted, 1988, England. *Education:* St. Cuthbart's High School; University of Keele; College of Law (B.A., with honors, 1988). Assistant Solicitor, Richard Butler, 1988-1994. Articled Clerk, 1986-1988. *PRACTICE AREAS:* Employment, Pensions, Commercial Litigation; Shipping Litigation; Commercial Property.

(For Complete Biographical Data on all Personnel, See Los Angeles, San Francisco, California; New York, N.Y.; St. Louis, Kansas City, Missouri and Washington, D.C. Professional Biographies)

SPEECHLY BIRCHAM

BOUVERIE HOUSE
154 FLEET STREET
LONDON EC4A 2HX, ENGLAND
Telephone: 0171-353-3290 International: +44 171 353 3290
Fax: 0171-353 4825; 0171-353 4992
DX: No. 54

FIRM PROFILE: Speechly Bircham is a City of London law firm whose core activities are in commercial property, corporate and litigation work servicing a broad range of domestic and international commercial clients. Within these areas are specialist teams advising on tax, banking, employment, environment, planning and construction. The firm also has a substantial private client and charity law practice.

PARTNERS

JOHN F. AVERY JONES, CBE, admitted, 1966. Internationally renowned as an authority in taxation law. Deputy-Special Commissioner and part-time VAT Tribunal Chairman. Visiting Professor, London School of Economics. Council Member, Institute for Fiscal Studies. Chairman, Board of Trustees, International Bureau of Fiscal Documentation, The Netherlands. Second Vice President, International Fiscal Association. *LANGUAGES:* English. *PRACTICE AREAS:* Taxation.

BRADLEY D. BROWN, admitted, 1958. *LANGUAGES:* English. *PRACTICE AREAS:* Litigation; Property; Leases and Leasing.

JOHN M. BRODIE, admitted, 1966. *LANGUAGES:* English. *PRACTICE AREAS:* Property; Real Estate.

RICHARD C. KIRBY, admitted, 1971. *LANGUAGES:* English. *PRACTICE AREAS:* Wills; Probate; Trusts and Estates.

ALAN J. JULYAN, admitted, 1974. *LANGUAGES:* English. *PRACTICE AREAS:* Labor and Employment.

MARK J. MUSGRAVE, admitted, 1977. *LANGUAGES:* English. *PRACTICE AREAS:* Wills; Probate; Trusts and Estates.

MERVYN D. COUVE, admitted, 1978. *LANGUAGES:* English and French. *PRACTICE AREAS:* Business Law; Commercial Law; Company Law; Corporate Law; Securities.

KENNETH E. CALCUTT, admitted, 1958. *LANGUAGES:* English. *PRACTICE AREAS:* Property; Real Estate; Leases and Leasing.

CHARLES D. PALMER, admitted, 1971. *LANGUAGES:* English. *PRACTICE AREAS:* Property; Real Estate.

RICHARD M. SCHMIDT, admitted, 1980. *LANGUAGES:* English and German. *PRACTICE AREAS:* Property; Real Estate; Leases and Leasing.

PAUL A. KAY, admitted, 1983. *LANGUAGES:* English. *PRACTICE AREAS:* Business Law; Commercial Law; Company Law; Corporate Law; Securities.

MICHAEL R. LINGENS, admitted, 1982. *LANGUAGES:* English and German. *PRACTICE AREAS:* Business Law; Commercial Law; Company Law; Corporate Law; Securities.

JOHN V. HUGHES, admitted, 1966. *LANGUAGES:* English and French. *PRACTICE AREAS:* Tax; Estates; Trusts; Charities; Wills and Probate.

TIMOTHY A. RAPER, admitted, 1981. *LANGUAGES:* English. *PRACTICE AREAS:* Construction Law.

NICK JANMOHAMED, admitted, 1985. *LANGUAGES:* English. *PRACTICE AREAS:* Business Law; Commercial Law; Company Law; Corporate Law; Securities.

D. JOHN M. WARD, admitted, 1983. *LANGUAGES:* English. *PRACTICE AREAS:* Charitable Organizations.

CHRISTOPHER J. MARTIN, admitted, 1977. *LANGUAGES:* English. *PRACTICE AREAS:* Property; Real Estate; Leases and Leasing.

NICHOLAS C. IVEY, admitted, 1981. *LANGUAGES:* English. *PRACTICE AREAS:* Property; Real Estate; Leases and Leasing.

ANTHONY C. G. CARTMELL, admitted, 1983. *LANGUAGES:* English. *PRACTICE AREAS:* Property; Real Estate; Leases and Leasing.

TIMOTHY M. VOAKE, admitted, 1983. *LANGUAGES:* English and French. *PRACTICE AREAS:* Property; Real Estate; Leases and Leasing.

(This Listing Continued)

SUSAN L. HAGGARD, admitted, 1985. *LANGUAGES:* English. *PRACTICE AREAS:* Property; Real Estate; Leases and Leasing.

BRIAN J. CONVERY, admitted, 1972. *LANGUAGES:* English. *PRACTICE AREAS:* Environmental Law; Zone, Planning and Land Use.

DAVID C. MASTERS, admitted, 1981. *LANGUAGES:* English. *PRACTICE AREAS:* Litigation; Property; Leases and Leasing.

ANTHONY R. WILSON, admitted, 1981. *LANGUAGES:* English. *PRACTICE AREAS:* Litigation; Intellectual Property; Patents; Trademarks.

MICHAEL G.S. JANNEY, admitted, 1981. *LANGUAGES:* English. *PRACTICE AREAS:* Construction Law.

JOHN H. LIDDINGTON, admitted, 1986. *LANGUAGES:* English. *PRACTICE AREAS:* Taxation.

STEPHEN D. ARMSTRONG, admitted, 1987. *LANGUAGES:* English. *PRACTICE AREAS:* Business Law; Commercial Law; Company Law; Corporate Law.

CONSULTANTS

JOHN R. BADDELEY, admitted, 1949. *LANGUAGES:* English. *PRACTICE AREAS:* Business Law; Commercial Law; Company Law; Corporate Law.

CHRISTINE M. HOUSTON, admitted, 1983. *LANGUAGES:* English and French. *PRACTICE AREAS:* Wills; Probate; Trusts and Estates.

RICHARD A. HULLAND, admitted, 1980. *LANGUAGES:* English. *PRACTICE AREAS:* Pensions.

SQUIRE, SANDERS & DEMPSEY

1 GUNPOWDER SQUARE
PRINTER STREET
LONDON EC4A 3DE, ENGLAND
Telephone: 011-44-171-830-0055
Fax: 011-44-171-830-0056

Cleveland, Ohio Office: 4900 Society Center, 127 Public Square, Cleveland, Ohio 44114-1304. Telephone: 216-479-8500. Fax's: 216-479-8780, 216-479-8781, 216-479-8787, 216-479-8795, 216-479-8777. 216-479-8793, 216-479-8776, 216-479-8788.

Columbus, Ohio Offices: 1300 Huntington Center, 41 South High Street, Columbus, Ohio 43215. Telephone: 614-365-2700. Fax: 614-365-2499.

Jacksonville, Florida Office: One Enterprise Center, Suite 2100, 225 Water Street, Jacksonville, Florida 32202. Telephone: 904-353-1264. Fax: 904-356-2986.

Miami, Florida Office: 201 South Biscayne Boulevard, Suite 2900 Miami Center, Miami, Florida 33131. Telephone: 305-577-8700. Fax: 305-358-1425.

New York, New York Office: 520 Madison Avenue, 32nd Floor, New York, New York 10022. Telephone: 212-715-4990. Fax: 212-715-4915.

Phoenix, Arizona Office: Two Renaissance Square, 40 North Central Avenue, Suite 2700, Phoenix, Arizona 85004-4441. Telephone: 602-528-4000. Fax: opier: 602-253-8129.

Washington, D.C. Office: 1201 Pennsylvania Avenue, N.W., P.O. Box 407, Washington, D.C. 20044. Telephone: 202-626-6600. Fax: 202-626-6780.

Brussels, Belgium Office: Avenue Louise, 165-Box 15, 1050 Brussels, Belgium. Telephone: 011-32-2-648-1717. Fax: 011-32-2-648-1064.

Prague Office: Adria Palace, Jungmannova 31/36, 11000 Prague 1, Czech Republic. Telephone: 011-42-2-231-5661. Fax: 011-42-2-231-5482.

Bratislava Office: Mudronova 37, 811 01 Bratislava, Slovak Republic. Telephone: 011-42-7-313-362; 011-42-7-315-370. Fax: 011-42-7-313-918.

Budapest, Hungary Office: Deak Ferenc Ut. 10, Office 304, H-1052 Budapest V., Hungary. Telephone: 011-36-1-266-2024. Fax: 011-36-1-226-2025.

Kiev, Ukraine Office: vul. Prorizna 9, Suite 20, Kiev 252035, Ukraine. Telephones: 011-7-044-244-3452, 011-7-044-244-3453, 011-7-044-228-8687. Fax: 011-7-044-228-4938.

General and International Practice.
(This Listing Continued)

RESIDENT PARTNER

MARK A. CUSICK, born Pittsburgh, Pennsylvania, 1948; admitted, 1975, Ohio. *Education:* Duquesne University (B.A., 1970); University of Virginia (J.D., 1975). Order of the Coif. Member, University of Virginia Law Review. *Member:* Cleveland, Ohio State and American (Member, Business Law and Law Practice Sections) Bar Associations. *PRACTICE AREAS:* Corporate; International.

(For Biographical Data on Cleveland and Columbus, Ohio, Miami and Jacksonville, Florida, New York, New York, Phoenix, Arizona, Washington, D.C., Brussels, Belgium, Prague, Czech Republic, Bratislava, Slovak Republic, Budapest, Hungary and Kiev, Ukraine Personnel, see Professional Biographies at those Points Respectively).

LAW OFFICES OF
LAWRENCE H. STEIN

Established in 1983

5TH FLOOR
10 EASTCHEAP
LONDON EC3M 1ET, ENGLAND
Telephone: (0171) 623 3229
Fax: (0171) 623 3227

General U.S. and International Practice, Legal aspects of Investing and Trading in the U.S. and EC, Intellectual Property and Computer Law, Commercial and Corporate Law, Business Immigration Law.
Firm engaged in American and International Law Practice, but not Authorized to appear before the English Courts or to act as Solicitors.

LAWRENCE H. STEIN, born New Jersey, U.S.A., November 15, 1954; admitted, 1980, Florida (Not admitted in England). *Education:* University of Florida (B.A., High Honors, 1976); University of Miami, School of Law (J.D., 1980); University of London, London School of Economics and Political Science (LL.M., 1983). *Member:* The Florida Bar; American and International Bar Associations; Computer Law Association; British Computer Society; American Immigration Lawyers Association; London Chamber of Commerce. *LANGUAGES:* English and French. *PRACTICE AREAS:* Intellectual Property/Computer Law; Business Immigration Law.

STEPHENSON HARWOOD

ONE, ST. PAUL'S CHURCHYARD
LONDON EC4M 8SH, ENGLAND
Telephone: (44) 0171 329 4422
Telex: 886789 SHSPC G
Fax: (44) 0171 606 0822

Brussels, Belgium Office: Avenue du Diamant 139, 1040. Telephone: (322) 735 9190. Fax: (322) 732 2237.

Guangzhou, People's Republic of China Associated Office: Stephenson Harwood & Lo, Room 516, China Hotel, Liu Hua Lu, 510015. Telephone: (8620) 669 3490. Telex: 44888 CHLGZ CN. Fax: (8620) 669 3479.

Hong Kong Associated Office: Stephenson Harwood & Lo, 18th Floor, Edinburgh Tower, The Landmark, 15 Queen's Road Central. Telephone: 852-2868 0789. Telex: 66278 SHL HX. Fax: 852-2868 1504.

Kuwait Associated Office: Al Sarraf, Al Ruwayeh & Stephenson Harwood, Salhiya Complex, Gate 1 3rd Floor, P.O. Box 1448, Safat 13015. Telephone: 965 240 0061/2/3. Fax: 965 240 0064.

Madrid, Spain Office: Fernando El Santo 15-3°, 28010. Telephone: (341) 319 1212. Fax: (341) 319 1940.

Banking, Trade Finance and Asset Finance, Commercial Agreements, Company Acquisitions and Disposals, Construction, Corporate Finance, Cross-Border Transactions and Joint Ventures, Employment and Pensions, Environment, European Community, Fraud and Business Crime, Fund Management and Financial Services, Information Technology, Insurance and Reinsurance, Intellectual Property, Inward Investment in the UK and Europe, Litigation, Arbitration and Alternative Dispute Resolution, Private Client (Matrimonial, Tax, Trusts, Probate), Property and Property Finance, Shipping and Ship Finance, Tax (Corporate and Personal).

FIRM PROFILE: Stephenson Harwood is a leading firm of solicitors which has been practising in the City of London for over 150 years. The firm has more than 70 partners and a total strength of over 500 lawyers
(This Listing Continued)

STEPHENSON HARWOOD, London—Continued

and support staff. The core of the firm's business is banking, corporate and litigation work which more often than not has an international element.

PARTNERS

ANTHONY ISAACS, born August 9, 1934; admitted, 1960. Senior Partner. *LANGUAGES:* English, French and Italian. *PRACTICE AREAS:* Corporate; Corporate Finance.

DONALD AMLOT, born September 29, 1933; admitted, 1961. *LANGUAGES:* English. *PRACTICE AREAS:* Commercial Property.

MICHAEL WILSON, born September 9, 1934; admitted, 1961. *LANGUAGES:* English. *PRACTICE AREAS:* Commercial Litigation.

JOHN BACH, born February 18, 1936; admitted, 1963. *LANGUAGES:* English and Russian. *PRACTICE AREAS:* Corporate; Commercial; International Transactions; Joint Ventures; Cross-border Mergers and Acquisitions.

MARK BAILY, born September 13, 1940; admitted, 1964. Head, Tax Department. *LANGUAGES:* English and French. *PRACTICE AREAS:* Estate Planning; Individual Tax Planning; Tax Shelters; Charitable Trusts and Foundations.

DAVID SLADE, born July 3, 1941; admitted, 1966. Head, Shipping Department. *LANGUAGES:* English and French. *PRACTICE AREAS:* Ship Finance; Ship Mortgages; Ship Registration.

MICHAEL JENNINGS, born November 25, 1944; admitted, 1969. *LANGUAGES:* English and French. *PRACTICE AREAS:* Individual Tax Planning; Tax Shelters; Trusts; Charitable Trusts and Foundations.

DESMOND MCCANN, born September 28, 1943; admitted, 1967. *LANGUAGES:* French and Spanish. *PRACTICE AREAS:* Mergers and Acquisitions; Corporate Finance; Hostile Takeovers; Securities Offerings.

TONY SCALES, born January 3, 1942; admitted, 1968. *LANGUAGES:* English. *PRACTICE AREAS:* International Transactions; Corporate; Corporate Finance; GEOGRAPHIC REGIONS: Middle East.

MICHAEL HODDINOTT, born December 12, 1944; admitted, 1970, England; 1979, Hong Kong. Senior Partner, Stephenson, Harwood & Lo, Hong Kong. *LANGUAGES:* English and French. *PRACTICE AREAS:* Corporate; Commercial; Trusts and Asset Protection; GEOGRAPHIC REGIONS: Asian-Pacific.

GEOFFREY WOOLF, born October 13, 1946; admitted, 1970. *LANGUAGES:* English. *PRACTICE AREAS:* Insolvency; Financial Restructuring; Corporate Restructuring; Property Finance.

KENNETH DUNCAN, born December 30, 1946; admitted, 1971. *LANGUAGES:* English, French and German. *PRACTICE AREAS:* Commercial Litigation; Property Litigation; Landlord and Tenant.

TONY STOCKWELL, born January 14, 1949; admitted, 1974. Head, Banking Department. *LANGUAGES:* English, French and Spanish. *PRACTICE AREAS:* Banking; International Banking; International Finance; Banking Regulation; Securitisation; Insolvency.

JOHN FORDHAM, born December 15, 1948; admitted, 1974. *LANGUAGES:* English and French. *PRACTICE AREAS:* Commercial Litigation; Banking; Insolvency Litigation; Multi-Jurisdictional Disputes; Asset Tracing Law.

ROGER BROWN, born May 10, 1949; admitted, 1974. *LANGUAGES:* English. *PRACTICE AREAS:* Commercial Litigation; Professional Indemnity.

STEVEN LOWE, born November 24, 1946; admitted, 1972. *LANGUAGES:* English. *PRACTICE AREAS:* Commercial Litigation; Insurance and Reinsurance; Marine Insurance.

CHRISTOPHER ELWEN, born September 14, 1944; admitted, 1976. *LANGUAGES:* English. *PRACTICE AREAS:* Commercial Litigation; Insurance and Reinsurance.

COLIN MACKENZIE-GRIEVE, born January 28, 1951; admitted, 1975. Head, Property Department. *LANGUAGES:* English and French. *PRACTICE AREAS:* Commercial Property; Landlord and Tenant.

PATRICK RODIER, born December 31, 1950; admitted, 1976. Head, Corporate Department. *LANGUAGES:* English. *PRACTICE AREAS:* International Transactions; Corporate Finance; Mergers and Acquisitions.

(This Listing Continued)

PETER FIDLER, born March 16, 1942; admitted, 1967. Licensed Insolvency Practitioner. *LANGUAGES:* English and French. *PRACTICE AREAS:* Banking; Insolvency; Corporate Restructuring; Bankruptcy.

RICHARD LIGHT, born January 30, 1953; admitted, 1977. *LANGUAGES:* English. *PRACTICE AREAS:* Commercial Property.

PAUL DISS, born November 30, 1951; admitted, 1976. *LANGUAGES:* English. *PRACTICE AREAS:* Banking; International Banking; International Finance; Insolvency.

JOHN CARRELL, born November 18, 1945; admitted, 1981. *LANGUAGES:* English, French and Spanish. *PRACTICE AREAS:* Corporate Tax; Tax Shelters; Individual Tax Planning.

RICHARD OLSEN, born June 15, 1943; admitted, 1969. *LANGUAGES:* English, French, German and Norwegian. *PRACTICE AREAS:* Admiralty; Marine Salvage Rights; Offshore Pollution; Casualties; Marine Disasters.

ANDREW SUTCH, born July 10, 1952; admitted, 1979. *LANGUAGES:* English, French and Russian. *PRACTICE AREAS:* Mutual Funds; Unit Trusts; Financial Services; Corporate Finance.

JONATHAN COPELAND, born July 10, 1951; admitted, 1976. *LANGUAGES:* English and German. *PRACTICE AREAS:* Commercial Property.

WILLIAM CORBETT, born April 7, 1951; admitted, 1979. Chief Executive. *LANGUAGES:* English. *PRACTICE AREAS:* Estate Planning; Tax Shelters Law; Trust Law; Charitable Trusts and Foundations.

JOHN PIKE, born January 10, 1953; admitted, 1978. *LANGUAGES:* English. *PRACTICE AREAS:* Commercial Property.

RICHARD GWYNNE, born March 9, 1955; admitted, 1979. *LANGUAGES:* English. *PRACTICE AREAS:* Commercial Litigation; Insurance Law; Lloyd's Litigation.

RICHARD UFLAND, born May 4, 1957; admitted, 1981. *LANGUAGES:* English and French. *PRACTICE AREAS:* Mergers and Acquisitions; Corporate Finance Law; Hostile Takeovers; Securities Offerings.

ROBERT PARTRIDGE, born July 6, 1952; admitted, 1978. *LANGUAGES:* English. *PRACTICE AREAS:* Administration of Estates; Probate Law; Succession, Wills.

MICHAEL WALTER, born May 6, 1956; admitted, 1981. *LANGUAGES:* English, French and German. *PRACTICE AREAS:* International Transactions; Corporate Finance; Mergers and Acquisitions; Hostile Takeovers; GEOGRAPHIC REGIONS: Asian-Pacific.

ANTONY MAIR, born December 27, 1946; admitted, 1976. *LANGUAGES:* English, French, German and Spanish. *PRACTICE AREAS:* International Transactions; Joint Ventures; European Community; Competition Law; GEOGRAPHIC REGIONS: Central and Eastern Europe; European Community.

NICHOLAS PHILLIPS, born May 13, 1953; admitted, 1977. *LANGUAGES:* English and French. *PRACTICE AREAS:* Charterparties and Bills of Lading; P&I Clubs; Marine Insurance; International Trade.

TREFOR JOHN, born August 19, 1954; admitted, 1979. *LANGUAGES:* English and French. *PRACTICE AREAS:* Corporate Tax Planning; Tax Shelters.

JOHN GALE, born February 1, 1958; admitted, 1982, England; 1983, Hong Kong. *LANGUAGES:* English. *PRACTICE AREAS:* Corporate Finance; Mutual Funds; Banking; GEOGRAPHIC REGIONS: Asian-Pacific.

ANDREW KEATES, born November 25, 1953; admitted, 1979. *LANGUAGES:* English. *PRACTICE AREAS:* P&I Clubs; Charterparties and Bills of Lading; Oil and Gas Law; International Trade.

GRAHAM BURNS, born August 9, 1958; admitted, 1983. *LANGUAGES:* English, French and German. *PRACTICE AREAS:* Ship Finance; Ship Mortgages; Ship Registration.

JONATHAN WALSH, born April 21, 1944; admitted, 1969. *LANGUAGES:* English. *PRACTICE AREAS:* Family and Matrimonial; Divorce; Child Custody; Child Dependency Proceedings.

MARK REED, born August 2, 1957; admitted, 1981. *LANGUAGES:* English and French. *PRACTICE AREAS:* Banking Law; International Banking; Finance Law; International Finance; Banking Regulation; Insolvency; Financial Restructuring.

(This Listing Continued)

BARRY JEEPS, born March 17, 1958; admitted, 1982. *LANGUAGES:* English. *PRACTICE AREAS:* Commercial Property; Property Development and Syndications; Land Use; Planning.

VICTORIA YOUNGHUSBAND, born July 14, 1954; admitted, 1984, England; 1991, Hong Kong. *LANGUAGES:* English and French. *PRACTICE AREAS:* Corporate Finance; Commercial; Financial Services.

KATHRYN NEWSOME, born March 3, 1960; admitted, 1984. *LANGUAGES:* English. *PRACTICE AREAS:* Commercial Litigation.

ROLAND FOORD, born June 6, 1958; admitted, 1984. *LANGUAGES:* English, French, German and Portuguese. *PRACTICE AREAS:* Commercial Litigation; Professional Indemnity.

GWENDOLINE GRIFFITHS, born April 30, 1955; admitted, 1979. *LANGUAGES:* English. *PRACTICE AREAS:* Banking; International Banking; International Finance; Securitisation.

CATHERINE BREARLEY, born January 12, 1957; admitted, 1989. Head, Employment and Pensions Group. *LANGUAGES:* English. *PRACTICE AREAS:* Employment; Employer/Employee Relations; Immigration; Employment Discrimination.

ROBERT NEWMAN, born March 31, 1959; admitted, 1984. *LANGUAGES:* English. *PRACTICE AREAS:* Commercial Property; Property Finance; Insolvency.

MARGARET COLE, born June 17, 1961; admitted, 1985. *LANGUAGES:* English. *PRACTICE AREAS:* Commercial Litigation; Securities Litigation; Insolvency.

KENNETH BONAVIA, born January 10, 1957; admitted, 1982. (Resident Partner, Madrid Office). *LANGUAGES:* English, French, Spanish and Italian. *PRACTICE AREAS:* Commercial; International Trade; International Transactions; Joint Ventures; GEOGRAPHIC REGIONS: Europe.

CHRISTOPHER STOAKES, born January 22, 1958; admitted, 1982. *LANGUAGES:* English and French.

CHRISTOPHER TITE, born December 22, 1959; admitted, 1985. *LANGUAGES:* English and French. *PRACTICE AREAS:* Corporate; Commercial; International Transactions; Joint Ventures; Privatisations; Cross-border Mergers and Acquisitions.

JILL WHITEHOUSE, born December 2, 1959; admitted, 1984. *LANGUAGES:* English and French. *PRACTICE AREAS:* Corporate Finance; Mergers and Acquisitions; Leveraged and Management Buyouts; Venture Capital.

MARCEL HANIFF, born July 20, 1959; admitted, 1984. *LANGUAGES:* English. *PRACTICE AREAS:* Commercial Property.

MICHAEL COWLEY, born July 20, 1954; admitted, 1984. *LANGUAGES:* English. *PRACTICE AREAS:* Pensions and Profit Sharing.

STEVEN WAIT, born June 23, 1959; admitted, 1984. Head, Construction Group. *LANGUAGES:* English and German. *PRACTICE AREAS:* Building and Construction; Building Contracts; International Construction Contracts.

DENIS PETKOVIC, born November 23, 1959; admitted, 1983, New South Wales, Australia; 1990, England, Wales and Hong Kong. *LANGUAGES:* English and Croatian. *PRACTICE AREAS:* Banking and Insolvency.

DAVID CUCKSON, born November 30, 1942; admitted, 1978. *LANGUAGES:* English. *PRACTICE AREAS:* Environmental Law; Environmental Liability; Hazardous Waste; Local Authorities; Public Sector.

MARION GILL, born November 1, 1952; admitted, 1990. *LANGUAGES:* English. *PRACTICE AREAS:* Commercial Litigation; Insurance; International Trade; Shipping.

MARK LEWIS, born September 14, 1954; admitted, 1991. *LANGUAGES:* English. *PRACTICE AREAS:* Information Technology; Telecommunications Contracts; Computer Regulation; Computer Software; Data Protection; Facilities Management; Public EC Procurement; Public and Administrative.

PAUL GODWIN, born April 6, 1949; admitted, 1974. (Resident Partner, Al Sarraf, Al Ruwayeh & Stephenson Harwood). *LANGUAGES:* English. *PRACTICE AREAS:* Banking; Commercial; International Construction Projects; GEOGRAPHIC REGIONS: Middle East.

JUDITH SHEPHERD, born September 13, 1961; admitted, 1987. *LANGUAGES:* English and French. *PRACTICE AREAS:* Corporate Fi-

(This Listing Continued)

nance; Mergers and Acquisitions; Leveraged and Management Buyouts; Hostile Takeovers; Securities Offerings; Venture Capital.

TAMASIN LITTLE, born March 29, 1960; admitted, 1985. *LANGUAGES:* English. *PRACTICE AREAS:* Mutual Funds; Unit Trusts; Financial Services; Securities Offerings.

PAOLO GHIRARDANI, born October 11, 1959; admitted, 1985. *LANGUAGES:* English and Spanish. *PRACTICE AREAS:* Commercial Litigation; Insurance; International Trade; Charterparties and Bills of Lading; P&I Clubs.

TIBOR GOLD, born January 26, 1942; admitted, 1993. *LANGUAGES:* English, French, German, Spanish and Hungarian. *PRACTICE AREAS:* Patent Applications; Trademark; Intellectual Property.

MALCOLM KEMP, born March 13, 1954; admitted, 1980, England and Wales; 1982, Hong Kong. *LANGUAGES:* English and German. *PRACTICE AREAS:* Litigation; Shipping.

ANDREW HART, born September 18, 1961; admitted, 1987, England and Wales; 1988, Hong Kong. *LANGUAGES:* English. *PRACTICE AREAS:* Litigation.

STIBBE SIMONT MONAHAN DUHOT

66 GRESHAM STREET
LONDON EC2V 7NH, ENGLAND
Telephone: (44 171) 600-4400
Telecopier: (44 171) 600-4411

Amsterdam, The Netherlands Office: Strawinskylaan 2001, P.O. Box 75640, 1070 AP. Telephone: (31) (20) 546 06 06. Cable Address "Mandatum. Telex: 16414 (Stib NL). Telecopier: (31) (20) 546 01 23.
Brussels, Belgium Office: Henri Wafelaertsstraat 47-51 (box 1), B-1060. Telephone: (32) (2) 533 52 11 . Telex: 24519. Telecopier: (32) (2) 533 52 12.
Paris, France Office: 154, Rue de l'Université, 75007. Telephone: (33) (1) 40 62 20 00. Telecopier: (33) (1) 40 62 20 62.
New York, New York Office: 335 Madison Avenue, 10017. Telephone: (1) (212) 972 40 00. Telecopier: (1) (212) 972 49 29.

General Practice of Netherlands, Belgian, French and Netherlands Antilles Law, including Commercial Law, Corporations, Mergers and Acquisitions, Tax, Banking, Securities and Finance, Insurance, Corporate Reorganization, Bankruptcy and Insolvency, Competition, Anti-trust, Contracts, Torts, and Product Liability, Computer Law, Public and Administrative Law, Environmental Law, Building and Construction, Building, Property, European Law, Distributorship, Agency and Franchising, Energy, Trademarks, Industrial and Intellectual Property, Human Rights, Employment and Labour, Arbitration and Litigation.

RESIDENT PARTNERS

JAAP WILLEUMIER, born 1953; admitted, 1979, Amsterdam. *Education:* University of Amsterdam (1979). *PRACTICE AREAS:* Corporate practice of Netherlands and Netherlands Antilles Law; Mergers and acquisitions; Banking and finance; securities; insolvency.

ASSOCIATES

JOOST J. VETTER, born 1964; admitted, 1989, Amsterdam. *Education:* University of Amsterdam (Tax Law, 1987). *PRACTICE AREAS:* Netherlands and international taxation.

STIKEMAN, ELLIOTT

COTTONS CENTRE
COTTONS LANE
LONDON SE1 2QL, ENGLAND
Telephone: 171-378-0880
Fax: 171-378-0344

Montreal, Quebec Office: 1155 René-Lévesque Boulevard West, 40th Floor, H3B 3V2. Telephone: 514-397-3000. Fax: 514-397-3222.
Toronto, Ontario Office: Commerce Court West, 53rd Floor, M5L 1B9. Telephone: 416-869-5500. Fax: 416-947-0866.
Ottawa, Ontario Office: 50 O'Connor Street, Suite 914, K1P 6L2. Telephone: 613-234-4555. Fax: 613-230-8877.
Calgary, Alberta Office: 855 - 2nd Street S.W., 1500 Bankers Hall, T2P 4J7. Telephone: 403-266-9000. Fax: 403-266-9034.
Vancouver, British Columbia Office: 666 Burrard Street, Suite 1700, Park Place, V6C 2X8. Telephone: 604-631-1300. Fax: 604-681-1825.

(This Listing Continued)

STIKEMAN, ELLIOTT, London—Continued

New York, New York Office: 126 East 56th Street, 11th Floor, Tower 56, 10022. Telephone: 212-371-8855. Fax: 212-371-7087.

Washington, D.C. Office: 1300 I Street, N.W., Suite 1210 West, 20005-3314. Telephone: 202-326-7555. Fax: 202-326-7557.

Paris, France Office: In Association with Société Juridique Internationale, 39, rue François Ier, 75008. Telephone: 33-1-40-73-82-00. Fax: 33-1-40-73-82-10.

Budapest, Hungary Office: Andrássy út 100, II Floor, H-1062. Telephone: 36-1-269-1790. Fax: 36-1-269-0655.

Hong Kong Office: 29 Queen's Road Central, Suite 1506, China Building. Telephone: 852-2868-9903. Fax: 852-2868-9912.

Hong Kong: In Association with Shum & Co., 29 Queen's Road Central, Suite 1103, China Building. Telephone: 852-2526-5531. Fax: 852-2845-9076.

Taipei, Taiwan Office: 117 Sec. 3 Min Sheng East Road, 8th Floor. Telephone: 886-2-719-9573. Fax: 886-2-719-4540.

Firm engaged in Canadian and International Law Practice, but not authorized to appear before the English Courts or to act as Solicitors.

RESIDENTS IN LONDON

MARC BARBEAU, born Arvida, Québec, September 27, 1961; admitted, 1986, Quebec; 1991, New York (Not admitted in England). *Education:* McGill University (B.C.L., 1984; LL.B., 1984); Paris 1, Paris, France (Panthon-Sorbonne) (D.E.A., 1985). University Scholar (McGill, 1984). *Member:* Comite consultatif de soquij sur l'informatisation des banques de données.

MICHELE J. BUCHIGNANI, born Trail B.C., Canada, November 20, 1963; admitted, 1990, Ontario (Not admitted in England). *Education:* University of British Columbia (B.A., with honors, 1985); University of Toronto (LL.B., 1988). *Member:* Canadian and International Bar Associations.

RICHARD J. HAY, born Ottawa, Ontario, July 2, 1954; admitted, 1979, Ontario; 1981, New York (Not admitted in England). *Education:* University of Toronto; Osgoode Hall (LL.B., 1977); Columbia University (LL.M., 1981). Law Clerk to Chief Justice of the Supreme Court of Ontario, 1979-1980. Assistant Professor of Tax and Corporate Law, University of Ottawa Law School, 1981-1984. Lecturer in International Taxation, National University of Singapore, 1984-1987. *Member:* Law Society of Upper Canada; Canadian Bar Association.

CALIN ROVINESCU, born Romania, September 16, 1955; admitted, 1979, Quebec; 1984, Ontario (Not admitted in England). *Education:* McGill University (D.E.C., 1974); University of Montreal (LL.L., 1978); University of Ottawa (LL.B., 1980). *Member:* Montreal, Quebec and Canadian Bar Associations; Law Society of Upper Canada.

WILLIAM A. SCOTT, born Shawinigan, Quebec, January 22, 1956; admitted, 1984, Ontario (Not admitted in England). *Education:* St. John's College, England (B.A. Hons., 1978); Queen's College, England (B.A. Hons., 1980); University of Toronto (LL.B., 1982). *Member:* Canadian Bar Association; Law Society of Upper Canada.

MARIANNE SUSSEX, born London, Ontario, July 2, 1949; admitted, 1977, Ontario (Not admitted in England). *Education:* University of Windsor (B.A., Hons., 1972); University of Western Ontario (LL.B., 1975); University of London (LL.M., 1981). *Member:* Canadian Bar Association. Law Society of Upper Canada.

(For biographical data on other personnel, see Professional Biographies at Montreal, Quebec, Toronto, Ontario, Ottawa, Ontario, Calgary, Alberta, Vancouver, British Columbia, New York, New York, Washington, D.C., Paris, France, Budapest, Hungary, Hong Kong and Taipei, Taiwan)

STONEHAM LANGTON & PASSMORE

8 BOLTON STREET
PICCADILLY
LONDON W1Y 8AU, ENGLAND
Telephone: 0171-499 8000
Fax: 0171-629 4460
Telex: 21640 Intlaw G DX: 37223 Piccadilly - 1

FIRM PROFILE: *The firm is a Commercial and Private Client Practice, which can trace its roots back to 1782. Although it is one of the oldest firms in the country, it has a progressive outlook, a considerable interna-*

(This Listing Continued)

---

tional element to its practice, and is highly approachable and responsive to the needs of all its clients. The firm's major areas of practice are in Corporate, Commercial Property, Private Client and Litigation work for a wide range of national and international clients.

The firm initiated a close network of European lawyers in the mid 1970s. The Private Association of Lawyers in Europe (PALS) has members in 26 European cities, and contacts throughout the world, allowing the firm to provide a fully international service to all its clients.

The firm is a founder member of QLG a national association of English and Scottish lawyers in most of the provincial centres in the U.K. The members are committed to Total Quality Management in legal practice and, as a first step on that road, have obtained registration under ISO 9001. The Group provides direct access to local high quality commercial legal services throughout England and Scotland.

PARTNERS

J. GRANT MIDDLETON. PRACTICE AREAS: Partnerships; Commercial and Residential Property.

STUART M. DUNCAN. PRACTICE AREAS: Litigation; Arbitration.

ROBERT J. EWING. PRACTICE AREAS: Commercial and Residential Property; Property Finance.

JOHN G. FOSTER. PRACTICE AREAS: Trusts and Estates; Probate.

ANDREW R. CHERRY. PRACTICE AREAS: International Law (Investments); Agency and Distributorships.

C.D.J. NELSON. PRACTICE AREAS: Commercial Property (Development and Finance); Commercial Leases.

PETER R. BRICKNELL. PRACTICE AREAS: Trusts and Estates; Commercial and Residential Property.

JULIET R. DAVIES. PRACTICE AREAS: Residential Real Estate; Conveyancing.

RUSSELL W. BELL. PRACTICE AREAS: Corporate Acquisitions and Sales; Corporate Finance.

W.R. FULCHER. PRACTICE AREAS: Commercial Real Estate; Landlord and Tenant.

ALINA T.J. NOSEK. PRACTICE AREAS: Banking (Asset-based Finance); Company Law.

JOHN N. CLARK. PRACTICE AREAS: Commercial Property (Development and Finance); Commercial Leases.

PAUL J. PENNEY. PRACTICE AREAS: Commercial and Residential Real Estate; Conveyancing.

C.I. MILLAR. PRACTICE AREAS: Bankruptcy; Commercial Litigation.

ANNE MARTIN. PRACTICE AREAS: Labour and Employment; Occupational Health and Safety.

TEJA PICTON HOWELL. PRACTICE AREAS: Company Law; Mergers, Acquisitions and Divestitures.

ALBERT PASSMORE. PRACTICE AREAS: Litigation; Intellectual Property.

CONSULTANTS

ROGER D. DOUGLAS-HUGHES. PRACTICE AREAS: Land and Landowners; Trusts and Estates.

STEVEN A. FRIEZE. PRACTICE AREAS: Bankruptcy; Insolvency.

PETER J. GROVES. PRACTICE AREAS: Intellectual Property.

Languages: English, Spanish, Portuguese, Polish, French and Japanese

---

JOHN C. STOTSENBURG

5, THE POSTERN, WOOD STREET
LONDON EC2Y 8BJ, ENGLAND
Telephone: 0171-628-6757
Telecopier: 0171-628-7529

New York, New York Office: Stotsenburg & Stotsenburg. 757 Third Avenue, 10017. Telephone: (212) 595-5963. Fax: (212) 755-6155.

General American and International Law Practice, but not Authorized to appear before the English Courts or to act as Solicitors.

(This Listing Continued)

General Practice, Corporate and Commercial Law, International Litigation, Software Licensing and Distribution, International Financing and Taxation, Acquisitions and Investments.

JOHN C. STOTSENBURG, born Camden, New Jersey, U.S.A., April 20, 1940; admitted, 1970, New York; 1974, U.S. Court of Appeals, Second Circuit and U.S. District Court, Southern District of New York; 1982, California; 1990, U.S. District Court, District of Arizona (Not admitted in England). *Education:* Cornell University (B.A., Government, 1962); Boalt Hall School of Law, University of California (J.D., 1969). *Member:* The Association of the Bar of the City of New York; American and International Bar Associations. (Also Member, Stotsenburg & Stotsenburg, New York, New York). *PRACTICE AREAS:* General Practice; Intellectual Property; Investments; Acquisitions; Taxation; Copyright Matters.

ASSOCIATES

FRANK H. WALSER, born Dunmore, Pennsylvania, U.S.A., March 14, 1964; admitted, 1992, Pennsylvania (Not admitted in England). *Education:* Muhlenberg College (B.A., Communications, 1989); Seton Hall University School of Law (J.D., cum laude, 1992); London School of Economics and Political Science (LL.M., 1993). Seton Hall Constitutional Law Journal, Member, 1990-1991; Managing Editor, 1991-1992. (Also Associate, Stotsenburg & Stotsenburg, New York, New York).

STURTIVANT & CO.

17 BULSTRODE STREET
LONDON W1M 5FQ, ENGLAND
Telephone: 0171 486 9524
Facsimile: 0171 224 3164

Specialist practice devoted exclusively to UK Immigration Law.

KAREN L. STURTIVANT, born Leicester; admitted, 1980, England. *Education:* College of Law, London (Solicitor's, 1978). Editor, Immigration and Nationality Law & Practice, Frank Cass & Co., Ltd., 1987/1988. *Member:* International Bar Association (Member, 1983—, Vice-Chair, 1986-1988, Immigration and Nationality Division); Law Society Immigration Law Subcommittee (Member, 1990—); Immigration Law Practitioners Association (Member, 1984—; Member, Executive Committee, 1985-1991; Co-Founder, International Sub Committee); American Immigration Lawyers Association (Member, 1985—).

TIM REED, born London; admitted, 1993, England. *Education:* The King's School Canterbury and College of Law, London. *Member:* Immigration Law Practitioners Association; Middle East Legal Practice Forum; British Legal Association.

SULLIVAN & CROMWELL

ST. OLAVE'S HOUSE
9A IRONMONGER LANE
LONDON EC2V 8EY, ENGLAND
Telephone: (011)(44171)710-6500
Telecopier: (011)(44171)710-6565

New York City Offices: 125 Broad Street, 10004-2498; Midtown Office: 250 Park Avenue, 10177-0021. Telephone: 212-558-4000. Telex: 62694 (International); 12-7816 (Domestic). Cable Address: "Ladycourt, New York". Telecopier: 125 Broad Street 212-558-3588; 250 Park Avenue 212-558-3792.

Washington, D.C. Office: 1701 Pennsylvania Avenue, N.W., 20006-5805. Telephone: 202-956-7500. Telex: 89625. Telecopier: 202-293-6330.

Los Angeles, California Office: 444 South Flower Street, 90071-2901. Telephone: 213-955-8000. Telecopier: 213-683-0457.

Paris Office: 8, Place Vendôme, Paris 75001, France. Telephone: (011)(331)4450-6000. Telex: 240654. Telecopier: (011)(331)4450-6060.

Melbourne, Australia Office: 101 Collins Street, Melbourne, Victoria 3000. Telephone: (011)(613)654-1500. Telecopier: (011)(613)654-2422.

Tokyo Office: Gaikokuho Jimu Bengoshi Office of Robert G. DeLaMater, a member of the firm of Sullivan & Cromwell, Tokio Kaijo Building Shinkan, 2-1, Marunouchi, 1-chome Chiyoda-ku, Tokyo 100, Japan. Telephone: (011)(813)3213-6140. Telecopier: (011)(813)3213-6470.

Hong Kong Office: 28th Floor, Nine Queen's Road, Central, Hong Kong. Telephone: (011)(852)826-8688. Telecopier: (011)(852)522-2280.

Not authorized to appear before the English Courts or to act as Solicitors.

(This Listing Continued)

PARTNERS IN LONDON

JOHN W. DICKEY, born Springfield, MO., 1927; admitted, 1954, Missouri; 1955, New York (Not admitted in England). *Education:* Univ. of Missouri (A.B., 1950); Oxford (B.A., 1952; M.A., 1956); Harvard (LL.B., 1954).

ROBERT M. OSGOOD, born Elmira, NY., 1942; admitted, 1968, New York (Not admitted in England). *Education:* Syracuse (A.B., 1963; J.D., 1968); Univ. London (D.EC Law, 1994).

WILLIAM A. PLAPINGER, born Washington, D.C., 1952; admitted, 1979, New York (Not admitted in England). *Education:* Vassar (A.B., 1974); New York University (J.D., 1978).

GEORGE H. WHITE, III, born Washington, D.C., 1955; admitted, 1984, New York (Not admitted in England). *Education:* Harvard (A.B., 1977; J.D., 1981).

RICHARD C. MORRISSEY, born Boston, MA., 1956; admitted, 1983, New York (Not admitted in England). *Education:* Harvard (B.A., 1978); Cambridge (LL.M., 1980); Univ. of Michigan (J.D., 1982).

SCOTT D. MILLER, born Redondo Beach, CA., 1961; admitted, 1987, California (Not admitted in England). *Education:* Arizona State Univ. (B.S.E., 1982); Columbia (J.D., 1985).

EUROPEAN COUNSEL IN LONDON

KATHRYN ANN CAMPBELL, born Washington, D.C., 1954; admitted, 1982, New York (Not admitted in England). *Education:* Montclair State (B.A., 1976); Rutgers (J.D., 1981); Oxford (B.C.L., 1983).

ASSOCIATES IN LONDON

MARK D. ALEXANDER, born Nashville, TN., 1967; admitted, 1993, New York (Not admitted in England). *Education:* Indiana Univ. (B.A., 1989); Cornell Univ. (J.D., 1992).

BARBARA A. BAYLISS, born Pittston, PA., 1953; admitted, 1989, California (Not admitted in England). *Education:* Michigan State University (B.A., 1974); University of San Francisco; Pepperdine University (J.D., 1989).

COREY R. CHIVERS, born Boise, ID., 1965; admitted, 1992, New York; 1994, District of Columbia (Not admitted in England). *Education:* Brigham Young Univ. (B.A., 1988); Columbia (J.D., 1991).

FRANCIS P. CRISPINO, born Toronto, Canada, 1965; admitted, 1992, New York (Not admitted in England). *Education:* Univ. of Toronto (B.A., 1988); Oxford Univ. (Bachelor of Laws, 1990); Univ. of Chicago (LL.M., 1991).

RICHARD A. ELY, born Queens, NY., 1957; admitted, 1988, New York (Not admitted in England). *Education:* Cornell (B.S., 1980); College of William & Mary (M.B.A., 1985); New York Univ. (J.D., 1988).

LAURA AYN HOLLEMAN, born Grand Rapids, MI., 1966; admitted, 1993, New York (Not admitted in England). *Education:* Michigan State Univ. (B.A., 1988); Ohio State Univ. (J.D., 1992).

DOUGLAS E. HOLTZ, born New York, NY., 1967; admitted, 1994, New York (Not admitted in England). *Education:* Harvard (A.B., 1989); Columbia (J.D., 1993).

CHRISTOPHER L. MANN, born Beaumont, TX., 1963; admitted, 1991, New York (Not admitted in England). *Education:* Harvard (A.B., 1985; J.D., 1989); Univ. of Cambridge (M.Phil., 1987).

MICHAEL B. MILLER, born Detroit, MI., 1965; admitted, 1992, New York (Not admitted in England). *Education:* Brown (A.B., 1987); Univ. of California, Berkeley (J.D., 1990).

STEVEN J. P. MILLER, born New Brunswick, NJ., 1959; admitted, 1987, New York (Not admitted in England). *Education:* Univ. of Pennsylvania (B.S., 1981; J.D., 1986).

NICOLAS A. PAGLIETTI, born Rome, Italy, 1965; admitted, 1991, Italy; 1993, New York (Not admitted in England). *Education:* LUISS, Rome, Italy (J.D., 1987); New York Univ. (LL.M., 1992).

DAVID B. ROCKWELL, born Honolulu, HI., June 13, 1964; admitted, 1990, New York (Not admitted in England). *Education:* University of California (A.B., 1986); Cambridge University (B.A., 1990); Harvard University (J.D., 1990).

(This Listing Continued)

SULLIVAN & CROMWELL, London—Continued

ADAM S. RUBINSON, born New York, NY., 1966; admitted, 1992, New York (Not admitted in England). *Education:* Columbia (B.A., 1988); Stanford (J.D., 1991).

(For Biographical Data on all Partners and Associates see Professional Biographies at New York, N.Y.).

STUDIO LEGALE SUTTI

Established in 1952

19 PRINCES STREET

LONDON W1R 7RE, ENGLAND

Telephone: +44 171 4091384

Telefax: +44 171 4091384

ISDN & Videoconference: +44 171 4933395

Main Office: Via Molino delle Armi 4, 1 20123, Milan, Italy. Telephone: +39 2 72022126 - 8693239. Fax: +39 2 8900732.

International Contracts, Foreign Investments, Distributorship, Agency and Franchise Law, EEC Law, Competition Law, Antitrust Law, Company Law, Banking Law, Bankruptcy, Product Liability Law, Entertainment Law, Industrial Property Dept.: Patent Litigation and Prosecution, Trademark Litigation, Copyright Law, Industrial Models, Licence Negotiation, Technology Transfer, General Patent and Intellectual Property Practice, Advertising Law, Labour Dept.: Employment Law, Employer's Liability, Pension Law, Industrial Relations.

FIRM PROFILE: Representative office of Studio Legale Sutti, an Italian firm based in Milan, which specializes in, inter alia, providing a full range of consultative, litigation and representational services concerning the above mentioned fields within the Italian jurisdiction to British law firms and their clients, also benefitting from the presence of English solicitors among its members.

RESIDENT ASSOCIATE

DAVIDE BRAGHINI, born Somma Lombardo, Italy, August 14, 1969. *Education:* University of Milan (J.D., 1992). Co-Author: "Guide to National Competition Laws of Europe - Italy," 1994. *Member:* Association Internationale des Jeunes Avocats (AIJA); International Bar Association; British Italian Law Association. *LANGUAGES:* Italian, English and French. *PRACTICE AREAS:* Antitrust Law; Company Law; Commercial and International Contracts; Construction Law; EEC Law.

(For a Complete List of Personnel and more information concerning the Firm, see Milan, Italy)

TAYLOR JOYNSON GARRETT

CARMELITE

50 VICTORIA EMBANKMENT

BLACKFRIARS

LONDON EC4Y 0DX, ENGLAND

Telephone: (44) 171 353 1234

Facsimile: (44) 171 936 2666

EC Office: 14 Rue Montoyer, 1040 Brussels, Belgium. Telephone: (32) 2 514 0402. Facsimile: (32) 2 514 0088.

Bucharest, Romania Office: Bd. Nicolae Titulescu Nr. 1, Bloc A7, Scara 3, Etaj 9, Apart. 88, Sector 1. Telephone: (401) 211 88 98. Facsimile: (401) 211 75 89.

Affiliated firms and offices:

Graham & James in San Francisco, Los Angeles, Newport Beach, Sacramento, Palo Alto, Washington DC, New York, Raleigh, Milan. Joint Offices in Bangkok, Guangzhou, Hanoi, Taipei, Beijing. Graham & James affiliated offices in Riyadh, Jeddah, Jakarta, Mexico City, Tokyo, Kuwait, Bahrain, Sydney, Brisbane, Melbourne, Perth, Canberra.

Deacons, Hong Kong.

Haarmann, Hemmelrath & Partner in Dusseldorf, Berlin, Munich, Frankfurt, Leipzig, Prague.

International Commercial Lawyers specializing in International Trade, EC Law, Taxation, Company Law, Mergers and Acquisitions, Biosciences, Corporate Finance, Environmental and Planning Law, Energy, Stock Exchange Listings, Banking and Securities, Corporate Recoveries, Pensions and Employee Benefits, Intellectual Property, Entertainment and Media, Employment Law, Insurance and Reinsurance, Shipping, Commodities,

(This Listing Continued)

EU340B

Commercial Litigation, Information Technology, Liability Claims, Construction, Commercial Property, Residential Property, Matrimonial and Family, Wills, Trusts and Probate.

SENIOR PARTNERS

Michael Morrison

PARTNERS

Martin Baker	**David Lester**
Christopher Belk	**Anthony Lewis**
Christopher Bell	**Beverley Lewis**
Peter Bond	**John Linneker**
Viscount Brentford	**Charles Lloyd**
Nicholas Briant	**Marcus Mackay**
Graham Briggs	**Tom Mackay**
David Brown	**Paul Manser**
Nicholas Burkill	**Richard Marsh**
Peter Clarke	**Paul Mitchell**
Elaine Colville	**Penelope Moore**
Martin Dillon	**Glyn Morgan**
Giles Dixson	**Gary Moss**
Peter Droop	**Martin Newey**
Rodney Dukes	**Philip Newhouse**
Timothy Eyles	**Kathryn Peat**
Sarah Faulder	**Richard Pertwee**
John Featherstone	**Richard Price**
Clare Ferguson	**Malcolm Ring**
James Ferguson	**Raman Sharma**
Mark Fletcher	**Peter Shepherd**
Colin Fraser	**James Sleightholme**
Michael Frawley	**Peter Smith**
Robert Gayford	**Michael Stanford-Tuck**
Martin Goodwin	**Deborah Stones**
Andrew Granger	**Stephen Stowell**
David Greig	**Declan Tarpey**
Paul Harrison	**Garry Turkie**
Ian Hunter	**David West**
Gordon Jackson	**Neil White**
Peter Kempe	**John Whitfield**
David Kent	**John Williams**

Kirk Wolley Dod

CONSULTANTS

Alan Grieve	**Rosina Harris**
David M. Findlay (Also Member,	**David Petterson**
Graham & James, London)	**Philippa Blake-Roberts**
Michael Hamilton	(Non Solicitor)

Hugh Young

Languages: French, German, Spanish, Italian, Portuguese, Greek, Punjabi, Hebrew, Arabic, Indonesian, Malay, Romanian and Japanese

THEODORE GODDARD

Established in 1902

150 ALDERSGATE STREET

LONDON EC1A 4EJ, ENGLAND

Telephone: (44) (171) 606 8855

Telex: 884678

Fax: (44) (171) 606 4390

Brussels, Belgium Office: 79 avenue de Cortenberg/Kortenberglaan 79, B-1040 Brussels. Telephone: (32) (2) 732 2700. Fax: (32) (2) 735 23 52.

St. Helier, Jersey, Channel Islands Office: Theodore Goodard Jersey, P.O. Box 344, Osprey House, 5 Old Street, St. Helier, Jersey JE4 8UZ. Telephone: (44) (534) 76085. Telex: 4192289. Fax: (44) (534) 35227.

Paris, France Office: Klein Goddard, 44 Avenue des Champs Elysées, 75008, Paris, France. Telephone: (33) (1) 44 95 20 00. Fax: (33) (1) 49 53 03 97.

Warsaw, Poland Office: Dewey Ballantine Theodore Goddard Sp.z o.o, ul. Klonowa 8, 00-591, Warsaw, Poland. Telephone: (48) (22) 49 32 88. Fax: (48) (22) 49 80 23. Satellite: (48) (39) 12 21 85.

Prague, Czech Republic Office: Dewey Ballantine Theodore Goddard, 6th Floor, Revolucni 13, 110 15 Prague 1. Telephone: (42) (2) 24810283. Fax: (42) (2) 231 0983.

(This Listing Continued)

Budapest, Hungary Office: Dewey Ballantine Theodore Goddard, Vadasz utca 31, H-1054 Budapest, Hungary. Telephone: (36) (1) 111 9620. Fax: (36) (1) 112 2272.

Associated offices in London, England: c/o Dewey Ballantine, 150 Aldersgate Street, London EC1A 4EJ. Telephone: (44) (171) 606 6121. Fax: (44) (171) 600 2754; New York, USA: c/o Dewey Ballantine, 1301 Avenue of the Americas, New York, NY 10019-6092. Telephone: (1) (212) 259 8000. Fax: (1) (212) 259 6333; Washington, USA: c/o Dewey Ballantine, 1775 Pennsylvania Avenue, N.W., Washington D.C., 20006-4605. Telephone: (1) (202) 862 1000. Fax: (1) (202) 862 1093; Los Angeles, USA: c/o Dewey Ballantine, 333 South Hope Street, Los Angeles, California, 90071. Telephone: (1) (213) 626 3399. Fax: (1) (213) 625 0562.

PARTNERS RESIDENT IN LONDON

W.H.S. May (Senior Partner)	S.N. Goodworth
W.S. Rogers	P.S. Cooke
M.J. Harris	P.M. Bulley
M.G. Chester	D.E.M. Janney
P. Grafton Green	P.R.M. Kavanagh
D. Guy	J.S. Smyth
D.S. Wilkinson	J.H. Taylor
R.M. Preston	G.A.M. Russell
D.W. Lewis	A.K. Walkling
J.S. Stubbings	D.F. Evans
M.C. Kramer	P.S. Laskey
G.I.F. Leigh	M. Westaway
C.J.J. Maples	R.J. MacCarthy
J.M. Lewis	J.A. Shellard
J.H. Lomas	C.E.G. Ashton
L.I. Jackson	H.J. Garety
M. Gilbert	J.G.M. Ballingall
C. Lerry	J.G. Clark
J.R. Kelleher	T.S. Sanders
J.H.K. Harman	D.M. Wilson
H.S. Porter	J.R. Patel
M.E. Hatchard	J.R. Barnes
	S.M. Jones

CONSULTANTS

W.H. Blackburn	D.P. Kerr
	C.D.S. Clogg

PARTNER RESIDENT IN WARSAW

B.W.C. McGregor

THOMAS COOPER & STIBBARD

52 LEADENHALL STREET
LONDON EC3A 2DJ, ENGLAND
Telephone: 0171-481 8851
Cable Address: "Recoup London"
Telex: 886334 RECOUP G
Facsimile: 0171-480 6097 (Groups II and III)

Firm engaged in English and International Law Practice.
Admiralty and Maritime Law, Litigation and International Arbitration, Transportation, Personal Injury, Commercial and Company Law, Insurance including Maritime Insurance and Real Estate.

FIRM PROFILE: *Established in 1825, Thomas Cooper & Stibbard originally made its name in Marine Law and over the years has diversified into many other areas of commercial law. The firm offers a wide variety of legal advice to shipowners, charterers, insurance companies, foreign governments and ministries, major oil companies, international traders, banks and financial institutions. The firm has 10 Partners and 20 Assistants, including French and Spanish speakers and 2 Master Mariners.*

MEMBERS OF FIRM

DAVID HEBDEN, admitted, 1971, England. *LANGUAGES:* English. *PRACTICE AREAS:* Charter Parties and Bills of Lading; Marine and Inland Marine; International Arbitration; Personal Injury.

STEPHEN SWABEY, admitted, 1972, England. *Education:* B.A. *LANGUAGES:* English. *PRACTICE AREAS:* Marine Insurance Law; Ship Finance; European Community Law; Reinsurance; Carriers and Transport.

TIMOTHY GOODE, born March 14, 1950; admitted, 1975, England. *Education:* M.A. *LANGUAGES:* English. *PRACTICE AREAS:* Charter

(This Listing Continued)

Parties and Bills of Lading; International Casualties; Maritime; Marine Insurance Law; Construction Law.

NICHOLAS GREEN, admitted, 1978, England. *Education:* M.A. (Oxon). *LANGUAGES:* English. *PRACTICE AREAS:* Charter Parties and Bills of Lading; Construction Law; Insurance; Civil Arbitration; Sale of Goods.

RUPERT STRANGE, born July 18, 1956; admitted, 1980, England. *Education:* LL.B. *LANGUAGES:* English and French. *PRACTICE AREAS:* Marine and Inland Marine; Medical Negligence; Personal Injury.

TIMOTHY KELLEHER, born March 7, 1959; admitted, 1985, England. *Education:* M.A. (Oxon). *LANGUAGES:* English, Russian and French. *PRACTICE AREAS:* Casualties; Marine Insurance Law; Civil Arbitration; Insolvency; Carriers and Transport.

DOUGLAS BATESON, born May 20, 1960; admitted, 1985, England. *Education:* B.A. *LANGUAGES:* English, Spanish and French. *PRACTICE AREAS:* Charter Parties and Bills of Lading; Casualties; Marine Insurance Law; International Arbitration; Oil and Gas.

WILLIAM KELLY, born September 9, 1960; admitted, 1986, England. *Education:* B.Sc. *LANGUAGES:* English. *PRACTICE AREAS:* Charter Parties and Bills of Lading; Casualties; Shipping P & I Clubs; Reinsurance.

ROBERT GORDON, born July 14, 1945; admitted, 1990, England. *Education:* LL.B., LL.M., Master Mariner. *LANGUAGES:* English. *PRACTICE AREAS:* Charter Parties and Bills of Lading; Casualties; Marine Disasters; Marine Salvage Rights; Seamen; Marine Insurance Law.

ELIZABETH MARSDEN, born September, 1964; admitted, 1988, England. *Education:* LL.B. *LANGUAGES:* English. *PRACTICE AREAS:* Charter Parties and Bills of Lading; Diving and Offshore Injuries; Casualties; Seamen; Litigation.

ASSOCIATES

G.R. Eldred
E.V. Fenwick
Miss K.E. Harrison
Miss M. Margossian
K.C. Wagland
J. Alegre-Climent
Miss C.S. Sheehan

CONSULTANTS

J.T. Jessup
F.D. Bateson
M.H. Jubber

THOMMESSEN KREFTING GREVE LUND

44/45 CHANCERY LANE
LONDON WC2A 1JB, ENGLAND
Telephone: 44 171 404 4825
Fax: 44 171 404 1471

In Alliance With: Vinge, Sweden and Kromann & Münter, Denmark.
Oslo, Norway Office: Tollbodgaten 27, P.O. Box 413 Sentrum, 0103 Oslo 1. Telephone: 47 22 42 18 10. Telefax: 47 22 42 35 57.
Bergen, Norway Office: Valkendorfsgate 1A, P.O. Box 349, 5000. Telephone: 47 55 31 13 50. Fax: 47 55 31 74 75.
Brussels, Belgium Office: Avenue Louise 475/B 12, 1050. Telephone: 32 2 646 3620. Fax: 32 2 646 4049.
Paris, France Representation Office: 21, Rue Jean Goujon, 75008. Telephone: 331 40.75.37.37. Fax: 331 45.63.05.49.
Hong Kong Representation Office: 20003 Hutchison House, 10 Harcourt Road Central. Telephone: 852 523 6149. Fax: 852 810 5343.

Firm engaged in Norwegian and International Law Practice, but not authorized to appear before the English Courts or to act as Solicitors.

RESIDENT PARTNER

BERIT STOKKE, born Stockholm, Sweden, December 21, 1956; admitted, 1983, Norway. *Education:* Candidate in Jurisprudence (1981); Diplome des Etudes Superieures d'Universite d'Aix-Marseille, France (1983). Co-author: "Ship-Owner and Financial Institutions from a Practical Point of View," Article published by Scandinavian Institute of Maritime Law, 1979; *Ship, Shipyard and Financial Institutions,* Book published by Scandinavian Institute of Maritime Law, 1980. Scientific Assistant, Scandinavian Institute of Maritime Law, 1979-1980. Lecturer in Private Law, Institute

(This Listing Continued)

THOMMESSEN KREFTING GREVE LUND, London— *Continued*

for Private Law, Oslo Law Faculty, 1982. Legal Consultant, Civil Servant, Ministry of Justice, 1981. *Member:* Norwegian Bar Association; Association Internationaux des Jeunes Avocats. *LANGUAGES:* Scandinavian, English and French. *PRACTICE AREAS:* Finance; Maritime; International Tax; Business Law.

RESIDENT ASSOCIATES

HANS CAPPELEN ARNESEN, born Norway, 1964. *Education:* Oslo College of Business and Economics, University of Oslo (Candidate in Jurisprudence, 1990). *Member:* Norwegian Bar Association. *LANGUAGES:* Scandinavian Languages and English. *PRACTICE AREAS:* Contracts; Mergers; Tax; Finance; Aviation Law.

(For biographical data on all personnel, see Professional Biographies at Oslo, Norway).

TITMUSS SAINER DECHERT

Established in 1938

2 SERJEANTS' INN

LONDON EC4Y 1LT, ENGLAND

Telephone: 0171 583 5353

Telex: 23823 Advice G

Facsimile: 0171 353 3683/2830

EU Office: Dechert Price & Rhoads, 65 Avenue Louise, 1050 Brussels, Belgium. Telephone: (32 2) 535 5411.

New York Office: Dechert Price & Rhoads, 477 Madison Avenue, New York, NY 10022-5891, USA. Telephone: (212) 326 350.

Philadelphia Office: Dechert Price & Rhoads, 4000 Bell Atlantic Tower, 1717 Arch Street, Philadelphia, PA, 19103-2793, USA. Telephone: (215) 994-4000.

Princeton Office: Dechert Price & Rhoads, Princeton Pike Corporate Center, P.O. Box 5218, Princeton, NJ 08543-5218, USA. Telephone: (609) 520-3200.

Washington Office: Dechert Price & Rhoads, 1500 K Street, N.W., Washington, D.C., 20005-1208, USA. Telephone: (202) 626-3300.

Boston Office: Dechert Price & Rhoads, Ten Post Office Square South, Boston, MA 02109-4603, USA. Telephone: (617) 728-7100.

Harrisburg Office: Dechert Price & Rhoads, Thirty North Third Street, Harrisburg, PA 17101-1603, USA. Telephone: (717) 237-2000.

Titmuss Sainer Dechert is a leading City of London law firm with a complement of over 280 lawyers and supporting staff and a strong international presence through its union with Dechert Price & Rhoads, one of the large U.S. law firms. The two practices offer an internationally resourced legal service with over 450 lawyers.

PARTNERS

MICHAEL SMITH, born 1945; admitted, 1970. *Education:* Sorbonne, Paris. *PRACTICE AREAS:* Insurance; Financial Services.

CHARLES CORMAN, born 1934; admitted, 1959. *Education:* University College, London (LL.B., Hons.; LL.M.); Berkeley, California. *PRACTICE AREAS:* Corporate Finance; Charities; Matrimonial.

DICK RUSSELL, born 1942; admitted, 1968. *Education:* University College, Oxford (B.A. Hons.). *PRACTICE AREAS:* Corporate Finance; Banking.

MICHAEL STEINFELD, born 1943; admitted, 1970. *Education:* Pembroke College, Oxford (B.A., Hons). *PRACTICE AREAS:* Corporate Finance; Mergers and Acquisitions; Venture Capital.

JOHN HUME, born 1945; admitted, 1970. *Education:* College of Law, Lancaster Gate. *PRACTICE AREAS:* Corporate Litigation; Partnership Disputes.

EDWARD L. KLING, born 1947, U.S.A.; admitted, 1974, California (Not admitted in England). *Education:* Babson College (B.S.); Oxford University (B.A., B.A., M.A.). (Also Partner, Dechert Price & Rhoads).

DAVID VOGEL, born 1948; admitted, 1972. *Education:* University College, London (LL.B.; LL.M.). *PRACTICE AREAS:* Corporate Finance; Mergers and Acquisitions; Venture Capital.

PAUL BERRY, born 1949; admitted, 1974. *Education:* Birmingham College of Commerce (LL.B., sec. Hons.). *PRACTICE AREAS:* Property Development; Landlord and Tenant.

(This Listing Continued)

DAVID TANDY, born 1944; admitted, 1975. *Education:* University of London; City of London College (LL.B.). *PRACTICE AREAS:* Tax; Estate Planning; Trusts; Charities.

BARRY THORNE, born 1946; admitted, 1970. *PRACTICE AREAS:* Commercial Property; Property Development and Investment; Landlord and Tenant.

STEVEN FOGEL, born 1951; admitted, 1976. *Education:* King's College, London (LL.B.; LL.M.; ACI Arb). *PRACTICE AREAS:* Commercial Leases; Rent Review; Property Development, Investment and Financing.

SIMON LEONARD, born 1944; admitted, 1969. *Education:* Durham University (B.A.). *PRACTICE AREAS:* Commercial Contracts; Information Technology.

PETER DRAPER, born 1952; admitted, 1976. *Education:* Warwick University (LL.B.). (Also Partner, Dechert Price & Rhoads).

MICHAEL HALLOWELL, born 1954; admitted, 1978. *Education:* Queens College, Cambridge (M.A.). *PRACTICE AREAS:* Property Development Investment and Financing; Landlord and Tenant.

DAVID BYRNE, born 1951; admitted, 1978. *Education:* Ealing College; King's College (B.A., Hons.; LL.M.). *PRACTICE AREAS:* Financial Services; Tax Investigations.

JEREMY GROSE, born 1950; admitted, 1977. *Education:* King's College, London (LL.B.; A.K.C.). *PRACTICE AREAS:* Commercial Litigation.

CHRISTOPHER EDWARDS, born 1955; admitted, 1980. *Education:* Leeds University (LL.B., Hons.). *PRACTICE AREAS:* Property Development, Investment and Construction.

GEOFFREY WALTERS, born 1951; admitted, 1975. *Education:* Leicester (LL.B.). *PRACTICE AREAS:* Corporate Finance; Mergers and Acquisitions; Venture Capital.

PAUL HARDING, born 1955; admitted, 1981. *Education:* London School of Economics (LL.B.). *PRACTICE AREAS:* Corporate Finance; Mergers and Acquisitions; Venture Capital.

REG MORTON, born 1951; admitted, 1975. *Education:* Birmingham University (LL.B.). *PRACTICE AREAS:* Financial Services; Insurance.

ANDREW HEARN, born 1957; admitted, 1982. *Education:* St. John's College, Oxon (B.A.). *PRACTICE AREAS:* Commercial Litigation; Intellectual Property; Defamation.

TAMSIN EASTWOOD, born 1960; admitted, 1984. *Education:* Guildford Law School. *PRACTICE AREAS:* Corporate Finance; Mergers and Acquisitions; Venture Capital.

DAVID WELLS, born 1950; admitted, 1976. *Education:* Queen Mary College, London (LL.B.). *PRACTICE AREAS:* Commercial Property; Banking; Insolvency.

GEORGINA KEANE, born 1954; admitted, 1988. *Education:* Inns of Court Law School; Bar examinations (Hons) 1975. *PRACTICE AREAS:* Employment Law; Share Incentives; Employee Benefits.

CAROL HOLMES, born 1947; admitted, 1971. *Education:* Nottingham University (LL.B.). *PRACTICE AREAS:* Commercial Property; Landlord and Tenant.

PATRICK GLOYENS, born 1953; admitted, 1977. *Education:* Bristol University (LL.B., 1974). *PRACTICE AREAS:* Commercial Property; Development; Landlord and Tenant.

WILLIAM FRYZER, born 1957; admitted, 1983. *Education:* Exeter University (LL.B.). *PRACTICE AREAS:* Commercial Property.

PETER CROCKFORD, born 1953; admitted, 1978. *Education:* King's College, London (LL.B., Hons). *PRACTICE AREAS:* Commercial Agreements; Competition Law; Intellectual Property.

IAN MARSH, born 1953; admitted, 1978. *Education:* Associate of the Institute of Taxation. *PRACTICE AREAS:* Tax.

GILLIAN BAXTER, born 1958; admitted, 1982. *Education:* King's College, London (LL.B., Hons). *PRACTICE AREAS:* Commercial Property; Development Investment and Financing.

ALAN KERFOOT, born 1959; admitted, 1983. *Education:* Kent University (B.A., Hons., LL.M.). *PRACTICE AREAS:* Employment; Financial Crime; Litigation.

(This Listing Continued)

DAVID FAIRFIELD, born 1957; admitted, 1984. *Education:* Kings College (LL.B.; A.K.C.). *PRACTICE AREAS:* Corporate Finance; Mergers and Acquisitions; Venture Capital.

KEITH CONWAY, born 1960; admitted, 1984. *Education:* City of London Polytechnic (LL.B.). *PRACTICE AREAS:* Banking; Insolvency Litigation.

CIARAN CARVALHO, born 1961; admitted, 1986. *Education:* Kent University (B.A., with Hons.). *PRACTICE AREAS:* Commercial Property; Landlord and Tenant.

ANDREW HUTCHINSON, born 1969; admitted, 1986. *Education:* Nottingham University (B.A., Law). *PRACTICE AREAS:* Commercial Property; Development; Investment and Property Finance.

KATHRYN SKOYLES, born 1958; admitted, 1988. *Education:* London School of Economics (LL.B., 1st class Hons.; LL.M., with distinction); Monash University (Ph.D.). *PRACTICE AREAS:* Insider Trading; DTI and SFO Investigations; Disciplinary Proceedings; Lloyd's related matters.

SALLY UNWIN, born 1952; admitted, 1977. *Education:* Manchester University (LL.B.). *PRACTICE AREAS:* Commercial Litigation; Insolvency.

JEREMY DUTTON, born 1961; admitted, 1986. *Education:* Leicester University (LL.B.). *PRACTICE AREAS:* Commercial Litigation.

BERNARD CAULFIELD, born 1954; admitted, 1981. *Education:* University of Hull (B.Sc., Econ.). *PRACTICE AREAS:* Litigation; Commercial; Insurance.

DUNCAN BLACK, born 1962; admitted, 1987. *Education:* Lincoln College, Oxford (B.A., Hons.). *PRACTICE AREAS:* Commercial Litigation; Intellectual Property; Defamation.

EVELYN SMITH, born 1958; admitted, 1987. *Education:* University College of Wales, Aberystwyth (LL.B., Hons.). *PRACTICE AREAS:* Commercial and Property Litigation.

MARTIN EDWARDS, born 1957; admitted, 1981. *Education:* University of Kent (B.A., Hons.). *PRACTICE AREAS:* Planning and Environmental Law.

PAUL GARDNER, born 1963; admitted, 1987. *Education:* Nottingham University (LL.B.). *PRACTICE AREAS:* Information Technology; Multi-Media; Entertainment Software.

ANDREW HOLDERNESS, born 1962; admitted, 1987. *Education:* Exeter University (LL.B.). *PRACTICE AREAS:* Lloyd's of London; Financial Services.

JAMES LEWIS, born 1963; admitted, 1987. *Education:* Manchester University (LL.B.). *PRACTICE AREAS:* Corporate Finance; Mergers and Acquisitions; Venture Capital.

KATE O'ROURKE, born 1959; admitted, 1991. *Education:* University of New South Wales (B.A.; LL.B.). Member of Institute of Trademark Agents. *PRACTICE AREAS:* Trademarks.

OTHER SPECIALISTS

*ROWAN BOSWORTH-DAVIES. PRACTICE AREAS: Financial Crime.

BARBARA COOKSON. PRACTICE AREAS: Patents and Designs.

MALACHY CORNWELL-KELLY. PRACTICE AREAS: Customs and Excise; EC Agriculture.

*JENNY LEWIS. PRACTICE AREAS: Pensions.

*GAVIN MCFARLANE. PRACTICE AREAS: Customs and Excise; VAT.

*Specialists not admitted as solicitors.

Languages: French, German, Italian, Spanish and Hebrew, Icelandic.

B.C. TOMS & CO.
64 LONDON WALL
LONDON EC2M 5TP, ENGLAND
Telephone: (44) (171) 638-7711
Fax: (44) (171) 382-9360

Kiev, Ukraine Office: 18 Proreznaya Street, Apts 1/2, 252034. Telephone: (7044) 228-1000, 225-2032. Fax: (7044) 228-6508.

(This Listing Continued)

Odessa, Ukraine Office: Ulitsa Kirova 47, Apt. 5, 270014. Telephone: (7) 0482-218 704. Fax: (7) 0482 259 265.

Paris, France Office: 44, Avenue d'Iena, 75116. Telephone: (33) (1) 47234724. Fax: (33) (1) 47239053.

Associated Offices: Minsk, Belarus; Milan, Italy; Moscow, Russia.

Acquisitions and Investments, Property, Construction and Project Finance, Ukrainian, Belorussian, Russian, Italian and French Law, Corporate, Banking, Securities, Privatisation, Arbitration, Litigation, Agency, Distribution, Licensing, Insolvency, EU and Intellectual Property Law.

BATE C. TOMS, III, born Virginia, U.S.A., 1949; admitted, 1975, Virginia; 1977, District of Columbia; 1982, France (as avocat) (Not admitted in England). *Education:* Institut d'Etudes Politiques de Paris-Soviet Studies (1969-1970); Washington and Lee University (B.A., magna cum laude, 1971); Cambridge University, Magdalene College (Law, 1972-1973); Yale Law School (J.D., 1975). Phi Beta Kappa. Editor: Yale Law Journal, 1975-1976; Journal of International Banking Law, 1986—; Oil and Gas Law and Taxation Review, 1984—. Author: "Ukrainian Real Estate Law," Butterworths' Central and East European Business Law J., March 1994. BOT and Non-Recourse Projects-Proceedings of the Second Int"l. Construction Projects Conference, 1989; "Privatisation in Ukraine," Euromoney IFLR, September 1992; "Ukrainian Oil and Gas Licensing," 13(2) Oil and Gas Law and Tax Rev., 1995; "Ukrainian Law," Interforum Books-1992-in Press, with Dr. F. Burchak, Legal Advisor to Ukrainian Pres.; "Ukrainian Law on Banking," J. of Int'l. Banking Law, June 1992; "Ukrainian Special Economic Zone: CCH Doing Business in Europe 1992—, Ukrainian Tax Law," November 1992— Interforum Conference on Doing Business in Ukraine; "Offshore Share Offerings," 1 J. Int'l Banking L. 36, 1986; "French Response to the Extraterritorial Application of U.S. Laws," 15 Int'l Law 585, 1982; "Compensating Shareholders in Two-Step Mergers," 78 Column L. Rev. 549, 1978; Practical Legal Considerations for Investing in Italy (1991 Fibex/Coopers & Lybrand Doing Business In Italy); "Belarussian Intellectual Property," Intel Prop News, November 1994, with N. Kandrusora. *Member:* District of Columbia Bar; Virginia State Bar; American and International Bar Associations.

COUNSEL

PETER FULLERTON, born UK, 1943; admitted, 1978, California. *Education:* Gonville & Caius College, Cambridge University (Tapp Major Scholar; 1st class honours; B.A., 1964; M.A., 1968) Yale University (Henry Fellow; M.A., 1968); Stanford Law School (J.D., 1978). Member, Board of Editors, Stanford Law Review. President Cambridge Union Society, 1965; Member, Gray's Inn.

LOUIS ELY O'CARROLL, born England, 1954; admitted, 1977, Solicitor, England. *Education:* Leeds University (B.A., Hons. Russian Studies, 1976); Kiev State Law School (LL.M., 1975), College of Law, (1976-1977).

VLADIMIR N. PETRINA, born Ukraine, 1956; admitted, 1990, Ukraine (Not admitted in England). *Education:* Kiev State University Law School (LL.B., 1982). Director of Kiev Centre for Legal Studies (Soros Foundation); Assoc. Professor of Law, Kiev State University. Member Advisory Council, Ukraine Institute of Bankers; Legal Counsel GradoBank, 1993-1994.

ASSOCIATES

LEIGH ANNA REICHENBACH, born Florida, USA, 1968; admitted, 1992, California (Not admitted in England). *Education:* Yale University (B.A. cum laude, 1989); Northwestern University School of Law (J.D. cum laude, 1992); London School of Economics (LL.M., 1994). Recipient, Charles Cheney Hyde Prize). *Member:* California Bar Association.

RONALD D.A. SALLOWS, born England, 1966; admitted, 1994, Solicitor, England. *Education:* University of London (B.Sc, Hons., 1988); London Guildhall University Law School (C.P.E., 1991).

DMITRIY A. SERDYUK, born Ukraine, 1973; admitted, 1995, Ukraine (Not admitted in England). *Education:* Kiev State University Law School (LL.B., 1995).

Languages: English, Russian, Ukrainian, Italian, French and German.

(For Additional Biographical Entries, see Kiev, Ukraine)

TORY TORY DesLAURIERS & BINNINGTON

Canadian Barristers and Solicitors

44/45 CHANCERY LANE

LONDON WC2A 1JB, ENGLAND

Telephone: 0171-831 8155

Facsimile: 0171-831 1812

Toronto, Ontario Office: Suite 3000, Aetna Tower, Toronto-Dominion Centre, P.O. Box 270, Toronto, Canada M5K 1N2. Telephone: 416-865-0040. Facsimile: 416-865-7380.

Hong Kong Office: Suite 1705, One Exchange Square, 8 Connaught Place, Central, Hong Kong. Telephone: (852) 868-3099. Facsimile: (852) 523-8140.

Affiliated with:

Desjardins Ducharme Stein Monast:

Montreal, Quebec Office: Bureau 2400, 600 rue de la Gauchetière West, H3B 4L8. Telephone: (514) 878-9411. Facsimile: (514) 878-9092.

Quebec City, Quebec Office: 1150, rue de Claire-Fontaine Bureau 300, G1R 5G4. Telephone: (418) 529-6531. Facsimile: (418) 523-5391.

Lawson Lundell Lawson & McIntosh:

Vancouver, British Columbia Office: 1600 Cathedral Place, 925 West Georgia Street, V6C 3L2. Telephone: (604) 685-3456. Facsimile: (604) 669-1620.

Yellowknife, Northwest Territories Office: Suite 204, 4817 - 49th Street, X1A 3S7. Telephone: (403) 669-9990. Facsimile: (403) 669-9991.

General Practice. Administrative, Aircraft Finance, Banking, Bankruptcy, Insolvency and Receivership, Competition, Commercial, Corporate, Corporate Finance, Computer and Technology, Criminal, Employment, Environmental, Estates, Euromarket, Foreign Investment, International, Labour, Litigation, Mergers and Acquisitions, Municipal, Negligence, Oil and Gas, Property Development and Financing, Real Property, Securities, Taxation.

RESIDENT IN LONDON

KATHLEEN L. KELLER-HOBSON, born Toronto, Ontario, August 8, 1956; admitted, 1981, Ontario. *Education:* University of Ottawa (LL.B., 1979). **PRACTICE AREAS:** Securities; General Corporate.

TRAVERS SMITH BRAITHWAITE

10 SNOW HILL

LONDON EC1A 2AL, ENGLAND

Telephone: 0171-248 9133; 0171-696 0998

Telex: 887117 TRAVER G

Facsimile: 0171-236 3728; 0171-696 9747

Douglas, Isle of Man Office: 4 Upper Church Street. Telephone: 0624 625515. Facsimile: 0624 624625.

FIRM PROFILE: The principal activity of Travers Smith Braithwaite is advising both UK and overseas based corporate clients in relation to a wide range of business requirements and transactions. Principal areas of work include company, corporate finance, mergers and acquisitions, takeovers, financial services, capital markets, venture capital, commercial, intellectual property, employment, pensions, energy, EC and competition, environment, finance, banking regulations, corporate insolvency and asset recovery, litigation, domestic and international arbitrations, commercial property, planning, construction and corporate tax.

A.C. HUMPHRIES O.B.E., Senior Partner. **PRACTICE AREAS:** Property.

A.M. KEAT. PRACTICE AREAS: Company.

C.C. BELL. PRACTICE AREAS: Company.

R.L. HARMAN Managing Partner. **PRACTICE AREAS:** Property.

M.P. COMBES. PRACTICE AREAS: Company.

J.W. KINGSTON. PRACTICE AREAS: Litigation.

O.W.A. BARNES. PRACTICE AREAS: Company.

W.N. CAMPION-SMITH. PRACTICE AREAS: Company.

J.C. LONGDON. PRACTICE AREAS: Company.

J. LESLIE. PRACTICE AREAS: Litigation.

F.J. PYM. PRACTICE AREAS: Company.

(This Listing Continued)

A.J. BARROW. PRACTICE AREAS: Property.

R.M.B. HOLMES. PRACTICE AREAS: Property.

A.F. DOUGLAS. PRACTICE AREAS: Tax.

C.J. CARROLL. PRACTICE AREAS: Company.

N.A.C. MURRAY. PRACTICE AREAS: Finance.

D.Y. ADAMS. PRACTICE AREAS: Company.

C.G. HALE. PRACTICE AREAS: Company.

G.A.O. WEDLAKE. PRACTICE AREAS: Finance.

J.L. BASS. PRACTICE AREAS: Finance.

D.I. STRANG. PRACTICE AREAS: Company.

P.D. HILL. PRACTICE AREAS: Company.

P.A.C. STANNARD. PRACTICE AREAS: Pensions.

N.D. MOORE. PRACTICE AREAS: Company.

R.J. STRATTON. PRACTICE AREAS: Tax.

P.M. HILL. PRACTICE AREAS: Property.

N.H.J. RAINEY. PRACTICE AREAS: Property.

S.J. PAGET-BROWN. PRACTICE AREAS: Litigation.

M.A. MOORE. PRACTICE AREAS: Company.

S. JAY. PRACTICE AREAS: Company.

M.J. PINSON. PRACTICE AREAS: Company.

M. CHAMBERLAIN. PRACTICE AREAS: Company.

S. BUCKINGHAM. PRACTICE AREAS: Finance.

D.M. HENDERSON. PRACTICE AREAS: Employment.

J.M.R. PINDER. PRACTICE AREAS: Company.

M.R. BARDELL. PRACTICE AREAS: Finance.

N.P.B. ALEKSANDER. PRACTICE AREAS: Tax.

W.S. PEARSON. PRACTICE AREAS: Insolvency.

J.M. WALSH. PRACTICE AREAS: Insolvency.

S.J. SMITH. PRACTICE AREAS: Pensions.

A.J. GRAHAM. PRACTICE AREAS: Litigation.

CONSULTANT

R.B.M. Quayle

TROWERS & HAMLINS

Established in 1784

6 NEW SQUARE, LINCOLN'S INN

LONDON WC2A 3RP, ENGLAND

Telephone: 0171 831 6292

Facsimile: 0171 831 8700

Telex: 21422

Manchester, England Office: Heron House, Albert Square, M2 5HD. Telephone: 061 833 9293. Facsimile: 061 834 5950. Telex: 667977.

Exeter, England Office: 8 Southernhay West, EX1 1JG. Telephone: 0392 221047. Facsimile: 0392 221047. Telex: 42766.

Ruwi, Muscat, Sultanate of Oman Office: B.B.M.E., Building, Muttrah Business District, P.O. Box 2991, Postcode 112. Telephone: 968 701 760. Facsimile: 968 794 685. Telex: 3061.

Dubai, United Arab Emirates Office: Rais Hassan Saadi Building, Mankhool Road, P.O. Box 23092. Telephone: 519201. Facsimile: 519205. Telex: 46598.

Abu Dhabi, United Arab Emirates Office: 6th Floor, Suite 1011, Al Aweidha Building, Liwa Street, P.O. Box 45628. Telephone: 9712 345411. Facsimile: 9712 393123. Telex: 46598.

Singapore Associated Office: Ann Tan & Associates. 14 Robinson Road, 09/02 Far East Finance Building, 0104. Telephone: 65 225 5822. Facsimile: 65 224 1515.

Company: General Commercial Law, Mergers and Acquisitions, Banking, Construction, Corporate Finance, Corporate Tax, EC Law, Joint Ventures. Property: Commercial Property, Local Authorities, Housing, Planning and Public Sector, Estates, Residential, Environment.

(This Listing Continued)

Litigation: Commercial, Construction, Administrative, Employment, Family, Insolvency, Intellectual Property, Personal Injury and Medical Negligence, Property.
Private Client: Tax, Trust and Trust Administration, Probate, Wills, Charities.

PARTNERS

D.W. JONES, born May 26, 1938; admitted, 1961. (Senior Partner). **PRACTICE AREAS:** General Commercial; International; Mergers and Acquisitions.

A.G.S. BARSTOW, born February 5, 1936; admitted, 1965. (Resident Partner, Abu Dhabi, United Arab Emirates Office). **PRACTICE AREAS:** Middle East.

J.W.S. CLARK, born November 1, 1943; admitted, 1966. **PRACTICE AREAS:** Housing; Voluntary Transfer of Housing Stock.

D.W.C. MORRISON, born January 26, 1935; admitted, 1961. **PRACTICE AREAS:** Private Client; Probate.

J.T.W. MARTIN, born March 27, 1943; admitted, 1967. **PRACTICE AREAS:** Commercial; Domicile and Residence; Transactions Involving Yachts and Racing Cars.

D.J. WHITE, born January 26, 1943; admitted, 1967. **PRACTICE AREAS:** Housing Associations; Local Authorities.

M.G. WILLIAMSON, born November 1, 1942; admitted, 1967. (Head of Private Client Service). **PRACTICE AREAS:** Probate and Heritage Property.

J.P.N. ADLINGTON, born April 26, 1949; admitted, 1973. (Head of Property Service). **PRACTICE AREAS:** Housing; Housing Finance; Commercial Property.

G.F. TURNER, born January 28, 1947; admitted, 1979. (Head of Manchester Office). **PRACTICE AREAS:** Housing.

N.H. HILLS, born December 9, 1947; admitted, 1979. (Resident Partner, Dubai, United Arab Emirates Office). **PRACTICE AREAS:** Middle East; International Project Financing; Joint Ventures.

D.G. MARSHALL, born March 29, 1943; admitted, 1979. **PRACTICE AREAS:** Commercial and Residential Conveyancing.

D.L. MOORHOUSE, born November 21, 1950; admitted, 1976. (Managing Partner). **PRACTICE AREAS:** Litigation; Construction.

R.T. KING, born December 24, 1952; admitted, 1977. **PRACTICE AREAS:** Commercial and Construction Litigation.

L.H. VALNER, born December 10, 1951; admitted, 1977. **PRACTICE AREAS:** Private Client; Trust and Tax.

P.H. KEULS, born May 24, 1952; admitted, 1977. (Head of Exeter Office). **PRACTICE AREAS:** Housing Associations.

A.F. BODE, born March 28, 1954; admitted, 1978. (Manchester Office). **PRACTICE AREAS:** Housing.

D. MOSEY, born October 28, 1954; admitted, 1980. (Head of Oman Office). **PRACTICE AREAS:** Commercial; Construction; Banking; New Ventures; Middle East.

R.A. PICKEN, born May 23, 1955; admitted, 1980. **PRACTICE AREAS:** Commercial; Banking; Housing Finance; Loan and Security Documentation.

J.D. DOLLIMORE (MISS), born March 26, 1948; admitted, 1972. **PRACTICE AREAS:** Probate; Charities.

A. TAN (MRS), born September 6, 1940; admitted, 1983. (Partner in Associated Office, Singapore). **PRACTICE AREAS:** General Commercial and Litigation; Conveyancing; Matrimonial; Probate.

J.H.A. MCHUGO, born July 13, 1951; admitted, 1982. **LANGUAGES:** French; German; Arabic. **PRACTICE AREAS:** International Boundary Disputes; Europe, Middle East, General Commercial.

J.W. LINWOOD, born July 8, 1956; admitted, 1980. (Head of Litigation Service). **PRACTICE AREAS:** General Litigation; Injunctions; Discovery.

J.M. GUBBINS (MRS), born January 18, 1958; admitted, 1982. **PRACTICE AREAS:** Housing Finance; General Commercial.

E. MCKIBBIN (MRS), born November 26, 1958; admitted, 1985. **PRACTICE AREAS:** Commercial Property.

(This Listing Continued)

J.A. WINROW (MRS), born May 13, 1958; admitted, 1982. (Manchester Office). **PRACTICE AREAS:** Housing; Property.

N.W. WHITE, born July 7, 1958; admitted, 1983. **PRACTICE AREAS:** Middle East; Commercial Litigation.

J. JOINER, born June 9, 1955; admitted, 1980. **PRACTICE AREAS:** Commercial Property.

M.R. AMISON, born September 4, 1958; admitted, 1983. **PRACTICE AREAS:** Middle East; Commercial; Construction.

R.D. HART (MRS), born April 5, 1954; admitted, 1978. **PRACTICE AREAS:** Housing; Shared Ownership; Secured Lending.

P.C. WARD, born November 8, 1955; admitted, 1982. **PRACTICE AREAS:** Commercial Conveyancing; Landlord and Tenant; Commercial Leases.

D. BIGGERSTAFF, born January 2, 1957; admitted, 1983. **PRACTICE AREAS:** Commercial and Property Litigation.

N. COHEN, born August 26, 1958; admitted, 1983. **PRACTICE AREAS:** Commercial and Private Client Tax.

I.D. GRAHAM, born July 22, 1960; admitted, 1986. **PRACTICE AREAS:** Housing.

N.C. EDMONDES, born March 31, 1962; admitted, 1986. (Resident Partner, The Sultanate of Oman). **PRACTICE AREAS:** Middle East; Commercial Finding; Insolvency; Commercial Property.

A.S. HASHEMI, born March 23, 1959; admitted, 1987. **PRACTICE AREAS:** Company and Commercial; Intellectual Property.

R.D. SIMPSON, born August 23, 1962; admitted, 1987. **PRACTICE AREAS:** Company and Commercial; Asset Acquisitions and Finance.

S.E. HAYES (MISS), born January 21, 1963; admitted, 1988. **PRACTICE AREAS:** Housing; Private Finance.

G.D. HALSALL, born October 3, 1962; admitted, 1988. (Manchester Office). **PRACTICE AREAS:** Housing; Property.

I.G. DOOLITTLE, born September 6, 1951; admitted, 1987. **PRACTICE AREAS:** Public Sector; Environmental.

A.J. CARTER, born September 5, 1963; admitted, 1989. **PRACTICE AREAS:** Housing Finance; General Commercial.

CONSULTANTS

A.G. TROWER, born July 12, 1921; admitted, 1950.

A.J. BATESON, born November 23, 1925; admitted, 1950.

T.R. LAYTON, born March 28, 1923; admitted, 1955.

P.H. MAITLAND, born November 17, 1929; admitted, 1952.

J.E. ROBINS, born November 8, 1926; admitted, 1953.

R.P. ROBINSON, born May 26, 1938; admitted, 1957.

E.A. PAYNE, born June 8, 1926; admitted, 1953.

TURNER KENNETH BROWN

100, FETTER LANE
LONDON EC4A 1DD, ENGLAND
Telephone: 0171-242 6006 (National)
+ 44 171 242 6006 (International)
Telex: 297696 TKBLAW G
Fax: Group 2 & 3 0171-242 3003

Reading, England Office: Abbot's House, Abbey Street, RG1 3BD.
Telephone: 0734-504700. Fax: 0734 505640.
Brussels, Belgium Office: 19 avenue des Arts, 1040. Telephone: 010 322 218 2188; 010 322 218 3322. Fax: 010 322 217 4895.

Company/Commercial, Litigation, Property, Dispute Resolution, Computers and Communications, Intellectual Property and Information Technology, Construction, Banking, Charities, Employment, Pensions, EC and Competition, Trusts and Estates, Wills, Probate, Tax.

MEMBERS OF FIRM

DAVID R. WIGHTMAN, SENIOR PARTNER, admitted, 1962. **PRACTICE AREAS:** Commercial Law; Corporate Law; Corporate Finance Law; Building and Construction.

(This Listing Continued)

TURNER KENNETH BROWN, London—Continued

PETER R. DAVIES, admitted, 1962. *PRACTICE AREAS:* Individual Tax Planning; Estate Planning.

JOHN B. WATKISS, admitted, 1961. *PRACTICE AREAS:* Commercial Property Law; Landlord and Tenant Law; Property Development.

ROSEMARY MARTIN-JONES, MANAGING PARTNER, READING, admitted, 1967. *PRACTICE AREAS:* Commercial Law; Corporate Law; Information Technology; High Technology.

DAVID P. O'CALLAGHAN, admitted, 1965. *PRACTICE AREAS:* Commercial Litigation; Libel and Slander; Professional Malpractice.

DOMINICK COSGROVE, admitted, 1968. *PRACTICE AREAS:* Commercial Property Law; Property Development.

ROBERT H. JACKSON, admitted, 1969. *PRACTICE AREAS:* Commercial Law; Corporate Law; European Community.

DAVID J. WRIGHT, admitted, 1971. *PRACTICE AREAS:* Commercial Property Law; Property Development.

IAN G. LEWIS, admitted, 1972. *PRACTICE AREAS:* Pensions; Charities; Individual Tax Planning; Tax Shelters.

NIGEL D. WILDISH, admitted, 1972. *PRACTICE AREAS:* Information Technology; Alternative Dispute Resolution; Computer Law.

MICHAEL J.B. VANN, admitted, 1971. *PRACTICE AREAS:* Property Finance; Project Finance; Banking Law.

JAMES F. EDMONDSON, MANAGING PARTNER, admitted, 1972. *PRACTICE AREAS:* Individual Tax Planning; Tax Shelters Law.

RICHARD A. BUTTLE, admitted, 1973. *PRACTICE AREAS:* Commercial Litigation; Insurance Law.

ANTHONY G. BAILES, admitted, 1975. *PRACTICE AREAS:* Intellectual Property; Data Protection; Information Technology; Alternative Dispute Resolution.

GEOFFREY R. PRESTON, admitted, 1975. *PRACTICE AREAS:* Pensions; Commercial Law.

RHIDIAN H.B. JONES, admitted, 1978. *PRACTICE AREAS:* Corporate Law; Leveraged and Management Buyout; Corporate Finance; Corporate Restructuring; Venture Capital.

JONATHAN R. BURCHFIELD, admitted, 1978. *PRACTICE AREAS:* Estate Planning; Individual Tax Planning; Tax Shelters Law; Charitable Trusts and Foundations.

ANDREW P. INKESTER, admitted, 1980. *PRACTICE AREAS:* Commercial Law; Corporate Law; Venture Capital; Leveraged and Management Buyouts; Building and Construction.

ADRIAN C. HALL, admitted, 1971. *PRACTICE AREAS:* Banking Law; Project Finance; International Banking.

NICHOLAS I. SHEPHERD, admitted, 1974. *PRACTICE AREAS:* Commercial Property; Property Development; Landlord and Tenant; Health and Hospital Law; VAT.

SARAH E. STOWELL, admitted, 1978. *PRACTICE AREAS:* Wills; Individual Tax Planning; Trust Law; Probate Law.

REEF T. HOGG, admitted, 1980. *PRACTICE AREAS:* Corporate Law; Mergers and Acquisitions; Securities Offerings; Corporate Finance Law.

PETER KAY, admitted, 1975. *PRACTICE AREAS:* Commercial Property Law; Property Development; Landlord and Tenant Law.

ANTHONY E. WALES, admitted, 1981. *PRACTICE AREAS:* Corporate Law; Venture Capital; International Practice; Asian/Pacific, Central and Eastern Europe.

EILEEN P. CARROLL, admitted, 1981. *PRACTICE AREAS:* Commercial Litigation; Lloyd's Litigation; Alternative Dispute Resolution; Insurance Law.

GERLANDO BUTERA, admitted, 1982. *PRACTICE AREAS:* Commercial Litigation; Building and Construction.

TIMOTHY C. CORNICK, admitted, 1982. *PRACTICE AREAS:* Unit Trusts; Securities Law; Financial Institutions Law.

JONATHAN M. HOGGETT, admitted, 1978. *PRACTICE AREAS:* Commercial Property; Property Development; Environmental Law.

(This Listing Continued)

KAREN E. FRIEBE, admitted, 1983. *PRACTICE AREAS:* Commercial Property.

RICHARD M. HARRISON, admitted, 1983. *PRACTICE AREAS:* Commercial Litigation; Directors and Officers Liabilities; Insolvency.

SIMON A. STAITE, admitted, 1983. *PRACTICE AREAS:* Commercial Property Law; Building and Construction.

GILES C. DIXON, admitted, 1968. *PRACTICE AREAS:* Engineering and Construction; Energy Projects and Infrastructure; Middle East.

NICHOLAS A.P. CHESHIRE, admitted, 1981. *PRACTICE AREAS:* Planning Law; Environmental Law; Commercial Property.

MICHAEL J. CANT, admitted, 1984. *PRACTICE AREAS:* Corporate Tax; Stamp Duties and VAT.

LYNDA A. FARMER, admitted, 1984. *PRACTICE AREAS:* Intellectual Property Law; Computer Law; Information Technology; Alternative Dispute Resolution.

VALMAI ADAMS, admitted, 1985. *PRACTICE AREAS:* Employment Law; Immigration Law; Share Option Schemes.

RICHARD C. HIERONS, admitted, 1983. *PRACTICE AREAS:* Corporate Law; Mergers and Acquisitions; Securities Offerings; Corporate Finance Law.

ROBERT S.K. BELL, admitted, 1989; called to Bar, 1982. *PRACTICE AREAS:* Competition Law; Antitrust Law; Unfair Competition Law; European Community Law.

CAROLINE A. KIRBY, admitted, 1977. *PRACTICE AREAS:* Estate Planning; Tax Shelters Law; Charitable Trusts and Foundations.

PETER A. SMITH, admitted, 1986. *PRACTICE AREAS:* Building and Construction; Arbitration Law.

ANDREW BOND, admitted, 1978. *PRACTICE AREAS:* Commercial Property; Planning Law.

Languages: French, German, Spanish, Swedish, Greek, Polish, Cantonese and Mandarin.

URÍA & MENÉNDEZ

Established in 1941

ROYEX HOUSE, ALDERMANBURY SQUARE
LONDON EC2V 7HR, ENGLAND
Telephone: (44) 171 600 36 10
Fax: (44) 171 600 17 18

Madrid, Spain Office: Hermosilla, 30, 28001. Telephone: 586.04.00. Telex: 48141 URME E. Fax: 586.04.04/03.
Barcelona, Spain Office: Diagonal, 514, 08036. Telephone: 415.50.05. Fax: 415.90.61.
Brussels, Belgium Office: Rue Bréderode, 13A, B-1000. Telephone: 505.02.11. Fax: 502.26.44.
New York, New York Office: 712 Fifth Avenue, 30th Floor, 10019. Telephone: 801-3460. Fax: 801-3465.
Prague, Czech Republic Office: Blanická, 28, CZ 120 00 Prague 2. Telephone: 20.70.50. Fax: 25.42.23.

General Practice in Spanish and EEC Law.

FIRM PROFILE: *Member of Alliance of European Lawyers (EEIG) which regroups six law firms from Continental Europe. The Alliance consists of De Bandt, van Hecke & Lagae at Brussels and Antwerp; De Brauw Blackstone Westbroek at The Hague, Amsterdam, Rotterdam and Eindhoven; Jeantet & Associés at Paris and Warsaw; Lagerlöf & Leman at Stockholm, Gothenburg and Malmö; Oppenhoff & Rädler at Berlin, Cologne, Frankfurt am Main, Leipzig and Münich; Uria & Menendez at Madrid and Barcelona.*

RESIDENT LAWYERS

JORGE MARTI MORENO, born 1962; admitted, 1986, Valencia; 1990, Madrid (Not admitted in England). *Education:* College of Europe, Bruges (Degree in EEC Law). Lecturer at Law Department, College of Europe, Bruges, 1986-1988. *LANGUAGES:* English and French.

TERESA PAZ-ARES, born 1969; admitted, 1991. (Not admitted in England). *LANGUAGES:* English.

(See Professional Biographies, Madrid and Barcelona, Spain)

VALLARINO, VALLARINO & RIVERA

20-21 TOOK'S COURT
LONDON EC4A 1LB, ENGLAND
Telephone: 0171-486-5324
Fax: 0171-480-7327

Panama, Republic of Panama Office: Via Espana No. 200, P.O. Box 6188. Telephone: 69-3100. Fax: 648458; 63-3098.

Formation of Panama Companies, Searches, Legal Opinions, Ship Registration.

PARTNERS

JUAN RAMÓN VALLARINO-LÓPEZ, born Washington D.C., U.S.A., March 3, 1942; admitted, 1964, Republic of Panamá. *Education:* University of Panamá Law School (LL.B., Sigma Lambda Honour Chapter, 1964); Tulane University (LL.M., 1965). Legal Counsellor, Ministry of Planning and Economic Policy, 1969-1978; President Rotary Club-Panamá Sur, 1989-1990. *Member:* Panamanian Bar Association; Maritime Bar Association. (Senior Partner). *LANGUAGES:* Spanish and English. *PRACTICE AREAS:* Commercial Law; Corporate Law; Banking Law; Financial; Tourism Investment.

FERNANDO VALLARINO, born Republic of Panamá, Panamá August 9, 1943; admitted, 1967, Republic of Panamá. *Education:* University of Panamá Law School (LL.B., 1967); University of Edinburgh (Postgraduate; Diploma in Criminology, 1970); Universidad Complutense, Madrid (Diploma Superior, 1973). Lecturer in Criminology, Faculty of Law, Universidad de Panamá, 1970-1972; Lecturer-Chair in Criminology, Universidad Santa María La Antigua, Panamá, 1970-1972. Legal Counsellor, Embassy of Panamá in London, 1978-1980. Vice Consul, Consulate General of Panamá in London, 1978-1980. Member, Overseas Lawyer Counsellor in Panamanian Law, U.K. Law Society, 1985—. *Member:* Panamanian Bar Association (1967—.). *LANGUAGES:* Spanish and English. *PRACTICE AREAS:* Commercial law; Shipping.

ASSOCIATES

ROLANDO GARCÍA-MARITANO P., born Republic of Panamá, PanamáCity, Panamá June 1, 1967; admitted, 1992, Republic of Panamá. *Education:* University of PanamáLaw School (LL.B., 1991); SESA Institute (B.A., 1990). *Member:* Panamanian Bar Association; Maritime Law Association of Panamá. *LANGUAGES:* Spanish and English. *PRACTICE AREAS:* Maritime and Admiralty Law; Corporate Law; Taxation.

ALEXIS CARLES BARRAZA, born PanamáCity, Panamá, July 1, 1965; admitted, 1991, Republic of Panamá. *Education:* Universidad Santa María La Antigua (LL.B., 1990). *Member:* Panamanian Bar Association. *LANGUAGES:* Spanish and English. *PRACTICE AREAS:* Patents and Trademarks; Litigation; Corporate Law; Commercial Law; Administrative Law.

JUAN RAMÓN VALLARINO-JAYNES, born Panamá City, Panamá, January 23, 1971; admitted, 1994, Republic of Panamá. *Education:* Universidad Santa María La Antigua (LL.B., 1994). *Member:* Panamanian Bar Association. *LANGUAGES:* Spanish, English and French. *PRACTICE AREAS:* Commercial; Corporate; Tourism Investment; Oil & Gas.

VEIL ARMFELT JOURDE

4 CARLTON GARDENS, PALL MALL
LONDON SW1Y 5AA, ENGLAND
Telephone: 44. 0171 930 8644
Fax: 44. 0171 321 0670

Paris, France Office: 69, avenue Victor Hugo, 75116. Telephone: 33.1. 44.17.50.50. Fax: 33.1. 45.01.77.21.
Cairo, Egypt Office: 4 Gaber Ibn Hayan Street, Dokki. Telephone: 20. 2 349 2217/2498/8678. Fax: 20.2 349 3655.

International Construction Law and Arbitration, Joint Ventures, Project Financing and General Commercial Law.

PARTNER IN CHARGE

ANDREW P. ARMFELT, admitted, 1970, Solicitor, Supreme Court of England and Wales; 1986, Avocat à la Cour de Paris.

RESIDENT

DENNIS R. BRAND (Legal Executive).

(For complete biographical data on personnel and for Firm Profile, see Professional Biographies at Paris, France)

VINGE

(In Alliance with: Kromann & Münter, Denmark and Thommessen Krefting Greve Lund, Norway)

44/45 CHANCERY LANE
LONDON WC2A 1JB, ENGLAND
Telephone: +44-171-404 4825
Telex: 25585 VINGE G
Telefax: +44-171-831 6860

Stockholm, Sweden Office: Smålandsgatan 20, P.O. Box 1703, S-111 87. Telephone: 08-6143000. Telex: 11150 VINGE S. Telefax: 08-6119037.
Gothenburg, Sweden Office: Nils Ericsonsgatan 17, P.O. Box 11025, S-404 21. Telephone: 031-80 51 00. Telex: 21119 VINGE S. Telefax: 031-15 88 11.
Malmö Sweden Office: Östergatan 30, P.O. Box 4255, S-203 13. Telephone: 040-748 40. Telex: 8305122 VINGE S. Telefax: 040-97 27 72.
Helsingborg, Sweden Office: Rådhustorget 6, P.O. Box 1064, S-251 10. Telephone: +46-24 80 80. Telex: 8335079 VINGE S. Telefax: 46 42-24 8085.
Paris, France Office: 21, rue Jean Goujon, 75008. Telephone:33-1-40 75 3737. Fax: 33-1-45 63 0549.
Hong Kong Office: 2109 Hutchison House, 10 Harcourt Road, Central. Telephone: +852-5-236149. Telex: 62250 VINGE HX. Telefax: +852-5-8105343.
Brussels, Belgium Office: Avenue Louise 475/B12, B-1050. Telephone: National (2) 646 36 20; (2) 646 36 80. International +32 2 646 36 20; +32 2 646 36 80. Telefax: National (2) 646 41 46. International: +32 2 646 41 46.

Firm engaged in Swedish and International Law Practice, but not authorized to appear before the English Courts or to act as Solicitors.

FIRM PROFILE: The firm specialises in Swedish and International Commercial Law, Company Law, Mergers and Acquisitions, International Banking and International Commercial Arbitration.

RESIDENT PARTNERS

HANS BAGNER, born 1937; (Not admitted in England). *Education:* University of Stockholm (juris kandidat/LL.M., 1959); University of Michigan Law School (Master of Comparative Law, 1963). Practised with: Grönbergs Advokatyrå, Stockholm, 1959-1962; Squire, Sanders & Dempsey, Cleveland, Ohio, 1963. Member of this firm since 1964. Instructor in Law, University of Stockholm Law School, 1964-1968. Lecturer in International Trade Law, Louisiana State University Law School, Fall, 1966. Panel of Arbitrators, American Arbitration Association, 1972. Associate Member, Chartered Institute of Arbitrators, London. *Member:* Swedish (1965) and International Bar Associations. *LANGUAGES:* Swedish, English and German. *PRACTICE AREAS:* Mergers and Acquisitions; Company and Commercial Law; International Commercial Arbitration.

ASSOCIATES

MIKAEL STENSTRÖM, born 1961; admitted, 1991, New York (Not admitted in England). *Education:* Lingnan College, Hong Kong (Business Administration, 1983); University of Lund (juris kandidat/LL.M., 1989); Duke in Denmark, 1987; Harvard Law School (LL.M., 1990). Practised with: Pennie & Edmonds, New York, 1990-1991. *LANGUAGES:* Swedish and English. *PRACTICE AREAS:* International Business Law; Corporate/Commercial; Contracts; Cross-border Insolvency; International Commercial Arbitration.

DAN HANQVIST, born 1965; (Not admitted in England). *Education:* University of Stockholm (German, 1985); Universities of Gothenburg and Lund (juris kandidat/LL.M., 1992); University of Lund (filosofie kandidat/B.Sc., 1992); Edinburgh University (LL.M., Dissertation: Maritime Salvage, 1993)). Author: Acta Societatis Juridicae Lundensis No. 115, Lund 1993. *LANGUAGES:* Scandinavian languages, English and German. *PRACTICE AREAS:* Contracts; Law of Transport; Maritime and Shipping Law; Labor Law; European Union Law; International Commercial Arbitration.

KARIN WINLÖF, born 1968; (Not admitted in England). *Education:* University of Uppsala (juris Kandidat; LL.M., 1992); University of Exeter (LL.M., 1994). Practice with the EFTA Surveillance Authority, 1994.

(This Listing Continued)

VINGE, London—Continued

LANGUAGES: Swedish, English, French. *PRACTICE AREAS:* European Union Law; Corporate/Commercial; Competition Law; Intellectual Property.

VINSON & ELKINS

Registered Foreign Lawyers and Solicitors

47 CHARLES STREET, BERKELEY SQUARE
LONDON W1X 7PB, ENGLAND
Telephone: (44-171)491-7236
Fax: (44-171)499-5320

Moscow, Russian Federation Office: 16 Alexey Tolstoy Street, Second Floor, Moscow, 103001 Russian Federation. Telephone: (70-95) 956-1995. Telecopy: (70-95) 956-1996.

Mexico City, Mexico Office: Aristóteles 77, 5°Piso, Colonia Chapultepec Polanco, 11560 Mexico, D.F. Telephone: (52-5) 280-7828. Fax: (52-5) 280-9223.

Singapore Office: 50 Raffles Place, #19-05 Shell Tower, Singapore, 0104. U.S. Voice Mailbox: 713-758-3500. Telephone: (65) 536-8300. Fax: (65) 536-8311.

Houston, Texas Office: 1001 Fannin, Suite 2300, 77002-6760. Telephone: 713-758-2222. Fax: 713-758-2346. Cable Address: "Vinelkins". International Telex: 6868314.

Washington, D.C. Office: The Willard Office Building, 1455 Pennsylvania Avenue, N.W., 20004-1008. Telephone: 202-639-6500. Fax: 202-639-6604. Cable Adress: "Vinelkins".

Dallas, Texas Office: 3700 Trammell Crow Center, 2001 Ross Avenue, 75201-2975. Telephone: 214-220-7700. Fax: 214-220-7716.

Austin, Texas Office: One American Center, 600 Congress Avenue, 78701-3200. Telephone: 512-495-8400. Fax: 512-495-8612.

Firm engaged in American, English and International Law Practice, including Energy and Natural Resources, Project and Structured Finance, Mergers and Acquisitions and Corporate and Commercial.

RESIDENT PARTNERS

PAUL C. DEEMER, born Bowling Green, Kentucky, February 19, 1947; admitted to bar, 1976. Texas; (Not admitted in England). *Education:* Vanderbilt University (B.A., 1969; J.D., 1975); University of Madrid. Vanderbilt Law Review, 1973-1975 (Special Projects Editor, 1974-1975). Order of the Coif. *PRACTICE AREAS:* International Law; Energy and Natural Resources Law; Project and Structured Finance Law; Corporate and Commercial Law.

JOHN C. LAMASTER, born South Bend, Indiana, March 14, 1959; admitted, 1986, Texas; 1988, Louisiana (Not admitted in England). *Education:* Vanderbilt University (B.A., 1981); Louisiana State University (J.D., 1986). Louisiana Law Review, 1984-1986 (Associate Editor, 1985-1986). Order of the Coif; Phi Delta Phi; Phi Kappa Phi. *PRACTICE AREAS:* International Law; Energy and Natural Resources Law; Project and Structured Finance Law; Corporate and Commercial Law.

A. SAM MACGIBBON, born New Zealand, February 21, 1963; admitted, 1985, New Zealand; 1994, England and Wales. *Education:* University of Otago, Dunedin, New Zealand (LL.B., 1984). *PRACTICE AREAS:* International Law; Energy and Natural Resources Law; Project and Structured Finance Law; Corporate and COmmercial Law.

(Other Offices at Houston, Texas; Austin, Texas; Dallas, Texas; Washington, D.C.; Moscow, Russian Federation, Mexico City, Mexico, Singapore)

WALLACE & PARTNERS

9 GREAT JAMES STREET
LONDON WC1N 3DA, ENGLAND
Telephone: 0171 404 4422
Facsimile: 0171 831 6850

FIRM PROFILE: Wallace & Partners is a young, energetic practice which is primarily concerned with the legal needs of companies and businesses. The firm specialises in corporate, commercial litigation and real estate work, with wide experience in international transactions and disputes.

(This Listing Continued)

PARTNERS IN THE FIRM

SIMON SEROTA, LL.B., born July 2, 1952; admitted, 1977, England. *Education:* Manchester University. *PRACTICE AREAS:* Commercial Litigation; Arbitration; Landlord and Tenant Disputes.

ADRIAN WALLACE, LL.B., born December 11, 1957; admitted, 1981, England. *Education:* University College, London. *PRACTICE AREAS:* Real Estate; Planning; Residential and Commercial Developments; Leases.

REX NEWMAN, LL.B., born November 16, 1957; admitted, 1981, England; 1987, New York. *Education:* University College, London. *PRACTICE AREAS:* Company Law; Commercial Law; Corporate Finance; Mergers and Acquisitions; Joint Ventures; Commercial Agreements.

NICHOLAS YAPP, LL.B., born February 21, 1957; admitted, 1981, England. *Education:* Reading University. *PRACTICE AREAS:* Commercial Litigation; Employment; Intellectual Property.

BARRY SHAW, LL.B., born December 8, 1960; admitted, 1986, England. *Education:* Downing College, Cambridge. *PRACTICE AREAS:* Real Estate; Wills and Probate; Personal Tax Planning.

RICHARD PIKE, LL.B., born December 19, 1961; admitted, 1987, England. *Education:* Bristol University. *PRACTICE AREAS:* Company Law; Commercial Law; Corporate Finance; Mergers and Acquisitions; Joint Ventures; Commercial Agreements.

ASSISTANTS

ANDREW GAFSEN, LL.B., born April 3, 1965; admitted, 1990, England. *Education:* Birmingham University. *PRACTICE AREAS:* Commercial Litigation; Landlord and Tenant Disputes.

CLIVE HALPERIN, B. Pharm., born April 16, 1967; admitted, 1994, England. *Education:* King's College, London. *PRACTICE AREAS:* Company Law; Commercial Law; Corporate Finance.

MARTIN OTVOS, B.A., born February 8, 1968; admitted, 1994, England. *Education:* Manchester Polytechnic. *PRACTICE AREAS:* Real Estate; Wills and Probate.

Languages: French and Hebrew

WANSBROUGHS WILLEY HARGRAVE

DRURY HOUSE
RUSSELL STREET
LONDON WC2B 5HA, ENGLAND
Telephone: 0171 497 3262
Fax: 0171 497 1210

Other London, England Office: Suite 670, Lloyd's Building, One Lime Street, EC3M 7DQ. Telephone: 071 327 4447. Fax: 071 327 4448.

Bristol, England Office: 103 Temple Street, BS99 7UD. Telephone: 0272 268981. Fax: 0272 291582.

Leeds, England Office: 7 Park Square East, LS1 2LW. Telephone: 0113 244 1151. Fax: 0113 243 6050.

Birmingham, England Office: 37 Temple Street, B2 5DP. Telephone: 0121 631 4099. Fax: 0121 631 3781.

Winchester Office: Southgate House, Southgate Street, SO23 9EH. Telephone: 01962 841444. Fax: 01962 843133.

FIRM PROFILE: National 48 partner law firm specializing in insurance litigation, particularly general property and casualty, professional indemnity, environmental and product liability, arson and fraud. The firm also offers a range of services to commercial clients including corporate and commercial law, property, planning, litigation, employment, debt recovery, insolvency, computer, EU and construction law.

A founder member of Insurolaw, a pan-European Group of complementary insurance law firms.

INTERNATIONAL CONTACT PARTNERS

CHRISTOPHER BLYTHE, Manager of Insurolaw. (Resident, London Office). *PRACTICE AREAS:* Insurance; General Corporate; Commercial.

PAUL REDFERN (Resident, Lloyd's Office). *PRACTICE AREAS:* Professional Indemnity.

ANDREW ROACH (Resident, Birmingham Office). *PRACTICE AREAS:* General Insurance.

(This Listing Continued)

TONY BROWN (Resident, Bristol Office). *PRACTICE AREAS:* General Insurance.

ROOHI SHEIKH-COLLINS (Resident, Leeds Office). *PRACTICE AREAS:* Professional Indemnity.

WARNER CRANSTON

Established in 1979

PICKFORDS WHARF
CLINK STREET
LONDON SE1 9DG, ENGLAND
Telephone: 0171-403-2900
Fax: 0171-403-4221
Telex: 9312133051 (WN G) DX: 39904 London Bridge South

Coventry, England Office: 62/64 Moor Street, Earlsdon, CV5 6EU. Telephone: 01203-691996. Fax: 01203-691820.

Manchester, England Office: Hanover House, 30-32 Charlotte Street, M1 4FB. Telephone: 0161-236 0560. Fax: 0161-236 5057.

Corporate Finance, Banking, Mergers and Acquisitions, Construction, Insurance, Litigation and Arbitration, Insolvency, Taxation, Employment & Trade Unions, Work Permits, Debt Recovery, Environmental Law and Commercial Property.

FIRM PROFILE: *Founded in 1979 by David C. Warner, the current Senior Partner. The firm is divided into the following departments: company commercial and finance, employment, general litigation, construction litigation and environmental law, insurance and debt recovery. Working predominantly for corporate clients the firm has established strong links with the USA and France and incorporates a French division of bi-lingual lawyers within its company commercial and finance department. Regulated by the Law Society in the Conduct of Investment Business.*

PARTNERS

DAVID CHARLES WARNER, born England, 1947; admitted, 1973, England. *Education:* Oxford University (M.A., 1968); College of Law, Guildford (Solicitor, 1970). *LANGUAGES:* English and French. *PRACTICE AREAS:* Employment Law; Commercial Law; Corporate Law.

MICHAEL DANIEL CRANSTON, born England, 1942; admitted, 1981, England. *LANGUAGES:* English. *PRACTICE AREAS:* International Financial Litigation; Finance and Recovery of Assets; Insolvency Law.

IAN BERNARD FAGELSON, born England, 1952; admitted, 1975, England. *Education:* Southampton University (LL.B., 1973); Oxford University (B.C.L., 1975). *LANGUAGES:* English. *PRACTICE AREAS:* Corporate Law; Banking and Finance Law; Commercial Law.

PETER RAFAEL ALFANDARY, born England, 1953; admitted, 1979, England. *Education:* University of Kent at Canterbury (B.A. Hons., 1974); London School of Economics (LL.M., 1977). *Member:* Chevalier Dans L'Ordre National du Merite (1991); French Chamber of Commerce (Deputy President, 1994). *LANGUAGES:* French, English and Italian. *PRACTICE AREAS:* French Inward Investment; Corporate Immigration Law.

CHRISTOPHER JOHN WRIGHT, born England, 1952; admitted, 1976, England. *Education:* Cambridge University (B.A., 1973; M.A., 1977); College of Law (1974). A Fellow of the Chartered Institute of Arbitrators, 1991. *LANGUAGES:* English. *PRACTICE AREAS:* Construction Litigation; Arbitration Law; Alternative Dispute Resolution.

NICHOLAS PAUL SPEED, born England, 1955; admitted, 1981, England. *Education:* Warwick University (LL.B., 1977); Guildford College of Law (1978). Member, Society of Construction Law, 1986. *LANGUAGES:* English. *PRACTICE AREAS:* Construction Law; Insurance Law; Product Liability Law.

WITOLD JAN GRYKO, born England, 1958; admitted, 1982, England. *Education:* Oxford University (B.A., 1979); College of Law, London (1980). *LANGUAGES:* English, French and Polish. *PRACTICE AREAS:* Commercial and Corporate Law; Banking and Finance Law; International Taxation.

MICHAEL PATRICK DILLON WESTON, born England, 1936; admitted, 1962, England. *Education:* Cambridge University (M.A., 1958). *LANGUAGES:* English. *PRACTICE AREAS:* Product Liability Law; Environmental Law; Health and Safety Legislation.

DAVID IAN DALGARNO, born Scotland, 1955; admitted, 1988, England. *Education:* Warwick University (LL.B., 1977); Inns of Court School

(This Listing Continued)

of Law (Barrister, 1978). *LANGUAGES:* English. *PRACTICE AREAS:* Employment Law; Compensation Law; Labour and Trade Union Matters.

PATRICIA A. MITCHELL, born England, 1957; admitted, 1981, England. *Education:* Durham University (B.A., 1978); Chester College of Law (1979). *LANGUAGES:* English. *PRACTICE AREAS:* Commercial Litigation; Banking, Finance and Commodity Litigation; Reinsurance Law.

LARRY COLTMAN, born England, 1958; admitted, 1984, England. *Education:* Leicester University (LL.B., 1980); Chester (1981). Member, Institute of Credit Management, 1990; Insolvency Lawyers Association, 1989. Associate, Chartered Institute of Arbitrators, 1992. *LANGUAGES:* English. *PRACTICE AREAS:* Commercial Litigation; Debt Collection Law; Insolvency Law.

ALASDAIR DUNCAN EDWARDS, born South Africa, 1956; admitted, 1988, England. *Education:* Natal University, Durban, South Africa (B.A., 1976; LL.B., 1979). *LANGUAGES:* English. *PRACTICE AREAS:* Commercial Property Law.

DAVID JAMES STUART HEARD, born New Zealand, 1958; admitted, 1985, New Zealand; 1990, England. *Education:* Canterbury University, New Zealand (1977); Université de Toulouse, France, (Diplôme des Études Francaises, 1980); Victoria University, New Zealand (LL.B. Hons., 1984). *LANGUAGES:* English and French. *PRACTICE AREAS:* Corporate Commercial Law; Financial Services Law; Insurance Law; Information Technology Law.

TIMOTHY G. FOSTER, born England, 1958; admitted, 1983, England. *Education:* Cambridge University (B.A., Hons., 1980); College of Law (1981). *LANGUAGES:* English. *PRACTICE AREAS:* Company and Commercial Law; Acquisitions and Disposals/Joint Ventures; International Commercial Contracts; Agency and Distribution; Intellectual Property Licensing.

EDWARD SAMUEL MILLER, born England, 1961; admitted, 1988, England. *Education:* Oxford University (B.A., 1982; M.A., 1985); Free University of Brussels (Licence Spéciale, 1983); Hebrew University of Jerusalem (LL.M., 1985); Manchester Polytechnic (1986). *LANGUAGES:* English and French. *PRACTICE AREAS:* Commercial Law; Corporate Law; Competition Law.

WATSON, FARLEY & WILLIAMS

15 APPOLD STREET
LONDON EC2A 2HB, ENGLAND
Telephone: (44-171) 814 8000
Telex: 8955707 WFW LON G
Fax: (44 171) 814 8141

New York, New York Office: 380 Madison Avenue, 10017. Telephone: 212-922-2200. Telex: 6790626 WFW NY Fax: 212-922-1512.

Paris, France Office: 19 Rue de Marignan, 75008 Paris. Telephone: (33 1) 45 63 15 15. Telex: WFW PAR 651096 F. Fax: (33 1) 45 61 09 01.

Oslo, Norway Office: Beddingen 8, Aker Brygge, 0250 Oslo. Telephone: (47 22) 83 83 08. Telex: 79209 WFW N. Fax: (47 22) 83 83 13.

Athens, Greece Office: Alassia Building, Defteras Merarchias 13, 185-35 Piraeus. Telephone: (30 1) 422 3660. Telex: 24 1311 WFW GR. Fax: (30 1) 422 3664.

Moscow, Russia Office: 36 Myaskovskovo Street, Moscow 121019. Telephone: +7 502 224 1700 (international only); +7 (095) 291 8046/5698. Fax: +7 502 224 1701 (international only); +7 (095) 202 9027. Copenhagen, Denmark Office: Lille Kongensgade 20, DK-1074 Copenhagen K. Telephone: +45 (33) 913303. Fax: +45 (33) 914912.

General International Practice, Corporate, Commercial and Financing, Shipping, Aviation, Banking, Taxation, Commercial Litigation and Arbitration, Bankruptcy, Real Property, European Community Law, Offshore Oil and Gas, Immigration, Employment.

PARTNERS

ALASTAIR H. FARLEY, born 1946; admitted, 1971, England. *Education:* Jesus College, Cambridge (M.A.). *Member:* City of London Solicitors' Company; International Bar Association; Worshipful Company of Shipwrights (Court of Assistants). (Senior and Founding Partner). *PRACTICE AREAS:* International Finance; General Commercial; Commercial Shipping; Ship Finance.

MARTIN A. WATSON, born 1946; admitted, 1971, England. *Education:* St. Catharine's College, Cambridge (B.A.). (Founding Partner). *PRACTICE AREAS:* International Finance; Project Finance; Ship Finance; Commercial Leasing; Banking and Asset Finance; Corporate Re-

(This Listing Continued)

WATSON, FARLEY & WILLIAMS, London—Continued

structuring; Admiralty; Maritime; Ship Mortgage Enforcement; Ship Registration; General Commercial.

GEOFFREY C. WILLIAMS, born 1944; admitted, 1970, England. *Education:* Dublin (B.A., LL.B.). (Founding Partner). *PRACTICE AREAS:* Asset and Project Finance; Domestic and Cross Border Leasing (particularly Ships and Aircraft); Aviation and Satellites; General Commercial; Tax Leasing.

DAVID J. WARDER, born 1950; admitted, 1976, England. *Education:* Trinity College, Cambridge (B.A.). *PRACTICE AREAS:* Ship, Asset and Project Finance; Ship Leasing; Ship Building; Commercial and Corporate Shipping; Ship Mortgage Enforcement; Ship Registration.

CHRISTOPHER A. L. PRESTON, born 1950; admitted, 1975, England. *Member:* Fellow of the Institute of Taxation; VAT Practitioners Group (Founder Member; Chairman, London Chapter); Law Society (Chairman, VAT Sub-Committee; Member: Revenue Law Committee; International Tax Law Sub-Committee; Representative, Joint VAT Consultative Committee (JVCC)). *PRACTICE AREAS:* Corporate Tax; International Tax Planning; VAT and Customs; Structural and Levy Finance.

CHARLES ST. C. SMALLWOOD, born 1949; admitted, 1979, England. *Education:* Trinity College, Oxford (M.A.). *Member:* British Maritime Law Association. *PRACTICE AREAS:* Shipping and Commercial Litigation and Arbitration.

WILLIAM G. FOSSICK, born 1940; admitted, 1966, England. *PRACTICE AREAS:* Corporate Finance; Management Buy-Outs; Corporate Restructuring; Directors' and Officers' Liabilities; Investment and Securities; Financial Services.

GEOFFREY L. WYNNE, born 1950; admitted, 1975, England. *Education:* Christ Church College, Oxford (M.A.). *Member:* International Bar Association. *PRACTICE AREAS:* Banking; Asset Finance; Project Finance; Debt Recovery; Equipment Leasing; Insolvency and Financial Restructuring; Bankruptcy; Leveraged and Management Buy-Outs; General Commercial; Corporate and International Finance; Syndicated Lending; Taking Security.

FRANCIS DUNNE, born 1956; admitted, 1980, England. *Education:* Downing College, Cambridge (M.A.). *PRACTICE AREAS:* Financing; Foreclosure; Workouts; Ship Financing; General Commercial.

NEIL D. CUTHBERT, born 1954; admitted, 1979, England. *Education:* Exeter (LL.B.). *Member:* International Bar Association. *PRACTICE AREAS:* Banking and Asset Finance; General Commercial; Insolvency and Financial Restructuring; Bankruptcy; Project Finance; Taking Security; Syndicated Lending.

SIMON R. CURTIS, born 1955; admitted, 1982, England. *Education:* Jesus College, Oxford (M.A.) (B.C.L.). Author: "The Law of Shipbuilding Contracts," Lloyds of London Press Ltd. (December, 1991). *PRACTICE AREAS:* Maritime; Insurance and Off-Shore Litigation and Arbitration; Shipbuilding; Conversion and Repair Contract Negotiation and Dispute Resolution.

DAVID N. OSBORNE, born 1956; admitted, 1981, England; 1993, New York. *Education:* Downing College, Cambridge (M.A.). (Also at New York Office). *PRACTICE AREAS:* International Finance; Ship and Aircraft Finance; General Commercial.

CHARLES M. H. WALFORD, born 1955; admitted, 1980, England. *Education:* Trinity Hall, Cambridge (M.A.). *Member:* City of London Solicitors Company. *PRACTICE AREAS:* Corporate Finance; Mergers and Acquisitions; Management Buyouts; Corporate Restructuring; Employment and Immigration; Joint Ventures; Facilities Management/Outsourcing Arrangements; Computer Licensing and Development; General Corporate and Commercial.

OONAGH A. WHITTY, born 1954; admitted, 1981, England. *Education:* London (B.S.). *PRACTICE AREAS:* Project and Asset Finance; Commercial Leasing; Aircraft Leasing; Corporate Tax; Cross Border Tax Based Finance; International Tax Planning.

NIGEL A. D. THOMAS, born 1956; admitted, 1981, England. *Education:* St. Catharine's College, Cambridge (M.A.). (Resident, Oslo Office from 1988-1993). *PRACTICE AREAS:* International Banking; Shipping and Asset Finance; General Commercial.

ANDREW H. WETTERN, born 1957; admitted, 1981, England. *Education:* Jesus College, Cambridge (B.A.). (Resident, Paris Office). *PRACTICE*

(This Listing Continued)

AREAS: Aviation and Shipping Finance; Banking; Asset Finance; Asset Based Lending; General Commercial; International Cross Border Finance.

MARIA M. LLEWELLYN, born 1957; admitted, 1981, England. *Education:* London (LL.B.). *PRACTICE AREAS:* Commercial Property; Property Finance; Secured Lending; Insolvency Related Property Matters; Leasing; Investment Property.

NIGEL R. D. MOSS, born 1947; admitted, 1973, England. *Education:* Exeter (B.A.). (Resident, Paris Office). *PRACTICE AREAS:* Aviation Finance; Banking; Asset Finance; Asset Based Lending; International Project Finance; Trade Finance.

RICHARD P. WHISH, born 1953; admitted, 1977, England. *Education:* Worcester College, Oxford (B.A., B.C.L.). Professor of Law, King's College, London. *Member:* Society of Public Teachers of Law; Centre of European Law, Kings College, London; Centre for the Study of Regulatory Industries, London. *PRACTICE AREAS:* European Community and Competition Law; Agency and Distribution Agreements; Franchise; Comparative Anti-Trust; Public Procurement; Air and Sea Transport Law; International Mergers and Joint Ventures.

J. ANTHONY VAUGHAN, born 1948; admitted, 1979, England. *Education:* East Anglia. *PRACTICE AREAS:* Media-Related Transactions and Sponsorship; Mergers and Acquisitions; Leveraged and Management Buy-Outs; Corporate Restructuring; Directors' and Officers' Liabilities; Venture Capital; General Commercial and Corporate; Corporate Finance.

MARK J. LAWSON, born 1960; admitted, 1984, England. *Education:* London. *PRACTICE AREAS:* Ship Finance; Asset Finance; Project Finance; Ship Building; Ship Registration; Commercial and Corporate Shipping.

MARK J. DAVIS, born 1959; admitted, 1985, England. *Education:* Nottingham (LL.B.). *PRACTICE AREAS:* Commercial Litigation; Banking; Fraud; Maritime; Tort; Insurance; Arbitration; Shipping.

ANDREW J. W. MURIEL, born 1952; admitted, 1988, England. *Education:* Southampton (LL.B.). *PRACTICE AREAS:* Banking; Asset Finance; Aviation Finance; Leasing; General Commercial; Aviation Regulatory.

JAMES A. D. WATTERS, born 1945; admitted, 1972, England. *Education:* Pembroke College, Oxford (B.A.). *Member:* International Bar Association; City of London Solicitors' Company; Law Society. *PRACTICE AREAS:* Banking and Commercial Leasing; Finance Law; Asset Finance; Aviation Finance; Equipment Leasing.

JAMES H. SURGEONER, born 1945; admitted, 1971, England. *Education:* Aberdeen (LL.B.). *PRACTICE AREAS:* Ship Finance; Ship Mortgage Enforcement; Charterparties and Bills of Lading; Ship Registration; General Commercial Shipping.

PETER J. FLINT, born 1956; admitted, 1983, England. *Education:* University College, Oxford (B.A.). *PRACTICE AREAS:* International Trade Regulation; Tort; Arbitration; Mortgage Enforcement; Maritime; Charterparties and Bills of Lading; Ship Finance; Marine Insurance.

JULIA M. KIRKLAND, born 1953; admitted, 1980, England. *Education:* Birmingham (LL.B.); Bar Finals (Hons.). *Member:* Insolvency Lawyers Association; Society of Practitioners of Insolvency. *PRACTICE AREAS:* Debt Recovery; Insolvency; Bankruptcy; Directors' and Officers' Liabilities; Fraud; White Collar Crime.

DAVID I. SYED, born 1964; admitted, 1992, France (Not admitted in England). *Education:* Exeter (LL.M.); Université de Rheims (License en Droit: Félicitations du Jury). *Member:* Ordre des Avocats à la Cour de Paris; Association Française des Avocats Conseils d'Entreprise; International Bar Association. (Avocats à la Cour de Paris) (Resident Paris Office). *PRACTICE AREAS:* Banking; Structured and Project Finance; International Joint Ventures; International Mergers and Acquisitions.

MICHAEL L. VERNELL, born 1951; admitted, 1975, England. (Resident, Oslo Office). *PRACTICE AREAS:* Shipping; Finance; Banking; Commercial; Capital Markets.

EDWARD J. NALBANTIAN, born Englewood, New Jersey, September 4, 1955; admitted, 1983, New York; 1990, California. *Education:* Georgetown University (A.B., cum laude, 1977; J.D., 1982); London School of Economics, England (M.Sc., 1978). Fulbright Scholar, 1977-1978. Staff member, 1980-1982, Topics Editor, 1981-1982, Law and Policy in International Business. Author: "The Constitutional Dilemma of State Tax Exemptions: Sears, Roebuck and Co. v. County of Los Angeles," 13 Law and Policy in International Business 811, 1981. Co-author: "Eurobonds," Supple-

(This Listing Continued)

ment Journal of International Banking and Financial Law, Butterworth's, December, 1987. Author: "Restructuring Junk Bonds: Bondholders Beware," International Financial Law Review, April, 1991. (Resident, Paris Office). *LANGUAGES:* French and Armenian. *PRACTICE AREAS:* International Capital Markets and Derivatives Transactions; Project and Structured Finance; General Corporate and Securities Matters.

J. DOUGLAS WARDLE, born 1960; admitted, 1986, England. *Education:* Keble College, Oxford (M.A.). *PRACTICE AREAS:* Privatisations in Central and Eastern Europe; Joint Ventures; Acquisitions; Corporate Transactions in the UK, Central and Eastern Europe; Institution Building; Inward Investment.

NICK A. TOWLE, born 1954; admitted, 1985, England. *Education:* St. Peter's College, Oxford (B.A.). *PRACTICE AREAS:* Privatisations; Corporate Transactions in the UK, Central and Eastern Europe; Mergers and Acquisitions; Joint Ventures.

MICHAEL G.S. GREVILLE, born 1962; admitted, 1990, England. *Education:* University of Bristol (LL.B. (Hons)). (Resident, Moscow Office). *PRACTICE AREAS:* Shipping; General Commercial; Oil and Gas Exploration and Production; Energy; Project Finance; Asset Finance; Russia and C.I.S..

DEBORAH CLARK, born 1961; admitted, 1988 (formerly Barrister, Gray's Inn 1984). *Education:* Caius College, Cambridge (B.A.). *PRACTICE AREAS:* Asset Finance and Aviation; Acting for Banks and Financial Institutions; Aircraft Operators; Manufacturers and Packagers.

MICHAEL A. KENNY, born 1952; admitted, 1978, England; 1986, Hong Kong. *Education:* Magdalen College, Oxford (B.A., M.A.). *LANGUAGES:* French, German. *PRACTICE AREAS:* International Banking and Asset Financing; Capital Markets; Project Finance; Trade Finance.

(For Biographical Data on additional partners, see Professional Biographies at Copenhagen, Denmark, Oslo, Norway, Paris, France, Pireaus, Greece and Moscow, Russia)

WEDLAKE BELL

Established in 1781

16 BEDFORD STREET, COVENT GARDEN
LONDON WC2E 9HF, ENGLAND
Telephone: (44) 171 379 7266
Fax: (44) 171 836 6117 DX: 40009 Covent Garden

St. Peter Port, Guernsey, Channel Islands Office: Wedlake Bell McKean. 1 Mignot Plateau. Telephone: (44) 481 710315. Fax: (44) 481 714443.
Brussels, Belgium Office: TELFA, Boulevard Brand Whitlock 114/5, B-1200. Telephone: (32) 2 735 0206. Fax: (32) 2 735 3713.

Public Issues, Mergers and Acquisitions, Banking Law, Intellectual Property and Trademarks, Real Estate and Planning, Environmental Law, Antitrust and EC Law, International and U.K. Taxation, Commercial and Corporate Matters, Commercial Litigation, Agricultural Marketing, Divorce, Trusts and Estates (including in Guernsey Off-Shore Trust Administration), Construction Law, Insolvency, Food Law, Pharmaceutical Law and specialist offshore property services.

FIRM PROFILE: Wedlake Bell is a law firm of 31 partners, approximately 40 assistant legal staff and more than 100 support staff. It is a commercial practice with well reputed clients and a history going back over 210 years. The firm's strategy is to provide a first class service to its clients and to maintain its reputation in corporate and commercial work, complex commercial property work, litigation and tax.

PARTNERS

Robert Dolman	Tim Piper
Barry Weatherill	Andrew Baker
Sir John Welch	John Cowlishaw
Richard Andersen	Clive Weber
Geoffrey Wheal	Richard Hewitt
Michael Butcher	Peter Whatmuff
Michael Nicol	Tim Cheshire
Geoffrey Waters	Suzanne Reeves
Quentin Spicer	Philip Matthews
Nigel Goodeve-Docker	Anthony Gubbins
Charles Hicks	John Fluker
Duncan Rabagliati	Jonathan Cornthwaite
Martin Walford	Patricia Taplin
Robert Salter	Peter Cull

(This Listing Continued)

David Earl

ST. PETER PORT, GUERNSEY PARTNERS

Michael McKean
David Harry

ASSOCIATES

Hugh Thomson
John Muncey
Martin Arnold
Richard Islam
Emma Loveday

CONSULTANTS

Fraser Bird

Member of TELFA (Trans European Law Firms Association) TELFA is an association of European law firms, whose members have offices in Arnhem, Barcelona, Brussels, Budapest, Copenhagen, Düsseldorf, Edinburgh, Geneva, Glasgow, Halle, London, Lisbon, Luxembourg, Madrid, Milan, Nijmegen, Paris and Vienna.
For more details see the TELFA entry under Brussels, Belgium.

Languages: English, French, German, Spanish, Dutch

WHITE & CASE

7-11 MOORGATE
LONDON EC2R 6HH, ENGLAND
Telephone: (44-171) 726-6361
Facsimile: (44-171) 726-4314; 726-8558

New York, New York: Telephone: 212-819-8200. Facsimile: 212-354-8113.
Washington, D.C.: Telephone: 202-872-0013. Facsimile: 202-872-0210.
Los Angeles, California: Telephone: 213-620-7700. Facsimile: 213-687-0758; 213-617-2205.
Miami, Florida: Telephone: 305-371-2700. Facsimile: 305-358-5744.
Mexico City, Mexico: Telephone: (52-5) 207-9717. Facsimile: (52-5) 208-3628.
Tokyo, Japan: Telephone: (81-3) 3239-4300. Facsimile: (81-3) 3239-4330.
Hong Kong: Telephone: (852) 2822-8700. Facsimile: (852) 2845-9070; Grice & Co., Solicitors, Telephone: (852) 2826-0333. Facsimile: (852) 2526-7166.
Singapore, Republic of Singapore: Telephone: (65) 225-6000. Facsimile: (65) 225-6009.
Bangkok, Thailand: Pacific Legal Group Ltd., In Association With White & Case, Telephone: (662) 236-6154/7. Facsimile: (662) 237-6771.
Hanoi, Viet Nam: Representative Office, Telephone: (84-4) 227-575/6/7. Facsimile: (84-4) 227-297.
Bombay, India: Telephone: (91-22) 282-6300. Facsimile: (91-22) 282-6305.
Paris, France: Telephone: (33-1) 42-60-34-05. Facsimile: (33-1) 42-60-82-46.
Brussels, Belgium: Telephone: (32-2) 647-05-89. Facsimile: (32-2) 647-16-75.
Stockholm, Sweden: Telephone: (46-8) 679-80-30. Facsimile: (46-8) 611-21-22.
Helsinki, Finland: Telephone: (358-0) 631-100. Facsimile: (358-0) 179-477.
Moscow, Russia: Telephone: (7-095) 201-9292/3/4/5. Facsimile: (7-095) 201-9284.
Budapest, Hungary: Telephone: (36-1) 269-0550; (36-1) 131-0933. Facsimile: (36-1) 269-1199.
Prague, Czech Republic: Telephone: (42-2) 2481-1796. Facsimile: (42-2) 232-5522.
Warsaw, Poland: Telephone/Facsimile: (48-22) 26-80-53; (48-22) 27-84-86. International Telephone/Facsimile: (48-39) 12-19-06.
Istanbul, Turkey: Telephone: (90-212) 275-68-98; (90-212) 275-75-33. Facsimile: (90-212) 275-75-43.
Ankara, Turkey: Telephone: (90-312) 446-2180. Facsimile: (90-312) 437-9677.
Jeddah, Saudi Arabia: Law Office of Hassan Mahassni, Telephone: (966-2) 651-3535. Facsimile: (966-2) 651-3636.
Riyadh, Saudi Arabia: Law Office of Hassan Mahassni, Telephone: (966-1) 476-7099. Facsimile: (966-1) 479-0110.
Almaty, Kazakhstan: Telephone: (7-3272) 50-7491/2. Facsimile: (7-3272) 61-0842.

General International Practice as Registered Foreign Lawyers.

(This Listing Continued)

WHITE & CASE, London—Continued

RESIDENT PARTNERS

JOHN M. H. BELLHOUSE, born Oxford, England, March 16, 1946; admitted, 1971, Solicitor, England and Wales; 1980, Solicitor, Hong Kong. *Education:* Trinity College, Cambridge, England (B.A., 1969).

WILLIAM E. BUTLER, born Minneapolis, Minnesota, October 20, 1939; admitted, 1967, District of Columbia (Not admitted in England). *Education:* Harvard University (J.D., 1966); Ph.D., 1970; LL.D., 1979).

PETER FINLAY, born Dublin, Ireland, May 4, 1955; admitted, 1979, Solicitor, Republic of Ireland; 1982, New York; 1992, Solicitor, England and Wales. *Education:* University College, Dublin, Ireland (B.A., 1976). *Member:* American Bar Association.

FRANCIS FITZHERBERT-BROCKHOLES, born Preston, England, September 18, 1951; admitted, 1978, New York; 1993, Registered Foreign Lawyer, England and Wales. *Education:* Corpus Christi College, Oxford University (B.A., 1973; M.A., 1982); The Inns of Court School of Law (1975). *Member:* American Bar Association.

BERNARD E. NELSON, born Miles City, Montana, May 9, 1950; admitted, 1976, New York; 1993, Registered Foreign Lawyer, England and Wales. *Education:* Yale University (B.A., 1972); Harvard University (J.D., 1975). *Member:* New York State and American Bar Associations; Union Internationale des Avocats; International Bar Association.

H. PHILIP T. STOPFORD, born Westminster, England, September 10, 1953; admitted, 1980, District of Columbia; 1981, New York; 1993, Registered Foreign Lawyer, England and Wales. *Education:* Brunel, Uxbridge, England (LL.B., 1977); University of Virginia (LL.M., 1978). *Member:* The District of Columbia Bar; New York State Bar Association.

RESIDENT ASSOCIATES

RUTH AMBROSE, born Hertfordshire, England, May 5, 1965; admitted, 1993, England and Wales. *Education:* University of Surry (B.Sc., 1990; L.S.F., 1991).

CAROLYN M. BRZEZINSKI, born Norwalk, Connecticut, May 10, 1966; admitted, 1992, California (Not admitted in England). *Education:* University of Connecticut (B.A. and M.A., 1988); University of Virginia (J.D., 1991).

JONATHAN M. CLARK, JR., born Charlottesville, Virginia, September 28, 1961; admitted, 1987, New York (Not admitted in England). *Education:* Yale University (B.A., 1983); University of Virginia (J.D., 1986).

GERARD N. CRANLEY, born Perth, Australia, October 20, 1961; admitted, 1985, Australia; 1991, England. *Education:* University of Western Australia (B. Juris, 1984; LL.B., 1985).

GREGORY J. HAMMOND, born Chelsfield, Kent, England, August 28, 1964; admitted, 1990, England. *Education:* St. John's College (B.A., 1986; M.A., 1990); Lancaster Gate College of Law (1987).

THOMAS A. HARTNETT, born Springfield, Massachusetts, July 4, 1964; admitted, 1990, New York (Not admitted in England). *Education:* University of Pennsylvania (B.A., 1986); New York University (J.D., 1989).

KAYA H. PROUDIAN, born Bloomington, Indiana, December 20, 1967; admitted, 1993, New York (Not admitted in England). *Education:* Indiana University (B.A., 1989); Harvard University (J.D., 1992).

JEFFREY A. WASHENKO, born Washington, D.C., August 10, 1961; admitted, 1990, New York (Not admitted in England). *Education:* Duke University (B.S., 1983); University of Virginia (M.B.A., 1989; J.D., 1989).

(For biographical data as to other locations, see Professional Biographies at New York, New York; Washington, D.C.; Los Angeles, California; Miami, Florida; Mexico City, Mexico; Tokyo, Japan; Hong Kong; Singapore, Republic of Singapore; Bangkok, Thailand; Hanoi, Viet Nam; Bombay, India; Paris, France; Brussels, Belgium; Stockholm, Sweden; Helsinki, Finland; Moscow, Russia; Budapest, Hungary; Prague, Czech Republic; Warsaw, Poland; Istanbul and Ankara, Turkey; Jeddah and Riyadh, Saudi Arabia; Almaty, Kazakhstan).

WHITMAN BREED ABBOTT & MORGAN

11 WATERLOO PLACE
LONDON SW1Y 4AU, ENGLAND
Telephone: 01-839-3226
Cable Address: "Whitsom London SW1"
Telex: 917881
Telecopier: 01-839-6741

New York, N.Y. Offices: 200 Park Avenue, 10166. Telephone: 212-351-3000.
Los Angeles, California Office: 633 West Fifth Street, 90071. Telephone: 213-896-2400.
Sacramento, California Office: Senator Hotel Building, 1121 L Street, 95814. Telephone: 916-441-4242.
Washington, D.C. Offices: 1215 17th Street, N.W. Telephone 202-887-0353; 1818 N Street, N.W. Telephone: 202-466-1100.
Greenwich, Connecticut Office: 2 Greenwich Plaza, 06830. Telephone: 203-869-3800.
Newark, New Jersey Office: One Gateway Center, 07102-5398. Telephone: 201-621-2230.
Palm Beach, Florida Office: 220 Sunrise Avenue. Telephone: 407-832-5458.
Tokyo, Japan Office: Suite 450, New Otemachi Building, 2-2-1 Otemachi, Chiyoda-Ku, Tokyo 100. Telephone: 81-3-3242-1289.
Associated with: Tyan & Associes, 22, La Sagesse Street, Beirut, Lebanon. Telephone: 337968. Fax: 200969. Telex: 43928.

Firm engaged in American and International Practice, but not authorized to appear before the English Courts or to act as Solicitors.

RESIDENT PARTNERS

GORDON L. JAYNES, born Spokane, Washington, 1929; admitted, 1954, Washington; 1964, California (Not admitted in England). *Education:* Whitman College (A.B., 1950); University of Washington (LL.B., 1954); University of London Academic Postgraduate Diploma in International Law (U.C.L., 1962). *Member:* Washington State and American Bar Associations; The State Bar of California; The International Bar Association (Chairman Emeritus, Committee on International Construction Contracts); The Law Society, London (Overseas Lawyer). Fellow, Chartered Institute of Arbitrators, London. *PRACTICE AREAS:* International Construction Projects; International Commercial Arbitration.

MICHAEL J. MCNULTY, born Buffalo, New York, 1932; admitted, 1958, New York (Not admitted in England). *Education:* Holy Cross College (A.B., 1953); Harvard University (LL.B., 1956); University of Munich (Comparative Law, 1958). Private Practice in New York City and Paris, 1958-1968. International Corporate Counsel, Reliance Group based in London, England, 1968-1981. *Member:* American Society of International Law. *LANGUAGES:* French and German. *PRACTICE AREAS:* U.S. Taxation of Foreign pension funds and European Acquisitions.

ELWOOD A. RICKLESS, born Rochester, New York, 1929; admitted, 1958, New York (Not admitted in England). *Education:* Harvard University (A.B., 1951; M.A. 1958; LL.B., 1958). *Member:* American Bar Association. *LANGUAGES:* French and German.

ELTON SHANE, born London, England, 1959; admitted, 1985, England. *Education:* Brunel University (LL.B. (Hons), 1983); Lancaster State law College (Solicitor's Final Exams, 1985). *PRACTICE AREAS:* Corporate and Commercial; Computer Law; Trade Financing; U.K. Financial Services; European Community Law.

RESIDENT ASSOCIATE

LUCINDA M. WILLIAMS, born Bristol, England, 1965; admitted, 1993, England. *Education:* University College Cardiff (B.A., Joint Hons. Law & English, 1989).

WIKBORG, REIN & CO.

Established in 1987

1, KNIGHTRIDER COURT, 2ND FLOOR
LONDON EC4V 5JP, ENGLAND
Telephone: 44 171 236 4598
Telefax: 44 171 236 4599
Telex: 915952

Oslo, Norway Office: Kronprinsesse Märthas Plass 1, P.O. Box 1513 Vika, 0117 Oslo. Telephone: 47 22827500. Telefax: 47 22827501.

(This Listing Continued)

Bergen, Norway Office: Handelens og Sjøfartens Hus, Olav Kyrresgate 11, 5014. Telephone: 47 55318116. Telex: 42516 WRCON. Telefax: 47 55310015.

Kobe, Japan Office: Wikborg & Rein, 1-1, 5-Chome Minatojima Nakamachi, Chuo-ku, 650. Telephone: (78) 303 1772. Telex: 5622404. Telefax: (78) 303 1781.

Firm engaged in Norwegian and International Law Practice, but not authorized to appear before the English Courts or to act as Solicitors.

RESIDENT PARTNER

Lars Olav Askheim

WILDE SAPTE

1, FLEET PLACE
LONDON EC4M 7WS, ENGLAND
Telephone: 0171-246-7000
Facsimile: 0171-246 7777
Telex: 887793 lde/cde 145

Brussels, Belgium Office: 27 Avenue des Arts, 1040. Telephone: (32-2) 280 1404. Facsimile: (32-2) 280 1764.

Hong Kong Office: 31st Floor, One Exchange Square. Telephone: (852) 2810 5081. Facsimile: (852) 2810 1295.

New York, New York Office: 19th Floor, 450 Lexington Avenue, 10017. Telephone: (212) 867 4530. Facsimile: (212) 557 4451.

Paris, France Office: 217 rue du Faubourg St. Honoré, 75008. Telephone: (33-1) 44 95 02 70. Facsimile: (33-1) 42 89 62 25.

Tokyo, Japan Office: 2nd Floor, AIG Building, 1-1-3 Marunouchi, Chiyoda-ku 100. Telephone: (81-3) 3215 3801. Facsimile: (81-3) 32153868.

Lloyd's Office: 40 Lime Street, London, EC3M 5DG. Telephone: 0171 246 7000. Fax: 0170 246 7722.

Banking, Corporate Lending, Acquisition Finance, Aviation, Shipping, Leasing, Work-outs, Trade Finance, Structured Finance, Project Finance, Insolvency, Property, Insurance, Employment, Charities, EC Law and Company and Commercial.

FIRM PROFILE: *Wilde Sapte is a commercial City firm handling a wide range of work for our UK and international clients.*

The practice is centered around the company and commercial, banking, property, insolvency, insurance and transport expertise, though smaller specialist groups, such as an intellectual property group and a Japanese unit, have been formed to serve particular client needs. It is a progressive and much respected firm which has tripled in size over the last decade. In the last year, in response to increasing international demands from the business communities, offices have been opened in Hong Kong, Tokyo and at Lloyd's to complement those existing in New York, Paris and Brussels. In addition, the practice has extensive connections with law firms in jurisdictions throughout the world.

SENIOR PARTNERS

Charles G.J. Leeming

MEMBERS OF FIRM

Malcolm Glover
Stephan G. Bird
Andrew M.S. Beer
Robert S. McCaw
Richard J.S. Bethell-Jones
Philip N. Brown
Adrian S. Miles
Mark B. Andrews
Andrew D. Collins
Richard H. Scopes
Andrew Campbell
Robert K. Dibble
Colin E.A. Thaine
Mary Bonar
James A. Curtis
Graham E.H. Paine
Miles H. Walton
Philip Rocher
Peter J. Sharp
Mark S. Gill
Ashley Burns (Contact Partner, Hong Kong)
(This Listing Continued)

Charles J. Jennings
George R. Sandars
Steven Blakeley (Contact Partner, Belgium)
Graham R.E. Smith
Richard F. Caird
Adrian Mecz (Not admitted in England)
Alan L. Jarvis
Justin T. Spendlove
D.W. Mark Menhennet
Jeremy J. Ogden
Thomas J. McDonald (Contact Partner, Paris)
Hugh R.S. O'Donovan
Rory McAlpine
Guy N. Fifield
David M.W. Smith
Stephen J. Brower
Richard Pell-Ilderton
Michael Ratcliff
Derek C. Tadiello
John K. Hull
Peter von Schwartz de Megyesi
Christopher A. Cardona (Contact Partner, New York)
Charlotte L. Sallabank
Ian M. Roberts
Gregory R. Kahn
Helen M. Cleaveland
Nigel D. Barnett
James Johnson
Rory Gallaher
Elisabeth Gaunt
Howard J. Barrie
Jeremey P. Gibb
Russell L. Jacobs
Philip Quirk (Contact Partner, Tokyo)
Lisa M. Marks
Pratap Amin
Ian Birchall
Brian M. Smith
Duncan McDonald
John Walker
Alastair J. Collett
Nicholas Syson
Richard W. Macklin
Jonathan Shann

WILLKIE FARR & GALLAGHER

3RD FLOOR
35 WILSON STREET
LONDON EC2M 25J, ENGLAND
Telephone: 011-44-171-696-9060
Fax: 011-44-171-417-9191

New York City Office: One Citicorp Center, 153 East 53rd Street, 10022-4669. Telephone: 212-821-8000. Fax: 212-821-8111. Telex: RCA 233780-WFGUR; RCA 238805-WFGUR.

Washington, D.C. Office: Three Lafayette Centre, 1155 21st Street, N.W., 6th Floor, 20036-3384. Telephone: 202-328-8000. Fax: 202-887-8979; 202-331-8187. Telex: RCA 229800-WFGIG; WU 89-2762.

Paris, France Office: 6, Avenue Velasquez 75008. Telephone: 011-33-1-44-35-44-35. Fax: 011-33-1-42-89-87-01. Telex: 652740 WFG Paris.

Firm engaged in American and International Law, but not authorized to appear before the English Courts or to act as Solicitor.

PARTNER

CHRISTOPHER E. MANNO, born New Rochelle, New York, November 22, 1954; admitted, 1980, New York (Not admitted in England). *Education:* Colgate University (B.A., 1976); St. John's University (J.D., 1979). Managing Editor, St. John's Law Review, 1978-1979. *Member:* American Bar Association. (Also: New York Office). *LANGUAGES:* French.

(This Listing Continued)

WILLKIE FARR & GALLAGHER, London—Continued

RESIDENT ASSOCIATES

WILLIAM H. GUMP, born New York, New York, March 22, 1963; admitted, 1990, New York (Not admitted in England). *Education:* Harvard University (B.A., 1985; J.D., 1989). Recipient: Ames Prize; John Harvard Scholar; Harvard Scholar, Aloan Prize. *Member:* American Bar Association.

JEFFREY R. POSS, born Livingston, New Jersey, January 17, 1966; admitted, 1991, New Jersey; 1992, New York (Not admitted in England). *Education:* University of Pennsylvania (B.A., 1988); Boston University (J.D., 1991). *Member:* New York State and American Bar Associations.

(For complete biographical data of all Partners and Counsel, see Professional Biographies at New York, N.Y.)

WILMER, CUTLER & PICKERING

Registered Foreign Lawyers and Solicitors

4 CARLTON GARDENS
LONDON SW1Y 5AA, ENGLAND
Telephone: (44 171) 839-4466
Facsimile: (44 171) 839-3537

Washington, D.C. Office: 2445 M Street, N.W., 20037-1420. Telephone: 202-663-6000. Facsimile: 202-663-6363. Internet: Law@Wilmer.Com.
Brussels, Belgium Office: Rue de la Loi 15 Wetstraat. B-1040. Telephone: (32 2) 231-0903. Facsimile: (32 2) 230-4322.
Berlin, Germany Office: Friedrichstrasse 95, D-10117. Telephone: (49 30) 2643-3601. Facsimile: (49 30) 2643-3630.

General Practice.
Firm engaged in English, European, American, and International Law Practice.

RESIDENT PARTNERS

GARY B. BORN, born Binghamton, New York, U.S.A., September 14, 1955; admitted, 1984, District of Columbia (Not admitted in England). *Education:* Haverford College (B.A., 1978); Phi Beta Kappa; University of Pennsylvania (J.D., summa cum laude, 1981). Articles Editor, University of Pennsylvania Law Review. Clerk to Hon. Henry J. Friendly, 2d Circuit; Clerk to Hon. William H. Rehnquist, U.S. Supreme Court, October Term, 1982. Co-author, *International Civil Litigation in United States Courts* (Kluwer 2d ed., 1992); Co-author, Extraterritorial Application of National Laws (Kluwer 1987). Author, *A Reappraisal of the Extraterritorial Reach of U.S. Law,* 24 Law and Policy in International Business 1 (1992); Author, *Reflections on Judicial Jurisdiction in International Cases,* 17 Georgia Journal of International and Comparative Law 1 (1987). Member of Executive Council, American Society of International Law, 1990. Visiting Lecturer (International Business Transactions), University College, London, 1991—; Adjunct Professor of Law (International Civil Litigation), Georgetown University, 1987-1992. Co-chair, Committee on International Aspects of Litigation, ABA International Section, 1988-1992.

DIETER G. F. LANGE, born Leipzig, Germany, January 6, 1943; admitted, Germany (Not admitted in England). *Education:* Universities of Heidelberg, Bonn and Oxford. First State Examination (1968); Second State Examination (1974). Chairman, ICC Committee on Extraterritorial Application of National Laws, 1984-1987. Co-author, *Recent Changes in English Arbitration Practice Widen Opportunity For More Effective International Arbitrations,* 35 The Business Lawyer 1621 (1980); Co-author, Civil Litigation in the United States: A Practical Guide for German Companies (1985) (published in Germany, 1987); Co-author, *Extraterritorial Application of National Laws* (Kluwer 1987).

ARTHUR L. MARRIOTT, born Blantyre, Scotland, March 30, 1943; admitted, as Solicitor, 1966, England and Wales; 1976, Hong Kong. *Education:* College of Law, London. Co-author, ADR Principles and Practice (1993); Co-author, *International Arbitration in the Aftermath of Socialism,* 10 Journal of International Arbitration 5 (1993). Author, *International Arbitration and the Adaptation of Contracts,* 4 International Arbitration Reporter 16 (1989); Author, *Arbitrating International Commercial Disputes in the United Kingdom,* 44 Arbitration Journal 3 (1989); Author, *Evidence in International Arbitration,* 5 Arbitration International 280 (1989). Member, Departmental Advisory Committee on Arbitration, 1992—; Fellow, Chartered Institute of Arbitrators. Advisory Council, Centre of Commercial Law Studies of Queen Mary and Westfield, University of London, 1990;

(This Listing Continued)

EU354B

Member, Court of Arbitration, London Court of International Arbitration, 1993.

ANDREW K. PARNELL, born London, England, August 19, 1953; admitted, as Solicitor, 1979, England and Wales. *Education:* Cambridge University (B.A., 1975). Author, *Enforcing United States Judgments Abroad -- England,* Enforcing Foreign Judgments in the United States and United States Judgments Abroad (Ronald A. Brand, Jr., ed., 1992).

SPECIAL COUNSEL

JOHN J. KALLAUGHER, born Springfield, Massachusetts, U.S.A., February 5, 1952; admitted, 1978, New York (Not admitted in England). *Education:* Harvard University (B.A., 1973); Cornell University (J.D., 1977). Research Editor, Cornell Law Review. German Academic Exchange Service Special Program for Foreign Lawyers in Germany, 1981-1982. Visiting Lecturer (EEC Competition Law), University College, London, 1985-1993; Visiting Professor, 1993—. Speech, *Recent Developments Affecting Distribution and Abuse of Dominant Position* (Institute of Advanced Legal Studies, London, 1993); Speech, *Legal and Economic Concepts in Article 86* (IBC Introductory Competition Law Programme, Luxembourg, June, 1993); Speech, *Article 3(f) and the Goals of EC Competition Law* (European Studies Conference, London, May, 1992); Speech, *The Relationship Between Article 86 and the EC Merger Regulation* (European Studies Conference, Brussels, November, 1992).

ASSOCIATES

ANGELA BEDFORD, born July 20, 1966; admitted, 1990, England and Wales. *Education:* University of Warwick (LL.B., 1987); University of Cambridge (LL.M., 1993); Inns of Court School of Law. Part-time Supervisor (Public International Law), London School of Economics, University of London, 1990-1991. Lecturer (Public International Law, European Community Law, and Armed Conflict and the Use of Force), King's College, University of London, 1989-1990. Supervisor (Armed Conflict and the Use of Force, Law of International Institutions, and Law of the Sea), University of Cambridge, 1988-1990. Part-time Lecturer (Armed Conflict and the Use of Force), King's College, University of London, 1988-1989.

MICHAEL R. HOLTER, born September 11, 1965; admitted, 1988, England and Wales. *Education:* Cambridge University (B.A., 1987). Tutor, Inns of Court School of Law, 1988-1989.

NEIL D. MIDGLEY, born July 5, 1968; admitted, 1992, England and Wales. *Education:* University of Oxford (B.A., 1989); College of Law, Chester. (Resident, European Office, London, England).

(For Complete Biographical Data on all Personnel, see Professional Biographies at Washington, D.C.)

WILSON, ELSER, MOSKOWITZ, EDELMAN & DICKER

141 FENCHURCH STREET
LONDON EC3M 6BL, ENGLAND
Telephone: (01) 623-6723
Telex: 885741
Facsimile: (01) 626-9774

New York, N.Y. Office: 150 East 42nd Street, 10017-5639. Telephone: 212-490-3000. Telex: 177679. Facsimile: 212-490-3038; 212-557-7801.
Los Angeles, California Office: Suite 2700, 1055 W. Seventh Street, 90017. Telephone: 213-624-3044. Telex: 17-0722. Facsimile: 213-624-8060.
San Francisco, California Office: 555 Montgomery Street, 94111. Telephone: 415-433-0990. Telex: 16-0768. Facsimile: 415-434-1370.
Washington, D.C. Office: The Colorado Building, Fifth Floor, 1341 "G" Street, N.W. 20005. Telephone: 202-626-7660. Telex: 89453. Facsimile: 202-628-3606.
Newark, New Jersey Office: One Gateway Center, 07102-5311. Telephone: 201-624-0800. Telex: 6853589. Facsimile: 201-624-0808.
Philadelphia, Pennsylvania Office: The Curtis Center, Independence Square West, 19106. Telephone: 215-627-6900. Telex: 6711203. Facsimile: 215-627-2665.
Baltimore, Maryland Office: 250 West Pratt Street, 21201. Telephone: 410-539-1800. Telex: 19-8280. Facsimile: 410-539-1820.
Miami, Florida Office: International Place, 100 Southeast Second Street, 33131. Telephone: 305-374-1811. Telex: 810845940. Facsimile: 305-579-0261.
Chicago, Illinois Office: 120 N. La Salle Street, 26th Floor, 60602. Telephone: 312-704-0550. Telex: 1561590. Facsimile: 312-704-1522.

(This Listing Continued)

White Plains, N.Y. Office: 925 Westchester Avenue. Telephone: 914-946-7200. Facsimile: 914-946-7897.

Dallas, Texas Office: 5000 Renaissance Tower, 1201 Elm Street, 75270. Telephone: 214-698-8000. Facsimile: 214-698-1101.

Albany, New York Office: One Steuben Place, 12207. Telephone: 518-449-8893. Fax: 518-449-8927.

Tokyo, Japan Office: AIU Building, 1-3 Marunouchi 1-chome, Chiyoda-Ku, 100. Telephone: 011-813-216-6551. Telex: 781-2227216. Facsimile: 011-813-216-6965.

Affiliate Office in Paris, France: Honig Bufffat Mettetal. 21 Rue Clément Marot. Telephone: 33 (1) 44.43.88.88. Fax: 33 (1) 44.43.88.77

Firm engaged in General American and International Law Practice but not authorized to appear before the English Courts or to act as Solicitors.

FIRM PROFILE: WILSON, ELSER, MOSKOWITZ, EDELMAN & DICKER *is a full service international law firm, ranking among the largest law firms in the United States with offices in eleven major cities in the United States. We have provided our clients with a full range of expert and innovative legal services for more than a quarter of a century. Our dramatic growth during this period has been a response to the emerging needs of existing clients and addition of new ones. Initially, ours was an insurance-related practice and we maintain a preeminent position with regard to all aspects of insurance law and the insurance/reinsurance industry serving insureds, brokers, insurers and reinsurers. As our clients have matured and broadened in scope, so have our services and expertise and we have expanded into the general corporate law, including creditors' rights and bankruptcy, trusts and estates and real estate transactions and regulatory work.*

RESIDENT PARTNER

THOMAS R. CHERRY, born Danbury, Connecticut, December 31, 1951; admitted, 1978, Washington; 1985, U.S. District Court, Western District of Washington; 1988, New York and Connecticut (Not admitted in England). *Education:* University of Bonn, Federal Republic of Germany; Syracuse University (B.A., 1974); University of Puget Sound (J.D., 1977); University of Amsterdam, The Netherlands (ICEI, 1978). Guest Lecturer: U.S. Product Liability Law, University of Bonn, 1986-1987; IFS, Frankfurt Federal Republic of Germany, 1986-1989. Deputy Prosecuting Attorney, King County, Washington, 1979-1983. *Member:* Internationales Fachinstitut fuer Steuer und Wirtschaftsrecht; International Bar Association; Defense Research Institute.

(For additional Biographical data, see Professional Biographies at New York, New York).

WINCKWORTH & PEMBERTON

Incorporating Sherwood & Co.

Established in 1788

35 GREAT PETER STREET, WESTMINSTER
LONDON SW1P 3LR, ENGLAND
Telephone: 0171-593-5000
Fax: 0171-593-5099
Telex: 8955719

Chelmsford, England Office: 54 New Street, Chelmsford, Essex CM1 1NG. Telephone 0245 262212. Fax 0245 252502.

Oxford, England Office: 16 Beaumont Street, Oxford, Oxon OX1 2LZ. Telephone: 0865 241974. Fax: 0865 726274.

Litigation - Building Contract Disputes, Intellectual Property Rights, Unfair Dismissal and Employment Matters, Liquor Licensing, Matrimonial Problems, Debt Collection, Personal Injury, Insurance Claims, Landlord and Tenant and Professional Conduct and Disciplinary Hearings.

Property - Acquisition and Disposal of Freehold and Leasehold Properties for Investment, Development of Operational Purposes, Housing Association Law, Town and Country Planning, Institutional and Agricultural Property, Tenant Block Purchase Schemes and Property Finance.

Company/Commercial - Company Formations, Restructuring, Taxation, Patents, Trademarks, Copyright and Industrial Design, Agency and Distribution Agreements, EC Law, Consumer Law, Insolvency, Trade Competitions and Lotteries, Advertising Standards and Codes.

Private Client - Capital Taxation and Estate Planning, the Creation, Administration and Winding-up of Trusts and Settlements, Probate, Deeds of Covenant, Offshore Trust and Tax Planning Operations and Court of Protection Work.

(This Listing Continued)

FIRM PROFILE: Ecclesiastical: *The firm has a long established connection with the Church of England. It provides registries for several Dioceses and advises on ecclesiastical matters and wider questions such as church property and the administration of ecclesiastical charities.*

Parliamentary - With the incorporation of Sherwood & Co. Parliamentary agents in 1991, the firm is now involved in the promotion and opposition of private and delegated legislation.

PARTNERS

R.W. Larard	N.F. Welch
F.E. Robson	R.H.A. MacDougald
H.W. Gamon	C.J. Tipping
K. Miller	J. Rees
B.J. Hood	P.J. Williams
D.K. Jenkins	A.J. Murray
N.A.F. Owston	C.M. Vine
P.C.E. Morris	P.C.M. Irving
A.J. Taylor	D.R. Fitton
M.C. Thatcher	C.M. Hand
A.M.H. Gorlov	A. Aisbett
H.S. Wiggs	P.J. Lawrence

CONSULTING PARTNER

D.W. Faull

CONSULTANTS

L. Grosse
M. Edwardes-Evans
J.M. Morgan
J.A. Foster
R.M. Milligan
C.R. Winser

ASSISTANT SOLICITORS

F. Carr	H. Stallard
C.C.M. Enfield	R. Williams
R. Harris	A. Calvert
R.C. Harrison	R. Botkai
T.M. Bullimore	L. Gardner
T.J. Watts	K. Jones
P.J. Manfield	C. Matthews
A. Marsh	A. Wells
A.M.K. Murray	N. Goode
A. Meek	

LEGAL SUPPORT PERSONNEL
PARALEGALS

S. Asser	E. Herbert
J.F. Chalmers	S.M. Jones
J. Dowler	B.H. Mandalia
B.A. Farrer	J. O'Reilly
A.J. Hammond	E. Okoro
J.M. Hussey	B.E. Paul
A.J. Robertson	

WINTHROP, STIMSON, PUTNAM & ROBERTS

2 THROGMORTON AVENUE
LONDON EC2N 2AP, ENGLAND
Telephone: 011-44171-628-4931
Telefax: 011-44171-638-0443
Cable Address: "Winstim, London EC2"
Telex: 8950511 ONEONE G BOX 24723001

New York Main Office: One Battery Park Plaza, New York, N.Y., 10004-1490. Telephone: 212-858-1000.

Stamford, Connecticut Office: Financial Centre, 695 East Main Street, P.O. Box 6760, 06904-6760. Telephone: 203-348-2300.

Washington, D.C. Office: 1133 Connecticut Avenue, N.W., 20036. Telephone: 202-775-9800.

Palm Beach, Florida Office: 125 Worth Avenue, 33480. Telephone: 407-655-7297.

(This Listing Continued)

WINTHROP, STIMSON, PUTNAM & ROBERTS,
London—Continued

Brussels Office: Rue Du Taciturne 42, B-1040 Brussels, Belgium. Telephone: 011-322-230-1392.

Tokyo, Japan Office: 608 Atagoyama Bengoshi Building 6-7, Atago 1-chome, Minato-ku, Tokyo 105 Japan. Telephone: 011-813-3437-9740.

Hong Kong Office: 2505 Asia Pacific Finance Tower, Citibank Plaza, 3 Garden Road, Central. Telephone: 011-852-530-3400.

Firm engaged in American and International Law Practice, but not authorized to appear before the English Courts or to act as Solicitors.

RESIDENT PARTNERS

PETER S. BROWN, born Jersey City, New Jersey, January 8, 1951; admitted, 1978, New York (Not admitted in England). *Education:* Drew University (B.A., 1974); Harvard Law School (J.D., 1977).

RESIDENT ASSOCIATES

STEFANIE L. ROTH, born New York, N.Y., March 23, 1946; admitted, 1983, New York (Not admitted in England). *Education:* New York University (B.A., 1967); Yale University (J.D., 1982).

WINWARD FEARON & CO.

Established in 1986

35 BOW STREET

LONDON WC2E 7AU, ENGLAND

Telephone: 0171-836 9081

Fax: 0171-836 8382

Telex: 267651

FIRM PROFILE: Established in 1986, Winward Fearon & Co. is one of London's fastest expanding commercial practices. The firm concentrates on giving specialist advice in its particular areas of expertise, namely construction law, corporate and project finance, insurance and property. At the same time, the departments regularly work together on major national and international projects in the energy, oil and gas and construction fields. The firm has 14 partners and 8 assistants, practising from offices in Central London. In addition, the firm is a member of a group of European lawyers firms with offices in Brussels, Cologne, Hamburg, Leipzig, Dresden and Paris.

NICHOLAS CARNELL, born Amersham, 1962; admitted, 1986, England and Wales. *Education:* University College, London (LL.B., Hons., 1983). Accredited mediator for Centre for Dispute Resolution (CEDR). *LANGUAGES:* English and German. *PRACTICE AREAS:* Construction Law (Building and Civil Engineering); Domestic and International Law; Arbitration and Litigation.

DAVID CORNES, born Stoke-on-Trent, 1944; admitted, 1979, England and Wales. *Education:* Kings College, University of London (B.Sc., Eng., 1966). AKC, Chartered Civil Engineer, Member of the Institution of Civil Engineers, 1971. Author: "Design Liability in the Construction Industry," Third Edition, Blackwell Scientific Publications, 1989. Co-author: "Collateral Warranties - A Practical Guide for the Construction Industry," Blackwell Scientific Publications, 1990. *Member:* Fellow of the Chartered Institute of Arbitrators. Accredited mediator for Centre for Dispute Resolution (CEDR). *LANGUAGES:* English and French. *PRACTICE AREAS:* Construction Law (Building and Civil Engineering); Domestic and International Law; Arbitration and Litigation.

JULIAN CRITCHLOW, born Liss, Hants, 1958; admitted, 1983, England and Wales. *Education:* University College, London (LL.B., MSc. Lond, 1981, ACI Arb.); Kings College, Chancery Lane College of Law. *LANGUAGES:* English, French, Spanish and Italian. *PRACTICE AREAS:* Construction Law (Building and Civil Engineering); Domestic and International Law; Arbitration and Litigation.

ROGER DOULTON, born Uppingham, Rutland, 1949; admitted, 1976, England and Wales. *Education:* St. Edmund Hall, Oxford (M.A., Oxon, 1971). Politics, Philosophy and Economics. Editor, British Insurance Law Association Journal. Member of the British Academy of Experts, Fellow of the Royal Society of Arts. Accredited mediator for Centre for Disputes Resolution (CEDR). *LANGUAGES:* English and Italian. *PRACTICE AREAS:* Insurance Law; Non-Marine Work; Coverage Disputes; Reinsurance; Professional Indemnity; Fidelity Claims and Personal Lines; Liability Work.

(This Listing Continued)

GUY FEARON, born London, 1955; admitted, 1980, England and Wales. *Education:* Milton Abbey. *LANGUAGES:* English. *PRACTICE AREAS:* Property Law; Commercial Property; Residential and Commercial Development; Acquisition of Investment; Residential Properties for Offshore Clients.

DAVID GWILLIM, born London, 1954; admitted, 1981, England and Wales. *Education:* University of Wales, Cardiff (LL.B., Hons., FCI Arb., 1978). *LANGUAGES:* English and German. *PRACTICE AREAS:* Construction Law (Building and Civil Engineering); Domestic and International Law; Arbitration and Litigation.

TIMOTHY GULLIVER, born Margate, 1952; admitted, 1983, England and Wales. *Education:* Trinity College, Oxford (M.A., Oxon, 1978). *LANGUAGES:* English. *PRACTICE AREAS:* Construction Law (Building and Civil Engineering); Domestic and International Law; Arbitration and Litigation.

CLIVE LEVONTINE, born London, 1961; admitted, 1988, England and Wales. *Education:* Birmingham University (Law and Politics, Hons., 1983). *LANGUAGES:* English. *PRACTICE AREAS:* Landlord and Tenant Law; Insurance Law; Property Claims; Personal Lines and Liability Work.

ADRIAN LUTO, born Farnham, Surrey, 1956; admitted, 1983, England and Wales; 1986, Hong Kong. *Education:* Downing College, Cambridge (M.A., Cantab, LL.B., 1979). *LANGUAGES:* English and French. *PRACTICE AREAS:* Energy Projects; Company Acquisitions; Joint Ventures; Corporate Finance.

DAVID RAFF, born Manchester, 1959; admitted, 1983, England and Wales. *Education:* University College, London (LL.B., 1980). *LANGUAGES:* English and French. *PRACTICE AREAS:* Company Acquisitions; Joint Ventures; Corporate Finance.

MAXIMILIAN WIELICZKO, born London, 1961; admitted, 1987, England and Wales. *Education:* University College, London (LL.B., Hons., 1983). *LANGUAGES:* English and Polish. *PRACTICE AREAS:* Construction Law (Building and Civil Engineering); Domestic and International Law; Arbitration and Litigation.

RICHARD WINWARD, born Manchester, 1947; admitted, 1972, England and Wales. *Education:* Sheffield University (LL.B., Hons.). Co-author: "Collateral Warranties - A Practical Guide for the Construction Industry," Blackwell Scientific Publications, 1990. *Member:* Fellow of the Chartered Institute of Arbitrators. Accredited mediator for Centre for Dispute Resolution (CEDR). *LANGUAGES:* English and French. *PRACTICE AREAS:* Construction Law (Building and Civil Engineering); Domestic and International Law; Arbitration and Litigation.

JUDITH RIXON, born High Wycombe, 1947; admitted, 1990, England and Wales. *Education:* Newnham College, Cambridge (M.A., Cantab, 1969); London University Institute of Education (PGCE, 1970). *LANGUAGES:* English and Italian. *PRACTICE AREAS:* Construction Law (Building and Civil Engineering); Domestic and International Law; Arbitration and Litigation.

BRIAN BANNISTER, born Barrow-in-Furness, 1957; admitted, 1988, England and Wales. *Education:* St. John's College, Cambridge (M.A., Cantab, 1979). *LANGUAGES:* English. *PRACTICE AREAS:* Company Acquisitions; Joint Ventures; Corporate Finance; Non-litigious Employment Law.

WITHERS

12 GOUGH SQUARE

LONDON EC4A 3DE, ENGLAND

Telephone: 0171-936 1000

Telex: 24213 Witherg

Fax: 0171-936 2589 DX: 160 London/Chancery Lane

Paris, France Office: Withers. 15, Rue de Marignan, 75008. Telephone: (33.1) 49.53.06.66. Telex: 640057F WAYLAND. Fax: (33.1) 49.53.05.76.

London, England Associated Office: Michael Soul & Associates. 12 Gough Square, London EC4A 3DE. Telephone: 0171-353 3358; 071-936 1000. Fax: 0171-936 2589.

Agricultural and Farming, Aviation, Charities, Company Law (UK and European), Commercial Litigation (including contentious property work), Employment, Environmental Law, Inheritance Planning and Succession, Insurance, Separation and Divorce, Probate (including contentious pro-

(This Listing Continued)

bate), Real Estate and Commercial Property, Shipping, Tax Planning (UK and International), Trusts (UK and Offshore).

FIRM PROFILE: Withers is a 30 partner firm based in Central London. Well-known for its private client activities including international asset management and tax planning for private individuals and their families, it has extended its range of services to include a highly personal commercial service to individuals and their companies both UK and International seeking access to the City of London's financial markets. Its commercial expertise is built on corporate finance and international shipping. In-house French and Spanish lawyers make up the European team in London which is complemented by French lawyers in Withers' Paris office.

CONSULTANTS

SIR ARTHUR COLLINS, KCVO, B.A. (Oxon.).

DAVID M. DIXON, CVO, B.A. (Oxon.).

PARTNERS

BRIAN T. J. STEVENS (Senior Partner).

EDWARD D. A. RAM, B.A. (Oxon.).

CHARLES E. DOUGHTY, B.A. (Oxon.).

PHILIP W. DURRANCE, B.A. (Oxon.).

ANTHONY J. THOMPSON, M.A., LL.B. (Cantab).

STEPHEN COOKE

MURRAY HALLAM, M.A. (Oxon.).

ANDREW E. H. GERRY, M.A. (Cantab).

ROBIN J. M. PAUL, M.A. (Oxon.).

KEITH J. BRUCE-SMITH, M.A. (Oxon.).

JONATHAN J. EASTWOOD (Resident, Paris, France Office).

THERESA J. GRANT PETERKIN, B.A.

DIANA C. PARKER, M.A., M.Phil. (Cantab).

DAVID BOWYER, M.A. (Cantab).

ANNABEL L. BRENTON, LL.B.

PETER W.J. DUFFIELD, M.A. (Oxon.).

JEREMY P. ARNOLD, M.A. (Cantab).

MARGARET ROBERTSON, B.A. (Oxon).

MICHAEL S.E. CARPENTER, LL.B.

MICHAEL MITCHELL, M.A. (Oxon.), M.A. (Cantab).

DAWN W.M. GOODMAN

MICHAEL J. SOUL

TIMOTHY J. TAYLOR, M.A. (Oxon).

ALISON J.S. PAINES, M.A. (Cantab).

TIMOTHY E. STOCKS, LL.B.

HENRY STUART, B.A.

CLAUDIA D. GIBBONS, B.A. (Oxon).

JUDITH INGHAM, M.A. (Oxon.).

JULIA ABREY, M.A. (Oxon.).

DAVID GEBBIE, LL.B.

ANDREW H. LANE, M.A. (Cantab).

Languages: French, Italian, Spanish, German, Dutch and Russian

YOUNGSTEIN & GOULD

Established in 1974

17 BULSTRODE STREET
LONDON W1M 5FQ, ENGLAND
Telephone: 0171-935 5372
Telefax: 0171-935 0860

U.S., U.K. and International Taxation, U.S. and International Business and Corporate Law, Cross-Border Mergers and Acquisitions, International Estate Planning.

(This Listing Continued)

Firm engaged in American and International Practice, but not authorized to appear before the English Courts or to act as Solicitors.

MEMBERS OF FIRM

HOWARD G. YOUNGSTEIN, born New York, N.Y., October 23, 1944; admitted, 1968, New York (Not admitted in England). *Education:* University of Pennsylvania (A.B., magna cum laude, with distinction, 1965); University of Florence, Italy; Columbia University (LL.B., 1968). Phi Beta Kappa. Fulbright Scholar. *LANGUAGES:* French and Italian.

JEFFREY L. GOULD, born Los Angeles, California, December 5, 1948; admitted, 1974, California (Not admitted in England). *Education:* Pomona College (B.A., magna cum laude, with distinction, 1970); Harvard University (J.D., cum laude, 1974). Phi Beta Kappa. Adjunct Professor of Taxation, University of Notre Dame London Law Centre, 1981-1985. *Member:* American Bar Association (Member, Tax Section). *LANGUAGES:* French.

ASSOCIATES

MARYANN CLEMENTE, born Nyack, New York, November 14, 1960; admitted, 1988, New York (Not admitted in England). *Education:* Bryn Mawr College (A.B., cum laude, 1982); New York University School of Law (J.D., 1987).

ZAPRUDER & ODELL THORSTEINSSONS

6 BROADGATE
LONDON EC2M 2QS, ENGLAND
Telephone: 44-171-972-0434
Fax: 44-171-972-0433

Washington, D.C. Office: Zapruder & Odell, 601 Thirteenth Street, N.W. Suite 800 South. Telephone: 202-508-9600. Fax: 202-508-9601.

Berwyn, Pennsylvania Office: Zapruder & Odell, 1235 Westlakes Drive, Suite 385. Telephone: 610-651-5600. Fax: 610-651-5605.

Design of Tax Sensitive Financial Products and Advice Concerning International Tax Planning.

FIRM PROFILE: Zapruder & Odell Thorsteinssons consists of two tax professionals located in London and the combined international tax resources of Zapruder & Odell in the United States and Thorsteinssons in Canada. The firm concentrates on the design of financial products to meet the tax needs of Western European and North American multinational corporations and international tax consulting services.

TAX PROFESSIONALS

RICHARD K. BRIFFETT, born Bristol, England, May 8, 1947. *Education:* University College London University (B.A., Hons, 1968, M.Phil., 1971). H.M. Inspector of Taxes, UK Inland Revenue, 1971-1979. Vice President and Senior Director, Continental Bank, 1979-1992. Vice President, Salomon Brothers International Limited, 1992-1994.

STUART E. HORWICH, born Los Angeles, California, April 14, 1961; admitted, 1986, Washington; 1991, District of Columbia. *Education:* University of California at San Diego (B.A., magna cum laude, 1982); University of Cambridge, Cambridge, England (LL.M., with honors, 1985); University of California at Berkeley (J.D., 1985). Law Clerk, Washington Supreme Court. Attorney, Tax Division, Department of Justice, 1987-1989. Senior Attorney, Securities and Exchange Commission, 1989-1990.

(For Complete Biographical Data on all Personnel, see Professional Biographies at Washington, D.C.)

ZELLERMAYER, PELOSSOF & SCHIFFER

Established in 1991

46 MOUNT STREET
LONDON W1Y 5RD, ENGLAND
Telephone: 44-171-629 1920
Fax: 44-171-408 0202

Tel Aviv, Israel Office: Zellermayer Pelossof, Advocates. Europe House, 37 Shaul Hamelech Blvd., 64928. Telephone: 03-6954222. Telecopier: 03-6952884.

General and International Law Practice, Banking, Commercial, Corporate and Project Finance, Property, International Litigation, Shipping, Arbitration and Mediation, Intellectual Property and European Community Law.

(This Listing Continued)

ZELLERMAYER, PELOSSOF & SCHIFFER, *London—*
Continued

RICHARD A. SCHIFFER, born Cleveland, Ohio, September 25, 1944; admitted, 1969, Illinois and U.S. District Court, 7th Circuit (Not admitted in England). *Education:* University of Michigan (B.A., 1966); Northwestern University School of Law (J.D., 1969); University of Amsterdam, Europa Institute (1972). General Counsel, Johananoff Group, 1971-1985. European Director, International Dispute Resolution Ltd., and Chairman, ADR Group Ltd., (Alternative Dispute Resolution), 1987. Arbitrator, International Commercial and Industrial Arbitration Court (CARICI), Geneva, 1987. Associate Member of the Chartered Institute of Arbitrators, 1988. Advisory Board Member, World Arbitration and Mediation Report (BNA). Member of the Association of Fellows and Legal Scholars of the Centre for International Legal Studies, Salzburg. Author: Computer Mediation, Business and Assets, July, 1988. Mediation - Effective Dispute Resolution, *Architects Liability* , September, 1988 and *Professional Liability Today* , October, 1988; "Mediation - less damage than the courts?" Director Magazine, February, 1989; The use of "Alternative Dispute Resolution," in Resolving Disputes Involving Electronic Data Interchange, *EDI and the Law* , Blenheim Online Ltd., August, 1989; Contract Journal, April 1990, "The Use of Mediation in the Construction Industry Dispute Prevention and Resolution;" The Comparative Law Yearbook of International Business - Vol. 12, "The Use of Alternative Dispute Resolution in International Trade." *Member:* Illinois State Bar Association; American Bar Association (Member, Section of International Law and Practice); International Bar Association (Member, Section on Business Law). *LANGUAGES:* French.

ASSOCIATES

BARRY PHILLIPS, born London, England, 1942; admitted, 1970, Solicitor of the Supreme Court of England and Wales. *Education:* London School of Economics (B.Sc., Econ., 1963). *PRACTICE AREAS:* Commercial Legal; Private Companies; Joint Ventures; Finance.

CHARLES B. GOTTLIEB, born Pittsburgh, Pennsylvania, July 1, 1963; admitted, 1989, Pennsylvania; 1994, Solicitor of the Supreme Court of England and Wales. *Education:* Indiana University (1985); University of Pittsburgh School of Law (J.D., 1988); The London School of Economics and Political Science (B.S.; LL.M., International Business Law, 1989). *Member:* Pennsylvania, American and International Bar Associations. *PRACTICE AREAS:* Intellectual Property; International Trade and Finance.

ADDLESHAW SONS & LATHAM

Established in 1873

DENNIS HOUSE

MARSDEN STREET

MANCHESTER M2 1JD, ENGLAND

Telephone: Nat. 061 832 5994

Int. + 44 61 832 5994

Fax: Nat. 061 832 2250

Int. + 44 61 832 2250

Company and corporate finance, EC Competition and Commercial, Commercial Property, Environmental, Joint Ventures, Acquisitions and Mergers, Corporate Tax, Intellectual Property, Commercial Litigation, Employment, Construction, Insolvency and Corporate Reconstruction, Debt Recovery, Banking and Finance, Venture Capital, Pensions.

FIRM PROFILE: Founded in Manchester in 1873, Addleshaw Sons & Latham is regarded as one of the premier non-London firms in the UK. The firm has associated international offices through its membership of the Norton Rose M5 Group of independent legal practices.

PARTNERS

DAVID J. TULLY, born India, 1942; admitted, 1965. Rylands Fletcher Law Prize, 1960. *Member:* Law Society of England and Wales; National Young Solicitors (Past Chairman); The Manchester Law Society (Past President). (Senior Partner). *LANGUAGES:* English. *PRACTICE AREAS:* Commercial Property Law; Personal Tax Law; Estate Planning Law; Administration Law.

FRANCIS R. SHACKLETON, born England, 1940; admitted, 1965. *Education:* Cambridge University (M.A.LL.M., 1962). *Member:* Law Society of England and Wales; National Association of Pension Funds; Association of Pension Lawyers. *LANGUAGES:* English. *PRACTICE AREAS:* Pensions Law; Trusts Law; Probate Law; Tax Planning Law.

(This Listing Continued)

DAVID R. WITHINGTON, born England, 1944; admitted, 1969. *Education:* Sheffield University (LL.B., 1966). *Member:* Law Society of England and Wales. *LANGUAGES:* English. *PRACTICE AREAS:* Commercial Property Law.

PAUL A. LEE, born England, 1946; admitted, 1970. *Education:* Cambridge University (M.A. LL.B., 1968). *Member:* Law Society of England and Wales; International Bar Association. (Managing Partner). *LANGUAGES:* English and French. *PRACTICE AREAS:* Corporate Law; Commercial Law.

ANTHONY G. KIRBY, born England, 1944; admitted, 1969. *Education:* Leeds University (LL.B., 1966). *Member:* Law Society of England and Wales; Licensed Insolvency Practitioner; Society of Practitioners of Insolvency. *LANGUAGES:* English. *PRACTICE AREAS:* Banking Law; Insolvency Law.

RICHARD W. HAYES, born England, 1947; admitted, 1972. *Education:* Cambridge University (B.A., 1969; LL.B., 1970). *Member:* Law Society of England and Wales. *LANGUAGES:* English. *PRACTICE AREAS:* Corporate Tax; Employee Share Schemes.

E. ANDREW NEEDHAM, born England, 1950; admitted, 1975. *Education:* Cambridge University (M.A. LL.B., 1972). *Member:* Law Society of England and Wales. *LANGUAGES:* English. *PRACTICE AREAS:* Company Law; Commercial Law; Corporate Finance Law.

DIANA M. CRAVEN, born England, 1950; admitted, 1974. *Education:* Nottingham University (LL.B., 1971). *Member:* Law Society of England and Wales. *LANGUAGES:* English. *PRACTICE AREAS:* Commercial Property Law; Secured Lending Law; Property Development Law.

T. KEITH JOHNSTON, born England, 1952; admitted, 1976. *Education:* London University (LL.B., 1973). *Member:* Law Society of England and Wales. *LANGUAGES:* English. *PRACTICE AREAS:* Corporate Finance Law; Corporate Law; Commercial Law; Local Authority Law.

GARTH LINDRUP, born South Africa, 1948; admitted, 1975. *Education:* Cambridge University (B.A., 1972; LL.M., 1978). Editor: Butterworths Competition Law Handbook. *Member:* Chairman, Solicitors' European Group; Law Society of England and Wales; International Bar Association; Ligue Internationale du Droit de la Concurrence. *LANGUAGES:* English, Italian and French. *PRACTICE AREAS:* UK and EEC Competition Law; Merger Control; Joint Ventures Law; Distribution Law; Franchising Law; Agency Agreements Law.

JOHN M. HEPPLESTONE, born England, 1947; admitted, 1971. *Education:* Cambridge University (M.A., 1969). *Member:* Law Society of England and Wales; Association Internationale des Jeunes Avocats. *LANGUAGES:* English and French. *PRACTICE AREAS:* Commercial and Residential Property Law.

JOHN K. GATENBY, born England, 1950; admitted, 1975; 1980, Barrister and Solicitor of New Zealand; Fellow, Chartered Institute of Arbitrators. *Education:* Cambridge University (M.A. LL.M., B.A., 1971; LL.B., 1972); Squire Law Studentship. Author: "Recovery of Money." *Member:* Law Society of England and Wales; Solicitors' European Group; International Bar Association; London Solicitors Litigation Association; Commonwealth Law Association; Institute of Credit Management. *LANGUAGES:* English, French and German. *PRACTICE AREAS:* Commercial Litigation; International Litigation; Arbitration Law.

SHÂN M. SPENCER, born Wales, 1953; admitted, 1977, Licensed Insolvency Practitioner. *Education:* Sheffield University (LL.B., 1974). *Member:* Law Society of England and Wales; Society of Practitioners of Insolvency; Insolvency Lawyers Association; Association Europeenne des Practiciens des Procedures Collectives. *LANGUAGES:* English. *PRACTICE AREAS:* Insolvency Law; Banking Law.

JOHN K. KELSEY, born England, 1949; admitted, 1972. *Member:* Law Society of England and Wales. *LANGUAGES:* English. *PRACTICE AREAS:* Commercial Litigation; Employment Law; Construction Law.

STEPHEN DEVLIN, born England, 1957; admitted, 1982. *Education:* Kingston-upon-Hull University (LL.B., 1978). *Member:* Law Society of England and Wales. *LANGUAGES:* English. *PRACTICE AREAS:* Corporate Law.

IAN O. GOULTY, born England, 1954; admitted, 1980. *Education:* Oxford University (M.A., 1976). *Member:* Law Society of England and Wales. *LANGUAGES:* English. *PRACTICE AREAS:* Commercial Property Law.

THERESA M. FENTON, born England, 1952; admitted, 1979. *Education:* Manchester Metropolitan University (B.A., 1973). *Member:* Law Soci-

(This Listing Continued)

ety of England and Wales; Insolvency Practitioners Association. *LANGUAGES:* English, French and Spanish. *PRACTICE AREAS:* Insolvency Law; Banking Law; Commercial Litigation.

NIGEL R.J. MADELEY, born England, 1956; admitted, 1983. *Education:* Oxford University (M.A., 1978). *Member:* Law Society of England and Wales. *LANGUAGES:* English. *PRACTICE AREAS:* Commercial Property Law; Residential Estate Development; Environmental Law.

RICHARD N.F. LEE, born England, 1959; admitted, 1984. *Education:* Cambridge University (M.A., 1980). *Member:* Law Society of England and Wales. *LANGUAGES:* English and French. *PRACTICE AREAS:* Corporate Law; Corporate Finance Law.

SHAUN J. REARDEN, born England, 1954; admitted December 1979. *Education:* London University (LL.B., 1975). *Member:* Law Society of England and Wales. *LANGUAGES:* English. *PRACTICE AREAS:* Banking Law; Asset Finance Law; Corporate Finance; Property Finance.

MICHAEL B. KENWORTHY, born England, 1956; admitted, 1981. *Education:* Keele University (B.A., 1978). *Member:* Law Society of England and Wales. *LANGUAGES:* English. *PRACTICE AREAS:* Town and Country Planning Law; Environmental Law; Local Government Law.

JOHN A. GOSLING, born England, 1959; admitted, 1984. *Education:* Durham University (B.A., 1981). *Member:* Law Society of England and Wales. *LANGUAGES:* English. *PRACTICE AREAS:* Commercial and Property Litigation.

JONATHAN R. SHORROCK, born England, 1953; admitted, 1985. *Education:* Manchester University (LL.B., 1982). *Member:* Law Society of England and Wales; International Bar Association. *LANGUAGES:* English. *PRACTICE AREAS:* Company Law; Commercial Law; Corporate Finance Law.

ANNABEL M. CARTER, born England, 1956; admitted, 1980. *Education:* Exeter University (LL.B., 1977). *Member:* Law Society of England and Wales. *LANGUAGES:* English. *PRACTICE AREAS:* Commercial Property Law.

ROBERT R. STOKER, born England, 1953; admitted, 1981. *Education:* Cambridge University (M.A., 1975). *Member:* Law Society of England and Wales; Licensing Executives Society; Solicitors' European Group; Law Society de la Concurrence; Society for Computers and Law. *LANGUAGES:* English. *PRACTICE AREAS:* Patents and Trademarks Law; Copyright and Design Law.

HELEN J. BURTON, born England, 1957; admitted, 1982. *Education:* Exeter University (LL.B., 1979). *Member:* Law Society of England and Wales. *LANGUAGES:* English. *PRACTICE AREAS:* Commercial Property Law.

GLENDA A. TURNER, born England, 1960; admitted, 1985. *Education:* Sheffield University (LL.B., 1981). Sheffield and District Incorporated Law Society Senior Prize. *Member:* Law Society of England and Wales. *LANGUAGES:* English. *PRACTICE AREAS:* Corporate Law; Commercial Law.

GREGORY J. MCMAHON, born England, 1960; admitted, 1985. *Education:* Manchester University (LL.B., 1982). *Member:* Law Society of England and Wales. *LANGUAGES:* English. *PRACTICE AREAS:* General Commercial Law; Corporate Law.

JULIA K. BURROWS, born England, 1956; admitted, 1980, Licensed Insolvency Practitioner. *Education:* Leicester University (LL.B., 1977). *Member:* Law Society of England and Wales; Society of Practitioners of Insolvency; Insolvency Lawyers Association. *LANGUAGES:* English. *PRACTICE AREAS:* Insolvency Law; Banking Law.

MALCOLM J. PIKE, born England, 1959; admitted, 1984. *Education:* Leicester University (LL.B., 1981). *Member:* Law Society of England and Wales; Industrial Law Society; Employment Lawyers' Association; IBA. *LANGUAGES:* English. *PRACTICE AREAS:* Employment Law.

TIMOTHY M. RAYNER, born England, 1960; admitted, 1985. *Education:* King's College, London (LL.B., 1982). *Member:* Law Society of England and Wales. *LANGUAGES:* English and French. *PRACTICE AREAS:* Insolvency and Corporate Law.

HUW BAKER, born England, 1962; admitted, 1987. *Education:* Cambridge University (M.A. (Cantab), 1984). *LANGUAGES:* English. *PRACTICE AREAS:* Construction Law.

STEPHEN P. CLARK, born England, 1961; admitted, 1987. *Education:* Cambridge University (M.A., 1984). *Member:* Law Society of England and

(This Listing Continued)

Wales. *LANGUAGES:* English and French. *PRACTICE AREAS:* Banking Law; Corporate Finance; Property Finance; Securitisation.

JEAN C. BOLDERO, born England, 1963; admitted, 1987. *Education:* Manchester University (LL.B., 1984). *Member:* Law Society of England and Wales; Society of Practitioners of Insolvency. *LANGUAGES:* English. *PRACTICE AREAS:* Insolvency Law; Banking Law.

JONATHAN W. DAVEY, born England, 1963; admitted, 1988. *Education:* Manchester University (LL.B., Hons., 1986). *Member:* Law Society of England and Wales; Manchester Law Society; NW Solicitors European Group; L'Association Internationale des Jeunes Avocats; CBI National Advisory Panel on Consumer Affairs. *LANGUAGES:* English. *PRACTICE AREAS:* Competition Law; Commercial Agreements; EC Law.

ALSOP WILKINSON

11 ST. JAMES'S SQUARE
MANCHESTER M2 6DR, ENGLAND
Telephone: 0161-834 7760
Telex: 667965
Fax: 0161-831 7515

London, England Office: 6 Dowgate Hill, EC4R 2SS. Telephone: 0171-248 4141. Telex: 885593. Fax: 0171-623 8286.

Liverpool, England Office: India Buildings, L2 0NH. Telephone: 0151-227 3060. Telex: 627369. Fax: 0151-236 9208.

Hong Kong Office: 4010 Jardine House, 1 Connaught Place, Central. Telephone: 852-524 2003. Fax: 852-810 1345.

New York, New York Office: 230 Park Avenue, Suite 1150, New York, New York, 10169. Telephone: (212) 499-7500. Fax: (212) 499-7505.

Brussels, Belgium Office: Avenue de Cortenberg, 79-81, 1040. Telephone: 2-732-36-00. Fax: 2-734-87-93.

Key Practice Areas: Banking, Commercial Litigation and Arbitration, Commercial Property, Construction, Corporate and Commercial, Corporate Fraud and Investigations, Corporate Taxation, Employee Benefits, Employment, Environment and Planning, Insolvency, Insurance and Reinsurance, Intellectual Property and Computer Law, Marine, Pensions, Private Client.

FIRM PROFILE: One of the largest commercial law practices in the U.K. Established 1821 and offering a full service to corporate and mercantile clients.

RESIDENT PARTNERS

Roger Lane-Smith (Chairman)	J. Procter
N.E.J. Kissack	S.R. Jackson
(Managing Partner)	A. Harris
R.H.C. Nichols	Kate Ive
D.S. Maples	P. Manning
Roy G. Beckett	Mary Clarke
Susan Molloy	Sally Wightman
T. Hamilton	W.J.A. Hyde
	Riaz Bowmer

RESIDENT ASSOCIATES

Hans Scheiwiller	Andrew Dawson
Gill Worthington	Tim Drew
A.B. Winterburn	Dermot Preston
J.M. Taylor	Antony S. Weightman
Jane A. Senior	Roger Gough

Member of The Legal Resources Group

(For the Names of Partners Resident in Other Offices, see Listings for Those Offices)

COBBETT LEAK ALMOND

SHIP CANAL HOUSE
KING STREET
MANCHESTER M2 4WB, ENGLAND
Telephone: Nat. 0161 833 3333
Int. +44 161 833 3333
Fax: Nat. 0161 833 3030
Int. +44 161 833 3030

FIRM PROFILE: Cobbett Leak Almond is one of the largest law firms in the North West of England with its beginnings in the early 19th Century. In 1987 two major Manchester firms, Cobbetts and Leak Almond Parkinson merged to create Cobbett Leak Almond. Our reputation rests on a

(This Listing Continued)

COBBETT LEAK ALMOND, Manchester—Continued

commitment to meet the different needs of each of our clients, whether they are large multinationals, growing entrepreneurial businesses or private individuals. Our own success is founded on our ability to help each and every one achieve its objectives locally, nationally and internationally.

To enable us to meet the changing needs of all our clients, we provide a complete and comprehensive range of expert legal services. The services provided include a full range of company and commercial services including advice on Corporate Finance, Acquisitions and Mergers, Banking, Commercial Property, Licensing, Planning, Employment, EC and UK Competition Law, Product Liability, Environmental, Intellectual Property, Construction and Insolvency.

Cobbett Leak Almond has 28 Partners and over 180 staff and is divided into four main departments.

PARTNERS

J. ANTHONY H. FIELDEN, born England, 1937; admitted, 1961, England. *Education:* Keble College Oxford (B.A., 1958). *Member:* Law Society of England and Wales. *PRACTICE AREAS:* Company and Commercial Partnerships.

W.A. DUNCAN BROCK, born England, 1937; admitted, 1963, England. *Education:* Clare College Cambridge (M.A., 1961). *Member:* Law Society of England and Wales; Manchester Law Society. *PRACTICE AREAS:* Commercial Property; Leisure Industry; Property Development.

MICHAEL RAWSTHORN, born England, 1943; admitted, 1967, England. *Education:* University College London (LL.B. Hons., 1964). *Member:* Law Society of England and Wales. *PRACTICE AREAS:* Probate; Commercial and Residential Property.

TIMOTHY J. BENOY, born England, 1942; admitted, 1968, England. *Education:* Oxford University (B.A., 1964). *Member:* Law Society of England and Wales. *PRACTICE AREAS:* Corporate; Commercial.

MICHAEL I. GRIERSON, born England, 1944; admitted, 1970, England. *Education:* Oxford University (B.A., Hons., 1966). *Member:* Law Society of England and Wales. *PRACTICE AREAS:* Commercial Law; Employment Law; Distribution Franchising and Agency.

PETER M.B. OLDHAM, born England, 1945; admitted, 1969, England. *Education:* University of Manchester (LL.B., Hons., 1966). *Member:* Law Society of England and Wales; The Law Society of Manchester. *PRACTICE AREAS:* Town and Country Planning; Retail and Commercial Property Development.

PHILIP HODSON, born England, 1944; admitted, 1969, England. *Education:* Oxford University (B.A., 1966; M.A., 1971). *Member:* Law Society of England and Wales; Solicitors Disciplinary Tribunal. *PRACTICE AREAS:* Litigation; Construction; Personal Injury.

ROBIN M. HAIG, born England, 1947; admitted, 1972, England. *Education:* Liverpool University (LL.B., 1969). *Member:* Law Society of England and Wales. *PRACTICE AREAS:* Commercial and Residential Property; Private Client.

GAVIN R. BUSHELL, born Germany, 1948; admitted, 1972, England. *Education:* Manchester University (LL.B., 1969). *Member:* Law Society of England and Wales; The Notaries Society. *PRACTICE AREAS:* Trust; Probate; Tax.

A. HENRY M. STONE, born England, 1948; admitted, 1973, England. *Education:* Fitzwilliam College Cambridge (B.A., 1970; M.A., 1974). *Member:* Law Society of England and Wales; The Notaries Society. *PRACTICE AREAS:* Commercial Litigation; Insolvency; Building.

ROGER S. HAWES, born England, 1949; admitted, 1974, England. *Education:* Sheffield University (LL.B., 1971). *Member:* Law Society of England and Wales. *PRACTICE AREAS:* Corporate Finance; Company; Employment.

STEPHEN J. WHITE, born England, 1949; admitted, 1974, England. *Education:* University College London (LL.B., 1971). *Member:* Law Society of England and Wales; American Bar Association (Associate Member). *PRACTICE AREAS:* Commercial Property; Secured Lending; Banking.

PETER J.W. STONE, born England, 1951; admitted, 1976, England. *Education:* Liverpool University (LL.B., 1973). *Member:* Law Society of England and Wales. *PRACTICE AREAS:* Property Litigation; Defamation.

(This Listing Continued)

JANET RICHMOND, born England, 1952; admitted, 1976, England. *Education:* Manchester Polytechnic (B.A., Hons., 1973). *Member:* Law Society of England and Wales; The Notaries Society. *PRACTICE AREAS:* Banking; Landlord and Tenant Litigation; Property Litigation.

HAMISH K. LAWSON, born England, 1951; admitted, 1978, England. *Education:* Oxford University (B.A., Oxon, 1971). *Member:* Law Society of England and Wales; Manchester Law Society. *PRACTICE AREAS:* Licensing and Entertainment Law; Food Law; Planning.

ALAN D. STURROCK, born England, 1953; admitted, 1977, England. *Education:* Liverpool University (LL.B., 1974). *Member:* Law Society of England and Wales; Society of Trust and Estate Practitioners. *PRACTICE AREAS:* Trusts; Probate and Personal Taxation.

PETER J. TAYLOR, born England, 1948; admitted, 1978, England. *Education:* Cambridge University (M.A., 1968). *Member:* Law Society of England and Wales. *PRACTICE AREAS:* Property Development.

SIMON D.A. JONES, born Wales, 1953; admitted, 1978, England. *Education:* Oxford University (B.A., 1975). *Member:* Law Society of England and Wales. *PRACTICE AREAS:* Licensing; Environmental Law.

STEPHEN J. BENSON, born England, 1955; admitted, 1980, England. *Education:* Manchester University (LL.B., 1977). *Member:* Law Society of England and Wales; American Bar Association (Associate Member). *PRACTICE AREAS:* Commercial Property; Leisure Industry; Licensed Trade.

ROBERT A. ROPER, born England, 1953; admitted, 1979, England. *Education:* University of Wales (Cardiff) (LL.B., Hons., 1976). *Member:* Law Society of England and Wales; Licensing Executives Society. *PRACTICE AREAS:* Intellectual Property; Competition and Commercial Litigation.

MICHAEL P. SHAW, born 1956; admitted, 1981, England. *Education:* Manchester Polytechnic (B.A., 1978). *Member:* Law Society of England and Wales. *PRACTICE AREAS:* Commercial Property; Banking.

JOHN R. HUNTER, born 1953; admitted, 1977, England. *Education:* King's College London (LL.B., 1974). *Member:* Law Society of England and Wales. *PRACTICE AREAS:* Commercial and Residential Property.

DAVID PICKERING, born England, 1955; admitted, 1980, England. *Education:* University College Cardiff (LL.B., Hons., 1977). *Member:* Law Society of England and Wales. *PRACTICE AREAS:* Matrimonial; Personal Injury.

DAVID P. ROGERS, born England, 1954; admitted, 1983, England. *Education:* Liverpool University (LL.B., 1977). *Member:* Law Society of England and Wales. *PRACTICE AREAS:* Commercial Litigation; Construction; Employment.

G. MARK WHITTELL, born England, 1957; admitted, 1982, England. *Education:* Sheffield University (LL.B., 1977). *Member:* Law Society of England and Wales. *PRACTICE AREAS:* Insolvency; Commercial Litigation.

ANTHONY FITZMAURICE, born England, 1958; admitted, 1984, England. *Education:* Birmingham University (LL.B., 1979). *Member:* Law Society of England and Wales. *PRACTICE AREAS:* Commercial Property; Landlord and Tenant; Licensed Premises.

ROBERT G. TURNBULL, born Bahrain, 1959; admitted, 1984, England. *Education:* Jesus College, Cambridge (B.A., M.A., 1981). *Member:* Law Society of England and Wales. *PRACTICE AREAS:* Corporate.

ROBIN J.C. HIGHAM, born England, 1956; admitted, 1980, England. *Education:* Birmingham University (LL.B., Hons., 1977). *Member:* Law Society of England and Wales. *PRACTICE AREAS:* Banking and Asset Finance.

Languages: French, Italian, Spanish and German

DAVIES ARNOLD COOPER

60 FOUNTAIN STREET
MANCHESTER M2 2FE, ENGLAND
Telephone: 161-839 8396
Facsimile: 161-839 8309

London, England Offices: 6-8 Bouverie Street, EC4Y 8DD. Telephone: 171-936 2222. Telex: 262894. Facsimile: 171-936 2020 and Room 991 Lloyd's Building, 1 Lime Street. Telephone: 171-283 8658. Facsimile: 171-283 8063.

(This Listing Continued)

Madrid, Spain Office: Serrano Anguita, 10-5 DCHA. Telephone: 1-446 3566. Facsimile: 1-445 1600.

International Practice including Corporate, Commercial, Banking, Financial Services, Taxation, Insolvency and Corporate Rescue, Competition and Anti-Trust Law, Entertainment Law, Computer Law, Intellectual Property, Employment, Commercial Property and Funding, Town Planning and Environmental Law, Construction, Commercial Litigation, Marine and Aviation, Insurance and Reinsurance, Product Liability, Personal Injury, Professional Indemnity, Disaster Litigation and Crisis Management.

RESIDENT PARTNERS

John Jackson	Michael Cover
Beth Wilkins	Paul Lockett
Andrew Willcock	Nicholas Rudgard
	John Webster

(For complete list of personnel, see Professional Biographies at London, England)

EVERSHEDS

LONDON SCOTTISH HOUSE
24 MOUNT STREET
MANCHESTER M2 3DB, ENGLAND
Telephone: (44) 161 832-6666
Fax: (44) 161 832 5337

Other Eversheds Offices:
Birmingham, Bristol, Cardiff, Derby, Ipswich, Leeds, London, Middlesbrough, Newcastle-upon-Tyne, Norwich, Nottingham, Berlin, Brussels, Jersey.

Acquisitions and Mergers, Agency/Distribution, Agriculture, Banking, Commercial Property, Company Law, Competition Law, Construction, Corporate Finance, Corporate Tax, EC Law, Employment, Environment, Entertainment, Information Technology, Franchising, Insolvency, Intellectual Property, Litigation, Management Buy-Outs, Pensions and Employee Benefits, Personal Tax & Financial Planning, Property Development, Shipping, Trading Contracts.
Partners within Eversheds: 273.

REGIONAL MANAGING PARTNERS

John Moody

MANCHESTER PARTNERS

G. Blower	M.R. Mattison
J.K. Boardman	D.J. Moody
A. Brearey	C.P. Norbury
P.G. Cole	D. Pine
R.C. Glithero	E.S. Pysden
A. Gold	E.M. Shepherd
R.H.J. Graham	H.H. Solomons
D.C.J. Hall	S.T. Sorrell
J.S. Knowles	J. Walsh
T. Leonard	N.G. Ward

HALLIWELL LANDAU

Established in 1975

ST JAMES'S COURT
BROWN STREET
MANCHESTER M2 2JF, ENGLAND
Telephone: Nat: 061-835-3003 Int: 44-61-835-3003
Facsimile: Nat: 061-835-2994 Int: 44-61-835-2994

FIRM PROFILE: Since its formation in 1975 Halliwell Landau is one of Manchester's leading commercial law firms. It acts for a comprehensive range of corporate, institutional and professional clients, providing a full range of company and commercial services including advice on corporate finance, acquisitions and mergers, banking law, taxation, insolvency, commercial property, commercial litigation, construction law, planning and the environment, construction law and banking, intellectual property, UK and

(This Listing Continued)

European competition law, trusts and estate planning. The firm has 22 partners and over 130 staff and is organized into seven main departments.

PARTNERS

Clive R. Garston	K. Awen Wright
David Stratton	Andrew J. Livesey
Roger Lancaster	Ian D. Austin
Geoffrey R. Marks	Stephen J. Hills
Paul A. Thomas	Stephen L. Goodman
Elizabeth Gardner	Richard J. White
Paul M. Rose	Stephen M. Houston
Geoffrey A. Shindler	Darryl J. Cooke
John M. Whatnall	Justin J. Ryan
Jonathan Moakes	Matthew Wightman
I. Alec Craig	Chris Phillips

DEPARTMENTAL CONTACTS

CLIVE R. GARSTON, born England, 1945; admitted, 1968, England. *Education:* Leeds University (LL.B.). Senior Partner and Head of the Corporate and Commercial Department. *Member:* Law Society of England and Wales; International Bar Association; Northwest Council of Confederation of British Industry. **LANGUAGES:** French. **PRACTICE AREAS:** Corporate Law; Corporate Finance.

DAVID STRATTON, born England, 1947; admitted, 1971, England. *Education:* Leeds University (LL.B.). Head of the Commercial Property Department. *Member:* Law Society of England and Wales. **PRACTICE AREAS:** Commercial Property.

ROGER LANCASTER, born England, 1951; admitted, 1975, England. *Education:* Leicester University (LL.B.). Head of the Planning and Environmental Law Department. *Member:* Law Society of England and Wales. **PRACTICE AREAS:** Planning and Environmental Law.

PAUL A. THOMAS, born England, 1954; admitted, 1978, England. *Education:* Aberystwyth University (LL.B.). Head of the Commercial Litigation Department. *Member:* Law Society of England and Wales. **PRACTICE AREAS:** Commercial Litigation.

GEOFFREY A. SHINDLER, born England, 1942; admitted, 1969, England. *Education:* Cambridge University (M.A., LL.M.). Head of the Trust and Estate Planning Department. *Member:* Law Society of England and Wales; International Bar Association; Society of Estate and Trust Practitioners (Council Member); Association of Pension Lawyers. **PRACTICE AREAS:** Personal, Financial and Estate Planning; Trusts and Pensions.

JONATHAN MOAKES, born England, 1960; admitted, 1984, England. *Education:* Cambridge University (M.A.). Head of the Intellectual Property Department. *Member:* Law Society of England and Wales; International Bar Association; Solicitors' European Group; Licensing Executives Society. **LANGUAGES:** French and German. **PRACTICE AREAS:** Intellectual Property; Computer Law; UK and European Competition Law.

ANDREW J. LIVESEY, born England, 1960; admitted, 1985, England. *Education:* Durham University (B.A.). Head of the Insolvency Department. *Member:* Law Society of England and Wales; Insolvency Lawyers' Association. **PRACTICE AREAS:** Insolvency.

HAMMOND SUDDARDS

TRINITY COURT
16 JOHN DALTON STREET
MANCHESTER M60 8HS, ENGLAND
Telephone: 0161 834 2222
Fax: 0161 834 2244

Leeds, England Office: 2 Park Lane. LS3 1ES. Telephone: 0113 234 3500. Fax: 0113 234 3600. Telex: 517201.
Brussels, Belgium Office: Avenue Louise 250, 1050. Telephone: 00 32 2 627 7676. Fax: 00 32 2 627 7686.
London, England Office: Moor House, 119 London Wall, London, EC2Y 5ET. Telephone: 0171 628 4767. Fax: 0171 628 6161.
Bradford, England Office: Pennine House. 39-45 Well Street. BD1 5NL. Telephone: 01274 734700. Fax: 01274 737547. Telex: 517201.

Corporate Finance including Acquisitions and Mergers, Corporate Finance, Commercial including Acquisitions and Mergers, Corporate Tax, Commercial including Joint Ventures, Pensions, Banks and Building Societies, Intellectual Property, Commercial Litigation, Town and Country Planning, Environmental Law, Commercial Property, European Community Law,

(This Listing Continued)

EU361B

HAMMOND SUDDARDS, Manchester—Continued

Information Technology Law, Employment, Utilities, Insurance Litigation, Media, Mortgage and Aviation Law.
Hammond Suddards has over 870 staff, including 58 partners, 100 Associates and 50 Legal Executive and Paralegals.

RESIDENT PARTNERS

LIAM BUCKLEY. PRACTICE AREAS: Commercial Property.

RICHARD BURNS. PRACTICE AREAS: Corporate Law.

NIGEL DALE. PRACTICE AREAS: Banking.

WILLIAM N. DOWNS. PRACTICE AREAS: Corporate Law.

DUNCAN R. HAYMES. PRACTICE AREAS: Insolvency.

SIMON KILLICK. PRACTICE AREAS: Corporate Law.

IAN MEREDITH. PRACTICE AREAS: Commercial Litigation.

DAVID MOSS. PRACTICE AREAS: Construction Litigation.

SUSAN C. NICKSON. PRACTICE AREAS: Employment.

MICHAEL L. SHEPHERD. PRACTICE AREAS: Commercial Litigation.

ANNE TAYLOR. PRACTICE AREAS: Pensions.

(For lists of other Members, see Professional Biographies at Leeds, London, Bradford and Brussels, Belgium)

PANNONE & PARTNERS

123 DEANSGATE
MANCHESTER M3 2BU, ENGLAND
Telephone: 0161-832 3000
Facsimile: 0161-834 2067

Part of the Pannone Law Group EEIG with Offices in Manchester, London, Paris, Lyon, Brussels, Milan, Barcelona, Madrid, Lisbon, Andorra, Stockholm and Geneva.

(For Details, see London, England Entry)

EVERSHEDS

PERMANENT HOUSE
91 ALBERT ROAD
MIDDLESBROUGH TS1 2PA, ENGLAND
Telephone: (44) 1642 247456
Fax: (44) 1642 240446

(For full details see entry for Eversheds, Newcastle-upon-Tyne).

EVERSHEDS

MILBURN HOUSE
DEAN STREET
NEWCASTLE-UPON-TYNE NE1 1NP, ENGLAND
Telephone: (44) 191 261 1661
Fax: (44) 191 261 8270

Middlesbrough, England: Permanent House, 91 Albert Road, TS1 2PA. Telephone: (44) 1642 247456. Fax: (44) 1642 240446.
Other Eversheds Offices:
Birmingham, Bristol, Cardiff, Derby, Ipswich, Leeds, London, Manchester, Norwich, Nottingham, Berlin, Brussels, Jersey.

Acquisitions and Mergers, Agency/Distribution, Agriculture, Banking, Commercial Property, Company Law, Competition Law, Construction, Corporate Finance, Corporate Tax, EC Law, Employment, Environment, Entertainment, Information Technology, Franchising, Insolvency, Intellectual Property, Litigation, Management Buy-Outs, Pensions and Employee Benefits, Personal Tax & Financial Planning, Property Development, Shipping, Trading Contracts.

(This Listing Continued)

Partners within Eversheds: 273.

REGIONAL MANAGING PARTNER

Nigel Robson

NEWCASTLE-UPON-TYNE AND MIDDLESBROUGH PARTNERS

R.L. Allison	*P.B. Puxon*
K.L. Andersen	*E.J. Pybus*
A.L. Dowie	*A. Reed*
T.J. Driver	*G. Ritzema*
G. Harrison	*N.R. Robson*
M.T. Herbert	*T.H. Tilly*
C.J. Hilton	*I. Ward*
C.J. Hugill	*D.J.M. Wilson*
R.M.V. Jones	*D.T. Wright*
R.J. Nankervis	*R.F.J. Wrighton*

SHOOSMITHS & HARRISON

Established in 1845

VICTORIA HOUSE
3 VICTORIA STREET
NORTHAMPTON NN1 3NR, ENGLAND
Telephone: 0604 31747; 0604 29977
Fax: 0604 234109

Acquisitions and Mergers, Agency/Distribution, Building Society, Commercial Property, Company Law, Competition Law, Corporate Finance, Employment, Environment, European Law, Franchising, Insolvency, Intellectual Property, Litigation, Pensions and Employee Benefits, Taxation, Trading Contracts, Planning and Property Development.

FIRM PROFILE: *Founded in 1845, Shoosmiths & Harrison is one of the country's largest regional firms of solicitors with seven offices offering a full range of legal services.*

CONTACT

C.M. St J. O'Grady

PARTNERS

Miss C.N. Bagley	*P. Llewellyn*
M.H. Banks	*A.G. Mackinlay*
D.J. Bispham	*L.J. Marshall*
N.P. Bradshaw	*J.W. Morton*
O.C. Brookshaw	*M.J. Murray*
D.M. Bunney	*G. New*
J. Castell	*S. Norcross-Webb*
R. Cooper	*C.M. St J. O'Grady*
C.J. Cox	*D.M. Orton-Jones*
K.J. Croft	*I.G. Pears*
B.J. Dobinson	*J.H. Peet*
Miss J.H. Dorkins	*A.J.K. Price*
P.E. Ellis	*Mrs. K.M. Reeve*
D. Endicott	*R.F. Reid*
S.R. Finn	*M.J.F. Roberts*
F.S. Garford	*J.P. Roche*
T. George	*Miss C.M. Rowe*
Miss M. Gibson	*R.F. Sherwood*
J.S.K. Hargreaves	*J.L. Spencer*
D.L. Harrison	*J.E. Spratt*
N.A. Haynes	*N. Stanbrook*
C.A. Hill	*J.C. Temple*
J.C. Hill	*J.F. Thorpe*
R.W. Horner	*A.R. Tubbs*
D.H. Inch	*W.J. West*
M.O. Leopold	*C.M. Whittington*
K.E. Lewington	*R.W.V. Wilson*

Mrs. M. Yeow

Languages: French, German, Spanish, Italian, Polish and Cantonese.

EVERSHEDS

HOLLAND COURT
THE CLOSE
NORWICH NR1 4DX, ENGLAND
Telephone: (44) 1603 272727
Fax: (44) 1603 610535

Ipswich, England: Churchgates House, Cutler Street, 1P1 1UR.
Telephone: (44) 1473 233433. Fax: (44) 1473 233666.
Other Eversheds Offices:
Birmingham, Bristol, Cardiff, Derby, Leeds, London, Manchester, Middlesbrough, Newcastle-upon-Tyne, Nottingham, Berlin, Brussels, Jersey.

Acquisitions and Mergers, Agency/Distribution, Agriculture, Banking, Commercial Property, Company Law, Competition Law, Construction, Corporate Finance, Corporate Tax, EC Law, Employment, Environment, Entertainment, Information Technology, Franchising, Insolvency, Intellectual Property, Litigation, Management Buy-Outs, Pensions and Employee Benefits, Personal Tax & Financial Planning, Property Development, Shipping, Trading Contracts.
Partners within Eversheds: 273.

REGIONAL MANAGING PARTNER

Colin Brown

NORWICH AND IPSWICH PARTNERS

B.M. Adam	D.M.H. Lloyd
S.D. Anderson	P.N. Matthews
C.S. Brown	R.M. McGurk
J. Cadywould	C.M. Medvei
J.R. Chapman	H.G. Noe
E.M. Clarke	P.R. Norton
R.J.M. Collier	B.J. Padfield
A.P.M. Croome	M.J. Partridge
J.F. Durrell-Walsh	J.F.C. Perowne
G.S. Field	M. Roessler
R.V. Gibbs	M.D. Savory
B.F. Gillery	I.R. Shann
C.J. Gillham	D.R. Sisson
B.R. Goodfellow	N.G. Sparrow
T.J. Gould	H.M.G. Speer
R.J.B. Halpin	A.C.K. Sword
S.K. Hamilton	P.J. Thompson
J.B. Hardman	K.A. Threlfall
C.H.W. Holloway	O.H. Warnock
J.E. Hurst	C. Watson
I.G. Inman	M.D. Willcox
A. Jackson	D.V. Woods
R.J. Jacob	R.J. Wortley
	T.J. Yates

MILLS & REEVE

Established in 1789

FRANCIS HOUSE
3-7 REDWELL STREET
NORWICH NR2 4TJ, ENGLAND
Telephone: +44 (0) 1603 660155
Fax: +44 (0) 1603 633027

Cambridge, England Office: Francis House 112 Hills Road, CB2 1PH.
Telephone: +44 (0) 1223 64422. Fax: +44 (0) 1223 355848.

Agriculture, Banking and Building Societies, Bloodstock, Building and Engineering, Charities and Legacies, Commercial Property, Commercial Litigation, Commercial Tax, Company, Corporate Finance, Debt Collection, Ecclesiastical Law, Education, Employment, Entertainment, European, Investment Services, Health and Public Authorities, Insolvency, Insurance, Landlord and Tenant, Licensing, Matrimonial and Family, Medical Litigation, Pensions, Personal Accident and Injury, Personal Tax and Estate Planning, Planning and Environment, Professional Negligence, Residential and Foreign Property, Trademarks, Copyright and Patents, Wills and Probate.

FIRM PROFILE: Founded in 1789, Mills & Reeve is one of the largest law firms outside London with over 100 lawyers and a total staff of around 400. Mills & Reeve has strong international links and has access to

(This Listing Continued)

international offices throughout its membership of the Norton Rose M5 Group of independent legal practices.

PARTNERS

MICHAEL ORR, born 1938; admitted, 1965, England. Education: M.A. (Oxon). Member: Law Society. (Senior Partner). LANGUAGES: English. PRACTICE AREAS: Contract Law; Commercial Property.

MARK JEFFRIES, born 1957; admitted, 1981, England. Education: M.A. (Cantab). Member: Law Society. (Managing Partner). LANGUAGES: English and French. PRACTICE AREAS: Contract Law; Commercial Law; Commercial Property Law.

JOHN KNIGHT, born 1933; admitted, 1957, England. Member: Law Society. LANGUAGES: English, French and Russian. PRACTICE AREAS: Commercial Property Law; Charity Law; Property Finance.

ANTHONY JORDAN, born 1938; admitted, 1960, England. Member: Law Society. LANGUAGES: English. PRACTICE AREAS: Professional Indemnity; Licensing Law.

BRUCE WILSON, born 1942; admitted, 1967, England. Education: LL.B., London. Member: Law Society; Solicitors Family Law Association. LANGUAGES: English. PRACTICE AREAS: Family; Divorce; Matrimonial Law.

JOHN HERRING, born 1946; admitted, 1971, England. Education: M.A. (Cantab). Member: Law Society; Ecclesiastical Law Association; Ecclesiastical Law Society. LANGUAGES: English. PRACTICE AREAS: Church; Ecclesiastical Law; Conveyancing; Property Law.

ALASDAIR DARROCH, born 1947; admitted, 1971, England. Education: M.A. (Cantab). Member: Law Society, Assistant Recorder. LANGUAGES: English, French and German. PRACTICE AREAS: Litigation; Tort Law; Business Crimes.

JONATHAN BARCLAY, born 1947; admitted, 1971, England. Education: University of East Anglia, B.A. Chairman of the Norton Rose M5 Group of independent legal practices. Member: Law Society; IBA. LANGUAGES: English, French, German and Italian. PRACTICE AREAS: Agriculture; Estate Planning; Individual Tax Planning; Tax Shelter Law; Successions; Heritage.

IAN ALEXANDER-SINCLAIR, born 1946; admitted, 1971, England. Education: M.A. (Oxon). Member: Law Society. LANGUAGES: English. PRACTICE AREAS: Corporate Law; Corporate Finance Law; Directors and Officer Liability; Venture Capital; Purchasing Law.

EDWARD CALLAGHAN, born 1950; admitted, 1974, England. Education: LL.B., Exeter. Member: Law Society. LANGUAGES: English. PRACTICE AREAS: Commercial Litigation; Alternative Dispute Resolution; Banking Litigation; Building and Engineering Litigation.

STEPHEN CHRISTY, born 1950; admitted, 1974, England. Education: LL.B., Southampton. Member: Law Society. LANGUAGES: English, French, German, Spanish and Malay. PRACTICE AREAS: Commercial Property Law; Environmental.

MATTHEW ARROWSMITH-BROWN, born 1951; admitted, 1976, England. Education: B.A., York. Member: Law Society; Sand and Gravel Association; Agricultural Law Association. LANGUAGES: English. PRACTICE AREAS: Agricultural Law; Estate Planning; Successions; Administration of Estates; Bloodstock.

RONALD SUTCLIFFE, born 1947; admitted, 1983, England. Member: Law Society. LANGUAGES: English. PRACTICE AREAS: Personal Injury; Insurance Law.

ROBERT HUTTON, born 1952; admitted, 1977, England. Education: M.A. (Oxon). Member: Law Society. LANGUAGES: English. PRACTICE AREAS: Commercial Property Law; Contract Law.

SUSAN JACK, born 1952; admitted, 1977, England. Education: M.A. (Oxon). Member: Law Society. LANGUAGES: English. PRACTICE AREAS: Trust Law; Administration of Estates; Probate Law; Wills.

COLIN TWEEDIE, born 1953; admitted, 1978, England. Education: M.A. (Cantab). Member: Law Society. LANGUAGES: English. PRACTICE AREAS: Employment Law; Employer/Employee Relations; Employment Discrimination; Employment Benefits Law; Industrial Tribunals.

GUY HODGSON, born 1954; admitted, 1979, England. Education: B. Econ. (Melbourne). Member: Law Society. LANGUAGES: English. PRACTICE AREAS: Professional Negligence; Insurance Law.

(This Listing Continued)

MILLS & REEVE, Norwich—Continued

NICOLAS FISCHL, born 1954; admitted, 1979, England. *Education:* M.A. (Cantab). *Member:* Law Society. *LANGUAGES:* English. *PRACTICE AREAS:* Corporate Law; Mergers and Acquisitions; Management Buyouts; Intellectual Property.

PETER FURNIVALL, born 1954; admitted, 1980, England. *Education:* M.A. (Oxon). *Member:* Law Society. *LANGUAGES:* English. *PRACTICE AREAS:* Tax Shelters; Revenue Law; VAT; Estate Planning; Individual Tax Planning.

JAMES FALKNER, born 1953; admitted, 1980, England. *Education:* LL.B. Hull. *Member:* Law Society. *LANGUAGES:* English. *PRACTICE AREAS:* Property Litigation; Landlord and Tenant Law; Agricultural; Commercial and Residential.

JAMES SAWER, born 1959; admitted, 1983, England. *Education:* LL.B., Birmingham. *LANGUAGES:* English. *PRACTICE AREAS:* Residential Property Law; Estate Planning; Tax Shelters Law; Trust Law; Probate Law.

IAN MAYERS, born 1956; admitted, 1981, England. *Education:* LL.B., Warwick. *Member:* Law Society. *LANGUAGES:* English. *PRACTICE AREAS:* Personal Injury; Insurance Law.

HARRY SCOTT, born 1955; admitted, 1980, England. *Education:* M.A. (Cantab). *Member:* Law Society; Association of Pension Lawyers. *LANGUAGES:* English and French. *PRACTICE AREAS:* Pensions.

RACHEL HIGGS, born 1960; admitted, 1984, England. *Education:* LL.B., Nottingham. *Member:* Law Society. *LANGUAGES:* English. *PRACTICE AREAS:* Commercial Litigation; Intellectual Property Litigation.

BRYONY FALKUS, born 1952; admitted, 1976, England. *Education:* Lanchester Polytechnic Coventry, B.A. (Hons). *Member:* Law Society. *LANGUAGES:* English. *PRACTICE AREAS:* Corporate Law; Corporate Restructuring; Insolvency Law; Venture Capital.

STEPHEN KING, born 1961; admitted, 1986, England. *Education:* Bristol Polytechnic, B.A. *Member:* Law Society. *LANGUAGES:* English. *PRACTICE AREAS:* Medical Negligence; Professional Negligence.

JUSTIN RIPMAN, born 1961; admitted, 1988, England. *Education:* M.A. (Cantab). *Member:* Law Society. *LANGUAGES:* English. *PRACTICE AREAS:* Estate Planning; Individual Tax Planning; Tax Shelter Law; Successions; Heritage.

EVERSHEDS

14 FLETCHER GATE
NOTTINGHAM NG1 2FX, ENGLAND
Telephone: (44) 1159 366 000
Fax: (44) 1159 366 001

Derby, England: 11 St. James Court, Friar Gate, DE1 1BT. Telephone: (44) 1332 360992. Fax: (44) 1332 371469.

Other Eversheds Offices:
Birmingham, Bristol, Cardiff, Ipswich, Leeds, London, Manchester, Middlesborough, Newcastle-upon-Tyne, Norwich, Berlin, Brussels, Jersey.

Acquisitions and Mergers, Agency/Distribution, Agriculture, Banking, Commercial Property, Company Law, Competition Law, Construction, Corporate Finance, Corporate Tax, EC Law, Employment, Environment, Entertainment, Information Technology, Franchising, Insolvency, Intellectual Property, Litigation, Management Buy-Outs, Pensions and Employee Benefits, Personal Tax & Financial Planning, Property Development, Shipping, Trading Contracts.
Partners within Eversheds: 273.

REGIONAL MANAGING PARTNER

William F. Whysall

NOTTINGHAM AND DERBY PARTNERS

H.P. Campion	V.W. Semmens
A.R.S. Cooper	N.R. Sharpe
R.G.L. Davis	B.S. Smith-Hillard
P.J. Hilsdon	P.D. Southby
L.M. Howard	N.P. Sternberg
S. Kitts	R.B. Stringfellow

(This Listing Continued)

G.A.C. Orton	W.F. Whysall
A.J. Pickin	C.E. Wigley
F.B. Raven	D.W. Wild
J.H. Sarginson	J.D.C. Young

SHOOSMITHS & HARRISON

Established in 1845
22A THE ROPEWALK
NOTTINGHAM NG1 5DT, ENGLAND
Telephone: 0602 474645
Fax: 0602 475556

(For full details, see entry for Northampton)

EASTLEYS

THE MANOR OFFICE
VICTORIA STREET
PAIGNTON, DEVON TQ4 5DW, ENGLAND
Telephone: 011 44 1803 559257
Fax: 011 44 1803 558625

Conveyancing, Probate, Trusts, Tax Planning; Financial Services including General Investment and Pensions Advice; Civil Litigation including Personal Injury; Matrimonial Litigation including Child Care.

FIRM PROFILE: Established about 150 years ago, the firm now has nine partners and six other solicitors undertaking a broad spread of private client work and, unlike most solicitors, also offering wide ranging financial services. Member of CONQUEST, a national network of independent quality assessed firms. Authorized by the Law Society of England and Wales to conduct investment business.

MEMBERS OF FIRM

ANDREW PRYCE. *PRACTICE AREAS:* Litigation and General Liaison with U.S. Firms.

JOHN HOPKINS. *PRACTICE AREAS:* Financial Services.

MARK SUMMERS. *PRACTICE AREAS:* Trusts, Probate and Tax Planning.

ROBERT LETCHER. *PRACTICE AREAS:* Conveyancing.

BOND PEARCE

BALLARD HOUSE
WEST HOE ROAD
PLYMOUTH PL1 3AE, ENGLAND
Telephone: 01752 266633
Fax: 01752 225350

Agriculture, Energy, Banking, Construction, Charities, Commercial Property, Commercial Tax, Company, Competition, Corporate Finance, Debt Collection, EC, Employment, Family and Matrimonial, Insolvency, Insurance, Intellectual Property, Landlord and Tenant, Licensing, Litigation, Pensions, Personal Injury, Personal Tax, Planning, Environment, Probate and Wills, Professional Indemnity, Trust Administration.

FIRM PROFILE: Founded in 1881, Bond Pearce is a leading regional practice with over 100 lawyers and a total staff of around 310. The practice is broadly based with integrated specialist skills applied across the full spectrum of legal services. As a founder member of The Norton Rose M5 Group of independent legal practices, Bond Pearce has significant international links.

PARTNERS

JONATHAN TRAFFORD, admitted, 1960. (Senior Partner). *LANGUAGES:* French. *PRACTICE AREAS:* Business Affairs; General Commercial Work.

JOHN PRICE, admitted, 1962. *LANGUAGES:* French. *PRACTICE AREAS:* Personal Injury Litigation.

RICHARD WEST, admitted, 1967. (Notary Public). *LANGUAGES:* French. *PRACTICE AREAS:* Private Chent; Partnerships.

KEITH DAVIES, admitted, 1971. (Notary Public). *LANGUAGES:* French. *PRACTICE AREAS:* Property Law; Secured Lending; Building Society Law.

(This Listing Continued)

HAMISH ANDERSON, admitted, 1973. *LANGUAGES:* French. *PRACTICE AREAS:* Insolvency; Banking; Asset Finance.

BRIAN STARKS, admitted, 1972. *LANGUAGES:* French. *PRACTICE AREAS:* Property Litigation; Business Tenancies; Agricultural Litigation; Mortgage Repossession; Partnership Litigation.

RICHARD CHALLANDS, admitted, 1975. *PRACTICE AREAS:* Professional Indemnity; Insurance; Product Liability; Litigation.

DAVID JAMES, admitted, 1974. *LANGUAGES:* French, German. *PRACTICE AREAS:* Tax and Agricultural Property.

ERIK SALOMONSEN, admitted, 1975. *LANGUAGES:* French, German. *PRACTICE AREAS:* Environmental Litigation; Licensing; Insurance; Professional Indemnity Litigation.

NIGEL THEYER, admitted, 1977. *LANGUAGES:* French, German. *PRACTICE AREAS:* Landlord and Tenant; Property Development and Investment Work.

JONATHAN NICHOLSON, admitted, 1968. *LANGUAGES:* French. *PRACTICE AREAS:* Probate; Trust Administration; Wills and Charity Law.

NIKKI DUNCAN, admitted, 1979. *LANGUAGES:* German, French. *PRACTICE AREAS:* Employment Law.

MICHAEL WILLIAMS, admitted, 1975. *PRACTICE AREAS:* Commercial Tax; Commercial Law.

ROGER ACOCK, admitted, 1980. *LANGUAGES:* French. *PRACTICE AREAS:* Corporate Finance; Environmental particularly Waste Management.

JULIAN TRAHAIR, admitted, 1980. *LANGUAGES:* French. *PRACTICE AREAS:* Bank Recovery and Insolvency Litigation.

WENDY BOYCE, admitted, 1980. *LANGUAGES:* French. *PRACTICE AREAS:* Family and Matrimonial Law.

ROBERT HECKFORD, admitted, 1974. *PRACTICE AREAS:* Professional Indemnity; Insurance; Landlord and Tenant Litigation.

DAVID GUNN, admitted, 1982. *LANGUAGES:* French, Russian. *PRACTICE AREAS:* Commercial Property.

MICHAEL VERITY, admitted, 1970. *LANGUAGES:* French. *PRACTICE AREAS:* General Property Work for Institutions.

WILLIAM EATON, admitted, 1981. *LANGUAGES:* French, German. *PRACTICE AREAS:* Property Development.

BETTINA RIGG, admitted, 1982. *LANGUAGES:* French. *PRACTICE AREAS:* Insurance Litigation.

MICHAEL FORD, admitted, 1984. *LANGUAGES:* German, French. *PRACTICE AREAS:* Construction; Professional Indemnity; Insurance Litigation.

JONATHAN COOPER, admitted, 1984. *LANGUAGES:* French. *PRACTICE AREAS:* Personal Injury Litigation Specialising in Industrial Disease Claims.

IAN DOWNING, admitted, 1984. *PRACTICE AREAS:* Family and Matrimonial Law.

SIMON RICHARDSON, admitted, 1983. *PRACTICE AREAS:* General Commercial Litigation Specialising in Employment Law.

VICTOR TETTMAR, admitted, 1985. *LANGUAGES:* French. *PRACTICE AREAS:* Non-Contentious Insolvency; Asset Realization; Security Enforcement and Auditing.

LUKE GABB, admitted, 1980. *PRACTICE AREAS:* Investment and Development Work; Energy.

MARCUS TRINICK, admitted, 1983. *PRACTICE AREAS:* Planning; Environment; Energy; Wind Farm/Development.

MARK THOMPSON, admitted, 1983. *PRACTICE AREAS:* Personal Injury; Medical Negligence Litigation.

IAN PEACOCK, admitted, 1984. *PRACTICE AREAS:* Professional Indemnity; Financial Services; Insurance Litigation.

STEPHEN HANKIN, admitted, 1985. *PRACTICE AREAS:* Professional Indemnity; Road Traffic Litigation.

JULIA ALLSOP, admitted, 1985. *LANGUAGES:* French. *PRACTICE AREAS:* Bank Recovery and Insolvency Litigation.

(This Listing Continued)

JULIAN KINSEY, admitted, 1984. *LANGUAGES:* French. *PRACTICE AREAS:* Banking; Asset Finance; Aviation Finance.

CHARMIAN LEATT, admitted, 1985. *PRACTICE AREAS:* Corporate Finance; General Practice.

ANDREW TOBEY, admitted, 1983. *PRACTICE AREAS:* Commercial Litigation; Employment Law.

SHOOSMITHS & HARRISON

Established in 1845

REGENTS GATE
CROWN STREET
READING RG1 2PQ, ENGLAND
Telephone: 0734 498765
Fax: 0734 498800

(For full details, see entry for Northampton)

SHOOSMITHS & HARRISON

Established in 1845

BLOXAM COURT
CORPORATION STREET
RUGBY CV21 2DU, ENGLAND
Telephone: 0788 573111
Fax: 0788 536651

(For full details, see entry for Northampton)

SHOOSMITHS & HARRISON

Established in 1845

RUSSELL HOUSE, 1550 PARKWAY
SOLENT BUSINESS PARK, FAREHAM HANTS
SOUTHAMPTON PO15 7AG, ENGLAND
Telephone: 0489 881010
Fax: 0489 881000

(For full details, see entry for Northampton)

MUNDAYS

Established in 1960

CROWN HOUSE, CHURCH ROAD
CLAYGATE, ESHER
SURREY KT10 0LP, ENGLAND
Telephone: +44 (0)1372 467272
Fax: +44 (0)1372 463782

Corporate and commercial advice, intellectual property and franchising, distribution and agency, European and EEC law, commercial property, litigation including commercial contract and employment disputes, family law including divorce, separation and financial matters, private client advice including property, wills, trusts - Members of Eurolink for Lawyers, American Chamber of Commerce (UK) and an affiliate of the British Franchise Association. Location: equidistant between Heathrow and Gatwick airports; near M25 motorway.

FIRM PROFILE: Well respected commercial practice with specially highly regarded international franchising team. Also offers private client services. Strong Emphasis on quality; targets substantial and established corporate clients at rates which are more attractive than those available in London but with similar quality lawyers. Members of Eurolink for Lawyers, American Chamber of Commerce (UK) and an affiliate of the British Franchise Association.

MEMBERS OF FIRM

PETER JAMES MUNDAY, born England, October 31, 1938; admitted, 1968, England. *Education:* College of Law, Guildford. Notary Public, 1975. *LANGUAGES:* English. *PRACTICE AREAS:* Corporate and Commercial.

RAYMOND DEREK WALLEY, born England, July 29, 1944; admitted, 1976, England. *Education:* Institute of Bankers (Trustee Diploma, Distinction; Certificate in Investment). Recipient, Robert Edmund Mellersh Prize, College of Law, Guildford. *Member:* Surrey European Business Asso-

(This Listing Continued)

MUNDAYS, Surrey—Continued

ciation and Institute of Directors. *LANGUAGES:* English and French. *PRACTICE AREAS:* Franchising; Distribution; Intellectual Property.

SIMON COURTENAY WITHERS, born England, June 15, 1954; admitted, 1978, England. *Education:* University of Leicester; College of Law Lancaster Gate. *LANGUAGES:* English and French. *PRACTICE AREAS:* Commercial Property.

MANZOOR GULAMHUSSEIN KASSAM ISHANI, born Nairobi, Kenya, October 6, 1949; admitted, 1976, England. *Education:* University of St. Andrews, Scotland (M.A.); College of Law, Guildford. Author: "The European Community." Co-Author: "Franchising in the U.K.,"; "Franchising in Europe,"; "Franchising in Canada,"; "Franchise Handbook." Legal Adviser, Franchise Consultants Association. *Member:* International Bar Association (Franchise Committee); American Bar Association (Forum Committee on Franchising); International Union of Lawyers (Committee on Franchising); International Association of Young Jurists (Working Commission on Franchising); Legal Committee of British Franchise Association; Association of Swiss Arbitrators; European Contributing Editor of World Franchise and Business report. *LANGUAGES:* English, Gujarati and French. *PRACTICE AREAS:* Intellectual Property; Franchising; Distribution.

RICHARD ANTHONY ROY ASHBY, born England, April 14, 1944; admitted, 1970, England. *Education:* College of Law, Lancaster Gate. *LANGUAGES:* English. *PRACTICE AREAS:* Residential Property.

FIONA RUTH MCALLISTER, born England, June 5, 1961; admitted, 1985, England. *Education:* University of Nottingham. *LANGUAGES:* English and Basic Russian. *PRACTICE AREAS:* Litigation.

MEHBOOB DHARAMSI, born Kampala, Uganda, March 26, 1955; admitted, 1987, England. *Education:* College of Law, Lancaster Gate. *LANGUAGES:* English and Katchi. *PRACTICE AREAS:* Probate; Trusts; Powers of Attorney; Receivership.

RICHARD ANDREW POWELL, born England, November 6, 1948; admitted, 1975, England. *Education:* College of Law, Guildford. *LANGUAGES:* English. *PRACTICE AREAS:* Corporate Finance; Company Commercial.

MINDELLE ISON, born England, April 6, 1934; admitted, 1973, England. *Education:* Liverpool University. Part-Time Chairman Social Security and Disability Tribunals. *LANGUAGES:* English. *PRACTICE AREAS:* Matrimonial and Child Care.

ROBERT ANTHONY BRUCE HARRIS, born England, February 19, 1947; admitted, 1973, England. *Education:* College of Law, Guildford. *LANGUAGES:* English. *PRACTICE AREAS:* Commercial Property.

VALERIE ANN TOON, born England, April 20, 1963; admitted, 1987, England. *Education:* University of Sussex; College of Law, Guilford. *LANGUAGES:* English. *PRACTICE AREAS:* Litigation.

KAREN LYNNE BARHAM, born England, September 14, 1962; admitted, 1988, England. *Education:* University of Hull; College of Law Lancaster Gate. *LANGUAGES:* English. *PRACTICE AREAS:* Matrimonial.

KAREN ANN CROSSLEY, born England, January 10, 1963; admitted, 1988, England. *Education:* St. Anne's College, Oxford; College of Law, Chester. *LANGUAGES:* English. *PRACTICE AREAS:* Commercial Property.

SUSAN EILEEN DRUSILLA POULTON, born England, May 21, 1946; admitted, 1992, England. *Education:* College of Law, Guildford. *LANGUAGES:* English. *PRACTICE AREAS:* Residential Conveyancing.

NATALIE JACOBS, born England, January 3, 1968; admitted, 1993, England. *Education:* King's College London, Paris La Sorbonne; College of Law, Lancaster Gate. *LANGUAGES:* English and French. *PRACTICE AREAS:* Franchising; Intellectual Property.

ROBIN EDWARDS, born England, June 19, 1965; admitted, 1992, England. *Education:* University of Leicester, University of Strasbourg; College of Law, Guildford. *LANGUAGES:* English, French and German. *PRACTICE AREAS:* Litigation.

(This Listing Continued)

STEPHEN HENRY MORRIS, born England, November 24, 1956; admitted, 1981, England. *Education:* Manchester University; College of Law, Lancaster Gate. *LANGUAGES:* English. *PRACTICE AREAS:* Litigation.

ESTONIA

LAW OFFICE AARE TARK

Established in 1991

VAIKE - KARJA 12
TALLINN EE0001, ESTONIA
Telephone: 372 2 44 92 96, 44 83 98
Telecopier: 372 2 44 36 61

Corporate, Business, Financial, Tax and Patent Law, Arbitration, Litigation, International Business Law, Real Property, General Practice Agreements and Contracts.

MEMBERS OF FIRM

AARE TARK, born Tallinn, Estonia, April 4, 1959; admitted, 1983, Estonia. *Education:* University of Tartu (LL.B., 1983). Audited at Indiana Vocational Technical College, USA, 1990- 1991. *Member:* Estonian Bar Association; International Bar Association; Estonian Academic Law Society. *LANGUAGES:* Estonian, English, Finnish and Russian. *PRACTICE AREAS:* General Company and Commercial Law; Business Law; Contracts; Litigation.

MART SUSI, born Tallinn, Estonia, April 11, 1965; admitted, 1989, Estonia. *Education:* University of Tartu (LL.B., 1988); University of Wisconsin-Madison (LL.M., 1992). Honorary Doctorate Degree, College of New Rochell, 1990. *Member:* Estonian Bar Association; International Bar Association; Estonian Academic Law Society. *LANGUAGES:* Estonian, English, Russian. *PRACTICE AREAS:* International Law; Corporate Law; International Litigation; Constitutional Law.

STEN LUIGA, born Tallinn, Estonia, January 20, 1968; admitted, 1992, Estonia. *Education:* University of Tartu (LL.B., 1992). *Member:* Estonian Bar Association; International Bar Association; Estonian Academic Law Society. *LANGUAGES:* Estonian, English, Russian, Finnish. *PRACTICE AREAS:* Taxation; Trademark Law; Business Law.

MARJU TARK, born Johvi, Estonia, July 10, 1960. *Education:* University of Tartu (LL.B., 1983). *Member:* Estonian Academic Law Society; International Bar Association. *LANGUAGES:* Estonian, English, Finnish, Russian. *PRACTICE AREAS:* Corporate Law; Real Property.

PRIIT KOTKAS, born Tallinn, Estonia, July 7, 1970; admitted, 1993, Estonia. *Education:* University of Tartu (LL.B., 1993). *Member:* Estonian Bar Association. *LANGUAGES:* Estonian, English, Finnish and Russian. *PRACTICE AREAS:* General Company and Commercial Law; Taxation; Business Law.

FOREIGN LAW OFFICE OF ESTONIA

Established in 1991

KINGA 10
P.O. BOX 425
EE0090 TALLINN, ESTONIA
Telephone: (372 2) 44 44 11
Fax: (372 2) 44 51 24

Civil, Family Law, Genealogical Researches, Inheritance and Wills, Missing Heirs, Real Estate.

FIRM PROFILE: The office is specialized in matters in which in addition to legal services it is necessary to find and collect information and proofs in Estonian as well as world archives such as e.g. inheritance matters in different states in which genealogical research is needed.

MEMBERS OF FIRM

Ivo Mahhov   *Ellinora Mänd*

Languages: English, German, Russian, Swedish, Finnish and Estonian.

LAW OFFICE HETA

Established in 1989

RÜÜTLI STR. 4

EE0001 TALLINN, ESTONIA

Telephone: 372-2-446990; 445820; 441710; 443862; 372-6313801

Telefax: 372-2-442889

General Practice, Corporate, Commercial, International, Company and Tax Law, Commercial Litigation and Arbitration, Corporate Insolvency.

MEMBERS OF FIRM

KAIDO PIHLAKAS, born Tallinn, Estonia, July 18, 1940; admitted, 1967, Estonia. *Education:* University of Tartu (LL.B., 1967). *Member:* Estonian Bar Association. *LANGUAGES:* Estonian, Finnish, English and Russian. *PRACTICE AREAS:* Corporation and Business Law; Civil Law; Civil Procedure; Administrative Law.

ÜLLAR TALVISTE, born Tallinn, Estonia, March 20, 1956; admitted, 1980, Estonia. *Education:* University of Tartu (LL.B., 1979). *Member:* Estonian Bar Association. *LANGUAGES:* Estonian, Finnish, English and Russian. *PRACTICE AREAS:* Corporation and Business Law; Civil Law; Civil Procedure; Administrative Law.

ANDRES AAVIK, born Pärnu, Estonia, June 2, 1957; admitted, 1990, Estonia. *Education:* University of Tartu (LL.B., 1980). *Member:* Estonian Bar Association. *LANGUAGES:* Estonian, Finnish, German and Russian. *PRACTICE AREAS:* General Practice; Corporate; Commercial; International; Company and Tax Law; Commercial Litigation; Arbitration; Corporate Insolvency.

ASSOCIATES

SIMON S. LEVIN, born Tallinn, Estonia, November 3, 1928; admitted, 1947, Estonia. *Education:* University of Tartu (LL.B., 1947; LL.D., 1974). *Member:* Estonian Bar Association. *LANGUAGES:* Estonian, French, German and Russian. *PRACTICE AREAS:* Civil; Criminal; Administrative Law.

ANDRES HALLMÄGI, born Pärnu, Estonia, June 3, 1957; admitted, 1993, Estonia. *Education:* University of Tartu (LL.B., 1980). *Member:* Estonia Bar Association. *LANGUAGES:* Estonian, Finnish, English, German and Russian. *PRACTICE AREAS:* General Practice; Corporate; Commercial; International; Company and Tax Law; Commercial Litigation; Arbitration; Corporate Insolvency.

MARGUS MUGU, born Tallinn, Estonia, December 23, 1966; admitted, 1992, Estonia. *Education:* University of Tartu (LL.B., 1992). *Member:* Estonian Bar Association. *LANGUAGES:* Estonian, Finnish, English and Russian. *PRACTICE AREAS:* General Practice; Corporate; Commercial; International; Company and Tax Law; Commercial Litigation; Arbitration; Corporate Insolvency.

AIVAR PIHLAK, born Tallinn, Estonia, January 17, 1966; admitted, 1993, Estonia. *Education:* University of Tartu (LL.B., 1992). *Member:* Estonian Bar Association. *LANGUAGES:* Estonian, Finnish, English and Russian. *PRACTICE AREAS:* General Practice; Corporate; Commercial; International; Company and Tax Law; Commercial Litigation; Arbitration; Corporate Insolvency.

JÜRI PLOOM, born Tartu, Estonian, December 24, 1970; admitted, 1994, Estonia. *Education:* University of Tartu (LL.B., 1994). *Member:* Estonian Bar Association. *LANGUAGES:* Estonian, Finnish, English and Russian. *PRACTICE AREAS:* General Practice; Corporate; Commercial; Company and Tax Law; Commercial Litigation; Arbitration; Corporate Insolvency.

INDREK KASELA, born Tallin, Estonia, December 10, 1971; admitted, 1994, Estonia. *Education:* University of Tartu (LL.B., 1994). *Member:* Estonian Bar Association. *LANGUAGES:* Estonian, Finnish, English and Russian. *PRACTICE AREAS:* General Practice; Corporate; Commercial; Company and Tax Law; Commercial Litigation; Arbitration; Corporate Insolvency.

LAW OFFICE KAASIK & CO.

Established in 1991

4 SUUR-KARJA

EE0001 TALLINN, ESTONIA

Telephone: 372-2-44-34-01; 6-31-31-66

Fax: 372-2-44-53-34

Firm engaged in Estonian, European and International Law practice. Entitled to plead before Estonian Courts.

FIRM PROFILE: "Kaasik & Co" is a representative office of the Scandinavian Business Law Group (SLG) - an integrated cooperation between five law offices in United Kingdom, Denmark, Norway, Sweden and Finland.

"Kaasik & Co" has a staff of 6 people having good knowledge of English, German, Russian, Finnish and Estonian. The law firm is particularly active in the fields of Privatization of Real Property, Legal Protection of Foreign Investments, Company Law, Contract Law, Banking Law, Intellectual Property Law and Competition Law, Mergers and Acquisitions, Litigation, and Arbitration with special focus on setting up foreign companies in Estonia. "Kaasik & Co" makes a point of ensuring that the legal advisory service is closely matched to the commercial considerations. Important services are the participation in negotiations and consultation on legal-commercial strategy.

MEMBERS OF FIRM

VIKTOR KAASIK, born Estonia, November 16, 1954; admitted, 1981, Estonia. *Education:* University of Tartu (Lawyer's Diploma, 1979). *Member:* Estonian Bar Association; International Bar Association. *LANGUAGES:* German, Finnish and Russian. *PRACTICE AREAS:* Privatization of Real Property; Foreign Investments; Company Law; Contract Law; Banking Law; Construction Law; Litigation; Arbitration.

DRAGAN PEROVIČ, born Estonia, June 9, 1968. *Education:* University of Tartu (Lawyer's Diploma, 1993). *LANGUAGES:* English, Finnish and Russian. *PRACTICE AREAS:* Privatization of Real Property; Mergers and Acquisitions; Real Property; Contract Law; Litigation; Arbitration.

HARRAS LÄÄN, born Estonia, April 1, 1962. *Education:* University of Tartu (Lawyer's Diploma, magna cum laude, 1990). *LANGUAGES:* English, Finnish and Russian. *PRACTICE AREAS:* European Community Law; Estonian Competition Law; Company Law; Contract Law; Administrative Law; Real Estate; Intellectual Property Law.

ANNELI URGE, born Estonia, September 5, 1971. *Education:* University of Tartu (Lawyer's Diploma, cum laude, 1994). Qualified Bankruptcy Administrator. *LANGUAGES:* English, Russian and Finnish. *PRACTICE AREAS:* Company Law; Contract Law; Mergers and Acquisitions; Competition Law; Real Estate.

TOOMAS LAANEMAA, born Estonia, December 31, 1971. *Education:* University of Tartu (Lawyer's Diploma, 1994). Qualified Bankruptcy Administrator. *LANGUAGES:* English and Russian. *PRACTICE AREAS:* Insolvency; Mergers and Acquisitions; Contract Law; Real Estate.

SANJAY JAANUS MODY, born Estonia, December 29, 1971. *Education:* University of Tartu (Lawyer's Diploma, 1994). Qualified Bankruptcy Administrator. *LANGUAGES:* English and Russian. *PRACTICE AREAS:* Litigation; Arbitration; Contract Law; Finance; Insolvency.

LAW OFFICE OF LEPIK & LUHAÄÄR

Established in 1990

5 LAI STREET

TALLINN EE0001, ESTONIA

Telephone: 372 2 444 861

Telefax: 372 2 441 597

Mobile phone: 372 2 248 543; 372 2 248 544

FIRM PROFILE: Lepik & Luhaäär was the first private law firm established by members of Estonian Bar Association in Estonia in 1990. General Practice, International Business and Commercial Law, Corporate Law, Litigation, Real Estate, Foreign Investments in the Republic of Estonia, Privatization projects.

MEMBERS OF FIRM

PEETER LEPIK, born Tallinn, Estonia, August 28, 1954; admitted, 1984, Estonia. *Education:* Pedagogical University of Tallinn (Faculty of Foreign Languages, 1977); University of Tartu (Faculty of Law, cum laude, 1984). *Member:* Estonian Bar Association. *LANGUAGES:* Estonian, English, Finnish and Russian. *PRACTICE AREAS:* General Company and

(This Listing Continued)

LAW OFFICE OF LEPIK & LUHAÄÄR, Tallinn— Continued

Commercial Law; Corporate Law; Foreign Investments in the Republic of Estonia.

TOOMAS LUHAÄÄR, born Türi, Estonia, April 24, 1957; admitted, 1983, Estonia. *Education:* University of Tartu - Faculty of Law. *Member:* Estonian Bar Association (Member of the Board). *LANGUAGES:* Estonian, Finnish, English and Russian. *PRACTICE AREAS:* General Company and Commercial Law; Corporate Law; Foreign Investments in the Republic of Estonia; Taxation.

ASSOCIATES

LIINA LINSI, born Tallinn, Estonia, January 9, 1961; admitted, 1984, Estonia. *Education:* University of Tartu (Faculty of Law cum laude, 1984). *Member:* Estonian Bar Association; International Bar Association. *LANGUAGES:* Estonian, English and Russian. *PRACTICE AREAS:* Business Law; Real Property; Litigation.

HASSO LEPIK, born Tallinn, Estonia, September 6, 1926; admitted, 1956, Estonia. *Education:* University of Tartu (1952). *Member:* Estonian Bar Association. *LANGUAGES:* Estonian and German. *PRACTICE AREAS:* Real Property; Litigation.

VESSE VÕHMA, born Tallinn, Estonia, July 24, 1963; admitted, 1994, Estonia. *Education:* University of Tartu (Faculty of Law, cum laude, 1986). *Member:* Estonian Bar Association. *LANGUAGES:* Estonian, English and Russian. *PRACTICE AREAS:* General Company and Commercial Law; Corporate Law.

MARTIN SIMOVART, born Tallinn, Estonia, December 8, 1970; admitted, 1994, Estonia. *Education:* University of Tartu (Faculty of Law, 1994). *Member:* Estonian Bar Association. *LANGUAGES:* Estonian, English and Russian. *PRACTICE AREAS:* General Company and Commercial Law; Corporate Law.

Member of Lawyers Associated Worldwide (LAW)

RAIDLA & PARTNERS
MOQUET BORDE DIEUX GEENS & ASSOCIES

10 PÄRNU STR.
EE 0001 TALLINN, ESTONIA
Telephone: (372) 640 58 36
Fax: (372) 640 58 38

Paris, France Office: 30 avenue de Messine, 75008 Paris. Telephone: (33-1) 42 99 04 50. Fax: (33-1) 45 63 91 49.

Lyon, France Office: 11 Place Bellecour, 69002 Lyon. Telephone: (33) 72 40 00 32. Fax: (33) 72 41 98 62.

Budapest, Hungary Office: Kossuth ter 16-17. III/2/A, H-1055 Budapest (1245 Budapest, P.O. Box 1228). Telephone: (36-1) 1531 255. Fax: (36-1) 1531 229.

Brussels, Belgium Office: Rue de la Bonté 5-7, B-1050. Telephone: (32-2) 538 6869. Fax: (32-2) 538-6867.

Estonian, Hungarian, EEC, French and General International Practice.

RESIDENT COUNSELS

JURI RAIDLA, born Pärnu, Estonia, July 2, 1957. Minister of Justice of the Republic of Estonia, 1990-1992. Head of Expert Commission on Elaborating the Constitution of the Republic of Estonia, 1992. *Education:* University of Tartu, Estonia (Master of law, cum laude, 1980) University of St. Petersburg (Ph.D., 1987). *LANGUAGES:* Estonian, English and Russian.

SVEN PAPP, born Tallinn, Estonia, January 5, 1963; admitted, 1987, Estonia. *Education:* University of Tartu (Master of Law, 1986); Stockholm University (LL.M., 1991). *LANGUAGES:* Estonian, English, Russian, Finnish and Swedish.

RESIDENT ASSOCIATES

MONIKA SEHVER, born Tallinn, Estonia, March 18, 1966. *Education:* University of Tartu, Estonia (Master of Law, cum laude, 1989). *LANGUAGES:* Estonian, English and Russian.

REET SAKS, born Tallinn, Estonia, June 2, 1962. *Education:* University of Tartu (Master of Law, 1986). *LANGUAGES:* Estonian, English, Russian and Finnish.

(This Listing Continued)

ASKO POHLA, born Tallinn, Estonia, August 10, 1964. *Education:* University of Tartu (Masters of Law, cum laude, 1989); Georgetown University (Master of Law, 1994). *LANGUAGES:* Estonian, English and Russian.

SCANDINAVIAN LAW OFFICES AS

RÜÜTLI 16
EE0001 TALLINN, ESTONIA
Telephone: +372-2-666689
Telefax: +372-6-313549

Helsinki, Finland Office: Eteläranta 8, 00130. Telephone: +358-0-171900. Telefax: +358-0-171950.

St. Petersburg, Russia Office: Proletarskaya Diktatura Sq. 6, Room 309, 193124. Telephone: +7-812-8502200 (Int'l.); +7-812-2744347. Telefax: +7-812-8502201 (Int'l.); +7-812-2741146.

Corporate, Contract, Business, Financial and Tax Law, International Business Transactions, East-West Trade, Arbitration and Litigation.

MEMBERS OF FIRM

ANDRES ALAS, born Tallinn, Estonia, March 15, 1961. *Education:* University of Tartu (LL.M., 1984). *LANGUAGES:* Estonian, English, Russian and Finnish.

AIVAR RAUDSIK, born Tallinn, Estonia, May 31, 1962. *Education:* University of Tartu (LL.M., 1985). *LANGUAGES:* Estonian, English, Russian and Finnish.

ANSSI JAANTI, born Helsinki, Finland, December 27, 1951; admitted, 1987, Finland (Not admitted in Estonia). *Education:* University of Helsinki (LL.M., 1981). *Member:* Finnish Bar Association. *LANGUAGES:* English, Finnish, Swedish and German.

MARKKU ROPPONEN, born Helsinki, Finland, August 26, 1961; (Not admitted in Estonia). *Education:* University of Helsinki (LL.M., 1989). *LANGUAGES:* English, Finnish, Swedish and German.

FINLAND

AHOLA, PENTZIN, RANTASILA & SOKKA

Established in 1993

ITÄLAHDENKATU 15-17
FIN-00210 HELSINKI, FINLAND
Telephone: 358-0-682 2399
Telecopy: 358-0-682 2404

Corporate and Business Law, Investment and Securities, Banking Law, Shipping Law, Contracts, International Business Transactions, Commercial Law, Real Estate Law, Bankruptcy and Insolvency, Taxation Law, Arbitration, Litigation, Industrial Property, Copyright Law, Marketing Legislation, Creditors Rights.

MEMBERS OF FIRM

JUHANI AHOLA, born Helsinki, Finland, February 5, 1943; admitted, 1976, Finland. *Education:* University of Helsinki (LL.M., 1968). Member, Board of Directors, Vice-Chairman, Tax and Law Committee, 1989—, Harbour Committee, 1992—; Helsinki Chamber of Commerce, 1985—; Secretary General, Board of the Finnish CMR-Insurers, 1986-1992; Vice President, 1979 and Treasurer, 1981, International Junior Chamber of Commerce. *Member:* International Bar Association (IBA); CMI; A.I.D.A.; Finnish Bar Association. *LANGUAGES:* Finnish, English, Swedish and German. *PRACTICE AREAS:* Corporate and Business Law; Shipping Law; International Business Transactions; Commercial Law; Taxation.

VIKING PENTZIN, born Helsinki, Finland, December 18, 1946; admitted, 1990, Finland. *Education:* University of Helsinki (LL.M., 1977). Referendary at the High Court of Justice, Finland, 1981-1984. Circuit Judge, 1980-1982. Manager, Bank of Helsinki Ltd., Legal and Tax Services, 1984-1986; Manager, Union Bank of Finland Ltd., Legal and Tax Services, 1986-1990; Partner, Ahola, Nenonen, Pokela & Rantasila, 1990-1993. *LANGUAGES:* Finnish, English, Swedish and French. *PRACTICE AREAS:* Banking; Arbitration; Litigation; Creditors Rights; Securities.

JUHA RANTASILA, born Pori, Finland, June 5, 1945; admitted, 1972, Finland. *Education:* University of Helsinki (LL.M., 1969). *LANGUAGES:* Finnish, Swedish, English and German. *PRACTICE AREAS:* Corporate

(This Listing Continued)

and Commercial Litigation; International Sales and Related Commercial Transactions; Creditors Rights; Reorganization; Insolvency; Bankruptcy; Contract and General Business Law; Investment and Securities; Real Estate Law.

OSSI SOKKA, born Helsinki, Finland, September 17, 1955; admitted, 1985, Finland. *Education:* University of Helsinki (LL.M., 1982). Municipal Court, 1984-1985. *Member:* Finnish Bar Association; Junior Chamber of Commerce; Law Committee of Espoo Chamber of Commerce (1988). *LANGUAGES:* Finnish, English and Swedish. *PRACTICE AREAS:* Contract; Company; Insolvency; General Business Law.

ASSOCIATES

LASSE LAGUS, born Helsinki, Finland, October 22, 1958; admitted, 1991, Finland. *Education:* University of Helsinki (LL.M., 1986); University of Uppsala, Department of Commercial Law (Extensive Course in Swedish Law); University of Amsterdam, School of International Relations, EC Business Law (LL.M., 1993). *LANGUAGES:* Finnish, English and Swedish. *PRACTICE AREAS:* Contract; Competition; Copyright and EC Law; Industrial Property.

JOHANNA NYLÄNDEN, born Hattula, Finland, July 3, 1966. *Education:* University of Helsinki (LL.M., 1990). *Member:* Finnish Legal Society. *LANGUAGES:* Finnish, Swedish and English. *PRACTICE AREAS:* General Business Law; Contract; Litigation.

LEENA PYYMÄKI, born Lahti, Finland, March 30, 1964; admitted, 1994, Finland. *Education:* University of Helsinki (LL.M., 1990). *Member:* The Finnish Legal Society. *LANGUAGES:* Finnish, English, French and Swedish. *PRACTICE AREAS:* Litigation; Creditors Right; Insolvency; Bankruptcy; Contract; General Business Law.

KRISTIINA RAIVIO, born Helsinki, Finland, November 18, 1964. *Education:* University of Helsinki (LL.M., 1991). *Member:* The Finnish Legal Society. *LANGUAGES:* Finnish, English, Swedish and German. *PRACTICE AREAS:* Litigation; Business Law; Bankruptcy.

Languages: Finnish, Swedish, English, German and French

ASIANAJOTOIMISTO
VEIKKO PALOTIE & CO OY

Established in 1951

MELKONKATU 28 E
SF-00210 HELSINKI, FINLAND
Telephone: 358-0-673 050
Telefax: 358-0-675 062

Admiralty and Maritime Law, Advertising and Marketing, Agency and Distributorship, Antitrust and Trade Regulation, Arbitration, Bankruptcy, Banks and Banking, Business Law, Charitable Organizations and Trusts, Commercial Law, Company Law, Construction Law, Consumer Law, Contracts, Corporate Law, Debtor and Creditor, Entertainment and The Arts, Environmental Law, Federal Tax, Finance and Leasing, Franchising, General Practice, Industrial and Intellectual Property, Labour and Employment, Litigation, Mergers and Acquisitions, Products Liability and Damages, Real Estate, Sports, Taxation, Transportation.

FIRM PROFILE: *The firm offers a full range of legal services for business community. The firm employs 20 people.*

MEMBERS OF FIRM

TAUNO PALOTIE, born Helsinki, Finland, December 29, 1947; admitted, 1972, Finland. *Education:* University of Helsinki (Master of Laws, 1972); University of Brussels (Master of Laws, 1978). *Member:* Finnish Bar Association; Finnish Industrial Property Society; Licensing Executive Society. *LANGUAGES:* Finnish, Swedish, English and German. *PRACTICE AREAS:* Agency and Distributorships; Business Law; Commercial Law; Company Law; Corporate Law; Mergers and Acquisitions.

MIKA PAKARINEN, born Helsinki, Finland, September 25, 1958; admitted, 1983, Finland. *Education:* University of Helsinki (Master of Laws, 1983). *Member:* Finnish Bar Association; AIJA - International Association of Young Lawyers. *LANGUAGES:* Finnish, Swedish, English and French. *PRACTICE AREAS:* Arbitration; Bankruptcy Law; Banks and Banking; Debtor and Creditor; Finance and Leasing; Litigation.

JYRI SARPANIEMI, born Helsinki, Finland, January 19, 1952; admitted, 1978, Finland. *Education:* University of Helsinki (Master of Laws, 1978). *Member:* Finnish Bar Association; AIJA - International Association

(This Listing Continued)

---

of Young Lawyers. *LANGUAGES:* Finnish, Swedish, English and German. *PRACTICE AREAS:* Corporate Law; Taxation.

TIMO VALSTA, born Lahti, Finland, May 23, 1952; admitted, 1980, Finland. *Education:* University of Helsinki (Master of Laws, 1980). *Member:* Finnish Bar Association; AIJA - International Association of Young Lawyers. *LANGUAGES:* Finnish, Swedish and English. *PRACTICE AREAS:* Construction Law; Environmental Law; Real Estate.

ASTA SIPONEN, born Nurmes, Finland, July 6, 1961; admitted, 1986, Finland. *Education:* University of Helsinki (Master of Laws, 1986); Leyden-Amsterdam-Columbia, Summer Program in American Law (1986). Deputy of the Registrar, County of Hollola, July, 1983. *Member:* Society of Finnish Young Lawyers. *LANGUAGES:* Finnish, Swedish, English and German. *PRACTICE AREAS:* Bankruptcy Law; Banks and Banking; Business Law; Construction Law; Debtor and Creditor; Environmental Law.

TERO ROUTAMO, born Helsinki, Finland, March 29, 1957; admitted, 1987, Finland. *Education:* University of Helsinki (Master of Laws, 1987). *Member:* Society of Finnish Young Lawyers. *LANGUAGES:* Finnish, Swedish and English. *PRACTICE AREAS:* Industrial and Intellectual Property; Debtor and Creditor.

JUHA PÖYTÄNIEMI, born Vaasa, Finland, July 17, 1959; admitted, 1987, Finland. *Education:* University of Helsinki (Master of Laws, 1987). *LANGUAGES:* Finnish, Swedish and English. *PRACTICE AREAS:* Commercial Law; Bankruptcy Law; Litigation; Debtor and Creditor.

ASSOCIATES

MARKKU MÄKINEN, born Oulu, Finland, August 9, 1966; admitted, 1990, Finland. *Education:* University of Helsinki (Master of Laws, 1990). *LANGUAGES:* Finnish, Swedish, English and German. *PRACTICE AREAS:* Admiralty and Maritime Law; Business Law; Litigation; Transportation.

PETER NYGÅRD, born Helsinki, Finland, July 6, 1965; admitted, 1993, Finland. *Education:* University of Helsinki (Master of Laws, 1993). *LANGUAGES:* Finnish, Swedish, English and German. *PRACTICE AREAS:* Debtor and Creditor.

TERO PÖYTÄNIEMI, born Vaasa, Finland, March 3, 1962; admitted, 1990, Finland. *Education:* University of Helsinki (Master of Laws, 1990). *LANGUAGES:* Finnish, Swedish, English. *PRACTICE AREAS:* Commercial Law; Bankruptcy Law; Litigation; Banks and Banking; Debtor and Creditor.

KIRSI VITIKKA, born Helsinki, Finland, September 1, 1953; admitted, 1980, Finland. *Education:* University of Helsinki (Master of Laws, 1980). *Member:* Finnish Bar Association. *LANGUAGES:* Finnish, Swedish, English. *PRACTICE AREAS:* Commercial Law; Debtor and Creditor; Litigation; Labor and Employment Law.

Languages: Finnish, English, Swedish and German

ATTORNEYS' HOUSE ANPR STENBÄCK
STREET

Established in 1988

STENBÄCKINKATU 26
FIN-00250 HELSINKI, FINLAND
Telephone: 358-0-474 21
Telecopier: 358-0-474 2323; 474 2222

Business Law, Business Organizations, Commercial Law, Corporate and Company Law, Contracts, Mergers, Acquisitions, Creditors Rights, Insolvency, Liquidation and Reorganizations, International Sales and Related Commercial Transactions, Domestic and International Tax Law, Securities, East-West Trade, International Construction, Joint Ventures, Transport, Patents, Trademarks and Intellectual Property, Competition and Antitrust Law, Banking, Litigation and Arbitration.

FIRM PROFILE: *The firm, a result of a 1988 merger between the law firms Ahola & Pokela and Nenonen & Rantasila, is among the larger law firms in Finland and provides a broad set of specialized services to national and international corporate clients.*

MEMBERS OF FIRM

JORGEN HAMMARSTROM, born Vasa, Finland, December 8, 1957; admitted, 1988, Finland. *Education:* University of Helsinki (LL.M., 1984). *Member:* Juridical Society of Finland; International and Comparative Law Center (Advisory Board); Academy of American and International Law

(This Listing Continued)

ATTORNEYS' HOUSE ANPR STENBÄCK STREET, Helsinki—Continued

Alumni Association (The Southwestern Legal Foundation); International Bar Association (IBA); Finnish Bar Association; Association of Private Sector Lawyers. *LANGUAGES:* Swedish, Finnish and English. *PRACTICE AREAS:* Business and Commercial Law; Company and Corporate Law; Contracts; Banking; Tax Law; Securities; Litigation; Arbitration.

HANNU HERKAMA, born Helsinki, Finland, July 31, 1950; admitted, 1981, Finland. *Education:* University of Helsinki (LL.M., 1977). *Member:* The Finnish Legal Society; Finnish Bar Association. *LANGUAGES:* Finnish, Swedish and English. *PRACTICE AREAS:* Commercial Law; Creditor's Rights; Bankruptcy; Litigation.

MATTI NENONEN, born Laukaa, Finland, February 24, 1945; admitted, 1971, Finland. *Education:* University of Helsinki (LL.M., 1967). *Member:* The Finnish Legal Society; Finnish Bar Association. *LANGUAGES:* Finnish, Swedish and English. *PRACTICE AREAS:* Business and Commercial Law; Company and Corporate Law; Contracts; Reorganizations; Tax Law.

HANNU POKELA, born Helsinki, Finland, February 15, 1952; admitted, 1979, Finland. *Education:* University of Helsinki (LL.M., 1975); Legal Scholar, Max-Planck-Institut for Industrial Property Rights, Munich (1979-1980). Member, ICC Commission on Intellectual and Industrial Property, 1981—. *Member:* Association International pour la Protection de la Propriété Industrielle (A.I.P.P.I.); International Bar Association (IBA); Finnish Bar Association. *LANGUAGES:* Finnish, English, Swedish and German. *PRACTICE AREAS:* Antitrust and Competition Law; Advertising and Marketing Law; Trademarks; Intellectual Property.

PEKKA PUHAKKA, born Helsinki, Finland, June 27, 1956; admitted, 1984, Finland. *Education:* University of Helsinki (LL.M., 1981). *Member:* The Finnish Legal Society; Finnish Bar Association (Auditor); Young Lawyers' International Association (AIJA, National Vice President); Society for Copyright Law; Association International pour la Protection de la Propriété Industrielle (A.I.P.P.I.). *LANGUAGES:* Finnish, Swedish, English, German and French. *PRACTICE AREAS:* Business Law; Company Law; Contracts; Labour Law; Intellectual Property; Product Liability; Litigation; Arbitration.

HEIMO SALAKORPI, born Helsinki, Finland, November 1, 1945; admitted, 1985, Finland. *Education:* University of Helsinki (LL.M., 1969). *Member:* The Finnish Legal Society; International Bar Association (IBA); Finnish Bar Association. *LANGUAGES:* Finnish, English and Swedish. *PRACTICE AREAS:* Construction Law; Project Exports; East West Trade; Environmental Law; Computers and Software.

ASSOCIATES

SATU TIIRIKKA, born Liperi, Finland, February 5, 1957; admitted, 1991, Finland. *Education:* University of Helsinki (LL.M., 1982). *Member:* Finnish Bar Association; Association of Private Sector Lawyers. *LANGUAGES:* Finnish, English and Swedish. *PRACTICE AREAS:* Business Law; Contracts; Labour Law; Litigation; Agency; Distributorship.

MARJA VALPOLA, born Espoo, Finland, June 29, 1965; admitted, 1993, Finland. *Education:* University of Helsinki (LL.M., 1989). *Member:* Finnish Bar Association; Young Lawyers Association. *LANGUAGES:* Finnish, Swedish, English and German. *PRACTICE AREAS:* Creditor's Rights; Bankruptcy; Litigation; Banking.

ANNE NENONEN, born Lapua, Finland, August 13, 1963; admitted, 1992, Finland. *Education:* University of Helsinki (LL.M., 1987). *Member:* Finnish Bar Association; Association of Private Sector Lawyers. *LANGUAGES:* Finnish, English and Swedish. *PRACTICE AREAS:* Competition Law; Public Procurement; Commercial Law; Litigation.

SAIJA KIVINEN, born Vaasa, Finland, October 14, 1967. *Education:* University of Turku (LL.M., 1990). *Member:* Young Lawyers Association; Association of Private Sector Lawyers. *LANGUAGES:* Finnish, Swedish, English and German. *PRACTICE AREAS:* Corporate Law; Contracts; Banking; Litigation.

VELI-PEKKA ELONEN, born Hämeenkyrö, Finland, July 29, 1965. *Education:* University of Helsinki (LL.M., 1991). *Member:* Young Lawyers Association; Association of Private Sector Lawyers. *LANGUAGES:* Finnish, Swedish, English and German. *PRACTICE AREAS:* Business Law; Insurance Law; Contracts; Litigation.

(This Listing Continued)

MINNA KURRU, born Helsinki, Finland, April 13, 1969. *Education:* University of Helsinki (LL.M., 1994). *Member:* Young Lawyers Association. *LANGUAGES:* Finnish, Swedish, English, German and French. *PRACTICE AREAS:* Business Law; Creditor's Rights; Litigation.

BACKSTRÖM & CO.
SÖDRA MAGASINSGATAN 4
FIN-00130 HELSINKI, FINLAND
Telephone: +358-0-175911
Fax: +358-0-177730

Commercial and Corporate Law, Industrial Property, Mergers and Acquisition, Licensing, Distributorship, Agency, Insolvency Law, Taxation and Inheritance Law.

FIRM PROFILE: Member of Eurojuris International

MEMBERS OF FIRM

PETER G. BACKSTRÖM, born Helsinki, October 16, 1947; admitted, 1973, Finland. *Education:* University of Helsinki (LL.B., 1969). *LANGUAGES:* English, Scandinavian, German and Finnish. *PRACTICE AREAS:* Trademarks; Patents; Competition; Corporate; Licensing.

HARRI HUTTUNEN, born Maaninka, September 22, 1964; admitted, 1993, Finland. *Education:* University of Turku (LL.B., 1989). *LANGUAGES:* English, Finnish and Swedish. *PRACTICE AREAS:* Corporate Law; Mergers and Acquisitions; Agency Law; Litigation; Insolvency.

OF COUNSEL

RALF BLOMQVIST, born Helsinki, March 11, 1945. *Education:* University of Helsinki (LL.B., 1969). Formerly Chief Legal Officer, Aktia Bank, Helsinki). *LANGUAGES:* English, Scandinavian and Finnish. *PRACTICE AREAS:* Corporate and Fiscal Law; Inheritance and Family Law.

BARDY & BOSTRÖM LAW OFFICE
ETELÄESPLANADI 22
FIN-00130 HELSINKI, FINLAND
Telephone: +358-0-607211
Fax: +358-0-601048

Company and Commercial Law, Maritime and Transport Law, Commercial Contracts and International Sales, Mergers, Acquisitions and Financings, Industrial Property Rights, Competition Law, Computer Law, Construction Law, Creditors Rights, Insolvency, Bankruptcy, Taxation, Litigation and Arbitration.

MEMBERS OF FIRM

JOHAN HENRIK BARDY, born Kotka, Finland, February 1, 1954; admitted, 1988, Finland. *Education:* University of Helsinki (LL.M., 1982); University of Oslo (Special Degree in Maritime Law, 1985). *Member:* Finnish and International Bar Associations; Comitè Maritime International, Finland (CMI); Legal Society of Finland. *LANGUAGES:* Finnish, Swedish and English.

CARL JOHAN BOSTRÖM, born Helsinki, Finland, December 19, 1950; admitted, 1982, Finland. *Education:* University of Helsinki (LL.M., 1979). *Member:* Finnish Bar Association; Finnish Industrial Property Rights Association; Legal Society of Finland. *LANGUAGES:* Finnish, Swedish, English and German.

ASSOCIATE

KIMMO REKOLA, born Helsinki, Finland, July 2, 1958. *Education:* University of Helsinki (LL.M., 1983). *Member:* Union of Finnish Lawyers; Computer Law Society of Finland. *LANGUAGES:* Finnish, Swedish, English, German and Russian.

BJÖRN PETER ENGSTRÖM, born Espoo, Finland, May 29, 1957. *Education:* University of Helsinki (LL.M., 1981). *Member:* Finnish Industrial Property Rights Association; Legal Society of Finland; Computer Law Society of Finland. *LANGUAGES:* Finnish, Swedish and English.

BORENIUS & KEMPPINEN

Established in 1911

YRJÖNKATU 13 A

SF-00120 HELSINKI, FINLAND

Telephone: 358-0-615 333

Telefax: 358-0-615 33499

Corporate, Commercial, Computer, Contract, Industrial Property, Patent and Licenses, Intellectual Property, Labor, Family, European Community, Agency, Franchise, Banking, Finance, Tax, Construction and Bankruptcy Law, Litigation, Arbitration, General Practice.

FIRM PROFILE: *The firm has a long tradition in providing a full range of services to institutional, corporate and individual clients both nationally and internationally.*

MEMBERS OF FIRM

SEPPO KEMPPINEN, born Kauhava, Finland, February 26, 1950; admitted, 1978, Finland. *Education:* University of Helsinki (LL.M., 1975). *Member:* Finnish Bar Association (Chairman of the Delegation); Legal Society of Finland; International Bar Association; Finnish Industrial Property Society; Association International pour la Protection de la Propriété Industrielle. *LANGUAGES:* Finnish, Swedish, English and German. *PRACTICE AREAS:* Industrial Rights; Intellectual Property; Corporate; Contracts.

RITVA-LIISA LUOMARANTA, born Muurame, Finland, May 20, 1948; admitted, 1975, Finland. *Education:* University of Helsinki (LL.M., 1972). *Member:* Finnish Bar Association; Legal Society of Finland. *LANGUAGES:* Finnish, Swedish and English. *PRACTICE AREAS:* Labor; Family; Corporate Law; Litigation.

SAKARI SORRI, born Loppi, Finland, August 13, 1954; admitted, 1984, Finland. *Education:* University of Helsinki (LL.M., 1978). *Member:* Finnish Bar Association; International Bar Association; Alumni Association of the Southwestern Legal Foundation, Dallas, Texas; Les Scandinavia (Licensing Executives Society); Institute for Transnational Arbitration, Houston, Texas; Guide to International Arbitration and Arbitrators, New York. *LANGUAGES:* Finnish, Swedish, English and German. *PRACTICE AREAS:* Contracts; Corporate; Bankruptcy; Liabilities.

JYRKI TÄHTINEN, born Helsinki, Finland, November 16, 1961; admitted, 1990, Finland. *Education:* University of Helsinki (LL.M., 1985); Helsinki School of Economics (M.B.A., 1989). *Member:* Finnish Bar Association; Finnish European Law Association; AIJA; International Association of Young Lawyers. *LANGUAGES:* Finnish, Swedish, English and German. *PRACTICE AREAS:* Banking; Commercial Contracts; Bankruptcy; Competition.

ASSOCIATES

MINNA SAARELAINEN, born Tampere, Finland, February 10, 1964; admitted, 1994, Finland. *Education:* University of Turku (LL.M., 1989). *Member:* Legal Society of Finland; Finnish Bar Association. *LANGUAGES:* Finnish, Swedish, English and German. *PRACTICE AREAS:* Labor Law; Corporate Law; Litigation.

MIKA SALONEN, born Turku, Finland, May 8, 1964; admitted, 1994, Finland. *Education:* University of Turku (LL.M., 1989); University of Amsterdam, European Community Business Law Course (LL.M.). *Member:* Finnish Bar Association; AIJA (International Association of Young Lawyers); Legal Society of Finland; Finnish Association of European Law (Board Member). *LANGUAGES:* Finnish, Swedish, English and French. *PRACTICE AREAS:* European Community Law; Computer Law.

CHRISTINA STENVALL, born Helsinki, Finland, November 9, 1964; admitted, 1993, Finland. *Education:* University of Helsinki (LL.M., 1989). *Member:* Finnish Bar Association; Legal Society of Finland; AIJA; International Association of Young Lawyers; International Fiscal Association. *LANGUAGES:* Swedish, Finnish, English, German and French. *PRACTICE AREAS:* Corporate Law; Tax Law; Securities.

JYRKI NIKULA, born Helsinki, Finland, February 8, 1965. *Education:* University of Helsinki (LL.M., 1992). *Member:* Legal Society of Finland; Young Lawyers Society of Finland (Board Member). *LANGUAGES:* Finnish, Swedish, English and German. *PRACTICE AREAS:* Immaterial Rights; Computer Law; Contracts and Litigation.

ARI-PEKKA SAANIO, born Tampere, Finland, April 30, 1965. *Education:* University of Helsinki (LL.M., 1994). *Member:* Legal Society of Finland. *LANGUAGES:* Finnish, Swedish, English, German, French and Spanish. *PRACTICE AREAS:* Insolvency Law; Private International Law.

(This Listing Continued)

TIMO RANKI, born Helsinki, Finland, September 27, 1966. *Education:* University of Turku (LL.M., 1993). *Member:* Legal Society of Finland. *LANGUAGES:* Finnish, Swedish, English and French. *PRACTICE AREAS:* Banking and Financial Services; Competition.

JARI VIKIÖ, born Oulu, Finland, July 2, 1968. *Education:* University of Turku (LL.M., 1994). *LANGUAGES:* Finnish, Swedish, English, German. *PRACTICE AREAS:* European Community Law; Contracts; Competition.

OF COUNSEL

KULLERVO KEMPPINEN, born Terijoki, Finland, June 24, 1921; admitted, 1958, Finland. *Education:* University of Helsinki (LL.M., 1947). *Member:* Finnish Bar Association (Board Member, 1972-1976); Legal Society of Finland (Board Member, 1984-1987). *LANGUAGES:* Finnish, Swedish, English and German. *PRACTICE AREAS:* Foundation Law; Trust Law; Copyright Law.

Member of the Intergrated Advisory Group.

BÜTZOW & CO.

Member of S.L.G.

(Scandinavian Business Law Group)

Copenhagen: Berning Schlüter Hald

Helsinki: Bützow & Co.

Oslo: Vogt & Co.

Stockholm: Tisell & Co.

Established in 1969

POHJOISESPLANADI 21 A

P.O. BOX 121

FIN-00101 HELSINKI, FINLAND

Telephone: +358-0-651 744

Facsimile: +358-0-665 417

Representative Offices: London, England and Tallinn, Estonia.

General Corporate and Business Law, Banking, Financing, Insurance Law, Intellectual Property, Maritime and Transportation Law, Licensing, Arbitration and Litigation in Civil Matters.

FIRM PROFILE: *The firm offers a full range of legal services for all corporate clients. The membership of Scandinavian Business Law Group gives the firm an extra strength in serving its clients also in other Scandinavian countries and in the Baltic states.*

HENRIK HÄSTÖ, born Helsinki, Finland, April 25, 1947; admitted, 1975, Helsinki. *Education:* University of Helsinki (LL.B., 1971). *Member:* Helsinki and Finnish (Member, Executive Committee, 1984-1992; Disciplinary Committee, 1992—) Bar Associations; Legal Society of Finland; Union of Finnish Lawyers. *LANGUAGES:* Finnish, Swedish, English and German. *PRACTICE AREAS:* Mergers and Acquisitions; Corporate Structuring; Tax Law; Corporate Law; Commercial Law.

MARTTI TIMGREN, born Juankoski, Finland, October 20, 1955; admitted, 1983, Helsinki. *Education:* University of Helsinki (LL.B., 1980). *Member:* Helsinki, Finnish and International Bar Associations; Young Lawyers' Association (AIJA); Legal Society of Finland; Union of Finnish Lawyers; Union International des Avocats; Licensing Executive Society (LES). *LANGUAGES:* Finnish, Swedish, English and French. *PRACTICE AREAS:* Contract Law; Mergers and Acquisitions; Commercial Disputes; Corporate Law; Construction Law.

HENRIK GAHMBERG, born Helsinki, Finland, May 12, 1949; admitted, 1987, Helsinki. *Education:* University of Helsinki (LL.B., 1973). Supervisory Board Member, Institute of Maritime and Commercial Law at the Åbo (Turku) Akademi University. *Member:* Helsinki, Finnish and International Bar Associations; European Maritime Law Organisation (EMLO); Comité Maritime International, Finland (CMI, Board Member). *LANGUAGES:* Finnish, Swedish, English and German. *PRACTICE AREAS:* Maritime Law; Transport Law; Air Law; Sales of Goods; Insurance Law; Liability Disputes; Commercial Disputes.

PETER BÜTZOW, born Helsinki, Finland, March 16, 1959; admitted, 1988, Helsinki. *Education:* University of Helsinki (LL.B., 1984). *Member:* Finnish Bar Association; Comité Maritime International, Finland (CMI); Young Lawyers' Association (AIJA); Legal Society of Finland. *LANGUAGES:* Finnish, Swedish and English. *PRACTICE AREAS:* Insolvency Law; Labour Law; Construction Law.

(This Listing Continued)

BÜTZOW & CO., Helsinki—Continued

PETER ANTHONI, born Helsinki, Finland, December 15, 1960; admitted, 1990, Helsinki. *Education:* University of Helsinki (LL.B., 1986). *Member:* Helsinki, Finnish and International Bar Associations; Legal Society of Finland. *LANGUAGES:* Finnish, Swedish, English and German. *PRACTICE AREAS:* Contract Law; Company Law; Banking Law; Commercial Disputes.

KAISA PERKKIÖ, born Helsinki, Finland, August 14, 1960; admitted, 1992, Helsinki. *Education:* University of Turku (LL.B., 1988). *Member:* Finnish Bar Association; Comité Maritime International (CMI) Finland; Young Lawyers' Association (AIJA); European Lawyers' Association (ELS). *LANGUAGES:* Finnish, Swedish, English and German. *PRACTICE AREAS:* Transport Law; Maritime Law; Insurance Law; Environmental Law.

REETTA HÄRKKI, born Harjavalta, Finland, February 23, 1965; admitted, 1993, Helsinki. *Education:* University of Helsinki (LL.B., 1989). *Member:* Helsinki and Finnish Bar Associations; Young Lawyers' Association (AIJA). *LANGUAGES:* Finnish, Swedish, English and German. *PRACTICE AREAS:* Company Law; Commercial Disputes; Contract Law; Agency and Distributorship Contracts.

KAI HAANPÄÄ, born Helsinki, Finland, February 15, 1963; admitted, 1993, Helsinki. *Education:* University of Helsinki (LL.B., 1990). *Member:* Finnish Bar Association. *LANGUAGES:* Finnish, Swedish and English. *PRACTICE AREAS:* Commercial Disputes; Company Law; Contract Law; Civil Law.

URSULA SCHILDT, born Sysmä, Finland, March 15, 1965; admitted, 1994, Helsinki. *Education:* University of Helsinki (LL.B., 1989). *Member:* Helsinki and Finnish Bar Associations; Finnish Association for Industrial Property Rights; Finnish Association for Copyright Law. *LANGUAGES:* Finnish, Swedish, English, German and French. *PRACTICE AREAS:* Intellectual Property; Contract Law.

KATARIINA ORA, born Mikkeli, Finland, August 1, 1966; admitted, 1995, Helsinki. *Education:* University of Helsinki (LL.B., 1990). *Member:* Finnish Bar Association. *LANGUAGES:* Finnish, Swedish, English and German. *PRACTICE AREAS:* EEC Law; Agency and Distributorship Contracts; Product Liability.

ANNA-KARIN LINDHOLM, born Helsinki, March 24, 1964; admitted, 1995, Helsinki. *Education:* University of Helsinki (LL.B., 1989); Universitet Brussel (LL.M., 1991). *Member:* Finnish Bar Association; Comité Maritime International, Finland (CMI); Legal Society of Finland. *LANGUAGES:* Finnish, Swedish, English, French and Russian. *PRACTICE AREAS:* Maritime Law; Transport Law; Tort Law.

PIA MIETTINEN, born Helsinki, April, 11, 1966. *Education:* University of Helsinki (LL.B., 1991). *LANGUAGES:* Finnish, Swedish, English and German. *PRACTICE AREAS:* EEC Law; Civil Law; Company Law; Contract Law.

MIKA ALANKO, born Jalasjärvi, December 18, 1966. *Education:* University of Turku (LL.B., 1991). *LANGUAGES:* Finnish, Swedish, English and German. *PRACTICE AREAS:* Company Law; Commercial Disputes; Mergers and Acquisitions; Environmental Law.

HERMAN LJUNGBERG, born Helsinki, Finland, May 30, 1968. *Education:* University of Helsinki (LL.B., 1993). *LANGUAGES:* Finnish, Swedish and English. *PRACTICE AREAS:* Maritime Law; Civil Law; Tax Law.

Languages: Finnish, Swedish, English, German, French and Russian

---

CASTRÉN & SNELLMAN

Established in 1888

EROTTAJANKATU 5A

00130 HELSINKI, FINLAND

Telephone: 358-0-228 581

Telefax: 358-0-655 919, 601 961

REVISERS OF THE FINLAND LAW DIGEST FOR THIS DIRECTORY.

St. Petersburg, Russia Office: Nevsky Prospekt 22-24/18, 191186. Telephone: 7-812-119 8085. Fax: 7-812-119 8086.

(This Listing Continued)

General Practice, Industrial Property Rights, Corporate, Commercial, International, Company and Tax Law, Insolvency Law, Mergers and Acquisitions, Arbitration and Litigation.

MEMBERS OF FIRM

BERTEL ÅKERMARCK, born Porvoo, Finland, June 8, 1933; admitted, 1958, Finland. *Education:* University of Helsinki (LL.B., 1958). *Member:* Finnish Bar Association; Union of Finnish Lawyers; Juridiska Föreningen i Finland. *LANGUAGES:* Finnish, Swedish, English and German.

EERO RELAS, born Helsinki, Finland, July 31, 1942; admitted, 1965, Finland. *Education:* University of Helsinki (LL.B., 1965). *Member:* Finnish Bar Association; Union of Finnish Lawyers. *LANGUAGES:* Finnish, Swedish, English, German, Estonian.

PEKKA SIRVIÖ, born Kajaani, Finland, January 27, 1945; admitted, 1968, Finland. *Education:* The Helsinki School of Economics and Business Administration (B.Sc. in Econ., 1971); University of Helsinki (LL.B., 1968). *Member:* Association of Finnish Attorneys. *LANGUAGES:* Finnish, Swedish, English and German.

JOUKO HUHTALA, born Tampere, Finland, November 26, 1950; admitted, 1973, Finland. *Education:* University of Helsinki (LL.B., 1973). *Member:* Finnish Bar Association; Union of Finnish Lawyers; Young Lawyers International Association (AIJA). *LANGUAGES:* Finnish, Swedish, English and German.

MIKAEL ASPELIN, born Espoo, Finland, October 21, 1954; admitted, 1980, Finland. *Education:* University of Helsinki (LL.B., 1980); Vrije Universiteit of Brussels (LL.M., 1986). *Member:* Finnish Bar Association; International Bar Association; Union of Finnish Lawyers; Juridiska Föreningen i Finland. *LANGUAGES:* Finnish, Swedish, English and German.

PEKKA JAATINEN, born Porvoo, Finland, May 30, 1956; admitted, 1983, Finland. *Education:* University of Helsinki (LL.B., 1983). *Member:* Young Lawyers International Association. *LANGUAGES:* Finnish, Swedish and English.

JAN KUHLEFELT, born Helsinki, Finland, June 10, 1955; admitted, 1985, Finland. *Education:* University of Helsinki (LL.B., 1985). *LANGUAGES:* Swedish, Finnish and English.

ASSOCIATES

JOHAN ÅKERMARCK, born Helsinki, Finland, January 10, 1960; admitted, 1987, Finland. *Education:* University of Helsinki (LL.B., 1987). *Member:* Association of Young Lawyers. *LANGUAGES:* Finnish, Swedish, English and German.

MARKO HENTUNEN, born Helsinki, Finland, March 3, 1962; admitted, 1987, Finland. *Education:* University of Helsinki (LL.B., 1987). *Member:* Union of Finnish Lawyers; Association of Private Sector Lawyers. *LANGUAGES:* Finnish, Swedish and English.

JUHA VÄYRYNEN, born Helsinki, Finland, July 16, 1964; admitted, 1988, Finland. *Education:* University of Helsinki (LL.B., 1988). *Member:* Union of Finnish Lawyers; Association of Private Sector Lawyers. *LANGUAGES:* Finnish, Swedish, English and German.

CLAUDIO BUSI, born Helsinki, Finland, September 4, 1958; admitted, 1984, Finland. *Education:* University of Helsinki (LL.B., 1984). *LANGUAGES:* Finnish, Swedish, English and Italian.

PAULIINA TENHUNEN, born Pihtipudas, Finland, February 15, 1966; admitted, 1990, Finland. *Education:* University of Helsinki (LL.B., 1990). *Member:* Union of Young Finnish Lawyers. *LANGUAGES:* Finnish, Swedish, English, German.

UWE UUSITALO, born Tampere, Finland, September 22, 1963; admitted, 1989, Finland. *Education:* University of Helsinki (LL.B., 1989). *Member:* Union of Finnish Lawyers. *LANGUAGES:* Finnish, German, English and Swedish.

OUTI ISOTALO, born Helsinki, Finland, April 28, 1961; admitted, 1988, Finland. *Education:* University of Helsinki (LL.B., 1988). *LANGUAGES:* Finnish, Swedish and English.

LENNART SIMONSEN, born Espoo, Finland, August 27, 1960; admitted, 1985, Finland. *Education:* University of Helsinki (LL.B., 1985). *LANGUAGES:* Swedish, Finnish and English.

SUVI LAHTINEN, born Helsinki, Finland, June 15, 1958; admitted, 1992, Finland. *Education:* University of Helsinki (LL.B., 1992). *LANGUAGES:* Finnish, Swedish and English.

(This Listing Continued)

ANNA MARIA FELLMAN, born Helsinki, Finland, September 16, 1965; admitted, 1993, Finland. *Education:* University of Helsinki (LL.B., 1993). *LANGUAGES:* Swedish, Finnish, English, German and French.

MIKA ILVESKERO, born Espoo, Finland, March 16, 1966; admitted, 1990, Finland. *Education:* University of Helsinki (LL.B., 1990). *Member:* Union of Young Lawyers; Union of Finnish Lawyers. *LANGUAGES:* Finnish, English, German and Swedish.

MERJA KIVELÄ, born Imatra, Finland, September 27, 1960; admitted, 1987, Finland. *Education:* University of Helsinki (LL.B., 1987). *Member:* Union of Finnish Lawyers. *LANGUAGES:* Finnish, Swedish, English and German.

MIKKO MALI, born Helsinki, Finland, May 21, 1964; admitted, 1990, Finland. *Education:* University of Helsinki (LL.B., 1990). *Member:* Union of Finnish Lawyers. *LANGUAGES:* Finnish, Swedish, English, French, Russian and Spanish.

NINA STANISLAVOVNA VASILJEVA, born Leningrad, USSR, October 8, 1966. *Education:* Leningrad State University (Law degree, 1989). *Member:* St. Petersburg Regional Bar Association. (Resident, St. Petersburg, Russia). *LANGUAGES:* Russian and English.

IGOR LIVSHITS, born Tallinn, Estonia, January 31, 1958. *Education:* University of St. Petersburg (Law degree, 1982). *Member:* Russian Sociological Association; Association of Finnish Lawyers. (Resident, St. Petersburg, Russia). *LANGUAGES:* Russian, English and Finnish.

ANNA KUUSNIEMI, born Tampere, Finland, October 14, 1970. *Education:* University of Helsinki (LL.B., 1994). *Member:* Union of Young Finnish Lawyers. *LANGUAGES:* Finnish, English and German.

Languages: Finnish, Swedish, English, German, Estonian, Italian, French and Russian

REVISERS OF THE FINLAND LAW DIGEST FOR THIS DIRECTORY.

DITTMAR & INDRENIUS

Established in 1899

POHJOISESPLANADI 25 A
FIN-00100 HELSINKI, FINLAND
Telephone: 358-0-661711
Telecopier: 358-0-652 406
Cable Address: "Dittmarindren"
Telex: 121974 dilaw sf

FIRM PROFILE: *The firm concentrates on Corporate and Commercial Law, Mergers and Acquisitions, Banking and Financial Services, Antitrust, Taxation, Intellectual Property and Commercial Litigation and Arbitration.*

The firm's clientele consists mostly of foreign multinational companies, foreign-controlled subsidiaries in Finland and Finnish medium-sized to large corporations engaged in activities in Finland and abroad. More than half of the firm's work relates to foreign companies.

The firm serves clients in English, French, German, Italian, Swedish and Finnish.

MEMBERS OF FIRM

TOM PETTERSSON, born Copenhagen, Denmark, June 12, 1949; admitted, 1977, Helsinki, Finland. *Education:* University of Helsinki (LL.B., 1973). *Member:* Finnish Bar Association; Legal Society of Finland; International Bar Association. *LANGUAGES:* Finnish, Swedish, English and German.

KARL MARKUS TROBERG, born Turku, Finland, April 5, 1951; admitted, 1977, Helsinki, Finland. *Education:* University of Helsinki (LL.B., 1974); Georgetown University Law Center, Washington, D.C. (1978); Southern Methodist University, Dallas, Texas (M.C.L., 1979); Swedish School of Economics and Business Administration in Helsinki (B.Sc., 1977). With Cleary, Gottlieb, Steen & Hamilton, 1979. *Member:* Finnish Bar Association; Legal Society of Finland; International Bar Association. *LANGUAGES:* Finnish, Swedish, English and German.

ANTTI KUUSIMÄKI, born Pielisjärvi, Finland, August 27, 1960; admitted, 1988, Helsinki, Finland. *Education:* University of Helsinki (LL.B., 1984). Legal Counsel with the Finnish Foreign Trade Association, 1984-1986. *Member:* Finnish Bar Association; Finnish Lawyers' Society; Finnish Association for European Law; International Bar Association. *LANGUAGES:* Finnish, Swedish, English, German and French.

(This Listing Continued)

MATTI S. KURKELA, born Helsinki, Finland, May 28, 1951; admitted, 1978, Helsinki, Finland; 1990, Paris, France. *Education:* University of Helsinki (LL.B., 1974; LL.Lic., 1981; LL.D., 1993); Harvard Law School (LL.M., 1983); Université de Paris (D.S.U. Paris II, 1990). Acting assistant professor of International Trade at the University of Helsinki, 1985. Docent of International Private Law and International Trade, University of Helsinki Law School. Legal advisor at the First National Bank of Boston (Boston), 1983 and 1989. With Chadbourne & Parke (New York), 1983-1984. Partner: Obstbaum, Harju & Kurkela, 1984-1988; Heikki Haapaniemi, 1988-1993. Author of several books and articles including "Letters of Credit under international trade law," Oceana, New York, 1985 and "Bank guarantees in International trade," 1993. *Member:* Finnish and French Bar Associations; International Bar Association. *LANGUAGES:* Finnish, Swedish, English, German, Italian and French.

ASSOCIATES

PETER ROOS, born Helsinki, Finland, February 13, 1960; admitted, 1989, Helsinki, Finland. *Education:* University of Helsinki (LL.B., 1983). *Member:* Finnish Bar Association; International Fiscal Association; International Bar Association. *LANGUAGES:* Finnish, Swedish, English and German.

RAIJA-LEENA OJANEN, born Helsinki, Finland, November 7, 1962; admitted, 1990, Helsinki, Finland. *Education:* University of Helsinki (LL.B., 1986). *Member:* Finnish Bar Association. *LANGUAGES:* Finnish, Swedish, English and German.

JAN SANDSTRÖM, born Porvoo, Finland, November 2, 1962; admitted, 1994, Helsinki, Finland. *Education:* University of Helsinki (LL.B., 1990). *Member:* Finnish Bar Association. *LANGUAGES:* Finnish, Swedish, English and German.

JAN OLLILA, born Helsinki, Finland, March 27, 1965. *Education:* University of Helsinki (LL.B., 1992). *Member:* International Fiscal Association. *LANGUAGES:* Finnish, Swedish and English.

PETTERI UOTI, born Helsinki, Finland, June 3, 1963; admitted, 1994, Helsinki, Finland. *Education:* University of Helsinki (LL.B., 1988). *Member:* Finnish Bar Association; Finnish Industrial Lawyers Association; Finnish Labor Law Association. *LANGUAGES:* Finnish, Swedish and English.

SEPPO NURMI, born Nurmijärvi, Finland, February 21, 1966. *Education:* University of Helsinki (LL.B., 1992). *LANGUAGES:* Finnish, Swedish, English, German and French.

HANNELE VON HERTZEN, born Espoo, Finland, April 3, 1965; admitted, 1994, Helsinki, Finland. *Education:* University of Helsinki (LL.B., 1990). *Member:* Finnish Bar Association. *LANGUAGES:* Finnish, Swedish, English, German and French.

JOHANNA JALAS, born Helsinki, Finland, March 18, 1970. *Education:* University of Helsinki (LL.B., 1992); College of Europe, Brugge (Master of European Legal Studies, LL.M., 1993). *LANGUAGES:* Finnish, Swedish, English, French and German.

KAARINA STÅHLBERG, born Helsinki, Finland, December 23, 1966. *Education:* University of Helsinki (LL.B., 1992). *LANGUAGES:* Finnish, Swedish, English and French.

ANTTI AALTONEN, born Marttila, Finland, March 1, 1964. *Education:* University of Turku (LL.B., 1991). *LANGUAGES:* Finnish, Swedish, English and German.

PETRI MÄNTYSAARI, born Äänekoski, Finland, October 15, 1962. *Education:* University of Helsinki (LL.B., 1988); University of Bristol (LL.M., 1989); University of Hamburg (Doctoral Student, 1992—). Visiting Scholar, Max-Planck-Institute for Foreign and Private International Law, Hamburg, 1992-1994. Author: "The Sale of Goods Act and the Liability of the Vendor of Shares for Breach of Contract," Defensor Legis, 1993, in Finnish; "The Sale of Shares and Breach of Contract Relating to the Shareholder's Rights," Defensor Legis, 1994, in Finnish. *LANGUAGES:* Finnish, Swedish, English and German.

TIMO LEIVO, born Helsinki, Finland, April 10, 1968. *Education:* University of Helsinki (LL.B., 1993); College of Europe, Brugge, Belgium (Master of European Legal Studies, LL.M., 1994). *LANGUAGES:* Finnish, Swedish, English, French and German.

FACT LAW GROUP

Asianajotoimisto Kyyrö

MECHELININKATU 15 B 32
00100 HELSINKI, FINLAND
Telephone: 358-0-446 500
Telefax: 358-0-441 633
24 Hour Answering Service: 358-0-445475

Washington, D.C. Office: The Capitol Hill Office Building, 412 First Street, S.E., Suite One -- Lobby Level, 20003. Telephone: 1-202-362-6900. Telefax:1-202-362-9699.

General Practice, Finnish-American Trade, including Corporate and Business Law, General Trial and Appellate Litigation in Courts and before Government Agencies, Arbitration, Contracts, Agency and Franchise, Product Liability, Trademarks and Copyrights, Antitrust, East-West Trade, Construction and Real Estate Law.

FIRM PROFILE: FACT -- the Finnish American Corporate Team -- is the first law firm to have established offices in both the United States and Finland. The firm's clients range from multinational corporations to government organizations to individuals.

ARI KYYRÖ, born Helsinki, Finland, October 22, 1952; admitted, 1986, Finland. *Education:* University of Helsinki (LL.M., 1982). *Member:* The Finnish Legal Society; Finnish Bar Association; Young Lawyer's International Association (AIJA). *LANGUAGES:* Finnish, English and Swedish.

TOM A. LIPPO, born Greensburg, Pennsylvania, October 6, 1955; admitted, 1982, District of Columbia; 1983, U.S. District Court for the District of Columbia and U.S. Court of Appeals for the District of Columbia Circuit. *Education:* Yale University (B.A., summa cum laude with distinction, 1978); University of Jyväskylä, Finland (M.A., summa cum laude, 1979); Stanford University (J.D., 1982). Psi Chi; Phi Beta Kappa. Fulbright Scholar. Rotary Foundation International Education Award. Law Clerk-Intern to Hon. Joyce Hens Green, U.S. District Court for the District of Columbia, 1981-1982. *Member:* The District of Columbia Bar. *LANGUAGES:* English and Finnish.

COUNSEL

JYRKI PEKKALA, born Rovaniemi, Finland, February 11, 1960. *Education:* University of Helsinki (LL.M., 1987). *Member:* Finnish Bar Association; Union of Finnish Lawyers. *LANGUAGES:* Finnish, English and Swedish.

CARROLL D. HAUPTLE, JR., born Wilmington, Delaware, August 18, 1954; admitted, 1987, Virginia, U.S. Court of Appeals, Fourth Circuit; 1988, District of Columbia; 1991, U.S. District Court, Eastern District of Virginia; 1992, U.S. District Court, District of Columbia (Not admitted in Finland). *Education:* Yale University (B.A., 1976); Washington College of Law at American University (J.D., 1987). Executive/Topics Editor, Administrative Law Journal, 1986-1987. Legal Editor, The Journal of Arts Management and Law, 1986-1987. *Member:* The District of Columbia Bar; Virginia State Bar; American Bar Association; Washington Area Lawyers for the Arts. *LANGUAGES:* English, French and German.

MINNAMARI MARTTILA, born Helsinki, Finland, May 3, 1967; admitted, 1994, Finland. *Education:* University of Helsinki (LL.M., 1994); University of Uppsala, Department of International Law (EC Law). *Member:* Finnish Bar Association; Young Lawyers Association. *LANGUAGES:* Finnish, English. Swedish and German.

REPRESENTATIVE CLIENTS: Finnair; Nokia Mobile Phones.

GILBERT, SEGALL AND YOUNG OY

POHJOISESPLANADI 33
00100 HELSINKI, FINLAND
Telephone: 358-0-177 300
Telecopier: 358-0-177 644

New York, New York Office: Gilbert, Segall and Young. 430 Park Avenue, 10022. Telephone: 212-644-4000. Telecopier: 212-644-4051.

General Practice.

RESIDENT ATTORNEY

SARNO LINDBERG, born Helsinki, Finland, October 1, 1960; admitted, 1994, Helsinki, Finland. *Education:* University of Helsinki (LL.M., 1985); Southern Methodist University (LL. M., 1986). Engaged in the Practice of Law Since 1986. *Member:* Finnish Bar Association; International Bar

(This Listing Continued)

Association; Legal Society of Finland; The Union of Finnish Lawyers. *LANGUAGES:* Finnish, English, Swedish and German.

(For complete biographical information on all personnel see Professional Biographies at New York, New York)

HEIKKI HAAPANIEMI

Established in 1958

MANNERHEIMINTIE 14 B
FIN-00100 HELSINKI, FINLAND
Telephone: 358-0-177 613
Telecopier: 358-0-653 873

Mailing Address: P.O. Box 232, 00101 Helsinki, Finland

Paris, France Branch Office: 148, Boulevard du Montparnasse, 75014. Telephone: 33-1-43.35.23.12. Telecopier: 33-1-43.35.19.58.

Corporate and Business Law, Investments and Securities, Banking Law and Corporate and Project Financing, International Contracts, Distributorship, Agency and Franchise Law, Licensing, International Business Transactions, Antitrust and Competition Law, Commercial Law, Industrial Property and Copyright Law, Media Law, Advertising and Marketing Law, Product Liability, Construction Law and Real Estates, Environmental Law, International Private Law, Taxation, Employment Law, Arbitration and Litigation.

FIRM PROFILE: Heikki Haapaniemi is one of the largest law firms in Finland specializing in Domestic and International Business Law. The Firm was established in 1958 and its main office is located in the financial and commercial center of Helsinki. The international aspects of the Firm's practice are of great importance. In order to meet the demands of the Firm's clientele engaged in international operations and to satisfy needs associated with the European integration process, Heikki Haapaniemi established a branch office in Paris on May 1, 1989, being at the present the only Finnish law firm registered as a member of the Paris Bar. The Firm presently consists of 26 lawyers, 13 of whom are partners and a support staff of approximately 20 employees.

MEMBERS OF FIRM

HEIKKI HAAPANIEMI (1920-1983).

MARTTI IKONEN, born Soanlahti, Finland, December 24, 1934; admitted, 1962, Finland. *Education:* University of Helsinki (LL.M., 1959). *Member:* Finnish Bar Association; The Bar Association of Helsinki (Chairman, 1980-1984); The Union of Finnish Lawyers (Board Member, 1988—); International Bar Association; Union Internationale des Avocats. *LANGUAGES:* Finnish, Swedish, English and German.

TIMO KORPIOLA, born Helsinki, Finland, May 8, 1945; admitted, 1973, Finland. *Education:* University of Helsinki (LL.M., 1970). *Member:* Finnish Bar Association; The Bar Association of Helsinki (Board Member, 1984-1990); The Union of Finnish Lawyers; Council of the Bars and Law Societes of the European Community (CCBE); Young Lawyers' International Association (AIJA, Member of the Executive Committee, 1980-1983; National Vice President, 1983-1987); International Bar Association. *LANGUAGES:* Finnish, Swedish, English and French.

EERO KAJANDER, born Helsinki, Finland, February 23, 1952; admitted, 1980, Finland. *Education:* University of Helsinki (LL.M., 1976). *Member:* Finnish Bar Association; The Bar Association of Helsinki (Board Member, 1990—); The Union of Finnish Lawyers; Young Lawyers' International Association (AIJA, Member of the Executive Committee, 1983-1987; National Vice President, 1987-1992). *LANGUAGES:* Finnish, Swedish, French and English.

MARJA TOMMILA, born Helsinki, Finland, March 18, 1950; admitted, 1980, Finland. *Education:* University of Helsinki (LL.M., 1974). *Member:* Finnish Bar Association; The Union of Finnish Lawyers; The Finnish AIPPI-Group; The Finnish Marketing Federation (President, 1989—); The Finnish Franchise Association (President, 1988-1989); International Bar Association. *LANGUAGES:* Finnish, Swedish, English, French and German.

KARI LAUTJÄRVI, born Espoo, Finland, January 8, 1955; admitted, 1984, Finland. *Education:* University of Helsinki (LL.M., 1981); Harvard Law School (LL.M., 1986). *Member:* Finnish Bar Association; The Union of Finnish Lawyers; International Bar Association. *LANGUAGES:* Finnish, Swedish, English and German.

JARI NIKUPAAVOLA, born Hämeelinna, Finland, January 29, 1959; admitted, 1988, Finland. *Education:* University of Helsinki (LL.M., 1984).

(This Listing Continued)

Member: Finnish Bar Association; The Union of Finnish Lawyers; Young Lawyers' International Association (AIJA). *LANGUAGES:* Finnish, Swedish, English, German and Italian.

VELI LEINONEN, born Keitele, Finland, May 24, 1952; admitted, 1989, Finland. *Education:* University of Helsinki (LL.M., 1982). *Member:* Finnish Bar Association; The Union of Finnish Lawyers; Finnish Lawyers Society. *LANGUAGES:* Finnish, Swedish, English and German.

LAURI TOLVANEN, born Helsinki, Finland, March 27, 1957; admitted, 1985, Finland. *Education:* University of Helsinki (LL.M., 1982). *Member:* Finnish Bar Association; The Union of Finnish Lawyers. *LANGUAGES:* Finnish, Swedish and English.

KRISTIINA LEHTONEN, born Helsinki, Finland, May 15, 1955; admitted, 1983, Finland. *Education:* University of Helsinki (LL.M., 1980). *Member:* Finnish Bar Association; The Union of Finnish Lawyers. *LANGUAGES:* Finnish, Swedish, English and German.

ARTO KUKKONEN, born Mäntyharju, Finland, July 9, 1959; admitted, 1991, Finland. *Education:* University of Helsinki (LL.M., 1986). *Member:* Finnish Bar Association; The Union of Finnish Lawyers; International Fiscal Association (IFA). *LANGUAGES:* Finnish, Swedish and English.

JARI SONNINEN, born Helsinki, Finland, April 21, 1957; admitted, 1990, Finland. *Education:* University of Rovaniemi (LL.M., 1985); Southern Methodist University (LL.M., 1987). *Member:* Finnish Bar Association; The Union of Finnish Lawyers; International Bar Association. *LANGUAGES:* Finnish, Swedish and English.

HEIKKI CANTELL, born Helsinki, Finland, March 9, 1959; admitted, 1992, Finland. *Education:* University of Helsinki (LL.M., 1987); University of Paris II (D.S.U., 1991). *Member:* Finnish Bar Association; Paris Bar Association; The Union of Finnish Lawyers; Young Lawyers' International Association (AIJA, Member of the Executive Committee, 1993—). (Resident, Paris, France Office). *LANGUAGES:* Finnish, Swedish, English, French, German and Italian.

RIKU PAANILA, born Kuhmo, Finland, July 9, 1961; admitted, 1991, Finland. *Education:* University of Helsinki (LL.M., 1986); University of Trier (M. Iur., 1988). *Member:* Finnish Bar Association; The Union of Finnish Lawyers; Young Lawyers' International Association (AIJA). *LANGUAGES:* Finnish, Swedish, English and German.

ASSOCIATES

PASI HAAPANIEMI, born Helsinki, Finland, July 6, 1957. *Education:* University of Helsinki (LL.M., 1988). *Member:* The Union of Finnish Lawyers. *LANGUAGES:* Finnish, Swedish, English and French.

TAINA TUOHINO, born Kemijärvi, Finland, December 21, 1958; admitted, 1993, Finland. *Education:* University of Helsinki (LL.M., 1982); Helsinki School of Economics (M.B.A., 1989). *Member:* Finnish Bar Association; The Union of Finnish Lawyers; Finnish MBA Association. *LANGUAGES:* Finnish, Swedish and English.

TAPANI MANNINEN, born Helsinki, Finland, November 12, 1961; admitted, 1993, Finland. *Education:* University of Helsinki (LL.M., 1987); Centre Européen Universitaire de Nancy (D.E.S.E., 1990). *Member:* Finnish Bar Association; The Union of Finnish Lawyers. *LANGUAGES:* Finnish, Swedish, English and French.

ILKKA RAHNASTO, born Seinäjoki, Finland, November 13, 1964; admitted, 1994, Finland. *Education:* University of Helsinki (LL.M., 1989). *Member:* Finnish Bar Association; The Union of Finnish Lawyers; The Finnish Association for the Protection of Industrial Property. *LANGUAGES:* Finnish, Swedish, English and German.

OLLI RAUSTE, born Joensuu, Finland, January 17, 1963. *Education:* University of Helsinki (LL.M., 1990); University of Pennsylvania (LL.M., 1993). *Member:* The Union of Finnish Lawyers. *LANGUAGES:* Finnish, Swedish, English and German.

JANNE JOKINEN, born Riihimäki, Finland, November 15, 1965; admitted, 1994, Finland. *Education:* University of Helsinki (LL.M., 1989). *Member:* Finnish Bar Association; The Union of Finnish Lawyers. *LANGUAGES:* Finnish, Swedish, English and German.

RISTO SIPILÄ, born Helsinki, Finland, September 21, 1965. *Education:* University of Helsinki (LL.M., 1991). *Member:* The Union of Finnish Lawyers. *LANGUAGES:* Finnish, Swedish and English.

KARIN COLLIN, born Helsinki, Finland, August 12, 1964. *Education:* University of Helsinki (LL.M., 1991). *Member:* The Union of Finnish Lawyers. *LANGUAGES:* Finnish, Swedish, English and French.

(This Listing Continued)

MIKKO HARJU, born Helsinki, Finland, March 4, 1966. *Education:* University of Helsinki (LL.M., 1991); University of Amsterdam (LL.M., 1994). *Member:* The Union of Finnish Lawyers. *LANGUAGES:* Finnish, Swedish, English, French and German.

KAISA VIRTANEN, born Rauma, Finland, April 12, 1966. *Education:* University of Turku (LL.M., 1991). *Member:* The Union of Finnish Lawyers. *LANGUAGES:* Finnish, Swedish, English, French and German.

HARRI SALMI, born Helsinki, Finland, January 6, 1964. *Education:* University of Helsinki (LL.M., 1991). *Member:* The Union of Finnish Lawyers. *LANGUAGES:* Finnish, Swedish, English, French and German.

JORI TAIPALE, born Helsinki, Finland, October 2, 1969. *Education:* University of Helsinki (LL.M., 1993). *Member:* The Union of Finnish Lawyers. *LANGUAGES:* Finnish, Swedish, English and French.

JUKKA MUHONEN, born Helsinki, Finland, June 8, 1968. *Education:* University of Helsinki (LL.M., 1994). *Member:* The Union of Finnish Lawyers. *LANGUAGES:* Finnish, Swedish, English and German.

HEDMAN LAW OFFICES

Established in 1975

LUOTSIKATU 7 A 4
00160 HELSINKI, FINLAND
Telephone: + 358-0-177 060
Telefax: + 358-0-629 759

St. Petersburg, Russia Office: 134, Nevsky Prospekt, 193036. Telephone: 7-812-274 3968; 274 4169. Fax: 7-812-274 4355.

Tallinn, Estonia Office: 5, Uus, EE0001. Telephone: 372-6-313 258. Fax: 372-6-313 257.

General Civil Practice, Litigation in all Courts, Corporation Law, Business, Commercial, Trade Secrets, Taxation and Real Property Law, Joint Ventures.

FIRM PROFILE: Established in 1975, Hedman Law Offices is based in the center of Helsinki. Specializing in providing tailormade services, Hedman Law Offices has served Finnish corporations, banks and institutions and a wide range of major US and European corporations for nearly twenty years. The firm has recently acquired special competence in EC and EEA legislation. Hedman Law Offices has a well established and prominent Eastern and Baltic law practice with branch offices in St. Petersburg and Tallinn and is regarded as a leading law firm in Scandinavia. With many years' experience in these areas, and with highly skilled lawyers, Hedman Law Offices has successfully represented foreign clients in Finland and Finnish clients abroad.

HARRY HEDMAN, born Helsinki, Finland, December 4, 1946; admitted, 1976, Finland. *Education:* University of Helsinki (LL.M., 1971). Court Practice, 1973-1975; Degree of Bench Training, 1975. Finnish Member, ICC Commission on International Arbitration, 1978-1991. Chairman, Tax and Legal Planning Committee, Espoo Chamber of Commerce. Board Member, Finnish American Club 1932. *Member:* Finnish Bar Association (Helsinki Section). *LANGUAGES:* Finnish, Swedish and English.

ASSOCIATES

KALLE PEDAK, born Tallinn, Estonia, March 15, 1960. *Education:* University of Tartu (LL.M., 1984). Practice: Lawyers in Estonian Union of Consumers Co-operatives (ETKVL), 1984-1989. Licensed Bankruptcy Estate Administrator, Estonia, 1993. Non-Resident Member, Estonian Bar Association, 1992. *LANGUAGES:* Estonian, Finnish, Russian, German and English.

ROGER LEHTONEN, born Loviisa, Finland, May 20, 1959. *Education:* University of Helsinki (LL.M., 1986). Court Practice, 1987-1988; Degree of Bench Training, 1988. EC Study Programme, Institute of International Marketing (Finland), 1993. Practice: Lawyer in Confederation of Finnish Construction Industries, 1988-1992. *LANGUAGES:* Finnish, Swedish, English and German.

AKU SORAINEN, born Helsinki, Finland, June 25, 1965. *Education:* University of Lapland (LL.M., 1993). Student at Helsinki School of Economics and Business Management. Author: "A Foreign investor in the Baltics," 1993. (Resident, Tallinn, Estonia Office). *LANGUAGES:* Finnish, English, Swedish, German and Estonian.

JUKKA-PEKKA NIEMELÄ, born Oulu, Finland, April 19, 1952. *Education:* University of Helsinki (LL.M., 1978); University of Wales (Post-

(This Listing Continued)

HEDMAN LAW OFFICES, Helsinki—Continued

graduate Diploma, 1980). Court Practice, 1983-1984; Degree of Bench Training, 1984. *LANGUAGES:* Finnish, Swedish, English and German.

PETER PYLKKÖNEN, born Kuopio, Finland, May 1, 1968. *Education:* University of Helsinki (LL.M., 1990). Court Practice, 1993-1994; Degree of Bench Training, 1994. *LANGUAGES:* Swedish, Finnish, English, Russian, German and French.

LAW OFFICES OF ERKKI KANNISTO

Established in 1985

YRÖNKATU 21 C 22

SF-00100 HELSINKI, FINLAND

Telephone: 385-0-602-006

Facsimile: 385-0-601-041

General Practice, Company Law, Family Law, Criminal Law, Bankruptcies and Taxation.

ERKKI KANNISTO, born Muurame, Finland, September 19, 1945; admitted, 1984, Finland. *Education:* The University of Helsinki (LL.M., 1970). Instructor: Aviation Law Courses for Air Traffic Controllers, National Board of Aviation; Aviation Institute of Finnair, 1973-1975. Assistant General Councel, National Board of Post and Telegraphs, 1971-1972. Legal Advisor, National Board of Aviation, 1972-1977. *Member:* The Finnish Bar Association; Licensing Executive Society. *LANGUAGES:* Finnish, Swedish, English and French.

AARO LIUKSIALA KY

MUSEOKATU 9 B

00100 HELSINKI, FINLAND

Telephone: 90-440 687

Cable Address: "Lexcom"

Fax: 408 807

Contracts, Corporate, Commercial, Trademark, Transportation and Tax Law.

AARO LIUKSIALA KY, born Tampere, Finland, December 27, 1949; admitted, 1972, Finland. *Education:* University of Helsinki (LL.B., 1972; B.Sc. Econ., 1983). *Member:* Bar Association of Helsinki; International Law Association; AIJA (Association Internationale Des Jeunes Avocats); Comite Maritime International. *LANGUAGES:* English, German, Swedish and Finnish.

ASSOCIATE

PIA STOOR, born Vasa, Finland, May 27, 1959. *Education:* University of Helsinki (LL.B., 1987). *LANGUAGES:* English, German, Swedish and Finnish.

Languages: English, German, Swedish and Finnish.

LINDGREN & CO.

POHJOISESPLANADI 33 A

00100 HELSINKI, FINLAND

Telephone: +358-0-669895

Fax: +358-0-669 576

General Corporate and Business Law, Taxation, Litigation and Arbitration, Insolvency.

JIMMY LINDGREN, born Helsinki, Finland, January 6, 1947; admitted, 1976, Finland. *Education:* University of Helsinki (LL.M., 1973; Lic., 1980). *Member:* Finnish Bar Association; International Fiscal Association (IFA). *LANGUAGES:* Finnish, Swedish, English, German.

BJÖRN HOLMING, born Vaasa, December 31, 1950; admitted, 1993, Finland. *Education:* Uppsala, Sweden (LL.M., 1981); University of Helsinki (LL.M., 1985). *Member:* Finnish Bar Association. *LANGUAGES:* Finnish, Swedish, English.

LENA MITTS, born Virtasalmi, April 25, 1961; admitted, 1993, Finland. *Education:* University of Helsinki (LL.M., 1986). *Member:* Finnish Bar Association. *LANGUAGES:* Finnish, Swedish, English, German.

PATRICK LINDGREN & CO OY AB

SALOMONKATU 17 A (AUTOTALO)

00100 HELSINKI, FINLAND

Telephone: 358-0-70019730

Telecopier: 358-0-685 2244

International and Domestic Corporate Law, Trade and Competition Law, Agency, Franchise and Licensing, Industrial Property Rights, Real Estate Law, Joint Ventures, Arbitration and Litigation.

PATRICK LINDGREN, born Helsingfors, Finland, April 29, 1952; admitted, 1983, Finland. *Education:* University of Helsinki (LL.M., 1980). General Counsel, Finnish Foreign Trade Association, 1984-1994. *Member:* International Bar Association; International Fiscal Association; Industrial Lawyers' Association; Finnish Europe Law Society. *LANGUAGES:* Swedish, Finnish, English and German.

LINDSTRÖM, RISTOLA, SIVENIUS & SUVANTO

POHJOINEN HESPERIANKATU 15A 11

HELSINKI 00260, FINLAND

Telephone: +358 0 440 185

Facsimile: +358 0 447 148; +358 0 406 298

Corporate, Commercial, Labor, Banking, Finance, Tax, Construction, Liability, Insurance and Insolvency.

MEMBERS OF FIRM

JORMA LINDSTRÖM, born Pielisensuu, November 12, 1950; admitted, 1980, Finland. *Education:* University of Helsinki (LL.M., 1977). *Member:* Finnish Bar Association. *LANGUAGES:* Finnish, Swedish and English. *PRACTICE AREAS:* Corporations; Contracts; Bankruptcy.

ANTTI RISTOLA, born Lahti, September 15, 1947; admitted, 1977, Finland. *Education:* University of Helsinki (LL.M., 1970). *Member:* Finnish Bar Association. *LANGUAGES:* Finnish, Swedish and English. *PRACTICE AREAS:* Corporations; Contracts; Bankruptcy; Family and Inheritance.

JUHA SIVENIUS, born Helsinki, November 15, 1949; admitted, 1978, Finland. *Education:* University of Helsinki (LL.M., 1975). *Member:* Finnish Bar Association. *LANGUAGES:* Finnish, Swedish and English. *PRACTICE AREAS:* Corporations; Contracts; Bankruptcy.

JUKKA SUVANTO, born Helsinki, January 1, 1950; admitted, 1987, Finland. *Education:* University of Helsinki (LL.M., 1974). *Member:* Finnish Bar Association; Finnish Insurance Lawyers Association (Member, Committee, 1988—). *LANGUAGES:* Finnish, English and Swedish. *PRACTICE AREAS:* Insurance; Product Liability; Liability; Environment; Corporations.

ASSOCIATES

ANN DAMSTRÖM, born Johnstone, Scotland, August 15, 1955; admitted, 1982, Finland. *Education:* University of Helsinki (LL.M., 1979). *Member:* Finnish Bar Association. *LANGUAGES:* Finnish, Swedish and English. *PRACTICE AREAS:* Corporations; Contracts; Bankruptcy.

JARMO HENRIKSSON, born Vihti, August 6, 1960; admitted, 1992, Finland. *Education:* University of Helsinki (LL.M., 1988). *Member:* Finnish Bar Association. *LANGUAGES:* Finnish and English. *PRACTICE AREAS:* Corporations; Contract; Labour; Employment; Bankruptcy.

OLLI HOPPU, born Espoo, February 2, 1965; admitted, 1993, Finland. *Education:* University of Helsinki (LL.M., 1989). *Member:* Finnish Bar Association. *LANGUAGES:* Finnish, Swedish and English. *PRACTICE AREAS:* Corporate; Contracts; Securities; Insurance; Liability.

JUHA TUOMAS YRJANA SARASTO, born January 15, 1957. *Education:* Helsinki University (LL.M., 1991). *LANGUAGES:* Finnish, Swedish and English. *PRACTICE AREAS:* General Practice.

MARKKU O. TUNTURI, born Helsinki, January 6, 1946; admitted, 1972, Finland. *Education:* University of Helsinki (LL.M., 1972; Licentiate in Laws, 1983). *LANGUAGES:* Finnish, Swedish and English. *PRACTICE AREAS:* Tax Law; Real Estate; Company Law.

JUKKA HILLO, born Helsinki, January 26, 1954. *Education:* University of Helsinki (LL.M., 1979). *LANGUAGES:* Finnish, Swedish and English. *PRACTICE AREAS:* Aviation; Maritime.

MERILAMPI, MARTTILA & LAITASALO

KALEVANKATU 9 A
00100 HELSINKI, FINLAND
Telephone: 358-0-680 1001
Fax: 358-0-680 1916

Tampere, Finland Office: Hämeenkatu 17 B, 33200. Telephone: 358-31-2141 100. Fax: 358-31-2141 103.

Corporate, Competition and Administrative Law, Civil Litigation, Mergers and Acquisitions, European Community Law, International Business Law and General Trade Law.

MEMBERS OF FIRM

PEKKA MERILAMPI, born Pori, Finland, April 6, 1948; admitted, 1975, Finland. *Education:* University of Helsinki (LL.M., 1972). *Member:* Finnish Bar Association. *LANGUAGES:* Finnish, Swedish and English.

TUOMO MARTTILA, born Kangasala, Finland, March 31, 1950; admitted, 1978, Finland. *Education:* University of Helsinki (LL.M., 1973). *Member:* Finnish Bar Association. (Resident, Tampere Office). *LANGUAGES:* Finnish, Swedish and English.

JUKKA LAITASALO, born Viiala, Finland, July 4, 1957; admitted, 1984, Finland. *Education:* University of Turku (LL.M., 1980). *Member:* Finnish Bar Association. *LANGUAGES:* Finnish, Swedish and English.

ARI KEINÄNEN, born Kemi, Finland, July 17, 1960; admitted, 1992, Finland. *Education:* University of Turku (LL.M., 1986). *Member:* Finnish Bar Association. *LANGUAGES:* Finnish, Swedish and English.

ASSOCIATES

ARI KANTOR, born Helsinki, Finland, July 18, 1964. *Education:* University of Helsinki (LL.M., 1990). *LANGUAGES:* Finnish, Swedish and English.

LASSI KETTULA, born Tampere, Finland, June 17, 1964. *Education:* University of Helsinki (LL.M., 1989). (Resident, Tampere Office). *LANGUAGES:* Finnish, Swedish and English.

MATTI YLÄ-MONONEN, born Helsinki, Finland, April 18, 1966. *Education:* University of Helsinki (LL.M., 1991). *LANGUAGES:* Finnish, Swedish and English.

NORDIC LAW, SUNDSTRÖM KY

MIKONKATU 2 D
00100 HELSINKI, FINLAND
Telephone: +358 0 648 711
Telefax: +358 0 605 043

Brussels, Belgium Office: 177 Avenue Louise, Bte 1, B-1050. Telephone: +32 2 640 0429. Telefax: +32 2 648 3439.
Stockholm, Sweden Office: Sky City, Box 182, S-190 45, Stockholm-Arlanda. Telephone: +46 8 600 04. Telefax: +46 8 600 05.
Gothenburg, Sweden Office: Mässansgata 14, P.O. Box 5043, S-402 21. Telephone: 46-31-815 100. Telefax: 46-31-208 252.
Lund, Sweden Office: Kungsgatan 2 C, S-223 50. Telephone: 46-46-151 000. Telefax: 46-46-189 440.
Geneva, Switzerland Office: 1 Carrefour de Rive, CH-1207. Telephone: +41 22 786 4266. Telefax: +41 22 786 4997.

Antitrust Law, Arbitration, Competition Law, Trade Law (anti-dumping), Acquisitions, Mergers and Joint Ventures, Corporate Transactions and Formations, Distributorship, Agency and Franchise Law, EEC and EEA Law, Product Liability Law, Tax Structuring, Industrial Rights, Environmental Law, Air Transportation Law, Maritime Law and Africa Practice.

MEMBERS OF FIRM

G. O. ZACHARIAS SUNDSTRÖM, born Helsinki, Finland, 1936; admitted, 1961, Finland. *Education:* University of Helsinki (LL.B., 1960; LL.M., 1961; LL.D., 1965); University of Chicago (M.C.L., 1963); Cambridge University (M.Litt., Cantab., 1966). Assistant Professor, University of Stockholm, 1966—. Visiting Professor, Haile Selassie University, Ethiopia, 1967-1969. Professor: Law, Turku University, Finland, 1972-1976; Law, University of Helsinki, Finland, 1976—. With, Haight, Gardner, Poor & Havens, New York, 1963. Acting Judge, Municipal Court of Helsinki, 1962. Legal Expert, Commission of the European Communities, 1971-1972. Counsel, Ministry of Finance, Lesotho, 1973-1974. Legal Consultant: United Nations Industrial Development Organization; United Nations

(This Listing Continued)

Conference on Trade and Development. Managing Partner, Nordic Law Attorneys-at-Law, 1972—. *Member:* Finnish Bar Association; International Bar Association; Finnish Association for European Law (President). *LANGUAGES:* Finnish, English, Swedish, German and French.

ASSOCIATES

PIA CONSEIL, born Paramé, France, 1951; admitted, France, CNTE; Heidelberg and Lund. *Education:* Sorbonne III, Paris, France (Translator and Interpreter's Diploma, 1974); ULB, Brussels (license en droit, 1978-1981); Sorbonne Panthéon, Paris (LL.B., 1982; LL.M. , 1984). Translator, Paris and Brussels; Commission of European Communities, 1974-1975. (Resident, Brussels Office). *LANGUAGES:* French, English, German, Swedish and Danish.

LENA SUNDSTRÖM, born Stockholm, Sweden, 1954; admitted, 1981, Sweden. *Education:* University of Stockholm (LL.M., 1981). *LANGUAGES:* Swedish, English, Finnish and French.

ULRIKA LARPES, born Åland, Finland, 1961; admitted, 1984, Sweden; 1990, Finland. *Education:* University of Lund (LL.M., 1984); University of Helsinki (LL.M., 1990). *LANGUAGES:* Swedish, Finnish, English, German and French.

JUHA MÄKELÄ, born Pori, Finland, 1962; admitted, 1991, Finland. *Education:* University of Turku (LL.M., 1991). *LANGUAGES:* Finnish, English, German and Swedish.

BENIAMIN COHEN, born Helsinki, Finland, 1966; admitted, 1992, Finland. *Education:* University of Helsinki (LL.M., 1992). *LANGUAGES:* Finnish, English and Swedish.

VELI SAINIO, born Helsinki, Finland, 1946; admitted, 1969, Finland. *Education:* University of Helsinki (LL.M., 1969); Centre Européenne Universitaire de Nancy (1970); New York University (1971). *LANGUAGES:* Finnish, English, Swedish, Spanish and French.

KIMMO TENHOVIRTA, born Helsinki, Finland, 1964; admitted, 1991, Finland. *Education:* University of Helsinki (LL.M., 1991; Intl. LL.M., 1992-1993). *LANGUAGES:* Finnish, Swedish, English and German.

OBSTBAUM & HARJU

Established in 1932

UUDENMAANKATU 25 A 5
SF-00120 HELSINKI, FINLAND
Telephone: 358-0-641 001
Telex: 123484 droit sf
Telecopier: (Group 3) 358-0-607686

Corporate, Business, Financial, Tax and Patent Law, Arbitration and Litigation, International Business Law, Intellectual Property, Mergers, Acquisitions.

FIRM PROFILE: The firm offers swift legal service especially in the field of Business Law.

MEMBERS OF FIRM

PETRIK OBSTBAUM, born Stockholm, Sweden, March 8, 1940; admitted, 1973, Finland. *Education:* Helsinki (LL.M., 1969). *Member:* Finnish Bar Association; LES; AIPPI; The International Association of Jewish Lawyers and Jurists. *LANGUAGES:* Swedish, Finnish, English and German. *PRACTICE AREAS:* Corporate Law; Patent Law; Tax Law; Intellectual Property; General Business.

PEKKA A. HARJU, born Helsinki, Finland, January 23, 1946; admitted, 1973, Finland. *Education:* Helsinki (LL.M., 1968). *Member:* Finnish Bar Association; Finnish Arbitration Association; AIJA. *LANGUAGES:* Finnish, English and German. *PRACTICE AREAS:* Corporate Law; Financial Law; Litigation.

ASSOCIATES

PETRI MORELIUS, born Helsinki, Finland, October 7, 1963. *Education:* Helsinki (LL.M., 1992). *LANGUAGES:* Swedish, Finnish, English and German. *PRACTICE AREAS:* General Corporate Law; Business Law.

Languages: Finnish, Swedish, English and German

PELTONEN, ÖRNDAHL, RUOKONEN & ITÄINEN

FREDRIKINKATU 48 A
00100 HELSINKI, FINLAND
Telephone: 358-0-694 4966
Telecopier: 358-0-694 4206

Corporate, Company and Business Law, Commercial Transactions and Contracts, Banks, Banking and Finance, Securities, Trade and Marketing, Franchises, Agency and Distributorship, Antitrust and Trade Regulations, Bankruptcy and Insolvency, Consumer Protection, Product Liability and Liability for Damages and Personal Injuries, Insurance, Labour and Employment, Intellectual Property, Patents, Trademarks and Copyrights, Media, Real Estate, Environment, Construction, Taxation, Administrative Law, International Private Law, General Practice, Arbitration and Litigation.

MEMBERS OF FIRM

JUKKA PELTONEN, born Tuusula, Finland, October 27, 1939; admitted, 1970, Finland. *Education:* University of Helsinki (LL.B., 1966). *Member:* The Finnish Bar Association (President, 1988-1992); The Union of Finnish Lawyers (Member of The Committee for Justice Policy, 1981-1988); International Bar Association (Council Member, 1992—). *LANGUAGES:* Finnish, Swedish and English. *PRACTICE AREAS:* General Corporate and Commercial Law; Banking and Finance; Ship Finance; Securities; Insurance.

PETER ÖRNDAHL, born Helsinki, Finland, September 27, 1942; admitted, 1969, Finland. *Education:* University of Helsinki (LL.B., 1966). *Member:* Finnish Bar Association. *LANGUAGES:* Finnish, Swedish, English and German. *PRACTICE AREAS:* Corporate Law; Commercial Transactions; Restructuring of Business Firms.

PEKKA RUOKONEN, born Savonlinna, Finland, May 9, 1946; admitted, 1975, Finland. *Education:* University of Helsinki (LL.B., 1972). *Member:* Finnish Bar Association. *LANGUAGES:* Finnish, Swedish, English and German. *PRACTICE AREAS:* General Corporate and Commercial Law; Labour and Employment; Insurance; Liability for Damages and Injuries; Bankruptcy and Insolvency.

LEIF ROLFSSON ITÄINEN, born Helsinki, Finland, May 11, 1955; admitted, 1983, Finland. *Education:* University of Helsinki (LL.B., 1980). *Member:* The Finnish Bar Association. *LANGUAGES:* Finnish, Swedish and English. *PRACTICE AREAS:* General Corporate and Commercial Law; Bankruptcy and Insolvency; Corporate Restructuring; Debtor and Creditor; Finance.

GERHARD AF SCHULTEN, born Helsinki, Finland, April 24, 1938; admitted, 1965, Finland. *Education:* University of Helsinki (LL.B., 1961) and Licentiate of Law, 1968. *Member:* Finnish Bar Association. *LANGUAGES:* Finnish, Swedish, English and German. *PRACTICE AREAS:* Corporate Law; Consumer Protection and Unfair Competition; Antitrust Law.

RISTO ROUVARI, born Vaala, Finland, March 22, 1958; admitted, 1988, Finland. *Education:* University of Turku (LL.B., 1984). *Member:* Finnish Bar Association; AIJA. *LANGUAGES:* Finnish, Swedish, English and German. *PRACTICE AREAS:* General Corporate and Commercial Law; Competition; Intellectual Property; Patents and Trademarks; General Practice and Litigation.

JUSSI MANNINEN, born Tampere, Finland, February 2, 1958; admitted, 1989, Finland. *Education:* University of Helsinki (LL.B., 1984). *Member:* Finnish Bar Association. *LANGUAGES:* Finnish, Swedish and English. *PRACTICE AREAS:* Labour and Employment Law; Financing Law; Civil Trial Practice.

ESA SALONEN, born Vaasa, Finland, January 27, 1958; admitted, 1988, Finland. *Education:* University of Helsinki (LL.B., 1983). *Member:* Finnish Bar Association; AIJA. *LANGUAGES:* Finnish, Swedish, English and German. *PRACTICE AREAS:* General Corporate and Commercial Law; Insurance; Liability for Damages and Injuries; Banking Litigation; Debtor and Creditor.

JUSSI SAVONEN, born Helsinki, Finland, November 18, 1961; admitted, 1992, Finland. *Education:* University of Helsinki (LL.B., 1987). *Member:* Finnish Bar Association. *LANGUAGES:* Finnish, Swedish, English and German. *PRACTICE AREAS:* General Corporate and Commercial Law; Banking Litigation; Bankruptcy and Insolvency; Reorganization; Debtor and Creditor.

(This Listing Continued)

MÅRTEN ASPELIN, born Espoo, Finland, May 9, 1963; admitted, 1992, Finland. *Education:* University of Helsinki (LL.B., 1988). *Member:* Finnish Bar Association. *LANGUAGES:* Finnish, Swedish, English and German. *PRACTICE AREAS:* General Commercial Law; Contract Law.

ASSOCIATES

HARRIET HANNELE LAGUS, born Kotka, Finland, March 3, 1961. *Education:* University of Helsinki (LL.B., 1985). *LANGUAGES:* Finnish, Swedish and English. *PRACTICE AREAS:* General Corporate and Commercial Law; Bankruptcy and Insolvency; Corporate Restructuring; Debtor and Creditor; Insurance.

JAN ÖRNDAHL, born Helsinki, Finland, May 24, 1966. *Education:* University of Helsinki (LL.B., 1991). *LANGUAGES:* Finnish, Swedish, English and German. *PRACTICE AREAS:* General Commercial Law; Debt Collection.

PETTERI SOTAMAA, born Helsinki, Finland, September 5, 1961. *Education:* University of Helsinki (1990). *LANGUAGES:* Finnish, Swedish and English. *PRACTICE AREAS:* General Corporate and Commercial Law; Insurance; Liability for Damages; Bankruptcy and Insolvency; Corporate Restructuring.

HANS SUNDBLAD, born Säynätsalo, Finland, April 1, 1956. *Education:* University of Turku (LL.B., 1978). *LANGUAGES:* Finnish, Swedish and English. *PRACTICE AREAS:* Contract Law; Corporate Law; Finance and Banking.

MATTI HUTTUNEN, born Lapua, Finland, October 20, 1966. *Education:* University of Turku (LL.B., 1992). *LANGUAGES:* Finnish, Swedish and English. *PRACTICE AREAS:* General Commercial Law.

Languages: Finnish, Swedish, English and German

PROCOPÉ & HORNBORG

Established in 1919

MANNERHEIMINTIE 20 B
00100 HELSINKI, FINLAND
Telephone: 358-0-694 4466
Telefax: 358-0-694 8651

Tampere, Finland Office: Hämeenkatu 12 A, 33100. Telephone: 358-31-2145 800. Telefax: 358-31-2148 078.

London, England Office: Burne House, 88/89 High Holborn, WC1V 6LS. Telephone: 44-71-831 0292. Telefax: 44-71-831 9074.

Commercial, Corporate, Contract, International Business, Banking, Intellectual Property, Competition and Insolvency Law. Litigation and Arbitration.

MEMBERS OF FIRM

OLAVI YLÄNKÖ, born Helsinki, Finland, October 26, 1940; admitted, 1969, Finland. *Education:* University of Helsinki (LL.M., 1963; LL., Lic., 1978). *Member:* Finnish and International Bar Associations; Union of Finnish Lawyers. *LANGUAGES:* Finnish, Swedish, English and German.

SATU JUUROLA, born Pusula, Finland, January 13, 1943; admitted, 1977, Finland. *Education:* University of Helsinki (LL.M., 1968). *Member:* Finnish and International Bar Associations; Union of Finnish Lawyers. *LANGUAGES:* Finnish, Swedish, German and English.

MARTTI HEINONEN, born Helsinki, Finland, September 27, 1945; admitted, 1976, Finland. *Education:* University of Helsinki (LL.M., 1970). *Member:* Finnish Bar Association; Union of Finnish Lawyers; Young Lawyers' International Association (AIJA). *LANGUAGES:* Finnish, Swedish, English and French.

ILMARI PÖYHÖNEN, born Kemijärvi, Finland, November 29, 1955; admitted, 1982, Finland. *Education:* University of Turku (LL.M., 1978). *Member:* Finnish Bar Association; Union of Finnish Lawyers. *LANGUAGES:* Finnish, Swedish, English and German.

OLLI HAPPONEN, born Tuusniemi, Finland, March 7, 1953; admitted, 1990, Finland. *Education:* Helsinki School of Economics (B.Sc. Econ., 1974); University of Helsinki (LL.M., 1980). *Member:* Finnish Bar Association; Union of Finnish Lawyers. (London, England Office). *LANGUAGES:* Finnish, English, Swedish and German.

TIINA FRENCH, born Helsinki, Finland, October 12, 1955; admitted, 1990, Finland. *Education:* University of Helsinki (LL.M., 1983). *Member:* Finnish Bar Association; Union of Finnish Lawyers; Young Lawyers Inter-

(This Listing Continued)

national Association (AIJA). *LANGUAGES:* Finnish, English, Swedish, French and German.

JUHA KOIVULA, born Tampere, Finland, April 4, 1958; admitted, 1990, Finland. *Education:* University of Turku (LL.M., 1985). *Member:* Finnish Bar Association; Union of Finnish Lawyers; Young Lawyers International Association (AIJA). (Tampere Office). *LANGUAGES:* Finnish, Swedish, German, English and Russian.

ASSOCIATES

JOHAN HEIKFOLK, born Närpes, Finland, August 12, 1963; admitted, 1992, Finland. *Education:* University of Helsinki (LL.M., 1987). *Member:* Finnish Bar Association; Union of Finnish Lawyers. *LANGUAGES:* Swedish, Finnish and English.

KIMMO PENTTILÄ, born Helsinki, Finland, September 8, 1963; admitted, 1993, Finland. *Education:* University of Helsinki (LL.M., 1988). *Member:* Finnish Bar Association; Union of Finnish Lawyers. *LANGUAGES:* Finnish, English, Swedish and German.

MATTI HAUTAKANGAS, born Kokkola, Finland, May 7, 1963; admitted, 1994, Finland. *Education:* University of Helsinki (LL.M., 1988). *Member:* Finnish Bar Association; Union of Finnish Lawyers. *LANGUAGES:* Finnish, Swedish, English and German.

PERTTU PESSA, born Lahti, Finland, November 13, 1963; admitted, 1994, Finland. *Education:* University of Helsinki (LL.M., 1988); London University Queen Mary Westfield College (LL.M., 1990). *Member:* Finnish Bar Association; Union of Finnish Lawyers; Finnish Computer Law Society; Computer Law Association (U.S.A.). *LANGUAGES:* Finnish, English, Swedish and German.

HELI PIKSILÄ-RANTANEN, born Noormarkku, Finland, February 8, 1963; admitted, 1992, Finland. *Education:* University of Turku (LL.M., 1987). *Member:* Finnish Bar Association; Union of Finnish Lawyers. (Tampere Office). *LANGUAGES:* Finnish, Swedish and English.

ISMO HENTULA, born Turku, Finland, October 22, 1960; admitted, 1994, Finland. *Education:* University of Helsinki (LL.M., 1985). *Member:* Finnish Bar Association; Union of Finnish Lawyers. *LANGUAGES:* Finnish, English, Swedish and German.

VESA TURKKI, born Salo, Finland, June 22, 1966. *Education:* University of Turku (LL.M., 1992). *Member:* Union of Finnish Lawyers. *LANGUAGES:* Finnish, Swedish, English and German.

CONSULTANT

ERIK SALVÉN, born Helsinki, Finland, January 25, 1914; admitted, 1959, Finland. *Education:* University of Helsinki (LL.M., 1938). *Member:* Finnish Bar Association; Union of Finnish Lawyers. (Tampere Office). *LANGUAGES:* Finnish, Swedish, English and German.

ROSCHIER-HOLMBERG & WASELIUS

Established in 1936

KESKUSKATU 7 A

00100 HELSINKI, FINLAND

Telephone: (0) 3580-228 551
Telex: 12 2310 ADVOX
Cable Address: "Cognitor"
Telefax: (0) 664 303; (0) 175 451
Teletex: 1000901

London, England Office: 36-38 Cornhill, EC3V 9DR. Telephone: 44-71-929 0966. Telefax: 44-71-929 0933.
Vaasa, Finland Office: Alatori, 65100 Vaasa. Telephone: 358-61-3179311. Fax: 358-61-3179377.

General Practice. International Financing, Commercial Banking, Industrial Property Rights, Trade and Market, Maritime, Aviation, Corporate, Establishing, Taxation and Real Estate Law, Litigation, EC Law.

FIRM PROFILE: The firm is one of the largest law firms in Finland with experienced specialist skills in all areas of Finnish and international business law, including EC law. The clients of the firm include large Finnish and foreign listed and non-listed corporations as well as medium sized and smaller businesses, international entities and states. The firm has special experience and knowledge of international transactions and maintains close ties to leading law practices in all jurisdictions with trade relations to Finland. The firm has served the Finnish and international business society for six decades and is one of the oldest law firms in Europe.

(This Listing Continued)

MEMBERS OF FIRM

JAN WASELIUS, born Vaasa, Finland, March 23, 1944; admitted, 1972, Finland. *Education:* University of Helsinki (LL.B., 1968). Honorary Legal Adviser to Her Britannic Majesty's Ambassador to Finland. Honorary Legal Adviser to Her Danish Majesty's Ambassador to Finland. Honorary Legal Adviser to His Swedish Majesty's Ambassador to Finland. *Member:* Finnish Bar Association; Legal Society of Finland; AIPPI; International Bar Association; International Fiscal Association; Economic Society of Finland. *LANGUAGES:* Finnish, Swedish, English and German. *PRACTICE AREAS:* Corporate Law; Finance Law.

ROBERT LILJESTRÖM, born Helsinki, Finland, August 17, 1945; admitted, 1973, Finland. *Education:* University of Helsinki (LL.B., 1970). *Member:* Finnish Bar Association; International Bar Association (Member, Business Section); AIPPI; ILA; Legal Society of Finland; Economic Society of Finland. *LANGUAGES:* Finnish, Swedish, English and German. *PRACTICE AREAS:* Litigation; Arbitration.

JAN AMINOFF, born Stockholm, Sweden, December 26, 1944; admitted, 1974, Finland. *Education:* University of Helsinki (LL.B., 1969). *Member:* Finnish Bar Association; International Bar Association; Legal Society of Finland; (CMI) Finnish Maritime Law Association (Board Member); Sea Transport Commission of International Chamber of Commerce (Finnish Branch). *LANGUAGES:* Finnish, Swedish, English and French. *PRACTICE AREAS:* Litigation; Arbitration; Transportation; Maritime Law; Insolvency; Insurance.

TOM SCHUBERT, born Helsinki, Finland, October 12, 1950; admitted, 1980, Finland. *Education:* University of Helsinki (LL.B., 1977). *Member:* Finnish Bar Association; Legal Society of Finland; International Bar Association; Association Internationale des Jeunes Avocats. *LANGUAGES:* Finnish, Swedish and English. *PRACTICE AREAS:* Corporate Law; Finance Law; Insolvency; Marketing.

TOMAS LINDHOLM, born Helsinki, Finland, January 20, 1953; admitted, 1983, Finland. *Education:* University of Helsinki (LL.B., 1975); The Swedish School of Economics in Helsinki (B.Sc. Econ., 1977). Member, Auditors Board, Central Chamber of Commerce in Finland. *Member:* Finnish Bar Association (Board Member, 1990—); International Bar Association; Licensing Executives Society (Board Member, LES Scandinavia, 1989; President, 1989-1990); AIPPI; Legal Society of Finland; Finnish Industrial Lawyers' Association. *LANGUAGES:* Finnish, Swedish, English and German. *PRACTICE AREAS:* Transactions; Projects Law.

CARITA CHRISTINA WALLGREN, born Tammisaari, Finland, October 2, 1953; admitted, 1983, Finland. *Education:* University of Helsinki (LL.B., 1979). *Member:* Finnish Bar Association; Legal Society of Finland; Association Internationale des Jeunes Avocats; International Bar Association; AIPPI. *LANGUAGES:* Finnish, Swedish, English and French. *PRACTICE AREAS:* Transactions; Projects Law; International Arbitration.

EVA NORDMAN, born Helsinki, Finland, July 19, 1953; admitted, 1985, Finland. *Education:* University of Helsinki (LL.B., 1982). *Member:* Finnish Bar Association; International Bar Association; AIPPI; Legal Society of Finland; Association Internationale des Jeunes Avocats. *LANGUAGES:* Finnish, Swedish and English. *PRACTICE AREAS:* Litigation; Arbitration; Labor Law.

RISTO OJANTAKANEN, born Helsinki, Finland, July 3, 1954; admitted, 1987, Finland. *Education:* University of Helsinki (LL.B., 1982); Southern Methodist University School of Law, Dallas, Texas (M.C.L., 1983). *Member:* Finnish Bar Association; International Bar Association; Legal Society of Finland; Licensing Executives Society (Vice President, LES Scandinavian Chapter, 1993—); The Union of Finnish Lawyers. *LANGUAGES:* Finnish, Swedish, English and German. *PRACTICE AREAS:* Corporate Law; Finance Law; Reorganization.

KAJ SWANLJUNG, born Helsinki, Finland, December 14, 1957; admitted, 1989, Finland. *Education:* University of Helsinki (LL.B., 1983); Swedish School of Economics in Helsinki (B.Sc. Econ., 1984). *Member:* Legal Society of Finland. *LANGUAGES:* Finnish, Swedish and English. *PRACTICE AREAS:* Corporate Law; Finance Law; Labor Law; Real Estate; Environmental Law.

CHRISTIAN WIK, born Helsinki, Finland, July 17, 1960; admitted, 1989, Finland. *Education:* University of Helsinki (LL.B., 1984); Southern Methodist University, Dallas Texas (LL.M., 1985). *Member:* Finnish Bar Association; Legal Society of Finland; Deutsch-Nordische Juristenvereinigung. *LANGUAGES:* Finnish, Swedish, English and German.

(This Listing Continued)

ROSCHIER-HOLMBERG & WASELIUS, Helsinki— Continued

PRACTICE AREAS: Transactions; Projects Law; EC-Law; Competition Law; Debtor and Creditor.

ASSOCIATES

INGA PŐNTYNEN, born Turku, Finland, March 17, 1951. *Education:* University of Helsinki (LL.B., 1975); Georgetown University Law School (International Licensing, 1985). Previous employment: Representative of the Finnish Chamber of Commerce in Brussels (specialist in EC law) 1990-1992. Member: The Union of Finnish Lawyers; Finnish Industrial Lawyers Association; Finnish Association for Industrial Property Rights and AIPPI. *LANGUAGES:* Finnish, Swedish and English. *PRACTICE AREAS:* Transactions; Projects Law; EC-Law; Competition Law.

RAINER HILLI, born Helsinki, Finland, October 30, 1960; admitted, 1991, Finland. *Education:* University of Helsinki (LL.B., 1986). *Member:* Legal Society of Finland. *LANGUAGES:* Finnish, Swedish, English and German. *PRACTICE AREAS:* Litigation; Arbitration; Intellectual Property.

GUNNAR WESTERLUND, born Mariehamn, Finland, November 22, 1955; admitted, 1983, Finland as Judge. *Education:* University of Helsinki (LL.B., 1980). *Member:* Legal Society of Finland; International Bar Association; International Fiscal Association. *LANGUAGES:* Swedish, Finnish and English. *PRACTICE AREAS:* Corporate Law; Finance Law; Taxation.

EEVA HAKORANTA, born Vaasa, Finland, July 21, 1964; admitted, 1993, Finland. *Education:* University of Helsinki (LL.B., 1989). *LANGUAGES:* Finnish, Swedish, English and German. *PRACTICE AREAS:* Transactions; Projects Law; Intellectual Property.

TARJA WIST, born Vantaa, Finland, September 25, 1965. *Education:* University of Helsinki (LL.B., 1989). *Member:* Legal Society of Finland. *LANGUAGES:* Finnish, Swedish, English and German. *PRACTICE AREAS:* Corporate Law; Finance Law; Securities.

KIRSI SWANLJUNG, born Turku, Finland, September 24, 1962; admitted, 1993, Finland. *Education:* University of Turku (LL.B., 1986). *Member:* Legal Society of Finland. *LANGUAGES:* Finnish, Swedish, English, German and Spanish. *PRACTICE AREAS:* Transactions; Projects Law.

ANNELI TAHVANAINEN, born Helsinki, Finland, April 11, 1961; admitted, 1993, Finland. *Education:* University of Helsinki (LL.B., 1986). *Member:* Legal Society of Finland. *LANGUAGES:* Finnish, Swedish and English. *PRACTICE AREAS:* Litigation; Arbitration.

ULF-HENRIK KULL, born Pietarsaari, Finland, July 19, 1964. *Education:* Abo Academy University (CM.Pol.Sc., 1987); University of Turku (LL.B., 1990). *LANGUAGES:* Swedish, Finnish and English. *PRACTICE AREAS:* Transactions; Projects Law.

MARTINA EHRSTRÖM, born Helsinki, Finland, October 22, 1966. *Education:* University of Helsinki (LL.B., 1990). *LANGUAGES:* Swedish, Finnish, English and German. *PRACTICE AREAS:* Transactions; Projects Law.

DIMITRIOS HIMONAS, born Helsinki, Finland, October 7, 1966. *Education:* University of Helsinki (LL.B., 1991). *LANGUAGES:* English Finnish, Swedish, German and French. *PRACTICE AREAS:* Corporate Law; Finance Law.

MAIJA VÄHÄNÄKKI, born Kajaani, Finland, January 29, 1966. *Education:* University of Helsinki (LL.B., 1990). *LANGUAGES:* Finnish, Swedish, English and French. *PRACTICE AREAS:* Litigation; Arbitration.

SATU RELANDER, born Pori, Finland, January 8, 1967. *Education:* University of Helsinki (LL.B., 1991). *LANGUAGES:* Finnish, Swedish, English and French. *PRACTICE AREAS:* Transactions; Projects Law.

PETRI TAIVALKOSKI, born Helsinki, Finland, November 7, 1966. *Education:* University of Helsinki (LL.B., 1990). *LANGUAGES:* Finnish, Swedish, English, French and German. *PRACTICE AREAS:* Litigation; Arbitration.

PIA VAPAAVUORI, born Helsinki, Finland, October 8, 1967. *Education:* University of Helsinki (LL.B., 1992). *LANGUAGES:* Finnish, Swedish, English and German. *PRACTICE AREAS:* Corporate Law; Finance Law.

(This Listing Continued)

ANTTI HEIKKILA, born Kuortane, Finland, March 8, 1962. *Education:* University of Helsinki (LL.B., 1990). *LANGUAGES:* Finnish, Swedish and English. *PRACTICE AREAS:* Litigation; Arbitration.

BERNT JUTHSTRÖM, born Vaasa, Finland, June 26, 1967. *Education:* University of Helsinki (LL.B., 1991). *LANGUAGES:* Swedish, Finnish, English and German. *PRACTICE AREAS:* Litigation; Arbitration.

JOUNI SNELLMAN, born Helsinki, Finland, March 14, 1965. *Education:* University of Helsinki (LL.B., 1992). *LANGUAGES:* Finnish, Swedish, English, German, Russian and Estonian. *PRACTICE AREAS:* Corporate Law; Finance Law.

SUSANNE MATTSON, born Helsinki, Finland, July 5, 1967. *Education:* University of Helsinki (LL.B., 1992). *LANGUAGES:* Swedish, Finnish and English. *PRACTICE AREAS:* Transactions; Projects Law.

JOAKIM ÅBERG, born Helsinki, Finland, August 24, 1968. *Education:* University of Helsinki (LL.B., 1994). *LANGUAGES:* Finnish, Swedish, English and German.

EVA FAGERHOLM, born Turku, Finland, April 11, 1968. *Education:* University of Helsinki (LL.B., 1994). *LANGUAGES:* Swedish, Finnish and English. *PRACTICE AREAS:* Legal Information Management.

CRAIG THOMPSON, born East Lansing, Michigan, U.S.A., October 5, 1961. *Education:* University of Helsinki (LL.B., 1994). *LANGUAGES:* English, Finnish, Swedish and Czechoslovakian. *PRACTICE AREAS:* Transactions; Projects Law.

KJELL RENLUND, born Pietarsaari, Finland, April 6, 1968. *Education:* University of Helsinki (LL.B., 1994). *LANGUAGES:* Finnish, Swedish, English and German.

MARINA MONTONEN, born Helsinki, Finland, January 27, 1968. *Education:* University of Helsinki (LL.B., 1994). *LANGUAGES:* Finnish, Swedish, English and German.

TIMO M. AIRISTO, born Helsinki, Finland, February 25, 1967. *Education:* University of Helsinki (LL.B., 1992); Columbia University, New York (LL.M., 1994). *LANGUAGES:* Finnish, Swedish, English and German.

SCANDINAVIAN LAW OFFICES

ETELÄRANTA 8
00130 HELSINKI, FINLAND
Telephone: +358-0-171900
Telefax: +358-0-171950
Telex: 125998 lawco fi

Tallinn, Estonia Office: Rüütli 16, EE0001. Telephone: +372-2-666689. Telefax: +372-6-313549.

St. Petersburg, Russia Office: Proletarskaya Diktatura Sq. 6, Room 309, 193124. Telephone: +7-812-8502200 (Int'l.); +7-812-2744347. Telefax: +7-812-8502201 (Int'l.); +7-812-2741146.

Corporate, Contract, Business, Financial and Tax Law, International Business Transactions, East-West Trade, Arbitration and Litigation.

MEMBERS OF FIRM

ANSSI JAANTI, born Helsinki, Finland, December 27, 1951; admitted, 1987, Finland. *Education:* University of Helsinki (LL.M., 1981). *Member:* Finnish Bar Association. *LANGUAGES:* English, Finnish, Swedish and German.

MARKKU ROPPONEN, born Helsinki, Finland, August 26, 1961. *Education:* University of Helsinki (LL.M., 1989). *LANGUAGES:* English, Finnish, Swedish and German.

ASSOCIATES

ANTTI ROUHESMAA, born Tampere, Finland, July 27, 1965. *Education:* University of Helsinki (LL.M., 1990); Swedish School of Economics and Business Administration, Helsinki (M.Sc., Econ., 1994). *LANGUAGES:* English, Finnish, Swedish and German.

JAANA KLINGA, born Lahti, Finland, August 19, 1968. *Education:* University of Helsinki (LL.M., 1991). *LANGUAGES:* English, Finnish, Swedish and German.

OLLI PELTOLA, born Kauniainen, Finland, September 21, 1966. *Education:* University of Helsinki (LL.M., 1993). *LANGUAGES:* English, Finnish, Swedish and German.

(This Listing Continued)

MARJA NAULAPÄÄ-SIPILÄ, born Helsinki, Finland, June 13, 1966. *Education:* University of Helsinki (LL.M., 1991). *LANGUAGES:* English, Finnish, Swedish and German.

Languages: English, Finnish, Swedish and German

ADVOKATBYRÅ HANNES SNELLMAN

ETELÄRANTA 8 (6TH FLOOR)
00130 HELSINKI, FINLAND
Telephone: 358-0-177 570
Fax: 358-0-177 393; 358-0-177 228

Mailing Address: P.O. Box 333, 00131 Helsinki, Finland

General Corporate and Business Law, International Transactions, Financing, Taxation, Litigation in Commercial Matters.

MEMBERS OF FIRM

ROBERT MATTSON, born Helsinki, Finland, March 3, 1936; admitted, 1962, Helsinki. *Education:* University of Helsinki. *Member:* The Bar Association of Finland; Legal Society of Finland. *LANGUAGES:* Finnish, Swedish, English and German.

JARL ENGBERG, born Helsinki, Finland, May 3, 1938; admitted, 1967, Helsinki. *Education:* University of Helsinki. *Member:* The Bar Association of Finland; Legal Society of Finland. *LANGUAGES:* Finnish, Swedish and English.

JOHAN G. SNELLMAN, born Helsinki, Finland, April 29, 1941; admitted, 1968, Helsinki. *Education:* University of Helsinki. *Member:* The Bar Association of Finland; Legal Society of Finland; International Bar Association. *LANGUAGES:* Finnish, Swedish, English and German.

BERNDT HEIKEL, born Helsinki, Finland, October 4, 1952. *Education:* University of Helsinki. *Member:* The Bar Association of Finland; Legal Society of Finland. *LANGUAGES:* Finnish, Swedish, English and German.

JUHANI MÄKINEN, born Helsinki, Finland, October 1, 1956. *Education:* University of Helsinki. *Member:* The Bar Association of Finland; Legal Society of Finland. *LANGUAGES:* Finnish, Swedish, German and English.

MAGNUS POUSETTE, born Helsinki, Finland, December 1, 1953. *Education:* University of Helsinki. *Member:* The Bar Association of Finland; Legal Society of Finland. *LANGUAGES:* Finnish, Swedish, English, Norwegian and German.

ANTTI HEIKINHEIMO, born Espoo, Finland, November 27, 1954. *Education:* University of Helsinki; University of Maryland. *Member:* The Bar Association of Finland; Legal Society of Finland. *LANGUAGES:* Finnish, Swedish and English.

MIKAEL DAMSTÉN, born Helsinki, Finland, April 24, 1958. *Education:* University of Helsinki. *Member:* The Bar Association of Finland; Legal Society of Finland. *LANGUAGES:* Finnish, Swedish and English.

ANTTI MÄKINEN, born Helsinki, Finland, June 8, 1961. *Education:* University of Helsinki. *Member:* The Bar Association of Finland; Legal Society of Finland. *LANGUAGES:* Finnish, Swedish, English and German.

JOHAN AALTO, born Helsinki, Finland, September 20, 1962. *Education:* University of Helsinki. *Member:* The Bar Association of Finland; Legal Society of Finland. *LANGUAGES:* Finnish, Swedish, English and German.

OF COUNSEL

HANS G. SNELLMAN, born Helsinki, Finland, September 28, 1910; admitted, 1942, Helsinki. *Education:* University of Helsinki. *Member:* The Bar Association of Finland (Board Member, 1962-1970); American Bar Association; Legal Society of Finland. *LANGUAGES:* Finnish, Swedish, English and German.

ASSOCIATES

JUHA LINDSTRÖM, born Espoo, Finland, April 22, 1962. *Education:* University of Helsinki. *Member:* The Bar Association of Finland; Legal Society of Finland. *LANGUAGES:* Finnish, Swedish and English.

PEKKA INKEROINEN, born Kotka, Finland, September, 18, 1957. *Education:* University of Helsinki; Southern Methodist University, Dallas, Texas (1988). *Member:* The Bar Association of Finland; New York State Bar Association. *LANGUAGES:* Finnish, Swedish, English and German.

(This Listing Continued)

OUTI RAITASUO, born Hartola, Finland, September 8, 1959. *Education:* University of Helsinki; University of Toronto (1989). *Member:* The Bar Association of Finland; Legal Society of Finland. *LANGUAGES:* Finnish, Swedish, English, French and German.

TEEMU KALLIALA, born Helsinki, Finland, October 23, 1958. *Education:* University of Helsinki. *Member:* The Bar Association of Finland; Legal Society of Finland. *LANGUAGES:* Finnish, Swedish, English and French.

IRMELI STADIGH, born Helsinki, Finland, May 26, 1964. *Education:* University of Helsinki. *Member:* The Bar Association of Finland; Legal Society of Finland. *LANGUAGES:* Finnish, Swedish, English and German.

LUCAS KRANCK, born Helsinki, Finland, October 31, 1964. *Education:* University of Helsinki. *Member:* The Bar Association of Finland; Legal Society of Finland. *LANGUAGES:* Finnish, Swedish, English and German.

PETER NYSTÉN, born Helsinki, Finland, July 20, 1965. *Education:* University of Helsinki. *Member:* The Bar Association of Finland; Legal Society of Finland. *LANGUAGES:* Finnish, Swedish, English and German.

HENRIK MATTSON, born Helsinki, Finland, March 26, 1961. *Education:* University of Helsinki. *Member:* Legal Society of Finland. *LANGUAGES:* Finnish, Swedish, English and German.

HELI TERÄVÄINEN, born Helsinki, Finland, October 12, 1966. *Education:* University of Helsinki. *Member:* Legal Society of Finland. *LANGUAGES:* Finnish, Swedish and English.

JARI TUKIAINEN, born Jyväskylä, Finland, June 28, 1963. *Education:* University of Turku. *Member:* Legal Society of Finland. *LANGUAGES:* Finnish, Swedish and English.

CARL-HENRIK WALLIN, born Vaasa, Finland, March 3, 1967. *Education:* University of Helsinki. *Member:* Legal Society of Finland. *LANGUAGES:* Finnish, Swedish, English and German.

MARKUS ENGBERG, born Helsinki, Finland, December 18, 1967. *Education:* University of Helsinki. *Member:* Legal Society of Finland. *LANGUAGES:* Finnish, Swedish and English.

TOMAS HOLMBERG, born July 23, 1965. *Education:* University of Helsinki. *Member:* Legal Society of Finland. *LANGUAGES:* Finnish, Swedish and English.

NINA HAKKARAINEN, born August 19, 1967. *Education:* University of Helsinki. *Member:* Legal Society of Finland. *LANGUAGES:* Finnish, English, Swedish and German.

Languages: Finnish, Swedish, English, German, Norwegian and French

---

LAW OFFICES OF VON KONOW & REHN

MANNERHEIMINTIE 20 A
00100 HELSINKI, FINLAND
Telephone: 358 0 644 806
Telefax: 358 0 644 643

Corporate, Tax, Financing, Foreign Clients, Trusts and Estates.

MEMBERS OF FIRM

KATE VON KONOW, born Helsinki, November 3, 1954; admitted, 1979, Finland. *Education:* University of Helsinki (LL.M., 1973). *LANGUAGES:* Swedish, Finnish and English.

BJÖRN-JOHAN VON KONOW, born Helsinki, September 25, 1953; admitted, 1978, Finland. *Education:* University of Helsinki (LL.M., 1978). *LANGUAGES:* Swedish, Finnish and English.

OLOF REHN, born Helsinki, Finland, September 23, 1961; admitted, 1988, Finland. *Education:* University of Helsinki (LL.M., 1987). *LANGUAGES:* Finnish, Swedish and English.

ASIANAJOTOIMISTO
WHITE & CASE OY

ETELARANTA 14
SF-00130 HELSINKI, FINLAND
Telephone: (358-0) 631-100
Facsimile: (358-0) 179-477

New York, New York: Telephone: 212-819-8200. Facsimile: 212-354-8113.

Washington, D.C.: Telephone: 202-872-0013. Facsimile: 202-872-0210.

Los Angeles, California: Telephone: 213-620-7700. Facsimile: 213-687-0758; 213-617-2205.

Miami, Florida: Telephone: 305-371-2700. Facsimile: 305-358-5744.

Mexico City, Mexico: Telephone: (52-5) 207-9717. Facsimile: (52-5) 208-3628.

Tokyo, Japan: Telephone: (81-3) 3239-4300. Facsimile: (81-3) 3239-4330.

Hong Kong: Telephone: (852) 2822-8700. Facsimile: (852) 2845-9070; Grice & Co., Solicitors, Telephone: (852) 2826-0333. Facsimile: (852) 2526-7166.

Singapore, Republic of Singapore: Telephone: (65) 225-6000. Facsimile: (65) 225-6009.

Bangkok, Thailand: Pacific Legal Group Ltd., In Association With White & Case, Telephone: (662) 236-6154/7. Facsimile: (662) 237-6771.

Hanoi, Viet Nam: Representative Office, Telephone: (84-4) 227-575/6/7. Facsimile: (84-4) 227-297.

Bombay, India: Telephone: (91-22) 282-6300. Facsimile: (91-22) 282-6305.

London, England: Telephone: (44-171) 726-6361. Facsimile: (44-171) 726-4314; (44-171) 726-8558.

Paris, France: Telephone: (33-1) 42-60-34-05. Facsimile: (33-1) 42-60-82-46.

Brussels, Belgium: Telephone: (32-2) 647-05-89. Facsimile: (32-2) 647-16-75.

Stockholm, Sweden: Telephone: (46-8) 679-80-30. Facsimile: (46-8) 611-21-22.

Moscow, Russia: Telephone: (7-095) 201-9292/3/4/5. Facsimile: (7-095) 201-9284.

Budapest, Hungary: Telephone: (36-1) 269-0550; (36-1) 131-0933. Facsimile: (36-1) 269-1199.

Prague, Czech Republic: Telephone: (42-2) 2481-1796. Facsimile: (42-2) 232-5522.

Warsaw, Poland: Telephone/Facsimile: (48-22) 26-80-53; (48-22) 27-84-86. International Telephone/Facsimile: (48-39) 12-19-06.

Istanbul, Turkey: Telephone: (90-212) 275-68-98; (90-212) 275-75-33. Facsimile: (90-212) 275-75-43.

Ankara, Turkey: Telephone: (90-312) 446-2180. Facsimile: (90-312) 437-9677.

Jeddah, Saudi Arabia: Law Office of Hassan Mahassni, Telephone: (966-2) 651-3535. Facsimile: (966-2) 651-3636.

Riyadh, Saudi Arabia: Law Office of Hassan Mahassni, Telephone: (966-1) 476-7099. Facsimile: (966-1) 479-0110.

Almaty, Kazakhstan: Telephone: (7-3272) 50-7491/2. Facsimile: (7-3272) 61-0842.

General and International Practice.

RESIDENT OF COUNSEL

PETRI YRJO JOHANNES HAUSSILA, born Jyväskylä, Finland, March 1, 1954; admitted, 1981, Finland; 1986, New York. *Education:* University of Helsinki (LL.M., 1978); Columbia University (LL.M., 1984). *Member:* Finnish, International and American Bar Associations.

RESIDENT ASSOCIATES

PIA T. HELLMAN, born Turku, Finland, June 8, 1967; admitted, 1995, New York (Not admitted in Finland). *Education:* Turku University, Finland (OT.K., 1992); Georgetown University (LL.M., 1993).

JAMES G. HUNT, born Teaneck, New Jersey, February 16, 1962; admitted, 1989, New Jersey; 1990, New York (Not admitted in Finland). *Education:* University of Southern California, Los Angeles (B.S., 1984); State University of New York at Buffalo (J.D., 1989).

PEKKA J. LEHTINEN, born Sotkamo, Finland, May 26, 1962; admitted, 1993, Finland. *Education:* Turku University, Finland (LL.M., 1987).

LAURA A. SUSI-GAMBA, born Hameenlinna, Finland, February 19, 1963; admitted, 1994, Finland; Admitted as Avocat, France. *Education:* University of Helsinki (J.D., 1986); Boston University (LL.M., 1989).

(This Listing Continued)

ALA MICHAEL TARAZI, born Kuwait City, Kuwait, July 6, 1967; admitted, 1994, New York (Not admitted in Finland). *Education:* Harvard University (B.A., 1989; J.D., 1993).

(For biographical data as to other locations, see Professional Biographies at New York, New York; Washington, D.C.; Los Angeles, California; Miami, Florida; Mexico City, Mexico; Tokyo, Japan; Hong Kong; Singapore, Republic of Singapore; Bangkok, Thailand; Hanoi, Viet Nam; Bombay, India; London, England; Paris, France; Brussels, Belgium; Stockholm, Sweden; Moscow, Russia; Budapest, Hungary; Prague, Czech Republic; Warsaw, Poland; Istanbul and Ankara, Turkey; Jeddah and Riyadh, Saudi Arabia; Almaty, Kazakhstan).

WREDE & CO

Established in 1976

P. ROOBERTINKATU 7
00130 HELSINKI, FINLAND
Telephone: 358-0-618 6416
Telefax: 358-0-602 595

General Practice. Corporate, Commercial, Contract, International, Trademark and Tax Law.

FIRM PROFILE: Established in 1976, the firm offers a full range of legal services for the business community. The client base is Scandinavian, European and North American in scope. The firm is a founding member of GLOBALAW, a group of about 50 independent law firms in 40 countries worldwide. The firm is also a founding member of EUROJURIST, a group of independent European based law firms specializing in European Community matters.

PARTNERS

R. KENNETH WREDE, born Turku, Finland, July 13, 1944; admitted, 1972, Finland. *Education:* Commercial School of Turku (B.B.A., 1963); University of Helsinki (LL.M., 1969); Diploma Export Business, Helsinki (1969); University of Illinois College of Law (Diploma, 1977). Honorary Consul for Jamaica in Finland, 1988. Legal Advisor to the US-Embassy in Helsinki, 1972—. *Member:* Finnish Bar Association; Helsinki Bar; Legal Society of Finland; International Bar Association (Business Section); AIPPI; LES-Scandinavia (Licensing Executives Society); International Fiscal Association; EEC Society of Finland; Asia-Pacific Lawyers Association; Association Europeenne des Avocats. *LANGUAGES:* Finnish, Swedish, English, French and German. *PRACTICE AREAS:* Corporate; Commercial; Contract; International; Trademark; Tax Law.

THOMAS C.W. WREDE, born Helsinki, Finland, March 27, 1939; admitted, 1988, Finland. *Education:* Diploma Hague Academy of International Law (1966); University of Helsinki (LL.M., 1967). *Member:* Finnish Bar Association; Economic Society of Finland. *LANGUAGES:* Finnish, Swedish and English. *PRACTICE AREAS:* Commercial; Tax; Estate; Collection Law.

OF COUNSEL

HEIKKI LEISVUORI, born Turku, Finland, 1950. *Education:* University of Turku (LL.M., 1977). *LANGUAGES:* Finnish, Swedish, English and German. *PRACTICE AREAS:* Commercial; Banking; Tax; Collection Law.

NEOVIUS LAW OFFICE

Established in 1989

NORRA ESPLANADGATAN 1
P.O. BOX 180
FIN-22100 MARIEHAMN, FINLAND
Telephone: +358-28-177 40
Fax: +358-28-177 46

Corporate and Competition Law, Civil Litigation, Mergers and Acquisitions, Shipping, International Banking and Business Law, General International Trade Law.

KENNETH NEOVIUS, born Ekenäs, Finland, April 3, 1947; admitted, 1980, Finland. *Education:* University of Helsinki (1973). *Member:* Finnish Bar Association. *LANGUAGES:* Swedish, Finnish, English and German.

(This Listing Continued)

ASSOCIATE

KRISTINA FAGERLUND, born Mariehamn, Finland, March 23, 1961; admitted, 1993, Finland. *Education:* University of Helsinki (1987). *Member:* Finnish Bar Association. *LANGUAGES:* Swedish, Finnish and English.

HOLMIA & VUORENPÄÄ OY

Established in 1978

OTAVALANKATU 3 A

P.O. BOX 466

33101 TAMPERE, FINLAND

Telephone: 358-31-2143333

Telecopier: 358-31-2132280

International and Domestic Tax Law, Commercial Contracts, Insurance, Mergers and Acquisitions, Civil Litigation and Insolvency Law.

STEN HOLMIA, born Tampere, Finland, January 10, 1946; admitted, 1978, Finland. *Education:* University of Helsinki (LL.M., 1973). *Member:* Finnish Bar Association.

ESA VUORENPÄÄ, born Lemu, Finland, May 11, 1956; admitted, 1993, Finland. *Education:* University of Turku (LL.M., 1984). Member: Tampere Chamber of Commerce; International Fiscal Association. *Member:* Finnish Bar Association. *LANGUAGES:* Finnish, Swedish, English, French and German. *PRACTICE AREAS:* Taxation; Insurance; International Contracts; Mergers and Acquisitions.

ROSCHIER-HOLMBERG & WASELIUS

ALATORI

VAASA 65100, FINLAND

Telephone: 358-61 3179311

Fax: 358-61 3179377

Helsinki, Finland Office: Keskuskatu 7 A, 00100. Telephone: (0) 3580-228 551. Telex: 12 2310 ADVOX. Cable Address: "Cognitor." Telefax: (0) 664 303; (0) 175 451. Teletex: 1000901. London, England Office: 36-38 Cornhill, EC3V 9DR. Telephone: 44-71-929 0966. Telefax: 44-71-929 0933.

General Practice. International Financing, Commercial Banking, Industrial Property Rights, Trade and Market, Maritime, Aviation, Corporate, Establishing, Taxation and Real Estate Law, Litigation, EC Law.

ASSOCIATES

STEFAN WIKMAN, born Sipoo, Finland, November 10, 1956. *Education:* University of Helsinki (LL.B., 1979). *LANGUAGES:* Swedish, Finnish and English.

JAN-ANDERS WIK, born Esse, Finland, February 29, 1964. *Education:* University of Helsinki (LL.B., 1988). *LANGUAGES:* Swedish, Finnish and English.

FRANCE

BIGNON & LEBRAY

3, COURS MIRABEAU

13100 AIX-EN-PROVENCE, FRANCE

Telephone: 78.37.03.17

Telecopier: 78.92.82.94

Paris, France Office: 4, rue Bayard, 75008. Telephone: 42.56.64.00. Telex: BIGLEX 649 526 F. Telecopier: 45.61.09.50.
Lyon, France Office: 29, rue Gasparin, 69002. Telephone: 78.37.03.17. Telecopier: 78.92.82.94.
Lille, France Office: 19, boulevard de la Liberté, 59800. Telephone: 20.57.90.90. Telecopier: 20.57.90.25.
Madrid, Spain Office: Castello 35, 28001. Telephone: (34.1) 577. 26.66. Telecopier: (34.1) 577.61.89.

General French, European Community and International Practice. Corporate, Reorganization, Real Estate, Construction, Commercial Leases, Banking, Financial, Securities, Stock Exchange Regulations, International Contracts, Antitrust, Unfair Competition, Distributorship, Agency, Franchise, Product Liability, Patent and Trademark, Environment, Labor, Taxation, Litigation, Arbitration. Admitted to appear before all French Courts and

(This Listing Continued)

The European Community Court of Justice. Some lawyers of the firm are admitted to appear before certain foreign courts.

FIRM PROFILE: Originally founded in 1982, Bignon & Lebray is dedicated to providing corporate law assistance. Composed of a multidisciplinary team, it renders legal advice and counselling or litigation in all branches of business law, from a domestic, European and international perspective.

The firm counsels and assists French and foreign corporations, comprising major groups as well as smaller competitive companies, with varied activities including industry, banking, finance, portfolio management, distribution, real estate, transportation, computer and tourism.

While the firm maintains an extensive network of correspondents in the rest of France and in most major foreign cities, it has began an expansion program to open branch offices in several major cities in France and in other countries of Europe. At present, it has three branch offices in France, in Lille, in Lyon and in Aix-en-Provence and one in Spain, in Madrid.

RESIDENT PARTNERS

REMI DE GAULLE, born Paris, France, May 3, 1952; admitted, 1978, Paris; 1979, Aix-en-Provence. *Education:* University of Grenoble (Maîtrise en Droit, 1975); University of Paris (D.E.A. in History of Law, 1977). President, Union des Jeunes Avocats, 1983; President, Fédération Nationale des Unions de Jeunes Avocats (F.N.U.J.A.), 1989-1990. Member, Conseil de l'Ordre, 1984-1986; 1991-1993. *LANGUAGES:* French and English. *PRACTICE AREAS:* Construction Law; Contracts; Labor Law; Commercial Litigation.

RESIDENT ASSOCIATES

EMMANUELLE FERRERI-SAPENE, born Rouen, France, March 18, 1965; admitted, 1989, Bordeaux; 1993, Aix en Provence. *Education:* Université de Bordeaux (Maîtrise en Droit, 1987). *Member:* Aix en Provence Bar Association. *LANGUAGES:* French and English. *PRACTICE AREAS:* Commercial Litigation.

(For List of Partners and Associates, see Professional Biographies at Paris, France)

SOKOL LAW OFFICES

Established in 1973

14, RUE PRINCIPALE, B.P. 3

13540 PUYRICARD

AIX-EN-PROVENCE, FRANCE

Telephone: 42-92-08-20

Telecopier: 42 92 14 51

FIRM PROFILE: Firm engaged in non-routine work wherein special expertise and understanding of French and U.S. legal systems and culture are brought to bear to help solve intractable problems. In addition to acting as counsel, Mr. Sokol has testified in the U.S. as an expert witness on French law and practice.

A typical client is an American, Canadian or English law firm with a problem in France, but the firm also represents French subsidiaries of two Fortune 500 companies, non-profit organizations, businesses and individuals.

Practice areas in which the firm has experience are French and transnational litigation, civil rights under U.S. constitutional law and under the European Convention on Human Rights, citizenship, nationality, extradition, business-related immigration problems in the U.S. and France, French labor law, problems related to inheritances and French estate administration, French real estate and construction problems, French personal injury cases, French bioethics laws, child custody and matrimonial problems in a transnational context, counseling American lawyers on tactics and strategy within the French legal environment, reviewing and supervising the work of other lawyers.

RONALD P. SOKOL, born Milwaukee, Wisconsin, March 23, 1939; admitted, 1962, Wisconsin; 1973, Conseil Juridique; 1992, Avocat, Aix-en-Provence, France. *Education:* Duke University; University of Mexico; University of Virginia (J.D., 1962; LL.M., 1963). Phi Delta Phi. Regional Delegate, American Chamber of Commerce for Marseille-Provence. Ex-Officio Director, American Chamber of Commerce in France. Director, American International School of the Cote d'Azur, 1979-1994. Director, U.S. Navy League, Marseille. Author: "A Handbook of Federal Habeas Corpus," Michie, 1965; "Language and Litigation," Michie, 1966; "The Political Trial: Courtroom As Stage, History As Critic," 2 New Literary History 495, 1971;

(This Listing Continued)

SOKOL LAW OFFICES, Aix-En-Provence—Continued

"Justice After Darwin," Michie, 1975; "French Taxation of Intercompany Transfer Arrangements: Article 57 v. Section 482," 12 International Lawyer 639, 1978; "Termination of French Labor Contracts," 14 International Lawyer 267, 1980; "Law-Making Process," The Legal System of France, Modern Legal Systems Cyclopedia, Wm. S. Hein (1990). "Reforming the French Legal Profession," 26 International Lawyer 1025, 1992. Director, Appellate Legal Aid and Lecturer in Law, University of Virginia School of Law, 1963-1966. *Member:* State Bar of Wisconsin; American Bar Association; Scientific Instrument Society. *LANGUAGES:* English, French and Japanese.

REPRESENTATIVE CLIENTS: Laboratories Pfizer; Rain Bird Europe.

ROBERT FLOYD
22-24, BOULEVARD ALEXANDRE III
06400 CANNES, FRANCE
Telephone: 93.43.32.56-93.43.93.55
Fax: 93.43.40.26

General and International Practice.

ROBERT FLOYD, born London, England, September 29, 1946; admitted, 1971, England; 1992, France. *Education:* London University (LL.B., 1969; LL.M., 1970); Université d'Aix, Marseille, France; Inns of Court School of Law (Barrister). *Member:* Association d'Avocats Inscrits à un Barreau Etranger, Paris; Association des Juristes Européens; I.B.A. *LANGUAGES:* French.

TREMBLAY LAW OFFICES
41 RUE DES VIEUX CAPUCINS
B.P. 193
28004 CHARTRES CEDEX, FRANCE
Telephone: (33) 37 28 59 68
Fax: (33) 37 35 73 72

Paris, France Office: 79 Avenue de Villiers, 75017 Paris. Telephone: (33) (1) 42 27 51 73. Fax: (33) (1) 46 22 06 24.

Banking, Bankruptcy & Reconstruction, Company, Employment, Commercial Property, Receivership.

FIRM PROFILE: General, Commercial and International Firm. Founders of the Unilegal Grouping EEIG.

Unilegal was created in order to offer full corporate legal services in the majority of EC states. Each member practices in his own country and is, therefore, best placed to advise on matters concerning the law of that country.

MEMBERS

JEAN-PIERRE TREMBLAY, born France, 1946; admitted, 1972, Chartres. *Education:* University of Paris, Assas-Panthéon (Maîtrise Private Law, 1970); Institut d'Etudes Judiciaires (Diploma, 1970). Co-Author: "Le Droit Communautaire & International devant le Juge du Commerce," ed. Epargne, 1989. *LANGUAGES:* French and English.

CLAUDE TREMBLAY, born France, 1949; admitted, 1975, Chartres. *Education:* University of Paris, Assas-Panthéon (Maîtrise Private Law, 1974); Institut d'Etudes Judiciaires (Diploma, 1974). *LANGUAGES:* French and English.

ASSOCIATES

CHRISTINE BORDET-LESUEUR, born France, 1961; admitted, 1990, Chartres. *Education:* University of Paris I (D.E.A. Business and Tax Law). *LANGUAGES:* French.

ELISABETH DE KREUZNACH, born France, 1965; admitted, 1993, Paris. *Education:* University of Paris X (D.E.A. Business Law, 1989). (Resident, Paris Office). *LANGUAGES:* French and English.

ISABELLE COUDERC, born France, 1965; admitted, 1989, Paris. *Education:* University of Tours (Maîtrise Private Law, 1986). (Resident, Paris Office). *LANGUAGES:* French and English.

CLAIRE GINISTY-MORIN, born France, 1966; admitted, 1994, Chartres. *Education:* University of Toulouse (D.E.S.S. Business Law, International, 1989). *LANGUAGES:* French and English.

RICHARD KLIEMAN, born Great Britain, 1966; admitted, Conseil Juridique Stagiaire; 1994, Chartres. *Education:* Manchester (LL.B., 1989);

(This Listing Continued)

University of Paris II (Maîtrise E.E.C. and International Law, 1991). *LANGUAGES:* English and French.

FABIENNE CHAGNY, born France, 1971; admitted, 1994, Chartres. *Education:* University of Paris X (Maîtrise Business Law, 1992). *LANGUAGES:* French and English.

MARIE-ANTOINE TAREAU-DROUET, born France, 1965; admitted, 1993, Paris; 1994, Chartres. *Education:* University of Antigua-Guyana (Maîtrise, 1986). *LANGUAGES:* French.

DIDIER POPIELA, born 1962; admitted, 1994, Chartres. *Education:* University of Lyon III (D.E.S.S.-D.J.C.E., Business and Tax Law, 1989). *LANGUAGES:* French and German.

ALEXIS LEGENS, born 1969; admitted, 1995, Chartres. *Education:* University of Poitiers (D.S.S.-D.J.C.E., Business Law, 1992). *LANGUAGES:* French and English.

IAN J. STOCK
53, ROUTE D'EPERNON
78125 HERMERAY, FRANCE
Telephone: (33)(1) 34 83 46 20
Fax: (33)(1) 34 83 46 10

International Commercial Practice, with an emphasis on International Acquisitions, Joint Ventures and Licenses in Europe.

IAN J. STOCK, born Buckinghamshire, England, December 7, 1952; admitted, 1982, California; 1984, New York; 1990, Paris. *Education:* Sir William Borlase's School, Marlow; University of California at Berkeley (A.B., summa cum laude, 1979); Yale University (J.D., 1982). Associate, Kronish Lieb Weiner & Hellman, New York, 1983-1986. Associate, 1987-1990 and Member, 1991-1992, Kevorkian & Partners, Paris. *Member:* Union Internationale des Avocats. (Also Of Counsel to Branche & Associés, Paris, France). *LANGUAGES:* English and French.

BIGNON & LEBRAY
19, BOULEVARD DE LA LIBERTE
59800 LILLE, FRANCE
Telephone: 20.57.90.90
Telecopier: 20.57.90.95

Paris, France Office: 4, rue Bayard, 75008. Telephone: 42.56.64.00. Telex: BIGLEX 649 526 F. Telecopier: 45.61.09.50.
Aix-en-Provence, France Office: 3 cours Mirabeau, 13100. Telephone: 42.38.58.38. Telecopier: 42.26.92.37.
Lyon, France Office: 29 rue Gasparin, 69002. Telephone: 78.37.03.17. Telecopier: 78.92.82.94.
Madrid, Spain Office: Castello 35, 28001. Telephone: (34.1) 577. 26.66. Telecopier: (34.1) 577.61.89.

General French, European Community and International Practice. Corporate, Reorganization, Real Estate, Construction, Commercial Leases, Banking, Financial, Securities, Stock Exchange Regulations, International Contracts, Antitrust, Unfair Competition, Distributorship, Agency, Franchise, Product Liability, Patent and Trademark, Environment, Labor, Taxation, Litigation, Arbitration. Admitted to appear before all French and The European Community Court of Justice. Some lawyers of the firm are admitted to appear before certain foreign courts.

FIRM PROFILE: Originally founded in 1982, Bignon & Lebray is dedicated to providing corporate law assistance. Composed of a multidisciplinary team, it renders legal advice and counselling or litigation in all branches of business law, from a domestic, European and international perspective.

The firm counsels and assists French and foreign corporations, comprising major groups as well as smaller competitive companies, with varied activities including industry, banking, finance, portfolio management, distribution, real estate, transportation, computer and tourism.

While the firm maintains an extensive network of correspondents in the rest of France and in most major foreign cities, it has began an expansion program to open branch offices in several major cities in France and in other countries of Europe. At present, it has three branch offices in France, in Lille, in Lyon and in Aix-en-Provence and one in Spain, in Madrid.

(This Listing Continued)

RESIDENT PARTNER

BERTRAND DEBOSQUE, born Lille, France, January 27, 1960; admitted, 1985, Paris; 1986, Lille. *Education:* University of Lille, Faculté de Droit (Maîtrise en Droit, 1980; D.E.A. de Droit des Affaires, 1982; Docteur en Droit, Thèse d'Etat, 1986); New York University, Institute of Comparative Law (M.C.J., 1984). Author: "Le choix de la monnaie dans les contrats privés," thesis, 1986. *Member:* Lille Bar Association. *LANGUAGES:* French and English. *PRACTICE AREAS:* Commercial Litigation; Monetary Law; Bankruptcy Law; Contracts; Criminal Law.

RESIDENT ASSOCIATES

PHILIPPE JOOS, born Lille, France, May 2, 1966; admitted, 1991, Lille. *Education:* University of Lille (Maîtrise en Droit Privé, 1989; D.E.S.S. - Certificat d'Aptitude à l'Adminsitration des Entreprises, 1990). *Member:* Lille Bar Association. *LANGUAGES:* French and English. *PRACTICE AREAS:* Commercial Litigation.

PHILIPPE LARIVIERE, born Lille, France, October 28, 1968; admitted, 1992, Lille. *Education:* University of Lille (Maîtrise de Droit Privé, 1989). *Member:* Lille Bar Association. *LANGUAGES:* French, English and German. *PRACTICE AREAS:* Commercial Litigation; Labor Law.

BÉATRICE PARMENTIER, born Lille, France, September 26, 1962; admitted, 1987, Paris. *Education:* University of Lille II (Maîtrise en Droit, 1984; D.E.A. de Droit Privé, 1985); Polytechnic of Central London (1988). *Member:* Paris Bar Association. *LANGUAGES:* French, English and German. *PRACTICE AREAS:* Labor Law; Commercial Litigation.

(For List of Partners and Associates, see Professional Biographies at Paris, France)

LEBAS-LEMISTRE ET ASSOCIES

Established in 1971

ESPACE JURIDIQUE

99 RUE NATIONALE

59000 LILLE, FRANCE

Telephone: (33) 20.12.56.70

Fax: (33) 20.12.56.52

Arbitration, Banking and Finance, Bankruptcy/Insolvency, Civil Litigation, Commercial, Administrative, Commercial Property, Company, Competition, Construction, Debt Recovery, Defamation, Distribution, Employment, Franchising, House Purchase, Insolvency, Insurance, Intellectual Property, International Investment and Financial Services, Labour Relations, Mergers and Acquisitions, Mortgages/Hypothecs, Partnerships, Personal Injury, Tax Company, Transports, Trusts, Wills and Probate.

FIRM PROFILE: The firm was established in 1971 and offers a full range of legal services. It is well known for its commercial and company law. This six partner firm has a legal support staff of seven consisting of Avocats and Legal Support Personnel.

The partners of LEBAS-LEMISTRE et ASSOCIES are also partners of the sarl ESPACE JURIDIQUE which is instituted with six notaries. The aim of ESPACE JURIDIQUE is to provide the best service to clients both in the traditional areas of legal work and also in new areas as they emerge.

MEMBERS OF FIRM

BERNARD LEBAS, born Calais, France, January 7, 1941; admitted, 1968, Lille. *Education:* Lauréat de la Faculté de Droit de Lille (Civil and Commercial). *Member:* Ancien Secrétaire de la Conference; l'Union des Jeunes Avocats of Lille (Former President); Fédération Nationale des Unions des Jeunes Avocats (Former Vice-President); Ancien Bâtonnier de l'Ordre des Avocats. *LANGUAGES:* French and German. *PRACTICE AREAS:* Arbitration, Banking and Finance; Bankruptcy/Insolvency; Commercial Property; Company; Composition; Distribution; Insurance; Intellectual Property; International; Investment and Financial Services; Business Crime; Mergers and Acquisitions; Partnerships; Company Tax Law.

BRUNO LEMISTRE, born Soissons, France, October 30, 1942; admitted, 1969, Lille. *Education:* Lauréat des Facultés de Droit (Civil); Diplôme d'etudes supérieures de droit privé et de sciences criminelles. *Member:* Ancien Premier Secrétaire de la Conférence; Faculté des Sciences Juridiques, Politiques et Sociales of Lille (Former Assistant). *LANGUAGES:* French and English. *PRACTICE AREAS:* Arbitration, Banking and Finance; Bankruptcy/Insolvency; Commercial; Commercial Property; Company; Competition; Construction; Distribution; Employment; Franchising; Busi-

(This Listing Continued)

ness Crime; Intellectual Property; Investment and Financial Services; Mergers and Acquisitions; Partnerships; Company Tax Law.

CHRISTINE PERRIN, born Roubaix, France, July 22, 1943; admitted, 1968, Lille. *Education:* Lauréate de la Faculté (Commercial). *Member:* Ancien Premier Secrétaire de la Conférence. *LANGUAGES:* French. *PRACTICE AREAS:* Insolvency; Civil Litigation; Commercial; Commercial Property; Competition; Defamation; Distribution; Family; House Purchase; Insurance; Matrimonial; Mortgages; Wills and Probate; Franchising.

PHILIPPE CHAILLET, born Valenciennes, France, May 29, 1953; admitted, 1979, Lille. *LANGUAGES:* French. *PRACTICE AREAS:* Civil Litigation; Commercial; Company; Construction; Defamation; Insolvency; Insurance; Transport; Administrative Law; Bankruptcy; Real Property.

OLIVIER TRESCA, born Dunkirk, France, November 14, 1955; admitted, 1983, Lille. *Member:* Union des Jeunes Avocats of Lille (Former President). *LANGUAGES:* French and English. *PRACTICE AREAS:* Civil Litigation; Commercial; Distribution; Employment; Labor law; Family; Franchising; Insolvency Insurance; Matrimonial; Transports; Wills and Probate; Personal Injury.

LAURENT HEYTE, born Haubourdin, France, July 19, 1962; admitted, 1985, Lille. *LANGUAGES:* French. *PRACTICE AREAS:* Civil Litigation; Commercial; Construction; Employment; Labor Law; Insolvency; Insurance Transport; Chattel Real.

FRANÇOISE AUQUE, born St. Quentin, France, July 10, 1948; admitted, 1977, Lille. *Education:* Doctorate en Droit (1977). Professeur des Facultés de Droit, 1979. *LANGUAGES:* French and English. *PRACTICE AREAS:* Commercial Law; Distribution Law; Company Competition.

ASSOCIATES

MARCEL DORWLING CARTER, Magistrat Honoraire à la Cour de Cassation, Avocat.

ROBERT DELTOUR, born Roncq, France, February 28, 1938; admitted, 1965, Lille. *LANGUAGES:* French and English. *PRACTICE AREAS:* Tax Law.

LETARTRE-FREYRIA-LEFEVRE & ASSOCIÉS

Société Civile Professionnelle d'Avocats

Established in 1970

72, AVENUE DU PEUPLE BELGE

59009 LILLE, FRANCE

Telephone: 20.55.92.37

Fax: 20.55.85.91

Corporate Law, Tax Law, Merger and Acquisitions, European Community Law, Banking Law, Admiralty and Transportation Law, Intellectual Property Law, National and International Litigation and Arbitration.

FIRM PROFILE: The firm has a strong reputation in the areas of Corporate and Reorganization Law, European Community Law, National and International Litigation. It is entitled to plead before all French Tribunals and Courts, to the exception of Cour de Cassation and Conseil d'Etat, as well as before the European Commission and European High Court of Justice. The firm has 16 partners, 7 associates and a secretarial staff of 30. It provides a full range of legal services and is particularly keen on representing clients from abroad. The foreign client base is mainly German, English and Dutch, as well as North American. The firm has reception offices in Paris with adequate legal and secretarial staff.

MEMBERS OF FIRM

JEAN LEFEBVRE, born Roubaix, France, September 25, 1939; admitted, 1966, Lille. *Member:* Regional Commission of Conseils Juridiques (Former President). *LANGUAGES:* French. *PRACTICE AREAS:* Corporate; Tax Law.

JACQUES DUTAT, born Lille, France, March 5, 1945; admitted, 1968, Cour d'Appel de Douai. *LANGUAGES:* French and English. *PRACTICE AREAS:* Administrative Law; Tax Litigation.

YVES LETARTRE, born Lille, France, November 29, 1947; admitted, 1970, Cour d'Appel de Douai. *Education:* Doctorate in Law, 1975. Maître de Conférences, University of Lille. *LANGUAGES:* French. *PRACTICE AREAS:* Bankruptcy Law; Banking Law.

(This Listing Continued)

LETARTRE-FREYRIA-LEFEVRE & ASSOCIÉS, Lille—Continued

JEAN-FRANCOIS THERY, born Quesnoy, France, February 16, 1948; admitted, 1974, Lille. *LANGUAGES:* French. *PRACTICE AREAS:* Corporate; Tax Law.

FLORENCE DESENFANS, born Boulogne-Billancourt, France, December 8, 1951; admitted, 1972, Cour d'Appel de Douai. *LANGUAGES:* French and English. *PRACTICE AREAS:* Commercial Law; Labour Law.

MICHEL LEFEVRE, born Saint-Just-en-Chausée, France, November 25, 1946. *LANGUAGES:* French and English. *PRACTICE AREAS:* Corporate; Tax Law.

JEAN-LOUIS FREYRIA, born Lille, France, March 29, 1954; admitted, 1977, Cour d'Appel de Douai. *Education:* Maître de Conférences Associé, University of Economics of Lille. Associate, Shearman and Sterling, New York, 1980-1981 and Mueller Weitzel Weisner, Frankfurt, 1981-1982. *LANGUAGES:* French, English and German. *PRACTICE AREAS:* International Litigation; Distribution Law; Intellectual Property Law.

FRANCIS BARROIS, born Lille, France, February 22, 1951; admitted, 1978, Lille. *LANGUAGES:* French. *PRACTICE AREAS:* Corporate; Tax Law.

JEAN-MARC DOMANIEWICZ, born Valenciennes, France, January 13, 1951; admitted, 1979, Cour d'Appel de Douai. *LANGUAGES:* French and German. *PRACTICE AREAS:* Employment; Labour Law.

BRUNO RICHE, born Valenciennes, France, March 30, 1954; admitted, 1982, Lille. *LANGUAGES:* French and German. *PRACTICE AREAS:* Corporate Law.

LUCETTE FRANKE, born Lomme, France, April 18, 1946; admitted, 1983, Cour d'Appel de Douai. *LANGUAGES:* French. *PRACTICE AREAS:* Inheritance Law; Family Law; Real Estate.

PHILIPPE GUIOT, born Relizane, Algerie, April 22, 1956; admitted, 1984, Cour D'Appel De Douai. *LANGUAGES:* French and Spanish. *PRACTICE AREAS:* Administrative Law; Tax Litigation; Insurance Law.

FLORENCE LEFEBVRE-AUBERT, born Escaudain, France, February 26, 1944; admitted, 1980, Cour d'Appel de Douai. *LANGUAGES:* French and Spanish. *PRACTICE AREAS:* Commercial Law; Employment Law.

FRANCIS DEFRENNES, born Lille, France, January 17, 1961; admitted, 1986, Lille. *LANGUAGES:* French. *PRACTICE AREAS:* Commercial Law.

GENEVIEVE SOLICH, born Bapaume, France, May 8, 1955; admitted, 1985, Lille. *LANGUAGES:* French and English. *PRACTICE AREAS:* Corporate Law.

ETIENNE CURTELIN, born Avesnes sur Helpe, France, September 11, 1960; admitted, 1990, Lille. *LANGUAGES:* French and English. *PRACTICE AREAS:* Corporate Law; Tax Law.

OF COUNSEL

CHARLES FREYRIA, born Marseille, France, October 20, 1921; admitted, 1943, France. *Education:* Doctorate en Droit (1944); Agrégation Droit Paris (1951). Professeur á la Faculté de Droit de l'Université de Lille, 1954—. Vice-Dean of the Faculté de Droit, 1960-1970. *LANGUAGES:* French and English. *PRACTICE AREAS:* Corporate Law; Criminal Business Law; Tax Law.

ASSOCIATES

MARIE-PIERRE DUTAT-MORSEAU, born Lille, France, February 3, 1950; admitted, 1978, Lille. *LANGUAGES:* French. *PRACTICE AREAS:* Administrative Law; Personal Injury Law.

ISABELLE BARROIS, born Bouar, République of Africa, March 19, 1962; admitted, 1989, Lille. *LANGUAGES:* French and English. *PRACTICE AREAS:* Commercial Law; Banking Law.

CHRISTOPHE LELART, born Lille, France, June 1, 1965; admitted, 1991, Lille. *LANGUAGES:* French and English. *PRACTICE AREAS:* European Community Law; Commercial Law.

HUGUES MAQUINGHEN, born Lille, France, July 27, 1965; admitted, 1991, Lille. *LANGUAGES:* French and English. *PRACTICE AREAS:* Employment; Labour Law.

(This Listing Continued)

EMMANUEL MASSON, born Saint-Denis, France, July 21, 1968; admitted, 1992, Lille. *LANGUAGES:* French. *PRACTICE AREAS:* Commercial Law.

BRIGITTE DELOBEL-BEFVE, born Cambrai, France, January 31, 1964; admitted, 1990, Lille. *LANGUAGES:* French and English. *PRACTICE AREAS:* Corporate Law.

BERTRAND WAMBEKE, born Lille, France, December 13, 1963; admitted, 1992, Lille. *PRACTICE AREAS:* Commercial and Labour Law.

Languages: French, English, German and Spanish

BERLIOZ & CO.

48, RUE DU PRÉSIDENT HERRIOT
69002 LYON, FRANCE
Telephone: (33) 78 38 12 79
Telefax: (33) 78 38 12 83

Paris, France Office: 68, Boulevard de Courcelles, 75017 Paris. Telephone: (33.1) 44 01 44 01. Telefax: (33.1) 44 15 94 15; 42 67 04 43.

Toulouse, France Office: 22, rue de la Dalbade, 31000 Toulouse. Telephone: (33) 61 53 01 56. Telefax: (33) 61 53 65 51.

Sophia Antipolis, France Office: Villantipolis n° 11, 473, route des Dolines, Sophia Antipolis, 06560 Valbonne. Telephone: (33) 93 65 42 50. Telefax: (33) 93 65 39 26.

London, England Office: 44-46 Kingsway, WC2B 6EN. Telephone: (44 71) 831-4022. Telex: 263 680 BERLAW. Telefax: (44 71) 831-8233.

Brussels, Belgium Office: 179 avenue Louise, 1050. Telephone: (32.2) 646.40.04. Telefax: (32.2) 644.14.88.

New York, New York Office: 655 Madison Avenue, 10021. Telephone: 212-486-6302. Telex: 3717883. Telefax: 212-486-8668.

Vilnius, Kalvariju Office: g. 276-36, 2021 VILNIUS. Telephone: (370.2) 62.46.04. Contact: Valentinas MIKELENAS.

General French and International Law Practice, Advertising Law, Aeronautical Law, Arbitration, Banking and Financial Law, Commercial Leasing, Competition Law, Computer Law, Construction Law, Consumer Protection, Corporate Law, Criminal Law, Distributorship Law, Entertainment Law, Agency and Franchise Law, EC Law, Food and Drug Regulations, Foreign Investments, Industrial Relations and Labor Law, Insurance Law, International Private Law, Licensing, Litigation, Maritime and Transport Law, Financial Engineering, Public Contracts, State Enterprises, Taxation, Tax Planning, Mergers and Acquisitions Law, Product Liability, Property, Real Estate, Rent and Lease Law, Securities Law, Trade Regulations, Patent, Trademark and Copyright Law, Tax, East-West Trade, North-South Trade, Audio-visual Law, Telecommunications.

PASCALE BISSUEL, born 1955; admitted, 1978, Lyon. *Education:* Université de Saint-Etienne (Licence et Maîtrise de Droit Privé, 1977). *Member:* AIPPI (Association Internationale pour la Protection de la Propriété Industrielle).

DOMINIQUE CHAPELLON LIEDHART, born 1967; admitted, 1991, Lyon. *Education:* Université de Lyon II (D.E.S.S. de Droit Social, 1990).

Languages: French, English, German, Italian, Spanish, Portuguese, Russian, Arabic, Malaysian

---

BIGNON & LEBRAY

29, RUE GASPARIN
69002 LYON, FRANCE
Telephone: 78.37.03.17
Telecopier: 78.92.82.94

Paris, France Office: 4, rue Bayard, 75008. Telephone: 42.56.64.00. Telex: BIGLEX 649 526 F. Telecopier: 45.61.09.50.

Aix-en-Provence, France Office: 3, cours Mirabeau, 13100. Telephone: 42.38.58.38. Telecopier: 42.26.92.37.

Lille, France Office: 19, boulevard de la Liberté, 59800. Telephone: 20.57.90.90. Telecopier: 20.57.90.25.

Madrid, Spain Office: Castello 35, 28001. Telephone: (34.1) 577. 26.66. Telecopier: (34.1) 577.61.89.

General French, European Community and International Practice. Corporate, Reorganization, Real Estate, Construction, Commercial Leases, Banking, Financial, Securities, Stock Exchange Regulations, International Contracts, Antitrust, Unfair Competition, Distributorship, Agency, Franchise,

(This Listing Continued)

Product Liability, Patent and Trademark, Environment, Labor, Taxation, Litigation, Arbitration. Admitted to appear before all French Courts and The European Community Court of Justice. Some lawyers of the firm are admitted to appear before certain foreign courts.

FIRM PROFILE: Originally founded in 1982, Bignon & Lebray is dedicated to providing corporate law assistance. Composed of a multidisciplinary team, it renders legal advice and counselling or litigation in all branches of business law, from a domestic, European and international perspective.

The firm counsels and assists French and foreign corporations, comprising major groups as well as smaller competitive companies, with varied activities including industry, banking, finance, portfolio management, distribution, real estate, transportation, computer and tourism.

While the firm maintains an extensive network of correspondents in the rest of France and in most major foreign cities, it has began an expansion program to open branch offices in several major cities in France and in other countries of Europe. At present, it has three branch offices in France, in Lille, in Lyon and in Aix-en-Provence and one in Spain, in Madrid.

RESIDENT PARTNER

ANTOINE ARMINJON, born Neuilly-sur-Seine, France, May 24, 1959; admitted, 1985, Paris; 1988, Lyon. Education: University of Lyon (Maître en Droit des Affaires, 1982). Member: Lyon Bar Association. LANGUAGES: French, English and German. PRACTICE AREAS: Banking Law; Commercial Litigation; Corporate Law; Labor Law.

RESIDENT ASSOCIATES

GHISLAINE ARNAUD-CROZAT, born October 19, 1962; admitted, 1991, Lyon. Education: University of Lyon (Maîtrise en Droit Privé, 1987; D.E.A. en Droit de la Famille, 1988; Diplôme de l'Institut de Droit Comparé, 1990). LANGUAGES: French, Spanish and English. PRACTICE AREAS: Commercial Litigation.

CATHERINE ROBIN, born Lyon, France, March 26, 1964. Education: University of Lyon (Maîtrise en Droit des Affaires, 1987); University of Montpellier (D.E.S.S. de Concurrent, Distribution, Consommation, 1988; Certificat de Gestion Commericale et Financière, 1989). LANGUAGES: French and English. PRACTICE AREAS: Competition; Distribution Law; EEC Law.

(For List of Partners and Associates, see Professional Biographies at Paris, France)

DMG

12, QUAI ANDRÉ LASSAGNE
69001 LYON, FRANCE
Telephone: (33) 72.00.76.76
Fax: (33) 78.29.69.57

Mergers and Acquisitions, Corporate and Individual Taxation, Tax Litigation, Foreign Taxation, National and International Tax Planning, Foreign Investments, Exchange Control Regulations, Customs and Excise Taxes, Securities Regulations and Law, Corporate Law, Corporate Litigation, Labour Law, Administrative Law, National and EC Competition, Contracts, Drafting, Distributorship, Agency, Franchise, Bankruptcy, Charitable Organizations.

PARTNERS

JEAN-PHILIPPE DELSOL, born Paris, France, February 24, 1950. Education: University of Lyon (Docteur En Droit, 1978). LANGUAGES: French and English. PRACTICE AREAS: Taxation Law; Corporate Law; Mergers, Acquisitions and Divestitures; Charitable Organizations; Administrative Law.

MICHEL DUQUAIRE, born Lyon, France, March 23, 1949. Education: University of Lyon (Des De Droit-IAE, 1973). LANGUAGES: French. PRACTICE AREAS: Tax Law; Tax Litigation.

MICHEL CHAPAS, born Lyon, France, January 4, 1949. Education: University of Lyon (Des De Sciences Economiques, 1969). LANGUAGES: French. PRACTICE AREAS: Corporate Law; Taxation Law; Labor Law; European Law; Competition Law; Computer and Software.

JÉRÔME BROSSETTE, born Ste. Foy Les Lyon, France, March 26, 1944. Education: University of Lyon (Licence Sciences Economiques-IAE, 1969). LANGUAGES: French. PRACTICE AREAS: Corporate Law; Business Transactions.

(This Listing Continued)

CORINNE MALAPERT, born Neufchateau, France, September 30, 1949. Education: University of Aix-en-Provence (Dess Droit Prive, 1975). LANGUAGES: French, Italian and English. PRACTICE AREAS: Corporate Law; Business Law; Taxation Law.

PAULETTE TRILLAT, born Belley, France, February 9, 1957. Education: University of Grenoble (Dess Droit Fiscal, 1980). LANGUAGES: French. PRACTICE AREAS: Tax Litigation; Taxation Law.

PHILIPPE WOERNER, born Die, France, October 10, 1954. Education: University of Lyon (Djce/Dess Droit Des Affaires et Fiscalite, 1983). LANGUAGES: French. PRACTICE AREAS: Corporate Law; Taxation Law; Contract Law; Mergers, Acquisitions and Divestitures.

CHRISTOPHE COCHET, born St. Fons, France, May 16, 1962. Education: University of Lyon (Djce/Dess Droit Des Affaires et Fiscalite, 1985). LANGUAGES: French and English. PRACTICE AREAS: Mergers, Acquisitions and Divestitures; Corporate Law; Commercial Law; Taxation Law.

THIERRY PERMEZEL, born Neuilly-sur-Seine, France, October 20, 1961. Education: University of Lyon (Dess Droit Des Affaires, 1984). LANGUAGES: French and English. PRACTICE AREAS: Corporate Law; Contract Law; Bankruptcy; Mergers, Acquisitions and Divestitures; International Business Law; Taxation Law.

ETIENNE JOULIE, born Valence, France, November 15, 1947. Education: University of Paris (Maitrise De Droit-IAE, 1970). LANGUAGES: French, English and German. PRACTICE AREAS: Insurance Law; Labor Law; Transportation Law; Litigation.

ALAIN RIPERT, born Avignon, France, September 14, 1950. Education: University of Aix-en-Provence (Maitrise, 1972, Eni). LANGUAGES: French. PRACTICE AREAS: Taxation Law; Tax Litigation.

GILLES BAZAILLE, born Oullins, France, October 13, 1962. Education: University of Dijon (Dess Droit Des Affaires et Fiscalite, 1988). LANGUAGES: French and English. PRACTICE AREAS: Taxation Law; Tax Planning Law; Mergers, Acquisitions and Divestitures; International Business Law; Corporate Law.

ASSOCIATES

Jean Marc Bernardin	*Guy De Foresta*
Philippe Dumez	*Pierre Malhiere*
Pierre Marie Durade Replat	*Marie Laetitia Pagnoni*
Isabelle Walet	

OFFICE JURIDIQUE FRANÇCAIS ET INTERNATIONAL

(O.J.F.I.)

Established in 1945

10, RUE STELLA
69002 LYON, FRANCE
Telephone: (33) 72.41.16.16
Fax: (33) 72.41.16.06

Paris, France: 374, rue Saint-Honoré; 75001 Paris.
Barcelona, Spain: Avenida Diagonal, 477; Torre de Barcelona, Planta 20; 08036 Barcelona.
Bristol, England: 30 Queen Charlotte Street; Bristol BS99 7QQ.
Brussels, Belgium: Avenue de Cortenberg 79/81; 1040 Bruxelles.
Copenhagen, Denmark: H.C. Andersens Boulevard 37; DK-1553 Copenhagen V.
Frankfurt, Germany: Westendstrasse 24; 60325 Frankfurt am Main.

General and International Practice. Corporate, Tax, Mergers and Acquisitions, Labor Law, Litigation, Arbitration, Real Estate, Commercial Leases, Foreign Investments, Industrial and Intellectual Property, Products Liability, Competition, Administrative Law.
Firm engaged in French, European and International Law practice and authorized to appear before the French and European Courts.

FIRM PROFILE: Established in 1945, the Firm's practice covers the entire spectrum of legal, judicial and tax specialties. The Firm regularly advises foreign companies, more particularly European, North American and Japanese companies, doing business in France as well as French companies and individuals doing business in North America. The Firm has formed a European Economic Interest Group, "Office Juridique: Osborne Clarke", with the English firm OSBORNE CLARKE, the Danish firm MOLLER

(This Listing Continued)

OFFICE JURIDIQUE FRANÇÇAIS ET INTERNATIONAL, Lyon—Continued

TVERMOES & HOFFMEYER and the Spanish firm DAGA & SAURET. The Firm has also a close relationship with YAMADA CONSULTING, S.L.

(For complete biographical data, see professional biographies at Paris, France)

LAMY, VÉRON, RIBEYRE & ASSOCIÉS

Established in 1965

40, RUE DE BONNEL

F-69484 LYON CEDEX 03, FRANCE

Telephone: (33) 78.62.14.00

Fax: (33) 78.62.14.99

Paris, France Office: 242 bis, Boulevard Saint-Germain, 75007.
Telephone: (1) 45 48 86 08. Fax: (1) 45 49 44 23.

Advertising, Antitrust, Arbitration, Banking, Bankruptcy, Competition, Construction, Corporate, Customs and Excise, Distributorship Agency and Franchise, EEC, Finance, Foreign Investments, Industrial Relations, Labor, Products Liability and International Contracts Law and Litigation. Intellectual Property, Patent, Merger and Acquisition, Tax Planning, Trademark and Copyright Litigation and Industrial Models Law.

FIRM PROFILE: *Established in 1965, LAMY, VERON, RIBEYRE & ASSOCIES has grown to become the biggest law firm in the southern part of France and is among the top ranking law firms in France.*

The firm offers the full range of French Business, Corporate and Trade Law and Litigation as well as quality service in different areas of specialization, and in European Community Law and International Law. Its members are entitled to plead before French Courts and the European Commission.

The firm has 16 partners and 21 associates practising in Lyon and a Paris office.

MEMBERS OF FIRM

BRUNO LAMY, born Lyon, France, May 2, 1941; admitted, 1965, Lyon. *Education:* Lyon III University (Docteur en Droit). Former Assistant, Lyon III University. *LANGUAGES:* French, English and Spanish. *PRACTICE AREAS:* Corporate Law; Company Law; Finance.

PIERRE VÉRON, born Roanne, France, July 20, 1947; admitted, 1969, Lyon. *Education:* Lyon III University (Laureat). Member, Council of the Bar of Lyon, 1977-1979. President, French Young Lawyers Association, 1977-1978. Member, Consultative Committee of the Bars and Law Societies of the European Community, 1977-1980. *Member:* I.B.A.; A.I.P.P.I. (President, Rhône-Alpes Group, 1989-1991; Vice President, Rhône-Alpes Center of Arbitration, 1992—). *LANGUAGES:* French, English, Italian and Spanish. *PRACTICE AREAS:* Arbitration; Intellectual Property; Litigation.

ALAIN RIBEYRE, born February 1, 1949; admitted, 1971, Lyon. *Education:* Lyon III University. *LANGUAGES:* French and English. *PRACTICE AREAS:* Bankruptcy; Banking; Litigation; Taxation.

FRANÇOIS BALSAN, born Valence, France, October 12, 1945; admitted, 1972, as Conseil Juridique en Droit des Sociétés; 1983, Lyon. *Education:* Lyon III University (Docteur en Droit); Institut d'Administration des Entreprises. *LANGUAGES:* French and English. *PRACTICE AREAS:* Corporate Law; Company Law; Taxation; Finance; Antitrust.

YVES BIZOLLON, born Bourgoin, France, October 24, 1957; admitted, 1981, Lyon. *Education:* Lyon III University (D.E.A. de Droit Privé; D.E.S.S. de Droit Notarial; Laureat). *Member:* Council of the Bar (1991—). *LANGUAGES:* French, English and Spanish. *PRACTICE AREAS:* Intellectual Property; Construction Law; Technology and Science; Environmental Law.

ANNE COVILLARD, born October 11, 1954; admitted, 1978, France. *Education:* University of Burgundy. Member: Council of the City of Dijon, 1983; Council of the Bar of Lyon, 1988-1990. Professor at CRFPA. *Member of U.J.A.; A.C.E. LANGUAGES:* French and English. *PRACTICE AREAS:* Agency and Distributorships; Commercial Law; Bankruptcy.

PHILIPPE GENIN, born Nantes, France, July 24, 1955; admitted, 1979, Lyon. *Education:* University of Lyon (Licence en Droit, 1976; Maîtrise en Droit, 1977; Diplôme d'Etudes Approfondies de Droit des Affaires, 1979). *LANGUAGES:* French and English. *PRACTICE AREAS:* Com-

(This Listing Continued)

mercial Law; Litigation; Antitrust; European Community Law; Corporate Litigation; Environmental Law.

GILLES BRIENS, born Lyon, France, December 3, 1955; admitted, 1980, Lyon. *Education:* Lyon Law School (Maîtrise de droit des Affaires, 1979; D.J.C.E., 1980; D.E.S.S., 1980). Author: "Business and the Law of Supplementary Social Insurance Coverage," Litec, 1990. Co-author: "La Retraite en Entreprise," 1994; "Intéressement, Participation, Plan d'É-pargne," 1993. Article, Collective Bargaining and Social Insurance Cover, Litec, 1987; Article, Social Security Retirement Benefits and Contributions, Assurance Française, 1990. *Member:* Bar of Lyon. *LANGUAGES:* French and English. *PRACTICE AREAS:* Labour and Employment; Social Welfare.

YVES FROMONT, born Saint Quentin, February 4, 1954; admitted, 1980, Lyon. *Education:* University of Lyon (D.J.C.E., 1978; D.J.C.E. in Business Legal Counsellor, 1979; Doctorate in Law, 1980). Author: "The Work Inspect of Experts of the Enterprise Committee," Liaisons Sociales, 1986 and 1987; "The Length of Work Restructuring the Enterprise," Liaisons Sociales, 1988 and 1989. Co-author: "Intéressement, Participation Plan d'Épargne," 1993. *LANGUAGES:* French, Spanish and English. *PRACTICE AREAS:* Labour and Employment; Social Welfare.

GERARD LEGRAND, born Verdun, France, August 15, 1958; admitted, 1986, Lyon. *Education:* University of Reims (Licence en Droit, 1980; Maîtrise en Droit, 1981); University of Paris, Panthéon Sorbonne (Diplôme d'Etude Approfondies Droit des Affaires, 1985); University of Paris René Descartes (Diplôme d'Audit de l'Entreprise, 1988). *LANGUAGES:* French and English. *PRACTICE AREAS:* Commercial Law; Banking; Taxation.

DOMINIQUE GRIVET, born Aubenas, France, November 24, 1949; admitted, 1992, Lyon. *Education:* University of Lyon (Maîtrise, 1971). *LANGUAGES:* French and English. *PRACTICE AREAS:* Corporate Law; Company Law; Taxation.

CHRISTOPH MARTIN RADTKE, born Reutlingen, West Germany, October 14, 1956; admitted, 1985, Tübingen, West Germany; 1992, Lyon. *Education:* University of Tübingen (Referendar, 1982; Assessor, 1985); London School of Economics (1980); Faculte Internationale Strasbourg (1981); University of Urbino (1983-1984). Author: "The Creation of a GmbH as a Subsidiary of a French Corporation in Germany," Petites Affiches, July 1988; "The Execution of Decisions under the Brussel's Convention," La Gazette du Palais, June 1988; The Control of Mergers in Germany, Le Monde, Sept., 1989. Co-Author: "The Company in the Face of Europe," Dunod-Bordas, 1989; "Business in Germany," CFCE Paris, 1993; "Corporations and Trusts in Europe," Juris, 1994. Professor: University of Paris X, Nanterre, 1987-1989; Center for the Professional Formation of the Paris Bar, 1986—. *Member:* German Bar Association; French-German Lawyers' Association; German-Italian Lawyers' Association; French-German Chamber of Commerce (Rhône-Alpes Representative); European Lawyers' Union; Centre d'Etudes Juridiques Européennes d'Urbino. *LANGUAGES:* German, French, English and Italian. *PRACTICE AREAS:* International Law; European Community Law.

ANNIE DAVID, born Morteau, France, May 31, 1953; admitted, 1975, Lyon. *Education:* Besançon University (Licence en droit, 1974); Dijon University (D.E.S., 1975; Laureat, 1975). *LANGUAGES:* French, English and Italian. *PRACTICE AREAS:* Banking Law; Bankruptcy; Industrial Relations and Labour Law; Litigation; Commercial Law.

ERIC BAROIN, born France, October 18, 1964; admitted, 1992, Lyon. *Education:* Lyon University Law School (Maîtrise de Droit des Affaires, 1986; D.J.C.E., 1987; Major D.E.S.S., Business Legal Counseling, 1987; Superior Certificate in Tax). Co-Author: "Guide to European Company Law," Sweet & Maxwell. *LANGUAGES:* French and English. *PRACTICE AREAS:* Corporate Law; Company Law; Taxation; Antitrust.

PHILIPPE CLEMENT, born 1959; admitted, 1987, Lyon. *Education:* University of Lyon. Instructor, University of Lyon. Co-author: "Intéressement, Participation, Plan d'Épargne," 1993. *LANGUAGES:* French and English. *PRACTICE AREAS:* Labour Law; Employment Law; Social Welfare.

CATHERINE MILLET-URSIN, born 1961; admitted, 1984, Lyon. *Education:* University of Lyon. Instructor, University of Lyon. Co-author: "La Retraite en Entreprise," 1994. *LANGUAGES:* French and English. *PRACTICE AREAS:* Labour; Employment Law; Social Welfare.

MARILYN FAVIER, born 1957; admitted, 1981, Lyon. *Education:* University of Lyon. Instructor, University of Lyon. Co-author: "Intéressement,

(This Listing Continued)

Participation, Plan d'Épargne," 1993. *LANGUAGES:* French and English. *PRACTICE AREAS:* Labour; Employment Law; Social Welfare.

ASSOCIATES

Blandine Tronel	Rémi LLinas
Christel Gomez	Béatrice Mounier-Bertail
Jérôme Letang	Hugues Pelissier
Véronique Gignoux	Sophie-Adrienne Forest
Catherine Leng	Yves Saunier
Olivier Ponchon De Saint Andre	Denis Laloux
Anne Bolland	Olivier Ellul
Agnès Perrin	Armelle Dechelette
Laurence César	Sophie Chassignolle
Jean-Guillaume Monin	Hervé Poquillon

Fabienne Chebroux

Languages: French, English, German, Spanish and Italian

MOQUET BORDE DIEUX GEENS & ASSOCIÉS

11 PLACE BELLECOUR
69002 LYON, FRANCE
Telephone: 72 40 00 32
Fax: 72 41 98 62

Paris, France Office: 30 Avenue de Messine, 75008. Telephone: (1) 42 99 04 50. Telex: 640 650 F. Fax: (1) 45 63 91 49.

Budapest, Hungary Office: Kossuth tér 16-17, III/2/a, H-1055 Budapest, (1245 Budapest, P.O. Box 1228). Telephone: (36-1) 1531 255. Fax: (36-1) 1531 229.

Tallinn, Estonian Office: 10 Pärnu str., EE 0001 Tallinn, Estonia. Telephone: (372) 6405836. Fax: (372) 6405838.

Brussels, Belgium Office: Rue de la Bonté 5-7, B-1050. Telephone: (32-2) 538 6869. Fax: (32-2) 538 6867.

French, EEC and International Law Practice.

RESIDENT MEMBER OF FIRM

Philippe Croizat

RESIDENT ASSOCIATES OF FIRM

Xavier Dequidt

(For Complete Biographical data on all Personnel, see Professional Biographies at Paris, France)

CABINET RATHEAUX

Société d'Avocats

Established in 1920

40, RUE DE BONNEL
69484 LYON CEDEX 03, FRANCE
Telephone: (33) 72 61 75 75
Fax: (33) 78 60 00 09

Member of the Association of European Lawyers which regroups leading law firms in the United Kingdom and Continental Europe.

Corporate and Individual Taxation, Tax Litigation, Foreign Taxation, National and International Tax Planning, Customs and Excise Taxes, Corporate Law, Securities Regulation, Mergers and Acquisitions, Reorganizations and Spin-offs, Banking, Antitrust, National and EEC Competition, Distributorship and Consumer Protection, Franchising, Venture Capital, Labor, Intellectual Property, Contract Drafting, Foreign Investments and Exchange Restrictions, Real Estate.

FIRM PROFILE: Since its foundation in Lyon in 1920 the firm has, over the years, participated in the creation and development of several large industrial French and foreign groups now expanding throughout Europe. This valuable experience enables the CABINET RATHEAUX to meet all the needs of the companies in each aspect of Business Law, especially in the dynamic region of economic growth.

PARTNERS

PIERRE COTE, born Lyon, France, May 17, 1945; admitted, as conseil juridique en droit des societes et droit fiscal (corporate law and tax counsel). *Education:* ESSEC (Ecole Superieure des Sciences Economiques et Commerciales); Institut d'Etudes Politiques de Paris (DES of private law,

(This Listing Continued)

Master of Laws). *LANGUAGES:* French and English. *PRACTICE AREAS:* Corporate Law; Mergers and Acquisitions Law; Venture Capital Law.

SERGE BERRETTONI, born Bron, France, February 11, 1960; admitted, 1989, as conseil fiscal (tax counsel). *Education:* University of Lyon (Maîtrise en droit, DESS droit des affaires et fiscalité des entreprises, Master of Law; Diplome de Juriste conseil d'entreprise). Part-time Assistant Lyon III University. *LANGUAGES:* French, English and Italian. *PRACTICE AREAS:* Taxation Law; Tax Planning Law; Management Buyouts Law; Offshore Corporations; Foreign Investments Law.

HENRI SAINT PERE, born Antibes, France, May 3, 1958; admitted, 1987 as conseil juridique en droit des societes (corporate law counsel). *Education:* Paris V University (Maîtrise en droit; diplome de juriste conseil d'entreprise). Part-time assistant Lyon III University. *Member:* Association Française des Avocats Conseils d'Entreprise (section Internationale). *LANGUAGES:* French and English. *PRACTICE AREAS:* Corporate Law; Antitrust Law; Intellectual Property Law; Settlement of Foreign Companies in France; International Business Law.

JACQUES MERLE, born Chalon sur Saone, France, January 4, 1936; admitted, 1972 as conseil fiscal (tax counsel). *Education:* University of Lyon (Maîtrise en droit); Ecole Nationale des Impots (former tax inspector). *LANGUAGES:* French. *PRACTICE AREAS:* Taxation Law.

GEORGES MOREL, born Lyon, France, March 16, 1944; admitted, 1972 as conseil fiscal (tax counsel). *Education:* University of Lyon (Maîtrise en droit); Ecole Nationale des Impots (former tax inspector). *LANGUAGES:* French. *PRACTICE AREAS:* Corporate Law; Mergers and Acquisitions; Securities Regulation Law.

MICHEL BELIN, born Saulxures, France, January 26, 1947; admitted, 1985 as conseil fiscal (tax counsel). *Education:* University of Clermont-Ferrand (Maîtrise en droit); Ecole Nationale des Impots (former tax inspector). Tax Specialist in an International firm (Rhone Poulenc, 1975-1984). *LANGUAGES:* French. *PRACTICE AREAS:* Mergers and Acquisitions; Tax Planning Law; Management Buyouts; Foreign Investments; Venture Capital Law.

MICHEL BOTTAZZI, born Annecy, France, August 29, 1957; admitted, 1988, as conseil en droit des societes (corporate law counsel). *Education:* University of Grenoble (Maîtrise en droit; Diplome d'Etudes Comptables Superieures, Decs). *LANGUAGES:* French and Italian. *PRACTICE AREAS:* Corporate Law; Mergers and Acquisitions; Spin-Offs; Bankruptcy Law.

GAËTAN DE LA BOURDONNAYE, born Lyon, France, September 8, 1961; admitted, 1988 as Conseil juridique en droit des societes (corporate law counsel). *Education:* University of Lyon (Maîtrise en droit, DESS Droit des Affaires et fiscalite des entreprises; diplome de juriste conseil d'entreprise). *LANGUAGES:* French and English. *PRACTICE AREAS:* Corporate Law; Securities Regulation Law; Mergers and Acquisitions.

CHRISTIAN MULLER, born Roanne, France, April 4, 1955; admitted, 1989 as conseil fiscal (tax counsel). *Education:* University of Lyon (Maîtrise en droit); graduate of the Ecole Nationale des Impots (former tax inspector); University of Urbino (European Law Diploma). *LANGUAGES:* French and Spanish. *PRACTICE AREAS:* Taxation Law; Tax Litigation; Tax Ruling.

ANDRÉ MONET, born Villeurbanne, France, November 15, 1952; admitted, 1979, as conseil fiscal et droit des sociétés (tax and corporate law counsel). *Education:* University of Lyon (Maîtrise en Économie; Maîtrise en droit; DESS droit des affaires et fiscalité). *LANGUAGES:* French and Spanish. *PRACTICE AREAS:* Taxation Law and Corporate Law.

ASSOCIATES

FRANCK BUFFAUD, born Lyon, France, December 19, 1961; admitted, 1989 as conseil en droit des societes (corporate law counsel). *Education:* University of Lyon (Maîtrise en droit; DESS droit des affaires et fiscalite des entreprises, Master of Laws; Diplome de juriste conseil d'entreprise). *LANGUAGES:* French and English. *PRACTICE AREAS:* Corporate Law; Mergers and Acquisitions; Settlement of Foreign Companies in France; Domestic and International Contracts Law; Bankruptcy Law.

ALEXIS VANDELET, born Lyon, France, April 4, 1959; admitted, 1989 as conseil en droit des societes (corporate law counsel). *Education:* University of Lyon (Maîtrise en droit; DEA droit des affaires et droit economique; CESMA, Certificat d'Etudes Superieures du Management); University Business School (Ecole Superieure de Commerce de Lyon).

(This Listing Continued)

CABINET RATHEAUX, Lyon—Continued

LANGUAGES: French and English. **PRACTICE AREAS:** Corporate Law; Mergers and Acquisitions.

FRANK DE VAUBLANC, born Marseille, France, March 7, 1955; admitted, 1988 as conseil en droit des societes (corporate law counsel). *Education:* University of Aix en Provence (Maîtrise en droit; DESS en gestion du personnel, Master of Laws). **LANGUAGES:** French. **PRACTICE AREAS:** Corporate Law; Securities Regulation Law; Banking Law.

GILLES VUARCHEX, born Lyon, France, April 8, 1959; admitted, 1982, as Avocat. *Education:* University of Lyon (Maîtrise en droit). **LANGUAGES:** French and English. **PRACTICE AREAS:** Commercial Law; Banking; Litigation; Real Estate Law; E.E.C. Regulations; Bankruptcy Law.

CHARLES SIMIAN, born Lyon, France, May 19, 1958; admitted, 1988 as conseil juridique. *Education:* University of Lyon (Maîtrise en droit; DESS droit des affaires et fiscalité). **LANGUAGES:** French. **PRACTICE AREAS:** Corporate Law; Mergers and Acquisitions.

JEAN-JACQUES LEVRAT, born Besancon, France, July 7, 1965; admitted, 1992, as Avocat. *Education:* University of Lyon (Maîtrise en droit; DESS droit des Affaires et fiscalite des entreprises, Master of Laws; Diplome de juriste conseil d'entreprise). **LANGUAGES:** French. **PRACTICE AREAS:** Corporate Law.

RODOLPHE MOSSE, born Chambery, France, July 6, 1968; admitted, 1994, as Avocat. *Education:* University of Grenoble (Maîtrise en droit; DESS droit fiscal, Master of Law). **LANGUAGES:** French. **PRACTICE AREAS:** Taxation Law.

PHILIPPE ROUSSELIN-JABOULAY, born Lyon, France, December 30, 1968. *Education:* University of Lyon (D.E.A. Droit Social; Master of Labor Law). **LANGUAGES:** French and English. **PRACTICE AREAS:** Labor Law; Litigation.

LAURENT SIMON, born Lyon, France, November 16, 1967; admitted, 1994, as Avocat. *Education:* University of Saint Etienne (Maîtrise en droit; DESS droit des affaires et fiscalité, Masters of Law); University of Lyon (Diplome de juriste conseil d'entreprise). **LANGUAGES:** French and English. **PRACTICE AREAS:** Domestic and International Contracts Law.

ISABELLE BOUVIER, born Lyon, France, June 25, 1968. *Education:* University of Lyon (DESS Droit International des Affaires). **LANGUAGES:** French and English. **PRACTICE AREAS:** Domestic and International Contract Law; E.E.C. Regulations.

CHRISTOPHE VIEUX-ROCHAS, born Saint Jean De Luz, France, August 18, 1964; admitted, 1992, as Avocat. *Education:* University of Lyon (Maîtrise en droit). **LANGUAGES:** French and Spanish. **PRACTICE AREAS:** Corporate Law.

CAROLE DAHAN, born Villeurbanne, France, October 28, 1967; admitted, 1994, as Avocat. *Education:* University of Lyon (DESS droit des affaires et fiscalité; diplôme de juriste conseil d'entreprise). **LANGUAGES:** French. **PRACTICE AREAS:** Corporate Law.

CHRISTOPHE BRACHET, born Paris, France, September 18, 1967. *Education:* University of Paris (DEA Droit des Affaires et Droit Economiques; DEA Droit Communautaire). **LANGUAGES:** French and English. **PRACTICE AREAS:** Litigation; Commercial Law; E.E.C. Regulations.

LEGAL SUPPORT PERSONNEL

MICHÉLE BRUN In charge of the Formalities Department; drafting of incorporation documents.

CHRISTIANE FATET In charge of the Formalities Department; drafting of incorporation documents.

SOULIER, REINHARD, AZÉMA & ASSOCIÉS

Established in 1960

51, AVENUE MARÉCHAL FOCH
69006 LYON, FRANCE
Telephone: 72.82.20.80
Telefax: 72.82.20.90

Mailing Address: P.O. Box 6067, 69412 Lyon Cédex 06
(This Listing Continued)

Paris, France Office: 10, rue Clément Marot, 75008. Telephone: (1) 44.43.80.55. Fax: (1) 40.70.05.43.

General French and International Law Practice, Advertising, Anti-trust, Arbitration, Banking, Bankruptcy, Civil, Communications and Entertainment, Competition, Construction, Consumer Protection, Corporate, Criminal, Customs and Excise, Distributorship, Agency and Franchise, EEC, Environmental, Food and Drug Regulations, Foreign Investments and Exchange Control Regulations, Health, Hospital and Malpractice, Industrial Relations and Labor, Insurance, Licensing, Litigation, Patent, Trademark and Copyright, Press, Product Liability, Property, Real Estate, Rent and Lease, Taxation and Trade Regulations.

FIRM PROFILE: *Founded in 1960, the law firm of Soulier, Reinhard, Azéma & Associés presently consists of fourteen attorneys, including four partners, with offices in Paris and Lyon. The firm specializes in French and international commercial matters, as well as all aspects of a traditional civil practice.*

ANDRÉ SOULIER, born Lyon, France, October 18, 1933; admitted, 1959, Lyon; 1989, Paris. *Education:* University of Lyon (Licence en Droit, 1956; Diplôme de l'Institut d'Etudes Politiques, 1956; Diplôme d'Etudes Supérieures d'Economie Politique, 1957). Co-Author: "International Environmental Law & Regulation," Chapter on France, Butterworth, 1991. Assistant Professor, Business Law, Institut de Préparation aux Affaires, University of Lyon, 1964-1966. Member, Comité Français de l'Arbitrage. *Member:* National Association of Lawyers (ANA); American Chamber of Commerce in France. **LANGUAGES:** French and English. **PRACTICE AREAS:** Commercial and Criminal Litigation and Arbitration.

JEAN-LUC SOULIER, born Lyon, France, March 29, 1955; admitted, 1977, Lyon; 1989, Paris. *Education:* University of Lyon (Licence en Droit, 1976; Maîtrise en Droit, 1977); University of Michigan (LL.M., 1980). Associate, Sullivan & Cromwell, New York, 1980-1981. Co-Author: "Guide Juridique et Fiscal de l'Exportateur," C.F.C.E., 1987; "International Environmental Law & Regulation," Chapter on France, Butterworth, 1991; "Creating and Structuring International Joint Ventures in France," International Business Lawyer, 1991. Author: "Les Instruments de l'Internationalisation Financière en Europe dans la Perspective du Marché Unique," C.J.F.E., 1988; "Le Marché Intérieur de 1992 : les Aspects Juridiques de la Coopération à Caractère Technique et Industriel : Contrats de Recherche et de Développement, Contrats de Spécialisation, de Savoir-faire," C.J.F.E., 1988. Professor, International Business Law, 1985-1989, and European Community Law, 1987-1991. University of Lyon. *Member:* American Chamber of Commerce in France; International Bar Association; European Lawyers Union. **LANGUAGES:** French and English. **PRACTICE AREAS:** International Business Law; European Community Law.

YVES REINHARD, born Lyon, France, February 20, 1947; admitted, 1988, Lyon; 1989, Paris. *Education:* University of Lyon (LL.B., 1969; Awarded LL.D., 1974). Awarded Agrégé des Facultés de Droit (Professor of Law), 1978. Author: "L'acte du Salarié et la Responsabilité Pénale du chef d'entreprise," 1974; "Droit Commercial," 1990. Contributor: Revue Trimestrielle de droit commercial et de droit économique, chronique des sociétés par actions, 1986-. Professor of Commercial Law, 1977-. Lectured on International Law: University of Yaounde, Cameroon, 1971-1972; University of Rabat, Morocco, 1978-1979; University of Minneapolis, U.S.A., 1982. Honorary Director of the Institute of Business Law, University of Lyon. *Member:* A.I.P.P.I. **LANGUAGES:** French and English. **PRACTICE AREAS:** Corporate Law.

JACQUES AZEMA, born Lyon, France, August 20, 1941; admitted, 1990, Lyon and Paris. *Education:* University of Lyon (LL.B., 1963; LL.D., 1968). Awarded Agrégé des Facultés de Droit (Professor of Law), 1969. Author: "La Durée des contrats successifs," LGDJ 1969; "Le Droit Francais de la Concurrence," PUF Coll. Thémis 2ème édition 1989; "Le Droit Pénal de la Pharmacie," LITEC 2ème édition 1990; "Le Droit de la Propriété Industrielle," LAMY Com.; Contributor: "Chronique de droit de la Concurrence," J.C.P. 1982—; "Chroniques de Propriété Industrielle," (Revue trimestrielle de Droit Commercial et de Droit Economiqué 1972—). Professor of Commercial Law, University of Lyon, 1969—. Director, Paul Roubier Center. Member, Commission de la Concurrence, 1983-1986. Member, Conseil de la Concurrence, 1987-1990. Member, Conseil Supérieur de la Propriété Industrielle, 1986—. *Member:* A.I.P.P.I. (President, French Group, 1986-1989; Honorary President 1990—). **LANGUAGES:** French, Spanish and English. **PRACTICE AREAS:** Intellectual Property Law; Competition Law.

GÉRARD CHANU, born Montbéliard, France, December 11, 1956; admitted, 1995, Lyon. *Education:* University of Lyon (Licence en droit, 1979; Maîtrise en droit, 1980; Diplôme d'Etudes Supérieures Supécialisées
(This Listing Continued)

en Droit des Affaires et Fiscalité, 1982; Diplôme de Juriste-Coneil d'Entreprises, 1982). Legal Counsel of companies listed on the Paris Stock Exchange. *LANGUAGES:* French, English and Spanish. *PRACTICE AREAS:* Security; Corporate Law; Tax Law; High Technology and software issues; International Trade.

CONSULTANTS

CHRISTIAN GABOLDE, born Lons-le-Saunier, France, September 19, 1924; admitted, 1989, Lyon; 1989, Paris. *Education:* University of Paris (Lauréat, 1945; Docteur en Droit, 1952; Licence de Lettres, 1946; Diplôme de l'Ecole Libre des Sciences Politiques, 1946); Ecole Nationale d'Administration (1946-1948). Author: "L'Urgence en Droit Administratif," 1952; "Les Etablissements dangereux, incommodes et insalubres," 1951; "Les Installations Classées pour la protection de l'Environnement," 1978; "La Procédure des Tribunaux Administratifs et des Cours Administratives d'Appel," 1988. Co-Author: "International Environmental Law & Regulation," Chapter on France, Butterworth, 1991. Contributor: Jurisclasseur Administratif, Encyclopédie DALLOZ. Breveté du Centre des Hautes Etudes Administratives, 1959. Président: Administrative Court of Caen, 1968; Administrative Court of Lyon, 1977-1982. Member of the Conseil d'Etat, 1982-1988. *LANGUAGES:* French and Spanish. *PRACTICE AREAS:* Administrative Law.

LAURENT MICHAUX, born Beaujeu, France, March 19, 1921. *Education:* Ecole de Notariat de Lyon (Notaire, 1947). *LANGUAGES:* French. *PRACTICE AREAS:* Property Law; Real Estate Law; Wills.

ASSOCIATES

MARC MICHEL, born Lyon, France, January 30, 1952; admitted, 1993, Lyon. *Education:* Maîtrise en droit privé, 1976; Certificat d'études supérieures de droit du travail et de la sécurité sociale, 1976; Diplômé de l'Ecole Nationale des Impôts, 1978. Senior French Tax Inspector, 1988-1992. *LANGUAGES:* French, English and Spanish. *PRACTICE AREAS:* Tax Law; Corporate Law.

VALERIE SPIGUELAIRE, born Blanc Mesnil, France, May 23, 1964; admitted, 1989, Paris; 1994, Lyon. *Education:* Diplôme de l'Institut d'Etudes Politiques de Paris, 1985; University of Paris I (Maîtrise en Droit Privé, 1987). *Member:* Institut Francais des Praticiens des Procédures Collectives (Bankruptcy); Association des anciens élèves de l'Institut d'Etudes Politiques. *LANGUAGES:* French and English. *PRACTICE AREAS:* Criminal Litigation; Business Law; Bankruptcy.

JOCELYNE FRESEL, born Lyon, France, May 8, 1964; admitted, 1992, Lyon. *Education:* University of Lyon (Maîtrise en Droit des Affaires, 1985); University of Aix-en-Provence (Diplôme d'Etudes Supérieures Spécialisées en Commerce Extérieur, 1987; Diplôme de Juriste-Conseil d'Entreprises, Option Internationale, 1987); Stevenson College of Edinburgh (Cambridge First Certificate, 1988; Oxford Higher, 1988). *LANGUAGES:* French and English. *PRACTICE AREAS:* Corporate Law.

ANDREW GARELECK, born Buffalo, New York, USA, April 4, 1964; admitted, 1993, New York (Not admitted in France). *Education:* University of Michigan, Ann Arbor (B.A., 1986); Vermont Law School (J.D., 1990); University of Paris I Panthéon, Sorbonne (Maîtri se en Droit International et Européen, 1992). *Member:* The Association of the Bar of the City of New York. *LANGUAGES:* English, French and Spanish. *PRACTICE AREAS:* International Contracts; Corporate Law.

KARINE ETIENNE, born Lyon, France, April 21, 1969; (Not admitted in France). *Education:* University of Lyon (Magistère de Droit des Affaires, 1990; Diplôme d'Etudes Supérieures Spécialisées en Droit des Affaires, 1991; Diplôme de Juriste Conseil d'Enterprises, 1991; Certificat d'Etudes Spécialisées en Droit Fiscal, 1991). *LANGUAGES:* French, English and Spanish. *PRACTICE AREAS:* Business Law; Tax Law.

STEPHANE LAPALUT, born Marseille, France, May 20, 1970; admitted, 1994, Lyon. *Education:* University of Lyon (Magistére de Droit des Affaires, 1993; Diplôme d'Etudes Supérieures Spécialisées en Droit des Affaires, 1993; Diplôme de Juriste-Conseil d'Entreprises, 1993). *LANGUAGES:* French and English. *PRACTICE AREAS:* Litigation.

Languages: French, English, German and Spanish

ANDRE, ANDRE & ASSOCIES

Established in 1983

89, AVENUE DU PRADO
13008 MARSEILLE, FRANCE
Telephone: (33) 91.80.44.22
Fax: (33) 91.80.49.80

Corporate Law, Mergers and Acquisitions, Tax Law and Tax Litigation, Bankruptcy, Labor Law, Civil Law and Administrative Law.

FIRM PROFILE: The firm was established in 1983 and offers a full range of business law services to companies and their managers. It is particularly known for its Merger and Acquisitions department and for its Tax Litigation. The client base is French and European. The firm is based on 2 partners and has the support of 6 associates.

MEMBERS OF FIRM

GUY E. ANDRE, born Djibouti, November 18, 1952; admitted, 1981, Marseille. *Education:* University of Law and Economic Sciences of Montpellier (Diplôme d'Etudes Supérieures de Droit des Affaires; Diplôme de Juriste Conseil d'Entreprise); Ecole Nationale Supérieure des Services Extérieurs du Trésor. Lecturer, Law, University of Aix-en-Provence. *Member:* International Bar Association; Fédération des Juristes Européens. *LANGUAGES:* French. *PRACTICE AREAS:* Corporate Law; Mergers and Acquisitions; Arbitration; Share Purchase Agreements; Share Sales; Share Agreements and Disputes; Business Law; Banks and Banking.

MARC ANDRE, born Djibouti, November 18, 1952; admitted, 1986, Marseille. *Education:* University of Law and Economic Sciences of Montpellier (Diplôme d'Etudes Approfondies de Droit Public); Ecole Nationale des Impôts. Lecturer, Law, University of Montpellier. Author: "Le droit du recouvrement de l'impôt," P.U.F., to be published. Co-Author: "La fiscalité du cheval de course," P.U.F., 1990; "Lamy Immobilier," 1994. *Member:* International Bar Association; Fédération des Juristes Européens. *LANGUAGES:* French. *PRACTICE AREAS:* Taxation; Tax Law; Tax Litigation; Administrative Law; Real Estate Law; Timeshares.

ALAIN BOFFARD, born Nîmes, France, March 23, 1957; admitted, 1985, Marseille. *Education:* University of Law and Economic Sciences of Montpellier (Maîtrise en Droit). *LANGUAGES:* French and English. *PRACTICE AREAS:* Corporate Law; la Bankruptcy Law; Labor Law; Social Law and Insolvency.

JULIETTE BROCHE-ANDRE, born Nîmes, France, December 10, 1953; admitted, 1987, Marseille. *Education:* University of Law and Economic Sciences of Montpellier (Maîtrise en Droit); University of Poitiers (Higher Degree, Financial and Accounting Techniques); Ecole Nationale Supérieure des Services Extérieurs du Trésor. *LANGUAGES:* French. *PRACTICE AREAS:* Corporate Law; Accounting Law; Financial Law.

PIERRE DI MALTA, born Bône, Algeria, January 13, 1929; admitted, 1987, Marseille. *Education:* University of Algiers. Professor of Public Law, University of Law and Economic Sciences of Montpellier; Director, Center of Preparation de General Administration. Author: "Droit pénal fiscal," P.U.F., 1992; "Droit fiscal comparé," to be published. Co-Author: "Droit budgétaire," Litec; "Droit fiscal," Litec; "La fiscalité du cheval de course," P.U.F., 1990. "Droit pénal fiscal," P.U.F., 1993. *LANGUAGES:* French. *PRACTICE AREAS:* Tax Law; Administrative Law.

ISABELLE ANDRE, born Wiesbaden, Germany, January 28, 1966; admitted, 1991, Marseille. *Education:* University of Law and Economic Sciences of Aix-en-Provence (Maîtrise en Droit public with distinction, 1987); University of Law and Economic Sciences of Montpellier (Maîtrise en Droit des Affaires with distinction, 1988). Co-author, "International Immigration and Nationality Law," Chapter on France, Nartinus Nijhoff. *Member:* International Bar Association (Vice-Chairman, Committee onMigration and Nationality Law, 1992). *LANGUAGES:* French and English. *PRACTICE AREAS:* Corporate Law; Foreign Investments.

CHRISTIAN CAVASINO, born Tunis, July 18, 1954; admitted, 1991, Marseille. *Education:* University of Law and Economic Sciences of Aix en Provence (Diplôme d'Etudes Approfondies en droit Privé, 1977); Ecole Nationale de la SantéPublique, Ecole Nationale des Imôts. *LANGUAGES:* French and Italian. *PRACTICE AREAS:* Taxation; Tax Controversies; Social Security.

JACQUES DOMINICI, born Marseille, France, July 7, 1946; admitted, 1974, Marseille. *Education:* University of Law and Economic Sciences of Aix en Provence (Diplome de Juriste Conseil d'Entreprise, 1972, Diplome d'Etudes Supérieures Spécialisées de Droit des Affaires et de Fiscalité des

(This Listing Continued)

ANDRE, ANDRE & ASSOCIES, Marseille—Continued

Entreprises, 1992). *LANGUAGES:* French, English. *PRACTICE AREAS:* Commercial Law; Business Law; Corporate Litigation; Banking Litigation.

LEGAL ASSISTANTS

SÉVERINE LASSERRE, born Casablanca (Morocco), November 15, 1963. *Education:* University of Bordeaux (Diplôme de Sciences Politiques, 1988); University of Toulon (Maîtrise de Droit Privé, 1992). *LANGUAGES:* French, English and Spanish. *PRACTICE AREAS:* Civil Litigation.

CAMMARATA & MONTFORT

Avocats au Barreau de Paris

Established in 1983

2, RUE HENRI BARBUSSE
13241 MARSEILLE CEDEX 01, FRANCE
Telephone: 91.90.90.00
Telefax: 91.56.17.22

Paris, France Office: 15 rue de la Baume, 75008. Telephone: (33-1) 53 75 21 21. Telefax: (33-1) 53 75 15.00.

General and International Law Practice.

MEMBERS OF FIRM

ARNAUD DE BARTHÈS DE MONTFORT, born Paris, France, June 10, 1953; admitted, 1978, Paris. *Education:* University of Paris (Baccalaureat, 1971; Licence en Droit, 1975; D.E.A. de Droit Commercial, 1976; D.E.A. de Droit Civil, 1978); Institut d'Etudes Politiques de Paris (Section Economique et Financiere, 1976). *LANGUAGES:* French and English.

GEORG ANDREAS HENN, born Stuttgart, Germany, April 14, 1956; admitted, 1985, Marseille. *Education:* University of Tubingen, Neusprachliche Fakultat, Germany (1980-1981); Tubingen Law School, Germany (LL.B., 1981); Aix-en-Provence Law School (LL.M., 1982); Institut de Droit des Affaires of Aix-en-Provence (Diplôme d'Études Supérieures Spécialisées, Diplôme Juriste Conseil d'Entreprise, 1983). *Member:* Fondation Internationale pour l'Enseignement du Droit des Affaires; Chambre Francoallemande du Commerce et de l'Industrie; Mediterranean Maritime Arbitration Association. *LANGUAGES:* German, French, English and Spanish.

ETIENNE DE PINS, born Saint-Gaudens, France, July 9, 1964; admitted, 1991, Paris. *Education:* University of Aix en Provence (Maîtrise en Droit des Affaires, 1986; D.E.S.S. de Juriste d'Affaires Internationales, 1987; Diplôme de Juriste Conseil d'Entreprises, 1987). *LANGUAGES:* French and English.

CALIXTE KONAN, born Abidjan, Cote d'Ivoire, February 16, 1966; admitted, 1992, Marseille. *Education:* University of Aix-en-Provence (Maîtrise en Droit des Affaires, 1988); Institut de Droit des Affaires of Aix-en-Provence (Magistère de Droit des Affaires Fiscalité et Comptabilité, D.E.S.S.; Droit et Fiscalité de l'Entreprise; Diplôme de Juriste Conseil d'Entreprises, D.J.C.E., 1989); Université Laval of Quebec (Stage de Formation au Commerce International, 1989). *LANGUAGES:* French and English.

VERONIQUE BENTOLILA, born Marseille, France, April 17, 1961; admitted, 1991, Marseille. *Education:* University of Aix-en-Provence (Maîtrise en Droit des Affaires, 1986); Institut de Droit des Affaires of Aix-en-Provence (D.E.A., Droit des Affaires, 1987). *LANGUAGES:* French and English.

(For Complete Biographical Data of Paris Personnel, see Professional Biographies at Paris, France).

RENARD-ALLEMAND-TASSY

Groupement d Intérêt Economique

Established in 1873

27, COURS PIERRE-PUGET
13006 MARSEILLE, FRANCE
Telephone: 91.37.74.30
Telecopier: 91.53.71.51

Paris, France Office: 95 Rue de Prony, 75017. Telephone: (16 1) 43 80 23 19. Telecopier: (16 1) 44 40 40 52.

General and International Law, Transportation Law (Shipping, Maritime, Admiralty, Fluvial, Road), Commercial, Corporate, Customs, Arbitration, Labor, E.E.C. Law, Merger, Banking, Corporation Law and Bankruptcy.

PARTNERS

JEAN-LÉOPOLD RENARD, born Marseilles, France, March, 1949; admitted, 1970, Marseilles. *Education:* University of Aix-Marseille (Licence en Droit, 1970). General Honorary Consul of Austria, 1983. Knight of Maritime Merit, 1990. *Member:* International Bar Association; Union Internationale des Avocats. (Resident, Paris, France Office). *LANGUAGES:* French, English and Italian.

HERVÉ TASSY, born Marseilles, France, 1949; admitted, 1979, Marseilles. *Education:* l'Institut d'Etudes Politiques d'Aix en Provence (Economy and Business Section, 1970); University of Aix en Provence (Licence de Sciences Economiques, 1970; Diplôme d'Etudes Supérieures de Droit Privé, 1972; Doctorate d'Etat, 1977). *Member:* Institut Méditerranéen de Transports Maritime (I.M.T.M.); Association Française de Droit Maritime; The Propeller Club of the United States. *LANGUAGES:* French and English.

WILLIAM ELLIS, born Marseilles, France, 1946; admitted, 1973, Marseilles. *Education:* Institut Politique d'Aix en Provence (Economy and Business Section, 1970); University of Aix en Provence (Licence de Sciences Economiques, 1970; Diplôme d'Etudes Supérieures de Droit Privé, 1972). *Member:* Institut Méditerranéen de Transports Maritimes (I.M.T.M.). *LANGUAGES:* French and English.

GILBERT ALLEMAND, born Marseilles, France, 1947; admitted, 1970, Marseilles. *Education:* University of Aix-Marseille (Licence en droit, 1970). Membre des Conseil de l'Ordre, 1990. *Member:* Young Lawyers' International Association (A.I.J.A.); Junior Economical Chamber. *LANGUAGES:* French, English and German.

ASSOCIATES

Béatrice Favarel-Veidig	Karen Benhamou-Koskas
Henri-Pierre Rivollet	Anne Marie Rosty Dupré
Geneviève Gallin-Lobell	Michel Amas
Emmanuelle Casanova	

Languages: French, English, Italian and German

SCP SCAPEL SCAPEL-GRAIL BONNAUD

Established in 1921

28, BOULEVARD PAUL PEYTRAL
13006 MARSEILLE, FRANCE
Telephone: 91.33.38.29 - 91.54.31.17
Telex: 441 413 F
Facsimile: 91.55.61.41

Commercial Law (Transport, Admiralty, Banking, Insurance), Civil Law (Property, Building and Town Planning), Family Law and Labor Law.

PARTNERS

CHRISTIAN SCAPEL, born Marseilles, France, 1945; admitted, 1970, France. *Education:* Diplomé I.E.P., Paris. Maître de Conférences à la Facultéde Droit et de Science Politique, d'Aix Marseille. Professeur à l'Institut de formation universitaire et de Recherche du transport aérien (IFURTA). Directeur du DESS Transport Aérien. Directeur de la Revue de Droit Français Commercial Maritime et Fiscal. Membre des Associations Françaises de Droit Aérien et de Droit Maritime. Administrateur de l'IMTM. *LANGUAGES:* French and English. *PRACTICE AREAS:* Commercial Law; Transportation Law; Maritime and Air Law.

RÉGINE SCAPEL-GRAIL, born Marseilles, France, 1943; admitted, 1966, France. Ancien membre du Conseil de l'Ordre des Avocats du barreau de Marseille. *LANGUAGES:* French and English. *PRACTICE AREAS:* Civil Law; Family Law; Banking Law; Labor Law.

(This Listing Continued)

JACQUES BONNAUD, born Marseilles, France, 1945; admitted, 1985, France. *Education:* Docteur en droit. Collaborateur du Dictionnaire Permanent du Droit des Affaires. Administrateur de l'IMTM. *LANGUAGES:* French and English. *PRACTICE AREAS:* Commercial Law; Transportation Law; Maritime Law.

JEAN-LOUIS BERGEL, born Marseilles, France, 1942; admitted, 1964, France. Agrégé des Facultés de Droit and Professeur à la Facultéde Droit et de Science Politique d'Aix Marseille. Président de l'Association Internationale de Méthodologie juridique (A.I.M.J.). *LANGUAGES:* French and English. *PRACTICE AREAS:* Civil Law; Property, Building and Town Planning Law.

ASSOCIATES

DOMINIQUE SARRAU-MICHEL, born Bône (Algérie), France, 1956; admitted, 1980, France.

CHRISTINE SCELLIER-FOURNIER, born Marseilles, France, 1959; admitted, 1985, France.

MICHEL-ROGER BERGEL, born 1970; admitted, 1994, France.

CONSULTANT

LOUIS SCAPEL, admitted, 1944, Marseille, France.

TREVES INTERNATIONAL LAW OFFICE

Avocats

Established in 1958

66, RUE SAINT-JACQUES
13006 MARSEILLE, FRANCE
Telephone: (33) 91.81.74.60
Telefax: (33) 91.37.69.12

French, EEC and International Law Practice.
Corporate Law, Company Law, Mergers and Acquisitions, Rent and Lease, Commercial Law, Taxation, Labour Law, International Contracts, International Private Law, Distributorship, Agency and Franchise Law, Foreign Investments, E.E.C. Law, Competition Law, Maritime Law, Aeronautical Law, Administrative Law, Environmental Law, Intellectual Property, Copyright, Arbitration, Conciliation and Litigation.
Firm also engaged in E.E.C., North American and Asian Practice.

FIRM PROFILE: The firm offers full range of services in business law. The client base includes individuals, small and medium-sized firms or industrial concerns located in the south of France and abroad. The law firm collaborates with a Notary's office and Accountant firm well known in Marseille.

MEMBERS OF FIRM

JACQUES TREVES, born Marseille, France, June 30, 1925; admitted, 1971, Marseille. *Education:* University of Aix-en-Provence; Polytechnic Notarial School of Paris. *Member:* Chambre Régionale d'Arbitrage Provence Alpes Côte-d'azur; Cour d'Arbitrage Européenne. *LANGUAGES:* French, Italian, Spanish.

ALBERT TREVES, born Marseille, France, October 20, 1958; admitted, 1990, Marseille. *Education:* University of Aix-en-Provence (Maître en Droit des Affaires). Author: Foreign Investments, Publications: Droit et Affaires C.E.E. International, L'Exportation Magazine, March-May, 1987; The Detection of the Difficulties of Companies, Publications: Dossier P.M.I., Ecosud, September-October, 1987. Lecturer, Constitutional and Administrative Law, Air Force Academy at Salon de Provence, 1981. Lecturer, Commercial, Fiscal, Labour Law and International Agreements, Chamber of Commerce, Marseille. *Member:* Cour d'Arbitrage Européenne; Centre Européen de Consultation et d'Assistance Juridique; International Department's Bureau of the French Association for Advocats in Business Law. *LANGUAGES:* French, English.

OF COUNSEL

JEAN DEBERGUE, born Marseille, France, July 25, 1924; admitted, 1951, Marseille. *Education:* University of Aix-en-Provence. *LANGUAGES:* French.

DANIÈLE CHALAND-GIOVANNONI, born Saint-Lo, France, May 7, 1954; admitted, 1986, Conseil Juridique et Fiscal et en Droit des Sociétés. *Education:* University of Paris I (D.E.S.S.); Orleans University (B.S. Political Science: I.E.P. of Paris). Lecturer: High School in Business Law, Grenoble University (1989-1991). *Member:* International Department Bureau of the French Association for Advocats in Business Law. *LANGUAGES:*

(This Listing Continued)

French, English. *PRACTICE AREAS:* Intellectual Property and Copyright Law.

CONSULTANTS

DIANE TREVES, born Marseille, France, May 16, 1967. *Education:* Notarial Law School, Marseille-Nice. *LANGUAGES:* French, English, Spanish, Italian.

CHRISTOPHE FOULON, born Marseille, France, April 20, 1959. *Education:* University of Aix-en-Provence (Maître en Droit des Affaires); Graduated of Higher Studies in International Trade, C.E.C.E. Marseille. Export Manager, Foulon & Partners. *LANGUAGES:* French, English.

Languages: French, English, Italian and Spanish

REFERENCES: Paribas Bank, Marseille; Commercial Chamber, Marseille.

CABINET CARLER

22, RUE MARÉCHAL JOFFRE
F-06000 NICE, FRANCE
Telephone: 33 93 88 88 96
Fax: 33 93 88 94 98

Stockholm, Sweden Office: Engelbrektsplan 2, S-114 34. Telephone: 46-8 6796360. Telex: 11900 CARLER S. Telefax: 46-8 6112605.
Gothenburg, Sweden Office: Engelbrektsgatan 28, S-411 37. Telephone: 46 31 18 02 50. Fax: 46 31 18 02 51.
Gävle, Sweden Office: P.O. Box 1346, S-801 38. Telephone: 46 26 12 51 30. Fax: 46 26 12 89 20.
Helsingborg, Sweden Office: Hamntorget 5, S-252 21. Telephone: 46-42.18 70 60. Telex: 721 40 Carler S. Telefax: 46.42.18 47 53.
Linköping, Sweden Office: Slattefors Herrgård, S-585 93. Telephone: 46-13 160350. Fax: 46-13 160355.
Paris, France Office: 36, rue Tronchet, F-75009. Telephone: 33-1 42661449. Telefax: 33-1 42665945.
Milan, Italy Office: Via Silvio Pellico 12, I-20121. Telephone: 39-2.86 09 68; 39-2.805 94 39. Telefax: 39-2.86 46 54 45.

International Business Law, Intellectual Property Law, European Community Law, Corporate, Competition and Administrative Law, Labor Law, Civil Litigation, Mergers and Acquisitions.

FIRM PROFILE: The firm was established in 1960 and offers services relating to International Business Law. The firm has 26 lawyers. Its offices are located in Stockholm, Gothenburg, Gävle, Helsingborg, Linkoping, Milan, Nice and Paris. Its objective is to improve the quality of business transactions thereby increasing the profitability of the client.

MEMBERS OF FIRM

JOHAN ROSENLUND, born 1936; admitted, 1971, Conseil Juridique; 1992, Avocat at Barreau de Nice. *Education:* LL.M. (Jur.kand.) 1962. District Court, 1963-1965. Private Legal Practice since 1965. *Member:* Swedish Bar Association; Barreau de Nice. *LANGUAGES:* Swedish, French and English.

NATHALIE COSSA, born 1964; Avocat at Barreau de Nice, 1993. *Education:* Maîtrise de droit; DEA. *LANGUAGES:* French and English.

(For Complete Biographical Data on all Personnel, see Professional Biographies at Stockholm, Sweden).

STUDIO LEGALE DE CAPOA - GUIDUCCI
ASSOCIATI - CABINET ORTS - AVO CAT

6 RUE DE LA TERRASSE
06300 NICE, FRANCE
Telephone: 33-93 80 92 32
Telefax: 33-93 80 63 72

Bologna, Italy Office: Via Albertazzi 22, 40137. Telephone: 39 61 343799; 346062; 348835. Telefax: 39 51 344125.
Brussels, Belgium Office: Square Ambirix 32, 1140. Telephone: 32-2-2308246.
Budapest, Hungary Office: Honved UT 38, 1065. Telephone: 36-1-1121683.
Milan, Italy Office: Corso Venezia 61. Telephone: 39-2-29510822. Telefax: 39-2-29510835.
Warsaw, Poland Office: Ul. Belwederska 14. Telephone: 48-22-412475. Telefax: 48-22-412475.

(This Listing Continued)

STUDIO LEGALE DE CAPOA - GUIDUCCI ASSOCIATI - CABINET ORTS - AVO CAT, Nice—Continued

G.E.I.E. with the firm Spitzweg & Partners, Munchen, Germany.

Los Angeles, California Associated Office: Forward & Dix, 2049 Century Park East, Suite 1200, 90067. Telephone: 310-785-2150. Telecopier: 310-785-2099.

International and Domestic Commercial Law, General and Civil Practice, Contracts, Litigation, Intellectual Property, EEC and Tax Law.

MEMBERS OF FIRM

Antonio de Capoa   Michel Orts
Elena Baroni   Faustin Ekollo

(For Complete Biographical Data on all Personnel, see Professional Biographies at Bologna, Italy)

EDEL - HAUTECOEUR - ROUCH - POGLIANO

2, RUE DU CONGRÈS
06046 NICE CEDEX 1, FRANCE
Telephone: (33) 93.16.36.90
Fax: (33) 93.16.36.92

Cagnes-sur-Mer, France Office: Villa Christine, Chemin des Petits Plans, 06800. Telephone: (33) 92.02.40.90. Fax: (33) 92.02.40.91.

General French Law Practice, Banking, Bankruptcy, Civil, Commercial, Construction, Corporate Law, Corporate Fraud, Family Law, Labor Law, Litigation, Real Estate Law.

FIRM PROFILE: The firm was established in 1985 and offers a full range of legal services. It is well known for Civil and Commercial Litigation. Its client base includes numerous banks, insurance companies, liquidators, notaries and real estate agents.

PARTNERS

ERIC MICHEL EDEL, born Toulouse, France, October 2, 1942; admitted, 1972, Nice. *Education:* Institut d'Etudes Politiques (Aix-en-Provence, 1964); Université d'Aix-en-Provence (Docteur d'Etat en Droit). Professor: Institut d'Etudes Politiques, Aix-en-Provence, 1964-1966; Université d'Aix-en-Provence, 1974-1976. Author: "Les Opérations à Terme de la Bourse des Valeurs," (Thèse). *Member:* Confédération Nationale des Avocats.

ALAIN HAUTECOEUR, born Cuffies, France, December 23, 1940; admitted, 1967, Draguignnan; 1985, Nice. *Education:* Université d'Aix-en-Provence (Licence en Droit Privé, 1964); Institut d'Etudes Politiques (Aix-en-Provence, 1964).

ANNIE ROUCH-POGLIANO, born Nice, France, August 15, 1949; admitted, 1982, Nice; 1988, Grasse. *Education:* Université de Nice (Licence en Droit Privé, 1975).

Languages: French, English, Italian and Spanish

CABINET PATRICK HERROU

Avocats au Barreau de Nice

Established in 1975

2 PLACE MASSÉNA
06000 NICE, FRANCE
Telephone: 33 93 62 33 80
Telefax: 33 93 62 32 29

Toulon, France Office: 126 rue des Remparis 83000. Telephone: 33 94 92 38 89.

General International Practice.

FIRM PROFILE: The firm was established in 1975 and offers a full range of legal services from two offices in Nice, (Alpes Maritimes) and Toulon (Var). It specializes in Tax law, Corporate, Business and Employment Law. The client base is South of France and Monaco in scope.

PATRICK YVES MARIE HERROU, born Coray, France, November 4, 1942; Avocat au Barreau de Nice, Ancien Conseil Juridique, Conseil Fiscal, Conseil en Droit des Sociétés; admitted, 1975. Ancien Inspecteur des Impôts. *Education:* Maîtrise es Sciences Economiques Faculté de Droit et Sciences Economiques Paris et Rennes: 1967. Ecole Nationale des Impôts

(This Listing Continued)

Paris: 1961-1966. *Member:* Commission Régionale des Conseils Juridiques près la Cour d'Appel (1975-1990); Association Nationale des Conseils Juridiques (Membre du Comité Directeur, 1989-1991, Vice-Président du Conseil Régional); Assemblée Permanente des Chambres des Professions Libérales (Conseil d'Administration, 1990); Chambre Régionale des Professions Libérales Provence-Côte d'Azur (Vice President, 1989); Chambre des Professions Libérales des Alpes Maritimes (Président, 1981-1991); Union des Anciens des Impôts; Association de Gestion Agréée des Alpes Maritimes (Administrateur, 1985); Chambre de Commerce et d'Industrie des Alpes Maritimes (Lecturer in Tax Law, 1992); Fédération Nationale du Droit de l'Entreprise (Lecturer in Commercial Law, 1992). *LANGUAGES:* French, English and Spanish. *PRACTICE AREAS:* French and International tax law; French Commercial and Corporate Law.

OF COUNSEL

CATHERINE GUITTARD, born Nice (France) 1965 Avocat au Barreau de Nice; admitted, 1994. *LANGUAGES:* French, English and Italian. *PRACTICE AREAS:* Trade Law; Civil Law.

CATHERINE JOSSERAND, born Tunis, Tunisia, 1961 Avocat au Barreau de Toulon; admitted, 1992. *LANGUAGES:* French, English, Spanish and Arabic. *PRACTICE AREAS:* Civil Law; Corporate Law.

LEGAL SUPPORT PERSONNEL

Janine Hassen-Herrou   Valérie Olivari

DONALD M. MANASSE

Established in 1986

2, RUE DU CONGRES
06000 NICE, FRANCE
Telephone: 93.16.36.80
Telefax: 93.16.36.81

Monte Carlo, Monaco Office: 4, Boulevard des Moulins. Telephone: 93.50.29.21. Telefax: 93.50.82.08.

General International Practice of Law.

DONALD M. MANASSE, born Milan, Italy, November 29, 1951; admitted, 1978, New York; 1979, Connecticut; 1986, Advocat, Nice. *Education:* Transylvania College (B.A., 1971); University of Missouri at Columbia (M.A., 1974); New York Law School (J.D., 1977). *Member:* Connecticut, New York State and American Bar Associations; International Bar Association; Compagnie des Conseils Juridiques; American Chamber of Commerce, Côte d'Azur Section (President, 1989, 1990); Monaco-U.S.A. Association; U.S. Trademark Association. *LANGUAGES:* English, Italian and French.

ASSOCIATES

CATHERINE TERRY, born France, May 7, 1958; admitted, 1991, Paris. *Education:* Paris (Doctorate in International Taxation, 1982). *Member:* American Chamber of Commerce (Côte d'Azur Section). *LANGUAGES:* French and English. *PRACTICE AREAS:* International Tax Law; Expatriate Tax Areas.

PATRICK RIZZO

Established in 1979

6, AVENUE DE VERDUN
06000 NICE, FRANCE
Telephone: 93.88.82.09
Fax: 93.87.59.92

Corporate and Business Law, International and National Tax Law, Accounting Services, Mergers and Acquisitions, Financial Transactions, Foundation and Liquidation of Companies, Structuring of Funds, Venture Capital, Management and Leveraged Buy-outs, National and Cross-border Leasing Transactions, Banking, International Law, Antitrust Law, Unfair Competition and Intellectual Property Rights Law, EEC Law, Real Estate Transactions, Penal Law, Common Law, Bankruptcy and International Bankruptcy, Labour Law, State/Political Affairs, European and International Law Practice.

FIRM PROFILE: Established in 1979, the firm has grown to have an international and especially a european vocation. It is particularly specialized in difficult and delicate affairs concerning Business Law, Penal Law, Common Law and Commercial Law.

(This Listing Continued)

Therefore the firm has some members who speak German, English and Italian.

The firm is working in collaboration with various firms established throughout the whole world.

DR. PATRICK RIZZO, born Nice, France; admitted, 1977, Nice. *Education:* University of Nice (Diploma Trustee Judicial). Consul of Austria. *Member:* International Association of Lawyers. *LANGUAGES:* French, English, Italian and German.

DR. JEAN-MICHEL RENUCCI, born Nice, France; admitted, 1990, Nice. *Education:* University of Nice. *LANGUAGES:* French and English. *PRACTICE AREAS:* Common Law; Business Law; Labour Law; International Law.

SCP WEISSBERG GAETJENS ZIEGENFEUTER

34, AVENUE HENRI MATISSE
06200 NICE, FRANCE
Telephone: (33) 93.18.83.50
Telecopier: (33) 93.18.83.51

Paris, France Office: 34, avenue Marceau, 75008. Telephone: (33) 1 47.20.22.48. Telecopier: (33) 1 47.20.21.59 and 47.20.21.64.

New York, New York Office: 270 Madison Avenue, 9th Floor, 10016. Telephone: (212) 545-4680. Telecopier: (212) 545-4675.

London, England Office: Chichester House, 278-283 High Holborn, WC1V 7HA. Telephone: (071) 242-2877. Telecopier: (071) 242-1431.

Toronto, Canada Office: 150 York Street, Suite 1902, Toronto, Ontario, M5H 355. Telephone: (416) 367-4100. Fax: (416) 367-0076.

General French and International Law Practice, Aviation and Maritime Law, Banking and Finance Law, Bankruptcy and Reorganization of Entreprises, Commercial Law, Competition Law, Corporate Law, Distribution, Franchise and License Agreements, European Community Law, Intellectual and Industrial Property, International Contracts, International and French Taxation, International Private Law including Inheritance Estates, Labor Law, Real Estate Transactions and Financing.

MEMBERS OF FIRM

Gerd O. Ziegenfeuter	*Sophie Dagannaud*
Kenneth Weissberg	*Leila Saber*
Kay Gaetjens	*Nicolas Flachet*
Robert H. Manley (Also	*Mark Zeindler*
Practicing Individually, Paris, France)	

OF COUNSEL

Sidney D. Bluming	*Robert R. Amsterdam*
Stephen Mayer	

Languages: French, English, German, and Persian

(For Complete Biographical Data on all Personnel, see Professional Biographies at Paris, France)

ROY GARY SPITZ

2 RUE DU CONGRÈS
06000 NICE, FRANCE
Telephone: (33) 93.16.36.90
Fax: (33) 93.16.36.92

General French and International Law Practice.

ROY GARY SPITZ, born Johannesburg, South Africa, May 16, 1966; admitted, 1991, Nice. *Education:* University of Nice (Licence en Droit, 1988; Maîtrise en Droit Privé-Droit des Affaires, 1989); Aix-en-Provence (CAPA, 1991). Author: "Monaco Law and Practice" in "Tax Havens Encyclopaedia", Butterworths, London; "English Law and Limitation of Liability Clauses in International Contracts." Professor of International Taxation, University of Southern Europe (Monaco). *Member:* International Bar Association. *LANGUAGES:* English and French.

ADER, JOLIBOIS & ASSOCIES

Established in 1962
26, BOULEVARD RASPAIL
75007 PARIS, FRANCE
Telephone: (1) 45.44.10.33
Cable Address: "Broderjo-Paris"
Telex: BRODERJ 201.482 F
Telefax: 45.48.80.27

General Practice. Corporation, Labor and Commercial Law. International Law. Arbitration, Press, Copyright, Financing, and Banking.

FIRM PROFILE: *The firm was established in 1962 and offers a full range of legal services with a staff of nearly 30 partners and other lawyers located in Paris.*

The firm is a general practice mainly involved in national and international corporate and commercial law.

Its principal fields of activity range from providing general legal advice to companies and their management to more complex matters including mergers and acquisitions, take-overs, foreign investment in France, agency, distribution and franchising agreements and EEC law.

The firm has also developed specialist units operating in banking, construction law, employment law, press and copyright law and unfair competition.

In addition Ader, Jolibois & Associés covers contentious work, mainly in national or international commercial disputes, whether in court or by arbitration, including arbitration submitted to the Court of Arbitration of the International Chamber of Commerce.

The firm is also a member of "Legalliance," a European Grouping of law firms established in various European cities such as London, Madrid, Barcelona, Valencia, Brussels, Berlin, Cologne, Frankfurt, Leipzig, Milano, Padova, Bologna and the Hague, which offers European coordination and cooperation through a single point of contact.

MEMBERS OF FIRM

HENRI ADER, born Paris, France, April 13, 1928; admitted, 1953, Paris. *Education:* Paris University Law School (Licentiate in Law, 1948; D.E.S., Public and Private Law, 1949); Paris Institut d'Etudes Politiques (1950); Harvard Law School (LL.M., 1951). Secretary, Conference du Stage, 1956-1957. *Member:* Paris Bar Association (Member, President-elect, 1989; President, 1990-1991); Association of Ancient Auditors of the Academy of International Law of The Hague. *LANGUAGES:* French and English. *PRACTICE AREAS:* Civil Litigation; Press Law; Family Law.

CHARLES JOLIBOIS, born Paris, France, October 4, 1928; admitted, 1953, Paris. *Education:* Paris University Law School (Licentiate in Law, 1948; D.E.S., Public and Private Law, 1949); Paris Institut d'Etudes Politiques (1950); Harvard Law School (LL.M., 1951). Secretary, Conference du Stage, 1955-1956. *LANGUAGES:* French and English. *PRACTICE AREAS:* Business Law; Commercial Law; Corporate Law.

GÉRARD DELAGRANGE, born February 3, 1939; admitted, 1965, Paris. *Education:* Paris University Law School (Licentiate in Law, 1963). Secretary, Conference du Stage, 1955-1956. *LANGUAGES:* French. *PRACTICE AREAS:* Computers and Software; Construction Law; Agency and Distributorships.

OLIVIER ROUX, born May 15, 1940; admitted, 1965, Paris. *Education:* Paris University Law School (Licentiate in Law; 1961; D.E.S., Private Law, 1962); Paris Institut d'Etudes Politiques (1963). First Secretary, Conference du Stage Supreme Court Lawyers, 1968-1969. *LANGUAGES:* French and English. *PRACTICE AREAS:* Business Law; Agency and Distributorships; Litigation.

MARC-NOËL LOUVET, born December 23, 1945; admitted, 1968, Paris. *Education:* Paris University Law School (Licentiate in Law, 1967); Paris Institut d'Etudes Politiques (1968). *LANGUAGES:* French. *PRACTICE AREAS:* Press Law; Labor Legislation; Communications and Media.

PIERRE LACAILLE, born March 11, 1939; admitted, 1966, Paris. *Education:* Paris University Law School (Licentiate in Law, 1966); Ecole Superieure de Commerce (1964); Deutsch-Franzoesische Handelskammer (1963); Paris Institut d'Etudes Politiques. *LANGUAGES:* French and German. *PRACTICE AREAS:* Commercial Dispute Resolution; Press Law; Labor Relations.

MICHEL LACORNE, born March 28, 1947; admitted, 1972, Paris. *Education:* Paris University Law School (Licentiate in Law, 1971; D.E.S., Public Law Major Field, E.E.C. Law, 1972). *LANGUAGES:* French and

(This Listing Continued)

ADER, JOLIBOIS & ASSOCIES, Paris—Continued

English. *PRACTICE AREAS:* Antitrust and Trade Regulations; Banks and Banking; Business Law.

GILLES DE MAILLARD, born September 1, 1945; admitted, 1973, Paris. *Education:* Paris University Law School (Licentiate in Law, 1969; D.E.S., Private Law, 1979). *PRACTICE AREAS:* Leases and Leasing; Bankruptcy; Construction Law.

GEORGES PETIT, born December 22, 1951; admitted, 1980, Paris. *Education:* Paris University Law School (Maîtrise, Commercial Law, 1977; D.E.A., Commercial Law, 1979). *PRACTICE AREAS:* Commercial Law; Communications and Media; Labor and Employment Law.

NATALIE CREISSELS, born April 16, 1958; admitted, 1981, Paris. *Education:* Paris University Law School (Maîtrise, Private Law, 1980; D.E.A., Criminal Law, 1981). *PRACTICE AREAS:* Labor and Employment; Litigation; Property Law.

JACQUES ROHAUT, born June 8, 1950; admitted, 1978, Paris. *Education:* Paris University Law School (Licentiate in Law, 1976; D.E.S., Legal Profession, 1978). *LANGUAGES:* French and English. *PRACTICE AREAS:* Art Law; Commercial Law; Construction Law.

SENIOR ASSOCIATES

JEAN-LUC DONNADOU, born May 30, 1952; admitted, 1977, Paris. *Education:* Paris University Law School (Maîtrise, Private Law, 1975; D.E.A., Commercial Law, 1976; Graduate in French History, 1979). *LANGUAGES:* French.

STÉPHANE LATASTE, born August 31, 1960; admitted, 1985, Paris. *Education:* Paris University Law School (Maîtrise, Private Law, 1984; D.E.A., Copyright Law, 1985). Secretary, Conference du Stage, 1987-1988. *LANGUAGES:* French and English.

YVES VIVIEZ DE CHATTELARD, born October 22, 1962; admitted, 1989, Paris. *Education:* Montpellier University Law School (Maîtrise, Private Law, 1985). *LANGUAGES:* French and English.

SOPHIE THOMAS-PLA, born October 20, 1966; admitted, 1990, Paris. *Education:* Paris University Law School (Maîtrise, Private and Commercial Law, 1988; D.E.S.S., Commercial Law, 1989). *LANGUAGES:* French and English.

BASILE ADER, born March 8, 1961; admitted, 1988, Paris. *Education:* Paris University Law School (Maîtrise, Private Law; D.E.S.S., Law and Administration of Communication). Secretary, Conference du Stage, 1993—. *Member:* Association des Secretaries et anciens, Secretaries du la Conference; Association du Droit du la Communication (Paris II). *LANGUAGES:* French and English.

HUGHES BERRY, born August 2, 1962; admitted, 1993, Paris. *Education:* Paris University Law School (Maîtrise, Private Law; Maîtrise, Public Law; D.E.S.S., Intellectual Property; D.E.A., International Law). *LANGUAGES:* French, English and Spanish.

JOCELYNE CLERC-KACZMAREK, born January 5, 1956; admitted, 1984, Paris. *Education:* Paris University Law School (Maîtrise, Private Law, 1979; D.E.S.S., Company Law, 1980). *LANGUAGES:* French and English.

NATHALIE KALESKI, born February 14, 1961; admitted, 1993, Paris. *Education:* Sorbonne (Maîtrise de Lettres Classiques, 1983); Paris Institut d'Etudes Politiques (1985); Paris University Law School (Maîtrise, Private Law, 1990; D.E.A., Private Law, 1992). *LANGUAGES:* English.

ALLEN & OVERY

1 AVENUE FRANKLIN D. ROOSEVELT
75008 PARIS, FRANCE
Telephone: (33 1) 49 53 06 37
Telex: 651079
Facsimile: (33 1) 49 53 91 52

London, England Office: One New Change, EC4M 9QQ. Telephone: 0171 330 3000. Facsimile: 0171 330 9999.
Beijing, China Office: Suite 3204, Jing Guang Centre, Hu Jia Lou, Chaoyang District, 100020. Telephone: (86 1) 501 4681. Facsimile: (86 1) 501 4682.
Brussels, Belgium Office: Rue de la Loi 99, Box 8, 1040. Telephone: (32 2) 230 27 91. Facsimile (32 2) 230 66 13.

(This Listing Continued)

Budapest, Hungary Office: Mádach Trade Center, Mádach Imre utca 13-14, H-1075. Telephone: (361) 268 1511. Facsimile: (361) 268 1515.
Dubai, United Arab Emirates Office: 501 Al Futtaim Tower,P.O. Box 3251, Deira. Telephone: (971 4) 282296. Facsimile: (971 4) 212860.
Frankfurt, Germany Office: Taunusanlage 11, 11th Floor, 60329. Telephone: (49 69) 242 6120. Facsimile: (49 69) 242 61220.
Hong Kong Office: 9th Floor, Three Exchange Square, 8 Connaught Place. Telephone: (852) 2840 1282. Telex: 68757. Facsimile: (852) 2840 0515.
Madrid, Spain Office: Antonio Maura 7, 6°, 28014. Telephone: (34 1) 521 2654. Facsimile: (34 1) 523 0458.
Moscow, Russia Office: 9 ul Tverskaya, Entrance No 5, 8th Floor, 103009. Telephone: (7 501) 940 4500. Facsimile: (7 501) 940 4501.
New York Office: Swiss Bank Tower, 10 East 50th Street, 10022. Telephone (1-212) 754 3340. Facsimile: (1-212) 754 7903.
Prague, Czech Republic Office: Jindřišská 34, 110 00 Prague 1. Telephone: (42 2) 2410 3317. Facsimile: (42 2) 2410 3235.
Singapore Office: 20 Raffles Place #08-03, Ocean Towers, 0104. Telephone: (65) 533 0988. Facsimile: (65) 533 1322.
Tokyo, Japan Office: NSE Building, 5th Floor, 1-7-1 Kanda Jinbo-cho, Chiyoda-ku Tokyo 101. Telephone (81 3) 3259 9898. Facsimile (81 3) 3259 9888.
Warsaw, Poland Office: ul. Kopernika 17, IV Floor, 00-359. Telephone: (48 22) 262 226. Facsimile: (48 22) 262 360.

Firm engaged in EC Law (including Antitrust and Dumping), International, Commercial and English Practice.

RESIDENT PARTNERS

David Sutton   **Paul Crook**
                    Andrew Wilson

(For Complete List of Firm Personnel, see Professional Biographies at London England).

CABINET AMALIEGADE NO. 42

Established in 1947

36, RUE TRONCHET
75009 PARIS, FRANCE
Telephone: 1-42 66 14 49
Telefax: 1-42 66 59 45

Copenhagen, Denmark Office: Amaliegade No. 42, DK-1256. Telephone: 33 11 33 99. Telefax: 33 32 46 25.

Firm engaged in International Law Practice and authorized to appear before the French courts only accompanied by a French Avocat.

FIRM PROFILE: Advokaterne Amaliegade 42, is a medium sized law firm concentrating on cross-frontier legal advice. We believe that the client shall decide what problems are important and our ambition is to offer solutions whether the problems concern his private life or that of his business. We consider that efficient advice cannot be given without a full understanding of the business of the client and his cultural background.

RESIDENT PARTNER

PATRICE CARON, born Rouen, France, August 11, 1951. *Education:* University of Rouen (Licence droit privé, 1973); University of Copenhagen (1974); University of Paris I (Certificate CUECE and DES Droit des Communautés Européennes, 1975). Admitted as advocate at the Bars in Paris and in Denmark. *Member:* A.I.J.A.; Paris Bar; Danish Bar Association. *LANGUAGES:* French, Danish and English. *PRACTICE AREAS:* Banking; Finance; Corporate Law; EEC Law; Mergers and Acquisitions; Tax Law.

(For complete biographical data on all associates, see biographical card: Copenhagen, Denmark).

ARCHIBALD ANDERSEN ASSOCIATION D'AVOCATS'

Avocats à la Cour
Established in 1883

TOUR GAN-CEDEX 13
16, PLACE DE L'IRIS
92082 PARIS LA DÉFENSE 2, FRANCE
Telephone: (33-1) 42.91.07.00
Telecopier: (33-1) 42.91.08.00

Lyon, France Office: Tour Crédit Lyonnais, 129 rue Servient, 69431.
Telephone: (33) 78.63.72.00. Telecopier: (33) 78.62.91.57.

French Tax Law, European Community Law and Antitrust Law, International Tax Law, Corporate and Commercial Law, Banking and Finance Law, Advertising Law, High Technology Law, Pharmaceutical Law, Worldwide Tax Efficiency Review, Implementation of Tax Planning and Monitoring Systems, Expatriate Policy Development (Labor, Social Security and Income Tax Laws), Establishment of In-House Legal and Tax Departments, Legal Analysis, Intragroup Transfer-Pricing Policy, Management Fee Contracts, Corporate Reorganizations, Joint Venture Structures, International Contracts, Intellectual and Industrial Property, International Services on a Contract Basis, Arbitration and Litigation, Insolvency Law, Government Services, Real Estate and Notarial Law, Management of Personal Assets.

MEMBERS OF FIRM

SIMONE AICARDI, born Paris, France, March 22, 1932; admitted, 1973, Paris. Education: University of Paris (Docteur en Droit, 1954); Diplôme de l'Institut de Droit Comparé (1954). (S.G. Archibald). LANGUAGES: English, French, Italian and Spanish. PRACTICE AREAS: General Corporate Law; Commercial Law; Competition Law; Pharmaceutical Law; Labor Law.

HERVÉ BIDAUD, born Nantes, France, February 17, 1950; admitted, 1980, France. Education: ESSEC (1974); Bar Exam (1975). Lecturer, International Taxation, ESSEC. Member: International Fiscal Association (I.F.A.). (Arthur Andersen International). LANGUAGES: French, English and German. PRACTICE AREAS: Tax Law; International Law; Real Estate Law.

PATRICK BIGNON, born Neuilly, France, August 8, 1954; admitted, 1986, France. Education: I.E.P. Paris (1976); Maîtrise de droit (1977); Certificat d'Aptitude à la Profession de Notaire (1984). (Arthur Andersen International). LANGUAGES: English and French. PRACTICE AREAS: Corporate Law.

ALAIN BRIOTTET, born Dijon, France, February 22, 1952; admitted, 1985, France. Education: Licence de droit (1975); Law Faculty of Dijon, France (D.E.S.S. of tax law). Senior Lecturer, Aix and Dijon Universities. (Arthur Andersen International). LANGUAGES: English and French. PRACTICE AREAS: Tax Law; Business Law.

RODNEY W. BURTON, born Detroit, Michigan, USA, November 1, 1943; admitted, 1970, Indiana; 1971, Ohio; 1982, Paris. Education: Purdue University (B.S., 1966). (S.G. Archibald). LANGUAGES: English and French. PRACTICE AREAS: U.S. and International Tax Law.

KATHIE D. CLARET, born New York, New York, USA, April 7, 1951; admitted, 1976, New York; 1980, Paris. Education: Harvard University (A.B., 1972); New York University (J.D., 1975). (S.G. Archibald). LANGUAGES: English, French and Russian. PRACTICE AREAS: General Corporate Law; Commercial Law; Intellectual Property Law; Arbitration.

SYLVIE DARIOSECQ, born Paris, France, August 17, 1956; admitted, 1979, Paris; 1983, New York. Education: University of Paris (Maîtrise de Droit Privé, 1977; D.E.A. de Droit Privé, 1978; D.E.A. de Droit International, 1979); Columbia University (LL.M., 1982). (S.G. Archibald). LANGUAGES: English and French. PRACTICE AREAS: General Corporate and Commercial Law.

FRÉDÉRIC DONNEDIEU DE VABRES, born Boulogne-Billancourt, France, January 2, 1956; admitted, 1988, Paris. Education: University of Paris (Graduated, 1981). (Arthur Andersen International). LANGUAGES: English and French. PRACTICE AREAS: Tax Law.

JEAN-PIERRE FIQUET, born Amiens, France, January 27, 1946; admitted, 1972, Paris. Education: University of Paris (Licence en Droit, 1967); University of Lille (D.E.S. de Droit Privé, 1969). (Arthur Andersen International). LANGUAGES: English and French. PRACTICE AREAS: Tax

(This Listing Continued)

Law; Real Estate Taxation Law; Tax Aspects of Mergers and Acquisitions Law; Private International Law.

CLAUDE GOLDMAN, born Paris, France, June 15, 1950; admitted, 1985, Paris. Education: University of Paris (D.E.S. de Sciences Economiques, 1973; Maîtrise de Droit des Affaires, 1982). (S.G. Archibald). LANGUAGES: English and French. PRACTICE AREAS: Banking Law; Finance Law; International Arbitration Law.

ANDRÉ GOURMELEN, born Achères, France, February 6, 1942; admitted, 1969, Paris. Education: University of Paris (D.E.S. in Economic Sciences); National Tax School. Former Lecturer, International Taxation, ESSEC. Member: Conseil de l'Ordre des Avocats, Hauts-de-Seine Bar Vice President Juri-Avenir - Institut des avocats conseils fiscaux; International Fiscal Association (I.F.A.). (Arthur Andersen International). LANGUAGES: English and French. PRACTICE AREAS: Tax Law.

THOMAS G. JAHN, born Tübingen, Germany, January 13, 1951; admitted, 1982, Hamburg and Paris; 1984, New York. Education: Universities of Heidelberg, Munich, Freiburg (First State Law Examination, 1974; Second State Law Examination, Hamburg, 1978); New York University (M.C.J., 1980). (S.G. Archibald). LANGUAGES: English, French and German. PRACTICE AREAS: General Corporate Law; Commercial Law; Mergers and Acquisitions Law; Joint Ventures.

XAVIER JASPAR, born Cotonou, Bénin, February 25, 1957; admitted, 1985, Paris. Education: University of Paris (D.E.S.S. de Droit des Affaires, 1981). (S.G. Archibald). LANGUAGES: English and French. PRACTICE AREAS: General Corporate Law; Commercial Law; Group Reorganizations; Mergers and Acquisitions Law.

KRISTINE E. KARSTEN, born Milwaukee, Wisconsin, USA, July 3, 1952; admitted, 1978, Illinois; 1981, Paris; 1985, New York. Education: Denison University (B.A., 1974); University of Michigan (J.D., 1977). (S.G. Archibald). LANGUAGES: English and French. PRACTICE AREAS: High-Tech and Computer Law; New Technologies Law; Project Financing; Construction Law.

YANN DE KERGOS, born Boulogne-Billancourt, France, April 18, 1951; admitted, 1983, Paris. Education: DES de droit privé - Maîtrise de droit privé - Certificat d'Etudes fiscales de la Fondation nationale pour le droit de l'entreprise. Author, book on tax aspects of software industry. French report on IFA congress, Amsterdam, 1988. Tax treatment of computer software. (Arthur Andersen International). LANGUAGES: English and French. PRACTICE AREAS: Tax Law.

HERVÉ LEHERISSEL, born Paris, France, May 7, 1953; admitted, 1991, Paris. Education: I.E.P. Paris (1973) - Licence en Droit; University of Paris II (1974); E.N.A. (1978). (Arthur Andersen International). LANGUAGES: French and English. PRACTICE AREAS: Tax Law; Public Law.

ANTOINE MORTEROL, born June 6, 1959; admitted, 1987, Paris. Education: University of Paris II (D.E.A. in Tax Law). (Arthur Andersen International). LANGUAGES: English and French. PRACTICE AREAS: Tax Law; International Mergers and Acquisitions.

LIONEL NENTILLE, born Lyon, France, November 30, 1956; admitted, 1987, Paris. Education: Lyon University III (Law Doctorate, 1981). Lecturer, ESSEC, Business Law School. (Arthur Andersen International). LANGUAGES: English, French and Spanish. PRACTICE AREAS: Tax Law; Real Estate Taxation Law; Financial Tax Law; Wealth Tax.

NICOLE POIRIER, born Paris, France, February 17, 1952; admitted, 1978, Paris. Education: Institut d'Etudes Politiques, Paris (1977); University of Paris (D.E.A., Droit des Affaires et Droit du Travail et de la Sécurité Sociale, 1976 and 1977). (S.G. Archibald). LANGUAGES: English and French. PRACTICE AREAS: General Litigation; Labor Law; Real Estate Law.

XAVIER DE SARRAU, born Toulouse, France, December 11, 1950. Education: H.E.C. (Doctorate in Taxation Law, 1973). (Arthur Andersen International). LANGUAGES: English, French and Spanish. PRACTICE AREAS: Tax Law; Private International Law.

BRUNO SCHRIMPF, born Dinard, France, July 31, 1958; admitted, 1984, Paris. Education: Institut Français de Presse (Licence, 1980); University of Paris (D.E.A., Private Law, 1982). (S.G. Archibald). LANGUAGES: English and French. PRACTICE AREAS: General Litigation; Commercial Law; Banking Law; Bankruptcy; Real Estate Law.

SOSTHÈNE DE VILMORIN, born Boulogne-Billancourt, France, April 14, 1933; admitted, 1957, Paris. Education: University of Paris (Licencié en Droit, 1958). Member: International Bar Association (SGP; Com-

(This Listing Continued)

ARCHIBALD ANDERSEN ASSOCIATION D'AVOCATS',
Paris—Continued

mittee E Banks; SBL; Former Chairman, Committee 20, Cultural Property); International Law Association (French Delegate to international Cultural Hertiage Law Committee). (S.G. Archibald). *LANGUAGES:* English and French. *PRACTICE AREAS:* Banking and Financial Markets; Cultural Property; Real Estate.

ALEXANDER P. WILSON, born London, England, July 6, 1939; admitted, 1965, Solicitor; 1980, Paris. *Education:* The Queen's College, Oxford (B.A., 1961). (S.G. Archibald). *LANGUAGES:* English and French. *PRACTICE AREAS:* General Corporate Law; Commercial Law.

ASSOCIATES

CLAIRE ACARD (Associate Tax - Arthur Andersen International).

JEAN-PASCAL AMOROS (Associate Tax - Arthur Andersen International).

LIONEL BENANT (Associate Tax - Arthur Andersen International).

LUCIE A. CARSWELL (Associate Legal - S.G. Archibald).

FRÉDÉRIC CHESNAIS (Associate Legal - Arthur Andersen International).

BÉNÉDICTE CHESNELONG (Associate Legal - S.G. Archibald).

ANNE COLMET-DAAGE (Associate Tax - Arthur Andersen International).

HERVÉ-ANTOINE COUDERC (Associate Tax - Arthur Andersen International).

ALAIN DECOMBE (Associate Legal - S.G. Archibald).

MARIE-THÉRÈSE DELIGNAT-LAVAUD (Associate Legal - Arthur Andersen International).

JEAN-PAUL DEMANGE (Associate Legal - Arthur Andersen International).

FLORENCE DEDIEU (Associate Legal - Arthur Andersen International).

DENIS FONTAINE-BESSET (Associate Tax - Arthur Andersen International).

ERIC FOUREL (Associate Tax - Arthur Andersen International).

YVELINE GALIEN-LEBRET (Associate Tax - Arthur Andersen International).

CHARLES GRANT (Not admitted in France; Associate Legal - S.G. Archibald).

JOËLLE HAELLING (Associate Legal - S.G. Archibald).

JEAN-NOËL IMBERT (Associate Tax - Arthur Andersen International).

DIANE JUZAITIS (Associate Tax - Arthur Andersen International).

BRUNO KERN (Associate Legal - Arthur Andersen International).

GILLIAN LEMAIRE (Not admitted in France; Associate Legal - S.G. Archibald).

KIRSTEN MCDONOUGH (Associate Legal - Arthur Andersen International).

SYLVIE MAGNEN (Associate Tax - Arthur Andersen International).

VÉRONIQUE MAILLEY (Associate Tax - Arthur Andersen International).

VÉRONIQUE MILLISCHER (Associate Tax - Arthur Andersen International).

MARIE-HÉLÈNE RAFFIN (Associate Tax - Arthur Andersen International).

NORO-LANTO RAVISY (Associate Tax - Arthur Andersen International).

VALÉRIE RAYNAUD (Associate Legal - S.G. Archibald).

MARK F. RICHARDSON (Associate Legal - S.G. Archibald).

ARNAUD DE ROUCY (Associate Tax - Arthur Andersen International).

(This Listing Continued)

CHRISTY RUSSELLO (Associate Tax - Arthur Andersen International).

ROLAND SCHNEIDER (Associate Tax - Arthur Andersen International).

JOSEPH J. SMALLHOOVER (Associate Legal - S.G. Archibald).

SABINE SMITH-VIDAL (Associate Legal - S.G. Archibald).

REBECCA SOUTHGATE (Associate Tax - Arthur Andersen International).

MONIQUE TARRERE (Associate Legal - S.G. Archibald).

BRIGITTE VERDIERRE (Associate Legal - S.G. Archibald).

OLIVIER VERGNIOLLE (Associate Tax - Arthur Andersen International).

Languages: French, English, German, Russian, Spanish and Italian

---

ARMAND, BOEDELS ET ASSOCIES

Avocats au Barreau de Paris

38, AVENUE HOCHE
75008 PARIS, FRANCE
Telephone: (1) 45 61 57 57
Telecopier: (1) 42 56 43 36

General and International Law Practice.

MEMBERS OF FIRM

GABRIEL ARMAND, born Setubal, Portugal, May 30, 1942; admitted, 1967, Paris. *Education:* Ecole Supérieure des Sciences Economiques et Commerciales (Diplôme, 1967); University of Paris (Maîtrise en Droit, 1967). *Member:* International Bar Association (Member, Committee on Commercial Banking, Section on Business Law). *LANGUAGES:* French, English and Portuguese.

JACQUES SIMON BOEDELS, born Paris, France, July 7, 1943; admitted, 1972, Paris. *Education:* Institut d'Etudes Politiques de Paris (Diplome, 1966); University of Paris (Maîtrise en Droit, 1968; D.E.S., 1970). *LANGUAGES:* French, English, German, Dutch and Spanish.

RUPERT BERNARD EDMUND WINDELER, born London, England, February 1, 1957; admitted, 1980, England and Wales; 1989, Paris. *Education:* Trinity College, Cambridge (French and Russian Languages, 1976; Law, 1978); Institute of European Studies, Free University of Brussels (Licence Speciale en Droit Europeen, 1979). *LANGUAGES:* English, French and Russian.

CHRISTOPHE DEVEAU, born Mantes, France, January 27, 1956; admitted, 1984, Paris. *Education:* University of Paris I (Maîtrise en Droit, 1980; D.E.A. in European Common Market Law, 1982). *Member:* EUROLEX; UAE. *LANGUAGES:* French and English.

FRANÇOIS DE GRANDMAISON, born Neuilly-Sur-Seine, France, July 3, 1962; admitted, 1992, France. *Education:* University of Paris II, ASSAS (Laureat de la Faculté; D.E.S. in Taxation Law). *LANGUAGES:* French and English.

HÉLÈNE DE SAINT GERMAIN-SAVIER, born Paris, France, December 18, 1965; admitted, 1990, France. *Education:* University of Paris II, ASSAS (Maîtrise en Droit; D.E.A., Droit des Affaires et de Droit économique. *LANGUAGES:* French and English.

ANNE MARICHEZ, born September 27, 1964; admitted, 1994, Paris. *Education:* University of Paris II (Maîtrise en Droit International et en Droit Européen, 1985); University of Paris I (Diplôme d'Etudes Approfondies-Droits Anglais et Nord-Américain des Affaires, 1986); New York University School of Law (LL.M., Corporate Law, 1989). Fulbright Scholar. *LANGUAGES:* French and English.

SHAILA-ANN RAO, born London, England, May 12, 1967; admitted, 1993, England and Wales (Not admitted in France). *Education:* University of Warwick (LL.B., Honours, 1989); College of Law (Law Society Final Exam, Honours, 1990). *Member:* Law Society of England and Wales. *LANGUAGES:* English and French.

MARIE-THÉRÈSE ARMAND-ALONSO, born Paris, France, May 28, 1967; admitted, 1993, Paris. *Education:* University of Paris II, ASSAS (Maîtrise en Droit Public et Maîtrise en Droit Privé; D.E.A. en Finances Publiques et Fiscalité). *LANGUAGES:* French, Spanish and English.

(This Listing Continued)

CATHERINE LECLERCQ, born Paris, France, July 19, 1966; admitted, 1994, Paris. *Education:* University of Paris V (Maîtrise en Droit des Affaires; D.E.S.S. in Tax Law). *LANGUAGES:* French, English and German.

GABRIEL BALLIF, born Paris, France, September 13, 1964; admitted, 1994, Paris. *Education:* University of Paris-Sorbonne (Licence d'Histoire, 1987); University of Panthéon-ASSAS (D.E.A. de Droit International Privé, 1993). *LANGUAGES:* French, English and German.

Languages: Dutch, English, French, German, Italian, Portuguese, Russian and Spanish

---

ASA - AVOCATS ASSOCIES

44, RUE FRANÇOIS 1ER
75008 PARIS, FRANCE
Telephone: (1) 44.43.48.88
Fax: (1) 40.70.18.32 / 44.43.81.60

Strasbourg Office: 22, Rue du Général de Castelnau, B.P. 395, 67010. Telephone: 88.56.56.49. Fax: 88.76.73.55. Telex: 890 229 F Asavoca.

Arbitration, Bank Law, International, Commercial Law, Taxation, Finance Law, General Practice.

MEMBERS OF FIRM

DOMINIQUE SCHMIDT, born Strasbourg, France, June 5, 1942; admitted, 1969, Strasbourg. *Education:* University of Strasbourg. Professeur Agrégé à la Faculté de Droit et des Sciences Politiques de Strasbourg. Author: "Les droits de la minorité dans la Société Anonyme"; "Droit des Sociétés Anonymes et des Sociétés à responsabilité limitée," with Mr. Ph. Gramling. *Member:* Association Droit et Commerce (President). *LANGUAGES:* French, English and German. *PRACTICE AREAS:* Securities; Stock Exchange; Finance Law; Company Law.

FRIEDRICH NIGGEMANN, born Frechen, Germany, September 18, 1946; admitted, 1975, Germany; 1986, France. *Education:* University of Cologne, Germany (1970); Strasbourg (Referendar, 1971). *Member:* Deutsche Institution für Schiedsgerichtswesen; International Bar Association. *LANGUAGES:* French, English and German. *PRACTICE AREAS:* Arbitration; International Commercial and Trade Law; Investments.

HUBERT ANDRES, born Strasbourg, France, November 20, 1950; admitted, 1976, France. *Education:* University of Strasbourg. *LANGUAGES:* French, German and English. *PRACTICE AREAS:* Banking Law; General Practice.

DOMINIQUE DOISE, born Basingstoke, United Kingdom, July 31, 1949; admitted, 1972, Paris. *Education:* University of Strasbourg. Contributor: Revue de Droit des Affaires Internationales, International Business Law Journal. *Member:* International Bar Association. *LANGUAGES:* French and English. *PRACTICE AREAS:* Banking Law.

PHILIPPE MATHURIN, born Paris, France, September 22, 1962; admitted, 1988, Paris. *Education:* University of Paris II. *LANGUAGES:* French and Spanish. *PRACTICE AREAS:* Banking Law; General Practice.

PASCALE TOLLITTE, born Laimont, France, May 5, 1962; admitted, 1990, Paris. *LANGUAGES:* French and Spanish. *PRACTICE AREAS:* General Practice; Banking.

XAVIER DE RYCK, born Elbeuf, France, May 16, 1966; admitted, 1991, Strasbourg. *PRACTICE AREAS:* Intellectual and Industrial Property; Transport Law.

THIERRY GONTARD, born Lyons, France, November 10, 1962; admitted, 1988, Paris. *Education:* University of Canterbury (Law, 1985); Faculté de droit (Maitrise, 1986; DESS, 1987); CFPA (CAPA, 1987). Co-Author: "Les Raltions Financiéres Avec l'Etranger," 1990, GLN, Joly Editions; "Joint Ventures in France," part of book "Joint Ventures in Europe," 1991, Butterworths. Chargé d'enseignement Université de Paris (1989—). *LANGUAGES:* English. *PRACTICE AREAS:* Stock Exchange Rules; Mergers and Acquisitions; Corporation Law; Foreign Investment in France.

ASHURST MORRIS CRISP

Established in 1990

8, RUE CLÉMENT MAROT
PARIS 75008, FRANCE
Telephone: (33-1) 47 20 0088
Fax: (33-1) 47 20 0093

London, England Office: Broadwalk House, 5 Appold Street, EC2A 2HA. Telephone: 0171-638-1111. Telex: 887067. Fax: 0171-972-7990.
Brussels, Belgium Office: Avenue Louise 65, 1050. Telephone: (32-2) 537 6895. Fax: (32-2) 537 4353.
Tokyo, Japan Office: Kioicho Building, 8th Floor, 3-12 Kioicho, Chiyoda-ku, 102. Telephone: (81-3) 5276 5900. Fax: (81-3) 5276-5922.
New Delhi, India Office: 6 Aurangzeb Road D-202, 110011. Telephone: (91 11) 301 4054. Facsimile: (91 11) 301 4089.

Firm engaged in French, English and General International practice.

RESIDENT PARTNERS

C.D. Crosthwaite   **T. Forschbach**

BAKER & McKENZIE

32 AVENUE KLEBER
75116 PARIS, FRANCE
Telephone: 44 17 53 00
Intn'l. Dialing: (33-1) 44 17 53 00
Cable Address: ABOGADOFRANCE
Telex: 643914F
Answer Back: ABOGA A643914F
Facsimiles: (33-1) 44 17 45 75

Associated Offices of Baker & McKenzie in: Almaty, Amsterdam, Bangkok, Barcelona, Beijing, Berlin, Bogotá, Brasília, Brussels, Budapest, Buenos Aires, Cairo, Caracas, Chicago, Dallas, Frankfurt, Geneva, Hanoi, Ho Chi Minh City, Hong Kong, Juárez, Kiev, London, Madrid, Manila, Melbourne, México City, Miami, Milan, Monterrey, Moscow, New York, Palo Alto, Prague, Rio de Janeiro, Riyadh, Rome, St. Petersburg, San Diego, San Francisco, São Paulo, Singapore, Stockholm, Sydney, Taipei, Tijuana, Tokyo, Toronto, Valencia, Warsaw, Washington, D.C. and Zürich.
Correspondent Law Firm: Hadiputranto, Hadinoto & Partners, Jakarta.

Firm engaged in advising on French Tax, Corporate and Business Law including advice on Litigation and Arbitration, American Law and International Practice

RESIDENT ATTORNEYS

WALLACE R. BAKER, born Chicago, Illinois, June 11, 1927; admitted, 1952, Illinois, U.S.A.; 1953, District of Columbia, U.S.A.; Avocat (France). *Education:* Harvard University (A.B., 1948); Harvard Law School (LL.B., 1952); University of Brussels Law School (Docteur en Droit, 1961); University of Paris (Licencié en Droit, 1972). *Member:* Chicago, Illinois State and American Bar Associations; District of Columbia Bar; French Avocat.

PIERRE-YVES BOURTOURAULT, born Trouhaut, France, May 14, 1949. Avocat (France). *Education:* Faculte de Droit de Dijon (Licence, D.E.S., Doctorate in Law). Lecturer on Law at Dijon Law School, 1974-1975. Teacher of Tax Law at Dakar, Senegal, 1972-1974.

JEAN-FRANÇOIS BRETONNIÈRE, born France, September 6, 1947. Avocat (France). *Education:* University of Toulouse Faculty of Law (Licencie en Droit, 1972; Docteur en Droit, 1977); Institut d'Etudes Politiques (1973); Sophia University (Jochi Daighaku), Tokyo, Japan (1974-1976). *LANGUAGES:* French, English, Japanese and Spanish.

RÉMY BRICARD, born Paris, France, July 21, 1960; Avocat (France); 1988, New York, U.S.A. *Education:* University of Paris Law School (Maîtrise en Droit, 1984).

JEAN-FRANCOIS BUISSON, born Sainte Helene, Lozere, France, June 6, 1934; Avocat (France). *Education:* University of Montpellier (Licencié en Droit, 1956); National Tax School. *Member:* Ordre des Conseils Fiscaux de France; Juris Consulta Internationaux.

JEAN-CLAUDE DEMOULIN, born Oran, Algeria, 1933; Avocat (France). *Education:* University of Paris (Licencié en Droit, 1958); National Tax School, Paris (1958).

(This Listing Continued)

BAKER & McKENZIE, Paris—Continued

ALEX DOWDING, born Walton On Thames, January 19, 1959; Avocat (France). *Education:* University of Paris Law School (Maîtrise en Droit, 1981; DESS Droit des Affaires et Fiscalitē, 1982).

LAURENT EPSTEIN, born Boulogne sur Seine, France, November 11, 1957. Avocat (France). *Education:* University of Paris Law School (Maitrise en Droit, 1980); Ecole des Hautes Etudes Commerciales, 1982 Diplome d'Etude Comptable Superieur DECS 1978. University of Temple, LLM. 1983.

CHRISTINE LAGARDE, born Paris, France, January 1, 1956. Avocat (France). *Education:* Institut d'Etudes Politiques (1977). University of Paris Law School, Maitrise en Droit 1979. *Member:* French National Association of Labor Law; National Federation on Distribution Law.

MONIQUE PETIT NION, born Brussels, Belgium, October 9, 1933; Avocat (France). *Education:* University of Louvain (Dr. Jur., 1956); Européen Centre of Nancy (Diplôme du Centre Européen Universitaire de Nancy, 1957); University of Chicago (Master of Comparative Law, 1965). *Member:* Licensing Executives Society.

PIERRE A. RAY, born Courpière, France, 1940; Avocat (France). *Education:* University of Clermond-Ferrand Law School (Licencie en Droit, 1964).

HENRY DE SUREMAIN, born Beaune, Cote d'Or, France, 1934; Avocat (France). *Education:* University of Dijon (Licencié en Droit), 1956; University of Michigan (M.C.L., 1958).

LOCAL PARTNER

REIDA S. GUENFOUD, born Tlemcen, Algeria, August 6, 1945; Avocat (France). *Education:* University Paris I - Maitrise en droit 1977.

OF COUNSEL

FRANÇOIS MEUNIER, born Paris, France, June 19, 1941; Avocat (France). *Education:* University of Paris Law School (Licence, 1964); Institut d'Etudes Politiques Dipl., 1964); University of Algiers Law School (D.E.S., 1968). Member of the Jury C.F.P.A. (Examination for Entry to the School for Young Lawyers), 1980-1994.

MICHEL PERIDIER, born Montpellier, France, January 25, 1928; Avocat (France). *Education:* University of Toulouse (License in Law, 1948); Institut Des Sciences Politiques; University of Paris I (DESS, 1950). *LANGUAGES:* French and English.

———————

LAURENT BARBARA, born, Paris, France, 1962; Avocat (France). *Education:* University of Paris Law School (Maitrise Droit des Affaires, 1984; DESS Banques et Finances, 1985).

MARIE-FRANÇOISE BRÉCHIGNAC, born Blois, France, June 23, 1962; Avocat (France). *Education:* Université de Paris Law School (Maîtrise en Droit, 1985); Institut Supérieur d'Interprétariat et de Traduction, Paris (Diplôme Trillingue, 1985); University of Kent at Canterbury (B.A., 1986). Lecturer, French Company Law, University of Kent, Canterbury, England, 1985-1986. *Member:* Association pour le Développement des Echanges Internationaux de Juristes.

DENISE BROUSSAL, born San Francisco, California, July 19, 1958; Avocat (France). *Education:* Université de Paris I Pantheon-Sorbonne, France (D.E.A., Droit International Privé et Droit du Commerce International, 1989, Maitrise de Droit des Affaires, 1985); Boalt Hall School of Law, University of California, Berkeley (LL.M., 1986). *LANGUAGES:* French and English.

VANESSA CARPANO, born Sallanches (Haute-Saudie), France, February 13, 1969; Avocat (France). *Education:* Lyon II; University of Assas, Paris II; Dauphine, Paris IX. *LANGUAGES:* French, English and Italian.

DOMINIQUE CLOUET D'ORVAL, born Tours, France, February 25, 1946; Avocat (France). *Education:* Université de Paris-I Panthéon-Sorbonne (Maîtrise en Droit des Affaires, 1978; D.E.A. en Droit Social, 1988).

CATHERINE DAOUD, born Paris, France, September 13, 1963; Avocat (France). *Education:* University of Paris X: Maîtrise de L.E.A. anglais, allemand, 1985; Droit des Affaires (Maîtrise, 1985); University of Paris I: Droit International Privé (D.E.A., 1986).

JEANNE DUBARD, born Dijon, France, September 22, 1963; Avocat (France). *Education:* D.E.C.F. (1987); Université de Dijon: DESS Droit

(This Listing Continued)

Fiscal (1988); Maîtrise Droit des Affaires (1987). *LANGUAGES:* French and English.

DAVID F. FREEDMAN, born Darby, Pennsylvania, August 26, 1959; admitted, 1987, New York, U.S.A.; 1990, U.S. Supreme Court; Avocat (France). *Education:* Northwestern University (B.S., Journalism, 1981); Columbia University School of Law (J.D., 1985). Notes and Comments Editor, Columbia Law Review, 1984-1985. Teaching Fellow, Civil Procedure and Property Law, Columbia University School of Law, 1984-1985. *Member:* American Bar Association. *LANGUAGES:* English and French.

SAPPHO S. GARELLI, born Kinshasa, Zaire, March 16, 1967; Avocat (France). *Education:* Paris I, Pantheon Sorbonne (D.E.U.G., 1988; License, 1989; Maitrise, 1990; D.E.A., 1991; CRFPP and D.C.A.P.A., 1993). *LANGUAGES:* English, Italian and French.

CLAUDIA M. HEINS, born Twistringen/Niedersachsen, Germany, 1963; admitted, 1991, Germany (Not admitted in France). *Education:* University of Hamburg (Rechtspraktikant, 1986); University of Montpellier/-France (1986-1987). Tutor, University of Hamburg (1984-1986, 1990-1991). *LANGUAGES:* German, English and French.

GILLES JOLIVET, born Alès, France, April 18, 1961; Avocat (France). *Education:* Paris-II, D.E.A. Droit du Travail et Protection Sociale, 1990; Montpellier I, Maîtrise de Droit des Affaires, 1984. *LANGUAGES:* French and English.

DELPHINE F. LAISNEY-DREUX, born Paris, France, April 23, 1964; Avocat (France). *Education:* University of Assas (Paris Licence and Master of Law, 1984-1985); University of Pantheon Sorbonne (Construction and Real Estate Law, 1986); CAPA, Paris, France (1987). *Member:* Paris Bar Association. *LANGUAGES:* French, English, Spanish and Japanese.

DENISE LEBEAU-MARIANNA, born Pondicherry, India, October 9, 1965; Avocat (France). *Education:* Université Paris I (Maitrise Droit des Affaires Internationales, 1988); Université Paris II (DEA Droit International Privé, 1989); Université Paris I (Maitrise Carrieres Judicial, 1992); Université Paris XI (DESS Droit de Informatique, 1993). *LANGUAGES:* English, Spanish and Tamil.

MATHIEU LESCOT, born Paris, France, January 14, 1964; Avocat (France). *Education:* Institut d'Etudes Politiques (Diploma, 1987); University of Paris Law School (Maîtrise de Droit des Affaires, 1985; DESS de Fiscalité Internationale, 1988).

CORINNE E. MATHEZ, born Sale, Morocco, March 17, 1968; Avocat (France). *Education:* Montpellier University (D.J.C.E., 1991); Northwestern University (LL.M., 1994). *LANGUAGES:* English and French.

WILLIAM C. PHILLIPS, born Greenwich, Connecticut, June 15, 1959; admitted, 1986, New York, U.S.A. (Not admitted in France). *Education:* Sarah Lawrence College (B.A., 1982); University of Paris-I (D.E.A., 1988); Brooklyn Law School (J.D., 1985). *Member:* New York State Bar Association. *LANGUAGES:* English and French.

ERIC POMONTI, born Neuilly Sur Seine, France, July 10, 1960; Avocat (France). *Education:* DESS Institut d'Administration des Entreprises (1990); Maîtrise en Droit des Affaires, Strasbourg (1983); DESS Droit des Affaires, Montpellier (1984). *LANGUAGES:* French, English and German.

ANNE-LAURE REVEILHAC, born Neuilly sur Seine, France, May 17, 1955; Avocat (France). *Education:* Université de Nanterre (Maîtrise en Droit Privé, 1978).

JEAN-DOMINIQUE TOURAILLE, born Suresnes, France, March 3, 1956; Avocat (France). *Education:* Faculté de Droit Clermont-Ferrand, Maître (1980); Faculté de Droit Paris-I Sorbonne (D.E.A.; C.A.P.A. Bar, 1982). *LANGUAGES:* English and French.

FRÉDÉRIC VALLET, born Paris, France, April 13, 1964; Avocat (France). *Education:* University of Paris II (DESS, 1987; Maitrise, 1986). *LANGUAGES:* English and French.

OLIVIER VASSET, born Fontainebleau, France, June 16, 1964; Avocat (France). *Education:* University of Paris Law School (Licence en Droit, 1986); Institut d'Etudes Politiques de Paris (Diploma, 1988). *LANGUAGES:* French and English.

BARDEHLE, PAGENBERG, DOST, ALTENBURG, FROHWITTER, GEISSLER & PARTNERS

7, BOULEVARD DE SÉBASTOPOL
75001 PARIS, FRANCE
Telephone: (1) 40 28 07 25
Telefax: (1) 40 28 06 29

Munich, Germany Office: Galileiplatz 1, 81633 Munich. Telephone: 49-89-92 80 50. Telefax: 49-89-98 97 63; 92 805 292.

Düsseldorf, Germany Office: Xantener Strasse 12, 40474 Düsseldorf. Telephone: 49-211-47 81 30. Telefax: 49-211-47 81 331.

Houston, Texas Office: Three Riverway, Suite 550, 77056. Telephone: 713-621 0703. Telefax: 713-622 1624.

Intellectual Property, Unfair Competition and Trade Law, Patent and Trademark Law, Copyright Law, EC Law, Commercial, Corporate, Common Market and International Practice, International Arbitration, Computer, Electronic Means of Payment and Entertainment Law.

RESIDENT PARTNERS

ANDRÉ R. BERTRAND, born Marrakech, Morocco, 1952; admitted, 1989, Paris as Avocat. *Education:* University of Dijon, Faculté de Droit de Dijon (Licence en Droit, 1975); Ecole des Hautes Etudes en Sciences Sociales (Ph.D. African Studies and Islamic Law, 1977); Boalt Hall School of Law, University of California, Berkeley (LL.M., 1978). Editor-in-Chief: SILEX, 1986; Expertises, 1987; DISEP, 1986-1988. Editorial Board Member: "Revue de la Propriété Intellectuelle", "Derecho de Alta Tecnologia", "Software Protection", "Computer Law Adviser", "World Intellectual Property Report." Author: "Computer Contracts," Award AFIN, 1983; "The Legal Protection of Software," 1984; "Copyright and Neighboring Rights," 1991; "Treaties on Patents, Trademarks and Designs," 1994. Co-Author: "The Law of Credit Cards and EFT Systems," 2nd 1989. President, 1986-1987 and Vice President, 1988—, French Computer Law Association, AFDI. President, International Center for Research and Studies in Computer and Telecommunication Law, CIREDIT, 1991—. Legal Counsel The Roche Group, 1981-1984. Country Counsel, NCR France; 1984-1985. Area Counsel, Europe, NCR Corp., 1986-1988. Lecturer, Copyright Law, University of Paris I, 1988—. *Member:* Paris Bar Association; AIPPI. *LANGUAGES:* French, English and German. *PRACTICE AREAS:* Patent, Trademark and Copyright Litigation; Licensing; International Distribution Agreements; Antitrust and Computer Law.

DOMINIQUE DUPUIS-LATOUR, (MR.), born Paris, France, 1954; admitted, 1989, Paris as Avocat. *Education:* Ecole Centrale, Lyons (Engineering Degree); University of Paris II (LL.M., Maîtrise en Droit, 1981; DESS in Industrial Property, 1982); Strasbourg University (CEIPI, 1985); Diplôme en Brevets d'Invention (1986). Consulting Auditor, D.P. Department of the French Ministry of Justice, 1977-1979. Lecturer, Physics and Chemistry, Casablanca, Morocco, 1979-1980. Associate Legal Counsel (Conseil Juridique) and Patent Counsel (Conseil en Brevets), Cabinet Regimbeau (Corre, Martin, Schrimpf, Warcoin & Ahner), Paris, 1981-1986. Independent practice, 1986-1992. Author, "La contrefaçon indirecte en droit français et en droit américain," 1982. *Member:* Paris Bar Association; AIPPI; LES. *LANGUAGES:* French and English. *PRACTICE AREAS:* Industrial Property Law; Patent Prosecution; Patent Infringement Litigation; Licensing; Auditing of Patent Portfolios.

RESIDENT ASSOCIATE

FRANCINE WAGNER, born Troyes, France, 1963; admitted, 1989, Paris as Avocat. *Education:* University of Paris II (LL.M.; DESS, Intellectual and Industrial Property, 1989). Author: "The Law of Fragrance," 1989; "The Enforcement in France of the Theory of Exhaustion of Rights of Trademark," IRPI, 1988. Associate as Avocat: Cabinet Courtois, Bouloy, Lebele et Associés, Paris, 1989; Cabinet Robert Collin et Associés, 1990-1992. *Member:* Paris Bar Association; LES-France (Board Member); APRAM; AIPPI. *LANGUAGES:* French and English. *PRACTICE AREAS:* Patent, Trademark and Copyright; Unfair Competition; Antitrust Law; EEC Law; Licensing; Litigation.

OF COUNSEL

CHARLES P. BONELLI, born Marseille, France, 1929; admitted, 1955, Marseille; 1992, Paris as Avocat. *Education:* University of Aix-en-Provence (Licence en Droit Privé). Judge, 1980-1991. Avocat, Member: Marseille Bar, France, 1955-1979; Paris Bar, 1992. *Member:* International Bar Association. *LANGUAGES:* French and English. *PRACTICE AREAS:* Pa-
(This Listing Continued)

tents, Trademarks and Copyright Litigation; Licensing; Know-How Agreements.

(For Biographical Data of the Munich Personnel, see Professional Biographies at Munich, Germany).

BARJON JOFFRE

Société d'Avocats
Established in 1990

36, RUE WASHINGTON
75008 PARIS, FRANCE
Telephone: (33-1) 45.62.35.00
Telecopier: (33-1) 43.59.52.05

Los Angeles, California Office: 11377 West Olympic Blvd., 90064-1638. Telephone: (1-310) 914-7979. Telecopier: (1-310) 914-7927.

French and International Entertainment Law and Practice, General, Commercial and International Practice.

FIRM PROFILE: *The firm is well known and offers a full range of legal services in specialized areas such as producing and financing Motion Pictures, Motion Picture Contracts, Theatres, Media and Entertainment, Sponsoring, Advertising, TV Production and Distribution, Networks, Video, Copyright, Press Law, Protection of Personality and French and EEC Business Law, Corporate Law and Labor and Employment.*

MEMBERS OF THE FIRM

JEAN-CHRISTOPHE BARJON, born Boulogne, France, January 26, 1955; admitted, 1978, Paris. *Education:* Université de Paris (Maîtrise en Droit, 1977). Chevalier des Arts et Lettres. *Member:* International Bar Association; A.C.E.E.C.C.A., Association des Conseils et Experts Européens du Cinéma et de la Communication Audiovisuelle; A.I.A.D.A.; A.A.D.A. *LANGUAGES:* French and English. *PRACTICE AREAS:* Entertainment Law; Intellectual Property Law; General Practice.

JEAN-FRANCOIS JOFFRE, born Paris, France, December 21, 1954; admitted, 1980, Paris. *Education:* Université de Paris (Licence Droit Privé; Licence Droit Public; Maîtrise en Droit, 1979). *Member:* International Bar Association; A.C.E.E.C.C.A., Association des Conseils et Experts Européens du Cinema et de la Communication Audiovisuelle, (Board of Directors); A.I.A.D.A.; A.A.D.A. *LANGUAGES:* French and English. *PRACTICE AREAS:* Corporate Law; Entertainment Law; Intellectual Property Law; Bankruptcy Law; Labour Law.

BARBERINE MARTINET DE DOUHET, born Dakar, Sénégal, June 13, 1962; admitted, 1989, Paris. *Education:* Université de Paris (Maîtrise en Droit des Affaires, 1983; D.E.S.S. de Droit des Affaires et Fiscalité, 1984; D.E.A. de Droit International Economique, 1986). *LANGUAGES:* French and English. *PRACTICE AREAS:* Entertainment Law; Intellectual Property Law; Corporate Law; Business Law; Enforcement Law; General Practice.

FRANÇOISE POUGET COURBIERES, born Paris, France, December 4, 1967; admitted, 1994, Paris. *Education:* Université de Paris (Maîtrise en Droit des Affaires; Maîtrise en Droit Privé; D.E.A. en Droit de la Propriété Littéraire et Artistique et Industrielle, 1993). *LANGUAGES:* French, English and German. *PRACTICE AREAS:* General Practice; Labour Law; Trademark; Intellectual Property Law.

BARSI DOUMITH PAVIE ET ASSOCIES

Established in 1989

186 AVENUE VICTOR HUGO
75116 PARIS, FRANCE
Telephone: (1) 45 03 16 26
Facsimile: 45 03 07 86

General French and International Law. Agency and Distributorships, Arbitration both Domestic and International. Unfair Competition, Aviation, Bankruptcy, Banking Law, Business Law, Children, Civil Law, Commercial Law, Media and Press Law, Company Law, Contracts, Copyrights, Corporate Law, Criminal Law, Debtor and Creditor, Entertainment and the Arts, European Community Law, Family Law, Finance, Franchises and Franchising, Fraud and Deceit, Intellectual Property, International Law, Investments, Labour and Employment, Leases and Leasing, Libel and Defamation, Litigation, Mergers and Acquisitions, Personal Injury, Professional Liability, Property, Securities, Social Law, Taxation, Trademarks, Transportation, White Collar Crime and Wills.

(This Listing Continued)

BARSI DOUMITH PAVIE ET ASSOCIES, Paris—Continued

MEMBERS OF FIRM

GUY BARSI, born April 22, 1941; admitted, 1966, France. *Education:* Université de Paris (Licence en Droit; D.E.S. en Droit Privé; D.E.C.S. Dîplome d'Etudes Comptables Supérieures). Author: "Les O.P.A. en France Droit et Pratique", Nathan, ed. 1988. *LANGUAGES:* French and English. *PRACTICE AREAS:* Mergers & Acquisitions; Business Law.

ROGER DOUMITH, born November 24, 1941; admitted, 1965, France. *Education:* Institute d'Etudes Politique de Paris (Doctorate, 1964); Faculte de Droit et des Sciences Economiques de Paris (D.E.A., 1964). Lecturer, Centre de Formation Professionnelle des Avocats a la Cour de Paris. Representative of the Paris Bar for the American Bar Association. *Member:* Ancien Membre du Conseil de l'Ordre. *LANGUAGES:* French, English and Arabic. *PRACTICE AREAS:* Criminal; Business Law; Litigation; Press Law; Unfair Competition.

PHILIPPE PAVIE, born November 11, 1944; admitted, 1969, France. *Education:* Faculte de Droit Paris (Licence, 1968); Institut Goethe, Paris. Lecturer, Centre de Formation Professionnelle des Avocats à la Cour de Paris. Former Chairman, Union des Jeunes Avocats. *Member:* Ancien Membre du Conseil de l'Ordre. *LANGUAGES:* English and French. *PRACTICE AREAS:* Banking; Press Law; Entertainment Law; Business Law; Criminal Business Law; Litigation.

BERNARD EME, born July 2, 1929; admitted, 1973, France. *Education:* Paris Sorbonne Ecole Nationale des Impôts (Licence, 1953). Member, Ministry of Finance, 1953-1973. *LANGUAGES:* French. *PRACTICE AREAS:* Domestic Tax Law.

ANNICK LUCAS, born September 2, 1950; admitted, 1976, France. *Education:* Paris I, Sorbonne CAPA (License, 1974). *Member:* Paris Bar Association. *LANGUAGES:* French and English. *PRACTICE AREAS:* Labor Law; Tenancy; Litigation.

JEAN LUC A. CHARTIER, born April 13, 1944; admitted, 1970, France. *Education:* Université de Paris (Licence en Droit, 1970; Doctorat en Droit, 1971). *LANGUAGES:* French and English. *PRACTICE AREAS:* Antitrust Laws; Trademark; Sports Law; Real Estate.

EVELYNE DOUMITH GEMAYEL, born October 31, 1944; admitted, 1979, France. *Education:* College Institute Notre Dame, Paris (1963); Faculte de Droit et des Sciences Economics Paris II (Licence, 1968). *LANGUAGES:* French, English, German and Arabic. *PRACTICE AREAS:* Family Law; Wills; Real Estate Law.

ASSOCIATES

AVRIL LEE, born November 12, 1962; admitted, 1986, England; 1992, Paris. *Education:* University of Kent (B.A. Hons., 1985); Council of Legal Education (Barrister-at-law, 1986); University of Paris II (DSU Droit Commercial). *LANGUAGES:* English, French and Chinese. *PRACTICE AREAS:* Commercial and Corporate Law; Industrial and Intellectual Property Law.

MYLÉNE BAILLY, born February 22, 1958; admitted, 1992, France. *Education:* National School of Taxation (1980). *LANGUAGES:* French. *PRACTICE AREAS:* Tax Law.

BRIGITTE VICTOR-GRANZER, born October 21, 1956; admitted, 1991, Austria, Rechtsanwalt (Not admitted in France). *Education:* Degree in Austrian Law. (Also Member of Lambert Grohmann Kerres & Deissenberger, Vienna, Austria). *LANGUAGES:* French, German and English. *PRACTICE AREAS:* Joint Venture; German and Austrian Law.

PHILIPPE GUILLUY, born January 24, 1964; admitted, 1992, France. *Education:* University of Paris I, Pantheon Sorbonne (D.E.S.S. Droit des Affaires; Diploma in EEC Law). *LANGUAGES:* French. *PRACTICE AREAS:* Competition Law; Bankruptcy Law.

DAVID VATEL, born April 28, 1968; admitted, 1992, France. *Education:* D.E.A., Business Law. *LANGUAGES:* French and English. *PRACTICE AREAS:* Commercial; Business Law; Financial Law.

MATHIAS LASSAILLY, born April 2, 1966; admitted, 1994, France. *Education:* Paris Law School; National Institute of Political Sciences; National Institute of Oriental Languages. *LANGUAGES:* English, French, German and Japanese. *PRACTICE AREAS:* Corporate Law.

OLIVIER BAHOUGNE, born December 13, 1962; admitted, 1994, France. *Education:* University of Bordeaux Law School (D.E.S.S. Business Law). *LANGUAGES:* French and English. *PRACTICE AREAS:* Unfair

(This Listing Continued)

Competition Law; Antitrust Law; Distribution Law; Contract Law; Trademark, Copyrights and Audio Visual Law.

OLIVIA DUFOUR, born December 31, 1969; (Not admitted in France). *Education:* University of Paris II (D.E.A. Philosophy in Law). *LANGUAGES:* French and English. *PRACTICE AREAS:* Civil Litigation; Private International Law; Family Law; Criminal Law.

BAUDEL GELINAS DELCLAUX LANDON & BENECH

69, AVENUE VICTOR HUGO
75783 PARIS CEDEX 16, FRANCE
Telephone: (33-1) 44 17 36 60
Telecopier: (33-1) 40 67 91 40

Nicosia, Cypres Office: Baudel Gelinas & Partners. Capital Center, Makarios Avenue. Telephone (357) 2 450790 Telefax (357) 2 45 0620.

General French, European Union and International Law Practice.

FIRM PROFILE: The firm is composed of French Avocats combining various international experience and foreign backgrounds. It serves French and foreign clients in France as well as abroad, mainly in the field of international joint ventures and business law, distribution and competition law, product liability, litigation and arbitration, mergers and acquisitions. Its other main specialization is the field of copyright, intellectual and industrial property law, including drafting, filing and processing patent and trademark applications.

MEMBERS OF FIRM

JULES-MARC BAUDEL, born Yvrencheux, France, April 18, 1938; admitted, 1961, Paris. *Education:* University of Paris Law School (Licence en droit, 1960; DES Histoire du droit, 1966; DES droit privé, 1973; Doctorat en droit, 1987); Institut d 'Etudes Politiques de Paris (Diploma, 1966); University of Chicago Law School (M.C.L., 1967). Author: "La législation des Etats-Unis sur le Droit d'auteur," Editions Frison-Roche, 1989. *Member:* Ancien Membre du Conseil de l'Ordre, Paris Bar; Union Internationale des Avocats. *LANGUAGES:* French and English. *PRACTICE AREAS:* International Litigation; International Arbitration; Distribution Law; Product Liability; Copyright Law; Intellectual Property Law.

PAUL-A. GÉLINAS, born la Tuque, Quebec, Canada, August 4, 1944; admitted, 1969, Quebec; 1978, Paris. *Education:* University of Montreal (B.A., 1965); McGill University (B.C.L., 1968). *Member:* Quebec, Canadian and International Bar Associations; Canadian Tax Foundation; Union Internationale des Avocats; I.C.C. Commission on International Arbitration; Council of the I.C.C. Institute of International Business Law and Practice; French National Committee of the I.C.C.; Court of International Arbitration (1974-1990); Arbitrator's Institute of Canada Inc.; Comité Francais de l'Arbitrage; Panel of Arbitration, American Arbitration Association. *LANGUAGES:* French and English. *PRACTICE AREAS:* International Joint Ventures; Construction; International Arbitration; Corporate Law; Business Law; International Trade; Agency and Distribution; Finance; Banking; Taxation; Customs.

PASCAL DELCLAUX, born Lille, France, August 5, 1955; admitted, 1981, France. *Education:* University Paris X (Maîtrise de droit des affaires, 1980; DEA de droit des affaires, 1981); University Paris I, Institut d'administration des entreprises (DESS, 1981). *LANGUAGES:* French and English. *PRACTICE AREAS:* Corporate Law; Mergers and Acquisitions.

ERICK LANDON, born Poissy, France, March 27, 1958; admitted, 1984, France. *Education:* University of Paris I (Maîtrise de droit des affaires - Carrières judiciaires, 1983; DEA de droit privé, 1984; DEA de droit économique et de droit des affaires, 1985). *Member:* APRAM (French Trademark and Model Property Lawyers Association, 1990; Member of the board, 1993). *LANGUAGES:* French and English. *PRACTICE AREAS:* Copyright Law; Industrial Property Law; Trademarks; Patents; Design and Utility Models; Varieties of Plants Protection; Publishing; Advertising; Mechanical Engineering; Nuclear Engineering; Electricity; Electronics; Software; Data Processing; Cinema.

FREDERIC BENECH, born Paris, France, January 19, 1954; admitted, 1992, European Patent Attorney; 1994, Paris. *Education:* Graduate Engineer of the Ecole Spéciale des Travaux Publics (ESTP), 1977; University of Paris I (Maîtrise d'economie, 1977; Licence en droit, 1980; Maîtrise de droit des affaires internationales, 1989). Practice: Seven years in Nuclear Engineering and ten years in Industrial Property. Co-Author: Global Economic Co-operation - A Guide to Agreements and Organizations, Editions United

(This Listing Continued)

Nations University Press, 1994; International Software Protection Hand Book (Fish et Richardson - AIPLA, 1992). Professor, ESTP, Faculté Jean Monnet (Paris Sud). *Member:* Ancien Conseil en Propriété Industrielle; EPI Institute of Professional Representative before the European Patent Office; SFEN Société Francaise de l'Energie Nucléaire. AIPPI, Association Internationale pour la Protection de la Propreté. *LANGUAGES:* French, English and German. *PRACTICE AREAS:* Copyright; Industrial Property Law; European and French Patent Applications and Prosecution; Trademarks; Design Infringements; Antitrust Litigation; Software Contracts.

ASSOCIATES

LAURENCE BENRUBI, born Boulogne-Billancourt, France, June 2, 1963; admitted, 1990, France. *Education:* University of Paris II (Maîtrise en droit des affaires et fiscalité, 1986; DESS de propriété littéraire et artistique, 1987); University of Paris I (DEA de droit communautaire et européen, 1988). *LANGUAGES:* French, English and German.

SOPHIE MENARD, born Saint-Louis, Sénégal, August 24, 1965; admitted, 1993, Paris. *Education:* University of Paris II (Maîtrise en droit général, 1988); University of Paris I (DESS de droit du Marché Commun, 1989). *LANGUAGES:* French and English.

SOPHIE CISTERNE-BLONDEAU, born Amiens, France, March 1, 1969; admitted, 1994, Paris. *Education:* University of Paris II (Maîtrise droit privé mention carrières judiciares, 1991; DEA de droit de la Propriété Intellectuelle, 1992). *LANGUAGES:* French and English.

XENIA KAZOLI, born Thessaloniki, Greece, July 5, 1968; admitted, 1993, New York and Athens. *Education:* George Washington University, National Law Center, Washington D.C. (LL.M., Trade and Patent Law, 1992); University of Athens (Juris Doctorate, 1990); University of Heidelberg, Germany (DAAD Scholarship, 1990). Consultant, Trade and Finance Technical Department, Latin America Division, The World Bank, Washington, D.C., 1992-1994. Publications: "Restructuring Peru's Regulatory Activities," Prom Peru, 1994. *Member:* American Intellectual Property Law; American Bar Association; New York Bar Association Society; Association Internationale des Jeunes Avocats. *LANGUAGES:* Greek, French, English, Spanish and German.

EMMANUELLE DEHECQ-MCGRATH, born Suresnes, France, May 22, 1966. *Education:* University of Paris II (Maîtrise de droit international privé, 1989); ENSAMAA (Diploma, 1989). *LANGUAGES:* French, English and Spanish.

CABINET ALAIN BENSOUSSAN

Established in 1978

29, RUE DU COLONEL-PIERRE-AVIA
75508 PARIS CEDEX 15
Telephone: (33.1) 41 33 35 35
Fax: (33.1) 41 33 35 36

Lyon, France Office: 194 bis, rue Garibaldi, 69428 Lyon Cedex 03. Telephone: (33) 78 60 10 21. Fax: (33) 78 60 08 42.

Grenoble, France Office: 27, rue Pierre Semard, 38000. Telephone: (33) 76 70 09 95. Fax: (33) 76 70 09 96.

Brussels, Belgium Office: 12A/15 avenue Brugmann, 1060. Telephone: (32.2) 343 63 01. Fax: (32.2) 343 47 33.

New York, New York Office: 45 West 45th Street, 10036. Telephone: (212) 840 00 80. Fax: (212) 944 04 87.

Montréal, Canada Office: 191 Avenue Mc Gill College Montreal. Telephone: 1-514-847-4747. Fax: 1-514-286-5474.

Computer and Telecommunications Law, Electronics Data Interchange Law, Data Protection Law, Space Law, Biotechnology Law, Communication Law, Direct Marketing Law, Intellectual Property, Copyright Law, Patents Law, Business and Labor Law.

MEMBERS OF FIRM

ALAIN BENSOUSSAN, born Relizane, Algeria, September 14, 1951; admitted, 1978, Paris. *Education:* Institut d'Etudes Politiques, Paris (Diploma in Economics and Finance, 1976); Economical Sciences University, Paris (Maîtrise in Econometrics, 1976); University of Paris (Maîtrise in Business Law, 1976; D.E.A. in Business Law, 1977). Lecturer, ENST, National Superior School of Telecommunications. Director of Publications: G.T.A. Trimestrial Special Number of Gazette du Palais; Memento-Guides and Guides-Juridiques Alain Bensoussan Collections. Author: Papers in "01 Informatique": L'intégration des systèmes: une nouveauté ancienne 1994, Droit du logiciel: La Révolution 1994, Déclarez votre autocommutateur," 1993, L'affaire Borland/Lotus; in "Vidéotex & RNIS/Solutions téléma-

(This Listing Continued)

tiques, "Téléphone, informatique et liberté," 1992, "Des écoutes téléphoniques aux écoutes de télécommunications," 1991; Papers in, "Les Echos": Fichiers illicites: les contraintes de la loi, 1994, Attention aux progiciels illicites, 1993, La France en retard, 1993. Publications: "Droit de l'informatique et de la télématique," Berger-Levrault, 1985; "La Protection des logiciels sous la loi de juillet 1985," Editions des Parques, 1986, Revue Alain Bensoussan Droit des Technologies Avancées. *Member:* AFDIT Association Française du Droit de l'Informatique et des Télécommunications (Vice President, 1988; President, 1993); UIA Union Internationale des Avocats (Treasury of the French section, 1993; President of the Commission on Telecommunication and Computer Law, 1993). (Senior Partner). *LANGUAGES:* French and English. *PRACTICE AREAS:* Intellectual Property and Copyright Law; Computer and Telecommunications Law; Space Law; Biotechnology Law; Direct Marketing and Communication Law.

ISABELLE DEMNARD-TELLIER, born Paris, France, June 24, 1954; admitted, 1980, Paris. *Education:* University of Paris X (Maîtrise in Law, 1979). Author: Papers in Expertises: "Formation des informaticiens," 1983; "Imputation des frais liés à l'implantation d'un système formatique," 1987; "Les expertises des systèmes d'information," 1988; "Introduction de nouvelles technologies," 1988; "Informatique et droit du travail," 1988; "Prud'Hommes ou TGI?", 1990; In Applicatique: "Le contrat de confiance fournisseur-utilisateur," 1988; "Le salaire de la peur," 1988. Co-Author: Publications, "Les Télécommunications et le Droit," 1992; "Le Facilities Management et le Droit," 1993; "L'informatique et le droit," 1994; Mémentos-Guides Alain Bensoussan. *LANGUAGES:* French and English. *PRACTICE AREAS:* Intellectual Property; Copyright and Patents Law; Computer Law; Labor Law.

PIERRE-YVES FAGOT, born Paris, France, September 16, 1952; admitted, 1977, Paris. *Education:* University of Paris X (Licence in Business Law, 1975; D.E.S.S. of Tax Law, 1976). Author: Papers in, "La Gazette du droit des technologies avancées": Impôts indirects. Papers in Expertises des Systems d'information: "Logiciel et crédit d'impôt," 1992. Co-Author: Publications, "Le Crédit d'impôt recherche," 1993, Guide juridique Alain Bensoussan; "Le Facilities management," Tax Law, 1993; "L'informatique et le droit" (la comptabilité), 1994; Memento-Guide Alain Bensoussan. *LANGUAGES:* French. *PRACTICE AREAS:* Business; Tax Law; Fusion-Acquisition.

DANIÈLE VERET, born Saint-Maur-des-Fossés, France, March 24, 1957; admitted, 1992, Paris. *Education:* University of Paris XII (Maîtrise in Law, 1981; Certificate of Legal English); University of Paris I (D.E.A. in Comparative Law, English and North American Business Law, 1982); Institute of Comparative Law of Paris (Certificate of Translating Legal English). Author of papers: La maintenance des logiciels in New AFSM and CXP Journal, 1994; La qualité des logiciels in CXP Journal, 1993; Les droits et obligations du directeur des Achats in Capital Etude, 1994; La vérification des outils de levage in IFTIM Entreprises, 1994; La garantie et la maintenance in Les Echos, 1994. Author: Papers in, "La Gazette du droit des technologies avancées": Contrat informatique CA Paris 25.02.93, 1993; Maintenance informtique CA Paris 20.11.92, 1993; Matériel informatique CA Paris 13.03.92, 1992; Maintenance informatique CA Bordeaux 30.-01.90, 1991. Papers in "Expertises des Systèmes d'Information": La Maintenance Internationale, 1990; Le dépôt international des programmes, 1990. Co-Author: Publications, "L'informatique et le droit," 1994; "La maintenance des systèmes informatiques et le Droit," 1993, "Les télécommunications et le droit," 1992, "L'échange de données informatisé et le droit," 1991, "Les contrats IBM," 1994; "Mémentos-guides Alain Bensoussan." Lecturer, MIAGE in University of Paris XII. *Member:* SYNTEC (Legal Commission); AFSM (Legal Commission); Association française du droit de l'informatique et dela télécommunication AFDIT; Association Française de Normalisation AFNOR. *LANGUAGES:* French, English and German. *PRACTICE AREAS:* Intellectual Property; Copyright Law; Computer and Telecommunications Law.

BRIGITTE VAN DORSSELAERE, born Paris, France, June 23, 1958; admitted, 1981, Paris. *Education:* University of Paris I (Maîtrise de Droit Privé , 1980). Author of Papers: "La protection juridique des programmes informatiques," l'Actualité Juridique Propriété Immobilière, 1983; "Le secret de fabrique," in Expertises, 1984; "La Copie des logiciels: un régime juridique en évolution," La Gazette du Palais, 1989; la décompilation, une incitation à la publication, 01 Informatique, 1994. Papers in "Les échos": contrat informatique: les obligations de l'utilisateur, 1994; le dépôt légal: les modalités sont fixées, 1994, la décompilation des logiciels autorisée, 1994. Papers in Le Monde Informatique depuis, 1984: Papers in Distributique (1988 to 1991) and Distributique Europe (1989 and 1990). Papers in Lamy Droit de l'Informatique: "La copie de sauvegarde," 1988, "La responsabilité du fait des produits défectueux: application au domaine informatique,"

(This Listing Continued)

CABINET ALAIN BENSOUSSAN, Paris—Continued

1989, "Commentaire de la proposition de directive du Conseil CEE concernant la protection juridique des programmes d'ordinateur, modifié par la Commission," 1990, "La distribution des copies de sauvegarde, des programmes plombés et de déplombage en Cour de Cassation," 1991, "La commercialisation des données publiques au regard du droit d'auteur et du droit de la concurrence," 1993, "La loi du 10 Mai 1994 sur la protection des logiciels," 1994. Author of Publications: "Guide Juridique de l'Informatique," Dunod-Bordas, awarded AFDIT, 1991. Co-Author of Publications: "Le Logiciel et le Droit, 1994," Mémento Guide, Alain Rensoussan, Revue Alain Bensoussan; "Droit des Technologies Avancées". *Member:* Association Française du Droit de l'Informatique et de la Télécommunication, AFDIT. *LANGUAGES:* French and English. *PRACTICE AREAS:* Computer and related matters; Intellectual Property; Copyright Law.

CATHERINE LATRY-BONNART, born Boulogne sur Seine, France, March 22, 1957; admitted, 1985, Paris. *Education:* University of Paris X (D.E.A. in Business Law). Lecturer: Institut de Management d'Informations, University of Compiegne. Miage maîtrise d'informatique appliquée à la gestion d'entreprise University of Evry. Author: Papers in, "La Gazette du droit des technologies avancées": Fraude informatique CA Paris 25.-11.92, 1993; Contrefaçon de logiciel CA Douai 07.10.92, 1992; Escroquerie au téléphone Cass. Crim. 13.12.90, 1991. Co-Author: Publications, "Les télécommunications et le droit," 1992, Mémento-guide Alain Bensoussan. *LANGUAGES:* French. *PRACTICE AREAS:* Computer and Telecommunications Law; Criminal Law; Intellectual Property; Copyright Law.

JEAN-PHILIPPE LECLERE, born Orléans, France, November 2, 1950; admitted, 1991, Paris. *Education:* University of Orleans - Tours (Licence in German, 1970); Institute of Comparative Law of Paris (Certificat of Translating Legal English); University of Paris I (D.E.S.S. International Public Law, 1975); University of Aix en Provence (D.E.S.S. International Business Law, 1979). Lecturer: ESCG Ecole Supérieure de Commerce de Grenoble. Author: Papers in, "l'Usine nouvelle": Le porte-monnaie électronique ne peut pas tout payer: il doit respecter les règlementations bancaires et informatiques, 1993; Archivage électronique et droit de la preuve: comment conserver les documents et combien de temps? 1993; Logiciels: toute utilisation n'est pas licite: déplombage, reproduction, transfert entre ordinateurs, 1993; Cartographie tout se complique: les activités liées à l'urbanisme et à l'environnement concernées en priorité, 1993; Des garanties pour les échanges de données tehcniques: un nouveau champ d'application du droit, 1993; Le dépôt légal appliqué aux nouvelles technologies: la réforme soulève de nombreuses difficultés pratiques, 1992; Papers in, "La Gazette du droit des technologies avancées": La protection et l'exploitation des données cartographiques (1st and 2nd part), 1993; La cartographie numérique et le droit, 1992; La protection de l'image générée par ordinateur, 1992. Co-Author: Publications, "Les télécommunications et le droit," 1992; "Les systèmes d'information géographique et le droit," 1993, Mémentos-Guides Alain Bensoussan. *Member:* World Trade Center GRENOBLE; Club Juridique du GREX. *LANGUAGES:* French, English and German. *PRACTICE AREAS:* Intellectual Property Law; Computer and Telecommunications Law.

FRANÇOIS BRUTE DE REMUR, born Soulom, France, July 12, 1944; admitted, 1992, Paris. *Education:* Institut d'Etudes Politiques de Paris, Etudes Supérieures de Sciences Economiques, CESA-Finance (4ème promotion). Author: Papers in Les Echos, "Contrats de FM: les précautions à prendre; in 01 INFORMATIQUE "Le FM et ses contracts," 1994; Publications, "Le désordre monétaire internationale, PUF, 1972. Co-Author: Publications, "Le Facilities Management et le Droit," 1992, "Les télécommunications et le droit," 1992, "L'informatique et le Droit," 1994. Mémentos-guides Alain Bensoussan. *LANGUAGES:* French, English and Italian. *PRACTICE AREAS:* Tort; Business Law; Computer Law.

DANIÈLE DELAVAL, born Sully, France, May 19, 1953; admitted, 1977, Paris. *Education:* Certificate in intellectual property and copyright law: University of Paris II (Maîtrise in Business Law). Author: Papers, "Los Echos: La Commercialisation des donne'es publiques et la protection l'investissement," 1994; "La Gazette du droit des technologies avancées": Le projet de directive relatif à la protection juridique des bases de données ou l'adaptation du droit d'auteur au traitement de l'information, 1993; La responsabilité du créateur de logiciel et ses limites, 1992. Papers in, "Solutions télématiques": L'emergence d'un droit d'accès aux données publiques, 1993; La création du Conseil Supérieur de la Télématique et du Comité de la Télématique Anonyme, 1993; Le nouveau contrat Télétel et le contrôle du kiosque, 1993; L'étatisation de l'information face au droit communautaire, 1993. Author: Publications, "L'audiotex ou la télématique vocale," 1993, Guide juridique Alain Bensoussan. Co-Author: "Les Systèmes d'Informa-

(This Listing Continued)

tion Géographique et le droit," 1993, Mémento-Guide Alain Bensoussan. *LANGUAGES:* French. *PRACTICE AREAS:* Intellectual Property; Copyright Law; Computer, Communication and Telecommunications Law.

CATHERINE CHABERT-PELTAT, born Lyon, France, October 12, 1959; admitted, 1992, Paris. *Education:* University of Lyon III (D.E.A. in Family Law); University of Paris X Nanterre (Maîtrise in Business Law). Author: Papers in, "La Gazette du droit des technologies avancées,": "La Carte-Santé-Aspects juridiques," 1994; "Commentaires des projets de lois sur la bioéthique," 1993; "La loi Huriet et le matériel médical," 1992; "La recherche biomédicale et la protection des personnes," 1992; "L'expérimentation sur l'être humain," 1991. Papers, "Le disque optique numérique, la solution juridique aux problémes de l'archivage, ARCHIMAG," 1991; "Le disque optique numérique et le droit de la preuve," "La prévention des risques informatiques," 1993; "Aspects juridiques du FM," 1993; "L'accord d'interchange," 1993; "La gestion des hommes," 1993; "La certification: arme ou contrainte," 1994; "Bulletin de liaison de l'ADIRA," 1991. Co-Author: Publications, "Les télécommunications et le droit," 1992; "Les cartes et le Droit," 1992; "Les biotechnologies et le droit," (A paraître) "Mémentos-guides Alain Bensoussan." Lecturer, University Lyon II (DESS OPSI). *Member:* AFDIT Association Française de Droit de l'Informatique et de la Télécommunication; GRAPI Groupement Rhône-Alps de la Propriété Industrielle; SEL Société de Droit et d' Ethique de la Santé; Sociétéd'imagerie medico légale, ADIRA, association ETHICA. *LANGUAGES:* French, English, Italian and Spanish. *PRACTICE AREAS:* Biotechnology Law; Intellectual Property; Copyright Law; Computer and Telecommunications Law; EDI (Electronics Data Interchange).

BRUNO DUCOULOMBIER, born Paris, France, August 23, 1958; admitted, 1981, Paris. *Education:* University of Paris II (Maîtrise in Business Law, European Law). Author: in "Le Guide de Chéque, 1994": "ie régime juridique du chèque," in "La Gazette du droit de technologies avancées," "Le Mécenat technologique. Co -Author: Publications, "Le Facilities Management et le Droit," 1992, Mémento-guide Alain Bensoussan. *LANGUAGES:* French, English and German. *PRACTICE AREAS:* Business Law.

THIERRY PIETTE-COUDOL, born Sainte Adresse, France, May 12, 1947; admitted, 1993, Paris. *Education:* Université de Haute Normandie (D.E.S.S. in Public Law; Doctorat in Hospitable Law). Author: Papers in, "La Gazette du droit des technologies avancées": Le remplacement de l'écrit par un message électronique: le cas de la facture 1st part, 1992, 3rd part, 1993, L'émergence d'un droit de la sécutité des technologies de la communication, 1992 "L'échange de données informatisées," EDI 1991. Papers in, "Expertises des Systèmes d'information.": "Un nouveau Système de preuve pour l'EDI basé sur la sécurité," mai 1994 - Chambre de Commerce internationale "de l'accord d'interchange au profil d'interchange," 1991-1992. Author: Publications: Co-Author "L'EDI pour les auditeurs et les vérificateurs," Editions du Quebec, 1991-1994; "L'échange de données informatisé et le droit," 1991; Mémentos-guide Alain Bensoussan; "La facture électronique EDI," 1992, Guide Juridique Alain Bensoussan; "Les microordinateurs," Unesco, 1983; "La législation hospitaliere," Unesco, 1978. Lecturer, Ecole Nationale d'Administration de Libereville, GABON, 1976-1978; Institut des sciences administration de ANNABA, Algérie, 1978-1980; Institut d'administration économique et sociale de Grenoble, France, 1982-1984; Faculté de Droit de Grenoble, France, 1986-1990. *Member:* ONU (WP4 EDI French delegation in Geneva); EDI-Avocat (General Delegate); Institut Européen de management de l'EDI (IEMEDI founder); USERS CLUB CREDIBLE (founder). *LANGUAGES:* French. *PRACTICE AREAS:* EDI (Electronics Data Interchange) Law; Computer and Telecommunications Law; Administrative Disputed Claims.

ARIANE MOLE, born Paris, France, July 17, 1958. *Education:* University of Paris X (DESS de Droit Public - Licence d'Anglais). Previously, Expert, EEC Commission, DG XIII, in charge of the proposal for a directive on the protection of individuals with regard to the processing of personal data. Author: Papers: "Directive Européenne, à quand l'adoption?,"le Géomarketing et les obligations de la loi informatique et libertés,"; "Direct," 1994; "Informatique et libertés: Les obligations de l'employeur,"; "Les échos," 1994; "Travail et libertés individuelles: l'evolution du droit," "la Gazette du Palais," 1994; "Au-delà de la loi informatique et liberté," "Droit social," 1992; "The Draft EC Directive on Data Protection, Computer Fraud and Security," 1991; "Ordinateurs, recruteurs et logiciels d'valuation," Semaine Sociale Lamy, 1990; "Aide à la décision, informatique et libertés, La Lettre de l'Intelligence Artificielle," 1989. *LANGUAGES:* French and English. *PRACTICE AREAS:* Data Protection Law.

JEAN-FRANÇOIS FORGERON, born Pau, France, October 17, 1959. *Education:* University of Bordeaux (DESS in Business Management); Uni-

(This Listing Continued)

versity of Pau (Maîtrise in Business Law, 1982). Author: Papers in, "La Gazette du droit des technologies avancées,": Le dépôt legal appliqué aux nouvelles technologies; la réforme du 20 juin 1992; Contrefaçon CA Lyon 28.-11.91, 1992. Propriétélittéraire et artistique CA Paris 9.03.93, 1994. Papers in, "La Lettre de l'intelligence artificielle,": La brevetabilité des réseaux neuronumériques; l'exemple américain, 1993; Le système expert en tant que logiciel; le cas des auteurs salariés, 1993; la réception d'un système expert; étape obligatoire de contrôle de conformité," 1993. Papers, "De la compétence du client, contrats types à revoir, Expertises, 1991; "A qui appartiennent les banques de données? Le Monde informatique," 1991; "Digitalisation," et échantillonnage numérique: quelques perspectives juridiques," LEGICOM, 1994; "La nouvelle loi sur la protection des logiciels: des précisions des modifications et une innovation," "Expertises," 1994. Co-Author: Publications, "Le Logical et le droit," 1994, "Les télécommunications et le droit," 1992; Mémento-guide Alain Bensoussan, 1992; "Le dépôt des logiciels,"Guide Juridique Alain Bensoussan, 1992. *LANGUAGES:* French, English and Spanish. *PRACTICE AREAS:* Intellectual Property; Copyright and Registered Trademarks Law; Computer and Telecommunications Law.

Members: Union Internationale des Avocats (UIA); SYNTEC; Association Française pour le Droit de l'Informatique et des Télécommunications (AFDIT); Association Française pour les Services de Maintenance (AFSM); CLUSIF; Union Française du Marketing Direct (UFMD); European Direct Marketing Association (EDMA); EDI-Avocat; EDI-FRANCE.
Co-Authors and Editors: Mémento-Guides Alain Bensoussan; Guides Alain Bensoussan.

BERLIOZ & CO.

Société d'Avocats

68 BOULEVARD DE COURCELLES
75017 PARIS, FRANCE
Telephone: (33.1) 44 01 44 01
Telefax: (33.1) 44.15.94.15; 42.67.04.43

Lyon, France Office: 48, rue du Président Edouard Herriot, 69002 Lyon. Telephone: (33) 78 38 12 79. Telefax: (33) 78 38 12 83.

Toulouse, France Office: 22, rue de la Dalbade, 3100 Toulouse. Telephone: (33) 61 25 06 97. Telefax: (33) 61 25 06 57.

Sophia Antipolis, France Office: Villantipolis n° 11, 473, route des Dolines, Sophia Antipolis, 06560 Valbonne. Telelphone: (33) 93 65 42 50. Telefax: (33) 93 65 39 26.

London, England Office: 44-46 Kingsway, WC2B 6EN. Telephone: (44.71) 831-4022. Telex: 263680 BERLAW. Telefax: (44.71) 831-8233.

Brussels, Belgium Office: 179 avenue Louise, 1050 Brussels. Telephone: (32.2) 646.40.04. Telefax: (32.2) 644.14.88.

New York, New York Office: 655 Madison Avenue, 10021. Telephone: 212-486-6302. Telex: 3717883. Telcfax: 212-486-8668.

Vilnius, Kalvariju Office: g. 276-36, 2021 VILNIUS. Telephone: (370.2) 62.46.04 - Contact: Valentinas MIKELENAS.

General French and International Law Practice, Advertising Law, Aeronautical Law, Arbitration, Banking and Financial Law, Commercial Leasing, Competition Law, Computer Law, Construction Law, Consumer Protection, Corporate Law, Criminal Law, Distributorship Law, Entertainment Law, Agency and Franchise Law, EC Law, Food and Drug Regulations, Foreign Investments, Industrial Relations and Labor Law, Insurance Law, International Private Law, Licensing, Litigation, Maritime and Transport Law, Financial Engineering, Public Contracts, State Enterprises, Taxation, Tax Planning, Mergers and Acquisitions Law, Product Liability, Property, Real Estate, Rent and Lease Law, Securities Law, Trade Regulations, Patent, Trademark and Copyright Law, Tax, East-West Trade, North-South Trade, Audio-visual Law, Telecommunications.

FIRM PROFILE: The firm: Founded in 1974, Berlioz rapidly expanded into the international arena, establishing offices in New York in 1983, London in 1985, Brussels in 1987, Lyon in 1990.

Types of work undertaken: Berlioz has always concentrated on commercial and financial work in both the international and domestic domains. The foreign offices work in conjunction with the Paris headquarters advising clients on French and foreign law. In close collaboration with its offices abroad, the firm advises on commercial activities and transactions, both in France and internationally, including acquisitions, national and international contracts, sale and restructuring of companies, debt collection and bankruptcy, distribution, computer law and telecommunication, transportation law, consumer matters, employment law and tax law. Anti-competition law, involving French and E.C. competition law, G.A.T.T. agreements, and international practices, is another field where the firm has particular skills.

(This Listing Continued)

In the financial law field, the firm advises companies, banks, and financial institutions on stock market transactions and on the financing of large projects and exports, handles all aspects of banking law, and assists in tax planning under both French and foreign tax regulations. There is an intellectual property division dealing with patents, trademarks, communication law, media, copyrights, and royalties. Commercial property work encompasses all aspects of complex development projects in France and internationally, including financing, purchase, town planning, environment, leasing, and sale. The firm has considerable expertise handling work in the litigation, consumer claims, advertising, penal business law, and debt collection, as well as arbitration and tribunal work.

Overall, the firm sees itself as efficient, competent, and quick to respond, with an internation outlook, also high technology equipment, as well as an open and friendly response to clients.

MEMBERS OF FIRM

GEORGES BERLIOZ, born 1943; admitted, 1969, Paris; 1991, Brussels. *Education:* University of California, Berkeley (B.A., physics, 1963); University of California, Boalt Hall (J.D., 1966); Université de Paris (Docteur en Droit, 1971). Maître de Conférences délégué des Facultés de droit, 1971-1974 and 1979-1981. Chargé d'enseignement de Droit du Commerce International, Université de Paris, 1979-1981, Droit de l'Informatique, Université de Paris IX, 1983-1985. Author, "Le Contrat d'Adhésion," 1973-1976 and Co-author of numerous articles on civil, commercial, and banking law. Editorial Adviser: "International Financial Law Review", "Réflexions Immobilières", "Marchés et Techniques Financières". Member, Comité d'Orientation, "Revue des Affaires Européennes". *Member:* International Bar Association; Union Internationale des Avocats (President, working group on Contracts); London Court of International Arbitration.

MICHEL CARDIN, born 1945; admitted, 1988, Paris. *Education:* Université de Paris (Doctorat d'Etat en Droit International Privé, 1973). In house lawyer for: TOTAL, 1972-1985; THOMSON, 1985-1987.

ALAIN-JEAN DAVID, born 1944; admitted, 1973, Paris. *Education:* Université de Paris (Diplôme d'Etudes Supérieures de Droit Privé, 1970; Docteur en Droit, 1976). Author: Rédacteur in "Revue trimestrielle de droit commercial et de droit économique". *Member:* American Chamber of Commerce in France; Belgo-Luxembourgeoise Chamber of Commerce.

LAURENT LUTZ, born 1948; admitted, 1973, Paris. *Education:* Université de Strasbourg (licence es-Sciences Economiques); Université de Paris (Diplôme d'Etudes Supérieures de Droit Privé, 1972). Assistant à la Faculté d'Alger, 1974-1976. Member, Co-trésorier national de l'Association des Avocats Conseils d'Entreprise ACE.

PASCALE GROS, born 1958; admitted, 1988, Paris. *Education:* Université de Lyon III (Maîtrise de Droit des Affaires, 1980); Université d'Aix-Marseille III (D.E.S.S. de Juriste d'Affaires Internationales, Diplôme de Juriste Conseil d'Entreprise, D.J.C.E., 1981); Université de Paris I (D.E.A. de Droit Nord-Américain et Anglais des Affaires, 1984). *Member:* AIPPI; ACE; Union Internationale des Avocats.

BRIGITTE BERLIOZ-HOUIN, born 1942. *Education:* Diplôme de l'Institut d'Etudes Politiques de Paris (1962); Diplôme de Droit Comparé de la Faculté Internationale pour l'Enseignement du Droit Comparé (1964); Doctorat en Droit (1973); Agrégée de Droit Privé et Sciences Criminelles (1973). Professeur agrégée des facultés de droit. Présidente Honoraire de l'Université Paris IX Dauphine, author of various articles on civil and commercial law. Chevalier de l'Ordre National du Mérite. Officier des Palmes Académiques.

DJAMAL LAKHDARI, Former Attorney at Law, Supreme Court of Algiers and Paris Bar.

MICHEL DURUPTY, born 1937; admitted, 1978, France. *Education:* Université de Paris (Doctor in Law and Political Science, 1964; Agrégé des Facultés de Droit, 1968). Professeur à l'Université de Paris I. Author "Traité des Entreprises Publiques," 1986; "Les Privatisations en France," 1988. Chevalier de la Légion d'Honneur. Chevalier des Palmes Académiques. Chevalier de l'Ordre National du Mérite.

ARNOLD GEWELBE, born 1948; admitted, 1972, Paris. *Education:* French German High School and College, Saarbrücken; Université de Paris Diplôme de l'Institut de Droit Comparé (MCL, 1970); DES de Traduction et d'Interprétariat Français, Allemand, Anglais (ISIT, 1970); Université de Paris II (D.E.S. de Droit Public et Sciences Politiques, 1972); Université Paris I (D.E.A. de Droit Communautaire, 1977). *Member:* International Bar Association; French-German Chamber of Commerce.

(This Listing Continued)

BERLIOZ & CO., Paris—Continued

PIERRE RODIERE. *Education:* Agrégé des Facultés de Droit (1980); Tulane University (LL.M.). Professeur: Université de Bourgogne, 1970-1985; Université de Paris I, 1985—. Author of numerous articles on labor law.

JOSÉ ROSELL, born 1950; admitted, 1978, Barcelona and Toulouse. *Education:* Maîtrise en Droit Privé (1977); Académie de Droit International, La Haye (Certificat, 1977); Université de Paris I (D.E.A. en Droit Commercial Approfondi, 1978). Chargé de cours: Université Paris I, 1977-1979; Université Paris X, 1980-1982; Université Paris V, 1985—. Author: "Interbanks Agreements are they Anti-Competitive?"; "Les Filiales Communes Sino-Etrangères"; "Le Tribunal Arbitral du Sport"; "Les Investissements Etrangers en Chine" and numerous articles on international law. *Member:* International Bar Association; Union Internationale des Avocats; Association Henri Capitant; Inter-Pacific Bar Association (Founder); Barcelona Bar (Former Member, Conseil de l'Ordre).

JEAN-LOUIS MEDUS, born 1962; admitted, 1993, Paris. *Education:* Université de Paris-Val de Marne (Licence d'Administration des Entreprises, 1984); Université de Paris XII (Maîtrise en Droit Privé, 1985, D.E.S.S. de Juriste d'Affaires, 1986); ISA (Groupe HEC-ISA; MBA, Majeure Finance, 1988) MBA Program Wharton Business School, Philadelphia, Pennsylvania, 1988; Docteur en Droit, 1992. Maître de conférences des universitiés, 1994. Prix du Meilleur Livre d'Economie Financière de l'année 1991 (Prix I.F.G./INTERFINANCES, "Michel DEVELLE") for "Ingéniere Financière et Opérations à effets de levier," 1991. Author: "Méthodes de valorisation d'une marque," 1990; "Pratiques et conditions de réussite du RES en France," 1990; "Goodwill et survaleur; plaidoyer pour une valorisation financière fondée," 1990; "La lettre de confort, thèse de doctorat, 1992; "L.B.O. et fusion rapide," 1992; "Engagements de ratios et garanties par la gestion," 1993; "Conventions de portage et information comptable et financière," Revue des sociétés, 1993; "Les Augmentations de capital," Economica, 1994; "Les Missions irrégulières d'une lettre de confort par une SA et sa sanction," Bull Joly 06/1993. Co-author: "Ingénierie Financière et mécanismes de flux intra-groupe," 1992.

JACQUES RANCHIN, born 1952; admitted, 1982, Lyon. *Education:* Diplôme de l'Institut d'Etudes Politiques, 1975; Université de Grenoble (Maîtrise de droit privé "Carrières Juridiques et Judiciaires", 1978).

PHILIPPE LEGENTIL, born 1964; admitted, 1993, Paris. *Education:* Université de Paris V (Maîtrise en Droit des Affaires, 1985, D.E.S.S. Banques et Finances, 1987, D.E.S.S Fiscalité Appliquée, 1988). Lecturer, Université de Paris IX - Dauphine, Université de Paris X 1993—. Author: "The use of limited liability companies in crossborder transactions," The LLC supplement, 1994-1995. Co-Author: "Ingénierie Financière et mécanismes de flux intra-groupe," 1992.

ASSOCIATES

THIERRY AMRAM, born 1964; admitted, 1994, Paris. *Education:* Université de Droit d'Aix-en-Provence (Maîtrise en Droit des Affaires; option fiscalité, 1986; D.E.A. Etudes Politiques, 1987); University of Pennsylvania (Master in Law LL.M., 1989).

THIERRY ARACHTINGI, born 1967; admitted, 1994, Paris. *Education:* Université de Paris X (D.E.S.S. de Droit du Commerce International, 1991); Université de Paris II (D.E.A. de Droit des Affaires et Droit Economique, 1991). Co-author: "Présentation Générale de l'Accord sur l'Espace Economique Européen (E.E.E.)," R.A.E., 1992.

ALEXANDRA BERTINI, born 1966. *Education:* Université de Paris X (Licence de Droit, 1991; Maîtrise de Droit Privé, 1993).

LÉA BIGIAOUI, born 1970. *Education:* Université de Paris I (D.E.A. de Droit Social, 1993). Lecturer, Université de Paris I, 1994.

PASCALE BISSUEL, born 1955; admitted, 1978, Lyon. *Education:* Université de Saint-Etienne (Licence et Maîtrise de Droit Privé, 1977). *Member:* AIPPI (Association Internationale pour la Protection de la Propriété Industrielle). (Lyon Office).

BERNARD BROUSSEAU, born 1965; admitted, 1994, Paris. *Education:* Diplômé de l'Institut d'Etudes politiques de Paris (1987); Université de Paris X Maîtrise de Droit des Affaires, 1990); Université de Paris IX - Dauphine (D.E.S.S. Affaires Internationales, 1990).

DOMINIQUE CHAPELLON LIEDHART, born 1967; admitted, 1991, Lyon. *Education:* Université de Lyon II (D.E.S.S. de Droit Social, 1990). (Lyon Office).

(This Listing Continued)

PHILIPPE COEN, born 1966; admitted, 1994, Paris. *Education:* International Law Academy, The Hague (Certificate of International Private Law, 1988); Université de Paris I (Diplôme de Droit Européen, 1989; Maîtrise en droit des Affaires, 1989); Harvard Law School (Master in Laws LL.M., 1991). Awarded, Lavoisier Scholarship, French Ministry of Foreign Affairs, 1991. Lecturer at Law (magistère de droit des activités économiques - Université de Paris I - Panthéon Sorbonne, 1995). *Member:* Harvard Club of Europe.

EMMANUELLE CORCOS, born 1971; (Not admitted in France). *Education:* Université de Paris II (Maîtrise droit des affaires et fiscalité, 1993); Université de IX- Dauphine (DEA droit économique et social, 1994).

FRÉDÉRIC COSME, born 1968; admitted, 1994, Paris. *Education:* Université de Paris II (Maîtrise de Droit des Affaires, 1991); Faculté de Droit de Poitiers (D.E.S.S. Juriste d'Affaires - DJCE Diplôme de Juriste Conseil d'Entreprise, 1992); Université de Montpellier (Certificat de spécialité en Droit Fiscal, 1992). Lecturer at Law (Maîtrise Sciences et Gestion - Ecole Supérieure des affairs, Université Paris Val de Marne, 1995).

ANNE V. DELAUNAY, born 1967. *Education:* Université de Paris I (DEA de Droit Communautaire, 1990).

NANCY DUNN, born 1968, California, USA. *Education:* Université de Paris I (Maîtrise de Droit, mention Droit International et Européen, 1991; D.E.A. de Droit Communautaire et Européen, 1992).

DOMINIQUE PAULE DUPARD, born 1959; admitted, 1986, Paris. *Education:* Université de Paris X (D.E.A de Droit des Affaires, 1985). Juriste à la Cour International de Justice de La Haye, 1983. Professeur de droit au Centre de Formation Professionnelle Bancaire, 1986-1987. Chargée de cours de Droit des Affaires à l'Université de Paris XIII, 1989-1992. Professeur auxiliaire à l'Université de Maasticht, 1987-1992. Ancienne Présidente de Juris-Essec.

SANDRINE MISRAHI, born 1968. *Education:* Facultéde Droit, Sceaux Paris XI (Maîtrise de droit des affaireset fiscalité, 1994).

CAROLINE PELLETIER, born 1971. *Education:* Université d' Aix-Marseille III (DEA droit privé, 1993). Lecturer at Law, Université de Paris XII, 1994—.

VINCENT RAMETTE, born 1965. *Education:* First Certificate of Cambridge; Université d'Angers (DEUG de Droit, 1985); Université de Paris V (DUT en Information-Communication, option Documentation, 1990). Author of various articles on Legal Documentation.

PAULINE ROESER, born 1970. *Education:* Université de Paris IX-Dauphine (Maîtrise de Gestion mention droit des affaires internationales, 1993); University of Exeter-England (Master in Law LLM, 1994).

MARIE-JEANNE SEICHEL, born 1950, Tunis, Tunisie; admitted, 1992, Paris. *Education:* Universitéde Grenoble (Licence de Russe, 1971); Université de Nanterre, Paris X (Maîtrise des Carrières Judiciaires, 1988; Maîtrise de Droit des Affaires, 1989).

VÉRONIQUE SENS-ANDRE, born 1966; admitted, 1993, Paris. *Education:* Université de Paris X (Maîtrise de Droit des Affaires, 1989); Université Paris II (Maîtrise de Droit des Affaires et Fiscalité, 1992).

KARINA SKAFF, born 1966. *Education:* Université de Paris II Assas (Maîtrise de Droit Privé Général, 1990; D.E.S.S. de Droit Notarial, 1991).

MANIAM SUBRAMANIAM, born Malaysia, 1947; admitted, 1982, Malaysia (Not admitted in France). *Education:* Lincoln's Inn, London (Barrister at Law, 1976); University of London (Bachelor of Law, 1978); City of London Polytechnic (M.A. in Business Law, 1979).

PATRICK VAN SURELL, born 1968. *Education:* Université de Paris II (Maîtrise de Droit des Affaires et Fiscalité, 1992); Université de Paris IX - Dauphine (DEA Droit Economique et Social, 1993).

Languages: French, English, German, Italian, Spanish, Portuguese, Russian, Arabic, Malaysian

BERNARD-HERTZ-BÉJOT

153, BOULEVARD HAUSSMANN
75008 PARIS, FRANCE
Telephone: (1) 42.56.30.80
Telex: 649045 F BTAVOC
Telecopier: (1) 45.63.25.25

General Corporate and International Practice.
(This Listing Continued)

MEMBERS OF FIRM

PATRICK BERNARD, born Neuilly-sur-Seine, France, May 7, 1950; admitted, 1976, Paris. *Education:* Institut d'Etudes Politiques (I.E.P.) Paris, Section Économique et Financière (1971-1974); University of Paris (Licence en Droit, 1972; D.E.S. Droit Privé, Droit Fiscal et des Affaires, 1976); University of Michigan Law School (M.C.L., 1977). Lecturer on International Financial Transactions, 1981 and on International Commercial Transactions, 1988-1994, University of Paris. Guest Speaker, "Taking Evidence in France for Use in Litigation in the United States," American Bar Association, Section of International Law and Practice, April, 1989. Co-Author: "What Legal Hurdles Persist in SEC/COB Cooperation?", International Financial Law Review, March 1993; "Peaceful Solutions: an international Guide to Commercial Arbitration: Special Report for France", International Financial Law Review, May 1993. *Member:* Comité Français de Droit International Privé; Commission on International Arbitration of the French Committee of the ICC; Comité Français de l'Arbitrage; International Law Association (French Branch); European Trade Law Association; Association Droit et Commerce. *LANGUAGES:* French, English and German.

MARIE-ELISABETH HERTZ, born Mulhouse, France, September 14, 1949; admitted, 1973, Paris. *Education:* University of Paris (Licence en Droit, 1970; EEC Law Certificate, 1971); Chambre de Commerce Franco-Allemande (German Language Certificate, 1971; D.E.S. Droit Privé, Droit des Affaires, 1971). *Member:* Chambre Franco-Allemande de Commerce et d'Industrie; Deutscher Anwalt-verein (Ausserordentliches Mitglied). *LANGUAGES:* French, German and English.

MICHEL BÉJOT, born Lons-le-Saunier, France, August 28, 1947; admitted, 1978, Paris. *Education:* University of Dijon, Faculté de Droit de Dijon (Doctorat en Droit, 1974); Centre d'administration des entreprises, Dijon (CAAE, 1971); Institut Für Arbeits-und Wirtschaftrecht, Cologne (1972); Max-Planck-Institut, Hamburg (1973); New York University (M.C.J., 1976). Author: "La Protection des Actionnaires Externes dans les Groupes de Sociétés en France et en Allemagne," Ets. Bruylant, 1976; "Einige Elemente der konzernrechtlichen Sonderregeln in Frankreich," Max-Planck-Institut Symposium, 1990. *LANGUAGES:* French, English and German.

ALEXANDER B. BLUMROSEN, born Montclair, New Jersey, August 7, 1960; admitted, 1987, New York; 1991, France. *Education:* Dartmouth College (A.B., cum laude, 1982); New York University (M.A., 1984); Georgetown University (J.D., 1986); University of Paris I Panthéon-Sorbonne (D.E.A. Droit International Economique, mention bien, 1990). Editor, American Criminal Law Review, 1985-1986. Co-Author: "What Legal Hurdles Persist in SEC/COB Cooperation?", International Financial Law Revies, March 1993; "Peaceful Solutions: Special Report for France", International Financial Law Review, May 1993. *Member:* American and International Bar Associations; Association of the Bar of the City of New York. *LANGUAGES:* English and French.

ASSOCIATES

EUGENIE BERTHET, born Chateauroux, France, June 23, 1968; admitted, 1992, Paris. *Education:* University of Paris II (Magistére de Droit des Affaires, DESS Droit Fiscal et Droit des Sociét__248 s, 1992), Cornell University (LLM, 1993). *LANGUAGES:* French and English.

LAURE GONTIER, born Suresnes, France, January 11, 1963; admitted, 1987, Paris. *Education:* University of Paris (Maître en Droit Carrières Judiciaires, 1984; D.E.A., English and North American Business Law, 1985). *LANGUAGES:* French, English and German.

NICOLA KÖMPF, born Heidelberg, Germany, October 17, 1967; admitted, 1993, Paris. *Education:* University of Paris (Maître en Droit des Affaires, 1990; D.E.A. droit des Affaires, 1991). *LANGUAGES:* German, French, English and Italian.

MARIE-ELISABETH MATHIEU, born Antony, France, April 20, 1969; admitted, 1994, Paris. *Education:* University of Paris II Maître de Droit International, 1990); Dipl. me de Droit Compar248 , 1990), University of Paris I (DEA de Droit International Priv298 , 1992), Academy of International Law, The Hague (Certificate, 1993).

SYLVAIN RIEUNEAU, born Grenoble, France, January 28, 1965; admitted, 1989, Grenoble; 1990, Paris. *Education:* University of Grenoble (Maître en Droit Privé, 1987); University of Kent at Canterbury (English Law Diploma, 1986). *LANGUAGES:* French, English and German.

CORINNE THIERACHE, born Dinan, France, February 28, 1968; admitted, 1994, Paris. *Education:* University of Nanterre (Maître en Droit des Affaires et Diplôme d'Etudes Juridiques Appliquées en Droit Alle-

(This Listing Continued)

mand, 1992); University of Paris I Panthéon-Sorbonne (DEA Droit des Affaires, 1993). Co-author: "Le Droit du Délit d'Initiéen Europe: analyse comparative des réglementations en Allemagne, France, Grande Bretagne, et Italie au reraud du droit communautaire", Cahiers Finance, Ethique, Confiance de l'Association d'Economie Financiére, 1994; "La faillite des banques en France", Revue d'Economie Financiére n° 28, Spring 1994; "Une introduction au droit du délit d'initié", Association d'Economie Financiére, June 1994. *LANGUAGES:* French, German and English.

CLAIRE VIDELIER, born Paris, France, March 10, 1970. *Education:* University of Paris XI (Maîtrise en Droit Privé, 1992), University of Paris X (DESS de Droit du Commerce International, 1993). *LANGUAGES:* French, English and Spanish.

Languages: French, English, German, Italian and Spanish

BERTAGNA - GRUIA DUFAUT

Avocats Associés

BERRYMANS EUROPE

EEIG

59, AVENUE MARCEAU
75116 PARIS, FRANCE
Telephone: (33.1) 47.23.05.09
Fax: (33.1) 47.23.04.09

Athens, Greece Office: Georgiadi. 79, rue Skoufa, 106 80.
Bucarest, Romania Office: B-dul Maresal Averescu 8-10.
London, England Office: Berrymans Solicitors. Salisbury House, London Wall, EC2M 5QN.

International and French Practice. Business, Commercial, Corporation, Investment, Tax and Labour Laws, International Contracts, Laws of the East European Countries, Insurance Law, Trusts, New Chinese and Russian Economic Laws, Agency/Franchise Law, Arbitration/Litigation and Bad Debt Collections, Property and Real Estate Law, Mergers and Acquisitions, Computer and Software Laws.

JEAN-JACQUES H.P. BERTAGNA, born London, England, March 12, 1951; admitted, 1976, Paris, France as Avocat. *Education:* Wiener International Hochschulkurse, Vienna University (1971); Paris University (Licence en Droit, 1973; DES Business Law, 1976); University of East Asia , Macau (Chinese Law Diploma, 1987); International Law Diploma (EFB, 1994). Author: "Les contrats économiques sino-étrangers," G.P., 1988; "Force Majeure & Hardship Clause in Drafting International Contracts," Euro Conferences, London, 1989; "Investing in France," European Handbook, London Society of Chartered Accountants, 1993; "Company Law in France," ibid, 1994. Co-Author: "Les Paradis Fiscaux-Les Iles Anglo-Normandes," Forum Droit des Affaires, Monte-Carlo, 1990. Former Overseas Advisory Editor, French Laws, The Company Lawyer, Longman, London, England. Former Tutor on Criminal Corporation Law, Institut National des Techniques Economiques et Comptables, Paris, 1979-1986. *LANGUAGES:* English, French and German. *PRACTICE AREAS:* International, Foreign and French Business; Commercial Law; Corporate Law; Contract Law; Trusts; New Chinese and Russian Economic Laws; Arbitration.

DANA GRUIA DUFAUT, born Romania, March 27, 1960; admitted, 1987, Paris, France as Avocat. *Education:* Paris University (Maîtrise en Droit, 1984; DEA, Construction Law, 1985; DEA, Business Law, 1986). Author: "Evolution du Cadre Juridique du Commerce en Roumanie depuis Décembre, 1989, Europa, January, 1991; "L'implantation des sociétés mixtes en Roumanie," CFCE, June, 1991; "Intervenir et travailler en Roumanie," Les Cahiers du Barreau de Paris, 1992; "La Roumanie à l'heure des privatisations," Les Cahiers juridiques de l'exportation, CFCE n° 2/1993; "Le cadre juridique des investissements étrangers en Roumanie," CNPF, February, 1993; "La transformation du secteur public et les investissements étrangers in Roumanie," CNPF-CFCE, 1994; "L'espace roumain, échanges et implantations juridiques," Graphein, 1994. Secretary General of the Commission of the Paris and Bucharest Bars. *Member:* International Union of Lawyers (for East European Countries, Secretary). *LANGUAGES:* French, Romanian and English. *PRACTICE AREAS:* Foreign Investments; East European Business and Investment Law; Industrial Relations; International Private Law; Litigation; International Tax Law.

GERVAS STEELE, born London, England, 1943; admitted, 1967, London, England as Solicitor. *Education:* College of Law (1967). Formerly Senior Partner, Steele & Co. (21 years); Practice of the Year, United King-

(This Listing Continued)

BERTAGNA - GRUIA DUFAUT, Paris—Continued

dom, 1992. **LANGUAGES:** English and French. **PRACTICE AREAS:** Corporate Finance; Mergers and Acquisitions; Expatriate Work.

PASCALE BEHERAY DERRIEN, born Rouen, France, August, 1964; admitted, 1992, Paris, France as Avocat. *Education:* Paris Law University (DEA in International Law, 1989); Comparative Law Institute (1990). **LANGUAGES:** French and English.

ZSUZSANNA MIHALY SALAMON, born Miercurea-Ciuc, Romania, November, 1960; admitted, 1983, Romania; 1993, Paris, France as Avocat. *Education:* University Babes-Bolyai, Cluj, Romania. **LANGUAGES:** Hungarian, Romanian, French and English.

EMMANUEL RENAULT, born Paris, France, April, 1967; admitted, 1994, Paris, France as Avocat. *Education:* Paris Law University (DEA in Private Law, 1991). **LANGUAGES:** French, English and Italian.

MARC SKREIKES, born Boulogne, France, September, 1966; admitted, 1993, Paris, France as Avocat. *Education:* Paris Law University (1991). **LANGUAGES:** French, English, Spanish.

IOANA LETCA, born Bucharest, Rumania, 1968; admitted, 1992, Bucharest. *Education:* Bucharest Law-University. **LANGUAGES:** Rumanian, French, English.

SANDRINE WEIL, born Paris, France, June 12, 1971; admitted, 1994, Paris, France as Avocat. *Education:* Paris Law University (1992; DEA in Business a Economical Law, 1993). **LANGUAGES:** French, English, Spanish, Hebrew.

LAVINIA DUGAY, born Paris, France, 1970; admitted, 1994, Paris, France as Avocat. *Education:* Paris University (English Diploma, 1991); Paris Law University (1992). **LANGUAGES:** French, English.

BIGLE, CARBONNIER, DE LAMAZE & RASLE

7, RUE BAYARD
75008 PARIS, FRANCE
Telephone: (33-1) 42.25.22.98
Fax: (33-1) 42.25.08.99

General and International Law Practice, Corporate, Administration Law, EEC, Contracts, Labor Law, Unfair Competition, Real Estate and Building, Taxation, Direct Investments and Exchange Control.
Entertainment, Copyright, Intellectual Property, Merchandising, Trademark, Art and Sport, Advertising, Computer and Software Law.
Litigation and Arbitration.

FIRM PROFILE: This dynamic international and general practice law firm, comprised of 4 partners and a staff of 15 associates and paralegals, effectively handles international legal matters, for a clientele which is primarily North-American and European.

MEMBERS OF FIRM

GERALD BIGLE, born Uccle, Belgium, June 12, 1947; admitted, 1972, Paris. *Education:* University of Paris X (Master of Law); Institut de Droit des Affaires; Harvard University (Summer Session, 1970). Professor, University of Paris, Villetaneuse and Panthéon-Sorbonne. Author: "Memento Guide Juridique de l'Audiovisuel"; "Guide des Droits de Musique dans le Cinéma et la Vidéo"; "Droits Dérivés, Licences et Character Merchandising"; "TELE-CONTRAT"; Co-Author: "Lexique Juridique de l'Audiovisuel." *Member:* French Law Associations for International Copyright Protection; International Center of Audiovisual and Communication Law (President, CIDAC). **LANGUAGES:** French, English and Spanish. **PRACTICE AREAS:** French and International Business Law; Intellectual Property; Entertainment and Communication Law; Media Law; Competition Law.

JEAN-HUGUES CARBONNIER, born Poitiers, France, August 14, 1951; admitted, 1978, Paris. *Education:* University of Paris II, Assas (Dr. Jur., 1975). Professor Law Faculty: University of Paris I, 1975-1989; Political Sciences Institute, 1989—. Author: "Gestion du Personnel et Droit du Travail," 1991. *Member:* Paris Bar Association. **LANGUAGES:** French and English. **PRACTICE AREAS:** Business Law; Administrative Law; Environment Law.

EDOUARD DE LAMAZE, born Germany, April 28, 1954; admitted, 1979, Paris. *Education:* University of Paris X, Nanterre (Master of Law). *Member:* Union of Young Lawyers of France (President). **LANGUAGES:**

(This Listing Continued)

English. **PRACTICE AREAS:** Business Law; Banking Law; Corporate Law.

MICHEL RASLE, born Paris, France, May 8, 1950; admitted, 1976 Paris. *Education:* University of Paris X, Nanterre (Economics); University of Paris I, Panthéon-Sorbonne (Master of Law); Institute of Political Studies of Paris. Author: "Droit Pénal de l'Entreprise." *Member:* Paris Bar Association; Association des Professeurs et Maîtres de Conférences de Sciences Po. **LANGUAGES:** English and German. **PRACTICE AREAS:** Business Law; Entertainment Law; Competition Law.

BIGNON & LEBRAY

Established in 1982

4, RUE BAYARD
75008 PARIS, FRANCE
Telephone: (1) 42.56.64.00
Telex: BIGLEX 649 526 F
Telecopier: (1) 45.61.09.50

Aix-en-Provence, France Office: 3, cours Mirabeau, 13100. Telephone: 42.38.58.38. Telecopier: 42.26.92.37.
Lille, France Office: 19, boulevard de la Liberté, 59800. Telephone: 20.57.90.90. Telecopier: 20.57.90.95.
Lyon, France Office: 29, rue Gasparin, 69002. Telephone: 78.37.03.17. Telecopier: 78.92.82.94.
Madrid, Spain Office: Castello 35, 28001. Telephone: (34.1) 577.26.66. Telecopier: (34.1) 577.61.89.

General French, European Community and International Practice. Corporate, Reorganization, Real Estate, Construction, Commercial Leases, Banking, Financial, Securities, Stock Exchange Regulations, International Contracts, Antitrust, Unfair Competition, Distributorship, Agency, Franchise, Product Liability, Patent and Trademark, Environment, Labor, Taxation, Litigation, Arbitration. Admitted to appear before all French Courts and The European Community Court of Justice. Some Lawyers of the firm are admitted to appear before certain foreign courts.

FIRM PROFILE: Originally founded in 1982, Bignon & Lebray is dedicated to providing corporate law assistance. Composed of a multidisciplinary team, itrenders legal advice and counselling or litigation in all branches of business law, from a domestic, European and international perspective.

The firm counsels and assists French and foreign corporations, comprising major groups as well as smaller competitive companies, with varied activities including industry, banking, finance, portfolio management, distribution, real estate, transportation, computer and tourism.

While the firm maintains an extensive network of correspondents in the rest of France and in most major foreign cities, it has began an expansion program to open branch offices in several major cities in France and in other countries of Europe. At present, it has three branch offices in France, in Lille, in Lyon and in Aix-en-Provence and one in Spain, in Madrid.

MEMBERS OF FIRM

JEAN-FRANCOIS ADELLE, born Saint-Avold, France, April 17, 1958; admitted, 1979, Nancy. *Education:* University of Nancy, Faculté de Droit (Maîtrise en Droit Privé, 1979; D.E.S.S. de Droit des Affaires et Fiscalité, 1980); University of Paris, Faculté de Droit (D.E.A. de Droit Communautaire et Européen , 1982); Institut d'Etudes Politiques de Paris (1981-1983); Institut de Droit Comparé (1984); University of Pennsylvania Law School, Wharton School (LL.M., 1986). *Member:* Paris Bar Association; European Lawyers Association; Association of Attenders and Alumni of the Hague Academy of International Law; Union Internationale des Avocats. **LANGUAGES:** French and English. **PRACTICE AREAS:** Banking Law; Stock Exchange Regulation; Financial and Securities Law; EEC Law; Computer Law; International Contracts.

ANTOINE ARMINJON, born Neuilly-sur-Seine, France, May 24, 1959; admitted, 1985, Paris; 1988, Lyon. *Education:* University of Lyon (Maîtrise en Droit des Affaires, 1982). (Resident, Lyon Office). **LANGUAGES:** French, English and German. **PRACTICE AREAS:** Banking Law; Commercial Litigation; Corporate Law; Labor Law.

JEAN-PAUL BIGNON, born Neuilly-sur-Seine, France, May 31, 1953; admitted, 1976, Paris; 1983, New York and U.S. District Court, Southern District of New York. *Education:* University of Paris (Licence en Droit, 1975; D.E.A. de Droit Civil, 1977); New York University (LL.M., 1982). *Member:* Paris Bar Association; Club des Avocats France-Amérique. **LANGUAGES:** French and English. **PRACTICE AREAS:** Banking Law; Real

(This Listing Continued)

Estate Law; Construction Law; International Contracts; Corporate Law; Commercial Litigation.

BERTRAND DEBOSQUE, born Lille, France, January 27, 1960; admitted, 1985, Paris; 1986, Lille. *Education:* University of Lille, Faculté de Droit (Maîtrise en Droit, 1980; D.E.A. de Droit des Affaires, 1982; Docteur en Droit, Thèse d'Etat, 1986); New York University, Institute of Comparative Law (M.C.J., 1984). Author: "Le choix de la monnaie dans les contrats privés," thesis, 1986. *Member:* Paris Bar Association. (Resident, Lille Office). *LANGUAGES:* French and English. *PRACTICE AREAS:* Commercial Litigation; Monetary Law; Bankruptcy Law; Contracts; Criminal Law.

REMI DE GAULLE, born Paris, France, May 3, 1952; admitted, 1978, Paris; 1979, Aix-en-Provence. *Education:* University of Grenoble (Maîtrise en Droit, 1975); University of Paris (D.E.A. in History of Law, 1977). President, Union des Jeunes Avocats, 1983; President, Fédération Nationale des Unions de Jeunes Avocats (F.N.U.J.A.), 1989-1990. Member, Conseil de l'Ordre, 1984-1986; 1991-1993. (Resident, Aix-en-Provence Office). *LANGUAGES:* French and English. *PRACTICE AREAS:* Construction Law; Contracts; Labor Law; Commercial Litigation.

DIDIER FAIZANT, born Paris, France, January 28, 1957; admitted, 1982, Paris. *Education:* University of Paris, Faculté de Droit (Maîtrise en Droit, 1980). *Member:* Paris Bar Association. *LANGUAGES:* French and English. *PRACTICE AREAS:* Competition; Distribution Law; Consumer Law; Product Liability; Industrial Property Law.

JACQUES GOYET, born Angers, France, January 3, 1960; admitted, 1985, Paris. *Education:* University of Rouen, Faculté de Droit (Licence en Droit, 1982); Ecole Supérieure de Commerce et d'Administration des Entreprises de Rouen (1982); University of Paris, Faculté de Droit (Maîtrise en Droit, 1984; D.E.A. de Droit Communautaire et European, 1985). *Member:* Paris Bar Association. *LANGUAGES:* French, English and German. *PRACTICE AREAS:* Mergers and Acquisitions; Corporate Law; Bankruptcy Law; Industrial Property Law.

XAVIER LEBRAY, born Amiens, France, February 27, 1950; admitted, 1981, Paris. *Education:* University of Lille, Faculté de Droit (I.A.E., 1973; Licence en Droit, 1973); University of Paris (D.E.S. de Droit des Affaires 1974; D.E.S. de Sciences Economiques, 1975); New York University (M.C.J., 1976). Conseil Member, St. Germain-en-Laye, 1989. *Member:* Paris Bar Association. *LANGUAGES:* French and English. *PRACTICE AREAS:* Mergers and Acquisitions; Corporate Restructuring; Bankruptcy Law; Labor Law; Commercial Arbitration.

OF COUNSEL

JEROME BIGNON, born Neuilly-sur-Seine, France, January 1, 1949; admitted, 1973, Paris. *Education:* University of Paris, Faculté de Droit (Licence en Droit, 1971; D.E.S. de Droit Public, 1972); Institut de Droit Européen (1972). Mayor of Bermesnil, Somme, 1980—. Member of Parliament (National Assembly), 1993. Vice-Chairman, Conseil Régional, Picardy, 1986—. *Member:* Paris Bar Association. *LANGUAGES:* French and English. *PRACTICE AREAS:* Commercial Leases; Real Estate Companies; Bankruptcy Law.

YVONNE JUNYENT, born Buenos Aires, Argentina, January 19, 1961; admitted, 1985, Buenos Aires; 1990, Madrid and Paris. *Education:* University of Buenos Aires, Faculty of Law and Social Sciences (1984); University of Paris II (D.E.A., Business and Economic Law, 1987); University of Paris V (D.E.S.S., Companies and Countries in Development, International Trade, 1989). *Member:* Paris, Madrid and Buenos Aires Bar Associations. *LANGUAGES:* Spanish, French, English and Italian. *PRACTICE AREAS:* International Contracts; International Commercial Arbitration; Argentinian Business Law; Spanish Business Law.

ASSOCIATES

GHISLAINE ARNAUD-CROZAT, born October 19, 1962; admitted, 1991, Lyon. *Education:* University of Lyon (Maîtrise en Droit Privé, 1987; D.E.A. en Droit de la Famille, 1988; Diplôme de l'Institut de Droit Comparé, 1990). (Resident, Lyon Office). *LANGUAGES:* French, Spanish and English. *PRACTICE AREAS:* Corporate Law; Commercial Litigation.

THIERRY BERNARD, born Suresnes, France, December 19, 1965. *Education:* Université de Paris II (Maîtrise en droit des affaires et fiscalité, 1987); Institut d'Etudes Politiques de Paris, 1990. *LANGUAGES:* French, English and German. *PRACTICE AREAS:* Corporate Law.

BRIGITTE BIGNON, born Rennes, France, May 7, 1950; admitted, 1972, Paris. *Education:* University of Paris, Faculté de Droit (Licence en Droit Public, 1972). Commission Nationale de l'Informatique et des Li-

(This Listing Continued)

bertés, 1980-1986. *Member:* Paris Bar Association. *LANGUAGES:* French and English. *PRACTICE AREAS:* Commercial Leases.

CONSTANCE BOURUET-AUBERTOT, born Paris, France, November 19, 1967; admitted, 1993, Paris. *Education:* University of Paris X (Maîtrise de Droit des Affaires, 1990); University of Paris I (D.E.S.S. de Droit Immobilier, 1992). *LANGUAGES:* French, English and German. *PRACTICE AREAS:* Commercial Litigation.

SYLVAINE BOUSSARD-LE-CREN, born Paris, France, April 7, 1960; admitted, 1989, Paris. *Education:* University of Poitiers (Licence en Administration Economique et Sociale, 1980); Institut d'Etudes Politiques de Paris, 1982; University of Paris (License en Droit, 1983; D.E.A. de Droit des Affaires et Droit Economique, 1985). *Member:* Paris Bar Association. *LANGUAGES:* French and English. *PRACTICE AREAS:* Real Estate Law; Commercial Leases; Commercial Law.

FLORENCE BOUTHILLIER, born Neuilly-sur-Seine, France, April 29, 1962; admitted, 1988, Paris. *Education:* University of Paris (Maîtrise en Droit des Affaires et de Fiscalité, 1987). *Member:* Paris Bar Association. *LANGUAGES:* French and English. *PRACTICE AREAS:* Real Estate Law.

PIERRE-OLIVIER BROUARD, born Versailles, France, February 27, 1969; admitted, 1994, Paris. *Education:* University of Paris II (Maîtrise in Business Law and Tax Law, 1991; D.E.A., Business and Economic Law). Teacher's Assistant, University of Paris II. *Member:* Paris Bar Association. *LANGUAGES:* French and English. *PRACTICE AREAS:* Business Law.

JACQUES BOUYSSOU, born October 10, 1965. *Education:* Institut d'Etudes Politiques de Toulouse, 1988; University of Paris V (Maîtrise de Droit des Affaires, 1989; D.E.S.S. de Juriste d'Affaires International, 1990). *LANGUAGES:* French, English and Spanish. *PRACTICE AREAS:* Commercial Law.

FRANCISCO JAVIER CARBONELL RODRIGUEZ, born Cartagena, Spain, December 14, 1958; admitted, 1982, Madrid. *Education:* University Autonome of Madrid (Licence in Law, 1982). *Member:* Madrid Bar Association. (Resident, Madrid, Spain Office). *LANGUAGES:* Spanish, French and English. *PRACTICE AREAS:* Commercial Law; Civil Law; Intellectual Property; Maritime Law; Bankruptcy Law.

LAURENCE DEFONTAINE, born Lille, France, April 6, 1966; admitted, 1992, Paris. *Education:* University of Paris (Maîtrise en Droit, des Affaires et de Fiscalité, 1988; Diplome I.D.A., 1988; Institut d'Etudes Politiques de Paris, 1990). *Member:* Paris Bar Association. *LANGUAGES:* French and English. *PRACTICE AREAS:* Corporate Law; Commercial Litigation.

CORINNE DEMAZURE-THOMAS, born Besny Loisy, France, October 31, 1962; admitted, 1989, Paris. *Education:* University of Paris, Faculté de Droit (Maîtrise en Droit, 1986 D.E.S.S. de Droit de l'Immobilier, 1987). *Member:* Paris Bar Association. *LANGUAGES:* French, Spanish and English. *PRACTICE AREAS:* Real Estate Law.

EMMANUELLE FERRERI-SAPENE, born Rouen, France, March 18, 1965; admitted, 1989, Bordeaux; 1993, Aix en Provence. *Education:* Université de Bordeaux (Maîtrise en Droit, 1987). *Member:* Aix en Provence Bar Association. (Resident, Aix-en-Provence Office). *LANGUAGES:* French and English. *PRACTICE AREAS:* Commercial Litigation.

MARIE-BÉRÉNICE GOSSOT, born Baden, Germany, May 4, 1964; admitted, 1993, Paris. *Education:* Université de Paris II (Maîtrise de droit des affaires, droit du commerce international, droit international privé, 1987). *Member:* Paris Bar Association. *LANGUAGES:* French and English. *PRACTICE AREAS:* Real Estate Law.

CHRISTOPHER C.H. IVES, born Newmarket, Ontario, Canada, May 25, 1963; admitted, 1991, Ontario, Conseil Juridique Stagiaire, Paris (Not admitted in France). *Education:* University of British Columbia (LL.B., 1988); Institute of International and Comparative Law, University of San Diego (Diploma in East-West Trade Law); Graduate Institute of International Studies, University of Geneva (D.E.S. Public International Law, 1991). *Member:* Law Society of Upper Canada; Canadian Bar Association. *LANGUAGES:* French and English. *PRACTICE AREAS:* Foreign Investment in France; International Contracts; Immigration Law (Canadian/-French).

PHILIPPE JOOS, born Lille, France, May 2, 1966; admitted, 1991, Lille. *Education:* University of Lille (Maîtrise en Droit Privé, 1989; D.E.S.S. - Certificat d'Aptitude à l'Adminsitration des Entreprises, 1990). (Resident, Lille Office). *LANGUAGES:* French and English. *PRACTICE AREAS:* Commercial Litigation.

(This Listing Continued)

BIGNON & LEBRAY, Paris—Continued

LEILLA KERCHOUCHE, born March 24, 1965; admitted, 1992, Paris. *Education:* University of Paris (Maîtrise d'Administration Economique et Sociale, 1987; D.E.S.S. d'Administration et Gestion de l'Emploi, 1988; Maîtrise Droit des Affaires, 1989; Maîtrise Carrières Judiciaires, 1989; D.E.S.S. deDroit Privé, 1990). *Member:* Paris Bar Association. *LANGUAGES:* French and English. *PRACTICE AREAS:* Real Estate Law.

PHILIPPE LARIVIERE, born Lille, France, October 28, 1968; admitted, 1992, Lille. *Education:* University of Lille (Maîtrise de Droit Privé, 1989). (Resident, Lille Office). *LANGUAGES:* French, English and German. *PRACTICE AREAS:* Commercial Litigation; Labor Law.

GILDAS LUNVEN DE CHANROND, born Paris, France, January 29, 1965; admitted, 1993, Paris. *Education:* ESCP, 1988; Maîtrise en Droit des Affaires et Fiscalité, 1990; D.E.A., 1981. *LANGUAGES:* French and English. *PRACTICE AREAS:* Corporate Law; Commercial Law; Banking Law.

BÉATRICE PARMENTIER, born Lille, France, September 26, 1962; admitted, 1987, Paris. *Education:* University of Lille II (Maîtrise en Droit, 1984; D.E.A. de Droit Privé, 1985); Polytechnic of Central London (1988). *Member:* Paris Bar Association. (Resident, Lille, France Office). *LANGUAGES:* French, English and German. *PRACTICE AREAS:* Labor Law; Commercial Litigation.

JEAN-PHILIPPE ROBE, born Lyon, February 24, 1963; admitted, 1993, Paris; 1993, New York and U.S. District Court, Southern District of New York. *Education:* University of Lyon (Diplôme de Terminologie Juridique Anglaise, 1984; Maîtrise en Droit des Affaires, 1985); University of Michigan Law School (Etat-Unis, LL.M., 1988); European University Institute of Florence, Italy (Ph.D., 1992). *Member:* New York State Bar Association. *LANGUAGES:* French, English and Italian. *PRACTICE AREAS:* Mergers and Acquisitions; Trade Law; EEC Law.

CATHERINE ROBIN, born Lyon, France March 26, 1964; admitted, 1993, Lyon. *Education:* University of Lyon (Maîtrise en Droit des Affaires, 1987); University of Montpellier (D.E.S.S. de Concurren, Distribution, Consommation, 1988; Certificat de Gestion Commericale et Financière, 1989). *Member:* Lyon Bar Association. (Resident, Lyon Office). *LANGUAGES:* French and English. *PRACTICE AREAS:* Competition; Distribution Law; EEC Law.

CHRISTINE SABAS-BIDEGAIN, born Boulogne-Billancourt, France, March 9, 1959; admitted, 1986, Paris. *Education:* Université de Paris XI (Maîtrise en droit privé, 1980); Université de Paris I (D.E.A. de Droit International Privé et Droit du Commerce International, 1981; D.E.A. de droits anglais et nord-américain des affaires, 1982); University of Illinois (M.C.L., 1983). *Member:* Paris Bar Association. (Resident, Madrid, Spain Office). *LANGUAGES:* French, Spanish and English. *PRACTICE AREAS:* Foreign Investments; Corporate law; Industrial Property Law; International Contracts.

CABINET COLETTE BIRNBAUM

Avocat à la Cour

77 AVENUE DES CHAMPS ELYSÉES
75008 PARIS, FRANCE
Telephone: (33.1) 47.55.00.67

London, England Office: 8 Welbeck Way, W1M 7PE. Telephone: 44.171.486.78.81. Fax: 44.171.935.05.00.

New York, New York Office: 1 Pennsylvania Plaza, 49th Floor, New York, NY 10119-0165, USA. Telephone: (1) 212 603 3222. Fax: (1) 212 465 1278.

General French and International Law Practice. Corporate, International Con tracts, Taxation, Foreign Investments, Industrial Relations Law, Immigration, Travel and Tourism Transactions, Media and Entertainment Law, Industrial and Intellectual Property, Communication and Advertising Law, Litigation and General Practice French Law. Attorney authorized to appear before French and European Community Courts.

COLETTE BIRNBAUM, born Constantine, Algeria, November 30, 1955; admitted, 1981, Paris. *Education:* University of Paris Panthéon Sorbonne (Maîtrise en Droit des Affaires Interntionales, 1980); Ecole des Hautes Etudes en Sciences Sociales (Diplôme de l'Ecole des Hautes Etudes en Sciences Sociales, 1974; DEA en Sciences de l'Information et de la Communication, 1977); Docteur en Sciences de l'Information et de la Communi-

(This Listing Continued)

cation (Ph.D., 1980). Lecturer, CELSA (Ecole des Hautes Etudes en Sciences de l'Information et de la Communication, Sorbonne, 1986—). *Member:* Paris Bar Association. *LANGUAGES:* French, English and Spanish.

BOCHET - CRAMER

9, AVENUE HOCHE
75008 PARIS, FRANCE
Telephone: 33 (1) 49.53.00.55
Fax: 33 (1) 49.53.00.64

General French practice, business law, corporate law, commercial law, criminal law, real estate, bankruptcy, industrial relations and labor law, litigation and arbitration, insurance law, patent trademark and copyright law, European and international practice, international private law, international contracts and negotiations.

FIRM PROFILE: Our firm was established in 1984 and now comprises a staff of six lawyers with various backgrounds and skills. The firm offers a full range of legal services in French, European and International Law to both a private and a corporate clientele.

PARTNER

HERVÉ BOCHET, born Neuilly, France, September 5, 1947; admitted, 1977, France. *Education:* Paris University-France (Master, 1972); New York University (M.C.J., 1983). Member, Association Internationale des Jurites d' Affaires, 1987-1989. *LANGUAGES:* English. *PRACTICE AREAS:* Business Law; Corporate Law; Commercial Law; Insurance Law; Real Estate Law; International Law; Contract Law.

ASSOCIATES

ARNAULT CHARRIERE, born Creteil, 1968; admitted, 1994, Paris. *Education:* University of Paris (Maitrise en Droit, 1991). *LANGUAGES:* English. *PRACTICE AREAS:* Corporate Law; Business Law; Labor Law; Bankruptcy Law; Litigation.

STEPHANIE M. PONSOT, born Dijon, May 4, 1966; admitted, 1995, France. *Education:* University of Paris (Maitrise en Droit Des Affaires, 1990). Consultant, World Bank Group, 1994; Former Legal Analyst, Law Library of Congress, Washington, D.C., 1991-1993. *Member:* Foreign Lawyers Forum, Washington, D.C.; Association des Avocats Conseils D' Enterprise, Paris. *LANGUAGES:* English, Italian and Spanish. *PRACTICE AREAS:* Commercial Law; Business Law; Labor Law; International Private Law; Patent, Trademark and Copyright.

JEAN-JACQUES DIEUMEGARD, born Neuilly, 1967. *Education:* University of Paris (Maitrise en Droit Prive Mention Carrieres Judiciaires, 1992; Maitrise en Droit Prive, Mention Droit des Affaires, 1991; DEA de Droit des Affaires et de Droit de l'Economie, 1993). *LANGUAGES:* English and Spanish. *PRACTICE AREAS:* Business Law; Corporate Law; Labor Law; Commercial Law; Real Estate.

CONSULTANTS

PETRA CRAMER, born Leidschendam, May 15, 1958; admitted, 1984, Rotterdam; 1992, Paris. *Education:* City of London Polytechnic (English Private, 1981); University of Leyden-Amsterdam (Master of Law, 1982); Aix en Provence and Nile (Master fo Law Degree, 1993). Former Associate, Loeff and Van der Ploegh, 1984-1985, Rotterdam. Legal Counsel, Cooper and Lybraud, 1986-1987, Paris. Chariman, Center D'Information Juridique Internationale, 1991-1993, France. Legal Specialist, European Parliament, Luxemberg, 1993-1995. *LANGUAGES:* Dutch, French, English and German. *PRACTICE AREAS:* EEC Law; Commercial Law; Patent, Trademark and Copyright Law; International Private Law; International Contract Law.

JACQUES LE GUIFFANT, born May 12, 1926; admitted, 1947, France. *Education:* Faculte De Droit De Paris. Tax Officer, Direction Generale des imports, Morocco, 1947-1962; France, 1962-1964; Tax Manager, Arthur Andersen Paris Office, 1965-1968; Lawyer, (Conseil Juridique et Fiscal, 1968-1992); Attorney, (Avocat, 1992—). Maitre de Seminaires de droit fiscal, Universite de Paris I Pantheon-Sorbonne; Conferencier at the International Management Association Brussels. *LANGUAGES:* English and Spanish. *PRACTICE AREAS:* Tax Law; International Tax Law; Corporate Law.

BOREL FADLALLAH MOQUIN

Established in 1964

52, RUE COPERNIC
75116 PARIS, FRANCE
Telephone: (1) 45.01.50.50
Telex: 649900 F
Fax: (1) 45.00.56.00

International Arbitration, Civil, Commercial, Criminal, Fiscal and International Law.

FIRM PROFILE: *The firm offers a full range of legal services. The client base is European, North American, Lebanese and Middle Eastern in scope.*

JACQUES BOREL, born Paris, France, January 13, 1931; admitted, 1964, Paris, France. *Education:* Faculté des Lettres de Bordeaux, France (Diplôme d'Etudes Littéraires Générales Classiques); Faculté de Droit de Paris (Licence en Droit; Diplôme d'Etudes Supérieures de Droit Privé). Author: "Opportunities for and Obstacles to Obtaining Evidence in France for Use in Litigation in the United States," The International Lawyer, Winter, 1979. Secrétaire de la Conférence de Stage des Avocats à la Cour de Paris, 1966-1967. *Member:* Association Française de Droit Maritime; Association Droit et Commerce; Chambre de Commerce Franco-Américaine. *LANGUAGES:* French and English. *PRACTICE AREAS:* National and International Business Law; Corporate Trade Litigation; Mergers and Acquisitions.

GEORGES FADLALLAH, born Zahlé, Liban, January 17, 1949; admitted, 1974, Liban; 1992, Paris, France. *Education:* Université de Beyrouth (Licence Française et Libanaise en Droit); Faculté de Droit de Paris II (Diplôme d'Etudes Supérieures de Droit Public; Diplôme d'Etudes Supérieures de Droit Privé). Lecturer at Law, Université de Beyrouth, 1976-1981. Lebanese Speaker for René Capitan Association. *Member:* French-Lebanese Lawyers Association (President); Euro-Arab Arbitration Chamber. *LANGUAGES:* French, Arab and English. *PRACTICE AREAS:* International Business and Tax Law; Corporate Law; Mergers and Acquisitions.

ARNAUD MOQUIN, born Neuilly-sur-Seine, France, March 11, 1958; admitted, 1981, Paris, France. *Education:* Faculté de Droit de Paris (Licence, Maîtrise de Droit Privé). Member, Junior Enterprises Association. *LANGUAGES:* French and English. *PRACTICE AREAS:* Business and Corporate Law; Non-Competition Law; Corporate Trade Law; Social Law and Litigation; Mergers and Acquisitions.

VERONIQUE GAGEY-DANDREL, born France, August 14, 1965; admitted, 1993, Paris, France. *Education:* Paris-Malakoff University (Maîtrise de Droit, 1987); University College of London (1987); Paris University (D.E.A. Droit Anglo-Américain des Affaires, 1988). *Member:* Club Convaincre; Commission Justice et Lois. *LANGUAGES:* French and English. *PRACTICE AREAS:* International Tax Law; Business Law.

GUILLAUME SIMON, born Annaba, Algérie, June 1963; admitted, 1993, Paris, France. *Education:* Paris University (Maîtrise de Droit, 1987). *LANGUAGES:* French and English. *PRACTICE AREAS:* Business Law; Corporate Law.

MARTINE VOIRIN-HAVEZ, born Nancy, France, July 29, 1952; admitted, 1989, Paris, France. *Education:* Nancy University (Licence es-lettres, 1976; Licence d'Anglais, 1979); Institut d'Administration des Entreprises I.A.E. (1986); Rheims University (Maîtrise de Droit, 1986); Paris-Assas University (D.E.A. de Droit Communautaire, 1992). *LANGUAGES:* French and English. *PRACTICE AREAS:* Commercial Law; Civil Law; Social Law.

JEAN-MARC WASILEWSKI, born Rheims, France, May 24, 1964; admitted, 1993, Paris, France. *Education:* Université de Paris-Panthéon-Sorbonne (Maîtrise de Droit, 1986; D.E.A. de Droit Social, 1987; D.E.A. de Droit Privé, 1988). Lecturer at Law, Université de Paris-Panthéon-Sorbonne. *LANGUAGES:* French, English and German. *PRACTICE AREAS:* Social Law; Civil Law; Commercial Law.

LEGAL SUPPORT PERSONNEL

EVELYNE BEAUVOIS, born Saint-Mandé, France, September 19, 1952. *Education:* Paris University (Licence en Droit). Corporate Law. *LANGUAGES:* French and English.

MYRIELLE ROCHER, born Douai, France, November 15, 1949. *Education:* Paris-Nanterre University (Capacité en Droit, 1984). Legal Research, Drafting, Client Correspondence. (Paralegal). *LANGUAGES:* French and English.

BORLOO, SAIGNE & ASSOCIÉS

Société Civile Professionnelle d'Avocats

4, RUE BRUNEL
75017 PARIS, FRANCE
Telephone: (1) 48.88.44.44
Fax: (1) 48.88.44.00
Telex: 642.733

General French and International Law, Acquisitions, Arbitration, International Transactions, Foreign Investment, Labor and Social Law, Construction Law, Public Projects and particularly Insolvency, Bankruptcy and Restructuring Work.

PARTNERS

JEAN-LOUIS BORLOO, born April 7, 1951; admitted, 1976, Paris. *Education:* Paris (Master of Laws, 1975); Institut Supérieur des Affaires (Jouy-en-Josas, 1976). Co-Author: with Gérard Proutheau, "How to Obtain Assistance and Financing Economica," Practical guide to Grants, Paris, 1987. Professor, Financial Analysis, Institut Supérieur des Affaires and Hautes Etudes Commerciales. Member, French Parliament, 1994—; Mayor, Valenciennes, 1994—. *LANGUAGES:* English.

JEAN-DOMINIQUE DAUDIER DE CASSINI, born July 6, 1957; admitted, 1992, Paris. *Education:* Ecole des Hautes Etudes Industrielles, Lille (Thermoengineering); Institut Supérieur des Affaires (Jouy-en Josas, 1982). *LANGUAGES:* English. *PRACTICE AREAS:* Insolvency Law; Acquisitions.

PHILIPPE LAYE, born April 13, 1960; admitted, 1988, Paris. *Education:* University of Paris (D.E.A. Advanced Degree in Business Law, 1985). *LANGUAGES:* English and Spanish. *PRACTICE AREAS:* Insolvency Law; Acquisitions; Arbitration; Commercial Litigation.

MARC LEFEVRE, born February 21, 1951; admitted, 1994, Paris. *Education:* University of Paris (Master of Laws, 1975; D.E.A. Advanced Degree in Business Law). Visiting Professor, D.E.S.S. Public Enterprise Law. Author: "Practical Guide to Public Contracts," 1994. General Legal Counsel, Société Centrale pour l'Equipment du Territoire. *LANGUAGES:* English. *PRACTICE AREAS:* Public Law.

JEAN-YVES MARQUET, born October 27, 1951; admitted, 1992, Paris. *Education:* University of Paris (Master of Laws, 1975; D.E.S.S. Advanced Degree in Private Law, 1977); Centre Supérieur d'Etudes Notariales (Graduate, 1976). *LANGUAGES:* English. *PRACTICE AREAS:* Insolvency Law; Acquisitions; Commercial Litigation.

PHILIPPE SAIGNE, born April 22, 1949; admitted, 1973, Paris. *Education:* University of Paris (D.E.S. Advanced Degree, Public Law; D.E.S. Advanced Degree, Political Science, 1972). *PRACTICE AREAS:* Insolvency Law; Acquisitions; Arbitration; Commercial Litigation.

PASCAL SIGRIST, born December 1, 1958; admitted, 1987, Paris. *Education:* University of Paris (Master of Laws, 1983; D.E.A. Advanced Degree in Business Law, 1984). *LANGUAGES:* English. *PRACTICE AREAS:* Commercial Law; Leasing Law; Litigation.

ASSOCIATES

PHILIPPE BERTEAUX, born August 15, 1967; admitted, 1992, Paris. *Education:* University of Paris (Master of Law, 1989; D.E.A. Advanced Degree in Patent and Trademark Law, 1990). *LANGUAGES:* English. *PRACTICE AREAS:* Commercial Law; Litigation.

JOELLE CATTAN, born July 23, 1967; admitted, 1994, Paris. *Education:* University of Paris (D.E.A. of Private Law, Advanced Degree in Private Law, 1991). *LANGUAGES:* English and Arabic. *PRACTICE AREAS:* Leasing Law; Commercial Law; Litigation.

CATHERINE GEOFFROY, born January 3, 1969; (Not admitted in France). *Education:* University of Paris II Panthéon Assas (Master of Business and Private Law, 1990; D.E.A. Advanced Degree in History of Law, 1991). *LANGUAGES:* English. *PRACTICE AREAS:* Leasing Law; Commercial Law.

STEPHANIE HIRSCH, born December 26, 1966; admitted, 1994, Paris. *Education:* University of Paris (D.E.A. Advanced Degree in International Law, 1989). *LANGUAGES:* German and English. *PRACTICE AREAS:* Insolvency Law; Acquisitions; Commercial Litigation.

PATRICIA LE MARCHAND, born November 25, 1969; (Not admitted in France). *Education:* Ecole Supérieure de Commerce de Toulouse (Business School of Toulouse); University of Toulouse (D.E.S.S., D.J.C.E. Ad-

(This Listing Continued)

BORLOO, SAIGNE & ASSOCIÉS, Paris—Continued

vanced Degree in Business Law). *LANGUAGES:* English and German. *PRACTICE AREAS:* Insolvency Law; Acquisitions.

ISABELLE MANSARD, born September 30, 1966; (Not admitted in France). *Education:* University of Paris (D.E.A. Advanced Degree in Public Law, 1990). *PRACTICE AREAS:* Commercial Law; Factoring; Leasing; Litigation.

MARTINE MALAIZE-VERDEAU, born May 8, 1965; (Not admitted in France). *Education:* University of Paris II Panthéon Assas (Master of Business and Tax Law, 1990); Institut des Hautes Etudes Internationales (Advanced Degree in International Law, 1987). *LANGUAGES:* English, German, Russian and Indonesian. *PRACTICE AREAS:* Insolvency Law; Leasing Law.

PAULINE PERRIN, born September 6, 1992; admitted, 1986, Paris. *Education:* University of Paris (D.E.A. Advanced Degree in Labor Law, 1985). *LANGUAGES:* English. *PRACTICE AREAS:* Labour Law.

MICHEL PETITDEMANGE, born April 17, 1954; admitted, 1981, Strasbourg. *Education:* University of Strasbourg. *LANGUAGES:* German and English. *PRACTICE AREAS:* Commercial Litigation.

JEAN-CHRISTOPHE ROUBAUT, born March 5, 1957; (Not admitted in France). *Education:* D.E.C.S. (Advanced Commerce/Accounting degree). *LANGUAGES:* English. *PRACTICE AREAS:* Financial Analysis; Acquisitions.

ANNE-MARIE ROUXEL, born August 15, 1962; admitted, 1993, Paris. *Education:* University of Paris (Master of Laws). *LANGUAGES:* English. *PRACTICE AREAS:* Construction Law; Litigation.

FRANCK SINGER, born December 14, 1961; admitted, 1985, Lille. *Education:* Université Lille (LL.M., 1987); Institut d'Etudes Judiciaires, Lille (LL.B., 1985). Premier Secrétaire de la Conférence, Lille, 1987. *LANGUAGES:* English and Italian. *PRACTICE AREAS:* Insolvency Law; Banking Law; Commercial Law; Litigation.

ANKER SORENSEN, born April 10, 1962; admitted, 1990, Paris. *Education:* Institut d'Etudes Politiques de Strasbourg (D.E.S.S. de Commerce Extérieur); Ecole de Management Européen, University of Strasbourg; University of Paris Pantheon-Sorbonne (Masters of Laws in International Business Law and Civil Procedure). *LANGUAGES:* English, German and Danish. *PRACTICE AREAS:* Insolvency Law; Acquisitions; Commercial Litigation.

ELISABETH VANDENHEEDE, born September 3, 1961; admitted, 1990, Paris. *Education:* University of Paris and Caen (D.E.A. Advanced Degree in Private Law, 1986). *LANGUAGES:* English, German. *PRACTICE AREAS:* Banking Law; Leasing; Litigation.

CHARLES WEIL, born July 27, 1962; admitted, 1988, Paris. *Education:* Institut d'Etudes Politiques de Paris (1986); University of Paris Panthéon-Sorbonne (D.E.A. Master of Business Law, 1992). *LANGUAGES:* English. *PRACTICE AREAS:* Construction Law; Administrative Law; General Commercial Law; Litigation.

Languages: English, German, French, Danish, Arabic, Russian and Indonesian

---

BOURGOING DUMONTEIL ET ASSOCIES

Société d'Avocats

Established in 1901

119, RUE DE LILLE
75007 PARIS, FRANCE
Telephone: (33-1) 45.55.90.45+
Telecopier/Fax: (33-1) 45.55.94.04

Brussels, Belgium Associated Office: Baetens & Associés, Avenue Jules César 2, 1150. Telephone: 19.32.2.771.20.23. Fax: 19.32.2.771.89.20. Telex: 24048.

Brazzaville, Congo, Africa Associated Office: Brudey and Andziel, B.P. 2041. Telephone: 19.242.83.12.01. Fax: 19.242.83.52.07.

Ouagadougou, Burkina Faso Associated Office: Dabire and Sorgho, B.P. 1026. Telephone: 19.226.30.45.93. Fax: 19.226.30.48.30.

Beyruth, Lebanon Associated Office: Maître Georges Jabre, B.P. 5512. Telephone: 19.961.380.011; 19.961.380.012. Telex: 43906.

Niamey, Niger Associated Office: Maître Kouaovi, B.P. 10191. Telephone: 19.227.73.43.49. Fax: 19.227.73.49.23.

(This Listing Continued)

Conakry, Guinea Associated Office: Maître Amadou Thidiane Kaba, B.P. 1767. Telephone: 19.224.44.39.45. Fax: 19.224.44.39.45.

General French, EEC and International Legal and Tax Practice. Litigation, Arbitration, Debt Collection. Law of the French speaking African Countries. French Nationality Law.

Firm admitted to appear before French, EEC and French Speaking Courts.

FIRM PROFILE: The Firm was established in 1901 by Charles Bourgoing Dumonteil, then was ran by Jean-Vincent Bourgoing Dumonteil and today by Vincent Bourgoing Dumonteil from 1960. It offers a full range of legal services. It is known for its practice in French Speaking African Countries.

MEMBERS OF FIRM

VINCENT BOURGOING DUMONTEIL, born St. Maur, France, December 24, 1937; admitted, 1962, Paris, France. *Education:* Institut d'Administration des Entreprises (1960); Paris University (Maîtrise en Droit et Sciences Economiques, 1960). Author: "Négotiation des Blocs d'Actions des Sociétés Anonymes," Les Petites Affiches 8 November 1974; "Droit au report des Déficits," LPA 16 April 1976; "IVORY COAST: The Reform of Company Law," (The Company Lawyer - LONDON - 1984 Vol. 5); "L'intérêt légal, complément substantiel d'indemnisation," (Les Gens de Robe, ABIDJAN, Ivory Coast N° 3 - 1986); "Exequatur, chronique d'application de l'Accord Franco-ivoirien de Coopération en matière de justice," (Ibidem N° 8/9 - 1987); "Modes de constatation de la Nationalité Française" (Française du Renouveau, ABIDJAN N° 5 - avril 1992). *PRACTICE AREAS:* International Practice; Laws of the French Speaking African Countries; French Nationality Law; Arbitration.

LAURENT BERNET, born Mâcon (Saône et Loire), France, December 30, 1966; admitted, 1994, Paris, France. *Education:* University of Lyon (Maîtrise en Droit des Affaires, 1989); University of Dijon (DESS Droit des Affaires et Fiscalité, 1990); University of Kent, Canterbury (LL.M., International Commercial Law, 1991). *PRACTICE AREAS:* International Practice; Litigation; Arbitration.

LUC CASTAGNET, born Limoges, France, April 27, 1966; (Not admitted to appear before the French Courts). *Education:* University of Paris II, Panthéon-Assas. Author: "La Reglementation fiscale en Cote d'Ivoire," (updating, C2A Editions), 1992 and 1993; Co-Author: "Bulletin de fiscalité Ivoirienne," (revue bi-mensuelle C2A Editions). Legal Consultant, Law Firm in Abidjan, Ivory Coast, 1991-1993. *PRACTICE AREAS:* Laws of the French Speaking African Countries; Business Law.

FLORENCE BRASSEUR, born Amiens, France, August 25, 1966; admitted, 1995, Paris. *Education:* University of Paris V (Maîtrise de droit privé, 1991). *PRACTICE AREAS:* Company Law; Commercial Law.

Languages: French, English and Spanish

BRANCHE & ASSOCIES

26, BOULEVARD RASPAIL
75007 PARIS, FRANCE
Telephone: (33)(1) 42 22 10 11
Fax: (33)(1) 45 44 91 17

Firm engaged in French and European General Practice and authorized to appear before French and EEC Courts. International Commercial Transactions. Litigation and Arbitration. Lawyers qualified in U.S., French and European Law.

J. MICHEL BRANCHE, born Poitiers, France, August 1956; admitted, 1983, Paris. *Education:* University of Paris I and II, Schools of Law; Institut d'Etudes Politiques de Paris (1982); Trainee, Commission of the European Economic Community (February 1985-July, 1985); University of Paris, Sorbonne (Diplôme d'Etudes Approfondies in European Law, 1986); New York University (M.C.J., 1987). Author: "EC Competition Policy: the 21st Report of the Commission", in "Cahiers Juridiques et Fiscaux a l'Exportation", CFCE, 1992 Member: NYU Club of Europe; TEAM EUROPE (Board Member for France). *LANGUAGES:* French and English.

KARIM MEDJAD, born Rabat, Morocco, May 4, 1962; admitted, 1990, Paris. *Education:* University of Paris I, Faculty of Law (D.E.A. International and EEC Law, 1985; Ph.D. in Economics, 1993); Harvard Law School (LL.M., 1986). Assistant Professor, Groupe HEC (Courses in International Contract Law and Corporate Law). *Member:* Harvard Club of France. *LANGUAGES:* French, English and Arabic.

VALERIE AMAND, born Paris, France, January 4, 1956; admitted, 1979, Paris. *Education:* University of Paris X, Faculty of Law (Master of

(This Listing Continued)

Business Law, 1977). *Member:* Association de Juristes Européens. *LANGUAGES:* French and English.

OF COUNSEL

IAN J. STOCK, born Buckinghamshire, England, December 7, 1952; admitted, 1982, California; 1984, New York; 1990, Paris. *Education:* University of California at Berkeley (A.B., summa cum laude, 1979); Yale University (J.D., 1982). *Member:* Union Internationale des Avocats. (Also, practicing individually, Hermeray, France). *LANGUAGES:* English and French.

GUY SOUSSAN, born December 4, 1958; admitted, 1993, Paris. *Education:* University of Nantes (D.E.A., Public Law, 1982); College of Europe, Bruges, Belgium (Diploma in Advanced European Legal Studies, 1984); New York University School of Law (M.C.J., 1987). *LANGUAGES:* French, Danish, English.

BRANDI DRÖGE PILTZ & HEUER

250 BIS, BOULEVARD SAINT-GERMAIN
75007 PARIS, FRANCE
Telephone: 33-1 49 54 90 37
Facsimile: 33-1 49 54 90 02

Bielefeld, Germany Office: Elsa-Brändström-Str. 1 and 3, 33602. Telephone: 49 521 96535-0. Telecopier: 49 521 96535-99.

Detmold, Germany Office: Lindenweg 2, 32756. Telephone: 49 5231 9857-0. Telecopier: 49 5231 9857-50.

Gütersloh, Germany Office: Hochstr. 19, 33332. Telephone: 49 5241 5 88 86. Telecopier: 49 5241 5 88 81.

Berlin, Germany Office: Seelenbinderstr. 124, 12555. Telephone: 49 30 6509465. Telecopier: 49 30 6565679.

Leipzig, Germany Office: Katharinenstr. 1-3, 04109. Telephone: 49 341 287550. Telecopier: 49 341 289162.

German-French Business Law, International and EEC Law

MEMBER OF FIRM

DR. HENNING HEUER, born Hannover, Germany, May 26, 1938; admitted, 1967, Germany; 1990, France. *Education:* Universities of Freiburg, Paris and Münster (Erstes Juristisches Staatsexamen, 1962; Doctor of Jurisprudence, 1964). Author: "Das richtige Bezugsobjekt des Adäquanzurteils," Dissertation 1964. *LANGUAGES:* German, French, English and Spanish. *PRACTICE AREAS:* German-French Business Law; International and EEC Law.

BREDIN PRAT

130 RUE DU FAUBOURG SAINT-HONORÉ
75008 PARIS, FRANCE
Telephone: 44 35 35 35
Telefax: 42 89 10 73; 43 59 70 01
Telex: 219000 Q53215-LEGIS

General French, American and International Practice, Mergers and Acquisitions, Securities Law, Litigation and Arbitration, EC and French Competition Law, Banking and Finance, Intellectual and Industrial Property, Property Law.

JEAN-DENIS BREDIN, born Paris, France, May 17, 1929; admitted, 1950, Paris. *Education:* University of Paris, Sorbonne; University of Paris Law School (Licence, 1949; Doctorat en Droit, 1950; Agrégé des Facultés de Droit, 1957). Author: "Traité de Droit du Commerce International," 1969. Professor of International Law: Rennes Law School, 1957-1967; Lille Law School, 1968; Paris Law School, 1969—. Lectured on International Law: University Tunis, Tunisia; Rabat, Morocco; Cairo, Egypt. Member: Bar of the Court of Appeal of Paris, 1953; Comité Français de Droit International; membre de l'Académie Française; Académie Française, 1990. Contributor: Journal de Droit International; Revue Critique de Droit International Privé; Revue Française de l'Arbitrage, Collections in honor of Professeur Goldman, Premier Président Bellet et Professeur Loussouarn. *LANGUAGES:* French and English.

JEAN-FRANÇOIS PRAT, born Caen, Calvados, France, October 10, 1941; admitted, 1966, Paris. *Education:* University of Aix; University of Paris Law School (Licence, 1963; Doctorat en Droit, 1969). Author: "L'harmonisation de l'imposition des revenus de capitaux mobiliers dans les pays du Marché commun," 1972. *LANGUAGES:* French, English and Italian.

(This Listing Continued)

ROBERT SAINT-ESTEBEN, born Ustaritz, France, April 26, 1942; admitted, 1975, Paris. *Education:* University of Paris; University of Paris Law School (Licence, 1964); Ecole Nationale des Impôts, 1964, Diplome d'Etudes Superieures de Droit Privé, 1965; Diplome d'Etudes Supérieures de Sciences Criminelles 1967, Diplome du Centre Universitaire d'Etudes des Communautés Europeennes, CEE, 1966. Author: "Droits Communautaires et Droits Nationaux," 1967; "Une Concentration Internationale d'Entreprises," L'Affaire Continental Can, 1972; "Chronique de droit communautaire: Developpements du droit communautaire de la concurrence," DPCI 667, 1988; Les Concentrations in Jurisclasseur Europe, I, 1991. Assistant Professor: in Common Market Regulations, University of Paris Law School. Member, Bar of the Court of Appeal of Paris, 1975. Contributor: Jurisclasseur Europe.

RICHARD SCHEPARD, born New York, N.Y., October 21, 1942; admitted, 1968, New York; 1971, U.S. Supreme Court; 1973, France; 1979, District of Columbia. *Education:* City College of the City University of New York (B.A., 1964); New York University (J.D., 1967). Order of the Coif. Fulbright Scholarship, Faculty of Law, University of Paris, 1967-1968. Editor, New York University Law Review, 1966-1967. Assistant General Counsel for Industry and Trade, U.S. Department of Commerce, Washington, D.C., 1977-1978. Special Consultant, U.S. Department of State, 1979-1983. *Member:* New York State and American Bar Associations. *LANGUAGES:* English and French.

CLAUDE BENDEL, born Paris, France, December 20, 1946; admitted, 1969, Paris. *Education:* University of Paris Law School (Licence, 1969). *LANGUAGES:* French, German and English.

DIDIER MARTIN, born Paris, France, August 30, 1952; admitted, 1977, Paris. *Education:* Faculté de Droit de Paris II (D.E.A., Private Law, 1976; D.E.A., Criminal Law, 1977). Author: "Les sociétés holdings," "Mergers & Acquisitions in France," "OPA-OPE.". *LANGUAGES:* French and English.

JEAN-PIERRE GRANDJEAN, born Bourg-la-Reine, France, April 22, 1959; admitted, 1985, Paris. *Education:* University of Paris Law School (Licence, 1979; Maîtrise, 1980; D.E.A. de Droit International, 1981; D.E.A. de droit Privé, 1983). *LANGUAGES:* French and English.

SYLVIE AMIEL-MORABIA, born Paris, France, September 26, 1957; admitted, 1984, Paris. *Education:* University of Paris, Sorbonne (Maîtrise, 1979); University of Paris Law School (Licence, 1981; Maîtrise, 1982; D.E.A. de Droit Privé, 1983). *LANGUAGES:* French and English.

ELENA M. BAXTER, born Cincinnati, Ohio, July 29, 1957; admitted, 1983, New York; 1989, France. *Education:* University of Tennessee (B.A., summa cum laude, 1979); University of Virginia (J.D., 1982). Phi Beta Kappa; Order of the Coif. *LANGUAGES:* English and French.

LOUIS CHRISTOPHE DELANOY, born Epinal, France, January 1, 1960; admitted, 1987, Paris. *Education:* Institut National des Langues et Civilisations Orientales (Russian, 1977-1978); Institut d'Etudes Politiques de Paris (1978-1981); Law School of Paris (Licence, 1982; Maîtrise, 1984; D.E.A., 1985). *LANGUAGES:* French, German, English and Russian.

PHILIPPE BEURIER, born Nantes, France, April 6, 1959; admitted, 1985, Paris. *Education:* University of Paris Law School (Licence, 1980; Maîtrise, 1981). *LANGUAGES:* French and English.

MARIA R. RUEGG, born Palo Alto, California, January 12, 1945; admitted, 1986, New York; 1988, France. *Education:* Cornell University (B.A., 1966); University of Paris; Yale University (M.Phil., 1971; Ph.D., 1976; J.D., 1984). *LANGUAGES:* English and French.

ERIC DEZEUZE, born Rognac, France, May 10, 1963; admitted, 1987, Aix-en-Provence. *Education:* University of Aix-en-Provence Law School (Maîtrise, 1985; D.E.A., Sciences Pénales et Criminologie, 1986). *LANGUAGES:* French, English and Italian.

ASSOCIATES

ANNE-CAROLINE BOCCARD, born Lyon, France, March 7, 1964; admitted, 1989, Lyon; 1992, Paris. *Education:* University Lyon III (DEA, droit des affaires 1986); College of Europe, Belgium (Diploma of European Legal Studies, 1989). Auxiliary, EC Commission, 1991-1992. *LANGUAGES:* French and English.

DOMINIQUE BOMPOINT, born March 12, 1966; admitted, 1989, Bordeaux. *Education:* Ecole Supérieure de Commerce de Bordeaux (DESCAF, 1987); Université de Bordeaux I (Diplôme d'Etudes Compatibles Supérieures, 1988; Diplôme d'Etudes Approfondies de Droit Privé, 1989). *LANGUAGES:* French, English and Spanish.

(This Listing Continued)

BREDIN PRAT, *Paris—Continued*

INÈS LEGRIS, born Montreal, Canada, February 3, 1967; admitted, 1990, Montreal; 1992, Paris. *Education:* Université de Montreal (LL.B., 1989). *Member:* Canadian Bar Association. *LANGUAGES:* French, English and Spanish.

FRANK LIPWORTH, born Johannesburg, South Africa, January 6, 1963; admitted, 1989, as Solicitor, United Kingdom; 1994, as Avocat, Paris (Not admitted in France). *Education:* University of Kent at Canterbury (BSc., 1983); Law School, United Kingdom (1986). *LANGUAGES:* English, French and Spanish.

PASCALE MORIN, born Rougemontier, France, February 14, 1965; admitted, 1991, Paris. *Education:* University of Rouen Law School (Licence, 1986; Maîtrise, 1987); University of Paris Law School, Sorbonne (D.E.A. Droit des Affaires et de l'Economie, 1988; D.E.A. Droit Communautaire et Européen, 1989). *LANGUAGES:* French, English and German.

JEAN REYNAUD, born Paris, France, October 2, 1960; admitted, 1992, Paris. *Education:* University of Paris, Sorbonne (Maîtrise in Lettres Modernes, 1982); University of Paris Law School (Maîtrise, 1984); Institut d'Etudes Politiques de Paris (Diploma, 1984). *LANGUAGES:* French and English.

ISABELLE SCHMITT, born Bombay, India, November 20, 1955; admitted, 1990, Counseil Juridique, France. *Education:* DEUG (Droit, 1976; Licence Droit, 1977; Maîtrise Droit, 1978; D.E.A. Droit Comparé, 1980; Doctorat en Droit, 1986). *LANGUAGES:* French and English.

GREGORY C. SHAFFER, born Cincinnati, Ohio, July 8, 1958; admitted, 1991, California; 1992, France. *Education:* Dartmouth College (B.A., magna cum laude, 1980); University of Madrid (Reynolds Fellowship, 1982-1983); Stanford University (J.D., 1988). Recipient, Carl Mason Franklin Prize in International Law, 1988. Editor, Stanford Law Review, 1987-1988. *LANGUAGES:* English, French and Spanish.

DIANE PASTUREL, born Neuilly sur Seine, France, February 4, 1967; admitted, 1989, Paris. *Education:* University of Paris Law School (Licence, 1987, Maîtrise, 1988, D.E.A., Droit des Affaires et Economic). Head of the Legal Department of the "Société de Bourse Française" (1992-1994). *LANGUAGES:* French, English, Spanish.

BEATRIZ DE SILVA, admitted, 1995, Paris. *Education:* Ecole Supérieure de Sciences Economiques et Sociales (ESSEC, 1992); University of Paris Law School, ASSAS (Maîtrise, 1993). *LANGUAGES:* French, English, Spanish and Portuguese.

BREITENSTEIN MEILLASSOUX HAUSER

Avocats au Barreau de Paris

Rechtsanwälte

Established in 1987

29, RUE DU FAUBOURG ST. HONORÉ

75008 PARIS, FRANCE

Telephone: (33) (1) 42 66 63 19
Telecopier: (33) (1) 42 66 64 81

General French, German, European Community and International Law, Arbitration, International Contracts, Construction, Corporate, Mergers and Acquisitions, Antitrust, Copyright, Computer, Entertainment, Trademark, Litigation, East European Joint Ventures.

DETLEV VON BREITENSTEIN, born Saarbrücken, Germany, October 21, 1937; admitted, 1974, Germany; 1977, France. *Education:* Universities of Berlin, Bonn, Tübingen (Referendar, 1961); University of Paris (D.E.S., 1963); University of Bonn (Doctor juris, 1966); University of Berlin (Assessor, 1967); Centre de Perfectionnement dans l'Administration des Affaires (C.P.A., 1974). Chairman, Permanent Court of Arbitration of the Franco-German Chambre of Commerce and Industry (COFACI), Paris. Arbitrator: Vienna Court of Arbitration, Federal Chamber of Commerce; Budapest Court of Arbitration, Hungarian Chamber of Commerce. *Member:* U.I.A. (President, Law and Technology Commission); I.B.A.; Deutsches Institut für Schiedsgerichtswesen (D.I.S.); Association française de l'Arbitrage (afa); Société française pour le Droit de l'Environnement (SFDE). *LANGUAGES:* German, French and English. *PRACTICE AREAS:* International Arbitration; Environmental Law; International Law; Corporate Law; Commercial Law; Competition Law; Products Liability Law; Commercial Litigation; German and Swiss Law.

(This Listing Continued)

ANDRÉ MEILLASSOUX, born Roubaix, France, January 16, 1958; admitted, 1983, France. *Education:* University of Paris II (Maîtrise en Droit, 1980); University of Paris-Sorbonne (Russian Literature); Paris Institute of Comparative Law. *LANGUAGES:* French, English, German and Russian. *PRACTICE AREAS:* Business Law; Corporate Law; International Law; Contracts; Mergers and Acquisitions; Intellectual Property; Computer Law; Construction Law; Labor Law; Leases; Commercial Litigation; Russian Ventures.

MARTIN H. HAUSER, born Frankfurt/Main, Germany, October 14, 1955; admitted, 1985, Germany; 1991, France. *Education:* Universities of Frankfurt/Main, Geneva, Freiburg im Breisgau (Referendar, 1979); University of Munich (Dr. jur., 1983; Assessor, 1985); New York University (M.C.J., 1986); European Community Lawyers Bar Examination (Paris, 1991). Author: "Der Patentlizenzvertrag im Französischen Recht im Vergleich zum Deutschen Recht," J. Schweitzer Verlag, Munich, 1984. Research Fellow, Foreign and International Patent Law, Copyright and Competition Law, Max-Planck Institute, Munich 1980-1983. *LANGUAGES:* German, French and English. *PRACTICE AREAS:* Copyright and Trademark Law; Intellectual Property; Computer Law; Entertainment Law; International Law; Mergers and Acquisitions; Competition Law; Business Law; Contracts; Commercial Litigation; EEC Law; German Law.

BARBARA S. BERTHOLET, born Lyon, France, May 20, 1967; admitted, 1991, Paris. *Education:* Paris Sorbonne (Licence d'Histoire, 1988), University of Paris II (Maîtrise Droit des Affaires, 1990; DESS Droit des Affaires et Fiscalité, 1991; Magistère de Juriste d' Affaire, 1991). *LANGUAGES:* French and German.

ALEXANDRE BRABANT, born Adelaide, Australia, January 8, 1964; admitted, 1991, New York (Not admitted in France). *Education:* Syracuse University (B.A., 1987); New England School of Law (J.D., 1990); Regent's College, London, Great Britain, 1989. *Member:* New York State and American Bar Associations. *LANGUAGES:* French and English.

SANDRINE M. LACHAZE, born Neuilly-sur-Seine, France, February 14, 1967; admitted, 1991, Paris. *Education:* University of Paris X (Maîtrise Droit des affaires, 1990); University of Paris Dauphine (Maîtrise de Gestion, 1990); University of Paris Sorbonne (DESS Droit du Commerce Exterieur, 1991); Franco-British Chamber of Commerce and Industry (Diploma in Business English, 1987). *LANGUAGES:* French, English and German.

HENRI PIEYRE DE MANDIARGUES, born Montpellier, France, October 10, 1968; admitted, 1993, Montpellier; 1994, Paris. *Education:* University of Montpellier (Magistère-DJCE de Droit des Affaires, 1992; DJCE, 1992; CES en Droit de la Distribution et en Droit Fiscal, 1992). *LANGUAGES:* French and English.

SANDRINE M. CONIN, born Montereau, France, October 20, 1967; admitted, 1994, Paris. *Education:* ISIT (Diplôme d'interprétariat et de Traduction, 1990); Paris Sceaux (Maîtrise Droit du Commerce International, 1990; DESS Droit Communautaire, 1991); Marburg, Germany (Magister Legum, LL.M., German Law, 1991); Sydney University, Sydney, Australia (LL.M., 1994). *LANGUAGES:* French, English and German.

BRIZAY LONDON

Established in 1990

28, RUE MESLAY

75003 PARIS, FRANCE

Telephone: (33-1) 42 77 11 54
Telecopier: (33-1) 42 77 11 40

Corporate, Bank and Finance, Foreign Investments, EEC and French Environment and Competition Law, International Trade, International Contracts, Human Rights, Arbitration.

JEAN-PIERRE BRIZAY, born Singapore, Singapore, January 31, 1935; admitted, 1974, Paris. *Education:* Paris University (Licence en Droit, 1956; D.E.S. Droit Privé, 1958; D.E.S. Histoire du Droit & Droit Romain, 1958); Harvard Law School (LL.M., 1960). Co-author: "Pratique des Contrats Internationaux," 1982. Author: "Joint Ventures in France," New York Institute of France's Acquisitions Yearbook, 1992/3. *Member:* International Bar Association; Confédération Syndicale des Avocats. *LANGUAGES:* French and English. *PRACTICE AREAS:* Corporate; Bank and Finance; Foreign Investments; International Contracts.

CAROLINE LONDON, born Neuilly-sur-Seine, France, May 8, 1954; registered, 1988 as Conseil Juridique; 1992, Avocat. *Education:* Faculté de

(This Listing Continued)

Droit, Nancy (Licence en droit, 1975; DEA droit Communautaire, 1976); Centre Européen Universitaire (Diplôme, 1976). Schuman Fellowship European Parliament, Luxembourg, 1977. Director and Co-Author: "Les Déchets," Lamy Environnement, 1994. Author: "Environnement et Stratégie de l'Entreprise," Ecoplanet - Apogée Publications, March 1993;"Le Secteur Bancaire au Regard du droit Communautaire," RTDE 593, 1987; "Fusions et acquisitions en droit communautaire," JCP 1988 §13320; "OPA/OPE: la voie communautaire?" JCP 1990 §15762; "L'heure des Choix," JCP 1991 §3512; "La prise en compte de l'environnement par l'entreprise," Petites Affiches No 64 29 May 1991; "Lenders' Ecological Liability-Myth or Reality," in EFMA letter no. 116, March 1992; "La Dynamique du Droit L'Environnement," in Revue des Affaires Européennes no. 3, 1992. Instructor, Competition and Environmental Law (French and EEC), University of Paris I Panthéon Sorbonne Law School, E.S.C.P. Paris, INSA Lyon, 1985—. *Member:* International Bar Association; Society of International Economic Law (President, 1988). *LANGUAGES:* French, English and German. *PRACTICE AREAS:* EEC Law; Environmental Law; Competition Law; Arbitration.

ASSOCIATES

VALÉRIE THIRÉ, admitted, 1994, Paris. *LANGUAGES:* French and English.

MICHAEL LLAMAS, admitted, 1994, Paris; 1990, as Barrister, England and Wales; 1994, Gibraltar. *LANGUAGES:* English, French, and Spanish.

CATHERINE BONNAFOUS. LANGUAGES: French and English.

CHRISTIAN BROGI

Notaire

Established in 1986

8 AV. DU PÈRE LACHAISE
75020 PARIS, FRANCE
Telephone: (1) 43 58 29 29
Fax: (1) 43 58 33 42

Residential & Commercial Property, Purchase, Sale, Leasing, Development & Funding, Conveyancing, Incorporation, Tax & Tax Planning, Marriage Contracts, Wills, Estates, Inheritance.

CHRISTIAN BROGI, born Neuilly-sur-Seine, France, 1948; admitted, 1979, Paris. *Education:* University of Paris (Maîtrise en Droit Privé, DSEN).

CAHILL GORDON & REINDEL

A Partnership including a Professional Corporation

Established in 1919

19 RUE FRANÇOIS 1ER
75008 PARIS, FRANCE
Telephone: 33.1-47.20.10.50
Facsimile: 33.1-47.23.06.38
Telex: 842-642331; CGR 642331F
Cable Address: "Cottofrank Paris"

New York City Office: 80 Pine Street, 10005. Telephone: 212-701-3000.
District of Columbia Office: 1990 K Street, N.W., Washington, D.C., 20006. Telephone: 202-862-8900.

General Practice.
Firm engaged in American, French and General International Practice, registered as Avocats in France and admitted to practice in French Courts reserved for Avocats.

EUROPEAN COUNSEL

FREDDY DRESSEN, born Courbevoie, France, October 12, 1946; admitted, 1978, France, Avocat. *Education:* Université de Paris (Licence en Droit, Certificat de l'Institut d'Etudes Judiciaires, 1970, Diplôme de l'Institut de Droit des Affaires, 1971); Cornell University (LL.M., 1972). *Member:* Association Française des Avocats Conseils d'Entreprises; Association Française d'Arbitrage. *LANGUAGES:* French and English.

(This Listing Continued)

ASSOCIATES

FRANÇOIS BONNIN, born Joigny, France, July 29, 1964; admitted, Conseil Juridique Stagiaire. *Education:* Université de Paris (Maîtrise en Droit des Affaires et Fiscalité, 1988; Diplôme d'Etudes Approfondies de Droit des Affaires, 1989); New York University (LL.M., 1992). *LANGUAGES:* French and English.

(For biographical data of the New York partners, see Professional Biographies at New York, N.Y.).

CAMMARATA & MONTFORT

Avocats au Barreau de Paris

Established in 1983

15 RUE DE LA BAUME
75008 PARIS, FRANCE
Telephone: (1) 53 75 21 21
Telefax: (1) 53 75 15 00

Marseille, France Office: 2, Rue Henri Barbusse, 13241, Cedex 01. Telephone: 91.90.90.00. Telefax: 91.56.17.22.

General and International Law Practice.

MEMBERS OF FIRM

CATALDO L. CAMMARATA, born Marseille, France, June 26, 1950; admitted, 1979, Paris. *Education:* University of Aix-Marseille (Baccalaureat); University College London (English Phonetics Degree, 1971); University of Aix-Marseille (B.A., 1972; M.A., 1973); Aix-en-Provence Law School (LL.M., 1976); Harvard Law School (LL.M., 1978). Harkness Foundation Fellow, 1978. *LANGUAGES:* French, Italian and English.

JEAN LATOURNERIE, born Paris, France, December 27, 1964; admitted, 1990, Paris. *Education:* Institut d'Etudes Politiques de Paris, (1988); University of Paris II (Maîtrise en Droit Public et Maîtrise en Droit des Affaires, 1986; D.E.A., Droit des Affaires, 1987). *LANGUAGES:* French, English and Italian.

ISABELLE MONIN LAFIN, born Paris, France, May 10, 1966; admitted, 1990, Paris. *Education:* Université de Paris (Maîtrise de droit des Affaires); Universitéde Paris I (D.E.A., Droit Privé, 1989). *LANGUAGES:* French, English and German.

FRANCK BERTHAULT, born Châlons-sur-Saône, France, June 18, 1963; admitted, 1991, Paris. *Education:* University of Montpellier Law School (Maîtrise de Droit des Affaires, 1987; D.E.S.S. Juriste d'Affairs, Diplôme de Juriste Conseil d'Entreprise, D.J.C.E.; Certificat de Spécialisation Droit Economique, 1988). Author: "Commentaire décision du Conseil de la concurrence relative au marché de la chaussure de sport haute et moyenne gamme," Lamy, 1990. Various articles in the newspaper "Les Echos". *LANGUAGES:* French and English.

OF COUNSEL

THIERRY S. RENOUX, born Nogaro Gers, France, December 8, 1953; admitted, 1983, Paris. *Education:* Lycee d'Etat de Toulouse; University of Paris I, Pantheon-Sorbonne; University of Aix-En-Provence-Marseille III; Maîtrise en Droit, Diplôme d'Etudes Approfondies de Droit Priveé (Droit Processuel); Diplôme d'Etudes Approfondies de Droit Public; Doctorat d'Etat en Droit. Professeur agrégé des Facultés de Droit, 1988. *LANGUAGES:* French and English.

(For Complete Biographical Data of Marseille Personnel, see Biographical Card at Marseille, France).

CAMPBELL, PHILIPPART & ASSOCIES

45 AVENUE MONTAIGNE
75008 PARIS, FRANCE
Telephone: (33)-1-47 23 64 82
Telecopier: (33)-1-47 23 37 74

French and EEC Corporate, Tax, Customs and Labor Law.

FIRM PROFILE: The firm was established in 1974 and offers a full range of business legal services to its clients, with particular emphasis on the legal and tax structuring of all forms of commercial investments and litigation. The firm has six partners and six associates.

(This Listing Continued)

CAMPBELL, PHILIPPART & ASSOCIES, Paris— Continued

MEMBERS OF FIRM

CHARLES G. G. CAMPBELL, born Lauder, Scotland, December 20, 1942; admitted, 1965, London, England; 1973, Paris. *Education:* Cambridge University, Cambridge, U.K. (B.A., 1964); Paris University Law Faculty (Certificate of Common Market Law, 1968). Author: "Tax Management, Business Operations in France-Regulation and Choice of Entity, Taxation," BNA, 1992. President, Cambridge University Law Society, 1964. *Member:* Franco-Irish Chamber of Commerce. (Also Counsel to Rand Rosenzweig Smith & Radley, New York, N.Y.). *LANGUAGES:* English and French. *PRACTICE AREAS:* Acquisitions; Real Estate Law; Mutual Funds.

ALAIN PHILIPPART, born Paris, France, February 23, 1945; admitted, 1970, Paris. *Education:* Law Faculty of Paris, Political Science Institute, Paris (Maîtrise en Droit, 1968; Certificat d'Aptitude à la Profession d'Avocat, 1969); College of Europe, Bruges, Belgium (1970). Author: "IR-SOFT Softwear for Income Revenue Calculation," Francis Lefebvre, 1985-1990; "Tax Management, Business Operations in France-Taxation," BNA, 1992. *Member:* Association Française des Avocats Fiscalistes. *LANGUAGES:* French and English. *PRACTICE AREAS:* Tax Law; Mergers and Acquisitions; Administrative Law.

JOCELYNE DELSOUILLER, born Geneva, Switzerland, September 24, 1949; admitted, 1974, Geneva, Switzerland; 1979, Paris. *Education:* Geneva University (Law Degree, 1972; Bar Examination, 1974). Author: "Tax Management, Business Operations in France-Regulation and Choice of Entity," BNA, 1992. *LANGUAGES:* French and English. *PRACTICE AREAS:* Company Law; Mergers and Acquisitions.

CLAIRE BONNET, born Paris, France, November 27, 1946; admitted, 1970, Paris. *Education:* Law Faculty of Paris (Law Degree, 1968); Business Institute for Law in Paris (Law Degree, 1970); Political Science Institute in Paris (Diploma, 1971). Author: "Tax Management," BNA, 1992. Chief Administrator, Directorate General of Indirect Taxes, Commission of the European Communities, 1979-1985. *LANGUAGES:* French and English. *PRACTICE AREAS:* Tax Law; Leveraged Buy-Outs; Personal Estate Planning.

HERVÉ LAIGO, born Nantes, France, September 26, 1946; admitted, 1971, Bordeaux; 1976, Paris. *Education:* Rennes University (Law Degree, 1969). Author: "Relations with Social Authorities," SYNCODS, 1975. *LANGUAGES:* French and English. *PRACTICE AREAS:* Labor Law; Distribution Law; Intellectual Property.

CHARLES SCHEER, born Paris, France, February 22, 1952; admitted, 1985, Paris. *Education:* L'Ecole des Hautes Etudes Commerciales (M.B.A., 1974; C.P.A., Commissaire aux Comptes, 1978; Expert Comptable, 1979); Law Faculty, Paris (Maîtrise en Droit, 1975; D.E.A., Tax Law, 1980). Author: "Tax Planning for International Executives." *Member:* International Fiscal Association; Franco-German Chamber of Commerce; H.E.C. Alumni Association (Real Estate and Finance Sections); Institut Français des Avocats spécialisés en Droit Fiscal; Association Française des Avocats Fiscalistes; Compagnie Nationale des Commissaires aux Comptes. *LANGUAGES:* French, English and German. *PRACTICE AREAS:* Tax Law; Cross Border Transactions.

Member of Telfa (Trans European Law Firms Association) in association with Interlega.
Telfa-Interlega is an association of European Law Firms, whose members have offices in Athens, Arnhem, Brussels, Budapest, Copenhagen, Dusseldorf, Edinburgh, Glasgow, London, Luxembourg, Madrid, Milan, Nijmegen, Paris and Vienna.
For more details see the Telfa-Interlega entry under Brussels.

CABINET CARLER

36, RUE TRONCHET
F-75009 PARIS, FRANCE
Telephone: 33-1-42661449
Telefax: 33-1-42665945

Nice, France Office: 22, rue Maréchal Joffre, F-06000. Telephone: 33 93 88 88 96. Fax: 33 93 88 94 98.
Stockholm, Sweden Office: Engelbrektsplan 2, S-114 34. Telephone: 46-8 6796360. Telex: 11900 CARLER S. Telefax: 46-8 6112605.
Gothenburg, Sweden Office: Engelbrektsgatan 28, S-411 37. Telephone: 46 31 18 02 50. Fax: 46 31 18 02 51.

(This Listing Continued)

Gävle, Sweden Office: P.O. Box 1346, S-801 38. Telephone: 46 26 12 51 30. Fax: 46 26 12 89 20.
Helsingborg, Sweden Office: Hamntorget 5, S-252 21. Telephone: 46-42.18 70 60. Telex: 721 40 Carler S. Telefax: 46.42.18 47 53.
Linköping, Sweden Office: Slattefors Herrgård, S-585 93. Telephone: 46-13 160350. Fax: 46-13 160355.
Milan, Italy Office: Via Silvio Pellico 12, I-20121. Telephone: 39-2.86 09 68; 39-2.805 94 39. Telefax: 39-2.86 46 54 45.

International Business Law, Intellectual Property Law, European Community Law, Corporate, Competition and Administrative Law, Labor Law, Civil Litigation, Mergers and Acquisitions.

FIRM PROFILE: *The firm was established in 1960 and offers services relating to International Business Law. The firm has 26 lawyers. Its offices are located in Stockholm, Gothenburg, Gävle, Helsingborg, Linkoping, Milan, Nice and Paris. Its objective is to improve the quality of business transactions thereby increasing the profitability of the client.*

MEMBERS OF FIRM

GUNNAR CARLER, born 1928; admitted, 1971, Conseil Juridique; 1992, Avocat at Barreau de Paris. *Education:* LL.M. (Jur.kand.) 1954. District Court, 1954-1956. Private Legal Practice, 1956-1960. Founder of Advokatfirman Carler, 1960. Appointed Chairman of Arbitral Tribunal by the International Chamber of Commerce, Paris. Chairman or Member, Board of Directors of Swedish Subsidiaries of foreign Companies such as Reynolds, Sharp Corporation, Marubeni Corporation, Rhône Poulenc, L'Oréal, Legrand, Essilor, Thomson and Legal Counsel for the French, Belgian and Italian Embassy in Stockholm. *Member:* Swedish Bar Association; Barreau de Paris. *LANGUAGES:* Swedish, French, English and German.

ASSOCIATES

ANNIKA ARVIDSSON, born 1946; admitted, 1983, Conseil Juridique; 1992, Avocat at Barreau de Paris. *Education:* LL.M. (Jur.kand.) 1971; The District Court, 1973-1975, Maîtrise de droit, Paris II, 1987. *Member:* Swedish Bar Association. Barreau de Paris. *LANGUAGES:* Swedish, French and English.

JACQUES MERRET, born 1963. admitted, 1991, Conseil Juridique; 1992, Avocat at Barreau de Paris. *Education:* Université de Paris II Maîtrise de droit des affaires de fiscalité . *LANGUAGES:* French, Swedish, English and German.

(For Complete Biographical Data on all Personnel, see Professional Biographies at Stockholm, Sweden).

CASANOVA & ASSOCIÉS

Established in 1980

250 BIS, BOULEVARD SAINT GERMAIN
75341 PARIS CEDEX 07, FRANCE
Telephone: (1) 44.39.89.89
Telex: THEMIS 270065 F
Telecopier: (1) 45.48.86.71

New York, New York Office: 600 Madison Avenue, 10022. Telephone: (212) 380-3500. Telex: 66146. Telecopier: (212) 380-3185.

General Practice. Civil, Commercial, Business, Construction, Company, Banking, Unfair Competition, Corporate Planning, Finance, Tax, International, Investment, Labor and Criminal Law. Trademark, Designs and Copyright, Licensing, EEC and International Private Law. Litigation.

MEMBERS OF FIRM

BERNARD CASANOVA, born Constantine, Algeria, 1949; admitted, 1973, Paris. *Education:* University of Paris Law School (Licence en Droit, Private Law); Diplôme de l'Institut d'Etudes Judiciaires, Certificat d'Aptitude à la Profession d'avocat (CAPA). *Member:* Confédération Nationale CNA des Avocats. *LANGUAGES:* French.

CHRISTIAN HENRI CHEMIN, born Chaumont, France, 1947; admitted, 1973, Paris. *Education:* University of Reims Law School (Licence en Droit, Private Law; DES, International Law); Diplôme Institut d'Etudes Judiciaires; Certificat d'aptitude à la Profession d'Avocat; University of Paris; Institut des Hautes Etudes Internationales. Lecturer on Law, 1972-1974 and Assistant Professor, Private Law, 1974-1980, University of Reims. *Member:* Association Française d' Étude de la Concurrence A.F.-.E.C.; International Bar Association (Business Law Section). *LANGUAGES:* French and English.

(This Listing Continued)

DANIEL OHL, born Strasbourg, France, 1951; admitted, 1975, France. *Education:* University of Strasbourg Law School (Licence en Droit, Business Law; CAPA); University of Montpellier Law School (Diplôme d'Etudes Supérieures de Droit Privé; Diplôme de Juriste Conseil d'Entreprise; Doctorat d'Etat en Droit). Author: "Les prêts et avances entre sociétés d'un même groupe", (Loans and Advances Among Affiliated Companies), Litec, 1982. Assistant Professor, Business Tax Law, Abidjan University Law School, Ivory Coast, 1976-1979. *Member:* International Fiscal Association (I.F.A., French Section); Chambre de Commerce Franco Allemande (COFACI). *LANGUAGES:* French, English and German.

GEORGES SOUCHON, born Tananarive, Madagascar, 1953; admitted, 1977, Paris. *Education:* University of Paris (Licence en Droit); Faculté co-gérée de droit et d'économie de Paris; Institut d'Etudes Politiques de Paris - CAPA. *LANGUAGES:* French and English.

CHANTAL MENARD DAUVERGNE, born Paris, France, 1951; admitted, 1977, Paris. *Education:* Hunter College of New York City (1973); University of Paris Law School (Licence and DES in Private Law, 1975); Institut d'Etudes Judiciaires (1976). Assistant Professor, Communication Law, University of Paris V and VII, 1982-1987. *LANGUAGES:* French and English.

OF COUNSEL

DIDIER SALAVERT, born Tarbes, France, 1952; admitted, 1978, Paris; 1985, New York. *Education:* Ecole Supérieure des Sciences Economiques et Commerciales (ESSEC, 1975); Sorbonne University (D.E.A., en Droit des Affaires, Diplôme d'Etudes Comptables Supérieures, 1978); Cornell University (LL.M., 1984). Adjunct Professor of Law, Sorbonne, 1979-1980. Professor of Law, Manhattan Institute of Management, 1984. Managing Editor, "Investissement/USA," 1986-1988. Member, Commercial Panel of Arbitrators, American Arbitration Association. *LANGUAGES:* French and English.

ASSOCIATES

BRUNO MARTIN, born Strasbourg, France, 1960; admitted, 1987, Paris. *Education:* University of Paris, Pantheon Sorbonne (Licence en droit, Public Law, 1982; Maîtrise en droit, Private Law, 1985). *LANGUAGES:* French and English.

ISABELLE FORTIN, born Paris, France, 1965; admitted, 1989, Paris. *Education:* University of Paris II (Maitrise de Droit Prive, 1987; DEA de Droit Prive General, 1988). *LANGUAGES:* English and German.

PASCAL TELLE, born Neuilly-sur-Seine, France, 1962; admitted, 1991, Hypokhâgne and Khâgne. *Education:* University of Paris X (DEA Lettres Modernes, Doctorat Lettres Modernes); University of Paris II (DEA de Propriété littéraire artistique et industrielle). *LANGUAGES:* French and English.

CLAUDE-NICOLE OHL, born Nancy, France, 1958; admitted, 1987, Paris. *Education:* University of Paris XII (Maîtrise de Droit, DEA de Droit Privé fondamental); University of Paris I (DEA de Droit international privé et Droit du commerce international); Certificat de fin de stage des avocats au Conseil d'Etat et à la Cour de Cassation. Lecturer on Law, Private Law and International Private Law, University of Paris II, 1982-1984. *LANGUAGES:* French and English.

ODILE LARY-BACQUAERT, born Marselle, France, 1958; admitted, 1985, Paris. *Education:* University of Paris, II (D.E.A. de Droit International), Criminology Institut of Paris; Universities of Columbia-Leyden (Summer Program in American Law), 1987, University of Cologue, Germany, (Sprachzeugnisse, Gesthic). *LANGUAGES:* French, German and English.

CAYOL & ROCHER

Société d'Avocats

85 BOULEVARD DE COURCELLES
75008 PARIS, FRANCE
Telephone: 47.66.02.15
Fax: 43.80.37.19

Paris La Defense, France Office: 4 Square Henri Régnault, 92400 Courbevoie La Defense 6. Telephone: 47.73.73.37. Fax: 47.73.61.80.

General and International Law Practice: Company and Commercial Law, Civil Law, Property and Real Estate, Construction Law, Rent and Lease Law, Administrative Law.

(This Listing Continued)

MEMBERS OF FIRM

DIDIER CAYOL, born Nice, France, January 19, 1936; admitted, 1962, Paris. *Education:* Institut Catholique of Paris (Licencié en Droit, Principal Clerc d'Avoué). Former Member, Conseil de l'Ordre; Former President: Union des Jeunes Avocats de Paris; Fédération Nationale de l'Union des Jeunes Avocats. *Member:* Commission Ministérielle de Réforme du Code de Procédure Civile; Conseil de Surveillance de la Caisse Autonomes des Règlements Pécuniaires des Avocats (President); l'Ordre National du Mérite (Officer).

DANIEL ROCHER, born Saint Malo, France, April 22, 1947; admitted, 1972, Paris. *Education:* Faculté de la Sorbonne (Maîtrise de Lettres); Faculté de Droit de Paris Assas (Licencié en Droit). *Member:* Conférence des Avocats à la Cour (Former Secretary); Association JUSTICE CONSTRUCTION.

JÉROME CAYOL, born Paris, France, January 5, 1960; admitted, 1985, Paris. *Education:* Université de Paris X (Maîtrise de Droit); Institut d'Etudes Politiques de Paris (Licencié en Philosophie). *Member:* European Lawyer Association, E.L.A.; Admissible E.N.A.

GUY CAYOL, born Nice, France, May 5, 1925; admitted, 1988, Hauts-de-Seine. *Education:* Faculté de Droit d'Aix-en-Provence (Licencié en Droit). Former Adjoint Director, Service Financier et Juridique d'ELECTRICITE DE FRANCE; Chevalier de l'Ordre National du Mérite; Chevalier du Mérite Agricole.

CEJEF
AMEDEE-MANESME - ATHENOSY - BINDER ET ASSOCIES

Established in 1978

94 BOULEVARD FLANDRIN
75116 PARIS, FRANCE
Telephone: 33 (1) 45.53.06.05.
Telefax: (33) (1) 45.53.05.10./47.55.96.05.

General French Law Practice, Arbitration, Litigations, Business Law Practice, Insurance Law Practice, Commercial Law Practice, Banking Law Practice, European Law Practice, Communication and Media Law Practice, Competition Law Practice, Consummation Law Practice, Distribution and Tax Law Practice, Intellectual Property Rights and Patents, Corporate Law, Mergers and Acquisitions, International Estates and Trusts.
Economical Fields: Chemistry, Pharmacy, Textile, Clothing, Leisure, Building, Transportation, Tourism, Services.

PARTNERS OF FIRM

GILLES AMÉDÉE-MANESME, born October 24, 1950, Avocat au barreau de Paris. *Education:* E.N.I. (1973); University of Clermont-Ferrand (Doctorat d' Etat en droit, 1977). Author: "Droit et pratique du droit fiscal et des affaires" Economica, 1990. Various tax law and distribution law articles (GP, RJC, professional reviews). Partner Lecturer, Law University of Paris XI, Sceaux. Member, I.F.A., Droit et Commerce. *PRACTICE AREAS:* Arbitration; Distribution Law; Tax Law; Corporate Law.

GEORGES ATHÉNOSY, born April 9, 1949, Avocat au barreau de Paris. *Education:* D.J.C.E. (1973); University of Montpellier (Doctorat d'Etat en droit, 1981). Author: "Banque Etrangère et fiscalitéfrancaise" Economica, 1982; "L'entreprise face à l'Europe" Referentiel DUNOD, 1990. Various patrimonial and fiscal law articles. Partner Lecturer, Ecole Supérieure de Commerce de Paris, E.S.C.P. Group. Member, I.F.A. Paris. *LANGUAGES:* French and English. *PRACTICE AREAS:* Commercial Law; Tax Law.

OLIVIER BINDER, born June 18, 1952, Avocat au barreau de Paris. *Education:* Paris University (1973); C.P.A. (Paris Chamber of Commerce). Author: "Chroniques en droit communautaire" cahiers juridiques et fiscaux de l'exportation (C.F.C.E.). Member of Directorate of Admical (Association of Business Sponsorship for the arts). A.I.J.A. past National Vice-Président for France, 1990-1994. Chairman, International Franchising and Distribution Standing Commission of the A.I.J.A. Chairman, Legal Commission of France-Israel Chamber of Commerce. *LANGUAGES:* French and English. *PRACTICE AREAS:* Business and Commercial Law; European Community Law; Intellectual Property Rights; Communication and Media Law; Competition and Distributor Law; Litigations.

MURIEL BLOCH-MAUREL, born January 19, 1948, Avocat au barreau de Paris. *Education:* Paris University (1969). Author: "Le travail tem-

(This Listing Continued)

CEJEF AMEDEE-MANESME - ATHENOSY - BINDER ET ASSOCIES,—Paris Continued

poraire", E.M.E., 1980. Various advertising articles (Strategie, 1985). *LANGUAGES:* French and German. *PRACTICE AREAS:* Business and Commercial Law; Distribution Law; Litigations.

SOPHIE BAILLIE DE SENILHES, born July 14, 1962, Avocat au barreau de Paris. *Education:* University of Paris II (Dess Droit des affaires et fiscalité); University of Paris XII (Lauréate 1st Prize, 1983). Former Associate, Coudert Frères, Paris (until 1988). *LANGUAGES:* French and English. *PRACTICE AREAS:* Business and Commercial Law; European Community Law; Competition and Distribution Law; Corporate Law; Mergers and Acquisitions; Corporate Restructurings; Reorganizations.

GILLES FLORES, born February 15, 1956, Avocat au barreau de Paris. *Education:* D.J.C.E. Aix - Marseille (1978). Author: Various corporate law articles (Revue des sociétés; Act Legislative Dalloz). Co-Author: Dictionnaire Permanent Droit des Affaires. *PRACTICE AREAS:* Business Law; Financial Law; Corporate Law; Mergers and Acquisitions; Corporate Restructurings; Reorganizations.

BRIGITTE VERGILINO, born May 9, 1958, Avocat au barreau de Paris. *Education:* University of Paris (D.E.S.S. de fiscalité appliquée, 1984); Chargee d'enseignement Institut de droit public des affaires. *PRACTICE AREAS:* Tax Law; Tax Dispute.

ASSOCIATES

VERONIQUE ROBIN-ILLOUZ, born October 28, 1962, Avocat au barreau de Paris. *Education:* University of Paris V (D.E.S.S. de fiscalité appliquée). *PRACTICE AREAS:* Tax Law.

PATRICK DE LA GRANGE, born February 9, 1964, Avocat au barreau de Paris. *Education:* I.E.P. University of Paris II (D.E.A. de droit Européen; D.E.A. Propriété Littéraire, Artistique et Commerciale). *PRACTICE AREAS:* Communication and Media Law; Intellectual Property Rights.

MARIE-ISABELLE DAVID-LAUSSINOTTE, born August 24, 1946, Avocat au de Paris. *Education:* University of Paris. *PRACTICE AREAS:* Commercial Property; International Estates; Litigations.

Member of G.I.E.E. "Cercle Juridique Européen" and of E.F.L. "Euro Franchise Lawyers".

CHAINTRIER, CAILLARD & ASSOCIES

Established in 1976

5, AVENUE GEORGE V

75008 PARIS, FRANCE

Telephone: (33.1) 47.23.00.09

Telex: 613.244

Fax: (33.1) 47.23.68.79

General French and International Practice, General Business Law, Mergers and Acquisitions, Taxation, European Law, Banking and Financial Law, Bankruptcy and Reorganizations, Franchising Licensing and Distribution, Media and Telecommunications, Environment, Real Estate, Foreign Investments, Litigation.

MEMBERS OF FIRM

MICHEL CAILLARD, born Bayonne, July 21, 1944; admitted, 1972, as Conseil Juridique; 1975, Paris Bar. *Education:* University of Paris Law School (Institut d'Etudes Juriciaires, 1969; Maîtrise en Droit, 1970); Centre d'Etudes des Communautés Européennes (1970); New York University, School of Business Administration (1972). *Member:* Paris Bar; Law Society of London; International Bar Association. *LANGUAGES:* French and English.

BERNARD CHAINTRIER, born Paris, July 18, 1946; admitted, 1976, as Conseil Juridique; 1989, Paris Bar. *Education:* University of Paris Law School (Maîtrise en droit, 1973); Paris Institut d'Etudes Politiques (Graduate, 1970). Vice President, Société de Caution Mutuelle des Conseils Juridiques, 1982-1989. Expert to the International Chamber of Commerce. *Member:* Paris Bar; International Bar Association. *LANGUAGES:* French and English.

PHILIPPE CHARHON, born Neuilly-sur-Seine, March 5, 1949; admitted, 1985, as Conseil Juridique; 1992, Paris Bar. *Education:* University of Paris Law School (Maîtrise en Droit, 1973); Paris Institut d'Etudes Politiques (Graduate, 1970). Expert to the International Chamber of Commerce. *Member:* Paris Bar; International Bar Association. *LANGUAGES:* French and English.

(This Listing Continued)

SOPHIE LESIEUR-CAZAVAN, born Boulogne, December 29, 1946; admitted, 1986, Paris Bar. *Education:* University of Paris Law School (Maîtrise en Droit Privé, 1967; D.E.S. de Droit Privé, 1970); Institut de Droit des Affaires (1975). *Member:* Paris Bar; International Bar Association. *LANGUAGES:* French, English and Spanish.

ASSOCIATES

MARC SAGE, born Beziers, June 22, 1956; admitted, 1981, Paris Bar. *Education:* University of Paris Law School (Institut d'Etudes Judiciaires, Maîtrise en Droit, 1979); New York University School of Law (1981). *Member:* Paris Bar. *LANGUAGES:* French, English and Spanish.

MICHEL DE MONT-MARIN, born Lorient, April 8, 1923; admitted, as Conseil Juridique et Fiscal, Paris Bar. *Education:* University of Paris Law School (Maîtrise en Droit, 1947). *LANGUAGES:* French and English.

GHISLAIN THERY, born Jallien, January 31, 1954; admitted, 1983, as Conseil Juridique; 1992, Paris Bar. *Education:* University of Grenoble Law School (Maîtrise en Droit, 1977). *Member:* Paris Bar. *LANGUAGES:* French.

JEAN-MARC DELAS, born Dieppe, July 8, 1953; admitted, 1980, Paris Bar. *Education:* University of Paris Law School (Maîtrise en droit, 1975); Paris Institut d'Etudes Politiques (Graduate, 1978). Ancien Secrétaire de la Conférence du Stage des Avocats. *Member:* Paris Bar. *LANGUAGES:* French and English.

PASCAL JARDIN, born Nogent-le-Rotrou, September 20, 1959; admitted, 1992, Paris Bar. *Education:* University of Paris II and IX Law Schools (Maîtrise en Droit des Affaires et Fiscalité, 1983; D.E.S.S. de Gestion Fiscale des Entreprises, 1984; Certificat Supérieur Juridique et Fiscal, 1985; Certificat Supérieur de Révision Comptable, 1988). *Member:* Paris Bar; International Fiscal Association (IFA). *LANGUAGES:* French and English.

CAROLINE LACAZE, born Talence, February 5, 1964; admitted, 1988, as Conseil Juridique; 1992, Paris Bar. *Education:* University of Paris Law School (Maîtrise en Droit des Affaires, 1986; D.E.S.S. en Fiscalité, 1987). *Member:* Paris Bar. *LANGUAGES:* French.

ROSELINE SAUSER, born Paris, April 9, 1958; admitted, 1984, Paris Bar. *Education:* CAPA 1983; D.E.A. Droit Privé, 1984; D.E.A. Droit Communautaire, 1984. *Member:* Paris Bar. *LANGUAGES:* French, German and English.

ALAIN HURBAL, born Montargis, December 11, 1943; Clerc de Notaire. (Not admitted in France). *LANGUAGES:* French and English. *PRACTICE AREAS:* Real Estate.

LENIE VERLEYE, born Argenteuil, October 14, 1955. (Not admitted in France). *LANGUAGES:* French and English. *PRACTICE AREAS:* General Corporate Law.

OF COUNSEL

XAVIER DELCROS, born Fez, Morocco, April 17, 1940. Professor Universites de Paris; Ecole Nationale d'Administration; Institut d'Etudes Politiques de Paris.

CHRISTOPH LIEBSCHER, born Salzburg, Austria, June 1, 1957; admitted, 1985, Bar Austria and Munich Tribunal; 1989, as Legal Counsellor in Austrian Law (Not admitted in France). *Education:* Doctor Juris, 1979; Rechtsanwaltsprütung, 1983; Master of Business Administration (INSEAD), 1986. Author: "Rechtsbruch nach Art. 1 UWG," Wirtschaftsrechtliche Blätter, May, 1990; "Country Report on Austria," in "European Coproduction in Film and Television," Nomos, 1989; "Investments in FRG," Seminar of the Austrian Chamber of Commerce, 1987; "Patents and the European Biotechnolgy lag: A Study of Large European Pharmaceutical Firms," Reinhard Angelmar-Christoph Liebscher, INSEAD Working Papers 87/88; "Austria and the EEC," Series of six articles, Austrian Chamber of Commerce, 1987. *Member:* A.I.J.A.; International Bar Association. *LANGUAGES:* German, English, French, Italian, Spanish and Russian.

The firm is a member of J.C.S. Group, comprising the English law firm of Eversheds Jaques & Lewis and the German law firm of Schmidt, Von Der Osten & Huber, as well as the Dutch law firm of Van Wijmen and Koedam in Rotterdam and Breda.

CHAMBAZ & SUERMONDT

Established in 1946

45 RUE RAFFET
75016 PARIS, FRANCE
Telephone: (331) 45 25 90 00
Telex: 648610
Telecopier: (331) 45 25 90 43

General and International Practice, Corporate, Tax, Administrative, Petroleum, Labor and Real Property Law, Litigation and Arbitration, Investment and Exchange Control Regulations, Trust Law.

FIRM PROFILE: The firm of Chambaz & Suermondt, since its foundation in 1946, has concentrated on all aspects of international business law, with emphasis on relations between the English-speaking and French-speaking business communities.

MEMBERS OF FIRM

MARCEL G. CHAMBAZ, born Evreux, France, September 17, 1920; Avocat a la Cour; admitted, 1973, Conseil Juridique. *Education:* Lycée Janson de Sailly; University of Paris (Docteur en Droit, 1945). Contrôleur de l'Enregistrement, 1941-1944. Professor of International Law, Ecole Polytechnique de Droit et de Notariat de Paris, 1945-1965 (now Honorary Professor). Former President, Association des Conseils Juridiques Docteurs et Licenciés en Droit. Vice President, Paris Chapter, Association Française des Avocats Conseils d'Entreprises (A.C.E.). Member of the Board of Directors, Association Française d'Arbitrage. Lecturer, University of Paris Law School, 1968-1985. *Member:* American Society of International Law; International Fiscal Association. *LANGUAGES:* French, English, German and Dutch. *PRACTICE AREAS:* Oil and Gas Law; Trusts and Estate Law; Civil and Tax Law; International Arbitration.

GUY R. SUERMONDT (1919-1966).

LAURENT G. CHAMBAZ, born Paris, France, December 25, 1947; Avocat a la Cour; admitted, 1973, Conseil Juridique. *Education:* Lycée Pasteur; University of Paris (Licencié en Droit, 1970, Laureate, Civil Law Contest). Member of Board of the Paris Bar Council (Conseil de l'Ordre). Member, French Delegation to the Council of the Bars and Law Societies of the European Community. General Secretary, Association Nationale des Conseils Juridiques, 1989-1992. First Vice President, French Chapter, Union Internationale des Avocats, 1991—. Country Representative for France, International Bar Association (IBA). *Member:* Association Française des Avocats Conseils d'Entreprises (A.C.E.). *LANGUAGES:* French, English and German. *PRACTICE AREAS:* Mergers and Acquisitions; International Contracts; International Arbitration; Trust Law.

JACQUES LE BLEVENNEC, born Lanvollon, France, October 11, 1946; Avocat a la Cour; admitted, 1973, Conseil Juridique. *Education:* St. Charles College, St. Brieuc, France; University of Clermont, France (Licencié en Droit, 1971); Ecole Nationale des Impôts (1971). *Member:* Association Française des Avocats Conseils d'Entreprises (A.C.E.). *LANGUAGES:* French and English. *PRACTICE AREAS:* International and Domestic Taxation (Corporate and Personal); Tax Litigation; Trust Law.

ANNIE L. LORTON, born Lyons, France, September 17, 1954; Avocat a la Cour; admitted, 1980, Conseil Juridique. *Education:* Lycée de Bourgoin-Jallieu, France; University of Lyons III (law); Lyons II (languages); Licenciée en Droit, 1976; D.E.S.S. Conseil Juridique 1977. *Member:* Association Française des Avocats Conseils d'Entreprises (A.C.E.). *LANGUAGES:* French, English and German. *PRACTICE AREAS:* Mergers and Acquisitions; Corporate Law.

NADINE L. ROUET, born Paris, France, May 7, 1956; Avocat a la Cour; admitted, 1985, Conseil Juridique. *Education:* Lycée Camille Sée, Paris, France; University of Paris (Maîtrise en Droit, 1980, D.E.S.S.; Conseil Juridique, 1982). *Member:* Association Française des Avocats Conseils d'Entreprises (A.C.E.). *LANGUAGES:* French, English and Spanish. *PRACTICE AREAS:* Industrial Relations Law; Consumer Law.

NICOLAS G. SCHAKOWSKOY, born Paris, France, September 25, 1964; admitted, 1992, Avocat a la Cour. *Education:* Lycée Gustave Monod, France; University of Paris (Maîtrise en Droit, 1986; D.E.S.S. Fiscalité, 1987; Diplôme de l'Institut du Droit des Affaires, 1987). Lecturer, University of Paris Law School. *Member:* Association Française des Avocats Conseils d'Entreprises (A.C.E.). *LANGUAGES:* French, English and German. *PRACTICE AREAS:* International and Domestic Taxation (Corporate and Personal); Tax Litigation.

DELPHINE D. DORON, born Levallois Perret, France, April 18, 1965; admitted, 1992, Avocat a la Cour. *Education:* Lycee Moliere, France; University of Paris I (Maîtrise en Droit, 1989; D.E.S.S. Conseil Juridique et Fiscal, 1990). Lecturer, University of Paris Law School. *Member:* Association Française des Avocats Conseils d'Entreprises (A.C.E.). *LANGUAGES:* French, English and German. *PRACTICE AREAS:* EEC Law; Antitrust Law; Franchise Law.

RICHARD J. ANÉ, born New York, New York, USA, September 13, 1961; admitted, 1992, Avocat a la Cour. *Education:* Fordham University (B.A., 1982); University of Aix-Marseilles III (Maît rise en Droit International, 1986); University of Paris I (D.E.A. Droits Anglais et Nord-Américain des Affaires, 1987); New York University Law School (LL.M., Corporate Law, 1989). *Member:* Association Française des Avocats Conseils d'Entreprise (A.C.E.). *LANGUAGES:* French, English and Spanish. *PRACTICE AREAS:* International Contracts; Corporate Law; EEC Law; Antitrust Law.

KARL H. BELTZ, born Wuppertal, Germany, September 17, 1954; admitted, 1984, Düsseldorf, Rechtsanwalt; 1992, Paris, Avocat à la Cour. *Education:* Bochum and Bonn Universities (1 & 2, Juristisches Staatsexamen). *Member:* Association Francaise des Avocats Conseils d'Entreprise (A.C.E.); Association Franco-Allemande de Juristes; French-German Chamber of Commerce. *LANGUAGES:* German, French and English. *PRACTICE AREAS:* EEC Law; International Contracts; Competition Law.

CHANEY CONNOR LEMETAIS & ASSOCIÉS

29 AVENUE HOCHE
75008 PARIS, FRANCE
Telephone: (1) 42 89 17 43
Telex: 260 953 F
Telecopier: (1) 45 63 70 73

General French and International Law Practice, Corporate and Commercial Matters, Cross-Border Contracts, Tax, Financial and Banking Law, Mergers and Acquisitions, Employment, Transport Law, Media Law, Technology Law.
All members are admitted in Paris and authorized to appear before the French courts as Avocats.

PARTNERS

CHRISTINE BAUDOIN, born Paris, France, October 30, 1950; admitted, 1981, Paris. *Education:* Lyons Faculty of Law (D.E.A., Business Law, 1981). *LANGUAGES:* French, English, Italian and Spanish. *PRACTICE AREAS:* Labour and Commercial Law.

STANLEY CHANEY, born Paris, France, November 6, 1945; admitted, 1973, Paris. *Education:* University of Paris (Licencié en Droit, 1970; D.E.S. Droit Privé, 1971); Centre Universitaire de Droit Européen Paris (1970). Lecturer, Institut Universitaire de Technologie Sceaux, Université de Paris Sud, 1975-1981. *Member:* International Bar Association. *LANGUAGES:* French, English and Italian. *PRACTICE AREAS:* Corporate and Commercial Law; Technology Law; Products Liability.

CHRISTIAN CONNOR, born Paris, France, October 27, 1952; admitted, 1977, Paris. *Education:* Faculty of Law, University of Strasbourg (Maîtrise en Droit, 1977). Lecturer, Institute of Preparation to Business Management, 1986-1987. Contributing Editor, Dictionnaire Permanent de Droit des Affaires (permanent dictionary of business law). *Member:* Association Internationale des Jeunes Avocats. *LANGUAGES:* French, German and English. *PRACTICE AREAS:* Transport Law; Franco German Cross-Border Contracts.

ANTOINE LEMETAIS, born Paris, France, April 16, 1955; admitted, 1980, Paris. *Education:* Ecole des Hautes Etudes Commerciales, Paris (H.E.C., 1976); University of Paris (Maîtrise en Droit, 1977); Diplôme d'Etudes Comptables Supérieures (DECS, 1977), Academy of American and International Law, Southwestern Legal Foundation, Dallas, Texas (1981). *LANGUAGES:* French, English, Spanish and Italian. *PRACTICE AREAS:* Corporate and Commercial Law; Mergers and Acquisitions; National and Cross-Border Contracts.

OLIVIER SAMYN, born Paris, France, May 31, 1959; admitted, 1982, Paris. *Education:* Faculty of Law, University of Paris (Maîtrise, 1981; D.E.A. Civil Law, 1982). Lecturer, Centre de Formation Professionnelle des Avocats. *LANGUAGES:* French and English. *PRACTICE AREAS:* Labour and Commercial Law; Media Law.

(This Listing Continued)

(This Listing Continued)

CHANEY CONNOR LEMETAIS & ASSOCIÉS, Paris—Continued

OF COUNSEL

JEAN HESS, born Paris, France, August 16, 1954; admitted, 1992, Paris. *Education:* University of Paris (D.E.A. Droit des Affaires et Droit Economique, 1981). *Member:* International Fiscal Association. **LANGUAGES:** French, English and Spanish. **PRACTICE AREAS:** Taxation; Corporate and Commercial Matters.

ASSOCIATES

MARIE-ADELAIDE CLEMENT, born Grenoble, France, January 15, 1968; admitted, 1993, Paris. *Education:* University of Paris I (D.E.A. Droit Anglo-Américain des Affaires, 1991); University of Canterbury, Kent, U.K. (English Law-Maîtrise Droit option droit anglais, Diploma, 1990). **LANGUAGES:** French, English and Spanish. **PRACTICE AREAS:** Corporate and Commercial Law.

JÉRÔME GERTLER, born Paris, France, May 27, 1963; admitted, 1992, Paris. *Education:* University of Paris (Maîtrise en Droit des Affaires, 1986, D.E.S.S. Fiscalité Internationale, Paris XI-HEC, 1988); University of Kent (B.A. in English Law, 1987). **LANGUAGES:** French, English and German. **PRACTICE AREAS:** Corporate and Commercial Law; Tax; Mergers and Acquisitions.

CHRISTOPHE HERY, born Saint-Brieuc, France, February 16, 1966; admitted, 1994, Paris. *Education:* University of Paris I (Maîtrise, 1988; DEA International Private and Business Law, 19 89); University of San Diego, Paris Summer Session (1988); The Hager Academy of International Law, Summer Session (1993). Lecturer, International Business Law, University Paris I, 1992-1994. *Member:* A.A.A. **LANGUAGES:** French and English. **PRACTICE AREAS:** Corporate and Commercial Matters; Contracts.

LOLA SCHAUFUSS, born Paris, France, October 5, 1964; admitted, 1991, Paris. *Education:* University of Paris II (Maîtrise en Droit des Affaires, 1988; Diplôme d'Etudes Approfondies de Droit Privé, 1989). Assistant Professor, German Law and Economics, University Créteil, 1991. **LANGUAGES:** French, German and English. **PRACTICE AREAS:** Commercial Law; Franco German Cross-Border Contracts.

VALÉRIE TROMAS, born Versailles, France, January 14, 1968; admitted, 1994, Paris. *Education:* University of Paris X (Maîtrise en Droit, 1991, Licence en Sciences Economiques, 1990). **LANGUAGES:** French and English. **PRACTICE AREAS:** Commercial and Labour Law.

Member of PANNONE LAW GROUP E.E.I.G., offices in Brussels, London, Manchester, Paris, Lyon, Madrid, Barcelona, Lisbon, Milan, Geneva, Andorra, Stockholm.

CHARDON, TARRADE & ASSOCIÉS

Notaires

83 BOULEVARD HAUSSMANN
75008 PARIS, FRANCE
Telephone: (1) 42.66.49.40
Fax: (1) 42.66.25.03

General French Notarial Practice, Real Estate, Construction, Mortgage Law, Family and Matrimonial Law, Settlement of Estates, Securities, Credit Law.

PAUL CHARDON, born 1926; admitted, 1957, France. *Education:* Paris University (license en droit, 1947); Insitut d'Etudes Politiques (1947); Institut des Hautes Etudes de Droit International Privé. Chairman, Institut d'Etudes Juridiques du Conceil Supérieur du Notariat. First Vice-Chairman, Union Internationale du Notariat Latin. Former President, Counseil Supérieur du Notariat Français.

BERTRAND CHARDON, born 1949; admitted, 1985, as Conseil Juridique, 1986 as Notaire, France. *Education:* Institut d'Etudes Politiques de Paris (1971); University of Paris (Diplôme d'Etudes Supérieures de droit public, 1973; doctorat d'état, 1981); Yale Law School (Master of Law, 1975). Author: "Governing Giant Cities: Paris, London, New York," 1983.

JEAN TARRADE, born 1948; admitted, 1981, France as Notaire. *Education:* University of Paris (Diplôme d'Etudes Supérieures de droit privé; Dilpôme supérieur du Notariat). *Member:* Chambre des Notaires de Paris.

MARIE-JOSEPH EXPERTON, born 1952; admitted, 1986, as Conseil Juridique, 1994, as Notaire, France. *Education:* University of Paris (Di-

(This Listing Continued)

plôme d'Etudes Supérieures de Droit Privé); Oxford University (B.A. in Jurisprudence - Worcester College, 1979-1982). Teaching: University of Paris (Company Law).

CHAZEAUX, PEYRON ET ASSOCIÉS

63, BD DES BATIGNOLLES
75008 PARIS, FRANCE
Telephone: (33-1) 42 94 20 00
Fax: (33-1) 42 94 15 14

Firm engaged in French, European and International general law practice. Entitled to plead before the EEC and French Courts.

FIRM PROFILE: The firm has a broadly based practice for offering a full range of quality legal services in three specific areas: Business law, Construction and Real Estate Law, Legislative and Public Affairs.

MEMBERS OF FIRM

OLIVIER DE CHAZEAUX, born Toulon, France, 1961; admitted, 1989, Paris. *Education:* University of Paris V (Maîtrise en Droit Privé, 1987); The American University, Washington D.C. (LL.M., International Law, 1988). Assistant Lecturer, International Law and Corporate Law, University of Paris V, 1989 and 1990; Lecturer, EEC Law and Arbitration Law, IPAG, Paris, 1992 and 1993. President, French Association of Young Political Leaders. **LANGUAGES:** French and English. **PRACTICE AREAS:** International and EEC Law; Corporate Law; Mergers and Acquisitions; Legislative and Public Affairs.

NATHALIE PEYRON, born Eaubonne, France, 1962; admitted, 1988, Paris. *Education:* University of Paris V (Maîtrise en Droit Privé, 1984); University of Paris II (D.E.A. en Droit Foncier et Immobilier, 1987); The American University, Washington D.C. (LL.M., International Law, 1988). Assistant Lecturer, Contract Law, University of Paris V, 1988-1989. **LANGUAGES:** French, English and Spanish. **PRACTICE AREAS:** Contract Law; Construction Law; Real Estate Law; Litigation.

JEROME HENRY, born Paris, France, 1959; admitted, 1984, Paris. *Education:* University of Paris II (Maîtrise en Droit, 1981). **LANGUAGES:** French and English. **PRACTICE AREAS:** Litigation; Commercial and Labour Law; Leases; Contracts and Torts; Intellectual Property.

JEAN-FRANCOIS MEYER, born Paris, France, 1949; admitted, 1983, Paris. *Education:* University of Paris II (Maîtrise en Droit Privé, 1973). Assistant Lecturer, Private Law, University of Paris II. *Member:* Swiss Chamber of Commerce, Paris. **LANGUAGES:** French, English and German. **PRACTICE AREAS:** International and Domestic Tax Law.

PASCALE INTER-NASTA, born Sauflieu (80), France, 1948; admitted, 1980, Paris. *Education:* University of Paris XI (Maîtrise en Droit Privé, 1974). **LANGUAGES:** French and Spanish. **PRACTICE AREAS:** Real Estate Law; Joint Ownership; Leases.

LAURENT CARPENTIER, born Paris, France, 1966; admitted, 1993, Paris. *Education:* University of Paris II Assas (Maîtrise en Droit des Affaires, 1988; D.E.S.S. Droit des Affaires et Fiscalité, 1989); University of Paris I, Institut d'Administration des Enterprises (D.E.S.S., Gestion, 1990). **LANGUAGES:** French and English. **PRACTICE AREAS:** Tax Law; Corporate Law; Mergers and Acquisitions.

BEATRICE FESSOL, born Neuilly, France, 1968; admitted, 1994, Paris. *Education:* University of Paris I (Maîtrise droit des Affaires et Droit Privé, 1991; DEA Droit Privé, 1992). **LANGUAGES:** French and English. **PRACTICE AREAS:** Real Estate Law; Lease.

OF COUNSEL

BERNARD DREYFUS, born Strasbourg, France, 1957; (Not admitted in France). *Education:* Institut d'Etudes Politiques de Strasbroug (M.C., 1978); University of Strasbourg (D.E.A., Public Law, 1980). Professor, Public Law, Conservatoire National Arts et Métiers, 1989—. Advisor: Minister of Transportation, 1980-1981; Minister of Overseas Territories, 1987-1988. International Vice-President, Atlantic Association of Young Political Leaders, 1988—. **LANGUAGES:** French, English and German. **PRACTICE AREAS:** Legislative and Public Affairs; Public Law.

CLEARY, GOTTLIEB, STEEN & HAMILTON

Established in 1946

41, AVENUE DE FRIEDLAND
75008 PARIS, FRANCE
Telephone: 33-1-4074-6800
Telex: 650021
Facsimile/Infotec: 33-1-45-63-35-09
Facsimile/Infotec: 33-1-45-63-66-37

New York, New York Office: One Liberty Plaza, New York, N.Y. 10006. Telephone: 212-225-2000.
Washington, D.C. Office: 1752 N Street, N.W., Washington, D.C. 20036. Telephone: 202-728-2700.
Brussels, Belgium Office: Rue de la Loi 23, Bte 5, 1040 Brussels, Belgium. Telephone: 32-2-287-2000.
London, England Office: City Place House, 55 Basinghall Street, London EC2V 5EH England. Telephone: 44-71-614-2200.
Hong Kong Office: 56th Floor, Bank of China Tower, One Garden Road, Hong Kong. Telephone: 852-521-4122.
Tokyo, Japan Office: Morgan Carroll Terai Gaikokuho Jimubengoshi Jimusho, 20th Floor, Shin Kasumigaseki Building, 3-2, Kasumigaseki 3-Chome, Chiyoda-Ku, Tokyo 100, Japan. Telephone: 81-3-3595-3911.
Frankfurt, Germany Office: Ulmenstrasse 37-39, 60325 Frankfurt am Main, Germany. Telephone: 49-69-971-03-0.

Firm engaged in French, American and General International Practice; admitted as Avocat and authorized to practice before the French courts.

COUNSEL

RICHARD H. MOORE, born Chester, Connecticut, January 23, 1918; admitted, 1947, Connecticut and New York; 1957, U.S. Supreme Court; 1992, Paris. *Education:* Bowdoin College (A.B., 1939); Yale University (LL.B., 1946). Phi Beta Kappa. Officier de la Légion d'Honneur. Member of the Executive Committee (Conseil de l'Ordre) of the Paris Bar. President, 1973-1976 and Director, American Chamber of Commerce in France. President, 1972-1973 and Director, American Club of Paris. Director: Fondation Foch; American Association for the International Commission of Jurists. *Member:* Association of the Bar of the City of New York; American and International Bar Associations; Union Internationale des Avocats; Association Française des Avocats Conseils d' Entreprise (Member, Paris Regional Council).

JEAN L. BLONDEEL, born Bruges, Belgium, September 9, 1921; admitted, 1946, Ghent; 1992, Paris. *Education:* Ghent University (Doctor of Laws, 1946); Harvard Law School (LL.M., 1949; S.J.D., 1952). Military Prosecuting Attorney, Ghent, 1946-1947. Associate Professor of Law, University of Ghent, 1955. Legal Advisor, European Coal & Steel Community, Luxembourg, 1953-1956. Special Counsel, International Bank for Reconstruction and Development and International Finance Corporation, 1956-1958. Chairman and President, Kredietbank (Suisse) S.A., 1980. Honorary Chairman and President, Kredietbank S.A. Luxembourgeoise, 1966-1991. Director, Société Anonyme des Produits et Engrais Chimiques du Portugal, Brown Shipley & Co., IB.SA. IBI, Intersec, Noveurop, Biermans-Lapôtre Foundation of the University of Paris. Member, Common Market Committee on Financial Markets, 1964-1966. Counsellor, Foreign Trade of the Kingdom of Belgium in France, 1966. *Member:* Monetary Committee of International Law Association.

HUBERT DE GRANDCOURT, born Nantes, France, July 27, 1932. Avocat Honoraire, Paris. *Education:* University of Rennes; Faculté de Droit de Rennes (Licence en Droit, 1954; D.E.S. Droit Privé, 1955; D.E.S. Droit Public, 1956); Columbia University (M.C.L., 1957).

DONALD L. HOLLEY, born Olustee, Oklahoma, December 19, 1931; admitted, 1960, New York; 1993, Paris. *Education:* University of Oklahoma (B.F.A., 1953); Columbia University (M.I.A., 1959; LL.B., 1959). Resident at: New York Office, 1959-1963; Paris Office, 1963-1967; Brussels Office, 1967-1991.

RESIDENT PARTNERS

ROGER J. BENRUBI, born Paris, France, April 11, 1928; admitted, 1950, Paris. *Education:* University of Paris; Faculté de Droit de Paris (Licence en Droit, 1948; D.E.S. Droit Privé, 1949); Harvard Law School (LL.M., 1950). *Member:* Association Française des Avocats Conseils d'Entreprise.

SYDNEY M. CONE, III, born Greensboro, North Carolina, November 30, 1930; admitted, 1959, North Carolina; 1960, District of Columbia (inac-

(This Listing Continued)

tive); 1970, New York; 1992, Paris. *Education:* Haverford College (A.B., 1952); Yale University (LL.B., 1959). Phi Beta Kappa. Editor-in-Chief, Yale Law Journal, 1958-1959. Lecturer, Yale Law School, 1975-1976. Special Consultant to the Under Secretary of State, 1961. Resident at: Washington Office, 1959-1962; Brussels Office, 1962-1966; Paris Office, 1966-1968; New York Office, 1968-1991. *Member:* Association of the Bar of the City of New York; New York State and American Bar Associations; International Law Association; American Society of International Law; Union Internationale des Avocats; Association Française des Avocats Conseils d'Entreprise.

BERNARD JOSIEN, born Paris, France, May 4, 1932; admitted, 1992, Paris. *Education:* University of Paris; Faculté de Droit de Paris (Licence en Droit, 1953; D.E.S. Droit Public, 1954; D.E.S. Droit Privé, 1955; D.E.S. Droit Romain et Histoire du Droit, 1956; Doctorat en Droit, 1957); University of Cambridge (Diploma of Comparative Legal Studies, 1957). *Member:* Association Française des Avocats Conseils d'Entreprise.

JEAN-MICHEL TRON, born Rabat, Morocco, June 22, 1940; admitted, 1992, Paris. *Education:* University of Paris; Institut d'Etudes Politiques (1962); Faculté de Droit de Paris (Licence en Droit, 1964; D.E.S. Droit Public, 1965); Harvard Law School (LL.M., 1968). *Member:* Association Française des Avocats Conseils d'Entreprise; International Fiscal Association.

JEAN-PIERRE VIGNAUD, born Reignac, France, May 5, 1946; admitted, 1992, Paris. *Education:* University of Paris; Institut d'Etudes Politiques (1967); Faculté de Droit de Paris (Licence en Droit, 1968; D.E.S. Droit Public, 1969); Cornell Law School (LL.M., 1970). *Member:* Association Française des Avocats Conseils d'Entreprise.

GILLES ENTRAYGUES, born Paris, France, July 7, 1946; admitted, 1992, Paris. *Education:* University of Paris; Institut d'Etudes Politiques (1966); Faculté de Droit de Paris (Licence en Droit, 1968). Co-Author: "Gestion Fiscale Internationale Des Entreprises," 1986. Lecturer, Institut d'Etudes Politiques, 1990. *Member:* Association Française des Avocats Conseils d'Entreprise; International Fiscal Association.

WILLIAM B. MCGURN, III, born New York, N.Y., April 3, 1943; admitted, 1973, District of Columbia; 1977, New York; 1992, Paris. *Education:* Yale University (B.A., 1965); Harvard Law School (J.D., cum laude, 1972). Resident at: Washington Office, 1972-1975, 1978-1985; Paris Office, 1975-1978. Member, Board of Governors, American Hospital of Paris. *Member:* The District of Columbia Bar; American Bar Association; Association Française des Avocats Conseils d'Entreprise.

ROBERT BORDEAUX-GROULT, born Neuilly-sur-Seine, France, November 10, 1953; admitted, 1975, Paris. *Education:* University of Paris; Faculté de Droit de Paris (Licence en Droit, 1975; D.E.A. Droit Privé, 1976); University of Chicago Law School (LL.M., 1977). *Member:* Association Française des Avocats Conseils d'Entreprise.

FRANÇOIS JONEMANN, born Fontès, France, April 20, 1951; admitted, 1992, Paris. *Education:* University of Paris; Institut d'Etudes Politiques (1972); Faculté de Droit de Paris (Licence en Droit, 1972; D.E.S. Droit Public, 1973); Faculté des Lettres de Paris (Licence en Sociologie, 1974; Licence ès Lettres, 1974); Boalt Hall School of Law, University of California (LL.M., 1976). *Member:* Association Française des Avocats Conseils d'Entreprise.

JEAN-MARCEL CHEYRON, born Paris, France, July 17, 1946; admitted, 1970, Paris. *Education:* University of Paris, Faculté de Droit de Paris (Licence en droit, 1969; D.E.S. Droit Privé, 1970).

DANIEL S. STERNBERG, born New York, N.Y., February 18, 1954; admitted, 1980, New York; 1993, Paris. *Education:* Yale University (B.A., 1976); Columbia University (J.D., 1979). Editor, Columbia Law Review, 1978-1979. Law Clerk to Judge Edward Weinfeld, U.S. District Court, Southern District of New York, 1979-1980. Resident at New York, 1980-1991.

LAURENT COHEN-TANUGI, born Tunis, Tunisia, February 8, 1957; admitted, 1984, New York; 1992, Paris. *Education:* Ecole Normale Supérieure (Agrégation de Lettres, 1979); Institut d'Etudes Politiques de Paris (1980); Faculté de Droit de Paris (Licence en Droit, 1980; Maîtrise en Droit, D.E.A. Droit Anglo-Américain, 1981); Harvard Law School (LL.M., 1982). Author: "Le droit sans L'Etat, Sur la démocratie en France et en Amérique," PUF, 1985; "La Metamorphose De La Democratie," Editions Odile Jacob, 1989; "L'Europe en Danger," Fayoud, 1992. *Member:* American Bar Association; Association Française des Avocats Conseils d' Entreprise.

(This Listing Continued)

CLEARY, GOTTLIEB, STEEN & HAMILTON, Paris—Continued

ARNAUD DE BROSSES, born Paris, France, August 13, 1959; admitted, 1992, Paris. *Education:* University of Paris II Assas (Maîtrise de Droit Fiscal, 1981). *Member:* Association Française des Avocats Conseils d'Entreprise.

JEAN-MARIE AMBROSI, born Chamalières, France, June 26, 1955; admitted, 1987, New York; 1992, Paris. *Education:* University of Aix-Marseilles, Faculté de Droit et de Science Politique (Maîtrise en Droit, 1976; D.E.S.S. Droit des Affaires, 1977; Doctorat en Droit des Affaires, 1979); Faculté de Sciences Economiques (Diplôme d'Etudes Comptables Supérieures, 1980); University of Pennsylvania (LL.M., 1985). *Member:* American Bar Association; Association Française des Avocats Conseils d'Entreprise.

ASSOCIATES

KARINE AUDOUZE, born Dieuze, France, May 22, 1967; admitted, 1991, New York; 1993, Paris. *Education:* University of Paris I (Maîtrise Droit International des Affaires, 1988); University of Paris II Assas (D.E.A. Droit des Affaires et Droit Economique, 1989); New York University (LL.M., 1990).

CAROLINE BERTIN, born Paris, France, June 2, 1963; admitted, 1992, Paris. *Education:* University of Paris II Assas (Maîtrise Droit des Affaires, 1984); University of Paris V René Descartes (D.E.S.S. Fiscalité, 1985); New York University (LL.M., 1987). *Member:* Association Française des Avocats Conseils d'Entreprise.

NATHALIE BIDERMAN, born Paris, France, July 28, 1966; admitted, 1990, Paris. *Education:* University of Paris II Assas (D.E.S.S. Droit des Affaires et Fiscalité Magistère de Juriste d'Affaires, 1989); University of Georgetown (LL.M., 1993).

PIERRE-MARIE BOURY, born Le Mans, December 10, 1965; admitted, 1994, Paris. *Education:* Ecole Normale Supérieure (1985); University of Paris IV Sorbonne (Licence, 1986; Maîtrise, 1987); University of London, Queen Mary & Westfield College (LL.M., 1992).

JOHN D. BRINITZER, born Wiesbaden, Germany, December 17, 1963; admitted, 1991, New York (Not admitted in France). *Education:* Amherst College (B.A., 1986); Harvard Law School (J.D., cum laude, 1990). Phi Beta Kappa. Harvard International Law Journal, Recent Developments Editor.

PIERRE-YVES CHABERT, born Nevers, France, March 1, 1962; admitted, 1987, Paris; 1989, New York. *Education:* Hautes Etudes Commerciales (H.E.C., 1985); Faculté de Droit de Paris (Doctorat en Droit, 1987); Harvard Law School (LL.M., 1988). Author: "Les Swaps Technique contractuelle et régime juridique," Masson, 1992. *Member:* Association Française des Avocats Conseils d'Entreprise.

ANNE CHRUN, born Phnom-Penh, Cambodia, December 1, 1964; admitted, 1991, Paris. *Education:* University of Paris II Assas (Maîtrise, mention Droit des Affaires, 1988; D.E.A. en Droit Privé Général, 1991); New York University School of Law (LL.M., 1993).

SERGE COHEN, born Boulogne-Billancourt, November 19, 1967; admitted, 1993, Paris. *Education:* University of Paris II Assas (Maîtrise en Droit Public, Maîtrise en Droit Privé, mention Carrières Judiciaires, 1989; DEA en Droit Privé Général, 1990); Institut d'Etudes Politiques de Paris (Diplôme de la Section Service Public, 1992); Ecole des Hautes Etudes Commerciales (H.E.C., 1993).

FRANCOIS FUNCK-BRENTANO, born Boulogne-Billancourt, France, June 7, 1961; admitted, 1988, New York; 1991, Paris. *Education:* Ecole Supérieure de Commerce de Paris (1983); University of Paris II Assas (Maîtrise en Droit, 1984); University of Paris I Panthéon Sorbonne (D.E.A. Droit des Affaires, 1985); Harvard Law School (LL.M., 1987). *Member:* New York State Bar Association.

JEAN-YVES GARAUD, born Paris, France, November 11, 1963; admitted, 1988, Paris; 1991, New York. *Education:* University of Paris II Assas (D.E.A. de Droit, 1985); Institut D'Etudes Politiques (1986); University of Paris II Assas (D.E.A., 1987); New York University (LL.M., 1990). *Member:* New York State Bar Association.

RAYMOND GIANNO, born Saint-Denis-sur-Seine, France, March 16, 1963; admitted, 1994, New York (Not admitted in France). *Education:* National Police School (qualified O.P.C., 1984); University of Paris II Assas (Maîtrise, mention Droit des Affaires, summa cum laude, 1989' D.E.S.S.,

(This Listing Continued)

Droit des Affaires et Fiscalité, cum laude, 1990); Harvard Law School (LL.M., 1992).

ANTOINE KIRRY, born La Tronche, France, December 28, 1958; admitted, 1983, Strasbourg; 1987, New York; 1992, Paris. *Education:* University of Strasbourg, School of Historical Sciences (Licence d'Histoire, 1982); University of Strasbourg, School of Law (Maîtrise en Droit Privé, 1981; D.E.A. en Droit Privé, 1983); Columbia University (LL.M., 1986). *Member:* Association Française des Avocats Conseils d'Entreprise.

FRÉDÉRIC LALANCE, born Tours, France, April 22, 1961; admitted, 1986, Paris. *Education:* University of Paris I Panthéon Sorbonne (Maîtrise Droit des Affaires, mention Carrières Judiciaires, 1983; D.E.A. Droit des Affaires et Droit Economique, 1985); Institute d'Etudes Judiciaires of Paris I Panthéon Sorbonne (1983).

MARGUERITE A. LAMPLEY, born New York, N.Y., December 30, 1964; admitted, 1991, New York (Not admitted in France). *Education:* University of California (B.A., 1986); Columbia Law School (J.D., 1990).

CARINE L'HOTE, born Montéeliard, France, March 7, 1966; admitted, 1993, Hauts-de-Seine; 1994, Paris. *Education:* Hautes Etudes Commerciales (H.E.C., 1990).

CARL L. LIEDERMAN, born Los Angeles, California, June 7, 1964; admitted, 1992, New York (Not admitted in France). *Education:* Pomona College (B.A., 1986); Yale Law School (J.D., 1991). Phi Beta Kappa. Co-Editor-in-Chief, Yale Journal of International Law.

CARINE PERRIER, born Bourges, October 15, 1964; admitted, 1994, Paris. *Education:* University of Paris IV Sorbonne (Licence en Russe, 1985); Ecole Normale Supérieure (Agrégation en Anglais, 1988); University of Paris I Panthéon-Sorbonne (Maîtrise en Droit, 1992).

XAVIER RENARD, born Paris, France, May 20, 1965; admitted, 1991, Paris. *Education:* University of Paris II Assas (Maîtrise en Droit des Affaires, 1987); Diplôme de l'Ecole Supérieure des Sciences Economiques et Commerciales (ESSEC, 1989).

ALAN M. RIFKIN, born New York, N.Y., March 18, 1964; admitted, 1991, New York and Massachusetts (Not admitted in France). *Education:* University of Pennsylvania (B.A., 1985; J.D., 1990); Johns Hopkins University, School of Advanced International Studies (M.A., 1987).

ISABELLE B. ROUX, born Marseilles, France, March 5, 1957; admitted, 1984, New York and U.S. District Court, Southern and Eastern Districts of New York; 1992, Paris. *Education:* University of Paris, France, Faculté de Droit de Paris II (Maîtrise de Droit Privé , summa cum laude, 1978; Diplôme d'Etudes Approfondies de Droit Privé Général, 1979); Tulane University School of Law (LL.M., 1982). *Member:* Association Française des Avocats Conseils d'Entreprise.

CHRISTOPHE A. SALAMON, born Marseilles, France, April 14, 1962; admitted, 1988, Paris; 1990, New York. *Education:* University of Paris I Panthéon Sorbonne (Maîtrise en Droit International des Affaires et du Commerce International, with distinction, 1984; D.E.A. de Droit International Privé et de Commerce International, 1985); University of Paris II (D.E.A. de Droit Privé, 1986); University of Chicago Law School (LL.M., 1989). *Member:* New York State, American and International Bar Associations.

FABIENNE SCHALLER, born Basel, Switzerland, August 15, 1960; admitted, 1986, Paris; 1993, New York. *Education:* University of Paris X Nanterre (Maîtrise en Droit Social, 1984; D.E.A. Droit Social, 1987); New York University (LL.M., 1992).

YVETTE P. TEOFAN, born Austin, Texas, July 17, 1963; admitted, 1989, New York (Not admitted in France). *Education:* Stanford University (B.A., 1985); Yale University (J.D., 1988). Phi Beta Kappa. Articles Editor, Yale Law Journal.

MARIE-LAURENCE TIBI, born Enghien-les-Bains, May 5, 1967; admitted, 1993, New York; 1994, Paris. *Education:* Ecole des Hautes Etudes Commerciales (H.E.C., 1988); University of Paris X Nanerre (Maîtrise en Droit, 1991); New York University School of Law (LL.M., 1992).

PASCALE TRAGER-LEWIS, born Birmingham, England, August 14, 1964; admitted, 1987, Paris, 1989, New York. *Education:* University of Paris X (Maîtrise, 1986; D.E.S.S. Droit du Commerce International, 1988); New York University School of Law (M.C.J., 1989).

(For biographical data of the partners resident in the New York, Washington, Brussels , London, Hong Kong, Tokyo and Frankfurt Offices, see Professional Biographies at New York, N.Y., Washington, D.C., Brussels, Belgium, London, England, Hong Kong, Tokyo, Japan and Frankfurt, Germany).

CLIFFORD CHANCE

Established in 1962

112 AVENUE KLÉBER
BP 163 TROCADÉRO
75770 PARIS CEDEX 16, FRANCE
Telephone: (33 1) 44 05 52 52
Fax: (33 1) 44 05 52 00

Amsterdam, The Netherlands Office: Apollolaan 171, 1077 AS, P.O. Box 7301, 1007 JH. Telephone: (31 20) 577 71 11. Fax: (31 20) 676 93 26.

Bahrain, Manama Associated Office: Law Office of Shaikh Isa bin Mohammed Al Khalifa. P.O. Box 20717. Telephone: (973) 531535; 531073. Fax: (973) 536272; 530608.

Barcelona, Spain Office: Pau Claris 102, 08009. Telephone: (34 3) 318 68 64. Fax: (34 3) 317 73 23.

Brussels, Belgium Office: Avenue Louise 65, Box 2, 1050. Telephone: (32 2) 533 59 11. Fax: (32 2) 533 59 59.

Budapest, Hungary Office: Köves & Partners, Clifford Chance. Madách Trade Center, Madách Imre Út 14, 1075. Telephone: (36 1) 268 1600. Fax: (36 1) 268 1610.

Dubai, United Arab Emirates Office: 18th Floor, Dubai World Trade Centre, P.O. Box 9380. Telephone: (971 4) 314333. Fax: (971 4) 313990; 314565.

Frankfurt/Main, Germany Office: Friedrichstraße 2-6, 60323. Telephone: (49 69) 971 4090. Fax: (49 69) 971 40977.

Hanoi, Vietnam Office: 52 Nguyen Binh Khiem. Telephone: (844) 229 182/3/4/5/6. Fax: (844) 229 190.

Hong Kong Office: 30th Floor, Jardine House, One Connaught Place. Telephone: (852) 2810 0229. Fax: (852) 2810 4708; 2810 4858; 2810 4743.

London, England Office: 200 Aldersgate Street, EC1A 4JJ. Telephone: (44 171) 600 1000. Fax: (44 171) 600 5555.

Madrid, Spain Office: Paseo de la Castellana 110, 28046. Telephone: (34 1) 562 7674. Fax: (34 1) 562 49 93.

Milan, Italy Associated Office: Grimaldi e Clifford Chance. Via Gesú, 3, 20121. Telephone: (39 2) 7600 8040. Fax: (39 2) 7600 4950.

Moscow, Russia Office: Ul. Sadovaya - Samotechnaya 24/27, 2nd Floor, 103051. Telephone: (7 501) 258 50 50. Fax: (7 501) 258 50 51.

New York, New York Office: Swiss Bank Tower, 10 East 50th Street, 10022. Telephone: (1 212) 750 1440. Fax: (1 212) 758 6625.

Riyadh, Saudi Arabia Associated Office: The Law Firm of Salah Al-Hejailan. P.O. Box 1454, 11431. Telephone: (966 1) 479 2200. Fax: (966 1) 479 1717.

Rome, Italy Associated Office: Grimaldi e Clifford Chance. Viale G. Rossini 7, 00198. Telephone: (39 6) 807 2251. Fax: (39 6) 807 8201.

Shanghai, People's Republic of China Office: Suite 898, Shanghai Centre, 1376 Nanjing Xi Lu, 200040. Telephone: (86 21) 279 8461. Fax: (86 21) 279 8462.

Singapore Office: 16 Collyer Quay #31-00, 0104. Telephone: (65) 535 1855. Fax: (65) 535 6855.

Tokyo, Japan Office: 6th Floor, South Hill Nagatacho Building, 11-30 Nagatacho 1-chome, Chiyoda-ku, 100. Telephone: (81 3) 3581 4311. Fax: (81 3) 3593 0651.

Warsaw, Poland Office: Warsaw Corporate Centre, ul. Emilii Plater 28, 00-688. Telephone: (48 2) 630 3344. Fax: (48 2) 630 3355.

International Banking and Finance including Project Finance, Aircraft Finance and Securitization, Regulatory Law, Environmental Law, Commercial Law, Competition Law, Commercial Property Law, Labour Law, Bankruptcy Law, Intellectual Property, Administration Law, Taxation, Litigation, Arbitration and Immigration.
Firm engaged in English, French and General International Practice.

PARTNERS RESIDENT

RONALD S. AUSTIN, Liverpool University (LL.B. Hons., 1967). Diplôme de Droit Comparé Faculté Internationale pour l'Enseignement de Droit Comparé, 1968. Solicitor, 1970. Avocat, 1973. *LANGUAGES:* English and French. *PRACTICE AREAS:* Sports Law; Property Tax; International Real Estate; Commercial Leases; Property Investment.

PIERRE BECHMANN, Maîtrise de Droit, Université de Paris. Avocat à la Cour. *LANGUAGES:* English and French. *PRACTICE AREAS:* Permit Litigation; Environmental Liability and Insurance; Biotechnology; Environmental Law.

(This Listing Continued)

OLIVIER BERTIN-MOUROT, Licence en Droit, Université de Paris, 1967. Institut d'Etudes Politiques, 1968. Avocat, 1974. *LANGUAGES:* English and French. *PRACTICE AREAS:* Banking and Finance Law; Stock Exchange Regulations; Securities; Mergers and Acquisitions; Asset Based Lending.

JOHN TREVOR BROWN, Cambridge University; Université de Paris. Admitted, 1965, Solicitor Supreme Court of England and Wales; Avocat, 1973. *LANGUAGES:* English and French. *PRACTICE AREAS:* Aeronautical Law; Finance; Aerospace Law; Banking Law; Energy.

THOMAS R. BUDGETT, Cambridge University (MA, 1969). Solicitor, 1972. *LANGUAGES:* English and French. *PRACTICE AREAS:* Asset Based Lending; Equipment Leasing; Ship Finance; Banking Law; Aviation Finance.

JEAN-JACQUES CAUSSAIN, Docteur en Droit, Université de Paris, 1965. Diplômé d'Etudes Supérieures de Droit Privé, 1966. Docteur en Droit, 1968. Avocat, 1975. *LANGUAGES:* English and French. *PRACTICE AREAS:* Securities; Joint Ventures; Stock Exchange Regulations; Venture Capital; Mergers and Acquisitions; Corporate Law.

BRIAN J. CORDERY, OBE, Solicitor, 1963. Avocat, 1973. (Administrative Partner). *LANGUAGES:* English and French.

JEAN-PIERRE DUFFOUR, Licence en Droit, 1969. Avocat au Barreau de Paris. *LANGUAGES:* English and French. *PRACTICE AREAS:* Insolvency; Personal Bankruptcy; Civil Arbitration; Litigation.

MICHAEL ELLAND-GOLDSMITH, Cambridge University (B.A., 1967; LL.B., 1968; M.A., 1971); Barrister, 1969. Avocat, 1978. Diplômé d'Etude Approfondies (Droit Privé Général, 1979); Solicitor, 1985. *LANGUAGES:* English and French. *PRACTICE AREAS:* Project Finance; Banking Law; Ship Financing; Equipment Leasing.

JOHN HAMILTON, Oxford University (M.A., 1981); Solicitor, 1983; Avocat, 1990. *LANGUAGES:* English and French. *PRACTICE AREAS:* Asset Based Lending; Securities; Banking Regulations; Banking Law.

CHRISTIAN LACHÈZE, Des en Droit, Université de Paris, 1972; Diplômé d'Etudes Supérieures de Droit Privé, 1973. Avocat, 1979. *LANGUAGES:* English and French. *PRACTICE AREAS:* Insolvency; Industrial and Intellectual Property; Employment Law; Environmental Law.

HENRY LAZARSKI, Edinburgh University (M.A., LL.B., 1966-1968). Solicitor, 1968. Avocat, 1973. *LANGUAGES:* English, French and Polish. *PRACTICE AREAS:* Real Estate-Commercial Law; Taxation; Complex Litigation; Acquisitions, Divestitures, Mergers.

FRANÇOIS ROUX, Avocat, 1987. *LANGUAGES:* English and French. *PRACTICE AREAS:* Property Litigation; Gaming Law; Commercial Property Law.

JEAN-MARC TIRARD, Licence en Droit, 1971, Lauréat de la Faculté de Droit de Dijon. Diplômé de l'Ecole Nationale des Impôts, 1971. Diplômé d'Etudes Comptables Supérieures, 1978. Avocat, 1989. *LANGUAGES:* English and French. *PRACTICE AREAS:* Tax on Individuals and Businesses; Taxation; Tax Controversies.

PIERRE R.N. VERKHOVSKOY, D.E.S. en Droit, 1968. D.E.S. Droit Public, des Sciences Politiques, Etudes Americaines. C.A.P.A. Lauréat de la Faculté de Droit de Paris; Lauréat du Concours Général des Facultés de Droit. Institut d'Etudes Politiques, 1969. Avocat, 1974. *LANGUAGES:* English and French. *PRACTICE AREAS:* Commercial Law; Water and Power; Banking Regulation; Joint Ventures.

YVES WEHRLI, Avocat, 1985. *LANGUAGES:* English and French. *PRACTICE AREAS:* Commercial Law; Computer Law; Sports Law; Business Acquisitions; Telecommunications Law.

AVOCATS

Arnaud Achard	Frédéric Gros
Catherine Astor-Veyres	Landry Guesdon
Olivier Barrat	Mark Henderson
Thomas Baudesson	Gilles Heude
Jean-Paul Bertolas	Richard Jadot
Jacques Bertran de Balanda	Sylvie Kande de Beaupuy
Francois Bloch	Bernard Lamon
Virginie Bouet	Gilles Lebreton
Sophie Boyer-Chammard	Hélène Malecot
Christine Carbonnel	Philippe Margraph (New York)
Eric Davoudet	François Mary
Laurent Develle (Tokyo)	Hélène Moisand-Florand
Laurent d'Hervé	Didier Moutard

(This Listing Continued)

CLIFFORD CHANCE, Paris—Continued

Cécile Duval
Sean Edwards
Hubert Fabre-Magnan
Marc Favero
Eric Ferguson
Olivier Gaillard
Dominique Gatti
Stephane Gazale
Catherine Gouesse
Walter Grandpré
Pierre Gromnicki (Warsaw)

Richard Parolai
Valérie Petitbois-Gastinel
Jean-Norbert Pontier
Clément Rouyer
Thierry Schoen
Christophe Sciot-Siegrist
Fabienne Sorin
Brigitte Soustiel
Viviane Stulz
Willem Wynaendts
Eric Zeller

JURISTES

Antoine Allez
Jacques Beaumont
Franck Blin
Françoise Blum
Alain Checri
Edouard Clément
Catherine Dawson
Sean Edwards
Stéphanie Faber
Richard Fellous
Solange Fougere
Jason Fry
Tina Fung

Angela Guinaudie
John Harrison
Ulrike Heidegger
Ann Hieu Ly-Ky
Sarah Jones
Felicity Kirk
Peter Kirk
Alexandre Lagarrigue
Sue Palmer
Christophe Pelet
Jacques Pickering
Anne-Sophie Ple
Rex Rosales

Nick Tidman

Languages: English, French, German, Spanish, Polish, Japanese and Italian

(For the names of Partners resident in other offices, see Professional Biographies for those offices).

COBLENCE ET ASSOCIES

Established in 1983

24, RUE CLÉMENT MAROT
75008 PARIS, FRANCE
Telephone: 1-47.20.74.50
Telex: JMCRD 613269 F
Telefax: 1-47.23.68.42

Lyon, France Associated Office: Alain Jakubowicz. 33, Av. Maréchal Foch, 69006. Telephone: 78.93.11.94. Fax: 78.94.19.64.

General French and International Law Practice. Arbitration, Corporate, Antitrust Banking, EEC Regulations, Copyright, Advertising, Labor Law, Unfair Competition, Foreign Investment and Real Estate.

MEMBERS OF FIRM

JEAN-MARC COBLENCE, born Paris, France, July 17, 1952; admitted, 1977, Paris and Paris Court of Appeals. *Education:* University of Paris Law School (Licence 1976, DEA Droit du Commerce International, 1977). *LANGUAGES:* French and English. *PRACTICE AREAS:* Arbitration Law; Advertising Law; Foreign Investment Law.

ROLAND DESPONDS, born Fribourg, Switzerland, December 11, 1953, nationality, French and Swiss; admitted, 1978, Paris and Paris Court of Appeals. *Education:* Diplôme de l'Institut d'Etudes Politiques de Paris, 1974, University of Paris, Law School (Licence 1975, DEA Droit Civil, 1976). *LANGUAGES:* French, English and German. *PRACTICE AREAS:* EEC Regulation Law; Unfair Competition Law; Antitrust Law.

ELISABETH LAHERRE, born Alger, Algeria, October 14, 1956; admitted, 1980, Paris; 1981, Paris Court of Appeals. *Education:* Ecole des Hautes Etudes Commerciales (1977); University Paris III (Licence, 1978, DEA Droit syndical et relation du Travail, 1982). *LANGUAGES:* French, English and German. *PRACTICE AREAS:* General Litigation; Labor Law.

CHANTAL GIRAUD-VAN GAVER, born Lille, France, November 22, 1949; admitted, 1976, Paris Court of Appeals. *Education:* University of Lille (Licence en droit, 1974); University of Paris (DES Droit du Travail, 1976). Contributor, European Labor Law, Lamy Social, 1988. *PRACTICE AREAS:* Labor Law; EEC Regulation Law; Copyright Law.

ANNIE GAUTHERON VEBRET, born Dijon, October 22, 1958; admitted, 1983, Paris Court of Appeal. *Education:* University of Bourgogne

(This Listing Continued)

Law School (Maîtrise, 1980, DESS Commerce International, 1981). *LANGUAGES:* French and German. *PRACTICE AREAS:* Advertising Law; Copyright; Unfair Competition.

ASSOCIATES

CÉCILE DELOCHE DE NOYELLE, born Paris, France, April, 1953; admitted, 1989, Paris and Paris Court of Appeals. *Education:* University of Paris Law School (Licence, 1975; DESS Conseil Juridique, 1976). *LANGUAGES:* French and English. *PRACTICE AREAS:* Medical Law.

ANNE-DOMINIQUE BOUSQUET, born Nantes, France, November 29, 1965; admitted, 1990, Paris and Paris Court of Appeals. *Education:* University of Nantes Law School (Maîtrise, 1987); University of Paris Law School (DEA Droit International, 1988). *LANGUAGES:* French and English. *PRACTICE AREAS:* Arbitration Law.

MARTINE RIOU, born L'Hay Les Roses, France, February 12, 1966; admitted, 1990, Paris and Paris Court of Appeals. *Education:* University of Sceaux Law School (Maîtrise, 1988). *PRACTICE AREAS:* Labor Law; Employment Law.

PHILIPPE BENAMOU, born Paris, France, September 21, 1960; admitted, 1991, Paris Court of Appeal. *Education:* University of Paris II Law School (Maîtrise, 1986). *LANGUAGES:* French and English. *PRACTICE AREAS:* Criminal Law.

MARLÈNE SAFAR-GAUTHIER, born Alger, Algeria, November 15, 1958; admitted, 1993, Paris and Paris Court of Appeal. *Education:* University of Rouen Law School (Maîtrise, 1980); University of Paris II Law School (DEA Droit Civil; Droit International Privé). *LANGUAGES:* French, English and Spanish. *PRACTICE AREAS:* General Litigation; Advertising Law; Unfair Competition; Copyright; Banking Law.

LUDOVIC DORES, born Saint-Germain-en-Laye, France, March 22, 1966; admitted, 1994, Paris and Paris Court of Appeal. *Education:* University of Nanterre Law School (Maîtrise, 1990); University of Paris Dauphine Management School (Maîtrise, 1990); University of Paris II Law School (DEA Droit Communautaire, 1991). *LANGUAGES:* French and English. *PRACTICE AREAS:* General Litigation; EEC Regulation Law; Business Law; Unfair Competition; Antitrust Law; Distributorship and Consumer Law.

COBLENCE & WARNER

69 AVENUE VICTOR HUGO
PARIS, FRANCE
Telephone: (1) 4417-50-50
Fax: (1) 4501-77-21

New York, N.Y. Office: 415 Madison Avenue. Telephone: 212-593-8000. Fax: 212-593-9058.

General Corporate, International Corporate and Tax, Mergers and Acquisitions, Entertainment, Licensing, Matrimonial. Civil and Criminal Litigation and Appellate Practice.

ALAIN COBLENCE, born New York, N.Y., April 6, 1948; admitted, 1970, France; 1975, New York and U.S. District Court, Southern and Eastern Districts of New York. *Education:* Institut d'Etudes Politiques; Faculté de Droit, France (Licence en Droit, with honors, 1970); Institut de Droit Comparé (Diplome, with honors, 1970); Institut d' Etudes Judiciaires (Diplome, with honors, 1970). *Member:* New York State and American Bar Associations; Ordre des Avocats au Barreau de Paris. *LANGUAGES:* French.

CONSTANT & CONSTANT

Solicitors and Avocats

190 BOULEVARD HAUSSMANN
75008 PARIS, FRANCE
Telephone: (1) 42 89 08 89
Fax: (1) 42 89 21 00

London, England Office: Sea Containers House, 20 Upper Ground Blackfriars Bridge, CDE Box No. 1067, SE1 9QT. Telephone: 0171-261 0006 (IDD: 44 71). 24 Hour Answering Service: 0171-638 3535. Fax: 0171-401 2161; 0171-401 2731 Groups 2/3. Telex: 927766 TWOCTS G.

Shipping, Corporate and Commercial, Banking and Finance, Property and Private Client.

(This Listing Continued)

ANDREW HOWARD CHARLIER, born Redhill, England, November 30, 1962; admitted, 1988, England and Wales; 1994, France. *Education:* University of Birmingham; Universite de Limoges (1985); College of Law, Guildford. *Member:* Law Society of England and Wales. *LANGUAGES:* English and French. *PRACTICE AREAS:* Shipping; Company; Commercial; Banking.

GILLES GAUTIER, born 1954; admitted, 1992, Paris; 1994, English Registered Foreign Lawyer. *Education:* Universite de Paris II (Maitrise de Droit des Affaires, 1977); Universite de Paris I (Diplome d'Etudes Specialisees Transport International, 1979). *Member:* Association Francaise de Droit Maritime. *LANGUAGES:* French and English. *PRACTICE AREAS:* Shipping; Insurance; Commercial Agreements; Litigation.

COOPERS & LYBRAND
CLC JURIDIQUE ET FISCAL

Avocats au Barreau de Paris

32, RUE GUERSANT
75017 PARIS, FRANCE
Telephone: (1) 45.72.83.40
Fax: (1) 45.72.87.01
Telex: 641415 COLYBRA

Lyon, France Office: 177 rue Garibaldi, 69328 LYON, Cedex 03.
Telephone: 72.60.52.52. Fax: 78.95.17.12.
Marseille, France Office: 141 avenue de Prado, 13008, MARSEILLE.
Telephone: 91.25.65.66. Fax: 91.25.66.67.

General Business Law, Corporate, Banking, Mergers and Acquisitions, Domestic and International Taxation, Labour and Social Law, Business Litigation and Arbitration, European Community Law.

FIRM PROFILE: Firm established in 1971 as CONSEIL JURIDIQUE et FISCAL, not admitted to the Paris Bar until 1992, when they were admitted as lawyers under the names of COOPERS & LYBRAND CLC JURIDIQUE et FISCAL. The French law firm offers a full range of legal and tax services for domestic as well as international clients. Besides the thirteen partners, the firm has a legal support staff of 110 associates, most of them being admitted to the Paris Bar.

MEMBERS OF FIRM

MARTIAL BUONO, born Paris, France, October 28, 1956; admitted, 1986, Paris. *Education:* University of Paris (D.E.S.S. in Business law, 1981). *LANGUAGES:* French and English. *PRACTICE AREAS:* Tax Law; Restructuring for international groups in France.

RAYMOND CANNARD, born Bourg, France, October 19, 1953; admitted, 1985, Paris. *Education:* University of Lyon (D.E.S.S. in Business Law and D.J.C.E., 1979). *LANGUAGES:* French and English. *PRACTICE AREAS:* Business Law; Corporate Law; Mergers and Acquisitions; Litigation and Arbitration.

DANIEL CHASSAGNE, born Saint-Sauves, France, August 10, 1950; admitted, 1991, Paris. *Education:* Ecole Nationale des Impôts (Masters in Law, 1971). Past Cabinet Ministre. *Member:* Direction Géneale des Impôts (Director); Chevalier de l'Ordre des Arts & Lettres.

ARNAUD CHASTEL, born Dakar, Senegal, October 27, 1959; admitted, 1990, Paris. *Education:* University of Paris (Graduate in Economics, 1983; Masters in Business Law, 1983; D.E.S.S. in Tax Law, 1984). *LANGUAGES:* French and English. *PRACTICE AREAS:* Tax Law; International Tax Law; Local Tax Law; Mergers and Acquisitions.

MICHEL COMBE, born Aubenas, France, March 6, 1959; admitted, 1990, Paris. *Education:* D.E.A. en Droit des Affaires, Aix en Provence (1982); Institut Superieur des Affaires, Paris (Groupe HEC, 1984). *LANGUAGES:* French, English and Spanish. *PRACTICE AREAS:* Corporate; National Law; International Tax Law; Social Law.

MARC CRETTE, born Saint-Maur-des-Fossés, France, March 27, 1960; admitted, 1990, Paris. *Education:* University of Paris (D.E.S.S. in International Tax Law, 1982). *LANGUAGES:* French and English. *PRACTICE AREAS:* Tax Law; Real Estate; Property Tax.

YANN KERGALL, born Paris, France, January 5, 1941; admitted, 1966, Paris. *Education:* Diplômé de l'Ecole des Hautes Etudes Commerciales, Paris, 1963; University of Paris (Masters in Law, 1966); Free University of Berlin, Germany. Co-Author: "Summary of French Company Law," 1976. Secretary General of Comité National des Conseillers du Commerce Extéricur de la France. *Member:* International Fiscal Association (I.F.A.).

(This Listing Continued)

LANGUAGES: French, English and German. *PRACTICE AREAS:* International Tax; Domestic Tax; Corporate Law; Mergers and Acquisitions.

ROBERT MAGNAN, born Marseille, France, May 5, 1951; admitted, 1981, Paris. *Education:* University of Paris (Masters in Economics, 1972; Masters in Law, 1975; D.E.A., Commercial Law, 1976); Ecole Nationale des Impôts. *LANGUAGES:* French and English. *PRACTICE AREAS:* Corporate Finance; Mergers and Acquisitions; International Tax Law.

GÉRARD NICOLAY, born Chamalières, France, July 27, 1946; admitted, 1974, Paris. *Education:* University of Paris (Masters in Law, 1974). *LANGUAGES:* French and English. *PRACTICE AREAS:* Tax Law; Corporate Law.

JEAN-LUC PIERRE, born Paris, France, August 5, 1953; admitted, 1985, Lyon. *Education:* Institut d'Etudes Politiques de Paris (cum laude 1974); University of Paris (D.E.A. de Finances Publiques et Fiscalité, 1977; Docteur en droit, 1979). Professor Associate of Law at the University of Lyon III. Author: "Fiscalité de la Recherche, de la propriété industrielle et des logiciels," 1993. Co-Author: Optimisation fiscale et abus de droit," 1990. *Member:* International Fiscal Association (IFA); International Bar Association (IBA); International Tax Planning Association (ITPA); Société Francaise de Droit Fiscal. *LANGUAGES:* French and English. *PRACTICE AREAS:* Tax Law; Business Law.

BERNARD PREUILH, born Dax, France, October 24, 1959; admitted, 1989, Lyon. *Education:* University of Montpellier (D.E.S.S. in Business Law and D.J.C.E., 1984). *LANGUAGES:* French, English and Spanish. *PRACTICE AREAS:* Business Law; Commercial; Distribution; Corporate Law; International Law; Mergers and Acquisitions.

DANIEL SIMONIN, born Toul, France, February 15, 1949; admitted, 1980, Paris. *Education:* University (Masters in Law, 1972); Ecole Nationale des Impôts. *LANGUAGES:* French and English. *PRACTICE AREAS:* Transfer Pricing; Tax Law; Mergers and Acquisitions.

DOMINIQUE SIZES, born Casablanca, Morocco, January 4, 1952; admitted, 1987, Paris. *Education:* University of Paris (Docteur en droit, 1987). *LANGUAGES:* French, English and Spanish. *PRACTICE AREAS:* Corporate; Commercial; European and International Law; Litigation.

MARIE SUPIOT, born Angers, France, January 2, 1957; admitted, 1991, Paris. *Education:* University of Paris (D.E.A., Commercial Law, 1979; I.A.E., 1982). *LANGUAGES:* French and English. *PRACTICE AREAS:* Business Law; Corporate Law.

JACQUES TAQUET, born Algiers, May 22, 1958; admitted, 1983, Paris. *Education:* University of Montpellier (D.J.C.E., 1980). *Member:* International Fiscal Association (I.F.A.). *LANGUAGES:* French and English. *PRACTICE AREAS:* International Tax Law; Insurance Law.

DOMINIQUE VILLEMOT, born Wimereux, France, January 31, 1954; admitted, 1991, Paris. *Education:* Institut d'Etudes Politiques de Paris, 1975, Ecole Nationale d'Administration, 1980. *LANGUAGES:* French, English, Italian and Greek. *PRACTICE AREAS:* Tax Law.

JOSE YBORRA, born Algiers, August 30, 1942; admitted, 1980, Marseille. *Education:* University (Masters in Law, 1968), Ecole National des Impôts (1968). Former Conseil Juridique en Droit et Fiscalité. *Member:* I.F.C.F. *LANGUAGES:* French, English and Spanish.

ALAIN CORNEC

Avocat á la Cour

11, RUE LINCOLN
75008 PARIS, FRANCE
Telephone: (33-1) 4561 4236
Fax: (33-1) 4561 4232

International Private Clients: Personalities' Law, Family Law, Child Abduction, Succession, Property, Entertainment and Sports.

ALAIN CORNEC, born 1949; admitted, 1973, Paris. *Education:* University of Paris; King's College, London (Docteur en droit, 1975). *Member:* International Academy of Matrimonial Lawyers; International Bar Association. *LANGUAGES:* French, English and Spanish.

ASSOCIATES

ANA MARTINS, born 1968; admitted, 1993, Paris. *Education:* Paris (D.E.A.). *LANGUAGES:* French, English, Portuguese and Spanish.

(This Listing Continued)

ALAIN CORNEC, Paris—Continued

MARIE HELÈNE CHAUDONNERET, born 1964. *Education:* Paris (Maîtrise en Droit des Affaires, 1988); England (LL.M., Company EEC Law, 1989). *LANGUAGES:* French and English.

OF COUNSEL

MAUREEN HOLM, born 1951; admitted, 1982, New York. *Education:* Fordham University, New York (J.D., 1981; LL.M. in International Business and Trade Law, 1991). *Member:* Association of the Bar of the City of New York (Committee Member, Foreign and Comparative Law; Eastern European Affairs). *LANGUAGES:* French, English and German. *PRACTICE AREAS:* Intellectual Property; Licensing and Distribution; International Law; Eastern European Commerce; Trade Law.

COUDERT FRÈRES

Avocats à la Cour

52, AVENUE DES CHAMPS ELYSÉES
75008 PARIS, FRANCE
Telephone: (33) 1 43590160
Cable Address: "Treduf"
Telex: 650164
Telecopier: (33) 1 43596655

REVISERS OF THE FRANCE LAW DIGEST FOR THIS DIRECTORY.

New York, New York 10036-7794: 1114 Avenue of the Americas.
Washington, D.C. 20006: 1627 I Street, N.W.
Los Angeles, California Office 90017: 1055 West Seventh Street, Twentieth Floor.
San Francisco, California 94111: 4 Embarcadero Center, Suite 3300.
San Jose, California 95113: Suite 1250, Ten Almaden Boulevard.
London, EC4M 7JP, England: 20 Old Bailey.
Brussels B-1050, Belgium: Tour Louise. 149 Avenue Louise-Box 8.
Beijing, People's Republic of China 100020: Suite 2708-29 Jing Guang Centre, Hu Jia Lou, Choa Yang Qu.
Shanghai, People's Republic of China 200002: Suite 1804, Union Building, 100 Yanan Road East.
Hong Kong: 25th Floor, Nine Queen's Road Central.
Singapore, 0104: Tung Centre, 20 Collyer Quay.
Sydney N.S.W. 2000, Australia: Suite 2202, State Bank Centre, 52 Martin Place.
Tokyo, 107 Japan: 1355 West Tower, Aoyama Twin Towers, 1-1-1 Minami-Aoyama, Minato-ku.
Moscow, Russia: Ulitsa Staraya Basmannaya 14.
01301 Sao Paulo, SP, Brazil: Machado, Meyer, Sendacz, e Opice, Advogados, Rua da Consolacao, 247, 8 Andar.
Bangkok 10500, Thailand: Chandler and Thong-Ek, Southeast Insurance Building, 315 Silom Road, 10th Floor.
Ho Chi Minh City, Vietnam: c/o Saigon Business Centre, 49-57 Dong Du Street, District 1.

General and International Law Practice. Corporation, Tax and Estate Law.
Authorized to appear before French and EEC Courts.

PARTNERS

JACQUES BUHART, born Mulhouse, France, July 11, 1950. Avocat à la Cour; admitted, 1977, Paris, France. *Education:* Ecole Sainte-Geneviève, Versailles; Ecole Supérieure de Commerce de Paris (1974); University of Paris, Faculty of Law (Licence en Droit des Affaires, 1975; Diplôme d'Etudes Supérieures Spécialisées, 1976); Institute of Comparative Law (1975); Academy of International Law, The Hague (1976). *Member:* International Bar Association (Chairman, Committee G, Business Organizations, 1992—); International Competition Law Association. *LANGUAGES:* French and English.

CATHERINE CHARPENTIER, born St. Nazaire, France, April 17, 1957; admitted, 1989, France. *Education:* Paris I Sorbonne (D.E.S.S., Tax Law/Corporate Law; Conseil Juridique & Fiscal, 1981; D.E.A., Anglo-Saxon Law, 1984). Professor, ESSEC - Paris - International Tax Law. Member, TGI Nanterre (Hauts-de-Seine), 1989 - Bar of Paris (1994). *LANGUAGES:* French and English.

WILLIAM LAURENCE CRAIG, born New York, N.Y., September 17, 1933; admitted, 1957, New York; 1960, District of Columbia; 1963, U.S. Supreme Court. 1973, Paris, France. *Education:* Williams College (A.B.,

(This Listing Continued)

1954); Harvard Law School (LL.B., cum laude, 1957); Faculty of Law, University of Paris (Docteur en droit de l'Université). Member: NATO Appeals Board, 1974-1977; Court of Arbitration of the International Chamber of Commerce, 1978-1984; Academic Council, ICC Institute of International Business Law and Practice, 1980-1991. Panel of Arbitrators: American Arbitration Association, Schiedsgericht Berlin (Arbitration Court Berlin), China International Economic and Trade Arbitration (CIETAC). Co-Author: International Chamber of Commerce Arbitration (2 Vols. 1st ed. 1984, 2d ed. 1990). *Member:* Bar Association of the District of Columbia; The Association of the Bar of the City of New York; American Bar Association; Chartered Institute of Arbitrators. *LANGUAGES:* English and French.

JEAN-PATRICE DE LA LAURENCIE, born Paris, France, April 2, 1943; admitted, 1990, Paris, France. *Education:* Institut d'Etudes Politiques, Paris, France (M.A., 1964); Faculte de Droit, Paris, France (M.A., 1966); Ecole Nationale d'Administration, Paris, France (Ph.D., 1970). Author: "Public Operators' Behavior Regarding Antitrust Rules," Les Petites Affiches, August 1988; "The Role of the French Administration Facing the New EEC Regulation on Franchising," La Semaine Juridique, March 1989; "Takeover Bids and Merger Control," Review of Competition and Consumer Affairs, September-October 1989 and International Business Law Journal, July 1989; "The New EC Merger Control Regulation: A Good Political Compromise but a Nest for Political Litigation," BNA Publication, February 23, 1990. Lecturer: Price and Competition Policies, Ecole Nationale Supérieuré d'Arts Et Métiers, University of Paris, 1978-1987; French and EEC Antitrust Rules, University of Paris-V, March to June 1989. Antitrust Law école Supérieuré de Commerce de Paris, 1992. Personal Advisor to French Minister of Finance, Jacques Delors, 1981-1982. Assistant Director and Deputy Director General of the Finance Ministry's Competition, Consumers and Anti-Fraud Department, 1982-1989. *Member:* Association Francaise D'Etude de La Concurrence; Union Internationale Des Avocats. *LANGUAGES:* French, English and Italian.

CHARLES KAPLAN, born Neuilly-S-Seine, France, December 26, 1958; admitted, 1980, England and Wales; 1992, Paris. *Education:* Trinity Hall, Cambridge (B.A., Philosophy and Law, 1979; M.A., 1984).

ERIC LAPLANTE, born Paris, France, May 23, 1957; admitted, 1987, New York and France. *Education:* I.E.P. Paris, France (Diplôme, 1977); University of Paris IX Dauphine, France (DEA in International Economics, 1980); University of Paris II Panthéon-Assas, France (DEA in Law, 1981); New York University (LL.M., 1984). Fulbright Scholar.

VAN KIRK REEVES, born New York, N.Y., May 14, 1939; admitted, 1964, New York; 1969, U.S. Supreme Court, U.S. Court of Appeals, 2nd Circuit and U.S. District Court, Southern District of New York; 1973, Paris, France. *Education:* Harvard University (B.A., 1960); Institut d'Etudes Politiques, University of Paris; Harvard Law School (LL.B., 1964). *Member:* American Foreign Law Association (Secretary, 1969-1970); American Society of International Law; New York State and American Bar Associations; The Association of the Bar of the City of New York; International Law Association. *LANGUAGES:* French and English.

ROBIN TREVOR TAIT, born New York, N.Y., February 5, 1929; admitted, 1957, New York; 1973, Paris, France. *Education:* Cornell University (A.B., 1951) Phi Beta Kappa; Cambridge University (B.A., 1953; M.A., 1956); Yale Law School (LL.B., 1956). Correspondent for France, International Banking and Financial Law Bulletin, 1987—. *Member:* The Association of the Bar of the City of New York; American Bar Association; International Bar Association; British Institute of International and Comparative Law. *LANGUAGES:* English and French.

JONATHAN M. WOHL, born Washington, D.C., August 18, 1949; admitted, 1976, New York and U.S. District Court, Southern District of New York; 1983, France. *Education:* Yale University (B.A., magna cum laude, 1971); Harvard Law School (J.D., cum laude, 1974). Phi Beta Kappa. Member, Harvard Law School Board of Student Advisors, 1972-1974. Law Clerk to Hon. Robert Braucher, Associate Justice, Massachusetts Supreme Judicial Court, 1974-1975. *Member:* American Bar Association.

GEORGE T. YATES, III, born Roanoke, Virginia, July 16, 1948; admitted, 1974, New York; 1984, California; 1992, France. *Education:* University of Virginia (B.A., 1970; J.D., 1973); Columbia University (LL.M., 1974); Universite de Paris II, 1974-1975. Phi Beta Kappa. Member, Board of Editors, Virginia Law Review, 1971-1973 and Virginia Journal of International Law, 1972-1973. Lecturer in Law, University of Virginia, 1976-1982. Co-editor, Limits to National Jurisdiction Over the Sea, 1974. Jervey Fellow in Foreign Law, 1973-1975. Author: "International Law and the Delimitation of Bays," N.C. Law Review, 1971; "The Rhodesian Chrome Statute: The

(This Listing Continued)

Congressional Response to United Nations Economic Sanctions Against Southern Rhodesia," Virginia Law Review, 1972; "Postwar Belgian International Claims: Their Settlement by Lump Sum Agreements," Virginia Journal of International Law, 1973; "Substantive Law Aspects of Enforcement of Foreign Judgments Between Foreigners in France: The Competence Question," The International Lawyer, 1975; "European Directives on Formation and Operation of Companies and the Role of the Lawyer," Harmonization of Laws in the European Communities, P. Herzog ed., 1983; "State Responsibility for Nonwealth Injuries to Aliens in the Postwar Era," International Law of State Responsibility for Injuries of Aliens, R. Lillich ed., 1983; "International Claims: Contemporary Belgian Practice," International Claims: Contemporary European Practice, R. Lillich and B. Weston ed., 1983. *Member:* The Association of the Bar of the City of New York; New York State and American Bar Associations; State Bar of California; American Society of International Law. *LANGUAGES:* English and French.

OF COUNSEL

HUBERT DE MAHUET, born Arraye, France, August 26, 1933.; admitted, 1973, Paris, France. *Education:* University of Nancy (Docteur en Droit, 1958).

DIDIER NEDJAR, born Neuilly Sur Seine, July 30, 1950; admitted, 1980, Paris. *Education:* Lycée Pasteur (Bacc, 1968); University of Paris II (Maîtrise, 1972; Doctorat, 1987); Harvard Law School (S.J.D., 1978). Instructor, Chargé d'Enseignements - Maître de Conférences Université de Paris I Panthéon Sorbonne (1987—) Maître de Conférences - Institut d'Etudes Politiques de Paris (1990-1991) - Visiting Expert IDL I Rome (1987—). *Member:* Societe Francaise De Droit International. (European Counsel). *LANGUAGES:* French, English and Spanish.

JEAN-CLAUDE PETILON, born Paris, France, June 13, 1942; admitted, 1973, Paris, France; 1975, District of Columbia. *Education:* Pennsylvania State University (A.B., 1964); George Washington University Law School (J.D., 1967); University of Paris, Faculty of Law (Diplôme d'Etudes Supérieures de Droit Privé, 1970). Legal Advisor to Republic of Zaire, 1975-1977.

ASSOCIATES

Delphine Abellard	Arnaud Guérin
Monique R. Beguiachvili	(Not admitted in France)
Jean-Mathieu Cot	Hélène Lepetit
Olivier de Précigout	Michael Polkinghorne
Laure Givry	Pascale Rouast-Bertier
Aline Gladiline	Catherine Santoul
(Not admitted in France)	Philippe Shin
Elisabeth Terron	

REVISERS OF THE FRANCE LAW DIGEST FOR THIS DIRECTORY.

(For biographical data of the Washington personnel, see Professional Biographies at Washington, D.C.).
(For biographical data of the San Francisco personnel, see Professional Biographies at San Francisco, California).
(For biographical data of the Los Angeles personnel, see Professional Biographies at Los Angeles, California).
(For biographical data of the San Jose personnel, see Professional Biographies at San Jose, California).
(For biographical data of the New York personnel, see Professional Biographies at New York, N.Y.).
(For biographical data of the Brussels personnel, see Professional Biographies at Brussels, Belgium).
(For biographical data of the London personnel, see Professional Biographies at London, England).
(For biographical data of the Tokyo personnel, see Professional Biographies at Tokyo, Japan).
(For biographical data of the Hong Kong personnel, see Professional Biographies at Hong Kong).
(For biographical data on Beijing personnel, see Professional Biographies at Beijing, People's Republic of China).
(For biographical data of the Singapore personnel, see Professional Biographies at Singapore).
(For biographical data of the Sao Paulo personnel, see Professional Biographies at Sao Paulo, Brazil).
(For biographical data of the Shanghai personnel, see Professional Biographies at Shanghai, People's Republic of China).
(For biographical data of the Sydney personnel, see Professional Biographies at Sydney, Australia).
(For biographical data of the Moscow personnel, see Professional Biographies at Moscow, U.S.S.R.).
(For biographical data on the Ho Chi Minh City personnel, see Professional Biographies at Ho Chi Minh City, Vietnam).

COURNOT ET ASSOCIÉS

Established in 1981

217 RUE DU FAUBOURG SAINT HONORÉ
75008 PARIS, FRANCE
Telephone: (1) 42.56.66.22
Telefax: (1) 42.56.72.68

General French Law Practice, Business Law, Corporate Law, Tax Law, Mergers and Acquisition, Commercial Law, Intellectual Property Rights, Communication and Media Law, Investments in the people's Republic of China.

FIRM PROFILE: Founded in 1981, the firm is member of Unilaw, an international group of law firms, and has a close association with DE BACKER & Associés, a leading law firm based in Belgium.

STÉPHANE J. COURNOT, born Rouen, France, 1947; admitted, 1968, Paris; 1981, District of Columbia. *Education:* University of Paris (Licence en Droit, 1968; Diplôme d'Etudes Supérieures, 1970); Georgetown Law School (M.C.L., 1979). *Member:* American Bar Association; Club des Avocats France-Amérique (President). *LANGUAGES:* French and English. *PRACTICE AREAS:* Company Law; Mergers and Acquisitions.

JEAN-PHILIPPE DESTREMAU, born Sfax, Tunisia, 1948; admitted, 1972, Paris. *Education:* Faculté de Droit de Paris (Licence, 1971). *LANGUAGES:* French and Spanish. *PRACTICE AREAS:* Labor Law; Litigation; Intellectual Property Law; Communications Law; Media Law.

CHRISTINE GUILLERM-KIRK, born Paris, France, 1948; admitted, 1972, Paris; 1977, New York. *Education:* University of Paris (Licenciée en Droit, 1970); Institut d'Etudes Politiques de Paris (Diplôme, 1969). Author: "Direct Investment Techniques for the U.S.A." (Kluwer-1983). French Editor: "Tax Notes International (U.S.A.). *Member:* International Fiscal Association; International Bar Association; Club des Avocats France-Amérique; Institut des Avocats Conseils Fiscaux. *LANGUAGES:* French and English. *PRACTICE AREAS:* Business Law; Corporate Law; Taxation Law.

GEORGES-MARIE DUCLOS, born La Rochelle, France, 1946; admitted, 1978, Paris. *Education:* University of Paris (Maîtrise en Droit, 1970; Diplôme d'Etudes Supérieures, 1971); Institut d'Administration des Entreprises de Paris (1971). *Member:* International Fiscal Association; Institut des Avocats Conseils Fiscaux (Treasurer). *LANGUAGES:* French, English and Spanish. *PRACTICE AREAS:* Business Law; Taxation Law.

PAUL RANJARD, born Paris, France, 1944; admitted, 1972, Paris. *Education:* Lycée Claude Bernard and Jeanson de Sailly, Paris (Baccalauréat, 1962); Faculté de Droit de Paris (Licence en droit, 1968; Diplôme d'Etudes Supérieures de Droit Privé, 1969). Co-Author: "Foreign Investment in China and the Special Economic Zones," 1982. *LANGUAGES:* French and English. *PRACTICE AREAS:* Civil Law; Business Litigation; Foreign Investment Law.

ARNAUD DE CORBIÈRE, born Chambery, France, 1960; admitted, 1993, Paris. *Education:* University of Paris (Maîtrise de Droit, 1984; Diplôme d'Etudes Approfondies, 1986). *LANGUAGES:* French and ?English. *PRACTICE AREAS:* Business Law; Corporate Law.

ASSOCIATES

LAURENCE PINCHOU, born Boulogne, France, 1960; admitted, 1984, Paris. *Education:* University of Paris (Maîtrise de Droit, 1983).

PATRICIA GILLOT, born Rouen, France, 1968; admitted, 1993, Paris. *Education:* University of Nanterre (Diplôme d'Etudes Supérieures Spécialisées, 1991). *LANGUAGES:* French and English.

YVES COURSIN, born Paris, France, 1960; admitted, 1987, Paris. *Education:* University of Paris (Maîtrise de Droit Privé, 1984). *LANGUAGES:* French and English.

JEAN-LUC PETIT, born Neuilly sur Seine, France, June 22, 1963; admitted, 1989, Paris. *Education:* University of Paris II (Diplôme d'Etudes Approfondies, 1987). *LANGUAGES:* French and English.

CHRISTOPHE JEAN, born Rennes, France, 1963; admitted, 1991, Paris. *Education:* University of Paris II (Maîtrise de Droit, 1987). *LANGUAGES:* French and English.

GUY LAMBOT, born Nantes, France, 1966; admitted, 1993, Paris. *Education:* University of Paris II (D.E.A., 1988). *LANGUAGES:* French and English.

(This Listing Continued)

COURNOT ET ASSOCIÉS, Paris—Continued

CYRILLE D'ESTIENNE DU BOURGUET, born Boulogue-Billancourt, France, 1968; admitted, 1993, Paris. *Education:* University of Paris II (Maître de Droit Privé, 1991); University o f Paris XI (D.E.S.S., 1992). *LANGUAGES:* French and English.

OF COUNSEL

FU JIANG BIN, born Shanxi, People's Republic of China, 1955; (Not admitted in France). *Education:* Graduate Institutes of Foreign Languages, Luoyang (English, 1976); Beijing (French, 1982). Ministry of Oil, Shenzen (Chinese Economic Law, 1983). Contract Negotiator, China National Offshore Oil Corporation, 1982-1985. *LANGUAGES:* Chinese, French and English. *PRACTICE AREAS:* Investment Law.

COUSTÉ

29, BOULEVARD RASPAIL
75007 PARIS, FRANCE
Telephone: (1) 42 22 46 11
Fax: 45 44 97 04

Copyright, Patent, and Trademark Law, Civil and Commercial Law, Computer, Electronic Means of Payment, Entertainment, Common Market and International Practice.

MEMBERS OF FIRM

MARINA COUSTÉ, born Paris, France, March 28, 1952; admitted, 1976, Paris. *Education:* University of Paris X (Licence en Droit, 1974; DEA de Droit Civil, 1975). Lecturer, Commercial Law, Institut Supérieur de Gestion, 1985-1987. President, International Center for Research and Studies in Computer and Telecommunication Law, CIREDIT, 1987—. *Member:* French Computer Law Association, AFDI; European Computer Law Association, AEPDI. *LANGUAGES:* French, English and German.

ELISABETH SCOTTO D'APOLLONIA, born Alger, Algérie, September 22, 1954; admitted, 1981, Paris. *Education:* University of Paris X (Licence en Droit, 1976). Contributor to Jurisclasseur Social Law. *LANGUAGES:* French and English.

LAURENT MERCIÉ, born Grenoble, France, May 10, 1967; admitted, 1992, Paris. *Education:* University of Paris X (Licence en Droit, 1989; Maîtrise en Droit des Affaires, 1990; Institut d'Etudes Judiciaires, 1990; C.A.P.A., 1991). *LANGUAGES:* French and English.

COUTARD & ASSOCIES

67-69, AVENUE VICTOR HUGO
75783 PARIS CEDEX 16, FRANCE
Telephone: (1) 45.01.57.50
Telefax: (1) 45.01.78.29

General French and International Law Practice.

MEMBERS OF FIRM

JEAN-PIERRE COUTARD, born La Flèche, France, January 16, 1949; admitted, 1974, Paris. *Education:* Prytanée Militaire (La Flèche); Lycée Louis Le Grand, Paris; University of Paris; Graduate Institute of Comparative Law. *Member:* International Bar Association. *LANGUAGES:* French and English.

DOMINIQUE DINOT-COUTARD, born Mantes-La-Jolie, May 11, 1949; admitted, 1983, Paris. *Education:* University of Paris (Diplôme d'Etudes Supérieures, 1973). *LANGUAGES:* French and English.

CHRISTIAN COSTE, born Paris, January 13, 1957; admitted, 1984, Paris. *Education:* Lycée Carnot; University of Paris. *LANGUAGES:* French and English.

ERIC HARM, born Paris, January 14, 1959; admitted, 1988, Paris. *Education:* University of Paris (Dîplome d'Etudes Approfondies de Droit International). *LANGUAGES:* French, German and English.

YANNICK AMSELLEM, born Marseille, March 22, 1963; admitted, 1988, Paris. *Education:* University of Paris (Diplôme d'Etudes Supérieures de Fiscalite Internationale). *LANGUAGES:* French and English.

COUTRELIS & ASSOCIES

55 AVENUE MARCEAU
75116 PARIS, FRANCE
Telephone: 44.43.91.30
Fax: 40.70.07.97

Brussels, Belgium Office: 235, Rue de la Loi, 1040. Telephone: 230.48.45. Fax: 230.82.06.

Arbitration, Lobbying, Counseling and Litigation (both before National Courts and before the Court of Justice in Luxembourg) on Free Movement of Goods, Common Agricultural Policy, Antitrust, State Aids, Banking and Financial Law, Products Liability, Customs and Tariff Law, Food and Drug Regulations, Consumer Law, Environmental Law, Patents, Trademarks, Designs, Copyrights, Licensing, Distribution and Franchising Law.

FIRM PROFILE: The firm is well known for its expertise in European Community Law as it is applied within EC countries, as well as for its work regarding the likely effects of EC Law as it will be applied by EFTA countries with the coming into force of the European Economic Area Agreement.

MEMBERS OF FIRM

ANDRÉ COUTRELIS, born Cairo, Egypt, April 15, 1944; admitted, 1982, Paris as Conseil Juridique; 1987, Paris, as Avocat. *Education:* University of Paris (Licence en Droit, 1969; Certificat du Centre Universitaire d'Etudes des Communautés Européennes, 1969; DES Droit Public, 1971); University of California at Berkeley (LL.M., 1973). Lecturer in Law, Faculty of Law and Economic Sciences of Paris, 1969-1972. Banque Nationale de Paris, 1975-1976; Baker & McKenzie, Paris, 1976-1977. *Member:* International Bar Association; International Association of Boalt Alumni (IABA); Association des Juristes Européens; Association des Juristes de Banque. *LANGUAGES:* French, English, Greek and Arabic. *PRACTICE AREAS:* European Community Law.

NICOLE COUTRELIS, born Toulon, France, August 28, 1950; admitted, 1985, Paris as Avocat. *Education:* University of Paris (Licence d'Histoire, 1970); University of Paris II (Licence en Droit, 1973). Office National Interprofessionel des Céréales, 1972-1978; Représentation Permanente de la France auprès de la CEE, 1978-1982; Legal Service, Commission of the European Communities, 1982-1985. Lecturer, Seminars on EC Law, EN-GREF (Ecole Nationale du Génie Rural, des Eaux et Forêts, Paris). *Member:* International Bar Association; Association des Juristes de Banque; Association des Juristes Européens; Association Française du Droit de l'Alimentation (AFDA); Secretary General of Association Internationale des Juristes pour le Droit de la Vigne et du Vin (AIDV) and of European Food Law Association (EFLA). *LANGUAGES:* French, English, Italian, Spanish and German. *PRACTICE AREAS:* European Community Law; Litigation; Food and Drug Regulation.

JOHN ANDREW JOHNSON, born Manchester, England, June 26, 1961; called to the Bar, 1983, Gray's Inn; (Not admitted in France). *Education:* University of Newcastle-Upon-Tyne (LL.B., Hons., 1982); Inns of Court School of Law (1982-1983); University of Amsterdam, Amsterdam School of International Relations (LL.M., European Community Business Law, 1993). Pupillage, 2 Harcourt Buildings, Temple, 1985-1986; Prosecutor, Crown Prosecution Service, Leeds, 1986-1987; Legal Advisor HM Government, 1987-1991. *Member:* Bar European Group; Council of the Bar and Law Societies of the European Community. *LANGUAGES:* English, French, German and Dutch. *PRACTICE AREAS:* European Community Law.

RACHIDA SEMAIL, born Villacourt, France, July 22, 1964; admitted, 1994, Paris as Avocat. *Education:* Université des Sciences Sociales, Toulouse (Licence en Droit, 1986; Maîtrise en Droit Public, Relations Internationales, 1987; DEA Droit Économique International et Communautaire, 1988; Doctorat en Droit, 1992). Thesis: "la dénomination des produits agricoles et des denrées alimentaires en droit communautaire." Certificat d'aptitude à la profession d'Avocat, 1993. *LANGUAGES:* French, English and Arabic. *PRACTICE AREAS:* European Community Law; Food and Drug Regulation.

OF COUNSEL

JEAN-CLAUDE MASCLET, born Neuilly-sur-Seine, France, January 15, 1943. Professeur Agrégé des Facultés de Droit; Professor Paris I; Honorary Dean, Faculté de Droit Jean Monnet at Sceaux; Director, DESS "Entreprise et Droit Communautaire" at Faculté de Droit Jean Monnet; President, Commission pour l'étude des Communautés Européennes (CEDECE). Chevalier de la Légion d'Honneur; Chevalier des Palmes Académiques. Deputy-Mayor, Montmorency. Member, Editorial Boards of

(This Listing Continued)

Revue Trimestrielle de Droit Européen and Revue Française de Droit Constitutionnel. *LANGUAGES:* French and English. *PRACTICE AREAS:* European Community Law; Constitutional Law; Administrative Law.

PIERRE-MARIE VINCENT, born Marseille, France, June 28, 1926. *Education:* Swiss Federal Institute of Technology, Zurich (M.Sc., Agronomy, 1953). Lecturer, Food Law, University Aix-Marseille III, 1988—. Director, Food Law, Educational Programme at CNAM, Paris, 1985—. Author: "La certification et la normalisation en France"; "Qualité de l'aliment. Législation et Réglementation"; "Industrial requirements in food safety"; "Sugars, Sweeteners and EC Regulations"; "Hemmnisse in grenzüberschreitenden Handel mit Lebensmitteln für eine besondere Ernährung". Manager, Plant Protection R & D, Pechiney-Progil, Lyons, 1954-1962; Monsanto Europe, Brussels, 1963-1972; Manager, Food Law Dept., Brooke Bond Liebig Continental Division, Schoten, Belgium, 1972-1977; Manager, Food Law Dept., Worldwide, Roquette Fréres, Lestrem, France, 1978-1990. Member: Chairman, French Food Law Association; Board Member, European Food Law Association; Board Member, Plant Protection and Environment Association; Board Member, Regional Center for Food Research, Innovation and Technology, Avignon; Chairman, Commission Générale des Méthodes d'Analyse. Member, Association Nationale des Industries Agroalimentaires. *LANGUAGES:* French, English, German, Italian and Spanish. *PRACTICE AREAS:* Food and Drug Regulation.

J. ET B. CREMADES ET ASSOCIÉS

51, AVENUE GEORGES MANDEL
75116 PARIS, FRANCE
Telephone: 45.53.55.50
Fax: 45.53.55.49

Madrid, Spain Office: J. y B. Cremades y Asociados, Goya 18, 2nd Floor, 28001. Telephone: 431.8354. Fax: 576.9794.
Brussels, Belgium Office: Av. Louise, 391, 1050. Telephone: 648.9840. Fax: 647.8351.

General Practice. Commercial, Corporate, Foreign Investment, Licensing, Insurance, Banking and Finance, Oil and Gas, Real Estate and Patent Law, Aeronautical/Transportation, Commercial Arbitration, EEC, Competition Law, Customs Regulations, Environmental Law, Public Procurement.

PARTNERS

JUAN ANTONIO CREMADES, born Zaragoza, Spain, January 1, 1940; admitted, 1961, Zaragoza; 1966, Madrid; 1986, Paris. *Education:* University of Zaragoza (Law Degree, 1960); University of Paris (Law Degree, 1960; Ph.D., 1968); International Faculty of Comparative Law (1961). President, Union Internationale des Avocats, 1990-1991; Representative of the Paris Bar, 1992; Chairman, Committee of Regulation of Contracts of the International Chamber of Commerce, 1979-1980; International Maritime Arbitration Organization (CMI-ICC), 1979-1980. President, Spanish Chamber of Commerce in France since 1987. *Member:* Madrid Bar Association; Ordre des Avocats à la Cour de Paris; ICC International Court of Arbitration since 1969; Honorary member, Zaragoza, Mexico and Dominican Republic Bar Associations. (Also at Madrid, Spain and Brussels, Belgium Offices). *LANGUAGES:* Spanish, French and English.

BERNARDO M. CREMADES, born Zaragoza, Spain, July 20, 1943; admitted, 1969, Madrid; 1986, Paris. *Education:* University of Cologne (Ph.D., German Law, 1967); University of Seville (Ph.D., Spanish Law, 1968). Author of Litigating in Spain (Kluwer, 1989). Professor, Law Faculty, University of Madrid, 1975—. Arbitration in Spain (Butterworths, 1991) and Business Law in Spain (Butterworths, 1992). *Member:* Madrid Bar Association; Avocat à la Cour de Paris; International Council of Commercial Arbitration; International Bar Association; American Bar Association. (Also at Madrid, Spain and Brussels, Belgium Offices). *LANGUAGES:* Spanish, French, German and English.

ISABEL ZIVY, born Mexico City, Mexico, July 25, 1946; admitted, 1969, Paris; 1992, Madrid. *Education:* University of Paris (Law Degree, 1968). Permanent Contributor for Latin America, Revue de Droit des Affaires Internationales, 1982; Revue Française de Droit Aérien, 1986. Representative of the Mexican Capítulo, Committee on Air Transport of the ICC, 1986; on Arbitration, 1992. *Member:* Instituto Iberoaméricano de Derecho Aeronáutico; Franco-Latin American Chamber of Commerce (Director, 1988—; President, Chilian Section); International Bar Association; International Association of Lawyers. *LANGUAGES:* French, Spanish and English.

(This Listing Continued)

MARIE-ANNICK VALLUIS, born St. Palais, France, June 26, 1946; admitted, 1969, Paris; 1992, Madrid. *Education:* University of Paris (Law Degree, 1968); Institut d'Etudes Judiciaires, Paris (Diploma, 1968); University of Paris (D.E.S., Private Law, 1969). Contributor: Droit et Pratique du Commerce International, 1982. Representative of the Mexican Capítulo, Committee on Regulations and Procedures in International Trade of the ICC 1986. *Member:* Chambre de Commerce Franco-Espagnole; Association Française des Avocats Conseils d'Entreprises (ACE); International Association of Lawyers. *LANGUAGES:* French, Spanish and English.

EDITH MARION, born Sens, France, April 19, 1948; admitted, 1976, Paris. *Education:* University of Dijon (Literature Degree, 1969); Spanish teacher at Academy of Dijon, 1969-1970; University of Reims (Law Degree, 1974); Institut d'Etudes Judiciaires Reims (Diploma, 1974); Private Law and Trade Law teacher, 1974-1976; University of Paris (D.E.S., Sciences Politiques, 1976); Institut de Droit des Affaires (First Degree, 1976); University of Brussels (Law Degree, 1987). *Member:* Droit et Commerce Association. *LANGUAGES:* French, Spanish and English.

BRUNO ROCA GRAU, born Paris, France, September 27, 1962; admitted, 1988, Valencia, Spain; 1991, Madrid; 1992, Paris. *Education:* University of Valencia (Law Degree, 1986); Institut de'Etudes Europeennes Université Libre de Bruxelles (Master in European Law, 1987). *LANGUAGES:* Spanish, French and English.

ALEJANDRO ALONSO DREGI, born Barcelona, Spain, June 11, 1964; admitted, 1988, Barcelona; 1991, Madrid; 1992, Paris. *Education:* University of Barcelona (Law Degree, 1987); Institut de'Etudes Europeennes Université Libre de Bruxelles (Master in European Law, 1988). Professor (Business Law), CEILA, University of Paris Sorbonne. *LANGUAGES:* Spanish, French, Italian and English.

ASSOCIATES

NATHALIE CAZEAU, born Libourne, France, June 6, 1963; admitted, 1987, Rennes, France. *Education:* University of Paris II (Third Degree, 1984); University of Rennes (Law Degr ee, 1985); Institut d'Etudes Judiciaires Rennes (1986); University of Renne s (DESS Private Law, 1986). President, International Commission of Union des Jeunes Avocats. *LANGUAGES:* French, English and Spanish.

ISABELLE ROMERO, born Madrid, Spain, November 29, 1966; admitted, 1990, Paris. *Education:* University of Paris II (Law Degree, 1988), University of Paris I (Master in European Law, 1989). *LANGUAGES:* French, Spanish and English.

MARIA DOLORES GARCIA-LUDEÑA, born Salamanca, Spain, April 7, 1962; admitted, 1986, Salamanca; 1990, Madrid. *Education:* University of Salamanca (Law Degree, 1986; Master in European Law, 1987). *LANGUAGES:* Spanish, French and English.

SYLVIA MESA, born Paris, France, September 10, 1964; admitted, 1989, Paris. *Education:* University of Paris (Law Degree, 1987; DESS in International Commercial Law). *LANGUAGES:* French, Spanish and English.

Languages: French, Spanish, English and German.

(For complete biographical data on all personnel, see Professional Biographies at Madrid, Spain)

CURTIS, MALLET-PREVOST, COLT & MOSLE

Established in 1830

8 AVENUE VICTOR HUGO
75116 PARIS, FRANCE
Telephone: 45-00-99-68
Telecopier: 45-00-84-06.

REVISERS OF THE ARGENTINA, BOLIVIA, BRAZIL, CHILE, COLOMBIA, COSTA RICA, DOMINICAN REPUBLIC, ECUADOR, EL SALVADOR, GUATEMALA, HONDURAS, MEXICO, NICARAGUA, PERU, URUGUAY AND VENEZUELA LAW DIGESTS FOR THIS DIRECTORY.

New York, New York Office: 101 Park Avenue, 10178. Telephone: 212-696-6000. Telecopier: 212-697-1559. Cable Address: " Migniard New York". Telex: 12-6811 Migniard; ITT 422127 MGND.
Newark, New Jersey Office: One Gateway Center, Suite 403. Telephone: 201-622-0605. Telecopier: 201-622-5646.

(This Listing Continued)

CURTIS, MALLET-PREVOST, COLT & MOSLE,
Paris—Continued

Washington, D.C. Office: Suite 1205L, 1801 K Street, N.W., 20006.
Telephone: 202-452-7373. Telecopier: 202-452-7333. Telex: ITT 440379
CMPUI.

Houston, Texas Office: 2 Houston Center, 909 Fannin Street, Suite 3725.
Telephone: 713-759-9555. Telecopier: 713-759-0712.

Mexico City, D.F., Mexico Office: Torre Chapultepec, Ruben Dario 281,
Col. Bosques de Chapultepec, 11530 Mexico, D.F. Telephone:
525-282-0444. Telecopier: 525-282-0637.

London, England Office: Two Throgmorton Avenue, EC2N 2DL.
Telephone: 71-638-7957. Telecopier: 71-638-5512.

Frankfurt am Main 1 Office: Staufenstrasse 42. Telephone: 069-971-4420.
Telecopier: 69-17 33 99.

General American and International Law Practice.
Firm engaged in Corporate and Business Law and International Arbitration, registered as Avocat and authorized to practice before the French Courts.

PARTNER

PETER M. WOLRICH, born New York, N.Y., September 4, 1946; admitted, 1974, New York; admitted as Avocat, France. *Education:* Temple University (A.B., 1968); Brown University (A.M., 1969); Georgetown University Law Center (J.D., 1973). Woodrow Wilson Fellow. Editor, Georgetown Law Journal, 1972-1973. *Member:* American Bar Association. *LANGUAGES:* English and French.

COUNSEL

JOHN M. COCHRAN, III, born New York, N.Y., June 26, 1941; admitted, 1967, New York; admitted as Avocat, France; 1974, California. *Education:* College of William & Mary (A.B., 1963); George Washington University (J.D., cum laude, 1967); University of Paris School of Law, France (1971-1973). Order of the Coif. Member, Foreign Barrister of Chambers of the Right Honorable The Lord Rippon of Hexham, Q.C., The Temple, London, England, 1978—. Member, Arbitration Committee, International Chamber of Commerce, 1983—. Member, Panel of Arbitrators, American Arbitration Association, 1985—. *Member:* The Association of the Bar of the City of New York; New York State, American and International Bar Associations. *LANGUAGES:* English and French.

RESIDENT ASSOCIATES

GEOFFROY P. LYONNET, born Paris, France, July 5, 1961; admitted as Avocat, France. *Education:* Ecole des Hautes Etudes commerciales H.E.C. (1983); University of Paris Law School (License en Droit, 1983. Maîtrise de Droit des Affaires, 1984); Georgetown University Law Center (LL.M., 1988). Languages: French and English.

LEILA S. ANGLADE, born Suresnes, France, December 1, 1962; admitted as Avocat, France. *Education:* Ecole Supéricere de Commerce de Lyon E.S.C.L. (1984); University of Paris School of Law (Licence en Droit des Affaires, 1985. Maitrise de Droit des Affaires, 1986. D.E.S.S. de Droit du Commerce Extérieur, 1987; D.E.A. de Droits Angiais ef Ameéricain des Affaires, 1989); C.A.P.A. 1988; Harvard Law School (LL.M., 1990). *LANGUAGES:* French, English and Spanish.

REVISERS OF THE ARGENTINA, BOLIVIA, BRAZIL, CHILE, COLOMBIA, COSTA RICA, DOMINICAN REPUBLIC, ECUADOR, EL SALVADOR, GUATEMALA, HONDURAS, MEXICO, NICARAGUA, PERU, URUGUAY AND VENEZUELA LAW DIGESTS FOR THIS DIRECTORY.

(For complete biographical data on all personnel, see Professional Biographies at New York, New York)

CABINET DAHAN

Established in 1981

6, PLACE ST GERMAIN DES PRÉS
75006 PARIS, FRANCE
Telephone: 33-1-45-49-16-16
Telecopier: 33-1-42-22-68-61

Office engaged in International Practice as well as in European practice: Specializing in Franco-American Matters.
Antitrust Affairs, Comparative Law, Contracts, Consumer Protection, Custom, Immigration, Intellectual Property, Joint Ventures, Key-on-Door-Factories, Labor Law, Product Liability, Banking and Shipping, Litigations.

(This Listing Continued)

FIRM PROFILE: Established PARIS, in 1981, the firm specializes in the resolution of transnational litigations and transactions. Clients are located worldwide with predomination from Belgium, France, Great-Britain, Ireland, Italy, Switzerland, United States and Gulf Countries. They include Major Banks, International Corporations, National Corporations, Individuals, Non-Profit Organizations and other Law Firms.

MAURICE M. DAHAN, born Tlemcen, Algeria, May 16, 1933, diplomed, 1958, Avocat, Paris France. *Education:* Faculté de Droit de PARIS-Sorbonne (Licence: 1956, DES Private Law: 1957, DES Public Law: 1958, DES History of Law and Roman Law: 1958, Doctorat d'Etat, 1961). Ex. Director of the Legal Service, French Board for Foreign Trade, 1966-1980. Assistant Professor, Law, Faculté de Droit de Paris, 1962-1965. Associate Lecturer, Commercial Law and International Tax Law, University of PARIS Sud, 1980-1982. Lecturer, International Contract Law, University of PARIS II Assas, 1975-1994. Founding Member: CARICI, International Arbitration Court, Geneva; Cahiers Juridiques et Fiscaux de l'Exportation. Arbitrator, International Commercial Chamber - ICC, PARIS. Author: "Sécurité Sociale et Responsabilté," LGDJ, 1961; "L'imputation des Libéralités sur la Quotité Disponible ou la Réserve," Dalloz, 1964; "Les droits successoraux de l'incapable majeur," Dalloz, 1964; "La surélévation des immeubles bâtis," Semaine Juridique, 1965; "Comparative Study on Investment in African Countries," Jeune Afrique, 1971; "Legal Developments on Transfer of technology to Developing Countries," Droit Economique PEDONE, 1977; "Investment in Egypt, Legal and Tax Problems," CJFE, 1-1980; "Yugoslavia investment regulation," CJFE, 1-1980; "Reservation Of Title In French Law," CJFE, 2-1980; "Legal Introduction to Chinese Market," CJFE 3-1980; "Companies Law, Comparative Analysis," CJFE 3-1980; "Agency Contract in International Business," CJFE 4-1980; "Housing and Building in Algeria," CJFE, 1981; "Investment in Greece, Tax and Legal Aspects," CJFE, 1981; "Product Liability in Comparative Law," CJFE, 1982; "LES Cessions d'Entreprise duns le Marché Commun," CJFE, 1993; "La Pratique Francaise du Commerce International," Editions du CFCE, 1993. *Member:* Paris Bar; CARICI, ROTARY. *LANGUAGES:* English and French. *PRACTICE AREAS:* Arbitration; Banking Law; International Contracts; International Litigation; Joint-Ventures; Shipping Law; Transfer of Technology; Foreign Investment.

AGNES B. DAIIAN-BITTON, born Paris, France, January 18, 1964; admitted, 1994, Avocat Paris, France. *Education:* University of PARIS-Assas, (Maîtrise Private Law: 1990); University of PARIS-Malakoff: DESS Business Law: 1991): Conseil Juridique: 1994: Avocat. *LANGUAGES:* English, French. *PRACTICE AREAS:* Commercial Litigation; Consumers Protection; Family Law; Fair-Trade; Intellectual Property; Labor Law and Torts.

ARIEL R. DAHAN, born Paris, Frace, May 26, 1968; admitted, 1994, Avocat, Paris, France. *Education:* University of Paris V, (Maîtrise of Business Law and International Law, 1991; DESS European Business Law: 1992); Conseil Juridique: 1992-1993. Legal Consultant Europe, French Board for Foreign Trade, Paris: 1994: Avocat. *LANGUAGES:* English, French and Spanish. *PRACTICE AREAS:* Anti-Trust; Comparative Law; Construction; Environment Law; Immigration; Labor and Shipping Law.

DAVIS POLK & WARDWELL

4, PLACE DE LA CONCORDE
75008 PARIS, FRANCE
Telephone: 011-331-40.17.36.00
Telecopier: 011-331-42.65.22.34
Cable Address: "Davispolk Paris"

New York, N.Y. Office: 450 Lexington Avenue, 10017. Telephone: 212-450-4000. Cable Address: "Davispolk New York". Telex: ITT-421341; ITT 423356. Telecopier: 212-450-4800.

Washington, D.C. Office: 1300 I Street, N.W., 20005. Telephone: 202-962-7000. Telecopier: 202-962-7111.

London, England Office: 1 Frederick's Place, EC2R 8AB. Telephone: 011-44-71-418-1300. Telex: 888238. Telecopier: 011-44-71-418-1400.

Tokyo, Japan Office: In Tokyo practicing as Reid Gaikokuho-Jimu-Bengoshi Jimusho. Tokio Kaijo Building Annex, 2-1, Marunouchi 1-Chome, Chiyoda-Ku, Tokyo 100, Japan. Telephone: 011-81-3-201-8421. Telecopier: 011-81-3-201-8444. Telex: 2224472 DPWTOK.

Frankfurt, Germany Office: MesseTurm, 60308 Frankfurt am Main, Federal Republic of Germany. Telephone: 011-49-69-97-57-03-0. Telecopier: 011-49-69-74-77-44.

(This Listing Continued)

Hong Kong Office: The Hong Kong Club Building, 3A Chater Road. Telephone: 852 533 3300. Fax: 852 533 3388.

American and General International Practice.
Firm engaged in American and General International Practice but not admitted to appear before the French Courts.

RESIDENT PARTNER

MARLENE J. ALVA, born Rochester, New York, April 6, 1948; admitted, 1975, New York; admitted as Conseil Juridique, 1979; 1989, France; admitted as avocat 1992 France. *Education:* Barnard College (B.A., 1970); Columbia University (J.D., 1974). *Member:* The Association of the Bar of the City of New York; American Bar Association; American Society of International Law.

ASSOCIATES

Kathleen de Carbuccia; Arthur P. Morin; M. Elizabeth Pauchet; Joseph S. Roslanowick (Not admitted in France); **Deborah Frank Shabecoff** (Not admitted in France); **Craig E. Sherman** (Not admitted in France); **Laurence Yansouni** (Not admitted in France).

(For Complete Biographical Data on all Personnel see Professional Biographies at New York City)

DEBEVOISE & PLIMPTON

Established in 1931

21 AVENUE GEORGE V
75008 PARIS, FRANCE
Telephone: (33-1) 40 73 12 12
Telecopier: (33-1) 47 20 50 82.
Telex: 648141F DPPAR

New York Office: 875 Third Avenue, 10022. Telephone: 212-909-6000. Telex: (Domestic) 148377 DEBSTEVE NYK. Telecopier: (212) 909-6836.

Washington, D.C. Office: 555 13th Street, N.W., 20004. Telephone: 202-383-8000. Telex: 405586 DPDC WUUD. Telecopier: (202) 383-8118.

Los Angeles, California Office: 601 South Figueroa Street, Suite 3700, 90017. Telephone: 213-680-8000. Telex: 401527 DPLA. Telecopier: 213-680-8100.

London, England Office: 1 Creed Court, 5 Ludgate Hill, EC4M 7AA. Telephone: (44-171) 329-0779. Telex: 884569 DPLON G Facsimile: (44-171) 329-0860.

Budapest, Hungary Office: 1065 Budapest, Révay Köz 2.III/2. Telephone: (36-1) 131-0845. Telecopier: (36-1)132-7995.

Hong Kong Office: 13/F Entertainment Building, 30 Queen's Road Central. Telephone: (852) 2810-7918. Fax: (852) 2810-9828.

Firm engaged in American, French and General International Practice.
FIRM PROFILE: OFFICE PROFILE: Opened in 1964, the Paris office provides a full range of American, French and international legal services in practice areas such as acquisitions and dispositions; general corporate, tax, antitrust, commercial and labor law advice in connection with the formation and ongoing operations of subsidiaries and joint ventures; banking, financings and financial services; Central and Eastern Europe; international tax planning; arbitration and litigation. The Paris office works closely with our offices in London and Budapest, our attorneys and affiliates based in Prague and Moscow and H ong Kong and our U.S. offices.

JAMES A. KIERNAN III, born October 20, 1944; admitted, 1972, N.Y.; 1984, Paris. *Education:* Harvard (B.A., magna cum laude, 1966; M.P.A., 1970; J.D., cum laude, 1971). Fulbright Scholar, Brazil, 1966-1967. *Member:* The Association of the Bar of the City of New York; American and International Bar Associations; Union Internationale des Avocats; Association Francaise des Avocats Conseils d' Entreprises. Fellow, American College of Investment Counsel.

GERALD M. SHEA, born November 10, 1942; admitted, 1968, N.Y.; 1975, Paris. *Education:* Yale (B.A., 1964); Columbia (J.D., 1967). *Member:* The Association of the Bar of the City of New York; International Bar Association; Association Française des Avocats Conseils d'Entreprises.

JAMES CECIL SWANK, born January 4, 1947; admitted, 1975, Massachusetts; 1978, Paris. *Education:* Harvard College (A.B., 1969); Harvard Law School (J.D., 1974). *Member:* Association Française des Avocats Conseils d'Entreprises.

(This Listing Continued)

SUSAN H. ABRAMOVITCH, born June 1, 1967; admitted, 1992, Quebec; 1994, New York (Not admitted in France). *Education:* McGill University (B.C.L., LL.B., first class honours, 1991).

ANN G. BAKER, born May 2, 1956; admitted, 1981, N.Y.; 1985, Paris. *Education:* Wellesley College (B.A., 1978); Tulane School of Law (J.D., 1981). *Member:* The Association of the Bar of the City of New York; American and International Bar Associations; Union Internationale des Avocats.

E. RAMAN BET-MANSOUR, born August 4, 1963; admitted, 1990, New York (Not admitted in France). *Education:* Johns Hopkins University (B.A., 1985); School of Advanced International Studies (M.A., 1986); Columbia University School of Law (J.D., 1989).

CÉCILE BOYER, born July 17, 1969; admitted, 1994, Paris. *Education:* E.S.S.E.C. (Diplôme, 1990); University of Paris II (Maîtrise en Droit des Affaires, 1993).

DEBORAH FRANK, born July 26, 1966; admitted, 1992, New York. *Education:* Yale College (B.A.); Harvard Law School (J.D., 1991).

VALÉRIE GAILLARD, born April 9, 1966; admitted, 1993, Paris. *Education:* Institut d'Etudes Politiques de Lyon (Diplôme, 1987); University Jean Moulin, Lyon (D.E.S.S. Droit des Affaires et Fiscalité , Diplôme de J uriste Conseil d 'Entreprise, 1989); Boalt Hall, University of California (LL.M., 1992). Fulbright Scholar. Lavoisier Scholar.

GERARD LACROIX, born September 20, 1957; admitted, 1986, Paris; 1987, N.Y. *Education:* Chicago (B.A., 1979); University of Paris I (Maîtrise, 1982; D.E.A., 1984); Institut d'Etudes Politiques, Paris (Diplôme, 1983); Boalt Hall, University of California (LL.M., 1986). Associate Editor, International Tax and Business Lawyer.

EMMANUEL LULIN, born January 7, 1960; admitted, 1988, Paris. *Education:* University of Paris I (Licence en Droit Public, 1982); Institut d'Etudes Politiques de Paris, Section Service Public (1982-1984); University of Paris II (Maîtrise en Droit Privé , 1986); The University of Chicago Law School (LL.M., 1989). Assistant Adjunct Professor, New York University School of Law, 1992. *Member:* Association Française des Avocats Conseils d'Entreprises.

JEAN-LOUIS MARTIN, born January 13, 1965; admitted, 1993, Hauts-de-Seine, 1994, Paris. *Education:* Faculté de Droit de Dijon (Maitrise de Droit des Affaires, 1987); Faculté de Droit de Montpellier (D.E.S.S. de Juriste d'Affaires, D.J.C.E., (Diplome de Juriste Conseil d'Entreprise) and C.E.S. de Techniques Fiscales, 1988); Columbia Law School (LL.M., 1994).

SYLVIE DEPARIS-MAZE, born February 7, 1956; admitted, 1990, Paris. *Education:* University of Paris I (Diplôme d'Etudes Approfondies - Droit Anglais et Nord-Américain des Affaires 1982; Doctorat en droit 1987) and University of Michigan (M.C.L., 1985). Chargée de Mission, Commission des Opérations de Bourse, 1987-89. *Member:* Association Française des Avocats Conseils d'Entreprises.

ANTOINE D'ORNANO, born February 1, 1949; admitted, 1980, Paris; 1988, N.Y. *Education:* University of Paris (Licence en Droit, 1971; D.E.S. Droit Privé, 1973); Faculty of Law, Cambridge University, United Kingdom (Diploma in International Law, 1976); New York University (M.C.J., 1985). Adjunct Professor, University of Paris V, 1988-1992. *Member:* Association Française des Avocats Conseils d'Entreprises.

PETER SHABECOFF, born April 14, 1962; admitted, 1992, N.Y. (Not admitted in France). *Education:* Wesleyan University (B.A., 1985); Kennedy School of Government at Harvard (M.P.P., 1991); Harvard University (J.D., 1991).

CLAUDE VUILLIEME, born October 31, 1966; admitted, 1994, Paris and New York. *Education:* University of Paris II (Maîtrise de Droit des Affaires et Fiscalité, 1988; D.E.A. 1989); Columbia Law School (LL.M., 1992).

(For Biographical Data of all Partners, see Professional Biographies at New York, N.Y.)

DEBOST & THIL

Established in 1982

2, RUE DE SFAX
75116 PARIS, FRANCE
Telephone: (1) 44.17.38.50
Telecopier: (1) 44.17.38.59

French Business Law including Corporations, Contracts, Labour and Bankruptcy; Commercial and Civil Litigation in French Courts including Personal Injury and Collections; French and International Arbitration.

MEMBERS OF FIRM

DENIS DEBOST, born Neuilly, France, December 2, 1929; admitted, 1959, New York; 1966, Paris. *Education:* University of California at Berkeley (A.B., 1952); Harvard Law School (J.D., 1955); University of Paris (Licence en Droit, 1959). *LANGUAGES:* French, English and Italian. *PRACTICE AREAS:* Business Law.

BERTRAND THIL, born Paris, France, May 6, 1952; admitted, 1977, Paris. *Education:* University of Paris (Licence en Droit, 1975; Diplôme d'Etudes Supérieures de Droit des Affaires, 1976; Diplôme de l'Institut de Droit Comparé, 1977). *LANGUAGES:* French and English. *PRACTICE AREAS:* Litigation.

DE CHAMBRUN & PARTNERS

Société d'Avocats

Established in 1933

52 AVENUE DES CHAMPS-ELYSÉES
75008 PARIS, FRANCE
Telephone: (1) 43.59.10.31
Telex: 640970 Chamlaw
Fax: (1) 45.62.59.02

General French, American and International Practice.

FIRM PROFILE: *The members of the firm are fluent in English. The firm is active in the various areas of Private International Law in the fields of Business, Personal and Tax Practice.*

MEMBERS OF FIRM

RENÉ DE CHAMBRUN, born 1906; admitted, 1933, Paris; 1934, New York. *Education:* University of Paris, Ecole des Sciences Politiques (Doctor of Law). Member, Knight of the Legion of Honor. President, French Chapter, Sons of the American Revolution. President, Cristalleries de Baccarat.

JOHN P. HEINZEN, born 1926; admitted, 1950, District of Columbia; 1962, U.S. Supreme Court; 1992, Paris. *Education:* University of Paris (Licencie en Droit, 1947); Harvard University (LL.D., 1950).

FERNAND COHEN, born 1931; admitted, 1952, Paris. *Education:* Universities of Toulouse and Paris; Institut d'Etudes Politiques, Paris.

FRANÇOISE LIFFARD-LAURIOL, (MRS.), born 1940; admitted, 1973, Paris. *Education:* University of Poitiers.

EMMANUEL DE SABOULIN BOLLENA, born 1951; admitted, 1980, Paris. *Education:* University of Paris.

GORDON J. ORENBUCH, born 1951; admitted, 1980, District of Columbia; 1982, Virginia; 1992, Paris. *Education:* Institut D'Etudes Politiques, Paris (C.E.P., 1973); Boston University (B.A., cum laude, 1974); George Washington University (J.D., 1980). *Member:* American Bar Association.

SERGE DIDIER, born 1951; admitted, 1978, Toulouse. *Education:* University of Toulouse.

PIERRE M. REYSS, born 1931; admitted, 1953, Dakar; 1988, Paris. *Education:* University of Paris.

MURIEL HEINZEN, born 1958; admitted, 1984, Paris. *Education:* University of Paris.

ANDREE CHATEL, born 1933; admitted, 1969, Paris. *Education:* University of Paris.

XAVIER LORÉAL, born 1965; admitted, 1993, Paris. *Education:* University of Rennes (D.J.C.E., 1988); University of Exeter (LL.M., 1989).

TAX COUNSEL

EDMOND-LUC HENRY, born 1950; (Not admitted in France). *Education:* University of Paris.

(This Listing Continued)

OF COUNSEL

ALLIN C. SEWARD, III, born 1943; admitted, 1970, New York; 1991, Michigan (Not admitted in France). *Education:* Yale University (B.A., cum laude, 1965); University of Michigan (J.D., 1969). *Member:* American Bar Association.

Languages: English, French, German and Spanish

DELOITTE & TOUCHE

185, AVENUE CHARLES DE GAULLE
NEUILLY-SUR-SEINE, CEDEX
92201 PARIS, FRANCE
Telephone: (33-1) 40 88 28 00
Telecopier: (33-1) 40 88 22 17

Litigation, Corporate, French and International Tax, Business, Advertising, Contracts, Mergers & Acquisitions, Bankruptcy, Finance, Securities, Insolvency, EEC, Civil, Labor, Immigration and Real Estate Law.

MANAGING PARTNER

DOMINIQUE LARTIGUE, born September 25, 1946; admitted, 1991, France. *Education:* University of Bordeaux (Master of Laws, 1973). Member, Hautes Etudes Commerciales (H.E.C.), International Fiscal Committee. *LANGUAGES:* French and English. *PRACTICE AREAS:* International Tax Law; Tax Litigation.

PARTNERS AND ASSOCIATES

CHRISTIAN BAILLON, born Marseilles, France, June 15, 1958; admitted, 1988, France. *Education:* University of Aix en Provence (DEA Droit Public; Lecturer). *LANGUAGES:* French and Italian. *PRACTICE AREAS:* Business Law; Administrative Law; Local Collectivities.

HERVE BARDON, born Montpellier, France, December 30, 1950; admitted, 1979, France. *Education:* University of Montpellier Law School (Maîtrise en Droit, 1974; D.E.S.S., 1975; DJCE, 1975) Ecole Nationale des Impots (1976). *LANGUAGES:* French and English.

VERONIQUE BEAL CHILD, born Reims, France, April 26, 1963; admitted, 1992, France. *Education:* University of Paris, School of Law (D.E.A., 1987); University of Montpellier (D.J.C.E., 1988). *LANGUAGES:* French, English and Spanish. *PRACTICE AREAS:* Labour Law; Business Law; EEC Law.

DOMINIQUE BERA, born Paris, France; admitted, 1990, France. *LANGUAGES:* French and English. *PRACTICE AREAS:* Mergers and Acquisitions; Tax Control; International Tax; Business Tax.

LAURENCE BERTHON, born Le Havre, France, February 16, 1964; admitted, 1994, France. *Education:* University of Dijon (DESS Droit des Affaires, 1987). *LANGUAGES:* French, English and Spanish. *PRACTICE AREAS:* Corporate Law; Business Law; Mergers and Acquisitions.

ISABELLE BEYER-MALLEZE, born Bône, Algeria, February 15, 1960; admitted, 1993, France. *Education:* University of Paris (DEA Strategy and International Relations; Master in Tax and Business Law; Master in International Strategy Major in the Asia and Pacific Ring Area; B.A. in English, French National Institute for Oriental Languages and Civilizations; B.A. in Chinese Language and Civilization). *LANGUAGES:* French, English and Chinese. *PRACTICE AREAS:* French and International Tax Law; Mergers and Acquisitions.

AMBROISE BRICET, born Rennes, France, February 18, 1949; admitted, 1980, France. *Education:* University of Rennes (Master, 1973). *LANGUAGES:* French and English. *PRACTICE AREAS:* Corporate Real Estate; Tax Law.

BRIGITTE CAMBOLY, born Besancon, France, January 11, 1959; admitted, 1990, France. *Education:* I.S.A./Wharton Business School (M.B.A., 1988); Paris Assas (D.E.S.S., 1982). *Member:* International Fiscal Association. *LANGUAGES:* English, Spanish and French. *PRACTICE AREAS:* International Tax Law; Financial Tax Law.

SUZANNE CINCAR, born Prague, Czechoslovakia, May 10, 1955; admitted, 1983, France. *Education:* Institut d'Etudes Politiques de Paris (Di-

(This Listing Continued)

ploma, 1977); University of Paris I (Master of Laws, 1979); Columbia University School of Law, USA (Master of Laws, 1980). *Member:* International Bar Association; Association des Juristes Europeens. *LANGUAGES:* French, English and Czech. *PRACTICE AREAS:* French & International Business Law; Mergers & Acquisitions; Banking & Finance Law.

ODILE COURJON, born Pau, France, June 27, 1960; admitted, 1990, France. *Education:* Institut of Business Law (Diplôme, 1983); University of Paris XII (D.E.S.S., 1984; Doctor in Law, summa cum laude, 1988); Boston University School of Law (LL.M., in Taxation, 1986); University of Paris VIII, Institut Charles V (Licence in U.S. Civilization, 1987). *LANGUAGES:* French, English and German. *PRACTICE AREAS:* Tax Law; Customs Law.

FRANCE CRESSENT, born Reims, France; admitted, 1992, France. *Education:* University of Paris X (Maîtrise en Droit Privé, 1986). *LANGUAGES:* French, English and Italian.

MAUD DAVENE, born Rennes, France, August 24, 1965; admitted, 1993, France. *Education:* University of Paris (Master of Law, 1987; D.E.S.S., in Tax Law, 1988). *LANGUAGES:* French, English and German. *PRACTICE AREAS:* Tax Law; Mergers & Acquisitions.

PIERRE-MARC DENAMIEL, born Bougie, Algeria, March 21, 1940; admitted, 1965, France. *Education:* University of Paris (DESS Droit Public, 1963); University of Algers (Licence en Droit, 1962); Institute d'Etudes Politiques of Algiers (Diplôme, 1962). Lecturer: Institut de Droit des Affaires d'Aix en Provence, France; Centre d'Etudes du Commerce Extérieur of Marseilles, France; Centre de Formation des Barreaux du Sud-Est, France. *LANGUAGES:* French and English. *PRACTICE AREAS:* Public Law; Business Law.

ERIC DESMORIEUX, born Hautin, France, March 26, 1963; admitted, 1991, France. *Education:* University of Burgundy (Master of Laws, 1985; D.E.S.S. in Tax Law, 1986). *LANGUAGES:* French and English. *PRACTICE AREAS:* Corporate Tax Law; Personal Tax Law.

FRANÇOISE DRAPPIER-FAURE, born Lyon, France, March 1, 1962; admitted, 1988, France. *Education:* University of Lyon (Diplôme de Juriste Conseil d'Entreprise, 1984; DESS Droit des Affaires, 1984); University nof Montepellier (Certificat Supérieur de Gestion du Personnel, 1984). *LANGUAGES:* French and English. *PRACTICE AREAS:* Labour Law; Social Security Law; Social Audit.

CARINE DUCHEMIN, born Orsay, France, April 24, 1964; admitted, 1993, France. *Education:* University of Paris V (Master of Law, 1987; D.E.S.S., of Tax). *LANGUAGES:* French and English. *PRACTICE AREAS:* Corporate; Tax Law; Customs.

FRANK DUMAS, born Marseilles, France, July 22, 1962; admitted, 1992, Paris. *Education:* University of Aix-en-Provence (Master of Law, 1985); University of Montpellier (Diplôme de Juriste Conseil d'Entreprise, 1986; Certificat Supérieur de Technique Fiscale, 1987). Teacher, Montpellier, Paris, Cergy-Pontoise and Lyon Universities. *Member:* ASSINJA (Business Lawyers International Association); ANDJCE. *LANGUAGES:* French, English and German. *PRACTICE AREAS:* Tax Law; Corporate Income Tax; International Tax; International Financing Schemes; Merger and Acquisition; VAT; Business Law; Corporate Law.

MARIE-LAURE FALLER-RAMIER, born Orleans, France, June 15, 1964; admitted, 1989, France. *Education:* University of Paris I (D.E.A. Droit Privé, 1987; D.E.A. Droit International Privé, 1988). *LANGUAGES:* French, English and German. *PRACTICE AREAS:* International Law; Commercial Law; Banking Law.

JEAN GONCALVES, born Portugal, June 24, 1965; admitted, 1993, France. *Education:* University of Paris I, Law School (Master of Private Law, 1988); University of Poitiers (D.E.S.S.; D.J.C.E., 1989). *Member:* Association Nationale des D.J.C.E. *LANGUAGES:* French, English, Spanish, Portuguese. *PRACTICE AREAS:* Tax Law.

HELENE HAQUIN, born Chantilly, France, December 2, 1955; admitted, 1991, France. *Education:* University of Paris (Master of Laws, 1980; D.E.S.S., 1981). *LANGUAGES:* French and English. *PRACTICE AREAS:* Mergers & Acquisitions; International Tax Planning; Corporate Law.

(This Listing Continued)

ISABELLA IVERSEN, born Nantes, France, June 15, 1962; admitted, 1987, France. *Education:* University of Lyon (Master of Law, 1985; CAPA, 1987); University of Brussels (IEE, diploma of European Law). *LANGUAGES:* French and English. *PRACTICE AREAS:* Litigation; Arbitration; Commercial Law.

ALAIN JOUAN, born Paris, France, December 10, 1963; admitted, 1994, France. *Education:* University of Paris II (Master in Tax and Business Law, 1988); University of Paris IX (DESS, 1989); University of Paris VII (Licence in French Language, 1987). *LANGUAGES:* French, English and German. *PRACTICE AREAS:* French and International Tax Law.

YVON LE FORESTIER, born Saint-Germain-en-Laye, France, January 1, 1956; admitted, 1983, France. *Education:* (Master of Law). *LANGUAGES:* French, English, Italian and German. *PRACTICE AREAS:* International Taxation; Tax Consolidation; Tax Audit; Litigation with Tax Authorities.

BLANDINE LEPORCQ, born Philippeville, Algeria, September 11, 1961; admitted, 1992, France. *Education:* University of Paris (Master of Laws, 1984; D.E.S.S., 1985). *LANGUAGES:* French and English. *PRACTICE AREAS:* Tax Law; Finance & Banking Law; Acquisitions & Takeover Law.

YVES LONG, born Forbach, France, March 20, 1948; admitted, 1991, France. *Education:* Aix-en-Provence (Licence en Droit, 1971); Paris Law University (D.E.S. Droit des Affaires, 1972; Institut d'Administration des Entreprises, 1973; Diplome Expert Comptable, 1981). Professor, Ecole des Hautes Etudes Commerciales. *Member:* International Fiscal Association. *LANGUAGES:* French, German and English. *PRACTICE AREAS:* International Tax Law; Mergers & Reorganizations.

ANNE MADON-TAUPIN, born Epinal, France, July 3, 1964; admitted, 1992, France. *Education:* University of Dijon (Master in Tax and Laws, 1987; Bachelor of Arts in Private Law, 1986). *LANGUAGES:* French, English. *PRACTICE AREAS:* Tax Law; Finance and Banking Law; Value added Tax.

MARIE MANUELLI, born Pointe Noire, Congo; admitted, 1991, France. *Education:* University of Paris (D.E.S.S., 1982). *LANGUAGES:* English and French. *PRACTICE AREAS:* Tax Law.

ANDRÉ MARSANDE, born Oullins, France, November 15, 1956; admitted, 1991, France. *Education:* University of Grenoble (master of Law, 1978); University of Lyon (Diplôme de Juriste Conseil d'Etreprise, 1979; DESS Carriére de Conseil Juridique, 1979). *LANGUAGES:* French and English. *PRACTICE AREAS:* Corporate Law; Corporate Tax; Individual Tax; Business Law; Agricultural Cooperation Law.

DOMINIQUE MIGNUCCI, born Paris, France, January 7, 1950; admitted, 1989, France. *Education:* University of Paris I (D.E.S.S., 1980). *LANGUAGES:* French, English and Italian. *PRACTICE AREAS:* Corporate Law; Mergers & Acquisitions; Securities Law.

MICHELLE MULLER-GAILLOT, born 1956; admitted, 1982, France. *Education:* (Master of Law; Diplôme de Juriste Conseil d'Entreprise, 1982). *LANGUAGES:* French. *PRACTICE AREAS:* Corporate Law.

NATHALIE PICHOT, born Paris, France, May 4, 1962; admitted, 1993, France. *Education:* University of Dijon (Master in Tax and Law, 1989); University of Paris, Sorbonne (Bachelor of Arts in Private Law; Bachelor of Arts in Foreign Languages-English and Russian). *LANGUAGES:* French, English, Russian. *PRACTICE AREAS:* Value added Tax; Tax; Mergers and Acquisitions.

JEAN-VICTOR PREVOST, born New York, August 13, 1953; admitted, 1988, New York; 1991, France. *Education:* Georgetown Law Center (J.D., 1987); University of Paris II (D.E.A., 1988). Order of the Coif, Georgetown Law Center. Author: "Copyright Problems in Mastermixes," Communications and the Law, 1987. *LANGUAGES:* French, English and Portuguese. *PRACTICE AREAS:* Corporate Law; Mergers & Acquisitions; Bankruptcy Law.

XAVIER RIBIERRE, born Limoges, France, July 2, 1955; admitted, 1994, France. *Education:* University of Paris I, Panthéon Sorbonne (Licence en Droit, 1980; Maîtrise en Droit des Affaires Internationales, 1981); University of Paris V, R ené Descartes (DESS Affaires Internationales, 1983); University of Pennsylvania, Philadephia, U.S.A. (Master of Law; LL.M., 1984). *LANGUAGES:* French and English. *PRACTICE AREAS:* Banking Law; Insurance Law; International Contracts; Arbitration.

SERGE ROGNON, born Blida, Alegeria, August 24, 1960; admitted, 1992, France. *Education:* University of Paris I, Panthéon Sorbonne (DESS in Notary Law, 1985; DEA in English and North American Corporate

(This Listing Continued)

DELOITTE & TOUCHE, *Paris—Continued*

Law, 1986). *LANGUAGES:* French and English. *PRACTICE AREAS:* General Corporate Law; Commercial Law; Mergers and Acquisitions.

PIERRICK SALLES, born Saint Germain en Laye, France, February 10, 1961; admitted, 1993, France. *Education:* University of Paris (Maîtrise en Droit, 1984; DEA, 1985). *LANGUAGES:* French and English. *PRACTICE AREAS:* International Tax Law; Corporate Law; Tax Law; Tax Litigation.

CLAUDE TISSERANT, born Givet, France, October 8, 1943; admitted, 1976, France. *Education:* Ecole de Commerce (1966); Reims (Licence de Droit, 1970; D.E.S. de Droit Public, 1972). *LANGUAGES:* French.

ANNE VAUCHER, born Orléans, France, March 3, 1964; admitted, 1994, France. *Education:* University of Paris II (DEA Droit International Privé, 1987); University of Paris I (DEA Droit International Economique, 1987; Maîtrise Droit des Affaires Module International Privé, 1986; Licence de Droit International, 1985). *LANGUAGES:* French and English. *PRACTICE AREAS:* Individual Tax Law; Inheritance; International Transfer Administration.

MARIE-FRANCE VERNAY, born France, 1949. *Education:* University of Paris Assas (Master of Private Law), Ecole Nationale des Impôts (Diploma). *LANGUAGES:* French, English and Spanish. *PRACTICE AREAS:* Private Law; Bank and Finance Law; Insurance Law.

DELVOLVÉ ROUCHE

Avocats au Barreau de Paris

5 RUE MARGUERITTE
F-75017 PARIS, FRANCE
Telephone: (1) 42 27 70 68
Telex: 649 188 ADVIN
Telecopier: (1) 43 80 27 89

General French, European Economic Community and International Law and Practice, Public and Administrative Law, International Construction Law, International Arbitration.

MEMBERS OF FIRM

JEAN-LOUIS DELVOLVÉ, born Paris, France, October 30, 1932; admitted, 1956, Paris. *Education:* University of Paris (Maîtrise en droit, 1954). First Secretary: Conférence du Stage des Avocats au Conseil d'Etat et à la Cour de Cassation, 1956; Conférence du Stage des Avocats à la Cour d'Appel de Paris, 1958. Ancien Membre du Conseil de l'Ordre. Member, The London Court of International Arbitration, LCIA London; President, European Users' Council, LCIA. *Member:* The Comité Français de Droit International Privé; I.B.A.; U.I.A. *LANGUAGES:* French, English and Italian.

JEAN RENÉ STÉPHANE ROUCHE, born Charleville, France, September 14, 1946; admitted, 1971, Paris. *Education:* University of Paris II (Maîtrise en droit). Ancien Secrétaire de la Conférence du Stage des Avocats à la Cour d'Appel de Paris. *Member:* A.I.J.A.; Confédération Syndicale des Avocats (Past President, Section Parisienne). *LANGUAGES:* French, English and German.

DEMOYEN & ASSOCIES

Société d'Avocats au Barreau de Paris

Established in 1970

17 AVENUE DE LAMBALLE
75016 PARIS, FRANCE
Telephone: (1) 45 24 46 30
Fax: (1) 45 24 47 08

General, Commercial and International Law Practice, Mergers and Acquisitions, Antitrust and Trade Regulation, Company Law, Contracts, Franchising.

FIRM PROFILE: The firm offers a full range of legal services, specialized in the corporate, business and international trade law. This 3 partner firm has a legal support staff of 8 consisting of legal and paralegal personnel.

(This Listing Continued)

MEMBERS OF FIRM

CHRISTIAN DEMOYEN, born Chaumont, France, December 29, 1939; admitted, 1970, Paris. *Education:* University of Paris (Docteur en Droit, 1964). *LANGUAGES:* French and English. *PRACTICE AREAS:* International Business Law; Mergers and Acquisitions; Antitrust and Trade Regulation.

PATRICE PINSSEAU, born Roanne, France, September 29, 1945; admitted, 1973, Paris. *Education:* Institut d'Etudes Politiques de Paris (Diploma, 1969); University of Paris (D.E.S., Public Law, 1969); Centre de Perfectionnement dans l'Administration des Affaires Paris (C.P.A., 1983). *LANGUAGES:* French and English. *PRACTICE AREAS:* Corporate Law; Commercial Litigation; European Community Law.

JEAN-YVES FOUCARD, born Oran, Algérie, December 17, 1952; admitted, 1977, Paris. *Education:* Haute Etudes Commerciales (H.E.C.; Diploma, 1974); Law University of Paris (D.E.A., Business, 1978). *LANGUAGES:* French, English and Spanish. *PRACTICE AREAS:* Corporate Law; Corporate Trade Litigation.

DE PARDIEU BROCAS MAFFEI & ASSOCIES

43/45, AVENUE KLÉBER
75116 PARIS, FRANCE
Telephone: (1) 53 70 24 24
Telecopier: (1) 53 70 24 00

General Corporate and International Practice. Mergers and Acquisitions, Banking and Finance, European Economic Community, Litigation and Arbitration, Real Estate, Commercial Contracts, Transfers of Technology, Labor Law, Antitrust, Environment.

MEMBERS OF FIRM

CHARLES-HENRI DE PARDIEU, born Paris, France, December 24, 1937; admitted, 1965, Paris. *Education:* University of Paris (Licence en Droit, 1963). Author: "Les Restructurations Internationales," 1981. *Member:* International Bar Association; Southwestern Legal Foundation (Advisory Board). *LANGUAGES:* French, English, German and Spanish.

THIERRY BROCAS, born Paris, France, June 29, 1946; admitted, 1971, Paris. *Education:* University of Paris (Licence en Droit, 1967; D.E.S., Droit Public, 1968); Institut d'Etudes Politiques, Paris (1967); Harvard Law School (LL.M., 1970). *LANGUAGES:* French and English.

ANTOINE MAFFEI, born Ixelles, Belgium, June 8, 1945; admitted, 1989, Paris. *Education:* University of Ghent, Belgium (Docteur en Droit, 1969); New York University (MCJ, 1970). *LANGUAGES:* French, English and Dutch.

DOMINIQUE LEFORT, born Sainte Adresse, France, July 29, 1950; admitted, 1987, Paris. *Education:* University of Paris (Licence en Droit, 1973; D.E.S. de Droit Privé Général, 1974; D.E.S. de Sciences Criminelles, 1974; Docteur d'Etat en Droit, 1981). Author: "La Rétractation des Actes Juridiques en Droit Français"; "La Forme du Mariage en Droit International Privé.". *LANGUAGES:* French and English.

JACQUES HENROT, born Neuilly-Sur-Seine, France, March 25, 1952; admitted, 1980, France. *Education:* Ecole Superieure de Commerce de Paris (Diploma, 1974); University de Paris II, Faculté de Droit (Licence en Droit, 1975); Harvard Law School (Master of Laws, 1976). Co-Author: "Drafting and enforcing contracts," Ed. Kluwer, 1986. Lecturer on Law, University of Paris XII, 1983-1985.

JACQUES DE TAISNE, born Paris, France, May 31, 1959; admitted, 1984, Paris. *Education:* University of Paris (Maîtrise de Carriéres Judiciaires, 1982; Maîtrise de Droit International et Européen, 1982); Institut d'Etudes Politiques, Paris (1981). Corporate Banking Officer, Paribas Limited, London, 1987-1989. *LANGUAGES:* French and English.

JEAN TIMSIT, born Tunis, Tunisia, April 28, 1961; Avocat à la Cour d'Appel de Paris. *Education:* Diplôme des Hautes Etudes Commerciales; Diplôme d'Etudes Comptables Supérieures; Paris University (Maîtrise en Droit International Privé, mention carriéres Judiciaires); Certificat d'Aptitude à la Profession d'Avocat. *LANGUAGES:* French, English and German. *PRACTICE AREAS:* Litigation; EC; Environment.

(This Listing Continued)

ASSOCIATES

PATRICK SERGANT, born Paris, France, September 8, 1962; admitted, 1992, Paris. *Education:* University of Paris (Maîtrise de Droit des Affaires, 1985; D.E.A. de Droit Communautaire, 1987; D.E.A. de Droit de la Propriété Littéraire, Artistique et Industrielle, 1988); Certificado de la Camara de Comercio Espanol (1984). *LANGUAGES:* French, English and Spanish.

NATHALIE WEYD, born Strasbourg, France, January 29, 1960; admitted, 1993, Paris. *Education:* University of Paris (Maîtrise de Droit, 1983; D.E.A. de Droit Anglais et Nord-Américain des Affaires, 1986; Docteur en Droit, 1990). With, Banque de Neuflize Schlumberger Mallet, International Department, 1983-1990. *LANGUAGES:* French, German, English and Spanish.

DIANE DE MOÜY, born Toulouse, France, January 16, 1963; admitted, 1988, Paris; 1991, New York. *Education:* University of Paris I (D.E.A., Droit Privé, 1986); McGeorge School of Law (LL.M., 1989). *LANGUAGES:* French and English.

CONSTANCE DE LA HOSSERAYE, born Paris, France, December 21, 1967; admitted, 1992, France. *Education:* DESS of domestic and European Litigation (1990). *LANGUAGES:* French and English.

MARIE-ANGE SEBELLINI, born Casablanca, Maroc, September 28, 1966; admitted, 1994, France. *Education:* University of Paris, DEA Private Law. *LANGUAGES:* French, English and Spanish.

BÉATRICE BOISSEAU, born Neuilly-Sur-Seine, France, February 24, 1970; admitted, 1995, France. *Education:* University of Paris; Maîtrise d'Histoire, 1992; Maîtrise de Droit des Affaires. Ecole Supérieure de Commerce de Paris, 1993. *LANGUAGES:* French, English and German.

IRÈNE CAMBOURAKIS, born Paris, France, December 18, 1962; admitted, 1989, France. *Education:* University of Paris; (Licence d'Anglais, 1984); Maîtrise en droit, 1987; DEA de droit anglais et Nord-American des Affaires, 1989. *LANGUAGES:* French, English and Modern Greek.

PAUL TALBOURDET, born Saint-Quentin, France, March 11, 1967; admitted, 1991, France. *Education:* Ecole Supérieure de Commerce de Paris, 1989; University of Paris; Maîtrise de droit, 1990. *LANGUAGES:* French, English and German.

ERIC GOURDIN SERVENIERE, born Paris, France, June 29, 1961; admitted, 1994, France. *Education:* Licence en droit Affaires, 1987; Maîtrise en droit Privé, 1988. *LANGUAGES:* French and English.

DEPREZ, DIAN, GUIGNOT & ASSOCIES

Established in 1987

21, RUE CLÉMENT MAROT
75008 PARIS, FRANCE
Telephone: (1) 47.20.05.74
Fax: (1) 47.20.05.52

General French, European and International Law Practice, Corporate, Tax Securities, Banking, Financing, Mergers and Acquisition, Labor Law, Arbitration, Wine Business, French and EEC Competition, Distribution, Licensing and Franchising Law, Transfer of Technology, Patents, Designs, Trademark, Food and Drug Law, Copyright, Entertainment, Art, Culture, Sponsoring, Advertising, Press, Media, Motion Pictures, Computer and new related matters.

FIRM PROFILE: The firm is well known and offers a full range of legal services in French, European and International business law.

The firm has developed skills in the above listed specialized areas.

PARTNERS

PIERRE DEPREZ, born 1953; admitted, 1979, Paris. *Education:* Institut d'Etudes Politiques de Paris (Sciences Po, 1976); University of Paris (D.E.A. Private Law, 1977); Institut Français de Presse (1977). Author: "Les limites de la uiation publicitaire," Legicom, 1994; "L'oeuvre Publicitaire, Jurisclasseur Propriété Litteraire et Artistique," November, 1991; "L'auteur salarié dans l'entreprise d'information: journalistes et banques de données," Editions LAMY, May, 1988. *Member:* Association Internationale de Droit d'Auteur; Association de droit de la Communication. *LANGUAGES:* French and English. *PRACTICE AREAS:* Advertising; Press; Media; Copyright; Trademark; Competition; Distribution.

PHILIPPE DIAN, born 1955; admitted, 1980, Paris. *Education:* University of Paris (Maîtrise in Business Law, 1979); Institut d'Etudes Politiques de Paris (Sciences Po, 1980). *LANGUAGES:* French and English. *PRAC-*

(This Listing Continued)

TICE AREAS: Mergers and Acquisitions; Bankruptcy; Commercial Litigation and Contracts; Media; Copyright; Competition; Distribution; Trade Secrets.

MICHEL GUIGNOT, born 1950; admitted, 1976, Paris. *Education:* University of Montpellier (Maîtrise, 1972); University of Paris I, Sorbonne (D.E.A. Public Law, 1973); Georgetown University Law School (Master, Comparative Law, 1975). Curator, Foundation 'Fortant de France' for the promotion of Mediterranean painting. *Member:* International Fiscal Association. *LANGUAGES:* French and English. *PRACTICE AREAS:* Tax; Banking and Financing; Corporate; International Contracts; Art and Culture; Wine Business; Arbitration.

ASSOCIATES

ANA PAULA REIS LOPES, born 1957; admitted, 1982, Lisbon; 1987, Paris. *Education:* University of Paris (D.E.A. European Law, 1981). *LANGUAGES:* French, English, Portuguese and Spanish. *PRACTICE AREAS:* Corporate; Bankruptcy; Labor Law; Tax.

STÉPHANE BOGORATZ, born 1964; admitted, 1990, Paris. *Education:* University of Paris II and I (D.E.A. English and North American Business Law, 1990). Author: "Les Acquisitions d'Entreprise," Forum Européen de la Communication Larcier, 1992. *LANGUAGES:* French, English and Spanish. *PRACTICE AREAS:* Labor Law; Social Security Law; Commercial Litigation.

CHRISTINE DAUPHIN, born 1966; admitted, 1993, New York (Not admitted in France). *Education:* University of Paris I, Sorbonne (D.E.S.S. International Business Law, 1990); Georgetown University (LL.M., 1992). *LANGUAGES:* French, English, Spanish, Russian. *PRACTICE AREAS:* International Business Law; International Private Law; Arbitration; Food and Drug Law; New Technologies; Multi-Media; General U.S. Law.

CORALIE BLUM, born 1967; admitted, 1993, Paris. *Education:* University of Paris II - Institut Français de Presse (1990; D.E.S.S. Business Law, 1991). *LANGUAGES:* French, English and German. *PRACTICE AREAS:* Entertainment Law; Intellectual Property Law.

OLIVIER CHOPIN, born 1966; admitted, 1993, Paris. *Education:* University of Montpellier, France (Magistere D.J.C.E; D.E.S.S. Corporation Law, 1993). *LANGUAGES:* French, English and Spanish. *PRACTICE AREAS:* Contracts; Tax; Corporation; Business Law; Litigation.

ANTOINE DEROT, born 1965; admitted, 1993, Paris. *Education:* University of Paris II (Maîtrise Business and Tax Law, 1989). *LANGUAGES:* French and English. *PRACTICE AREAS:* Tax; Corporation Law; Bankruptcy; Financing; Torts.

MARC SUSINI, born 1964; admitted, 1991, Paris. *Education:* University of Paris II (D.E.A. Business Law and Economic Law, 1989). *LANGUAGES:* French and English. *PRACTICE AREAS:* Commercial Litigation; Banking; Measures of Execution.

DIDIER THEOPHILE, born 1964; admitted, 1993, Paris. *Education:* Institut d'Etudes Politiques de Strasbourg (Diploma, 1986); University of Strasbourg (D.E.S.S. Industrial Property, 1989); College of Europe, Brugge, Belgium, (Diploma of Advanced Legal European Studies, 1990). Author: "Football et droits de retransmission télévisée: les limites de l'exclusivité," La Semaine Juridique, Supplement no. 5, Edition Entreprise, October, 1992; "La commercialisation des données publiques," Lamy informatique, 1993. *LANGUAGES:* French, English and German. *PRACTICE AREAS:* French and EEC Competition; Antitrust; Distribution; Intellectual Property; Advertising; Contracts.

DERAINS & ASSOCIÉS

Established in 1984

167 BIS, AVENUE VICTOR HUGO
75116 PARIS, FRANCE
Telephone: (33-1) 45 53 38 38
Telex: 640 236 DER GEL
Telefax: (33-1) 45 53 63 48

International Commercial Practice, Construction, Mineral Resources, Agency and Distribution, Sales, Transfer of Technology, Transfer of Corporate Participation, Private International Law, International Commercial Arbitration.

FIRM PROFILE: The firm offers a full range of legal services in France and especially internationally, whether in French Law, international private Law or commercial Law. It is particularly involved in international arbitration. Its clients are of worldwide origin.

(This Listing Continued)

DERAINS & ASSOCIÉS, Paris—Continued

PARTNERS

YVES DERAINS, born Paris, France, March 14, 1945; admitted, 1982, Paris. *Education:* Université de Paris (D.E.S. de Droit Privé, 1970). Former Secretary General of the Court of Arbitration of the International Chamber of Commerce. *Member:* International Council for Commercial Arbitration; Council of the ICC Institute of International Business Law and Practice; ICC Commission on International Arbitration; Union Internationale des Avocats; International Bar Association; French Committee for International Private Law; Comité Français de l'Arbitrage; Greek Arbitration Association; Editorial Advisory Board of Arbitration International; International Consultant of the Court of Arbitration of the National and International Chamber of Commerce of Milan; Panels of Arbitrators of the American Arbitration Association, of the Cairo and Kuala Lumpur Regional Centers for Commercial Arbitration, of the Indian Council of Arbitration, Hong Kong International Arbitration Center, of the Arbitration Court of the Polish Chamber of Commerce. *LANGUAGES:* French, English, Spanish, Italian and Portuguese. *PRACTICE AREAS:* International Arbitration; International Private Law; International Trade and Construction; Agency and Distribution; Finance and Banking.

ROSABEL E. GOODMAN-EVERARD, born The Hague, the Netherlands, April 28, 1953; admitted, 1993, Paris. *Education:* University of Leyden, the Netherlands (Meester in de Rechten, 1979). Former Legal Staff Member, Iran-U.S. Claims Tribunal, The Hague, the Netherlands; Former Legal Counsel, American Arbitration Association, New York, U.S.A.; Former Head of International Arbitration Department, T.M.C. Asser Institute, The Hague, the Netherlands. Author: "International Commercial Arbitration in New York," with J. Stewart McClendon, Transnational Publishers Inc., New York, 1986. *Member:* Netherlands Arbitration Journal (Board of Editors); Commercial Panel of Arbitrators; American Arbitration Association. *LANGUAGES:* Dutch, English, French and German. *PRACTICE AREAS:* International Arbitration; International Private Law; International Trade and Construction; Agency and Distribution; Finance and Banking.

LAURENCE KIFFER, born Strasbourg, France, December 13, 1961; admitted, 1991, Paris. *Education:* Centre de Droit du Commerce International, Tours, France (1986); University of Tours (Droit du Commerce Extérieur, D.E.S.S., 1987). *LANGUAGES:* French, English, German and Spanish. *PRACTICE AREAS:* International Arbitration; International Private Law; International Trade and Construction; Agency and Distribution; Finance and Banking.

DESCHAMPS, LEONZI & MEYER
D, L & M LAWROPE

147 RUE DE RENNES
75006 PARIS, FRANCE
Telephone: 33 1 44 39 00 80
Telecopier: 33 1 40 49 07 44

Brussels, Belgium Office: 50 boulevard de la Révision 1070 Bruxelles. Telephone: (32) 2.521.81.62. Fax: (32) 2.521.80.69.

Montreal, Canada Office: 1 place Ville Marie, 37c étage, Montreal (Quebec) H3B 3P4. Telephone: (514) 878.9641. Fax: (514) 878.1450.

Business Law, Commercial Law, Company Law, Securities, Bankruptcy, Corporate Law, Intellectual Property, Trademarks, Copyrights, Franchises and Franchising, Agency and Distributorships, Antitrust and Trade Regulation, Labour and Employment, Taxation, Construction Law, Administrative Law, Litigation, Arbitration and Mediation, White Collar Crime, Debtor and Creditor. Commercial Real Estate Development, Commercial Leases and Leasing.

Firm engaged in French, EEC and International Law Practice; admitted as Advocate and authorized to practice before the French and EEC Courts.

FIRM PROFILE: The firm is founding member of LAWROPE, grouping of european lawyers (France, Belgium, Spain, Great-Britain, Greece, Italy, Netherlands, Portugal, Switzerland, Germany, Austria).

MEMBERS OF FIRM - PARTNERS

OLIVIER DESCHAMPS, born Saint Raphaël, France, 1957; admitted, 1980, Paris. *Education:* University of Nice. *Member:* administrator ANAAFA. *Member:* Expert College of the Federation Francaise De La Franchise; International Bar Association; A.E.A. *LANGUAGES:* French,

(This Listing Continued)

English. *PRACTICE AREAS:* Franchising; Distribution; Antitrust; Intellectual Property; Labour.

YVES LEONZI, born Paris, France, 1957; admitted, 1980, Paris. *Education:* University of Paris. *Member:* AEDBF. *LANGUAGES:* French, English. *PRACTICE AREAS:* Bankruptcy; Company Law; Construction Law.

OLIVIER MEYER, born Neuilly sur Seine, France, 1957; admitted, 1980, Paris. *Education:* University of Paris. *Member:* LAWROPE (President); A.J.F.B.L.S; International Bar Association. *LANGUAGES:* French, English. *PRACTICE AREAS:* Labour; Administrative; White Collar Crime; Debtor and Creditor.

ASSOCIATES

ERICK BELZIC, born 1957; admitted, 1992, Paris. *Education:* Ecole Nationale des Impôts. *LANGUAGES:* French, English. *PRACTICE AREAS:* Taxation.

PHILIPPE RINCAZAUX, born 1966; admitted, 1990, Paris. *Education:* University of Paris. Lecturer: ESSEC and University Panthéon - Sorbonne. *LANGUAGES:* French, English. *PRACTICE AREAS:* Antitrust; Arbitration; Securities; Intellectual Property; White Collar Crime.

PHILIPPE GLASER, born 1966; admitted, 1992, Paris. *Education:* University of Paris. *LANGUAGES:* French. *PRACTICE AREAS:* Company Law; Bankruptcy.

ERIC LENARD, born 1966; admitted, 1993, Paris. *Education:* University of Paris. *LANGUAGES:* French, Italian, English. *PRACTICE AREAS:* Intellectual Property.

OLIVIER FRATICELLI, born 1954; admitted, 1981, Paris. *LANGUAGES:* French, English. *PRACTICE AREAS:* (Head of Montreal's Office).

MARIE-HÉLÈNE FOURNIER, born 1969; admitted, 1995, Paris. *Education:* University of Paris. *LANGUAGES:* French, English. *PRACTICE AREAS:* Labour.

LEGAL SUPPORT PERSONNEL

CONSULTANT

YVES MAYNE, born 1961; admitted, 1985, Brussels; 1991, Paris. *Education:* University of Brussels. *LANGUAGES:* French, Dutch, English. *PRACTICE AREAS:* Distribution; Commercial Real Estate Development; Commercial Leases and Leasing.

LAW OFFICES OF
JEAN-PIERRE DIEHL

Established in 1975

7, RUE BAYARD
75008 PARIS, FRANCE
Telephone: (1) 42 25 22 98, (1) 42 89 39 01
Telefax: (1) 45 63 42 78

General Commercial Practice. International Law.
Firm engaged in General Practice authorized to appear before the French Courts as Avocats.

JEAN-PIERRE DIEHL, born Néris-les-Bains, France, November 4, 1940; admitted, 1966, France. *Education:* Institut d'Etudes Politiques Strasbourg, France (Diplôme, 1962); Strasbourg, France (Licence en Droit, 1963); Harvard Law School (LL.M., 1966). *LANGUAGES:* French, English and German.

ULLA VASBY DIEHL, born Copenhagen, Denmark, July 6, 1940; admitted, 1988, France. *Education:* University of Paris (Maîtrise de Droit, 1979). *LANGUAGES:* French, English, Danish and German.

ASSOCIATES

FRANÇOIS REBOUL, born Saint-Etienne, France, August 25, 1963; admitted, 1993, France. *Education:* University of Paris (Maitrise de Droit, 1987); European College of Bruges, Belgium (1989). *LANGUAGES:* French and English.

LAW OFFICES OF
HARRY CHARLES DONKERS

Member, Groupe Thésis (E.I.G.)

14, RUE DE BASSANO
75116 PARIS, FRANCE
Telephone: (33.1) 40.70.15.58
Fax: (33.1) 47.20.15.27

General and International Law Practice, Corporate, Tax and Administrative Law, International Arbitration, EEC Competition Regulations, Licensing, Franchising and Industrial Property Law, Mergers and Acquisitions, International Joint Ventures.

FIRM PROFILE: Firm engaged in American, European and General International Practice. Member of Groupe Thésis, a French Economic Interest Group comprising four law firms.

HARRY CHARLES DONKERS, born Lima, Peru, 1931; admitted, 1961, California; 1980, Conseil Juridique, France; 1992, Avocat, France. *Education:* University of Oregon (B.S., 1954); Stanford University (J.D., 1960). Author: "A U.S. Company Licenses Into Europe", The Law and Business of Licensing, Vol. 2, p. 734, 39 (Licensing Executives Society), 1977; "The Evolution of Licensing Law in the EEC", The Law and Business of Licensing, Vol. 3, p. 384, 161 (Licensing Executives Society), 1977; "Exclusive License Agreements in EEC, The Quest for Legitimacy", Journal of the Licensing Executives Society, Vol. 14, No. 3, p. 129, September, 1979; "The Effects of Governmental Sanctions on Trade Relations and Transfers of Technology-A European View", Journal of the Licensing Executives Society, Vol. 15, No. 4, P. 234; December, 1980; The Extraterritorial Application of U.S. Technology Export Controls-Will the Siberian Pipeline Caper Restrict the Flow of Technology Transfer". Journal of the Licensing Executives Society, Vol. XVIII, No. 3, September, 1983; "EC Policy-Where Licensing Stands" Journal of the Licensing Executives Society, Vol. 19, No. 3, September 1984. *Member:* American and International (Member, Business Law Section) Bar Associations; State Bar of California; American Society of International Law; Licensing Executives Society. *LANGUAGES:* English, French, Dutch, German and Spanish. *PRACTICE AREAS:* International Mergers and Acquisitions; International Transfers of Technology; International Joint Ventures; Industrial Franchising; European Competition Law; French Environmental Law; International Arbitration; International Group Reorganizations.

CHRISTINA M. HALSTEAD, born Pasadena, California, October 26, 1960; admitted, 1986, California and U.S. District Court, Central District of California; 1987, District of Columbia (Not admitted in France). *Education:* University of California at Irvine (B.A., 1982); Pepperdine University School of Law (J.D., 1985); McGeorge School of Law, Salzburg (Advanced Degree International law and Transnational Business, 1990). *Member:* Los Angeles County Bar Association; State Bar of California; The District of Columbia Bar; The American Bar Association. *LANGUAGES:* English and French. *PRACTICE AREAS:* U.S. and French Corporate Law; French Labor Law; U.S. Taxation and Tax Treaties; International Family Law.

OTHER MEMBERS OF THE GROUPE THESIS

GÉRARD BEAUVAIS, admitted, 1966, France as Conseil Juridique, Avocat since January 1992. (Partner, Cabinet Thésis). *LANGUAGES:* French and Spanish. *PRACTICE AREAS:* Business Law; Commercial Law; Leases; Real Property Law.

BERNARD FOREST, admitted, 1948, France as Conseil Juridique, Avocat since January 1992. (Partner, Cabinet Thésis). *LANGUAGES:* French. *PRACTICE AREAS:* Business Law; Joint Ventures; Company Law; Commercial Law.

ALAIN HOLLANDE, admitted, 1964, France as Conseil Juridique, Avocat since January 1992. (Partner, Cabinet Thésis). *LANGUAGES:* French and English. *PRACTICE AREAS:* Computers and Software; Commercial and Company Law; Mergers and Acquisitions.

JEAN-PIERRE PINTO, admitted, 1967, France as Conseil Juridique, Avocat since January 1992. (Partner, Cabinet Thésis). *LANGUAGES:* French and Spanish. *PRACTICE AREAS:* Environmental Law; Commercial Acquisitions and Financings; Public Administration; Tourism.

JEAN-LOUIS TROUSSET, admitted, 1974, France as Conseil Juridique, Avocat since January 1992. (Partner, Cabinet Thésis). *LANGUAGES:* French. *PRACTICE AREAS:* Corporate Law; Mergers and Acquisitions; Estate Planning; Inheritance Tax.

(This Listing Continued)

JEAN BERTOLAS, admitted, 1950, France as Avocat. Former member of Conseil de l'Ordre. (Partner, Cabinet Bertolas). *LANGUAGES:* French. *PRACTICE AREAS:* Litigation.

MONIQUE BERTOLAS, admitted, 1950, France as Avocat. (Partner, Cabinet Bertolas). *LANGUAGES:* French. *PRACTICE AREAS:* Litigation.

GERARD DELALOYE, admitted, 1961, France as Conseil Juridique, Avocat since January 1992. (Partner, Cabinet Thesis). *LANGUAGES:* French. *PRACTICE AREAS:* Business and Corporate Law; Arbitration, Bankruptcy, Mergers, Tax, Wills.

MARIE-FRANCE MOREAU, admitted, 1970, France as Conseil Juridique, Avocat since January 1992. *LANGUAGES:* French. *PRACTICE AREAS:* Corporate and Company Law; Leases.

CAROLINE THOMELET, admitted, 1981, France as Conseil Juridique, Avocat since January 1992. *LANGUAGES:* French. *PRACTICE AREAS:* Labor Law; Social Security.

CLAUDE BRUNO, admitted, France as Conseil Juridique, Avocat since January 1992. *LANGUAGES:* French. *PRACTICE AREAS:* Taxation.

JOSEPH BANCEL, admitted, France as Conseil Juridique, Avocat since January 1992. *LANGUAGES:* French. *PRACTICE AREAS:* Taxation; Public Law.

MARIE-CHRISTINE CHAUSSON, admitted, France as Conseil Juridique, Avocat since January 1992. *LANGUAGES:* French and English. *PRACTICE AREAS:* Company Law; Taxation; Estate Planning.

MARIE-CLAUDE MOLLARD, admitted, France as Conseil Juridique, Avocat since January 1992. *LANGUAGES:* French. *PRACTICE AREAS:* Company Law; Commercial Distribution; Trademarks.

BRUNO FOREST, admitted, France as Conseil Juridique, Avocat since January 1992. *LANGUAGES:* French. *PRACTICE AREAS:* Company Law.

MURIEL FOREST-VERGEE, admitted, France as Conseil Juridique, Avocat since January 1992. *LANGUAGES:* French. *PRACTICE AREAS:* Commercial Leases.

DONOVAN LEISURE NEWTON & IRVINE

130 RUE DU FAUBOURG SAINT-HONORÉ
75008 PARIS, FRANCE
Telephone: 1-42-25-47-10
Telecopier: 011-33-1-42-56-08-06

New York, New York Office: 30 Rockefeller Plaza, 10112. Telephone: 212-632-3000. Cable Address: "Donlard, N.Y." Telecopiers: 212-632-3315; 212-632-3321; 212-632-3322.

Washington, D.C. Office: 1250 Twenty-Fourth Street, N.W., 20037-1124. Telephone: 202-467-8300. Telecopier: 202-467-8484.

Los Angeles, California Office: 333 South Grand Avenue, 90071. Telephone: 213-253-4000. Cable Address: "Donlard, L.A." Telecopier: 213-617-2368; 213-617-3246.

Palm Beach, Florida Office: 450 Royal Palm Way. Telephone: 407-833-1040. Telecopier: 407-835-8511.

Firm engaged in American and General International Practice and registered as Avocats à la Cour de Paris.

PARTNERS

WILLIAM J. T. BROWN, born South Haven, Michigan, November 15, 1941; admitted, 1967, Michigan; 1968, New York; 1973, U.S. Supreme Court; 1992, Avocat, France. *Education:* University of Wisconsin (B.A., 1963); Harvard Law School (LL.B., magna cum laude, 1966). Phi Beta Kappa. Member, Harvard Law Review, 1964-1966. *Member:* The Association of the Bar of the City of New York; New York State Bar Association; State Bar of Michigan.

RENÉ DE MONSEIGNAT, born Principality of Monaco, April 17, 1946; admitted, Avocat, France. *Education:* University of Nice, University of Paris, Faculté de Droit (Licence en Droit, 1969; D.E.S. Droit Public, 1970; D.E.S. Droit Privé, 1971); Institut d'Études Politiques, 1971; Sorbonne, Licence és Lettres, 1971).

(This Listing Continued)

DONOVAN LEISURE NEWTON & IRVINE, Paris—
Continued

COUNSEL

REID L. FELDMAN, born New York, New York, April 17, 1947; admitted, 1971, District of Columbia; 1979, Avocat, France. *Education:* Columbia University (B.A., 1968); Yale University (J.D., 1971); Oxford University, England (M.Litt., 1981). Member, Board of Editors, Yale Law Journal, 1969-1971. Author: "Les Aspects Juridiques des Affaires aux États-Unis," CFCE, 1990. Member, Panel of Arbitrators, American Arbitration Association. *Member:* The District of Columbia Bar; Union Internationale des Avocats.

ASSOCIATES

SANDRINE M. BONNET, born Saint-Denis, France, October 14, 1966; admitted, 1994, France. *Education:* University of Paris Assas (Maîtrise des Affaires, 1988); University of Paris Panthéon-Sorbonne (D.E.A. Droit des Affaires et de l'Économie, 1989); C.F.P.P. (Paris 1989).

D.S., PARIS
ASSOCIATION D'AVOCATS

Established in 1973

46 RUE DE BASSANO
75008 PARIS, FRANCE
Telephone: 53-67-50-00
Telefax: 47-20-78-76; 53-67-50-03

Taipei, Taiwan, Republic of China, Associated Office: D.S. Forman & Partners. 6th Floor, No. 85 Jen Ai Road. Telephone: (886-2) 778-3427. Fax: (886-2) 778-3428.

Seoul, Korea, Associated Office: Kim, Shin & Yu. 12th Fl. Leema Building, 146-1, Susong-Dong, Chongro-Ku, 110-140. Telephone: 735-5833. Fax: (82-2) 739-6606.

In Association in Singapore with:
Thümmel, Schütze & Partner and Setterwall, Kleberg & Co., 9 Battery Road, #17-08, Straits Trading Building. 0104. Telephone: (65) 535-3112. Fax: (65) 535-7409.

Beijing, People's Republic of China, Associated Office: D.S. Meyer & Partners. Kun Lun Hotel, Suite 317-321. 10004. Telephone: (86-1) 500-3073. Fax: (86-1) 500-3073.

Hanoi, Vietnam, Associated Office: D.S. Pollack & Partners. 76 Hang Trong, Hanoi, SR. Vietnam. Telephone: (84-4) 250-218. Fax: (84-4) 260-260.

In Association in Thailand with:
Pollack & Co. Ltd. Diamond Tower 138 427/162 Silom Road, Bangrak, Bangkok 10500. Telephone: (66-2) 231-5005. Fax: (66-2) 231-5535.

National and International Litigation. Company, Real Estate, Building, Transportation (Road and Air), EEC, Tax (International and Domestic), Tourism and Travel, Arbitration Law, Intellectual Property, Labour, Banking, Mergers and Acquisitions, Bankruptcy.
Member of GLOBALEX

MEMBERS OF FIRM

DENIS DE RICCI (1922-1993).

GEORGES SELNET, born Algiers, May 28, 1934; admitted, 1959, Paris. *Education:* Graduate, Institut d'Etudes Politiques; Paris and Nice (Docteur en Droit). Author: "Development and Investments in Malaysia," Nice University, 1974. *LANGUAGES:* French and English.

JEAN POSSOZ, born Paris, France, July 18, 1928; admitted, 1968, Paris. *Education:* Paris (Licence en Droit - DES droit privé). *Member:* Confédération Syndicale des Avocats; CSA; U.I.A. *LANGUAGES:* French and German.

PATRICK MONTIER, born Le Havre, France, June 20, 1952; admitted, 1976, Paris. *Education:* Rouen (Licence en Droit); Paris (DEA, droit des affaires, Business Law). *Member:* CSA; A.I.J.A.; Eurolex. *LANGUAGES:* French and English.

DANIEL CHAUSSE, born Perigueux, France, August 27, 1953; admitted, 1980, Paris. *Education:* Graduate, Institut Judiciaire - Paris; Institut d'Etudes Politiques - Grenoble. *LANGUAGES:* French and English.

OLIVIER FAGES, born Montpellier, France, March 21, 1953; admitted, 1985, Paris. *Education:* Paris II (Maîtrise Droit des Affaires). *LANGUAGES:* French, English and Spanish.

(This Listing Continued)

JEAN PIERRE THUILLANT, born Paris, France, April 15, 1947; admitted, 1972, Paris. *Education:* Paris (Licence en Droit); Institut d'Etudes Judiciaires. *LANGUAGES:* French, English and Spanish.

JEAN-MARC OLIVIER LEONELLI, born Bourron-Marlotte, France, June 25, 1944; admitted, 1972, Paris. *Education:* University of Paris (Licence en Droit, 1968; D.E.S. en Droit Privé, cum laude, 1970; Institute of Comparative Law, cum laude, 1970); Cornell Law School (LL.M., 1972). *Member:* Paris Bar Association. *LANGUAGES:* French, English and Spanish.

ASSOCIATES

Marie-Pierre Alix; Jean-François Bizet; Jean-Daniel Bretzner; Anne Calligaro; François Dauchy (Not admitted); **Renaud Dufeu; Benjamine Fiedler; Denis Forman** (Also at D.S. Forman & Partners); **Gilles Grinal; Frédéric Lévy; Philippe Li** (Also at Kim, Shin & Yu, Seoul, Korea); **Emmanuelle Llop; Xavier Maucande; Marie-Christine Mergny; Clément Ponczek; Frédéric Selnet; Olivier Suares.**

OF COUNSEL

JEAN-JACQUES LIZAMBARD, born Neuilly Sur-Seine, France, May 3,1948; Conseil Juridique et Fiscal, 1976; admitted, 1992. *Education:* Diplôméde l'Ecole des Hautes Etudes Commerciales, Paris, 1971. *LANGUAGES:* French, English and German.

ANNE-MARIE FILIPPINI, born Paris, France, April 30, 1963; admitted, 1994. *Education:* DESS Droit des Affaires et Fiscalite, Paris, 1994. *LANGUAGES:* French, English and Italian.

BERTRAND POTOT, born Poitiers, France, November 1, 1958; admitted, 1984. *Education:* DEA droit privé, Paris, 1983; Institut de development industriel, Paris , 1984. *LANGUAGES:* French and English.

CATHERINE BRUN-LORENZI, born Lyon, France, August 17, 1951; admitted, 1973. *Education:* Licence en Droit, Grenoble, 1972. *LANGUAGES:* French and English.

LAURENCE COULON-PETITFRERE, born Paris, France, September 24, 1951; admitted, 1973. *Education:* Licence en Droit, Paris, 1973; Institut de Etudes Judiciaires. *LANGUAGES:* French and English.

Languages: French, English, German, Spanish and Italian.

DUBARRY, LEVEQUE, LE DOUARIN & VEIL

Established in 1984

9, RUE LE TASSE
75116 PARIS, FRANCE
Telephone: (1) 45.27.39.00
Telex: 612160 F
Telecopier: (1) 45.27.31.20

Brussels, Belgium Office: 55, Avenue de Tervueren, B-1040. Telephone: (32-2) 736.40.90. Telecopier: (32-2) 735.87.14.

Firm engaged in French, Belgian and International Practice and admitted to appear before French, Belgian and European Economic Community Courts.
Commercial, Contracts, Banking, Corporate, Litigation, Arbitration, EEC, Trademark and Patent, Labor Law and Bankruptcy.

MEMBERS OF FIRM

JEAN-CLAUDE DUBARRY, born Neuilly, France, May 15, 1936; admitted, 1963, Paris. *Education:* University of Paris Law School; Institute of Comparative Law; University of Paris II School of Law. Professor, Institut de Droit des Affaires, 1970. Lecturer on Contracts Law for Doctorate Candidates, 1984—. Secrétaire de la Conference du Stage, 1965-1966. *Member:* Association Henri Capitant.

PIERRE LEVEQUE, born Paris, France, December 29, 1951; admitted, 1975, Paris. *Education:* University of Paris I School of Economics (Maîtrise, 1973); University of Paris II School of Law (Maîtrise, C.A.P.A., 1975). *Member:* A.I.J.A.; U.I.A. *LANGUAGES:* French and English.

YANN LE DOUARIN, born Vannes, France, December 2, 1953; admitted, 1977, Rennes, 1979, Paris. *Education:* Rennes University School of Law (Maîtrise, C.A.P.A., 1976); University Paris I Sorbonne; Business Administration Institute (I.A.E.; DESS, 1983). Lecturer in Law, University of Paris I Sorbonne, Institut d'Administration des Entreprises, 1984-1986. *LANGUAGES:* French and English.

(This Listing Continued)

PIERRE-FRANÇOIS VEIL, born Paris, France, March 16, 1954; admitted, 1979, Paris. *Education:* Institut d'Etudes Politiques de Paris (Diplômé, 1976); University of Paris I Sorbonne (Maîtrise; C.A.P.A., 1978). Secrétaire de la Conférence du Stage, 1979-1980. *Member:* I.B.A. *LANGUAGES:* French, English and Hebrew.

DOMINIQUE MENARD, born Merrey s/Arce, France, June 5, 1949; admitted, 1974, Paris. *Education:* University Paris X Nanterre School of Law (Maîtrise, 1974; I.E.T., 1974; C.A.P.A., 1974). *Member:* U.S.T.A.; A.I.P.P.I. *LANGUAGES:* French and English.

ALAIN FRÉVILLE, born Lyon, France, January 15, 1963; admitted, 1988, Paris. *Education:* University of Paris XI (Maîtrise, 1986, C.A.P.A., 1987). Lecturer in Law, University of Paris XI, 1986-1990, I.P.E.S.U.P. (1987-1989).

STÉPHANE WOOG, born Neuilly, France, June 1, 1958; admitted, 1988, Paris. *Education:* University of Paris II (Maîtrise, C.A.P.A., 1988); Ecole des Hautes Etudes Commerciales (H.E.C., 1984); Maître de conférences à H.E.C. (1987). *LANGUAGES:* French and English.

OF COUNSEL

ERIC LOQUIN, born Dijon, France, May 17, 1949. *Education:* University Dijon (Doctorat d'Etat, 1978; Agrégation Droit Privé, 1985). *Member:* Comité Français de Droit International Privé; Comité Français de l'Arbitrage, Association Internationale de Droit. *LANGUAGES:* French.

CHARLEY HANNOUN, born Constantine, Algérie, June 6, 1953; admitted, 1980, Paris. *Education:* University of Paris I, Sorbonne, et Paris X Nanterre, Schools of Law and Economics (Doctorat en droit, 1988; Habilitation à diriger des recherches, 1988; Licence ès sciences économiques, 1978; C.A.P.A., 1979); Maître de conférences, University Paris V - René Descartes, School of Law. *Member:* Association Internationale de Droit Économique.

LAW OFFICES DEREK ELLIOTT

67-69 AVENUE VICTOR HUGO
75116 PARIS, FRANCE
Telephone: (1) 45.01.57.50
Telefax: (1) 45.01.78.29

Construction Law, Joint Ventures, Arbitration.

DEREK ELLIOTT, born London, September 13, 1946; called to Bar, England and Wales, 1971; admitted, 1994, Paris. *Education:* Cambridge University; University of Paris. *LANGUAGES:* English and French.

NEIL KEARNEY, born San Diego, California, April 9, 1959; admitted, 1987, California; 1994, Paris. *Education:* Yale College (B.A., cum laude, 1983); University of California at Berkeley (J.D., 1987). *LANGUAGES:* English and French.

ANNE O'KELLY, born Belfast, Northern Ireland, August 1, 1955; called to bar, 1980, Northern Ireland; admitted, 1994, Paris. *Education:* Queen's University, Belfast, Northern Ireland. *LANGUAGES:* English and French.

FALQUE, CARPENTIER, BARBÉ ET ASSOCIÉS (DSH)

Established in 1974

14, AVENUE GOURGAUD
75017 PARIS, FRANCE
Telephone: (1) 44.15.61.00
Telex: 641'206 F
Telefax: (1) 44.15.91.81

French and EEC Commercial Law particularly Banking and Finance, Construction, Companies and Securities, Insurance, Oil and Gas, Taxation, French and International Arbitration.

MEMBERS OF FIRM

DOMINIQUE FALQUE, born Paris, France, October 30, 1940; admitted, 1963, Paris. *Education:* University of Paris (Licence en Droit, 1964; Doctorat en Droit, 1970). *LANGUAGES:* French, English and German. *PRACTICE AREAS:* International Business Law; Corporate Trade Litigation; International Arbitration.

(This Listing Continued)

MARIE-PIERRE CARPENTIER, born Ribécourt, France, June 11, 1944; admitted, 1967, Paris. *Education:* University of Paris (Licence en Droit, 1966). *LANGUAGES:* French and English. *PRACTICE AREAS:* French and EEC Mergers and Acquisitions; Commercial and Banking Law.

MARC-FRANÇOIS BARBÉ, born Paris, France, September 8, 1947; admitted, 1972, Paris. *Education:* University of Paris (Licence en Droit, 1971; Diplôme d'Etudes Supérieures de Droit des Affaires, 1972). *LANGUAGES:* French and English. *PRACTICE AREAS:* Mergers and Acquisitions; Banking and Finance; Taxation.

JEAN-FRANÇOIS BOUCLY, born Saint-Cloud, France, January 14, 1949; admitted, 1970, Paris. *Education:* University of Paris (Licence en Droit, 1970; Diplôme d'Etudes Supérieures de Droit Privé, 1971). *LANGUAGES:* French and English. *PRACTICE AREAS:* French and EEC Commercial Law; Oil and Gas; International Arbitration.

JEAN-PHILIPPE THIBAULT, born Nevers, France, October 22, 1957; admitted, 1984, Paris. *Education:* Universities of Dijon and Paris (Maîtrise en Droit, 1979). *LANGUAGES:* French and English. *PRACTICE AREAS:* Corporate Finance; Property Development; Taxation.

ANNICK LECOMTE, born Paris, France, July 13, 1956; admitted, 1983, Paris. *Education:* University of Paris (Maîtrise en Droit, 1979; Diplôme d'Etudes Approfondies de Droit International Privé et de Droit de Commerce International, 1980). *LANGUAGES:* French and English. *PRACTICE AREAS:* Intellectual Property; Patent Law.

JUAN-CARLOS GROENER, born Bogota Colombia, December 20, 1956; admitted, 1983, Paris. *Education:* University of Paris-Sorbonne (Licencèes Lettres, 1979); University of Paris Panthéon-Sorbonne (Maîtrise en Droit, 1981; Diplôme de'Etudes Approfondies de Droit International Privé et Droit du Commerce International, 1982). *LANGUAGES:* French, English, German, Portuguese and Spanish. *PRACTICE AREAS:* International Business Law; Corporate Trade Litigation.

FISCHER, TANDEAU DE MARSAC, GROS & ASSOCIES

Avocats au Barreau de Paris

Established in 1985

44, AVENUE D'IÉNA
75116 PARIS, FRANCE
Telephone: (1) 47.23.47.24
Facsimile: (1) 47.23.30.53

General Corporate Practice, International Contracts, Arbitration and Litigation, Pre-trial Procedure and Judicial Proceedings.

MEMBERS OF FIRM

CÉDRIC FISCHER, born Paris, July 4, 1958; admitted, 1980, Paris. *Education:* University of Paris II, ASSAS (Maîtrise en Droit, 1980; DEA Droit Privé, 1982). *Member:* Association Française pour la Protection de l' Eau (Legal Committee); Confédération Nationale des Avocats; Droit et Commerce.

SILVESTRE TANDEAU DE MARSAC, born Paris, January 4, 1961; admitted, 1984, Paris. *Education:* University of Paris II, ASSAS (Maîtrise Droit des Affaires et Fiscalité, 1982; DEA en Droit Privé Général, 1983). First Secretary of Conference des Avocats à la Cour d'Appel de Paris, 1987. Author: "Les Obligations contractuelles Intermédaires Financiers: Le Devoir de Conseil" in les actes du colloque "Les marchés financiers et les valeurs mobilières," 1990. *Member:* UJA; AIJA; International Bar Association; Association Franco-Chinoise pour le Droit Economique; ELTA; YLD of ABA (Honorary Member). *LANGUAGES:* French and English. *PRACTICE AREAS:* Banks and Banking; International Law.

HENRI DELMONT, born Paris, December 3, 1907; admitted, 1929, Paris. *Education:* University of Paris (Licence). Secretary, Conference des Avocats à la Cour d'Appel de Paris, 1934-1935. Member, Conseil de l'Ordre des Avocats à la Cour d'Appel de Paris, 1952-1956. *Member:* Association Nationale des Avocats ANA (President, 1967-1969); International Bar Association (Conseil d'administration, 1967-1984); Caisse Nationale des Barreaux Français (Honorary President, 1957-1959); Confederation Syndicale des Avocats (Honorary President).

JEAN-LEO GROS, born Paris, September, 1956. *Education:* University of Paris (Maitrise). Author: "L'Orchestre Solitaire.".

(This Listing Continued)

FISCHER, TANDEAU DE MARSAC, GROS & ASSOCIES, Paris—Continued

DANIÈLE BARUCHEL-BEURDELEY, born Alexandrie, May 6, 1956; admitted, 1979, Paris. *Education:* University of Paris X (Nanterre) (Maîtrise, 1978).

ASSOCIATES

KATHERINE M. ACAMPORA, born Staunton, Virginia, October 17, 1950; admitted, 1988, Virginia; 1989, District of Columbia (Not admitted in France). *Education:* College of William & Mary (B.A., 1969); Georgia State University (M.A., 1979); Georgetown University Law Center (J.D., 1988). *Member:* American Bar Association; The District of Columbia Bar. *LANGUAGES:* English and French. *PRACTICE AREAS:* Arbitration; Mediation.

FABIENNE MOUREAU, born Juvisy Sur Orge, August 16, 1965; admitted, 1990, Paris. *Education:* University of Paris II, ASSAS (Maîtrise en Droit, 1987; DEA Droit Privé, 1988). *LANGUAGES:* French and English.

FODOR MASSON PIERON SWARTZ & BEAUCOURT

6, RUE JEAN GOUJON
75008 PARIS, FRANCE
Telephone: (33-1) 42 56 06 32
Facsimile: (33-1) 42 56 09 89

Firm engaged in French, EEC and General International Business Practice, including Securities Regulations, Corporate Finance, French and International Taxation, Acquisitions, Mergers, Competition, Distribution, Real Estate and Labor Law, Litigation and Arbitration. Admitted to plead before French and EEC Courts.

MEMBERS OF FIRM

EMMANUEL DE BEAUCOURT, born Paris, France, September 23, 1952; admitted, 1977, Paris. *Education:* University of Paris II (Maîtrise en Droit, 1974; D.E.S. Droit Public, 1976); University of Paris I (D.E.S.S. Relations Commerciales Internationales, 1976); University of Illinois (M.C.L.). *Member:* Paris Bar Association. *LANGUAGES:* French and English. *PRACTICE AREAS:* Mergers and Acquisitions; Litigation and Arbitration.

CAROLINE FODOR, born Neuilly-sur-Seine, France, April 18, 1954; admitted, 1987, Paris. *Education:* University of Paris X Law School (Maîtrise en Droit, option Droit des Affaires, 1981; D.E.A. de Droit des Affaires); Harvard Law School-Program of Instruction for Lawyers (1990). Author: "Les Stock Options en Droit Americain," Cahiers du Barreau de Paris, 1990. *Member:* Association Internationale des Jeunes Avocats (A.I.J.A.); Union Internationale des Avocats (U.I.A.). *LANGUAGES:* French and English. *PRACTICE AREAS:* Industrial Joint Ventures; International Commercial Contracts; Transfers of Technology; French Corporate Law and Litigation.

FRANCIS D. MASSON, born Verdun, France, September 6, 1952; admitted, 1981, Paris. *Education:* German Studies Sarrebruck (Bachelor, 1972); University of Paris II (Maîtrise en Droit des Affaires, 1975). Translator Interpreter in Ottawa, Canada, Federal Court and Federal Parliament, 1976. Program of German Law, Dusseldorf, 1977. *LANGUAGES:* French, English and German. *PRACTICE AREAS:* Real Estate; Corporate Finance; Taxation.

CHARLES PIERON, born Brétigny s/Orge, France, September 3, 1946; admitted, 1978, Paris. *Education:* University of Paris II (Maîtrise en Droit, 1970); Institut d'Etudes Politiques de Paris (Service Public, 1971). *LANGUAGES:* French and English. *PRACTICE AREAS:* French and International Taxation; Mergers and Acquisitions; Securities.

SALLI A. SWARTZ, born Philadelphia, Pennsylvania, USA, August 23, 1952; admitted, 1977, Pennsylvania, State Courts and the Middle District Federal Court; 1981, Paris. *Education:* University of Massachusetts (B.A., magna cum laude, Phi Beta Kappa, 1974); Syracuse University College of Law, International Legal Studies Program (J.D., 1977). Editor, Syracuse Journal of International Law and Commerce, 1976-1977. Contributor, *Doing Business in France,* two volumes published by Matthew Bender, 1987. *Member:* American Bar Association. *LANGUAGES:* French and English. *PRACTICE AREAS:* International Joint Ventures; Labor Law; French Corporate Law; International Commercial Contracts.

(This Listing Continued)

MARIE-PIERRE GAY, born Paris, France, May 31, 1966; admitted, 1989, Paris. *Education:* University of Paris I (D.E.A. de Droit de l'Environnement, 1993); University of Paris II (Maîtrise de Droit des Affaires, 1987). *LANGUAGES:* French and English.

RENA SPIEGELSTEIN, born Munich, Germany, February 2, 1967; admitted, 1993, Paris. *Education:* Institute of European Studies, Geneva (1988); University of Munich (Law Degree, 1989); University of Paris XI (Maîtrise en Droit, 1991; D.E.S.S. Droit International, 1991); Institut d'Etudes Politiques de Paris (1992). *LANGUAGES:* German, French, English, Italian and Hebrew.

CABINET PIERRE FONTANEAU

ATTORNEY AT LAW

Established in 1948

28 RUE DE FRANQUEVILLE
75116 PARIS, FRANCE
Telephone: (1) 45.03.03.40
Telex: 630069 FONTANE
Telefax: (1) 45.03.08.14

Nice, France Office: Villa Maraval, Avenue du Parc de Cimiez, 06000 Nice, France. Telephone: 93.81.01.27. Telex: 461682. FAX: 93.53.66.28.
Brussels, Belgium Office: 45 Bd Saint Michel, 1040 Brussels, Belgium. Telephone: (2) 736.59.44. Telex: 64797 FOBLEX. FAX: (2) 736.58.68.

General French, International and Common Market, Legal and Tax Practice. Antitrust, Banking, Bankruptcy, Competition, Corporate, Customs and Excise, Entertainment, Expatriation, Foreign Investments, International Contracts, Health, Hospital, Intellectual Property, Sport, Research and Development, Venture Capital.

PIERRE FONTANEAU, Docteur d'Etat en Droit; Docteur d'Etat en Sciences Economiques. Professeur Agrégé en Sciences Economiques. Author: "Fiscalité Européenne", (France-Germany-Belgium-Italy-Luxemburg-Monaco-Netherlands-UK-Spain), updated quarterly; "La Fiscalité de l'Innovation et du Capital-Risque dans la C.E.E." and "L'Impôt Français sur la Fortune," (Collection Gestion du Patrimoine), updated semi-annually.

Languages: French, English, Spanish, Italian, German and Portuguese

FOUCAUD, TCHÉKHOFF, POCHET ET ASSOCIÉS

1 BIS AVENUE FOCH
75116 PARIS, FRANCE
Telephone: (1) 4500.86.20
Telex: 611221
Fax: (33-1) 44.17.41.65; 45.01.98.20; 45.00.08.19

Budapest, Hungary Office (F.C.C. Associated): 4 Tars Utca, 1118. Telephone: (36-1) 267.11.66. Fax: (36-1) 267.11.70.

General French and International Law Practice. Arbitration, E.E.C. Legislation, Antitrust, Banking, Finance, Mergers and Acquisitions, Common Market Regulations, Corporate, Taxation, Commercial Contracts, Public Supply Agreements, Copyright, Entertainment, Labor Law, Litigation, Patents, Trademarks, Unfair Competition.

MEMBERS OF FIRM

PROF. ALAIN GÉRARD BERCHEBRU DE FOUCAUD ET D'AURE, born France, March 26, 1940; admitted, 1972, Paris. *Education:* University of Paris Law School; University of Paris II Assas (Docteur en Droit). Inspector of the French Treasury, 1968. Honorary Consul, 1979. Author: *Les Investissements Directs des Etats-Unis en France sous forme d'établissements Stables* (1972); *"Les Investissements Francais a l'Etranger"* (1991). Advisor, Centre de Développement Industriel de la Communauté Européenne et Pays ACP, Brussels (1978). Professor of Law (Corporate Law), University of Paris-XIII. *Member:* International Lawyers Club (Founder, 1979); Chevalier de l'Ordre National de la Légion d'Honneur (Conseiller Général, 1992). *LANGUAGES:* French and English.

SERGE ANTOINE TCHÉKHOFF, born France, November 25, 1950; admitted, 1975, Paris. *Education:* University of Paris-X Law School (D.E.S. in Business Law, 1974); Certificat d'Études fiscales (1974); University of

(This Listing Continued)

Michigan Law School (LL.M., 1975). Author: *Le Régime Fiscal des Marchands de Biens* (1974); *A Comparative Study of Franchising in French, EEC and U.S. Law* (1975). Assistant Professor, University of Paris V. *LANGUAGES:* French, English and Spanish.

PHILIPPE BERNARD POCHET, born France, April 26, 1950; admitted, 1976, Paris. *Education:* University of Paris Law School (D.E.S. in Private Law, 1974); Paris Institute of Political Science, Section of Economy and Finance (1973); University of California at Los Angeles, Business Administration (1976); University of California at Los Angeles Law School (1978). Author: *La Télévision par Câble et la Convergence des Télécommunications aux Etats-Unis* (1981); *Les Obstacles Juridiques aux Echanges de Programmes de Télévision en Europe* (1983). Cultural Attache at the French Consulate General Los Angeles, 1978-1981. Lecturer in Communication Law, University of Paris-Sorbonne, 1982—. *LANGUAGES:* French and English.

PROF. JEAN-FRANÇOIS CÉCIL PRÉVOST, born France, April 4, 1946; admitted, 1978, Paris. *Education:* University of Paris Law School; D.E.A. in Political Science (1969) ; Doctorat d'Etat des Facultés de Droit (1973); Professeur Agrégé des Facultés de Droit (1979). Author: *Les Effets des Traités Conclus entre Etats à l'Égard des Etats Tiers* (1973); *A la Recherche du Critère du Contrat Administratif* (RDP, 1971); Professor, University of Paris-XII, 1979. *LANGUAGES:* French and English.

MICHÈLE JAUDEL-CHAPPE, born France, June 7, 1954; admitted, 1978, Paris. *Education:* University of Paris Law School (D.E.S.S., Copyright, Patents and Trademarks). *LANGUAGES:* French, English, Spanish and German.

PHILIPPE LEPEK, born Switzerland, May 16, 1956; admitted, 1979, Paris. *Education:* University of Paris Law School (D.E.A. in International Private Law). Lecturer: University of Paris-X, 1981-1982. Adjunct Professor of Tax Law at Centre de Formation des Avocats à la Cour d'Appel de Paris. *LANGUAGES:* French, German and Spanish.

CÉCILE DELATTRE, born France, June 13, 1952; admitted, 1988, Paris. *Education:* University of Paris I, Law School (Masters in International Law, 1974; DESS in Political Science, 1977); University of Paris VII (DEA, Chinese Language, 1977); University of Peking (Certificate, 1976); Fudan University, Shanghai (Certificate, 1978). C G E E Alsthom's in-house Counsel, 1978-1988. *LANGUAGES:* French, English and Chinese.

MICHÈLE MORANGE DE LAMBERTYE, born France, November 24, 1949; admitted, 1986, Paris. *Education:* Paris Institute of Political Science (1978); University of Paris, Law School (Masters in Business Law, International Public and Private Law, 1980). *LANGUAGES:* French, English and German.

ISABELLE SIMOND, born France, March 26, 1959; admitted, 1981, Paris. *Education:* University of Paris V Law School (Masters in Law, 1981; C.A.P.A., 1981; D.E.S.S. de juriste d'affaires, 1982). Adjunct Professor at Francis LEFEBVRE FORMATION (1988) and at ESA3 (1990). Author in the Review, Eclipses (1988). *LANGUAGES:* French and English.

ISABELLE VAUGON, born France, May 14, 1961; admitted, 1989, Paris. *Education:* University of Paris I Law School (Masters in Public Law, 1986; D.E.S.S. in E.E.C. Law, 1987; Masters in Private Law, 1988). *LANGUAGES:* French, English and Spanish.

ROBERT CORCOS, born Morocco, May 1, 1960; admitted, 1990, Paris. *Education:* University of Paris I Law School (Masters in International Law, 1983 and D.E.A. in English and American Business Law, 1984). *LANGUAGES:* French and English.

BÉATRICE DE CHAIGNON, born France, January 14, 1964; admitted, 1990, Paris. *Education:* University of Paris II Law School (Masters in Public Law, 1986); University of Paris I (Masters in European Law, 1986; D.E.A. in E.E.C. Law, 1987). *LANGUAGES:* French and English.

IAN M.G. ROSS, born England, August 20, 1942; admitted, 1966, England as Solicitor; 1992, Paris. *Education:* Universities of London, Munich and Madrid (LL.B., London, 1965; M.B.A., INSEAD Fontainebleau, 1969). Solicitor, Slaughter & May, London. President, Association of International Banks and Trust Companies of the Bahamas, 1981. Member: Young Presidents' Organization (YPO), 1982; Crédit Lyonnais, (International Accountants). General Manager, CKL Europe, 1989. *LANGUAGES:* English, French and German.

PIERRE SOUVILLE, born Algiers, August 20, 1931; admitted, 1992, Paris. *Education:* Universities of Algiers and Paris (Licence en droit, 1957); École Nationale des Impôts (Degree, 1957). Inspector and Deputy to the Head of Accounts, Compagnie d'Assurances "Le Monde," Paris, 1960-1965.

(This Listing Continued)

Tax Advisor, 1965-1971, and Manager, 1971-1979, FIDAL-KPMG. Conseil Juridique and Head of Tax Department, 1979-1981. Fonde de Pouvoirs, Caisse Nationale de Crédit Agricole, 1981-1991. Manager, SOGEQUIP SA, 1989-1991.

PAUL DANDURAND, born France, July 11, 1923. *Education:* Alumnus of l'Ecole Polytechnique (Promo 44); Harvard University (Ph.D., 1950). Directeur Juridique Bouygues, 1976-1988. Board Director for la Compagnie Française d'Entreprises since 1983 (affiliated with la Compagnie Financière de Suez). Co-director of GIE Insere Savoie Autoroutes (I.S.A.) since 1986. Advisor for contractual questions to Transmanchelink (A grouping of the ten franco-british entrepreneurs in charge of the tunnel under the English Channel 86-88) and since July 15, 1989.

AXELLE DE BORGER, born Belgium, October 19, 1962; admitted, 1991, Paris. *Education:* University of Paris II Law School (Masters of Private Law, 1988). *LANGUAGES:* French and English.

JEAN-EMMANUEL KUNTZ, born France, August 4, 1966; admitted, 1993, Paris. *Education:* Paris Institute of Political Science (1988); University of Paris II Law School (Magistere of Commercial Law and D.E.S.S. of Commercial and Tax Law, first in class, 1992). *LANGUAGES:* French and English.

FRANÇOIS DESLIERRES, born Quebec, Canada, April 27, 1951; admitted, 1977, Quebec; 1985, Paris. *Education:* College Saint-Viateur, University of Montreal (LL.L., 1974); University of Paris, Law School, Institut des Hautes Etudes Internationales (LL.M. in Public International Law, 1978). Author: "Investing in France," Paris, 1986. Co-author: "Investing in Canada," 1987; "Investing in Ontario," 1989. Director, Board of Directors, of the France-Canada Chamber of Commerce, Paris, 1986-1989. Canadian Representative to Commissions on Banking Practice and on Law of Competition, International Chamber of Commerce, Paris. Conseiller du Commerce Extérieur du Québec (Appointed by the Prime Minister of the Province of Quebec), 1987. *LANGUAGES:* English and French.

ALAIN FRÉCON

91 AVENUE DE WAGRAM
75017 PARIS, FRANCE
Telephone: 33-1-42-27-01-87
Fax: 33-1-40-54-00-65

Minneapolis, Minnesota, United States Office: 902 Foshay Tower, 821 Marquette Avenue South. 55402-2908. Telephone: 612-338-6868. Fax: 612-338-6878.

International Business, Trademark, Unfair Competition and Arbitration.

ALAIN FRÉCON, born Casablanca, Morocco, 1946; admitted, 1969, Paris, France; 1982, Minnesota. *Education:* University of Paris (Diplome, 1969); Faculté de Droit Paris II (Licence en Droit, cum laude, 1972); Stanford University (J.S.M., 1976); William Mitchell College of Law (J.D., 1982). Author: "Practical Considerations in Drafting F.O.B. Terms in International Sales," International Tax & Business Lawyer, Vol. 3, Winter, 1986, No. 2. Guest Lecturer, International Intellectual Property, William Mitchell College of Law. Nominated Foreign Trade Advisor to France by decree of March 2, 1988. National (U.S.) Secretary, 1990. Honorary Consul of France in Minnesota, 1994. Past Chair of International Business Law Section, Minnesota State Bar Association, 1991-1992. President, French American Chamber of Commerce, Minneapolis-St. Paul, 1988, 1989, 1990, 1993. Chair: Subcommittee of International Intellectual Property, American Bar Association, 1992, 1993; "Global Markets and the Law," MILE, 1989, 1990, 1991, 1993, 1994; International Advisory Committee, American Arbitration Association, Minneapolis, 1994. Member, Advisory Committee, William Mitchell College of Law, Intellectual Property Studies, 1994. *LANGUAGES:* French. *PRACTICE AREAS:* International Business.

FRERE CHOLMELEY

Established in 1968

42 AVENUE DU PRÉSIDENT WILSON
75116 PARIS, FRANCE
Telephone: (33) (1) 44 34 71 00
Fax: (33) (1) 44 34 71 11

London, England Office: 4 John Carpenter Street, London EC4Y 0NH. Telephone: 0171-615 8000. Fax: 0171-615 8080. Telex: 27623. LDE: DX 140.

(This Listing Continued)

FRERE CHOLMELEY, Paris—Continued

Rome, Italy Office: and Studio Legale Associato, 47, Viale Bruno Buozzi, 00197. Telephone: (39) (6) 808 0133. Fax: (39) (6) 808 0134.

Milan, Italy Office: and Studio Legale Associato, Piazza Castello 24, 20121 Milan. Telephone: (39) (2) 720 03 457. Fax: (39) (2) 720 03 469.

Monte Carlo, Monaco Office: "Est Ouest" 24 Boulevard Princesse Charlotte, MC 98000. Telephone: (33) (93) 50 85 70. Fax: (33) (93) 50 22 10.

Berlin, Germany Office: im Internationalen Handelszentrum, Friedrichstrasse, 95, 10117. Telephone: (49) (30) 26 43 2000. Telex: 305996 Kbihzd. Fax: (49) (30) 2643 1900.

Moscow, Russia Office: ul. Sadovaya-Samotyochnaya 24/27, 103051 Moscow. Telephone: (7) 095 258 5058. Fax: (7) 095 258 5060. Telex: 412348 ALM SU.

Dubai, United Arab Emirates Office: Suite 802, EBIL Building, PO Box 2510, Deira, Dubai. Telephone: (9714) 267085/268336. Fax: (9714) 260206. Telex: 45493 LAWMC EM.

The principal areas of practice in the Paris Office are Public and Private International Law, French and International Commercial Transactions and Commercial Arbitration. The office has a particular expertise in the handling of International Boundary Disputes. Clients include not only French Companies but Multinational Corporations doing business in France as well as several sovereign States.

RESIDENT PARTNERS

TIMM T. RIEDINGER, born Darmstadt, Germany, 1940; admitted, 1972, Hamburg, Germany. *Education:* Universities of Heidelberg, Munich, Wuerzburg (1962-1966); New York University, School of Law (M.C.J., 1967); Formerly Member of the Max-Planck Institute. *Member:* The German-French Lawyers Association (Member of the Board).

RICHARD MEESE, born Lisieux, France, 1949; admitted, 1980, Paris. *Education:* University of Caen (Licence on Droit, 1972); University of Paris (D.E.S., de Droit des Affaires, 1973; Docteur en Droit, 1977). *Member:* International Law Association; Société Française de Droit International.

RODMAN R. BUNDY, born Boston, U.S.A., 1951; admitted, 1982, New York; 1987, Paris. *Education:* Yale University (B.A., 1976); Georgetown University (J.D., 1979). Director, Geopolitics and International Boundaries Research Centre, University of London, School of Oriental and African Studies. *Member:* American and International Bar Associations; Royal Institute of International Affairs.

HENRI-XAVIER ORTOLI, born Paris, France, 1954; admitted, 1982, New York; 1986, Paris. *Education:* University of Paris II-Assas (Maîtrise, 1976). *Member:* Société Française de Droit International; American Bar Association; International Bar Association.

JEAN-PHILIPPE BERTHET, born Buenos Aires, Argentina, 1957; admitted, 1982, New York; 1986, Paris. *Education:* Harvard College (A.B., 1978); Georgetown University (J.D., 1981). *Member:* American and International Bar Associations.

ANN C. ABBOUD, born New Jersey, USA, 1952; admitted, 1982, Paris. *Education:* Vassar College; University of Paris II (DEUG, cum laude, 1979; Maîtrise, magna cum laude, 1981). *Member:* International Bar Association; Franco-British Lawyers Society.

DR. MICHAEL BÜHLER, born Munich, Germany, 1956; admitted, 1985, Dusseldorf; 1987, New York; 1991, Paris. *Education:* Universities of Bonn and Geneva (Dr. Jur., 1983); Columbia University School of Law (LL.M., 1985). Counsel of the ICC Court of Arbitration, Paris, 1985-1988. *Member:* ICC Commission on International Arbitration; German American Lawyers Association; International Bar Association.

CONSULTANT

WALTER D. SOHIER, born Boston, U.S.A., 1924; admitted, 1952, New York; 1966, District of Columbia (Not admitted in France). *Education:* University of Chicago and Harvard University (A.B., 1949); Columbia University Law School (LL.B., 1951).

RESIDENT ASSOCIATES

HELEN CONYBEARE-WILLIAMS, born Burton-Upon-Trent, England, 1966; admitted, 1992, Solicitor, England and Wales. *Education:* Oxford University (M.A., 1992).

FRANCOIS HUGONIN, born Clermont-Ferrand, France, 1957; admitted, 1990, Paris. *Education:* University of Clermont-Ferrand (Maîtrise

(This Listing Continued)

Droit des Affaires 1983; DESS Finances, Fiscalité Droit des Affaires, 1984; IAE, 1982). *PRACTICE AREAS:* Taxation; International Taxation.

BERNARD M. HUSSON, born Mount Vernon, USA, 1965; admitted, 1993, Paris. *Education:* University of Paris II (Maîtrise Droit des Affaires et Fiscalité des Entreprises; LL.M., 1987); University of Panthéon Sorbonne (D.E.A. Droit International Privié et Droit du Commerce International).

LORETTA MALINTOPPI, born Rome, Italy, 1956; admitted, 1990, Rome; 1993, Paris. *Education:* University of Rome (Laurea in Guirisprudenza, 1978); Georgetown University (LLM, 1986).

NANETTE E. PILKINGTON, born Ulverston, England, 1955; admitted, 1991, Paris. *Education:* University College London (B.A., 1977); University of Paris II (Maîtrise en Droit, 1987).

THOMAS M. SCHRADE, born Villingen, Germany, 1956; admitted, 1991, Konstanz; 1992, Berlin. *Education:* University of Tubingen, Freiburg (1976-1982).

DAVID S. SELLERS, born Birkenhead, England, 1961; admitted, 1987, Solicitor, England and Wales. *Education:* Edinburgh University (M.A., 1983).

SAM WORDSWORTH, born Oxford, England, 1964; admitted, 1991, Solicitor England and Wales; 1994, France. *Education:* University College London (B.A., 1986).

NATALIE JANNIN, born Aix-en-Provence, France, 1965; admitted, 1994, Paris. *Education:* University of Paris V René Descartes (Maîtrise Droit des Affaires, 1989); Queen Mary College, London (LL.M., 1990).

ANNE LUCCHINI, born Carthage, Tunisia, 1968; admitted, 1994, Paris. *Education:* University of Paris I (DEA Droit communautaire, 1990).

CHRISTINE MENGUE, born Jouy-en-Josas, France, 1964; admitted, 1994, Paris. *Education:* University of Paris II Assas (Maîtrise de Droit, 1987); Institut de Droit Comparé (1986). *LANGUAGES:* English.

LAURENCE NAJARIN, born Montpellier, France, 1963; admitted, 1994, Paris. *Education:* University of Montpellier (Maîtrise Droit de l'Entreprise, 1985), University College London (LL.M., 1989).

INÈS BALAŸ, born Lyon, France, 1969; admitted, 1994, Paris. *Education:* University of Paris II Assas (Maîtrise de Droit des Affaires, 1991); University of Paris I Sorbonne (DESS de Droit des Affaires et Fiscalité, 1992). Paris Bar Exam, 1993.

EDITH BOUCAYA, born Paris, France, 1970; admitted, 1995, Paris. *Education:* University of Paris X Nanterre (Maîtrise de Droit des Affaires et Diplôme d'Etudes Jurisiques Appliquées mention droit anglo-américain Niveau 2, 1991); University of Paris X Nanterre (DEA de Droit des Affaires, 1993). Versailles Bar Exam, 1994.

Languages: English, French, German, Spanish and Italian

FRESHFIELDS

69 BOULEVARD HAUSSMANN
75008 PARIS, FRANCE
Telephone: (33 1) 44 56 44 56
Fax: (33 1) 44 56 44 00
G4 Fax: (1) 44 51 18 88

Other Offices in: Bangkok, Barcelona, Brussels, Frankfurt, Hanoi, Hong Kong, London, Madrid, Moscow, New York, Singapore and Tokyo.

Firm engaged in English, French, EC and General International Practice.

PARTNERS

ANTONIN BESSE, born Aden, South Yemen, March 5, 1958; admitted, as Solicitor and Avocat à la Cour. *Education:* Worcester College, Oxford (B.A., Jurisprudence). *LANGUAGES:* English and French. *PRACTICE AREAS:* Banking; Capital Markets; Securitization; Structured Finance.

JEAN-CLAUDE COTONI, born Paris, France, October 12, 1958; admitted, Avocat à la Cour. *Education:* Paris University (Maîtrise en Droit des Affaires et Fiscalité; Institut du Droit des Affaires; DESS de Droit des Affaires et Fiscalité). *LANGUAGES:* French and English. *PRACTICE AREAS:* Mergers and Acquisitions; Joint Ventures; Commercial; Cooperation Agreements.

HUGH CRISP, born London, England, January 28, 1958; admitted, as Solicitor and Avocat à la Cour. *Education:* Christ Church, Oxford (M.A., Jurisprudence). *LANGUAGES:* English and French. *PRACTICE AREAS:*

(This Listing Continued)

Mergers and Acquisitions; Joint Ventures; Commercial; Cooperation Agreements.

JEAN DE HAUTECLOCQUE, born Bruges, Belgium, September 11, 1954; Avocat à la Cour. *Education:* Paris University (Maître en Droit des Affaires; DESS de Droit des Affaires); Certificat d'Aptitude á la Profession d'Avocat (1979). *Member:* Association Internationale des Jeunes Avocats; International Bar Association. *LANGUAGES:* French and English. *PRACTICE AREAS:* Litigation; Arbitration.

YVES HUYGHE DE MAHENGE, born Uccle, Belgium, November 11, 1948; admitted, Avocat à la Cour. *Education:* Aix-en-Provence University (Licence en Droit; Diplôme d'Etudes Supérieures de Droit Privé; DJCE; Diplôme d'Etudes Supérieures de Sciences Criminelles; Docteur d'Etat en Droit, summa cum laude). Teaching Assignment, Institut de Droit des Affaires d'Aix-en-Provence; INSEAD. *Member:* International Bar Association; Fondation Internationale pour le Droit de l'Entreprise; Association Nationale des Conseils Juridiques. *LANGUAGES:* French, English and Italian. *PRACTICE AREAS:* International Commercial Law; Banking.

HERVÉ KENSICHER, born Dijon, France, February 3, 1960; admitted as Avocat. *Education:* Paris University (Maîtrise en Droit International Privé); Institut Supérieur d'Interprétariat et de Traduction de Paris; School of Public Affairs. Indiana University (Certificate of Public Management). *Member:* New York State Bar Association; International Bar Association. *LANGUAGES:* French, English, German and Russian. *PRACTICE AREAS:* Corporate Law; Aviation Finance; International Finance; Energy Law; Arbitration.

ISABELLE MACELHONE, born Boulogne, France, May 20, 1959; admitted, Avocat à la Cour. *Education:* Paris University (Maître en Droit Privé; DEA de Droit Privé Général). *Member:* Association Nationale des Conseils Juridiques; International Bar Association. *LANGUAGES:* French, English and Spanish. *PRACTICE AREAS:* Domestic and International Acquisitions; Domestic and International Joint Ventures; Commercial; Cooperation Agreements; Energy Law.

GLENN MATHESON, born West Kirby, England, December 21, 1960; admitted, as Solicitor and Avocat à la Cour. *Education:* Oriel College, Oxford (B.A.). *LANGUAGES:* English, French and German. *PRACTICE AREAS:* Asset and Project Finance; Capital Markets; Banking.

JEAN-LUC MICHAUD, born Chambéry, France, August 3, 1954; admitted, Avocat à la Cour. *Education:* Lyon University (Maîtrise en Droit; DESS; DJCE); Minnesota University (Master's Degree in Law). *Member:* Franco-British Lawyers Society; Association Europeéne pour le droit Bancaire et Financière (AEDBF); International Bar Association. *LANGUAGES:* French and English. *PRACTICE AREAS:* Finance; Banking; Acquisitions.

JAN PAULSSON, born Nyköping, Sweden, November 5, 1949; admitted, Connecticut and Avocat à la Cour. *Education:* Harvard (A.B.); Yale (J.D., Board of Editors, Yale Law Journal); Paris University (DESS). Co-Author: International Chamber of Commerce Arbitration (2 vols. 2d ed. 1990); Arbitration International (General Editor); Revue de l'Arbitrage (main contributor) *Member:* London Court of International Arbitration (Vice President). *LANGUAGES:* English, French and Swedish. *PRACTICE AREAS:* International Arbitration.

MICHEL QUÉRÉ, born Boulogne, France, April 27, 1957. *Education:* Paris University (Maîtrise en Droit); University of Kent (B.A. in Law). *Member:* Association pour le Développement des Echanges Internationaux de Juristes (Chairman); Association Nationale des Juristes de Banques. *LANGUAGES:* French, English and German. *PRACTICE AREAS:* Aircraft Finance; Specialist Finance; Mergers and Acquisitions; Leasing.

CHRISTIAN N.R. SALBAING, born Montréal, Quebec, January 23, 1950; admitted, 1971, Quebec; 1974, California and U.S. District Court, Northern District of California; 1979, France. *Education:* Stanislas College (B.A., 1967); University of Montreal (LL.L., 1970); University of San Francisco (J.D., 1974). Editorial Board Member, "Canadian Lawyer" Magazine, Toronto, 1988—. Editor, Company Law and Partnership Law in Selected Asian Countries, 1987. Author: Chapter on: Company Law in the People's Republic of China," International Bar Association, 1986; Dispute Resolution in the People's Republic of China, "Doing Business in China," Matthew Bender, 1989. President, 1984-1985 and Governor, 1984-1987, The Canadian Chamber of Commerce, Hong Kong. Member, Hong Kong Law Reform Commission Sub Committee on Legal Effects of Age, 1983-1986. *Member:* Canadian, American and International Bar Associations; Asia-Pacific Lawyers Association; International Fiscal Association (French Branch).

(This Listing Continued)

ERIC THOMAS, born Saint-Mande, France, June 30, 1958; admitted, Avocat à la Cour et Fiscal. *Education:* Paris University (DESS de Droit des Affaires et Fiscalité). *LANGUAGES:* French and English. *PRACTICE AREAS:* Domestic and International Tax; Capital Markets; Specialist Finance.

JAMES VAUDOYER, born Levallois-Perret, France, April 5, 1951; admitted, Avocat à la Cour. *Education:* Paris University (Maîtrise en Droit des Affaires; DESS de Juriste d'Affaires, Option Fiscalité). *LANGUAGES:* French and English. *PRACTICE AREAS:* Corporate Tax; Mergers and Acquisitions; Joint Ventures; Commercial; Cooperation Agreements.

ASSOCIATES

FRANK AUCKENTHALER, born Bordeaux, France, January 7, 1963; admitted, Avocat à la Cour. *Education:* Montpellier University (Doctorat d'Etat DJCE, DESS - Affaires et Fiscalité); Paris University (Maîtrise en Droit; Diplome de Institut d'Etudes Politiques); Bordeaux University. *LANGUAGES:* French and English. *PRACTICE AREAS:* Asset Finance; Banking; Capital Markets.

NATHALIE BADETZ, born Paris, France, August 4, 1968; admitted, Avocat à la Cour. *Education:* Paris University (DESS de Droit des Affaires et Fiscalité, Magistère); University of California, Berkeley (LL.M.). *LANGUAGES:* French and English. *PRACTICE AREAS:* Environmental Law; Litigation.

CHRISTOPHE BERKANI, born Neuilly sur Seine, France, August 1, 1969; admitted, Avocat à la Cour. *Education:* Paris University (Maîtrise en Droit des Affaires et Fiscalité; Maîtrise en Droit Privé; DEA de Droit des Affaires et Droit Économique). *LANGUAGES:* French and English.

STÉPHANE BOUJNAH, born Albertville, France, April 11, 1964. *Education:* Diplôme de l'Institut d'Etudes Politiques de Paris; Paris University (Maîtrise en Droit des Affaires; DEA de Droit International Economique); University of Kent, Canterbury (LL.M.); INSEAD - M.B.A. *LANGUAGES:* French, English, Hebrew and Spanish. *PRACTICE AREAS:* Mergers and Acquisitions; Capital Markets; International Industrial Company Operation Agreements.

XAVIER BUFFET DELMAS D'AUTANE, born Manosque, France, September 13, 1960. *Education:* Strasbourg University, Centre d'Etudes Internationales de la Propriété Industrielle (Diplôme d'Etudes Internationales des Marques, Dessins et Modèles); Paris University (DEA en Droit de la Propriété Litéraire, Artistique et Industrielle). *Member:* International Trademark Association (INTA); Association Internationale pour la Protection de la Propriét éIndustrielle (AIPPI); Association des Spécialistes en Marques et Dessins et Modèles. *LANGUAGES:* French, English and Spanish. *PRACTICE AREAS:* Intellectual Property; Competition Law; Commercial Law.

IRIS CHOI-BELLANGER, born Hong Kong, May 29, 1958; admitted, Avocat à Cour. *Education:* University of Hong Kong (B.A., Degree, English and Comparative Literature); Ecole Supérieure d'Interprète et de Traducteurs (Diploma in French-Chinese translation); University of Paris II (Maîtrise en Droit Privé); CAPA (1993). *LANGUAGES:* Chinese (Mandarin, Cantonese, Fujianese), English and French. *PRACTICE AREAS:* Foreign Investments in China.

CÉLINE COASNES, born Hyères, France, August 14, 1968. *Education:* Aix-Marseille University (DESS de Droit de Commerce Extérieru; DJCE, Magistère de Droit des Affaires, Fiscalité et Comptabilité). *LANGUAGES:* French and English. *PRACTICE AREAS:* EC Law; Competition Law; Commercial Law; Company Law.

FREDERIC COHEN, born Mortagne au Perche, France, September 10, 1964; admitted, Avocat à la Cour. *Education:* Paris University: (Maîtrise en droit des Affaires-Diplôme de l'Institut de Droit des Affaires-Certificat d'Aptitude àl'Administration des Entreprises); Strasbourg University (Certificat de Droit Européen). *LANGUAGES:* French, English and Spanish. *PRACTICE AREAS:* Mergers and Acquisitions; Company and Commercial Law.

VERONIQUE COLLIN, born Paris, France, January 2, 1962; admitted, Avocat à la Cour. *Education:* Paris University (Maîtrise en Droit des Affaires); Indiana University (Master's in Public and International Affairs). *LANGUAGES:* French, English, German and Japanese. *PRACTICE AREAS:* Aircraft and Project Finance; Mergers and Acquisitions.

GRAHAM COOP, born London, England, July 31, 1965; admitted, as Solicitor, and to the New Zealand Bar, as Barrister and Solicitor. *Education:* University of Auckland, New Zealand (LL.B., honors; B.Sc.). *LAN-*

(This Listing Continued)

FRESHFIELDS, Paris—Continued

GUAGES: English, French and German. PRACTICE AREAS: International Arbitration; Intellectual Property.

JULIETTE DESLANDRES, born Lons-Le-Saunier, France, August 12, 1968. Education: Paris University (Maîtrise en Droit des Affaires, DESS de Droit de la Construction et de l'Urbanisme, Licence d'Anglais). LANGUAGES: French, English and German. PRACTICE AREAS: Construction Law; Town Planning.

CLOTILDE DIRNAT, born Oran, Algeria, 1959; admitted, 1986, Avocat, France. Education: Université Paris I Panthéon-Sorbonne (Maîtrise en Droit des Affaires Internationales; DEA Droit International Privé, 1984). LANGUAGES: French, English and Spanish. PRACTICE AREAS: Finance; Mergers and Acquisitions.

PHILIPPE DURAND, born Vichy, France, September 6, 1963; admitted, 1990, New York; Avocat à la Cour. Education: Diplôme de l'Institut d'Etudes Politiques de Paris, Public Service Section; Paris University (Maîtrise en Droit des Affaires et Fiscalité; Georgetown University Law Center, Washington, D.C., USA (LL.M.); Strasbourg University (E.C. Business Law Diploma). Member: American Bar Association; New York State Bar Association. LANGUAGES: French and English. PRACTICE AREAS: Joint Venture; Company and Commercial Law; Special Contract; Employment Law; Litigation.

SOPHIE GARGARO, born Tours, France, June 9, 1963; admitted, Avocat à la Cour. Education: Montpellier University (DJCE, DESS en Droit des Affaires et Fiscalité, Certificat du Droit de la Distribution); Tours University (Maîtrise de Droit Privé et Diplôme du Centre du Commerce International). LANGUAGES: French and English. PRACTICE AREAS: Property and Commercial Leases.

DANIEL GOGEK, born Toronto, Canada, November 5, 1957; admitted, New York; Avocat à la Cour. Education: Columbia University (LL.M.); Mc Gill University (B.C.L., LL.B.); Institut d'Etudes Politiques de Paris; University of Toronto (B.Comm.). Member: Union des Jeunes Avocats de Paris; American Bar Association; Canadian Bar Association. LANGUAGES: English, French, Russian and Spanish. PRACTICE AREAS: Foreign Investments; Joint Venture Projects in Eastern Europe and CIS.

PHILIPPE HAMEAU, born Vernon, France, April 26, 1960; admitted, Avocat à la Cour. Education: Paris University (DEA de Droit Privé Général); Institut de Droit des Affaires de Paris. Assignment: Facultéde Droit, Paris II; Facultéde Droit, Paris V. Member: Ancien premier secrétaire de la conférence du stage des avocats au conseil d'Etat et à la Cour de Cassation. LANGUAGES: French and English. PRACTICE AREAS: Commercial and Civil Litigation.

JOSEPH HUSE, born Cleveland, Ohio, November 9, 1955; admitted, Avocat à la Cour. Education: Boston College (J.D.; M.B.A.); Paris University (DESS). LANGUAGES: English and French. PRACTICE AREAS: Construction; Project Finance; Environmental Law; International Arbitration.

DIDIER LASAYGUES, born Angoulême, France, September 15, 1956; admitted, Avocat à la Cour. Education: Paris University (Maîtrise en Droit des Affaires, mention Carriéres Judiciaires); Diplôme d'Aptitude aux Fonctions de Notaire. LANGUAGES: French and English. PRACTICE AREAS: Property Law.

VÉRONIQUE LE GALL, born Versailles, France, May 18, 1967; admitted, Avocat à la Cour. Education: Paris University (Maîtrise en Droit des Affaires); Strasbourg University (DJCE; DESS Juriste d'Affaires); Montpellier University (Certificat de Fiscalité). LANGUAGES: French and English. PRACTICE AREAS: French and International Tax.

JEAN L'HOMME, born Rose Hill, Mauritius, November 1, 1961; admitted, Avocat à la Cour. Education: Paris University (Maîtrise en Droit des Affaires; DESS de Droit des Affaires et Fiscalité). LANGUAGES: French and English. PRACTICE AREAS: Asset Finance; Finance.

ABDEL-HAMID MAZOUZ, born Bedjaia, Algeria, June 4, 1967. Education: Lille University (Maîtrise en Droit des Affaires; DESS en Finance et Fiscalité Internationales); Warwick University (Certificate in English Law). LANGUAGES: French and English. PRACTICE AREAS: Capital Markets.

DOMINIQUE MONDOLONI, born Montreal, Canada, November 12, 1964; admitted, Avocat à la Cour. Education: Aix-Marseille University (Maîtrise en Droit des Affaires); Paris University (DESS de Commerce Ex-

(This Listing Continued)

térieur). Co-Author: "France Encyclopedia of International Litigation," ed. Sir Anthony Coleman. LANGUAGES: French, English and Spanish. PRACTICE AREAS: Commercial and Civil Litigation; Insolvency.

THIERRY MOURRUAU, born Papeete, Tahiti, February 15, 1966. Education: Paris University (Maîtrise en Droit des Affaires; DESS Fiscalité Internationale). LANGUAGES: French, English and German. PRACTICE AREAS: International Tax.

JONATHAN NABARRO, born Johannesburg, South Africa, January 20, 1962; admitted, Avocat à la Cour. Education: Montpellier University (DESS de Juristes d'Affaires; DJCE); Gonville and Caius College, Cambridge (Ph.D.). LANGUAGES: English, French, Spanish and Afrikaans. PRACTICE AREAS: Project Finance; Asset Finance.

DAVID NEWTON, born London, England, May 15, 1959; admitted, as Solicitor. Education: London University (LL.B.); Chester College of Law (SFE). LANGUAGES: English and French. PRACTICE AREAS: International Arbitration.

DOMINIQUE PAILLUSSEAU, born Lorient, France, May 19, 1960; admitted, Avocat à la Cour. Education: Rennes University (Maîtrise en Droit des Affaires et Fiscalité; DESS de Droit des Affaires et Fiscalité; DJCE); Montpellier University (Certificat Supérieur de Fiscalité). LANGUAGES: French and English. PRACTICE AREAS: Property.

FRANCE PELLETIER, born Lyon, France, January 27, 1968; admitted, Avocat à la Cour. Education: Lyon University (Maîtrise de Droit Public); University of Missouri (M. A. in Political Science); Paris University (DEA de Droit des Affaires; DESS de Droit Immobilier), Certificat d'Aptitude àla Profession d'Avocat. LANGUAGES: French and English. PRACTICE AREAS: Property Law; Litigation; Company Law.

CHRISTOPHE PERCHET, born Roubaix, France, October 5, 1966. Education: Strasbourg University (Maîtrise en Droit des Affaires; Diplôme de l'Institut d'Etudes Politiques; DESS de Juriste d'Affaires; DJCE). LANGUAGES: French, English and German.

ARNAUD PERES, born Rouen, France, August 15, 1964; admitted, Avocat à la Cour. Education: Bordeaux University (Maîtrise en Droit Privé, Droit des Affaires; DEA de Droit Privé). LANGUAGES: French and English. PRACTICE AREAS: Acquisitions; Company Law; Commercial Law.

PATRICK PERTEGNAZZA, born Nice, France, July 8, 1965; admitted, Avocat à la Cour. Education: Paris University (Maîtrise de Droit des Affaires, DESS Droit et Commerce Extérieur). (Also at Hanoi Office). LANGUAGES: French, English and Italian. PRACTICE AREAS: Litigation.

CATHERINE PEULVE, born Neuilly-sur-Seine, France, March 28, 1967; admitted, Avocat à la Cour. Education: Paris University (Maîtrise en Droit des Affaires et Fiscalité; Maîtrise en Droit International et Droit Européen; DEA de Droits des Affaires et Droit Economique). LANGUAGES: French and English. PRACTICE AREAS: Commercial and Civil Litigation; International Law; Arbitration.

HILARY PLATT, born Belfast, Northern Ireland, July 16, 1968; admitted, Solicitor. Education: Merton College, Oxford (B.A., Law). LANGUAGES: English and French. PRACTICE AREAS: Finance.

PASCALE RAHMAN, born Ajmer, India, April 3, 1960; admitted, Barrister. Education: Paris University (Licence en droit); Lincoln College, Oxford (B.A., Law); Columbia University (Diploma in Comparative Law). LANGUAGES: English, French and Spanish. PRACTICE AREAS: Commercial and Telecommunications.

VICTORIA RIGBY, born York, England, January 2, 1969; admitted, as Solicitor. Education: St. Hilda's College, Oxford (M.A., Jurisprudence). LANGUAGES: English, German and French. PRACTICE AREAS: Finance.

PHILIPPE ROYOU, born Petit-Quevilly, France, January 6, 1962; admitted, Avocat à la Cour. Education: Rouen University (Maîtrise en Droit Privé Général); Paris University (DESS de Droit des Affaires et Fiscalité). LANGUAGES: French and English. PRACTICE AREAS: Domestic and International Tax; Mergers and Acquisitions.

BRIAN J. SCHWAB, born Berkeley, California, July 18, 1964; admitted, California (Not admitted in France). Education: Cornell University, Ithaca, New York (B.A., History and Government); University of California at Los Angeles (Juris Doctor); Rijksuniversiteit Limburg, Maastricht, The Netherlands (M.A., Comparative and European Community Law).

(This Listing Continued)

LANGUAGES: English and French. *PRACTICE AREAS:* Construction Law; International Arbitration; Project Finance.

GRAHAM SCOTT, born Newcastle-upon-Tyne, England, March 5, 1962; admitted, as Solicitor and Avocat à la Cour. *Education:* University of Bristol (LL.B.). *LANGUAGES:* English, French and German. *PRACTICE AREAS:* Banking; Capital Markets; Derivatives; Structured Finance.

MARTIN WRIGHT, born Glastonbury, England, September 20, 1963; admitted, as Solicitor and Avocat à la Cour. *Education:* King's College, Cambridge (B.A. in Modern Languages and Law; M.A.). *LANGUAGES:* English, French, German, Spanish and Italian. *PRACTICE AREAS:* Mergers and Acquisitions; Joint Ventures; Commercial.

HONG WU CHEN, born Beijing, China, May 3, 1961. *Education:* Beijing Foreign Languages University (Bachelor of Arts Degree, 1983); Political Science and Law University of China (Masters in Law, 1986); Paris University (since 1991 for a Doctorat de Droit International Privé); CAPA of China (1988). Lecturer in Law at the Political Science and Law University in China, 1986-1990. Publications: "Application of Laws of International Commercial Cont racts," published in Beijing, 1980; "The Law of Armed Conflicts by Charles Rousseau," translation into Chinese, published in Beijing, 1987; "Private International Law by Batiffol and Lagard," translation into Chinese, published in Beijing, 1989. *LANGUAGES:* Chinese, French and English. *PRACTICE AREAS:* Private International Law; Commercial Law; Foreign Investment Law in China; Real Estate Law in China.

OF COUNSEL

CHRISTIAN LARROUMET, born Talence, France, September 23, 1939. *Education:* Bordeaux University (Licence en Droit; Diplôme d'Etudes Supérieures de Droit Privé; Diplôme d'Etudes Supérieures d'Histoire du Droit; Docteur d'Etat en Droit); Agrégé des Facultés de Droit. Professeur à l'Université de Panthéon-Assas. Author: "Droit Civil Introduction," 1984; "Droit des Biens," 2nd ed., 1988; "Droit des Contrats," 2nd ed., 1990 and various contributions to Law Reviews in France and abroad in Civil and Commercial Law. *LANGUAGES:* French, English and Spanish.

FRIED, FRANK, HARRIS, SHRIVER & JACOBSON

Correspondance Organique

7, RUE ROYALE
PARIS 75008, FRANCE
Telephone: (+331) 40 17 04 04
Fax: (+331) 40 17 08 30

New York, New York Office: One New York Plaza, 10004. Telephone: 212-859-8000. Cable Address: "Steric New York." W.U. Int. Telex: 620223. W.U. Int. Telex: 662119. W.U. Domestic: 128173. Telecopier: 212-859-4000 (Dex 6200).

Washington, D.C. Office: Suite 800, 1001 Pennsylvania Avenue, N.W., 20004-2505. Telephone: 202-639-7000.

Los Angeles, California Office: 725 South Figueroa Street, 90017. Telephone: 213-689-5800.

London, England Office: 4 Chiswell Street, London EC1Y 4UP. Telephone: 011-44-171-972-9600. Fax: 011-44-171-972-9602.

PARTNER

ERIC M. CAFRITZ, born 1954; admitted, New York; Paris. *Education:* University of California at Berkeley (A.B., with highest honors, 1977); Yale Law School (J.D., 1980). Phi Beta Kappa. Member, Yale Law Journal, 1978-1979.

ASSOCIATES

JEAN-PHILIPPE LAMBERT, born 1963; admitted, Paris. *Education:* University of Paris II, Pantheon-Assas (Maîtrise in Business and Taxation Law, with Honors, 1985); University of Paris V (D.E.S.S. in International Business Law, with Honors, 1986).

JEAN-PIERRE HYUN LEE, born 1965; admitted, New York; Paris. *Education:* University of Paris II, Pantheon-Assas (Maîtrise with High Honors, 1986, D.E.A. with Honors, 1987; Laureat de l'Universite, 1985 and 1986); Columbia University School of Law (LL.M., 1989).

SYLVIE A. MONGELOUS, born 1958; admitted, Paris. *Education:* University of Paris II, Pantheon-Assas (Maîtrise in International and EEC Law, 1980); University of Paris I, Pantheon-Sorbonne (D.E.A. in English and Northern American Commercial Law, 1981); New York University School of Law (LL.M., 1984).

(This Listing Continued)

(For Biographical Data of New York, New York, Personnel, see Professional Biographies at New York, New York).
(For Biographical Data of Washington, D.C. Personnel, see Professional Biographies at Washington, D.C.).
(For Biographical Data of Los Angeles, California Personnel, see Professional Biographies at Los Angeles, California).
(For Biographical Data of London Personnel, see Professional Biographies at London, England).

FUNCK-BRENTANO & PARTNERS

Established in 1954

198, AVENUE VICTOR HUGO
75116 PARIS, FRANCE
Telephone: (33-1) 45.04.61.73
Telefax: (33-1) 45.04.41.43

Brussels, Belgium Office: Avenue de la Joyeuse Entrée 1, Boîte 16, B-1040 Bruxelles. Telephone: (32) (2) 230.46.69. Telefax: (32) (2) 231.00.35.

Cologne, Germany Office: Salierring 42, D-50677 Köln. Telephone: (49) (221) 208070. Telex: 8883 360. Telefax: (49) (221) 239255.

Hamburg, Germany Office: Poststrasse 9 A, D-20354 Hamburg. Telephone: (49) (40) 359220. Telefax: (49) (40) 344573. Telex: 211 729 MOD D.

Dresden, Germany Office: Winterbergstrasse 2, D-01277 Dresden. Telephone:(49) (351) 2516024. Telefax: (49) (351) 2513722.

Leipzig, Germany Office: Katharinenstrasse 15, D-04109 Leipzig. Telephone: (49) (341) 2114606. Telefax: (49) (341) 281073.

General Practice, Commercial, Banking, Corporation, Unfair Competition, International Arbitration. EEC and ECSC Law, Dumping, Agricultural Common Policy, Free Movements of Goods.

MEMBERS OF FIRM

ROLAND FUNCK-BRENTANO, born Paris, France, July 30, 1929; admitted, 1954, Paris. *Education:* Paris University (D.E.S. Civil Law; D.E.S. History and Roman Law). Ancien Secrétaire de la Conférence du Barreau de Paris, 1956-1957. Member, Editorial Staff, French Arbitration Review, 1978—. *Member:* Paris Bar; International Chamber of Commerce. *LANGUAGES:* French and English.

LISE FUNCK-BRENTANO, born Saarbrücken, Germany, August 21, 1929; admitted, 1954, Paris. *Education:* Paris University (Maîtrise en droit); Frankfurt a.m., Germany (Doctor Juris). *Member:* Paris Bar; Hamburg Bar Association; European Lawyers Association (Secretary General, 1978-1987; President, 1988—); A.F.E.C. (French Association for Competition Study); International League Against Unfair Competition; Grür (Deutsche Vereinigung Für Gewerblichen Urheberschutz und Urheberrecht, Germany). (Also Member, Graf von Westphalen & Modest, Hamburg, Germany). *LANGUAGES:* French, German and English.

CHRISTIAN E. ROTH, born Strasbourg, France, March 20, 1955; admitted, 1979, Paris. *Education:* University of Saarbrücken, Germany (M.A., German Lit. and Civilization, 1976); University of Strasbourg (Maîtrise en Droit, 1979). Lecturer of EEC Law, University of Paris, Sorbonne, 1987—. *Member:* Paris Bar; European Lawyers Association (Deputy Secretary General, 1984-1987; Secretary General, 1988—); Union of European Attorneys (Treasurer, 1993—). *LANGUAGES:* German, English and French.

MARTINE SCHMITT, born Sarreguemines, France, October 16, 1958; admitted, 1987, Paris. *Education:* University Saarbrücken, Germany; University of Paris (Maîtrise en Droit, 1982; Ph.D., 1987). *Member:* Paris Bar; Deutscher-Rheinischer Juristenverein. *LANGUAGES:* French, German and Italian.

XAVIER FORTY DE LAMARRE, born Montmorency, France, September 7, 1959; admitted, 1985, Paris. *Education:* University of Paris (Maîtrise en Droit, 1982; D.E.A., Business Law, 1984; D.E.A. EEC Law, 1986). *Member:* Paris Bar. *LANGUAGES:* French and English.

CATHERINE NELKEN, born Versailles, France, January 30, 1965; admitted, 1988, Paris. *Education:* University of Paris (Maîtrise en droit, 1986). *Member:* Paris Bar. *LANGUAGES:* French.

ANNE NAKOU, born Athens, Greece, August 27, 1966; (Not admitted in France). *Education:* University of Athens, Greece (Maîtrise en droit, 1988); University of Lyon, France (D.E.A., EEC Law, 1990); University of Paris, Sorbonne (D.E.S.S., EEC Law, 1991). *Member:* Athens Bar Association; Jeunes Européens Fédéralistes. *LANGUAGES:* Greek, French, English and German.

(This Listing Continued)

FUNCK-BRENTANO & PARTNERS, Paris—Continued

OF COUNSEL

PIERRE MATHIJSEN, born Tilburg, Netherlands, March 7, 1924; (Not admitted in France). *Education:* University of Minnesota (M.A., Economics, 1952); University of Leyden (M.A., 1951; Ph.D., 1957). Assistant Professor, Law School, University of Michigan, 1961-1962. Professor: Law Faculty, University of Nijmegen, Netherlands, 1967-1985; Law Faculty, University of Brussels, Belgium, 1986—. Attaché, ECSC Court of Justice, 1953-1958. Legal Adviser, EAEC Commission, 1958-1967. Director, DG IV Competition, EEC Commission, 1968-1977. Director General for Regional Policy, EC Commission, 1977-1986. Member of the Board, European Investment Bank, 1977-1986. Delegate General, CIAA, Brussels, Belgium, 1986-1989. Author: "A Guide to European Community Law," London/New York, 1972, 6. Edition, 1993. Member, Editorial Staff, "Encyclopedia of European Community Law," and "European Law Review," 1973—. *LANGUAGES:* Dutch, French, English and German.

KLAUS LANDRY, born Zittau, Germany, November 1, 1938; admitted, 1968, Hamburg (Not admitted in France). *Education:* Universities of Munich, Heidelberg, London (University College), Frankfurt and Kiel (Doctor Juris, 1966). *Member:* Hamburg Bar (President) and International Bar Associations; GRUR; German Institute for Arbitration; German Association for Food Law; German Association of Comparative Law. (Also Member, Graf von Westphalen & Modest, Hamburg, Germany). *LANGUAGES:* German and English.

FRIEDRICH GRAF VON WESTPHALEN, born Aussig/CSFR, July 23, 1940; admitted, 1969, Germany (Not admitted in France). *Education:* Universities of Münster, Heidelberg, Cologne, Bonn, Washington (1965-1966). Industrial Commercial experience, until 1973. Publications: The Munich Handbook of Contract: Comments on Banking Law, Legal Aspects of Export Financing, 1987; Product Liability, 1989; Commentary on the General Terms and Conditions of Business, 1985; Law of Leasing, 1992; Bonds and Bank-Guarantees in International Trade, 1990; Contracts of Sale in Europe, (ed.) 1992. (Also Member, Graf von Westphalen & Modest, Cologne, Germany). *LANGUAGES:* German and English.

CHRISTIAN-ERNST OSTERMANN, born Bad Oeynhausen, Germany, May 3, 1945; admitted, 1978, Germany (Not admitted in France). *Education:* Universities of Cologne, Hamburg. Publications: Commentary on Property Management, Competition Law, Insurance Law. *Member:* German Association for the Protection of Industrial Property; German-Italian Lawyer's Association. (Also Member, Graf von Westphalen & Modest, Cologne, Germany). *LANGUAGES:* German, French and English.

Member of Eurolegal

GIBSON, DUNN & CRUTCHER

Established in 1890

104 AVENUE RAYMOND POINCARE
75116 PARIS, FRANCE
Telephone: 011-33-1-45-01-93-83
Telecopier: 011-33-1-45-00-69-59
Cable Address: GIBTRAK PARIS

Los Angeles, California Office: 333 South Grand Avenue, 90071-3197. Telephone: 213-229-7000. Telex: 188171 GIBTRASK LSA (TRT), 674930 GIBTRASK LSA (WUT). Telecopier: 213-229-7520. Cable Address: GIBTRASK LOS ANGELES.

General and International Law Practice.
Firm engaged in American and General International Practice and registered as Avocats in France.

FIRM PROFILE: Gibson, Dunn & Crutcher, originating in Los Angeles, has been providing legal services to clients since 1890. Today, the firm has grown to one of the largest law firms in the world with approximately 650 attorneys in 17 offices situated in most of the world's important business centers. The firm has experts in virtually every area of the law, particularly those which relate to commercial transactions and disputes, and has more effective geographical coverage in the United States than any other major firm. The firm's lawyers and staff are dedicated to providing quality service on a timely and cost effective basis.

The Paris office is positioned to serve our clients throughout the growing European market. It is staffed with a majority of European lawyers, with extensive experience in transnational transactions. This office provides both U.S. and non-U.S. clients with a full range of legal services in connection

(This Listing Continued)

---

with a variety of corporate operations, litigations and transactions, including transnational mergers, acquisitions, mining activities and general joint ventures, international financings and international commercial transactions—from licensing and distribution to trade dispute matters. In addition to providing significant tax planning advice required for such transactions, these offices also have a well-developed practice advising individuals and families on complex tax, estate planning and corporate and investment matters, and on the developing law of the European Economic Community and the new free market systems emerging in Central and Eastern Europe.

PARTNERS

WENDY M. SINGER, born February 5, 1950; admitted, 1975, New York; 1981, Avocat, Paris; 1994, England and Wales (Not Practicing as a Solicitor). *Education:* Harvard University (A.B., magna cum laude, 1970; J.D., cum laude, 1974). Phi Beta Kappa. *Member:* Association Françaisé des Avocats Conseils d'Entreprises. (London, England and Paris, France Offices). *LANGUAGES:* English, French. *PRACTICE AREAS:* Taxation; International Law.

BERNARD GRINSPAN, born November 5, 1956; admitted, 1979, France; 1983, New York. *Education:* Lycée Henri IV, France (Baccalauréat Mathematics, 1975); University of Paris II, France (Master of Law, with very high honors, 1979); Institut d'Etudes Politiques, France (Diploma, with high honors, 1981); Harvard University (LL.M., 1983). *Member:* New York State and American Bar Associations; Ordre Des Avocats Au Barreau De Paris. *LANGUAGES:* French and English.

ASSOCIATES

FRÉDÉRIQUE SAUVAGE, born November 25, 1965; admitted, 1993, France. *Education:* Panthéon Sorbonne, Paris, France (Maîtrise droit privé, 1988;DESS droit des affaires et fiscalite, 1989); Kings College, London, England (LL.B., 1988). *LANGUAGES:* French and English.

BERYL LEMAIGRE-DUBREUIL, born September 27, 1963; (Not admitted in France). *Education:* University of Bordeaux, France (DESS of Wine and Winerie, 1988); University of Paris II, France (DEA des Affaires et Droit Economique, 1989). *LANGUAGES:* French and English.

(For information on firm personnel, address and telephone information regarding the firm's offices located in Century City, Irvine, San Diego, Menlo Park and San Francisco, California; Denver, Colorado; Washington, D.C.; New York, N.Y.; Dallas, Texas; Seattle, Washington; London, England; Hong Kong; Tokyo, Japan and Jeddah and Riyadh, Saudi Arabia (Affiliated Offices), see professional biographies at Los Angeles, California)

GIDE LOYRETTE NOUEL

26, COURS ALBERT 1ER
75008 PARIS, FRANCE
Telephone: (1) 40.75.60.00
Cable Address: "3 Avocagidva Paris 86"
Telex: 651261F GILOY
Telecopier: (1) 43.59.37.79

New York, New York Office: Swiss Bank Tower, 10 East 50th Street, 10022. Telephone: (1-212) 644-1201. Telex: 424353 GIDE. Telecopier: (1-212) 644-1205.

Brussels, Belgium Office: Rue de la Loi 99.101, B-1040. Telephone: (32.2) 231.11.40. Telecopier: (32.2) 231.11.77.

Warsaw, Poland Office: Ul. Kopernika 17, 00-359. Telephone: (48.22) 26.22.21. Telecopier: (48.22) 26.03.02.

Riyadh, Saudi Arabia Office: P.O. Box 4615, 11412. Telephone: (966.1) 476.60.39. Telex: 401677 NASHWA. Telecopier: (966.1) 476.18.96.

Tokyo, Japan Office: Homei Building 3F, 3-19 Akasaka 1-Chome, Minato-Ku, 107. Telephone: (81.3) 55.62.03.01. Telecopier: (81.3) 55.62.03.06.

Beijing, People's Republic of China Office: Suite 3309 A, Jing Guang Centre, Hu Jia Lou, Chaoyang District, 100020. Telephone: (86.1) 501 4511. Telecopier: (86.1) 501 4551.

Prague, Czech Republic Office: 34 Jindrisska, 11207. Telephone: (42.2) 24.21.34.65;24.21.36.50. Telecopier: (42.2) 24.21.09.12;24.22.58.53.

St. Petersburg, Russia Office: 34 Souvorovsky Prospect, App 45, P.O. Box 172, 193015. Telephone by satellite: (7.812) 850.16.85. Telecopier by satellite: (7.812) 850.16.86.

Moscow, Russia Office: 9, Ulitsa Tverskaya - App 66, 103009. Telephone by satellite: (7.501) 940.45.00. Telecopier by satellite: (7.501) 940.45.01.

(This Listing Continued)

Budapest VII, Hungary Office: EMKE Building, Rákóczi út 42, BP 409, 1072. Telephone: (36.1) 268.1236;268.1237;268.1238. Telecopier: (36.1) 268.1239.

Madrid, Spain Office: Antonio Maura 7, 6°, 28014. Telephone: (34.1) 531.25.01. Telecopier: (34.1) 531.35.30.

Hanoi, Vietnam Office: Hanoi Business Centre, 51 Ly Thai To. Telephone: (84.42) 66.122.3. Telecopier: (84.42) 66.030.1.

General French European Community and International Practice, Admiralty, Antitrust, Banking, Civil, Copyright, Corporation Financing, Engineering Contracts, Labor, Law Practice Litigation and Arbitration, Mining, Patent, Taxation, Trademark, Reorganization, Unfair Competition.
Avocats à la Cour d'Appel de Paris, Firm Admitted to appear before French and European Community Court.

MEMBERS OF FIRM

P. GIDE (1886-1964).

JEAN LOYRETTE, born May 1, 1927; admitted, 1950, Paris. *Education:* University of Paris (Licentiate in Law, 1948); School of Political Sciences (Diplome, 1948; D.E.S., 1949); Oxford University, England (Doctor of Letters, 1952).

PHILIPPE NOUEL, born July 21, 1926; admitted, 1954, Paris. *Education:* University of Paris (Licentiate in Law, 1947; D.E.S., Private Law, 1948; D.E.S., Public Law, 1948). Barrister-at-Law, Lincoln's Inn, 1953. C.P.A., Paris Chamber of Commerce, 1957. Member, Council of the Bar of Paris, 1982.

BERNARD BUISSON, born July 3, 1936; admitted, 1961, Paris. *Education:* University of Paris (Licentiate in Law, 1957; Doctor of Law, 1959); Institute of Comparative Law, New York University, U.S.A.

XAVIER DE ROUX, born December 4, 1940; admitted, 1962, Paris. *Education:* University of Paris (Licentiate in Law, 1961). Author: "Les contrats franco-soviétiques de biens d'equipements," 1970, Ed. Joly; "Le droit de la concurrence des Communautés Européennes," 4ème èd., 1982, Ed Joly; "Le droit français de la concurrence et de la consommation," 4ème Ed., 1986, Ed. Joly; Dictionnaire Joly-Concurrence, 1988, Ed. Joly; "L'acte unique européen," 1989. Secretary, Conférence du Stage, 1964-1965; Member of Parliament.

JACQUES GRANDBOIS DE VILLENEUVE, born August 8, 1937; admitted, 1962, Paris. *Education:* University of Paris (Licentiate in Law, 1957; Doctor of Law, 1960; D.E.S. in Economics, 1961); McGill University, Montreal, Quebec (Master of Law, 1962). Lecturer, University of Cameroon, Africa, 1963-1964.

BERTRAND NOUEL, born June 12, 1939; admitted, 1966, Paris. *Education:* University of Paris (Licentiate in Law, 1963; D.E.S., Private Law, 1964).

JACQUES TERRAY, born October 1, 1937; admitted, 1965, Paris. *Education:* University of Paris (Licentiate in Law, 1960; D.E.S., Private Law, 1961); Columbia University, U.S.A. (M.C.L., 1965). Author: "La titrisation des crédits," 1990.

FRANKLIN RIST, born July 14, 1942; admitted, 1965, Paris. *Education:* University of Paris (Licentiate in Law, 1964; D.E.S., Private Law, 1965).

BERNARD CAILLAUD, born July 17, 1937; admitted, 1972, Paris. *Education:* University of Bordeaux, (Licentiate in Law, 1959; Doctor of Law, 1965).

GERARD TAVERNIER, born January 11, 1942; admitted, 1969, Lyon; 1970, Paris. *Education:* University of Lyon (Licentiate in Law, 1964; D.E.S., Private Law, 1965; Doctor of Law, 1967); Institut d'Etudes Politiques (1962).

DOMINIQUE VOILLEMOT, born May 12, 1939; admitted, 1967, Paris. *Education:* University of Paris (Licentiate in Law, 1965; D.E.S., Private Law, 1966); Institut d'Etudes Politiques (Diplome, 1966); des hautes Etudes Internationales (Diplome, 1966). Author: "Le droit de la concurrence des Communautés Européennes," 4ème éd., 1982, Ed. Joly; "Le droit français de la concurrence et de la consummation" 4ème Ed., 1986, Ed. Joly; Dictionnaire Joly-Concurrence, 1988, Ed. Joly; "Le Règlement CEE antidumping," 1989, Ed. Joly.

JEAN-MARIE BURGUBURU, born August 4, 1945; admitted, 1966, Paris. *Education:* University of Paris (Licentiate in Law, 1966; D.E.S., Private Law, 1967; D.E.S., Criminal Law, 1968). *Member:* AFPPI; AIPPI; APRAM (Secretary of the French National Group).

(This Listing Continued)

MARC DONATO, born August 21, 1948; admitted, 1970, Paris. *Education:* University of Nice (Licentiate in Law, 1970).

THIERRY JACOMET, born October 27, 1944; admitted, 1970, Paris. *Education:* Faculté Droit de Paris (Licentiate in Law, 1966); Columbia University, U.S.A. (M.C.L., 1967; D.E.S., Droit Privé; Licence d'Anglais, 1968). Co-Author: "Les Relations financières avec l'étranger," Ed. Joly; "Joint-ventures in Europe," Butterworths.

NOËL CHAHID-NOURAÏ, born Teheran, Iran, December 24, 1942; admitted, 1992, Paris. *Education:* Institut d'Etudes Politiques, Paris (1962); DES de Droit Public (1964); Ecole Nationale d'Administration, Paris (1967-1969). Co-Author: "Fiscalité internationale," Ed. E.F.E.; "Optimisation fiscale et abus de droit," Ed. E.F.E. Technical Advisor, Minister of Information, 1973-1974. Deputy Director and Deputy Director General, National Cinematographic Center, 1977-1982. Legal Advisor, Minister of Foreign Affairs, 1974-1977. Principal Private Secretary to Mr. Jobert, Minister of External Trade, 1982-1983. Government Commissioner, Taxation Commissions, Financial Section, 1984. Principal Reporter, Taxation of Inheritances, Aicardi Commission, 1986-1987. Member, Taxation Advisory Council, 1991.

EMMANUEL FONTAINE, born June 3, 1944; admitted, 1973, France. *Education:* University of Paris Law School (Diplome d'etudes supérieures, 1968); Institut d'Etudes Politiques Paris (Diplome, 1968); University of California at Berkeley (LL.M., 1971).

JEAN-MICHEL LUCHEUX, born October 11, 1944; admitted, 1971, France. *Education:* Faculté de Droit, Paris (Docteur en Droit); Institut d'Etudes Politiques, Paris (Diplomé); Institut de droit des Affaires, Paris (Diplomé). Chargé de cours à l'Ecole National d'administration d'Alger, 1969-1970.

RICHARD BEAUVAIS, born April 27, 1946; admitted, 1974, France. *Education:* University of Caen (Licenciate in Law, 1969); University of Paris (Des droit privé Honour, 1971); Southwestern Legal Foundation, Dallas, Texas (1978); Cambridge CPE (1969). Author: "Taxation in France of Real Property Held by Non Reside Tax Management," International Journal, November, 1979. Lecturer: University of Arts, Business Institute IDA, 1972-1978; ESLSCA, 1976—; Seminar Service International, Taxation, 1979—; Institut de commerce International, Taxation. *Member:* International Fiscal Association. *LANGUAGES:* English and Spanish.

BRUNO DE CAZALET, born July 8, 1947; admitted, 1973, France. *Education:* Institut d'Administration des Enterprises, I.A.E. (Docteur en droit, licence es-sciences Economiques); Southwestern Legal Foundation, Dallas, Texas. Lecturer on Law, Institut de Commerce International. CIF-Export-Institut Francais d'Ingenierie. *Member:* Fondation International pour l'Enseignement du droit des Affaires (FIEDA). *LANGUAGES:* English and Spanish.

PHILIPPE DEROUIN, born Saint Germain en Laye, France, March 27, 1948; admitted, 1973, Paris. *Education:* Institut d'Etudes Politiques de Paris (Licencié in Economy, 1968); Paris University (Doctor of Law, 1976). Author: "La taxe sur la valeur ajoutée dans la C.E.E.," 1970; Co-Author: "Droit pénal de la fiscalité," 1989. Lecturer on Law, University of Lille, France, 1976-1982 and Paris XII, Saint Maur, 1979-1983. *Member:* International Bar Association; International Fiscal Association; Association Henri Capitant. *LANGUAGES:* French, English and Spanish.

FRÉDÉRIC WAPLER, born July 12, 1946; admitted, 1973, France. *Education:* University of Lille (Licenciate in Law, 1969); University of Paris (D.E.S., Public Law, 1970; D.E.S., Private Law, 1971); Institut d'Etudes Politiques (Diplome, 1971). Author: "Approche juridique du marché saoudien," DPCI, 1985; "Commerce et Implantation en Arabie Saoudite," Ed. Joly, 1989. Lecturer on Law, University of Paris, 1970-1972. *Member:* International Bar Association.

GILLES DUQUET, born Coulommiers, France, October 16, 1950; admitted, 1974, France. *Education:* University of Paris (Licentiate in Law, 1971; D.E.S. Droit Privé Affaires, 1973).

THIERRY VASSOGNE, born Paris, France, May 13, 1951; admitted, 1973, France. *Education:* University of Paris (Licentiate in Law, 1973).

HUBERT FLICHY, born June 13, 1949; admitted, 1974, France. *Education:* D.E.S. de Droit des Affaires, 1972. *LANGUAGES:* French and English.

PIERRE RAOUL-DUVAL, born September 30, 1950; admitted, 1976, Paris; Licensed Legal Consultant, 1985, New York. *Education:* University of Paris (License en Droit, 1972); London School of Economics (LL.M., 1973). *Member:* American Bar Association (Council Member, Section of

(This Listing Continued)

GIDE LOYRETTE NOUEL, Paris—Continued

International Law and Practice, 1986-1969); The Association of the Bar of the City of New York (Member, Foreign and Comparative Law Committee, 1986-1989); International Bar Association.

EDOUARD DIDIER, born Paris, France, May 12, 1948; admitted, 1972, Paris. *Education:* University of Paris; Institut de droit Comparé (Licentiate in Law, 1972; DES droit prive, 1974). Co-Author: with Thierry Jacomet, "Les Relations Financières avec l'étranger," Editions July, 1982. *LANGUAGES:* French and English.

FRANCOIS KROTOFF, born Orléans, France, January 12, 1952; admitted, 1978, Paris. *Education:* Institut d'Etudes Politiques (Diplôme, 1975); University of Aix-en-Provence (Licentiate in Law, 1976). Co-Author: "Investir en Europe centrale et orientale," GLN.JOLY, 1992. Lecturer, Business Institute IDA, University of Paris. 1978-1979.

MATTHIEU DE BOISSESON, born Oloron, France, January 2, 1950; admitted, 1977, Paris. *Education:* Paris, Sorbonne (Agrégation de Lettres, 1974; Maîtrise de Philosophie, 1972) Institut d'Etudes Politiques (Diplôme, 1973); Paris II (Maîtrise de Droit, 1976). Author: "Le droit français de l'arbitrage interne et international," Ed. Joly, 1983-1990; Co-Author: "International commercial litigation," Butterworths, 1990. *Member:* Association Française d'arbitrage.

OLIVIER D'ORMESSON, born Rabat, Morocco, September 26, 1953; admitted, 1978, Paris; Licensed Legal Consultant, 1989, New York. *Education:* Ecole Supérieure de Commerce de Rouen (Degree in Finance, Accountancy, 1976; D.E.C.S., 1977); University of Paris (Maîtrise en droit, 1977). Author: "L'achat par des étrangers d'actions de sociétés privatisées au regard du droit français et du droit communautaire," Revue de droit des affaires internationales, 1987; "The commercial law of France," Digest of commercial laws of the world, 1991. Resident at New York Office, 1990-1992; Resident at Brussels Office, 1993—. *Member:* The Association of the Bar of the City of New York; New York State and American Bar Associations; AIJA. (Resident Partner, Brussels Office).

PHILIPPE XAVIER-BENDER, born Leopoldville, Zaire, April 1, 1949; admitted, 1974, Paris; Licensed Legal Consultant, 1993, New York. *Education:* University of Paris Nanterre (Licentiate in Law, 1972); Institut de Droit Comparé (Diplôme, 1973); Institut d'Etudes Politiques (1974). *Member:* The Association of the Bar of the City of New York; New York State and American Bar Associations; International Association of Young Lawyers (AIJA); International Bar Association. (Resident Partner, New York Office). *LANGUAGES:* English and German.

PIERRE-MARIE ROSSIGNOL, born Lyon, France, February 1, 1948; admitted, 1975, France. *Education:* University of Lyon (Licentiate in Law); Certificat d'Aptitude à la Profession D'Avocat (C.A.P.A) Paris. *Member:* Association Francaise de Droit Maritime.

PAUL-ANDRÉ NIVAULT, born Nice, France, January 21, 1954; admitted, 1981, Paris. *Education:* Faculté de Droit de Poitiers (Maîtrise Droit des Affaires, 1975; D.E.S. Droit Notarial, 1976); George Washington University, Washington, D.C. (M.C.L., 1979). Author: "L'Assurance crédit," 1990.

JEAN THIBAUD, born Neuilly-Sur-Seine, France, October 7, 1952; admitted, 1978, Paris. *Education:* University of Paris XII Sceaux (Maîtrise en Droit, 1977); University of Paris II (Certificat d'Etudes Judiciaires, 1977); Southwestern Legal Foundation, Dallas, Texas (1984). *Member:* The Association of the Bar of the City of New York. *LANGUAGES:* French and English.

CHARLES-HENRI LEGER, born Paris, France, April 29, 1956; admitted, 1981, Paris. *Education:* Ecole des Mines de Paris (Civil Engineer, 1978); University of Paris II (Maîtrise, 1980; Diplome d'Etudes Approfondies Droit International, 1982); INALCO (Diplome de Chinois, 1982). Charge de Cours (Lecturer), Commerciales (HEC), Ecole des Hautes Etudes, 1986—. *Member:* Paris Bar. *LANGUAGES:* English and Chinese (Mandarin).

ARNAUD MICHEL, born Cameroons, June 5, 1956; admitted, 1980, Paris. *Education:* University of Paris II (Degree in International Public Law; Master in International Private Law) Law School of Paris, University of Paris II (Degree, 1979). Lecturer on French Law, Exeter University, 1979-1980 and Law Society of London. *Member:* AIPPI (French Group); APRAM, Trademark Law Practitioners. *LANGUAGES:* French and English.

MICHEL PITRON, born Nice, France, August 19, 1954; admitted, 1981, France. *Education:* Paris (Diplome d'Etude Approfondie de Droit des

(This Listing Continued)

Affaires and Diplome de l'Institut d'Etudes Politiques, 1978); Southwestern Legal Foundation, Dallas (1985). Author: "Investir en Indochine," Ed. Joly, 1993. (Partner in Charge, Hanoi Office). *LANGUAGES:* French and English.

SYLVIE AZOULAY, admitted, 1972, Paris.

GRÉGOIRE TRIET, born May 4, 1954; admitted, 1980, Paris. *Education:* University of Paris II (Licenciate in Law, 1978; Master in Law, 1979); Institut d'Etudes Judiciaires (Certificate, 1979).

THIERRY BALLET, born Paris, France, June 22, 1953; admitted, 1981, Paris. *Education:* Université de Paris XI (Maîtrise); Institut d'Etudes Politiques de Paris; Université de Paris I (D.E.S.S., 1981); Columbia University, New York (A.L.P., 1984). Lecturer on Law, Université de Paris I, 1985-1988. *LANGUAGES:* French, English and German.

PHILIPPE GEORGIADES, born June 11, 1954; admitted, 1979, Paris. *Education:* Universite Paris I (Maîtrise de droit des affaires, 1977). *LANGUAGES:* French and English.

JEAN-JACQUES RAQUIN, born November 27, 1957; admitted, 1981, Paris. *Education:* Universite Paris II (Maîtrise). *LANGUAGES:* English and Spanish.

LAURENT J. DERUY, born Bethune, France, May 5, 1956; admitted, 1989, Paris. *Education:* Ecole Normale Supérieure (1978-1982); Institut d'Etudes Politiques de Paris (1979); Université de Paris II (Maîtrise in public law; Maîtrise in private law, 1980); Diplôme d'Etudes Approfondies in public law , 1982; Agrégation de Philosophie, 1981; Ecole Nationale d'Administration (1983-1985). Lecturer: Université de Paris II; Institut d'Etudes Politiques de Pari s. Conseiller référendaire à la Cour des Comptes (Court of Accounts), 1985-1989. Special Counsellor to the Directeur Général of the Conseil Supérieur de l'Audiovisuel, 1988-1989. Member, Board of Auditors of the United Nations, New York, 1986-1988. *Member:* Paris Bar; International Bar Association (Vice-Chairman, Committee of Administration Law); Association pour le Droit Public de l'Entreprise (ADPE). *LANGUAGES:* French, English and German.

DIDIER LAIGO, born January 15, 1954; admitted, 1984, Paris. *Education:* University of Rennes (Maîtrise en Droit; Diplôme d'Etudes Approfondies en Droit des Affaires); Law School of Saarbruecken, University of Saar, Germany (Degree). *LANGUAGES:* French, English and German.

BAUDOUIN DE MOUCHERON, born April 27, 1956; admitted, 1983, Paris. *Education:* Université de Paris II (Maîtrise); Institut d'Etudes Judiciaires, Paris; Centre de Formation Professionnelle des Barreaux du Ressort de la Cour d'Appel de Paris (1981). Former Secrétaire de la Conférence, Paris Bar, 1989.

KAMEL BEN SALAH, born Tunis, Tunisia, July 17, 1953; admitted, 1985, Tunisia; 1992, Paris. *Education:* University of Tunis (Maîtrise in Private Law, 1978); University of Paris II (Diplôme d'Etudes Approfondies (graduate degree) in General Private Law, 1980; Diplôme d'Etudes Approfondies (graduate degree) in Criminal Law, 1981). *LANGUAGES:* French, English and Arabic.

OLIVIER COUSI, born Paris, France, June 2, 1959; admitted, 1985, Paris. *Education:* Institut d'Etudes Politiques (Diplôme, 1983); University of Paris II (Diplôme d'Etudes Approfondies in Public Law, 1983); Institut Français de Presse (Diplôme, 1980); Institut Multi-Medias (Promotion Louis Lumiere, 1992). Former Secrétaire de la Conférence, Paris Bar, 1987. Co-Founder of the "Ligue d'Improvisation" of the Paris Bar, 1989. *LANGUAGES:* French and English.

JEAN-MARC DESACHE, born January 30, 1959; admitted, 1987, Paris. *Education:* Hautes Etudes Commerciales (Finance option) 1982; University of Paris I (Licenciate in Law; DECS and Certificat Supérieur de Relations Economiques, 1984; Diplôme d'Etudes Approfondies (graduate degree) in Private Law, 1987). *LANGUAGES:* French, English and German.

JEAN-GUILLAUME D'HEROUVILLE, born March 16, 1959; admitted, 1985, Paris; 1990, New York. *Education:* Institut d'Etudes Politiques, Paris (1980); University of Paris II (Licenciate in Law, 1980; Diplôme d'Etudes Approfondies (graduate degree) Droit des Affaires, 1982); Georgetown University (Master of Law, 1984). *LANGUAGES:* French, English and German.

YOUSSEF DJEHANE, born Tunis, Tunisia, December 4, 1959; admitted, 1987, Paris. *Education:* University of Paris I, Panthéon Sorbonne (Maîtrise de Droit Privé; D.E.A. Droit Privé, 1985). *LANGUAGES:* English.

(This Listing Continued)

ERIC GINTER, born Paris, France, December 17, 1953; admitted, 1992, Paris. *Education:* Institut d'Etudes Politiques, Paris (Diplôme, 1974); University of Paris (Licence d'histoire, 1975; Maîtrise de Sciences Economiques, 1976; Maîtrise en Droit, 1976). Ancien Élève de l'Ecole Nationale d'Administration, 1982.

GILBERT LADREYT, born Privas, France, August 29, 1958; admitted, 1985, Paris. *Education:* University of Strasbourg (Maîtrise de Droit des Affaires, 1980; Diplôme d'Etudes Comptables Supérieures, 1983; Certificat Supérieur Juridique et Fiscal, 1984). Member: Southwestern Legal Foundation, Dallas, 1987.

FRÉDÉRIC NOUEL, born Paris, France, June 8, 1961; admitted, 1985, Paris. *Education:* University of Paris X, Dauphine (Maîtrise Finances et Fiscalité, 1983); University of Paris X, Nanterre (Maîtrise de Droit); University of Paris I (D.E.A.; Droit des Affaires, 1985). *LANGUAGES:* English.

JEAN-CHRISTOPHE VALETTE, born Paris, France, March 17, 1959; admitted, 1985, Paris. *Education:* University of Paris II (Maîtrise en Droit, 1982; D.E.S.S. en Droit des Affaires et Fiscalité, 1984). *LANGUAGES:* German and English.

ASSOCIATES

Lamia Abillama; Nathalie Andrieux (Resident Associate, St. Petersburg Office); **Charles-Henri Arminjon; Olivier Assant** (Resident Associate, Brussels Office); **Ana Atallah; Isabelle Ayache; Daniel Azan** (Resident Associate, Prague Office); **Renaud Baguenault; Eliska Barthelemy** (Resident Associate, Prague Office); **Christophe Barut; Valérie Batigne; Astrid Baumgardner** (Resident Associate, New York Office); **Andréa Bayer** (Resident Associate, Budapest Office); **Hubert Bazin; Frédéric Beccaria; Aurélia Bejinariu; Emmanuelle Bely; Elyes Ben Mansour; Sandrine Besnard; Florence de Beughem d'Halluin; Nicolas Bichot; Antoine Bonnasse; Christophe Bornes; Eric Borysewicz; Andreï Bushev** (Resident Associate, St. Petersburg Office); **Jean-Pierre Bouère; Kiril Bougartchev; Aurélien Boulanger; Pierre Bourguignon** (Resident Associate, Brussels Office); **Didier Bracchi; Eva Branecka** (Resident Associate, Warsaw Office); **Grégoire Brizay; Hubert de Broca; Jean-Pascal Bus; Claire de Bussy; Lucie Buxtorf; Carole Cacheux; Laurent Caillaud** (Resident Associate, Brussels Office); **Christian Camboulive; Eric Cartier-Millon; Catherine Cathiard-Guillermin; Marc Chevallier; Antoine Choffel; Xavier Cledat; Vincent Cohen-Steiner; Antoine Colonna d'Istria; Laurence Costantini; Chautal Couteaux** (Resident Associate, Moscow Office); **Iwona Czarnecka; Philippe Dalpayrat** (Resident Associate, Tokyo Office); **Olivier Dauchez** (Resident Associate, Beijing Office); **Helen Davey; Olivier Diaz; Patrice Doat** (Resident Associate, Budapest Office); **Thierry Dor; Laurent Dubois** (Resident Associate, Tokyo Office); **Pierre Duprey; Arnaud Duhamel; Serge Durox; Stanislas Dwernicki** (Resident Associate, Warsaw Office); **Christophe Eck; Emmanuel Eslami; Philippe Esposito** (Resident Associate, Madrid Office); **Jean-Jacques Essombe; Mathieu Fabre-Magnan** (Resident Associate, Moscow Office); **Anne-Laure Fantova** (Resident Associate, Prague Office); **Emmanuel Fatome; Rémy Fekete; Véronique Froding; Sophie Gaignard; Marielle Garot; Marie-France Gaujal-Joseph; Isabelle Gavanon; Mathieu Geny** (Resident Associate, Tokyo Office); **Pierre Gissinger; Bruno Gloaguen** (Resident Associate, Riyadh Office); **Grégoire Goussu; Stéphane Grand** (Resident Associate, Beijing Office); **Joël Grangé; Marek Grodek** (Resident Associate, Warsaw Office); **Michel Guenaire; Katia Guendzekhaze** (Resident Associate, Moscow Office); **Jacques-Philippe Gunther** (Resident Associate, Brussels Office); **Benoît Herault; Dan Huang** (Consultant, Beijing Office); **Zhen Huang; Marie-Pia Hutin; Christophe Jacomin; Valerie Jamot; Gerard Jeanpierre; Dominique Jolivet; Xavier de Kergommeaux; Helena Kheifets** (Resident Associate, Moscow Office); **Christine Korsbaek; Arnaud de La Cotardiere; Pascale Lagesse-Cotty; Ruth Lansner** (Consultant, New York Office); **Amina Larbi; Emmanuel Larère; Charlotte Lavedrine; Nathalie Legendre; Emeric Lepoutre; Marc Loy; Fabrice de La Morandiere; Pierre-Yves Lucas; Stéphane Luo** (Resident Associate, Beijing Office); **Carole Malinvaud; Eric Malinvaud** (Resident Associate, New York Office); **Frédéric Marchand; Benoît Marcilhacy; Didier G. Martin; Eric Martin-Imperatori; Hugues Mathez** (Resident Associate, New York Office); **Philippe Matignon; Marzena Matuszyk** (Resident Associate, Warsaw Office); **Lucie Maurel-Aubert; Arwid Mednis** (Resident Associate, Warsaw Office); **Philippe Mezin; Geneviève Milhau; Philippe Montanier; Siamak Mostafavi; Michaëla Mozerova** (Resident Associate, Prague Office); **Alexandra Nesterenko** (Resident Associate, St. Petersburg Office); **Philippe Netto; Xavier Perinne; Benoît Philippe; Cécile Pinaire; Dominique Pinault; Hervé Pisani; Ilana Polne; Hugues de Pommereau; François Poudelet; David Preat; Olivier Puech; Philippe Rames; Jean-Claude Rivalland; Jean Rossi; Guillaume Rougier-Brierre** (Resident Associate, Warsaw Office);

(This Listing Continued)

Piotr Sadownik (Resident Associate, Warsaw Office); **Rachid Safa; Gilles Saint-Marc; Joëlle Salzmann; Hugues Scalbert** (Resident Associate, Riyadh Office); **Jacques de Servigny** (Resident Associate, Budapest Office); **Yves Sexer; Jean-Emmanuel Skovron; Denis Sukhanov** (Resident Associate, Moscow Office); **Guenhaëlle Surpas-Lemonnier; Anne Syrota; Gérard Tantin; Nicolas de la Taste** (Resident Associate, Prague Office); **Claire Thomassin; Anna Tomaszewska; Dariusz Tokarczuk** (Resident Associate, Warsaw Office); **François Veit; Stéphane Verney; Antoine Vignial; Anne Wachsmann** (Resident Associate, Brussels Office); **Natasha Wauthion; Frédérique Weber de Chambure; Lan Yan; Sabine Yu; Nicole Zerah.**

GINESTIE & ASSOCIES

Established in 1982

8, RUE MURILLO
75008 PARIS, FRANCE
Telephone: (33-1) 47.54.92.92
Telecopier: (33-1) 46.22.25.08; 46.22.59.14

French, EC and International Business Law, Litigation, Arbitration, Corporate Law, Tax Law, Legal Organization of Corporate Control and Management Power, Mergers and Acquisitions, Investment Funds, Financing and Banking Law, Stock Exchange Law, Insurance Law, Intellectual Property Law, Trademarks, Medical Law, Civil Law and Competition Law, Extradition, Human Rights and International Criminal Law.

MEMBERS OF FIRM

PHILIPPE GINESTIE, born Montpellier, France, January 1, 1943; admitted, 1982, Paris. *Education:* University of Montpellier (Licence en Droit, 1964; Diplôme d'Etudes Supérieures de Sciences Economiques, 1967; Diplôme d'Etudes Supérieures de Droit, 1977)); Institut de Préparation aux Affaires (CAAE, 1964); Paris Ecole des Hautes Etudes Commerciales (Diplôme, 1966); Harvard Business School (MBA, 1973); Harvard Law School (International Tax Program, 1973). Lecturer, Business and Law, University of La Paz, Bolivia, 1967-1968. Legal Adviser, 1973-1982. *LANGUAGES:* French, English and Spanish.

CATHERINE PALEY-VINCENT, born Paris, France, May 12, 1945; admitted, 1967, Paris. *Education:* University of Paris I Panthéon-Sorbonne (Licence en Droit, 1967). Premier Secrétaire de la Conférence des Avocats à la Cour d'Appel de Paris, 1971-1972; Member, Conseil de l'Ordre des Avocats à la Cour d' Appel de Paris, 1989-1991. Président de la Commission de Déontologic de l'Ordre des Avocats, 1990-1991. *LANGUAGES:* French.

FRANCOISE CIAUDO-GINESTIE, born Beirut, Lebanon, February 19, 1947; admitted, 1977, Paris. *Education:* University of Lyon (Licence en Droit, 1968). *LANGUAGES:* French, English, Italian and German.

GATIENNE BRAULT, born Saint-Cloud, France, November 10, 1960; admitted, 1986, Paris. *Education:* University of Paris IX (Maîtrise en Droit des Affaires, 1983); Institut Supérieur d'Interprétariat et de Traduction (Diplôme, 1983); University of Paris I Panthéon-Sorbonne (Diplôme d'Etudes Approfondies de Droit des Affaires, 1984). *LANGUAGES:* French, English, German.

ANNE DABEZIES, born Paris, France, July 17, 1958; admitted, 1981, Paris. *Education:* Institut d'Etudes Politiques de Paris (Diplôme, 1978) University of Paris II (Maîtrise en Droit Privé, 1980); University of Paris I Panthéon-Sorbonne (Diplôme d'Etudes Approfondies de Droit Anglais et Américain des Sociétés, 1981); Georgetown Law School (Summer Program, 1982). *LANGUAGES:* French and English.

CATHERINE OTTAWAY, born Saint-Cloud, France, May 14, 1960; admitted, 1984, Paris. *Education:* University of Paris II (Maîtrise en Droit Privé, 1982; Diplôme d'Etudes Supérieures Spécialisées de Droit des Assurances, 1983). *LANGUAGES:* French and English.

RICHARD RENAUDIER, born Le Mans, France, October 7, 1960; admitted, 1988, Paris. *Education:* University of Montpellier (Maîtrise en Droit Privé, 1984); University of Aix-en-Provence (Diplôme de Juriste Conseil d'Entreprise, 1985; Diplôme d'Etudes Supérieures Spécialisées de Droit des Affaires et Fiscalité, 1985). *LANGUAGES:* French and English.

DANY COHEN, born Cairo, Egypt, 1953; admitted, 1975, Paris. *Education:* University of Paris XIII, Paris I and II (Diplôes d'études approfondies de droit public, 1976; de droit de l'environnement, 1977 et de droit privé général 1979; Docteur en droit, 1984). Lauréat de la Chancellerie des Universités de Paris; Secrétarie-rédacteur à la Conférence de la Haye de droit international privé, 1982-1985. Agrégé des Facultés de droit, 1984; Professeur à l'Université Paris XIII. Author: *La cour de cassation et la séparation des autorités administrative et judiciaire* (Economica, 1987). *Member:*

(This Listing Continued)

GINESTIE & ASSOCIES, Paris—Continued

L.L.A., Association internationale de droit pénal. *LANGUAGES:* French and English.

ASSOCIATES

SIMONE ARRIGHI DE CASANOVA, born Nîmes, France, March 16, 1942; admitted, 1988, Paris. *Education:* University of Montpellier (Certificats de Biologie et de Géologie, 1962); University of Paris II (Maîtrise en Droit Privé et des Affaires, 1974). *LANGUAGES:* French.

BRIGITTE BERDUGO, born Meknes, Morocco, March 7, 1955; admitted, 1989, France. *Education:* University of Angers (Maîtrise en Droit des Affaires, 1981); University of Paris V (Diplôme d'Etudes Supérieures Spécialisées de Fiscalité Appliquée, 1986). *LANGUAGES:* French, Hebrew and English.

JEAN-LUC BLEIN, born Bordeaux, France, October 21, 1963; admitted, 1991, Paris. *Education:* University of Bordeaux (Diplôme d'Etudes Supérieures Spécialisées de Droit des Affaires et Fiscalité, 1986); University of Montpellier (Diplôme de Juriste Conseil d' Entreprise, 1987; Diplôme d'Etudes Supérieures Spécialisées de Juriste d'Affaires, 1987; Certificat Supérieur de Techniques Fiscales, 1987). *LANGUAGES:* French and English.

PASCALE FROSSARD, born Sallanches, France, April 14, 1963; admitted, 1993, Paris. *Education:* University of Lyon III (Maîtrise en Droit des Affaires, 1985); Institut des Relations Internationales, Dijon (Diplôme d'Etudes Supérieures Spécialisées des Carrières Juridiques du Commerce International, 1986); Institut d'Administration des Enterprises de Lyon II (Diplôme d'Etudes Supérieures Spécialisées, Certificat d'Aptitude à l'Administration des Entreprises, 1987). *LANGUAGES:* French and English.

DANIELE GANEM, born Paris, France, August 18, 1969. *Education:* University of Paris V (Maîtrise en Droit des Affaires, 1991; Diplôme d'Etudes Supérieures Spécialisées de Fiscalité Appliquée, 1993). *LANGUAGES:* French.

JEAN-CHRISTOPHE VIDAL, born Montpellier, France, March 20, 1961; admitted, 1986, Paris. *Education:* University of Paris II (Maîtrise en Droit Privé, 1982); University of Paris IX (Diplôme d'Etudes Supérieures Spécialisées de Fiscalité de l'Entreprise, 1984); Ecole des Hautes Etudes Commerciales HEC Paris (Diplôme, 1984); Ecole Supérieure de Sciences Economiques et Commerciales ESSEC Paris (Mastère de Techniques Financières, 1987). *LANGUAGES:* French, English and Italian.

LAURENT JOURDAN, born Paris, France, July 26, 1969; admitted, 1994, Paris. Docteur en droit, 1994. *Education:* University of Paris I, Panthéon-Sorbonne (Maîtrise en Droit des Affaires Internationales, 1991; Diplôme d'Etudes Approfondies de Droit des Affaires, 1992); Universities of Paris (Chargé d'Enseignement en Droit des Procédures Collectives since 1992). *LANGUAGES:* French.

ODILE PAOLETTI, born Boulogne, France, January 9, 1964; admitted, 1989, Paris. *Education:* University of Paris I Panthéon-Sorbonne (Maîtrise Carrières Judiciaires, 1985; Maîtrise en Droit Fiscal, 1986; Diplôme d'Etudes Supérieures Spécialisées de Droit des Affaires et Fiscalité, 1987). *LANGUAGES:* French and English.

SYLVIE VALLEIX, born Brive, France, August 5, 1964; admitted, 1992, Paris. *Education:* University of Paris II (Maîtrise Carrières judiciaires, 1987). Author: "Sociétés de personnes (SNC - SCS) : les associés" Jurisclasseur Editions Techniques - Droit des Sociétés, 1992. *LANGUAGES:* French and English.

CATHERINE LE GUEN, born Paris, France, August 4, 1960; admitted, 1986, Paris. *Education:* Maîtrise en Droit, 1982; Diplôme d'Etudes Approfondies de Droit des Affaires et Fiscalité, 1983; Diplôme de l'Institut de Droit des Affaires de Paris II, 1983. *Member:* Institut Francais des Practiciens des Procédures Collectives. *LANGUAGES:* French and English.

JEAN-MARC THOMAS, born Rabat, Morocco, March 12, 1962; admitted, 1992, Haut de Seine. *Education:* University of Lyon III (Maîtrise en Droits des Affaires, 1983; Diplôme de Terminologie Juridique Anglaise, 1983; Diplôme d'Etudes Supérieures Spécialisées Droit des Affaires et Fiscalité, 1984); Institut d'Administration des Entreprises Aix en Provence (Diplôme d'Etudes Supérieures Spécialisées: Certifcat d'Aptitude àl'Administration des Entreprises, 1986). *LANGUAGES:* French and English.

S.C.P. GIRARD - BOURNILHAS - CITRON

25 AVENUE DE L'OPÉRA
75001 PARIS, FRANCE
Telephone: (33-1) 42.96.16.33
Fax: (33-1) 42.96.17.34

General Business Law - Corporation, Tax and Customs. Arbitration and Investment Law. Mergers and Acquisitions.

JEAN-FRANÇOIS BOURNILHAS, born Courpiere (Puy De Dome), May 19, 1944; admitted, 1968, Paris, France. *Education:* Baccalauréat (1961); University of Clermont Ferrand (Licence en Droit, 1965); University of Paris (DES Droit Public, 1967; DES Droit Privé, 1968). Lecturer on Taxation Law, Orléans University (I.U.T. Bourges) and Institut National des Techniques Economiques et Comptables, Paris. *LANGUAGES:* French. *PRACTICE AREAS:* Tax Law; Customs Law; International Contracts Law; Corporation Law; Mergers and Acquisitions Law.

FRANÇOIS CITRON, born Paris, France, December 15, 1952; admitted, 1988, France. *Education:* University of Paris (Baccalauréat, 1972); University of Paris I (DEUG in Philosophy, 1974); University of Paris X (Licence en droit, 1984); University of Aix-en-Provence (Maîtrise en Droit, 1985; DEA de Droit Privé, 1986). *LANGUAGES:* French and English. *PRACTICE AREAS:* Customs Law; Transportation Law; General Business Law.

GIROUX, BUHAGIAR & ASSOCIES

Established in 1973

32 AVENUE GEORGES MANDEL
75116 PARIS, FRANCE
Telephone: (1) 44.05.38.90
Cable Address: "Counsel" Paris
Telex: 630922 F
Telecopier: (1) 44.05.38.70 - 44.05.38.71

French and General International Practice. Avocats à la Cour de Paris. Firm engaged in French and General International Practice and admitted to appear before French and European Economic Community Courts.

FIRM PROFILE: Established in 1973, the firm acts as corporate counsel both for French and foreign companies. The firm advises in each area of business law (including tax and litigation...) and has a special experience in banking, finance and securities law.

MEMBERS OF FIRM

PHILIPPE GIROUX, born Paris, France, January 7, 1929; admitted, 1953, France. *Education:* Stanislas College, University of Paris Law School (Licencié en Droit, 1950; Diplôme d'Etudes Supérieures, 1952); Paris Institut des Hautes Etudes Internationales. *Member:* International Bar Association. *LANGUAGES:* French and English. *PRACTICE AREAS:* Banking; Securities and Finance; Mergers and Acquisitions.

MARIE-FRANCE MISEREY-SAULGRAIN, born Courville, September 22, 1941; admitted, 1963, France. *Education:* Lycee Pasteur and University of Caen Law School (Licencié en Droit, 1963). *Member:* International Bar Association. *LANGUAGES:* French. *PRACTICE AREAS:* Employment; Labour Law; Litigation.

JEAN-LOUP MONTIGNY, born Paris, France, August 3, 1934; admitted, 1969, France. *Education:* University of Paris Law School (Docteur en Droit). *LANGUAGES:* French and English. *PRACTICE AREAS:* Arbitration; Litigation.

OLIVIER EDWARDS, born Neuilly-sur-Seine, France, November 14, 1947; admitted, 1969, France. *Education:* University of Paris Law School (Licencié en Droit, 1968); City of London Polytechnic (Master of Arts, Business Law, 1973). *LANGUAGES:* French and English. *PRACTICE AREAS:* Corporate Mergers; Acquisitions.

PATRICK SINGER, born Boulogne-sur-Seine, France, May 11, 1951; admitted, 1976, France. *Education:* University of Paris Humanities and Law Schools (Licencié en Droit, 1971). *LANGUAGES:* French and English. *PRACTICE AREAS:* Banking; Securities and Finance; Tax; Mergers and Acquisitions.

PATRICK BONVARLET, born Paris, France, August 21, 1952; admitted, 1981, France. *Education:* University of Paris Law School (Maîtrise de Droit Privé, 1975; Diplôme d'Etudes Approfondies de Droit du Commerce International, 1976); Institut d'Etudes Judiciaires, Paris (1977). *LAN-*

(This Listing Continued)

GUAGES: French and English. **PRACTICE AREAS:** Banking; Securities and Finance; Mergers and Acquisitions.

PATRICK LE NEZET, born Paris, France, July 27, 1951; admitted, 1978, France. *Education:* University of Paris Law School (Maîtrise en Droit, 1974); Institut d'Etudes Politiques (1974-1976); Institut d'Etudes Judiciaires, Paris (1977). **LANGUAGES:** French and English. **PRACTICE AREAS:** Arbitration; Litigation.

JACQUELINE DUTHEIL DE LA ROCHERE, born Nîmes, France, December 18, 1940; admitted, 1962, France. *Education:* University of Paris Law School (D.E.S. de Droit Public; D.E.S. de Sciences Politiques); Institut d'Etudes Politiques (1960), Docteur en Droit (1967), Agrégée de Droit Public (1969). Professor and Honorary Dean, Faculté de Droit de l'Universite René Descartes, Paris V. *Member:* International Law Association. **LANGUAGES:** French and English. **PRACTICE AREAS:** Competition; European Community Law.

NICOLAS BOMBRUN, born Soisy-sous-Montmorency, France, February 26, 1958; admitted, 1988, France and New York. *Education:* University of Lyon, Law School (Licence en Droit, 1980; Maitrise de Droit des Affaires, 1981; D.E.S.S. de Droit des Affaires et de Fiscalité, 1982; D.J.C.E., 1982); New York University School of Law (Master of Comparative Jurisprudence, 1984). **LANGUAGES:** French and English. **PRACTICE AREAS:** Corporate; Mergers and Acquisitions.

CHRISTIAN NOUEL, born Paris, France, April 26, 1956; admitted, 1989, France as Tax Lawyer. *Education:* University of Economics, Paris (Maîtrise d'Economie Appliquée, 3ème cycle de gestion financière, Dauphine); Diplôme d'Etudes Comptables Supérieures (1984). **LANGUAGES:** French and English. **PRACTICE AREAS:** Tax.

ASSOCIATES

CATHERINE MUYL, born Vincennes, France, April 5, 1962; admitted, 1988, France. *Education:* University of Paris and London King's College (double degree in English and French law, 1985); Diplôme d'Etudes Approfondies de Droit des Affaires (1986). **LANGUAGES:** French and English. **PRACTICE AREAS:** Corporate; Intellectual Property.

CAROLE SANDÈRE-TERTRAIS, born Paris, France, July 6, 1959; admitted, 1984, Paris. *Education:* University of Paris Law School (Institut de Droit des Affaires, Section Expertise-Comptable, 1980; Maîtrise en Droit Fiscal des Affaires, 1981; D.E.S.S. Droit Fiscal, 1982; D.E.A. Droit Anglais et Nord-Américain des Affaires, 1984); Institut des Hautes Etudes Internationales, 1984. **LANGUAGES:** French and English. **PRACTICE AREAS:** Corporate; Mergers and Acquisitions.

ANTON THEODORE COMMISSARIS, born Auckland, New Zealand, February 27, 1961; admitted, 1985, New Zealand; 1991, United Kingdom; 1993, France. *Education:* University of Auckland (LL.B., Hons., 1984); University of Montpellier (Maîtrise de Droit Privé, mention Droit de l'Entreprise, 1991). **LANGUAGES:** French and English. **PRACTICE AREAS:** Banking; Securities and Finance; Mergers and Acquisitions.

Languages: French, English, German and Italian

J.C. GOLDSMITH & ASSOCIES

Société d'Avocats

Established in 1967

4, AVENUE VAN DYCK

75008 PARIS, FRANCE

Telephone: (1) 47.66.51.19

Telex: 290081 FRANL

Telecopier: (1) 46.22.53.98

General French, E.E.C. and International Law and Tax Practice including in particular International Contracts, Investments, Mergers and Acquisitions, Joint Ventures, Financing, Banking, Bankruptcy, Antitrust, Intellectual Property, Advertising, Entertainment, Trusts, Real Estate, Timeshare, Transfers of Technology, Tax Planning, Labor Law, Litigation and Arbitration.

Firm authorized to appear before French and E.E.C. Courts as Avocats à la Cour.

FIRM PROFILE: *Founded in 1967, the Firm specializes in international business and its various legal and tax dimensions. Its client base ranges from medium-sized companies to large corporations and multinational groups, also including private individuals faced with complex transnational problems. All members of the Firm work equally well in French and at*

(This Listing Continued)

---

least one of the following languages: English, German, Italian and Spanish.

JEAN-CLAUDE GOLDSMITH, born Paris, France, July 7, 1924; admitted, 1948, Paris, France. *Education:* University of Paris (Diplôme d'Etudes Supérieures in Mathematics, 1944; Master of Laws, 1946; Doctor of Laws, 1951). *Member:* International Arbitration Commission of the International Chamber of Commerce; The Chartered Institute of Arbitrators; Panel of Arbitrators, American Arbitration Association; London Court of International Arbitration; International Bar Association (Chairman of the Committee on Taxes, Section of Business Law, 1970-1982; Chairman of the Working Group on Mergers, Acquisitions and Takeovers, 1984-1986); International Fiscal Association; International Academy of Estate and Trust Law. Representative of the French Bar on the CCBE Special Committee for EEC Company Law. **LANGUAGES:** French and English. **PRACTICE AREAS:** International Contracts; Finance; Banking; International Taxation; Mergers and Acquisitions; Trusts; Timeshare; Intellectual Property; Litigation; International Arbitration.

ALAIN DE FOUCAUD, born Neuilly-sur-Seine, France, April 12, 1952; admitted, 1977, Paris. *Education:* University of Paris (Master of Laws, 1975); Centre d'Etudes Judiciaires (1975); Institut d'Etudes Politiques de Paris (1976). Lecturer, Chargé de Travaux Dirigés, University of Paris, 1980-1982. Associated with: Winthrop, Stimson, Putnam & Roberts, New York, 1982-1983; Hughes Hubbard & Reed, New York and Paris, 1983-1986. *Member:* Bureau de l'Association des Avocats-Conseils d'Entreprises; International Bar Association. **LANGUAGES:** French and English. **PRACTICE AREAS:** International Law; Finance; Mergers and Acquisitions; Joint Ventures; Bankruptcy; Corporate Litigation.

SERGE LAZAREFF, born Paris, France, November 8, 1926; admitted, 1946, readmitted, 1988, Paris. *Education:* University of Paris (Master of Laws, 1946; Doctor of Laws, 1948); Harvard Law School (Master of Laws, 1949). Author: "Le Statut des Forces de l'OTAN et son Application en France," 1964; "Status of Military Forces Under Current International Law," 1971. Legal Adviser to Commander-in-Chief NATO Allied Forces, Central Europe, 1952-1967. Pechiney, General Counsel-International Operations, Vice President Asia Pacific, 1967-1983. Counsel to Rogers & Wells, Paris, 1983-1988. Foreign Trade Adviser to French Government (Conseiller du Commerce Extérieur de la France). *Member:* International Arbitration Commission of the International Chamber of Commerce (Chairman, French International Arbitration Commission); Institute of International Business Law and Practice (Corresponding Member); American Arbitration Association Panel; Harvard Law School Association of Europe (Former President). **LANGUAGES:** French, English and Spanish. **PRACTICE AREAS:** International Contracts; Joint Ventures; International Arbitration.

ISABELLE SMITH MONNERVILLE, born Paris, France, March 4, 1959; admitted, 1984, Paris. *Education:* Institut d'Etudes Politiques de Paris (1980; Diplôme d'Etudes Supérieures Spécialisées in Foreign Trading, 1981); University of Paris (Master of Laws, 1982). *Member:* International Bar Association; AIPPI; ICC (Intellectual and Industrial Property French Commission; Commercial Practice International Commission). **LANGUAGES:** French and English. **PRACTICE AREAS:** Commercial and Corporate Law; Competition; Intellectual Property; International Contracts; Litigation.

THIERRY GILLOT, born Mazingarbe, France, July 19, 1958; admitted, 1992, Paris. *Education:* University of Paris (Master of Laws, 1981; Diplôme d'Etudes Approfondies in Private International Law, 1983). *Member:* International Bar Association. **LANGUAGES:** French and English. **PRACTICE AREAS:** International Contracts; Commercial and Corporate Law; Joint Ventures; Mergers and Acquisitions; Labor Law; Advertising; Entertainment Law.

ANTOINE FOURMENTIN, born Boulogne-sur-Mer, France, October 31, 1962; admitted, 1990, France. *Education:* University of Paris (Master of Laws, 1985; Diplôme d'Etudes Supérieures Spécialisées in International Business Law, 1987); Institut d'Administration des Entreprises de Paris (1987). **LANGUAGES:** French and English. **PRACTICE AREAS:** Commercial Law; Joint Ventures; Mergers and Acquisitions.

NICOLAS LE QUINTREC, born Paris, France, July 13, 1960; admitted, 1988, Paris. *Education:* University of Paris (Master of Laws, 1983; Diplôme d'Etudes Approfondies in Private International Law, 1984). **LANGUAGES:** French, English and German. **PRACTICE AREAS:** Commercial Law; International Contracts; Labor Law; Litigation.

FERDI M. TONGSIR, born Istanbul, Turkey, December, 1957; admitted, 1987, New York. *Education:* University of Paris (Master of Laws,

(This Listing Continued)

J.C. GOLDSMITH & ASSOCIES, Paris—Continued

1981); Harvard Law School (Master of Laws, 1983). French-Turkish Judge, United States Court of Appeals for the Fifth Circuit; Associated with: White & Case, New York, New York. *Member:* International Arbitration Commission of the International Chamber of Commerce; Commission on Multinational Enterprises and International Investment of the ICC; Harvard Law School Association of Europe; Association of Former Students of Lycée Henri IV, Paris. [J.A.G. Corps, U.S. Air Force, 1988-1991]. *LANGUAGES:* French, English and Turkish.

JANE WILLEMS, born Enghien, France, April 19, 1964; admitted, 1991, France. *Education:* University of Paris (Master of Laws, 1989; Diplôme d'Etudes Supérieures Spécialisées in International Business Law, 1990); Institut National des Langues Orientales (Licence in Chinese Language, 1986). *LANGUAGES:* French, English and Chinese Mandarin. *PRACTICE AREAS:* International Arbitration; Litigation.

PHILIPPE THOMAS, born Lyon, France, July 31, 1963; admitted, 1990, Paris. *Education:* University of Paris II (Master of Laws, 1986); Georgetown University (LL.M., 1990). *LANGUAGES:* French and English.

GERALDINE PEREZ, born Casablanca, Morocco, June 20, 1965; admitted, 1990, Paris. *Education:* University of Paris (Master of Laws, 1988; Diplôme d'Etudes Approfondies in Business Law, 1989; Diplôme d'Etudes Supérieures Spécialisées in Management of Public Enterprises, 1989). *LANGUAGES:* French, English and Italian.

CHRISTOPHE HUET, born Hennebont, France, March 7, 1961; admitted, 1991, Nanterre. *Education:* University of Rennes (Master of Laws, 1984; Diplôme d'Etudes Supérieures Spécialisées in Business Law, 1985; Diplôme de Juris Conseil d'Enterprise, 1985). Associated with: KMPG-Peat Marwick, 1987-1992. *LANGUAGES:* French and English. *PRACTICE AREAS:* International Taxation.

XAVIER SCULFORT, born Le Havre, France, September 1, 1965; admitted, 1994, Paris. *Education:* University of Paris (Master of Laws, 1989; Diplôme d'Etudes Approfondies in Business Law, 1990). *LANGUAGES:* French and English.

CLAUDE AMARDEIL, born Paris, France, August 14, 1967; admitted, 1993, Paris. *Education:* University of Paris (Master of Laws, 1990; Diplôme d'Etudes Supérieures Spécialisées in Business and Tax Law, 1991; Diplôme du Magistère de Juriste d'Affaires, 1991); University of Leiden (Erasmus International Exchange Program, 1991). *LANGUAGES:* French, English and German.

ANN CARY DANA, born New York, New York, July 23, 1948. *Education:* Mills College (Bachelor of Arts, 1970); Middlebury College (Master of Arts, 1971); University of Aix-en-Provence (Master of Laws, 1991); University of Exeter (Erasmus International Exchange Program, 1991). *LANGUAGES:* English, French and German.

CELINE PLANTARD, born Aix-en-Provence, France, March 9, 1967. *Education:* University of Aix-en-Provence (Master of Laws, 1989; Diplôme d'Etudes Supérieures, Spécialisées in International Business Law, 1990; Diplôme du Magistère de Droit des Affaires et Fiscalité Comptabilité, 1990); University of London (Master of Law, 1991). Associated with: Herbert Smith, London, 1991-1992. *LANGUAGES:* French and English.

YVES BARBERY, born Hennebont, France, June 25, 1964. *Education:* University of Paris (Master of Laws, 1986; Diplôme d'Etude Supérieures Spécialisées in Foreign Trade, 1987); Columbia University (Master of Laws, 1991). *LANGUAGES:* French and English.

HERVE BLATRY, born Paris, France, May 11, 1965; admitted, 1990, Paris. *Education:* University of Paris (Master of Laws, 1988); University of Kent at Canterbury (Bachelor of Arts in English Law, 1990). *LANGUAGES:* French and English.

MARTIN LABASTIE, born Boulogne-Billancourt, France, March 12, 1960; admitted, 1992, Paris. *Education:* University of Paris (Master of Laws, 1987; Diplôme d'Etudes Supérieures Spécialisées in International Taxation, 1988). Associated with: Coopers & Lybrand CLC Juridique et Fiscal, 1988-1993. *LANGUAGES:* French and English. *PRACTICE AREAS:* International Taxation.

GOODMAN PHILLIPS & VINEBERG
PARIS, FRANCE

(See Montreal, Quebec, Canada or Toronto, Ontario, Canada)

GOODRICH, RIQUELME Y ASOCIADOS

Established in 1971

15 RUE GREUZE
75116 PARIS, FRANCE
Telephone: (33 1) 47 27 0310
Fax: (33 1) 47 27 3781

Mexico, D.F., Mexico Office: Paseo de la Reforma 355 06500 México, D.F., México, P.O. Box 93-Bis, 06000 México, D.F., México . Telephone: (525) 533 00 40 to 55. Cable Address: "Godal". Telex: 17-61278 GRAME. Fax: (525) 525 12 27.

Tijuana, Baja California, Mexico Office: German Gedovius No. 10489-201, Zona del Río, 22320. Telephone: (52 66) 84 72 61; 84 29 43. Fax: (52 66) 84 03 82. U.S.A. Mailing Address: P.O. Box 43 4307 San Diego, California 92143-4307.

London, England Associated Office: Bomchil, Castro, Goodrich, Claro, Arosemena & Associates. 3rd Floor, Globe House, 4 Temple Place, WG2R 3HP. Telephone: (44 71) 240 17 55. Fax: (44 71) 240 18 08.

All Aspects of Mexican Law, French Corporate and Commercial Law, European Economic Community Law.
Admitted to practice in France as Avocats a la Cour de Paris.

FIRM PROFILE: *Goodrich, Riquelme y Asociados was founded in 1934, committed to serving the needs of Mexican and international business. It is one of Mexico's largest firms serving a broad international clientele and leading Mexican companies in every facet of manufacturing, agriculture, commerce and service industries. A number of our attorneys have lived, trained and are qualified to practice in other countries and are prepared to assist foreign business people to better understand "doing business in Mexico", and to help Mexican business people and government officials comprehend and evaluate foreigner's objectives. We take pride in our firm's role in Mexico's past and look forward to participating in Mexico's dynamic future.*

PARTNERS

David H. Brill, Jr.
Luis Capin Lopez

RESIDENT ASSOCIATE

Dulce Almeida

(For all Attorneys, see Professional Biographies at México, D.F., Mexico).

CABINET D'AVOCATS
EMILE E. GOUIRAN

Avocat à la Cour d'Appel

Attorney at Law

Of Counsel to U.S. Law Firms

146, RUE DU CHÂTEAU
75014 PARIS, FRANCE
Telephone: (33-1) 45.43.71.82
Fax: (33-1) 45.43.10.89 Modem: (33-1) 45.43.91.95

Civil and Criminal Litigation Practice. General French and American Law.

FIRM PROFILE: *Mr. Gouiran, a French citizen, has an extensive experience in the American and French trial courts and practices from his office in Paris. American and British clients primarily include those with interests in France and Europe. The firm houses complete French and American legal libraries, LEXIS, NEXIS, Jurisdata, LEXPAT and customized billing and reporting capabilities.*

(This Listing Continued)

EMILE E. GOUIRAN, born Washington, D.C., March 14, 1949; admitted, 1984, Paris. *Education:* The City University of New York (B.S., cum laude, 1980); New York Law School (J.D., cum laude, 1981). *Member:* International Bar Association. **LANGUAGES:** French and English. **PRACTICE AREAS:** Litigation; Banks and Banking; Corporate Law; Real Estate; Finance; Business Law; Criminal; Labor and Unemployment; Arbitration and Mediation; International Law.

ABEL SOUHAIR, born Morocco, December 31, 1956; admitted, 1986, Paris as Avocat à la Cour. *Education:* University of Bordeaux (Doctor of Law, Droit Privé, 1986; Doctor of French Literature, 1987). Curriculum Director and Instructor, Mans University of Law, 1992-1993. Groupe ESSEC, Ecole Supériore de Sciences Economiques, 1993-1994. *Member:* National Association of Doctors of Law. **LANGUAGES:** French and Arabic. **PRACTICE AREAS:** Labor Law; Immigration Law.

DONNA HOPE LINSK, born Denville, New Jersey, September 1, 1966; admitted, 1992, California. *Education:* University of California, Santa Barbara (B.A., 1988); Hastings College of Law (J.D., 1991). *Member:* State Bar of California. **LANGUAGES:** English and French. **PRACTICE AREAS:** Litigation; Criminal; Communications Law.

LAW OFFICES OF DAVID P. GRIFF

75 BOULEVARD MALESHERBES
75008 PARIS, FRANCE
Telephone: (331) 45.22.93.52
Telecopier: (331) 45.22.18.40

General Commercial Practice. International Law.

DAVID P. GRIFF, born Monticello, New York, USA, August 16, 1940; admitted, 1968, New York; 1975, France (Conseil Juridique); 1992, France (Avocat). *Education:* Princeton University (A.B., 1962); Institut d'Etudes Politiques de Paris (Diplôme, 1964); Harvard Law School (LL.B., 1967). Author: "Le Venture Capital et l'Experience américaine," 1974, Le Financement de l'Innovation et le Capital Risque, published by Chambre Nationale des Conseillers Financiers. **LANGUAGES:** French and English.

GÉRARD GUILLOT
PARS ASSOCIATES

Established in 1979

33 RUE DE LA BIENFAISANCE
75008 PARIS, FRANCE
Telephone: 33.1.43 59 15 70
Fax: 33.1.42 56 14 80

Tehran, Iran Office: Pars Associates. 12 Moghan Street, 4th Street, Zartosht Avenue, P.O. Box 11365-6665. Telephone: 98.21.651169. Fax: 98.21.657197. Telex: 212107 MATN IR.

International Business and Tax Laws. Iranian, Islamic, Middle East Laws. Foreign Investments, International Litigation, International Successions, Fiduciary Activities.

FIRM PROFILE: Firm established in 1979 in Tehran and in 1980 in Paris. The main office is in Tehran. The Paris branch developed activities with the Middle East and Islamic countries in general. It has correspondents in the Gulf area. Editor of the Iranian codes and of a weekly legal and tax bulletin in English.

MEMBERS OF FIRM IN PARIS

Gérard Guillot   Marie Patrice Lassauzet

MEMBERS OF FIRM IN TEHRAN

Zoreh Majdzadeh   Reza Matine
                M. Khajeh Nouri

HANOTIAU, BRUYNS ET ASSOCIATES

14, AVENUE GOURGAUD
F-75017 PARIS, FRANCE
Telephone: 33-1-44 156100
Fax: 33-1-44 159181

Brussels, Belgium Office: 391, Avenue Louise (B-11), B-1050. Telephone: 32-2-640 3525. Fax: 32-2-648 5086.

(This Listing Continued)

General EEC, International and National Commercial Practice, Taxation, Corporate, Mergers and Acquisitions, Banking, Commercial Arbitration and Litigation, Competition, Computer Law, Trademarks, Patents and Copyright Law, Real Estate.

MEMBERS OF FIRM

BERNARD HANOTIAU, born Charleroi, Belgium, August 10, 1947; admitted, 1975, Brussels; 1988, Paris. *Education:* University of Louvain (Dr. Juris, 1970; Special Degree in Labour Law, 1972; Ph.D., Private International Law, 1979); Southern Methodist University Academy of American and International Law (1971); Columbia University School of Law (LL.M., 1973). Author: "Les Problèmes de Sécurité Sociale des Travailleurs Migrants," 1973, Le Droit International Privé Americain, 1979. Co-Author: "Le Droit des Contrats Informatiques," 1983. Professor of Law, Universities of Louvain-La-Neuve and Namur. **LANGUAGES:** English, French and Flemish. **PRACTICE AREAS:** Arbitration; International Commercial Law; Banking Law.

STANISLAS VAN WASSENHOVE, born Leuven, Belgium, September, 1958; admitted, 1981, Brussels; 1990, Paris. *Education:* University of Louvain (Dr.Jr., 1981: Dr. Jr. in International public affairs, 1982). **LANGUAGES:** English, French and Flemish. **PRACTICE AREAS:** Labour and Social Security Law.

HELDENSTEIN

7, RUE ROYALE
75008 PARIS, FRANCE
Telephone: 33-1-42 65 03 71
Telecopier: 33-1-42 65 03 88

Luxembourg, Luxembourg Office: 5 Boulevard Royal, L-2449 Telephone: 352- 22 05 82. Fax: 352-22 05 83.

The firm handles both matters in Luxembourg and French law, mainly in the financial area.
Securities and Negotiable Instruments, Financial Futures and other Derivative Products, Banking, Stock Market Regulation, Tax Planning, Formation of Investment Funds, Investment Trusts and Holding Companies, International Trade and Financial Litigation.

GEORGES HELDENSTEIN, born Luxembourg, Luxembourg, December 22, 1951; admitted, 1976, Luxembourg; 1986, Paris. *Education:* Faculté de Droit de l'Université Paris II (Maîtrise, 1975); Institut d'Etudes Politiques de Paris (Diplôme, 1975); Harvard Business School (M.B.A., 1978). *Member:* Belgium-Luxembourg Chamber of Commerce in France (Director). **LANGUAGES:** English, French and German. **PRACTICE AREAS:** Securities; Commodities Futures Law; Brokerage Law; Banking Law; Taxation of Individuals and Business Entities.

HÉLÈNE HELWASER

52, RUE ETIENNE MARCEL
75002 PARIS, FRANCE
Telephone: (33-1) 40 28 09 00; (33-1) 42 21 15 98
Fax: (33-1) 40 28 09 75

General French and International Law Practice, Civil and Commercial Law, Acquisitions, Copyright, Patent and Trademark Law, Relations and Labor Law, Bankruptcy, Agency and Franchise Law, Contracts Law, Litigation, Commercial Lease Law.

HÉLÈNE HELWASER, born Paris, France, November 23, 1946; admitted, 1985, Paris and Bar of the Court of Appeal of Paris. *Education:* Ecole de Haut Enseignement Commercial pour Jeunes Filles (HEC JF, 1968); Diplôme d'Etudes Comptables Supérieures (DECS, 1981); University of Paris Law School (LL.B., 1981; LL.M., 1982); Diplôme d'Etudes Approfondies (D.E.A., Commercial and Economic Law, 1985). Author: "La Publicité à la Télévision"; "l'Alimentation Infantile," 1968; "Un Investissement Communautaire en France," 1984. **LANGUAGES:** French and English.

CATHERINE ETIEVE, born Argenteuil, France, November 20, 1961; admitted, 1990, Paris and Bar of the Court of Appeal of Paris. *Education:* University of Paris Law School (LL.B., 1982; LL.M., 1984); Diplôme d'Etudes Approfondies (D.E.A., Commercial and Economic Law). Author: "Les clauses abusives," 1984; "L'escroquerie aux ASSEDIC," 1989. **LANGUAGES:** French, English and German.

(This Listing Continued)

HÉLÈNE HELWASER, Paris—Continued

VÉRONIQUE HABIBOU, born Dugny, France, April 25, 1964; admitted, 1991, Paris and Bar of the Court of Appeal of Paris. *Education:* University of Paris Law School (LL.M., 1987); Diplôme d'Etudes Approfondies (D.E.A., Commercial and Economic Law, 1988). Author: "La rémunération des Agents Immobiliers," 1990. *LANGUAGES:* French, English and Hebrew.

AXIELLE DREVON, born Laval, France, November 22, 1964; admitted, 1992, Paris and Bar of the Court of Appeal of Paris. *Education:* University of Paris Law School (LL.M., 1987); Diplôme d'Etudes Approfondies (D.E.A., Commercial and Economic Law, 1988). Author: "La rupture du contrat de franchise," 1988. *LANGUAGES:* French, English and Spanish.

CABINET YVES P. HENAFF

Avocat à la Cour, Attorney at Law

27, AVENUE KLÉBER
75116 PARIS, FRANCE
Telephone: (33-1) 44 05 08 98
Telex: HENLAW 644777 F
Fax: (33-1) 44 05 09 18

French and International Business Law, Commercial Contracts and Corporate Law, Counsel, Negotiation, Litigation and Arbitration. International Investments, Foreign Corporations, Conflict of Laws, Aviation and Aircraft Law, Banking and Financing, Trademarks, Licensing and Distribution, Unfair Competition and Antitrust, Computers and Software, Products Liability, Industrial Property and Liability, Criminal Law, Labor Law, Bankruptcy, Environmental Law, Common Market.

YVES P. HENAFF, born Courbevoie, France, June 19, 1951; admitted, 1981, Paris; 1984, New York. *Education:* University of Paris I Panthéon-Sorbonne (Masters of Law, 1979; D.E.A. in Business Law, 1980); Institute of Criminology of Paris (Certificate of Criminology, 1980; Certificate of Criminal Sciences, 1980); Institute of International and Comparative Law, University of San Diego, School of Law, Paris Center (1980); Institute of Comparative Law of Paris University (1982). New York University School of Law (Visiting Scholar, International Law, LL.M. Division, 1980-1981). Co-author, "Aircraft Finance, Registration, Security and Enforcement," Longman editor, London. Lecturer, University of Paris I, Panthéon-Sorbonne, Chargé de Travaux Dirigés, Business and Corporate Law, 1982-1985. *Member:* New York State Bar; Bar of the Court of Appeals of Paris; International Commission of the Paris Bar Committee. *LANGUAGES:* French and English.

HENRY SAUTEREAU

8 RUE DE MONDOVI
75001 PARIS, FRANCE
Telephone: 33 1 42 96 15 12
Telecopier: 33 1 40 20 99 12

General French, European Economic Community and International Law Practice.

MEMBERS OF FIRM

HELENE HENRY, born Paris, France, May 9, 1950; admitted, 1976, Paris. *Education:* AFS International Scholarships (1969); Institut d'Etudes Politiques de Paris, section Ecofi (1972), University of Paris (Licence en droit, 1975). *Member:* International Bar Association; Union Internationale des Avocats. *LANGUAGES:* French and English. *PRACTICE AREAS:* Corporate Law; Trademark Law; Commercial Litigation.

GERARD SAUTEREAU, born Paris, France, April 30, 1948; admitted, 1972, Paris. *Education:* AFS International Scholarships (1966), University of Paris (Licence en droit, 1972), Centre d'Etudes des Communautés Européennes (1972). Member, Advisory Editorial Board, "Journal of International Franchising & Distribution Law." *Member:* International Bar Association; Union Internationale des Avocats. *LANGUAGES:* French, English and Spanish. *PRACTICE AREAS:* Distribution Law; Franchising Law; Commercial Litigation.

HERBERT SMITH

41 AVENUE GEORGE V
75008 PARIS, FRANCE
Telephone: 3314-723-9124
Telex: 219602
Fax: 3314-720-9213

London, England Office: Exchange House, Primrose Street, EC2A 2HS. Telephone: 071-374-8000. Telex: 886633. Fax: 071-496-0043.
Hong Kong Office: 17th Floor, Edinburgh Tower, 15 Queen's Road Central. Telephone: 852-8456639. Telex: 72266. Fax: 852-8459099.
Brussels, Belgium Office: 15, Rue Guimard, 1040. Telephone: 322-511 7450. Fax: 322-511 7772.

Firm engaged in English and General International Law Practice. All resident partners are authorized to appear before the French Courts as Advocats.

RESIDENT PARTNERS

N.J. Brimson	P.M.C. Trosset
I.F.B. Gosling	A.R. Morley

(For List of Partners see Professional Biographies at London, England)

HEUKING KÜHN CELESTINE & ASSOCIÉS

3, AVENUE DU PRESIDENT WILSON
F-75116 PARIS, FRANCE
Telephone: 33(1) 40 70 91 90
Fax: 33(1) 40 70 92 11

Düsseldorf, Germany Office: Heuking Kühn Kunz Wojtek, Elisabethstrasse 16, D-40217. Telephone: 49 211 38 95 01. Telex: 8 588 247 jurad. Telefax: 49 211 37 06 44.
Frankfurt/Main, Germany Office: Heuking Kühn Kunz Wojtek, Lindenstrasse 37, D-60325. Telephone: (49) 69-975610. Fax:(49) 69-97561200.
Hamburg, Germany Office: Heuking Kühn Kunz Wojtek, Bleichenbrücke 9, D-20354. Telephone: 49 40 355 280 0. Telefax: 49 40 355 280 80.
Berlin, Germany Office: Karl-Liebknecht-Strasse 33, D-10178. Telephone: 49 30 238 616 1. Telecopier: 49 30 238 616 6.
Chemnitz, Germany Office: Heuking Kühn Kunz Wojtek, Weststr. 49, D-09112. Telephone: 49 371 902345. Fax: 49 371 902348.

Corporate, Banking, Tax, National and EC Antitrust, Mergers, Acquisitions, Intellectual Property, Unfair Competition and Trade Law, Commercial and International Law, EC Law, Environmental Law, Administrative Law, International Arbitration, Litigation, General Practice.

RESIDENT PARTNER

PATRICK CELESTINE, born Agen, France, August 25, 1950; admitted, 1975, Paris, France (Avocat à la Cour); 1990, Düsseldorf (Member Chamber of Bar). *Education:* Universities of Paris and Strasbourg, France (Maîtrise en Droit, Certificat d'Aptitude à la Profession d'Avocat, 1974; Diplôme d'Etudes Supérieures Spécialisées de Droit des Relations Commerciales, Industrielles et Financières Internationales, 1976); German Academic Exchange Service, Program of Legal Studies, Tübingen and Düsseldorf, 1974, 1975; Institut de Droit Comparé de Paris, 1979. Conseiller du Commerce Extérieur de la France (appointed by Government Decree, 1987). Author: "Die Stille Gesellschaft in Frankreich," 1979; "Die französische Gesellschaft bürgerlichen Rechts," 1980; "Gundstückserwerb in Frankreich," 1981: all in Internationale Wirtschaftsbriefe. Co-author: Die Garantie auf erstes Anfordern in der französischen Gerichtspraxis," Recht der Internationalen Wirtschaft, 1989; "La Pratique du Marché Allemand," 1980; "German Business Enterprises France," 1991. *LANGUAGES:* French, German and English. *PRACTICE AREAS:* Corporate Law; General Commercial Law; Mergers and Acquisitions.

OF COUNSEL

NICOLAS CHAMOZZI, born Paris, France, June 3, 1955; admitted, Paris, France; Avocat à la Cour. *Education:* University of Paris II Assas. Diplomas: (maîtrise en droit privé, 1977; D.E.A. de droit fiscal 1978); Graduate Tax Academy, 1979. 1980-1984, Tax Inspector: Direction de Vérifications nationales et internationales; Tax consultant since 1984. Chargé de cours (Adjunct Faculty) droit fiscal; Institut du droit des Affaires Université de Paris II Assas, 1986-1988; Université de Paris X Nanterre, 1988-

(This Listing Continued)

1990; since 1991, Chargé d'enseignement (Adjunct Faculty) Université de Paris Dauphine. *LANGUAGES:* French, English and German.

JEAN-GABRIEL CASTEL, O.C., Q.C., admitted, 1960, Ontario (Not admitted in France). *Education:* University of Paris (LL.B., 1950); University of Michigan (Juris Doctor, 1953); University of Harvard (Doctor Science Jurisprudence, 1957). Diplomas: Institute of Comparative Law, Paris; Institute of Comparative Law, Mexico. Fulbright Scholar; Commonwealth Scholar; Fellow of the Royal Society of Canada; Killam Senior Research Fellowship. LL.D. Honoris Causa, University Aix-Marseille, France, 1988. Appointed Queen's Counsel, 1980. Professor of Law, The Osgood Hall Law School of York University, 1959—. Editor of the Canadian Bar Review, 1957-1983. Canadian Editor, Journal du Droit International, Paris, 1970—. Member, Board of Editors, Canadian Yearbook of International Law, 1963—. Author: *Canadian Conflict of Laws,* Butterworth, 1986. Co-Author, *International Business Transactions and Economic Relations,* Emond Montgomery, 1987. Arbitrator for the Court of Arbitration of the International Chamber of Commerce, Paris, 1970—. Executive of Canadian Human Rights Foundation, 1982—. Member, Panel of Arbitrators, American Arbitration Association. Associate Member of the International Academy of Comparative Law; Académie du Var; Regional Centre for Commercial Arbitration, Kuala, Lumpur; Regional Center for Commercial Arbitration, Cairo. *LANGUAGES:* French, English, Italian.

(For Biographical Data of Düsseldorf Office, see Professional Biographies at Düsseldorf, Germany).

HOGAN & HARTSON L.L.P.

PARIS, FRANCE

(See Cabinet Wolfram)

General Practice, including International Public and Private Financings, Acquisitions, Commercial Transactions, Strategic Investments and Joint Ventures, and Litigation and Arbitration.

HOLMAN, FENWICK & WILLAN

3 RUE LA BOETIE
75008 PARIS, FRANCE
Telephone: 44-94-40-50
Telex: 281699F HFWPA A
Telefax: 42-65-46-25

London, England Office: Marlow House, Lloyds Avenue, EC3N 3AL. Telephone: 0171-488-2300. Telex: 8812247 HFWLON. Telefax: 0171 481 0316.
Hong Kong Office: 1418 Two Pacific Place, 88 Queensway. Telephone: 2522 3006. Telex: 63536 HFWHK HX. Telefax: 2887 8110.
Singapore Office: 10 Collyer Quay #08-02, Ocean Building, Singapore, 0104. Telephone: 534 0195. Telex: HFWSIN RS 26188. Telefax: 534-5864.
Piraeus, Greece Office: 6th Floor, 86 Filonos Street. Telephone: 429-3978. Telefax: 429-3118.
Rouen, France Office: 47 Avenue Gustave Flaubert, 76000. Telephone: 32 08.18.60. Telefax: 35.89.90.54.

Admiralty, all aspects of Maritime Law, International Trade, Commodities, Transportation, Insurance and Reinsurance, Ship Finance, Company and Commercial Matters and Aviation.

RESIDENT PARTNERS

TIMOTHY P. CLEMENS-JONES (Solicitor and Avocat à la Cour). *PRACTICE AREAS:* Admiralty and Maritime Law; Commodities; Contracts; International Law; Litigation.

OLIVER M. PURCELL (Solicitor and Avocat à la Cour). *PRACTICE AREAS:* Admiralty and Maritime Law; Insurance; Commercial Law; Litigation; Contracts.

GUILLAUME BRAJEUX (Avocat à la Cour). *PRACTICE AREAS:* Admiralty and Maritime Law; Commercial Law; Commodities; Contracts; Transportation.

JEAN-JACQUES OLLU (Avocat à la Cour). *PRACTICE AREAS:* Admiralty and Maritime Law; Commodities; International Law; Products Liability; Transportation.

(This Listing Continued)

Languages: Cantonese, English, French, German, Italian, Mandarin, Polish, Russian and Swedish

(For Complete List of Partners see Professional Biographies at London, England).

HONIG BUFFAT METTETAL

Established in 1979

21, RUE CLÉMENT MAROT
75008 PARIS, FRANCE
Telephone: (33.1) 44.43.88.88
Telex: 219876 AVOPARI
Telecopier: (33.1) 44.43.88.77

General French Law Practice, Arbitration, Aviation, Construction, Environment, Hotel and Restaurant Commercial Development, Insurance and Reinsurance Claims and Regulation, Labor Law, Products Liability, Real Estate, Trade and Commodity Financing.
Avocats à la Cour d'Appel de Paris, admitted to appear before the French and EEC Courts.

FIRM PROFILE: The firm was established in 1979. Honig Buffat Mettetal is associated with Wilson, Elser, Moskowitz, Edelman & Dicker, an American Law Firm.

MEMBERS OF THE FIRM

GÉRARD HONIG, born July 2, 1946; admitted, 1970, Paris. *Education:* University of Paris II (Master in Law, 1969; D.E.S., Private Law, 1970); New York University (LL.M., Comparative Law, 1974). *Member:* Avocat au Barreau de Paris; International Bar Association. *LANGUAGES:* French and English. *PRACTICE AREAS:* Insurance Law; Products Liability; Aviation Law.

CHRISTIAN BUFFAT, born February 13, 1946; admitted, 1969, Paris. *Education:* University of Paris II (Master in Law, 1969; D.E.S., Private Law, 1970). *Member:* Avocat au Barreau de Paris. *LANGUAGES:* French. *PRACTICE AREAS:* International Hotel Transactions; Airplane Crash Litigation.

BERNARD METTETAL, born January 30, 1947; admitted, 1972, Paris. *Education:* University of Paris II (Master in Law, 1970; D.E.S., Private Law, 1971; D.E.S., Criminal Law, 1972). Lecturer on Commercial Law, University of Paris X (1975-1990). *Member:* Avocat au Barreau de Paris; International Bar Association. *LANGUAGES:* French and English. *PRACTICE AREAS:* Insurance Law; Directors & Officers Liability; Construction Contract Law.

FRÉDÉRIC BARTET, born November 24, 1958; admitted, 1989, Paris. *Education:* University of Paris XII (Master in Law, 1984). *Member:* Avocat au Barreau de Paris. *LANGUAGES:* French. *PRACTICE AREAS:* Products Liability.

LAURENCE BIACABE, born December 20, 1952; admitted, 1979, Paris. *Education:* University of Pau (Master in Law, 1977). *Member:* Avocat au Barreau de Paris. *LANGUAGES:* French. *PRACTICE AREAS:* Products Liability.

ALAIN PERRONNET, born January 19, 1951; admitted, 1980, Paris. *Education:* University of Paris II (1979); Diplôme d'Etudes d'Architecture, 1972; Diplôme d'Etudes Approfondies Droit Immobilier, 1982 (D.E.A., Sociologie Politique, 1983; Master in Law, 1979). *Member:* Avocat au Barreau de Paris. *LANGUAGES:* French. *PRACTICE AREAS:* Construction Defect Litigation.

ELISABETH PESSAYRE-BUFFAT, born March 10, 1947; admitted, 1972, Paris. *Education:* University of Paris II (Master in Law, 1969; D.E.S., Private Law, 1970). Collaboratrice d'Avocat á la Cour de Cassation, 1971-1985. *Member:* Avocat au Barreau de Paris. *LANGUAGES:* French and Spanish. *PRACTICE AREAS:* Construction Insurance; Construction Law.

CLAUDE-ANNE ROMEFORT-LEHEUZEY, born June 11, 1947; admitted, 1980, Paris. *Education:* University of Paris II (Master in Law, 1980). *Member:* Avocat au Barreau de Paris. *LANGUAGES:* French. *PRACTICE AREAS:* Labor Law.

FABIENNE OUDART, born June 8, 1963; admitted, 1989, Paris. *Education:* University of Lille (Master in Law, 1986); University of Warwick (Certificate in English, 1987). *Member:* Avocat au Barreau de Paris and Solicitor. *LANGUAGES:* French and English. *PRACTICE AREAS:* International Law.

(This Listing Continued)

HONIG BUFFAT METTETAL, Paris—Continued

LAURENCE THOMAS RIOUALLON, born December 24, 1958; admitted, 1980, Paris. *Education:* (Maîtrise en Droit Privé, 1980; D.E.A., Droit Pénal, 1981). *Member:* Avocat au Barreau de Paris. *LANGUAGES:* French.

VALERIE ANNETTE, born March 25, 1966; admitted, 1994, Paris. *Education:* (D.E.A., Droit Public, 1989; Master of Laws, 1993). *LANGUAGES:* French, English and Spanish.

HSD ERNST & YOUNG

Member of Ernst & Young International

Limited Company Incorporated in 1984

Established in 1984

TOUR MANHATTAN, 6, PLACE DE L'IRIS
92095 PARIS, LA DEFENSE 2, FRANCE
Telephone: (33-1) 46.93.70.00
Fax: (33-1) 47.67.01.06
Telex: 615200

Lyons, France Office: Tour Ernst & Young Lyons, 113, boulevard Stalingrad, 69626 Villeurbanne CEDEX. Telephone: (33) 72 44 19 19. Fax: (33) 72 44 18 20.

Lille, France Office: 35, avenue de la Marne, 59293 Wasquehal. Telephone: (33) 20 27 42 42. Fax: (33) 20 27 78 42.

Nantes, France Office: 10, rue du Président-Herriot, 44000. Telephone: (33) 40 35 44 45. Fax: (33) 40 89 55 09. Telex: 720336.

Toulouse, France Office: Le Compans, 1, place Alphonse-Jourdain, 31000. Telephone: (33) 62 15 43 43. Fax: (33) 62 22 86 00.

Other Offices: Gabon, Ivory Coast, Monaco, Sénépal.

Commercial Law, Banking, Stock Exchange and Financial Law, Corporate Law, Taxation, Customs Duties and Negotiable Instruments, Competition Law, Distribution and Consumption, Realty Law, Computer Law and Intellectual Property, Labor Law, EC Law. Specific Foreign Law: Francophone North Africa and West Africa.

FIRM PROFILE: With 30 Partners and 208 Jurists and Tax Attorneys, combining rigor and imagination, the firm stands behind the solutions it proposes and assures their implementation. It has both generalists and specialists at its disposal.

PARTNERS

PIERRE ALAIN MOLINIER, born 1950. *Education:* University of Paris I (M.A., Economics, 1973); Certified Public Accountant (1979). Partner, 1985 (Paris). Auditor, 1973; Tax Consultant, 1977, HSD Ernst & Young. *Member:* Bar of Nanterre. *LANGUAGES:* English and French. *PRACTICE AREAS:* International Corporate Taxation; Mergers and Acquisitions.

JACK ANDERSON, born 1946. *Education:* University of Denver (M.B.A.; J.D., 1972); New York University (LL.M., Tax Law, 1980); Certified Public Accountant, New York and California. Partner, 1986 (Paris). Manager and Partner, Audit and Legal Firm, United States; Consultant, Anglo-Saxon multinationals; Coordinator of US Legal and Taxation activity, HSD Ernst & Young. Author: "Investissement en France; La nouvelle formule pour les expatriés: Tax planning in France," tax column, International Herald Tribune. Member: Board of Directors, Foch Foundation; American Foundation; American Library in Paris. *Member:* Bar of Nanterre (France); State Bar of California; New York State Bar Association; Colorado and American Bar Associations; AICPA. *LANGUAGES:* English and French. *PRACTICE AREAS:* International Taxation; Design of Expatriate Policies; Tax Planning and Social Security for Directors and Executives of International Companies.

EVELYNE BATAILLE, born 1953. *Education:* Orléans (M.A., Business Law, 1976); University of Paris IX (DESS, International Taxation, 1984). Partner, 1993 (Paris). Tax Inspector, Assistant to BNP Tax Director, Director of Tax Service of Barclays Bank France; HSD Ernst & Young, 1992—. Author: "Banque et Droit" review, articles. *Member:* Bar of Nanterre. *LANGUAGES:* English and French. *PRACTICE AREAS:* Banking and Financial Law; Taxation.

FRANCOIS BEGLIN, born 1952. *Education:* University of Paris I (DEA, Public Finance and Taxation, 1976); University of Pennsylvania (LL.M., 1978). Partner, 1989 (Toulouse). Dart Industries, 1979-1981; Deloitte, Haskins & Sells, 1981-1984; Attaché to the Finance Committee of the

(This Listing Continued)

National Assembly, 1984-1987; HSD Ernst & Young, 1987—. *Member:* Bar of Toulouse. *LANGUAGES:* English and French. *PRACTICE AREAS:* Corporate and Personal Taxation.

DENIS BOISNARD, born 1949. *Education:* University of Paris (Degree in Private Law). Partner, Paris. 10 years experience in the Human Resources Department of a large group and as consultant. Legal Consultant for French and foreign companies on Social Security and Labour Law issues. Social Law Specialist, HSD Ernst & Young. *Member:* Bar of Nanterre. *PRACTICE AREAS:* Labour Law; Social Audits; Mergers and Acquisitions; Restructuring Operations; Retirement Plans; Profit-Sharing and Participation Plans.

JEAN-BERNARD CAUMONT, born 1952. *Education:* University of Paris, IEP (DEA, Tax Law); Certified Public Accountant. Partner, 1991 (Paris). Legal and Tax Consultant and Attorney, HSD Ernst & Young. Author: "Option Finances." *Member:* Bar of Nanterre; Franco-Japanese Chamber of Commerce in France. *LANGUAGES:* English and French. *PRACTICE AREAS:* Tax Law; Corporate Law; Restructuring Operations; Mergers and Acquisitions; Internal Financial and Economic Flows Operations.

CHRISTIAN CLOCHER, born 1950. *Education:* M.A., Public Law and Political Science (1973); Ecole nationale des Impôts (1974). Partner, 1985 (Lyons). Sub-editor, DGI, 1976-1980; Consultant, Arthur Andersen International, 1980-1982; Attorney and Partner, HSD Ernst & Young, 1982—. Author: "Guide juridique et fiscal de l'exportateur," Ed. BFCE. *Member:* Bar of Lyons. *LANGUAGES:* English and French. *PRACTICE AREAS:* Taxation of Restructuring Operations; Taxation of Risk Capital Ventures.

BERNARD COLLIN, born 1957. *Education:* Licence in Public Law (1978); M.A., Private Law (1979); DESS, Tax and Public Finance (1981); Ecole Nationale des Impôts (1981); CAPA (1983). Partner, 1993 (Paris). Tax Inspector, DGI, 1982; HSD Ernst & Young, 1986. Author: "Sports Marketing Europe, Taxation Aspects France," Ed. Kluwer, 1993. *Member:* Bar of Nanterre; UIA. *LANGUAGES:* English and French. *PRACTICE AREAS:* Tax, Customs Duties and Exchange Control Regulations; Taxation of Communication, Sport and Art, and Tourism Sectors.

NIELS DEJEAN, born 1959. *Education:* M.A., Law, (1982); DESS, Taxation (1983). Partner, 1991 (Paris). Tax Consultant, HSD Ernst & Young, 1988-1992. Author: "Tax Planning International" and "The International Tax Review," articles. *Member:* Bar of Nanterre. *LANGUAGES:* English and French. *PRACTICE AREAS:* International Taxation; Corporate Restructuring and Reconciliations; Hybrid Structures; Transfer Pricing; Marketing Plans; Financial Products; Cross-Borders LBOS.

DOMINIQUE DERVEAUX, born 1948. *Education:* University of Paris X (M.A., Economics, 1970); Ecole Nationale des Impôts (1971). Partner, 1987 (Paris). Computer Analyst, DGI, Computer Services Department, 1973-1976; Tax Inspector, DGI, DVNI, 1976-1978; Tax Consultant, HSD Ernst & Young, 1983—. *Member:* Bar of Nanterre. *LANGUAGES:* English and French. *PRACTICE AREAS:* Realty Taxation.

JEAN-JACQUES DUFLOS, born 1950. *Education:* University of Paris X (M.A., Law; DESS, Legal Studies, 1975). Partner, 1993, (Lyons). Legal Director, Castorama; Partner, Cabinet Ratheaux, Lyons, 1985-1990; HSD Ernst & Young, 1990—. Author: "Guide Formulaire du comité d'entreprise," Ed. Litec, 1992. *Member:* Bar of Lyons. *LANGUAGES:* English and French. *PRACTICE AREAS:* Corporate; Labor Law.

ANNE ERMEL, born 1948. *Education:* University of Paris II (M.A., Public Law); University of Dijon (DESS, Corporate Law and Taxation, 1984). Partner, 1990 (Paris). Gillette Co. and St. Dupont, 1978-1984; HSD Ernst & Young, 1984—. Author: "VAT in Europe," 1989; "International VAT," 1991. *Member:* Bar of Nanterre. *LANGUAGES:* English and French. *PRACTICE AREAS:* Corporate Taxation; Customs Duties and Exchange Control Regulations.

DOMINIQUE GAVEAU, born 1955. *Education:* DESS, Corporate Law; DEA, Finance; Certified Public Accountant. Partner, 1985 (Paris). Certified Public Accountant and Statutory Auditor, National and International Groups, 1977-1989; Tax Consultant and Attorney, specializing in Tax Law, French and International Corporate Taxation, 1989—. Editor: "La stratégie fiscale des entreprises," publication of the Certified Public Accountancy Society, article in the review Acts Pratiques: "Les fusions par confusion du patrimoine." *Member:* Bar of Nanterre. *LANGUAGES:* English and French. *PRACTICE AREAS:* Corporate and Personal Taxation.

DOMINIQUE GERRY, born 1947. *Education:* University of Paris II (Phd., Law, 1981). Partner, (Paris). Chambaz & Leblond, 1976-1982; Le Villeguérin Conseils, 1982-1989; HSD Ernst & Young, 1989—. Author:

(This Listing Continued)

"Actes pratiques," articles, Ed. Techinques. *Member:* Bar of Nanterre; ANSA (Legal Committee). *LANGUAGES:* English and French. *PRACTICE AREAS:* Banking Law; Securities and Financial Law; Corporate Law; Taxation.

JEAN-CLAUDE GRANGER, born 1937. *Education:* University of Paris (M.A., Law and Humanities, 1960; DESS, Economics, 1961); Ecole Nationale des Impôts. Partner, 1988 (Paris). Legal and Tax Consultant and Director General, La Villeguérin Conseils; HSD Ernst & Young, 1988—. *Member:* Bar of Nanterre; IFA; ANSA; IADF; Legal Workshop of Mercatel (President). *LANGUAGES:* French. *PRACTICE AREAS:* Tax and Corporate Law; Mergers and Acquisitions; Distributions; Commercial Law; Banking Law; Securities and Finance; Realty Law; Rental Leases-Personal, Professional and Commercial.

LUC JULIEN SAINT-AMAND, born 1958. *Education:* Ph.D. European Law, DECS, M.A. Economic Science. Partner, 1994 (Frankfurt). Ernst & Young, 1984—. Publications: Ph.D. thesis on Corporate European Law. *Member:* Bar of Nanterre. *PRACTICE AREAS:* Franco-German Relations, currently detached in Frankfurt.

PIERRE KNOEPFLER, born 1942. *Education:* University of Paris, Toulouse (M.A., Law, 1965; Lauréat of the faculty of law); Ecole Nationale des Impôts. Partner, 1986 (Paris). Tax Inspector and Chief Tax Inspector, 1961-1975; Touche-Ross, Partner, 1975-1985; HSD Ernst & Young, 1985—. *Member:* Bar of Nanterre. *LANGUAGES:* English, French and German. *PRACTICE AREAS:* International Corporate Taxation; Mergers and Restructuring of Groups and Companies.

DIDIER LANGLOIS, born 1951. *Education:* Rouen (DESCAF; ESC, 1975; DECS). Partner, 1990 (Paris). Legal Consultant and Attorney, HSD Ernst & Young. *Member:* Bar of Nanterre. *LANGUAGES:* English and French. *PRACTICE AREAS:* Taxation of Restructuring Operations; Mergers and Acquisitions in High Tech Industry; Customs Duties and Foreign Exchange Regulations.

FRÉDÉRIC LAUREAU, born 1954. *Education:* Paris 2 (M.A., Business Law, 1979). Partner, 1991 (Paris). Arthur Anderson International: Consultant, 1980; Director, 1985; Partner, 1990. Partner, HSD Ernst & Young, 1994. Publications: La Synthèse Financière, Marchés et Techniques Financières. *Member:* Bar of Nanterre. *PRACTICE AREAS:* Finance Law; Long Term Financing Taxation; Banking Law; International Taxation.

CHRISTIAN LEROY, born 1955. *Education:* University of Paris, IEP (M.A., Economics). Partner, 1991 (Lyons). Legal and Tax Consultant, 1987; Certified Public Accountant, 1989; Attorney, 1991. Author: "La revue de Banque" and "Les Petits Affiches," articles. *Member:* Bar of Nanterre; IADF. *LANGUAGES:* English and French. *PRACTICE AREAS:* Corporate Law; Taxation.

ROGER MARTIN, born 1933. *Education:* Licence in Law (1954); Faculté de Droit de Paris; Statutory Auditor and Certified Public Accountant. Partner, 1988 (Paris). Chief Tax Inspector, 1965-1968; Expert for Court of Appeals, 1981-1992; Expert for Administrative Courts of Paris, 1975—; Expert for European Arbitration Court at Versailles, 1992—; Legal and Tax Consultant, HSD Ernst & Young, 1988—. *Member:* Bar of Nanterre. *LANGUAGES:* French.

BERNARD MERMILLON, born 1957. *Education:* License in Public Law (1980); ENI (1981). Partner, 1994 (Paris). Tax Inspector, 1982-1990, HSD Ernst & Young, 1990. Publications: L'argus journal international de l'assurance. *Member:* Bar of Nanterre. *PRACTICE AREAS:* Tax Law; Insurance Law.

THIERRY MEUNIER, born 1957. *Education:* M.A., Public Law, 1976; Ecole Nationale des Impôts (1977). Partner, 1988 (Nantes). Tax Inspector, 1976-1985; Legal and Tax Consultant for French and foreign companies implanted in France; Attorney, HSD Ernst & Young, 1985-1992. *Member:* Bar of Nantes. *LANGUAGES:* English and French. *PRACTICE AREAS:* Banking Law; Security Regulations; Health Regulations.

PIERRE MICHAUX, born 1947. *Education:* Clermont-Ferrand (licence in Economics, 1970). Partner, 1977 (Dakar). Tax Inspector, 1970-1974; Tax Consultant, FFA, Dakar; Manager, FFA HSD Ernst & Young, Dakar. *Member:* Ordre des experts et évaluateurs agrées of Senegal (Association of Legal and Tax Consultants and Appraisers). *LANGUAGES:* English and French. *PRACTICE AREAS:* Tax Law; Corporate Law; West African Law.

MARC POURBAIX, born 1946. *Education:* Lille (DESS, Private Law, 1968). Partner, 1992 (Lille). Legal and Tax Consultant, 1967—; CEO, Fiduciare du Nord Juridique et fiscal, 1984—. *Member:* Bar of Lille; IADF.

(This Listing Continued)

LANGUAGES: English and French. *PRACTICE AREAS:* Corporate Law; Taxation.

BERNARD SCHAMING, born 1956. *Education:* Strasbourg (DESS, Intellectual Property Rights, 1979); University of Paris II (DEA, Corporate Law and Economics, 1984). Partner, 1986 (Paris). Law Office of Weinstein, 1979-1986; La Villeguérin Conseils, 1986-1988; HSD Ernst & Young, 1988—. Author: "Le droit du logiciel," Ed. La Villeguérin, 1990. *Member:* Bar of Nanterre; AFEC; APRAM; LES FRANCE; AIPPI. *LANGUAGES:* English, French and German. *PRACTICE AREAS:* Intellectual Property Rights; Competition Law; Mergers and Acquisitions.

JEAN CLAUDE SERVIGNAT, born 1951. *Education:* University of Paris, ESC (Higher Certificate of Accounting). Partner, 1989 (Monaco). Auditor, Arthur Young & Co., 1974-1977; Financial Director, French subsidiary of US Company; Chemical and Computer Industries, 1978-1985; Legal and Tax Consultant, HSD Ernst & Young, 1985-1993. *LANGUAGES:* English and French. *PRACTICE AREAS:* Mergers and Acquisitions; Banking; International Taxation.

DANIEL TAPIN, born 1951. *Education:* M.A., Law (1975); DESS, Tax Law. Partner, 1993 (Paris). Specialist in African Law and Taxation, HSD Ernst & Young, 1979—. *Member:* Bar of Nanterre. *LANGUAGES:* English and French. *PRACTICE AREAS:* West African and North African (Maghreb) Law.

ROBERT TARIKA, born 1949. *Education:* Certified Public Accountant (1974); Statutory Auditor (1974). Partner, 1979 (Paris), Ernst & Young Management Consulting, Managing Director (Medium and Large Enterprises). Arthur Young, 1968, in charge of Legal and Tax Activity; HSD Ernst & Young, 1979, legal counsel, 1984. *Member:* Bar of Nanterre (France); National Commission for Legal Council (1991); Franco-American Chamber of Commerce in France (Tax Committee); Juri-Avenir (Vice President). *LANGUAGES:* English, French and German. *PRACTICE AREAS:* International Taxation; Mergers and Acquisitions; Computer and Franchising.

Firm Publications: "Doing Business in France, EC Brief," Revue et Mementos, "Fiscalité Africaine," "US Tax and Legal Update, la lettre juridique Fiscale."

Languages: French, English, German, Spanish, Italian and Dutch

---

HUGHES HUBBARD & REED

47, AVENUE GEORGES MANDEL
75116 PARIS, FRANCE
Telephone: 33.1.44.05.80.00
Cable Address: "Hughreed, Paris"
Telex: 645440
Telecopier: 33.1.45.53.15.04.

New York, New York Office: One Battery Park Plaza, 10004. Telephone: 212-837-6000. Cable Address: "Hughreed, New York." Telex: 427120. Telecopier: 212-422-4726.

Los Angeles, California Office: 350 S. Grand Avenue, Suite 3600, 90071-3442. Telephone: 213-613-2800. Telecopier: 213-613-2950.

Miami, Florida Office: 801 Brickell Avenue, 33131. Telephone: 305-358-1666. Telex: 51-8785. Telecopier: 305-371-8759.

Washington, D.C. Office: 1300 I Street, N.W., Suite 900 West, 20005. Telephone: 202-408-3600. Telex: 89-2674. Telecopier: 202-408-3636.

Berlin, Germany Office: Kurfürstendamm 44, D-1000 Berlin 15. Telephone: 030-880008-0. Telefax: 030-880008-65. Telex: 185803 KNAPA D.

General Practice.
Firm engaged in American, French and General International Practice and authorized to appear before the French Courts reserved for Avocats.

RESIDENT PARTNERS

JOËL ALQUEZAR, born Dijon, France, May 16, 1952; admitted, 1979, Paris. *Education:* Institut d'Études Politiques de Paris (Diploma, 1973); Faculté de Droit et des Sciences Economiques, University of Paris (D.E.A., Droit Fiscal, 1975; D.E.A., Sciences Économiques, 1977). Professor, International Taxation, University of Paris V. *Member:* Groupement des Avocats Fiscalistes. (Partner). *LANGUAGES:* English, French and Spanish. *PRACTICE AREAS:* Litigation; Corporate Law; Tax Law.

CLAIRE S. AYER, born Paris, France, June 1, 1947; admitted, 1977, France. *Education:* University of Paris (D.E.S., 1970). (Partner). *LANGUAGES:* English and French. *PRACTICE AREAS:* Real Estate and Franchising.

(This Listing Continued)

HUGHES HUBBARD & REED, Paris—Continued

AXEL H. BAUM, born Berlin, Germany, July 14, 1930; admitted, 1957, Connecticut; 1958, New York; 1972, France; 1976, U.S. Supreme Court. *Education:* Amherst College (B.A., cum laude, 1952); Yale University (LL.B., 1957). Managing Editor, Yale Law Journal, 1955-1957. Delegate, International Chamber of Commerce Commission on International Arbitration, 1985—. Member: Panel of International Mediators, CPR, 1992—; Board of Directors, American Chamber of Commerce in France, 1991—. Member, Panel of Arbitrators, American Arbitration Association. *Member:* American and International Bar Associations. (Partner). *LANGUAGES:* English, French and German. *PRACTICE AREAS:* International Business Transactions; International Arbitration; International Acquisitions.

JAMES J. LIGHTBURN, born New York, N. Y., September 28, 1943; admitted, 1968, New Jersey; 1973, France. *Education:* Columbia University (B.A., 1965); New York University (J.D., 1968). (Partner). *LANGUAGES:* English and French.

DOMINIQUE MENDY, born Paris, France, October 27, 1953; admitted, 1981, France. *Education:* University of Tours (Maître en Droit, 1974; Droit des Affaires C.D.C.I., 1975); City of London Polytechnic (M.A., 1977). (Partner). *LANGUAGES:* English and French. *PRACTICE AREAS:* Corporate; Labor.

JONATHAN A. SCHUR, born New York, N.Y., October 31, 1953; admitted, 1979, New York; 1982, France. *Education:* Harvard University (B.A., cum laude, 1975; J.D., cum laude, 1978). *Member:* Union International des Avocats (Administrative Director, 1987-1989); Association of Americans Resident Overseas (Director, 1992—). (Partner). *LANGUAGES:* English and French. *PRACTICE AREAS:* International Commercial; Corporate; Litigation; Real Estate; Pharmaceutical.

VINCENT SOL, born Brive, France, December 30, 1957; admitted, 1988, France. *Education:* Institut d'Etudes Politiques de Paris (Diplome 1980); Universite of Paris, Faculté de Droit (Licence 1977, Maitrise 1978, DEA de Droit International, 1984). Member, European Sub-Committee on Environmental Law of the International Bar Association, Société Francaise pour le droit de l'Environnement (French Association for Environmental Law). (Partner). *LANGUAGES:* French and English. *PRACTICE AREAS:* Environmental (Regulatory, Transactional and Litigation Aspects).

THOMAS HENRY WEBSTER, born Owen Sound, Ontario, Canada, August 4, 1951; admitted, 1979, Ontario; 1980, New York; 1982, England and France. *Education:* University of Alberta, Canada (B.A., 1971); University of Toronto (LL.B., 1974); Cambridge University (LL.M., 1976); University of Paris (D.E.A. Droit des Communautés Européennes, 1977). Delegate, ICC Commission on International Commercial Arbitration, 1992—. Member, Panel of Arbitrators, American Arbitration Association. (Partner). *LANGUAGES:* English, French and German. *PRACTICE AREAS:* International Arbitration; International Acquisitions; Joint Ventures; Commercial.

OF COUNSEL

GEORGE W. BALKIND, born New York, N.Y., April 22, 1931; admitted, 1956, New York; 1972, France. *Education:* Williams College (B.A., 1952); Yale University (J.D., 1955). *LANGUAGES:* English and French.

CLAUDE SULEYMAN, born Paris, France, July 19, 1926; admitted, 1952, France. *Education:* University of Paris (License en Droit, 1946; D.E.S., 1947); Harvard (LL.M., 1950; LL.B., 1952). *LANGUAGES:* English and French.

RESIDENT ASSOCIATES

EVELINE BELTZUNG, born Clermont (Oise), France, January 2, 1944; admitted, 1986, France. *Education:* University of Paris (License en Droit, 1980; Maitrise en Droit, 1981). *LANGUAGES:* French and English.

BOUZIANE BEHILLIL, born Bretigny Sur Orge, France, February 15, 1967; admitted, 1992, France. *Education:* University of Paris, Panthéon - Sorbonne (Magistère de Droit des Affaires, 1991; D.E.S.S. de Droit des Affaires, 1991). *LANGUAGES:* French, English, Italian, Dutch and Arabic.

LAURE COLLI-PATEL, born Momtbeliard, France, June 4, 1965; admitted, 1989, France. *Education:* University of Paris II (Maître en Droit des Affaires, 1987; DEA en Droit des Affaires et Droit économique, 1988). *LANGUAGES:* French and English.

LAURENCE DUMURE-LAMBERT, born Fontenay sous Bois, France, March 22, 1966; admitted, 1989, France. *Education:* University of

(This Listing Continued)

Paris II-Assas (Maîtrise Droit des Affaires, 1987; Magistère de Juriste d'Affaires, 1988). Instructor, French Law Program, American University of Paris Institute for Paralegal Studies, 1991-1992. *LANGUAGES:* French and English.

ALEXANDRE DE GOÜYON MATIGNON, born Paris, France, March 22, 1957; admitted, 1985, France. *Education:* University of Panthéon-Sorbonne (Maîtrise Droit Européen, 1982; DEA Economie Internationale, 1982; DEA Droit Européen, 1984). *LANGUAGES:* French, English and Spanish.

JOHN G. HEARD, born New Orleans, Louisiana, October 11, 1967; admitted, 1992, Maryland; 1993, District of Columbia. *Education:* University of Richmond (B.A., magna cum laude, 1989); Georgetown University Law Center (J.D., cum laude, 1992). *LANGUAGES:* English and French.

JOELLE HERSCHTEL, born Neuilly-sur-Seine, France, January 29, 1963; admitted, 1988, Paris. *Education:* University of Paris X (Maîtrise en Droit, 1985; D.E.A., Droit des Affaires, 1987; German Licence, 1987); Institut d'Etudes Politiques, Paris (Diploma , 1986). *LANGUAGES:* French, English and German.

THEODOR W. KRAUSS, born New York, N.Y., June 8, 1961; admitted, 1989, New York and District of Columbia; 1992, France. *Education:* Boston College (B.A., 1983); Université de Nice (Faculté de Droit, 1985); Georgetown University (M.S.F.S., 1988; J.D., 1988). *LANGUAGES:* English, French and Italian.

WINSTON J. MAXWELL, born Portland, Oregon, December 18, 1960; admitted, 1986, New York; 1989, France. *Education:* Oregon State University (B.A., 1982); Cornell University (J.D., 1985). *Member:* Licensing Executives Society. *LANGUAGES:* English and French.

LAURE MOTTET, born Neuilly, France, April 14, 1969; admitted, 1994, France. *Education:* University of Paris II (Maitrise Droit Prive, 1991); University of Paris I (D.E.A. Droit Prive, 1992); E.S.C.P. (Mastere, 1993); C.F.P.P. (C.A.P.A., 1993). *LANGUAGES:* French, English and German.

FLORENCE PERROT, born Issy-Les-Moulinëaux, France, October 31, 1966; (admission pending). *Education:* Lycée Victor Dury (Bac. D., 1984); University of Paris II-Assas (Maîtrise en Droit, 1988); Institut d'Études Politiques (Diploma 1990); University of Paris Nanterre (DESS, 1991). *LANGUAGES:* French and English.

BERTRAND THOUNY, born Paris, France, February 27, 1962; admitted, 1993, France. *Education:* University of Paris XII (License en Droit, 1985; Maîtrise en Droit, 1988; D.E.S.S., 1989). *LANGUAGES:* French and English.

(For biographical data of the New York, N.Y. partners, see Professional Biographies at New York, N.Y.).

JEANTET & ASSOCIES

87, AVENUE KLÉBER
75784 PARIS CEDEX 16, FRANCE
Telephone: (33) 1 45 05 80 08
Fax: (33) 1 47 04 20 41; (33) 1 47 55 95 10

London, England Office: Royex House, Aldermanbury Square, EC2V 7HR. Telephone: (44) 171 600 36 08. Fax: (44) 171 600 17 18.

Brussels, Belgium Office: Rue Brederode 13 A, B, 1000. Telephone: (32) 2505 02 11. Fax: (32) 2502 26 44.

New York, New York Office: 712 Fifth Avenue, 10019. Telephone: (212) 801 3440. Fax: (212) 801 3445.

Prague, Czech Republic Office: Blanicka 28, 12000. Telephone: (42) 2 256 251. Fax: (42) 2 254 233.

Budapest, Hungary Office: Szemere Utca 17.IV./1, 1054. Telephone: (36) 2 203 40759. Fax: (36) 2 201 63 79.

Bucarest, Romania Office: Strada Docentilor 7, Sector 1. Telephone: (40) 1 312 99 36. Fax: (40) 1 312 97 56.

Warsaw, Poland Office: Ul. Wiejska 12a, PL 00-490. Telephone: (48) 2/628 24 12. Fax: (48) 2/628 24 11.

Moscow, Russia Correspondent Office: Krasnopresnenskaya NAB, 12, International Trade Center, Office 2009, CEI - 123610. Telephone: (7) 502 253 00 41. Fax: (7) 502 253 20 42.

General Practice in French, EEC and International Business Law (i.e. Interalia Corporate, Tax, Mergers and Acquisitions, Securities, Banking, Patent and Trademarks, Labor, Finance, Litigation, International Estates, Arbitration, Computer Law, French and European Economic Community Antitrust, Insurance and Product Liability Law, Distribution, Consumer, Transportation Law).

(This Listing Continued)

Member of Alliance of European Lawyers (EEIG) which regroups six law firms from Continental Europe. The Alliance consists of De Bandt, van Hecke & Lagae at Brussels and Antwerp; De Brauw Blackstone Westbroek at The Hague, Amsterdam, Rotterdam and Eindhoven; Jeantet & Associés at Paris and Warsaw; Lagerlöf & Leman at Stockholm, Gothenburg and Malmö; Oppenhoff & Räat Berlin, Cologne, Frankfurt am Main, Leipzig and Münich; Uria & Menendez at Madrid and Barcelona.

MEMBERS OF FIRM

FERNAND-CHARLES JEANTET, born Tlemcen, Algeria, September 7, 1912; admitted, 1937, Paris. *Education:* Algiers (Licence); Paris (D.E.S., Histoire du Droit, Droit Privé, Droit Public, Doctorat, 1939). Author: "Le Code des Prix," Montchrestien, 1949; "Le Droit des Affaires," Montchrestien, 1957. *Member:* Comité Consultatif de Legislation Commerciale des Ministres de l'Economie Nationale et de la Justice (1970-1980); Association Nationale des Avocats de France (Vice President, 1963-1965; President, Section Internationale, 1960-1965); Conseil d'Administration de l'Association Francaise d'Arbitrage (AFA); I.F.A.; I.B.A.; U.I.A.; Comité Francais de Droit International; Association des Juristes Europeens; Association Francaise de l'Etude de la Concurrence (AFEC) (President Honoraire, 1989). *LANGUAGES:* French and English.

ROGER L'ELEU, born Le Mans, France, October 1, 1917; admitted, 1947, Paris. *Education:* Ecole Libre des Sciences Politiques, Paris (1938); Sorbonne (1939); Paris Law School (Licence, 1937; D.E.S. Droit Privé and Droit Public, 1938). *LANGUAGES:* French, English and German.

JEAN-PIERRE LE GALL, born Hazebrouck, France, May 4, 1937; admitted, 1957, Paris. *Education:* Grenoble Law School (Licence, 1957; D.E.S. Droit Privé and D.E.S. Dro it Public, 1958; D.E.S. Droit Romain, 1959); Paris Law School (Doctorat, 1963, Premier Prix de Thése). Author: "French Company Law," 1974; "La Fiscalite Internationale des Eurocredits," "Les Suretés sur Aeronefs," "Fiscalité et exportation," The Journal of International Business Law (taxation). Contributor to Encyclopedia of Comparative Law. Editor of Fiscalité Internationale (DPCT). Professeur Agrégé des Facultés de Droit, 1964. Professor of Commercial, Company and Tax Law, Paris II Law School. *Member:* IFA; IBA. *LANGUAGES:* French and English.

GERARD MAZET, born Aix-en-Provence, France, May 17, 1942; admitted, 1966, Paris. *Education:* Harrow School; Law Schools of Aix-en-Provence, Paris (Licence, 1964) and Montpellier (D.E.S., Droit Privé, 1966); Institut d'Etudes Politiques (1963) ; Ecole des Hautes Etudes Commerciales (HEC, 1965). Articles and Lectures on: Securities Law; Mergers and Acquisitions; International joint ventures; Banking law, Leasing. *Member:* IBA. *LANGUAGES:* French and English.

JACQUELINE JAEGER, born Lagrave, France, January 3, 1930; admitted, 1955, Paris. *Education:* Paris Law School (Licence, 1951; D.E.S. Droit Romain, 1952; D.E.S. Droit Privé, 1953). *LANGUAGES:* French and English.

PIERRE LENOIR, born Saint-Quentin, France, March 28, 1948; admitted, 1972, Paris. *Education:* Paris Law School (Maitrise, 1972); Centre Universitaire d'Etudes des Communautés Européennes (1972). *Member:* AFPPI; IAPIP. *LANGUAGES:* French and English.

CLAUDE LAZARUS, born Paris, France, May 5, 1945; admitted, 1976, Paris. *Education:* Ecole des Hautes Etudes Commerciales (HEC, 1967); Institut d'Etudes Politiques, Paris (1969); Paris Law School (Licence, 1968; D.E.S. Droit Public, 1969; D.E.S. Science Politique, 1971). Lecturer, HEC-ISA. Assistant Editor, Institute of International Law. *Member:* IBA; AFEC. *LANGUAGES:* French and English.

GEORGES TERRIER, born Grasse, France, March 29, 1946; admitted, 1980, Paris. *Education:* Nice Law School (Licencié Es Sciences Economiques, 1968; Lauréat de la Faculté); Paris Law School (Maîtrise en Droit, D.E.S. Sciences Economiques, 1971); Institut d'Etudes Politiques, Paris (1971). In-house Counsel, Goodyear France, 1973-1979. *LANGUAGES:* French and English.

PHILIPPE SARRAILHE, born Dakar, Senegal, September 29, 1949; admitted, 1972, Paris. *Education:* Law Schools of Paris X (Licence en Droit and Diplôme Institut d'Etudes Judiciaires, 1972); Paris I (D.E.S.S. Commerce International, 1976); Paris X (D.E.A. Droit des Affaires, 1980); University of Pennsylvania (LL.M., 1978). Author: "Contracts and Investments in Venezuela", "Product Liability (France)," Oceana. Panelist: Mergers and Acquisitions, Joint Ventures, Banking, EEC Law. Assistant Lecturer, EEC Law and International Trade Law, University of Paris II Law School, 1982-1985. *Member:* ABA; IBA; NYSBA; Association of the Bar of the City of New York; American Foreign Law Association (Vice-President). (Also at

(This Listing Continued)

London, England Office). *LANGUAGES:* French, English, Spanish, Italian and Portuguese.

JEAN NERET, born Neuilly-sur-Seine, France, February 18, 1947; admitted, 1977, Paris. *Education:* Paris II Law School (D.E.S. Sciences Criminelles, 1971; D.E.S. Droit Privé, 1973); Doctorat, 1977 Prix Léon Julliot de la Morandiére. Author: "Le sous-contrat," 1979; Contributor to: Juris-Classeur, Business and Labor Law; Gazette du Palais, Labor Law. Professeur Agrégé des Facultes de droit, 1981. Professor at the Institut des Relations Internationales. Professor of Private Law, Paris XII Law School. *LANGUAGES:* French, Italian and English.

FRANCIS LOUVARD, born Abbeville, France, June 30, 1952; admitted, 1982, Paris. *Education:* Paris Law School (D.E.A. Fiscalité et Finances Publiques, 1977); Institut d'Etudes Politiques, Paris (1977); Institut National des Langues et Civilisations Orientales (Russian, 1976). Former Banking Representative, U.S.S.R. Professor, Institut Technique de Banque. *Member:* IBA. *LANGUAGES:* French, English and Russian.

ANNE CIRET, born Marseilles, France, September 3, 1951; admitted, 1976, Paris. *Education:* Bordeaux Law School and Institut d'Etudes Politiques, Paris I Law School (Licence, 1972; DES Droit Européen, 1973); Deutsche Akademische Austauschendienst, Düsseldorf, Hamburg (1973-1975). *LANGUAGES:* French, English and German.

BRUNO LEURENT, born Roncq, France, April 25, 1945; admitted, 1972, Paris. *Education:* Law Schools of Lille (Licence, 1966; D.E.S. Droit Public, 1967); Paris (D.E.S. Droit Privé, 1968); Institut d'Etudes Politiques, Paris (1968). Lecturer, Secrétaire Rédacteur at the Hague Conference on Private International Law (13th and 14th Sessions). Legal Advisor to the Iran US Claims Tribunal, 1982-1984. *Member:* AFA. *LANGUAGES:* French and English.

CHANTAL MOMEGE, born Voiron, France, July 16, 1948; admitted, 1974, Lyons; 1984, Paris. *Education:* Lyon Law School (Licence, 1974); Lyon Institut d'Etudes Politiques (Diplômée de l'Institut d'Etudes Judiciaires de Lyon). Co-Author: "1993: Tomorrow's Europe: companies restructuring and competition law," Brussels 1989. Lecturer, Business Law, HEC, 1985-1988. Lecturer, European Law, Paris II, 1988. In-house Counsel, Radar, Paris, 1979-1984. *Member:* AFEC. *LANGUAGES:* French and English.

PASCAL COUDIN, born Neuilly-sur-Seine, France, June 4, 1959; admitted, 1987, Paris. *Education:* Paris Law School XI (Maître, 1984). Author: "Taxation of Seller's Guaranty in Shares Acquisition Transactions." Co-Author: "Legal Consequences of the Use of a Subsidiary's Deficits in a Tax Consolidated Group"; "Tax Aspects of the Ordonnance of October 21, 1986, Relative to Employees' Profit Sharing"; "Comparative Tax Study of French and Dutch Holdings." Contributing Editor, International Tax Report. *Member:* IBA; American Tax Institute. *LANGUAGES:* French and English.

CHRISTIAN BOUCKAERT, born Calonne, France, October 10, 1945; admitted, 1975, Paris. *Education:* Paris Law School (Licence, 1969; D.E.S., Droit des Affaires, 1973); Institut d'Etudes Politiques, Paris (1971). *Member:* IBA; International Association of Defence Counsel; Defense Research Institute. *LANGUAGES:* French and English.

PHILIPPE BLAQUIER-CIRELLI, born Libreville (Gabon), January 13, 1959; admitted, 1982, Lille; 1985, Paris. *Education:* Lille Law School (Maîtrise, 1980; D.E.A. Droit Privé, 1983); Institut d'Etudes Judiciaires (1981); Paris I Law School (D.E.A. Droit International Privé, 1984); The Hague Academy of International Law (1985); Academy Center for Studies and Research in International Law and International Relations; Institut d'Etudes Politiques de Paris (Master of Conferences in International Law, 1990—). *Member:* Hague Academy of International Law (Secretaire Redacteur); Union des Jeunes Avocats; Association of Attenders and Alumni of the Hague Academy of International Law; Association des juristes franco-britanniques. *LANGUAGES:* French and English.

HENRY LESGUILLONS, born Paris, France, May 26, 1938. *Education:* Paris Law School (Licence, 1962; D.E.S. Droit Public and Doctorat, 1963; D.E.S. Sciences Politiques, 1964). Professeur Agrégé des Facultés de Droit. Author: Interalia: "Régime Communautaire de Protection contre le Dumping et les subventions." Professor, EEC Law and Trade Law, Paris X Law School. *LANGUAGES:* French and English.

PATRICK DIBOUT, born St. Malo, France, October 14, 1950; admitted, 1988, Paris. *Education:* Reims Law School (Licence, 1971; D.E.S., 1972; Doctorat, 1975; D.E.A., Sciences Politiques, 1976). Professeur Agrégé des Facultés de Droit. Professor, Tax Law, Paris XI Law School. *Member:* IBA; IFA. *LANGUAGES:* French and English.

(This Listing Continued)

JEANTET & ASSOCIES, Paris—Continued

PAUL COCCHIELLO, born Paris, France, October 23, 1956; admitted, 1981, Paris. *Education:* University of Paris XI Law School (Master in Private Law, 1978); University of Paris I Law School Institute of Legal Studies (June 1978). *LANGUAGES:* French, English.

PASCAL MARTIN, born June 16, 1958. *Education:* University of Paris X Law School (Maitrise de Droit Public, 1983). Assistant Lecturer, Droit Public, University of Paris XI Law School. *LANGUAGES:* French and English.

YASMINE TARASEWICZ, born Neuilly sur Seine, France, June 16, 1958; admitted, 1985, Paris. *Education:* University of Paris V (D.E.A. Droit Privé, 1983). Author: "Le statut du dirigeant social," Cahiers sociaux, Barreau de Paris. *LANGUAGES:* French and English.

LORAINE DONNEDIEU DE VABRES, born Neuilly sur Seine, France, October 19, 1961; admitted, 1985, Paris. *Education:* D.E.A. of Business Law and of French and Community Economic Law. Author: "L'Etude des Lois essentielles sur la concurrence dans les 10 pays membres de la CEE," 1984, updated in 1992; "La concentration dans la distribution cinématographique," 1985. *LANGUAGES:* French and English.

YVON DREANO, born Pontivy, France, October 1, 1961; admitted, 1989, Paris. *Education:* Law Schools of Saarbrücken, Germany, Rennes and Paris II (Maître, 1984; Institut d'Etudes Judiciares, 1987); Institut d'Etudes Politiques, Paris (1986). Lecturer, Maître de Conférences, Institut d'Etudes Politiques, Paris. *Member:* IBA; ABA; New York State Bar Association; Association of the Bar of the City of New York; American Foreign Law Association. (Resident, New York, New York Office). *LANGUAGES:* French, English and German.

OF COUNSEL

*GENEVIÈVE BURDEAU, born Lyon, France, April 10, 1946. *Education:* Paris Law School (License, 1967; D.E.S. Droit Public, 1969; D.E.S. Science Politiques, 1969; D.E.S. Droit Privé, 1970; Doctorat d'Etat, 1974); Institut d'Etudes Politiques, Paris (1968); Ecole Nationale des Langues et Civilisations Orientales (Russe). Professeur Agrégée des Facultés de Droit, 1974. Author: Inter alia: "Les successions de systèmes monétaires en droit international"; "Die französischen Verstaatlichungen"; "Les accords entre organismes publics de pays differents". Contributor, Annuaire Français de Droit International, Journal du Droit International. Professor of Public and Economic International law, Dijon Law School, 1974–; Institut d'Etudes Politiques, Paris, 1984—; Hague Academy of International Law, 1989. *Member:* International Law Association; Société Française pour le Droit International; Association Internationale du Droit Economique. *LANGUAGES:* French, English, Italian and Polish.

*CLAUDE DUCOULOUX-FAVARD, born Belfort, France, October 5, 1930; admitted, 1956, Bordeaux. *Education:* Bordeaux Law School (Licence en Droit, 1956; D.E.S. Droit Privé, 1957; D.E.S. Droit Public, 1958; Doctorat, 1961). Master of Conferences, Paris IX Law School, 1969—. Lecturer, Luis Private Law School, Milan. Co-Author Dictionnaire Permanent du Droit des Affaires et Droit des Affaires Européennes. Regular Correspondent, "Revista delle Societá," Milan, Giuffré Publication. Author: inter alia: "Droit Pénal des Affaires," 1987; "Droit de la Vente," 1990; "Sociétés et Marché Commun (Aktien Gesellschaft, societa per azioni, Société anonyme)," 1991. *LANGUAGES:* French, Italian and German.

*HENRI FROMENT-MEURICE, AMBASSADEUR DE FRANCE, born Paris, June 5, 1923. *Education:* Paris Sorbonne (Licence es-letters); Ecole libre des Sciences Politiques; Ecole Nationale d'Administration (1948). Head of the Economic and Financial Department, Quai d'Orsay, 1975-1979. Ambassador in Moscow, 1979-1981 and Bonn, 1982-1983. Author: inter alia: "Une puissance nommée Europe," 1984 (Ventinck Award); "Europe 1992," 1988. *Member:* Franco-Soviet Committee on Joint Ventures (Chairman). *LANGUAGES:* French, English, German and Russian.

*LAURENCE IDOT, born Versailles, France, November 7, 1952. *Education:* Paris Law School (D.E.S. Droit Privé, 1974; D.E.S. de Droit Public, 1975; Diplôme du Centre Universitaire d'Etudes des Communautés Européennes, 1976); Institut d'Etudes Politiques, Paris, (1975). Professeur Agrégée des Facultés de Droit, 1982. Research Scholar, University of Michigan Law School, 1978. Author: "L'application extra-territoriale du droit européen de la concurrence," 1976; "Le contrôle des pratiques restrictives de concurrence dans les échanges internationaux," 1981; "Le guide juridique de la Côte d'Ivoire," 1988. Professor: Paris V Law School, 1988—; National Ivory Coast Law School, 1983-1988. *LANGUAGES:* French and English.

(This Listing Continued)

*VERONIQUE SELINSKY, born Montpellier, France, April 21, 1946. *Education:* Montpellier Law School (Licence, 1969; Maîtrise, 1970; DES des Droit Privé, 1971; Diplôme de Juriste Counseil d'Entreprise, 1971; DES Sciences Criminelles, 1972). Lecturer: Montpellier Law School; Montpellier School for Business Law. Chargée de mission à la Commission de la Concurrence, 1985. Rapporteur extérieur du Counseil de la Concurrence, 1986-1987. Author: "L'entente prohibée, 1979. Co-Author: with Professor Mousseron, Le droit français nouveau de la concurrence," 1989. *Member:* AFEC; AIDE. *LANGUAGES:* French and English.

SENIOR ASSOCIATES

Marie-Emmmanuelle Amphoux	Christophe Leguevaques
Yves Ardaillou	Nathalie Levasseur
Marion Barbier	Virginie Lisfranc-Galesne
Catherine Bastide	*Guillaume Loriot
Gauthier Blanluet	Philippe Losappio
Antoine Bolze	Jérôme Mailhé
Thierry Brun	*Gerald Matlofsky
Marie-Cécile de la Chapelle	Nathalie Meyer Fabre
Nicolas Charbit	*Karim Missaoui
Michelle Colas	Silvana Morandi
*Susan Coles	Pierre Mousseron
*Alexis Constantin	Pascal Ormen
Isabelle Damay	Carole Philippe
Marie-Pierre Dambly	Anne-Marie Pecoraro
Pascal Demko	Olivier Piquemal-Pradere
Amaury d'Everlange	Ilinca Popovici
Philippe Dubois	Philippe Portier
*Christine Fortea	Sébastien Prat
Dominique Gaffuri	Sonia Reeb
Jérôme Gandon	*Liubomir Rogleff
Jérôme Gaudin	Edouard Roty
Caroline Gravisse	*Diane Sénéchal
Béatrice Harichaux	Gilles Serreuille
Dominique Jardin	*Nicolas Telesnine
Katia Joffroy	Régis Turrini
*Anthony Lacoudre	Pascal Valance
Sandrine Lalardie	Catherine Verneret
Thierry Laloum	Valérie Vitu
Valérie Landes	Alexandre Vuchot
Benoît Laurin	*Laurent Xardel
Thierry Lauriol	François Zimeray

*Not authorized to appear before the French Courts as Avocats.

(For a list of Partners and Counsel of the respective Member Firms see Professional Biographies at: Oppenhoff & Rädler at Munich, Cologne, Frankfurt/Main and Berlin, Germany; De Bandt van Hecke & Lagae at Brussels, Belgium; De Brauw Blackstone Westbroek at The Hague, Rotterdam and Amsterdam, The Netherlands; Jeantet & Associés, at Paris, France; Uria & Menendez at Madrid and Barcelona, Spain).

JOBARD, CHEMLA & ASSOCIÉS

AVOCATS A LA COUR

Association d'Avocats

50 BOULEVARD DE COURCELLES
75017 PARIS, FRANCE
Telephone: (33-1) 42 67 11 70
Telecopier: (33-1) 42 67 11 83

General French and International Law Practice, Corporate, Mergers and Acquisitions, International Contracts, Banking, Agency, Franchise, Licensing, Copyright, Computer, Real Estate, Construction, Labor and Tax Law, Bankruptcy, Litigation and Arbitration.

MEMBERS

PIERRE-EMMANUEL JOBARD, born Paris, 1947; admitted, 1975, Paris. *Education:* Ecole Supérieure de Commerce de Paris, ESCP (Graduate, 1970); University of Paris (Licencié en Droit, 1971; Diplômé d'Etudes Comptables Supérieures, 1971; Certificat Supérieur de Relations Economiques Internationales, 1973; ; Diplômé d'Etudes Supérieures de Droit, 1975); Institut Auguste Comte, IAC (1981). *Member:* International Bar Association (IBA, Committees M,S,T); Union Internationale des Avocats (UIA); International Association of Young Lawyers - Former-President, Committee of representatives to International Organizations (AIJA); Association Française Pour l'Etude du Droit de la Concurrence (AFEC); Inter-Pacific Bar Association (IPBA) (Member, Executive Council). *LAN-*

(This Listing Continued)

GUAGES: French and English. *PRACTICE AREAS:* Acquisitions; Distribution Law; Intellectual Property; Real Estate; Litigation and Arbitration.

CHANTAL CHEMLA, born Tunis, 1952; admitted, 1980, Paris. *Education:* University of Paris (Maîtrise en Droit des Affaires, 1978). *LANGUAGES:* French and English. *PRACTICE AREAS:* Acquisitions; Corporate; Computer Law; International Contracts.

MARIE-LAURE LABAT-OLIVEAU, born Paris, 1949; admitted, 1973, Paris. *Education:* University of Paris (Licenciée en Droit, 1971). *Member:* International Association of Young Lawyers (AIJA). *LANGUAGES:* French and English. *PRACTICE AREAS:* Acquisitions; Corporate; Labor Law.

ERIC LEFEUBVRE, born Rennes, France, 1964; admitted, 1994, Paris. *Education:* University of Paris II - Assas (Maîtrise de Droit Privé, 1990). *Member:* Union des Jeunes Avocats (UJA). *LANGUAGES:* French, English. *PRACTICE AREAS:* Banking Law; Distribution Law; Bankruptcy; Litigation.

ANNE-MARIE SANSELME, born 1964; admitted, 1992, Paris. *Education:* University of Montpellier, Maîtrise en Droit Priveé, Droit des Affaires (1986); Diplomée d'Etudes Supérieures de Droit Economique (1987); University of Lyon, Diplôme de Juriste Conseil d'Entreprise (1987); Certificat d'Etudes Supérieures de Gestion du Personnel (1988). *LANGUAGES:* French, English, German. *PRACTICE AREAS:* Corporate; Labor Law; Intellectual Property; Distribution Law; Litigation.

LUC MOREAU, born 1966; admitted, 1992, Paris. *Education:* University of Paris, Licenciéen Droit (1987) Maîtrise de droit des affaires et de fiscalité (1988); DEA de droit des affaires (1989); Esole Supérieure de Commerce de Paris (ESCP) (1992). *LANGUAGES:* French, English. *PRACTICE AREAS:* Banking Law; Mergers and Acquisitions; Corporate; Litigation.

OF COUNSEL

GILLES CELIMENE, born Strasbourg, France, 1957; admitted, 1990, Paris. *Education:* University of Paris (Maîtrise en Droit des Affaires et Fiscalité, 1983); National Tax School (ENI). Tax House Officer (1986-1990). Maître de Conférences of Tax Law, Institut d'Etudes Politiques de Paris; Lecturer: University of Paris V in Tax Law. *Member:* Institut des Avocats Conseils Fiscaux. International Bar Association (IBA) (Committee N). *LANGUAGES:* French, English. *PRACTICE AREAS:* Tax Law.

MARIE-NOELLE JOBARD-BACHELLIER, born 1948. *Education:* University of Paris (Doctorat d'Etat en Droit, 1982; Agrégée des Facultés de Droit, 1984). Professor of Civil Law and International Law, University of Nanterre Paris X; Lecturer: University of Paris I Sorbonne. Author of Chronicles in Revue Critique de Droit International Privé. *Member:* Comité Français de Droit International Privé. *LANGUAGES:* French and English. *PRACTICE AREAS:* International Law.

JOHNS & ASSOCIATES

LAW OFFICES

2, AVENUE HOCHE
75008 PARIS, FRANCE
Telephone: (33.1) 44 40 46 46
Fax: (33.1) 44 40 46 47; (33.1) 44 40 46 49; (33.1) 44 40 46 50; (33.1) 44 40 46 51

Saint Tropez, France Office: 1, Place des Lices. Telephone: (16) 94 97 22 44. Fax: (16) 94 97 49 47.

Amsterdam, The Netherlands Associated Office: Herengracht 268, 1016. Telephone: (31.20) 627 2088. Fax: (31.20) 623 7129.

London, England Associated Office: 2 Carlos Place, Mount Street, W1Y 5AE. Telephone: (44.71) 499-8921. Fax: (44.71) 629-7720.

New York Office: 425 Park Avenue, New York, NY, 10022. Telephone: (212) 754-9400. Fax: (212) 754-6262.

General French, European and International Business and Commercial Law Practice. Corporate, Tax, International Tax Planning, Mergers and Acquisitions, Contract, Distribution and Franchising, Banking, Labour Law, Immigration, Litigation, Oil Trading, Arbitration, Property and Construction Law, Commercial Law, Bankruptcy Law, EEC Law, Aviation Law, Cross-border Insolvency, Intellectual Property and Private Clients.

FIRM PROFILE: The firm's experience is in providing service to foreign corporate and private clients in contact with the French legal system and to help our French clients market their abilities abroad, especially when meeting the English or American markets.

(This Listing Continued)

The lawyers and staff are fully bilingual in French and English and most speak other languages such as: German, Italian, Spanish, Greek, Turkish, Arabic, Luxemburg and Japanese.

PETER A. JOHNS, born 1947; admitted, 1977, Paris. *Education:* Universities of Paris and Nice (Maîtrise de Droit, 1972). Law Professor, Paris Bar Council. Lecturer: "How to Invest in England"; "Company law and Investments in France." Articles: "Cross border Mergers and Acquisitions"; "Company in the United Kingdom," Les Echos; "Mergers and Acquisitions in France." *Member:* International Bar Association; Inter Pacific Bar Association; American Bar Association; Association Internationale des Jeunes Avocats; Lawyers Associated Worldwide. *LANGUAGES:* French, English and German. *PRACTICE AREAS:* Mergers & Acquisitions; Arbitration; Company & Foreign Investment Law; Tax Law; Contracts; EEC Law; Commercial Litigations.

FRANÇOISE LALANNE, born 1956; admitted, 1985, Paris. *Education:* Université Paul Sabatier, Toulouse (Licence en Sciences Mathématiques, 1977); Université des Sciences Sociales de Toulouse (Maîtrise de Droit, carriére judiciaire, 1982). Assistant Professor, Université Paris-Malakoff, 1989-1990. Lecturer, "The French Agent Commercial." Author: "Droits des Femmes," First. Co-Author with Marie-Michèle Blouin: "200 Questions à mon Avocat," Marabout; "L'Avocat À Votre Service," First. *LANGUAGES:* French, English and Spanish. *PRACTICE AREAS:* Commercial; Civil Litigation.

MARIE-MICHÈLE BLOUIN, born 1955; admitted, 1987, Quebec (Not admitted in France). *Education:* York University, Toronto, Canada (Bachelor in Sciences, 1976); Université Laval, Québec, Canada (Licence en Droit, 1986). Co-Author with Françoise Lalanne: "200 Questions à mon Avocat," Marabout; "L'Avocat À Votre Service," First . *Member:* Quebec Bar Association; Canadian Bar Association; Association des Avocats du Barreau du Québec en France. *LANGUAGES:* French and English. *PRACTICE AREAS:* International Commercial Matters.

FRANÇOISE LUC-JOHNS, born 1950; admitted, 1983, Paris. *Education:* University of Nice (Maîtrise de Droit, 1972). *LANGUAGES:* French, English, German and Luxemburg. *PRACTICE AREAS:* Commercial; Civil Litigation; Building and Construction Law.

JOSETTE ROULOT, born 1949; admitted, 1993, Paris. *Education:* University of Nanterre Paris X (Maîtrise Droit des Affaires, 1972). *PRACTICE AREAS:* General Business Law.

ANNE-CAROLE TANGUY, born 1966; admitted, 1995, Paris. *Education:* University Paris (Maîtrise de Droit 1991-D.E.S.S. Droit du Commerce Extérieur 1992-Licence Lettres 1987). *LANGUAGES:* French, English and German. *PRACTICE AREAS:* International Business Law.

ROSALIE BEGA, born 1965. *Education:* Law University Reunion (D.E.S.S. Law 1987-Banking and Financial Law 1988); London Chamber of Commerce (Accounting 1990). *LANGUAGES:* French and English. *PRACTICE AREAS:* Banking; Tax; Corporate Law.

LEGAL SUPPORT PERSONNEL

SUZANNE NICOLA, born 1935. *Education:* Certificats ISSEC/ESSEC, Paris (Droit Général des Affaires, Droit des Sociétés, Droit du Travail, 1980); Certificate in Business Management (Gestion des Enterprises), University of Paris II (1982). (Paralegal). *LANGUAGES:* French, English, Italian, Greek and Turkish. *PRACTICE AREAS:* Immigration and Labour Law.

JONES, DAY, REAVIS & POGUE

62, RUE DU FAUBOURG SAINT-HONORE
75008 PARIS, FRANCE
Telephone: 33-1-44-71-3939
Cable Address: "Surgoe Paris"
Telex: 290156 Surgoe
Telecopier: 33-1-49-24-0471

In Atlanta, Georgia: 3500 One Peachtree Center, 303 Peachtree Street, N.E. Telephone: 404-521-3939. Cable Address: "Attorneys Atlanta". Telex: 54-2711. Telecopier: 404-581-8330.

In Brussels, Belgium: Avenue Louise 480, 7th Floor. B-1050 Brussels. Telephone: 32-2-645-14-11. Telecopier: 32-2-645-14-45.

In Chicago, Illinois: 77 West Wacker. Telephone: 312-782-3939. Telecopier: 312-782-8585.

(This Listing Continued)

JONES, DAY, REAVIS & POGUE, Paris—Continued

In Cleveland, Ohio: North Point, 901 Lakeside Avenue. Telephone: 216-586-3939. Cable Address: "Attorneys Cleveland." Telex: 980389. Telecopier: 216-579-0212.

In Columbus, Ohio: 1900 Huntington Center. Telephone: 614-469-3939. Cable Address: "Attorneys Columbus." Telecopier: 614-461-4198.

In Dallas, Texas: 2300 Trammell Crow Center, 2001 Ross Avenue. Telephone: 214-220-3939. Cable Address: "Attorneys Dallas." Telex: 730852. Telecopier: 214-969-5100.

In Frankfurt, Germany: Triton Haus, Bockenheimer Landstrasse 42, 60323 Frankfurt am Main. Telephone: 49-69-9726-3939. Telecopier: 49-69-9726-3993

Geneva, Switzerland: 20, rue de Candolle. Telephone: 41-22-320-2339. Telecopier: 41-22-1232.

In Hong Kong: 1501 One Exchange Square, 8 Connaught Place. Telephone: 852-2526-6895. Telecopier: 852-2810-5787.

In Irvine, California: 2603 Main Street, Suite 900. Telephone: 714-851-3939. Telex: 194911 Lawyers LSA. Telecopier: 714-553-7539.

In London, England: One Mount Street. Telephone: 44-71-493-9361. Cable Address: "Surgoe London WI." Telecopier: 44-71-493-9666.

In Los Angeles, California: 555 West Fifth Street, Suite 4600. Telephone: 213-489-3939. Telex: 181439 UD. Telecopier: 213-243-2539.

In New York, New York: 599 Lexington Avenue. Telephone: 212-326-3939. Cable Address: "JONESDAY NEWYORK." Telex: 237013 JDRP UR. Telecopier: 212-755-7306.

In Pittsburgh, Pennsylvania: 500 Grant Street, 31st Floor. Telephone: 412-391-3939. Cable Address: "Attorneys Pittsburgh". Telecopier: 412-394-7959.

In Riyadh, Saudi Arabia: Law Offices of Saud M.A. Shawwaf, P.O. Box 2700. Telephones: (966-1) 465-6543, (966-1) 464-8534 or (966-1) 464-8540. Telex: 401831 SAUCON SJ. Telecopier: (966-1) 464-8480.

In Taipei, Taiwan: 8th Floor, 2 Tun Hwa South Road, Section 2. Telephone: (886-2) 704-6808. Telecopier: (886-2) 704-6791.

In Tokyo, Japan: Toranomon MT Building, 4th Floor, 10-3, Toranomon 3-Chome, Minato-Ku, Tokyo 105 Japan. Telephone: 81-3-3433-3939. Telecopier: 81-3-5401-2725.

In Washington, D.C.: Metropolitan Square, 1450 G Street, N.W. Telephone: 202-879-3939. Cable Address: "Attorneys Washington." Telex: 89-2410 ATTORNEYS WASH. Telecopier: 202-737-2832.

Firm engaged in American and General International Practice and registered as Avocats in France as of January 1, 1992.

MEMBERS OF FIRM IN PARIS

JOHN F. CRAWFORD, born New York, New York, September 23, 1937. admitted to bar, 1965, District of Columbia; Avocat, 1973, Paris, France. *Education:* Haverford College (B.A., 1958); Fletcher School of Law and Diplomacy (M.A., 1959); Institut d'Etudes Politiques and Faculté des Lettres, University of Paris (1959-1961); Columbia University (J.D., 1964). Assistant to Director-General, International Labor Office, 1968-1970. President, American Chamber of Commerce in France, 1985-1988. Chairman, European Council of American Chambers of Commerce, 1987-1990.

DAVID F. CLOSSEY, born Cleveland, Ohio, January 31, 1944; admitted, 1968, Ohio; 1981, Texas (Not admitted in France). *Education:* Georgetown University (A.B., 1965); Cornell University (J.D., 1968). Order of the Coif.

PIERRE ULLMANN, born Neuilly sur Seine, France, May 6, 1950; admitted, Avocat, 1975, Paris, France. *Education:* Institut d'Etudes Politiques de Paris (1971); University of Paris (Maitrise en Droit, 1973- DES Droit des Affaires, 1974). Lecturer, Tax Law, University of Paris. *Member:* Institut Français des Conseils Fiscaux; International Fiscal Association (I.F.A.); International Bar Association (I.B.A.).

PHILIPPE BILLOT, born Paris, France, December 17, 1950; admitted, Avocat, 1991, Paris, France. *Education:* Universite de Paris X (Maitrise in Private Law, 1976); Center for Advanced Notarial Studies, Paris, France (1976). Qualified as Notary, 1980. *Member:* International Bar Association.

ANNE C. BOILEAU, born Neuilly-sur-Seine, France, March 29, 1952; admitted, Avocat, 1984, Paris, France. *Education:* University of Paris, Faculté de Droit (Licence en Droit, 1975; D.E.A. Droit International Public et Privé, 1977); University of Michigan (M.C.L., 1977).

WESLEY R. JOHNSON, JR., born Westport, Connecticut, June 17, 1954; admitted to bar, 1982, California; Avocat, 1991, Paris, France. *Education:* University of Michigan (B.A., 1975); Cambridge University (B.A., 1977; M.A., 1982); Harvard University (M.A., 1978; J.D., 1982).

(This Listing Continued)

LAURENT FAUGÉROLAS, born Périgueux, France, December 28, 1957; admitted, Avocat, 1989, Paris, France. *Education:* Institut d'Etudes Politiques, University of Bordeaux (Diplôme, 1982); Institute Supérieur des Affaires (M.B.A., 1986); University of Bordeaux (Do ctorat en Droit, 1988).

GAEL P. SAINT OLIVE, born Paris, France, March 22, 1960; admitted, Avocat, 1988, Paris, France. *Education:* Ecole Normale Supérieure (1983); Universite de Paris, Faculté de Droit (Licence, 1981, Maitrise 1983, DESS de Droit des Affaires et Fiscalité, 1983), and Faculté des Lettres (DEA d'Histoire, 1982); Institut d'Etudes Politiques de Paris (Diplome, 1983); Georgetown University (LL.M., 1985).

PETER R. STERNBERG, born Brussels, Belgium, March 14, 1961; admitted to bar, 1986, New York; Avocat, 1991, Paris, France. *Education:* University of Pennsylvania (B.A., 1982); New York University (J.D., 1985).

SENIOR ATTORNEY

MARIE-LAURE LARGET-BOZONNET, born St. Germain en Laye, France, April 25, 1948; admitted, Avocat, 1982, Paris, France. *Education:* University of Paris, Faculté des Lettres (Sociology Degree, 1968) and Faculté de Droit (Licence en Droit, 1970), Institut des Hautes Etudes Internationales, (1968-1970); New York University (Institute of Comparative Law Degree, 1973; M.C.J., 1975).

ASSOCIATES

NATHALIE GARNIER, born Boulogne-Billancourt, France, May 18, 1966; admitted, Avocat, 1993, Paris, France. *Education:* University of Paris XI and II (Maitrise en Droit, 1988; DEA, 1990).

SOPHIE HAGÈGE, born Bagneux, France, March 22, 1965. Avocat Stagiaire, Paris, France. *Education:* Institut d'Etudes Politiques de Paris (1987); Faculte de Droit de Sceaux (Maitrise, 1989); Duke University (LL.M., 1990).

AGNÈS L. FÉREY, born Cherbourg, France, May 18, 1966; admitted to bar, 1991, New York; Avocat, 1993, Paris, France. *Education:* University of Paris II (Maîtrise de Droit Privé, 1987); University of Paris IX (D.E.S.S. de Fiscalité de l'entreprise, 1988); University of Paris I (D.E.A. de Droit Américain des Affaires, 1989); New York University (LL.M., 1990).

ETIENNE MOUTHON, born Paris, France, February 27, 1966. admitted to bar, 1993, New York. Avocat Stagiaire, Paris, France, *Education:* Université Paris XI, Faculté de Droit de Sceaux (Licence en Droit, 1988); Université Paris XI, Faculté de Droit de Sceaux, (Maîtrise Droit des Affaires, option droit fiscal, 1989); Université Paris XI/H.E.C., Faculté de Droit de Sceaux, Ecole des Hautes Etudes Commerciales (DESS de Droit Fiscal International, 1990); New York University (LL.M., 1993).

ARNAUD G. VANBREMEERSCH, born Amiens, France, January 4, 1967; Avocat Stagiaire, Paris, France. *Education:* University of Paris II (Maîtrise de Droit des Affaires et Fiscalité , 1991); Institut de Droit des Affaires de Paris, 1991; University of Paris II (D.E.S.S. de Droit des Affaires et Fiscalité , 1992); University of Paris XI/HEC (D.E.S.S. de Droit Fiscal International, 1992). Lecturer in Tax Law, University of Paris II.

PIERRE-NICOLAS FERRAND, born Lyon France, July 29, 1965. *Education:* University of Paris 2 - Assas (DEA, 1990); Catholic Institute of Paris (DEA, 1991); University of Chicago (LL.M., 1992).

FRANÇOIS R. BONTEIL, born Paris, France, January 10, 1963; admitted, 1989, Paris, France; 1992, New York. *Education:* Lycee Janson de Sailly (Baccalaureat, 1982); Universite de Paris II - Assas (Maîtrise en Droit des Affaires-Fiscalite, 1986); Universite de Paris I - Sorbonne (Diplome D'etudes Approfondies en Droit Anglais et Nord-Americain des Affaires, 1987); New York University (Master of Comparative Jurisprudence, 1991).

ANTOINE ECHARD, born Châteauroux, France, April 12, 1968. *Education:* University of Paris II (Maitrise en Droit des Affaires et Fiscalité, 1990; D.E.A. Droit des Affaires, 1991); London University Queen Mary and Westfield College (Master of Laws in International Business Law, 1992).

Languages: English, French, German, Italian, Russian, Spanish, Swedish.

OFFICE JURIDIQUE FRANÇAIS ET INTERNATIONAL

(O.J.F.I.)

Established in 1945

374, RUE SAINT-HONORÉ

75001 PARIS, FRANCE

Telephone: (33-1) 42.86.57.57

Fax: (33-1) 42.86.57.58

Lyon, France: 10, rue Stella; 69002 Lyon.

Barcelona, Spain: Avenida Diagonal, 477; Torre de Barcelona, Planta 20 08036 Barcelona.

Bristol, England: 30 Queen Charlotte Street; Bristol BS99 7QQ.

Brussels, Belgium: Avenue de Cortenberg 79/81; 1040 Bruxelles.

Copenhagen, Denmark: H.C. Andersens Boulevard 37; DK-1553 Copenhagen V.

Frankfurt, Germany: Westendstrasse 24; 60325 Frankfurt am Main.

General and International Practice. Corporate, Tax, Mergers and Acquisitions, Labor Law, Litigation, Arbitration, Real Estate, Commercial Leases, Foreign Investments, Industrial and Intellectual Property, Products Liability, Competition, Administrative Law.

Firm engaged in French, European and International Law practice and authorized to appear before the French and European Courts.

FIRM PROFILE: Established in 1945, the Firm's practice covers the entire spectrum of legal, judicial and tax specialties. The Firm regularly advises foreign companies, more particularly European, North American and Japanese companies, doing business in France as well as French companies and individuals doing business in North America. The Firm has formed a European Economic Interest Group, "Office Juridique: Osborne Clarke Europe EEIG", with the English firm OSBORNE CLARKE, the Danish firm MOLLER TVERMOES & HOFFMEYER, the Belgian firm LEFEVRE & DOUTAELGPONT and the Spanish firm DAGA & SAURET. The Firm has also a close relationship with YAMADA CONSULTING, S.L.

MEMBERS OF FIRM

ANNICK BÉNT, born 1956; admitted, 1978, Lyon. *Education:* University of Lyon III (Masters Degree in Private Law). *LANGUAGES:* Spanish. *PRACTICE AREAS:* General Litigation; Commercial and Tax Litigation; Family Law; Civil Law.

JEAN-CLAUDE CAVAILLE, born 1947; admitted, 1981, Lyon. *Education:* University of Lyon III (Masters Degree in Law); Ecole Nationale des Impôrs (Diploma); Diploma of Advanced Accounting Studies. *PRACTICE AREAS:* Tax Advise and Litigation; Corporate Reorganization; Business Disposals and Acquisitions; Accounting Law; Law Relating to Local Authorities.

PATRICK GENTIL, born 1951; admitted, 1982, Paris. *Education:* University of REIMS (Masters Degree in Business Law); Institut Supérieur de Gestion, Paris (Diploma). *LANGUAGES:* English. *PRACTICE AREAS:* Corporate Law; Mergers and Acquisitions; Corporate Reorganization; Commercial Law; Real Estate Transactions and Commercial Leases; Intellectual Property Law; Bankruptcy Law; French and European Economic Law; Arbitration.

GEORGES LE MOIGN, born 1940; admitted, 1971, Paris. *Education:* University of Paris-Sorbonne (Masters Degree in Private Law and Diploma of Advanced Studies in Private Law). Former Partner at Ernst & Young, 1969-1977. *PRACTICE AREAS:* Real Estate Transactions and Commercial Leases; Commercial Law; Corporate Reorganization; Distribution Law.

DANIEL MARMOND, born 1948; admitted, 1978, Lyon. *Education:* University of Lyon III (Masters Degree in Labor Law, Diploma of Advanced Studies in Labor Law and Doctorate Degree); Cambridge University, U.K. (Diploma); Diploma from the Center for Further Business Studies (Centre de Perfectionnement aux Affaires - CPA); Agrégé de lettres. Professor of Law, Catholic University of Lyon and Lyon Business School, 1986—. *LANGUAGES:* English. *PRACTICE AREAS:* Labor Law; Economic Law.

FRANÇOISE MEPILLAT, born 1961; admitted, 1983, Lyon. *Education:* University of Lyon III (Masters Degree in Private Law, Diploma of Advanced Study in Economic and Business Law). Associate, Ernst & Young, 1983-1992. *LANGUAGES:* English. *PRACTICE AREAS:* Labor Law and Social Relations.

(This Listing Continued)

REMI J. TURCON, born 1963; admitted, 1988, Paris; 1991, California; 1993, New York. *Education:* University of Aix-Marseille III (Masters Degree in Private Law and Diploma of Advanced Studies in Public Law); Diploma from the Institute of Litigation Study, Aix en Provence; Doctorate in Public International Law, University of Aix-Marseille III; University of California, Los Angeles (LL.M., in International Law). Author: Foreign Direct Investment in the United States, Sweet & Maxwell, 1993; Investir aux Etats-Unis, Dalloz, 1994; Grundlagen des US-amerikanischen Gesellschafts-, Wirtschafts-, Steuerund-Fremdenrechts, C.H. Beck, 1994. Associate, Graham & James, Los Angeles, 1989-1991; Associate, Rogers & Wells, New York, 1991-1993. *Member:* Paris Bar Association; State Bar of California; New York State and American Bar Associations. *LANGUAGES:* English, Spanish. *PRACTICE AREAS:* French and U.S. Corporate Law; French and U.S. Commercial Law; Real Estate Transactions and Commercial Leases; Mergers and Acquisitions; International Transactions; Corporate Litigation.

VINCENT VERVANDIER, born 1953; admitted, 1980, Lyon. *Education:* University of Dijon (Masters Degree in Private Law and Diploma of Further Studies in Tax Law); Lauréat of University of Dijon. Lecturer, University of Dijon, 1975-1976. Lecturer, Universities of Lyon II and Lyon III. *LANGUAGES:* German. *PRACTICE AREAS:* Tax Advice and Contentious Tax Work; Corporate Reconstruction and Business Acquisitions and Disposals; Succession Law and Law Relating to Gifts.

LAURENT VIENOT, born 1947; admitted, 1974, Lyon. *Education:* University of Paris Sorbonne (Masters Degree in Private Law, Diploma of Further Studies in Law). *LANGUAGES:* English. *PRACTICE AREAS:* Commercial Law; Corporate Law; Arbitration; Corporate Reconstruction; Bankruptcy Law.

OF COUNSEL

JEAN-MARC LANDAULT, born 1952; admitted, 1976, Paris. *Education:* University of Paris (Masters Degree in Law and Diploma of Advanced Studies in Law). *PRACTICE AREAS:* General Litigation; Construction Law; Distribution and Competition Law.

PATRICK MUSSAT, born 1944; admitted, 1971, Paris. *Education:* University of Paris (Masters Degree in Law). Vice President of Centre d'Arbitrage pour les Entreprises. Correspondant Member of Association des Responsables Juridiques d'Entreprises. *Member:* Association Francaise de Droit Maritime; Cercle de la Finance. *PRACTICE AREAS:* Maritime and Industrial Litigation; Construction and Real Estate Litigation; Financial Litigation; White Collar Crimes.

ASSOCIATES

Nathalie Bergeron-Lanier; Eric Boyadjian; Francois-Noël Buffet; Jean-Pierre Coic; Nicole Estrabaud; Véronique Fournier; Sylvie Michel; Fabienne Regis.

DANIEL P. KAHN & ASSOCIÉS

35, AVENUE MAC MAHON

75017 PARIS, FRANCE

Telephone: (33-1) 42 67 03 20

Telecopier: (33-1) 42 67 03 24

French and International Practice. General Business and Corporate Law, Computer and New Technologies Related Matters, Aviation Law, Labor Law, Immigration Law, Litigation in French Courts, Arbitration.

DANIEL P. KAHN, born Strasbourg, France, December 12, 1957; admitted, 1980, France, Avocat a la Cour. *Education:* University of Strasbourg, Faculté de Droit (Licence en Droit, 1978; Maîtrise en Droit, 1979); Lauréat de la Faculté de Droit de L'Université des Sciences Juridiques, Politiques et Sociales de Strasbourg; Northwestern University School of Law (LL.M., 1980); C.A.P.A., 1980. *Member:* Computer Law Association.

RAPHAEL NACCACH

DIANE HEDARY

MARIE-LAURE DE CORDOVEZ

ISABEL DANINOS

AGNES GRENARD

(This Listing Continued)

DANIEL P. KAHN & ASSOCIÉS, Paris—Continued

Editor of the "Doing Business in France" Guide, Published by Credit Lyonnais Group.

Languages: French, English, Italian and Portuguese

"List of Representative Clients will be furnished upon request".

LAW OFFICES OF
PHILIP KAPLAN

2, RUE DE VILLERSEXEL
75007 PARIS, FRANCE
Telephone: (33.1) 44.39.10.00
Fax: (33.1) 45.49.39.69

International Sales, Distribution and Agency Contracts, International Debt Collection, Resolution and Litigation of Sales Disputes, French and International Banking Law, Bankruptcy Law.

PHILIP KAPLAN, born Newton, Massachusetts, October 24, 1945; admitted, 1985, Paris, Avocat, licensed to practice before all French Courts. *Education:* Harvard (B.A., 1967); Université de Paris, Sorbonne (Certificat C 1, 1968); University of Chicago (M.A., 1969); Harvard (Ed.D., 1977); Université de Paris II (Masters of Law, 1983). Certified Specialist in Commercial Law, Paris Bar. *Member:* Paris Bar Association; Harvard Club of France; French-Portuguese Chamber of Commerce; French-American Chamber of Commerce of New England. *LANGUAGES:* English, French, Portuguese and German. *PRACTICE AREAS:* Agency and Distributorships; International Banking; Bankruptcy; Sale of Goods; Debtor and Creditor Collections.

LAW OFFICES OF
PETER F. KENTON

16 RUE PUTEAUX
75017 PARIS, FRANCE
Telephone: (33-1) 42942059
Telecopier: (33-1) 42942049

General and International Practice, particularly Corporate, Taxation, Wills and Estates, Industrial Property, Product Liability, Real Estate, Insurance. Not authorized to plead before French Courts reserved for Avocats.

PETER F. KENTON, born New York, N.Y., 1926; admitted, 1953, New York (Not admitted in France). *Education:* Ohio State University; Brown University (A.B., 1949); Columbia University School of Law (J.D., 1952); New York University School of Law (LL.M., Comparative Law, 1959); University of Paris, Faculty of Law. Phi Alpha Delta. Special Mission, United Nations, 1957. Conseil Juridique in France, 1959-1972. *Member:* International Bar Association; American Foreign Law Association; American Chamber of Commerce in France. *LANGUAGES:* English, French, German and Hungarian.

KETCHEDJIAN & BAYLE

19 BIS, BD DELESSERT
75016 PARIS, FRANCE
Telephone: (33-1) 40 50 31 13
Telecopier: (33-1) 40 50 31 61

Saint-Denis (La Réunion), Indian Ocean Office: 1 rue des Hibiscus, 97400.

General Business Practice including Litigation before the French Courts. Corporate, Local and International Tax including related Litigation, Mergers and Acquisitions and Foreign Investments. Public Law Practice.

PARTNERS

DENIS KETCHEDJIAN, born Marseilles, France, April 26, 1940; admitted, 1974, Conseil Juridique, Paris; 1979, Nanterre; Avocat. *Education:* Graduate Political Studies Institute, University of Aix-en-Provence (1961); University of Paris, Faculty of Law (Licence en Droit, 1962; Diplôme d'Etudes Supérieures de Droit Public, 1963; Diplôme d'Etudes Supérieures de Science Politique, 1964; Docteur en Droit, mention très bien, 1972). Co-Author: "Rapport sur les Problèmes Juridiques Relatifs à une Société: Internationale pour la Contruction et l'Exploitation du Tunnel sous la Manche," Paris, 1965; "Mémoire au Conseil Constitutionnel sur la Non-

(This Listing Continued)

---

conformité à la Constitution de la Loi de Nationalisation de 1981," Paris, 1981. Author: "La personnalité morale au regard du droit fiscal," Paris, 1972; "L'entreprise individuelle et le droit fiscal: un nouveau sujet de droit?" Revue de Science Financière, 1974; "Le contrat de transfert fiduciaire de valeurs mobilières," Actes du Colloque de l'Unione Fiduciaria, Venice, 1976; "La récupération des déchets et le droit fiscal," Séminaire FEDUCI, Paris, 1984; "Les PME et les obligations fiscales," Colloque de l'Association Internationale de droit Economique, Nice, 1985. Professor, Faculty of Law, University of Paris (Teaching since 1963). Doctoral Candidate Lecturer in Real Estate Tax Law and International Tax Law, Fiduciaire Parisienne Juridique et Fiscale, 1973-1979. Associate, Arnaud Lyon-Caen, 1973-1978, Jean Labbé, 1979-1985, Avocats before the Conseil d'Etat, Cour de Cassation. Of Counsel, 1985-1986 and Partner, 1987-1990, Kevorkian & Rawlings. *Member:* Paris Bar. *LANGUAGES:* French and English.

CHRISTIAN BAYLE, born Salonique, Greece, February 4, 1961; admitted, Paris as Avocat. *Education:* University of Paris I, Faculty of Law (Licence en droit (Public), 1981; Maîtrise en droit des Affaires, 1982; Diplôme d'Etudes Supérieures Spécialisées en Droit des Affaires et Fiscalité, 1983). With: Clifford-Turner, 1983; Attaché French Embassy, Thailand, 1983-1985; Kevorkian & Rawlings, 1985-1990. *LANGUAGES:* French and English.

ASSOCIATES

FRANÇOIS BAYLE, born Geneva, Switzerland, September 23,1967. *Education:* University of Paris II, Faculty of Law (Maîtrise en Droit des Affaires et Fiscalité, 1989; Diplôme d'Etudes Supérieures Spécialisées en Droit des Affaires et Fiscalité, 1990). *LANGUAGES:* French and English.

FRANÇOIS CHAPTAL DE CHANTELOUP, born Avignon, France, May 8, 1966. *Education:* University of Paris II, Faculty of Law (Licence information et communication, 1988; Maîtrise Droit des Affaires et Fiscalité, 1989; Maîtrise Droit Public, 1989; DEA Droit des Affaires et Droit Economique, 1990; DESS de Défense, 1991); University of Paris I, Sorbonne (DESS Droit du Commerce Extérieur, 1991). *LANGUAGES:* French, English and Italian.

RICHARD GROCH, born Champigny s/Marne, France, April 14,1965. *Education:* University of Paris I, Sorbonne (Maîtrise Droit des Affaires et Fiscalité, 1989); University of Paris XII (DESS Fiscalité Appliquée option Internationale). *LANGUAGES:* French and English.

ERIC BACHELERIE, born Paris, France, December 19, 1965. *Education:* University of Paris II, Faculty of Law (Maîtrise en Droit des Affaires et Fiscalité, 1989; Diplôme d'Etudes Approfondies en Droit des Affaires, 1990); University of Paris I, Faculty of Law (Diplôme d'Etudes Supérieures Spécialisées en Droit des Assurances, 1990). *LANGUAGES:* French, German and English.

OF COUNSEL

CHARLES HAGGAI, born Mostaganem, Algeria, June 6, 1934; admitted, 1956, Paris as Avocat. *Education:* University of Alger (Licence en droit; DES de droit privé, 1955). Lecturer: CAPA, 1971-1977; "La Protection des Cours d'Eau Intérieurs en Droit Français," Conférence Internationale de Royan sur la Protection de l'Environnement, 1970; "Communauté Européenne, Convention de Lomé et Développement Economique de l'Ile de la Réunion," conférences du Conseil Economique et Social, 1989. Contribution to Study on, "Emprunts Euro-obligataires," with Professor Kahn, 1971. Secrétaire de la Conférence du stage, 1958; Vice President, Union des Jeunes Avocats, Paris, 1960. (Resident, Saint-Denis de la Réunion Office).

KEVORKIAN & PARTNERS

46, AVENUE D'IÉNA
75116 PARIS, FRANCE
Telephone: 40.69.50.00
Telecopier: 47.20.54.64

New York, New York Office: 135 E. 57th Street, 10022. Telephone: (212) 838 5600. Telecopier: (212) 753 6971. Telex: 238725.

London, England Office: 38 Hertford Street, W1Y 7TG. Telephone: 0171-355-2051. Fax: 0171-355-4975.

General and International Law Practice.
Firm engaged in American and General International Practice, and registered as Conseils Juridiques in France since 1966, and as Avocats since January, 1992.

(This Listing Continued)

MEMBERS OF FIRM

ARAM J. KEVORKIAN, born Philadelphia, Pennsylvania, December 31, 1928; admitted, 1953, District of Columbia; 1959, New York; Conseil Juridique, France; 1992, Avocat. *Education:* University of Pennsylvania (B.A., 1950); Harvard Law School (J.D., magna cum laude, 1953); University of Strasbourg (1953-1954). Phi Beta Kappa. Editor, Harvard Law Review, 1951-1953. Author: "Quelques Critiques Pragmatiques de la Loi Française sur les Sociétés Commerciales," and "Descartes, Symétrie, et Justice," Gazette du Palais, 1968; "Montaigne et Descartes," Les Petites Affiches, 1984; "Le Droit Antitrust Américain et les Brevets d'Invention," Gazette du Palais, 1976; Legal Newsletter from France, September 1978—. Lecturer, U.S. Antitrust Law, University of Strasbourg, 1976-1980. Associate, Dewey, Ballantine, Bushby, Palmer & Wood, 1954, 1958-1961. Associate, 1961-1963 and Member, 1964-1966, Coudert Frères, Paris, France. Visiting Professor of Law, New York University, 1969. *Member:* Association of the Bar of the City of New York; New York County Lawyers' Association. [J.A.G. Corps, U.S. Army, 1955-1957]. *LANGUAGES:* English, French and Armenian.

SYLVIE KAISERMANN, (MRS.), born Cairo, Egypt, May 1, 1936; admitted, 1973, Conseil Juridique, France; 1992, Avocat. *Education:* University of Oxford (General Certificate of Education, 1951); Faculté des Lettres University of Paris (Maitrise es-Lettres, 1959); Faculty of Law, University of Paris (Maitrise en Droit, 1971). *LANGUAGES:* English and French.

PATRICK ZAMBEAUX, born Lille, France, August 20, 1950. *Education:* Faculty of Law, Université de Paris X-Nanterre (Licence en Droit, 1972; D.E.S., 1974); Fondation Nationale pour le Droit de l'Entreprise (Diplôme d'Etudes fiscales et commerciales, 1974). *LANGUAGES:* French and English.

JAMES A. LOUGHRAN, born New York, N.Y., 1931; admitted, 1959, New York; 1960, Connecticut (Not admitted in France). *Education:* Fordham University (A.B., 1953); University of Pennsylvania (LL.B., 1958); Columbia University (M.I.A., 1959). Fulbright Scholar, Argentina 1963. Author: "Some Reflections on the Argentine Problem," Journal of Inter-American Economic Affairs, 1964; "Britain-Banking Capital of the World," 1980. *Member:* Law Society of England and Wales as Overseas Lawyer; American Bar Association; Chartered Institute of Arbitrators, London (Associate Member). [1st Lieut., U.S. Marine Corps, 1953-1955]. (Resident Partner, London Office). *LANGUAGES:* English, Spanish, French and Italian.

ASSOCIATES

EMMANUEL ASMAR, born Abidjan, Ivory Coast, March 15, 1969; admitted, 1994, Avocat. *Education:* University of Paris I - Panthéon-Sorbonne (Maitrise en droit des affaires, 1991 et DEA en droit des affaires et droit économique, 1993). *LANGUAGES:* French and English.

THIERRY FORTIER-DUGUAY, born Montréal, Canada, June 18, 1962; admitted, 1988, California (Not admitted in France). *Education:* University of California Los Angeles (B.A., 1985); Loyola Law School at Los Angeles (J.D., 1988); Institut d'Administration des Entreprises de Montpellier, France (C.A.A.E., 1991). *LANGUAGES:* English, French and Spanish.

LAURENCE TOUATI, born Paris, France, July 26, 1969; admitted, 1994, Avocat. *Education:* University of Paris X - Nanterre (Maîtrise en Droit des Affaires, 1990); McGill University, Montréal, Canada (LL.M., 1992). *LANGUAGES:* French and English.

OF COUNSEL

MARC DAMELINCOURT, born Libercourt, France, May 15, 1952; admitted, 1976, Paris, France, Avocat. *Education:* Graduate Political Studies Institute, Paris, (1973); University of Paris II (Licence en Droit, 1975); Institute d'Etudes judiciaires (1975); D.E.S.S. Droit des Affaires, 1976). Associate: Cabinet Biaggi, Paris, France, 1973-1975; Thomas et Associés, Paris, France, 1979-1980. Member, Thomas et Associés, 1981-1985. *Member:* Paris Bar; ANASED (Association Nationale des Avocats pour la Sauvegarde des Enterprises et leur développement). *LANGUAGES:* French and English.

ARMAND COHEN, born Casablanca, Morocco, December 3, 1951. *Education:* University of Paris II, Faculty of Law, Legal and Economic Science Degree, (1975);. Arthur Anderson Tax Department, 1977-1980. Partner in charge of FAE International for legal and Tax advise in France, 1980-1990. *LANGUAGES:* French and English.

PAUL CORIAT, born Oran, France, August 28, 1933. *Education:* University of Paris (Licence en Droit, 1957); Institut du Droit des Affaires,

(This Listing Continued)

Paris (1957). Associate and European Counsel, Coudert Frères, Paris, 1961-1970. Partner, International Affairs, Francis Lefebvre, Paris, 1971-1981. Senior Partner, Fides Partner, Geneva Switzerland. Senior Partner, Legal & Business Consulting, Geneva, Switzerland, 1992—. Member, Credit Suisse Group, 1981-1992. *LANGUAGES:* French, English, Italian and Spanish.

KIMBROUGH & ASSOCIES

A PROFESSIONAL CORPORATION

72, BOULEVARD SAINT GERMAIN
75005 PARIS, FRANCE
Telephone: (33) (1) 43.25.15.05
Telefax: (33) (1) 43.29.98.38
Telex: KHV 205 672 F

General and International Commercial Law Practice, Corporate Law, International Investments (acquisition and joint ventures), Banking and Project Financing, European Community Law, Real Estate and Construction Law, International Arbitration and French Court Litigation, Intellectual Property, Registered in France.

PHILIP R. KIMBROUGH, born Waxahachie, Texas, July 23, 1956; admitted, 1980, Texas; 1984, Conseil Juridique, Paris; 1992, avocat, Paris Bar. *Education:* Texas Christian University (B.A., 1977) Phi Beta Kappa; Université de Paris I, undergraduate certificate in French language and culture (1976); Harvard Law School (J.D., 1980); Université de Paris I, Panthéon-Sorbonne, Law School (D.E.S.S. in Foreign Trade, 1983). Co-Author: "Esprit de Géométrie, esprit de finesse ou l'acception du mot 'raisonnable' dans les contrats de droit privé américain," IX, I *Droit et Pratique du Commerce International,* pp. 43-56, 1983. Author: "Singapore Report," XI *Yearbook Commercial Arbitration,* pp. 29-52, 1986; "General Viability of Arbitration in Singapore: Singapore's Accession to the New York Convention Fills the Last Gap," *Revue de Droit des Affaires Internationales,* N°8, pp. 783-798, 1986. President, Harvard International Law Society, 1979-1980; President, Harvard Club of France, 1989—. *Member:* American and International Bar Associations; State Bar of Texas; Singapore Institute of Arbitrators. *LANGUAGES:* English and French.

YVES GAUBIAC, born Paris, France, February 2, 1952; Avocat, Paris Bar. *Education:* Université de Paris II, Law School (License in Business Law, 1976; D.E.A. in literary, artistic and industrial property, 1977; Doctorat d'Etat, 1980). Consultant for the Chambre de Commerce et d'Industrie de Paris, Paris, France, 1980-1983. Consultant for UNESCO Paris offices, 1983-1987. Director of the Section of Rights to Mechanical Reproduction in the Legal Department of SACEM, the French entity in charge of the collective administration of the rights of composers and publishers of musical works, Paris (1988-1991). Author: "The new Technical Means of Reproduction and Copyright," 122 Revue Internationale du Droit d'Auteur, pp. 22-144 and 123 RIDA pp. 107-177, 1984; "Renumeration of private copies of phonograms and videograms according to the French Act of July 3, 1985," 4 Revue trimestrielle de droit commercial et de droit économique, pp. 491-512, 1986. Lecturer, Université de Paris II Panthéon Assas Law School. Editor in Chief, *Revue Internationale du Droit d'Auteur.* *Member:* International Literary and Artistic Association; International League of Competition Law; International Association for the Protection of Industrial Property; International Association for the Advancement of Teaching and Research in Intellectual Property. *LANGUAGES:* French and English.

KLEIN-GODDARD ASSOCIÉS

44, AVENUE DES CHAMPS-ELYSEES
75008 PARIS, FRANCE
Telephone: 44.95.20.00
Paris Telecopier: 49.53.03.97

Abidjan, Cote d'Ivoire Office: 01 BP 3586 Abidjan 01, Le Jeceda F32.
Telephones: (225) 21-28-52; (225) 21-28-64. Telecopier: (225) 21-28-43.
Other Offices: London, Brussels, Budapest, Jersey, Prague, Warsaw, Los Angeles, New York, Washington, D.C., Tel Aviv.

International, Corporate, Taxation, Foreign Investments and Real Estate Law, Banking, Securities, Stock Exchange, Bankruptcy, Competition, EC Law, Environmental Law, Contracts, Commercial, Intellectual Property Law, Arbitration and Litigation, English and Scottish Law, Laws of West Africa.
Firm authorized to appear before French Courts as Avocats à la Cour.

FIRM PROFILE: The firm was created in 1993 following the merger of Klein et Associés, and Theodore Goddard, Paris.

(This Listing Continued)

KLEIN-GODDARD ASSOCIÉS, Paris—Continued

PARTNERS

THEODORE KLEIN, born Paris, France, June 25, 1920; admitted, 1945, Paris; 1970, Israël. *Education:* University of Paris (Licence en Droit, diplôme de l'Ecole des Sciences Politiques, 1945). *Member:* Paris Bar Association; Israël Bar Association. *LANGUAGES:* French, German, Hebrew and English. *PRACTICE AREAS:* Adviser to Corporations and their Executives; International Relations; Law of Contracts; Arbitration and Litigation.

STÉPHANE BACRIE, born Suresnes, France, September 28, 1960; admitted, 1988, Paris. *Education:* University of Paris (Maîtrise Droit des Affaires, 1985); University of Miami Law School (M.C.L., 1986); C.A.P.A. (1987). *Member:* Paris Bar Association. *LANGUAGES:* French, English and Spanish. *PRACTICE AREAS:* Corporate and Commercial Law; Litigation; Law of Contracts; Distribution Law; Broadcasting Law.

JEAN-FRANÇOIS CHAUVEAU, born Paris, France, April 19, 1948; admitted, 1983, Paris. *Education:* Paris (D.E.S. droit public, 1973); Centre des Communautés Européennes (Paris, 1971); C.A.P.A. (1982). *Member:* Paris Bar Association. *LANGUAGES:* French and English. *PRACTICE AREAS:* Administrative and Public Business Law; International Relations Law; Law of Contracts; Law of the States of West Africa.

PHILIPPE GOLD, born Paris, France, August 7, 1940; admitted, 1974, Paris. *Education:* University of Paris, Eastern Languages School, Paris (Russian), Political Sciences Institute (Diploma, 1965); University of Paris (Faculté de Droit, Licence, 1964, et Diplôme d'Etudes Supérieures, 1966); C.A.P.A. (1971). *Member:* Paris Bar Association. *LANGUAGES:* French, English and Spanish. *PRACTICE AREAS:* Property (public and private law); Banking Law; Arbitration and Litigation.

FRANÇOIS KLEIN, born Paris, April 21, 1951; admitted, 1976, Paris. *Education:* University of Nanterre (D.E.A. Droit des Affaires); Institut d'Etudes Politique s de Paris. *Member:* Paris Bar Association. *LANGUAGES:* French and English. *PRACTICE AREAS:* Intellectual Property Law; Litigation; Employment Law; Competition Law; Law of Contracts; Bankruptcy Law.

BERNARD LAURENT-BELLUE, born Laval, France, November 11, 1958; admitted, 1988, Paris. *Education:* Institut d'Etudes Politiques de Paris I (1980); University of Paris (Maîtrise en Droit, 1982; D.E.A. en Droit Comparé, 1983); Doctorat en Droit, magna cum laude, 1992; University of California at Berkeley (LL.M., 1987). Lecturer on Law, University of Paris I. *Member:* Paris Bar Association. *LANGUAGES:* French and English. *PRACTICE AREAS:* Corporate Law; Financial and Stock Exchange Law; Mergers and Acquisitions.

DOMINIC MCCLUSKEY, born Glasgow, Great Britain, January 31, 1939; admitted, 1961, as Solicitor, Scotland; 1992, Paris. *Education:* University of Edinburgh (Bachelor of Laws). *Member:* Paris Bar Association. *LANGUAGES:* English and French. *PRACTICE AREAS:* Property Law; Private International Law; Commercial Law.

JOHN G. SELL, born Radlett, Great Britain, May 19, 1945; admitted, 1970, as Solicitor, England; 1992, Paris. *Education:* University of Cambridge (1967); Centre Universitaire d'études des Communautés européennes, University of Paris (1971); D.E.S.S. Conseil juridique et fiscal d'entreprises (1976). *Member:* Paris Bar Association. *LANGUAGES:* English and French. *PRACTICE AREAS:* Corporate Law; Mergers and Acquisitions; Tax; International Law.

LAURENT XAVIER SIMONEL, born Brazzaville, Congo, July 13, 1955; admitted, 1986, Paris. *Education:* Institut d'Etudes Politiques de Paris, University of Paris (D.E.A. Droit International Public; Maîtrise de Droit Public), C.A.P.A. (1986). *Member:* Paris Bar Association. (Resident, Abidjan Office). *LANGUAGES:* French and English. *PRACTICE AREAS:* Public Law; Law of Contracts; International Law; International Relations Law.

DUNCAN B. STAPYLTON-SMITH, born Tunbridge Wells, Great Britain, May 1, 1958; admitted, 1983, as Solicitor, England; 1992, Paris. *Education:* University of Leicester (LL.B., 1981). *Member:* Paris Bar Association. *LANGUAGES:* French and English. *PRACTICE AREAS:* Property Law and Property Tax; Construction Law.

SERGE WILINSKI, born Paris, July, 1962; admitted, 1992, Paris. *Education:* University of Paris (D.E.S.S. de droit du commerce extérieur, 1985). *Member:* Paris Bar Association. *LANGUAGES:* French and English.

(This Listing Continued)

PRACTICE AREAS: International Business Law; Mergers and Acquisitions; Corporate Law.

OF COUNSEL

AMI BARAV, born September 18, 1946; admitted, 1992, Paris. *Education:* University of London (M.Se (Econ.) Politics (1971); LL.M. (1973), Doctorat d'Etat, University of Strasbourg (1983). *LANGUAGES:* French, English, Hebrew. *PRACTICE AREAS:* European Community Law.

PATRICK BERJAUD, born Casablanca, Morocco, July 13, 1961; admitted, 1988, Paris. *Education:* University of Paris (Maîtrise du Droit des affaires, 1984); C.A.P.A. (1987). *Member:* Paris Bar Association. *LANGUAGES:* French and English. *PRACTICE AREAS:* Employment Law.

PHILIP WOOLFSON, born Glasgow, Scotland, December 23, 1955; admitted, 1982, as Solicitor, Scotland; 1992, Paris. *Education:* University of Glasgow (M.A., 1976; B.L., 1979); Certificat de hautes études européennes, Collège d'Europe de Bruges. *Member:* Paris Bar Association. (Resident, Brussels Office). *LANGUAGES:* English and French. *PRACTICE AREAS:* Corporate Law; Mergers and Acquisitions; European Community Law.

ASSOCIATES

JEAN-LUC BOUTON, born September 27, 1954; admitted, 1992, Paris. *Education:* Tax Specialist Certificate, Licence de sciences économiques, University of Nancy (1978); National School of Tax (1978). *Member:* Paris Bar Association. *LANGUAGES:* French and English. *PRACTICE AREAS:* French and International Tax.

MICHÈLE DAUVOIS, born Pithiviers, France, April 6, 1961; admitted, 1989, Paris. *Education:* University of Paris I (Maîtrise en Droit, 1984; D.E.A. en Droit des Affaires, 1985); University of London, King's College (LL.B., in French and English Law, 1984). *Member:* Paris Bar Association. *LANGUAGES:* French and English. *PRACTICE AREAS:* Corporate and Commercial Law; Litigation.

RAPHAËLE FRANCOIS-PONCET, born Paris, France, August 12, 1962; admitted, 1992, Paris. *Education:* Political Science Institute, Paris; University of Paris I; Institute of Comparative Law. *Member:* Paris Bar Association. *LANGUAGES:* French and English. *PRACTICE AREAS:* Corporate Law; Financial and Stock Exchange Law; Mergers and Acquisitions.

NARINA GREWAL, born London, Great Britain, August 29, 1967; admitted, 1994, as Solicitor, England. *Education:* University of Oxford, 1989; College of Law, England, 1991. *LANGUAGES:* French, German and English. *PRACTICE AREAS:* Corporate Law.

JULIE JACOB, born Neuilly, France, February 4, 1971; admitted, 1994, Paris. *Education:* University of Paris X (D.E.S.S. de Droit des affaires et fiscalité, 1993); C.A.P.A. (1993). *Member:* Paris Bar Association. *LANGUAGES:* French and English. *PRACTICE AREAS:* Trademark Law; Employment Law; Civil and Commercial Litigation.

OLIVIER MAES, born Berck/Mer, France, September 2, 1963; admitted, 1992, Paris. *Education:* University of Lille (Maîtrise de droit des affaires, 1985); University of Warwick (Diplôme de droit anglais, 1986). *Member:* Paris Bar Association. *LANGUAGES:* French and English. *PRACTICE AREAS:* Corporate and Commercial Law.

LAURENCE MIGUEL-CHESTERKINE, born Neuilly, France, February 11, 1960; admitted, 1992, Paris. *Education:* University of Paris (Maîtrise de droit "carriéres judiciaires," 1983; Diplôme de l'Institut d'Etudes Judiciaires, 1983; Certificat d'Aptitude à la Profession d'Avocat, 1984). *Member:* Paris Bar Association. *LANGUAGES:* French, English and Spanish. *PRACTICE AREAS:* Law of Contracts; Commercial Law; Litigation.

LAWRENCE PARDOE, born Birmingham, Great Britain, March 30, 1958; admitted, 1983, as Solicitor, England; 1992, Paris. *Education:* University of Manchester (1979). *Member:* Paris Bar Association. *LANGUAGES:* French, English and Spanish. *PRACTICE AREAS:* Asset Finance; Commercial Law.

FRANCOIS-LUC PONTHIEU, born Algeria, March 22, 1962; admitted, 1992, Israel; 0994, Paris. *Education:* Imoversotu pf Aix-en-Provence (Maîtrise de Droit public (1983); Diplôme Institut Etudes Politiques (1983); C.A.P.A. (1990). *Member:* Paris Bar Association and Israel Bar Association. *LANGUAGES:* French, English, Spanish and Hebrew. *PRACTICE AREAS:* Intellectual Property.

RACHEL ROBINSON - SALOMON, born Boulogne-sur-Seine, France, October 27, 1968; admitted, 1993, Paris. *Education:* University of Paris II (D.E.A. de Propriét é Littéraire, artistique et industrielle (1991);

(This Listing Continued)

C.A.P.A. (1992). *Member:* Paris Bar Association. *LANGUAGES:* French, English. *PRACTICE AREAS:* Intellectual Property.

ANDRÉE SASSON, born Manchester, Great Britain, September 16, 1965; admitted, 1992, Paris. *Education:* University of Paris (Maîtrise de Droit Privé, 1987). *Member:* Paris Bar Association. *LANGUAGES:* French and English. *PRACTICE AREAS:* Property and Private International Law.

FRANÇOISE SEILLER, born Issy les Moulineaux, France, October 31, 1959; admitted, 1990, Paris. *Education:* Paris University of Sceaux (Maîtrise en Droit Public et Européen, 1984; D.E.S.S. de Diplomatie et Administration des Organisations Internationales, 1985). *Member:* Paris Bar Association. *LANGUAGES:* French and English. *PRACTICE AREAS:* Property Litigation.

ERIC SITBON, born Paris, France, May 9, 1968; admitted, 1995 Paris. *Education:* Paris X University, D.E.A. de Droit des Affaires (1993); Diploma in English and American Law (1991);. Visiting Scholar at Columbia University School of Law, New York, U.S.A. (1991-1992); C.A.P.A. (1994); Lecturer, at Paris X University (Civil Law). *Member:* Paris Bar Association. *LANGUAGES:* French, English and German. *PRACTICE AREAS:* European Community Law; Corporate Law; Contract Law.

TRAINEES

HÉLÈNE GUERIN, born Bourges, France, December 18, 1965. *Education:* University of London (LL.M., 1989); University of Paris (D.E.S.S. de droit des affaires, 1992). (Trainee). *LANGUAGES:* French, English and German. *PRACTICE AREAS:* Corporate and Commercial Law.

LIONEL SCOTTO LE MASSESE, born Paris, France, April 5, 1965. *Education:* University of Kent (B.A., in Law, honors, 1991); University of Paris (D.E.S.S. de droit des affaires, 1992). (Trainee). *LANGUAGES:* French, English, German. *PRACTICE AREAS:* Corporate Law.

FRANCOIS VALLEE, born May 13, 1965. *Education:* University of Paris (D.E.A. de propriété artistique et industrielle, 1990), Diploma in English law; University of Kent (1987); London School of Ecnomics (LL.M., 1991). (Trainee). *LANGUAGES:* English, German.

LAW OFFICES OF WM. JAMES KOPACZ

Established in 1984

83 AVENUE FOCH
75116 PARIS, FRANCE
Telephone: (1) 47 04 61 74
Fax: (1) 47 55 67 81

Engaged in General Patent, Trademark and Copyright Practice specializing in litigation before the French and European Courts. Registered to practice before the European Patent Office and U.S. Patent Office.

WILLIAM J. KOPACZ, born Chicago, Illinois, September 24, 1941; admitted, 1969, Virginia; 1970, California; 1979, Conseil Juridique; 1992, France (Avocat); registered to practice before U.S. Patent and Trademark Office, European Patent Office and French Patent and Trademark Office. *Education:* University of Illinois (B.S.E.E., 1964); Georgetown University (J.D., 1968). Examiner, U.S. Patent and Trademark Office, 1964-1968. Research Fellow, Max Planck Institute for Foreign and International Industrial Property Law, Munich, 1974-1976. *Member:* Paris Bar; Virginia State Bar; State Bar of California. *LANGUAGES:* French and German. *PRACTICE AREAS:* Patent; Trademark Law; Litigation; Data Processing Law.

M-P DAUQUAIRE

M. BOBONE

H. FRASSON-GARRET

P. PETIT

All attorneys are members of the Paris Bar (Avocats).

REPRESENTATIVE CLIENTS: Motorola; Visa International; Medtronic; Porsche; Levi Strauss; Dolby Labs; Harris Corp.; Thomson CSF; Quantum Corp.; Stanford University; Pro-Log Corp.; Stratus Computer; Colburn Optical; Emmanuelle Khanh; La Vie Claire; SunDisk Corp.; Cummins Engine; Den-Mat Corp.; Lloyd Loom; Baker & MacKenzie; Dorsey & Whitney; Graham & James; Haverstock, Medlen; Howard, Rice; Dike Bronstein; Lahive & Cockfield; Townsend & Townsend; Owen, Wickersham; Rudnick & Wolf; Majestic, Parsons; Limbach & Limbach; Heller, Ehrman.

KPMG FIDAL PEAT INTERNATIONAL

47, RUE DE VILLIERS
92200 NEUILLY-SUR-SEINE
PARIS, FRANCE
Telephone: (1) 46 39 40 40
Telecopier: (1) 47 59 00 78

General French, EU and International Practice: Mergers & Acquisitions, Banking, International Business Transactions and Contracts, Formation of Companies, Exchange Control Regulations, Labor and Social Security Law, Corporate and Individual Tax, Tax Planning and Litigation, Real Estate, Entertainment, Insurance, Oil, Transportation, High Technology.

FIRM PROFILE: *Resulting from the merger in 1988 of Peat Marwick France and Fidal's International Law Division, with approximately 50 Lawyers, the Firm offers a complete range of legal and tax services to French and multinational companies. All firm members are admitted to the practice of law, Paris Bar or Hauts-de-Seine Bar. It is a division of Fiduciaire Juridique et Fiscale de France (FIDAL), the largest and among the oldest French law firms providing the most extensive national coverage through over 100 offices.*

MEMBERS OF FIRM

LOÏC STEUNOU, Law Degree, University of Paris, 1961; Real Estate, Pharmaceutical, Agro-Business.

MICHEL ALBESSARD, Law Degree, University of Dijon, 1975: Banking, Financial Instruments, Investment Funds, Real Estate, High Technology.

JEAN-FRANÇOIS BLOUET, Law Degree, University of Paris, 1969: EU and Tax Law, International Tax Structures and Reorganization, Manufacturing, Distribution, Retailing.

FRANÇOIS BON, Law Degree, University of Montpellier, 1979, Accounting Degree: Banking, Transportation, Publishing, Advertising.

PHILIPPE BRETON, Tax Law Degree, University of Dijon, 1985: Banking, Financial Services, Agro-Business, Group Taxation.

SERGE BROCHE, Law Degree, National Tax School, 1969: Oil and Gas, Transportation.

GUILLAUME DE BRONDEAU, Law Degree, University of Paris, 1967, Graduate Business School: Banking, Financial Services, Luxury Products.

NATHALIE CORDIER-DELTOUR, Business Law Degree, University of Montpellier, 1984: Transportation, Publishing, Restructuring, Group Taxation.

KRISTIN DEFERT, Born in United States, Law Degree, Rutgers University, 1978, Law Review, Member of Pennsylvania Bar: Corporate, Contract and Commercial Law, Mergers and Acquisitions.

JEAN-PIERRE DUMAZAUD, Business and Tax Law Degree, University of Paris I, 1982: Insurance, Distribution, Mergers and Acquisitions, Group Taxation.

GILLES GALINIER-WARRAIN, Law Degree, University of Paris, 1975, Degree, Political Sciences Institute: Leasing, Banking, Oil and Gas, International Corporate Tax, High Technology.

PHILIPPE HUTCHINGS, Law Degree, University of Paris II, 1979: Transportation, Distribution, High Technology, Restructuring, Group Taxation.

NORBERT MAJERHOLC, Business Law Degree, University of Paris I, 1983: Chemical and Pharmaceutical, Restructuring and Group Taxation, Mergers and Acquisitions.

FRANÇOIS-RÉGIS PASCAL, Law Degree, University of Paris, 1972: Company Law, Mergers and Acquisitions, Restructuring, Financial and Stock Exchange Law.

(This Listing Continued)

KPMG FIDAL PEAT INTERNATIONAL, Paris—
Continued

LIONEL REBILLY, Law Degree, National Tax School, 1971: Local and Real Estate, Taxes, Restructuring, High Technology, Pharmaceutical.

SENIOR ASSOCIATES - CORPORATE LAW SECTION

Anne-Sophie Cornette de St-Cyr	Stéphane Jaffrain
Catherine Husson	Helene Krautter
Patrice Meunier	

SENIOR ASSOCIATES - TAX LAW SECTION

Antoine Badinier	Alexandre Ippolito
Pascal Bourdarias	Béatrice Rabattu
Jean-Pierre Collet	Regine Landes
Pascal Dewavrin	Yves Robert
Olivier Ferrari	Olivier Schmitt
Xavier Stoclet	

ASSOCIATES

Jean-François Aubert	Bénédicte Menigaux
Arnaud Bouin	Pascale Oblekowski
Olivier Charpentier	Odile Prévot
Marc Dumon	George T. Rigo, Jr.
Frédéric Lafond	Grietje Van De Wiel
Olivia Lê Horovitz	Philippe De Saint-Bauzl
Catherine Tykoczinski	

Languages: French, German and English

LACOURTE & BALAS

109, BOULEVARD MALESHERBES
75008 PARIS, FRANCE
Telephone: 42-89-27-10
Fax: 42-89-27-20

General French, European Community and International Corporate, Commercial, Financial and Tax Practice, Mergers and Acquisitions, Corporate Restructurings and Reorganizations, Real Estate, Construction, Banking, Trusts, Estates, Bankruptcy, Litigation and Arbitration.
The Firm has two Partners and eight Associates.

MEMBERS OF FIRM

THIERRY LACOURTE, born Neuilly-sur-Seine, France, June 22, 1946; admitted, 1985, Paris. *Education:* Ecole Supérieure de Sciences Economiques et Commerciales (ESSEC Graduate, 1969); University of Paris (Licence en Droit, 1970, Diplômé Notaire, 1976). *LANGUAGES:* French and English. *PRACTICE AREAS:* Construction; Bankruptcy; Corporate Law.

JEAN-CLAUDE BALAS, born Toulouse, France, August 31, 1948; admitted, 1988, Paris. *Education:* University of Toulouse (Licence en Droit, 1969); National Tax School of Clermont Ferrand (Ecole Nationale des Impots). *LANGUAGES:* French, English and Spanish. *PRACTICE AREAS:* Taxation, Mergers and Acquisitions.

ASSOCIATES

EMILLA BULICH, born Formia, Italy, January 28, 1958; admitted, 1984, Conseil Juridique, Nanterre; 1990, Paris. *Education:* University of Paris XII Sceaux (Maîtrise en Droit des Affaires, 1979). *LANGUAGES:* French and Italian. *PRACTICE AREAS:* Mergers and Acquisitions; Corporate Restructurings and Reorganizations.

JEROME DURAND, born Paris, France, December 21, 1966; admitted, 1995, Paris. *Education:* Ecole Supérieure des Sciences Economiques et Comerciales (ESSEC Graduate, 1990). *LANGUAGES:* French and English.

AGNES DE L'HAMAIDE, born Givet, France, September 18, 1956; admitted, 1994, Paris. *Education:* Institut d'Etudes Politiques, Grenoble (Graduate, 1979); University of Grenoble II (Maîtrise en droit, 1982). *LANGUAGES:* French and English. *PRACTICE AREAS:* Real Estate; Construction.

STEPHANE ILLOUZ, born Neuilly-sur-Seine, France, May 26, 1968; admitted, 1995, Paris. *Education:* Ecole Supérieure des Sciences Economiques et Commerciales (ESSEC Graduate, 1989); University of Paris II (Maîtrise en droit, 1990); Institut d'Etudes Politiques de Paris (Graduate, 1991). *LANGUAGES:* French, English and Spanish.

(This Listing Continued)

SOPHIE MESNIER TEISSEDRE, born Paris, France, July 28, 1964; admitted, 1992, Paris. *Education:* University of Paris II (Maîtrise, 1987). *LANGUAGES:* French.

CHRISTINE DE SANDOR, born Vaux-sur-Mer, France, January 3, 1958; admitted, 1992, Paris. *Education:* University of Paris I (Maîtrise en Droit des Affaires, 1990); University of Paris II (DESS de Droit Immobilier et de la Construction, 1991). *LANGUAGES:* French and Hungarian. *PRACTICE AREAS:* Construction.

CATHERINE SCHILANSKY, born Paris, France, May 4, 1970; admitted, 1995, Paris. *Education:* University of Paris II (DESS de Droit des Affaires et Fiscalité, 1994; Magistère de Juriste d'affaires, 1994). *LANGUAGES:* French and English.

MARTINE SEROR, born Sarreguemines, France, June 22, 1961; admitted, 1994, Paris. *Education:* Ecole Supéricure de Commerce de Paris (ESCP Graduate, 1983); Diplôme d'Etudes Comptables Supérieures (1984); University of Paris I (DESS de droit des Affaires et Fiscalité, 1984); Diplômée Notaire (1990). *LANGUAGES:* French and English.

LAFARGE, FLECHEUX, REVUZ

Avocats à La Cour

17 AVENUE DE LAMBALLE
75016 PARIS, FRANCE
Telephone: 45.24.43.50
Telex: 610858 F Alorm
Telecopier: 42 88 97 15

General French and International Law Practice. Administrative, Admiralty, Arbitration, Banking, Bankruptcy, Commercial, Competition, Construction, Copyright, Corporate, Corporate Fraud, EEC Law, Engineering Contracts, Environmental, Family Law, Industrial Relations and Labor Law, Real Estate, Licensing, Litigation, Maritime, Mining, Reorganization, Stock Exchange, Taxation, Trademark.

MEMBERS OF FIRM

GEORGES FLECHEUX, born Nice, France, January 28, 1929; admitted, 1954, Paris. *Education:* University of Aix en Provence (Licencié en Droit, 1954; Docteur en Droit, 1958). Lecturer, à la Faculté de Droit de Paris, 1960-1968. Battonier de l'ordre de des Avocats à La Cour de Paris, 1992-1993; Conseil de la Concurrence, 1986—. Président de la Société de Législation Comparée; Honorary Member, Law Society of England and Wales. *Member:* I.B.A.; U.I.A.

PHILIPPE LAFARGE, born Paris, France, February 14, 1934; admitted, 1956, Paris. *Education:* University of Paris (Docteur en Droit). Author: "Les responsabilités du chef d'entreprise EDEC 1982; Droit Pénal du travail," Sirey, 1985. Chargé de Cours à l'Ecole des H.E.C., 1963-1973. Member: Conseil de l'Ordre des Avocats à la cour de Paris, 1976-1979; Batonnier de l'ordre des Avocats, a la Cour de Paris, 1988-1989.

FRANCINE MARIERE-LAMBERT, born Paris, France, March 22, 1942; admitted, 1967, Paris. *Education:* University of Paris (Licenciée en droit, 1965).

PAUL NEMO, born Vichy, France, August 1, 1944; admitted, 1968, Paris. *Education:* University of Paris (DES Droit Public des Sciences Politiques); Institut d'Etudes Politiques (Diplôme Service Public, 1965); Institut des Hautes Etudes Défense Nationale. Co-Author: "Promotion Des Ventes," Delmas, Maître Conférence I.E.P., 1973-1977. Professor, Institut Supérieur du Marketing. Member, Conseil de l'Ordre des Avocats à la cour de Paris, 1988-1990. *Member:* U.I.A.

FRANÇOISE FLEURY-MAZEAUD, born Cherbourg, France, January 6, 1930; admitted, 1970, Paris. *Education:* University of Paris (Licencié en Droit).

GUILLAUME LE FOYER DE COSTIL, born Paris, France, January 13, 1953; admitted, 1973, Paris. *Education:* University of Paris (Licencié en Droit, 1973). Lecturer, University of Paris VII Tolbiac, 1978-1979. Lecturer, Institut de droit des Affaires University of Paris II, 1985—. Member, Board of the Confédération Nationale des Avocats (C.N.A.).

DOMINIQUE RENAUDIN, born Paris, France, March 24, 1953; admitted, 1976, Paris. *Education:* University of Paris (Licencié en Droit, 1975; D.E.A. Business Law, 1976); Business Law Institute, University of Paris (1975).

MICHEL BAZEX, born Toulouse, France, May 28, 1939; admitted, 1977, Paris. *Education:* Institut d'Etudes Politiques de Toulouse (Diplomé,

(This Listing Continued)

1960); University of Toulouse (Doctorat d'Etat, 1967); Académie de Droit International de la Haye (Diplomé, 1961); Agrégé des Facultés de Droit (Droit Public, 1974). Author: "L'extension du secteur public, 1981-1982," J.C.P. 1983, I. 3127, en Association avec M. Guyon; "Chroniques de Droit Public économique," (réglementation des prix, concurrence, entreprises publiques) à l'Actualité Juridique, Droit Administratif depuis, 1983; de droit des mines et des carrières à la Revue juridique de l'environnement depuis, 1985; de droit Financier Européen à la Revue Trimestrielle de droit Européen depuis, 1986. Professor of Public Law, University of Rouen, 1974-1982. Professor of Public Law, University of Paris X, 1982.

PIERRE BRUEDER, born Neuilly-sur-Seine, France, November 14, 1949; admitted, 1977, Paris. *Education:* Institut d'Etudes Politiques de Paris (Diplome Economie et Finances, 1973); University of Paris (Licencié en Droit, 1972); Kings College, London (Foreign Lawyers' Course, 1979). Lecturer, University of Paris, 1980-1982. *Member:* I.B.A.; UIA.

JEAN CHARLES GUILLARD, born Neuilly-sur-Seine, France, November 5, 1953; admitted, 1978, Paris. *Education:* University of Paris (Licencié en Droit, 1976; DEA Droit Civil, 1979).

RENÉE LAFARGE-BOYER CHAMMARD, born Paris, France, December, 1940; admitted, 1980, Paris. *Education:* University of Paris II (Maîtrise en droit).

OLIVIER BEJAT, born June 14, 1954; admitted, 1978, Paris. *Education:* University of Sceaux (Licencié en Droit, 1976); Institut d'Etudes Politiques, Paris (1977); Institut de Droit Comparé, Paris (1976).

ISABELLE HAUTOT-CRUSET, born Toulon, France, July 29, 1953; admitted, 1981, Paris. *Education:* Institut d'Etudes Politiques (Diplomé Economie et Finance, 1973); University of Aix en Provence (D.E.S. Droit Prive, 1975); Institut Supérieur de Droit des Affaires (1975). In House Counsel, 1976-1981. Lecturer, University of Paris, 1982-1983. *Member:* Institut de Criminologie.

FREDERIC SICARD, born Versailles, France, December 26, 1960; admitted, 1985, Paris. *Education:* University of Paris II (DEA de Droit Prive, 1983); University of Paris I (DEA Droit Social, 1984).

DOMINIQUE BRETAGNE-JAEGER, born Neuilly Sur Seine, February 28, 1953; admitted, 1978, Paris. *Education:* University of Paris (licenciée en Droit 1974; DES Droit Civil, 1975; DES Sciences Criminelles, 1975).

OLIVIER FLECHEUX, born Paris, April 10, 1959; admitted, 1988, Paris. *Education:* University of Sceaux (Maîtrise en Droit, 1984); University of Paris (DESS de Droit d'auteur, 1985; DEA de Droit des Affaires, 1987). Lecturer Hautes Etudes Commerciales (HEC) 1993.

XAVIER FLECHEUX, born Paris, May 4, 1960; admitted, 1989, Paris. *Education:* University of Paris (Maîtrise en Droit; DEA Droit des Affaires et Droit Economique).

GRÉGOIRE LAFARGE, born Boulogne-Billancourt, April 4, 1959; admitted, 1985, Paris. *Education:* University of Paris (Maîtrise en Droit, 1982). Secrétaire Conférence du Stage des Avocats á la Cour de Paris, 1988-1989.

HÉLÈNE HALPERIN-KATZ, born Neuilly Sur Seine, June 19, 1960; admitted, 1985, Paris. *Education:* University of Paris II (Maîtrise en Droit, 1982; DEA Droit Privé, 1 984).

Languages: French, English, Italian and Spanish

LAGERLÖF & LEMAN
87 AVENUE KLÉBER
F 75116 PARIS, FRANCE
Telephone: 33-1-45 05 1208
Telefax: 33-1-47 55 0975

Stockholm, Sweden Office: Strandvägen 7 A, P.O. Box 5402, S-114 84 Stockholm. Telephone: Int. 46-8-665 66 00. Telefax: Int. 46-8-667 68 83. Telex: 17715 Laglaw S.
Gothenburg, Sweden Office: Västra Hamngatan 24, P.O. Box 2252, S-403 14, Gothenburg. Telephone: Int. 46-31-17 10 00. Telefax: Int. 46-31-13 56 62. Telefax Maritime department: Int. 46-31-11 65 37.
Malmö, Sweden Office: Stortorget 8, S-211 34, Malmö. Telephone: Int. 46-40-704 50. Telefax: Int. 46-40-97 19 17.
London, England Office: Royex House, Aldermanbury Square, London EC2V 7HR. Telephone: Int. 44-171-606 17 15. Telefax: Int. 44-171-600 17 18.
Berlin, Germany Office: Meinekestrasse 13, D-10719 Berlin. Telephone: Int. 49-30-884 710. Telefax: Int. 49-30-882 4852

(This Listing Continued)

New York, N.Y. Office: 712 Fifth Avenue, 30th Floor, New York, New York, 10019-4102 U.S.A. Telephone: Int. 1-212-801-3450. Telefax: Int. 1-212-801-3455.

Corporate and Commercial law, including Tax, Banking, Financing, Insurance, Real Estate, Computer, Patent, Trademark, Copyright, Labor, Trade Regulation and Antitrust Law. International Legal Transactions. Arbitration and Litigation in Civil Matters. EC Law. International Private Law. Maritime and Admiralty Law.
Member of Alliance of European Lawyers (EEIG).

PARTNER

SIGVARD JARVIN, born Stockholm, Sweden, 1942. *Education:* University of Stockholm (juris kandidat LL.M., 1966). Service with Swedish Courts; Judgeship, Stockholm Administrative Court of Appeal, 1969-1971. Author: "Guide to ICC Arbitration," ICC publishing SA; "Commercial Arbitration", "Law in Asia and the Pacific," Oceana, New York; "Collection of ICC Arbitral Awards," ICC/Kluwer, Amsterdam. General Counsel to the ICC Court of Arbitration, 1982-1987. *Member:* Swedish and Paris Bar Associations. **LANGUAGES:** Swedish, English, French and German. **PRACTICE AREAS:** International Arbitration Law; French Law; Swedish Law.

ASSOCIATES

ISABELLE SORGENT, born France, 1964. *Education:* University of Dijon (Maîtrise en Droit Privé , 1990). **LANGUAGES:** English, French, Swedish and German. **PRACTICE AREAS:** French Corporate and Commercial Law.

LA GIRAUDIERE, LARROZE ET ASSOCIÉS
Member of French GIE Clausen Miller & Dutaret, Europe

58, RUE DE MONCEAU
75008 PARIS, FRANCE
Telephone: 33.1.44.95.25.25
Telex: 649622 F
Facsimile: 33.1.44.95.25.00

Brussels, Belgium Office: Avenue des Arts, 53, 1040. Telephone: (2) 511 44 66. Facsimile: (2) 514 56 62.
Chicago, Illinois Associated Office: Clausen, Miller, Gorman, Caffrey and Witous. 10, South La Salle Street, 60603-1098. Telephone: (312) 855-1010. Facsimile: (312) 606-7777.
New York, New York Associated Office: Clausen, Miller, Gorman, Caffrey and Witous. 100 Maiden Lane, Suite 1600, 10038. Telephone: (212) 504-6020. Facsimile: (212) 504-6015.

General and International Practice, Corporations, E.U. Law, Environment, Arbitration, Banking, Intellectual Property, Copyright, Insurance, Mergers and Acquisitions.

MEMBERS OF FIRM

ANN-PHILIPPE DE LA GIRAUDIERE, born Paris, France, February 4, 1959; admitted, 1983, France. *Education:* University of Paris; Université Paris I (Maîtrise en Droit, 1981; Diplôme d'Etudes Approfondies, 1982). Author, "L'assurance du risque pollution," 1994. Member: European Economic Community, 1984-1985; Commission of The European Communities. *Member:* French Environmental Lawyers Association; European Environmental Lawyers Association. **LANGUAGES:** French and English. **PRACTICE AREAS:** Business Law; Corporate Law; Mergers and Acquisitions; Computer Law; European Law; Environmental Law.

CHARLES LARROZE, born Boulogne-Billancourt, France, March 21, 1958; admitted, 1984, France. *Education:* Université Paris II (Maîtrise en Droit, 1981). **LANGUAGES:** French and English. **PRACTICE AREAS:** International Law; Environment Law; Insurance; General Corporate Practice.

DENY-PIERRE ROSEN, born Paris, France, June 2, 1962; admitted, 1988, France. *Education:* University of Paris-Sorbonne (D.E.A., Corporate and Economic Law, 1987; M.B.A., Sorbonne, 1989). **LANGUAGES:** French, English and Spanish. **PRACTICE AREAS:** Corporate Law; Commercial Law; Mergers and Acquisitions.

PHILIPPE GUMERY, born Agen, Paris, France, August, 17, 1964; admitted, 1991, France. *Education:* University of Paris (Maîtrise, Business, Tax Law and International Law, 1988); University of Paris, Dauphine (D.E.A. Economic Law). **LANGUAGES:** French and English. **PRACTICE AREAS:** Commercial and Corporate Law; Stock Exchange Law; Computer Law.

(This Listing Continued)

LA GIRAUDIERE, LARROZE ET ASSOCIÉS, Paris— Continued

SOPHIE GABAI, born Tours, France, December 17, 1965; (Not admitted in France). *Education:* Université Paris II (Maîtrise, Private Law and E.E.C. Law, 1990; D.E.A., Environmental Law, 1991). Author, "L'assurance du risque pollution," 1994. *LANGUAGES:* French and English. *PRACTICE AREAS:* Environmental Law.

ASSOCIATES

EILEEN BARRINGTON, born Dublin, Ireland, July 12, 1966; admitted, 1990, Ireland; 1995, France. *Education:* Trinity College, Dublin (LL.B., 1988); College of Europe, Bruges (Diploma of Advanced Legal European Studies, 1991); King's Inns, Dublin (Barrister, 1990). *LANGUAGES:* English and French. *PRACTICE AREAS:* E.U. Law; International Law.

VÉRONIQUE DESBROSSES, born Lyon, France, January 26, 1960; (Not admitted in France). *Education:* College of Europe, Bruges (Diploma, 1984); University of Lyon (D.E.A., 1983). Consultant: International Labour Office (ILO), Geneva, 1985; Commission of the European Communities, 1986-1988. (Resident, Brussels Office). *LANGUAGES:* French, English and Spanish. *PRACTICE AREAS:* E.U. Law.

MARTINE REZZI, born Oran, Algeria, October 11, 1956; (Not admitted in France). *Education:* College of Europe, Bruges (1984); University of Aix en Provence (Ph.D., 1984). Author: "Action de la Communauté dans le domaine de la recherche agricole," Agence Européenne d'Information, 1986; "Le sucre dans la CEE," Agence Européenne d'Information, 1987. Attachée de recherches, University of Aix en Provence, 1980-1982. Consultant, Commission of the European Communities, 1983-1987. (Resident, Brussels Office). *LANGUAGES:* French, English and Italian. *PRACTICE AREAS:* E.U. Law.

HONG KANG ZHANG, born Shanghai, China, July 1, 1956; (Not admitted in France). *Education:* Université Paris I (D.E.A., 1988). Author: "Droit Général de la Communauté Européenne," Cosmos Book, 1991. *LANGUAGES:* Chinese and French. *PRACTICE AREAS:* EEC Law; Trademark Law; Chinese Law.

CELINE LUGAGNE DELPON, born Béziers, France, October 1, 1962; admitted, 1989, France. *Education:* Université de Montpellier (D.E.S.S., Maîtrise in Private Law, 1987; D.E.S.S. Real Property Law, 1988); Institute of Insurance Law (Diploma, 1987). *LANGUAGES:* French, English and Spanish. *PRACTICE AREAS:* Commercial Law; Insurance Law; Real Property Law.

DAVID GABRIEL, born Paris, France, July 25, 1966; (Not admitted in France). *Education:* University of Paris (Maîtrise, Business and Tax Law, 1990); University of Paris, Sorbonne (Diplôme Etudes Approfondies, Environmental Law, 1992; Diplôme en Droit et Economie Immobiliers du CERCOL, 1992). Author: "Les sources du droit international de l'environnement," Techniques du jurisclasseur, 1993; "Les organisations internationales et l'environment," Jurisclasseur, 1994. *LANGUAGES:* French and English. *PRACTICE AREAS:* Commercial Law; Environmental Law.

CHARLOTTE MEINNIER, born La Celle St. Cloud, France, May 9, 1968; admitted, 1994, France. *Education:* University of Paris II (Maîtrise en droit des affaires et fiscalité, 1990; D.E.A., Corporate and Economic Law, 1991). *LANGUAGES:* French, English and Spanish. *PRACTICE AREAS:* Commercial Law; Litigation.

CHRISTOPHE ADRIEN, born Saint-Germain-en-Laye, France, June 22, 1967; admitted, 1993, France. *Education:* University of Paris X (D.E.A., Business Law, 1990). *LANGUAGES:* French and English. *PRACTICE AREAS:* Litigation.

AGATHE C. JAGIELLA, born Besançon, France, November 19, 1964; admitted, 1993, Belgium. *Education:* University of Montpellier (Maîtrise Corrière Judiciaire, 1990); George Washington University (LL.M., International and Comparative Law, 1991). *LANGUAGES:* English and French. *PRACTICE AREAS:* E.U. Law; Corporate Law.

LEBRAY, GAILLOT & GRAVEL

Established in 1990

4, RUE BAYARD
75008 PARIS, FRANCE
Telephone: (1) 42.89.24.48
Telecopier: (1) 42.89.88.35; 42.89.55.25

General French, EEC and International Practice.

FIRM PROFILE: *Firm engaged in General International, French and Canadian Business Law practice with the following areas of concentration: International Arbitration, Antitrust and Competition Law, Mergers and Acquisitions, International Financing.*

MEMBERS OF FIRM

PHILIPPE LEBRAY, born Amiens, France, March 4, 1948; registered 1975 as Conseil Juridique, Paris; admitted, 1982, Paris. *Education:* University of Lille, Faculté de Droit (Licence en Droit, 1970; DES Droit Privé, 1971); University of Paris, Institut d'Etudes Politiques (1973); New York University (Institute of Comparative Law, 1973); University of Abidjan, Ivory Coast, Faculté de Droit (CAPA, 1974). *Member:* Paris Bar Association; International Bar Association; Union Internationale des Avocats. *LANGUAGES:* French and English.

LAURENT GAILLOT, born Paris, France, March 29, 1950; admitted, 1979, New York and U.S. District Court, Southern District of New York; 1980, Paris. *Education:* University of Paris (Licence en Droit, 1972; D.E.S. Droit Privé, Droit Fiscal et des Affaires, 1973; D.E.S. Sciences Criminelles, 1974; Institute of Comparative Law, 1976-1977); University of Cambridge, England, Summer Law Courses (1974); Harvard Law School (LL.M., 1978). Co-Author: "French Nationalizations and Foreign Banks," International Financial Law Review, June, 1982; "French Nationalizations: The Decisions of the French Constitutional Council and their Aftermath," Volume 17, N°1, The George Washington Journal of International Law and Economics, 1982. Author: "What to Look for in a French Legal Opinion," International Financial Law Review, July, 1986. *Member:* American Bar Association; International Bar Association; Harvard Law School Association of Europe. *LANGUAGES:* French and English.

SERGE GRAVEL, born Montreal, Canada, November 12, 1948; admitted, 1974, Quebec; 1978, Paris. *Education:* University of Montreal (B.A., 1969; LL.L., 1972); Harvard Law School (LL.M. , 1974); University of Paris II (1975); Institut Universitaire de Hautes Etudes Internationales, Geneva (Diploma, 1976). Canadian Representative, ICC International Court of Arbitration, 1991—. Author: "French Law and Arbitration Clauses, Distinguishing Scope from Validity: Comment on ICC Case n° 6519 Final Award," 37 McGill L.J. 515, 1991; "Arbitration within the NAFTA area (Canada, Mexico, U.S.A.): current difficulties and future trends," The ICC International Court of Arbitration Bulletin, Vol. 4, n° 2, October, 1993, p. 22. *Member:* Union Internationale des Avocats; International Bar Association; Swiss Arbitration Association; International Fiscal Association; Association des Avocats Conseils d'Entreprises; Canadian Bar Association; Harvard Law School Association of Europe. *LANGUAGES:* French, English, German, Spanish and Italian.

ASSOCIATES

MARTINE BARAGAN, born Chamalieres, France, May 11, 1960; admitted, 1984, Paris. *Education:* University of Paris, Faculté de Droit (Maîtrise en Droit des Affaires Internationales, 1982). *Member:* Paris Bar Association. *LANGUAGES:* French and English.

PHILIPPE TOISON, born Douai, France, July 31, 1961; admitted, 1988, Paris. *Education:* University of Lille, Faculté de Droit (Maîtrise en Droit Privé, 1984); University of Paris, Institut d'Etudes Politiques (1986); Faculté de Droit (D.E.A. Droit des Affaires et de l'Economie, 1987). *Member:* Paris Bar Association. *LANGUAGES:* French and English.

ANNE GRANGER, born Bagneux, France, November 4, 1966; admitted, 1992, Paris. *Education:* University of Paris I (Maîtrise en Droit des Affaires, 1988; D.E.A. Droit International Privé et du Commerce International, 1989). *LANGUAGES:* French and English.

STEPHANE BONIFASSI, born Neuilly-sur-Seine, France, October 12, 1963; admitted, 1991, Paris. *Education:* Institut d'Etudes Politiques de Paris (1984); University of Paris II (Maîtrise de Droit Privé, 1989). *Member:* Paris Bar Association. *LANGUAGES:* French and English.

HUGUES VILLEY-DESMESERETS, born Caen, France, September 21, 1964; admitted, 1993, Paris. *Education:* University of Paris, Institut

(This Listing Continued)

d'Etudes Politiques (1986); Faculté de Droit (D.E.A., Droit Communautaire, 1989). *LANGUAGES:* French and English.

PIERRE MAUGUE, born Saint-Cloud, France, October 11, 1967; admitted, 1993, Paris. *Education:* University of Paris II (Magistère de Juriste d'Affaires, 1991; D.E.S.S. Droit des Affaires et Fiscalité, 1991). *LANGUAGES:* French and English.

MARC RIGHENZI DE VILLERS, born Paris, France, December 13, 1966; admitted, 1993, Paris. *Education:* University of Paris II (Maîtrise en Droit des Affaires, 1989); Ecole des Hautes Etudes Commerciales (1991). *Member:* Paris Bar Association. *LANGUAGES:* French and English.

SOPHIE MUYARD, born Dijon, France, April 12, 1969; admitted, 1994, Paris. *Education:* University of Paris II (D.E.A. de Droit Privé Général, 1992; D.E.S.S. de Contentieux et d'Arbitrage, 1993). *LANGUAGES:* French and English.

DAPHNE COUSINEAU, born Montréal, Canada, October 28, 1966; admitted, 1992, Québec. *Education:* University of Montréal (LL.B., 1991); University of Nice (Licence de Philosophie, 1988). *LANGUAGES:* French and English.

LAURA ARMSTRONG, born Toronto, Canada, July 1, 1962; admitted, 1993, Ontario. *Education:* University of Ottawa (LL.B., 1991); University of Toronto (B.A., Honours, 1985). *LANGUAGES:* English and French.

BUREAU FRANCIS LEFEBVRE

Avocats

Established in 1925

3, VILLA EMILE BERGERAT
92522 NEUILLY-SUR-SEINE, CEDEX
PARIS, FRANCE
Telephone: (33.1) 47 38 55 00
Telex: 620 971 LEFEB A
Fax: (33.1) 47 38 55 55

Berlin, Germany Office: Rankestrasse 21. Telephone: (49.30) 214.96.223. Fax: (49.30) 214.96.100.

Brussels, Belgium Office: avenue de Tervueren 270, b. 13. Telephone: (32.2) 772.30.60. Fax: (32.2) 772.28.44.

Buenos Aires, Argentina Office: Avenida Corrientes 587, Piso 4. Telephone: (56.1) 394.38.40. Fax: (56.1) 393.42.76.

Düsseldorf, Germany Office: Immermannstrasse 15. Telephone: (49.211) 1.64.00.11. Fax: (49.211) 1.64.04.11.

London, England Office: Royex House, 14th Floor, Aldermanbury Square. Telephone: (44.71) 606.05.81. Fax: (44.71) 606.05.82.

Madrid, Spain Office: Velazquez, 51. Telephone: (34.1) 578.06.43. Fax: (34.1) 431.21.52.

Moscow, Russia Office: 22, rue Herzen Bur, 18. Telephone: (7.095) 202.11.70. Fax: (7.095) 975.26.65.

New York, United States Office: 712 Fifth Avenue. Telephone: (1.212) 246.80.45. Fax: (1.212) 246.29.51.

Taxation, Company Law, Mergers and Acquisitions, Contracts, Competition, Labour Law, Estate Planning, Customs Regulations, Foreign Investments and Cross-Border Corporate Finance, E.C. Law and Litigation.

FIRM PROFILE: Established in 1925, Bureau Francis Lefebvre is constantly developing its areas of competence and adapting the nature of its activities to the needs of corporate clients.

The firm is present in all areas of law, and in particular company law, labour law and tax legislation.

Its services include the organization and the negotiation of complex transactions, as well as the defense of its clients before the courts.

With offices in major business capitals, and as a member of the Loyens Lefebvre Rädler (LLR) European tax network, the firm grants an increasing part of its expertise to international activities.

MANAGEMENT BOARD

ROBERT BACONNIER, born April 15, 1940; admitted, 1991. *Education:* Licencié en Lettres (1960); diplômé de l'Institut d'Etudes Politiques de Paris (1962); ancien élève de l'E.N.A. (1965-1967). *Member:* International Fiscal Association (Permanent Scientific Committee and Management Board of French Branch); Institut des Avocats Conseils Fiscaux. *LANGUAGES:* German and English.

HENRI BARDET, born July 1, 1944; admitted, 1977. *Education:* University of Paris (Masters in Law); diplômé d'Etudes Comptables Supéri-

eures. Former Inspector of Taxes, French Tax Administration. *Member:* Institut des Avocats Conseils Fiscaux; International Fiscal Association (I.F.A.). *LANGUAGES:* German. *PRACTICE AREAS:* Direct Taxes.

CHRISTIAN LAVABRE, born October 6, 1945; admitted, 1977. *Education:* University of Montpellier (Doctor in Law, 1970). Chargé d'Enseignement à la Faculté de Montpellier. *PRACTICE AREAS:* Contracts; Competition and Consumer Protection Law.

PHILIPPE PEYRAMAURE, born June 20, 1942; admitted, 1969. *Education:* Diplômé de l'Institut de Droit des Affaires (1968); University of Paris (D.E.S. in Law, 1969). Président d'honneur de l'Association Nationale des Avocats Conseils d'Entreprises. Vice-Président du Conseil National des Barreaux; Vice-Président de la Chambre Nationale des Experts Financiers et de la Fondation Nationale du Droit de l'Entreprise. *Member:* Institut des Avocats Conseils Fiscaux; Union Internationale des Avocats (U.I.A.); International Fiscal Association (I.F.A.). *PRACTICE AREAS:* Company Law; Mergers and Acquisitions; Registration Duties.

SUPERVISORY BOARD

ETIENNE BARBIER, born September 27, 1931; admitted, 1957. *Education:* Diplômé de l'Ecole des Hautes Etudes Commerciales (1954); University of Paris (Masters in Law, 1973). *Member:* Institut des Avocats Conseils Fiscaux; International Fiscal Association (I.F.A.). *PRACTICE AREAS:* Direct Taxes.

INTERNATIONAL DEPARTMENT
PARTNERS

JEAN-NICOLAS ANDRIEU-GUITRANCOURT, born March 10, 1933; admitted, 1982. *Education:* University of Paris (Doctor in Law, 1966). *Member:* Institut des Avocats Conseils Fiscaux; International Fiscal Association (I.F.A.); International Bar Association (I.B.A.). *LANGUAGES:* English and German. *PRACTICE AREAS:* International Taxation.

JEAN-PIERRE ANDRIEUX, born April 24, 1946; admitted, 1976. *Education:* Diplômé de l'Ecole Supérieure de Commerce de Paris (1969). Co-Author: Dossiers Internationaux Francis Lefebvre: Algérie, Afrique Centrale. *Member:* Comité National des Conseillers du Commerce Extérieur; Institut des Avocats Conseils Fiscaux; International Fiscal Association (I.F.A.). *PRACTICE AREAS:* International Taxation.

GENEVIÈVE BOUCHARD, born February 11, 1938; admitted, 1963. *Education:* University of Paris (D.E.S. in Law, 1962). *Member:* Institut des Avocats Conseils Fiscaux; International Fiscal Association (I.F.A.). *LANGUAGES:* Spanish. *PRACTICE AREAS:* International Taxation.

PIERRE-JEAN DOUVIER, born May 31, 1954; admitted, 1987. *Education:* University of Paris (D.E.A. in Law, 1981). Author: Dossiers Internationaux Francis Lefebvre: Monaco. Chargé d'Enseignement à l'Ecole des Hautes Etudes Commerciales et à la Faculté de Paris II. *Member:* Institut des Avocats Conseils Fiscaux; Union Internationale des Avocats (U.I.A.); International Fiscal Association (I.F.A.); International Bar Association (I.B.A.). *LANGUAGES:* English and German. *PRACTICE AREAS:* International Taxation; Cross-Border Transactions; Financial Instruments; Reorganizations.

MARC FRILET, born March 23, 1949; admitted, 1980. *Education:* University of Aix-en-Provence (D.E.S. in Law, 1972,) diplômé de l'Institut d'Etudes Politiques de Paris (1973); McGill University, Montréal (Masters in Law, 1974). *Member:* Inter-Pacific Bar Association; Institut des Avocats Conseils Fiscaux; International Bar Association (I.B.A.) (Vice-Chairman, Committee T). *LANGUAGES:* English. *PRACTICE AREAS:* International Construction; Oil Contracts; International Arbitration and Sponsoring.

BRUNO GOUTHIERE, born October 14, 1957; admitted, 1989. *Education:* Diplômé de l'Institut d'Etudes Politiques de Paris (1978); University of Paris (Masters in Law, 1980); ancien élève de l'E.N.A., (1982-1984). Author: Dossiers Internationaux Francis Lefebvre: les Impôts dans les affaires internationales. Chargé d'Enseignement à l'Ecole des Hautes Etudes Commerciales. *Member:* Institut des Avocats Conseils Fiscaux; International Fiscal Association (I.F.A.). *LANGUAGES:* English. *PRACTICE AREAS:* International Taxation.

JEAN-JACQUES LECAT, born August 17, 1950; admitted, 1979. *Education:* University of Rennes (D.E.S. in Law, 1973). Co-author: Dossiers Internationaux Francis Lefebvre: Afrique Centrale. *Member:* International Bar Association (I.B.A.). (Partner, Moscow Office). *LANGUAGES:* English. *PRACTICE AREAS:* International Contracts; Foreign Investments; French Investments in non-OECD countries, Eastern Europe and Vietnam.

(This Listing Continued)

(This Listing Continued)

BUREAU FRANCIS LEFEBVRE, Paris—Continued

PASCAL MAYEUR, born April 10, 1948; admitted, 1971. *Education:* University of Paris (D.E.S. in Law, 1975) Chargé d'Enseignement à la Faculté de Paris X. Bâtonnier du Barreau des Hauts-de-Seine. *Member:* New York State Bar Association; Union Internationale des Avocats (U.I.A.); International Bar Association (I.B.A.) (Chairman, Committee E). *LANGUAGES:* English. *PRACTICE AREAS:* International Contracts; Arbitration; Banking; Corporate Finance; Cross-Border Acquisitions.

CARINA LEVINTOFF, born February 5, 1951; admitted, 1973, Belgium; 1983, New York (Not admitted in France). *Education:* Free University of Brussels (J.D., summa cum laude, 1973). *Member:* The Association of the Bar of the City of New York; New York State Bar Association. (Partner, New York Office). *LANGUAGES:* English and Dutch. *PRACTICE AREAS:* U.S. Corporate Law.

PIERRE-SÉBASTIEN THILL, born April 1, 1956; admitted, 1988. *Education:* University of Aix-En-Provence (D.E.S.S. in Law, 1980). *Member:* Institut des Avocats Conseils Fiscaux; International Fiscal Association (I.F.A.); International Bar Association (I.B.A.) (Partner, New York Office). *LANGUAGES:* German and English. *PRACTICE AREAS:* International Taxation.

WOLFHARD TILLMANNS, born November 26, 1943; admitted, 1975, Germany; 1991, France; Steuerberater, 1978. *Member:* International Fiscal Association (I.F.A.). (Partner, Düsseldorf Office). *LANGUAGES:* German. *PRACTICE AREAS:* German Taxation; Corporate Law.

SENIOR ASSOCIATES

TATIANA DESJOBERT, born July 11, 1958; admitted, 1981, France; 1985, Louisiana. *Education:* C.A.P.A.; University of Paris (D.E.A. in Law, 1981); University of Tulane (LL.M., 1984). (Moscow Office). *LANGUAGES:* Russian and English. *PRACTICE AREAS:* Foreign Investments in Eastern Europe.

GILLES DUBOIS, born May 2, 1951; admitted, 1983, Germany; 1991, France. *Education:* Germany (Assessor Jur., 1983; Rechsanwalt, 1983). Arbitre au Comité National Français de la Chambre de Commerce Internationale. *Member:* Comité National des Conseillers du Commerce Extérieur. (Düsseldorf Office). *LANGUAGES:* German. *PRACTICE AREAS:* German Business Law; Arbitration.

LIONEL FOREST, born January 24, 1961; admitted, 1986. *Education:* University of Paris (Masters in Law, 1983); C.A.P.A. *Member:* International Bar Association (I.B.A.). (Brussels Office). *LANGUAGES:* English. *PRACTICE AREAS:* Distribution; Competition; Trademark Law; Litigation.

PASCAL GASTINEAU, born February 24, 1962; admitted, 1991. *Education:* Diplômé de l'Institut d'Etudes Politiques de Paris (1983); diplômé de l'Ecole Supérieure des Sciences Economiques et Commerciales (1987); University of Paris (Masters in Law, 1988). *Member:* International Fiscal Association (I.F.A.). (Madrid Office). *LANGUAGES:* English and Spanish. *PRACTICE AREAS:* International Taxation.

MICHÈLE HERVOCHES, born December 7, 1948; admitted, 1981. *Education:* University of Paris (Masters in Law, 1974). *LANGUAGES:* English. *PRACTICE AREAS:* International Contracts; Foreign Investments; Cross-Border Acquisitions.

JEAN DE LA HOSSERAYE, born June 29, 1957; admitted, 1988. *Education:* University of Paris (D.E.A. in Law, 1980). *Member:* European Lawyers Association. *LANGUAGES:* English. *PRACTICE AREAS:* International Contracts; Foreign Investments; Cross-Border Acquisitions.

PHILIPPE JUILHARD, born August 29, 1961; admitted, 1989, New York; 1990, France. *Education:* University of Paris (D.E.A. in Law, 1985); Georgetown University, Washington (Masters in Law, 1988). (London Office). *LANGUAGES:* English. *PRACTICE AREAS:* International Taxation.

PATRICK PATELIN, born September 3, 1956; admitted, 1991. *Education:* University of Bordeaux (Masters in Law, 1979); Iowa University (Masters in Law, 1983). *Member:* International Bar Association (I.B.A.). (Buenos Aires Office). *LANGUAGES:* English and Spanish. *PRACTICE AREAS:* International Contracts; Foreign Investments; Cross-Border Acquisitions.

MARIE-FRANCE ROEDERER, born April 7, 1947; admitted, 1988. *Education:* University of Paris (Masters in Law, 1987). *Member:* Institut des Avocats Conseils Fiscaux. *LANGUAGES:* English. *PRACTICE AREAS:* International Taxation.

(This Listing Continued)

DOMESTIC DEPARTMENT
PARTNERS

JEAN-CLAUDE ANISTEN, born November 14, 1954; admitted, 1983. *Education:* University of Paris (D.E.A. in Law, 1977). *Member:* International Bar Association (I.B.A.). *LANGUAGES:* English. *PRACTICE AREAS:* Labour Law.

OLIVIER BENOIT, born June 30, 1950; admitted, 1981. *Education:* University of Paris (D.E.S.S. in Law, 1973). *Member:* Conseil de l'Ordre des Avocats-Barreau des Hauts-de-Seine. *LANGUAGES:* English. *PRACTICE AREAS:* Contracts; Competition and Consumer Protection Law; Customs Regulations.

MARCEL BISSERET, born March 17, 1936; admitted, 1963. *Education:* Capacitaire en Droit. *PRACTICE AREAS:* Direct Taxes.

JEAN-CLAUDE BOUCHARD, born May 8, 1942; admitted, 1966. *Education:* University of Paris (Masters in Law, 1970); diplômé d'Etudes Supérieures d'Anglais; Chargé d'Enseignement à la Faculté de Paris IX. *Member:* Institut des Avocats Conseils Fiscaux; International Fiscal Association (I.F.A.); International Bar Association (I.B.A.) (Chairman, Committee N.I.). *LANGUAGES:* English. *PRACTICE AREAS:* Value-Added Tax; Indirect Taxes; Customs Regulations.

FRANCOIS CHARPAIL, born November 16, 1950; admitted, 1988. *Education:* University of Paris (D.E.S.S. in Law, 1976). Former Inspector of Direct Taxes, French Tax Administration. *LANGUAGES:* English. *PRACTICE AREAS:* Direct Taxes.

ANNE CHARVÉRIAT, born February 7, 1946; admitted, 1986. *Education:* University of Paris (Masters in Law, 1968). Author: Editions Francis Lefebvre: défaillances d'entreprises. Chargée d'Enseignement à l'Ecole des Hautes Etudes Commerciales. *Member:* Institut des Avocats Conseils Fiscaux. *PRACTICE AREAS:* Research Department.

NICOLE COURRECH DU PONT, born October 24, 1943; admitted, 1968. *Education:* University of Paris (D.E.S. in Law, 1969). *Member:* Institut des Avocats Conseils Fiscaux. *PRACTICE AREAS:* Company Law; Mergers and Acquisitions; Registration Duties.

COLETTE DE BACKER, born October 20, 1949; admitted, 1978. *Education:* University of Paris (D.E.S. in Law, 1969). *Member:* Conseil de l'Ordre des Avocats-Barreau des Hauts-de-Seine; Institut des Avocats Conseils Fiscaux.

FRANCIS DELBARRE, born March 27, 1939; admitted, 1965. *Education:* Diplômé de l'Ecole Supérieure de Commerce de Lille (1963). *LANGUAGES:* English. *PRACTICE AREAS:* Contracts; Competition and Consumer Protection Law.

LOUIS DEPARIS, born March 10, 1933; admitted, 1964. *Education:* Masters in Law. Former Inspector of Taxes, French Tax Administration. *Member:* Institut des Avocats Conseils Fiscaux. *PRACTICE AREAS:* Company Law; Mergers and Acquisitions; Registration Duties.

FRANÇOIS EBRARD, born May 14, 1948; admitted, 1978. *Education:* University of Paris (Masters in Law). Professor of Tax Law, Ecole Supérieure des Sciences Economiques et Commerciales. *Member:* Institut des Avocats Conseils Fiscaux. *LANGUAGES:* English. *PRACTICE AREAS:* Value-Added Tax; Indirect Taxes; Customs Regulations.

DIDIER GINGEMBRE, born May 26, 1949; admitted, 1980. *Education:* University of Paris (D.E.S. in Law, 1973); diplômé de l'Institut d'Etudes Politiques de Paris (1973). *Member:* Institut des Avocats Conseils Fiscaux. *LANGUAGES:* English. *PRACTICE AREAS:* Direct Taxes.

DOMINIQUE GODET, born March 13, 1954; admitted, 1985. *Education:* University of Montpellier (D.E.S.S. in Law, 1980). Chargé d'Enseignement à la Faculté de Montpellier. *LANGUAGES:* English. *PRACTICE AREAS:* Direct Taxes.

PATRICK GUILLET, born April 7, 1949; admitted, 1977. *Education:* University of Paris (D.E.S. in Law, 1973); diplômé de l'Institut d'Etudes Politiques de Paris (1973). *Member:* Institut des Avocats Conseils Fiscaux. *PRACTICE AREAS:* Direct Taxes.

JEAN GUILMOTO, born January 13, 1952; admitted, 1983. *Education:* University of Paris (Masters in Law, 1978). Chargé d'Enseignement à l'Ecole des Hautes Etudes Commerciales. *Member:* Institut des Avocats Conseils Fiscaux. *LANGUAGES:* English. *PRACTICE AREAS:* Direct Taxes.

JEAN-CLAUDE GUINARD, born March 12, 1939; admitted, 1977. *Education:* University of Paris (Doctor in Law, 1973). Chargé d'Enseignement à la Faculté de Montpellier. *Member:* Institut des Avocats Conseils

(This Listing Continued)

Fiscaux; International Fiscal Association (I.F.A.). *PRACTICE AREAS:* Value-Added Tax; Indirect Taxes; Customs Regulations.

PHILIPPE JANIN, born December 28, 1931; admitted, 1955. *Education:* Masters in Law; diplômé de l'Institut de Droit des Affaires. Co-Author: Mémento Pratique Francis Lefebvre sur les Sociétés Commerciales, Mémento Pratique Francis Lefebvre sur les Sociétés Civiles. *Member:* Institut des Avocats Conseils Fiscaux. *PRACTICE AREAS:* Research Department.

MICHEL JEHANNIN, born May 22, 1942; admitted, 1967. *Education:* University of Paris (Doctor in Law, 1966). *Member:* Institut des Avocats Conseils Fiscaux. *LANGUAGES:* English. *PRACTICE AREAS:* Direct Taxes.

GÉRARD KLING, born February 11, 1954; admitted, 1982. *Education:* University of Montpellier (D.E.S.S. in Law, 1978). *Member:* International Bar Association (I.B.A.). *LANGUAGES:* English and German. *PRACTICE AREAS:* Corporate; Property Finance.

PIERRE LE ROUX, born November 21, 1958; admitted, 1986. *Education:* University of Montpellier (D.E.S.S. in Law, 1981). Chargé d'Enseignement à la Faculté de Paris II et de Montpellier. Maître de Conférences à l'Institut d'Etudes Politiques de Paris. *PRACTICE AREAS:* Direct Taxes.

FRANÇOIS-XAVIER MATTEOLI, born February 27, 1949; admitted, 1976. *Education:* University of Paris (Masters in Law, 1976); diplômé de l'Institut d'Etudes Judiciaires, 1976; CAPA. Vice Président de l'U.N.A.P.L. *Member:* Délégation Française du Conseil des Barreaux Européens; Conseil de l'Ordre des Avocats-Barreau des Hauts-de-Seine. *PRACTICE AREAS:* Litigation.

JEAN-MARIE MAZALON, born February 15, 1941; admitted, 1966. *Education:* Ecole de Notariat de Lyon. *PRACTICE AREAS:* Company Law; Mergers and Acquisitions; Registration Duties.

JEAN-YVES MERCIER, born September 15, 1948; admitted, 1976. *Education:* Diplômé de l'Institut d'Etudes Politiques de Paris; University of Paris (Masters in Law). *Member:* Vice-Président de l'Institut des Avocats Conseils Fiscaux. *PRACTICE AREAS:* Research Department.

JACQUES NICOLAS, born February 16, 1949; admitted, 1978. *Education:* University of Montpellier (D.E.S. in Law, 1974). Chargé d'Enseignement à la Faculté de Montpellier. *PRACTICE AREAS:* Labour Law.

BRUNO PEILLON, born December 3, 1951; admitted, 1981. *Education:* University of Montpellier (D.E.S.S. in Law, 1975). *Member:* Institut des Avocats Conseils Fiscaux. *PRACTICE AREAS:* Company Law; Mergers and Acquisitions; Registration Duties.

PHILIP SERVAJEAN, born January 9, 1952; admitted, 1983. *Education:* University of Nice (Masters in Law, 1972). Former Inspector of Indirect Taxes, French Tax Administration. *Member:* Institut des Avocats Conseils Fiscaux. *LANGUAGES:* English. *PRACTICE AREAS:* Value-Added Tax; Indirect Taxes; Customs Regulations.

NICOLAS DE SEVIN, born March 24, 1958; admitted, 1987. *Education:* Diplômé de l'Institut d'Etudes Politiques de Paris (1981); University of Paris (D.E.A. in Law, 1983); Chargé d'Enseignement à l'Institut de Droit des Affaires. *Member:* International Bar Association (I.B.A.). *LANGUAGES:* English. *PRACTICE AREAS:* Labour Law.

EDOUARD SICOT, born August 16, 1948; admitted, 1977. *Education:* Diplômé de l'Ecole des Hautes Etudes Commerciales (1971); University of Paris (Masters in Law, 1973). *Member:* Institut des Avocats Conseils Fiscaux. *LANGUAGES:* English. *PRACTICE AREAS:* Direct Taxes.

BRUNO SOLLE, born October 8, 1956; admitted, 1983. *Education:* University of Paris (Doctor in Law, 1981). *Member:* Institut des Avocats Conseils Fiscaux. *LANGUAGES:* English. *PRACTICE AREAS:* Company Law; Mergers and Acquisitions; Registration Duties.

ALAIN STIEFBOLD, born February 27, 1945; admitted, 1975. *Education:* University of Paris (Masters in Law, 1969); diplômé du Centre Supérieur d'Etudes Notariales (1968). *Member:* Institut des Avocats Conseils Fiscaux. *PRACTICE AREAS:* Company Law; Mergers and Acquisitions; Registrations Duties.

RENAUD STREICHENBERGER, born June 3, 1940; admitted, 1967. *Education:* University of Lyons (D.E.S. in Law, 1964). *Member:* Institut des Avocats Conseils Fiscaux; International Fiscal Association (I.F.A.). *LANGUAGES:* English. *PRACTICE AREAS:* Direct Taxes.

JEAN-LUC TIXIER, born April 27, 1958; admitted, 1985. *Education:* University of Paris (Doctor in Law, 1994). Chargé d'Enseignement à la

(This Listing Continued)

Faculté de Paris I. *LANGUAGES:* English. *PRACTICE AREAS:* Contracts; Competition and Consumer Protection Law.

FRANÇOIS VIGNERON, born April 20, 1948; admitted, 1982. *Education:* University of Paris (Masters in Law, 1971); diplômé Expert-Comptable (1980). Former Inspector of Taxes, French Tax Administration. *Member:* Institut des Avocats Conseils Fiscaux. *LANGUAGES:* English. *PRACTICE AREAS:* Direct Taxes.

FRÉDÉRIC WINKLER, born October 28, 1950; admitted, 1978. *Education:* University of Paris (D.E.S. in Law, 1972). *Member:* Institut des Avocats Conseils Fiscaux. *LANGUAGES:* English. *PRACTICE AREAS:* Direct Taxes.

SENIOR ASSOCIATES

ARIANE BEETSCHEN, born January 18, 1958; admitted, 1985. *Education:* Diplômée de l'Ecole Supérieure des Sciences Economiques et Commerciales (1986). *Member:* Institut des Avocats Conseils Fiscaux. *LANGUAGES:* English. *PRACTICE AREAS:* Value-Added Tax; Indirect Taxes.

HUBERT BRESSON, born April 13, 1957; admitted, 1987. *Education:* University of Paris (D.E.S.S. in Law, 1982). *LANGUAGES:* English. *PRACTICE AREAS:* Direct Taxes.

DANIEL CARTON, born November 24, 1953; admitted, 1981. *Education:* University of Paris (D.E.A. in Law, 1979); C.A.P.A. Chargé d'Enseignement à la Faculté de Paris II. *LANGUAGES:* English. *PRACTICE AREAS:* Company Law; Mergers and Acquisitions.

LAURENT CESBRON, born June 21, 1962; admitted, 1991. *Education:* University of Angers (D.E.S.S. in Law, 1987). *PRACTICE AREAS:* Company Law; Mergers and Acquisitions; Registrations Duties.

CHRISTINE CLÉMENT, born July 21, 1943; admitted, 1978. *Education:* University of Paris (D.E.S.S. in Law, 1970). *LANGUAGES:* English. *PRACTICE AREAS:* Value-Added Tax; Indirect Taxes.

MARYLINE DANIS-DRAY, born December 7, 1956; admitted, 1987. *Education:* University of Toulouse (Doctor in Law, 1983). *Member:* Institut des Avocats Conseils Fiscaux. *PRACTICE AREAS:* Direct Taxes.

PATRICK DANIS, born January 13, 1960; admitted, 1987. *Education:* University of Paris (D.E.A., 1983). *PRACTICE AREAS:* Value-Added Tax; Indirect Taxes.

MARTINE EBRARD-GRELLETY, born September 24, 1954; admitted, 1988. *Education:* Diplômée de l'Institut d'Etudes Politiques de Paris (1976); diplômée d'Etudes Comptables Supérieures; diplômée Expert-Comptable (1983). *LANGUAGES:* English. *PRACTICE AREAS:* Direct Taxes.

GERARD EYSSAUTIER, born October 11, 1948; admitted, 1987. *Education:* University of Paris (D.E.A. in Law, 1978). Former Inspector of Taxes, French Tax Administration. *LANGUAGES:* Spanish. *PRACTICE AREAS:* Direct Taxes.

BRIGITTE GAUCLÈRE, born November 5, 1957; admitted, 1985. *Education:* University of Montpellier (D.E.S.S. in Law, 1981). *PRACTICE AREAS:* Contracts; Competition and Consumer Protection Law.

FRANÇOISE GENOT-DELBECQUE, born August 26, 1942; admitted, 1992. *Education:* Diplômée de l'Institut d'Etudes Politiques de Paris (1968); University of Paris (Masters in Law, 1970). *LANGUAGES:* English. *PRACTICE AREAS:* Litigation and Arbitration.

ANNE GROUSSET, born October 19, 1961; admitted, 1987. *Education:* University of Paris (Masters in Law, 1983). Chargée d'Enseignement à la Faculté de Paris IX et de Montpellier. *LANGUAGES:* English. *PRACTICE AREAS:* Value-Added Tax; Indirect Taxes.

PHILIPPE GROUSSET, born August 8, 1959; admitted, 1989. *Education:* University of Montpellier (D.E.S.S. in Law, 1985). Chargé d'Enseignement à l'Ecole des Hautes Etudes Commerciales et à la Faculté de Montpellier. *LANGUAGES:* English. *PRACTICE AREAS:* Direct Taxes.

CHARLES-ETIENNE GUDIN, born October 1, 1946; admitted, 1977. *Education:* University of Paris (Doctor in Law, 1977). Chargé d'Enseignement à la Faculté de Bordeaux. Directeur de la Revue des Affaires Européennes. *Member:* Inter-Pacific Bar Association; International Bar Association (I.B.A.). *LANGUAGES:* English. *PRACTICE AREAS:* E.C. Law and Litigation.

JACQUES ISNARD, born February 14, 1955; admitted, 1993. *Education:* University of Paris (Masters in Law, 1977). *LANGUAGES:* English

(This Listing Continued)

BUREAU FRANCIS LEFEBVRE, Paris—Continued

and Spanish. *PRACTICE AREAS:* Mergers and Acquisitions; General Company Matters.

CHANTAL JORDAN, born January 6, 1956; admitted, 1983. *Education:* University of Paris (D.E.S.S. in Law, 1988). *PRACTICE AREAS:* Company Law; Mergers and Acquisitions.

FRANÇOIS LACROIX, born May 6, 1956; admitted, 1983. *Education:* University of Paris (D.E.S.S. in Law, 1979). *LANGUAGES:* English. *PRACTICE AREAS:* Direct Taxes.

GEORGES LATIL, born November 30, 1954; admitted, 1986. *Education:* University of Paris (D.E.S.S. in Law, 1980). *LANGUAGES:* English. *PRACTICE AREAS:* Company Law; Mergers and Acquisitions.

LIONEL LENCZNER, born November 19, 1955; admitted, 1990. *Education:* University of Paris (D.E.A. in Law, 1982). Former Inspector of Taxes; French Tax Administration. *LANGUAGES:* English. *PRACTICE AREAS:* Direct Taxes.

SYLVIE LE TANNEUR, born June 4, 1961; admitted, 1988. *Education:* Diplômée de l'Ecole des Hautes Etudes Commerciales (1982); University of Paris (Masters in Law, 1984). *LANGUAGES:* English. *PRACTICE AREAS:* Direct Taxes.

JEAN-PHILIPPE MABRU, born June 12, 1961; admitted, 1988. *Education:* University of Paris (D.E.S.S. in Law, 1984); diplômé du Centre Supérieur d'Etudes Notariales (1986). *LANGUAGES:* English. *PRACTICE AREAS:* Estate Planning; Trust and Estate Law.

LAURENT MARQUET DE VASSELOT, born July 28, 1961; admitted, 1991. *Education:* Diplômé de l'Institut d'Etudes Politiques de Paris (1984); University of Paris (Doctor in Law, 1991). Chargé d'Enseignement à la Faculté de Paris II. *LANGUAGES:* English. *PRACTICE AREAS:* Labour Law.

LAURENT MION, born February 11, 1964; admitted, 1989. *Education:* University of Montpellier (D.E.S.S. in Law, 1986). *LANGUAGES:* English. *PRACTICE AREAS:* Contracts; Competition and Consumer Protection Law.

CHRISTIAN PEYROU, born July 9, 1959; admitted, 1989. *Education:* University of Paris (D.E.S.S. in Law, 1985). *LANGUAGES:* English. *PRACTICE AREAS:* Direct Taxes.

MICHEL-LOUIS PIZZORNO, born October 31, 1949; admitted, 1986. *Education:* University of Aix-en-Provence (Masters in Law, 1973). Former Inspector of Taxes; French Tax Administration. Chargé d'Enseignement à la Faculté de Montpellier. *LANGUAGES:* English. *PRACTICE AREAS:* Value-Added Tax; Indirect Taxes.

PIERRE PRADIÉ, born December 24, 1954; admitted, 1987. *Education:* University of Paris (Masters in Law). Former Inspector of Taxes; French Tax Administration. Chargé d'Enseignement à la Faculté de Paris II. *LANGUAGES:* English. *PRACTICE AREAS:* Direct Taxes.

AGNÈS RIVIÈRE-DURIEUX, born March 27, 1957; admitted, 1986. *Education:* University of Paris (Masters in Law, 1979); diplômée de l'Ecole Supérieure des Sciences Economiques et Commerciales (1981). *LANGUAGES:* English. *PRACTICE AREAS:* Direct Taxes.

CAROLE ROMETTI, born January 4, 1962; admitted, 1988. *Education:* University of Montpellier (D.E.S.S. in Law, 1983). *PRACTICE AREAS:* Labour Law.

JEAN-MARIE ROCHEFORT, born July 9, 1947; admitted, 1982. *Education:* University of Paris (Masters in Law, 1970). *PRACTICE AREAS:* Company Law; Mergers and Acquisitions.

MARIE-PIERRE SCHRAMM, born March 18, 1961; admitted, 1988. *Education:* University of Paris (D.E.A. in Law, 1984). *PRACTICE AREAS:* Labour Law.

PIERRE-JEAN SINIBALDI, born December 21, 1958; admitted, 1989. *Education:* University of Paris (D.E.A. in Law, 1983). *PRACTICE AREAS:* Labour Law.

JACQUELINE SOLLIER, born May 27, 1954; admitted, 1984. *Education:* University of Paris (D.E.S.S. in Law, 1981). *LANGUAGES:* English. *PRACTICE AREAS:* Direct Taxes.

LAURENCE TELLIER, born November 27, 1954; admitted, 1981. *Education:* University of Rennes (D.E.S.S. in Law, 1977). *LANGUAGES:*

(This Listing Continued)

English. *PRACTICE AREAS:* Contracts; Competition and Consumer Protection Law.

PHILIPPE TOURNÈS, born September 10, 1958; admitted, 1987. *Education:* University of Paris (D.E.S.S. in Law, 1984). *PRACTICE AREAS:* Value-Added Tax; Indirect Taxes.

PHILIPPE ZOUBRITZKY, born June 28, 1962; admitted, 1987. *Education:* University of Paris (Masters in Law, 1984); diplômé d'Etudes Comptables Supérieures (1983). Chargé d'Enseignement à l'Ecole des Hautes Etudes Commerciales. *PRACTICE AREAS:* Direct Taxes.

LEFEVRE PELLETIER & ASSOCIÉS

Established in 1983

56, AVENUE VICTOR HUGO
75116 PARIS, FRANCE
Telephone: 44.17.14.14
Fax: 44.17.14.14

FIRM PROFILE: The firm LEFEVRE PELLETIER & ASSOCIES was created from the merger in 1993 of two firms, with complementary activities:

LEFEVRE, DE MALLMANN, CHARDIGNY, founded in 1983

PELLETIER, DUGUEYT, VAISSIE, founded in 1988.

Its main fields of activities are, commercial law, international matters, real estate investments and developments.

The firm has presently eleven partners and approximately twenty lawyers and paralegal assistants.

It is able to provide services in French, English, Dutch, German, Italian and Spanish.

PARTNERS

PHILIPPE LEFEVRE, born 1945; admitted, 1970. *Education:* University of Paris (Post Graduate in Business Law); Hautes Etudes Commerciales (H.E.C. Graduate). Former Secretary of the Paris Bar Conference. *Member:* Paris Bar. *LANGUAGES:* French and English. *PRACTICE AREAS:* Real Estate; Insurance.

PHILIPPE PELLETIER, born 1949; admitted, 1983. *Education:* University of Paris (Post Graduate in General Private Law and Crime Sciences). *LANGUAGES:* French. *PRACTICE AREAS:* Notarial Law; Liability.

CYRILLE DE MALLMANN, born 1947; admitted, 1978. *Education:* University of Paris (Post Graduate in Business Law). *Member:* Paris Bar. *LANGUAGES:* French and English. *PRACTICE AREAS:* Competition Law; Industrial Property; Business Law.

MARIE-ODILE VAISSIE, born 1951; admitted, 1981. *Education:* University of Paris, ISIT (Post Graduate in Compared Law and Interpretership, ISIT); Polytechnic School of Law, London. *Member:* Paris Bar. *LANGUAGES:* French, English and German. *PRACTICE AREAS:* Leaser and Leasing.

ROBERT BIJLOOS, born 1947; admitted, 1988. *Education:* University of Leyden (Post Graduate in Labor Law. *Member:* Amsterdam Bar. *LANGUAGES:* French, Dutch, English, German, Italian and Spanish. *PRACTICE AREAS:* Property Law; Company Law.

HUBERT DUGUEYT, born 1949; admitted, 1978. *Education:* University of Paris; Institut d'Etudes Politiques de Paris (Post Graduate in Crime Sciences and graduate). *Member:* Paris Bar. *LANGUAGES:* French. *PRACTICE AREAS:* Banking Law; Litigation.

DENIS CHARDIGNY, born 1954; admitted, 1978. *Member:* Paris Bar (Former Secretary, Paris Bar Conference). *LANGUAGES:* French. *PRACTICE AREAS:* Leaser and Leasing.

FRANCOISE PELLETIER, born 1950; admitted, 1973. *Education:* University of Paris (Post Graduate in General Private Law). *Member:* Paris Bar. *LANGUAGES:* French. *PRACTICE AREAS:* Labor Law.

JEAN-PIERRE DANIEL, born 1954; admitted, 1989. *Member:* Paris Bar. *LANGUAGES:* French. *PRACTICE AREAS:* Administrative Law; Taxation.

PASCALINE DECHELETTE-TOLOT, born 1956; admitted, 1987. *Education:* University of Paris (Post Graduate in Property Law). *Member:* Paris Bar. *LANGUAGES:* French. *PRACTICE AREAS:* Property Law Litigation.

(This Listing Continued)

PIERRE POPESCO, born 1954; admitted, 1993. *Education:* University of NICE (Post graduate in General Private Law). Former Director, Legal Department Espace Promotion (Groupe Arc Union-Unibail). *LANGUAGES:* French and English. *PRACTICE AREAS:* Property; Commercial Property.

ASSOCIATES

PIERRE APPREMONT. LANGUAGES: French and English. *PRACTICE AREAS:* Taxation.

CATHERINE BACROT. LANGUAGES: French. *PRACTICE AREAS:* Corporate Law.

THIERRY BENAROUSSE. LANGUAGES: French. *PRACTICE AREAS:* Construction Law.

PHILIPPE BENSUSSAN. LANGUAGES: French. *PRACTICE AREAS:* Litigation.

PIERRE-JEAN BRENIER. LANGUAGES: French and English. *PRACTICE AREAS:* Commercial Law.

OLIVIER CABON. LANGUAGES: French and English. *PRACTICE AREAS:* Property Law; Litigation.

ISABELLE CHEVALIER. LANGUAGES: French. *PRACTICE AREAS:* Labor Law.

ODILE DHAVERNAS. LANGUAGES: French and English. *PRACTICE AREAS:* Litigation.

MARYSE DIOCOS. LANGUAGES: French and English. *PRACTICE AREAS:* Real Estate Law; Banking Law.

MARIE HELENE DUPOUX. LANGUAGES: French, English, Italian and Spanish. *PRACTICE AREAS:* Corporate Law.

NATHALIE GAULTIER DE LA FERRIERE. LANGUAGES: French and English. *PRACTICE AREAS:* Insurance; Private Law.

PASCAL GOURDAULT-MONTAGNE. LANGUAGES: French and English. *PRACTICE AREAS:* Real Estate Law; Environmental Law; Commercial Litigation.

OLIVIER JOSSET. LANGUAGES: French. *PRACTICE AREAS:* Commercial Law.

MARIE CHRISTINE PEYROUX. LANGUAGES: French and English. *PRACTICE AREAS:* Insurance.

SOPHIE POUGET CHARDIGNY. LANGUAGES: French and English. *PRACTICE AREAS:* Leaser and Leasing.

VERONIQUE PREVOST LEYGONIE. LANGUAGES: French. *PRACTICE AREAS:* Administration Law.

LAURENCE RENAUD. LANGUAGES: French. *PRACTICE AREAS:* Commercial Law.

JOCELYNE SERGHERAERT. LANGUAGES: French. *PRACTICE AREAS:* Leaser and Leasing.

ANNE SEUGE. LANGUAGES: French and English. *PRACTICE AREAS:* Private Law.

VALERIE VINCENOT. LANGUAGES: French and English. *PRACTICE AREAS:* Real Estate Law; Corporate Law.

STEPHANE VITAL-DURAND. LANGUAGES: French and English. *PRACTICE AREAS:* Intellectual Property Law; Acquisition.

MARTINE WALLIMANN. LANGUAGES: French and English. *PRACTICE AREAS:* Mergers and Acquisitions; Corporate; Finance; Joint Venture; Business Law.

LETTE & ASSOCIÉS

3, RUE DU BOCCADOR
75008 PARIS, FRANCE
Telephone: (1) 47 23 62 03
Telefax: (1) 47 20 76 79

Montreal, Quebec Office: Lette & Associates, 615 René-Lévesque Blvd. West, Suite 1010, H3B 1P9. Telephone: 514-871-3838. Telefax: 514-876-4217.

Ottawa, Ontario Office: 100 Sparks St., Suite 1000, K1P 5B7. Telephone: 613-237-6430. Telefax: 613-563-7671.

(This Listing Continued)

Toronto, Ontario Office: Lette, Whittaker, 20 Queen Street West, Suite 2800, P.O. Box 33, M5H 3R3. Telephone: 416-971-4848. Telefax: 416-971-4849.

Milano, Italy Office: Via G. Serbelloni 1 - 20122 Milano. Telephone: (39-2) 76009099. Telefax: (39-2) 76014407.

Roma, Italy Office: Via di Villa Grazioli 13 - 00198 Roma. Telephone: (39-6) 84 11 753. Telefax: (39-6) 84 11 702.

International and General Practice, Corporation, Taxation, Banking and Finance Law, Litigation, Trademark Agents (Canada and U.S.A.).
Firm engaged in Canadian and General International Practice and, except as noted (*), all are Members of the Paris Bar and are authorized to appear before the French Courts as Avocats.

PHILIPPE J. LETTE, admitted to bar, 1969, Quebec and France. *Education:* Stanislas College, McGill University (B.C.L., 1968); University of Bordeaux, France (LL.B., 1969); University of Paris (D.E.S. de Droit Privé Comparé, 1969); International Faculty of Comparative Law (LL.M., 1970). Certified by the Bar of Paris as a specialist in fiscal and economic law. Canada Council Scholar. Conseiller du Commerce Extérieur de la France (Appointed by Government Decree, 1982). Chevalier dans l'Ordre National du Mérite (1990). Legal Counsel: Canadian Embassy in Paris; Swiss Embassy in Paris. President of France-Canada Chamber of Commerce, 1990—. Visiting Professor, University of Florida College of Law. Professor of International Business Law, Institut d'Etudes Politiques, Paris, France. Member, Canadian Council for International Business, International Arbitrator appointed by ICC and Polish Chamber of Commerce. Contributing Author: International Financial Law Review. *Member:* Montreal, Quebec and Canadian Bar Associations; German Bar Association (Ausserordentliches Mitglied des Deutschen Anwaltvereins, 1978); Canadian Tax Foundation; French Tax Lawyers' Association. (Also at Montreal, Quebec Office).

BERNARD LETTE, admitted to bar, 1979, Quebec and France; 1984, Ontario. *Education:* Stanislas College (B.A., 1974); McGill University (B.C.L., 1978; LL.B., 1981); University of Bordeaux, France (LL.M., 1979). Certified by the Bar of Paris as a specialist in fiscal and economic law. President, The French Chamber of Commerce in Canada (Ontario), 1988-1992, (Director, 1986—). President, (1993-1994), (Director, 1987), Swiss-Canadian Chamber of Commerce (Ontario) Inc. President, 1991-1992 and Director, 1987-1993, The Ontario Club. Chairperson, 1987-1988, International Law Section, Canadian Bar Association, Ontario. Member, Legal Committee, Canadian Exporters Association, 1987-1988. Conseiller du Commerce Extérieur de La France, (Appointed by Government Decree, 1989). Honorary Vice-Consul of the Republic of San Marino, 1987—. Co-Author: column on International Business Law in "Action France Canada" and "The Link" published by the French Chamber of Commerce in Canada. *Member:* Paris, France, Montreal, Quebec and Canadian Bar Associations; Law Society of Upper Canada; German Bar Association (Ausserordentliches Mitglied des Deutschen Anwaltvereins); Ontario Club; Canadian Tax Foundation; Canadian Council on International Law; International Fiscal Association; International Association of Lawyers. (Also at Montreal, Quebec and Toronto, Ontario Offices).

THIERRY FOURNO, admitted to bar, 1978, France. *Education:* University of Paris (LL.B., 1977; LL.M., 1978); Diplôme de l'Institut de Droit des Affaires et de l'Institut d'Etudes Judiciaires de l'Université de Paris, Lauréat des Facultés de Droit et de Sciences Sociales de Paris. *Member:* Association Internationale pour la Protection de la Propriété Industrielle. (Resident).

ENRICO CASTALDI, admitted to bar, 1986, Rome, Italy; 1992, France. *Education:* University of Rome (J.D., magna cum laude, 1983); City of London Polytechnic (Seminar in English Business Law, 1984); McGill University (Institute of Comparative Law, 1985). Professor of Italian Law, University of Paris at Nanterre, 1992—. Co-Author: "Doing Business in Canada (I.C.E.)," 1988; "Doing Business in France (I.C.E.)," 1990. Vice President, Italian Chamber of Commerce in France, 1993. Legal Counsel, French Chamber of Commerce in Italy, 1990. (Also at Milan and Rome, Italy Offices).

ALEXIS MOURRE, admitted to bar, 1988, Paris. *Education:* University of Paris I (LL.M., 1985; DESS International Business Law, 1986). Former Member of the Board, World University Service, University of Paris I. *Member:* International Union of Lawyers; Italian Chamber of Commerce in France. (Resident).

CATHERINE PAUL-REYNAUD DE LA ROZIERE, admitted to bar, 1992, France. *Education:* Institut d'Etudes Politiques and University of Paris II (LL.M., 1990). (Resident).

(This Listing Continued)

LETTE & ASSOCIÉS, Paris—Continued

LAURENT FAURE, admitted to bar, 1992, France. *Education:* University of Paris (LL.M., 1990); Institut d'Etudes Judiciaires. (Resident).

VERONIQUE LENOIR, admitted to bar, 1992, France. *Education:* University of Paris X (LL.M., 1980; D.E.A. Political Sciences, 1981); Ecole Nationale des Impôts (1984). Formerly Inspector, Department of Taxation, France. (Resident).

LASZLO BARTOK, admitted to bar, 1994, France. *Education:* University of Paris II (LL.M., 1990; D.E.A. Philosophy of Law, 1991; D.E.A. Business Law, 1992). Faculty of Law, University of Bologna (Italy) (Erasmus Programme, 1990). (Resident).

NAIR SENGHOR, admitted to bar, 1994, France. *Education:* University of Paris II, Assas (Magistère de juriste d'Affaires and D.E.S.S. in Commercial and Tax Law, 1989); University of California at Berkeley, Boalt Hall School of Law (LL.M., 1991). (Resident).

Languages: English, French, German and Italian.

(For complete biographical data on all personnel, see Professional Biographies at Montreal, Quebec, Canada)

LEVINE & OKOSHKEN

51 AVENUE MONTAIGNE
75008 PARIS, FRANCE
Telephone: (1) 44 13 69 20
Telecopier: (1) 45 63 24 96

Lyon, France Office: 59, Rue de l'Abondance. Telephone: 78717923. Telecopier: 78717899.

General French, United States and International Commercial and Corporate Law. United States and International Tax Practice. Litigation and Arbitration, European Community Law, Mergers and Acquisitions, Joint Ventures, Licensing, Franchising and Distribution. Foreign Investment. Matrimonial Law. Wills and Estates. Labor Law.

MEMBERS OF FIRM

KENNETH LEVINE, born New York, N.Y., February 5, 1941; admitted, 1965, New York; 1967, Paris. *Education:* Johns Hopkins University (B.A., 1962); New York University (J.D., 1965; LL.M. in Comparative Law, 1966); Faculty of Law, University of Paris, 1966-1967. Editor, New York University Law Review, 1963-1965. Author: "L'Investissement Commercial Aux Etats-Unis, FEDUCI, 1980." *Member:* The Association of the Bar of the City of New York; American Bar Association.

SAMUEL H. OKOSHKEN, born New York, N.Y., May 1, 1942; admitted, 1966, New York; 1974, Paris and U. S. Tax Court. *Education:* Brown University (A.B., 1962); New York University (LL.B., 1965; LL.M. in Taxation, 1967). Phi Alpha Delta. Member, New York University Intramural Law Review, 1966. Special Memorandum Editor, 1965 and Member, Advisory Board, 1979—, American Tax Institute, Paris. French Correspondent, Bureau of National Affairs, Tax Management Series, 1980. *Member:* American Bar Association. *LANGUAGES:* English and French.

ALAIN SPILLIAERT, born Boulogne Billancourt, France, January 28, 1957; admitted, 1983, Paris. *Education:* Paris II, University Law School (Maîtrise en Droit, 1980); Institute de Droit des Affaires (1980); Certificat d'Aptitude á la Profession d'Avocat (1982). *Member:* Young Lawyers Association of Paris. *LANGUAGES:* French, English and German.

ROLLAND VERNIAU, born Macon, France, October 13, 1947; admitted, 1973, Lyon. *Education:* University of Lyon (Licence en Droit Privé, 1971). Lecturer, Antitrust Law, University of Montpellier. (Resident Partner, Lyon Office).

ALAIN ARFI, born Ain-El-Arba, Algeria, October 13, 1948; admitted, 1989, Lyon. *Education:* University of Lyon (Maîtrise de Droit Privé, 1972; D.E.S., Sciences Sociales, 1972; D.E.s. Gestion des Entreprises, 1986). Inspecteur Principal, Police Judiciaire, Affaires Economiques et Financières, 1976-1988,. (Resident Partner, Lyon Office).

ASSOCIATES

MARIE-CHRISTINE GARDE, born Paris, France, September 9, 1966; admitted, 1994, Paris. *Education:* Université de Paris, Panthéon-Sorbonne (Maîtrise in Business Law, 1989; D.E.A. en Droit Privé, 1990; D.E.A. en Droit des Affaires et de l'Economie, 1992). *LANGUAGES:* French, English and German.

(This Listing Continued)

EU476B

OF COUNSEL

DIDIER FERRIER, born Toulon, France, August 25, 1945; (Not admitted in France). *Education:* University of Toulouse (Doctorat en Droit, 1973); University of Aix-En-Provence (D.E.A. Sciences Criminelles, 1976). Author: "Traité de Droit de la Consommation," P.U.F., 1983; "Traité Je Droit Economique," en collaboration, Lamy, 1988; "Le Contrat de Distribution dans la CEE," Encyclopédie Dalloz, 1992;" La Franchise Inteanationale," Revue de Droit Internationale Clunet, 1988. Professor of Civil Law and Business Law, University of Montpellier, 1980. [Capt., French Naval Reserve]

LINKLATERS & PAINES

Established in 1973
21, BOULEVARD DE LA MADELEINE
75001 PARIS, FRANCE
Telephone: 44 55 54 54
Telex: 214042
Fax: 42 96 00 99

London, England Office: Barrington House, 59-67 Gresham Street, EC2V 7JA. Telephone: 0171-606-7080. Cable Address: Linklaters, London, EC2V 7JA. Telegrams: Linklaters, London. Telex: 884349. Fax: 0171-606-5113.

Integrated French and English law and language service. Corporate (mergers and acquisitions, listings and securities transactions, investment funds, arbitration, labor law), Finance (international finance, banking projects and asset finance), Property, Tax.
Firm of avocats à la Cour d'appel de Paris and English solicitors.

PARTNERS

Michael W. Canby	Jean-Marc Lefèvre
Gilles R.L. Endréo	Eryl M. Besse
Roberto Cristofolini	Dorothée Bontoux
Bertrand L. Andriani	

(For full list of offices see entry at London, England)

LOEFF CLAEYS VERBEKE

1, AVENUE FRANKLIN D. ROOSEVELT
75008 PARIS, FRANCE
Telephone: 33-1-49539125
Telecopier: 33-1-42891460

Amsterdam, The Netherlands Office: 15 Apollolaan, P.O. Box 75088, 1070 AB. Telephone: 31-20-5741200. Telex: 14292 LEX NL. Telecopier: 31-20-6718775.

Brussels, Belgium Office: 268 A Avenue de Tervueren, A-1150. Telephone: 02-778.22.11. Telecopier: 02-763.21.85.

Antwerp, Belgium Office: "De Hertoghe," 8th Floor, 92 Desguinlei, B.8, B-2018. Telephone: 32.3.2385656. Telex: 72748 (EURLAWB). Telecopier: 32.3.2387877.

Liege, Belgium Office: 13, Rue Simonon, (Place de Bronckart), B-4000. Telephone: 32-41-527722. Telecopier: 32-41-527511.

New York, New York Office: Swiss Bank Tower, 23rd Floor, 10 East 50th Street, 10022. Telephone: 212-759-9000. Fax: 212-759-9018.

Rotterdam, The Netherlands Office: 70 Weena, P.O. Box 74, 3000 AB. Telephone: 31-10-4034777. Telex: 23395 (LEX NL). Telecopier: 31-10-4149388.

Singapore Office: 20 Raffles Place, #08-03, Ocean Towers, Singapore 0104. Telephone: 65-5335332. Fax: 65-5330313.

Tokyo Office: NSE Building, 5th Floor, 1-7-1 Kanda Jinbo-cho, Chiyoda-ku, Tokyo 101, Japan. Telephone: 81-3-32599831. Fax: 81-3-32599888.

Barcelona, Spain Office: 550, 4° 1A, Av. Diagonal, 08021. Telephone: 34-3-2007117. Telecopier: 34-3-2023098.

Madrid, Spain Office: Balañá Eguía, Antonio Mauor 7, 5°, 28014. Telephone: 34-1-5312501. Telecopier: 34-1-5313530.

Jakarta, Indonesia Associated Office: Ali Budiardjo, Nugroho, Reksodiputro, Niaga Tower, 24th floor, Jalan Jenderal Sudirman Kav. 58, 12920. Telephone: 62.21.2505125/2505136. Telecopier: 62.21.2505121/2505001.

Luxembourg, Luxembourg Office: Zeyen Beghin Feider. 67, Rue Ermesinde, P.O. Box 5017, 1050. Telephone: 352.468946. Telex: 60736 (zflaw lu). Telecopier: 352.468947.

(This Listing Continued)

Dutch Attorneys may represent clients before all Dutch Courts respectively, before the European Court of Justice and the Benelux Court of Justice, and are admitted to plead before all Courts of the Memberstates of the Common Market (EEC).

RESIDENT PARTNERS

ALBERT A. BAKHUYS ROOZEBOOM, born 1937; admitted, 1973, Rotterdam, The Netherlands (Not admitted in France). *Education:* University of Amsterdam (1961); New York University (1964). *Member:* International Bar Association.

ALFRED J.M. HOOGVELD, born 1950; admitted, 1976, Rotterdam, The Netherlands (Not admitted in France). *Education:* Nijmegen University (1976); Université Paris I (1976). *Member:* International Bar Association; Union Internationale des Avocates; Association Européenne pour le Droit Bancaire et Financier.

(For Personnel and other data, see Professional Biographies at Amsterdam, Antwerp, Barcelona, Brussels, Liège, New York, Rotterdam, Singapore and Tokyo)

LOVELL WHITE DURRANT

37 AVENUE PIERRE 1ER DE SERBIE
75008 PARIS, FRANCE
Telephone: (1) 49 52 04 26
Fax: (1) 47 23 96 12

London, England Office: 65 Holborn Viaduct, EC1A 2DY. Telephone: 0171 236 0066. Fax: 0171 248 4212; 236 0084; 248 7273. Telex: 887122 LWD G.

New York, New York Office: 527 Madison Avenue, 10th Floor, 10022. Telephone: (212) 758 3773. Fax: (212) 486 0367.

Brussels, Belgium Office: Avenue Louise 523, Bte 24, 1050. Telephone: (2) 647 0660. Fax: (2) 647 1124.

Prague, Czech Republic Office: U Prasne brany 3, State Mesto, 1. Telephone: (2) 2481 1672. Fax: (2) 2481 1608.

Ho Chi Minh City, Vietnam Office: 141 Vo Van Tan Street, District 3. Telephone: (848) 298 787. Fax: (848) 392 868.

Hong Kong Office: 11th Floor, Peregrine Tower, Lippo Centre, Queensway. Telephone: 2810 4770. Fax: 2868 4051.

Beijing, Republic of China Office: Office 5D, CITIC Building, 19 Jianguomenwai Dajie, 100004. Telephone: (861) 506 3588. Fax: (861) 500 1972.

Tokyo, Japan Office: Shin-Kasumigaseki Building, 20th Floor, 3-3-2 Kasumigaseki, Chiyoda-ku, 100. Telephone: (3) 3503 2571. Fax: (3) 3503 0699.

Shanghai, People's Republic of China Associated Office: Room 1703, Shanghai International Trade Centre, 2200 Yan An Road (W). Telephone: (21) 219 4419. Fax: (21) 219 5462.

Arbitration, Aviation, Banking, Building and Engineering, China, Collective Investment Schemes, Commercial, Commodities, Competition and Trade Regulation, Computers, Construction, Corporate Finance, Corporate Law, East-West Trade, EEC, Employment, Energy, Environmental Law, Financial Services, Fraud and Asset Recovery, Insolvency, Insurance, Intellectual Property, Litigation, Management Buy-Outs and Venture Capital, Media Law, Mergers and Acquisitions, Pensions, Planning, Product Liability, Property, Rating, Shipping, Taxation, Trusts and Estate Planning.

RESIDENT PARTNERS

John Cooper
Robert P. Follie
R. Mark Huleatt-James

All Partners in the Firm are Solicitors except R. Follie.
J. Cooper and R. Follie are Avocats au Barreau de Paris.

(For List of Partners see Professional Biographies at London, England)

LUSSAN BROUILLAUD

Société Advocats
Established in 1932

250 BIS, BOULEVARD SAINT GERMAIN
75341 PARIS CEDEX 07
Telephone: (1) 49 54 90 00
Telex: 204 413 F
Telecopier: (1) 49 54 90 01

Bordeaux, France Office: 16 Cours de Verdun, 33082. Telephone: (16) 56 44 66 90. Fax: (16) 56 81 74 82.

Corrispondent, Bielefeld, Germany Office: Brandi Droge, Piltz et Heuer. 4800. (RFA), Elsa Brandstrom-Str 1U 3. Telephone: (05 21) 96 53 500. Fax: (05 21) 96 53 599.

London, England Office: Boodle Hatfield. 43 Brook Street, WIY2BL. Telephone: 071 629 7411. Fax: 071 629 26 21.

Madrid, Spain Office: Lupicinio Rodriguez, Abogados. Vilanueva, 29, Madrid 28001. Telephone: 577 5502. Fax: 431 0413.

Hanoï, Vietnam Office: 1 rue Yet-Kieu. Telephone: 22 82 62. Fax: 22 82 63.

Banking, Financing, Acquisitions, Commercial, Urban, Copyright, Civil Law, Communications, Environmental and International Law.

FIRM PROFILE: Established in 1932. The firm has 22 lawyers with experience in Property Law, Tax Law, Stock and Finances, Mergers and Acquisitions, Finance and Corporation , Law, Competition Law, Distribution and Consumption, Real Estate and Urban Law,Estate, Copyright, Art, Civil Law, Insurance Law, Communication Law, Environmental Law and International Law.

MEMBERS OF FIRM

ROBERT BROUILLAUD, born 1924; admitted, 1944, Bordeaux; 1978, Paris. *Education:* Bordeaux (licence en droit, 1944; doctorats en droit privé, droit public et histoire du droit, 1944, 1945 and 1946). Bâtonnier du barreau de Bordeaux, 1969-1971. Membre, du Conseil de l'Ordre, 1960-1965, 1968-1969, 1971-1974, 1976-1977. Président de la CARPA, 1972-1977, 1978. Association professionelle: Confédération syndicale des Avocats. **PRACTICE AREAS:** Criminal Business Law; Banking, Corporate and Commercial Law; Succession Law.

PHILIPPE CHAULET, born 1941; admitted, 1969, Paris. *Education:* Institut Etudes Judiciares, Paris (licence en droit). **PRACTICE AREAS:** Insurance Law; Civil Liability; Law of Transports; Construction Law.

JEAN-YVES DUPEUX, born 1948; admitted, 1976, Paris. *Education:* Bordeaux (IEP, 1971; licence en droit, 1972) Paris I (DES en droit public, mention études européennes,1973; DES en droit privé, mention droit des affaires, 1974). Member, du conseil de l'Ordre des avocats à la cour d'appel de Paris, 1991-1993. *Member:* CNA; UIA. **LANGUAGES:** English. **PRACTICE AREAS:** Competition Law and Regulations; Distribution and Consumer Law; Price and Trade Regulations; French and EEC Trade Regulations; Media and Communication Law; Criminal Business Law.

MARIE-ANNE GALLOT LE LORIER, born 1945; admitted, 1969, Paris. *Education:* (Maîtrise en droit, 1967). Membre: du Conseil de l'Ordre des Avocats à la Cour d'Appel de Paris, 1991-1993; Secrétaire Général de la Conférence Internationale des Barreaux, 1992-1993; Membre, de la Commission de Communication de l'Ordre des Avocats àla Cour d'Appel de Paris. **LANGUAGES:** English. **PRACTICE AREAS:** Civil Liability; Environment Law; Insurance Law; Intellectual Property.

CLAUDE LUSSAN, born 1910; admitted, 1932, Paris. *Education:* IEP (licence et doctorat en droit). Bâtonnier de l'Ordre des avocats de Paris, 1967. Président, CARPA, 1975. Administrateur, Fondation nationale des sciences politiques. Commandeur de la Légion d'honneur. *Member:* UIA (Président, 1969). **PRACTICE AREAS:** Commercial Law; Banking; Finance and Stock Market Law; Criminal Business Law; Arbitration.

LUCIEN M. MARTIN, born 1931; admitted, 1952, Bordeaux; 1979, Paris. *Education:* Bordeaux (doctorat en droit, 1956). Chargé de cours, faculté de droit, Bordeaux, 1957-1961. Directeur juridique adjoint, BNP, 1962-1979. Publications: "Pratique bancaire et droit," 1983; "Chronique juridique Revue Banque," 1971-1984; "Banques et bourses," Montchrestien, 1991. **PRACTICE AREAS:** Banking; Finance and Stock Market Law; Bankruptcy; Corporate.

FRANCOIS MARTINEAU, born 1951; admitted, 1976, Paris. *Education:* IEP, Paris (licence en philosophie, maîtrise en droit). Secrétaire de la conférence, 1981. Chargé d'enseignement en procédure civile, Paris I, 1985.

(This Listing Continued)

LUSSAN BROUILLAUD, Paris—Continued

Publications: "Fripons, gueux et loubards, histoire de la délinquance de 1750 à nos jours," 1986; "Abrégé de raisonnement contentieux," éd. Montpensier, 1989; "Le discours polémique," Quai Voltaire, 1990; "Redressement et liquidation judiciaire," Le Nouvel Economiste, 1993. *LANGUAGES:* English. *PRACTICE AREAS:* Banking; Commercial Law; Bankruptcy; Criminal Business Law; Public Law; Labour Law.

THIERRY MASSIS, born 1947; admitted, 1972, Paris. *Education:* Paris II (DES en droit privé général, 1972; doctorat d'Etat en droit, 1980). Chargé d'enseignement, Paris II, 1990-1992. Publications: "Le contrat préliminaire dans la vente d'immeubles à construire," thèse Paris II. *Member:* UIA. *LANGUAGES:* English. *PRACTICE AREAS:* Real Estate, Conveyancing and Financing; Media and Communication Law; Succession Law.

FRANCOISE MONOD, born 1938; admitted, 1967, Paris. *Education:* Paris (Maîtrise en droit, 1960); Harvard Law School (LL.M., Master of Laws, 1961). Publications: "Vers un capital risque sans frontière," publication collective, éd. Siparex. "Capital développement Pactes d'Actionnaires," éd. Capital Finance. *Member:* Association Française des Investisseurs en capital AFIC. *LANGUAGES:* English and Spanish. *PRACTICE AREAS:* Venture Capital; Foreign Investments in France; Mergers and Acquisitions; Corporate Law.

MICHEL PUISAIS-JAUVIN, born 1942; admitted, 1992, Paris. *Education:* (DES de droit public et DES de Sciences Politiques, licence en droit public). Formerly "Conseil Juridique.". *LANGUAGES:* English. *PRACTICE AREAS:* Commercial Law; Corporate Law; Mergers and Acquisitions; Agency; Representation; Public Contracts; Commercial Lease Regulations.

DIDIER SKORNICKI, born 1952; admitted, 1975, Paris. *Education:* (Maîtrise en droit privé, DES en droit privé général, DES en droit pénal, licence en philosophie). Chargé d'enseignement, université de Sceaux, 1980-1986, Paris II, 1986-1990. *PRACTICE AREAS:* Corporate Law; Stock Market and Finance Regulations; Media Law; French and International Arbitration; Criminal Business Law.

ASSOCIATES

VALERIE D'ABRIGEON, born 1959; admitted, 1985, Paris. *Education:* Université de Paris V René Descartes (D.E.A., 1984). *LANGUAGES:* Anglais and Espanol. *PRACTICE AREAS:* Civil Law; Family Law; Media Law; Real Estate Law.

CHRISTOPHE BIGOT, born 1965; admitted, 1990, Paris. *Education:* Université de Paris (DEA droit privé, 1987). *PRACTICE AREAS:* Press Law; Advertising; Competition Law.

MARIE-PIERRE BLANC, born 1963; admitted, 1988, Paris. *Education:* Faculté d'Aix en Provence (maîtrise, 1986). *LANGUAGES:* English and Spanish. *PRACTICE AREAS:* Criminal Business Law; Civil Law (contracts); Commercial Law.

PHILIPPE DUGLUE, born 1960; admitted, 1992, Paris. *Education:* Faculté de droit de Rennes (maîtrise, 1992); Ecole Nationale des Impôts (1985). *LANGUAGES:* English. *PRACTICE AREAS:* Corporate Tax Law; Taxation; Taxation Proceedings; Mergers and Acquisitions.

CORINNE HAREL, born 1962; admitted, 1990, Paris. *Education:* Université de Paris V René Descartes (DESS, 1987). *PRACTICE AREAS:* Banking; Civil Law; Leasing Regulations.

ALAIN HAZAN, born 1966; admitted, 1990, Paris. *Education:* Université Paris II - Pathéon Assas (DEA Propriét é Littéraire Artistique et Industrielle, 1990). *LANGUAGES:* English. *PRACTICE AREAS:* Intellectual Property; Advertising Law; Competition Regulation; Unfair Competition Actions; European Community and Trade Law.

ELISABETH MAS, born 1960; admitted, 1987, Paris. *Education:* Université de Pau et des Pays de l'Addour (CAPA, 1985). *LANGUAGES:* Espanol. *PRACTICE AREAS:* Banking; Commercial Law.

LAURENT PETTITI, born 1958; admitted, 1986, Paris. *Education:* Paris X Nanterre, Paris I Panthéon (DEA). *PRACTICE AREAS:* European Law.

MARIE PIARD, born 1954; admitted, 1992, Paris. *Education:* Université de Paris II Panthéon-Assas (DEA de droit public, 1977); Harvard Law School (LL.M., master of laws, 1980). *LANGUAGES:* English and Russian. *PRACTICE AREAS:* Financial and Banking Law; Corporate Law.

(This Listing Continued)

MARIE LAURE ROUQUET, born 1966; admitted, 1990, Paris. *Education:* Université de Paris II Panthéon-Assas (DEA, propriétélittéraire artistique et industrielle, 1988). *LANGUAGES:* English. *PRACTICE AREAS:* Civil Law; Intellectual Property; Criminal Business Law.

R. ALEXANDRE SIAD, born 1958; admitted, 1985, Paris. *Education:* Université de Paris XII St Maur (DESS de justiste d'affaires, DEA de droit privé, 1985). *LANGUAGES:* English. *PRACTICE AREAS:* Commercial Law; Civil Law; Law of Contracts; Insurance Law.

STEPHANIE STEIN, born 1965; admitted, 1988, Paris. *Education:* Université Paris X Nanterre, Sorbonne (DEA, 1989). *LANGUAGES:* English. *PRACTICE AREAS:* Labor Law.

MANDEL, NGO & PARTNERS

45, AVENUE MONTAIGNE
75008 PARIS, FRANCE
Telephone: 4720 92 92
Telecopier: 47.23.91.55 (1st Floor) and 47.23.53.21 (3rd Floor)

Hanoi, Vietnam Office: Business Center, Hotel Pullman Metropole, 15, Ngo Quyen Street. Telephone: (84.4).269.975; (84.4).266.919. Fax: (84.4).244.809.

General Business Practice including Litigation before the French Courts. International Arbitration, Corporate, Tax, Foreign Investments, Labor, Estate, Intellectual Property and EC Law, Immigration.

MEMBERS

AIMÉ D. MANDEL, born Vincennes, April 20, 1948; admitted, 1973, Paris; 1975, California. *Education:* Faculté de Droit (Licence en Droit, 1969; D.E.S. de Droit Privé, 1971; et d'histoire du droit, 1973); Boalt Hall School of Law, University of California at Berkeley (LL.M., 1971; J.D., 1973). Co-author: with Gerard Ngo, "Doing Business in France," Tokyo Seminar by J.E.T.R.O. (Japan External Trade Organization) May, 1983; "Collecting debts in France," C.F.C.E.; "Cahiers juridiques et fiscaux de l'exportation," N° 3, 1986. Assistant Lecturer, Bankruptcy, University of Paris at Nanterre, 1973-1976. *Member:* State Bar of California; Inter-Pacific Bar Association (International Law Section); Paris Bar; Franco-British and Japanese Chamber of Commerce in Paris. *LANGUAGES:* English.

GÉRARD V.L. NGO, born Hanoi, Vietnam, August 18, 1948; admitted, 1977, Paris. *Education:* Academy of Paris (Baccalauréat, 1967); University of Paris, Institut d'Etudes Politiques (Diplôme, 1973); Faculté de Droit (Licence en Droit, 1972); D.E.S. de Droit Privé (1973); Boalt Hall School of Law, University of California at Berkeley (LL.M., 1975). *Member:* Paris Bar; Japanese Chamber of Commerce in Paris. [Defense Officer, French Army]. *LANGUAGES:* English.

LUC A. MIGUÉRÈS, born Algiers, Algeria, July 25, 1952; admitted, 1975, Paris. *Education:* Paris (Baccalauréat, Philosophie, 1971); University of Paris (Bachelor of Arts; Licence, 1974; Maitrise, 1975; D.E.A. in Labor Law. Co-Author: with Aimé Mandel, "Aspects of French Law," Tokyo Seminar by J.E.T.R.O., April, 1986. Author: "Quelques aspects de l'implantation d'une entreprise etrangere en France," April, 1987 and "Incitations à l'investissement en France," September, 1987, Journal of the Italian Chamber of Commerce in Paris, France. Lecturer, Business and Bankruptcy Law, University of Paris, 1979-1983. Legal Counsel, The Italian Chamber of Commerce in Paris. *Member:* Paris Bar. *LANGUAGES:* English and Italian.

PIERRE JUNG, born Chartres, France, May 24, 1959 (Swiss national); admitted, 1988, Paris. *Education:* University of Paris (Licence, 1983; Maîtrise, 1984). *Member:* Paris Bar. (Resident, Hanoi, Vietnam Office). *LANGUAGES:* English and German.

MONIQUE PELLETIER, born Trouville sur Mer, July 25, 1926; admitted, 1946, Paris, France. *Education:* Lycée Racine, Paris (Bacalauréat, 1942); University of Paris, Faculté de Droit (Licence en Droit, 1946). Co-Author: "Le Droit Dans Ma Vie," published by Stock, 1973. Secrétaire d'Etat à la Justice, 1978. Ministre de la Condition Féminine et de la Famille, 1978-1981. Officier de la Légion d'Honneur. *Member:* Paris Bar. *LANGUAGES:* English.

AKIRA HASHIMOTO, born Hiroshima-Ken, Japan, August 27, 1947; admitted, 1973, Japan; 1984, New York; 1992, Paris. *Education:* Tokyo University (LL.B., 1970); Legal Research and Training Institute, Supreme Court of Japan (1971-1973); University of Paris (D.S.U., Droit Commercial, 1974; Docteur en droit, 1980); Harvard Law School (LL.M., 1982). *Member:* Tokyo Bar Association; New York State Bar Association. *LANGUAGES:* Japanese, English and French.

(This Listing Continued)

ASSOCIATES

NICOLE CHABRUX, born Paris, France, September 9, 1953; admitted, 1979, Paris. *Education:* University of Paris (Baccalaureat, Sciences, 1971; Licence, 1978; D.E.A. Business Law, 1983). *Member:* Paris Bar. *LANGUAGES:* English and Spanish.

DOMINIQUE MILLE, born Lausanne, Switzerland, March 26, 1951; admitted, 1977, Paris. *Education:* University of Paris, Faculte de droit (Licence en droit, D.E.S. de droit International Public); Institut d'Etudes Politiques (Diplôme, 1973); Oxford Brasenose College (Diploma in Law, 1975). Counsel, Paris Chamber of Commerce et d'Industrie, Direction des Relations Internationales. *Member:* Paris Bar. *LANGUAGES:* English and Spanish.

ALINE GANDILLON, born Boulogne-Billancourt, France, October 8, 1965; admitted, 1991, Paris. *Education:* University of Paris (Maîtrise, 1988; D.E.A. de Droit privé, 1989); Institut des Langues orientales "INALCO" (Diplôme de langue russe, 1988); Institut de Droit comparé (diplôme de terminologie juridique russe, 1989). *Member Paris Bar. LANGUAGES:* Russian and English.

FREDERIC MANDEL, born Perigueux, France, October 1, 1964; admitted, 1991, Paris. *Education:* University of Bordeaux (Maîtrise, 1987; D.E.S.S. de Droit des affaires et fiscalité, 1988). *Member:* Paris Bar. *LANGUAGES:* English.

LIONEL BOCHURBERG, born Paris, France, January 25, 1968; admitted, 1992, Paris. *Education:* University of Paris (Maîtrise, 1989; D.E.A. en droit des Affaires, 1990; Docteur en Droit, Mention "Très honorable:, 1992). Author: "The Right of Fair Use Under the French Laws of Copyright, a Comparative Approach," Doctoral Thesis. *LANGUAGES:* English.

MARTINE BOURRY D'ANTIN, born Lagny, France, January 2, 1956; admitted, 1979, Paris. *Education:* University of Paris XII (Maîtrise, 1979; D.E.A. de droit international public, mention droit européen, 1981). Secrétaire de la Conférence du stage des Avocats à la Cour d'Appel de Paris, 1986; Prix d'improvisation Marcel Poignard, 1986; Prix du Barreau de Montréal, 1986. Co-Author, with Godin Raymond Harris Thomas of Montréal, Québec: "Investir au Canada" and "Lettre des Investissements France-Canada." *Member:* Institut France-Canada (General Secretary); Association des anciens Avoués de la Seine. *LANGUAGES:* English and Spanish.

JACK M. BUSSY, born Paris, France, October 13, 1955; admitted, 1981, Paris. *Education:* University of Paris (Maîtrise , 1980) National Institute of Oriental Studies "INALCO" (Masters Degree in Japenese language, 1982); INSEAD (M.B.A., 1986). Resident Associate, Nakagawa Law Office, Tokyo, 1983-1985. Vice-President, M & A Department, Crédit Commercial de France, 1987-1989. Author or Co-Author: "Dépôt des brevets et protection du savior-faire au Japon", France-Japon Eco, 1984; "La propriété industrielle au Japon", MOCI, 1984; "Dossier juridique pratique : statut fiscal et social de l'expatriéau Japon", France-Japon Eco, 1985; "Protection de l'expatrié", MOCI, 1986: *Member:* Paris Bar. *LANGUAGES:* English, Japanese and Italian.

YVES MIGUÉRÈS, born Algiers, August 14, 1949; admitted, 1975, Paris. *Education:* University of Paris (License en Droit, 1975). Former Teaching Assistant, University of Paris at Sceaux. *LANGUAGES:* English.

PAOLA GARNIER, born Milano, Italy, April 26, 1961; admitted, 1986, Italy (Not admitted in France). *Education:* University of Milano (Doctor, summa cum laude, 1985);. Auditor: City of London Polytechnic Summer, 1985 and 1989; Columbia University, 1990-1991. Author: "The Recovery of Damages in Case of Patent Infringement," Doctoral Thesis, 1985. *LANGUAGES:* French, Italian, English and Spanish.

CLAIRE PIOLÉ, born Quessy, France, March 22, 1968; admitted, 1992, Paris. *Education:* University of Paris (Maîtrise, 1990; D.E.S.S. Juriste Affaires International, 1992). *LANGUAGES:* English and German.

FRANÇOIS BARRY, born June 21, 1963; admitted, 1989, Paris. *Education:* University of Paris (Maîtrise, 1987; D.E.S.S. de FiscalitéAppliquée, 1988); New York University (LL.M., 1991). *LANGUAGES:* English.

LAURENCE MARTINET, born September 28, 1964; admitted, 1992, Paris. *Education:* University of Paris (Maîtrise, 1988; D.E.A. de Droit Privé, 1989; D.E.A. de Droit Anglais et Nord-Américain des Affaires, 1990). Teaching Assistant, University of Paris. *LANGUAGES:* English and Spanish.

PHILIPPE LEBAUVY, born August 12, 1966; admitted, 1991, Paris. *Education:* University of Paris (Maîtrise en Droit Privé "Carrières judi-

(This Listing Continued)

ciaires", 1989; D.E.A. de Droit Privé, 1990). *LANGUAGES:* French, English and German.

EMMANUEL MOULIN, born Montpellier, December 3, 1966; admitted, 1994, Paris. *Education:* University of Montpellier (Maîtrise en Droit des Affaires, 1990); Institut Supérieur de Gestion, Paris (M.B.A., 1992). *LANGUAGES:* French and English.

GUILLAUME ROCHEMAURE, born Paris, May 18, 1963; admitted, 1994, Paris. *Education:* University of Paris (Maîtrise en Droit des Affaires et en fiscalité des Entreprise, 1989; Certificat en Droit communautaire de la concurrence, 1990). *Member:* Paris Bar. *LANGUAGES:* English and German.

MIYAKO IKUTA, born Kyoto, Japan, August 4, 1966; admitted, 1994, Paris. *Education:* University of Ritsumeika - Japan (Master of Law, 1989); University of Paris (D.S.U. de Droit Commercial, 1990, D.E.A. de Droit des Afaires et de Droit Economique, 1992, D.E.S.S. de PropriétéIndustrielle, 1993). *LANGUAGES:* Japanese, English and French.

NICOLAS AUDIER, born Boulogne-Billancourt, France, October 24, 1961; admitted, 1992, Paris. *Education:* University of Paris X, Faculté de Droit et de Sciences Politiques (Maîtrise en Droit des Affaires, 1984; D.E.S.S. en Droit des Affaires Internationales, 1986, high honors); New York University School of Law (M.C.J., 1989).

OF COUNSEL

PATRICE JOURDAIN, born Paris, July 2, 1951. *Education:* Baccalaureat 1970; University of Paris (Maîtrise en Droit, 1974; D.E.S. de Droit privé, 1976; D.E.A. de Droit social, 1978); admitted as Docteur en droit, 1982. (doctoral dissertation, "Recherche sur l'imputabilité en matière de responsabilité civile et pénale," mention très bien, Prix Dupin Ainé). Professeur agrégé de droit privé, 1986; appointed University of Paris at Sceaux and Université du Maine, 1987.

CORINA CADENA, born Mexico, February 16, 1961; admitted, 1986, Mexico (Not admitted in France). *Education:* Mexico at University Anahuac Law School (graduated, 1985); University of Paris (D.E.A., Droit International Public, 1987). Formerly Assistant, The Mexican Senate. *LANGUAGES:* Spanish and English.

ROBERT H. MANLEY

Attorney at Law

Avocat à la Cour

Established in 1953

127 BOULEVARD MALESHERBES
75017 PARIS, FRANCE
Telephone: 33 (1) 47.63.74.07
Telecopier: 33 (1) 43.80.92.72

Associated Office: Weissberg Gaetjens Ziegenfeuter, 34 avenue Marceau, 75008 Paris, France. Telephone: (33.1) 47.20.22.48. Fax: (33.1) 47.20.21.59.

General French and US Corporate Practice, International Foreign Investments, Estate, Entertainment Law, Banking Law, Tax Planning.

ROBERT H. MANLEY, born Paris, France, July 17, 1922; admitted, 1951, Massachusetts and Paris as Avocat à la Cour. *Education:* University of Aix en Provence, France (1942); Boston College Law School, Boston (LL.B., 1951). President, Association of Attorneys Members of Foreign Bars. *Member:* Massachusetts Bar Association, Paris Bar Association. (Also Member, Weissberg Gaetjens Ziegenfeuter, Paris, France). *LANGUAGES:* French and English. *PRACTICE AREAS:* International Corporate Law; Entertainment Law; Wills and Trusts; Estate Planning; Real Property; Contracts; Distribution Agreements.

ALAIN HENRI MARKON

Established in 1977

68 BD DE COURCELLES
75017 PARIS, FRANCE
Telephone: 47 66 02 12
Telecopier: 46 22 48 10

General French, American and International Law Practice. Avocat à la Cour de Paris, admitted to practice before the French Courts.

(This Listing Continued)

ALAIN HENRI MARKON, Paris—Continued

ALAIN HENRI MARKON, born Toulouse, France, June 13, 1941; admitted, 1968, District of Columbia; 1971, New York and U.S. Supreme Court; 1974, California and Paris. *Education:* Colgate University (B.A., cum laude, 1962); Columbia Law School (J.D., 1965); University of Paris (Licence en Droit, 1968). Lecturer, Ecole des Hautes Etudes Commerciales, 1986-1991. Corporate Counsel, Schlumberger Limited, Paris, France, 1968-1973. International Counsel, Hewlett-Packard Company, Palo Alto, California, 1974-1976. *Member:* American Bar Association (Member, Sections of: Banking, Corporation and Business Law; International Law); The District of Columbia Bar; The State Bar of California. *LANGUAGES:* English, French and Russian.

MARTIN & MAYNADIER

Established in 1983

198, AVENUE VICTOR HUGO
75116 PARIS, FRANCE
Telephone: (33) (1) 45.04.84.84
Telefax: (33) (1) 45.04.87.22

New York, New York Office: 324 East 51st Street, 10022. Telephone: (212) 754-3390. Telefax: (212) 754-3397.

Madrid, Spain Office: C. Raimundo Fernandez Villaverde, 30, 28003. Telephone: 34-1-535-37-64; 34-1-535-38-07. Telefax: 34-1-554-73-91.

General French, American, European Community and International Corporate, Commercial, Financial and Tax Practice. Mergers, Acquisitions, Joint Ventures, Corporate Restructurings and Reorganizations, Intellectual Property Rights, Trademark and Technology Transfers, Real Estate, Banking and Trusts and Estates. Litigation and Arbitration.

MEMBERS OF FIRM

FRANÇOIS MARTIN, born Paris, France, March 28, 1935; admitted, 1958, Paris; Licensed Legal Consultant, New York. *Education:* University of Paris (Licence en Droit, 1958; D.E.S. Economie Politique; D.E.S. Sciences Politiques; D.E.S. Droit Public); Institut des Sciences Politiques de Paris; Centre de Perfectionnement dans l'Administration des Affaires (C.P.A.; Diplôme, 1971). Member, Board of Trustees, University of Paris-Sorbonne, 1989—. *Member:* Confédération Nationale des Avocats; Union Internationale des Avocats (President, 1985-1987); Association of the Bar of the City of New York; American Bar Association (Member, Section on International Law and Practice). *LANGUAGES:* French and English. *PRACTICE AREAS:* Mergers and Acquisitions; Joint Ventures; Corporate Restructuring and Reorganization; Takeovers.

ALAIN MAYNADIER, born Limoges, France, April 8, 1946; admitted, 1968, Paris; 1989, Madrid. *Education:* University of Poitiers (Licence en Droit, 1968); University of Paris (Doctorat d'Etat en Droit, 1977); Institut des Hautes Etudes d'Amérique Latine. Recipient: Laureat du Concours Général des Facultés de Droit de France, 1966; Premier Prix de Droit International Privé de la Faculté de Droit de Poitiers, 1968. Professor of Contract Law, Faculté Autonome de Paris, 1972-1978. Lecturer in Private International Law, Faculté de Droit de Nanterre, France, 1969. Lecturer, Universidad Trias de Bes de Barcelona, 1985. *Member:* Confédération Nationale des Avocats; Union Internationale des Avocats. *LANGUAGES:* French, English and Spanish. *PRACTICE AREAS:* Intellectual Property Rights; Trademarks and Technology Transfers; Banking; Contracts; Licensing and Distribution.

FRANÇOISE NAMIN-MARTIN, born Paris, France, May 14, 1933; admitted, 1958, Paris. *Education:* Institut des Sciences Politiques de Paris (1952-1953); University of Paris (Licence en Droit, 1958). *Member:* Confédération Nationale des Avocats. *LANGUAGES:* French and English. *PRACTICE AREAS:* Litigation; Contracts; Family Law; Trusts and Estates; Franchising.

ASSOCIATES

ARNAUD BURG, born Agen, France, March 24, 1964; admitted, 1989, Paris. *Education:* University of Toulouse (Maîtrise en Droit Privé, 1985; Certificat Préparatoire á la Maîtrise de Sciences Techniques de Comptabilité Financière, 1987). *LANGUAGES:* French and English. *PRACTICE AREAS:* Corporate and Business Law.

MARIO CELAYA, born Madrid, Spain, December 7, 1958; admitted, 1989, Madrid (Not admitted in France). *Education:* Paris University (Licence en Droit, Maîtrise en Droit Communautaire, D.E.A. en Droit Com-

(This Listing Continued)

munautaire, 1983); Institut d'Etudes Politiques de Paris (1983). *LANGUAGES:* Spanish, French, English. *PRACTICE AREAS:* European Community and International Corporate Contracts; Trademarks and Technology Transfers.

MARGUERITE NOUGUÉ-SANS, born Tlemcen, Algeria, December 1, 1957; admitted, 1985, New York (Not admitted in France). *Education:* University of Paris II (License en Droit; Maîtrise en Droit Administratif; D.E.A., Sciences Politiques, 1980); New York University (LL.M., 1984). *Member:* American Bar Association; Association of the Bar of the City of New York. *LANGUAGES:* French and English. *PRACTICE AREAS:* Intellectual Property; Trademarks; Corporate Law; Contracts; Real Estate.

Languages: French, English and Spanish

CABINET REGIMBEAU
MARTIN, SCHRIMPF, WARCOIN, AHNER

Established in 1931

26, AVENUE KLÉBER
75116 PARIS, FRANCE
Telephone: (33) 45009202
Cable Address: "Brevregi, Paris, 034"
Telex: 640890 F BREVR
Fax: (1) 45.00.46.12

Patents, Trademarks and Designs Law. Application, Prosecution and Maintenance, Conduct of Actions for Infringement, Legal Opinions, Agreements under French and Common Market Laws, Antitrust Regulations, Copyright Laws.

FIRM PROFILE: Established in 1931 by Pierre Regimbeau, the firm has become one of the major patent and trademark firms in Europe, with a strength of more than 70, including French Industrial Property Counsels and European Patent Attorneys. It offers French and foreign clients a full range of services in intellectual matters, including patents, trade-marks, designs, licensing, etc., with particular emphasis on pharmacy, biotechnology and computers.

PARTNERS OF FIRM

JEAN JACQUES MARTIN, born 1936. *Education:* Ecole Nationale Supérieure des Mines (Engineer); Massachusetts Institute of Technology, U.S.A. (M.S., 1959). Patent, Trademark and Design Counsel (Registered Industrial Property Counsel). European Patent Attorney. Formerly registered Legal Counsel. *LANGUAGES:* French, English and German. *PRACTICE AREAS:* French, European and International Patent, Trade-Mark and Design Laws; Litigations.

ROBERT SCHRIMPF, born 1934. *Education:* Ecole Supérieure de Physique et de Chimie Industrielles (Engineer). Doctor of University. Patent, Trademark and Design Counsel (Registered Industrial Property Counsel). European Patent Attorney. Formerly registered Legal Counsel. *LANGUAGES:* French, English and German. *PRACTICE AREAS:* French, European and International Patent, Trade-Mark and Design Laws; Litigations.

JACQUES WARCOIN, born 1946. *Education:* Ecole Nationale Superieure de Chimie de Toulouse (Engineer); Diplôme du Centre d'Etudes Internationales de la Propriété Industrielle (CEIPI, 1974). Patent, Trademark and Design Counsel (Registered Industrial Property Counsel). European Patent Attorney. *LANGUAGES:* French, English and German. *PRACTICE AREAS:* French, European and International Patent, Trade-Mark and Design Laws; Litigations.

FRANCIS AHNER, born 1946. *Education:* Ecole Nationale Supérieure de Chimie de Strasbourg (Engineer); Diplôme du Centre d'Etudes Internationales de la Propriété Industrielle (CEIPI, 1971). Patent, Trademark and Design Counsel (Registered Industrial Property Counsel). European Patent Attorney. *LANGUAGES:* French, English and German. *PRACTICE AREAS:* French, European and International Patent, Trade-Mark and Design Laws; Litigations.

CHRISTIAN TEXIER, born 1956. *Education:* University of Angers (Master of Sciences and Technology, 1979); Diplôme du Centre d'Etudes Internationales de la Propriété Industrielle (CEIPI, 1980). Patent, Trademark and Design Counsel (Registered Industrial Property Counsel). European Patent Attorney. Formerly Registered Legal Counsel. *LANGUAGES:* French, English, German. *PRACTICE AREAS:* French, European and International Patent, Trade-Mark and Design Laws; Litigation.

(This Listing Continued)

ERIC LE FORESTIER, born 1957. *Education:* Ecole Nationale Supérieure des Mines de Paris (Engineer, 1980); Diplôme du Centre d'Etudes Internationales de la Propriété Industrielle (CEIPI, 1987). Patent, Trademark and Design Counsel (Registered Industrial Property Counsel). European Patent Attorney. *LANGUAGES:* French, English, German. *PRACTICE AREAS:* French, European and International Patent, Trade-Mark and Design Laws; Litigations.

Officially appointed under N.A.T.O. secrecy regulations. Members: French Company of Counsels in Industrial Property; International Federation of Industrial Property Attorneys (FICPI); International Association for the Protection of Industrial Property (AIPPI); United States Trademark Association; Union of European Practitioners in Industrial Property; Institut of Professional Representatives before the European Patent Office; International League of Competition Law; Licensing Executives Society (LES); Association Litteraire et Artistique Internationale (ALAI).

MARTINET & ASSOCIÉS

Société d'Avocats

Established in 1980

L'ATRIUM

15 RUE GALVANI

75017 PARIS, FRANCE

Telephone: (33-1) 40.55.16.00

Telecopier: (33-1) 40.55.16.01

Firm authorized to appear before French and European Economic Community Courts.

General Practice in French, EEC and International Business Law (inter alia Corporate, Tax, Mergers and Acquisitions, Securities, Banking, Patents and Trademarks, Labor, Finance, Litigation, International Estates, Arbitration, Computer Law, French and European Economic Community Antitrust, Insurance and Product Liability, Distribution, Consumer, Transportation, Environment Law.

MEMBERS OF FIRM

MARTINE BARBERON, born Paris, France, January 12, 1952; admitted, 1976, Paris. *Education:* University of Paris II (Bachelor of Law, 1975; C.A.P.A., 1976). *Member:* Association des femmes de carriëre juridique, Association Française des Avocats Conseils d'Entreprise (A.C.E.); Association Française des Ingénieurs et Techniciens pour l'Environnement (A.F.-.I.T.E.). *LANGUAGES:* French and English. *PRACTICE AREAS:* Litigation; Commercial law; Environment.

JEAN-JACQUES BATAILLON, born Versailles, France, May 29, 1948; admitted, 1978, Paris. *Education:* University of Paris X (Bachelor of Law, 1972; Diplôme d'Etudes Supérieures, 1973; Certificate of Economy - DECS, 1977). Author: "La T.V.A. Immobiliére," "Summary of French Tax System (ordered by French Development Agency)." Co-Author: "Guide Fiscalo-Comptable," "Tax Implications of Confidentiality Law." Lecturer in International Tax Law, University of Paris V. *Member:* Association Franco-Vietnamienne de Commerce et d'Industrie (President); Union Internationale des Avocats (Tax Committee); American Chamber of Commerce in France; International Fiscal Association (National Reporter, 1990); Association Française des Avocats Fiscalistes (Former Chairman); Association Française des Avocats Conseils d'Entreprise (A.C.E.) (President, Tax Section). *LANGUAGES:* French and English. *PRACTICE AREAS:* National and International Restructuration and Planification; Strategy of Investments; Mergers and Acquisitions.

VIRGINIE MARRER, born Paris, France, August 1, 1961; admitted, 1993, Paris. *Education:* University of Paris II (Master of Law, 1983; D.E.S.S. in Business Law and Taxation, 1984). *Member:* International Fiscal Association; Association Internationale des Jeunes Avocats. *LANGUAGES:* French, English and Spanish. *PRACTICE AREAS:* Taxation Law; Mergers and Acquisitions; Corporate Law.

CONSULTANT

BASIL BARAN, born London, England, June 17, 1958. U.S. Corporate and Individual Tax Consultant. *LANGUAGES:* French and English.

ASSOCIATES

VERONIQUE BURNIER, born Sallanches, France, March 2, 1959; admitted, 1987, Paris. *Education:* University of Montpellier (DESS in Business Law, 1984; Diplôme de Juriste Conseil d'Entreprise, 1984). *LANGUAGES:* French and English. *PRACTICE AREAS:* Intellectual Property Law; Litigation; Commercial Law.

(This Listing Continued)

ISABELLE DE SILVA, born Paris, France, June 26, 1964; admitted, 1989, Paris. *Education:* University of Paris X (Bachelor of Law, 1987; Master of Corporate Law, 1988). *LANGUAGES:* French, English and German. *PRACTICE AREAS:* Business Law; Litigation and Contracts.

VALERIE DUBAILE, born Paris, France, June 5, 1966; Registered: Conseil Juridique stagiaire. *Education:* University of Paris XII (Bachelor of Law, 1989; Master of Law, 1990; DESS Droit des Affaires, 1991). *LANGUAGES:* French and English. *PRACTICE AREAS:* Labour Law; Business Law; Contracts.

HERVE JEGOU, born Antony, France, March 18, 1967; admitted, 1994, Paris. *Education:* University of Paris-Dauphine (DEA droit privé, 1990; DEA droit anglis et nord-américain des affairs, 1991; CAPA, 1994). *LANGUAGES:* French and English. *PRACTICE AREAS:* Corporate Law; Contracts; Litigation; Commercial Law.

KATHLEEN JOHNSON, born Antony, France, March 20, 1967; admitted, 1994, Paris. *Education:* University of Paris I-Panthéon-Sorbonne (Bachelor of Law, 1988; Master of European Law, 1989; Diplôme d'Etudes Approfondies, 1990, first of the year). *LANGUAGES:* French, English and German. *PRACTICE AREAS:* Corporate Finance Law; Bankruptcy Law; Contracts.

JEAN-BASTIEN PASQUINI, born Sarlat, France, July 25, 1965; admitted, 1995, Paris. *Education:* University of Montpellier (Magistère droit des affaires, 1990; DESS droit des Affaires, 1992; DJCE, 1992; DEA accords industriels et commerciaux, 1993; CAPA, 1994). *LANGUAGES:* French and English. *PRACTICE AREAS:* Taxation Law; Mergers and Acquisitions; Corporate Law.

OLIVER PAUL, born Paris, France, August 24, 1967; admitted, 1995, Paris. *Education:* University of Paris V-RenéDescartes (DESS droit des affaires, 1965). *LANGUAGES:* French, German and English. *PRACTICE AREAS:* Business Law; Contracts.

CHRISTOPHE THERON, born Paris, France, April 13, 1964; admitted, 1989, Paris. *Education:* University of Paris I-Panthéon-Sorbonne (Diplôme d'Etudes Approfondies, 1988). *LANGUAGES:* French and English. *PRACTICE AREAS:* Banking Law; Bankruptcy Law; Contracts; Litigation.

OF COUNSEL

ODILE LAJOIX, born St. Cloud, France, October 7, 1950; admitted, 1977, Paris; 1990, Brussels. *Education:* University Grenoble (Licence en droit, 1973); Tulane University (LL.M., 1974); University of Paris (D.E.S. in EEC Law, 1975; C.A.P.A., 1977). Co-Author, "Banking Secrecy in France." Co-Editor, Revue de l'A.C.E. *Member:* International Bar Association; American Bar Association; Association Internationale des Jeunes Avocats; Association française des Avocats Conseils d'Entreprises (A.C.E.). *LANGUAGES:* French and English. *PRACTICE AREAS:* Commercial Transactions; Business Law; International Law; Litigation; Arbitration.

MARYAN GREEN AND PAPAIOANNOU

205, BOULEVARD SAINT GERMAIN

75007 PARIS, FRANCE

Telephone: 1 44 39 29 19

Fax: 1 44 39 29 18

London, England Office: 4, Breams Buildings, EC4. Telephone: 71 353 5835.

Athens, Greece Office: Constantinidou-Papaioannou Law Offices. 19-21 Arahovis Str. & Ippokratous, 10680. Telephone: 36 36 567.

General Practice, International Contracts, Companies, Commercial Law, Employers and Employees Law, Public Works, Family Law, Social Law, Human Rights, Private and Public International Law, EEC Law.

PARTNERS

NEVILLE MARYAN GREEN, born London, England, October 3, 1936; admitted, 1962, England; 1978, France. *Education:* Cambridge University, England (Master of Arts, 1960; Bachelor of Laws, 1962) Hague Academy (Diploma, 1963); University of Paris (Law Degree, 1976). Author: "International Law," Pitmans 3rd Edition, 1987. Lecturer in Law, University of Sheffield, 1963-1964. Lecturer on EEC Law, International Faculty of Comparative Law, Strasbourg, 1968-1970. Official in Legal Department of Council of Europe, Strasbourg, 1966-1973. *Member:* International Law Association; A.A.A.; I.B.A.; Institut Français de Droit International,

(This Listing Continued)

MARYAN GREEN AND PAPAIOANNOU, Paris—
Continued

Comité Français de Droit International Privé. (Also Counsel, Constantinidou-Papaioannou Law Offices, Athens, Greece).

VASSILIKI PAPAIOANNOU, born 1955; admitted, 1981, Greece; 1989, France. *Education:* Athens University (Master's Degree in Law, 1977); Paris University (Master's Degree in Sociology, 1981; DEA in Employment Law, 1983). (Also Member, Constantinidou-Papaioannou Law Offices, Athens, Greece).

ASSOCIATES

VÉRONIQUE STEVENSON DELHOMME, born 1952; admitted, 1980, Paris.

LAURENCE ITIE, born 1966; admitted, 1990, Paris.

VÉRONIQUE HERVAULT, born 1963; admitted, 1993, Paris.

ISABELLE LE COQ, born 1966; admitted, 1994, Paris.

Languages: French, English, German and Greek

MEADE & NABIAS

Established in 1970

85, RUE DE COURCELLES
75017 PARIS, FRANCE
Telephone: (1) 42.67.14.89
Fax: (1) 42.67.06.08
E Mail: C'Serve 100451,3613

London, England Associated Office: Pollecoff Rangeley, 123/125 City Road, WC1V 1JB. Telephone: (71) 608.2568. Fax: (71) 608.2751.
Bogotá, Colombia Associated Office: Cavelier Abogados. Edificio Siski, Carrera 4a. # 72-35, 8. Telephone: 2120100. Fax: 2358850.

General French, EEC, American and International Practice. Corporate, Labor, Arbitration, Litigation, Trade and Customs.

RICHARD C. MEADE, born Philadelphia, Pa., April 20, 1939; admitted, 1965, France, Avocat, New York, U.S. Court of International Trade and U.S. Court of Appeals for the Federal Circuit; 1968, District of Columbia. *Education:* Cornell University (A.B., 1960); University of Paris Law School; Columbia University (J.D., 1964). Lecturer, EEC Customs Law. Member: International Chamber of Commerce Commission on International Arbitration, 1982—; AAA Panel of Arbitrators. *LANGUAGES:* English, French.

ASSOCIATES

FRANCE GUÉNET, born Neuilly-sur-Seine, France, May 11, 1967; admitted, 1993, France, Avocat. *Education:* University of Paris Law School. *LANGUAGES:* French, English.

OF COUNSEL

JAMES C. PLOWDEN-WARDLAW, born Oneonta, New York, September 22, 1936; admitted, 1965, New York; 1971-1980 France, conseil juridique. *Education:* University of Virginia (B.A., 1959); Columbia University (J.D., 1964); Institut d'Etudes Politiques, Paris France; University of Madrid, Madrid, Spain;. (Also Practicing Individually). *LANGUAGES:* English, French and Spanish.

MEYOHAS COHEN MEYER CHOUCHANA
MEILICHZON

49/53 AVENUE DES CHAMPS ELYSÉES
75008 PARIS, FRANCE
Telephone: 40.75.40.75
Telefax: 40.75.40.40; 40.75.40.65

Mergers and Acquisitions, Foreign Investments, Taxation, Companies and Groups, Construction, Building, Banking, Securities and Finance, Entertainment, Trademarks and Intellectual Property, Commercial Law, Arbitration and Litigation, Bankruptcy and Insolvency.

(This Listing Continued)

MEMBERS OF FIRM

ANDRÉ COHEN, born Oran, Algeria, November 1, 1927; admitted, 1973, Paris as Conseil Juridique; 1992, Paris. *Education:* University of Montpellier (Licence en Droit, 1950); Ecole Nationale des Impôts. *Member:* International Fiscal Association. *LANGUAGES:* French and English.

MICHEL MEYER, born Paris, France, April 5, 1946; admitted, 1973, Paris as Conseil Juridique; 1992, Paris. *Education:* University of Paris (Licence en Droit, 1968). *LANGUAGES:* French, English and Spanish.

JEAN-PAUL CHOUCHANA, born Constantine, Algeria, October 20, 1944; admitted, 1977, Paris as Conseil Juridique; 1979, Paris. *Education:* University of Nice Law School (Licence en Droit, 1971); Mention Fiscalité Internationale (D.E.S., 1972); Institut d'Administration des Entreprises (1972). Recipient, Deutscher Akademischer Austauschdienst Scholarship, Bonn, Germany, 1973. *Member:* International Fiscal Association. *LANGUAGES:* French, English and German.

ROBERT MEILICHZON, born Neuilly-sur-Seine, France, July 21, 1947; admitted, 1977, Paris. *Education:* Paris University (Licence en Droit, 1972; D.E.S. Droit Privé-Maîtrise Droit des Affaires, 1974); Diplôme de l'Institut d'Etudes Politiques, Paris, 1973. *LANGUAGES:* French and English.

MARIE-CHRISTINE GRINDA, born Toulon, France, December 30, 1941; admitted, 1987, Paris as Conseil Juridique; 1992, Paris. *Education:* University of Paris (Licence en Droit, 1977). *LANGUAGES:* French and English.

PASCALE GUYARD, born Boulogne Billancourt, France, April 14, 1960; admitted, 1987, Paris. *Education:* University of Paris II, Assas (Maîtrise); University of Paris I, Panthéon (D.E.A., 1982). *LANGUAGES:* French and English.

FRÉDÉRIC POLI, born Boulogne Billancourt, France, April 27, 1962; admitted, 1990, Paris as Conseil Juridique; 1992, Paris. *Education:* University of Paris (Maîtrise en Droit, 1985). *LANGUAGES:* French, English and Italian.

CHRISTIAN SMIDA, born Antony, France, July 19, 1963. *Education:* Université de Paris (D.E.S.S. de Droit du Commerce Extérieur, 1988); Harvard University (C.S.S. in Management and Business Administration, 1990); Boston University School of Law (LL.M., 1990). *LANGUAGES:* French and English.

CAMILLE GLEIZE, born Neuilly-sur-Seine, France, April 8, 1964. *Education:* University of Tours (Maîtrise en Droit, 1989; Diplôme du Centre de Droit et Commerce International). *LANGUAGES:* French and English.

NINON RAUH, born Strasbourg, France, September 23, 1965; admitted, 1993, Paris. *Education:* University of Strasbourg Law School (Maîtrise en Droit des Affaires, 1988); University of Pennsylvania Law School (LL.M., 1989). *LANGUAGES:* French, English and German.

MEYRIER RENTMEESTERS FAYOUT
LACOSTE

3, RUE ALBÉRIC MAGNARD
75116 PARIS, FRANCE
Telephone: 45 27 81 10
Fax: 45 20 45 66

French and International Law Practice. Avocats a la Cour d'Appel de Paris. Admitted to Appear before French and European Community Courts.

MEMBERS OF FIRM

FRANCIS MEYRIER, born Neuilly-sur-Seine, France, 1946; admitted, 1969, Paris. *Education:* University of Paris; Worcester College, Oxford; Institut de Droit Comparé, Paris. Partner, Shearman & Sterling, 1981-1988. *LANGUAGES:* French and English.

LUC RENTMEESTERS, born Louvain, September 22, 1949; admitted, 1992, Paris. *Education:* Université Catholique de Louvain (Docteur en droit, 1973); Ecole Supérieure des Sciences Fiscales, Université de Bruxelles (1974). *LANGUAGES:* French, English and Dutch.

FRÉDÉRIC FAYOUT, born Montreuil-sous-Bois, November 17, 1962; admitted, 1989, Paris. *Education:* University of Paris. *LANGUAGES:* French, English and Spanish.

(This Listing Continued)

THIERRY C. LACOSTE, born Paris, France, June 19, 1959; admitted, 1992, Paris. *Education:* University of Paris; George Washington University, Washington, D.C., U.S.A. *LANGUAGES:* French and English.

MEZZULLO & McCANDLISH

A PROFESSIONAL CORPORATION

37, RUE GALILÉE
75116 PARIS, FRANCE
Telephone: (33-1) 47-20-30-01
Telex: 649545 F GALILEX
Telecopier: (33-1) 47-20-06-01

Richmond, Virginia Office: 1111 East Main Street, Suite 1500, P.O. Box 796. Telephone: 804-775-3100. Telecopier: 804-775-3800. Telex: 49608502-MEZMCC RICHMD.

Norfolk, Virginia Office: 1160 Town Point Center, 23510. Telephone: 804-640-7102. Fax: 804-640-7117.

Affiliated with Michel Normand, François Sarda et Associes, Paris, France.

International Law, Taxation, Patent and Trademark, Commercial, Products Liability, Construction and General Civil Litigation, Labor and Bankruptcy Law.

All lawyers in Paris Office are admitted to practice before courts of France, all member-states of European Economic Community and European Court of Justice.

All are members of the Ordre des Avocats à La Cour d'Appel de Paris and of the Confederation Syndicale des Avocats and all speak English and French.

RESIDENT COUNSEL

Michel Normand	Pascal Paillard
François Sarda	Georges Holleaux
Xavier Normand-Bodard	Ralph Boussier

(For complete biographical data on all personnel, see Professional Biographies at Richmond, Virginia)

MONAHAN & DUHOT

PARIS, FRANCE

(See Stibbe Simont Monahan Duhot)

MOQUET BORDE DIEUX GEENS & ASSOCIÉS

30 AVENUE DE MESSINE
75008 PARIS, FRANCE
Telephone: (1) 42 99 04 50
Telex: 640 650 F
Fax: (1) 45 63 91 49

Lyon, France Office: 11 Place Bellecour, 69002. Telephone: 72 40 00 32. Fax: 72 41 98 62.

Budapest, Hungary Office: Kossuth tér 16-17. III/2/a, H-1055 Budapest, (1245 Budapest, P.O. Box 1228). Telephone: (36-1) 1531 255. Fax: (36-1) 1531 229.

Tallinn, Estonian Office: 10 Pärnu str., EE 0001 Tallinn, Estonia. Telephone: (372) 640 58 36. Fax: (372) 640 58 38.

Brussels, Belgium Office: Rue de la Bonté 5-7, B-1050. Telephone: (32-2) 538-6869. Fax: (32-2) 538-6867.

French, EEC and International Law Practice.

RESIDENT MEMBERS OF FIRM

ANDRÉ MOQUET, born Vierzy, France, June 24, 1937; admitted, 1962, Paris. *Education:* University of Paris (Maîtrise en Droit with honors, 1959); IMEDE, Lausanne, (Master of Business Administration, 1969). *LANGUAGES:* French and English.

DOMINIQUE BORDE, born Rouen, France, October 27, 1941; registered 1966 as Conseil Juridique, Paris; admitted, 1976, Paris. *Education:*

(This Listing Continued)

University of Paris (Maîtrise en Droit, 1963); Columbia University (M.C.L., 1966). *Member:* ICC Institute of International Business Law and Practice; Legal Committee of the Conseil National du Patronat Français (Confederation of French Industries and Services); Arbitration with The International Court of Arbitration of ICC. *LANGUAGES:* French and English.

DANIEL HURSTEL, born Strasbourg, France, December 12, 1955; admitted, 1980, Paris. *Education:* Ecole des Hautes Etudes Commerciales, H.E.C. (Master of Business Administration, 1977); University of Paris (Maitrise en Droit, 1979; DEA Droit des Communautés Européennes, 1980). Lecturer at HEC-ISA. *Member:* International Bar Association (Co-Chairman, Sub committee Q3, "Euromarkets", Section of Business Law). *LANGUAGES:* French, English and German.

JEAN LEYGONIE, born Paris, France, June 1, 1943; practiced as Conseil Juridique in Paris and Brussels, 1972-1984; Vice President and General Counsel Pechiney, 1984-1990; admitted, 1991, Paris. *Education:* Institut d'Etudes Politiques de Paris (1968); University of Paris (Maitrise en Droit, 1968; D.E.S. Droit Public, 1969); Columbia University (LL.M., 1971). *LANGUAGES:* French and English.

HENRI DE FEYDEAU, born Saint-Junien, France, May 21, 1947; registered as Conseil Juridique, 1985; admitted, 1990, Paris. *Education:* Institut d'Etudes Politiques de Paris (1969); University of Paris (D.E.S. ès Sciences Economiques, 1971). Co-Author: "Optimisation fiscale et abus de droit", 1990. *Member:* Institut Avocats Specialistes du Droit Fiscal, International Fiscal Association (IFA); International Tax Planning Association (ITPA). *LANGUAGES:* French and English.

FREDERIQUE DUPUIS-TOUBOL, born Paris, France, March 24, 1959; admitted, 1983, Paris. *Education:* University of Paris X (Doctor in Law, 1985). Author: "Le logiciel, analyse juridique." Member of Editorial Committee: Computer and Telecom Law Review; ICC French Data Processing, Telecommunications and Information Committee. IBA. *LANGUAGES:* French and English.

ALINE PONCELET, born Paris, France, April 5, 1961; admitted, 1987, Paris. *Education:* University of Paris (Maîtrise en Droit, Paris II 1982; D.E.A., Droit des Affaires, Paris, 1983); Ecole des Hautes Etudes Commerciales, H.E.C. (Master of Business Administration, 1985). *LANGUAGES:* French and English.

PHILIPPE CROIZAT, born Lyon, France, November 5, 1940; admitted, 1965, Lyon. *Education:* University of Lyon (Docteur en droit, 1965); New York University (M.C.J., 1966). General Counsel and Member of the Management Committee, Michelin et Cie, 1973-1994. *LANGUAGES:* French and English.

PIERRE KIRCH, born Santa Barbara, California, January 8, 1956; registered as Conseil Juridique, 1991; admitted, 1991, Paris. *Education:* Dartmouth (B.A., 1979); University of Paris (Maîtrise en Droit, 1987; D.E.A. Droit International Privé et Droit du Commerce International, 1988). Lecturer at H.E.C. *LANGUAGES:* English, French, Italian and Spanish.

BUDAPEST RESIDENT COUNSEL

ANDRAS SZECSKAY, born Kecskemet, Hungary, December 3, 1948; admitted, 1975, Budapest (Not admitted in France). *Education:* University of Szeged (Master of Law, 1973). *Member:* Presidium of the Budapest Bar; Hungarian Association for the Protection of Industrial Property; Licensing Executives Society. *LANGUAGES:* Hungarian and English.

ESTONIA RESIDENT COUNSEL

JURI RAIDLA, born Pärnu, Estonia, July 2, 1957. Minister of Justice of the Republic of Estonia, 1990-1992. Head of Expert Commission on Elaborating the Constitution of the Republic of Estonia, 1992. *Education:* University of Tartu, Estonia (Master of law, 1980) University of St. Petersburg (Ph.D., 1987). *LANGUAGES:* Estonian, English and Russian.

OF COUNSEL

ANDRÉ VILLEREY, born Beaujeu, France, December 20, 1925; admitted, 1990, Paris. *Education:* University of Dijon (Maîtrise en droit, 1947). Former General Counsel of Société Générale.

FRANÇOIS VERGNE, born Paris, France, July 20, 1957; admitted, 1987, Paris. *Education:* Institut d'Etudes Politiques de Paris (1980); University of Paris II (Maîtrise en Droit, 1980); University of Paris I (D.E.A., Droit Anglais et Nord Américain des Affaires, 1983); University of Pennsylvania (LL.M., 1984, Fulbright Scholar). Lecturer at l'Institut d'Etudes Politiques de Paris. *LANGUAGES:* French and English.

(This Listing Continued)

MOQUET BORDE DIEUX GEENS & ASSOCIÉS,
Paris—Continued

ASSOCIATES

MARIE-FRANCOISE GABARRE, born Paris, France, June 8, 1957; admitted, 1988, Paris. *Education:* Institut d'Etudes Politiques de Paris (1978); University of Paris I (Maîtrise en Droit, 1980); Institut d'Administration des Entreprises (1981); New York University (M.C.J., 1986, Fulbright Scholar). *LANGUAGES:* French and English.

XAVIER DEQUIDT, born Lezennes, France, February 3, 1956; admitted, 1992, Paris. *Education:* University of Reims (Maîtrise en Droit); University of Paris (D.E.A., Droit Communautaire, 1982). Lecturer at l'Institut d'Etudes Politiques de Lyon. (Resident, Lyon, France Office). *LANGUAGES:* French and English.

JOELLE HANNELAIS, born Paris, February 2, 1961; admitted, 1987, Paris. *Education:* Institut National des Langues et Civilisations Orientales (1980-1982); University of Paris (Maîtrise en Droit des Affaires, 1984; D.E.A. de Droit International Privé, 1985). *LANGUAGES:* French, English and Russian.

SYLVIE GAUTRON MAGNAVAL, born Paris, France, October 14, 1964; admitted, 1989, Paris. *Education:* University of Paris (Maîtrise en Droit Privé, 1986; D.E.A. de Droit Privé, 1988). *LANGUAGES:* French, English and Spanish.

ELIE KLEIMAN, born Paris, France, November 12, 1963; admitted, 1990, Paris. *Education:* University of Paris (Maîtrise en Droit, Paris X, 1986; D.E.A. Droit International, Paris II, 1987). *LANGUAGES:* French and English.

XAVIER MATHARAN, born Toulouse, France, August 21, 1962; admitted, 1993, Paris. *Education:* Institut d'Etudes Politiques de Paris (1985); Ecole Nationale de la Magistrature (1985); University of Paris IV (Licence en Histoire, 1983); Univerity of Paris II (D.E.S.S., Droit de l'environnement, des travaux publics et des collectivés locales, 1985). Author: "Comment Défendre votre Environnement," 1993; Co-Author: "La Justice et l'Environnement," 1992. Lecturer, University of Paris I. Deputy Public Procedure, 1987-1992. Cabinet of the Environmental Secretary of State, 1992-1993. *LANGUAGES:* French and English.

ANNETTE PERON, born Reinbeck, Germany, April 28, 1964; admitted, 1992, Paris. *Education:* University of Kent-Canterbury (Diploma of English Law, 1986); University of Paris XI (Maitrise en Droit des Affaires, 1987); I.S.I.T. Paris (Diplôme de traductrice et d'interpréte de liaison Anglais et Allemand, 1987); HEC University of Paris XI (D.E.S.S. Fiscalité Internationale, 1989). *LANGUAGES:* French, English and German.

LAURENT MABILAT, born Antibes, France, May 30, 1966; admitted, 1994, Paris. *Education:* University of Nice (Maîtrise en Droit des Affaires, 1987; D.E.A. Droit et Economie du Dévelopement, 1989); Ecole Supérieure de Commerce du CERAM - Sophia Antipolis (1988); Ecole Supérieure des Sciences Economiques et Commerciales (Mastére Spécialisé en Techniques Financières, 1989). *LANGUAGES:* French, English and Spanish.

PATRICE LEFEVRE, born Paris, France, March 22, 1966; admitted, 1992, Paris. *Education:* University of Paris II (Maîtrise en droit, 1988; D.E.S.S. de Droit des affaires et fiscalité des Enterprises, 1989); University of Lyon (Diplôme de Juriste Conseil d'Entreprises, 1989); University of Montpellier (Certificat Superieur de Fiscalité, 1989). *LANGUAGES:* French and English.

MARIE-CHRYSTEL DANG-TRAN, born Paris, France, July 16, 1966; admitted, 1992, Paris. *Education:* University of Paris II (Maîtrise en Droit des Affaires et Fiscalite des Entreprises, 1989); Maîtrise en Droit Européen et Droit International, 1989); H.E.C.-University of Paris XI; D.E.S.S. Fiscalité Internationale (1990). *LANGUAGES:* French and English.

MARIE-HELENE TONNELLIER, born La Ferté-Macé, France, April 21, 1965; admitted, 1990, Paris. *Education:* University of Paris I (Maîtrise en Droit des Affaires, 1987; D.E.A. de droit des Affaires, 1988); University of Paris II (D.E.S.S. de Droit Notarial, 1989). *LANGUAGES:* French and English.

GISELA SUESS, born Ansbach, West Germany, June 8, 1962; admitted, 1990, Germany; 1993, France. *Education:* University of Würzburg (First State Examination in Law, 1987; Doctor of Law, 1988); University of Caen, France (1984-1985); Second State Examination in Law (1990); Ecole Nationale d'Administration (1989-1990). *LANGUAGES:* French, English and German.

(This Listing Continued)

MICHEL LEQUIEN, born Haiti, June 20, 1964; admitted, 1991, Paris. *Education:* University of Paris II (Maîtrise en Droit Public, 1986; D.E.A. Droit Communautaire, 1987; Maîtrise Carrières Judiciaires, 1988); German Academic Exchange Service, Program of Legal Studies, Tübingen and Düsseldorf (1988-1989). *LANGUAGES:* French, English and German.

SOFIA BENGANA, born Algiers, August 13, 1965; admitted, 1991, Paris. *Education:* University of Paris I (Maîtrise en droit des affaires, 1988; D.E.A. de droit des affaires et de l'économie, 1989). *LANGUAGES:* French, English and Arabic.

BEATRICE HONORAT, born Bourganeuf, France, October 19, 1967; admitted, 1993, Paris. *Education:* Ecole des Hautes Etudes Commerciales, H.E.C. (Master of Business Administration, 1990); University of Paris XI (Maîtrise en Droit, 1990); College of Europe, Bruges (Advanced European Legal Studies, 1991). *LANGUAGES:* French, English, German and Italian.

ISABELLE FRANCOU, born Grenoble, France, April 10, 1967. *Education:* Ecole des Hautes Etudes Commerciales, H.E.C. (Master of Business Administration, 1991); University of Paris II (Maîtrise en Droit, 1993). *LANGUAGES:* French, English and Spanish.

OLIVIER DEREN, born Paris, France, March 23, 1966; admitted, 1992, Paris. *Education:* Institut d'Etudes Politiques de Paris (1987); University of Paris II (Maîtrise en Droit, 1990). *LANGUAGES:* French, English and German.

CHANTAL CORDIER-VASSEUR, born Dunkerque, France, October 24, 1967; admitted, 1993, Paris. *Education:* University of Lille II (Maîtrise en Droit, 1989); University of Paris I (D.E.A. Droit International Privé et Droit du Commerce International, 1990). *LANGUAGES:* French, English and Spanish.

ANNE TOLILA, born Paris, France, May 29, 1967; admitted, 1993, Paris. *Education:* Institut d'Etudes Politiques de Paris (1991); University of Paris II (Maîtrise en Droit, 1989); H.E.C. University of Paris XI (D.E.S.S. Fiscalité Internationale, 1992). *LANGUAGES:* French and English.

PHILIPPE DIDIER, born Clermont-Ferrand, France, September 12, 1966; admitted, 1993, New York; 1994, Paris. *Education:* University of Clermont-Ferrand (Maîtrise en Droit, 1988; D.E.A. Droit des Affaires, 1989); New York University (LL.M., 1992). *LANGUAGES:* French and English.

PASCALE GELLY, born Grenoble, France, April 4, 1966. *Education:* University of Paris II (Maîtrise en Droit, 1988; D.E.S.S. Droit de la propriété littéraire, Artistique et Industrielle, 1990); Columbia University (LL.M., 1992). *LANGUAGES:* French and English.

YVON MARTINET, born Chambery, France, June 4, 1966; admitted, 1989, Paris. *Education:* University of Paris I (Maîtrise en Droit, 1988, D.E.A. Droit Privé, 1989). Premier Secretaire de la Conference du Stage des Avocats a la Cour de Paris (Chairman of the Young Lawyers' Association of the Paris Bar), 1991; Columbia University (LL.M., Sp. S., 1992-1993). *LANGUAGES:* French, English and Spanish.

BENEDICTE BREMOND, born Laxou, France, February 14, 1970. *Education:* Ecole Superieure des Sciences Economiques et Commerciales (E.S.S.E.C., 1991); University of Paris II (Maîtrise en Droit des Affaires, Maîtrise de Carrières Judiciaires, 1992). *LANGUAGES:* French and English.

FLORENCE GUTHFREUND-ROLAND, born Nancy, France, September 3, 1966; admitted, 1993, Paris. *Education:* University of Nancy (Maîtrise en Droit, 1989); Institut d'Etudes Politiques de Paris (1990); University of Paris I (D.E.S.S. de Droit du Marché Commun, 1991). *LANGUAGES:* French, English, German and Spanish.

TATIANA NOURISSAT, born Ixelles, Belgium, January 3, 1969. *Education:* University of Paris Dauphine (Maîtrise des Sciences de Gestion, 1991; D.E.A. Droit Economique et Social, 1992); University of Paris II (Maîtrise en Droit, 1991). *LANGUAGES:* French, English and Russian.

MARIE PISANTE, born Saint-Maur-des-Fossés, France, May 7, 1968; admitted, 1994, Paris. *Education:* Institut d'Etudes Politiques de Paris (1993); University of Paris II (D.E.S.S. de Droit des Affaires et Fiscalité). *LANGUAGES:* French and English.

PHILIPPE NONE, born Paris, France, June 16, 1965. *Education:* University of Paris X (Maîtrise en droit des affaires, 1987); University of Paris IX (D.E.A. économique et social, 1989); University of Georgetown (LL.M., Master of Laws, 1994). *LANGUAGES:* French and English.

LAURENT A. NIDDAM, born Fés, Morocco, January 23, 1960; admitted, 1995, Paris. *Education:* University of Paris II (Maîtrise en Droit Privé

(This Listing Continued)

Général, 1991; D.E.A. Droit International, 1992); Columbia University (LL.M., 1994, Harlan Fiske Stone Scholar). Author: "L'exécution des des sanctions arbitrales Internationales aux Etats-Unis," 1993. *LANGUAGES:* French and English.

AIDA TAMER, born Beirut, Lebanon, July 7, 1964; admitted, 1991, Paris. *Education:* University of Paris II (Maîtrise en Droit des Affairs, 1986); Fletcher School of Law and Diplomacy, Tufts-Harvard (Master of Arts, 1988); St. Joseph University of Beirut (Licence en droit, 1993). *LANGUAGES:* French, English and Arabic.

MARY ANN CARPENTER-PECQUET, born San Francisco, California, September 26, 1961; admitted, 1992, California and U.S. District Court, Southern District of California (Not admitted in France). *Education:* University of California at Santa Barbara (B.A., 1978); Boston University (M.A. in International Relations, 1989); California Western School of Law (J.D., 1992). Law Clerk to John S. Rhodes, 1991. *Member:* California and American Bar Asociations. *LANGUAGES:* French, English and Spanish.

ANDRÉ FARACHE, born Casablanca, Morocco, December 6, 1965; admitted, 1992, Paris. *Education:* University of Paris I (Maîtrise en Droit, 1989); University of Paris II (D.E.A. de Droit de la Propriété Littéraire, Artistique et Industrielle, 1990); Ecole Supérieure de Commerce de Paris (E.S.C.P., 1993). *LANGUAGES:* French and English.

STEPHANE LEMARCHAND, born Paris, France, March 4, 1967; admitted, 1993, Paris. *Education:* University of Paris XI (Maîtrise en Droit, 1989; D.E.S.S. en Droit, Informatique et Technologies nouvelles, 1990); University of Paris II (D.E.S.S. en Droit de la Propriété Industrielle, 1991). *LANGUAGES:* French, English, Italian and German.

MARY-ELIZABETH GIUFFRA, born New York, N.Y., March 22, 1961; admitted, 1995, New York. *Education:* Smith College (B.A., 1984); University of Aix-en-Provence (D.E.S.U. Comparative Law, 1991); Institute of International and Comparative Law, University of San Diego, London and Paris (Certificate in International and Comparative Law, 1993); Benjamin N. Cardozo Law School (J.D., 1994). *LANGUAGES:* English and French.

CHARLES GUIEN, born Marseille, France, December 28, 1965; admitted, 1993, Paris. *Education:* University of Paris I (Maîtrise en Droit des Affaires et Fiscalité, 1989; D.E.A. en Droit des Affaires et de l'Economie, 1990); Ecole Supérieure de Commerce de Paris, E.S.C.P. Masters of Business Administration, 1993; Institut d'Etudes Poliques de Paris, 1993. *LANGUAGES:* French and English.

ANDREA GEIGER, born Munich, Germany, March 4, 1965. *Education:* University of Munich (First State Examination in Law, 1990; Second State Examination in Law, Ph.D. in Law, 1994). *LANGUAGES:* French, English and German.

ANNE-NOELLE CHARVILLAT, born Bourg-en-Bresse, France, October 10, 1969; admitted, 1995, Paris. *Education:* University of Paris II (Maîtrise em Droit des Affaires, 1992; DESS de Droit des Affaires et Fiscalité , 1993; Magistére de Juriste d'Affaires, DJCE); University of King's College London (LL.M. in International Business Law, 1994). *LANGUAGES:* French, English and German.

JEAN-DAVID SICHEL, born Strasbourg, France, September 5, 1969; admitted, 1995, Paris. *Education:* Ecole Supérieure des Science Economiques et Commerciales (ESSEC, 1992); University of Paris II (Maîtrise de Droit, 1993; D.E.A. Droit des Affaires, 1994). *LANGUAGES:* French, English and Spanish.

JEROME BROSSET, born Challans, France, August 1, 1970. *Education:* Institu d'Etudes Politiques de Paris (1991); Ecole des Hautes Etudes Commerciales, H.E.C. (Master of Business Administration, 1993); University of Paris XI (Maîtrise en Droit des Affaires, 1994). *LANGUAGES:* French and English.

Co-Authors and Editors of "Doing Business in France," a Matthew Bender publication.

MORAY & ASSOCIÉS

Société d'Avocats
12-14 AVENUE VICTOR HUGO
75116 PARIS, FRANCE
Telephone: (33) (1) 45 00 02 03
Fax: (33) (1) 45 00 60 99

Company Law, EU Law (Monitoring, Lobbying, Aid Applications, Competition Law, etc.), Property Law, Tax Law, Banking and Finance Transactions, White Collar Crime, Mergers and Acquisitions, Employment Law, Insurance Law, Transportation Law, Intellectual Property Law, International Private Law and location of business partners (Member of the EU's B.C. Net).

FIRM PROFILE: *The firm specialises in international transactions and EU Law and is part of the EUROLAW E.E.I.G. which is made up of law firms specializing in international business law from the entire European Economic Area. The law firm also undertakes all aspects of French law, but specializes particularly in business and commercial Law.*

MEMBERS OF FIRM

YVES-MARIE MORAY, born Brussels, Belgium, June 17, 1955; admitted, 1983, Brussels; 1986, Paris. *Education:* Saint Louis University, Brussels (Candidate en Droit, 1976); Catholic University of Louvain (Licence en Droit 1979, Licence en Droit Communautaire, 1985); Royal University of Leyden (Certificat en Droit International, 1981); Academy of International Law of The Hague (1979-1980); International Institute of Human Rights of Strasbourg (1983); University Center of European and International Research (Grenoble, 1984). Former member of the European Parliament Legal Service, General Directorate of Research and Documentation, 1981-1983 and General Directorate IV of the European Community (Competition Law), 1985. Lecturer, European Business Law, Universities of Paris and Zurich. *LANGUAGES:* French, German, English and Dutch. *PRACTICE AREAS:* French and Belgian Business Law; European Community Law (Competition Law, Auditing, Monitoring, Community Lobbying); and International Joint Ventures.

JEAN-JACQUES ZANDER, born Blois, France, June 12, 1954; admitted, 1991, Sweden; 1993, Paris and Brussels. *Education:* University of Stockholm (LL.M., 1978); François Rabelais University, Tours (Maitrise en Droit International, 1979); Centre de Droit de Commerce International, Tours (Diplôme Droit International, 1980). Author: "How to successfully invest in Sweden". Member of the Legal Department of the French Chamber of Commerce in Sweden, 1980-1982. Member of the Board French Chamber of Commerce for Sweden, Legal Adviser to the French Embassy in Stockholm. Founder and senior partner of the Zanders Advokatbyrå AB in Stockholm, Sweden. *LANGUAGES:* French, Swedish and English. *PRACTICE AREAS:* French and International Business Law; International Arbitration; Foreign Investment in Nordic Countries.

JEAN-PIERRE PIN, born Boulogne Billancourt, France, January 1, 1949; admitted, 1992, Paris, Former Conseil Juridique. *Education:* University of Paris Panthéon-Sorbonne (Licence en Droit, 1973, D.E.S.S. Droit des Affaires, 1974). *LANGUAGES:* French. *PRACTICE AREAS:* Company Law; Corporate Tax; Bankruptcy; International Trade Litigation.

OF COUNSEL

PATRICE FARRAS, born Montauban, France, March 11, 1944; admitted, 1992, Paris, Former Conseil Juridique. *Education:* University of Toulouse (Licence en Droit, Certificat de Droit Privé, 1967). *LANGUAGES:* French. *PRACTICE AREAS:* Company Law; Tax Law.

JEAN-MICHEL BARGIARELLI, born Bordeaux, France, June 22, 1943; admitted, 1970, Bordeaux. *Education:* University of Bordeaux (Maitrise en Droit, 1968, D.E.S.S. de Droit Privé, 1970). Former Lecturer, E.N.A. in Tchad, 1968-1970. *LANGUAGES:* French, English, Spanish. *PRACTICE AREAS:* Business Law; Trade Law; Tax Law.

B. NEIL S. CLARKE, born Newcastle-upon-Tyne, England, August 2, 1957; admitted, 1988, California; 1990, New York (Not admitted in France). *Education:* Duke (J.D., 1988); Stanford Law School (1988); University of Connecticut (M.A. Econ., 1985); University of London (B.A. Hons, 1979). Founder and senior partner of Clarke & Associates in New York, New York. *LANGUAGES:* English, French. *PRACTICE AREAS:* International Business Law; U.S. Company; Securities and Financial Law.

GÉZA SIMONFAY, born Budapest, Hungary, May 26, 1949; admitted, Austria (Not admitted in France). *Education:* University of Vienna (Lic. jur. 1972, Dr. jur., 1974); Vienna Diplomatic Academy (Diploma, 1976). Former member of the Legal Department Mobil Oil Austria, former Head

(This Listing Continued)

MORAY & ASSOCIÉS, Paris—Continued

of Legal Department Steyr-Daimler-Puch, Austria. Founder and senior partner of Simonfay & Ranzenhofer in Vienna, Austria. *LANGUAGES:* German, Hungarian, English, French. *PRACTICE AREAS:* International Business Law; Austrian Commercial Law; Litigation and Property Law; Acquisitions and Joint Ventures in Austria and Hungary.

NATHALIE FANAIE, born Ispahan, Iran, September 16, 1964; admitted, 1993, Brussels (Not admitted in France). *Education:* University of Paris II, Assas (Licence en Droit, 1989, Maitrise en Droit International et Européen, 1990, D.E.S.S. en Droit de Commerce International, 1991). *LANGUAGES:* French, English, Persian. *PRACTICE AREAS:* Company Law; European Business Law; Contract Law; Private International Law; International and Domestic Labor Law.

MORRIS, LENDAIS, HOLLRAH & BROWN

A PROFESSIONAL CORPORATION

Established in 1991

167 BIS AVE. VICTOR HUGO
PARIS 75116, FRANCE
Telephone: 33-1 4553 3838
Fax: 331 4553 6348

Houston, Texas Office: 1980 Post Oak Boulevard 77056, Suite 700. Telephone: 713-966-7200. Facsimile: 713-966-7729.

General Civil Practice. International Business Transactions and Litigation, Creditors Rights, Mortgage Lending, Domestic Relations, Banking, Corporate, Business and Commercial Law, Bankruptcy, Taxation, Real Estate, Construction Law. General Civil Litigation, Probate, Immigration, Personal Injury.

JEAN-PIERRE LENDAIS, born Oran, France, June 1, 1937; admitted, 1961, France; 1975, Louisiana and U.S. District Court, Western District of Louisiana; 1976, U.S. Court of Appeals, Fifth Circuit; 1983, U.S. District Court, Southern District of Texas; 1984, Texas; 1987, District of Columbia. *Education:* Ecole Polytechnic Notariat, Paris, France (Diploma, 1958); University of Paris-Sorbonne, Paris, France (License, 1961). Who's Who in American Law, 1992-1993. *Member:* Houston (Member, Section on International Law), Louisiana State and American (Member, Section on International Law) Bar Associations; State Bar of Texas (Member, Section on International Law); District of Columbia Bar; Secretaire de la Conference des Avocats a la Cour de Paris; Foreign Trade Advisor to the French Government; French-American Chamber of Commerce. *LANGUAGES:* French. *PRACTICE AREAS:* International Law; Commercial Law; Construction Law; International Arbitration.

(For Complete Biographical Data on all Personnel, see Professional Biographies at Houston, Texas)

MUDGE ROSE GUTHRIE ALEXANDER & FERDON

(Mudge, Stern, Baldwin & Todd)
(Caldwell, Trimble & Mitchell)

12, RUE DE LA PAIX
75002 PARIS, FRANCE
Telephone: 42.61.57.71
Cable Address: "Baltuchins, Paris"
Telecopier: 42.61.79.21

New York City Office: 180 Maiden Lane, New York, N.Y., 10038. Telephone: 212-510-7000. Telecopier: 212-248-2655/57.
Los Angeles, California Office: 21st Floor, 333 South Grand Avenue, 90071. Telephone: 213-613-1112. Telecopier: 213-680-1358.
Washington, D.C. Office: 1200 19th Street, N.W., Suite 400, 20037. Telephone: 202-973-1200. Telecopier: 202-429-9367.
West Palm Beach, Florida Office: Suite 900, 515 North Flagler Drive, 33401. Telephone: 407-650-8100. Telecopier: 407-833-1722.
Parsippany, New Jersey Office: Morris Corporate Center Two, Building D, 1 Upper Pond Road, 07054-1075. Telephone: 201-335-0004. Telecopier: 201-402-1593.
Tokyo, Japan Office: Infini Akasaka, 8-7-15 Akasaka, Minato-Ku, Tokyo 107, Japan. Telephone: (03) 3423-3970. Fax: (03) 3423-3971.

(This Listing Continued)

EU486B

General Practice.
Firm engaged in French, EC and General International Practice including Corporate Law, Banking and Financial Law, Commercial Law, Tax Law, Civil Law, Labor Law, Industrial and Intellectual Property Law, European Community Law, Estate Law, Energy Law, Environmental Law, Aribtration and Litigation and Civil Procedure. Avocats à la Cour admitted to appear before French Courts.

RESIDENT PARTNERS

ALAN F. CARIDDI, born Cairo, Egypt, April 25, 1949; admitted, 1974, New York; 1977, France; 1984, District of Columbia; Avocat à la Cour. *Education:* Georgetown University (A.B., magna cum laude, 1970); Columbia University (J.D., 1973). Phi Beta Kappa. Harlan Fiske Stone Scholar. Member, Advisory Board, The American Tax Institute in Europe, 1985-1992. *Member:* New York State, American (Member, Sections on: Business Law; International Law and Practice) and International Bar Associations. *LANGUAGES:* French, English and Portuguese.

BRUCE C. MEE, born Mineola, New York, January 11, 1954; admitted, 1982, New York; 1986, France. *Education:* Harvard University (A.B., magna cum laude, 1977); Universitéde Paris I (Maîtrise ès Lettres, 1978); Ecole Normale Supérieure de Paris (1977-1978); Columbia University (J.D., 1981). Harlan Fiske Stone Scholar. *Member:* New York State and American Bar Associations. *LANGUAGES:* French, English and German.

FABRICE RUÉ, born Chartres, France, February 12, 1954; admitted, 1984, France. *Education:* Université de Paris, I (Maîtrise en Droit Public, 1977; Licence d'Histoire, 1978; D.E.A. Fiscalité-Finances Publiques, 1979; Maîtrise en Droit Privé, 1980); Institut d'Etudes Politiques (1978); University of Michigan Law School (LL.M., 1985). *Member:* Paris Bar Association (Member, Tax Committee); International Bar Association; International Fiscal Association; American Tax Institute in Europe (Member, Advisory Board, 1992—); International Trademark Association (Member, International Committee, Information Resources Group, 1994—). *LANGUAGES:* French, English.

INTERNATIONAL COUNSEL

VUONG VAN BAC, born Bac Ninh, North Vietnam, September, 1927; admitted, 1952, Hanoi; 1954, Saigon; 1977, France; 1992, France, as Avoc at. *Education:* Faculte de Droit de l'Universite de Hanoi (Licence en Droit, 1952); Diplome s d'Etudes Superieures de Droit Prive, 1953 and de Droit Public, 1954. Treasurer, Saigon Bar Council, 1963-1969. Author: "Cautionnement bancaire et garantie bancaire à première demande," Revue Droit et Affaires, (Paris, Sept. 1986). *LANGUAGES:* French, English and Vietnamese.

ASSOCIATES

CHRISTINE BOUGIS, born Nantes, France, May 23, 1966. *Education:* Université de Paris II, Magistére de Juriste d'Affaires (Maîtrise, 1987; D.E.S.S. de Droit des Affaires et Fiscalité , 1988); Université de Paris I (D.E.A. de Droit Communautaire et Européen, 1989); University of Virginia (LL.M., 1990). *LANGUAGES:* French and English.

MICHAEL S. CARTER, born Minneapolis, Minnesota, August 5, 1961; admitted, 1987, New York; 1991, France. *Education:* Bowdoin College (B.A., magna cum laude, 1983); Columbia University (J.D., 1986). Phi Beta Kappa. Harlan Fiske Stone Scholar. Articles Editor, Columbia Journal of Law and Social Problems, 1985-1986. Author: "Ethnic Minority Groups and Self-Determination: The Case of the Basques," 20 Col. J.L. & Soc. Probs. 55 (1986). *Member:* The Association of the Bar of the City of New York; American Bar Association (Member, Section on International Law and Practice). *LANGUAGES:* French and English.

HERVÉ DE KERVASDOUÉ, born Paris, France, July 13, 1968. *Education:* Universiteé Paris, Pantheon-Assas (D.E.A., 1992); Cornell University (LL.M., 1994). *LANGUAGES:* French, English.

BIJAN-EMMANUEL EGHBAL, born Paris, France, January 20, 1963; admitted, 1992, France. *Education:* Université de Paris II (Maîtrise, 1986); George Washington University (M.C.L., 1988). *LANGUAGES:* French and English.

CAROL A. UMHOEFER, born Stroughton, Wisconsin, January 6, 1967; admitted, 1993, New York (Not admitted in France). *Education:* University of Wisconsin (B.A., 1988); Université de Paris III, Centre d'Etudes Critiques (Jan.-June 1989); Harvard University (J.D., cum laude, 1992). Phi Beta Kappa. Thesis: "History and Analysis of the Mandatory Tender Offer in France"; Author: "Towards a United Nations Solution in Cambodia," 21 Har. Intl. L.J. 275 (1991); "Reassessing Aspiration Levels in Negotiation,"

(This Listing Continued)

Workshop Readings, Harvard Program on Negotiation. Co-author: Le Délit d'Initié : Insider Trading Law in France," 30 Col. J. Transnatl. L. 89 (1992). *LANGUAGES:* French and English.

NAUTA DUTILH

Attorneys, Civil Law Notaries, Tax Advisers

77, AVENUE RAYMOND POINCARÉ
F-75116 PARIS, FRANCE
Telephone: (33-1) 44344747
Telecopier: (33-1) 44344748; 44344749

MEMBERS OF FIRM ATTORNEYS AT LAW

GUY-MARTIAL A.X. WEIJER, born 1945; admitted, 1980, The Netherlands. *Education:* Amsterdam University.

JACQUES P. PRATS, born 1944; admitted, 1986, France. *Education:* Paris University (I) Panthéon Sorbonne Paris.

CÉLINE M. MOITRY, born 1948; admitted, 1979, France. *Education:* Paris University (II), Assas.

FRANÇOIS L.B. LUCAS DE BOURGEREL, born 1950; admitted, 1979, France. *Education:* Paris University (II), Assas.

SIERK BRUNA, born 1954; admitted, 1983, The Netherlands. *Education:* Utrecht University.

ASSOCIATES ATTORNEYS AT LAW

JAN WILLEM G.M. VAN LOTRINGEN, born 1956; admitted, 1985, The Netherlands (Not admitted in France). *Education:* Utrecht University.

ROGIER I. LOOSEN, born 1963; admitted, 1988, The Netherlands (Not admitted in France). *Education:* Nijmegen University.

ANN TOUZET, born 1943; admitted, 1971, France. *Education:* Paris University.

NADINE VOISIN, born 1957; admitted, 1993, France. *Education:* Paris University.

ODILE B. PLÉGAT, born 1956; admitted, 1983, France. *Education:* Paris and New York Universities.

MARINKA J.C. SCHILLINGS, born 1960; admitted, 1985, France. *Education:* Paris University.

MIRJAM BERG, born 1959; admitted, 1993, France. *Education:* Tours University.

RÉGINE G. GOURY, born 1963; admitted, 1990, France. *Education:* Paris University.

NATHALIE CHARPENTIER, born 1962; admitted, 1989, France. *Education:* Paris University.

SYLVIE ADIJES, born 1963; admitted, 1989, France. *Education:* Paris University.

DIANE T.N.B. TU NGOC BAO, born 1967; admitted, 1991, France. *Education:* Paris University.

JACQUES T. ASSCHER, born 1962; admitted, 1994, France. *Education:* Lyon University.

MICHEL LIBERMANN, born 1944; admitted, 1994, France. *Education:* Paris University.

(For Complete Biographical Data on all Personnel, see Professional Biographies at Rotterdam, The Netherlands)

CABINET NEHRING

Established in 1976

229, BOULEVARD PÉREIRE
75017 PARIS, FRANCE
Telephone: (33.1) 45 74 59 00
Fax: (33.1) 45 74 59 01

São Paulo, Brazil Office: Nehring e Associados - Advocacia. Av. Paulista, 1159-17° Andar, 01311. Telephone: 2882577. Fax: 2882071.

General Civil and International Practice. Taxation, Commercial, Real Estate, Investments, Technology and Informatics Legislation.

FIRM PROFILE: *The firm offers a full range of legal services, related to the Brazilian legislation. The client base is European and North American.*

(This Listing Continued)

MEMBERS OF FIRM

CARLOS NEHRING NETTO (Not admitted in France; Also Member, Nehring e Associados - Advocacia, São Paulo, Brazil).

TANIA MARA FERREIRA (Not admitted in France; Also Member, Nehring e Associados - Advocacia, São Paulo, Brazil).

SUELI A.S. AVELLAR FONSECA (Not admitted in France; Also Member, Nehring e Associados - Advocacia, São Paulo, Brazil).

Languages: Portuguese, English, French, Spanish and Italian

(For Complete Biographical Data on all Personnel, see Professional Biographies at São Paulo, Brazil).

MICHEL NORMAND, FRANÇOIS SARDA ET ASSOCIES

Established in 1950

37, RUE GALILÉE
75116 PARIS, FRANCE
Telephone: 33.1.47.20.30.01
Fax: 33.1.47.20.06.01

Business Law, Taxation, Commercial Litigation, Product Liability and Industrial Accidents, Environmental Law, Patent and Trademark Litigation, Construction Law, Real Estate Law, EEC Legislation and Litigation, Medical Liability, Administrative Law, Labor Law and Litigation, Tax, Corporate and Financial Criminal Litigation, Intellectual Property Law, Media and Communication Law.

FIRM PROFILE: *The firm was established in 1950 and offers a full range of legal services. It is well known for Tax, Corporate and Financial Criminal Litigation, Intellectual Property Law, Media and Communication Law, Commercial, Taxation, Construction, Product Liability Law. This 6 partner firm has a legal support staff of 12 associates. The firm is affiliated with MEZZULLO & McCANDLISH law firm in RICHMOND, Virginia. The firm is a member of ACL (Association of Commercial lawyers), a worldwide network of law firms.*

MEMBERS OF FIRM

MICHEL NORMAND, born Les Sables d'Olonne, France, July 12, 1925; admitted, 1950, France. *Education:* University of Paris (Licence en Droit, 1949; Certificat d'Aptitude à la Profession d'Avocat, 1949). President, Confederation Syndicale des Avocats, 1984-1985. Member of Conseil de L'Ordre (Executive Committee) des Avocats à la Cour d'Appel de Paris, 1978-1980. Administrator, 1985, Vice President, 1989, Caisse Nationale des Barreaux Francais. Honorary President, Confederation Nationale des Avocats. *Member:* Conseil National des Barreaux. *LANGUAGES:* French and English. *PRACTICE AREAS:* Taxation; Business Law; Environmental Law.

FRANÇOIS SARDA, born Perpignan, France, November 13, 1929; admitted, 1951, France. *Education:* University of Paris (Licence en Droit, 1951; Certificat d'Aptitude à la Profession d'Avocat, 1951; Diplôme d'Etudes Supérieures de Droit, 1952). First Secretary, Conference du Stage des Avocats à la Cour d'Appel de Paris, 1955. *Member:* Legal Advisory Board, City of Paris, 1967; Civil Proceedings Reform Committee, 1969-1972; Criminal Code Reform Committee (particularly on white-collar offenders), 1974-1981; Avocat of "Agence Judiciaire du Trésor" (State's Judicial defence), 1981; Henri Capitant International Association - Friends of French legal culture (rapporteur of the Canada Convention, 1987 and the Japan Convention, 1994). *LANGUAGES:* French and elementary knowledge in English and Spanish. *PRACTICE AREAS:* Corporate and Criminal Corporate Law; Civil and Professional Liabilities; Intellectual Property Law; Media and Communication Law; Medical Liability Law.

XAVIER NORMAND-BODARD, born Paris, France, March 17, 1952; admitted, 1973, France. *Education:* University of Paris (Licence en Droit, 1973; Certificat d'Aptitude à la Profession d'Avocat, 1973; Diplôme d'Etudes Supérieures de Droit Fiscal, 1974). Secretary, Conférence du Stage des Avocats à la Cour d'Appel de Paris, 1977. Lecturer, Fiscal Law, Centre de Formation Professionnelle des Avocats à la Cour d' Appel de Paris, 1979. Editor-in-Chief: Barreau de France, 1983; C.C.B.E. (Council of the Bars and Law Societies of the European Community) Journal, 1988-1990. Treasurer, 1990 and Vice Président, 1992, Confederation Nationale des Avocats. *Member:* Conseil de l'Ordre (Executive Committee) des Avocats à la Cour d'Appel de Paris. *LANGUAGES:* French and English. *PRACTICE AREAS:* Taxation; Distribution and Competition Law; Patent and

(This Listing Continued)

MICHEL NORMAND, FRANÇOIS SARDA ET ASSOCIES, Paris—Continued

Trademark Litigation; Construction; Real Estate Law; Enforcement of Judgements.

PASCAL PAILLARD, born Neuilly Sur Seine, France, August 22, 1950; admitted, 1976, France. *Education:* University of Paris (Licence en Droit, with honors, 1973; Certificat d'Aptitude à la Profession d'Avocat, 1973; Licence es-Lettres, 1973; Diplôme d'Etudes Supérieures de Droit Fiscal, 1974); Institut d'Etudes Politiques de Paris (Diplôme, 1975). Member, Confederation Nationale des Avocats. Lecturer, Committee on Continuing Legal Education of the Virginia Law Foundation, Williamsburg, 1990 and Monte Carlo, 1991. *LANGUAGES:* French and English. *PRACTICE AREAS:* Business Law; Product Liability; Industrial Accidents; Commercial Litigation and Arbitration; Labor Law; Litigation.

GEORGES HOLLEAUX, born Paris, France, November 11, 1958; admitted, 1985, France. *Education:* Institut d'Etudes Politiques de Paris (with honors, 1979; Examen Probatoire de Comptabilité, 1980); University of Paris (Maitrise en Droit, 1982; Certificat d'Aptitude à la Profession d' Avocat, 1984). Secretary, Conference du Stage des Avocats à La Cour d'Appel de Paris, 1988-1989. Author: "La Politique Monétaire Allemande," Institut d'Etudes Politiques, 1979; "La Responsabilité Juridique de l'Infirmière," 1989. In charge of Legal Chronicle, Interbloc (Surgery Nurses Professional Journal) 1982-1990. Trainee, EEC Court of Justice, 1987. *Member:* Confederation Nationale des Avocats; European Lawyers' Union. *LANGUAGES:* French and English. *PRACTICE AREAS:* Medical Liability; Administrative Law; Environmental Law; Economic Crimes Law; EEC Legislation and Litigation.

RALPH BOUSSIER, born Neuilly Sur Seine, France, February 24, 1959; admitted, 1986, France. *Education:* University of Paris (Maitrise en Droit, 1984); Certificat d' Aptitude à la Profession d'Avocat (1985). Treasurer, 1987 and Vice President, 1988, Union des Jeunes Avocats de Nanterre. Secretary, Conférence du Stage des Avocats au Barreau des Hauts de Seine, 1988. *LANGUAGES:* French, Spanish and English. *PRACTICE AREAS:* Bankruptcy; Construction Law.

NORTON ROSE
35 RUE LA BOÉTIE
75008 PARIS, FRANCE
Telephone: +33 1 40 76 03 06
Fax: +33 1-40 76 03 18; +33 1 40 76 03 17

Other Offices: London, Bahrain, Brussels, Hong Kong, Moscow, Piraeus, Prague and Singapore.

FIRM PROFILE: Norton Rose is a leading City and International law firm with its principal office in the City of London. The firm provides a wide range of legal services primarily to the business and financial communities as well as to a number of sovereign governments and state organizations. We are known particularly for our corporate and debt finance, banking, company and commercial law, natural resources, insurance, property development, aerospace and maritime practices and wide-ranging expertise on tax matters. Norton Rose has a major litigation department handling all forms of commercial dispute resolution.

In Paris the firm specialises in aerospace finance; banking; capital markets; company and commercial; international arbitration; joint ventures; management buyouts; marine finance and project finance, under both English and French law.

RESIDENT PARTNERS

G. FRANCIS CHRONNELL, admitted, 1962, England and Wales. *Education:* Manchester (LL.B.); London (LL.M.). *LANGUAGES:* English and French. *PRACTICE AREAS:* Banking and Finance; Export Finance; Capital Markets; Project Finance; Central and Eastern Europe.

MARTIN GDANSKI, admitted, 1977, New York; 1981, Paris as Conseil Juridique; 1992, Paris as Avocat. *Education:* New York University (B.A., 1973); Yale Law School (J.D., 1976). *LANGUAGES:* English and French. *PRACTICE AREAS:* Banking and Financial; Capital Markets; Company and Commercial; Mergers and Acquisitions.

KENNETH J.G. GRAY, admitted, 1983, Barrister; 1989 England and Wales; 1993, Paris as Avocat. *Education:* Cambridge (M.A. (Hons)). *LANGUAGES:* English, French and Spanish. *PRACTICE AREAS:* Banking and Finance; Aerospace and Asset Finance.

(This Listing Continued)

W. NIGEL T. WARD, admitted, 1982, England and Wales; 1993, Paris as Avocat. *Education:* London (B.A. Hons SOAS). *LANGUAGES:* English and French. *PRACTICE AREAS:* Banking and Finance; Aerospace, Marine and Asset Finance.

(For Complete Biographical Data on all Personnel, see Professional Biographies at London, England).

NOVAMARK / NOVAPAT
63 BIS, BOULEVARD BESSIERES
75017 PARIS, FRANCE
Telephone: (1) 44 85 80 00 (Grouped lines)
Telex: 280984 F
Telecopier: (1) 42 29 02 02

Geneva, Switzerland Office: Novamark SA, 9 rue du Valais, CH-1202. Telephone: 41-22/732 52 40. Telex: 423553 CH. Fax: 41-22/731 33 84.

Other Geneva, Switzerland Office: Novapat SA, 9 rue du Valais, CH-1202. Telephone: 41-22/732 52 66. Telex: 423553 CH. Fax: 41-22/731 33 84.

London, England Office: Castle International, Canterbury House, Syndenham Road 2-6, Croydon CRO 9XE. Telephone: 181/688 34 90. Fax: 181/680 12 25.

Brussels, Belgium Office: Novamark SA, 8-10 avenue Guillaume Pools, 1160. Telephone: 32 2/675 57 07. Fax: 32 2/675 06 22.

Law Offices specializing in Industrial Property Rights in all countries, Patent and Trademark Causes, Designs, Application, Prosecution and Maintenance, Licenses, Agreements, Arbitrations and Litigations and especially direction of Infringement cases, Legal and Technical Opinions, Common Market Regulations, Investigations and Searches with an Information Service on the latest developments of the Patent and Trademark Law and Practice.

Registered on the list of French Qualified Patent Agents, Admitted to Practice under N.A.T.O. Secrecy Regulations, under the Patent Cooperation Treaty PCT and before European Patent Office as European Patent Attorneys.

Not Authorized to Appear before the French Courts as Avocats.

MEMBERS OF FIRM

PIERRE LOUIS CHEREAU, born Paris, France, 1936. Registered on the List of Qualified Patent Attorneys before the French Patent Office. European Patent Attorney. *Education:* St. Andrews University (M.A.). (Resident in Geneva).

WILHELM M. HRANITZKY, born Vienna, Austria, 1932. Patent and Trademark Attorney before the Swiss Patent Office; European Patent Attorney. *Education:* Polytechnic University of Vienna, Austria (Graduated Engineer). Former Senior Examiner at the Search Division of the European Patent Office (formerly, I.I.B.).

JOHAN VAN DEN BOSSCHE, born Gramont, Belgium, 1951. *Education:* University of Louvain (M.A., 1971); University of Brussels (Post Graduate Diploma in International Law, 1972). Guest Lecturer, University of Strasbourg. Member, Brussels Bar, 1972-1976. Legal Counsel and Industrial Relations Manager, MDS-International, 1977-1980. Director, Legal and Industrial Property Department, Adidas-France, 1980-1987. *Member:* AIPPI; LES.

BERNHARD A. KÜGELE, born Mariahof, Austria, 1947. Patent Attorney before the French Patent Office and the Swiss Patent Office. European Patent Attorney. *Education:* Vienna University, Austria (Ph.D., Physics, 1974).

DAVID W. J. CASTLE, born Carshalton, Surrey, England, 1952. *Education:* Moorgate Polytechnic (General Legal Diploma, 1974). Member: Institute of Trademark Agents (England); MITMA, 1980; ECTA; PTMG (Pharmaceutical Trade Mark Group). (Resident in Croydon, England).

JEAN RIEU, born France, 1925. Patent Attorney. *Education:* Higher Electricity School, Paris (Graduate Engineer, 1948).

STÉPHANE LYNDE, born Saint-Cloud, France, 1961. *Education:* Strasbourg University (Master of Law, 1983; LL.M., Post Graduate Diploma in Industrial Property, 1984).

FRANCK SOUTOUL, born Rochefort, France, 1961. *Education:* University of Poitiers (Master of Law and International Trade, LL.M., Post Graduate Diploma in Management, 1985).

(This Listing Continued)

ERIC SCHAHL, born Levallois-Perret, France, 1961. *Education:* University of Strasbourg (Master of Law, LL.M., Post Graduate Diploma in Industrial Property, 1986).

STEPHANIE FUCHS-SCHAHL, born France, 1961. *Education:* University of Paris (Master of Law, LL.M., Post Graduate Diploma in Industrial Property, 1986). Formerly, Assistant Manager of the Trademark Department of SANOFL.

Members of the Union des Conseils en Brevets Européens, French and International Associations for the Protection of Industrial Property, Chartered Institute of Patent Agents (London), Institute of Trademark Agents (London), Patent and Trademark Institute of Canada, Institute of Patent Attorneys of Australia, American Bar Association, American Industrial Property Law Association, Licensing Executives Society, American Arbitration Association, U.S. Trademark Association and International Chamber of Commerce.

Languages: French, English, German, Spanish, Dutch and Arabic

---

OPPENHEIMER WOLFF & DONNELLY

53 AVENUE MONTAIGNE
PARIS 75008, FRANCE
Telephone: (33/1) 44 95 03 50
FAX: (33/1) 44 95 03 40

Brussels, Belgium Office: Avenue Louise 250, Box 31, 1050. Telephone: 32-2-647-4060. FAX: 32-2-648-6554.

Chicago, Illinois Office: Two Prudential Plaza, 45th Floor, 183 North Stetson Avenue, 60601. Telephone: 312-616-1800. FAX: 312-616-5800.

Minneapolis, Minnesota Office: 3400 Plaza VII, 45 South Seventh Street, 55402. Telephone: 612-344-9300. FAX: 612-344-9376.

New York, N.Y. Office: Citicorp Center, 153 East 53rd Street, 10022. Telephone: 212-826-5000. FAX: 212-486-0708.

St. Paul, Minnesota Office: 1700 First Bank Building, 55101. Telephone: 612-223-2500. FAX: 612-223-2596.

Washington, D.C. Office: 1020 Nineteenth Street, N.W., Suite 400, 20036. Telephone: 202-293-6300. FAX: 202-293-6200.

General and International Corporate and Tax Law, European Community Law, International Trade Law, International Commercial Arbitration, EC/U.S./Asia Trade Relations and Investments.

RESIDENT PARTNERS

BOYNTON M. RAWLINGS, born December 6, 1935; admitted, 1962, California; 1973, Conseil Juridique, France; 1980, District of Columbia; 1992, Avocat à la Cour, Paris, France. *Education:* Princeton University (A.B., 1958); Stanford University (LL.B., 1961); Graduate Institute of International Studies, University of Geneva (1962); Institute of Comparative Law and Economics, University of Strasbourg (Diplome, 1963). *LANGUAGES:* English and French. *PRACTICE AREAS:* Corporate; Tax; Arbitration.

W. PAUL BISHOP, born February 14, 1948; admitted, 1974, Georgia; 1975, District of Columbia; 1991, Avocat a La Cour de Paris; 1992, France. *Education:* University of Virginia (B.A., 1970); George Washington University (M.S.A., International Commerce, 1977); University of Georgia (J.D., 1974). *LANGUAGES:* English and French. *PRACTICE AREAS:* International Corporate Law; Commercial Law; Transactional Law; Arbitration Law.

JENNY VACHER-DESVERNAIS, born October 19, 1952. *Education:* IEP (1975); Law Degree (1978); CAPA (1983); Avocat. *LANGUAGES:* French and English. *PRACTICE AREAS:* International Transactions; Corporate Law; Commercial; Tax; Intellectual Property; Computer Law; Arbitration and Litigation.

RESIDENT ASSOCIATE

LAURENT SEGAL, born March 5, 1965; admitted, 1994, France. *Education:* Paris-Sorbonne I, France (Licence en Droit, 1987; Maitrise en Droit des Affaires, 1988); Washington College of Law, American University (LL.M., 1991). *PRACTICE AREAS:* French and International Corporate and Contract Law; Anti Money Laundering Regulation; Taxation.

ALEXANDRE DENIS BRUE, born February 24, 1964; admitted, 1989, France. *LANGUAGES:* French, English. *PRACTICE AREAS:* Commercial Law.

(This Listing Continued)

RESIDENT OF COUNSEL

ALAIN B. MAGNE, born September 22, 1938; admitted, 1988, Conseil Juridique. *Education:* Lycée d'Etat, Perigueux (B.A., 1957); Institut d'Etudes Politiques (M.A., 1962); Université de Bordeaux (J.D., summa cum laude, 1966). *Member:* Association Nationale des Docteurs en Droit. *PRACTICE AREAS:* International Law; French Corporate Law.

OSLER RENAULT

4, RUE BAYARD
75008 PARIS, FRANCE
Telephone: 1.42.89.00.54
Fax: 1.42.89.51.60

London, England Office: 20 Little Britain, London, EC1A 7DH. Telephone: 071-606-0777. Fax: 071-606-0222.

New York, N.Y. Office: 200 Park Avenue, Suite 3217, 10166-0193. Telephone: 212-867-5800. Fax: 212-867-5802.

Hong Kong Office: Suite 1708, One Pacific Place, 88 Queensway. Telephone: 011-852-2877-3933. Fax: 011-852-2877-0866.

Singapore Office: 65 Chulia Street, #40-05 OCBC Centre, Singapore 0104. Telephone: (65) 538-2077. Fax: (65) 538-2977.

Osler Renault is an international partnership of Osler, Hoskin & Harcourt and Ogilvy Renault.

Osler, Hoskin & Harcourt has offices at: P.O. Box: 50, 1 First Canadian Place, Toronto, Ontario, Canada M5X 1B8. Telephone: 416-362-2111. Fax: 416-862-6666 and 50 O'Connor Street, Suite 1500, Ottawa, Ontario, Canada K1P 6L2. Telephone: 613-235-7234. Fax: 613-235-2867.

Ogilvy Renault has offices at: 1981 McGill College Avenue, Suite 1100, Montreal, Quebec, Canada H3A 3C1. Telephone: 514-847-4747. Fax: 514-286-5474 and Suite 1600, 45 O'Connor Street, Ottawa, Ontario, Canada K1P 1A4. Telephone: 613-780-8661. Fax: 613-230-5459 and 500 Grande-Allée Est, Suite 520, Quebec, Quebec G1R 2J7. Telephone: 418-640-5000. Fax 418-640-1500.

Engaged in Canadian and General International Practice but not authorized to appear before the French Courts as Avocats.

RESIDENT IN PARIS

SERGE GRAVEL, born Montreal, Quebec, 1948; admitted, 1974, Quebec; 1978, France as Conseil Juridique. *Education:* Université of Montréal (B.A., 1969; LL.L., 1972); Harvard Law School (LL.M., 1974); Université de Paris II (1975); Graduate Institute of International Studies, Geneva (Diploma, 1976).

PAUL, WEISS, RIFKIND, WHARTON & GARRISON

199, BOULEVARD SAINT-GERMAIN
75007 PARIS, FRANCE
Telephone: (33-1) 45.49.33.85
Telex: 269940F
Facsimile: (33-1) 42-22-64-38

New York, N.Y. Office: 1285 Avenue of the Americas, 10019-6064. Telephones: (212) 373-3000, TDD 212-373-2000. Cable Address: "Longsight, New York". Telex: WUI 666-843. Facsimile: 212-757-3990.

Washington, D.C. Office: 1615 L Street, N.W., Suite 1300, 20036-5694. Telephones: 202-223-7300, TDD 202-223-7490. Telex: 248237 PWA UR. Facsimile: 202-223-7420. Cable Address: "Longsight, Washington".

Tokyo, Japan Office: 11th Floor, Main Tower, Akasaka Twin Tower, 17-22 Akasaka 2-chome, Minato-Ku. 107. Telephone: (81-3) 3505-0291. Facsimile: (81-3) 3505-4540. Telex: 02428120 PWRWGT.

Beijing, People's Republic of China Office: Suite 1910, Scite Tower, 22 Jianguomenwai Dajie, 10004. Telephones: (86-1) 5123628-30, (86-1) 5122288X.1910. Telex: 210169 PWRWG CN. Facsimile: (86-1) 5123631.

Hong Kong Office: 13th Floor, Hong Kong Club Building, 3A Chater Road, Central Hong Kong. Telephone: (011-852) 2536-9933. Facsimile: 011 (852) 2536-9622.

General Practice.
Firm engaged in French, EEC, American and General International Practice; admitted as Avocat and authorized to practice before the French and EEC Courts.

(This Listing Continued)

PAUL, WEISS, RIFKIND, WHARTON & GARRISON, Paris—Continued

RESIDENT PARTNERS

DOMINIQUE FARGUE, born Lyon, France, May 8, 1943; admitted, 1977, Paris, France. *Education:* University of Grenoble (Licence en Droit, 1968; Diplôme d'Etudes Judiciaires, 1968). *Member:* The Association of the Bar of the City of New York; International Bar Association; Franco-British Lawyers Society; Association Francaise des Avocats Conseils d'Entreprises; Comité National Francais de la Chambre de Commerce Internationale. *LANGUAGES:* French and English.

STEVEN E. LANDERS, born New York, N.Y., May 23, 1947; admitted, 1974, New York; 1975, U.S. District Court, Southern District of New York; 1981, U.S. District Court, Eastern District of New York; 1982, District of Columbia; 1993, Paris, France. *Education:* Antioch College (B.A., 1969); Harvard University (J.D., 1973). General Counsel, New York State Executive Advisory Committee on Sentencing, 1978-1979. Secretary, New York State Advisory Commission on the Administration of Justice, 1981-1983. Member, Departmental Disciplinary Committee, First Department, 1980-1984. *Member:* The Association of the Bar of the City of New York; The District of Columbia Bar; International Bar Association. *LANGUAGES:* French and English.

COUNSEL

RICHARD DEHÉ, born Paris, France, June 11, 1952; admitted, 1983, Paris, France. *Education:* University of Paris (Licence en Droit Public, 1974; Diplôme d'Etu des Supérieures de Droit Fiscal et des Affaires, 1976); Georgetown University (M.C.L., 1979). *LANGUAGES:* French and English.

JOSEPH S. ISEMAN, born New York, N.Y., May 29, 1916; admitted, 1941, New York; 1970, District of Columbia; 1986, Conseil Juridique, Paris, France. *Education:* Harvard University (A.B., magna cum laude, 1937); Yale University (LL.B., 1941). Phi Beta Kappa. Article and Book Review Editor, Yale Law Journal, 1940-1941. Counsel, Charles F. Kettering Foundation, 1965-1984. Director, Secretary and General Counsel: Academy for Educational Development, 1966—. Trustee, 1969-1981 and Acting President, 1976, Bennington College. Trustee, 1988— and Vice Chairman, 1989—, The American University of Paris. Trustee, The Scherman Foundation, 1973-1986. Chairman of the Board, Metropolitan Assistance Corporation, Victims' Services and Travelers' Aid, 1984-1985. Member, Board of Visitors, Wake Forest College, 1983-1986. Woodrow Wilson Visiting Fellow: College of William & Mary, 1977; Ripon College, 1979; Rollins College, 1980; DePauw College, 1980; Fisk University, 1981; Albright College, 1982; Hood College, 1983; Southwestern University, 1984. Member, Board of Zoning Appeals, Rye, New York, 1978-1984. *Member:* The Association of the Bar of the City of New York; New York State and American Bar Associations.

PHILIPPE JAMBRUN, born Paris, France, February 7, 1955; admitted, 1986, Paris, France. *Education:* University of Paris (Maîtrise en Droit International Public et Droit International Privée 1977; Diplome d'Etudes Approfondics de Droit International Privée et Droit du Commerce International, 1979); University of Michigan (M.C.L., 1981). Teaching Assistant, University of Paris Law School, 1980. *LANGUAGES:* French and English.

PIERRE E. PETIT, born Casablanca, Maroc, October 25, 1951; admitted, 1982, Paris, France. *Education:* University of Reims (Maîtrise en Droit, 1975). *LANGUAGES:* French and English.

EEC LAW COUNSEL

ANTHONY MCCLELLAN, born Liverpool, England, April 12, 1925; admitted, 1958, England and Wales; 1974, European Court. *Education:* Clare, Cambridge (Council of Legal Education, 1958). Member, Overseas Civil Service, 1959-1967. District Officer and Magistrate - Nigeria and Sarawak Commission of the EEC, 1974-1990, Principal Legal Adviser. *Member:* International Bar Association; Bar European Group; Bar Association for Commerce, Finance and Industry (BACFI, 1965; General Committee, 1965-1974). *LANGUAGES:* English and French.

RESIDENT ASSOCIATES

KATIA CHÉRON, born Metz, France, February 22, 1964; admitted, 1992, Paris, France. *Education:* University of Aix-en-Provence (Maîtrise en Droit des Affaires, 1986); Institut Droit des Affaires (DESS de Droit des Affaires Internationales; DJCE de Commerce Extérieur, 1987); University of Aix-en-Provence (DEA de Droit International et de Droit Com-

(This Listing Continued)

munautaire, 1988); C.A.P.A., 1988. *LANGUAGES:* French, English, German.

HENRI GLASER, born Cairo, Egypt, October 25, 1928; admitted, 1989, Paris, France. *Education:* University of Paris (Licence en Droit, 1968). *LANGUAGES:* French and English.

VALÉRIE MASSET-BRANCHE, born Paris, France, January 3, 1962; admitted, 1984, Paris, France. *Education:* University of Paris (Licence en Droit Social et Droit des Affaires, 1983; MaîTrise en Droit Fiscal et des Affaires, 1984; D.E.S.S. d'Economie et Droit des Transports et Distribution, 1985; Doctorat d'Economie des Transports, 1987). *LANGUAGES:* French and English.

DOMINIQUE M. RYDER, born London, England, June 20, 1962; admitted, Solicitor, 1988, London, England; 1992, Paris, France. *Education:* University of Aix-en-Provence; University of Exeter (LL.B., 1985); Guilford College of Law. *LANGUAGES:* English and French.

(For Biographical Data of other Personnel, see Professional Biographies at New York, Tokyo, Japan, Beijing, People's Republic of China, and Hong Kong)

PENNINGTONS

Established in 1791

140 AVENUE VICTOR HUGO
75116 PARIS, FRANCE
Telephone: (1) 47 27 57 55
Fax: (1) 47 27 36 05

London, England Office: Royex House, 5 Aldermanbury Square, London EC2V 7HD. Telephone: 0171-457 3000. Fax: 0171-457 3240. Telex: 951567 Penshp G.

Basingstoke, England Office: Clifton House, Bunnian Place, Basingstoke, Hampshire RG21 1QY. Telephone: 01256.469091. Fax: 01256.479425.

Bournemouth, England Office: 70 Richmond Hill, Bournemouth Dorset BH2 6JA. Telephone: 01202.551991. Fax: 01202.295403.

Godalming, England Office: Highfield, Brighton Road, Godalming, Surrey GU7 1NS. Telephone: 01483 423003. Fax: 01483 424177.

Newbury, England Office: Phoenix House, 9 London Road, Newbury, Berkshire RG13 1JL. Telephone: 01635.523344. Fax: 01635.523444.

Firm engaged in English and General International Law Practice.

RESIDENT PARTNER

Henry C.M. Page (Avocat à la Cour)

(For complete personnel, see Biographical Card, London, England)

PETIT-FRECHE-LOMBARD

Avocats associes au Barreau de Paris

21, AVENUE VICTOR HUGO
75116 PARIS, FRANCE
Telephone: (33-1) 44 17 13 13
Fax: (33-1) 44 17 13 00

General French European Economic Community and International Practice, Administrative Law, Aeronautical Law, Banking and Finance, Bankruptcy, Commercial, Competition Law, Computer Law, Construction Law, Corporate Law, Corporate Fraud, Copyright, Criminal Law, Engineering Contracts, Environmental Law, General Litigation, Industrial Relations and Labor Law, Insurance Law, Intellectual Property, Joint Ventures, New Technologies, Patent and Trademark, Real Estate, Rent and Lease Law, Rural Law, Tax.
All members are Avocats à la Cour d'Appel de Paris and authorized to appear before the French and EEC Courts.

MEMBERS OF FIRM

PIERRE PETIT, born 1951; admitted, 1975, Paris. *Education:* Université de Nanterre, Paris X (Maîtrise de Droit Privé, 1974; D.E.S. de Droit Fiscal et des Affaires, 1977); Institut d'études Politiques de Paris (Economic and Financial Section, 1976). In Charge of Conferences, Centre de Perfectionnement de l'Assurance, C.P.A., 1980-1983. *Member:* Association GESICA, Avocats Européens (Vice-President). *LANGUAGES:* English.

ALAIN FRECHE, born 1961; admitted, 1988, Paris. *Education:* Université de Paris II (Maîtrise de Droit Public, 1983; Maîtrise de Droit Privé, 1984; D.E.A. de Droit Public, 1985). Professor in Charge, Université de

(This Listing Continued)

Paris I-Sorbonne. *Member:* Commission de Droit Administratif du Conseil de l'Ordre des Avocats de Paris. *LANGUAGES:* English.

MARTINE LOMBARD, born 1953; admitted, 1992, Paris. *Education:* E.N.A. (1973); Université de Strasbourg (Doctorat en Droit, 1978; Agrégée des Facultés de Droit, 1979). Professor, Université de Paris IX-Dauphine. Legal Director of the Group, Air France, 1989-1993. *LANGUAGES:* English.

RÉMY DOUARRE, born 1951; admitted, 1977, Paris. *Education:* Université de Nanterre-Paris X (Maîtrise de Droit Privé, 1975). Professor in Charge, Procédure Pénale et Droit Pénal, Centre de Formation Professionnelle des Avocats de Paris (C.F.P.P.); Secretary of the Conférence, 1981. *Member:* Union des Jeunes Avocats (Président, 1989; President of Honor); Commission Pénale de l'Ordre des Avocats de Paris. *LANGUAGES:* English and Spanish.

ASSOCIATES

GAELLE DADEZ-BASSERES, born 1960; admitted, 1987, Paris. *Education:* Université de Paris II (Maîtrise de Droit Public et Européen, 1982); Institut d'Etudes Politiques de Paris (Political, Economic and Social Section, 1984); Université de Paris I-Sorbonne (D.E.A. de Droit Privé, 1987). *LANGUAGES:* English.

YVES-MARIE HERROU, born 1964; admitted, 1989, Paris. *Education:* Université de Nanterre-Paris X (Maîtrise Carrières Judiciaires, 1986; Maîtrise de Droit des Affaires, 1988; D.E.A. de Droit Privé, 1988). *LANGUAGES:* English.

DIDIER BRUERE-DAWSON, born 1964; admitted, 1993, Paris. *Education:* Université de Paris I-Sorbonne (Maîtrise de Science de Gestion, 1988; Maîtrise de Droit des Affaires, 1989); Université de Paris II, Institut des Hautes Etudes Internationales (1988; D.E.A. de Droit des Affaires et de l'Economie, 1990). Professor in Charge, Université de Paris II. *LANGUAGES:* English.

CONSULTANTS

CATHERINE PUIGELIER, born 1957; admitted, 1984, Paris. *Education:* Université de Paris II (D.E.A. Droit du Travail et de la Sécurité Sociale, 1982); Université de Paris XIII (D.E.A. de Droit des Affaires, 1983; Doctorat en Droit, 1983). Lecturer and Director on Thesis. Recipient, Lauréat prix, "Henri Capitant," 1984. *LANGUAGES:* English.

PHILLIPS & GIRAUD

Established in 1977

49 BOULEVARD DE COURCELLES
75008 PARIS, FRANCE
Telephone: 42 27 22 51
Telex: 641 525 Philex
Cable Address: "Philex"
Telecopier: (331) 42 27 90 85; (331) 47 64 36 84

General and International Law Practice. Corporate, Commercial, Labor, Tax and Banking Law. Arbitration, Trademark and Intellectual Property Law, Law of European Communities and of French Speaking Countries of Africa.

FIRM PROFILE: The firm was established in 1977 and engages in a general business law practice centered in France. It is experienced in assisting foreign clients from both common law and civil law jurisdictions in connection with investments and commercial or financial transactions involving France and is particularly well known for its expertise in transactions and investments involving Japanese clients or co-contracting parties. The firm consists of three partners, three associates and three paralegals.

MEMBERS OF FIRM

LAFOREST PHILLIPS, born Palo Alto, California, June 4, 1934; admitted, 1958, California; 1974, France (former Conseil Juridique); 1976, District of Columbia. *Education:* Stanford University (B.A., 1955; LL.B., 1957); University of Lyon, France. *LANGUAGES:* English, French, Italian and German.

MARC GIRAUD, born Izmir, Turkey, May 25, 1943; admitted, 1974, France (former Conseil Juridique). *Education:* École des Roches (Baccalauréat, 1962); Faculté de Droit de Paris (Licencié en Droit, 1967; D.E.S. Droit Privé, 1969; Doctorate, 1971). *LANGUAGES:* French and English.

VALÈRIE NAUD, born Paris, January 10, 1957; admitted, 1987, France (former Conseil Juridique). *Education:* University of Paris (Licence en Droit Privé, 1978; Maîtrise de Droit des Affaires, 1979; D.E.A. Droit des Af-

(This Listing Continued)

faires, 1980); Tulane University (LL.M., 1982). *LANGUAGES:* French and English.

ASSOCIATES

ETIENNE GLORIAN, born Lille, France, January 9, 1948; admitted, 1992, France. *Education:* University of Lausanne (Licence en droit Français, 1973); University of Paris (D.E.S. de Droit de la Propriété Industrielle, 1981). *LANGUAGES:* French, English, German and Dutch. *PRACTICE AREAS:* Intellectual Property; Trademarks.

CATHERINE SENET-LARSON, born Albertville, France, March 5, 1964; admitted, 1992, France. *Education:* University of Orléans (Maîtrise de Droit Privé, 1986; D.E.A. de Droit des Affaires, 1988); University of South Dakota, School of Law, (1987). *LANGUAGES:* French, English and Spanish.

MICHÉLE STERN, born Oran, Algeria, March 10, 1959; admitted, 1991, France (former Conseil Juridique). *Education:* University of Paris (Maîtrise en Droit, 1981); University of Nancy (D.E.A., D.E.S. de Droit Européen, 1982). *LANGUAGES:* French, English and Spanish.

OF COUNSEL

NICOLAS ROUMIANTZOFF, born Neuilly-sur-Seine, France, March 31, 1956; admitted, 1991, France. *Education:* University of Paris (Licence en Droit Privé, 1981); Fordham University School of Law (M.C.J., 1982). *LANGUAGES:* French, English and Spanish.

LAW OFFICES OF SAMUEL PISAR

Established in 1962

68 BOULEVARD DE COURCELLES
75017 PARIS, FRANCE
Telephone: 47.66.02.12
Cable Address: "Parlaw Paris"
Telex: 280 885 F
Telecopier: 46.22.82.03

General European Community and International Law Practice. Corporate, Tax, Estate, Real Estate, Banking, Competition Entertainment, Communication and East-West Trade Law. Commercial and Civil Litigation. International Arbitration.

Firm engaged in American and General International Practice and registered as Avocats à la Cour in France, authorized to appear before all French Courts.

FIRM PROFILE: The firm was established in 1962 and offers a full range of legal services. It is well known for its international, corporate, European Community and East European law, as well as its wide range of experience in commercial litigation and arbitration. The client base is North American and European.

SAMUEL PISAR, born March 18, 1929; admitted, 1961, District of Columbia; 1962, California; 1982, New York; in England, 1966, Gray's Inn London (Barrister-at-Law); in France as Avocat à la Cour. *Education:* Queen's College and University of Melbourne (LL.B., 1953); Harvard Law School (LL.M., 1955; S.J.D., 1959); University of Paris (Doctor of Law, 1966). Adviser, Joint Economic Committee of Congress, 1961-1962. Member, President's Task Force on Foreign Economic Policy, 1961. Consultant, Committee on Foreign Commerce, U.S. Senate, 1960. Author: "Coexistence and Commerce," McGraw-Hill Inc., 1970; "Of Blood and Hope," Little, Brown and Company, 1980. *Member:* American Bar Association.

ROBERT L. SIMPSON, JR., born Jacksonville, Florida, November 6, 1943; admitted, 1970, New York and in France as Avocat à la Cour. *Education:* Institut d'Etudes Politiques and Sorbonne, Paris (1963-1964); Duke University (B.A., 1965; J.D., 1968). Phi Beta Kappa. Member, Faculty of Law, University of Paris III (Sorbonne Nouvelle), 1975-1976.

DOMINIQUE BLANCO, born 1946; admitted, 1974, France. *Education:* University of Paris Sorbonne Law School (DES Doctorat, 1968); Institut d'Etudes Politiques (Diploma, 1968); Lauréat du Concours Général National des Facultés de Droit, Harvard Law School (LL.M., 1970). Professor, International Business Law, Institut d'Etudes Politiques, 1985—. Author: "Negotiating and Drafting International Contracts," 1993.

CHI-WOON WON, born October 9, 1969. *Education:* Ecole Active Bilingue, Paris (Baccalauréat, 1987); Ecole de Hautes Etudes Commerciales du Nord (Diplôme EDHEC, 1992); University of Lille (Licence en droit des Affaires, 1993).

(This Listing Continued)

LAW OFFICES OF SAMUEL PISAR, Paris—Continued

ANTHONY J. BLINKEN, born New York City, N.Y., April 6, 1962; admitted, 1989, New York; 1991, District of Columbia. *Education:* Ecole Bilingue Paris (Baccalaureat, 1980) Harvard College (B.A., magna cum laude, 1984); Columbia University (J.D., 1988). Author: "Ally Versus Ally; America, Europe and the Siberian Pipeline Crisis," (Praeger, 1987).

OF COUNSEL

DANIEL DIEDLER, born May 23, 1951; admitted, 1980, France as Avocat à la Cour. *Education:* University of Paris (Maîtrise de Droit, 1972; Certificate D'Etudes Judiciaires, 1972; D.E.S. de Droit Prive, 1973; D.E.S. d'Histoire de Droit, 1974). Assistant Professor of Law, University of Paris, 1974-1979.

OLIVIER DE LA ROBERTIE, born October 8, 1956; admitted, 1981, France as Avocat à la Cour. *Education:* University of Paris (Maîtrise de Droit, 1979; D.E.S. de Droit Immobilier, 1981; Doctor of Law, 1984).

Languages: French, English, German, Spanish, Russian, Polish and Korean

REPRESENTATIVE CLIENTS: Apple Computers; Givenchy Couture; Heinz Food; International Olympic Committee; Louis-Dreyfus; Mead Corporation; Newmont Mining; Dai-Nippon-Sun Chemical; Starkist Foods; Warnaco; Weight Watchers; William Morris Agency.

POITRINAL & ASSOCIÉS/GALEXIA

Established in 1989

53 AVENUE VICTOR HUGO
75116 PARIS, FRANCE
Telephone: (33-1) 45 00 61 61
Telecopier: (33-1) 45 00 38 88

General French and International Practice, Mergers and Acquisitions and Divestitures, Corporate, Securities Regulation, Banking and Financing, Taxes, EEC Law, Litigation and Arbitration.

FIRM PROFILE: The firm specializes in the legal and tax aspects of transactions involving mergers and acquisitions.

FRANÇOIS-DENIS POITRINAL, born Boulogne, France, December 29, 1958; admitted, 1986, New York; 1988, Paris. *Education:* Institut d'Etudes Politiques de Paris (Diploma, 1980); Ecole Supérieure des Sciences Economiques et Commerciales (M.B.A., 1984); University of Paris I, Panthéon-Sorbonne (Maîtrise en Droit, 1982; D.E.A. en Droit Comparé, 1983); Columbia University Law School (LL.M., 1985). Lecturer on Law, Université de Paris II, Assas, 1988-1992 and on Corporate Law, Ecole des Hautes Etudes Commerciales, 1989-1995. *Member:* New York State and American Bar Associations. *LANGUAGES:* French and English. *PRACTICE AREAS:* Mergers and Acquisitions; Corporate Law; Securities; International Business Law.

ALEX BURRI, born Saint Chamond, France, December, 1956; admitted, 1986, Dijon. *Education:* Ecole Supérieure de Commerce de Dijon (Diploma, 1978; D.E.C.S., 1982); University of Dijon (Diploma in Tax Law, 1982). *LANGUAGES:* French and English. *PRACTICE AREAS:* Tax Law.

LAURENCE REINER-SACAU, born Paris, France, November, 1962; admitted, 1988, Paris. *Education:* University of Paris X, Nanterre (Maîtrise en Droit, 1984; D.E.A., Droit des Affaires et Droit Economique, 1985). *LANGUAGES:* French and English. *PRACTICE AREAS:* Labor Law; Litigation.

JÉRÔME LOMBARD-PLATET, born Lima, Peru, May, 1961; admitted, 1988, Lyon; 1990, Paris. *Education:* University of Lyon III (Maîtrise en Droit, Private Law, 1983; D.E.A., EEC Law, 1985). Lecturer on Law, Université de Paris II, Assas, 1992-1995. *LANGUAGES:* French, Spanish and English. *PRACTICE AREAS:* Mergers and Acquisitions; Corporate Law; Litigation; Arbitration.

GILLES BIGOT, born Dieppe, France, July, 1964; admitted, 1990, Paris. *Education:* University of Paris II, Assas (Maîtrise en Droit, Business and Tax Law, 1988); University of Rouen (D.E.S.S., Business Administration, 1989; D.E.S.S., Trust and Estate Law, 1989). *LANGUAGES:* French

(This Listing Continued)

---

and English. *PRACTICE AREAS:* Business Law; Litigation; Civil Law; Securities.

ASSOCIATES

Fabien Bartczak

Marie-Ange Miquel

Corinne d'Agrain

Anne Gaughan Lechartier

David Duchosal

CABINET POLIER

4 RUE DE MARIGNAN
75008 PARIS, FRANCE
Telephone: (33)(1) 47-23-41-51
Telecopier: (33)(1) 47-23-37-93

New York, New York Office: Wolfson & Carroll, 233 Broadway. Telephone: (212) 233-0314. Telecopier: (212) 227-6534.

Communications, Business, Contracts, Corporate, International Practice, Franchising, Copyright, Matrimonial, Estates, Wills, Trusts, Intellectual Property, Real Estate and Trademark Law. Litigation in all Courts.

OF COUNSEL

JONATHON WISE POLIER, born 1941; admitted, 1971, New York; 1974, Connecticut; 1992, Paris, as Avocat à la Cour (Ancien Conseil Juridique). *Education:* Oberlin College (B.A., with honors, 1964); University of California at Berkeley (M.A., Political Science, 1965); National Foundation of Political Science in Paris, France (M.A., Political Science, 1967); University of Paris, France (Ph.D., in Political Science, 1968); Columbia Law School (J.D., 1970). Harlan Fiske Stone Scholar. *Member:* The Association of the Bar of the City of New York; Connecticut Bar Association; Paris Bar Association. (Also Of Counsel, Wolfson & Carroll, New York, N.Y.). *LANGUAGES:* French and English.

(For Complete Biographical Data on all Personnel see Professional Biographies at New York, New York, U.S.A.)

POPINEAU, FRÉMY, HAYAUX DU TILLY

Avocats à la Cour de Paris

Established in 1976

69, AVENUE VICTOR HUGO
75783 PARIS CEDEX 16, FRANCE
Telephone: (1) 45.01.93.50
Fax: (1) 45.01.24.71

French and International Business Practice. Banking and Finance, Corporate, Mergers and Acquisitions, International and Domestic Litigation and Arbitration, Taxation, Labor Law, EEC Law, Distribution and Franchising, Competition Law, Environmental Law and Bankruptcy Law.
Firm engaged in French and International Practice and admitted to appear in French and European Economic Community Courts.

PARTNERS

JEAN-FRANÇOIS POPINEAU, born Strasbourg, France, August 15, 1934; admitted, 1977, Paris. *Education:* Institut d'Etudes Politiques de Paris (Diploma 1958); University of Paris (Licentiate in Law, 1955; Lauréat de la Faculté de Droit de Paris); British Institute (1954). Former Deputy General Counsel of the Crédit Lyonnais. *Member:* International Bar Association. *LANGUAGES:* French, English and German. *PRACTICE AREAS:* Corporate; Bank and Finance; Mergers and Acquisitions; Domestic Litigation; Taxation Law.

RENÉ FRÉMY, born La Rochelle, France, April 24, 1946; admitted, 1971, Paris. *Education:* University of Paris Law School (Licentiate in Law, 1970; D.E.S. in Private Law, 1971; post graduate studies in Public Law, 1971). Member of the Paris Bar Council. Judge at the Paris Labor Court. Treasurer, 1986-1989 and Vice-President, International Section, 1988-1990, Confédération Syndicale des Avocats. *Member:* Union Internationale des Avocats. *LANGUAGES:* French and English. *PRACTICE AREAS:* Corporate; Domestic Litigation; French and International Labor Law; Bankruptcy Law.

EMMANUEL HAYAUX DU TILLY, born Paris, France, July 28, 1946; admitted, 1975, Paris. *Education:* Institut d'Etudes Politiques de Paris (graduate in Economics and Finance, 1966); University of Paris Law School (Licentiate in Law, 1971; post graduate studies in Management, 1972). Honorary Secretary General, Association Internationale des Jeunes Avocats. *Member:* Association Française d'Etude de la Concurrence. *LAN-*

(This Listing Continued)

GUAGES: French, English and Spanish. PRACTICE AREAS: Corporate; Mergers and Acquisitions; International Litigation; EEC Law; Distribution and Competition Law; Environmental Law.

TAX DEPARTMENT

GÉRARD ZOVIGHIAN, born Beirut, Lebanon, August 25, 1947; admitted, 1992, Paris. Education: Ecole Supérieure des Sciences Économiques et Commerciales, ESSEC (graduate in Finance and Accounting, 1970); University of Paris (graduate in Law, 1970). Member, National Chamber of Financial Experts and Advisors. LANGUAGES: French, English and Arabic. PRACTICE AREAS: Taxation; Corporate Law; Bank and Finance; Mergers and Acquisitions.

Languages: French, English, German and Spanish

PORTER & DUNHAM

Established in 1966

5, RUE CAMBON
75001 PARIS, FRANCE
Telephone: (1) 42 61 55 77
Telefax: (1) 42 86 94 07

Private International, Commercial, Corporate, Tax and Estate Law. Firm engaged in American and General International Practice. Authorized to appear before the French Courts as Avocats.

MEMBERS OF FIRM

RUSSELL M. PORTER, born Paris, France, July 31, 1924; admitted, 1950, Louisiana; 1958, U.S. Supreme Court; 1992, Paris. Education: University of New Mexico; Tulane University of Louisiana (LL.B., 1950); Faculté de Droit, University of Paris (Diplome d'Etudes Supérieures, 1951). Member: Louisiana State Bar Association; Société du Droit Civil. LANGUAGES: French and English. PRACTICE AREAS: Trust and Estate Law.

GUY H. DUNHAM, born Paris, France, January 13, 1921; admitted, 1950, New York; 1955, District of Columbia; 1992, Paris. Education: University of Virginia (B.A., 1941); Columbia Law School (LL.B., 1949); Faculté de Droit de Paris. Member: Federal and American Bar Associations. LANGUAGES: French, Spanish and English. PRACTICE AREAS: International Corporate Law.

ASSOCIATE

TIMOTHY P. RAMIER, born Lafayette, Louisiana, February 1, 1960; admitted, 1989, Louisiana; 1992, Paris. Education: University of Southwestern Louisiana (B.A., 1985); University of Lyon, Faculté de Droit (Certificat de Droit Comparé , 1988); Loyola University School of Law (J.D., 1989). Assistant Professor, Faculty of Law, Université de Paris II. Member: Louisiana State and American Bar Associations. LANGUAGES: English, French and Spanish. PRACTICE AREAS: International Art Law; Trust and Estate Law.

LEGAL SUPPORT PERSONNEL

C. RAJAKARUNA, born Sri Lanka, August 2, 1942. Certified Accountant (U.K.). PRACTICE AREAS: U.S. and French Taxation.

PRICE WATERHOUSE JURIDIQUE ET FISCAL

Established in 1979

TOUR AIG, PLACE DES COROLLES, 34
92908 PARIS - LA DEFENSE, FRANCE
Telephone: (33-1) 41 26 40 00
Fax: (33-1) 41 26 41 26

Corporate and Individual Taxation, International Taxation, European Community Law, International Banking and Business Law, Corporate, Mergers and Acquisitions and U.S. Taxation.

FIRM PROFILE: The firm was established in 1979 and offers a full range of tax and legal services. It is a member of Correspondent Law Firms of Price Waterhouse EEIG and cooperates with member firms and Price Waterhouse firms to render legal services throughout Europe, where appropriate on a multidisciplinary basis. The client base is European, North American and Francophone African in scope. This 15 partner firm has a legal support staff consisting of 90 Associates and 50 Administrative Staff.

(This Listing Continued)

MEMBERS OF FIRM

ANNE BERTSCH, born Paris, France; admitted, 1970, France. Education: University of Paris Law School, Institut d'Etudes Judiciare (1967). Member: International Bar Association; Union des Avocats Européens. LANGUAGES: French and English. PRACTICE AREAS: Business Law; Mergers and Acquisitions.

LAURENT PIERRE BORET, born Nantes, France, September 10, 1947; admitted, 1980, France. Education: University of Rennes (Doctorat en Droit). Counsellor, Commerce Extérieur of France in Africa. LANGUAGES: French and English. PRACTICE AREAS: African Tax Law; Business Law.

PIERRE BOURON, born Surgères, France, March 14, 1944; admitted, 1979, France. Education: University of Poitiers (Masters Degree, Economic Science). Member: International Fiscal Association. LANGUAGES: French and English. PRACTICE AREAS: Corporate Tax.

MICHEL-PIERRE BOUTIN, born La Rochelle, France, July 24, 1948; admitted, 1979, France. Education: Law University of Poitiers (Master Degree, 1973). Author: "Guide Fiscal International," 1988, 1991. Member: Paris Bar Association; International Fiscal Association. LANGUAGES: French and English. PRACTICE AREAS: International Tax.

STEPHEN HUGH DALE, born England, July 12, 1955. Education: Manchester University (B.A., Honors, 1976). Chartered Accountant. LANGUAGES: English and French. PRACTICE AREAS: Value Added Taxes in the European Community; Customs Duties; United Kingdom Taxation.

GILLES FOREST, born Grasse, France, September 22, 1947; admitted, 1981, France. Education: University of Nice (Business Administration, 1970; Doctorat in Law, 1973). LANGUAGES: French and English. PRACTICE AREAS: Corporate Tax; Corporate Law; Mergers and Acquisitions.

JEAN GAIGNON, born Le Mans, France, September 22, 1947; admitted, 1981, France. Education: Ecole Nationale des Impots (Law Degree, 1968); University of Strasbourg (Doctorate, Finance and Management, 1972). Member: Paris Bar Association. LANGUAGES: French and English. PRACTICE AREAS: Corporate Tax; International Tax; Banking Law.

GILLES Y. HERREMAN, born Albi, France, June 14, 1951; admitted, 1986, France. Education: University of Paris (Masters, Law, 1974; Business Law, 1976). LANGUAGES: French and English. PRACTICE AREAS: Corporate Tax Law.

MICHAEL S. JAFFE, born Los Angeles, California, March 11, 1954; admitted, 1979, California; 1984, New York; 1991, Paris. Education: University of California at Los Angeles (B.A., 1976); Loyola School of Law, Los Angeles (J.D., 1979); University of Paris II (Droit International, 1980). Member: State Bar of California; New York State Bar Association; Paris Bar Association. LANGUAGES: French and English. PRACTICE AREAS: Individual Taxation; International Transfers of Personnel.

MICHEL LECERF, born Cancale, France, July 18, 1949; admitted, 1977, France. Education: University of Rennes (Masters Degree, Law, Diplôme de Juriste Conseil d'Entreprise, 1972). LANGUAGES: French and English. PRACTICE AREAS: Economic Law; Privacy Law; Agriculture; Francophone African Law.

PHILIPPE MOISAND, born March 17, 1939; admitted, 1991, France. Education: University of Paris, Law School (1962). Member: Paris Bar Association. LANGUAGES: French and English. PRACTICE AREAS: Tax Law.

BERNARD PIGALLE, born July 16, 1944; admitted, 1991, France. Education: University of Paris, Law School (1962). Member: Paris Bar Association. LANGUAGES: French and English. PRACTICE AREAS: International Tax.

PHILIPPE VAYSSE, born Châtillon-sur-Seine, France, July 28, 1954; admitted, 1991, Paris. Education: University of Dijon (Legal and Tax, 1977). Chartered Accountant. Member: Paris Bar Association. LANGUAGES: French, English and German. PRACTICE AREAS: Financial Industry Law; International Tax.

RENAUD JOUFFROY, born September 27, 1957; admitted, 1983, France. Education: University of Dijon (Masters in Law, 1979; Business and Finance Degree, 1979; Higher Tax Degree, 1980). Member: Paris Bar Association. LANGUAGES: French and English. PRACTICE AREAS: Corporate Tax; International Law.

STEPHANE BRABANT, born October 22, 1956; admitted, 1991, France. Education: LL.M. in Private Law (1979); Institut d'Etudes Judi-

(This Listing Continued)

PRICE WATERHOUSE JURIDIQUE ET FISCAL,
Paris—Continued

ciares (1980; Graduate, Diploma of International Law, 1981). *LAN-GUAGES:* French and English. *PRACTICE AREAS:* Oil, Gas and Mineral Resources Law; Taxation.

ASSOCIATES

AZIZ BELAYACHI, born Morocco, November 15, 1957; admitted, 1991, Paris. *Education:* University of Paris (M.A., Private Law, 1982; M.A., Insurance Law, 1985; Doctorate in Private Law, 1987). *LANGUAGES:* French, Arabic, English. *PRACTICE AREAS:* Insurance Law; Information Technology Law; Competition Law.

ISABELLE D'AUBENTON-CARAFA, born Paris, France, March 14, 1950; admitted, 1991, Paris. *Education:* University of Paris VII (Degree in History and Geography, 1974; Professional Diploma Civil, Fiscal and Commercial Law). *Member:* Paris Bar Association. *LANGUAGES:* French and English. *PRACTICE AREAS:* Social Security.

PASCAL FISSELIER, born Saint Malo, France, November 12, 1962; admitted, 1991, Paris. *Education:* University of Rennes (Degree in Law; Masters Degree, Business Law and Taxation; Diplôme de Juriste Conseil d'Entreprise; Post-graduate, Business Law and Taxation). *Member:* Paris Bar Association. *LANGUAGES:* French, German and English. *PRACTICE AREAS:* Business Law; Corporate Tax in Africa and France.

CLAUDIA JONATH, born March 12, 1960; admitted, 1991, Paris. *Education:* University of Paris (M.A., International and European Law; Droit International Prive/Droit du Commerce International). *LANGUAGES:* French, German, English. *PRACTICE AREAS:* Labor Law; Company Law.

CHRISTOPHER JOSEPH MESNOOH, born New York, USA, December 13, 1958; admitted, 1985, New York; 1989, Washington DC; 1992, Paris. *Education:* Columbia University (B.A., 1980); Yale University (J.D., 1983); Columbia University (Masters of International Affairs, 1986). Author: "Law and Business in France," Kluwen, 1994. *Member:* District of Columbia Bar; New York State and Paris Bar Associations. *LANGUAGES:* English, French and Arabic. *PRACTICE AREAS:* French and International Corporate Law.

LAURENCE MICHEL, born Paris, France. *Education:* University of Paris (Modern Languages, 1970; Degree in Law, 1982). *Member:* Paris Bar Association. *LANGUAGES:* French, English and Spanish. *PRACTICE AREAS:* Business Law; Financial Law; Restructuring Law.

XENIA MINIC, born France, September 9, 1959. *Education:* University of Paris I (Masters Degree, Law). *Member:* Paris Bar Association. *LANGUAGES:* French and English. *PRACTICE AREAS:* Corporate and Commercial Law; Mergers and Acquisitions.

PHILIPPE PUECH, born Paris, France, July 10, 1960; admitted, 1991, Paris. *Education:* University of Paris X (Masters Degree, Business Law, 1986); University of Paris I, Sorbonne (Third Cycle Degree, Business Law, 1987); HEC (1970); Columbia University (M.B.A., 1973). *Member:* Paris Bar Association. *LANGUAGES:* French, English, German, Swedish, Serbo-Croat. *PRACTICE AREAS:* Financial; Corporate; Commercial Law.

PIERRE OGER, born Paris, France, October 12, 1946; admitted, 1974, Paris. *Education:* D.E.S.S. de droit (1980). *Member:* Paris Bar Association. *LANGUAGES:* French, German and English. *PRACTICE AREAS:* Business Law; Mergers and Acquisitions; Economic Recovery Law; Restructuring Law.

FRANCISCO RAMIREZ-VASCO, born March 6, 1954; admitted, 1977, Santa Fé Bogota; Columbia (Not admitted in France). *Education:* Colegio Mayor de Nuestra Senora des Rosario, (Doctor en Jurisprudencia, wit h honors, 1977; Specialization in Economic Law (with honours, 1977); French Government Scholar (1978-1980); University of Paris (Constitutional Law, 1979; Political Science, 1980). Member, International Court of Arbitration of the International Chamber of Commerce in Paris, 1991—. *LANGUAGES:* English, French, Spanish, Italian and Portuguese. *PRACTICE AREAS:* International Investments and Contracts; Banking and Finance; Arbitration.

JEAN-MARC SAINSARD, born Le Touquet, France, January 19, 1958; admitted, 1987, Paris. *Education:* University of Paris (Maîtrise de droit public, 1980; D.E.A. de relations internationales, 1982); University of

(This Listing Continued)

EU494B

Montpelier (C.E.S. gestion du personnel, 1983). *Member:* Paris Bar Association. *LANGUAGES:* French and English. *PRACTICE AREAS:* Labour Law.

PROSKAUER ROSE GOETZ & MENDELSOHN LLP

9 RUE LE TASSE
75116 PARIS, FRANCE
Telephone: (33-1) 45 27 43 01
FAX: (33-1) 40.50.36.71

New York, New York Office: 1585 Broadway. Telephone: 212-969-3000.
Washington, D.C. Office: 1233 Twentieth Street, N.W., Suite 800. Telephone: 202-416-6800.
Los Angeles, California Office: 2121 Avenue of the Stars, Suite 2700. Telephone: 310-557-2900.
San Francisco, California Office: 555 California Street, Suite 4604. Telephone: 415-956-2218.
Boca Raton, Florida Office: One Boca Place, Suite 340 West, 2255 Glades Road. Telephone: 407-241-7400.
Clifton, New Jersey Office: 1373 Broad Street. P.O. Box 4444. Telephone: 201-779-6300.

General Practice.

WILLIAM E. KRISEL, born Los Angeles, California, USA, May 24, 1954; admitted, 1981, New York; 1988, France. *Education:* Harvard University (A.B., summa cum laude, 1976; J.D., cum laude, 1980). *LANGUAGES:* French and English. *PRACTICE AREAS:* French and EC Antitrust Law; Arbitration; French Corporate Law; Real Property Law; Securities Law.

DELIA SPITZER, born Buenos Aires, Argentina, April 7, 1957; admitted, 1983, New York; 1992, France. *Education:* Catholic University of Cordoba (B.A., 1978); Columbia University (J.D., 1982). Harlan Fiske Stone Scholar. *LANGUAGES:* French, English and Spanish. *PRACTICE AREAS:* U.S. Corporate and Securities Law; International Law; Mergers and Acquisitions.

S.C.P. RAFFIN, RAFFIN-COURBE, GOFARD & ASSOCIÉS

77, RUE BOISSIÈRE
75116 PARIS, FRANCE
Telephone: (1) 44-17-48-00
Telex: 620565F
Cable Address: AVORAFFIN PARIS
Telecopier: (1) 45-01-86-41

Toulouse, France Office: Raffin-Course Gofard. 61 Bvd Carnot, 31000. Telephone: (61) 234877. Telecopier: (61) 23 14 18.
New York, New York Associated Office: Stairs Dillenbeck Kelly & Merle. 330 Madison Avenue, Suite 2900, 10017-5090. Telephone: (1) (212) 697-2700. Telex: 237372. Cable Address: MULTILEX, NEW YORK. Telecopier: (1) (212) 687-3523.
Montreal, Canada Associated Office: Guy et Gilbert. 770 Rue Sherbrooke Ouest, Bureau 2200, H3A 1G1. Telephone: (1) (514) 281-1766. Telex: EUREKA MTL 055-60053. Telecopier: (1) (514) 281-1059.
Brussels, Belgium Associated Office: De Diego, Carreira & Benalal. 194 Avenue Brugmann, 1180. Telephone: (32) 23-46-58-51. Fax: (32) 23-46-19-00.
London, England Associated Office: Kennedys. Longbow House, 4th Floor, 14-20 Chiswell Street, EC1Y 4TY. Telephone: (44) (71) 638-3688. Telex: 886120 KENEDY G. Telecopier: (44) (71) 638-2212.
Madrid, Spain Office: Raffin-Raffin Courbe-Gofard. Diego de Leon, 32-5° 1, 28006. Telephone: (34) (1) 564 56 03. Fax: (34) (1) 411 07 80. Telex: 45326 DIXAN E.

General French and International Law Practice, E.E.C. Law, Corporate Law, Taxation, Antitrust, Mergers and Acquisitions, Company Law, Financing, Unfair Competition, Construction Law, Builders Liability, Insurance, Professional Liability, Labour and Employment, Litigation and Arbitration.
Avocats admitted to appear before French and European Communities Courts.

(This Listing Continued)

MEMBERS OF FIRM

JACQUES RAFFIN (1928-1992).

FRANCOISE RAFFIN-COURBE, born Paris, France, March 4, 1940; admitted, 1960, France. *Education:* Lycée Fénelon, Paris, France (Baccalauréat, 1956); Faculté de Droit, Paris, France (Diploma in Comparative Law, 1959; License en Droit, 1960). Partner, S.C.P. Raffin, Raffin-Courbe, Gofard & Associés and predecessor firms, Paris, France, 1960—. *Member:* Paris Bar Association; Union Internationale des Avocats. *LANGUAGES:* French, English, Italian and Spanish. *PRACTICE AREAS:* Insurance Law; Construction Law.

JEAN-CLAUDE GOFARD, born Paris, France, July 23, 1951; admitted, 1977, France; 1992, Spain. *Education:* Paris Business School (Diplôme de l'Ecole Supérieure de Commerce de Paris, 1973); University of Paris (Licence en Droit, 1976). Auditor, KPMG Peat Marwick Main & Co., Paris, France and Barcelona, Spain, 1973-1975. Partner Gofard & Cussac, Paris, France, 1976-1987. Corporate Secretary, Elysées Investissements, Paris, France, 1987-1989. Partner, S.C.P. Raffin, Raffin-Courbe, Gofard & Associés, Paris, France, 1989. *Member:* Paris and Madrid Bar Associations. *LANGUAGES:* French, English and Spanish. *PRACTICE AREAS:* Corporate Law; Mergers and Acquisitions; E.E.C. Regulations; Commercial Litigation; Leaseholds; Arbitration; Contracts; Insurance Litigation; Labour and Employment.

CATHERINE RAFFIN, born Paris, France, February 6, 1966; admitted, 1987, France. *Education:* Faculté de Droit, Paris II-Assas; Boalt Hall School of Law University of California at Berkeley (1988-1990). *Member:* Paris Bar Association; Union Internationale des Avocats. *LANGUAGES:* French and English. *PRACTICE AREAS:* International Contracts; EDP Contracts; Construction Law; Commercial Litigation; Product Liability; Arbitration.

MATTHIEU PATRIMONIO, born Honfleur, France, December 22, 1966; admitted, 1992, France. *Education:* Faculté de Droit, Paris II (DEA Droit Privé Général). *Member:* Paris Bar Association. *LANGUAGES:* French and English. *PRACTICE AREAS:* Insurance Law; Professional Liability; Construction Law; Product Liability; Professional Liability.

ASSOCIATES

PATRICIA LE TOUARIN-LAILLET, born Le Havre, France, May 8, 1953; admitted, 1981, France. *Education:* Faculté de Droit de Bordeaux (Maîtrise Droit Privé). *Member:* Paris Bar Association. *LANGUAGES:* French and English. *PRACTICE AREAS:* Construction Law; Insurance Litigation; Commercial Litigation.

CATHERINE MAUDUY-DOLFI, born Neuilly sur Seine, France, October 23, 1959; admitted, 1984, France. *Education:* Faculté de Droit, Paris II (DESS Transport International). *Member:* Paris Bar Association. *LANGUAGES:* French. *PRACTICE AREAS:* Construction Law; Insurance Law.

BRIGITTE AUBRY-GLAIN, born Paris, France, June 5, 1961; admitted, 1987, France. *Education:* University of Paris II-Assas and Paris I (D.E.S.S. Insurance Law, Diplôme d'Etudes Supérieures Spécialisées). *Member:* Paris Bar Association. *LANGUAGES:* French. *PRACTICE AREAS:* Insurance Law; Consulting; Labor Law; Commercial Litigation; Distribution; E.E.C. Regulations.

CATHERINE COURTEILLE, born February 10, 1958; admitted, 1987, France. *Education:* Faculté de Droit de Paris, DEA Droit de Affaires, 1985; DEA Droit privé Général, 1986. *LANGUAGES:* French. *PRACTICE AREAS:* Construction Law; Insurance Litigation.

CLAUDE ROYER D'ELLOY, born Grenoble, France, June 24, 1964; admitted, 1989, France. *Education:* University of Law of Grenoble (Doctorat Droit Civil, 1994). *Member:* Paris Bar Association. *LANGUAGES:* French, English and Russian. *PRACTICE AREAS:* Insurance Law; Contracts; Professional Liability.

PASCAL MURZEAU, born Angers, France, September 16, 1963; admitted, 1989, France. *Education:* University of Paris II (D.E.A. Droit de l'Environnement). *Member:* Paris Bar Association; Société de Droit de l'Environnement. *LANGUAGES:* French and English. *PRACTICE AREAS:* Commercial Litigation; Contracts; Environmental Law; Distribution; EEC Regulation.

STEPHANE LAUNEY, born Caen, France, November 20, 1964; admitted, 1990, France. *Education:* Faculté de Droit, Caen (Maîtrise Droit Privé). *Member:* Paris Bar Association. *LANGUAGES:* French and English. *PRACTICE AREAS:* Construction Law; Insurance Litigation; Arbitration.

(This Listing Continued)

ISABELLE PEYREDIEU DU CHARLAT, born Toulon, France, June 17, 1966; admitted, 1992, France. *Education:* Maîtrise de Droit Privé, 1989; DEA de Droit Privé, 1990. *LANGUAGES:* French, English and Spanish. *PRACTICE AREAS:* Construction Law; Insurance Litigation; Commercial Litigation; Leaseholds.

OF COUNSEL

IVAN V. KERNO, born Geneva, Switzerland, July 28, 1928; admitted, 1957, District of Columbia and U.S. Court of Appeals for the District of Columbia Circuit; 1964, U.S. Supreme Court (Not admitted in France). *Education:* Faculté des Lettres, Université de Dijon (Baccalauréat, cum laude, 1947); Harvard University (B.A., cum laude, 1950); Harvard Law School (J.D., 1953). Associate Attorney and Partner, Meyers & Batzell, Washington, D.C., 1955-1965. General Counsel, Mobil Oil Française, Paris, France, 1965-1969. Managing Director, Mobil North and West Africa Group, Paris, France, 1969-1971; Managing Director, Mobil Oil Denmark, Copenhagen, Denmark, 1972-1974. General Counsel, Mobil Europe, Inc., London, England, 1974-1982. Assistant General Counsel-International, Mobil Oil Corporation, New York, New York, 1982-1985. Of Counsel, Stairs Dillenbeck Kelly & Merle, New York, New York, 1989. *Member:* The District of Columbia Bar; American Bar Association; American Society of International Law; International Law Association; French-American Chamber of Commerce in the United States. [With U.S. Army, 1953-1955]. (Resident New York, New York Associated Office, Stairs Dillenbeck Kelly & Merle).

MAXO BENALAL BENDRIHEM, born Madrid, Spain, 1961; admitted, 1988, Spain; 1989, France. *Education:* University of Montpellier I (Master, Business Law; Master, International Legal Studies; Postgraduate, Honors, Labor Law); University of Madrid (Law Degree); Spanish Institute of Technology (Systems Engineer). *Member:* European and International Labour Law Institute of Montpellier (Board of Trustees). *LANGUAGES:* Spanish, French, English, Portuguese and Italian.

Languages: French, English, German, Spanish, Portuguese and Italian

(For Biographical Data of the New York, London, Montreal and Brussels Personnel, see Professional Biographies at New York, N.Y., London, England, Quebec, Canada and Brussels, Belgium).

RENARD-ALLEMAND-TASSY

Groupement d Intérêt Economique

95, RUE DE PRONY
75017 PARIS, FRANCE
Telephone: (16 1) 43 80 23 19
Telecopier: (16 1) 44 40 40 52

Marseille, France Office: 27, cours Pierre-Puget, 13006. Telephone: 91.37.47.30. Telex: 401 457 F (RENAR F). Telecopier: 91.53.71.51.

General and International Law, Transportation Law (Shipping, Maritime, Admiralty, Fluvial, Road), Commercial, Corporate, Customs, Arbitration, Labor, E.E.C. Law, Merger, Banking, Corporation Law and Bankruptcy.

JEAN-LÉOPOLD RENARD, born Marseilles, France, March, 1949; admitted, 1970, Marseilles. *Education:* University of Aix-Marseille (Licence en Droit, 1970). General Honorary Consul of Austria 1983. Maritime Merit, 1990. *Member:* International Bar Association; Union Internationale des Avocats; The Propeller Club of the United States. *LANGUAGES:* French, English and Italian.

(For Biographical data on all Personnel, see Professional Biographies at Marseille, France)

LAW OFFICES OF WILLIAM J. REZAC

Established in 1979

49 AVENUE FRANKLIN D. ROOSEVELT
75008 PARIS, FRANCE
Telephone: (1) 45.62.32.04
Telex: 642786
Telecopier: (1) 42.56.01.81

Trademarks, Designs, Copyright, Unfair Competition, Antitrust, Licensing and Common Market Law.
Firm engaged in French and International Practice.

WILLIAM J. REZAC, born Tisnov, Czech Republic, July 25, 1927; admitted, 1960, New York; 1973, France; Admitted to practice before the European Patent Office in Munich, Germany. *Education:* Ecole des Hautes

(This Listing Continued)

LAW OFFICES OF WILLIAM J. REZAC, Paris— Continued

Etudes Commerciales (Académie Commerciale), Paris, France (Certificat d'Etudes Commerciales Supérieures, 1949); University of California at Los Angeles (B.S. in Chemistry, with honors, 1955); New York University (J.D., 1960). *Member:* American and Paris Bar Associations. *LANGUAGES:* English, French and German.

RICHARDS BUTLER
134 RUE DU FAUBOURG SAINT HONORÉ
75008 PARIS, FRANCE
Telephone: 1-44 13 63 53
Fax: 1-42 89 20 60

London, England Office: Beaufort House, 15 St Botolph Street, EC3A 7EE. Telephone: 0171-247 6555. Telex: 949494 RBLAW G. Fax: 0171-247 5091.
Abu Dhabi, United Arab Emirates Office: Al-Sayegh Richards Butler. P.O. Box 46904, Saif Bin Ghobash Building, Zayed the Second Street. Telephone: 2-725561. Telex: 22261 RBLAW EM. Fax: 2-778630.
Hong Kong Office: Alexandra House, Twentieth Floor, 16-20 Chater Road. Telephone: 810 8008. Telex: 62554 RBLAWHX. Fax: 810 0664.
Brussels, Belgium Office: Avenue de la Renaissance 1, Bte 11, 1040. Telephone: 2-732 20 55. Fax: 2-735 46 91.

RESIDENT PARTNER

Michael A. Mackenzie-Smith

(For Complete List of Partners, see Professional Biographies at London, England)

ROBERT-MOREAU-BERNARD & ASSOCIÉS
3, RUE LA BOÉTIÉ
75008 PARIS, FRANCE
Telephone: (33-1) 42 66 10 11
Fax: (33-1) 42 66 33 33

Member of Cyrus Ross International Association of Law Firms: with offices in Netherland, Greece, Germany, Denmark, Ireland, Switzerland, Cyprus, Great Britain, Spain, Norway, Austria.

General French and International Law Practice. Arbitration, Corporate Law, Business Law, Finance, Banks and Banking, Bankruptcy, Labor and Employment, Construction Law, Contracts, Competition, Distribution, Transportation Law, Admiralty and Maritime Law, Aviation and Aerospace, Insurance, Property Law and Litigation.

PARTNERS

JEAN ROBERT (1903-1992).

BERTRAND MOREAU, born Paris, France, 1936; admitted, 1960, Paris. *Education:* Académie de Paris. Co-Author: with Jean Robert "L'Arbitrage," Dalloz; with Thierry Bernard, "L'Arbitrage en Droit Interne et en Droit International," Delmas Masson. Member, Conseil de l'Ordre, 1981-1984. *Member:* Association Européenne de Droit Bancaire et Financier; International Bar Association; Association Suisse d'Arbitrage; Association Française d'Arbitrage; Comité Français de l'Arbitrage (President). *LANGUAGES:* French and English. *PRACTICE AREAS:* Arbitration; Banking Law; Commercial Disputes.

HERVÉ ROBERT, born Boulogne Billancourt, France, November 27, 1943; admitted, 1968, Paris. *Education:* University of Dijon (Licence, 1968). *Member:* Association des Juristes Français et Allemands; Association Française d'Etude de la Concurrence; Ligue Internationale du Droit de la Concurrence. *LANGUAGES:* French and English. *PRACTICE AREAS:* Real Estate; Competition; Distribution.

THIERRY BERNARD, born Boulogne Billancourt, France, April 26, 1955; admitted, 1978, Paris. *Education:* University of Paris II, Faculty of Law (Licence en Droit Privé, 1976; Maîtrise en Droit des Affaires, 1977); Chambre de Commerce et d'Industrie de Paris, Centre de Perfectionement aux Affaires (C.P.A., 1989). Co-Author: with Bertrand Moreau "L'Arbitrage en Droit Interne et en Droit Internationale," Delmas-Masson; "La Gazette d'Arbitrage," Association Internationale des Jeunes Avocats. *Member:*

(This Listing Continued)

Comité Français de l'Arbitrage (Secretary General); Association Française d'Arbitrage; Association Française de Droit Maritime; Association Internationale du Droit de l'Assurance; Association Internationale des Jeunes Avocats. *LANGUAGES:* French and English. *PRACTICE AREAS:* Corporate Law; Business Law; Litigation; Arbitration; Transport Law; Maritime Law; Labor and Employment.

BRUNO AMIGUES, born Paris, France, December 2, 1961; admitted, 1987, Paris. *Education:* University of Paris (D.E.A., 1985); Institut of Comparative Law. *Member:* Association Nationale des Juristes de Banques. *LANGUAGES:* French and English. *PRACTICE AREAS:* Banking Law; Corporate Trade Law and Litigation; Commercial Disputes.

NEILLY DARMON, born France, June 12, 1963; admitted, 1987, Paris. *Education:* University of Burgundy (D.E.S.S., International Commerce, 1985); Centre de Formation Professionelle de Paris (C.A.P.A., 1986). *Member:* Paris Bar Association; Association des Juristes d'Affaires Internationales. *LANGUAGES:* French and English. *PRACTICE AREAS:* International Business Law; Banking Law; Arbitration.

ASSOCIATES

ANDRÉ ROULLEAUX-DUGAGE, born Brest, France, September 29, 1961; admitted, 1989, Paris. *Education:* University of Paris X, Nanterre (Master IV, with distinction 1987). *Member:* Paris Bar Association. *LANGUAGES:* French and English. *PRACTICE AREAS:* Commercial Law; Insurance Law; Labor Law.

CHRISTINE BEZARD-FALGAS, born Boulogne, France, July 23, 1964; admitted, 1990, Paris. *Education:* University of Paris I; Ecole d'Avocats (C.A.P.A., 1990). *LANGUAGES:* French. *PRACTICE AREAS:* Real Estate.

BERTRAND CHAMBREUIL, born Limoges, France, April 2, 1963; admitted, 1991, Paris. *Education:* Faculté de Droit et Sciences et Economiques de Limoges (Maîtrise, 1986; O.E.S.S. International Commerce and Finance, 1988); Faculté Strasbourg (Diplome cycle Droit Compere, 1988); University of Paris I, Pantheon-Sorbonne (D.E.A., Droit International Privé et Droit du Commerce International, 1989). *LANGUAGES:* French and English. *PRACTICE AREAS:* Banking Law; Commercial Law; Arbitration.

CECILE DE LA FOREST-DIVONNE, born Saint Remy, France, November 30, 1966; admitted, 1991, Paris. *Education:* University of Dijon (D.E.A., Diplome d'Etudes Approfondies in Business Law, 1988); Ecole d'Avocats de Paris (C.A.P.A., 1990). *LANGUAGES:* French. *PRACTICE AREAS:* Business Law; Litigation; Labor Law.

MURIEL WASSERMANN, born Enghien Les Bains, France, February 6, 1960; admitted, 1992, Paris. *Education:* University of Paris XIII, Paris-Nord (D.E.A. d'Etudes Approfondies, 1986); Center de Formation Professionelle de Paris (C.A.P.A., 1991). *LANGUAGES:* French. *PRACTICE AREAS:* Business Law.

NATHALIE LEROY-LEPAGE, born Paris, France, January 4, 1964; admitted, 1993, Paris. *Education:* University of Nantes (D.E.A., 1988). *LANGUAGES:* French. *PRACTICE AREAS:* Transportation Law; Admiralty; Maritime Law; Aviation; Aerospace.

AGNÉS DUBRUEL, born Lorient, France, May 7, 1968; admitted, 1993, Paris. *Education:* University of Paris V (D.E.S.S. Business Law, 1992). *LANGUAGES:* French and English. *PRACTICE AREAS:* Corporate Law; Business Law; Litigation.

BÉNÉDICTE BURY, born Québec, Canada, January 2, 1967; admitted, 1992, Paris. *Education:* University of Paris II (D.E.A. Private Law, 1993). *LANGUAGES:* French and English. *PRACTICE AREAS:* Contract Law; Banking Law; Commercial Law; Litigation.

MICHÈLE PEREZ, born Paris, France, 1963; admitted, 1988, Paris. *Education:* University of Paris X (D.E.A. Business Law, 1987; D.E.A. European Law, 1988). *LANGUAGES:* French, German and English. *PRACTICE AREAS:* Commercial Law; Labor Law; Construction Law.

ROGERS & WELLS

47, AVENUE HOCHE
75008 PARIS, FRANCE
Telephone: 33-1-44-09-46-00
Facsimile: 33-1-42-67-50-81
Telex: 651617 EURLAW

REVISERS OF THE NEW YORK LAW DIGEST FOR THIS DIRECTORY.

New York, New York Office: Two Hundred Park Avenue, New York, N.Y., 10166-0153. Telephone: 212-878-8000. Facsimile: 212-878-8375. Telex: 234493 RKWUR.

Washington, D.C. Office: 607 Fourteenth Street, N.W., Washington, D.C. 20005-2011. Telephone: 202-434-0700. Facsimile: 202-434-0800.

Los Angeles, California Office: 444 South Flower Street, Los Angeles, California 90071-2901. Telephone: 213-689-2900. Facsimile: 213-689-2999.

London, England Office: 58 Coleman Street, London EC2R 5BE, England. Telephone: 44-71-628-0101. Facsimile: 44-71-638-2008. Telex: 884964 USLAW G.

Frankfurt, Germany Office: Lindenstrasse 37, 60325 Frankfurt/Main, Federal Republic of Germany. Telephone 49-69-97-57-11-0. Facsimile: 49-69-97-57-11-33.

General Practice.
Firm engaged in French, American and general international law practice; licensed as Avocats in France and authorized to appear before the French Courts.

PARTNERS

PHILIPPE X. LEDOUX, born Meaux, France, April 24, 1946; admitted, 1974, France. *Education:* University of Paris (Licence en Droit, 1969; graduate, Institut de Droit Comparé, Centre des Communautés Européennes); University of Michigan (M.C.L., 1970). *LANGUAGES:* French, English.

ALEXANDER MARQUARDT, born Bad Nauheim, Germany, August 31, 1945; admitted, 1974, France; 1976, New York. *Education:* Universities of Munich and Vienna (Dr. iur., 1969); Columbia University (LL.M., 1970); University of Paris. Senior Editor, East/West Executive Guide. *Member:* American and International Bar Associations; Deutsch-Amerikanische Juristenvereinigung. *LANGUAGES:* English, German, French.

CHRISTIAN ORENGO, born Constantine, Algeria, November 10, 1947; admitted, 1970, France. *Education:* University of Paris-Panthéon (LL.B., 1968; LL.M. private law, 1969). Former First Secretary of the Conference of the Attorneys admitted to the Conseil d'Etat and the Cout de Cassation; former Secretary of the Conference of the Court of Appeal of Paris. *LANGUAGES:* French, English.

ANTOINE PASZKIEWICZ, born Neuilly-sur-Seine, France, June 20, 1953; admitted, 1977, France (as Avocat); 1980, New York; 1985, U.S. Supreme Court. *Education:* University of Paris (Licence en Droit, 1976; Diplôme d'Etudes Supérieures Spécialisées en Fiscalité, 1977); Columbia University (LL.M., 1979). *Member:* New York State Bar Association. *LANGUAGES:* French, English.

CONSULTANT

SOUHAM EL HARATI, born, Dakar, Senegal; admitted, 1972, Beirut; 1993, France. *Education:* University of Lyon, France, Faculty of Law: Law Degree (Maîtrise; Private Law, 1971) Faculty of Law, St. Joseph University, Beirut (Law Degree in Private Law and Lebanese Law, 1971). *Member:* Beirut Bar Association. Languages: Arabic, English, French.

ASSOCIATES

SERVANE BONNET, born Greenwich, Connecticut, U.S.A., May 31, 1962; admitted, 1990, New York; 1992, France. *Education:* Université de Droit de Paris II (Masters in European Law, 1983; D.E.A., 1985); Institut d'Etudes Politiques (Diploma, 1986); Columbia University (LL.M., 1988). Teaching Assistant, University of Paris II, 1982-1986. *Member:* American Bar Association. *LANGUAGES:* English, French.

ELLEN H CLARK, born Hartford, Connecticut, March 24, 1962; admitted, 1987, New York and Connecticut; 1993, France. *Education:* Brown University (A.B., magna cum laude, 1984); University of Edinburgh, Scotland; New York University (J.D., 1987). Author: "First Amendment II," Annual Survey of American Law, 1986, issue No. 2; "United States - Regulation of Investment Companies," April Supplement, 1990. *Member:* Ameri-

(This Listing Continued)

can (Member, Section on Business Law) and International (Member, Section on Business Law) Bar Associations. *LANGUAGES:* English and French.

MARIE-CHRISTINE FOURNIER-GILLE, born Saint Maur des Fossés, France, March 27, 1968; admitted, 1993, France. *Education:* University of Paris XII (LL.B. business law, 1990; DESS business law, 1991). *LANGUAGES:* French, English, German.

CORINNE HERSHKOVITCH, born Draveil, France, July 20, 1966; admitted, 1992, France. *Education:* University of Paris I (LL.B. business law, 1990); University of Paris II (DEA intellectual property, 1991). *LANGUAGES:* French, English, German.

GERALDINE KANTOR-LERNER, born Boulougne-sur-Scinc, France, June 27, 1968; admitted, 1992, France. *Education:* University of Paris II-Assas (LL.B. business law, 1990); University of Paris-Panthéon (DEA business law, 1991). *LANGUAGES:* French, English, Spanish.

GÉRALDINE MASPETIOL-LUNVEN, born Neuilly-sur-Seine, France, January 17, 1968; admitted, 1992, France. *Education:* University of Paris II (LL.B. private law, 1989; DEA business law, 1990; DESS industrial property law, 1991). *LANGUAGES:* French, English, Spanish.

PASCALINE NEVEU, born Issoudun, France, August 19, 1959; admitted, 1985, France. *Education:* University of Tours (LL.B. private law, 1981). *LANGUAGES:* French, English, Italian.

ODILE I. RENNER, born Saarlouis, Germany, July 17, 1966; admitted, 1993, France. *Education:* Centre D'Etudes Juridiques Francaises, University of Saarbrucken, Germany (D.E.U.G., 1985); University of Paris I, Pantheon-Sorbonne (Maîtrise Droit des Affaires Internationales, 1987); Benjamin Cardozo School of Law, New York; University of Strasbourg, France (D.E.A. Droit International, 1990). *LANGUAGES:* French, German, English.

WADIE SANBAR, born Beirut, Lebanon, June 9, 1965; admitted, 1994, France. *Education:* University of Paris II (ASSAS) Maîtrise de Droit Privé General, summa cum laude, 1988; Diplôme D'Etudes Approfondies (D.E.A.) de Droit des Affaires et Droits Economiques, cum laude, 1989; D.E.A. de Droit Penal et Sciences Penales, magna cum laude, 1990. Assistant Professor and Lecturer on Law at Paris II University (ASSAS) and at The Institute of Criminology of Paris, 1990—. *LANGUAGES:* French, English, Arabic.

JOHN A. STEVENSON, born Atlanta, Georgia, August 12, 1962; admitted, 1988, New York; 1993, France. *Education:* Princeton University (B.A., magna cum laude, 1984); Harvard University (J.D., cum laude, 1987). *LANGUAGES:* English and French.

MARIKA TOURRES, born Sainte Adresse, France, April 24, 1964; admitted, 1993, France. *Education:* University (Maître de Droit Privé, Mention Droit International Privé, 1987). *LANGUAGES:* French, Spanish, Modern Greek, English.

Languages: English, French, German and Arabic.

REVISERS OF THE NEW YORK LAW DIGEST FOR THIS DIRECTORY.

(For biographical data of all partners, see Professional Biographies at New York, New York)

SALANS HERTZFELD & HEILBRONN

Established in 1978

9, RUE BOISSY D'ANGLAS
75008 PARIS, FRANCE
Telephone: 42.68.48.00
Telex: 280990 PARILEX
Fax: 42.68.15.45; 42.68.15.46; 42.68.15.47

New York, N.Y. Office: 750 Lexington Avenue, 10022. Telephone: 212.644.0800. Fax: 212.644.1003.

London, England Office: 103 Mount Street. W1Y-5HE. Telephone: 44.171.491.3735. Fax: 44.171.408 0843.

Moscow, Russia Office: Gazetnyi Pereulok, 17/9, (Ex. UL. Ogareva). 103009. Telephone: 7.501.940.2944. Fax: 7.501.940.2806.

Warsaw, Poland Office: ul. Podwale 7, 00-252. Telephone: 48.22 31.96.88; 31.25.72; 31.29.20. Fax: 48.22 31.39.32; 31.15.65.

St. Petersburg, Russia Office: Dom Zhurnalistov, 70 Nevskii Prospekt. 191 025. Telephone: 7.812.272.4572; 273.6844. Fax: 7.812.273.6844.

(This Listing Continued)

SALANS HERTZFELD & HEILBRONN, Paris— Continued

Other St. Petersburg, Russia Office: 6 Inzhenernaya Ulitsa, 191011. Telephone: 7.812.850.1504; 210.4040; 210.4447; 210.4008; 210.4032; 210.4005; 210.4348; 210.4812. Fax: 7.812.850.1505; 210.4114. Office move planned for March 15, 1995.

Kiev, Ukraine Office: Ukrainskii Dim, Vul. Kreshchatik 2 (4th Floor), 252601. Telephone: 7.044.228.5451. Fax: 7.044.228.6398.

Almaty, Kazakhstan Office: 10A Abaya Prospect, Corner "Furmanova," 11th Floor, Suite 5, 480013. Telephone: 7 3272 634 053; 634 049.

Other Almaty, Kazakhstan Office: 86 Gogol Street, 5th Floor, 480091. Office move planned for April 1, 1995.

General and International Practice. Corporate, Tax, Mergers and Acquisitions, Banking, Labor Law, Industrial and Intellectual Property, Litigation, Arbitration, East-West Trade, EC Law, Competition Law, Foreign Investments, Entertainment Law, Real Estate, Administrative Law. Firm engaged in French, American and General International Practice.

MEMBERS OF FIRM

ODILE CARON, born Seclin, France, February 24, 1942; Avocat. *Education:* University of Paris II (Maître de Droit, 1977; Certificat d'études Judiciaires, 1977; Diplomes d'études approfondies: Droit Privé General, 1978; Droit Européen, 1980; Histoire du Droit, 1981). Instructor in Civil Law, University of Paris II, 1977-1984. *PRACTICE AREAS:* Corporate and Commercial Law.

BERNARD CHESNAIS, born Paris, France, September 7, 1945; Avocat. *Education:* Universities of Rennes and Clermont Ferrend (Licencié en Droit, 1969); Lauréat de Faculté; Ecole Nationale des Impôts (Graduate). *PRACTICE AREAS:* Taxation.

GENE E. DYE, born Valparaiso, Indiana, October 26, 1942; admitted, 1968, New York; Avocat. *Education:* Wittenberg University (B.S., 1963); University of Chicago Law School (J.D., 1967). Lecturer, Faculty of Law, University of Paris, 1984—. Fellow, Columbia University Law School, 1967-1968. Order of the Coif. Member, University of Chicago Law Review, 1964-1965. *PRACTICE AREAS:* Corporate; Commercial; Real Estate.

BRIGITTE FUNEL, born Cauderan, France, October 29, 1955; Avocat. *Education:* Université de Paris I (Maîtrise de Droit Commercial, 1978; D.E.A., Droit Commercial, 1979); Vice-President of the Association Nationale des Avocats. *PRACTICE AREAS:* Litigation; Labor and Employment Law.

BENOIT GIRAUX, born Caen, France, July 22, 1954; Avocat. *Education:* Institut d'Etudes Politiques de Paris; University of Paris II (Maîtrise en Droit Privé, 1978). Professor, Institut d'Etudes Politiques de Paris. *PRACTICE AREAS:* Taxation.

ELIANE HEILBRONN, born Paris, France, April 14, 1925; Avocat. *Education:* University of Paris (PCB, 1946); New York Law School (LL.B., 1958). *PRACTICE AREAS:* Corporate; Commercial.

JEFFREY M. HERTZFELD, born Philadelphia, Pennsylvania, U.S.A. March 26, 1942; admitted, 1966, Delaware; 1969, New York; 1978, District of Columbia; 1992, Avocat. *Education:* University of Pennsylvania (B.A., 1963); Harvard University (J.D., 1966). Articles Editor, Harvard International Law Journal, 1965-1966. Law Clerk, Delaware Supreme Court, 1966-1967. Associate Law Faculty, University of Leiden, 1967-1968. Consultant to the World Bank on legal aspects of joint ventures in Russia. Member, International Chamber of Commerce Advisory Group on the C.I.S and Economies in Transition and of the I.C.C. Task Force on Soviet Joint Ventures and Corporate Law. *Member:* New York State and American Bar Associations. *PRACTICE AREAS:* Eastern European Commerce; Arbitration.

JAMES E. HOGAN, born Albany, New York, May 16, 1960; admitted, 1984, District of Columbia; Avocat. *Education:* University of Michigan (A.B., 1979); Pushkin Institute, Moscow (1980-1981); University of Texas (J.D., 1984). Coordinating Articles Editor, Texas International Law Journal, 1983-1984. *PRACTICE AREAS:* Eastern European Commerce.

MARIE-CLAIRE LACHAUD, born Clermont-Ferrand, France, September 13, 1935; Avocat. *Education:* Cours Levé (Baccalauréat, 1953); University of Paris (Licenciée en Droit, 1956; D.E.S. Droit Privé, 1957); Harvard University. *PRACTICE AREAS:* Corporate; Commercial; Mergers and Acquisitions.

JEAN-LOUIS MAGNIER, born Choisy-la-Victoire, France, May 18, 1949; Avocat. *Education:* Institut d'Etudes Politiques de Paris, 1971; University of Paris (Licencié en Droit, 1971; D.E.S. de Droit Privé, 1972). *PRACTICE AREAS:* Labor and Employment.

LAWRENCE C. MAISEL, born Boston, Massachusetts, March 2, 1948; admitted, 1973, California; 1974, District of Columbia; Avocat. *Education:* Harvard University (B.A., in Economics, 1969); Stanford University (J.D., 1972). Lecturer on Antitrust Law, University of Paris. *PRACTICE AREAS:* Corporate; Commercial; Mergers and Acquisitions.

THEODORE P. MATHENY, born Louisville, Kentucky, June 26, 1954; admitted, 1982, District of Columbia; Avocat. *Education:* Brown University (B.A., 1977); Leningrad State University, USSR, 1977; Harvard University (J.D., 1982). Associate Editor, Harvard International Law Journal, 1981. Co-author: "Ivory Coast in Legal Aspects of Doing Business in Africa," Vol. 4, International Business Series, Kluwer, 1985. *PRACTICE AREAS:* Eastern European Commerce.

PAUL MOREL, born Saint-Erme, France, September 13, 1954; Avocat. *Education:* University of Reims (Maîtrise en Droit Privé Général, 1976); University of Paris II Panthéon (D.E.A. en Droit Social, 1977); University of Paris I Panthéon Sorbonne (D.E.A. en Droits des Affaires Anglo-Américains, 1978); University of Paris IV Sorbonne (Licence Es Lettres, Histoire, 1978); George Washington University (M.C.L., 1980); University of Paris I Panthéon Sorbonne (Doctorat d'Etat en Droit Privé, 1984). *PRACTICE AREAS:* Mergers and Acquisitions; Finance.

PHILIPPE PECH DE LACLAUSE, born Narbonne, France, October 22, 1956; Avocat. *Education:* University of Montpellier (Maîtrise en Droit Privé, 1980; D.E.A., Droit Public, 1982). Executive Secretary to the Conference of the Avocat au Barreau de Paris. *PRACTICE AREAS:* Litigation.

GEORGE S. PINKHAM, born New York, N.Y., May 16, 1947; admitted, 1977, New York; Avocat. *Education:* Dartmouth College (B.A., 1969); Stanford University (M.S., 1972; J.D., 1976). *Member:* Association Française des Investisseurs en Capital; European Venture Capital Association (Member, Tax and Legal Committee); International Fiscal Association. *PRACTICE AREAS:* Finance; Mergers and Acquisitions; Taxation.

PASCALE POUPELIN, born Paris, France, March 30, 1959; Avocat. *Education:* University of Paris I (Maîtrise de Droit Public, 1980); University of Paris II (D.E.A., Droit Pénal, 1983). *PRACTICE AREAS:* Litigation; Administrative Law; Criminal Law.

CARL F. SALANS, born Chicago Heights, Illinois, March 13, 1933; admitted, 1957, Illinois; 1974, District of Columbia; Avocat. *Education:* Harvard University (A.B., 1954); Trinity College, Cambridge University, England (M.A., 1956; LL.B., 1958); University of Chicago Law School (J.D., 1957). Office of Legal Adviser, Department of State, 1959-1972. Member of Board, 1977-1988, American Chamber of Commerce in France. Substitute Arbitrator, United States - Iran Claims Tribunal at the Hague. Member, Commercial Panel, American Arbitration Association. *PRACTICE AREAS:* Arbitration; Corporate; Commercial.

JOHN G. SPEERS, born Montclair, New Jersey, February 19, 1955; admitted, 1982, New York; Avocat. *Education:* Princeton University (A.B., 1977); University of Chicago Law School (J.D., 1981). *PRACTICE AREAS:* Mergers and Acquisitions; Banking; Finance; Eastern European Commerce.

JEAN-PIERRE STENGER, born Boulogne-Billancourt, France, January 4, 1934; Avocat. *Education:* Institut Commercial de Nancy (1955); University of Nancy and Paris (Docteur en Droit, 1964); University of Michigan Law School (Master of Comparative Law, 1961). Author: "Infringement Actions and Sanctions for Infringements," Juris Classeur (Patents), 1991. Vice-President of the French Group of the International Association for the Protection of Industrial Property. *PRACTICE AREAS:* Litigation; Intellectual and Industrial Property.

SYLVIE VANSTEENKISTE, born Linselles, France, November 11, 1956; Avocat. *Education:* University of Lille I (Maîtrise de Sciences économiques, 1980; D.E.A. Economie du Travail, 1981); Ecole Nationale des Impôts (Graduate). *PRACTICE AREAS:* Taxation.

FRANÇOIS VIGNAUD, born Paris, France, March 5, 1950; Avocat. *Education:* Institut d'Etudes Polituques de Paris (I.E.P.) (1971); University of Paris II (Licence en Droit des Affaires, 1972; D.E.S. de Droit des Affaires, 1974); University of Michigan Law School (LL.M., 1974). *PRACTICE AREAS:* Corporate; Commercial; Mergers and Acquisitions.

(This Listing Continued)

ASSOCIATES

ALIX D' ANGLEJAN-CHATILLON, born La Jolla, California, March 17, 1962; admitted, 1989, Quebec; Avocat. *Education:* Queen's University (B.A., 1984); McGill University (LL.B., 1987; B.C.L., 1988). *Member:* Canadian Bar Association. *PRACTICE AREAS:* Corporate; Commercial.

NATASHA AZAIS, born Kiev, Ukraine, February 24, 1969; (Not admitted in France). *Education:* University of Paris I (Maîtrise Droit des Affaires Internationales avecmention, 1991); Institut d'Administration des Enterprises de Paris (DESS, Certificat d'Aptitude àl'Administration des Entreprises, 1993). *PRACTICE AREAS:* Corporate; Commercial; Eastern European Commerce.

FRÉDÉRIC BAILLY, born Neuilly-sur-Seine, France, December 17, 1962; Avocat. *Education:* University of Paris II (Maîtrise de Fiscalité des Affaires, 1985; D.E.S.S. de Droit Notarial, 1987). *PRACTICE AREAS:* Corporate; Real Estate.

PASCAL BATHMANABANE, born March 27, 1961; Avocat. *Education:* Université de Montpellier (D.E.A. Droit privé, 1984; Docteur en droit, 1992). Conseiller prud'hommes, Paris, 1987-1989. Publications: "L'abus du droit syndical," 1992. *PRACTICE AREAS:* Labor Law.

MARC A. CHANTEDUC, born Vienna, Austria, August 12, 1960; Avocat. *Education:* University of Paris (Maître en Droit Privé, 1984). *PRACTICE AREAS:* Corporate; Commercial.

FLORENCE COLY, born Lille, France, February 12, 1960; Avocat. *Education:* University of Paris II (DESS de Droit Notarial, 1982. *PRACTICE AREAS:* Commercial.

CÉLINE COSTE, born Rouen, France, February 1, 1966. *Education:* Université de Nanterre, Paris X (Maîtrise de Droit Civil, mention Droit du Travail, 1989; D.E.S.S. de Droit Social et Relations Professionelles, 1990). *PRACTICE AREAS:* Labor Law.

DOMINIQUE DEDIEU, born Compiègne, France, June 7, 1964; Avocat. *Education:* University of Paris II (Maîtrise de Droit, 1986; D.E.A., Droit International Privé, 1987). *PRACTICE AREAS:* Litigation.

CLAIRE DESPORTES, born Boulogne-Billancourt, France, June 10, 1962; Avocat. *Education:* University of Paris II (Maîtrise de Droit Privé, 1984); Université de Paris I (D.E.A., Droit anglais et nord-américain des Affaires, 1985). *PRACTICE AREAS:* Litigation.

SARAH FRANÇOÍS-PONCET, born New York, N.Y., June 16, 1958; admitted, 1985, New York; Avocat. *Education:* Brown University (B.A., 1980); Fordham University (J.D., 1984); University of Paris (DESS, Droit des Affaires et Fiscalité, 1988). *PRACTICE AREAS:* Arbitration; Corporate; Commercial.

FRANÇOISE GOSSET, born Paris, France, June 26, 1944; (Not admitted in France). *Education:* Conservatoire National des Arts et Métiers (ICH, 1977); Techniques Financières et Comptables des Entreprises et Droit Commercial, 1982). *PRACTICE AREAS:* Corporate.

JEAN-CHRISTOPHE HONLET, born St. Cloud, France, November 16, 1967; (Not admitted in France). *Education:* University of Paris II (Licence de Droit, 1990; Maîtrise de Droit Privé, 1991); University of Paris I (D.E.A. Droit Privé, 1992); University of Oxford (Lavoisier scholar, 1994).

JOHANNES JONAS, born Aachen, Germany, May 3, 1960; admitted, 1990, Germany and New York; 1993, France. *Education:* University of Geneva, IUEE, IUHEI, Switzerland (1983); University of Passau, University of Munich, Germany (Dr. jur., 1987); University of Chicago (LL.M., 1989). *Member:* DAJV; DJT. *PRACTICE AREAS:* Commercial Law; Corporate Law; German-French Transactions.

ANNE-MATHILDE LAMY, born Clermont-Ferrand, France, November 5, 1965; Avocat. *Education:* University of Clermont-Ferrand (Maîtrise de Droit des Affaires, 1987); University of Montpellier (DESS, Droit des Affaires, DJCE, 1988). *PRACTICE AREAS:* Labor and Employment Law.

PIERRE LAPORTE, born Saint Germain-en-Laye, France, August 17, 1961; Avocat. *Education:* Institut d'Etudes Politiques de Paris (1983); University of Paris X (Maîtrise de Droit, 1984); University of Paris I (D.E.A., Droit des Affaires, 1985); Georgetown University Law Center (LL.M., 1988). *PRACTICE AREAS:* Corporate; Commercial; Audiovisual.

PATRICK MARTOWICZ, born Metz, France, June 3, 1965 (not admitted in France). *Education:* University of Social Sciences of Toulouse I (Maîtrise en Droit des Affaires); Diplôme de l'Institut d' Etudes Politiques de Toulouse; DESS Droit des Affaires Internationales; DEA de Droit Privé; Certificat d'Etudes Judiciaires; University of Young Lawyers in Germany;

(This Listing Continued)

Institut Max Planck. *PRACTICE AREAS:* Intellectual Property; Corporate; Commercial.

CÉDRIC MEILLER, born Saint-Cloud, France, January 24, 1967; Avocat; admitted, 1994, France. *Education:* Université de Paris I (Maîtrise de Droit International, Certificat du Centre Universitaire d'Etudes Communautaires, 1989); University College London (LL.M., Commercial and Corporate Law, 1990). *PRACTICE AREAS:* Industrial Property.

JULIEN E. NAGINSKI, born Princeton, New Jersey, June 28, 1965; (Not admitted in France). *Education:* Columbia College (B.A., 1987); Université de Paris VII (Jussieu); Tufts University (M.A.L.D., 1993); Cornell Law School (J.D., 1994).

FREDERIC PINET, born Boulogne-Billancourt, France, May 12, 1966 (not admitted in France). *Education:* University of Paris II (Maîtrise de Droit des Affaires et Fiscalité, 1989; DESS Droit des Affaires et Fiscalité, 1990). *PRACTICE AREAS:* Corporate; Commercial.

ANNE PONCY D'HERBES, born February 22, 1963; Avocat. *Education:* Université de Paris II (Maîtrise de Droit Privé, 1987). *PRACTICE AREAS:* Litigation; Labor and Employment Law.

THIERRY RENAUD DE LA FAVERIE, born Paris, France, September 29, 1955; Avocat. *Education:* Faculté de Droit, Université de Paris XIII (Maîtrise en Droit, 1983). *PRACTICE AREAS:* Corporate.

CHRISTINE SÉVÈRE, born Brest, France, May 23, 1960; Avocat. *Education:* University of Paris II (Maîtrise de Droit Public, 1982; Maîtrise de Droit International et Européen, 1982); Université de Paris I (D.E. S.S., Droit International Maritime et Aérien, 1983); Université de Paris II (Maîtrise Carrières Judiciaires de Droit Privé, 1984). *PRACTICE AREAS:* Litigation.

MELANIE THILL-TAYARA, born Luxembourg, July 27, 1960; Avocat. *Education:* University of Munich (Diploma of Political Sciences, 1980); University of Paris I (Maîtrise de Droit International et Européen, Certificate du Centre Universitaire d'Etudes Communautaires, 1984; D.E.A. de Droit International Privé et Droit du Commerce International, 1985). *PRACTICE AREAS:* Anti-Trust; Common Market Law; Commercial Law.

SOPHIE UETTWILLER, born Sannois, France, April 5, 1968; Avocate; admitted, 1994, France. *Education:* Université de Paris II Panthéon-Assas (Maîtrise de Droit Privé mention Droit des Affaires et Fiscalité, 1990; Maîtrise de Droit International et Européen, 1990). *PRACTICE AREAS:* Labor Law.

BERTRAND VEZIN, born Paris, France, March 7, 1944; Avocat. *Education:* University of Paris II (Maîtrise de Droit Privé, 1971); Institut d'Etudes Judiciaires (Diplôme, 1971). *PRACTICE AREAS:* Intellectual Property; Trademarks.

ARMELLE WALTERS-RENAUD, born Vesoul, France, January 10, 1962; Avocat. *Education:* University of Strasbourg (DESS de Droit des Affaires, DJCE, 1986). *PRACTICE AREAS:* Corporate; Commercial.

OF COUNSEL

KAREN E. NELSON, born Evanston, Illinois, 1946; admitted, 1978, New York; Avocat. *Education:* University of Illinois (B.S., 1968); Yale University (M.A., 1970); University of Chicago (M.S., 1971); Columbia University (J.D., 1977). *PRACTICE AREAS:* Corporate and Commercial; Arbitration.

FRANCOISE TOSTAIN-BERTOT, born Grandcamp-les-Bains, France, December 23, 1925; Avocat. *Education:* University of Paris (Licence de Droit, 1948; D.E.S. Droit Privé, 1949; D.E.S. Droit Romain, 1951; Docteur en Droit, 1953). *PRACTICE AREAS:* Banking; Finance; Corporate; Mergers and Acquisitions.

Languages: French, English, German, Spanish, Russian, Dutch, Ukrainian and Italian

---

SALÈS VINCENT & ASSOCIÉS

Société d'Avocats

Established in 1977

43, RUE DU FAUBOURG SAINT-HONORÉ
75008 PARIS, FRANCE
Telephone: (33-1) 42-66-50-31
Fax: (33-1) 42-66-58-95

General French, EEC and International Law Practice.

(This Listing Continued)

SALÈS VINCENT & ASSOCIÉS, Paris—Continued

MEMBERS OF FIRM

JACQUES SALÈS, born Port-au-Prince, Haiti, March 12, 1942; registered 1967 as Conseil Juridique, Paris; admitted, 1977, Paris. *Education:* University of Haiti (Licence en Droit, 1963); University of Paris Law School (D.E.S. Droit Privé, 1964; Doctorat en Droit, 1966); Harvard Law School (LL.M., 1967). Author: "Droit uniforme et conflits de lois," 1966; "Termination of Sales Agents and Distributors in France," International Lawyer, Fall, 1983. *Member:* Harvard Law School Association of Europe, President (1986-1989); Harvard Law School Association, Council (1989-1993), Executive Committee (1990-1993) and Vice-President (1993—); Union Internationale des Avocats; International Bar Association. *LANGUAGES:* French and English.

ALAIN L. VINCENT, born Lyon, France, November 4, 1945; registered 1971 as Conseil Juridique, Paris; admitted, 1978, Paris. *Education:* University of Paris Law School (Licence en Droit, 1969); New York University Law School (Institute of Comparative Law, 1971; M.C.J., 1973). Author: "Favorable Ruling for Selective Distribution," International Financial Law Review, August 1987. *Member:* International Bar Association. *LANGUAGES:* French and English.

JEAN-YVES MARTIN, born Saint-Mandé, France, January 27, 1953; admitted, 1992, Paris. *Education:* University of Paris Law School (Licence en Droit, 1974; D.E.S. Droit Privé, 1976; Doctorat en Droit, 1981); University of Chicago Law School (M.C.L., 1977). Lecturer, Ecole Supérieure des Sciences Economiques et Commerciales, Paris, 1992—. Co-Author: "Les moyens de défense anti-OPA en France," La Revue Banque, October 1990; "Les offres publiques," Encyclopédic Dalloz, 1991. *LANGUAGES:* French and English.

YANN COLIN, born Vichy, France, November 7, 1955; admitted, 1979, Paris. *Education:* University of Paris Law School (Maîtrise en Droit, 1977). *Member:* Association Internationale des Jeunes Avocats. *LANGUAGES:* French and English.

JODIE M. COHEN-TANUGI, born Ridgewood, New Jersey, April 8, 1957; admitted, 1982, District of Columbia; registered 1986 as Conseil Juridique, Paris; admitted, 1992, Paris. *Education:* Princeton University (A.B., magna cum laude, 1978); Harvard Law School (J.D., cum laude, 1982). *Member:* American Bar Association; District of Columbia Bar. *LANGUAGES:* English and French.

ALEXANDRE MARQUE, born Paris, France, January 31, 1959; admitted, 1987, Paris. *Education:* University of Paris Law School (Maîtrise en Droit Public, 1981; D.E.A. de Droit Public, 1983; D.E.A. de Droit International, 1984); Institut d'Etudes Politiques de Paris (Diploma, 1983). *LANGUAGES:* French and English.

YAM ATALLAH, born Paris, France, March 9, 1962; admitted, 1985, New York; 1990, Paris. *Education:* University of Nancy Law School (Maîtrise en Droit des Affaires, 1983); Institut d'Etudes Politiques de Paris (Diploma, 1983); University of Paris Law School (D.E.S.S. Banques et Finances, 1984); Georgetown University Law School (LL.M., 1985). *LANGUAGES:* French and English.

BRADLEY L. JOSLOVE, born Milwaukee, Wisconsin, August 6, 1961; admitted, 1986, Massachusetts; 1988, District of Columbia; 1992, Paris. *Education:* University of Kansas (B.A., 1983); University of Bordeaux, Talence, France; Harvard Law School (J.D., 1986). Phi Beta Kappa. *Member:* American Bar Association; District of Columbia Bar. *LANGUAGES:* English and French.

ADRIAN PETER GONZALEZ, born Port-of-Spain, Trinidad, May 29, 1956; admitted, 1987, New York; 1992, Paris. *Education:* Sarah Lawrence College (B.A., magna cum laude, 1980); Harvard Law School (J.D., 1985); University of Paris Law School (Maîtrise en Droit des Affaires, 1991). Co-Author: Special Report on France in "Ideas as Assets: A Guide to Intellectual Property Worldwide," International Financial Law Review, May, 1991. *Member:* Association of the Bar of the City of New York; New York State and American Bar Associations; American Foreign Law Association. *LANGUAGES:* English, Spanish and French.

ASSOCIATES

MURIEL DE COURRÈGES, born Paris, France, June 2, 1963; admitted, 1989, Paris. *Education:* University of Paris Law School (Maîtrise en Droit, 1984; Maîtrise de Sciences Politiques, 1984; D.E.A. de Droit Communautaire, 1985; D.E.A. de Finances Publiques et Fiscalité, 1988); Georgetown University Law School (LL.M., 1986). Author: "European

(This Listing Continued)

Product Liability," (chapter dedicated to French Law), Butterworths, 1992. *LANGUAGES:* French, English, Spanish and Russian.

CONSTANTIN ACHILLAS, born Paris, France, January 1, 1964; admitted, 1989, Paris. *Education:* University of Paris Law School (Maîtrise en Droit des Affaires et Fiscalité, Maîtrise en Droit Public, 1985); Institut d'Etudes Politiques de Paris (Diploma, 1987); Ecole Supérieure des Sciences Economiques et Commerciales (ESSEC) (Mastère Spécialisé en Techniques Financières, 1988). *LANGUAGES:* French and English.

FABIENNE HAAS, born Neuilly-sur-Seine, France, November 5, 1959; admitted, 1985, Paris. *Education:* University of Paris Law School (Maîtrise en Carrières Judiciaires, 1982; Maîtrise en Droit Public, 1982; D.E.A. de Droit des Affaires et Economie, 1983); New York University Law School (LL.M., 1986). *LANGUAGES:* French and English.

MARIE-LAURE MCHANETZKI, born Neuilly-Sur-Seine, France, February 5, 1963; admitted, 1992, Paris. *Education:* University of Paris Law School (Maîtrise en Droit des Affaires et Fiscalité, 1987; D.E.S.S. de Fiscalité des Entreprises, 1988). *LANGUAGES:* French, English and Russian.

EMMANUELLE BARBARA, born Boulogne, France, July 12, 1966; admitted, 1993, Paris. *Education:* University of Paris Law School (Maîtrise en Droit des Affaires et Fiscalité, 1988; D.E.S.S. de Droit des Affaires et Fiscalité, 1989). *LANGUAGES:* French, English and Italian.

JÉRÔME MICHEL, born Ankara, Turkey, January 10, 1965; admitted, 1993, Paris. *Education:* Institut d'Etudes Politques de Paris (Diploma, 1985); University of Paris Law School (Maîtrise de Droit des Affaires et de Fiscalité, 1988). *LANGUAGES:* French and English.

VÉRONIQUE BOUVIER, born Epinal, France, August 6, 1965; admitted, 1994, Paris. *Education:* Ecole Supérieure des Sciences Economiques et Commerciales (ESSEC) (Diploma, 1988; D.E.A. Stratégie et Management, 1989); University of Paris Law School (Maîtrise de Droit des Affaires, 1990); Diplôme d'Etudes Supérieures Comptables et Financières, 1992. *LANGUAGES:* French and English.

RYAD GHALI, born Hama, Syria, August 15, 1961; admitted, 1991, Damascus. *Education:* University of Paris Law School (Maîtrise en Droit, 1987); University of Damascus Law School (Maîtrise en Droit, 1992). *LANGUAGES:* Arabic, French and English.

ISABELLE ARMAND, born Paris, France, February 20, 1966; admitted, 1991, Paris. *Education:* University of Paris Law School (Maîtrise en Droit Civil Administratif, 1988; Maîtrise en Droit des Affaires et Fiscalité, 1988; D.E.S.S. Immobilier, 1989). *LANGUAGES:* French and English.

STEFAN NAUMANN, born Geneva, Switzerland, October 10, 1963; admitted, 1992, California; 1993, Paris. *Education:* Harvard University (B.A., 1986); Boalt Hall School of Law, University of California (J.D., 1990); University of Paris Law School (Maîtrise en Droit Privé, 1991). Author: "Issues in Computer-Assisted Contracting, a Review of II Contratto Concluso Mediante Computer," High Technology Law Journal, Fall, 1989. *Member:* AIPPI. *LANGUAGES:* English, French, German, Italian and Spanish.

PAUL OKEL, born Columbus, Ohio, October 17, 1966; admitted, 1992, California. *Education:* University of Chicago (B.A., 1988); Institut d'Etudes Politiques de Paris (D.E.A. en Etudes Politiques, 1989); University of Chicago Law School (J.D., 1992). *LANGUAGES:* English and French.

FRANÇOIS SERRES, born Toulouse, France, May 5, 1965; admitted, 1994, Paris. *Education:* University of Toulouse Law School (Maîtrise, 1987); Institut d'Etudes Politiques de Paris (Diploma, 1990); Harvard Law School (LL.M., 1992). *LANGUAGES:* French and English.

SÉBASTIEN DAVESNE, born Neuilly-sur-Seine, France, January 1, 1967; admitted, 1994, Paris. *Education:* University of Paris Law School (Maîtrise en Droit Public, 1988; D.E.A. de Droit Communautaire, 1991); Institut d'Etudes Politiques de Paris (Diploma, 1990). *LANGUAGES:* French and English.

JEAN-FRANÇOIS TOURNEUR, born Lille, France, March 23, 1969. *Education:* University of Paris Law School (Maîtrise en Droit des Affaires, 1992; D.E.A. de Droit International Privé et Droit du Commerce International, 1993). *LANGUAGES:* French and English.

DANIEL SALMON

205 BOULEVARD SAINT-GERMAIN
75007 PARIS 75007, FRANCE
Telephone: (1) 42.22.45.01
Telecopier: (1) 42.22.36.33

French and International Private Law, General Practice including Litigation before the Courts.

DANIEL SALMON, born Paris, France, April 9, 1946; admitted, 1972, Paris; 1986, New York. *Education:* University of Paris (Licence en Droit; Maîtrise d'Histoire de l'Art et d'Archéologie); Cambridge University (LL.B.). *Member:* New York State Bar Association; The Association of the Bar of the City of New York.

SCHÜRMANN & PARTNERS

Established in 1976

12, RUE D'ASTORG
F-75008 PARIS, FRANCE
Telephone: 01-4451-0570
Telefax: 01-4266-3368

Frankfurt/Main, Germany Office: Friedrich-Ebert-Anlage 14, 60325, P.O. Box 11 16 33, 60051. Telephone: 069-7 54 90. Telefax: 7549 290.
Berlin, Germany Office: Karl-Liebknecht-Strasse 32, 10178. Telephone: 030-247-5960. Telefax: 030-238-6032.
Bonn, Germany Office: Philosophenring 94, 53177 Bonn. Telephone: 0228-328-055, Telefax: 0228-311-863.
Brussels, Belgium Office: Avenue de la Raquette 24, B-1150. Telephone: 02-770-0878. Telefax: 02-770-0878.
Dresden, Germany Office: Schnorrstrasse 70, 01069. Telephone: 0351-477-770. Telefax: 0351-477-7799.
Leipzig, Germany Office: Gustav-Adolf-Strasse 30 04105 Leipzig. Telephone: 0341-211-0622. Telefax: 0341-211-0625.
Milan, Italy Office: Via Gabrio Casati, 1, I-20123. Telephone: 02-809131/32. Telefax: 02-809-133.
New York, New York Office: 250 Park Avenue, 10177. Telephone: 212-972-3300. Telefax: 212-972-9374.

General Practice. Corporation, Trade, Banking, International and German Tax Law. Labor Law. Law on Mergers, Acquisitions. Fair Trade, Antitrust and EU Law, Administrative Law. Notary Public. Litigation Department.

JOHANNES VIEGENER, born Haan, Germany, January 21, 1939; admitted, 1971, Germany; 1986, France. *Education:* Universities of Bonn and Paris. *LANGUAGES:* German, French and English.

HUGUES TROUSSET, born Angoulême, France, November 8, 1953; admitted, 1980, France. *Education:* Universities of Limoges and Paris II. *LANGUAGES:* French and German.

CHRISTIAN KLEIN, born Bonn, Germany, January 3, 1959; admitted, 1991, Germany. *Education:* University of Bonn. *LANGUAGES:* German, French and English.

FRANK LAUTENBACH, born Bonn, Germany, February 14, 1964; admitted, 1993, France (Not admitted in France). *Education:* University of Dijon. *LANGUAGES:* German, French and English.

THOMAS FÜHRLBECK, born Düsseldorf, Germany, December 8, 1959; admitted, 1989, Germany; 1992, Tax Advisor (Not admitted in France). *Education:* University of Nuremberg. *LANGUAGES:* German, French and English.

Languages: German, English, French, Spanish and Italian.

(For complete biographical data on all Personnel, see Professional Biographies at Frankfurt/Main, Germany)

SCP WEISSBERG GAETJENS ZIEGENFEUTER

34, AVENUE MARCEAU
75008 PARIS, FRANCE
Telephone: (33) 1 47.20.22.48
Telecopier: (33) 1 47.20.21.59 and 47.20.21.64

Nice, France Office: 34, Avenue Henri Matisse, 06200. Telephone: (33) 93.18.83.50. Telecopier: (33) 93.18.83.51.

(This Listing Continued)

New York, New York Office: 270 Madison Avenue, 9th Floor, 10016. Telephone: (212) 545-4680. Telecopier: (212) 545-4675.
London, England Office: Chichester House, 278-283 High Holborn, WC1V 7HA. Telephone: (071) 242-2877. Telecopier: (071) 242-1431.
Toronto, Canada Office: 150 York Street, Suite 1902, Toronto, Ontario M5H 355. Telephone: (416) 367-4100. Fax: (416) 367-0076.

General French and International Law Practice. Aviation and Maritime Law, Banking and Finance Law, Bankruptcy and Reorganization of Enterprises, Commercial Law, Competition Law, Corporate Law, Distribution, Franchise and License Agreements, European Community Law, Intellectual and Industrial Property, International Contracts, International and French Taxation, International Private Law including Inheritance Estates, Labor Law, Real Estate Transactions and Financing.

MEMBERS OF FIRM

KENNETH WEISSBERG, born Paris, France, May 24, 1952; admitted, 1979, Paris; 1991, Nice. *Education:* University of Nice (Maîtrise en Droit, 1977); New York University (LL.M., International Law, 1979). Registered Legal Consultant in New York, 1986. *Member:* American Foreign Law Association; French-American Chamber of Commerce (Paris Chapter); Franco-British Lawyers' Society. *LANGUAGES:* French and English.

KAY GAETJENS, born Hamburg, Germany, February 6, 1952; former Conseil Juridique; admitted, 1991, Paris. *Education:* University of Tübingen (1974); University of Nice (Maîtrise en Droit, 1977). *Member:* Franco-German Chamber of Commerce in Paris; Association Française des Avocats Conseils d'Entreprise (ACE). *LANGUAGES:* French, German and English.

GERD O. ZIEGENFEUTER, born Dortmund, Germany, December 16, 1948; admitted, 1978, Nice; 1991, Paris. *Education:* University of Münster (LL.B., 1973); University of Nice (Maîtrise en Droit, 1977). *Member:* Franco-German Chamber of Commerce in Paris; German-Thai Chamber of Commerce in Bangkok; Consul of the Federal Republic of Germany in Nice (1984—). *LANGUAGES:* French, German and English.

ROBERT H. MANLEY, born Paris, France, July 17, 1922; admitted, 1951, Massachusetts and Paris as Avocat à la Cour. *Education:* University of Aix en Provence, France (1942); Boston College Law School, Boston (LL.B., 1951). President, Association of Attorneys Members of Foreign Bars. *Member:* Massachusetts Bar Association, Paris Bar Association. (Also Practicing Individually, Paris, France). *LANGUAGES:* French and English. *PRACTICE AREAS:* International Corporate Law; Entertainment Law; Wills and Trusts; Estate Planning; Real Property; Contracts; Distribution Agreements.

SOPHIE DAGANNAUD, born Saint Quentin, France, May 18, 1962; admitted, 1987, Paris. *Education:* University of Paris (Maîtrise en Droit, 1984; D.E.A. de Droit de la Propriété Littéraire Artistique et Industrielle, 1985). *Member:* European Lawyers Association. *LANGUAGES:* French and English.

LEILA SABER, born Teheran, Iran, December 30, 1965; admitted, 1991, Nice. *Education:* University of Nice (Maîtrise en Droit, 1988). *LANGUAGES:* French, English and Persian.

NICOLAS FLACHET, born Suresnes, France, April 21, 1966; Conseil Juridique Stagiaire. *Education:* University of Paris (Maîtrise en Droit, 1989); University College, London (LL.B., 1989). *LANGUAGES:* French and English.

MARK ZEINDLER, born Walenstadt, Switzerland, May 5, 1958; admitted, 1989, Zurich. *Education:* University of Berne (lic. jur., 1985). *LANGUAGES:* French, German and English.

LAURENCE DI FILIPPO, born Paris, France, July 23, 1967; Conseil Juridique Stagiaire. *Education:* University College of London (1989); University of Paris (Maîtrise en Droit des Affaires, 1990); IAE Sorbonne (D.E.S.S. en Administration des Entreprises, 1991). *LANGUAGES:* French and English.

OF COUNSEL

SIDNEY D. BLUMING, born New York, New York, 1944; admitted, 1968, New York; U.S. District Court, Southern and Eastern Districts of New York; U.S. Court of Appeals, Second Circuit (Not admitted in France). *Education:* Queens College (B.A., Accounting, 1965); Brooklyn Law School (J.D., 1968). *Member:* Association of the Bar of the City of New York; American Bar Association (Member, Corporate Law Section). Fellow: American Bar Foundation; Licensing Executives Society. (Also Member, Wolf Haldenstein Adler Freeman & Herz, New York, New York). *LANGUAGES:* English.

(This Listing Continued)

SCP WEISSBERG GAETJENS ZIEGENFEUTER,
Paris—Continued

STEPHEN MAYER, M.A., admitted, 1974, Law Society of England and Wales. (Also Member, Reynolds Porter Chamberlain, London, England).

ROBERT R. AMSTERDAM, born 1956; admitted, 1980, Ontario (Not admitted in France). *Education:* Carleton University, Ottawa (B.A., 1975); Queens University, Kingston (LL.B., 1978). (Also Member, Amsterdam & Peroff, Toronto, Canada). *LANGUAGES:* English, German and French.

SERRA MICHAUD & ASSOCIES

2, RUE DE LA BAUME
75008 PARIS, FRANCE
Telephone: 33 1 4421 97 97
Facsimile: G3-33 1 4289 57 90

General French, EEC and International Business Practice, Banking, Corporate, Taxation, Foreign Investments, Telecommunications and Media, Licensing and Technology Transfers.

MEMBERS AND ASSOCIATES OF FIRM

CLAUDE SERRA, born Carthage, Tunisia, June 6, 1956; admitted, 1978, Paris. *Education:* University of Aix-en-Provence (Licence en Droit, 1977; Maîtrise en Droit, Master of Law, 1978). *Member:* International Bar Association. *LANGUAGES:* French and English. *PRACTICE AREAS:* Corporate; Telecommunications and Media.

PATRICK J. MICHAUD, born Neuilly-sur-Seine, France, March 15, 1947; admitted, 1970, Paris. *Education:* Ecole Nationale des Impôts (1966); Institut d'Etudes Politiques (1970); Paris University (Maîtrise en Droit, 1968); Academy of American International Law, Dallas, Texas. Graduate of the Centre de Perfectionnement des Affaires (1978). Author: "Relations fiscales franco-suisses," 1977; "Régime fiscal de l'implantation internationale d'entreprises," 1978; "Régime d'imposition des sociétés immobilières en France," 1980; "Prevéntion contre la fraude fiscale internationale," 1982. *Member:* Conseil de l'Ordre (Bar Council); International Bar Association; International Fiscal Association. *LANGUAGES:* French and English. *PRACTICE AREAS:* Taxation.

JAMES LEAVY, born Dublin, Ireland, November 4, 1947; admitted, 1976, Quebec, Canada; 1990, Paris. *Education:* University College Dublin (B.A., 1968); McGill University, Montréal (LL.B., 1972; B.C.L., 1973); College of Europe, Bruges (Diploma in European Law, 1975); Université de Montréal (LL.M., 1980); Université de Paris XI (Maîtrise en Droit, 1990). Lecturer, Department of Economics, Concordia University, Montreal, 1969-1974 and Chargé de Cours, Law Faculty, Université de Montréal, 1980-1982. *Member:* Canadian, International (I.B.A.) and Inter-American Bar Associations; Licensing Executives Society. *LANGUAGES:* English, French and Spanish. *PRACTICE AREAS:* Financial Law; Licensing and Technology; Latin America.

LUCIEN RAPP, born Toulouse, France, July 16, 1954; admitted, 1977, Paris. *Education:* University of Toulouse I, Institut d'Etudes Politiques (1975; Master of Public Law, 1976; Doctor of Public Law, 1982; French "Agrégation de droit public," 1983). Recipient: French Award for the Best Thesis (1982); Toulouse Bar Award (Gold Medal) (1979). Professor of International Economic Law and Administrative Economic Law at the Faculty of Law of Toulouse. Legal consultant to the Commission of the European Communities and of the United Nations (I.L.O., World Bank, W.H.O.). Author: "Les filiales des entreprises publiques," LGDJ, 1983; "Techniques de privatisation des entreprises publiques," Litec, 1986; "La privatisation des compagnies aériennes publiques en Europe," ITA, 1987; "Contrats des collectivités locales," Editions Francis Lefebvre, 1989. Co-Author: "Lamy Droit de l'Informatique," Lamy, (6ème ed.) 1992. Several recent publications on Air Law and Telecommunications Law. *Member:* IBA (International Bar Association); ISASI (International Society of Air Safety Investigators); Association Française des Juristes d'Entreprises; Société Française de Droit Aérien et Spatial. *LANGUAGES:* French and English. *PRACTICE AREAS:* Telecommunications; Administrative Law; Air Transport Law.

NADINE STERN, born Neuilly-sur-Seine, France, February 11, 1955; admitted, 1979, Paris. *Education:* Paris I University, Sorbonne (Maîtrise en Droit, 1977; D.E.A. Business Law, 1978); University of Paris IX, Dauphine (D.E.S.S. Gestion fiscale de l'entreprise, 1986). Chargé de Cours (Lecturer) in Law, University of Paris I, Sorbonne, 1978-1983. *Member:* Paris Bar As-
(This Listing Continued)

sociation. *LANGUAGES:* French and English. *PRACTICE AREAS:* Corporate; Commercial Litigation.

FREDERIC CAZALS, born Fontenay-aux-Roses, France, February 2, 1966; admitted, 1992, Paris. *Education:* University of Paris II, Assas (Maîtrise en Droit, 1987); Institut d'Etudes Politiques de Paris (1989). *LANGUAGES:* French and English. *PRACTICE AREAS:* Corporate Law.

EMMANUEL DRAI, born Champigny, France, November 25, 1965; admitted, 1993, Paris. *Education:* University of Paris XIII (Maîtrise en Droit Public, mention Droit International, 1989); University of Paris II Assas (Maîtrise en Droit des Affaires et Fiscalité, 1989); University of Paris I Sorbonne (D.E.A. de Droit Communautaire, 1990; D.E.A. de Droit des Affaires, 1991). *LANGUAGES:* French and English. *PRACTICE AREAS:* EEC Law; Competition Law.

FRANCOIS-XAVIER ROBICHET, born December 9, 1958; admitted, 1984, Paris. *Education:* University of Paris I (Maîtrise en Droit, 1981); University of Paris XII (D.E.S.S. Applied Taxation, 1983). *Member:* Paris Bar Association. *LANGUAGES:* French and English. *PRACTICE AREAS:* Taxation.

PASCALE BEAUCHAMP, born Montreal, Canada, May 31, 1963; admitted, 1992, Paris. *Education:* McGill University, Montreal (Economics and Finance, Honours, 1983); Faculty of Law (1984); Université de Genève (Licence en Droit, 1988). *Member:* Canadian Bar Association; American Bar Association; Licensing Executives Society. *LANGUAGES:* French and English. *PRACTICE AREAS:* Corporate Law; Financial Law.

AGNES LANREZAC, born Boulogne-Billancourt, France, May 10, 1966. *Education:* University of Paris I, Sorbonne (Maîtrises en Droit, International Business Law, 1988; Internal Tax Law, 1989; D.E.S.S. International Law, 1990). *LANGUAGES:* French and English. *PRACTICE AREAS:* Taxation.

ODILE CASSIOT, born Neuilly-sur-Seine, France, September 30, 1966; admitted, 1992, Paris. *Education:* University of Paris XIII; University of Paris II (Maîtrise en Droit, International, Business and Tax Law, 1989); University of Paris I (D.E.A. Business and EEC Law, 1991). *Member:* Paris Bar Association. *LANGUAGES:* French and English. *PRACTICE AREAS:* Litigation; Administrative Law.

ANDRÉ SERRERO

Avocat au Barreau de Paris

Established in 1973

19 RUE FRANÇOIS IER
75008 PARIS, FRANCE
Telephone: (33-1) 47.20.10.50
Facsimile: (33-1) 47.23.06.38

French and International Business Practice, Banking and Finance, Corporate, Mergers and Acquisitions, International and Domestic Litigation and Arbitration, Taxation, Labor Law, Distribution and Agency, EEC Law, Competition Law, Countertrade Transactions, Air and Space Law.
Firm engaged in French and International Practice and admitted to appear in French and European Economic Community Courts.

FIRM PROFILE: The firm has an overall expertise and experience in the handling of international business transactions and in the resolution of international disputes.

ANDRÉ SERRERO, born Casablanca, Morroco, September 15, 1927; admitted, 1947, Paris. *Education:* Ohio State University, College of Law; University of Paris, Law School (Docteur en Droit et Lauréat de la Faculté de Droit de Paris, 1951). Author "La Protection des Oeuvres Littéraires et Artistiques Étrangères aux Etats-Unis," published by L.G.D.J., 1953. *Member:* International Bar Association; The Law Society's Solicitors' European Group. *LANGUAGES:* French and English. *PRACTICE AREAS:* Corporate; Mergers and Acquisitions; Banking and Finance; International Litigation and Arbitration.

SHEARMAN & STERLING

12 RUE D'ASTORG
75008 PARIS, FRANCE
Telephone: (33-1) 44-71-17-17
Telex: 282964 Royale
Fax: (33-1) 44-71-01-01

New York, N.Y. Office: 599 Lexington Avenue, New York, New York 10022-6069 and Citicorp Center, 153 East 53rd Street, New York, New York 10022-4676. Telephone: (212) 848-4000. Telex: 667290 Num Lau. Fax: 599 Lexington Avenue: (212) 848-7179. Citicorp Center: (212) 848-5252.

Abu Dhabi, United Arab Emirates Office: P.O. Box 2948. Telephone: (971-2) 324477. Fax: (971-2) 774533.

Beijing, People's Republic of China Office: Suite #2205, Capital Mansion, No. 6, Xin Yuan Nan Road. Chao Yang District Beijing, 100004. Telephone: (861) 465-4574. Fax: (861) 465-4578.

Budapest, Hungary Office: Szerb utca 17-19, 1056 Budapest. Telephone: (36-1) 266-3522. Fax: (36-1) 266-3523.

Düsseldorf, Federal Republic of Germany Office: Königsallee 46, D-40212 Düsseldorf. Telephone: (49-211) 13 62 80. Telex: 8 588 294 NYLO. Fax: (49-211) 13 33 09.

Frankfurt, Federal Republic of Germany Office: Bockenheimer Landstrasse 55, D-60325 Frankfurt am Main. Telephone: (49-69) 97-10-70. Fax: (49-69) 97-10-71-00.

Hong Kong, Hong Kong Office: Standard Chartered Bank Building, 4 Des Voeux Road Central, Hong Kong. Telephone: (852) 2978-8000. Fax: (852) 2978-8099.

London, England Office: 199Bishopsgate, London EC2M 3TY. Telephone: (44-71) 920-9000. Fax: (44-71) 920-9020.

Los Angeles, California Office: 725 South Figueroa Street, 21st Floor, 90017-5421. Telephone: (213) 239-0300. Fax: (213) 239-0381, 614-0936.

San Francisco, California Office: 555 California Street, 94104-1522. Telephone: (415) 616-1100. Fax: (415) 616-1199.

Taipei, Taiwan Office: 7th Floor, Hung Kuo Building, 167 Tun Hwa North Road. Telephone: (886-2) 545-3300. Fax: (866-2) 545-3322.

Tokyo, Japan Office: Shearman & Sterling (Thomas Wilner Gaikokuho-Jimu-Bengoshi Jimusho), Fukoku Seimei Building, 5th Fl. 2-2-2,Uchisaiwaicho, Chiyoda-ku, Tokyo 100, Japan. Telephone: (81 3) 5251-1601. Fax: (81 3) 5251-1602.

Toronto, Ontario, Canada Office: Commerce Court West, Suite 4405, P.O. Box 247, M5L 1E8. Telephone: (416) 360-8484. Fax: (416) 360-2958.

Washington, D.C. Office: 801 Pennsylvania Avenue, N.W., Suite 900, 20004-2604. Telephone: (202) 508-8000. Fax: (202) 508-8100.

General Practice.
Firm engaged in American, French and General International Practice and authorized to appear before the French Courts.

FIRM PROFILE: *Shearman & Sterling, founded in 1873, has more than 500 lawyers in 15 offices throughout the world. The firm's practice encompasses most major areas of business law, including: Antitrust and Trade Regulation; Banking; Bankruptcy and Corporate Reorganization; Compensation and Benefits; Environmental; Finance (including Corporate Finance, Domestic Private Finance, Financial Institutions, International Private Finance and Project Finance); Individual Clients, Trusts and Estates; Insurance; International Trade and Government Relations; Litigation and Arbitration; Mergers and Acquisitions; Oil and Gas; Privatizations; Real Estate; and Tax. The Firm is also engaged in the practice of French, German and Hungarian law through its offices in France, Germany and Hungary.*

RESIDENT PARTNERS

HUBERTUS V. SULKOWSKI, born Csikeszereda, Hungary, 1943; admitted, 1971, New York; 1981, U.S. Supreme Court; admitted in France. *Education:* Trinity College (B.A., 1966); Boston College (J.D., 1969). (Managing Partner). *LANGUAGES:* English, French and Hungarian.

JOHN J. MADDEN, born New York, N.Y., 1946; admitted, 1976, New York (Not admitted in France). *Education:* University of Pennsylvania (B.A., 1968); Fordham University (J.D., 1975). (Managing Partner, Europe). *LANGUAGES:* English and French.

(This Listing Continued)

OF COUNSEL

ROBERT A. MACCRINDLE, born Glasgow, United Kingdom, 1928; called to bar of England and Wales, 1952; Queens Counsel, 1963; Member of Hong Kong bar; Bencher of Gray's Inn, 1970; admitted in France. *Education:* London University (LL.B., 1948); Cambridge University (LL.M., 1951). Fellow, American College of Trial Lawyers. *LANGUAGES:* English and French.

DAVID T. MCGOVERN, born New York, N.Y., 1928; admitted, 1955, New York; admitted in France. *Education:* Yale University (B.S., 1949); Columbia University (LL.B., 1955). *LANGUAGES:* English and French.

EUROPEAN COUNSEL

NORBERT ANDREAE, born La Réole, France, 1946; admitted in France. *Education:* University of Saarbrucken, Germany; University of Bordeaux I (Docteur en Droit, 1971). Member, International Fiscal Association, 1989—. *LANGUAGES:* French, English and German.

EMMANUEL GAILLARD, born Chambéry, France, 1952; admitted in France. *Education:* University of Paris (J.D., 1975; D.E.A. in Private Law, 1976; D.E.A. in Criminal Law, 1977); Agrégé des Facultés de Droit (1982). Professor of Law, University of Paris XII, 1987—. Visiting Professor of Law, Harvard Law School, 1984. *LANGUAGES:* French and English.

ANDREA K. MULLER, born Detroit, Michigan, 1959; admitted, 1986, New York; admitted in France. *Education:* Georgetown University (B.S.F.S., 1981; J.D., 1985); College d'Europe, EEC Studies, 1982. *LANGUAGES:* English and French.

ROBERT C. TREUHOLD, born New York, N.Y., 1957; admitted, 1984, New York; admitted in France. *Education:* University of Montpellier (Diplôme, 1975); Georgetown University (B.S., 1978); New York University (J.D., 1983). *LANGUAGES:* English and French.

FRENCH COUNSEL

HERVÉ LETRÉGUILLY, born Rouen, France, 1962; admitted in France. *Education:* University of Haute Normandie (J.D., 1983); University of Paris I -Pantheon -Sorbonne (D.E.A., in English and North American Corporate Law, 1986).

CONSULTANT

DOMINIQUE CARREAU, born Neuilly-sur-Seine, France, 1939; (Not admitted in France). *Education:* University of Michigan (M.C.L., 1967); Agrégé des Facultés de Droit (1970). Professor at: University of Paris X, 1970-1976; University of Paris V, 1976-1979; University of Paris I, Panthéon-Sorbonne, 1979—. Head of Department of International Studies, University of Paris I (Panthéon-Sorbonne), 1982-1989. *LANGUAGES:* French and English.

RESIDENT ASSOCIATES

CHRISTOPHER ARMENIADES, born Boston, Massachusetts, 1962. admitted, 1991, New York; admitted in France. *Education:* University of Oregon (B.A., 1984); Fulbright Scholar, Faculté de Droit de Nancy, France, 1985; Harvard University (J.D., 1989). *LANGUAGES:* English and French.

ISABELLE CHAUVET, born Boulogne, Seine, France, 1960; admitted in France. *Education:* University of Paris V (D.E.S.S. in Tax Law, 1986); University of Paris X (D.E.S.S. in International Commercial Law, 1987). *LANGUAGES:* French, English and Spanish.

MICHAEL J. COLEMAN, born Exeter, Canada, 1963; admitted, 1992, New York (Not admitted in France). *Education:* University of Toronto (B.A.Sc., 1987); University of Waterloo (LL.B., 1991). *LANGUAGES:* English and French.

ALESSANDRO C. DE GIORGIS, born New York, N.Y., 1967; admitted, 1994, New York. *Education:* Columbia University (B.A., 1989; J.D., 1993).

CHRISTOPHE DUGUÉ, born La Ciotat, France, 1958; admitted in France. *Education:* University of Law of Aix-en-Provence (J.D. in International Law, 1980; D.E.S.S. and D.J.C.E. in International Business Law, 1982). *LANGUAGES:* French and English.

PETER GRIFFIN, born Dublin, Ireland, 1969; (Not admitted in France). *Education:* Kings' College, London (LL.B., 1991); University of Paris I (Maitrise en droit, 1991; D.E.A. in Trade Law, 1992). *LANGUAGES:* English and French.

MICHÈLE HULIN, born Paris, France, 1948; admitted in France. *Education:* University of Paris-Nanterre (Maîtrise in English, 1970); Ecole Na-

(This Listing Continued)

SHEARMAN & STERLING, Paris—Continued

tionale des Lángues Orientales (Diplôme de 1'ENLOV in Russian, 1971); University of Paris II (J.D., 1981). **LANGUAGES:** French and English.

NITSCH MARIANNA, born Vienna, Austria, 1968. *Education:* University of Vienna Law Faculty (Master, 1991; D.E.A. in International Economique Law, 1992). **LANGUAGES:** English, German, French and Italian.

MICHÈLE F. MOSS, born New York, N.Y., 1948; admitted, 1975, Pennsylvania; 1976, District of Columbia; 1984, New York; admitted in France. *Education:* Harvard University (B.A., 1971); University of Pennsylvania (J.D., 1975); University of Paris II (D.E.S.S in International Commercial Law, 1991). **LANGUAGES:** English, French and Italian.

LEE D. NEUMANN, born Cincinnati, Ohio, 1958; admitted, 1991, New York (Not admitted in France). *Education:* Princeton University (B.S.E., magna cum laude, 1981); London School of Economics, England (M.S., 1984); Columbia University (J.D., 1990). **LANGUAGES:** French.

PHILIPPE PINSOLLE, born Dax, France, 1968. admitted in France. *Education:* École Supérieure des Sciences Economiques et Commerciales--ESSEC (Diplome, 1989); Université de Paris-II (J.D., 1991). **LANGUAGES:** French, English and Spanish.

PHILIPPE ROSENPICK, born Paris, France, 1962. admitted in France. *Education:* University of Grenoble II (Maître en droit, 1984); University of Aix-Marseille (D.E.S.S. in International Corporate Law and D.J.C.E., 1988). **LANGUAGES:** French, English and Spanish.

JOHN SAVAGE, born Poole, England, 1967; admitted, 1993, England and Wales (Not admitted in France). *Education:* King's College, London (LL.B., 1990); Guildmall University (L.S.F., 1991).

LESLEY SIMMONS, born New York, N.Y., 1962. ; admitted, 1989, New York; admitted in France. *Education:* Brown University (B.S., 1984); Fordham University (J.D., 1988). **LANGUAGES:** English, French and Italian.

ERIC TEYNIER, born Neuilly-sur-Seine, France, 1956; admitted in France. *Education:* University of Nanterre (J.D., 1978; D.E.A. in Labor Law, 1980). **LANGUAGES:** French and English.

SAMI L. TOUTOUNJI, born Beirut, Lebanon, 1964; admitted, 1990, New York (Not admitted in France). *Education:* Georgetown University (B.S.B.A., 1986; J.D., 1989). **LANGUAGES:** English and French.

(For Biographical data of the New York partners, see Professional Biographies at New York, N.Y.)

SHUBERT & DUSAUSOY

Established in 1990

190 BOULEVARD HAUSSMANN
75008 PARIS, FRANCE
Telephone: (33) (1) 40 76 01 43
Telecopier: (33) (1) 40 76 01 44

General French, American and International Legal Practice, Commercial, Corporate, Mergers and Acquisitions, Industrial Property and Copyright, Computer Law, Labor Law, Litigation, Immigration and EEC Law.

MEMBERS OF FIRM

GARY MICHAEL SHUBERT, born Cleveland, Ohio, May 25, 1948; admitted, 1981, New York; 1985, Conseil Juridique; 1992, Paris. *Education:* University of California at Los Angeles (B.A., 1970); University of Wisconsin (M.A., 1972); Boalt Hall School of Law, University of California at Berkeley (J.D., 1980); Harvard Law School (1979-1980). Phi Beta Kappa; Order of the Coif. Member, Board of Directors, American Center for Students and Artists, Paris, France, 1986—. *Member:* Association of the Bar of the City of New York; New York State and American Bar Associations; Union Internationale des Avocats; American Immigration Lawyers Association. **LANGUAGES:** French and English.

PATRICE-MARIE DUSAUSOY, born Saint-Omer, France, March 17, 1953; conseil juridique stagiaire, 1980; admitted, 1984, Paris. *Education:* University of Lille School of Economics (Maîtrise de Sciences Economiques, 1977); University of Lille (Maîtrise de Droit, 1977); Boalt Hall School of Law, University of California at Berkeley (LL.M., 1978). *Member:* French Computer Law Association (A.F.D.I.). **LANGUAGES:** French and English.

(This Listing Continued)

ASSOCIATE

CLAIRE FOUGEA, born Boulogne, France, May 1, 1964; admitted, 1989, Paris. *Education:* University of Paris V (Maîtrise de Droit Privé, 1986; Certificate of Advanced Studies, Civil and Commercial Law, 1987); Washington College of Law, American University (LL.M., 1988). **LANGUAGES:** French and English.

SIMÉON & ASSOCIÉS

5, AVENUE PERCIER
75008 PARIS, FRANCE
Telephone: (1) 40 75 08 08
Fax: (1) 40 75 04 50

Brussels, Belgium Office: Avenue de Tervuren 13, B-1040. Telephone: (2) 732 69 69. Fax: (2) 732 70 71.

Warsaw, Poland Office: Siméon Karniol Malecki, Aleje Jerozolimskie 30. 00024. Telephone: (48) 22 27 04 64. Fax: (48) 22 27 48 08; 39 12 32 01.

Hanoi, Vietnam Office: 13 Tran Hung Dao. Telephone: (84 4) 251 588; (84 4) 244 345. Fax: (84 4) 251 514.

Ho Chi Minh Ville, Vietnam Office: IBC Centre. 1A Me Linh Square. Telephone: (84) 8 294 890. Fax: (84) 4 294 876.

French, EEC and International Law Practice.

MEMBERS OF FIRM

CHRISTIAN BELLOIN, born Beauvais, France, January 24, 1955; admitted, 1980, Paris. *Education:* University of Paris (Maîtrise en Droit, 1977; DEA, Droit Commercial, 1979); Tulane University (LL.M., 1980). **LANGUAGES:** French, English and German.

BERNARD CARREZ, born Saint-Quentin, France, October 16, 1946; admitted, 1971, Paris. *Education:* University of Paris, Sorbonne (Licencés en Philosophie et en Histoire, 1968); University of Paris Law School (Licencié en Droit, 1971; DES Droit Privé, DES Droit Public, 1972); Institut d'Etudes Politiques de Paris (Service Public, 1971). **LANGUAGES:** French, English and Spanish.

JEAN MARIE DUCHEMIN, born Algiers, Algeria, September 2, 1951; admitted, 1977, Paris. *Education:* University of Paris (Licencié en Droit, 1975; DEA Droit Européen, 1977); Institut d'Etudes Politiques de Paris, 1975. **LANGUAGES:** French and English.

JACQUES EPSTEIN, born April 19, 1952; admitted, 1977, Paris. *Education:* Baccalauréat 1970; Paris I (Panthéon-Sorbonne) Maîtrise 1974; Paris I - Panthéon-Sorbonne D.E.S. de Droit Privé 1975, D.E.S. de Droit Public/Droit Européen) 1975; Columbia LL.M. 1976. Author: "Le Contrôle des Concentrations," Dalloz, 1978; "Pratique de la Commission des Communautés Européennes en matierè de concurrence, "Revue du Marché Commun, 1980; "French Takeovers: Control and Concert, "International, Financial L. Review, Nov., 1991. *Member:* Association Francaise des Avocats Conseils d' Entreprises.

JEAN-PIERRE LANGLAIS, born Rennes, France, August 30, 1948; admitted, 1974, Paris. *Education:* Institut d'Etudes Politiques de Paris, 1973; University of Rennes (Licencé en Droit, 1971; DES Droit Privé, 1972); University of Paris (DES Droit Public, 1973). **LANGUAGES:** French and English.

PIERRE DE MONTALEMBERT, born Paris, France, November 9, 1953; admitted, 1978, Paris; 1982, New York. *Education:* University of Paris I (Maîtrise en Droit, 1978; DEA Droit International Privé et Droit du Commerce International, 1979); Ecole Supérieure de Commerce de Paris (1976); New York University (M.C.J., 1981). *Member:* Paris Bar Council. **LANGUAGES:** French, English and Italian.

ERIC MORGAN DE RIVERY, born Tours, France, August 18, 1952; admitted, 1978, Paris. *Education:* University of Tours (Licencié en Droit, 1973); University of Paris (DES Droit des Affaires, 1974); Harvard Law School (LL.M., 1977). **LANGUAGES:** French and English.

CYRILLE NIEDZIELSKI, born Cairo, Egypt, December 16, 1948; admitted, 1973, Paris. *Education:* University of Paris (Licencé en Droit, 1971); Columbia Law School (LL.M., 1977). **LANGUAGES:** French, English and Portuguese.

BERNARD SIMÉON, born Tulle, France, July 25, 1936; admitted, 1966, Paris. *Education:* University of Paris (Doctorat en Droit, 1964). Author: "Le Reglement n° 17 de la CEE," 1964; "Les Fusions et Scissions de Sociétés," Dunod, 1971. **LANGUAGES:** French and English.

(This Listing Continued)

ALEXIS TERRAY, born Boulogne-Billancourt, France, December 8, 1962; admitted, 1988, Paris. *Education:* Institut d'Etudes Politiques de Paris (1983); University of Paris (Maîtrise en Droit, 1985). *LANGUAGES:* French and English.

JACQUES WANTZ, born Talence, France, June 24, 1955; admitted, 1977, Paris. *Education:* University of Bordeaux (Maîtrise en Droit, 1977); University of Pennsylvania Law School (LL.M., 1980). (Resident, Ho Chi Minh City, Vietnam). *LANGUAGES:* French and English.

ASSOCIATES

ELISA BARDAVID, born Versailles, France, August 13, 1968; admitted, 1995, Paris. *Education:* Institut d'Etudes Politiques de Paris (1990); University of Paris I (Maîtrise en Droit des Affaires, 1992; DEA Droit International Privé et Droit du Commerce International, 1993). *LANGUAGES:* French, English and German.

CAROLINE BERGERON, born Angers, France, April 13, 1971; admitted, 1995, Paris. *Education:* Institut d'Etudes Politiques de Paris (1991); University of Paris (Licencé en droit, 1993; DESS de Fiscalité Internationale, 1993); Ecole des Hautes Etudes Commerciales (H.E.C., 1993). *LANGUAGES:* French, English and German.

OLIVIER BLUCHE, born Paris, France, August 14, 1969; admitted, 1992, Paris. *Education:* University of Paris II (Magistère de Juriste d'Affaires et DESS Droit des Affaires et Fiscalité, 1992); New York University (M.C.J., 1994). *LANGUAGES:* French, English and Italian.

SOPHIE BOROWSKY, born Boulogne-Billancourt, France, May 17, 1965; admitted, 1990, Paris. *Education:* University of Paris X (Maîtrise Carrières Judiciaires, 1987); University of Paris II (DEA de Droit International Privé, 1988); New York University School of Law (M.C.J., 1994). *LANGUAGES:* French, English and Spanish.

JOËL CATHERIN, born Bagneux, France, March 28, 1969; admitted, 1995, Paris. *Education:* University of Paris II (Maîtrise en Droit des Affairs er Droit Fiscal, Maîtrise en Carrières Judiciaires, 1991); University of Panthéon Assas Paris II (D.J.C.E.-D.E.S.S. de Droit des Affaires et Fiscalité, 1993); ESSEC (1994). *LANGUAGES:* French, English and German.

CHRISTOPHE CLERC, born Uccle, Belgium, June 11, 1966; admitted, 1993, Paris. *Education:* Institut d'Etudes Politiques de Paris (1989); University of Paris II (Maîtrise en Droit International et Communautaire, 1989); University of Paris I, Sorbonne (DEA Droit des Affaires, 1990). *LANGUAGES:* French, English and German.

MONICA CUNNINGHAM, born Cambridge, United Kingdom, March 21, 1969; admitted, 1995, Brussels (Not admitted in France). *Education:* King's College, University of London (LL.B., English and French Law, 1991); University of Paris I (Maîtrise en Droit Privé, 1991); College of Europe, Bruges (LL.M., European Law, 1994). *LANGUAGES:* English, French and Dutch.

JACQUES DERENNE, born Marche-en-Famenne, Belgium, April 16, 1964; admitted, 1991, Brussels; 1994, Paris. *Education:* University of Liege (Licencé en Droit, 1987) and College of Europe (Diploma in Advanced European Legal Studies, 1988). (Resident, Brussels, Belgium Office). *LANGUAGES:* French and English.

VINCENT FAUCHOUX, born Nantes, France, February 6, 1965; admitted, 1990, Paris. *Education:* University of Paris I (Maîtrise en Droit, 1987); University of Paris II (DEA Droit International Privé, 1988). *LANGUAGES:* French, English and Polish.

MICHAEL E. FREUNDLICH, born Minneapolis, Minnesota, September 8, 1961; admitted, 1991, New York; 1992, Washington D.C. (Not admitted in France). *Education:* Oberlin College (A.B., 1984); Universidad Pontificia, Salamanca, Spain; University of Miami School of Law (J.D., cum laude, 1990); University of Paris I (DESS, Droit du Marché Commun, 1992). *LANGUAGES:* English, French and Spanish.

EVELYNE FRIEDEL, born Paris, France, May 19, 1963; admitted, 1993, Paris. *Education:* University of Paris II (Maîtrise de Droit International et Européen, 1985; DEA de Droit Communautaire, 1986); University of Paris I (DESS de Droit du Commerce Extérieur, 1987); Georgetown University Law Center (LL.M., 1 989); University of Paris II (Doctorat en Droit, 1992). *LANGUAGES:* French and English.

PIERRE DE GIRARD VAN COEHORN, born Paris, France, June 4, 1964; admitted, 1988, Paris. *Education:* Institut d'Etudes Politiques de Paris, 1987; University of Paris (Maîtrise en Droit, 1986). *LANGUAGES:* French and English.

(This Listing Continued)

CLAIRE GUIONNET-MOALIC, born Paris, France, February 17, 1965; admitted, 1993, Paris. *Education:* University of Paris II (Maîtrise en Droit Privé, 1987; DESS de Fiscalité Internationale); H.E.C. Sceaux (1988); Institut d'Etudes Politiques de Paris (1990). *LANGUAGES:* French and English.

MARC HENRY, born Paris, France, January 9, 1964; admitted, 1988, Paris. *Education:* University of Paris I (Maîtrise en Droit, 1985; DEA Droit International Privé et DEA Droit des Affaires, 1986). *LANGUAGES:* French, English and German.

ARNAUD LATSCHA, born Boulogne, France, October 10, 1965; admitted, 1991, Paris. *Education:* Institut d'Etudes Politiques de Paris (1990); University of Paris I (Maîtrises en Droit, 1987). *LANGUAGES:* French and English.

LUCAS DE LE BARROIS D'ORGEVAL, born Cannes, France, August 7, 1969; admitted, 1995, Paris. *Education:* Commercial University of Milano (1991); ESSEC (Majeure Finance, 1992); University of Paris II (Maîtrise de droit privé, 1993). *LANGUAGES:* French, English, Italian and German.

GAËLLE LE BRETON, born Boulogne Billancourt, France, July 25, 1968; admitted, 1995, Paris. *Education:* University of Paris I (D.E.A. de Droit Privé, 1990); Collège d'Europe, Bruges (Diplôme de Hautes Etudes Juridiques Européennes, 1992); Institut Universitaire Européen, Florence (Diplôme d'Etudes Juridiques Comparatives, Internationales et Européennes (LL.M.), 1993). *LANGUAGES:* French, English, Italian and German.

JOHANN LE FRAPPER, born Hennebont, France, April 20, 1968; admitted, 1994, Paris. *Education:* University of Rennes (Licencé de Droit); University of Paris II (Maîtrise en Droit des Affaires et Fiscalité, 1990; DEA de Droit des Affaires, 1991); McGill University (LL.M. in International Business Law, 1993). *LANGUAGES:* French and English.

LUC LEJEUNE, born Brest, France, November 3, 1965. *Education:* University of Aix-Marseille III (Maîtrise en Droit, 1987); University of Paris V (DESS, 1989); Institut d'Etudes Politiques de Paris (1990). (Resident, Hanoi, Vietnam Office). *LANGUAGES:* French, English, German, Italian and Vietnamese.

EMMANUELLE PEYRAUD, born Saint-Cloud, France, June 1, 1970; admitted, 1995, Paris. *Education:* University of Sceaux Paris XI (DESS de Fiscalité Internationale, 1993); HEC (Majeure Stratégie Juridique et Fiscale Internationale, 1993); University of Nanterre Paris X (Licence en Droit, 1994). *LANGUAGES:* French, English and German.

CHRISTOPHER EDWARD POTTER, born Geneva, Switzerland, May 21, 1970; admitted, 1993, Paris. *Education:* King's College, London (LL.B., 1989); University of Paris I (Maîtrise en Droits français et anglais, 1992; DEA Droit Fiscal, 1993). *LANGUAGES:* English and French.

THOMAS ROUHETTE, born Tananarive, Madagascar, December 20, 1966; admitted, 1992, Paris. *Education:* Institut d'Etudes Politiques de Paris (1987); University of Paris II (Maîtrises en Droit Privé et en Droit Public, 1990); University of Paris I (DEA Droit International Privé et Droit du Commerce International, 1991). *LANGUAGES:* French and English.

PATRICIA SALOMON, born Suresnes, France, March 28, 1966; admitted, 1991, Paris. *Education:* University of Paris X - Nanterre (Maîtrise en Droit des Affaires, 1988; DESS, Droit du Commerce International, 1989). *LANGUAGES:* French, English and Spanish.

Co-Authors and Co-Editors of "Doing Business in France," a Matthew Bender publication.

SIMMONS & SIMMONS

Avocats à la Cour and Solicitors

Established in 1988

2, AVENUE BUGEAUD
75116 PARIS, FRANCE
Telephone: 33-1-45016767
Telecopier: 33-1-45012232
Telex: TRANSAV 649381F

London, England Office: 21 Wilson Street, EC2M 2TQ. Telephone: 44-171-628 2020; 44-171-528 9292. Facsimile: 44-171-628 2070. Telex: 888562SIMMON G.

Brussels, Belgium Office: Rue d'Arlon 118, 1040. Telephone: 32-2-280 16 70. Telecopier: 32-2-280 04 84.

(This Listing Continued)

SIMMONS & SIMMONS, Paris—Continued

Lisbon, Portugal Office: Rua Castilho, n° 32-9°, 1250. Telephone: 351-1-352 1318. Telecopier: 351-1-352 1418.

Milan, Italy Office in joint practice with Studio Avv. Eugenio Grippo: Via Dei Boschetti 1, 20121. Telephone: 39-2-76003012. Telecopier: 39-2-782770.

Abu Dhabi Office: The Blue Tower, Khalifa Street. P.O. Box 5931. Telephone: 971 2 347882. Telecopier: 971 2 347832.

Hong Kong Office: 24th Floor, Jardine House, One Connaught Place, Central. Telephone: 852-28681131. Telecopier: 852-28105040. Telex: 75888 SANDS HX.

New York, New York Office: 115 East 57th Street, 10022. Telephone: 1-212-688-6620. Telecopier: 1-212-355-3594.

French, English, EC and International Law Practice.

RESIDENT PARTNERS

CHRISTOPHER WATSON, Avocat à la Cour, Solicitor; born Swansea, Wales, 1957; admitted, 1983, England and Wales; 1993, Paris. *Education:* New College, Oxford (M.A.). *LANGUAGES:* English, French, German and Italian. *PRACTICE AREAS:* Company; Commercial Law; Competition (all French and English Law) and European Community Law.

HARVEY CHALMERS, Solicitor; born Glasgow, Scotland, 1947; admitted, 1974, Scotland; 1978, England and Wales. *Education:* University of Glasgow (LL.B., Hons); Magdalene College, Cambridge (Ph.D.). *Member:* Law Society; Law Society of Scotland. *LANGUAGES:* English and French. *PRACTICE AREAS:* Banking.

NICHOLAS WILLIAMS, Avocat à la Cour, Solicitor; born London, England, 1957; admitted, 1985, England and Wales; 1993, Paris. *Education:* University of Warwick (B.A., Hons.). *LANGUAGES:* English, French and Spanish. *PRACTICE AREAS:* International Commercial Law; Employment Law; Insolvency.

MARIE-CAROLINE MOISSINAC, Avocat à la Cour; born Neuilly-sur-Seine, France, 1959; admitted, 1984, Paris. *Education:* University of Paris. *LANGUAGES:* French and English. *PRACTICE AREAS:* Litigation; Arbitration.

COLIN MILLAR, Avocat à la Cour, Solicitor; born Ayr, Scotland, 1960; admitted, 1989, England and Wales; 1993, Paris. *Education:* Exeter College, Oxford (B.C.L., M.A., Hons). *LANGUAGES:* English, French and German. *PRACTICE AREAS:* Banking; Asset Finance; Financial Services; Mergers and Acquisitions; Capital Markets.

ASSISTANTS

LAURENT ARCHAMBAULT, Avocat à la Cour; born, Neuilly-sur-Seine, France, 1968; admitted, 1992, Paris. *Education:* University of Kent (Master of International Commercial Law); University of Lyon. *LANGUAGES:* French, English and German. *PRACTICE AREAS:* International Commercial Law.

SARAH BAILEY, Solicitor; Conseil Juridique Stagiaire; born Lincolnshire, England, 1964; admitted, 1992, England and Wales. *Education:* University of Kent (B.A. in English and French Law); University of Paris (D.E.S.S.). *LANGUAGES:* English and French. *PRACTICE AREAS:* Company Law; Commercial Law; Intellectual Property; Financial Services.

IVAN DE GOULLARD D'ARSAY, Avocat à la Cour; born, 1967; admitted, 1994. *Education:* London School of Economics (LL.M.); University of Paris (D.E.S.S.). *LANGUAGES:* French, English and Russian. *PRACTICE AREAS:* Commercial Law.

MARY GRAYSTON, Avocat à la Cour, Solicitor; born Canterbury, England, 1963; admitted, 1990, England and Wales; 1993, Paris. *Education:* University of Buckingham (LL.B.); University of Aix-Marseille. *LANGUAGES:* English and French. *PRACTICE AREAS:* Company Law; Commercial Law; Environmental Law; Real Estate Law.

ERIC HAZA, Avocat à la Cour; born La Rochelle, France, 1968; admitted, 1994, Paris. *Education:* University of Poitiers (D.E.A.). *LANGUAGES:* French and English. *PRACTICE AREAS:* Litigation; Commercial Law.

GENEVIEVE HUSSENOT-LABIC, Avocat à la Cour; born Rognac, France, 1944; 1966 Conseil Juridique Paris; admitted to bar, 1992, Paris. *Education:* University of Paris. *LANGUAGES:* French and English. *PRACTICE AREAS:* Tax Law; Company Law; Commercial Law; Administrative Law; Insolvency; Mergers and Acquisitions.

(This Listing Continued)

FRANCOIS LEFEBVRE, Avocat à la Cour; born, 1959; admitted, 1992, Paris. *Education:* Ecole Supérieure de Commerce, Lyon (M.B.A.); University of Lillie. *LANGUAGES:* French, English, German and Chinese. *PRACTICE AREAS:* Commercial Law; Litigation.

JACQUELINE LUESBY, Solicitor; Conseil Juridique Stagiaire; born Swineshead, England, 1958; admitted, 1983, England and Wales. *Education:* Hertford College, University of Oxford (M.A., Hons.). *LANGUAGES:* English and French. *PRACTICE AREAS:* Tax and Trust Law.

VALERIE RAMOS, Avocat à la Cour; born Narbonne, France, 1966; admitted, 1992, Paris. *Education:* University of Montpellier (D.E.S.S.; Magistère D.J.C.E.); London School of Economics (LL.M.). *LANGUAGES:* French and English. *PRACTICE AREAS:* Company Law; Commercial Law; EC and French Competition Law.

STEPHEN WALTERS, Solicitor; born Cardiff, Wales, 1964; admitted, 1988, England and Wales. *Education:* University of Warwick (LL.B.). *LANGUAGES:* English and French. *PRACTICE AREAS:* Company Law; Commercial Law.

LAURE JONCOUR, Avocat à la Cour, born La Garenne Colombes, France, 1967; admitted, 1994, Hauts de Seine. *Education:* University of Paris X Nanterres. *LANGUAGES:* French and English. *PRACTICE AREAS:* Employment Law.

(For List of other Partners, see Professional Biographies at London, England).

SKADDEN, ARPS, SLATE, MEAGHER & FLOM

105 RUE DU FAUBOURG SAINT-HONORÉ
75008 PARIS, FRANCE
Telephone: 011-33-1-40-75-44-44
Fax: 011-33-1-49-53-09-99

New York, New York Office: 919 Third Avenue, 10022. Telephone: 212-735-3000. Fax: 212-735-2000; 212-735-2001. Telex: 645899 Skarslaw.

Boston, Massachusetts Office: One Beacon Street, 02108. Telephone: 617-573-4800. Fax: 617-573-4822.

Washington, D.C. Office: 1440 New York Avenue, N.W., 20005. Telephone: 202-371-7000. Fax: 202-393-5760.

Wilmington, Delaware Office: One Rodney Square, 19899. Telephone: 302-651-3000. Fax: 302-651-3001.

Los Angeles, California Office: 300 South Grand Avenue, 90071. Telephone: 213-687-5000. Fax: 213-687-5600.

Chicago, Illinois Office: 333 West Wacker Drive, 60606. Telephone: 312-407-0700. Fax: 312-407-0411.

San Francisco, California Office: Four Embarcadero Center, 94111. Telephone: 415-984-6400. Fax: 415-984-2698.

Houston, Texas Office: 1600 Smith Street, Suite 4460, 77002. Telephone: 713-655-5100. Fax: 713-655-5181.

Newark, New Jersey Office: One Riverfront Plaza, 07102. Telephone: 201-596-4440. Fax: 201-596-4444.

Tokyo, Japan Office: 12th Floor, The Fukoku Seimei Building, 2-2-2, Uchisaiwaicho, Chiyoda-ku, 100. Telephone: 011-81-3-3595-3850. Fax: 011-81-3-3504-2780.

London, England Office: 25 Bucklersbury EC4N 8DA. Telephone: 011-44-0171-248-9929. Fax: 011-44-0171-489-8533.

Hong Kong Office: 30/F Peregrine Tower, Lippo Centre, 89 Queensway, Central. Telephone: 011-852-820-0700. Fax: 011-852-820-0727.

Sydney, New South Wales, Australia Office: Level 26-State Bank Centre, 52 Martin Place, 2000. Telephone: 011-61-2-224-6000. Fax: 011-61-2-224-6044.

Toronto, Ontario Office: Suite 1820, North Tower, P.O. Box 189, Royal Bank Plaza, M5J 2J4. Telephone: 416-777-4700. Fax: 416-777-4747.

Brussels, Belgium Office: 523 avenue Louise, Box 30, 1050. Telephone: 011-32-2-648-7666. Fax: 011-32-2-640-3032.

Frankfurt, Germany Office: MesseTurm, 27th Floor, 60308. Telephone: 011-49-69-9757-3000. Fax: 011-49-69-9757-3050.

Beijing, China Office: 1605 Capital Mansion Tower, No. 6 Xin Yuan Nan Road, Chao Yang District, 100004. Telephone: 011-86-1-466-8800. Fax: 011-86-1-466-8822.

Budapest, Hungary Office: Mahart Building, H-1052 Apáczai Csere János u.11, Vl.em. Telephone: 011-36-1-266-2145. Fax: 011-36-1-266-4033.

Prague, Czech Republic Office: Revolu_ni 16, 110 00. Telephone: 011-42-2-231-75-18. Fax: 011-42-2-231-47-33.

(This Listing Continued)

Moscow, Russia Office: Pleteshkovsky Pereulok 1, 107005. Telephone: 011-7-501-940-2304. Fax: 011-7-501-940-2511.

Firm engaged in general practice as Avocats.

ISAAC SHAPIRO, born Tokyo, Japan, 1931; admitted, 1957, New York; 1991, France. *Education:* Columbia University (A.B., 1954); Columbia Law School (LL.B., 1956); University of Paris, 1956-1957. Editor, Columbia Law Review. (Also at New York, New York Office).

CHRISTOPHER L. BAKER, born Lake Forest, Ill., 1958; admitted, 1984, New York; 1989, Conseil Juridique, France; 1993, France. *Education:* Harvard University (B.A., magna cum laude, 1979); University of Chicago (J.D., 1983); New York University (LL.M., Taxation, 1986).

(For Biographical data on other Personnel, see New York, New York Professional Biographies).

SLAUGHTER AND MAY

Solicitors of the Supreme Court of England and Wales

Avocats au Barreau de Paris

112 AVENUE KLÉBER
75116 PARIS, FRANCE
Telephone: (1) 44.05.60.00
Telex: 642514
Fax: (1) 44.05.60.60; (1) 44 06 60 99 (G-4)

London, England Office: 35 Basinghall Street, EC2V 5DB. Telephone: (0171) 600 1200. Telex: 883486; 888926. Fax: (0171) 726 0038; (0171) 600 0289; (0171) 600 1455 (G-4).

Brussels, Belgium Office: Rue D'Arlon 69/71, 1040. Telephone: (2) 230 5631. Fax: (2) 230 7699.

Frankfurt am Main, Germany Office: Westend-Carree Grüneburgweg 16, D-60322 Frankfurt am Main. Telephone: (69) 9551370. Fax: (69) 5964126.

Hong Kong Office: 27th Floor, Two Exchange Square. Telephone: (852) 521 0551. Telex: HX 86230. Fax: (852) 845 2125; (852) 845 9079.

Tokyo, Japan Office: Mitsui Asahi Building, 1-1 Kanda Sudacho, Chiyoda-ku, 101. Telephone: (3) 3258 5700. Telex: 2227208. Fax: (3) 3258 5708.

New York, New York Office: 126 East 56th Street, 10022-3613. Telephone: (212) 888-1112. Fax: (212) 888-1170; (212) 832-2021; (212) 832 0075 (G-4).

General and International Law Practice.

RESIDENT PARTNERS

P.J.L. Kett	**A.A. Maggiar**
P.L.R. Deckers	**P.J.W. Boys**

SOCIÉTÉ JURIDIQUE INTERNATIONALE

(Associated Office of Stikeman, Elliott)

39, RUE FRANÇOIS IER
75008 PARIS, FRANCE
Telephone: 33-1-40-73-82-00
Fax: 33-1-40-73-82-10

Montreal, Quebec Office: 1155 René-Lévesque Boulevard West, 40th Floor, H3B 3V2. Telephone: 514-397-3000. Fax: 514-397-3222.

Toronto, Ontario Office: Commerce Court West, 53rd Floor, M5L 1B9. Telephone: 416-869-5500. Fax: 416-947-0866.

Ottawa, Ontario Office: 50 O'Connor Street, Suite 914, K1P 6L2. Telephone: 613-234-4555. Fax: 613-230-8877.

Calgary, Alberta Office: 855 - 2nd Street S.W., 1500 Bankers Hall, T2P 4J7. Telephone: 403-266-9000. Fax: 403-266-9034.

Vancouver, British Columbia Office: 666 Burrard Street, Suite 1700, Park Place, V6C 2X8. Telephone: 604-631-1300. Fax: 604-681-1825.

New York, New York Office: 126 East 56th Street, 11th Floor, Tower 56, 10022. Telephone: 212-371-8855. Fax: 212-371-7087.

Washington, D.C. Office: 1300 I Street, N.W., Suite 1210 West, 20005-3314. Telephone: 202-326-7555. Fax: 202-326-7557.

London, England Office: Cottons Centre, Cottons Lane, SE1 2QL. Telephone: 71-378-0880. Fax: 71-378-0344.

Budapest, Hungary Office: Andrássy út 100, II Floor, H-1062. Telephone: 36-1-269-1790. Fax: 36-1-269-0655.

Hong Kong Office: 29 Queen's Road Central, Suite 1102, China Building. Telephone: 852-2868-9903. Fax: 852-2868-9912.

(This Listing Continued)

Hong Kong: In Association with Shum & Co., 29 Queen's Road Central, Suite 1506, China Building. Telephone: 852-2868-9903. Fax: 852-2868-9912.

Taipei, Taiwan Office: 117 Sec. 3 Min Sheng East Road, 8th Floor. Telephone: 886-2-719-9573. Fax: 886-2-719-4540.

Taxation, Corporation, Tariff, Insurance, Freight Rates and Marine Law. Trials and General Practice. Labour Law.

PARTNERS

ROBERT COUZIN, born Chicago, Illinois, November 27, 1945; admitted, 1974, Quebec; 1977, Ontario; 1986, Alberta (Not admitted in France). *Education:* Princeton University and University of Chicago (A.B., 1967; A.M., 1968); McGill University (B.C.L., Gold Medalist, 1972). Co-Author: "Business Operations in Canada," published by Tax Management Inc. Lecturer in Taxation, McGill University Faculty of Law, 1974-1977; Faculty of Law, University of Toronto, 1987-1989. Governor, Canadian Tax Foundation, 1987-1990. General Editor, Canada Tax Service. Vice-Chairman, Fair Tax Commission of Canada, 1991—. *Member:* Canadian Bar Association; Law Society of Upper Canada; International Fiscal Association (President, Canada, 1992-1993). (Also at Montreal Office).

(For biographical data on other personnel, see Professional Biographies at Montreal, Quebec, Toronto, Ontario, Ottawa, Ontario, Calgary, Alberta, Vancouver, British Columbia, New York, New York, Washington, D.C., London, England, Budapest, Hungary, Hong Kong and Taipei, Taiwan)

SOKOLOW, DUNAUD, MERCADIER & CARRERAS

100 BOULEVARD MALESHERBES
75017 PARIS, FRANCE
Telephone: (33-1) 44 29 11 00
Telecopier: (33-1) 44 40 45 08; (1) 44 40 45 09

New York, New York Office: 1675 Broadway, 25th Floor, 10019. Telephone: 19 1 212 484 39 00. Telecopier: 19 1 212 484 39 90.

International and French General Practice. Corporate. Securities, Mergers and Acquisitions, Privatization, Project Finance, Media Law, Telecommunications and Competition Law (French and EEC). Litigation and Arbitration. Authorized to plead before French and European Courts.

PARTNERS

NICOLAS SOKOLOW, born Barranquilla, Colombia, December 9, 1949; admitted, 1977, Paris France. *Education:* Institut D'Etudes Politiques de Paris (Diplôme Economie et Finances, 1971); Faculté de Paris (Licencié en Droit des Affaires, 1972); Institut des Langues Orientales de Paris (Diplôme Russe, 1972); University of Michigan (Master of Comparative Law, 1973). *LANGUAGES:* French, English, Russian and Spanish.

PATRICK DUNAUD, born September 22, 1955; admitted, 1980, Paris, (Conseil Juridique, 1983-1986). *Education:* Institut d'Études Politiques, University of Bordeaux (Diploma, 1976); Faculté de Droit, University of Bordeaux (D.E.A., droit International et de droit Communautaire, 1978). *Member:* International Bar Association, Association Française d'Etude de la Concurrence; International Law Association. *LANGUAGES:* French and English.

JEAN-FRANCOIS MERCADIER, born Paris, France, August 23, 1956; admitted, 1985, Paris, France. *Education:* Lycée Janson De Sailly (B.A., 1975); Universite de Paris I, Pantheon-Sorbonne (Maîtrise en Droit Public, 1979; Maîtrise en Droit Des Affaires, 1980; Diplôme d'Etudes Supérieures Spécialisées en Droit Commercial International, 1981). *LANGUAGES:* French and English.

PATRICIA ELSEN, born Luxembourg, April 25, 1958; admitted, 1987, Paris. *Education:* Université Paris I Panthéon-Sorbonne, Paris (Maîtrise de Droit des Affaires, 1981; DEA de Droit des Affaires et de Droit Economique, 1982; Maîtrise de Gestion, 1982). *LANGUAGES:* French, English and German.

JEAN-MICHEL ISCOVICI, born November 8, 1954; admitted, 1986, Paris, France. *Education:* University of Paris II (Licence en droit public, 1976; Maîtrise en droit européen, 1977); Institut d'Etudes politiques of Paris (Section Service Public, 1977). *LANGUAGES:* French.

STEPHEN MONTRAVERS, born September 12, 1963; admitted, 1989, Paris. *Education:* Faculté de Droit, University of Dijon (Maîtrise en droit, 1986; D.E.S.S., droit fiscal, 1988). *LANGUAGES:* French.

(This Listing Continued)

SOKOLOW, DUNAUD, MERCADIER & CARRERAS,
Paris—Continued

NEIL ROBERTSON, born Nairobi, Kenya, March 25, 1962; admitted, 1987, England; 1992, Paris, France. *Education:* University of Durham; Guildford College of Law. *Member:* Law Society of England and Wales; Franco-British Lawyers Association; Law Society Solicitors' European Group. *LANGUAGES:* English, French, Spanish.

OF COUNSEL

HUBERT DE MAHUET, born Arraye, France, August 26, 1933; admitted, 1973, Paris, France. *Education:* University of Nancy (Docteur en Droit, 1958). *LANGUAGES:* French, English and German.

JEAN-CHRISTOPHE GALLOUX, born Beaune, France, March 11, 1959; admitted, 1984, Dijon, France. *Education:* University of Dijon (Maîtrise de Droit Privé, 1983); European University Institute, Florence (LL.M., European and Comparative Law, 1988); University of Bordeaux (Doctorat en droit et habilitation, 1988); Paris, Agrégation de Droit Privé (1991). Professor, Law Faculty, University of Reims. *Member:* International Association for the Protection of Industrial Property; Organisation de l'Industrie Biotechnologique; Association Internationale pour le Droit des Biotechnologies. *LANGUAGES:* French and English.

RESIDENT ASSOCIATES

SANDRA BENOIT, born Paris, October 1, 1968; admitted, 1995, France. *Education:* University of Paris II (DEA de Droit Privé Gén éal, 1991). *LANGUAGES:* French, English and Spanish.

HERVÉ CASTELNAU, born Paris, France, December 27, 1963. *Education:* University of Paris II, Assas (Maîtrise en Droit des Affaires/Fiscal, 1985); University of Paris I, Panthéon-Sorbonne (D.E.A., Droit Communautaire et Européen, 1986); Institut d'Etudes Politiques de Paris, 1988; New York University (L.L.M., Corporate Law, 1990). *LANGUAGES:* French, English, Spanish and Portuguese.

CÉCILE DEBIN, born Courbevoie, France, November 26, 1966; admitted, 1990, France. *Education:* University of Paris II ASSAS (Maîtrise en Droit Privé, 1988; DEA, de Droit Privé, 1989). *LANGUAGES:* French, English, Russian and Hungarian.

PASCALE GALLIEN, born Condrieu, France, December 3, 1962; admitted, 1990, France. *Education:* University of Paris, Panthéon-Sorbonne (D.E.A., Private International Law; D.E.A., Commercial Law; Maîtrise, Commercial Law). *LANGUAGES:* French and English.

AGNÈS GOREUX, born Boulogne, France, February 18, 1968. *Education:* University of Paris X Nanterre (Maîtrise Droit des Affaires 1991, DESS de Droit Immobilier, Paris I Sorbonne, 1992). *LANGUAGES:* French and English.

ALAIN MALEK, born Châlons s/Marne, France, December 1, 1965. *Education:* University of Paris II ASSA (Maîtrise en Droit des Affaires et Fiscalitédes Enterprises, 1990; DEA de Droit des Affaires et Droit Economique, 1992); Institut d'Etudes Politiques de Paris (DEA de Science Politiques, 1993-1995). *LANGUAGES:* French, Arabic and English.

XAVIER NYSSEN, born November 23, 1961; admitted, 1992, Brussels; 1993, Paris, France. *Education:* University of Liège, Belgium (License en droit, 1986); University of Gent (License spéciale en droit européen). *LANGUAGES:* French, English, Dutch and French.

ONDREJ PETERKA, born Prague, Czechoslovakia, August 2, 1969; admitted, 1995, Paris. *Education:* University of Reims (Maîtrise en Droit Privé, 1991); University of Paris I (DEA de Droit International Privé et de Commerce International, 1992); University of Prague (International Law, 1994). *LANGUAGES:* French, Czech and English.

(For biographical data of the New York personnel, see biographies at New York, N.Y.)

SONIER & ASSOCIES

Established in 1971

69 AVENUE VICTOR HUGO
75116 PARIS, FRANCE
Telephone: (33.1) 45.01.17.17
Fax: (33.1) 45.01.26.65

Corporate, Commercial, Banking, Bankruptcy, International, Real Estate, Intellectual Property, EEC, and Litigation.

(This Listing Continued)

EU508B

MEMBERS OF FIRM

GABRIEL SONIER, born Cannes, France, April 29, 1943; admitted, 1971, Paris, France. *Education:* University of Paris (Licence en Droit; Diplôme d'Etude Supérieures de Droit Privé); Diplôme de l'Institut de Droit Comparé de Paris. Contributing Author: "Revue de Jurisprudence Commerciale." *Member:* Association des Praticiens de Procédure Collective; Association Nationale des Juristes de Banque. *LANGUAGES:* French, English and Spanish.

BERTRAND CHAUCHAT, born Paris, France, April 15, 1951; admitted, 1977, Paris, France. *Education:* University of Paris (Maîtrise en Droit Privé). *Member:* Association des Praticiens de Procédure Collective; Association Nationale des Juristes de Banque. *LANGUAGES:* French and English.

CORINNE BENICHOU, born Boulogne Billancourt, France, September 3, 1965; admitted, 1989, Paris, France. *Education:* University of Paris (Maîtrise spécialité carrières judiciaires; Diplôme d'Etudes Approfondies de Droit Anglais et Nord-Américain des Affaires). *Member:* Association Nationale des Juristes de Banque; Association des Praticiens de Procédure Collective. *LANGUAGES:* French, English and Spanish.

AYMAR DE MAULEON DE BRUYERES, born Revel, France, July 16, 1961; admitted, 1988, Paris, France. *Education:* University of Toulouse (Maîtrise Droit des Affaires); University of Aix en Provence (Diplôme d'Etudes Supérieures Spécialisées de Droit des Affaires); University of The West Indies, Guyan (Diplôme d'Etudes Approfondies d'Economie Politique dans Les Caraibes). *LANGUAGES:* French and English.

LAURE MICHEL, born Boulogne Billancourt, France, October 2, 1959; admitted, 1985, Paris, France. *Education:* University of Paris (Maitrise spécialité carrieres judiciaires; Diplome d'Etudes supérieures spécialisées de droit et pratique des contrats internationaux). *LANGUAGES:* French, English and Italian.

GUILHEM BREMOND, born Béziers, France, January 5, 1968; admitted, 1994, Paris. *Education:* Ecole Supérieure des Sciences Economiques el Commerciales, ESSEC (1990) (Master of Business Administration); University of Paris, La Sorbonne (Maîtrise en droit des affaires internationales). *LANGUAGES:* French, English, Portugese and German.

SOULIER, REINHARD, AZÉMA & ASSOCIÉS

Established in 1960

10, RUE CLÉMENT MAROT
75008 PARIS, FRANCE
Telephone: (1) 44.43.80.55
Telefax: (1) 40.70.05.43

Lyon, France Office: 51, Avenue Maréchal Foch, 69006. Telephone: 72.82.20.80. Telefax: 72.82.20.90.

General French and International Law Practice, Advertising, Anti-trust, Arbitration, Banking, Bankruptcy, Civil, Communications and Entertainment, Competition, Construction, Consumer Protection, Corporate, Criminal, Customs and Excise, Distributorship, Agency and Franchise, EEC, Environmental, Food and Drug Regulations, Foreign Investments and Exchange Control Regulations, Health, Hospital and Malpractice, Industrial Relations and Labor, Insurance, Licensing, Litigation, Patent, Trademark and Copyright, Press, Product Liability, Property, Real Estate, Rent and Lease, Taxation and Trade Regulations.

FIRM PROFILE: Founded in 1960, the law firm of Soulier, Reinhard, Azéma & Associés presently consists of fourteen attorneys, including five partners, with offices in Paris and Lyon. The firm specializes in French and international commercial matters, as well as all aspects of a traditional civil practice.

ANDRÉ SOULIER, born Lyon, France, October 18, 1933; admitted, 1959, Lyon; 1989, Paris. *Education:* University of Lyon (Licence en Droit, 1956; Diplôme de l'Institut d'Etudes Politiques, 1956; Diplôme d'Etudes Supérieures d'Economie Politique, 1957). Co-Author: "International Environmental Law & Regulation," Chapter on France, Butterworth, 1991. Assistant Professor, Business Law, Institut de Préparation aux Affaires, University of Lyon, 1964-1966. Member, Comité Français de l'Arbitrage. *Member:* National Association of Lawyers (ANA); American Chamber of Commerce in France. *LANGUAGES:* French and English. *PRACTICE AREAS:* Commercial and Criminal Litigation and Arbitration.

(This Listing Continued)

JEAN-LUC SOULIER, born Lyon, France, March 29, 1955; admitted, 1977, Lyon; 1989, Paris. *Education:* University of Lyon (Licence en Droit, 1976; Maîtrise en Droit, 1977); University of Michigan (LL.M., 1980). Associate, Sullivan & Cromwell, New York, 1980-1981. Co-Author: "Guide Juridique et Fiscal de l'Exportateur," C.F.C.E., 1987; "International Environmental Law & Regulation," Chapter on France, Butterworth, 1991; "Creating and Structuring International Joint Ventures in France," International Business Lawyer, 1991. Author: "Les Instruments de l'Internationalisation Financière en Europe dans la Perspective du Marché Unique," C.J.F.E., 1988; "Le Marché Intérieur de 1992 : les Aspects Juridiques de la Coopération à Caractère Technique et Industriel : Contrats de Recherche et de Développement, Contrats de Spécialisation, de Savoir-faire," C.J.F.E., 1988. Professor, International Business Law, 1985-1989, and European Community Law, 1987-1991, University of Lyon. *Member:* American Chamber of Commerce in France; International Bar Association; European Lawyers' Union. *LANGUAGES:* French and English. *PRACTICE AREAS:* International Business Law; European Community Law.

YVES REINHARD, born Lyon, France, February 20, 1947; admitted, 1988, Lyon; 1989, Paris. *Education:* University of Lyon (LL.B., 1969; Awarded LL.D., 1974). Awarded Agrégé des Facultés de Droit (Professor of Law), 1978. Author: "L'acte du Salarié et la Responsabilité Pénale du chef d'entreprise," 1974; "Droit Commercial," 1990. Contributor: Revue Trimestrielle de droit commercial et de droit économique, chronique des sociétés par actions, 1986—. Professor of Commercial Law, 1977—. Lectured on International Law: University of Yaounde, Cameroon, 1971-1972; University of Rabat, Morocco, 1978-1979; University of Minneapolis, U.S.A., 1982. Honorary Director of the Institute of Business Law, University of Lyon. *Member:* A.I.P.P.I. *LANGUAGES:* French and English. *PRACTICE AREAS:* Corporate Law.

JACQUES AZEMA, born Lyon, France, August 20, 1941; admitted, 1990, Lyon and Paris. *Education:* University of Lyon (LL.B., 1963; LL.D., 1968). Awarded Agrégé des Facultés de Droit (Professor of Law), 1969. Author: "La Durée des contrats successifs," LGDJ 1969; "Le Droit Francais de la Concurrence," PUF Coll. Thémis 2ème édition 1989; "Le Droit Pénal de la Pharmacie," LITEC 2ème édition 1990; "Le Droit de la Propriété Industrielle," LAMY Com. Contributor: "Chronique de Droit de la Concurrence," J.C.P. 1982—; "Chroniques de Propriété Industrielle," (Revue Trimestrielle de Droit Commercial de Droit Economique, 1972—). Professor of Commercial Law, University of Lyon, 1969—. Director, Paul Roubier Center. Member, Commission de la Concurrence, 1983-1986. Member, Conseil de la Concurrence, 1987-1990. Member, Conseil Supérieur de la Propriété Industrielle, 1986—. *Member:* A.I.P.P.I. (President, French Group, 1986-1989; Honorary President, 1990—). *LANGUAGES:* French, Spanish and English. *PRACTICE AREAS:* Intellectual Property Law; Competition Law.

GÉRARD CHANU, born Montbéliard, France, December 11, 1956; admitted, 1995, Lyon. *Education:* University of Lyon (Licence en droit, 1979; Maîtrise en droit, 1980; Diplôme d'Etudes Supérieures Supécialisées en Droit des Affaires et Fiscalité, 1982; Diplôme de Juriste-Coneil d'Entreprises, 1982). Legal Counsel of companies listed on the Paris Stock Exchange. *LANGUAGES:* French, English and Spanish. *PRACTICE AREAS:* Security; Corporate Law; Tax Law; High Technology and software issues; International Trade.

CONSULTANTS

CHRISTIAN GABOLDE, born Lons-le-Saunier, France, September 19, 1924; admitted, 1989, Lyon; 1989, Paris. *Education:* University of Paris (Lauréat, 1945; Docteur en Droit, 1952; Licence de Lettres, 1946; Diplôme de l'Ecole Libre des Sciences Politiques, 1946); Ecole Nationale d'Administration (1946-1948). Author: "L'Urgence en Droit Administratif," 1952; "Les Etablissements dangereux, incommodes et insalubres," 1951; "Les Installations Classées pour la protection de l'Environnement," 1978; "La Procédure des Tribunaux Administratifs et des Cours Administratives d'Appel," 1988. Co-Author: "International Environmental Law & Regulation," Chapter on France, Butterworth, 1991. Contributor: Jurisclasseur Administratif, Encyclopédie DALLOZ. Breveté du Centre des Hautes Etudes Administratives, 1959. Président: Administrative Court of Caen, 1968; Administrative Court of Lyon, 1977-1982. Member of the Conseil d'Etat, 1982-1988. *LANGUAGES:* French and Spanish. *PRACTICE AREAS:* Administrative Law.

LAURENT MICHAUX, born Beaujeu, France, March 19, 1921. *Education:* Ecole de Notariat de Lyon (Notaire, 1947). *LANGUAGES:* French. *PRACTICE AREAS:* Property Law; Real Estate Law; Wills.

(This Listing Continued)

ASSOCIATES

MARC MICHEL, born Lyon, France, January 30, 1952; admitted, 1993, Lyon. *Education:* Maîtrise en droit privé, 1976; Certificat d'études supérieures de droit du travail et de la sécurité sociale, 1976; Diplômé de l'Ecole Nationale des Impôts, 1978. Senior French Tax Inspector, 1988-1992. *LANGUAGES:* French, English and Spanish. *PRACTICE AREAS:* Tax Law; Corporate Law.

NANCY COSSON, born Toulon, France, April 15, 1966; admitted, 1990, Paris. *Education:* University of Paris II (Licence en Droit, 1986: Maîtrise en Droit, 1987, D.E.A. de Droit Privé, 1988). *LANGUAGES:* French and English. *PRACTICE AREAS:* Litigation.

Languages: French, English, German and Spanish

(For Biographical Data on all Firm Personnel, see Professional Biographies at Lyon, France).

LAW OFFICES OF JOAN SQUIRES-LIND

6 RUE DU FOIN
75003 PARIS, FRANCE
Telephone: (33-1) 44 59 82 57; 44 59 82 58
Facsimile: (33-1) 44 59 82 69
Compu Serve: 100125,103

General and International Practice. Corporate, Commercial, Litigation, Arbitration, Business Immigration, Intellectual and Artistic Property.

JOAN SQUIRES-LIND, born Berkeley, California, May 2, 1941; admitted, 1978, New York; 1988, France, as Conseil Juridique; 1990, U.S. Supreme Court; 1992, France, as Avocat. *Education:* Stanford University (B.A., 1962, Special Honors in Humanities); Graduate Program in Communications (1969-1971); Cornell University (J.D., 1977). Nathan Burkan Copyright Prize, 1977. Thaler & Thaler, Ithaca, New York, Associate, 1977-1980 and Partner, 1980-1986. Private practice, Paris, 1986—. Member, Panel of Arbitrators, American Arbitration Association. *Member:* American, International and New York State Bar Associations; American Immigration Lawyers Association; Association of the Bar of the City of New York; Computer Law Association. *LANGUAGES:* English and French. *PRACTICE AREAS:* Corporate; International Business.

STEHLIN & ASSOCIES

Established in 1989

10, AVENUE DE MESSINE
75008 PARIS, FRANCE
Telephone: (33-1) 42.89.53.33
Telecopier: (33-1) 42.89.53.89

Corporate, Mergers and Acquisitions, Tax, Commercial, Contract, Financial, Banking, Brokerage, Securities, Civil, European, Intellectual Property, International, Labor, Litigation, Pharmaceutical and Environmental Law.

MEMBERS OF FIRM

MARC PIERRE STEHLIN, born Washington, D.C., June 27, 1954; admitted, 1977, Paris; 1979, New York. *Education:* University of Paris (Maîtrise en Droit des Affaires, 1975; D.E.A. Droit Européen, 1977); Columbia University (LL.M., 1978). *Member:* New York State and Paris Bar Associations. *LANGUAGES:* French, English and German. *PRACTICE AREAS:* International Transactions; Corporate Law; Mergers and Acquisitions; Banking Law; European Law.

JACQUES BARROT, born Yssingeaux, France, February 3, 1937; admitted, 1969, Paris. *Education:* University of Paris (Licence en Droit; D.E.S. en Sociologie; Diplôme I.E.P.). Mayor of Yssingeaux. Member, National Assembly. President of the Conseil Général de la Haute Loire. *LANGUAGES:* French and English. *PRACTICE AREAS:* European Law; Pharmaceutical Law.

ARMELLE KWIATKOWSKI-MAÎTRE, born Montbard, France, May 24, 1963; admitted, 1986, Paris. *Education:* University of Paris II, Assas (Maîtrise en Droit des Affaires, 1984); University of Paris I, Pantheon-Sorbonne (D.E.A. Droit des Affaires, 1985). *LANGUAGES:* French and English. *PRACTICE AREAS:* Corporate Law; Mergers and Acquisitions; Corporate Tax; Commercial Law.

ANNICK VISCHEL-KANTOROWICZ, born Mulhouse, France, July 28, 1957; admitted, 1987, France. *Education:* Universite Dijon (D.E.C.S., 1979; Maîtrise en Droit, 1980; D.E.S.S. Droit Fiscal, 1981). *LAN-*

(This Listing Continued)

STEHLIN & ASSOCIES, Paris—Continued

GUAGES: French and English. **PRACTICE AREAS:** Corporate Tax; Individual Tax Planning; International Tax.

CLAUDE MERKIN, born Paris, France, September 1, 1945; admitted, 1990, Paris. *Education:* University of Paris (Docteur en Droit, Honorable Mention, 1971). Assistant Professor, University of Paris II, 1971-1990. General Counsel, Paris Stock Exchange, 1972-1989. Consulting Activities for Foreign Exchanges, Mauritius Island, Tunisia, Ukraine and Lithuania, 1986-1988, 1992—. *LANGUAGES:* French and English. *PRACTICE AREAS:* Financial Institutions Law; Securities Law; Brokerage Law; Banking Regulations; Commercial Law.

ASSOCIATES

CATHERINE BROUSSOT-MORIN, born Angers, France, December 3, 1963; admitted, 1988, Paris. *Education:* University of Paris II (D.E.A. de Droit des Affaires, 1986; D.E.A. de Droit Public, 1986). *LANGUAGES:* French and English. *PRACTICE AREAS:* Labor Law; Litigation; Corporate Law; Intellectual Property.

FRÉDÉRIC LECOMTE, born Tours, France, April 15, 1963; admitted, 1992, France. *Education:* Université de Tours (Maîtrise de Droit privé Mention Commerce International; D.E.S.S., du Commerce Extérieur); Diplôme du Centre de Droit du Commerce International de Tours. *LANGUAGES:* French and English. *PRACTICE AREAS:* Commercial Law; Banking Law; Environmental Law.

RÉMY WILNER, born Paris, France, March 3, 1960; admitted, 1987, Paris; 1993, New York. *Education:* University of Paris X (Maîtrise en Droit des Affaires, 1982); University of Paris I (D.E.A. Droit Anglo et Nord-Americain des Affaires, 1983); New York University (M.C.J., 1988). *LANGUAGES:* French and English. *PRACTICE AREAS:* Contract Law; Litigation; International Transactions.

BEATRICE BENFREDJ, born Nice, France, 1966; admitted, 1989, Paris. *Education:* University of Paris I Panthéon (Maîtrise en Droit des Affaires). *LANGUAGES:* French and English. *PRACTICE AREAS:* Commercial Law; Financial Law; Civil Law; Litigation.

LAURENT RIBES, born Neuilly-sur-Seine, France, June, 1964; admitted, 1994, Paris. *Education:* Ecole Spéciale des Travaux Publics (Civil Engineer); University of La Sorbonne (Licence Economie d'Entreprise); ESSEC Management School (Diplôme de l'ESSEC). *LANGUAGES:* French and English. *PRACTICE AREAS:* Corporate Tax; Individual Tax; International Tax; V.A.T.; Real Estate Taxation Law; Tax Planning.

LEGAL SUPPORT PERSONNEL

MANUELLA BARRAILLER, born Mont-de-Marsan, France, August 1, 1954. *Education:* Ecole des Secretaires de Direction (B.T.S.S.); University of Paris I (D.E.U.G. Droit des Affaires). (Legal Secretary). *LANGUAGES:* French and English.

STIBBE SIMONT MONAHAN DUHOT

154 RUE DE L'UNIVERSITÉ
75007 PARIS, FRANCE
Telephone: 1-40 62 20 00
Telex: 204 298 F MONALAS
Telecopier: 1-40 62 20 62

Amsterdam, The Netherlands Office: 'Stibbe Toren' Strawinskylaan 200l, P.O. Box 75640, 1070 AP. Telephone: (20) 546 06 06. Telefax: (20) 546 01 23. Telex: 16414.

Brussels, Belgium Office: Rue Henri Wafelaerts, 47-51, B-1060. Telephone: (32-2) 533 52 11. Telecopier: (32-2) 533 5212. Telex: 24519.

London, England Office: 66 Gresham Street, EC2V 7NH. Telephone: (44 171) 600-4400. Telecopier: (44 171) 600-4411.

New York, New York: 335 Madison Avenue, 10017. Telephone: (1-212) 972 40 00. Telecopier: (1-212) 972 49 29.

General French and International Practice, Corporation, Mergers and Acquisitions, Banking and Financing, International Arbitration, Oil and Gas, Taxes, EC Law, Litigation.

FRANÇOIS DUHOT, born Paris, France, April 17, 1934; admitted, 1958, Paris. *Education:* University of Paris (Licence en Droit, 1956; DES, 1958); Columbia Law School (M.C.L., 1958). *LANGUAGES:* French and English.

(This Listing Continued)

PATRICK BEAUVISAGE, born Valenciennes, France, March 26, 1944; admitted, 1968, Paris. *Education:* University of Paris (Licence en Droit, 1967; DES, 1968). *LANGUAGES:* French and English.

YVES SICARD, born Versailles, France, January 18, 1940; admitted, 1966, Paris. *Education:* University of Paris (Licence en Droit, 1964; DES, 1965); Harvard Law School (LL.M., 1969). *LANGUAGES:* French and English.

ALAIN GEORGES, born Lyon, France, May 23, 1946; registered 1974 as Conseil Juridique, Paris; admitted, 1981, Paris. *Education:* Ecole Supérieure des Sciences Economiques et Commerciales (ESSEC, 1968); University of Paris (Licence en Droit, 1969; DES Droit Privé, 1970; Doctorat en Droit, 1974). *Member:* Union des Avocats Européens. *LANGUAGES:* French and English.

DANIEL AUBRY, born Autun, France, September 13, 1939; admitted, 1966, Paris. *Education:* University of Paris (Licence en Droit, 1963; DES, 1967). *LANGUAGES:* French and English.

DOMINIQUE BASDEVANT, born Vichy, France, March 10, 1943; admitted, 1968, Paris. *Education:* Institut d'Etudes Politiques de Paris, 1968; University of Paris (Licence en Droit, 1967; DES, 1968). *LANGUAGES:* French and English.

RICHARD VILANOVA, born Paris, France, October 19, 1950; admitted, 1979, Paris. *Education:* University of Paris (Licence en Droit, 1972; DES, 1973); Harvard Law School (LL.M., 1975). *LANGUAGES:* French and English.

PIERRE J. DESCHEEMAEKER, born Neuilly-sur-Seine, France, January 7, 1947; registered 1973 as Conseil Juridique, Paris; admitted, 1984, Paris. *Education:* University of Paris (Licence en Droit, 1969; DES Droit Privé, 1970; Institut de Droit Comparé, 1971); Cornell Law School (LL.M., 1973). *LANGUAGES:* French and English.

DOMINIQUE BERLIN, born Lyon, France, October 16, 1952; admitted, 1990, Paris. *Education:* Agrégé in Public Law (1985). Author: "Droit Fiscal Communautaire" (European Tax Law), 1988; "Controle Communautaire des Concentrations" (EC Merger Control), 1992. Professor, University of Paris, Paris I Law School. Director of EC Law Graduate Courses. *Member:* French Committee on International Private Law (1982—); C.E.D.E.C.E. (European Law, 1985—). *LANGUAGES:* French and English.

OLIVIER HOEBANX, born Neuilly, France, June 4, 1951; admitted, 1975, France. *Education:* University of Paris (Diplôme d'Etudes Approfondies en Droit de l'Entreprise, 1977). *LANGUAGES:* French and English.

VALERIE BOUAZIZ-TORRON, born Oujda, Morocco, October 8, 1959; admitted, 1986, Paris. *Education:* University of Paris (Maîtrise de Droit International, 1981; DEA de Droit International Public, 1982; DEA de Droit International Privé et du Commerce International, 1983). *LANGUAGES:* French and English.

LAURENT JAEGER, born Paris, France, April 15, 1957; admitted, 1986, Paris; 1987, New York. *Education:* University of Paris (Maîtrise en Droit des Affaires, 1984; DEA de Droit International Privé et du Commerce International, 1985). *LANGUAGES:* French and English.

AGNÈS CLOAREC-MÉRENDON, born Paris, France, September 4, 1954; admitted, 1976, Paris. *Education:* University of Paris (Maîtrise en Droit Privé, 1976); Institut Britannique (1975). *LANGUAGES:* French and English.

LAURENCE PINOT, born Paris, France, April 8, 1961; admitted, 1985, Paris. *Education:* University of Paris (Maîtrise en Droit International, 1982; Maîtrise en Droit des Affaires, 1983; DEA de Droit International Privé et du Commerce International, 1984; DEA de Droit des Affaires, 1985); Harvard Law School (LL.M., 1987). *LANGUAGES:* French and English.

HUGUES CALVET, born Rodez, France, April 13, 1958; admitted, 1992, Paris. *Education:* University of Toulouse (Maîtrise en Droit Privé, 1978; DEA en Droit Privé, 1979); Ecole Nationale de la Magistrature (1981-1983). Appointments: Official, French Ministry of Justice, 1985-1987; Law Clerk (Référendaire), European Court of Justice, 1987-1992. *Member:* Union des Avocats Européens. *LANGUAGES:* French, English and Italian.

MARTIN J.F. IN DE BRAEKT, born Heerlen, The Netherlands, May 31, 1962; admitted, 1988, Amsterdam; 1992, Paris. *Education:* Leyden University (Dutch Law, 1985; Tax Law, 1988). *LANGUAGES:* Dutch, French, English and German.

(This Listing Continued)

OF COUNSEL

OLIVIER DELATTRE, born March 12, 1955; admitted, 1985, Paris. *Education:* University of Paris (DES, 1980). *Member:* International Fiscal Association (I.F.A.); International Bar Association (I.B.A.). *LANGUAGES:* French and English.

YANN FRANCOIS, born Paris, France, November 14, 1947; admitted, 1974, Paris. *Education:* University of Paris (Maîtrise en Droit, 1971); Institute for Comparative Law, Paris, (1971); University of Mainz, Düsseldorf (Special Program of German Legal Studies for Foreign Lawyers, DAAD, 1971-1972); Graduate of higher studies of Business Law, Paris (DES, 1973-1974). *LANGUAGES:* French, German and English.

JEANNE-MARIE HENRIOT BELLARGENT, born Compiegne, France, 1951; admitted, 1973, France. *Education:* University of Paris (Licence en Droit, 1972). *LANGUAGES:* French, German and English.

CAMILLE VILLETTE, born Paris, France, August 3, 1922; admitted, 1985, Paris. *Education:* University of Paris (Licence en Droit). *LANGUAGES:* French and English.

ASSOCIATES

LUCILE AUBERTY JACOLIN, born Paris, France, July 6, 1967; admitted, 1992, Paris. *Education:* University of Paris (Maîtrise Carrières Judiciaires, 1989; DEA de Droit Privé Général, 1990). *LANGUAGES:* French and English.

CORALIE AUGUET, born Paris, France, May 11, 1965; admitted, 1989, Paris. *Education:* Ecole des Hautes Etudes Commerciales (HEC, 1987); University of Paris (Maîtrise en Droit, 1988). *LANGUAGES:* French and English.

EMMANUEL BAUD, born Grenoble, France, July 27, 1967; admitted, 1992, Paris. *Education:* University of Paris (Maîtrise en Droit des Affaires, 1989; DESS de Droit Immobilier et de la Construction, 1990); Cornell University (LL.M., 1993). *LANGUAGES:* French, English and German.

MARIE-HÉLÈNE BENSADOUN, born Paris, France, December 7, 1964; admitted, 1991, Paris; 1992, Madrid. *Education:* University of Madrid (Diploma en Derecho Español, 1987); University of Paris (Maîtrise de Droit Fiscal des Affaires, 1988). *LANGUAGES:* French and Spanish.

CLAIRE BRUNET, born Paris, France, May 12, 1968; (Not admitted in France). *Education:* University of Paris (Maîtrise en Droit Privé, Mention "Droit des Affaires et Fiscalité," 1990; DEA de Droit Social, 1991). *LANGUAGES:* French and English.

JEAN-BAPTISTE CACHERA, born Paris, France, March 5, 1962; admitted, 1992, Paris. *Education:* University of Paris (Maîtrise en Droit des Affaires et Fiscalité, 1984; DESS Juriste d'Affaires International, 1986). *LANGUAGES:* French and English.

DENIS S. CHEMLA, born Paris, France, May 21, 1964; admitted, 1986, Paris; 1991, New York. *Education:* University of Paris (Maîtrise en Droit Privé , 1985; DEA de Droit International, 1986); New York University Law School (LL.M., 1990). *LANGUAGES:* French, English and Italian.

MARTINE DALET, born Algiers, Algeria, September 28, 1959; admitted, 1990, Paris. *Education:* University of Aix Marseille (Maîtrise de Droit International et Droit Communautaire, 1981; Maîtrise en Droit des Affaires, 1982); Institut de Droit des Affaires (DESS Droit des Affaires Internationales, 1983); McGill University, Montreal, Canada (LL.B., B.C.L., 1989). *LANGUAGES:* French and English.

HERVE DIOGO AMENGUAL, born Saint-Rémy, France, May 21, 1965; admitted, 1994, Paris. *Education:* ISIT (Trilingual Translator Diploma, 1988; Trilingual Conference Interpretor Diploma, 1990); University of Paris (Maîtrise en Droit des Affaires, 1989; DEA de Droit Privé, 1991); Ecole des Hautes Etudes Commerciales (HEC, 1992). *LANGUAGES:* French, English and Spanish.

PATRICK DONSIMONI, born Marseille, France, July 12, 1964; admitted, 1992, Paris. *Education:* University of Paris (Maîtrise en Droit des Affaires et Fiscalité, 1987; DESS de Fiscalité des Entreprises, 1988; DESS de Juriste d'Affaires, 1988). *LANGUAGES:* French, English and Spanish.

JUDITH FARGEOT, born Paris, January 1, 1970; (Not admitted in France). *Education:* Ecole des Hautes Etudes Commerciales (HEC, 1992); University of Paris (Maîtrise de Droit des Affaires, 1993; DEA de Droit International Privé, 1994). *LANGUAGES:* French, German and English.

CHRISTEL DE GANAY D'INDY, born Neuilly-sur-Seine, France, February 11, 1963; admitted, 1988, Paris. *Education:* University of Paris

(Maîtrise en Droit, Mention "Carrières Judiciaires," 1985; DEA de Droit Privé, 1986). *LANGUAGES:* French and English.

ETIENNE GENTIL, born Rueil-Malmaison, France, February 3, 1963; admitted, 1988, England as Solicitor of Supreme Court of England and Wales; 1992, Paris. *Education:* University of Paris (Maîtrise en Droit des Affaires, 1984); King's College of London, England (LL.B., 1984). *LANGUAGES:* French, English and German.

JAN B. HEIJMEIJER, born Lugano, Switzerland, February 12, 1964; admitted, 1990, Paris. *Education:* University of Paris (Maîtrise en Droit, 1986; DEA in English and American Business Law, 1987); Columbia University Law School (LL.M., 1991). *LANGUAGES:* French, Dutch and English.

ANNE-LAURE JESTIN, born Suresnes, France, October 3, 1965; admitted, 1991, Paris. *Education:* King's College of London, England (LL.B., 1986); University of Paris (Maîtrise en Droit des Affaires, 1988; DEA de Droit International Privé et du Commerce International, 1989). *LANGUAGES:* French and English.

OLIVIER LÉONARD DE JUVIGNY, born Versailles, France, December 11, 1967; admitted, 1991, Paris. *Education:* University of Paris (Maîtrise en Droit des Affaires, 1990; DESS en Droit des Affaires et de Fiscalité, 1991); Ecole Supérieure des Sciences Economiques et Commerciales (ESSEC, 1992). *LANGUAGES:* French and English.

MARC LAUBREAUX, born Paris, France, July 13, 1962; admitted, 1989, Paris. *Education:* University of Paris (Maîtrise en Droit International et Européen, 1985; DESS de Droit du Commerce International, 1988). *LANGUAGES:* French and English.

MARCO LENZ, born Brussels, Belgium, July 31, 1966; admitted, 1993, Paris. *Education:* University of Strasbourg (Magistàre "Juristes d'affaires franco-allemands," 1989); Hautes Etudes Commerciales (HEC, 1991). *LANGUAGES:* French, German and English.

DENIS MARCHETREAU, born Chateau-Gontier, April 20, 1969; (Not admitted in France). *Education:* University of Paris (Maîtrise en Droit des Affaires et Fiscalité, 1992). *LANGUAGES:* French, English and Spanish.

ANTOINE MARTIN, born Brive, France, September 22, 1962; admitted, 1987, Paris. *Education:* University of Paris (Maîtrise en Droit Privé, 1986; DEA English and American Business Law, 1987); ISA, Institut Supérieur des Affaires (Master, Business Administration, 1990). *LANGUAGES:* French and English.

ALEXANDRA DE LA MARTINIÈRE, born Paris, France, May 11, 1964; admitted, 1990, Paris. *Education:* University of Paris Law School (Maîtrise en Droit, Mention "Carrières Judiciaires," 1987; DEA de Droit Privé, 1988). *LANGUAGES:* French and English.

VALERIE MEIMOUN, born Tunis, Tunisia, August 16, 1966; admitted, 1991, Paris. *Education:* Institut d'Etudes Politiques de Paris, 1988; University of Paris (Maîtrise en Droit des Affaires et Fiscalité , 1989; Maîtrise en Droit International et Européen, 1989; DEA de Droit des Affaires et de l'Economie, 1990). *LANGUAGES:* French, Italian and English.

BENEDICTE MONCELET, born Nantes, France, May 6, 1968; (Not admitted in France). *Education:* University of Nantes (Maîtrise de Droit des Affaires, 1991; DEA de Droit Social, 1992). *LANGUAGES:* French and English.

OLIVIER DU MOTTAY, born Strasbourg, France, May 3, 1969; (Not admitted in France). *Education:* Ecole Supérieure des Sciences Economiques et Commerciales (ESSEC, 1990); University of Paris (Maîtrise en Droit des Affaires, 1992). *LANGUAGES:* French, English and Spanish.

FLORENCE NOVELLA, born Cap-Haitien, Haiti, January 11, 1963; admitted, 1989, Paris. *Education:* University of Paris (Maîtrise en Droit Privé Général, 1985); Institut Supérieur de Gestion (Diploma, 3ème Cycle de Gestion, 1986). *LANGUAGES:* French, English and Spanish.

STEPHAN PAETZOLD, born Saarbrücken, Germany, February 21, 1969; admitted, 1993, Paris. *Education:* University of Paris (Maîtrise en Droit des Affaires et Fiscalité, 1991; DESS de Droit des Affaires et Fiscalité, 1992; Magistère de Juristes d'Affaires, 1992). *LANGUAGES:* French, English and German.

ESTELLE DE LA ROCHEFOUCAULD, born Boulogne, France, January 12, 1968; admitted, 1993, Paris. *Education:* University of Paris (Maîtrise en Droit Privé Général, 1989; DEA de Propriété Littéraire, Artistique et Industrielle, 1992); University of London (Information Technology Law, European Comparative Law, European Internal Market, 1991). *LANGUAGES:* French and English.

(This Listing Continued)

(This Listing Continued)

STIBBE SIMON MONAHAN DUHOT, Paris—Continued

ROBERT E. ROEDER, born North Platte, Nebraska, USA, September 27, 1964; admitted, 1991, New York; 1992, Nebraska; 1992, U.S. District Court, Southern District of New York; 1992, U.S. District Court, Eastern District of New York; 1994, Paris. *Education:* Vassar College (B.A., 1987); Institut d'Etudes Politiques de Paris (C.E.P., 1988); University of Nebraska College of Law (J.D., 1990); University of Paris (DESS Juriste d' Affaires International, 1992). *LANGUAGES:* English and French.

SANDRINE ROUBIN DEVRIENDT, born Paris, France, February 2, 1965; admitted, 1989, Paris. *Education:* University of Paris (Maîtrise en Droit des Affaires et Fiscalité, 1987; Magistère de Juriste d'Affaires, 1988; DESS Droit des Affaires et Fiscalité, 1988). *LANGUAGES:* French and English.

ALEXANDRE STYLIOS, born Paris, France, September 3, 1967; admitted, 1993, Paris. *Education:* University of Paris (Maîtrise de Droit des Affaires et Fiscalité, 1989; DEA de Droit des Affaires et Droit Economique, 1990; DESS de Droit Immobilier et Droit de la Construction, 1991); Institut de Droit Public des Affaires, 1991; Cornell University (LL.M., 1994). *LANGUAGES:* French, Greek and English.

LAURENT SZUSKIN, born Asnières, France, June 23, 1964; admitted, 1989, Paris. *Education:* University of Paris (Maîtrise en Droit des Affaires, 1986; DEA de Droit des Affaires, 1987). *LANGUAGES:* French, English and Italian.

MARIE THÉODORIDÈS, born Bordeaux, France, September 13, 1966; (Not admitted in France). *Education:* University of Bordeaux Law School (Maîtrise en Droit Privé, 1988); Université Libre de Bruxelles, Institut d'Etudes Européennes (Licence Spéciale en Droit Européen, 1990). *LANGUAGES:* French, English and Greek.

JEAN-CHRISTOPHE TRISTANT, born Suresnes, France, June 1, 1963; admitted, 1989, Paris. *Education:* Institut d'Etudes Politiques de Paris (Diploma, 1986); University of Paris (Maîtrise en Droit Privé, 1987; D.E.A. de Droit Communautaire et Européen, 1988). *LANGUAGES:* French, English and German.

HUGUES VALLETTE VIALLARD, born Paris, France, January 6, 1969; admitted, 1993, Paris. *Education:* University of Paris (Maîtrise en Droit Privé, 1990; DEA de Droit Privé Général, 1991; DESS de Droit des Affaires Internationales, 1992). *LANGUAGES:* French and English.

EMMANUEL VARIN, born Saint Lô, France, April 22, 1969; (Not admitted in France). *Education:* University of Paris (Maîtrise en Droit des Affaires et Fiscalité, 1992; DEA de Droits Anglais et Nord-Américain des Affaires, 1993); Ecole des Hautes Etudes Commerciales (HEC, 1992). *LANGUAGES:* French and English.

NICOLAS VIVIEN, born Villeneuve-Saint-Georges, France, December 15, 1961; admitted, 1992, Paris. *Education:* University of Paris (Licence en Droit Public, 1983); Institut d'Etudes Politiques de Paris (Service Public, 1985); University of Paris (DESS Affaires Internationales, 1987); Cornell University (LL.M., 1990). Assistant Adjunct Professor, New York University School of Law, 1991. *Member:* Association Française des Avocats Conseils d'Entreprise. *LANGUAGES:* French and English.

IAN J. STOCK

PARIS, FRANCE

(See Ian J. Stock, Hermeray, France)

International Commercial Practice, with an emphasis on International Acquisitions, Joint Ventures and Licenses in Europe.

SULLIVAN & CROMWELL

8, PLACE VENDÔME
75001 PARIS, FRANCE
Telephone: (011)(331)4450-6000
Telex: 240654
Telecopier: (011)(331)4450-6060

New York City Offices: 125 Broad Street, 10004-2498; Midtown Office: 250 Park Avenue, 10177-0021. Telephone: 212-558-4000. Telex: 62694 (International); 12-7816 (Domestic). Cable Address: "Ladycourt, New

(This Listing Continued)

York". Telecopier: 125 Broad Street 212-558-3588; 250 Park Avenue 212-558-3792.

Washington, D.C. Office: 1701 Pennsylvania Avenue, N.W., 20006-5805. Telephone: 202-956-7500. Telex: 89625. Telecopier: 202-293-6330.

Los Angeles, California Office: 444 South Flower Street, 90071-2901. Telephone: 213-955-8000. Telecopier: 213-683-0457.

London Office: St. Olave's House, 9a Ironmonger Lane, London EC2V 8EY, England. Telephone: (011)(44171)710-6500. Telecopier: (011)(44171)710-6565.

Melbourne, Australia Office: 101 Collins Street, Melbourne, Victoria 300. Telephone: (011)(613)654-1500. Telecopier: (011)(613)654-2422.

Tokyo Office: Gaikokuho Jimu Bengoshi Office of Robert G. DeLaMater, a member of the firm of Sullivan & Cromwell, Tokio Kaijo Building Shinkan, 2-1 Marunouchi, 1-chome Chiyoda-ku, Tokyo 100, Japan. Telephone: (011)(813)3213-6140. Telecopier: (011)(813)3213-6470.

Hong Kong Office: 28th Floor, Nine Queen's Road, Central, Hong Kong. Telephone: (011)(852)826-8688. Telecopier: (011)(852)522-2280.

Not authorized to appear before the French Courts.

PARTNERS IN PARIS

RICHARD G. ASTHALTER, born New York, NY., 1944; admitted, 1973, New York; 1979, Paris. *Education:* Yale (B.A., 1966; J.D., 1971); Oxford (M.Litt., 1968).

DAVID F. MORRISON, born Jeffersonville, IN., 1952; admitted, 1980, New York; 1984, Paris. *Education:* Yale (B.A., 1974); Univ. of California, Los Angeles (J.D., 1978).

EUROPEAN COUNSEL IN PARIS

PIERRE SERVAN-SCHREIBER, born Paris, France, 1955; admitted, 1979, Paris; 1981, New York. *Education:* University Paris I Panthéon-Sorbonne (Maîtrise, C.A.P.A., 1978); Columbia University (LL.M., 1980). Chairman, Club des Avocats France Amérique, 1989—.

ASSOCIATES IN PARIS

ARI ASSAYAG, born Casablanca, Morocco, 1969; admitted, 1995, Paris. *Education:* Lycee Marie-Curie (B.A.C., 1987); University of Paris-Nanterre (Maitrise, 1991; Deja, 1992); University of Reading (UK) (LL.M., 1992); Ecole Superieure de Commerce de Paris (C.A.P.A., 1993).

MICHAL DLOUHY, born Prague, Czechoslovakia, 1961; admitted, 1991, New York (Not admitted in France). *Education:* McGill University (B.A., 1984); Fordham (J.D., 1990).

NANCY C. JACKSON, born Philadelphia, PA., 1958; admitted, 1986, California; 1992, Paris. *Education:* Princeton University (B.A., 1981); University of California, Boalt Hall School of Law (J.D., 1986).

SUSAN SILVERMAN LIAUTAUD, born Oakland, CA., 1962; admitted, 1990, New York (Not admitted in France). *Education:* Stanford University (B.A., 1986; M.A., 1986); Columbia (J.D., 1989).

MATHIAS TURCK, born Saint Germain en Laye, France, 1970; admitted, 1995, Paris. *Education:* Institut D'Etudes Politiques, Paris (Section Economique et Financier, 1991); University of Montpellier (D.E.A., 1992; D.E.S.S. - D.J.C.E., 1993; C.A.P.A., 1994).

DIMITRI NIKOLAKAKOS, born London, Canada, 1963; admitted, 1992, New York (Not admitted in France). *Education:* Univ. of Western Ontario (B.A., 1987); Univ. of Toronto (LL.B., 1991).

JEAN RABY, born Quebec, Canada, 1964; admitted, 1988, New York; 1991, Quebec (Not admitted in France). *Education:* Laval (LL.B., 1986); Cambridge (M.Phil., 1988); Harvard (LL.M., 1989).

(For Biographical Data on all Partners and Associates see Professional Biographies at New York, N.Y.)

THIEFFRY ET ASSOCIÉS

Established in 1977

23 AVENUE HOCHE
75008 PARIS, FRANCE
Telephone: (1) 45.62.45.54
Telex: "THIEFRY 640 689 F"
Telefax: (1) 42.25.80.07

New York, N.Y. Office: 780 Third Avenue, 10017. Telephone: 212-750-0080. Telefax: 212-750-0054.

(This Listing Continued)

Brussels, Belgium Office: 100, Avenue de Tervueren, 1040. Telephone: (2) 733.97.15. Telefax: (2) 733.97.16.

Hong Kong Office: Bank of China Tower, 21st Floor, 1 Garden Road. Telephone: (852) 25 23 4833. Telefax: (852) 25 24 6438.

Shanghai, People's Republic of China Office: Room 1406 Ruijin Building, 205 Maoming Nan Lu, 200020. Telephone: (86-21) 472 79 93; 472 70 96. Fax: (86-21) 472 43 92.

Associated Offices: Shenzhen, People's Republic of China; Beirut, Lebanon; Cairo, Egypt; Jeddah, Saudi Arabia.

Transnational Arbitration, Litigation and Transactions (Acquisitions, Transfers of Technology, Joint Ventures, General Corporate, Tax and Contractual Practice, Environmental and Intellectual Property Law).
Firm engaged in French, European Union and International Law Practice, authorized to appear in the courts of the European Union, France and other European Union Member States, and composed of lawyers admitted in various European Union, United States and other jurisdictions.

JEAN THIEFFRY, born Tournai, Belgium, November 14, 1931; admitted, 1956, Brussels; 1977, Paris. *Education:* Louvain University (Docteur en Droit, 1955). Arbitrator, International Chamber of Commerce. Author: "L'exécution des Sentences Arbitrales - Eléments de Droit Comparé," Revue de l'Arbitrage, No. 4, 1983. Co-author: "La Vente Internationale," C.F.C.E., 1992 (2nd Edition); "L'entreprise face a l'Europe," Dunod, 1989; *Maître de Conferences,* Ecole des Hautes Etudes Commerciales (HEC). *Member:* Commission Internationale de l'Ordre des Avocats du Barreau de Paris; International Bar Association. *LANGUAGES:* French and English.

CHRISTINE LECUYER-THIEFFRY, born Paris, France, August 26, 1954; admitted, 1979, Paris. *Education:* Paris II University (D.E.A. de Droit de la Société Internationale, 1979; Laureate, 1977). Co-Author: "Le Réglement des Litiges Civils et Commerciaux Avec les Etats-Unis," 399 pages, Ed. Jupiter, Paris, 1986; "Negotiating Settlement of Disputes Provisions in International Business Contracts: Recent Developments in Arbitration and Other Processes," 45 Bus. Law., 577 (1990). Arbitrator: American Arbitration Association; International Chamber of Commerce. *Member:* American Bar Association; Société de Législation Comparée. *LANGUAGES:* French and English.

PATRICK THIEFFRY, born Paris, France, October 21, 1955; admitted, 1979, Paris, France; 1983, New York; 1984, Georgia. *Education:* Paris II University (D.E.A. en Economie Européenne et Internationale, 1979; D.E.A. de Droit International Privé et de Droit du Commerce International, 1980). Special Student, Emory University School of Law (1982). Recipient, American Jurisprudence Award. Author: "European Integration and Transnational Litigation," 13 Boston College Int'l and Comp. L.Rev. 339 (1990); "The New EC Merger Control Regulation," 24 Int'l Law, 543 (1990); "Le Réglement des Litiges Civils et Commerciaux avec les Etats-Unis," 399 pages, Ed. Jupiter, Paris 1986; "The E.C.'s Regulation and Control of Waste and the Adoption of Civil Liability," 14 Hastings Int'l & Comp. L.R. 949 (1991). *Member:* American Chamber of Commerce in France; City of New York, New York State and American Bar Associations; State Bar of Georgia; Société de Législation Comparée. Arbitrator, American Arbitration Association. *LANGUAGES:* French and English.

CHANTAL GRANIER, born La Garenne, France, January 11, 1954; admitted, 1980, Paris. *Education:* Paris X University (D.E.A. de Droit des Affaires, 1978; D.E.A. de Droit International, 1979). Co-Author: "La Vente Internationale," C.F.C.E., 2nd ed., 1992. *LANGUAGES:* French and English.

SHEILA O'DONNELL, born Buffalo, New York, U.S.A., August 20, 1959; admitted, 1986, New York; 1992, Paris; 1993, U.S. District Court, Southern District of New York. *Education:* Union College (B.A., 1981); Pace University School of Law (J.D., 1984); Centre Européen Universitaire of Nancy (Diplome d'Etudes Superieures Europeennes, 1985); Legal Trainee, Commission of the European Communities, D.G. IV for Competition (1986). Co-Author: "Arbitration Centers in Europe," Int'l Corp. Law, June 1992. *Member:* New York State and American Bar Associations; Copyright Society of the US; Licensing Executives Society. *LANGUAGES:* English, French and Russian.

VINCENT MERCIER, born Nice, France, May 24, 1960; admitted, 1988, Paris. *Education:* Paris II University (D.E.A. de Droit Privé Général, 1985); Paris I University (D.E.S.S. de Droit du Commerce Exterieur, 1987). *Member:* American Bar Association (Vice Chair, TIPS-International Torts and Insurance Practice Committee, 1991-1992). (Also at Hong Kong and People's Republic of China Offices). *LANGUAGES:* French and English.

ZHAO HUA WANG, born Sichuan, People's Republic of China, August 16, 1963; admitted, 1995, Paris. *Education:* Université of Robert Schuman

(This Listing Continued)

de Strasbourg (D.E.A. de Droit International, 1987; Doctorat en Droit, 1992). *LANGUAGES:* Mandarin Chinese, French and English.

AUGUSTIN ROBERT, born Paris, France, December 8, 1966. *Education:* Institut d'Etudes Politiques de Paris (Diploma of Economics and Finance, 1988); Paris IX University (D.E.S.S. en Gestion des Organismes Bancaires et Financiers, 1989); Paris II University (Maîtrise de Droit Privé, 1990). *LANGUAGES:* French, English and Spanish.

ANNE-CÉLINE JEAN, born Reims, France, February 7, 1967; admitted, 1993, Paris. *Education:* Paris X University (DEA de Droit Privé, 1991). *LANGUAGES:* French, English and German.

LAURENCE BENOIT, born Boulogne, France, July 20, 1969; admitted, 1995, Paris. *Education:* Paris XII University (DESS de Fiscalité Appliquée, 1994); Paris I University (DEA de Droit Privé International et de Droit du Commerce International, 1993); Institut d'Etudes Politiques de Paris (Diploma in Public Administration, 1990). *LANGUAGES:* French, English and German.

FRANCOIS PH. THOMAS

Avocat à la Cour

16, RUE DE NAPLES
75008 PARIS, FRANCE
Telephone: (33/1) 42 94 13 00
Telefax: (33/1) 42 94 14 04

Taxation, Company Law including Mergers and Acquisitions, Foreign Investments, International Contracts, Agency and Distribution, Transfer of Technology, Intellectual Property, Advertising, Travel and Tourism, Entertainment Law, Unfair Competition, Litigation and Arbitration.

FRANCOIS PH. THOMAS, born Saint-Cloud, France, November 19, 1963. *Education:* Collège in Buenos-Aires, Argentina (1974-1978); University of Paris II (Institut de Droit Comparé, 1985; Maîtrise en Droit Public, 1986; Maîtrise en Droit des Affaires, 1986; D.E.A. de Fiscalité, 1988); Ecole Nationale des Impôts (1988). Author: "La qualification des flux financiers, technique d'optimisation fiscale des contrats internationaux," La Revue du Financier, 1992; "La TVA Intra-communautaire au 1er Janvier, 1993 dans l'Ordre Juridique Français: Présentation des Nouveaux Mécanismes," Cahiers Juridiques et Fiscaux de l'Exportation, 1993. Co-Author: "Dealing with Irak and Kuwait," International Corporate Law Review, 1991; "Guide des Sociétés dans la Communauté Économique Européenne," CFCE, 1992; "Le Guide du Propriétaire: Fiscalité," L'information Immobiliére, 1993. *Member:* International Bar Association; Union Internationale des Avocats; Union des Anciens des Impôts; Association des Conseils et Experts Européens du Cinéma et de la Communication Audiovisuelle; Comité Français de l'Arbitrage. *LANGUAGES:* French, English, Spanish and Italian.

THOMAS & ASSOCIÉS

43-47 AVENUE DE LA GRANDE ARMÉE
75116 PARIS, FRANCE
Telephone: (1) 44-17-68-00
Telex: 630 985 F THOMSIL
Telecopier: (1) 44-17-68-68

Brussels, Belgium Office: 66 Avenue Louise, 1050 Bruxelles. Telephone: (2) 511 94 17. Telecopier: (2) 511 70 58.

General French and International Law Practice, in particular, Mergers and Acquisitions, Public Takeovers, Corporate and Commercial Law, Corporate Restructuring, Business Purchases. Litigation and Arbitration. Financial Services and Stock Exchange Regulation; Venture Capital. EEC Law. Entertainment Telecommunications and Media and related Intellectual Property Law. Public and Administrative Law. Environmental and Planning Law. Competition Law. Tax. Private and Public International Law. Trademarks, Distribution, Franchising, Agency. Labour Law. Industrial and Commercial Agreement both National and International. Construction.

FIRM PROFILE: Founded in 1979, Thomas & Associés currently has more than 40 lawyers and is at the forefront of French commercial law firms.

The firm's involvement may be in either contentious or non-contentious matters. The firm has regular involvement in various states of the CIS. Our clients belong to all sectors of the economy. They include French and foreign companies, both private or public.

The firm maintains an extensive network of correspondents in France and

(This Listing Continued)

THOMAS & ASSOCIÉS, Paris—Continued

abroad, including: United Kingdom, Eire, Benelux, West Germany, Switzerland, Italy, Spain, Portugal, Scandinavia, North America, Brazil, French-speaking Africa, Australia, Hong-Kong and Japan.

Overall, the firm sees itself as efficient, competent and quick to respond, with an international outlook, as well as an open and friendly response to clients.

MEMBERS OF FIRM

JEAN-BERNARD THOMAS, born Paris, France, March 1, 1947; admitted, 1971, Paris. *Education:* University of Paris, Faculté de Droit de Paris (Licence en Droit, LL.M.; D.E.S., Postgraduate Degree, Business Law, 1971); Institut de Droit Comparé (Graduate); Institut de Droit des Affaires (Graduate). Former Member of Paris Bar Council, UIA, AIJA. President, French Association of Business Lawyers. *LANGUAGES:* French, English. *PRACTICE AREAS:* Mergers and Acquisitions and Corporate Restructuring; Venture and Development Capital; Contracts and International Trade Law; Banking and Finance; Stock Exchange Regulations; Commercial Arbitration; Corporate Law.

ERIC LAUVAUX, born Paris, France, December 13, 1950; admitted, 1977, Paris. *Education:* Ecole des Hautes Etudes Commerciales, (H.E.C. Graduate, 1971); University of Paris, Faculté de Droit de Paris (Licence en Droit, LL.M., 1974; D.E.S., Postgraduate Degree, Business Law, 1974). *LANGUAGES:* French, English, German. *PRACTICE AREAS:* Communications Law; Intellectual Property Law; Computer Law; Contract Law.

MARY-DAPHNÉ FISHELSON, born Nicosia, Cyprus, February 2, 1949; admitted, 1975, Paris. *Education:* University of Melbourne (B.A., 1972); University of Paris, Faculté de Droit (LL.M., 1973). *Member:* French Labour Law Association; French Maritime Law Association; UIA. *LANGUAGES:* French, English, Russian, Hebrew, German. *PRACTICE AREAS:* Labour Law; Maritime Law; Contracts and International Trade Law; Computer Law.

CHRISTIAN HAUSMANN, born Bergzabern, Germany, June 9, 1946; registered as Conseil Juridique, 1978; admitted, 1986, Paris. *Education:* Tulane University, New Orleans (Political Science, 1968) University Laureate, 1967; License en Droit, 1968; D.E.S. Postgraduate Degree, Administrative Law, 1970; New York University School of Law (MCJ, Master Program, 1972). Fulbright Fellow, 1971. Lecturer, Facultéde Droit et de Sciences Politiques, Strasbourg-DJCE, 1985—. Listed Arbitrator, National Committee, International Arbitration Court of ICC. *LANGUAGES:* French, German, English, Spanish. *PRACTICE AREAS:* Contracts and International Trade Law; Banking and Finance; Corporate Law; Industrial Cooperation Agreements; Commercial Arbitration; Venture and Development Capital; Mergers and Acquisitions.

JANINE FRANCESCHI-BARIANI, born Abidjan, Ivory-Coast, October 20, 1946; admitted, 1976, Paris. *Education:* University of Paris II (Licence en Droit, LL.M., Business Law; D.E.A., Postgraduate Degree, Political Sciences; D.E.S., Postgraduate Degree, State Administration); Institut d'Etudes Politiques, Paris (Graduate, 1969). Former Member, Paris Bar Council. *Member:* National Bar Council. *LANGUAGES:* French, Italian. *PRACTICE AREAS:* Litigation and Arbitration; Cinematographic, Media and Communications Law; Engineering and Construction Contracts; Unfair Competition/Restraint of Trade; Stock Exchange/Financial Services Law.

MONIQUE SENTILLES-DUPONT, born Vic en Bigorre, France, June 30, 1953; admitted, 1978, Toulouse. *Education:* University of Toulouse (Maîtrise de Droit Privé, LL.M., 1977); Faculté Internationale de Droit Comparé, Strasbourg (Graduate). *LANGUAGES:* French, English, Spanish. *PRACTICE AREAS:* Stock Exchange and Finance Law; Mergers and Acquisitions and Corporate Restructuring; Venture and Development Capital; Corporate Law.

MICHEL DE GUILLENCHMIDT, born Paris, France, August 19, 1941; admitted, 1979, Paris. *Education:* Ecole Nationale d'Administration (ENA, 1965-1967); Institute d'Etudes Politiques (Political Science); Facult248 de Droit de Paris (Licence en Droit, LL.M., Public Law and Economy); University of Paris, Sorbonne (Graduate in Russian). Author: Numerous articles published on tax law and public and administrative law in legal and administrative reviews. Professor, Public Law, Taxation, European Community Law, University of Paris V, René Descartes. Former Member of the Conseil de'Etat (Administrative Supreme Court and Legal Adviser to the French Government). *LANGUAGES:* French, Russian and English. *PRACTICE AREAS:* European Community Law; Environmental

(This Listing Continued)

and Planning Law; Tax; Public and Administrative Law (particularly local authority and public contracts law); Russian Law and CIS Law.

FRANÇOIS MIRIKELAM, born Paris, France, April 30, 1958; admitted, 1985, Paris. *Education:* University of Paris II (Maîtrise en Droit, LL.M.; D.E.A., Postgraduate Degree, Business Law, 1983); Institut Supérieur des Affaires (I.S.A., 1984). Lecturer, Hautes Etudes Commerciales, H.E.C. *LANGUAGES:* French, English, German. *PRACTICE AREAS:* Media and Communications; Corporations.

CHRISTOPHE PECNARD, born Paris, France, December 28, 1959; admitted, 1985, Paris. *Education:* University of Paris I (D.E.A., Postgraduate Degree, Business and Economic Law; D.E.A., Postgraduate Degree, International Law). Lecturer, University of Paris X, Nanterre and Sup de Pub Campus. Articles on: Distribution Law (Gazette du Palais, Petites Affiches); Advertising Law (J.C.P. Edition Entreprises, Petites Affiches and Revue de Droit des Affaires Internationales). *LANGUAGES:* French and English. *PRACTICE AREAS:* Distribution; Competition and Consumer Law; Advertising Law; Contract Law.

ASSOCIATES

ALEXANDRA NERI, born Athens, Greece, April 18, 1959; admitted, 1984, Athens; 1992, Paris. *Education:* University of Salonica, Greece (LL.M.); University of Paris I (D.E.A., Postgraduate Degree, Philosophy; LL.M. in Telecommunications); University of Paris II (LL.M. in Criminal Sciences). Lecturer, University of Paris, Sup de Pub Campus. *Member:* Athens Bar Association. *LANGUAGES:* Greek, French, English, Italian and German.

COLETTE SALAMA-HAUSMANN, born Oran, Algeria, November 4, 1945; admitted, 1992, Paris. *Education:* University of Strasbourg (Maîtrise en droit, LL.M., 1968; Diplôme d'Etudes Supérieures en Droit, 1970). *LANGUAGES:* French, English and Spanish.

MARIE-AIMÉE PEYRON, born Alger, Algeria, June 19, 1960; admitted, 1989, Paris. *Education:* University of Paris II (Maîtrise en Droit, LL.M., Private Law, 1983); University of Paris III (Diplôme de l'Institut National des Langues et Civilisations Orientales, Russian, 1981). *LANGUAGES:* French, Russian and English.

PHILIPPE TORRE, born Versailles, France, November 8, 1964; admitted, 1991, Paris. *Education:* University of Panthéon-Assas, Paris II (Maîtrise en Droit, LL.M., Business Law, 1986; D.E.S.S., Postgraduate Degree, Business Law and Tax Law, 1987). Co-Author of Memorandum, Gide-Loyrette-Nouel "Commerce et implantation en Arabie-Saoudite.". *LANGUAGES:* French and English.

MARIE-LOUISE GORRIS, born Paris, France, August 21, 1954; (Not admitted in France). *Education:* University of Paris I (Masters Degree). *LANGUAGES:* French and Italian.

ISABELLE VAUTRIN-BURG, born Nancy, France, October 19, 1964; admitted, 1990, Paris. *Education:* University of Toulouse I (Maîtrise en Droit, LL.M., 1987; D.E.S.S., Postgraduate Degree, Business Law, 1989); University of Paris II (D.E.A., Postgraduate Degree, International Law, 1988). *LANGUAGES:* French and English.

STÉPHANIE MOUQUET-DARMON, born Neuilly sur Seine, France, August 19, 1964; admitted, 1993, Paris. *Education:* University of Paris X, Nanterre (Maîtrise en Droit, LL.M., 1986); University of Montpellier (D.J.C.E., Graduate of Juriste Conseil d'Entreprise, 1987; D.E.S.S., Postgraduate Degree, Business Law, 1987). *LANGUAGES:* French and English.

LAURENT MARTINET, born Paris, France, November 27, 1964; admitted, 1990, Paris. *Education:* University of Paris II, Assas (Maîtrise en Droit, LL.M., Business and Tax Law, 1986; D.E.A., Postgraduate Degree, 1989); Institut d'Etudes Politiques de Paris, Economic and Financial Section (Graduate). *LANGUAGES:* French and English.

CAROLINE LACAZEDIEU, born Mont de Marsan, France, December 4, 1959; registered as Conseil Juridique et Fiscal, 1991; admitted, 1992, Paris. *Education:* University of Toulouse (Maîtrise en Droit Privé, LL.M., Business Law, 1983; D.E.S.S., Postgraduate Degree, Business and Tax Law, 1984). *LANGUAGES:* French and English. *PRACTICE AREAS:* Tax Law.

LISE TIFFANEAU, born Poitiers, France, April 28, 1967; admitted, 1995, Paris. *Education:* University of Poitiers (D.E.S.S., Postgraduate Degree, Communications Law, 1991). *LANGUAGES:* French and English.

(This Listing Continued)

CHRISTOPHER WILDE, born Solihull, United Kingdom, December 25, 1962; admitted, 1989, as Solicitor, England and Wales (Not admitted in France). *Education:* University of London, King's College (LL.B., 1989); University of Paris I (Maîtrise en Droit, LL.M., 1986). *LANGUAGES:* English, French and German. *PRACTICE AREAS:* Mergers and Acquisitions; Venture Capital; Company Law.

NATASCIA RUBINIC, born Casalmaggiore, Italy, October 31, 1966; admitted, 1992, Paris. *Education:* University of Paris X, Nanterre (Maîtrise, LL.M., Business Law, 1989); University of Paris V, René Descartes (D.E.S.S., Postgraduate Degree, International Business Law, 1990). *LANGUAGES:* French, Italian, English, German and Spanish.

OLIVIER SARFATI, born Tunis, Tunisia, May 26, 1964; admitted, 1993, Paris. *Education:* University of Paris I Panthéon-Sorbonne (Maîtrise in Business Law, LL.M., 1990; D.E.A., Postgraduate Degree, Business Law, 1991). *Member:* Association de Droit des Affaires et des Juristes Européen (ADAJE). *LANGUAGES:* French and English.

JEAN-FRANÇOIS POURDIEU, born Paris, France, July 6, 1968; admitted, 1994, Paris. *Education:* Ecole Supérieure des Sciences Economiques et Commerciales (Graduate, 1990); University of Paris II Assas (Maîtrise, Business Law, LL.M., 1991). *LANGUAGES:* French, English and German.

CHRISTOPHE HENIN, born La Rochelle, France, April 18, 1968; admitted, 1994, Paris. *Education:* University of Paris II, Assas (Maîtrise, LL.M.); University of Paris I, Sorbonne (D.E.A., Postgraduate degree in International Private Law and International Business Law). *LANGUAGES:* French, English, German, Spanish.

STÉPHANIE ROHLFING, born Berlin, Deutschland, July 15, 1962; admitted, 1993, Darmstadt (Germany); 1994, Paris. *Education:* University of Paris, Nanterre (D.E.A., Postgraduate degree in Business Law, 1987); University of Frankfurt sur Main (Doctorat in Law, 1989); Ecole Nationale d'Administration (E.N.A., 1990-1991); University of Paris, Pantheon Sorbonne (Doctorat in Competition Law, 1993). *LANGUAGES:* German, French, English.

RAYMOND RUDIO, born Lynchburg, USA, December 14, 1965; admitted, 1991. *Education:* University of Lille II; University of Paris II (Maîtrise LL.M., EEC Law, 1988). *LANGUAGES:* French, English.

CATHERINE VERGNE-MOITRY, born Troyes, France, October 6, 1964; admitted, 1991. *Education:* University of Paris II (D.E.A., Postgraduate degree, International Private Law, 1988; Maîtrise LL.M., 1987; D.E.A., Postgraduate degree, English and American Business Law, 1989). *LANGUAGES:* French, English.

OLIVIER ORTEGA, born Montpellier, France, January 8, 1967; admitted, 1993. *Education:* University of Paris II (Maîtrise LL.M., public Law, 1988; D.E.A., Postgraduate degree, Finance and Tax, 1990; Doctorat, Ph.D. in Finance Law); Institut d'Etudes Politiques, Paris, (Graduate, 1990); London School of Economics (Introduction to English Law, 1989); HEC (Graduate, Hautes Etudes Commerciales). Lecturer, University of Paris II. *LANGUAGES:* French, English.

ISABELLE CAMUS, born Paris, France, July 9, 1961; admitted, 1993. *Education:* University of Paris II (Maîtrise LL.M., Intellectual Property); Business Law Institut; Institut des Hautes Etudes Internationales; European Young Lawyer Program Certificate. *Member:* European Lawyers Association (ELA); International Bar Association; Association des Juristes Franco-Britanniques. *LANGUAGES:* French, English.

BENOÎT PRUVOST, born Talence, France, September 29, 1969; admitted, 1993. *Education:* University of Montpellier I (DESS, Postgraduate degree, Business Law, 1993; Magistère DJCE, Business legal advisor diploma, 1993; CES of distribution law, 1993; Maîtrise LL.M., business law, 1992). *LANGUAGES:* French, English, German.

MAXENCE BLOCH, born Nancy, France, July 22, 1968. *Education:* University of Nancy II (magistère Business Law, 1991; D.E.A., EC Law, 1993); University of Sheffield (Diplôme in English Legal Studies, 1991). Lecturer in Law, University of East Anglia and University of Sheffield. *LANGUAGES:* French, English, German.

LAURENT BAUER, born Paris, France, November 15, 1962. *Education:* University of Paris X (Maitrîse en droit, Business Law); University of Paris II (D.E.S.S., Postgraduate Degree, Intellectual Property Law). *LANGUAGES:* French, English.

ANTOINE JUARISTI, born Paris, France, December 2, 1960; admitted, 1994, Paris. *Education:* University of Paris IV, Paris-Sorbonne (Licence, Arts, 1983, Maîtrise); Institut d'Etudes Politiques de Paris (Gradu-

(This Listing Continued)

ate 1988); University of Paris I, Panthéon-Sorbonne (Maîtrise en Droit, LL.M., Business Law, 1991); Institut de Droit Comparé (Graduate, 1992); University of Paris V René Descartes (DEA, Postgraduate Degree, Comparative Law, 1993). *LANGUAGES:* French, Spanish and English.

MATHIEU HANAUT, born Nice, France, July 17, 1968; admitted, 1995, Paris. *Education:* University of Pantheon-Assas, Paris II (Maîtrise en Droit, LL.M., Business Law, 1991; DESS, Postgraduate Degree Business Law and Tax Law, 1992); Institut de Droit des Affairs (Graduate, 1991);. Lecturer, University of Pantheon-Assas (Paris II). *Member:* Association Droit des Affairs et Fiscalité(A.D.A.F.). *LANGUAGES:* French, English, Spanish.

FREDERIC SAFFROY, born Geneva, Switzerland, February 5, 1969; admitted, 1995, Paris. *Education:* Institut d'Etudes Politiques de Paris, (Economic and Financial Section Graduate, 1991); University of Paris II, Assas (Maîtrise, LL.M., 1992; D.E.A., Postgraduate Degree in EC Law , 1993). *LANGUAGES:* French, English.

HELENA DELABARRE, born Paris, France, February 7, 1969; admitted, 1995, Paris. *Education:* University of Paris X (Maitrise, LL.M., Business Law, 1990); University of Paris I Panthéon-Sorbonne (D.E.A. Postgraduate Degree, Business and Economic Law, 1991). *LANGUAGES:* French, English.

OF COUNSEL

JEAN-CLAUDE BIGNON, born Bais, France, September 18, 1951; admitted, 1992, Paris. *Education:* University of Rennes (Licence en droit, LL.M.; D.E.S.S., Postgraduate degree in Applied Taxation). *LANGUAGES:* French, English. *PRACTICE AREAS:* Business Tax Law; Taxation applicable to Mergers and Acquisitions; Personal Tax Planning; Tax Law in Insurance Sector.

ANNE-MARIE HATCHONDO, born Begles, France, December 30, 1957; admitted, 1982, Paris. *Education:* University of Paris I, Pantheon Sorbonne (D.E.S.S., Postgraduate degree in Foreign Trade); Institute of Political Science (Economics and Finance) in Toulouse. *LANGUAGES:* French, English. *PRACTICE AREAS:* Corporate Tax Law; Personal Tax Planning; Taxation applicable to Mergers and Acquisitions.

THÜMMEL, SCHÜTZE & PARTNER

Established in 1987

46, RUE DE BASSANO
F-75008 PARIS, FRANCE
Telephone: (0033) 1-53 67 50 00
Telefax: (0033) 1-47 20 78 76

Stuttgart, Germany Office: Landhausstraße 90, 70190 Stuttgart. Telephone: (0711) 1667-0, Telefax: (0711) 286 44 66, 2 62 69 10.

Singapore Office: 9, Battery Road, #16-01 Straits Trading Building, Singapore 0104. Telephone: (00 65) 53 53 112. Telefax: (00 65) 53 43 100.

Dresden, Germany Office: Friedrichstraße 33, 01067 Dresden, Telephone: (0351) 496 5302. Telefax: (0351) 496 5346.

Berlin, Germany Office: Lützowstraße 33/36, 10785 Berlin. Telephone: (030) 2 61 11 31. Telefax: (030) 2 61 90 49. Telex: 3 01304.

Frankfurt, Germany Office: Eschersheimer Landshraße 10 60322 Frankfurt. Telephone: (069) 9591350. Telefax: (069) 95913530.

Brussels Office: Avenue des Arts, 41 B-1040 Brussels. Telephone: (0032) 2-512 7846. Telefax: (0032) 2-512 7023.

Firm engaged in International Law Practice, but not authorized to appear before the French Courts or to act as French Advocates and Solicitors.

RESIDENT PARTNER

PROF. DR. JUR. ROLF A. SCHÜTZE, born Castrop-Rauxel, Germany, December 12, 1934; admitted, 1962, Germany. (Not admitted in France).

(For Complete Biographical Data on all Personnel, see Professional Biographies at Stuttgart, Germany).

TREGOUET, PIGOT & ASSOCIES

Established in 1972

16 AVENUE DE FRIEDLAND
75008 PARIS, FRANCE
Telephone: 45.63.81.60
Fax: 45.63.62.70

Commercial Law, Corporate Law, Banking Law, Leasing Contracts, General International Trade Law, Labour Law, Bankruptcy Law, Administrative Law and Litigation.

FIRM PROFILE: The firm was established in 1972 and offers a full range of legal services. The client base is European and North American in scope.

MEMBERS OF FIRM

JACQUES-ALEXANDRE TREGOUET, born Falaise, France, April 21, 1943; admitted, 1967, Paris. *Education:* Faculté de Droit de Paris, DES Droit Privé (1965); DES Droit Public (1966); Institut d'Etudes Politiques de Paris (Diplomé, 1963). *LANGUAGES:* French and English. *PRACTICE AREAS:* Commercial Law; Banking Law; Leasing Contracts; Labour Law; Litigation.

DOMINIQUE PIERRE PIGOT, born St. Mande, France, December 12, 1958; admitted, 1984, Paris. *Education:* Faculté de Droit de Paris I, DESS Droit du Marché Commun (1985); E.E.C., DGIII, (Internal Market, 1984). *LANGUAGES:* French and English. *PRACTICE AREAS:* Banking Law; Leasing Contracts; Bankruptcy Law; Administrative Law; EEC Law; Litigation.

ERIC SEGOND, born Oran, Algerie, December 1, 1961; admitted, 1986, Paris. *Education:* Faculté de Droit de Paris I, DEA Droit Privé (1984). Secrétaire de la Conférence du Stage, 1992. *LANGUAGES:* French and English. *PRACTICE AREAS:* Labour Law; Criminal Law; Litigation.

MARTINE BONSOM-DELUCCA, born Ivry Sur Seine, France, November 13, 1957; admitted, 1987, Paris. *Education:* Faculté de Droit de Paris II, DESS Droit Banques et Finances. Secrétaire de la Conférence du Stage, 1993. *LANGUAGES:* French and English. *PRACTICE AREAS:* Corporate Law; Banking Law; Leasing Contracts; Bankruptcy Law; Litigation.

HABIB GHERARI, born Souk-Abras, Algeria, April 18, 1955; admitted, 1991, Paris. *Education:* University of Paris Law School; DEA Etudes Internationales et Européennes (1981); DESS Droit de l'Energie (1982); Doctorat d'Etat Droit International (1987). Author: "Les organisations régionales africaines" et "la Guerre du Golfe: le dossier d'une crise internationale," 1990-1992. Lecturer, International Economics Law and Investment Law, University of Paris X; Institut d'Etudes Politiques de Paris. *LANGUAGES:* French, English and Arabic. *PRACTICE AREAS:* Labour Law; International Economic Law; Administrative Law; CEE Law; Litigation.

TREMBLAY LAW OFFICES

79 AVENUE DE VILLIERS
75017 PARIS, FRANCE
Telephone: (33) 1 42 27 51 73
Fax: (33) 1 46 22 06 24

Chartres, France Office: 41 rue des Vieux Capucins, B.P. 193, 28004 Chartres Cedex. Telephone: (33) 37 28 59 68. Fax: (33) 37 35 73 72.

Banking, Bankruptcy & Reconstruction, Company, Employment, Commercial Property, Receivership.

RESIDENT ASSOCIATES

ELISABETH DE KREUZNACH, born France, 1965; admitted, 1993, Paris. *Education:* University of Paris X (D.E.A. Business Law, 1989). *LANGUAGES:* French and English.

ISABELLE COUDERC, born France, 1965; admitted, 1989, Paris. *Education:* University of Tours (Maîtrise Private Law, 1986). *LANGUAGES:* French and English.

(For complete biographical data on all personnel, see Professional Biographies at Chartres, France)

TROY & ASSOCIES

147, AVENUE DE MALAKOFF
75116 PARIS, FRANCE
Telephone: (1) 40.67.91.21
Fax: (1) 40.67.17.08

General Practice in French, EEC and International Business Law (Corporate, Tax, Mergers and Acquisitions, Patent and Trademarks, Labor, Finance, Litigation, Arbitration, French and European Economic Community Antitrust, Distribution, Consumer).

FIRM PROFILE: Member of Lawspan International (EEIG) which regroups twelve law firms from Continental Europe. The network consists of Association Gregoire at Brussels, Groenback & Hansen at Randers in Denmark, Roiter Zucker at London, Grossman & Partner at Frankfurt, Dr. Abel & Partner at Schleswig in Germany, Takis G. Kommatas at Athens, Teekens at Leiderdorp in Holland, O'Flynn Exhams & Partners at Dublin, Cera & Cappelletti at Milan, Schiltz & Delaporte at Luxembourg, Artur Reis e Sousa at Lisboa, Carretero at Marbella.

MEMBERS OF FIRM

GEORGES TROY, born Espelette, France, April 24, 1948; admitted, 1983, Paris. *Education:* Aix-en-Provence Law School (Licence, 1970); Paris Law School (DES Droit Privé, 1974; DES Conseil Juridique et Fiscal d'Entreprise, 1976; Doctorat d'Etat de Droit Privé, 1977); École Nationale des Impôts; Expert Comptable Diplômé. *Member:* International Fiscal Association. *LANGUAGES:* French and English. *PRACTICE AREAS:* Mergers and Acquisitions; Corporate Law; Taxation; Corporate Trade Litigation; Corporate Finance.

ROLLAND TROY, born Lafitte, France, May 24, 1939. *Education:* Aix en Provence Law School (Licence, 1961); Paris Law School (DES, Public Law, 1965); École Nationale d'Administration. *LANGUAGES:* French, English and Italian. *PRACTICE AREAS:* Mergers and Acquisitions; Corporate Law; Administrative Law; Labor Law; Building Law.

LAURENT GUILLOU, born Bondy, France, October 12, 1959; admitted, 1988, Paris. *Education:* Paris Law School (Licence, 1982). *LANGUAGES:* French and English. *PRACTICE AREAS:* Litigation; Commercial Law.

ASSOCIATES

RÉMI LANGLOIS, born Montpellier, France, October 12, 1964; admitted, 1991, Paris. *Education:* Montpellier Law School (Maîtrise de Droit de l'Entreprise, 1988); University of Montpellier (DEA Droit des Affaires et des Accords Industriels, 1989); University of Tulane, New Orleans, USA (Master of Law, 1992). *LANGUAGES:* French, English and Spanish. *PRACTICE AREAS:* Litigation; Commercial Law.

NICOLAS JENNEPIN, born Paris, France, September 25, 1964; admitted, 1993, Paris. *Education:* University of Paris I (Maîtrise de Droit, 1987); University of Exeter, United Kingdom (Master of Law, 1988). *LANGUAGES:* French, English and Spanish. *PRACTICE AREAS:* Litigation; Commercial Law.

YVES CLAISSE, born Paris, France, December 6, 1966. *Education:* University of Paris II Assas (Maîtrise de Droit, 1988); Institut d'Etudes Politiques de Paris (Mention: Lauréat, 1989); University of Paris II Assas (DEA de Droit Public, 1990; DEA de Droit Public Interne, 1991). First Secretary, Conference du Stage des Avocats au Conseil d'Etat et à la Cour de Cassation. *LANGUAGES:* French and English. *PRACTICE AREAS:* Administrative Law.

U G G C

(UETTWILLER, GRELON, GOUT, CANAT & ASSOCIES)

Société Civile Professionnelle

68, BOULEVARD DE COURCELLES
75017 PARIS, FRANCE
Telephone: 48.88.89.00
Telefax: 48.88.05.50

Brussels, Belgium Office: U G L D (Uettwiller, Grelon, Lippens, Dekeyser & Associés) 73, avenue Vandendriessche, 1150. Telephone: (32-2) 772.87.50. Fax:(32-2) 772.87.52.

Litigation/Arbitration, Corporate, Commercial Law, Distribution Law, Computer Law, Construction Law, Food and Drug Regulations, Banking and Finance, Tax, EC Law, Representation of Public Bodies, Environmental Law, Cultural Property Law, Intellectual Property, Contract Law (do-

(This Listing Continued)

mestic and international), Labour Law, Employee Benefits, Health Law, Real Estate, Transportation Law, Bankruptcy Law, Teaching Duties, Foreign Law: Belgium, Eastern Europe, French speaking African Countries, Italy, Spain, USA.

FIRM PROFILE: Jean-Jacques Uettwiller, Bernard Grelon, Michel Gout, Jean-François Canat, Alain Ménard et Thierry Monteran have created a law firm, UGGC. With their former associates and clients, UGGC comprises initially 50 persons and will offer all the legal services needed for business. UGGC is developing its international orientation, having an office in Brussels, and has concluded international alliances with Paisner & Co. (U.K.), Mc Dermott, Will & Emery (U.S.A.) and other major law firms.

PARTNERS

JEAN-JACQUES UETTWILLER, born 1945; admitted, 1986, Paris. *Education:* University of Paris X (Civil Law Laureate, 1970; General Private Law Doctorate, 1973). Lecturer, Commercial Law, Ecole Supérieure des Sciences Commerciales Appliqués. General Counsel: Revillon Group, 1975-1982; Bongrain Group, 1982-1986; Berlioz & Co., 1986-1993. *Member:* Brussels Bar Association (Foreign Lawyer); Union Internationale des Avocats; Association Française des Avocats Fiscalistes.

BERNARD GRELON, born 1945; admitted, 1978, Paris. *Education:* University of Paris (Literature Diploma, 1964; Doctorate in Law, 1976; Law Faculties Agrégé, 1980). Lecturer, Commercial Law, University of Paris, 1976-1987. Professeur, Paris-Dauphine University. Author: "Les Entreprises de Services," 1978. Co-Author: "Entreprise et Pouvoir," 1983. Author: "Informatique et Relations de Travail," 1986; "Actualité de la Charte d'Amiens," 1987; "Contrats et Crise du Golfe," Journal de Droit International, 1991. Editor, "Revue Trimestrielle de Droit Commercial et Economique." Editorial Adviser, "Revue Internationale de Droit Economique." *Member:* Association Internationale de Droit Economique; Société de Legislation Comparée; Association H. Capitant; Union Internationale des Avocats; Brussels Bar Association (Foreign Lawyer).

MICHEL GOUT, born 1943; admitted, 1967, Paris. *Education:* University of Paris (Law Degree, 1965); Urbino University, Compared Law Institute (Italian Law Certificate, 1967). Former National President, Union des Jeunes Avocats, 1980-1981. Former Member, Conseil de L'Ordre des Avocats de Paris, 1983-1985. *Member:* Bureau de L'Institut de Droit International des Transports, Rouen; EC Bar Council (Head of French Delegation).

JEAN-FRANCOIS CANAT, born 1947; admitted, 1972, Paris. *Education:* University of Paris X (Masters Degree in Law, 1970; Doctorate in Business Law, 1971). Lecturer, Superior School of Notaries. Arbitrator, Franco-Polish Chamber of Commerce, Warsaw, Poland. *Member:* International Bar Association.

ALAIN MÉNARD, born 1957; admitted, 1982, Paris. *Education:* University of Paris (Masters Degree in Law). Director, Labour Law Section, publication "Droit et Patrimoine." Secretary, Versailles Bar Conference, 1984. *Member:* Young Lawyers Association (President).

THIERRY MONTERAN, born 1953; admitted, 1980, Paris. *Education:* University of Paris I (Masters Degree in Law). *Member:* Franco-Egyptian Chamber of Commerce; Institut Français des Praticiens des Procédures Collectives.

ASSOCIATES

LAURENCE AMIEL, born 1967. *Education:* University of Montreal (Masters Degree in Business Law); University of Paris I (Doctorate in Business and Economic Law, with honors, 1990; Doctorate in English and American Business Law, 1991); CFPA (1991). Lecturer, Labour Law.

NURIA BOVE-ESPINALT, born 1965; admitted, 1989, Barcelona. *Education:* Barcelona University (Law Degree, 1988); Victoria University (International Law Course, 1989); (Masters Degree in International Commerce and Legislation, 1991); University of Paris II (Post-graduate Degree in French Commercial Law, 1993). Spanish Ministry of Foreign Affairs, Official Diploma of Sworn Translator, English/Spanish, 1991. *Member:* Commission des Assises Européennes des Professions Juridiques et Judiciaires.

JEAN-PHILIPPE CROT, born 1963; admitted, 1994, Paris. *Education:* University of Paris II (Masters Degree in Business and Tax Law, 1985); Mc Gill University, Institute of Comparative Studies, Montreal, Canada (LL.M., Masters Degree in International Commercial Law, 1988). Lecturer, Masters Degree of Science and Management, Business Law Option, University of Paris-Dauphine, 1992—.

(This Listing Continued)

EMMANUELLE HELLOT-CINTRACT, born 1966; admitted, 1990, Paris. *Education:* University of Paris X (Doctorate in Labour Law; Magistère in Social Law); Law Practice Certificate (CAPA, 1989).

EDOUARD HELIOT, born 1967. *Education:* University of Paris I, Sorbonne (Masters Degree in Law, Tax and Business Law, 1990). Lecturer, Masters Degree of Science and Management, Business Law Option, University of Paris-Dauphine, 1991—.

VANESSA JAEGER, born 1970. *Education:* University of Paris II-Assas (B.A. in Law, 1990; Masters Degree in Tax and Business Law, with honors, 1991; Doctorate in Business and Economic Law, with honors, 1992).

ANTOINETTE LEGALL, born 1962; admitted, 1988, Paris. *Education:* Nantes University (Masters Degree in Private Law, Legal Careers Option, 1984); Mc Gill University, Montreal, Canada (LL.M., 1986); Law Practice Certificate (CAPA, 1987).

HENRI LARMARAUD, born 1965. *Education:* University of Paris XI-Sceaux (Law Diploma, 1987; B.A. in General Private Law, 1989); University of Paris II-Assas (Masters Degree in Private Law, Tax and Business Law Option, 1991).

PATRICK LARRIVE, born 1965. *Education:* University of Lyon (General Law Degree, 1988; Private Law Degree, 1989; Masters Degree in Business and Tax Law, 1990; Ecole Supérieure Libre des Sciences Commerciales Appliquées ESLSCA Paris (J.D. in Financial Engineering, 1991); University of Paris I-Panthéon Sorbonne (Doctorate in Business and Tax Law). Lecturer, Masters Degree Course in Science and Management, University of Paris-Dauphine, 1992—.

FRANCE LEMAITRE-BASSET, born 1961; admitted, 1985, Paris. *Education:* University of Paris II (Masters Degree in Law, Legal Careers, 1983); Law Practice Certificate (CAPA, 1984).

SOPHIE LEPICARD, born 1966; admitted, 1992, Paris. *Education:* University of Paris IX-Sceaux (Masters Degree in Private Law, Legal Careers Option, with honors, 1989); University of Paris I-Panthéon Sorbonne (Doctorate in Private Law, with honors, 1990); Law Practice Certificate (CAPA, 1991).

ELIZABETH LOGEAIS, born 1957; admitted, 1990, New York; 1993, Paris. *Education:* Rouen University (B.A., Law, with honors, 1978); Paris Political Studies Institute (Diploma, 1980); University of Paris-Panthéon Sorbonne (Doctorate in British and American Business Law, with honors, 1988; Doctorate in International Law in Trade, 1982); New York University (LL.M., Trade Regulation, 1990). Author: "Paramount v. Videobroadcasting," case comment on the unauthorized addition of video ads in recorded video tapes, ESC Entertainment Law Review, 1990. French Correspondent, "Entertainment Law Review." *Member:* Ligue Internationale du Droit de la Concurrence; Licensing Executives Society; International Bar Association; American Bar Association.

JOËLLE MARTEAU-PERETIÉ, born 1962. *Education:* University of Paris X-Nanterre (Masters Degree in Labour Law, 1986; Doctorate in Social and Professional Law, Pshychosociology of Organizations, International Labour Law, 1988).

CLAIRE MAURICE, born 1959; admitted, 1988, Paris. *Education:* University of Paris Sorbonne-Censier (Degree in Modern Literature, 1981); University of Paris I-Panthéon Sorbonne (Masters Degree in International Business Law, 1984; Masters Degree in Business Law, Legal Carrers Option, 1986; Doctorate in Anglo-American Business Law, 1987); Law Practice Certificate (CAPA, 1987).

ARIANE PALIES CHATEAUX, born 1963; admitted, 1992, Paris. *Education:* University of Paris II-Assas (Masters Degree in Private Law, Business Law Option, with honors, 1986; Doctorate in Business and Tax Law, 1987).

DAVID DE PARIENTE, born 1968. *Education:* University of Paris II-Assas (Masters Degree in Tax and Company Law, Company Business Lawyer Magistère). Lecturer, Company Law, University of Paris IX-Dauphine. Author, Report for ACAVI (Association des Cabinets d'Avocats à Vocation Internationale) on changes in the legal profession due to legal needs of companies.

MICHEL PONSARD, born 1962; admitted, 1991, Paris. *Education:* University of Paris V (Doctorate, International Business Lawyer, 1988); University of Brussels (Special European Law Degree, 1990). Author, "Company Law" chapter in *1992, Tomorrow is Europe,* private publishing. *Member:* Association des Juristes d'Affaires Internationales.

(This Listing Continued)

*U G G C (UETTWILLER, GRELON, GOUT, CANAT & ASSOCIES),
Paris—Continued*

JEAN-BAPTISTE SCHROEDER, born 1966; admitted, 1993, Paris. *Education:* University of Paris (Masters Degree in Law and History).

LAETITIA SQUERCIONI, born 1967. *Education:* Montpellier University (Diploma in Private Accounting, 1988; B.A., Private Law, with honors, 1989; Masters Degree in Company Law, with honors, Special Certificate in Distribution Law, with honors, 1990; Company Business Lawyer Diploma, 1991; Doctorate in Business and Company Law, 1991; Company Business Lawyer Magistère, 1991).

PASCAL SQUERCIONI, born 1967; admitted, 1992, Paris. *Education:* University of Paris II-Assas (Law Diploma, 1988; Masters Degree in Law, Business and Tax Law, with honors, 1989; Doctorate in Business Law, 1990); Law Practice Certificate (CAPA, 1991).

MICHEL TURON, born 1961; admitted, 1989, Nice; 1992, Paris. *Education:* University of Paris I-Panthéon Sorbonne (Masters Degree in Business Law; Doctorate in Business and Tax Law). Lecturer, International Tax Law: University of Paris IX-Dauphine; University of Paris II-Assas. Author: "The Post Acquisition Merger: Tax Aspects" (Option Finance); "The Netherlands Tax Regime" (Moci); "Real Estate Investment in France" (Journal de Sophia Antipolis).

SYLVIE WELSCH, born 1959; admitted, 1986, Paris. *Education:* University of Paris XI (Masters Degree in Private Law, Legal Careers Option); University of Paris I (Doctorate in Private Law; Doctorate in Social Law); Law Practice Certificate (CAPA, 1985).

CONSULTANTS

THIERRY DAL FARRA, born 1961; admitted, 1993, Paris. *Education:* Ecole Nationale d' Administration (1987); University of Paris II-Panthéon Assas (Doctorate in Advanced Public Law); Paris Institute of Political Studies (Public Service Diploma). Lecturer, Paris Superior School of Commerce, 1989—. Author: "EC Law Directives in National Litigation Cases," Revue Trimestrielle de Droit Européen, 1992; "Questions of Public Law Today," Masson, 1989. Co-Author with Bernard Stirn and Yves Gaudemet: "The Major Opinions of the State Council," Dalloz.

JEAN MOISSENET, born 1941; admitted, 1989, Paris. *Education:* University of Paris (Law Diploma, 1960; B.A., Law, 1963); Paris Institute of Political Studies (Diploma, 1962). General Counsel, Bureau de Recherches Géologiques et Minieres (BRGM), 1978-1985. Head of Securities and Affiliates Department, Compagnie Générale des Établissements Michelin, 1986-1988.

Languages: French, English, German, Italian, Spanish, Dutch, Japanese and Russian

---

VAISSE LARDIN ET ASSOCIES

Established in 1966

51, AVENUE MONTAIGNE
75008 PARIS, FRANCE
Telephone: (1) 43.59.39.66
Telex: VAISSE 660 862 F
Telecopier: (1) 45.63.78.73

General French and International Law Practice, Advertising and Marketing, Agency and Distributorships, Arbitration, Banking, Bankruptcy and Reorganization, Business Law, European Community Law, Communications and Media, Corporate, Mergers and Acquisitions, Entertainment and the Arts, Intellectual and Industrial Property, Labor, Antitrust and Trade Regulations, Products Liability, Trust and Estates, White Collar Crime, Litigation.

MEMBERS OF FIRM

SAUVEUR VAISSE, born Algiers, France, February 9, 1933; admitted, 1954, Algiers. *Education:* University of Algiers Law School (Licence 1954, Honor); Lauréat des Facultés de Droit (1954); Diplome d'Etudes Supérieures de Droit Privé (1955); Diplome d'Etudes Supérieures de Droit Public (1955); Diplome d'Etudes Supérieures de Droit Romain (1956); Diplome d'Etudes Supérieures d'Histoire du Droit (1956); University of Paris Law School (Doctorat d'Etat en Droit Privé, 1967; Agregation, 1970). Author: "La loi de la majorité dans les Sociétés Anonymes," 1967. Lecturer on Law, Institute of Comparative Law, 1963-1966. Professor, University of Caen Law School, 1966-1973. Professor of Commercial Law, University of Paris X, 1973-1976; University of Paris V, 1976—. Dean of the Institute of Legal

(This Listing Continued)

Proceedings, University of Paris V, 1981-1991. Director of the DESS (Doctorate) of Business Lawyer. Member, Panel of Legal Advisors, Ministry of Justice. 1er Secrétaire de la Conférence du Stage des Avocats á la Cour d'Alger, 1956. *Member:* World Council of I.A.J.L.J.; International Bar Association; Association Droit et Commerce. **LANGUAGES:** French, English and Spanish. **PRACTICE AREAS:** Banking; Bankruptcy; Intellectual Property; Business Law; Litigation; European Community Law; Commercial Law; Commercial Arbitration; White Collar Crime.

MARIE-ODILE LARDIN, born Neufchateau, France, November 20, 1942; admitted, 1965, Paris. *Education:* University of Nancy Law School (Licence, 1964). Secrétaire de la Conférence, Paris, 1967-1968. **LANGUAGES:** French and English. **PRACTICE AREAS:** Company Law; Commercial Law; Bankruptcy; Commercial Mergers and Acquisitions; Business Law; Litigation.

CHRISTIAN BREMOND, born Alfortville, France, October 11, 1951; admitted, 1973, Paris. *Education:* University of Paris Law School (Licence en Droit, 1973); Diplome d'Etudes Supérieures en Droit Privé Général (1975); Diplome d'Etudes Supérieures de Sciences Criminelles (1977, Honor); Lauréat de la Faculté de Droit et Science Politique de Paris XII (1973). Lecturer, International and Commercial Law, University of Paris, 1975-1981. **LANGUAGES:** French, English and Spanish. **PRACTICE AREAS:** Commercial Law; Agency and Distributorship; Consumer Law; Intellectual Property; European Community Law; Computer Law; Litigation.

DANIEL DU PUCH, born Tunis, Tunisia, September 30, 1948; admitted, 1982, Paris. *Education:* University of Paris Law School (Licence en Droit, 1970) Diplome d'Etudes Supérieures de Droit International (1972); Institute of Comparative Law Degree (1970). Lecturer University of Paris Law School, Financial Instruments in International Trade, 1984. **LANGUAGES:** French, English, Spanish and Oriental Arabic. **PRACTICE AREAS:** Banking; Finance; Labor and Employment; Commercial Arbitration; Construction Law; Litigation.

MARIE-AIMÉE BICH, born Neuilly, France, September 12, 1958; admitted, 1983, Paris. *Education:* University of Paris Law School (Maîtrise, 1981). **LANGUAGES:** French and English. **PRACTICE AREAS:** Company Law; Commercial Mergers and Acquisitions; Commercial Property; Litigation.

ANNE VAISSE, born Algiers, France, March 18, 1961; admitted, 1986, Paris. *Education:* University of Paris Law School (Maîtrise, 1983); Diplôme d'Etudes Approfondies de Propriete Litteraire, Artistique et Industrielle (1985). **LANGUAGES:** French, English and Danish. **PRACTICE AREAS:** Intellectual Property; Entertainment and the Arts; Advertising and Marketing; Agency and Distributorship; Consumer Law; Litigation.

HERVÉ CABELI, born Paris, France, August 4, 1960; admitted, 1987, Paris. *Education:* University of Paris Law School (Maîtrise, 1984); Diplôme d'Etudes Approfondies de Droit Comparé et Droits Etrangers (1985); Diplôme d'Etudes Approfondies de Droit Privé (1985). **LANGUAGES:** French and English. **PRACTICE AREAS:** Company Law; Commercial Law; Commercial Mergers and Acquisitions; Business Law; Communications and Media; Litigation.

ASSOCIATES

SOPHIE MERLIN, born Toulouse, France, July 18, 1959; admitted, 1987, Paris. *Education:* University of Paris Law School (Maîtrise 1981); Diplôme d'Etudes Approfondies de Propriété Littéraire, Artistique et Industrielle (1982). **LANGUAGES:** French and English.

SYLVIE MOREL, born Geneva, Switzerland, February 18, 1965; admitted, 1988, Geneva (Not admitted in France). *Education:* University of Geneva Law School (Licence en Droit, 1987); King's College, University of London, Department of Law (LL.M., 1988). **LANGUAGES:** French, English and German.

ANNE BIMAR, born Lille, France, December 4, 1968; admitted, 1994, Paris. *Education:* University of Paris Law School (Maîtrise, 1991; D.E.S.S. Contentieux et Arbitrage, 1993). **LANGUAGES:** French and English.

SANDRA MALICBEGOVIC, born Paris, France, December 28, 1968; admitted, 1992, Paris. *Education:* University of Paris Law School (Magistère de Droit des Affaires et de Fiscalité, 1991; D.E.S.S. de Droit des Affaires et de Fiscalité, 1991). **LANGUAGES:** French, English and Serbo-Croatian.

(This Listing Continued)

OF COUNSEL

GERAUD DE GEOUFFRE DE LA PRADELLE, born Le Mans, France, August 1, 1935; admitted, 1958, Paris. *Education:* University of Paris Law School (Licence, 1956; Diplome d'Etudes Superieures de Droit Privé et Sciences Criminelles, 1957; Diplome d'Etudes Superieures d'Histoire du Droit et Droit Romain, 1958; Diplome d'Etudes Superieures de Droit Public, 1959; Doctorat en Droit, 1965; Agregation, 1969); Institute of High International Studies of the University of Paris (Degree, 1960). Author: "Les conflits de lois en matiere de nullites," Dalloz, 1967; "L'homme juridique," P.U.G.-Maspero, 1979; "Droit international prive," avec D. Holleaux et J. Foyer, Masson, 1987; "Essai d'introduction au droit français," Erasme, 1990; various chronicles and commentaries on case law published in Repertoire Dalloz de Droit International, Jurisclasseur de Droit International, Journal du Droit International, Revue Critique de Droit International Prive etc. Assistant, University of Paris Law School, 1962-1965. Lecturer on Law, University of Caen Law School, 1965-1969. Maître de Conference Agrege, University of Caen Law School, 1969-1972. Professor, University of Paris X Nanterre Law School, 1972—. *LANGUAGES:* French and English.

CABINET VAN HAGEN

Avocats à la Cour

Established in 1981

6, AVENUE GEORGE V

75008 PARIS, FRANCE

Telephone: (33 1) 47.20.00.64

Fax: (33 1) 47.20.25.09

Avocats à la Cour d'Appel de Paris, firm admitted to appear before all French Courts.

General French and International Law Practice. Commercial Law, Commercial Property Law, Competition Law, Labour Law, Bankruptcy Law, Intellectual Property, Administration Law, Taxation, Litigation, Arbitration.

FIRM PROFILE: Established in 1981, Cabinet Van Hagen is a Paris based independent international law firm, specialised in advising foreign clients doing business in France.

Our clients are principally European and North American companies; we also provide a service for private clients requiring international tax planning and advice in connection with their personal status and investments in France. As a founder member of the Eu-Lex International Practice Group, with 55 legal and accounting member firms throughout Europe, we are able to provide advice on the European legal issues and business opportunities arising out of the Single European Market.

MEMBERS OF FIRM

ANTHONY VAN HAGEN, born 1950; admitted, France as Avocat à la Cour; United Kingdom as Barrister. *Education:* Trent Polytechnic, Nottingham (B.A. Hons., Law); College of Law, London; Articled to Coudert Brothers, Paris. Former Counsel Member, Junior Franco-British Chamber of Commerce, Paris, 1980-1982. *Member:* Association des Avocats Inscrits à un Barreau Etranger (Association of Foreign Lawyers); International Bar Association. *LANGUAGES:* English and French. *PRACTICE AREAS:* Establishment of Foreign Corporations in France; Mergers and Acquisitions; Commercial Litigation; Commercial and Residential Real Estate Development and Finance; Finance Law.

MARGARET J. HOWARD, born 1953; admitted, United Kingdom as Barrister (Not admitted in France). *Education:* Birmingham University (LL.B.). *LANGUAGES:* English. *PRACTICE AREAS:* Insurance Archaeology; Product Liability; Environmental Pollution Litigation; Insurance Coverage; London Market Policies; Secondary Evidence Coverage for US Corporations.

OF COUNSEL

ALAIN BOITUZAT, born 1946; admitted, France as Avocat à la Cour. *Education:* University of Paris (Doctorat en Droit). *LANGUAGES:* French and English. *PRACTICE AREAS:* Commercial Litigation.

ROLAND BLAVIER, born 1938; admitted, France as Avocat à la Cour. *Education:* University of Strasbourg (Doctorat en Droit). *LANGUAGES:* French, English and German. *PRACTICE AREAS:* Tax Litigation.

VEIL ARMFELT JOURDE

69, AVENUE VICTOR HUGO

75116 PARIS, FRANCE

Telephone: 33.1.44.17.50.50

Fax: 33.1.45.01.77.21

London, England Office: 4 Carlton Gardens, Pall Mall, SW1Y 5AA. Telephone: 44. 0171 930 8644. Fax: 44. 0171 321 0670.
Cairo, Egypt Office: 4 Gaber Ibn Hayan Street, Dokki. Telephone: 20. 2 349 2217/2498/8678. Fax: 20. 2 349 3655.

Corporate Law and Mergers and Acquisitions, Trade and Competition Law, Finance and Banking Law, Construction Law and International Arbitration, Intellectual Property Law, Media, Commercial and Civil Litigation, Taxation and Administrative Law, Labour Law, Stock Exchange Regulations, Insolvency and Financial Criminal Litigation, Transfer of Technology.

FIRM PROFILE: The firm in its present form was established in 1990 through the merging of four separate practices. It is a partnership between French and English Lawyers with branch offices in London and Cairo. It currently has nine partners and a legal support staff of 12.

MEMBERS OF FIRM

JEAN VEIL, born 1947; admitted, 1972, Paris. *Education:* Université de Paris II (Licence en Droit, 1971); Conférencier à l'Université de Paris I (1975-1979). *LANGUAGES:* French and English. *PRACTICE AREAS:* Mergers, Acquisitions and Divestitures; Corporate Law; Stock Exchange Regulation; Commercial and Financial Criminal Litigation.

ANDREW P. ARMFELT, born 1948; admitted, 1970, Solicitor of the Supreme Court of England and Wales; 1986, Paris. *Education:* Law Society Finals (1969, with distinction in Accounts); Paris Bar exam (1986). *LANGUAGES:* English and French. *PRACTICE AREAS:* Mergers, Acquisitions and Divestitures; Construction Law; Transfer of Technology; Project Financing and Joint Ventures; International Arbitration.

ALAIN FRENKEL, born 1946; admitted, 1970, Paris. *Education:* Université de Paris II (Licence en Droit, 1967, D.E.S. de Droit Public, 1968, D.E.S. Droit Privée, 1970, Docteur en Droit, 1976, Lauréat de l'Université, Institut d'Etudes Politique, 1968). Professor, Université de Paris X, in Administrative Law, 1969-1974, in Tax Law, 1974-1987. Author: "La Genèse de la T.V.A.," 1976; "La Taxation d'Office à l'Impôt sur le Revenu," 1980; "Don Manuel et Contrôle des Revenus," 1991. *Member:* Institut des Avocats conseils fiscaux (Vice President), IFA. *LANGUAGES:* French and English. *PRACTICE AREAS:* Taxation.

PATRICIA GHOZLAND, born 1946; admitted, 1970, Paris. *Education:* Université de Paris II (Licence en Droit with honours, 1968, D.E.S. de Droit Privé with honours, 1970, D.E.S. Sciences Criminelles, 1970); Institut d'Etudes Politiques (1969); Ancien Assistant à l'Université de Droit de Paris II. *LANGUAGES:* French, English and Italian. *PRACTICE AREAS:* International Arbitration; Trade and Competition Law; Computer Hardware and Software Contracts (financing, engineering and marketing); Corporate Law; International Insolvency; Commercial Litigation.

GEORGES JOURDE, born 1945; admitted, 1969, Paris. *Education:* Université de Paris II (Licence en Droit Privé, 1969; Licence en Sciences Economiques, section économétrie, 1969; D.E.S. Droit Privé, 1970); Ancien Assistant à l'Université de Droit de Paris II. *PRACTICE AREAS:* Trade and Competition Law; Corporate Law; Commercial Litigation.

MARIE ALICE JOURDE, born 1954; admitted, 1981, Paris. *Education:* Université de Paris II (Maîtrise Droit Privé, 1977); Conférencier en Droit du Travail et de la Sécurité Social à l'Université de Paris II (1987-1992), Formation des Adultes en Droit du Travail. *PRACTICE AREAS:* Labour Law; Social Security Regulations.

DOMINIQUE DE LA GARANDERIE, born 1943; admitted, 1968, Paris. *Education:* Université de Paris II (Licence en Droit Privé, 1968; D.E.S. Droit Privé with high honours, 1969). Chargé de Séminaires en Doctorat du Droit du Travail, Université de Paris II, 1976-1979; Chargé d'Enseignement en Droit du Travail à l'Ecole Supérieure de Commerce de Paris, 1976-1979. Editorial Committee, "Cahiers Sociaux des Barreaux de Paris." Author: "Le Conseil des Prud'hommes," in Jurisclasseur, 1982; "Le travailleur français expatrié à l'étranger," in "Traité du Droit du Chef d'Entreprise," 1993; "Le doute dans le Droit du Travail," in "Le Doute et le Droit," 1994. *Member:* National Bar Council; Paris Bar Council (Former Chairman of the Labour Law Committee Board, 1987-1990); Union Intanationale des Avocats, Chairman of the Social Committee; Confederation Nationale des

(This Listing Continued)

VEIL ARMFELT JOURDE, Paris—Continued

Avocats-Employers, Chairman. **PRACTICE AREAS:** Labour Law; Social Security Regulations.

GUILLAUME KUPERFILS, born 1961; admitted, 1985, Paris. *Education:* Université de Paris II (Maîtrise en Droit, with honours and high honours, 1983, D.E.A. du Droit de la Propriété Intellectuelle, 1985); Institut Supérieur des Affaires, Groupe HEC (M.B.A., 1993); Conférencier en Droit Civil, Université de Paris I (1991); Conférencier en Droit des Affaires,Université de Paris II (1992). *LANGUAGES:* French and English. **PRACTICE AREAS:** Mergers, Acquisitions and Divestitures; Corporate Law; Competition and Trade Law; Commercial Litigation.

PATRICK JAIS, born 1959; admitted, 1987, Paris. *Education:* Université de Paris X (Maîtrise en Droit, Carrières judiciaires, 1984; D.E.A. de Droit des Affaires, with honours, 1985); Conférencier en Droit des Affaires, Université de Paris X (1986-1988). *LANGUAGES:* French and English. **PRACTICE AREAS:** Mergers and Acquisitions; Stock Exchange Regulations; Corporate Law; Finance; Joint Ventures.

HENRI BRANDFORD-GRIFFITH, born 1961; admitted, 1988, Paris. *Education:* Université de Paris II (Maîtrise en Droit, with honours, 1985); Certificat d' Aptitude á la Profession d'Avocat (Bar exam, 1987). *LANGUAGES:* French and English. **PRACTICE AREAS:** Stock Exchange; Mergers and Acquisitions; Privatisations; Corporate Law; Finance and Banking Law; Civil and Commercial Litigation.

VILLENEAU ROHART SIMON & ASSOCIES

Avocats à la Cour

Established in 1978

12 BOULEVARD DE COURCELLES
75017 PARIS, FRANCE
Telephone: (1) 46 22 51 73
Facsimile: (1) 47 66 06 37; (1) 47 54 90 78

Admiralty, Maritime Law, Marine Insurance, Air and Land Transportation, International Trade, Customs and Sale of Goods Law, Product Liability, Litigation, French and International Arbitration.

PARTNERS

JEAN-SERGE ROHART, born Lille, France, March 15, 1945; admitted, 1972, Paris. *Education:* University of Lille, (Licence en Droit, 1967); University of Paris (Diplome d'Etudes Superieures de Droit Public, 1968; Diplome d'Etudes Superieures d'Histoire Du Droit, 1969). Lecturer, Maritime Law, University of Paris, Nanterre, 1972-1975. Contributor: "Registration of Vessels," Kluwer, 1983 and "Arrest of Vessels," Kluwer, 1987, I.B.A.'s Handbook on Maritime Law. *Member:* Association Francaise de Droit Maritime (Treasurer, 1989—); International Bar Association (Chairman, Committee "A", Section on Business Law, 1992—); Comite Maritime International. *LANGUAGES:* French, English and German.

PATRICK D. SIMON, born Paris, France, November 16, 1949; admitted, 1973, Paris. *Education:* University of Paris (Licence de Droit, 1971; Doctorat d'Etat en Droit, 1976); Institut d'Etudes Comparees, Paris (1972). Author: "La reparation Civile des Dommages causes en mer par les Hydrocarbures," These, Paris, 1976; "Essai, d'Interpretation des Clauses obscures ou Ambigues dans les Chartes - Parties," D.M.F., 1975. "Le Droit, arme politique, 1988. "La main invisible et le droit," Les Belles Lettres, 1992. *Member:* Association Francaise de Droit Maritime; International Bar Association. *LANGUAGES:* French and English.

BENOÎT PINCEMIN, born April 28, 1958; admitted, 1992, Paris. *Education:* University of Nantes (Diplome d'Etudes Approfondies en Droit Maritime et Aerien, 1983). *Member:* Association Francaise de Droit Maritime. *LANGUAGES:* French and English.

ASSOCIATES

CATHERINE CAYREL-COUTURIER, born June 28, 1949; admitted, 1972, Paris. *Education:* University of Paris II (Licence en Droit, 1972); College of Law, Chancery Lane, London (1978-1980). Lecturer on French Law, Surrey University, Guilford, U.K., 1978-1980. *Member:* Association Francaise de Droit Maritime. *LANGUAGES:* French, English and German.

SIMON OVADIA, born Safi, Morocco, November 28, 1956; admitted, 1991, Paris. *Education:* University of Aix-en-Provence and Paris (D.E.S.S.

(This Listing Continued)

Droit des Transports; Doctorat d'Université en Droit, 1986). *LANGUAGES:* French and English.

CLAUDINE BOQUIN, born August 2, 1965; admitted, 1994, Paris. *Education:* University of Paris (D.E.A. Droit Privé, 1991). *Member:* Association Francaise de Droit Maritime. *LANGUAGES:* French, Norwegian and English.

ANNE-LAURENCE MICHEL, born February 1, 1955; admitted, 1993, Paris. *Education:* University of Aix-Marseille (D.E.S.S. Maritime and Aviation Transport Law, 1982; Doctorat d'Université en Droit, 1986). Lecturer, International Trade, Transport Insurance Law and Aviation Law, University of Rouen, 1991—. *Member:* Association Francaise de Droit Maritime. *LANGUAGES:* French and English.

NATALIE LIARDET, born April 28, 1968. *Education:* University of Paris II, Institut de Droit Comparé (1989; Diplôme d'Etudes Approfondies en Droit International Privé et en Droit de Commerce International, 1991); University of Paris II (D.E.S.S. de Droit du Commerce Extérieur). *LANGUAGES:* French and English.

ADVOKATFIRMAN VINGE

21, RUE JEAN GOUJON
F-75008 PARIS, FRANCE
Telephone: +33-1-40 75 37 37
Telefax: +33-1-45 63 05 49

Stockholm, Sweden Office: Smalandsgatan 20, P.O. Box 1703, S-111 87. Telephone: +46-8-614 30 00. Telex: 11150 VINGE S. Telefax: +46-8-611 90 37.

Gothenburg, Sweden Office: Nils Ericsonsgatan 17, P.O. Box 11025, S-404 21. Telephone: +46-31-80 51 00. Telex: 21119 VINGE S. Telefax: +46-31-15 88 11.

Malmö, Sweden Office: Östergatan 30, P.O. Box 4255, S-203 13. Telephone: +46-40-748 40. Telex: 8305122 VINGE S. Telefax: +46-40-97 27 72.

Helsingborg, Sweden Office: Råhustorget 6, P.O. Box 1064, S-251 10. Telephone: +46-42-24 80 80. Telex: 8335079 VINGE S. Telefax: +46- 42-24 80 85.

London, England Office: 44/45 Chancery Lane, WC2A 1JB. Telephone: +44-171-404 48 25. Telex: 25585 VINGE G. Telefax: +44-171-831 68 60.

Hong Kong Office: 2003 Hutchison House, 10 Harcourt Road, Central. Telephone: +852-2523 61 49. Telex: 62250 VINGE HX. Telefax: +852-2810 5343.

Brussels, Belgium Office: Avenue Louise 475/B12, B-1050. Telephone: +32-2-646 36 20; +32-2-646 36 80. Telefax: +32-2-646 41 46.

Swedish and International Law Practice, Contracts, Corporate, Transport. Foreign Investments in Scandinavia. Arbitration.

MEMBERS

BJÖRN PALM-JENSEN, born April 27, 1930. *Education:* University of Stockholm (juris kandidat, LL.B., 1955). Service in Swedish Courts, 1955-1957. Practised with: Nils Setterwalls Advokatbyra, 1957-1966; Björn Palm-Jensens Advokatbyra, 1966-1970; Advokatfirman Palm-Jensen & Roos, 1970-1983. Member of this firm since 1983. *Member:* Swedish Bar Association (1961); Board of Stockholm Bar (1971-1976).

ANDERS ÅBERG, born April 18, 1943. *Education:* University of Lund, Sweden (juris kandidat, LL.B., 1970; Master of Science Business Administration, Commercial Law with Fiscal Law, 1971); Collège d'Europe, Bruges, Belgium (Master of Law EEC-law, 1972); Stanford Business School, USA (Stanford Executive Program SEP, 1983). Service in Swedish Courts, 1967-1969; Swedish Chamber of Commerce, Brussels; The Commission of the European Communities, Brussels; The Law firm De Bandt, Van Hecke & Lagae, Brussels, Belgium, 1972-1975; Swedish Match, Brussels and Stockholm, 1975-1988; Trygg-Hansa SPP Holding/Home Holsings,, Stockholm, Sweden and New York, General Counsel, Secretary and Ex Vice President, 1989-1994. Member of this firm since 1994.

KURT MARK, born 1929. *Education:* University of Uppsala (juris kandidat, LL.B., 1954). *Member:* Swedish Bar Association (1960).

(This Listing Continued)

ASSOCIATES

SABINE VON UTHMANN, born April 20, 1961. *Education:* University of Stockholm (juris kandidat, LL.B., 1987); University of Paris X (Maîtrise en Droit des Affaires, LL.B., 1989). Service with Swedish Courts, 1987-1988. Associated with this firm since 1989.

Languages: Swedish, French and English

VOGEL & VOGEL

6, AVENUE PIERRE 1 ER DE SERBIE
75116 PARIS, FRANCE
Telephone: (33.1) 53.67.76.20
Telecopier: (33.1) 53.67.76.75

Brussels, Belgium Office: Avenue du Diamant, 139, B-1040. Telephone: (32) 2.735.34.28. Fax: (32) 2.735.49.30.
Frankfurt/Main, Germany Office: Kettenhofweg 29, D-60325. Telephone: (49) 69.71.036.16. Fax: (49) 69.72.27.26.

Antitrust Law, European Community Law, International Business Law, International Investment Law, Mergers and Acquisitions, Agency and Distributorships, Products Liability Law, Unfair Competition Law.

FIRM PROFILE: *The firm offers a full range of legal services especially in the fields of French and EEC Antitrust Law, Distribution and General Business Law.*

LOUIS VOGEL, born Saarbrücken, Germany, October 22, 1954; admitted, 1981, Paris; 1990, New York. *Education:* Institut d'Etudes Politiques de Paris (Diplômé, 1976); Yale Law School (LL.M., 1982); University of Paris I (Panthéon-Sorbonne) and Paris II Law School (Panthéon-Assas), Doctor of Law (1985); Agrégé des Facultés de Droit (1989). Author: "Droit commercial européen," with B. Goldman and A. Lyon-Caem, 835p., Dalloz, 1994; "Le droit européen des affaires," Dalloz, 128 p., 2nd ed., 1994; "Droit de la concurrence et concentration économique," 427 p., Economica, 1988; "Chronique du droit de la concurrence," Revue du Marché Commun, 1991—; "Chronique Concurrence," Revue Contrats Concurrence Consummation, 1991—; "Chronique de jurisprudence communautaire," Semaine juridique, 1990—; "French Merger Law," Fordham Corporate Law Institute, 1990. Professor of Law, University of Paris Law School. Director, Juris Classeurs de droit international et de droit comparé. Director, Encyclopédie Dalloz de Droit Commercial. *Member:* American Bar Association; Comité Français de Droit International Privé; International Law Association; Société de Législation Comparée; Union des Avocats Européens; Association des juristes franco-allemands, Deutscher Anwaltverein. (Also at Brussels, Belgium Office). *LANGUAGES:* French, English and German. *PRACTICE AREAS:* Antitrust Law; European Community Law; International Business Law.

JOSEPH E. VOGEL, born Saarbrücken, Germany, December 5, 1959; admitted, 1985, Paris; 1990, New York. *Education:* Institut d'Etudes Politiques de Paris (Diplômé, 1980); Ecole des Hautes Etudes Commerciales (Diplômé HEC, 1982); Diplômé d'Etudes Comptables Superieures (1982); University of Paris I (Panthéon-Sorbonne) and Paris II Law School (Panthéon-Assas); DEA in Business Law, 1983. Author: "Le droit européen des officiires," with Louis Vogel, Dalloz, 128p., 2nd ed., 1994. *Member:* American Bar Association; Association des juristes franco-allemands, Deutscher Anwaltverein. *LANGUAGES:* French, English and German. *PRACTICE AREAS:* Product Distribution Law; European Community Law.

CHARLES S. FAHRNER, born Boulogne-sur-Seine, France, April 7, 1961; admitted, 1988, Paris. *Education:* University of Toulon (Maîtrise en droit, 1986). *Member:* Association des juristes franco-allemands. *LANGUAGES:* French, English and German. *PRACTICE AREAS:* Products Liability Law; Unfair Competition Law.

EDITH BACCHICHETTI, admitted, 1991, Paris. *Education:* University of Paris II, Pantheon-Assas (Maîtrise en droit, 1989; DEA, Business Law, 1990; CFPA, 1991). *LANGUAGES:* French and English. *PRACTICE AREAS:* Product Distribution Law; Litigation.

XAVIER HENRY, admitted, 1992, Paris. *Education:* University of Paris XII (Maîtrise, Business Law, 1989; DEA, Private Law, 1990; DESS, City Planning and Real Estate Law, 1991; CFPA, 1991). *LANGUAGES:* French and English. *PRACTICE AREAS:* Litigation.

EMMANUELLE BERKOVITS, admitted, 1993, Paris. *Education:* University of Paris I (DEA, Business Law, 1990; DESS, Common Market Law, 1991; CFPA, 1992). *LANGUAGES:* French and English. *PRACTICE AREAS:* Distribution Law; Litigation; General Business Law.

(This Listing Continued)

CATHERINE LEPETZ, admitted, 1994, Paris. *Education:* University of Paris XII (DEA, Private Law, 1990). *LANGUAGES:* French and English. *PRACTICE AREAS:* Distribution Law; Litigation; General Business Law; Arbitration.

LAW OFFICES OF SYLVIE J. VOLNAY

44 RUE DES BELLES FEUILLES
PARIS 75016, FRANCE
Telephone: (1) 45 53 19 19
Fax: (1) 47 55 17 85

Trademark and Intellectual Property Law, Franchising, European Community Law, Antitrust, Distribution, Unfair Competition, Economic Regulations, Environment, General Commercial and Trade Law, Commercial and Contract Law, International, Litigation.

SYLVIE J. VOLNAY, born Paris, France, July 13, 1946; admitted, 1972, France. *Education:* Paris University of Law (Law Degree, 1968; D.E.S., in Law, 1970); Graduate European Economic Community Law. Author of articles among which: "The new french antitrust legislation," 1986; "Franchising and antitrust," 1987; "Free movement of goods in the European Economic Community," 1987; "The new trademark regulations," 1991; "New trademark law and competition law," 1991. *Member:* A.C.E. (Association Française des Avocats Conseils d'entreprises); AFEC (Association pour l'Etude de la Concurrence); U.A.E. (Union des Avocats Européens); U.I.A. (Union Internationale des Avocats); I.B.A. (International Bar Association). *LANGUAGES:* French, English and Spanish.

ASSOCIATES

PIERRE CUSSAC, born February 2, 1965; admitted, 1990, Paris. *Education:* Paris University of Law (B.A., in Economics; M.A., in Business Law; D.E.A. of European Economic Community Law). *LANGUAGES:* French, English and German.

Counsel for French Federation of Franchising, for Conseil National du Commerce, and for Major French and Multinational Corporations.

Languages: French, English, Spanish and German

S.C.P. VOVAN & ASSOCIES

7, RUE DE MADRID
75008 PARIS, FRANCE
Telephone: (1) 47.90.17.10
Facsimile: (1) 44.70.01.64
Telex: 280.012 F VOLEX

General Practice, Construction, Computer, Aviation, Engineering Contracts, Commercial, Labor, Reorganization, French and International Corporation, Distributorship, Agency and Franchise, Licenses and Transfer of Technology, Foreign Investments, Administrative Law, Trademark and Patents, Competition and Antitrust Law, Taxation, Constitutional Law, Human Rights, EEC Law, Litigation and French and International Arbitration.
Firm engaged in French and General International practice and admitted to appear in French and European Economic Communities Courts.

MEMBERS OF FIRM

PATRICK VOVAN, born Biarritz, France, July 12, 1946; admitted, 1970, Paris, France. *Education:* Faculté de Droit de Paris, France (Master, 1969); Diplome du Centre d'Etudes des Communautés Européennes (1969); New York University, Institute of Comparative Law (Diploma of Comparative Jurisprudence, 1973). Partner, Raffin-Raffin-Courbe-Vovan, France, 1972-1986. Associate, Leaf, Deull and Drogin, New York, New York, 1974-1984. *LANGUAGES:* French, English, Spanish and Italian.

DANIEL GIORGETTI, born Paris, France, May 8, 1944; admitted, 1970, Paris, France. *Education:* Economics and Trade Management School (1961-1969); University of Paris II (Master, 1969); Judicial Studies Institute (1968-1969); Political Studies Institute (1968-1970). With Justice Department, 1969-1970. *LANGUAGES:* French and Italian.

PHILIPPE LHUMEAU, born Nogent Sur Marne, France, February 23, 1953; admitted, 1978, Paris, France. *Education:* University of Paris II (Master, 1978). Lecturer, Commercial and Comparative Law, University of Paris XI, 1982-1983. *Member:* Union of Young Lawyers (Member of Permanent Commission, 1979-1982). *LANGUAGES:* French and English.

MICHEL AURILLAC, born Marseille, France, July 11, 1928; admitted, 1988, Paris, France. *Education:* Faculté de Droit de Paris; Institut d'Etudes

(This Listing Continued)

S.C.P. VOVAN & ASSOCIES, Paris—Continued

Politiques de Paris; Ecole Nationale d'Administration (Promotion Paul Cambon, 1953). Author: *Reflexions Sur La Defense*, Editions De La Nation, 1979; *La France, Une Et Indivisible*, Economica, 1983; *Liberer La Communication*,Albatros, 1984; *Le Royaume Oublie*, Olivier Orban, 1986; *L'Afrique A Coeur*, Berger-Levrault, 1988. Conseiller Général de Châteauroux, 1985. Ancien Ministre de la Cooperation, 1986-1988. Ancien Deputé, 1978-1981; 1986-1988. Conseiller d'Etat honoraire. Co-Writer, French Constitution of 1958. President, Administrative and Account Section, Supreme Court of Senegal - Personal Advisor of Mr. Leopold Sedar Senghor, President, Republic of Senegal, 1960. Advisor for Mr. Georges Pompidou, French Prime Minister, 1963. Political Advisor for Mr. Messmer, French Prime Minister, 1974. Chief of Staff for Mr. Michel Poniatowski, State Minister, Interior Minister, 1974-1976. Conseiller Général de Châteauroux, 1985-1992. *Member:* French Arbitration Association. *LANGUAGES:* French and English.

ANTOINE BIDET, born Angers, France, June 23, 1954; admitted, 1984, Paris, France. *Education:* Faculté de Droit d'Angers, France (Master, 1980); Faculté de Droit de Rennes, Centre de Droit des Affaires, France (Diplôme d'Etudes, Supérieures Spécialisées de Droit des Affaires et Ficalité; Diplôme de Juriste Conseil d'Entreprises, 1981). *LANGUAGES:* French and English.

JEAN-FRANCOIS SANTACROCE, born Chalons sur Marne, France, April 11, 1956; admitted, 1981, Paris, France. *Education:* University of Paris II (Master, 1978); University of Paris I (Institut d'Etudes Judiciaires, 1979); University of Paris II (Centre Interuniversitaire de Formation à la Fonction Personnel, 1989). *LANGUAGES:* French and English.

CHRISTOPHE PETTITI, born Paris, France, December 30, 1959; admitted, 1986, Paris, France. *Education:* University of Paris X and Paris I (Master, 1983; D.E.A., Labor Law, 1984); Urbino University, Italy (Diploma of Comparative Law and EEC Law); Strasbourg International Institute of Human Rights, France, 1981. Member, Expert Network of EEC Commission on the application of the Equalities Directives. Co-Author: Equality in law between men and women in the European Community, French law publication commission of the European Community. Contributor: Gazette du Palais - "Revenue trimestrielle des droits de l'Homme.". *LANGUAGES:* French, English.

ARMELLE JARLAUD, born Paris, France, December 13, 1959; admitted, 1992, France. *Education:* University of Paris II (Master of Business Law and Fiscality, 1982). Former Consulting and Tax Lawyer. Registered, 1986. *LANGUAGES:* French and English.

ASSOCIATES

SARAH XERRI, born Orléans, France, October 24, 1966; admitted, 1992, Paris, France. *Education:* University of Paris X and IX (Master, 1989; DESS, Business Law and Fiscality, 1990). *LANGUAGES:* French and English.

CATHERINE BOURGI, born Paris, France, January 16, 1950; admitted, 1977, Cotonou, Benin; 1978, Nouakchott, Mauritania; 1979, Abidjan, Côte d'Ivoire; 1989, Paris, France. *Education:* University of Nice (Master, 1972); Law Institute, Paris (1973). *LANGUAGES:* French.

SEBASTIAN VAN TESLAAR, born Neuilly, France, October 6, 1958; admitted, Conseil Juridique Stagiaire. *Education:* University of Paris II (M.A., Business and Tax Law, 1988); University of Paris XI-HEC (D.E.S.S., International Tax Law, 1989); Paris Beaux-Arts (1984). *LANGUAGES:* French, English and Spanish.

FRÉDÉRIC DOCEUL, born Bois-Colombes, France, November 26, 1964; admitted, 1992, Paris, France. *Education:* University of Paris II (Master, 1987; D.E.S.S., Industrial Property Law, 1988). *LANGUAGES:* French and English.

FRANCK VEISSE, born Paris, France, September 1, 1963; admitted, 1990, France as Conseil Juridique Stagiaire; 1993, Paris, France. *Education:* University of Montpellier (M.A., Business Law, 1987; D.E.A., Business Law, 1989; C.E.S., Distribution Law, 1989). Co-Author: "Distribution of TOTAL Corporation Oil Products and Hydrocarbon," 1987. *LANGUAGES:* French and English.

(This Listing Continued)

LAURENT SALAAM-CLARKE, born August 4, 1964; admitted, 1993, Paris, France. *Education:* University of Paris I-Sorbonne (Maîtrise de Droit International Privé, 1989); Institut d'Etudes Judiciaires (1990). *LANGUAGES:* French and English.

Languages: French, English, Spanish, Italian and German

WATSON, FARLEY & WILLIAMS

19 RUE DE MARIGNAN
75008 PARIS, FRANCE
Telephone: (33-1) 45 63 15 15
Telex: WFW PAR 651096 F
Fax: (33-1) 45 61 09 01

London, England Office: 15 Appold Street, London EC2A 2HB. Telephone: (44 171) 814 8000. Telex: 8955707 WFW LON G. Fax: (44 171) 814 8141.
New York, New York Office: 380 Madison Avenue, 10017. Telephone: 212-922-2200. Telex: 6790626 WFW NY. Fax: 212-912-1512.
Oslo, Norway Office: Beddingen 8, Aker Brygge, 0250 Oslo. Telephone: (47 22) 83 83 08. Telex: 79209 WFW N. Fax: (47 22) 83 83 13.
Athens, Greece Office: Alassia Building, Defteras Merarchias 13, 185-35 Piraeus. Telephone: (30 1) 422 3660. Telex: 24 1311 WFW GR. Fax: (30 1) 422 3664.
Moscow, Russia Office: 36 Myaskovskovo Street, Moscow 121019. Telephone: (7 502) 224 1700 (international only); (7 095) 291 8046/5968. Fax: (7 502) 224 1701 (international only); (7 095) 202 9027.
Copenhagen, Denmark Office: Lille Kongensgade 20 DK-1074 Copenhagen K. Telephone: (45 33) 91 33 03. Fax: (54 33) 91 49 12.

Firm engaged in General International Practice, Corporate, Commercial and Financing, Shipping, Aviation, Banking, Taxation, Commercial Litigation and Arbitration and European Community Law.

RESIDENT PARTNERS

Andrew H. Wettern　　　　**Edward J. Nalbantian** (Admitted
Nigel R. D. Moss　　　　　to the Bar in New York and
David I. Syed　　　　　　California)
(Avocats à la Cour de Paris)

(For Biographical Data on additional partners, see Professional Biographies at Copenhagen, Denmark, London, England, Oslo, Norway, Pireaus, Greece and Moscow, Russia)

WEINSTEIN LAW OFFICES

Established in 1934

20, AVENUE DE FRIEDLAND
75008 PARIS, FRANCE
Telephone: (1) 45.63.22.31
Fax: (1) 45 62 04 23
Telex: 280 241 POPRI

Munich, West Germany Office: Normannenplatz 29, 8000 Munich 80.

Patents, Trademarks, Designs, Copyrights, Unfair Competition, Valuation, Arbitration, Computer and Software, European Community Law, Franchising, Transfer and Licensing.
Not authorized to appear before the French Courts as Avocats.

FIRM PROFILE: The firm was founded in 1934 by Zinovi Weinstein (1906-1991) as a one partner firm. Its activity was interrupted during World War II in 1939 and resumed in 1945. The firm has a staff of 80 among which 22 associate lawyers of which 12 lawyers have a technical background in different fields (chemistry, biology, electronics, computers, mechanics). All lawyers know perfectly French and English and some of them German and Russian. The firm has specialized non lawyer support personnel, is internationally known and has a reputation as a specialist in the fields of Intellectual and Industrial property rights. It has a great experience in trial work in France and Belgium. Has also a subsidiary in Belgium.

MEMBERS OF FIRM

DOMINIQUE FRANCOIS, born Paris, France, September 3, 1945; admitted, 1973, France; Patent Attorney before the European Patent Office. *Education:* University of Paris, University of Strasbourg, Bachelor of Laws (Paris), Master of Laws (Paris), 1972, Degree of High Legal Education; Degree of the International Institute of Industrial Property Right (CEIPI), 1974. Lecturer at the University of Paris. Lecturer at the Law Faculty Uni-

(This Listing Continued)

versity of Paris, High School of Commerce (HEC). *Member:* Chamber of French Trademark and Design Attorneys (President, 1978-1980); National Association of Industrial Property Attorneys; United States Trademark Association; Institute of Professional Representatives before the European Patent Office; A.I.P.P.I. *LANGUAGES:* French and English. *PRACTICE AREAS:* Trademark Law; Copyright Law; Unfair Competition Law; Designs Law; EEC Regulations; Valuation of Trademarks and Patents.

GEORGES BEAUCHAMPS, born Berlin, Germany, October 4, 1924; admitted, 1960, France; Patent Attorney before the European Patent Office. *Education:* Superior Degree of General Mathematics (1947); Engineer High School of Lyon (1949); High School of Aeronautics (1957). *Member:* National Association of Industrial Property Attorneys; Institute of Professional Representatives before the European Patent Office; A.I.P.P.I. *LANGUAGES:* French, English and German. *PRACTICE AREAS:* Patent Law; Copyright Law; Unfair Competition.

YVES DURAND, born La Roche-sur-Yon, France, January 4, 1937; admitted, 1968, France; Patent Attorney before the European Patent Office. *Education:* Master of Sciences; Degree of High Legal Education; Degree of the International Institute of Industrial Property Right (CEIPI). *Member:* National Association of Industrial Property Attorneys; Institute of Professional Representatives before the European Patent Office; A.I.P.P.I. *LANGUAGES:* French, English. *PRACTICE AREAS:* Patent Law; Copyright Law; Unfair Competition.

HELMUT BERGER, born Germany, March 27, 1939; admitted, 1971, France; Patent Attorney before the European Patent Office. *Education:* Technical High School of Braunschweig (Germany); Degree of the International Institute of Industrial Property Right (CEIPI). *Member:* National Association of Industrial Property Attorneys; Institute of Professional Representatives before the European Patent Office. *LANGUAGES:* French, German, English. *PRACTICE AREAS:* Patent Law; Copyright Law; Unfair Competition.

STEPHANIE CHAST, born Baltersweiler, Germany, April 6, 1952; admitted, 1992, France. *Education:* High School of Commerce Neunkirchen (Germany); University of Law of Paris. *Member:* National Association of Industrial Property Attorneys. *LANGUAGES:* French, German, English. *PRACTICE AREAS:* Trademark Law; Copyright Law.

MICHEL THINAT, born Bourges, France, April 11, 1955; admitted, 1980, France; Patent Attorney before the European Patent Office. *Education:* Superior Degree of Technologies (1977); Master of Sciences and Technics (1979); Degree of the International Institute of Industrial Property Right (CEIPI). *Member:* National Association of Industrial Property Attorneys; Institute of Professional Representatives before the European Patent Office. *LANGUAGES:* French, English. *PRACTICE AREAS:* Patent Law; Copyright Law; Unfair Competition.

CHANTAL NOEL, born Morocco, October 19, 1956; admitted, 1992, France. *Education:* High School of Chemical Engineer; Degree of the International Institute of Industrial Property Right. *LANGUAGES:* French, English. *PRACTICE AREAS:* Patent Law; Copyright Law; Unfair Competition.

CHRISTIAN FRICK, born Colmar, France, December 5, 1958; admitted, 1988, France. *Education:* High Degree of European Law (Strasbourg); High Degree of Licensing and Franchising (Strasbourg); High Degree of Industrial Property (Paris). *Member:* National Association of Industrial Property Attorneys. *LANGUAGES:* French, English. *PRACTICE AREAS:* Trademark Law; Copyright Law; Unfair Competition; EEC Regulations.

MARION LEFRANC, born Paris, France, January 1, 1964; admitted, 1986, France. *Education:* High Degree of Fiscal Policy; High Degree of Industrial Property. *Member:* National Association of Industrial Property Attorneys. *LANGUAGES:* French, English. *PRACTICE AREAS:* Trademark Law; Copyright Law; Unfair Competition.

ISABELLE POUJADE, born Saint-Mandé, France, January 24, 1964; admitted, 1988, France. *Education:* High Degree of Trade and Commerce Law (Paris); High Degree of Copyright and Industrial Property (Paris). *Member:* National Association of Industrial Property Attorneys. *LANGUAGES:* French, English. *PRACTICE AREAS:* Trademark Law; Copyright Law; Unfair Competition.

MARTINE BLOCH-WEILL, born Strasbourg, France, January 28, 1964; admitted, 1986, France. *Education:* High Degree of Trade and Commercial Laws (Strasbourg); High Degree of Industrial Property (Strasbourg). *Member:* National Association of Industrial Property Attorneys.

(This Listing Continued)

LANGUAGES: French, English. *PRACTICE AREAS:* Trademark Law; Copyright Law; Unfair Competition.

JEAN-MARIE ALGOUD, born Paris, France, December 12, 1965; admitted, 1990, France. *Education:* Master of Laws (Paris); High Degree of Industrial Property (Paris). *LANGUAGES:* French, English. *PRACTICE AREAS:* Trademark Law; Copyright Law; Unfair Competition.

WHITE & CASE
11, BOULEVARD DE LA MADELEINE
75001 PARIS, FRANCE
Telephone: (33-1) 42-60-34-05
Facsimile: (33-1) 42-60-82-46

New York, New York: Telephone: 212-819-8200. Facsimile: 212-354-8113.
Washington, D.C.: Telephone: 202-872-0013. Facsimile: 202-872-0210.
Los Angeles, California: Telephone: 213-620-7700. Facsimile: 213-687-0758; 213-617-2205.
Miami, Florida: Telephone: 305-371-2700. Facsimile: 305-358-5744.
Mexico City, Mexico: Telephone: (52-5) 207-9717. Facsimile: (52-5) 208-3628.
Tokyo, Japan: Telephone: (81-3) 3239-4300. Facsimile: (81-3) 3239-4330.
Hong Kong: Telephone: (852) 2822-8700. Facsimile: (852) 2845-9070; Grice & Co., Solicitors, Telephone: (852) 2826-0333. Facsimile: (852) 2526-7166.
Singapore, Republic of Singapore: Telephone: (65) 225-6000. Facsimile: (65) 225-6009.
Bangkok, Thailand: Pacific Legal Group Ltd., In Association With White & Case, Telephone: (662) 236-6154/7. Facsimile: (662) 237-6771.
Hanoi, Viet Nam: Representative Office, Telephone: (84-4) 227-575/6/7. Facsimile: (84-4) 227-297.
Bombay, India: Telephone: (91-22) 282-6300. Facsimile: (91-22) 282-6305.
London, England: Telephone: (44-171) 726-6361. Facsimile: (44-171) 726-4314; (44-171) 726-8558.
Brussels, Belgium: Telephone: (32-2) 647-05-89. Facsimile: (32-2) 647-16-75.
Stockholm, Sweden: Telephone: (46-8) 679-80-30. Facsimile: (46-8) 611-21-22.
Helsinki, Finland: Telephone: (358-0) 631-100. Facsimile: (358-0) 179-477.
Moscow, Russia: Telephone: (7-095) 201-9292/3/4/5. Facsimile: (7-095) 201-9284.
Budapest, Hungary: Telephone: (36-1) 269-0550; (36-1) 131-0933. Facsimile: (36-1) 269-1199.
Prague, Czech Republic: Telephone: (42-2) 2481-1796. Facsimile: (42-2) 232-5522.
Warsaw, Poland: Telephone/Facsimile: (48-22) 26-80-53; (48-22) 27-84-86. International Telephone/Facsimile: (48-39) 12-19-06.
Istanbul, Turkey: Telephone: (90-212) 275-68-98; (90-212) 275-75-33. Facsimile: (90-212) 275-75-43.
Ankara, Turkey: Telephone: (90-312) 446-2180. Facsimile: (90-312) 437-9677.
Jeddah, Saudi Arabia: Law Office of Hassan Mahassni, Telephone: (966-2) 651-3535. Facsimile: (966-2) 651-3636.
Riyadh, Saudi Arabia: Law Office of Hassan Mahassni, Telephone: (966-1) 476-7099. Facsimile: (966-1) 479-0110.
Almaty, Kazakhstan: Telephone: (7-3272) 50-7491/2. Facsimile: (7-3272) 61-0842.

General International Practice.
Firm engaged in American, French and International Law Practice and registered as "Avocats."

RESIDENT PARTNERS

STEPHEN R. BOND, born New York, New York, July 5, 1943; admitted, 1969, New York. Admitted as Avocat, Paris, France, 1992. *Education:* Brown University (A.B., 1965); Columbia University (J.D., 1968). Member, ICC International Court of Arbitration, 1994-1996. *Member:* American and International Bar Associations; Chartered Institute of Arbitrators; Institute for Transactional Arbitration; Panels of Arbitrators, American Arbitration Association; Federal Economic Chamber; Court of Arbitration, Polish Chamber of Commerce; Hong Kong International Arbitration Centre; U.S. Council for International Business.

JEAN-LUC BOUSSARD, born Orléans, France, December 27, 1942. Admitted as Avocat, 1973, Paris, France. *Education:* University of Paris

(This Listing Continued)

WHITE & CASE, Paris—Continued

(Licence en Droit, 1964; Diplôme d'Etudes Supérieures de Droit Public, 1966; Diplôme d'Etudes Supérieures de Science Politique, 1968); University of London, Kings College.

ANTHONY GIUSTINI, born Pittsburgh, Pennsylvania, December 25, 1958; admitted, 1985, New York; 1988, District of Columbia; Admitted as Avocat, France. *Education:* Princeton University (A.B., 1981); Harvard University (J.D., 1984); European University Institute, Florence, Italy (LL.M., 1985). *Member:* New York State and American Bar Associations.

ROSINE LOROTTE, born Avallon, France, February 1, 1940. Admitted as Avocat, France. *Education:* University of Paris (Licence és Lettres, 1960; Diplôme d'Etudes Supérieures de Lettres, 1961; Licence en Droit, 1963); Harvard University (LL.M., 1965).

GILLES PEIGNEY, born Boulogne Billancourt, France, November 12, 1951. Admitted as Avocat, France. *Education:* University of Paris (Licence en Droit, 1973; Diplôme de l'Institut d'Etudes Politiques de Paris, 1974; Diplôme d'Etudes Supérieures de Droit des Affaires, 1975; Diplôme d'Etudes Supérieures de Droit Public, 1978).

JOHN H. RIGGS, JR., born Plainfield, New Jersey, November 21, 1936. Admitted, 1965, New York. Admitted as Avocat, France. *Education:* Yale University (B.A., 1958); University of Virginia (LL.B., 1964). *Member:* The Association of the Bar of the City of New York; American Bar Association; American Society of International Law; Union Internationale des Avocats; International Bar Association.

CHRISTOPHER R. SEPPALA, born Guildford, England, October 18, 1941. Admitted, 1970, New York. Admitted as Avocat, France. *Education:* Harvard University (B.A., 1963); Columbia University (J.D., 1967). Member, Panel of Arbitrators: American Arbitration Association; European International Contractors; Indian Institute of Arbitration. *Member:* American and International Bar Associations.

RESIDENT COUNSEL

NICHOLAS BUDD, born Milwaukee, Wisconsin, August 18, 1945 Admitted 1970, California; 1975, Colorado. Admitted as Avocat, France. *Education:* University of California, Berkeley (B.A., 1967); University of California, Los Angeles (J.D., 1970). *Member:* State Bar of California; Colorado and International Bar Associations; British Institute of Comparative Law; European Maritime Law Organization.

PIERRE-YVES CORRIEU, born Oran, Algeria, March 17, 1942. Admitted as Avocat, France. *Education:* University of Paris (Licence en Droit Privé, 1965); Ecole Nationale des Impôts.

RESIDENT ASSOCIATES

PAULE BIENSAN, born Oran, Algeria, December 12, 1956. Admitted as Avocat, France. *Education:* Université de Paris X (1985); Universit'48 de Paris I (1987).

ROBERT BRADA, JR., born Kansas City, Missouri, June 7, 1965. Admitted, 1990, California; (Not admitted in France). *Education:* University of Kansas, (B.A., 1987); University of Southern California (J.D. , 1990). *Member:* State Bar of California.

BERTRAND CARADET, born Neuilly-sur-Seine, France, January 30, 1959. Admitted as Avocat, France. *Education:* Université de Paris II (B.A., 1976; Maîtrise en Droit, 1982; DEA/ DESS, 1984).

RÉMY COTTAGE-STONE, born Amiens, France, January 5, 1967. Admitted as Avocat, France. *Education:* Ecole Supérieure de Commerce de Paris (ESCP) (Diploma, 1989); University of Paris Law School (Maîtrise en Droit Privé, Mention Droit des Affaires, 1990).

DR. REINHARD DAMMANN, born Harsewinkel, Westfalia, Germany, July 9, 1959. Admitted as Avocat, France. *Education:* Aix - Marseille III (Maîtrise en Droit, 1985); Institut d'Etudes Politiques d' Aix-Marseilles III (1985).

JEAN-CHARLES DE DARUVAR, born Sassandra, Ivory Coast, October 2, 1955. Admitted as Avocat, France. *Education:* Université de Paris X (1982); Université de Paris IX (1983); University of Pennsylvania (LL.M., 1985).

PHILIPPE DENEUX, born September 3, 1966. Admitted as Avocat, France. *Education:* Institut d'Etudes Politiques de Paris (Diploma, 1990); University of Paris II (Ms.L., 1991).

CARROLL S. DORGAN, born Ponca City, Oklahoma, August 18, 1949. Admitted 1988, California; 1989, District of Columbia. Admitted as

(This Listing Continued)

Advocat, France. *Education:* Harvard University (A.B., 1971); London School of Economics and Political Science (M.S., 1982); University of California, Berkeley, Boalt Hall School of Law (J.D., 1988).

SUZANNE DURDEVIC, born Suresnes, France, October 21, 1966. Admitted as Avocat, France. *Education:* Université Paris II (1990, 1991, 1992); Paris Law School (EFB; C.A.P.A., 1993).

FRANÇOIS FARMINE, born Teheran, Iran, July 18, 1967. Admitted as Avocat, France. *Education:* Université de Paris II (Maîtrise en Droit, 1990, 1991).

PIERRE FORGET, born Boulogne Billancourt, France, March 31, 1966. Admitted as Avocat, France. *Education:* Université de Paris II (Maîtrise en Droit, 1989); Institut d'Etudes Politiques de Paris (1991); Université de Paris (1991); Université de Paris II (1992).

ERIC GASTINEL, born Aix-les-Bains, France, June 11, 1964. Admitted as Avocat, France. *Education:* Université de Lyon III (DEA Droit Communautaire, 1987); Université d'Aix-Marseille III (1988); Université de Lyon III (1990).

RONALD E. M. GOODMAN, born Ancon, Panama Canal Zone, October 25, 1950. Admitted, 1987, New York; 1989, District of Columbia. Admitted as Avocat, France. *Education:* Cornell University (B.A., 1971); Princeton University (Ph.D., 1978); Columbia University (J.D., 1986).

CLIFFORD J. HENDEL, born Boston, Massachusetts, November 11, 1957. Admitted, 1983, Connecticut; 1984, New York; (Not admitted in France). *Education:* Wesleyan College (B.A., 1979); University of Connecticut (J.D., 1983).

CAROLINE KAHN, born Toulouse, France, January 2, 1962. Admitted, 1987, New York. Admitted as Avocat, France. *Education:* University of Paris (Maîtrise, 1983); University of London, Kings College (LL.B., 1983); New York University School of Law (M.C.J., 1985).

JEAN-FRANCOIS LECORRE, born Vannes, France, January 19, 1962. Admitted as Avocat, France. *Education:* University de Rennes (M.A., 1984); Institut D'Etudes Politiques de Paris (Diplome, 1989); Université de Paris-Dauphine (DESS, 1989).

ANNE-FRANCE MARMOT, born Suresnes, France, May 28, 1968. Admitted as Avocat, France. *Education:* Notre Dame de Boulogne (B.A., 1986); University Patheon-Assas-Paris II (Maîtrise en droit privé, 1991; 1992); University Paris-IX-Dauphine (1992).

PHILIPPE METAIS, born Lucon, Vendee, France, December 29, 1960. Admitted as Avocat, France. *Education:* Paris I Pantheon - Sorbonne (D.E.A., 1986).

MARK G. MILFORD, born Paris, France, January 25, 1967. Admitted, 1991, New York; Barrister-At-Law, England, Wales and Northern Ireland; (Not admitted in France). *Education:* University of London (LL.B., 1987); Universite de Paris I, Patheon-Sorbonne (Maîtrise, 1989).

VINCENT MORIN, born Surenes, France, April 7, 1963. Admitted, 1989, New York. Admitted as Avocat, France. *Education:* Ecole des Hautes Etudes Commerciales (M.B.A., 1985); University of Paris IX (J.D., 1985); University of Chicago (LL.M., 1989).

MARIE-HELENE PERES, born Boulogne, Billacourt, France, February 23, 1967. Admitted as Avocat, France. *Education:* University of Paris II-Assas (Maîtrise en droit, 1990; 1991).

LAURA RESTELLI, born Milan, Italy, November 8, 1962; admitted, 1991, Milan, Italy (Not admitted in France). *Education:* Universita Degli Studi Di Milano (Law, 1986); Columbia University Law School (LL.M., 1992).

MARK B. RICHARDS, born Salt Lake City, Utah, October 14, 1964; admitted, 1993, New York (Not admitted in France). *Education:* Brigham Young University (B.A., 1988); New York University (J.D., 1992).

PETER ROSHER, born London, England, January 26, 1964. Admitted as Solicitor, 1990, England. *Education:* Leicester University, England (LL.B., 1987); University of London, King's College (M.Sc., 1992); London Law School (J.D., 1988).

STEWART ROBERT SHACKLETON, born Ontario, Canada, November 29, 1958; admitted, 1993, Ontario; 1994, Admitted as Avocat, France. *Education:* University of Western Ontario (B.A., 1983; LL.B., 1987); University of Paris I Sorbonne-Panthéon (D.E.A., 1989).

(This Listing Continued)

(For biographical data as to other locations, see Professional Biographies at New York, New York; Washington, D.C.; Los Angeles, California; Miami, Florida; Mexico City, Mexico; Tokyo, Japan; Hong Kong; Singapore, Republic of Singapore; Bangkok, Thailand; Hanoi, Viet Nam; Bombay, India; London, England; Brussels, Belgium; Stockholm, Sweden; Helsinki, Finland; Moscow, Russia; Budapest, Hungary; Prague, Czech Republic; Warsaw, Poland; Istanbul and Ankara, Turkey; Jeddah and Riyadh, Saudi Arabia; Almaty, Kazakhstan).

WILDE SAPTE

217 RUE FAUBOURG ST. HONORÉ
75008 PARIS, FRANCE
Telephone: (33-1) 44 95 02 70
Facsimile: (33-1) 42 89 62 25

London, England Office: 1, Fleet Place, EC4M 7WS. Telephone: 0171-246 7000. Facsimile: 0171-246 7777. Telex: 887793 lde/cde 145.
Brussels, Belgium Office: 27 Avenue des Arts, 1040. Telephone: (32-2) 280 1404. Facsimile: (32-2) 280 1764.
Hong Kong Office: 31st Floor, One Exchange Square. Telephone: (852) 2810 5081. Facsimile: (852) 2810 1295.
New York, New York Office: 19th Floor, 450 Lexington Avenue, 10017. Telephone: (212) 867 4530. Facsimile: (212) 557 4451.
Tokyo, Japan Office: 2nd Floor, AIG Building, 1-1-3 Marunouchi, Chiyoda-ku 100. Telephone: (81-3) 3215 3801. Facsimile: (81-3) 3215 3868.
Lloyd's Office: 40 Lime Street, London, EC3M 5DG. Telephone: 0171 246 7000. Fax: 0171 246 7722.

Banking, Corporate Lending, Acquisition Finance, Aviation, Shipping, Leasing, Work-outs, Trade Finance, Structured Finance, Project Finance, Insolvency, Property, Insurance, Employment, Charities, EC Law and Company and Commercial.

FIRM PROFILE: Wilde Sapte are a leading City law firm representing UK and overseas clients on a worldwide basis from London, Brussels, Hong Kong, New York, Paris and Tokyo. The Paris office is a full service practice and can offer advice in both French and English law with particular specialization in the fields of aviation, banking, asset finance and corporate finance.

CONTACT PARTNERS

Thomas J. McDonald

(For complete list of all personnel, see Professional Biographies at London, England)

WILLKIE FARR & GALLAGHER

6, AVENUE VELASQUEZ
75008 PARIS, FRANCE
Telephone: 011-33-1-44-35-44-35
Fax: 011-33-1-42-89-87-01
Telex: 652740-WFG Paris

New York City Office: One Citicorp Center, 153 East 53rd Street, 10022-4669. Telephone: 212-821-8000. Fax: 212-821-8111. Telex: RCA 233780-WFGUR; RCA 238805-WFGUR.
Washington, D.C. Office: Three Lafayette Centre, 1155 21st Street, N.W., 6th Floor, 20036-3384. Telephone: 202-328-8000. Fax: 202-887-8979; 331-8787. Telex: RCA 229800-WFGIG; WU 89-2762.
London, England Office: 35 Wilson Street, 3rd Floor. EC2M 25J. Telephone: 011-44-171-696-9060. Fax: 011-44-171-417-9191.

General Practice.
Firm engaged in French American and General International Practice and registered as Avocats in France authorized to appear before the French Courts.

RESIDENT PARTNERS

JEAN-LUC CUADRADO, born Casablanca, Morocco, August 13, 1952; admitted, France as Avocat (Tax Law). *Education:* University of Lyon (Licence en Droit, 1974); University of Aix en Provence (D.E.S.S. de Droit des Affaires, 1975; D.J.C.E., 1975); University of Paris X (Docteur en Droit Fiscal, 1977). *Member:* International Fiscal Association and International Bar Association. *LANGUAGES:* French, English.

ERIC J. FLEURY, born Lille, France, January 9, 1954; admitted, 1986, New York; France as Avocat. *Education:* University of Lyon (D.E.S.S. Droit des Affaires et Fiscalité, 1982; D.J.C.E., 1982); New York University

(This Listing Continued)

School of Law (LL.M., 1984). *Member:* American Bar Association. *LANGUAGES:* French, English.

MICHEL FRIEH, born Lyon, France, June 17, 1957; admitted, France as Avocat. *Education:* Institut d'Etudes Politiques de Paris (I.E.P., 1979); University of Paris I (Maîtrise en Droit, 1980); Ecole Nationale de la Magistrature (1980-1982). Judge at the Tribunal de Grande Instance of Hazebrouck, 1983-1985. *LANGUAGES:* French, English.

JAY F. LEARY, born Glen Ridge, New Jersey, November 8, 1938; admitted, 1963, New York; France as Avocat. *Education:* Harvard University (A.B., 1960; LL.B., 1963). Phi Beta Kappa. *Member:* The Association of the Bar of the City of New York. *LANGUAGES:* English, French.

BERNARD LE-PEZRON, born Constantine, Algeria, February 6, 1949; admitted, in France as Avocat (Tax Law). *Education:* University of Bordeaux (Licencié es Sciences Economiques, 1971); Ecole Nationale des Impôts , 1972. Tax Inspector, 1973-1977. Professor, Ecole Nationale des Impôts, 1977-1981.

DANIEL PAYAN, born Paris, France, June 29, 1947; admitted, France as Avocat. *Education:* Institut d'Etudes Politiques de Paris (I.E.P., 1969); University of Paris (Licence en Droit, 1970; D.E.S. Droit Privé, 1971). (Also of Counsel to Law Offices of Dr. Mujahid M. Al-Sawwaf, Jeddah, Saudi Arabia). *LANGUAGES:* French, English.

EMMANUEL ROSENFELD, born Neuilly-sur-Seine, France, February 8, 1954; admitted, France as Avocat. *Education:* Alumnus of Ecole Normale Supérieure (B.A., in History, 1975); Agrégation in French Literature (1977); Ecole Nationale d'Administration (E.N.A., 1983); M.A., in Private Law, (1984). Honorary Fellow, Ezra Stiles College, Yale University. Judge in the Administrative Courts, 1983-1984. *LANGUAGES:* French, English, Spanish.

KRISTEN VAN RIEL, born Paris, France, November 28, 1950; admitted, France as Avocat. *Education:* Lycée Janson de Sailly (Baccalauréat, 1968); Institut d'Etudes Politiques de Paris (Diplôme, 1974); University of Paris (Licence en Droit, 1975); New York University Law School (LL.M., 1979). *LANGUAGES:* French, English.

SPECIAL COUNSEL

ANNA DE NERCIAT-LASCAR, born New York, N.Y., July 12, 1948; admitted, 1973, New York; 1978, California; France as Avocat. *Education:* Barnard College (B.A., magna cum laude, 1969); Yale Law School (J.D., 1972); University of Paris (D.E.S.S., Droit des Affaires, 1977). *LANGUAGES:* English and French.

ASSOCIATES

THOMAS W. BARK, born Baton Rouge, Louisiana, April 17, 1965; admitted, 1991, New York. *Education:* Louisiana State University (B.S., 1987); University of Virginia (J.D., 1990).

GUY BENDA, born Uccle, Belgium, July 19, 1967; admitted, France as Avocat. *Education:* Ecole des Hautes Etudes Commerciales (H.E.C., 1989); University of Paris II (Maîtrise, 1991). *LANGUAGES:* French, English, German.

ALEXANDRA BIGOT, born Paris, France, March 18, 1968; admitted, France as Avocat. *Education:* Ecole des Hantes Etudes Commerciales (H.E.C., 1990); University of Paris XI (D.E.S.S. Fiscalite Internationale, 1990). *LANGUAGES:* French, English and German.

ADRIEN CADIEUX, born Brussels, Belgium, August 13, 1969; (Not admitted in France). *Education:* Ecole des Hautes Etudes Commerciales (HEC Paris, 1992); Université de Paris XI (D.E.S.S. de Fiscalité Internationale, 1993). *LANGUAGES:* French, English, Spanish.

JEAN-CHRISTOPHE CASTERA, born Pau, France, August 18, 1960; admitted, 1988, New York; France as Avocat. *Education:* University of Paris II (D.E.S.S., Droit Fiscal Et Droit Des Affaires, 1984) ; Columbia University (LL.M., 1986). *Member:* American Bar Association. *LANGUAGES:* French, English.

PASCAL CHADENET, born Paris, France, December 26, 1956; admitted, France as Avocat. *Education:* University of Paris X Nanterre (Maîtrise de Philosophie, 1978); University of Paris VII Jussieu (Maîtrise de Mathématiques, 1979); University of Paris I Panthéon-Sorbonne (Licence en Droit, 1987); Georgetown University Law School (LL.M., 1988). *LANGUAGES:* French, English.

FRANCK COURMONT, born Abbeville, France, March 1, 1965; admitted, France as Avocat. *Education:* University of Picardie (Licence en Droit, 1985); Institut d'Etudes Politiques de Paris (I.E.P., 1987); University of Paris II Assas (Maîtise en Droit des Affaires, Maîtrise en Droit Interna-

(This Listing Continued)

WILLKIE FARR & GALLAGHER, Paris—Continued

tional et Européen, 1988); DukeUniversity School of Law (LL.M., 1991). **LANGUAGES:** French, English.

ALLARD DE WAAL, born Amsterdan, The Netherlands, August 8, 1962; admitted, France as Avocat. *Education:* Ecoles des Hautes Etudes Commerciales, Paris (H.E.C., 1986); University of Paris XI, Sceaux (D.E.S.S., Fiscalité Internationale, 1986). **LANGUAGES:** French, Dutch, German, English.

RENAUD DUBOIS, born Paris, France, May 2, 1965; admitted, France as Avocat. *Education:* University of Paris I Panthéon-Sorbonne (D.E.A. de Droit Privé, 1989). **LANGUAGES:** French, English.

CLAIRE DUVAL, born Versailles, France, July 8, 1954; admitted, France as Avocat. *Education:* University of Paris XI, Sceaux (Maîtrise en Droit Privé , 1976); Institut d' Etudes Economiques et Juridiques Appliquées è la Construction (I.C.H., 1983). **LANGUAGES:** French, English.

JOHN R. FLANIGAN, born Cincinnati, Ohio, November 15, 1957; admitted, 1986, New York; France as Avocat. *Education:* University of Cincinnati (B.A., summa cum laude, 1981); New York University; University of North Carolina (J.D., 1985). Phi Beta Kappa. Recipient, Louise Taft Semple Scholarship in the Classics. Staff Member, North Carolina Law Review, 1983-1984. *Member:* The Association of the Bar of the City of New York; American Bar Association. **LANGUAGES:** English, French.

JEFFREY W. FOUTS, born Washington, D.C., May 9, 1957; admitted, 1984, New York; France as Avocat. *Education:* University of Virginia (B.A., 1979); Columbia Law School of New York (J.D., 1983). *Member:* Association Internationale des Jeunes Avocats. **LANGUAGES:** English and French.

CATHERINE JEANCOLAS, born Nancy, France, August 18, 1952; admitted, France as Avocat; Paris. *Education:* University of Paris II Panthéon-Assas (Licence en Droit, 1974; D.E.S. Droit Public, 1975; D.E.S. Droit Privé, 1976); Institut d'Etudes Politiques,Paris (I.E.P., 1973). **LANGUAGES:** French and English.

PIERRE KARPIK, born Paris, France, July 10, 1967; (admission pending). *Education:* Ecole des Hantes Etudes Commerciales (HEC Paris, 1990); University of Paris II (Maîtrise, 1991); University of Paris XI (D.E.S.S. de Fiscalité Inter nationale, 1990). **LANGUAGES:** French, English.

JONATHAN E. MARSH, born Boston, Massachusetts, July 12, 1964; admitted, 1990, Wisconsin; 1991, New York (Not admitted in France). *Education:* University of Wisconsin (B.A., 1986; J.D., cum laude, 1990). Order of the Coif. Senior Articles Editor, *Wisconsin Law Reivew. Member:* State Bar of Wisconsin. **LANGUAGES:** English, French.

DIDIER PENOT, born Angers, France, July 24, 1964; admitted, France as Avocat. *Education:* University of Paris I Panthéon-Sorbonne (Maîtrise Mention "Droit des Affaires," Module "Affaires Internationales," 1986-1987; D.E.A. "Droit des Affaires et de l'Economie, 1988-1989). Author: "Différents Aspects Juridiques des Opérations Réalisées sur le Monep,". *Member:* Union des Jeunes Avocats de Paris. **LANGUAGES:** French, English.

MURIEL SERRE-PREVOST, born Croix, France, January 23, 1968; admitted, France as Avocat. *Education:* University of Paris X, Nanterre (Maîtrise Droit des Affaires, 1991); University of Paris II, Panthéon-Assas (D.E.A. Droit Communautaire, 1992). **LANGUAGES:** French, English, German.

CHRISTOPHE GARAUD, born Paris, France, May 2, 1966; admitted, 1992, France as Avocat. *Education:* Université de Paris II (D.E.S.S., Droit des Affaires et Fiscalité , 1992); New York University (Masters Corporate Law, 1994). **LANGUAGES:** French, English.

(For complete biographical data on all Partners and Counsel, see Professional Biographies at New York, N.Y.)

WITHERS

15, RUE DE MARIGNAN
75008 PARIS, FRANCE
Telephone: (33.1) 49.53.06.66
Telex: 640057F WAYLAND
Fax: (33.1) 449.53.05.76

London, England Office: Withers. 12 Gough Square, London EC4A 3DE. Telephone: 0171-936 1000. Fax: 0171-936 2589. Cable Address: "Notaires, London". Telex: 24213 WITHER G.

(This Listing Continued)

Agricultural and Farming, Aviation, Charities, Company Law (UK and European), Commercial Litigation (including contentious property work), Employment, Environmental Law, Inheritance Planning and Succession, Insurance, Matrimonial and Divorce, Probate (including contentious probate), Real Estate and Commercial Property, Shipping, Tax Planning (UK and International), Trusts (UK and Offshore).
Firm engaged in English and General International Law Practice, and staff are authorized to appear before the French Courts as Avocats.

FIRM PROFILE: *The Paris branch office of London firm Withers was established in 1985. The dual qualified staff are supported by a 20 lawyer associate firm who work from the same offices allowing Withers to offer a full range of corporate, private client and maritime services involving cross boarder issues.*

RESIDENT MEMBERS

Jonathan J. Eastwood

Languages: French and German

CABINET WOLFRAM

(In affiliation with Hogan & Hartson)

14, RUE CHAUVEAU-LAGARDE
75008 PARIS, FRANCE
Telephone: (33-1) 44.71.97.00
Fax: (33-1) 47.42.13.56

Washington, D.C. Office: Hogan & Hartson L.L.P., Columbia Square, 555 13th Street, N.W., 20004. Telephone: 202-637-5600. Telex: 89-2757. Cable Address: "Hogander Washington". Fax: 202-637-5910.
Brussels, Belgium Office: Hogan & Hartson L.L.P., Avenue des Arts 41, 1040. Telephone: (32.2) 505.09.11. Fax: (32.2) 502.28.60.
London, England Office: Hogan & Hartson L.L.P., Veritas House, 125 Finsbury Pavement, London EC2A 1NQ. Telephone: (44 171) 638.9595. Fax: (44 171) 638.0884.
Moscow, Russia Office: 33/2 Usacheva Street, Building 3, 119048. Telephone: (7095) 245-5190. Fax: (7095) 245-5192.
Prague, Czech Republic Office: Hogan & Hartson L.L.P., Opletalova 37, 110 00. Telephone: (42-2) 2422-9009. Fax: (42-2) 2421-5105.
Warsaw, Poland Office: Hogan & Hartson L.L.P., Marszalkowska 6/6, 00-590. Telephone: (48 2) 628 0201; Int'l (48) 3912 1413. Fax: (48 2) 628 7787; Int'l (48) 3912 1511.
Baltimore, Maryland Office: Hogan & Hartson L.L.P., 111 South Calvert Street, 16th Floor. Telephone: 410-659-2700. Fax: 410-539-6981.
Bethesda, Maryland Office: Hogan & Hartson L.L.P., Two Democracy Center, Suite 720, 6903 Rockledge Drive. Telephone: 301-564-5000. Fax: 301-493-5169.
Colorado Springs, Colorado Office: Hogan & Hartson L.L.P., 518 North Nevada Avenue, Suite 200. Telephone: 719-635-5900. Fax: 719-635-2847.
Denver, Colorado Office: Hogan & Hartson L.L.P., One Tabor Center, Suite 1500, 1200 Seventeenth Street. Telephone: 303-899-7300. Fax: 303-899-7333.
McLean, Virginia Office: Hogan & Hartson L.L.P., 8300 Greensboro Drive. Telephone: 703-848-2600. Fax: 703-448-7650.

General Practice, including International Public and Private Financings, Acquisitions, Commercial Transactions, Strategic Investments and Joint Ventures, and Litigation and Arbitration.

AVOCATS A LA COUR
(MEMBERS OF PARIS BAR)

STEVEN L. WOLFRAM, born Dallas, Texas, April 28, 1949; admitted, 1975, New York; 1992, Paris. *Education:* Harvard University (A.B., magna cum laude, 1971; J.D., 1974). *Member:* The Association of the Bar of the City of New York. **LANGUAGES:** English and French.

FREDERIQUE SCHLUMBERGER, born Paris, France, July 25, 1949; admitted, 1983, New York; 1993, Paris. *Education:* University of Paris, Maîtrise en Droit (1970); New York University (LL.M., 1980). **LANGUAGES:** English and French.

COUNSEL

MARK E. MAZO, born Philadelphia, Pennsylvania, January 12, 1950; admitted, 1975, District of Columbia (Not admitted in France). *Education:* Princeton University (A.B., 1971); Harvard University (J.D., 1974). Phi Beta Kappa. *Member:* District of Columbia Bar. (Also Member, Washington, D.C. Office). **PRACTICE AREAS:** Domestic and International Cor-

(This Listing Continued)

porate and Strategic Transactions; Securities and Finance Law; International Commercial Law.

LORRAINE SOSTOWSKI, born Scranton, Pennsylvania, November 11, 1953; admitted, 1977, Massachusetts; 1986, District of Columbia (Not admitted in France). *Education:* Tufts University (A.B., magna cum laude, 1974); Harvard Law School (J.D., 1977). *Member:* District of Columbia Bar; American Bar Association (Member, Sections on: Business Law; International Law). *LANGUAGES:* English and French.

RESIDENT ASSOCIATES

KATE VICKERS ROMAIN, born Houston, Texas, January 21, 1964; admitted, 1991, Texas (Not admitted in France). *Education:* University of Colorado (B.A., 1986); University of Texas (J.D., with honors, 1991). *Member:* State Bar of Texas. *LANGUAGES:* English and French.

DAVID W. SMAIL, born St. Paul, Minnesota, May 30, 1965; admitted, 1991, Minnesota; 1992, District of Columbia (Not admitted in France). *Education:* Macalester College (B.A., summa cum laude, 1987); Harvard Law School (J.D., cum laude, 1991). Phi Beta Kappa. Co-Author: "Privatizations: Ouverture du marché Americain?" *Banque* n° 543, Dec. 1993, p. 30. *Member:* District of Columbia Bar; Minnesota State Bar Association. *LANGUAGES:* English and French. *PRACTICE AREAS:* Commercial Law.

(For complete biographical data on all personnel, see Professional Biographies at Washington, D.C.)

RENAUD DELUBAC

43, RUE JEAN LECANUET
76000 ROUEN, FRANCE
Telephone: 35 88 16 52
Fax: 35 88 79 78

Civil Litigation, Commercial Litigation, Road Traffic Accidents; EEC Law, French and German Business Law and Arbitration.

RENAUD DELUBAC, born 1943; admitted, 1969, Rouen. *Education:* Austin, Texas; University of Freiburg (GFR) Caen, France Maîtrise en droit (magna cum laude, 1966); D.E.S. de Science Politique (1967); Doctorat d'Erat de droit (magna cum laude, 1969). Author: Le Financement des Paris Politiques PUF Paris, 19 Articles in "Le Monde ", "30 Jours d'Europe,", "La Gazette du Palais", La Vie Juridique", " Revue de Droit Public"; "Revue Trimestrielle de Droit european". Lecturer: Rouen University in EEC Law. *Member:* Union des Avocats europeans; Association des juristes franco-allemands; Union internationale des Avocats; Deutscher Anwaltverein; French-German Chamber of Commerce. *LANGUAGES:* French, German and English.

ASA - AVOCATS ASSOCIES

22, RUE DU GÉNÉRAL DE CASTELNAU
B.P. 395
67010 STRASBOURG CEDEX, FRANCE
Telephone: 88.56.56.49
Fax: 88.76.73.55
Telex: 890 229 F Asavoca

Paris, France Office: 44, Rue François 1er. Telephone: (1) 44.43.48.88. Fax: (1) 40.70.18.32 / 44.43.81.60.

Arbitration, Bank Law, International, Commercial Law, Taxation, Finance Law, General Practice.

PARTNERS

JEAN-CLAUDE AMBACH, born August 3, 1933; admitted, 1957, Strasbourg. *LANGUAGES:* French and German.

NICOLAS WILTBERGER, born August 26, 1937; admitted, 1960, Strasbourg. *LANGUAGES:* French and German.

GENEVIÈVE SCHMIDT, born November 13, 1943; admitted, 1966, Strasbourg. *LANGUAGES:* French.

RÉMY SEGUIN, born January 28, 1950; admitted, 1971, Strasbourg. *LANGUAGES:* French.

PHILIPPE HOEPFFNER, born June 22, 1947; admitted, 1972, Strasbourg. *LANGUAGES:* French.

DANY KRETZ, born May 2, 1950; admitted, 1972, Strasbourg. *LANGUAGES:* French.

(This Listing Continued)

FRANÇOIS RUHLMANN, born July 2, 1949; admitted, 1971, Strasbourg. *LANGUAGES:* French, English and German.

NOËL VAILLANT, born December 26, 1949; admitted, 1976, Strasbourg. *LANGUAGES:* French and English.

PHILIPPE GRAMLING, born March 23, 1952; admitted, 1979, Strasbourg. *LANGUAGES:* French and German.

BRUNO HUCK, born September 15, 1956; admitted, 1979, Strasbourg. *LANGUAGES:* French and English.

PAUL LUTZ, born July 1, 1948; admitted, 1980, Strasbourg. *LANGUAGES:* French, German and English.

LILYANE ANSTETT-GARDEA, born May 18, 1956; admitted, 1981, Strasbourg. *LANGUAGES:* French, English and German.

PATRICK PEGUET, born January 25, 1960; admitted, 1984, Strasbourg. *LANGUAGES:* French and English.

REINERT, APPY & PARTNER

Avocats / Rechtsanwälte
66, RUE MARCHÈ-GARE
F-67200 STRASBOURG, FRANCE
Telephone: (033) 88-261426
Telecopier: (0033) 88-268840

Karlsruhe, Germany Office: Steinhäuserstrasse 17, 76135. Telephone: (0721) 812024. Telécopier: (0721) 818738.
Dresden, Germany Office: Selliner Strasse 1, 01109 Dresden/Saxony. Telephone: 0351/4604353. Telecopier: 0351/460352. Mobile Phone: 0049 161-3719355.
Washington, D.C. Office: Suite 1004, 1101 Seventeenth Street, N.W., 20036-4798. Telephone: (202) 293-5555. Telecopier: (202) 293-9035.

General Practice and Litigation. Corporate, Commercial, Banking, Business, Antitrust, Trademark, Computer, Copyright, Tax, Unfair Competition, Civil Aviation, International and EC Law, Administrative Law.

MEMBERS OF FIRM

DAMIEN WEDRYCHOWSKI, born Orleans, France, 1947; admitted, 1978, France. *Education:* Universities Orleans and Strasbourg (Licence en Droit, 1969; Diplome Etudes Superieures, Private Law, 1972). Assistant, Universities of Heidelberg and Strasbourg, 1973-1977. Lecturer, University of Heidelberg, 1974—; University of Freiburg/Breisgau, 1989—. *Member:* French Bar Association; Club d'Affaires Franco-Allemand, Germany. *LANGUAGES:* German, English and French.

(For complete biographical data on all personnel, see Professional Biographies at Karlsruhe, Germany)

WACHSMANN, MEYER, HECKER BARRAUX, HOONAKKER

Société d'Avocats
14 AVENUE DES VOSGES
67000 STRASBOURG, FRANCE
Telephone: 88 21 10 20
Fax: (33) 88 25 03 20

General French and International Law Practice. Administrative Law, Arbitration, Banking and Financial Law, Bankruptcy, Competition Law, Construction Law, Corporation Law, Criminal Law, Distributorship Law, Environmental Law, Fluvial and Rhenish Law, Franchise Law, EEC Law, Fiscal Law, Foreign Investments, Human Rights, Labor Law. Insurance Law, Property, Rent and Lease Law. Patent, Trademark and Copyright Law.

MEMBERS OF FIRM

JEAN-PAUL WACHSMANN, born 1935; admitted, 1957, Strasbourg. *Education:* University of Strasbourg (Licence en Droit, Lauréat de la Faculté). *Member, Bâtonnier de L'Ordre des Avocats de Strasbourg (1980-1981). Président du Centre de Formation des Avocats d'Alsace, 1986-1988. Co-Président du Comité d'Organisation du Congrès de L'Union Internationale des Avocats, 1990. LANGUAGES:* French, English and German.

MARC MEYER, born 1936; admitted, 1961, Strasbourg. *Education:* University of Strasbourg, Diplômé du Droit de la Pollution et des nuisances (1974). Président de L'Union Départementale des Associations Familiales

(This Listing Continued)

WACHSMANN, MEYER, HECKER BARRAUX, HOONAKKER, Strasbourg—Continued

du Bas-Rhin. *Member:* Comité Economique et Social d'Alsace. *LANGUAGES:* French.

JEAN-LOUIS HECKER, born 1947; admitted, 1968, Strasbourg. *Education:* University of Strasbourg (Lauréat de la Faculté, 1966; D.E.S. Droit Privé, 1969; D.E.S. de Sciences Criminelles et Pénitentiaires, 1970); Chargé de Cours à l'Institut Europeéen d'Enseignement Commercial Supérieur (Université Robert Schuman de Strasbourg). Arbitre à la Cour Européenne d'Arbitrage. *Member:* Droit et Commerce; FIEDA (Fondation Internationale pour l'Enseignement du Droit des Affaires); ANASED (Association Nationale des Avocats Spécialistes des entreprises en difficultés). *LANGUAGES:* French, German and English.

PATRICK BARRAUX, born 1948; admitted, 1976, Strasbourg. *Education:* University of Strasbourg (Licence et Diplôme Supérieur d'Histoire, 1972; Maîtrise en Droit, 1974; Diplômé de l'Institut Universitaire des Hautes Etudes Européennes). Conseiller Prud'hommes depuis 1983 (ancien Président et Vice-Président de la Section des Activités Diverses du Conseil de Prud'hommes de Strasbourg). *LANGUAGES:* French.

MARTIN MEYER, born 1954; admitted, 1976, Strasbourg. *Education:* University of Strasbourg (Lauréat de la Faculté de Droit de Strasbourg; Maîtrise en Droit, 1975). *Member:* ASTRAFI (Association des Jeunes Avocats pour le Droit Administratif et Fiscal). *LANGUAGES:* French and German.

PHILIPPE HOONAKKER, born 1959; admitted, 1985, Strasbourg. *Education:* University of Strasbourg (Docteur en Droit, 1988); Chargé d'Enseignement à l'Université Robert Schuman de Strasbourg. *Member:* ANDD (Association Nationale des Docteurs en Droit). *LANGUAGES:* French and German.

ASSOCIATES

Régine Steibel; Christine Guyon; Jean-René Kopp; Isabelle Huet; Luc Strohl; Marie-Laurence Lang.

COURET - DELAHAIE - DUPUY - MANAUD
GIVRY - MORVILLIERS - SENTENAC
SOCIETE D'AVOCATS

24, PLACE DES CARMES
31000 TOULOUSE, FRANCE
Telephone: 61.52.03.57
Fax: 61.52.16.58

General and International Practice, Patents, Trademarks, Copyrights, Unfair Competition, Arbitration, Technology Transfer, Joint Ventures, Know-How, Mergers and Acquisitions, Banking, Finance, Insurance, Labour Law.

FIRM PROFILE: The firm offers a full range of legal services. It is well known for its international, commercial and company law practice. The firm is a member of the network GIE LEXTEAM with members in all important cities in France.

MEMBERS OF FIRM

ALAIN COURET, born Agen, France, 1949; admitted, 1992, Toulouse. *Education:* University of Toulouse (Maîtrise en droit; Docteur en droit, Augmentation de capital); University of Strasbourg (Droit comparé). Professor of Law, University of Toulouse. Author: "L'Ingenierie Financiere," Editions Liaisons, 1991; "Les O.P.A.," 1992; "Les Sociétiés Holdings," 1992; "La Maîtrise du Risque dans les Cessions d'Actions," GLN-JOLY, 1994; "La Sociétié par Actions Simplifeée," GLN-JOLY, 1994. Director, Finance, Lamy. *LANGUAGES:* French and English. *PRACTICE AREAS:* Finance Law; Mergers and Acquisitions; Corporate Law.

ANNIE DELAHAIE, born France, 1947; admitted, 1977, Perpignan; 1978, Toulouse. *Education:* University of Paris Sorbonne (Maîtrise en Philosophie); University of Paris Assas (Maîtrise en Droit). *LANGUAGES:* French, English and Catalan. *PRACTICE AREAS:* Labour and Employment; Family Law; Civil Practice; Criminal Law.

JEAN-DENIS DUPUY-MANAUD, born Talence, France, 1954; admitted, 1993, Toulouse. *Education:* University of Paris Assas (Maîtrise en

(This Listing Continued)

Droit); Ecole Supérieure de Commerce of Paris (1977). Author: "Copyright on Space Imagery," 1991; "Technology Transfer," 1992. Legal Counsel, Spot Image, 1982-1988. *Member:* European Center Space Law. *LANGUAGES:* French and English. *PRACTICE AREAS:* International Law; Intellectual and Industrial Property; Business Law; Commercial Law; Space Law; Computer and Software; Pharmaceutical Law.

MICHEL GIVRY, born Casablanca, Morocco, 1948; admitted, 1988, as Conseil Juridique; 1990, as Avocat, Toulouse. *Education:* Institut d'Etudes Politiques Paris (1970); University of Toulouse (DES Droit des Affaires, 1973). Professor, International Contracts, DJCE Law School, Toulouse. *Member:* Association des Avocats Conseils d'Entreprise (President, Regional Association); Association des Anciens Eleves de Sciences Politiques de Paris; Centre Régional de Formation des Avocats (Board member). *LANGUAGES:* French, English and Spanish. *PRACTICE AREAS:* General Practice; International Practice; Corporate; Investment; Exchange Control Regulations; International Arbitration; Joint Venture; Telecommunications; Aeronautics.

NICOLAS MORVILLIERS, born Rouen, France, 1962; admitted, 1988, Toulouse. *Education:* Universities of Saarbrücken and Tübingen, Germany; University of Toulouse. Author: "Les Honoraires de l'Avocat Allemand." *Member:* European Network, Brussels; Rheinische Internationale Juristenvereinigung, Düsseldorf. *LANGUAGES:* French, German, English and Italian. *PRACTICE AREAS:* Intellectual Property; Pharmaceutical Law; Unfair Competition; General Practice.

GUY-ALAIN DE SENTENAC, born Toulouse, France, 1951; admitted, 1983, as Conseil Juridique; 1992, as Avocat, Toulouse. *Education:* Institut d'Etudes Politiques (1974; DEA Droit des Affaires, 1978). Associate Professor, University of Toulouse. Legal Counsel: Peat-Marwick KPMG, 1978-1982; Kevorkian, 1983-1985; Remy Martin, 1985-1987. *Member:* Association des Anciens Elèves de Sciences Politiques. *LANGUAGES:* French and English. *PRACTICE AREAS:* International Tax Law; French Tax Law; Corporate Law; Mergers and Acquisitions.

ASSOCIATES

DR. RAINER BECKMANN, born Ahnsen, Germany, 1962; admitted, 1993, Stuttgart; 1994, Toulouse. *Education:* University of Tübigen, Germany (State Exams, 1988 and 1993; Dr.Jur., 1989); Ecole Nationale d'Administration, Paris (1989). Lecturer, Law, University of Tübingen, 1988, 1990-1993. Airbus Lawyers Trainee Program, 1992. *Member:* Association des Anciens Elèves de l'ENA. *LANGUAGES:* German, French and English. *PRACTICE AREAS:* German Law; International Commercial Law; European Community Law; Alternative Dispute Resolution.

MURIELLE FREUND, born Paris, France, 1969. *Education:* University of Toulouse (DESS Droit des Affaires, DJCE, 1992). *LANGUAGES:* French and English. *PRACTICE AREAS:* Corporate Law; Business Law.

XAVIER LASSUS, born Saint-Gaudens, France, 1966; admitted, 1991, as Conseil Juridique Stagiaire; 1994, as Avocat, Toulouse. *Education:* University of Toulouse (DESS, Droit des Affaires Internationales, 1991). Author: "L'Organisation Africaine de la Propriété Intellectuelle," 1991. *LANGUAGES:* French, English and Spanish. *PRACTICE AREAS:* Corporate Law; Contracts; Intellectual Property; Computer and Software.

CLAUDE YEPONDE, born Pointe-à-Pitre, Guadeloupe, 1962; admitted, 1993, Toulouse. *Education:* DESS, Droit Fiscal; Certificate d'Etudes Judiciaires. *Member:* Groupement des Avocats Africains et Antillais de France. *LANGUAGES:* French and English. *PRACTICE AREAS:* Bankruptcy; Civil Practice; Tax Law.

GERMANY

FRIEDHOFF, MAUER & PAMPFER

WILHELMSTRAβE 61
D-52070 AACHEN, GERMANY
Telephone: (0241) 502095
Telefax: (0241) 511067

A Member of AdvoSelect EEIG, a network of law firms pooling their resources in special fields and cross border cases, specializing in business law for middle sized companies. AdvoSelect is represented in 51 cities throughout Europe.

(This Listing Continued)

MEMBERS OF FIRM

HEINRICH C. FRIEDHOFF, born Aachen, Germany, 1946; admitted, 1976, Germany. *Education:* University School, Shaker Heights, Ohio (1964); Universities of Bonn, Munich and Geneva (1972). *Member:* Deutscher Anwaltsverein. *LANGUAGES:* German, English and French. *PRACTICE AREAS:* Commercial and Corporate Law; Insolvency Law; Copyright and Publishing Law; International Civil Law.

ALBRECHT MAUER, born Aachen, Germany, 1952; admitted, 1981, Germany. *Education:* University of Cologne (1979). *Member:* Deutscher Anwaltsverein. *LANGUAGES:* German and English. *PRACTICE AREAS:* Debt Collection; Traffic Regulations and Accident Claims; Planning and Building Laws and Regulations; Landlords and Tenants Law.

DIETER PAMPFER, born Aachen, Germany, 1955; admitted, 1983, Attorney-at-Law, Germany; 1990, Chartered Book Accountant, Germany. *Education:* Universities of Bonn and Cologne. *Member:* Deutscher Anwaltsverein. *LANGUAGES:* German and English. *PRACTICE AREAS:* Commercial and Corporate Law; Insolvency Law; Labor Law; Tax Law.

RALPH SCHMITZ, born Aachen, Germany, 1961; admitted, 1992, Germany. *Education:* University of Münster. *Member:* Deutscher Familiengerichtstages eV German Family Law Association. *LANGUAGES:* German, English and French. *PRACTICE AREAS:* Family and Divorce Law and Matrimonial Affairs; Administrative Law; Immigration Law; EC Law.

GABRIELE HESEN, born Krefeld, Germany, 1965; admitted, 1993, Germany. *Education:* University of Trier. *Member:* Deutsch-Niederländische Juristenvereinigung German-Dutch Law Association. *LANGUAGES:* German, English and Dutch. *PRACTICE AREAS:* Commercial and Corporate Law; Tax Law; Competition Law; Dutch Law.

SCHULTZE & BRAUN

Established in 1975

EISENBAHNSTR. 19-23

77855 ACHERN, GERMANY

Telephone: 07841-7080

Telefax: 07841-70301

Dresden, Germany Office: Boltenhagener Platz 9, 01109. Telephone: 0351/8808046. Telefax: 0351/8808040.

Leipzig, Germany Office: Brahest.8, D-04347. Telephone: 0341/244340. Telefax: 0341/2443439.

General International Practice including Restructuring and Bankruptcy, Finance and Banking, International Transactions, Corporate, Investment, Settlement, Competition, Construction and Employment Law, Debt Collection, Foreign Investment, Shareholders and Agency Agreements, Unfair Competition, Taxes, Tax-Planning, Cross Boarder-Tax Questions, Cross Boarder Insolvencies.

FIRM PROFILE: The firm is specialised in reorganization and bankruptcy law and all kind of business, bank and corporate law. Partners are lawyers and accountants, partly double qualified.

DR. EBERHARD BRAUN, born Heidenheim, Baden-Württemberg, Germany, June 11, 1947; admitted, 1975, Germany. *Education:* University of Freiburg (Dr.Jur.). Author: "Die Prüfung von Sanierungskonzepten"; "Betriebswirtschaftliche Checkliste zur Prüfung der Sanierungsfähigkeit von Unternehmen"; "Kapitalersetzende Maßnahme i. S. v. §32 a Abs. 3 GmbHG durch Pachtverträge in der Betriebsaufspaltung?"; "Sanierung und Insolvenz"; "Die Ableitung der Kreditunwürdigkeit gem. §32 a GmbHG aus dem Jahresabschluß der Gesellschaft"; "Sanierung im gerichtlichen Gesamtvollstreckungsverfahren der DDR." *Member:* Freiburg Bar (Vice President); Chairman, Restructuring and Insolvency Committee IDW; Deutscher Anwaltsverein; Arbeitskreis Sanierung und Insolvenz; A.E.P.P.C.; IBA; Arbeitskreis für Insolvenzrecht; Arbeitskreis f. Insolvenz- und Schiedsgerichts e.V.; Arbeitsgemeinschaft f. Internationalen Rechtsverkehr im DAV. *LANGUAGES:* English, French and Italian. *PRACTICE AREAS:* Bankruptcy; Banks and Banking; Corporate Law.

THEO NAENDRUP, born Münster, Westfalia, Germany, May 15, 1950. *Education:* University of Freiburg. *Member:* Deutscher Anwaltsverein; Arbeitsgemeinschaft der Verkehrsrechtsanwälte und der Strafverteidiger i. Deutschen Anwaltsverein. *LANGUAGES:* English. *PRACTICE AREAS:* Environmental Law; Criminal Law; Government.

BARBARA MEIDER, born Bad Mergentheim, Germany, June 14, 1951. *Education:* Universities of Freiburg and Mainz. *Member:* Deutscher

(This Listing Continued)

Anwaltsverein. *LANGUAGES:* English and French. *PRACTICE AREAS:* Family Law; Labour and Employment.

CLAUDIA WOLF, born Heidelberg, Germany, December 6, 1955. *Education:* University of Freiburg. President, Anwaltsverein Baden-Baden. *Member:* Deutscher Anwaltsverein; Arbeitsgemeinschaft der Verkehrsrechtsanwälte und für privates Baurecht. *LANGUAGES:* English and Italian. *PRACTICE AREAS:* Construction Law; Contracts; Criminal Law.

DR. FERDINAND KIEßNER, born Bad Köngishofen i. Gr. Unterfranken, Germany, November 25, 1952. *Education:* Universities of Würzburg and Freiburg (Dr.Jur). *Member:* Deutscher Anwaltsverein; Arbeitskreis für Insolvenzrecht. *LANGUAGES:* English. *PRACTICE AREAS:* Bankruptcy.

BERTRAM WOLF, born Obergrombach, Bruchsal, Germany, May 29, 1958. *Education:* University of Heidelberg. *Member:* Deutscher Anwaltsverein. *LANGUAGES:* English and French. *PRACTICE AREAS:* Commercial Law; Labour and Employment Law.

THOMAS KIND, born Coburg, Germany, November 5, 1960. *Education:* University of Würzburg. *Member:* Deutscher Anwaltsverein; Arbeitskreis für Insolvenzrecht. *LANGUAGES:* English and Italian. *PRACTICE AREAS:* Bankruptcy; Torts.

MARTINA CHARLOTTE DIETRICH, born Frankfurt, Germany, June 17, 1959. *Education:* University of Frankfurt. *Member:* Deutscher Anwaltsverein. *LANGUAGES:* English and French. *PRACTICE AREAS:* Business Law; Commercial Law; Company Law.

DR. PETER DE BRA, born Essen, Germany, December 3, 1958. *Education:* University of Freiburg (Dr. jur.). *Member:* Deutscher Anwaltsverein. *LANGUAGES:* English and French. *PRACTICE AREAS:* International Law; Business Law; Banks and Banking.

STEPHANO BUCK, born Cologne, Germany, August 27, 1961. *Education:* Universities of Konstanz, München and Freiburg. *Member:* Deutscher Anwaltsverein. *LANGUAGES:* English. *PRACTICE AREAS:* Bankruptcy.

JUDITH FRANZ, born Hofweier, Offenburg, Germany, August 22, 1961. *Education:* University of Freiburg. *Member:* Deutscher Anwaltsverein. *LANGUAGES:* English and French. *PRACTICE AREAS:* General Practice.

HARALD KROTH, born Mespelbrunn, Aschaffenburg, Germany, January 11, 1961. *Education:* University of Würzburg. *Member:* Deutscher Anwaltsverein. *LANGUAGES:* English. *PRACTICE AREAS:* Bankruptcy.

DETLEF SPECOVIUS, born Gelsenkirchen, Germany, July 1, 1961. *Education:* University of Münster. *Member:* Deutscher Anwaltsverein. *LANGUAGES:* English. *PRACTICE AREAS:* Bankruptcy.

DR. RAINER RIGGERT, born Frankfurt a. Main, Germany, February 4, 1962. *Education:* University of Freiburg. *Member:* Deutscher Anwaltverein. *LANGUAGES:* English. *PRACTICE AREAS:* Government; Commercial Law; Constitutional Law.

CHRISTIAN FORCHER, born Baden-Baden, Germany, November 22, 1964. *Education:* University of Heidelburg. *Member:* Deutscher Anwaltverein und Arbeitsgemeinschaft der Verkehrsrechtsanwälte. *LANGUAGES:* English. *PRACTICE AREAS:* General Practice; Criminal Law.

URSULA RÖRIG, born Baden-Baden, Germany, July 26, 1963. *Education:* University of Freiburg. *Member:* Deutscher Anwaltverein und Arbeitsgemeinschaft der Verkehrsrechtsanwälte. *LANGUAGES:* English. *PRACTICE AREAS:* General Practice.

Languages: English, French, German and Italian.

SEITZ WECKBACH FENT

ANNASTRASSE 36A

POSTFACH 10 23 44

86013 AUGSBURG, GERMANY

Telephone: 0821/ 3 45 85-0

Telefax: 0821/ 3 45 85-33

General Practice, Corporate, Tax, Labor, Unfair Competition, Estate Planning, Probate Law, Family Law and Arbitration.

(This Listing Continued)

SEITZ WECKBACH FENT, Augsburg—Continued

MEMBERS OF FIRM

DR. THEODOR SEITZ, born Augsburg, Germany, November 9, 1951; admitted, 1982, Bavaria; 1983, New York. *Education:* University of Augsburg (Dr.jur., 1980); Harvard Law School (LL.M., 1981). Author: "Effective Legal Protection in Labor Law," Athenäum Verlag, 1978; "Annotations to District Court Düsseldorf, Decision of December 10, 1986," CR 33, 1986; "Annotation to District Court Karlsruhe, Decision of October 7, 1983," CR 549, 1986; "Annotation to Federal Tax Court, Decision of July 20, 1988," CR 291, 1989. With Shearman & Sterling, 1981-1982. Assistant Professor, 1978-1980 and Lecturer on Corporate and Commercial Law, 1988—, University of Augsburg. Lecturer at the Verwaltungs and Wirtschaftsakademie, Augsburg, 1986, 1990 and 1994. *Member:* Bavarian Bar Association; New York Bar; Harvard Law School Association of Europe; German Society for Data Processing Law; German Arbitration Society; Young Lawyers Association (AIJA). *LANGUAGES:* German and English.

DR. THOMAS WECKBACH, born Augsburg, Germany, June 1, 1956; admitted, 1986, Bavaria. *Education:* University of Augsburg (Dr.jur., 1986);. Author: Annotations to Labour Appeal Court decision of 20.06.85, CR 480/1986., "The Binding Effect of the Prohibition of Estate Partition", Duncker & Humblot, Berlin, 1987; "The Works Council's Right to Information on the Introduction of Electronic Data Processing in Personnel Administration", NZA 1988, 305. Book Review, "Collective Commentary on the Law relating to Part-time Work", Becker, Danne et al 1987, CR 551/1989. Assistant Professor, 1983-1986 and Lecturer, 1988, 1992, and 1994. University of Augsburg. *Member:* Bavarian Bar Association; German Society for Data Processing Law; German Labor Court Association. *LANGUAGES:* German, English and Italian.

MICHAEL FENT, born Burgau, Germany, July 12, 1956; admitted, 1982, Bavaria. *Education:* University of Augsburg. Assistant Professor, University of Augsburg, 1979-1982. *Member:* Bavarian Bar Association; Young Lawyers Association (AIJA); Kiwanis Club. *LANGUAGES:* German and English.

HANS-PETER BERNHARD, born Augsburg, Germany, July 8, 1962; admitted, 1993, Bavaria. *Education:* University of Augsburg. *Member:* Bavarian Bar Association. *LANGUAGES:* German and English.

DR. RUDOLF WITTMANN, born Nuremberg, Germany, October 25, 1960; admitted, 1994, Bavaria. *Education:* Universities of Bayreuth and Augsburg (Dr.jur., 1992). Author: "Views and Nature of Tax Depreciation," FR 540, 1988; "Paths to Taxation Law. Festschrift for Wolfgang Jakob," Wittmann, Augsburg, 1991; "Market Income - Legal and Constitutional Concept of Income Taxation?" Wittmann, Augsburg, 1992; "Changes in Real-Estate Taxation under the Mißbrauchsbekämpfungsgesetz," BB 255, 1994. Assistant Professor, 1986-1994 and Lecturer on Taxation Law, 1994, University of Augsburg. Lecturer, Verwaltungs und Wirtschaftsakademie, Augsburg, 1994. *Member:* Bavarian Bar Association; German Society for Taxation Law. *LANGUAGES:* German and English.

WÖRLEN & ZIEGELMEIR

Lawyers at the Landgericht Augsburg, the Oberlandesgericht München and the Bayerisches Oberstes Landesgericht

Established in 1975

MARKTPLATZ 4/I
86720 AUGSBURG (NÖRDLINGEN), GERMANY
Telephone: 09081/3011
Telefax: 09081/22983
Fu: 01 61 19 15 844 (w) / 01 61 18 07 346 (z)

General practice, consultation and litigation, real estate, building and construction (private and public law), labour law, insurance law and damage liability, family law, inheritance law.

FIRM PROFILE: *The firm was founded in 1975 by Mr. Wörlen who left at this time the career of a notary public. It is collaborating with the county's Corporation of Masons and other artisans where Mr. Wörlen is also working in the legal training of the corporation members. Mr. Ziegelmeir is a chartered labor lawyer. The firm is a member of AdvoSelect EEIG, a network of law firms pooling their resources in special fields and crossborder cases, specializing in business law for middle-sized companies. AdvoSelect is represented in 51 cities throughout Europe.*

(This Listing Continued)

EU530B

FRIEDRICH WÖRLEN, born Nördlingen, 1945; admitted, 1975 (1980, OLG München and BayObLG). *Education:* Universities of Tübingen, Geneva and Munich. Notary's assessor, 1974. *Member:* German Bar Association (President, Local Branch; Member of the Board, Construction Law Committee, Bavarian Branch); German Association for Inheritance Law. *LANGUAGES:* German, French, English, Italian and Latin. *PRACTICE AREAS:* Civil Litigation; Construction; Architecture; Real Estate; Zoning, Planning and Land Use; Wills; Family Law; Inheritance; Companies and Partnerships; Arbitration.

JOHANNES ZIEGELMEIR, born Nördlingen, 1961; admitted, 1990. *Education:* University of Munich. Chartered Labor Lawyer. *Member:* German Bar Association (Traffic Law Committee). *LANGUAGES:* German and English. *PRACTICE AREAS:* General Practice; Labor; Liability and Insurance; Real Estate; Leases and Leasing.

LUTZ KAISER

HARDÄCKERSTRASSE 5
76530 BADEN-BADEN, GERMANY
Telephone: 07221-392523
Fax: 07221-392523

General Practice.

LUTZ KAISER, born Northeim, Germany, August 10, 1961; admitted, 1992, District Court of Baden-Baden, Germany. *Education:* University of Freiburg, Germany. *Member:* International Bar Association; German-American Lawyers Association; German-Latin-American Lawyers Association. *LANGUAGES:* German, English and Spanish. *PRACTICE AREAS:* Taxation; Restitution Claims (in former GDR); Successions.

VOIGTLÄNDER-TETZNER & PARTNER

Established in 1989

KAISER-FRIEDRICH-PROMENADE 9-11
P.O. BOX 2411
BAD HOMBURG v.d.H.
Telephone: (06172) 25226
Fax: (06172) 20111

Dresden, Germany Office: Grossenhainer Straße 198.
Berlin, Germany Office: Friedrichstraße 180.

Mergers and Acquisitions, Corporate Law, Litigation and Arbitration, Business and Trade Law, Unfair Competition, International Medical Regulations, Real Estate and Construction Law, German Unification and Privatization, European Community Law, Eastern European Legal Systems.

CHRISTOPH SCHALAST, born Frankfurt am Main, Germany, December 13, 1960; admitted, 1991, Frankfurt am Main. *Education:* Universities of Gießen, Lausanne (Switzerland) and Frankfurt am Main (Referendar, 1987); Faculté Internationale de Droit Comparé Strasbourg (Diplome Supérieure de Droit Comparé, 1988); University of Saarbrücken (Certificate of European Studies, 1990). Trainee, European Parliament, 1989. Attorney with Albert, Flad & Schlosshan, 1991-1992. Author: "German Electricity Industry and the EC Internal Market for Energy," Luxembourg, 1989; "Tax Reduction Procedure for Contributables with Limited Income," FR 1990; "Internal Market for Energy and System for Advancement of Coal Supported Electricity in Germany," RdE 1991. *Member:* Frankfurt/Main Lawyers' Association; Comparative Law Association; International Bar Association (Member, Energy Law Section); Club des Affaires de la Hesse. *PRACTICE AREAS:* European Community Law; Mergers and Acquisitions; Corporate Law; Energy Law.

Languages: English, French, Russian, Dutch and Greek

(For Biographical Data on additional personnel, see Professional Biographies at Dresden, Germany)

RECHTSANWÄLTE DR. KROLL & PARTNER

Established in 1994

FRIEDRICHSTR. 57
D-72336 BALINGEN, GERMANY
Telephone: (07433) 90160
Fax: (07433) 901632

Reutlingen, Germany Office: Eberhardstr.1, D-72764. Telephone: 07121/324-0. Fax: 07121/324-10.

Stuttgart, Germany Office: Vaihinger Straβ24, D-70567. Telephone: (0711) 161770. Fax: (07 11) 71 00 34.

All fields of law, except Maritime Law.

FIRM PROFILE: *The firm was established in 1953 and offers a full range of legal services and tax-advising, with offices in Reutlingen, Stuttgart and Balingen. In 1990 association with attorneys' offices Villingen-Schwenningen (Black Forest), Schmalkalden (Thuringia) and Saverne (France) under the name of C.A.P. EWIV Cooperation Anwaltspartner, legal domicile Stuttgart.*

The Reutlingen office consists of 10 attorneys and a staff of 20 employees.

MEMBER OF FIRM

DR. KLAUS GEKELER, born Stuttgart, Germany, 1957; admitted, 1991, Germany. *Education:* University of Tübingen, Bankkaufmann. Author: "Der personengesellschaftliche Konzern im Licht des aktienrechtlichen Konzernmodells." *Member:* German Lawyers Association. *LANGUAGES:* German, English and French. *PRACTICE AREAS:* Unfair Competition; Business Law; Civil Law; Commercial Law; International Trademarks.

ACKERMANN & SCHULTZE-ZEU

Established in 1972

KANTSTRAβE 13
D-10623 BERLIN, GERMANY
Telephone: 030-313 02 41
Telefax: 030-313 13 64

Commercial and Corporate Law, International Contracts, East West Law, License Agreements, Arbitration, Copyright, Real Estate, Competition, Antitrust, Labor, Tenancy, Divorce, Inheritance, Environmental and Administration Law, Restitution Law in Connection with Expropriation in the former Eastern-Bloc.

FIRM PROFILE: *The firm was established in 1972 and offers individual and practical legal counselling for both the corporate and individual client in all areas of civil and commercial law in a national and international context. Furthermore, it offers all notary services.*

MEMBERS OF FIRM

PETER R. ACKERMANN, born Berlin, West Germany, February 12, 1939; admitted, 1967, Notary Public, Berlin; 1979, United States Court in Berlin. *Education:* Universities of Berlin, Munich, Fribourg (Switzerland), Göttingen (Referendar, 1963); Strasbourg (France, Diploma of EEC Law). Scholarship Student, California, 1956. Author: "Aviation Law," Publications of the University of Göttingen, 1963; "Selling and Buying under the New Civil Code at the German Democratic Republic," Schriftenreihe Recht und Wirtschaft; "Foreign Trade Laws of German Democratic Republic," Chase World Information Corporation, New York, 1977. Co-author: "The New Civil Code of the GDR," Berlin, 1978. *Member:* Berlin and German Bar Associations; American Chamber of Commerce in Germany; German Chamber of Industry and Commerce, London; Deutsches Institut für Schiedsgerichtswesen e. V. *LANGUAGES:* German, English and French. *PRACTICE AREAS:* International Arbitration; Business and Corporate Law; Mergers and Acquisitions; Formation of Companies; Partnerships and Joint Ventures.

DR. DIETER SCHULTZE-ZEU, born Cottbus, Germany, May 15, 1934; admitted, 1964, Germany, Notary Public, Berlin. *Education:* Universities of Frankfurt, Berlin and Kiel (Referendar, Berlin and Kiel, 1961). District Judge, Mainz, 1962. Author, "Die Rechtstellung des Internationalen Beamten," Kiel, 1961; "Contracts in East-West-Trade," Ost-Wirtschaftsreport, 1975; "Technologie-Transfer im Ost-West Handel," Heidelberg, 1988; "Patentrecht der DDR," Verlag für Recht und Wirtschaft Heidelberg, August, 1989. *Member:* Berlin and German Bar Associations; American Chamber of Commerce in Germany; Debelux Chamber of Com-

(This Listing Continued)

merce, Bruxelles. *LANGUAGES:* German, English and French. *PRACTICE AREAS:* International Business Law; Corporate and Contract Law; Mergers and Acquisitions; Formation and Ongoing Maintenance of Corporations; Partnerships; Joint Ventures; Business Organizations; Real Estate Law; Restitution & Compensation in connection with Expropriations in Eastern Bloc countries.

DIETGER FEDER, born Breslau, Germany, February 26, 1939; admitted, 1968, Germany; Notary Public, Berlin. *Education:* Universities of Freiburg, Berlin, Kiel (Referendar, 1963); Hamburg (Assessor, 1967). *Member:* Berlin and German Bar Associations; Association for Real Estate; Handelskammer Deutschland-Schweiz, Zürich. *LANGUAGES:* German, English, French and Spanish. *PRACTICE AREAS:* Labour and Family Law; Residential and Commercial Premises Law; Real Estate and Corporate Law.

DETLEF P. EULITZ, born Berlin, Germany, November 17, 1948; admitted, 1975, Germany; Notary Public, Berlin. *Education:* University of Berlin (Referendar, 1973; Assessor, 1975). *Member:* Berlin and German Bar Associations. *LANGUAGES:* German, English and French. *PRACTICE AREAS:* Competition and Copyright Law; Civil Building and Architectural Law; Family and Divorce Law; Restitution & Compensation in connection with Expropriations in Eastern Bloc countries.

DR. GERHARD GÖTZ, born Erbach, Germany, September 5, 1947; admitted, 1977, Germany. Author: "Verbundbildung bei den Einkaufsgenossenschaften des Lebensmittelshandels und einzelgenossenschaftlicher Förderauftrag," Marburger Schriften zum Genossenschaftswesen, Band 54, Vandenhoeck & Ruprecht. *Member:* Berlin and German Bar Associations. *LANGUAGES:* German, English, French and Polish. *PRACTICE AREAS:* General Civil Law; Commercial, Labour and Competition Law; Securities and Commodity Futures Law; Medical and Health Service Law.

MARTIN SCHRADER, born Berlin, Germany, December 31, 1955; admitted, 1983, Germany. *Education:* Universities of Berlin, Münster (Referandar, 1980; Assessor, 1983). *Member:* Berlin and German Bar Associations; German-Swedish Chamber of Commerce, Stockholm. *LANGUAGES:* German, English, Swedish and Norwegian. *PRACTICE AREAS:* National and International Business Law; Trade and Corporate Law; Leasing and Real Estate Law; Computer Law; National and International Inheritance Law.

DR. NIKOLAUS WÜRTZ, born Viersen, Germany, October 25, 1951; admitted, 1983, Germany. *Education:* Universities of Freiburg, Heidelberg, Würzburg (Referendar 1977, Assessor 1983). Author: "The Law of Swap-Arrangements," 1984. *Member:* Berlin and German Bar Associations. *LANGUAGES:* German and English. *PRACTICE AREAS:* General Civil Law; Transport Law; Labour Law; Tenancy Law; Family Law; Criminal Law.

BEITEN BURKHARDT MITTL & WEGENER

Rechtsanwälte

KURFÜRSTENSTRASSE 72-74
D-10787 BERLIN, GERMANY
Telephone: (0 30) 264 71-0
Telefax: (0 30) 264 71-123

Munich, Germany Office: Leopoldstrasse 236, D-80807. Telephone: (089) 35065-00. Telefax: (089) 35065-123.

Frankfurt/Main, Germany Office: Arndtstrasse 28, D-60325 Frankfurt/Main. Telephone: (0 69) 75 60 95-0. Telefax: (0 69) 75 60 95-12.

Nürnberg, Germany Office: Obere Turnstrasse 8, D-90429 Nürnberg. Telephone: (09 11) 2 79 71-0. Telefax: (09 11) 2 79 71-99.

Leipzig, Germany Office: Käthe-Kollwitz-Strasse 54, D-04109 Leipzig. Telephone: (03 41) 4 77 25 97. Telefax: (03 41) 4 77 25 99.

Potsdam, Germany Office: Heinrich-Mann-Allee 105 B, D-14473 Potsdam. Telephone: (0331) 33 43 06. Telefax: (0331) 33 43 29.

Hof, Germany Office: Oberer Torplatz 1, D-95028 Hof. Telephone: (09281) 80 23. Telefax: (09281) 1 65 69.

Plauen, Germany Office: Lindenstrasse 5, D-08523 Plauen. Telephone: (03741) 22 35 11; 22 49 62. Telefax: (03741) 22 49 62.

New York, New York Office: 215 East 73rd Street, New York, NY 10021. Telephone: (212) 570-2141. Telefax: (212) 734-7011.

London, England Office: Swedenborg House, 21 Bloomsbury Way, London, WC1A 2TH. Telephone: (0171) 2 42 44 66. Telefax: (0171) 2 42 44 67.

(This Listing Continued)

BEITEN BURKHARDT MITTL & WEGENER, Berlin—Continued

Moscow, Russia Office: Ul. Alekseja Tolstovo D.30/1, 103001 Moscow. Telephone and Telefax: (095) 202 37 60; 290 05 56.

Prague, Czech Republic Office: Na Bojišti 24, 120 00 Prague 2. Telephone: (2) 24 91 5808. Telefax: (2) 24 91 5804.

Budapest, Hungary Office: József Nádor Tér 9, H-1051 Budapest. Telephone: (1) 2 66 18 10. Telefax: (1) 2 66 18 11.

Hong Kong Office: 605 B, Sixth Floor, Peregrine Tower, Lippo Centre, 89 Queensway. Telephone: (852) 2524 6468. Telefax: (852) 2524 7028.

Beijing, People's Republic of China Office: Unit 10, 29th Floor, Jing Guang Centre, Hu Jia Lou, Chao Yang Qu, 100020. Telephone: (86-1) 501 4569; 501 3388 Ext. 2910. Telefax: (86-1) 501 3034.

Commercial Law, Company Law, M & A, Joint Ventures, Finance, Banking, Leasing, Domestic and International Tax, Antitrust, EC Law, Real Property and Private Construction, Electronic Data Processing (Protection and Licensing), Media, Publishing, Unfair Competition, Trademarks, Copyright, Labour, General and Special Administrative Law Particularly Public Construction and Planning Regulations and Public International Law, Environmental Law, Agricultural Law, Privatization and Restitution (former GDR), Probate, Family and Estate Planning, Insolvency and Sports, Insurance, Automobile Accidents and Injuries.

FIRM PROFILE: BEITEN BURKHARDT MITTL & WEGENER is a nation-wide and international law firm with 108 lawyers. The firm's head office is in Munich. All the firm's offices provide a comprehensive range of services in the main areas of civil and commercial law.

FEDOR SEIFERT, born Bad Pyrmont, 1946; admitted, 1976, Germany. *Education:* Universities of Frankfurt a.M. and Freiburg (law degree, 1972; Dr. jur., 1976). Notary Public, 1986. Author: "From Homer to Richard Strauss - Copyright in Stories and Figures," 1989. Co-author: "Introduction into Copyright of Music," 1982. *Member:* German Association for the Protection of Industrial Property and Copyright (GRUR); International Society of Copyrights (INTERGU). *LANGUAGES:* German and English. *PRACTICE AREAS:* Press Law; Publishing and Radio; Unfair Competition; Copyrights; Advertising and Marketing; Labour and Employment.

ROLAND STEINMEYER, born Augsburg, 1954; admitted, 1983, Germany. *Education:* University of Augsburg (law degree, 1979); University of Würzburg (Dr. jur., 1985) and Cape Town, South Africa (LL.M., 1980). Lecturer in law, University of Augsburg, 1981-1983. Member: Bundesverband der Deutschen Industrie e.V. (Committee on Contract Clauses), 1988—; Supervisory Board, Westerwald AG, 1989-1993; Travel Hotel GmbH, 1992-1993; Elektrokohle Lichtenberg AG, 1993—. *LANGUAGES:* German, English and French. *PRACTICE AREAS:* Company Law; Acquisitions and Sales; Restructuring; Financial Services; Expropriation and Restitution; Insolvency; Liquidations.

WOLF WEGENER, born Berlin, 1933; admitted, 1960, Germany. *Education:* Universities of Freiburg/Breisgau, Geneva, Kiel, Paris and Berlin (law degree, 1957; Dr. jur., 1957). Notary Public, 1974. Bank Executive, 1961-1964. General Counsel of ADAC (German Automobile Association). Deputy Chairman of the Supervisory Board of ADAC-Verlag GmbH. *Member:* ADAC-Rechtsschutz-Versicherungs-AG; ADAC Beteiligungs-und Wirtschafts GmbH (Supervisory Board); Deutsche Bank AG (Advisory Board); Volkswagen AG (Advisory Board Berlin); Deutsche Akademie für Verkehrswissenschaft, Hamburg (Board Member). *LANGUAGES:* German, English and French. *PRACTICE AREAS:* Tax Planning; Pensions; Insurance; Automobile Accidents and Injuries; Sports.

ULRICH HUSCHKE, born Seddin, 1938; admitted, 1967, Germany. *Education:* University of Berlin (law degree, 1963). Notary Public, 1990. General Counsel of ADAC (German Automobile Association), Berlin-Brandenburg. *LANGUAGES:* German. *PRACTICE AREAS:* Real Estate; Construction Law; Insurance; Automobile Accidents and Injuries.

RALF WITTKOWSKI, born Quedlinburg/Harz, 1957; admitted, 1986, Germany. *Education:* University of Berlin (law degree, 1983). Co-author: "Deutsch-Deutsche Rechtsfragen," 1993. *LANGUAGES:* German and English. *PRACTICE AREAS:* Public, Administrative and Environmental Law; Ecclesiastical Law; Zoning, Planning and Land Use; Insurance; Automobile Accidents and Injuries; Sports.

FRANK OBERMANN, born Frankfurt am Main, 1959; admitted, 1989, Germany. *Education:* University of Frankfurt a.M. (law degree, 1985). Staff Member, University of Frankfurt a.M., 1982-1983. Member of the Supervisory Board, Neue Deutsche Spielcasino GmbH, 1994. *LANGUAGES:* German and English. *PRACTICE AREAS:* Company Law; Acquisitions and

(This Listing Continued)

Sales; Restructuring; Real Estate; Construction Law; Labour and Employment; Expropriation and Restitution.

BERNHARD SCHULTZ, born Dahn, 1959; admitted, 1989, Germany. *Education:* University of Munich (law degree, 1985; Dr. jur., 1991). Associate with a major law firm in Luxembourg, 1989-1990. *LANGUAGES:* German, English and French. *PRACTICE AREAS:* Financial Services; Labour and Employment; Expropriation and Restitution.

BERND FIESSLER, born Frankfurt a.M., 1960; admitted, 1992, Germany. *Education:* University of Frankfurt a.M. (law degree, 1989). *LANGUAGES:* German. *PRACTICE AREAS:* Real Estate; Construction Law.

HOLGER KÜHL, born Hamburg, 1959; admitted, 1991, Germany. *Education:* Universities of Munich, Bonn (law degree, 1986; Dr. jur., 1993) and Cape Town, South Africa (LL.M., 1987). Trainee, EEC Commission, Brussels, 1989. *LANGUAGES:* German, English and French. *PRACTICE AREAS:* Expropriation and Restitution; European Community Law.

KARIN HELD, born Zwickau, 1952; admitted, 1982, Germany. *Education:* University of Kiel (law degree, 1980). *LANGUAGES:* German and English. *PRACTICE AREAS:* Labour and Employment; Insurance; Automobile Accidents and Injuries.

CHRISTIANA UPMANN, born Osnabrück, 1961; admitted, 1991, Germany. *Education:* University of Würzburg and Freiburg (law degree, 1987). *LANGUAGES:* German. *PRACTICE AREAS:* Insurance; Automobile Accidents and Injuries.

MARIO-ULRIK OLOWSON, born Hamburg, 1961; admitted, 1993, Germany. *Education:* University of Hamburg (law degree, 1989). *LANGUAGES:* German, English and Italian. *PRACTICE AREAS:* Labour and Employment; Insurance; Automobile Accidents and Injuries.

CHRISTOPH V. ARNIM, born Frankfurt a.M., 1962; admitted, 1993, Germany. *Education:* Universities of Mainz and Freiburg (law degree, 1990). *LANGUAGES:* German and English. *PRACTICE AREAS:* Insolvency; Liquidations; Real Estate; Construction Law.

STEFAN KOBES, born Bochum, 1960; admitted, 1989, Germany. *Education:* Universities of Kiel, Lausanne, Freiburg; University of Public Administration Speyer (law degree, 1989; Dr. jur., 1993). Staff Member, Institute for Foreign and International Private Law, University of Freiburg, 1986-1987. *LANGUAGES:* German, French and English. *PRACTICE AREAS:* Public; Administrative and Environmental Law; Zoning; Planning and Land Use; European Community Law.

HUGUES LAINE, born Lille, France, 1966; admitted, 1994, as Avocat à la Cour de Paris. *Education:* University of Tours, France (Maîtrise en Droit, Institute for International Commercial Law, 1990; Diplôme d'Etudes Supérieures Spécialisées, D.E.S.S., 1991; Docteur en Droit, 1993); University of Passau, Germany (1989). In-house Counsel with Ciments Français Berlin, 1992-1993. Lecturer, University of Berlin, 1994—. *Member:* German-French Jurists' Association. *LANGUAGES:* French, German and English. *PRACTICE AREAS:* Company Law; Acquisitions and Sales; Restructuring; European Community Law; Cartels.

ARNOLD WENDORFF, born Düsseldorf, 1962; admitted, 1994, Germany. *Education:* Universities of Passau and Berlin (law degree, 1991). *LANGUAGES:* German, English and Russian. *PRACTICE AREAS:* Insurance; Automobile Accidents and Injuries; Public and Administrative Law.

SUSANNE REMES, born Dorsten/Westfalen, 1962; admitted, 1994, Germany. *Education:* Universities of Marburg, Lausanne and Munich (law degree, 1988). In-house Counsel with Treuhandanstalt Berlin, 1991-1993. *LANGUAGES:* German, English and French. *PRACTICE AREAS:* Company Law; Acquisitions and Sales; Restructuring; Real Estate; Construction Law; Labour and Employment; Expropriation and Restitution.

ANGELIKA RÜBELING, born Bremerhaven, 1963; admitted, 1994, Germany. *Education:* Universities of Hamburg and Bayreuth (law degree, 1989). *LANGUAGES:* German, English and Spanish. *PRACTICE AREAS:* Automobile Accidents and Injuries; Public and Administrative Law; Zoning; Planning and Land Use.

REGINA ROGGE, born Berlin, 1962; admitted, 1993, Germany. *Education:* University of Berlin (law degree, 1990). *LANGUAGES:* German, English, Czech and French. *PRACTICE AREAS:* Insurance; Automobile Accidents and Injuries; Expropriation and Restitution; Probate and Family Law.

CLAUDIA MUMMENHOFF, born Cologne, 1960; admitted, 1991, Germany. *Education:* University of Cologne (law degree, 1987). In-house

(This Listing Continued)

Counsel with Treuhandanstalt Berlin/Treuhandliegenschaftsgesellschaft Berlin, 1991-1994. *LANGUAGES:* German and English. *PRACTICE AREAS:* Company Law; Acquisitions and Sales; Restructuring; Real Estate; Construction Law; Labour and Employment; Expropriation and Restitution.

BENDER ZAHN TIGGES

KÜRFURSTENDAMM 170
10707 BERLIN, GERMANY
Telephone: (0 30) 883 23 98
Telefax: (0 30) 8 82 45 52

Düsseldorf, Germany Office: Thyssen-Haus, August-Thyssen-Straβe 1, 40211. Telephone: 0211/86 87-0. Telex: 8 588 246 bend. Telefax: 0211/86 87-100.

Chemnitz, Germany Office: Straβe der Nationen 37, 09111 Chemnitz. Telephone: (0371/428946/47). Telefax: (0371/428949).

Warsaw, Poland Office: ul.Piekna 66a, 00-072 Warsaw. Telephone: (00482) 628-02-11. Fax: (00482) 628-47-66.

General and International Practice, Corporate and Securities, Banking, Commercial, Bankruptcy, Insolvency and Reorganization, Taxation, Real Estate, Antitrust, Intellectual Property, Environmental and Administrative, Insurance, Litigation, International Trusts, Family and Inheritance Law. Privatization in the former German Democratic Republic. Restitution Claims in the former German Democratic Republic. Commercial and Business Law in Poland.

MEMBERS - BERLIN

WOLFGANG ZAHN, born Bärtorf, Germany, 1940; 1972, Germany. *Education:* Universities of Tübingen, Hamburg and Göttingen. Appointed Notary, 1983. Former Junior Barrister with Ramdohr-Plön Law Firm, Santiago, Chile. *LANGUAGES:* German and English.

DR. THOMAS PUFFE, born 1958; admitted, Landesgericht Berlin. *Education:* Free University of Berlin; Columbia University, New York (1984). Associate, Kärgel, Poppendorf & Vollhardt, Berlin, 1982-1990. *LANGUAGES:* German and English.

CARSTEN PÜTGER, born Hameln, Germany, 1961; admitted, 1992, Germany. *Education:* University of Giessen and University of Hannover. Law Department, Hoechst A.G., 1991. Attorney, Treuhandanstalt, Berlin, 1992-1993. *LANGUAGES:* German and English.

STEPHAN EIDEN, born Dortmund, Germany, 1958; admitted, 1993, Germany. *Education:* University of Regensburg. Attorney, Treuhandanstalt, Berlin, 1991-1992. Co-author, "Arbeitsrecht und Privatisierung von Unternehmen durch die Treuhandanstalt," AuA 1/91. *LANGUAGES:* German and English.

CHRISTOPH GERMER, born Gieβen, Germany, 1961; admitted, 1993, Germany. *Education:* Justus-Liebig University, Gieβen. *LANGUAGES:* German and English.

Languages: German, English, French, Italian, Polish and Japanese

BODEN OPPENHOFF RASOR RAUE

BERLIN, GERMANY

(See Oppenhoff & Rädler)

BOESEBECK, BARZ & PARTNER

Established in 1990

SCHLUETERSTRASSE 37
10629 BERLIN, GERMANY
Telephone: (49) (30) 88 57 45-0
Telecopier: (49) (30) 88 57 45-99

REVISERS OF THE GERMAN LAW DIGEST FOR THIS DIRECTORY.

Frankfurt am Main, Germany Office: Darmstaedter Landstrasse 125, 60598 Frankfurt am Main. Telephone: (49) (69) 96 236-0. Telefax: (49) (69) 96 236-100.

(This Listing Continued)

Dresden, Germany Office: Heideparkstrasse 4, 01099 Dresden . Telephone: (49) (351) 56 70 550. Telecopier: (49) (351) 50 23 476.

Vienna, Austria Office (Sprechstelle) Graben 29A, 1010 Vienna. Telephone: (43) (1) 53 55 744. Telecopier (43) (1) 53 50 649.

Warsaw, Poland Office: ul. Wspólna 25, 00519 Warsaw. Telephone: (48) (2) 62 83 029. Telecopier: (48) (22) 29 41 05.

Zagreb, Croatia Office: Trg bana J. Jelacica 3, 4100 Zagreb. Telephone: (385) (41) 42 71 16. Telecopier: (385) (41) 42 87 99.

Commercial, Corporation, Contracts, Mergers and Acquisitions, Banking, Tax, Antitrust, Unfair Competition, Distributorship Agency and Franchising, Patents and Trademarks, Arbitration and Litigation, Product Liability, International Public and Private Law, EEC-Law, Property and Real Estate, Foreign Investments, Administrative, Environmental, Trade Regulations, Food and Drug Regulations, Notaries.

MEMBERS OF FIRM

NIKOLAUS M. LEY, born Frankfurt/Main, Germany, January 20, 1950; admitted, 1979, West Germany; 1984, Fachanwalt für Steuerrecht. *Education:* Universities of Frankfurt, Geneva (Switzerland), Tuebingen, New York (New York University, Master of Comparative Jurisprudence, 1981). Author: "Inclusion and valuation of debtor's assets under the balance sheet test," a study of ll U.S.C. §101 (26) (A), 1981; "Die zivilrechtlichen Beziehungen der Parteien des Spendenvertrages," 1982; "Investitionsvorranggesetz." Notary, 1989. *LANGUAGES:* German, English and French. *PRACTICE AREAS:* Property and Real Estate; Inheritance Law and Estates; Tax; Mergers and Acquisitions; Corporate; Foreign Investments; Restitution.

KLAUS RACKY, born Rangoon, Burma, March 31, 1958; admitted, 1987, West Germany. *Education:* University of Bonn. Author: "Investitionsvorranggesetz," 1993. *LANGUAGES:* German, English and Spanish. *PRACTICE AREAS:* Licensing; Banking; Financial Institutions; Stock Exchange; Tax; Product Liability; Litigation; Corporate; East German Investments and Matters related to the German Unification.

DR. THOMAS LINDEMANN, born Hannover, Germany, November 16, 1959; admitted, 1989, Germany. *Education:* Universities of Tuebingen and Goettingen (Doctor of Jurisprudence). Author: "Wann unterliegt die Aufhebung bzw. Änderung von Verträgen der Form des §313 BGB?,". Diss. Gottingen, 1989. *LANGUAGES:* German, English and French. *PRACTICE AREAS:* Corporate; Mergers and Acquisitions; International Trade and Transactions; Antitrust; Licensing; Product Liability; Insolvency; Litigation.

NICKLAS OSTERMANN, born Hamburg, Germany, April 22, 1960; admitted, 1992, Germany. *Education:* University of Berlin and New York University (LL.M., 1989). *LANGUAGES:* German, English and Spanish. *PRACTICE AREAS:* Corporate; Mergers and Acquisitions; International Trade and Transactions; Antitrust; Licensing; Product Liability; Litigation; Tax; Restitution.

REVISERS OF THE GERMAN LAW DIGEST FOR THIS DIRECTORY.

BRUCKHAUS WESTRICK STEGEMANN

FRIEDRICHSTRASSE 95 (IHZ)
10117 BERLIN, GERMANY
Telephone: (030) 26 43-3303
Telefax: (030) 26 43-3366

Düsseldorf Office: Freiligrathstrasse 1, 40479 Düsseldorf. Telephone: (0211) 49 79-0. Telefax: (0211) 49 79-103. Telex: 858 7027 JUS D.

Frankfurt Office: Taunusanlage 11, 60329 Frankfurt am Main. Telephone: (069) 27308-0. Telefax: (069) 232664. Telex: 41 49 17 WEST C D .

Hamburg Office: Alsterarkaden 27, 20354 Hamburg. Telephone: (040) 36 90 60. Telefax: (040) 36 906-155. Telex: 212 522 EURO D.

Leipzig Office: Grimmaische Strasse 25, 04109 Leipzig. Telephone: (0341) 127230. Telefax: (0341) 1272333.

Brussels, Belgium Office: Rue de la Loi 99/101, B-1040 Brussels. Telephone: 32-2 2 87 26 11. Telefax: 32-2 2 30 39 03.

Tokyo, Japan Office: Ark Mori Building, 22F, 12-32, Akasaka 1-chome, Minato-ku, Tokyo 107. Telephone: (81-3) 55610-236. Telefax: (81-3) 55610-238.

New York, New York Office: 767 Fifth Avenue, GM Building, New York 10153. Telephone: (212) 486-1100. Telefax: (212) 759-3151.

(This Listing Continued)

BRUCKHAUS WESTRICK STEGEMANN, Berlin—
Continued

Moscow, Russia Office: Malyj Gnezdnikovskij per. 9 No. 2, 103990
Moscow. Telephone: (7-503) 9562300; (7-501) 9401200. Telefax:
(7-503) 9562301; (7-501) 9401211.

*Corporate Law, Commercial Law, Mergers, Acquisitions and Divestitures,
Joint Ventures, Banks and Banking, Finance, Securities, Capital Markets,
Leases and Leasing, Equipment Finance, Aircraft Finance and Leasing,
Antitrust and Trade Regulation, German and EC Cartel Law, Competi-
tion, Unfair Trade, Intellectual Property (trademarks, patents, copyrights),
Taxation, Property, Real Estate, Energy, Natural Resources, Environmen-
tal Law, Administrative Law, Computers and Software, Food and Drug,
Biotechnology, Labour and Employment, Products Liability, Insurance,
Litigation, Arbitration, Broadcasting, Telecommunications, Aviation, Subsi-
dies and State Aids, Construction Law, Zoning, Planning and Land Use,
Customs and Foreign Trade Law, European Community Law, German-
French Investments, Russian and Post Soviet Commerce.*

MEMBERS OF FIRM

GERT KRÜGER, born Berlin, Germany, December 26, 1940; admitted,
1968, Germany. *Education:* Universities of Tübingen and Hamburg. Associate of the Institute for German and International Tax Law, University of
Nürnberg/Erlangen, 1965 and Heidelberg, 1966. *LANGUAGES:* German
and English. *PRACTICE AREAS:* Corporate Law; Commercial Law;
Joint Ventures.

DR. MICHAEL SCHÜTTE, born Bremen, Germany, January 10, 1952;
admitted, 1981, Germany. *Education:* Universities of Freiburg im Breisgau
and Heidelberg; University of California, Berkeley; University of Hamburg
(Dr. jur., 1985); Max-Planck-Institute for Foreign and International Private
Law (Research Assistant, 1979-1981). (Resident, Brussels Office). *LAN-
GUAGES:* German, English and French. *PRACTICE AREAS:* Corporate
Law; Commercial Law; Antidumping; EC Law.

DR. JAN WILLISCH, born Stommeln/Cologne, Germany, October 3,
1952; admitted, 1984, Germany. *Education:* Universities of Kiel and Oxford
(D. Phil., Oxon), Cecil Rhodes Scholarship. *LANGUAGES:* German and
English. *PRACTICE AREAS:* Corporate Law; Commercial Law; Mergers,
Acquisitions and Divestitures; Company Law.

DR. HANS-MICHAEL GIESEN, born Berlin, Germany, May 20,
1957; admitted, 1984, Germany; 1986, New York. *Education:* Universities
of Freiburg im Breisgau and Münster (Dr. jur., 1983); University of Michigan (LL.M., 1985). *LANGUAGES:* German, English and French. *PRAC-
TICE AREAS:* Corporate Law; Company Law; Commercial Law; Mergers, Acquisitions and Divestitures.

DR. MATTHIAS BENECKE, born Hamburg, Germany, January 5,
1958; admitted, 1988, Germany. *Education:* University of Hamburg (Dr.
jur., 1986). *LANGUAGES:* German and English. *PRACTICE AREAS:*
Corporate Law; Commercial Law.

MARTIN WIEMANN, born Bonn, Germany, January 28, 1957; admit-
ted, 1989, Germany. *Education:* Universities of Bonn and Paris, Columbia
University, New York (LL.M., 1987). *LANGUAGES:* German, English,
French and Italian. *PRACTICE AREAS:* Real Estate; Corporate Law;
Commercial Law.

DR. GERHARD BRAND, born Hannover, Germany, April 25, 1946;
admitted, 1990, Berlin, Germany. *Education:* University in Leipzig and
University for Economic Affairs Berlin (Dr. jur., 1974); Institute for Foreign Law Potsdam (Dr.sc.jur., 1988). Practising company lawyer since
1974. *LANGUAGES:* German and English. *PRACTICE AREAS:* Corporate Law; Commercial Law; GDR Law.

DR. JOCHEN LESSMANN, born Düsseldorf, Germany, March 9,
1963; admitted, 1993, Germany. *Education:* University of Cologne (Dr.
jur., 1991). *LANGUAGES:* German and English. *PRACTICE AREAS:*
Labor Law; Commercial Law.

MALTE DIESSELHORST, born Wissen/Sieg, Germany, January 24,
1963; admitted, 1993, Germany. *Education:* Universities of Marburg, Lausanne (Switzerland) and Freiburg. *LANGUAGES:* German, English and
French. *PRACTICE AREAS:* Corporate Law; Commercial Law.

DR. ANNEDORE STREYL, born Münster, Germany, December 12,
1960; admitted, 1993, Germany. *Education:* Universities of Münster, Tübingen, Munich and Bonn (Dr. jur., 1991). *LANGUAGES:* German and
English. *PRACTICE AREAS:* Corporate Law; Commercial Law.

(This Listing Continued)

DR. THOMAS WINKEMANN, born Plettenberg, Germany, July 8,
1963; admitted, 1993, Germany. *Education:* Gymnasium, Plettenberg (Abitur, 1982); University of Lausanne (1985-1986); University of Heidelberg
(Staats Examen, 1990). Author: "Die Fahrlaessigkent Im Umwelt Strafrecht," Peter Lang, 1991. Research Felloe, University of Heidelberg, 1986-
1989. *Member:* Frankfurt Bar Association. *LANGUAGES:* German, English and French. *PRACTICE AREAS:* International Taxation; Corporate
Taxation; Corporate Law; Mergers and Acquisitions.

DANIEL REICHERT-FACILIDES, born Hamburg, Germany, March
22, 1965; admitted, 1994, Germany. *Education:* University München, Munich, Germany (J.D., 1990); Paris II (LL.M., 1991). *LANGUAGES:* German, English, French. *PRACTICE AREAS:* General Prwactice; International Litigation; East German Restitutions.

BRUSS & PARTNER
MARKT 12/13
13597 BERLIN, GERMANY
Telephone: 030/3 33 74 40
Telefax: 030/3 33 76 98

*Family Law, Labor Law, Commercial Law, Corporate Law and Real Es-
tate Law.*

ISOLDE BRUSS, born Bad Pyrmont, Germany, 1947; admitted, 1975,
Diepholz; 1985, Notare. *Education:* Free University of Berlin (1974). Refer-
endar and Assessor, Berlin, Lebanon and France, 1974. Worked for the
Anti-trust Authorities, 1975-1979. *Member:* International Bar Association
(Section, Business Law); Berlin Bar Association; German Bar Association;
Deutsche Anwaltsverein. *LANGUAGES:* German, English and French.
PRACTICE AREAS: Family Law; Labor Law; Commercial Law; Corpo-
rate Law; Real Estate Law.

BURCHERT & PARTNER

Established in 1971

OTTO-SUHR-ALLEE 29
10585 BERLIN, GERMANY
Telephone: (030) 341 6006
Telefax: (030) 342 5032

*General Practice, Commercial, Unfair Competition, Trademark, Antitrust,
Food, Drug, Labor, Real Estate Law, Real Estate Transactions, Trusts
and Estates.*

*FIRM PROFILE: Founded by Manfred Burchert, Burchert & Partner
concentrates chiefly on unfair competition law and general practice. The
law firm represents one of Germany's leading competition associations authorized under German law to bring unfair competition actions. Burchert
& Partner is also experienced in providing legal counseling on advertisement and marketing, including food and drug law. Two members of the
law firm are notaries public, authorizing them to certify, among others,
company and real estate contracts. The firm's well-established contacts
with law firms across the country and in every major city enable it to meet
its clients' needs throughout Germany.*

MEMBERS OF FIRM

MANFRED BURCHERT, born May 30, 1942; admitted, 1971, Germany; 1981, Notary Public. *Education:* Universities of Göttingen and Berlin (Law Degree, 1966). Berlin Appellate Court, 1976. *Member:* Vereinigung für gewerblichen Rechtsschutz und Urheberrecht (Association for
Industrial Property Rights and Copyright). *LANGUAGES:* German, English and Spanish. *PRACTICE AREAS:* Unfair Competition; Commercial
Law.

JÖRN RICHTER, born August 27, 1943; admitted, 1973, Germany;
1984, Notary Public. *Education:* University of Hamburg (Law Degree,
1970). Berlin Appellate Court, 1978. *Member:* Berlin Bar Association.
LANGUAGES: German, English and Spanish. *PRACTICE AREAS:* Real
Estate Transactions; Contracts; Trusts and Estates.

ROLAND JAHN, born May 15, 1962; admitted, 1991, Germany. *Education:* Universities of Munich and Freiburg (Law Degree, 1988). *Member:*
German American Lawyers Association; Berlin Bar Association. *LAN-
GUAGES:* German and English. *PRACTICE AREAS:* Unfair Competition; Commercial; Food and Drug Law.

(This Listing Continued)

JÖRG ALBIG, born June 6, 1960; admitted, 1991, Germany. *Education:* Free University of Berlin (Law Degree, 1987). *Member:* Berlin Bar Association. *LANGUAGES:* German and English. *PRACTICE AREAS:* Unfair Competition; Commercial Law.

CARLOS CLAUSSEN & PARTNER

Established in 1980

JOSEF-ORLOPP-STRASSE 89-91
10365 BERLIN, GERMANY
Telephone: 0049 172 309 03 10
Fax: 0049 30 558 81 16

Hamburg, Germany Office: Mönckebergstraße 31, 20095 Hamburg. Telephone: 0049-40-30 96 40-0. Fax: 0049-40-30 96 40-99.
Potsdam, Germany Office: Benkertstraße 13, 14467 Potsdam. Telephone: 0049-331-28 46 90. Fax: 0049-331-280 48 31.

Commercial, Corporation, Common Market, Unfair Competition, Admiralty, Insurance, Trademark, Copyright, International Private Law, Litigation and Arbitration, Banking Law, Probate, East-European Law, Property Law (Restitution of Property Rights), Labour Law.

FIRM PROFILE: *The firm was established in 1980 in Hamburg, Germany and has now offices as well in Potsdam, Germany as in Berlin, Germany. It offers a full range of legal services and is a member of the EULEX-IPG Group, Europe with their professional service. The client base is European and North American in scope.*

(For Complete Biographical Data on all Personnel, see Professional Biographies at Hamburg, Germany)

THOMAS CRASEMANN

SOPHIE-CHARLOTTEN STR. 57/58, 4TH FLOOR
14057 BERLIN, GERMANY
Telephone: 030/3215834
Fax: 030/3224016

Landlord and Tenant Law, Family Law, Criminal Law, Traffic Law, Estate Cases, Trade Disputes and Criminal Cases.

THOMAS CRASEMANN, born Hamburg, Germany, 1947; admitted, 1977, Berlin. *Education:* University of Heidelberg (Law Degree, 1973). Assessor in Berlin, 1974-1976. *Member:* Berlin and German Bar Associations. *LANGUAGES:* English, French and German.

CYRUS, MAKOWSKI & PARTNER

AUGUSTE-VIKTORIA-ALLEE 2
13403 BERLIN, GERMANY
Telephone: 030/412 30 56
Telefax: 030/413 72 30

Hamburg, Germany Office: Ost-West-Straße 61, 20457. Telephone: 040/36 33 43. Telefax: 040/374 37 91. Telex: 21 321 699 HS D.
Rostock, Germany Office: Grosse Wasserstrasse 2/3, 18055. Telephone: 0381/499 60 60. Telefax: 0381/499 63 51.

Members of CYRUS ROSS INTERNATIONAL (E.E.I.G.) Association of Law Firms: Alphen (NL), Athens, Berlin, Brussels, Copenhagen, Dublin, Hamburg, Limassol, London, Madrid, Nicosia, Oslo, Padua, Paris, Rostock, Sion, Vienna.

RESIDENT PARTNERS

THOMAS JASTER, born 1956; admitted, 1984, Berlin. *Education:* University of Berlin. *Member:* Berlin Bar Association; German Association for the Protection of Industrial Property; Berlin Retailers' Association (Adviser). *PRACTICE AREAS:* Competition Law; Copyright Law; Industrial Property; Company Law; Banking Law; Labour Law; Trade Law.

REINKE DUHME, born 1953; admitted, 1983, Hamburg. *Education:* Universities Hamburg and Geneva; Emory University, Atlanta (M.C.L.). Member, Round Table on Science and Economics of the BDI (National Federation of German Industries), BDA (National Federation of German Employer Associations) and DIHT (Federation of German Chambers of Industry and Commerce). *PRACTICE AREAS:* Foreign Trade; Mercantile

(This Listing Continued)

Law; Transport Law; Banking Law; Insurance Law; Construction Law; Tenancy and Hire Law; Restitution Law.

Languages: German, English, French and Spanish

(For Complete Biographical Data on all Personnel, see Professional Biographies at Hamburg, Germany)

DSH DERKS • STAR BUSMANN

BERNADOTTESTRAßE 66
14195 BERLIN, GERMANY
Telephone: +49-30-831 63 00
Fax: +49-30-831 65 28

International Business Law, Commercial Property Law, Computers & Software Law, Taxation, International Mergers & Acquisitions, Dutch-German Business Law.

FIRM PROFILE: *Derks • Star Busmann is a member of DSH, a European grouping of firms (EEIG) with more than 160 attorneys at law, civil law notaries and tax advisors. The members have offices in The Netherlands, (head office Utrecht), Belgium (Brussels), France (Paris) and Germany (Berlin).*

The Berlin office is specialized in offering a full range of legal services for foreign companies doing business in Germany and Eastern Europe.

RESIDENT PARTNERS

DR. MANFRED BOCK, born Berlin, Germany, January 15, 1940; admitted, 1976, Germany. *Education:* Universities of Frankfurt and Munich (1966); Opal University of Princeton (1986); University of Virginia (LL.M., 1969). Chartered Expert in Tax Law, Finance Dept. E.l. Pont de Nemours, Wilmington, Delaware and Düsseldorf, Germany, 1975. General Counsel and Board Member, Gerling Insurance Group, Cologne, Germany, 1975-1988. Advisor Privatization, Treuhand Anstalt, Berlin, 1990. *Member:* Berlin and German-American Bar Associations. *LANGUAGES:* German, English and French. *PRACTICE AREAS:* Commercial Property Law; Taxation; International Mergers and Acquisitions; Restitution Law; Insurance Law; Environmental Law.

MARTIKA JONK, born The Netherlands, December 19, 1959; admitted, 1986, The Netherlands (Not admitted in Germany). *Education:* University of Amsterdam (Law Degree, 1986). Foreign Legal Consultant, Palmer & Dodge, Boston, Massachusetts, 1991. *Member:* Dutch Bar Association; International Bar Association. *LANGUAGES:* Dutch, German, English and French. *PRACTICE AREAS:* International Business Law; Commercial Property Law; Property Development and Finance; Computer Law; Licensing and Distribution; High Technology Law; Dutch-German Business Law.

ASSOCIATES

MURK MULLER, born The Netherlands, 1962; admitted, 1987, The Netherlands (Not admitted in Germany). *Education:* University of Leiden (Law Degree, 1984). Trainee, American Law Firms in San Francisco, Houston, New York, 1984-1985. Co-author: "Legal Aspects of Investments in the Czech and Slovak Federal Republic.". *LANGUAGES:* Dutch, German, French, English, Spanish and Russian. *PRACTICE AREAS:* Transport, Trade and Telecommunications in the Netherlands; Germany and Eastern European Commerce; Dutch-German Business Law.

DÖSER AMERELLER NOACK

(Baker & McKenzie)

KLEISTSTRASSE 23-26
D-10787 BERLIN, GERMANY
Telephone: (030) 214990-0
Intn'l Dialing: (49-30) 214990-0
Facsimile: (49-30) 214990-99

Frankfurt/Main, Germany Office: Bethmannstrasse 50-54, D-60311 Frankfurt/Main. Telephone: (069) 299080. Facsimile: (069) 29908108.

Administrative Law, Antitrust Law, Arbitration, Banking and Finance, Commercial Law, Company Law, Computer Law, Corporate Finance, Employment and Labour Law, Environmental Law, European Community Law, Food and Drug Law, Franchising, Industrial and Intellectual Property, Litigation, Mergers and Acquisitions, Multinational Business Transactions, Product Liability, Real Estate/Conveyancing, Taxation, Telecommunications Law, Trademarks, Unfair Competition Law.

(This Listing Continued)

DÖSER AMERELLER NOACK, Berlin—Continued

*CARL H. ANDRES, born Bad Kreuznach, Germany, 1945; admitted, 1974, Germany; 1989, California, U.S.A. *Education:* Universities of Heidelberg and Bonn (Referendar, 1971); University of Michigan, Ann Arbor (M.C.L., 1975). *LANGUAGES:* German, English and French. *PRACTICE AREAS:* Mergers and Acquisitions; Corporate and Partnership Law; Real Estate Law.

*WILHELM B. HEBING, born Anholt/Westphalia, Germany, 1949; admitted, 1979, Germany. *Education:* Universities of Bonn and Göttingen (Referendar, 1973); University of Michigan, Ann Arbor. Tax Attorney. *LANGUAGES:* German and English. *PRACTICE AREAS:* Mergers and Acquisitions; Taxation; Corporate and Partnership Law.

*ULRICH HENNINGS, born Lüneburg, Germany, 1958; admitted, 1988, Germany. *Education:* Universities of Freiburg and Munich (Referendar, 1982); University of Freiburg (Dr. jur., 1987); University of Miami School of Law (LL.M., 1988). *LANGUAGES:* German and English. *PRACTICE AREAS:* Mergers and Acquisitions; Corporate and Partnership Law; Real Estate Law.

OF COUNSEL

REINHARD PÖLLATH, born Marktredwitz, Germany, 1948; admitted, 1977, Germany. *Education:* University of Regensburg (Referendar, 1973); Harvard Law School (LL.M., 1974). *LANGUAGES:* German, English and French. *PRACTICE AREAS:* Taxation; Mergers and Acquisitions; Banking and Finance; Real Estate Law; Trust, Probate and Estate Planning.

ASSOCIATES

GREGOR FRANK, born Ravensburg, Germany, 1960; admitted, 1989, Germany. *Education:* University of Konstanz (Rechtspraktikant, 1982); University of Berlin, Assistant Lecturer 1985-1989 (Dr. jur., 1990); Indiana University (LL.M., 1989). *LANGUAGES:* German, English and French. *PRACTICE AREAS:* Corporate and Partnership Law; Intellectual Property Law; Computers and Technology Law; Labor and Employment Law; Mergers and Acquisitions.

MAX B. GUTBROD, born Stuttgart, Germany, 1960; admitted, 1990, Germany. *Education:* Universities of Tübingen and Munich (Referendar, 1986; Dr. jur., 1992). *LANGUAGES:* German, English, French, Portuguese, Spanish and Italian. *PRACTICE AREAS:* Corporate and Partnership Law; Mergers and Acquisitions; Oil and Gas/Mining; Construction and Property Development.

ANDRE SAYATZ, born Lübbenau, Germany, 1962; admitted, 1990, Germany. *Education:* Friedrich-Schiller-University of Jena (Diploma, 1986). *LANGUAGES:* English and Russian. *PRACTICE AREAS:* German Restitution Law; Real Estate Law; Labor and Employment Law; Mergers and Acquisitions.

ANDRES SCHOLLMEIER, born Münster, Germany, November 22, 1960; admitted, 1991, Germany. *Education:* Westfälische Wilhelms-Universität Münster (initial bar examination, 1985; qualifying bar examination, 1989). Assistant at Institute of Tax Law, University of Münster, 1989-1991. Lecturer on Law, Finanz hochschule Münster, 1990-1991. Lecturer on Law, Verwaltungsakademie Münster, 1989-1991. *LANGUAGES:* German and English. *PRACTICE AREAS:* Taxation; Mergers and Acquisitions; Corporate and Partnership Law; Securities and Financial Products.

FRANK-RAINER TÖPFER, born Leipzig, Germany, 1955; admitted, 1990, Germany. *Education:* Martin-Luther-University, Halle-Wittenberg (Diploma, 1982); University of Economics, Berlin (Dr. jur., 1985). Lecturer on Law, 1982-1990. *LANGUAGES:* German, English and Russian. *PRACTICE AREAS:* Real Estate Law; Administrative Law; Construction and Property Development.

FRANK VOGEL, born Berlin, Germany, 1965; admitted, 1994, Germany. *Education:* University of Berlin (Referendar, 1989; Dr. jur., 1993; University of Cambridge, GB (LL.M., 1991). *LANGUAGES:* German and English. *PRACTICE AREAS:* Commercial Litigation; Civil Litigation; Corporate and Partnership Law.

HEIDEMARIE WAGNER, born Lübeck, Germany, 1957; admitted, 1986, Germany. *Education:* University of Kiel. Tax Advisor (Steuerberaterin). *LANGUAGES:* German, English and Russian. *PRACTICE AREAS:* Taxation; Corporate and Partnership Law.

HUBERTUS WELSCH, born Hildesheim, Germany, 1957; admitted, 1989, Germany. *Education:* University of Göttingen (Referendar, 1983; Dr. jur., 1986). Assistant Lecturer, University of Göttingen; EEC-Consultant,

(This Listing Continued)

1987-1988. *LANGUAGES:* German, English and French. *PRACTICE AREAS:* Commercial Litigation; Civil Litigation; Arbitration and Dispute Resolution; Corporate and Partnership Law; Labor and Employment Law.

PETER WESSELS, born Münster, Germany, 1963; admitted, 1992, Germany. *Education:* Universities of Münster (Dr. jur., 1991), Berlin and Guilford/Surrey (Referendar, 1988). *LANGUAGES:* German, English, French and Russian. *PRACTICE AREAS:* Corporate and Partnership Law; Construction and Property Development; Real Estate Law; Commercial Litigation.

*Also Partner of Baker & McKenzie, Chicago, Illinois, U.S.A.

(For offices in other countries, see Chicago, Illinois, U.S.A. listing for Baker & McKenzie)

DROSTE

The Merged Firms of Droste, Pietzcker, Sprick, Ohlgart & Klosterfelde; Triebel & Weil; Strobl, Killius & Vorbrugg

KURFÜRSTENDAMM 54-55
10707 BERLIN, GERMANY
Telephone: (030) 88 24 300
Telefax: (030) 88 24 393

Düsseldorf, Germany Office: Berliner Allee 48, 40212 Düsseldorf. Telephone: (0211) 13 680. Telecopier: (0211) 32 44 39.
Hamburg, Germany Office: Wargurgstrasse 50, 20354 Hamburg. Telephone: (040) 4 1993-0. Telecopier: (040) 4 1993 200.
Munich, Germany Office: Marstallstrasse 8, 80539 Munich. Telephone: (089) 290120. Telecopier: (089) 29012 222. Telex: 524 973 skv.
Frankfurt/Main, Germany Office: Schaumainkai 91, 60596 Frankfurt/Main. Telephone: (069) 63 00 89-0. Telecopier: (069) 630089-99.
Brussels, Belgium Office: Avenue des Gaulois 9, B-1150 Brussels. Telephone: 02-7358945. Telecopier: 02-7352251.

General and International Practice. Commercial Law, Corporate, Banking, Finance, Tax, Mergers and Acquisitions, EU Law, Antitrust, Unfair Competition, Trademarks, Copyright, Patents, Licensing, Food and Drug Law, Law of the Press, Products Liability, Environmental Law, Labor Law, Real Estate, Estate Planning, International Construction, Contracts, Commercial Litigation and Arbitration, Bankruptcy, Administrative Law.

FIRM PROFILE: Droste is engaged in the practice of corporate and commercial law. The firm is the result of the merger of Droste, Pietzcker, Sprick, Ohlgart & Klosterfelde in Hamburg (formed in 1887), Strobl, Killius & Vorbrugg in Munich (formed in 1961) and Triebel & Weil in Düsseldorf (formed in 1951). The firm's traditional areas of practice are: corporate law, including mergers and acquisitions; industrial property law, including copyright, unfair competition and anti-trust law; trademark law; tax law, both domestic and international; real estate law. Further areas of particular expertise include banking and finance, computer and software law, environmental law, labour law, EU law and commercial litigation and arbitration.

RESIDENT PARTNERS

DR. ROLF SCHULTZ-SÜCHTING, born Hamburg, Germany, September 11, 1944; admitted, 1971, Germany. *Education:* Universities of Berlin and Hamburg (Law Degree, 1967; Doctor of Laws, 1971). *Member:* International Association for the Protection of Industrial Property. *LANGUAGES:* German and English. *PRACTICE AREAS:* Patent Law; Unfair Competition Law.

DR. BENEDIKT BRÄUTIGAM, born Düsseldorf, Germany, March 9, 1956; admitted, 1984, Germany. *Education:* University of Hamburg (Law Degree, 1980; Doctor of Laws, 1985). *Member:* Union of European Advocats. *LANGUAGES:* German and English. *PRACTICE AREAS:* Corporate Law; Commercial Litigation; Mergers and Acquisitions; Unfair Competition Law; Law of the Press and Antitrust Law.

DR. JOHANNES MEINEL, born Dresden, Germany, September 17, 1957; admitted, 1989, Germany. *Education:* University of Freiburg (Law Degree, 1983; Doctor of Laws, 1987); University of Reims, France and Harvard University (M.P.A., 1985). *LANGUAGES:* German and English. *PRACTICE AREAS:* General Corporate and Commercial Law; Mergers and Acquisitions; Environmental Law.

HEINZ WINKLER, born Meinsdorf, Germany, May 11, 1953; admitted, 1990, East Germany; 1991, Germany. *Education:* University of Halle

(This Listing Continued)

(Law Exam and Diploma 1975). *LANGUAGES:* German and English.. *PRACTICE AREAS:* Real Estate Law; Law of the former GDR.

DR. PETER RIES, born Munich, Germany, March 29, 1961; admitted, 1990, Germany. *Education:* Universities of Würzburg and Munich (Law Degree, 1987; Doctor of Law, 1989); London School of Economics, United Kingdom. *LANGUAGES:* German and English. *PRACTICE AREAS:* Contracts; Corporate Law; Arbitration.

ASSOCIATES

Dr. Peter Ries

Languages: German, English, French, Spanish, Russian, Italian, Portuguese, Latvian, Chinese and Japanese.

(For list of personnel at Düsseldorf, Frankfurt/Main, Hamburg, Munich and Brussels, see Professional Biographies at those locations)

EGGERS

FASANENSTRASSE 74
10719 BERLIN, GERMANY
Telephone: 49-30-884 78 10
Telefax: 49-30-8847 81 30

Corporate Law, Mergers and Acquisitions, Real Estate Transactions, Banking, Securities, Investments in the Former GDR, Notarizations.

MEMBERS OF FIRM

BERNHARD AUST, born Forst, Germany, September 13, 1943; admitted, 1974, Germany. *Education:* University of Berlin (1966-1971). *Member:* Berlin Bar Association; Berlin Lawyers Society. *LANGUAGES:* German, English.

CARSTEN R. EGGERS, born Cincinnati, Ohio, December, 7, 1957; admitted, 1984, Germany; 1986, New York. *Education:* Universities of Frankfurt am Main, Munich and Cologne (1977-1981); Boalt Hall School of Law, University of California, Berkeley (1984-1985). Associate, Kaye, Scholer, Fierman, Hays & Handler, New York (1985-1987). Partner, Feddersen Laule Scherzberg & Ohle Hansen Ewerwahn, Berlin (1987-1992). Co-Author: "Business Transactions in Germany." *Member:* Berlin and New York Bar Associations; German-American Law Association; International Bar Association. *LANGUAGES:* German, English, French.

STEFAN J. SIHLER, born Munich, Germany, June 7, 1962; admitted, 1994, Germany. *Education:* University of Munich (1983-1988). Munich Reinsurance Group, New York (1990-1991). Head of Legal Department, Treuhandanstalt, Berlin Branch (1991-1994). *LANGUAGES:* German, English.

FEDDERSEN LAULE SCHERZBERG & OHLE HANSEN EWERWAHN

KURFUERSTENDAMM 185
D-10707 BERLIN, GERMANY
Telephone: 49-30-88 57 16 0
Fax: 49-30-88 57 16 50

Frankfurt/Main, Germany Office: Stiftstraße 9-17, P.O. Box 100836, D-60313 Frankfurt am Main. Telephone: 49-69-29994-0. Telefax: 49-69-282615. Telex: 41 33 96 fls d.

Hamburg, Germany Office: Jungfernstieg 51 (Prien-Haus), D-20354 Hamburg. Telephone: 49-40-35 00 50. Telex: 21 27 99 99 lawt d. Telefax: 49-40-35 00 51 11.

Dresden, Germany Office: Königsbrücker Straße 17, D-01099 Dresden. Telephone: 49-03 51-567 02 77. Telefax: 49-03 51-567 02 79.

Brussels, Belgium Office: 118, Rue d'Arlon, B-1040 Brussels. Telephone: 32-2-280-1544. Telefax: 32-2-280-0703.

Prague, Czech Republic Office: Spanĕlská 2, CZ-120 00 Prague 2. Telephone: 42-2-268203; 268229. Telefax: 42-2-260310.

General Practice, Administrative Law, Admiralty, Antitrust, Arbitration, Aviation, Banking, Commercial and Corporate Law, Environmental Law, Entertainment Law, Estate Planning, EC and International Law, Insurance, Labor Law, License, Merger and Acquisition, Patent, Trade Mark and Copyright, Real Estate, Securities Law, Tax, Transportation, Unfair Competition, Litigation.

FIRM PROFILE: The firm offers a full range of legal services. It is well known for its commercial, corporate, banking and tax law and its practice in the field of merger and acquisitions, real estate and environmental law.

(This Listing Continued)

The firm has a broad national as well as international client base with a focus on Europe, the United States and Japan. The firm has 79 attorneys at law (8 of whom are notaries public) and 5 tax advisors.

MEMBERS OF FIRM

DR. CLAUS HEUCHEMER, born Bad Ems, Germany, June 12, 1943; admitted, 1974, Frankfurt. *Education:* Universities of Bonn, Geneva and Munich (Dr. jur., 1974). Tax Counsel, 1980. Legal Counsel, Kraftwerk Union AG, 1974-1978. *Member:* Berlin and German Bar Associations; Association of Tax Consels (Arbeitsgemeinschaft Fachanwälte für Steuerrecht); German Lawyer's Conference (Deutscher Juristentag): Banking Law Association-Scientific Society for Banking Law, Institute for Finance and Taxes: International Bar Association; German-Chinese Lawyers Association; German-American Lawyers Association; American Chamber of Commerce; British Chamber of Commerce; Suisse-German Chamber of Commerce; Swedish Chamber of Commerce in Germany. *LANGUAGES:* German, English, French. *PRACTICE AREAS:* Real Estate Law; Merger and Acquisition Law; Corporate Partnership Law; Tax Law; Banking Law.

WILFRIED VOEMEL, born Prague, Czechoslovakia, November 4, 1929; admitted, 1961, Germany. Notary Public, 1973. Trustee lawyer of the Israelian Embassy in Bonn, 1964-1970. *LANGUAGES:* German. *PRACTICE AREAS:* Real Estate Law; Commercial Law.

WINFRIED JOPEN, born Essen, Germany, October 1, 1959; admitted, 1989, Bonn. *Education:* University of Bonn. *LANGUAGES:* German. *PRACTICE AREAS:* Insurance; Commercial; Corporate Law; Banking Law; Litigation.

ENDRIK LETTAU, born Büsum, Germany, September 12, 1959; admitted, 1988, New York; 1992, Berlin. *Education:* University of Kiel (First State Examination, 1986); University of Miami (Master of Law, 1987). DAAD Fellowship, 1986-1987. Recipient, Fulbright Scholarship, 1986. Master of Law, 1986. Foreign Associate, Law Firm Washington, D.C., 1987-1988. Lawyers Wilmer, Cutler & Pickering, London, 1991-1992. *Member:* Berlin and New York Bar Associations. *LANGUAGES:* German, English. *PRACTICE AREAS:* International Transactions; Commercial Law; Property Development; Construction Law; Architect Law.

DR. JÜRGEN CHR. JENCKEL, born Lüneburg, Germany, November 24, 1957; admitted, 1989, Cologne; 1990, Berlin. *Education:* Universities of Gottingen (Dr. jur., 1990) and Geneva (Switzerland). *Member:* German Bar Association. *LANGUAGES:* German and English. *PRACTICE AREAS:* International Transactions; Mergers and Acquisitions; Corporate Law; Real Estate Law; Tax Law; Restitution Law; Copyright and Telecommunication Law.

DR. ANDREAS POCHHAMMER, born Potsdam, Germany, July 21, 1947; admitted, 1976. *Education:* University of Berlin. Specialized in Tax Law. *LANGUAGES:* German and English. *PRACTICE AREAS:* Mergers and Acquisitions; Fiscal Offences Law; Tax Law; Corporate/Partnership Law.

DR. MARGARETE MUEHL-JAECKEL, born Goettingen, Germany, July 27, 1950. *Education:* Universities of Mainz, Freiburg/Breisgau and Tuebingen, Munich (Dr. jur., 1981); Harvard Law School (LL.M., 1978). *Member:* German-American Lawyers' Association; Gesellschaft Für Rechtsvergleichung. *LANGUAGES:* German, English, French and Italian. *PRACTICE AREAS:* Administrative Law; Zoning, Planning and Land Use Law; Environmental Law; Public Road Traffic Law; Constitutional Law.

ASSOCIATES

DR. RAINER MARKFORT, born Oberhausen, Germany, June 10, 1961; admitted, 1992, Berlin. *Education:* Universities of Muenster and Paris, Maîtrise en Droit, 1984. *LANGUAGES:* German, French, English, Italian.. *PRACTICE AREAS:* Litigation; Insolvency Law; Labor Law; Tax Law; Civil Procedure; Arbitration.

DR. CELIA ISABEL GAISSERT, born Hamburg, Germany, November 29, 1955; admitted, 1993, Berlin. *Education:* Universities of Bonn (Dr. jur., 1987) and Hamburg. Legal Counsel, Bayerische Hypotheken- und Wechsel-Bank AG, 1988-1991. *LANGUAGES:* German, English, French, Italian, Spanish, Russian and Hebrew. *PRACTICE AREAS:* European Community Law; Banking Law; Law of the New Laender (former GDR).

(For Complete Biographical Data on all Personnel, see Professional Biographies at Hamburg, Germany)

FIEDLER & FORSTER

BONNER STRASSE 172-176
50968 COLOGNE, GERMANY
Telephone: (0049) (221) 937 050-0
Telefax: (0049) (221) 937 050-50

Berlin, Germany Office: Oranienburger Strasse 69, D-10117 Berlin.
Telephone: (0049) (30) 283 2418. Telefax: (0049) (30) 283 2420.
Frankfurt/Main, Germany Office: Opernplatz 2, D-60313
Frankfurt/Main. Telephone: (0049) (69) 298930. Telefax: (0049) (69)
29893299.
Leipzig, Germany Office: Grimmaische Str. 25, 04109 Leipzig. Telephone:
(0049) (341) 2115112. Telefax: (0049) (341) 9602530.
Munich, Germany Office: Brienner Strasse 12/III, D-80333 Munich.
Telephone: (0049) (89) 23980. Telefax: (0049) (89) 2398259.
Stuttgart, Germany Office: Gänsheidestr. 68, D-70184. Telephone: (0049)
(711)-16445-0. Fax: (0049) (711) 16445-11.
Paris, France Office: Tour Fiat la Dèfense 6, F-92084. Telephone:
33-1-47 76 28 10. Fax: 33-1-47 96 63 63.

*Commercial, Banking, Corporate, Mergers and Acquisitions, International
Business Transactions, Antitrust and Unfair Competition, Employment and
Labor, Taxation and Litigation, Building and Planning Law, Real Property,
Computer Law, Intellectual Property, Franchising, Air Law.*

MEMBERS OF FIRM

BIRGIT KORSCH, born December 11, 1953; admitted, 1991, Berlin;
1991, Notary. *Education:* Humboldt University of Berlin. **LANGUAGES:**
German and Russian.

ASSOCIATES

DR. FRANK HAMMEL, born Essen, Germany, March 30, 1960; admitted,
1991, Düsseldorf; 1993, Berlin. *Education:* Universities of Bonn,
Bochum, Cologne (Dr. jur., 1992). Author: "Legal Assistance in Canada,"
Canada Journal, 5-6, 1991. *Member:* Wirtschaftsjunioren (Economic Juniors),
Berlin; Canadian German Lawyers' Association. **LANGUAGES:**
German, English and French.

FLICK GOCKE SCHAUMBURG

Attorneys-at-Law, Auditors, Tax Consultants

Established in 1971

NÜRNBERGER STR. 67
10787 BERLIN, GERMANY
Telephone: (030) 217 6843
Telefax: (030) 218 4686

Bonn, Germany Office: Johanna-Kinkel-Str. 2-4, 53175 Bonn. Telephone:
(0-228) 9594-0. Telefax: (0-228) 9594-100.

*National and International Tax Law, Corporate Law, M & A, Joint Ventures,
International Trust and Corporate Structures, Investment, Real
Property, Estate Planning, Wills and Trusts, Auditing.*

RESIDENT PARTNER

DR. LENHARD JESSE, born Dörpe, 1953; admitted, 1991, Germany;
Certified Tax Consultant. *Education:* University of Cologne (Doctor of
Law, 1991). Author: "Inheritance Tax and Income Tax," (Germ.), 1991.
PRACTICE AREAS: International Tax Planning; Joint Ventures; Holding
Companies; Corporate Restructuring; Investments.

ASSOCIATES

DIRK REMUSS, Attorney-at-Law.

FRERE CHOLMELEY

Established in 1990

IM INTERNATIONALEN HANDELSZENTRUM
FRIEDRICHSTRASSE 95
10117 BERLIN, GERMANY
Telephone: (49) (30) 26 43 2000
Telex: 305996 Kbihxd
Fax: (49) (30) 26 43 1900

London, England Office: 4 John Carpenter Street, London EC4Y 0NH.
Telephone: 0171-615 8000. Fax: 0171-615 8080. Telex: 27623. LDE:
DX 140.

(This Listing Continued)

Paris, France Office: 42 Avenue du Président Wilson, 75116. Telephone:
(33) (1) 44 34 71 00. Fax: (33) (1) 44 34 71 11.
Rome, Italy Office: and Studio Legale Associato, 47, Viale Bruno Buozzi,
00197 . Telephone: (39) (6) 808 0133. Fax: (39) (6) 808 0134.
Milan, Italy Office: and Studio Legale Associato, Piazza Castello 24,
20121 Milan. Telephone: (39) (2) 720 03 457. Fax: (39) (2) 720 03
469.
Monte Carlo, Monaco Office: "Est Ouest", 24 Boulevard Princesse
Charlotte, MC 98000. Telephone: (33) (93) 50 85 70. Fax: (33) (93) 50
22 10.
Moscow, Russia Office: ul. Sadovaya Samotyochna 24/27, 103051
Moscow. Telephone: (7) 095 258 5058. Fax: (7) 095 258 5060. Telex:
412348 ALM SU.
Dubai, United Arab Emirates Office: Suite 802, EBIL Building, PO Box
2510, Deira, Dubai. Telephone: (9714) 267085/268336. Fax: (9714)
260206. Telex: 45493 LAWMC EM.

*FIRM PROFILE: The firm's Berlin office is staffed by East and West
German Lawyers who are experienced in handling international commercial
transactions and in dealing with East European jurisdictions. The clients
include major international companies as well as companies involved
in a range of sectors from retail and aviation to heavy industry and construction.
Specialisations of this office include advising on transactions involving
foreign investment in newly formed businesses and the creation of
joint venture and other investment vehicles.*

ASSOCIATES

BÄRBEL LUTHER, born Quedlinburg, Germany, 1941. Legal Adviser
since 1969; Rechtsanwalt since 1990. *Education:* Humboldt-Universität of
Berlin. **PRACTICE AREAS:** Property Law,; Industrial and Business Development;
Construction Law.

DR. GÜNTHER WILLMA, born Berlin, Germany, 1940. Legal Adviser
since 1969; Rechtsanwalt and Notar since 1990. *Education:* Humboldt-
Universität of Berlin, Hochschule fur ökonomie, Berlin. **PRACTICE
AREAS:** Notary; Property Law.

DR. WOLFGANG BUCHHOLZ, born Berlin, Germany, 1955. Legal
Adviser since 1985; Rechtsanwalt since 1990. *Education:* Karl-Marx-
Universität of Leipzig. **PRACTICE AREAS:** Company Law; Commercial
Law.

GERD BAIERLEIN, born Dresden, Germany, 1954. Legal Adviser
since 1979; Rechtsanwalt since 1990. *Education:* Martin-Luther-Universität
of Halle. **PRACTICE AREAS:** Property Law; Litigation; Labour Law.

PROF. DR. ELMAR M. GIEMULLA, born Gerolzhofen, Germany,
1950. Attorney-at-Law, New York. *Education:* University of Cologne.
PRACTICE AREAS: Aviation Law; Administration Law.

DR. RUDOLF VON HANSTEIN, born Bonn, Germany, 1955. Rechtsanwalt
since 1986. *Education:* Universities of Göttingen, Geneva, Switzerland
and Bonn. **PRACTICE AREAS:** Company Law; Commercial Law.

THOMAS KEXEL, born Düsseldorf-Mettmann, Germany, 1960.
Rechtsanwalt since 1989. *Education:* Philipps Universität of Marburg, Ludwig-Maximilians
University, Munich. **PRACTICE AREAS:** Property Law;
Litigation.

DR. HEIKO VAN SCHYNDEL, born Halle, Germany, 1963. Advocat,
Woronesh, Russia, since 1992. *Education:* Martin-Luther Universität of
Halle, State University of Woronesh, Russia, Humboldt-Universität of Berlin.
PRACTICE AREAS: Aviation Law; Russian Law.

Languages: German, English, Russian and French

(For a full list of the Partners see Professional Biographies, London,
England Office)

GAEDERTZ VIEREGGE QUACK KREILE

Rechtsanwälte

KURFÜRSTENDAMM 157, P.O.B. 311120
D-10709 BERLIN, GERMANY
Telephone: (30)-89005-0
Telex: 17 30 8815 qkp
Teletex: 30 8815 qkp
Telefax: (30) 892 26 06

Cologne, Germany Office: Theodor-Heuss-Ring 19-21, D-50668 Cologne.
Telephone: (221)77 16-0. Telefax: (221)77 16-110. Teletex: 221 43 76
Olga d. Telex: 8885 143 Olga d.

(This Listing Continued)

Frankfurt/Main, Germany Office: Airport Center, Hugo-Eckener-Ring, D-60549 Frankfurt/Main. Telephone: (69)69 48 52. Telefax: (69)69 48 60. Telex: 40 32 145 zibr d.

Leipzig, Germany Office: August-Bebel-Str. 38, D-04275 Leipzig. Telephone: (341) 477 83 81/83. Telefax: (341) 477 83 88.

Munich, Germany Office: Widenmayerstrasse 32, D-80538. Munich. Telephone: (89)212147-0. Telefax: (89)228 55 62.

Wiesbaden, Germany Office: Kaiser-Friedrich-Ring 65, D-65185 Wiesbaden. Telephone: (611)88 05-0. Telefax: (611)81 03 09. Telex: 41 86 295 gaed d.

Brussels, Belgium Office: Avenue de Tervuren 35, B-1040 Brussels. Telephone: (2) 736 07 97. Telefax: (2) 732 69 12.

Prague, Czech Republic Office: Betlémska 1, CR-11000 Prague 1. Telephone: (2) 24 22 94 98. Telefax: (2) 232 12 29.

General Practice. Commercial, Corporate, Antitrust and Tax Law. Mergers and Acquisitions, Unfair Competition, Industrial Property Rights, Labor Law and Environmental Law. Real Estate. International Construction and Joint Venture Contracts. Arbitration and Litigation. Notaries (Berlin, Frankfurt/Main and Wiesbaden).

FIRM PROFILE: *The law firm Gaedertz Vieregge Quack Kreile is the result of a merger between 4 partnerships: Heydt Vieregge & Partner, Cologne; Gaedertz Henn & Partner, Wiesbaden; Quack Kühn & Partner, Berlin; Prof. Kreile & Partner, Munich.*

Gaedertz Vieregge Quack Kreile is one of the major German based law firms representing domestic and foreign clients in all fields of law that are relevant for national and international enterprises. An important part of the practice are the legal aspects of transnational transactions especially in EC. The firm advises not only German clients in international matters but also foreign enterprises about all implications of doing business in Germany. Thus many attorneys and also members of the support staff are fluent in English. Other languages such as French, Spanish, Portuguese, Italian, Russian, and Dutch are also spoken.

In addition, the offices in Cologne and Wiesbaden have the specialized capacity to administer large trademark portfolios worldwide including registration and litigation of trademarks and registered designs.

Clients of the firm include many well-known German and foreign companies active in a wide variety of businesses. Gaedertz Vieregge Quack Kreile also represents various trade associations as well as German federal, state and local governmental authorities.

In the Berlin, Wiesbaden and Frankfurt/Main offices, there are 10 attorneys qualified to act as "Notar," specially licensed to prepare and execute documents relating to incorporation of companies, real estate matters and other important commercial transactions where a special form of document is prescribed.

Gaedertz Vieregge Quack Kreile has more than 70 attorneys, including 42 partners, plus a support staff of approximately 150 people, working in the eight different offices.

The offices have for the most part city centre locations. The Frankfurt office is situated at the Airport-Centre of the Rhein-Main Airport.

MEMBERS OF FIRM

KARLHEINZ QUACK, born Berlin, Germany, 1926; admitted, 1954, Berlin, notary public. *Education:* University of Berlin. Co-author, Frankfurter Kommentar zum GWB (commentary on Law against Restraints of Competition). Various publications regarding Corporate and antitrust law. Lectureship at Freie Universitat Berlin (Free University of Berlin). *Member:* Berlin Bar Association; Lawyers Society Berlin; International Bar Association; German Association for Industrial Property Rights and Copyright. *LANGUAGES:* English, French. *PRACTICE AREAS:* Business Law; Corporate and German/EC Antitrust Law; Industrial Property Rights and Copyright Law; EC Law; Arbitration.

ELISABETH QUACK, born Berlin, Germany, 1926; admitted, 1954, Berlin, notary public. *Education:* Universities of Berlin and Heidelberg. *Member:* Berlin Bar Association; Lawyers Society Berlin; German Association for Industrial Property Rights and Copyright. *LANGUAGES:* English, French. *PRACTICE AREAS:* Succession, Notarial Acts.

FRIEDRICH BECKER, born Stavenhagen/Mecklenburg, Germany, 1938; admitted, 1968, Hamburg, notary public. *Education:* University of Hamburg. *Member:* Berlin Bar Association; Lawyers Society Berlin (Vice-President); German Association for Industrial Property Rights and Copyright. *LANGUAGES:* English. *PRACTICE AREAS:* Investment in the New Federal States (former GDR), Litigation.

(This Listing Continued)

DR. WOLFGANG ROSENER, born Berlin, Germany, 1934; admitted, 1965, Berlin, notary public. *Education:* Universities of Frankfurt/Main, Munich and Berlin (Dr. jur.). Co-author: Münchener Vertragshandbuch, vol. 2 Wirtschaftsrecht (Business Law), Contracts for the international construction business; Chapter on Germany in "Business Law in Europe"; Various publications on German and International Business and Corporate Law. *Member:* Berlin Bar Association; Lawyers Society Berlin; German Association for Industrial Property Rights and Copyright; International Bar Association; (Section on Business Law, Committee T: Construction Contracts; Committee C: Antitrust Law and Monopolies); German-Chinese Lawyers Association; Association Européenne d'Etudes Juridiques et Fiscales. *LANGUAGES:* English, Italian. *PRACTICE AREAS:* Business Law; Corporate and Contract Law; International Construction Law; Arbitration; Investment in the New Federal States (former GDR); Notarial Acts.

KAY JACOBSEN, born Nordstrand, Schleswig-Holstein, Germany, 1950; admitted, 1978, Munich, notary public. *Education:* University of Munich. *Member:* Berlin Bar Association; Lawyers Society Berlin; German Association for Industrial Property Rights and Copyright; Association for the Study of Cartel Law. *LANGUAGES:* English. *PRACTICE AREAS:* Business Law; Antitrust and Competition Law; Investment in the New Federal States (former GDR).

DR. FRANK ROITZSCH, born Berlin, Germany, 1954; admitted, 1980, Berlin, notary public. *Education:* University of Berlin and Tübingen (Dr. jur.). Degree in economics. Author, "Minority Rights in Corporate Law / Der Minderheitenschutz im Verbandsrecht". *Member:* Berlin Bar Association; Lawyers Society Berlin; German Association for Industrial Property Rights and Copyright. *LANGUAGES:* English, French, Italian. *PRACTICE AREAS:* Business Law; Corporate and Real Estate Law; Investment in the New Federal States (former GDR); Notarial Acts.

THOMAS RIEDEL, born Berlin, Germany, 1953; admitted, 1980, Berlin, notary public. *Education:* University of Berlin. *Member:* Berlin Bar Association; Lawyers Society Berlin; German Association for Industrial Property Rights and Copyright. *LANGUAGES:* English. *PRACTICE AREAS:* Litigation; Business Law; Industrial Property Rights and Copyright.

EVA LANGNER, born Fulda/Hessen, Germany, 1948; admitted, 1984, Berlin. *Education:* University of Berlin. *Member:* Berlin Bar Association; Lawyers Society Berlin. (Expert Lawyer (Fachanwalt) in Labor Law). *PRACTICE AREAS:* Labour Law; Environmental Law; Family Law.

GEORG GRAF ZU CASTELL-CASTELL, born Castell, Germany, 1956; admitted, 1989, Berlin. *Education:* University of Bonn. Diplomized banker. *Member:* Berlin Bar Association; Lawyers Society Berlin. *LANGUAGES:* English.

ULRICH QUACK, born Berlin, Germany 1959; admitted, 1989, Berlin. *Education:* University of Berlin. *Member:* Berlin Bar Association; Lawyers Society Berlin; German Association for Industrial Property Right and Copyright. *LANGUAGES:* English.

THOMAS SCHMIDT, born Saarbrücken, Germany 1957; admitted, 1985, Berlin, Notary Public. *Education:* University of Saarbrücken. *Member:* Berlin Bar Association; Lawyers Society Berlin. *LANGUAGES:* English.

REEMT REEMTSMA, born Hamburg, Germany 1960; admitted, 1990, Berlin. *Education:* Universities of Kiel and Hamburg. *Member:* Berlin Bar Association; Lawyers Society Berlin. *LANGUAGES:* English.

ASSOCIATES

ULRIKE DÖRR, born Berlin, Germany, 1963; admitted, 1990, Berlin. *Education:* Universities of Berlin and Lausanne. *Member:* Berlin Bar Association; Lawyers Society Berlin; German Association for Industrial Property Rights and Copyright. *LANGUAGES:* English, French.

DR. LIANE THAU, born Eisenhüttenstadt, Germany, 1964; admitted, 1990, Berlin. *Education:* University of Leipzig (Dr. jur.). *Member:* Berlin Bar Association; Lawyers Society Berlin; German Association for Industrial Property Rights and Copyright. *LANGUAGES:* Russian.

ALEXANDER KOLLMORGEN, born Berlin, Germany, 1964; admitted, 1991, Berlin. *Education:* University of Berlin. *Member:* Berlin Bar Association; Lawyers Society Berlin. *LANGUAGES:* English.

MICHAEL MENK, born Haiger, Germany, 1958; admitted, 1989, Karlsruhe; 1993, Berlin. *Education:* Universities of Erlangen, Nürnberg and Freiburg. *Member:* Berlin Bar Association; Lawyers Society Berlin; German Society for Law and Informatic (DGRI). *LANGUAGES:* English.

(This Listing Continued)

GAEDERTZ VIEREGGE QUACK KREILE, Berlin—Continued

THOMAS MEYER, born Aachen, Germany, 1964; admitted, 1994, Berlin. *Education:* Universities of Regensburg and Berlin. *Member:* Berlin Bar Association. *LANGUAGES:* English and Spanish.

KLAUS SCHUBERT, born Frankfurt/Main, Germany, 1962; admitted, 1993, Berlin. *Education:* University of Hamburg. *Member:* Berlin Bar Association. *LANGUAGES:* English.

MARTIN SUKOWSKI, born Wanne-Eickel, Germany, 1960; admitted, 1990, Berlin. *Education:* University of Berlin. *Member:* Berlin Bar Association; Lawyers Society Berlin. *LANGUAGES:* English.

Languages: German, English, French, Italian, Spanish and Russian.

(For complete biographical data on personnel at Cologne, Frankfurt/Main, Leipzig, Munich and Wiesbaden, Germany Offices as well as Brussels, Belgium and Prague, Czech Republic Offices, see Professional Biographies at those locations).

GLEISS LUTZ HOOTZ HIRSCH & PARTNERS

Established in 1949

CLARA-ZETKIN-STRASSE 16
D-10117 BERLIN, GERMANY
Telephone: (49) (30) 20 17 14-0
Telefax: (49) (30) 207 12 06
Cellular Telefax: 0161/271 00 45

Stuttgart (Head Office), Germany Office: Maybachstrasse 6, D-70469 Stuttgart. Telephone: (49) (711) 89 97-0. Telefax: (49) (711) 85 50 96. Telex: 722 439 jura d.

Frankfurt/Main, Germany Office: Eschersheimer Landstr. 19-21, D-60322 Frankfurt/Main. Telephone: (69) 955 14-0. Telefax: (69) 955 14-198; 955 14-199. Telex: 414 292glhcc d.

Brussels, Belgium Office: Avenue Louise 475, Bte. 13, B-1050 Brussels. Telephone: (32) (2) 647 63 74. Telefax: (32) (2) 640 92 31. Telex: 65348 jura b.

Prague, Czech Republic Office: Jugoslávská 29, CR-120 00 Prague 2. Telephone: (42) (2) 24007-510. Telefax: (42) (2) 24007-555.

German, EC and International Practice, in particular Administrative, Anti-Dumping, Anti-Trust, Arbitration, Banking, Capital Markets, Competition, Commercial, Copyright, Corporate/Company, Corporate Finance, Environmental, Finance, Foreign Investment, Industrial Property Rights, Insurance, Labour, Litigation, Media, Mergers and Acquisitions, Real Property, Regulated Industries, Securities, Tax, Telecommunications, Trade, Trademark, Unfair Competition, Zoning.

FIRM PROFILE: The firm was established in 1949 in Stuttgart and developed from a German and later EC competition and anti-trust law boutique to a corporate practice with the full range of corporate legal services. The firm opened its Brussels office in 1987, its Berlin and Frankfurt offices in 1990, and its Prague office in 1992. It employs in total 85 lawyers and expects to grow in Central Europe in particular.

PARTNERS

DR. DETLEF SCHMIDT, born Hannover, 1952; admitted, 1984, Germany. *Education:* University of Göttingen (State Exams, 1977, 1982; Dr. jur., 1984). Author: "Die Unterscheidung von privatem und öffentlichem Recht" (Distinguishing between Private and Public Law), 1985. Lecturer on Law, University of Göttingen, 1976-1981. *Member:* German Bar Association. *LANGUAGES:* German and English. *PRACTICE AREAS:* Corporations; Commercial; Litigation; Privatizations; Product Liability.

CHRISTIAN STEINKE, born Berlin, 1963; admitted, 1991, Germany. *Education:* University of Berlin (State Exams, 1988, 1991). Assistant, University of Berlin, 1989-1991. *Member:* German Bar Association. *LANGUAGES:* German and English. *PRACTICE AREAS:* Commercial; Litigation; Privatizations; Product Liability; Real Property.

DR. STEFAN LINGEMANN, born Eschweiler, 1958; admitted, 1986, Germany. *Education:* Universities of Giessen, Bonn and Tübingen (State Exams, 1983, 1986; Dr.jur., 1991). Author: "Der Wahrheitsbeweis beim Widerruf Ehrkränkender Behauptungen" (The Burden of Proof in Actions for a Withdrawal of Libellous Allegations), 1990. Lecturer on Law, University of Tübingen, 1984-1986. *Member:* German and International Bar Associations; German Lawyers' Association. *LANGUAGES:* German, English

(This Listing Continued)

and French. *PRACTICE AREAS:* Co-Determination; Commercial; Commercial Litigation; Labor; Pensions.

FRED WENDT, born Stuttgart, 1965; admitted, 1993, Germany. *Education:* University of Tübingen (State Exams, 1989, 1992). Assistant, University of Tübingen, 1989-1990. *Member:* German Bar Association. *LANGUAGES:* German, English and French. *PRACTICE AREAS:* Civil; Commercial; Construction; Corporations; Mining.

COUNSEL

DIPL. JUR. SABINE QUARG, born Leipzig, 1953; admitted, 1977, East Germany. *Education:* University of East Berlin (Dipl. jur., 1976). *Member:* Association of Lawyers of East Germany. *LANGUAGES:* German, English and Russian. *PRACTICE AREAS:* Corporations; Commercial; GDR Law; Litigation; Real Property.

GOEBELS, POKORNY, KÄHLER & PARTNER

Established in 1991

LINDENSTR. 54 A
10117 BERLIN, GERMANY
Telephone: 030/2384128
Telefax: 030/2071890

Krefeld, Germany Office: 47800 Krefeld, Wilhelmshofallee 79-18. Telephone: 02151/507-0. Telefax: 02151/599608.

Administrative Law, Antitrust, Banking and Financial Services, Common Market Law, Construction and Engineering Contracts, Corporate Matters, Environmental Law, Industrial and Intellectual Property, Labor Law, Litigation and Arbitration, Mergers and Acquisitions, Procurement Contracts, Product Liability, Taxation, High Technology and Telecommunication, Trade Law, Unfair Competition.

RESIDENT PARTNERS

MANFRED WALTHER, born Panchim, Germany, September 24, 1948; admitted, 1984. *Education:* University of Halle/Wittenberg. Notary, 1991. *LANGUAGES:* German and English.

ASSOCIATES

NICOLE BESSLING, born Düsseldorf, Germany, April 4, 1965; admitted, 1993. *Education:* University of Bayreuth. *LANGUAGES:* German, English and Spanish.

(For biographical data on Krefeld, Germany personnel, see Professional Biographies at that location)

GSCHWENDTNER, REGEL, TREMPEL & PARTNER

Wirtschaftspruefer, Steuerberater, Rechtsanwaelte, Chartered Public Accountants, Tax Advisors, Lawyers

Established in 1987

SPICHERNSTRASSE 15
D-10777 BERLIN, GERMANY
Telephone: 49 (0) 30-212486-0
Fax: 49 (0) 2185432; 21248630

Hanoi, Vietnam Representative Office: 12 Hai Ba Trung. Telephone: 844-254435. Fax: 844-267707.

Member Office of the: International Lawyers, Chartered Public Accountants, Tax Advisors, IASW-EWIV (Frankfurt/Main, Rotterdam).

General Practice, Litigation and Arbitration, Corporate Law and Finance, Financing and Reorganisation, EC, International Law, Unfair Competition, Investments, Mergers and Acquisitions, International and Domestic Tax Law, Accounting and Auditing, International Construction, Joint Venture Contracts (USSR and it's Republics, CSFR, Poland, Hungary, China, Vietnam), Controlling, Marketing Audit, Management Consulting.

FIRM PROFILE: The 1987 established firm specializes in mergers and acquisitions, reorganisation and privatization of central planned systems, economics and companies in eastern Europe, China, Vietnam and the Asia-Pacific-Region.

(This Listing Continued)

WOLFGANG GSCHWENDTNER, born 1949, Wirtschaftsprüfer. *Education:* Free University of Berlin (Master of National Economy; MBA Law). Chartered Public Accountant, Steuerberater/Tax Advisor, 1982 —. *Member:* Institute of Certified Public Accountants. *LANGUAGES:* German and English. *PRACTICE AREAS:* Mergers and Acquisitions.

KLAUS REGEL, born 1955; admitted, 1986 as Certified Tax Law Attorney. *Education:* Free University of Berlin. *Member:* German-Brazilian Lawyers Association. *LANGUAGES:* German and English. *PRACTICE AREAS:* Tax Law; Corporate Law; Reconstruction; Mergers and Acquisitions.

EBERHARD J. TREMPEL, born 1955; admitted, 1986 as Certified Tax Law Attorney. *Education:* Free University of Berlin. Stage at the Camara de Industria e Commercio Brazil-Aleanha São Paulo, Brazil. Author: "Das Exportförderungssaystem Brasiliens," Schriftenreihe des Deutsch-Brasilianischen Handelskammer, São Paulo, Brazil; "China Handbook," Berlin, 1985, 1987, 1989; "Investment Handbook Vietnam," Berlin, 1992. *Member:* German-Chinese Lawyers Association; German Bar Association; German-Japanese Lawyers Association. *LANGUAGES:* German, English, French, Portuguese and Spanish. *PRACTICE AREAS:* Corporate Law; Joint Venture Contracts.

DR. MANFRED KREISSL, born 1929; admitted, 1966. *Education:* Business School Dresden; School of Finance of the Ministry of Finance, Dresden; Ilmenau, Radebeul, Dr. rer, oec. University of Economy, Berlin (1986). Director: Ministry of Industry; Ministry of Finance. *LANGUAGES:* German and English. *PRACTICE AREAS:* Tax Law.

BERND SCHULTZ, born 1959. *Education:* Humboldt University, Berlin. *LANGUAGES:* German, English and Russian. *PRACTICE AREAS:* East European Law; Corporate Law; Business Law; Arbitration and Litigation.

GOTA GUERIN, born 1960; admitted, 1990. *Education:* Free University, Berlin; Maximilian University of Wuerzburg. Stages in Switzerland, 1987. Ministry of Commerce, 1988. Trier, Rheinland-Pfalz, Speyer Law School for Administrative and Public Law, Ministry of Commerce, Berlin, 1992. *LANGUAGES:* English, French and German. *PRACTICE AREAS:* Reorganisation; Bankruptcy; Liquidations; Commercial Law; Privatizations.

GURLAND & LAMBSDORFF

ZIMMERSTRASSE 86-91
D-10117 BERLIN, GERMANY
Telephone: 30-2291018
Telefax: 30-2385878

Also offices in Cologne, Frankfurt and Leipzig.

General Business and International Practice, Corporate, Company, Commercial, Unfair Competition, Acquisitions and Mergers, Distribution, Unsolved Property Questions, Restitution Law, GDR Law, Law on Foreign Trade between former COMECON states.

MEMBERS OF FIRM

PROF. DR. RUDOLF STREICH, born 1938; admitted, 1991, Germany. *Education:* Hochschule für Ökonomie, Berlin. Dr. of Law, HfÖ. Publications: Wirtschafts-und Aussenwirtschaftsrecht, Berlin, 1977 and 1987; Wirtschaftsrecht, Berlin, 1979; Verträge in Wissenschaft und Technik, Berlin, 1980; EDV in der Wirtschaftsleitung, Berlin, 1982; Wirtschaftsrechtsverhältnisse, Berlin, 1985; Lehrbuch Wirtschaftsrecht, Berlin, 1988 and many and various essays and publications. University Lecturer, Hfö, Berlin. Professor, Commercial Law, Hfö. Lecturer: Humboldt University, Berlin; University of Rostock; University of Leipzig; Plechanow Institute, Moscow; University of Rostow/Don. *LANGUAGES:* German, Russian and English.

ASSOCIATES

KLAUS KRÜGER, born 1947; admitted, 1990, Germany. *Education:* Humboldt University, Berlin. Co-Author: "Aspects of Intention or Negligence in White Collar Crime," Berlin. *LANGUAGES:* German and Russian.

CARMEN-SYLVIA SPREER, born 1953; admitted, 1993, Germany. *Education:* Humboldt University, Berlin, (Diplom-Jurist, 1988). *Member:* Berlin Bar Association. *LANGUAGES:* German and English.

DR. UTA KENSY, born 1943; admitted, 1990, Germany. *Education:* Humboldt University, Berlin (Dr.jur., 1986). Publications: "Protection of Computer Software". *Member:* German Bar Association; Association of

(This Listing Continued)

Computer Information Systems. *LANGUAGES:* German, Russian and French.

Member of LEGALLIANCE EEIG (Association of European Law Firms): ADER, JOLIBOIS & ASSOCIES, Paris; BAILEYS, SHAW & GILLETT, London; SARDA, CALOMARDE, CASTELO Y ASOCIADOS, Barcelona/Valencia/Madrid; SCAMONI E ASSOCIATI, Milano/Bologna/Padova; WILLEMART & ASSOCIES, Brussels/Tongres/-Namur; BARENTS & KRANS, The Hague/Brussels; VERUM ADVOKATFIRMAN, Stockholm.

HAARMANN, HEMMELRATH & PARTNER

BUDAPESTER STRASSE 40A
D-10787 BERLIN, GERMANY
Telephone: (030) 264 73-0
Telefax: (030) 264 73-133

Munich Office: Effnerstrasse 38, D-81925 München. Telephone: (089) 924 00-0. Telefax: (089) 92400-133. Telex: 5 23 900 Hup d.
Düsseldorf Office: Martin-Luther-Platz 26, D-40212 Düsseldorf. Telephone: (0211) 8399-0. Telefax (0211) 8399-133.
Frankfurt Office: Neue Mainzer Strasse 75, D-60311 Frankfurt/Main. Telephone: (069) 920 59-0. Telefax: (069) 920 59-133.
Leipzig Office: Neumarkt 24, D-04109 Leipzig. Telephone: (0341) 1263-0. Telefax: (0341) 1263-133.
Tokyo Office: Shiroyama JT Mori Building, 8F, 3-1 Toranomon 4-chome, Minato-ku, Tokyo 105. Telephone: 81-3-34 59 54 85. Fax: 81-3-35 78 89 56.
Prague Office: Cermàkova 7, CZ-1200 00 Prague 2, Czech Republic. Telephone: 42-2-24 23 90 36. Telefax: 42-2-24 23 88 42.

Corporate and Business Law, International and National Tax Law, Banking, Commercial Law, Labour Law, all Areas of Mergers and Acquisitions, Financial Transactions, International Law, Antitrust Law, Unfair Competition and Intellectual Property Rights Law, EEC Law, Real Estate Transactions, Management and Leveraged Buy-outs, National and Cross-border Leasing Transactions, Structuring of Funds, Accounting Services.

FIRM PROFILE: The firm, established in 1987, has strongly developed as a multi-disciplinary firm in Germany with seven offices. The firm is affiliated with Graham & James (US, Italy, Japan and China), Taylor Joynson Garrett (UK) and Deacons (Hong Kong and Southeast Asia) and is a member of the international tax and audit network RSM International.

RESIDENT MEMBERS OF FIRM

DETLEF OLUFS, born Bruxelles, Belgium, September 7, 1942; admitted, 1980, Berlin; Fachanwalt Für Steuerrecht, 1983. *Education:* Universities of Vienna and Göttingen (J.D., 1976). *Member:* Deutscher Juristentag e.V. *LANGUAGES:* German and English. *PRACTICE AREAS:* Corporate; Tax; Mergers and Acquisitions, Real Estate, Commercial.

DR. WOLFGANG JANKA, born Augsburg, Germany, May 12, 1957; admitted, 1988, Frankfurt. *Education:* Universities of Regensburg and Freiburg (J.D., 1983; M.B.A., 1988; Doctor at Law, 1989). Certified Public Accountant, USA, 1991; Wirtschaftsprüfer (Certified Public Accountant, Germany, 1992. Author: various publications in German and International periodicals. *Member:* Foreign American Law Association; Institute of German Chartered Accountants (IDW); AICPA. *LANGUAGES:* German, English and French. *PRACTICE AREAS:* Corporate; Tax; Bankruptcy; Business Law; Finance.

THOMAS SANTÜNS, born Berlin, Germany, August 16, 1959; admitted, 1989, Berlin. *Education:* University of Berlin. *LANGUAGES:* German and English. *PRACTICE AREAS:* Real Estate; Company; Commercial; Bankruptcy; Building Law.

DR. KLAUS HERKENROTH, born Shelters, Germany, June 22, 1956; admitted, 1987, New York; 1988, Frankfurt; 1992, Steuerberater (Certified Tax Advisor);1994, Berlin Court of Appeals (Kammergericht). *Education:* Universities of Marburg and Giessen (J.D., 1983; Doctor at Law, 1992); University of Michigan Law School (LL.M., 1986). *Member:* Berlin, New York and American Bar Associations; German-American Bar Association; German-American Lawyers Association. *LANGUAGES:* German, English and Spanish. *PRACTICE AREAS:* Corporate and Commercial Law; Corporate and Individual Taxation; Tax Planning; Mergers and Acquisitions; Corporate Restructurings.

DR.DR. CHRISTIAN DIERKS, born Johannesburg, South Africa, April 10, 1960; admitted, 1991, Munich. *Education:* Universities of Regensburg and Hamburg (M.D., General Practitioner, 1987); Universities of Re-

(This Listing Continued)

HAARMANN, HEMMELRATH & PARTNER, Berlin—Continued

gensburg and Munich (Doctor at Law, 1992). Author: "Datenschutz und Schweigepflicht im Gesundheitswesen," 1992. Member: German Society of Medical Law (DGMR); Medicine and Ethics; South African Medical and Dental Council. *Member:* American Society of Law; German-South African Lawyers Association (Chairman). *LANGUAGES:* German and English. *PRACTICE AREAS:* Medical Law; Health Insurance Law; Pharmaceutical Law; Malpractice Law.

Languages: German, English, French, Dutch, Spanish, Japanese, Slovakian, Russian, Czech and Mandarin.

(For Biographical Data on all other Members of Firm See Professional Biographies at Munich, Düsseldorf, Frankfurt and Leipzig, Germany, Tokyo, Japan and Prague, Czech Republic).

DR. VOLKER HENCKEL

Established in 1965

BASELER STRASSE 12
12205 BERLIN, GERMANY
Telephone: 030-8338132
Telefax: 8332158

Labor, Corporation, Business, Bankruptcy, Bank, Probate and Family Law.

FIRM PROFILE: *The firm was established in 1968 to offer civil legal services to a small selected clientele and remained small in order to be able to provide personal and individual attention to them.*

The Firm maintains strong relationships and cooperation with law firms in the U.S., England and Western Europe.

DR. VOLKER HENCKEL, born Stettin, Germany, January 2, 1934; admitted, 1968, Berlin. *Education:* Universities of Cologne, Munich and Berlin (Referendar); Columbia University; New York University; University of Cologne (Doctor of Laws); Kammergericht Berlin (Assessor). Author: "The Legal Nature of the American Collective Bargaining Agreement and Its Enforceability," Dissertation, Cologne, 1966; "The Present and the Future of the Law of Microfilming in West Germany," Journal of Microphotography, Tokyo, Vol. 10, No. 2, 1971; "Is the Ascertainment of Debt in the German Bankruptcy Proceedings a Final and Conclusive Judgment in England?", AWD des Betriebsberaters, March, 1972; "The Legal Aspects of Microfilming in Germany," Journal of Micrographics, USA, April, 1972; "Introduction to the Japanese Bankruptcy Law," Zeitschrift für Konkurs-, Treuhand- und Schiedsgerichtswesen, July, 1973; "Nos Amenaza la Servidumbre del Computador?" (Will We Become Computer Slaves?), Revista Jurídica Boletín, Universidad Nacianal de Colombia, Bogotá, August, 1978; "The Japanese Legal System: The Law of Insolvency," 1979. Lecturer of Civil Law, Fachhochschule für Wirtschaft (College of Economics), Berlin, 1970-1972. Sworn Interpreter for the Courts of Berlin. *Member:* Berlin Bar Association (Rechtsanwaltskammer Berlin); Lawyers Society (Anwaltsverein); German-American Legal Association (Deutsch-Amerikanische Juristen-Vereinigung e.V.); American Chamber of Commerce in Germany; British-German Jurists' Association. *LANGUAGES:* English, German, French and Spanish.

HENGELER MUELLER WEITZEL WIRTZ

Rechtsanwälte

KURFÜRSTENDAMM 54/55
D-10707 BERLIN, GERMANY
Telephone: (030) 882 76 47
Telefax: (030) 882 71 44

Düsseldorf, Germany Office: Trinkausstrasse 7, D-40213 Düsseldorf. Telephone: (0211) 8304-0. Telefax: (0211) 13 26 41 & 8 04 61. Telex: 85 87 300 whds d.
Frankfurt/Main, Germany Office: Bockenheimer Landstrasse 51, D-60325 Frankfurt/Main. Telephone: (069) 170 95-0. Telefax: (069) 72 57 73 & 7239 83. Telex: 41 45 95 Jura D.
Brussels, Belgium Office: Boulevard du Régent 50, Bte. 6, B-1000 Brussels. Telephone: (02) 511 41 15. Telefax: (02) 514 02 12.
Budapest, Hungary Office: Teréz krt. 38, H-1066. Telephone: (1) 1323121. Telefax (1) 2690098.
New York Office: 712 Fifth Avenue, New York, New York, 10019. Telephone: (212) 586-4600. Telefax: (212) 586-4481.

(This Listing Continued)

Commercial, Corporate, International, Banking, Finance and Underwriting, Taxation, Arbitration, EEC, Antitrust, Merger Control, Fair Trade, Patent, Trademark, Litigation, Labor, Administrative, Constitutional, Environmental and Planning Law.

PARTNERS

DR. BERNHARD WIRTZ, born Düsseldorf, Germany, 1927; admitted, 1959, Berlin. *Education:* Universities of Bonn, Cologne and Munich (Dr. jur.).

DR. JULIUS BUDDE, born Woldegk, Germany, 1950; admitted, 1977, Berlin. *Education:* Universities of Heidelberg, Bonn, Tübingen and Göttingen (Dr. jur.). Foreign Associate, New York Law Firm, 1978-1979.

DR. CORD-GEORG HASSELMANN, born Hamburg, Germany, 1956; admitted, 1987, Berlin. *Education:* Universities of Munich and Hamburg (Dr. jur.); Georgetown University, Washington, D.C. (LL.M.).

DR. ULRICH BLECH, born Königstein/Taunus, Germany, 1959; admitted, 1990, Berlin. *Education:* University of Bonn (Dr. jur.); University of Chicago Law School (LL.M.).

JOHN FLÜH, born Flensburg, Germany, 1962; admitted, 1991, Berlin. *Education:* Universities of Kiel and Surrey (U.K.); Harvard University (M.B.A.). Associate, McKinsey & Company, Inc., 1990-1991.

Languages: German, English and French

(For biographical data of the members of the firm admitted to the bar in Düsseldorf and Frankfurt/Main, see Professional Biographies at Düsseldorf and Frankfurt/Main)

HERZOG, MEYER, WILL

SCHLÜTERSTRAßE 54
10629 BERLIN, GERMANY
Telephone: +49 30 8857040
Telefax: +49 30 8824821

Krefeld, Germany Office: Sollbrüggenstrasse 52, 47800 Krefeld. Telephone: +49 2151 589501. Telefax: +49 2151 598110.
Moers, Germany Office: Haagstraße 12, 47441 Moers. Telephone: +49 2841 25207. Telefax: +49 2841 28384.

General Practice, Commercial, Corporation, Securities, Property, Taxation, International and Unfair Law. Antitrust Law. Labour Law. Air Law.

MEMBERS OF FIRM

GERTRUD WEBER, born Cologne, Germany, October 6, 1956; admitted, 1990, Krefeld. *Education:* Universities of Marburg and Gießen. *Member:* German Bar Association. *LANGUAGES:* German, English, French and Spanish.

DR. ROLF RAHM, born Münster, Germany, September 24, 1956; admitted, 1986, Münster. *Education:* Universities of Münster; Strasbourg, France; Lausanne, Switzerland; Padua, Italy (Doctor of Laws, 1989). Author: "Internationales Gesellschaftsrecht." *Member:* German Bar Association. *LANGUAGES:* German, English, Italian, French and Spanish.

ASSOCIATES

HARALD SCHLEICHER, born Singen, Germany, October 10, 1963; admitted, 1992, Hamburg. *Education:* University of Constance. German Trade Office, Taipei, 1991. With Heuking Kühn Herold Kunz Wojtek, 1992-1993. *Member:* German Bar Association; German-American Lawyers Association. *LANGUAGES:* German and English.

ASTRID POCKRANDT, born Bielefeld, Germany, June 15, 1964; admitted, 1994, Berlin. *Education:* University of Bonn. *Member:* German Bar Association. *LANGUAGES:* German, English and French.

(For Complete Biographical Data on all Personnel, see Professional Biographies at Krefeld, Germany)

HEUKING KÜHN KUNZ WOJTEK

KARL-LIEBKNECHT-STRASSE 33
D-10178 BERLIN, GERMANY
Telephone: 49 30 238 6161
Telefax: 49 30 238 6166

Other Offices: Düsseldorf, Frankfurt, Hamburg (Germany); Paris (France)

Real Estate, Corporate, Banking, Tax, National and EC Antitrust, Mergers, Acquisitions, Intellectual Property, Unfair Competition and Trade Law, Commercial and International Law, EC Law, Environmental Law, Administrative Law, International Arbitration, Litigation, General Practice.

FIRM PROFILE: *All Attorneys are Members of Denton International and of the Berlin Bar Association. Languages spoken are English, German, French and Russian.*

MEMBER OF FIRM

CHRISTIAN R. BRAUN, born Mainz, Germany, September 8, 1959; admitted, 1987, Germany; Certified Counsel for Administrative Law. *Education:* University of Berlin (Referendar, 1984; Assessor, 1987). *Member:* (German) Environmental Law Society. **PRACTICE AREAS:** Administrative and Environmental Law; General Commercial Law; Real Estate.

ASSOCIATES

INGEBURG LÖSEKANN, born Brake, Germany, September 12, 1950; admitted, 1981, Germany. *Education:* University of Bremen (1974-1980). Research Fellow, European University Institute, Florence, Italy, 1981-1984. Research Assistant, University of Louvain-La-Neuve, Belgium, 1984-1985. Counsel on European Law and Economics, Brussels, Belgium, 1985-1991. **PRACTICE AREAS:** EC Law; General Commercial.

DR. GÜNTER TEUPEL, born Leipzig, Germany, November 24, 1928; admitted, 1990, Germany. *Education:* University of Leipzig (Referendar, 1950, Assessor, 1952, Doctor of Law, 1963, Mechanical Engineer, 1959). Legal Adviser Tractor Factory Brandenburg, 1953-1961. Lawyer Ministry of Machines, 1962-1984. Deputy Commissioner of Office of Legal Protection of the GDR, 1984-1990. Deputy Commissioner of the Government, 1990-1991.

HERMANN MEYNEN, born Kiel, Germany, June 11, 1961; admitted, 1994, Germany. *Education:* University of Marburg and Bonn (Referendar 1990, Assessor, 1993). **PRACTICE AREAS:** Civil Law; Commercial Law; Construction Law.

HEUSSEN BRAUN VON KESSEL & PARTNER

SCHLÜTERSTR. 37
10629 BERLIN, GERMANY
Telephone: 030-88 57 68 - 0
Fax: 030-88 87 68 - 30

Munich, Germany Office: Briennerstrasse 9, D-80333. Telephone: 089-290 97 - 0. Telex: 5-216 022 ADVO D. Telefax: 089-22 85 117.

General International Practice.

DR. BENNO HEUSSEN, born Stuhlingen, Germany, May 18, 1944; admitted, 1973, Germany. *Education:* Free University of West Berlin, Freiburg, Munich (Dr.jur., 1972). *Member:* German-Japanese Association; German and American Lawyers Association; German-British Chamber of Commerce; German-Japanese Chamber of Commerce. **LANGUAGES:** German and English.

(For Complete Biographical Data on all Personnel, see Professional Biographies at Munich, Germany)

HOFFMANN, LIEBS, FRITSCH & PARTNER

KURFÜRSTENDAMM 11
10719 BERLIN, GERMANY
Telephone: 0 30/88 44 17 60
Telex: 0 30/88 44 17 63

Düsseldorf, Germany Office: Rotthäuser Weg 12, 40629. Telephone: 0211/9284 (0). Telefax: 0211/9284-100.

(This Listing Continued)

Chemnitz, Germany Office: Augustusburger Strasse 331, 09127. Telephone: 03 71/72 90 31 34. Telefax: 03 71/72 04 46.
Halle, Germany Office: Wilhelm-Külz-Strasse 13, 06108. Telephone: 0345/50 27 24 26. Telefax: 0345/50 27 08.

(For Complete Biographical Data on all Personnel, see Professional Biographies at Düsseldorf, Germany)

HÖLTERS & ELSING

Established in 1989

WIELANDSTRASSE 23
10707 BERLIN, GERMANY
Telephone: (030) 885 74 20
Telecopier: (0211) 35 39 28

Düsseldorf, Germany Office: Immermannstrasse 40, 40210. Telephone: (0211) 36 78 70. Telefax: (0211) 35 39 28.
Leipzig, Germany Office: Nordstrasse 23, 04105. Telephone: (0341) 98 24 60. Telefax: (0341) 98 24 612.

General and International Practice, Business Organizations, Commercial Law, Corporate Banking, Finance, Mergers and Acquisitions, Bankruptcy and Reorganization, Labor, Antitrust, Unfair Competition, National and International Commercial Litigation and Arbitration, Consumer Affairs, Advertising, Product Liability, Real Estate, Estate Planning, International Construction Contracts, Trademark, Licensing, Franchise and Distribution Law, International and National Tax Planning and Tax Counselling, Protection of Intellectual Property, Administrative and Company Law, European Community Law.

RESIDENT MEMBER

DR. NORBERT IMPELMANN, born Spellen/Niederrhein, Germany, 1960; admitted, 1989, Germany. *Education:* Universities of Bonn and Cologne (Doctor of Law, 1990). Co-author, "Kanadisches Handels- und Wirtschafrecht" (Canadian Commercial and Business Law), 1992. *Member:* British-German Jurists Association; Association Internationale des Jeunes Avocats. **LANGUAGES:** German and English.

(For biographical data on personnel, see Professional Biographies at Düsseldorf and Leipzig, Germany)

HUGHES HUBBARD & REED

KURFÜRSTENDAMM 44
D-1000 BERLIN 15, GERMANY
Telephone: 030-880008-0
Telefax: 030-880008-65
Telex: 185803 KNAPA D

New York, New York Office: One Battery Park Plaza, 10004. Telephone: 212-837-6000. Cable Address: "Hughreed, New York." Telex: 427120. Telecopier: 212-422-4726.
Los Angeles, California Office: 350 S. Grand Avenue, Suite 3600, 90071-3442. Telephone: 213-613-2800. Telecopier: 213-613-2950.
Miami, Florida Office: 801 Brickell Avenue, 33131. Telephone: 305-358-1666. Telex: 51-8785. Telecopier: 305-3718759.
Washington, D.C. Office: 1300 I Street, N.W., Suite 900 West, 20005. Telephone: 202-408-3600. Telex: 89-2674. Telecopier: 202-408-3636.
Paris, France Office: 47, Avenue Georges Mandel, 75116. Telephone: 33.1.44.05.80.00. Telex: 645440. Telecopier: 33.1.45.53.15.04.

General Practice.

(For biographical data of the New York, N.Y. partners, see Professional Biographies at New York, N.Y.).

KÄRGEL VOLLHARDT & PARTNER

KURFÜRSTENDAMM 36
POSTFACH 15 07 86
10669 BERLIN, GERMANY
Telephone: 030/885 77 10
Telecopier: 030/881 13 08

Administrative, Banking and Finance, Bankruptcy/Insolvency, Civil Litigation, Commercial, Commercial Property, Company, Competition, Construction, Corporate, Debt Recovery, Employment, Environment, European Community, Import/Export, Insurance, International, Mergers and Acquisitions, Mortgages/Hypothecs, Notaries, Partnerships, Real Estate Purchase, Transport, East European Investments and Business.

(This Listing Continued)

KÄRGEL VOLLHARDT & PARTNER, Berlin—
Continued

MEMBERS OF FIRM

UWE KÄRGEL, born Gladbeck, December 9, 1942; admitted, 1971, Germany. *Education:* Universities of Münster, Innsbruck, Cologne and Bonn. Notary, 1981. *Member:* I.B.A.; U.I.A.; U.A.E. (Honorary Member); Berlin Bar Association (President, 1989—); German Bar Association (Member of Board). *LANGUAGES:* German, English, French and Spanish. *PRACTICE AREAS:* Real Estate; Corporate Law; International Contracting; Notarizations.

JÜRGEN J. VOLLHARDT, born Bielefeld, August 13, 1928; admitted, 1961, Germany. *Education:* Universities Frankfurt/Main and Mainz. Long Term Chief Executive Officer of a German Commercial Bank, retired, 1989. Chairman and Member of Supervisory Boards in Industrial, Banking and Housing Corporations. *Member:* Association of Berlin Industrialists and Businessmen, Committee for Berlin's Economic Integration at the Chamber of Commerce, Berlin; East-West Trade Magazine (Advisory Board to the Editors). *LANGUAGES:* German, English and French. *PRACTICE AREAS:* Banking; Finance; Mergers and Acquisitions; Real Estate; International Contracting.

DIRK MICHAELSEN, born Schleswig, December 13, 1955; admitted, 1983, Germany; 1993, Notary. *Education:* University of Göttingen. *LANGUAGES:* German and English. *PRACTICE AREAS:* Employment Law; Real Estate Law; Notarizations.

JULIA EIS, born Berlin, July 12, 1955; admitted, 1987, Germany; 1993, Notary. *Education:* Universities of Berlin and Bonn. *LANGUAGES:* German and English. *PRACTICE AREAS:* Real Estate Law; General Commercial Law; Notarizations.

TORSTEN BLOCH, born Paderborn, August 20, 1961; admitted, 1990, Germany. *Education:* Universities of Regensburg and Berlin. *LANGUAGES:* German and English. *PRACTICE AREAS:* Corporate Law; Real Estate Law.

SEBASTIAN PÖTTER, born Berlin, March 1, 1962; admitted, 1989, Germany. *Education:* Free University of Berlin. *Member:* German-American Lawyers Association; German-Polish Lawyers Association. *LANGUAGES:* German, English, French and Russian. *PRACTICE AREAS:* Corporate Law; Insurance Defense.

PROF. DR. ROSWITHA SVENSSON, born Wollersleben, August 25, 1950; admitted, 1990, Germany. *Education:* Humboldt University, Berlin (Dr. jur., 1977; Dr. sc. jur., 1986). Professor, Academy of Sciences, Berlin, 1987-1990. *LANGUAGES:* German and Russian. *PRACTICE AREAS:* Communist Expropriation; Restitution; East European Business Law; Family Law.

VOLKER NITSCHKE, born Kiel, May 14, 1960; admitted, 1991, Germany. *Education:* University of Kiel. *LANGUAGES:* German and English. *PRACTICE AREAS:* Administrative Law; Bankruptcy; Insolvency Law.

GERO VOLLHARDT, born Düsseldorf, January 20, 1960; admitted, 1992, Germany. *Education:* Free University of Berlin. *LANGUAGES:* German and English. *PRACTICE AREAS:* Employment Law; Public and Private Construction Law.

INES RÖDER, born Jena, December 22, 1963; admitted, 1993, Germany. *Education:* Humboldt University, Berlin. *LANGUAGES:* German, English and Russian. *PRACTICE AREAS:* Communist Expropriation; Restitution; Inheritance Law.

ALEXANDER VON STAHL, born Berlin, July 10, 1939; admitted, 1989-1990 and 1993, Germany. *Education:* Universities of Münster and München. Long Term Secretary of State of the Berlin Ministry of Justice. General Prosecutor of the Federal Republic of Germany, 1990-1993. *LANGUAGES:* German and English. *PRACTICE AREAS:* Company Law; Administrative; Criminal Law.

A Member of European Law Firm (ELF) which is a European Economic Interest Group. It has offices in Belgium, France, Germany, Great Britain, Holland, Luxembourg, Ireland, Italy, Portugal and Spain. Associate offices in Austria, Sweden and U.S.A.

Languages: English, French, German, Russian and Spanish

KLEINER & KÜGEL
KLEISTSTRAβE 35
10787 BERLIN, GERMANY
Telephone: 030/217 64 91
Telefax: 030/217 69 47

Stuttgart, Germany Office: Silberburgstraβe 187, 70178. Telephone: 0711/640 20 66. Telefax: 0711/6 494 222.

Patent, Trademark, Copyright, Unfair Competition, Corporation, Labour Law, Commercial, Antitrust, Private International Law, Administrative Law, Environmental and Pollution, Waste and Disposal, Zoning and Construction, Food and Drugs, Litigation.

RESIDENT PARTNERS

DR. THOMAS MILLER, born Ulm, Germany, February 7, 1959; admitted, 1989, Germany. *Education:* University of Münster; University of Berlin (Referendar, 1986; Assessor, 1989; Doctor of Jurisprudence, 1992). Author: "Die Mehrfachabmahnung im Wettbewerbsrecht," Berlin, 1992. *Member:* German Bar Association; German Association for the Protection for Industrial Property and Copyright; Lawyers' Society Berlin; German-American Lawyers' Association. *LANGUAGES:* German, French and English. *PRACTICE AREAS:* Patent; Trademark; Copyright; Unfair Competition; Corporation; Labour Law; Food and Drugs; Pharmacy Law; Litigation.

DR. KNAUTHE & PARTNER

Rechtsanwälte und Notare
Established in 1969
KURFÜRSTENDAMM 44
10719 BERLIN, GERMANY
Telephone: 030-880008-0
Telefax: 030-880008-65
Telex: 185803 KNAPA D

Other Berlin, Germany Office: Clara-Zetkin-Strasse 80, 10117 Berlin. Telephone: 030-22086-0. Telefax: 030-2292026.
Potsdam, Germany Office: Eisenhart Str. 2, 14469 Potsdam. Telephone: 0331-2803590. Telefax: 0331-2803592.
Dresden, Germany Office: Ostra-Allee 25, 01067 Dresden. Telephone: 0351-4860165. Telefax: 0351-4860166.

Corporation, Building and Planning, Real Estate and Zoning, Construction, Mergers and Acquisitions, Joint Ventures, Common Market, Investment, Banking, Company, Commercial, Insurance, Trademark and Copyright, Labor, Family, Housing, Estates, Wills, Trusts, Restitution, Communist Expropriation, Investment in East Germany and Eastern Europe, Litigation, Notaries.

MEMBERS OF FIRM

DR. KARLHEINZ KNAUTHE, born Berlin, April 8, 1941; admitted, 1969, Berlin; Notary. *Education:* Free University of Berlin (Dr.jur., 1968). Author: "Causal Legal Thought," Doctoral Thesis, 1968. President: Grundkredit Bank, Berlin. *Member:* Berlin Bar Association; American Chamber of Commerce; Advisory Board Carl Hofer Gesellschaft. *LANGUAGES:* German and English. *PRACTICE AREAS:* Corporation; Investment.

HANS-DIETER BECKER, born Lublin, September 5, 1942; admitted, 1971, Berlin. *Education:* Free University of Berlin. *Member:* Berlin Bar Association. *LANGUAGES:* German. *PRACTICE AREAS:* Family; Wills.

WOLFGANG A. GUSTAVUS, born Weixlbaum, October 19, 1945; admitted, 1975, Berlin; Notary. *Education:* Free University of Berlin and Freiburg. *Member:* Berlin Bar Association (Executive Board); Federal Association for Loan Employment. *LANGUAGES:* German and English. *PRACTICE AREAS:* Labor; Housing.

WERNER F. SCHROTH, born Konstanz, February 12, 1945; admitted, 1975, Berlin; Notary. *Education:* Universities of Erlangen and Berlin. *Member:* Berlin Bar Association; British Chamber of Commerce. *LANGUAGES:* German and English. *PRACTICE AREAS:* Commercial; Banking.

FRIEDER SONNTAG, born München, April 9, 1942; admitted, 1969, Berlin; Notary. *Education:* Universities of Freiburg and Hamburg. *Member:* Berlin Bar Association. *LANGUAGES:* German and French. *PRACTICE AREAS:* Estates; Trusts.

(This Listing Continued)

ERNST VOGEL, born Neustadt am Rübenberg, August 7, 1943; admitted, 1975, Berlin; Notary. *Education:* Universities of München, Saarbrücken and Münster. *Member:* Berlin Bar Association. *LANGUAGES:* German and English. *PRACTICE AREAS:* Building and Planning; Construction.

DR. FRANK H. WALTER-VON GIERKE, born Kassel, August 3, 1960; admitted, 1989, Berlin. *Education:* University of Göttingen (Dr.jur., 1988). Author: "Equality of Men and Women in the Premium and Benefit Systems of Private Pension Schemes," Doctoral Thesis, 1988. *Member:* Berlin Bar Association. *LANGUAGES:* German and English. *PRACTICE AREAS:* Mergers and Acquisitions; Company.

ASSOCIATES

MARION RUHL, born Stuttgart, November 21, 1959; admitted, 1988, Berlin. *Education:* University of Freiburg. *Member:* Berlin Bar Association; German-Brasilian Law Association. *LANGUAGES:* German, English and Portuguese. *PRACTICE AREAS:* Housing; Labor.

DR. MARTIN F. FLECKENSTEIN, born Freiburg, February 26, 1959; admitted, 1987, Freiburg; 1991, Berlin. *Education:* Universities of Göttingen and Freiburg. Author: "Egypt Import Regulations," 1986; "Execution of German Titles in Egypt," 1986. *Member:* Berlin Bar Association. *LANGUAGES:* German and English. *PRACTICE AREAS:* Real Estate and Zoning; Corporation.

DR. UWE RITTER, born Hildesheim, August 25, 1957; admitted, 1991, Berlin. *Education:* University of Göttingen; Fachhochschule für Verwaltung und Rechtspflege Hildesheim (Judicial Officer-Rechtspfleger). Author: "Interlocutory Relief in Matters of Noncontentious Litigation," Doctoral Thesis, 1991. *Member:* Berlin Bar Association. *LANGUAGES:* German, English and Spanish. *PRACTICE AREAS:* Company; Commercial.

DR. JEANNETTE WEISS, born Berlin, October 22, 1963; admitted, 1992, Berlin. *Education:* Free University of Berlin (Dr.jur., 1993). Author: "The Development of the Legal Protection of Tenants," Doctoral Thesis, 1993. *Member:* Berlin Bar Association. *LANGUAGES:* English and French. *PRACTICE AREAS:* Property; Construction Law.

DR. KAI MERTENS, born Neumünster, August 20, 1965; admitted, 1994, Berlin. *Education:* Universities of Kiel (Dr. jur., 1993) and Surrey. Author: "Reconstructions, Transformations and Amalgamations under German Company Law," Doctoral Thesis, 1993; "The Transfer of Property and Liabilities under Revised German Company Law," 1994. *Member:* Berlin Bar Association. *LANGUAGES:* German and English. *PRACTICE AREAS:* Company; Anti-Trust and Competition; Litigation.

(For Biographical Data at Other Berlin, Germany Office, Potsdam and Dresden Offices, see Professional Biographies at Berlin, Potsdam and Dresden, Germany)

DR. KNAUTHE & PARTNER

Rechtsanwälte und Notare

Established in 1969

CLARA-ZETKIN-STR. 80
10117 BERLIN, GERMANY
Telephone: 030-22086-0
Telefax: 030-2292026

Other Berlin (Head), Germany Office: Kurfürstendamm 44, 10719 Berlin. Telephone: 030-880008-0. Telefax: 030-880008-65; Telex: 18503 KNAPA D.
Potsdam, Germany Office: Eisenhart Str. 2, 14469 Potsdam. Telephone: 0331-2803590. Telefax: 0331-2803592.
Dresden, Germany Office: Ostra-Allee 25, 01067 Dresden. Telephone: 0351-4860165. Telefax: 0351-4860166.

Corporation, Building and Planning, Real Estate and Zoning, Construction, Mergers and Acquisitions, Joint Ventures, Common Market, Investment, Banking, Company, Commercial, Insurance, Trademark and Copyright, Labor, Family, Housing, Estates, Wills, Trusts, Restitution, Communist Expropriation, Investment in East Germany and Eastern Europe, Litigation, Notaries.

MEMBERS OF FIRM

DR. KLAUS RIEBSCHLÄGER, born Berlin, August 17, 1940; admitted, 1990, Berlin. *Education:* Free University of Berlin (Dr.jur., 1968). Author: "Die Freirechtsbewegung," Doctoral Thesis, 1968; "Vor Ort-Blicke in die Berliner Politik," 2nd ed., 1983. Former Minister of Finance, Berlin. *Member:* Berlin Bar Association; Berlin Parliament; Verband der Konsum-

(This Listing Continued)

---

genossenschaften, Berlin (Deputy President). *LANGUAGES:* German and English. *PRACTICE AREAS:* Real Estate; Zoning; Joint Ventures.

HOLGER SIEVERSEN, born Berlin, March 24, 1948; admitted, 1984, Berlin. *Education:* Free University of Berlin. *Member:* Berlin Bar Association; Federal Revenue Academy. (Tax Counsellor). *LANGUAGES:* German and English. *PRACTICE AREAS:* Taxation; Trusts and Estates.

DETLEV NEUSETZER, born Göttingen, July 1, 1946; admitted, 1975, Berlin; Notary. *Education:* Free University of Berlin. *Member:* Berlin Bar Association; German-Finnish Society. *LANGUAGES:* German, Finnish and English. *PRACTICE AREAS:* Insurance.

ASSOCIATES

ERMBRECHT RINDTORFF, born Recklinghausen, April 11, 1958; admitted, 1986, Berlin. *Education:* Free University of Berlin. *Member:* Berlin Bar Association. *LANGUAGES:* German, Italian, French, English and Spanish. *PRACTICE AREAS:* Common Market; Trademark; Copyright.

DR. HARALD WESTPHAL, born Rostock, September 5, 1957; admitted, 1990, Berlin. *Education:* University of Leipzig; Akademie für Staats und Rechtswissenschaft, Potsdam-Babelsberg (Dr.jur., 1987). Author: "International Legal Regulations for the Registration of Ships," Doctoral Thesis, 1987. *Member:* Berlin Bar Association; German Maritime Law Association. *LANGUAGES:* German and English. *PRACTICE AREAS:* Communist Expropriation; Restitution.

MICHAEL HAVERS, born Hamm, March 19, 1962; admitted, 1992, Berlin. *Education:* University of Münster. *Member:* Berlin Bar Association. *LANGUAGES:* German, English and French. *PRACTICE AREAS:* Restitution; Corporation; Company.

DR. STEPHAN SÜDHOFF, born Holte, January 13, 1962; admitted, 1993, Berlin. *Education:* Universities of Passau, Lausanne, Geneva and Heidelberg (Dr.jur., 1994). Author: "The Claim to Remedial Action as a Basis for a Ban on Utilization in Administrative Procedures," Doctoral Thesis, 1994. *Member:* Berlin Bar Association. *LANGUAGES:* German, English and French. *PRACTICE AREAS:* Administrative Law; Property; Real Estate.

BERNHARD KALTENBACH, born Biberach, July 23, 1959; admitted, 1993, Berlin. *Education:* Universities of Konstanz, Heidelberg and Munich. *Member:* Berlin Bar Association. *LANGUAGES:* German, English and French. *PRACTICE AREAS:* Restitution; Contracts; Commercial Law.

(For Biographical Data at Other Berlin (Head), Germany Office, Potsdam and Dresden Offices, see Professional Biographies at Berlin, Potsdam and Dresden, Germany)

KOBLITZ LAW OFFICE

RANKESTRASSE 9
10789 BERLIN, GERMANY
Telephone: (49 30) 883-3047
Fax: (49 30) 883-3317

Brandenburg Office: Dorfstrasse 36, 14548 Ferch. Telephone: (49 33209) 71636.

General Business Practice, Aviation, Restitution, Property Claims, Real Estate and Music.

DONALD KOBLITZ, born New York, July 15, 1953; admitted, 1979, New York; 1981, Washington, D.C.; 1992, Berlin, FRG (as Rechtskundiger). *Education:* Stanford (J.D., M.A) and Columbia (B.A.). Clerk, William B. Bryant. Chief Judge, U.S. District Court, Washington, D.C., 1979-1981. State Department legal service, 1982-1990. Legal Adviser, Berlin, 1985-1989. Legal Adviser, German Reunification Negotiations, 1990. *LANGUAGES:* English, German, Japanese and French.

KÜBLER, ROGIER & PARTNER

EINEMSTRASSE 24
D-10785 BERLIN, GERMANY
Telephone: (030) 264768-0
Telefax: (030) 264768-40

Cologne, Germany Office: Aachener Strasse 217, D-50931. Telephone: (0221) 400770. Telefax: (0221) 4007720.
Dresden, Germany Office: Antonstrasse 10, D-01097. Telephone: (0351) 44 879-0. Telefax: (0351) 44 879-99.

(This Listing Continued)

KÜBLER, ROGIER & PARTNER, Berlin—Continued

Bankruptcy, Banking, Corporate, Commercial, Creditors' Rights, Industrial Relations and Labor Law, Insolvency and Reorganization, International Private, Property and Real Estate, Taxation, Unfair Competition, General Practice and Litigation.

RESIDENT PARTNERS

THOMAS SIERING, born Essen, Germany, November 18, 1952; admitted, 1983, Berlin; 1988, Court of Appeals, Berlin. *Member:* Berlin Bar Association and Lawyers Association. *LANGUAGES:* German, English, French.

DR. DIETER KÜHNE, born Hannover, Germany, July 4, 1957; admitted, 1986, München; 1994, Berlin and Berlin Court of Appeals. *Education:* University of Göttingen, Germany; University of Lausanne (Switzerland); University of Münster, Germany (Doctor of Law, 1984). *Member:* Bar Association. *LANGUAGES:* German, English, French.

ANDRÉ LÖFFLER, born Bernau, Germany, November 9, 1962; admitted, 1990, Berlin. *Member:* Berlin Bar Association and Lawyers Association. *LANGUAGES:* German, English, Russian.

(For complete biographical data on Personnel at Cologne and Dresden, Germany Offices, see Professional Biographies at those locations)

LAGERLÖF & LEMAN

MEINEKESTRASSE 13
D-10719 BERLIN, GERMANY
Telephone: Int. 49-30-884 710; 884 712 90
Telefax: Int. 49-30-882 4852

Stockholm, Sweden Office: Strandvägen 7A, P.O. Box 5402, S-114 84, Stockholm. Telephone: Int. 46-8-665 66 00. Telefax: Int. 46-8-667 68 83. Telex: 17715 Laglaw S.

Gothenburg, Sweden Office: Västra Hamngatan 24, P.O. Box 2252, S-403 14, Gothenburg. Telephone: Int. 46-31-17 10 00 Telefax: Int. 46-31-13 56 62. Telefax Maritime department: Int. 46-31-11 65 37.

Malmö, Sweden Office: Stortorget 8, S-211 34, Malmö. Telephone: Int. 46-40-704 50. Telefax: Int. 46-40-97 19 17.

London, England Office: Royex House, Aldermanbury Square, London EC2V 7HR. Telephone: Int. 44-171-606 1715. Telefax: Int. 44-171-600 1718.

Paris, France Office: 87 Avenue Kléber, F-75116 Paris. Telephone: 33-1-45 05 1208. Telefax: 33-1-47 55 0975.

New York, N.Y. Office: 712 Fifth Avenue, 30th Floor, New York, N.Y. 10019-4102 U.S.A. Telephone: Int. 1-212-801-3450. Telefax: Int. 1-212-801-3455.

Corporate and Commercial law, including Tax, Banking, Financing, Insurance, Real Estate, Computer, Patent, Trademark, Copyright, Labor, Trade Regulation and Antitrust Law. International Legal Transactions. Arbitration and Litigation in Civil Matters. EC Law. International Private Law. Maritime and Admiralty Law.
Member of Alliance of European Lawyers (EEIG).

PARTNERS

VERNER THORSEN, born Copenhagen, Denmark, 1933. *Education:* Lund University (juris kandidat, LL.M., 1959). Service with Swedish Courts. Bank Lawyer and Manager of International Department, Skånska Banken, 1961-1970. General Counsel, Alfa Laval AB, 1970-1981. *Member:* Swedish Bar Association. *LANGUAGES:* Swedish, English, German, French and Danish. *PRACTICE AREAS:* Commercial Law; Corporate Law; Alternative Dispute Resolution.

TOMAS SETTERBERG, born Gothenburg, Sweden, 1945. *Education:* Lund University (juris kandidat, LL.M., 1971). *Member:* Swedish and International Bar Associations; Association Internationale de Jeunes Avocats. *LANGUAGES:* Swedish, English and German. *PRACTICE AREAS:* Commercial Law; Corporate Law; Real Estate Law.

LÜER & GÖRG

Established in 1974
KURFÜRSTENDAMM 54/55
D-10707 BERLIN, GERMANY
Telephone: (030) 884503-0
Telecopier: (030) 8827150

Cologne, Germany Office: Konrad-Adenauer-Ufer 21, D-50668 Cologne. Telephone: (0221) 916 44 0. Telecopier: (0221) 916 44 30.

General and International Law Practice, Corporate and Commercial Law, Banking, Insurance and Reinsurance, Bankruptcy and Insolvency Law, Mergers and Acquisitions, Litigation and Arbitration, Labor and Co-determination Law, Antitrust, Unfair Competition and Intellectual Property Law, Private International Law, EEC Law and Environmental Law, Tax Law.

RESIDENT MEMBERS OF FIRM

DR. ROLAND HOFFMANN, born Bielefeld, Germany, March 8, 1960; admitted, 1991, Cologne; 1993, Berlin. *Education:* Universities of Passau and Freiburg (Dr. jur., 1991). Author: "Verfahrensgerechtigkeit," 1992; "Bankers Liability in Germany," in: "Bankers Liability: Risks and remedies," ed. D. Campbell/R. Merani, 1993, 221-230. Assistant: University of Freiburg i.Br., 1987-1988; University of Cologne, Institute for Banking Law, 1988-1991. *Member:* International Bar Association; Association of Fellow and Legal Scholars of the Center for International Legal Studies; Deutsche Sektion der Internationalen Juristen-Kommission e.V.; Deutsche Stiftung für internationale rechtliche Zusammenarbeit e.V.; Deutsche Gesellschaft für Gesetzgebung e.V.; Deutsch-Deutsche Juristische Vereinigung; Deutsch-Türkische Juristenvereinigung e.V. *LANGUAGES:* German, English and French. *PRACTICE AREAS:* Corporate and Commercial Law; Banking Law; Mergers and Acquisitions.

HANS PETER PIETZ, born Haan/Rheinland, Germany, January 21, 1955; admitted, 1982, Berlin. Tax Advisor, 1990. Notary, 1995. *Education:* University of Berlin. *LANGUAGES:* English and French. *PRACTICE AREAS:* Tax Law; Real Estate Law; Corporate Law; Law of Successions.

CHRISTIAN PIETZ, born Berlin, Germany, September 9, 1963; admitted, 1993, Berlin. *Education:* University of Berlin. *LANGUAGES:* English and French. *PRACTICE AREAS:* Unfair Competition Law; Construction Law; Labor Law.

ASSOCIATES

JOBST-FRIEDRICH VON UNGER, born Essen, Germany, September 23, 1962; admitted, 1993, Berlin. *Education:* Universities of Bonn, Geneva and Speyer. Author: "Öffentlich-rechtliche Vorgaben für die Treuhandanstalt," in: Fischer/Hax/Schneider: Die Treuhandanstalt - das Unmögliche wagen, 1993 (with Prof. Dr. Michael Kloepfer). *Member:* Deutsch-Amerikanische Juristen-Vereinigung. Associate, Treuhandanstalt, Berlin, 1991-1992. *LANGUAGES:* German, English and French. *PRACTICE AREAS:* Corporate and Commercial Law; Public Law; East German Law.

(For Complete Biographical Data on all Personnel, see Professional Biographies at Cologne, Germany)

LUTHER & PARTNER

HARDENBERGSTRASSE 12
D-10623 BERLIN, GERMANY
Telephone: (030) 315 956-0
Telefax: (030) 21 82 612

Hamburg, Germany Office: Hermannstrasse 46, D-20095 Hamburg. Telephone: (040) 32 81 180. Telefax: (040) 32 73 57.

German, EEC and International Practice with an emphasis on Corporate Law: For details see the entry under HAMBURG.

FIRM PROFILE: Luther & Partner is a steadily growing law firm with offices in Hamburg and Berlin. The origin of the firm goes back into the 1930's. Various lawyers of the firm, in addition to their legal training, have worked as research associates at renowned universities and have received legal training in the United States, other European countries and/or with the EEC-Commission in Brussels. Several lawyers of the firm have published books and articles on topics relating to their fields of expertise. All partners are members of specialized professional associations.

The firm's lawyers have broad experience in domestic and international business law including EEC law with a special emphasis on corporate and

(This Listing Continued)

corporate-related matters. The firm handles corporate issues and, through various specialized departments, all business related areas of law.

In its major fields of practise, the firm represents and renders its services to well-known German and international companies.

RESIDENT PARTNERS

DETLEV STOECKER, born Bonn, Germany, April 29, 1954; admitted, 1981, Germany; notary, 1991. *Education:* University of Berlin; Referendar Göteborg, Sweden, 1980. Author: Besonderes Handels- und Wirtschaftsrecht, in: Unternehmensgründung, München, 1980. Lecturer, Constitutional Law, Berlin, 1979. *Member:* Berlin Bar Association; Swedish Chamber of Commerce in Germany; Deutscher Juristentag; German-Nordic Lawyers' Association. *LANGUAGES:* German, English and Swedish.

DR. KLAUS VON GIERKE, born Heidelberg, Germany, October 2, 1954; admitted, 1982, New York; 1984, Germany. *Education:* Universities of Freiburg (Dr.jur., 1983) and Geneva; Tulane University of Louisiana, School of Law, New Orleans (LL.M., 1980). Author: Die Dritthaftung des Rechtsanwalts, 1984, (on lawyer's Liability). *Member:* German-American Lawyers' Association. *LANGUAGES:* German, English and French.

DR. EVA HUNTEMANN, born Bremen, Germany, May 18, 1960; admitted, 1990, Germany. *Education:* Universities of Erlangen-Nürnberg and Göttingen (Dr. jur. 1988). Author: Die Endlagerung radioaktiver Abfälle, 1988, (on radioactive waste). Research Assistant, Institute for International Law, University of Göttingen 1985-1986 and Institute for Criminal Law, University of Hamburg 1986-1989. *Member:* Hamburg Bar Association; Hamburg Lawyers Association; Deutsch-Deutsche Juristengesellschaft. *LANGUAGES:* German, English and Spanish.

CLEMENS SCHOLZ, born Essen, Germany, August 2, 1961; admitted, 1990, Germany. *Education:* Universities of Bonn, Marburg, Lausanne (Switzerland) and Munich. *Member:* Berlin Bar Association. *LANGUAGES:* German and English.

CHRISTIAN GRAF VON BROCKDORFF, born Kiel, Germany, June 26, 1960; admitted, 1991, Germany. *Education:* Universities of Hamburg and Munich; Temple University School of Law (LL.M., 1989). Author: "Örtliche oder sachliche Zuständigkeitsnormen?" (on questions of jurisdiction), Zeitschrift für Wirtschaftsrecht, ZIP 1993, 980-987. *Member:* Hamburg Bar Association. *LANGUAGES:* German and English.

ASSOCIATES

RAINER KLINGENFUSS, born Kassel, Germany, July 7, 1959; admitted, 1992, Germany. *Education:* Universities of Marburg and Berlin. *Member:* German Lawyers Association. *LANGUAGES:* German and English.

HANS JOACHIM BÜSSELBERG, born Wilhelmshaven, Germany, February 4, 1965; admitted, 1994, Germany. *Education:* University of Freiburg (First State Exam, 1990). *LANGUAGES:* German, English and French.

DR. ILONA A. MURATI, born Hamburg, Germany, August 28, 1965; admitted, 1994, Germany. *Education:* Universities of Freiburg, Bonn, Cologne and Bielefeld (Dr. jur., 1993). Author: "Gläubigerschützende Massnahmen zur Sicherung der Kapitalaufbringung und der Kapitalerhaltung im spanischen Aktienrecht," (on Spanish and European Stock Company Law). *Member:* German-Spanish Lawyers Association. *LANGUAGES:* German, English, Spanish and French.

Languages: German, English, French, Spanish, Italian and Swedish.

(For Complete Listing and Biographical data on further Personnel, see Biographical Card at Hamburg, Germany)

MANQUEN & LOKAU

Established in 1983

RHEINSTR. 45

12161 BERLIN, GERMANY

Telephone: (030) 8520371
Telefax: (030) 8515951

Business Law, Family Law, Immigration and Naturalization, Inheritance, International Private Law, Labor and Employment, Probate, Property, Real Estate, Taxation, Trusts and Estates, Wills.

FIRM PROFILE: Established in 1983. Two partners. Close co-operation with firms in southern and eastern Germany as well as the United States. Specialized in international cases and in particular US German cases.

(This Listing Continued)

MEMBERS OF FIRM

TIMOTHY D. MANQUEN, born Detroit, Michigan, March 30, 1947; admitted, 1983, Germany. *Education:* Free University, Berlin; University of Maryland. *Member:* Berlin Bar Association; American Chamber of Commerce in Germany. *LANGUAGES:* English, German and Spanish. *PRACTICE AREAS:* Business Law; Labor and Employment; Probate; Property; Real Estate; Taxation; Trusts and Estates.

VIKTORIA LOKAU, born Karlsruhe, Germany, February 8, 1954; admitted, 1983, Germany. *Education:* Free University, Berlin; University of Lausanne, Switzerland. *Member:* Berlin Bar Association. *LANGUAGES:* German, English and French. *PRACTICE AREAS:* Family Law; Immigration and Naturalization; International Private Law; Labor and Employment; Inheritance Law; Wills.

MAYER, BROWN & PLATT

SPREEUFER 5
BERLIN 10178, GERMANY
Telephone: 011-49-30-240-7930
Facsimile: 011-49-30-240-79344

Chicago, Illinois Office: 190 South LaSalle Street, 60603-3441. Telephone: (312) -782-0600. Pitney Bowes: (312) 701-7711. Telex: 190404. Cable: LEMAY.

Washington, D.C. Office: 2000 Pennsylvania Avenue, N.W., 20006-1882. Telephone: (202) 463-2000. Pitney Bowes: (202) 861-0484, Pitney Bowes: (202) 861-0473. Telex: 892603. Cable: LEMAYDC

New York, New York Office: 787 Seventh Avenue, Suite 2400, 10019-6018. Telephone: (212) 554-3000. Pitney Bowes: (212) 262-1910. Telex: 701842. Cable: LEMAYEN.

Houston, Texas Office: 700 Louisiana Street, Suite 3600, 77002-2730. Telephone: (713) 221-1651. Pitney Bowes: (713) 224-6410. Telex: 775809. Cable: LEMAYHOU.

Los Angeles, California Office: 350 South Grand Avenue, 25th Floor, 90071-1503. Telephone: (213) 229-9500. Pitney Bowes: (213) 625-0248. Telex: 188089. Cable: LEMAYLA.

London, England Office: 162 Queen Victoria Street, EC4V 4DB. Telephone: 011-44-71-248-1465. Fax: 011-44-71-329-4465. Telex: 8811095. Cable: LEMAYLDN.

Tokyo, Japan Office: (Kawachi Gaikokuho Jimu Bengoshi Jimusho) Urbannet Otemachi Building 13F 2-2, Otemachi 2-chome, Chiyoda-ku, Tokyo 100. Telephone: 011-81-3-5255-9700. Facsimile: 011-81-3-5255-9797.

Brussels, Belgium Office: Square de Meeûs 19/20, Bte. 4, 1040. Telephone: 011-32-2-512-9878. Fax: 011-32-2-511-3305. Telex: 20768 MBPBRU B.

Mexico City, Mexico, D.F., Mexico Correspondent: Jáuregui, Navarrete, Nader y Rojas, S.C., Abogados, Paseo de la Reforma 199, Pisos 15, 16 & 17, 06500. Telephone: 011-525-591-16-55. Fax: 011-525-535-80-62, 011-525-703-22-47. Cable: JANANE.

General Practice.
Firm engaged in American and General International Practice but not authorized to appear before the German Courts.

PARTNER

C. MARK NICOLAIDES, born Detroit, Michigan, February 11, 1954; admitted, 1981, New York and U.S. District Court, Southern and Eastern Districts of New York; 1983, U.S. Court of Appeals, Second Circuit (Not admitted in Germany). *Education:* Cornell University (B.A., 1976); University of Virginia (J.D., 1980). Phi Beta Kappa; Phi Kappa Phi. Lyle Moot Court Winner. Author: "Overview of 1986 ISDA Rate Swap Code," Butterworths Journal of International Banking and Financial Law, September, 1986; "Documentation of LDC Asset Transfers," Butterworths Journal of International Banking and Financial Law, August, 1987; "A Survey of Lender Liability in the United States," Journal of International Banking Law, Vol. 3, Issue 4, 1988; "Priorities For Subordinated Debt," Butterworths Journal of International Banking and Financial Law, June, 1989. Co-Author: "Fraudulent Conveyance Aspects of Leveraged Buyouts," International Financial Law Review, April, 1986; "Coping With Cross-Border Securitization," International Financial Law Review, November, 1991. *Member:* Association of the Bar of the City of New York; American Bar Association (Member, Section of Corporation, Banking and Business Law).

ASSOCIATE

Richard L. Bjelde (Not admitted in Germany)

MELCHERS, SCHUBERT, STOCKER, STURIES

Established in 1973

SCHIFFBAUERDAMM 17
D-10117 BERLIN, GERMANY
Telephone: (49-30) 2252 2133
Telecopier: (49-30) 2252 2108

Heidelberg, Germany Office: Slevogtstrasse 6, D-69126 Heidelberg. Mailing Address: P.O. Box 10 52 22, D-69042 Heidelberg. Telephone: (49-6221) 39 91 01. Telefax: (49-6221) 37 91 00; 37 40 69.

Zwickau, Germany Office: Kolpingstrasse 28, D-08058 Zwickau. Telephone: (49-375) 294023/4/5. Telecopier: (49-375) 521629.

Frankfurt/Main, Germany Office: Beethovenstrasse 29, D-60325 Frankfurt/Main, Telephone: (49-69) 9757 3227. Telecopier: (49-69) 9757 3220.

Administrative Law, Banking, Commercial, Contracts, Corporate, EC-Law, Environmental Law, General Practice, Inheritance, Intellectual Property and Trade Marks, Arbitration, International Private Law, Investment, Labour Law, Mergers and Acquisitions, National and EC Antitrust, National and International Tax Law, Real Estate, Trade and Trade Show Law, Unfair Competition.

FIRM PROFILE: *The law firm was founded in 1973 as a multidisciplinary partnership of lawyers, certified public accountants and tax advisors. Today, 31 professionals, of which 24 are lawyers, offer services and advice in the firm's offices in Berlin, Frankfurt/Main, Heidelberg and Zwickau. The multidisciplinary combination of legal services provides clients with comprehensive advice in the fields of business law, tax law, business administration and auditing.*

RESIDENT PARTNERS

ULRICH SCHUBERT, born Danzig, July 17, 1943; admitted, 1971, Germany. *Education:* Universities of Bonn and Freiburg. Author: "Konkursfenster beim Konkurs des gewerblichen Zwischenanmieters," in: Probleme der Rechts- und Steuerberatung in mittelständischen Unternehmen, Köln, 1988. *Member:* German and Berlin Bar Associations. *LANGUAGES:* German, English and French. *PRACTICE AREAS:* Insolvency Law; Reorganization; Mergers and Acquisition; Company Law; Commercial Law.

ASSOCIATES

STEFAN TRÄUMER, born Heidelberg, June 8, 1957; admitted, 1990, German Tax Courts; 1992, Germany. *Education:* University of Heidelberg. Certified Public Accountant, Germany 1992. *Member:* Institute of C.P.A., Germany (I.d.W.); German and Berlin Bar Associations. *LANGUAGES:* German and English. *PRACTICE AREAS:* National and International Tax Law; Auditing and Valuation; Commercial Law; Company Law.

DR. JUR. CHRISTOPH RIESE, born Oberhausen/Rheinland, January 25, 1964; admitted, 1992, Germany. *Education:* University of Bonn. Author: Der Maßgabebeschluß des Bundesrates bei zustimmungsbedürftigen Rechtsverordnungen. *Member:* German and Berlin Bar Associations; Bundesvereinigung Öffentliches Recht. *LANGUAGES:* German and English. *PRACTICE AREAS:* Commercial Law; Administrative Law.

DR. JUR. PETRA HILGERS, born Holzheim, March 15, 1964; admitted, 1993, Germany. *Education:* University of Freiburg. Author: "Besitzlose Mobillarsicherheiten im Absonderungsverfahren unter besonderer Berücksichtigung der Verwertungsprobleme." *Member: German and Berlin Bar Associations. PRACTICE AREAS:* Company Law; Real Estate; Contracts.

FRANK SCHULKAMP, born January 18, 1961; admitted, 1991, Germany. *Education:* University of Freiburg. *Member:* German and Berlin Bar Associations. *LANGUAGES:* German, English and French. *PRACTICE AREAS:* Competition and Intellectual Property.

CERTIFIED PUBLIC ACCOUNTANTS AND TAX ADVISORS

ARMIN GROTHE, born Eberswalde, April 28, 1942; admitted, 1972, German Tax Courts. Tax Advisor, Germany, 1972. Certified Public Accountant, Germany, 1977. *Education:* University of Saarbrücken (Dipl.-Kfm.). *Member:* Institute of C.P.A. in Germany (I.d.W.). *LANGUAGES:* German and English. *PRACTICE AREAS:* National and International Tax Law; Auditing and Valuation.

(For complete biographical data on Personnel at Frankfurt/Main, Heidelberg and Zwickau offices see Professional Biographies at those locations)

MENOLD HERRLINGER REINKING & PARTNER

FRAUNHOFER STRAßE 33-36
D-10587 BERLIN, GERMANY
Telephone: (0049 30) 34 78 68 11
Telefax: (0049 30) 34 78 68 35

Dresden Office: Uhlandstraße 39, 01069 Dresden. Telephone: (0049 351) 478-71-0. Telefax: (0049 351) 478 71 15.

Düsseldorf Office: Am Wehrhahn 50, 40211 Düsseldorf. Telephone: (0049 211) 93 52 300. Telefax: (0049 211) 93 52 683.

Stuttgart Office: Mittlerer Pfad 15, 70499 Stuttgart. Telephone: (0049 711) 1386 800. Telefax: (0049 711) 1386 808.

Corporate, Commercial, Tax and Business Law Practice, including: Mergers & Acquisitions, Antitrust and Unfair Competition Law, Intellectual and Industrial Property Law, Reorganization and Bankruptcy, Labor Law and Redundancy Plans (Sozialpläne), Private Wealth Planning, Trusts, Foundations and Estate Law, Environmental, Waste and Administrative Law, the Laws of the East European Countries, Business Law for Japanese clients (Düsseldorf), Restitution of Property in the East German federal states (Dresden), General Civil Law and Civil Litigation, European Community Law.

FIRM PROFILE: *The firm springs from a merger of the law firms Menold Herrlinger Maulbetsch Schick & Oltmanns (Stuttgart), Bezler & Partner (Stuttgart), Reith & Battke (Dresden) and Reinking, Frings & Drude (Düsseldorf).*

MEMBERS OF FIRM

CHRISTIAN REINKING, born Darmstadt, Germany, 1952; admitted, 1982, Germany. *Education:* Universities of Heidelberg, Tübingen, Germany and Cambridge (Trinity Hall), United Kingdom as a scholar of the "Studienstiftung des Deutschen Volkes" (State Exams, 1978, 1982). *Member:* Association for the Study of Antitrust Law; IBA; AIJA. *LANGUAGES:* German and English. *PRACTICE AREAS:* Corporate Law; Mergers & Acquisitions; Antitrust; Real Estate Transactions; Intellectual Property.

DR. THOMAS KAPP, born Stuttgart, Germany, 1958; admitted, 1987, Germany. *Education:* University of Tübingen (State Exams, 1981, 1986; Doctor of Law, 1984); University of California, Los Angeles (Master of Laws, 1983). Assistant Lecturer, University of Tübingen, 1984-1985. Internship with Hughes, Hubbard & Reed, Los Angeles, 1983 and Paris, 1985. Partner, Law Firm Bezler & Partner, 1991-1993. Author: "Wettbewerbsbeschränkungen durch vertikale Vertriebsbindungen?" 1984; numerous Articles on Antitrust and Business Law Matters. *Member:* German Bar Association; German Lawyers Association; German-American Lawyers Association; German-French Lawyers Association. *LANGUAGES:* German, English and French. *PRACTICE AREAS:* Corporate Law; Antitrust and Trade Regulation; Distributorships; Mergers and Acquisitions.

NÖRR, STIEFENHOFER & LUTZ

Established in 1993

SCHLÜTERSTRAßE 36
D-10629 BERLIN, GERMANY
Telephone: 49-30-8836700
Telecopier: 49-30-8835052

Munich, Germany Office: Brienner Str. 28, 80333 Munich, Postfach 101121, 80085 Munich. Telephone: 49-89-280111. Telecopier: 49-89-280110.

Frankfurt/Main, Germany Office: Freiherr-vom-Stein-Straße 11, 60323 Frankfurt/Main. Telephone: 49-69-172917. Telecopier: 49-69-172916.

Dresden, Germany Office: Böhmertstraße 3, 01099 Dresden. Telephone: 49-351-5671188, 49-351-5671187. Telecopier: 49-351-5671186.

Prague, Czech Republic Office: Masarykovo nábřeži 30, 11000 Prague 1. Telephone: 42-2-24913396, 42-2-24913882. Telecopier: 42-2-24911836.

Budapest, Hungary Office: Becsi utca 5/1. 1-2, 1052 Budapest V. Telephone: 36-1-1174905; 36-1-1378293. Telecopier: 36-1-1184035.

Warsaw, Poland Office: Kancelaria Adwokacka Sp. Z o. o. UL. Nowogrodzka 50, 00950 Warsaw. Telephone: 48-2-6216232. Telecopier: 48-2-6251976.

Brussels, Belgium EEC Office: 106 Avenue Louise, 1050 Brussels. Telephone: 32-2-6470650. Telecopier: 32-2-6464729.

(This Listing Continued)

Moscow, Russia Office: Ul. Levoberezhnaya, 32. 125475. Telephone: 7-095-4585822; 7-095-4585792. Telecopier: 7-095-4585782.

German and International Practice, Media, Telecommunication, Corporate, Commercial, Mergers and Acquisitions, Finance and Banking, Tax, EEC, Public and Constitutional Law, Antitrust, Real Estate, Construction, Labor, Insurance, Landlord-Tenant, Leasing, Product Liability, Aviation, Law of Succession, Industrial Property, Copyright, Trademarks, Unfair Competition, Advertising, Administrative and Planning Law, Litigation and Arbitration, Joint Ventures, Appellate, Civil, Federal, Legislative, Trial Practice, Advice to Legislative Institutions in Eastern Europe, Eastern European Law.

RESIDENT PARTNERS

DR. RONALD FROHNE, born Bremen, Germany, March 21, 1945; admitted, 1975, Germany; 1979, Tax Lawyer; Certified Public Accountant, 1988. *Education:* Universities of Paris (Sorbonne) and Munich. With Metropolitan Trust Company, Toronto, Canada, 1969. Assistant Lecturer, University of Augsburg, 1973-1975. Managing Director, Beta/Taurus Group, 1984-1987. *Member:* International and German Bar Associations. *LANGUAGES:* German, English and French. *PRACTICE AREAS:* Entertainment; Media; Telecommunications; Tax; Corporate Law.

DR. HANS CHRISTOPH SCHIMMELPFENNIG, born Lüneburg, Germany, September 28, 1957; admitted, 1989, Germany. *Education:* Universities of Berlin and Munich. *Member:* Berlin Bar Association. *LANGUAGES:* German and English. *PRACTICE AREAS:* Corporate and Tax; Commercial and Public Law; Mergers and Acquisitions.

ASSOCIATES

DR. ASTRID FRENSE, born Indonesia, February 22, 1962; admitted, 1991, Germany. *Education:* Universities of Erlangen and Bonn. Assistant Lecturer, University of Bonn, 1990-1991. *Member:* Berlin Bar Association. *LANGUAGES:* German, English and French. *PRACTICE AREAS:* Commercial Law; Company Law; Real Estate; Landlord-Tenant; Leasing; Product Liability.

FLORIAN HARTL, born Munich, July 28, 1963; admitted, 1994, Germany. *Education:* University of Munich. *LANGUAGES:* German and English. *PRACTICE AREAS:* Company Law; Tax Law; Public Law.

Languages: German, English, French and Italian.

OPPENHOFF & RÄDLER

MEINEKESTR. 13
D-10719 BERLIN, GERMANY
Telephone: (030) 88471-0
Telecopier: (030) 88471-200

Other Berlin, Germany Office: Rankestr. 21, D-10789. Telephone: (030) 21496-0. Telecopier: (030) 21496-100.

Munich, Germany Office: Prinzregentenplatz 10, D-81675. Telephone: (089) 41808-0. Telecopier: (089) 41808-100.

Cologne, Germany Office: Hohenstaufenring 62, D-50674. Telephone (0221) 2091-0. Telecopier: (0221) 2091-435. Telex: 8 882 294 bos. Teletex: 2627 221 4054BOS.

Frankfurt/Main, Germany Office: Bockenheimer Landstr. 51-53, D-60325. Telephone: (069) 170003-0. Telecopier: (069) 170003-33.

Frankfurt/Main, Germany Office: Myliusstr. 33-37, D-60323. Telephone: (069) 17093-0. Telecopier: (069) 17093-444.

Leipzig, Germany Office: Kommandant-Trufanow-Str. 14, D-04105. Telephone: (0341) 56649-0. Telecopier: (0341) 56649-99.

Brussels, Belgium Office: Rue Brederode 13A, B-1000. Telephone: (2) 5050211. Telecopier: (2) 5022644.

London, England Office: Royex House, Aldermanbury Square, GB-London EC2V 7HR. Telephone: (171) 600 3609. Telecopier: (171) 600 1718.

New York, New York Office: 712 Fifth Avenue, 30th Floor, 10019, USA. Telephone: (212) 801 3410. Telecopier: (212) 801 3415.

New York, New York Office: 712 Fifth Avenue, 29th Floor, 10019, USA. Telephone: (212) 397 7580/7546. Telecopier: (212) 397 4292.

Prague, Czech Republic Office: Alliance Prague, Jachymova 2, CZ-11000 Prague 1. Telephone: (2) 232 1130. Telecopier: (2) 232 6371.

FIRM PROFILE: Oppenhoff & Rädler has been created by a merger of two large German firms, Boden Oppenhoff Rasor Raue and Rädler Raupach Bezzenberger. The firm at present has more than 90 partners and comprises together some 200 lawyers and tax advisers.

Oppenhoff & Rädler acts for domestic and for international clients. The

(This Listing Continued)

firm offers a comprehensive range of legal services, including: General Corporate and Commercial; Taxation; Banking, Finance and Securities; Mergers and Acquisitions; Real Estate; Litigation and Arbitration; Intellectual Property and Trademarks; Construction Law; Antitrust and European Community Law; Administrative and Environmental Law; Media, Communications and Entertainment Law; Technology and Computer Law; Food, Drug and Chemistry; Family Law; Wills.

Oppenhoff & Rädler is a member of the ALLIANCE OF EUROPEAN LAWYERS EEIG (members: Oppenhoff & Rädler, Germany; De Bandt, van Hecke & Lagae, Belgium; De Brauw Blackstone Westbroek, The Netherlands; Jeantet & Associés, France; Lagerlöf & Leman, Sweden; Uria & Menendez, Spain) and of the LLR EEIG (members: Loyens & Volkmaars, The Netherlands; Bureau Francis Lefebvre, France; Oppenhoff & Rädler, Germany).

RESIDENT PARTNERS AND JUNIOR PARTNERS

DR. GEROLD BEZZENBERGER, born Königsberg, Germany, March 13, 1930; admitted, 1956, Germany. *Education:* Universities of Munich, Hamburg and Heidelberg (Dr.jur.); University of Stuttgart. *LANGUAGES:* German, English. *PRACTICE AREAS:* Corporate Law; Company Law; Mergers, Acquisitions and Divestitures.

PROF. DR. PETER RAUE, born Munich, Germany, February 4, 1941; admitted, 1971, Germany. *Education:* University of Berlin (Dr.jur.). *LANGUAGES:* German, English. *PRACTICE AREAS:* Art Law; Civil Law; Copyrights; Entertainment and the Arts.

KLAUS MOCK, born Berlin, Germany, August 9, 1939; admitted, 1968, Germany. *Education:* University of Berlin. *LANGUAGES:* German, English. *PRACTICE AREAS:* Corporate Law; Company Law; Mortgages; Property; Real Estate.

DR. RUDOLF CÖLLE, born Celle, Germany, February 26, 1941; admitted, 1968, Germany. *Education:* Universities of Geneva, Münster and Cologne (Dr. jur.). *LANGUAGES:* German, English. *PRACTICE AREAS:* Corporate Law; Company Law; Employee Benefits; Labour and Employment; Mergers, Acquisitions and Divestitures.

DR. LUTZ ZIESCHE, born Baerwalde/Neumark, Germany, July 19, 1944; admitted, 1973, Germany. *Education:* Universities of Lausanne, Berlin and Cologne (Dr.jur.). *PRACTICE AREAS:* Construction Law.

DR. MAX BRAEUER, born Münden, Germany, October 17, 1950; admitted, 1979, Germany. *Education:* Universities of Göttingen, Geneva and Heidelberg (Dr.jur.). *LANGUAGES:* German, French. *PRACTICE AREAS:* Family Law; Litigation; Real Estate.

KLAUS-MICHAEL HAPPE, born Berlin, Germany, September 30, 1939; admitted, 1967, Germany. *Education:* Universities of Freiburg and Berlin (Dipl.-Kfm./M.B.A.). *PRACTICE AREAS:* Civil Law; Family Law; Wills.

DR. WOLFGANG KUHLA, born Hamburg, Germany, May 20, 1953; admitted, 1983, Germany. *Education:* Universities of Berlin, Lausanne, Tübingen (Dr.jur.). *LANGUAGES:* German, English, French. *PRACTICE AREAS:* Administrative Law; Construction Law; Labour and Employment; Real Estate; Zoning; Planning and Land Use.

NIKOLAUS BRENDLE, born Konstanz, Germany, December 6, 1949; admitted, 1978, Germany. *Education:* Universities of Heidelberg and Berlin. *LANGUAGES:* German, English. *PRACTICE AREAS:* Company Law; Real Estate.

GEORG MIGGEL, born Duisburg, Germany, August 31, 1958; admitted, 1987, Germany. *Education:* Universities of Giessen and Berlin. *LANGUAGES:* German, French. *PRACTICE AREAS:* Civil Law; Construction Law; Litigation.

HANS-HERMANN RÖSCH, born Hemmingstedt, Germany, February 7, 1950; admitted, 1980, Germany. *Education:* University of Berlin. *LANGUAGES:* German, English, Spanish. *PRACTICE AREAS:* Business Law; Corporate Law; Commercial Law; Company Law; Mergers, Acquisitions and Divestitures.

DR. STEFAN LÜTJE, born Hamburg, Germany, April 20, 1959; admitted, 1987, Germany. *Education:* Universities of Bayreuth and Munich (Dr.jur.). *LANGUAGES:* German, English. *PRACTICE AREAS:* Copyrights; Communications and Media; Entertainment and the Arts; Intellectual Property.

DR. THOMAS TÖBEN, born Varel, Germany, October 10, 1955; admitted, 1987, Germany, Tax Advisor (Steuerberater). *Education:* Universities of Marburg/Lahn and Hamburg (Dipl.-Kfm./M.B.A.; Dr.rer.pol.).

(This Listing Continued)

OPPENHOFF & RÄDLER, Berlin—Continued

(Resident Partner, New York Office). *LANGUAGES:* German, English. *PRACTICE AREAS:* Taxation; German Taxation Law; Taxation in Eastern-Bloc Countries Law; International Tax Aspects of Executive Remuneration Law.

DR. KAI-UWE PRITZSCHE, born Frankfurt, Germany, June 24, 1957; admitted, 1988, Germany. *Education:* Universities of Bonn, Freiburg, Geneva and Cologne (Dr.jur.); University of California at Berkeley (LL.M.). *LANGUAGES:* German, English, French. *PRACTICE AREAS:* Corporate Law; Energy; Mergers, Acquisitions and Divestitures.

KLAUS JUNG, born Berlin, Germany, November 9, 1949; admitted, 1976, Germany. *Education:* Universities of Freiburg and Berlin. *LANGUAGES:* German, English, French. *PRACTICE AREAS:* Contracts; Real Estate.

HANNS-WILLIAM MÜLSCH, born Darmstadt, Germany, October 5, 1959; admitted, 1988, Germany. *Education:* University of Berlin. *LANGUAGES:* German, English, French. *PRACTICE AREAS:* Business Law; Civil Law; Contracts; Corporate Law; Energy; Litigation; Property.

THOMAS SCHADE, born Bamberg, Germany, October 30, 1954; admitted, 1989, Germany. *Education:* University of Berlin. *LANGUAGES:* German, French. *PRACTICE AREAS:* Construction Law; Environmental Law; Zoning, Planning and Land Use.

DR. RAIMUND KÖRNER, born Wedel/Holstein, Germany, August 24, 1958; admitted, 1989, Germany. *Education:* Universities of Berlin and Bielefeld (Dr. jur.). *LANGUAGES:* German, English and French. *PRACTICE AREAS:* Administrative Law; Environmental Law; Intellectual Property.

DR. GERNOD MEINEL, born Berlin, Germany, March 22, 1960; admitted, 1988, Germany. *Education:* University of Berlin (Dr.jur.). *LANGUAGES:* German, English. *PRACTICE AREAS:* Corporate Law; Labour and Employment; Mergers, Acquisitions and Divestitures.

DR. DETLEV SCHUSTER, born Bünde, Germany, October 23, 1957; admitted, 1987, Germany. *Education:* University of Kiel (Dr.jur.); Indiana University, USA (J.D.). *LANGUAGES:* German, English. *PRACTICE AREAS:* Banks and Banking; Corporate Law; Company Law.

DR. KORNELIUS KLEINLEIN, born Munich, Germany, May 11, 1959; admitted, 1990, Germany. *Education:* Universities of Munich, Würzburg and Berlin (Dr. jur.). *LANGUAGES:* German, English. *PRACTICE AREAS:* Administrative Law; Environmental Law; Real Estate; Wills.

DR. WALTER L. RUST, born Donaueschingen, Germany, May 20, 1957; admitted, 1986, Germany. *Education:* Universities of Geneva, Freiburg i. Br. and Constance (Dr.jur.); Georgetown University, Washington, D.C. (Master of Laws). *LANGUAGES:* German, English, French. *PRACTICE AREAS:* Antitrust and Trade Regulations; Business Law; Environmental Law; European Community Law.

DR. CHRISTOPH WAGNER, born Berlin, Germany, February 4, 1962; admitted, 1991, Germany. *Education:* University of Berlin (Dr.jur.); University of Bologna. *LANGUAGES:* German, English, Italian. *PRACTICE AREAS:* Contracts; Communications and Media; Entertainment and the Arts; Mergers, Acquisitions and Divestitures.

WOLFRAM H. GANZLEBEN, born Eichberg, Germany, October 9, 1960; admitted, 1990, Germany. *Education:* Universities of Bayreuth and Würzburg. *LANGUAGES:* German, English. *PRACTICE AREAS:* Construction Law; Corporate Law; Real Estate; Zoning, Planing and Land Use.

DR. MICHAEL BEST, born München, Germany, December 17, 1959. *Education:* University of München (Dipl. Kfm/M.B.A.; Dr.jur.). Tax Advisor. *LANGUAGES:* German, English, Spanish. *PRACTICE AREAS:* Mergers, Acquisitions and Divestitures; Real Estate; Taxation.

ALEXANDER EBERT, born Leipzig, Germany, October 18, 1941; admitted, 1970, Germany. *Education:* Universities of Berlin and Saarbrücken. *LANGUAGES:* German, English, French. *PRACTICE AREAS:* Banks and Banking; Civil Law; Commercial Law.

DR. WERNER MARTIN, born Genthin, Germany, July 30, 1942; admitted, 1970, Germany. *Education:* Universities of Würzburg and Berlin (Dr.jur.). *LANGUAGES:* German, English.

PREU, BOHLIG & PARTNERS
MAUERSTRASSE 77
D-10117 BERLIN, GERMANY
Telephone: 30-6 09 36 60
Telefax: 30-6 09 36 64

Munich, Germany Office: Seestrasse 13, D-80802 Munich. Telephone: 89-381 59 60. Telex: 05 215 591. Telefax: 89-39 25 22.

General Commercial and Corporate Practice. Patents, Trademarks, Models, Copyright, Unfair Competition, Advertising, Press and Media Law, Entertainment Law, Food and Drug Law, Computer Law, R & D Law, Construction Law, Product Liability Law, Labor Law, Corporations, Taxation, Antitrust, Franchising, Mergers and Acquisitions, Banking and Securities, International Trade, EEC-Law, Licensing, Litigation, Transactions, Arbitration Proceedings, International, Agency and Distribution, Biotechnology, Business Law.

DR. JÜRGEN WOLTZ, born Eisenach, Germany, May 12, 1939; admitted, 1990, Germany. *Education:* University of Halle-Wittenberg Law School (Diplom-Jurist; Dr. jur.). Inhouse Counsel, State Enterprises, 1963-1966. Government Executive, Department of Justice. Lecturer of Law, Humbold-University, Berlin, 1989—. Author: "Tradenames of Business Entities," Berlin, 1982; "Unfair Competition Law," Berlin, 1988; "GmbH Short-Commentary," Berlin, 1990; "Product Liability," Berlin, 1990. *Member:* German Association for Industrial Property and Copyright (GRUR); Association Internationale pour la Protection de Propriété Industrielle (AIPPI). *LANGUAGES:* German and English.

DR. LUDWIG VON ZUMBUSCH, born Munich, Germany, October 2, 1956; admitted, 1989, Germany and New York. *Education:* Bank Trainee, Bank Official's Degree (Bankkaufmann); Studies of Law: University of Tuebingen, Freiburg Law Schools (Referendar); Law School of the University of Texas, Austin (M.C.J., 1987); University of Munich (Dr.jur., 1990). Research Fellow, Max Planck Institute for Foreign and International Patent, Copyright and Unfair Competition Law, 1984-1987. Foreign Associate, Kirkpatrick & Lockhart, Washington, D.C., 1987-1988. Author: "Arbitrability of Antitrust Claims under US, EEC and German Law: The 'International Transaction,' Criterion and Public Policy," 22 Texas Int'l Law Journal, 1987, 291- GRUR Int. 1988, 541; "The Designation of Wines under German and EEC Labelling Provisions," Munich 1990. *Member:* International Bar Association; American Bar Association; German-American Jurists' Association (DAJV). *LANGUAGES:* German and English.

(For Complete Biographical Data on other Personnel, see Professional Biographies at Munich, Germany)

PÜNDER, VOLHARD, WEBER & AXSTER
KATHARINA-HEINROTH-UFER
10787 BERLIN, GERMANY
Telephone: (49)(30) 2546 5800
Fax: (49)(30) 2546 5900

Frankfurt/Main, Germany Office: Mainzer Landstrasse 46, 60325 Frankfurt/Main. Telephone: (49)(69) 71 99-01. Fax: (49)(69) 71 99-4000. Telex: 414 827.

Düsseldorf, Germany Office: Cecilienallee 6, 40474 Düsseldorf. Telephone: (49)(211) 43 55-0. Fax: (49)(211) 43 55-600.

Leipzig, Germany Office: Burgplatz 7, 04109 Leipzig. Telephone: (49)(341) 21 49-0. Fax: (49)(341) 21 49-600.

Beijing, People's Republic of China Office: Suite C 603, Beijing Lufthansa Center, 50 Liangmaqiao Road, Beijing 100 016. Telephone: (86)(1) 465 15 68; (86)(1) 465 18 08; (86)(1) 465 13 45. Fax: (86)(1) 467 12 56.

Brussels, Belgium Office: Rue d'Arlon 92, 1040 Bruxelles. Telephone: (32)(2) 230 90 11. Fax: (32)(2) 231 19 55.

Budapest, Hungary Office: Endrödy Sandor utca 48, 1026 Budapest. Telephone: (36) 60 33 26 18 international; (6) 60 33 26 18 national. Fax: (36) 60 33 26 17 international; (6) 60 33 26 17 national.

Moscow, Russia Office: ul. Wolchonka, 18/2, 121 019 Moskwa. Telephone: (7)(095) 202 64 90; (7)(095) 202 65 12; (7)(543) 708 00 900 from Germany; (49)(7545) 893 42 from other countries. Fax: (7)(095) 202 65 14; (7)(543) 708 00 990 from Germany; (49)(7545) 893 43 from other countries.

New York, New York Office: 152 West 57th Street, Carnegie Hall Tower, New York, N.Y. 10019. Telephone: (1)(212) 582 28 28. Fax: (1)(212) 582 24 24.

(This Listing Continued)

Warsaw, Poland Office: ul. Jasna 1, 00-013 Warszawa. Telephone: (48) 39 12 21 41. Fax: (48)(22) 27 15 29.

Administrative Law; Antitrust Law; Arbitration; Auditing and Valuations; Banking, Securities and Finance; Bankruptcy; Building Law; Chinese Law; Commercial Crime; Computer Law; Construction Law; Corporate Law; EU Law; Energy Law; Environmental Law; Franchising; Industrial Property Law; Insolvency; Intellectual Property Law; International and German Business Law; Labor and Employment Law; Litigation; Media Law; Mergers and Acquisitions; Pharmaceutical Law; Privatizations; Product Law; Public Law; Real Estate; Reorganizations; Russian Law; Tax Law; Telecommunications; Unfair Trade Law.

FIRM PROFILE: *Member of PÜNDER GROUP*

Members:

- *BURUMA MARIS, The Hague, Rotterdam*

- *CERHA, HEMPEL & SPIEGELFELD, Wien*

- *COPPENS, VAN OMMESLAGHE, HORSMANS & FAURES, Bruxelles.*

- *DE PARDIEU-LACOURTE G.I.E., Paris*

- *PÜNDER, VOLHARD, WEBER & AXSTER, Frankfurt/Main, Düsseldorf, Berlin, Leipzig*

- *STOFFEL & PARTNER, Zürich, Genève.*

Joint Offices of PÜNDER GROUP:

Beijing - Bruxelles - Budapest - Moskwa - New York - Warszawa

MEMBERS OF FIRM

JENS-PETER LACHMANN, born Schubin "Warthegau", July 12, 1941; admitted, 1972, Berlin; 1982, Notary. *Education:* Exchange Student (American Field Service), Universities of Berlin, Geneva, Kiel, postgraduate studies European Institute of the University of Saarbrücken. *Member:* German Association for the Protection of Industrial Property and Copyright. Judge, Disciplinary Court, Berlin, 1979-1983. Judge, Disciplinary Court of Appeals, Berlin, 1983-1987. Judicial Examination Board (Justizprüfungsamt) 1975—. *Member:* German Bar Association (Chairman, Information Law Committee). *LANGUAGES:* German, English and French. *PRACTICE AREAS:* Corporate Law; Real Estate; Business Law.

HELGA DEBES, born Verden/Aller, September 12, 1940; admitted, 1976, Berlin; Notary. *Education:* Universities of Göttingen and Berlin. *Member:* German Bar Association. *LANGUAGES:* German and English. *PRACTICE AREAS:* Building Law; Real Estate.

DR. CHRISTIAN OSTERRIETH, born Freiburg, Germany, May 30, 1957; admitted, 1984, Freiburg; 1986, Düsseldorf; 1990, Berlin. *Education:* University of Constance; University of Paris, Université de droit, d'Economie et des Science Sociales. Author: "Die Neuordnung des Rechts des internationalen Technologietranfers," 1986. *Member:* German Association for the Protection of Industrial Property and Copyright; American Chamber of Commerce; AIJA; Licensing Executive Society; L.E.S., Germany (Board Member). *LANGUAGES:* German, English and French. *PRACTICE AREAS:* Industrial Property Law; Litigation; Business Law.

ELKE HOLTHAUSEN-DUX, born Herten, Germany, March 20, 1958; admitted, 1988, Frankfurt/Main; 1992, Berlin. *Education:* University of Bonn. Court Clerk, 1979-1980. *Member:* German Bar Association. *LANGUAGES:* German, English and French. *PRACTICE AREAS:* Real Estate; Building Law; Planning Law.

ROMAN BÄRWALDT, born Berlin, Germany, October 2, 1962; admitted, 1990, Berlin. *Education:* Free University of Berlin. *Member:* German Bar Association. *LANGUAGES:* German, English and French. *PRACTICE AREAS:* Corporate Law; Business Law.

DR. JÖRG KRAFFEL, born Berlin, Germany, August 20, 1963; admitted, 1990, Berlin. *Education:* Free University of Berlin (Dr. jur.). Author: "Rechtsgrundlage bei Bürgschaft und Schuldanerkenntnis," 1990. *Member:* German Bar Association. *LANGUAGES:* German and English. *PRACTICE AREAS:* Corporate Law; Business Law.

DR. ECKART PUTZIER, born Taipei, Taiwan, October 19, 1956; admitted, 1985, Hamburg; 1992, Berlin. *Education:* Universities of Geneva, Switzerland and Freiburg (Dr. jur., 1986); University of Pennsylvania, Philadelphia (LL.M., 1982). Author: "Die Ermächtigungen des Außenwirtschaftsgesetzes," 1987. *Member:* German Bar Association; German-American Lawyers' Association; AIJA. *LANGUAGES:* German, English and French. *PRACTICE AREAS:* Real Estate; Building Law; Foreign Trade Law; International Private Law.

(This Listing Continued)

ASSOCIATES

BARBARA WEIDLICH, born Zwickau, Germany, November 23, 1940; admitted, 1990, Berlin. *Education:* Humboldt-University, Berlin. *LANGUAGES:* German. *PRACTICE AREAS:* Real Estate.

MARTIN WÖRLE, born Baden-Baden, Germany, October 24, 1961; admitted, 1991, Frankfurt/Main; 1992, Berlin. *Education:* University of Freiburg. Assistant of the Institute of Commercial and Labor Law, University of Freiburg, 1988-1991. *Member:* German Bar Association. *LANGUAGES:* German, English and French. *PRACTICE AREAS:* Labor and Employment Law; Commercial Law.

JAN LINDNER-FIGURA, born Düsseldorf, Germany, July 18, 1962; admitted, 1991, Berlin. *Education:* University of Berlin. *Member:* German Bar Association. *LANGUAGES:* German, English and Italian. *PRACTICE AREAS:* Real Estate; Business Law.

SABINE HACKER-FUNK, born Cologne, Germany, October 8, 1961; admitted, 1992, Frankfurt/Main; 1994, Berlin. *Education:* Free University Berlin, Germany. Judge, Civil Court, 1991. *Member:* German Bar Association. *LANGUAGES:* German, English and French. *PRACTICE AREAS:* Real Estate; Commercial Leases; Building and Planning Law; Construction Law.

MARCUS HERRMANN, born Schwäbisch Gmünd, Germany, September 13, 1960; admitted, 1992, Berlin. *Education:* University of Frankfurt-/Main, Germany. Research Fellow at the Law Faculty, University of Frankfurt/Main. *Member:* German Bar Association; German Association for the Protection of Industrial and Property Rights. *LANGUAGES:* German, English and French. *PRACTICE AREAS:* Intellectual Property Law; Litigation.

GINA MASCHKE, born Lübeck, Germany, January 15, 1963. *Education:* University of Berlin. *LANGUAGES:* German and English. *PRACTICE AREAS:* Tax Law.

EWALD VOLHARD, born Bad Homburg v.d.H., Germany, August 4, 1960; admitted, 1992, Berlin. *Education:* Universities of Munich and Frankfurt/Main, Germany. *LANGUAGES:* German and English. *PRACTICE AREAS:* Real Estate; Corporate Law.

DR. JUSTUS SCHMIDT-OTT, born Berlin, Germany, August 1, 1961; admitted, 1993, Berlin. *Education:* Universities of Freiburg and Cologne. Author: "Pauli Quaestiones - Eigenart und Textgeschichte einer spätklassischen Juristenschrift", 1993. *Member:* Berlin Bar Association. *LANGUAGES:* German, English, French, Spanish and Russian. *PRACTICE AREAS:* Real Estate; Corporate Law.

UWE AMENDA, born Munich, Germany, November 9, 1963; admitted, 1994, Berlin. *Education:* Universities of Münster, Heidelberg and Munich. Legal Trainee, Cape Town, South Africa, and London, 1992-1993. *Member:* German Bar Association. *LANGUAGES:* German, English and French. *PRACTICE AREAS:* Real Estate; Commercial Leases; Construction Law; Planning Law.

TOBIAS GEERLING, born Tübingen, Germany, June 8, 1961; admitted, 1991, Berlin. *Education:* Universities of Regensburg and Munich. *Member:* German Bar Association. *LANGUAGES:* German and English. *PRACTICE AREAS:* German and International Tax Law.

AXEL SOMMER, born Ulm/Donau, Germany, December 23, 1961; admitted, 1994, Berlin. *Education:* University of Freiburg; Legal Department of Deutsche Bank AG. *Member:* German Bar Association. *LANGUAGES:* German, English and Portuguese. *PRACTICE AREAS:* Real Estate; Private and Public Building Law; Litigation.

ULRICH REBLIN, born Berlin, Germany, March 30, 1963; admitted, 1991, Berlin. *Education:* Free University of Berlin, University of Exeter (LL.M., 1989). *LANGUAGES:* German and English. *PRACTICE AREAS:* Real Estate.

TAX ADVISORS

BENNO STRATMANN, born Frankfurt/Main, Germany, November 8, 1936; 1966, Tax Advisor. *Education:* University of Frankfurt. *LANGUAGES:* German and English. *PRACTICE AREAS:* Auditing and Valuations.

DR. DETLEF HARITZ, born Rostock, Germany, August 31, 1949; admitted, 1985, Berlin; 1986, Tax Adviser. *Education:* Universities of Kiel and Berlin. Author: Commentary on "Treuhandspaltungsgesetz.". *LANGUAGES:* German and English. *PRACTICE AREAS:* German and International Tax Law; Mergers and Acquisitions; Real Estate Taxation.

(This Listing Continued)

PÜNDER, VOLHARD, WEBER & AXSTER, Berlin—
Continued

(For complete biographical data on personnel at Frankfurt/Main, Düsseldorf and Leipzig Germany, Brussels, Belgium, Moscow, Russia, Warsaw, Poland, New York, New York and Beijing, People's Republic of China, see Professional Biographies at those locations)

QUACK, KUHN & PARTNER

BERLIN, GERMANY

(See Gaedertz Vieregge Quack Kreile, Berlin, Germany)

RÄDLER RAUPACH BEZZENBERGER

BERLIN, GERMANY

(See Oppenhoff & Rädler)

RAU, VAN DORP & PARTNER

LIETZENSEEUFER 10
14057 BERLIN, GERMANY
Telephone: (030) 32 25 023
Telefax: (030) 32 21 018
Telex: 185607

Munich, Germany Office: Widenmayerstrasse 38, D-80538 Munich. Telephone: (089) 21 12 13-0. Telefax: (089) 21 12 13-40.
Dresden, Germany Office: Niederwaldstr. 23, 01277 Dresden. Telephone: (0351) 44 11 207. Telefax (0351) 44 11 210.
Leipzig, Germany Office: Gustav Adolf Str. 12, 04105 Leipzig. Telephone: (0341) 27 12 29. Telefax: (0341) 27 12 29.
Budapest Hungary Office: Békés-Németh-Vékás & Tásai, Ügyvédi Iroda, Egyetem tér 1-3, H-1053 Budapest. Telephone: (01) 117-4930. Telefax: (01) 117-4930.
Trento, Italy Office: Via Grazloli 6, I-38100 Trento. Telephone: (0461) 98 00 51. Telefax: (0461) 98 52 57.

General European and International Practice, European Community Law. Corporate, Commercial, Intellectual and Industrial Property Rights, Patents. Trademarks, Copyright, Unfair Competition, Antitrust, Computer Law, Press Law, Entertainment Law, Franchising, Licensing, Insurance, Product Liability, Real Estate, Construction, Labor Law, Trusts and Estates, International Private Law, Administrative Law, Litigation, Arbitration.

DIP. ING. MICHAEL RAU, born Berlin, Germany, December 11, 1939; admitted, 1992, Berlin, Germany. *Education:* University (Fachhochschule) for Textile-Chemistry of Reutlingen (Dipl.-Ing., 1970); University of Berlin (Referendar, 1989; Assessor, 1992). Research Assistant, Institut for Textile-Technique of Reutlingen, 1970-1985. Faculty Member of Humboldt University, Berlin. *Member:* German Bar Association; German Lawyers Association (DAV); German Association for the Protection of Industrial Property and Copyright (GRUR); International Association for the Protection of Industrial Property Right (AIPPI). *LANGUAGES:* German and English.

ROSENBERG

BERLIN, GERMANY

(See Weiss & Hasche)

RÜCKEL, TRENKNER & COLLEGEN

KURFÜRSTENDAMM 132 A
10711 BERLIN, GERMANY
Telephone: (030) 896 6920
Fax: (030) 8966 9244

Atlanta, Georgia Office: Ten Piedmont Center, Suite 350, 3495 Piedmont Road, 30305. Telephone: (404) 266-1008. Fax: (404) 266-0205.
Dresden, Germany Office: Bautzner Straße 14, 01099. Telephone: (0351) 502 43 00. Fax: (0351) 502 43 02.
Leipzig, Germany Office: Marperger Straße 20, 04229. Telephone: (0341) 401 13 41. Fax: (0341) 401 14 54.
Frankfurt/Main, Germany Office: Bockenheimer Anlage 13, 60322. Telephone: (069) 55 07 31. Fax: (069) 596 39 94.
Munich, Germany Office: Karollnenstraße 4, 80538. Telephone: (089) 212 38 70. Fax: (089) 212 38 75 0.

International Business Transactions, Real Estate (including restitution of property rights), Tax Law, General Practice, Litigation and Commercial Law, Corporate Law, Employment Law.

FIRM PROFILE: The firm is a member of LAWORLD. LAWORLD is an international organization of law firms who coordinate and share information with other member firms in Brussels, Budapest, Hong Kong, Jerusalem, Lausanne, London, Moscow, New York, Padova, Stockholm, Taipei, Tel Aviv, Vancouver, Warsaw, Zagreb and Zug.

MEMBERS OF FIRM

MICHAEL MINDERJAHN, born Aachen, Germany, March 1, 1961; admitted, 1991, Germany. *Education:* Gymnasium Schongau (1980); University of Augsburg (1989). Member, Berlin Seminar for Tax Law, Trust Management and Accounts, Wustrau Association Insolvency. *LANGUAGES:* English and French. *PRACTICE AREAS:* Corporate Law; Real Estate; Tax Law; Civil Law; Law Enforcement.

WOLFRAM HUBNER, born Berlin, Germany, February 26, 1940; admitted, 1969, Germany. *Education:* University of Berlin (Referendar, 1965). Member, American Chamber of Commerce in Germany, 1988—. *LANGUAGES:* German and English. *PRACTICE AREAS:* Civil Law; Penal Law; Notary.

ASSOCIATES

KLAUS-DIETER FROST, born Berlin, Germany, May 20, 1960; admitted, 1992, Germany. *Education:* University of Leipzig (1986). *PRACTICE AREAS:* Property Law; Landlord and Tenant Law; Employment Law; Real Estate Law; Restitution of Property Rights.

JOHANNES JEEP, born Hamburg, Germany, October 22, 1962; admitted, 1994, Germany. *Education:* Ratsgymnasium Bielefeld (1982); University of Heidelberg; University of Berlin (1991). *Member:* German-Polish Lawyers Association. *LANGUAGES:* English and French. *PRACTICE AREAS:* Commercial Law; Insolvency; Public Law; Arbitration.

NIKLAS GRAF VON BERNSTORFF, born Tübingen, Germany, September 13, 1959; admitted, 1993, Germany. *Education:* University of Heidelberg (1982); University of Münster (1986). *Member:* German-Polish Lawyers Association. *LANGUAGES:* English and French. *PRACTICE AREAS:* Civil Law; Commercial Law; Litigation; Corporate Law.

(For biographical data on additional personnel, see Professional Biographies at Munich, Germany)

SCHÄFER WIPPRECHT SCHICKERT

SCHLÜTERSTRASSE 39
D-10629 BERLIN, GERMANY
Telephone: (49-30- 88 45920
Telecopy: (49-30) 88 459222

Düsseldorf, Germany Office: Bankstr. 1, D-40476. Telephone: (49-211) 49340. Telecopy: (49-211) 4920097.

General Practice. Corporate, Commercial, Banking, Labor, Tax, EEC, Antitrust, Unfair Competition, Insurance, Construction, Licensing, Product Liability, Trademark, Copyright, Litigation and Arbitration, Mergers

RESIDENT MEMBERS

DR. GERD KRIEGER, born Essen, Germany, November 21, 1950; admitted, 1979, Germany. *Education:* Universities of Münster, Bonn (Doctor of Laws, 1980). Author: "Personalentscheidungen des Aufsichtsrats," 1981; "Kapitalmaßnahmen" and "Konzernrecht des Aktiengesetzes," in Münch,

(This Listing Continued)

Hdb. des Gesellschaftsrechts, 1988. Co-Author: "Rechte und Pflichten des Aufsichtsrats," 3rd Edition, 1993. *LANGUAGES:* German and English.

DR. DIETMAR RAHLMEYER, born Bad Oeynhausen, Germany, June 14, 1957; admitted, 1986, Germany. *Education:* Universities of Freiburg and Bonn (Doctor of Laws, 1991). Author: "Die Spürbarkeitsprüfung im Rahmen des § 1 GWB," 1991. *LANGUAGES:* German and English.

ASSOCIATES

Torsten Feldkamp

German and English

SCHEELE, SCHWARTZ, ZIELCKE & PARTNER

ALT-MOABIT 101A
10559 BERLIN, GERMANY
Telephone: 030 3992750
Fax: 030 399275-303; 030 399275-404

Munich, Germany Office: Prinzregentenplatz 15, 81675. Telephone: 089/470 10 02. Fax: 089/470 10 06.

FIRM PROFILE: Scheele, Schwartz, Zielcke & Partner is an international law firm advising business clients and public institutions on all domestic and overseas corporate and commercial matters. The firm specializes in Eastern European and C.I.S. matters. Currently the firm is representing a broad range of clients in Europe, North America, South America, Asia and Africa.

(For biographical data and areas of practice see listing at Munich, Germany)

SCHLUTIUS, ESPEY & PARTNER

Established in 1990

FRIEDRICHSTRASSE 105B
10117 BERLIN, GERMANY
Telephone: XX 49/30/229 90 20; 282 35 58
Telefax: XX 49/30/283 41 17

Hamburg, Germany Office: 20095 Hamburg, Spitalerstrasse 4/Kurze Mühren 2, Telephone: XX 49/40/33 40 10. Telefax: XX 49/40/33 68 69.

Commercial, Corporation, Labor, Unfair Competition, Trademarks, Copyright, German and EEC Antitrust Law, Tax and Duty, Antidumping, Customs, Arbitration, Environmental Law, Law of the former GDR, Privatization, Restitution, Family Law, Inheritance and General Practice.

FIRM PROFILE: Schlutius, Espey & Partner is a nation wide and international orientated lawyer's office concentrating on the advice needs of business clients with offices in Hamburg and Berlin.

The circle of clients consists mainly of medium-sized businesses from industry, trade and the service sector.

With their respective specialized fields the firm's partners cover the complete range of Commercial Law. The key focal points are Mercantile and Company Law, Competition and Unfair Trade Practices Law, Protection of Industrial Property Rights and Copyright, Labour and Industrial Relations Law, International Law of Contract, Family and Inheritance Law, Tariff Legislation and EC Law.

The firm acts chiefly in advisory capacity.

Partners resident in the Hamburg office will in matters concerning their specialized fields be available in the Berlin office by arrangement.

RESIDENT PARTNERS

DR. JÖRG LOCKE, born Gauernitz/Kreis Meissen, Germany, November 19, 1949; admitted, 1990, Berlin; 1991, Notary, Berlin. *Education:* Humboldt-University, Berlin (Dipl.-Jurist 1972; Dr. Jur., 1978). Judge at different civil courts, 1972-1990. Author: "The publication of scientific works in Universities," (Die Herausgabe von wissenschaftlichen Werken im Hochschulwesen), 1978. *Member:* Berlin Bar Society; Berlin Notary Society; Berlin Bar Association. *LANGUAGES:* German. *PRACTICE AREAS:* Real Estates; Matters of Privatisation and Expropriation in the new Länder (former GDR); Law of the former GDR; Notary Public.

HANNELORE STEINERT, born Ascheraleben, Germany, September 4, 1951; admitted, 1990, Germany. *Education:* Martin-Luther-University,

(This Listing Continued)

Halle (Dipl.-Juristin 1974). In-house Lawyer in Public owned Companies of the former GDR, 1974-1990. *Member:* Berlin Bar Society; Berlin Bar Association. *LANGUAGES:* German. *PRACTICE AREAS:* Matters of Privatisation and Expropriation in the new Länder (former GDR); Law of the former GDR; Labour Law.

Languages: German and English

(For Complete Listing and Biographical data on all Personnel, see Hamburg, Germany Biographical Card).

SCHMIDT-SIBETH ZIRNGIBL
LANGWIESER HEISSE

LEIPZIGER STRAßE 63
10117 BERLIN, GERMANY
Telephone: 030/20 22 73
Telefax: 030/20 22 7426

Munich, Germany Office: Maximiliansplatz 5, 80333 Munich. Telephone: 089/54 56 5-0. Fax: 089/54 56 5-201.

Erfurt, Germany Office: Anger 23, 99084 Erfurt (Thuringia). Telephone: 0361/6 42 12 36. Fax: 0361/6 42 25 04.

General Practice, Corporate, Commercial, E.E.C., International Law, Trademarks, Copyright, Unfair Competition, Real Estate, Construction and Building Law, Labor Law, Legal Affairs in former East Germany.

CARSTEN BRÜNINGHAUS, born Berlin, Germany, November 17, 1962; admitted, 1991, Munich. *Education:* Freie Universität Berlin. Research Assistant, Institute for Corporate Law, Freie Universität Berlin (1988-1990). *LANGUAGES:* German, English and French.

ECKART VON LOJEWSKI, born Hannover, Germany, February 24, 1962; admitted, 1993, Munich. *Education:* Universities of Munich and Freiburg. Assistant, Institute of Criminal Law, University of Konstanz. *LANGUAGES:* German, English and French.

JÖRG ZEISE, born Essen, Germany, July 11, 1965; admitted, 1995, Berlin. *Education:* University of Bonn. *LANGUAGES:* German and English.

(For complete biographical data on Personnel at Berlin, Munich and Erfurt, Germany Offices, see Professional Biographies at Munich, Germany)

SCHMIDT, VON DER OSTEN & HUBER

MOMMSENSTRAßE 73
D-10629 BERLIN, GERMANY
Telephone: 030-8844900
Telecopier: 030-88449090
Teletex: 030-2627-20149 SOH

Essen, Germany Office: Haumannplatz 28/30, 45130 Essen.

FIRM PROFILE: Established in 1952, Schmidt von der Osten & Huber has grown to become one of Germany's leading commercial law firms in the Ruhr area concentrating on legal advice for entrepreneurs, business men and professional persons, the firm has also an effective litigation department.

The firm has nine partners and further associates in two offices, Essen and Berlin. The firm provides also services in Brussels, London and Paris together with its partners Jaques & Lewis in London, Brussels, the Isle of Man and Jersey; Chaintrier, Caillard & Associés in Paris and van Wijmen & Koedam in Rotterdam and Breda.

DR. JÜRGEN HABICH, born Hannover, Germany, July 2, 1956; admitted, 1986, Germany. *Education:* Universities of Hannover and Göttingen (Second Legal Examination, 1986). *LANGUAGES:* German and English. *PRACTICE AREAS:* Labor Law; Collective Labor Law; Law of Competition; Corporate Law of Eastern Europe; Tax Law.

DR. ANDREAS KEIL, born Bochum, Germany, August 10, 1960; admitted, 1992, Essen; 1994, Berlin. *Education:* Universities of Bochum (Dr. jur., 1991), Geneva and Freiburg; University of Georgia School of Law, Athens, Georgia (LL.M., 1988). Assistant, Institute of Foreign and Private International Law, University of Freiburg, 1985-1987. Foreign Legal Consultant, Glass, McCullough, Sherill & Harrold, Atlanta, Georgia, 1991. Author: "Die Haftungsbefreiung des Schuldners im UN-Kaufrecht," 1993. *Member:* German-American Lawyers Association; Canadian-German Lawyers Association. *LANGUAGES:* German, English and French. *PRAC-*

(This Listing Continued)

SCHMIDT, VON DER OSTEN & HUBER, Berlin—
Continued

TICE AREAS: Commercial and Corporate Law; Unfair Competition Law; Intellectual Property Law; International Private Law.

Schmidt, von der Osten & Huber is a member of the JCS Group which comprises Schmidt, von der Osten & Huber in Essen and Berlin; Jacques & Lewis in London, Brussels, the Isle of Man and Jersey; Chaintrier, Caillard in Paris; and Van Wijmen & Koedam in Rotterdam and Breda.
The JCS Group is an integrated group of law firms providing a comprehensive range of legal services to international clients.

(For complete Biographical Data on all Personnel, see Professional Biographies at Essen)

•

SCHÖN NOLTE FINKELNBURG & CLEMM

KURFÜRSTENDAMM 29
D-10719 BERLIN, GERMANY
Telephone: (30) 880 910
Telex: 182999
Telecopier: (30) 882 35 37

Other Offices: Hamburg and Dresden, Germany; Brussels, Belgium.

General Corporate and Commercial Practice, Administrative and Constitutional Law.

MEMBERS OF FIRM

PROF. DR. KLAUS FINKELNBURG, born Bonn, Germany, 1935; admitted, 1966, Berlin. *Education:* Universities of Bonn and Berlin (Dr. jur., 1963). Co-editor, Neue Zeitschrift für Verwaltungsrecht (NVWZ). Professor of Public and Administrative Law, 1971—. Member, Berlin Parliament, 1985-1992. President of Berlin Constitutional Court, 1992—. *LANGUAGES:* German and English. *PRACTICE AREAS:* Administrative Law; Constitutional Law; Construction Law; Environmental Law; Zoning, Planning and Land Use.

PROF. DR. NILS CLEMM, born Berlin, Germany, 1941; admitted, 1971, Berlin. *Education:* Free University of Berlin (Dr. jur., 1968). Professor of Construction Law, Technical University of Berlin, 1988—. *LANGUAGES:* German and English. *PRACTICE AREAS:* Construction Law; Family Law; White Collar Crime.

DR. CHRISTIAN BRÖSE, born Wittenberg, Germany, 1946; admitted, 1975, Berlin. *Education:* Free University of Berlin (Dr. jur., 1977). *LANGUAGES:* German and English. *PRACTICE AREAS:* Banks and Banking; Construction Law; Insurance; Professional Liability; Real Estate.

DR. JOST VON TROTT ZU SOLZ, born Bellers, Germany, 1944; admitted, 1976, Berlin. *Education:* Free University of Berlin (Dr. jur., 1972). *LANGUAGES:* German and English. *PRACTICE AREAS:* Administrative Law; Business Law; Contracts; Zoning, Planning and Land Use.

DR. ERNESTO LOH, born Berlin, Germany, 1945; admitted, 1974, Berlin. *Education:* Universities of Berlin and Freiburg (Dr. jur., 1972). *LANGUAGES:* German, English, French and Italian. *PRACTICE AREAS:* Labour and Employment; Antitrust and Trade Regulation; Intellectual Property; Communications and Media.

CHRISTIAN RAHNS, born Berlin, Germany, 1948; admitted, 1976, Berlin. *Education:* Free University of Berlin. *LANGUAGES:* German and English. *PRACTICE AREAS:* Company Law.

MELANIE ARNDT, born Berlin, Germany, 1958; admitted, 1985, Berlin. *Education:* Free University of Berlin. *LANGUAGES:* German and English. *PRACTICE AREAS:* Construction Law; Environmental Law; Food and Drug Regulation.

DR. KLAUS ARLT, born Berlin, Germany, 1921; admitted, 1982, Berlin; 1984, as Tax Adviser. *Education:* Universities of Brussels and Berlin (Dr. jur., 1944). President of the Berlin Regional Tax Office, 1970-1979. *LANGUAGES:* German and English. *PRACTICE AREAS:* Taxation.

DR. ULRICH CARLHOFF, born Reutlingen, Germany, 1956; admitted, 1988, Berlin. *Education:* Justus Liebig University, Gießen (Dr. jur., 1988). Co-Author: "Frankfurter Kommentar zum GWB". *LANGUAGES:* German and English. *PRACTICE AREAS:* Corporate Law; Mergers, Acquisitions and Divestitures; Antitrust; Trade Regulation; Estates.

(This Listing Continued)

DR. KARL-CHRISTOPH VON HÜLSEN, born Düsseldorf, Germany, 1958; admitted, 1988, Berlin. *Education:* Universities of Heidelberg and Freiburg (Dr. jur., 1989). *LANGUAGES:* German and English. *PRACTICE AREAS:* Labour and Employment; Leases and Leasing.

BIRGITTA THUROW, born Essen, Germany, 1959; admitted, 1989, Berlin. *Education:* Universities of Berlin and Bochum. *LANGUAGES:* German and English. *PRACTICE AREAS:* Administrative Law; Construction Law; Building Permits; Town Planning.

LOTHAR HÜTTENHEIN, born Oldenburg, Germany, 1950; admitted, 1990, Berlin. *Education:* University of Tübingen. *LANGUAGES:* German and English. *PRACTICE AREAS:* Administrative Law; Constitutional Law.

SASKIA THEUERKAUF, born Langenhagen, Germany, 1959; admitted, 1988, Berlin. *Education:* Free University of Berlin. *LANGUAGES:* German and English. *PRACTICE AREAS:* Family Law.

BRIGITTE WAGNER, born Berlin, Germany 1937; admitted, 1973, Berlin. *Education:* Universities of Berlin and Hamburg. Assistant Professor, Free University of Berlin, 1965-1973. *LANGUAGES:* German, English and French. *PRACTICE AREAS:* Property; Real Estate.

CHRISTIAN WIRTH, born Berlin, Germany, 1963; admitted, 1992, Berlin. *Education:* Free University of Berlin. *LANGUAGES:* German, English and French. *PRACTICE AREAS:* Real Estate; Construction Law; Professional Liability; Banks and Banking; Insurance.

Languages: German, English, French, Italian and Russian

SCHÜRMANN & PARTNERS

Established in 1990

KARL-LIEBKNECHT-STRASSE 32
10178 BERLIN, GERMANY
Telephone: 030-247-5960
Telefax: 030-238-6032

Frankfurt/Main, Germany Office: Friedrich-Ebert-Anlage 14, 60325, P.O. Box 11 16 33, 60051. Telephone: 069-7 54 90. Telefax: 7549 290.
Bonn, Germany Office: Philosophenring 94, 53177 Bonn. Telephone: 0228-328-055, Telefax: 0228-311-863.
Brussels, Belgium Office: Avenue de la Raquette 24, B-1150. Telephone: 02-770-0878. Telefax: 02-770-0878.
Dresden, Germany Office: Schnorrstrasse 70, 01069. Telephone: 0351-477-770. Telefax: 0351-477-7799.
Leipzig, Germany Office: Gustav-Adolf-Strasse 30 04105 Leipzig. Telephone: 0341-211-0622. Telefax: 0341-211-0625.
Milan, Italy Office: Via Gabrio Casati, 1, I-20123. Telephone: 02-809131/32. Telefax: 02-809-133.
New York, New York Office: 250 Park Avenue, 10177. Telephone: 212-972-3300. Telefax: 212-972-9374.
Paris, France Office: 12, rue d'Astorg F-75008 Paris. Telephone: 01-4451-0570. Telefax: 01-4266-3368.

General Practice. Corporation, Trade Banking, International and German Tax Law. Labor Law. Law on Mergers, Acquisitions, Fair Trade, Antitrust and EU Law, Administrative Law. Notary Public. Litigation Department.

(For complete biographical data on all Personnel, see Biographical Card at Frankfurt/Main, Germany)

AXEL SCHWARZBERG

LEIBNIZSTRASSE 47
10629 BERLIN, GERMANY
Telephone: 030/3234014/15
Fax: 030/3237515

Media Law including Music, Video, Film, Press and Libel Law.

FIRM PROFILE: The firm was established in 1987 and practices mainly in entertainment law representing international recording artists, film and theatre actors and fine artists. The practice also involves representation of producers and production companies in the areas of film, video, stage, festival and concert.

AXEL SCHWARZBERG, born Bonn, Germany, September 14, 1943; admitted, 1978, Notary; 1989, Germany. *Education:* Free University of Berlin. *LANGUAGES:* German and English.

SEGELKEN & SUCHOPAR

Established in 1949

ZIMMERSTRASSE 86-91
10117 BERLIN (MITTE), GERMANY
Telephone: (030) 229 41 81
Telefax: (030) 391 44 34

Hamburg, Germany Office: Baumwall 7, "Uberseehaus", 20459 Hamburg 11. Telephone: (040) 37 68 050. Telefax: (040) 36 20 71. Telex: 213 094 sesu d.

General Practice, National and International Business Law, Insurance and Liability Law, Transportation including Admiralty Law, Aviation, Road and Rail, Corporate and Contract Law, Insolvency and Bankruptcy, Competition and Anti-Trust Law, Construction, E.C. Law, Litigation, Arbitration.

FIRM PROFILE: *The firm was established in 1949 and offers a full range of legal service. It is well-known for its commercial and transportation/maritime law.*

RESIDENT MEMBERS

DR. THOMAS REICHELT, born Frankfurt, September 17, 1959; admitted, 1987, Hamburg. *Education:* University of Gießen. Author: "Der Vorbescheid im Verwaltungsverfahren"; "Neuere Tendenzen im Wettbewerbsrecht der Apotheker." Lecturer in Law, Academy of Advertising, Hamburg. Research Assistant, University of Gießen, 1981-1984. *Member:* Berlin Bar Associations. *LANGUAGES:* German, English and French.

DR. RALF GROTE, born Höxter, Germany, April 2, 1963; admitted, 1994, Berlin. *Education:* University of Göttingen. Trainee, Rowcliff, London. *LANGUAGES:* German and English. *PRACTICE AREAS:* Company Law; Business Law; Transportation; Construction; Litigation.

(For Complete Biographical Data on Other Personnel, See Professional Biographies at Hamburg)

SIGLE, LOOSE, SCHMIDT-DIEMITZ & PARTNERS

FRIEDRICHSTRASSE 130 A
10117 BERLIN, GERMANY
Telephone: 030-308792-0
Telefax: 030-2385849

Stuttgart, Germany Office: Schöttlestr. 8, P.O. Box 70 02 65, D-70572 Stuttgart (Degerloch). Telephone: 0711-9764-0. Telefax: 0711-9764-900.
Leipzig, Germany Office: August-Bebel-Strasse 38, 04275 Leipzig. Telephone: 0341-3912007. Fax: 0341-391-2085.
Frankfurt/Main, Germany Office: Schumannstrasse 62, 60325 Frankfurt/Main. Telephone: 069-975849-0. Telefax: 069-9758 4997.
Chemnitz, Germany Office: Barbarossastraße 46, 09112 Chemnitz. Telephone: 0379-36974-0. Telefax: 0379-3697429.
Moscow, Russia Office: Sadovaja Samotjotschnaja, 103 051. Telephone: 007/095/258 50 55. Fax: 007/095/258 51 55.

Commerical, Corporation, Mergers and Acquisitions, Banking, Investment, Common Market, Antitrust, Unfair Competition, Copyright, Patent and Trademark, License Agreements, Press, Transportation, Insurance, Product Liability, Real Estate, Construction, Probate, Labor, Administrative, Tax, International, Litigation and Arbitration.

RESIDENT PARTNER

DR. WOLF-GEORG FREIHERR VON RECHENBERG, born Bad Gandersheim, Germany, 1954; admitted, 1982, Freiburg. *Education:* Universities of Göttingen, Lausanne and Freiburg (Doctor of Law, 1986). Tax Consultant, 1987. With Carter, Ledyard & Milburn, New York, 1989-1990. Author: "The Stock Holders Meeting as the Highest Organ of the Joint-Stock Company," 1986; Succession in Family Owned Enterprises, 1991. Co-Author: Manual for the Examen of Public Accountante, 1987; Practice Manual for Public Accountants, 1989; The European Economic Interest Grouping, 1991. Succession in family owned enterprises, 1991; Business practice in the New German States, 1992. Assistant Lecturer, Freiburg Law School, 1983-1988. Member of Supervisory Board: REIK Schleifmittel-werke Dresden GmbH, Dresden, NILES Werkzeugmaschinen GmbH, Berlin. *Member:* German Bar Association; German Tax Law Association; German Association of Tax Consultants; German American Chamber of Commerce; American Bar Association. *LANGUAGES:* German, English and

(This Listing Continued)

French. *PRACTICE AREAS:* Corporate Law; Corporate Taxation; International Taxation; Mergers and Acquisitions.

RESIDENT ASSOCIATES

JOACHIM ELSNER, born Waltershausen, Germany, 1949; admitted, 1990, Notary Public; 1991, Berlin. *Education:* University of Jena. Co-Author: Business practice in the new German States, 1992. *Member:* German Bar Association. *PRACTICE AREAS:* Corporate Law; Property and Real Estate Law.

DR. BARBARA MITSCHKE, born Mügeln, Germany, 1945; admitted, 1990, Berlin. *Education:* University of Leipzig (Doctor of Law, 1971; Habilitation, 1978). Co-Author: Business practice in the new German States, 1992. *Member:* German Bar Association; German-German Juridical Association. *LANGUAGES:* German and English. *PRACTICE AREAS:* Property and Real Estate Law; Law of Expropriation and Compensation; Administrative Law.

DR. HERMANN STAPENHORST, born Goettingen, Germany, 1961; admitted, 1991, Berlin. *Education:* Universities of Goettingen and Freiburg (Doctor of Law, 1993). With Wiley, Rein & Fielding, Washington, D.C., 1990. *Member:* German Bar Association; German-American Lawyers Association. *LANGUAGES:* German, English and French. *PRACTICE AREAS:* Corporate Law; Mergers and Acquisitions; Real Estate Law; Construction.

MARION WOELK, born Luckau, Germany, 1958; admitted, 1990, Berlin; 1991, Notary Public. *Education:* University of Halle. *Member:* German Bar Association. *LANGUAGES:* German, English and Russian. *PRACTICE AREAS:* Corporate Law; Property and Real Estate Law.

MARKUS LIECK, born Berlin, Germany, 1964; admitted, 1992, Berlin. *Education:* Free University of Berlin; University of Geneva, Switzerland. Assistant Lecturer, Free University of Berlin, Institute of Energy Law, 1989-1992. *Member:* German Bar Association. *LANGUAGES:* German, English and French. *PRACTICE AREAS:* Corporate Law; Antitrust Law; Energy Law.

THÜMMEL, SCHÜTZE & PARTNER

Established in 1989

LÜTZOWSTRAßE 33/36
10785 BERLIN, GERMANY
Telephone: (030) 2 61 11 31
Telefax: (030) 2 61 90 49
Telex: 3 01304

Stuttgart Office: Landhausstraße 90, 70190 Stuttgart. Telephone: (0711)1667-0, Telefax: (0711) 286 44 66, 2 62 69 10.
Dresden Office: Friedrichstraße 33, 01067 Dresden. Telephone: (0351) 496 5302. Telefax: (0351) 496 5346.
Frankfurt Office: Eschersheimer Landshraße 10 60322 Frankfurt. Telephone: (069) 9591350. Telefax: (069) 95913530.
Brussels Office: Avenue des Arts, 41 B-1040 Brussels. Telephone: (0032) 2-512 7846. Telefax: (0032) 2-512 7023.
Paris, France Office: 46, Rue de Bassano, F-75008 Paris. Telephone: (0033) 1-53 67 50 00. Telefax: (0033) 1-47 20 78 76.
Singapore Office: 9, Battery Road, #16-01 Straits Trading Building, Singapore 0104, Telephone: (00 65) 53 53 112. Telefax: (00 65) 53 43 100.

Corporate, Commercial, Antitrust, Unfair Competition, Banking, Taxation, Trademark, Copyright, Media, Estate, Food Law, International, EEC Law, General Practice and Litigation.

EBERHARD DIEPGEN, born Berlin, West Germany, November 13, 1941. *Education:* University of Berlin (Referendar, 1967; Assessor, 1972; 1984-1989, Government of Berlin). (On Leave). *LANGUAGES:* German and English.

LUTZ VON PUFENDORF, born February 8, 1942; admitted, 1989, Germany. *Education:* Universities of Bonn and Freiburg. Secretary of State in Berlin, 1984-1989. *LANGUAGES:* German and English.

DR. JUR. GERHARD BOLLMANN, born Sulingen, August 12, 1957. *Education:* Georg-August-University, Göttingen (Referendar, 1983; Assessor, 1986). *LANGUAGES:* German, English, French and Dutch.

DR. JUR. CHRISTINA MITSCH, born Fulda, West Germany, December 5, 1961; admitted, 1990, Germany. *Education:* Universities of Munich and Würzburg (Referendar 1986; Assessor 1990). Assistant, University of Würzburg, 1986-1987. *LANGUAGES:* German and English.

(This Listing Continued)

THÜMMEL, SCHÜTZE & PARTNER, Berlin—Continued

DR. JUR. KLAUS KEMEN, born Viersen, Germany, February 22, 1962; admitted, 1993, Germany. *Education:* Universities of Cologne and Freiburg i.Br. (Referendar, 1988; Assessor, 1993). Assistant, University of Freiburg i.Br. 1988-1990. Doctor of Jurisprudence 1992. *LANGUAGES:* German, English.

(For Complete Biographical Data on all Personnel, see Professional Biographies at Stuttgart, Germany).

WALTER & PARTNER

Established in 1979

MARTIN LUTHER STRASSE 19
10777 BERLIN, GERMANY
Telephone: 030-2119092
Telefax: 030-2119094

Heidelberg, Germany: Lessingstrasse 24, P.O. Box 103466, 69024 Heidelberg 1. Telephone: 06221/12002. Telefax: 06221/20378.
Dessau, Germany Office: Kavalierstr. 35-39, 06844. Telephone: 0340-2207285. Telefax: 0340-213280.

General Business and Civil Practice, Antitrust and Trade Regulation, Bankruptcy, Business, Civil Law, Commercial Law, Company and Corporate Law, Computer and Software, Consumer Law, Contracts, Copyrights, European Competition Law, Family Law, Insurance, Intellectual Property, Investments, East Europe, Labour and Employment, Leasing, Professional and Product Liability, Property, Real Estate, Trademarks.

FIRM PROFILE: *The Berlin Office of Walter & Partner was founded as an independent law firm by Mr. Gert Kietzmann in 1979. The firm has been associated with Walter & Partner in 1993. The office offers full legal service and a Notary in Public. The Berlin office especially offers services for foreign investment and cases with the Treuhandanstalt.*

RESIDENT PARTNERS

GERT KIETZMANN, born Berlin, Germany, January 30, 1946; admitted, 1974, Germany. *Education:* Free University of Berlin. *Member:* Various Trade Associations. *LANGUAGES:* English, Swedish and German.

REINHARD WALTER, born Heidelberg, Germany, February 3, 1954; admitted, 1982, Germany. *Education:* Universities of Mannheim and Heidelberg. Co-Author: "Rechtskunde für Kaufleute". Member of the Board, Lions Club Mittlere Bergstraße, 1982—. *Member:* German and European Bar Association; German Association for the Protection of Industrial Property and Copyright; International Association for the Protection of Industrial Property (AIPPI); American Chamber of Commerce; German Industrial Commerce Association (Member, Legal Committee, 1986—). *LANGUAGES:* English, French and German.

DR. BERND GRÜBER, born Ingelbach, Germany, September 28, 1959; admitted, 1988, Germany. *Education:* Finanz-Fachhochschule Rhineland-Palatinate (special tax-college); University of Mannheim (Doctor of Law, 1990). Training at the European Communities, Brussels. Author: "Die missbräuchliche Abmahnung und Verfahrenseinleitung im Wettbewerbsrecht (abuse of law in unfair competition)". *Member:* German Chamber of Commerce. *LANGUAGES:* English and German.

GERHARD SCHELLER, born Blieskastel, Germany, July 17, 1948; admitted, 1976, Germany, District Court Berlin and Court of Appeal. *Education:* University of Saarbrücken. Chief, Department of Liquidation Treuhandanstalt Suhl, Internal Revision Treuhandanstalt, Main Office Berlin. *Member:* Wirtschaftsprüferkammer, Dusseldorf. *LANGUAGES:* English, French and German.

(For Complete List of Firm Personnel and Specialties, see Walter & Partner at Heidelberg, Germany)

WEISS & HASCHE

A Merger of the law firms Hasche Albrecht Fischer, Hamburg, Ott Weiss Eschenlohr & Partner, Munich and Rosenberg, Berlin.

MEINEKESTRASSE 13
10719 BERLIN, GERMANY
Telephone: (030) 881 97 83
Telefax: (030) 882 34 79

Hamburg, Germany Office: Valentinskamp 88, 20355 Hamburg. Telephone: (040) 35 00 20. Cable Address: "Lawyers" Telex: 215461 LAWY D. Teletex: 402276 LAWY D. Telefax: (040) 35 00 21 52.
Munich, Germany Office: Brienner Strasse 11/V (Luitpoldblock), 80333 Munich. Telephone: (089) 23 80 70. Cable Address: "Interlaw" Munich. Telex: 5 22957 Law. Telefax: (089) 23 80 71 10.
Leipzig, Germany Office: Karl-Tauchnitz-Strasse 10 B, 04107 Leipzig. Telephone: (0341) 216 720. Telefax: (0341) 216 72 33.
Prague, Czech Republic Office: Dělnická 30, 170 00 Prague 7. Telephone: (2) 683 40 23. Telefax: (2) 683 40 23.

Commercial, International Trade, Maritime, Transport, Forwarding, Shipbuilding, Shipfinancing, Tax, Banking, Corporation, Mergers and Acquisitions, Antitrust, Unfair Competition, Industrial Property, Real Estate, Environment, Common Market, Insurance, Aviation, Arbitration, Media, Administrative, Labor, Computer, German Reunification, Litigation.

MEMBER OF FIRM
(BERLIN OFFICE)

VIKTOR ROSENBERG, born Reval, Estonia, May 25, 1933; admitted, 1970, Germany; 1984, Notar. *Education:* Universities of Erlangen, Frankfurt am Main and Berlin (Referendar, 1967; Assessor, 1970). *LANGUAGES:* German.

ASSOCIATES

DR. CHRISTOPHER FRANTZEN, born Krefeld-Uerdingen, Germany, July 19, 1959; admitted, 1992, Germany. *Education:* University of Bonn (Referendar, 1986; Assessor, 1991; Dr. jur., 1992). *Member:* German-American Lawyers Association; German Association for the Protection of Stockholders (DSW). *LANGUAGES:* German, English and French.

ANDREAS J. ROQUETTE, born Offenbach/Main, Germany, June 15, 1962; admitted, 1992, Germany; 1993, New York. *Education:* Universities of Regensburg, Mainz, Paris and Munich (Referendar, 1988; Assessor, 1991); New York University Law School (LL.M.). *Member:* German-American Lawyers Association; American Council on Germany; German-French Lawyers Association; International Bar Association; American Foreign Law Association; German Institute for Arbitration. *LANGUAGES:* German, English and French.

Languages: German, English and French

WESSING BERENBERG-GOSSLER ZIMMERMANN LANGE

SPREEUFER 5
10178 BERLIN, GERMANY
Telephone: 030-238 45 45
Telefax: 030-238 45 34

Munich, Germany Office: Vilshofener Str. 8, D-81679 Munich, P.O. Box 86 08 67, D-81635 Munich. Telephone: 49-89-98 28 021. Telefax: 49-89-98 12 14.
Düsseldorf, Germany Office: Königsallee 92 A, D-40212 Düsseldorf, P.O. Box 10 53 61, D-40044 Düsseldorf. Telephone: 49-211-83 87-0. Telex: 858 19 14 wess d. Cable Address: "Wegolex". Telefax: 49-211-32 36 16.
Hamburg, Germany Office: Neuer Wall 46, D-20354 Hamburg. Telephone: 49-40-36 80 30. Cable Address: "Unilaw". Telex: 2-14111 Jura d. Teletex: 40 32 91 Unilaw. Telefax: 49-40-36 80 32 80.
Frankfurt, Germany Office: Freiherr-Vom-Stein-Strasse 24-26, D-60323 Frankfurt. Telephone: 49-69-971300. Telefax: 49-69-97130100.
Leipzig, Germany Office: Ferdinand-Rhode-Strasse 16, D-04107 Leipzig. Telephone: 49-341-213 13 80. Fax: 49-341-213 13 88.
Dresden, Germany Office: Heinrichstrasse 16, D-01097 Dresden. Telephone: 49-351-567 12 12. Telefax: 49-351-567 12 13.
Brussels, Belgium Office: Avenue Louise 149, Box 42, B-1050 Brussels. Telephone: +32 (2) 537 01 86. Telefax: +32 (2) 534 25 31.

(This Listing Continued)

General Practice. Corporate, Commercial, Banking, Tax, International, EEC and Antitrust Law, Unfair Competition, Industrial Property, Copyright and Patent Infringement, Labor Law, Business Offenses. Notary Public.

RESIDENT MEMBERS

JOST-THIEL HECKER, born Duesseldorf, September 25, 1928; admitted, 1958, Duesseldorf, Northrhein-Westfalia; 1959, Regional Court Stuttgart; 1962, Regional Court and Court of Appeals, Munich; 1991, Regional Court and Court of Appeals, Berlin, Germany. *Education:* University of Cologne. Posts of Honor: Vice-Chairman LEBENSHILFE für geistig und körperlich Behinderte, Kreisvereinigung Starnberg E.V., 1972   ; Chairman and Executive Officer, ISAR-WÜRM-LECH IWL Werkstätten für Behinderte gemeinn. GmbH, 1979—. *Member:* Deutsche Vereinigung für Gewerblichen Rechtsschutz und Urheberrecht e.V.; AIPPI; International Bar Association. *LANGUAGES:* German, English and French. *PRACTICE AREAS:* General Practice; Corporate; Mergers and Acquisitions; Commercial; Tax; International; EEC and Antitrust Law; Unfair Competition; Industrial Property; Copyright and Patent Infringement; Business Offenses; German Reunification and Restitution Law; Arbitration.

VOLKER G. HEINZ, born Kassel, Germany, May 23, 1943; admitted, 1973, Germany (Berlin Bar); Notary Public (Berlin Bar); Barrister-at-Law, England and Wales (The Honourable Society of the Inner Temple). *Education:* Universities of Heidelberg, Bonn and Berlin, Germany, and London, England; First State Bar Examination, Cologne 1969; Second State Bar Examination, Hamburg 1972; Diploma in Law (The City University), London 1988. Author: Section on Germany in Sheridan & Cameron's EC Legal Systems, An Introductory Guide, Butterworths, 1992. *Member:* Berlin Attorneys' Association; British-German Jurists' Association; Commercial Chambers (3c Gray's Inn Place London, Associate Member); German-Australian Association; German-Czech Jurists' Association; European Lawyers' Union; Inter-Pacific Bar Association; The Commonwealth Lawyers' Association; International Bar Association; Seldon Society; The Association of the Friends of the Hamburg-Max-Planck-Institute for Foreign and International Private Law; The German Institute for Arbitration (DIS); The Berlin Court of Arbitration; The London Court of International Arbitration; Swiss Arbitration Association (ASA). *LANGUAGES:* German, English and French. *PRACTICE AREAS:* German and English Business Law; German Real Estate Law; German Law of Restitution; Mergers and Acquisitions; International Joint Ventures; Trusts and Wills; International Aviation; International Commercial Arbitration; Litigation in Germany, England and Wales.

VICENTE VOIGT DE OLIVEIRA, born Berlin, May 27, 1963; admitted, 1992, Regional Court, Berlin, Germany. *Education:* University of Berlin. *LANGUAGES:* German, Portuguese, English and French. *PRACTICE AREAS:* General Practice; Corporate; Commercial; Labor Law; Business Offenses; German Reunification and Restitution Law.

KONSTANTIN GRAF LAMBSDORFF, born Frankfurt/Main, May 17, 1963; admitted, 1992, Regional Court, Berlin, Germany. *Education:* University of Munich. *LANGUAGES:* German and English. *PRACTICE AREAS:* General Practice; Corporate; Commercial; Tax; Business Offenses; German Reunification and Restitution Law.

WESTPHAL & VOGES

KURFÜRSTENDAMM 46
10707 BERLIN, GERMANY
Telephone: 030/883 40 04/05
Telefax: 030/882 57 26

Rostock Office: Lange Strasse 1 A, 18055. Telephone: 0381/4 58 20 70, Telefax: 0381/4 58 20 71.
Hamburg Office: Esplanade 41. Telephone: 040-356100. Telecopier: 040-35610-180.

Banking, Stock Markets and Securities, Commercial Law, Competition and Anti-Trust Law, Computer Law, Corporate Law, Environmental Law, European and International Private Law, General Contractual Terms and Conditions, Inheritance Law, Wills and Succession, Insolvency Law, Insurance and Re-Insurance, Intellectual Property, Labour Law, Media Law, Mergers and Acquisitions, Property and Construction law, Property Rights in the New Federal States, Public and Administrative Law, Shipping-/Maritime Law, Tax Law.

(This Listing Continued)

RESIDENT PARTNER

DR. CHRISTIAN F. FRIEHE, born November 20, 1940; admitted, 1974, Berlin. *Education:* Free University of Berlin (Dr. jur). Public Notary, 1991—. Research Assistant, Free University of Berlin, Institute for Civil, Commercial and Corporate Law, 1969-1974. *PRACTICE AREAS:* Intellectual Property; Competition and Anti-trust Law; Corporate Law.

ASSOCIATE

HARTMUT LESCHKE, born Berlin, November 22, 1964; admitted, 1993, Berlin. *Education:* Free University of Berlin. Research Assistant, Free University of Berlin, Institute for Civil and Insurance Law. *Member:* Berlin Bar Association. *LANGUAGES:* German and English.

Languages: German, English and French.

WILMER, CUTLER & PICKERING

FRIEDRICHSTRASSE 95
D-10117 BERLIN, GERMANY
Telephone: (49 30) 2643-3601
Facsimile: (49 30) 2643-3630

Washington, D.C. Office: 2445 M Street, N.W., 20037-1420. Telephone: 202-663-6000. Facsimile: 202-663-6363. Internet: Law@Wilmer.Com.
London, England Office: 4 Carlton Gardens, London, SW1Y 5AA. Telephone: (44 171) 839-4466. Facsimile: (44 171) 839-3537.
Brussels, Belgium Office: Rue de la Loi 15 Wetstraat, B-1040. Telephone: (32 2) 231-0903. Facsimile: (32 2) 230-4322.

General Practice.
Firm engaged in German, European, American, and International Law Practice.

RESIDENT PARTNERS

DR. MANFRED BALZ, born December 22, 1944; admitted, 1993, Germany. *Education:* Universities of Tübingen and Munich. First State Examination (1968); Second State Examination (1971). Universities of Leningrad and Moscow; Harvard University (LL.M., 1973); University of Tübingen (Dr. jur., 1979). German Federal Ministry of Justice, 1974-1990. General Counsel of Treuhandanstalt, 1990-1993.

BRYAN SLONE, born July 29, 1957; admitted, 1983, Nebraska (Not admitted in Germany). *Education:* University of Nebraska (B.S., 1979; J.D., 1983). Assistant to the Commissioner (Legislative Liaison), Internal Revenue Service, 1987-1989. Tax Counsel to Rep. Hal Daub, 1985-1986.

ASSOCIATES

DR. NATALIE LÜBBEN, born December 22, 1961; admitted to bar, 1990 Germany. *Education:* Free University of Berlin; University of Geneva. First State Examination (1987); Second State Examination (1990); Free University of Berlin (Dr. jur., 1992). Author, "Das Recht auf freie Benutzung des Luftraums," (Duncker & Humblot, 1993).

JUTTA VON FALKENHAUSEN, born March 18, 1963; admitted to bar 1993, Germany. *Education:* Harvard University (M.P.A., 1990); Freie Universität Berlin. First State Examination (1988). Kammergericht Berlin. Second State Examination (1993).

HENNING MENNENOEH, born December 29, 1957; admitted to bar 1990, Germany. *Education:* Ernst-Moritz-Arndt-Gymnasium (Arbitur, 1976). First State Examination, 1984. University of Bon (Dr. jur. 1989); University of Illinois (LL.M., 1986). Research and Teaching Assistant (Introduction to Civil Law, Contracts), University of Bonn (1984-1987). *Member:* German-American Lawyers Association; Association Internationale des Jeunes Avocats; International Bar Association.

(For Complete Biographical Data on all Personnel, see Professional biographies at Washington, D.C.)

WOLLMANN & PARTNER

Established in 1920

KURFÜRSTENDAMM 237
10719 BERLIN, GERMANY
Telephone: 0049 30 884 10 90
Fax: 0049 30 884 10 930/39

Brandenburg, Germany Office: Neustädtische Wassertorstraße 13, 14776. Telephone: 0049 3381 52 770. Fax: 0049 3381 52 7777.
Potsdam, Germany Office: Dortustraße 73, 14467. Telephone: 0049 331 27 19 70. Fax: 0049 331 27 19 755.

(This Listing Continued)

WOLLMANN & PARTNER, Berlin—Continued

General Practice, Commercial, Corporate, Real Estate, Building and Planning, Construction, Mergers and Acquisitions, Joint Ventures, Investment, Insurance, Labor, Family, Housing, Estates, Restitution, Investment in East Germany and Eastern Europe, Trademark and Copyright, Unfair Competition, Litigation, Notary.

MEMBERS OF FIRM

ERNST-JÜRGEN WOLLMANN, born Berlin, January 1, 1929; admitted, 1956, Berlin; 1967, Notary Public. *Education:* Free University of Berlin. President: Chamber of Notaries Berlin; Anton Schmittlein Baunternehmen AG; EUWO Holding AG. Member of Supervisory Board, Berlinische Lebensversicherung AG. *Member:* Berlin Bar Association. *LANGUAGES:* German and English. *PRACTICE AREAS:* Real Estate; Corporate Law; Notarizations; Business Law.

ERNST-RÜDIGER WOLLMANN, born Berlin, October 21, 1932; admitted, 1960, Berlin; 1973, Notary Public. *Education:* Free University of Berlin. *Member:* Berlin Bar Association. *PRACTICE AREAS:* Unfair Competition; Trademarks; Copyright; Insurance; Family.

DR. JOACHIM BÖRNER, born Wolfenbüttel, July 22, 1950; admitted, 1979, Berlin; 1988, Notary Public. *Education:* Georg-August-Universität of Göttingen (Dr. jur., 1984). Author: "Sportstätten-Haftungsrecht," Berlin, 1985. *Member:* Berlin Bar Association; German Bar Association. *LANGUAGES:* German, English and French. *PRACTICE AREAS:* Real Estate; Corporate Law; Investment; Commercial; Labor; Sports and Sports Association Law.

FRANK LEITHOLD, born Frankfurt/Main, March 12, 1953; admitted, 1981, Berlin; 1991, Notary Public. *Education:* University of Frankfurt/Main; Free University of Berlin. *Member:* Berlin Bar Association; Association for Industrial Property Rights and Copyright. *LANGUAGES:* German and English. *PRACTICE AREAS:* Real Estate; Corporate Law; Private Construction Law; Contracts; Architects and Engineers; Unfair Competition.

ASSOCIATES

GERT ROSENTHAL, born August 29, 1958; admitted, Landesgericht (District Court) Berlin. *Education:* Berlin Bank (Traineeship as Bank Clerk); Free University of Berlin (Law). *LANGUAGES:* German and English. *PRACTICE AREAS:* Real Estate; Banking Law; Transport Law; Corporate Law.

MICHAEL CH. BSCHORR, born Munich, December 9, 1961; admitted, 1991, Berlin. *Education:* Ludwig-Maximilians-Universität of Munich. *LANGUAGES:* German and English. *PRACTICE AREAS:* Private Construction Law; Landlord and Tenant; Housing.

CLAUDIA CARL, born Marburg/Lahn, December 3, 1963; admitted, 1992, Berlin. *Education:* Free University of Berlin. *LANGUAGES:* German and English. *PRACTICE AREAS:* Labor Law.

MICHAEL SCHUDNAGIES, born Hamburg, September 3, 1963; admitted, 1993, Berlin. *Education:* University of Heidelberg, University of Tübingen, Free University of Berlin. *LANGUAGES:* German and English. *PRACTICE AREAS:* Restitution Claims; Real Estate; Investment; Unfair Competition.

ZENK TIPPENHAUER OSMER SCHROETER SCHMIDT-DECKER BERGMANN

Established in 1973

PANORAMASTR. 1/ALEXANDERPLATZ
10178 BERLIN, GERMANY
Telephone: (030) 2425698
Fax: (030) 2424555

Hamburg, Germany Office: Hartwicusstr. 5, 22087 Hamburg. Telephone: (040) 220 10 61. Fax: (040) 220 18 05.

Commercial, Corporation, Mergers and Acquisitions, Joint Ventures, Antitrust, Unfair Competition, Intellectual Property (Trademark, Copyright), EC Law (including CAP), Admiralty, Customs, Transport, Food and Drug, Product Liability, Environmental and Administrative, Labour, Real Estate, Leasing, Probate, Property Law (Restitution of Property Rights in East

(This Listing Continued)

Germany), Taxation, Banking and Financing, Arbitration, Litigation, General Practice.

FIRM PROFILE: Established as a general practice in 1973, the firm has since grown to offer the full range of legal services for commercial matters. The Berlin office particularly deals with investment and restructuring in the former GDR.

Jürgen Zenk

(For Complete Biographical Data on all Personnel, see Professional Biographies at Hamburg, Germany)

BRANDI DRÖGE PILTZ & HEUER

ELSA-BRÄNDSTRÖM-STR. 1 U 3
33602 BIELEFELD, GERMANY
Telephone: 49 521 9 65 35-0
Facsimile: 49 521 9 65 35-99

Detmold, Germany Office: Lindenweg 2, 32756. Telephone: 49 5231 9857-0. Telecopier: 49 5231 9857-50.

Gütersloh, Germany Office: Hochstr. 19, 33332. Telephone: 49 5241 58886. Telecopier: 49 5241 58881.

Berlin, Germany Office: Seelenbinderstr. 124, 12555. Telephone: 49 30 6509465. Telecopier: 49 30 6565679.

Leipzig, Germany Office: Katharinenstr. 1-3, 04109. Telephone: 49 341 287550. Telecopier: 49 341 289162.

Paris, France Office: 250 bis, Boulevard Saint-Germain, 75007. Telephone: 33-1 49549037. Telecopier: 33-1 49549002.

Company Law, Unfair Competition, Commercial Law, Labor Law, Banking Law, Environmental Law, Family Law, Notary.

MEMBERS OF FIRM

CLAUS V. ZITZEWITZ, born Zitzewitz (County Stolp/Pommern), Germany, August 9, 1923; admitted, 1953, Germany. *Education:* University of Göttingen (Erstes Juristisches Staatsexamen, 1949). *LANGUAGES:* German. *PRACTICE AREAS:* Notary; National Family Law.

DR. HENNING HEUER, born Hannover, Germany, May 26, 1938; admitted, 1967, Germany; 1990, France. *Education:* Universities of Freiburg, Paris and Münster (Erstes Juristisches Staatsexamen, 1962; Doctor of Jurisprudence, 1964). Author: "Das richtige Bezugsobjekt des Adäquanzurteils," Dissertation 1964. *LANGUAGES:* German, French, English and Spanish. *PRACTICE AREAS:* German-French Business Law; Family Law; Law of Succession; Conveyancing; Mortgages.

DR. AXEL BRANDI, born Dortmund, Germany, May 6, 1936; admitted, 1967, Germany. *Education:* Universities of Freiburg, Munich and Münster (Erstes Juristisches Staatsexamen, 1962; Doctor of Jurisprudence, 1965). Author: " Bereicherung aus fremdem Vertrag," Dissertation 1965. Lecturer, University of Bielefeld, 1989—. *Member:* Board Rechtsanwaltskammer (Chamber of Attorneys) for the Judicial District of Hamm, 1984-1991; Board Notarkammer (Chamber of Notaries), for the Judicial District of Hamm, 1981—; Federal Chamber of Notaries (Committee, Commercial and Company Law). *LANGUAGES:* German and English. *PRACTICE AREAS:* Company Law; Unfair Competition; Conveyancing; Mortgages.

DR. HEINRICH SIEMENS, born Lemgo, Germany, October 19, 1944; admitted, 1975, Germany. *Education:* Universities of Hamburg and Münster (Erstes Juristisches Staatsexamen, 1970; Doctor of Jurisprudence, 1974). Author: "Wandel in der Rechtsprechung bezüglich der Sittenwidrigkeit von Geliebtentestamenten unter Berücksichtigung soziologischer Aspekte," Dissertation 1974. *Member:* German Bar Association; German Association for Building Law. *LANGUAGES:* German and English. *PRACTICE AREAS:* Construction Contracts; Building Law; Contracts for Work and Services; Banking Law.

DR. HANS-JÜRGEN HIEKEL, born Plettenberg, Germany, April 25, 1954; admitted, 1981, Germany. *Education:* University of Bielefeld (Examination, 1981; Doctor of Jurisprudence, 1985). Author: "Der Ausgleichsanspruch des Handelsvertreters und Vertriebshändlers." Dissertation 1985. *LANGUAGES:* German and English. *PRACTICE AREAS:* Labor Law; Commercial Agency Law; Law of Independent Dealers; Contracts for Managing Directors and Members of the Board; Franchising.

DR. JÖRG KÖNIG, born Stuttgart, Germany, November 22, 1957; admitted, 1986, Germany. *Education:* University of Bielefeld (Examination, 1984; Doctor of Jurisprudence, 1987). Author: "Rechtsverhältnisse und Rechtsprobleme bei der Darlehnsvalutierung über Notaranderkonto," Dissertation 1988. Assistant Professor, Civil and Trade Law, University of

(This Listing Continued)

Bielefeld, 1984-1986. *Member:* Bielefeld and German Bar Associations; German Association for the Protection of Industrial Property and Copyright Law. *LANGUAGES:* German and English. *PRACTICE AREAS:* Protection of Industrial Property; Unfair Competition; Landlord and Tenant Law; Insurance Law; Bankruptcy.

ANDREAS KÖNIG, born Bielefeld, Germany, August 15, 1959; admitted, 1992, Germany. *Education:* University of Cologne (Erstes juristisches Staatsexamen, 1978). *Member:* Bielefeld and German Bar Associations. *LANGUAGES:* German, English. *PRACTICE AREAS:* Transportation Law; Contracts for Work and Services; Building Law.

DR. IRENE VLASSOPOULOU, born Athens, Greece, 1954; admitted, 1983, Greece; 1991, Germany. *Education:* University of Athens Law School (Examination, 1977); University of Tübingen (Doctor of Jurisprudence, 1982). Author: "Der eheliche Hausrat im Familien-und Erbrecht," Berlin, 1983; "Das neue griechische Ehegüterrecht im Übergang-Altehen und Zugewinnausgleich nach neuem Recht," IPRax 1988, 189, and several other articles on Family Law. *Member:* Athens Bar Association; German Bar Association. *LANGUAGES:* Greek, German, French and English. *PRACTICE AREAS:* Family Law; International Private Law; International Civil Procedure.

STREITBOERGER, MAASS & STANGE

Established in 1970

ARTUR-LADEBECK-STRASSE 51
33617 BIELEFELD, GERMANY
Telephone: 0521/150015
Telefax: 0521/140733

International Law (U.S.A., U.K., France, Italy, Eastern European Countries); Company Law, Acquisition and Sale of Companies, Mergers; Competition Law, Trademarks, Copyright; Product Liability; Insolvency; Labour; Administrative, Construction, Environmental, Licenses for Industrial Plants; Commercial Law, Bank, General Business Conditions, Insurance, Transportation; Tax-Law; Reunification Law (former GDR); Litigation.

MEMBERS OF FIRM

DR. MANFRED STREITBOERGER, born 1928; admitted, 1960, Bielefeld, West Germany. *Education:* University of Muenster (Dr. jur. 1957); First State Examination (1952); Second State Examination (1956). Judge, 1956-1960. Member, Advisory Board of the Institute for German, European, and International Business Law, University of Bielefeld. *LANGUAGES:* German and English. *PRACTICE AREAS:* Law of Succession-especially succession in companies; Mergers; Company Law.

WALTER MAASS, born 1938; admitted, 1970, Bielefeld, West Germany. *Education:* Free University of Berlin, First State Examination (1964); Second State Examination (1967). Judge, 1967-1969. *LANGUAGES:* German and English. *PRACTICE AREAS:* Competition Law; Trade Mark Law; Copyright Law; Company Law.

DR. HARTMUT STANGE, born 1940; admitted, 1969, Bielefeld, West Germany. *Education:* University of Cologne (Dr. jur., 1967); First State Examination (1963); Second State Examination (1968). Research Assistant of the German Lower House of Parliament, 1964. *LANGUAGES:* German and English. *PRACTICE AREAS:* Insolvency Law; Labour Law; Company Law; Acquisition and Sale of Companies; Real Estate Law.

DR. HERMANN GOERDES, born 1950; admitted, 1978, Bielefeld, West Germany. *Education:* University of Bielefeld (Dr. jur. 1976); First State Examination (1974); Second State Examination (1978). Member, Advisory Board of the Institute for Environmental Law, University of Bielefeld. Certified Specialist for Administrative Law. *LANGUAGES:* German and English. *PRACTICE AREAS:* Business-Related Administrative Law; Construction Law; Environmental Law; Licenses for Industrial Plants on the Occasion of Industrial Plant Siting.

FRIEDERIKE STREITBOERGER, born 1960; admitted, 1985, Bielefeld, West Germany. *Education:* London University (Master of Laws, 1986); Final State Examination, 1985; Intermediate State Examination (1983). *LANGUAGES:* German, English and Italian. *PRACTICE AREAS:* International Law (Great Britain/Italy); Labour Law; General Business Conditions; Family Law; Reunification Law (former GDR); Litigation.

DR. NORBERT WESTHOFF, born 1956; admitted, 1986, Bielefeld, West Germany. *Education:* University of Bielefeld (Dr. jur., 1983); First State Examination (1980); Second State Examination (1985); Institute for

(This Listing Continued)

State & Law, Moscow. Certified Specialist for Labour Law. *LANGUAGES:* German, Russian and English. *PRACTICE AREAS:* Labour Law; Insolvency Law; Commercial Law; Company Law; International Law (Eastern European Countries).

PETRA WESTERWELLE, born 1959; admitted, 1986, Bielefeld, West Germany. *Education:* Intermediate State Examination (1981); Final State Examination (1986). *LANGUAGES:* German, French and English. *PRACTICE AREAS:* International Law (France); Family Law; Reunification Law (former GDR); Litigation.

DR. PETER MEYER, born 1958; admitted, 1987, Bielefeld, West Germany. *Education:* University of Bayreuth (Dr. jur., 1987); Intermediate State Examination (1984); Second State Examination (1986). *LANGUAGES:* German, French and English. *PRACTICE AREAS:* Company Law; Transportation Law; Competition Law; Bank Law; Litigation.

DR. BERTRAM SCHACKER, born 1958; admitted, 1987, Bielefeld, West Germany; 1989, New York, N.Y. *Education:* Intermediate State Examination (1984); Second State Examination (1986); University of Bayreuth (Dr. jur. 1986); University of Georgia, School of Law (Master of Laws, 1988); Graduate Assistantship/Scholarship of the German Academic Exchange Service (DAAD). *LANGUAGES:* German and English. *PRACTICE AREAS:* International Law (USA); Company Law; Acquisition and Sale of Companies; Commercial Law; Bank Law.

JOST HINRICH STREITBÖRGER, born 1964; admitted, 1991, Bielefeld, West Germany. *Education:* University of San Diego (Master of Comparative Law, 1993); Final State Examination (1991); Intermediate State Examination (1989). *LANGUAGES:* German and English. *PRACTICE AREAS:* Business-Related Administrative Law; Environmental Law; Commercial Law.

DR. MATTHIAS ROSE, born 1956; admitted, 1985, Bielefeld, West Germany. *Education:* University of Bielefeld (Dr. jur., 1988); Final State Examination (1985); Intermediate State Examination (1983). Certified Specialist for Administrative Law. *LANGUAGES:* German and English. *PRACTICE AREAS:* Business-Related-Administrated Law; Environmental Law; Licenses for Industrial Plants; Reunification Law (former GDR).

AULINGER, BOTTKE, KNÄLMANN

Established in 1948

ABC-STRASSE 5
D-44787 BOCHUM, GERMANY
Telephone: 0234/68779-0
Teletex: 234334 (Dufhues) (from
Telex: 17234334)
Fax: 0234/680 642

Leipzig, Germany Office: Goethestrasse 1, 04109 Leipzig. Telephone: 0341/9600910. Telecopier: 0341/9601169.
Dresden, Germany Office: St. Petersburger Str. 15, O1069 Dresden. Telephone: 0351/4872419. Fax: 0351/4873327.
Erfurt, Germany Office: Kleine Arche 1, 99084 Erfurt. Telephone: 0361/5667808. Fax: 0361/5667810.

General Practice. Corporate, Commercial, Banking, Antitrust, Unfair Competition, Real Estate, Merger and Acquisition, Products Liability, Labor, Co-Determination, Tax, Arbitration, Administrative and Public, Building and Planning, Notaries. Reversion of nationalized enterprises and real estate to private ownership in the eastern parts of Germany.

FIRM PROFILE: The firm was established in 1948 by the late J.H. Dufhues (former Minister of State North Rhine-Westphalia) and offers a full range of legal services at the offices in Bochum, Dresden, Erfurt and Leipzig.

MEMBERS OF FIRM

DR. LEONHARD AULINGER, born Bochum, Germany, February 25, 1930; admitted, 1958, Bochum; Notary. *Education:* Universities of Bamberg and Munich (Dr. jur., 1954). Fachanwalt: Tax Law. Author: "Die atypische stille Gesellschaft (The non-typical Silent Partnership); Verdeckte Sacheinlagen im GmbH-Recht (Non-cash capital contribution in limited companies). *Member:* Association of Tax Lawyers; German Association of Industrial Property and Copyright, Several Supervisory Boards. *LANGUAGES:* German, English.

MANFRED BOTTKE, born Bochum, Germany, May 15, 1937; admitted, 1966, Bochum; Notary. *Education:* Universities of Marburg (English and French) and Münster (Laws). Fachanwalt: Labor Law and Adminis-

(This Listing Continued)

AULINGER, BOTTKE, KNÄLMANN, Bochum—Continued

trative Law. *Member:* Deputies-boards. *LANGUAGES:* German, English, French.

REINHARD KNÄLMANN, born Steinfeld/Oldb., Germany, June 18, 1939; admitted, 1970, Bochum; Notary. *Education:* Universities of Freiburg and Münster. Fachanwalt: Tax Law. *Member:* Association of Tax Lawyers; Several Supervisory Boards. *LANGUAGES:* German, English.

HANS-JOCHEN HÜTTER, born Dorsten, Germany, September 27, 1949; admitted, 1977, Bochum; Notary. *Education:* University of Münster. Fachanwalt: Tax Law. *Member:* German Association of Building Law; German Lawyer's Association (Family Law and Private Building Law Study Groups). *LANGUAGES:* German, English.

DR. KARLHEINZ LENKAITIS, born Essen, Germany, October 12, 1950; admitted, 1977, Essen; 1980, Bochum; Notary. *Education:* University of Bochum, Assistant at University of Bochum, 1974-1977 (Dr. jur.). Fachanwalt: Tax Law. Author: "Krankenunterlagen aus juristischer, insbesondere zivilrechtlicher Sicht" (Legal problems of Medical Records), 1979. *Member:* Association of Banking Law; Association of Tax Lawyers. *LANGUAGES:* German, English, French.

DR. EGON A. PEUS, born Bochum, Germany, October 8, 1951; admitted, 1979, Bochum; Notary. *Education:* Universities of Bochum (Referendar, Assessor, 1978, Dr. jur., 1982) and Bielefeld (Assistant). Fachanwalt: Tax Law and Administrative Law. Author: "Der Aufsichtsratsvorsitzende - seine Rechtsstellung nach dem Aktiengesetz und dem Mitbestimmungsgesetz," (The Chairman of the supervisory board of corporations; his legal position under corporation law and co-determination law, 1983). *Member:* German Federal Association of Public Law. *LANGUAGES:* German, English.

DR. MATTHIAS KOCH, born Münster/Westf., Germany, March 23, 1956; admitted, 1984, Bochum. *Education:* University of Münster (Dr. jur.); Assistant, University of Münster, 1982-1985. Fachanwalt: Tax Law. Author: "Sittenwidrigkeit von Unterhaltsverzichten" (Immorality of Waivers of Alimony), self-published (Dissertation), 1985. *Member:* Association of Traffic Lawyers. *LANGUAGES:* German, English.

DR. ANDREAS EICKHOFF, born Rheda, Germany, March 1, 1958; admitted, 1987, Bochum. *Education:* University of Bonn (Dr. jur.); Assistant, Universities of Bonn (1983-1984), Bochum (1985-1987). Author: "Die Gesellschafterklage im GmbH-Recht" (The Shareholder's derivative suit under the law of limited companies), 1988. *LANGUAGES:* German, English.

GERALD BAUSCH, born Halle, Germany, January 10, 1953; admitted, 1980, Leipzig. *Education:* University of Berlin (Humboldt-University). (Leipzig Office). *LANGUAGES:* German, Russian.

MICHAEL HOESELER, born Recklinghausen, Germany, March 28, 1957; admitted, 1990, Bochum. *Education:* University of Bochum; School of Administration, Speyer. (Erfurt Office). *LANGUAGES:* German, English.

KARL FRIEDRICH NOLTING, born Herford, Germany, September 12, 1959; admitted, 1992. *Education:* University of Munich. (Dresden Office). *LANGUAGES:* German, English and French.

BENEDIKT GALLE, born Münster, Germany, January 4. 1958; admitted, 1990, Hamburg. *Education:* Universities of Bochum and Münster. (Leipzig Office). *LANGUAGES:* German, English and French.

ASSOCIATES

DR. VOLKER WEINREICH, born Plettenberg, Germany, May 11, 1961; admitted, 1991, Bochum. *Education:* University of Bochum (Dr. jur.). Assistant at University of Bochum, 1985-1987. Fachanwalt: Tax Law. Author: "Probleme des Verlustausgleichs über die Grenze." (Problems of the Loss Compensation across the Border), 1994. *LANGUAGES:* German and English.

DR. ULRICH DALL, born Lingen/Ems, Germany, September 5, 1963; admitted, 1994, Bochum. *Education:* Universities of Bayreuth and Bonn. Assistant, University of Bonn, 1990-1991. Author: "Das Preisgegenüberstellungsverbot gemäß§ 6 e UWG - Problematik und Kritik der Auslegung dieser Norm in Rechtsprechung und Literatur," (Prohibition on Price Comparison in Sec. 6 e. of the German Act Against Unfair Competition - Issues and review of the construction by case law and legal literature of this provision), 1992. *LANGUAGES:* German, English and French.

(This Listing Continued)

DR. MARTIN ALBERTS, born Essen, Germany, March 23, 1965; admitted, 1994, Bochum. *Education:* University of Freiburg (Laws and Political Economy Science, 1984-1987); University of Münster (Dr. jur., 1987-1991). Assistant, University of Münster, 1990-1991. Author: "Die Gesellschaft Bürgerlichen Rechts im Umbruch" (The Partnership under the German Civil Code in Upheaval). *LANGUAGES:* German, English and French.

DR. HANS-JOACHIM DAVID, born Dülmen/Westf., Germany, August 21, 1964; admitted, 1994, Bochum. *Education:* University of Münster (Referendar, Assessor, 1994, Dr. jur., 1992). Assistant, University of Münster. Author: "Der Jugendhilfeausschuß, Zusammensetzung, Verfahren und Kompetenzen aus verwaltungs- und verfassungsrechtlicher Sicht," 1993 ("The committee for youth welfare, the structure, procedure and competence from the view of administrative law and constitutional law"). *LANGUAGES:* German, English and French.

EIMER • HEUSCHMID • MEHLE

Established in 1973

FRIEDRICH-BREUER-STR. 104-112
53225 BONN, GERMANY
Telephone: 01149-228-466025
Fax: 01149-228-460708

Cologne, Germany Office: Hohenstaufenring 44-46, 50674 Cologne.
  Telephone: 01149-221-235555. Fax: 01149-221-236121.
Halle, Germany Office: Rudolf-Breitscheid-Str. 92, 06108 Halle.
  Telephone: 01149-345-29392. Fax: 01149-345-29392.

Civil, Commercial and Company Law, Patents and Trade Marks, Family Law and Estate Administration, Labour Law, Private International and EC Law, Insurance and Medical Malpractice Law, Criminal Law, Serious Fraud, Tax and Environmental Offences.

FIRM PROFILE: The firm was established in 1973 and offers a full range of services including litigation in all judicial branches. It is well known for its wide-ranging commercial, family and specialized criminal law. Its client base is European. The firm is a member of a European Economic Interest Grouping (AVRIO), the partners of which are well-known firms throughout Europe; close cooperation and advice on European scale is offered.

MEMBERS OF FIRM

RICHARD B. EIMER, born Istanbul, August 3, 1941; admitted, 1973, Bonn. *Education:* Bonn University (Law and Economics). *Member:* German Bar Association; Board of Bonn Bar Association; Commission of Competition Law; Union des Avocats Européens. *LANGUAGES:* German, French and English. *PRACTICE AREAS:* Civil Law; Commercial Law; Company and Economic Law; European Competition Law; Patents and Trade Marks; Labour Law; Agency Law; Insolvency Law; German Unification and East German Property Law.

DR. HERMANN HEUSCHMID, born Rheydt, August 14, 1943; admitted, 1973, Bonn. *Education:* Universities of Freiburg and Bonn (Dr. jur., 1971). Author: "Pactes sur successions futures," 1971. *Member:* German Association of Family Lawyers; German Bar Association; Union des Avocats Européens. *LANGUAGES:* German, English and French. *PRACTICE AREAS:* Civil Law; Family Law; Law of Succession; Private International Law.

DR. VOLKMAR MEHLE, born Zschopau/Saxonia, November 11, 1944; admitted, 1976, Germany. *Education:* Universities of Lausanne and Bonn (Dr. jur., 1981). Author: "Einschränkende Tendenzen im Bereich der absoluten Revisionsgründe (S 338 StPO)," 1981; "Anmerkungen zum Alternativ-Entwurf aus anwaltlicher Sicht," in: Neue Zeit-schrift für Strafrecht (NStZ) 1982, 309; "Entkriminalisierung der fahrlässigen Körperverletzung?," in: Anwaltsblatt 1983, 381; Anmerkung zum Beschluß des Kammergerichts vom 05.07.1982 - 1 AR 460/82 -in: NStZ 1983, 557; "Der Verteidiger - Ein Korrektiv auch zu Lasten des Beschuldigten?," in: Festgabe für Karl Peters (Heidelberg, 1984) S. 201; "Die Entziehung des Wortes in der Hauptverhandlung," in: Schriftenreihe der Arbeitsgemeinschaften des Deutschen Anwaltvereins, Arbeitsgemeinschaft Strafrecht, Heft 1, 1984, S. 67; "Anmerkungen zur Unerreichbarkeit von Zeugen," in: Schriftenreihe der Arbeitsgemeinschaft des Deutschen Anwaltsvereins, Arbeitsgemeinschaft Strafrecht, Band 3, S. 133; Anmerkung zum Urteil des BGH vom 24.-06.1986 - 5 StR 114/86 -, in: Strafverteidiger 1987, 93; "Einige Anmerkungen zum gegenwärtigen Stand der Diskussion uber die Fernwirkung des Verwertungsverbots nach S 136 a Abs. 3 Satz 2 StPO," in: Schriftenreihe der Arbeitsgemeinschaften des Deutschen Anwaltvereins, Arbeitsgemeinschaft

(This Listing Continued)

Strafrecht, Band 6, S. 172; "Strafvereitelung durch Wahrnehmung prozessualer Rechte? - Einige Anmerkungen zum Umfang mit Zeugen," in: Strafverteidigung im Strafprozeß, Festgabe für Ludwig Koch (Heidelberg, 1989) S. 179; Anmerkung zum Beschluß des BGH vom 03.03.1989 - 2 ARs 54/89 - in: NStZ 1990, 92; "Das Erfordernis des Beruhens im Revisionsrecht - die ungewisse Hürde für den Revisionsführer," - in: Schriftenreihe der Arbeitsgemeinschaften des Deutschen Anwaltvereins, Arbeitsgemeinschaft Strafrecht, Heft 7, S. 47; "Warum das alle angeht," in: Anwaltsblatt 1990, 138; "Rehabilitierung und Kassay Kassation - Beseitigung von Justizunrechten der DDR," - (with: Amelung/Brüssow/Keck/Kemper), Seminarschriften der Deutschen Anwaltsakademie, Band 25 (München, 1991). Reader, Criminal Law, German Lawyers' Academy. Member, Board of Examiners, Court of Appeal, Cologne. Disciplinary Judge, Cologne Bar Council. *Member:* Association of Criminal Lawyers; German Bar Association (Deputy Chairman). *LANGUAGES:* German, English and French. *PRACTICE AREAS:* Criminal Law; Commercial Law; Corporate Law; Tax and Environmental Offences; Medical Malpractice Law.

PETER BLUMENTHAL, born Bonn, March 31, 1949; admitted, 1978, Bonn. *Education:* Universities of Freiburg and Bonn. *Member:* German Bar Association's Commission on Traffic Law. *LANGUAGES:* German and English. *PRACTICE AREAS:* Civil Law; Insurance Law; Medical Malpractice Law; Transportation Law; Accident Regulation Law; Traffic and Transport Offences.

WERNER REINLEIN, born Königswinter, November 20, 1951; admitted, 1981, Bonn. *Education:* Bonn University. *LANGUAGES:* German and English. *PRACTICE AREAS:* Civil Law; Commercial Law; Land and Tenancy Law; Competition Law; Intellectual Property Law.

MANFRED BECKER, born Cologne, April 22, 1955; admitted, 1984, Bonn. *Education:* Universities of Cologne and Bonn. *LANGUAGES:* German and English. *PRACTICE AREAS:* Civil Law; Commercial Law; Construction Law; Labour Law; Insolvency Law.

ULRICH KUDOWEH, born Neuss, June 30, 1961; admitted, 1989, Cologne. *Education:* Bonn University. *Member:* German Bar Association; Association of Criminal Lawyers. (Resident, Cologne Office). *LANGUAGES:* German and English. *PRACTICE AREAS:* Civil Law; Commercial Law; Criminal Law.

ANDREAS FRÄNKEN, born Mönchengladbach, February 9, 1961; admitted, 1991, Bonn. *Education:* Bonn University. *Member:* German Bar Association; Deutscher Familiengerichtstag. *LANGUAGES:* German and English. *PRACTICE AREAS:* Civil Law; Commercial Law; Family Law; Criminal Law.

WOLFGANG JOHANNES, born Darmstadt, December 15, 1960; admitted, 1992, Bonn. *Education:* Bonn University. *Member:* German Bar Association. *LANGUAGES:* German and English. *PRACTICE AREAS:* Civil Law; Commercial and Company Law; Private International Law; German Unification and East German Property Law.

FLICK GOCKE SCHAUMBURG

Attorneys-at-Law, Auditors, Tax Consultants

Established in 1971

JOHANNA-KINKEL-STR. 2-4
53175 BONN, GERMANY
Telephone: (0-228) 9594-0
Telefax: (0-228) 9594-100

Berlin, Germany Office: Nürnberger Str. 67, 10787 Berlin. Telephone: (030) 217 6843. Telefax: (030) 218 4686.

National and International Tax Law, Corporate Law, M & A, Joint Ventures, International Trust and Corporate Structures, Investment, Real Property, Estate Planning, Wills and Trusts, Auditing.

MEMBERS OF FIRM

DR. HANS FLICK, born Wuppertal, 1927; admitted, 1961, Germany; Tax Lawyer. *Education:* University of Cologne (Doctor of Law, 1956). Former Deputy General Manager of the Federation of German Chambers of Industry and Commerce (DIHT); Member, Board of International Fiscal Association-German Section. Author: "Methods to Prevent International Double Taxation," (Germ.), Mitchell B. Carroll Award of IFA,1962; "Tax Treatment of Transfer of Technology-Know-How, Patents and Other Intangibles," German Report to 1975 IFA Congress, London; "Planning of Succession in Enterprises (Germ.), 4th ed. 1992. Co-Author: "Commentary on the VAT Act," (Germ., 5 vol.), 1967/1991 ff; "Commentary on the For-

(This Listing Continued)

eign Tax Relations Act," (Germ., 3 vol.), 1973/1992 ff; "Commentary on the German-Swiss Double Taxation Treaty," (Germ., 2 vol.), 1981/1989 ff. *PRACTICE AREAS:* International Tax Planning; International Trusts and Estates; Wills; Partnerships.

RUDOLF GOCKE, born Paderborn, 1937; C.P.A., Certified Tax Consultant. *Education:* Universities of Berlin and Münster (Dipl.-Kfm., 1963). Author: "Unilateral Measures to Prevent Double Taxation," German Report to IFA Congress 1981, Berlin. Co-Author: "Reflections on Establishing a Foreign Holding Company," IWB 1989, p. 87. *PRACTICE AREAS:* International Tax Planning; International Corporate Restructuring; Holding Companies; Audits.

PROF. DR. IIARALD SCHAUMBURG, born Königswinter, 1944; admitted, 1967, Germany; Tax Lawyer. *Education:* University of Cologne (Doctor of Law, 1973). Honorary Professor of Tax Law, University of Cologne. Author: "International Tax Law," (Germ.), 1993. Co-Author: "Standard Agreements and Forms Manual for Tax Purposes," (Germ.), 2nd ed. 1992. *PRACTICE AREAS:* International Tax Planning; Joint Ventures; Holding Companies; Mergers and Acquisitions; Corporate Restructuring.

DR. KARL-DIETER WINGERT, born Ratibor, 1944; admitted, 1973, Germany; Tax Lawyer. *Education:* Universities of Cologne, Tübingen, Bonn (Doctor of Law, 1973). Author: "Rules for Determining Income and Expenses as Domestic or Foreign," German Report to IFA Congress 1980, Paris. Co-Author: "Commentary on the German-Swiss Double Taxation Treaty," (Germ., 2 vol.), 1981/1989 ff.; "Commentary on Selected Double Taxation Treaties," 1993. *PRACTICE AREAS:* International Tax Planning; International Trusts and Estates; Wills; Partnerships; Investments.

KLAUS KAPPE, born Hilden, 1950; admitted, 1980, Germany; Tax Lawyer. *Education:* Universities of Cologne, Freiburg and Bonn. *PRACTICE AREAS:* International Tax Planning; International Trusts and Estates; International Mergers and Acquisitions; Investments; International Corporate Law.

HERMANN-J. HÜRHOLZ, born Bad Münstereifel, 1951; C.P.A., Certified Tax Consultant. *Education:* Universities of Bonn (Dipl.-Vw., 1974) and Würzburg. *PRACTICE AREAS:* International Tax Planning; Accounting; Audits.

DR. HUBERTUS BAUMHOFF, born Welschen Ennest, 1954; C.P.A., Certified Tax Consultant. *Education:* Universities of Münster (Dipl.-Kfm., 1980) and Hamburg (Doctor of Economics, 1985). Author: "Intercompany Pricing for Services," (Germ.), 1986. Co-Author: "Commentary on the German-Swiss Double Taxation Treaty," (Germ., 2 vol.), 1992; "Tax Incentives for Investments in the New Länder," (Germ.), 1992. *PRACTICE AREAS:* International Tax Planning; Corporate Restructuring; Holding Companies; Investment; Accounting; Audits.

PROF. DR. DETLEV J. PILTZ, born Bärwalde, 1944; admitted, 1975, Germany; Tax Lawyer. *Education:* Universities of Freiburg, Bonn, Mannheim (Doctor of Law, 1980). Honorary Professor of Tax Law, University of Mannheim. Author: "German Civil Law," (Germ.), 1975; "Partnerships in International Tax Law," (Germ.), 1981; "Court Practice on Valuation of Enterprises," (Germ.), 3rd ed. 1993. Co-Author: "Taxation of Transnational Enterprises," (Germ.), 1992. *PRACTICE AREAS:* International Tax Planning; International Trusts and Estates; Wills; Corporate Restructuring; Partnerships.

DR. BERND NOLL, born Kassel, 1956; admitted, 1988, Germany; Tax Lawyer. *Education:* University of Göttingen (Doctor of Law, 1992). Co-Author: "The New VAT System in the Common Market," (Germ.), 1991. *PRACTICE AREAS:* International Tax Planning; Joint Ventures; Holding Companies; Investment; Value Added Tax (VAT).

DR. JÖRG W. LÜTTGE, born Bochum, 1955; admitted, 1987, Germany; Certified Tax Consultant. *Education:* Universities of Berlin, Bochum, Geneva (Switzerland) and Bielefeld (Doctor of Law, 1989). Author: "Restraints of Competition in the European Steel Market," (Germ.), 1989; "New Options For Non-Resident Investors," International Tax Review 1993, p. 91. *PRACTICE AREAS:* International Tax Planning; Holding Companies; Corporate Restructuring; International Corporate Law; Customs Law.

DR. THOMAS RÖDDER, born Lüdinghausen, 1962; Certified Tax Consultant. *Education:* University of Cologne (Doctor of Economics, 1991). Author: "In Search of Income Tax Advantages," (Germ.), 1 991; Co-Author: "The New VAT System in the Common Market," (Germ.), 1992; "Tax Incentives for Investments in the New Länder," (Germ.), 1992. *PRACTICE AREAS:* International Tax Planning; Holding Companies; Corporate Restructuring; Investments; Audits.

(This Listing Continued)

FLICK GOCKE SCHAUMBURG, Bonn—Continued

ASSOCIATES

THOMAS BRINKMEIER, Certified Tax Consultant.

BERTHOLD FELDMANN, Certified Tax Consultant.

DR. LAMBERTUS FUHRMANN, Attorney-at-Law.

DR. OLIVER HÖTZEL, Certified Tax Consultant.

CHRISTIAN HOPPEN, Certified Tax Consultant.

DR. MARC JÜLICHER, Attorney-at-Law.

DR. CHRISTIAN VON OERTZEN, Attorney-at-Law.

VERA PIOTROWSKY-HERMANN, C.P.A., Certified Tax Consultant.

FRAUKE RUNGS, C.A., Certified Tax Consultant.

DR. STEPHAN SCHAUHOFF, Attorney-at-Law.

ROLF SCHEIBLER, Certified Tax Consultant.

VALENTIN SEIDENFUS, Attorney-at-Law.

LYDIA WETTER, C.P.A., Certified Tax Consultant.

Languages: German, English, French

KREUTZBERG, GROSSE-WILDE & BURCHARD

Established in 1980

KAISERSTR. 15

D-53113 BONN, GERMANY

Telephone: 0228/211460

Fax: 0228/211734

A Member of AdvoSelect EEIG, a network of law firms pooling their resources in special fields and cross border cases, specializing in business law for middle-sized companies. AdvoSelect is represented in 51 cities throughout Europe.

Commercial, Company, Tax, Competition, Contract, Labour, Construction, Family, Product Liability, Medical Negligence, Intellectual Property and Publishing.

MEMBERS OF FIRM

ALFRED KREUTZBERG, born Marktbreit, Germany, 1947; admitted, 1980, Bonn. *Education:* Universities of Munich and Bonn. *Member:* German Bar Association; Deutscher Juristentag. *LANGUAGES:* German and English. *PRACTICE AREAS:* Commercial; Association; Administrative.

FRANZ GROSSE-WILDE, born Bottrop, Germany, 1953; admitted, 1984, Bonn. *Education:* University of Bonn. *Member:* German Bar Association; Association of Inheritance Law; National Association of Administrative Law. *LANGUAGES:* German, English and Italian. *PRACTICE AREAS:* Commercial; Company; Tax; Construction; Probate; Administrative; Aviation; Medical Negligence; Intellectual Property; Publishing.

MARTINA GROSSE-WILDE, born Luenen, Germany, 1955; admitted, 1987, Bonn. *Education:* University of Bonn. *Member:* German Bar Association; German Society for Family Law. *LANGUAGES:* German, English and French. *PRACTICE AREAS:* Labour; Contract; Family; Construction; Product Liability; Competition; Medical Negligence.

MEILICKE & PARTNER

Established in 1933

POPPELSDORFER ALLEE 106

53115 BONN, GERMANY

Telephone: 0228-631635

Telex: 8869340

Telecopier: 0228-659306

Taxation, Corporation, Reorganization, Mergers and Acquisitions, International Business Law, Anti-Trust, EEC Law, Competition, Civil Litigation, Labor Law, Environmental and Banking, Media Law.

FIRM PROFILE: *The firm offers a full range of legal services. It is well known for its Tax and Commercial Law. The client base is European and North American in scope.*

(This Listing Continued)

PARTNERS OF FIRM

PROF. DR. HEINZ MEILICKE, born Berlin, Germany, December 25, 1904; admitted, 1933, Berlin. *Education:* Universities of Berlin and Graz (Dr. jur., 1928). Author: *D-Markbilanzen,* 1949; *Lastenausgleichsgesetz,* 1953; Steuerrecht, Allgemeiner Teil, 1965. Co-author with Böttcher-Hohlfeld: *Umwandlung und Verschmelzung von Kapitalgesellschaften,* 5th Edition, 1958. Professor of Tax and Corporation Law, Free University of Berlin, 1951-1969. Co-author with Wienand Meilicke: Kommentar zum Mitbestimmungsgesetz 1976, first and second edition. *LANGUAGES:* German, English and French. *PRACTICE AREAS:* Taxation; Corporation; Reorganization.

DR. WIENAND MEILICKE, born Seilershof, Germany, July 11, 1945; admitted, 1975, Bonn. *Education:* Weberbank Berlin, 1965-1966; Bonn and Berlin Law Schools (Dr. jur., 1970); Aix-en-Provence Law School, France (Licencié en Droit Français, 1971); New York University (LL.M., Taxation, 1976). Lawyer with Shearman & Sterling, New York and Paris, 1973-1975. Fachanwalt für Steuerrecht. Author: Rechtsgrundsätze zur Unternehmensbewertung 1975; Die "verschleierte" Sacheinlage, 1989. Co-author with Heinz Meilicke: Kommentar zum Mitbestimmungsgesetz, 1976. *LANGUAGES:* German, English and French. *PRACTICE AREAS:* Taxation; Corporation; Mergers and Acquisitions; International Business Law; EEC Law.

DR. JÜRGEN HOFFMANN, born Troisdorf, Germany, March 9, 1954; admitted, 1982, Bonn. *Education:* Bonn Law School (Dr. jur., 1989). Fachanwalt für Steuerrecht. Vereidigter Buchprüfer. Author: Verhaltenspflichten der Banken und Kreditversicherungsunternehmen, 1990. *LANGUAGES:* German, English and French. *PRACTICE AREAS:* Corporation; Taxation; Competition; Banking; Environment; Law relating to German unification.

DR. STEPHAN PAULY, born Bonn, Germany, December 1, 1958; admitted, 1987, Bonn. *Education:* Bonn Law School (Dr. jur., 1986). Fachanwalt für Arbeitsrecht. *LANGUAGES:* German and English. *PRACTICE AREAS:* Labor; Litigation; Competition; Law regarding Fiscal Offenses; General Commercial and Civil Law.

DR. THOMAS HEIDEL, born Berlin, Germany, July 27, 1956; admitted, 1988, Bonn. *Education:* Kiel and Freiburg Law Schools (Dr. jur., 1987). Fachanwalt für Steuerrecht. Author: Verfassungsfragen der Finanzierung von Privatfunk durch Werbung, 1988. *LANGUAGES:* German and English. *PRACTICE AREAS:* Taxation; Corporation; Media Law; General Commercial and Civil Law; Litigation.

ASSOCIATES

HERBERT KRUMSCHEID, born Setterich, Germany, February 28, 1960; admitted, 1990, Bonn. *Education:* Bonn Law School. *LANGUAGES:* German, English and Dutch. *PRACTICE AREAS:* Civil Litigation; Rent and Lease; Law of Succession.

GEORG ERDMANN, born Bochum, Germany, March 30, 1958; admitted, 1991, Bonn. *Education:* Bonn Law School. DG Bank, Frankfurt, 1991-1992. *LANGUAGES:* German and English. *PRACTICE AREAS:* Banking; Law relating to German unification; General Commercial and Civil Law; Corporation.

Languages: German, English, French and Dutch.

REDEKER SCHÖN DAHS & SELLNER

Established in 1929

OXFORDSTRASSE 24

53111 BONN, GERMANY

Telephone: (0228) 7 26 25 0

Telefax: (0228) 65 04 79

Cologne, Germany Office: Kaiser-Wilhelm-Ring 22, 50672 Cologne, Telephone: (0221) 912 8680. Telefax: (0221) 912 86838.

Hamburg, Germany Office: Büschstrasse 12, 20354 Hamburg. Telephone: (040) 342737/8. Telefax: (040) 352144.

Leipzig, Germany Office: Mozartstr. 1, 04107 Leipzig. Telephone: (0341) 213780. Telefax: (0341) 2137830.

London, England Office: 43 Brook Street, London, W1Y 2BL. Telephone: (0171) 3225823. Telefax: (0171) 6292621.

Administrative, Anti-Trust, Aviation, City Planning, Civil, Corporate and Commercial, Constitutional and Parliamentary, Construction, Criminal, Environmental, European Community Law, Family, Health, Insurance,

(This Listing Continued)

Labour, Media and Copyright, Medical Malpractice, Domestic and International Tax, Trade, Transportation Law, Litigation and Appeals.

MEMBERS OF FIRM

PROF. DR. KONRAD REDEKER, born Mühlheim, Ruhr, June 21, 1923; admitted, 1954, Bonn (Fachanwalt für Verwaltungsrecht). *Education:* University of Hamburg (Dr. jur., 1949). Recipient, Hans-Dahs-Award of the German Lawyers' Association, 1985. Co-Editor, "Neue Juristische Wochenschrift" (NJW) and the Publication Series of the NJW. Co-Author: "Kommentar zur Verwaltungsgerichtsordnung," 10th ed., Kohlhammer-Verlag, 1991. Honorary Professor, University of Bonn, 1978—. Member, 1964-1976 and Chairman, 1966-1970, Permanent Delegation of the German Lawyers' Congress. President, 1968-1970 and Honorary Member, 1986—, German Lawyers' Congress. *Member:* German Lawyers' Association (Member of the Board, 1971-1981; Vice President, 1975-1981; Chairman: Administrative Law Committee, 1968-1982; Environmental Committee, 1974-1978); German-Israeli Lawyers' Association.

DR. KURT SCHÖN (1928-1986).

PROF. DR. HANS DAHS, born Bonn-Beuel, November 1, 1935; admitted, 1964, Bonn. *Education:* Universities of Bonn, Munich, Freiburg i.Br. and Zurich (Dr. jur, 1963). Co-Editor: "Neue Zeitschrift für Strafrecht," and "Neue Entscheidungssammlung für Strafrecht," Co-Author: "Grosskommentar zur Strafprozessordnung," de Gruyter, 1986 and 1987; "Handbuch des Strafverteidigers," 5th ed., Schmidt-Verlag, 1983; "Revision im Strafprozess," 5th ed., Beck-Verlag, 1993. Honorary Professor, University of Bonn, 1983—. Lecturer, German Lawyers' Academy, 1985—. Member: State Board of Law Examiners, Cologne Section. *Member:* National Bar Association (Chairman, Criminal Law Committee).

DR. DIETER SELLNER, born Wuppertal, January 11, 1935; admitted, 1968, Bonn (Fachanwalt für Verwaltungsrecht); registered as foreign lawyer in England and Wales. *Education:* Universities of Cologne, Munich, Bonn, and Zurich (Dr. jur., 1961). Co-Editor: "Neue Zeitschrift für Verwaltungsrecht", "Immissionsschutzrecht und Industrieanlagen," 2d ed. Beck-Verlag, 1988. Chairman, Lawyers' Administrative Law Committee, Northrhine-Westfalian Section. Member, Board of the Environmental Association, Berlin. *Member:* German Lawyers' Association (Chairman, Environmental Law Committee). *LANGUAGES:* German and English.

DR. KLAUS D. BECKER, born Wuppertal, October 17, 1942; admitted, 1972, Bonn (Fachanwalt für Verwaltungsrecht); registered as foreign lawyer in England and Wales. *Education:* Universities of Cologne, Bonn and Bochum (Dr. jur., 1977); University of Göttingen. *Member:* Board of the Bonn Association of Politics and Law; German Lawyers' Education Association; Law Committee, Bonn Chamber of Commerce; German-Israeli Lawyers' Association; German-German Lawyers' Association; German-British Jurists' Association; State Board of Law Examiners, Northrhine-Westfalian Section. *LANGUAGES:* German and English.

ULRICH KELLER, born Wesel/Rhine, November 18, 1943; admitted, 1973, Bonn (Fachanwalt für Arbeitsrecht). *Education:* Universities of Freiburg and Bonn. *Member:* German Association of Labor Lawyers; Association for the Protection of Industrial Property Rights.

ULRIKE BÖRGER, born Munich, February 1, 1949; admitted, 1976, Bonn. *Education:* Universities of Freiburg, Geneva and Bonn. Author: "Eheliches Güterrecht," Nomos-Verlag, 1989. *Member:* International Academy of Matrimonial Lawyers (IAML). *LANGUAGES:* German, English and French.

DR. FRIEDWALD LÜBBERT, born Westerkappeln/Westfalen, May 18, 1953; admitted, 1982, Bonn. *Education:* University of Bonn (Dr. jur., 1981). *Member:* Board of Directors, Bonn Lawyers' Association; State Board of Law Examiners, Northrhine-Westfalian Section.

HANNS W. FEIGEN, born Oberhausen, March 13, 1949; admitted, 1982, Bonn. *Education:* Universities of Heidelberg and Bonn. *LANGUAGES:* German and English.

DR. KAY ARTUR PAPE, born Wuppertal, February 7, 1950; admitted, 1983, Bonn (Fachanwalt für Verwaltungsrecht). *Education:* Universities of Bochum and Bonn (Dr. jur., 1984). *Member:* Lawyers' Administrative Law Committee, Northrhine Westfalian Section; Environmental Law Association; German-German Lawyers' Association.

DR. CHRISTIAN-DIETRICH BRACHER, born Berlin, September 22, 1954; admitted, 1982, Bonn (Fachanwalt für Verwaltungsrecht). *Education:* University of Bonn (Dr. jur., 1986). Author: "The Convention on Third Party Liability in the Field of Nuclear Energy (Paris Convention)," 1981; "Gefahrenabwehr durch Private," 1987. Co-Author, Frankfurter Kommen-

(This Listing Continued)

tar zum Gesetz gegen Wettbewerbsbeschränkungen, 3rd ed. 1993. *Member:* Federal Bar Association (Member, Constitutional Law Committee); German Lawyers' Association (Member, Administrative Law Committee). *LANGUAGES:* German, English and French.

DR. ANDREAS FRIESER, born Teublitz, June 20, 1957; admitted, 1984, Bonn. *Education:* University of Regensburg (Dr. jur., 1986). Author; "Der Bereicherungswegfall in Parallele zur hypothetischen Schadensentwicklung," (1987); "Guter Rat in Erbrechtsfragen," (Bd.1, 1992); "Was Tun im Erbfall," 1993. *Member:* Association for the Protection of Industrial Property Rights; Association for Inheritance Law; German-German Lawyers' Association. *LANGUAGES:* German and English.

DR. BURKHARD MESSERSCHMIDT, born Bad Schwartau, July 24, 1953; admitted, 1982, Münster; 1985, Bonn. *Education:* University of Hamburg (Dr. jur., 1986). Editor in Chief, "Handbuch der deutschen Rechtspraxis," Beck-Verlag, 1990. Co-Editor: "Rechtshandbuch Vermögen und Investitionen in der ehemaligen DDR," Beck-Verlag 1991; "Zeitschrift für Vermögen und Investitionen in den neuen Bundesländern," Zeitschrift Wirtschatsrechtliche Beratung. *Member:* German-German Lawyers' Association (Vice Chairman); German Society of Construction Law; German Association for the Protection of Industrial Property Rights.

DR. JÜRGEN LÜDERS, born Essen, January 2, 1955; admitted, 1983, Bonn (Fachanwalt für Steuerrecht; vereidigter Buchprüfer); registered as foreign lawyer in England and Wales. *Education:* Universities of Bonn and Speyer (Dr. jur., 1986). Author: "Der Zeitpunkt der Gewinnrealisierung im Handelsbilanz und Steuerbilanzrecht". *Member:* German-American Lawyers' Association; German Association of Tax Lawyers; German-British Jurists' Association. *LANGUAGES:* German and English.

THOMAS THIERAU, born Hagen, Westfalen, July 14, 1955; admitted, 1986, Köln; 1991, Bonn. *Education:* University of Bonn. *Member:* German Society of Construction Law; German-German Lawyers' Association. *LANGUAGES:* German and English.

DIETER MERKENS, born Heinsberg, October 27, 1960; admitted, 1989, Bonn. *Education:* University of Bonn. *Member:* German-German Lawyers' Association; Bonn Association of Politics and Law. *LANGUAGES:* German and English.

DR. THOMAS MAYEN, born Augsburg, December 16, 1957; admitted, 1991, Bonn. *Education:* Universities of Bonn and Cologne (Dr. jur., 1991). Author: "Der grundrechtliche Informationsanspruch des Forschers gegenüber dem Staat," (1992). *Member:* German Lawyers' Association (Member, Constitutional Law Committee); Environmental Law Association; German-Israeli Lawyers' Association. *LANGUAGES:* German and English.

DR. OLAF REIDT, born Gelsenkirchen, June 20, 1964; admitted, 1992, Bonn. *Education:* Universities of Bochum and München (Dr. iur., 1989). Author: "Rundfunkwerbung im lokalen Rundfunk," Nomos-Veslag, 1990. *Member:* German Lawyers' Association (Administrative Law Committee); Bonn Association of Politics and Law.

KLAUS WALPERT, born Hagen, March 26, 1956; admitted, 1991, Bonn. *Education:* University of Bonn. *Member:* German Association of Tax Lawyers. *LANGUAGES:* German and English.

DR. HEIKE GLAHS, born Dortmund, February 22, 1963; admitted, 1993, Bonn. *Education:* University of Bochum (Dr. jur., 1993). *LANGUAGES:* German and English.

Languages: German, English and French.

SCHMITZ KNOTH WUELLRICH MARQUARDT

Established in 1953

WILHELMSTRASSE 38
53111 BONN, GERMANY
Telephone: (0228) 98 509-0
Telefax: (0228) 98 509-33

Cologne, Germany Office: Bonner Strasse 327, 50968, Cologne. Telephone: (0221) 93 70 45-0; Telefax: (0221) 93 70 45-20.

General Practice, International Litigation and Arbitration. International Civil, Commercial, Corporate, Antitrust, Tax, Media, Computer and Technology Law. Unfair Competition. Industrial Property Rights. Labor Relations. White Collar Crime. Public Procurement and Government Contracts.

(This Listing Continued)

SCHMITZ KNOTH WUELLRICH MARQUARDT,
Bonn—Continued

Construction Law. International Joint Ventures. Transportation. Aviation and Aerospace.

MEMBERS OF FIRM

DR. KARL SCHMITZ, born Homécourt, France, 1917; admitted, 1953, Bonn. *Education:* Universities of Bonn, Mainz and Cologne (Dr. jur.). Author: "Staatsbürger und Staatsvolk," Cologne 1950. *Member:* German Association of Industrial Property and Copyright; Court of Honour Cologne Bar Association. *PRACTICE AREAS:* Commercial Law; Industrial Property Rights.

KARL HEINZ KNOTH, born Olbernhau, Germany, 1930; admitted, 1960, Bonn. *Education:* Academy of Wilhelmshaven and Universities of Cologne and Bonn. *Member:* German Association of Industrial Property and Copyright. *PRACTICE AREAS:* Family Law; Estates; Labor Relations.

DR. MICHAEL WUELLRICH, born Gelsenkirchen, Germany, 1946; admitted, 1975, Bonn. *Education:* Universities of Freiburg, Cologne and Bonn (Assistant, Dr. jur.). Author: "Das groupement d'intéret d'économique, ein Modell auf dem Weg zur europäischen Integration im Gesellschaftsrecht," Bonn 1975. *Member:* German Association of Industrial Property and Copyright; State Court of Honour, Nordrhein-Westfalen. *PRACTICE AREAS:* Commercial Law; Unfair Competition; Construction Law.

DR. NORBERT KNUEPPEL, born Dortmund, Germany, 1953; admitted, 1987, Bonn. *Education:* Banque Petrofigaz S.A., Paris; Universities of Berlin, Paris (Sorbonne) and Bonn (Assistant, Dr. jur.). Author: "Zwingendes materielles Recht und internationale Schuldverträge," Bonn 1988. *Member:* International Bar Association; American Bar Association; German Association of Industrial Property and Copyright. *PRACTICE AREAS:* Corporate Law; International Litigation and Arbitration; International Civil Law.

DR. CLAUS RECKTENWALD, born Bonn, Germany, 1959; admitted, 1990, Bonn. *Education:* Dresdner Bank AG, Cologne; Universities of Freiburg and Bonn (Dr. jur. - Antitrust Law); Bundeskartellamt Berlin; Law Offices Röhm International, P.C. (N.Y./N.Y.). *Member:* Bonn Lawyers' Association (Member, Board of Directors); German Association of Industrial Property and Copyright; German Association of Tax Lawyers. *PRACTICE AREAS:* Antitrust Law; Tax Law; Public Procurement and Government Contracts.

ASSOCIATES

NORBERT KNITTLMAYER, born Memmingen, Germany, 1964; admitted, 1994, Bonn. *Education:* Universities of Berlin, Bonn, Cologne; The Johns Hopkins University, School of Advanced International Studies, Bologna, Italy. Visiting Legal Specialist, Office of the General Counsel, National Aeronautics and Space Administration, Washington, D.C. Author: "Patentschutz bei Tätigkeiten im Weltraum," Recht der Internationalen Wirtschaft 1991, 823. *Member:* American and International Bar Associations; American Institute of Aeronautics and Astronautics (Associate); German American Lawyers Association; European Centre for Space Law. *PRACTICE AREAS:* International Joint Ventures; Transportation; Aviation and Aerospace.

All Members of Firm are Members of Cologne Bar and Cologne Lawyers Society.

Languages: German, English and French.

WENZEL & DR. SIEG'L

KURSTRASSE 62
14776 BRANDENBURG H, GERMANY
Telephone: 49 3381 224516
Fax: 49 3381 223778

New Address Effective July 1, 1995: Lindenstrasse 23, 14776 Brandenburg.

Commercial Law (including Corporation Trade, Unfair Competition and Labour), Contracts, Commercial Litigation and Arbitration, Real Estate, Construction, Medical and Family Law.

FIRM PROFILE: *The firm was established in 1991. It offers a full range of legal services in the commercial field. The firm is a member of the AdvoSelect EEIG, a European network of independent law firms being represented in 51 cities throughout Europe, pooling their resources in special fields and crossborder cases.*

(This Listing Continued)

MEMBERS OF FIRM

GEORG WENZEL, born Regensburg, Germany, August 7, 1960; admitted, 1991, Cologne. *Education:* University of Cologne. *Member:* German Bar Association (Commission for Family Law). *LANGUAGES:* German and English. *PRACTICE AREAS:* Commercial; Real Estate; Family and Medical Law.

DR. CHRISTIAN SIEG'L, born Cologne, Germany, March 24, 1959; admitted, 1991, Cologne. *Education:* University of Cologne (Dr. of Law, 1991). *Member:* German Bar Association (Commission for Construction Law). *LANGUAGES:* German and English. *PRACTICE AREAS:* Commercial and Construction Law; Communist Expropriation.

WOLLMANN & PARTNER

Established in 1920

NEUSTÄDTISCHE WASSERTORSTRAßE 13
14776 BRANDENBURG, GERMANY
Telephone: 0049 3381 52 770
Fax: 0049 3381 52 7777

Berlin, Germany Office: Kurfürstendamm 237, 10719. Telephone: 0049 884 10 90. Fax: 0049 884 10 930/39.
Potsdam, Germany Office: Dortustraße 73, 14467. Telephone: 0049 331 271970. Fax: 0049 331 2719755.

General Practice, Commercial, Corporate, Real Estate, Building and Planning, Construction, Mergers and Acquisitions, Joint Ventures, Investment, Insurance, Labor, Family, Housing, Estates, Restitution, Investment in East Germany and Eastern Europe, Trademark and Copyright, Unfair Competition, Litigation, Notary.

MARTIN CH. GROSSE, born Hanover, Germany, October 24, 1958; admitted, 1988, Berlin; 1995, Brandenburg, Brandenburgisches Oberlandesgericht. *Education:* Free University of Berlin (Dr. jur. 1990). Legal adviser Deutsche Interhotel GmbH, 1992-1994. *LANGUAGES:* German, English and Italian. *PRACTICE AREAS:* Litigation; Commercial Law; Corporate Law; Real Estate; Restitution Claims; Unfair Competition; Building and Planning.

STEUERBERATUNGS UND ANWALTSKANZLEI GEMMER & GEMMER

Established in 1988

MANNHEIMSTRASSE 14
D-38112 BRAUNSCHWEIG, GERMANY
Telephone: 49 (0) 531-311071
Fax: 49 (0) 531-311750

Magdeburg, Germany Office: Moritzplatz 6, D-39124. Telephone and Telefax: 49 (0) 391-5614056.
Wernigerode, Germany Office: Nöschenröder Straße 80 D-38855. Telephone and Telefax: 49 (0) 3943-23306.

FIRM PROFILE: *Member-office of the IASW-EWIV (Frankfurt/M.)*

East German consulting offices of tax advisor Traudel Gemmer:

TRAUDEL GEMMER, born 1949. Tax advisor since 1975, Managing Partner of the Gemmer & Gemmer, Treuhand-, Wirtschaftsberatungs-, Steuerberatungsgesellschaft mbH in Magdeburg. *Member:* Board of the Chamber of Tax advisors in the Lower Saxony, 1983—; Board of the Tax Advisors' Association in Braunschweig, 1984—. *LANGUAGES:* German and English. *PRACTICE AREAS:* Commercial Tax; Fiscal Law; Tax Planning.

JÜRGEN GEMMER, born 1954; admitted, 1985. *Education:* University of Giessen. Managing Partner of the Treuhand-, Wirtschaftsberatungs-, Steuerberatungsgesellschaft in Magdeburg. President of the MIT (Medium-sized Firms' Association) of the East German Saxony-Anhalt. *LANGUAGES:* German and English. *PRACTICE AREAS:* Company Commercial Law; Commercial Crime; Fiscal Law.

AHLERS & VOGEL

CONTRESCARPE 21
28203 BREMEN, GERMANY
Telephone: +49 421 33340
Cable Address: "Klient"
Telex: 245301 legal d
Telefax: +49 421 3334111

Mailing Address: P.O. Box 103527, D-28035

Hamburg, Germany Office: (Dr. Holtappels, H. Sager, A.v. Knobelsdorff) Schaartor 1, D-20459. Telephone: +49 40 371075. Fax: +49 40 371092.

Rostock, Germany Office: (S. Hischer, W. Dierks, B. Rinck) Wielandstrasse 7, D-18055. Telephone: +49 381 455892. Fax: +49 381 455879.

General Practice. Taxation, Commercial, Company and Corporation, Bankruptcy, Public Administration, Labor, Traffic, Construction and Real Estate, Shipping and Admiralty Law, Unfair Competition Law.

MEMBERS OF FIRM

DR. DIETER AHLERS, born Bremen, September 1, 1921; admitted, 1950, Bremen. Notary Public. *Education:* University of Hamburg (Doctor of Jurisprudence, 1948). *Member:* American Arbitration Association. *LANGUAGES:* German. *PRACTICE AREAS:* Company Law; Commercial Law; Inheritance Law.

DR. HELLMUT VOGEL, born Marburg, September 20, 1919; admitted, 1951, Bremen. Notary Public. *Education:* Universities of Munich and Frankfurt (Doctor of Jurisprudence, 1948). *Member:* Maritime Law Association; International Lawyers Association. *LANGUAGES:* German and English. *PRACTICE AREAS:* Commercial Law; Bankruptcy Law.

VOLKMAR SCHOTTELIUS, born Bremen, March 22, 1925; admitted, 1954, Bremen. Notary Public. *Education:* Universities of Kiel and Hamburg; University of Chicago Law School. *LANGUAGES:* German and English. *PRACTICE AREAS:* Public Administration Law; Labor Law.

DR. HANS URBAN BULLING, born Bremen, March 1, 1935; admitted, 1964, Bremen. Notary Public. *Education:* Universities of Tübingen, Berlin and Munich (Doctor of Jurisprudence); London School of Economics and Political Science. *LANGUAGES:* German and English. *PRACTICE AREAS:* Taxation Law; Inheritance Law; Civil Law.

DR. PETER HOLTAPPELS, born Hamburg, July 13, 1935; admitted, 1989, Bremen; 1992, Hamburg. *Education:* Universities of Munich and Hamburg (Doctor of Jurisprudence, 1965). *Member:* Maritime Law Association; German Maritime Arbitration Association (Chairman). *LANGUAGES:* German, English and French. *PRACTICE AREAS:* Shipping Law; Admiralty Law; Commercial Law.

HEIKO GOTTWALD, born Fürstenwalde, February 18, 1937; admitted, 1971, Bremen. Notary Public. *Education:* Universities of Berlin and Bonn. *Member:* Maritime Law Association; German Maritime Arbitration Association; German Society of Construction Law. *LANGUAGES:* German and English. *PRACTICE AREAS:* Construction Law; Admiralty Law.

DR. GERD JUSTUS ALBRECHT, born Heppenheim, January 31, 1940; admitted, 1969, Bremen. Notary Public. *Education:* Universities of Cologne, Munich and Kiel (Doctor of Jurisprudence). Member, CCBE - Council of the Bars and Law Societies of the European Community, 1980-1987. *Member:* Maritime Law Association; American Arbitration Association. *LANGUAGES:* German, English, French and Italian. *PRACTICE AREAS:* Civil Law; Commercial Law; Shipping Law; Transport Law.

WALTER BEHRENS, born Bremen, November 19, 1951; admitted, 1980, Bremen. Notary Public. *Education:* University of Hamburg. *LANGUAGES:* German and English. *PRACTICE AREAS:* Family Law; Inheritance Law.

DR. RÜDIGER LEYKAM, born November 5, 1952; admitted, 1981, Bremen. Notary Public. *Education:* University of Freiburg (Doctor of Jurisprudence). *LANGUAGES:* German and English. *PRACTICE AREAS:* Taxation; Banking; Company Law; Commercial Law.

DR. GERHARD LOHFELD, born Sulingen, April 2, 1953; admitted, 1982, Bremen. *Education:* University of Hamburg College of Agriculture (Graduate Engineer of Agriculture); University of Hamburg (Doctor of Jurisprudence, 1990). *LANGUAGES:* German. *PRACTICE AREAS:* Labor Law; Public Administration Law.

(This Listing Continued)

BURKHARD KLÜVER, born Bremen, July 24, 1955; admitted, 1986, Bremem. Notary Public. *Education:* University of Kiel. *Member:* Maritime Law Association; German Society of Transport Law. *LANGUAGES:* German and English. *PRACTICE AREAS:* Company Law; Commercial Law; Shipping Law; Admiralty Law; Transport Law.

WOLFGANG DIERKS, born Stuttgart, May 22, 1953; admitted, 1989, Bremen; 1993, Rostock. *Education:* Universities of Erlangen and Berlin. *LANGUAGES:* German, English, French and Spanish. *PRACTICE AREAS:* Shipping Law; Admiralty Law; Transport Law.

SUSANA HISCHER, born Hamburg, August 31, 1956; admitted, 1985, Hamburg; 1990, Rostock. *Education:* Universities Hamburg and Bonn. *LANGUAGES:* German and English. *PRACTICE AREAS:* Commercial Law; Construction Law; Unfair Competition Law.

DR. JAN-MARTIN ZIMMERMANN, born Bremen, April 26, 1961; admitted, 1992, Bremen. *Education:* University of Kiel (Doctor of Jurisprudence, 1990). *LANGUAGES:* German and English. *PRACTICE AREAS:* Construction Law; Company Law; Taxation Law.

ASSOCIATES

ANTJE THOMAS, born Bremen, March 17, 1963; admitted, 1992, Bremen. *Education:* Universities of Regensburg and Goettingen. *LANGUAGES:* German and English. *PRACTICE AREAS:* Civil Law; Rent Law; Lease Law.

DR. RALPH MEYER IM HAGEN, born Bremen, May 18, 1960; admitted, 1994, Bremen. *Education:* University of Kiel (Doctor of Jurisprudence). *LANGUAGES:* German and English. *PRACTICE AREAS:* Civil Law; Commercial Law; Unfair Competition Law.

HERBERT STAPPERT-ENGLERT, born Soergeloch, October 12, 1953; admitted, 1994, Bremen. *Education:* University of Bremen. *LANGUAGES:* German. *PRACTICE AREAS:* Real Estate; Probate; Company Law.

BETTINA RINCK, born Hamburg, February 26, 1958; admitted, 1993, Rostock. *Education:* University of Hamburg. *LANGUAGES:* German and English. *PRACTICE AREAS:* Commercial Law; Civil Law.

HARTMUTH SAGER, born Hamburg, July 27, 1964; admitted, 1993, Bremen; 1994, Hamburg. *Education:* Universities of Hamburg, Lausanne (Switzerland), Bonn and Berlin. *LANGUAGES:* German, English and French. *PRACTICE AREAS:* Labor Law.

ARIANE D. VON KNOBELSDORFF, born Hamburg, March 4, 1964; admitted, 1993, Hamburg. *Education:* Universities of Hamburg and London (England). *LANGUAGES:* German and English. *PRACTICE AREAS:* International Civil Law; International Commercial Law; Company Law; Taxation Law.

BLAUM, DETTMERS, RABSTEIN

AM WALL 153-156
D-28195 BREMEN, GERMANY
Telephone: 421/366010
Telex: 244030 delaw d
Cable Address: Elfad Bremen
Telecopier: 421 36 60 151

Mailing Address: P.O. Box 10 64 40, Bremen, D-28064

Maritime, Admiralty, Transport, Commercial, Company, Corporation, Tax, Unfair Competition, Insurance, Bank and Administration Law. General Practice, EEC Law, Real Estate. Notary's Office.

FIRM PROFILE: The firm was established more than 100 years ago and covers all areas of commercial law with special emphasis on company and corporate law, maritime, transportation and insurance law. It offers a full range of legal service including that of Notaries Public.

MEMBERS OF FIRM

DR. OTTO DETTMERS (1892-1986).

*DR. DR. RUDOLF BLAUM, born Bremen, Germany, March 14, 1915; admitted, 1948, Bremen. *Education:* Heidelberg, Munchen, Hamburg and Berlin (Doctor of Laws; Doctor of Philosophy). Chartered Expert of Tax Law. *Member:* Bremen Bar and German Lawyers Society; International Bar Association. *LANGUAGES:* German, English, French, Spanish and Portuguese. *PRACTICE AREAS:* Company; Tax.

*EDZARD DETTMERS, born Bremen, Germany, August 13, 1929; admitted, 1958, Bremen. *Education:* Marburg, Innsbruck and Hamburg.

(This Listing Continued)

BLAUM, DETTMERS, RABSTEIN, Bremen—Continued

Member: Bremen Bar and German Lawyers Society; German International Maritime Law Association; International Bar Association. *LANGUAGES:* German and English. *PRACTICE AREAS:* Maritime; Company; Environment; Insurance.

*DR. KLAUS RABSTEIN, born Gumbinnen, Germany, December 12, 1940; admitted, 1968, Bremen. *Education:* Kiel and Saarbrücken (Doctor of Laws). *Member:* Bremen Bar and German Lawyers Society. *LANGUAGES:* German and English. *PRACTICE AREAS:* Company; Bank; Unfair Competition.

*DR. LUTZ WEIPERT, born Hamburg, Germany, July 19, 1938; admitted, 1972, Bremen. *Education:* Hamburg and Bonn (Doctor of Laws). Chartered Expert of Tax Law. *Member:* Bremen Bar and German Lawyers Society; German International Maritime Law Association. *LANGUAGES:* German and English. *PRACTICE AREAS:* Company; Tax; Maritime; Arbitration.

*DR. FRIEDRICH STRUBE, born Bremen, Germany, January 10, 1942; admitted, 1971, Bremen. *Education:* Tübingen and Berlin (Doctor of Laws). *Member:* Bremen Bar and German Lawyers Society; German International Maritime Law Association; International Bar Association. *LANGUAGES:* German, English, French and Spanish. *PRACTICE AREAS:* Maritime; Transport; Insurance; Arbitration.

*DR. JOACHIM F. BARTELS, born Hamburg, Germany, August 2, 1942; admitted, 1971, Hamburg; 1977, Bremen. *Education:* Hamburg (Doctor of Laws). *Member:* Bremen Bar and German Lawyers Society; German International Maritime Law Association; International Bar Association; Supporting Member, LMAA, London. *LANGUAGES:* German, English and French. *PRACTICE AREAS:* Maritime; Transport; Insurance; Arbitration.

*DR. EBERHARD LOHMANN, born Bremen, Germany, July 26, 1949; admitted, 1977, Kleve; 1978, Bremen. *Education:* Munster (Doctor of Laws). *Member:* Bremen Bar and German Lawyers Society. *LANGUAGES:* German and English. *PRACTICE AREAS:* Labour; Co-Determination; Intellectual Property.

DR. FRIEDRICH-MARTIN HOHRMANN, born Bremen, Germany, April 17, 1953; admitted, 1982, Bremen. *Education:* Münster (Doctor of Laws). *Member:* Bremen Bar and German Lawyers Society. *LANGUAGES:* German, English and Spanish. *PRACTICE AREAS:* Company; EC Law; Law of Succession.

ASSOCIATES

HARTWIN HEITMANN, born Brilon Wald, Germany, September 7, 1954; admitted, 1985, Bremen. *LANGUAGES:* German and English. *PRACTICE AREAS:* Transportation; Commercial Law.

THOMAS ADLER, born Wolfenbüttel, Germany, January 17, 1958; admitted, 1987, Bremen. *LANGUAGES:* German. *PRACTICE AREAS:* Labour; Commercial Law.

CLAUS HOLZHÜTER, born April 16, 1959; admitted, 1993, Bremen. *LANGUAGES:* German and English. *PRACTICE AREAS:* Maritime; Transportation; Commercial Law.

THOMAS BEHRENS, born August 6, 1964; admitted, 1993, Bremen. *LANGUAGES:* German and English. *PRACTICE AREAS:* Unfair Competition; Intellectual Property; Trademarks.

*Also Notary Public

Languages: German, English, French, Spanish and Portuguese.

BÜSING, MÜFFELMANN & THEYE

Established in 1961

MARKTSTRASSE 3, BÖRSENHOF C
28195 BREMEN, GERMANY
Telephone: (0421) 36600-0
Telex: 2 45 551 advo
Telecopier: (0421) 36600-366

Frankfurt/Main, Germany Office: Freiherr-vom-Stein-Strasse 11, 60323 Frankfurt/Main. Telephone: (069) 17 23 24 - 26. Telecopier: (069) 725958.

Firm engaged in Corporate, Tax, Commercial, Mergers and Acquisitions, Media and Entertainment Law, EEC and International Law, Antitrust, Industrial and Intellectual Property Rights, Unfair Competition, Advertis-

(This Listing Continued)

ing, Admiralty and Maritime, Arbitration, Transportation, Real Estate, Litigation, General Practice, Notary's Office.

MEMBERS OF FIRM

ARTHUR BÜSING, born Bremen, Germany, February 14, 1928; admitted, 1954, Germany. *Education:* University of Mainz. Notary Public, Chartered Expert in Tax Law. *Member:* Bremen Bar Association; Society of Bremen Lawyers; Institute of the Chartered Experts of Tax Law in Germany. *LANGUAGES:* German and English.

DR. HERBERT MÜFFELMANN, born Bremen, Germany, September 24, 1934; admitted, 1965, Germany. *Education:* Universities of Hamburg (Dr. jur., 1965), Göttingen and Marburg. Notary Public. Chartered Expert in Tax Law. Deputy Member of the Court of Constitution of the State of Bremen. *Member:* Bremen Bar Association; Society of Bremen Lawyers; Institute of the Chartered Experts of Tax Law in Germany. *LANGUAGES:* German and English.

DR. JOACHIM THEYE, born Bremen, Germany, April 5, 1940; admitted, 1969, Germany. *Education:* Universities of Munich, Berlin and Hamburg (Dr. jur., 1968). Notary Public. Chartered Expert in Tax Law. *Member:* Bremen Bar Association, Bremen; Society of Bremen Lawyers; Institute of the Chartered Experts of Tax Law in Germany. *LANGUAGES:* German and English.

GERHARD SCHUMANN, born Chemnitz, Germany, December 23, 1927; admitted, 1965, Germany. *Education:* Universities of Berlin and Münster. Notary Public. *Member:* Bremen Bar Association; Society of Bremen Lawyers. *LANGUAGES:* German and English.

DR. JÜRGEN FRISINGER, M.C.L., born Köln, Germany, January 8, 1940; admitted, 1972, Germany. *Education:* Universities of Freiburg and Hamburg (Dr. jur., 1967); practical legal education in Paris, French Law Firm, 1966; State University of Illinois, U.S.A. (M.C.L., 1971). Notary Public. *Member:* Bremen and International Bar Associations; Society of Bremen Lawyers; Industrial and Copyright Association; Comparative Law Association. *LANGUAGES:* German, English and French.

DR. HANS-RÜDIGER HINTZE, born Bitterfeld, Germany, February 2, 1944; admitted, 1974, Germany. *Education:* University of Göttingen (Dr. jur., 1973). Chartered Expert in Tax Law. Notary Public. *Member:* Bremen Bar Association; Bremen Society of Lawyers; Institute of the Chartered Experts of Tax Law in Germany. *LANGUAGES:* German and English.

JÖRG ZIMMER, born Hamburg, Germany, December 22, 1945; admitted, 1975, Germany. *Education:* Universities of Tübingen and Hamburg. Notary Public. *Member:* Bremen and International Bar Associations; Society of Bremen Lawyers; Industrial and Copyright Association. *LANGUAGES:* German and English.

CONSTANTIN FRICK, born Bremen, Germany, June 11, 1946; admitted, 1976, Germany. *Education:* Universities of Lausanne and Freiburg i.Br. Notary Public. *Member:* Bremen and International Bar Associations; Bremen Society of Lawyers. *LANGUAGES:* German, English and French.

DIETRICH GORNY, born Schneidemühl, Pomerania, August 11, 1937; admitted, 1969, Germany. *Education:* Universities of Berlin, Freiburg and Hamburg. *Member:* Frankfurt Bar Association; Society of Frankfurt Lawyers; European Food Law Association (Council); International Association for the Protection of Industrial Property; Federation for Food Law and Food Science; Scientific Society for Food Law. (Resident Partner, Frankfurt Office). *LANGUAGES:* German, English, French and Italian.

HEINZ-WERNER EHLGEN, born Hachenburg, Germany, April 13, 1950; admitted, 1981, Germany. *Education:* University of Frankfurt. *Member:* Frankfurt Bar Association; Society of Frankfurt Lawyers. (Resident Partner, Frankfurt Office). *LANGUAGES:* German and English.

DR. MONIKA BECKMANN-PETEY, born Köln, Germany, December 2, 1958; admitted, 1988, Germany. *Education:* Universities of Köln, Clermont-Ferrand (France) and Belgrade (Dr.jur., 1989). *Member:* Breman Bar Association; Bremen Society of Lawyers; German-Brazilian Law Association; German Association for East-European Studies. *LANGUAGES:* German, English, French, Portuguese, Italian, Serbo-Croatian and Russian.

DIETER JANßEN, born Bremen, Germany, January 4, 1958; admitted, 1988, Germany. *Education:* Universities of Gießen and Münster. *Member:* Bremen Bar Association; Society of Bremen Lawyers; German Society for Transportation Law (Deutsch Gesellschaft für Transportrecht). *LANGUAGES:* German and English.

DR. SIEGFRIED EDEN, born Abbehausen, Germany, April 27, 1949; admitted, 1980, Germany. *Education:* University of Hamburg (Dr.rer.pol.,

(This Listing Continued)

1981). Chartered Accountant. *Member:* Bremen Bar Association; Society of Bremen Lawyers; Institut der Wirtschaftsprüfer (IDW). *LANGUAGES:* German and English.

ASSOCIATES

Hermann Ströver	Dr. Christian Jacobs
Reinhard Schneider	Jochen Kaufmann (Resident Associate, Frankfurt Office)

HORN, VOIGT & PARTNER

Established in 1969

WACHTSTRASSE 17
D-28195 BREMEN, GERMANY
Telephone: (0421) 36 60 60
Telefax: (0421) 36 60 6-30

Mailing Address: P.O. Box 10 06 03, 28006 Bremen, Germany

General German and International Practice, Commercial, Bankruptcy, Corporate, Tax, Labor, Banking, Litigation, Arbitration, Real Estate, Notaries.

MEMBERS OF FIRM

DR. ADOLF J. HORN, born Germany, 1942; admitted, 1969, Germany; 1971, as Chartered Expert in Tax Law; 1977, Notary Public. *Education:* Universities of Hamburg, Freiburg, Lausanne (Switzerland) and Cologne (Dr. jur., 1968). Member, German Committee of Bankruptcy Law (Fachkreis für Insolvenzrecht). *LANGUAGES:* German, English and Spanish. *PRACTICE AREAS:* Tax; Banking; Mergers and Acquisition; Bankruptcy.

DR. AREND VOIGT, born Germany, 1947; admitted, 1975, Germany; 1984, as Chartered Expert in Tax Law; 1985, Notary Public. *Education:* Universities of Freiburg, Hamburg, Kiel (Dr. jur., 1976). *Member:* German Committee of Bankruptcy Law (Fachkreis Für Insolvenzrecht). *LANGUAGES:* German and English. *PRACTICE AREAS:* Bankruptcy.

HANS-CHRISTOPH NEUMANN, born Germany, 1951; admitted, 1979, Germany; 1989, Notary Public. *Education:* University of Tübingen. *LANGUAGES:* German and English. *PRACTICE AREAS:* Real Estate; Litigation; Arbitration; Commercial.

DR. KARL GÖBEL, born Germany, 1951; admitted, 1981, Germany; 1991, Notary Public. *Education:* University of Bremen (Dr. jur., 1980). Author: "Prozesszweck der AGB-Klage und Herkömmlicher Zivilprozeβ," Königstein/Ts. (Purpose of Legal Action in the German Law Governing Standard Business Conditions). *Member:* German Committee of Bankruptcy Law (Fachkreis für Insolvenzrecht). *LANGUAGES:* German and English. *PRACTICE AREAS:* Labor; Corporate; Banking; Bankruptcy.

RÜDIGER THOLEN, born Germany, 1952; admitted, 1992, Germany. *Education:* University of Bremen. *LANGUAGES:* German, French and English.

All Members of the Firm are Members of the Bremen Bar Association and Lawyers Society.

KRAFT RASCH & PARTNER

KURFÜRSTENALLEE 4
28211 BREMEN 1, GERMANY
Telephone: (0421) 32 52 25; 3 49 12 36
Telefax: (0421) 3 49 12 38

Rostock, Germany Office: Saarplatz, 18057. Telephone: (0381) 45 93 422. Telefax: (0381) 45 93 422.

General Practice, Litigation, Commercial, Corporate, Tax, Acquisitions, Mergers and Entertainment Law, Unfair Competition, Insurance, Arbitration, Transportation, Advertising, Real Estate, EEC and International Law, Industrial and Intellectual Property Rights.

MEMBERS OF FIRM

THOMAS H. KRAFT, born Heidelberg, Germany, July 1, 1952; admitted, 1979, Germany. *Education:* Universities of Heidelberg and Göttingen. *Member:* Mecklenburg-Vorpommern Bar Association and Lawyers Society. *LANGUAGES:* German, English and French.

(This Listing Continued)

WULFHARDT J. RASCH, born Bremen, Germany, February 18, 1930; admitted, 1960, Germany. *Education:* University of Kiel. Notary Public. *Member:* Bremen Bar Association and Lawyers Society.

DR. SCHACKOW & PARTNER

DOMSHOF 17
28195 BREMEN 1, GERMANY
Telephone: (0421) 36990
Cable Address: "Doctores"
Telex: 174 212 248; 244412 dres d
Teletex: 4212248
Telecopier: (0421) 3699144

Rostock, Germany Office: Strandstrasse 25, 18055. Telephone: (0381) 49 23440; 49 23750. Telecopier: (0381) 49 23262. Telex: 398145 dresrd.

Maritime, Company, Tax, Commercial, Transport, Aviation, Bank, Unfair Competition, Labor, EEC Law. Real Estate and General Practice. Notaries.

MEMBERS OF FIRM

DR. ALBRECHT SCHACKOW, born Bremen, Germany, October 19, 1907; admitted, 1934, Bremen. Notary Public. *Education:* Universities of Freiburg, Munich and Goettingen (Dr. jur.). Chairman, Advisory Board of Deutsche Schiffahrtsbank AG, Minverva Versicherungs-AG, Sloman Neptun Schiffahrts-AG. *Member:* Bremen Bar Association. *LANGUAGES:* German and English. *PRACTICE AREAS:* Company Law; Bank Law.

DR. GÜNTER KOEHLER, born Ritterhude, Germany, December 14, 1927; admitted, 1957, Bremen. Notary Public. *Education:* Universities of Kiel and Freiburg (Dr. jur.). *Member:* Bremen Bar Association. *LANGUAGES:* German and English. *PRACTICE AREAS:* Maritime Law; Company Law; Commercial Law; Bank Law.

DR. RALPH HARNISCH, born Bremen, Germany, December 18, 1931; admitted, 1961, Bremen. Notary Public. *Education:* University of Hamburg (1st State Examination, 1957; 2nd State Examination, 1961; Doctor Degree, 1963). Legal Teacher in Deutsche Aussenhandels und Verkehrsschule in Bremen. *Member:* Bremen Bar Association. *LANGUAGES:* German and English. *PRACTICE AREAS:* Maritime Law; Company Law; Commercial Law; Transport Law.

DR. HANS-EDGAR SCHUETTE, born Koethen/Anhalt, Germany, November 5, 1942; admitted, 1972, Bremen. Notary Public. *Education:* Universities of Berlin, Freiburg, Munich (1st State Examination, 1968), Regensburg (Doctor Degree, 1969) and Hamburg (2nd State Examination, 1972). *Member:* Bremen Bar Association. *LANGUAGES:* German, English and French. *PRACTICE AREAS:* Company Law; Commercial Law; Real Estate; General Practice.

REINHARD SCHALE, born Brandenburg, Germany, July 2, 1941; admitted, 1973, Bremen. Notary Public. *Education:* Universities of Berlin, Freiburg and Cologne (State Examinations). *Member:* Bremen Bar Association. *LANGUAGES:* German and English. *PRACTICE AREAS:* Maritime Law; Commercial Law; Transport Law.

JÜRGEN BREITHAUPT, born Delmenhorst, Germany, January 14, 1945; admitted, 1974, Bremen. Notary Public. *Education:* Hamburg University (Civil-Service Examinations of Law). *Member:* Bremen Bar Association. *LANGUAGES:* German and English. *PRACTICE AREAS:* Company Law; Commercial Law; Transport Law; Aviation; Real Estate.

DR. HANS-GEORG FRIEDRICHS, born Hannover, Germany, December 17, 1949; admitted, 1979, Bremen. Notary Public. *Education:* University of Göttingen (1st State Examination, 1977; 2nd State Examination, 1979; Doctor Degree, 1980). *Member:* Bremen Bar Association. *LANGUAGES:* German and English. *PRACTICE AREAS:* Company Law; Commercial Law; Labor Law.

DR. JULIUS DRUMM, born Neunkirchen, Germany, November 23, 1954; admitted, 1985, Bremen. *Education:* Nautical College Bremen (B.Sc. in Nautical Science, Diplom Nautiker and master mariner foreign going (AG) 1979); University of Bremen (State Examination 1985, Doctor Degree, 1986). *Member:* Bremen Bar Association. *LANGUAGES:* German and English. *PRACTICE AREAS:* Maritime Law; Commercial Law; Transport Law.

DR. DETLEV GROSS, LL.M., born Bremen, Germany, June 11, 1957; admitted, 1987, Bremen. *Education:* Universities of Erlangen and Paris I (Sorbonne); London School of Economics and Political Science, Göttingen (1st State Examination, 1983; Doctor Juris, 1987); Institution of Higher

(This Listing Continued)

DR. SCHACKOW & PARTNER, Bremen—Continued

Education for Administrative Sciences, Speyer (2nd State Examination, 1987); University of Cambridge (Master of Laws, 1988). *Member:* British German Lawyer's Association; Bremen Bar Association. *LANGUAGES:* German, English and French. *PRACTICE AREAS:* Company Law; Commercial Law; International Law; EEC Law.

DR. THOMAS BRINKMANN, LL.M., born Lueneburg, Germany, August 28, 1957; admitted, 1989, Bremen. *Education:* Universities of Munich and Hamburg (1st State Examination, 1983; 2nd State Examination, 1988; Doctor Degree, 1991); Tulane Law School, New Orleans (LL.M., Admiralty, 1988. *Member:* Bremen Bar Association. *LANGUAGES:* German and English. *PRACTICE AREAS:* Maritime Law; Commercial Law; Transport Law; Unfair Competition.

ASSOCIATES

DR. GERHARD LIENING, born Bremen, Germany, July 18, 1962; admitted, 1989, Lüneburg. *Education:* University of Passau (first state examination, 1986, second state examination, 1989, Doctor degree, 1992). *Member:* Bremen Bar Association; European Lawyers Association (Brussels). *LANGUAGES:* German and English. *PRACTICE AREAS:* Company Law; Commercial Law; Tax Law; Administrative Law.

DR. v. EINEM & PARTNER

SCHLACHTE 3-5
28195 BREMEN, GERMANY
Telephone: 49/421/36 50 50
Fax: 49/421/32 46 15; 32 55 67

FIRM PROFILE: Established in 1924, Dr. v. Einem & Partner is a law firm in Bremen with 10 partners and 5 associates. The members of the firm are specializing in commercial and corporate law as well as in real estate, mergers and acquisitions, tax, banking, unfair competition, industrial property, labour, family and international private law. General Practice. Notary's Office.

In addition, the firm has close cooperation partners in the Netherlands (Vos, Seidel & Plas, Groningen) and in Spain (Espada Gerlach, Barcelona).

MEMBERS OF FIRM

DR. FRIEDRICH-WILHELM V. EINEM, born Dresden, Germany, November 22, 1920; admitted, 1951, Germany. *Education:* Universities of Munich and Göttingen (Doctor of Jurisprudence, 1953). Notary Public. *Member:* Bremen Bar Association; German Lawyers Society. *LANGUAGES:* German and English.

KLAUS-PETER DUCHROW, born Halle/Saale, Germany, December 3, 1929; admitted, 1960, Germany. *Education:* University of Göttingen. Notary Public. Chartered Expert in Tax Law. *Member:* Bremen Bar Association; German Lawyers Society. *LANGUAGES:* German and English. *PRACTICE AREAS:* Taxation; Real Estate; Successions.

DR. HANS-JÜRGEN NÖLLE, born Bremen, Germany, January 12, 1934; admitted, 1962, Germany. *Education:* Universities of Tübingen and Hamburg (Doctor of Jurisprudence, 1959). Notary Public. Member, Board of Bremen Stock Exchange. Director, German Association for the Protection of Property, Bremen District. *Member:* Bremen Bar Association; German Lawyers Society. *LANGUAGES:* German. *PRACTICE AREAS:* Business Law; Successions; Family Law; Administrative Law.

HANS-GEORG SCHOTTE, born Bremen, Germany, July 15, 1939; admitted, 1969, Germany. *Education:* Universities of Marburg and Munich. Notary Public. *Member:* Bremen Bar Association; German Lawyers Society. *LANGUAGES:* German and English. *PRACTICE AREAS:* Business Law; Successions.

DR. KLAUS EISSING, born Wilhelmshaven, Germany, June 22, 1938; admitted, 1969, Germany. *Education:* Universities of Freiburg, Munich, Münster and Kiel (Doctor of Jurisprudence, 1967). Notary Public. *Member:* Bremen Bar Association; German Lawyers Society; German Dutch Lawyers Conference. *LANGUAGES:* German, Dutch and English. *PRACTICE AREAS:* Commercial Law; Business Law; Successions; International Private Law.

HANFRIED BOEHNCKE, born Ostercappeln, Germany, November 16, 1939; admitted, 1969, Germany. *Education:* Universities of Göttingen and Munich. Notary Public. *Member:* Bremen Bar Association; German

(This Listing Continued)

Lawyers Society. *LANGUAGES:* German and English. *PRACTICE AREAS:* Family Law; Successions; Real Estate.

HANS MÖLLER, born Walsrode, Germany, January 13, 1947; admitted, 1974, Germany. *Education:* University of Kiel. Notary Public. *Member:* Bremen Bar Association; German Lawyers Society. *LANGUAGES:* German and English. *PRACTICE AREAS:* Business Law; Construction Law.

DR. BURKARD PLENGE, born Sulingen, Germany, February 12, 1944; admitted, 1975, Germany. *Education:* Universities of Göttingen, Lausanne (Switzerland), Münster and Kiel (Doctor of Jurisprudence, 1975). Notary Public. *Member:* Bremen Bar Association; German Lawyers Society. *LANGUAGES:* German and English. *PRACTICE AREAS:* Business Law; Commercial Law; Real Estate; International Private Law.

DR. JOACHIM V. EINEM, born Bremen, Germany, June 4, 1947; admitted, 1977, Germany. *Education:* Universities of Freiburg and Göttingen (Doctor of Jurisprudence, 1978). Notary Public. Director of Arbeitsgemeinschaft Industrie Bremen-Nord. Chartered Expert in Tax Law, 1980. Accountant with Arthur Andersen & Co., 1977-1979. Attorney, O'Melveny & Myers, Los Angeles, California, 1979. *Member:* Bremen Bar Association; German Lawyers Society; German American Law Association; German Association of Chartered Experts in Tax Law. *LANGUAGES:* German and English. *PRACTICE AREAS:* Business Law; Taxation; Real Estate; International Private Law.

DR. CHRISTOPH FÖRSTER, born Bremen, Germany, June 4, 1956; admitted, 1985, Germany. *Education:* University of Münster (Doctor of Jurisprudence, 1985). Expert in Labour Law. Notary Public. *Member:* Bremen Bar Association (Board Member); German Lawyers Society. *LANGUAGES:* German and English. *PRACTICE AREAS:* Labour Law; Commercial Law; Business Law.

ASSOCIATES

DR. LAMBERT GROSSKOPF, born Bremen, Germany, March 1, 1954; admitted, 1991, Germany. *Education:* University of Bremen (Doctor of Jurisprudence, 1993). Managing Director, HiFly South Africa Ltd., Cape Town, 1983. *Member:* Bremen Bar Association; German Lawyers Society. *LANGUAGES:* German and English. *PRACTICE AREAS:* Commercial Law; Communications and Media; Common Market Law.

DR. THOMAS RINNE, born Nienburg, Germany, March 17, 1960; admitted, 1991, Germany. *Education:* Universities of Würzburg, Lausanne (Switzerland) and Freiburg (Doctor of Jurisprudence, 1992). *Member:* Bremen Bar Association; German Lawyers Society; German Spanish Lawyers Conference. *LANGUAGES:* German, English, French, Spanish. *PRACTICE AREAS:* Commercial Law; Taxation; International Private Law.

JÖRG JARCHOW, born Bremen, Germany, January 1, 1959; admitted, 1992, Germany. *Education:* University of Kiel. *Member:* Bremen Bar Association; German Lawyers Society. *LANGUAGES:* German and English. *PRACTICE AREAS:* Taxation; Civil Law.

FRANK WITTE, born Bremen, Germany, May 13, 1962; admitted, 1993, Germany. *Education:* Universities of Passau and Kiel. *Member:* Bremen Bar Association; German Lawyers Society. *LANGUAGES:* German and English. *PRACTICE AREAS:* Taxation; Commercial Law; Civil Law.

DR. TORSTEN KÖHNE, born Bremerhaven, Germany, January 21, 1964; admitted, 1994, Germany. *Education:* Universities of Osnabrück (Doctor of Jurisprudence, 1993) and Leyden (The Netherlands). *Member:* Bremen Bar Association; German Lawyers Society; Canadian German Lawyers Association. *LANGUAGES:* German and English. *PRACTICE AREAS:* Administrative; Environmental and European Law.

BENDER ZAHN TIGGES

STRAße DER NATIONEN 37
09111 CHEMNITZ, GERMANY
Telephone: (0371) 428946/47
Telefax: (0371) 428949

Düsseldorf, Germany Office: Thyssen-Haus, August-Thyssen-Straße 1, 40211. Telephone: 0211/86 87-0. Telex: 8 588 246 bend. Telefax: 0211/86 87-100.

Berlin, Germany Office: Kurfurstendamm 170, 10707 Berlin. Telephone: (0 30) 883 23 98/99. Telefax: (0 30) 8 82 45 52.

Warsaw, Poland Office: ul.Piekna 66a, 00-072 Warsaw. Telephone: (00482) 628-02-11. Fax: (00482) 628-47-66.

(This Listing Continued)

General and International Practice, Corporate and Securities, Banking, Commercial, Bankruptcy, Insolvency and Reorganization, Taxation, Real Estate, Antitrust, Intellectual Property, Environmental and Administrative, Insurance, Litigation, International Trusts, Family and Inheritance Law. Privatization in the former German Democratic Republic. Restitution Claims in the former German Democratic Republic. Commercial and Business Law in Poland.

MEMBERS - CHEMNITZ

GERD TIEGELKAMP, born Haan, Germany; admitted, 1981, Germany. *Education:* Cologne University. *Member:* Society for the Legal Protection of Industrial Property rights; West-East German Law Society; German-French Law Society. *LANGUAGES:* German, English and French.

RAIMUND SCHAFMEISTER, born Warendorf, Germany, 1962; admitted, 1992, Germany. *Education:* University of Bonn and University of Münster. Assistant, Institute for Labor and Economics Law, University of Münster, 1987-1988. Associate, Munro Lays & Co., Suva, Fiji, 1991. *LANGUAGES:* German, English and French.

HARALD KOLLRUS, born Kempten, Germany, 1965; admitted, 1993, Germany. *Education:* University of Regensburg. *LANGUAGES:* German and English.

Languages: German, English, French, Italian, Polish and Japanese

---

FAHR-BECKER, JAKUBOWICZ & PARTNER

REICHENHAINER STR. 34-36
D-09126 CHEMNITZ, GERMANY
Telephone: 49-371-445281
Telefax: 49-371-445285

Munich, Germany Office: Prinzregentenstr. 79, 81675. Telephone: 49-89-4707042. Telefax: 49-89-479011.

London, England Associated Office: Curry, Ch. Hausmann, Popeck, Solicitors, 17 A, Welbeck Way, GB-London W1M 7PD. Telephone: 44-71-2246633. Telefax: 44-71-9354042.

FIRM PROFILE: *Firm established in 1990. The firm has a broadly-based practice concentrating on a full range of civil legal services. The firm has concentrated on European Commercial and Corporate Law, General Civil Law and advising Multinational Corporations in European and German activities. In addition the firm has a close association with Central Treuhand AG, a Tax Advising and Auditing company with numerous offices in Germany.*

MEMBERS OF FIRM

DR. SITTIG FAHR-BECKER, born Heidelberg, Germany, August 23, 1940. "Doktor Juris" 1969, admitted, 1972. *Education:* University of Frankfurt and Würzburg. *LANGUAGES:* German, English and French. *PRACTICE AREAS:* National and International Business Law; Contracts for Civil Engineering; Contracting and Turn Key Projects; Restitution Law for the New Federal States of Germany; General Civil Law.

ASSOCIATES

ULRIKE HERMANN, born Hertigswalde, Germany, July 6, 1949; admitted, 1990. *Education:* University of Halle/Wittenberg, Germany. *LANGUAGES:* German, English and Russian. *PRACTICE AREAS:* Civil Law; Business Law; Labour Law.

MARKUS FAIT, born Wiesbaden, Germany, July 1, 1964; admitted, 1994. *Education:* Universities of Mainz an Freiburg. *LANGUAGES:* German and English. *PRACTICE AREAS:* Civil Law; Tax Law; Administrative Law.

(For Complete Biographical Data on all Personnel, see Professional Biographies at Munich, Germany)

HEUKING KÜHN KUNZ WOJTEK

WESTSTR. 49
D-09112 CHEMNITZ, GERMANY
Telephone: 49 371 902345
Telefax: 49 371 902348

Other Offices: Düsseldorf, Frankfurt, Hamburg, Berlin (Germany); Paris (France).

Corporate, Banking, Tax, National and EC Antitrust, Mergers, Acquisitions, Intellectual Property, Unfair Competition and Trade Law, Commercial and International Law, EC Law, Environmental Law, Administrative Law, International Arbitration, Litigation, General Practice.

FIRM PROFILE: *All Attorneys are Members of Denton International and of the Chemnitz Bar Association. Languages spoken are English, German and French.*

MEMBER OF FIRM

DR. ARMIN FRHR V. GRIESSENBECK, born Frankfurt/Main, Germany, October 20, 1961; admitted, 1990, Germany. *Education:* Universities of Regensburg, Munich, Salzburg (Austria) and Cape Town (South Africa) (Referendar 1987, doctorate in company law, 1988, Assessor, 1990). Publications: "Liability arising from errors in shareholders' prospectuses under the prospectus liability regulations in the German Federal High Court" in: Osterreichische Juristenzeitung 1989, pp. 166-173, "The applicability of Section 98 of the Commercial Code to issuing bodies in the sale of shares in a public limited company" in: Betriebsberater 1988, pp. 2188-2192; "The concept of "Parents' domicile" in Section 12 para 2 of the Federal Education Promotion Act for children born out of wedlock and of age" in: Familienrechtszeitung 1989, pp. 352-355; Legal requirements for investments in the Soviet Union, Hungary, Poland, Czechoslovakia and the GDR," in: Manager Magazine 1990, pp 24-24, 28, 34, 39, 43; "Legal Developments in the Privatization of companies in the former GDR," in: Eastern European Forum Magazine 1991, pp. 2-4. *Member:* German-Japanese Law Association. *PRACTICE AREAS:* Commercial Law; Properties; Construction; Restitutional Law.

ASSOCIATES

ANNEMARIE ROTT, born Munich, Germany, September 14, 1962; admitted, 1992, Germany (BG Chemnitz). *Education:* University of Munich (Referendar, 1989; Assessor, 1992). *PRACTICE AREAS:* Civil Law; Commercial Law; Labor Law; Restitutional Law.

MICHAEL UTECHT, born Essen, Germany, August 3, 1995; admitted, 1994, Germany. *Education:* University of Passau (Referendar 1991, Assessor 1994). *PRACTICE AREAS:* Civil Law; Corporate Law; Construction; Private International Law.

SIGLE, LOOSE, SCHMIDT-DIEMITZ & PARTNERS

BARBAROSSASTRAßE 46
09112 CHEMNITZ, GERMANY
Telephone: 0371-36974-0
Telefax: 0371-3697421

Stuttgart, Germany Office: Schöttlestr. 8, P.O. Box 70 02 65, D-70572 Stuttgart (Degerloch). Telephone: 0711-9764-0. Telefax: 0711-9764-900.

Berlin, Germany Office: Friedrichstrasse 130 a, 10117 Berlin. Telephone: 030-308792-0. Telefax: 030-2385849.

Leipzig, Germany Office: August-Bebel-Strasse 38, 04275 Leipzig. Telephone: 0341-3912007. Telefax: 0341-391-2085.

Frankfurt/Main, Germany Office: Schumannstraße 62, 60325 Frankfurt/Main. Telephone: 069-975841-0. Telefax: 069-97584117.

Moscow, Russia Office: Sadovaja Samotjotschnaja, 103 051. Telephone: 007/095/258 50 55. Fax: 007/095/258 51 55.

DR. HARTMUT HAMANN, born Karlsruhe, Germany, 1962; admitted, 1990, Stuttgart. *Education:* Universities of Freiburg (Doctor of Law, 1991) and Geneva. Author: "Das Unternehmen als Täter im europäischen Wettbewerbsrecht" (The Criminal Responsibility of Companies under European Competition Law), 1991. *Member:* German Bar Association. *LANGUAGES:* German, English, French and Spanish. *PRACTICE AREAS:* Corporate Law; Commercial Law; Property and Real Estate Law.

BACHEM & PARTNER

LUXEMBURGER STR. 186
D-50937 COLOGNE, GERMANY
Telephone: 221-41 10 85
Telefax: 221-41 73 84

Companies, Corporations, Commercial (general), Mergers and Acquisitions, Unfair Competition, Trademarks, Industrial and Intellectual Property, Product-Piracy and Liability, Insurance, Banking, Employment, Labour and Temporary Work Law, Property, Real Estate, Family and Matrimonial Law, Law of Succession, Contracts, Medical Practitioner's Liability, Debt Collection (EC and Germany).

DR. RUPERT BACHEM (1954-1989).

WALTER J. SCHAUSEIL, born Cologne, Germany, 1939; admitted, 1970, Cologne. *Education:* Universities of Freiburg/Br., Cologne (1959-1965); Cornell University, It haca, N.Y.; Institute of World Affairs, Salisbury, Conn. (1961); Institute of Public Administration, Speyer/Germany (1968); Legal Training at Commission on Human Rights and Legal Department of Council of Europe, Strasbourg, France (1969). Head of Legal Department of Private Company, 1972. *Member:* German Bar Association; German Association for the Protection of Industrial Property Rights, German-American Lawyers Association; Subgroup for International and Foreign Law of the German Bar Association; IBA; UIA. *LANGUAGES:* German and English. *PRACTICE AREAS:* Unfair Competition; Labour Law.

WERNER LUTHMANN, born Haan/Rhld, Germany, 1954; admitted, 1984, Cologne. *Education:* University of Cologne. Research Assistant, Institute of Labour and Social Law, University of Cologne, 1982-1983. *Member:* German Bar Association; Law Society Cologne. *LANGUAGES:* German, English and French. *PRACTICE AREAS:* Insurance Law; Family and Matrimonial Law.

BODEN OPPENHOFF RASOR RAUE

COLOGNE, GERMANY

(See Oppenhoff & Rädler)

DERINGER TESSIN HERRMANN & SEDEMUND

HEUMARKT 14
D-50667 COLOGNE, GERMANY
Telephone: 49-221-205070
Telefax: 49-221-2050790
Telex: 8 881 356 ELAW D

Brussels, Belgium Office: Place Des Barricades 13, B-1000 Brussels. Telephone: 32-2-219 82 50. Telefax: 32-2-219 88 32.

Frankfurt/Main, Germany Office: Bockenheimer Landstraβe 51-53, D-60325 Frankfurt a.M. Telephone 49-69-971090-0. Telefax: 49-69-971090-90.

Leipzig, Germany Office: Burgplatz 2, D-04109 Leipzig. Telephone: 49-341-711590. Telefax: 49-341-7115999.

Moscow, Russia Office: ul. Bolschaja Ordynka 21, RF-113035 Moscow. Telephone: 7-095-2332450, 2345403. Telefax: 7-095-2334355.

German and EEC Antitrust Law. Corporate, Commercial, Tax, General EEC, Mergers and Acquisitions, Media and Entertainment, Banking and Finance, Arbitration, Pharmaceutical and Foodstuffs, Telecommunication, Insurance and Labor Law. Unfair Competition, Industrial Property Rights, Trademarks, Environmental, Construction, Administrative Law. General International Practice.

PARTNERS

PROF. ARVED DERINGER, born Neustuttgart, Russia, June 4, 1913; admitted, 1953, Stuttgart; 1962, Cologne, Court of Appeals. *Education:* Universities of Tübingen, Berlin, Kiel and Geneve. Co-author with: Dr. Claus Tessin, "The Competition Law of the European Economic Community," German edition, 1962-1965, French edition, 1963-1965 and English edition, CCH, 1968; Co-author: Mueller-Henneberg-Schwartz, "Commentary German Competition Law," 1963. Author: "Urheberrecht," 1965. Member, German Federal Diet, 1957-1969 (Member: Economic Committee, 1957-1965; Legal Committee, 1957-1969; Finance Committee, 1968-1969). Member, European Parliament, 1958-1970 (Member, Economic Committee, 1958-1970; Chairman, Legal Committee, 1966-1970; Rapporteur for Regulation No. 17 on European Economic Community Antitrust Law, 1962). Honorary Title of Professor, 1977. *Member:* German and International (Chairman, Committee on Restrictive Trade Practices and Monopolies, 1968-1980) Bar Associations; Deutscher Juristentag; Studienvereinigung Kartellrecht (Vice-Chairman, 1964-1988); International Law Association; German Association for the Protection of Industrial Property and Copyright; British Institute of International and Comparative Law; German Society for European Law (Member of Board, 1988). *LANGUAGES:* German, English, French and Russian.

DR. CLAUS TESSIN, born Schwaan, Germany, July 28, 1927; admitted, 1961, Stuttgart; 1962, Bonn; 1970, Cologne, Court of Appeals. *Education:* University of Hamburg (Dr. jur., 1958); Oxford University, England. Co-author with Arved Deringer: "The Competition Law of the European Economic Community," German edition, 1962-1965. French edition, 1963-1965 and English edition, CCH, 1968. *Member:* German and International Bar Associations; Studienvereinigung Kartellrecht; German and International Association for the Protection of Industrial Property and Copyright. *LANGUAGES:* German, English and Spanish.

DR. HANSJÜRGEN HERRMANN, born Düsseldorf, Germany, September 18, 1933; admitted, 1965, Bonn, Germany; 1970, Cologne, Court of Appeals. *Education:* University of Cologne (Referendar, 1958; Dr. jur., 1969); University of Freiburg; Washington University, St. Louis, Missouri, U.S.A. (Fulbright Scholarship). Author: "Mergers and the Cartel Prohibition of Sec. 1 German Cartel Law," 1966; "No Attack Clauses Regarding Industrial Property Rights and Related Problems," 1969; "Competition and Antitrust Law," in Concise Dictionary on Insurance, 1987. Member: German and International Bar Associations; Studienvereinigung Kartellrecht; German and International Associations for the Protection of Industrial Property and Copyright; German American Lawyers Association. *LANGUAGES:* German, English and French.

JOCHIM SEDEMUND, born Elmshorn, Germany, August 8, 1935; admitted, 1967, Bonn. *Education:* Universities of Kiel, Cologne and Hamburg. Stagiaire with EC-Commission, Brussels. Author: "Verhältnis des EWG-Kartellrechts zu den Nationalen Patentrechten," 1968; "Development of Community Law," Periodical Articles in NJW on "European Community Law," 1969-1988; "The Procedural Rules of EEC Antitrust Law," Eüroparecht, pp. 306-327, 1974; "The Impact of Amendments to German Cartel Law," ECLR 1980. Co-Author: "Doing Business in Germany", "Handbook on Mergers and Acquisitions"; "Lawyers' Handbook on EEC Economic Law." *Member:* International Bar Association, (Vice-Chairman, 1979-1986 and Chairman, 1986-1987, Committee on Antitrust Law); Union International des Avocats; Society of Comparative Law; German American Lawyers Association; Studienvereinigung Kartellrecht; German and International Association for the Protection of Industrial Property and Copyright. *LANGUAGES:* German, English and French.

DR. WILHELM DANELZIK, born Marl-Hüls, Germany, April 3, 1946; admitted, 1977, Cologne; 1979, Cologne Court of Appeals. *Education:* Universities of Bochum and Bonn (Referendar 1972; Dr. jur., 1976). *Member:* German and International Bar Associations; German and International Association for the Protection of Industrial Property and Copyright; German-Spanish and German-Italian Lawyers Associations; Studienvereinigung Kartellrecht. *LANGUAGES:* German, English, French, Italian and Spanish.

DR. JOACHIM PFEFFER, born Wiesbaden, Germany, September 11, 1947; admitted, 1978, Cologne; 1980, Court of Appeals. *Education:* Universities of Mainz, London, Göttingen (Dr. jur., 1976). Author: "Legal Framework of East-West-Trade," 1978; "Reorganization of Car Dealer Agreements," in NJW, pp. 1241-1247, 1985; "Buyer Power in Germany - Recent Case Law," in ECLR, pp. 1-8, 1986; "International Competition and Definition of the Relevant Market," in WuW, pp. 851-863, 1986; "Fifth Amendment of the German Act Against Restraints of Competition," ECLR, 1991, pp. 95-102. *Member:* German and International Bar Associations; Studienvereinigung Kartellrecht; German Association for the Protection of Industrial Property and Copyright; German-Hungarian Lawyers Association (General Secretary). *LANGUAGES:* German, English, French and Russian.

DR. GERHARD PICOT, born Hemer/Iserlohn, Germany, March 7, 1945; admitted, 1979, Cologne. *Education:* Universities of Freiburg and Bonn (Dr. jur., 1977). Research Assistant, Institute of Company and Labour Law, University of Cologne, 1977-1979. Lecturer, Insurance Academy

(This Listing Continued)

(This Listing Continued)

of Cologne, 1977-1987. Author inter alia: "Redistribution of Profits and Constitutional Law," 1978; "Social Protection of Employees," RdA 1979 pp. 16-23; "Closure of Plants and Other Operational Changes of Companies in West Germany," International Business Lawyer 1988, pp. 59-62; "Liability of GmbH-Shareholders for capital-replacing loans," BB1991, pp. 1360-1363; "Mergers and Acquisitions in East Germany," International Business Lawyer 1991, pp. 396-400; "Majority and Minority Votes in Partnerships," BB1993, pp. 13-21; "Reorganization of Companies in Germany," International Business Lawyer 1993. *Member:* German and International Bar Associations; German Japanese Lawyers Association; German British Lawyers Association. *LANGUAGES:* German, English and French.

DR. JÜRGEN SIEGER, born Bonn, Germany, September 22, 1952; admitted, 1983, Cologne. *Education:* Universities of Tübingen, Bonn (Referendar, 1978); Hamburg, Cologne, Assistant Professor at the Institute of Insurance Law (Dr. jur., 1983). Author: "The Legal Status of the English Insurance Broker," 1983. With: Rye and Partners, Toronto, 1979; White & Case, New York, 1984. *Member:* German and International Bar Associations; German-American Lawyers Association. *LANGUAGES:* German and English.

DR. FRANK MONTAG, born Siegen, Germany, June 25, 1957; admitted, 1986, Cologne. *Education:* United World College of the Atlantic, Wales (I.B., 1976); University of Bonn (Referendar, 1981; Dr. jur., 1984); University of Georgia, U.S.A. (LL.M., 1982). Author: "International Agreements with Preliminary Effects," Berlin, 1986; "International Organizations for the Research and Exploitation of Outer Space," Kaiser/v. Welck (eds.); "Outer Space and International Politics," Bonn, 1987; "The External Dimension of the Internal Market," EuZW, pp. 112-117,1990; "Basic Principles of EC-Merger Control," IWB, pp. 681-690, 1990; "Common Market Merger Control of Third-Country Enterprises," Comparative Law Yearbook of International Business, pp. 47-64, 1991; Periodical articles with J. Sedemund, "European Community Law," NJW, 1987-1991. Research Assistant, Institute for Public International and European Law, University of Bonn, 1982-1985. *Member:* German and International Bar Associations; German-American Lawyers Association; German Society for Foreign Affairs; European Air Law Association (Member, Management Committee); European Trade Law Association; Studienvereinigung Kartellrecht; Union des Avocats Européens (Member, Executive Committee). (Resident, Brussels, Belgium Office). *LANGUAGES:* German, English and French.

ANDREAS RÖHLING, born Essen, Germany, June 13, 1952; admitted, 1986, Cologne. *Education:* Deutsche Bank AG (Bankkaufmann, 1974); Universities of Bielefeld and Bonn (Referendar, 1980). Author: "Unsolved Questions of European Merger Control," ZIP 1990, pp. 1179-1186; "Options under German and European Antitrust Law," Festschrift Quack, 1990 (with Cl. Tessin); Articles "Prohibition of Discrimination" and "Energy Law" in: Encyclopedia of the Law. With, Federal Cartel Office of Germany, Berlin, 1983-1985. *Member:* German Bar Association; Studienvereinigung Kartellrecht; Union des Avocats Européens (German Coordinator of the Commission on Intellectual Property Rights); German Association for the Protection of Industrial Property and Copyright. *LANGUAGES:* German and English.

HEINZ JOACHIM KUMMER, born Berlin, Germany, January 28, 1960; admitted, 1988, Cologne. *Education:* University of Cologne (Referendar, 1984); Academy of Public Administration, Speyer. Author: "Games of Chance in Germany," 1986; "Liability Law including Product Liability" in: Deutsche Rechtspraxis, 1991; "The Project and Development Plan in Local Zoning Laws within the New German States" in: OV-Spezial 1992; "Construction Planning Law: Possible Forms and their Realization" in: "Immobilienhandbuch Ost," 1993. *Member:* German Bar Association (Member, Administrative Law Committee); Deutscher Juristentag; Deutsch-Deutsche Juristische Vereinigung; Environmental Law Association; Administrative Law Association. *LANGUAGES:* German and English.

DR. LUDWIG LEYENDECKER, born Brühl, Germany, August 1, 1958; admitted, 1989, Cologne. *Education:* University of Bonn (Referendar, 1984; Dr. jur., 1987); University of Geneva, Switzerland; Institut Universitaire de Hautes Etudes Internationales; Georgetown University, Washington, D.C. (LL.M., 1985). Author: "Foreign Debts and International Law," Frankfurt, 1988; "Civil Litigation in the US," von Boehmer (ed.), Deutsche Unternehmen auf dem amerikanischen Markt, Stuttgart, 1988 (w. D.Lange). With: Wilmer, Cutler & Pickering, London, 1985, 1988, Washington, D.C., 1988; White & Case, Paris, 1991. *Member:* German Bar Association; German-American Lawyers Association (Board Member); Association Internationale des Jeunes Avocats. *LANGUAGES:* German, English, French and Spanish.

(This Listing Continued)

DR. CHRISTIAN BORRIS, born Bottrop, Germany, June 5, 1956; admitted, 1989, Cologne. *Education:* Universities of Giessen, Cologne (Referendar, 1982; Dr. jur., 1986); University of Miami, USA (LL.M., 1983). Author: "International Commercial Arbitration in the USA," 1987. Legal Assistant, Institute of International and Foreign Private Law, Cologne, 1983-1985. Stagiaire with International Chamber of Commerce Court of Arbitration, Paris, 1985. With Iran-United States Claims Tribunal, The Hague, 1987-1988. *Member:* German Bar Association; German Institute of Arbitration; German-American Lawyers Association. *LANGUAGES:* German, English and French.

DR. HELMUT BERGMANN, born Nürnberg, Germany, June 20, 1961; admitted, 1991, Cologne. *Education:* Universities of Würzburg, Geneva, Switzerland (Institute Universitair e d'Etudes Européennes) and Tübingen (Referendar, 1987; Dr. jur., 1989). Author: "Buying Power and Merger Control," Berlin, 1989; "Settlements in EC Merger Control Proceedings: A Summary of EC Enforcement Practice and a Comparison with the United States," Antitrust Law Journal, Vol. 62, Issue 1. Stagiaire with EC-Commission, Brussels, 1990. Research Assistant, Institute of Commercial and Economic Law, University of Bonn, 1987-1991. With: White & Case, New York, 1992-1993. *Member:* German Bar Association; German-American Lawyers Association; Studienvereinigung Kartellrecht. *LANGUAGES:* German, English, French and Spanish.

DR. KLAUS HEINEMANN, born Aachen, Germany, March 31, 1959; admitted, 1991, Cologne. *Education:* University of Cologne (Referendar, 1983; Dr. jur., 1988); McGill University, Montreal, Canada (LL.M., 1989). Author: "Burden of Proof in Case of Breach of Contract," Cologne, 1988; "Pre-Incorporation Transactions," Cologne, 1990; "Donation of Partnership Interests and its Revocation," DB 1990, 1649-1655 (Co-Author); "Shareholders Hanging by a Thread," ZHR 1991, 447-470; "EC Harmonization of Service Liability Rules," ZIP 1991, pp. 1193-1204; "The Case Law of European Merger Control," ZIP 1992, pp. 1367-1379 (Co-Author). Research Assistant, 1987-1988, and Assistant Professor, 1989-1991, Institute for Labour and Business Law, University of Cologne. *Member:* German Bar Association; Studienvereinigung Kartellrecht; German-French Lawyers' Association; Canadian-German Lawyers' Association. (Resident, Brussels, Belgium Office). *LANGUAGES:* German, French and English.

GERALD SCHUBERT, born Hünfeld, October 26, 1953; admitted, 1981, Cologne. *Education:* Universities of Würzburg, Geneva, London and Bonn (Referendar, 1978). (Resident, Brussels, Belgium Office). *LANGUAGES:* German, French and English.

DR. STEPHAN EILERS, born Bonn, Germany, October 7, 1959; admitted, 1989, Cologne. *Education:* Universities of Bonn and Geneva (Referendar, 1984; Dr. jur., 1987; Assessor, 1989); New York University (LL.M., tax, 1990). Specialized Tax Lawyer (Fachanwalt für Steuerrecht) 1992. Author: "The Tax Secret as Limit to the International Exchange of Information in Tax Matters," Cologne, 1987; "Override of Tax Treaties Under Domestic Legislation of the U.S. and Germany," 1990; "Reserves for Environmental Liabilities," Munich 1993. *Member:* German Bar Association; German-American Lawyers Association; International Fiscal Association (National Reporter Barcelona 1991). *LANGUAGES:* German, English and French. *PRACTICE AREAS:* Domestic and International Tax Law.

KLAUS JAKOB BEUCHER, born July 7, 1961; admitted, 1992, Cologne. *Education:* University of Saarbrücken; Bonn University; University of Wisconsin (LL.M., 1988). Research Assistant, Institute for Public Law, University of Bonn, 1987. Author: "U.S. Punitive Damages and the XIV. Amendment," RIW 1992, pp. 893-900; "The Evolving European Media System and the Law of the European Communities" in: Die Einflüsse europarechtlicher Entwicklungen auf das Bund-Länder-Verhältnis im Rundfunkwesen, 1992. Co-author: "Financing of Broadcasting under Judicial Review," AfP 1989, pp. 708-716; "Public Broadcasters and Publishers Competing in the area of Publishing TV Guides," Rundfunk und Fernsehen 1990, pp. 184-200; "United States Punitive Damage Awards in German Courts: The Evolving German Position on Service and Enforcement," 23 Vanderbilt J. of Transntl. L. 1991, pp. 967-991. With: Wilmer, Cutler & Pickering, London, 1988. *Member:* German Bar Association; German-American Lawyers Association; Institute of European Media Law. *LANGUAGES:* German, English and French.

DR. KARSTEN MÜLLER-EISING, born Hanover, Germany, November 15, 1960; admitted, 1992, Cologne. *Education:* University of Würzburg; Hull University, United Kingdom; University of Bonn (Referandar, 1987; Dr. jur., 1992). Author: "The Hidden Contribution in Kind," Munich, 1993. Research Assistant, Institute for Commercial and Economic Law, University of Bonn, 1987-1988. *LANGUAGES:* German and English.

(This Listing Continued)

DERINGER TESSIN HERRMANN & SEDEMUND,
Cologne—Continued

DR. ANDREA NOWAK-OVER, born Cologne, Germany, December 16, 1960; admitted, 1992, Cologne. *Education:* University of Cologne (Dr. iur., 1990). Author: Auslegung und rechtliche Zulâssigkeit von Serienschadensklauseln in der Haftpflicht und Vermögenschadenhaftpflichtversicherung, 1991. Research Assistant, Institute for Insurance Law of the University of Cologne, 1988. *LANGUAGES:* German and English.

KIRSTEN FLOSS, born Münster, Germany, April 11, 1963; admitted, 1993, Cologne. *Education:* University of Münster (Germany), Strasbourg (France), Geneva (Switzerland); Institute Universitaire d'Etudes Européennes, Geneva; Pushkin-Institut, Moscow. Consultant of EC Commission, Brussels, 1990, Stagiaire with Russian Chamber of Commerce, Moscow, 1992; Stagiaire with White & Case, New York, 1992. *Member:* German Bar Association. (Resident, Moscow, Russia Office). *LANGUAGES:* German, English, French and Russian.

OF COUNSEL

DR. KARL-HEINZ NARJES, born Soltau, Germany, January 1, 1924; admitted, 1990, Cologne. *Education:* University of Hamburg (degrees in law and economics, 1948; Dr. jur., 1953). Senior Civil Servant, Internal Revenue Service, Bremen, 1953. Career Officer, German Foreign Office, 1955. Member, Cabinet of the President of the EC Commission, Walter Hallstein, deputy head, 1958-1963, head, 1963-1967; Director-General of the EC Commission for Press and Information, 1968; Minister of Economic Affairs and Transport in the Land Schleswig-Hostein, 1969-1973; Member of the Bundestag and Member of the Steering Committee of the CDU/CSU parliamentary group, 1972-1981; Chairman of the Bundestag Committee of Economic Affairs, 1972-1976; CDU/CSU Spokesman for Energy and Economic Relations, Member of the Foreign Affairs Committee of the Bundestag, 1976-1980. Member, EC Commission for the Internal Market and Customs Union, Environment, Consumer Protection and Innovation, 1981-1985; Vice-President, EC Commission for Industry and Industrial Innovation, Science, Research and Development and Joined Research Centres, Telecommunication, 1985-1989. *Member:* German Bar Association; German Society for Foreign Affairs; Trilateral Commission. (Resident, Brussels, Belgium Office). *LANGUAGES:* German, English and French.

ASSOCIATES

DR. THORSTEN KLEINE, born Oberhausen, Germany, November 4, 1961; admitted, 1992, Cologne. *Education:* University of Münster (Referendar, 1987; Dr. jur., 1993). Stagiaire with German-Australian Chamber of Industry & Commerce, Sydney, 1991. Author: "Co-determination in Supervisory Boards of Cooperatives," 1993. *Member:* German Bar Association; Studienvereinigung Kartellrecht. *LANGUAGES:* German, English and French.

DR. LUDGER GIESBERTS, born Geldern, Germany, January 24, 1961; admitted, 1991, Düsseldorf; 1993, Cologne. *Education:* University of Bonn, University of Trier (Dr. jur., 1989); Academy of Public Administration Speyer (Magister Rerum Publicarum, 1990); London School of Economics and Political Science (LL.M., 1991) Ministry for Environment and Health of the State Rhineland-Palatinate, 1990. Research and Teaching Assistant in Public, Environmental, Technology and Constitutional Law, University of Trier. Author: "The Just Distribution of Costs among Polluters of the Environment - Choice and Compensation in Environmental Damage Cases," Berlin 1990; "Commercial Waste Management by Companies in Germany," Taiwan Commercial Times, August 1992; "Review of the Draft Ordinances on Electronic Scrap, Batteries, Old Cars and Used Paper," BB 1993, pp. 1376-1381; "Environmental Liability for Industrial Installations in Germany," International Business Lawyer, January, 1994, pp. 14-19; "Emission Control by Strict Environmental Liability Rules in Germany," Journal of Taipei Bar Association, February, 1994, pp. 71-76; "Marketing Hazardous Substances in the EC," International Business Lawyer, April, 1994, pp. 183-184. *Member:* German Bar Association; German-British Lawyers Association; German-American Lawyers Association; European Environmental Lawyers Association; International Bar Association. *LANGUAGES:* German, English and Dutch.

DR. KATHARINA SPECHT-JONEN, born Bremen, Germany, February 3, 1964; admitted, 1993, Cologne. *Education:* University of Bonn (Dr. jur., 1992). Research Assistant, University of Bonn, 1988-1991. Author: "Excessive Judicial Review of General Business Terms"; "Rights of Local Communities concerning Abandoned Military Bases." *Member:* German Bar Association. *LANGUAGES:* German and English.

(This Listing Continued)

DR. PAUL PAEZ-MALETZ, born Cologne, Germany, March 14, 1964; admitted, 1993, Cologne. *Education:* University of Cologne (Referendar, 1988; Dr. jur., 1992); Cornell University, Ithaca, New York (LL.M., 1989). Author: "Barriers to Entry in the Natural Gas Market in EC Member States," (with J.F. Baur), Baden-Baden, 1990; "Reliance on the Formation of Contracts in American and German Law," Karlsruhe, 1992. Research Assistant, Institute for Energy Law, University of Cologne, 1990-1992. *Member:* German-American and German-Spanish Lawyers Associations; Cornell Law Association. *LANGUAGES:* German, English and Spanish.

UTE PLOCH-KUMPF, born Sinn, December 6, 1961; admitted, 1993, Cologne. *Education:* University of Trier; University of Cologne (Referendarin, 1989). Author: "Attachment of Credit Lines," DB 1986, pp. 1961-1965. Research Assistant: Institute for European Law, University of Cologne, 1988-1991; Institute for Professional Conduct of Lawyers, University of Cologne, 1992-1993. *LANGUAGES:* German and English.

ULRICH BORMANN, born Cologne, October 28, 1960; admitted, 1993, Cologne. *Education:* University of Cologne (Referendar, 1989); Academy of Public Administration, Speyer, 1991. Co-Author: with Gerhard Picot, "Obstacles for Investment Relating to the Purchase of Former GDR Companies," BFUP 1991, pp. 23-46. Police Officer, 1979-1983. Teaching Assistant, University of Cologne, 1989-1990. Stagiaire with Davis, Shelton & Rainey, Oklahoma City, 1992. *Member:* German Bar Association. *LANGUAGES:* German, English and Italian.

DR. REGINE NOWACK, born September 18, 1962; admitted, 1989-1991, Frankfurt. *Education:* University of Munich (Referendar, 1986; Assessor, 1989); Academy of Public Administration Speyer (1987-1988). Research and Teaching Assistant, Institute for Tax Law, University of Bamberg (Dr. jur., 1994). *LANGUAGES:* German, English, French and Italian. *PRACTICE AREAS:* Domestic and International Tax Law.

DR. DOMINIK SCHNICHELS, born Arnsberg, Germany, December 7, 1962; admitted, 1994, Cologne. *Education:* University of Passau, King's College London; University of Munich (Referendar, 1990; Dr.jur., 1993; Assessor, 1994). Author: "The Right of Establishment in EC-Law," 1993. Co-Author: "The Case Law of the European Institutions," 1994. *LANGUAGES:* German and English.

WALDEMAR JOSCHKO, born June 9, 1962; admitted, 1994, Cologne. *Education:* University of Giessen (Referendar, 1990; Assessor, 1994). *LANGUAGES:* German, Polish, English and Russian.

DR. THOMAS MERREM, born August 2, 1965; admitted, 1994, Cologne. *Education:* University of Trier (Referendar, 1991; Dr.jur., 1994). Author: "Sicherung vertraglicher Verfugungsverbote," JR 1993, 53-60 ; "Ist der Besitz ein die Veräußerung hinderndes Recht im Sinne des § 771 ZPO?," 1994. *LANGUAGES:* German and English.

EIMER • HEUSCHMID • MEHLE
HOHENSTAUFENRING 44-46
50674 COLOGNE, GERMANY
Telephone: 01149-221-235555
Fax: 01149-221-236121

Bonn, Germany Office: Friedrich-Breuer-Str. 104-112, 53225 Bonn. Telephone: 01149-228-466025. Fax: 01149-228-460708.
Halle, Germany Office: Rudolf-Breitscheid-Str. 92, 06108 Halle. Telephone: 01149-345-29392. Fax: 01149-345-29392.

Civil, Commercial and Company Law, Patents and Trade Marks, Family Law and Estate Administration, Labour Law, Private International and EC Law, Insurance and Medical Malpractice Law, Criminal Law, Serious Fraud, Tax and Environmental Offences.

FIRM PROFILE: The firm was established in 1973 and offers a full range of services including litigation in all judicial branches. It is well known for its wide-ranging commercial, family and specialized criminal law. Its client base is European. The firm is a member of a European Economic Interest Grouping (AVRIO), the partners of which are well-known firms throughout Europe; close cooperation and advice on European scale is offered.

RESIDENT PARTNER

ULRICH KUDOWEH, born Neuss, June 30, 1961; admitted, 1989, Cologne. *Education:* Bonn University. *Member:* German Bar Association; Association of Criminal Lawyers. *LANGUAGES:* German and English. *PRACTICE AREAS:* Civil Law; Commercial Law; Criminal Law.

GEORG N. FELLMANN

Rechtsanwalt

HAUPTSTR. 89
POSTFACH 50 13 04
D-50996 COLOGNE, GERMANY
Telephone: 0221-354866; 354764
Telefax: 0221-351752

General Practice, Corporate, Commercial, Trade, Unfair Competition and International Private Law, Litigation and Traffic Law.

GEORG N. FELLMANN, born Cologne, West Germany, September 7, 1948; admitted, 1979, Cologne. *Education:* University of Cologne; University of Geneva; University of Bonn; King's College, London (LL.M., 1982). Lecturer on Law: Polytechnic of Central London, 1982; Gesellschaft für wirtschaftsbervFliche Bildung mbH & Co., 1988-1989. *Member:* Deutscher Anwaltsverein; English Law Society; German-American Lawyers Association; German-Chinese Lawyers Association; European Lawyers Association (General Secretary, 1986-1990); British-German Jurists Association; German-Mexican Jurists Association. *LANGUAGES:* German, English and French.

FIEDLER & FORSTER

BONNER STRASSE 172-176
50968 COLOGNE, GERMANY
Telephone: (0049) (221) 937 050-0
Telefax: (0049) (221) 937 050-50

Berlin, Germany Office: Oranienburger Strasse 69, D-10117 Berlin. Telephone: (0049) (30) 283 2418. Telefax: (0049) (30) 283 2420.
Frankfurt/Main, Germany Office: Opernplatz 2, D-60313 Frankfurt/Main. Telephone: (0049) (69) 298930. Telefax: (0049) (69) 29893299.
Leipzig, Germany Office: Grimmaische Str. 25, 04109 Leipzig. Telephone: (0049) (341) 2115112. Telefax: (0049) (341) 9602530.
Munich, Germany Office: Brienner Strasse 12/III, D-80333 Munich. Telephone: (0049) (89) 23980. Telefax: (0049) (89) 2398259.
Stuttgart, Germany Office: Gänsheidestr. 68, D-70184. Telephone: (0049) (711)-16445-0. Fax: (0049) (711) 16445-11.
Paris, France Office: Tour Fiat la Défense 6, F-92084. Telephone: 33-1-47 76 28 10. Fax: 33-1-47 96 63 63.

Bankruptcy, Banking, Business Law, Civil Law, Commercial Law, Company Law, Corporate Law, Debtor and Creditor, Family Law, Labor and Employment, Leasing.

MEMBERS OF FIRM

HANNELORE KRÜGER-KNIEF, born Bromberg, Germany, December 28, 1942; admitted, 1974, Cologne. *Education:* Universities of Münster and Bonn. *LANGUAGES:* German.

ASSOCIATES

DR. CHRISTIANE VAN ZWOLL, born Dortmund, Germany, November 3, 1961; admitted, 1992, Dortmund; 1993, Cologne. *Education:* Universities of Münster and Hamburg (Dr.jur., 1993). *LANGUAGES:* German and English.

DR. DIETMAR RENDELS, born Eitorf/Sieg, Germany, April 26, 1962; admitted, 1991, Bonn; 1993, Cologne. *Education:* University of Bonn (Dr.jur., 1993). *LANGUAGES:* German and English.

DR. HANS-JÜRGEN STREICHER, born Essen, Germany, January 21, 1959; admitted, 1992, Düsseldorf; 1993, Cologne. *Education:* Universities of Bonn and Berlin (Dr.jur., 1994). *LANGUAGES:* German, English and Spanish.

GAEDERTZ VIEREGGE QUACK KREILE

Rechtsanwälte

THEODOR-HEUSS-RING 19-21
D-50668 COLOGNE, GERMANY
Telephone: (221)77 16-0
Telex: 888 5143 olga d
Teletex: 221 4376 olga d
Telefax: (221)77 16-110

Berlin, Germany Office: Kurfürstendamm 157, D-10709 Berlin. Telephone: (30)890 05-0. Telefax: (30)892 26 06. Teletex: 30 88 15 qkp d. Telex: 17 30 88 15 qkp d.
Frankfurt/Main, Germany Office: Airport Center, Hugo-Eckener-Ring, D-60549 Frankfurt/Main. Telephone: (69)69 48 60. Telefax: (69)69 48 52. Telex: 40 32 145 zibr d.
Leipzig, Germany Office: August-Bebel-Str. 38, D-04275 Leipzig. Telephone:(341) 477 83 81/83. Telefax: (341) 477 83 88.
Munich, Germany Office: Widenmayerstrasse 32, D-80538 Munich. Telephone: (89)212147-0. Telefax: (89)228 55 62.
Wiesbaden, Germany Office: Kaiser-Friedrich-Ring 65, D-65185 Wiesbaden. Telephone: (611)88 05-0. Telefax: (611)81 03 09. Telex:41 86 295 gaed d.
Brussels, Belgium Office: Avenue de Tervuren 35, B-1040 Brussels. Telephone: (2) 736 07 97. Telefax: (2) 732 69 12.
Prague, Czech Republic Office: Betlémska 1, CR-11000 Prague 1. Telephone: (2) 24 22 94 98. Telefax: (2) 232 12 29.

General Practice, Commercial, Corporate, Antitrust, Unfair Competition, Trademarks, Labour Law, Insurance, Construction, Administrative Law, Food and Drug Law, Banking, EC Law.

FIRM PROFILE: The law firm Gaedertz Vieregge Quack Kreile is the result of a merger between 4 partnerships: Heydt Vieregge & Partner, Cologne; Gaedertz Henn & Partner, Wiesbaden; Quack Kühn & Partner, Berlin; Prof. Kreile & Partner, Munich.

Gaedertz Vieregge Quack Kreile is one of the major German based law firms representing domestic and foreign clients in all fields of law that are relevant for national and international enterprises. An important part of the practice are the legal aspects of transnational transactions especially in EC. The firm advises not only German clients in international matters but also foreign enterprises about all implications of doing business in Germany. Thus many attorneys and also members of the support staff are fluent in English. Other languages such as French, Spanish, Portuguese, Italian, Russian, and Dutch are also spoken.

In addition, the offices in Cologne and Wiesbaden have the specialised capacity to administer large trademark portfolios worldwide including registration and litigation of trademarks and registered designs.

Clients of the firm include many well-known German and foreign companies active in a wide variety of businesses. Gaedertz Vieregge Quack Kreile also represents various trade associations as well as German federal, state and local governmental authorities.

In the Berlin, Wiesbaden and Frankfurt/Main offices, there are 11 attorneys qualified to act as "Notar," specially licensed to prepare and execute documents relating to incorporation of companies, real estate matters and other important commercial transactions where a special form of document is prescribed.

Gaedertz Vieregge Quack Kreile has more than 70 attorneys, including 42 partners, plus a support staff of approximately 150 people, working in the eight different offices.

The offices have for the most part city centre locations. The Frankfurt office is situated at the Airport-Centre of the Rhein-Main Airport.

MEMBERS OF FIRM

DR. ERICH KÖHLER, born Gelenau, 1916; admitted, 1952, Cologne. *Education:* Universities of Leipzig, Debrecen (Hungary) and Gottingen. *Member:* Cologne Bar Association (Member, Board of Directors, 1975-1987). *PRACTICE AREAS:* Civil Law; Law of Succession; Compensation and Indemnification Law.

DR. RALF VIEREGGE, born Lorenzdorf/Schlesien, 1925; admitted, 1957, Cologne. *Education:* Universities of Tübingen, Mainz, Münster and Cologne (Dr. jur.). *Member:* Cologne Bar Association; German Association for Industrial Property Rights and Copyright (Member, Board of Directors); German Lawyers Society; Studienvereinigung Kartellrecht; International Bar Association. *LANGUAGES:* English. *PRACTICE AREAS:* Business Law; Company Law; Antitrust Law; Intellectual Property Rights.

(This Listing Continued)

GAEDERTZ VIEREGGE QUACK KREILE, Cologne—
Continued

DR. KURT BAUER, born Düren, 1936; admitted, 1966, Cologne. *Education:* Universities of Freiburg, Munich and Cologne (Dr. jur.). Co-author, Kommentar "Furler, Geschmacksmusterrecht". *Member:* Cologne Bar Association; Federal Association of Pharmaceutical Producers (Member, Legal Committee); German Association for Industrial Property Rights and Copyright. *LANGUAGES:* English. *PRACTICE AREAS:* Antitrust Law; Unfair Trade Practices; Trademarks; Copyright; Licensing; Food and Drug Law.

PROF. DR. RAINER JACOBS, born Jena, 1941; admitted, 1971, Cologne. *Education:* Universities of Tübingen (Dr. jur.) and Cologne. Editor of Magazine "Gewerblicher Rechtsschutz und Urheberrecht". Co-author, "Handbuch des Wettbewerbsrechts"; Co-Editor and Author of "Großkommentar zum UWG;" Co-Author of Aust/Jacobs Expropriation Law. *Member:* Cologne Bar Association; German Association for Industrial Property Rights and Copyright; International Bar Association. *LANGUAGES:* English. *PRACTICE AREAS:* Business Law, in particular Intellectual Property; Copyright; Company Law; Expropriation Law.

PROF. DR. JÜRGEN SALZWEDEL, born Frankfurt/Oder, 1929; admitted, 1994, Cologne. *Education:* Universities of Berlin and Cologne (Dr. jur.). Habilitation, Cologne. Professor, Public Law, Bonn University, 1961-1994. Director, Water Resources Law Institute, 1978-1987. Member Chairman, Council of Environmental Advisers, 1981-1985. Lecturer: Tulane University, New Orleans; Cornell University. Ithaka; University of Tennessee, Knoxville; Université Paris II. *Member:* German Association for Environmental Law (Chairman); Association of German Constitutional Law Professors; Association of German Water Protection; Study Group for Environment. *LANGUAGES:* English and French. *PRACTICE AREAS:* Environmental Law; Administrative Law.

LUDWIG STIEGLER, born Parsberg, 1944; admitted, 1976, Cologne. *Education:* Universities of Cologne and Munich. Chairman, Sub-committee on European Law, Vice-Chairman of Legal Committee and Member, 1980—, Bundestag (Lower House of the German Federal Parliament). *LANGUAGES:* English. *PRACTICE AREAS:* Construction Law.

DR. ALBRECHT PILTZ, born Poessneck, 1948; admitted, 1976, Cologne. *Education:* University of Bonn (Dr. jur.). *Member:* Cologne Bar Association; German Association for Industrial Property Rights and Copyright; German-Czech-Slowakian Jurists Association; German-Polish Jurists Association; German-Bulgarian Jurists Association. *LANGUAGES:* English. *PRACTICE AREAS:* Business Law, in particular Intellectual Property; Labour Law; Copyright and Publishing Law.

DR. MICHAEL LOSCHELDER, born Freiburg, 1945; admitted, 1978, Cologne. *Education:* Universities of Munich and Bonn (Dr. jur.). *Member:* Cologne Bar Association; German Association for Industrial Property Rights and Copyright (Member, Board of Directors). *LANGUAGES:* English, French. *PRACTICE AREAS:* Business Law, in particular Intellectual Property; Company Law.

DR. WILFRIED RÜFFER, born Haan, 1951; admitted, 1981, Cologne. *Education:* University of Bonn (Dr. jur.). *Member:* Cologne Bar Association; German Association for Industrial Property Rights and Copyright. *LANGUAGES:* English. *PRACTICE AREAS:* Insurance Law; Transport Law; Antitrust Law.

DR. YORK STROTHMANN, born Hamburg, 1951; admitted, 1983, Cologne. *Education:* University of Bonn (Dr. jur.). *Member:* Cologne Bar Association; German Association for Industrial Property Rights and Copyright; German-Dutch Lawyers' Conference; International Bar Association. *LANGUAGES:* English, Dutch. *PRACTICE AREAS:* Business Law, in particular Commercial and Company Law; Banking; Industrial Property; International Law.

DR. JÜRGEN LAUER, born Trier, 1956; admitted, 1985, Cologne. *Education:* Universities of Bonn and Geneva (Dr. jur.); Diplome d'Etudes Superieures en droit. *Member:* Cologne Bar Association; Lawyers Society Cologne; Study Group for Administrative Law; Legal Society Cologne; German Society for Construction Law. *LANGUAGES:* French, English. *PRACTICE AREAS:* Construction Law; Administrative Law.

DR. RALPH G. DROUVEN, born Cologne, 1958; admitted, 1987, Cologne. *Education:* Universities of Cologne and Geneva (Dr. jur.). *Member:* Cologne Bar Association; German-Chinese Law Society (Secretary-General); International Bar Association; German Association for Industrial Property Rights and Copyright. *LANGUAGES:* English, French. *PRAC-*

(This Listing Continued)

TICE AREAS: Business Law, in particular Mergers and Acquisitions; Company Law; Tax Law; International Law; Law of the former GDR.

DR. MATTHIAS KAPPUS, born Wuppertal, 1955; admitted, 1988, Cologne. *Education:* University of Cologne (Dr. jur.). Co-author, "Handbuch des EG-Rechts". *Member:* Cologne Bar Association; Lawyers Society of Cologne; German Association for Industrial Property Rights and Copyright. *LANGUAGES:* English. *PRACTICE AREAS:* Business Law, in particular Labour Law.

DR. ROBERT BUDDE, born Cologne, 1956; admitted, 1987, Cologne. *Education:* University of Cologne (Dr. jur.). *Member:* Cologne Bar Association; Lawyers Society of Cologne; German-Italian Lawyers' Association. *LANGUAGES:* Italian, English.

ASSOCIATES

DR. WINFRIED SCHNEPP, born Wuppertal, 1960; admitted, 1991, Cologne. *Education:* Universities of Saarbrücken and Cologne (Dr. jur.). *Member:* Cologne Bar Association; Lawyers Society of Cologne; German Association for Industrial Property Rights and Copyrights; German Institute for Protection of Geographical Indications of Origin (Managing Director). *LANGUAGES:* English and Dutch.

GORDIAN N. HASSELBLATT, born Bühlertal, 1961; admitted, 1992, Cologne. *Education:* Universities of Giessen, Bonn and Hamburg. With Murray & Ass. San Francisco, USA, 1991. *Member:* Cologne Bar Association; German-American Lawyers' Association. *LANGUAGES:* English.

DR. HENNING W. WAHLERS, born Kaltenkirchen, 1960; admitted, 1992, Cologne. *Education:* University of Bonn (Dr. jur.). *Member:* Cologne Bar Association. *LANGUAGES:* English, French.

DR. FRANK THILO KLINGBEIL, born Braunfels/Lahn, Hessen, September 2, 1959; admitted, 1992, Cologne. *Education:* University of Freiburg; University of Paris (Dr. jur.). *Member:* Cologne Bar Association. *LANGUAGES:* French, English.

DR. HERBERT WIEHE, born March 11, 1962; admitted, 1992, Cologne. *Education:* University of Bonn (Dr. jur.). *Member:* Cologne Bar Association; Cologne Lawyers Association.

DETLEF GRIMM, born Cologne, Germany, 1958; admitted, 1991, Cologne. *Education:* University of Cologne. *Member:* Cologne Bar Association; Cologne Lawyers Association. *LANGUAGES:* English.

DR. ARSÈNE VERNY, (M.E.S.), born Aussig Elbe, Czech Republic, 1956; admitted, 1993, Cologne. *Education:* Universities of Mainz, Cologne, RWTH-Aachen and Budapest (University of Economic Sciences). Co-Editor and Author: "Handbuch Wirtschaft und Recht in Osteuropa," "Zur Umsetzung von EG-Recht." *Member:* Association for the Study of Cartel Law; German-Czech-Slowakian Economy Association; German-Polish Jurists Association; German-Bulgarian Jurists Association. *LANGUAGES:* Czech, Slovaki, English, German and Russian.

MICHAEL JÜRGEN WERNER, born Krefeld, Germany, 1962; admitted, 1991, Düsseldorf. *Education:* University of Bonn; University of London/King's College (LL.M., 1992). *Member:* German-British Lawyers Association; European Air Law Association. *LANGUAGES:* English and French.

DR. WALTER KLEIN, born Remagen, Germany, 1964; admitted, 1994, Cologne. *Education:* University of Bonn (Dr. jur.). *Member:* Cologne Bar Association; Cologne Lawyer's Association.

MARTIN GRABLOWITZ, born Aachen, Germany, 1965; admitted, 1994, Cologne. *Education:* University of Bonn. *Member:* Cologne Bar Association. *LANGUAGES:* English and French.

Languages: German, English, French, Italian and Dutch.

(For complete biographical data on personnel at Berlin, Frankfurt/Main, Leipzig, Munich and Wiesbaden, Germany Offices as well as Brussels, Belgium and Prague, Czech, Republic Offices, see Professional Biographies at those locations).

GRAF VON WESTPHALEN & MODEST

SALIERRING 42
50677 COLOGNE, GERMANY
Telephone: (0221) 20807-0
Telex: 8883 360
Telefax: (0221) 239255

Dresden, Germany Office: Winterbergstraße 2, 01277. Telephone and Fax: 0351-2516 024 or 2516032.

(This Listing Continued)

Hamburg, Germany Office: Poststraße 9 A, 20354. Telephone: (040) 35922-0. Fax: (040) 344573. Telex: 211 729 MOD D.

Leipzig, Germany Office: Katharinenstraße 15, 04109. Telephone: (0341) 281073. Telefax: (0341) 281073.

Brussels, Belgium Office: Avenue de la Joyeuse Entrée 1, Boite 16, B-1040. Telephone: (02) 2304669. Fax: (02) 2310035.

Paris, France Office: 198, Avenue Victor Hugo, F-75116. Telephone: (01) 45046173. Fax: (01) 45044143.

National and International Contract Law, National and International Trade and Finance Law, Insurance Law, Construction Law, Corporate Law, Banking Law, Antitrust Law, Competition Law. Distributor Contracts, General Conditions of Contract, Labour Law, Tax Law, Administration Law, Reprivatization of Companies and Property, Environmental Law, Medical Law and the Law of Succession, Aviation Law, Leasing and Data Protection.

MEMBERS OF FIRM

DR. FRIEDRICH GRAF VON WESTPHALEN, born Aussig, July 23, 1940; admitted, 1969. *Education:* Universities of Münster, Heidelberg, Cologne, Bonn, Washington (1965-1966). Industrial Commercial experience, until 1973. Publications: The Munich Handbook of Contract: Comments on Banking Law, Legal Aspects of Export Financing, 1987; Product Liability, 1989; Commentary on the General Terms and Conditions of Business, 1985; Law of Leasing, 1992; Bonds and Bank-Guarantees in International Trade, 1990; Contracts of Sale in Europe, (ed.) 1992; Standard Business Conditions: A Handbook 1993. (Also Of Counsel, Funck-Brentano & Partners, Paris, France).

DR. HANS-RUDOLF EBEL, born Berlin, September 19, 1935; admitted, 1974. *Education:* Universities of Frankfurt and Innsbruck. Professional Experience: Federal Cartel Authority (until 1966); Federal Ministry of Economic Affairs (1966-1971); Managing Director of a federal association at Bonn (1971-1975). Publications: Energy Supply Contracts, 1991. Thesis in commercial and tax law, several publications on restrictive agreements of cartels; commentary on Antitrust-Law. Co-Author: Handbook of Mergers and Acquisitions (to be published in 1995).

DR. FRANZ-CHRISTIAN GENZOW, born Bad Salzungen, December 22, 1947; admitted, 1974. *Education:* Universities of Münster, Geneva, Cologne, Cornell (Ithaca/USA). Publications: Law of General Terms and Conditions of Business, Law of Authorized Dealers, Labour Law and Competition Law. Founding Member of the German-American Lawyers' Association.

DR. CHRISTIAN-ERNST OSTERMANN, born Bad Oeynhausen, May 3, 1945; admitted, 1978. *Education:* Universities of Cologne, Hamburg. Publications: Commentary on Property Management, Competition Law, Insurance Law. *Member:* German Association for the Protection of Industrial Property; German-Italian Lawyer's Association; Canadian-German Lawyers Association. (Also Of Counsel, Funck-Brentano & Partners, Paris, France).

RENATE RENÉE GENZOW, born Cologne, March 1, 1955; admitted, 1983. *Education:* University of Cologne. AKF-Leasing Bank, 1983. *Member:* German-American Lawyer's Association.

JÜRGEN K. FRIEDRICH, born Dresden, December 7, 1951; admitted, 1983. *Education:* University of Cologne. Publications on the Law of Leasing. Legal Adviser in the Banking and Leasing Department of the AKF Leasing-Bank, 1983. Founding Member of the Union of West and East German Business Lawyers.

WOLFRAM MICHAEL BRÜCK, born Cologne, February 27, 1937; admitted, 1989. *Education:* Universities of Cologne and Freiburg. Attorney at Law until 1970. Clerk of Federal Parliament until 1977. Commissioner, City of Frankfurt, 1977-1986; Mayor, City of Frankfurt, 1986-1989. General Director of Treuhand, Berlin, 1990-1991. Managing Director, Der Grüne Punkt Duales System Deutschland GmbH, 1991—.

STEFAN RIZOR, born Hannover, July 8, 1961; admitted, 1990. *Education:* Universities of Würzburg and McGill (LL.M., 1990). Publications: Commentary on the draft EEC Directive on Packaging and Packaging Waste. *Member:* German-American Lawyers Association; Canadian-German Lawyers Association (Board).

HELMUT KRÜGER, born Hannover, April 21, 1957; admitted, 1990, Germany. *Education:* Universities of Bielefeld and Bonn. *Member:* German-American Lawyers Association.

RALPH STOCK, born Cologne, October 19, 1962; admitted, 1991. *Education:* University of Cologne. Legal Department of Arthur Anderson &

(This Listing Continued)

Co., 1990-1991. *Member:* German-Portuguese and German-Brazilian Lawyers Associations.

JÖRG M. PÖSCHL, born Velbert, February 27, 1960; admitted, 1992. *Education:* University of Bonn. Associate in the Dresden Office, 1990-1992. *Member:* German-American Lawyers Association.

RALF SCHLÖSSER, born Münster, July 22, 1959; admitted, 1992, Tax Advisor (Steuerberater). *Education:* University of Münster. Member, Tax Department, Arthur Andersen & Co., 1990-1992. *Member:* German-British Lawyers Association.

RUDOLF HÜBNER-WEINGARTEN, born Kiel, January 23, 1953; admitted, 1983, Tax Counsel (Fachanwalt für Steuerrecht). *Education:* Universities of Innsbruck, Munich and Kiel. Judge, District Court of Munich until 1982. Partner of major law offices (Munich and Cologne). *Member:* Tax Law Council (Cologne Bar Association).

MARCUS SACRE, born Wuppertal, May 5, 1962; admitted, 1993. *Education:* University of Cologne, Law, History, English Literature and Latin (M.A., 19 87). Publication: Theodore Roosevelt and American Judicial Reforms During the Progressive Era 1993; public relation department of Bayer AG, Leverkusen. *Member:* German-American Lawyers Association.

DR. TOBIAS LENZ, born Mettmann, November 20, 1961; admitted, 1993. *Education:* University of Cologne. Research Assistant, Institute for Insurance Law of the University of Cologne, 1989. Publications in national and international Insurance Law including Die Kulanzleistung des Versicherers, 1993.

Member of Eurolegal

Languages: German, English, French and Portuguese.

GURLAND & LAMBSDORFF

EUGEN-LANGEN STRASSE, 12
D-50968 COLOGNE, GERMANY
Telephone: 221-937071-0
Telefax: 221-937071-99

Also offices in Berlin, Frankfurt and Leipzig.

General Business and International Practice, Corporate, Company, Commercial, Unfair Competition, Acquisitions and Mergers, Distribution and Franchise Law, Antitrust, EEC, Trademark, Computer and Copyright Law, Insolvency, Collective and Individual Labour Law, Food Stuffs, Wine and Spirits and Environmental Law.

FIRM PROFILE: *The law firm of GURLAND & LAMBSDORFF is the result of a merger between GURLAND & PARTNERS, in Cologne, and LAMBSDORFF & PARTNERS, in Frankfurt, in 1990. The separate firms and now the firm GURLAND & LAMBSDORFF were and are one of the German law firms representing domestic foreign clients in all fields of commercial, business and both national and international law. An important part of the practice is the legal aspects of transnational business, especially within the EEC. GURLAND & LAMBSDORFF not only advises German clients in international matters but also foreign enterprises and clients on doing business in Germany and elswhere. The majority of lawyers and members of the support-staff are fluent in English, French and other foreign languages.*

Clients of the firm are many well-known German and foreign companies in a wide variety of businesses.

In the Frankfurt office there are 2 partners whoare also qualified to act as notaries and are specially licensed to prepare and execute documents relating to the incorporation of companies, real estate, probate matters and other important commercial transactions requiring, in German law, a notarial form of document.

In GURLAND & LAMBSDORFF there are more than 20 attorney, including 9 partners, and a support-staff of more than 50 people, working in the 4 offices.

MEMBERS OF FIRM

DR. HARRO GURLAND, born 1931; admitted, 1961, Germany; 1993, Paris, France. *Education:* Universities of Tübingen (Dr. of Law, 1960) and Paris. Lecturer, University of Strasbourg (France), Franchise Law. *Member:* German Bar Association; Association for the Protection of Industrial Property and Copyright; Association of European Advocates; International Union of Advocates; International Chamber of Commerce; International Association of Young Lawyers (Honorary President, 1976). *LANGUAGES:* German, French and English.

(This Listing Continued)

GURLAND & LAMBSDORFF, Cologne—Continued

DIETER P. ZENZ, born 1934; admitted, 1963, Germany. *Education:* Universities of Freiburg, Lausanne and Cologne. *Member:* German Bar Association; Association of Practitioners in Insolvency and Arbitration Law; ICC-International Chamber of Commerce; Bank Law Society/Academic Society on the Law of Banking and Stock Exchange. *LANGUAGES:* German, French and English.

DR. ULRICH WACKERHAGEN, born 1942; admitted, 1973, Germany. *Education:* Universities of Munich and Lausanne; Regensburg (Dr. of Law, 1974). Chairman: Alumni Association of Salem; Linden Foundation for Pre-School Education under the auspices of the Stifterverband. Member of the Board, Kurt Hahn Foundation under the auspices of the Stifterverband. *Member:* The German Chamber of Industry and Commerce in the United Kingdom; Anglo-German Jurists' Association; Cologne (Committee for Employment and Labour Law) and German Bar Associations; Federal Association of Young Businessmen. *LANGUAGES:* German, English and French.

ULRICH C. FELDMANN, born 1942; admitted, 1971, Germany. *Education:* Universities of Bonn, Berlin and Cologne; INSEAD Fontainebleau/France (M.B.A. INSEAD, 1969). Author: "Lebensmittelwerberecht," in RWW, 1988. *Member:* German Bar Association; European Food Law Association; Academic Society of Food Law; German-British Jurists' Society; German-French Jurists' Society; German-Belgium Jurists' Society; Association of European Advocates; International Union of Advocates; International Bar Association; International Association of Young Lawyers (Honorary Vice-President 1987). *LANGUAGES:* German, English and French.

ASSOCIATES

DR. WERNER THELEN, born 1956; admitted, 1986, Germany. *Education:* University of Cologne (Dr. of Law, 1988). *Member:* Banking Law Association-Academic Society for Banking Law; The German-Japanese Jurists' Association; Society for Transport and Carriage of Goods Law. *LANGUAGES:* German and English.

Member of LEGALLIANCE EEIG (Association of European Law Firms): ADER, JOLIBOIS & ASSOCIES, Paris; BAILEYS, SHAW & GILLETT, London; SARDA, CALOMARDE, CASTELO Y ASOCIADOS, Barcelona/Valencia/Madrid; SCAMONI E ASSOCIATI, Milano/Bologna/Padova; WILLEMART & ASSOCIES, Brussels/Tongres/-Namur; BARENTS & KRANS, The Hague/Brussels; VERUM ADVOKATFIRMAN, Stockholm.

HECKER, WERNER & HIMMELREICH

Rechtsanwälte

Established in 1969

BRABANTER STRASSE 53

D-50672 COLOGNE, GERMANY

Telephone: (0221) 5 79 99-0

Telefax: (0221) 57 999-200

Leipzig, Germany Office: Richard-Lehmann-Straße 31, D-04275. Telephone: (0341) 477 83 77-79. Telefax: (0341) 477 82 10.

Berlin, Germany Office: Kurfürstendamm 66, D-10707. Telephone: (030) 8 85 26 05. Telefax: (030) 8 86 07 91.

General Practice, Company, Commercial, Banking, Competition, Labor, Construction, Real Property, Road Traffic, Insurance, Medical Malpractice and Administrative Law, Arbitration and Litigation, Mergers and Acquisitions.

MEMBERS OF FIRM

PAUL F. HECKER, born Cologne, Germany, December 18, 1936; admitted, 1968, Cologne; 1983, Cologne Court of Appeal. *Education:* Universities of Bruxelles, Vienna and Cologne. Co-Author: Hecker/Tschöpe, "Der Arbeitsgerichtsprozess," 1989; Sattler/Hecker, "So kaufen Sie eine Firma oder eine Beteiligung," 1992. Lecturer, Legal Academy of the German Bar Association, 1983-1992; Haus der Technik e.V. Essen, 1989—; Technische Akademie Esslingen (TAE), 1990—; Württembergische Verwaltungs- und Wirtschaftsakademie, 1991—. *Member:* German Bar Association (Member, International Law Committee). (Also at Leipzig Office). *LANGUAGES:* German, French and English. *PRACTICE AREAS:* Mergers and Acquisitions.

DR. ULRICH WERNER, born Berlin, Germany, May 14, 1940; admitted, 1968, Cologne. *Education:* Universities of Cologne (Dr. jur., 1967) and

(This Listing Continued)

Freiburg. Co-Author: Werner/Pastor, "Der Bauprozess," 1993; Werner/-Pastor, "Lexikon des Baurechts," 1991; Werner/Pastor, "Rechtsfragen beim Bauen," 1993. Lecturer, University of Aachen, 1987—. *Member:* German Association of Construction Law. *LANGUAGES:* German and English. *PRACTICE AREAS:* Construction; Real Property; Arbitration.

DR. KLAUS HIMMELREICH, born Cologne, Germany, October 2, 1937; admitted, 1968, Cologne. *Education:* Universities of Freiburg and Cologne (Dr. jur., 1969). Co-Author: Himmelreich/Hentschel, "Fahrverbot/Führerscheinentzug"; Himmelreich/Klimke/Bücken, "Kfz-Schadensregulierung,"; Himmelreich/Bücken, "Musterschriftsätze Verkehrsrecht,"; Himmelreich/Bücken, "Verkehrsunfallflucht,"; Himmelreich-/Janker MPU-Begutachtung. Publisher and Editor of German Legal Journal for Motorists, 1988—. Lecturer, Legal Academy of the German Bar Association, 1978—. *Member:* German Road Traffic Law Academy; German Association of Public Defenders. *LANGUAGES:* German and English. *PRACTICE AREAS:* Road Traffic; Criminal Law.

HANS-GEORG KURELLA, born Neukirchen-Vluyn, Germany, July 13, 1946; admitted, 1977, Cologne. *Education:* University of Cologne. *Member:* German Family Law Council; German Bar Association; Original President of "Deutscher Jagdrechtstag". *LANGUAGES:* German and English. *PRACTICE AREAS:* Family; Marital; Probate Law; Hunting Law.

DR. CARL GUSTAV CREMER, born Düsseldorf, Germany, September 7, 1938; admitted, 1976, Cologne. *Education:* Universities of Freiburg, Munich and Bonn; Assistant, Cologne Institute of Criminal Science (Dr. jur., 1972). Lecturer, TÜV-Academy, Cologne. *Member:* German Bar Association (Member, Road Traffic Law Committee); German Association of Public Defenders. *LANGUAGES:* German, English and French. *PRACTICE AREAS:* Road Traffic; Criminal Law.

MICHAEL BÜCKEN, born Aachen, Germany, September 3, 1951; admitted, 1980, Cologne. *Education:* University of Cologne. Co-Author: Himmelreich/Bücken, "Musterschriftsätze Verkehrsrecht" ; Himmelreich-/Bücken, "Verkehrsunfallflucht"; Himmelreich/Klimke/Bücken "Kfz-Schadensregulierung." Lecturer, Legal Academy of the German Bar Association, 1984—. *Member:* German Bar Association (Member, Road Traffic Law Committee); German Association of Public Defenders. *LANGUAGES:* German and English. *PRACTICE AREAS:* Insurance; Road Traffic; Medical Malpractice.

GERD RAGUSS, born Cologne, Germany, September 30, 1952; admitted, 1981, Cologne. *Education:* University of Cologne. Lecturer, TÜV-Academy, Cologne. *Member:* German Bar Association (Member, Labor Law Committee). *LANGUAGES:* German and English. *PRACTICE AREAS:* Labor; Law on Agency.

LORENZ KNEER, born Arnsberg, Germany, September 20, 1949; admitted, 1983, Cologne. *Education:* University of Cologne. Lecturer, TÜV-Academy, Cologne. *Member:* German Bar Association; Bundesvereinigung Öffentliches Recht e.V. *LANGUAGES:* German and English. *PRACTICE AREAS:* Administrative Law; Construction; Industrial Property.

PETRA CHRISTIANSEN-GEISS, born Hanover, Germany, October 28, 1955; admitted, 1984, Cologne; 1987, Cologne Court of Appeal. *Education:* Universities of Bonn and Cologne. *LANGUAGES:* German and English. *PRACTICE AREAS:* Construction; Real Property; Medical Malpractice.

HEINZ-PETER VERSPAY, born Moers, Germany, November 3, 1950; admitted, 1983, Cologne; Vereidigter Buchprüfer (Certified Public Accountant). *Education:* University of Cologne. Co-author: Sattler/Verspay, "Der Ingenieur als GmbH-Geschäftsführer," 1993. Lecturer, Haus der Technik e.V., Essen. *Member:* German Bar Association (Member, International Law Committee); German-French Lawyers Association; Belgian-German Lawyers Association. *LANGUAGES:* German, English and French. *PRACTICE AREAS:* Tax; Company; Mergers and Acquisitions.

WERNER GROSSPIETSCH, born Leverkusen, Germany, April 29, 1955; admitted, 1986, Cologne; 1991, Cologne Court of Appeal. *Education:* University of Cologne. Lecturer, Legal Academy of the German Bar Association, 1992. *Member:* German Bar Association (Member, Labor Law Committee). *LANGUAGES:* German and English. *PRACTICE AREAS:* Labor Law.

ULRICH DÖLLE, born Düren, Germany, March 16, 1957; admitted, 1988, Cologne. *Education:* University of Cologne. *Member:* German Bar Association. *LANGUAGES:* German and English. *PRACTICE AREAS:* Construction; Real Property.

HILTRUD KOHNEN, born Willich-Anrath, Germany, May 30, 1960; admitted, 1992, Cologne. *Education:* Universities of Nürnberg (Erlangen)

(This Listing Continued)

and Cologne. *LANGUAGES:* German, English and French. *PRACTICE AREAS:* Labor Law; Contract of Sales; Leasing Law.

DR. HANS DIETER MONTAG, born Cologne, Germany, October 29, 1959; admitted, 1993, Berlin. *Education:* Universities of Regensburg and Cologne (Dr. jur., 1993). *Member:* German-British Lawyers Association; German-American Lawyers Association; International Bar Association. *LANGUAGES:* German and English. *PRACTICE AREAS:* Commercial and Company; Banking; Real Property.

CHANTAL ZALANE, born Brussels, Belgium, March 19, 1963; admitted, 1990, Brussels (Avocat au barreau de Bruxelles); 1992, Cologne. *Education:* University of Bruxelles. *Member:* Belgian-German Lawyers Association; Belgian Business Club (Cologne); Debelux; German-Israelian Lawyers Association. *LANGUAGES:* German, French and English. *PRACTICE AREAS:* Belgian and International Law.

CHR. MANFRED KLETTE

KAISER-WILHELM-RING 2
50672 COLOGNE, GERMANY
Telephone: 49-221-132041
Telefax: 49-221-132045

Competition, Copyright, Industrial Property Rights, Unfair Competition, Trade Marks, Food and Drug Law, General International Practice.

CHR. MANFRED KLETTE, born Zwickau, Germany, September 1, 1941; admitted, 1977, Cologne; 1979, Cologne Court of Appeals. *Education:* Universities of Tübingen and Bonn, Harvard University (LL.M., 1970). Publications: Numerous Articles and Papers on Industrial Property Rights, Unfair Competition and Constitutional Law. *Member:* International Bar Association (Vice-Chairman, 1988-1991, and Chairman, 1992-1995, Committee on Products Liability, Advertising, Unfair Competition and Consumer Affairs); German and International Association for the Protection of Industrial Property (AIPPI); Studienvereinigung Kartellrecht, European Communities Trade Mark Association (ECTA); German-American Lawyers-Association. *LANGUAGES:* German, English and French.

KLUMPE & PARTNER

Rechtsanwälte

LUXEMBURGER STRASSE 282 E
D-50937 COLOGNE, GERMANY
Telephone: Int. 49 (221) 94 20 94 - 0
Telefax: Int. 49 (221) 94 20 94 - 25
Telex: 8 883 021 RAWK

Investments, Contracts, Corporate Law, Commercial Law, Criminal Law, Banks and Banking, Securities and Capital Markets, Building, Real Estate, Construction Law, Leases and Leasing, Communications and Media, Family Law, Labor and Employment, Bankruptcy, Unfair Competition, Trusts and Estates, General Practice, Appellate Practice.

MEMBERS OF FIRM

WERNER KLUMPE, born Duisburg, Germany, March 31, 1948; admitted, 1976, Germany. *Education:* University of Cologne. Author: "Haftung und Besteuerung des Vermögensberaters"; "Immobilienfonds." Co-editor: "Recht und Praxis der Kapitalanlage (RPK)"; "Handbuch der Bauinvestitionen und Immobilienkapitalanlagen (HdB)." *Member:* German Bar Association. *LANGUAGES:* German and English. *PRACTICE AREAS:* Investments; Trust Planning; Corporate Real Estate.

MARTIN JAGNER, born Travemuende, Germany, July 13, 1951; admitted, 1981, Germany. *Education:* University of Cologne. *Member:* German Bar Association (Criminal Law Committee); Deutsche Gesellschaft f. Baurecht, German-American Lawyers' Association; Institut für Baurecht Freiburg im Breisgau e.V. *LANGUAGES:* German and English. *PRACTICE AREAS:* Criminal Law; White Collar Crime; Building; General Practice.

ALEXANDER KIESSLING, born Cologne, Germany, April 21, 1950; admitted, 1982, Germany. *Education:* University of Bonn. Co-author: "Handbuch d. Bauherrengemeinschaften zu Prospekthaftung/Vertriebsprovision." *Member:* German Bar Association. *LANGUAGES:* German and English. *PRACTICE AREAS:* Labour and Employment; Appellate Practice; Agency.

(This Listing Continued)

ACHIM WERNER, born Cologne, Germany, August 28, 1955; admitted, 1984, Germany. *Education:* University of Cologne. *Member:* German Bar Association; Institut für Baurecht Freiburg im Breisgau e.V. *LANGUAGES:* German and English. *PRACTICE AREAS:* Real Estate Investment; Heritage; Executry.

WOLFGANG R.W. ARNDT, born Cologne, Germany, May 4, 1951; admitted, 1983, Germany. *Education:* Universities of Cologne and Bonn. *Member:* German Bar Association. *LANGUAGES:* German and French. *PRACTICE AREAS:* Bankruptcy; Commercial Law; Banking; Unfair Competition.

FRANZ-JOSEF SCHROEDER, born Cologne, Germany, October 22, 1955; admitted, 1984, Germany. *Education:* University of Cologne. Author: "Die Gesellschaft Bürgerlichen Rechts mit Haftungsbeschränkung - eine sinnvolle Gestaltungsvariante?" *Member:* German Law Association; Deutscher Juristentag e.V. *LANGUAGES:* German and English. *PRACTICE AREAS:* Investments; Trusts; Corporate Law; Mutual Funds.

MONIKA FINK-PLÜCKER, born Butzbach, Germany, August 29, 1957; admitted, 1985, Germany. *Education:* Universities of Giessen and Marburg. *Member:* German Bar Association. *LANGUAGES:* German and English. *PRACTICE AREAS:* Leases; Family Law; Condominium Law.

INGRID KÜHNAU, born Cologne, Germany, July 29, 1954; admitted, 1987, Germany. *Education:* University of Cologne. Co-author: "Handbuch der Bauinvestitionen und Imobilienkapitalanlagen (HdB)." *Member:* German Bar Association. *LANGUAGES:* German and French. *PRACTICE AREAS:* Banking; Capital Markets; Press Law.

DIPL. KFM JÜRGEN MÜLLER, born Hurth, Germany, January 22, 1957; admitted, 1990, Germany. *Education:* University of Cologne. *Member:* German Bar Association. *LANGUAGES:* German and English. *PRACTICE AREAS:* Media Law; Contract Law; Construction Law.

ULRICH A. NASTOLD, born Bad Mergentheim, Germany, April 11, 1960; admitted, 1990, Germany. *Education:* Universities of Heidelberg and Saarbrücken. Author: "Rechtshandbuch Ost-Immobilien"; "Immobilienfonds"; "Ausgewählte rechtliche Probleme beim Einsatz von Beratungstechnologien im Finanzdienstleistungsbereich." *Member:* German Bar Association; German-American Lawyers' Association; Institut für Baurecht Freiburg im Breisgau e.V. *LANGUAGES:* German, English and French. *PRACTICE AREAS:* Investments; Corporate Real Estate; Corporate Contracts.

DR. THOMAS ZACHER, born Cologne, Germany, July 27, 1961; admitted, 1993, Germany. *Education:* University of Cologne (Dr.jur., 1991). Author: "Schuldrecht Allgemeiner Teil"; "Kapitalsicherung und Haftung in der GmbH & Co. KG." *Member:* German Bar Association; German-Czech Jurists Association ; Verein zur Förderung der Rechtswissenschaft. *LANGUAGES:* German and English. *PRACTICE AREAS:* Securities; Corporate Law; Taxation.

JOERG FISCHER, born Zweibrücken, Germany, September 3, 1963; admitted, 1994, Germany. *Education:* Universities of Saarbrücken and Cologne. *Member:* German Bar Association; German-American Lawyers' Association. *LANGUAGES:* German, English and French. *PRACTICE AREAS:* White Collar Crime; Corporate Law; Litigation.

KÜBLER, ROGIER & PARTNER

AACHENER STRASSE 217
D-50931 COLOGNE, GERMANY
Telephone: 0221/400 770
Telefax: 0221/400 7720

Berlin, Germany Office: Einemstrasse 24, D-10785. Telephone: (030) 264768-0. Telefax: (030) 264768-40.
Dresden, Germany Office: Antonstrasse 10, D-01097. Telephone: (0351) 44 879-0. Telefax: (0351) 44 879-99.

Bankruptcy, Banking, Corporate, Commercial, Creditors' Rights, Industrial Relations and Labor Law, Insolvency and Reorganization, International Private, Property and Real Estate, Taxation, Unfair Competition, General Practice and Litigation.

MEMBERS OF FIRM

DR. BRUNO M. KÜBLER, born Düsseldorf, Germany, April 6, 1945; admitted, 1970, Cologne; 1974, Cologne Court of Appeals. *Education:* Universities of Cologne (Doctor of Law, 1969), Fribourg (Switzerland) and Munich. Publisher and Managing Editor-in-Chief, "Zeitschrift für Wirtschaftsrecht" (ZIP) and "Entscheidungen zum Wirtschaftsrecht" (EWiR).

(This Listing Continued)

KÜBLER, ROGIER & PARTNER, Cologne—Continued

Editor: "Neuordnung des Insolvenzrechts", 1989; "Das Gesamtvollstreckungsrecht in den neuen Bundesländern," 1992. Co-Editor: "Beiträge zum Insolvenzrecht". Partner and Managing Director of Kübler & Weber Unternehmensberatung GmbH Wirtschaftsprüfungsgesellschaft Steuerberatungsgesellschaft. *Member:* Bar Association and Lawyers Association of Cologne; Institute of Chartered Accountants (IdW); International Bar Association; European Association of Insolvency Practitioners, AEPPC (President); International Fiscal Association; Union Internationale des Avocats; German American Lawyers Association; German-British Jurist's Association; German Association for the Protection of Industrial Property Rights; Deutscher Juristentag; Cologne Legal Society. *LANGUAGES:* German, English and French.

DR. JOACHIM ROGIER, born St. Annaberg, Germany, March 21, 1947; admitted, 1976, Cologne; 1979, Cologne Court of Appeals. *Education:* Universities of Münster and Munich (Doctor of Law, 1981). Legal Assistant, Cologne University, 1975-1982. *Member:* Bar Association and Lawyers Association of Cologne; German Association for the Protection of Industrial Property Rights. *LANGUAGES:* German and English.

HORST E. MÜLLER-WÜSTEN, born Cologne, Germany, May 11, 1942; admitted, 1974, Cologne; 1981, Cologne Court of Appeals. *Education:* Universities of Cologne, Bonn and Speyer. Assistant Corporate Counsel, New York, 1970. Assistant at the Institute for Banking Law, Cologne University, 1975-1979. *Member:* Bar Association and Lawyers Association of Cologne; German American Lawyers Association; European Association of Insolvency Practitioners, AEPPC; Deutscher Juristentag; Cologne Legal Society. *LANGUAGES:* German and English.

DR. CHRISTOPH JUNKER, born Iserlohn, Germany, March 13, 1954; admitted, 1983, Düsseldorf; 1985, Cologne. *Education:* Universities of Münster (Doctor of Law, 1981) and London. Legal Assistant, Münster University, 1977-1980. *Member:* Bar Association and Lawyers Association of Cologne; European Association of Insolvency Practitioners, AEPPC; Cologne Legal Society. *LANGUAGES:* German, English and French.

DIPL.-KFM. RICHARD WEBER, born Dresden, Germany, October 5, 1923. *Education:* University of Cologne, Germany (Diploma in Economic Science, 1951). Certified Public Accountant, Germany, 1958. Certified Tax Advisor, Germany, 1965. *Member:* Certified Public Accountants Association, Düsseldorf; Association of Tax Advisors. *LANGUAGES:* German, English.

ASSOCIATE

DR. HANS-GEORG KNOTHE, born Lodz, Poland, March 6, 1943; admitted, 1987, Cologne. *Education:* Law studies in Bonn; Doctor of Law, 1980. Author: "Die Geschäftsfähigkeit der Minderjährigen in geschichtlicher Entwicklung," 1983; "Die Rücknahme von Widersprüchen gegen Errichtungsgenehmigungen von Kraftwerken gegen Entgelt - BGHZ 79, 131, in: JuS 1983, 18; "Umfunktionierte' Klassiker-Aufführung ohne Hinweis - vertragsgemässe Theaterleistung?, in NJW 1984, 1074; "Das Erbbaurecht," 1987. Judge, 1974-1976. Assistant: Institute of Roman Law and Civil Law, University of Cologne, 1976-1987. Lecturer: University of Cologne. *Member:* Zivilrechtslehrervereinigung. *LANGUAGES:* German and English.

(For complete biographical data on Personnel at Berlin and Dresden, Germany Offices, see Professional Biographies at those locations)

DR. GINO LÖRCHER

Established in 1979

THEODOR-HEUSS-RING 62
D-50668 COLOGNE, GERMANY
Telephone: (49 221) 13 62 01
Fax: (49 221) 13 62 72 (Groups II & III)

Commercial and Corporate Law. International Contracts. Patent and Know-How Licensing, Agency and Distribution. Franchising. Joint Ventures. Arbitration, Legal Opinions.

FIRM PROFILE: Advising foreign corporations in English, French and Italian, on basis of 15 years as in-house counsel in international groups and 10 years spent in England, France, Italy and Belgium.

DR. GINO LÖRCHER, born Stuttgart, Germany, January 31, 1933; admitted, 1972, Germany. *Education:* University of Tübingen (Doctor-at-Law; First State Examination); University of Grenoble, France (1954-1955); The Johns Hopkins Bologna Center, Italy (1958-1959); EEC

(This Listing Continued)

Trainee, Brussels, 1961-1962 and Second State Examination of Law. Author: "RFA. L'arbitrage commercial," Moniteur du Commerce International, 1984, pp. 161 ss.; "L'Arbitrato Commerciale in Germania," Il Commercio Italo-Germanico, 10/1985. "Übernahme des UNCITRAL-Modellgesetzes?" Zeitschrift für Rechtspolitik 1987, pp. 230 ss. "Le Choix du Lieu de l'Arbitrage: Allemagne." Union Internationale des Avocats, Rapports de la Commission Arbitrage International, 1991, pp. 12 ss. Book on *"Treaty-Making Power of the Three European Communities (EEC, etc.),"* Bouvier, Bonn, 1965, 265 pp. In-house Counsel, 1964-1979. Senior Legal Officer-International, Inco Europe in London. General Counsel, Girmes-Werke, AG, Oedt. Chief Legal and Patents Officer and Director of Demag AG, Duisburg. Chief Legal and Patents Officer and Vice-President, Schmalbach-Lubeca GmbH, Braunschweig (Subsidiary of The Continental Group, Inc., New York). Arbitrator, International and Commercial Panel of Arbitrators, American Arbitration Association, World Intellectual Property Organization. Chairman, International Lawyers' Group, 1980-1987. Secretary, Working Group on Franchising, Union Internationale des Avocats, 1987—. *Member:* German Arbitration Institute; The Chartered Institute of Arbitrators, London (Fellow); ICC Institute of International Business Law and Practice, Paris (Corresponding Member) Associazione Giuristi di Lingua Italiana, Milan. *LANGUAGES:* English, German, French and Italian. *PRACTICE AREAS:* Distribution; Commercial Arbitration; International Commercial Law; Company Acquisitions and Sale; Breach of Contracts; International Contracts; Incorporation; Franchise Agreements; Intellectual Property Licensing; Conflict of Laws; International Trade Arbitration.

LÜER & GÖRG

Established in 1974

KONRAD-ADENAUER-UFER 21
D-50668 COLOGNE, GERMANY
Telephone: (0221) 916440
Telex: 8 885 109 JUS D;
Telex: 2627-2214263 JUSD;
Telecopier: (0221) 916 44 30

Berlin, Germany Office: Kurfürstendamm 54/55, D-10707 Berlin.
Telephone: (030) 884503-0. Telecopier: (030) 8827150.

General and International Law Practice, Corporate and Commercial Law, Banking, Insurance and Reinsurance, Bankruptcy and Insolvency Law, Mergers and Acquisitions, Litigation and Arbitration, Labor and Co-determination Law, Antitrust, Unfair Competition and Intellectual Property Law, Private International Law, EEC Law and Environmental Law, Tax Law.

MEMBERS OF FIRM

DR. HANS-JOCHEM LÜER, born Stuttgart, Germany, March 20, 1938; admitted, 1974, Cologne; 1992, Court of Appeals. *Education:* Universities of Tübingen, Bonn, Cologne (Dr. iur., 1968); University of California at Berkeley, School of Law (LL.M., 1964). Author: "The Lex Loci Delicti in Single Contact Cases," Nederlands Tijdschrift voor International Recht, 1965, 124; "Die Begrenzung der Haftung bei fahrlässig begangenen unerlaubten Handlungen," 1969; "Devisenhandel und Bankenaufsicht," WM, 1977, Sonderbeilage Nr. 1; "Einzelzwangsvollstreckung im Ausland bei inländischen Insolvenzverfahren," KTS, 1978, 200, 1979, 12; "Börsentermingeschäftsfähigkeit und Differenzeinwand," JZ, 1979, 171; "Einheitliches Insolvenzrecht innerhalb der Europäischen Gemeinschaften-Die Quadratur des Kreises?" KTS, 1981, 147; "Reform des deutschen Insolvenzrechts und europäische Rechtsvereinheitlichung," Der Deutsche Rechtspfleger 1984, 209; "Non-Contractual Liabilities of Related Third Parties in Bankruptcy of a Legal Entity," in Challenges to the Legal Profession (Lucknow, India 1984) 352-374; "Comments on German International Bankruptcy Law," in Kuhn-Uhlenbruck, Konkursordnung, 10th ed., 1986, 1949-1988; "Deutsch-Amerikanischer Justizkonflikt," Produkthaftpflicht International 1987, 166-177; "Allgemeine Wirkungen des Konkurses," in Vorschläge und Gutachten zum Entwurf eines EG-Konkursübereinkommens (1988) 341-355; "German Court Decisions Interpreting and Implementing the New York Convention," 7 Journal of International Arbitration (1990) 127-138; "Überlegungen zu einem künftigen deutschen Internationalen Insolvenzrecht, KTS, 1990, 377-402. Banking Secrecy in Germany, The Comparative Law Year Book of International Business 12 (1990), 211-225. "Zur Neuordnung des deutschen Internationalen Insolvenzrechts," in: Stellungnahmen und Gutachten zur Reform des deutschen Internationalen Insolvenzrechts (1992) 96-143. *Member:* International Bar Association; Deutscher Juristentag. *LAN-*

(This Listing Continued)

GUAGES: German and English. *PRACTICE AREAS:* Banking and Insurance Law; Corporate Law; Mergers and Acquisitions; Insolvency Law.

DR. KLAUS HUBERT GÖRG, born Düsseldorf, Germany, November 27, 1940; admitted, 1972, Cologne. *Education:* Universities of Marburg, Munich, Cologne (Dr. iur., 1970). Author: "Nachträgliche Leistungsstörungen im Bereich arbeitsrechtlicher Wettbewerbsverbote," Cologne, 1970; "Zur Konkurrenz von Sachhaftung und persönlicher Haftung bei der Feststellung des Ausfalls nach § 64 KO oder § 27 VglO," KTS 1987, 191. *Member:* Deutscher Juristentag. *LANGUAGES:* German and English. *PRACTICE AREAS:* Insolvency Law; Corporate Law; Banking Law.

DR. HANS-JOACHIM GOLLING, born Cologne, Germany, December 28, 1942; admitted, 1971, Cologne, Tax Advisor. *Education:* Universities of Marburg and Cologne (Dr. iur., 1968). Author: "Manufacturer's Liability," Modern Law and Society, 1968, 135; "Zum Abschluss von Wärmelieferungsverträgen," BB, 1970, 324; "Die Verantwortlichkeit der Vorstandsmitglieder für ihre Geschäftsführung gemäss §93 Akt. Gesetz," 1969. *LANGUAGES:* German, French and English. *PRACTICE AREAS:* Insolvency Law; Corporate Law; Banking Law.

DR. ARNOLD SCHULTZE-VON LASAULX, born Jena, Germany, February 2, 1939; admitted, 1975, Cologne; 1992, Court of Appeals. *Education:* Universities of Hamburg (Dr. iur., 1976), Munich and Paris; Institut de Droit Comparé (Diplôme de Droit Comparé, 1965). Author: "Die Vertragsaufhebung im Haager Einheitlichen Kaufgesetz-System und Kritik," 1977; "Gilt für Änderungen des Gesellschaftsvertrages einer GmbH & Co. KG das Verbot des Selbstkontrahierens?: Zeitschrift für Unternehmens-und Gesellschaftsrecht, 1976, 33 (with Bernstein). *Member:* Deutscher Juristentag. *LANGUAGES:* German, French and English. *PRACTICE AREAS:* Insurance Law; Private International Law; Litigation.

DR. STEFAN T. SIEGEL, born Berlin, Germany, April 16, 1943; admitted, 1977, Cologne; Certified Specialist in Tax Law. *Education:* Universities of Würzburg, Lausanne and Freiburg (Dr. iur., 1975). *Member:* Deutsche Steuerjuristische Gesellschaft. *LANGUAGES:* German, French and English. *PRACTICE AREAS:* Tax Law; Corporate Law.

BERT JÜRGEN BOSTEN, born Cologne, Germany, November 28, 1947; admitted, 1977, Cologne. *Education:* University of Cologne. Author: "Zur kartellrechtlichen Zulässigkeit der Gemeinschaftswerbung, Archiv für Presserecht," 3/1974, 640-642; "Zur Einführung der Dienstleistungsmarke-Anwendung im Pressebereich," Archiv für Presserecht, 1980, 22; "Zur Haftung der Beteiligten bei einer wettbewerbswidrigen Gemeinschaftswerbung," Wettbewerb in Recht und Praxis, 1981, 1; Abgrenzungsprobleme zwischen Arzneimitteln und Kosmetika, Pharma Recht 1989, 214-217; Comment on BGH, June 22, 1989 - I ZR 39/87 - Archiv für Presserecht 1989, 666 (with Dr. Prinz); Wettbewerbsrechtlicher Titelschutz durch Titelschutzanzeige, Archiv für Presserecht 1991, 361-365 (with Dr. Prinz). *Member:* Deutsche Vereinigung für gewerblichen Rechtsschutz und Urheberrecht; Bund für Lebensmittelrecht und Lebensmittelkunde; Bundesfachverband der Arzneimittel-Hersteller; Deutscher Juristentag. *LANGUAGES:* German and English. *PRACTICE AREAS:* Unfair Competition Law; Food Law; Drug Law; Intellectual Property.

DR. WILHELM MOLL, born Gevelsberg, Germany, October 31, 1949; admitted, 1982, Cologne; Certified Specialist in Labor Law. *Education:* Universities of Marburg, Cologne (Dr. iur., 1977); University of California at Berkeley, School of Law (LL.M., 1981). Author: "Die Mitbestimmung des Betriebsrats beim Entgelt," 1977; "Der Tarifvorrang im Betriebsverfassungsgesetz," 1980; "Künstliche Beschäftigung im Kollektivvertragsrecht der USA und der Bundesrepublik Deutschland," 1982; "Zum Verhältnis von Streik und kollektiv ausgeübten Zurückbehaltungsrechten," RdA, 1976, 100-107; "Zur Insolvenzsicherung der Betriebsrenten von Gesellschafter-Geschäftsführern," ZIP, 1980, 422-425; "Zur Begründung von Rechtsansprüchen gegen betriebliche Unterstützungskassen," ZIP, 1980, 497-506; "Zur Einstandspflicht des Arbeitgebers bei Insolvenz betrieblicher Unterstützungskassen," ZIP, 1980, 733-741; "Dienstvergütung bei persönlicher Verhinderung", RdA, 1980, 138-155; "Anlegerschutz und Gläubigerschutz", BB, 1982, Beilage 3; "Telefondatenerfassung und betriebliche Mitbestimmung", Der Betrieb, 1982, 1722-1726; "Betriebliche Mitbestimmung beim Einsatz computergestützter Bildschirmarbeitsplätze", ZIP, 1982, 889-899; "Die außerordentliche betriebsbedingte (Änderungs-) Kündigung", Der Betrieb, 1984, 1346-1350; "Arbeitsrechtsvergleichung", RdA, 1984, 223-236; "Wie unbefangen ist der politische Richter?", Zeitschrift für Rechtspolitik, 1985, 244-247; "Zur Entscheidungsfrist der Hauptfürsorgestelle bei außerordentlichen Kündigungen gegenüber Schwerbehinderten", NZA, 1987, 550-552; "Der Ablösungsgedanke im Verhältnis zwischen Vertragsregelung und Betriebsvereinbarung", NZA, 1988, Beilage 1, 17-30; "Altersversorgung in Form von Direktzusagen als Sozialeinrichtung?", BB, 1988,

(This Listing Continued)

400-402. "Schadenersatzansprüche für unkündbare Arbeitnehmer nach §22 II KO bei Betriebsstillegungim Konkurs?" KTS , 1990, 563-570; "Betriebsübergang und Arbeitsverhältnisse," Anwaltsblatt, 1991, 282-298; "Altersgrenzen in Kollektivverträgen," Der Betrieb, 1992, 475-478; "Die Rechtsstellung des Arbeitnehmers nach einem Betriebsübergang," NJW, 1993, 2016-2023; "Altersgrenzen am Ende?", NJW, 1994, 499-501. Co-Author: "Aushilfs- und Teilzeitbeschäftigung," 1990; "Das Beschwerdeverfahren nach dem Betriebsverfassungsgesetz 1972," RdA, 1973, 361-369; "Der persönliche Geltungsbereich des Gesetzes zur Verbesserung der betrieblichen Altersversorgung," RdA, 1977, 13-25. *Member:* Deutscher Juristentag; Deutscher Arbeitsgerichtsverband; Deutsch-Amerikanische Juristenvereinigung; Internationale Gesellschaft für das Recht der Arbeit und der Sozialen Sicherheit; International Bar Association; International Association of Boalt Hall Alumni; Boalt Hall Alumni Association. *LANGUAGES:* German and English. *PRACTICE AREAS:* Labor Law; Corporate Law; Mergers & Acquisitions.

DR. THOMAS VON PLEHWE, born Duisburg, Germany, March 2, 1956; admitted, 1985, Bonn; 1990, Court of Appeals; Certified Specialist in Tax Law. *Education:* St. Paul's School, London; University of Bonn (Dr.iur., 1987). Author: "Besitzlose Warenkreditsicherheiten im Internationalen Privatrecht," 1987; "Leitfaden zum Europäischen Gerichtsstands-und Vollstreckungsübereinkommen," 1990 (with S. Reich and H. Tagaras). *Member:* European Lawyers Union; Association of German and Italian Lawyers; British Institute of International and Comparative Law; International Bar Association; Deutsche Vereinigung für gewerblichen Rechtsschutz und Urheberrecht. *LANGUAGES:* German, English and Italian. *PRACTICE AREAS:* Private International Law; International Procedural Law; Anti-Trust Law; Tax Law.

DR. GÜNTHER STEIN, born Coswig (b. Dresden), Germany, January 2, 1956; admitted, 1984, Cologne. *Education:* University of Cologne (Dr. iur., 1982). Author: "Die Inhaltskontrolle vorformulierter Verträge des allgemeinen Privatrechts," 1982; "Zur Bestimmung des zahlungpflichtigen Kunden bei Hausanschlüssen mit mehreren angeschlossenen Verbrauchern", Recht der Elektrizitätswirtschaft 1988, 22-27; "Die Treuhandanstalt im einstweiligen Verfügungsverfahren," ZIP 1992, 893. *LANGUAGES:* German and English. *PRACTICE AREAS:* East German Law; Environmental Law; Banking Law; Litigation.

DR. ULRICH JÜNGST, born Rheinberg, Germany, July 6, 1953; admitted, 1982, Cologne. *Education:* University of Cologne (Dr.iur., 1981). Author: "Der Missbrauch organschaftlicher Vertretungsmacht," 1981; "Der "Ehrenvorsitzende" in der Aktiengesellschaft," BB, 1984, 1583. *Member:* International Bar Association; Deutsch-Britische Juristenvereinigung. *LANGUAGES:* German and English. *PRACTICE AREAS:* Corporate Law; Commercial Transactions; Labor Law.

DR. CHRISTIAN WENNER, born Giessen, Germany, February 21, 1956; admitted, 1989, Cologne. *Education:* Universities of Marburg and Bonn (Dr.jur., 1990). Author: "Gleitender und fester Rang der Grundpfandrechte im deutschen, schweizerischen und österreichischen Recht," 1990; "Auslandskonkurs und Inlandsprozess: Rechtssicherheit contra Universalität im deutschen Internationalen Konkursrecht?" IPRax, 1989, 144-148 (with Dr. Ackmann); "Inlandswirkung des Auslandskonkurses: Verlustscheine und Restschuldbefreiungen," IPRax, 1990, 209-214 (with Dr. Ackmann); "Ausländisches Sanierungsverfahren, Inlandsarrest und § 238 KO," KTS 1990, 429-436; "Internationale Architektenverträge, insbesondere das Verhältnis Schuldstatut-HOAI," BauR 1993, 257-270. *Member:* International Bar Association; Deutsche Gesellschaft für Baurecht. *LANGUAGES:* German and English. *PRACTICE AREAS:* Domestic and International Architects and Construction Law; Computer Law; International Insolvency Law; Private International Law.

DR. WOLFGANG PRINZ, born Essen, Germany, March 3, 1958; admitted, 1989, Cologne. *Education:* Universities of Göttingen, Freiburg and Cologne (Dr. jur., 1988). Author: "Der gutgläubige Vormerkungserwerb" 1989; Comment on BGH, June 22, 1989 - I ZR 39/87 - Archiv für Presserecht 1989, 666 (with Bosten); Wettbewerbsrechtlicher Titelschutz durch Titelschutzanzeige, Archiv für Presserecht 1991, 361-365 (with Bosten). *Member:* Deutsche Vereinigung für gewerblichen Rechtsschutz und Urheberrecht. *LANGUAGES:* German and English. *PRACTICE AREAS:* Unfair Competition Law; Food Law; Drug Law; Copyright Law; Press Law; Trademark Law.

HANS-GERD H. JAUCH, born Bad Honnef, Germany, March 10, 1953; admitted, 1990, Cologne. *Education:* Universities of Cologne and Bonn. Author: "Die nicht getrennt gehaltene Kaution im Konkurs des Vermieters," WuM, 1989, 277; "Kündigung einer widerruflichen Direktversicherung durch den Konkursverwalter bei unverfallbarer Anwartschaft,"

(This Listing Continued)

LÜER & GÖRG, Cologne—Continued

KTS, 1989, 809; "Die Schnecke im Salat: Zur Wandelung bei verbrauchsbestimmten Sachen," JuS, 1990, 706; "Foreign and Multinational Business Insolvency in Germany," in: Multinational Commercial Insolvency, ABA Publication, 1993 (with Dr. Lüer), Internship with Kilpatrick & Cody, Atlanta,Georgia, USA, 1989. *Member:* Bund Katholischer Unternehmer (Association of Catholic Entrepreneurs, Board Member); International Bar Association. *LANGUAGES:* German and English. *PRACTICE AREAS:* Insolvency Law; Real Estate Law.

ROLF WEIDMANN, born Gelsenkirchen, Germany, May 31, 1955; admitted, 1986, Cologne. *Education:* Universities of Kiel and Bonn. *LANGUAGES:* German, English and French. *PRACTICE AREAS:* Insolvency Law; Corporate Law.

DR. MARTIN STOCKHAUSEN, born Dortmund, Germany, November 19, 1959; admitted, 1990, Cologne. *Education:* Universities of Cologne, Lausanne/Switzerland, Freiburg, Mainz and Hamburg, (Dr. jur., 1989). Author: "Ärztliche Berufsfreiheit und Kostendämpfung," 1992. *LANGUAGES:* German, French and English. *PRACTICE AREAS:* Banking Law; Extrajudicial Liquidation and Reorganization; Landlord and Tenant Law.

DR. MICHAEL DOLFEN, born Linnich, Germany, July 25, 1957; admitted, 1987, Cologne. *Education:* University of Cologne (Dr.iur., 1991). Author: "Der Verkehr im Europäischen Wettbewerbsrecht," 1991; "Der kombinierte Verkehr im Europäischen Recht der Wettbewerbsbeschränkungen," Euromodal, 1992; "Verkehrs-und Transportrecht," Handbuch des EG-Wirtschaftsrechts (with Basedow), 1993; Nacherhebung. Erstattung und Erlaß von Abgaben nach dem neuen Zollkodez, EuZW, 1993; "Europäisches Privatrecht im Werden," Festschrift Rheinische Justiz, Geschichte und Gegenwart, 175 Jahre Oberlandesgericht Köln, 1994, 257. *Member:* Studienvereinigung Kartellrecht e.V. *LANGUAGES:* German and English. *PRACTICE AREAS:* EC-Commercial Law; Transport Law; Corporate Law.

ASSOCIATES

DR. CHRISTOF SIEFARTH, born Cologne, Germany, December 13, 1959; admitted, 1989, Cologne; 1992, New York. *Education:* University of Cologne (Dr. jur., 1990); Lausanne, University of Georgia, School of Law (LL.M., 1986). Author: "Motion Pictures in American and International Copyright Law," 1986; "US-amerikanisches Filmurheberrecht," 1990. Associate, Kilpatrick & Cody, Atlanta, Georgia, 1991. *Member:* Deutsch-Amerikanische Juristen-Vereinigung; Deutsche Vereinigung für gewerblichen Rechtsschutz and Urheberrecht. *LANGUAGES:* German, English and French. *PRACTICE AREAS:* Intellectual Property Law; Media Law; Private International Law; Computer Law.

DR. RALF HOTTGENROTH, born Essen, Germany, August 30, 1961; admitted, 1991, Cologne. *Education:* Universities of Mannheim and Cologne, (Dr. jur., 1989). Author: "Die Verhandlungspflicht der Tarifvertragsparteien", 1990. *Member:* Deutscher Arbeitsgerichtsverband. *LANGUAGES:* German and English. *PRACTICE AREAS:* Corporate Law; Labor Law.

DR. BEATE BERGER, born Gelsenkirchen-Buer, Germany, May 2, 1961; admitted, 1987, Ulm; 1993, Cologne. *Education:* University of Bielefeld (Dr. iur., 1993). Author: "Warranty for Software, An International Problem," The Comparative Law Year Book of International Business, 1990, 247 et seq. (with Dr. Günter Knorr); "Die fehlerhafte Steuerungssoftware," JA 1992 (with Dr. Klaus Peter Berger); "Principles of German Insolvency Law," published in: International Corporate Insolvency Law, 1992 (with Dr. Günter Knorr, Eberhard Knorr and Luise Widmaier-Müller); "Das Pflichtenheft im Spiegel der Rechtsprechung," CR 1993, 329 ss.; "Mängelgewährleistung für Standardsoftware," 1993. *Member:* EDV & Recht, Union International des Avocates; Deutsche Vereinigung für gewerblichen Rechtsschutz und Urheberrecht. *LANGUAGES:* German, English, French and Spanish. *PRACTICE AREAS:* Computer Law; Unfair Competition; Intellectual Property Law.

DR. PAUL-MARTIN SCHULZ, born Hamm, Germany, August 12, 1957; admitted, 1989, Cologne. *Education:* University of Bonn (Dr. jur., 1990). Author: "Die Gründung der Internationalen Kommission zum Schutz der Elbe (IKSE)," N+R, 1993, 483; "Klärschlamm: Abfall oder Wirtschaftsgut?" KA 1993, 1006; Buchbesprechung von: Krieger, Stephan; Normkonkretisierung im Recht der wassergefährdenden Stoffe, ZfW 1993. 188; "Vorschriften für den Umgang mit wassergefährdenden Stoffen," EP 1993, 734; "Anforderungskatalog für Betriebe der Schrottwirtschaft," Rohstoff-Rundschau 1993, 450 und 491; Urteilsanmerkung zu VG Köln 09.-

(This Listing Continued)

02.1993 - 14 K 3595/91 - ZfW 1994, 315; "Haftung bei Anlagen zum Umgang mit wassergefährdenden Stoffen," EP 1994, 315; "Die 4. Novelle des Abwasserabgabengesetzes," KA 1994, 1613. *LANGUAGES:* English. *PRACTICE AREAS:* Administrative Law; Environmental Law; Building Permits; Government Liability.

DR. EUGÈNE BEAUCAMP, born Frankfurt am Main, Germany, March 8, 1960; admitted, 1994, Cologne. *Education:* Universities of Trier and Cologne (Dr. jur., 1994). With, Revenue Authorities, Northrine-Westphalia, 1992-1994. *LANGUAGES:* English. *PRACTICE AREAS:* Corporate Law; Commercial Law; Tax Law; Tax Crimes.

DR. WOLFGANG MÜLLER, born Cologne, Germany, August 17, 1961; admitted, 1991, Cologne; 1989, New York. *Education:* Universities of Cologne and Geneva; University of Illinois, School of Law (LL.M., 1988). Author: "Bankruptcy in Rem Jurisdication Redefined within the Constitutional Boundaries Set by Shaffer v. Heitner," American Bankruptcy Law Journal, 1990. *Member:* Deutsch-Amerikanische Juristen-Vereinigung; Deutsch-Spanische Juristenvereinigung; University of Illinois Alumni Association. *LANGUAGES:* German, English, French and Spanish. *PRACTICE AREAS:* Corporate Law; Private International Law.

ELISABETH MÜLLER, born Ravensburg, Germany, May 31, 1963; admitted, 1993, Cologne. *Education:* Universities of Passau, Freiburg i.Br., Münster; American University in Cairo, Egypt (Diploma in Middle East Studies, 1989). *Member:* Deutscher Juristinnenbund; Deutsche Gesellschaft für Rechtsvergleichung; Deutsch-Arabische Gesellschaft. *LANGUAGES:* German, English, Spanish and Arabic. *PRACTICE AREAS:* Private International Law; Commercial and Family Law of the Arabic Countries.

VERENA HOENE, born Cologne, Germany, November 29, 1966; admitted, 1995, Cologne. *Education:* Universities of Trier and Washington School of Law (LL.M., 1994). *LANGUAGES:* English. *PRACTICE AREAS:* EC-Commercial Law; Unfair Competition Law; Administrative Law.

DR. PÄR JOHANSSON, born Kiel, Germany, April 17, 1966; admitted, 1994, Cologne. *Education:* Universities de Paris X (licencié en droit, 1990); University of Bonn, Cologne (Dr. jur., 1994). Author: "Handbuch des Rechts der Schausteller, des Markt- und Reisegewerbes," 2. Auflage, 1993; "Gesetzliches Pfand- und Zurückbehaltungsrechte nach schwedischem Recht," 1994. *LANGUAGES:* English, French, Swedish and Spanish. *PRACTICE AREAS:* Private International Law; Corporate Law.

All attorneys are member of Deutscher Anwaltverein (German Bar Association)

MATRAY UND PARTNER

Avocats au Barreau de Liege

Established in 1987

FRIESENPLATZ, 17A
D-50672 COLOGNE, GERMANY
Telephone: (49) (221) 52 25 13
Telex: 888 5 332 heid
Telecopier: (49) (221) 52 52 60

Liege, Belgium Office: Matray, Matray et Hallet. 34/24, Boulevard Frère-Orban, 4000. Telephone: (32) (41) 52 70 68. Telex: MACOHA 42330. Telecopier: (32) (41) 52 08 57.
Brussels, Belgium Office: Matray, Matray et Hallet. Avenue Louise, 500/9, 1050. Telephone: 32-2-647.79.80. Telecopier: 32-2-640.70.71.

General and International Practice, Commercial, Corporation, Labor Law, Tax, EEC, International Arbitration.

MEMBERS OF FIRM

LAMBERT MATRAY, born Liege, Belgium, June 6, 1921; admitted, 1944, Liege (Not admitted in Germany). *Education:* University of Liege (Dr. Jur., 1944). *LANGUAGES:* French, German and Dutch. *PRACTICE AREAS:* Commercial Law; Company Law; Commercial Arbitration.

DIDIER MATRAY, born Liege, Belgium, June 5, 1951; admitted, 1973, Liege (Not admitted in Germany). *Education:* University of Liege (Lic. Dr., 1973). *LANGUAGES:* French, German, English and Italian. *PRACTICE AREAS:* Commercial Law; Finance; Corporate Law; Commercial Arbitration; Banking; Mergers and Acquisitions.

OPPENHOFF & RÄDLER

HOHENSTAUFENRING 62
D-50674 COLOGNE, GERMANY
Telephone: (0221) 2091-0
Telecopier: (0221) 2091-435
Telex: 8 882 294 bos
Teletex: 2627 221 4054BOS

Munich, Germany Office: Prinzregentenplatz 10, D-81675. Telephone: (089) 41808-0. Telecopier: (089) 41808-100.

Berlin, Germany Office: Meinekestr. 13, D-10719. Telephone: (030) 88471-0. Telecopier: (030) 88471-200.

Berlin, Germany Office: Rankestr. 21, D-10789. Telephone: (030) 21496-0. Telecopier: (030) 21496-100.

Frankfurt/Main, Germany Office: Bockenheimer Landstr. 51-53, D-60325. Telephone: (069) 170003-0. Telecopier: (069) 170003-33.

Frankfurt/Main, Germany Office: Myliusstr. 33-37, D-60323. Telephone: (069) 17093-0. Telecopier: (069) 17093-444.

Leipzig, Germany Office: Kommandant-Trufanow-Str. 14, D-04105. Telephone: (0341) 56649-0. Telecopier: (0341) 56649-99.

Brussels, Belgium Office: Rue Brederode 13A, B-1000. Telephone: (2) 5050211. Telecopier: (2) 5022644.

London, England Office: Royex House, Aldermanbury Square, GB-London EC2V 7HR. Telephone: (171) 600 3609. Telecopier: (171) 600 1718.

New York, New York Office: 712 Fifth Avenue, 30th Floor, 10019 USA. Telephone: (212) 801 3410. Telecopier: (212) 801 3415.

New York, New York Office: 712 Fifth Avenue, 29th Floor, New York 10019, USA. Telephone: (212) 397 7580/7546. Telecopier: (212) 397 4292.

Prague, Czech Republic Office: Alliance Prague, Jachymova 2, CZ-11000 Prague 1. Telephone: (2) 232 1130. Telecopier: (2) 232 6371.

FIRM PROFILE: *Oppenhoff & Rädler has been created by a merger of two large German firms, Boden Oppenhoff Rasor Raue and Rädler Raupach Bezzenberger. The firm at present has more than 90 partners and comprises together some 200 lawyers and tax advisers.*

Oppenhoff & Rädler acts for domestic and for international clients. The firm offers a comprehensive range of legal services, including: General Corporate and Commercial; Taxation; Banking, Finance and Securities; Mergers and Acquisitions; Real Estate; Litigation and Arbitration; Intellectual Property and Trademarks; Construction Law; Antitrust and European Community Law; Administrative and Environmental Law; Media, Communications and Entertainment Law; Technology and Computer Law; Food, Drug and Chemistry; Family Law; Wills.

Oppenhoff & Rädler is a member of the ALLIANCE OF EUROPEAN LAWYERS EEIG (members: Oppenhoff & Rädler, Germany; De Bandt, van Hecke & Lagae, Belgium; De Brauw Blackstone Westbroek, The Netherlands; Jeantet & Associés, France; Lagerlöf & Leman, Sweden; Uria & Menendez, Spain) and of the LLR EEIG (members: Loyens & Volkmaars, The Netherlands; Bureau Francis Lefebvre, France; Oppenhoff & Rädler, Germany).

RESIDENT PARTNERS AND JUNIOR PARTNERS

DR. WALTER OPPENHOFF, born Aachen, Germany, May 26, 1905; admitted, 1930, Germany. *Education:* University of Cologne (Dr.jur.). *Member:* German Bar Association (President, 1959-1963); German Association for the Protection of Industrial Property Rights (President, 1968-1981); International Bar Association (Chairman Emeritus, Section on Business Law). *LANGUAGES:* German, English, French.

PETER SAMBUC, born Berlin, Germany, July 6, 1930; admitted, 1960, Germany. *Education:* Universities of Berlin, Freiburg and Kiel; New York University Law School. *Member:* German Association for the Protection of Industrial Property Rights (Co-Chairman, Chapter West, 1979—; Member, Competition and Trademark Law Committee). *LANGUAGES:* German, English. *PRACTICE AREAS:* Antitrust and Trade Regulations; European Community Law; Intellectual Property; Trademarks.

DR. HENNING RASNER, born Hilden, Germany, April 2, 1930; admitted, 1960, Germany. *Education:* Universities of Münster, Marburg, Bonn (Dr.jur.); University of Paris. *Member:* German Bar Association (Member, Business Law Committee); Commission Spéciale "Droit de Société" of the Commission Consultative des Barreaux Européens. *LANGUAGES:* German, English, French. *PRACTICE AREAS:* Business Law; Commercial Law; Company Law; Corporate Law; Mergers, Acquisitions and Divestitures.

(This Listing Continued)

MICHAEL OPPENHOFF, born Cologne, Germany, November 10, 1937; admitted, 1967, Germany. *Education:* Universities of Lausanne, Munich, Freiburg and Cologne; New York University Law School. *LANGUAGES:* German, English. *PRACTICE AREAS:* Corporate Law; Company Law; Mergers, Acquisitions and Divestitures.

GERHILD BUCHHOLZ-SZILÁGYI, born Berlin, Germany, March 5, 1936; admitted, 1966, Germany. *Education:* Universities of Cologne, Freiburg and Berlin. *LANGUAGES:* German, English, French. *PRACTICE AREAS:* Intellectual Property; Trademarks.

HANS-JÜRGEN PRINZ, born Wuppertal, Germany, August 2, 1936; admitted, 1967, Germany. *Education:* Universities of Cologne and Munich. Vice President, German Committee on UNICEF. *LANGUAGES:* German, English. *PRACTICE AREAS:* Communications and Media; Labour and Employment; Intellectual Property; Litigation.

MONIKA WENZ, born Dortmund, Germany, September 22, 1941; admitted, 1971, Germany. *Education:* University of Frankfurt. *LANGUAGES:* German, English. *PRACTICE AREAS:* Intellectual Property; Trademarks.

DR. KLAUS GÜNTHER, born Halle, Germany, December 16, 1941; admitted, 1970, Germany. *Education:* Universities of Munich and Cologne (Dr. jur.); University of California at Berkeley (LL.M.). *Member:* German American Lawyers Association (President). *LANGUAGES:* German, English, French. *PRACTICE AREAS:* Agency and Distributorship; Arbitration and Mediation; Aviation and Aerospace; Copyrights; Corporate Law; Mergers, Acquisitions and Divestitures.

DR. HANNO GOLTZ, born Berlin, Germany, September 2, 1940; admitted, 1972, Germany. *Education:* Universities of Bonn, Lausanne and Cologne (Dr. jur.). *LANGUAGES:* German, English, French. *PRACTICE AREAS:* Company Law; Corporate Law; Equipment Finance and Leasing; Insurance; Mergers, Acquisitions and Divestitures.

HANS GEORG BORNHEIM, born Cologne, Germany, July 28, 1946; admitted, 1975, Germany. *Education:* Universities of Bonn, Munich and Cologne. *LANGUAGES:* German, English. *PRACTICE AREAS:* Agency and Distributorships; Civil Law; Intellectual Property; Litigation.

RICHARD BÖCKING, born Baumholder, Germany, March 7, 1947; admitted, 1976, Germany. *Education:* Universities of Cologne, Geneva and Bonn. *LANGUAGES:* German, English. *PRACTICE AREAS:* Civil Law; Construction Law; Litigation.

PETER KLAPPICH, born Herne, Germany, September 1, 1950; admitted, 1978, Germany. *Education:* Universities of Heidelberg and Cologne. *LANGUAGES:* German, English. *PRACTICE AREAS:* Chemicals and Chemistry; Commercial Law; Environmental Law; Food and Drugs Law; Insurance; Licensing; Litigation; Products Liability.

DR. THOMAS VERHOEVEN, born Duisburg, Germany, May 20, 1947; admitted, 1978, Germany. *Education:* Universities of Cologne and Bielefeld (Dr.jur.). (Resident Partner, New York Office). *LANGUAGES:* German, English. *PRACTICE AREAS:* Antitrust and Trade Regulations; Banks and Banking; Business Law; Corporate Law; Company Law; Finance; Labour and Employment; Mergers, Acquisitions and Divestitures; Securities.

MICHAEL ABELS, born Bad Homburg, Germany, February 8, 1948; admitted, 1979, Germany. *Education:* University of Cologne. *LANGUAGES:* German, English. *PRACTICE AREAS:* Copyrights; Computer and Software; Communications and Media; Technology and Science.

DR. DIRK SCHROEDER, born Darmstadt, Germany, November 21, 1953; admitted, 1981, Germany. *Education:* University of Cologne (Dr.jur.); Ecole Nationale d'Administration, Paris. (Resident Partner, Brussels Office). *LANGUAGES:* German, English, French. *PRACTICE AREAS:* Antitrust and Trade Regulations; European Community Law.

HANS-JOSEF BUSCH, born Birgden-Gangelt, Germany, March 2, 1953; admitted, 1981, Germany. *Education:* University of Cologne. *LANGUAGES:* German, English. *PRACTICE AREAS:* Construction Law; Leases and Leasing; Real Estate.

DR. JOACHIM WESSEL, born Cologne, Germany, February 9, 1954; admitted, 1981, Germany. *Education:* University of Cologne (Dr.jur.). *LANGUAGES:* German, English. *PRACTICE AREAS:* Advertising and Marketing; Copyright; Communications and Media; Intellectual Property; Product Liability.

KARL-DIETMAR COHNEN, born Geilenkirchen, Germany, February 14, 1953; admitted, 1982, Germany. *Education:* Universities of Bonn and

(This Listing Continued)

OPPENHOFF & RÄDLER, Cologne—Continued

Freiburg. *LANGUAGES:* German, English. *PRACTICE AREAS:* Copyrights; Labour and Employment; Litigation.

GERT DITTERT, born Koblenz, Germany, February 11, 1957; admitted, 1986, Germany. *Education:* University of Cologne. *LANGUAGES:* German, English. *PRACTICE AREAS:* Advertising and Marketing; Communications and Media; Intellectual Property; Antitrust and Trade Regulations.

DR. AXEL BÖDEFELD, born Wuppertal, Germany, June 12, 1957; admitted, 1988, Germany. *Education:* Fachhochschule fur Finanzen, Nordkirchen; Universities of Bochum (Dr.jur.); University of Mannheim. *LANGUAGES:* German, English. *PRACTICE AREAS:* Taxation.

ROLF KOERFER, born Bensberg, Germany, September 26, 1957; admitted, 1988, Germany. *Education:* Universities of Cologne and Tübingen. *LANGUAGES:* German, English. *PRACTICE AREAS:* Company Law; Corporate Law; Mergers, Acquisitions and Divestitures.

DR. STEPHAN KÖNIG, born Luxembourg, September 30, 1957; admitted, 1986, Germany. *Education:* Universities of Cologne and Munich (Dr.jur.); University of Geneva. *LANGUAGES:* German, English, French. *PRACTICE AREAS:* Banks and Banking; Company Law; Corporate Law; Finance; Mergers, Acquisitions and Divestitures; Securities.

DR. MICHAEL LAPPE, born Bochum, Germany, August 17, 1957; admitted, 1987, Germany. *Education:* University of Bochum (Dr.jur.); University of Münster. (Resident Partner, London Office). *LANGUAGES:* German, English. *PRACTICE AREAS:* Company Law; Corporate Law; Finance; Mergers, Acquisitions and Divestitures; Securities.

HEINZ ZIMMERMANN, born Osberghausen, Germany, May 18, 1947; admitted, 1980, Certified Tax Advisor (Steuerberater); 1983, Certified Public Accountant (Wirtschaftsprüfer); 1987, Germany. *Education:* University of Saarbrücken. *LANGUAGES:* German, English, Spanish. *PRACTICE AREAS:* Business Law; Corporate Law; Taxation.

GEORG STURMBERG, born Bensberg, Germany, November 5, 1957; admitted, 1987, Germany. *Education:* University of Cologne. *LANGUAGES:* German, English. *PRACTICE AREAS:* Civil Law; Construction Law; Litigation; Zoning, Planning and Land Use.

DR. GILBERTH WURTH, born Leverkusen, Germany, October 17, 1958; admitted, 1988, Germany. *Education:* University of Cologne (Dr.jur.). *LANGUAGES:* German, English. *PRACTICE AREAS:* Agency and Distributorship; Company Law; Labour and Employment.

KAY-UWE JONAS, born Bremen, Germany, September 20, 1960; admitted, 1990, Germany. *Education:* University of Cologne. *LANGUAGES:* German, English. *PRACTICE AREAS:* Antitrust and Trade Regulations; Intellectual Property; Trademarks.

ROSEMARIE PORTNER, born Oberviechtach, Germany, March 5, 1952; admitted, 1993, Germany. *Education:* Universities of Bonn, Mainz, Graz and Harvard University (LL.M.). *LANGUAGES:* German, English, French. *PRACTICE AREAS:* Taxation.

DR. ULRICH PRINZ, born Oberhausen, Germany, June 25, 1955; admitted, 1985, Germany, Tax Advisor (Steuerberater); 1990, Certified Public Accountant (Wirtschaftsprüfer). *Education:* University of Cologne (Dipl.-Kfm./M.B.A.; Dr.rer.pol.). *LANGUAGES:* German, English, French. *PRACTICE AREAS:* Taxation.

THOMAS OERTER, born Cologne, Germany, April 6, 1958; admitted, 1988, Germany. *Education:* University of Cologne. *LANGUAGES:* German, English, French. *PRACTICE AREAS:* Agency and Distributorship; Company Law; Computer and Software; Commercial Law.

DR. CHRISTIAN HEY, born Hamburg, Germany, October 5, 1960; admitted, 1990, Germany. *Education:* University of Hamburg (Dr.jur.). *LANGUAGES:* German, English, French, Italian, Spanish. *PRACTICE AREAS:* Agency and Distributorship; Corporate Law; Communications and Media; Leases and Leasing.

DR. KLAUS MARINUS HOENIG, born Bad Honnef, Germany, September 23, 1959; admitted, 1990, Germany. *Education:* University of Bonn (Dr.jur.); University of Miami (LL.M.). *LANGUAGES:* German, English, French. *PRACTICE AREAS:* Company Law; Corporate Law; Mergers, Acquisitions and Divestitures.

MICHAEL BONSAU, born Essen, Germany, September 16, 1959; admitted, 1990, Germany. *Education:* Universities of Bielefeld and Cologne.

(This Listing Continued)

LANGUAGES: German, English, Spanish. *PRACTICE AREAS:* Civil Law; Intellectual Property; Leases and Leasing; Litigation.

JUTTA WITTLER, born Lohr, Germany, October 9, 1961; admitted, 1990, Germany. *Education:* University of Würzburg. *LANGUAGES:* German, English. *PRACTICE AREAS:* Civil Law; Construction Law; Contracts.

DR. GESA SIMON, born Wiesbaden, Germany, August 25, 1962; admitted, 1991, Germany. *Education:* University of Freiburg (Dr.jur.); University of Geneva. *LANGUAGES:* German, English, French. *PRACTICE AREAS:* Antitrust and Trade Regulations; Intellectual Property; Civil Law; Litigation.

DR. HEINRICH WATERMEYER, born Datteln, Germany, December 16, 1956; admitted, 1987, Germany. *Education:* Fachhochschule für Finanzen, Nordkirchen; University of Bochum (Dr.jur.). *LANGUAGES:* German, English. *PRACTICE AREAS:* Taxation.

DR. WOLFGANG DESELAERS, born Kempen, Germany, June 29, 1961; admitted, 1991, Germany. *Education:* University of Münster (Dr.jur.); Universities of Lausanne and Constance. *LANGUAGES:* German, English, Spanish. *PRACTICE AREAS:* Agency and Distributorship; Antitrust and Trade Regulations; European Community Law.

DR. RUDOLF BODEN (1900-1984).

JOHN MICHAEL OWENS

Established in 1991

BREITE STR. 100
50667 COLOGNE, GERMANY
Telephone: (0221) 258-3345
Fax: (0221) 258-3626

From Outside Germany, dial your international long distance access code, plus: Telephone: 49-221-258-3345. Fax: 49-221-258-3626.

Transnational Trade and Direct Investment, Transnational Civil Litigation, Arbitration and White Collar Criminal Matters, U.S. Immigration, Transnational Tax, Estate and Family Law Matters.

JOHN MICHAEL OWENS, born Tarboro, North Carolina, 1948; admitted, 1977, North Carolina; 1979, Florida; Admitted to practice in Germany as Foreign Legal Expert for United States Law (not admitted as a German Attorney). *Education:* University of North Carolina at Chapel Hill (B.A., Political Science, 1973); Wake Forest University (J.D., 1977); Georgetown University (LL.M., International and Comparative Law, 1990). Assistant United States Attorney, E.D.N.C., 1977-1980. Special Attorney, U.S. Department of Justice, Criminal Division, Organized Crime and Racketeering Section, Miami Strike Force, 1980-1987. *Member:* North Carolina and Florida State Bars; American, German-American and International Bar Associations. [With U.S. Army, 1968-1971]. *LANGUAGES:* English and German. Reading ability: French and Spanish. *PRACTICE AREAS:* Antitrust and Trade Regulation; Business Law; Computers and Software; Family Law; Trusts and Estates.

PELKA, NIEMANN, HOLLERBAUM, ROHDE

Established in 1976

STOLBERGER STRAβE 92
D-50933 COLOGNE, GERMANY
Telephone: (0221) 546780
Fax: (0221) 544028

Taxation Law, Corporation Law, Trade and Commercial Law, Auditing Law, Labour Law, Property and Real Estate Law, Taxation Penal Law, Mergers and Acquisitions, Subsidy Law.

FIRM PROFILE: Established in 1981, Pelka, Niemann, Hollerbaum, Rohde, has grown to become on e of Germany's well known tax- and commercial-law firms, offering a full range of legal-, bookkeeping- and auditing-services. The firm is practicing in four offices (Cologne, Berlin, Zwickau and Erfurt)

MEMBERS OF FIRM

DR. JÜRGEN PELKA, born Biebrich, Germany, October 11, 1944; admitted, 1976. *Education:* Cologne University (Dr. jur., 1973). Editor: "Beck'sches Rechtshandbuch für Steuerberater," Ch. Beck, Muenchen; Editor/Co-Author (i.a.): "Beck'sches Steuerberaterhandbuch," Ch. Beck,

(This Listing Continued)

Muenchen; Author (i.a.): "Recht der steuerbegünstigten Kapitalanlagen," Stollfuss Verlag, 1985; "Das Rechtsschutzsystem im Besteuerungsverfahren," RWS Verlag, Koeln. Co-Author: "Praxis der Rechnungslegung in Insolvenzverfahren," RWS Verlag, Koeln, 1987. Executive Secretary and Board Member, "Deutsche Steuerjuristische Gesellschaft e.V." (Association of Tax Law Experts). *LANGUAGES:* German and English. *PRACTICE AREAS:* Taxation Law; Corporation Law.

DR. WALTER NIEMANN, born Heidenheim, Germany, September 15, 1943; admitted, 1973; 1976, Tax Advisor; 1979, Auditor. *Education:* Muenster University (Dr. jur., 1972). Editor/Co-Author: "Beck'sches Steuerberaterhandbuch," Ch. Beck, Muenchen; Co-Author: "Beck'sches Rechtshandbuch für Steuerberater," Ch. Beck, Muenchen; "Praxis der Rechnungslegung in Insolvenzverfahren," RWS Verlag, Koeln, 1987. Editor: "Handbuch des Wirtschaftsrechts," Ch. Beck, Muenchen. *LANGUAGES:* German and English. *PRACTICE AREAS:* Taxation Law; Trade, Commercial and Corporation Law; Arbitration.

DR. ALEXANDER HOLLERBAUM, born Pfaffenhofen/Ilm, Germany, July 16, 1945; admitted, 1977; 1981, Tax Advisor. *Education:* Cologne University (Dr. jur., 1981). Co-Author: "Beck'sches Steuerberaterhandbuch," Ch. Beck, Muenchen. *LANGUAGES:* German, English and French. *PRACTICE AREAS:* Trade and Commercial Law; Labour Law; Taxation Penal Law.

WOLF-GEORG ROHDE, born Cologne, Germany, January 11, 1956; admitted, 1984, Tax Advisor; 1987, Auditor. *Education:* Cologne University (Dipl. Kfm, 1978). Co-Author: "Beck'sches Steuerberaterhandbuch," Ch. Beck, Muenchen. *LANGUAGES:* German and English. *PRACTICE AREAS:* Taxation Law; Auditing.

DR. JOACHIM WÜST, born Cologne, Germany, October 1, 1959; admitted, 1988; 1994, Tax Advisor. *Education:* Cologne University (Dr. jur., 1994). Co-Author:"Beck'sches Rechtshandbuch für Steu-erberater," C.H. Beck, München. *LANGUAGES:* German, English and French. *PRACTICE AREAS:* Taxation Law; Corporation Law; Trade and Commercial Law; Labour Law.

REDEKER SCHÖN DAHS & SELLNER

Established in 1929

KAISER-WILHELM-RING 22

50672 COLOGNE, GERMANY

Telephone: (0221) 912 8680

Telefax: (0221) 912 86838

Bonn, Germany Office: Oxfordstrasse 24, 53111. Telephone: (0228) 7 26 25 0. Telefax: (0228) 65 04 79.

Hamburg, Germany Office: Büschstrasse 12, 20354 Hamburg. Telephone: (040) 342737/8. Telefax: (040) 352144.

Leipzig, Germany Office: Mozartstr. 1, 04107 Leipzig. Telephone: (0341) 213780. Telefax: (0341) 2137830.

London, England Office: 43 Brook Street, London, W1Y 2BL. Telephone: (0171) 3225823. Telefax: (0171) 6292621.

Administrative, Anti-Trust, Aviation, City Planning, Civil, Corporate and Commercial, Constitutional and Parliamentary, Construction, Criminal, Environmental, European Community Law, Family, Health, Insurance, Labour, Media and Copyright, Medical Malpractice, Domestic and International Tax, Trade, Transportation Law, Litigation and Appeals.

PARTNERS

MARTIN REUTER, born Unna-Westfalen, October 7, 1954; admitted, 1984, Bochum; 1985, Bonn; 1993, Cologne and Court of Appeal (Oberlandesgericht). *Education:* University of Bochum. *LANGUAGES:* German and English.

AXEL GROEGER, born Dortmund, May 20, 1960; admitted, 1987, Berlin; 1993, Cologne and Bonn. *Education:* Universities of Berlin and Tübingen. *Member:* German Lawyers' Association; German Association of Labour Lawyers. *LANGUAGES:* German and English.

(For data on all firm personnel see Professional Biographies at Bonn)

SCHLÜTTER & DEBATIN

STADTWALDGURTEL 77

D-50935 COLOGNE, GERMANY

Telephone: (02 21) 9 40 50 60

Telefax: (02 21) 9 40 50 620; (02 21) 9 40 50 66

General and International Law Practice, Taxation, Corporate and Commercial, Mergers and Acquisition, Litigation and Arbitration, Labor and Co-determination Law, Publishing, Antitrust, Unfair Competition, Environmental Law.

DR. EGON SCHLÜTTER, born Cologne, Germany, September 18, 1932; admitted, 1966, Cologne. *Education:* University of Cologne (Dipl. Kfm., 1957; Dr. iur., 1966). Author: "Uncitral: Its Origin and Prospectus," The American Journal of Comparative Law, XV, 626 (with John Carey); "Die Bewertung von verdeckten Gewinnausschüttungen bei Vermietung von sog. Repräsentationsvillen, Finanzrundschau 1970, 548," Tax Management International Journal, September, 1976; "Czechoslovakia: Taxation of Foreign Companies"; "Steuerliche Aspekte der Devisen, Gold-und Warenterminspekulation," Der Betrieb, 1976, 1253 (with Dr. Lüer); "Einkommenbesteuerung von Devisen, Gold-und Warenspekulationsgeschäften," Betriebsberater, 1978, 606 (with Dr. Lüer); "Handelsrechtliche und Steuerrechtliche Behandlung der Gewinnanteile der Komplementäre einer Kommanditgesellschaft auf Aktien," Steuer und Wirtschaft, 1978, 295; Tax Management International Journal, September, 1979; Germany: New Tax Developments; Die Sondervergütungen eines Mitunternehmers im Aussensteuerrecht, Jahrbuch der Fachanwälte für Steuerrecht, 1979-1980, page 152; "Marktmiete oder Kostenmiete bei Überlassung eines Einfamilienhauses," Der Betrieb, 1981, 1851; "Personengesellschaft oder Körperschaft? - Aktuelle Qualifikationsfragen - ", in: (K. Vogel), Grundfragen des Internationalen Steuerrechts, 1985, 215; "Anforderungen und Tätigkeitsbereiche des Anwalts in Steuersachen," - Anwaltsblatt, 1987, page 379; "How to Minimize Foreign Tax Liabilities with the Major US Trading Partners after the Tax Reform Act of 1986 - The German Viewpoint," International Tax Review, May, 1988, 131. Steuerprobleme des Unternehmenskaufs, Neue Juristische Wochenschrift 1993, 2023. Assistant, Institute of Taxation of the University of Cologne, 1970-1971. With Coudert Brothers, New York, 1966-1967. *Member:* German Bar Association; Deutscher Anwaltsverein; Deutsche Vereinigung für Internationales Steuerrecht; Deutsch - Amerikanische Juristenvereinigung; Deutsche Steuerjuristische Gesellschaft; International Bar Association; International Fiscal Association. *LANGUAGES:* English and French. *PRACTICE AREAS:* German and International Taxation; Corporate Law; Mergers and Acquisitions.

PROF. DR. HELMUT F. DEBATIN, born Konstanz, Germany, September 26, 1926; admitted, 1956, Cologne; 1984, New York; 1985, Tax Consultant. *Education:* Germany; University of Freiburg, Germany (Dr. Jur., 1950); Harvard University (LL.M., 1956). Certified Public Tax Advisor, Hamburg, Germany, 1984. Author: "Handbook on the United States-German Tax Convention"; "Commentary on German International Tax Convention Law"; "The Role of Tax Treaties as an Instrument of Economic Cooperation between "Capitalist" and "Socialist" Countries - Bulletin for International Fiscal Documentation, Amsterdam," Vol. 39, No. 8/9, 1985; (Choice) "Debatin In: Korn-Debatin, Doppelbesteuerung, Commentary on all German Double Taxation Treaties, The New German Double Taxation Convention, 1990. Deputy Director General at German Finance Ministry, 1961-1973. Assistant Secretary General of the U.N., 1974-1979. Under-Secretary General at U.N., 1979-1984. Honorary Professorship at University of Mainz, 1974. Professor emeritus for International Finance and Tax Law. *Member:* German, New York State, American and International Bar Associations; International Fiscal Association; Deutsche Vereinigung Für Internationales Steuerrecht; Steuerberaterkammer, Steuerberaterverein. *LANGUAGES:* German and French. *PRACTICE AREAS:* German and International Taxation; Tax Treaties; Finance; Corporate Law.

DR. THOMAS KURTH, born Cologne, Germany, September 24, 1957; admitted, 1989, Cologne; 1990, New York. *Education:* New York University School of Law (M.C.J., 1986); Universities of Cologne, Heidelberg (Dr. jur., 1987). *Member:* New York State Bar Association, American Foreign Law Association, International Bar Association, Deutscher Anwaltsverein. *LANGUAGES:* English and French. *PRACTICE AREAS:* Corporate and Tax Law.

SCHMITZ KNOTH WUELLRICH MARQUARDT

Established in 1953

BONNER STRASSE 327
50968 COLOGNE, GERMANY
Telephone: (0221) 93 70 45-0
Telefax: (0221) 93 70 45-20

Bonn, Germany Office: Wilhelmstrasse 38, 53111 Bonn. Telephone: (0228) 98 509-0. Telefax: (0228) 98 509-33.

General Practice, International Litigation and Arbitration. International Civil, Commercial, Corporate, Antitrust, Tax, Media, Computer and Technology Law. Unfair Competition. Industrial Property Rights. Labor Relations. White Collar Crime. Public Procurement and Government Contracts. Construction Law. International Joint Ventures. Transportation. Aviation and Aerospace.

MEMBERS OF FIRM

DR. KARL-AUGUST HERTEL, born Mönchengladbach, Germany, 1921; admitted, 1954, Bonn. *Education:* Universities of Freiburg and Bonn (Dr. jur.). Author: "Die Rechtsstellung der bei einem objektiven Verfahren übergangenen Interessenten," Bonn 1952; "Rechtsgeschäfte im Vorfeld eines Projekts," Betriebsberater, 1983, 1824; "Öffentliches Auftragswesen; Vergütung im potentiellen Wettbewerb," Betriebsberater 1983, 1315; "Die Preisbildung und das Preisprüfrecht bei öffentlichen Aufträgen," Hamburg 1988; "Der Öffentliche Auftrag," Hamburg 1992. *PRACTICE AREAS:* Public Procurement and Government Contracts.

DR. HANNO MARQUARDT, born Bad Oldesloe, Germany, 1951; admitted, 1979, Bonn. *Education:* Universities of Kiel, Geneva, Bonn and Mannheim (Assistant, Dr. jur.). Author: "Die Entwicklung des Legalitätsprinzipes, ein historisch-empirischer Beitrag zur Gesetzgebung," Mannheim 1982. *Member:* German-Austrian-Swiss Bar Association; German Association of Industrial Property and Copyright. *PRACTICE AREAS:* White Collar Crime; Tax Crimes; Tax Law.

ASSOCIATES

JOERG NOA, born Burscheid, Germany, 1963; admitted, 1993, Cologne. *Education:* University of Cologne. *Member:* German American Lawyers Association. *PRACTICE AREAS:* Computer and Technology Law; Media Law.

All Members of Firm are Members of Cologne Bar and Bonn Lawyers Society.

Languages: German, English and French.

(For Complete Biographical Data on all Personnel, see Professional Biographies at Bonn, Germany)

SCHWEND, ADENAUER & PARTNER

SACHSENRING 75
50677 COLOGNE 1, GERMANY
Telephone: (49) 221-314068
Telefax: (49) 221-324162

Paris, France Office: 69, Avenue Victor Hugo, F-75016. Telephone: 33 (1) 44 17 50 50. Telefax: 33 (1) 45 01 77 21.

General and International Law Practice, Corporate and Commercial Law, Mergers and Acquisitions, Antitrust, EEC Law, Banking, Insurance, Unfair Competition, Industrial Property, International Arbitration, Litigation.

A. GERARD SCHWEND, born Cologne, Germany, 1951; admitted, 1979, Cologne; 1990, Paris. *Education:* Universities of Freiburg, Cologne and Dijon. *Member:* International League of Competition Law; German and International Industrial Property Law Association; German Institution of Arbitration; Paris Bar Association; Lawyers Association of Cologne (Board Member, 1984-1990). *LANGUAGES:* French, English and Spanish. *PRACTICE AREAS:* Corporate Law; Unfair Competition Law; Industrial Property Law; Mergers and Acquisitions; Litigation.

JENS BREDOW, born Bremen, Germany, 1948; admitted, 1980, Cologne. *Education:* University of Cologne. Co-Author: "Das Schiedsgericht in der Praxis," Glossner, Bredow, Bühler, 1990; " Übernahme des UNCITRAL-Modellgesetzes über die internationale Handelsschiedsgerichtsbarkeit in das deutsche Recht," 1989; "Incoterms 1990 - Wegweiser für die Praxis," Bredow/Seiffert, 1990. New York Convention on the Recognition and Enforcement of Foreign Arbitral Awards, Commenting in: Bülow-

(This Listing Continued)

Böckstiegel, Internationaler Rechtsverkehr, 1993. *Member:* German Institution of Arbitration (Secretary General); ICC Commission on International Arbitration; Wissenschaftliche Vereinigung für intern. Verfahrensrecht. *LANGUAGES:* English. *PRACTICE AREAS:* Corporate Law; Commercial Law; International Arbitration; Litigation.

DR. PETER ADENAUER, born Cologne, Germany, 1950; admitted, 1977, Heidelberg and Mannheim; 1988, New York. *Education:* Universities of Lausanne (Switzerland), Edinburgh (Scotland), Heidelberg and Münster (Dr.jur., 1981). Author: "Raumplanung und Enteignung in England," 1981. *Member:* American Bar Association; New York State Bar Association. *LANGUAGES:* English and French. *PRACTICE AREAS:* Corporate Law; Banking Law; Commercial Law; International Private Law; EEC Law; Antitrust Law; Litigation.

JOACHIM W. KLEIN, born Cologne, Germany, 1951; admitted, 1977, Cologne. *Education:* Universities of Cologne and Freiburg. Research Assistant, Institute of Insurance Law, University of Cologne, 1974-1978. *LANGUAGES:* French and English. *PRACTICE AREAS:* Insurance Law; Corporate Law; Commercial Law.

STOFFEL, PIETZKO & STRUNDEN

Established in 1957

NEUE WEYERSTRASSE 9
50676 COLOGNE, GERMANY
Telephone: 0221/921 22 80
Telefax: 0221/921 22 86; 0221/921 22 85

General Practice, Commercial, Merger and Acquisition, Corporate, Unfair Competition, Media and Copyright, Probate, Administrative Law, Planning, Construction, Environmental Law, Litigation.

FIRM PROFILE: Founded in 1957 by Dr. Michael Stoffel, the current Senior Partner. The firm is divided into the following departments: merger, company, commercial, employment, general litigation, construction, copyrights, entertainment, environmental, public law and debt recovery. Working predominantly for corporate clients, we have close relationships with many other international law firms in USA and European Countries. Our reputation rests on a commitment to meet the different needs of each of our clients.

MEMBERS OF FIRM

DR. MICHAEL STOFFEL, born Cologne, Germany, November 8, 1929; admitted, 1957, Cologne. *Education:* Universities of Cologne (Dr. jur.); State of Nordrhein-Westfalen (2nd jur. Staatsexamen). Author: "Der deliktsrechtliche Schutz der Ehe nach Amerikanischem, Englischem, Französischem und Deutschem Recht," 1953. *Member:* Lawyers Association of Cologne; Association of Insolvency Law; German American Lawyers Association. *LANGUAGES:* German and English. *PRACTICE AREAS:* Commercial; Corporate; Merger and Acquisition; Probate; Construction Law.

DR. JOACHIM PIETZKO, born Cologne, Germany, November 12, 1959; admitted, 1989, Cologne. *Education:* Universities of Cologne (Dr. jur.), Lausanne and Geneva; State of Nordrhein-Westfalen (2nd jur. Staatsexamen). Author: "Zur Zulässigkeit der Änderung einer Gegendarstellung nach Rechtshängigkeit," AfP, 1985; "Die Werbung mit dem Doppelgänger eines Prominenten," AfP, 1988; "Der Tatbestand des § 613 a BGB," 1988. Co-Author: "Das Recht der Presse," 4th Ed. 1988. *Member:* Lawyers Association of Cologne. *LANGUAGES:* German, English and French. *PRACTICE AREAS:* Unfair Competition; Copyrights and Media Law; Product Liability; Employment.

DR. STEFAN STRUNDEN, born Cologne, Germany, September 23, 1960; admitted, 1989, Cologne. *Education:* Universities of Konstanz and Cologne (Dr. jur.); State of Nordrhein-Westfalen (2nd jur. Staatsexamen). Author: "Altlasten-Ansprüche des Grundstückseigentümers im Spannungsfeld zwischem öffentlichem und zivilem Recht," 1991. Co-Author: "Gesetzliche Prospekthaftung," HdB 4520, 1989; "Haftung des Anlagevermittlers," HdB 4340, 1989; "Haftung des Anlageberaters," HdB 4345, 1989; "Immobilien (-kapitalanlagen) und Eintrittspflicht von Rechtsschutzversicherungen," HdB 5630, 1989. *Member:* Lawyers Association Cologne. *LANGUAGES:* German and English. *PRACTICE AREAS:* Environmental; Construction Law; General Practice; Litigation.

DR. RICHARD DETTE, born Dingelstaedt, Germany, April 25, 1928; admitted, 1990, Germany. *Education:* Universities of Jena and Cologne (Dr. jur., 1964). Judge, Administrative Court. Head of Department for Environment and Traffic, Regierungspräsident Cologne. *Member:* Lawyers' Association of Cologne. *LANGUAGES:* German and English. *PRACTICE*

(This Listing Continued)

AREAS: Administrative Law; Planning; Construction; Environmental Law.

KLAUS MATHY (1983-1993).

DR. GABRIELE PIETZKO, born Cologne, Germany, October 6, 1959; admitted, 1994, Cologne. *Education:* University of Cologne (Dr. Jur.) State of Nordrhein-Westfalen (2nd jur. Staatsexamen). Author: "Der materiell-rechtliche Folgenbeseitigungsanspruch," 1994. Co-Author: "Verwaltungsverfahren und Widerspruchsverfahren," 3nd. Ed. 1993. *Member:* Lawyers Association of Cologne. *LANGUAGES:* German, English and French. *PRACTICE AREAS:* General Practice; Administrative Law; Domestic Relations Law.

WEBER & PARTNER

Established in 1981

DÜRENER STR. 341

50935 COLOGNE, GERMANY

Telephone: 0221/466757
Telefax: 0221/466750

General Practice, Corporate, Commercial, Labour, Press and Publishing Law, Unfair Competition.

MEMBERS OF FIRM

ULRICH WEBER, born Gummersbach, 1948; admitted, 1981, Germany. *Education:* University of Cologne (State Exams, 1973 and 1976). Certified Labour Attorney. Author: "Der Anstellungsvertrag des Managers," 1991; "Rechtsberater für Manager," 1993; "Rechtsgrundlagen für GmbH-Geschäftsführer," 1993; "Kündigung und Kündigungsschutz," 1994; "Arbeitsrecht für Arbeitnehmer," 1994. Columnist: "Manager Magazine", "Welt am Sonntag". *Member:* German Bar Association; German-Italian Law Association. *LANGUAGES:* German and English. *PRACTICE AREAS:* Labour; Co-Determination; Services; Contracts.

CLAUDIA KOTHE-HEGGEMANN, born Bielefeld, 1954; admitted, 1986, Germany. *Education:* University of Bielefeld and Bonn (State Exams, 1983 and 1986). Certified Labour Attorney. Co-Author: "Rechtsextremismus und Strafrechtspflege," 1985. Author: "Kündigung und Kündigungsschutz," 1994; "Arbeitsrecht für Arbeitnehmer," 1994. Columnist, "Manager Magazine". *LANGUAGES:* German, English and French. *PRACTICE AREAS:* Labour; Contracts.

HUBERT JANSEN, born Erkelenz, 1957; admitted, 1991, Germany. *Education:* University of Cologne (State Exams, 1987 and 1991). Certified Labour Attorney. Author: "Gezielte Personalanpassung," 1994. Columnist: "Top-Business", "Welt am Sonntag". *LANGUAGES:* German. *PRACTICE AREAS:* Labour; Co-Determination; Pensions.

DR. AXEL HOβ, born Remscheid, 1963; admitted, 1993, Germany. *Education:* University of Cologne (State Exams, 1989 and 1993; Dr. jur., 1993). Hochschule für Verwaltungswissenschaften Speyer. Certified Labour Attorney. Author: "Gezielte Personalanpassung," 1994. Columnist: "Top Business". *LANGUAGES:* German and English. *PRACTICE AREAS:* Labour; Unfair Competition.

BEATRICE WREDE, born Darmstadt, 1963; admitted, 1994, Germany. *Education:* University of Passau, Tübingen and Cologne (State Exams 1988 und 1993). *Member:* Canadian-German Lawyers Association. *LANGUAGES:* German, English and French. *PRACTICE AREAS:* Labour; European Community Law; Press and Publishing Law.

WALTER & PARTNER

Established in 1990

KAVALIERSTR. 35-39

06844 DESSAU, GERMANY (EAST)

Telephone: 0340-2207285
Telefax: 0340-213280

Heidelberg, Germany Office: Lessingstrasse 24. P.O. Box 10 34 66, 69024 Heidelberg 1. Telephone: 06221/12002. Telefax: 06221/20378.
Berlin, Germany Office: Martin Luther Strasse 19, 10777. Telephone: 030-2119092. Telefax: 030-2119094.

Firm engaged in formations purchasing and advising of companies.

FIRM PROFILE: The Dessau Office was established in East Germany, January 1990, just three months after the fall of the Berlin Wall. It helped transforming communist enterprises into private companies and got

(This Listing Continued)

very special knowledge of theory and especially practice of communist enterprises. Today it can offer this knowledge referring to other former communist states. Now the Dessau Office also offers full legal service.

RESIDENT PARTNERS

DR. LUDWIG FEDERHEN, born Dortmund, April 24, 1929; admitted, 1964, Stuttgart, now District Court Dessau and Court of Appeal, Naumburg, Federal Patent Court Munich. *Education:* University of Cologne, London School of Economics, ESA École superieure d'Administration, Speyer (Doctorate, 1962). Author: Thesis on comparative law, various publications in the field of industrial property rights and law on unfair competition. *Member:* German Bar Association; GRUR, AIPPI, ICC. *LANGUAGES:* English, French, Spanish, Italian, Turkish and German.

HARALD KASPER, born Nurnberg, Germany, October 2, 1955; admitted, 1987, Germany, District Court Berlin and Court of Appeal, Naumburg. *Education:* Universities of Erlangen and Bonn. *LANGUAGES:* English and German.

KONRAD SCHNEIDER, born Hartha, Germany, March 10, 1949; admitted, 1994, District Court Dessau. *Education:* Humboldt University of Berlin. *LANGUAGES:* Russian and German.

(For Complete List of Firm Personnel and Specialties, see Walter & Partner at Heidelberg, Germany).

BRANDI DRÖGE PILTZ & HEUER

LINDENWEG 2

32756 DETMOLD, GERMANY

Telephone: 49 5231 98 57-0
Telecopier: 49 5231 98 57 50

Bielefeld, Germany Office: Elsa-Brändström-Str. 1 and 3, 33602. Telephone: 49 521 96535-0. Telecopier: 49 521 96535-99.
Gütersloh, Germany Office: Hochstr. 19, 33332. Telephone: 49 5241 58886. Telecopier: 49 5241 58881.
Berlin, Germany Office: Seelenbinderstr. 124, 12555. Telephone: 49 30 6509465. Telecopier: 49 30 6565679.
Leipzig, Germany Office: Katharinenstr. 1-3, 04109. Telephone: 49 341 287550. Telecopier: 49 341 289162.
Paris, France Office: 250 bis, Boulevard Saint-Germain, 75007. Telephone: 33-1 49549037. Telecopier: 33-1 49549002.

Commercial Law, Tax Law, Corporations and General Company Law, Unfair Competition, Labor Law.

MEMBERS OF FIRM

DR. HELMUT DRÖGE, born Magdeburg, Germany, 1934; admitted, 1962, Bochum; 1973, Detmold. *Education:* Universities of Marburg, Münster and Berlin (Erstes juristisches Staatsexamen, 1957; Doctor of Jurisprudence, 1960). Managing Director, Textile Company, 1964-1973. Author: "Die 'drohende Gefahr' und ihre Auswirkungen auf die Rechtsstellung der Zivilperson gegenüber der öffentlichen Gewalt," Dissertation 1960. *Member:* German and International Bar Associations; Tax Lawyers Association. *LANGUAGES:* German, English, French and Spanish. *PRACTICE AREAS:* Commercial Law; Company Law; Tax Law; Unfair Competition; Trade Law.

DR. BERNHARD KÖNIG, born Paderborn, Germany, February 12, 1954; admitted, 1986, Detmold. *Education:* University of Münster (Erstes juristisches Staatsexamen, 1979; Doctor of Jurisprudence, 1985). Author: "Befristete Arbeitsverträge im Hochschulbereich," Dissertation, 1985. Assistant Professor, Labor and Commercial Law, University of Münster, 1982-1985. *Member:* German Bar Association; Deutscher Juristentag. *LANGUAGES:* German and English. *PRACTICE AREAS:* Commercial Law; Labor Law; Company Law; Unfair Competition.

DR. BURKHARD SCHÜTTE, LL.M., born Oetinghausen, Germany, October 22, 1960; admitted, 1990, Hamburg; 1992, Detmold. *Education:* University of Bielefeld (Examination, 1987; Doctor of Jurisprudence, 1992; Diplom Volkswirt - Master of Economics, 1988); University of Michigan, U.S.A. (LL.M., 1989). Author: "Die Dividendenentscheidung in der Aktiengesellschaft," Dissertation 1991. *Member:* German Bar Association. *LANGUAGES:* German and English. *PRACTICE AREAS:* Commercial Law; Company Law; General Practice.

HIMMELMANN, POHLMANN, KUNST & POHLMANN

Established in 1979

ROSENTAL 1
44135 DORTMUND, GERMANY
Telephone: 49-231-52 88 37
Fax: 49-231-52 90 24

Staten Island, New York Office: Corash & Hollender. 60 Bay Street, 10301. Telephone: 1-718-442-4424. Fax: 1-718-273-4847.

General Practice, Litigation, and Debt Collection, Corporate Law, Tax Law, Bankruptcy, Labor Law, Contractors, Architects and Engineers, Agriculture, Mining Damage, Administration, Real Estate Transfer, Financing, International Hotel Investment, Joint Ventures, Torts.

MEMBERS OF FIRM

DR. WERNER HIMMELMANN, born Hannover, 1939; admitted, 1966, Germany; Notary. *Education:* Universities of Freiburg, Munich and Münster (Dr. jur., 1965). Lehrbeauftragter (lecturer) at the Ruhr University Bochum. Author: "Die Ersatzherausgabe nach § 281 BGB," 1965. *Member:* German-Israel Lawyers Association (Co-Founder and President). *LANGUAGES:* German, English and French. *PRACTICE AREAS:* Business Law; Corporate Law; Tax Law; Family Law.

AXEL POHLMANN, born Rimberg, 1943; admitted, 1969, Germany; Legal Consultant (Foreign Law) New York, 1992; Notary. *Education:* Universities of Münster and Hamburg (1963-1967). Author: "Aktivlegitimation der Landtagsfraktion," DVBl., 1972; "Zur Stundengebühr des Architekten," BauR, 1973, Urteilsanmerkung NJW, 1973; "Fälligkeit nach der Bauträgerverordnung," BauR, 1978. *LANGUAGES:* German, English and French. *PRACTICE AREAS:* Business Law; Corporate Law; Real Estate; Inheritance; Hotel Investment; Bankruptcy Law (Insolvency); Contractors; Architects; Engineers.

HEINRICH KUNST, born Dortmund, 1949; admitted, 1975, Germany; Notary. *Education:* University of Münster (1967-1972). *LANGUAGES:* German, English and French. *PRACTICE AREAS:* Labor Law; Mining Damages; Agriculture.

HANS-JOACHIM POHLMANN, born Bremen, 1954; admitted, 1984, Germany. *Education:* University of Bochum (1975-1981). *LANGUAGES:* German, English and French. *PRACTICE AREAS:* Administrative Law; Municipal Law.

ASSOCIATES

JOST ZUPKE, born Hamm, 1959; admitted, 1993, Germany. *Education:* University of Bochum (1984-1990). *LANGUAGES:* German and English. *PRACTICE AREAS:* General Practice; Torts.

MICHAEL TOLKSDORF, born Lünen, 1964; admitted, 1994, Germany. *Education:* University of Münster (1985-1990). *LANGUAGES:* German and English. *PRACTICE AREAS:* General Practice; Civil Law; Litigation.

All Partners are Members of the German Bar Association, Dortmund Lawyers' Association and German-American Chamber of Commerce.

SPIEKER, HOLTERMANN, DUVERNELL, DIECKHÖFER & PARTNER

Established in 1904

KLEPPINGSTR. 9 - 11
4600 DORTMUND 1, GERMANY
Telephone: 49 231 9 58 58-0
Telex: 04 775 313 455 SHDD A
Facsimile: 49 231 9 58 58-48

General Practice and Litigation. Commercial Law, Corporate Matters, Banking, Unfair Competition, International and EEC Law, Copyright, Tax Law, Environmental Law, Construction and Engineering Contracts, Franchise and Factoring, Industrial and Intellectual Property Rights, Debt Collection. Notaries.

MEMBERS OF FIRM

JOCHEN SPIEKER, born Dortmund, Germany, February 5, 1942; admitted, 1969, Germany. *Education:* Tuebingen and Munich (Erstes Juristisches Staatsexamen, 1966). Board Member, Rechtsanwaltskammer (Chamber of Attorneys) for the Judicial District of Hamm, 1984——. Mem-

(This Listing Continued)

ber: German Construction Law Association. *LANGUAGES:* German and English. *PRACTICE AREAS:* General Practice; Litigation; Construction Law; Products Liability Law.

DIRK HOLTERMANN, born Bochum, Germany, June 15, 1942; admitted, 1970, Germany. *Education:* Freiburg and Muenster (Erstes Juristisches Staatsexamen, 1967). *Member:* German Bar Association; Dortmund Lawyers Association. *LANGUAGES:* German and English. *PRACTICE AREAS:* Corporations Law; Trade Law.

LUTZ DUVERNELL, born Moenchengladbach, Germany, April 14, 1943; admitted, 1973, Germany. *Education:* Freiburg and Bonn (Erstes Juristisches Staatsexmen, 1969). Assistant Professor of Law, Ruhr-University in Bochum, 1970-1971. Board Member, Dortmund Bar Association, 1978-1990. *Member:* German Bar Association; German Association for the Protection of Industrial and Intellectual Property; Association of Tax Attorneys. *LANGUAGES:* German and English. *PRACTICE AREAS:* Trade Law; Corporations Law; Unfair Competition Law; Labor Law; Tax Law.

HANS DIECKHÖFER, born Bassum, Germany, June 7, 1944; admitted, 1973, Germany. *Education:* Tuebingen, Bonn (Erstes Juristisches Staatsexamen, 1969) London. Board Member, Dortmund Bar Association, 1988——. *Member:* German Bar Association; Deutscher Juristentag. *LANGUAGES:* German and English. *PRACTICE AREAS:* Trade Law; Banking Law; Industrial and Intellectual Property Rights Law; Unfair Competition Law; Brokerage Law; Domestic Relations Law; Wills Law.

DR. CHRISTIAN TILSE, born Gummerscbach, Germany, January 9, 1947; admitted, 1978, Germany. *Education:* Freiburg, Geneva, Bonn (Erstes Juristisches Staatsexamen, 1973; Doctor of Jurisprudence, 1978). Author: "Der allgemeine Küudigungschutz des Arbeitnehmers im gerichtlichen Vergleichsverfahren des Arbeitgebers," Dissertation, 1977. Counsel of Dortmund Section of German Red Cross, 1982-1988. *Member:* German Bar Association; Dortmund Lawyers Association; German-German Lawyers Association. *LANGUAGES:* German, English and French. *PRACTICE AREAS:* Labor Law; Real Estate Law; Construction Law; Lease Law.

DR. LUTZ ADERHOLD, born Magdeburg, Germany, March 28, 1951; admitted, 1981, Germany. *Education:* Cologne and Bielefeld (Erstes Juristisches Staatsexamen, 1975; Doctor of Jurisprudence, 1980). Author: "Das Schuldmodell der BGB-Gesellschaft," 1981; "Comments on §§741 - 758, 1008 - 1011 Civil Code and on the German Marital Law"; in: Erman's Comments on Civil Code, Aschendorff 1993, 9th Edition; "Culpa in Contrahendo beim Unternehmenskauf, DStR 1991, 844." Assistant Professor for Civil and Trade Law, Banking Law and International Law, University of Bielefield, 1975-1978. *Member:* Association for Banking Law. *LANGUAGES:* German, English and French. *PRACTICE AREAS:* Banking Law; Stock Exchange Law; Corporations Law; Trade Law; Antitrust Law; Bankruptcy Law; Leasing Law; Factoring Law; Franchise Law; Computer Law.

DR. DETLEF GÖTZ, born Dortmund, Germany, May 6, 1955; admitted, 1984, Germany. *Education:* Bochum (Erstes Juristisches Staatsexmen, 1980; Doctor of Jurisprudence, 1988). Author: "Untersuchungen zum Befangenheitsrecht, die Richterablehnung gem. §24 II StPO," Dissertation, 1988. Lecturer for Penal Law, University Bochum, 1981-1982. *Member:* German Bar Association; Association of Dortmund Lawyers. *LANGUAGES:* German and English. *PRACTICE AREAS:* Criminal Law; Environmental Law; Construction Law; Traffic Law; Insurance Law; Breweries Law; Catering Law.

DR. WOLFGANG NOCKELMANN, born Schwerte, Germany, August 6, 1957; admitted, 1990, Germany and New York. *Education:* Bochum (Erstes Juristisches Staatsexamen, 1987; Doctor of Jurisprudence, 1992); Ruhr-University, Bochum and St. Louis University (One year joint programme). Assistant for Commercial, Civil and European Law, Ruhr-University in Bochum, 1987-1988. Author: "Das Durchsuchungsrecht der EG-Kommission im kartellrechtlichen Nachprüfungsverfahren," Dissertation 1992. Legal Internship with Phillips, Lytle, Hitchcock, Blaine and Huber, Buffalo (N.Y.) *Member:* German-American Lawyers Association; German-Swiss-Liechtenstein Lawyers Associations; Association Internationale des Jeunes Avocats; Canadian-German Lawyers Association (President). *LANGUAGES:* German, English, French and Russian. *PRACTICE AREAS:* International Law; European Community Law; Contracts Law; Commercial Law; Transportation Law; Unfair Competition Law; Arbitration.

MARKUS STRÄTER, born Bochum, Germany, September 7, 1962; admitted, 1991, Germany. *Education:* Bochum (Erstes Juristisches Staat-

(This Listing Continued)

sexamen, 1987). *Member:* German Bar Association (Traffic Law Section and Public Law Section). Legal Advisor of State Environmental Center Dortmund; Lecturer for Environmental Law at Professional School. *LANGUAGES:* German and English. *PRACTICE AREAS:* Traffic Law; Construction Law; Public Law; Debt Collection Law; Environmental Law.

ASSOCIATES

ANJA BERNINGHAUS, born Versmold, Germany, June 18, 1953; admitted, 1981, Germany. *Education:* Freiburg, Muenster (Erstes Juristisches Staatsexamen, 1978). Assistant at Muenster Law School, Public and Penal Law, 1978-1981. Counsel to Regional Section of German Red Cross. *Member:* Association of Dortmund Lawyers. *LANGUAGES:* German, English and French. *PRACTICE AREAS:* Domestic Relations Law; Wills Law; Lease Law; Travel Contracts Law.

ROSE-MARIE SCHAEFERS, born Bochum, Germany, March 13, 1961; admitted, 1992, Germany. *Education:* Bochum (Erstes Juristisches Staatsexamen, 1988). *Member:* Dortmund Bar Association. *LANGUAGES:* German and English. *PRACTICE AREAS:* Domestic Relations; Lease; Food Processing and Distribution Law.

MANFRED EHLERS, born Cologne, Germany, May 28, 1962; admitted, 1993, Germany. *Education:* Münster (Erstes Juristisches Staatsexamen, 1990). Lecturer for Review Courses. Assistant, Institut for Labor Law and Civil Procedure, Münster University, 1990-1991. Lecturer, Special Courses for Lawyers from former East Germany, 1991-1992. *LANGUAGES:* German, French and English. *PRACTICE AREAS:* Commercial Law; Corporate Matters; Contracts.

DR. GUNTHER LEHLEITER, born Saulgau, Germany, May 3, 1964; admitted, 1993, Germany. *Education:* Bonn, Munich, Cambridge, U.K. (LL.M., 1988; Erstes Juristisches Staatsexamen, 1990; Doctor of Jurisprudence, 1994). Author: "Der rechtswidrige verbindliche Befehl," Dissertation, 1994. Lecturer for Review Courses, 1990-1993. *Member:* German-British Lawyers Association. *LANGUAGES:* German, English and French. *PRACTICE AREAS:* Commercial Law; Corporate Matters; International and EEC Law; Contracts.

ABTMEYER & FRICKE

Established in 1991

DOHNAER STRASSE 111
D-01239 DRESDEN, GERMANY
Telephone: +49-351 2816161
Fax: +49-351 2816165
Telex: 47-75313944 ABFR A

Corporate, Commercial and Administrative Law, Real Estate and Construction, Banking, Securities and Bankruptcy Law, Mergers and Acquisitions, EEC Law, Labor and Employment, Intellectual Property, Computers and Software, Media and Arts, Restitutions, Litigation.

MEMBERS OF FIRM

HANS H. ABTMEYER, born Stuttgart, Germany, September 27, 1958; admitted, 1986, Stuttgart; 1992, Oberlandesgericht Dresden. *Education:* University of Freiburg. Chambre Franco-Allemande de Commerce et de l'Industrie, Paris, 1988-1989. Chairman of the Board, Gebr. Friese AG, Dresden, 1992—. *Member:* German-American Lawyers Association; German Lawyers Association; Deutscher Juristentag. *LANGUAGES:* German, English and French. *PRACTICE AREAS:* Commercial and Corporate Law; Banking; Securities and Bankruptcy Law; EEC Law; Intellectual Property; Computers and Software; Media and Arts.

ANNETTE FRICKE, born Essen, Germany, December 15, 1960; admitted, 1989, Nürnberg; 1994, Oberlandesgericht Dresden. *Education:* Universities of Erlangen-Nürnberg and Passau. Assistant Notary Public, Erlangen, 1985-1986. *Member:* German-Czechoslovakian Law Society; German Lawyers Association (Committee Member, Construction Law); German Female Lawyers Association (Board Member). *LANGUAGES:* German and English. *PRACTICE AREAS:* Commercial and Corporate Law; Mergers and Acquisitions; Contracts; Labor and Employment; Real Estate and Construction Law; Restitutions.

ELISABETH WEITZELL-KNOLL, born Duisburg, Germany, October 7, 1959; admitted, 1989, Düsseldorf; 1994, Oberlandesgericht Dresden. *Education:* University of Münster. Assistant, Institute of Criminal Law, University of Münster, 1983-1987. *Member:* German Female Lawyers Association. *LANGUAGES:* German and English. *PRACTICE AREAS:* Real Estate; Restitutions; Intellectual Property; Media and Arts; Economic Offences; Litigation.

(This Listing Continued)

RAINER A. PESCH, born Dortmund, Germany, February 27, 1964; admitted, 1994, Dresden. *Education:* University of Bochum. *Member:* German Lawyers Association; German Tax Law Association. *LANGUAGES:* German and English. *PRACTICE AREAS:* Taxation; Restitutions; Labor and Employment; Insurance; Medical Malpractice; Litigation.

Languages: German, English and French

ARETZ SCHMALZ BÖNING

Established in 1993

ARNDSTRAßE 11
01099 DRESDEN, GERMANY
Telephone: 0351-5022450
Telefax: 0351-5023107

Frankfurt/Main, Germany Office: Stresemannallee 3, 60596. Telephone: 069-963700. Telefax: 069-96370100.

Commercial Litigation and Arbitration, Corporate, Contracts and Commercial Law, International Joint Ventures, Real Estate, Banking, Mergers and Acquisitions, Antitrust, Intellectual Property Law, Entertainment, Unfair Competition, Environmental Law, Labor Law and Industrial Relations.

FIRM PROFILE: *The firm was founded in 1993 by former partners of three renowned international corporate and business law firms in Frankfurt/Main and offers a full range of legal services. Currently Aretz Schmalz Böning is representing a variety of international commercial clients, among them banks, companies in the computer and electronics industry, automotive industry, food and beverage industry, private investors, Asian trading houses, press and publishing as well as advertising agencies.*

PARTNERS OF THE FIRM

DR. JUR. MEINULF DREGGER, born Fulda, Germany, January 18, 1958; admitted, 1991, Dresden. *Education:* Universities of Fribourg (Switzerland), Würzburg and Freiburg (Dr. jur., 1988). *LANGUAGES:* German, English and French. *PRACTICE AREAS:* Corporate and Commercial Law; Restitution and Real Property Law; Litigation.

ASSOCIATES

DR. JUR. SYLVIA HEYSER, born Hannover, Germany, July 1, 1958; admitted, 1985, Frankfurt/Main; 1994, Dresden. *Education:* Universities of Freiburg and Lausanne (Switzerland) (Dr. jur., 1989). *LANGUAGES:* German, English and French. *PRACTICE AREAS:* Corporate and Commercial Law; Antitrust and Unfair Competition Law; Insurance Law; Litigation.

Languages: German, English, French and Portuguese

AULINGER, BOTTKE, KNÄLMANN

ST. PETERSBURGER STRASSE 15
01069 DRESDEN, GERMANY
Telephone: (0351) 4 87 24 19
Fax: (0351) 4 87 33 27

Bochum, Germany Office: ABC-Strasse 5, D-44787 Bochum. Telephone: (0234) 68779-0. Teletex: 234 334 (Dufhues) (from Telex: 17234334). Fax: (0234) 68 06 42.

Erfurt, Germany Office: Kleine Arche 1, 99084 Erfurt. Telephone: 0361/5667808. Fax: 0361/5667810.

Leipzig, Germany Office: Goethestrasse 1, 04109, O-7010 Leipzig. Telephone: (0341) 9600910. Fax: (0341) 9601169.

General Practice. Corporate, Commercial, Banking, Antitrust, Unfair Competition, Real Estate, Merger and Acquisition, Products Liability, Labor, Co-Determination, Tax, Arbitration, Administrative and Public, Building and Planning. Reversion of nationalized enterprises and real estate to private ownership.

MEMBER OF FIRM

KARL FRIEDRICH NOLTING, born Herford, Germany, September 12, 1959; admitted, 1992. *Education:* University of Munich. *LANGUAGES:* German, English and French.

(For Complete Biographical data on all Personnel, see Professional Biographies at Bochum)

BAPPERT, WITZ & SELBHERR

BERGGARTENSTRASSE 7
D-01309 DRESDEN, GERMANY
Telephone: (0049) 351/4606131
Telecopier: 351/4655376

Freiburg, Germany Office: Leo-Wohleb-Strasse 6, D-79098. Telephone:
(0049) 761/218080. Telecopier: (0049) 761/2180821.
Brussels, Belgium Office: 176, Avenue Louise, B-1050. Telephone: (0032)
2/6473300. Telecopier: (0032) 2/6476539.

RESIDENT PARTNERS

DR. EKKEHARD NOLTING, born Hannover, Germany, April 21,
1955; admitted, 1988, Freiburg. *Education:* Universities of Göttingen, Lausanne, Switzerland and Freiburg (Dr.jur., 1995). *Member:* German Bar
Association; Association Internationale des Jeunes Avocats. *LAN-
GUAGES:* German, English, French and Spanish.

ASSOCIATES

Burghard von Bargen

(For complete biographical data see Professional Biographies at
Freiburg, Germany)

BERNET, WEITNAUER & PARTNER

ANTON-GRAFF-STRASSE 15
01309 DRESDEN, GERMANY
Telephone: 0357-447 6280
Telecopier: 0357-447 6289

Munich, Germany Office: Möhlstraße 10/I, 81675. Telephone: 089-470
90 14. Telecopier: 089-470 74 27.
Leipzig, Germany Office: Roscherstr. 17-21, 04105. Telephone: 0341-564
6766. Telecopier: 0341-566 0981.

BIRGIT FRANZ, born Munich, Germany, December 16, 1962; admit-
ted, 1991, Germany. *Education:* University of Munich (Referendar, 1988;
Assessor, 1991). Stagiaire, German-Canadian Chamber of Industry and
Commerce, Toronto, 1990-1991. *LANGUAGES:* German, English and
French. *PRACTICE AREAS:* Commercial and Corporate Law; Litigation;
Investment and Restitution of Property in East Germany.

BOESEBECK, BARZ & PARTNER

Established in 1990

HEIDEPARKSTRASSE 4
01099 DRESDEN, GERMANY
Telephone: (49) (351) 56 70 550
Telecopier: (49) (351) 50 23 476

Frankfurt am Main, Germany Office: Darmstaedter Landstrasse 125,
60598, Frankfurt am Main. Telephone: (49) (69) 96 236-0. Telefax:
(49) (69) 96 236-100.
Berlin, Germany Office: Schlueterstrasse 37, 10629, Berlin. Telephone:
(49) (30) 88 5745-0. Telecopier: (49) (30) 88 57-45-99.
Vienna, Austria Office (Sprechstelle): Graben 49A, 1010 Vienna.
Telephone: (43) (1) 53 55 744. Telecopier: (43) (1) 53 50 649.
Warsaw, Poland Office: ul. Wspólna 25, 00519 Warsaw. Telephone: (48)
(2) 62 83 029. Telecopier: (48) (22) 2941 05.
zAGREB, cROATIA oFFICE: tRG BANA j. jELACICA 3, 41000
zAGREB. tELEPHONE: (385) (41) 42 71 16. tELECOPIER: (385)
(41) 42 87 99.

*Commercial, Corporation, Contracts, Mergers and Acquisitions, Banking,
Tax, Antitrust, Unfair Competition, Distributorship Agency and Franchising, Computer, EDP, Patents and Trademarks, Capital Markets Financial
Services, Arbitration and Litigation, Product Liability, International Public
and Private Law, EEC-Law, Property and Real Estate, Foreign Investments, Administrative, Environmental, Trade Regulations, Food and Drug
Regulations, Notaries.*

MEMBERS OF FIRM

DR. VOLKMAR JESCH, born Tuebingen, Germany, March 7, 1958;
admitted, 1989, Germany. *Education:* University of Heidelberg (Doctor of
Jurisprudence). Author: "Das kartellrechtliche Schriftformgebot (§34
GWB)," Diss. Heidelberg, 1989; "Investitionsvorranggesetz," 1993. *LAN-
GUAGES:* German, French and English. *PRACTICE AREAS:* Mergers
and Acquisitions; Antitrust; Unfair Trade Practices; Industrial and Intellec-

(This Listing Continued)

tual Property Rights; Distributorship; Agency; Licensing; Litigation; Property and Real Estate; East German Investments and Matters related to the
German Unification.

BERNHARD KUHN, born Berlin, Germany, December 12, 1963; admitted, 1991, Germany. *Education:* University of Berlin. Author: "Investitionsvorranggesetz," 1993. *LANGUAGES:* German and English. *PRAC-
TICE AREAS:* Environment; Administration; Building and Zoning Property and Real Estate; East German Investments and Matters related to the
German Unification.

JOERG KRUEGER, born Zossen, Germany, May 10, 1962; admitted,
1990, Germany. *Education:* University of Leipzig. *LANGUAGES:* German,
English and Russian. *PRACTICE AREAS:* Civil and Commercial Law;
Corporate, Labour and Employment Law; Litigation; East German Investments and Matters related to the German Unification.

FRANK PRÜFKE, born Berlin, Germany, April 7, 1964; admitted,
1992, Germany. *Education:* University of Leipzig. *LANGUAGES:* German,
English and Russian. *PRACTICE AREAS:* Civil and Commercial Law;
Corporate, Labour and Employment Law; Litigation; East German Investments and Matters related to the German Unification.

FEDDERSEN LAULE SCHERZBERG &
OHLE HANSEN EWERWAHN

KOENIGSBRUECKER STR. 17
01099 DRESDEN, GERMANY
Telephone: 49 03 51 567 02 77
Telefax: 49 03 51 567 02 79

Frankfurt/Main, Germany Office: Stiftstraße 9-17, P.O. Box 100836,
D-60313 Frankfurt am Main. Telephone: 49-69-29994-0. Telefax:
49-69-282615. Telex: 41 33 96 fls d.
Hamburg, Germany Office: Jungfernstieg 51 (Prien-Haus), D-20354
Hamburg. Telephone: 49-40-35 00 50. Telex: 21 27 99 99 lawt d.
Telefax: 49-40-35 00 51 11.
Berlin, Germany Office: Kurfürstendamm 185, D-10707 Berlin.
Telephone: 49-30-88 57 16 0. Telefax: 49-30-88 57 16 50.
Brussels, Belgium Office: 118, Rue d'Arlon, B-1040 Brussels. Telephone:
32-2-280-1544. Telefax: 32-2-280-0703.
Prague, Czech Republic Office: Spanělská 2, CZ-120 00 Prague 2.
Telephone: 42-2-268203; 268229. Telefax: 42-2-260310.

*General Practice, Administrative Law, Admiralty, Antitrust, Arbitration,
Aviation, Banking, Commercial and Corporate Law, Environmental Law,
Entertainment Law, Estate Planning, EC and International Law, Insur-
ance, Labor Law, License, Merger and Acquisition, Patent, Trade Mark
and Copyright, Real Estate, Securities Law, Tax, Transportation, Unfair
Competition, Litigation.*

FIRM PROFILE: *The firm offers a full range of legal services. It is well
known for its commercial, corporate, banking and tax law and its practice
in the field of merger and acquisitions, real estate and environmental law.
The firm has a broad national as well as international client base with a
focus on Europe, the United States and Japan. The firm has 79 attorneys
at law (8 of whom are notaries public) and 5 tax advisors.*

MEMBERS OF FIRM

DR. AXEL BAUER, born Hamburg, December 1, 1946; admitted, 1976,
Germany. *Education:* Universities of Freiburg and Geneva, Switzerland
(Dr. jur., 1976). *Member:* GRUR; German Association of Comparative
Law; DRRI, Juris-Member of Expert Council. *LANGUAGES:* German,
English and French. *PRACTICE AREAS:* Corporate Law; Partnership
Law; EC Law; Technical Contracts; Computer Law.

DR. WOLFGANG STORM, born Frankfurt/Main, Federal Republic of
Germany, December 27, 1939; admitted, 1970, Frankfurt/Main; 1989, No-
tary. *Education:* Universities of Frankfurt/Main and Freiburg i.Br.;
Georgetown University, Washington, D.C. *Member:* Frankfurt/Main Law-
yers Association (Member of Board). *LANGUAGES:* English and German.
PRACTICE AREAS: Corporate Law; Real Property Law; Labor Law;
Litigation; General Practice.

ASSOCIATES

GUIDO REKER, born Meschede, Germany, October 14, 1961; admitted, 1991, Stuttgart; 1992, Dresden. *Education:* University of Passau (Bavaria, Germany); University of Angers (France) (State Exam, 1988). Assistant Lecturer, French Center of Law Studies at the University of Saarland.
Chair of French Public Law, Saarbruecken, Germany. *Member:* Dresden

(This Listing Continued)

Lawyers Association. *LANGUAGES:* English, French and German. *PRACTICE AREAS:* Law Pertaining to the German Reunification; Real Property Law; Litigation; General Practice.

JENS-CHRISTIAN POSSELT, born Essen, Germany, December 2, 1960; admitted, 1993, Dresden. *Education:* University of Kiel. Assistant to Professor at University of Kiel and Hamburg. Civil Servant, Feder al Maritime and Hydrographic Institute, Hamburg. *LANGUAGES:* German and English. *PRACTICE AREAS:* Public Law; International Law of the Sea; Litigation; General Law.

FINGERHUT, KARG & PARTNERS

HUEBLERSTRASSE 3-5
D-01309 DRESDEN, GERMANY
Telephone: 0351-33 01 19
Fax: 0351-3 55 71

Munich, Germany Office: Potsdamer Straße 12, D-80802. Telephone: 089-360 80 00. Fax: 089-361 77 63.

Administrative Law, Air Traffic, Antitrust, Banking, Commercial, Construction, Copyright, Criminal, European Union, Family Law, Foreclosure, General Practice, Insolvency, Insurance, Intellectual Property, Labour, Law pertaining to Property Claims in the former GDR, Licensing, Litigation, Medical, Mergers and Acquisitions, National and International Arbitration, Pharmaceutical, Product Liability, Tax Law, Trademark, Transportation, Trust and Estate, Unfair Competition.

MEMBERS OF FIRM

THOMAS MAUL, born Bad Wildungen, Germany, February 21, 1960; admitted, 1991, Germany. *Education:* Universities Würzburg, Munich (Referendar, 1988; Assessor, 1991). Co-Author: Nath/Schilling/Fingerhut, "Formbook on Contracts," 8, Edition, Heymanns Verlag Köln, 1994. *Member:* Dresden and German Bar Associations. *LANGUAGES:* German and English.

ASSOCIATES

SABINE KARG, born Stuttgart, Germany, March 7, 1958; admitted, 1985, Germany. *Education:* Universities of Tübingen and Munich (Referendar, 1982; Assessor, 1990). Stage at Peat Marwick, Munich, 1985-1989. *Member:* Dresden Bar Association. *LANGUAGES:* German, English, French and Italian.

INGO SAWITZKI, born Bremen, Germany, July 31, 1960; admitted, 1990, Germany. *Education:* University of Würzburg (Referendar, 1987; Assessor, 1990). *Member:* Dresden and German Bar Associations. *LANGUAGES:* German and English.

(For Complete Biographical Data on all Personnel, See Professional Biographies at Munich, Germany)

GRAF von WESTPHALEN & MODEST

WINTERBERGSTRAßE 2
01277 DRESDEN, GERMANY
Telephone and Fax: 0351-2516 024 or 2516032

Cologne, Germany Office: Salierring 42, 50677. Telephone: (0221) 10807-0. Telex: 8883 360. Telefax: (0221) 239255.
Hamburg, Germany Office: Poststraße 9 A, 20354. Telephone: (040) 35922-0. Fax: (040) 344573. Telex: 211 729 MOD D.
Leipzig, Germany Office: Katharinenstraße 15, 04109. Telephone: (0341) 281073. Telefax: (0341) 281073.
Brussels, Belgium Office: Avenue de la Joyeuse Entrée 1, Boite 16, B-1040. Telephone: (02) 2304669. Fax: (02) 2310035.
Paris, France Office: 198, Avenue Victor Hugo, F- 75116. Telephone: (01) 45046173. Fax: (01) 45044143.

National and International Contract Law, National and International Trade and Finance Law, Insurance Law, Construction Law, Corporate Law, Banking Law, Antitrust Law, Competition Law, Distributor Contracts, General Conditions of Contract, Labour Law, Tax Law, Administration Law, Reprivatization of Companies and Property, Environmental Law, Medical Law and the Law of Succession, Aviation Law, Leasing and Data Protection.

DR. HEINZ-JÖRG ENGELS, born Cologne, December 25, 1957; admitted, 1992. *Education:* University of Würzburg. Dresdner Bank AG, Cologne, Gummersbach, Madgeburg, 1989-1991.

(This Listing Continued)

HORST WITTEK, born Beuthen, June 18, 1933; admitted, 1969. *Education:* Universities of Frankfurt, Speyer and Straßburg (Law, History and Philosophy). Head of the legal department, Deutsche Lufthansa until 1993. Publications: Handbook on computer law, numerous publications.

Member of Eurolegal

Languages: German, English, French and Portuguese.

(For Complete Biographical Data on all Personnel, see Professional Biographies at Cologne, Germany)

GREUNER WICKER HUBER HANF

BERGMANNSTRASSE 22
01309 DRESDEN, GERMANY
Telephone: (0351) 3400 814
Facsimile: (0351) 3400 815

Frankfurt/Main, Germany Office: Goethestraße 31-33, 60313. Telephone: (49 69) 298 00 80. Telex: 416 395 Notar D. Facsimile: (49 69) 29 80 08 29.
Milan, Italy Office: Corso di Porta Romana, 6, 20121, Telephone: (39-2) 865394. Facsimile: (39-2) 865480.

Labour, Corporate, Real Estate Law.

ASSOCIATES

KARL WOSCHNAGG, born Ludvika, Sweden, October 17, 1961; admitted, 1990, Germany. *Education:* Universities of Tübingen, Munich and Uppsala. *Member:* Swedish Chamber of Commerce in Germany. Author: "Das neue schwedische Kaufrecht," 1991. *LANGUAGES:* German, Swedish, English and French.

KERSTIN RITTER, born Bahrendorf, Germany, April 2, 1964; admitted, 1992, Germany. *Education:* University of Leipzig. *LANGUAGES:* German and English.

GRUNENBERG & HELMKE-BECKER

Rechtsanwälte

Established in 1990

SCHILLERPLATZ 7
D-01309 DRESDEN, GERMANY
Telephone: 49351-3361090/1
Fax: 49351-3361092

Frankfurt/Main, Germany Office: Brüder-Grimm-Str. 50, D-60385. Telephone: 4969-432932/439526. Fax: 4969-439818.

Trade Law, Private International Law, Administrative Law, Company Law, Competition Law, Landlord and Tenant, Conveyancing, Contract Law, Building and Construction Law, Probate and Trusts.

THOMAS HELMKE-BECKER, RECHTSANWALT UND NOTAT, born Fulda, Germany, July 2, 1947; admitted, 1975, Germany. *Education:* Universities of Frankfurt and Würzburg. *Member:* International Bar Association; German Bar Association. *PRACTICE AREAS:* Landlord and Tenant; Conveyancing; Company; Trade and Contract Law.

(For Complete Biographical Data on all Personnel and Firm Profile, see Professional Biographies at Frankfurt/Main, Germany)

HAVER & MAILAENDER

Established in 1965

BAUTZNER STRASSE 23-25
D-01099 DRESDEN, GERMANY
Telephone: 0351-51955
Telecopier: 0351-53538

Stuttgart, Germany Office: Lenzhalde 83, D-70192. Telephone: (0711) 227440. Cable Address: "Intertax", Stuttgart. Telex: 721738 advo d. Telecopier: (0711) 2991935.
Frankfurt, Germany Office: Beethovenstrasse 4, D-60325. Telephone: 069-740190. Telecopier: 069-740247.
Brussels, Belgium Office: Av. de la Renaissance 1, 1040 Brussels. Telephone: 02-7366375. Telecopier: 02-7360571.

Commercial, Corporation, Banking and Financial Services, Mergers and Acquisitions, High Technology and Telecommunication, Transportation and Aviation, Construction and Engineering Contracts, Antitrust, EEC-

(This Listing Continued)

HAVER & MAILAENDER, Dresden—Continued

Law, Licensing, Patent, Trademark, Copyright, Trade Law and Product Liability, International and Tax Law, Litigation and Arbitration.

FIRM PROFILE: The firm was established in Stuttgart in 1965 and opened its Dresden Office in 1991. The firm offers the full range of legal services for commercial matters. The Dresden Office concentrates on restitution matters and on investments in the new federal states of Eastern Germany.

MEMBER OF FIRM

BERND HEILENZ, born Dresden, 1938; admitted, 1990, Dresden. General Counsel of Zeiss-Pentacon, 1966-1985, Central Institute of Nuclear Research till 1990. Member: German Association for the Protection of Industrial Property and Copyright. LANGUAGES: German and English.

(For complete list of Partners, see Professional Biographies at Stuttgart, Germany and Brussels, Belgium)

HESS WIENBERG FREUND & PARTNER

LOSCHWITZER STRAße 7
01309 DRESDEN, GERMANY
Telephone: 49/351/34085-0
Fax: 49/351/34085-5

Mainz Office: Wilhelm-Theodor-Römheld-Str. 14, 55130. Telephone: 49/6131/2850-0. Fax: 49/6131/285028.
Berlin Office: Friedrichstraße 180, 10117. Telephone: 49/30/22073-133. Fax: 49/30/22073-150.
Chemnitz Office: Treffurthstraße 17, 09120. Telephone: 49/371/590450-0. Fax: 49/371/590450-5.
Alzey Office: Antoniterstraße 65, 55232. Telephone: 49/6731/3066. Fax: 49/6731/3104.
Wiesbaden Office: Abeggstraße 2, 65193. Telephone: 49/611/52303-1. Fax: 49/611/52303-3.

Bankruptcy, Liquidation, Banking, Business Law, Partnerships, Limited Partnerships, Civil Law, Company Law, Contracts, Debtor and Creditor, Labour and Employment, Mergers and Acquisitions.

(For complete Biographical Data on all Personnel, see Professional Biographies at Mainz)

DR. KNAUTHE & PARTNER

Rechtsanwälte

Established in 1969

OSTRA-ALLEE 25
01067 DRESDEN, GERMANY
Telephone: 0351-4860165
Telefax: 0351-4860166

Berlin (Head), Germany Office: Kurfürstendamm 44, 10719 Berlin. Telephone: 030-880008-0. Telefax: 030-880008-65. Telex: 185803 KNAPA D.
Other Berlin, Germany Office: Clara-Zetkin-Strasse 80, 10117 Berlin. Telephone: 030-22086-0. Telefax: 030-2292026.
Potsdam, Germany Office: Eisenhart Str. 2, 14469 Potsdam. Telephone: 0331-2803590. Telefax: 0331-2803592.

Corporation, Building and Planning, Real Estate and Zoning, Construction, Mergers and Acquisitions, Joint Ventures, Common Market, Investment, Banking, Company, Commercial, Insurance, Trademark and Copyright, Labor, Family, Housing, Estates, Wills, Trusts, Restitution, Communist Expropriation, Investment in East Germany and Eastern Europe, Litigation, Notaries.

RESIDENT ASSOCIATES

FRIEDRICH CRAMER, born Rheda, June 25, 1960; admitted, 1993, Dresden. Education: Universities of Erlangen and Cologne. Member: Saxony Bar Association. LANGUAGES: German, English and French. PRACTICE AREAS: Restitution; Company Law; Real Estate.

KAI-THOMAS BUSMANN, born Soest, August 14, 1964; admitted, 1993, Dresden. Education: University of Münster. Member: Saxony Bar Association. LANGUAGES: German, English and French. PRACTICE AREAS: Labor and Employment; Construction Law; Criminal Law.

(This Listing Continued)

THOMAS DEFFNER, born Boston, USA, May 2, 1961; admitted, 1994, Dresden. Education: University of Munich. Member: Saxony Bar Association. LANGUAGES: German, English and French. PRACTICE AREAS: Administrative Law; Bankruptcy; Corporate Law.

(For Biographical Data at Berlin (Head), Germany Office, Other Berlin and Potsdam Office, see Professional Biographies at Berlin and Potsdam, Germany)

KOCH, HARTTMANN, FUCHS & ARNECKE

GOETHEALLEE 13
01309 DRESDEN, GERMANY
Telephone: 0351 33 78 18
Telefax: 0351 33 78 19

Frankfurt, Germany Office: Hamburger Allee 2, 60486. Telephone: 069 77 01 41. Telefax: 069 77 01 41. Telex: 41 42 51.

Antitrust, Banking and Financial Services, Corporation, Environmental Protection Law, Labor Law, Mergers and Acquisitions, Pharmaceutical Law, Tax, Unfair Competition, General Practice.

MEMBERS OF FIRM

DR. VOLKER M. FUCHS, born Polaun, CSFR, February 24, 1945; admitted, 1976, Frankfurt. Education: Universities of Frankfurt, Berlin and Giessen (Dr. jur., 1979). Specialized Tax Counsel. Author: "Warranty in Leasing Contracts in the Light of the Law Concerning Standard Business Conditions," 1979; "Retention of Title under German Law," 1981. Member: German Bar Association. (Also at Frankfurt Office). LANGUAGES: German and English.

THOMAS KNÖPFLE, born Königstein/Taunus, Germany, June 4, 1963; admitted, 1993, Dresden. Education: University of Freiburg. LANGUAGES: German, English and French.

(For Complete Biographical Data on all Personnel, see Professional Biographies at Frankfurt, Germany)

DR. KREUZER & COLL.

Anwaltskanzlei

HÜBLERSTR. 2
01309 DRESDEN, GERMANY
Telephone: 0351/337413
24h-Tel-Service under Nürnberg office: 0911/209103
Fax: 0351/337415

Mailing Address: P.O. Box 53 01 10, 01291

Nürnberg, Germany Office: Lorenzer Platz 3a, 90402. Mailing Address: P.O. Box 26 33, 90012. Telephone: 0911-209103. Telex: 047753/2633 Krpaa. Datex-P: 44/9110/40363. Telefax: 0911/226781; 0911/2059879.

Member of International Jurists EEIG
General Practice, Wills, Unfair Competition, Company, Commercial, Banking, Bankruptcy, Personal Injury, Insurance, Employment, Family, Criminal, Construction, Product Liability, Patent and Trademark Law, Environmental Law.

FIRM PROFILE: Since the firm's establishment in 1976 there has been broad expansion notably with the establishment of our second office in Dresden in 1990. The firm, as a whole (nine lawyers), is able to offer a comprehensive range of legal services. Individually, each lawyer has his own legal field of specialization.

We have a particularly healthy interest in international matters and were able to formalise this by the formation of "International Jurists" a European Economic Interest Grouping (EEIG).

International co-operation also features heavily in our activities as we feel the need, in order to be able to offer the optimal service to our clients, to keep abreast of issues within the fast moving realm of international law.

STEFAN KREUZER. PRACTICE AREAS: Labour Law; Company and Commercial Law; Competition Law; Co-Determination; Environmental Law; International Law; Construction Law.

UWE HAUCK. PRACTICE AREAS: Family Law; Maintenance; General Civil Law; Road and Traffic Law; Landlord and Tenant Law; Administrative Law.

(This Listing Continued)

KATRIN ZEIGER. PRACTICE AREAS: Social Security Law; Criminal Law; Road and Traffic Law; Landlord and Tenant Law; General Practice.

(For Compete Biographical Data on all Personnel, See Professional Biograpies at Nürnberg, West Germany)

KÜBLER, ROGIER & PARTNER

ANTONSTRASSE 10
D-01097 DRESDEN, GERMANY
Telephone: (0351) 44 879-0
Telefax: (0351) 44 879-99

Cologne, Germany Office: Aachener Strasse 217, D-50931.
   Telephone:(0221) 400770. Telefax: (0221) 4007720.
Berlin, Germany Office: Einemstrasse 24, D-10785. Telephone: (030)
   264768-0. Telefax: (030) 264768-40.

Bankruptcy, Banking, Corporate, Commercial, Creditors' Rights, Industrial Relations and Labor Law, Insolvency and Reorganization, International Private, Property and Real Estate, Taxation, Unfair Competition, General Practice and Litigation.

RESIDENT PARTNERS

DR. CHRISTOPH MÖLLERS, born Bochum, Germany, January 26, 1959; admitted, 1989, Germany. *Education:* University of Bochum, Germany (2. State Exam, 1989); University of Münster, Germany; University of Strasburg, France; Lander College, Greenwood, South Carolina. Member of Board of Ziegelwerke Halle GmbH, Halle/Saale, 1990-1992. *LANGUAGES:* German, English, French.

KLAUS-DIETER BARTH, born Bonn, Germany, October 18, 1957; admitted, 1987, Cologne; 1993, Dresden. *Education:* University of Bonn. *Member:* Bar Association and Lawyers Association of Dresden. *LANGUAGES:* German, English.

DIPL.-FINANZWIRT MICHAEL STAUDINGER, born Cologne, Germany, March 31, 1957. *Education:* College of Finance, Münster. Certified Tax Advisor, Germany. 1988. *Member:* Association of Tax Advisors, Cologne. *LANGUAGES:* German, English.

MICHAEL SCHMIDT, born Karlsruhe, Germany, August 30, 1962; admitted, 1993, Berlin; 1994, Dresden. *Education:* University of Heidelborg and Freiburg. *Member:* Bar Association. *LANGUAGES:* German and English.

ROBERT K. SCHULTE, born Düsseldorf, Germany, March 12, 1962; admitted, 1992, Cologne. *Education:* University of Bonn, Germany. *Member:* Bar Association; Lawyers Association of Dresden; German Bar Association; Canadian-German Lawyers Association (Co-Founder). *LANGUAGES:* German and English.

ALEXANDRA STEINECKE, born Bonn, Germany, January 9, 1963; admitted, 1990, Bonn; 1994, Dresden. *Education:* University of Passau, Germany. *Member:* Bar Association; Lawyers Association of Dresden. *LANGUAGES:* German, English and French.

(For complete biographical data on Personnel at Cologne and Berlin, Germany Offices, see Professional Biographies at those locations)

LICHTENSTEIN, KÖRNER & PARTNERS

LEIPZIGER STR. 1
01097 DRESDEN, GERMANY
Telephone: 0351-54040
Fax: 0351-54040

Stuttgart, Germany Office: Heidehofstrasse 9, 70184. Telephone: 0711/4 89-79-0. Cable Address: "Interjus, Stuttgart" Telex: 723251 ijus d. Telecopier: Group 3: 0711/4815 77; 0711/4873 65.

Patent, Trademark, Copyright, Unfair Competition, Company, Commercial, Antitrust, Tax and Private International Law.

DR. VERONIKA FREY, born Herrenberg, Germany, January 13, 1962; admitted, 1990, West Germany. *Education:* University of Tübingen (Referendar, 1985; Doctor of Law, 1987; Assessor, 1990). Author: "Der Schutz des Seelischen Kindeswohls," Tübingen, 1987. *Member:* Stuttgart Bar Association; German Association for the Protection of Industrial Property and

(This Listing Continued)

Copyright. *LANGUAGES:* German, English and French. *PRACTICE AREAS:* Family Law; Corporate Law.

Languages: German, English, French and Dutch

(For Complete Biographical Data on all Personnel, see Professional Biographies at Stuttgart, Germany)

MENOLD HERRLINGER REINKING & PARTNER

UHLANDSTRASSE 39
D-01069 DRESDEN, GERMANY
Telephone: 0049/351/478 71-0
Telefax: 0049/351/478 71-15

Berlin Office: Fraunhofer Straße 33-36, D-10587 Berlin. Telephone:
   (0049 30) 34 78 68 11. Telefax: (0049 30) 34 78 68 35.
Düsseldorf Office: Am Wehrhahn 50, 40211 Düsseldorf. Telephone: (0049
   211) 93 52 300. Telefax: (0049 211) 93 52 683.
Stuttgart Office: Mittlerer Pfad 15, 70499 Stuttgart. Telephone: (0049
   711) 13 86 800. Telefax: (0049 711) 13 86 808.

Corporate, Commercial, Tax and Business Law Practice, including Mergers and Acquisitions, Antitrust and Unfair Competition Law, Intellectual and Industrial Property Law, Reorganization and Bankruptcy, Labor Law and Redundancy Plans (Sozialpläne), Private Wealth Planning, Trusts, Foundations and Estate Law, Environmental, Waste and Administrative Law, The Laws of the East European Countries, Business Law for Japanese Clients (Düsseldorf), Restitution of Property in the East German Federal States, General Civil Law and Civil Litigation, European Community Law.

FIRM PROFILE: The firm springs from a merger of the law firms Menold Herrlinger Maulbetsch Schick & Oltmanns (Stuttgart), Bezler & Partner (Stuttgart), Reith & Battke (Dresden) and Reinking, Frings & Drude (Düsseldorf).

MEMBERS OF FIRM

DR. STEFAN SCHICK, born Stuttgart, Germany, 1954. *Education:* University of Tübingen (State Exams, 1978, 1981; Doctor of Law, 1985). Co-Author with E. Rüd: "Stiftung und Verein als Unternehmensträger," 1988; with Alfred Gleiss: "Facetten des Anwaltsberufs," 1989. Author of numerous articles, speeches and seminars on Charitable Organizations. *Member:* German Bar Association. *LANGUAGES:* German and English. *PRACTICE AREAS:* Corporate Law; Business Law; Environmental Law (Waste Disposal); Charitable Organizations; Hospitals.

JÖRG-DIETER BATTKE, born Göttingen, Germany, 1958; admitted, 1988, Germany. *Education:* University of Münster (State Exams, 1985, 1988). Associate with Arneth, Rechtsanwälte, Baden-Baden, 1988-1991. Author: Numerous articles, seminars and speeches on Company Law. *Member:* German Bar Association. *LANGUAGES:* German and English. *PRACTICE AREAS:* Business Law; Corporate Law; Company Law; Taxation.

DR. ULLA FINDEISEN, born Arnsdorf/Dresden, Germany, 1952. *Education:* University of Leipzig (Graduate Lawyer, 1974); University of Economy of Berlin (Doctor of Law, 1984). Author: "Die Vervollkommnung des Systems der materiellen Verantwortlichkeit in den Allgemeinen Lieferbedingungen des RGW"; numerous Articles in the journal "Recht im Außenhandel der DDR.". *LANGUAGES:* German, English and Russian. *PRACTICE AREAS:* Privatization; Company Law; Labor.

REINHARDT STIEHL, born Schongau, Germany, 1960; admitted, 1994, Germany. *Education:* University of Augsburg; University of Munich (State Exams, 1991 and 1994). *LANGUAGES:* German and English. *PRACTICE AREAS:* General Civil Law; Civil Litigation; Labor Law.

NÖRR, STIEFENHOFER & LUTZ

Established in 1990

BÖHMERTSTRAßE 3
01099 DRESDEN, GERMANY
Telephone: 49-351-5671188, 49-351-5671187
Telecopier: 49-351-5671186

Munich, Germany Office: Brienner Str. 28 80333 Munich, Postfach 101121, 80082 Munich. Telephone: 49-89-280111. Telecopier: 49-89-280110.

(This Listing Continued)

NÖRR, STIEFENHOFER & LUTZ, Dresden—Continued

Frankfurt/Main, Germany Office: Freiherr-vom-Stein-Straße 11, 60323
Frankfurt/Main. Telephone: 49-69-172917. Telecopier: 49-69-172916.
Berlin, Germany Office: Schlüterstraße 36, D-10629 Berlin. Telephone:
49-30-8836700. Telecopier: 49-30-8835052.
Prague, Czech Republic Office: Masarykovo nábřeži 30, 11000 Prague 1.
Telephone: 42-2-24913396, 42-2-24913882. Telecopier: 42-2-24911836.
Budapest, Hungary Office: Becsí utca 5/I. 1-2, 1052 Budapest V.
Telephone: 36-1-1174905; 36-1-1378293. Telecopier: 36-1-1184035.
Warsaw, Poland Office: Kancelaria Adwokacka Sp. Z o. o. UL.
Nowogrodzka 50, 00950 Warsaw. Telephone: 48-2-6216232.
Telecopier: 48-2-6251976.
Brussels, Belgium EEC Office: 106 Avenue Louise, 1050 Brussels.
Telephone: 32-2-6470650. Telecopier: 32-2-6464729.
Moscow, Russia Office: Ul. Levoberezhnaya, 32. 125475. Telephone:
7-095-4585822; 7-09504585792. Telecopier: 7-095-4585782.

German and International Practice, Corporate, Commercial, Mergers and
Acquisitions, Finance and Banking, Tax, EEC, Public and Constitutional
Law, Antitrust, Real Estate, Construction, Labor, Insurance, Landlord-
Tenant, Leasing, Product Liability, Estate, Aviation, Energy, Health, Food
and Drugs, Industrial Property, Copyright, Trademarks, Unfair Competition, Media, Telecommunications, Advertising, White Collar Crime, Administrative and Planning Law, Environmental and Waste Law, Litigation
and Arbitration, Joint Ventures, Appellate, Civil, Federal, Legislative, Trial
Practice, Advice to Legislative Institutions in Eastern Europe, Eastern European Law, Law of Restitution Claims.

RESIDENT PARTNERS

DR. DIETER SCHENK, born Munich, Germany, August 4, 1952; ad-
mitted, 1980, Germany; as Tax Advisor, 1985. *Education:* Universities of
Munich, Geneva, Freiburg and Tuebingen. Assistant Lecturer, Institute of
International Law, University of Munich, 1977-1980. *LANGUAGES:* Ger-
man, English and French. *PRACTICE AREAS:* Tax Law; Corporate Law;
Aviation Law.

OTTO STOLBERG-STOLBERG, born Frankfurt am Main, Germany,
March 6, 1955; admitted, 1983, Germany. *Education:* University of Mu-
nich. *LANGUAGES:* German and English. *PRACTICE AREAS:* Real
Estate Law; Landlord-Tenant Law; Corporate and Commercial Law; East
German Law; Law of Restitution Claims.

ASSOCIATES

DETLEV STEFAN STRÄSSER, born Ellwangen/Jagst, Germany,
June 25, 1961; admitted, 1991, Germany. *Education:* Universities of Munich, Passau, Freiburg and Moscow. *LANGUAGES:* German, English and
Russian. *PRACTICE AREAS:* Commercial Law; Real Estate; East German Law.

ROBERT MATTHES, born Germany, December 11, 1962; admitted,
1991, Germany. *Education:* Universities of Augsburg and Speyer. *LAN-
GUAGES:* German and English. *PRACTICE AREAS:* Administrative and
Planning Law.

FRANZ LUDWIG DANKO, born Gelnhausen, Germany, April 2, 1961;
admitted, 1991, Germany. *Education:* Johann-Wolfgang Goethe University
of Frankfurt/Main. *LANGUAGES:* German, English, Spanish. *PRAC-
TICE AREAS:* Labor Law; Corporate Law; Arbitration.

SYLVIA BELKA, born Dingelstadt, Germany, June 18, 1956; admitted,
1994, Germany. *Education:* University of East Berlin. *LANGUAGES:* German, Russian and English. *PRACTICE AREAS:* Commercial Law; East
German Law.

MICHAEL EGGERT, born Kaufbeuren, Germany, June 3, 1963; admit-
ted, 1993. *Education:* University of Heidelberg; University of Florenz
(EUI), Italy (LL.M., 1990). *LANGUAGES:* German, English, French.
PRACTICE AREAS: Law of Restitution Claims; Administrative Law;
Commercial law; Law of former GDR.

NIELS PETERSEN, born Kiel, Germany, January 14, 1962; admitted,
1993, Germany. *Education:* University of Passau and Munich. *LAN-
GUAGES:* German and English. *PRACTICE AREAS:* Construction Law;
Landlord-Tenant Law; Insolvency Law.

Languages: German, English, French, Spanish and Russian.

RAU, VAN DORP & PARTNER

NIEDERWALDSTR. 23
01277 DRESDEN, GERMANY
Telephone: (0351) 44 11 207
Telefax: (0351) 44 11 210

Munich, Germany Office: Widenmayerstrasse 38, D-80538 Munich.
Telephone: (089) 21 12 13-0. Telefax: (089) 21 12 13-40.
Berlin, Germany Office: Lietzenseeufer 10, 14057 Berlin. Telephone: (030)
32 25 023. Telefax: (030) 32 21 018. Telex: 185607.
Leipzig, Germany Office: Gustav Adolf Str. 12, 04105 Leipzig.
Telephone: (0341) 27 12 29. Telefax: (0341) 27 12 29.
Budapest Hungary Office: Békés-Németh-Vékás & Tásai, Ügyvédi Iroda,
Egyetem tér 1-3, H-1053 Budapest. Telephone: (01) 117-4930. Telefax:
(01) 117-4930.
Trento, Italy Office: Via Grazloli 6, I-38100 Trento. Telephone: (0461) 98
00 51. Telefax: (0461) 98 52 57.

General European and International Practice, European Community Law.
Corporate, Commercial, Intellectual and Industrial Property Rights, Patents. Trademarks, Copyright, Unfair Competition, Antitrust, Computer
Law, Press Law, Entertainment Law, Franchising, Licensing, Insurance,
Product Liability, Real Estate, Construction, Labor Law, Trusts and Estates, International Private Law, Administrative Law, Litigation, Arbitration.

HANS JOACHIM HERZOG, born Dresden, Germany, December 23,
1957; admitted, 1990, Dresden, Germany. *Education:* University of Leipzig
(Dipl. jur., 1983). General Counsel, Saxonian Office of Engineering for
Above and Below Ground Construction, Dresden, Germany, 1985—.
Member: German Bar Association (Dresden). *LANGUAGES:* German,
English and Russian.

DR. AXEL SCHOBER, born Bayreuth, Germany, October 23, 1961;
admitted, 1993, Dresden, Germany. *Education:* Universities of Würzburg,
Bayreuth and Bordeaux/France (Referendar, 1986; Assessor, 1990; Dr.
jur., 1990). Research Assistant, University of Bayreuth, Chair for Private,
International Private and Private Comparative Law, 1986-1987. Activities:
Solicitor in Paris, France, 1990-1991. Lecturer at Dresden University for
Private Law, 1991-1992. Judge at the Civil Court (Kreisgericht) at Dresden,
1991-1992 and at the Landgericht Munich, Chamber for Private Construction Law, 1992-1993. Author: "Possibilities of Integrating Third Persons
into the Course of a Current Procedure-Analysis of French, German and
European Civil Procedural Law," Diss., 1990. *Member:* German Bar Association (Dresden). *LANGUAGES:* German, English and French.

REINERT, APPY & PARTNER

Rechtsanwälte

SELLINER STRASSE 1
01109 DRESDEN, GERMANY
Telephone: 0351/4604353
Telecopier: 0351/460352
Mobile Phone: (0049) 161-3719355

Karlsruhe, Germany Office: Steinhäuserstrasse 17, 76135. Telephone:
(0721) 812024. Telecopier: (0721) 818738.
Strasbourg, France Office: 66, Rue Marchè-Gare, F-67200. Telephone:
0033 88-261426. Telecopier: 00330 88-268840.
Washington, D.C. Office: Suite 1004, 1101 Seventeenth Street, N.W.,
20036-4798. Telephone: (202) 293-5555. Telecopier: (202) 293-9035.

General Practice and Litigation. Corporate, Commercial, Banking, Business, Antitrust, Trademark, Computer, Copyright, Tax, Unfair Competition, Civil Aviation, International and EC Law, Administrative Law.

MEMBERS OF FIRM

LEONHARD BAUR, born Ulm, Germany, October 15, 1949; admitted,
1986, Germany; 1991, Dresden/Saxony (LG and OLG). *Education:* Lud-
wig-Wilhelm-Gymnasium Rastatt (1966); Hotel Management Training
Baden-Baden and Berlin (1967-1969); College for Business Administration
Heidelberg (Dipl. Betriebswirt FH, 1976); Freiburg University Law School
(Referendar, 1982). Hotel Manager, 1969-1973. Developer, Holiday Center
for Handicapped Persons near Rome, Italy, 1976-1978. Assessor, District
Court, Baden-Baden, 1986. *Member:* German Bar Association. *LAN-
GUAGES:* German, English and Italian.

HELMUT BECKER, born Rastatt, Germany, June 2, 1941; admitted,
1974, West Germany; 1994, Dresden (LG and OLG) Court of Appeal. *Ed-*
(This Listing Continued)

ucation: Ludwig-Wilhelm-Gymnasium, Rastatt (Abitur, 1962); Universities of Heidelberg and Geneva, Switzerland (Referendar, 1968); LG Baden-Baden (Assessor, 1972);. Consultant, Insurance Group in France, 1972-1974. *Member:* German Bar Association. *LANGUAGES:* German, English and French.

(For complete biographical data on all personnel, see Professional Biographies at Karlsruhe, Germany)

RÜCKEL, TRENKNER & COLLEGEN

BAUTZNER STRAßE 14
01099 DRESDEN, GERMANY
Telephone: (03 51) 502 43 00
Fax: (03 51) 502 43 02

Atlanta, Georgia Office: Ten Piedmont Center, Suite 350, 3495 Piedmont Road, 30305. Telephone: (404) 266-1008. Fax: (404) 266-0205.
Berlin, Germany Office: Kurfürstendamm 132 A, 10711. Telephone: (030) 896 6920. Fax: (030) 8966 9244.
Leipzig, Germany Office: Marperger Straße 20, 04229. Telephone: (0341) 401 13 41. Fax: (0341) 401 14 54.
Frankfurt/Main, Germany Office: Bockenheimer Anlage 13, 60322. Telephone: (069) 55 07 31. Fax: (069) 596 39 94.
Munich, Germany Office: Karollnenstraße 4, 80538. Telephone: (089) 212 38 70. Fax: (089) 212 38 75 0.

General Practice, Litigation and Commercial Law, International Business Transactions, Real Estate (including restitution of property rights), Corporate.

FIRM PROFILE: The firm is a member of LAWORLD. LAWORLD is an international organization of law firms who coordinate and share information with other member firms in Brussels, Budapest, Hong Kong, Jerusalem, Lausanne, London, Moscow, New York, Padova, Stockholm, Taipei, Tel Aviv, Vancouver, Warsaw, Zagreb and Zug.

MEMBERS OF FIRM

THOMAS ZEEH, born Stuttgart, Germany, August 11, 1959; admitted, 1990, Germany. *Education:* Ernst Sigle Gymnasium (Abitur, 1978); Ludwig-Maximilians University (1st State Exam, 1987; 2nd State Exam, 1990). *Member:* Deutsch Israelische Juristenvereinigung. *LANGUAGES:* German and English. *PRACTICE AREAS:* Reunification Law; Corporate Law; Bankruptcy; Insolvency.

(For biographical data on additional personnel, see Professional Biographies at Munich, Germany)

SCHAFFRATH & METZMACHER

LORTZINGSTRAßE 37
D-01307 DRESDEN, GERMANY
Telephone: 0351/4426234
Telecopier: 0351/4426268

Düsseldorf, Germany Office: Rosenstr. 11, D-40479. Telephone: (211) 49 222-0. Telecopier: (211) 49 82 408.
Görlitz, Germany Office: Berliner Str. 20, D-02826. Telephone: (3581) 406396. Telecopier: (3581) 403750.

Administrative Law, Antitrust, Construction and Engineering Contracts, Corporate, Environmental Law, European Law, Family Law, Industrial and Intellectual Property, Labor Law, Litigation and Arbitration, Mergers and Acquisitions, Property Law of New German States, Trade Law, Transportation and Aviation, Unfair Competition.

MEMBERS OF FIRM

PETER SCHAFFRATH, born Hamburg, Germany, March 30, 1944; admitted, 1974, Germany. *Education:* University of Cologne. Legal Advisor, Free State of Saxonia, 1993—. *Member:* IBA; German Association for the Protection of Industrial Property and Copyright Law; Industrieclub Düsseldorf. *LANGUAGES:* German, English and French. *PRACTICE AREAS:* Corporate Finance; Labor Law; Mergers and Acquisitions; Commercial Property Law; Tax Controversies.

EIKE TAESLER, born Darmstadt, Germany, November 30, 1966; admitted, 1994, Germany. *Education:* University of Bayreuth (1986-1991). Assistant, Institute for European and German Technology and Environmental Law, 1994. *Member:* German-American Jurists Association. *LANGUAGES:* German, English and French. *PRACTICE AREAS:* Litigation; Labor; Environmental.

SCHILLING, ZUTT & ANSCHÜTZ

Established in 1991

HOHE STRASSE 12
D-01069 DRESDEN, GERMANY
Telephone: 49-351 472 47 61
Telecopier: 49-351 472 47 66

Mailing Address: P.O. Box 579, D-01067

Mannheim, Germany Office: Otto-Beck-Straße 42, D-68165. Mailing Address: P.O. Box 10 27 50, D-68027. Telephone: 49-621 42 57-0. Telecopier: 49-621 42 57 280. Cable Address: "Advocat"

Commercial Law, Company Law, Employment and Labour Law, Environmental Law, Industrial and Intellectual Property, Litigation, Mergers and Acquisitions, Privatization of Companies, Product Liability, Property Claims, Real Estate, Trademarks, Unfair Competition Law, Administrative Law.

CARSTEN A. SALGER, born Karlsruhe, Germany, March 31, 1959; admitted, 1988, Germany; 1991, Dresden. *Education:* University of Freiburg (1982); University of Illinois (Master of Laws, 1984). Lecturer, Commercial Law, Labor Law and Civil Procedure, Professional Academy Baden-Württemberg, 1983-1985. *Member:* German-American Lawyers' Association; German Association for the Protection of Industrial Property and Copyright; Studienvereinigung Kartellrecht. *LANGUAGES:* German and English.

EVA-MARIA KRETZSCHMAR, born Dresden, Germany, April 21, 1948; admitted, 1992, Dresden. *Education:* University of Leipzig. In-house Counsel, 1982-1990. Office for Settlement of Unsolved Property Matters, 1990-1991. *LANGUAGES:* German.

DR. CHRISTINE TEICHMANN, born Hamburg, Germany, June 1, 1961; admitted, 1990, Germany. *Education:* University of Hamburg (1981). Author: "Der Verbesserungs- und Förderungsbeitrag im Sinne des Artikel 85 Abs. 3 EWGV in der Freistellungspraxis der EG-Kommission.". *LANGUAGES:* German, English and French.

DR. MARTIN ABEND, born Heilbronn, Germany, March 16, 1963; admitted, 1993, Germany. *Education:* Universities of Lausanne and Heidelberg (Dr. iur., 1992); Cornell University (LL.M., 1989). Author: "Die lex validitatis im internationalen Vertragsrecht," Heidelberg, 1994; "Produkthaftpflicht ausländischer Hersteller und internationale Zuständigkeit der Gerichte in Massachusetts," 9 IPRax 325 (1989). Assistant Lecturer on Law, University of Heidelberg, 1989-1991. Associate, De Bandt, van Hecke & Lagae, Brussels, 1992. *Member:* German-American Lawyers Association; Belgian-German Lawyers Association. *LANGUAGES:* German, English, French and Spanish.

(For Complete Biographical Data on all Personnel, see Professional Biographies at Mannheim, Germany)

SCHÖN NOLTE FINKELNBURG & CLEMM

BERLINER STRASSE 3
D-01067 DRESDEN, GERMANY
Telephone: (351) 496 5128
Telecopier: (351) 496 5228

Other Offices: Hamburg and Berlin, Germany; Brussels, Belgium.

General Corporate and Commercial Practice.

PARTNER IN CHARGE

DR. WOLFGANG G.M. KAU, born Bonn, Germany, 1958; admitted, 1988, Hamburg; 1992, England and Wales as Solicitor. *Education:* Universities of Bonn and Freiburg i.Br. *LANGUAGES:* German and English. *PRACTICE AREAS:* Commercial Law; Restitution; Corporate Law; International Law.

SCHULTZE & BRAUN

Established in 1992

BOLTENHAGENER PLATZ 9
01109 DRESDEN, GERMANY
Telephone: 0351/8808046
Telefax: 0351/8808040

Achern, Germany Office: Eisenbahnstr. 19-23, D-77855. Telephone: 07841-708-0. Telefax: 07841-708-301.

Leipzig, Germany Office: Brahestr.8, D-04347. Telephone: 0341/244340. Telefax: 0341/2443439.

General International Practice. Restructuring and Bankruptcy. Finance and Banking. International Transactions. Corporate. Investment. Settlement. Competition. Construction and Employment Law.

FIRM PROFILE: The firm is specialized in reorganization and bankruptcy law and all kinds of business, bank and corporate law.

HARALD BUßHARDT, born Freiburg, Germany, October 6, 1956. *Education:* Universities of Freiburg and Lausanne, Switzerland. *Member:* Deutscher Anwaltsverein; Arbeitskreis für Insolvenzrecht. **LANGUAGES:** English, French and German. **PRACTICE AREAS:** Bankruptcy; Banks and Banking; Corporate Law.

GRIT SPERNAU, born Gera, Thüringen, Germany, November 1, 1966. *Education:* University of Halle-Wittenberg. *Member:* Deutscher Anwaltverein. **LANGUAGES:** Russian, German and French. **PRACTICE AREAS:** Bankruptcy.

SCHÜRMANN & PARTNERS

Established in 1990

SCHNORRSTRASSE 70
01069 DRESDEN, GERMANY
Telephone: 0351-477-770
Telefax: 0351-477-7799

Frankfurt/Main, Germany Office: Friedrich-Ebert-Anlage 14, 60325, P.O. Box 11 16 33, 60051. Telephone: 069-7 54 90. Telefax: 7549 290.

Berlin, Germany Office: Karl-Liebknecht-Strasse 32, 10178. Telephone: 030-247-5960. Telefax: 030-238-6032.

Bonn, Germany Office: Philosophenring 94, 53177. Telephone: 0228-328-055. Telefax: 0228-311-863.

Brussels, Belgium Office: Avenue de la Raquette 24, B-1150. Telephone: 02-770-0878. Telefax: 02-770-0878.

Leipzig, Germany Office: Gustav-Adolf-Strasse 30 04105 Leipzig. Telephone: 0341-211-0622. Telefax: 0341-211-0625.

Milan, Italy Office: Via Gabrio Casati, 1, I-20123. Telephone: 02-809131/32. Telefax: 02-809-133.

New York, New York Office: 250 Park Avenue, 10177. Telephone: 212-972-3300. Telefax: 212-972-9374.

Paris, France Office: 12, rue d'Astorg F-75008 Paris. Telephone: 01-4451-0570. Telefax: 01-4266-3368.

General Practice. Trade, Banking, International and German Tax Law. Labor Law. Law on Mergers, Acquisitions. Fair Trade, Antitrust and EU Law, Administrative Law. Notary Public. Litigation Department.

(For complete biographical data on all Personnel, see Biographical Card at Frankfurt/Main, Germany)

SCHWARZ KURTZE SCHNIEWIND KELWING WICKE RECHTSANWÄLTE

MÜNZGASSE 10
01067 DRESDEN, GERMANY
Telephone: (0351) 498 91 66
Telefax: (0351) 498 91 68

Munich, Germany Office: Wittelsbacherplatz 1, 80333 Munich. Telephone: (089) 235 00 40. Telefax: (089) 280 94 32.

Berlin, Germany Office: Kurfürstendamm 220, 10719 Berlin. Telephone: (030) 885 92 70. Telefax: (030) 882 22 60.

Potsdam, Germany Office: Gregor-Mendel-Straße 14, 14469 Potsdam. Telephone: (0331) 280 07 06. Telefax: (0331) 280 07 76.

(This Listing Continued)

Copyright, Intellectual and Industrial Property, Media and Entertainment, Financing (Media, Construction and Real Estate), Banking, Unfair Competition and Antitrust, Corporate, Labour, Mergers & Acquisitions, Trademarks, Securities, Privatization and Restitution (East Germany), International Investment and Trade Matters, International Contracts, Arbitration & Litigation.

RESIDENT PARTNER

MATTHIAS MATZKA, born Riesa, Germany, October 7, 1962; admitted, 1990, Germany. **LANGUAGES:** German, English and Russian. **PRACTICE AREAS:** Property and Real Estate Law; Restitution Law; Litigation.

THÜMMEL, SCHÜTZE & PARTNER

Established in 1990

FRIEDRICHSTRAßE 33
01067 DRESDEN, GERMANY
Telephone: (0351) 496 5302
Telefax: (0351) 496 5346

Stuttgart Office: Landhausstraße 90, 70190 Stuttgart. Telephone: (0711)1667-0, Telefax: (0711) 286 44 66, 2 62 69 10.

Berlin Office: Lützowstraße 33/36, 10785 Berlin. Telephone: (030) 2 61 11 31. Telefax: (030) 261 90 49. Telex: 3 01304.

Frankfurt Office: Eschersheimer Landshraße 10 60322 Frankfurt. Telephone: (069) 9591350. Telefax: (069) 95913530.

Brussels Office: Avenue des Arts, 41 B-1040 Brussels. Telephone: (0032) 2-512 7846. Telefax: (0032) 2-5127023.

Paris, France Office: 46, Rue de Bassano, F-75008 Paris. Telephone: (0033) 1-53 67 50 00. Telefax: (0033) 1-47 2078 76.

Singapore Office: 9, Battery Road, #16-01 Straits Trading Building, Singapore 0104, Telephone: (00 65) 53 53 112. Telefax: (00 65) 53 43 100.

Corporate, Commercial, Antitrust, Unfair Competition, Banking, Taxation, Trademark, Copyright, Media, Estate, Food Law, International, EEC Law, General Practice and Litigation.

DR.JUR. DIRK PLAGEMANN, born Wuppertal, Germany, February 24, 1953; admitted, 1983, West Germany. *Education:* University of Bonn and Freiburg i. Br. (Referendar, 1978; Assessor, 1981). Associate, Max-Planck-Institute for Foreign and International Criminal Law, Freiburg i. Br., 1979-1983, Doctor of Jurisprudence, 1984. *Member:* German Bar Association. **LANGUAGES:** German, English, French and Spanish.

UWE WUNDERLICH, born Dornreichenbach/GDR, April 22, 1954. *Education:* Karl-Marx-Universität Leipzig (Diplom-Jurist, 1978). *Member:* Sächsischer Anwaltverein e.V. **LANGUAGES:** German, English and Russian.

HEINZ-ULRICH GISSELMANN, born Dorsten, West Germany, February 8, 1959; admitted, 1992, Germany. *Education:* Universities of Berlin and Cologne (Referendar, 1987; Assessor, 1990); Säxonian State Department of Economics, Dresden (1991-1992). **LANGUAGES:** German, English and French.

(For Complete Biographical Data on all Personnel, see Professional Biographies at Stuttgart, Germany).

VOIGTLÄNDER-TETZNER & PARTNER

GROßENHAINER STRAßE 198
P.O. BOX 230112
01111 DRESDEN, GERMANY
Telephone: (0351) 570442
Telefax: (0351) 570933
C-Netz
Telephone: (0161) 2609409
Telefax: (0161) 2644522

Bad Hamburg v.d.H., Germany Office: Kaiser-Friedrich Promenade 9-11, P.O. Box 2411, 61294. Telephone: (06172) 25226. Fax: (06172) 20111

Berlin, Germany Office: Friedrichstraße 180.

Mergers and Acquisitions, Corporate Law, Litigation and Arbitration, International Banking, Business and Trade Law, Unfair Competition, International Medical Regulations, Real Estate and Construction Law, Administrative Law, Environmental Law, German Unification and Privatization, European Community Law, Eastern European Legal Systems.

(This Listing Continued)

FIRM PROFILE: The firm focuses its legal services on German and international corporate matters. From the outset the firm has been deeply involved in the process of the German reunification. Its size and structure enables the firm to provide the highest quality legal services at excellent values to its clients. The firm serves its private and corporate clients as well as municipalities on a nationwide service.

ANDREAS R. VOIGTLÄNDER-TETZNER, born Hanau am Main, Germany, December 1, 1957; admitted, 1987, Frankfurt am Main. *Education:* University of Freiburg. Assistant to the Board of Directors, Fresenius AG, 1987. Senior Advisor, Schöller Bank AG, Vienna, 1989; Managing Partner, GIB Gesellschaft für industrielle Beteiligung, Frankfurt am Main/Budapest/Wien, 1990. Director of Legal Department, KDT, Engineers Association, Berlin, 1990-1993. Chairman of the Board, Thüringer, Ziegelwerke and Dieselmotorwerke, Cunewalde, 1990-1992, until privatization. Member of the Board, Flanschenwerk Bebitz and Brauerei Dessau, 1991-1992, until privatization. Member: Legal Committee, National Sports Association Saxony and Equestrian Sports Association Saxony. Legal Advisor, BVMW e V. Bonn. General Manager: Interbrevipharm GmbH, Oberursel; Miller of Golden Square , Ltd., London. Chairman of the Board, IBAG, Industrie Beteiligungen AG. *Member:* American Chamber of Commerce; Wirtschaftsrat der CDU; Ostausschuß des Deutschen Anwaltsvereins. **PRACTICE AREAS:** Mergers and Acquisitions; International Trade and Medical Regulations; International Banking Law.

MATTHIAS SCHMIDT, born Frankfurt am Main, Germany, February 2, 1960; admitted, 1992, Frankfurt am Main. *Education:* Universities of Marburg/Lahn and Frankfurt (Referendar, 1989). Traineeship with Attorney Augusto Weil, Malaga (Spain), 1989). Lecturer, "Bildungswerk der Hessischen Wirtschaft e.V.," (educational institution operated by the Association for Economy, Hessen, 1990). Attorney with Heinrich & Lang, Frankfort (-1990). Judge at the District Court Usingen and Regional Court, Frankfort am Main (-March, 1993). **PRACTICE AREAS:** Civil Law; Enforcement Law; Competition Law; Bankruptcy Law.

WOLF-DIETER HALLERVORDEN, born Frankfurt am Main, Germany, February 10, 1965; admitted, 1992, Dresden. *Education:* University of Mannheim (1984-1989). Traineeship with Dinsmore & Shohl, Cincinnati, Ohio, U.S.A., 1991. *Member:* German-American Lawyers Association. **PRACTICE AREAS:** Labor Law; Private and Public Planning; Building Laws and Regulations; Mergers and Acquisitions.

Languages: English, French, Russian, Dutch and Greek

(For Biographical Data on additional personnel, see Professional Biographies at Bad Homburg v.d.H., Germany)

VON **PANDER WILLFORT & PARTNER**

BERGGARTEN 11
D-01277 DRESDEN, GERMANY
Telephone: (0351) 33 607-12
Telefax: (0351) 33 607-14

Munich, Germany Office: Arnulfstrasse 25, D-80335. Telephone: (089) 55 14 84 50. Telefax: (089) 55 14 84 80.

Leipzig, Germany Office: Mozart Strasse 1, D-04107. Telephone: (0341) 21 376-0. Telefax: (0341) 21 376-10.

New York, New York Office: Two Park Avenue, 10016. Telephone: (212) 685-55 09. Telefax: (212) 685-88 62.

The present structure of the firm is the result of a merger in April 1993 between the two partners who work together with seven other associate lawyers in offices located in Munich, Leipzig, Dresden and New York. The firm offers highly specialized legal services tailored to the needs of the individual commercial clients of an international clientele in the following areas: General European and International Practice, European Community Law, Corporate, Commercial, Intellectual and Industrial Property Rights, Copyright, Unfair Competition, Antitrust, Computer Law, Press Law, Entertainment Law, Franchising, Licensing, Insurance, Product Liability, Real Estate and Construction Law, Labor Law, Bank Law, Trusts and Estates, International Private Law, Administrative Law, Litigation, Arbitration, Transport Law. The offices in Leipzig and Dresden allow cooperative legal services in matters of restitution and investments in the new federal states of Germany.

ASSOCIATE

HELMUT KNAPP, born Berlin, Germany, July 21, 1939; admitted, 1980, Stuttgart. *Education:* Universities of Saarbrücken and Geneva (Referendar, 1964; Assessor, 1968). General Counsel, Werner & Pfleiderer, Stuttgart, 1972-1980. *Member:* German Bar Association (Dresden); International Bar Association (IBA) (Member, Section on Business Law); Deutscher Juristentag; German Association for the Protection of Industrial Property and Copyright (GRUR). *LANGUAGES:* German, English and French. **PRACTICE AREAS:** Corporate Law; Contract Law; Banks and Banking Law; Business Law.

WESSING BERENBERG-GOSSLER ZIMMERMANN LANGE

HEINRICHSTRASSE 16
01097 DRESDEN, GERMANY
Telephone: 49-351-567 12 12
Telefax: 49-351-567 12 13

Munich, Germany Office: Vilshofener Str.. 8, D-81679 Munich, P.O. Box 86 08 67, D-81635 Munich. Telephone: 49-89-98 28 021. Telefax: 49-89-98 12 14.

Düsseldorf, Germany Office: Königsallee 92 A, D-40212 Düsseldorf, P.O. Box 10 53 61, D-40044 Düsseldorf. Telephone: 49-211-83 87-0. Telex: 858 19 14 wess d. Cable Address: "Wegolex". Telefax: 49-211-32 36 16.

Hamburg, Germany Office: Neuer Wall 46, D-20354 Hamburg. Telephone: 49-40-36 80 30. Cable Address: "Unilaw". Telex: 2-14111 Jura d. Teletex: 40 32 91 Unilaw. Telefax: 49-40-36 80 32 80.

Frankfurt, Germany Office: Freiherr-Vom-Stein-Strasse 24-26, D-60323 Frankfurt. Telephone: 49-69-971300. Telefax: 49-69-97130100.

Berlin, Germany Office: Spreeufer 5, D-10178 Berlin. Telephone: 49-30-238 45 45. Telefax: 49-30-238 45 34.

Leipzig, Germany Office: Ferdinand-Rhode-Strasse 16, D-04107 Leipzig. Telephone: 49-341-213 13 80. Fax: 49-341-213 13 88.

Brussels, Belgium Office: Avenue Louise 149, Box 42, B-1050 Brussels. Telephone: +32 (2) 537 01 86. Telefax: +32 (2) 534 25 31.

General Practice. Commercial, Corporation, International, Tax, Economic Criminality, Antitrust, Unfair Competition, Patent, Press, Copyright and Trademark Law, Estate, EEC-Law, Bank Law, International Arbitration Proceedings, Environmental Law, German Reunification and Restitution Law.

PETER PRINZ ZU HOHENLOHE-OEHRINGEN, born Altenstadt-/Iller, Germany, October 1, 1945; admitted, 1974, Germany. *Education:* Universities of Munich and Cologne. *Member:* German Bar Association; Arbeitskreis für Insolvenzrecht im Deutschen Anwaltsverein (team specialized in insolvency law in the German Bar Association); Bankrechtliche Vereinigung - wissenschaftliche Gesellschaft für Bankrecht e.V. (scientific Association for bank law). *LANGUAGES:* German and English. **PRACTICE AREAS:** Civil Law; Commercial Law; Insolvency Law; Real Estate; East German Law; Restitution Claims Law.

HELMUT SCHWARZ, born Hamburg, Germany, August 7, 1961; admitted, 1991, Germany. *Education:* Universities of Hamburg (Immediate Diploma in Economics) and Freiburg (Dr. juris, 1992); Fordham University, New York (LL.M.). *Member:* German Bar Association. *LANGUAGES:* German, English, French and Spanish. **PRACTICE AREAS:** Commercial Law; Corporation Law; Tax Law.

WOEDTKE RESZEL & PARTNER

KÖNIGSBRÜCKER STRAßE 62
01099 DRESDEN, GERMANY
Telephone: 03 51/8011893
Telefax: 03 51/53631

Düsseldorf, Germany Office: Königsallee 12, 40212. Telephone: 0211/86477-0. Telefax: 0211/86477-30. Telex: 8 582 088 WRD.

Hamburg, Germany Office: Zippelhaus 4, 20457. Telephone: 040/321266. Telefax: 040/323037.

FIRM PROFILE: The firm was established in 1986 and offers a full range of legal and business services. It is well known for General Practice, Corporate, Company, Commercial Taxation, Customs, Unfair Competition, Antitrust, EEC, Trademark and Copyright Law. The client base is Europe, North America, Japan and Scandinavia. The firm has a legal support staff of 22 consisting of attorneys, paralegal assistants and an office administrator.

DR. MICHAEL MÜGGE, born Uelzen, Germany, September 3, 1958; admitted, 1988, Germany. *Education:* Universities of Hamburg, Freiburg and Leyden, NL (J.D., 1987; Doctor of Laws, 1992). (Resident, Dresden,

(This Listing Continued)

WOEDTKE RESZEL & PARTNER, *Dresden—Continued*

Germany Office). *LANGUAGES:* German and English. *PRACTICE AREAS:* German-German Law; Bankruptcy Law; Business Law.

DR. MARKUS MÄRTENS, born December 1, 1962. *Education:* University of Göttingen. *LANGUAGES:* English. *PRACTICE AREAS:* Competition Law; Labour Law; Real Estate Law.

GRÜTER, HANISCH, HOLSCHBACH

Established in 1902

ANGERSTRAβE 14-16
D-47051 DUISBURG, GERMANY
Telephone: 0203 - 30 50 9-0
Telex: 855688 gruha d
Telecopier: 0203 - 34 33 31

Mailing Address: 10 06 52, D-47006 Duisburg

General Practice, Corporate, Commercial, Mergers and Acquisitions, Real Estate, Banking, Antitrust, International, Product Liability, Labor Law, Unfair Competition, Environmental and Administrative Law, Trademark, Litigation and Arbitration, Notarial Services.

MEMBERS OF FIRM

HELMUT GRÜTER, born Duisburg, August 9, 1920; admitted, 1959, Duisburg; Notary Public. *Education:* University of Bonn. *Member:* German Bar Association. *LANGUAGES:* German and English. *PRACTICE AREAS:* Notarial Services; Real Estate; Successions; Litigation.

DR. ERICH GRÜTER, born Duisburg, June 4, 1931; admitted, 1959, Duisburg; Notary Public. *Education:* Universities of Bonn and Geneva (Dr.jur.). *Member:* German Bar Association. *LANGUAGES:* German, English and French. *PRACTICE AREAS:* Commercial Law; Corporate Law; Mergers and Acquisitions; International Law; Antitrust Law; Arbitration; Notarial Services.

ERNST-ETZEL HANISCH, born Duisburg, August 29, 1932; admitted, 1965, Duisburg; Notary Public. *Education:* Universities of Cologne, Bonn and Heidelberg, Faculté de Droit Paris (Licence en Droit). *Member:* German Bar Association; German-French Lawyers Association; German-Spanish Lawyers Association; International Union of Lawyers. *LANGUAGES:* German, English, French and Spanish. *PRACTICE AREAS:* Litigation; International Law; Notarial Services.

DR. ULRICH HOLSCHBACH, born Hennef, August 3, 1945; admitted, 1974, Duisburg; Notary Public. *Education:* Universities of Münster, Geneva and Bonn (Dr.jur.). *Member:* German Bar Association; German Union for protection of industrial property and copyright. *LANGUAGES:* German, English and French. *PRACTICE AREAS:* Litigation; Corporate Law; Real Estate; Unfair Competition; International Law; Notarial Services.

BERND MICHAEL STOCK, born Duisburg, July 11, 1948; admitted, 1978, Duisburg. *Education:* Universities of Hamburg, Freiburg and Bonn. Training in Banking Business. *Member:* German Bar Association. *LANGUAGES:* German and English. *PRACTICE AREAS:* Litigation; Commercial Law; Corporate Law; Banking; Transportation; Labor; Environmental and Administrative Law.

DR. ACHIM BISCHOFF, born Bamberg, September 10, 1948; admitted, 1979, Duisburg. *Education:* Universities of Bonn, Freiburg and Cologne (Dr.jur.). *Member:* German Bar Association. *LANGUAGES:* German, English and French. *PRACTICE AREAS:* Commercial Law; Corporate Law; Agency and Distributorships; Licensing; Mergers and Acquisitions; International Law; Banking; Product Liability; Arbitration.

JÜRGEN SCHLICHTING, born Münster, May 21, 1954; admitted, 1983, Duisburg. *Education:* Universities of Bonn and Saarbruecken. *Member:* German Bar Association. *LANGUAGES:* German and English. *PRACTICE AREAS:* Litigation; Commercial Law; Corporate Law; Mergers and Acquisitions; Labor Law; Banking; Family Law.

DR. WERNER KIESGEN, born Velbert, October 10, 1923; admitted, 1954, Wuppertal; 1987, Duisburg; Notary Public. *Education:* Universities of Bonn, Göttingen and Cologne (Dr.jur.). *Member:* German Bar Association. *LANGUAGES:* German and English. *PRACTICE AREAS:* Real Estate; Successions; Execution Proceedings.

JENS HEUPGEN, born Bad Honnef, February 2, 1958; admitted, 1989, Duisburg. *Education:* University of Bochum. Training in Banking Business.

(This Listing Continued)

Member: German Bar Association. *LANGUAGES:* German, English and French. *PRACTICE AREAS:* Litigation; Labor Law; Construction Law; Banking; Administrative Law.

DR. INA-MARIA BÖNING, born Krefeld, May 29, 1963; admitted, 1991, Duisburg. *Education:* Universities of Freiburg and Lausanne (Dr. jur.). *Member:* German Bar Association. *LANGUAGES:* German, English and French. *PRACTICE AREAS:* International Law; Products Liability; Mergers and Acquisitions; Successions; Litigation.

DR. THOMAS ALTENBACH, born Euskirchen, June 28, 1963; admitted, 1993, Duisburg. *Education:* University of Bonn (Dr. jur.). *Member:* German Bar Association. *LANGUAGES:* German, English and French. *PRACTICE AREAS:* Administrative Law; Environmental Law; Trademarks; Transportation; Litigation.

MANTELL, HOFMANN, SPRENKER

Established in 1904

KÖNIGSTRAβE 49
P.O. BOX 100928
D-47009 DUISBURG, GERMANY
Telephone: 0203/332011
Telex/BTX: 0203/337211
Telefax: 0203/334983

General Practice, Corporation, Taxation, Commercial, Real Estate, Antitrust, Unfair Competition, International, Labor Law, Litigation.

MEMBERS OF FIRM

KARL MANTELL, born Duisburg, Germany, December 19, 1926; admitted, 1955, Duisburg; 1968, Notary Public. *Education:* University of Münster. *Member:* German Bar Association.

DR. GEORG HOFMANN, born May 24, 1940; admitted, 1971, Duisburg; 1980, Notary Public. *Education:* Universities of Munich, Salzburg and Münster (Dr. jur.). *Member:* German Bar Association. *LANGUAGES:* English.

MATTHIAS SPRENKER, born February 21, 1954; admitted, 1981, Duisburg. *Education:* University of Münster. *Member:* German Bar Association. *LANGUAGES:* English.

CHRISTOPH MANTELL, born Marburg, November 2, 1963; admitted, 1992, Duisburg. *Education:* Universities of Passau and Bonn. *Member:* German Bar Association. *LANGUAGES:* English and French.

ABRELL WENDLER NACKE & PARTNER

GRAF-RECKE-STRAβE 82
D-40239 DÜSSELDORF, GERMANY
Telephone: 0211/96 15 04
Telefax: 0211/96 15 674

Frankfurt/Main, Germany Office: Holzhausenstr. 22, D-60322. Telephone: 49-(0) 69-5 96 40 11. Telefax: 49-(0) 69-55 53 99.
Munich, Germany Office: Martiusstrasse 5/11, 80802. Telephone: 089/34 90 70. Telex: 5213222. Facsimile: 089/33 72 93.
Dresden, Germany Office: Bautznerstr. 22, 01099. Telephone: 0351/555 15. Facsimile: 0351/516 39.

General Corporate Practice, International Law, Mergers and Acquisitions, Banking, Computer, Administrative Law, Patents, Trademarks, Copyright, Unfair Competition, Cartel Law, Litigation, Taxation.

MEMBERS OF FIRM

MICHAEL WENDLER, born Germany, 1951; admitted, 1981, Germany. *Education:* Universities of Cologne and Bonn. *LANGUAGES:* German, English and French.

DR. REINHARD NACKE, born Germany, 1951; admitted, 1980, Germany. *Education:* University of Münster (Dr.jur., 1981). Special Tax Counsel. *LANGUAGES:* German, English, French, Spanish and Dutch.

DR. WOLFGANG SASS, born Germany, 1957; admitted, 1990, Germany. *Education:* University of Cologne (Dr.jur., 1992); University of Speyer. *LANGUAGES:* German, English and French.

DR. BARBIER AND PARTNER

HOHE STRASSE 46
40213 DÜSSELDORF, GERMANY
Telephone: 32 78 89
Telex: 858 1906 ius d
Fax: 0211 328470

General Practice, Commercial, Corporation, International, Taxation, Reorganization, Merger and Acquisitions, Joint Ventures, Arbitration, Banking and Financing, Antitrust, EEC, Insolvency and Labor Law.

MEMBERS OF FIRM

DR. RAINER BARBIER, born Frankfurt, Germany, September 30, 1946; admitted, 1976, Germany. *Education:* Frankfurt University (Dr. jur.); New York University Law School (M.C.J., 1974). Steuerberater (Tax Advisor), 1981. Wirtschaftspruefer (CPA), 1984. *Member:* German and International Bar Association; German Institute for Commercial Arbitration e.V.; German Group of International Chamber of Commerce; American Chamber of Commerce in Germany; Industrie-Club e.V. *LANGUAGES:* German, English (Certified Interpreter) and French.

MARITA BARBIER, born Muenster, Germany, April 30, 1948; admitted, 1981, Germany. *Education:* Universities of Bonn and Munich, Speyer, London School of Economics (LSE); Paris (Stagiaire); New York University Law School (M.C.J., 1977). Recipient, Scholarship for Studies on Multinational Corporations at United Nations, 1977. Traineeship at Deutsche Bank AG, Frankfurt, 1979-1981. *Member:* German and International Bar Association. *LANGUAGES:* German, English and French.

DR. HANS STRUCK, born Muenster, Germany, June 12, 1913; admitted, 1982, Germany. *Education:* University of Muenster (Dr. jur.). Ministerial Counsel of Federal Ministry of Economics, Bonn, Germany, 1948-1978. *Member:* German Bar Association. *LANGUAGES:* German and English.

Languages: German, English and French

BARDEHLE, PAGENBERG, DOST, ALTENBURG, FROHWITTER, GEISSLER & PARTNERS

XANTENER STR. 12
40474 DÜSSELDORF, GERMANY
Telephone: (211) 47 81 30
Telefax: (211) 47 81 331

Paris, France Office: 7, Boulevard De Sébastopol, 75001. Telephone: (1) 40 28 07 25. Telefax: (1) 40 28 06 29.
Houston, Texas Office: Three Riverway, Suite 550, 77056. Telephone: (713) 621-07030. Fax: (713) 622-1624.
Munich, Germany Office: Galileiplatz 1; 81679, Mailing Address: P.O. Box 86 06 20, 81633. Telephone: (89) 92 80 50. Telefax: (89) 98 97 63; 92 805 292.

Industrial and Intellectual Property Law, Patent, Trademark, Copyright, Design, Antitrust and Computer Law, Licensing and Unfair Competition.

FIRM PROFILE: The firm was established in 1978 as a combined partnership of attorneys and patent attorneys specialized exclusively in the field of industrial and intellectual property law and litigation before all German courts, licensing and prosecution before the European and the German Patent Office. Clients were primarily U.S., Japanese, French and German companies. In 1992, offices were founded in Paris, Düsseldorf and Houston with altogether 10 partners in the 4 offices and a total staff of approximately 90 legal and technical persons as well as office administrators.

PARTNERS

HERMANN H. KAHLHÖFER, born 1954; admitted, 1985, European Patent Office; 1990, German Patent Bar. *Education:* Universities of Bonn and Cologne. *Member:* PAK; epi; VPP. *LANGUAGES:* German, English and French. *PRACTICE AREAS:* German and International Industrial Property Law; Patent Prosecution; Nuclear Physics; Mechanical Engineering.

REINHARDT SCHUSTER, born Bildegg, Rumania, July 23, 1962; admitted, 1990, Munich. *Education:* University of Munich (Referendar, 1987; Assesor, 1990). *Member:* Düsseldorf Bar; Max-Planck-Institute for International Patent Law, Munich; AIPPI; LES; GRUR; German-Hungarian Lawyer's Association. *LANGUAGES:* German, English, Hungarian and Rumanian. *PRACTICE AREAS:* German and International

(This Listing Continued)

Intellectual Property Law; Patent Litigation; Licensing; Antitrust and Unfair Competition Law; European Community Law.

ASSOCIATES

DITMAR JENDRYSSEK-NEUMANN, born Krapkowice, Poland, June 25, 1960; admitted, 1991, German Patent Bar. *Education:* Technical University Aachen. *Member:* PAK; GRUR; FICPI. *LANGUAGES:* German, English and Polish. *PRACTICE AREAS:* German and International Industrial Property Law; Patent Prosecution; Mechanical Engineering; Power Plants.

(For Biographical Data of the Munich, Germany Personnel, see Professional Biographies at Munich, Germany and Paris, France Personnel, see Professional Biographies at Paris, France)

BELLINGER PRIEBE FELL

AM WEHRHAHN 24
40211 DÜSSELDORF, GERMANY
Telephone: (02 11) 35 03 55-7
Telefax: (02 11) 35 30 07

General Practice, Commercial, Corporation, Taxation, Labor, Unfair Competition, Intellectual Property, Computer and Software, Insurance, Construction, Family Law.

MEMBERS OF FIRM

DR. BERNHARD BELLINGER, born Berlin, Germany, March 14, 1953; admitted, 1981, Germany; 1993, Steuerberater (Certified Tax Advisor). *Education:* University of Bochum (Dr. of Law, 1987). Special Counsel for Tax Law.

DR. MICHAEL PRIEBE, born Siegen, Germany, January 12, 1954; admitted, 1984, Germany. *Education:* University of Bochum (Dr. of Law, 1987). Special Counsel for Tax Law. *Member:* International Bar Association.

DR. WOLFGANG FELL, born Köln, Germany, December 8, 1958; admitted, 1988, Germany. *Education:* University of Cologne (Dr. of Law, 1994). Special Counsel for Labor Law.

Languages: German, English and French

BELLSTEDT & PARTNER

Established in 1975

ROSS-STRASSE 130
D-40476 DÜSSELDORF, GERMANY
Telephone: 0211-4709001/2/3/4
Telecopier: 0211-4543102

Corporations, Taxation, International Taxation, EC Anti-dumping Commercial Law. Antitrust, Contracts.

FIRM PROFILE: The firm was established in 1975 and offers a full range of legal services. The client base is Japanese, European and North American.

DR. CHRISTOPH BELLSTEDT, born Durban, South Africa, November 27, 1933; admitted, 1962, Heidelberg; 1964, Frankfurt; 1971, Düsseldorf. *Education:* Universities of Hamburg, Geneva, Heidelberg (Bar Exam.; Dr. jur., 1961); Harvard University, U.S.A. Lecturer on Government (U.S. Political System), Heidelberg University, 1961-1962. Author: "The Tax as a Policy Instrument-A Comparative Analysis of US and German Tax Policy" (1964); The Taxation of Internationally Operating Companies", 3rd edition, 1973; "Aussensteuergesetz and Administration Principles on Income Allocation", 3rd edition 1987; "A German Tax Practitioner's View on the White Paper", Intertax 2-3 (1989) p. 108-114. *Member:* International Bar Association; International Fiscal Association; The Licensing Executives Society; Board of Directors, Swedish Chamber of Commerce in Germany; JUROPA EEIG Group of Lawyers. *LANGUAGES:* English, French, Japanese and German. *PRACTICE AREAS:* International Taxation Law.

HERWARD BEISE, born Arnsberg, Germany, May 28, 1947; admitted, 1972, Düsseldorf. *Education:* Universities of Bochum and Cologne (Bar Exam., 1972). Publications on Commercial Law and Banking Law. *LANGUAGES:* English and German. *PRACTICE AREAS:* Unfair Trade; Corporate Trade Litigation.

Languages: English, French, Japanese and German.

BENDER ZAHN TIGGES

THYSSEN-HAUS
AUGUST-THYSSEN-STRAβE 1
40211 DÜSSELDORF, GERMANY
Telephone: 0211/86 87-0
Telex: 8 588 246 bend
Telefax: 0211/86 87-100

Berlin, Germany Office: Kurfürstendamm 170, 10707 Berlin. Telephone: (0 30) 883 23 98/99. Telefax: (0 30) 8 82 45 52.

Chemnitz, Germany Office: Straße der Nationen 37, 09111 Chemnitz. Telephone: (0371/428946/47). Telefax: (0371/428949).

Warsaw, Poland Office: ul. Piekna 66a, 00-072 Warsaw. Telephone: (00482) 628-02-11. Fax: (00482) 628-47-66.

General and International Practice, Corporate and Securities, Banking, Commercial, Bankruptcy, Insolvency and Reorganization, Taxation, Real Estate, Antitrust, Intellectual Property, Environmental and Administrative, Insurance, Litigation, International Trusts, Family and Inheritance Law. Privatization in the former German Democratic Republic. Restitution Claims in the former German Democratic Republic. Commercial and Business Law in Poland.

MEMBERS - DÜSSELDORF

KLAUS W. BENDER, born Ratingen, Germany, 1947; admitted, 1977, Germany. *Education:* Cologne University (Business, Economics; Law). Academic Assistant, Department of Civil and International Law, Cologne University. Co-Author: "Competition Law in the Federal Republic of Germany," a contribution to "Competition Law in Western Europe and the U.S.A.," Kluwer/Deventer, The Netherlands, 1980. *Member:* International Bar Association; Studienvereinigung Kartellrecht (Society for the Study of Cartel Law); Society for the Legal Protection of Property Rights; German-Spanish Law Society. *LANGUAGES:* German, English and Italian.

DR. MICHAEL TIGGES, born Hagen, Germany, 1954; admitted, 1986, Germany. *Education:* Münster University (Law; Doctorate, 1986). Assistant: Institute for International Private Law; University for Administrative Law, Speyer. With Boodle Hatfield, London, 1985. Author: "History and Development of State Supervision of Insurance Companies," Karlsruhe, 1985. Co-Author: "Deutsche Rechtspraxis," München, 1991. *Member:* International Bar Association; Young Lawyers' International Association; West-East German Law Society; German-Japanese Law Society; Society for Banking Law; German-Polish Law Society. (Also at Warsaw, Poland Office). *LANGUAGES:* German and English.

DR. EHRENFRIED SAUTER, born Bürladingen, Germany, 1926; admitted, 1991, Germany. *Education:* University of Freiburg (Doctorate, 1952). Gerichtsassessor, Landgericht Hechingen, 1954. Companies audit section leader, Department of Taxation, State of North Rhine-Westphalia, 1955-1960. Member, Ministerial Council, Director and Senate Chairman, Landesrechnungshof, and Vice-President, State Accounting Office, State of North Rhine-Westphalia, 1960-1991. Member, Judicial Disciplinary Court, Oberlandesgericht Hamm, 1974-1987. Periodic lecturer, University of Münster, Hochschule Speyer, and joint section on continuing education for the Federal and State Accounting Offices. Holder of the Greater Federal Service Cross. *LANGUAGES:* German and English. *PRACTICE AREAS:* Taxation.

KLAUS SIEMON, born Kehl, Germany, 1959; admitted, 1988, Germany. *Education:* Universities of Regensburg, Cologne and Münster. Author, "The Avoidance of Gifts in Fictitious Profit Distribution in Commodities Futures Trading," Heidelberg, 1991; "Interruption of the Time Limit for Avoiding an Adjudicated Bankrupt's Transactions Only After Pendency?" Cologne, 1991. *Member:* Arbeitskreis Insolvenzrecht e.V. (Member, Working Group on Insolvency Law); Wustrauer Arbeitskreis e.V. *LANGUAGES:* German, English and Spanish. *PRACTICE AREAS:* Bankruptcy; Insolvency.

EDWARD M. STADUM, born Fargo, North Dakota, U.S.A., 1938; admitted, 1966, California; licensed in Germany as Rechtskundiger for U.S. Law, 1993 (Not admitted in Germany). *Education:* Stanford University (B.A., 1962); Harvard University (J.D., 1965); University of Konstanz (LL.M., 1992). Author, "Salmann, Trustee and Treuhänder," ZVgIRWiss 1994. Co-Author, "Die Sekuritisierung und ihre Zukunft in Deutschland," RIW 1991. *LANGUAGES:* English and German.

PETER M. HAVER, born Los Angeles, California, U.S.A., 1955; admitted, 1981, California; admitted as Avocat, France (Not admitted in Germany). *Education:* University of California (Santa Cruz) (B.A., 1977); University of Vienna (1976); Institut Universitaire de Hautes Etudes Internatio-

(This Listing Continued)

nale, Geneva (1983-1984); University of Virginia School of Law (J.D., 1981). Author: "Antitrust: New Developments (Non-Price Problems)," California Continuing Education of the Bar, 1982; "The Mandate of the U.N. Sub-Commission on the Prevention of Discrimination and Protection of Minorities," 21 Columb. J. Trans. L. 103 (1982); "The Status of Interim Measures of the International Court of Justice After the Iranian Hostage Crisis," Calif. W. Intl.J. 515 (1981). *LANGUAGES:* English, French and German.

PETRA TIGGES, born Dortmund, Germany, 1955; admitted, 1990, Germany. *Education:* Münster University (Romance Languages; Law). *Member:* German Society for Family Law; German-French Law Society. *LANGUAGES:* German, English and French.

FRANK BÜSER, born Dortmund, Germany, 1961; admitted, 1991, Germany. *Education:* Rühr University, Bochum. Law Office of Dr.Geyer, Schwarzhof and Partners, Essen, 1987-1991. With Law Offices of Martin J. Barab, Beverly Hills, California, 1989. *LANGUAGES:* German and English.

DR. GUIDO HOLLER, born Münster, Germany, 1962; admitted, 1991. *Education:* University of Heidelberg and University of Konstanz (Doctorate, 1992). Assistant, Faculty of Law, University of Konstanz, 1988-1991. Referendariat, BDO Binder Hamlyn, London, 1990. Tax Department, KPMG DTG, Düsseldorf, 1991-1992. *LANGUAGES:* German and English.

CARSTEN FUNDER, born Bielefeld, Germany, 1962; admitted, 1993, Germany. *Education:* University of Bielefeld. Assistant, Prof. Dr. Lampe, University of Bielefeld, 1988-1991. Reitaku University, Kashiva, Japan, 1991-1992. Associate, SLS Japan Consult Ltd., Tokyo, Japan (Tokyo office of Sigle, Loose, Schmidt-Diemitz, Stuttgart), 1992. *Member:* German-Japanese Jurists Association; Deutsch-Japanische Gesellschaft am Niederrhein e.V. *LANGUAGES:* German, English, French and Japanese.

MARC ANDRÉ GIMMY, born Munich, Germany, 1965; admitted, 1993, Germany. *Education:* University of Konstanz. Co-author: "Eigenkapitalersatz und Unternehmensfinanzierung," ZVgLRWiss, 1993. *Member:* German-Spanish Lawyers' Association. *LANGUAGES:* German, Spanish and English.

DR. GERHARD NÖSSER, born Cologne, Germany, 1960; admitted, 1993, Germany. *Education:* Universities of Bonn and Münster (Doctorate, 1991). *LANGUAGES:* German, English and French.

WOLFGANG MÜLLENSIEFEN, born Bottrop, Germany, 1963; admitted, 1993, Germany. *Education:* Ruhr University, Bochum. Lecturer in Environmental Law, North Rhine-Westphalia College of Public Administration, 1992-1993. *LANGUAGES:* German and English.

STEPHAN MITLEHNER, born Berlin, Germany, 1962; admitted, 1993, Germany. *Education:* Universities of Berlin and Bonn. Attorney, Treuhandanstalt, Berlin, 1992-1993. *LANGUAGES:* German and English.

DR. MARTIN VIEFHUES, born Lingen, Germany, 1962; admitted, 1993, Germany. *Education:* Universities of Passau and Bonn. Assistant, Prof. Dr. Wulf-Henning Roth, University of Bonn, 1989-1992; Internship, Popham, Haik, Schnobrich & Kaufmann, Washington, D.C., 1993. *LANGUAGES:* German and English.

NORMAN B. THOT, born Los Angeles, California, U.S.A., 1965; admitted, 1991, California (Not admitted in Germany). *Education:* University of California (Santa Barbara) (B.A., 1987); University of California, Hastings College of the Law (J.D., 1991); University of the Pacific, McGeorge School of Law (LL.M., 1992). *LANGUAGES:* English and German.

ANDREAS SCHWARZ, born Neuss, Germany, 1964; admitted, 1994, Germany. *Education:* University of Cologne. With, Abberley Kooiman Marcellino and Clay, New York, 1987-1988; With, Palmer Cowen, London, 1993. *LANGUAGES:* German and English. *PRACTICE AREAS:* Litigation; Commercial.

STEPHANIE MÖLLER, born Berlin, Germany, 1964; admitted, 1994, Germany. *Education:* University of Berlin; University of Administrative Law, Speyer. *LANGUAGES:* English, French and German.

WALTER SCHEERBARTH, born Cologne, Germany, 1963; admitted, 1994, Germany. *Education:* University of Cologne. Academic Assistant, Professor Dr. Arnulf Schmitt-Kammler, University of Cologne, 1992-1993. *LANGUAGES:* German and English.

Languages: German, English, French, Spanish, Italian, Polish and Japanese

BÖRNER & BÖRNER

Established in 1990

KÖNIGSALLEE 48
D-40212 DÜSSELDORF, GERMANY
Telephone: 0211/13 44 71
Fax: 0211/13 44 75
Telex: 8584024

EC and International, Corporate, Commercial and Civil, Antitrust and Unfair Competition, Intellectual Property, Banking, Insurance and Energy Law.

MEMBERS OF FIRM

DR. ACHIM-RÜDIGER BÖRNER, born Hamburg, Germany, April 1, 1955; admitted, 1981, Cologne. *Education:* Universities of Cologne and Bonn (J.D., 1977; Doctor of Laws, 1979). Author: "The Latest Judicial Development of Art. 9 Uniform Commercial Code, U.S.", Diss. Bonn, 1979. Legal Counsel to Ruhrgas AG, Essen, 1982-1984. Head of Legal Department of Aachener und Münchener Versicherung AG, Aachen, 1984-1987. *Member:* International Bar Association; German-American Law Association; German-South African Law Association; German Association for Comparative Law; German Association for European Law; Schmalenbach Association for Research in Business Administration. *LANGUAGES:* German, English and French.

PROFESSOR DR. BODO BÖRNER (1922-1994).

DR. RALF OEHMKE, born Krefeld, Germany, March 8, 1961; admitted, 1991, Cologne. *Education:* Commerzbank AG (Bankkaufmann,1982); University of Cologne (Referendar, 1986; Dr. jur., 1989). Author: "Protection for the Insured through Guaranty Funds in Non-Regulated Insurance Markets," Karlsruhe, 1990; "Basic Principles of German Corporate Law," Messerschmidt (ed), Munich 1991. With: Metabap S.A., Paris, 1980; micropac industries inc., Dallas, Texas, 1982; Aachener und Münchener Beteiligungs-Aktiengesellschaft, Aachen, 1987-1989. *LANGUAGES:* German, English and French.

BROCKMANN, SCHREINER AND PARTNER

BERLINER ALLEE 34 - 36
40212 DÜSSELDORF, GERMANY
Telephone: 0211/32 30 121
Telex: 8584092
Fax: 0211/13 25 30

General Practice, Commercial, Corporation, International, Taxation, Reorganization, Arbitration, Banking, Labor, Family, Contractual, Competition, Copyright, Transport, Employee - Invention, Patents and Trade Marks, Succession, Insurance Law.

MEMBERS OF FIRM

DR. LAMBERT BROCKMANN, born Cologne, Germany, August 26, 1940; admitted, 1970, Germany. *Education:* Freiburg and München University (Dr.jur.); Paris University (Sciences Politiques); Steuerberater (Tax Advisor, 1972); Wirtschaftsprüfer (CPA, 1974). *Member:* German and International Bar Association; International Union Lawyers; Industrie-Club e.V.; Fédération des Experts Comptables Euro- péens, Bruxelles. *LANGUAGES:* German, English, French and Italian.

DR. HELMUT SCHREINER, born Landau, Germany, August 9, 1943; admitted, 1971, Germany. *Education:* Heidelberg and München University (Dr.jur.); Lausanne University. *Member:* European Association of Lawyers; Association of Italian Foreign Chambers of Commerce; German-French Chambers of Commerce. *LANGUAGES:* German, English, French and Italian.

ROLF-MICHAEL MÜLLEJANS, born Düsseldorf, Germany, August 17, 1957; admitted, 1987, Germany. *Education:* Saarbrücken and Bonn University; Lausanne University. *Member:* International Association of Young Lawyers; Association des Juristes Belgo-Allemands. *LANGUAGES:* German, English, French and Italian.

ASSOCIATES

DR. HANS-JOACHIM VITS, born Wuppertal, Germany, November 23, 1935; admitted, 1984, Germany. *Education:* München and Münster University (Dr.jur.). *LANGUAGES:* German, English, Spanish and French.

(This Listing Continued)

KLAUS VON WERNEBURG, born Hagen-Hohenlimburg, Germany, October 3, 1942; admitted, 1973, Germany. *Education:* Göttingen, Würzburg and Münster Universities. *Member:* Rechtsausschuss des BvDI. *LANGUAGES:* German and English.

KLAUS LOCHMANN, born Düsseldorf, Germany, April 20, 1959; admitted, 1989, Germany. *Education:* Bonn University. *LANGUAGES:* German and English.

KAY SCHUSTER, born Mettmann, March 14, 1958; admitted, 1992, Germany. *Education:* Köln University. *LANGUAGES:* German and English.

JENS GRAF, born Cologne, Germany, September 3, 1956; admitted, 1988, Germany. *Education:* Cologne University. *LANGUAGES:* German and English.

LEGAL SUPPORT PERSONNEL

JOACHIM ZAKSEK, born Duisburg, Germany, May 31, 1939; Wirtschaftsprüfer (CPA, 1974). *Education:* Cologne University (Diploma, Business Administration, 1964). *Member:* Institut of Tax Advisors. *LANGUAGES:* German, English and French.

THEODOR VAN STIGT, born Emmerich, Germany, February 26, 1944; admitted Steuerberater (Tax Advisor, 1978). *Education:* Mönchengladbach University (Diploma, Business Administration, 1967). *Member:* Association of Tax Advisors. *LANGUAGES:* German and English.

BRUCKHAUS WESTRICK STEGEMANN

FREILIGRATHSTRASSE 1
40479 DÜSSELDORF, GERMANY
Telephone: (02 11) 49 79-0
Telefax: (02 11) 49 79-1 03 and 4 98 12 21
Telex: 858 7027 JUS D

Frankfurt Office: Taunusanlage 11, 60329 Frankfurt am Main. Telephone: (069) 27308-0. Telefax: (069) 232664. Telex: 41 49 17 WEST CD.
Hamburg Office: Alsterarkaden 27, 20354 Hamburg. Telephone: (040) 36 90 60. Telefax: (040) 36 906-155. Telex: 212 522 EURO D.
Berlin Office: Friedrichstrasse 95 (IHZ), 10117 Berlin. Telephone: (030) 26 43-3303. Telefax: (030) 26 43-3366.
Leipzig Office: Grimmaische Strasse 25, 04109 Leipzig. Telephone: (0341) 127230. Telefax: (01341) 1272333.
Brussels, Belgium Office: Rue de la Loi 99/101, B-1040 Brussels. Telephone: (32-2) 2 87 26 11. Telefax: (32-2) 2 30 39 03.
Tokyo, Japan Office: Ark Mori Building, 22F, 12-32, Akasaka 1-chome, Minato-ku, Tokyo 107. Telephone: (81-3) 55610-236. Telefax: (81-3) 55610-238.
New York, New York Office: 767 Fifth Avenue, GM Building, New York 10153. Telephone: (212) 486-1100. Telefax: (212) 759-3151.
Moscow, Russia Office: Malyj Gnezdnikovskij per. 9 No. 2, 103009 Moscow. Telephone: (7-503) 9562300; (7-501) 9401200. Telefax: (7-503) 9562301; (7-501) 9401211.

Corporate Law, Commercial Law, Mergers, Acquisitions and Divestitures, Joint Ventures, Banks and Banking, Finance, Securities, Capital Markets, Leases and Leasing, Equipment Finance, Aircraft Finance and Leasing, Antitrust and Trade Regulation, German and EC Cartel Law, Competition, Unfair Trade, Intellectual Property (trademarks, patents, copyrights), Taxation, Property, Real Estate, Energy, Natural Resources, Environmental Law, Administrative Law, Computers and Software, Food and Drug, Biotechnology, Labour and Employment, Products Liability, Insurance, Litigation, Arbitration, Broadcasting, Telecommunications, Aviation, Subsidies and State Aids, Construction Law, Zoning, Planning and Land Use, Customs and Foreign Trade Law, European Community Law, German-French Investments, Russian and Post Soviet Commerce.

MEMBERS OF FIRM

DR. HANNS H. WINKHAUS, born Essen, Germany, March 24, 1928; admitted, 1957, Germany. *Education:* Universities of Erlangen, Munich and Cologne (Dr. jur., 1955); Académie de Droit International, The Hague; Institute for Foreign and International Trade Law, Georgetown University. *LANGUAGES:* German, English and French. *PRACTICE AREAS:* Corporate Law; Commercial Law.

DR. OTFRIED LIEBERKNECHT, born Düsseldorf, Germany, April 20, 1927; admitted, 1954, Germany. *Education:* Universities of Bonn, Frankfurt am Main (Dr. jur., 1952); Harvard Law School. Faculty Assistant, Law Faculty, and Associate, Institute of Foreign and International

(This Listing Continued)

BRUCKHAUS WESTRICK STEGEMANN, Düsseldorf— Continued

Civil and Economic Law, University of Heidelberg, 1959-1963. LANGUAGES: German and English. PRACTICE AREAS: German and EC Cartel Law; Antitrust Law; Commercial Law; Unfair Competition; Industrial Property Law; Arbitration.

DR. GÜNTER BECKMANN, born Herford, Germany, September 17, 1935; admitted, 1966, Germany. Education: Universities of Kiel, Freiburg im Breisgau, Paris, Bonn (Dr. jur., 1964). LANGUAGES: German and English. PRACTICE AREAS: Corporate Law; Mergers, Acquisitions and Divestitures; Real Estate.

PETER M. KORSCH, born Berlin, Germany, June 23, 1935; admitted, 1967, Germany. Education: Universities of Lausanne (Switzerland), Cambridge (UK) and Berlin, E.E.C. Commission, 1962-1963. LANGUAGES: German, English and French. PRACTICE AREAS: Company Law (Corporate Law and Partnerships); Commercial Law (Distribution and Agency); Mergers, Acquisitions and Divestitures; Joint Ventures.

DR. BERND KUNTH, born Gleiwitz, Germany, June 22, 1943; admitted, 1971, Germany. Education: University of Fribourg (Switzerland) (2 Degréde l'Institut Français), Bonn and Heidelberg (Dr. jur., 1971). LANGUAGES: German, French and English. PRACTICE AREAS: Energy; Natural Resources; Environmental Law; Arbitration.

DR. CORNELIS CANENBLEY, born Loga, Germany, January 16, 1942; admitted, 1970, Germany. Education: Universities of Freiburg im Breisgau, Lausanne (Switzerland) Marburg (Dr. jur., 1970). E.E.C. Commission, 1968-1969 and Institute for International and Foreign Trade Law, Georgetown University, Washington, D.C. 1971. (Resident, Brussels Office). LANGUAGES: German, English and French. PRACTICE AREAS: German and EC Cartel Law; Antitrust Law; Competition; Unfair Trade; EC Law.

DR. GÜNTER H.W. STRATMANN, born Gelsenkirchen-Buer, Germany, May 12, 1941; admitted, 1972, Germany. Education: Universities of Frankfurt am Main, Göttingen (Dr. jur., 1971); Princeton and Harvard Law School (LL.M., 1968). Faculty Assistant, Institute for International Law, University of Göttingen, 1966-1967. LANGUAGES: German, English and French. PRACTICE AREAS: Corporate Law; Mergers, Acquisitions and Divestitures; Corporate Tax Law; Joint Ventures.

DR. WOLF-D. KRAUSE-ABLASS, born Kiel, Germany, January 9, 1940; admitted, 1972, Germany. Education: Universities of Tübingen, Geneva, Kiel (Dr. jur., 1970); Harvard Law School (LL.M., 1969). E.E.C. Commission, 1970-1971. LANGUAGES: German, English and French. PRACTICE AREAS: Corporate Law; Commercial Law; Mergers, Acquisitions and Divestitures; Company Law.

KARLHEINZ MOOSECKER, born Düsseldorf, Germany, November 5, 1943; admitted, 1972, Germany. Education: Universities of Cologne, Marburg, Geneva (Switzerland) and Münster. Assistant, Institute for Constitutional Law, University of Münster, 1967-1968. LANGUAGES: German, English and French. PRACTICE AREAS: German and EC Cartel Law; Antitrust Law; Competition; Unfair Trade.

DR. AXEL EPE, born Remscheid, Germany, April 28, 1950; admitted, 1977, Germany. Education: Universities of Munich and Tübingen (Dr. jur., 1978). Faculty Assistant, University of Tübingen, Law Faculty, 1976-1977. LANGUAGES: German and English. PRACTICE AREAS: Corporate Law; Commercial Law; Mergers, Acquisitions and Divestitures; Tax Law.

ULF DOEPNER, born Eberswalde, Germany, October 22, 1943; admitted, 1973, Germany. Education: Universities of Berlin, Munich, and Freiburg im Breisgau. E.E.C Commission, 1971-1972. LANGUAGES: German, English and French. PRACTICE AREAS: Intellectual Property; Copyright; Food and Drug Law; Competition; Unfair Trade.

DR. GERHARD WIEDEMANN, born Stolzenau/Weser, Germany, December 5, 1949; admitted, 1981, Germany. Education: Universities of Hamburg and Heidelberg (Dr. jur., 1980). Faculty Assistant, Institute of Company and Economic Law, University of Heidelberg, 1977-1980. (Traveling Partner, Düsseldorf and Brussels Office). LANGUAGES: German and English. PRACTICE AREAS: German and EC Cartel Law; Antitrust Law; Subsidies and State Aids; EC Law.

DR. HEINZ JOSEF WILLEMSEN, born Kranenburg, Germany, April 26, 1953; admitted, 1983, Germany. Education: University of Cologne (Dr. jur., 1979). Faculty Assistant, Institute of Labor and Economic

(This Listing Continued)

Law, University of Cologne, 1976-1978, 1981-1983. LANGUAGES: German and English. PRACTICE AREAS: Labor and Employment Law.

DR. ULRICH VON SCHÖNFELD, born Bonn, Germany, August 15, 1954; admitted, 1982, Germany. Education: University of Bonn (Dr. jur., 1982). Faculty Assistant, Institute for Public Law, University of Bonn, 1979. LANGUAGES: German, English and French. PRACTICE AREAS: Corporate Law; Commercial Law; Banks and Banking.

DR. PETER RHEINBAY, born Koblenz, Germany, September 26, 1953; admitted, 1983, Germany. Education: Universities of Munich and Freiburg im Breisgau (Dr. jur., 1982). Assistant, Institute for Civil and Comparative Law, University of Freiburg im Breisgau, 1979-1982. LANGUAGES: German and English. PRACTICE AREAS: Corporate Law; Company Law; Mergers, Acquisitions and Divestitures; Joint Ventures; Computer and Software Law.

DR. THOMAS KREIFELS, born Düsseldorf, Germany, February 13, 1957; admitted, 1983, Germany. Education: University of Bonn (Dr. jur., 1983). LANGUAGES: German and English. PRACTICE AREAS: Litigation; Arbitration; Products Liability; Commercial Law; Real Estate.

DR. RALPH WOLLBURG, born Kiel, Germany, February 16, 1956; admitted, 1984, Germany. Education: Universities of Freiburg im Breisgau and Munich (Dr. jur., 1984). LANGUAGES: German, English and French. PRACTICE AREAS: Corporate Law; Mergers, Acquisitions and Divestitures; Joint Ventures.

DR. BURKHARD BASTUCK, born Friedrichsthal/Saar, Germany, October 14, 1953; admitted, 1984, Germany and New York. Education: Universities of Saarbrücken, Lausanne (Switzerland) Bonn (Dr. jur., 1986); University of Pennsylvania Law School (LL.M., 1979). (Resident, New York Office). LANGUAGES: German, English and French. PRACTICE AREAS: Corporate Law; Commercial Law; Mergers, Acquisitions and Divestitures.

ACHIM KIRCHFELD, born Mülheim/Ruhr, Germany, February 15, 1955; admitted, 1985, Germany. Education: Universities of Cologne and Münster. LANGUAGES: German and English. PRACTICE AREAS: Corporate Law; Commercial Law; Real Estate.

DR. ALEXANDER GOEPFERT, born Northeim, Germany, September 3, 1956; admitted, 1986, Germany. Education: Universities of Göttingen and Heidelberg (Dr. jur., 1989). Faculty Assistant, Law Faculty, University of Cologne, 1982-1985. LANGUAGES: German and English. PRACTICE AREAS: Real Estate; Construction Law; Commercial Law; Litigation.

DR. BURKHARD RICHTER, born Hamm, Germany, March 9, 1954; admitted, 1987, Germany. Education: University of Münster (Dr. jur., 1986). Faculty Assistant, Institute of Civil and Company Law, University of Münster, 1982-1986. University Assistant, Centre of National and International Cartel Law and Institute of Energy Law, University of Berlin, 1986-1987. LANGUAGES: German and English. PRACTICE AREAS: German and EC Cartel Law; Antitrust Law; Corporate Law.

DR. WOLF FRIEDRICH SPIETH, born Stuttgart, Germany, November 6, 1958; admitted, 1988, Germany. Education: Universities of Tübingen and Freiburg im Breisgau (Dr. jur., 1991). LANGUAGES: German and English. PRACTICE AREAS: Environmental Law; Administrative Law.

DR. JOCHEN LÜDICKE, born Duisburg, Germany, December 29, 1958; admitted, 1985, Germany; Certified Tax Adviser, Ministry of Finance, Hessen, 1986. Education: University of Würzburg (Dr. jur., 1985). Faculty Assistant, Institute for Commercial and Tax Law, University of Würzburg, 1981-1985. Lectureship for International Tax Law, University of Würzburg, 1987—. LANGUAGES: German, English and French. PRACTICE AREAS: National and International Tax Law; Leasing.

DR. CHRISTIAN E. DECHER, born Bonn, Germany, February 11, 1958; admitted, 1989, Germany. Education: University of Cologne (Dr. jur., 1989). Faculty Assistant, Institute of Labor and Economic Law, University of Cologne, 1985-1989. LANGUAGES: German and English. PRACTICE AREAS: Corporate Law; Commercial Law; Real Estate.

RALF-DIETRICH TIESLER, born Detmold, Germany, December 6, 1959; admitted, 1991, Germany. Education: University of Marburg. Faculty Assistant, Institute of Trade, Economic and Labor Law, University of Marburg, 1985-1988. LANGUAGES: German and English. PRACTICE AREAS: Labor and Employment Law.

DR. CHRISTIAN FRANZ, born Herten, Germany, April 11, 1962; admitted, 1991, Germany. Education: Universities of Saarbrücken, Bonn (Dr. jur., 1993) and Nancy (France) (Maîtrise en Doit and Diplôme d'Etudes Approfondies, 1988). Faculty Assistant, University of Bonn, Institute

(This Listing Continued)

of Commercial and Economic Law, 1988-1991. *LANGUAGES:* German, English and French. *PRACTICE AREAS:* Corporate Law; Commercial Law.

DR. MICHAEL PFLUGRADT, born Düsseldorf, Germany, October 8, 1959; admitted, 1991, Germany. *Education:* Universities of Saarbrücken and Cologne (Dr. jur., 1989). Faculty Assistant, Institute of Labor and Economic Law, University of Cologne, 1987-1989. Federal Ministry for Economics, Bonn, 1989-1991. *LANGUAGES:* German, English and French. *PRACTICE AREAS:* Corporate Law; Commercial Law.

DR. ANDREA LENSING-KRAMER, born Bocholt, Germany, January 23, 1963; admitted, 1992, Germany. *Education:* University of Cologne (Dr. jur., 1990). *LANGUAGES:* German and English. *PRACTICE AREAS:* Intellectual Property; Competition Law; Unfair Trade.

DR. ANDRÉ KOWALSKI, born Burscheid, Germany, October 2, 1963; admitted, 1992, Germany. *Education:* Universities of Cologne and Geneva (Switzerland) (Dr. jur., 1989). *LANGUAGES:* German, English and French. *PRACTICE AREAS:* Corporate Law; Commercial Law.

DR. ANSELM RADDATZ, born Bochum, August 15, 1962; admitted, 1992, Germany. *Education:* Universities of Bochum and Münster (Dr. jur., 1991). Faculty Assistant: Institute for Commercial Law, University of Münster, 1985-1989; University of Bochum, Institute for German and European Commercial Law, 1989-1990. *LANGUAGES:* German, English and French. *PRACTICE AREAS:* Commercial Law; Corporate Law.

MARTIN KLUSMANN, born Duisburg, Germany, September 2, 1965; admitted, 1993, Germany. *Education:* Universities of Hamburg and Bochum. Faculty Assistant, Institute of Commercial and Economic Law, University of Bochum, 1989-1993. *LANGUAGES:* German and English. *PRACTICE AREAS:* German and EC Cartel Law; Antitrust Law; Unfair Trade.

CHRISTIAN GEHLING, born Paderborn, Germany, March 11, 1960; admitted, 1993, Germany. *Education:* Universities of Trier and Münster. Assistant, Institute of Commercial and Economic Law, Universities of Bonn. *LANGUAGES:* German and English. *PRACTICE AREAS:* Commercial Law; Corporate Law.

DR. HERBERT POSSER, born Essen, Germany, September 27, 1962; admitted, 1993, Germany. *Education:* University of Münster (Dr. jur., 1993) and Göttingen. Faculty Assistant, Institute of Administrative Law, University of Münster, 1988-1992. *LANGUAGES:* German, English and French. *PRACTICE AREAS:* Administrative Law; Environmental Law; Broadcasting; Telecommunications; EC Law.

MICHAEL J. ESSER, born Cologne, Germany, June 6, 1962; admitted, 1993, Germany. *Education:* Universities of Berlin and Bonn; Max-Planck-Institute for Foreign and International Private Law, Hamburg (1989-1992); University of Pennsylvania Law School (LL.M., 1988). *LANGUAGES:* German, English and French. *PRACTICE AREAS:* German and EC Cartel Law; Antitrust Law; Broadcasting; Telecommunications.

DR. EBERHARD SEYDEL, born Celle, Germany, April 29, 1965; admitted, 1993, Germany. *Education:* University of Bayreuth (Dr. jur., 1993). Faculty Assistant, Institute of Commercial and Economic Law, University of Bayreuth, 1991-1993. *LANGUAGES:* German and English. *PRACTICE AREAS:* Corporate Law; Commercial Law.

ARND EUGEN SIELING, born Bremen, Germany, March 1, 1962; admitted, 1993, Germany. *Education:* University of Bonn. Faculty Assistant, Institute of Tax Law, University of Bonn, 1988-1992. *LANGUAGES:* German, English and French. *PRACTICE AREAS:* German; EC and International Tax Law; Corporate Law; Mergers, Acquisitions and Divestitures.

MANFRED UNGEMACH, born Kiel, Germany, June 22, 1962; admitted, 1993, Germany. *Education:* University of Giessen and University of Wisconsin, Madison (LL.M., 1991). *LANGUAGES:* German, English and French. *PRACTICE AREAS:* Commercial Law; Energy Law; Arbitration; EC Cartel Law; Antitrust Law.

STEPHAN ANDREAS MECHNIG, born Worms, Germany, January 15, 1963; admitted, 1993, Germany. *Education:* Universities of Mainz and Marburg; University of Texas at Austin Law School (M.C.J., 1991). *LANGUAGES:* German and English. *PRACTICE AREAS:* Intellectual Property Law.

KONSTANTIN GÜNTHER, born Stuttgart, Germany, July 12, 1963; admitted, 1990, New York; 1994, Germany. *Education:* Universities of Tübingen, Geneva (Switzerland) and Feiburg im Breisgau; University of Penn-

(This Listing Continued)

sylvania Law School (LL.M., 1989). *LANGUAGES:* German, English and French. *PRACTICE AREAS:* Corporate Law.

DR. KLAUS BENNER, born Ludwigsburg, Germany, January 27, 1963; admitted, 1994, Germany. *Education:* Universities of Passau, Angers (France), Freiburg im Breisgau (Dr. jur., 1992); University of Surrey (Great Britain). University Assistant, Institute of Commercial and Economic Law, University of Freiburg im Breisgau, 1990-1991. *LANGUAGES:* German, English and French.

CHRISTIAN SCHRÖDER, born Bielefeld, Germany, May 7, 1963; admitted, 1994, Germany. *Education:* Universities of Münster, Geneva (Suisse). University Assistant, Institute of Mining and Energy Law, University of Münster, 1987-1992. *LANGUAGES:* German, English and French.

DR. WOLFGANG KIRCHHOFF, born Dortmund, Germany, January 20, 1959; admitted, 1989, Germany. *Education:* Universities of Bonn, Freiburg im Breisgau, Lausanne and Munich (Dr. jur., 1989). Faculty Assistant, International and European Law, University of Freiburg im Breisgau, 1982-1984. *LANGUAGES:* German and English.

HILDEGARD BISON, born Duisburg, Germany, May 21, 1963; admitted, 1990, New York; 1994, Germany. *Education:* University of Bonn; University of Chicago Law School (LL.M., 1989). Research Assistant, Institute for Commercial and Economic Law, University of Bonn, 1988. *LANGUAGES:* German, English and French.

DR. CHRISTIAN H.A. JUNG, born Munich, Germany, August 21, 1962; admitted, 1990, New York; 1995, Germany. *Education:* Faculté Internationale de Droit Comparé, Strasburg (1989); Southern Methodist University, School of Law, Dallas, Texas (LL.M., 1989); Universities of Munich and Augsburg (Dr. Jur., 1994). Research Assistant, Institute for Civil Law and International Business Law, University of Augsburg, 1992-1994. *LANGUAGES:* German, English and French.

THOMAS DURCHLAUB, born Mannheim, Germany, October 21, 1966; admitted, 1995, Germany. *Education:* University of Bochum (Dr. Jur., 1992). Research Assistant, Institute for Tax Law, University of Bochum, 1992-1994. *LANGUAGES:* German and English. *PRACTICE AREAS:* Tax Law.

DEHNEN & PARTNER

Established in 1985

PRINZ-GEORG-STRASSE 91

P.O. BOX 10 20 12

40011 DÜSSELDORF, GERMANY

Telephone: 211-48 45 61
Facsimile: 211-48 41 94

German/International Tax, International Business, Corporate, EEC Law.

FIRM PROFILE: The law firm was established in 1985 and is well known for its tax and accounting expertise, particularly with respect to transfer pricing audits and competent authority proceedings. This 4 partner firm has 10 lawyers in total working in three departments: International, Corporate and Commercial. The firm is the legal arm and international representative of the WRS Verbund, an independent association of German CPAs and tax advisors employing approximately 250 professionals in more than 20 cities throughout Germany.

MEMBERS OF FIRM

PETER H. DEHNEN, born Duisburg, Germany, January 1, 1956; admitted, 1982, Germany. *Education:* University of Bochum (1979). *Member:* International Fiscal Association; International Bar Association; German Tax Lawyer's Association; American Chamber of Commerce in Germany (Member, Tax Committee). *LANGUAGES:* German and English. *PRACTICE AREAS:* Taxation; Corporate and International Business Law.

ANDREAS POMMERIN, born Hameln, Germany, March 14, 1951; admitted, 1986, Germany. *Education:* University of Bonn (Diploma in Economic Studies, 1975). *Member:* German Tax Lawyers Association; Association Internationale des Jeunes Avocats; British Bar Association for Commerce, Finance and Industry. *LANGUAGES:* German, English and Dutch. *PRACTICE AREAS:* Taxation; Commercial Law.

KLAUS RESING, born Herne, Germany, December 1, 1957; admitted, 1991, Germany. *Education:* Technical College of Nordkirchen (Diploma of Fiscal Studies, 1981); Ruhr University of Bochum (1986). *LANGUAGES:* German and English. *PRACTICE AREAS:* Taxation; Company Succession.

(This Listing Continued)

DEHNEN & PARTNER, Düsseldorf—Continued

MARTIN KESSEMEIER, born Recklinghausen, Germany, January 12, 1958; admitted, 1991, Germany. *Education:* Ruhr University of Bochum. *LANGUAGES:* German and English. *PRACTICE AREAS:* Company Law; Taxation.

DROSTE

The Merged Firms of Droste, Pietzcker, Sprick, Ohlgart & Klosterfelde;

Triebel & Weil; Strobl, Killius & Vorbrugg

BERLINER ALLEE 48
40212 DÜSSELDORF, GERMANY
Telephone: (0211) 13 680
Telecopier: (0211) 32 44 39

Hamburg, Germany Office: Warburgstrasse 50, 20354 Hamburg. Telephone: (040) 4 1993-0. Telecopier: (040) 4 1993 200.

Munich, Germany Office: Marstallstrasse 8, 80539 Munich. Telephone: (089) 290120. Telecopier: (089) 29012 222. Telex: 524 593 skv.

Frankfurt/Main, Germany Office: Schaumainkai 91, 60596 Frankfurt/Main. Telephone: (069) 63 00 89-0. Telecopier: (069) 6300899-99.

Berlin, Germany Office: Kurfürstendamm 54-55, 10707 Berlin. Telephone: (030) 88 24 300. Telefax: (030) 88 24 393.

Brussels, Belgium Office: Avenue des Gaulois 9, B-1150 Brussels. Telephone: 02-7358945. Telecopier: 02-7352251.

General and International Practice. Commercial Law, Corporate, Banking, Finance, Tax, Mergers and Acquisitions, EU Law, Antitrust, Unfair Competition, Trademarks, Copyright, Patents, Licensing, Food and Drug Law, Law of the Press, Products Liability, Environmental Law, Labor Law, Real Estate, Estate Planning, International Construction, Contracts, Commercial Litigation and Arbitration, Bankruptcy, Administrative Law.

FIRM PROFILE: Droste is engaged in the practice of corporate and commercial law. The firm is the result of the merger of Droste, Pietzcker, Sprick, Ohlgart& Klosterfelde in Hamburg (formed in 1887), Strobl, Killius & Vorbrugg in Munich (formed in 1961) and Triebel & Weil in Düsseldorf (formed in 1951). The firm's traditional areas of practice are: corporate law, including mergers and acquisitions; industrial property law, including copyright, unfair competition and anti-trust law; trademark law; tax law, both domestic and international; real estate law. Further areas of particular expertise include banking and finance, computer and software law, environmental law, labour law, EU law and commercial litigation and arbitration.

RESIDENT PARTNERS

DR. VOLKER B. TRIEBEL, born Hildburghausen, Germany, October 25, 1941; admitted, 1972, Germany; called to the English Bar, 1976. *Education:* Universities of Bonn, Würzburg (Law Degree, 1965), Oxford (United Kingdom) and Munich (Doctor of Laws, 1974). Honorary Legal Adviser to the British Consul General. German Member of the Court of Arbitration of the International Chamber of Commerce, Paris (1985-1990). Fellow of the Chartered Institute of Arbitrators, London. *Member:* International Bar Association. *LANGUAGES:* German, English, French and Russian. *PRACTICE AREAS:* Commercial and Corporate Law; Banking Law; German and International Arbitration Law; Mergers & Acquisition.

DR. KURT G. WEIL, born Hamburg, Germany, July 23, 1936; admitted, 1968, Germany. *Education:* Universities of Munich, Hamburg (Law Degree, 1960) and Paris (France, Doctor of Laws, 1966). *Member:* Court of Arbitration, Milan (Council Member); European Lawyer's Association (Board Member); International Bar Association; International Union of Lawyers; German-French Jurists' Association; International Association of Jewish Lawyers; German-Italian Jurists' Association. *LANGUAGES:* German, English, French and Italian. *PRACTICE AREAS:* Corporate Law; Commercial Law; Mergers, Acquisitions and Divestitures.

DR. ULRICH WESTERMANN (1951-1993).

DR. ECKART PETZOLD, born Hamburg, Germany, July 15, 1956; admitted, 1983, Germany. *Education:* Universities of Freiburg (Law Degree, 1980), Lausanne (Switzerland) and Konstanz (Doctor of Laws, 1986). *Member:* German-Italian Jurists' Association; Association of Italian Speaking Lawyers (Member of the Board); International Association of Young Advocats. *LANGUAGES:* German, English, Italian and French. *PRACTICE AREAS:* Commercial Law, in particular Law of Distribution Agree-
(This Listing Continued)

ments, International Sale of Goods; Corporate Law; Mergers, Acquisitions and Divestitures.

DR. MICHAEL W. LEISTIKOW, born Frankfurt, Germany, October 15, 1956; admitted, 1986, Germany. *Education:* Universities of Bonn (Law Degree, 1982; Doctor of Laws, 1987) and Aix-Marseille. *Member:* German-Italian Jurists' Association. *LANGUAGES:* German, English, Italian and French. *PRACTICE AREAS:* Corporate Law; Futures and Options; Mergers and Acquisitions.

DR. WINFRIED F. SCHMITZ, born Cologne, Germany, April 19, 1954; admitted, 1985, Germany; 1988, New York and Connecticut. *Education:* Universities of Cologne, Freiburg, Lausanne (Switzerland), Bonn (Law Degree, 1980; Doctor of Law, 1986), Strasbourg (France) and New York University (M.C.J., 1987). *Member:* German-American Lawyers' Association; German-British Jurists' Association; International Association of Young Advocats; International Bar Association. *LANGUAGES:* German, English and French. *PRACTICE AREAS:* Mergers and Acquisitions; Transnational Contracts; Finance and Unfair Competition.

DR. ROLAND BOMHARD, born Munich, Germany, August 23, 1960; admitted, 1989, Germany. *Education:* Universities of Nuremberg-Erlangen (Law Degree, 1984; Doctor of Laws, 1988) and Lausanne, Switzerland. *Member:* AIJA; Spanish Chamber of Commerce. *LANGUAGES:* German, English, Spanish, French and Italian. *PRACTICE AREAS:* Real Estate; Construction Law; Commercial Law.

DR. THOMAS JESTAEDT, born Belgrade, Yugoslavia, July 1, 1956; admitted, 1981, Germany. *Education:* Universities of Bonn and Munich (Law Degree, 1979; Doctor of Laws, 1984); The University of Michigan Law School (LL.M., 1985). *Member:* European Lawyers' Union; German Association of Competition Lawyers; Licensing Executives Society; German-American Lawyers' Association. (Resident Partner, Brussels, Belgium Office). *LANGUAGES:* German, English, French, Dutch and Portuguese. *PRACTICE AREAS:* European Union Law; Competition Law; Joint Ventures; Licensing Executives Society.

DR. ULRIKE A. SCHÄFER, born Göttingen, Germany, April 4, 1958; admitted, 1990, Germany. *Education:* University of Göttingen (Law Degree, 1982; Doctor of Laws, 1991); University of California, Los Angeles (LL.M., 1985). *Member:* German-American Lawyers Association; Study Group for Insolvency and Arbitration. *LANGUAGES:* German, English and Spanish. *PRACTICE AREAS:* Commercial Law; Bankruptcy, Litigation and Arbitration.

DR. HANS-MICHAEL POTT, born Solingen, Germany, November 21, 1949; admitted, 1987, Germany ; 1989, Specialist (Fachanwalt) on Tax Law. *Education:* Universities of Bonn (Law Degree, 1974; Doctor of Laws, 1981) Kiel and Cologne. *Member:* International Fiscal Association; German Tax Law Society; German Tax Lawyers' Association; German Lawyers' Institute (Chairman, EC and International Law Division). *LANGUAGES:* German, English and French. *PRACTICE AREAS:* German and International Tax Law; European Community Law; Charitable Organizations.

DR. WOLFGANG KELLENTER, born Aachen, Germany, May 18, 1961; admitted, 1990, Germany; 1992, England (Solicitor). *Education:* Universities of Erlangen, Bayreuth (Law Degree, 1987; Doctor of Law, 1989); London School of Economics (LL.M., 1991). *Member:* German Association for the Protection of Industrial Property and Copyright; German-/British Jurists' Association. *LANGUAGES:* German and English. *PRACTICE AREAS:* Intellectual Property Law; Unfair Competition Law; Commercial Law.

ASSOCIATES

Christoph Brandts
Dr. Georg Müller, LL.M.
Dr. Hanns Jochen Siegrist, LL.M.
Dr. Michael J. Schmidt

Languages: German, English, French, Spanish, Russian and Italian.

(For list of personnel at Berlin, Frankfurt/Main, Hamburg, Munich and Brussels, see Professional Biographies at those locations)

ENGEL TILMANN & PARTNER

ELBERFELDER STRASSE 2
D-40213 DÜSSELDORF, GERMANY
Telephone: 49 (0) 211-84414
Telecopy: 49 (0) 211-32 72 65

Corporate, Commercial, Labor, Taxation, Unfair Competition, Antitrust, EEC Law, Real Estate, Building, Insurance, Product Liability, Patents, Trademark, Copyright, M&A, Banking, Litigation.

MEMBERS OF FIRM

DR. SIEGFRIED ENGEL, born Aalen, Germany, December 25, 1943; admitted, 1974, West Germany. *Education:* University of Tübingen (Dr. jur.). *LANGUAGES:* German and English.

ALBERT M. TILMANN, born Nordhorn, Germany, June 15, 1948; admitted, 1976, Certified Tax Law Attorney. *Education:* Universities of Freiburg, Munich and Münster. *Member:* Duits-Nederlandse Kamer van Koophandel. *LANGUAGES:* German, English, French and Dutch.

MICHAEL HECKMANN, born Oberhausen, Germany, August 15, 1952; admitted, 1981, Germany. *Education:* University of Kiel. *LANGUAGES:* German and English.

HANS-JOSEF ENGELS, born Düren, Germany, November 30, 1947; admitted, 1983, West Germany. *Education:* Universities of Cologne and Geneva, Switzerland. *Member:* Belgian-German Lawyers' Association. *LANGUAGES:* German, French and English.

RUDOLF KÜSTER, born Dortmund, Germany, July 31, 1951; admitted, 1980, Certified Tax Law Attorney. *Education:* University of Münster. *Member:* Bund Junger Unternehmer (BJU); Arbeitsgemeinschaft Selbständiger Unternehmer (ASU). *LANGUAGES:* German, English and French.

MICHAEL FISCHER, born Düsseldorf, Germany, August 8, 1960; admitted, 1990, Germany. *Education:* University of Bonn. *LANGUAGES:* German and English.

ASSOCIATE

DORIS MÜCKE, born Salzgitter, Germany, May 16, 1958; admitted, 1989, Germany. *Education:* University of Göttingen. *LANGUAGES:* German, English and French.

DR. FRIEDRICHS & PARTNER

Rechtsanwälte

STEINSTRAßE 27
D-40210 DÜSSELDORF, GERMANY
Telephone: (0211) 323 0108-9
Telefax: (0211) 32 6147

Leipzig, Germany Office: Paul-List-Str. 22, D-O4103. Telephone: 0341-9600659. Fax: 0341-9600659.

Commercial, Corporate and Business Law, Unfair Competition, Intellectual Property, International and German Law of Contracts, Tax Law, Transportation, Planning Law, Reprivatization, Litigation, Arbitration, Medical Malpractice, Family Law and Criminal Defense, Real Estate, Conveyancing, Construction Law.

MEMBERS OF FIRM

DR. CHRISTOPH FRIEDRICHS, born 1950; admitted, 1978, Germany. *Education:* Universities of Freiburg, Münster, Hamburg, UC Berkeley and London (Kings College, London School of Economics) (Dr. jur.). Author: "Chancen der Aktiengesellschaft und des Aktionärs," Tax Attorney (FA f.SteuerR). *Member:* German Bar Association; German-American Lawyers Association; German British Lawyers Association; Association International des Jeunes Advocats; AG Internationaler Rechtsverkehr im DAV. *LANGUAGES:* German and English.

DR. HEINZ HERMANN RÖMER, born 1948; admitted, 1978, Germany. *Education:* Universities Freiburg, Lausanne, Münster and Paris (Dr. jur.). Author: "Der gutgläubige Mobiliarerwerb im französischen Recht," Tax Attorney (FA f.SteuerR). *Member:* German Bar Association. *LANGUAGES:* German, English and French.

DR. HELMUT NASE, born 1951; admitted, 1991, Germany. *Education:* University Leipzig. *Member:* German Bar Association. (Resident Partner, Leipzig, Germany Office). *LANGUAGES:* German, English and Russian.

(This Listing Continued)

KAI-UWE MÄCHEL, born 1960; admitted, 1992, Germany. *Education:* University Cologne. *Member:* German Bar Association. *LANGUAGES:* German, English and French.

MARTINA THELEN, born 1965; admitted, 1994, Germany. *Education:* University of Bonn. *Member:* German Bar Association. *LANGUAGES:* German, Spanish and English.

MICHAEL SCHMIDT, born 1962; admitted, 1994, Germany. *Education:* University of Bonn and Cologne. Author: "Das Un-Übereinkommen über den internationalen Warenkauf," 1991; "Rundfunk- und Fernsehempfang durch Parabol-Antennen," 1991. *Member:* German Bar Association; German-American Lawyers Association. *LANGUAGES:* German, English and French.

GODEFROID, PIELORZ & PARTNER

GRAFENBERGER ALLEE 87
40237 DÜSSELDORF, GERMANY
Telephone: (02 11) 66 61 43
Telecopier: (02 11) 66 45 43
Teletex: 211 4259-CGMP

Mailing Address: P.O. Box 10 26 41, 40017

General Practice, Commercial, Corporate, Banking, Mergers and Acquisitions, Antitrust, Unfair Competition, Licensing, Labour, Product Liability, Bankruptcy and Reorganization, European Community Law, Environmental Law, Construction Law, Litigation and Arbitration.

MEMBERS OF FIRM

DR. CHRISTOPH GODEFROID, born West Berlin, Germany, 1948; admitted, 1980, Düsseldorf. *Education:* Universities of West Berlin, Tübingen and Bonn (Doctor of Laws, 1980). Author: "Bilaterale Staatsverträge zum internationalen Privat-oder Verfahrensrecht zwischen Vertragspartnern multilateraler Abkommen," 1980; "Zur Kündigung und Beendigung von Leasingverträgen nach dem Verbraucherkreditgesetz", BB Enclosure to Nr. 12/93, 15-19; "Leasing und Verbraucherkreditgesetz - Eine Zwischenbilanz," BB Enclosure to Nr. 12/94, 14-21. Assistant, Institute for Civil Law and Law of Civil Procedure, University of Bonn, 1975-1979. *Member:* International Bar Association; German Institute of Arbitration; Bankrechtiche Vereinigung; German-American Lawyers' Association; German-Japanese Lawyers' Association; German Association for the Protection of Industrial Property and Copyright. *LANGUAGES:* German, English, French and Italian.

DR. MICHAEL PIELORZ, born West Berlin, Germany, 1948; admitted, 1980, Düsseldorf. *Education:* Universities of West Berlin, Tübingen and Bonn (Doctor of Laws, 1977). Author: "Auslandskonkurs und Disposition über das Inlandsvermögen," 1977; "Wende im Deutschen Internationalen Insolvenzrecht," IPRax 1984. Assistant, Institute for Civil Law and Law of Civil Procedure, University of Bonn, 1974-1980. *Member:* Bankrechtiche Vereinigung; Arbeitskreis für Insolvenz- und Schiedsgerichtswesen, Cologne. *LANGUAGES:* German and English.

DR. KLAUS RELLERMEYER, born Duisburg, Germany, 1953; admitted, 1982, Bonn; 1984, Düsseldorf. *Education:* Universities of Bochum and Bonn (Doctor of Laws, 1985). Author: "Aufsichtsratsausschüsse" ("Committees of the supervisory board"), 1986; "Der Aufsichtsrat" ZGR 1993, 77-103; "Objektive Bezugsgrößen für die Bewertung von Kreditsicherheiten - Ist das Wirksamkeitserfordernis des Bundesgerichtshofs erfüllbar?", WM 1994, 1009-1021, 1053-1062. Assistant, Institute for Commercial Law and Business Law, University of Bonn, 1980-1984. *Member:* Bankrechechtiche Vereinigung; German-American Lawyers' Association; Deutscher Juristentag. *LANGUAGES:* German and English.

DR. ANETTE FROHN-STEINERT, born Essen, Germany, 1955; admitted, 1986, Düsseldorf. *Education:* Universities of Bochum and Berlin (Doctor of Laws, 1993). Author: "Die Gestaltung des Einzelbesuchsvertrages für Bühnenveranstaltungen durch Allgemeine Geschäftsbedingungen", 1993. With: RIAS Berlin, Legal Department, West Berlin, 1985-1986. *Member:* German-Japanese Lawyers' Association. *LANGUAGES:* German, English and French.

DR. WERNER HOLTKAMP, born Essen, 1958; admitted, 1989, Düsseldorf. *Education:* Universities of Bonn and Darmstadt (Doctor rer. pol., 1993). Author: "Die Genossenschaft als herrschendes Unternehmen im Konzern", 1993. *Member:* Association for the Study of Cartel Law. *LANGUAGES:* German and English.

DR. CHRISTIAN SALM, born Dortmund, Germany, 1961; admitted, 1991, Düsseldorf. *Education:* University of Bochum (Doctor of Laws,

(This Listing Continued)

GODEFROID, PIELORZ & PARTNER, *Düsseldorf—*
Continued

1990). Author: "Die Bundesanstalt Technisches Hilfswerk - eine organisations und statusrechtliche Untersuchung," 1991; various papers on Environmental law, ZAU (Zeitschrift für Angewandte Umweltforschung) 1991. Assistant, Institute for Public Law, University of Bochum, 1986-1991. *Member:* Society for Environmental Law. *LANGUAGES:* German and English.

ASSOCIATES

RALF SCHMIEDEL, born Düsseldorf, Germany, 1961; admitted, 1993, Düsseldorf. *Education:* University of Bonn. *LANGUAGES:* German and English.

DR. CHRISTOPH DIERKES, born Bottrop, Germany, 1963; admitted, 1993, Düsseldorf. *Education:* University of Bochum (Doctor of Laws, 1994). Author: "Die Grundpflichten bei der Einstellung des Betriebes genehmigungspflichtiger Anlagen gemäß § 5 Absatz 3 Bundes-Immissionsschutzgesetz," 1994. Assistant: Chair for Public and European Law (Professor Jarass), University of Bochum, 1989-1993. *Member:* Society for Environmental Law. *LANGUAGES:* German and English.

MICHAEL INTVEEN, born Düsseldorf, Germany, 1960; admitted, 1993, Düsseldorf. *Education:* University of Cologne. *Member:* Arbeitskreis EDV und Recht, Cologne. *LANGUAGES:* German and English.

MARTINA KERN, born Düsseldorf, Germany, 1964; admitted, 1994, Düsseldorf. *Education:* Universities of Würzburg and Cologne.

GRAHAM & JAMES

MARTIN-LUTHER-PLATZ 26
40212 DÜSSELDORF, GERMANY
Telephone: 011-49-211-839-9200
Telecopier: 011-49-211-839-9209

Other offices located in: San Francisco, Los Angeles, Newport Beach, Palo Alto, Sacramento and Fresno, California; Washington, D.C.; New York, New York; Milan, Italy; Beijing, China; Tokyo, Japan; London, England; Taipei, Taiwan.
Associated Offices: Deacons in Association with Graham & James, Hong Kong; Sly and Weigall, Sydney, Melbourne, Brisbane, Perth and Canberra, Australia.
Affiliated Offices: Graham & James in Affiliation with Taylor Joynson Garrett, London, England, Bucharest, Romania and Brussels, Belgium; Hanafiah Soeharto Ponggawa, Jakarta, Indonesia; Deacons and Graham & James, Bangkok, Thailand; Haarmann, Hemmelrath & Partner, Berlin, Munich, Leipzig, Frankfurt and Dusseldorf, Germany; Mishare M. Al-Ghazali & Partners, Kuwait; Sly & Weigall Deacons in Association with Graham & James, Hanoi, Vietnam and Guangzhou, China; Gallastegui y Lozano, S.C., Mexico City, Mexico; Law Firm of Salah Al-Hejailan, Jeddah and Riyadh, Saudi Arabia.

Firm engaged in American and International Law Practice, but admitted to appear before German Courts and to act as German Attorneys.

WOLFGANG M. KAU, born Frauental, West Germany, 1950; admitted, 1979, West Germany; 1981, California; 1982, U.S. Court of Appeals, Ninth and Eleventh Circuits. *Education:* Stadt. Emil-Fischer Gymnasium, Euskirchen, West Germany (Bacca Laurente, 1969); Rhein. Friedrich Wilhelm University, Bonn, West Germany (J.D., 1975); Southwestern University, Los Angeles. Author: "Venture Capital & Going Public - Unternehmensfinanzierung in den USA", Carl Heymanns Verlag, Cologne, 1984; "Zahlung mit Check," Recht der Internationale Wirtschaft, June, 1989; "Handelsblatt", April, 1984; "Venture Capital in den USA", June, 1984; "U.S. Installment Sales Tax (March 1982); "The U.S. Economic Recovery Tax Act of 1981." Co-Author: "Products Liability in Asset Acquisitions," "Acquisitions of Closely-Held Companies," "Registrierung einer California Corporation. als Gesellschafterin einer deutschen GmbH" Recht der Internationalen Wertschaft Jan. 1991. PLI 1982. *Member:* Los Angeles County, American and International Bar Associations; Düsseldorf Bar Association; German American Lawyers Association. (Also at Los Angeles Office). *LANGUAGES:* German and French. *PRACTICE AREAS:* International Business Law; Corporate Law.

JOHANNES GROOTERHORST

HEINRICH-HEINE-ALLEE 20
40213 DÜSSELDORF, GERMANY
Telephone: 0211/86.46.70
Fax: 0211/13.13.42

General and International Practice, Business Organizations, Commercial Law, Mergers and Acquisitions, Bankruptcy and Reorganization, Labor, Antitrust, Unfair Competition, National and International Commercial Litigation, Real Estate, Estate Planning, Construction Contracts, Licensing, Franchise and Distribution Law, Administrative and Company Law, European Community Law.

DR. JOHANNES GROOTERHORST, born Straelen, July 29, 1955; admitted, 1986, West Germany. *Education:* Universities of Münster (Doctor of Law, 1986) and Lausanne (Switzerland); Premier cycle de Droit Comparé, Faculté Internationale de Droit Comparé, Straßburg, 1979; Fachanwalt für Verwaltungsrecht (Specialized Attorney for Administrative Law). Author: "Die Wirkung der Ziele der Raumordnung und Landesplanung gegenüber Bauvorhaben nach § 34 BBauG," (The Effects of the Aims of Regional Planning and Land Planning to Building Projects pursuant to § BBauG), 1985. *Member:* German Lawyers' Association; German French Group AIJA, UIA; Club des Affaires en Rhénanie du Nord Westphalie e.V., Industrie-Club Düsseldorf. *LANGUAGES:* German, French, English and Spanish. *PRACTICE AREAS:* Company Law; Mergers, Acquisitions and Divestitures; Zoning, Planning and Land Use; Property; Commercial Law.

ASSOCIATES

DR. URSULA GROOTERHORST, born March 14, 1957; admitted, 1986, West Germany. *Education:* Universities of Münster (Doctor of Law, 1986) and Lausanne (Switzerland). Author" Der Geltungsverlust von Bebauungsplänen durch die nachträgliche Veränderung der tatsächlichen Verhältnisse," (1988). *LANGUAGES:* German, French and English. *PRACTICE AREAS:* Commercial Law; Administrative Law; Litigation.

FLORIAN FISCHER, born Düsseldorf, February 8, 1965; admitted, 1994, Düsseldorf. *Education:* University of Cologne. *LANGUAGES:* German and English. *PRACTICE AREAS:* Industrial and Intellectual Properties; Media Law; Entertainment; Unfair Competition.

DR. DIRK JOHANNES ELVERFELD, born Bremen, July 4, 1963; admitted, 1994, Germany. *Education:* University of Münster (1989). *LANGUAGES:* German and English. *PRACTICE AREAS:* Construction Law; European Community Law; Labour and Employment; Commercial Mergers and Acquisitions; Commercial Law.

HAARMANN, HEMMELRATH & PARTNER

MARTIN-LUTHER-PLATZ 26
D-40212 DÜSSELDORF, GERMANY
Telephone: (0211) 8399-00
Telefax: (0211) 8399-133

Munich Office: Effnerstrasse 38, D-81925 München. Telephone: (089) 924 00-0. Telefax: (089) 92400-133. Telex: 5 23 900 HUP D.
Berlin Office: Budapester Strasse 40a, D-10787 Berlin. Telephone: (030) 264 73-0. Telefax: (030) 264 73-133.
Frankfurt Office: Neue Mainzer Strasse 75, D-60311 Frankfurt/Main. Telephone: (069) 920 59-0. Telefax: (069) 920 59-133.
Leipzig Office: Neumarkt 24, D-04109 Leipzig. Telephone: (0341) 1263-0. Telefax: (0341) 1263-133.
Tokyo Office: Shiroyama JT Mori Building, 8F, 3-1 Toranomon 4-chome, Minato-ku, Tokyo 105. Telephone: 81-3-34 59 54 85. Fax: 81-3-35 78 89 56.
Prague Office: Cermàkova 7, CZ-1200 00 Prague 2, Czech Republic. Telephone: 42-2-24 23 90 36. Telefax: 42-2-24 23 88 42.

Corporate and Business Law, International and National Tax Law, Banking, Commercial Law, Labour Law, all Areas of Mergers and Acquisitions, Financial Transactions, International Law, Antitrust Law, Unfair Competition and Intellectual Property Rights Law, EEC Law, Real Estate Transactions, Management and Leveraged Buy-outs, National and Cross-border Leasing Transactions, Structuring of Funds, Accounting Services.

FIRM PROFILE: The firm, established in 1987, has strongly developed as a multi-disciplinary firm in Germany with seven offices. The firm is affiliated with Graham & James (US, Italy, Japan and China), Taylor Joynson

(This Listing Continued)

Garrett (UK) and Deacons (Hong Kong and Southeast Asia) and is a member of the international Tax and audit network RSM international.

RESIDENT MEMBERS OF FIRM

DR. BERND SAGASSER, born Munich, Germany, May 16, 1956; admitted, 1985, Munich; 1988, Steuerberater (Certified Tax Advisor). *Education:* University of Munich (J.D., 1982; Doctor at Law, 1986). Author: "Sondervorteile bei der Gründung von Aktiengesellschaften," VVF, 1986. Co-Author: "Handbuch des Kapitalanlagerechts," Verlag Beck, 1990. *Member:* International Bar Association; Deutsche Steuerjuristische Gesellsdraft; Deutsch-Mexikanische Juristenvereinigung e.V.; German-Japanese Lawyers Association. *LANGUAGES:* German, English, French and Spanish. *PRACTICE AREAS:* Mergers and Acquisitions; Corporate; Tax EC Law; Finance; EC Law.

DR. UDO W. HENKEL, born Münster, Germany, May 17, 1955; admitted, 1984, Hamburg; 1991, Steuerberater (Certified Tax Advisor). *Education:* Universities of Münster and Freiburg (J.D., 1981; Doctor at Law, 1988). Author: "Auslandsverluste im nationalen und internationalen Steuerrecht der Bundesrepublik Deutschland." Co-Author: Mössner, Steuerrecht international tätiger Unternehmen," Verlag Dr. Otto Schmidt, 1992. Learned Assistant, University of Hamburg, 1985-1987. *Member:* Deutsche Steuerjuristische Gesellschaft; Charity of International Tax Institute; University of Hamburg. *LANGUAGES:* German and English. *PRACTICE AREAS:* Banking; Corporate; Tax; Business Law; Finance.

THOMAS BULA, born Wuppertal, Germany, August 29, 1952; admitted, 1979, Steuerberater (Certified Tax Advisor), Wirtschaftsprüfer (Certified Public Accountant). *Education:* University of Münster (Business Administration, 1979). *Member:* Institute of German Chartered Accountants (IDW). *LANGUAGES:* German and English. *PRACTICE AREAS:* Audit; Tax; Finance.

CHRISTINE VOGEL, born Gierath, Germany, October 3, 1954; admitted, 1987, Steuerberater (Certified Tax Advisor). *Education:* Universities of Cologne and Düsseldorf. *LANGUAGES:* German and English. *PRACTICE AREAS:* Tax.

DR. FRANZ-JOSEF SCHÖNE, born Balve, Germany, July 26, 1958; admitted, 1991, Essen. *Education:* Universities of Berlin and Münster (Doctor at Law, 1989). Author: "Freedom to Provide Services within the EC and the German Economic Law," Köln, 1989. Faculty Assistant, University of Münster, 1985-1990; Assistant Professor, University of Applied Science for Public Law, Münster, 1990-1991. *Member:* International Bar Association; Association of Comparative Law and EC-Law. *LANGUAGES:* German and English. *PRACTICE AREAS:* Public Law; Environmental and Waste Disposal; Corporate; Commercial; Labor; European Union.

HARALD PLEWKA, born Essen, Germany, September 19, 1953; admitted, 1994, Düsseldorf. *Education:* University of Münster. Fiscal Administration in North-Rhine, Westfalia, 1983-1986. Judge at the Fiscal Court in Düsseldorf, 1987-1989. Researcher at the Federal Fiscal Court in Munich and Judge at the Fiscal Court, 1990-1993. *Member:* International Tax Law Association, Rhine Ruhr. *LANGUAGES:* German and English. *PRACTICE AREAS:* German and International Tax Law; Accounting Law.

Languages: German, English, French, Japanese, Dutch, Spanish, Italian, Slovakian, Czech, Russian and Mandarin.

(For Biographical Data on other Members of Firm See Professional Biographies at Munich, Berlin, Leipzig and Frankfurt, Germany, Tokyo, Japan and Prague, Czech Republic).

HENGELER KURTH WIRTZ

DÜSSELDORF, GERMANY

(See Hengeler Mueller Weitzel Wirtz)

HENGELER MUELLER WEITZEL WIRTZ

Rechtsanwälte
TRINKAUSSTRASSE 7
D-40213 DÜSSELDORF, GERMANY
Telephone: (0211) 8304-0
Telefax: (0211) 13 26 41 & 8 04 61
Telex: 85 87 300 whds d

Frankfurt/Main, Germany Office: Bockenheimer Landstrasse 51, D-60325 Frankfurt/Main. Telephone: (069) 17095-0. Telefax: (069) 72 57 73 & 72 39 83. Telex: 41 45 95 jura d.

Berlin, Germany Office: Kurfürstendamm 54/55, D-10707 Berlin. Telephone: (030) 882 76 47. Telefax: (030) 882 7144.

Brussels, Belgium Office: Boulevard du Régent 50, Bte. 6, B-1000 Brussels. Telephone: (02) 511 41 15. Telefax: (02) 514 02 12.

Budapest, Hungary Office: Teréz krt. 38, H-1066. Telephone: (1) 1323121. Telefax: (1) 2690098.

New York Office: 712 Fifth Avenue, New York, New York, 10019. Telephone: (212) 586-4600. Telefax: (212) 586-4481.

Commercial, Corporate, International, Banking, Finance and Underwriting, Taxation, Arbitration, EEC, Antitrust, Merger Control, Fair Trade, Patent, Trademark, Litigation, Labor, Administrative, Constitutional, Environmental and Planning Law.

PARTNERS

DR. HEINZ-BERND KURTH, born Essen, Germany, 1928; admitted, 1955, Germany. *Education:* University of Bonn (Dr. jur.).

ALBERT HEUSCH, born Aachen, Germany, 1931; admitted, 1961, Düsseldorf. *Education:* Universities of Lausanne, Perugia, Paris, Southern California at Los Angeles, Bonn and Cologne.

DR. KLAUS BÖHLHOFF, born Berlin, Germany, 1934; admitted, 1965, Düsseldorf. *Education:* Universities of Marburg, Berlin, Hamburg and Bonn (Dr. jur.). Foreign Associate, New York Law Firm, 1963-1964. (Also at New York, New York Office).

DIETER GERHARDT, born Berlin, Germany, 1934; admitted, 1965, Düsseldorf. *Education:* Universities of Marburg, Munich and Münster.

DR. HERMANN MENZEL, born Hirschberg/Schlesien, 1935; admitted, 1967, Germany. *Education:* Universities of Münster, Berlin, Freiburg and Fribourg/Switzerland (Dr. jur.).

HANS PETER HENGELER, born Düsseldorf, Germany, 1937; admitted, 1971, Düsseldorf. *Education:* Universities of Heidelberg, Freiburg, Bonn and Cologne. Co-Author: Beck Standard Forms and Agreements Manual for Commercial and Business Law, 7th ed. 1991.

DR. MICHAEL HOFFMANN-BECKING, born Magdeburg, Germany, 1943; admitted, 1971, Düsseldorf. *Education:* Universities of Freiburg, Munich and Münster (Dr. jur.). Editor and Co-Author: Munich Corporate Law Manual, Vol. 4, Stock Corporation, 1988. Co-Editor and Co-Author: Munich Contracts Manual, Vol. 7: Corporate Law, 2nd ed. 1985; Co-Author: Beck Standard Forms and Agreements Manual for Commercial and Business Law, 7th ed. 1991.

JOCHEN BURRICHTER, born Waltrop/Westfalen, 1941; admitted, 1973, Düsseldorf. *Education:* Universities of Münster and Freiburg. (Also at Brussels, Belgium Office).

DR. AXEL SCHMIDT-HERN, born Münster, Germany, 1942; admitted, 1970, Düsseldorf. *Education:* Universities of Freiburg and Münster (Dr. jur.). Co-Author: Beck Standard Forms and Agreements Manual for Commercial and Business Law, 7th ed. 1991.

DR. AXEL BAUMANNS, born Düsseldorf, Germany, 1950; admitted, 1981, Düsseldorf. *Education:* Universities of Cologne, Freiburg and Münster (Dr. jur.). Foreign Associate, New York Law Firm, 1979-1980.

DR. GEORG WIESNER, born Lübeck, Germany, 1948; admitted, 1982, Düsseldorf. *Education:* Universities of Hamburg and Heidelberg (Dr. jur.). Co-Author: Munich Corporate Law Manual, Vol. 4, Stock Corporation, 1988.

DR. MATTHIAS BLAUM, born Bremen, Germany, 1955; admitted, 1983, Düsseldorf. *Education:* Universities of Bern (Switzerland), Munich and Freiburg (Dr.jur.). Foreign Associate, New York Law Firm, 1982-1983.

DR. BARBARA WEITZ, born Niederaussem, Germany, 1955; admitted, 1984, Düsseldorf; 1986, New York. *Education:* Universities of Cologne,

(This Listing Continued)

HENGELER MUELLER WEITZEL WIRTZ,
Düsseldorf—Continued

Freiburg and Michigan (Dr.jur; LL.M.). Foreign Associate, Los Angeles Law Firm, 1983-1984.

DR. THOMAS L. SCHMIDT-KÖTTERS, born Gelsenkirchen, Germany, 1953; admitted, 1983, Düsseldorf. *Education:* Universities of Münster and Freiburg (Dr.jur.). Co-Author: Die Freiheit der Baugestaltung - Freedom of Construction Design, 1989.

DR. MAXIMILIAN SCHIESSL, born Cologne, Germany, 1960; admitted, 1986, Düsseldorf. *Education:* University of Munich (Dr. jur.); Harvard Law School (LL.M.). Foreign Associate, New York Law Firm, 1987-1988. Co-Author: "Due Diligence, Disclosures and Warranties in the Corporate Acquisition Practice," 2nd ed. 1992.

DR. ADALBERT UELNER, born Olpe/Westfalen, Germany, 1927; admitted, 1990, Düsseldorf. *Education:* Universities of Cologne and Bonn (Dr. jur.). Co-Editor and Co-Author: Blümich, Commentary on the Income Tax Act, the Corporation Tax Act and the Trade Tax Act.

DR. MATTHIAS HENTZEN, born Frankfurt/Main, Germany, 1960; admitted, 1990, Düsseldorf. *Education:* Universities of Saarbrücken and Münster (Dr. jur.); Georgetown University, Washington D.C. (LL.M.). Foreign Associate, Brussels Law Firm, 1989.

DR. ANDREAS AUSTMANN, born Herford, Germany, 1959; admitted, 1990, Düsseldorf; 1992, New York. *Education:* Universities of Heidelberg and Münster (Dr. jur.); Harvard Law School (LL.M.).

DR. GERD SASSENRATH, born Dormagen, Germany, 1960; admitted, 1990, Düsseldorf. *Education:* Universities of Bonn (Dr. jur.) and Lausanne (Switzerland). Foreign Associate, Los Angeles Law Firm, 1991.

DR. DANIEL WILM, born Hamburg, Germany, 1959; admitted, 1990, Düsseldorf. *Education:* Universities of Regensburg and Bonn (Dr. jur.). Foreign Associate, New York Law Firm, 1991-1992.

Languages: German, English and French

(For biographical data of the members of the firm admitted to the bar in Frankfurt/Main and Berlin, see Professional Biographies in Frankfurt/Main and Berlin)

HEUKING KÜHN KUNZ WOJTEK

ELISABETHSTRASSE 16
D-40217 DÜSSELDORF, GERMANY
Telephone: 49 211 389 501
Telex: 8 588 247 jura d
Telefax: 49 211 370 644

Other Offices: Frankfurt, Hamburg, Berlin, Chemnitz (Germany); Paris (France).

Corporate, Banking, Tax, National and EC Antitrust, Mergers, Acquisitions, Intellectual Property, Unfair Competition and Trade Law, Commercial and International Law, EC Law, Legal Assistance to Governments, Environmental Law, Administrative Law, Telecommunications and Media Law, Insurance Law, Product Liability, International Arbitration, Litigation, General Practice.

FIRM PROFILE: All Attorneys are Members of Denton International and of the Düsseldorf Bar Association. All speak English and German, other languages include French, Japanese, Spanish and Swedish.

MEMBERS OF FIRM

DR. HANS GÜNTER HEUKING, born Bottrop, Germany, February 2, 1938; admitted, 1969, Germany. *Education:* Universities of Tübingen and Münster (Referendar, 1961; Doctor of Law, 1968). Research and Teaching Assistant, University of Bochum, 1966-1969. Author: "Competency and Limited Competency to Enter into Employment Contracts," Bochum, 1968. *Member:* Industrial Property Rights and Copyrights Association. *PRACTICE AREAS:* Corporate Law; Mergers and Acquisitions.

DR. WOLFGANG KÜHN, born Zagreb, December 21, 1941; admitted, 1971, Germany. *Education:* Universities of Munich and Münster (Referendar, 1968; Assessor, 1971; Doctor of Law, 1971). Author: "Practical Experiences with English Arbitration Proceedings," 1987; "Antitrust Law and Arbitration in the Federal Republic of Germany," 1987; "Appeal of Arbitration Awards under the New Swiss Private International Law," 1988. "Rico Claims in International Arbitration and Their Recognition in Germany,"

(This Listing Continued)

1994. " With: Westfalenbank AG. 1962-1964; Buckeridge & Braune, London, 1971. *Member:* Court of Arbitration ICC; International Bar Association (Vice Chairman, Arbitration Committee); German Institute of Arbitration (Board Member). *PRACTICE AREAS:* Corporate; Mergers and Acquisitions; International Arbitration.

PROF. DR. WALTER KOLVENBACH, born Düsseldorf, Germany, January 28, 1922; admitted, 1952, Germany. *Education:* Universities of Cologne and Frankfurt/Main (Referendar, 1948; Doctor of Law, 1949; Assessor, 1952). General Counsel, Henkel KGaA, 1972-1985. Author: "Workers Participation in Europe," 1977; "Employee Councils in European Companies," 1978; "Cooperation between Management and Labor," 1982 (Italian Translation, 1984); "Handbook on European Employee Co-Management," 1987; "Private Law Protection for Foreign Investments," 1985 (Revised English Version, 1988). Co-Publisher: "Frankfurt Commentary on German Antitrust Law," 1986. Lecturer on Law, Universities of Bonn and Cologne, 1982-1988. Professor of Law, University of Cologne, 1988—. *Member:* International Bar Association (Chairman, Section on General Practice, 1988-1990); Treasurer, 1990-1994, German Chemical Association (Member, Legal Committee; Chairman, 1977-1985); Düsseldorf Chamber of Commerce (Member, Legal Committee, 1974—; Chairman, 1987—); European Company Lawyers Association (Past President, 1984-1987). *PRACTICE AREAS:* Corporate Law.

DR. MICHAEL KUNZ, born Berlin, Germany, July 16, 1938; admitted, 1973, Germany; Tax Advisor, 1972; Certified Public Accountant, 1974, Germany. *Education:* Universities of Würzburg and Cologne (Referendar, 1967; Doctor of Law, 1966; Assessor, 1973). Research Assistant at University of Würzburg, Germany, 1964-1966, International Supreme Court, The Hague, 1961. Recipient Scholarship for the Université Internationale, Luxembourg. Lecturer: Private University of Witten Itterdecke. *Member:* Düsseldorf Certified Public Accountants Association; Alumni University Salzburg Seminar in American Studies; Association des Auditeurs de l'Academie de Droit Internationale de la Haye. *PRACTICE AREAS:* Tax Law; Audit; Corporate Law.

DR. KATHARINA JANK-DOMDEY, born Frankfurt, Germany, February 10, 1949; admitted, 1975, Germany. *Education:* University of Frankfurt (Assessor, 1975; Doctor of Law, 1979). Author: "Private Claims for Promulgation of Statutory Law and their Enforcement before the Courts;" "Marriage and Divorce: Estate Planning Problems and Opportunities." *Member:* International Bar Association (Chairman, Family Law Committee). Designated Fellow, International Academy of Matrimonial Lawyers (Member, Management Committee, European Chapter). *PRACTICE AREAS:* Estate Planning; Wills; Trusts and Succession; Family Law.

PATRICK CELESTINE, born Agen, France, August 25, 1950; admitted, 1970, Düsseldorf Bar (Avocat); 1975, Paris, France (Advocat à la Cour). *Education:* Universities of Paris and Strasbourg, France (Maîtrise en Droit, Certificat d'Aptitude à la Profession d'Avocat, 1974; Diplôme D'Etudes Supérieures Spécialisées de Droit des Relations Commerciales, Industrielles et Financières Internationales, 1976); German Academic Exchange Service, Program of Legal Studies, Tübingen and Düsseldorf, 1974, 1975; Institut de Droit Comparé de Paris, 1979. Conseiller du Commerce Extérieur de la France (appointed by Government Decree, 1987). Author: "Die Stille Gesellschaft in Frankreich," 1979; "Die französiche Gesellschaft bürgerlichen Rechts," 1980; "Grundstückserwerb in Frankreich," 1981: all in Internationale Wirtschaftsbriefe; "Die Garantie auf erstes Anfordern in der französischen Gerichts-praxis," Recht der Internationalen Wirtschaft, 1989. Co-author: "La Pratique du Marché Allemand," 1980. (Resident Partner, Paris, France Office). *PRACTICE AREAS:* Corporate Law; General Commercial Law; Mergers and Acquisitions.

DR. PETER KAMPHAUSEN, born Rheydt, Germany, August 30, 1954; admitted, 1981, Germany; Certified Tax Counsel, 1981; Certified Counsel for Administrative Law, 1987. *Education:* University of Bochum (Referendar, 1978; Assessor, 1981; Doctor of Law, 1983). Co-Author: "Legal Problems Relating to the Provision of Information by Administrative Officials," Dissertation, 1983; "Legal Problems Relating to the Protection and Preservation of Historical Monuments," DWW, p. 246, 1985; "Amendment to the Air Pollution Regulations," DB, p. 1267, 1986. Co-author: "Eliminating Industrial Environmental Damage: Liability for Contaminated Sites, Legal Protection, Insurance Protection, Tax Consequences," DB, suppl. 3187, 8/1987; "Privatizing Public Facilities for Waste and Sewage Disposal," StuGR, p.215, 1988. Research Assistant, University of Bochum, 1979-1981. Lecturer on Law, University of Bochum, 1981-1984. *Member:* Deutscher Juristentag e.V.; Arbeitsgemeinschaft für Verwaltungsrecht im Deutschen Anwaltsverein; (German) Environmental Law Society; Arbeitsgemeinschaft der Fachanwälte für Steuerrecht e.V. *PRACTICE*

(This Listing Continued)

AREAS: Public and Environmental Law; Constitutional Law; Real Property; Acquisitions.

DR. DIETER BOHNERT, born Heilbronn, Germany, December 19, 1948; admitted, 1981, Germany; Certified Tax Counsel, 1985. *Education:* University of Heidelberg (Referendar, 1971; Assessor, 1975; Doctor of Law, 1981). Author: "US Tax Reform and the German-American Tax Treaty," Recht der Internat. Wirtschaft, p. 87, 1987. State of Baden-Wuerttemberg Revenue Service, 1975-1980. Head of Tax Department, Beiersdorf AG, 1980-1984 and Bertelsmann AG, 1984-1986. *Member:* International Fiscal Association (National Reporter for Germany at the 1990 IFA Congress); International Bar Association; Deutscher Juristentag e.V.; Arbeitsgemeinschaft der Fachanwaelte fuer Steuerrecht e.V.;. **PRACTICE AREAS:** Tax Law; Mergers and Acquisitions.

DIRK W. KOLVENBACH, born Düsseldorf, Germany, May 18, 1955; admitted, 1984, Germany. *Education:* University of Cologne (Referendar, 1979; Assessor, 1984). Author: "The Checking Law in Great Britain," 1980. Co-author: "Eliminating Industrial Environmental Damage," DB 87, suppl. *Member:* German-British Jurists Association; German-American Lawyers Association; German-French Lawyers Association; International Bar Association; (German) Environmental Law Society. **PRACTICE AREAS:** General Commercial; Labor Law; Mergers and Acquisitions.

DIETRICH MERKISCH, born Königsberg, Germany, July 15, 1926; admitted, 1955, Germany. *Education:* University of Erlangen (Referendar, 1952; Assessor, 1955). Director, Insurance Department, Henkel KGaA, 1970-1988. *Member:* German Insurance Coverage Association (Executive Board Member, 1978-1989); German Industry Association (Chairman, Insurance Committee, 1986-1988); Chemical Industry Association (Chairman, Insurance Committee, 1977-1987). **PRACTICE AREAS:** Insurance Law.

HIRONAGA KANEKO, born Tokyo, Japan, October 26, 1956; admitted, 1987, Germany. *Education:* University of Cologne (Referendar, 1984; Assessor, 1987). Research Assistant University of Cologne, 1980-1981, 1985. *Member:* Düsseldorf Bar Association; German-Japanese Lawyers Association. **PRACTICE AREAS:** General Commercial Law; Labor Law; Japanese Investments in Germany.

MICHAEL SCHMITTMANN, born Recklinghausen, August 21, 1958; admitted, 1989, Germany. *Education:* Universities of Cologne and Geneva, Switzerland (Referendar, Düsseldorf, 1983; Assessor, Stuttgart, 1987); British Institute of International and Comparative Law, London (1980); International Law Institute, Georgetown University, Washington, D.C. (1988);. Consultant to the EC-Commission, DG III (Internal Market and Industrial Affairs), Directorate Approximation of Laws, Freedom on Establishment, Freedom to Provide Services, Brussels, 1988-1989. Author: "L'Europe ádeux vitesses? EC and Council of Europe Struggle for Regulations on Transfrontier Television," Markenartikel 1989, p. 532, "TV Programmes of Law and Medium Power-Satellites and German Law," Zeitschrift für Urheber - und Medienrecht1990, p. 263; "The EC Directive of 21 December 1989 on the Coordination of the Laws Relating to the Application of Review Procedures to the Award of Public Supply and Public Work Contracts," Europäische Zeitschrift für Wirtschaftsrecht 17/1990; "Proprietary Rights Affecting Interoperability and Harmonization," Competition and Cooperation in the Changing Environment, ITU - Proceedings of the 6th World Telecommunication Forum, Part 3, Geneva 1991. Co-Author (with W. Vonnemann): "Mergers and Acquisitons in Europe 1993: the new merger control regulation and its effects on national merger control in Germany," The Antitrust Bull, 1992, p. 1025-1046. Co-Authorship with Gregory Thwaite "The Dualism of German and EC Competition Law - Some Progaostic Observations," Co-Authorship with Inge de Vries "An Oveview of the Aplication of European and National Competition Law in the Field of Tececommunication," Telecommunications & Space Journal 1994. *Member:* International Bar Association; German-American Lawyers Association; German-Spanish Lawyers Association; European Center of Space Law; VIVA Fernsehen Gmbtt (Member of the Board). **PRACTICE AREAS:** German and EC Competition Law; Telecommunications Law; Entertainment Law; Broadcasting Law; General Commercial Law.

THOMAS KERKHOFF, born Düsseldorf, Germany, July 10, 1959; admitted, 1989, Germany. *Education:* University of Cologne (Referendar, 1985; Assessor, 1989). *Member:* International Association for the Protection of Property Rights (AIPPI); Studienvereinigung Kartellrecht (German Antitrust and Unfair Trading Association). **PRACTICE AREAS:** Intellectual Property; Litigation.

HANS STEFAN KORSCH, born Düsseldorf, Germany, April 8, 1954; admitted, 1983, Germany. *Education:* Universities of Cologne and Tübingen, Germany and Cambridge, Great Britain (Referendar, 1979; Assessor,

(This Listing Continued)

1982). **PRACTICE AREAS:** Corporate Law; Labour Law; General Commercial Law; Litigation.

DR. UTE JASPER, born Bielefeld, Germany, September 24, 1962; admitted, 1991, Germany. *Education:* Universities of Saarbrücken and Münster, Germany and Cambridge, Great Britain Scholarship; German Academic Exchange Servicee (DAAD) (Referendar, 1986, Doctor of Law, 1988; Assessor, 1991). Author: "Associated Companies in German and British Group Accounts, 1989." Co-Author: "Conflicts of Interest of Members of the GmbH Supervisory Board," 1992; "Die Bilantierung von Genussrechts Kapital," Wib 1994, p. 102; "Kapitalerstrande Gebraushiuber Lassing," WiB 1994, p.12. **PRACTICE AREAS:** Corporate; Commercial Law.

DR. HANS GUMMERT, born Essen, Germany, August 18, 1961; admitted, 1990, Germany. *Education:* Universities of Tübingen, Germany and Bonn, Germany (Referendar, 1987; Assessor, 1990; Doctor of Law, 1991); College of Public Administration, Speyer. Author, "Liability and Limitations on Liability of the German Civil Partnership and its Partners - Principles of Liability Affecting the Civil Partnership," Bonn, 1991; Zur Zulassigkeit einseitiger Haftungsbeschrankungen auf das Vermogen der BGB-Außengesellschaft, ZIP 93, p. 1063; "Haftung in gualitsicken taktischen GmGH Lonzen," Wib a994, P.217. Co-Author: "Munchener Handbuch fur Gesellschaftsrecht" ; Kapitalerschende Gedrauchsiuberlassung,: WiB 1994, P.12. **PRACTICE AREAS:** Corporate; Commercial; Litigation.

DR. HANS HENNING PFEIFFER, born Chemnitz, Germany, February 18, 1934; admitted, 1968, Germany. *Education:* Universities of Munich, Berlin and Bonn (Referendar, 1959; Assissor, 1963; Doctor of Law, 1965). General Counsel, Rheinnmetall Berlin AG/Rheinmetall GmbH, 1975-1994. **PRACTICE AREAS:** International Contracts; Corporate Law; General Commercial Law; Government Contracting.

ASSOCIATES

ULRIKE GROEGER, born Calw, Germany, August 7, 1961; admitted, 1992, Germany. *Education:* Universities of Tübingen/Germany, Fribourg/-Switzerland, Freiburg/Germany (Referendar, 1988; Assessor, 1992). **PRACTICE AREAS:** Labour Law.

DR. JOHANNES KOLBECK, born Steinfeld, Germany, February 10, 1957; admitted, 1978, Tax Inspector; 1992, Germany; 1993, Tax Advisor. *Education:* Lower Saxony College for Financing, Universities of Freiburg-/Germany, Grenoble/France (Referendar, 1987; Assessor, 1990; Doctor of Law, 1990). Author: "The Tax Treatment of Payments to Troublesome Shareholders"; "The Definition of the Capital Account under Section 15A Income Tax Code." With: Tax Authorities of the State of Lower Saxony, 1975-1981; Tax Department of Price Waterhouse, 1990-1991. *Member:* Association of Tax Advisors. **PRACTICE AREAS:** Tax Law.

BERNHARD HARTMANN, born Sevelen, Germany, May 31, 1963; admitted, 1993, Germany. *Education:* Universities of Erlangen and Münster, Germany (Referander, 1989; Assessor, 1993). **PRACTICE AREAS:** Public Law.

INGRID L. LENHARDT, born Kitchener, Canada, December 12, 1959; admitted, 1987, California and U.S. District Court, Central District of California. *Education:* Indiana University (B.S., with highest distinction, 1982); Technische Universität, Berlin (1982-1983); Northwestern University School of Law (J.D., 1986); Christian-Albrechts-Universität, zu Kiel (LL.M., 1987). Editorial Board, Journal of International Law and Business, 1985-1986. With: O'Melveny & Myers, Los Angeles, 1987-1989; Author: "Legal Ethics as Market-Interference the German Residency Requirements, 1994. Authorized German/English Translators, 1994. Lecturer, Rheinische Friedrich-Wilhelms-Universität, Bonn, 1991—. Deutscher Akademischer Austauschdienst (DAAD) Scholarship, Berlin, 1982-1983; Fulbright Full Grant Scholarship, Kiel, 1986-1987; Robert Bosch Foundation Fellowship for Young American Leaders, Bonn, Karlsruhe, Cologne and Düsseldorf, 1990-1991. Certified Public Accountant, Illinois, 1982. *Member:* German-American Lawyers Association (DAJV); Los Angeles County Bar and American Bar Associations.

WOLFRAM MEVEN, born Dusseldorf, Germany, September 21, 1956; admitted, 1991, Germany; Tax Advisor, 1994. *Education:* University of Cologne (Referendar, 1988, Assessor, 1991). **PRACTICE AREAS:** Tax Law.

HOLGER LINDERHAUS, born Hilden, Germany, February 8, 1962; admitted, 1993, Germany. *Education:* University of Bonn and Lausanne/-Switzerland (Referendar, 1989; Assessor, 1993). *Member:* Dusseldorf Bar Association; German-American Lawyer's Association; German-Japanese Lawyer's Association. **LANGUAGES:** German, English and French.

(This Listing Continued)

HEUKING KÜHN KUNZ WOJTEK, Düsseldorf—
Continued

TAX ADVISORS

DR. MICHAEL HÜCHTEBROCK, born Gelsenkirchen, Germany, April 9, 1954. Certified Public Accountant, 1989, Germany; Tax Advisor, 1986, Germany. *Education:* University of Bochum (Diploma in Business Administration, 1978; Doctor of Economics, 1982). Research Assistant, University of Bochum, 1978-1983. Author: "Depreciation and Investment Theory," 1983. *Member:* Association of Certified Public Accountants; Association of Tax Advisors.

CLAUS CHRISTMANN, born Karlsruhe, German, April 22, 1943. Certified Public Accountant, 1978, Germany; Tax Advisor, 1980, Germany. *Education:* Business School, Düsseldorf (Diploma in Business Administration, 1966). *Member:* Association of Certified Public Accountants.

HEINZ-WERNER ORTJOHANN, born Detmold, Germany, April 27, 1950. Tax Advisor, 1981, Germany. *Education:* Business School, Detmold. *Member:* Association of Tax Advisors.

EVA M. WALCH, born Munich, Germany, June 15, 1952. Tax Advisor, 1983, Germany. *Education:* University of Cologne (Diploma in Business Administration, 1976); Scholarship, University of Colorado, Boulder, U.S.A. (1977-1978). *Member:* Association of Tax Advisors.

THOMAS W. KARCH, born Saarbrücken, Germany, October 9, 1953. Tax Advisor, 1983. *Education:* University of Cologne (Diploma in Business Administration, 1979; Vereidigter Buchpruter, 1991). Author: "Introduction to Tax Law, Neue Wirtschaftsbriefe," 1983; "Tax Law I," Beck-Verlag, 1988. *Member:* Association of Tax Advisors. *PRACTICE AREAS:* VAT in cross-border transactions.

FRIEDHELM NOHL, born Freckhausen, Germany, March 9, 1947; admitted, 1982, Tax Advisor; 1983, Certified Public Accountant. *Education:* University of Cologne (Diploma in Business Administration, 1977). Author: "Group Financial Reporting and Transfer Pricing," 1983. *Member:* Association of Certified Public Accountants; Association of Tax Advisors.

HOFFMANN, LIEBS, FRITSCH & PARTNER

ROTTHÄUSER WEG 12
40629 DÜSSELDORF, GERMANY
Telephone: 0211/9284 (0)
Telefax: 0211/9284-100

Berlin, Germany Office: Kurfürstendamm 11, 10719. Telephone: 0 30/88 44 17 60. Telefax: 0 30/88 44 17 63.

Chemnitz, Germany Office: Augustusburger Strasse 331, 09127. Telephone: 03 71/72 90 31-34. Telefax: 03 71/72 04 46.

Halle, Germany Office: Wilhelm-Külz-Straße 13, 06108. Telephone: 0345/50 27 24-26. Telefax: 0345/50 27 08.

Business, Corporation, German and EC-Antitrust, Energy, European Community, Unfair Competition, Trademark and Copyright, Co-determination, Labor, Administrative, Environmental and Banking Law, Acquisition Consulting.

FIRM PROFILE: *The firm Hoffmann, Liebs, Fritsch & Partner has been established in 1973. By its membership in LOGOS - group of European law firms - it has access to a network of regular cooperation partners with offices in important economic and administrative centres in all member states of the European Community as well as to the LOGOS common office in Brussels. The main areas of practice are corporate law, co-determination, banking, environmental, labour and antitrust law.*

MEMBERS OF FIRM

DR. DIETRICH HOFFMANN, born Bernburg, Germany, 1925; admitted, 1955. *Education:* University of Göttingen (Dr. jur., 1952). Special Tax Counsel. Author, among other publications: "Der Aufsichtsrat, Handbuch für die Praxis," 1984 (Supervisory Board Manual). *Member:* German-Chinese Lawyers Association; German-Korean Commerce Association; German-Australian Chamber of Commerce. *LANGUAGES:* German, English and French (Read Only). *PRACTICE AREAS:* Corporation Law; Co-determination Law; Antitrust Law.

DR. RÜDIGER LIEBS, born Köthen, Germany, 1939; admitted, 1976. *Education:* Universities of Heidelberg, Geneva, Tübingen and Freiburg (Dr. jur., 1973). Assistant Professor Commercial and Corporate Law, University

(This Listing Continued)

---

of Freiburg, 1970-1972. Author, among other publications: "Wettbewerbsbeschränkende Vertriebsverträge und unerlaubte Handlung," 1973 (Monograph on German Antitrust Law and Tort). *Member:* Deutsche Vereinigung für Gewerblichen Rechtsschutz und Urheberrecht e.V. (GRUR). *LANGUAGES:* German, English and French (Read Only). *PRACTICE AREAS:* Corporate Law; Banking Law; Accounting Law; Insolvency Law.

DIPL.-ING. KLAUS FRITSCH, born Berlin, Germany, 1948; admitted, 1985. *Education:* Technical Academy of Berlin (Dipl.-Ing. Chemistry); University of Berlin (Law). Author, among other publications: "Die Neuregelungen des Wasserrechts in Nordrhein-Westfalen," DVBl, 1989. *Member:* Committee of Advisers on Environmental Affairs in the Association of the Chemical Industry. *LANGUAGES:* German and English. *PRACTICE AREAS:* Administrative Law; Environmental Law.

DR. HABIL. PETER PREU, born Darmstadt, Germany, April 15, 1951; admitted, 1989. *Education:* University of Göttingen (Dr.jur., 1981, Dr. habil, 1990). Assistant Professor, University of Göttingen. *LANGUAGES:* German and English. *PRACTICE AREAS:* Administrative Law; Corporation Law; Privatisation Law; Restitution of Property Law; Investment in Eastern Germany Law.

WOLFGANG BUCKSCH, born Bodenburg, Germany, 1955; admitted, 1986. *Education:* University of Göttingen. Adjunct Professor, Institute for Labor Law. *Member:* German Bar Association (Member, Committee of Attorneys specialized in Labor Law); German Labor Court Association. *LANGUAGES:* German and English. *PRACTICE AREAS:* Labor Law; Co-determination Law; Trademark Law.

PROF. DR. CARSTEN P. CLAUSSEN, born Berlin, Germany, 1927; admitted, 1965. *Education:* Universities of Mainz, Cologne and Berlin (Dr. jur., 1954). Assistant Professor, Georgetown University, Washington, D.C. Honorary Professor, University of Hamburg. Former Member of the Board, German banks. Co-Author: "Cologne Commentary on the German Joint Stock Companies Act." *Member:* Banking Law Association; Swedish Chamber of Commerce, Düsseldorf (Management Board). *LANGUAGES:* German, English and Swedish. *PRACTICE AREAS:* Company Law including Tax Law; Banking Law and Capital Market Law; Accounting Law; Mergers and Acquisitions; Admission of Companies to the Stock Exchange.

DR. DIETER SCHOTTELIUS, born Bremen, Germany, 1922; admitted, 1949. *Education:* Universities of Göttingen, Munich, Freiburg and Harvard Law School (1954). Author, among other publications: Kohlhammer's Commentary on the Law of Chemicals. Lecturer on Environmental Law at the University of Heidelberg. Former Managing Director of the Association of the Chemical Industry and of Chemie-Umweltberatungs GmbH, Frankfurt on Main. (Resident, Halle Office). *LANGUAGES:* German and English. *PRACTICE AREAS:* Environmental Law; Law of Technology.

DR. ROLAND ERNE, born Radolfzell, Germany, 1960; admitted, 1989. *Education:* University of Konstanz. Author: "Die Swapgescháfte der Banken," 1992. *LANGUAGES:* German, English and French. *PRACTICE AREAS:* Banking Law; Corporation Law; Securities Law.

HANS-JÜRGEN MÜGGENBORG, born Aachen, Germany, 1959; admitted, 1990. *Education:* University of Trier. Author, among other publications: "Offentlich-rechtliche und zivilrechtliche Verantwortlichkeit für Altlasten", 1992. (Resident, Halle Office). *LANGUAGES:* German, English and French. *PRACTICE AREAS:* Administrative Law; Environmental Law; Law of Technology.

DR. RUDOLF STREICH, born Insterburg, Germany, 1942; admitted, 1972. *Education:* University of Munich (Dr. jur., 1973); tax consultant (1978). Long standing executive positions in the energy-producing industry in the fields of law, finance and business management. *LANGUAGES:* German and English. *PRACTICE AREAS:* Energy Law; Atomic Energy Law; Antitrust Law; Company Law.

KARSTEN KOCH, born Gorlitz, Germany, 1955; admitted, 1990,. *Education:* University of Leipzig. *PRACTICE AREAS:* German Democratic Republic Law; Labour Law; Civil Law.

CHRISTOPH PAUS, born Essen, Germany, 1961; admitted, 1989. *Education:* Universities of Freiburg and Heidelberg. Adjunct Professor, Institute for Finance and Tax Law, University of Heidelberg. *LANGUAGES:* English. *PRACTICE AREAS:* Trade Law; Company Law; Civil Law; German Democratic Republic Law.

(This Listing Continued)

ANGELA KOCH, born Chemnitz, Germany, 1958; admitted, 1991. *Education:* University of Leipzig. *PRACTICE AREAS:* Civil Law; Labour Law; Insolvency Law.

ASSOCIATES

Dr. Michael Hoffmann
Dr. Thomas M. Bentler, LL.M., U.S.A.
Silvia Radtke-Bonk
Martina Groth
Dr. Annette Ruoff
Anja Kühlborn

HÖLTERS & ELSING

Established in 1989

IMMERMANNSTRAßE 40

40210 DÜSSELDORF, GERMANY

Telephone: (0211) 36 78 70

Telex 8587142 HE D Telecopier: (0211) 35 39 28

Leipzig, Germany Office: Nordstrasse 23, 04105. Telephone: (0341) 98 24 60. Telefax: (0341) 98 24 612.

Berlin, Germany Office: Wielandstraße 23, 10707. Telephone: (030) 885 74 20. Telefax: (030) 885 74 2-20.

General and International Practice, Business Organizations, Commercial Law, Corporate Banking, Finance, Mergers and Acquisitions, Bankruptcy and Reorganization, Labor, Antitrust, Unfair Competition, National and International Commercial Litigation and Arbitration, Consumer Affairs, Advertising, Product Liability, Real Estate, Estate Planning, International Construction Contracts, Trademark, Licensing, Franchise and Distribution Law, International and National Tax Planning and Tax Counselling, Protection of Intellectual Property, Administrative and Company Law, European Community Law.

MEMBERS OF FIRM

DR. WOLFGANG HÖLTERS, born Cologne, Germany, 1947; admitted, 1974, Germany. *Education:* University of Cologne (Dr. jur.). Fachanwalt für Steuerrecht (Specialized Attorney for Tax Law). Author: "Legal and Contractual Obligations in Tariff Agreements," Berlin, 1973; "The Advisory Board of the GmbH and GmbH & Co. KG," Cologne, 1979; Form Book for the *Stock Corporation*, Munich, 3rd ed. 1991; *Handbuch des Unternehmens- und Beteiligungskaufs*, (Handbook for Mergers and Acquisitions), Cologne, 3rd ed. 1991 (contributory editor). *Member:* American Chamber of Commerce in Germany; International Bar Association; German Finnish Chamber of Commerce. *LANGUAGES:* German and English.

DR. SIEGFRIED H. ELSING, born Essen, 1950; admitted, 1979, Germany; 1983, New York. *Education:* Universities of Freiburg, Lausanne, Münster (Doctor of Law, 1976); Yale Law School (LL.M., 1979). Author: "Erweiterte Kommanditistenhaftung und atypische Kommanditgesellschaft," (Extended Limited Partner Liability and Atypical Limited Partnership), 1977; "U.S.-Amerikanisches Handels-und Wirtschafts recht," (US-American Commercial and Business Law), 1985. *Member:* German Bar Association; American Bar Association; International Bar Association; German-American Lawyers' Association; Association Internationale des Jeunes Avocats (President, 1990-1991). *LANGUAGES:* German, English, French and Portuguese.

DR. RAINER VELTEN, born Essen, Germany, 1958; admitted, 1988, Germany. *Education:* Universities of Erlangen/Nurnberg, Lausanne (Switzerland), Bonn and Kiel (Doctor of Law, 1986); University of Illinois Law School (LL.M., 1988). Author: "Die Anwendung des Völkerrechts auf State Contracts in der Internationalen Schiedsgerichtsbarkeit," (The Application of Public International Law on State Contracts in International Arbitration), 1987. *Member:* German Bar Association; German-American Lawyers' Association; Union des Avocats Européens. *LANGUAGES:* German, English and French.

DR. MARKUS SONDERMANN, born Witten/Ruhr, Germany, 1962; admitted, 1990, Germany. *Education:* University of Münster (Doctor of Law, 1989). *LANGUAGES:* German and English.

DR. PETER ZIMMERMANN, born Bensberg, Germany, 1960; admitted, 1991, Germany. *Education:* Universities of Cologne (Doctor of Law, 1990) and Lausanne (Switzerland). *Member:* DACH Europâische Anwaltsveveingung e.V. *LANGUAGES:* German, French and English.

ASSOCIATES

DR. BARBARA DEILMANN, born Münster, Germany, 1961; admitted, 1991, Germany. *Education:* University of Münster (Doctor of Law, 1988). *LANGUAGES:* German, English and Dutch.

(This Listing Continued)

THOMAS M. LAUDAGE, born Essen, Germany, 1963; admitted, 1993, Germany. *Education:* University of Bonn. Associate, German Ministry of Environmental Affairs, 1989-1990. Analyst, Economic Cooperation Matters, Information Service of the German Federal Parliament. *Member:* DACH Europâische Anwaltsveveingung e.V. *LANGUAGES:* English and German.

DR. GERHARD KERCKHOFF, born Meppen, Germany, 1965; admitted, 1994, Germany. *Education:* University of Trier, Germany (Doctor of Law, 1992) and Nancy (France). *LANGUAGES:* German, English, French and Portuguese.

DR. MICHAEL ALBERTS, born Essen, Germany, 1958; admitted, 1988, Essen. *Education:* Universities of Regensburg, Lausanne (Switzerland) and Freiburg (Dr.jur.). Author: "Der Einfluss von Waehrungsschwankungen auf Zahlungsansprueche nach deutschem und englischem Recht", 1986; "Schadensersatz und Fremdwaehrungsrisiko", NJW 1989, 609. *Member:* Essen and German Lawyers' Associations; German-American Lawyers' Association; Association Internationale des Jeunes Avocats. *LANGUAGES:* German, English and French.

DR. HARTWIG STIEBLER, born Melle, Germany, 1957; admitted, 1989, Germany. *Education:* Universities of Augsburg, Marburg, Göttingen, Osnabrück (Dr. jur., 1986). *LANGUAGES:* German and English.

LUKAS LENZ, born Hamburg, Germany, 1963; admitted, 1994, Germany. *Education:* Universities of Munich and Hamburg. Research Assistant, Max-Planck-Institute for Foreign and International Private Law, 1989-1992. *LANGUAGES:* German and English.

OF COUNSEL

MAXIMILIAN BISSINGER, (DOCTEUR EN DROIT), born Munich, Germany, 1946; admitted, 1981, Germany; 1988, France. *Education:* Universities of Munich and Paris II. *Member:* American Foreign Law Association; Association Internationale des Jeunes Avocats; Franco-German Chamber of Commerce; German Institute for Arbitration. *LANGUAGES:* German, French and English.

DR. RICHARD WOLTERECK, born Hamburg, Germany, 1938; admitted, 1993, Germany. *Education:* Universities of Freiburg/Breisgau and Hamburg (Doctor of Law, 1965). With Gerling-Konzern Insurance Group, Cologne, 1966. Member of Executive Board, Gerling-Konzern. Chief Executive Office, Gerling-Konzern Globale Reinsurance Company. *LANGUAGES:* German and English.

PROFFESSOR DR. OTTO SANDROCK, born Sontra, Germany, 1930; admitted, 1994, Germany. *Education:* Universities of Göttingen, Lyon, France; Yale Law School (LL.M., 1956). Author: inte ralia "Vertikale Konzentrationen im U.S.-amerikanischen Anti-trust Recht" (Vertical Restraints in U.S.-Americn Anti-Trust Law), Heidelberg, 1984; "Handbuch der internationalen Vertragsgestaltung" (Handbook for Drafting International Contracts), Heidelberg, 1980; "Kartellrecht und Genossenschaften" (Anti-Trust Law and Cooperatives), Tübingen, 1976; "Die Einheit der Wirtschaftsordnung" (Unity in the Legal Regulation of the Economy), Frankfurt, 1971; "Grundbegriffe des Gesetzes gegen Wettbewerbsbeschräkungen" (Basic Terms of the Anti-Trust Law), Munich, 1968; over 100 Law Review Articles. Law Professor, Universities of Münster and Bochum. *Member:* Deutscher Rat für internationales Privatrecht (German Council for International Private Law); Vizepräsident des Schiedszentrums der Offiziellen Deutsch-Französischen Industrie fund Handelskammer in Paris (Vice President of the Arbitration Court at the German-French Chamber of Industry and Commerce in Paris); Panel of Arbitrators of the American Arbitration Association, of the German Arbitration Association and Swiss Arbitration Association, New York. *LANGUAGES:* German, English and French.

KARBOWSKI, MASLING, HEGER & PARTNERS

Attorneys-at-Law and Notaries Public

Established in 1974

KAISER-WILHELM-RING 43

40545 DÜSSELDORF, GERMANY

Telephone: 49-211-55-57-17

Telefax: 49-211-55-57-85

Essen, Germany Office: Huyssenallee 86-88, 45128. Telephone: 0049-201-17580. Telefax: 0049-201-1758400.

(This Listing Continued)

KARBOWSKI, MASLING, HEGER & PARTNERS, Düsseldorf—Continued

Leipzig, Germany Office: Gohliser Strasse 7, 04105. Telephone: 0049-341-5662860; 0049-341-5662861. Telefax: 0049-341-5662862.

Administrative Law. Advertising Law. Banking Law. Bankruptcy. Competition Law. Constitutional Law. Consumer Protection Law. Customs and Excise Law. Distributorship, Agency and Franchise Law. EEC Law. Employer's Liability. Environmental Law. Family Law. Foreign Investments. International Contracts. International Private Law. Product Liability Law. Property and Real Estate Law. Rent and Lease. General Legal Practice. International Taxation. General Commercial and Corporate Law. Industrial Labor and Shop Constitution Law on behalf of Management. International Trade Law. Antitrust and Unfair Trade Practices.

FIRM PROFILE: *The firm was established in 1974. It has a sophisticated and extensive commercial practice, with strong concentrations in general corporate, antitrust and unfair trade practices, labor law and business-related civil litigation. The firm maintains branch offices in Düsseldorf and Leipzig/Germany.*

MEMBERS OF FIRM

E. ALEXANDER KARBOWSKI, born Gotha, Germany, February 16, 1945; admitted, 1974, Essen. Notary Public, 1984. *Education:* University of Münster (LL.B., 1971). Author: Periodical articles on national and international trade and company law. Co-Author: "Die Europäische Wirtschaftliche Interessenvereinigung," (european company law), 44 Wertpapier Mitteilungen 1313-1356 (1990). *Member:* Essen Bar Association; American Chamber of Commerce in Germany and New York. **LANGUAGES:** German, English and French. **PRACTICE AREAS:** Corporate Law; Banks and Banking; International Law; Company Law; Mergers, Acquisitions and Divestitures.

JÜRGEN MASLING, born Warnemünde, Germany, March 10, 1945; admitted, 1977, Hamburg; 1978, Essen. Notary Public, 1989. *Education:* Universities of Freiburg and Münster (LL.B., 1974). *Member:* Essen Lawyers Association; American Chamber of Commerce in Germany. **LANGUAGES:** German and English. **PRACTICE AREAS:** Labor and Employment.

KLAUS G. HEGER, born October 19, 1934, Chemnitz, Germany; admitted, 1968, Essen; 1970, Düsseldorf. *Education:* Universities of Tübingen, Hamburg and Münster (LL.B., 1964). *Member:* German Bar Association; International Bar Association; Industrieclub Düsseldorf. **LANGUAGES:** German and English. **PRACTICE AREAS:** Company Law; Mergers, Acquisitions and Divestitures; International Commercial Contracts.

DR. MARTIN HAMM, born Bonn, Germany, May 5, 1948; admitted, 1976, Cologne; 1984, Essen. *Education:* Universities of Freiburg and Cologne (LL.B., 1976); Freiburg (LL.D., 1976). Notary Public, 1990. Author: "Vorteilsausgleichung und Schadensminderungspflicht im Rahmen des § 844 BGB," (compensation and duty to prevent further damage), 1976. *Member:* Essen Lawyers Association. **LANGUAGES:** German and English. **PRACTICE AREAS:** Property; Real Estate; Labor and Employment; Commercial Law.

KLAUS BECKMANN, born Ennigloh, Germany, August 11, 1944; admitted, 1977, Essen. *Education:* University of Cologne. Parliamentary State Secretary to Federal Minister for Economics, 1989—. **LANGUAGES:** German and English. **PRACTICE AREAS:** Commercial Law.

BEATRIX EICKHOFF, born Legden, Germany, February 3, 1958; admitted, 1985, Essen. *Education:* University of Bonn (LL.B., 1982). *Member:* Essen Lawyers Association. **LANGUAGES:** German and English. **PRACTICE AREAS:** Contracts; Civil Law; Rent and Lease.

DR. CHRISTIAN GLORIA, born Lünen, Germany, June 9, 1957; admitted, 1989, Essen. *Education:* University of Bochum (LL.B., 1982; LL.D., 1987) and London. Author: "Das steuerliche Verständigungsverfahren und das Recht auf diplomatischen Schutz - zugleich ein Beitrag zur Auslegung der Doppelbesteuerungsabkommen," (study on the competent authority procedure under tax treaties), 1988; "Der subjektive Faktor" bei der Frage des Vorliegens einer verschleierten Handelsbeschränkung i. S. des Art. 36 Satz 2 EWG-Vertrag," (study on trade restrictions under the EEC-Treaty), 29 Recht der Internationalen Wirtschaft 898 - 905, 1983; "Die Doppelbesteuerungsabkommen der Bundesrepublik Deutschland und die Bedeutung der Lex-Fori-Klausel für ihre Auslegung," (study on the interpretation of tax treaties), 32 Recht der Internationalen Wirtschaft 970 - 978, 1986; "Verfassungsrechtliche Anforderungen an die gerichtlichen Geschäftsverteilungspläne," (due process of law under the Basic Law), 41 Die Öffentliche

(This Listing Continued)

Verwaltung 849 - 858, 1988; "Die Verwirklichung des Rechts auf den gesetzlichen Richter im Prozess," (due process of law), 42 Neue Juristische Wochenschrift 445 - 446, 1989; "Die Stellplatzpflicht nach den Landesbauordnungen," 9 Neue Zeitschrift für Verwaltungsrecht 305 - 314, 1990; "Der Anspruch auf Erschließung," 10 Neue Zeitschrift für Verwaltungsrecht 720-728, 1991. Co-Author: Der "finale Todesschuß" im Landesrecht Nordrhein-Westfalens," (legality of shooting to kill), 3 Nordrhein-Westfälische Verwaltungsblätter 37 - 45, 1989; "Die Europäische Wirtschaftliche Interessenvereinigung," (european company law), 44 Wertpapier Mitteilungen 1313 - 1356, 1990. Ipsen, Völkerrecht, 3rd ed. (treatise on public international law; inter alia chapters on international law of the sea and on international economic law), 1990. *Member:* German American Lawyers Association. **LANGUAGES:** German, English and French. **PRACTICE AREAS:** Administrative Law; Antitrust and Trade Regulation; Competition; European Community Law; International Law; Commercial Law; Company Law; International Contracts; International Joint Ventures; International Business.

DR. PETER M. MOMBAUR, born December 12, 1938, Solingen, Germany; admitted, 1991, Düsseldorf. *Education:* Universities of Marburg, Bonn and Cologne (LL.B., 1963; LL.D., 1964). Editor of several legal journals. Author: Bundeszwang und Bundestreue, 1964. Member, Committee of Energy, Technology and Research of the European Parliament. Deputy Judge, Northrhine-Westfalian Constitutional Court. **LANGUAGES:** German, English and French. **PRACTICE AREAS:** Administrative Law; Energy Regulation.

PROF. DR. MANFRED MÜLLER, born Rattwitz, Germany, October 2, 1926; admitted, 1990, Leipzig, Saxonia. *Education:* University Halle (Saale); University of Leipzig, 1950 (LL.D., 1959); Habilitation, 1969. Legal Adviser in Industry and Foreign Trade, 1952-1967. Member of the Institute for Foreign and Comparative Law, Potsdam, 1967-1990. Full Professor, 1975—. Publications on legal questions of international cooperation in science and technology and in the field of protection of intellectual property. Consultant on World Intellectual Property Organization, Geneva. **LANGUAGES:** German, English and French. **PRACTICE AREAS:** Intellectual Property.

ECKHARD H. POTT, born Essen, February 22, 1959; admitted, 1991, Essen. *Education:* University of Bochum (LL.B., 1987). **LANGUAGES:** German and English. **PRACTICE AREAS:** Contracts; Civil Law.

CHRISTOPH PESCH, born Essen, Germany, December 24, 1964; admitted, 1994, Essen. *Education:* University of Bochum (LL.B., 1990). **LANGUAGES:** German and English. **PRACTICE AREAS:** Commercial Law; Civil Law.

MARCUS HELF, born Essen, Germany, April 10, 1965; admitted, 1994, Essen. *Education:* Universities of Bochum and Münster (LL.B., 1991). **LANGUAGES:** German and English. **PRACTICE AREAS:** Labor and Employment; Civil Litigation.

PETER H. KORT

Established in 1973

KAISERSWERTHER STR. 239
D-40474 DÜSSELDORF, GERMANY
Telephone: +49 211 478010
Fax: +49 211 4780114
Telex: +47 858 4596 kort d

Intellectual Property (Trademark Law), Transportation Law, Commercial Law, International and National Law.

PETER H. KORT, born Dortmund, 1938; admitted, 1968, Düsseldorf. *Education:* Abitur, Timmendorferstrand (1958); Hamburg, Berlin and Strasbourg (Diplôme d'Etudes Superieures de Droit Comparé) Law Schools (1958-1964). Trainee: German Ship Owners Association, Hamburg, Berlin and French Attorney, Paris. *Member:* Legal Committees, German Forwarders and Road Transporters Associations; Pharmaceuticals Trade Mark Group; International Trademark Association; International Anticounterfeiting Coalition.

Languages: German, English, French, Spanish and Russian

KRIEGER, GENTZ, MES & GRAF VON DER GROEBEN

Established in 1929

AM BONNESHOF 6
40474 DÜSSELDORF, GERMANY
Telephone: (0211) 45 07 11
Telex: 8 588 509 mos d
Telefax: (02 11) 437 07 07

Mailing Address: P.O. Box 300843, 40408 Düsseldorf

Patent, Trademark and Copyright Law, Design Patents, Unfair Competition, Press, EEC and Antitrust Law, Litigation and Legal Advice.

FIRM PROFILE: *The firm was originally established in 1929 in Berlin by Richard Moser von Filseck, and moved to Düsseldorf in 1949. Specialities of the firm are Litigation and Legal Advice in Patent, Trademark and Copyright Law, Design Patents, Unfair Competition, Press, EEC and Antitrust Law, Corporate Law.*

MEMBERS OF FIRM

ULRICH KRIEGER, born Berlin, April 6, 1928; admitted, 1958. *Education:* Universities of Berlin and Munich. Co-Editor of the Monthly Review Gewerblicher Rechtsschutz und Urheberrecht (Industrial Property and Copyright Law). *Member:* International Association for the Protection of Industrial Property and Copyright, AIPPI (Former President of German Group). *LANGUAGES:* German, English and French. *PRACTICE AREAS:* Patent; Trademark; Copyright Law; Unfair Competition; Litigation; Legal Advice.

DR. GÜNTHER GENTZ, born Düsseldorf, April 11, 1930; admitted, 1962. *Education:* University of Cologne (Dr. jur.). *Member:* German Association for the Protection of Industrial Property and Copyright, AIPPI. *LANGUAGES:* German, English and French. *PRACTICE AREAS:* Patent; Trademark; Copyright Law; Unfair Competition; Litigation; Legal Advice.

DR. PETER MES, born Cologne, June 1, 1943; admitted, 1973. *Education:* Universities of Cologne and Munich (Dr. jur.). *Member:* German Association for the Protection of Industrial Property and Copyright, AIPPI (Secretary, German Group); International Bar Association. *LANGUAGES:* German, English and French. *PRACTICE AREAS:* Patent; Trademark; Copyright Law; Unfair Competition; Litigation; Legal Advice.

CARL-CHRISTOPH GRAF VON DER GROEBEN, born Bad Harzburg, July 14, 1947; admitted, 1975. *Education:* Universities of Bonn and Munich. *Member:* German Association for the Protection of Industrial Property and Copyright, AIPPI. *LANGUAGES:* German, English and French. *PRACTICE AREAS:* Patent; Trademark; Copyright Law; Unfair Competition; Litigation; Legal Advice.

GEREON ROTHER, born Bonn, April 4, 1956; admitted, 1985. *Education:* Universities of Freiburg and Munich. *Member:* German Association for the Protection of Industrial Property and Copyright, AIPPI; German-Italian Jurists' Association. *LANGUAGES:* German, English and Italian. *PRACTICE AREAS:* Patent; Trademark; Copyright Law; Unfair Competition; Litigation; Legal Advice.

WOLF GRAF VON SCHWERIN, born Hagen-Hohenlimburg, October 28, 1956; admitted, 1987. *Education:* Universities of Münster and Speyer. *Member:* German Association for the Protection of Industrial Property and Copyright, AIPPI. *LANGUAGES:* German and English. *PRACTICE AREAS:* Patent; Trademark; Copyright Law; Unfair Competition; Litigation; Legal Advice.

ASSOCIATE

JOCHEN BÜHLING, born Bochum, September 15, 1961; admitted, 1992. *Education:* University of Münster. *Member:* German Association for the Protection of Industrial Property and Copyright, AIPPI; German-American Jurists' Association. *LANGUAGES:* German, English and French. *PRACTICE AREAS:* Patent; Trademark; Copyright Law; Unfair Competition; Litigation; Legal Advice.

Languages: German, English, French and Italian

LANG & LANDWEHRMANN

Established in 1985

CECILIENALLEE 54
D-40474 DÜSSELDORF, GERMANY
Telephone: (0211) 43 90 2-0
Telefax: (0211) 43 90 2-69

General Practice, Corporate, Commercial, Mergers and Acquisitions, International Law, Product Liability, Insurance, Commercial Litigation and Arbitration.

MEMBERS OF FIRM

DR. HELMAR LANG, born Lörrach, Germany, 1935; admitted, 1965, Germany; 1989, Paris, France. *Education:* Universities of Freiburg/Breisgau, Paris, Bonn (J.D., 1959; Doctor of Laws, 1965). Author: "Der Einfluß der öffentlichen Hand auf gemischtwirtschaftlicheAktiengesellschaften," 1964; "La GmbH - Guide Pratique de la S.A.R.L. Allemande," 1974. *Member:* Union Internationale des Avocats (German Vice President); CCBE Company Law (Special Committee). *LANGUAGES:* German, English and French. *PRACTICE AREAS:* Corporate Law; Mergers and Acquisitions; Commercial Law; Products Liability Law.

DR. DETLEF RAHMANN, born Solingen, Germany, 1958; admitted, 1987, Germany; 1991, New York. *Education:* University of Cologne (J.D., 1981; Doctor of Laws, 1984); Cornell Law School (LL.M., 1982). Research Assistant, Institute for Foreign and International Private Law, Cologne. Author: "Deutsches und US-amerikanisches Recht der Gerichtsstands- und Schiedsvereinbarungen," 1984; "Investing in Eastern Germany," 18 IBL 507, 1990. *Member:* International Bar Association; Association Internationale des Jeunes Avocats; German Association of Industrial Property and Copyright Law; German Institution of Arbitration. *LANGUAGES:* German, English and French. *PRACTICE AREAS:* Corporate Law; Mergers and Acquisitions; Intellectual Property Law; Products Liability Law.

DR. OTTMAR PETER, born Bad Kreuznach, Germany, 1952; admitted, 1980, Germany. *Education:* Universities of Berlin, West (J.D., 1977; Doctor of Laws, 1986) London and Salzburg. Author: "Employees' Participation in and Financial Assistance to the Company," 1986. Lecturer, University of Berlin, West, 1980-1985. *Member:* German Bar Association. *LANGUAGES:* German and English. *PRACTICE AREAS:* Mergers and Acquisitions; Corporate Law; Taxation and Labor Law.

CARL-PETER FORSCHBACH, born Cologne, Germany, 1939; admitted, 1992, Germany. *Education:* University of Freiburg/Breisgau, Cologne and Bonn. With City of Cologne and Legislature, State of Northrhine-Westfalia, 1972-1990. Member, City Council, Krefeld, Germany, 1981. Legal Councel, Ministry for Protection of the Environment and Super-Regional Planning, State of Brandenburg, 1991. *LANGUAGES:* German, English and French. *PRACTICE AREAS:* Public Building Law; Practical Realization of Investment Projects.

OF COUNSEL

DR. FRIEDRICH G. LANDWEHRMANN, born Bad Pyrmont, Germany, 1945; admitted, 1974, Germany. *Education:* Universities of Freiburg/Breisgau, Münster (J.D., 1968; Doctor of Laws, 1970); Harvard Law School (LL.M., 1973). Faculty Assistant, Institute of International and Foreign Private and Commercial Law, University of Münster, 1971-1972. Staff Member, International Tax Program, Harvard Law School, 1972-1973. Author: " 'Zeit ist Geld'. Probleme des Schadenersatzes bei Freizeitbeeinträchtigung," 1970; "Legislative Development of International Corporate Taxation in Germany," 15 Harvard International Law Journal, 1974. *Member:* International Fiscal Association. *LANGUAGES:* German and English. *PRACTICE AREAS:* Mergers and Acquisitions; Investment Banking; Corporate Law and Taxation.

ASSOCIATES

DR. BERTHOLD KREMM, born Düsseldorf, Germany, 1963; admitted, 1993, Germany. *Education:* University of Mainz; University for Administrative Research in Speyer. Author: "Aims of State Planning as Basis for Individual Rights of Cities," 1993. *LANGUAGES:* German and English. *PRACTICE AREAS:* Public Building; Planning Law; Litigation; Public Law.

WEIF HAEGER, born Bochum, June 15, 1962; admitted, 1994, Germany. *Education:* University of Bochum; University of Bonn; University of Münster; University of Hagen (Micro Economics). Author, "The Basic
(This Listing Continued)

LANG & LANDWEHRMANN, Düsseldorf—Continued

Right for Supply with Broadcasting Services." Worked with German-American Chamber of Commerce, New York. *LANGUAGES:* German and English. *PRACTICE AREAS:* Corporate Law; Mediation Law.

LAUENROTH & PARTNERS

Rechtsanwälte

GNEISENAUSTRASSE 8
40477 DÜSSELDORF, GERMANY
Telephone: 49-211 495 010
Telefax: 49-211 498 2391

Berlin, Germany Office: Witzlebenplatz 4-5, 14057. Telephone: 49-30 321 2077. Fax: 49-30 325 6263.

Moscow, Russia Office: Okskaja Uliza 20, Block 2, Suite 13, 109117. Telephone and Fax: (International) 007-501 883 2499; (Local) 095 913 2499.

Paris, France Office: 60, Rue la Boetie, 75008. Telephone: 1-4289 1055. Fax: 1-4074 0758.

National and International Construction Law, Construction Contracts and Arbitration, Public Works, Town Planning, Environmental Law and Liability, Waste Management, Hazardous Materials, Insurance, Joint Ventures, Mergers and Acquisitions, East-West Trade, Company Contracts and Formation, EC Antitrust Law, Unfair Competition, Products Liability, Real Estate, Property Finance.

FIRM PROFILE: Lauenroth & Partners was established in 1959. The firm is engaged in German, French, Russian and Eastern European practice both as lawyers and arbitrators. It is a founding member of the ADVOC-network of independent lawyers in Europe with partners worldwide.

MEMBERS OF FIRM

DR. HANS-DIETER LAUENROTH, born Düsseldorf, Germany, 1927; admitted, 1959, Germany. *Education:* Universities of Köln, Bonn and München. Arbitrator, Wirtschaftsvereinigung Bauindustrie, Construction Industry Association, Nordrhein-Westfalen. *Member:* European International Arbitrators Board. *LANGUAGES:* German, English and French. *PRACTICE AREAS:* Construction Law; Corporate Law; International Finance; Company Takeovers; EC Antitrust Law; Mergers; Cartels; Commercial Arbitration; Investment in Eastern Europe.

DR. MICHAEL WOLFGANG MÜTZE, born Köln, Germany, 1952; admitted, 1981, Germany. *Education:* Universities of Strasbourg, München and Köln. *LANGUAGES:* German, English and French. *PRACTICE AREAS:* Construction Law; Corporate Law; Company Takeovers; International Arbitration; Antitrust Law; Design Rights; Intellectual Property; Telecommunications; Commercial Arbitration; International Commercial Contracts.

PAUL SCHULTE-BORBERG, born Dortmund, Germany, 1935; admitted, 1975, Germany. *Education:* Universities of Tübingen, Bonn and Köln. Assistant, Treuarbeit, auditing company, 1967-1969. *LANGUAGES:* German and English. *PRACTICE AREAS:* Construction Law; Construction Insurance; Corporate Law; Commercial Finance; Commercial Litigation; Company Takeovers; Management Labor and Employment; Commercial Leasing; Medical Malpractice; Property Development.

DR. WOLFRAM KESSELER, born Düsseldorf, Germany, 1930; admitted, 1976, Germany. *Education:* Universities of Köln and Freiburg/Breisgau. Civil Servant; Deputy Clerk; City Treasurer. *LANGUAGES:* German and English. *PRACTICE AREAS:* Public Finance; Taxation; Construction Contracts; Corporate Law; Commercial Finance; Company Takeovers; Commercial Leases; Medical Malpractice; Banking Litigation.

WERNER MAXEM, born Eiweiler, Germany, 1958; admitted, 1987, Germany. *Education:* University of Saarbrücken; University of Paris (Diplome Supérieur de l'Université. *LANGUAGES:* French, German and English. *PRACTICE AREAS:* Construction Law; Construction Contracts; Corporate Law; International Law; Company Takeovers; Labor Relations; Management Labor and Employment; International Commercial Litigation; Property Development; Unfair Competition.

EDITH RAUTENBACH, born Düsseldorf, Germany, 1956; admitted, 1990, Germany. *Education:* Fachhochschule für offentiliche Verwaltung Nordrhein-Westfalen in Gelsenkirchen (Diplom-Verwaltungswirt, 1978). Administration, Düsseldorf City, 1975-1980. *LANGUAGES:* German and English. *PRACTICE AREAS:* Construction Law; Construction Contracts;

(This Listing Continued)

Construction Insurance; Corporate Law; Commercial Finance; Company Takeovers; Management Labor and Employment; Commercial Leases; Medical Malpractice; Property Development.

DR. RALF LEINEMANN, born Gütersloh, Germany, 1962; admitted, 1992, Germany. *Education:* Universities of Würzburg, Köln; State University of New York (B.A., 1985). *LANGUAGES:* German and English. *PRACTICE AREAS:* International Construction Law; International Arbitration; Environmental Law; Waste Management; Mergers and Acquisitions; Antitrust Law; Urban Planning; Insurance Coverage; Communications and Media; Intellectual Property Protection.

CLAUS-PETER CRAMER, born Liegnitz, Germany, 1943; admitted, 1975, Germany. *Education:* Universities of Tübingen, München and Köln. *LANGUAGES:* German and English. *PRACTICE AREAS:* Civil Appeals; Medical Malpractice; Insurance; Construction Contracts; Products Liability; Banking; Litigation; Corporate Law; Commercial Litigation; Traffic Laws.

MENOLD HERRLINGER REINKING & PARTNER

AM WEHRHAHN 50
D-40211 DÜSSELDORF, GERMANY
Telephone: 0049/211/93 52 300
Telefax: 0049/211/93 52 683

Berlin Office: Fraunhofer Straße 33-36, D-10587, Berlin. Telephone: (0049 30) 34 78 68 11. Telefax: (0049 30) 34 78 68 35.

Dresden Office: Uhlandstraße 39, 01069 Dresden. Telephone: (0049 351) 478 71 0. Telefax: (0049 351) 478 71-15.

Stuttgart Office: Mittlerer Pfad 15, 70499 Stuttgart. Telephone: (0049 711) 13 86 800. Telefax: (0049 711) 13 86 808.

Corporate, Commercial, Tax and Business Law Practice, including Mergers and Acquisitions, Antitrust and Unfair Competition Law, Intellectual and Industrial Property Law, Reorganization and Bankruptcy, Labor Law and Redundancy Plans (Sozialpläne), Private Wealth Planning, Trusts, Foundations and Estate Law, Environmental, Waste and Administrative Law, The Laws of the East European Countries, Business Law for Japanese Clients, Restitution of Property in the East German Federal States (Dresden), General Civil Law and Civil Litigation, European Community Law.

FIRM PROFILE: The firm springs from a merger of the law firms Menold Herrlinger Maulbetsch Schick & Oltmanns (Stuttgart), Bezler & Partner (Stuttgart), Reith & Battke (Dresden) and Reinking, Frings & Drude (Düsseldorf).

MEMBERS OF FIRM

DR. ARNO FRINGS, born Bielefeld, Germany, 1958; admitted, 1986, Germany. *Education:* Universities of Bielefeld, Munich, Münster and Berlin, Germany (State Exams, 1983, 1986; Doctor of Law, 1989). Author: "Amtshaftung für fehlerhafte Bebauungspläne" (Public Liability for Defective Development Plans). *LANGUAGES:* German and English. *PRACTICE AREAS:* Labor; Commercial Law; Corporate Law; Administrative Law.

DR. JOACHIM DRUDE, born Düsseldorf, Germany, 1959; admitted, 1988, Germany. *Education:* University of Munich, Germany; University of Naples, Italy (State Exams, 1985, 1988; Doctor of Law, 1990). Author: "Die Zulässigkeit und Durchsetzbarkeit selektiver Vertriebsbindungssysteme im italienischen Zivil- und Wettbewerbsrecht" (Legal Aspects of Commercial Distribution in Italy). *Member:* Association of German and Italian Lawyers. *LANGUAGES:* German, English, Italian and French. *PRACTICE AREAS:* Commercial Law; Corporate/Company Law; Corporate Finance; Mergers and Acquisitions.

DONNA SHOOK-WIERCIMOK, born Holyoke, Massachusetts, 1954; admitted, 1981, Massachusetts. *Education:* Western New England College School of Law, Massachusetts; University of Exeter, United Kingdom; University of Strasbourg, France. *Member:* American Bar Association; Massachusetts Bar Association; IBA; AIJA. *LANGUAGES:* English, German and French. *PRACTICE AREAS:* German/American Commercial and Corporate Law.

MASAYO JINNO, born Kanazawa, Japan, 1969. *Education:* Keio University, Tokyo (LL.B., 1991); Columbia University, New York; University of Tübingen (LL.M., 1992); University of Cologne, Germany. *LAN-*

(This Listing Continued)

GUAGES: Japanese, German and English. *PRACTICE AREAS:* Japanese/German Commercial and Corporate Law.

DR. THOMAS HAUSS, born Düsseldorf, Germany, 1965; admitted, 1994, Germany. *Education:* Universities of Cologne and Bonn, Germany (State Exams, 1990, 1993; Doctor of Law, 1993). Research Assistant, Institute for Public Welfare Law, University of Cologne, Institute for Civil, Labor and Economic Law and Professional Responsibility, University of Cologne. Author: "Grenzüberschreitende Betriebsverfassung in Europa," (Cross-border Employees' Representation in Europe). *LANGUAGES:* German and English. *PRACTICE AREAS:* Environmental Law; Administrative Law; Labor and Commercial Law.

PICOZZI & UTZEL

Established in 1986

DÜSSELDORFER STR. 101
D-40545 DÜSSELDORF, GERMANY
Telephone: (0211) 572173
Telefax: (0211) 576025

Commercial, Corporations, Trademarks, Copyright, Computer Law, Leasing, Unfair Competition, Labor, Tax, Real Estate, Family Law.

FIRM PROFILE: *Picozzi & Utzel is a member of AdvoSelect EEIG, a network of law firms pooling their resources in special fields and crossborder cases, specializing in business law for middle sized companies. AdvoSelect is represented in 51 cities throughout Europe.*

DR. MARCO PICOZZI, born Wuppertal, 1952; admitted, 1979, Düsseldorf. *Member:* German Bar Association; Working-Committee "EDP and Law" e.V., Cologne. *LANGUAGES:* German, English and French. *PRACTICE AREAS:* Leasing; Tax; Trademark; Unfair Competition.

MECHTILD UTZEL, born Borken, 1961; admitted, 1990, Düsseldorf. *Member:* German Bar Association. *LANGUAGES:* German and English. *PRACTICE AREAS:* Labor; Family; Real Estate.

FRANZ FRENGER, born Neuss, 1964; admitted, 1995, Düsseldorf. *LANGUAGES:* German and English. *PRACTICE AREAS:* Copyright; Computer; Commercial; Corporations.

POHLE, PESCHEL & BURGER

Established in 1928

FREILIGRATHSTRASSE 34
D-40479 DÜSSELDORF, GERMANY
Telephone: (0211) 49 91 21
Telefax: (0211) 49 91 30

Dresden, Germany Office: Eisenstuckstraße 46, D-1069. Telephone: 0351/47 27 664. Telefax: 0351/47 27 507.

General Practice. Commercial, Corporate, Banking, Descent and Distribution, Tax, Insurance, Liability, Real Estate, Construction, Labour Law, Arbitration.

MEMBERS OF FIRM

ERIK POHLE, born Düsseldorf, Germany, May 30, 1932; admitted, 1960. *Education:* Universities of Tübingen and Cologne. Special Tax Counsel. Associate Arnold & Porter, Washington, D.C., 1960-1961. *LANGUAGES:* German, English and French. *PRACTICE AREAS:* Corporate; Commercial; Tax Law; Arbitration.

DR. KLAUS PESCHEL, born Dresden, Germany, December 2, 1929; admitted, 1958. *Education:* University of Cologne (Dr.jur.). *LANGUAGES:* German and English. *PRACTICE AREAS:* Litigation; Liability; Insurance.

DR. HERBERT BURGER, born Düsseldorf, Germany, August 8, 1931; admitted, 1960. *Education:* Universities of Cologne, Bonn, F.U. Berlin and Syracuse, New York. (Special Tax Counsel). *LANGUAGES:* German, English and French. *PRACTICE AREAS:* Civil Law; Tax Law; Administrative Law.

HORST-DIETER KOMANEK, born Duisburg, Germany, December 4, 1950; admitted, 1982. *Education:* University of Bonn. *LANGUAGES:* German, English and Italian. *PRACTICE AREAS:* Banking; Labour Law.

DR. HANS HERBERT MOEHREN, born Viersen, Germany, August 15, 1954; admitted, 1987. *Education:* University of Bonn. Assistant to the President, German Steel Federation, Düsseldorf, 1989-1990. *LAN-*

(This Listing Continued)

GUAGES: German and English. *PRACTICE AREAS:* Construction; Commercial; Descent and Distribution.

ARMIN ALEXANDER DICK, born Stuttgart, Germany, June 25, 1959; admitted, 1991. *Education:* Universities of Tübingen and Kiel. *LANGUAGES:* German and English. *PRACTICE AREAS:* Corporate; Insurance; Insolvency.

PÜNDER, VOLHARD, WEBER & AXSTER

CECILIENALLEE 6
40474 DÜSSELDORF, GERMANY
Telephone: (49)(211) 43 55-0
Fax: (49)(211) 43 55-600

Frankfurt/Main, Germany Office: Mainzer Landstrasse 46, 60325 Frankfurt/Main. Telephone: (49)(69) 71 99-01. Fax: (49)(69) 71 99-4000. Telex: 414 827.

Berlin, Germany Office: Katharina-Heinroth-Ufer, 10787 Berlin. Telephone: (49)(30) 2546 5800. Fax: (49)(30) 2546-5900.

Leipzig, Germany Office: Burgplatz 7, 04109 Leipzig. Telephone: (49)(341) 21 49-0. Fax: (49)(341) 21 49-600.

Beijing, People's Republic of China Office: Suite C 603, Beijing Lufthansa Center, 50 Liangmaqiao Road, Beijing 100 016. Telephone: (86)(1) 465 15 68; (86)(1) 465 18 08; (86)(1) 465 13 45. Fax: (86)(1) 467 12 56.

Brussels, Belgium Office: Rue d'Arlon 92, 1040 Bruxelles. Telephone: (32)(2) 230 90 11. Fax: (32)(2) 231 19 55.

Budapest, Hungary Office: Endrödy Sandor utca 48, 1026 Budapest. Telephone: (36) 60 33 26 18 international; (6) 60 33 26 18 national. Fax: (36) 60 33 26 17 international; (6) 60 33 26 17 national.

Moscow, Russia Office: ul. Wolchonka, 18/2, 121 019 Moskwa. Telephone: (7)(095) 202 64 90; (7)(095) 202 65 12; (7)(543) 708 00 900 from Germany; (49)(7545) 893 42 from other countries. Fax: (7)(095) 202 65 14; (7)(543) 708 00 990 from Germany; (49)(7545) 893 43 from other countries.

New York, New York Office: 152 West 57th Street, Carnegie Hall Tower, New York, N.Y. 10019. Telephone: (1)(212) 582 28 28. Fax: (1)(212) 582 24 24.

Warsaw, Poland Office: ul. Jasna 1, 00-013 Warszawa. Telephone: (48) 39 12 21 41. Fax: (48)(22) 27 15 29.

Administrative Law; Antitrust Law; Arbitration; Auditing and Valuations; Banking, Securities and Finance; Bankruptcy; Building Law; Chinese Law; Commercial Crime; Computer Law; Construction Law; Corporate Law; EU Law; Energy Law; Environmental Law; Franchising; Industrial Property Law; Insolvency; Intellectual Property Law; International and German Business Law; Labor and Employment Law; Litigation; Media Law; Mergers and Acquisitions; Pharmaceutical Law; Privatizations; Product Law; Public Law; Real Estate; Reorganizations; Russian Law; Tax Law; Telecommunications; Unfair Trade Law.

FIRM PROFILE: *Member of PÜNDER GROUP*

Members:

- *BURUMA MARIS, The Hague, Rotterdam*

- *CERHA, HEMPEL & SPIEGELFELD, Wien*

- *COPPENS, VAN OMMESLAGHE, HORSMANS & FAURES, Bruxelles*

- *DE PARDIUE-LACOURTE G.I.E., Paris*

- *PÜNDER, VOLHARD, WEBER & AXSTER, Frankfurt/Main, Düsseldorf, Berlin, Leipzig*

- *STOFFEL & PARTNER, Zürich, Genève.*

Joint Offices of PÜNDER GROUP:

Beijing - Bruxelles - Budapest - Moskwa - New York - Warszawa

MEMBERS OF FIRM

DR. PAUL SPICKERNAGEL, born Düsseldorf, Germany, August 6, 1907; admitted, 1935, Düsseldorf. *Education:* Universities of Tübingen and Cologne (Dr.jur.). Author: "Die gefährliche Körperverletzung als gesetzgeberisches Problem.". *LANGUAGES:* German and French. *PRACTICE AREAS:* Arbitration Law; Pharmaceutical Law.

DR. ALBRECHT PÜNDER, born Berlin, Germany, March 24, 1924; admitted, 1949, Frankfurt; 1952, Notary. *Education:* Universities of Berlin and Erlangen (Doctor juris utriusque, 1947). Author: "Die Bedeutung der Übergabe bei der vertraglichen Fahrnisübereignung in den Rechten der modernen Welt," 1947. *Member:* German Bar Association. *LANGUAGES:* German and English. *PRACTICE AREAS:* Arbitration Law.

(This Listing Continued)

PÜNDER, VOLHARD, WEBER & AXSTER,
Düsseldorf—Continued

DR. JOSEF HOUBEN, born Düsseldorf, Germany, October 3, 1922; admitted, 1959, Düsseldorf. *Education:* Universities of Bonn, Marburg and Cologne (Dr. jur.). Author: "Der Aufsichtsrat der kapitalistischen Kommanditgesellschaft.". *LANGUAGES:* German, English and Spanish. *PRACTICE AREAS:* Medical Malpractice Law; Commercial Law; Litigation.

OLIVER AXSTER, born Berlin, Germany, July 27, 1931; admitted, 1961, Düsseldorf. *Education:* University of Texas, University of Chicago (J.D.); Universities of Bonn and Cologne. Author: Volume on Licensing Agreements of the "Gemeinschaftskommentar," (Text Book on German and EC Antitrust Laws). *Member:* Association for Antitrust Law Studies (Board Member); German and International Association for the Protection of Industrial Property and Copyright (Member, Board of German Association); International Bar Association; American Chamber of Commerce in Germany; L.E.S. Licensing Executive Society International (International President). *LANGUAGES:* German and English. *PRACTICE AREAS:* Antitrust Law; EU Law; Industrial Property Law.

WERNER METZNER, born Coburg, Germany, January 24, 1928; admitted, 1961, Düsseldorf. *Education:* University of Marburg. *Member:* German Bar Association. *LANGUAGES:* German and English. *PRACTICE AREAS:* Public Planning Law; Commercial Leases; Litigation.

HANSGEORG GREUNER, born Leipzig, Germany, June 28, 1939; admitted, 1967, Düsseldorf. *Education:* Universities of Geneva, Munich and Heidelberg. Co-author: "Münchener Vertragshandbuch," (Section on Trademark Agreements). *Member:* German and International Association for the Protection of Industrial Property and Copyright; Association for Antitrust Law Studies. *LANGUAGES:* German, English and French. *PRACTICE AREAS:* Business Law; Corporate Law; Industrial Property Law.

DR. F. GEORG MILLER, born Berlin, Germany, November 27, 1936; admitted, 1968, Düsseldorf. *Education:* Universities of Freiburg, Geneva, Münster, Berlin, Luxemburg (Diplome en Droit Comparé). Author: "Wechsel and Grundforderung," 1969. Co-Author: "The German Turnover Tax Law," 1980; "GmbH-Gesetz," (Commentary on GmbH-Law), 1987. *Member:* German and International Bar Association. *LANGUAGES:* German, English, French and Italian. *PRACTICE AREAS:* International and German Corporate and Business Law; Mergers and Acquisitions.

DR. THOMAS REIMANN, born Breslau, Germany, November 27, 1943; admitted, 1973, Düsseldorf. *Education:* Universities of Munich and Bonn (Dr. jur.). Co-author: "Münchener Vertragshandbuch," (Section on Trademark Agreements and on Franchising Agreements); "Richtiges Verhalten bei Kartellamtsermittlungen." Author: "Zur Lehre vom rechtsordnungslosen Vertrag," 1970. *Member:* International Bar Association; International Trademark Association; German and International Association for the Protection of Industrial Property and Copyright; Association for Antitrust Law Studies; L.E.S. Germany; German and International Association for the Protection of Industrial Property and Copyright, Chairman of Patent and Utility Patent Law Committee. *LANGUAGES:* German and English. *PRACTICE AREAS:* Industrial Property Law; Unfair Competition; Franchising Law; Litigation.

DR. RAINER MASCHMEIER, born Gniesno, Poland, January 13, 1944; admitted, 1975, Düsseldorf. *Education:* Universities of Berlin, Geneva, Würzburg, Caen (France) and Münster (Dr. jur.). Lecturer, Law School of Warwick University, Coventry, U.K., 1972-1973. Author: "Die Einantwortung der Verlassenschaft nach österreichischem Recht durch deutsche Nachlaßgerichte," 1972. *Member:* Board of Düsseldorf Bar and Düsseldorf Lawyers' Association; German-Italian Association of Commerce. (Also at Warsaw, Poland Office). *LANGUAGES:* German, French and English. *PRACTICE AREAS:* International and German Business Law; Corporate Law; Construction Law; Real Estate; Privatizations.

THOMAS WEBER, born Duisburg, Germany, July 26, 1950; admitted, 1977, Düsseldorf. *Education:* Universities of Freiburg, Hamburg and Bonn. *Member:* International Bar Association; German Association for the Protection of Industrial Property and Copyright; Association for Antitrust Law Studies; European Telecommunication Forum. *LANGUAGES:* German and English. *PRACTICE AREAS:* Unfair Competition Law; Antitrust Law; Pharmaceutical Law; Media Law; Telecommunications; Litigation.

DR. WOLFGANG FLEHINGHAUS, born Hanover, Germany, March 20, 1937; admitted, 1966, Düsseldorf. *Education:* Universities of Cologne,

(This Listing Continued)

Paris, Munich (Dr. jur.). Author: "Die Subventionsverwaltung". *Member:* German Bar Association; Legal Committee of Düsseldorf Chamber of Commerce; American Chamber of Commerce in Germany. *LANGUAGES:* German and English. *PRACTICE AREAS:* Construction and Building Law; Real Estate; Corporate Law.

HOLGER F. WISSEL, born Oldenburg, Germany, May 6, 1950; admitted, 1979, Düsseldorf. *Education:* University of Münster. Assistant to the Law Faculty of the University of Münster, 1976-1978. Co-Author: Volume on Merger Control of the "Gemeinschaftskommentar;" "Vertikale Verträge : US-Guidelines 1985 und EG-Kartellrecht," 1986; "Environmental Liabilities and Regulation in Europe," 1993. Counsel to the Central Organization of the Advertising Industry, 1978-1981. Counsel to the Antitrust Department of the Federation of German Industry, 1981-1988. *Member:* German Association for the Protection of Industrial Property and Copyright; Association for Antitrust Law Studies; Federal Association of Pharmaceutical Manufacturers. *LANGUAGES:* German and English. *PRACTICE AREAS:* Antitrust Law; EU Law; Pharmaceutical Law; Environmental Law.

DR. ROLF GIEBELER, born Bonn, Germany, July 5, 1957; admitted, 1988, Frankfurt/Main; 1990, Düsseldorf. *Education:* University of Bonn (Dr. jur., 1990); University of Pittsburgh; Harvard University (M.P.A., 1987). Author: "Verfahren und Maßstäbe bei der Setzung von Umweltstandards in den USA," 1990. *Member:* German Bar Association; German-American Lawyers' Association; International and Environmental Law Association. *LANGUAGES:* German, English and French. *PRACTICE AREAS:* International Business Law; Corporate Law; Mergers and Acquisitions; Privatizations; Environmental Law.

DR. JOACHIM FELDGES, born Mönchengladbach, Germany, September 8, 1958; admitted, 1987, Düsseldorf. *Education:* Universities of Würzburg and Geneva (diplôme d'études supérieures en droit, docteur en droit). Assistant to the Law Faculty of the University of Geneva, 1982-1984. Author: "Konsumentenschutz durch private Normen," 1987. *Member:* German Association for the Protection of Industrial Property and Copyright; L.E.S. Germany; German and International Association for the Protection of Industrial Property and Copyright, Registered Design Law Committee. *LANGUAGES:* German, French, English and Italian. *PRACTICE AREAS:* Industrial Property Law; Litigation.

ALFRED HERDA, born Hürth, Germany, January 5, 1959; admitted, 1987, Düsseldorf. *Education:* University of Cologne. *Member:* Working Party for International Legal Relationships of German Bar Association; German-American Lawyers' Association; German Institute for Arbitration. *LANGUAGES:* German, English and French. *PRACTICE AREAS:* Business Law; Corporate Law; Product Liability Law.

DR. DAMIAN HECKER, born Neuss, Germany, September 21, 1958; admitted, 1990, Düsseldorf. *Education:* Universities of Freiburg, Washington, D.C., Berlin and Speyer (Dr. jur.). Author: "Eigentum als Sachherrschaft," 1990. Assistant at the Institute for Public Law of the University of Freiburg, 1984-1987. *LANGUAGES:* German, English and French. *PRACTICE AREAS:* Business Law; Corporate Law; Real Estate; Litigation.

ASSOCIATES

MARTIN WISSMANN, born Hamburg, Germany, April 20, 1961; admitted, 1991, Düsseldorf. *Education:* Universities of Frankfurt/Main and Georgetown, Washington, D.C. (LL.M., 1992). *LANGUAGES:* German and English. *PRACTICE AREAS:* Industrial Property Law; Telecommunications; Antitrust Law; EU Law; Business Law.

DR. KERSTIN KOPP, born Nürnberg, Germany, August 19, 1963; admitted, 1991, Düsseldorf. *Education:* University of Bonn. Author: "Die vollstreckbare Urkunde Aspekte der prozessualen Unterwerfungserklärung einerseits und des materiellen Anspruchs andererseits.". *LANGUAGES:* German, Italian, English and French. *PRACTICE AREAS:* International Business Law; Corporate Law; Mergers and Acquisitions.

DR. JOACHIM SCHÜTZE, born Duisburg, Germany, August 18, 1960; admitted, 1992, Düsseldorf. *Education:* Universities of Tübingen and Münster. Author: "Der Europäsche Stromverbund im Lichte des EG-Rechts," 1992. Co-Author: "Environmental Liabilities and Regulation in Europe," 1993. Assistant at the Institutes for Labor Law and Commercial Law and for International Commercial Law at the University of Münster, 1987-1991. *LANGUAGES:* German and English. *PRACTICE AREAS:* EU Law; Antitrust Law; Business Law; Environmental Law.

ULRICH LEMBECK, born Wuppertal, Germany, March 12, 1961; admitted, 1990, Düsseldorf. *Education:* Universities of Würzburg and Bonn.

(This Listing Continued)

LANGUAGES: German and English. **PRACTICE AREAS:** Corporate Law; International Tax Law; Real Estate.

DR. THORSTEN VORMANN, born Essen, Germany, September 18, 1961; admitted, 1991, Düsseldorf. *Education:* University of Frankfurt-/Main and McGill University, Montreal (LL.M., 1991). Author: "Kulturelle Souveränität und Fernsehen - Rechtsvergleich der Maßnahmen zur Sicherung der kulturellen Identität in Kanada und den Europäischen Gemeinschaften, unter besonderer Berücksichtigung der Quotenregelungen im Fernsehen," 1993. **LANGUAGES:** German, English and French. **PRACTICE AREAS:** Industrial Property Law; Media Law; EU Law; Business Law; Litigation.

MARTIN SCHULTE, born Duisburg, Germany, July 29, 1962; admitted, 1992, Düsseldorf; 1992, New York. *Education:* Universities of Cologne and Lausanne/Switzerland; University of California, Berkeley (LL.M., 1990). Assistant at the Institute for International and Foreign Private Law of the University of Cologne, 1988-1989. *Member:* German, American, International and New York State Bar Associations; German-American Lawyers' Association. **LANGUAGES:** German, English, French and Spanish. **PRACTICE AREAS:** International and German Commercial and Corporate Law; Contracts; Mergers and Acquisitions.

DR. THOMAS STOHLMEIER, born Essen, Germany, September 1, 1960; admitted, 1991, Düsseldorf. *Education:* University of Hamburg (Dr. jur., 1989); Tulane University, School of Law, New Orleans (LL.M., 1991). Author: "Die inhaltliche und zeitliche Reichweite der Sperrwirkung nach Art. 72 Abs. 1 GG," 1989. *Member:* German Bar Association; International Bar Association; German-American Lawyers' Association. **LANGUAGES:** German, English and Swedish. **PRACTICE AREAS:** International Business Law; Corporate Law; Mergers and Acquisitions.

DR. PETER DASZKOWSKI, born Gdansk, Poland, June 29, 1961; admitted, 1993, Düsseldorf. *Education:* Free University of Berlin (1986); University of Warsaw (Master of Law, 1988); University of Trier (Master of Law, 1989; Dr. jur., 1993). Konrad Adenauer Scholar, 1991-1993. Author: "Der internationale Schadenversicherungsvertrag im EG-Binnenmarkt." **LANGUAGES:** German, Polish, English and Russian. **PRACTICE AREAS:** Intellectual Property Law; Commercial Law; Real Estate.

REINHARD F. SCHEER-HENNINGS, born New York, New York, June 15, 1961; admitted, 1992, New York; 1993, Frankfurt/Main; 1994, Düsseldorf. *Education:* University of Munich; New York University School of Law (M.C.J., 1990). *Member:* American Bar Association; New York State Bar Association. **LANGUAGES:** German and English. **PRACTICE AREAS:** Real Estate; Litigation.

JAN F. WREDE, born Düsseldorf, Germany, December 30, 1962; admitted, 1990, New York; 1992, California; 1994, Düsseldorf. *Education:* Universities of Mannheim and Kiel; Indiana University School of Law, Bloomington; University of California School of Law, Los Angeles (J.D., 1990). Order of the Coif. *Member:* German Bar Association; German-American Lawyers' Association; State Bar of California. **LANGUAGES:** German and English. **PRACTICE AREAS:** International and German Business and Corporate Law; Mergers and Acquisitions; International Financing Transactions; Tax Law.

THOMAS WEIMANN, born Muelheim, Germany, March 10, 1964; admitted, 1994, Düsseldorf. *Education:* Universities of Münster, Osnabrück and Bonn. **LANGUAGES:** German and English. **PRACTICE AREAS:** Litigation; Business Law; Commercial and Private Lease Law; Bankruptcy Law.

DR. PETRA HÖFNER, born Frankfurt/Main, Germany, June 29, 1962; admitted, 1994, Düsseldorf. *Education:* University of Osnabrück. *Member:* German-American Lawyers' Association. **LANGUAGES:** German and English. **PRACTICE AREAS:** EU Law; Antitrust Law; Business Law; Environmental Law.

ANDREA HEGGEN, born Viersen, Germany, September 22, 1962; admitted, 1994, Düsseldorf. *Education:* Universities of Bonn and Cologne. **LANGUAGES:** German and English. **PRACTICE AREAS:** Industrial Property Law; Litigation.

DR. PETER DIENERS, born Monschau, Germany, May 24, 1962; admitted, 1992, Frankfurt/Main; 1994, Düsseldorf. *Education:* Universities of Saarbrücken, Bonn and Frankfurt/Main. Assistant of the Institutes for Public Law at the Universities of Bonn and Frankfurt/Main. Author: "Das Duell und die Sonderrolle des Militärs," 1992. *Member:* German Bar Association. **LANGUAGES:** German and English. **PRACTICE AREAS:** Business Law; Competition Law; Labor and Employment Law; Environmental Law.

(This Listing Continued)

LUDGER SPINDELDREIER, born Hirschberg/Westfalen, Germany, August 22, 1958. *Education:* University of Münster; 1986, Tax Advisor. **LANGUAGES:** German, English and French. **PRACTICE AREAS:** National and International Tax Law.

HORST LINDEN, born Düsseldorf, Germany, July 6, 1963. *Education:* FH Nordkirchen. **LANGUAGES:** German and English. **PRACTICE AREAS:** German Tax Law.

TAX ADVISORS

HEINZ-GÜNTER GONDERT, born Trier, Germany, April 30, 1949; 1978, Tax Advisor; admitted, 1983, Mainz; 1992, Frankfurt. *Education:* Universities of Freiburg/Breisgau and Bonn. Revenue service, 1975-1977. Member of the board of a leasing company, 1983-1986. Senior executive in a banking group, 1986-1992. *Member:* German Bar Association; German Tax Law Association. **LANGUAGES:** German and English. **PRACTICE AREAS:** Corporate Law; Banking and Financial Instruments; Tax Law and Auditing; Reorganizations.

WOLFGANG OHO, born Rüdesheim/Rhein, Germany, April 13, 1951; 1980, Tax Advisor. *Education:* University of Giessen (Master of Business Administration, 1974). *Member:* Frankfurter Finanzforum e.V. **LANGUAGES:** German, English and French. **PRACTICE AREAS:** International and German Tax Law; Reorganizations; Tax Structuring; Leasing.

(For complete biographical data on personnel at Frankfurt/Main, Berlin and Leipzig, Germany, Brussels, Belgium, Moscow, Russia, Warsaw, Poland, New York, New York and Beijing, People's Republic of China, see Professional Biographies at those locations)

ROTTHEGE WASSERMANN & PARTNER

WASSERSTRAßE 7
D-40213 DÜSSELDORF, GERMANY
Telephone: 49-211-867900
Fax: 49-211-132785

Essen, Germany Office: Heinrich-Held-Straße 16, 45133 Essen. Telephone: (49) (201) 842190. Fax: (49) (201) 8421922.

Berlin, Germany Office: Internationales Handelszentrum, Friedrichstraße 95, 10117 Berlin. Telephone: (49) (30) 26432749. Fax: (49) (30) 26432343.

Corporate, Mergers and Acquisitions, Tax, Real Estate, Construction/-Building, Banking, Commercial, Labor and Litigation.

FIRM PROFILE: *Rotthege Wassermann & Partner is counted among Germany's young and rapidly growing law firms engaged in international practice with a reputation for offering a full range of quality legal services. The combination of legal, accounting and tax services offered provides German and international clients with specialized advice in all areas of business law.*

MEMBERS OF FIRM

DR. GEORG ROTTHEGE, born Münster, Germany, June 22, 1951; admitted, 1978, Germany; Certified Tax Counsel, 1981. *Education:* University of Münster (Referendar, 1975; Assessor, 1978; Doctor of Law, 1981). Author: "Cartels and Co-operative Societies in Historical Perspective," Tübingen, 1982; "Recourse to German Guarantors in Case of Foreign Exchange Restrictions in the Country of the Debtor," 1983; "The Liability of Tax Advisors in Case of Capital Investment Recommendations," 1989. Research and Teaching Assistant, University of Münster, 1978-1980. Legal Department, Trinkaus & Burkhardt, Midland Bank Group, London, 1980-1982. *Member:* International Bar Association; Düsseldorf Bar Association; International Fiscal Association; DIS Deutsche Institution für Schiedsgerichtsbarkeit e.V.; Federal Association of Young Entrepreneurs (BJU) (Chairman, 1990-1992). **LANGUAGES:** German, English and French. **PRACTICE AREAS:** Corporate Law; Insolvency; Mergers and Acquisitions; Real Estate; Banking.

MICHAEL SPÖNEMANN, born Aachen, Germany, March 16, 1953; admitted, 1980, Germany. *Education:* Universities of Saarbrücken and Freiburg (Referendar, 1976; Assessor, 1980). With Balcke-Dürr AG, 1982-1983. **LANGUAGES:** German, English and French. **PRACTICE AREAS:** Litigation; Corporate; Commercial; Labor.

DR. JÖRG ZERHUSEN, born Düsseldorf, Germany July 26, 1960; admitted, 1990, Germany. *Education:* Universities of Osnabrück/Germany, Lausanne/Switzerland and Bonn/Germany (Referendar, 1987; Assessor, 1990; Doctor of Law, 1993). Author: "Reserves for Environmental Risks in the Tax Balance Sheet," 1993. **LANGUAGES:** German and English. **PRACTICE AREAS:** Building; Corporate; Tax; Construction.

(This Listing Continued)

ROTTHEGE WASSERMANN & PARTNER,
Düsseldorf—Continued

DR. FRIEDRICH KÖSTERS, born Rüthen, Germany, January 31, 1962; admitted, 1992, Germany. *Education:* Universities of Münster, Germany, Geneva, Switzerland, Paris-Sorbonne, France; London School of Economics and Political Science, Great Britain (Referendar, 1989; Assessor, 1992; Doctor of Law, 1991; Diplôme Supérieur de Droit Comparé, 1985). Author, "The Application of Foreign Public Law (lois de police) under French Private International Law," 1991. *Member:* Düsseldorf Bar Association; AIJA Association Internationale des Jeunes Avocats. *LANGUAGES:* German, English and French. *PRACTICE AREAS:* Banking; Corporate; Mergers and Acquisitions; Construction.

ASSOCIATES

THOMAS NONN, born Duisburg, Germany, March 3, 1962; admitted, 1992, Germany. *Education:* Universities of Münster, Germany and Cologne (Referendar, 1988; Assessor, 1991; Dr. of Law, 1995). Author: "Obligations of Corporate Shareholders to Consent," 1995. Research Assistant, University of Cologne, 1988-1989. *LANGUAGES:* German and English. *PRACTICE AREAS:* Commercial and Corporate Law; Trusts and Estates; Wills; Foundations and Endowments; Mergers and Acquisitions; Tax.

DR. SEBASTIAN BIEDENKOPF, born Wiesbaden, Germany, April 21, 1964; admitted, 1994, Germany. *Education:* University of Freiburg, Germany (Referendar, 1991; Assessor, 1994; Doctor of Law, 1994). Author: "Social Redundancy Plans in the Neue Bundesländer," Berlin, 1994. With Treuhandanstalt, Berlin, 1991-1992 (Privatization of Public Utilities). *LANGUAGES:* German and English. *PRACTICE AREAS:* Corporate; Labor; Energy; Insolvency.

BERND HARTMANN, born Wuppertal, Germany, June 9, 1958; admitted, 1994, Germany. *Education:* University of Freiburg, Germany (Referendar, 1988; Assessor, 1991). With C & L Treuhand-Vereinigung Deutsche Revision, Banking Team, 1991-1992; Department of Internal Revision of Treuhandanstalt, Berlin, 1992-1994. *LANGUAGES:* German and English. *PRACTICE AREAS:* Commercial; Environmental; Construction; Tax.

OF COUNSEL

BARBARA WARD-BÜHLING, born Plainfield, New Jersey, July 9, 1959; admitted, 1987, Massachusetts; 1988, New Jersey (Not admitted in Germany). *Education:* Mount Holyoke College (A.B., 1981); Williams College; Suffolk University Law School (J.D., cum laude, 1987. *LANGUAGES:* English and German.

JOANNA ZMUDA, born Krasnik, Poland, May 8, 1964; admitted, 1993, Poland (Not admitted in Germany). *Education:* Faculty of Law and Administration in Maria Curie-Sklodowska University of Lublin (Master of Law, 1987). *Member:* Polish Bar Association; German-Polish Law Society. *LANGUAGES:* Polish, German, Russian and English. *PRACTICE AREAS:* Business and Commercial Law; Joint Ventures; Foreign Investments Law.

TAX ADVISORS

KARLHEINZ SCHULTE, born Essen, Germany, February 4, 1925; admitted, 1962, Germany, Tax Advisor. *Education:* University of Cologne (Diploma in Business Administration, 1960). *Member:* Association of Tax Advisors.

DR. BERND WASSERMANN, born Essen, Germany, September 12, 1950; admitted, 1979, Germany, Tax Advisor; 1989, Certified Public Accountant. *Education:* Universities of Bochum and Cologne; Pennsylvania State University (Doctor of Business Administration, 1977). Author: "The Interest Rate as a Factor of Evaluation in the Tax Balance Sheet," Köln, 1979. *Member:* Association of Tax Advisors; Association of Certified Public Accountants. *LANGUAGES:* German and English. *PRACTICE AREAS:* Evaluation of Firms; Corporate Taxation; Audit.

WOLFGANG DAMASCHKE, born Moenchengladbach, Germany, May 15, 1960; admitted, 1991, Germany, Tax Advisor. *Education:* University of Nordkirchen, Germany (Diploma in Financial Economy, 1982). *Member:* Association of Tax Advisors. *LANGUAGES:* German, French and English. *PRACTICE AREAS:* Corporate Tax Law; Real Estate Tax Law.

LUDWIG BETTAG, born Bonn, Germany, August 21, 1957; admitted, 1991, Germany, Tax Advisor; 1993, Certified Public Accountant. *Education:* University of Cologne, Germany (Diploma in Business Administra-

(This Listing Continued)

tion, 1986). *Member:* Association of Tax Advisors. *LANGUAGES:* German and English. *PRACTICE AREAS:* Audit; Corporate Taxation; Evaluation of Firms; Management Accountancy.

SCHÄFER WIPPRECHT SCHICKERT

BANKSTRASSE 1
40476 DÜSSELDORF, GERMANY
Telephone: (49-211) 49340
Telex: 8 584 245 swsd
Telecopy: (49-211) 4920097

Berlin, Germany Office: Schlüterstrasse 39, D-10629. Telephone: (49-30) 8845920. Telecopy: (49-30) 88459222.

General Practice. Corporate, Commercial, Banking, Labor, Tax, EEC, Antitrust, Unfair Competition, Insurance, Construction, Licensing, Product Liability, Trademark, Copyright, Litigation and Arbitration, Mergers and Acquisitions.

MEMBERS OF FIRM

DR. GERD SCHÄFER, born Düsseldorf, Germany, April 25, 1939; admitted, 1968, Germany. *Education:* Universities of Bonn, Berlin, Münster (Doctor of Laws, 1967). Special Counsel for Labor Law. Author: "Grundsätze des gutgläubigen Mobiliarerwerbs im englischen Recht unter besonderer Berücksichtigung des Marktkaufs," 1967; "Das Arbeitsverhältnis im Konzern," 1987. *LANGUAGES:* German and English.

DR. WALTER WIPPRECHT, born Düsseldorf, Germany, June 25, 1938; admitted, 1969, Germany. *Education:* Universities of Köln, Bonn, Freiburg (Doctor of Laws, 1973). Special Counsel for Tax Law. Author: "Die Änderung der Rechtsprechung mit Wirkung nur für künftige Fälle. Eine rechtsvergleichende Untersuchung zum US-amerikanischen und deutschen Recht unter Berücksichtigung des englischen und schweizerischen Rechts," 1973. *LANGUAGES:* German, English and French.

WOLFGANG SCHICKERT, born Göttingen, Germany, November 23, 1942; admitted, 1973, Germany. *Education:* Universities of Kiel, Tübingen, Marburg. *LANGUAGES:* German, English and French.

DR. THOMAS SPIRITUS, born Mühlhausen/Thüringen, Germany, January 27, 1944; admitted, 1975, Germany. *Education:* Universities of Köln, München (Doctor of Laws, 1973). Author: "Haftungsbeeinflussende Nachlaßteilung zugleich mit erbrechtlicher Nachfolge in eine Personalhandelsgesellschaft?" 1974. *LANGUAGES:* German.

MARIE-LUISE KAUFFMANN-LAUVEN, born Bardenberg, Germany, January 26, 1949; admitted, 1976, Germany. *Education:* Universities of Bonn, Marburg. Special Counsel for Labor Law. *LANGUAGES:* German and English.

THOMAS CHRISTIAN MAY, born Düsseldorf, Germany, September 20, 1947; admitted, 1981, Germany. *Education:* Universities of Freiburg, München. Special Counsel for Tax Law. *LANGUAGES:* German and English.

DR. HELMUT BORNGRÄBER, born Breslau, Germany, March 26, 1943; admitted, 1974, Germany. *Education:* Universities of Köln, Kiel (Doctor of Laws, 1977). Author: "Arbeitsverhältnis bei Betriebsübergang," 1977; "Insolvenzschutz für Ruhegeldzusagen bei Anrechnung von Vordienstzeiten?" 1978. *LANGUAGES:* German and English.

DR. MICHAEL BRÜCK, born Hagen, Germany, April 13, 1954; admitted, 1982, Germany. *Education:* Universities of Pamplona, Köln, Cambridge (Doctor of Laws, 1989). Author: "Der strafrechtliche Schutz des Geschäfts- und Betriebsgeheimnisses in Spanien," 1989. *Member:* Deutsch-Spanische Juristenvereinigung e.V.; IBA International Bar Association; Deutsche Gesellschaft für Baurecht; Deutsch-Spanische Handelskammer; Càmara Official Española de Comercio en Alemania. *LANGUAGES:* German, English, Spanish and French.

DR. RAINER KIENAST, born Göttingen, Germany, October 25, 1955; admitted, 1983, Germany. *Education:* University of Göttingen (Doctor of Law, 1982). Special Counsel for Labor Law. Author: "Der Tod des ausgleichspflichtigen Ehegatten im schuldrechtlichen Versorgungsausgleich," 1982. *LANGUAGES:* German and English.

MONIKA MERTENS-MARL, born Isselburg, Germany, August 26, 1955; admitted, 1982, Germany. *Education:* University of Münster. *LANGUAGES:* German and English.

DR. BERND KÖSTER, born Dortmund, Germany. August 1, 1947; admitted, 1979, Germany. *Education:* Universities of Tübingen, Münster,

(This Listing Continued)

Darmstadt (Doctor rer. pol., 1981). Special Counsel for Tax Law. Author: "Anfechtungs—und Nichtigkeitsklage gegen Gesellschafterbeschlüsse bei oHG und KG," 1981. *LANGUAGES:* German, English and French.

JÖRG SCHULZE ZUR WIESCHE, born Düsseldorf, August 23, 1938; admitted, 1968, Germany. *Education:* Universities of Köln, München and Bonn. Author "Der Schutz der Farbe oder farbigen Aufmachung durch § 25 WZG," 1965, 1966; "Zum Benutzungszwang bei Warenzeichen," 1968, 1970; "Werberechtliche Probleme des Selbstbedienungsgroßhandels," 1975. *LANGUAGES:* German and English.

ALMUTH SCHULZE ZUR WIESCHE, born Kleve, Germany, July 25, 1938; admitted, 1975, Germany. *Education:* Universities of Bonn, Köln and München. *LANGUAGES:* German and English.

DR. THOMAS MANDERLA, born Köln, Germany, July 7, 1956; admitted, 1986, Germany. *Education:* University of Köln (Doctor of Laws, 1991). Author: "Die Rechtmäßigkeit der Verweigerung von Streikarbeit durch Arbeitnehmer," 1990; "Das Joint-Venture-Gesetz in Polen," 1991. *LANGUAGES:* German and English.

ASSOCIATES

Dr. Gabriele Post-Pawelleck
Dr. Jürgen Frodermann
Dr. Dirk Eckhardt
Dr. Dirk Jannott
Leo Mathias Waltermann

TAX ADVISOR

HARALD EWIG, born Behlingen, Germany, June 9, 1949. Certified Public Accountant, Germany, 1988. Tax Advisor, Germany, 1982. *Education:* University of Cologne (Diploma in Business Administration, 1977). *Member:* Association of Certified Public Accountants; Association of Tax Advisors. *LANGUAGES:* German and English.

Languages: German, English, French and Spanish

SCHAFFRATH & METZMACHER

ROSENSTR. 11
D-40479 DÜSSELDORF, GERMANY
Telephone: (211) 49 222-0
Telecopier: (211) 49 82 408

Görlitz, Germany Office: Berliner Str. 20, D-02826. Telephone: (3581) 406396. Telecopier: (3581) 403750.
Dresden, Germany Office: Lortzingstraße 37, D-01307, Dresden. Telephone: 0351/4426234. Telecopier: 0351/4426238.

Administrative Law, Antitrust, Construction and Engineering Contracts, Corporate, Environmental Law, European Law, Family Law, Industrial and Intellectual Property, Labor Law, Litigation and Arbitration, Mergers and Acquisitions, Property Law of New German Member States, Trade Law, Transportation and Aviation, Unfair Competition.

MEMBERS OF FIRM

FALK METZMACHER, born Seilershof, Germany, September 30, 1944; admitted, 1974, Germany. *Education:* University of Cologne. *Member:* German Association for the Protection of Industrial Property and Copyright Law. *LANGUAGES:* German and English. *PRACTICE AREAS:* Construction and Engineering Contract; Industrial and Intellectual Property; Antitrust; Transportation and Aviation; Unfair Competition; Litigation.

DR. MARIUS KUSCHKA, born Darmstadt, Germany, June 30, 1960; admitted, 1988, Germany. *Education:* University of Münster (Dr. jur. 1988); European University Institute, Florence (LL.M., 1986). Assistant, Institute for International Private and Business Law, Münster, 1984. Author: "Amerikanische Exportkontrollen und deutsches Kollisionsrecht," 1989; "Competition Law: The German Law of Merger Control," in The Company Lawyer, 1989. *Member:* International Association of Young Lawyers; Union International des Avocats; German-Italian Lawyers Association. *LANGUAGES:* German, English, French and Italian. *PRACTICE AREAS:* International Commercial Law; Commercial Contracts; Corporate Partnerships; Mergers and Acquisitions; Antitrust.

SCHINDLER, SCHLENGER, JACOBSEN

KÖNIGSALLEE 40
40212 DÜSSELDORF, GERMANY
Telephone: 0211/3230601-5
Telex: 858 7711 VSSJ D
Fax: 0211/131801

General Practice. International, Corporation, Commercial, Banking, Insurance, Customs, Unfair Competition, Trademark, Antitrust, Industrial Property, Copyright and Labor Law.

MEMBERS OF FIRM

GERHARD VETTER (1931-1984).

LUDWIG SCHLENGER, born Düsseldorf, Germany, July 14, 1930; admitted, 1962, West Germany. *Education:* University of Köln; University of Bonn. *LANGUAGES:* German and English.

DR. DIETER SCHINDLER, born Berlin, Germany, March 8, 1942; admitted, 1969, West Germany. *Education:* University of Munich; University of Cologne. Author: "Die Behandlung der Seeuntüchtigkeit in der Seekaskoversicherung". *LANGUAGES:* German, English and French.

HANS WERNER JACOBSEN, born Hamburg, Germany, March 7, 1938; admitted, 1967, West Germany. *Education:* University of Kiel. *LANGUAGES:* German and English.

KLAUS OTTO LITTAU, born Gera, Germany, November 26, 1943; admitted, 1973, West Germany. *Education:* University of Frankfurt; University of Giessen. *LANGUAGES:* German and English.

Languages: German, English and French.

SCHMITZ & WICHER

Rechtsanwälte
SIMROCKSTRASSE 64
40235 DÜSSELDORF, GERMANY
Telephone: (0211) 68 12 49
Fax: (0211) 6 80 15 16

General Business Law Practice, concentrating on Contracts, Corporate Law, Mergers and Acquisitions, Banking and Financing, Environmental Law, Civil and Commercial Litigation.

DR. THOMAS SCHMITZ, born Düsseldorf, Germany, March 16, 1956; admitted, 1982, Düsseldorf. *Education:* University of Cologne (Doctor of Laws, 1986). Author: "Umfang der Freizeichnung des Herstellers bei Versicherung," Diss. Cologne, 1986. Faculty Assistant, Institute of Criminal Law, University of Cologne, 1979. *Member:* German Bar Association; International Bar Association; German American Lawyers Association. *LANGUAGES:* German, English and French.

THOMAS WICHER, born Arnsberg, Germany, May 3, 1955; admitted, 1984, Düsseldorf. *Education:* University of Cologne. *Member:* German Bar Association; German American Lawyers Association. *LANGUAGES:* German, English and French.

SCHOLZ, KRAATZ, DITTMANN & PARTNER

Member of TELFA (Trans European Law Firms Association).

TELFA is an association of European Law Firms, whose members have offices in Athens, Arnhem, Barcelona, Brussels, Budapest, Kopenhagen, Düsseldorf, Edinburgh, Geneva, Glasgow, Halle, Lisbon, London, Luxemburg, Madrid, Milan, Nijmegen, Paris and Vienna.

For more details see the TELFA entry under Brussels.

KÖNIGSALLEE 100
D-40215 DÜSSELDORF, GERMANY
Telephone: +49 211-3 88 00-0
Telefax: +49 211 37 36 78
Telex: 8 587 246 skd d

Halle, Germany Office: Bernburger Strasse 9, D-06108. Telephone: +49-345-50 12 71. Telefax: +49-345-5 50 17 84.

(This Listing Continued)

SCHOLZ, KRAATZ, DITTMANN & PARTNER, Düsseldorf—Continued

Toronto, Ontario, Canada Affiliated Office: Dale & Dingwall. Commercial Union Tower, Toronto-Dominion Centre, Suite 2000, M5K 1E7.

General Practice of Commercial Law including Corporate, Tax, Finance, Banking, Unfair Competition, German and EEC Antitrust, Labor, Bankruptcy, Commercial Litigation and Arbitration, Trademark, Licensing, Mergers, Acquisitions, International Construction Contracts.

FIRM PROFILE: The Firm is an established practice which emerged from the former firm of Farnborough & Partner, founded in 1953. Specializing in all areas of commercial and business law as well as tax law, the Firm advises a wide variety of clients, from renowned national and international enterprises to small businesses. In addition to being practicing attorneys, several of the Firm's members are chartered accountants and/or tax advisers. This additional expertise is particularly valuable in the structuring of highly complex cross-border transactions as well as in advising local and national clients in their day-to-day operations.

MEMBERS OF FIRM

DR. CHRISTIAN G. SCHOLZ, born Berlin, May 10, 1942; admitted, 1969, West Germany; admitted as Tax Counsel, 1973; as Chartered Accountant, 1975. *Education:* Universities of Cologne and Munich (Doctor of Law, 1967). *LANGUAGES:* German, English and French. *PRACTICE AREAS:* Corporate Law; Commercial Law; Tax and International Tax Law; Law of Succession; Arbitration Law; International Contract Law.

KLAUS DITTMANN, born Plauen, March 24, 1928; admitted, 1959, West Germany. *Education:* University of Würzburg. Co-Author: "Commentary on the German Standard Business Conditions Act," 1977. Author: "Der rechtliche Charakter von Einschüssen bei Warentermingeschäften," 1977. *LANGUAGES:* German. *PRACTICE AREAS:* Standard Terms and Conditions; Commercial Law; Traffic Law; Product Liability; Insurance Law; Commercial Landlord-Tenant Law; Labour Law; Transport Law; Commodities Transactions.

DR. HENNING STAHL, born Weidenau, September 30, 1943; admitted, 1974, West Germany. *Education:* American University of Cairo; Universities of Innsbruck and Münster (Doctor of Law, 1971). Co-Author: "Commentary on the German Standard Business Conditions Act," Wiesbaden, 1977. *LANGUAGES:* German and English. *PRACTICE AREAS:* Arbitration Law; Standard Terms and Conditions; Commercial Law; Labour Law; Law of Competition; Personnel Leasing.

DR. PETER KRAATZ, born Hamburg, July 12, 1942; admitted, 1971, West Germany; admitted as Tax Counsel, 1975; as Chartered Accountant, 1977. *Education:* Universities of Hamburg and Bonn (Doctor of Law, 1971). *LANGUAGES:* German and English. *PRACTICE AREAS:* Corporate Law; Commercial Law; Tax and International Tax Law; International Contract Law; Auditing.

SABINE SCHMIDT-MENSCHNER, born Rheydt, September 17, 1949; admitted, 1977, West Germany. *Education:* Universities of Bonn and Freiburg; University of Missouri Law School, Kansas City, Missouri. *LANGUAGES:* German, English and Italian. *PRACTICE AREAS:* Labour Law; Employee Co-determination and Representation Law.

HEINRICH CLEV, born Cologne, December 28, 1955; admitted, 1985, West Germany; admitted as Tax Counsel, 1989. *Education:* University of Bonn. *LANGUAGES:* German, Dutch and English. *PRACTICE AREAS:* Corporate Law; Commercial and Business Law; German and International Tax Law.

KURT G. SONDERMANN, born Bandung, Indonesia, November 7, 1940; admitted, 1980, West Germany; admitted as Tax Counsel, 1977; admitted as Chartered Accountant, 1979. *Education:* Universities of Bonn, Paris and Cologne. *LANGUAGES:* German, English and French. *PRACTICE AREAS:* Tax and International Tax Law; Corporate Law; Commercial and Business Law; Auditing.

DR. BURKHARD FIRNHABER, born Hamburg, January 3, 1934; admitted, 1967, West Germany. *Education:* Universities of Marburg, Bonn and Cologne (Doctor of Law, 1962). Author: "Die strafbefreiende Selbstanzeige im Steuerrecht," (Exempting Self-Accusation in Tax Law), 1962. Board of Directors, Emschergenossenschaft/Lippeverband (Water Associations), Essen, 1967-1978. Senior Legal Counsel/Head of Legal Department, Ruhrkohle Aktiengesellschaft, Essen, 1978-1989. *Member:* International Bar Association (Section Energy and Natural Resources Law); German Bar Association (Working Group for In-House Counsel); Federal Association

(This Listing Continued)

of German Industry (Legal Committee); Association of German Chambers of Industry and Commerce (Legal Committee); Wirtschaftsvereinigung Bergbau (Chairman, Legal Committee, 1978—); Weserbergland-Klinik Foundation (Supervisory Board); Chamber of Commerce, Essen (Legal Committee, 1978-1990). *LANGUAGES:* German and English. *PRACTICE AREAS:* General Business Law; Corporate and Antitrust Law; Energy Law; Mining Law; Environmental Law; Water Law; Business and Commercial Law in the new German Länder (states).

DR. CHRISTIAN QUACK, born Büderich, April 4, 1956; admitted, 1985, West Germany. *Education:* Universities of Munich and Bonn (Doctor of Law, 1985); McGill University, Montreal, Canada (LL.M., 1983). Author: "Die Personalistische Kapitalgesellschaft im Kanadischen Gesellschaftsrecht," (Close Corporations in Canadian Corporate Law), 1985. Co-Author: "Die Gründung einer Tochtergesellschaft in Kanada," (Forming a Subsidiary in Canada), 1994. *Member:* German-American Lawyers' Association; Canadian-German Lawyers Association. *LANGUAGES:* German, English and French. *PRACTICE AREAS:* Corporate Law; Competition and Antitrust Law; Commercial Law; Business Law; Distribution Law; Arbitration Law.

ASSOCIATES

JACQUELINE RUMMEL, born March 2, 1961; admitted, 1989, West Germany. *Education:* Universities of Mainz and Cologne. *LANGUAGES:* German, English, French and Dutch. *PRACTICE AREAS:* Landlord-Tenant Law; General Contract Law; Commercial Law; Family Law; Labour Law; Private International Law.

HANS-PETER PALENBERG, born Düsseldorf, December 8, 1955; admitted, 1991, Germany. *Education:* University of Cologne. Legal Counsel, Victoria Insurance Group, Berlin and Düsseldorf, 1986-1991. *LANGUAGES:* German and English. *PRACTICE AREAS:* Business Law; Corporate Law and Affiliated Company Law; Employee Co-determination Law; Commercial and Insurance Law; Bank Law.

DR. MARKUS ROHNER, born Korschenbroich, October 12, 1961; admitted, 1991, Germany. *Education:* University of Bonn (Dr. of Law, 1991). *Member:* German-American Lawyers' Association; German (West)-German (East) Lawyers' Association. (Resident, Halle, Germany Office). *LANGUAGES:* German, English and French. *PRACTICE AREAS:* International Private and Civil Procedure Law; Commercial Sales Law; Law of Warranties; Real Property Law; Corporate Law; Law of Associations; Tax Law.

DR. THEO RAUH, born Erkelenz, December 21, 1961; admitted, 1993, Germany. *Education:* University of Trier (Doctor in Law, 1992); University of East Anglia, Norwich (LL.M., 1990). Author, "Leistungserschwerungen im Schuldvertrag," (Difficulties in Performing Contractual Obligations), 1992. *LANGUAGES:* German, English and French. *PRACTICE AREAS:* Business Law; General Contract Law; Private International Law.

DIETER G. PAPE, born Düsseldorf, August 23, 1961; admitted, 1993, Germany. *Education:* University of Cologne. *LANGUAGES:* German, English and Italian. *PRACTICE AREAS:* Labour Law; General Contract Law; Employee Co-determination and Representation Law; Corporate Law; Commercial Law.

ANDREAS ENGELBRECHT, born Cologne, May 13, 1964; admitted, 1993, Germany. *Education:* University of Bonn. *LANGUAGES:* German and English. *PRACTICE AREAS:* Commercial Law; General Contract Law; Civil Procedure Law; Traffic Law; Real Property Law; Insurance Law; Landlord-Tenant Law.

AILSA MCLAGGAN, born Edinburgh, July 15, 1967; admitted, 1991, Scotland. *Education:* University of Edinburgh (LL.B., Hons., with German 1989, Dip. L.P., 1990). *Member:* Law Society of Scotland; British-German Jurists' Association. *LANGUAGES:* English, German and French. *PRACTICE AREAS:* Scottish Commercial Law; Corporate Law; Private International Law.

KLAUS-JÖRG DEHNE, born Hildesheim, April 30, 1961; admitted, 1994, Germany. *Education:* University of Bonn. *LANGUAGES:* German and English. *PRACTICE AREAS:* German and International Tax Law; Corporate Law; Commercial and Business Law.

(This Listing Continued)

COUNSEL

DR. REZA TONKABONI, born Kazvin, Iran, January 30, 1935; admitted, 1963, Iran; Sworn and Officially Licenced Expert for Iranian Corporate, Trademark and Patent Law; admitted as Legal Expert on Iranian Law in West Germany. *Education:* University of Munich (Doctor of Law, 1961). Author: "Der Parlamentarismus im Iran," 1961. *LANGUAGES:* German and Farsi. *PRACTICE AREAS:* Iranian Law.

SHEARMAN & STERLING
KÖNIGSALLEE 46
D-40212 DÜSSELDORF, GERMANY
Telephone: (49-211) 13 62 80
Telex: 8 588 294 NYLO
Fax: (49-211) 13 33 09

New York, N.Y. Office: 599 Lexington Avenue, New York, New York 10022-6069 and Citicorp Center, 153 East 53rd Street, New York, New York 10022-4676. Telephone: (212) 848-4000. Telex: 667290 Num Lau. Fax: 599 Lexington Avenue: (212) 848-7179. Citicorp Center: (212) 848-5252.

Abu Dhabi, United Arab Emirates Office: P.O. Box 2948. Telephone: (971-2) 324477. Fax: (971-2) 774533.

Beijing, People's Republic of China Office: Suite #2205, Capital Mansion, No. 6, Xin Yuan Nan Road. Chao Yang District Beijing, 100004. Telephone: (861) 465-4574. Fax: (861) 465-4578.

Budapest, Hungary Office: Szerb utca 17-19, 1056 Budapest. Telephone: (36-1) 266-3522. Fax: (36-1) 266-3523.

Frankfurt, Federal Republic of Germany Office: Bockenheimer Landstrasse 55, D-60325 Frankfurt am Main. Telephone: (49-69) 97-10-70. Fax: (49-69) 97-10-71-00.

Hong Kong, Hong Kong Office: Standard Chartered Bank Building, 4 Des Voeux Road Central, Hong Kong. Telephone: (852) 2978-8000. Fax:(852) 2978-8099.

London, England Office: 199 Bishopsgate, London EC2M 3TY. Telephone: (44-171) 920-9000. Fax: (44-171) 920-9020.

Los Angeles, California Office: 725 South Figueroa Street, 21st Floor, 90017-5421. Telephone: (213) 239-0300. Fax: (213) 239-0381, 614-0936.

Paris, France Office: 12 rue d'Astorg, 75008. Telephone: (33-1) 44-71-17-17. Telex: 282964 Royale. Fax: (33-1) 44-71-01-01.

San Francisco, California Office: 555 California Street, 94104-1522. Telephone: (415) 616-1100. Fax: (415) 616-1199.

Taipei, Taiwan Office: 7th Floor, Hung Kuo Building, 167 Tun Hwa North Road. Telephone: (886-2) 545-3300. Fax: (866-2) 545-3322.

Tokyo, Japan Office: Shearman & Sterling (Thomas Wilner Gaikokuho-Jimu-Bengoshi Jimusho), Fukoku Seimei Building, 5th Fl. 2-2-2, Uchisaiwaicho, Chiyoda-ku, Tokyo 100, Japan. Telephone: (81 3) 5251-1601. Fax: (81 3) 5251-1602.

Toronto, Ontario, Canada Office: Commerce Court West, Suite 4405, P.O. Box 247, M5L 1E8. Telephone: (416) 360-8484. Fax: (416) 360-2958.

Washington, D.C. Office: 801 Pennsylvania Avenue, N.W., Suite 900, 20004-2604. Telephone: (202) 508-8000. Fax: (202) 508-8100.

Firm engages in German, EEC, American and General International Practice.

FIRM PROFILE: Shearman & Sterling, founded in 1873, has more than 500 lawyers in 15 offices throughout the world. The firm's practice encompasses most major areas of business law, including: Antitrust and Trade Regulation; Banking; Bankruptcy and Corporate Reorganization; Compensation and Benefits; Environmental; Finance (including Corporate Finance, Domestic Private Finance, Financial Institutions, International Private Finance and Project Finance); Individual Clients, Trusts and Estates; Insurance; International Trade and Government Relations; Litigation and Arbitration; Mergers and Acquisitions; Oil and Gas; Privatizations; Real Estate; and Tax. The Firm is also engaged in the practice of French, German and Hungarian law through its offices in France, Germany and Hungary.

RESIDENT PARTNERS

GEORG F. THOMA, born Trier, Germany, 1944; admitted, 1975, Germany. *Education:* Universities of Freiburg and Bonn. (Managing Partner, Dusseldorf and Frankfurt).

MICHAEL GRUSON, born Berlin, Germany, 1936; admitted, 1969, New York (Not admitted in Germany). *Education:* University of Mainz, Germany (LL.B., 1962); Columbia University (M.C.L., 1963; LL.B., 1965);

(This Listing Continued)

Freie Universität, Berlin, Germany (Dr.iur., 1966). Vice Chairman, Committee on Banking Law, 1984-1989 and Chairman, Subcommittee on Legal Opinions, 1985—, International Bar Association.

RESIDENT ASSOCIATES

DR. ANTON KLÖSTERS, born Kranenburg, Germany, 1964; admitted, 1992, Germany. *Education:* Universities of Saarbrücken, Münster and Utrecht; University of Münster (Dr. Jur., 1993).

DR. ALFRED L. KOSSMANN, born Bochum, Germany, 1961; admitted, 1989, Germany; 1991, New York. *Education:* Universities of Freiburg and Bonn; Duke University (LL.M., 1990); University of Bonn (Dr.Jur., 1994).

DR. HENNING H. KRAUSS, born Kaiserslautern, Germany, 1958; admitted, 1986, Germany. *Education:* Ludwig-Maximilians University, Munich; Duke University School of Law (LL.M., 1991).

DR. HANS JÜRGEN MEYER-LINDEMANN, born Frankfurt am Main, Germany, 1956; admitted, 1986, New York; 1988, Frankfurt am Main; 1989, Düsseldorf. *Education:* Universities of Bonn, Geneva and Strasbourg; New York University (M.C.J., 1983); University of Bonn (Dr.jur., 1986).

WANDA KIM, born 1969; admitted, 1989, New York (Not admitted in Germany). *Education:* Harvard University (B.A., 1982); Columbia University (J.D., 1988).

Languages: German, English, French, Dutch, Spanish and Portuguese.

(For Biographical data of all Partners, see Professional Biographies at New York, New York).

THOMAS STEIN
WILLICHER STRAβE 15
D-40547 DÜSSELDORF, GERMANY
Telephone: 0049/211/52 42 22 0
Telefax: 0049/211/59 42 98

German and International Tax Law; Share Valuation; Accounting Regulations; Corporate Law.

FIRM PROFILE: The firm was established in 1975 and cooperated since then closely with tax consulting and auditing firms. It also cooperated with bigger law firms. At present it concentrates on engagements exploiting its special experiences.

THOMAS STEIN, born Düsseldorf, Germany, February 16, 1942; admitted, 1975, Düsseldorf; 1976, Tax Advisor; 1977, Chartered Accountant. *Education:* Universities of Freiburg, Kiel and Bonn. *Member:* Institute of Chartered Public Accountants; American Chamber of Commerce in Germany, Nederlands-Duitse Kamer van Koophandel. *LANGUAGES:* German, English and Dutch. *PRACTICE AREAS:* German and International Tax Law; Share Valuation; Accounting Regulations; Corporate Law.

DR. ERNEST STIEFEL
FREILIGRATHSTRASSE 1
40479 DÜSSELDORF, GERMANY
Telephone: 0211-49790
Fax: (0211) 4979 103

New York, New York Office: The Grace Building. 1114 Avenue of the Americas. N.Y. 10036. Telephone: 212-626-4600. Fax: (212) 626-4120. Cable Address: "Ernstiefel." New York.

Corporation, Commercial, Estates and Trusts, Foreign and International Law.

Dr. Stiefel is authorized to practice before German Courts as Rechtsanwalt.

ERNST C. STIEFEL, admitted, 1944, New York; 1952, U.S. District Court, Southern District of New York; 1971, District of Columbia. Member of German Bar, 1932. Member of the English Bar (Honourable Society of the Middle Temple, London), 1938. *Education:* University of Heidelberg (Doctor of Laws, 1929); University of Paris (Licencié en Droit, 1934); University of Strasbourg (Diplôme d'Etudes Supérieures, 1935). Professor of Law, Adjunct, New York Law School, 1975—. Author: "German Commercial Law," New York, 1963; "Pitfalls in U.S. Common Market Joint Ventures," 1961; "As They See Us: Typische Rechtsprobleme bei Amerikanischen Investitionen in Deutschland," 1976; "Discovery Problems under the Hague Convention and German-American Legal Assistance," (in German), 1979 and 1983. Co-author: "Doing Business in Germany," 8th Edition,

(This Listing Continued)

DR. ERNEST STIEFEL, Düsseldorf—Continued

1978; "Shareholder's Rights in German Corporations," 1961; "The New German Stock Corporation Law," 1967; "Tendencies in Product Liability in Europe and the U.S.," 1981, 1989 and 1990. Consultant: Office of Economic Warfare, Washington, D.C., 1942-1943; Department of State, Washington, D.C. and American Legation, Berne, Switzerland, 1945-1946; War Department, Office of Military Government, Germany, 1946-1947. Member, Commission on Double Taxation Problems, German Ministry of Finance, 1955—. Chairman, Regulations on Mutual Funds in Europe, American Foreign Law Association, 1970. Panelist: Colloquium on Enforcement of Foreign Judgments, University of Virginia, 1977; Symposium on Foreign Investment in the U.S., 1979, on U.S. Investment in Europe, 1980, on U.S. Investment in Eastern Europe, 1989, on German Unification, 1990. Member, National Panel of Arbitrators, American Arbitration Association, 1969—. Member, Advisory Board Recht der Internationalen Wirtschaft, Heidelberg, 1979—. Versicherungsrecht (Insurance Law) 1975—. Faculty Advisor, Journal of Comparative and International Law, New York Law School, 1981—. Member, International Cartel Conference, Berlin, 1984—. Member, Advisory Board, German-American Association of Jurists, Bonn, 1985—. Member, Stiftung Heidelberg University, 1986—. Honorary Director, German-American Chamber of Commerce, USA, 1980—. *Member:* The Association of the Bar of the City of New York (Member, Committee on Foreign and Comparative Law); American Bar Association (Member, Corporation, Banking and Business Law Section); American Foreign Law Association (Director, 1986). [U.S. Army, active duty, 1943-1945]. (Also Senior Counsel to Coudert Brothers, New York City). *PRACTICE AREAS:* International Law.

TEMME VISÉ GÜNTHER & PARTNERS

LINDEMANNSTRAßE 47
40237 DÜSSELDORF, GERMANY
Telephone: 0211-66 60 31
Telecopier: 0211-66 69 97

Wuppertal, Germany Office: Günther Liesegang Temme & Partners, Döppersberg 19, 42103. Telephone: 0202-45 03 51. Telecopier: 0202-45 56 76.

General Business Practice, Forwarding and Transport Law, Corporate Law, Banking Law, Competition Law, Labor Law, Real Estate Transactions, Law of Inheritance, Insurance, Medical Malpractice, EEC Law, Litigation.

MEMBERS OF FIRM

DR. JÜRGEN TEMME, born Kassel, Germany, April 3, 1958; admitted, 1988, Germany. *Education:* University of Göttingen (Dr. jur., 1987). Author: "Haftung des Selbsteintretenden Spediteurs im Straßengüterfernverkehr," Verlag Versicherungswirtschaft, Karlsruhe, 1988. Co-Author: "Kommentar zur CMR," Verlag Recht und Wirtschaft, Heidelberg, 1994. Assistant Professor, Trade, Corporation, Competition and Antitrust Law, Göttingen University, 1984-1985. *Member:* German Association for Transport Law. *LANGUAGES:* German and English. *PRACTICE AREAS:* Forwarding and Transport Law; Corporate Law; Banking Law; Competition Law.

JOACHIM H. VISÉ, born Düsseldorf, Germany, May 19, 1959; admitted, 1991, Germany. *Education:* University of Cologne. *LANGUAGES:* German and English. *PRACTICE AREAS:* Labor Law; Commercial and Business Law; Corporate Law; Real Estate Transactions.

PETER WELBERS, born Düsseldorf, Germany, January 8, 1962; admitted, 1991, Germany. *Education:* Universities of Bonn and Münster. *Member:* German Lawyers' Association. *LANGUAGES:* German, English and French. *PRACTICE AREAS:* Law of Inheritance; Insurance; Medical Malpractice; EEC; Corporate Law.

ANNETTE LIESEGANG, born Cologne, Germany, January 31, 1950; admitted, 1980, Germany. *Education:* Universities of Cologne and Bochum. *LANGUAGES:* German and English. *PRACTICE AREAS:* Business Law; Commercial Law.

Languages: German, English and French

THOMAS & WESSING II

Rechtsanwälte
WASSERSTRASSE 13
40213 DÜSSELDORF 1, GERMANY
Telephone: 0211/32 06 41
Telefax: 0211/32 06 32

International Criminal Law, White Collar Crime, Environmental Law and Fiscal Offences.

MEMBERS OF FIRM

RÜDIGER DECKERS, born 1947; admitted, 1976, Germany. *Education:* Universities of Münster, Lausanne and Bochum. Author: Numerous Publications Regarding Criminal Law and Criminal Procedure. Co-Author: "Defence Counsels Handbook." *Member:* DAV German Lawyers Association; Arbeitsgemeinschaft Strafrecht DAV; German Lawyers Association (Committee for Criminal Law). *LANGUAGES:* German, English, French and Spanish.

DR. SVEN THOMAS, born 1947; admitted, 1978, Germany. *Education:* Universities of Münster and Bochum. Assistant at University of Bochum, 1976-1978. Lecturer for Criminal Law, University of Düsseldorf. Author: Numerous Publications Regarding Criminal Law and Criminal Procedure. *Member:* German Lawyers Association (Vice President). *LANGUAGES:* English and German.

DR. ANNE WEHNERT, born 1958; admitted, 1988, Germany. *Education:* University of Cologne (Dr. jur.). Author: "Rechtliche und rechtstatsächliche Aspekte des Klageerzwingungsverfahrens," *Member:* DAV, Arbeitsgemeinschaft Strafrecht DAV. *LANGUAGES:* English and German.

DR. JÜRGEN WESSING, born 1950; admitted, 1982, Germany. *Education:* Universities of Bonn, Cologne, Münster (First and Second State Examinations) and Washington (State of Washington). Author: "Die Kommunikation des Verteidigers mit seinem Mandanten - Eine rechtshistorische und aktuelle Untersuchung mit Ausblick auf Osterreich und die Schweiz". *Member:* International Bar Association; DAV; Arbeitsgemeinschaft Strafrecht DAV; Verein zur Förderung der Rechtswissenschaft. *LANGUAGES:* German, English and French.

ASSOCIATES

THOMAS ELSNER, born 1964; admitted, 1993, Germany. *Education:* Universities of Saarbrücken and Bonn. *Member:* DAV; Arbeitsgemeinschaft Strafrecht DAV. *LANGUAGES:* English and German.

DR. GRAF VON DER GOLTZ DR. WESSING & PARTNER

DÜSSELDORF, GERMANY

(See Wessing Berenberg-Gossler Zimmermann Lange)

General Practice. Commercial, Corporation, International, Tax, Economic Criminality, Antitrust, Unfair Competition, Patent, Press, Copyright and Trademark Law. Foreign Investments in Brazil, Portugal and Mexico. Estate, EEC-Law, Bank Law, International Arbitration Proceedings.

VON ROSPATT • VON DER OSTEN • PROSS

Established in 1950
KAISER-FRIEDRICH-RING 56
P.O. BOX 110935
40509 DÜSSELDORF, GERMANY
Telephone: 211-571051
Fax: 211-572048

Intellectual Property, Competition and Antitrust Law, Product Liability, Licensing, Civil Litigation.

FIRM PROFILE: The firm was founded 1950 by the late Georg Gewiese and offers the full range of legal services with respect to intellectual property and related matters. It handles in particular patent, trademark, copyright and design protection litigation before the District Court Düsseldorf which is internationally well-known for its competence in patent infringement matters. The client base is European and North American in scope.

(This Listing Continued)

MEMBERS OF FIRM

PETER VON ROSPATT, born Berlin, Germany, January 19, 1932; admitted, 1960, District Court of Düsseldorf, Germany. *Education:* Universities of Tuebingen and Bonn. Author: "German Patent Litigation," 1990, a revised version of a manuscript which the author used as faculty member for his lecture at the Foreign Patent Litigation Seminar held by the Practising Law Institute in 1983 in New York City. *Member:* AIPPI (International Association for the Protection of Intellectual Property). *LANGUAGES:* German, English and French (ability to read). *PRACTICE AREAS:* Litigation; Licensing; Patent Law; Trademark Law; Copyright Law; Competition Law.

DR. HORST VON DER OSTEN, born Berlin, Germany, July 31, 1932; admitted, 1962, District Court of Düsseldorf, Germany. *Education:* Universities of Cologne and Bonn (Doctor of Jurisprudence); Columbia University Law School, New York (Master of Comparative Law). Author: "Die Verkehrsgeltung im Warenzeichen- und Wettbewerbsrecht," (The Legal Protection of the Publicity of a Trademark), 1973. *Member:* AIPPI (International Association for the Protection of Intellectual Property); International Bar Association. *LANGUAGES:* German, English and French (ability to read). *PRACTICE AREAS:* Litigation; Licensing; Patent Law; Trademark Law; Copyright Law; Competition Law.

DR. ULRICH PROSS, born Herdecke, Germany, April 16, 1942; admitted, 1972, District Court of Düsseldorf, Germany. *Education:* Universities of Lausanne, Bonn and Cologne (Doctor of Jurisprudence). *Member:* AIPPI (International Association for the Protection of Intellectual Property); LES (Licensing Executives Society). *LANGUAGES:* German, English and French (ability to read). *PRACTICE AREAS:* Litigation; Licensing; Patent Law; Trademark Law; Copyright Law; Competition Law.

STEPHAN VON PETERSDORFF-CAMPEN, born Hannover, Germany, July 21, 1953; admitted, 1983, District Court of Düsseldorf, Germany. *Education:* Universities of Bonn and Göttingen. *Member:* UAE (European Lawyers's Association); AIJA (Young Lawyers' International Association). *LANGUAGES:* German, English and French. *PRACTICE AREAS:* Litigation; Licensing; Patent Law; Trademark Law; Copyright Law; Competition Law; Fashion and Design Law.

BERNWARD ZOLLNER, born Berlin, Germany, May 12, 1956; admitted, 1984, District Court of Berlin; 1988, District Court of Düsseldorf, Germany. *Education:* Free University of Berlin; Georgetown University, Washington, D.C. (LL.M.). *Member:* DAJV (German American Lawyers Association). *LANGUAGES:* German, English and French. *PRACTICE AREAS:* Litigation; Licensing; Patent Law; Trademark Law; Copyright Law; Competition Law.

WESSING BERENBERG-GOSSLER ZIMMERMANN LANGE

KÖNIGSALLEE 92 A
D-40212 DÜSSELDORF, GERMANY
Telephone: 49-211-83 87-0
Telex: 858 19 14 wess d
Cable Address: "Wegolex"
Telefax: 49-211-32 36 16

Mailing Address: P.O. Box 10 53 61, D-40044 Düsseldorf, Germany

Munich, Germany Office: Vilshofener Str. 8, D-81679 Munich, P.O. Box 86 08 67, D-81635 Munich. Telephone: 49-89-98 28 021. Telefax: 49-89-98 12 14.

Hamburg, Germany Office: Neuer Wall 46, D-20354 Hamburg. Telephone: 49-40-36 80 30. Cable Address: "Unilaw". Telex: 2-14111 Jura d. Teletex: 40 32 91 Unilaw. Telefax: 49-40-36 80 32 80.

Frankfurt, Germany Office: Freiherr-Vom-Stein-Strasse 24-26, D-60323 Frankfurt. Telephone: 49-69-971300. Telefax: 49-69-97130100.

Berlin, Germany Office: Spreeufer 5, D-10178 Berlin. Telephone: 49-30-238 45 45. Telefax: 49-30-238 45 34.

Leipzig, Germany Office: Ferdinand-Rhode-Strasse 16, D-04107 Leipzig. Telephone: 49-341-213 13 80. Fax: 49-341-213 13 88.

Dresden, Germany Office: Heinrichstrasse 16, D-01097 Dresden. Telephone: 49-351-567 12 12. Telefax: 49-351-567 12 13.

Brussels, Belgium Office: Avenue Louise 149, Box 42, B-1050 Brussels. Telephone: +32 (2) 537 01 86. Telefax: +32 (2) 534 25 31.

General Practice. Corporate, Commercial, Banking, Tax, International, EEC and Antitrust Law, Unfair Competition, Industrial Property, Copyright and Patent Infringement, Labor Law, Business Offenses.

(This Listing Continued)

MEMBERS OF THE FIRM IN DÜSSELDORF

DR. RÜDIGER GRAF VON DER GOLTZ (1894-1976).

DR. KURT WESSING, born 1927; admitted, 1955, Germany. *Education:* Universities of Munich, Erlangen, Bonn and Cologne (Dr. jur.). Author: "Der Wechselbereichungsanspruch," (Compensation Claim for Uncollectible Cheque Against Drawer). *Member:* International Bar Association; Association for the Protection of Industrial Property and Copyright; Association of German Chambers of Industry and Commerce; Legal Committee of the Chamber of Commerce, Düsseldorf. *LANGUAGES:* English. *PRACTICE AREAS:* Corporate; Commercial; Mergers and Acquisitions; Contracts; Arbitration.

ARNOLD GRAF VON DER GOLTZ, born 1939; admitted, 1970, Germany. *Education:* Universities of Cologne, Munich and Bonn. *Member:* Association for the Protection of Industrial Property and Copyright. *LANGUAGES:* English and Spanish. *PRACTICE AREAS:* General Civil Law; Commercial; Construction; Litigation.

DR. ELMAR LENZEN, born 1939; admitted, 1967, Germany. *Education:* University of Cologne (Dr. jur.). Author: "Mieterträge aus Bruchteilseigentum," (Leases for Co-Owned Property). *Member:* Deutsche Gesellschaft für Baurecht (German Society for Civil Construction). *LANGUAGES:* English and French. *PRACTICE AREAS:* General Civil Law; Construction; Real Estate; Insolvency; Insurance; Litigation.

WOLFGANG VON MEIBOM, born 1944; admitted, 1973, Germany. *Education:* Universities of Bonn, Berlin, Fairfield University, Connecticut, 1966. *Member:* International Bar Association; Association for the Protection of Industrial Property and Copyright. *LANGUAGES:* English and French. *PRACTICE AREAS:* Intellectual Property; Patent; Trademark; Copyright; Competition; Antitrust Law; EC Law.

DR. OTTO GRAF LAMBSDORFF, born 1926; admitted, 1960, Germany. *Education:* Universities of Bonn and Cologne (Dr. jur., 1952). Federal Minister of Economics, 1977-1984. Member of Parliament, 1972—. Federal Chairman of the Free Democratic Party, 1989-1993. *LANGUAGES:* English. *PRACTICE AREAS:* Corporate and Commercial; Constitution.

JÖRG SCHLEIFER, born 1939; admitted, 1968, Germany. *Education:* Universities of Munich, Berlin and Hamburg. Fachanwalt für Steuerrecht (Special Tax Counsel, 1974). Fachanwalt für Arbeitsrecht (Special Counsel for Labour Law). *LANGUAGES:* English. *PRACTICE AREAS:* Labour; Corporate; Real Estate.

DR. HORST MITTELSTAEDT, born 1922; admitted, 1974, Germany. *Education:* Universities of Mainz and Cologne (Dr. jur.). Author: "Gemeinschaftseinrichtungen Kreisangehoeriger Gemeinden," (Joint Institutions of County-Integrated Municipalities). Regierungsvizepräsident in Duesseldorf, 1967-1979. Staatssekretaer of Northrhine-Westfalia, 1970-1973. *LANGUAGES:* English. *PRACTICE AREAS:* Administration Law.

DR. DIETRICH H. MAX, born 1947; admitted, 1977, Germany. *Education:* University of Göttingen (Dr. jur.). Assistant at University of Göttingen, 1974-1976. Author: "Sittenverstoss bei Ausnutzung nicht geschützter gewerblicher Leistungen," (Unfair Exploitation of Unprotected Industrial Property). Fachanwalt für Steuerrecht (Special Tax Counsel, 1980). *LANGUAGES:* English. *PRACTICE AREAS:* General Civil Law; Corporate; Commercial; Mergers and Acquisitions; Litigation and Arbitration.

DR. ALEXANDER LOOS, born 1950; admitted, 1978, Germany. *Education:* Universities of Münster and Marburg (Dr. jur.). Author: "Arbeitskampfhilfeabkommen der Arbeitgeber im Wettbewerbs-und Arbeitsrecht" (Anti-Strike Associations under German Antitrust-and Labour Law). *Member:* German-Brasilian Lawyers Association; International Bar Association. *LANGUAGES:* English and Portuguese. *PRACTICE AREAS:* Commercial; Corporate; Mergers and Acquisitions; Agency; Joint Ventures; Computer Law; Arbitration.

KLAUS-JÜRGEN MICHAELI, born 1943; admitted, 1973, Germany. *Education:* University of Giessen; Georgetown Law School, Washington D.C. Assistant at University of Giessen, 1971-1973. *Member:* International Bar Association; Association for the Protection of Industrial Property (Chairman of the Board, Section West); Prof. h.c. (BG). *LANGUAGES:* English. *PRACTICE AREAS:* Intellectual Property; Patent; Trademark; Copyright; Food and Drug; Trade Regulation; EC Law; Media and Press Law.

DR. WOLFGANG GAEBELEIN, born 1925; admitted, 1955, Germany. *Education:* Universities of Jena and Frankfurt/Main. Author: "Die Grenzen der Abänderbarkeit von Entscheidungen nach §18 FGG", 1951.

(This Listing Continued)

WESSING BERENBERG-GOSSLER ZIMMERMANN LANGE, Düsseldorf—Continued

Member: Federal Association of German Industry, BDI (Chairman, Legal Committee, 1978). *LANGUAGES:* English and Portuguese. *PRACTICE AREAS:* Corporate; Antitrust; EC Law.

CHRISTIANE HOERDEMANN, born 1956; admitted, 1982, Germany. *Education:* University of Cologne. *Member:* Wirtschaftsjunioren IHK Mittlerer Niederrhein, DAV. *LANGUAGES:* English and French. *PRACTICE AREAS:* General Civil Law; Construction; Commercial Litigation.

PETER H. DAWIRS, born 1952; admitted, 1981, Germany. *Education:* Universities of Freiburg and Münster. *Member:* DAV, German-American Law Association; Deutsche Gesellschaft für Baurecht (German Society for Civil Construction). *LANGUAGES:* English. *PRACTICE AREAS:* Commercial; Commercial; Construction; Insolvency; Litigation; Insurance.

GUSTAF-RUDOLF SCHLIEPER, born 1952,; admitted, 1983, Germany; 1984, New York. *Education:* Universities of Freiburg and Münster; Temple University Law School, Philadelphia, Pennsylvania (LL.M., 1983). *Member:* American and International Bar Associations. *LANGUAGES:* English and French. *PRACTICE AREAS:* Commercial; Corporate; Mergers and Acquisitions; Joint Ventures.

DR. MICHAEL SAMER, born 1956; admitted, 1987, Germany. *Education:* Universities of Freiburg (Dr. jur.) and Geneva. Author: "Beherrschungs-und Gewinnabführungsverträge gem. § 291 Abs. 1 AKtG in Konkurs und Vergleich der Untergesellschaft," (Control Agreements and Profit Transfer Agreements Pursuant to Section 291, Subsection 1 Corporation Law in Bankruptcy and Composition of the Subsidiary). *Member:* German Association for Intellectual Property Law. *LANGUAGES:* English, French, Spanish, Italian. *PRACTICE AREAS:* Intellectual Property; Patent; Trademark; Copyright; Food and Drug; Media and Press Law; Licensing; Competition; Antitrust Law; Software Law.

DR. WOLFGANG A. GALONSKA, born 1957; admitted, 1986, Germany. *Education:* Universities of Lausanne, Göttingen, Freiburg, Würzburg (Dr. jur.). *LANGUAGES:* English and French. *PRACTICE AREAS:* General Civil Law; Construction Law; Real Estate; Litigation.

DR. KIRSTEN ANDEREGG, born 1962; admitted, 1989, Germany. *Education:* University of Hamburg (Dr. jur.); Max-Planck-Institut of Hamburg, 1985-1988. Author: "Foreign Peremptory Norms in Private International Law of Contracts". *LANGUAGES:* French and English. *PRACTICE AREAS:* Commercial; Corporate; Mergers and Acquisitions; Law of Succession.

DR. WALTER POTTHAST, born 1957; admitted, 1988, Germany. *Education:* University of Cologne (Dr. jur.). Author: "Dissolution of the federal parliament under Art. 68 GG". *LANGUAGES:* English. *PRACTICE AREAS:* Environmental and Administrative Law.

DR. KLAUS GROSSMANN, born 1960; admitted, 1990, Germany. *Education:* University of Cologne, 1979-1984 (Dr. jur.). *Member:* German-American Lawyers Association, JBA. *LANGUAGES:* English and French. *PRACTICE AREAS:* Commercial; Corporate; Mergers and Acquisitions; Joint Ventures; Banking and Financing.

DR. HEINRICH STALLKNECHT, born 1958; admitted, 1990, Germany. *Education:* Tax School Nordkirchen (Graduate, Financial Economist, Dipl. Finanzwirt, 1980); University of Bochum (Dr. jur.). Author: "Licenses and License fees - Constitutional Aspects of LAbfG NW. *LANGUAGES:* English. *PRACTICE AREAS:* General Civil Law; Corporate; Commercial; Tax Law.

STEPHAN L. PRINZ ZUR LIPPE, born 1959; admitted, 1988, Germany. *Education:* Universities of Bonn and Miami (LL.M.). Co-Author: (Dutch Publication) "Doing Business in Germany," Commentary on DM-Bilanzgesetz, Munich, 1991. Tax advisor (Steuerberater), Member: Fulbright Alumni. *LANGUAGES:* English and French. *PRACTICE AREAS:* Commercial; Corporate; Mergers and Acquisitions; Tax Law.

DR. PETRA MALSBENDEN, born 1962; admitted, 1992, Germany. *Education:* University of Passau (Dr. jur.). Author: Matrimonial Property Regimes in the 19th Century. *LANGUAGES:* English and French. *PRACTICE AREAS:* Commercial; Corporate; Mergers and Acquisitions; Agency.

UTE ZINSMEISTER, born 1962; admitted, 1992, Dusseldorf and before the Court of Justice and the Court of First Instance of the European Communities in Luxembourg. *Education:* University of Munich. *Member:*

(This Listing Continued)

Belgian-German Association of Jurists; European Association of Lawyers. *LANGUAGES:* English and French. *PRACTICE AREAS:* EC Law.

FRANZ JANSSEN, born 1960; admitted, 1991, Germany. *Education:* University of Bonn. *LANGUAGES:* English.

ASSOCIATES

GUIDO WIESEN, born 1963; admitted, 1994, Germany. *Education:* University of Münster. *Member:* DAV (German Law Association). *LANGUAGES:* English and French. *PRACTICE AREAS:* Corporate; Commercial; Civil Law.

DR. MICHAEL F. PEHLKE, born 1960; admitted, 1993, Germany. *Education:* Universities of Kiel, Freiburg im Breisgau, Munich, Surrey, England and Berlin (Dr.Jur.). Author: "Die Souveränität der Bundesrepublik Deutschland im westlichen Bündis," (The Sovereignty of Germany within the Western Treaty Organization). *LANGUAGES:* English. *PRACTICE AREAS:* Commercial; Corporate; Mergers and Acquisitions; Computer Law; Arbitration.

DR. JAN BYOK, born 1961; admitted, 1994, Germany. *Education:* Universities of Hamburg and Edinburgh (LL.M., 1990); University of Vienna (Dr.iur.). Author: "Britische Fusionskontrolle und Europäische Integration," (British Merger-Control and European Integration). *Member:* German-British Law Association. *LANGUAGES:* English and Spanish. *PRACTICE AREAS:* German and European Competition; Cartel Law; Intellectual Property.

DR. ALEXANDER SCHRÖDER-FRERKES, born 1960; admitted, 1992, Germany. *Education:* University of Cologne (Dr.jur.); University of Leuven and Belgium (LL.M., 1992). Author: "Konfliktbeilegungsmechanismen in der Rechtsschutzversicherung: ein europäischer Ländervergleich und Vorschlag eines Schiedsverfahrens," (Conflict Solving Mechanisms within the Field of Legal Cost Insurances: An European Study and Draft of an Arbitration Proceeding). President, Club of Leuven. *Member:* International Lawyers Association; DAV (German Law Association). *LANGUAGES:* English. *PRACTICE AREAS:* Banking; Financing; Corporate; Mergers and Acquisitions; International; Insurance Law.

Languages: German, English, French, Italian, Spanish and Portuguese

---

WOEDTKE RESZEL & PARTNER

Established in 1986

KÖNIGSALLEE 12
40212 DÜSSELDORF, GERMANY
Telephone: 0211/86477-0
Telefax: 0211/86477-30

Dresden, Germany Office: Königsbrücker Straße 62, 01099. Telephone: 03 51/8011893. Telefax: 03 51/53631.

Hamburg, Germany Office: Zippelhaus 4, 20457. Telephone: 040/321266. Telefax: 040/323037.

FIRM PROFILE: The firm was established in 1986 and offers a full range of legal and business services. It is well known for General Practice, Corporate, Company, Commercial Taxation, Customs, Unfair Competition, Antitrust, EEC, Trademark and Copyright Law. The client base is Europe, North America, Japan and Scandinavia. The firm has a legal support staff of 22 consisting of attorneys, paralegal assistants and an office administrator.

PARTNERS OF FIRM

DR. PETER VON WOEDTKE, born Lüneburg, Germany, July 31, 1950; admitted, 1977, Germany. *Education:* Universities of Bielefeld, Heidelberg, Bonn (J.D., 1974); University of Bielefeld (Doctor of Laws, 1977). *LANGUAGES:* German, English and French. *PRACTICE AREAS:* Corporate Law; Reorganization and Rehabilitation of Enterprises; International Business Law; Labour Law; Customs Law.

DR. PETER C. RESZEL, born Kattowitz, Poland, January 27, 1956; admitted, 1984, Germany. *Education:* Universities of Geneva and Bonn (J.D., 1981); University of Osnabrück (Doctor of Laws, 1986). Author: "Die Feststellung der Schädigung im Antidumping - und Subventionsrecht der Europäischen Gemeinschaften," 1987. *LANGUAGES:* German, English and French. *PRACTICE AREAS:* Competition Law; European Community Law; Leasing, Factoring and Franchising; Real Estate Law.

(This Listing Continued)

ASSOCIATES

DR. ROLAND SIMON, born Münster, Germany, October 6, 1955; admitted, 1985, Germany. *Education:* University of Münster (J.D., 1982; Doctor of Laws, 1990). *LANGUAGES:* German and English. *PRACTICE AREAS:* Banking Law; Labour Law; Landlord and Tenant Law.

REINHARD MELERROSE, born Darmstadt, Germany, December 29, 1951; admitted, 1979, Germany. *Education:* University of Bonn (J.D., 1975). *LANGUAGES:* German, English and French. *PRACTICE AREAS:* Corporate Law; Reorganization and Rehabilitation of Enterprises; International Business Law; Real Estate Law.

PETER ALTENBURGER, born Münster, Germany, September 22, 1961; admitted, 1993, Germany. *Education:* University of Munich and Münster (J.D., 1990). *LANGUAGES:* German and English. *PRACTICE AREAS:* Labour Law; Corporate Law; Medicine Law.

ULRICH HOCKER, born Bonn, Germany, November 6, 1950; admitted, 1983, Germany. *Education:* University of Bonn (J.D., 1976). *LANGUAGES:* German and English. *PRACTICE AREAS:* Banking Law; Stock Exchange Law.

AULINGER, BOTTKE, KNÄLMANN

KLEINE ARCHE 1
99084 ERFURT, GERMANY
Telephone: (0361) 5667808
Fax: (0361) 5667810

Bochum, Germany Office: ABC-Strasse 5, D-44787 Bochum. Telephone: (0234) 68779-0. Teletex: 234 334 (Dufhues) (from Telex: 17234334). Fax: (0234) 68 06 42.

Dresden, Germany Office: St. Petersburger Str. 15, 01069 Dresden. Telephone: (0351) 4 87 24 19. Fax: (0351) 4 87 33 27.

Leipzig, Germany Office: Goethestrasse 1, 04109 Leipzig. Telephone: (0341) 9600910. Fax: (0341) 9601169.

General Practice. Corporate, Commercial, Banking, Antitrust, Unfair Competition, Real Estate, Merger and Acquisition, Products Liability, Labor, Co-Determination, Tax, Arbitration, Administrative and Public, Building and Planning. Reversion of nationalized enterprises and real estate to private ownership.

MEMBER OF FIRM

MICHAEL HOESELER, born Recklinghausen, Germany, March 28, 1957; admitted, 1990, Bochum. *Education:* University of Bochum; School of Administration, Speyer. *LANGUAGES:* German, English.

(For Complete Biographical data on all Personnel, see Professional Biographies at Bochum)

SCHMIDT-SIBETH ZIRNGIBL
LANGWIESER HEISSE

ANGER 23
99084 ERFURT (THURINGIA), GERMANY
Telephone: 0361/6 42 12 36
Fax: 0361/6 42 25 04

Munich, Germany Office: Maximiliansplatz 5, 80333 Munich. Telephone: 089/54 56 5-0. Fax: 089/54 56 5-201.

Berlin, Germany Office: Leipziger Straße 63, 10117 Berlin. Telephone: 030/20 22 73. Telefax: 030/20 22 7426.

General Practice, Corporate, Commercial, E.E.C., International Law, Trademarks, Copyright, Unfair Competition, Real Estate, Construction and Building Law, Labor Law, Legal Affairs in former East Germany.

DR. MATTHIAS HEISSE, born Frankfurt/Main, Germany, July 28, 1960; admitted, 1989, Munich. *Education:* University of Munich (Dr. jur., 1988). *LANGUAGES:* German and English.

DR. WOLFGANG WEISSKOPF, born Stuttgart, Germany, December 11, 1959; admitted, 1991, Munich. *Education:* Universities of Regensburg and Tübingen (Dr. jur., 1992). *LANGUAGES:* German and English.

DR. KATHRIN THIELE, born Magdeburg, Germany, November 13, 1959; admitted, 1991, Munich. *Education:* University of Magdeburg (Dr. jur., 1987). *LANGUAGES:* German, Russian and English.

(This Listing Continued)

AXEL METZNER, born Düsseldorf, Germany, October 3, 1964; admitted, 1994, Düsseldorf. *Education:* Universities of Freiburg and Münster. *LANGUAGES:* German and English.

(For complete biographical data on Personnel at Berlin, Munich and Erfurt, Germany Offices, see Professional Biographies at Munich, Germany)

HORLITZ, von MENGES u. PARTNER

Established in 1973

RÜTTENSCHEIDER PLATZ 4 (AM MARKT)
D-45130 ESSEN, GERMANY
Telephone: 0049-201-77 70 44
Telefax: 0049-201-77 08 68

Potsdam, Germany Office: Behlertstraße 27a, D-14469. Telephone: 0049-331-27 15 30. Telefax: 0049-331-271 53 39.

General and International Practice, Antitrust, Banking, Bankruptcy, Commercial, Construction, Corporate, EC, Energy and Natural Resources, Environmental, Foreign Investments, International Trade Matters, Intellectual Property, Labor, Mergers and Acquisitions, Partnership, Real Estate, Taxation, Unfair Competition, Litigation and Arbitration, Notaries, Business Law, Co-Determination, Company Law, Estates, Family Law, Industrial Relations, Inheritance, Insurance, International Commercial Law, International Labor Law, Management Labor and Employment, Personal Injury, International Sale of Goods, Products Liability, Probate, Property, Services Contracts.

MEMBERS OF FIRM

HORST HORLITZ, born Tilsit/East Prussia, December 21, 1921; admitted, 1963, Essen. *Education:* University of Munich. Notary, 1972. Author: "Betrachtungen zur Verantwortung und Haftung des Aufsichtsrats (Beirats, Verwaltungsrats)," 2nd Edition, 1989. Board of Directors: Verein pro Brandenburg, 1990—. Supervisory Board: Stahl- und Walzwerk Riesa AG, 1991-1993. Advisory Committee: Anke GmbH & Co. KG Oberflächentechnik, 1986—. *LANGUAGES:* German and French. *PRACTICE AREAS:* Real Estate; Corporate Law; Mergers and Acquisitions; Foreign Investments.

DR. DIETRICH WILHELM VON MENGES, born Wangritten/East Prussia, October 26, 1909; admitted, 1975, Essen. *Education:* Universities of Königsberg, Berlin and Göttingen (Dr. jur.). Author: "Unternehmensentscheide," 1976; and numerous other publications. Board of Directors: Ferrostaal Aktiengesellschaft, 1947-1966 (Chairman, 1949-1966); Gutehoffnungshütte Aktienverein, 1965-1975 (Chairman, 1966-1975). Supervisory Board: Gutehoffnungshütte Aktienverein, 1975-1983. President: Chamber of Industry & Commerce for Essen, Mülheim and Oberhausen, 1969-1978 (Honorary President, 1978—). Vice President, German-Swedish Chamber of Industry & Commerce, Stockholm, 1958-1983 (Honorary Vice President, 1983—). Member of the Corporate Strategic Planning Council, International Management and Development Institute (IMDI), Washington, D.C., 1979—. *LANGUAGES:* German and English.

ELLEN POLLMANN-TACKEN, born Duisburg, April 14, 1955; admitted, 1983, Essen. *Education:* University of Bonn. *LANGUAGES:* German and English. *PRACTICE AREAS:* Insurance; Personal Injury; Family Law; General Practice; Products Liability.

DR. STEFAN KEITH, born Essen, November 18, 1953; admitted, 1983, Essen. *Education:* Universities of Freiburg and Münster (Dr. jur., 1983). Teaching Assistant, University of Münster, Institute for International Trade and Commercial Law, 1979-1983. Board of Directors: Essener Anwalt- und Notarverein e.V. *LANGUAGES:* German, English and French. *PRACTICE AREAS:* Antitrust; Bankruptcy; Business Law; Company Law; Commercial; Construction; Energy and Natural Resources; Environment; Limited Partnership; Taxation.

DR. HENNRICH DEMUTH, born Bielefeld, May 30, 1945; admitted, 1978, Essen. *Education:* Universities of Bonn, Münster and Gießen (Dr. jur., 1980). Notary, 1988. Assistant Professor, University of Bochum, 1974-1978. Co-Author: "Die besondere Bedeutung des Gesetzes über Ordnungswidrigkeiten für Betriebe und Unternehmen," Der Betriebsberater, 1970. *LANGUAGES:* German and English. *PRACTICE AREAS:* Estates; Family Law; Inheritance; Mortgages; Property.

DR. WOLF-HEINRICH GEISSEL, born Bielefeld, February 27, 1964; admitted, 1992, Essen. *Education:* Universities of Freiburg and Münster (Dr. jur., 1992). *LANGUAGES:* German, English and French. *PRAC-*

(This Listing Continued)

HORLITZ, VON MENGES U. PARTNER, Essen—
Continued

TICE AREAS: Business Law; Commercial Law; Company Law; General Practice.

DR. UWE JULIUS FAUSTMANN, born Solingen, July 4, 1958; admitted, 1992, Essen. *Education:* University of Bonn (Dr. jur., 1990). *LANGUAGES:* German and English. *PRACTICE AREAS:* Co-Determination; Industrial Relations; International Labor Law; Management Labor and Employment; Services Contracts.

DR. CHRISTIAN-F. BOLLMANN, born Kiel, October 18, 1960; admitted, 1993, Essen. *Education:* Universities of Kiel, Vancouver, Munich and Mainz (Dr. jur., 1994). *Member:* International Bar Association (Business Law Section); German-American Lawyer's Association; German Chamber of Industry and Commerce in the United Kingdom; Ghorfa. *LANGUAGES:* German, English and French. *PRACTICE AREAS:* Banking; European Community Law; International Commercial Law; International Sale of Goods; International Trade.

Languages: German, English, French, Spanish and Russian

(For Biographical Data on other Personnel, see Biographies at Potsdam, Germany)

KARBOWSKI, MASLING, HEGER & PARTNERS

Attorneys-at-Law and Notaries Public

Established in 1974

HUYSSENALLEE 86-88

45128 ESSEN, GERMANY

Telephone: 0049-201-17580
Telefax: 0049-201-1758400

Leipzig, Germany Office: Gohliser Strasse 7, 04105. Telephone: 0049-341-5662860; 0049-341-5662861. Telefax: 0049-341-5662862.

Dusseldorf, Germany Office: Kaiser-Wilhelm-Ring 43, 40545. Telephone: 49-211-55-57-17. Telefax: 49-211-55-57-85.

Administrative Law. Advertising Law. Banking Law. Bankruptcy. Competition Law. Constitutional Law. Consumer Protection Law. Customs and Excise Law. Distributorship, Agency and Franchise Law. EEC Law. Employer's Liability. Environmental Law. Family Law. Foreign Investments. International Contracts. International Private Law. Product Liability Law. Property and Real Estate Law. Rent and Lease. General Legal Practice. International Taxation. General Commercial and Corporate Law. Industrial Labor and Shop Constitution Law on behalf of Management. International Trade Law. Antitrust and Unfair Trade Practices.

FIRM PROFILE: The firm was established in 1974. It has a sophisticated and extensive commercial practice, with strong concentrations in general corporate, antitrust and unfair trade practices, labor law and business-related civil litigation. The firm maintains branch offices in Düsseldorf and Leipzig/Germany.

MEMBERS OF FIRM

E. ALEXANDER KARBOWSKI, born Gotha, Germany, February 16, 1945; admitted, 1974, Essen. Notary Public, 1984. *Education:* University of Münster (LL.B., 1971). Author: Periodical articles on national and international trade and company law. Co-Author: "Die Europäische Wirtschaftliche Interessenvereinigung," (european company law), 44 Wertpapier Mitteilungen 1313-1356 (1990). *Member:* Essen Bar Association; American Chamber of Commerce in Germany and New York. *LANGUAGES:* German, English and French. *PRACTICE AREAS:* Corporate Law; Banks and Banking; International; Company Law; Mergers, Acquisitions and Divestitures.

JÜRGEN MASLING, born Warnemünde, Germany, March 10, 1945; admitted, 1977, Hamburg; 1978, Essen. Notary Public, 1989. *Education:* Universities of Freiburg and Münster (LL.B., 1974). *Member:* Essen Lawyers Association; American Chamber of Commerce in Germany. *LANGUAGES:* German and English. *PRACTICE AREAS:* Labor and Employment.

KLAUS G. HEGER, born October 19, 1934, Chemnitz, Germany; admitted, 1968, Essen; 1970, Düsseldorf. *Education:* Universities of Tübingen, Hamburg and Münster (LL.B., 1964). *Member:* German Bar Association; International Bar Association; Industrieclub Düsseldorf. *LANGUAGES:*

(This Listing Continued)

German and English. *PRACTICE AREAS:* Company Law; Mergers, Acquisitions and Divestitures; International Commercial Contracts.

DR. MARTIN HAMM, born Bonn, Germany, May 5, 1948; admitted, 1976, Cologne; 1984, Essen. *Education:* Universities of Freiburg and Cologne (LL.B., 1976); Freiburg (LL.D., 1976). Notary Public, 1990. Author: "Vorteilsausgleichung und Schadensminderungspflicht im Rahmen des § 844 BGB," (compensation and duty to prevent further damage), 1976. *Member:* Essen Lawyers Association. *LANGUAGES:* German and English. *PRACTICE AREAS:* Property; Real Estate; Labor and Employment; Commercial Law.

KLAUS BECKMANN, born Ennigloh, Germany, August 11, 1944; admitted, 1977, Essen. *Education:* University of Cologne. Parliamentary State Secretary to Federal Minister for Economics, 1989—. *LANGUAGES:* German and English. *PRACTICE AREAS:* Commercial Law.

BEATRIX EICKHOFF, born Legden, Germany, February 3, 1958; admitted, 1985, Essen. *Education:* University of Bonn (LL.B., 1982). *Member:* Essen Lawyers Association. *LANGUAGES:* German and English. *PRACTICE AREAS:* Contracts; Civil Law; Rent and Lease.

DR. CHRISTIAN GLORIA, born Lünen, Germany, June 9, 1957; admitted, 1989, Essen. *Education:* University of Bochum (LL.B., 1982; LL.D., 1987) and London. Author: "Das steuerliche Verständigungsverfahren und das Recht auf diplomatischen Schutz - zugleich ein Beitrag zur Auslegung der Doppelbesteuerungsabkommen," (study on the competent authority procedure under tax treaties), 1988; "Der subjektive Faktor" bei der Frage des Vorliegens einer verschleierten Handelsbeschränkung i. S. des Art. 36 Satz 2 EWG-Vertrag," (study on trade restrictions under the EEC-Treaty), 29 Recht der Internationalen Wirtschaft 898 - 905, 1983; "Die Doppelbesteuerungsabkommen der Bundesrepublik Deutschland und die Bedeutung der Lex-Fori-Klausel für ihre Auslegung," (study on the interpretation of tax treaties), 32 Recht der Internationalen Wirtschaft 970 - 978, 1986; "Verfassungsrechtliche Anforderungen an die gerichtlichen Geschäftsverteilungspläne," (due process of law under the Basic Law), 41 Die Öffentliche Verwaltung 849 - 858, 1988; "Die Verwirklichung des Rechts auf den gesetzlichen Richter im Prozess," (due process of law), 42 Neue Juristische Wochenschrift 445 - 446, 1989; "Die Stellplatzpflicht nach den Landesbauordnungen," 9 Neue Zeitschrift für Verwaltungsrecht 305 - 314, 1990; "Der Anspruch auf Erschließung," 10 Neue Zeitschrift für Verwaltungsrecht 720-728, 1991. Co-Author: Der "finale Todesschuß" im Landesrecht Nordrhein-Westfalens," (legality of shooting to kill), 3 Nordrhein-Westfälische Verwaltungsblätter 37 - 45, 1989; "Die Europäische Wirtschaftliche Interessenvereinigung," (european company law), 44 Wertpapier Mitteilungen 1313 - 1356, 1990. Ipsen, Völkerrecht, 3rd ed. (treatise on public international law; inter alia chapters on international law of the sea and on international economic law), 1990. *Member:* German American Lawyers Association. *LANGUAGES:* German, English and French. *PRACTICE AREAS:* Administrative Law; Antitrust and Trade Regulation; Competition; European Community Law; International Law; Commercial Law; Company Law; International Contracts; International Joint Ventures; International Business.

DR. PETER M. MOMBAUR, born December 12, 1938, Solingen, Germany; admitted, 1991, Düsseldorf. *Education:* Universities of Marburg, Bonn and Cologne (LL.B., 1963; LL.D., 1964). Editor of several legal journals. Author: Bundeszwang und Bundestreue, 1964. Member, Committee of Energy, Technology and Research of the European Parliament. Deputy Judge, Northrhine-Westfalian Constitutional Court. *LANGUAGES:* German, English and French. *PRACTICE AREAS:* Administrative Law; Energy Regulation.

PROF. DR. MANFRED MÜLLER, born Rattwitz, Germany, October 2, 1926; admitted, 1990, Leipzig, Saxonia. *Education:* University Halle (Saale); University of Leipzig, 1950 (LL.D., 1959); Habilitation, 1969. Legal Adviser in Industry and Foreign Trade, 1952-1967. Member of the Institute for Foreign and Comparative Law, Potsdam, 1967-1990. Full Professor, 1975—. Publications on legal questions of international cooperation in science and technology and in the field of protection of intellectual property. Consultant on World Intellectual Property Organization, Geneva. *LANGUAGES:* German, English and French. *PRACTICE AREAS:* Intellectual Property.

ECKHARD H. POTT, born Essen, February 22, 1959; admitted, 1991, Essen. *Education:* University of Bochum (LL.B., 1987). *LANGUAGES:* German and English. *PRACTICE AREAS:* Contracts; Civil Law.

CHRISTOPH PESCH, born Essen, Germany, December 24, 1964; admitted, 1994, Essen. *Education:* University of Bochum (LL.B., 1990). *LANGUAGES:* German and English. *PRACTICE AREAS:* Commercial Law; Civil Law.

(This Listing Continued)

MARCUS HELF, born Essen, Germany, April 10, 1965; admitted, 1994, Essen. *Education:* Universities of Bochum and Münster (LL.B., 1991). *LANGUAGES:* German and English. *PRACTICE AREAS:* Labor and Employment; Civil Litigation.

KORDT + PARTNER

GIRARDET HAUS
GIRARDETSTRASSE 2-38
D-45131 ESSEN, GERMANY
Telephone: 0201-872620
Telefax: 0201-8726252

Paris, France Office: 16, Quai d'Orléans, F-75004 Paris. Telephone: 01-43.29.01.41. Telefax: 01-43.25.88.03.
London, England Office: 9, Kingsway, GB-London WC2B 6YF. Telephone: 071-379.51.14. Telefax: 071-836.49.74.
The firm is a member of AdvoSelect EEIG, a network of law firms pooling their resources in special fields and crossborder cases, specializing in business law for medium-sized companies. AdvoSelect EEIG is represented in 51 cities throughout Europe.

Commercial and International Law Practice, Corporate, Construction Law, Large Scale Industrial and Turn Key Projects, Banking and Financing, Arbitration, Litigation and General Practice. The firm offers a full range of legal consultancy for Domestic and International Commercial Matters.

PARTNERS OF FIRM

WERNER KORDT, born Münster/Westf., Germany, April 23, 1949; admitted, 1977, Essen; 1986, Notary Public. *Education:* University of Bielefeld. *Member:* IBA; UIA; Presiding Committee of the Arab German Chamber of Industry and Commerce. *LANGUAGES:* German, English and French. *PRACTICE AREAS:* Commercial and Construction Law; Company Law; International Private Law.

PETRA BLÜMEL, born Iserlohn, Germany, July 30, 1960; admitted, 1988, Essen. *Education:* University of Bochum. *Member:* Canadian German Chamber of Industry and Commerce. *LANGUAGES:* German, English and French. *PRACTICE AREAS:* Civil Law; Business and Commercial Law; International Private Law.

ASSOCIATES

JEAN-CLAUDE CIROTTEAU, born Niort, France, February 6, 1940; admitted, 1964, Paris, Avocat à la Cour; Germany, Legal Consultant in the field of French Law. *LANGUAGES:* French, German and English.

STEPHEN BAISTER, born Crawley, Sussex, England, February 15, 1952; admitted, 1981, London; Germany, Legal Consultant in the field of English Law. *Education:* B.A., Law, M.A., Solicitor. *LANGUAGES:* English, German and French.

SALEH MAJID, born Iraq, May 2, 1938; admitted, Germany, Legal Consultant in the fields of Business and Commercial Law of the Arab countries and Islamic Law. *Education:* B.A., Law (Baghdad), Postgrad., Dip. Law (London). *LANGUAGES:* Arabic, English and German.

KRAMEYER, v. FALKENHAUSEN, HANKE & PARTNERS

Established in 1952

GILDEHOFSTRAßE 1
P.O. BOX 102031
D-45020 ESSEN, GERMANY
Telephone: 0201-82015-0
Telefax: 0201-8201510

Halle, Germany Office: Hansering 4, D-06108 Halle. Telephone: 0345-28053; 0345-21669. Telefax: 0345-21669.
Brussels, Belgium Office: 6, Drève des Renards, B-1180 Brussels. Telephone: 02/3749200. Telefax: 02/3754525.

General Practice, Contracts, Company, Commercial, Construction and Engineering, Corporation, Banking, Antitrust Law and Unfair Competition, Labor, Patent and Trademark, Intellectual Property, Law of the former GDR, Product Liability, Real Estate, Insurance, Family, Inheritance, Environment, Energy and Natural Resources, Taxes, European Community, Arbitration, Administration, Notaries.

(This Listing Continued)

FIRM PROFILE: *The firm was established in 1952 in Essen and offers the full range of legal services. It is well known for its practice in all fields of commercial law. The client base is European and North American. The firm has two branch offices in Halle (former GDR) and in Brussels (Belgium).*

MEMBERS OF FIRM

DR. BERNARD FREIHERR VON FALKENHAUSEN, born Königsberg, Germany, May 10, 1927; admitted, 1960, Essen. *Education:* Universities of Freiburg and Bonn, Cornell Law School (LL.B., 1952); Dr. jur. Author: "Verfassungsrechtliche Grenzen der Mehrheitsherrschaft nach dem Recht der Kapitalgesellschaften (AG und GmbH)," 1967. Deputy Member, Constitutional Court of Northrhine-Westphalia, 1971—. Member, Advisory Council, Cornell Law School. *Member:* Essen and German Lawyers' Associations; Deutsche Gesellschaft für Rechtsvergleichung; American Society of International Law; Cornell Law Association. *LANGUAGES:* German and English. *PRACTICE AREAS:* International Business and Trade; Banking; Company; Commercial.

DR. REINHARD HANKE, born Hohenlimburg, Germany, May 4, 1940; admitted, 1971, Essen. Notary Public, 1981. *Education:* Universities of Goettingen, Munich and Muenster (Dr. jur.). Author: "Das Selbstkontrahieren des Stellvertreters im französischen und angle-amerikanischen Recht verglichen mit dem deutschen Recht", 1966. *Member:* Essen and German Lawyers' Associations; Deutsche Vereinigung für Baurecht; International Bar Association (Section on Energy & Natural Resources Law). *LANGUAGES:* German and English. *PRACTICE AREAS:* General Practice; Company; Contracts; Banking; Law of the former GDR; Energy and Natural Resources.

RAINER KLOTZBACH, born Masserberg, Germany, May 12, 1945; admitted, 1975, Essen; 1985, Notary Public; 1990, Brussels. *Education:* Universities of Munich and Muenster. *Member:* Essen and German Lawyers' Associations; Deutsche Vereinigung für Baurecht; Deutsche Vereinigung für gewerblichen Rechtschutz und Urheberrecht; Deutsch-deutsche Juristenveninigung. *LANGUAGES:* German, English and French. *PRACTICE AREAS:* General Practice; Company; Construction and Engineering; Antitrust and Unfair Competition; Product Liability; European Community.

DR. ANDREAS URBAN, born Dessau, Germany, February 28, 1956; admitted, 1983, Essen. *Education:* Universities of Bochum and Münster (Dr. jur.). Author: "Prognoseentscheidungen im Kartellrecht", 1982. *Member:* Essen and German Lawyers' Associations; German-American Lawyers' Association; Deutsche Vereinigung für gewerblichen Rechtschutz und Urheberrecht. *LANGUAGES:* German and English. *PRACTICE AREAS:* Chartered Expert in Labor Law; Company; Commercial; Antitrust and Unfair Competition; Intellectual Property; Product Liability.

IMKE GLUECKS, born Essen, Germany, July 12, 1961; admitted, 1990, Essen. *Education:* Universities of Regensburg, Bonn and Muenster. *Member:* Essen and German Lawyers Associations. *LANGUAGES:* German, English and French. *PRACTICE AREAS:* General Practice; Commercial; Labor; Family; Inheritance; Real Estate.

DR. ARNDT BEGEMANN, born Flensburg, Germany, June 5, 1961; admitted, 1992, Essen. *Education:* University of Kiel (Dr.jur.). Author: "Die Beziehung zwischen Maklertätigkeit und Abschluss des Hauptvertrages nach § 652 Abs. 1 Satz 1 BGB", 1989; "Gewahrsam bei Bewusstlosigkeit bis zum Eintritt des Todes", JUS 1987, 592; "Retention of Title Securing Payment from Foreign Buyer, in: Credit Manual of Commercial Laws, 1992. *Member:* Essen and German Lawyers Associations; German-American Association; Kieler Doctores Jures; Deutscher Juristen-Tag. *LANGUAGES:* German, English and Italian. *PRACTICE AREAS:* General Practice; Commercial; Patent and Trademark; Intellectual Property; Real Estate; Administration; European Community.

PETER KOENIG, born Herne, Germany, October 7, 1960; admitted, 1991, Frankfurt, 1993, Essen. *Education:* Universities of Bochum and Bonn. *Member:* Essen and German Lawyers' Associations; German-American Lawyers Association. *LANGUAGES:* German and English. *PRACTICE AREAS:* General Practice; Company; Corporate; Commercial; Labor Law; Banking.

ULRICH HOTZE, born Duisburg, Germany, September 29, 1962; admitted, 1992, Essen. *Education:* University of Bonn. *Member:* Essen and German Lawyers' Associations; German-American Lawyers' Association;

(This Listing Continued)

KRAMEYER, V. FALKENHAUSEN, HANKE & PARTNERS, Essen—Continued

German-Canadian Association; German-Poland Lawyers' Association. *LANGUAGES:* German and English. *PRACTICE AREAS:* General Practice; Company; Corporate; Commercial; Labor Law; Insurance.

Languages: German, English, French, Italian and Russian.

KÜMMERLEIN, SIMON & PARTNERS

HUYSSENALLEE 58 - 64
W-45128 ESSEN, GERMANY
Telephone: 02 01/23 33 57
Telefax: 02 01/23 53 76

Mailing Address: P.O. Box 102153, W-45021 Essen, Germany

Commercial, Corporate, Mergers and Acquisitions, Unfair Competition, Antitrust, Copyright, Trademark, License Agreements, Press, Insurance, Product Liability, Real Estate, Construction, Probate, Labor, Administrative, Tax, International Law, Litigation and Arbitration.

MEMBERS OF FIRM

DR. JÜRGEN SIMON, born Lübeck, 1930; admitted, 1959, Essen. *Education:* Universities of Marburg and Kiel (Dr. iur., 1953). Notary Public, 1971. *LANGUAGES:* German and English. *PRACTICE AREAS:* Corporate; Commercial; Tax Law.

MARGOT MÜHLE, born Rastenburg, 1936; admitted, 1964, Essen. *Education:* Universities of Freiburg i.Br. (Graz and Munich). Notary Public, 1973. *LANGUAGES:* German, English and French. *PRACTICE AREAS:* Corporate; Commercial; Probate Law.

DR. WALTER GÜNTHER, born Balingen, 1936; admitted, 1967, Essen. *Education:* Universities of Tübingen and Berlin (Dr. iur., 1964). Notary Public, 1978. Research Assistant, Institute for Commercial, Labor and Business Law, University of Tübingen, 1963-1967. Co-Author: "Munich Contracts Manual," (3rd ed., 1993). *LANGUAGES:* German and French. *PRACTICE AREAS:* Mergers and Acquisitions; Corporate; Commercial; Antitrust Law.

DR. PETER ISING, born Herford, 1941; admitted, 1969, Essen. *Education:* Universities of Freiburg i.Br. and Cologne (Dr. iur., 1969). Notary Public, 1979. *LANGUAGES:* German. *PRACTICE AREAS:* Mergers and Acquisitions; Corporate and Commercial Law; Tax Law.

FRANK J. SCHEUTEN, born Essen, 1947; admitted, 1974, Essen. *Education:* University of Tübingen. Notary Public, 1985. *Member:* German Atomic Forum; Society for Environmental Law. *LANGUAGES:* German. *PRACTICE AREAS:* Environmental Law; Atomic Energy Law; Administrative Law.

HEINZ F. HAHN, born Mülheim/Ruhr, 1951; admitted, 1981, Essen. *Education:* Universities of Bochum, Tübingen and Bielefeld. Notary Public, 1991. Research Assistant, Institute for Constitutional and International Law, University of Bielefeld, 1979-1981. *LANGUAGES:* German and English. *PRACTICE AREAS:* Administrative Law; Unfair Competition; Litigation.

MARTINA VOLMARI, born Essen, 1955; admitted, 1982, Essen. *Education:* University of Bochum. *LANGUAGES:* German, English and French. *PRACTICE AREAS:* Rental Law; Standard Form Contracts; Insolvency Law; Litigation.

MICHAEL M. SCHACKE, born Emsdetten, 1958; admitted, 1989, Essen. *Education:* University of Münster. Research Assistant, Institute for Labor and Commercial Law, University of Münster. *LANGUAGES:* German, English and French. *PRACTICE AREAS:* Mergers and Acquisitions; Corporate and Commercial Law; Distribution and License Agreements; Intellectual Property; International Law.

DR. ELKE VAN ARNHEIM, born Bielefeld, 1959; admitted, 1991, Essen. *Education:* Universities of Bielefeld and Münster (Dr. iur., 1990); London School of Economics and Political Science (LL.M., 1991). Research Assistant, Institute for International Business Law, University of Münster, 1989-1990. *Member:* German-British Lawyers' Association. *LANGUAGES:* German, English and French. *PRACTICE AREAS:* Commercial and Corporate Law; Antitrust; Successions; International Law.

DR. MARTIN MÖNKS, born Höxter, 1962; admitted, 1991, Essen. *Education:* University of Münster (Dr. iur., 1990). *LANGUAGES:* German

(This Listing Continued)

---

and English. *PRACTICE AREAS:* Labor and Social Law; Construction Law; Distribution Agreements.

BETTINA KEIENBURG, born Essen, 1963; admitted, 1993, Essen. *Education:* Universities Bochum and Cologne. *LANGUAGES:* German and English. *PRACTICE AREAS:* Administrative Law; Atomic Energy Law; Environmental Law.

DR. ULRICH IRRIGER, born Herford, 1962; admitted, 1993, Essen. *Education:* University of Münster (Dr. iur., 1991). *LANGUAGES:* German and English. *PRACTICE AREAS:* Mergers and Acquisitions; Corporate; Commercial Law.

SCHMIDT, VON DER OSTEN & HUBER

HAUMANNPLATZ 28/30
P.O. BOX 103231
D-45032 ESSEN, GERMANY
Telephone: 0201-72002-0
Telecopier: 0201-7200234; 0201-7200241; 0201-7200250; 0201-7200259;
0201-7200247
Teletex: 2627-20149 SOH

Berlin, Germany Office: Mommsenstraße 73, D-10629 Berlin. Telephone: 030-8844900. Telecopier: 030-88449090. Teletex: 309029 SOH.

FIRM PROFILE: Established in 1952, Schmidt von der Osten & Huber has grown to become one of Germany's leading commercial law firms concentrating on legal advice for entrepreneurs, business men and professional persons, the firm has also an effective litigation department.

The firm has nine partners and further associates in two offices, Essen and Berlin. The firm provides also services in Brussels, London and Paris together with its partners Jaques & Lewis, Chaintrier, Caillard & Associés and van Wijmen & Koedam.

MEMBERS OF FIRM

DR. KARL RONKEL (1912-1992).

DR. GERHARD SCHMIDT, born Halle, Germany, May 4, 1919; admitted, 1949, Germany. Notary. *Education:* Universities of Halle (Second Legal Examination, 1949); Lausanne and Leipzig. University Assistant, 1939-1940. Member of the foundation board of the world Economic Forum, Genf (WEF), chairman of foundations in Germany. *LANGUAGES:* German, English and French. *PRACTICE AREAS:* Corporate Law; Law of Foundations; Commercial Law.

DR. DINNIES VON DER OSTEN, born Hildesheim, Germany, October 18, 1939; admitted, 1969, Germany. Notary. Tax Adviser. *Education:* Universities of Munich, Berlin and Göttingen (Second Legal Examination, 1967). Author of different publications in GmbH Rundschau regarding (international) tax questions and corporate Law. Member of the Verein für Schiedsgerichtswesen. *LANGUAGES:* German, English and French. *PRACTICE AREAS:* Corporate Law; Tax Law; Law of Contracts, Distribution Agreements and Licensing; Law of Trusts.

DR. JOCHEN SCHMIDT, born Essen, Germany, September 9, 1947; admitted, 1974, Germany. Notary. *Education:* Universities of Lausanne, Freiburg and Münster. Member of supervisory boards of companies. *LANGUAGES:* German, English and French. *PRACTICE AREAS:* Corporate Law; Law of Succession; Commercial Law; Real Estate Law.

DR. EMIL HUBER, born Hoberge/Bielefeld, April 23, 1944; admitted, 1975, Germany. Notary. *Education:* University of Göttingen (Second Legal Examination, 1974). Legal adviser to several European businesses in the manufacturing, food and retail industries and member of their Advisory Board. *LANGUAGES:* German and English. *PRACTICE AREAS:* Corporate Law; Collective Labor Law; Commercial Law.

DR. BERND KLEIN, born Lemgo/Lippe, Germany, April 4, 1945; admitted, 1975, Germany. Notary. *Education:* Universities of Bonn and Freiburg (Second Legal Examination, 1973); University of California, Berkeley (LL.M.). *Member:* German-American Lawyers' Association; German-British Jurists' Association. *LANGUAGES:* German and English. *PRACTICE AREAS:* Corporate Law; Law of Foundations; Computer Law; Software Law.

DR. MANFRED FRIEDRICH, born Krefeld-Hüls, Germany, August 28, 1949; admitted, 1977, Germany. Notary. *Education:* University of Bochum (Second Legal Examination, 1977). Research Assistant, Institute for Civil Law, International Private Law and Comparative Law, 1976-1977. Author of different publications regarding Antitrust Law. *Member:* Verein zur Förderung der Rechtswissenchaft e.V. (Board of Directors); Gesell-

(This Listing Continued)

schaft für Gewerblichen Rechtsschutz und Urheberrecht e.V.; Studienvereinigung Kartellrecht e.V. *LANGUAGES:* German and English. *PRACTICE AREAS:* Corporate Law; Antitrust Law; Real Estate Law; Commercial Litigation.

DR. FRANZ-JOSEF DAHM, born Bochum, Germany, May 12, 1947; admitted, 1980, Germany. Notary. *Education:* Universities of Münster and Bochum (Second Legal Examination, 1976). Civil and Criminal Judge, 1976-1979. *LANGUAGES:* German and French. *PRACTICE AREAS:* Administrative Law; Environmental Law; Medical and Hospital Law; Food and Drug Law.

DR. JÚRGEN HABICH, born Hannover, Germany, July 2, 1956; admitted, 1986, Germany. *Education:* Universities of Hannover and Göttingen (Second Legal Examination, 1986). *LANGUAGES:* German and English. *PRACTICE AREAS:* Labor Law; Collective Labor Law; Law of Competition; Corporate Law of Eastern Europe; Tax Law.

DR. CARL-OTTO STUCKE, born Bramsche/Osnabrück, Germany, March 17, 1958; admitted, 1987, Germany. *Education:* Universities of Kiel and Hamburg (Second Legal Examination, 1986). *LANGUAGES:* German and English. *PRACTICE AREAS:* Construction Law; Corporate Law; Banking Law; Commercial Law.

DR. CHRISTIANE WILKENING, born Essen, Germany, December 11, 1963; admitted, 1993, Germany. *Education:* Universities of Bayreuth and Münster (Second Legal Examination, 1992, Dr. jur. 1992). *LANGUAGES:* German, English and French. *PRACTICE AREAS:* Private Law; Public Law esp. General Administrative Law; Environmental Law; Building License Law.

DR. ANDREAS KEIL, born Bochum, Germany, August 10, 1960; admitted, 1992, Essen; 1994, Berlin. *Education:* Universities of Bochum (Dr. jur., 1991), Geneva and Freiburg; University of Georgia School of Law, Athens, Georgia (LL.M., 1988). Assistant, Institute of Foreign and Private International Law, University of Freiburg, 1985-1987. Foreign Legal Consultant, Glass, McCullough, Sherill & Harrold, Atlanta, Georgia, 1991. Author: "Die Haftungsbefreiung des Schuldners im UN-Kaufrecht," 1993. *Member:* German-American Lawyers Association; Canadian-German Lawyers Association. *LANGUAGES:* German, English and French. *PRACTICE AREAS:* Commercial and Corporate Law; Unfair Competition Law; Intellectual Property Law; International Private Law.

Schmidt, von der Osten & Huber is a member of the JCS Group which comprises Schmidt, von der Osten & Huber in Essen and Berlin; Jacques & Lewis in London, Brussels, the Isle of Man and Jersey; Chaintrier, Caillard in Paris; and Van Wijmen & Koedam in Rotterdam and Breda. The JCS Group is an integrated group of law firms providing a comprehensive range of legal services to international clients.

Languages: German, English and French.

VON ALBERT & RICHTER

Established in 1982

ROLANDSTRASSE 11

D-45128 ESSEN, GERMANY

Telephone: (0201) 24 54 60

Fax: (0201) 23 89 01

Mailing Address: P.O. Box 10 02 30, D-45002 Essen, Germany

General Practice, Commercial, Corporation, Real Estate, Inheritance.

HANS-GERNOT VON ALBERT, born Berlin, Germany, February 12, 1937; admitted, 1967, Berlin; 1968, Essen; 1977, Notary Public. *Education:* Charlottenburger Gymnasium, Berlin; Free University of Berlin. Recipient, American Field Service Scholarship, 1954-1955. Member, Board of Trustees, American Field Service, 1968-1971. *Member:* Essen and German Lawyers' Associations; District Bar Association (Member, Board of Directors, 1977-1986). *LANGUAGES:* German and English.

MICHAEL RICHTER, born Meppen, Germany, November 14, 1956; admitted, 1985, Essen. *Education:* Heisenberg-Gymnasium, Gladbeck; Ruhr-University, Bochum. *LANGUAGES:* German and English.

ABRELL WENDLER NACKE & PARTNER

HOLZHAUSENSTR. 22

D-60322 FRANKFURT/MAIN, GERMANY

Telephone: 49 (0) 69-5 96 40 11

Telefax: 49 (0) 69-55 53 99

Dusseldorf, Germany Office: Graf-Recke-Straße 82, D-40239. Telephone: 0211/96 15 04. Telefax: 0211/96 15 674.

Munich, Germany Office: Martiusstrasse 5/11, 80802. Telephone: 089/34 90 70. Telex: 5213222. Facsimile: 089/33 72 93.

Dresden, Germany Office: Bautznerstr. 22, 01099. Telephone: 0351/555 15. Facsimile: 0351/516 39.

General Corporate Practice, International Law, Mergers and Acquisitions, Banking, Computer, Administrative Law, Patents, Trademarks, Copyright, Unfair Competition, Cartel Law, Litigation, Taxation.

MEMBERS OF FIRM

DR. MATTHIAS ABRELL, born Germany, 1948; admitted, 1978, Germany. *Education:* University of Mannheim (M.B.A., 1973; Dr. jur., 1978). Special Tax Counsel. Lecturer, Business Administration Law, University of Mannheim, 1975-1977. *Member:* German Bar Association. (Also at Tremml, Sholz, Bihler & Partners, Munich, Germany). *LANGUAGES:* German, English and French. *PRACTICE AREAS:* Corporate; Mergers and Acquisitions; Industrial Property Rights; Litigation; Taxation.

GOTTFRIED BLINDOW (1945-1991).

DR. KLAUS DUDEL, born Germany, 1928; admitted, 1960, Germany. *Education:* Universities of Berlin and Cologne (Laws, 1953; Dr. jur., 1958). *Member:* German Bar Association. *LANGUAGES:* English, French, Spanish and Portuguese. *PRACTICE AREAS:* Corporate.

FRANK METZ, born Germany, 1962; admitted, 1993, Germany. *Education:* Universities of Frankfurt am Main and Edinburgh (LL.M.). *Member:* German American Law Association. *LANGUAGES:* German, English and French. *PRACTICE AREAS:* EC Law; EC Competition; Litigation.

JOACHIM KNAPP, born Germany, 1956; admitted, 1982, Germany. *Education:* University of Konstanz (Steuerberater, 1988). Tax Consultant. Member, Official State Examination Board for Tax Consultants. *Member:* German Bar Association; German-Czech Economic Association. *LANGUAGES:* German and English. *PRACTICE AREAS:* Corporate Tax; Real Estate Tax; Double Taxation.

DUSSELDORF OFFICE

MICHAEL WENDLER, born Germany, 1951; admitted, 1981, Germany. *Education:* Universities of Cologne and Bonn. *LANGUAGES:* German, English and French.

DR. REINHARD NACKE, born Germany, 1951; admitted, 1980, Germany. *Education:* University of Münster (Dr.jur., 1981). Special Tax Counsel. *LANGUAGES:* German, English, French, Spanish and Dutch.

DR. WOLFGANG SASS, born Germany, 1957; admitted, 1990, Germany. *Education:* University of Cologne (Dr.jur., 1992); University of Speyer. *LANGUAGES:* German, English and French.

MUNICH OFFICE

WOLFGANG SCHUH (1973-1992).

DR. BERND TREMML, born Germany, 1944; admitted, 1974, Germany. *Education:* University of Munich (Dr.jur., 1975); University of Texas, Law School (M.C.J., 1977). (Also at Tremml, Scholz, Bihler & Partners, Munich, Germany). *LANGUAGES:* German, English and French.

DR. DR. GEORG SCHOLZ, born Germany, 1929; admitted, 1959, Germany. *Education:* University of Würzburg (Ph.D. in Economics, 1957; Dr.jur., 1961). (Also at Tremml, Scholz, Bihler & Partners, Munich, Germany). *LANGUAGES:* German and English.

DR. MICHAEL BIHLER, born Germany, 1950; admitted, 1979, Germany. *Education:* University of Munich (Dr.jur., 1979). Lecturer of International Law, University of Munich, 1974-1979. (Also at Tremml, Scholz, Bihler & Partners, Munich, Germany). *LANGUAGES:* German, English, French and Italian.

DR. LUDWIG SÖLDNER, born Germany, 1926; admitted, 1955, Germany. *Education:* University of Munich (Dr.jur., 1956). Legal Consultant to Austrian and Belgian General Consulates. (Also at Tremml, Scholz, Bihler & Partners, Munich, Germany). *LANGUAGES:* German, French and English.

(This Listing Continued)

ABRELL WENDLER NACKE & PARTNER,
Frankfurt/Main—Continued

WOLF SCHENK, born Germany, 1944; admitted, 1974, Germany. *Education:* University of Hamburg (1963-1965); University of Lausanne (1965); University of Munich (1966-1968); King's College, London (1973-1974). (Also at Tremml, Scholz, Bihler & Partners, Munich, Germany). *LANGUAGES:* German, English and French.

OF COUNSEL

DR. KLAUS HAHNZOG, born Germany, 1936; admitted, 1965, Germany. *Education:* University of Frankfurt am Main (Dr. jur., 1962). Member, Bavarian State Supreme Court, 1978—. Mayor, City of Munich, 1984-1990.

DRESDEN OFFICE

DR. ULRICH WIEDEMANN, born Germany, 1958. *Education:* Universities of Heidelberg, Tübingen and Berlin (Dr. jur., 1992). Berlin Court of Appeals, 1983-1986. (Also at Tremml, Scholz, Bihler & Partners, Dresden, Germany). *LANGUAGES:* German, French, Serbo-Croation, Russian and Polish.

MICHAEL S. ACKERMAN
GUIOLLETTSTRASSE 25
60325 FRANKFURT/MAIN, GERMANY
Telephone: (069) 726510
Telefax: (069) 172246

Personal Injury, Wrongful Death, Medical Legal. Insurance Matters involving Members of the U.S. Forces in Europe. Government Contracts, East-West Trade and Investments and International Law.

MICHAEL S. ACKERMAN, born Germany, June 13, 1947; admitted, 1972, New Jersey; admitted as Rechtsbeistand 1979, West Germany; 1987, Pennsylvania; 1992, Florida. *Education:* University of Pennsylvania, Wharton School of Finance and Commerce (B.S., in Econ., 1969); Temple University (J.D., 1972). *Member:* New Jersey, Pennsylvania, Florida and American Bar Associations; German-American Lawyers Association. *LANGUAGES:* English and German.

ALBERT, FLAD & SCHLOSSHAN
CRONSTETTENSTRASSE 66
D-60322 FRANKFURT/MAIN, GERMANY
Telephone: 49-69-55 02 26
Telex: 416314 coun d
Telecopier: 49-69-55 46 99

Leipzig, Germany Office: Gottschedstrasse 41, D-04109. Telephone: 49-341-211 36 16; 49-341-211 42 52. Telecopier: 49-341-211 42 82.

Commercial and Corporate Law with emphasis on Mergers and Acquisitions, Contracts, Corporate Taxation, Real Estate, Zoning, Planning and Land Use, Unfair Competition and Antitrust, EC Law, Intellectual Property, Computer, Telecommunications, Product Liability, Labor and Social Security, Banking and Securities, Administrative Law, Private and Public Construction, Environmental Law, Food and Drug, Insolvency, Expropriations and Restitution, Litigation and Arbitration.

FIRM PROFILE: The firm, whose roots can be traced back to Berlin and Dresden of the early 1930's, was founded under the present name in Frankfurt/Main in 1967; it was among the first to open a branch office in Leipzig in 1990 after the collapse of the Communist regime in East Germany. The firm provides comprehensive legal services covering all areas of modern business and public services. Most of the work is internationally related. The clientele ranges from large multinational industrial corporations and financial institutions to medium-sized trading companies and public law bodies.

MEMBERS OF FIRM

DR. FRITZ ALBERT (1902-1982).

DR. HUBERT FLAD (1929-1990).

DR. BODO SCHLOSSHAN, born Fulda, Germany, May 22, 1929; admitted, 1962, Germany; 1966, New York, U.S.A. *Education:* Universities of Mainz, Göttingen, Heidelberg and Marburg/Lahn (Referendar, 1952; Dr. jur., 1962); Harvard Law School, U.S.A. (LL.M., 1955). Research Assistant to Professor A.T. von Mehren of Harvard Law School, in writing:

(This Listing Continued)

The Civil Law System, (1957), 1955-1956. *Member:* The Association of the Bar of the City of New York; German, American and International Bar Associations; International Fiscal Association; Union Internationale des Avocats; Harvard Law School Association of Europe. *PRACTICE AREAS:* Mergers and Acquisitions; Joint Ventures; Corporate Taxation; Corporate and Commercial Law; Arbitration; Antitrust.

DR. JOACHIM MICHAEL, born Stuttgart, Germany, August 16, 1936; admitted, 1969, Germany. *Education:* Universities of Tübingen and Berlin (Referendar, 1963; Dr. jur., 1969); New York University School of Law, U.S.A. (M.C.J., 1967). Notary Public. *Member:* German and International Bar Associations; German Association for the Protection of Industrial Property and Copyright; Studienvereinigung Kartellrecht. *PRACTICE AREAS:* Mergers and Acquisitions; Antitrust; Competition; Product Liability; Agrochemicals; Corporate and Commercial Law; EC Law.

DR. HANS HOFMANN, born St. Georgenthal, Germany, February 19, 1946; admitted, 1974, Germany. *Education:* University of Frankfurt/Main (Referendar, 1969; Dr. jur., 1971). Notary Public. *PRACTICE AREAS:* Corporate and Commercial Law; Commercial Real Estate; Commercial Leases; Mergers and Acquisitions; Arbitration.

WERNER LUTZKE, born Lackenbach, Germany, May 21, 1949; admitted, 1982, Germany. *Education:* University of Munich (Referendar, 1974). Tax Consultant (Steuerberater), 1981. *Member:* Hesse Tax Consultants' Association. *PRACTICE AREAS:* Mergers and Acquisitions; Joint Ventures; Taxation; Corporate and Commercial Law; Labor Law.

DR. WERNER BLAU, born Hildesheim, Germany, June 11, 1952; admitted, 1981, Germany. *Education:* Universities of Frankfurt/Main and Freiburg/Breisgau (Referendar, 1978; Dr. jur., 1984). Chairman, Arbitration Board for the Settlement of Unfair Competition Disputes, Leipzig Chamber of Commerce. *Member:* German Association for the Protection of Industrial Property and Copyright; Asia-Pacific Lawyers' Association; German-Korean Lawyers' Association. (Also at Leipzig Office). *PRACTICE AREAS:* Competition; Antitrust; EC Law; Intellectual Property; Expropriations and Restitution.

DR. MARK C. HILGARD, born Duisburg, Germany, November 30, 1956; admitted, 1984, Germany. *Education:* University of Freiburg/Breisgau (Referendar, 1980; Dr. jur., 1985). *Member:* German-American Lawyers' Association; German-British Jurists' Association; Young Lawyers' International Association; Union Internationale des Avocats. *PRACTICE AREAS:* Corporate and Commercial Law; Banking and Securities; Mergers and Acquisitions; Product Liability; Litigation; Labor Law.

DR. RALF HESDAHL, born Frankfurt/Main, Germany, August 8, 1957; admitted, 1988, Germany. *Education:* University of Gießen (Referendar, 1984; Dr. jur., 1992). *Member:* Society for Environmental Law. *PRACTICE AREAS:* Corporate and Commercial Law; Administrative Law; Litigation; Construction Law; Environmental Law; Food and Drug.

DR. JÖRG MICHAEL LANG, born Frankfurt/Main, Germany, July 10, 1957; admitted, 1988, Germany. *Education:* University of Frankfurt/Main (Referendar, 1984; Dr. jur., 1989). *Member:* German-American Lawyers' Association; Banking Law Association. (Also at Leipzig Office). *PRACTICE AREAS:* Commercial and Corporate Law; Banking; Commercial Real Estate; Expropriations and Restitution.

BERND THALMANN, born Thedinghausen, Germany, June 30, 1959; admitted, 1989, Germany. *Education:* Universities of Hamburg, Gießen (Referendar, 1985); University of Georgia, Athens, U.S.A. (LL.M., 1987). *Member:* German-American Lawyers' Association; German-British Jurists' Association; LL.M. Alumni Association of the University of Georgia (President). *PRACTICE AREAS:* Banking; Mergers and Acquisitions; Bankruptcy; Environmental Law; Labor Law.

DR. JOACHIM HARTLE, born Freiburg/Breisgau, Germany, October 24, 1955; admitted, 1992, Germany. *Education:* University of Frankfurt/Main (Referendar, 1989), (Legal); Fachhochschule für Wirtschaft, Pforzheim (Betriebswirt, grad., 1977); University of Frankfurt/Main (Diplom-Kaufmann, 1979; Dr. rer. pol., 1984), (Business Administration). Academic Assistant to Professor Dr. Ordelheide, University of Frankfurt/Main, 1979-1984. Lecturer, University of Frankfurt/Main. Tax Consultant, (Steuerberater), 1987. *Member:* Association for Economic and Social Science-Society for Social Policy; Hesse Tax Consultants' Association. *PRACTICE AREAS:* Taxation; Mergers and Acquisitions; Litigation; Labor Law; Corporate and Commercial Law; Computers and Software.

DR. BARBARA SCHMIDT, born Coburg, Germany, February 25, 1962; admitted, 1990, Germany. *Education:* University of Würzburg (Referendar, 1987, Dr. jur., 1989). (At Leipzig Office). *PRACTICE AREAS:*

(This Listing Continued)

Commercial Real Estate; Commercial and Corporate Law; Expropriations and Restitution; Litigation.

ASSOCIATES

ANDREAS HILFRICH, born Frankfurt/Main, Germany, August 3, 1960; admitted, 1990, Germany. *Education:* University of Frankfurt/Main (Referendar, 1987). *PRACTICE AREAS:* Commercial and Corporate Law; Zoning, Planning and Land Use; Construction Law; Computers and Software; Arbitration.

JUTTA KURTH, born Frankfurt/Main, Germany, October 6, 1962; admitted, 1991, Germany. *Education:* University of Frankfurt/Main (Referendar, 1989). *PRACTICE AREAS:* Commercial Law; Competition; Antitrust; EC Law; Litigation.

DR. ANJA SCHÜMANN, born Kiel, Germany, April 13, 1964; admitted, 1993, Germany. *Education:* University of Bayreuth (Referendar, 1988; Dr. jur., 1992), (Legal); University of Bayreuth (Diplom-Kaufmann, 1988), (Business Administration). *PRACTICE AREAS:* Labor and Social Security; Commercial and Corporate Law; Litigation; EC Law.

WALTHER NEUSSEL, born Bad Kreuznach, Germany, October 18, 1963; admitted, 1993, Germany; 1993, New York, U.S.A. *Education:* Universities of Freiburg/Breisgau and Münster/Westfalen (Referendar, 1988); Fordham University, New York, U.S.A. (LL.M., 1992). *PRACTICE AREAS:* Commercial and Corporate Law; Expropriations and Restitution; Antitrust; Conflicts.

COUNSEL

PROF. DR. JOACHIM JEDZIG, born Drommershausen, Germany, May 13, 1949; admitted, 1976, Germany. *Education:* Universities of Frankfurt/Main and Freiburg/Breisgau (Referendar, 1973; Dr. jur., 1984). Lecturer, Fachhochschulen Wiesbaden and Frankfurt/Main, 1980-1987. Professor, Fachhochschule Bielefeld. *PRACTICE AREAS:* Labor and Social Security.

Languages: German, English and French

ALLEN & OVERY

TAUNUSANLAGE 11
11TH FLOOR
60329 FRANKFURT/MAIN, GERMANY
Telephone: (49 69) 242 6120
Facsimile: (49 69) 242 61220

London, England Office: One New Change, EC4M 9QQ. Telephone: 0171 330 3000. Facsimile: 0171 330 9999.

Beijing, China Office: Suite 3204, Jing Guang Centre, Hu Jia Lou, Chaoyang District, 100020. Telephone: (86 1) 501 4681. Facsimile: (86 1) 501 4682.

Brussels, Belgium Office: Rue de la Loi 99, Box 8, 1040. Telephone: (32 2) 230 27 91. Facsimile (32 2) 230 66 13.

Budapest, Hungary Office: Mádach Trade Center, Mádach Imre utca 13-14, H-1075. Telephone: (361) 268 1511. Facsimile: (361) 268 1515.

Dubai, United Arab Emirates Office: 501 Al Futtaim Tower,P.O. Box 3251, Deira. Telephone: (971 4) 282296. Facsimile: (971 4) 212860.

Hong Kong Office: 9th Floor, Three Exchange Square, 8 Connaught Place. Telephone: (852) 2840 1282. Telex: 68757. Facsimile: (852) 2840 0515.

Madrid, Spain Office: Antonio Maura 7, 6°, 28014. Telephone: (34 1) 521 2654. Facsimile: (34 1) 523 0458.

Moscow, Russia Office: 9 ul Tverskaya, Entrance No 5, 8th Floor, 103009. Telephone: (7 501) 940 4500. Facsimile: (7 501) 940 4501.

New York Office: Swiss Bank Tower, 10 East 50th Street, 10022. Telephone (1-212) 754 3340. Facsimile: (1-212) 754 7903.

Paris, France Office: 1 Avenue Franklin D. Roosevelt, 75008. Telephone (33-1) 49 53 06 37. Telex: 651079. Facsimile: (33-1) 49 53 91 52.

Prague, Czech Republic Office: Jindřišská 34, 110 00 Prague 1. Telephone: (42 2) 2410 3317. Facsimile: (42 2) 2410 3235.

Singapore Office: 20 Raffles Place #08-03, Ocean Towers, 0104. Telephone: (65) 533 0988. Facsimile: (65) 533 1322.

Tokyo, Japan Office: NSE Building, 5th Floor, 1-7-1 Kanda Jinbo-cho, Chiyoda-ku Tokyo 101. Telephone (81 3) 3259 9898. Facsimile (81 3) 3259 9888.

Warsaw, Poland Office: ul. Kopernika 17, IV Floor, 00-359. Telephone: (48 22) 262 226. Facsimile: (48 22) 262 360.

(This Listing Continued)

Firm engaged in English and International Practice.

RESIDENT PARTNERS

Carl Sheldon

(For Complete List of Firm Personnel, see Professional Biographies at London England).

ARETZ SCHMALZ BÖNING

Established in 1993

STRESEMANNALLEE 3
60596 FRANKFURT/MAIN, GERMANY
Telephone: 069-963700
Telefax: 069-96370100

Dresden, Germany Office: Arndstraße 11, 01099. Telephone: 0351-5022450. Telefax: 0351-5023107.

Commercial Litigation and Arbitration, Corporate, Contracts and Commercial Law, International Joint Ventures, Real Estate, Banking, Mergers and Acquisitions, Antitrust, Intellectual Property Law, Entertainment, Unfair Competition, Environmental Law, Labor Law and Industrial Relations.

FIRM PROFILE: The firm was founded in 1993 by former partners of three renowned international corporate and business law firms in Frankfurt/Main and offers a full range of legal services. Currently Aretz Schmalz Böning is representing a variety of international commercial clients, among them banks, companies in the computer and electronics industry, automotive industry, food and beverage industry, private investors, Asian trading houses, press and publishing as well as advertising agencies.

PARTNERS OF THE FIRM

ALF ARETZ, born Velbert, Germany, October 17, 1948; admitted, 1977, Frankfurt/Main. *Education:* Universities of Frankfurt/Main and Georgetown, Washington D.C. (Fellow, Konrad Adenauer Foundation). *LANGUAGES:* German and English. *PRACTICE AREAS:* International Contract Law; Distribution and Agency; Commercial Law; Intellectual Property Law; Antitrust Law; Food and Drug Regulation; Arbitration and Litigation.

GERHARD SCHMALZ, born Schlüchtern, Germany, July 23, 1953; admitted, 1982, Frankfurt/Main. *Education:* University of Würzburg. *Member:* Verein der Fachanwälte für Arbeitsrecht; Deutsche Gesellschaft für Erbrecht; Verein "Anwälte für Ärzte.". *LANGUAGES:* German and English. *PRACTICE AREAS:* Insurance Law; Medical Liability; Restitution; Trust and Estates; Estate Planning; Labor Law.

DR. JUR. PETER BÖNING, born Chemnitz, Germany, April 7, 1944; admitted, 1976, Frankfurt/Main. *Education:* Universities of Marburg and Frankfurt/Main (Dr. jur., 1978). *LANGUAGES:* German and English. *PRACTICE AREAS:* Banking and Financing; Real Estate; Corporate Law; Bankruptcy and Litigation.

AXEL WEBER, born Hanover, Germany, February 10, 1953; admitted, 1981, Frankfurt/Main. *Education:* Universities of Marburg and Frankfurt-/Main; Fachanwalt für Arbeitsrecht (1987). Co-Editor: Deutsche Wirtschaftsdienste. *Member:* Verein der Fachanwälte für Arbeitsrecht; German-Brazilian Jurists' Association. *LANGUAGES:* German, English and Portuguese. *PRACTICE AREAS:* Labor Law; Industrial Relations.

DR. PHIL. NAT. KLAUS-DIETER KUPKA, born Giessen, Germany, May 5, 1948; admitted, 1986, Frankfurt/Main. *Education:* University of Frankfurt/Main (Law and Physics; Dr. of Natural Sciences, 1977). Lecturer, Environmental Law, Frankfurt/Main School of Engineering. *Member:* Deutsche Vereinigung für Gewerblichen Rechtsschutz und Urheberrecht. *LANGUAGES:* German and English. *PRACTICE AREAS:* Antitrust and Unfair Competition Law; Intellectual Property Law; Entertainment Law; Environmental Law; Food and Drug Regulation; Commercial Law.

DR. JUR. JÜRGEN BREITENSTEIN, born Bad Homburg, Germany, August 24, 1956; admitted, 1986, Frankfurt/Main. *Education:* University of Giessen (Dr. jur., 1987); Fachanwalt für Arbeitsrecht (1993). *LANGUAGES:* German and English. *PRACTICE AREAS:* Corporate and Commercial Law; Copyrights; Labor Law; Antitrust and Unfair Competition Law.

(This Listing Continued)

ARETZ SCHMALZ BÖNING, *Frankfurt/Main—*
Continued

ASSOCIATES

RAINARD CLAUS, born Paderborn, Germany, April 20, 1962; admitted, 1992, Frankfurt/Main. *Education:* University of Marburg. *LANGUAGES:* German. *PRACTICE AREAS:* Litigation; Labor Law.

OF COUNSEL

GAYLE ELLEN HANLON, born New York, New York, November 21, 1950; admitted, 1978, New York; 1988, Virginia (Not admitted in Germany). *Education:* Stanford University; University of Denver, College of Law. *LANGUAGES:* English, German, Italian and French. *PRACTICE AREAS:* International Contract Law; Joint Ventures; Intellectual Property; Antitrust and Unfair Competition; Corporate Law; Computer Law.

Languages: German, English, French and Portuguese

DR. PETER K.-D. BARANDT, LL.M.

Rechtsanwalt and Attorney at Law

AN DEN PAPPELN 14
60388 FRANKFURT/MAIN, GERMANY
Telephone: (06109) 33081-83
International: 49-6109-33081-83
Telefax: 49-6109-31552

International Corporate, Business and Tax Law, Transnational Litigations, Establishing Subsidiaries and Branches, Labor Law, Estate Planning and Probate Law, Mergers and Acquisitions, Expropriation Matters and Other Legal Transactions in Former East Germany.

FIRM PROFILE: Specializing exclusively in bilateral German-American cross-border transactions based on double bar admission in both jurisdictions.

DR. PETER K.-D. BARANDT, LL.M., born Bamberg, Germany, September 21, 1951; admitted, 1983, Frankfurt am Main; 1988, New York; 1985, Bar-Approved Specialist in Tax Law (Fachanwalt für Steuerrecht), Frankfurt am Main; 1988, Certified and Sworn Court Interpreter, Frankfurt am Main; 1989, Certified Public Accountant, Frankfurt am Main. *Education:* Fürstenberg-Gymnasium, Donaueschingen, West Germany (B.A., 1970); Universities of Erlangen/Nuremberg and Munich (J.D., 1975); University of Cologne (M.B.A., Diplom-Kaufmann, 1978); Universities of Speyer and Passau (S.J.D., Dr. iur., 1985); Southern Methodist University, Dallas (LL.M., 1987). Author: "Betriebs-Berater", German Business Law Journal, 1983, p. 1293 et seq. (Leading Article); "Deutsche Steuer-Zeitung", German Tax Law Journal, 1983, p. 429 et seq.; "Der Betrieb", German Business Law Journal, 1984, p. 1702 et seq.; "Rückwirkung im Steuerrecht unter besonderer Berücksichtigung der steuerlichen Rückwirkung von Verträgen" (Retroactivity in Tax Law under Specific Consideration of Retroactivity of Contracts), published by Nomos Verlagsgesellschaft, Baden-Baden, West Germany, 1985, ISBN 3-7890-1153-3. Assistant Professor, University of Bonn, 1981. Clerk (Rechtsreferendar), Department of Justice, Mainz, West Germany, 1980-1982. With: R & I Bank of Western Australia, Perth, 1976; B.F. Goodrich Canada Ltd., Kitchener, Ontario, Canada, 1977; Coopers & Lybrand, New York, N.Y., 1978-1979; Arthur Andersen, Düsseldorf, 1979-1980; German-Brazilian Chamber of Commerce, Rio de Janeiro, 1982; Ernst & Whinney, Frankfurt am Main, 1983-1986; Storey, Armstrong, Steger & Martin, Dallas, Texas, 1987; Jupiter Hospital Corporation, Long Beach, California, 1988. *Member:* New York State and American Bar Associations; German-American Lawyers Association; German-Brazilian Lawyers Association; International Institute of Tax and Business Law. Fraternity: Phi Alpha Delta. *LANGUAGES:* German, English, French, Spanish and Portuguese. *PRACTICE AREAS:* International Law; Litigation; Probate Law; Real Estate Law; Trust and Estate Law.

BAUER GRONEN KIESGEN

Established in 1976

SCHUMANNSTRASSE 34 B
60325 FRANKFURT/MAIN, GERMANY
Telephone: 0049 69 975 57200
Telefax: 0049 69 975 57299

Milan, Italy Office: Studio Legale Gronen. Via Lavagna 24, I-20137.
Telephone: 0039 2 761 0907. Telefax: 0039 2 761 0732.

(This Listing Continued)

General Civil and Notarial Practice including Real Estate and International Inheritance Law, German and International Business Law, Labour and Employment Law, Industrial and Intellectual Property, Product Liability, Insurance Law, Mergers and Acquisitions.

MEMBERS OF FIRM

DR. HEINZ L. BAUER, born Jena, Germany, November 7, 1939; admitted, 1968, Germany. *Education:* Universities of Frankfurt am Main, Geneva and Göttingen (Law Degree, 1963; Dr.jur., 1969). Notary Public, 1978. Author: "Conflict of Laws in the Field of Employee's Inventions," RIW, 1970; "Uniform Law on Sale of Goods," RIW, 1980; "Manual Notarial: Dispositions Successorales," Ed., Luxembourg, 1991. *Member:* German-Italian Lawyers Association (Member of Board); Italian Chamber of Commerce for Germany; German-Spanish Lawyers Association; German Association for Intellectual Property and Copyright Law; Learned Society of International Procedure Law. *LANGUAGES:* German, Italian, French and English. *PRACTICE AREAS:* Company Law; Unfair Competition; International Commercial Law.

DR. PETER GRONEN, born Como, Italy, November 26, 1944; admitted, 1973, Germany; 1983, Italy. *Education:* Universities of Freiburg and Göttingen (Law Degree, 1973); University of Milan (Law Degree, 1972; Dr.jur., 1972). Author: "The Italian Tax Reform," RIW, 1975; "Italian Subsidiaries of German Companies," IWB, 1980, 1991; Co-Author: "German Enterprises in Italy," 1993. *Member:* German-Italian Lawyers Association; German-Italian Chamber of Commerce; Italian Chamber of Commerce for Germany. *LANGUAGES:* German, Italian, English and French. *PRACTICE AREAS:* International Business Law; Commercial Law; Mergers and Acquisitions.

PETER KIESGEN, born Kirchen, Germany, September 17, 1955; admitted, 1987, Germany. *Education:* Commercial Traineeship, Siemens AG, Munich; University of Bochum (Law Degree, 1983). Lecturer, Bundeswehrhochschule Siegen, Credit and Banking Law, 1983-1984. *Member:* AIJA; German Association for Insurance Science. *LANGUAGES:* German, French and English. *PRACTICE AREAS:* Labour Law; Commercial Law.

DIETRICH STÖHR, born Wiesbaden, Germany, October 24, 1959; admitted, 1991, Germany. *Education:* Universities of Marburg, Lausanne and Frankfurt am Main (Law Degree, 1991). *Member:* German-Italian Lawyers Association; German Association for Insurance Science. *LANGUAGES:* German, English and Italian. *PRACTICE AREAS:* International Business Law; Insurance Law.

BAUMGARTEN, BARON v. PUTTKAMER, SACHSE & TEN HÖVEL

GOETHEPLATZ 1-3
60313 FRANKFURT/MAIN, GERMANY
Telephone: 69-281 724
Telefax: 69-292 076
Telex: 4189064

Acquisitions, Air, Antitrust, Arbitration, Banking, Commercial, Corporate Finance, Corporation, EEC, Foreign Trade, Incentive Plans, Insurance, International, Labor, Mergers, Product Liability, Real Estate, German and International Tax, Trademarks, Unfair Competition and Transportation Law. Notaries. Litigation.

MEMBERS OF FIRM

KLAUS BAUMGARTEN, born Berlin, Germany, March 9, 1931; admitted, 1959, Frankfurt am Main. *Education:* University of Frankfurt am Main (Referendar, 1955); University of Paris, France. Notary, 1968—. *LANGUAGES:* German, English and French.

BOGISLAV BARON V.PUTTKAMER, born Leipzig, Germany, November 9, 1934; admitted, 1968, Frankfurt am Main. *Education:* University of Bonn (Referendar, 1963). Notary, 1987—. Banker, Dresdner Bank, Hamburg, 1956-1958. *LANGUAGES:* German, English and French.

ECKHARD SACHSE, born Zierenberg/Kassel, Germany, May 17, 1945; admitted, 1974, Frankfurt am Main. *Education:* University of Frankfurt am Main (Referendar, 1971). Notary, 1988—. Teaching Assistant to Professor Dr. Günter Püttner, 1970-1972. Head of Mergers and Acquisitions, Schröder, Münchmeyer, Hengst & Co. Bank, 1974-1979. Senior General Manager, "Die Zeit", 1980-1981. Senior General Manager and Head of Legal Department, Trinkaus & Burkhardt/Midland Bank Group, London, 1982-1985. *Member:* IBA; German-American Lawyers' Association. *LANGUAGES:* German, English and French. *PRACTICE AREAS:* Banks and

(This Listing Continued)

Banking; Business Law; Company Law; Corporate Law; Investments; Management Labor and Employment; Mergers, Acquisitions and Divestitures; Securities.

CLAUS TEN HÖVEL, born Wiesbaden, Germany, April 22, 1950; admitted, 1978, Frankfurt am Main. *Education:* Universities of Mainz, Freiburg/Breisgau, Frankfurt am Main (Referendar, 1975). Teaching Assistant to Professor Dr. Manfred Zuleeg, 1979-1984. *LANGUAGES:* German, English, French and Italian.

DR. ANNA-MARIA BEESCH, born Dreieich, Germany, October 10, 1954; admitted, 1986, Frankfurt am Main. *Education:* Universities of Frankfurt am Main and Lausanne, Switzerland (Referendar, 1982; Dr.jur., 1989). Scientific Staff Member, Institute for Foreign and International Trade Law (AIW), Research Project on International Transportation Law, University of Frankfurt am Main, 1985-1988. *LANGUAGES:* German, English and French.

Languages: German, English, French and Italian.

BEITEN BURKHARDT MITTL & WEGENER

Rechtsanwälte

ARNDTSTRASSE 28
D-60325 FRANKFURT/MAIN, GERMANY
Telephone: (0 69) 75 60 95-0
Telefax: (0 69) 75 60 95-12

Munich, Germany Office: Leopoldstrasse 236, D-80807. Telephone: (089) 35065-00. Telefax: (089) 35065-123.

Berlin, Germany Office: Kurfürstenstrasse 72-74, D-10787 Berlin. Telephone: (0 30) 264 71-0. Telefax: (0 30) 264 71-123.

Nürnberg, Germany Office: Obere Turnstrasse 8, D-90429 Nürnberg. Telephone: (09 11) 2 79 71-0. Telefax: (09 11) 2 79 71-99.

Leipzig, Germany Office: Käthe-Kollwitz-Strasse 54, D-04109 Leipzig. Telephone: (03 41) 4 77 25 97. Telefax: (03 41) 4 77 25 99.

Potsdam, Germany Office: Heinrich-Mann-Allee 105 B, D-14473 Potsdam. Telephone: (0331) 33 43 06. Telefax: (0331) 33 43 29.

Hof, Germany Office: Oberer Torplatz 1, D-95028 Hof. Telephone: (09281) 80 23. Telefax: (09281) 1 65 69.

Plauen, Germany Office: Lindenstrasse 5, D-08523 Plauen. Telephone: (03741) 22 35 11; 22 49 62. Telefax: (03741) 22 49 62.

New York, New York Office: 215 East 73rd Street, New York, NY 10021. Telephone: (212) 570-2141. Telefax: (212) 734-7011.

London, England Office: Swedenborg House, 21 Bloomsbury Way, London, WC1A 2TH. Telephone: (0171) 2 42 44 66. Telefax: (0171) 2 42 44 67.

Moscow, Russia Office: Ul. Alekseja Tolstovo D.30/1, 103001 Moscow. Telephone and Telefax: (095) 202 37 60; 290 05 56.

Prague, Czech Republic Office: Na Bojišti 24, 120 00 Prague 2. Telephone: (2) 24 91 5808. Telefax: (2) 24 91 5804.

Budapest, Hungary Office: József Nádor Tér 9, H-1051 Budapest. Telephone: (1) 2 66 18 10. Telefax: (1) 2 66 18 11.

Hong Kong Office: 605 B, Sixth Floor, Peregrine Tower, Lippo Centre, 89 Queensway. Telephone: (852) 2524 6468. Telefax: (852) 2524 7028.

Beijing, People's Republic of China Office: Unit 10, 29th Floor, Jing Guang Centre, Hu Jia Lou, Chao Yang Qu, 100020. Telephone: (86-1) 501 4569; 501 3388 Ext. 2910. Telefax: (86-1) 501 3034.

Commercial Law, Company Law, M & A, Joint Ventures, Finance, Banking, Leasing, Domestic and International Tax, Antitrust, EC Law, Real Property and Private Construction, Electronic Data Processing (Protection and Licensing), Media, Publishing, Unfair Competition, Trademarks, Copyright, Labour, General and Special Administrative Law Particularly Public Construction and Planning Regulations and Public International Law, Environmental Law, Agricultural Law, Privatization and Restitution (former GDR), Probate, Family and Estate Planning, Insolvency and Sports, Insurance, Automobile Accidents and Injuries.

FIRM PROFILE: BEITEN BURKHARDT MITTL & WEGENER is a nation-wide and international law firm with 108 lawyers. The firm's head office is in Munich. All the firm's offices provide a comprehensive range of services in the main areas of civil and commercial law.

HANS-JÜRGEN STERNER, born Schweidnitz, 1927; admitted, 1958, Germany. *Education:* University of Frankfurt (law degree, 1955; Dr. jur., 1958). Notary Public, 1968. *Member:* Executive Committee of the Frankfurt a.M. Bar Association (1968—). *LANGUAGES:* German and English.

(This Listing Continued)

PRACTICE AREAS: Press Law; Publishing and Radio; Real Estate; Construction Law; Probate and Family Law; Insurance; Automobile Accidents and Injuries.

THILO KRAUSE-PALFNER, born Insterburg, 1942; admitted, 1972, Germany. *Education:* University of Frankfurt (law degree, 1968; Dr. jur., 1973). Notary Public, 1987. Author: "The Proceeding of Laws to Become Unconstitutional," 1972. *Member:* German-Portuguese Chamber of Commerce, Lisbon. *LANGUAGES:* German and English. *PRACTICE AREAS:* Company Law; Acquisitions and Sales; Restructuring; Press Law; Publishing and Radio; Real Estate; Construction Law; Sports.

GERHARD SCHMIDT, born Lauf an der Pegnitz, 1957; admitted, 1986, Germany. *Education:* Universities of Erlangen-Nürnberg, Lausanne and Strasbourg (law degree, 1982; Dr.jur., 1984); Institut Européen d'Administration des Affaires, INSEAD (Business Administration Studies); Fontainebleau, France (M.B.A., 1984). Licensed as Steuerberater (Tax Advisor), 1988. Professor, University ("Fachhochschule") Mainz II. Publications on Public Law. Member of the Supervisory Board: Sappi Europe AG; Hannoversche Papierfabriken Alfeld-Gronau AG. *Member:* German-Czech Jurists' Association (Vice President). *LANGUAGES:* German, English and French. *PRACTICE AREAS:* Company Law; Acquisitions and Sales; Restructuring; Tax Planning; Financial Services.

BERTRAND H. PRELL, born Carshalton/Surrey, England, 1954; admitted, 1988, Germany; 1993 as Solicitor, England and Wales. *Education:* University of Munich (degrees in Theology, 1978 and law degree, 1980). Contracts Manager at the Fraunhofer-Gesellschaft, Munich, 1983-1984. Lecturer in Law at the University of East Anglia, Norwich, England, 1984-1988. Associate: Rechtsanwälte Stumm & Klein, Munich, 1988-1989. *Member:* British-German Jurists' Association; Institute of International and Comparative Law, London; German Chamber of Commerce, London. *LANGUAGES:* German and English. *PRACTICE AREAS:* Company Law; Acquisitions and Sales; Restructuring; Financial Services.

HEINER DRÜKE, born Soest, 1958; admitted, 1990, Germany. *Education:* Universities of Bonn and Berkeley, California (law degree, 1984; Dr.jur., 1989). Publications on Public Law. Legislative Aide to Member of the German Parliament, 1986-1988. *LANGUAGES:* German and English. *PRACTICE AREAS:* Company Law; Acquisitions and Sales; Restructuring; Financial Services.

STEPHAN GRAUKE, born Eltville/Rhein, 1959; admitted, 1991, Germany. *Education:* Universities of Mainz and Dijon, France (law degree, 1987). Member of Supervisory Board, BFM Unternehmensbeteiligungsgesellschaft für den Mittelstand AG. *Member:* German-British Jurists' Association. *LANGUAGES:* German, English and French. *PRACTICE AREAS:* Company Law; Acquisitions and Sales; Restructuring; Financial Services.

THOMAS P. HERTL, born Frankfurt, 1963; admitted, 1991, Germany. *Education:* Universities of Giessen and Frankfurt (law degree, 1987). Trainee with US law firm (main subject - Patent, Trademark and Copyright), San Francisco, 1990. *Member:* German-American Jurists' Association; German Association for the Protection of Industrial Property and Copyright (GRUR). *LANGUAGES:* German, English and French. *PRACTICE AREAS:* Company Law; Acquisitions and Sales; Restructuring; Unfair Competition; Copyrights; Advertising and Marketing.

WOLFGANG HOHENSEE, born Cologne, 1965; admitted, 1994, Germany. *Education:* University of Cologne (law degree, 1989; Dr.jur., 1993). Author: "Joint Ownership of a Company by Coheirs," 1994. Research Assistant, Institute for Civil Law, Labour Law and Commercial Law, University of Cologne, 1990-1994. Trainee, Heuking Kühn Celestine Weil, Paris, 1993. *Member:* German-French Jurists' Association. *LANGUAGES:* German, English and French. *PRACTICE AREAS:* Company Law; Acquisitions and Sales; Restructuring; Probate and Family Law; Sports.

ROBERT M. PEELER, born Dallas, Texas, 1958; admitted, 1986, Texas (Not admitted in Germany). *Education:* University of North Texas (M.B.A., 1982); Baylor University, School of Law (J.D., 1986). *Member:* American Bar Association (Corporate, International Section); American-German Chamber of Commerce. *LANGUAGES:* English and German. *PRACTICE AREAS:* Company Law; Acquisitions and Sales; Restructuring; Financial Services.

(For Complete Biographical Data on all Personnel, see Munich, Germany Biographical Card)

BODEN OPPENHOFF RASOR RAUE

FRANKFURT/MAIN, GERMANY

(See Oppenhoff & Rädler)

BOESEBECK, BARZ & PARTNER

Established in 1919

DARMSTAEDTER LANDSTRASSE 125

60598 FRANKFURT AM MAIN, GERMANY

Telephone: (49) (69) 96 236-0
Cable Address: "Legal"
Telex: 4 11 060 (legal d)
Telecopier: (49) (69) 96 236-100

Mailing Address: P.O. Box 70 01 26, D-60551 Frankfurt AM Main, Germany

REVISERS OF THE GERMAN LAW DIGEST FOR THIS DIRECTORY.

Berlin, Germany Office: Schlueterstrasse 37, 10629 Berlin. Telephone: (49) (30) 88 57 45-0. Telecopier (49) (30) 88 57 45-99.

Dresden, Germany Office: Heideparkstrasse 4, 01099 Dresden. Telephone: (49) (351) 56 70 550. Telecopier: (49) (351) 50 23 476.

Vienna, Austria Office (Sprechstelle): Graben 29A, 1010 Vienna. Telephone: (43) (1) 53 55 744. Telecopier: (43) (1) 53 50 649

Warsaw, Poland Office: ul. Wspólna 25, 00519 Warsaw. Telephone: (48) (2) 62 83 029. Telecopier: (48) (22) 29 41 05.

Zagreb, Croatia Office: Trg bana J. Jelacica 3, 41000 Zegreb. Telephone: (385) (41) 42 71 16. Telecopier: (385) (41) 42 87 99.

Commercial, Corporation, Contracts, Mergers and Acquisitions, Banking, Tax, Antitrust, Unfair Competition, Distributorship Agency and Franchising, Capital Markets Financial Services, Patents and Trademarks, Computer (EDP Law), Arbitration and Litigation, Product Liability, International Public and Private Law, EEC-Law, Property and Real Estate, Foreign Investments, Administrative, Environmental, Trade Regulations, Food and Drug Regulations, Notaries.

MEMBERS OF FIRM

DR. ERNST BOESEBECK (1892-1972).

DR. CARL HANS BARZ (1909-1975).

DR. WILLY PAUL (1909-1981).

ALBRECHT STOCKBURGER, born Denkendorf/Esslingen (Neckar), Germany, September 28, 1932; admitted, 1962, Germany. Education: Universities of Tübingen and Frankfurt am Main. Notary, 1973—. LANGUAGES: German and English. PRACTICE AREAS: Real Estate; Administrative; Construction; Zoning and Building; Corporate; Notary.

DR. GEORG HOHNER, born Heilbronn, Germany, October 26, 1942; admitted, 1970, Germany. Education: Universities of Munich and Frankfurt (Doctor of Jurisprudence). Notary, 1980. Author: Several Sections in Hachenburg, Grosskommentar on GmbH-Law (Limited Liabilities Company Act), 1977 (sections 33, 34) and 1980 (sections 65-77); Handbuch der Unternehmenszusammenschlüsse, Aktienrecht, 1972. LANGUAGES: German, English and French. PRACTICE AREAS: Corporate Reorganizations; Joint Ventures; Antitrust; Commerce; Litigation; Arbitration; Notary.

ECKART WILCKE, born Berlin, Germany, January 22, 1943; admitted, 1970, Germany. Education: Universities of Lausanne, Freiburg, Berlin and Frankfurt am Main. Notary, 1989. LANGUAGES: German, English and French. PRACTICE AREAS: Banking; Capital Markets; Financial Services; International Trade and Transactions; Antitrust; Distributorship; Agency; Litigation; Notary.

DR. GÜNTER PAUL, born Frankfurt, Germany, February 14, 1941; admitted, 1970, Germany. Education: Universities of Frankfurt and Hamburg. Notary, 1982. Author: "Auskunftshaftung in der neueren Rechtsprechung," Diss. Frankfurt/Main, 1973. Member: Institut der Steuerberater e.V.; International Bar Association. LANGUAGES: German, French and English. PRACTICE AREAS: Tax; Antitrust; Corporate; Industrial Intellectual Property; Media; Litigation; Notary.

(This Listing Continued)

DR. RICHARD H. STERZINGER, born Kassel, Germany, September 15, 1945; admitted, 1974, Germany. Education: Universities of Marburg, Darmstadt (Dr. rer. pol.) and Miami (Master of Comparative Law, 1977). Author: "Schadensrechtliche Auswirkungen des gesellschaftsrechtlichen Trennungsprinzips," 1976. Member: American Society of International Law. LANGUAGES: German and English. PRACTICE AREAS: International Trade and Transactions; Mergers and Acquisitions; Joint Ventures; Banking; Investment Funds; Project Finance; Capital Markets; Computer; Licensing; Notary.

DR. HARALD G. SEISLER, born Mosbach, Germany, January 23, 1953; admitted, 1981, Germany. Education: University of Mannheim (Doctor of Jurisprudence). Author: "Der Anspruch des Minderheitsaktionärs auf angemessene Abfindung im Verfahren nach §§ 306 AktG, 30 ff. UmwG," Diss. Mannheim, 1983. LANGUAGES: German and English. PRACTICE AREAS: Mergers and Acquisitions; Antitrust; Unfair Trade Practices; Industrial and Intellectual Property Rights; Tax; Distributorship; Agency; Licensing; Litigation.

DR. CLAUDIUS DECHAMPS, born Stuttgart, Germany, June 10, 1954; admitted, 1986, Germany. Education: University of Tübingen (Doctor of Jurisprudence). Author: "Wertrechte im Effekten-Giroverkehr," Köln, 1988. LANGUAGES: German and English. PRACTICE AREAS: Computer Law (EDP Law); Licensing; Banking; Financial Institutions; Stock Exchange; Tax; Product Liability; Litigation.

DR. HINRICH THIEME, born Saarbrücken, Germany, March 8, 1958; admitted, 1986, Germany. Education: Universities of Freiburg and Göttingen (Doctor of Jurisprudence); London School of Economics (LL.M., 1986). Author: "Das Verhältnis der Parlamentarischen Untersuchungsausschüsse zur Exekutive," Diss. Göttingen, 1983. Member: German-British Jurists' Association. LANGUAGES: German and English. PRACTICE AREAS: Zoning and Building; Construction; Environment; Real Estate; Administrative Law; Subsidies; EC Law; Litigation.

DR. RAINER BOMMERT, born Wanne-Eickel, Germany, June 1, 1958; admitted, 1989, Germany. Education: University of Gießen (Doctor of Jurisprudence). Author: "Verdeckte Vermögensverlagerungen im Aktienrecht," 1989. LANGUAGES: German and English. PRACTICE AREAS: Corporate; Mergers and Acquisitions; Joint Ventures; Antitrust; Banking; Finance; Litigation.

INGO WINTERSTEIN, born Frankfurt am Main, Germany, April 3, 1959; admitted, 1989, Germany. Education: University of Frankfurt am Main. Author: "Investitionsvorranggesetz," 1993. LANGUAGES: German and English. PRACTICE AREAS: Environment; Administration; Building and Zoning; Property and Real Estate; Constuction Litigation.

DR. GISELHER RÜPKE, born Bederkeda, Germany, May 23, 1934; admitted, 1975, Germany. Education: Universities of Muenchen, Goettingen (Doctor of Jurisprudence), Chicago (Master of Comparative Law), Freiburg. Author: "Gesetzgeberisches Ermessen und richterliches Prüfungsrecht in der Rechtsprechung des Bundesverfassungsgerichts, zum Gleichheitssatz," 1961/1964; "Schwangerschaftsabbruch und Grundgesetz," 1975; "Der verfassungsrechtliche Schutz der Privatheit," 1976. Lecturer on Law (Privatdozent) University of Frankfurt am Main, 1974—. Chairman, Committee on Data Protection of the Federal Bar Association. LANGUAGES: German and English. PRACTICE AREAS: Zoning and Building; Administrative; Data Protection.

URSULA HOLLER, born Berchtesgaden, Germany, January 13, 1948; admitted, 1987, Germany. Education: University of Frankfurt am Main. LANGUAGES: German and English. PRACTICE AREAS: Unfair Trade Practices; Industrial and Intellectual Property Rights; Consumer; Product Liability; Litigation.

DR. ROLF JOERKE, born Ludwigsburg, Germany, December 23, 1955; admitted, 1987, Germany. Education: University of Tuebingen (Doctor of Jurisprudence). Author: "Akteneinsicht als Voraussetzung effektiver Verteidigung. Zur Sicherung der Informationsrechte des Beschuldigten im Strafverfahren," 1987. LANGUAGES: German and English. PRACTICE AREAS: Commercial Penal Law; Food and Drug; Product Liability; Litigation.

IRIS LAUTH, born Koblenz, Germany, May 14, 1958; admitted, 1990, Germany. Education: University of Frankfurt am Main. LANGUAGES: German and English. PRACTICE AREAS: Litigation; Unfair Trade Practices; Industrial Rights and Intellectual Property Rights; Insurance; Transport.

DR. ALEXANDER VON NEGENBORN, born Hamburg, Germany, June 29, 1958; admitted, 1990, Germany. Education: Universities of Dues-

(This Listing Continued)

seldorf and Munich (Doctor of Jurisprudence). Author: "Kooperativer Grundrechtsschutz durch die Bundesländer am Beispiel des Satellitenrundfunks.". **LANGUAGES:** German, English and French. **PRACTICE AREAS:** Construction; Real Estate; Zoning and Building; Environment; Administrative; Litigation.

OLIVER FELSENSTEIN, born Hannover, Germany, June 9, 1960; admitted, 1990, Germany. *Education:* Universities of Freiburg and Miami (LL.M., Comparative Law). **LANGUAGES:** German, English and French. **PRACTICE AREAS:** Corporate; Finance; Banking; Investment Funds; Joint Ventures; International Trade and Transactions.

MICHAEL WAHL, born Dillenburg, Germany, June 6, 1964; admitted, 1992, Germany. *Education:* University of Gießen. **LANGUAGES:** German and English. **PRACTICE AREAS:** Labour and Industrial Relations; Litigation.

WERNER MICHAEL WALDECK, born Eggenfeld, Germany, February 20, 1945; admitted, 1992, Germany. *Education:* Universities of Bonn, Munich, University for Public Administration Speyer. Official at Federal Ministry of Finance, 1975-1986 (in charge of: stock exchange matters, banking supervision legislation, banking structure, government borrowings and foreign credit relations, law coordination for capital markets in the EC). Chief Executive Officer, Frankfurt Stock Exchange AG, 1987-1992. **LANGUAGES:** German and English. **PRACTICE AREAS:** Banking; Financial Institutions; Capital Market; Investment Funds; Corporate Law; Stock Exchange; Mergers and Acquisitions.

DR. UTA COYM, born Frankfurt, Germany, September 3, 1952; admitted, 1983, Germany. *Education:* University of Frankfurt, 1975, Doctor of Jurisprudence. Author: "Konsumentenkredit und Datenschutzprobleme in Kanada und der Bundesrepublik, 1978;" "German Bond Markets," Euromoney, London, 1986. In charge of euro-bond issues and syndicated loans, Commerzbank, Frankfurt, International New Issues and Syndicate Department, 1978-1983. **LANGUAGES:** German and English. **PRACTICE AREAS:** Capital Markets; Finance Institutions; Investment Funds; Mergers and Acquisitions; International Trade and Transactions.

DR. FRANK MICHEL, born Frankfurt am Main, October 20, 1960; admitted, 1993, Germany. *Education:* Universities of Giessen and Marburg (Doctor of Jurisprudence). Author: "Die Kommanditanteilsübertragung auf einen Dritten.". **LANGUAGES:** German and English. **PRACTICE AREAS:** Commercial; Corporate; Contracts; Litigation; Property and Real Estate.

OF COUNSEL

DR. ROLF BERNINGER, born Saarbrücken, Germany, June 29, 1927; admitted, 1957, Germany. *Education:* University of Frankfurt am Main (Doctor of Jurisprudence). Author: *Das Namensrechtliche Element der Firma.* Notary, 1965—. **LANGUAGES:** German and English. **PRACTICE AREAS:** Corporate; Real Estate; Litigation; Arbitration; Notary.

KLAUS H. ROQUETTE, born Königsberg, Germany, May 20, 1926; admitted, 1956, Germany. *Education:* Universities of Tübingen and Erlangen. Notary, 1965—. *Member:* International Union of Advocates (Member, Common Market Committee, 1960—). *Member:* American Chamber of Commerce in Germany; British Trade Council in Germany e.V. **LANGUAGES:** German, English and French.

REVISERS OF THE GERMAN LAW DIGEST FOR THIS DIRECTORY.

BRANDT KESTLER LAPPAT SCHÜTT & PARTNER

BOCKENHEIMER LANDSTRAßE 98-100
60323 FRANKFURT/MAIN, GERMANY
Telephone: (069) 75617-0
Telefax: (069) 75617-222

General Practice, Commercial, Antitrust, Corporate Partnership, Merger and Acquisition, National and International Contract Law, Real Estate, Administrative Law, Litigation and Arbitration, Labour, Family Law, Tax, EC, Environmental, Unfair Competition, Leasing, Computer, Law of Succession, Copyright, Banking and Finance Law, Aviation and Aerospace, Criminal Law.

(This Listing Continued)

MEMBERS OF FIRM

GERALD I. BRANDT, born Lübeck, Germany, August 8, 1949; admitted, 1980, Germany. *Education:* Universities of Frankfurt am Main and Saarbrücken. Tax Law Specialist, 1982. *Member:* German Bar Association; Tax Lawyers Association. **LANGUAGES:** German and English. **PRACTICE AREAS:** Aviation and Aerospace; National and International Contract; Taxation.

HUBERTUS W. KESTLER, born Bad Königshofen, Germany, October 17, 1952; admitted, 1981, Germany. *Education:* Universities of Frankfurt am Main and Paris; Fachhochschule für Verwaltungswissenschaften Speyer (School for Science of Administration). Notary Public, 1988. *Member:* German Bar Association. **LANGUAGES:** German, English and French. **PRACTICE AREAS:** Property; Corporate Law; Company Law; Real Estate; Antitrust.

HANS-JÜRGEN LAPPAT, born Frankfurt/Main, Germany, August 28, 1953; admitted, 1988, Germany. *Education:* University of Frankfurt am Main, Economics. Tax Consultant, 1985. Certified Public Accountant, 1991. *Member:* German Bar Association; Steuerberaterkammer Frankfurt am Main; Wirtschaftsprüferkammer, Düsseldorf. **LANGUAGES:** German and English. **PRACTICE AREAS:** Company Law; Corporate Law; Finance; Mergers; Acquisition and Divestitures; Taxation.

REINHART SCHÜTT, born Siedenburg, Germany, July 27, 1950; admitted, 1979, Germany. *Education:* University of Marburg. Tax Consultant, 1985. Certified Public Accountant, 1989. *Member:* German Bar Association; Steuerberaterkammer Frankfurt am Main; Wirtschaftsprüferkammer Düsseldorf. **LANGUAGES:** German and English.

HANS-JOACHIM OTTO, born Heidelberg, Germany, October 30, 1952; admitted, 1983, Germany. *Education:* Universities of Heidelberg, Munich and Frankfurt am Main. Scientific Assistant, Frankfurt University, 1980-1983. Member of National Parliament (Deutscher Bundestag). *Member:* German Bar Association. **LANGUAGES:** German, English and French. **PRACTICE AREAS:** Communications and Media; Law of Succession.

ALEXANDER SCHMID, born Frankfurt/Main, Germany, December 17, 1956; admitted, 1987, Germany. *Education:* University of Frankfurt (Economics). *Member:* German Bar Association. **LANGUAGES:** German, English and French. **PRACTICE AREAS:** Liquidation; Labour and Employment.

JOACHIM WINTER, born Kaiserslautern, Germany, October 20, 1956; admitted, 1986, Germany. *Education:* Universities of Frankfurt am Main and Urbino (European Law). *Member:* German Bar Association; Association Internationale de Jeunes Advocats; Italian Chamber of Trade for Germany. **LANGUAGES:** German, English, French and Italian. **PRACTICE AREAS:** Business Law; Corporate Law; Real Estate; European Community Law.

ASSOCIATES

CHRISTINE REICHLER-BRANDT, born Karlsruhe, Germany, August 14, 1956; admitted, 1982, Germany. *Education:* University of Munich. **LANGUAGES:** German, English and French. **PRACTICE AREAS:** Computers and Software; Leases and Leasing; Copyright.

HANS-PETER GRIMM, born Düsseldorf, Germany, October 21, 1956; admitted, 1987, Germany. *Education:* University of Mannheim. Lecturer, Berufsakademie Mannheim, State Academy of Studies. *Member:* German Bar Association. **LANGUAGES:** German and English. **PRACTICE AREAS:** Litigation and Arbitration; Criminal Law; Unfair Competition.

RAINER VENINO, born Frankfurt/Main, Germany, July 21, 1961; admitted, 1991, Germany. *Education:* University of Frankfurt. *Member:* German Bar Association. **LANGUAGES:** German and English. **PRACTICE AREAS:** Competition; Labour and Employment; Commercial.

SIBYLLE BIRKRKENFELD-OTTO, born Frankfurt/Main, Germany, December 19, 1953; admitted, 1981, Germany. *Education:* University of Frankfurt and Fachhochschule für Verwaltungswissenschaften Speyer (School for Science of Administration). *Member:* German Bar Association. **LANGUAGES:** German, English and Italian. **PRACTICE AREAS:** Family Law; General Practice.

RÜDIGER FREIHERR VON REITZENSTEIN, born Bamberg, Germany, March 19, 1942; admitted, 1989, Germany. *Education:* University of Heidelberg. *Member:* German Bar Association. **LANGUAGES:** German and English.

(This Listing Continued)

BRANDT KESTLER LAPPAT SCHÜTT & PARTNER,
Frankfurt/Main—Continued

FRANZ NEUKIRCH, born Stuttgart, Germany, April 26, 1963; admitted, 1993, Germany. *Education:* Universities of Heidelberg, Frankfurt am Main and Hochschule für Verwaltungswissenschaften, Speyer (School for Science of Administration). *Member:* German Bar Association. *LANGUAGES:* German and English. *PRACTICE AREAS:* Civil Law; Commercial Law; Administration and Environmental Law.

NINA HERZOG, born Germany, 1961; admitted, 1992, Germany. *Education:* Universities of Mainz and Frankfurt am Main. *Member:* German Bar Association. *LANGUAGES:* German, English and French. *PRACTICE AREAS:* Commercial Law; Family Law; Law of Succession; Law of Execution.

PETER MEIDES, born Frankfurt am Main, Germany, July 27, 1955; admitted, 1993, Germany. *Education:* University of Frankfurt. *Member:* German Bar Association. *LANGUAGES:* German, English and French.

DR. PEDRO FRÖLICH-PEREIRA, born Lisbon, Portugal, August 28, 1964; admitted, 1994, Germany. *Education:* University of Frankfurt am Main; Dissertation on Product Liability in Portuguese Law. *Member:* German Bar Association; German-Portuguese Law Association. *LANGUAGES:* German, English and Portuguese. *PRACTICE AREAS:* Civil Law; German Product Liability; International Product Liability; Commercial Law.

BRUCKHAUS WESTRICK STEGEMANN

TAUNUSANLAGE 11

60329 FRANKFURT/MAIN, GERMANY

Telephone: (069) 27308-0

Telefax: (069) 232664

Telex: 41 49 17 WEST C D

Düsseldorf Office: Freiligrathstrasse 1, 40479 Düsseldorf. Telephone: (02 11) 49 79-0. Telefax: (02 11) 49 79-1 03; 4 98 12 21. Telex: 858 7027 JUS D.

Hamburg Office: Alsterarkaden 27, 20354 Hamburg. Telephone: (040) 36 90 60. Telefax: (040) 36 906-155. Telex:212 522 EURO D.

Berlin Office: Friedrichstrasse 95 (IHZ), 10117 Berlin. Telephone: (030) 26 43-3303. Telefax: (030) 26 43-3366.

Leipzig Office: Grimmaische Strasse 25, 04109 Leipzig. Telephone: (0341) 127230. Telefax: (0341) 1272333.

Brussels, Belgium Office: Rue de la Loi 99/101, B-1040 Brussels. Telephone: (32-2) 2 87 26 11. Telefax: (32-2) 2 30 39 03.

Tokyo, Japan Office: Ark Mori Building, 22F, 12-32, Akasaka 1-chome, Minato-ku, Tokyo 107. Telephone: (81-3) 55610-236. Telefax: (81-3) 55610-238.

New York, New York Office: 767 Fifth Avenue, GM Building, New York 10153. Telephone: (212) 486-1100. Telefax: (212) 759-3151.

Moscow, Russia Office: Malyj Gnezdnikovskij per. 9 No. 2, 103009 Moscow. Telephone: (7-503) 9562300; (7-501) 9401200. Telefax: (7-503) 9562301; (7-501) 9401211.

Corporate Law, Commercial Law, Mergers, Acquisitions and Divestitures, Joint Ventures, Banks and Banking, Finance, Securities, Capital Markets, Leases and Leasing, Equipment Finance, Aircraft Finance and Leasing, Antitrust and Trade Regulation, German and EC Cartel Law, Competition, Unfair Trade, Intellectual Property (trademarks, patents, copyrights), Taxation, Property, Real Estate, Energy, Natural Resources, Environmental Law, Administrative Law, Computers and Software, Food and Drug, Biotechnology, Labour and Employment, Products Liability, Insurance, Litigation, Arbitration, Broadcasting, Telecommunications, Aviation, Subsidies and State Aids, Construction Law, Zoning, Planning and Land Use, Customs and Foreign Trade Law, European Community Law, German-French Investments, Russian and Post Soviet Commerce.

MEMBERS OF FIRM

DR. KLAUS WESTRICK, born Berlin, Germany, July 22, 1930; admitted, 1958, Germany. *Education:* Universities of Frankfurt am Main and Munich (Dr. jur., 1955). (Resident, New York Office). *LANGUAGES:* German, English and French. *PRACTICE AREAS:* Corporate Law; Commercial Law; Banks and Banking; Finance.

DR. GERHARD HESS, born Schenklengsfeld, Germany, December 13, 1937; admitted, 1966, Germany. *Education:* Universities of Frankfurt am Main and Munich (Dr. jur., 1966). *LANGUAGES:* German and English.

(This Listing Continued)

PRACTICE AREAS: Corporate Law; Commercial Law; Banks and Banking; Finance.

DR. HARALD VOSS, born Posen, Germany, May 28, 1939; admitted, 1970, Germany. *Education:* Universities of Göttingen, Berlin and Bonn (Dr. jur., 1968); Yale University. *LANGUAGES:* German and English. *PRACTICE AREAS:* Corporate Law; Commercial Law; Mergers, Acquisitions and Divestitures; Joint Ventures; Leases and Leasing; Aircraft Finance and Leasing.

DR. PETER SCHMIDT ZUR NEDDEN, born Cologne, Germany, September 2, 1937; admitted, 1969, Germany. *Education:* Universities of Hamburg and Heidelberg (Dr. jur., 1967). *LANGUAGES:* German and English. *PRACTICE AREAS:* Real Estate; Property; Corporate Law; Commercial Law.

REINHART H. DENSCH, born Munich, Germany, April 14, 1942; admitted, 1972, Germany. *Education:* Universities of Kiel, Berlin, Bonn and University of Michigan (LL.M., 1972). *LANGUAGES:* German and English. *PRACTICE AREAS:* Litigation; Arbitration; Commercial Law; Conflicts of Laws.

DR. ULRICH MANNSFELDT, born Stettin, Germany, February 14, 1938; admitted, 1969, Germany. *Education:* Universities of Heidelberg, Munich, Hamburg and Montpellier (France) (Dr. jur., 1967). *LANGUAGES:* German, English and French. *PRACTICE AREAS:* Corporate Law; Commercial Law; Joint Ventures; Leasing; German-French Investments; Company Law.

DR. NORBERT MEISTER, born Münster/Westf., Germany, March 26, 1941; admitted, 1973, Germany; 1974, Tax Adviser. *Education:* Universities of Münster (Dr. jur., 1969), Lausanne (Switzerland), Nice (France) and Chicago. *LANGUAGES:* German, English and French. *PRACTICE AREAS:* Corporate Law; Commercial Law; Mergers, Acquisitions and Divestitures; Tax Law.

HANS-CHRISTIAN NETZEL, born Leun, Germany, April 21, 1947; admitted, 1976, Germany. *Education:* Universities of Frankfurt am Main and Geneva (Switzerland). *LANGUAGES:* German, English and French. *PRACTICE AREAS:* Labor and Employment Law.

RALPH KÄSTNER, born Offenbach/Main, Germany, March 15, 1948; admitted, 1974, Germany. *Education:* Universities of Hamburg, Tübingen, Munich, Bonn and Nice (France). *LANGUAGES:* German, English and French. *PRACTICE AREAS:* Corporate Law; Commercial Law; Mergers, Acquisitions and Divestitures; Joint Ventures.

DR. GERHARD LIMBERGER, born Hofgeismar, Germany, August 14, 1952; admitted, 1980, Germany. *Education:* University of Frankfurt am Main (Dr. jur., 1982). *LANGUAGES:* German and English. *PRACTICE AREAS:* Environmental Law; Zoning; Planning and Land Use; Administrative Law; EC Law; Telecommunications; Broadcasting; Biotechnology.

DR. WOLFGANG HAUSER, born Geislingen an der Steige, Germany, August 3, 1952; admitted, 1980, Germany. *Education:* Universities of Göttingen and Frankfurt am Main (Dr. jur., 1982); Harvard Law School (LL.M., 1978). *LANGUAGES:* German, English and French. *PRACTICE AREAS:* Corporate Law; Commercial Law; Banks and Banking; Finance; Company Law.

DR. ANDREAS KÖNIG, born Berlin, Germany, June 1, 1953; admitted, 1983, Germany. *Education:* Universities of Frankfurt am Main and Konstanz (Dr. jur., 1983); University of Miami (M.C.L., 1981). *LANGUAGES:* German and English. *PRACTICE AREAS:* Banks and Banking; Finance; Securities; Capital Markets.

DR. KLAUS-ALBERT BAUER, born Aschaffenburg, Germany, September 8, 1954; admitted, 1981, New York; 1984, Germany. *Education:* Universities of Würzburg, Geneva (Switzerland) and Tübingen (Dr. jur., 1984); Columbia University (LL.M., 1979). (Resident, Moscow Office). *LANGUAGES:* German, English and French. *PRACTICE AREAS:* Securities; Capital Markets; Computer and Software Law; Russian and Post Soviet Commerce.

DR. KONSTANTIN METTENHEIMER, born Frankfurt am Main, December 5, 1955; admitted, 1987, Germany; 1991, Tax Adviser. *Education:* Universities of Frankfurt am Main, Geneva (Switzerland) and Freiburg im Breisgau (Dr. jur., 1987); Wharton School, University of Pennsylvania (M.B.A., 1983). *LANGUAGES:* German, English and French. *PRACTICE AREAS:* Corporate Law; Commercial Law; Tax Law.

CHRISTIAN BUNSEN, born Hamburg, Germany, July 12, 1956; admitted, 1982, Germany; 1985, New York. *Education:* University of Hamburg; Columbia University, New York (LL.M., 1984). (Resident, Tokyo,

(This Listing Continued)

Japan Office). *LANGUAGES:* German and English. *PRACTICE AREAS:* Corporate Law; Commercial Law; Securities and Capital Markets.

DR. DIRK SCHMALENBACH, born Essen, Germany, March 14, 1958; admitted, 1987, Germany. *Education:* Universities of Marburg and Göttingen (Dr. jur., 1986). *LANGUAGES:* German and English. *PRACTICE AREAS:* Corporate Law; Commercial Law; Leasing; Aircraft Finance and Leasing.

CAROLINE BITSCH, born Saarbrücken, Germany, May 10, 1958; admitted, 1987, Germany. *Education:* University of Frankfurt am Main. *LANGUAGES:* German, English and French. *PRACTICE AREAS:* Labor and Employment Law.

DR. ANDREAS FABRITIUS, born Düsseldorf, Germany, December 15, 1957; admitted, 1984, Germany; 1987, New York. *Education:* University of Michigan (LL.M., 1985); University of Bonn (Dr. jur., 1987); European University Institute, Florence, Italy. *LANGUAGES:* German, English and Italian. *PRACTICE AREAS:* Corporate Law; Mergers, Acquisitions and Divestitures; Joint Ventures; Investment Funds; Company Law.

DR. PETER CHROCZIEL, born Nürnberg, Germany, February 23, 1957; admitted, 1983, Germany; 1987, New York. *Education:* University of Erlangen and Munich (Dr. jur., 1985); New York University Law School (M.C.J., 1986); Max-Planck-Institute for Foreign and International Patent, Copyright and Competition Law, Munich; University of Brussels, Center for European Studies. *LANGUAGES:* German and English. *PRACTICE AREAS:* Intellectual Property; Corporate Law; Licensing.

MICHAEL KNOSPE, born Stuttgart, Germany, January 25, 1959; admitted, 1988, Germany. *Education:* Universities of Freiburg im Breisgau and Munich, Max-Planck-Institute for Foreign Law and International Patent, Copyright and Competition Law, Munich. *LANGUAGES:* German and English. *PRACTICE AREAS:* Intellectual Property; Competition and Unfair Trade; Computers and Software.

RONALD BAUER, born Frankfurt am Main, Germany, July 7, 1954; admitted, 1984, Germany. *Education:* University of Frankfurt am Main. *LANGUAGES:* German, English and French. *PRACTICE AREAS:* Litigation; Arbitration.

DR. ROLF A. TRITTMANN, born Frankfurt am Main, Germany, May 11, 1958; admitted, 1986, Germany. *Education:* Universities of Frankfurt am Main (Dr. jur., 1988) and Berkeley, California (LL.M., 1987). Research Assistant, University of Munich. *LANGUAGES:* German, English and French. *PRACTICE AREAS:* Litigation; Arbitration; Products Liability; Conflicts of Laws.

DR. THOMAS R. TSCHENTSCHER, born Bonn, Germany, March 21, 1960; admitted, 1989, Germany. *Education:* Universities of Bonn (Dr. jur., 1988); Munich and Virginia (LL.M., 1989). *LANGUAGES:* German, English and French. *PRACTICE AREAS:* Environmental Law; Administrative Law; EC Law; Aviation Law; Customs and Export Law; Broadcasting.

DR. GERD HENNING OESTERHAUS, born Mannheim, Germany, May 23, 1960; admitted, 1990, Germany and New York. *Education:* Universities of Mannheim, Munich and Heidelberg (Dr., jur., 1990); University of Texas at Austin (M.C.J., 1989). *LANGUAGES:* German and English. *PRACTICE AREAS:* Corporate Law; Commercial Law; Mergers, Acquisitions and Divestitures; Joint Ventures; Company Law.

DR. PETER E. HEIN, born Mettmann, Germany, April 17, 1960; admitted, 1989, Germany. *Education:* University of Cologne and Bonn (Dr. jur., 1987). Research Assistant, University of Bonn. *LANGUAGES:* German and English. *PRACTICE AREAS:* Commercial Law; Lease and Leasing; Equipment Finance; Aircraft Finance and Leasing.

DR. WALBURGA KULLMANN, born Hochheim/Main, Germany, March 24, 1961; admitted, 1990, Germany. *Education:* Universities of Mainz (Dr. jur., 1987), Kiel, Dijon, London, Bloomington (Indiana) (LL.M., 1986). Deutsche Bank AG, Frankfurt am Main, 1989-1990. *LANGUAGES:* German, English and French. *PRACTICE AREAS:* Securities; Capital Markets; Banks and Banking; Finance.

DR. MARKUS FISSELER, born Dortmund, Germany, December 8, 1956; admitted, 1986, Germany; 1990, New York. *Education:* Universities of Berlin and Würzburg (Dr. jur., 1985), Harvard University. *LANGUAGES:* German and English. *PRACTICE AREAS:* Corporate Law; Mergers, Acquisitions and Divestitures; Joint Ventures; Company Law.

DR. ERNST THOMAS EMDE, born Gummersbach, Germany, October 17, 1950; admitted, 1988, Germany. *Education:* Universities of Freiburg im Breisgau (Dr. jur., 1986), Heidelberg, Lausanne (Switzerland) and Mu-

nich. Senior Legal Counsel and Senior Manager, Investment Banking Division, DG Bank, 1984-1990. *LANGUAGES:* German and English. *PRACTICE AREAS:* Commercial Law; Banks and Banking; Finance; Investment Funds; Bank Regulation.

DR. MATTHIAS-GABRIEL KREMER, born Karlsruhe, Germany, April 22, 1957; admitted, 1991, Germany. *Education:* Universities of Freiburg im Breisgau (Dr. jur., 1987) and Geneva (Switzerland). Personal Assistant to a Member of the Board of Managing Directors of Deutsche Bank AG, Frankfurt am Main, 1988-1991. *LANGUAGES:* German, English, French and Spanish. *PRACTICE AREAS:* Banks and Banking; Finance; Corporate Law; Commercial Law.

DR. BRITTA ZIERAU, born Siegen, Germany, November 10, 1960; admitted, 1991, Germany. *Education:* Universities of Saarbrücken and Frankfurt am Main (Dr. jur., 1990). Research Assistant, Centre d'Etudes Juridiques Française, University of Saarbrücken, 1988-1991. *LANGUAGES:* German, French and English. *PRACTICE AREAS:* Commercial Law; Corporate Law; German-French Investments.

THOMAS JÖRGENS, born Bonn, Germany, January 24, 1960; admitted, 1991, Germany. *Education:* Universities of Bonn, Geneva (Switzerland) and University of Chicago (LL.M., 1987). *LANGUAGES:* German and English. *PRACTICE AREAS:* Real Estate; Property; Commercial Law.

NICOLE ENGESSER MEANS, born Tiengen, Germany, May 21, 1961; admitted, 1990, Germany. *Education:* University of Würzburg and Freiburg. *LANGUAGES:* German, English, French, Italian and Chinese (Mandarin). *PRACTICE AREAS:* Labor Law; Commercial Law.

DR. ANDREAS VON WERDER, born Stuttgart, Germany, June 11, 1961; admitted, 1991, Germany. *Education:* Universities of Marburg (Dr. jur., 1991), Geneva (Switzerland), Strasbourg (France); University of Illinois, Urbana-Champaign (LL.M., 1988). *LANGUAGES:* German, English and French. *PRACTICE AREAS:* Corporate Law; Mergers, Acquisitions and Divestitures.

DR. MATTHIAS KUHN, born Ludwigshafen/Rhein, Germany, January 4, 1963; admitted, 1991, Germany. *Education:* Universities of Munich (Dip.-Kfm., 1992) and Regensburg (Dr. jur., 1991). Tax Advisor. *LANGUAGES:* German and English. *PRACTICE AREAS:* Corporate Law; Mergers, Acquisitions and Divestitures; Tax Law.

YORCK JETTER, born Bad Homburg, Germany, December 22, 1961; admitted, 1992, Germany. *Education:* University of Tübingen and College of Europe, Bruges, Belgium (Diploma of Advanced European Legal Studies, 1990). (Resident, Moscow Office). *LANGUAGES:* German, English and French. *PRACTICE AREAS:* Securities; Capital Markets; Banks and Banking; Finance.

DR. ALFRIED HEIDBRINK, born Mönchengladbach, Germany, July 17, 1964; admitted, 1992, Germany. *Education:* Universities of Bonn (Dr. jur., 1989) and Geneva (Switzerland); University of Miami (LL.M., 1992). (Resident, New York Office). *LANGUAGES:* German, English, French, Spanish and Italian. *PRACTICE AREAS:* Corporate Law; Commercial Law; Banks and Banking; Finance.

DR. JOHANNES BRUSKI, born Arnsberg, Germany, July 20, 1962; admitted, 1992, Germany. *Education:* University of Bonn (Dr. jur., 1990); McGill University, Montreal (LL.M., 1989). *LANGUAGES:* German, English, Italian and French. *PRACTICE AREAS:* Real Estate; Property; Commercial Law; Construction Law.

DR. THOMAS WAGNER, born Limburg/Lahn, Germany, 1960; admitted, 1991, Germany. *Education:* University of Giessen (Dr. jur., 1991). Faculty Assistant, Department of Public, International and EEC Law. *LANGUAGES:* German and English. *PRACTICE AREAS:* Environmental Law; Administrative Law; EC Law; Zoning, Planning and Land Use; Construction Law; Food and Drug Regulation.

GUNHILD SCHÄFER, born Munich, Germany, June 10, 1963; admitted, 1993, Germany and New York. *Education:* University of Munich, Temple University Pennsylvania (LL.M., 1992). *LANGUAGES:* German and English. *PRACTICE AREAS:* Litigation; Arbitration; Criminal Law.

HANNS ARNO MAGOLD, born Biberach/Riss, Germany, November 15, 1959; admitted, 1991, New York; 1993, Germany. *Education:* Universities of Saarbrücken and Mannheim; University of Miami (LL.M., 1990). *LANGUAGES:* German and English. *PRACTICE AREAS:* Commercial Law; Corporate Law.

DR. GERWIN JANKE, born Frankfurt am Main, Germany, July 27, 1962; admitted, 1993, Germany. *Education:* University of Freiburg (Dr. jur., 1993); London School of Economics; University of Virginia (LL.M.,

(This Listing Continued)

(This Listing Continued)

BRUCKHAUS WESTRICK STEGEMANN,
Frankfurt/Main—Continued

1989). *LANGUAGES:* German and English. *PRACTICE AREAS:* Litigation; Arbitration; International Private Law.

DR. ANGELA MAUHS, born Duisburg, Germany, February 3, 1964; admitted, 1992, Germany. *Education:* Universities of Frankfurt am Main, Munich and Freiburg im Breisgau (Dr. Jur., 1991). *LANGUAGES:* German and English. *PRACTICE AREAS:* Intellectual Property; Trademark; Patent; Copyright; Computers and Software.

MARIETTA LIENHARD, born Hannover, Germany, February 21, 1966; admitted, 1994, Germany. *Education:* Free University of Berlin. *LANGUAGES:* German and English. *PRACTICE AREAS:* Commercial Law; Banks and Banking; Finance; Investment Funds; Bank Regulation.

IRENE ENGEL, born Branaul, former USSR, June 29, 1960; admitted, 1993, Germany. *Education:* University of Würzburg. (Resident, Moscow Office). *LANGUAGES:* German, English and Russian. *PRACTICE AREAS:* Russian Law; Russian and Post Soviet Commerce.

KONRAD SCHOTT, born Steinbach/Ts., Germany, September 27, 1965; admitted, 1994, Germany. *Education:* University of Gießen; University of Wisconsin-Madison, Law School. *LANGUAGES:* German and English. *PRACTICE AREAS:* Corporate Law; Commercial Law; Banking.

BERNHARD KAISER, born Ludwigshafen/Rhein, Germany, January 24, 1959; admitted, 1993, New York and Germany. *Education:* Universities of Mannheim and Heidelberg (Germany); Columbia University School of Law, New York (LL.M., 1991). Research Associate, Institute of Law and Technology, University of Heidelberg, 1985-1990. *LANGUAGES:* German and English. *PRACTICE AREAS:* Corporate Law; Capital Market.

DR. FRIEDRICH HEILMANN, born Hockenheim, Germany, October 21, 1959; admitted, 1990, Germany. *Education:* University of Heidelberg (Dr. Jur., 1991). Research Assistant, Institute of Finance and Tax Law, University of Heidelberg, 1983-1989. *LANGUAGES:* German and English. *PRACTICE AREAS:* Commercial Law; Tax Law; Real Estate; Mining Law.

EVA BETTINA MESSER, born Eltville, Germany, July 30, 1965; admitted, 1993, Germany. *Education:* Johannes Gutenberg University, Hainz; New York University (M.C.J., 1994). *Member:* Frankfurt Bar Association; German-American Lawyers Association. *LANGUAGES:* German, English and French. *PRACTICE AREAS:* International and German Litigation; Arbitration; Distribution Law.

TOBIAS MÜLLER-DEKU, born Cologne, Germany, June 18, 1962; admitted, 1994, Germany. *Education:* University of Würzburg (1986); Cambridge University, Cambridge, UK (LL.M., 1987). *LANGUAGES:* German, English and Japanese. *PRACTICE AREAS:* Corporate Law; Banks, Banking and Finance.

GOETZ NEUMANN, born Bautzen, Germany, April 8, 1959; admitted, 1994, Germany. *Education:* University of Munich (LL.B., 1990); Harvard University, Cambridge Massachusetts, U.S.A. (1991); Referendariat, Munich (2.Ex., 1993); University of San Diego (M.C.L., 1994). *Member:* German Bar Association; German-American Lawyers Association; American Society for International Law. *LANGUAGES:* German and English. *PRACTICE AREAS:* Intellectual Property; Licensing; Patent Law; International Sales; Corporate Law.

MIKIO TANAKA, born Kobe, Japan, October 16, 1958; admitted, 1989, Japan and Germany ad Rechtskundiger. *Education:* Hitotsubashi University (LL.B., 1987); Cambridge University, Cambridge, UK (Diploma in International Law, 1994). Author: "German Securities Trading Act," Kokusa: Shiohomu, 1994 Issue; "A Landmark Decision on a Product Liability Case," European Lawyers' Association Newsletter, Autumn, 1994. *Member:* German-Japanese Lawyers' Association; Russo-Japanese Lawyers Association. *LANGUAGES:* Japanese, English and German. *PRACTICE AREAS:* Japanese Corporate Law; Finance and International Banking Law; EC/EEA Law.

DR. GUNNAR SCHUSTER, born Buenos Aires, Argentina, December 6, 1960; admitted, 1994, Germany. *Education:* Reidelberg (Staats Examen, 1987 and 1991); University of Chicago (LL.M., 1989). Lecturer, University of Mannheim School of Law , 1992—. Research Fellow, Max-Planck-Institute for Comparative Public Law and International Law, 1991-1994. *Member:* Frankfurt Bar Association. *LANGUAGES:* English, Spanish and French. *PRACTICE AREAS:* Banking and Securities Law; Corporate Law; European Communities Law.

(This Listing Continued)

DR. THOMAS BÜCKER, born Bad Nauheim, Germany, August 21, 1963; admitted, 1994, Germany. *Education:* University of Exeter, Exeter, England (1988/1989); University of Frankfurt, Frankfurt, Germany (Staatsexamen; Dr. Jur., 1991). Author: "Finanzimmovationen and Kommunale Schuldwirtschaft Nomas-Verlag," 1993. *LANGUAGES:* English, French, Spanish. *PRACTICE AREAS:* Corporate and Commercial Law.

JOHAN MORTIMER MENTZEL, born Washington, D.C., U.S.A., July 16, 1968; admitted, 1994, England and Wales (Not admitted in Germany). *Education:* London School of Economics (LL.B.); College of Law, Guldford (Law Society Finals). *Member:* The Law Society of England and Wales. *LANGUAGES:* German, English and French. *PRACTICE AREAS:* Asset Finance.

BRYAN CAVE

A Partnership including a Professional Corporation

In Cooperation with Rossbach & Partner

Established in 1873

STRESEMANNALLEE 33

D-6000 FRANKFURT/MAIN, GERMANY

Telephone: 011-49-69-631 50 24
Facsimile: 011-49-69-631 31 64

St. Louis, Missouri Office: One Metropolitan Square, 211 North Broadway, Suite 3600, 63102-2750. Telephone: (314) 259-2000. Facsimile: (314) 259-2020.

Washington, D.C. Office: 700 Thirteenth Street, N.W., 20005-3960. Telephone: (202) 508-6000. Facsimile: (202) 508-6200.

New York, N.Y. Office: 245 Park Avenue, 10167-0034. Telephone: (212) 692-1800. Facsimile: (212) 692-1900 and Other New York, N.Y. Office: 575 Lexington Avenue, 10022. Telephone: (212) 371-1660. Facsimile: (212) 593-0243.

Kansas City, Missouri Office: 3300 One Kansas City Place, 1200 Main Street, 64141-6914. Telephone: (816) 374-3200. Facsimile: (816) 374-3300.

Overland Park, Kansas Office: 7500 College Boulevard, Suite 1100, 66210-4035. Telephone: (913) 338-7700. Facsimile: (913) 338-7777.

Phoenix, Arizona Office: 2800 North Central Avenue, Twenty-First Floor, 85004-1098. Telephone: (602) 230-7000. Facsimile: (602) 266-5938.

Los Angeles, California Office: 777 South Figueroa Street, Suite 2700, 90017-5418. Telephone: (213) 243-4300. Facsimile: (213) 243-4343.

Santa Monica, California Office: 120 Broadway, Suite 500, 90401-2305. Telephone: (310) 576-2100. Facsimile: (310) 576-2200.

Irvine, California Office: 18881 Von Karman, Suite 250, 92715-1500. Telephone: (714) 757-8100. Facsimile: (714) 757-8106.

London, England Office: 29 Queen Anne's Gate, SW1H 9BU. Telephone: 011-44-171-222-0511. Facsimile: 011-44-171-222-1240.

Riyadh 11465 Saudi Arabia Office: In Cooperation with Kadasah Law Firm, P.O. Box 20883. Telephones: 011-966-1-465-1371 and 1165. Facsimile: 011-966-1-464-3789.

Dubai, U.A.E. Office: Al-Mehairi-Bryan Cave, Holiday Centre, Commercial Tower, Suite 1103, P.O. Box 13677, UAE. Telephone: 011-971-4-314-123. Facsimile: 011-971-4-318-287.

Hong Kong Office: Suite 2106, Lippo Tower, 21/F, Lippo Centre, 89 Queensway. Telephone: 011-852-2522-2821. Facsimile: 011-852-2522-3830.

General International and Business Law.

RESIDENT PARTNER

FREDERICK W. BARTELSMEYER, born Illinois, 1957; admitted, 1983, Missouri; 1984, Illinois; 1987, New York; Licensed to Practice as Rechtskundiger for U.S. Law in Federal Republic of Germany. *Education:* University of Illinois (B.S., Acct., with high honors, 1979; J.D., magna cum laude, 1983). Order of the Coif. Member and Associate Editor, University of Illinois Law Review, 1981-1983. Certified Public Accountant, Illinois, 1979. *LANGUAGES:* German and English.

BUECHNER & RUEDT v. COLLENBERG

SCHLOSSERSTR. 25
60322 FRANKFURT/MAIN, GERMANY
Telephone: 011 4969 591060
Fax: 011 4969 551137

U.S. Investment, Immigration, U.S. Government Contract and Commercial Law, German Corporation, Labor, Construction, Real Estate Law.

RICHARD H. BUECHNER, born Syracuse, New York, October 21, 1931; admitted, 1957, Florida; 1960, admitted in Germany as Rechtskundiger. *Education:* Syracuse University (A.B., 1953); University of Munich, 1960-1962; Syracuse University Law School (J.D., 1956). Phi Alpha Delta (President, 1956). Litton Industries, 1968-1970. Counsel, European Real Estate Department, Zurich, Switzerland. Lecturer, International Public Law, University of Southern California— Overseas Graduate Program. *Member:* The Florida Bar; Association of American Lawyers in Germany (Vice-President, 1982-1989). [Capt., Airborne J.A.G.C., U.S.A.R., 1960-1965]. *LANGUAGES:* German and English. *PRACTICE AREAS:* U.S. Securities; Real Estate; Immigration Law.

BENEDETTA RUEDT VON COLLENBERG, born Freiburg, Germany, 1948; admitted, 1984, Germany. *Education:* University of Frankfurt. *Member:* German Bar Association. *LANGUAGES:* German, English, French and Italian.

BÜSING, MÜFFELMANN & THEYE

FREIHERR-VOM-STEIN-STRASSE 11
60323 FRANKFURT/MAIN, GERMANY
Telephone: (069) 17 23 24 - 26
Telecopier: (069) 725958

Bremen, Germany Office: Marktstrasse 3, Börsenhof C, 28195 Breman. Telephone: (0421) 36600-0. Telex: 2 45 551 advo. Telecopier: (0421) 36600-366.

Firm engaged in Corporate, Tax, Commercial, Mergers and Acquisitions, Media and Entertainment Law, EEC and International Law, Antitrust, Industrial and Intellectual Property Rights, Unfair Competition, Advertising, Admiralty and Maritime, Arbitration, Transportation, Real Estate, Litigation, General Practice, Notary's Office.

RESIDENT PARTNERS

DIETRICH GORNY, born Schneidemühl, Pomerania, August 11, 1937; admitted, 1969, Germany. *Education:* Universities of Berlin, Freiburg and Hamburg. *Member:* Frankfurt Bar Association; Society of Frankfurt Lawyers; European Food Law Association (Council); International Association for the Protection of Industrial Property; Federation for Food Law and Food Science; Scientific Society for Food Law. *LANGUAGES:* German, English, French and Italian.

HEINZ-WERNER EHLGEN, born Hachenburg, Germany, April 13, 1950; admitted, 1981, Germany. *Education:* University of Frankfurt. *Member:* Frankfurt Bar Association; Society of Frankfurt Lawyers. *LANGUAGES:* German and English.

ASSOCIATES

Jochen Kaufmann

(For complete biographical data of all partners see Professional Biographies at Bremen)

CLEARY, GOTTLIEB, STEEN & HAMILTON

Established in 1946

ULMENSTRASSE 37-39
60325 FRANKFURT/MAIN, GERMANY
Telephone: 49-69-971 03-0
Facsimile: 49-69-971 03 199

New York, New York Office: One Liberty Plaza, New York, N.Y. 10006. Telephone: 212-225-2000.
Washington, D.C. Office: 1752 N Street, N.W., Washington, D.C. 20036. Telephone: 202-728-2700.
Paris, France Office: 41, Avenue de Friedland, 75008 Paris, France. Telephone: 33-1-4074-6800.

(This Listing Continued)

Brussels, Belgium Office: Rue de la Loi 23, Bte 5, 1040 Brussels, Belgium. Telephone: 32-2-287-2000.
London, England Office: City Place House, 55 Basinghall Street, London EC2V 5EH England. Telephone: 44-71-614-2200.
Hong Kong Office: 56th Floor, Bank of China Tower, One Garden Road, Hong Kong. Telephone: 852-521-4122.
Tokyo, Japan Office: Morgan Carroll Terai Gaikokuho Jimubengoshi Jimusho, 20th Floor, Shin Kasumigaseki Building, 3-2, Kasumigaseki 3-Chome, Chiyoda-Ku, Tokyo 100, Japan. Telephone: 81-3-3595-3911.

Firm engaged in German, American and International Law Practice; authorized to practice before the German courts.

RESIDENT PARTNERS

RUSSELL H. POLLACK, born Lancaster, Pennsylvania, November 20, 1951; admitted, 1980, New York; 1992, Paris (Not admitted in Germany). *Education:* Cornell University (B.A., 1973); European Institute of Business Administration (INSEAD) (M.B.A., 1975); University of Virginia (J.D., 1978). Order of the Coif. Member, Board of Editors, Virginia Law Review, 1976-1978. Law Clerk to Robert A. Ainsworth, Jr., U.S. Court of Appeals, Fifth Circuit, 1978-1979. Resident at: New York Office, 1979-1980 and 1984-1988; Paris Office, 1981-1984 and 1988-1992. *Member:* Association of the Bar of the City of New York; American Bar Association; Association Française des Avocats Conseils d'Entreprise.

CHRISTOF VON DRYANDER, born Wuppertal, Germany, September 26, 1953; admitted, 1980, Germany; 1982, District of Columbia. *Education:* University of Freiburg (First State Examination, 1977; Second State Examination, 1980); Yale University (LL.M., 1981). Resident at: Brussels Office, 1982-1985; London Office, 1985-1991.

THOMAS M. BUHL, born Konstanz, Germany, May 2, 1955; admitted, 1980, Germany; 1992, Paris. *Education:* University of Konstanz (First and Second State Examinations, 1980); University of Chicago (LL.M., 1982). Resident at: New York Office, 1982-1983; Paris Office, 1983-1991. *Member:* German-American Lawyers Association; Association Française des Avocats Conseils d'Enterprise.

ASSOCIATES

GABRIELE APFELBACHER, born Weiden i.d. Opf., Germany, August 23, 1963; admitted, 1991, Germany. *Education:* University of Regensburg (First State Examination, 1988; Second State Examination, 1991; Dr. jur., 1992); Frankfurt Stock Exchange, 1992; Columbia University (LL.M., 1994). Resident at: New York Office, 1994.

STEPHAN BARTHELMESS, born Erlangen, Germany, September 30, 1959; admitted, 1987, Germany; 1988, New York; 1992, Paris. *Education:* Universities of Munich and Erlangen-Nuremberg (First State Examination, 1982; Second State Examination, 1985; Dr. jur., 1987); University of Michigan (LL.M., 1986). Resident at: New York Office, 1986-1987; Brussels Office, 1987-1989; Paris Office, 1989-1992. *Member:* German-American Lawyers Association; Association Française des Avocats Conseils d'Enterprise.

WARD A. GREENBERG, born Huntington, New York, May 7, 1963; admitted, 1990, New York (Not admitted in Germany). *Education:* Dartmouth College (A.B., 1985); University of Michigan (J.D., 1988). Note Editor, Michigan Law Review. Law Clerk to J. Edward Lumbard, Jr., U.S. Court of Appeals, Second Circuit, 1988-1989. Resident at: New York Office, 1989-1991.

SUSANNE HALSTRICK, born Bonn, Germany, March 7, 1962; admitted, 1990, Germany. *Education:* University of Bonn (First State Examination, 1985; Second State Examination, 1989); College of Europe, Bruges (Diploma of Advanced European Studies, 1990). Resident at: Paris Office, 1990-1991.

REINHARD HERMES, born Cologne, Germany, August 29, 1957; admitted, 1989, New York; 1990, Germany. *Education:* Universities of Regensburg, Kiel and Hamburg (First State Examination, 1981; Second State Examination, 1986; Dr. jur., 1988); Harvard University, Kennedy School of Government (M.P.A., 1988). Assistant, Law of the Sea and Maritime Law Institute, University of Hamburg, 1983-1986. Resident at: Brussels Office, 1990-1994.

WERNER MEIER, born Schötmar, Germany, April 20, 1963; admitted, 1992, New York and Germany. *Education:* University of Bielefeld (First and Second State Examinations, 1989; Diploma in Business Administration, 1990); Columbia University (LL.M., 1991).

FRANCESCA M. MORETTI, born Venice, Italy, April 10, 1964; admitted, 1991, Brussels; 1992, Bologna, Italy (Not admitted in Germany). *Education:* University of Bologna (Lic. Jur., 1988); Harvard Law School

(This Listing Continued)

CLEARY, GOTTLIEB, STEEN & HAMILTON,
Frankfurt/Main—Continued

(LL.M., 1990). Resident at: New York Office, 1990; Brussels Office, 1991-1994.

RALF M. NITSCHKE, born Bonn, Germany, February 5, 1962; admitted, 1993, Germany. *Education:* Universities of Bonn and Geneva (First State Examination, 1986; Second State Examination, 1993); Indiana University (LL.M., 1988). Federal Ministry of Defense, Bonn, 1989-1990.

BRENDAN J. ROSS, born Queens, New York, December 10, 1967; admitted, 1993, New York (Not admitted in Germany). *Education:* Stanford University (A.B., 1989); Duke University (J.D., LL.M., International Law, 1992). Resident at: New York Office, 1992-1994.

CHRISTIAN OSCAR ZSCHOCKE, born Cologne, Germany, December 7, 1960; admitted, 1990, Germany. *Education:* The London School of Economics and Political Science, 1983, 1989; University of Bonn (First State Examination, 1985; Second State Examination, 1990); Universidad Catolica de Buenos Aires, 1986. Resident at: London Office, 1989-1990; Brussels Office, 1990-1994.

(For biographical data of the partners resident in the New York, Washington, Brussels , London, Hong Kong, Tokyo and Paris Offices, see Professional Biographies at New York, N.Y., Paris, France, Washington, D.C., Brussels, Belgium, London, England, Hong Kong and Tokyo, Japan).

CLIFFORD CHANCE
Established in 1990

FRIEDRICHSTRAβE 2-6
60323 FRANKFURT/MAIN, GERMANY
Telephone: (49 69) 971 4090
Fax: (49 69) 971 40977

Amsterdam, The Netherlands Office: Apollolaan 171, 1077 AS, P.O. Box 7301, 1007 JH. Telephone: (31 20) 577 71 11. Fax: (31 20) 676 93 26.

Bahrain, Manama Associated Office: Law Office of Shaikh Isa bin Mohammed Al Khalifa. P.O. Box 20717. Telephone: (973) 531535; 531073. Fax: (973) 536272; 530608.

Barcelona, Spain Office: Pau Claris 102, 08009. Telephone: (34 3) 318 68 64. Fax: (34 3) 317 73 23.

Brussels, Belgium Office: Avenue Louise 65, Box 2, 1050. Telephone: (32 2) 533 59 11. Fax: (32 2) 533 59 59.

Budapest, Hungary Office: Köves & Partners, Clifford Chance. Madách Trade Center, Madách Imre Út 14, 1075. Telephone: (36 1) 268 1600. Fax: (36 1) 268 1610.

Dubai, United Arab Emirates Office: 18th Floor, Dubai World Trade Centre, P.O. Box 9380. Telephone: (971 4) 314333. Fax: (971 4) 313990; 314565.

Hanoi, Vietnam Office: 52 Nguyen Binh Khiem. Telephone: (844) 229 182/3/4/5/6. Fax: (844) 229 190.

Hong Kong Office: 30th Floor, Jardine House, One Connaught Place. Telephone: (852) 2810 0229. Fax: (852) 2810 4708; 2810 4858; 2810 4743.

London, England Office: 200 Aldersgate Street, EC1A 4JJ. Telephone: (44 171) 600 1000. Fax: (44 171) 600 5555.

Madrid, Spain Office: Paseo de la Castellana 110, 28046. Telephone: (34 1) 562 7674. Fax: (341) 562 49 93.

Milan, Italy Associated Office: Grimaldi e Clifford Chance. Via Gesú, 3, 20121. Telephone: (39 2) 7600 8040. Fax: (39 2) 7600 4950.

Moscow, Russia Office: Ul. Sadovaya - Samotechnaya 24/27, 2nd Floor, 103051. Telephone: (7 501) 258 50 50. Fax: (7 501) 258 50 51.

New York, New York Office: Swiss Bank Tower, 10 East 50th Street, 10022. Telephone: (1 212) 750 1440. Fax: (1 212) 758 6625.

Paris, France Office: 112 avenue Kléber, BP 163 Trocadéro, 75770 Paris Cedex 16. Telephone: (33 1) 44 05 52 52. Fax: (33 1) 44 05 52 00.

Riyadh, Saudi Arabia Associated Office: The Law Firm of Salah Al-Hejailan. P.O. Box 1454, 11431. Telephone: (966 1) 479 2200. Fax: (966 1) 479 1717.

Rome, Italy Associated Office: Grimaldi e Clifford Chance. Viale G. Rossini 7, 00198. Telephone: (39 6) 807 2251. Fax: (39 6) 807 8201.

Shanghai, People's Republic of China Office: Suite 898, Shanghai Centre, 1376 Nanjing Xi Lu, 200040. Telephone: (86 21) 279 8461. Fax: (86 21) 279 8462.

Singapore Office: 16 Collyer Quay #31-00, 0104. Telephone: (65) 535 1855. Fax: (65) 535 6855.

(This Listing Continued)

Tokyo, Japan Office: 6th Floor, South Hill Nagatacho Building, 11-30 Nagatacho 1-chome, Chiyoda-ku, 100. Telephone: (81 3) 3581 4311. Fax: (81 3) 3593 0651.

Warsaw, Poland Office: Warsaw Corporate Centre, ul. Emilii Plater 28, 00-688. Telephone: (48 2) 630 3344. Fax: (48 2) 630 3355.

International Banking, Securities and Finance, Leasing and Asset-based Finance, Mergers and Acquisitions, Joint Ventures, Corporate Law and Commercial Law.
Firm engaged in English and General International Practice.

PARTNERS

JAN TER HAAR, Advocat (The Netherlands). *LANGUAGES:* Dutch, English and German. *PRACTICE AREAS:* Corporate Finance; Project Finance; Loan Workouts; Venture Capital; Equipment Leasing.

RIKO K. VANEZIS, Solicitor. *LANGUAGES:* English, German and French. *PRACTICE AREAS:* Banking; Corporate Finance; Asset Based Finance; Aircraft Finance and Leasing; Mergers and Acquisitions.

DR. MICHAEL WELLER, Rechtsanwalt (Germany). *LANGUAGES:* German and English. *PRACTICE AREAS:* Capital Markets; Management Buyouts; Contracts; Banking; Bank Security.

(For the names of Partners resident in other offices, see Professional Biographies for those offices)

CURTIS, MALLET-PREVOST, COLT & MOSLE
Established in 1830

STAUFENSTRASSE 42
60323 FRANKFURT/MAIN 1, GERMANY
Telephone: 069-971-4420
Telecopier: 69-17 33 99

REVISERS OF THE ARGENTINA, BOLIVIA, BRAZIL, CHILE, COLUMBIA, COSTA RICA, DOMINICAN REPUBLIC, ECUADOR, EL SALVADOR, GUATEMALA, HONDURAS, MEXICO, NICARAGUA, PERU, URUGUAY AND VENEZUELA LAW DIGESTS FOR THIS DIRECTORY.

New York, New York Office: 101 Park Avenue, 10178. Telephone: 212-696-6000. Telecopier: 212-697-1559. Cable Address: " Migniard New York". Telex: 12-6811 Migniard; ITT 422127 MGND.

Newark, New Jersey Office: One Gateway Center, Suite 403. Telephone: 201-622-0605. Telecopier: 201-622-5646.

Washington, D.C. Office: Suite 1201L, 1801 K Street, N.W., 20006. Telephone: 202-452-7373. Telecopier: 202-452-7333. Telex: ITT 440379 CMPUI.

Houston, Texas Office: 2 Houston Center, 909 Fannin Street, Suite 3725. Telephone: 713-759-9555. Telecopier: 713-759-0712.

Mexico City, D.F., Mexico Office: Torre Chapultepec, Ruben Dario 281, Col. Bosques de Chapultepec, 11530 Mexico, D.F. Telephone: 525-282-0444. Telecopier: 525-282-0637.

London, England Office: Two Throgmorton Avenue, EC2N 2DL. Telephone: 71-638-7957. Telecopier: 71-638-5512.

Paris, France Office: 8 Avenue Victor Hugo. Telephone: 45-00-99-68. Telecopier: 45-00-84-06.

International Corporate, Commercial and Financial Practice.

RESIDENT COUNSEL

CHARLES E. STEWART, III, born Hartford, Connecticut, February 16, 1949; admitted, 1980, New York; 1988, Germany. *Education:* St. Louis University (A.B., 1971); Georgetown University (J.D., 1977; M.S.F.S., 1979); University of Frankfurt (First German Law Examination, 1985; Second German Law Examination, 1988). Rechtsreferendar in Germany, 1985-1988. Fulbright Fellow, 1972-1973. Alexander von Humboldt Fellow, 1977-1979. Lecturer in Law, University of Frankfurt. Co-Author: "Die Merger Guidelines des U.S. - Department of Justice", 29 RIW 906, 1983; "Betriebsverfassungsgesetz/Labor Management Relations Act", 3rd ed., 1983; 4th ed., 1993; "German Commercial Law", Business Transactions in Germany (FRG), 1st ed. 1983, 2nd ed., 1993. Author: "Recent Development: New Egyptian Foreign Investment Law", 7 Law & Pol'y Int'l Bus. 959, 1975; "International Decision: (German) Land Reform Decision," 85 Am.J. Int'l L. 690 (1991). *Member:* American and International Bar Associations; German-American Lawyers Association; Internationales Fachinstitut für Steuer- und Wirtschaftsrecht. *LANGUAGES:* English, German, French.

(This Listing Continued)

RESIDENT ASSOCIATES

ALBRECHT S. MÜNCH, born Frankfurt am Main, Germany, May 12, 1966; admitted, 1993, Germany. *Education:* University of Frankfurt (First German Law Examination, 1990); Rechtsreferendar in Germany, 1990-1993; Second German Law Examination, 1993). *Member:* Deutscher Anwaltverein. *LANGUAGES:* English, German.

UTE TÜNNERMANN-KASCH, born Kelkheim, Germany, December 20, 1960; admitted, 1991, Germany. *Education:* Universities of Würzburg and Frankfurt (First State Examination, 1986; Second State Examination, 1990). *Member:* Frankfurt Bar Association; Frankfurt Attorneys Union. *LANGUAGES:* German and English.

REVISERS OF THE ARGENTINA, BOLIVIA, BRAZIL, CHILE, COLUMBIA, COSTA RICA, DOMINICAN REPUBLIC, ECUADOR, EL SALVADOR, GUATEMALA, HONDURAS, MEXICO, NICARAGUA, PERU, URUGUAY AND VENEZUELA LAW DIGESTS FOR THIS DIRECTORY.

(For complete biographical data on all personnel, see Professional Biographies at New York, New York)

DAVIS POLK & WARDWELL

MESSETURM
60308 FRANKFURT AM MAIN
FEDERAL REPUBLIC OF GERMANY
FRANKFURT/MAIN, GERMANY
Telephone: 011-49-69-97-57-03-0
Telecopier: 011-49-69-74-77-44

New York, N.Y. Office: 450 Lexington Avenue, 10017. Telephone: 212-450-4000. Cable Address: "Davispolk New York". Telex: ITT-421341; ITT-423356. Telecopier: 212-450-4800.

Washington, D.C. Office: 1300 I Street, N.W., 20005. Telephone: 202-962-7000. Telecopier: 202-962-7111.

Paris, France Office: 4, Place de la Concorde, 75008. Telephone: 011-331-40.17.36.00. Telecopier: 011-331-42.65.22.34. Cable Address: "Davispolk Paris".

London, England Office: 1 Frederick's Place, EC2R 8AB. Telephone: 011-44-171-418-1300. Telecopier: 011-44-171-418-1400.

Tokyo, Japan Office: In Tokyo practicing as Reid Gaikokuho-Jimu-Bengoshi Jimusho. Tokio Kaijo Building Annex, 2-1, Marunouchi 1-Chome, Chiyoda-Ku, Tokyo 100, Japan. Telephone: 011-81-3-201-8421. Telecopier: 011-81-3-201-8444. Telex: 2224472 DPWTOK.

Hong Kong Office: The Hong Kong Club Building, 3A Chater Road. Telephone: 852 533 3300. Fax: 852 533 3388.

General Practice.

RESIDENT PARTNER

PATRICK S. KENADJIAN, born New York, N.Y., August 15, 1947; admitted, 1976, New York; registered in Germany as Rechtskundiger for U.S. Law, 1991, but not admitted as Rechtsanwalt in Germany (Not admitted in Germany). *Education:* Yale University (A.B., 1970); University of Virginia (J.D., 1975).

RESIDENT ASSOCIATES

Hannah L. Buxbaum (Not admitted in Germany); **Richard A. Kahn** (Not admitted in Germany); **Mark G. Strauch** (Not admitted in Germany).

(For Complete Biographical Data on all Personnel see Professional Biographies at New York City)

DERINGER TESSIN HERRMANN & SEDEMUND

BOCKENHEIMER LANDSTRAβE 51-53
D-60325 FRANKFURT/MAIN, GERMANY
Telephone: 49-69-971090-0
Telefax: 49-69-971090-90

Cologne, Germany Office: Heumarkt 14, D-50667 Cologne. Telephone: 49-221-205070. Telefax: 49-221-2050790. Telex: 8 881 356 ELAW D.

Leipzig, Germany Office: Burgplatz 2, D-04109 Leipzig. Telephone: 49-341-711590. Telefax: 49-341-7115999.

Brussels, Belgium Office: Place Des Barricades 13, B-1000 Brussels. Telephone: 32-2-219 82 50. Telefax: 32-2-219 88 32.

(This Listing Continued)

Moscow, Russia Office: Ul. Bolschaja Ordymka 21, RF-113035 Moscow. Telephone: 7-095-2332450, 2315403. Telefax: 7-095-2334355.

General German and International Practice. Banking and Finance, Mergers and Acquisitions, Corporate, Commercial, Foodstuffs and Pharmaceutical, Administrative Law.

PARTNERS

DIETMAR KNOPP, born Trier, Germany, March 26, 1951; admitted, 1977, Cologne; 1979, Cologne Court of Appeals; 1992, Frankfurt Court of Appeals. *Education:* University of Bonn. *Member:* German and International Bar Associations; German Administrative Law Association; German Association for the Protection of Industrial Property and Copyright. *LANGUAGES:* German, English, French and Spanish.

DR. WOLFGANG FEURING, born Hellersen, Germany, December 13, 1952; admitted, 1981, Duesseldorf; 1982, Hagen; 1985, Frankfurt/Main. *Education:* Universities of Goettingen, Lausanne and Hamburg, Assistant Professor at the Institute for International and Foreign Private and Business Law of the University of Goettingen (Dr. jur., 1980). Author: "Merger Control in the European Coal and Steel Community," 1980; "Merger Control pursuant to Art, 66 EGKSV compared to the German Antitrust Law," WuW 1981, pp. 401-410; "Application of the German Antitrust Law to mergers," WuW 1982, pp. 517-522. Co-Author: "The New Banking Law of the European Economic Community," The International Lawyer, 1991, pp. 1-40. Counsel: Legal Department of Deutsche Bank AG, Luxembourg, 1982-1985; Frankfurt/Main, 1985-1991. *Member:* German and International Bar Associations. *LANGUAGES:* German, English and French.

DR. HANS-JOACHIM PRIEβ, born Bremerhaven, Germany, February 19, 1958; admitted, 1988, Hamburg; 1991, Cologne. *Education:* Kiel University (Dr. jur, 1988); Freiburg i.Brsg., Lausanne, Switzerland; Indiana University School of Law (LL.M., 1984); Harvard Law School. Author: "International Administrative Tribunal and Appeal Boards," Berlin, 1989; "The Development of the EC-Law Pertaining to Maritime Transport," Europarecht 1989, pp. 369-378; "The Protection of the External and Internal Trade of the European Communities Against Dumping and Subsidies," JuS 1991, pp. 629-634; "The European Community as a Member of a Customs Union," Europarecht 1991, pp. 187-195. Contributor: Wolfrun (ed.), Handbook United Nations, Munich 1991, pp. 635-640 (Civil Service International) and 1002-1007 (Administrative Tribunals, International); "Combatting Fraud in the EC," EuZW 1994, pp. 297-304; "Public Procurement in the EU," Cologne et al., 1994. Research and Teaching Assistant, Institute for International Law at Kiel University, 1983. Lecturer, EC Law, College for Public Administration, Cologne, 1992. *Member:* German Bar Association; German-American Lawyers Association; Deutscher Juristentag e.V.; Fulbright Alumni e.V. (Also at Brussels, Belgium Office). *LANGUAGES:* German, English and French.

ECKHARD MARTIN, born Hannover, Germany, November 10, 1959; admitted, 1991, Germany and New York. *Education:* Universities of Munich, Lausanne and Goettingen (First State Examination, 1984; Second State Examination 1988); University of Illinois (LL.M., 1990). *LANGUAGES:* German and English.

ASSOCIATES

DR. THOMAS SCHRÖER, born Darmstadt, Germany, January 23, 1964; admitted, 1992, Frankfurt. *Education:* University of Frankfurt (Referendar, 1988; Dr. iur., 1991). Teaching Assistant, University of Frankfurt, 1988-1991. *LANGUAGES:* German and English.

GREGOR DORNBUSCH, born Cologne, Germany, November 23, 1963; admitted, 1992, Frankfurt. *Education:* Universities of Frankfurt and London. *LANGUAGES:* German and English.

(For complete biographical data on all personnel, see Professional Biographies at Cologne, Germany)

DÖSER AMERELLER NOACK

(Baker & McKenzie)

BETHMANNSTRASSE 50-54
D-60311 FRANKFURT/MAIN, GERMANY
Telephone: (069) 299080
Intn'l Dialing: (49-69) 299080
Cable Address: ABOGADO
Telex: 414239
Answer back: 414239a BM D
Facsimile: (49-69) 29908108

Berlin, Germany Office: Kleiststrasse 23-26, D-10787 Berlin. Telephone: (030) 214990-0. Facsimile: (030) 214990-99.

Administrative Law, Antitrust Law, Arbitration, Banking and Finance, Commercial Law, Company Law, Computer Law, Corporate Finance, Employment and Labour Law, Environmental Law, European Community Law, Food and Drug Law, Franchising, Industrial and Intellectual Property, Litigation, Mergers and Acquisitions, Multinational Business Transactions, Product Liability, Real Estate/Conveyancing, Taxation, Telecommunications Law, Trademarks, Unfair Competition Law.

PARTNERS

*HORST AMERELLER, born Munich, Germany, 1934; admitted, 1964, Germany. *Education:* University of Munich (Referendar, 1957); European Research Institute, University of Saarbrücken (Diploma, 1958; Dr. jur., 1964); Harvard Law School (LL.M., 1960). Notary. *LANGUAGES:* German, English and French.

*CHRISTIAN BRODERSEN, born Kiel, Germany, 1948; admitted, 1975, Germany. *Education:* Universities of Geneva and Frankfurt (Referendar, 1972); London School of Economics (LL.M., 1978). Notary, Tax Advisor (Steuerberater), Hon. Legal Advisor to the British Consul-General. *LANGUAGES:* German, English and French. *PRACTICE AREAS:* Taxation; Mergers and Acquisitions; Securities and Financial Products; Banking and Finance; Corporate and Partnership Law.

*WULF H. DÖSER, born Stuttgart, Germany, 1933; admitted, 1961, Germany. *Education:* Universities of Hamburg and Tübingen (Referendar, 1956; Dr. jur., 1959); University of Chicago (M.C.L., 1962). Notary, Tax Attorney, Lecturer in Law, University of Frankfurt. *LANGUAGES:* German, English and French. *PRACTICE AREAS:* Corporate and Partnership Law; Banking and Finance; Securities and Financial Products; Taxation; Antitrust Law.

*HANS-GEORG FEICK, born Berlin, Germany, 1940; admitted, 1970, Illinois, U.S.A.; 1972, Germany. *Education:* Universities of Frankfurt, Freiburg and Munich (Referendar, 1963); University of California at Berkeley (LL.M., 1966); ITT-Chicago Kent College of Law (J.D., 1970). Notary. *LANGUAGES:* German, English and French. *PRACTICE AREAS:* Corporate and Partnership Law; Mergers and Acquisitions; Banking and Finance; Aviation and Aerospace Technology.

*PETER FICHT, born Dortmund, Germany, 1936; admitted, 1964, Germany. *Education:* Universities of Münster and Erlangen (Referendar, 1960); Princeton University and University of California at Berkeley (LL.M., 1966). Notary. *LANGUAGES:* German, English and French. *PRACTICE AREAS:* Corporate and Partnership Law; Mergers and Acquisitions; Labor and Employment Law; Trade; Real Estate Law.

*WOLFGANG FRITZEMEYER, born Heidelberg, Germany, 1949; admitted, 1979, New York, U.S.A.; 1980, Germany; 1990, New South Wales, Australia. *Education:* Universities of Freiburg and Heidelberg (Referendar, 1973), Cornell Law School (LL.M., 1977); University of Konstanz (Dr. jur., 1983). Hon. Legal Advisor to the Australian Consul-General. *LANGUAGES:* German, English and French. *PRACTICE AREAS:* Computers and Technology Law; Mergers and Acquisitions; Franchise Law; EC Competition and Trade; Australian and U.S. Law.

*GÜNTHER HECKELMANN, born Wiesbaden, Germany, 1954; admitted, 1985, Germany. *Education:* University of Mainz (Referendar, 1981); University of California at Berkeley. Attorney for Labour Law. *LANGUAGES:* German, English, French and Spanish. *PRACTICE AREAS:* Labor and Employment Law; Executive Transfers; Employee Benefits.

*WALTER HENLE, born Munich, Germany, 1955; admitted, 1983, Germany. *Education:* University of Munich (Referendar, 1979; Dr. jur., 1984); New York University (LL.M., 1986). *LANGUAGES:* German, English and French. *PRACTICE AREAS:* Mergers and Acquisitions; Corporate and Partnership Law; Banking and Finance; Securities and Financial Products.

(This Listing Continued)

EU640B

*MATTHIAS G. JALETZKE, born Ludwigshafen am Rhein, Germany, 1960; admitted, 1988, Germany. *Education:* University of Mannheim (Referendar, 1983; Dr. jur., 1988); International Faculty for Comparative Law, Strasbourg (Diploma, 1984). *LANGUAGES:* German and English. *PRACTICE AREAS:* Mergers and Acquisitions; EC Competition and Trade; Antitrust Law; Corporate and Partnership Law.

*KARL-LUDWIG KOENEN, born Euskirchen, Germany, 1939; admitted, 1968, Germany. *Education:* Universities of Munich, Bonn and Cologne (Referendar, 1964; Dr. jur., 1967). Notary. *LANGUAGES:* German, English and French. *PRACTICE AREAS:* Corporate and Partnership Law; Real Estate Law; Trade (China, Russia); Construction and Property Development.

*RAINER A. MAGOLD, born Biberach, Germany, 1955; admitted, 1986, Germany. *Education:* Universities of Geneva and Mannheim (Referendar, 1981; Dr. jur., 1986); Tulane University (LL.M., 1982). *LANGUAGES:* German, English and French. *PRACTICE AREAS:* Banking and Finance; Securities and Financial Products; Corporate and Partnership Law; Mergers and Acquisitions.

*WERNER MÜLLER, born Schweinshaupten, Germany, 1945; admitted, 1972, Germany. *Education:* Universities of Erlangen, Geneva and Munich, Academy of Administration, Speyer (Referendar, 1968; Dr. jur., 1974). Notary. *LANGUAGES:* German, English, French and Portuguese. *PRACTICE AREAS:* Commercial Litigation; Civil Litigation; Intellectual Property Law; Arbitration and Dispute Resolution; Brazilian Law.

*HILMAR NOACK, born Berlin, Germany, 1929; admitted, 1956, Germany. *Education:* Free University of Berlin (Referendar, 1951); University of Cologne (Dr. jur., 1960). Notary, Tax Advisor (Steuerberater), C.P.A. (Wirtschaftsprüfer). *LANGUAGES:* German and English. *PRACTICE AREAS:* Taxation; Corporate and Partnership Law; Mergers and Acquisitions; Real Estate Law.

*ULRICH RÄNSCH, born Ludwigshafen am Rhein, Germany, 1952; admitted, 1984, Germany. *Education:* Universities of Frankfurt and Bremen (Diplom-Kaufmann, 1977; Dr. jur., 1986). Foreign Associate, German Trade Office in Auckland, New Zealand (1982); Tax Advisor (Steuerberater). *LANGUAGES:* German and English. *PRACTICE AREAS:* Taxation; Mergers and Acquisitions; Corporate and Partnership Law; Bankruptcy, Insolvency and Reorganization.

*ANDREAS RODIN, born Frankfurt/Main, Germany, 1956; admitted, 1986, Germany. *Education:* University of Munich (Referendar, 1983; Dr. jur., 1987, Munich). *LANGUAGES:* German and English. *PRACTICE AREAS:* Taxation; Mergers and Acquisitions; Securities and Financial Products; Corporate and Partnership Law.

*JOACHIM SCHERER, born Darmstadt, Germany, 1953; admitted, 1981, Germany. *Education:* Universities of Lausanne and Frankfurt (Referendar, 1976; Dr. jur., 1979); Columbia University Law School (LL.M., 1977). Assistant Professor and University Lecturer, 1981-1989, University of Frankfurt; Professor for Public Law, University of German Federal Armed Forces at Munich, 1990. Attorney for Administrative Law. *LANGUAGES:* German, English and French. *PRACTICE AREAS:* Environmental Law; Communications and Media Law; Administrative Law; Regulatory Law; Public Contracts and Utilities.

*RAINER STACHELS, born Münster, Germany, 1940; admitted, 1970, Germany. *Education:* Universities of Vienna, Freiburg and Cologne (Referendar, 1964; Dr. jur., 1967); Princeton University, University of California at Berkeley (LL.M., 1966); The Hague Academy of International Law. Notary. *LANGUAGES:* German, English and French. *PRACTICE AREAS:* Computers and Technology Law; Corporate and Partnership Law; Mergers and Acquisitions; Construction and Property Development; Real Estate Law.

*JOACHIM TREECK, born Unna, Germany, 1938; admitted, 1970, Germany. *Education:* Leibniz Kolleg, Tübingen; Universities of Freiburg and Münster (Referendar, 1963); University of Tübingen (Dr. jur., 1968); Harvard Law School (LL.M., 1969). Notary. *LANGUAGES:* German, English and French. *PRACTICE AREAS:* Corporate and Partnership Law; Antitrust Law; EC Competition and Trade; Mergers and Acquisitions.

*FRANZ J. WALTERMANN, born Münster, Germany, 1937; admitted, 1966, Germany. *Education:* Universities of Münster and Marburg (Referendar, 1961; Dr. jur., 1968). Notary. *LANGUAGES:* German and English. *PRACTICE AREAS:* Commercial Litigation; Arbitration and Dispute Resolution; Intellectual Property Law; Civil Litigation; Bankruptcy, Insolvency and Reorganization.

(This Listing Continued)

ASSOCIATES

MICHAEL A. FAMMLER, born Frankfurt/Main, Germany, 1962; admitted, 1990, Germany. *Education:* University of Konstanz (Rechtspraktikant, 1984); Dr. jur., 1989); Southern Methodist University, Dallas (LL.M., 1990). Assistant Lecturer, University of Konstanz, 1987-1989. *LANGUAGES:* German and English.

BERND J. GÖTZE, born Zittau, Germany, 1950; admitted, 1981, Germany. *Education:* University of Freiburg, Law and Japanology (Referendar, 1978; Dr. jur., 1991). *LANGUAGES:* German, Japanese, English and French. *PRACTICE AREAS:* Construction and Property Development; Environmental Law; Japan Law; Trade (Japan); Mergers and Acquisitions.

SEBASTIAN GRONSTEDT, born Goslar, Germany, 1957; admitted, 1990, Germany. *Education:* Universities of Tübingen, Geneva and Kiel (Referendar, 1984); Indiana University School of Law (LL.M., 1986); University of Regensburg (Dr. jur., 1993). Tutorial Teacher, University of Kiel, 1985. *LANGUAGES:* German, English and French. *PRACTICE AREAS:* German Law; Mergers and Acquisitions; EC Competition and Trade; Corporate and Partnership Law; Securities and Financial Products.

AXEL HAMM, born Wiesbaden, Germany, 1951; admitted, 1979, Germany. *Education:* Universities of Mainz and Frankfurt/M. (Initial Bar Examination, 1977). *Member:* Vereinigung für Gewerblichen Rechtsscnutz und Urheberrecht. *LANGUAGES:* German, English and French. *PRACTICE AREAS:* Commercial Litigation; Civil Litigation; Intellectual Property Law.

ANDREAS HOFFMANN, born Frankfurt/Main, Germany, 1964; admitted, 1993, Germany. *Education:* University of Frankfurt (Referendar, 1990). *LANGUAGES:* German and English.

INGRID M. KALISCH, born Amorbach/Odw., Germany, 1959; admitted, 1990, Germany. *Education:* Georgetown University, Washington, D.C.; University of Frankfurt (Referendar, 1985). *LANGUAGES:* German and English. *PRACTICE AREAS:* Banking and Finance; Securities and Financial Products; Mergers and Acquisitions; Corporate and Partnership Law.

MARKUS O. KAPPENHAGEN, born Soest, Germany, 1960; admitted, 1991, Germany. *Education:* Universities of Munich and Münster (Referendar, 1986; Dr. jur., 1991). Teaching Assistant, University of Münster, 1987-1988. *LANGUAGES:* German and English. *PRACTICE AREAS:* Labor and Employment Law; Executive Transfers; Employee Benefits.

JÖRG K. KIRCHNER, born Arnsberg, Germany, May 4, 1961; admitted, 1991, Germany and New York, U.S.A. *Education:* University of Munich (Dr., 1989); George Washington University Law School, Washington, D.C. (LL.M., 1991). *LANGUAGES:* German, English and French. *PRACTICE AREAS:* Corporate and Partnership Law; Mergers and Acquisitions; Communications and Media Law; Intellectual Property Law; Entertainment, the Arts and Sports Law.

MICHAEL MACK, born Frankfurt, Germany, 1954; admitted, 1981, Germany. *Education:* University of Frankfurt/Main. *LANGUAGES:* German and English. *PRACTICE AREAS:* Taxation; Corporate and Partnership Law; Mergers and Acquisitions.

JÜRGEN MARK, born Iserlohn, Germany, 1958; admitted, 1990, Germany. *Education:* University of Münster (Referendar, 1984); McGill University, Montreal (LL.M., 1987). *LANGUAGES:* German and English. *PRACTICE AREAS:* Commercial Litigation; Civil Litigation; Arbitration and Dispute Resolution.

GRACE NACIMIENTO, born New York, N.Y., April 22, 1962; admitted, 1993, Germany. *Education:* Deutsch-Franz. Gymnasium (Abitur, 1981); Sarah Lawrence University; Ruprecht-Karls University (Ref., 1988); Emory University (LL.M., 1989). *LANGUAGES:* German, Spanish, English and French. *PRACTICE AREAS:* Administrative Law; Environmental Law; Immigration Law; Public Contracts and Utilities.

SIBILLA NAGEL, born Stuttgart, Germany, July 31, 1962; admitted, 1994, Germany. *Education:* Economics (University) (Diploma, 1987); Ludwig-Maximilians Universität (1st State Exam, 1991); Practice District Court (2nd State Exam, 1994). *LANGUAGES:* German, English, French, Italian and Russian. *PRACTICE AREAS:* Corporate and Partnership Law; Intellectual Property Law; Antitrust Law; EC Competition and Trade.

HANSJÖRG PIEHL, born Düsseldorf, Germany, 1961; admitted, 1992, Germany. *Education:* Universities of Bochum, Lausanne and Münster (Referendar, 1987; Dr. jur., 1990); Duke Law School (LL.M., 1989). Research Assistant, University of Münster, 1987-1988 and 1989-1990. *LAN-*

(This Listing Continued)

GUAGES: German, English and French. *PRACTICE AREAS:* Corporate and Partnership Law; Mergers and Acquisitions.

THILO RÄPPLE, born Hildesheim, Germany, 1959; admitted, 1989, Germany. *Education:* University of Göttingen (Referendar, 1984; Dr. jur., 1991). Assistant Lecturer, Free University of Berlin, 1985-1987. *LANGUAGES:* German and English. *PRACTICE AREAS:* Health Care and Hospital Law; Regulatory Law; Intellectual Property Law.

ACHIM SCHÄFER, born Nürtingen, Germany, 1967; admitted, 1994, Germany. *Education:* Universities of Tübingen, Heidelberg and Johns Hopkins University Bologna Center (Referendar, 1991; Dr. jur., 1992; M.A. in History and Economics, 1994). *LANGUAGES:* German, English, French and Italian. *PRACTICE AREAS:* Banking and Finance; Corporate and Partnership Law; Securities and Financial Products; Insurance Law; Mergers and Acquisitions.

MATTHIAS P. SCHOLZ, born Hilden/Rhld., Germany, 1961; admitted, 1990, Germany. *Education:* University of Freiburg (Referendar, 1986; Dr. jur., 1988); University of Reims, France (Licencié en Droit, 1983); Tulane Law School (LL.M., 1992). *LANGUAGES:* German, English and French. *PRACTICE AREAS:* Computers and Technology Law; Communications and Media Law; Intellectual Property Law; EC Competition Law; U.S.A. Law.

JÖRG-MARTIN SCHULTZE, born Münster, Germany, 1957; admitted, 1989, Germany; 1991, New York, U.S.A. *Education:* University of Münster (Referendar, 1982; Dr. jur., 1988); Southern Methodist University, Dallas (LL.M., 1989). Assistant Lecturer, University of Münster, 1983-1988. *LANGUAGES:* German and English. *PRACTICE AREAS:* Antitrust Law; EC Competition and Trade; Mergers and Acquisitions; Corporate and Partnership Law; Commercial Litigation.

PETER SIGEL, born Engstingen, Germany, April 22, 1960; admitted, 1990, Germany. *Education:* University of Freiburg; University of Tübingen (Referendar, 1985; Dr. jur., 1987; Qualifying bar exam, 1990); London School of Economies and Political Science (LL.M., 1991). *LANGUAGES:* German and English. *PRACTICE AREAS:* Mergers and Acquisitions; Corporate and Partnership Law; Taxation; Trust, Probate and Estate Planning.

STEPHAN J. SPEHL, born Heidelberg, Germany, 1961; admitted, 1989, Germany; 1991, New York, U.S.A. *Education:* Universities of Munich, Geneva and Freiburg (Referendar, 1985; Dr.jur., 1988); University of Miami School of Law (LL.M., 1989). *LANGUAGES:* German and English. *PRACTICE AREAS:* Commercial Litigation; Civil Litigation; Intellectual Property Law; Arbitration and Dispute Resolution; Entertainment, the Arts and Sports Law.

LEOKADIA SZALKIEWICZ-ZARADZKA, born Mieszkonice, Poland, 1962; admitted, 1994, Germany. *Education:* University of Torun (Poland), University of Mainz (Referendar, 1989). *LANGUAGES:* Polish, German and English. *PRACTICE AREAS:* Corporate and Partnership Law; Civil Litigation; Commercial Litigation.

CONSTANZE ULMER-EILFORT, born Stuttgart, Germany, 1962; admitted, 1990, New York, U.S.A.; 1993, Germany. *Education:* Universities of Regensburg, Munich (Referendar, 1987) and Berlin; University of Pennsylvania Law School (LL.M., 1989). *LANGUAGES:* German, English and Italian. *PRACTICE AREAS:* Intellectual Property Law; Corporate and Partnership Law; Entertainment, the Arts and Sports Law; Computers and Technology Law.

ULF WAUSCHKUHN, born Elmshorn, 1963; admitted, 1992, Germany. *Education:* University of Hamburg (Referendar, 1988); University of Tübingen (Dr. jur., 1990). *LANGUAGES:* German and English. *PRACTICE AREAS:* Commercial Litigation; Civil Litigation; Arbitration and Dispute Resolution; Insurance Law.

*Also Partner of Baker & McKenzie, Chicago, Illinois, U.S.A.

(For offices in other countries, see Chicago, Illinois, U.S.A. listing for Baker & McKenzie)

DROSTE

The Merged Firms of Droste, Pietzcker, Sprick, Ohlgart & Klosterfelde;
Triebel & Weil; Strobl, Killius & Vorbrugg

SCHAUMAINKAI 91
60596 FRANKFURT/MAIN, GERMANY
Telephone: (069) 63 00 89-0
Telecopier: (069) 630089-99

Düsseldorf, Germany Office: Berliner Allee 48, 40212 Düsseldorf.
  Telephone: (0211) 13 680. Telecopier: (0211) 32 44 39.
Hamburg, Germany Office: Warburgstrasse 50, 20354 Hamburg.
  Telephone: (040) 4 1993-0. Telecopier: (040) 4 1993 200.
Munich, Germany Office: Marstallstrasse 8, 80539 Munich. Telephone:
  (089) 290120. Telecopier: (089) 29012 222. Telex: 524 973 skv.
Berlin, Germany Office: Kurfürstendamm 54-55, 10707 Berlin.
  Telephone: (030) 88 24 300. Telefax: (030) 88 24 393.
Brussels, Belgium Office: Avenue des Gaulois 9, B-1150 Brussels.
  Telephone: 02-7358945. Telefax: 02-7352251.

General and International Practice. Commercial Law, Corporate, Banking, Finance, Tax, Mergers and Acquisitions, EU Law, Antitrust, Unfair Competition, Trademarks, Copyright, Patents, Licensing, Food and Drug Law, Law of the Press, Products Liability, Environmental Law, Labor Law, Real Estate, Estate Planning, International Construction, Contracts, Commercial Litigation and Arbitration, Bankruptcy, Administrative Law.

FIRM PROFILE: Droste is engaged in the practice of corporate and commercial law. The firm is the result of the merger of Droste, Pietzcker, Sprick, Ohlgart& Klosterfelde in Hamburg (formed in 1887), Strobl, Killius & Vorbrugg in Munich (formed in 1961) and Triebel & Weil in Düsseldorf (formed in 1951). The firm's traditional areas of practice are: corporate law, including mergers and acquisitions; industrial property law, including copyright, unfair competition and anti-trust law; trademark law; tax law, both domestic and international; real estate law. Further areas of particular expertise include banking and finance, computer and software law, environmental law, labour law, EU law and commercial litigation and arbitration.

RESIDENT PARTNERS

DR. THOMAS FÖRSTERLING, born Riga, Latvia, December 28, 1943; admitted, 1975, Germany. *Education:* University of Munich (Law Degree, 1972); University of Perugia (Italy) and University of Aix-Marseille (Licencié and Doctor of Laws, 1974). *Member:* International Union of Lawyers; German-British Jurists' Association; German-French Jurists' Association; German-Italian Jurists' Association; American Foreign Law Association. *LANGUAGES:* German, English, French and Italian. *PRACTICE AREAS:* Commercial Litigation; Corporate Law; Company Law; Arbitration and Mediation; International Law.

DR. HANNS-CHRISTIAN SALGER, born Karlsruhe, Germany, April 9, 1955; admitted, 1982, Germany; 1986, New York. *Education:* University of Freiburg (Law Degree, 1978; Doctor of Laws, 1984); University of Illinois College of Law (LL.M., 1980). Lecturer, University of Frankfurt. *Member:* Society for Comparative Law; American Bar Association; German-American Lawyers' Association; German-British Jurists' Association; Canadian-German Lawyers' Association; International Bar Association; International Union of Lawyers (EEC-Section). *LANGUAGES:* German and English. *PRACTICE AREAS:* Contracts; Mergers and Acquisitions; Antitrust; Unfair Competition Law.

DR. CLAUDIA SEIBEL, born Heidelberg, Germany, March 1, 1955; admitted, 1982, Germany. *Education:* Universities of Würzburg, Geneva (Switzerland) and Munich (Law Degree, 1978; Doctor of Laws, 1987). *Member:* International Association of Young Advocats. *LANGUAGES:* German, English, French and Latvian. *PRACTICE AREAS:* Real Property Law; Construction and Construction Design Law; Commercial Leases; Administrative Law.

WENDELIN ACKER, born Tübingen, Germany, April 27, 1953; admitted, 1982, Germany. *Education:* University of Freiburg (Law Degree, 1978). *Member:* German Society for Construction Law; German-Spanish Jurists Association. *LANGUAGES:* German, English and Spanish. *PRACTICE AREAS:* Real Estate; Construction and Construction Design Law; Insurance Law, including Litigation.

THOMAS UBBER, born Frankfurt, Germany, March 6, 1961; admitted, 1990, Germany. *Education:* University of Frankfurt (Law Degree, 1986). *LANGUAGES:* German, English and Spanish. *PRACTICE*

(This Listing Continued)

AREAS: General Corporate and Commercial Law; Labour Law; Unfair Competition Law.

DR. MANUEL LORENZ, born Bad Homburg, November 2, 1959; admitted, 1991, Germany. *Education:* University of Frankfurt (Law Degree, 1983; Doctor of Laws, 1991); University of Geneva (Switzerland); University of Illinois (LL.M., 1986). *Member:* Society for Comparative Law; German-American Lawyers' Association. *LANGUAGES:* German, English and French. *PRACTICE AREAS:* International Corporate and Commercial Law; Banking; Computer and Software Law; Franchising.

ASSOCIATES

Stephanie K. Thompson (Not admitted in Germany)
Dr. Michael Hauf

Languages: German, English, French, Spanish, Russian, Italian, Portuguese, Latvian, Chinese and Japanese.

(For list of personnel at Berlin, Düsseldorf, Hamburg and Munich, see Professional Biographies at those locations)

ANWALTSKANZLEI
DR. DR. ULFERT ENGELS

In charge of the Statutory Management of the IASW-EWIV

International Attorney's Tax Counsel's and CPA's EEIG

Court Registered: HRA 26625 Amtsgericht Frankfurt a.M.

KLINGERSTR. 24
D-60313 FRANKFURT/MAIN, GERMANY
Telephone: 069-28.11.39
Fax: 069-28.35.12

Kassel, Germany Office: Wilhelmsstr. 11, D-34117. Telephone: 0561-709.83-0. Fax: 0561-71.10.71.
Rotterdam, The Netherlands Office: Engels & Jongeneel Advocaten, Westersingel 92, NL 3015 LC. Telephone: (31-10) 436.07.88. Fax: (31-10) 436.78.44.

(For concentration areas and bibliographical data of the Anwaltskanzlei see office located at Kassel)

FAEGRE & BENSON

Professional Limited Liability Partnership

Established in 1991

WESTENDSTRASSE 24
6000 FRANKFURT
FRANKFURT AM MAIN 1, GERMANY
Telephone: 49-69-1743 43
Facsimile: 49-69-1743 49

REVISERS OF THE MINNESOTA LAW DIGEST FOR THIS DIRECTORY.

Minneapolis, Minnesota Office: 2200 Norwest Center, 90 South Seventh Street, 55402-3901. Telephone: 612-336-3000. Facsimile: 612-336-3026.
Denver, Colorado Office: 2500 Republic Plaza, 370 Seventeenth Street, 80202-4004. Telephone: 303-592-5900. Facsimile: 303-592-5693.
Des Moines: Iowa Office: 400 Capital Square, 400 Locust Street, 50309-2335. Telephone: 55-248-9000. Facsimile: 515-248-9010.
Washington, D. C. Office: The Homer Building, Suite 450 North, 601 Thirteenth Street, N.W. 20005-3807 Telephone: 202-783-3880. Facsimile: 202-783-3899.
London, England Office: 10 Eastcheap. Telephone: 44-171-623-6163. Facsimile: 44-171-623-3227.

General Practice.

RESIDENT MEMBER

PHILIP B. HALEEN, born Minneapolis, Minnesota, 1949; admitted, 1974, Minnesota (Not admitted in Germany). *Education:* Stanford University (B.A., 1971); University of Minnesota (J.D., 1974).

RESIDENT ASSOCIATES

RALPH W. HUMMEL, born Weinheim, Germany, 1956; admitted, 1985, Germany. *Education:* Johannes-Gutenberg-University in Mainz (1982); Qualification as Tax Consultant.

(This Listing Continued)

VINZENZ BÖDEKER, born Ottemhaughen, Germany, 1958; admitted, 1987, Germany. *Education:* University of Bielefeld (Law Degree, 1986); Indiana University (LL.M., 1994).

EASTERN EUROPEAN COUNSEL

OLGA ILIANA BACHVAROVA, born Sofia, Bulgaria, 1947; admitted, 1970, Bulgaria (Not admitted in Germany). *Education:* University of Sofia, Law School, 1969. Faculty Member, University of Sofia, Law School for Civil and Commercial Law, 1974-1981. *LANGUAGES:* German, English, Russian, Bulgarian.

REVISERS OF THE MINNESOTA LAW DIGEST FOR THIS DIRECTORY.

(For complete Biographical Data on all personnel, see Professional Biographies at Minneapolis, Minnesota)

FEDDERSEN LAULE SCHERZBERG & OHLE HANSEN EWERWAHN

STIFTSTRASSE 9-17
P.O. BOX 100836
D-60313 FRANKFURT/MAIN, GERMANY
Telephone: 49-69-29994-0
Telex: 41 33 96 fls d
Telefax: 49-69-28 26 15

Hamburg, Germany Office: Jungfernstieg 51 (Prien-Haus), D-20354 Hamburg. Telephone: 49-40-35 00 50. Telex: 21 27 99 99 lawt d. Telefax: 49-40-35 00 51 11.
Berlin, Germany Office: Kurfürstendamm 185, D-10707 Berlin. Telephone: 49-30-88 57 16 0. Telefax: 49-30-88 57 16 50.
Dresden, Germany Office: Königsbrücker Straße 17, D-01099 Dresden. Telephone: 49-03 51-567 02 77. Telefax: 49-03 51-567 02 79.
Brussels, Belgium Office: 118, Rue d'Arlon, B-1040 Brussels. Telephone: 32-2-280-1544. Telefax: 32-2-280-0703.
Prague, Czech Republic Office: Spanĕlsk á 2, CZ-120 00 Prague 2. Telephone: 42-2-268203; 268229. Telefax: 42-2-260310.

General Practice, Administrative Law, Admiralty, Antitrust, Arbitration, Aviation, Banking, Commercial and Corporate Law. Environmental Law, Entertainment Law, Estate Planning, EC and International Law, Insurance, Labor Law, License, Merger and Acquisition, Patent, Trade Mark and Copyright, Real Estate, Securities Law, Tax, Transportation, Unfair Competition, Litigation.

FIRM PROFILE: The firm offers a full range of legal services. It is well known for its commercial, corporate, banking and tax law and its practice in the field of merger and acquisitions, real estate and environmental law. The firm has a broad national as well as international client base with a focus on Europe, the United States and Japan. The firm has 79 attorneys at law (8 of whom are notaries public) and 5 tax advisors.

MEMBERS OF FIRM

PROF. DR. DIETER FEDDERSEN, born Kiel, Germany, April 22, 1935; admitted, 1964, Braunschweig; 1971, Wiesbaden; 1974, Frankfurt. *Education:* University of Kiel (Dr. jur.); Berlin. Tax Counsel, 1971—. Notary Public, 1974—. Lecturer on Tax Law, Heidelberg, 1986. Honorary Professor, University of Heidelberg, 1991. Chairman: Board of Drägerwerk A.G., Lübeck, 1979—; Board of Wilhelm Schimmel Pianofortefabrik GmbH, Braunschweig, 1971—. Member, Board of Draeger Foundation, Munich, 1980—. Member, Board of Elfriede Draeger Memorial Foundation, New York, 1981—. Chairman, Board of Fuba Hans Kolbe & Co., Hildesheim, 1979—. Chairman, Board of Dr. Joachim Schmidt GmbH & Co. KG Gesellschaft für Industriebeteiligungen, Ilsede 1973—. Chairman, Board of Karl Munte Bauunternehmung, Braunschweig, 1983. Member, Board of YMOS AG, Obertshausen, 1984. Chairman, Board of Lindauer Dornier GmbH, Lindau, 1985. Chairman, Board of Sommer-Allibert Industrie AG, Frankfurt/Main, 1985. Member, Board of SGZ-Bank, Suedeutsche Genossenschafts-Zentralbank AG, 1994. *Member:* Studienvereinigung Kartellrecht; Deutsche und Internationale Vereinigung für gewerblichen Rechtsschutz und Urheberrecht; German American Lawyers Association; IFA, International Fiscal Association; Deutsche Steuerjuristische Gesellschaft; Arbeitsgemeinschaft Fachanwälte für Steuerrecht. *LANGUAGES:* German, English. *PRACTICE AREAS:* Corporate Partnership Law; Merger and Acquisition Law; Tax Law.

PROF. DR. GERHARD LAULE, born Potsdam, Germany, May 26, 1935; admitted, 1968, Frankfurt. *Education:* Universities of Freiburg/Breisgau, Bonn and Cologne (Dr. jur., 1961). Lecturer on Tax Law, University

of Heidelberg till 1978 now University of Saarbrücken. Professor, University of Saarbrücken, 1982. Tax Counsel, 1970. Corporate Counsel, 1964-1970; Tax Counsel and Managing Director, National and International Tax Department, 1970-1974; Managing Director, Accounting and Planning Department, 1974-1977, AEG-Telefunken. Member Advisory Board GBG-Verwaltungs- und Verwertungsgesellschaft für Grundbesitz mbH, Mannheim, 1989. Chairman, Board of AVA Allgemeine Handelsgesellschaft der Verbraucher Aktiengesellschaft, Bielefeld, 1990; Chairman of the Supervisory Board of DSL Holding AG, Bonn and First Deputy Chairman of the Supervisory Board of DSL Bank Deutsche Siedlungs- und Landesrentenbank, Bonn, Member of the Supervisory Board of Autania AG. *Member:* International Fiscal Association (Board Member, 1986); International Law Association (German Branch); Gesellschaft für Finanzwirtschaft in der Unternehmensführung; Deutsche Steuerjuristische Gesellschaft; Saarbruecker Rechtsforum. *LANGUAGES:* German, English, French. *PRACTICE AREAS:* Corporate Partnerships Law; Mergers and Acquisitions Law; EC Law.

DR. ROLF-RÜDIGER STROTH, born Leipzig, Germany, October 4, 1914; admitted, 1948, Frankfurt. *Education:* Universities of Heidelberg, Munich and Jena (Dr. jur., 1938). Notary Public, 1958. Tax Counsel, 1962. Recipient: Special Merit Award, April, 1986; Federal Service Cross, December 1992. Member of Board: American Chamber of Commerce in Germany, 1970—; Member, USO Council of Germany, 1976—. Chairman, Legal Committee American Chamber of Commerce in Germany, 1977—. Columnist, writing "Law Digest" in every Issue of "Commerce in Germany", Magazine, 1979—. *Member:* International Academy of Trial Lawyers (Board Member); Deutsche Vereinigung für gewerblichen Rechtsschutz und Urheberrecht; German American Lawyers Association; British Chamber of Commerce in Germany. *LANGUAGES:* German, English, French. *PRACTICE AREAS:* Copyright Law; Unfair Competition Law; Film Law; Antitrust Law.

HANS-JUERGEN HUESKER, born Trier, Germany, November 21, 1941; admitted, 1970 Göttingen; 1976, Frankfurt/Main. *Education:* Universities of Göttingen and Berlin (State Examination, 1965); University of Paris (1961-1962); Ministry of Justice, Hannover (German Bar Examination, 1970). Assistant Lecturer, Penal Law, University of Göttingen, 1971-1976. *Member:* Deutscher Juristentag e.V.; Anwaltsverein Frankfurt; Club des Affaires de la Hesse; Deutsche und Internationale Vereinigung für gewerblichen Rechtsschutz und Urheberrecht. *LANGUAGES:* German, English, French. *PRACTICE AREAS:* General Practice; Litigation; Unfair Competition Law.

DR. H.W. KORNICKER, born Sorrent, Italy, September 7, 1935; admitted, 1965, Ludwigshafen; 1973, Paris, France; 1978, Frankfurt. *Education:* Universities of Bonn (Dr. jur.), Munich and Paris. Avocat a la Cour. Member, Board of NORD-FRANCE S.A. Contributor to the Encyclopedia "JURISCLASSEUR DROIT COMPARE," Country reports for the Federal Republic of Germany. *LANGUAGES:* German, French, Italian and English. *PRACTICE AREAS:* Construction.

PETER LATSCHA (1946-1994).

KLAUS M. KÜBEL, LL.M., born Düsseldorf, Germany, December 15, 1945; admitted, 1975, Frankfurt. *Education:* Universities of Bonn and Frankfurt (State Examination, 1971); University of California, Berkeley, California (LL.M., 1973); Ministry of Justice, Wiesbaden German Bar Examination (1975). Notary. Assistant Lecturer, Institute for Foreign and International Law on Economics, University of Frankfurt, 1973-1974. Corporate Counsel, Altana Industrie-Aktien und Anlagen AG, 1983-1985. *Member:* Studienvereinigung Kartellrecht; Deutsche und Internationale Vereinigung für gewerblichen Rechtsschutz und Urheberrecht; International Bar Association. *LANGUAGES:* German and English. *PRACTICE AREAS:* Mergers and Acquisitions Law; Unfair Competition Law; Copyright Law.

DR. CARL-HEINZ HEUER, born Werne/Lippe, Germany, February 10, 1954; admitted, 1985, Frankfurt/Main. *Education:* Universities of Münster (Dr. jur., 1982); Heidelberg Administrative Law School of Speyer (1983-1984). Assistant Staff Member, General and Textile Free-market Economy Research, University of Münster, 1980-1981. Assistant Lecturer, Institute for Financial and Tax Law, University of Heidelberg, 1981-1984. Tax Counsel, 1987. *Member:* Deutsche Steuerjuristische Gesellschaft (German Tax Law Society); International Bar Association, London. *LANGUAGES:* German. *PRACTICE AREAS:* Antitrust Law; Mergers and Acquisitions Law; Tax Law; Taxation of Art.

DR. ANDREAS MEYER-LANDRUT, born Düsseldorf, Germany, June 21, 1959; admitted, 1987, Frankfurt. *Education:* University of Bonn

(This Listing Continued)

(This Listing Continued)

FEDDERSEN LAULE SCHERZBERG & OHLE HANSEN EWERWAHN, Frankfurt/Main—Continued

(Dr. jur., 1988). *LANGUAGES:* German, English, French. *PRACTICE AREAS:* General Practice; Unfair Competition Law; Stock Corporation.

MATTHIAS KASCH, born Frankfurt/Main, Germany, September 25, 1960; admitted, 1989, Frankfurt. *Education:* Universities of Freiburg/Breisgau and Frankfurt/Main. Assistant in Legal Department, Frankfurter Hypothekenbank AG, 1985-1987. Staff Assistant to Board of Directors, C&L Treuhand Vereinigung Deutsche Revision AG, 1988. *LANGUAGES:* German, English. *PRACTICE AREAS:* Mergers and Acquisitions Law; Corporate Partnerships Law; Antitrust Law; Banking Law; German Securities Law.

DR. WOLFGANG STORM, born Frankfurt/Main, Federal Republic of Germany, December 27, 1939; admitted, 1970, Frankfurt/Main. *Education:* Universities of Frankfurt/Main and Freiburg i.Br.; Georgetown University, Washington, D.C. Notary. *Member:* Frankfurt/Main Lawyers Association (Member of Board). *LANGUAGES:* English, German. *PRACTICE AREAS:* Corporate Law; Real Property Law; Labor Law; Litigation; General Practice.

DR. EKKEHARD MOESER, born Giessen, Germany, July 20, 1947; admitted, 1981, Frankfurt/Main. *Education:* Universities of Giessen, Marburg, Michigan (Ann Arbor) and Augsburg (Degree in Economics (Diplom-Oekonom); Master of Comparative Law). Research Assistant, University of Marburg. Civil Servant at the Federal Ministry of Economics in Bonn. *LANGUAGES:* German, English. *PRACTICE AREAS:* Business Law; Corporate Law; Partnership Law; Unfair Competition; Food Law; Real Estate Law; Transportation Law; General Practice.

DR. KLAUS PRASSEL, born Frankfurt/Main, Germany, May 29, 1929; admitted, 1961, Frankfurt. *Education:* Textiltechnikum Reutlingen; Universities of Munich and Frankfurt/Main (Dr. Jur., 1961). Tax Consultant, Wiesbaden, 1967. Notary Public, 1971. *Member:* Ausschuss für Steuerrecht bei der Bundesnotarkammer, Koeln; Pruefungsausschuss für Steuerberater, Wiesbaden; Ehrengericht fuer Steuerberater, Frankfurt; Institut für Steuerberater, Frankfurt. *LANGUAGES:* German. *PRACTICE AREAS:* General Practice; Tax Law; Corporate Partnership Law; Real Estate Law; Law of Descent; Trusts; Administration of Estate.

HERBERT HALBIG, born Frankfurt/Main, Germany, October 22, 1934; admitted, Frankfurt/Main. *Education:* University of Frankfurt/Main. Notary Public, 1974. *LANGUAGES:* German. *PRACTICE AREAS:* General Practice; Litigation; German Securities Law; Commercial Law.

ANDREAS RUDOLF STILCKEN, born Frankfurt/Main, Federal Republic of Germany, November 19, 1959; admitted, 1990, Germany. *Education:* University of Frankfurt (2.State Exam, 1989), American Law and Legal Institutions, Salzburg Seminar, 1987; Summer Program, London School of Economics, 1983; Internship, Law Firm Ballard, Spahr, Andrews & Ingersal, Philadelphia, 1988. *Member:* German-American Lawyers Association. *LANGUAGES:* German, English. *PRACTICE AREAS:* Corporate Law; Contract Law; Intellectual Property.

MARKUS HAUPTMANN, born Leverkusen, Federal Republic of Germany, January 11, 1959; admitted, 1991, Germany. *Education:* University of Cologne (1. State Exam, 1985); Summer Program London School of Economics 1983; Legal Internship Program in Cologne and Phoenix, AZ (2. State Exam, 1990). Assistant to Professor Dr. Wiedemann, University of Cologne, 1985-1989 and 1990. *Member:* German-American Lawyers Association. *LANGUAGES:* German, English. *PRACTICE AREAS:* Corporate Law; Contract Law; Banking Law; Law of the New Laender (former GDR).

DR. JOSEF L. SCHULTE, born Scheda, Federal Republic of Germany, December 31, 1953; admitted, 1983 (as Dr. jur.), Germany. *Education:* Westfälische Wilhelms Universität (1. State Exam 1979; 2. State Exam, 1983); Legal Internship in Münster and Hagen, 1981. Assistant to Professor Dr. P. Kirchhof, 1979-1982. Legal Expert of the German Monopolies Commission, 1986-1990. *LANGUAGES:* German, English. *PRACTICE AREAS:* Merger Control; Antitrust; Tax Law.

DR. PETER WENDT, born Duisburg, Germany, December 31, 1937; admitted, 1973, Frankfurt. *Education:* University of Freiburg/Breisgau, Hamburg, Muenster (Dr. jur.) State Examination 1968. Corporate Counsel, 1968-1980; Manager, Central Management Staff, 1984-1988; Member: Equity Finance Division, 1988-1991; Corporate Finance Division, 1991-1993, BHF-Bank. Managing Director, Installment Loan Bank, 1982-1984. Advi-

(This Listing Continued)

sory-Supervisory Board: Visloux Electronic GmbH., Berlin 1989; BNL Beteiligungsgesellschaft Neue Laender, Berlin 1993; Halder Beteiligungsberatung, Frankfurt 1993; Vice Chairman, Shareholder's Committee, Schmutz GmbH, Weil 1992. *LANGUAGES:* German and English. *PRACTICE AREAS:* Corporate and Partnership Law; Mergers and Acquisitions; Banking Law.

ASSOCIATES

HERMANN ARMIN KELLER, born Frankfurt/Main, Germany, March 18, 1961; admitted, 1992, Germany. *Education:* University of Frankfurt/Main (2nd State Exam, 1992). *LANGUAGES:* German and English. *PRACTICE AREAS:* Public Law; Law of the New Laender (former GDR); Bankruptcy; Administrative Law; General Practice.

DR. ANNE-MARIE PETER, born Mannheim, Germany, April 20, 1963; admitted, 1991, Germany. *Education:* University of Munich (1982-1987); Trainee Program in Munich (2. State Exam, 1990). Research Assistant, University of Munich, 1986-1991 (Dr. jur., 1991). Author: "Arbeitsteilung im Krankenhaus aus strafrechtlicher Sicht. Voraussetzungen und Grenzen des Vertrauensgrundsatzes," 1992. *LANGUAGES:* German, French and English. *PRACTICE AREAS:* Business Law; Copyrights; General Practice; Intellectual Property; Medical Malpractice.

DETLEV OSTERLOH, born Saarbruecken, Germany, August 31, 1959; admitted, 1992, Germany. *Education:* Universities of Mainz and Heidelberg (1979-1984); Summer Program, London School of Economics, 1992. Consultant to the State of Hamburg for Environmental, Construction and Public Administration Law (1989-1992). *Member:* German American Lawyer's Association. *LANGUAGES:* German, English, Spanish. *PRACTICE AREAS:* Public Law; Environmental Law; Construction Law; Law of the New Laender.

DR. ANDREAS KNEBEL, born Bruchsal, Germany, October 14, 1961; admitted, 1991, Frankfurt/Main. *Education:* Universities of Heidelberg and Dijon; Summer Program, London School of Economics, 1986; Research Assistant, University of Heidelberg, 1991-1992 (Dr. jur., 1993). Author: "Der Aufwendungsersatzanspruch des Leasinggebers nach der UNIDROIT Leasing Convention.". *LANGUAGES:* German, French and English. *PRACTICE AREAS:* Commercial and Trade Law; Corporate Law; Partnership Law; Litigation.

DR. KARIN L. PILNY, born Munich, Germany, August 16, 1962; admitted, 1990, Germany; 1992, New York; 1993, U.S. District Court, Southern District of New York. *Education:* Universities of Munich (Referendar, 1986; Assessor, 1989; Dr. jur., 1993), Geneva (Certificat d'etudes européennes), Strasbourg (Faculté Internationale de Droit Comparé); London School of Economics, University of Chicago Law School (M.C.L.). Research Fellow, Max-Planck-Institute for Foreign and International Patent, Trademark, Copyright and Competition Law, Munich, 1986-1987. Associate, Rogers & Wells, New York, 1990-1992. Management Consultant Intern, McKinsey & Co., Munich/Frankfurt, 1992. Author: "Präjudizienrecht im anglo-amerikanischen und im deutschen Recht." *Member:* International Fiscal Association; International Bar Association; German American Lawyers Association. *LANGUAGES:* German, English, French, Italian, Spanish. *PRACTICE AREAS:* Domestic and International Tax Law; Corporate Law; Mergers and Acquisitions.

DR. ROGER KIEM, born Langenthal, Switzerland, March 17, 1962; admitted, 1994, Germany. *Education:* University of Marburg (Dr. jur., 1990); London School of Economics (LL.M., 1990). Research Assistant, University of Marburg, 1988-1989. Author, "Die Eintragung der angefochtenen Verschmelzung, 1991. *Member:* German-American Lawyers Association. *LANGUAGES:* German and English. *PRACTICE AREAS:* Corporate Law; Tax Law; Antitrust; Banking Law.

DR. WOLFGANG GOTTWALD, born January 24, 1962; admitted, 1992, Cologne; 1994, Frankfurt/Main. *Education:* University of Erlangen/-Nuremberg and Munich (Referendar 1987; Assessor 1990; Dr. jur. 1992); New York University (M.C.J., 1992). Trainee, German Chamber of Commerce in Japan (Tokyo, 1990). Stagiaire, EC-Comm ission (Brussels, 1990). Research Assistant, Institute of Comparative Law, University of Munich (1990-1991). *LANGUAGES:* German, English, French and Spanish. *PRACTICE AREAS:* Corporate and Employment Law; International Law; General Practice and Litigation.

HERBERT HENSCHEN, born Lienen, Germany, July 2, 1961; admitted, 1994, Germany. *Education:* Universities of Erlangen and Rennes (France). *LANGUAGES:* French and English. *PRACTICE AREAS:* Corporate Law; Antitrust; EEC Law.

(This Listing Continued)

OLIVER HABIGHORST, born Bielefeld, Germany, February 1, 1963; admitted, 1994, Germany. *Education:* University of Bielefeld. *LANGUAGES:* German and English. *PRACTICE AREAS:* Company Law; Groups of Companies; Trade Law; EEC Law.

Languages: German, English, French, Italian and Spanish.

FIEDLER & FORSTER

OPERNPLATZ 2
60313 FRANKFURT/MAIN, GERMANY
Telephone: (0049) (69) 298930
Telefax: (0049) (69) 29893299

Berlin, Germany Office: Oranienburger Strasse 69, D-10117 Berlin. Telephone: (0049) (30) 283 2418. Telefax: (0049) (30) 283 2420.
Cologne, Germany Office: Bonner Strasse 172-176, D-50968 Cologne. Telephone: (0049) (221) 937050-0. Telefax: (0049) (221) 937050-50.
Leipzig, Germany Office: Grimmaische Str. 25, 04109 Leipzig. Telephone: (0049) (341) 2115112. Telefax: (0049) (341) 9602530.
Munich, Germany Office: Brienner Strasse 12/III, D-80333 Munich. Telephone:(0049) (89) 23980. Telefax: (0049) (89) 2398259.
Stuttgart, Germany Office: Gänsheidestr. 68, D-70184. Telephone: (0049) (711) 16445-0. Fax: (0049) (711) 16445-11.
Paris, France Office: Tour Fiat la Dèfense 6, F-92084 Paris. Telephone: 33-1-47 76 28 10. Fax: 33-1-47 96 63 63.

Commercial, Banking, Corporate, Mergers and Acquisitions, International Business Transactions, EC Law, Antitrust and Unfair Competition, Employment and Labor, Taxation and Litigation, Building and Planning Law, Real Property, Computer Law, Intellectual Property, Franchising, Air Law, Telecommunications.

MEMBERS OF FIRM

DR. PETER FORSTER, born Baden-Baden, Germany, July 29, 1937; admitted, 1967, Frankfurt; 1977, Notary. *Education:* University of Frankfurt. Professorial Assistant, Institute for Public Law, University of Frankfurt, 1963-1966. *Member:* Frankfurt Bar Association. *LANGUAGES:* German and English.

HELMUT HEIDE, born Warnsdorf, Germany, May 25, 1940; admitted, 1973, Frankfurt; 1988, Notary. *Education:* Universities of Frankfurt, Saarbrücken, Grenoble (France). Author: "Comment assurer de la bonne fin des créances commerciales en Allemagne Fédérale," 1985; "L'entreprise Francaise en Allemagne," 1985. *Member:* Frankfurt Bar Association; Club des Affaires de la Hesse; Chevalier de l'Ordre National du Mérite. *LANGUAGES:* German, French and English.

MANFRED IHLE, born Schwäbisch Hall, Germany, January 8, 1941; admitted, 1974, Frankfurt; 1990, Notary. *Education:* Universities of Munich, Lausanne, Würzburg, Strasbourg, Bordeaux (Dr. de l'Université de Bordeaux). Author: "La banque et l'entreprise en difficulte," La Revue Banque, 1989; "Les Procedures Collectives en République fédérale d'Allemagne," Revue des Affaires Internationales, 1989. *Member:* Frankfurt Bar Association; Club des Affaires de la Hesse. *LANGUAGES:* German, French and English.

HANS WILHELM PARTMANN, born Bochum, Germany, September 12, 1937; admitted, 1969, Frankfurt; 1979, Notary; 1981, Specialist for Tax Law (Fachanwalt für Steuerrecht). *Education:* Universities of Hamburg and Heidelberg. *Member:* Frankfurt Bar Association; German-American Lawyers' Association; Association of Tax Attorneys. *LANGUAGES:* German and English.

HANS-PETER HANSEN, born Wiesbaden, Germany July 30, 1954; admitted, 1983, Frankfurt; 1986, Specialist for Tax Law (Fachanwalt für Steuerrecht). *Education:* Universities of Frankfurt and Freiburg; King's College, London. *Member:* Frankfurt and International Bar Associations; German-British Lawyers' Association (Deutsch-Britische Juristenvereinigung); International Fiscal Association; Association of Tax Attorneys (Arbeitsgemeinschaft der Fachanwälte für Steuerrecht). *LANGUAGES:* German and English.

ROLF HALBIG, born Frankfurt, Germany, January 9, 1956; admitted, 1984, Frankfurt. *Education:* University of Frankfurt. Author: "L'injonction de Payer," Moniteur du Commerce International, 1987. *Member:* Frankfurt Bar Association; Wissenschaftliche Gesellschaft für Lebensmittelrecht (Society for Food Law); GRUR (German Association for Intellectual Property and Copyright); Bund für Lebensmittelrecht und Lebensmittelkunde. *LANGUAGES:* German and English.

(This Listing Continued)

BERND CHRISTIAN HAAGER, born Nürnberg, Germany, December 10, 1950; admitted, 1980, Germany, Attorney at Law and Special Tax Counsel; 1988, Frankfurt Court of Appeal. *Education:* Universities of Frankfurt, Munich, Mainz. Assistant Professor, Civil Law, University of Mainz, 1975-1976. Author: "Neuregelung durch das Markengesetz, Deutscher Sparkassenverlag," 1994. Former General Counsel of F & F Burda Holding, 1988-1990. *Member:* GRUR (German Association for Intellectual Property and Copyright); Studienvereinigung Kartellrecht (Association for Antitrust Law); Bankrechtliche Vereinigung (Association for Banking Law). *LANGUAGES:* German, English and Swedish.

WALTRAUD LANGENBRUCH, born Gießen, Germany, March 17, 1957; admitted, 1989, Frankfurt. *Education:* University of Gießen. *LANGUAGES:* German and English.

WERNER GAUS, born Stuttgart, Germany, January 26, 1955; admitted, 1988, New York; 1989, Frankfurt. *Education:* Universities of Augsburg, Lausanne, Freiburg i. Br., Tulane University, New Orleans (LL.M. with distinction, 1986). Co-Author: "Haftung des ausländischen Investors für Umweltschäden unter dem Superfund Gesetz bei Geschäften in den USA," RIW 846, 1988. Author: "Réglement des opérations des initiés au niveau de la Communauté Européenne," droit et pratique du commerce international, 1989; "Le réglement allemand en matière de réduction des emballages ("Verpackungsverordnung"), contact hors serie No. 1, 1992. Foreign Trainee and Associate with: Alexander & Green, 1986; Walter, Conston, Alexander & Green, P.C., New York, New York, 1987-1988. Lecturer in International Commercial Law at the "Akademie für Welthandel," Frankfurt, 1991—. *Member:* American Bar Association; German-American Lawyers' Association. *LANGUAGES:* German, French and English.

CHRISTIANE LEFFERS, born Lindau/Bodensee, Germany, April 24, 1958; admitted, 1987, Frankfurt. *Education:* Universities of Frankfurt and Paris (France). Co-Author: "Employee Share Schemes in United Kingdom, France and Germany," European Taxation 322, 1993. *LANGUAGES:* German, English and French.

ASSOCIATES

MATTHIAS VOLKMANN, born Gießen, Germany, January 11, 1963; admitted, 1991, Frankfurt. *Education:* University of Gießen. *Member:* Association of Tax Attorneys. *LANGUAGES:* German and English.

DR. STEPHAN K. RIPPERT, born Hamburg, Germany, September 16, 1962; admitted, 1990, Frankfurt. *Education:* Universities of Mainz (Dr. jur., 1993), Munich and Mc George School of Law, University of the Pacific, California (LL.M., 1992). Author: "The American pre-trial discovery procedure," RIW 626, 1993. *Member:* Frankfurt Bar Association; German Bar Association; American Chamber of Commerce in Germany. *LANGUAGES:* German, English and French.

AXEL BRAUN, born Sieglar, Germany, April 25, 1959; admitted, 1991, Cologne; Labor Law Specialist (Fachanwalt für Arbeitsrecht). *Education:* Universities of Cologne and Geneva. *Member:* German Bar Association; Arbeitsgemeinschaft der Fachanwälte für Arbeitsrecht. *LANGUAGES:* German, English, French and Spanish.

HEINZ BENESCH, born Münster, Germany, December 8, 1962; admitted, 1993, Frankfurt. *Education:* Universities of Münster, Geneva and Strasbourg. *Member:* Frankfurt Bar Association. *LANGUAGES:* German, French, English and Spanish.

DR. CORINNA RALLE, born Delmenhorst, Germany, June 17, 1964; admitted, 1994, Frankfurt. *Education:* Universities of Kiel and Heidelberg (Dr.jur., 1994). Assistant Professor, Comparative Law, Civil Law, University Panthéon-Assas of Paris, France, 1990-1991. *Member:* Frankfurt Bar Association; Club des Affaires de la Hesse; German-French Lawyers' Association. *LANGUAGES:* German, French, English and Italian.

SUSANNE BOLLER, born Frankfurt/Main, Germany, November 24, 1962; admitted, 1991, Frankfurt. *Education:* University of Frankfurt. *Member:* Frankfurt Bar Association. *LANGUAGES:* German and English.

Languages: German, English and French

FRESHFIELDS

MESSETURM
FRIEDRICH-EBERT-ANLAGE 49
60327 FRANKFURT/MAIN, GERMANY
Telephone: (49 69) 975 70101
Fax: (49 69) 748917/748918

Other Offices in: Bangkok, Barcelona, Brussels, Hanoi, Hong Kong, London, Madrid, Moscow, New York, Paris, Singapore and Tokyo.

General and International Law Practice. Firm engaged in German, English and General International Practice.

PARTNERS

NIKOLAS D. TARLING, born England, 1941; admitted, 1966, England. *Education:* Jesus College, Oxford. *Member:* Law Society; International Bar Association. *LANGUAGES:* French, German, Italian and English.

DR. PETER OPITZ, Born Berlin, Germany, July 7, 1940; admitted, 1975. *Education:* Free University Berlin (Referendar, 1963; Dr.Jur., 1968); Université de Sciences Comparées Luxembourg 1964. Assistant (Chair of Commercial and Civil Law) Free University Berlin, 1964-1969, Second State Examination 1969. General Counsel, Managing Partner, BHF-Bank, 1969-1990. *Member:* German-American Lawyers Association (Member); International Bar Association. *LANGUAGES:* German, English and French.

MARK TRAPNELL, born England, 1956; admitted, 1982, England as Solicitor; 1985, Hong Kong. *Education:* Christ Church, Oxford. *LANGUAGES:* English.

DR. CHRISTOPH VON BÜLOW, born Hanover, Germany, March 16, 1957; admitted, 1986. *Education:* Universities of Freiburg/Brsg., Hamburg and Göttingen (Dr. jur., 1983). *Member:* EC Lawyers Society (London). *LANGUAGES:* German and English.

ASSOCIATES

LUCILLE A. BARALE, born Chicago, Illinois, March 31, 1950; admitted, 1980, District of Columbia (Not admitted in Germany). *Education:* Georgetown University (B.S., 1972); University of Hawaii (M.A., 1974); George Washington University (J.D.,1980). Author: "China's Investment Implementing Regulations," China Business Review, March-April 1988; "China Before Tiananmen: Economic Background to a Political Disaster," East Asian Executive Reports, October, 1989; "Wholly Foreign - Owned Enterprises in the PRC," China Business Review, January-February 1990; "U.S. MFN Renewal For China: The Jackson-Vanik Amendment," East Asian Executive Reports, June, 1990; Editor, Joint Ventures in Eastern Europe, (Author) Chapters on Poland and Yugoslavia, Euromoney Books, 1990; "Filling in the Details on Wholly Foreign-Owned Enterprises in the PRC," China Business Review, May-June, 1991. *Member:* The District of Columbia Bar; American (Member, Section on International Law and Practice, Steering Committee Eastern Europe) and International Bar Associations. *LANGUAGES:* English, Chinese, French and Russian.

DR. JOACHIM KAFFANKE, born Bückeburg, Germany, August 6, 1960; admitted, 1992. *Education:* Universities of Tübingen, UC Berkeley, CA and Mainz (Dr. jur., 1988). *Member:* German-American Lawyers Association. *LANGUAGES:* German and English.

THOMAS SCHRELL, born Hameln, Germany, March 22, 1963; admitted, 1993. *Education:* Universities of Hamburg and London (LL.M., 1990). *LANGUAGES:* German, English and French.

JAMES HEALY, born Dublin, Ireland, June 16, 1962; admitted, 1987, Solicitor, Ireland; 1990, England and Wales (Not admitted in Germany). *Education:* University College, Dublin (B.C.L., 1982); European University Institute, Florence (LL.M., 1987). Tutor and Part-time Lecturer in Law, University College, Dublin, 1983-1988. *Member:* The British Italian Law Association; The Irish Solicitors in London Bar Association. *LANGUAGES:* Irish, Italian, French, German and English.

CHRISTOF GAUDIG, born Cologne, Germany, January 24, 1964; admitted, 1994. *Education:* Universities of Cologne and Freiburg/Brsg. *Member:* German-Portuguese Lawyers Association. *LANGUAGES:* German, English and Portuguese.

ANDREAS BARTSCH, born Bogota, Colombia, January 10, 1959; admitted, 1989; Qualified as Steuerberater (Tax Counsel), 1991; Wirtschaftspüfer (Accountant), 1993. *Education:* University of Hamburg (1978-1984); Second State Examination (1987). Gellart Wirtschaftsprüfung GmbH,

(This Listing Continued)

1987-1989. KpmG-Peat Marwick Treuhand GmbH, Frankfurt, 1989-1991. *LANGUAGES:* German and English.

GEORG PHILIPP COTTA, born Berlin, Germany, March 16, 1964; admitted, 1994. *Education:* University of Munich (1990); University of Leyden (1992); London School of Economics (1994). *LANGUAGES:* German, English, Spanish and French.

DR. ALEXANDER MENTZ, born Wiesbaden, Germany, June 20, 1944. *Education:* Universities of Frankfurt am Main, Freiburg/Brsg. and Tübingen (Dr.jur., 1972). Inhouse Counsel, Head of Primary Production Division, Member of Management Board, DEGUSSA AG, 1973-1994. *LANGUAGES:* German, English, French and Spanish.

ALEXANDER W. FAUST, born Kaufbeuren, Germany, October 18, 1961; admitted, 1991, Germany; 1993, New York. *Education:* Ludwig-Maximilian University, Munich (Referendar, 1987; Second State Examination, Munich, 1990; New York University (LL.M., 1992). HYPO-Bank, Legal Department, 1990-1991; Intern/Attorney-at-Law, New York, 1992 -1994. *Member:* Deutsch-Amerikanische Juristenvereinigung; American Bar Association. *LANGUAGES:* German, English, French and Italian.

TORSTEN STEINHAUS, born Bad Oldesloe, Germany, January 22, 1963; admitted, 1994; qualified as Steuerberater (Tax Counsel), 1993. *Education:* University Erlangen (1981); University of Munich (1986; Second Law State Examination, 1990). KPMG Peat Marwick, 1991-1994. *LANGUAGES:* English and German.

(For List of Partners see Professional Biographies at London, England)

FRITZE, WEIGEL, BORNEMANN, ARNOLD & KELM

ESCHERSHEIMER LANDSTRAβE 25-27
60322 FRANKFURT/MAIN, GERMANY
Telephone: 069/959 57 0
Telefax: 069/959 57 166

Mailing Address: Postfach 10 18 23, 60018 Frankfurt, Germany

Erfurt, Germany Office: Rechtsanwalt Jörg Walendy Schlachthofstr. 45, 99085. Telephone: 0361-6430754. Fax: 0361-6430754.

EEC Cooperation with: SCP Charrière-Bournazel, Champetier de Ribes, Spitzer, Attorneys at Law, Paris; Giuseppe Minieri, Attorneys at Law, Milan; Angel Lacambra, Attorneys at Law, Barcelona; Jean-Pierre Vander Borght, Attorneys at Law, Brussels.
Administrative, Advertising, Antitrust, Arbitration, Banking, Commercial, Computer, Construction, Copyrights and Publishing, Corporations, EEC-Law, Environmental, Employees' Inventions, Family Law, General Practice, Industrial and Intellectual Property, International Business Transactions, Insurance, Insolvency, Labour Law, Litigation, Mergers and Acquisitions, Nuclear Energy Law, Product Liability, Real Estate, Tax Law, Television and Broadcasting, Unfair Competition.

MEMBERS OF FIRM

DR. ULRICH FRITZE, born Kyritz, Germany, March 2, 1926; admitted, 1957, Frankfurt am Main. *Education:* University of Frankfurt a.M. (Doctor of Jurisprudence). Notary, 1965. Member of the Board of the German Association for the Protection of Industrial Property and Copyright Law (GRUR) and of the Executive Committee of the International Association for the Protection of Industrial Property (IAPIP-AIPPI). *Member:* IBA; International Chamber of Commerce (ICC). *LANGUAGES:* German, English and French. *PRACTICE AREAS:* Copyrights and Publishing; Corporations, Television and Broadcasting; Industrial and Intellectual Property; Insurance; Litigation; Unfair Competition.

THEODOR WEIGEL, born Giessen, Germany, October 28, 1930; admitted, 1960 Frankfurt. *Education:* Universities of Marburg, Berlin (FU), Frankfurt am Main. Notary, 1969. Vice President, Rechtsanwaltskammer Frankfurt am Main. *Member:* IBA; International Chamber of Commerce (ICC); Bankrechtliche Vereinigung. *LANGUAGES:* German and English. *PRACTICE AREAS:* Arbitration; Banking; Construction; Litigation.

KLAUS BORNEMANN, born Frankfurt am Main, Germany, March 11, 1933; admitted, 1964, Frankfurt a.M. *Education:* Universities of Tübingen, Berlin and Frankfurt am Main. Notary, 1974. Fachanwalt für Verwaltungsrecht. *Member:* Gesellschaft für Umweltrecht. *LANGUAGES:* German and English. *PRACTICE AREAS:* Administrative; Environmental; Nuclear Energy Law; Real Estate.

(This Listing Continued)

KARL-HEINZ ARNOLD, born Frankfurt am Main, Germany, November 20, 1937; admitted, 1967, West Germany. *Education:* University of Frankfurt am Main. Notary, 1979. *LANGUAGES:* German, English and Italian. *PRACTICE AREAS:* Construction; Computer; Real Estate.

BRIGITTE KELM, born Frankfurt am Main, Germany, August 1, 1939; admitted, 1972, West Germany. *Education:* Universities of Frankfurt, Freiburg, State University of New York at Buffalo (Ph.D. and M.A.). *LANGUAGES:* German, English and French. *PRACTICE AREAS:* Construction; Family Law.

WOLFGANG MAUTZ, born Kronberg, Germany, May 6, 1949; admitted, 1976, Frankfurt. *Education:* University of Frankfurt am Main. Notary, 1991. Fachanwalt für Arbeitsrecht. *Member:* Frankfurt Bar Association; Deutsche Vereinigung für Gewerblichen Rechtsschutz und Urheberrecht (GRUR). *PRACTICE AREAS:* Advertising, Copyrights and Publishing; Industrial and Intellectual Property; Labour Law; Litigation; Unfair Competition.

DR. REINHARD PATZINA, born Groß-Gerau, Germany, November 9, 1948; admitted, 1980, Frankfurt am Main. *Education:* Universities of Frankfurt am Main, McGill, Montreal, Canada, Georgetown, Washington, D.C. Scientific Staff Member, Institute for Foreign and International Trade Law, Frankfurt am Main. Scientific Staff Member, Institute for Foreign and International Trade Law, Georgetown University, Washington, D.C. Teaching Assistant to Prof. Dr. Günther Jaenicke, Frankfurt am Main, Dr. jur., 1980. Author: "Rohstofferschließungsvorhaben in Entwicklungsländern (Mining ventures in developing countries), Co-author part I, Frankfurt am Main, 1977; Mining ventures in developing countries I: Interests, bargaining process, legal concepts (co-author), Deventer and Frankfurt am Main, 1979; Rechtlicher Schutz ausländischer Privatinvestoren gegen Enteignungsrisiken in Entwicklungsländern (Legal protection of foreign private investment against expropriation in developing countries, Heidelberg, Hamburg, 1981; Mitautor des Münchner Kommentars zur Zivilprozeßordnung, Internationale Zuständigkeit und §§ 12 bis 40 Zivilprozeßordnung (Co-author of the Munich commentary on German rules of civil procedure, international jurisdiction and §§ 12 - 40). Fachanwalt für Steuerrecht (tax lawyer). *Member:* Frankfurt and International Bar Association; Prüfungssausschuß für Wirtschaftsprüfer und vereidigte Buchprüfer (Committee of examiners for accountants and auditors). *LANGUAGES:* German and English. *PRACTICE AREAS:* Banking; EEC Law; Mergers and Acquisitions; Tax Law; Corporation; Conflicts of Law; International Law.

RICHARD CREMER, born Langen, Germany, January 26, 1950; admitted, 1978, West Germany. *Education:* Universities of Mainz and Frankfurt. *Member:* Frankfurt Bar Association; German Association for the Protection of Industrial Property and Copyright Law (GRUR); International Association for the Protection of Industrial Property (IAPIP). *LANGUAGES:* German and English. *PRACTICE AREAS:* Industrial and Intellectual Property; Unfair Competition.

DR. FRIEDRICH W. KLINKERT, born Frankfurt, Germany, November 8, 1951; admitted, 1980, Frankfurt am Main. *Education:* University of Frankfurt (Doctor of Jurisprudence). Author: Code of Ethics and Antitrust Law-Germany and France, Diss. Frankfurt, 1984. *Member:* Frankfurt Bar Association; Association for Studies of Antitrust Law; German Association for the Protection of Industrial Property and Copyright Law (GRUR); International Association for the Protection of Industrial Property (IAPIP); German-Chinese Association of Lawyers; Vice-President Union des Avocats Européen. *LANGUAGES:* German, English and French. *PRACTICE AREAS:* Antitrust, Copyrights and Publishing; Industrial and Intellectual Property; Television and Broadcasting; Unfair Competition; Product Liability.

DR. ERNST FISCHER, born Oberdorla/Thüringen, Germany, February 20, 1921; admitted, 1957, Frankfurt am Main. *Education:* University Kiel (Law); University Frankfurt (Chemistry). Metallgesellschaft, Patent Department, 1954-1986. Member of the board and Honorary Chairman of Patent Committee of Deutsche Vereinigung für Gewerblichen Rechtsschutz und Urheberrecht. *LANGUAGES:* German and English. *PRACTICE AREAS:* Employee' Inventions; Industrial Property; Patent Law.

DR. KLAUS SCHNEIDER, born Flörshein/Main, Germany, April 28, 1957; admitted, 1986, Germany. *Education:* University of Frankfurt am Main (Doctor of Jurisprudence, 1986). *Member:* Frankfurt Bar Association. *LANGUAGES:* German and English. *PRACTICE AREAS:* Administrative; Construction; Environmental; Insurance.

ANDREAS BOCK, born Frankfurt am Main, Germany, October 27, 1957; admitted, 1990, Germany. *Education:* University of Frankfurt. *Member:* Frankfurt Bar Association; German Association for the Protection of

(This Listing Continued)

Industrial Property and Copyright (GRUR). *LANGUAGES:* German, English and Italian. *PRACTICE AREAS:* Advertising, Copyrights and Publishing; Industrial and Intellectual Property; Television and Broadcasting; Unfair Competition.

DR. UWE VOLKMANN, born Lunen/Westf., Germany, December 31, 1960; admitted, 1990, Germany. *Education:* University of Marburg (Doctor of Jurisprudence, 1993). *Member:* Frankfurt Bar Association. *LANGUAGES:* German and English. *PRACTICE AREAS:* Administrative; Computer; Environmental.

VOLKER SERTH, born Frankfurt am Main, Germany, October 16, 1962; admitted, 1991, Germany. *Education:* University of Frankfurt. *Member:* Frankfurt Bar Association. *LANGUAGES:* German and English. *PRACTICE AREAS:* Labour Law.

DIETMAR AIGNER, born Gelsenkirchen, Germany, April 10, 1959; admitted, 1992, Germany. *Education:* University of Marburg. *Member:* Frankfurt Bar Association; German and Copyright law (GRUR); International Association for the Protection of Industrial Property (IAPIP). *LANGUAGES:* German and English. *PRACTICE AREAS:* Copyrights and Publishing; Industrial and Intellectual Property; Unfair Competition.

THORSTEN LOTZ, born Bad Hersfeld, Germany, July 15, 1962; admitted, 1992, Germany. *Education:* Universities of Bayreuth and Frankfurt. Fachanwalt für Steuerrecht. *Member:* Frankfurt Bar Association. *LANGUAGES:* German and English. *PRACTICE AREAS:* Banking, Copyrights and Publishing; EEC Law; International Business Transactions; Tax Law.

DR. STEFAN REINHART, born Frankfurt am Main, Germany, December 26, 1962; admitted, 1992, Germany. *Education:* University of Frankfurt; University of Exeter, England (Doctor of Jurisprudence, 1994). Author: "Cross-border Problems of Company Rescues." *Member:* Frankfurt Bar Association; German-British Jurists Association. *LANGUAGES:* German and English. *PRACTICE AREAS:* Corporations; International Business Transactions; Insolvency; International Insolvencies.

JÖRG WALENDY, born Steglitz, Germany, November 23, 1947; admitted, 1977, Germany. *Education:* Universities of Mainz and Heidelberg. *Member:* Erfurt Bar Association. *LANGUAGES:* German, English and French. *PRACTICE AREAS:* Construction; General Practice; Litigation; Real Estate.

GAEDERTZ VIEREGGE QUACK KREILE

Rechtsanwälte

AIRPORT-CENTER, HUGO-ECKENER-RING
D-60549 FRANKFURT/MAIN, GERMANY
Telephone: (69) 69 48 52
Telex: 40 32 145 zibr d.
Telefax: (69) 69 48 60

Berlin, Germany Office: Kurfürstendamm 157, D-10709 Berlin. Telephone: (30) 890 05-0. Telefax: (30) 892 26 06. Teletex: 30 88 15 qkp d. Telex: 17 30 88 15 qkp d.
Cologne, Germany Office: Theodor-Heuss-Ring 19-21, D-50668 Cologne. Telephone: (221) 77 16-0. Telefax: (221) 77 16-110. Teletex: 221 43 76 olga d. Telex: 88 85 143 olga d.
Leipzig, Germany Office: August-Bebel-Str. 38, D-04275 Leipzig. Telephone: (341) 477 83 81/83. Telefax: (341) 477 83 88.
Munich, Germany Office: Widenmayerstrasse 32, D-80538 Munich. Telephone: (89) 212147-0. Telefax: (89) 228 55 62.
Wiesbaden, Germany Office: Kaiser-Friedrich-Ring 65, D-65185 Wiesbaden. Telephone: (611) 88 05-0. Telefax: (611) 81 03 09. Telex: 41 86 295 gaed d.
Brussels, Belgium Office: Avenue de Tervuren 35, B-1040 Brussels. Telephone: (2) 736 07 97. Telefax: (2) 732 69 12.
Prague, Czech Republic Office: Betlémska 1, CR-11000 Prague 1. Telephone: (2) 24 22 94 98. Telefax: (2) 232 12 29.

General Practice. Commercial, Corporate, Banking, Real Property, German and EEC Antitrust Law, Unfair Competition, Distribution and Franchise, Food and Drug Law, Industrial Property Rights, Intellectual, Trademarks, Designs, Investment East Germany and Eastern Europe, EC Law, Copyright, Notaries (Berlin, Frankfurt/Main and Wiesbaden).

FIRM PROFILE: The law firm Gaedertz Vieregge Quack Kreile is the result of a merger between 4 partnerships: Heydt Vieregge & Partner, Cologne; Gaedertz Henn & Partner, Wiesbaden; Quack Kühn & Partner, Berlin; Prof. Kreile & Partner, Munich.

(This Listing Continued)

GAEDERTZ VIEREGGE QUACK KREILE,
Frankfurt/Main—Continued

Gaedertz Vieregge Quack Kreile is one of the major German based law firms representing domestic and foreign clients in all fields of law that are relevant for national and international enterprises. An important part of the practice are the legal aspects of transnational transactions especially in EC. The firm advises not only German clients in international matters but also foreign enterprises about all implications of doing business in Germany. Thus many attorneys and also members of the support staff are fluent in English. Other languages such as French, Spanish, Portuguese, Italian, Russian, and Dutch are also spoken.

In addition, the offices in Cologne and Wiesbaden have the specialized capacity to administer large trademark portfolios worldwide including registration and litigation of trademarks and registered designs.

Clients of the firm include many well-known German and foreign companies active in a wide variety of businesses. Gaedertz Vieregge Quack Kreile also represents various trade associations as well as German federal, state and local governmental authorities.

In the Berlin, Wiesbaden and Frankfurt/Main offices, there are 10 attorneys qualified to act as "Notar," specially licensed to prepare and execute documents relating to incorporation of companies, real estate matters and other important commercial transactions where a special form of document is prescribed.

Gaedertz Vieregge Quack Kreile has more than 70 attorneys, including 42 partners, plus a support staff of approximately 150 people, working in the eight different offices.

The offices have for the most part city centre locations. The Frankfurt office is situated at the Airport-Centre of the Rhein-Main Airport.

MEMBERS OF FIRM

JOHANNES ZINDEL, born Ruedesheim, Germany, 1950; admitted, 1976, Frankfurt/Main. *Education:* University of Mainz. Assistant Lecturer, University of Mainz, 1973-1977. *Member:* German Bar Association; Association for the Study of Cartel Law; Association for the Protection of Industrial Property Rights; Scientific Association for the Study of Food Law; Association Internationale des Jeunes Avocats. *LANGUAGES:* English. *PRACTICE AREAS:* Corporate Law; German and EEC Antitrust Law; Investment in East Germany; Copyright.

ULRICH BRÜCKMANN, born Giessen, Germany, 1951; admitted, 1979, Frankfurt/Main. *Education:* University of Giessen; University of Paris I (1973-1974). With Woodham Smith, Solicitors, London, 1976-1977. Lecturer, Academy for Marketing and Communication, Frankfurt, 1986-1989. *Member:* German Bar Association; International Bar Association; European Food Law Association; Scientific Association for the Study of Food Law; German-British Jurist's Association; German Association for Industrial Property Rights and Copyright. *LANGUAGES:* English, French. *PRACTICE AREAS:* Commercial; Unfair Competition; Distribution and Franchise; Trademarks; Food and Drug Law; EEC Law.

WOLFGANG LEIP, born Bonn-Bad Godesberg, Germany, 1951; admitted, 1982, Frankfurt/Main. *Education:* American High School, Rio de Janeiro, Brazil; Universities of Heidelberg and Berlin; University of Arts, Berlin; University of the Pacific, Sacramento, California (LL.M., 1984). Author: "Zur Beurteilung langfrister Liefervertraege zwischen Wettbewerbern nach deutschem Kartellrecht," (Long-term Dealing Agreements between Competitors under German Antitrust Law), WUW, 1986. Co-Author: "Securing Purchase Price and Bank Financing in Transnational Trade under German Law," in "Survey of the International Sale of Goods," Deventer, 1986. *Member:* German Bar Association; AIJA; German Association for Industrial Property Rights and Copyright; Association for Antitrust Law; German-Brazilian Chamber of Commerce, Rio de Janeiro, Brazil. *LANGUAGES:* English, Portuguese, Spanish. *PRACTICE AREAS:* Commercial Law; Banking; German and EEC Antitrust Law; Unfair Competition; Industrial Property.

DETLEF KUNATH, born Frankfurt, Germany, 1953; admitted, 1982, Wiesbaden. *Education:* University of Nurnberg. *Member:* German Lawyers Association; German Association for Industrial Property Rights and Copyright. *LANGUAGES:* English. *PRACTICE AREAS:* Commercial; Unfair Competition; Distribution; Franchising; Trademarks; Copyright.

BARBARA OPITZ-DACH, born Lauenburg/Elbe, Germany, 1953; admitted, 1982, Bremen; 1986, Frankfurt/Main, Notary Public. *Education:* University of Saarbrücken, Frankfurt/Main, Berlin. *Member:* German Bar Association; German Association for Industrial Property Rights and Copy-

(This Listing Continued)

right; AIPPI; Association for the Study of Cartel Law. *LANGUAGES:* English, French. *PRACTICE AREAS:* Antitrust Law; Unfair Competition Law; Intellectual Property Law; Business Law.

ASSOCIATES

GEORG ALBRECHTSKIRCHINGER, born Munich, 1930; admitted, 1959, Munich, subsequently Frankfurt/Main. *Education:* Harvard University, University of Munich. Co-Editor of European Journal of Business Law. Until 1991, Member of the Executive Board, General Council and European Coordinator of the Chemical Industry Association. *Member:* Board of the German Association for Industrial Property Rights and Copyright; German Group of the Association Internationale pour la Protection de la Propriété Intellectuelle; Licensing Executives Society. *LANGUAGES:* English, French. *PRACTICE AREAS:* EEC Law; Food and Drug Law; Commercial Law.

PETER BARTH, born Wiesbaden, Germany, 1962; admitted, 1992, Frankfurt/Main. *Education:* University of Mainz. *Member:* German Bar Association; German Association for Industrial Property Rights and Copyright. *LANGUAGES:* English.

DR. ROGER MANN, born Hagen/Westfalen, Germany, 1964; admitted, 1993, Frankfurt/Main. *Education:* Universities of Bochum, London and Hagen (Dr.jur.). *Member:* German Bar Association; German Association for Industrial Property Rights and Copyright; Canadian-German Lawyers Association; Canadian-German Chamber of Commerce; International Association of Young Lawyers (AIJA). *LANGUAGES:* English.

KLAUS NIEDING, born Rheinbach/Bonn, 1964; admitted, 1993, Stuttgart. *Education:* University of Bochum. *Member:* German Lawyers Association; German Bar Association; Association for Banking Law; German-American Lawyers Association; German Association for Industrial Property Rights and Copyright. *LANGUAGES:* English.

Languages: German, English, French, Portuguese and Spanish.

(For complete biographical data on personnel at Berlin, Cologne, Leipzig, Munich and Wiesbaden, Germany Offices as well as Brussels, Belgium and Prague, Czech, Republic Offices, see Professional Biographies at those locations).

GLEISS LUTZ HOOTZ HIRSCH & PARTNERS

Established in 1949

ESCHERSHEIMER LANDSTR. 19-21
D-60322 FRANKFURT/MAIN, GERMANY
Telephone: (49) (69) 955 14-0
Telefax: (49) (69) 955 14-198; 955 14-199
Telex: 414 292glhcc d

Stuttgart (Head Office), Germany Office: Maybachstrasse 6, D-70469 Stuttgart. Telephone: (49) (711) 89 97-0. Telefax: (49) (711) 85 50 96. Telex: 722 439 jura d.

Berlin, Germany Office: Clara-Zetkin-Strasse 16, D-10117 Berlin. Telephone: (49) (30) 20 17 14-0. Telefax: (49) (30) 207 12 06.

Brussels, Belgium Office: Avenue Louise 475, Bte. 13, B-1050 Brussels. Telephone: (32) (2) 647 63 74. Telefax: (32) (2) 640 92 31. Telex: 65348 jura b.

Prague, Czech Republic Office: Jugoslávská 29, CR-120 00 Prague 2. Telephone: (42) (2) 24007-510. Telefax: (42) (2) 24007-555.

German, EC and International Practice, in particular Administrative, Anti-Dumping, Anti-Trust, Arbitration, Banking, Capital Markets, Competition, Commercial, Copyright, Corporate/Company, Corporate Finance, Environmental, Finance, Foreign Investment, Industrial Property Rights, Insurance, Labour, Litigation, Media, Mergers and Acquisitions, Real Property, Regulated Industries, Securities, Tax, Telecommunications, Trade, Trademark, Unfair Competition, Zoning.

FIRM PROFILE: The firm was established in 1949 in Stuttgart and developed from a German and later EC competition and anti-trust law boutique to a corporate practice with a full range of corporate legal services. The firm opened its Brussels office in 1987, its Berlin and Frankfurt offices in 1990, and its Prague office in 1992. It employs in total 85 lawyers and expects to grow in Central Europe in particular.

(This Listing Continued)

PARTNERS

DR. MARTIN HIRSCH, born Stuttgart, 1933; admitted, 1960, Germany. *Education:* University of Heidelberg (State Exams, 1956, 1960; Dr. jur., 1959). Co-author: "EWG-Kartellrecht" (EC Antitrust Law), Vol. 1, 4th ed., 1993. *LANGUAGES:* German and English. *PRACTICE AREAS:* Commercial; Corporations; German and EC Antitrust; German and EC Merger Control; Mergers and Acquisitions.

DR. HANS SCHLARMANN, born Ankum, 1950; admitted, 1978, Germany. *Education:* Universities of Munich, Bochum, Freiburg, Geneva/Switzerland and Münster (State Exams, 1975, 1977; Dr. jur., 1980). Co-author: "Kommunale Umweltverträglichkeitsprüfung" (Municipal Environmental Impact Assessment), 1988. Author: "Regionale Differenzierung von Instrumenten im Abwassersektor" (Regional Regulatory Differences in Sewage Disposal), 1985. Co-author: "Rechtskontrolle von Planungen in der Bundesrepublik Deutschland" (Judicial Control of Planning in Germany), 1982. Author: "Zur Durchsetzung von Umweltbelangen im Bereich der Räumlichen Planung" (Enforcing Environmental Protection in Regional Planning), 1982; "Rechtsschutz gegen die Planung von Strassen und anderen Verkehrsanlagen" (Judicial Control in Planning Roads and other Transportation Facilities), 1981; "Das Verhältnis der Privilegierten Fachplanung zur Kommunalen Bauleitplanung" (Relationship Between Privileged Specialized Planning and the Municipal Planning Authority), 1980. Co-editor, "Umwelt Kommunal" (Environment and the Municipality). Research Fellow, Central Institute for Regional Planning at the University of Münster, 1977-1981. Lecturer on Law, Fachhochschule Münster, 1978-1982, and University of Bayreuth, 1992—. *Member:* Permanent Commission on Law and Technology, Union Internationale d'Avocats, 1984—; German Bar Association; German Lawyers' Association; German Society of Environmental Law; Institute of Zoning Law (Freiburg); German Society for Building Law. (Certified Administrative Law Attorney). *LANGUAGES:* German, English and French. *PRACTICE AREAS:* Constitutional; Environmental; Media and Telecommunications; Real Property; Zoning.

DR. UWE EYLES, born Frankfurt/Main, 1961; admitted, 1990, Germany. *Education:* University of Konstanz (State Exams 1985, 1988; Dr. jur., 1990). Author: "Das Niederlassungsrecht der Kapitalgesellschaften in der Europäischen Gemeinschaft - Die Überlagerung des deutschen Gesellschaftsrechts und Unternehmenssteuerrechts durch Europäisches Gemeinschaftsrecht" (Freedom of Establishment for Corporate Entities in the European Economic Community - The Impact of EEC-Law on German Company and Tax Law), 1990. Lecturer on Law, University of Konstanz, 1988-1990. Banking Trainee, Deutsche Bank AG, Frankfurt/Main, 1980-1982. *Member:* German and American Bar Associations. *LANGUAGES:* German, English and French. *PRACTICE AREAS:* Arbitration and Litigation; Banking; Financial Services; Real Estate Law; Securities.

DR. BERNHARD BUSCH, born Olsberg, 1960; admitted, 1992, Germany. *Education:* University of Munster (State Exams, 1986, 1992; Dr.jur., 1991). Author: "Das Verhältnis des Artikel 80 Absatz 1 Satz 2 Grundgesetz zum Gesetzes - und Parlamentsvorbehalt" (The Interrelationship between Article 80 Paragraph 1 Sentence 2 of the German Constitution and the Principle of Formal Legality and Democracy), 1992. *Member:* German Bar Association. *LANGUAGES:* German and English. *PRACTICE AREAS:* Building and Planning; Constitutional; Environmental; Media and Telecommunications; Real Property.

DR. MICHAEL MARQUARDT, born Mannheim, 1958; admitted, 1988, Germany. *Education:* Universities of Heidelberg and Geneva/Switzerland (State Exams, 1983, 1988; Dr. jur., 1987). Author: "Das Streitbeilegungssystem im Rahmen des Tiefseebodenregimes" (Dispute Settlement under the Deep Seabed Regime), 1988. Research Assistant and Lecturer on Law, Max-Planck Institute of Foreign and International Public Law in Heidelberg, 1986-1988. Senior Managing Consultant of the KPMG, Leipzig branch, 1992. *Member:* Heidelberg Association of Foreign and International Public Law; German-Japanese Lawyers' Association. (Certified Tax Advisor). *LANGUAGES:* German, English and French. *PRACTICE AREAS:* Corporations; Mergers and Acquisitions; Real Estate; Restructuring; Tax Law; Tax Planning.

ANGELIKA KRUG, born Kassel, 1960; admitted, 1990, Germany. *Education:* Universities of Würzburg and Munich (State Exams, 1983, 1987). *Member:* German Bar Association. *LANGUAGES:* German, English and French. *PRACTICE AREAS:* Building and Planning; Commercial Leases; Construction; Project Development and Finance; Real Estate.

(This Listing Continued)

COUNSEL

PROF. DR. THEODOR HEINSIUS, born Hamburg-Altona, 1926; admitted, 1957, Germany. *Education:* University of Hamburg (State Exams, 1952, 1956; Dr. jur., 1955). Co-Author: "Depotgesetz" (Securities Deposit Act), 1975; "Aktienrecht und Mitbestimmung" (Corporation Law and Codetermination), 1989. General Counsel, Dresdner Bank AG, 1974-1991. Professor of Law, University of Frankfurt, 1980—. *Member:* Supervisory Board of Pott-Racke-Dujardin GmbH & Co. KG; Th. Heinsius Goldleisten-GmbH; Ploenzke AG (Chairman). *Member:* German and International Bar Associations. *LANGUAGES:* German and English. *PRACTICE AREAS:* Banking; Corporations; Commercial; Financial Services; Securities.

JUN HAO, born Beijing, People's Republic of China, 1963; (Not admitted in Germany). *Education:* Peking University (Beida), Department of Law/Economic Law (LL.B., 1985); University of Trier (LL.M., 1991). Experience: Freelance and consultant for German companies for Joint Venture projects in China, 1992-1993; The State Economic Commission/The State Planning Commission of the People's Republic of China, 1985-1988. *LANGUAGES:* German, Chinese (Mandarin and diverse dialects) and English. *PRACTICE AREAS:* Chinese Law; Financial Services; Joint Ventures; Intellectual Property; Taxation.

RONG R. YAN, born Xian, People's Republic of China, 1961; (Not admitted in Germany). *Education:* Northwest Institute of Political Science & Law, Xian/China (LL.B., 1984); New York University School of Law, USA (M.C.J., 1994). Lecturer on Law, China University of Political Science & Law, 1985-1987. Experience: Legal Counsel, China International Film Cooperative Production Company, 1984-1985; Lawyer, The Second Law Firm of Shaanxi Province, 1988-1989. *LANGUAGES:* English and Chinese. *PRACTICE AREAS:* Chinese Law; Commercial; Joint Ventures; Chinese Securities Regulations.

DR. DR. OTTOARNDT GLOSSNER

Rechtsanwalt

LUDWIG-SAUER-STRASSE 33
D-61476 FRANKFURT/MAIN (KRONBERG), GERMANY
Telephone: 06173/640 440
Facsimile: 06173/640 670

Commercial, Corporate Contract Law, Arbitration.

DR.DR. OTTOARNDT GLOSSNER, born Nürnberg, Germany, December 23, 1923; admitted, 1952, Germany. *Education:* Universities of Erlangen (Doctor at Law), Paris (Doctor at Law) and Liverpool. Dec: Chevalier de la Légion d' Honneur, Great Cross Order of Merit (Germany). Publications: Commercial Arbitration in the Federal Republic of Germany, Kluwer 1984, Das Schiedsgericht in der Praxis Glossner-Bredow-Bühler, Verlag Recht und Wirtschaft, 1990. Jahrbuch für die Praxis der Schiedsgerichtsbarkeit (1) 1987, (2) 1988, (3) 1989, (4) 1990 (Ed.). Corporate Counsel, 1952-1977, Honorary Director, 1975-1977, Legal Committee, Fed. of German Industries. Chairman, ICC Commission on International Arbitration, 1960—. President, German Institution for Arbitration, 1970-1994. Director, German Branch ILA, 1960-1994. Honorary Chairman, Committee D SBL, IBA, 1987—. Member, ICCA, London Court of International Arbitration. Accredited Arbitrator with: ICSID, AAA, Vienna Arbitration Court, Cairo and Kuala Lumpur Arbitration Centers. *LANGUAGES:* German, English, French and Italian.

GREUNER WICKER HUBER HANF

GOETHESTRAßE 31-33
60313 FRANKFURT/MAIN, GERMANY
Telephone: (49 69) 298 00 80
Telex: 416 395 Notar D
Facsimile: (49 69) 29 80 08 29

Dresden, Germany Office: Bergmannstrasse 22, 01309. Telephone: (49-351) 3400 814. Facsimile: (49-351) 3400 815.

Milan, Italy Office: Corso di Porta Romana, 6, 20121. Telephone: (39-2) 865394 Facsimile: (39-2) 865480.

Mergers and Acquisitions, Corporate Law, Real Estate, Taxation, Banking Law, Aviation Law.

(This Listing Continued)

GREUNER WICKER HUBER HANF, *Frankfurt/Main—*
Continued

MEMBERS OF FIRM

DR. HANS GREUNER, born Berlin, Germany, May 16, 1930; admitted, 1957, Germany; as a Notary, 1967. *Education:* Universities of Göttingen, Munich and Frankfurt/Main (Dr.jur., 1955). Author: "Beurkundungsfragen im Bauherrenmodell," 1983. *LANGUAGES:* German and English.

RAIMUND WICKER, born Warburg, Germany, January 29, 1943; admitted, 1973, Germany; as a Notary, 1978. *Education:* University of Frankfurt/Main.

HANS-GEORG FENDRICH, born Wissmar, Germany, May 2, 1949; admitted, 1978, Germany; as a Tax Lawyer, 1982; as a Notary, 1984. *Education:* University of Frankfurt/Main; Freie Universität Berlin. *LANGUAGES:* German, English and French.

CHRISTIAN HUBER, born Berlin, Germany, November 5, 1950; admitted, 1979, Germany. *Education:* Universities of Frankfurt, Bonn and Milan. *Member:* German-Italian Lawyers Association; German Italian Chamber of Commerce. *LANGUAGES:* German, Italian and English.

WOLFGANG HANF, born Frankfurt/Main, Germany, September 3, 1957; admitted, 1986, Germany; 1991, as a Notary. *Education:* University of Frankfurt/Main. *LANGUAGES:* German and English.

ASSOCIATES

KARL WOSCHNAGG, born Ludvika, Sweden, October 17, 1961; admitted, 1990, Germany. *Education:* Universities of Tübingen, Munich and Uppsala. *Member:* Swedish Chamber of Commerce in Germany. Author: "Das neue schwedische Kaufrecht", 1991. *LANGUAGES:* German, Swedish, English and French.

STEFAN OBERMANN, born Frankfurt/Main, Germany, September 1, 1961; admitted, 1990, Germany. *Education:* University of Frankfurt/Main. *LANGUAGES:* German and English.

DR. ULF SCHULER, born Tübingen, Germany, February 23, 1959; admitted, 1989, Germany; as a Tax Lawyer, 1992. *Education:* Universities of Tübingen, Aix-en-Provence, Konstanz (Dr.jur. 1990). Author: "Steuerrechtliche Auswiskungen auf den Internationalen Forderungshandel", 1990. *LANGUAGES:* German, English and French.

JOHANNA MASSER, born Schenklengsfeld, Germany, February 12, 1962; admitted, 1992, Frankfurt am Main. *Education:* University of Mainz. *Member:* German Bar Association. *LANGUAGES:* German, English and French.

FRANZISKUS GRAF VON PLETTENBERG, born Bad Kreuznach, Germany, May 8, 1961; admitted, 1990, Germany. *Education:* Universities of Freiburg/Breisgau and Bonn. *LANGUAGES:* German and English.

DR. FRANZ HAMMERSCHMIDT, born Frankfurt am Main, Germany, May 16, 1951; admitted, 1980, Germany. *Education:* Universities of Freiburg, Frankfurt am Main, Rome and Macerata, Italy. Author: "Law Practice in the European Communities," 1980. *Member:* German Bar Association; German Lawyers Association. *LANGUAGES:* German, English, French and Italian.

GRUNENBERG & HELMKE-BECKER

Rechtsanwälte and Notare
BRÜDER-GRIMM-STR. 50
D-60385 FRANKFURT/MAIN, GERMANY
Telephone: 4969-432932/439526
Fax: 4969-439818

Dresden, Germany Office: Schillerplatz 7, D-01309. Telephone: 49351-3361090/1. Fax: 49351-3361092.

Trade Law, Private International Law, Administrative Law, Company Law, Competition Law, Landlord and Tenant, Conveyancing, Contract Law, Building and Construction Law, Probate and Trusts.

FIRM PROFILE: The firm is one that has been long established in Frankfurt. It was founded in 1928 and has a broad based practice. Today there are three solicitors and more than seven staff working in the office, which is equipped with all the necessary up to date equipment. The firm also has a representative office in Chicago.

In recent years the development of the practice has been in connection with

(This Listing Continued)

the commercial and international activities of both corporate and private clients.

JOHANNES GRUNENBERG, born Königsberg, Germany, June 21, 1935; admitted, 1963, Germany. *Education:* Universities of Frankfurt, Freiburg and Cologne. *Member:* Frankfurt Home and Land Owners Association. *PRACTICE AREAS:* Landlord and Tenant; Conveyancing; Administrative Law; Contract and Competition Law.

THOMAS HELMKE-BECKER, born Fulda, Germany, July 2, 1947; admitted, 1975, Germany. *Education:* Universities of Frankfurt and Würzburg. *Member:* International Bar Association; German Bar Association. *PRACTICE AREAS:* Landlord and Tenant; Conveyancing; Company; Trade and Contract Law.

Languages: German, English and French

GRÜTZMACHER, GRAVERT & PARTNER

BROßSTRAßE 6
60487 FRANKFURT/MAIN, GERMANY
Telephone: 069/979 61-0
Fax: 069/979 61100

Hamburg, Germany Office: Herrengraben 3, 20459. Telephone: 040/36 96 33-0. Fax: 040/36 96 33 33.
Leipzig, Germany Office: Lessingstraße 17, 04109. Telephone: 0341-20 98 69/79. Fax: 0341-20 98 59.
Berlin, Germany Office: Kurfürstendamm 216, 10719. Telephone: 030/882 66 04. Fax: 030/882 17 63.

Law: Company Law, Business and Economic Legislation, Company Purchasing, LBO/MBO, Mergers and Acquisitions, Company Succession (Laws of Succession), Competition and Licensing Legislation, Anti-Trust Law, Law of Commerce and Marketing, Franchising, Labor Legislation, EDP Law, Legislation governing Real Estate, Private Building Law.
Taxation: German and International Taxation Legislation (esp. US Tax Law), Fiscal Planning, Counselling on Taxation Concepts, Legislation regulating the Transformation of Companies in Fiscal and Commercial Terms, Balance Sheet Planning and Dividend Schedules, Taxation Counselling for New Enterprises, Representation at Financial Courts of Law, Tax Litigation, Legislation regarding Fiscal Offences, Administration of Property.
Auditing: Annual Audits, Auditing Work such as required on the Banking Sector, support given in clarifying matters of Business Management particularly in the new German Länder, Counselling on Privatization, Company Reorganization, drawing up of expert opinions.

DR. ROLF GRÜTZMACHER, born Hamburg, Germany, December 28, 1940; admitted, 1972, Germany; 1973, Tax Consultant; 1990, Auditor. *Education:* University of Marburg, University of Göttingen and University of Munich (Dr.jur.). *Member:* International Fiscal Association; International Bar Association. *LANGUAGES:* German and English. *PRACTICE AREAS:* Corporate; Commercial; Merger and Acquisitions; Tax and Accounting Law.

DR. KLAUS GRAVERT, born Wilhelmshaven, Germany, April 18, 1942; admitted, 1971, Germany; 1974, Tax Advisor. *Education:* University of Göttingen and Munich (Dr.jur., 1971). With Arthur Andersen & Co., 1971-1978. (Resident, Hamburg Office). *LANGUAGES:* German and English. *PRACTICE AREAS:* Tax Law; International Taxation; Commercial Law; Merger Law; Tax Litigation.

DR. ANDREAS RICHARD BITTNER, born Frankfurt/Main, Germany, July 31, 1955; admitted, 1984, Germany. *Education:* University of Frankfurt/Main (Dr.jur., 1986). *Member:* German and Frankfurt Bar Association. *LANGUAGES:* German and English. *PRACTICE AREAS:* Commercial Business; Unfair Competition; Real Estate; Notarial Recording; Competition and Licensing Legislation.

DR. ROLAND STANGER, born Sindelfingen, Germany, November 1, 1954; admitted, 1987, Tax Advisor; 1989, Auditor. *Education:* Heidelberg University (Dr.rer.pol., 1981). *LANGUAGES:* German and English. *PRACTICE AREAS:* Commercial Annual Audit; International Audit; Consultant on Matters of Business Administration; Consultant to former GDR enterprises undergoing restructure; Taxation.

WOLFGANG SCHNEIDER, born Waldfischbach, Germany, August 17, 1953; admitted, 1987, Tax Consultant; 1989, Auditor. *Education:* University of Pforzheim (Dipl.Bw, 1987). *LANGUAGES:* German and English. *PRACTICE AREAS:* Counselling on Taxation Concepts; Legislation

(This Listing Continued)

relating to Succession and Company Inheritance Issues; Investigation and Counselling on Matters of Business Administration.

DR. GEORG FAERBER, born Freiburg, Germany, July 2, 1954; admitted, 1982, Germany. *Education:* University of Freiburg, Germany and University of Lausanne, Switzerland (Dr.jur., 1988). *Member:* German-British Lawyers' Association. (Resident, Hamburg Office). *LANGUAGES:* German, English and French. *PRACTICE AREAS:* Company Law; Commercial and Business Law; Real Property; EDP Law; Labor Taxation.

CHRISTOF ULRICH FRANZ, born Haiger, Germany, September 11, 1958; admitted, 1989, Germany. *Education:* University of Gießen (1986). *Member:* German Bar Association. (Resident, Leipzig Office). *LANGUAGES:* German and English. *PRACTICE AREAS:* Corporation Law; Employee Law; Tax Law; Insolvency Law; Civil Law; Commercial Law.

DR. KAY JEß, born Kiel, Germany, December 4, 1957; admitted, 1991, Germany; 1993, Tax Consultant. *Education:* University of Kiel, Germany; University of Lausanne, Switzerland (Dr.jur., 1991). (Resident, Hamburg Office). *LANGUAGES:* German, English and French. *PRACTICE AREAS:* Tax Law; International Taxation; Commercial Law; Merger Law; Tax Litigation.

GURLAND & LAMBSDORFF

FÜRSTENBERGER STRASSE 10-12
D-60322 FRANKFURT/MAIN, GERMANY
Telephone: 69-9552340
Telefax: 69-95523450

Also offices in Berlin, Cologne and Leipzig.

General, Business and International Practice, Corporate, Company, Commercial, Competition, Acquisitions and Mergers, Distribution and Franchise Law, Trademark, Labour Law, General Conditions of Sale and Delivery, Advertising and Agency Law, also Notarial Practice.

FIRM PROFILE: *The law firm of GURLAND & LAMBSDORFF is the result of a merger between GURLAND & PARTNERS, in Cologne, and LAMBSDORFF & PARTNERS, in Frankfurt, in 1990. The separate firms and now the firm GURLAND & LAMBSDORFF were and are one of the German law firms representing domestic and foreign clients in all fields of commercial, business and both national and international law. An important part of the practice is the legal aspects of transnational business, especially within the EEC. GURLAND & LAMBSDORFF not only advises German clients in international matters but also foreign enterprises and clients on doing business in Germany and elsewhere. The majority of lawyers and members of the support-staff are fluent in English, French and other foreign languages.*

Clients of the firm are many well-known German and foreign companies in a wide variety of businesses.

In the Frankfurt office ther are 2 partners who are also qualified to act as notaries and are specially licensed to prepare and execute documents relating to the incorporation of companies, real estate, probate matters and other important commercial transactions requiring, in German law, a notarial form of document.

In GURLAND & PARTNERS there are more than 20 attorneys, including 9 partners, and a support-staff of more than 50 people, working in the 4 offices.

MEMBERS OF FIRM

HANS GEORG GRAF LAMBSDORFF, born 1931; admitted, 1960, Germany. *Education:* Universities of Göttingen and Marburg. Author: Handbuch des Eigentunsvorbehalts im deutschen und ausländischen Recht, 1974; Handbuch des Werbeagenturrechts, 1975; Werbung mit Schutzrechtshinweisen, 1977; Mängelhaftungnach den Bedingungen der Textil-und Begleitungsindustrie, 1981; Eigentumsvorbehalt und AGB-Gesetz, 1982; Umweltwerberecht, 1993. *Member:* German Association for Intellectual Property and Copyright; German Society for Comparative Law; German-Hungarian Jurists' Association. *LANGUAGES:* German and English.

BERND SKORA, born 1940; admitted, 1969, Germany; 1987, Notary. *Education:* Universities of Berlin, Würzburg and Frankfurt. Author of (together with Hans Georg Graf Lamssdorff): Handbuch des Eigentumsvorbehalts im deutschen und ausländischen Recht, 1974; Handbuch des Werbeagenturrechts, 1975; Werbung mit Schutzrechtshinweisen, 1977. *Member:* German Association for Intellectual Property and Copyright Law. *LANGUAGES:* German and English.

(This Listing Continued)

MARION BROCKMANN-SKORA, born 1942; admitted, 1972, Germany; 1988, Notary. *Education:* Universities of Lausanne and Bonn. *Member:* German Association for Intellectual Property and Copyright Law. *LANGUAGES:* German, English and French.

ASSOCIATES

MARTIN MENZEL, born 1957; admitted, 1992, Germany. *Education:* Universities of Mainz and Paris. *Member:* German Bar Association; German-Spanish Law Association. *LANGUAGES:* German, English and French.

THOMAS GIES, born 1961; admitted, 1994, Germany. *Education:* University of Frankfurt. *Member:* German Bar Association. *LANGUAGES:* German, English and French.

Member of LEGALLIANCE EEIG (Association of European Law Firms): ADER, JOLIBOIS & ASSOCIES, Paris; BAILEYS, SHAW & GILLETT, London; SARDA, CALOMARDE, CASTELO Y ASOCIADOS, Barcelona/Valencia/Madrid; SCAMONI E ASSOCIATI, Milano/Bologna/Padova; WILLEMART & ASSOCIES, Brussels/Tongres/Namur; BARENTS & KRANS, The Hague/Brussels; VERUM ADVOKATFIRMAN, Stockholm.

HAARMANN, HEMMELRATH & PARTNER

NEUE MAINZER STRASSE 75
D-60311 FRANKFURT/MAIN, GERMANY
Telephone: (069) 920 59-0
Telefax: (069) 920 59-133

Munich Office: Effnerstrasse 38, D-81925 Munich. Telephone: (089) 924 00-0. Telefax: (089) 92400-133. Telex: 5 23 900 HUP D.

Düsseldorf Office: Martin-Luther-Platz 26, D-40212 Düsseldorf. Telephone: (0211) 8399-00. Telefax (0211) 8399-133. Telex: 1631 Btx d 0211 16 450.

Berlin Office: Budapester Strasse 40a, D-10787 Berlin. Telephone: (030) 264 73-0. Telefax: (030) 264 73-133.

Leipzig Office: Neumarkt 24, D-04109 Leipzig. Telephone: (0341) 1263-0. Telefax: (0341) 1263-133.

Tokyo Office: Shiroyama JT Mori Building, 8F, 3-1 Toranomon 4-chome, Minato-ku, Tokyo 105. Telephone: 81-3-34 59 54 85. Fax: 81-3-35 78 89 56.

Prague Office: Cermàkova 7, CZ-1200 00 Prague 2, Czech Republic. Telephone: 42-2-24 23 90 36. Telefax: 42-2-24 23 88 42.

Corporate and Business Law, International and National Tax Law, Banking, Commercial Law, Labour Law, all Areas of Mergers and Acquisitions, Financial Transactions, International Law, Antitrust Law, Unfair Competition and Intellectual Property Rights Law, EEC Law, Real Estate Transactions, Management and Leveraged Buy-outs, National and Cross-border Leasing Transactions, Structuring of Funds, Accounting Services.

FIRM PROFILE: *The firm, established in 1987, has strongly developed as a multi-disciplinary firm in Germany with seven offices. The firm is affiliated with Graham & James (US, Italy, Japan and China), Taylor Joynson Garrett (UK) and Deacons (Hong Kong and Southeast Asia) and is a member of the international tax and audit network RSM International.*

RESIDENT MEMBERS OF FIRM

DR. WILHELM HAARMANN, born Hagen/Westf., Germany, May 24, 1950; admitted, 1977, Hagen; 1979, Munich; 1981, Steuerberater (Certified Tax Advisor); 1983, Wirtschaftsprüfer (Certified Public Accountant). *Education:* Universities of Münster and Freiburg (J.D., 1973; Doctor at Law, 1979). Author: *Wegfall der Geschäftsgrundlage bei Dauerrechtsverhältnissen,* 1979. *Member:* International Bar Association; International Fiscal Association; Institute of German Chartered Accountants (IDW); Deutscher Anwaltsverein; German British Lawyers Association; German-Japanese Lawyers Association. *LANGUAGES:* German and English. *PRACTICE AREAS:* Corporate; Finance; Banks and Banking; Tax; Aviation.

EUGEN BOGENSCHÜTZ, born Hechingen, Germany, October 9, 1950; admitted, 1982, Wiesbaden, Steuerberater (Certified Tax Advisor); 1987, Wirtschaftsprüfer (Certified Public Accountant). *Education:* Fachhochschule of Frankfurt (Business Administration, 1979). *Member:* Institute of German Certified Public Auditors. *LANGUAGES:* German and English. *PRACTICE AREAS:* Tax; Mergers and Acquisitions.

DR. WOLFGANG THEOBALD, born Zell/Mosel, Germany, December 20, 1953; admitted, 1980, Giessen. *Education:* Universities of Giessen

(This Listing Continued)

HAARMANN, HEMMELRATH & PARTNER,
Frankfurt/Main—Continued

(Doctor at Law, 1983) and Exeter (LL.M.). Author: "Vor-GmbH und Gründerhaftung," 1984. *LANGUAGES:* German and English. *PRACTICE AREAS:* Corporate; Commercial; Unfair Competition; Mergers and Acquisitions; Labour.

WOLFGANG JAMIN, born Dillenberg, Germany, June 26, 1952; admitted, 1988, Steuerberater (Ceritified Tax Advisor); 1990, Wirtschaftspüfer (Certified Public Accountant). *Education:* Universities of Frankfurt and Bielefeld. *LANGUAGES:* Geerman, English and French. *PRACTICE AREAS:* Mergers and Acquisitions; Valuation of Companies.

BARBARA BUSCH, born Fulda, Germany, April 27, 1958; admitted, 1989, Munich; 1991, Steuerberater (Certified Tax Advisor). *Education:* University of Munich (J.D., 1986). *Member:* Chamber of Lawyers; Chamber of Tax Advisors. *LANGUAGES:* German and English. *PRACTICE AREAS:* Tax; Real Estate; Property; Finance.

Languages: German, English, French, Japanese, Mandarin, Dutch, Spanish, Italian, Russian, Czech and Slovakian.

(For Biographical Data on other Members of Firm and Firm Profile, See Professional Biographies at Munich, Berlin, Düsseldorf, Leipzig, Germany, Tokyo, Japan and Prague, Czech Republic).

HAVER & MAILAENDER

Established in 1965

BEETHOVENSTRASSE 4

D-60325 FRANKFURT/MAIN, GERMANY
Telephone: 069-740190
Telecopier: 069-740247

Stuttgart, Germany Office: Lenzhalde 83, D-70192. Telephone: (0711) 227440. Cable Address: "Intertax", Stuttgart. Telex: 721738 advo d. Telecopier: (0711) 2991935.
Dresden, Germany Office: Bautzner Strasse 23-25, D-01099. Telephone: 0351-51955. Telecopier: 0351-53538.
Brussels, Belgium Office: Av. de la Renaissance 1, B-1040. Telephone: 02-7366375. Telecopier: 02-7360571.

Commercial, Corporation, Banking and Financial Services, Mergers and Acquisitions, High Technology and Telecommunication, Transportation and Aviation, Construction and Engineering Contracts, Antitrust, EEC-Law, Licensing, Patent, Trademark, Copyright, Trade Law and Product Liability, International and Tax Law, Litigation and Arbitration.

FIRM PROFILE: The firm was established in Stuttgart in 1965 and opened its Frankfurt office in 1990. The firm offers the full range of legal services for commercial matters. The Frankfurt office concentrates on Banking and Securities Law.

MEMBER OF FIRM

DR. GÜNTER KRUMSCHEID, born Bad Godesberg, 1939; admitted, 1973, Frankfurt/Main. *Education:* University of Bonn (Doctor of Law, 1971). Author: "Die Anwendung von Voelkerrecht im Spanischen Recht nach der Verfassung der 2. Republik von 1931 und im gegenwaertigen Staat," 1971. *Member:* Frankfurt and German Bar Associations; International Bar Association (Member, Business Law Section). *LANGUAGES:* German, English, French, Spanish and Italian.

(For complete list of Partners, see Professional Biographies at Stuttgart, Germany and Brussels, Belgium)

HEBERER, REINMÜLLER & PARTNER

Established in 1976

MYLIUSSTRAβE 14

60323 FRANKFURT/MAIN, GERMANY
Telephone: (069) 97 10 97-0
Telefax: (069) 72 35 99

Associated German Offices:
Düsseldorf, Germany Office: Brockmann, Schreiner & Partner, Berliner Allee 34-36, 40212 Düsseldorf.
Hamburg, Germany Office: Curschmann, Rollenhagen & Partner, Baumwall 7, 20457 Hamburg.
Berlin, Germany Office: Hackenberger, Dr. Schmidt & Partner, Uhlandstraβe 171/172, 10719 Berlin.

(This Listing Continued)

Stuttgart, Germany Office: Koch-Heintzeler, Widmann & Partner, UHandstraβe 11, 70182 Stuttgart.
Dresden, Germany Office: Koch-Heintzeler, Widmann & Partner, Albertstraβe 34, 01097 Dresden.
Munich, Germany Office: Dr. Zoglmann, Dr. Kainz & Partner, Maximiliansplatz 18, 80333 Munich.

General and International Practice, Commercial Law, Corporate, Banking, Unfair Competition, Trade Marks, Copyright, Patents, Licensing, Law of the Press, Labour Law, Real Estate, Estate Planning, Construction, Contracts, Commercial Litigation and Arbitration, Bankruptcy, Inheritance.

MEMBERS OF FIRM

JÜRGEN M. HEBERER, born Frankfurt, May 17, 1942; admitted, 1974. *Education:* Universities of Frankfurt am Main (Law Degree, 1972); Training in Barcelona. Notary Public, 1984. *Member:* German Lusithanian Law Association. *LANGUAGES:* German, English, Spanish and Portuguese. *PRACTICE AREAS:* Real Estate; Investment; Company Law.

DR. BERND REINMÜLLER, born Friedewald, Germany, May 23, 1948; admitted, 1979. *Education:* Universities of Mainz (Dr. iur., 1976) and Aix-en-Provence (1974-1975). Assistant Manager, International Department, Deutsche Bank AG, 1978-1979. Lecturer: Comparative and German Civil Law, University of Paris II, Institute de Droit Comparé, 1982-1983; International Procedure Law, Heidelberg since 1992. *Member:* Union Internationale des Avocats (Member of Board); Committee, Internationales Zivilprozeβrecht, Bundesrechtsanwaltskammer; Club des Affaires de la Hesse. *LANGUAGES:* German, French and English. *PRACTICE AREAS:* Conflict of Laws; Commercial Law; Labour Law.

ADOLF M. SEFFER, born Celle, February 1, 1959; admitted, 1990. *Education:* Chemistry Frankfurt (1979-1980), Law Regensburg, Frankfurt, Munich (Law Degree, 1985), Military Degree, (Captain), 1987; Training in International Law in London, Strasbourg and Barcelona. *Member:* AIJA; German Association for Industrial Property and Copyright; LES Licence Executive Society; DGIR German Association of Computer Law. *LANGUAGES:* German, Spanish, English and French. *PRACTICE AREAS:* Unfair Competition Law; Law of the Press; Intellectual Property; Trade Mark; Computer Law.

ASSOCIATES

KLAUS BEINE, born Frankfurt a.M., August 19, 1961; admitted, 1993, Germany. *Education:* Deutsche Bank AG, 1981-1983; Universities of Mainz and Frankfurt a.M. (law degree, 1989). *Member:* ARGE Baurecht im Deutschen Anwaltsverein. *LANGUAGES:* German and English. *PRACTICE AREAS:* Commercial Law; Building Law.

STEPHAN MENZEMER, born Frankfurt a.M., October 23. 1964; admitted, 1994. *Education:* Universities of Frankfurt am Main, Aix en Provence and Marseille (law degree, 1990). Teaching Assistant, Institute of Civil Law and Law History, University of Frankfurt, 1988-1993. Training with Wilson-Daumas-Wilson, Marseille, 1987. Articled to Winckworth & Pemberton, London, 1994. *Member:* German-French Society; German-English Law Society. *LANGUAGES:* German, English and French. *PRACTICE AREAS:* Commercial Law; Litigation.

CONSULTANT

HILDEGARD MASSARI, born Frankfurt a.M. Main, July 15, 1964; admitted, 1994. *Education:* Universitá degli Studi, Milano (Law Degree, 1990); Research Scholar, University of Frankfurt (1991-1993). Publications: Rivista di diritto processuale 1992, 1995. *Member:* Ordine degli Avvocati e Procuratori di Milano; German-Italian Law Society. *LANGUAGES:* Italian, German, English and French. *PRACTICE AREAS:* Civil Procedure; Law of Torts; Insurance Law.

PROF. HEIERMANN, FRANKE, MÜLLER, KNIPP & PARTNER

Established in 1971

KETTENHOFWEG 126

D-60325 FRANKFURT/MAIN, GERMANY
Telephone: (0 69) 975 82 20
Telefax: (0 69) 74 70 83

Dresden, Germany Office: Strehlener Straβe 10, D-01069 Dresden. Telephone: (03 51) 46 65 - 3 10. Telefax: (03 51) 46 65 - 312.
Berlin, Germany Office: Carmerstraβe 2, D-10623 Berlin. Telephone: (030) 3152054. Telefax: (030) 3152056.

(This Listing Continued)

Brussels, Belgium Office: Rue de la Tourelle 37, B-1040 Brussels.
  Telephone: (02) 2 30 09 24. Telefax: (02) 2 30 09 01.

In Cooperation with: Watt, Tieder & Hoffar, 7929 Westpark Drive, Suite
  400, McLean, Virginia 22 102, U.S.A.

*Specialists in Construction Law, Contracts, Engineering, Civil Law, Public
Construction Law, Labour Law, Property Law, Leases and Leasing, Land-
lord and Tenant, Real Estate Law, International Law, European Law,
Law of Civil Procedure.*

PROF. W. HEIERMANN, born Stolp, Germany, January 8, 1935. *Education:* University of Tübingen (1956-1958) and Munich (1958-1960). Professor, University of Dortmund, 1982—. Author: Hauptkommentar zur VOB (Teil A und B), 7th publication, 1994; Kommentar zur VOB Teil C DIN 18451 and DIN 18 299 Gerüstarbeiten; Kommentar zur VOB/A-SKR; Kommentar zur Schiedsgerichtsordnung für das Bauwesen. Co-Author: "Zeitschrift für deutsches und internationales Baurecht(ZfBR)"; "Schriftenreihe der Deutschen Gesellschaft für Baurecht"; various publications concerning national and international construction law. Member, board of "Deutscher Verdingungsausschür Bauieistungen" (DAV;German Institution for Arbitration (DIS). Chairman, Institute for German and International Construction Law, Humboldt University of Berlin. *Member:* German and International Association of Construction Law (President); European Association for Arbitration of Construction Law. *LANGUAGES:* German and English.

HORST FRANKE, born Koblenz, Germany, February 20, 1949; admitted, 1976, Mainz; 1978, Bonn; 1994, Frankfurt. *Education:* University of Mainz. Assistant Professor of Construction Law, University GH of Wuppertal. Co-Author: Handbuch für die Baupraxis, VOB-Praxis, Die Europäische Herausforderung, Europäische Vergaberegeln im Bauwesen, Kommentar zur VOB/A-SKR; various publications concerning construction law and construction industry. *Member:* Frankfurt Bar; German Association of Construction Law (Board); Europäische Vereinigung für das Schiedsgerichtswesen Bau-und Anlagenbau; Deutsch-Tschechische Gesellschaft; Institut Für Deutsches und Internationales Baurecht (Board); Ausschufür Anwendungsfragen der VOB auf Bundesebene (VOB-Ausschuß) and Vergabeüberwachungsausschu des Bundes. *LANGUAGES:* German, French and English. *PRACTICE AREAS:* European Law; Construction Law; Contracts; International Law.

MANFRED MÜLLER, born Schmalkalden, Germany, October 23, 1956; admitted, 1988, Frankfurt. *Education:* University of Erlangen (1975-1978), Bologna (1979-1980) and Frankfurt (1981-1982). Assistant Professor, Construction Law, Technical University of Cotthus. Author: Kommentar zur VOB/A-SKR, various articles in Baurecht and Bauwirtschaft. *Member:* German Lawyers Association; German Association of Construction Law; Frankfurt Bar; International Bar; Deutsche Gesollschapt für Baurecht. *LANGUAGES:* German, French, English and Italian. *PRACTICE AREAS:* International Law; European Law; Construction Law; Contracts; Public Procurement.

BERND KNIPP, born Korbach, Germany, November 16, 1958; admitted, 1987, Frankfurt. *Education:* University of Marburg. Author: "Bauvertragliche Klauseln im Blickwinkel des AGB-Gesetzes," articles in ABC-Kolumne "Beratende Ingenieure." *Member:* Frankfurt Bar. *LANGUAGES:* German, English and French. *PRACTICE AREAS:* Construction Law; Contracts and Engineering; Law of Civil Procedure.

WOLFGANG SCHLUMBERGER, born Mannheim, Germany, June 21, 1955; admitted, 1985, LG Dresden; 1993, OLG Dresden. *Education:* University of Heidelberg (1976). *Member:* Frankfurt Bar; German Association of Construction Law. *LANGUAGES:* German and French. *PRACTICE AREAS:* Construction Law; Property Law; Labour Law.

TURID SCHARF, born Braunschweig, Germany, December 7, 1964; admitted, 1992, Frankfurt. *Education:* University of Frankfurt. *Member:* Frankfurt Bar; DAV; ARGE Construction Law (DAV). *LANGUAGES:* German, French and English. *PRACTICE AREAS:* Construction Law; Contracts; Leases and Leasing.

CHRISTIAN ZANNER, born Munich, Germany, January 26, 1962; admitted, 1993, Berlin. *Education:* University of Munich (LMU) and Berlin (FU). *Member:* Berlin Bar. *LANGUAGES:* German, English and Italian. *PRACTICE AREAS:* Construction Law.

GABRIELE FUNKE, born Frankfurt, Germany, November 20, 1964; admitted, 1993, Frankfurt. *Education:* University of Passau (1983-1985), Bonn (1985-1987) and Cologne (1987-1989). *Member:* German-French Lawyers Association; German-Japanese Association. *LANGUAGES:* German, French and English. *PRACTICE AREAS:* Construction Law.

(This Listing Continued)

URSULA BLAUERTZ, born Cologne, Germany, March 10, 1957; admitted, 1990, Heilbronn; 1993, Wiesbaden. *Education:* University of Bonn (1980). *LANGUAGES:* German, French, English and Spanish. *PRACTICE AREAS:* International Construction Law.

MATTHIAS WIENHOLD, born Germersheim, Germany, September 22, 1964; admitted, 1994, Frankfurt. *Education:* University of Mainz (1984-1989). Representative, firm in EDIBAU e. V. and CALS-study group of the National Association of German Industries e. V. *Member:* Frankfurt Bar. *LANGUAGES:* German, English, Spanish and Italian. *PRACTICE AREAS:* Construction Law; Contracts and Engineering; Computer and Software Law; General Terms and Conditions.

HENGELER MUELLER WEITZEL WIRTZ

Rechtsanwälte

BOCKENHEIMER LANDSTRASSE 51
D-60325 FRANKFURT/MAIN, GERMANY
Telephone: (069) 17095-0
Telefax: (069) 725773 & 723983
Telex: 41 45 95 Jura D

Düsseldorf, Germany Office: Trinkausstrasse 7, D-40213 Düsseldorf.
  Telephone: (0211) 8304-0. Telefax: (0211) 13 26 41 & 8 04 61. Telex: 85 87 300 whds d.
Berlin, Germany Office: Kurfürstendamm 54/55, D-10707 Berlin.
  Telephone: (030) 882 76 47. Telefax: (030) 882 7144.
Brussels, Belgium Office: Boulevard du Régent 50, Bte. 6, B-1000
  Brussels. Telephone: (02) 511 41 15. Telefax: (02) 514 02 12.
Budapest, Hungary Office: Teréz krt. 38, H-1066. Telephone: (1) 1323121. Telefax: (1) 2690098.
New York Office: 712 Fifth Avenue, New York, New York, 10019.
  Telephone: (212) 586-4600. Telefax: (212) 586-4481.

Commercial, Corporate, International, Banking, Finance and Underwriting, Taxation, Arbitration, EEC, Antitrust, Merger Control, Fair Trade, Patent, Trademark, Litigation, Labor, Administrative, Constitutional, Environmental and Planning Law.

PARTNERS

DR. RUDOLF MUELLER, born Darmstadt, Germany, 1904; admitted, 1947, Frankfurt/Main. *Education:* Amherst College; Heidelberg University (Dr. jur.). Co-Author: with Evan G. Galbraith, *The German Stock Corporation Law - The German Law on the Accounting by Major Enterprises Other Than Stock Corporations,* 2nd (revised) edition, 1976; with Horst Brücher and Ernst Stiefel, *Doing Business in Germany,* 8th (revised) edition, 1978; with Martin Heidenhain and Hannes Schneider, *German Antitrust Law,* 3rd edition, 1984. Minister of Economics and Transport, Hesse, 1945-1946. Chairman of Council and Executive Head, German Economic Administration of the Combined British and U.S. Zones of Occupation, 1946-1947.

DR. HORST BRÜCHER, born Altenburg, Germany, 1928; admitted, 1961, Frankfurt/Main. *Education:* Frankfurt University (Dr. jur.; Paris University, Sorbonne (Diplome of Comparative Law); Georgetown University, Washington, D.C. Co-author: with Rudolf Mueller and Ernst Stiefel, *Doing Business in Germany,* 8th (revised) edition, 1978; with Dieter Pulch, *The German Law of Foreign Investment Shares,* 1969.

DR. HEINZ WETTERKAMP, born Remscheid, Germany, 1930; admitted, 1961, Frankfurt/Main. *Education:* Universities of Munich and Erlangen (Dr. jur.).

DR. MICHAEL THOMA, born Trier, Germany, 1936; admitted, 1965, Frankfurt/Main. *Education:* Universities of Freiburg, Munich, Bonn and Cologne (Dr. jur.). Foreign Associate, New York Law Firm, 1967-1969.

DR. MARTIN HEIDENHAIN, born Berlin, Germany, 1936; admitted, 1969, Frankfurt/Main. *Education:* Universities of Berlin, Hamburg and Tübingen (Dr. jur.); Yale Law School (LL.M.). Co-Author: with Hannes Schneider, *German Antitrust Law,* 4th edition, 1990; with Burkhardt W. Meister, *German Law Concerning the Companies with Limited Liability - GmbH Law,* 5th edition, 1988; Business Transactions in Germany (FRG), Chapter on Antitrust Law.

DR. HANS-JÜRGEN HELLWIG, born Saarbrücken, Germany, 1940; admitted, 1970, Frankfurt/Main. *Education:* Universities of Marburg, Lausanne, Switzerland, Bonn (Dr. jur.); Georgetown University, Washington, D.C. Foreign Associate, Washington Law Firm, 1968. Co-Author with Hannes Schneider and David Kingsman, *The German Banking System,* 4th edition, 1986.

(This Listing Continued)

HENGELER MUELLER WEITZEL WIRTZ,
Frankfurt/Main—Continued

DR. HANNES SCHNEIDER, born Bad Rappenau/Heidelberg, 1936; admitted, 1970, Frankfurt/Main. *Education:* Universities of Heidelberg, Göttingen, Freiburg, Grenoble/France and Bonn (Dr. jur.). Foreign Associate, New York Law Firm, 1969-1970. Co-Author: with David Kingsman. *The German Co-Determination Act,* 2nd edition, 1982; with Hans-Jürgen Hellwig and David Kingsman, *The German Banking System,* 4th edition, 1986; with Martin Heidenhain, *German Antitrust Law,* 4th edition, 1990; Business Transactions in Germany (FRG), Chapter on Banking.

DR. BURKHARDT W. MEISTER, born Annaberg, Germany, 1940; admitted, 1971, Frankfurt/Main. *Education:* Universities of Würzburg and Munich (Dr. jur.); Faculté Internationale pour L'Enseignement de Droit Comparé, Strassburg/France (Diplôme de Droit Comparè); Harvard Law School (LL.M.). Co-Author: with Martin Heidenhain, *German Law Concerning the Companies with Limited Liability-GmbH Law,* 5th edition, 1988; Business Transactions in Germany (FRG), Chapter on Limited Liability Company.

DR. BERNHARD M. MAASSEN, born Munich, Germany, 1946; admitted, 1976, Frankfurt/Main. *Education:* Universities of Kiel, Freiburg and Bonn (Dr. jur.); University of California, Berkeley (LL.M.). Foreign Associate, Washington Law Firm, 1975. (Also at Brussels, Belgium Office).

DR. OLAF FREDERIK NISSEN (1944-1992).

DR. DIETER BEINERT, born Freiburg, Germany, 1949; admitted, 1978, Frankfurt/Main. *Education:* Universities of Freiburg, Saarbrücken and Bonn (Dr. jur.). Foreign Associate, New York Law Firm, 1980-1981. Co-Author: "Corporate Acquisitions & Mergers in Germany," 1991. (Also at New York, N.Y. Office).

DR. OLEG DE LOUSANOFF, born Frankfurt/Main, Germany, 1952; admitted, 1981, Frankfurt/Main. *Education:* University of Freiburg (Dr. jur.); London School of Economics; Keio University, Tokyo, Japan; Boalt Hall School of Law, University of California, Berkeley (LL.M.). Co-Author: with Benoit Laurin, *La GmbH - Loi sur la Société à Responsabilité Limitée de Droit Allemand,* 1988.

DR. PETER HECKEL, born Kulmbach, Germany, 1952; admitted, 1981, Frankfurt/Main. *Education:* University of Erlangen (Dr. jur.). Foreign Associate, New York Law Firm, 1983-1984.

DR. INGO KLÖCKER, born Cologne, Germany, 1955; admitted, 1983, Frankfurt/Main. *Education:* University of Freiburg (Dr. jur.); University of Texas at Austin School of Law (M.C.J.).

DR. MICHAEL BAUMGARTL, born Bad Homburg, Germany, 1957; admitted, 1985, Frankfurt/Main. *Education:* University of Gießen (Dr. jur.); College of Law, University of Illinois, Urbana-Champaign (M.C.L.).

DR. GERHARD LANG, born Straubing, Germany, 1956; admitted, 1984, Frankfurt/Main. *Education:* Universities of Munich and Freiburg (Dr. jur.); London School of Economics. Foreign Associate, Washington Law Firm, 1986-1987. (Also at Budapest, Hungary Office).

DR. HANS-JOACHIM LIEBERS, born Hameln, Germany, 1952; admitted, 1983, Frankfurt/Main. *Education:* University of Göttingen (Dr. jur.); University of California at Los Angeles, Law School (LL.M.).

PROF. DR. WILHELM A. KEWENIG (1934-1993).

DR. HENDRIK HAAG, born Frankfurt/Main, Germany, 1956; admitted, 1985, Frankfurt/Main. *Education:* Universities of Mannheim, Lausanne (Switzerland), Heidelberg and Freiburg (Dr. jur.). Foreign Associate, Atlanta Law Firm, 1987.

DR. HORST SATZKY, born Baden-Baden, Germany, 1954; admitted, 1987, Frankfurt/Main. *Education:* Universities of Berlin and Kiel (Dr.jur.). Official Federal Cartel Office, Berlin, Federal Ministry of Economics, Bonn, 1985-1987. Foreign Associate, New York Law Firm, 1989-1990. (Also at Brussels, Belgium Office).

FRIEDHELM JACOB, born Würzburg, Germany, 1948; admitted, 1992, Frankfurt/Main. *Education:* Universities of Marburg, Geneva (Switzerland) and Bielefeld. Associate International Tax Counsel, German Federal Ministry of Finance, 1977-1986. Fiscal Counselor of German Embassy, Washington, 1986-1991.

DR. KLAUS-DIETER STEPHAN, born Villingen, Germany, 1960; admitted, 1989, Frankfurt/Main. *Education:* University of Freiburg (Dr. jur.). Foreign Associate, London Law Firm, 1991.

(This Listing Continued)

EU654B

DR. CHRISTOF JÄCKLE, born Lahr, Germany, 1959; admitted, 1990, Frankfurt/Main. *Education:* Universities of Freiburg (Dr. jur.) and Geneva (Switzerland); University of Michigan Law School (LL.M.). Foreign Associate, Los Angeles Law Firm, 1986; Associate, McKinsey & Company, Inc., 1989-1990.

DR. PETER WEYLAND, born Mainz, Germany, 1960; admitted, 1991, Frankfurt/Main. *Education:* University of Freiburg (Dr. jur.). Foreign Associate, Atlanta Law Firm, 1990.

DR. STEFAN KRAUSS, born Wiesbaden, Germany, 1958; admitted, 1989, Frankfurt/Main. *Education:* Universities of Mainz, Aix-en-Provence (France) and Freiburg (Dr. jur.). Foreign Associate, New York Law Firm, 1992.

DR. BIRGIT SPIESSHOFER, born Aalen, Germany, 1960; admitted, 1989, Frankfurt/Main. *Education:* Universities of Tübingen and Freiburg (Dr. jur.); New York University School of Law (M.C.J.).

DR. EDGAR WALLACH, born Krefeld, Germany, 1958; admitted, 1991, Frankfurt/Main. *Education:* Universities of Munich (Economics) and Cologne (Dr.jur.). Foreign Associate, New York Law Firm, 1990 and 1993-1994.

THOMAS MUELLER, born Augsburg, Germany, 1963; admitted, 1991, Frankfurt/Main. *Education:* University of Augsburg. Foreign Associate, New York Law Firm, 1993.

DR. STEFAN RICHTER, born Soltau, Germany, 1961; admitted, 1991, Frankfurt/Main. *Education:* Universities of Berlin and Heidelberg (Dr.jur.). Foreign Associate, Washington Law Firm, 1993-1994.

DR. TORSTEN BUSCH, born Berlin, Germany, 1960; admitted, 1991, Frankfurt/Main. *Education:* University of Hamburg (Dr.jur.). Foreign Associate, New York Law Firm, 1993-1994.

DR. JOACHIM ROSENGARTEN, born Hamburg, Germany 1962; admitted, 1991, Frankfurt/Main. *Education:* University of Hamburg (Dr.jur.); University of Lausanne, Switzerland; Boalt Hall School of Law, University of California at Berkeley (LL.M.). Author: "Punitive Damages and Recognition and Enforcement in Germany," 1994.

Languages: German, English and French

(For biographical data of the members of the firm admitted to the bar in Düsseldorf and Berlin, see Professional Biographies at Düsseldorf and Berlin)

HEUKING KÜHN KUNZ WOJTEK

LINDENSTRASSE 37
D-60325 FRANKFURT/MAIN, GERMANY
Telephone: (49) 69-975610
Fax: (49) 69-97561200

Other Offices: Düsseldorf, Hamburg, Berlin, Chemnitz (Germany); Paris (France).

Corporate, Banking, Tax, National and EC Antitrust, Mergers, Acquisitions, Intellectual Property, Unfair Competition and Trade Law, Commercial and International Law, EC Law, Legal Assistance to Governments, Environmental Law, Administrative Law, International Arbitration, Litigation, General Practice.

FIRM PROFILE: All Attorneys are Members of Denton International and of the Frankfurt Bar Association. All listed speak English and German, other languages include French, Spanish, Italian and Farsi.

MEMBERS OF FIRM

RUDOLF DU MESNIL DE ROCHEMONT, born Marburg/Lahn, Germany, July 23, 1944; admitted, 1973, Germany, Licensed Legal Consultant, State of New York, USA, 1976. *Education:* Waldorf School of Adelphi College, Garden City, N.Y., 1960-1961; Universities of Marburg/Lahn, Berlin, Fribourg (Switzerland), Frankfurt/Main (Referendar, 1970; Assessor, 1973). With: Alexander & Green, New York, 1975-1976. Publications: Articles and Papers relating to Intellectual Property Law and Licensing. *Member:* The Association of the Bar of the City of New York; International Bar Association (Committee on Patents, Trademarks, Copyrights); German-American Lawyers Association (Past President); International Association for the Protection of Industrial Property (AIPPI); Deutscher Juristentag e.V. *PRACTICE AREAS:* Intellectual Property; Entertainment; Communication; Licensing; Corporate; International Commercial Law.

(This Listing Continued)

ULRICH P. HENSSEN, born Düsseldorf, Germany, January 19, 1951; admitted, 1982, Germany. *Education:* Universities of Bonn, Paris (Sorbonne), Munich (Referendar, 1979; Assessor, 1981). U.S. Professional Training, 1981-1982. *Member:* Young Lawyers' International Association (AIJA; Chairman, Committee on Environmental Law); International Bar Association; International Union of Lawyers (UIA). *LANGUAGES:* German, English and French. *PRACTICE AREAS:* Corporate and Commercial Law; Mergers and Acquisitions.

DR. ULF R. SIEBEL, born Düsseldorf, Germany, April 16, 1923; admitted, 1950, Germany. *Education:* University of Bonn (Referendar 1947, Assessor, 1950); Law Society, London (Doctor of Law, 1950). With Deutsche Bank AG, 1950-1969 (Int'l Loans and Bond Issues, Project Financing); Richard Daus & Co. Bankers, Frankfurt, General Partner, 1970-1984. Chief Executive, 1984-1988, Board since 1988; Arab Banking Corp Daus & Co GmbH, Board; Hypothekenbank in Essen AG, Board Vice Chairman; Krupp Lonrho GmbH, Board Vice Chairman; Hypothekenbank in Berlin AG, Board; Vice Chairman CDI Brussels, Board; Africa Assn, Hamburg, Vice Chairman; Assn. Developing Countries, Vice Chairman; German Ghanaian Economic Assn., President; Private Investment Protection Assn., Cologne, President; Frankfurt Stock Exchange, Member, Listing Commission, Insider Commission; Frankfurt Chamber of Industry and Commerce. Member, Foreign Trade Council; ICSID, Int'l Center for the Settlement of Investment Disputes, Washington, D.C., Member, Conciliator Panel. Author: Harmonization of Company law, 1954, German Restrictions on Capital Transactions with Foreigners, 1973, Equity and Quasi Equity of Credit Institutions, 1980, Foreign Trade Law of the Federal Republic of Germany, 1989. *Member:* Frankfurt Law Society; Frankfurt Law Association; German Institute on Comparative Law; German Association for International Law (ILA); International Bar Association (IBA); American Society of International Law, Washington, D.C. *PRACTICE AREAS:* Banking Law; Corporate Law; Foreign Trade Law; Public International Law.

DR. JÜRGEN PESCH, born Bitburg, Germany, March 19, 1946; admitted, 1986, Germany. *Education:* Universities of Geneva, Switzerland and Freiburg, Germany (Referendar 1971, Doctor of Law, 1975; Assessor, 1975). With Deutsche Bundesbank, 1975-1984; The Royal Bank of Canada AG, 1985-1986; Deutsche Anlagen Leasing GmbH, 1987-1990. Author: "Banking in Germany - The Legal Framework," in Butterworths Journal of International Banking and Financial Law, 8/1991. Co-Author (with Gregory Thwaite): "German Commercial Law Firms in Transition," International Legal Practitioner Vol. 17, No. 3, September, 1992; "Some Aspects of German Merger and Acquisition Law Explained for Foreign Counsel," International Business Lawyer Vol. 20, No. 11, December 1992; "Deciphering the Code," Capital Account, February, 1993. *Member:* International Bar Association. *PRACTICE AREAS:* Banking Law; General Commercial Law; Mergers and Acquisitions.

MATTHIAS PALM, born Blankenstein, Germany, August 13, 1948; admitted, 1990, Germany. *Education:* Universities of Cologne and Bochum (Referendar 1977; Assessor 1979). With BEB Erdgas und Erdöl GmbH, 1979-1990. Author: Expropriation under the old and new German Mining Law, 1981, Building and Operation of Plants of the Mining and Energy Industry in East Germany, 1990. *Member:* International Bar Association (Section on Business Law; Committee on Utility Law; Section on Energy and Natural Resources). *PRACTICE AREAS:* Public and Environmental Law; Mining and Energy Law.

MICHAEL PRINZ ZU LÖWENSTEIN, born December 20., 1950; admitted, 1978, Germany. *Education:* Universities of Freiburg and Bonn, Germany (Referendar 1975, Assessor, 1978). With Sullivan & Cromwell, New York, 1982; Stegemann, Sieveking & Lutteroth (Hamburg) 1978-1987. Legal Advisor to President's Office Republic of Niger, 1987-1990. *PRACTICE AREAS:* Banking Law; Corporate Law; General Commercial Law.

WOLFGANG BREHM, born Aschaffenburg, January 8, 1952; admitted, 1982, Germany. *Education:* Universities of Marburg, Munich and Frankfurt (Referendar, 1978; Assessor, 1982). *Member:* International Bar Association; German Association for Industrial Property Protection and Copyright (GRUR). *PRACTICE AREAS:* Copyright and Entertainment Law.

DR. ANNA-DOROTHEA POLZER, born Bonn, Germany, December 27, 1953; admitted, 1985, West Germany. *Education:* Universities of Tuebingen, Cologne and Geneva (Referendar, 1977; Assessor, 1980; Doctor of Law, 1987); University of Illinois, Champaign-Urbana (Master of Law, 1983). Research and Teaching Assistant, University of Cologne, 1983-1985. *PRACTICE AREAS:* General Commercial Law; Intellectual Property.

(This Listing Continued)

OF COUNSEL

GREGORY J. THWAITE, born Auckland, New Zealand, December 8, 1954; admitted, 1978, New Zealand; 1987, California; 1990, England and Wales; 1993, Germany Rechtskundiger auf dem Gebiet des Rechts der Vereinigten Staaten von Amerika. *Education:* University of Auckland, New Zealand (B.A., 1978; LL.B. (Hons), 1980); Harvard Law School (LL.M., 1986). Part-time tutor, University of Auckland, 1979-1980. With Buddle, Weir & Co., Solicitors, New Zealand, 1978-1980; with Chapman Tripp & Co., Solicitors, New Zealand, 1981-1985; with Allen Matkins Leck Gamble & Mallory, Attorneys, Los Angeles, California, 1986-1987; with Kelley, Drye & Warren, Attorneys, Los Angeles, California, 1987-1990. Author: "Litigation in America - As Welcome as Sickness or Death," in: International Business Lawyer, Vol. 19, No. 4, April 1991. Co-Author (with Dr. Jürgen Pesch); "German Commercial Law Firms in Transition," International Legal Practitioner Vol. 17, No. 3, September, 1992; "Some Aspects of German Merger and Acquisition Law Explained for Foreign Counsel," International Business Lawyer, Vol. 20, No. 11, December, 1992; "Deciphering the Code," Capital Account, February, 1993. Member, Panel of Arbitrators, American Arbitration Association. American Bar Association; International Bar Association. *PRACTICE AREAS:* Intern, Litigation and Arbitration; Intern, Business Transactions.

SHIRIN A. ENTEZARI, J.D., M.C.L., admitted, 1977, Illinois; 1979, Iran; 1984, District of Columbia (Not admitted in Germany). *Education:* Chicago Kent College of Law (J.D., 1977); Georgetown University Law Center (Master of Comparative Law, 1974); National University of Teheran (LL.B., 1971); International Private Law Program, The Hague (1975). Adjunct Professor of Middle East Law, George Washington University. With Baker & McKenzie, Chicago, 1975-1977; Dr. Kordestani & Associates, Teheran, 1978-1980; Powers & Hall, Washington, D.C., 1981-1982. Member, Board of Governors, Washington Foreign Law Society, 1966-1988. Member, Panel of Arbitrators, American Arbitration Association. Publications: "Middle East Executive Reports." *Member:* American Bar Association; American Society of International Law; The Middle East Institute; Young Lawyers International Association.

JONES, DAY, REAVIS & POGUE

TRITON HAUS
BOCKENHEIMER LANDSTRASSE 42
60323 FRANKFURT AM MAIN, FEDERAL REPUBLIC OF GERMANY
Telephone: 49-69-9726-3939
Telecopier: 49-69-9726-3993.

In Atlanta, Georgia: 3500 One Peachtree Center, 303 Peachtree Street, N.E. Telephone: 404-521-3939. Cable Address: "Attorneys Atlanta". Telex: 54-2711. Telecopier: 404-581-8330.

In Brussels, Belgium: Avenue Louise 480, 7th Floor. B-1050 Brussels. Telephone: 32-2-645-14-11. Telecopier: 32-2-645-14-45.

In Chicago, Illinois: 77 West Wacker. Telephone: 312-782-3939. Telecopier: 312-782-8585.

In Cleveland, Ohio: North Point, 901 Lakeside Avenue. Telephone: 216-586-3939. Cable Address: "Attorneys Cleveland." Telex: 980389. Telecopier: 216-579-0212.

In Columbus, Ohio: 1900 Huntington Center. Telephone: 614-469-3939. Cable Address: "Attorneys Columbus." Telecopier: 614-461-4198.

In Dallas, Texas: 2300 Trammell Crow Center, 2001 Ross Avenue. Telephone: 214-220-3939. Cable Address: "Attorneys Dallas." Telex: 730852. Telecopier: 214-969-5100.

In Geneva, Switzerland: 20, rue de Candolle. Telephone: 41-22-320-2339. Telecopier: 41-22-320-1232.

In Hong Kong: 1501 One Exchange Square, 8 Connaught Place. Telephone: 852-2526-6895. Telecopier: 852-2810-5787.

In Irvine, California: 2603 Main Street, Suite 900. Telephone: 714-851-3939. Telex: 194911 Lawyers LSA. Telecopier: 714-553-7539.

In London, England: One Mount Street. Telephone: 44-171-493-9361. Cable Address: "Surgoe London WI." Telecopier: 44-171-493-9666.

In Los Angeles, California: 555 West Fifth Street, Suite 4600. Telephone: 213-489-3939. Telex: 181439 UD. Telecopier: 213-243-2539.

In New York, New York: 599 Lexington Avenue. Telephone: 212-326-3939. Cable Address: "JONESDAY NEWYORK." Telex: 237013 JDRP UR. Telecopier: 212-755-7306.

In Paris, France: 62, rue du Faubourg Saint-Honore. Telephone: 33-1-44-71-3939. Cable Address: "Surgoe Paris." Telex: 290156 Surgoe. Telecopier: 33-1-49-24-0471.

(This Listing Continued)

JONES, DAY, REAVIS & POGUE, Frankfurt/Main— Continued

In Pittsburgh, Pennsylvania: 500 Grant Street, 31st Floor. Telephone: 412-391-3939. Cable Address: "Attorneys Pittsburgh". Telecopier: 412-394-7959.

In Riyadh, Saudi Arabia: Law Offices of Saud M.A. Shawwaf, P.O. Box 2700. Telephones: (966-1) 465-6543, (966-1) 464-8534 or (966-1) 464-8540. Telex: 401831 SAUCON SJ. Telecopier: (966-1) 464-8480.

In Taipei, Taiwan: 8th Floor, 2 Tun Hwa South Road, Section 2. Telephone: (886-2) 704-6808. Telecopier: (886-2) 704-6791.

In Tokyo, Japan: Toranomon MT Building, 4th Floor, 10-3, Toranomon 3-Chome, Minato-Ku, Tokyo 105, Japan. Telephone: 81-3-3433-3939. Telecopier: 81-3-5401-2725.

In Washington, D.C.: Metropolitan Square, 1450 G Street, N.W. Telephone: 202-879-3939. Cable Address: "Attorneys Washington." Telex: 89-2410 ATTORNEYS WASH. Telecopier: 202-737-2832.

Firm engaged in General International Transactions, Mergers and Acquisitions, Joint Ventures and International Financings, but not authorized (except where indicated) as Rechtsanwälte and not authorized to appear before the German courts or to act as German Lawyers.

MEMBERS OF FIRM IN FRANKFURT

KARL G. HEROLD, born Munich, Germany, February 3, 1947; admitted, 1972, Ohio; 1985, New York; 1990, Conseil Juridique, France; 1991, Rechtskundiger, Germany; 1992, Avocat, France (Not admitted as Rechtsanwalt in Germany). *Education:* Bowling Green State University (B.S., 1969); Case Western Reserve University (J.D., 1972). Order of the Coif.

DR. NORBERT KOCH, born Hamburg, Germany, May 25, 1927; admitted, Rechtsanwalt, Frankfurt/Main, Germany, 1990. *Education:* Marburg and Hamburg Universities (Referendar, 1951; Dr. Jur., 1953). Hamburg Referendariat (Assessor, 1955). Leitender Reg. Direktor, Federal Cartel Office, 1958-1990. Legal Adviser, E.C. Commission, 1959-1990. Hilfsreferent, Ministry of Economics, Antitrust Division, 1957. (Resident, Brussels, Belgium).

RICHARD H. KREINDLER, born New York, New York, April 23, 1959; admitted, 1986, New York; 1991, Conseil Juridique, France; 1992, Avocat, France; 1992, Rechtskundiger, Germany (Not admitted as Rechtsanwalt in Germany). *Education:* Harvard University (A.B., 1980); Ludwig-Maximilians-Universitaet, Munich (Magister, 1982); Columbia University (J.D., 1985). Corresponding Member, International Chamber of Commerce Institute of International Business Law and Practice, 1994—.

OF COUNSEL

DR. HELGA ELIZABETH KROEGER, born Winnipeg, Canada, October 26, 1954; admitted, 1984, Frankfurt, Germany; 1987, California. *Education:* University of Freiburg (First Staatsexamen Law, 1978); State of Baden-Württemberg (Second Staatsexamen Law, 1981); University of Freiburg (Dr. iur, 1983); University of California, Berkeley (Boalt Hall) (LL.M., 1986).

ASSOCIATES

OLIVER PASSAVANT, born Wuerzburg, Germany, April 21, 1956; admitted, 1988, New York and Ohio; 1991, Georgia (Not admitted in Germany). *Education:* Heidelberg University (Staatsexamen Law, 1984); Universite de Lausanne; Harvard University (M.P.A., 1987).

ANSGAR C. REMPP, born Karlsruhe, Germany, October 23, 1962; admitted, 1991, Frankfurt, Germany. *Education:* University of Heidelberg (First Staatsexamen Law, 1988); University of Speyer (M.P.A., 1991); New York University (M.C.J., 1993). Law Clerk Baden-Württemberg District Court Appellate Division (Second Staatsexamen Law, 1991).

DOUGLAS J. WHIPPLE, born Rochester, Pennsylvania, February 4, 1957; admitted, 1989, New York (Not admitted in Germany). *Education:* New York University (B.A., 1984); Georgetown University (M.S.F.S., 1988; J.D., 1988). Phi Beta Kappa.

PHILLIP H. SCHMANDT, born Paris, France, January 9, 1962; admitted, 1990, Texas (Not admitted in Germany). *Education:* Johns Hopkins University (B.A., 1983); University of Texas (J.D., 1990). Phi Beta Kappa; Order of the Coif.

(This Listing Continued)

ANTJE WESTPHAL, born Freiburg, Germany, January 14, 1966; admitted, 1991, Connecticut; 1992, New York; 1994, District of Columbia (Not admitted in Germany). *Education:* Duke University (A.B., 1987); Georgetown University (J.D., 1991).

Languages: English, French, German, Italian, Russian, Spanish.

KAPPUS & HARTMANN

Established in 1947

FRIEDENSSTRASSE 2

D-60311 FRANKFURT/MAIN 1, GERMANY

Telephone: (069) 2 01 86

Telecopier: (069) 29 59 53

Telex: 41 48 53 kaha d

Company Law/Mergers and Acquisitions. Banking Law, Unfair Competition and Antitrust Law. Tax Law, Environmental Law, Aviation Law, Labour Law.

MEMBERS OF FIRM

DR. GEORG KAPPUS (1909-1991).

DR. KLAUS-DIETER HARTMANN, born Frankfurt am Main, Germany, June 17, 1930; admitted, 1958, Germany; 1966, Notary. *Education:* J. W. Goethe University, Frankfurt (Dr. jur., 1952). President of the Chamber of Notaries Public, Frankfurt am Main, 1989—. *Member:* Frankfurt am Main Lawyers Association. *LANGUAGES:* German, English and French. *PRACTICE AREAS:* Mergers and Acquisitions; Company Law; Notarial Services.

DR. KLAUS ENGFER, born Berlin, Germany, September 5, 1937; admitted, 1968, Germany; 1978, Notary. *Education:* J. W. Goethe University, Frankfurt am Main, University of Geneva (Dr. jur., 1970). *Member:* Frankfurt am Main Lawyers Association. *LANGUAGES:* German, English and French. *PRACTICE AREAS:* Banking Law; Aviation Law; Notarial Services.

DR. HANS-JÜRGEN KION, born Berlin, Germany, January 6, 1939; admitted, 1976, Germany, Tax Law Specialist; 1991, Notary. *Education:* J. W. Goethe University, Frankfurt am Main (Dr. jur., 1970). Professor, Tax Law, Technical University of Frankfurt. *Member:* Frankfurt am Main Lawyers Association; German Tax Lawyers Association. *LANGUAGES:* German and English. *PRACTICE AREAS:* Company Law; Tax Law; Notarial Services.

DR. HANS GEORG FISCHER, born Bremen, Germany, April 15, 1951; admitted, 1982, Germany. *Education:* Albert Ludwigs University, Freiburg/Breisgau (Dr. jur., 1983). *LANGUAGES:* German and English. *PRACTICE AREAS:* Litigation.

DR. PETER HOH-MALEWSKI, born Frankfurt am Main, Germany, September 22, 1957; admitted, 1986, Germany. *Education:* J. W. Goethe University, Frankfurt am Main (Dr. jur., 1994). *LANGUAGES:* German, English and Spanish. *PRACTICE AREAS:* Competition and Antitrust Law; Environment Law.

ULRICH HARTMANN, born Frankfurt am Main, Germany, April 29, 1961; admitted, 1989, Germany. *Education:* J. W. Goethe University, Frankfurt am Main. *Member:* German-Spanish Lawyers Association. *LANGUAGES:* German, English and Spanish. *PRACTICE AREAS:* Competition Law; Trademarks.

ASSOCIATES

GREGOR SEGNER, born Frankfurt am Main, Germany, December 12, 1961; admitted, 1991, Germany. *Education:* J.W. Goethe University, Frankfurt am Main. *LANGUAGES:* German and English. *PRACTICE AREAS:* Administrative Law; Tax Law.

CATRIN RAANE, born Düsseldorf, Germany, September 15, 1964; admitted, 1992, Germany. *Education:* Justus-Liebig-University Giessen and University Warwick, Great Britain. *LANGUAGES:* German, English and French. *PRACTICE AREAS:* Labour Law.

ANNETTE RUTH, born Hanau, Germany, May 29, 1961; admitted, 1992, Germany. *Education:* J.W. Goethe University, Frankfurt. *LANGUAGES:* German, English, Russian and French. *PRACTICE AREAS:* Company Law; Competition Law.

(This Listing Continued)

FRIEDRICH WERK, born Bielefeld, Germany, March 15, 1961; admitted, 1988, Germany. *Education:* University Bielefeld; University Lausanne, Switzerland. *LANGUAGES:* German, English and French. *PRACTICE AREAS:* International Law; Antitrust Law.

Languages: German, English, French, Spanish.

KENYON & KENYON

Established in 1879

BOCKENHEIMER LANDSTRASSE 97-99
60325 FRANKFURT
FRANKFURT/MAIN, GERMANY
Telephone: 69-97-58-05-0
Telecopier: 69-97-58-05-99

New York, N.Y., Office One Broadway. 10004. Telephone: 212-425-7200. Telecopier: (212) 425-5288.
Washington, D.C. Office: 1025 Connecticut Avenue, N.W. 20036. Telephone: 202-429-1776. Washington, D.C.". Telecopier: (202) 429-0796.

Intellectual Property Practice. Patents, Trademarks, Copyrights, Trade Secrets, Unfair Competition, Computer Law, Licensing and related Trade Regulation, Antitrust and International Trade Matters, Sports Marketing, Entertainment Law. Trials, Appeals and Arbitration.

FIRM PROFILE: Kenyon & Kenyon, founded in 1879, specializes in the practice of law relating to intellectual property. Our practice includes the procurement and enforcement of legal rights relating to patents, trademarks and copyrights. This involves counseling clients on intellectual property matters, negotiating and drafting agreements, trial and appellate litigation in the Federal and State Courts in all areas of the country and before the International Trade Commission, as well as preparing applications to obtain patents, trademark registrations, and copyright registrations, and guiding these applications through the appropriate administrative bodies in Washington, D.C. The firm also renders advice and representation in closely allied fields, such as antitrust, trade protection, franchising, entertainment, computer law and product advertising and marketing.

RESIDENT PARTNER

PATRICK J. BIRDE, born New York, N.Y., July 25, 1951; admitted, 1983, New York (Not admitted in Germany). *Education:* Herbert Lehman College of the City University of New York (B.S., 1977); St. John's University (J.D., 1982). *Member:* New York State Bar Association, New York Intellectual Property Law Association; American Intellectual Property Law Association. *PRACTICE AREAS:* Intellectual Property.

RESIDENT ASSOCIATES

JEFFREY M. BUTLER, born 1962; admitted, 1989, Connecticut; 1990, New York; 1991, District of Columbia (Not admitted in Germany). *Education:* Trinity College (B.S., 1984); George Washington University (J.D., 1989). *Member:* The Association of the Bar of the City of New York; American Bar Association (Member, Sections on: Business Law; International and Practice Law). *PRACTICE AREAS:* Intellectual Property.

WILLIAM C. GEHRIS, admitted, 1993, New York (Not admitted in Germany). *Education:* Princeton University (B.S., magna cum laude, 1988); Columbia University (J.D., 1992). Phi Beta Kappa; Tau Beta Pi. *PRACTICE AREAS:* Intellectual Property.

(For Biographical data on all Personnel, see Professional Biographies at New York, New York)

KOCH, HARTTMANN, FUCHS & ARNECKE

HAMBURGER ALLEE 2
(PLAZA CENTER)
60486 FRANKFURT/MAIN, GERMANY
Telephone: 069-77 01 41
Cable Address: "INTLA"
Telex: 41 4251 (intla d)
Telefax: 069-70 02 70

Dresden, Germany Office: Goetheallee 13, 01309. Telephone: 0351 33 78 18. Telefax: 0351 33 78 19.

(This Listing Continued)

Antitrust, Banking and Financial Services, Corporation, Environmental Protection Law, Labor Law, Mergers and Acquisitions, Pharmaceutical Law, Tax, Unfair Competition, General Practice.

MEMBERS OF FIRM

HERMANN KOCH, born Reval, Estonia, February 11, 1923; admitted, 1956, Hessen. *Education:* University of Frankfurt. Notary Public. *Member:* Frankfurt Bar Association; German Bar Association; American Chamber of Commerce in Germany; Association Litteraire et Artistique Internationale (ALAI); British-German Trade Council; German-American Lawyers' Association; International Bar Association (Member, Section on Business Law, Committee W-Communications and Entertainment Law, 1982—). *LANGUAGES:* German and English.

DIETER E. HARTTMANN, born Trier, Germany, August 9, 1929; admitted, 1961, Frankfurt. *Education:* Free University of Berlin; Tulane University, New Orleans, Louisiana (M.C.L., 1956). Notary. *Member:* German British Jurists' Association; American Chamber of Commerce in Germany; German-American Lawyers' Association; Association Litteraire et Artistique Internationale. *LANGUAGES:* German, English and French:

DR. VOLKER M. FUCHS, born Polaun, CSFR, February 24, 1945; admitted, 1976, Frankfurt. *Education:* Universities of Frankfurt, Berlin and Giessen (Dr. jur., 1979). Specialized Tax Counsel. Author: "Warranty in Leasing Contracts in the Light of the Law Concerning Standard Business Conditions," 1979; "Retention of Title under German Law," 1981. *Member:* German Bar Association. (Also at Dresden Office). *LANGUAGES:* German and English.

GEORG ARNECKE, born Berlin, Germany, November 7, 1939; admitted, 1968, Frankfurt. *Education:* Universities of Berlin and Munich. Notary. Member of the Board, 1976-1982 and Managing Director, 1983-1985, F.W. Woolworth Co., GmbH, Frankfurt. *Member:* German Bar Association. *LANGUAGES:* German and English.

KARL-FRIEDRICH SCHAUHOFF, born Hilden/Rhld., Germany, January 18, 1957; admitted, 1985, Düsseldorf. *Education:* University of Munich; Southern Methodist University (LL.M., 1989). Phi Alpha Delta. *Member:* American Bar Association (Member, Sections on International and Business Law; Forum Committee on the Entertainment and Sports Industries); German-American Lawyers' Association. *LANGUAGES:* German, English and French.

LANGE & von BRAUNSCHWEIG

FRANKFURT/MAIN, GERMANY

(See Wessing Berenberg-Gossler Zimmermann Lange)

Commercial Law, Corporations, German and E.C. Antitrust, Trademark and Copyright, Computer Law, Labor, Administration, Environmental, Product Liability, Banking, Insurance, Real Property, Estate, Tax Law, Litigation, Conveyancing, General Practice. Civil Law Notaries.

LEIPNITZ & PARTNER

Associated with Pannell Kerr Forster, Frankfurt am Maim

Established in 1976

FEUERBACHSTRAßE 8
60325 FRANKFURT/MAIN, GERMANY
Telephone: (069) 17000017
Telecopier: (069) 17000027
Cable Address: "fraius"

Administrative, Banking, Commercial, Company, Corporation, Customs, EC, Entertainment, Intellectual Property, International Public, Labor, Real Property, Tax, Antitrust and Unfair Competition Law. Mergers and Acquisitions. Litigation. Notary.

MEMBERS OF FIRM

WERNER LEIPNITZ, born Nördlingen, Germany, October 6, 1948; admitted, 1976, West Germany; 1984, Frankfurt Court of Appeals; 1986, Notary. *Education:* University of Frankfurt (1967-1972). Referendar, 1972. Assessor, 1976. Chairman of Supervisory Board of BITAG Aktiengesellschaft - Beteiligungen in Industrie und Technik and of Marek Lieberberg Konzertagentur GmbH. Author: "Intellectual Property Under the GATT Treaty and Industrial Property Rights in Germany," 1994. Co-Author: "Combating Counterfeits in Germany," 1992; "Manual for Investment Counseling and Property Management," 1994. *Member:* Frankfurt Bar As-

(This Listing Continued)

LEIPNITZ & PARTNER, *Frankfurt/Main—Continued*

sociation; Association International de Jeunes Advocates; Deutsche Vereinigung für gewerblichen Rechtsschutz und Urheberrecht (German Association for Intellectual Property and Copyright); German-British Jurists' Association. *LANGUAGES:* German and English. *PRACTICE AREAS:* Corporation Law; EC Law; Intellectual Property Law; EC Antitrust Law; Unfair Competition Law.

DR. ERICH HARTMANN, born Heidelberg, Germany, April 3, 1923; admitted, 1989, West Germany. *Education:* Universities of Berlin (1941) and Heidelberg (1945-1948); University of Chicago Law School (1950). Referendar, 1948. Assessor, 1952. Government Official, Federal Debt Administration, 1953-1973. Member of City Government, Bad Homburg, 1973-1979. Consultant for foreign companies, Rhein-Main-Area, 1982—. Author: "Fragen des Klassischen Völkerrechts im Urteil des Internationalen Militärtribunals," 1952 (Dissertation). *Member:* Frankfurt Bar Association. *LANGUAGES:* German, French and English. *PRACTICE AREAS:* Administrative Law; Public International Law; Real Property Law.

DAGOBERT BELAU, born Königsberg, Germany, August 19, 1932; admitted, 1978, West Germany. *Education:* Universities of Tübingen (1952-1954) and Freiburg (1954-1958); Johns Hopkins Center, Bologna (1964-1965). Referendar, 1959. Assessor, 1964. Head of Legal Department, Kalle AG, 1966-1968. Legal Advisor, Videothek Programm GmbH, 1970-1973. Legal Advisor, CBS Schallplatten GmbH, 1974-1984. Managing Director, German Anti-Piracy Association e.V., 1984-1985. *Member:* Frankfurt Bar Association. *LANGUAGES:* German, English, Italian, French and Spanish. *PRACTICE AREAS:* Entertainment Law; Intellectual Property Law; Litigation.

DR. CHRISTIAN PABST, born Duisburg-Rheinhausen, Germany, May 16, 1963; admitted, 1993, Frankfurt. *Education:* Friedrich-Wilhelm-Universität of Bonn (1983-1989); Referendar, Berlin (1990-1993); (Dr. jur., 1994). Author: "Chances for More Flexible Working Hours - A Comparison of the Framework Collective Agreements for the Area of North-Württemberg/ North-Baden from 1984-1990," 1994; General Conditions regarding Commencement and Termination of Employment Relationships," 1994. *Member:* Frankfurt Bar Association. *LANGUAGES:* German and English. *PRACTICE AREAS:* European and German Labor Law; Litigation; Unfair Competition Law; Intellectual Property Law.

Member of LAWROPE-Association of European Law Firms

LEISSE & LEISSE

Established in 1972

OPERNPLATZ 6
60313 FRANKFURT
FRANKFURT/AM MAIN, GERMANY
Telephone: (0 69) 20 472
Telefax: (0 69) 20 474

General Civil and Notarial Practice, Litigation including Appellate Courts, Commercial, Corporate, Domestic Relations, Industrial and Intellectual Property, Labor and Employment, Wills and Estates, Real Estate and Unfair Competition Law.

MEMBERS OF FIRM

DR. GERD LEISSE, born Trier, Germany, March 18, 1930; admitted, 1964, Cologne; 1967, Frankfurt am Main; 1980, Notar. *Education:* Haverford College, Philadelphia (Political Science, Fulbright Scholar, 1954); Institut d'Etudes Politiques, Paris (1957); University of Frankfurt am Main (Doctor of Law, 1960). Author: "Die Gründe der mangelnden Regierungstabilität im Frankreich der IV. Republik und die verfassungsrechtlichen Möglichkeiten zu ihrer Behebung " (The Reasons for the Ministerial Instability in the Fourth French Republic and the Constitutional Possibilities for their Removal - Diss.); "Schadensersatz durch befristete Unterlassung " (Damage Compensation through Temporary Ceasing and Desisting) in Festschrift für Fritz Traub, 1994 and several articles on unfair competition and compensation topics, published in Gewerblicher Rechtsschutz und Urheberrecht (GRUR). Executive Board Member, Phywe AG, Göttingen, 1965-1967. President, Recognition Equipment International, Inc., Dallas/-Frankfurt am Main, 1968-1971. *Member:* International Bar Association; German-American Lawyers' Association; German Bar Association; German Association for the Protection of Industrial Property and Copyright Law; Frankfurt Society for Commerce, Industry and Science. *LANGUAGES:* German, English and French. *PRACTICE AREAS:* Industrial

(This Listing Continued)

and Intellectual Property; Commercial; Corporate; Unfair Competition; Labor and Employment.

LISETTE LEISSE, born Frankfurt am Main, Germany, December 27, 1932; admitted, 1964, Frankfurt am Main; 1974, Notar. *Education:* University of Frankfurt am Main; Institut d'Etudes Politiques, Paris. *LANGUAGES:* German, French and English. *PRACTICE AREAS:* Domestic Relations; Real Estate; Wills and Estates Law.

LINKLATERS & PAINES

Established in 1992

GRÜNEBURGWEG 14
D-60322 FRANKFURT/MAIN, GERMANY
Telephone: (69) 59 01 25
Fax: (69) 597 45 02

London, England Office: Barrington House, 59-67 Gresham Street, EC2V 7JA. Telephone: 0171-606 7080. Cable Address: Linklaters, London, EC2V 7JA. Telegrams: Linklaters, London. Telex: 884349. Fax: 0171-606 5113.

English and General International Law Practice.

RESIDENT PARTNER

A.G. Hickinbotham

(For full list of offices see entry at London, England)

ANWALTSBÜRO LOTZ & PARTNER

Established in 1986

STRESEMANNALLEE 41
60596 FRANKFURT/MAIN, GERMANY
Telephone: 069/63 20 52
Fax: 069/63 53 33

General Business Practice, International Joint Venture and Construction, Company, Labour, Competition, Business Contracts, Landlord-Tenant, European Community, International, Real Estate, Notaries, Litigation and International Arbitration, Environmental Law.

MEMBERS OF FIRM

BURKARD LOTZ, born Somborn, March 9, 1955; admitted, 1984, Frankfurt (Court of Appeal-Oberlandesgericht). *Education:* University of Freiburg i. Br.; University of Munich. Member: Canadian-German Chamber of Industry and Commerce, Montreal, 1981; Legal Department of Philipp Holzmann Aktiengesellschaft, Frankfurt, 1982-1986. *Member:* Frankfurt, German and International Bar Associations; German Association for Construction Law; American Chamber of Commerce in Germany; Deutsch-Österreichisch-Schweizerisch-Liechtensteinische Anwaltsvereinigung e.V.; Stellaner Vereinigung Deutschlands e.V. *LANGUAGES:* German, English and French. *PRACTICE AREAS:* National/International Construction Law; Business Law; Commercial Law; National/International Arbitration; Appellate Practice.

NICOLA LOTZ, born Düsseldorf, November 3, 1959; admitted, 1988, Frankfurt. *Education:* University of Heidelberg; University of Frankfurt. *LANGUAGES:* German, English and French. *PRACTICE AREAS:* Civil Law; Leases and Leasing.

ARNE GUTH, born Marburg, March 10, 1964; admitted, 1994, Frankfurt/Main. *Education:* Justus Liebig Universitat, Gießen. *LANGUAGES:* German and English. *PRACTICE AREAS:* Company Law; Labour Law; Wills; Environmental Law.

MATTHEWS LAW OFFICES

Counsellor and Attorney at Law

JUSTINIANSTRASSE 22
60322 FRANKFURT/MAIN, GERMANY
Telephone: 069-95515230
International: (49) 69-95515230
Telecopy: 069-95515230
International: (49) 69-595770

International Commercial Transactions, Corporate Financing and International Trade, Mergers and Business Consolidations, International Private Investments emphasizing Acquisition, Finance and Capital Venture Place-

(This Listing Continued)

ments, Business Law and International Contracts, Arbitration Disputes, US Civil and Criminal Law, EEO and Military Law, Complex Civil Litigation, Immigration Law, Federal Employment and Tort Claims.

LEODIS C. MATTHEWS, born Eloy, Arizona, June 20, 1949; admitted, 1973, Oregon; 1979, District of Columbia; 1982, California; U.S. Supreme Court (Not admitted in Germany). *Education:* Lewis and Clark College (B.S., 1970); Northwestern School of Law (Juris Doctor, 1973). Deputy District Attorney, Oregon, 1973-1977; Senior Counsel, U.S. House of Representatives, Select Committee on Assassinations, 1977-1979. Senior Assistant United States Attorney, Southern District of California, San Diego, California. Senior Trial Attorney, U.S. Department of Justice, Criminal Division, Organized Crime and Racketeering Section; Civil Division, Commercial and International Trade Litigation Sections, 1979-1984. Who's Who in American Law, 1989-1993. *Member:* Oregon State Bar; District of Columbia Bar (Member, Government Contracts and International Law Committees); Bar Association of the District of Columbia; State Bar of California; American Arbitration Association; Society of Professionals in Dispute Resolution; National Association of Criminal Defense Attorneys; President, Bar Association of American Lawyers in Germany (BAALG), 1990-1992. *LANGUAGES:* English and German.

MELCHERS, SCHUBERT, STOCKER, STURIES

Established in 1973

BEETHOVENSTRASSE 29
D-60325 FRANKFURT/MAIN, GERMANY
Telephone: (49-69) 9757 3227
Telecopier: (49-69) 9757 3220

Heidelberg, Germany Office: Slevogtstrasse 6, D-69126 Heidelberg. Mailing Address: P.O. Box 10 52 22, D-69042 Heidelberg. Telephone: (49-6221) 39 91 01. Telefax: (49-6221) 37 91 00; 37 40 69.
Berlin, Germany Office: Schiffbauerdamm 17, D-10117 Berlin. Telephone: (49-30) 2252 2133. Telecopier: (49-30) 2252 2108.
Zwickau, Germany Office: Kolpingstrasse 28, D-08058 Zwickau. Telephone: (49-375) 294023/4/5. Telecopier: (49-375) 521629.

Administrative Law, Banking, Commercial, Contracts, Corporate, EC-Law, Environmental Law, General Practice, Inheritance, Intellectual Property and Trade Marks, Arbitration, International Private Law, Investment, Labour Law, Mergers and Acquisitions, National and EC Antitrust, National and International Tax Law, Real Estate, Trade and Trade Show Law, Unfair Competition.

FIRM PROFILE: *The law firm was founded in 1973 as a multidisciplinary partnership of lawyers, certified public accountants and tax advisors. Today, 31 professionals, of which 24 are lawyers, offer services and advice in the firm's offices in Berlin, Frankfurt/Main, Heidelberg and Zwickau. The multidisciplinary combination of legal services provides clients with comprehensive advice in the fields of business law, tax law, business administration and auditing.*

RESIDENT PARTNERS

IMMO PETERSEN, born Hamburg, October 20, 1946; admitted, 1977, Germany; Sworn Auditor, Germany, 1991. *Education:* Universities of Munich, Giessen; University of California/Berkeley. Research and Teaching Assistant at the Institute for Trade and Commercial Law. University of Giessen (1971-1973). *Member:* German Association for the Protection of Industrial Property Rights; German and Frankfurt Bar Associations. *LANGUAGES:* German, English and French. *PRACTICE AREAS:* National and International Tax Law; Auditing and Valuation; Mergers and Acquisitions; Corporate and Company Law; Arbitration; International Law.

GERHARD BOSS, born Frankfurt, Germany, November 4, 1956; admitted, 1986, West Germany. *Education:* University of Frankfurt am Main. *Member:* German Association for the Protection of Industrial Property Rights (GRUR); German and Frankfurt Bar Associations. *LANGUAGES:* German and English. *PRACTICE AREAS:* Commercial Law; Unfair Competition; Intellectual Property; Trade Show Law.

ASSOCIATE

DR. IUR. UTR. THORSTEN HEYNE, born Frankfurt/Main, December 8, 1959; admitted, 1991, Germany. *Education:* Universities of Heidelberg, Mainz and Edinburgh (Master of Laws). *Member:* German and Frankfurt/Main Bar Associations. *LANGUAGES:* German, English and

(This Listing Continued)

French. *PRACTICE AREAS:* Intellectual Property; Commercial; International Private Law.

CERTIFIED PUBLIC ACCOUNTANTS AND TAX ADVISORS

PROF. DR. RER. POL. WINFRIED GAIL, born Koblenz, December 22, 1931; admitted, 1966, German Tax Courts. Tax Advisor, Germany, 1966. Certified Public Accountant, Germany, 1968. *Education:* University of Mannheim (Dipl.-Kfm., Dr. rer. pol.). *Author: Handbuch der Familienunternehmen,* Köln, 1977-1981. Co-Author: "Auswirkungen des Aktiengesetzes 1965 auf die Kommanditgesellschaft auf Aktien," Die Wirtschaftsprüfung 1966, p. 425; "Gemeinsamkeiten und Abweichungen zwischen Handels- und Steuerbilanz in der Bundesrepublik Deutschland," Journal UEC 1973, S. 2; "Bindung der Finanzverwaltung an die Rechtsprechung der Steuergerichte," Steuerberater-Jahrbuch 1978 - 1979, p. 461; "Gibt es eine Maßgeblichkeit der Steuerbilanz für die Handelsbilanz (umgekehrte Maßgeblichkeit)?", in: Probleme der Rechts-und Steuerberatung in mittelständischen Unternehmen, Köln 1988. Professor at the Faculty of Law and Economics at Technische Hochschule Darmstadt. *Member:* Institute of C.P.A. in Germany, Member of the Administrative Board (I.d.W.); Institute of Tax Advisors. *LANGUAGES:* German, English and French. *PRACTICE AREAS:* National and International Tax Law; Auditing and Valuation.

(For complete biographical data on Personnel at Berlin, Heidelberg and Zwickau offices see Professional Biographies at those locations).

MORGAN, LEWIS & BOCKIUS

SIESMAYERSTRAßE 44
FRANKFURT/MAIN 60323, GERMANY
Telephone: 069-72-6711
Telecopy: 069-72-6781
MCI Mail: 6333674
CompuServe: 100317.2557

Philadelphia, Pennsylvania Office: 2000 One Logan Square, 19103-6993. Telephone: 215-963-5000.
Washington, D.C. Office: 1800 M Street, N.W., 20036. Telephone: 202-467-7000.
New York, New York Office: 101 Park Avenue, 10178. Telephone: 212-309-6000.
Los Angeles, California Office: 801 South Grand Avenue, 90017-3189. Telephone: 213-612-2500.
Miami, Florida Office: 5300 First Union Financial Center, 200 South Biscayne Boulevard, 33131-2339. Telephone: 305-579-0300.
Harrisburg, Pennsylvania Office: One Commerce Square, 417 Walnut Street, 17101-1904. Telephone: 717-237-4000.
Princeton, New Jersey Office: 100 Overlook Center, 08540. Telephone: 609-520-6600.
Newport Beach, California Office: 4675 MacArthur Court, Suite 740, 92660. Telephone: 714-851-6333.
London, England Office: 4 Carlton Gardens, Pall Mall. Telephone: 0171-839-1677.
Brussels, Belgium Office: Rue Guimard 7, B-1040. Telephone: 32-2/512.55.01.
Tokyo, Japan Office: CS Tower, 1-11-30 Akasaka, Minato-ku. Telephone: 81-3-587-2900.

FIRM PROFILE: *Morgan, Lewis & Bockius is an international law firm with 750 lawyers and a diverse practice. Founded in 1873, the Firm was one of the first to develop an intergrated, multicity practice.*

The Firm's practice areas include antitrust; arbitration and ADR proceedings; banking, thrift and consumer financial services; bankruptcy and reorganization; business and corporate; construction; customs; energy regulation; environmental; executive compensation and employee benefits; food, drug and cosmetics regulation; foreign direct investment in the United States; government contracts; government regulation; immigration; insurance and reinsurance; intellectual property and technology, including patent, trademark and copyright; international financings; international trade; labor and employment; legislation and government relations; leveraged lease and project financings; litigation; mergers and acquisitions; municipal finance; personal law; products liability; public utilities; real estate; securities; tax; and transportation law.

(This Listing Continued)

MORGAN, LEWIS & BOCKIUS, *Frankfurt/Main—*
Continued

MEMBERS OF FIRM IN FRANKFURT/MAIN

ROBERT V. DALY, born November 7, 1938; admitted, 1967, Michigan; admitted in Germany as Rechtsbeistand. *Education:* Georgetown University (A.B., 1960; J.D., 1965). Fellow, Institut Fuer Auslaendisches und Internationales Wirtschaftsrecht, Frankfurt/Main, 1965-1966. *Member:* German-American Lawyers Association.

CHRISTOPHER C. KING, born February 16, 1961; admitted, 1983, New York; 1986, California; 1991, Pennsylvania; 1992, Rechtskundiger. *Education:* Georg-August-Universität (1978); University of California, Los Angeles (B.A., 1979; J.D., 1982).

PETER Y. SOLMSSEN, born January 24, 1955; admitted, 1980, Pennsylvania; 1987, Frankfurt, Federal Republic of Germany (Rechtskundiger). *Education:* Harvard University (A.B., 1976); Oxford University (Brasenose College); University of Pennsylvania Law School (J.D., 1980). Law Clerk to U.S. District Court Judge Clarence C. Newcomer, 1980-1982.

OF COUNSEL

HERMANN J. BOLTEN, born September 27, 1944; admitted, 1975-1979, Celle, Federal Republic of Germany; 1993, Frankfurt am Main, Federal Republic of Germany. *Education:* University of Bond (Referendar, 1971); Hamburg (Assessor, 1974).

Members of the Firm, Counsel, Of Counsel and Associates in Philadelphia and Harrisburg, Pennsylvania, Washington, D.C., New York, New York, Los Angeles and Newport Beach, California, Miami, Florida, Princeton, New Jersey, Brussels, Belgium and Tokyo, Japan are listed in the Biographical Section respectively.

MUELLER WEITZEL WEISNER

FRANKFURT/MAIN, GERMANY

(See Hengeler Mueller Weitzel Wirtz)

NAAB SKARNICEL SCHUBERT

Established in 1959

HOLBEINSTRASSE 74
D-60596 FRANKFURT/MAIN, GERMANY
Telephone: 49-69-63 40 61
Telefax: 49-69-63 93 82

Public and Private Building Law, National Tax Law, Labour Law, EDP and Data Protection Law, Real Estate, Cartel Law, Company Law, Unfair Competition, Industrial Property Law, Public Law, Administrative Law, Medical Profession Law, Liability Law, State Liability and Public Compensation Law.
A Member of AdvoSelect EEIG, a network of law firms pooling their resources in special fields on crossborder cases, specializing in business law for middle sized companies. AdvoSelect is represented in 51 cities throughout Europe.

MEMBERS OF FIRM

MICHAEL NAAB, born Dahn, Germany, October 18, 1943; admitted, 1972, Germany; 1987, Notary. *Education:* Universities of Heidelberg and Freiburg (Germany).

PETER SKARNICEL, born Munich, Germany, February 15, 1956; admitted, 1983, Germany. *Education:* University of Frankfurt.

HANS G. SCHUBERT, born Offenbach, Germany, May 3, 1960; admitted, 1990, Germany. *Education:* Universities of Würzburg and Frankfurt.

WOLFGANG E. TRAUTNER, born Hanau, Germany, October 1, 1958; admitted, 1991, Germany. *Education:* Washington High School, Tacoma, Washington; University of Frankfurt.

ASSOCIATES

DOROTHEA MARX, born Munich, Germany, December 22, 1957; admitted, 1988, Germany. *Education:* University of Frankfurt; Institute for Labour, Commercial and Civil Law (1981-1984). *Member:* Parliament (Deutscher Bundestag).

(This Listing Continued)

PETER J. HADASCH, born Augsburg, Germany, October 22, 1952; admitted, 1984, Syndikusanwalt. *Education:* University of Frankfurt.

JAN-HENRIK WETTERS, born Bremerhaven, Germany, February 18, 1960; admitted, 1993, Germany. *Education:* Universities of Kiel and Frankfurt.

HAGEN VIETZ, born Frankfurt, Germany, December 24, 1963; admitted, 1994, Germany. *Education:* Newport Hills High School, Bellevue, Washington; University of Frankfurt.

Languages: German and English

LESLIE I. NIMS

MÜNZENBERGER STRASSE 4
D-60389 FRANKFURT/MAIN 60, GERMANY
Telephone: (069) 467096 *International:* 011-49-69-467096
Telefax: (069) 467097 *International:* 011-49-69-467097

Indianapolis, Indiana Office: 10 West Market Street, 500 Market Tower, 46204. Telephone: (317) 464-5309. Fax: (317) 464-8252. Voice Mail: (317) 786-8759. E-Mail: (317) 786-0830.

Litigation in Civil and Criminal Defense Matters before U.S. Civil and Military Tribunals in Europe, Business Management Consultations, Computer Applications. Admitted to all military courts and tribunals as individual defense counsel.

LESLIE I. NIMS, born New Haven, Connecticut, April 4, 1940; admitted, 1973, Indiana and U.S. District Court of the Southern District of Indiana; 1979, U.S. Tax Court, U.S. Court of Military Appeals; 1981, U.S. Court of International Trade and West Berlin. *Education:* Indiana University (B.A., Journalism, 1966); Indiana University School of Law (J.D., 1973). Research Fellowship and Research Assistantship, Mass Communications Research, Indiana University Graduate School 1968-1969. With: E.J. Bellen Law Offices, Germany, 1973. Lecturer: Central Texas College, Hanau, Germany, 1975; Law Enforcement and Business Management, City College of Chicago, Wiesbaden, Germany, 1980; University of Maryland, Heidelberg, Germany, 1983. Program Manager, Central Texas College, Law Enforcement and Business Management, West Berlin and Northern Germany, 1977. Adjunct Professor, Programs leading to MBA and DBA in Industrial Management, Pacific States University, Salzburg and Graz, Austria and Uxbridge, England, 1979-1983. *Member:* Indiana, New York, American and International Bar Associations; Bar Association of American Lawyers in Germany; International Union of Lawyers. *LANGUAGES:* English and German.

NÖRR, STIEFENHOFER & LUTZ

Established in 1989

FREIHERR-VOM-STEIN-STRAßE 11
60323 FRANKFURT/MAIN, GERMANY
Telephone: 49-69-172917
Telecopier: 49-69-172916

Munich, Germany Office: Brienner Str. 28, 80333 Munich, Postfach 101121, 80085 Munich. Telephone: 49-89-280111. Telecopier: 49-89-280110.
Berlin, Germany Office: Schlüterstraße 36, D-10629 Berlin. Telephone: 49-30-8836700. Telecopier: 49-30-8835052.
Dresden, Germany Office: Böhmertstraße 3, 01099 Dresden. Telephone: 49-351-5671188, 49-351-5671187. Telecopier: 49-351-5671186.
Prague, Czech Republic Office: Masarykovo nábřeži 30, 11000 Prague 1. Telephone: 42-2-24913396, 42-2-24913882. Telecopier: 42-2-24911836.
Budapest, Hungary Office: Becsí utca 5/I. 1-2, 1052 Budapest V. Telephone: 36-1-1174905; 36-1-1378293. Telecopier: 36-1-1184035.
Warsaw, Poland Office: Kancelaria Adwokacka Sp. Z o. o. UL. Nowogrodzka 50, 00950 Warsaw. Telephone: 48-2-6216232. Telecopier: 48-2-6251976.
Brussels, Belgium EEC Office: 106 Avenue Louise, 1050 Brussels. Telephone: 32-2-6470650. Telecopier: 32-2-6464729.
Moscow, Russia Office: Ul. Levoberezhnaya, 32. 125475. Telephone: 7-095-4585822; 7-095-4585792. Telecopier: 7-095-4585782.

German and International Practice, Corporate, Commercial, Mergers and Acquisitions, Finance and Banking, Tax, EEC, Public and Constitutional Law, Antitrust, Real Estate, Construction, Labor, Insurance, Landlord-Tenant, Leasing, Product Liability, Estate, Aviation, Energy, Health, Food and Drugs, Industrial Property, Copyright, Trademarks, Unfair Competi-

(This Listing Continued)

tion, Media, Telecommunications, Advertising, White Collar Crime, Administrative and Planning Law, Environmental and Waste Law, Litigation and Arbitration, Joint Ventures, Appellate, Civil, Federal, Legislative, Trial Practice, Advice to Legislative Institutions in Eastern Europe, Eastern European Law.

PARTNERS

DR. THOMAS SCHÜRRLE, born Stuttgart, Germany, March 20, 1956; admitted, 1985, Germany; 1988, New York. *Education:* Universities of Heidelberg and Montpellier; University of Michigan Law School (LL.M., 1987). Assistant Lecturer, University of Heidelberg, 1980-1983. (Also Partner in charge of Brussels Office). *LANGUAGES:* German, English and French. *PRACTICE AREAS:* Corporate Law; Mergers and Acquisitions Law; Antitrust Law; EEC Law.

DR. THOMAS BERGMANN, born Altenburg, Germany, August 26, 1950; admitted, 1980, Germany. *Education:* University of Frankfurt am Main; European University Institute Florence. Assistant Lecturer, University of Frankfurt am Main, 1978-1979. *LANGUAGES:* German, English and Italian. *PRACTICE AREAS:* Corporate Law; Commercial Law; Litigation.

DIPL.-KFM. MICHAEL BÖTTCHER, born Hanau, Germany, March 9, 1953; admitted, 1983, Germany; as Notary Public, 1990. *Education:* University of Frankfurt/Main. *LANGUAGES:* German, English and Spanish. *PRACTICE AREAS:* Commercial Law; Real Estate; Litigation.

ASSOCIATES

KERSTIN MAST, born Stuttgart, Germany, 1964; admitted, 1993, Germany. *Education:* University of Cologne. *LANGUAGES:* German, English and French. *PRACTICE AREAS:* Mergers and Acquisitions; Corporate Law; Commercial law; Tax Law.

ALEXANDER DOMINIK WENDEL, born Hochheim/Main, November 22, 1964; admitted, 1994, Germany. *Education:* University of Passau. *LANGUAGES:* German, English, French and Japanese. *PRACTICE AREAS:* Commercial Law; Civil Law.

OF COUNSEL

DR. HANS-JÜRGEN MARTENS, born Hamburg, Germany, August 8, 1930; admitted, 1973, Frankfurt, Germany; as Certified Public Accountant, 1963. *Education:* Universities of Freiburg, Bonn and Paris. With KPMG Deutsche Treuhandgesellschaft Wirtschaftsprüfungsgesellschaft, Frankfurt and Paris, 1957-1982; Member of Management Board (Vorstand) of Adidas AG, 1983-1991. *Member:* Institut der Wirtschaftsprüfer (Association of Certified Public Accountants). *LANGUAGES:* German, French, English, Spanish. *PRACTICE AREAS:* Mergers and Acquisitions; Financial and Banking Law; Tax Law.

DR. ULRICH KRISZELEIT, born Insterburg, Germany, August 30, 1912; admitted, 1950, Germany. *Education:* Universities of Munich and Marburg. Retired since 1990.

Languages: German, English, French, Italian and Spanish.

OPPENHOFF & RÄDLER
BOCKENHEIMER LANDSTR. 51-53
D-60325 FRANKFURT/MAIN, GERMANY
Telephone: (069) 170003-0
Telecopier: (069) 170003-33

Other Frankfurt/Main, Germany Office: Myliusstr. 33-37, D-60323. Telephone: (069) 17093-0. Telecopier: (069) 17093-444.
Munich, Germany Office: Prinzregentenplatz 10, D-81675. Telephone: (089) 41808-0. Telecopier: (089) 41808-100.
Berlin, Germany Office: Meinekestr. 13, D-10719. Telephone: (030) 88471-0. Telecopier: (030) 88471-200.
Berlin, Germany Office: Rankestr. 21, D-10789. Telephone: (030) 21496-0. Telecopier: (030) 21496-100.
Cologne, Germany Office: Hohenstaufenring 62, D-50674. Telephone (0221) 2091-0. Telecopier: (0221) 2091-435. Telex: 8 882 294 bos. Teletex 2627 221 4054BOS.
Leipzig, Germany Office: Kommandant-Trufanow-Str. 14, D-04105. Telephone: (0341) 56649-0. Telecopier: (0341) 56649-99.
Brussels, Belgium Office: Rue Brederode 13A, B-1000. Telephone: (2) 5050211. Telecopier: (2) 5022644.
London, England Office: Royex House, Aldermanbury Square, GB-London EC2V 7HR. Telephone: (171) 600 3609. Telecopier: (171) 600 1718.

(This Listing Continued)

New York, New York Office: 712 Fifth Avenue, 30th Floor, 10019, USA. Telephone: (212) 801 3410. Telecopier: (212) 801 3415.
New York, New York Office: 712 Fifth Avenue, 29th Floor, New York 10019, USA. Telephone: (212) 397 7580/7546. Telecopier: (212) 397 4292.
Prague, Czech Republic Office: Alliance Prague, Jachymova 2, CZ-11000 Prague 1. Telephone: (2) 232 1130. Telecopier: (2) 232 6371.

FIRM PROFILE: Oppenhoff & Rädler has been created by a merger of two large German firms, Boden Oppenhoff Rasor Raue and Rädler Raupach Bezzenberger. The firm at present has more than 90 partners and comprises together some 200 lawyers and tax advisers.

Oppenhoff & Rädler acts for domestic and for international clients. The firm offers a comprehensive range of legal services, including: General Corporate and Commercial; Taxation; Banking, Finance and Securities; Mergers and Acquisitions; Real Estate; Litigation and Arbitration; Intellectual Property and Trademarks; Construction Law; Antitrust and European Community Law; Administrative and Environmental Law; Media, Communications and Entertainment Law; Technology and Computer Law; Food, Drug and Chemistry; Family Law; Wills.

Oppenhoff & Rädler is a member of the ALLIANCE OF EUROPEAN LAWYERS EEIG (members: Oppenhoff & Rädler, Germany; De Bandt, van Hecke & Lagae, Belgium; De Brauw Blackstone Westbroek, The Netherlands; Jeantet & Associés, France; Lagerlöf & Leman, Sweden; Uria & Menendez, Spain) and of the LLR EEIG (members: Loyens & Volkmaars, The Netherlands; Bureau Francis Lefebvre, France; Oppenhoff & Rädler, Germany).

RESIDENT PARTNERS AND JUNIOR PARTNERS

DR. DIETER SCHNEIDER, born Cologne, Germany, March 28, 1927; admitted, 1955, Germany. *Education:* University of Cologne (Dr.jur.); New York University Law School. *Member:* German Bar Association (Business Law Committee). *LANGUAGES:* German, English. *PRACTICE AREAS:* Arbitration; Banks and Banking; Corporate Law.

PROF. DR. MANFRED SCHIEDERMAIR, born Bad Godesberg, Germany, July 6, 1932; admitted, 1961, Germany. *Education:* Universities of Bonn and Frankfurt (Dr.jur.); Georgetown University. *Member:* German Bar Association (Committee for Legal Education). *LANGUAGES:* German, English. *PRACTICE AREAS:* Art Law; Corporate Law; Company Law; Real Estate.

ROGER ZÄTZSCH, born Meissen, Germany, February 18, 1939; admitted, 1967, Germany; 1975, Tax Adviser. *Education:* Universities of Frankfurt and Würzburg. Secretary, Deutsche Schutzvereinigung für Wertpapierbesitz (Protective Association for Security Holders), Hesse and Rhineland-Palatinate. *PRACTICE AREAS:* Corporate Law; Mergers, Acquisitions and Divestitures; Taxation.

DR. GEORG BAMBACH, born Bensheim, Germany, March 30, 1934; admitted, 1964, Germany. *Education:* University of Frankfurt (Dr.jur.). *LANGUAGES:* German, English, French. *PRACTICE AREAS:* Family Law; Real Estate.

DR. WELF MÜLLER, born Oberstdorf, Germany, November 22, 1935; admitted, 1972, Germany, Tax Advisor (Steuerberater); 1983, Certified Public Accountant (Wirtschaftsprüfer). *Education:* Universities of München and Lausanne (Dr.jur.). *LANGUAGES:* German, English. *PRACTICE AREAS:* Corporate Law; Company Law; Mergers, Acquisitions and Divestitures; Taxation.

DR. GEORG MAIER-REIMER, born Berlin, Germany, November 30, 1940; admitted, 1968, Germany. *Education:* Universities of Lausanne, Munich, Bonn and Tübingen (Dr. jur.); Harvard University (LL.M.). *LANGUAGES:* German, English. *PRACTICE AREAS:* Banks and Banking; Corporate Law; Finance; Mergers, Acquisitions and Divestitures; Securities.

DR. MANFRED ORTH, born Ruppertenrod, Germany, August 19, 1948. *Education:* University of Giessen (Dr.jur.). *LANGUAGES:* German, English. *PRACTICE AREAS:* Charitable Organizations; Mergers, Acquisitions and Divestitures; Taxation.

DR. WOLFGANG MATSCHKE, born Reinerz, Germany, September 28, 1937; admitted, 1966, Germany. *Education:* Universities of Freiburg and Frankfurt (Dr.jur.). *Member:* Frankfurt Bar Association (Board Member). *LANGUAGES:* German, English. *PRACTICE AREAS:* Charitable Organizations; Appellate Practice; Litigation; Real Estate; Wills.

HERMANN EBER-HUBER, born Neustadt/Weinstraße, Germany, March 26, 1951; admitted, 1980, Germany, Tax Advisor (Steuerberater);

(This Listing Continued)

OPPENHOFF & RÄDLER, *Frankfurt/Main—Continued*

1986, Certified Public Accountant (Wirtschaftsprüfer). *Education:* Bankkaufmann, University Mannheim (Dipl.-Kfm./M.B.A.). *LANGUAGES:* German, English. *PRACTICE AREAS:* Finance; Investments; Real Estate; Taxation.

LOTHAR THÜR, born Frankfurt, Germany, May 7, 1954; admitted, 1985, Germany. *Education:* Universities of Mainz and Freiburg. *LANGUAGES:* German, English. *PRACTICE AREAS:* Civil Law; Labour and Employment; Litigation.

DR. HERMANN SCHLINDWEIN, born Karlsdorf, Germany, August 21, 1954; admitted, 1986, Germany. *Education:* University Heidelberg (Dr.jur.). *LANGUAGES:* German, English. *PRACTICE AREAS:* Labour and Employment; Mergers, Acquisitions and Divestitures; Sports Law; Taxation.

HANS-DIETER SCHULZ-GEBELTZIG, born Solingen, Germany, January 4, 1956; admitted, 1983, Germany. *Education:* Universities of Cologne and Lausanne. *LANGUAGES:* German, English. *PRACTICE AREAS:* Construction Law; Contracts; Environmental Law; Litigation; Real Estate.

RALF E. HESS, born Luxembourg, March 27, 1944; admitted, 1978, Tax Advisor (Steuerberater); 1984, Germany; 1988, Certified Public Accountant (Wirtschaftsprüfer). *Education:* Universities of Marburg and Giessen. *LANGUAGES:* German, English. *PRACTICE AREAS:* Business Law; Civil Law; Contracts; Corporate Law; Mortgages; Real Estate; Taxation; Wills.

JOCHEN WINTER, born Braunschweig, Germany, June 4, 1956; admitted, 1984, Germany. *Education:* Universities of Cologne and Speyer; University of Georgia at Athens (LL.M.). *LANGUAGES:* German, English. *PRACTICE AREAS:* Antitrust and Trade Regulations; Corporate Law; Commercial Law; Mergers, Acquisitions and Divestitures; Transportation.

CHRISTOPHER AREND, born San Diego, California, U.S.A., November 16, 1951; admitted, 1981, California; 1984, Germany. *Education:* University of California at Berkeley (LL.M.); University of Frankfurt. *LANGUAGES:* German, English. *PRACTICE AREAS:* Business Law; Corporate Law; Computer and Software.

PETER ERWE, born Frankfurt am Main, Germany, April 21, 1957; admitted, 1985, Germany. *Education:* University of Frankfurt. *LANGUAGES:* German, English. *PRACTICE AREAS:* Banks and Banking; Company Law; Mergers, Acquisitions and Divestitures.

DR. BERTHOLD KUSSEROW, born Offenbach, Germany, April 27, 1956; admitted, 1984, Germany. *Education:* University of Frankfurt (Dr.jur.); McGill University, Montreal (LL.M.). *LANGUAGES:* German, English. *PRACTICE AREAS:* Banks and Banking; Corporate Law; Finance; Mergers, Acquisitions and Divestitures; Securities.

DR. PETER GAMON, born Osnabrück, Germany, September 30, 1955; admitted, 1985, Germany. *Education:* University of Frankfurt (Dr.jur.); University of Lausanne. *LANGUAGES:* German, English. *PRACTICE AREAS:* Company Law; Mortgages; Real Estate.

PETER ERBACHER, born Frankfurt am Main, Germany, March 5, 1957; admitted, 1988, Germany. *Education:* Universities of Erlangen and Frankfurt. *LANGUAGES:* German, English. *PRACTICE AREAS:* Agency and Distributorships; Corporate Law; Mergers, Acquisitions and Divestitures.

DR. MICHAEL WEIGEL, born Frankfurt am Main, Germany, November 3, 1958; admitted, 1989, Germany. *Education:* University of Frankfurt (Dr.jur.). Assistant Professor, University of Frankfurt, 1986-1989. *LANGUAGES:* German, English. *PRACTICE AREAS:* Appellate Practice; Contracts; Commercial Law; Insurance; Professional Liability.

DR. ANDREAS LUBBERGER, born Hamburg, Germany, November 18, 1957; admitted, 1989, Germany. *Education:* University of Frankfurt (Dr.jur.). *LANGUAGES:* German, English. *PRACTICE AREAS:* Administrative Law; Agency and Distributorship; Consumer Law; Constitutional Law; Intellectual Property; Trademarks.

DR. HARTWIG GRAF VON WESTERHOLT, born Schwaebisch Hall, Germany, June 18, 1944; admitted, 1973, Germany. *Education:* Universities of Bonn, Berlin and Munich (Dr.jur.). *LANGUAGES:* German, English, French. *PRACTICE AREAS:* Advertising and Marketing; Copyrights; Computer and Software; Technology and Science.

(This Listing Continued)

ULRICH H. WOLFF, born Karlsruhe, Germany, January 25, 1962; admitted, 1991, Germany. *Education:* Universities of Tübingen and Freiburg; Université de Montrèal. *LANGUAGES:* German, English, French. *PRACTICE AREAS:* Banks and Banking; Finance; Corporate Law; Mergers, Acquisitions and Divestitures.

ROBERT H. LEITERMANN, born Munich, Germany, March 11, 1961; admitted, 1990, Germany. *Education:* University of Munich. *LANGUAGES:* German, English. *PRACTICE AREAS:* Business Law; Contracts; Company Law; Investments; Mergers, Acquisitions and Divestitures.

DR. GÖTZ EILMANN, born Hannover, Germany, November 4, 1960; admitted, 1991, Germany. *Education:* University of Frankfurt (Dr.jur.). *LANGUAGES:* German, English. *PRACTICE AREAS:* Corporate Law; Commercial Law; Company Law; Litigation.

DR. EVA REUDELHUBER, born Munich, Germany, May 26, 1964; admitted, 1992, Germany. *Education:* University of Munich (Dr.jur.). *LANGUAGES:* German, English. *PRACTICE AREAS:* Banks and Banking; Corporate Law; Company Law.

DR. THOMAS PAUL, born Hilchenbach/Westfalen, Germany, 1959; admitted, 1990, Frankfurt/Main. *Education:* University of Marburg (Dr.jur.); University of Lausanne, Switzerland; Tulane Law School (LL.M.). *LANGUAGES:* English, German. *PRACTICE AREAS:* Banks and Banking; Investments; Securities.

PAUL, PAUL & SCHMITT

Established in 1947

ESCHERSHEIMER LANDSTRASSE 27
60322 FRANKFURT/MAIN, GERMANY
Telephone: 069/95 95 90
Telecopier: 069/55 77 99

Dresden, Germany Office: Bergmannstr. 21, O-8010.

General Practice. Contracts, Banking, Mergers and Acquisitions, Inheritance, Investment, Family, Tax, Corporate, Business, Labour, Aviation, Unfair Competition and Antitrust, Product Liability Law, Civil Litigation, Real Estate, Eastern European Law, Bankruptcy Proceedings and Notarial Recording.

FIRM PROFILE: Paul, Paul & Schmitt was founded in 1947 by Professor Dr. Rudolf Paul. The company was fast to develop into one of Germany's respected economic law offices.

Its activities center around the advice and representation of businessmen and enterprises. Here again, our work focuses on the sectors of company law, real estate law, economic law in its broadest sense as well as insolvency proceedings and the reorganization of enterprises. In case of legal action Paul, Paul & Schmitt appear before all courts. Paul, Paul & Schmitt have established relations with other law offices in every larger town at home and abroad. We have deliberately decided against any firm cooperations or "partnerships". Directed at the specific requirements of the client we choose the law office that is most qualified to serve that individual client. Under the overall control of Paul, Paul & Schmitt the client is then represented. We also have our own law office in Dresden.

MEMBERS OF FIRM

DR. DR. ALBERT PAUL, born Foerderstedt, October 11, 1914; admitted, 1946, Germany, Tax Law Specialist, Notary. *Education:* Universities of Jena and Breslau (Dr. jur. and Dr. rer. pol.). *PRACTICE AREAS:* Business Law; Corporate Law.

DR. HANS GEORG SCHMITT, born Loerrach, July 6, 1931; admitted, 1961, Germany, Notary. *Education:* Universities of Freiburg, Heidelberg, and Basel, Switzerland (Dr. jur.). *PRACTICE AREAS:* Business Law; Corporate Law; Banking Law; Real Estate.

KRISTINA GRAEFIN PILATI-BORGGREVE, born Eisenach, May 9, 1948; admitted, 1977, Germany, Notary. *Education:* Universities of Munich and Hamburg. *PRACTICE AREAS:* Family Law; Inheritance Law.

DR. THOMAS HEINZ, born Frankfurt, February 15, 1956; admitted, 1983, Germany. *Education:* University of Frankfurt a.M. (Dr. jur.). *PRACTICE AREAS:* Litigation; Aviation; Corporations Law.

DR. ROBIN L. FRITZ, born Frankfurt, August 13, 1955; admitted, 1984, Germany. *Education:* University of Frankfurt, School of Economics and Political Science, London (Dr. jur.). *Member:* Foreign Law Associa-

(This Listing Continued)

tion. *PRACTICE AREAS:* Business Law; Corporate Law; Labour Law; Unfair Competition; Eastern European Law.

HELMUT BRAUN, born Schwaebisch-Gmuend, April 9, 1958; admitted, 1987, Germany. *Education:* University of Heidelberg. *PRACTICE AREAS:* Banking; Bankruptcy Proceedings.

GORDON RAPP, born Bad Wimpfen, June 17, 1957; admitted, 1986, Germany. *Education:* University of Heidelberg. *Member:* AIJA. *PRACTICE AREAS:* Bankruptcy Proceedings; Mergers and Acquisitions.

ASSOCIATES

JOERG LAMERS, born Frankfurt a.M., April 25, 1960; admitted, 1987, Germany, specialized in Product Liability. *Education:* Universities of Frankfurt and Regensburg. *PRACTICE AREAS:* Business Law; Labour Law; Unfair Competition Law.

ANDRÉ Y. HORNSTEIN, born Paris, October 19, 1959; admitted, 1991, Germany. *Education:* Universities of Frankfurt and Hagen. *PRACTICE AREAS:* Economics Law; Litigation; Administrative Law.

GUNTHER PIEFKE, born Munich, September 11, 1963; admitted, 1993, Germany. *Education:* University of Heidelberg. *PRACTICE AREAS:* Business Law; Corporate Law; Public Law.

The firm has other employees who are specialized in various fields.
All the lawyers of the firm are members in the Frankfurt Bar Association.

Each of the above named members of the firm has already published several treatises in his particular field.
The firm maintains good connections with the municipality, the local chamber of industry and commerce and the relevant economic associations.
Languages: German, English and French.

PELTZER & RIESENKAMPFF

NIEDENAU 68

60325 FRANKFURT/MAIN, GERMANY

Telephone: 49-69-71 73 66
Cable Address: "Peljus, Frankfurt"
Telecopier: 49-69- 7 24 10 63; 72 48 64.
Telex: 416 307 pejus d.
Teletex: 6997628 pejus.

Brussels, Belgium Office: Avenue du Diamant 139, B-1040. Telephone: 32-2-735 34 28. Telecopier: 32-2-735 26 78.

Leipzig, Germany Office: Gottschedstrasse 44, 04109 Leipzig. Telephone: 341-28 21 46; 341-28 21 68. Telecopier: 341-980 04 18.

Banking, Corporate Finance, Commercial Business, Mergers and Acquisitions, Unfair Competition, Antitrust, Foreign Exchange, Labor Law, Arbitration, Industrial Property Rights, Environmental Law, Real Property. Reprivatization of Assets in the Former GDR.

MEMBERS OF FIRM

DR. MARTIN PELTZER, born Krefeld, Germany, February 28, 1931; admitted, 1962, Germany, Notary. *Education:* Universities of Paris, Freiburg, Madrid and Basel (Doctor of Law, 1958). Executive of Deutsche Bank, 1961-1965. Chief Financial and Administrative Officer of Zellstofffabrik Waldhof, Mannheim, 1965-1970. Author: "The Labor Management Relations Act," Fritz Knapp-Verlag, Frankfurt, 3rd Edition, 1983; "Banking in Germany," Fritz Knapp-Verlag, Frankfurt, 1973; "Co-Determination Act, 1976," Verlag Dr. Otto Schmidt KG, Köln, 2nd Edition, 1976; "German Insolvency Laws," Verlag Dr. Otto Schmidt KG, Köln, 1975; "German Banking Law," Dr. Otto Schmidt KG, Köln, 3rd Edition, 1990. Co-Author: "U.S.-Business Law/U.S.-Amerikanisches Wirtschaftsrecht," Verlag Dr. Otto Schmidt KG, Köln, 2nd Edition, 1990; "German Commercial Code/-Handelsgesetzbuch," Verlag Dr. Otto Schmidt KG, Köln, 1980; "Law Pertaining to Companies with Limited Liability/GmbH - Gesetz," Verlag Dr. Otto Schmidt KG, Köln, 2nd Edition, 1986; "Produzentenhaftpflicht in USA und Deutschland/Product Liability in Germany and the USA," German American Chamber of Commerce, Inc., New York, 3rd Edition, 1985. *Member:* German Bar Association; International Bar Association. *LANGUAGES:* German, English, French and Spanish.

DR. ALEXANDER RIESENKAMPFF, M.B.A., born Riga, April 16, 1936; admitted, 1970, Germany, Notary; 1978, Pennsylvania. *Education:* Columbia University Graduate School of Business, New York (Master of Business Administration, 1961); Universities of Munich, Bonn and Cologne (Doctor of Law, 1966); University of Pennsylvania. Legal Counsel, Chevron Erdoel Deutschland GmbH, 1967-1972. Lecturer on Business Law, University of Freiburg/Br., 1986—. Co-Author: "German Merger Controls:

(This Listing Continued)

The Role of Company Assurances," The Antitrust Bulletin, 1977; "Die kartellrechtliche Anmeldepflicht nach dem Hart-Scott-Rodino-Act - ein Neues Hindernis für Ausländische Investitionen in den USA," Wettbewerb in Recht und Praxis, März 1979; "Law Against Restraints of Competition with 1980 Amendments," Dr. Otto Schmidt KG, Koeln, 1980; "Antitrust Law in Germany and the USA," German-American Chamber of Commerce 1982. *Member:* German Bar Association, Studienvereinigung Kartellrecht e.V.; International Bar Association; American Bar Association; Pennsylvania Bar Association; Inter-Pacific Bar Association. *LANGUAGES:* German, English and French.

JOACHIM GRES, born Hameln/Westfalia, March 1, 1947; admitted, 1974, Germany, Notary; Member of the German Federal Parliament since 1990. *Education:* Universities of Heidelberg and Bonn. Author: "Handbook of German Employment Law," Alfred Metzner Verlag, Frankfurt, 1983. Co-Author: "The German Law Governing Standard Business Conditions," Dr. Otto Schmidt KG, Köln, 1977; "Law Against Restraints of Competition with 1980 Amendments," Dr. Otto Schmidt KG, Köln, 1980; "Starting Business Operations in Germany," Alfred Metzner Verlag, Frankfurt, 1984. *Member:* German Bar Association; International Bar Association; Deutsche Vereinigung für gewerblichen Rechtsschutz e.V.; German Federal Parliament (1990—). *LANGUAGES:* German and English.

DR. KONRAD WERNICKE, born Ratibor, Germany, November 15, 1905; admitted, 1947, Germany. *Education:* Universities of Tübingen and Breslau (Doctor of Law, 1928). *Member:* German Bar Association. *LANGUAGES:* German.

DR. HARALD JUNG, born Düsseldorf, May 31, 1948; admitted, 1978, Germany. *Education:* Universities of Munich and Marburg (Doctor of Law, 1977). Author: "Das Englische Hire-Purchase Law und das Deutsche Abzahlungsrecht," Alfred Metzner Verlag, Frankfurt, 1977; "Handbook of German Employment Law," Alfred Metzner Verlag, Frankfurt, 1993; "Starting Business Operations in Germany", Alfred Metzner Verlag, Frankfurt, 1984; "German Banking Act, German-English Commentary," Alfred Metzner Verlag, Frankfurt, 1988. *Member:* German Bar Association; Gesellschaft für Rechtsvergleichung; German American Lawyers Association; International Financial Management Association e.V.; Inter-Pacific Bar Association. *LANGUAGES:* German and English.

DR. CHRISTOPH SCHÜCKING, born Kassel, November 5, 1951; admitted, 1981, Germany. *Education:* Universities of Geneva and Freiburg (Doctor of Law, 1980). Author: "Importkreditsicherung", Fritz-Knapp-Verlag, Frankfurt, 1980. Co-Author: "Product Liability in Germany and the USA", 3rd ed. 1985. *Member:* German Bar Association; Gesellschaft für Rechtsvergleichung; Deutscher Juristentag. *LANGUAGES:* German, English and French.

DR. HEINZ-JOACHIM FREUND, born Frankfurt, Germany, September 5, 1953; admitted, 1984, Germany. *Education:* University of Frankfurt (Doctor of Law, 1985); Ecole Nationale d'Administration, Paris. *Member:* German Bar Association; Association des anciens éléves de l'ENA. *LANGUAGES:* German, French and English.

ALEXANDER VON REDEN, born Hannover, Germany, June 5, 1956; admitted, 1987, Germany. *Education:* Universities of Göttingen, Geneva, Kiel and Hamburg. *LANGUAGES:* German, English and French.

THEODOR SIMON, born Pruem, Germany, August 22, 1932; admitted, 1986, Germany. *Education:* Universities of Bonn and Cologne (Law and Economics). With Deutsche Bundesbank, Frankfurt, 1962. Executive of Deutsche Bank, 1964-1966. Chairman of the Board, Stadtsparkasse Trier, 1967-1969. Member of the Board, Vice Chairman, Landesbank Rheinland-Pfalz, 1969-1986. *LANGUAGES:* German, French and English.

KNUT MÜLLER, born Cottbus, Germany, August 14, 1929; admitted, 1988, Germany. *Education:* Universities of Marburg and Berlin. Assistant, Institut für öffentliches Recht, 1959-1964. Assistant, Federal Constitutional Court, 1964-1967. Advisor of Hessian Ministry of the Interior, Wiesbaden, 1967-1970. Police President of the City of Frankfurt, 1970-1980. President of the Government of Middle Hessia at Giessen, 1980-1987. *LANGUAGES:* German.

REINER KURSCHAT, born Uelzen, November 28, 1954; admitted, 1988, Germany. *Education:* University of Marburg. *LANGUAGES:* German and English.

GUNTHER BÜLOW, DIPLOM-JÚRIST, born Zerbst, February 17, 1959; admitted, 1990, Germany. *Education:* Martin Luther University of Halle/Wittenberg. In-House Counsel of TAKRAF-Förderanlagen-und Kranbau Köthen 1984-1990. *LANGUAGES:* German.

(This Listing Continued)

PELTZER & RIESENKAMPFF, Frankfurt/Main—Continued

MARTIN BELL, born Brühl/Cologne, February 13, 1961; admitted, 1991, Germany. *Education:* University of Bonn. *LANGUAGES:* German and English.

DR. THOMAS LINK, born Seligenstadt, December 9, 1963; admitted, 1992, Germany. *Education:* University of Würzberg. *LANGUAGES:* German, English.

DR. HEIKE WAGNER, born Aschaffenburg, July 16, 1962; admitted, 1990, Germany. *Education:* University of Würzburg (1981-1986). *LANGUAGES:* German and English.

GUDRUN HARTUNG, born Wolfsburg, December 21, 1959; admitted, 1992, Germany. *Education:* University of Göttingen (1982-1988). *LANGUAGES:* German, English and French.

HEIKE GÜNTHEL, born Rodewisch, June 16, 1963; admitted, 1992, Germany. *Education:* University of Leipzig (1982-1986). *LANGUAGES:* German, Russian and English.

ANDREA ZIEGLER, born Hamburg, April 10, 1960; admitted, 1993, Germany. *Education:* University of Hamburg, Göttingen and Lausanne (1980-1986). *LANGUAGES:* German, French and English.

DR. HUBERTUS KOLSTER, born Essen, December 7, 1962; admitted, 1993, Germany. *Education:* Universities of Göttingen and Munich. Author: "Die Qualität der Rücktrittsbemühungen des Täters beim beendeten Versuch," Peter Lang Verlag, Frankfurt, 1993. *LANGUAGES:* German and English.

DR. ULRICH ZIEGLER, born Frankfurt, January 25, 1964; admitted, 1992, Germany. *Education:* University of Munich. Author: "Leistungsstörungsrecht nach dem UN-Kaufrecht," Nomos Verlag, Baden Baden. *LANGUAGES:* German and English.

DR. KLAUS HEUVELS, born Düsseldorf, December 16, 1950; admitted, 1986, Germany. *Education:* University of Marburg. Co-Author: "Praxishandbuch Betriebliches Umweltmanagement," WEKA Fachverlag für technische Führungskräfte, Augsburg. *LANGUAGES:* German and English.

PÜNDER, VOLHARD, WEBER & AXSTER

MAINZER LANDSTRASSE 46
60325 FRANKFURT/MAIN, GERMANY
Telephone: (49)(69) 71 99-01
Fax: (49)(69) 71 99-4000
Telex: 414 827

Düsseldorf, Germany Office: Cecilienallee 6, 40474 Düsseldorf. Telephone: (49)(211) 43 55-0. Fax: (49)(211) 43 55-600.
Berlin, Germany Office: Katharina-Heinroth-Ufer, 10787 Berlin. Telephone: (49)(30) 2546 5800. Fax: (49)(30) 2546 5900.
Leipzig, Germany Office: Burgplatz 7, 04109 Leipzig. Telephone: (49)(341) 21 49-0 Fax: (49)(341) 21 49-600.
Beijing, People's Republic of China Office: Suite C 603, Beijing Lufthansa Center, 50 Liangmaqiao Road, Beijing 100 016. Telephone: (86)(1) 465 15 68; (86)(1) 465 18 08; (86)(1) 465 13 45. Fax: (86)(1) 467 12 56.
Brussels, Belgium Office: Rue d'Arlon 92, 1040 Bruxelles. Telephone: (32)(2) 230 90 11. Fax: (32)(2) 231 19 55.
Budapest, Hungary Office: Endrödy Sandor utca 48, 1026 Budapest. Telephone: (36) 60 33 26 18 international; (6) 60 33 26 18 national. Fax: (36) 60 33 26 17 international; (6) 60 33 26 17 national.
Moscow, Russia Office: ul. Wolchonka, 18/2, 121 019 Moskwa. Telephone: (7)(095) 202 64 90; (7)(095) 202 65 12; (7)(543) 708 00 900 from Germany; (49)(7545) 893 42 from other countries. Fax: (7)(095) 202 65 14; (7)(543) 708 00 990 from Germany; (49)(7545) 893 43 from other countries.
New York, New York Office: 152 West 57th Street, Carnegie Hall Tower, New York, N.Y. 10019. Telephone: (1)(212) 582 28 28. Fax: (1)(212) 582 24 24.
Warsaw, Poland Office: ul. Jasna 1, 00-013 Warszawa. Telephone: (48) 39 12 21 41. Fax: (48)(22) 27 15 29.

Administrative Law; Antitrust Law; Arbitration; Auditing and Valuations; Banking, Securities and Finance; Bankruptcy; Building Law; Chinese Law; Commercial Crime; Computer Law; Construction Law; Corporate Law; EU Law; Energy Law; Environmental Law; Franchising; Industrial Prop-

(This Listing Continued)

EU664B

erty Law; Insolvency; Intellectual Property Law; International and German Business Law; Labor and Employment Law; Litigation; Media Law; Mergers and Acquisitions; Pharmaceutical Law; Privatizations; Product Law; Public Law; Real Estate; Reorganizations; Russian Law; Tax Law; Telecommunications; Unfair Trade Law.

FIRM PROFILE: Member of PÜNDER GROUP

Members:
- BURUMA MARIS, The Hague, Rotterdam
- CERHA, HEMPEL & SPIEGELFELD, Wien
- COPPENS, VAN OMMESLAGHE, HORSMANS & FAURES, Bruxelles
- DE PARDIEU-LACOURTE G.I.E., Paris
- PÜNDER, VOLHARD, WEBER & AXSTER, Frankfurt/Main, Düsseldorf, Berlin, Leipzig
- STOFFEL & PARTNER, Zürich, Genève.

Joint Offices of PÜNDER GROUP:

Beijing - Bruxelles - Budapest - Moskwa - New York - Warszawa

MEMBERS OF FIRM

DR. RÜDIGER VOLHARD, born Frankfurt/Main, Germany, September 24, 1931; admitted, 1964, Frankfurt/Main; 1971, Notary. *Education:* University of Frankfurt (Dr. jur.). Editor and Co-Author: "Real Property in Germany, Legal and Tax Aspects of Development and Investment," 4th ed., 1991, 1st French ed., 1992, 1st Japanese ed., 1993. *Member:* International Bar Association; German and International Association for the Protection of Industrial Property and Copyright; Association for Antitrust Law Studies. *LANGUAGES:* German and English. *PRACTICE AREAS:* Banking Law; Corporate Law; Real Estate; Litigation.

DOLF WEBER, born Frankfurt/Main, Germany, March 31, 1936; admitted, 1963, Frankfurt/Main; 1973, Notary; 1976, Tax Lawyer. *Education:* University of Frankfurt. Editor, "Real Property in Germany, Legal and Tax Aspects of Development and Investment," 4th ed., 1991, 1st French ed., 1992, 1st Japanese ed., 1993. Presiding Judge, Court for Lawyers' Affairs, Frankfurt, 1971-1979. *Member:* German (Member, Committee on Disciplinary Law, 1979-1991) and International Bar Associations; German Chamber of Commerce in the United Kingdom; International Fiscal Association; British Trade Council; German-American Chamber of Commerce; German Notaries' Association (Member, Committee on International Law, 1981—). *LANGUAGES:* German and English. *PRACTICE AREAS:* Corporate Law; Real Estate; Banking Law; Arbitration.

JÜRGEN KICKER, born Cloppenburg, Germany, January 17, 1935; admitted, 1965, Hamburg; 1971, Frankfurt/Main; 1976, Notary. *Education:* University of Hamburg. Western Electric Company, Patent Division, New York, N.Y., 1963-1964. *Member:* German and American Bar Associations; German and International Association for the Protection of Industrial Property and Copyright (Member, Board of Frankfurt Association, Drug and Food Law Committee). *LANGUAGES:* German and English. *PRACTICE AREAS:* Industrial Property Law; Product Law; Unfair Trade Law; Telecommunications.

KARLA KÖHLER, born Leipzig, Germany, March 27, 1932; admitted, 1960, Frankfurt/Main; 1972, Notary; 1987, Labor Lawyer. *Education:* University of Berlin. Member of the Board, Frankfurt Bar. *Member:* German Bar Association. *LANGUAGES:* German and English. *PRACTICE AREAS:* Labor and Employment Law; Litigation; Aviation Law.

WOLFGANG USINGER, born Alsfeld, Germany, May 21, 1944; admitted, 1972, Frankfurt/Main; 1986, Notary. *Education:* Universities of Marburg and Geneva. Editor and Co-Author: "Real Property in Germany, Legal and Tax Aspects of Development and Investment," 4th ed., 1991, 1st French ed., 1992 and 1st Japanese ed., 1993. Judge, Court for Lawyer's Affairs, Frankfurt, 1979-1983. Associate Judge, Court of Appeals, Frankfurt, 1983-1991. *Member:* German Bar Association; Deutsche Gesellschaft für Baurecht. *LANGUAGES:* German, English and French. *PRACTICE AREAS:* Real Estate; Building Law; Planning Law; Construction Law.

DR. KLAUS SOMMERLAD, born Grossen-Buseck, Germany, November 6, 1944; admitted, 1975, Frankfurt/Main; 1990, Notary. *Education:* Universities of Freiburg and Marburg (Dr. jur.). Author: "Die innerprozessuale Bindung an vorangegangene Urteile der Rechtsmittelgerichte," 1974. Co-Author: "RWW Rechtsfragen in Wettbewerb und Werbung," 1982; "Pre-Trial and Pre-Hearing Procedures Worldwide," 1990; "Outsourcing, eine strategische Allianz besonderen Typs," 1993. *Member:* German Bar Association; German and International Association for the Protection of Industrial Property and Copyright; Association for Antitrust Law Studies; Ger-

(This Listing Continued)

man-Chinese Lawyers' Association. *LANGUAGES:* German, English and French. *PRACTICE AREAS:* Commercial Law; Product Liability Law; Industrial Property Law; Antitrust Law; Law of Competition; Telecommunications; Computer Law.

MANFRED BENKERT, born Cologne, Germany, May 21, 1942; admitted, 1971, Frankfurt/Main; 1975, Tax Adviser. *Education:* Universities of Berlin, Münster/Westf. and Würzburg (Master of National Economics, 1969). Co-Author: "Real Property in Germany, Legal and Tax Aspects of Development and Investment," 4th ed., 1991, 1st French ed., 1992, 1st Japanese ed., 1993. *Member:* German Bar Association; International Bar Association; Deutscher Juristentag; German Tax Law Association; Verein für Versicherungswissenschaft; International Fiscal Association. *LANGUAGES:* German and English. *PRACTICE AREAS:* German and International Tax Law; Mergers and Acquisitions; Corporate Law.

EIKE MAASS, born Gernrode/Harz, Germany, August 29, 1943; admitted, 1970, Hamburg; 1978, Frankfurt/Main; 1985, Notary. *Education:* Universities of Hamburg and Münster/Westfalen. Author: "Haftungsrecht des Notars," 1994. Co-Author: "Real Property in Germany, Legal and Tax Aspects of Development and Investment," 4th ed., 1991, 1st French ed., 1992, 1st Japanese ed., 1993. *Member:* German Bar Association; German Notaries' Association (Member of Committee on Procedure Law, 1994—); Member of the Board, Frankfurt Chamber of Notaries (1993—). *LANGUAGES:* German and English. *PRACTICE AREAS:* Real Estate including Commercial Leases Law; Bankruptcy Law.

DR. HANS-JOSEF SCHNEIDER, born Frankfurt/Main, Germany, May 25, 1950; admitted, 1978, Frankfurt/Main; 1987, Qualified Specialised Attorney-at-Law for Administrative Law; 1991, Notary. *Education:* University of Frankfurt (Dr. jur.); University Fellow of the Faculty of University of Frankfurt, 1976-1977. Author: "Nebenbestimmungen und Verwaltungsprozess". Co-Author: "Real Property in Germany, Legal and Tax Aspects of Development and Investment, 4th ed., 1991, 1st French ed., 1992, 1st Japanese ed., 1993. *Member:* German Bar Association. *LANGUAGES:* German and English. *PRACTICE AREAS:* Public Law; Administrative Law; Environmental Law; Real Estate; Building Law; Planning Law.

IRENE THIELE-MÜHLHAN, born Bad Salzdetfurth, Germany, September 4, 1948; admitted, 1980, Frankfurt/Main; 1991, Notary. *Education:* University of Göttingen. Co-Author: "Real Property in Germany, Legal and Tax Aspects of Development and Investment, 4th ed., 1991, 1st French ed., 1992, 1st Japanese ed., 1993. *Member:* German Bar Association; Deutscher Juristentag; Deutsche Gesellschaft für Baurecht. *LANGUAGES:* German, English and French. *PRACTICE AREAS:* Real Estate including Commercial Leases; Construction Law.

DR. THOMAS GASTEYER, born Frankfurt/Main, Germany, May 25, 1952; admitted, 1979, Frankfurt/Main; 1982, New York; 1982, Tax Lawyer. *Education:* University of Frankfurt (Dr. jur.); Columbia University Law School (LL.M., 1981). Teaching Fellow of the Law Faculty of University of Frankfurt, 1976-1979. Author: "Der mehrstufige internationale Konzern," 1981. Co-Author: "Real Property in Germany," Legal and Tax Aspects of Development and Investment, 4th ed., 1991, 1st French ed., 1992, 1st Japanese ed., 1993. *Member:* German, American, International and New York State Bar Associations. *LANGUAGES:* German, English and French. *PRACTICE AREAS:* Mergers and Acquisitions; International Law; Corporate Law; Banking Law.

DR. FABIAN VON SCHLABRENDORFF, born Berlin, December 23, 1944; admitted, 1982, Frankfurt/Main. *Education:* Universities of Tübingen, Berlin, Geneva and Chicago (M.A., 1975) and Frankfurt (Dr. jur., 1987). Author: "The Impact of the National Environmental Policy Act and the Federal Water Pollution Control Act on the Licensing of Nuclear Power Plants," 1975; "The Legal Structure of Transnational Forest-Based Investments in Developing Countries," 1987. Co-author: "Mining Ventures in Developing Countries," 1979 part 1, 1981 part 2,; "Bibliography on Transnational Law of Natural Resources," 1981. *Member:* German and International Bar Association; Inter-Pacific Bar Association; Bi-national Lawyers' Associations. *LANGUAGES:* German, English, French and Spanish. *PRACTICE AREAS:* Mergers and Acquisitions; Corporate Law; Banking and Securities Law; Litigation.

DR. WOLFGANG KAREHNKE, born Frankfurt/Main, Germany, November 7, 1953; admitted, 1981, Frankfurt/Main. *Education:* University of Frankfurt (Dr. jur.); Assistant of the Law Faculty of University of Frankfurt, 1981-1984. Author: "Die rechtsgeschäftliche Bindung kommunaler Bauleitplanung," 1983. *Member:* German Bar Association. *LANGUAGES:* German, English and French. *PRACTICE AREAS:* Corporate Law; Privatizations; Litigation.

(This Listing Continued)

DR. KERSTEN VON SCHENCK, born Hamburg, Germany, November 10, 1951; admitted, 1985, Frankfurt/Main. *Education:* Universities of Freiburg and Münster (Dr. jur.); New York University School of Law (M.C.J., 1979). Assistant Notary (Notarassessor), Hamburg, 1982-1985. Author: "Die Tätigkeit deutscher Wertpapier-Investmentgesellschaften in den Vereinigten Staaten," 1982. Co-Author: "Real Property in Germany, Legal and Tax Aspects of Development and Investment," 4th ed., 1991, 1st French ed., 1992, 1st Japanese ed., 1993. *Member:* German and International Bar Associations; Young Lawyers' International Association. *LANGUAGES:* German, English and French. *PRACTICE AREAS:* Banking and Securities Law; Capital Market Transactions; Corporate Law; Mergers and Acquisitions.

DR. SABINE STRICKER, born Frankfurt/Main, Germany, April 1, 1956; admitted, 1983, Frankfurt/Main. *Education:* University of Munich (Dr. jur.); University of Geneva; Harvard Law School (LL.M., 1983). University Fellow of the Institute of International Law, Munich, 1979-1982. Resident Lawyer at Beijing Office, 1985-1991. Author: "Die Substitution im Internationalen Privatrecht," 1983. Co-Author: "Wirtschaftsrecht und Außenwirtschaftsverkehr der Volksrepublik China". *Member:* German Bar Association; German Association for Chinese Law; German-Chinese Lawyers' Association; German-Chinese Business Association; German-Italian Lawyers' Association. *LANGUAGES:* German, English, Mandarin, French and Italian. *PRACTICE AREAS:* Chinese, German and International Business Law; Chinese, German and International Tax Law.

WOLFGANG TISCHBIREK, born Kiel, Germany, December 2, 1950; admitted, 1983, Frankfurt/Main; 1987, Tax Adviser. *Education:* Universities of Cologne, Geneva and Freiburg i. Br.; University of California, Berkeley (LL.M., 1979). Internship, Commission of the EEC, Tax Division, Brussels, 1975. University Fellow of the Institute of International Tax Law, University of Munich, 1979-1983. Co-author: "DBA-Doppelbesteuerungsabkommen," 2nd ed., 1990; "Double Taxation Conventions," 1991; "Chinas Wirtschaft zu Beginn der 90er Jahre," 1989; "Wirtschaftsrecht und Außenwirtschaftsverkehr der Volksrepublik China", 1988; "Real Property in Germany, Legal and Tax Aspects of Development and Investment," 4th ed., 1991, 1st French ed., 1992, 1st Japanese ed., 1993. *Member:* German Bar Association; International Fiscal Association; Tax Advisers' Association. *LANGUAGES:* German, English and French. *PRACTICE AREAS:* International and German Tax Law.

DANIELA WEBER-REY, born Frankfurt/Main, Germany, November 18, 1957; admitted, 1984, Frankfurt/Main; 1986, New York. *Education:* Universities of Frankfurt and Geneva; Columbia University Law School (LL.M., 1985). *Member:* German, American and International Bar Associations; German-American Lawyers' Association; German-French Lawyers' Association. *LANGUAGES:* German, English and French. *PRACTICE AREAS:* Corporate Law; Corporate Finance; Mergers and Acquisitions; Securities Law; Capital Market Transactions; International Law.

DR. DIRK OLDENBURG, born Kiel, Germany, July 19, 1957; admitted, 1985, Frankfurt/Main. *Education:* Universities of Munich and Kiel (Dr. jur., 1985). Author: "Die Keinmann-GmbH - Ein unmögliches Rechtsgebilde?" 1985. *Member:* German Bar Association. *LANGUAGES:* German and English. *PRACTICE AREAS:* Insolvency Law; Mergers and Acquisitions; Corporate Law; Commercial Crime.

DR. ANDREAS JUNIUS, born Dortmund, Germany, September 15, 1954; admitted, 1983, New York; 1986, Frankfurt/Main. *Education:* Universities of Bochum and Bonn (Dr jur.); Columbia University Law School (LL.M., 1982). Assistant of the Law Faculty of Bonn University, 1981. Lecturer on Law, Morin Center for Banking Law Studies, Boston University School of Law, 1989—. Author: "The United Nations Council for Namibia," 1988. Co-author: "Gründen und Führen einer US-Unternehmung, Handbuch für Direktinvestitionen in den USA," 1984; "Die Richtlinien des US-Justizministeriums zu vertikalen Wettbewerbsbeschränkungen," 1985. *Member:* German, American, International and New York State Bar Associations; Association of the Bar of the City of New York; German-American Lawyers' Association. (Also at New York, NY Office). *LANGUAGES:* German, English, French, Spanish and Italian. *PRACTICE AREAS:* International Law; Corporate Law; Mergers and Acquisitions; Banking and Securities Law.

DR. ULF HEIL, born Wuppertal, Germany, February 14, 1954; admitted, 1981, Bochum; 1988, Frankfurt/Main. *Education:* University of Bochum (Dr. jur.). Assistant to the Faculty of Bochum University, 1978-1980. Author: "Die Bindung der Gerichte an Entscheidungen anderer Gerichte," 1983. *Member:* German Bar Association; AIPPI; German Association for the Protection of Industrial Property and Copyright; Deutscher Juristentag.

(This Listing Continued)

PÜNDER, VOLHARD, WEBER & AXSTER,
  Frankfurt/Main—Continued

LANGUAGES: German and English. **PRACTICE AREAS:** Intellectual Property Law; Commercial Law; Product Liability Law; Litigation.

DR. KLAUS MINUTH, born Hanau, Germany, November 22, 1957; admitted, 1987, Frankfurt/Main. *Education:* University of Frankfurt/Main (Dr jur., 1988); University of Montpellier. Author: "Besitzfunktionen beim gutgläubigen Mobiliarerwerb im deutschen und französischen Recht," 1990. *Member:* German Bar Association; Deutsche Gesellschaft für Baurecht e.V. **LANGUAGES:** German, English and French. **PRACTICE AREAS:** Real Estate; Building Law; Planning Law.

DR. BERND-WILHELM SCHMITZ, born Neuwied/Rhein, Germany, August 2, 1956; admitted, 1984, Koblenz; 1989, Frankfurt/Main. *Education:* Universities of Giessen, Geneva and Bonn (Dr. jur., 1987). Author: "Die Haftung der Europäischen Wirtschaftsgemeinschaft für Verordnungsunrecht im Abgaben- und Beihilferecht," 1987. *Member:* German Bar Association. **LANGUAGES:** German, English and French. **PRACTICE AREAS:** Litigation; Mergers and Acquisitions; Privatizations; Business Law; Corporate Law.

PETER NÄGELE, born Frankfurt/Main, Germany, September 5, 1957; admitted, 1987, Frankfurt/Main; 1988, New York. *Education:* University of Frankfurt. Assistant to the Max Planck Society, Institute for European Legal History, Frankfurt, 1984-1985. Lecturer, Institute for Electronic Data Processing and Business Administration, Frankfurt/Main, 1982-1987. *Member:* German Bar Association; German-American Lawyers' Association; Banking Law Society; International Bar Association. **LANGUAGES:** German and English. **PRACTICE AREAS:** International Business Law; Capital Market Transactions; Banking Law.

BERNT GACH, born Hamburg, Germany, August 2, 1946; admitted, 1975, Hamburg; 1990, Frankfurt/Main. *Education:* University of Hamburg. Assistant Lecturer on Civil Law and Roman Historical Law, University Hamburg, 1973-1975; Lecturer on Labor Law, Wirtschaftsakademie (Commercial Academy), Hamburg, 1986-1987. *Member:* German Bar Association, Deutscher Juristentag. **LANGUAGES:** German and English. **PRACTICE AREAS:** Commercial Law; Labor and Employment Law; Construction Law.

HEINZ-GÜNTER GONDERT, born Trier, Germany, April 30, 1949; 1978, Tax Adviser; admitted, 1983, Mainz; 1992, Frankfurt/Main. *Education:* Universities of Freiburg/Breisgau and Bonn. Revenue service, 1975-1977. Member of the board of a leasing company, 1983-1986. Senior executive in a banking group, 1986-1992. *Member:* German Bar Association; German Tax Law Association. **LANGUAGES:** German and English. **PRACTICE AREAS:** Corporate Law; Banking and Financial Instruments; Tax Law and Auditing; Reorganizations.

DR. GERD LENGA, born Stuttgart, Germany, July 8, 1947; admitted, 1988, Stuttgart; 1993, Frankfurt/Main; 1977, sworn Translator for Russian and Polish. *Education:* Universities of Tübingen, Warsaw and Leningrad. Co-Editor: "WiRO - Wirtschaft und Recht Osteuropas," München 1992 ff. *Member:* German-Russian Forum; Society for Russian-German Economic Law; Society for East European Studies. (Also at Moscow, Russia Office). **LANGUAGES:** German, English, Russian, Polish and French. **PRACTICE AREAS:** Law of the Commonwealth of Independent States; Commercial and Corporate Law; Competition and Antitrust Law; Real Estate; Telecommunications; Energy Law.

DR. WOLFGANG RICHTER, born Fürth/Bayern, Germany, October 8, 1957; admitted, 1989, Frankfurt/Main. *Education:* Universities of Erlangen, Freiburg, Geneva; Harvard University, Kennedy School of Government (M.P.A., 1986). Author: "Gentechnologie als Regelungsgegenstand des technischen Sicherheitsrechts," 1989. *Member:* German Bar Association. **LANGUAGES:** German, English and French. **PRACTICE AREAS:** International Business Law; Corporate Law; Administrative Law.

MARTIN BECHTOLD, born Pforzheim, Germany, August 2, 1957; admitted, 1989, Frankfurt/Main. *Education:* University of Heidelberg; Federal Cartel Office, Berlin (1986-1989). *Member:* German Bar Association; Association for Antitrust Law Studies; German Association for the Protection of Industrial Property and Copyright. **LANGUAGES:** German and English. **PRACTICE AREAS:** Antitrust Law; Industrial Property Law; Law of Competition.

DR. ANDREAS DIETZEL, born Freiburg im Breisgau, Germany, June 14, 1959; admitted, 1988, Freiburg; 1990, Frankfurt/Main. *Education:* Universities of Freiburg and Geneva. Author: "Untergang statt Fortbestand-

(This Listing Continued)

Zur Abgrenzung der unvererblichen Rechtsbeziehungen im Schuldrecht," 1991. *Member:* German Bar Association. **LANGUAGES:** German, English and French. **PRACTICE AREAS:** Corporate Law; Commercial Law; Business Law.

DR. HORST SCHLEMMINGER, born Eppertshausen, Germany, November 4, 1959; admitted, 1988, Frankfurt/Main; Qualified Specialised Attorney-at-Law for Administrative Law. *Education:* University of Frankfurt. Assistant, Law Faculty of the University of Frankfurt, 1986-1987. Author: "Die gesetzliche Form der langfristigen Mietverträge über Grundstücke und Räume," 1994. Co-Author: "Environmental Liabilities and Regulation in Europe," 1993. *Member:* German Bar Association. **LANGUAGES:** German and English. **PRACTICE AREAS:** Real Estate; Building Law; Environmental Law.

UWE HORNUNG, born Darmstadt, Germany, November 15, 1960; admitted, 1989, Frankfurt/Main. *Education:* University of Frankfurt, Germany. *Member:* German Bar Association. **LANGUAGES:** German and English. **PRACTICE AREAS:** Litigation; Corporate Law; Business Law.

DR. JÜRGEN TASCHKE, born Niederrodenbach, Germany, August 2, 1956; admitted, 1986, Frankfurt/Main. *Education:* University of Frankfurt/Main (Dr. jur., 1988). Assistant to the Criminal Institute at the Law Faculty of Frankfurt University, 1982-1989. Author: "Die behördliche Zurückhaltung von Beweismitteln im Strafprozeß," Frankfurt/Main, Bern, New York, 1989. Co-editor: "Die Rechtsprechung zum Strafverfahrensrecht," 1989—. Editor: "Max Alsberg - Gesammelte Werke," 1992. *Member:* Board of Deutsche Strafverteidiger; Hessische Strafverteidiger; German Bar Association. **LANGUAGES:** German, English and French. **PRACTICE AREAS:** Commercial Crime; Bank Fraud.

PETER SCHERER, born Frankfurt/Main, Germany, June 17, 1958; admitted, 1990, Frankfurt/Main. *Education:* Frankfurt University and Indiana University, Bloomington (LL.M., 1989). *Member:* German and American Bar Associations; German-American Lawyers' Association; German Association for the Protection of Industrial Property and Copyright; Association for Antitrust Law Studies; Banking Law Society. **LANGUAGES:** German, English and French. **PRACTICE AREAS:** EU Law; Banking Law; Antitrust.

DR. HERMANN W. SCHMITT, born Kassel, Germany, May 15, 1961; admitted, 1989, Frankfurt/Main. *Education:* Universities of Marburg and Giessen. Judge, Civil Court, 1989-1990. Author: "Die Einrede des Schiedsvertrags im Verfahren des einstweiligen Rechtsschutzes," 1987; "Einstweiliger Rechtsschutz gegen drohende Gesellschafterbeschlüsse in der GmbH?" 1992. Co-Author: "Privatization in Eastern Germany: Legal Concepts and their Possible Value to Others," 1993. *Member:* International Bar Association; Society for Russian-German Economic Law. **LANGUAGES:** German, English and Russian. **PRACTICE AREAS:** Company Law; Arbitration; Privatizations; Mergers and Acquisitions; Project Finance.

DR. DIETRICH F.R. STILLER, born Braunschweig, Germany, April 15, 1960; admitted, 1990, Frankfurt/Main. *Education:* University of Bonn (Dr.jur.) and Yonsei University, Seoul. Zeuna Stärker GmbH & Co. KG, Assistant of the Managing Director, 1988-1990. Author: "Das internationale Zivilprozeßrecht der Republik Korea," 1989. *Member:* German-Korean Lawyers' Association. **LANGUAGES:** German, English and Korean. **PRACTICE AREAS:** Corporate Law; International Business Law; Private International Law; Privatizations.

DR. JOACHIM SCHREY, born Recklinghausen, Germany, April 4, 1961; admitted, 1990, Frankfurt/Main. *Education:* University of Mannheim, Germany. Assistant to the Chair for Public Law and Tax Law, University of Mannheim, 1986-1990. Author: "Wettbewerbsrechtliche Probleme beim Bildschirmtext," 1989. **LANGUAGES:** German and English. **PRACTICE AREAS:** Industrial Property Law; Computer Law; Distribution Contracts; Law on Standard Terms and Conditions; Law of Competition.

DR. ARNDT STENGEL, born Herne, Germany, February 25, 1963; admitted, 1991, Frankfurt/Main. *Education:* University of Trier (Dr. jur., 1992). Author: "Stiftung und Personengesellschaft," 1993. Co-Author: "Praxis der Gemeindeverwaltung (Stiftungsweren in Hessen)," 1994. *Member:* German Bar Association; AIJA. **LANGUAGES:** German, English and French. **PRACTICE AREAS:** Reorganizations and Insolvency; Corporate Law; Commercial Law; Foundations and Charities; Non-Profit Organizations.

(This Listing Continued)

ASSOCIATES

DR. ANNEGRET BÜRKLE, born Dortmund, Germany, February 2, 1958; admitted, 1987, Frankfurt/Main. *Education:* University of Frankfurt/Main. Author: "Rechte Dritter in der Satzung der GmbH," 1990. Assistant of the Institute for Foreign and International Business Law, Frankfurt, 1980 and of the Law Faculty of University of Frankfurt, 1983-1984. *Member:* German Bar Association. *LANGUAGES:* German and English. *PRACTICE AREAS:* Corporate Law; Business Law.

DR. ULRIKE BREIDENSTEIN, born Frankfurt/Main, Germany, July 28, 1958; admitted, 1988, Frankfurt/Main. *Education:* University of Frankfurt/Main. Author: "Grenzen der Regelungskompetenz des Betriebsrates beim Abschluß von Betriebsvereinbarungen zur Datenverarbeitung," 1991. *Member:* German Bar Association. *LANGUAGES:* German and English. *PRACTICE AREAS:* Labor Law; Business Law.

CHRISTINE KOZICZINSKI, born Hannover, Germany, March 18, 1960; admitted, 1990, Frankfurt/Main. *Education:* Universities of Würzburg, Freiburg and Heidelberg; European University Institute, Florence (LL.M., 1988). Author: "Mehr Macht der Kommission - Die legislativen Kompetenzen der EG-Kommission bei Untätigkeit des Rates," 1989. *Member:* German Bar Association, Vereinigung deutscher und italienischer Juristen zum Gedankenaustausch E.V. *LANGUAGES:* German, English and Italian. *PRACTICE AREAS:* Corporate and Business Law; EU Law.

DR. JOSEF BRINKHAUS, born Warendorf, Germany, January 20, 1960; admitted, 1991, Frankfurt/Main. *Education:* Universities of Münster and Cambridge/UK. Author: "Das britische Abwehrgesetz von 1980 - Alte und neue Methoden zur Abwehr amerikanischer Ansprüche auf extraterritoriale Jurisdiktionshoheit," Frankfurt/ Main et al., 1989. *Member:* German Bar Association; German-American Lawyers' Association. *LANGUAGES:* German and English. *PRACTICE AREAS:* International and German Tax Law; Corporate Law.

HANS GÜNTHER SCHMITT, born Gadernheim, Germany, November 27, 1957; admitted, 1991, Frankfurt/Main. *Education:* Universities of Mannheim (Master of Business Administration, 1983) and Munich. *LANGUAGES:* German, English and French. *PRACTICE AREAS:* German and International Tax Law; Corporate Law.

DR. ANDREA TIEDEMANN, born Hamburg, Germany, October 5, 1958; admitted, 1988, Hamburg; 1991, Frankfurt/Main. *Education:* University of Hamburg (Dr. jur., 1992); London School of Economics and Political Science. Research Assistant at the Max-Planck-Institute for Foreign and Private International Law, Hamburg, 1985-1988. Author: "Internationales Erbrecht in Deutschland und Lateinamerika," 1992. *Member:* Argentine-German Law Association (Member of Board, 1988—); German-Brazilian Law Association. *LANGUAGES:* German, English, Spanish, Portuguese and French. *PRACTICE AREAS:* International and German Business Law; Corporate Law; Litigation.

DR. STEFANIE TETZ, born Göttingen, Germany, April 16, 1960; admitted, 1991, Frankfurt/Main. *Education:* Universities of Bonn (Dr. jur.), Geneva, Beijing (Beida) and Shanghai (Fudan). Author: "Abschluß und Wirksamkeit von Verträgen in der Volksrepublik China," 1994. *Member:* German Bar Association; European Association for Chinese Law; German Association for Chinese Law. *LANGUAGES:* German, English and Mandarin. *PRACTICE AREAS:* Chinese Business Law; Commercial Law; Corporate and Business Law.

BEATE RÜDIG, born Hardert, Germany, January 11, 1957; admitted, 1987, Koblenz; 1992, Frankfurt/Main. *Education:* University of Bonn. *Member:* German Bar Association. *LANGUAGES:* German and English. *PRACTICE AREAS:* International and German Tax Law; Corporate Law.

UTE GÖRNER, born Frankfurt/Main, Germany, December 4, 1961; admitted, 1991, Frankfurt/Main. *Education:* Universities of Frankfurt/Main and Lausanne. *Member:* German Bar Association. *LANGUAGES:* German, English and French. *PRACTICE AREAS:* Labor and Employment Law; Commercial Law.

ANNETTE KESPOHL, born Bad Salzuflen, Germany, March 21, 1958; admitted, 1985, Hamburg; 1988, Bonn; 1991, Frankfurt/Main. *Education:* Universities of Münster and Bonn. Managing Director, German Bar Association, 1988-1991. *Member:* German Bar Association; Young Lawyers' International Association; German-American Lawyers' Association. *LANGUAGES:* German, English and French. *PRACTICE AREAS:* Corporate Law; Mergers and Acquisitions.

DR. MARTIN SCHÖDERMEIER, born Bensberg, Germany, July 27, 1959; admitted, 1990, Cologne; 1992, Düsseldorf; 1994, Frankfurt/Main. *Education:* University of Cologne (Dr. jur., 1989); Harvard Law School

(This Listing Continued)

(LL.M., 1985); University of Brussels; University of Paris I (D.E.A., European Community Law, 1987). Author: "Sonderprivatrecht für Internationale Wirtschaftsverträge," 1989. Co-Author: Chapters on "Selective Distribution "and" Exclusive Distribution and Exclusive Purchasing "in" *Juris-classeur Europe,"* (French Text Book on EU Law); Volume on "Specialisation and Research Development Agreements" of the "Gemeinschaftskommentar" (Textbook on German and EU Antitrust Laws). *Member:* German-American Lawyers' Association; Association for Antitrust Law Studies. *LANGUAGES:* German, English, French and Dutch. *PRACTICE AREAS:* Antitrust Law; EU Law; Banking and Corporate Law.

HANS-ULLRICH HAHN, born Hanau, Germany, September 21, 1962; admitted, 1992, Frankfurt/Main. *Education:* University of Frankfurt/Main. *Member:* German Bar Association. *LANGUAGES:* German and English. *PRACTICE AREAS:* Corporate Law; Banking and Securities Law.

JENNIFER MARLOW, born Nottingham, England, January 28, 1957; admitted as solicitor 1981, England; 1983, Hong Kong (Not admitted in Germany). *Education:* University of Bristol (LL.B., Hons.). *Member:* Law Society of England; Law Society of Hong Kong. *LANGUAGES:* English, German and French. *PRACTICE AREAS:* Corporate Law.

DR. CLAUS-PETER MARTENS, born Freiburg-Breisgau, Germany, September 11, 1960; admitted, 1991, Frankfurt/Main. *Education:* University of Bochum (Dr. jur.); University of Cambridge/U.K. (LL.M., 1989). Assistant at the Chair for Public Law and European Law, 1991, Bochum University. Author: "Die wesentliche Änderung im Sinne des §15 Bundes-Immissionsschutzgesetz unter besonderer Berücksichtigung des umfänglichen Anlagenbegriffs," 1993. Co-Author: "Environmental Liabilities and Regulation in Europe," 1993. *Member:* German Bar Association; International Bar Association. *LANGUAGES:* German, English and French. *PRACTICE AREAS:* Administrative Law; Environmental Law; Real Estate; EU Law.

THOMAS C. MAHLICH, born Berlin, Germany, March 7, 1959; admitted, 1989, Frankfurt/Main; 1991, Arizona. *Education:* University of Frankfurt, Germany; McGeorge School of Law (LL.M., 1990). *Member:* German Bar Association. *LANGUAGES:* German and English. *PRACTICE AREAS:* Litigation; Corporate Law.

JUTTA SCHNEIDER, born Solingen, Germany, October 16, 1961; admitted, 1992, Frankfurt/Main and New York. *Education:* University of Marburg; University of Virginia School of Law (LL.M., 1991). *Member:* German-American Lawyers' Association. *LANGUAGES:* German, English and Russian. *PRACTICE AREAS:* International and German Tax Law.

DR. PATRICK BIAGOSCH, born Paris, France, February 25, 1965; admitted, 1992, Munich; 1993, Frankfurt/Main. *Education:* Universities of Tübingen, Munich, Cologne (Dr. jur.). Author: "Europäische Dienstleistungsfreiheit und deutsches Versicherungsvertragsrecht," 1991. *Member:* German Bar Association. *LANGUAGES:* German, English and French. *PRACTICE AREAS:* Corporate and Tax Law.

MICHAEL MÜLLER, born Lahnstein, Germany, February 16, 1964; admitted, 1993, Frankfurt/Main. *Education:* Universities of Bonn and Berlin. *Member:* Society for Russian-German Economic Law. *LANGUAGES:* German, English, French and Russian. *PRACTICE AREAS:* Russian Economic Law.

DR. ANKE SESSLER, born Neustadt/Weinstraße, Germany, February 19, 1965; admitted, 1993, Frankfurt/Main. *Education:* University of Freiburg (Dr. jur.). Author: "Die Lehre von den Leistungsstörungen - Eine Untersuchung der schuldrechtlichen Lehren Heinrich Stolls unter besonderer Berücksichtigung seiner Lehre der Interessenjurisprudenz," 1993. *Member:* German Bar Association. *LANGUAGES:* German, English and French. *PRACTICE AREAS:* Corporate Law; Litigation.

DR. FRANK STELLMANN, born Rotenburg, Germany, July 18, 1961; admitted, 1993, Frankfurt/Main. *Education:* University of Kiel (Dr. jur.). Bank Clerk, Kiel, 1991-1993. Author: "Die Einziehung des Wertersatzes, §74 c StGB," 1991. *LANGUAGES:* German and English. *PRACTICE AREAS:* Real Estate; Construction Law.

ULRICH JACOB, born Bonn, Germany, April 18, 1962; admitted, 1993, Frankfurt/Main. *Education:* University of Mainz. *LANGUAGES:* German and English. *PRACTICE AREAS:* German and International Business Law; Labor and Employment Law.

MANFRED HEEMANN, born Mettingen, Germany, April 16, 1963; admitted, 1993, Frankfurt/Main. *Education:* University of Münster; University of Chicago Law School (LL.M., 1993). Assistant at the Institute of

(This Listing Continued)

PÜNDER, VOLHARD, WEBER & AXSTER,
Frankfurt/Main—Continued

Roman Law, Münster, 1992. *Member:* German-American Lawyers' Association; German-British Lawyers' Association; Deutscher Juristentag. *LANGUAGES:* German and English. *PRACTICE AREAS:* German and International Business Law; Corporate Law; Banking Law; Capital Market Transactions.

DR. STEFAN BEHRENS, born Essen, Germany, December 18, 1962; admitted, 1994, Frankfurt/Main. *Education:* University of Passau. *LANGUAGES:* German, English, French, Spanish and Russian. *PRACTICE AREAS:* Tax Law; Corporate Law.

FRANK OPRÉE, born Offenbach/Main, Germany, March 19, 1966; admitted, 1994, Frankfurt/Main. *Education:* University of Frankfurt. *LANGUAGES:* German and English. *PRACTICE AREAS:* Real Estate.

MARKUS PFÜLLER, born Frankfurt, Germany, November 24, 1960; admitted, 1992, Frankfurt/Main. *Education:* University of Freiburg. *Member:* British-German Lawyers' Association. *LANGUAGES:* German, English and French. *PRACTICE AREAS:* Corporate Law; Banking and Securities Law.

DR. STEFAN MENNER, born Überlingen, Germany, May 24, 1962; admitted, 1990, München; 1994, Frankfurt/Main. *Education:* University of Konstanz (Dr.jur.); University of Houston Law Center (LL.M., 1993). Author: "Die Umsatzsteuerharmonisierung in der Europäischen Gemeinschaft," 1992. Co-Author: "Federal Tax System." Editor, German Experience, Vosgerau, European Integration in the World Economy, 1992. *Member:* German-American Lawyers' Association; Vereinigung zur wissenschaftlichen Pflege des Umsatzsteuerrechts; International Fiscal Association. *LANGUAGES:* German and English. *PRACTICE AREAS:* National and International Tax Law; Corporate Law.

DR. LUTZ HORN, born Kamen, Germany, August 30, 1963; admitted, 1994, Frankfurt/Main. *Education:* Universities of Saarbrücken and Marburg (Dr.jur.). Research Assistant, Institute for Public Law, University of Marburg, 1988-1991. Author: "Die Anwendung militärischer Gewalt auf zivile Passagierflugzeuge im Friedensvölkerrecht und ihre Rechtsfolgen," 1992. *Member:* German Bar Association. *LANGUAGES:* German, English and French. *PRACTICE AREAS:* Administrative Law; Planning Law; Environmental Law; Government Employees' Law; EU-Procurement Procedures Law.

VOLKER KAMMEL, born Viernheim, Germany, July 8, 1964; admitted, 1994, Frankfurt/Main. *Education:* University of Heidelberg. *LANGUAGES:* German, English and Afrikaans. *PRACTICE AREAS:* Corporate Law; Insolvency Law; Tax Law.

THOMAS REICH, born Frankfurt/Main, April 18, 1966; admitted, 1994, Frankfurt/Main. *Education:* University of Würzburg; Open University Hagen. University Fellow, Institute of Commercial and Tax Law, Würzburg, 1991-1994. *LANGUAGES:* German and English. *PRACTICE AREAS:* German and International Tax Law.

DR. FRANK SCHOLDERER, born Frankfurt/Main, Germany, January 6, 1963; admitted, 1994, Frankfurt/Main. *Education:* University of Frankfurt (Dr.jur.). Assistant, Law Faculty of Frankfurt, 1988-1990. Author: "Rechtsbeugung im demokratischen Rechtsstaat," 1993. *LANGUAGES:* German, English and French. *PRACTICE AREAS:* Corporate Law.

ANDREAS JÜRGENS, born Wolfsburg, Germany, September 6, 1965; admitted, 1994, Frankfurt/Main. *Education:* Universities of Münster and Göttingen. *Member:* German Bar Association. *LANGUAGES:* German and English. *PRACTICE AREAS:* Corporate Law.

SIMONE MACKEPRANG, born Wiesbaden, Germany, July 17, 1962; admitted, 1994, Frankfurt/Main. *Education:* University of Passau. *Member:* German Bar Association; German-French Lawyers' Association. *LANGUAGES:* German, English and French. *PRACTICE AREAS:* Corporate Law; International Law.

DR. UWE MURMANN, born Sprendlingen, Germany, January 13, 1963; admitted, 1994, Frankfurt/Main. *Education:* University of Frankfurt/Main. Author: "Die Nebentäterschaft im Strafrecht," 1993. *LANGUAGES:* German and English. *PRACTICE AREAS:* Commercial Crime; Bank Fraud.

DR. GÜNTHER BREDOW, born Garmisch, Germany, July 17, 1962; admitted, 1993, Munich; 1994, Frankfurt/Main; 1994, International and Corporate Lawyer. *Education:* University of Munich, New York University, School of Law (LL.M., 1994); Universidad de Salmanca (Spain). Author: "Spanisches Werberecht." 1990; "Das neue spanische Markenrecht," 1994. *Member:* German Bar Association. *LANGUAGES:* German, English and Spanish. *PRACTICE AREAS:* Corporate Law; Mergers and Acquisitions; Antitrust Law.

GEORG RÜTZEL, born Bocholt i.W., Germany, March 3, 1964; admitted, 1994, Frankfurt/Main. *Education:* Universities of Freiburg i.Br. and Münster i.W. *LANGUAGES:* German, English and Dutch. *PRACTICE AREAS:* Tax Law.

STEFAN RÜTZEL, born Hosenfeld, Germany, July 15, 1962; admitted, 1994, Frankfurt/Main. *Education:* Universities of Frankfurt/Main and Speyer, University of Georgia School of Law (LL.M., 1994). Assistant, University of Frankfurt/Main, 1989/1990. Author: "Snitching for the Common Good: In Search of Response to the Legal Problems Posed by Environmental Whistleblowing," 1994. *Member:* German Bar Association; German-American Lawyers' Association. *LANGUAGES:* German and English. *PRACTICE AREAS:* Corporate Law.

DR. JOSEF MARIA WODICKA, born Frankfurt, Germany, August 16, 1961; admitted, 1994, Frankfurt/Main. *Education:* University of Heidelberg. Author: "Untreue - § 266 StGB - zum Nachteil der GmbH," 1993. *LANGUAGES:* German, English and French. *PRACTICE AREAS:* Real Estate.

DR. YORK-GERO VON AMSBERG, born Hamburg, May 19, 1963; admitted, 1994, Frankfurt/Main. *Education:* University of Heidelberg, Munich and Frankfurt am Main (Dr. jur.). Author: Anspruchskonkurrenz, Cumul and Samenloop-Das Verhältnis von Ersatz ansprüchen aus Vertrag und Delikt im deutschen, belgischen und niederländischen Recht, Frankfurt 1994. *LANGUAGES:* German, English, French, Dutch and Spanish. *PRACTICE AREAS:* Commercial Law; Intellectual Property Law; Law of Competition.

CORNELIA PIEHLER, born Hamburg, Germany, September 6, 1966; admitted, 1994, Frankfurt/Main. *Education:* University of Erlangen-Nürnberg. *Member:* German Bar Association. *LANGUAGES:* English, French, Italian. *PRACTICE AREAS:* Construction Law; Planning Law; Administrative Law.

DR. WOLFGANG HESS, born Cologne, Germany, April 7, 1963; admitted, 1994 Frankfurt/Main. *Education:* Universities of Bonn and Cologne (Dr.jur.). Teaching Fellow of the Law Faculty of University of Cologne, 1991-1994. Author: Verfassungsreschtliche Probleme der Gebährenfinanzierung im dualen "Rundfunksystem" 1994. *Member:* German Law Association. *LANGUAGES:* German, English and French. *PRACTICE AREAS:* Public Law; Planning and Building Law; Public Service Contracts; Environmental Law; Media and Telecomunication Law.

GUDULA LOOMAN, born Hamburg, Germany, January 20, 1966; admitted, 1994, Frankfurt/Main. *Education:* University of Frankfurt am Main. *LANGUAGES:* German, English, French. *PRACTICE AREAS:* Public Law; Planning and Building Law; Environmental Law; Competition Law.

TAX ADVISORS

HEINZ VESELY, born Reichenberg, CSFR, January 14, 1930; 1962, Tax Advisor. *Education:* University of Frankfurt (Master of National Economics, 1955). *Member:* American Tax Institute; International Fiscal Association. *LANGUAGES:* German, English and French. *PRACTICE AREAS:* International Tax Law; German Corporate Tax Law.

JÜRGEN MÜHLHÄUSER, born Frankfurt/Main, Germany, April 25, 1939; 1970, Tax Advisor. *Education:* Universities of Darmstadt and Mannheim (M.B.A., 1964). *Member:* Chamber of Tax Advisors. *LANGUAGES:* German and English. *PRACTICE AREAS:* German Tax Law; Auditing and Valuations.

WOLFGANG OHO, born Rüdesheim/Rhein, Germany, April 13, 1951; 1980, Tax Advisor. *Education:* University of Giessen (Master of Business Administration, 1974). *Member:* Frankfurter Finanzforum e.V. *LANGUAGES:* German, English and French. *PRACTICE AREAS:* International and German Tax Law; Reorganizations; Tax Structuring; Leasing.

HEINZ SCHÄFER, born Darmstadt, Germany, April 11, 1942; 1977, Tax Advisor (Not admitted to bar). *Education:* University of Frankfurt. *Member:* Chamber of Tax Advisors. *LANGUAGES:* German, English and French. *PRACTICE AREAS:* Tax Law; Auditing and Valuations.

MARTIN STARK, born Daun, Germany, November 22, 1956; 1987, Tax Advisor (Not admitted to bar). *Education:* FH Mainz II. *LANGUAGES:* German and English. *PRACTICE AREAS:* Tax Law.

(This Listing Continued)

(This Listing Continued)

JUTTA AICHELE, born Worms, Germany, June 21, 1961; 1990, Tax Advisor. *Education:* FH Mainz II. *LANGUAGES:* German and English. *PRACTICE AREAS:* Tax Law; Auditing.

ALEXANDER SCHNEIDER, born Achern/Baden, Germany, June 2, 1962; 1992, Tax Advisor (Not admitted to bar). *Education:* FH Mainz II. *LANGUAGES:* German and English. *PRACTICE AREAS:* Tax Law; Auditing.

(For complete biographical data on personnel at Düsseldorf, Berlin and Leipzig, Germany, Brussels, Belgium, Moscow, Russia, Warsaw, Poland, New York, New York and Beijing, People's Republic of China, see Professional Biographies at those locations)

RÄDLER RAUPACH BEZZENBERGER

FRANKFURT/MAIN, GERMANY

(See Oppenhoff & Rädler)

PAUL D. REINSDORF

Established in 1989

FEUERBACHSTRASSE 5

60325 FRANKFURT/MAIN, GERMANY

Telephone: (069) 725899 International: 011-49-69-725899
Telefax: (069) 172319; International: 011-49-69-172319

International Civil Litigation. Business Venture Advisement.

PAUL D. REINSDORF, born Anaheim, California, March 14, 1961; admitted, 1987, Massachusetts; 1988, U.S. District Court for the District of Massachusetts; 1989, Rechtskundiger des Rechts der U.S.A., Frankfurt-/Main. *Education:* Syracuse University (B.A., cum laude, 1982); Northeastern University School of Law (J.D., 1987); London School of Economics and Political Science (1982). Judicial Extern, The Honorable William W Schwarzer, U.S. District Court, Northern District of California, 1986. With Owens & Associates, Boston, MA, 1988. Lecturer, University of Maryland in Europe, 1989. *Member:* American Bar Association; The Association of Trial Lawyers of America. *LANGUAGES:* English and German. *PRACTICE AREAS:* Contracts.

OF COUNSEL

SALOMON J. AUGAPFEL, born St. Blasien, Germany, September 27, 1948; admitted, 1976, Frankfurt/Main. *Education:* Johann Wolfgang Goethe Universität, 1967-1973. Research Assistant, International Private and Comparative Law, Johann Wolfgang Goethe Universität, 1977-1982. With Dr. E. Klimowsky, Tel Aviv, Israel, Referendar, 1974-1975. Member: Rechtsanwaltkammer Frankfurt/Main; German-Israel, Chamber of Commerce. *LANGUAGES:* German, English, French and Hebrew. *PRACTICE AREAS:* International Trade; Corporate Law; Probate.

CONSULTANT

FREDERICK H. GERLACH, born Milwaukee, Wisconsin, August 9, 1938. *Education:* University of Wisconsin (B.A., cum laude, 1961); Bonn University, Germany (Bonn-Wisconsin exchange scholar, 1959-1960); Columbia University (M.I.A., 1963; Ph.D., 1968). Foreign Service Officer, Department of State, 1966-1987; Deputy Chief of Mission/Chargé d'Affaires, Abu Dhabi, United Arab Emirates, 1985-1987; Deputy Director, Energy Office, Department of State, 1982-1985; Officer-in-Charge, U.S. Embassy Liaison Office, Riyadh, Saudi Arabia, 1978-1982. Consultant, Frankfurt, Germany, 1988—. Lecturer, Boston University Overseas Program, 1991—. *Member:* American Foreign Service Association; Diplomatic and Consular Officers, Retired; Middle East Institute; American Chamber of Commerce in Germany; Nah- und Mittelost Verein e.V. *LANGUAGES:* English, German, French and Arabic. *PRACTICE AREAS:* International Trade; Privatization; Strategy.

RITTERSHAUS, WISSMANN & VON ROSENSTIEL

Established in 1993

LEERBACHSTRASSE 58

D-60322 FRANKFURT/MAIN, GERMANY

Telephone: (0) 69/17 41 91
Fax: (0) 69/17 43 51

Mannheim, Germany Office: Theodor-Heuss-Anlage 2, D-68165. Telephone: (0) 621/4256-0. Fax: (0)621/4256-250.

Commercial Law and Contracts, Corporate Law, Mergers and Acquisitions, Unfair Competition, Taxation, Arbitration, Banking, Notary, General Practice, Real Estate, Construction Law, Divorce, Entertainment and Sports.

MEMBERS OF FIRM

RAINER DIETMANN, born Bonn, October 15, 1956; admitted, 1985, Germany. *Education:* University of Mannheim; London School of Economics. Assistant Lecturer on Law, University of Heidelberg, 1980-1982. *LANGUAGES:* German, French and English. *PRACTICE AREAS:* Commercial Acquisitions; Leveraged and Management Buyouts; Commercial Tax; Holding Companies; Contracts; Entertainment and Sports.

WENDELIN FREIHERR VON KETELHODT, born Wolfsburg, September 2, 1954; admitted, 1985; Notary, 1991, Germany. *Education:* University of Frankfurt. Assistant Lecturer on Law, University of Frankfurt, 1981-1985. *LANGUAGES:* German and English. *PRACTICE AREAS:* Corporate Law; Real Estate; Construction Law; Contracts.

HELLA FREIFRAU VON KETELHODT, born Wiesbaden, November 18, 1944; admitted, 1984, Germany. *Education:* University of Frankfurt. *LANGUAGES:* German and English. *PRACTICE AREAS:* Divorce.

DR. BERND-MICHAEL ZINOW, born Stade, June 27, 1963; admitted, 1993, Germany. *Education:* University of Mannheim (Dr. jur., 1991). Author: "Rechtsprobleme der grenzüberschreitenden Durchleitung von Strom in einem EG-Binnenmarkt für Energie," 1991; "Zu den Rechtsansprüchen der Städte und Gemeinden der neuen Bundesländer bei der Gründung von Stadtwerken," LKV 1992, 1 ff. *Member:* International Bar Association (Member, Section of Energy and Natural Resources Law). *LANGUAGES:* German and English. *PRACTICE AREAS:* Law of the European Communities; Energy Law.

Languages: German, English, French, Spanish and Italian.

(For Complete Biographical Data on all Personnel, see Professional Biographies at Mannheim, Germany)

ROGERS & WELLS

LINDENSTRASSE 37

60325 FRANKFURT/MAIN, GERMANY

Telephone: 49-69-97-57-11-0
Facsimile: 49-69-97-57-11-33

REVISERS OF THE NEW YORK LAW DIGEST FOR THIS DIRECTORY.

New York, New York Office: Two Hundred Park Avenue, New York, N.Y. 10166-0153. Telephone: 212-878-8000. Facsimile: 212-878-8375. Telex: 234493 RKWUR.

Washington, D.C. Office: 607 Fourteenth Street, N.W., Washington, D.C. 20005-2011. Telephone: 202-434-0700. Facsimile: 202-434-0800.

Los Angeles, California Office: 444 South Flower Street, Los Angeles, California 90071-2901. Telephone: 213-689-2900. Facsimile: 213-689-2999.

London, England Office: 58 Coleman Street, London EC2R 5BE, England. Telephone: 44-171-628-0101. Facsimile: 44-171-638-2008. Telex: 884964 USLAW G.

Paris, France Office: 47, Avenue Hoche, 75008-Paris, France. Telephone: 33-1-44-09-46-00. Facsimile: 33-1-42-67-50-81. Telex: 651617 EURLAW.

General Practice.

PARTNERS

JOHANNES K. GÄBEL, born Munich, Germany, April 20, 1952; admitted, 1978, Germany; 1983, New York; 1984, U.S. District Court, Southern and Eastern Districts of New York. *Education:* Karlsgymnasium, Munich (Abitur, 1971); University of Munich (Rechtsreferendar, 1976; Dr. jur., 1983); Oberlandesgericht, Munich (Assessor, 1978); International As-

(This Listing Continued)

EU669B

ROGERS & WELLS, *Frankfurt/Main—Continued*

sociation of Comparative Law (Diplôme de Droit Comparé, 1979); Cornell University (J.D., cum laude, 1982). Author: "Das venezolanische Arbeitsrecht," 1977; "Neuere Probleme zur Aufrechnung im internat. Privatrecht," 1983; "Verbraucherschutz in den USA und die Auswirkungen auf deutsche Unternehmen," RIW/AWD, 1984, p. 253; (with Klaus H. Jander); "Neuere Entwicklungen der verschuldensunabhängigen Haftung im Produkthaftpflichtrecht der USA," ZVgl RWiss 1989, 352 (with Werner Gaus); "Das Ende des Streites um Parallelimporte in den USA," ZVgl RWiss 1990, 97; "Listing and Issuing Securities in Germany," Corporate Finance 2/1992; "Dividend Stripping," The International Tax Journal, 1994, 8. Member, Panel of Arbitrators, American Arbitration Association. *Member:* Association of the Bar of the City of New York; American and International Bar Associations; German-American Law Association. (Also at New York, N.Y. Office). *LANGUAGES:* German and Spanish.

KLAUS H. JANDER, born Glogau, Germany, May 17, 1940; admitted, 1964, New York; 1969, U.S. Supreme Court; 1980, District of Columbia (Not admitted in Germany). *Education:* Germany and Queens College of the City University of New York (B.A., 1961); Germany and Cornell University (J.D., 1964). Member, Panel of Arbitrators, American Arbitration Association. Author or Co-Author: "Public Offerings of Securities by Foreign Companies in the U.S.A.," New York/Bonn, 1984; "Zur Gruendung und Fuehrung von Tochtergesellschaften in den USA," Deutsch-Amerikanische Handelskammer New York/Bonn, 1982; "Anerkennung von Gerichtsstandsvereinbarungen in den U.S.A.," "Die Forderungssicherung unter dem Uniform Commercial Code im Handel mit den U.S.A.," "Amerikanische Sozialversicherung, insbesondere bei deutschen Arbeitnehmern mit Treaty Trader- (E-1) Visum," "Das neue Gesetz zur Lieferantengarantie in den U.S.A.," "Die Legal Opinion im Verkehr mit den U.S.A.," "Hart-Scott Rodino-Antitrust Improvements Act of 1976," all in Aussenwirtschaftsdienst, p. 437, 1972; p. 181, 1973; p. 281, 1975; pp. 78 and 332, 1976; p. 204, 1977, respectively; "Vermoegensuebertragungen im Erbschaftssteuer und Schenkungssteuerrecht der U.S.A.," Internat. Wirtschaftsbriefe, p. 359, 1977; "Verjaehrungsprobleme im internationalen Privatrecht der U.S.A.," "Steuerliche Aspekte bei Investitionen von Auslaendern in US-Amerikanischen 'Corporations' und 'Partnerships'," "Die Besteuerung von Einkuenften einer auslaendischen Gesellschaft, deren Anteile sich im wesentlichen in U.S.-Haenden befinden, durch die U.S.A.," "Uebersicht ueber das neue amerikanische Konkursrecht," "Uebersicht ueber gesetzliche Grundlagen und Anwendungsbereich US-amerikanischer Exportrestriktionen," "Verbraucherschutz in den USA und die Auswirkungen auf deutsche Unternehmen," "US-Steuerliche Aspekte amerikanischer Forschungsund Entwicklungsausgaben," Grey Market Imports in die USA; Kuendigungsschutz im amerikanischen Arbeitsrecht - Das Ende der Employee-at-Will Doktrin?; Neue Methoden bei Unternehmenskaeufen in den USA; Anti-Dumping und Ausgleichszollverfahren in den USA; Erstellung und Aufbewahrung von innerbetrieblichen Akten im Prozess- und Produkthaftpflichtrecht in den USA; Recht der Internat. Wirtschaft/Aussenwirtschaftsdienst, pp. 358 and 592, 1978; p. 398, 1979; p. 744, 1981; p. 778, 1982, p. 253 and p. 793, 1984, p. 325, 1986; p. 25, 1988; p. 582, 1991; p. 105, 1992, respectively; Promissory Note and Bill of Exchange - Amerikanische Wechsel? p. 410, 1988; Zeitschrift fuer Verfgleichende Rechtswissenschaft; Eastern Germany: An Investment Road Map, p. 33, 1991; The Journal of Business Strategy; "Business Opportunities in the United States," Price Waterhouse, Richard D. Irwin, Inc., 1992. *Member:* The Association of the Bar of the City of New York; New York State and International Bar Associations; New York County Lawyers Association (Member, Committee on Foreign and International Law, 1976—); Deutscher Anwaltsverein, e.V.; German-American Law Association. [Judge Advocate, U.S. Air Force, active duty, 1965-1968; Col., USAFR, 1968—]. (Also at New York, N.Y. Office). *LANGUAGES:* German and French.

COUNSEL

DIETER G. ZWICKER, born Goeppingen, Germany, August 9, 1946; admitted, 1980, Germany; 1989, Frankfurt. *Education:* University of Munich in Tuebingen, Hochschulefur Verwaltungswissenschaften, Speyer. Corporate Lawyer (Syndic), Suedwestdeutsche Landesbank Stuttgart, 1976-1993. Corporate Finance Department, Westdeutsche Landesbank Duesseldorf. Associate General Counsel, Hitachi Data Systems London. Head of Legal Department, Deutsche Leasing AG, Bad Homburg vdh. *LANGUAGES:* German, English.

DR. MICHAEL F. GRIESBECK, born Bamberg, Germany, January 28, 1947; admitted, 1978, Frankfurt. *Education:* Julius Maximilian University Würzburg (Referendar 1972, Assessor 1976, Dr. juris utriusque 1979); Université de Caen (France) 1973; The Hague Academy of International

(This Listing Continued)

Law 1979. Author: "venire contra factum proprium im Zivil- und Zivilrprozeßrecht," 1979; "Nacheheliche Unterhaltspflicht und Ordre Public," FamRZ 1983, 961. *LANGUAGES:* German, English, French, Spanish.

ASSOCIATES

JOACHIM A. BAST, born Steinfeld, February 23, 1957; admitted, 1988, Frankfurt. *Education:* Economics, University Hagen, 1980-1986; Free University of Berlin, Ruprecht Karls University School of Law, Heidelberg (Referendar, with honors, 1983). Author: "Nichtigkeit von Steuerbescheiden," RIW, 1990, 382 (Invalidity of Tax Assessment Notes); "GATT-Streitschlichtungsver-fahren," RIW, 1991, 929 (GATT Dispute Settlement Procedure); "Zum Verhältuis der Einreihungsvorschriften zur Schraubenzieherverordnung," ZfZ 1992, 1 (Relationship of the Tariff Classification Rules to the Screwdriver Regulation); "Der Grundsatz des rechtlichen Gehörs im Gemeinschaftsrecht," RIW 1992, 742 (The Principle of the Right of a Fair Hearing in Community Law); "Beihilfen in der EG und Rechtsschutzmöglichkeiten für Wettbewerber," WuW 93, 181 (Aid in the European Community and Legal Protection for Competitors). Associate, Arthur Andersen & Co., Frankfurt, 1987-1990. Associate, EC-Commission Legal Service, 1990-1991. *LANGUAGES:* German and English.

PROF. DR. MICHAEL H. MEUB, born Hanau am Main, Germany, September 18, 1949; admitted, 1978, Frankfurt. *Education:* Hochschule für Verwaltungswissenschaften, Speyer; Goethe University (1983). Author: Comparative Law book on maritime transport liability, Peter Lang, 1982; The international automotive industry and the GATT - rules, Handelsblatt, 1990; The North American Free Trade Agreement NAFTA, EuZW 1993. Full professor, Fachhochschule für Technik und Wirtschaft Mittweida (Saxonia). *LANGUAGES:* German, English, French, Italian.

STEFAN KUGLER, born Landshut, Germany, November 15, 1962; admitted, 1992, Germany; 1994, New York. *Education:* Munich, Lausanne and Hamburg Universities; Munich University (State Exam, 1992); Southern Methodist University (LL.M., 1992). *LANGUAGES:* English, French.

Languages: English, French, German and Portuguese

REVISERS OF THE NEW YORK LAW DIGEST FOR THIS DIRECTORY.

(For biographical data of all partners, see Professional Biographies at New York, New York)

ROSSBACH & PARTNER

Established in 1973

STRESEMANNALLEE 33
D-60596 FRANKFURT/MAIN, GERMANY
Telephone: 069-63 11 021
Telex: 41 49 78
Telefax: 069-63 75 00

General Civil and Notarial Practice, Antitrust, Aviation, Banking, Bankruptcy, Corporations, Entertainment, Environmental, Estate Planning, Industrial and Intellectual Property, International, Labour, Mergers and Acquisitions, Probate, Real Estate, Taxation, Transportation, Unfair Competition, General Civil Trial and Appellate as well as Arbitration Practice.

FIRM PROFILE: The firm was established in 1973 and offers a full range of legal services including those of a German notary public. Currently the firm is representing a broad variety of commercial clients based in Europe, North America and Asia, including foreign as well as domestic banks, companies in the electronics and construction industry, a major courier service and advertising agencies.

The firm is cooperating with Bryan Cave, St. Louis, Missouri, USA.

MEMBERS OF FIRM

JOHANN-ANDREAS ROSSBACH, born Erfurt, Germany, January 19, 1939; admitted, 1967, Frankfurt; 1973, Notary. *Education:* Universities of Frankfurt, Lausanne, Munich, Bonn and Cornell Law (Teaching and Research Fellowship, 1964). *LANGUAGES:* English, French and German. *PRACTICE AREAS:* International and German Corporate; Commercial and Business Law; Arbitration; Real Property Law; Antitrust Law; Mergers and Acquisitions.

BERND MOHR, born Frankfurt am Main, Germany, November 25, 1961; admitted, 1993, Frankfurt am Main. *Education:* University of Frankfurt am Main. *LANGUAGES:* English and German. *PRACTICE AREAS:* General Commercial Law; Competition Laws; Industrial Property Rights; Litigation.

(This Listing Continued)

SALOMON GRÜNBERG, born Munich, Germany, May 28, 1959; admitted, 1991, Frankfurt am Main. *Education:* Universities of Munich and Frankfurt am Main. Intern, Slotnick & Baker, New York, 1990. *Member:* German/American Law Association. *LANGUAGES:* German, English and Hebrew. *PRACTICE AREAS:* General Corporate Law; Commercial Law; International Business Law; EC Law.

DR. MATTHIAS MENKE, born Cologne, Germany, September 28, 1962; admitted, 1994, Frankfurt am Main. *Education:* Universities of Munich and Frankfurt am Main (Dr. Jur., 1993). Intern Bryan Cave, Saint Louis, 1993. *LANGUAGES:* English, Spanish and German. *PRACTICE AREAS:* General Corporate Law; Commercial Law; International Business Law; EC Law.

RÜCKEL, TRENKNER & COLLEGEN

BOCKENHEIMER ANLAGE 13
60322 FRANKFURT/MAIN, GERMANY
Telephone: (069) 55 07 31
Fax: (069) 596 39 94

Atlanta, Georgia Office: Ten Piedmont Center, Suite 350, 3495 Piedmont Road, 30305. Telephone: (404) 266-1008. Fax: (404) 266-0205.
Berlin, Germany Office: Kurfürstendamm 132 A, 10711. Telephone: (030) 896 6920. Fax: (030) 8966 9244.
Dresden, Germany Office: Bautzner Straße 14, 01099. Telephone: (0351) 502 43 00. Fax: (0351) 502 43 02.
Leipzig, Germany Office: Marperger Straße 20, 04229. Telephone: (0341) 401 13 41. Fax: (0341) 401 14 54.
Munich, Germany Office: Karollnenstraße 4, 80538. Telephone: (089) 212 38 70. Fax: (089) 212 38 75 0.

General Practice, Litigation and Commercial Law, International Business Transactions, Real Estate, Corporate.

FIRM PROFILE: *The firm is a member of LAWORLD. LAWORLD is an international organization of law firms who coordinate and share information with other member firms in Brussels, Budapest, Hong Kong, Jerusalem, Lausanne, London, Moscow, New York, Padova, Stockholm, Taipei, Tel Aviv, Vancouver, Warsaw, Zagreb and Zug.*

MEMBERS OF FIRM

HAGEN TRENKNER, born Hannover, Germany, January 30, 1939; admitted, 1970, Germany; 1985, Notary Public. *Education:* University of Berlin (1960); University of Hamburg (1962); University of Saarbrücken (1963); University of Würzburg (1964). Author: "Competition Law in Europa," article; "Financing-Leasing-Factoring," quarterly journal of an Association of Banks. Lecturer, Transborder Data Flow in Europe; Differences between European Countries concerning Data Protection Law. Honorary Legal Adviser and Member of Council, British Chamber of Commerce in Germany. *Member:* Frankfurt Bar Association. *LANGUAGES:* English and French. *PRACTICE AREAS:* Business Law; Company Law; Data Protection Law.

LUTZ W.J. WALLRAVEN, born Berlin, Germany, April 5, 1941; admitted, 1970, Germany; 1988, High Court of Appeal; 1989, Notary Public. *Education:* J.W. Goethe University (1967). Author: "Prevention against Bribery," Basics of Criminology, Vol. 13/2; "Competition Law in Theory and Practice," Ebner Verlag Ulm, 1987; "Wettbewerb in Recht und Praxis," Essays. *Member:* Frankfurt Bar Association; Frankfurt Notaries Association; German Society on Industrial Property Protection and Copyright; International League for Competition Law. *LANGUAGES:* French and English. *PRACTICE AREAS:* Industrial Property Rights; Copyright; Company Law; Business Law.

FRED ALBRECHT, born Gifhorn, Germany, May 23, 1949; admitted, 1980, Germany. *Education:* University of Marburg/Lahn (1970; 1st State Exam, 1977; 2nd State Exam, 1980). *Member:* German Law Society (Construction Law Section). *LANGUAGES:* English and French. *PRACTICE AREAS:* Business Law; Criminal Law; Insurance Law; Building Law.

HANS HELLWAG (1950-1991), Rechtsanwalt and Notary.

(For biographical data on additional personnel, see Professional Biographies at Munich, Germany)

SCHEIBER & PARTNER

METZLERSTRAßE 39
60594 FRANKFURT/MAIN, GERMANY
Telephone: (069) 61 80 41
Fax: (069) 61 80 46

Berlin, Germany Office: Frankfurter Allee 69, 10247 Berlin. Telephone: (030) 2386938. Telefax: (030) 2082050.

General Practice, Commercial, Company, Corporations, Unfair Competition, Government Contracts, Real Estate, Environmental Law, Transportation, Insurance Law, Estate Planning, International Law, Notary's Office.

FIRM PROFILE: *The firm was established in 1959 and provides qualified legal service on a personal basis.*

MEMBERS OF FIRM

PETER SCHEIBER, admitted, 1975, Frankfurt. *Education:* Universities of Göttingen, Bonn and Frankfurt. Notary Public, 1984. *Member:* Association of Insurance and Economy; Institute for Tax and Economy Law. *PRACTICE AREAS:* Commercial Law; Product Liability; Real Estate.

SOLVEIG STOCK, admitted, 1988, Frankfurt. *Education:* University of Erlangen. *LANGUAGES:* French. *PRACTICE AREAS:* Estate Planning and Probate; Administrative Law; International Law; Unfair Competition.

JÜRGEN PEITZ, admitted, 1987, Bielefeld; 1989, Frankfurt. *Education:* University of Bielefeld; University Fellow of the Institute for Criminology and Penal Law. *PRACTICE AREAS:* Penal Law; Law of Freight and Forwarders; Litigation.

UWE ZIMMER, admitted, 1990, Berlin. *Education:* University of Leipzig. Judge, Contract-Court, Berlin. *Member:* Berlin Bar Association. (Resident Partner at Berlin). *LANGUAGES:* Russian. *PRACTICE AREAS:* Real Property Law; Environmental Law.

ASSOCIATES

CARL W. KIEFER, admitted, 1976, Frankfurt. *Education:* University of Frankfurt. *PRACTICE AREAS:* Real Estate; Sports Law; Notary Public.

PETER WOLF, admitted, 1956, Essen; 1968, Frankfurt. *Education:* Universities of Köln and Bonn. Author: "Allgemeine Deutsche Spediteur-Bedingungen," German Forwarder, Standard Terms and Conditions, 15th ed., 1992. *Member:* Advisory Fiata Association (Intern. Federation of Freight and Forwarders; Deputy Chairman); D.T.V. (German Transport Insurance Association). *PRACTICE AREAS:* German and International Law of Freight and Forwarders; Carriers and Transport with respective Insurance Covers.

JOACHIM HEFFINGER, admitted, 1987, Hanau; 1990, Frankfurt. *Education:* University of Frankfurt. *Member:* German Society for Building Law. *PRACTICE AREAS:* Building and Planning Law; Banking.

MATTHIAS LOTZ, admitted, 1990, Frankfurt. *Education:* University of Frankfurt. *PRACTICE AREAS:* Real Estate Law; Insurance Law; Product Liability Law; Environmental Law.

DR. GERD MERKE, admitted, 1986, Munich; 1992, Frankfurt. *Education:* Universities of Augsburg, Munich, Grenoble, Madrid and Illinois, Chicago/Champlain. Author: Interstate Commerce, 1985; Free Trade US-/EC, 1987. *Member:* German/American Lawyer's Association. *LANGUAGES:* French and Spanish. *PRACTICE AREAS:* International Trade; EC Law.

PETER KLEMISCH, admitted, 1993, Frankfurt. *Education:* University of Regensburg. *PRACTICE AREAS:* German and International Law of Freight and Forwarders; Labour Law.

PETER MADEL, admitted, 1993, Frankfurt. *Education:* University of Mainz. *PRACTICE AREAS:* Tax Law; Company Law.

CHRISTINE YAZDANI, admitted, 1993, Frankfurt. *Education:* University of Freiburg. *PRACTICE AREAS:* International Law; Real Estate.

All lawyer personnel are members of the German Bar Association

Languages: German, English and French

SCHÜRMANN & PARTNERS

Established in 1957

FRIEDRICH-EBERT-ANLAGE 14

60325 FRANKFURT/MAIN, GERMANY

Telephone: 069-7 54 90

Telefax: 7549 290

Mailing Address: P.O. Box 11 16 33, 60051 Frankfurt/Main, Germany

Berlin, Germany Office: Karl-Liebknecht-Strasse 32, 10178. Telephone: 030-247-5960. Telefax: 030-238-6032.

Bonn, Germany Office: Philosophenring 94, 53177 Bonn. Telephone: 0228-328-055, Telefax: 0228-311-863.

Brussels, Belgium Office: Avenue de la Raquette 24, B-1150. Telephone: 02-770-0878. Telefax: 02-770-0878.

Dresden, Germany Office: Schnorrstrasse 70, 01069. Telephone: 0351-477-770. Telefax: 0351-477-7799.

Leipzig, Germany Office: Gustav-Adolf-Strasse 30 04105 Leipzig. Telephone: 0341-211-0622. Telefax: 0341-211-0625.

Milan, Italy Office: Via Gabrio Casati, 1, I-20123. Telephone: 02-809131/32. Telefax: 02-809-133.

New York, New York Office: 250 Park Avenue, 10177. Telephone: 212-972-3300. Telefax: 212-972-9374.

Paris, France Office: 12, rue d'Astorg F - 75008 Paris. Telephone: 01-4451-0570. Telefax: 01-4266-3368.

General Practice. Corporation, Trade, Banking, International and German Tax Law. Labor Law. Law on Mergers, Acquisitions. Fair Trade, Antitrust and EU Law, Administrative Law. Notary Public. Litigation Department.

WALTER SCHÜRMANN, born Hagen, Germany, July 27, 1924; admitted, 1954, Germany; 1956, as Tax Advisor; 1963, as Notary. *Education:* Universities of Frankfurt and Mainz (Diploma in Economics and Diploma in Business Administration). *LANGUAGES:* German and English.

DR. ARNULF WEIGEL, born Ulm, Germany, January 8, 1934; admitted, 1965, Germany; 1975, as Notary. *Education:* Universities of Frankfurt and Munich (Dr. jur.). Teaching Assistant, University of Frankfurt, 1961-1963. *LANGUAGES:* German, English and French.

DR. JAN ROHLS, born Limburg/Lahn, Germany, January 2, 1939; admitted, 1969, Germany; 1974, as Tax Lawyer; 1979, as Notary. *Education:* University of Frankfurt (Dr. jur.). *LANGUAGES:* German, French and English.

HANS-DIETER STOLLEY, born Kiel, Germany, June 16, 1940; admitted, 1970, Germany; 1974, as Tax Advisor; 1981, as Notary. *Education:* Universities of Kiel, Tübingen, Munich and Hamburg. With Cole, Corette & Abrutyn, Washington, D.C., 1976. *LANGUAGES:* German and English.

DR. AXEL HOFMANN, born Prague, Czechoslovakia, January 12, 1943; admitted, 1971, Germany; 1988, as Notary. *Education:* University of Frankfurt (Doctor of Jurisprudence). *LANGUAGES:* German, English, French and Spanish.

WOLFGANG ALTHAUS, born Wuppertal, Germany, October 20, 1939; admitted, 1972, Germany; 1966, as Conseil Juridique, Paris; 1972, as Tax Advisor; 1987, as Notary. *Education:* Universities of Frankfurt, Lausanne, Freiburg/Breisgau and Paris. *LANGUAGES:* German, French, English and Italian.

DR. BERNHARD MIELERT, born Gera, Germany, February 21, 1941; admitted, 1971, Germany, 1981, as Notary. *Education:* Universities of Geneva and Frankfurt (Dr. jur.). Foreign Associate, Arnold & Porter, Washington, D.C., 1970-1971. *LANGUAGES:* German, English and French.

HINRICH GLASHOFF, born Elmshorn, Germany, May 28, 1929; Tax Advisor Only. German Federal Customs Administration, 1950-1964. In Chemical Industry, 1965-1971. *LANGUAGES:* German and English.

ELMAR GROH, born Breslau, Germany, April 23, 1937; admitted, 1967, Germany; 1977, Tax Advisor and Notary. *Education:* University of Frankfurt. *LANGUAGES:* German, English and French.

MICHAEL FOGEL, born Butzbach, Germany, November 24, 1944; admitted, 1974, Germany. *Education:* University of Frankfurt. *LANGUAGES:* German and English.

HUBERT HESSE, born Brilon, Germany, March 18, 1947; admitted, 1974, Germany; 1988, Notary. *Education:* Universities of Bochum, Geneva

(This Listing Continued)

and Bonn. Lecturer, Academy for Economics and Politics, Hamburg, 1972-1974. *LANGUAGES:* German, English and French.

DR. GERALD BEYER, born Grünmorsbach, Germany, September 22, 1950; admitted, 1978, Germany; 1982, as Tax Advisor. *Education:* University of Würzburg (Dr. jur.; Diploma in Business Administration). *LANGUAGES:* German and English.

RAINER JACOB, born Hamburg, Germany, June 26, 1952; admitted, 1981, Germany. *Education:* Universities of Bremen, Grenoble and Ecole Nationale d' Administration (ENA) Paris. Foreign Associate, Arnold & Porter, Washington, D.C., 1982. *LANGUAGES:* German, French and English.

MATTHIAS MÜLLER, born Chemnitz, Germany, March 22, 1950; admitted, 1981, Germany. *Education:* University of Frankfurt. *LANGUAGES:* German, English and French.

JOHN A. FAYLOR, born Allentown, Pennsylvania, September 27, 1945; admitted, 1980, Munich, 1983, Essen, West Germany; 1984, Pennsylvania USA. *Education:* Bard College (B.A., 1967); University of Heidelberg (1st and 2nd State Bar Examinations, 1977); University of Michigan Law School (LL.M., 1979). *LANGUAGES:* German and English.

DR. WULF MERKEL, born Bad Homburg, Germany, September 10, 1956; admitted, 1985, Germany. *Education:* Universities of Heidelberg and Mannheim (Doctor of Jurisprudence). *LANGUAGES:* German, English and French.

KARL-ERICH STENGER, born Frankfurt am Main, Germany, September 7, 1946. Tax Advisory only. *LANGUAGES:* German and English.

REINHARD EYRING, born Frankfurt, Germany, October 27, 1958; admitted, 1988, Germany. *Education:* University of Freiburg. *LANGUAGES:* German, English, Spanish and French.

MICHAEL MAGOTSCH, born Berlin, Germany, July 13, 1956; admitted, 1984, Germany. *Education:* University of Munich; Georgetown University Law Center, Washington, D.C. (LL.M., 1985). Foreign Associate: Slaughter & Redinger, Charlottesville, Virginia, 1983-1984; Wilmer, Cutler & Pickering, Washington, D.C. and London, 1985-1986. *LANGUAGES:* German and English.

DR. KARL MARIA WALTER, born Oberkirch, Germany, July 10, 1959; admitted, 1991, Germany. *Education:* Universities of Heidelberg, Geneva and Mainz. *LANGUAGES:* German, English and French.

DR. LARS NEVIAN, born Mainz, Germany, December 23, 1962; admitted, 1992, Germany. *Education:* University of Mainz. Foreign Associate, Rogers & Wells, New York, 1991. *LANGUAGES:* German, English and Spanish.

DR. WERNER FRANKE, born Munich, Germany, November 17, 1959; admitted, 1989, Germany. *Education:* Universities of Munich and Regensburg; University of Illinois (LL.M., 1990). *LANGUAGES:* German and English.

DR. MARK OLIVER KERSTING, born Mainz, Germany, October 1, 1961; admitted, 1993, Germany. *Education:* Universities of Mainz, Aix-en-Provence and New Haven (LL.M. (Yale), 1992). *LANGUAGES:* German, English, French and Spanish.

JÖRG BAUSCH, born Darmstadt, Germany, August 18, 1964; admitted, 1993, Germany. *Education:* University of Frankfurt am Main. *LANGUAGES:* German and English.

JÖRG-PETER WINGLER, born Freiburg, Germany, October 21, 1963; admitted, 1992, Germany. *Education:* University of Freiburg. *LANGUAGES:* German and English.

DR. WERNER MIELKE, born Stuttgart, Germany, January 9, 1959; admitted, 1988, Germany. *Education:* Universities of Mannheim, Freiburg and Georgia (LL.M., 1984). *LANGUAGES:* German and English.

FEDERICO PAPPALARDO, born San Teodoro, Italy, April 28, 1964; admitted, 1993, Germany. *Education:* Universities of Mainz and Dijon. *LANGUAGES:* German, Italian, French and English.

KLAUS U. EYBER, born Mainz, Germany, August 5, 1964; admitted, 1993, Germany. *Education:* University of Mainz. *LANGUAGES:* German and English.

(This Listing Continued)

BERLIN OFFICE

DR. RÜDIGER BOERGEN, born Burgörner, Germany, February 10, 1941; admitted, 1971, Germany; 1979, Notary. *Education:* Universities of Berlin and Tübingen. *LANGUAGES:* German, English, French and Italian.

DIETER BETHGE, born Berlin, Germany, September 9, 1954; admitted, 1983, Germany. *Education:* University of Berlin. *LANGUAGES:* German and English.

DR. ROLF RABE, born Penig, Germany, November 13, 1928; admitted, 1968, Germany. *Education:* Humboldt University, Berlin. *LANGUAGES:* German and English.

DR. STEFAN BAUER, born Braunschweig, Germany, April 30, 1960; admitted, 1989, Germany. *Education:* Universities of Berlin and Frankfurt am Main. *LANGUAGES:* German, Italian, English and French.

BONN OFFICE

DR. PHILIPP NAU, born Mainz, Germany, November 30, 1930; admitted, 1991, Germany. *Education:* University of Mainz (Dr. jur.); Harvard University Graduate School of Public Administration, Cambridge/USA (M.P.A., 1963). Senior Government Officer, Federal Ministry of Transportation, 1960-1991. *LANGUAGES:* German, English and French.

DR. GEORG W. REHM, born Hannover, Germany, April 2, 1927; admitted, 1983, Germany. *Education:* Universities of Mainz and Marburg (Diploma in Economics). Senior Government Officer, Director General of Civil Aviation and State Secretary, Federal Ministry of Transportation, 1959-1982. *LANGUAGES:* German, English and French.

BRUSSELS OFFICE

KAREN ERDMENGER, born Hamburg, Germany, August 7, 1935; admitted, 1962, Germany. *Education:* Universities of Hamburg and Lausanne. *LANGUAGES:* German, French and English.

DRESDEN OFFICE

MICHAEL J. SADLO, born Ravensburg, Germany, August 29, 1957; admitted, 1985, Germany. *Education:* University of Freiburg. *LANGUAGES:* German and English.

HANS-JOACHIM HÖNIG, born Munich, Germany, June 26, 1959; admitted, 1989, Germany. *Education:* University of Berlin. *LANGUAGES:* German and English.

MARKUS HASELIER, born Oberhausen, Germany, September 28, 1961; admitted, 1993, Germany. *Education:* Universities of Tübingen, Aix-en-Provence and Hamburg. *LANGUAGES:* German, French and English.

DETLEV CORNELIUS, born Koblenz, Germany, June 21, 1960; admitted, 1991, Germany. *Education:* University of Freiburg. *LANGUAGES:* German and English.

CHRISTOPHER LANDEL, born Wuppertal, Germany, February 15, 1963; admitted, 1994, Germany. *Education:* University of Tübingen. *LANGUAGES:* German and English.

SVEN B. GROSSE, born Wiesbaden, Germany, December 17, 1965; admitted, 1994, Germany. *Education:* Universities of Saarbrücken and Mainz. *LANGUAGES:* German, English and Dutch.

LEIPZIG OFFICE

DR. HABIL. ANGELA SCHNABL, born Unterschönau, Germany, July 28, 1955; admitted, 1990, Germany. *Education:* University of Leipzig. *LANGUAGES:* German, English and Russian.

OLAF KÖHLER, born Delmenhorst, Germany, May 18, 1963; admitted, 1993, Germany. *Education:* Universities of Freiburg and Munich. *LANGUAGES:* German, English and French.

MILAN OFFICE

WOLF MICHAEL KÜHNE, born Kassel, Germany, November 29, 1963; admitted, 1991, Germany. *Education:* Universities of Würzburg and Padua. *LANGUAGES:* German, Italian and English.

FEDERICO SUTTI, born Milan, Italy, January 6, 1965; admitted, 1992, Italy (Not admitted in Germany). *Education:* University of Milan. *LANGUAGES:* Italian, English and French.

PETER SCHIMMANN, born Essen/Kettwig, Germany, June 26, 1965; admitted, 1993, Germany (Not admitted in Germany). *Education:* Universities of Freiburg and Munich. *LANGUAGES:* German, Italian, English and French.

(This Listing Continued)

FRANCO RINDONE, born Milan, Italy, April 12, 1965; admitted, 1993, Italy (Not admitted in Germany). *Education:* University of Milan. *LANGUAGES:* Italian and English.

NEW YORK OFFICE

JOHN A. FAYLOR, born Allentown, Pennsylvania, September 27, 1945; admitted, 1980, Munich, 1983, Essen, West Germany; 1984, Pennsylvania USA. *Education:* Bard College (B.A., 1967); University of Heidelberg (1st and 2nd State Bar Examinations, 1977); University of Michigan Law School (LL.M., 1979). *LANGUAGES:* German and English.

MICHAEL MAGOTSCH, born Berlin, Germany, July 13, 1956; admitted, 1984, Germany. *Education:* University of Munich; Georgetown University Law Center, Washington, D.C. (LL.M., 1985). Foreign Associate: Slaughter & Redinger, Charlottesville, Virginia, 1983-1984; Wilmer, Cutler & Pickering, Washington, D.C. and London, 1985-1986. *LANGUAGES:* German and English.

ROBERT M. PEERS, born New York, N.Y., September 14, 1923; admitted, 1950, New York (Not admitted in Germany). *Education:* Trinity School, New York (1940); Princeton University (A.B., cum laude, 1947); Columbia Law School (LL.B., 1950). *LANGUAGES:* English, French and German.

MCNEILL WATKINS, born Buenos Aires, Argentina, November 9, 1925; admitted, 1951, North Carolina; 1968, New York; 1974, Florida; 1951, U.S. District Court, Middle District of North Carolina; 1971, U.S. Supreme Court; 1975, U.S. District Court, Southern District of Florida and U.S. Court of Appeals, Fifth Circuit; 1981, U.S. Court of Appeals, Eleventh Circuit (Not admitted in Germany). *Education:* Wake Forest University (B.S., 1949); Wake Forest University School of Law (LL.B., 1951; J.D., 1971); American Graduate School of International Management (B.F.T., 1954); Columbia University, Parker School of Foreign and Comparative Law (1960). *LANGUAGES:* English, Spanish and Portuguese.

PETER L. HESSELLUND-JENSEN, born Stockholm, Sweden, March 27, 1945; admitted, 1976, New York (Not admitted in Germany). *Education:* Columbia University School of Law (LL.M., 1972); University of Copenhagen, School of Law (Cand. Jur., 1971). *LANGUAGES:* English, Danish, Norwegian and Swedish.

PARIS OFFICE

JOHANNES VIEGENER, born Haan, Germany, January 21, 1939; admitted, 1971, Germany; 1986, France. *Education:* Universities of Bonn and Paris. *LANGUAGES:* German, French and English.

HUGUES TROUSSET, born Angouléme, France, November 8, 1953; admitted, 1980, France (Not admitted in Germany). *Education:* Universities of Limoges and Paris II. *LANGUAGES:* French and German.

CHRISTIAN KLEIN, born Bonn, Germany, January 3, 1959; admitted, 1991, Germany. *Education:* University of Bonn. *LANGUAGES:* German, French and English.

FRANK LAUTENBACH, born Bonn, Germany, February 14, 1964; admitted, 1993, France (Not admitted in Germany). *Education:* University of Dijon. *LANGUAGES:* German, French and English.

THOMAS FÜHRLBECK, born Düsseldorf, Germany, December 8, 1959; admitted, 1989, Germany; 1992, Tax Advisor. *Education:* University of Nuremberg. *LANGUAGES:* German, French and English.

Languages: German, English, French, Spanish and Italian.

SHEARMAN & STERLING
BOCKENHEIMER LANDSTRASSE 55
D-60325 FRANKFURT AM MAIN, GERMANY
Telephone: (49-69) 97-10-70
Fax: (49-69) 97-10-71-00

New York, N.Y. Office: 599 Lexington Avenue, New York, New York 10022-6069 and Citicorp Center, 153 East 53rd Street, New York, New York 10022-4676. Telephone: (212) 848-4000. Telex: 667290 Num Lau. Fax: 599 Lexington Avenue: (212) 848-7179. Citicorp Center: (212) 848-5252.

Abu Dhabi, United Arab Emirates Office: P.O. Box 2948. Telephone: (971-2) 324477. Fax: (971-2) 774533.

Beijing, People's Republic of China Office: Suite #2205, Capital Mansion, No. 6, Xin Yuan Nan Road. Chao Yang District Beijing, 100004. Telephone: (861) 465-4574. Fax: (861) 465-4578.

(This Listing Continued)

SHEARMAN & STERLING, Frankfurt/Main—Continued

Budapest, Hungary Office: Szerb utca 17-19, 1056 Budapest. Telephone: (36-1) 266-3522. Fax: (36-1) 266-3523.

Düsseldorf, Federal Republic of Germany Office: Königsallee 46, D-40212 Düsseldorf. Telephone: (49-211) 13 62 80. Telex: 8 588 294 NYLO. Fax: (49-211) 13 33 09.

Hong Kong, Hong Kong Office: Standard Chartered Bank Building, 4 Des Voeux Road Central, Hong Kong. Telephone: (852) 2978-8000. Fax: (852) 2978-8099.

London, England Office: 199 Bishopsgate, London EC2M 3TY. Telephone: (44-171) 920-9000. Fax: (44-171) 920-9020.

Los Angeles, California Office: 725 South Figueroa Street, 21st Floor, 90017-5421. Telephone: (213) 239-0300. Fax: (213) 239-0381, 614-0936.

Paris, France Office: 12 rue d'Astorg, 75008. Telephone: (33-1) 44-71-17-17. Telex: 282964 Royale. Fax: (33-1) 44-71-01-01.

San Francisco, California Office: 555 California Street, 94104-1522. Telephone: (415) 616-1100. Fax: (415) 616-1199.

Taipei, Taiwan Office: 7th Floor, Hung Kuo Building, 167 Tun Hwa North Road. Telephone: (886-2) 545-3300. Fax: (866-2) 545-3322.

Tokyo, Japan Office: Shearman & Sterling (Thomas Wilner Gaikokuho-Jimu-Bengoshi Jimusho), Fukoku Seimei Building, 5th Fl. 2-2-2, Uchisaiwaicho, Chiyoda-ku, Tokyo 100, Japan. Telephone: (81 3) 5251-1601. Fax: (81 3) 5251-1602.

Toronto, Ontario, Canada Office: Commerce Court West, Suite 4405, P.O. Box 247, M5L 1E8. Telephone: (416) 360-8484. Fax: (416) 360-2958.

Washington, D.C. Office: 801 Pennsylvania Avenue, N.W., Suite 900, 20004-2604. Telephone: (202) 508-8000. Fax: (202) 508-8100.

Firm engages in German, EEC, American and General International Practice.

FIRM PROFILE: Shearman & Sterling, founded in 1873, has more than 500 lawyers in 15 offices throughout the world. The firm's practice encompasses most major areas of business law, including: Antitrust and Trade Regulation; Banking; Bankruptcy and Corporate Reorganization; Compensation and Benefits; Environmental; Finance (including Corporate Finance, Domestic Private Finance, Financial Institutions, International Private Finance and Project Finance); Individual Clients, Trusts and Estates; Insurance; International Trade and Government Relations; Litigation and Arbitration; Mergers and Acquisitions; Oil and Gas; Privatizations; Real Estate; and Tax. The Firm is also engaged in the practice of French, German and Hungarian law through its offices in France, Germany and Hungary.

RESIDENT PARTNERS

WILLIAM J. WIEGMANN, born Plainfield, New Jersey, 1953; admitted, 1978, New Jersey; 1979, New York (Not admitted in Germany). *Education:* Rutgers University (A.B., 1975); New York University (J.D., 1978). Law Clerk to Hon. J. D. Fuchsberg, New York Court of Appeals, 1978-1980.

MICHAEL GRUSON, born Berlin, Germany, 1936; admitted, 1969, New York (Not admitted in Germany). *Education:* University of Mainz, Germany (LL.B., 1962); Columbia University (M.C.L., 1963; LL.B., 1965); Freie Universität, Berlin, Germany (Dr.iur., 1966). Vice Chairman, Committee on Banking Law, 1984-1989 and Chairman, Subcommittee on Legal Opinions, 1985—, International Bar Association.

RESIDENT ASSOCIATES

JONATHAN S. BERCK, born New York, N.Y., 1959; admitted, 1986, New Jersey; 1987, New York; 1988, District of Columbia (Not admitted in Germany). *Education:* Swarthmore College (B.A., 1981); University of Tübingen (Fulbright Scholar, 1981-1982); Columbia University (M.A., 1983); Harvard Law School (J.D., 1986).

DR. HERBERT HARRER, born Munich, Germany, 1961; admitted, 1992, Germany and New York. *Education:* University of Munich (Dr.Jur., 1989; Hanns-Seidel Scholar); Columbia University (LL.M., 1991; Fulbright Scholar).

DR. STEPHAN HUTTER, born Bregenz, Austria, 1961; admitted, 1987, New York (Not admitted in Germany). *Education:* University of Vienna (Dr. jur., 1984); University of Illinois at Champaign-Urbana (LL.M., 1986; Fulbright Scholar).

(This Listing Continued)

DR. THOMAS N. KÖNIG, born Munich, Germany, 1959; admitted, 1991, Germany; 1992, New York. *Education:* University of Munich (Dr. jur., 1988); New York University Law School (M.C.J., 1990).

MICHAEL A. LEPPERT, born Burghausen, Bavaria, Germany, February 20, 1963; admitted, 1994, Germany. *Education:* University of Munich; New York University (LL.M., 1993).

JOHANN GEORG MÜHLMANN, born Verden, Germany, 1960; admitted, 1993, New York and Germany. *Education:* University of Bonn; New York University Law School (M.C.J., 1991).

PETRA J. PELLICANO, born Amityville, New York, June 30, 1961; admitted, 1991, Connecticut; 1992, New York; 1994, District of Columbia (Not admitted in Germany). *Education:* New York Institute of Technology (B.F.A., 1986); St. John's University School of Law (J.D., 1991).

TITUS J. WEINHEIMER, born Düsseldorf, Germany, 1965; admitted, 1994, Germany. *Education:* University of Heidelberg; University of Munich.

DR. JOHANNES WEISSER, born Munich, Germany, 1959; admitted, 1991, Germany. *Education:* Albert-Ludwigs-Universität, Freiburg, Germany; Université de Genève, Switzerland (DAAD-Scholar); Rheinische Friedrich-Wilhelms-Universität, Bonn, Germany (Dr. jur., 1990); University of Miami (LL.M., 1988; Fulbright Scholar).

Languages: German, English and French

(For Biographical data of all Partners, see Professional Biographies at New York, New York).

SIGLE, LOOSE, SCHMIDT-DIEMITZ & PARTNERS

SCHUMANNSTRASSE 62
60325 FRANKFURT/MAIN, GERMANY
Telephone: 069-976849-0
Telefax: 069-975849-97

Stuttgart, Germany Office: Schöttlestr. 8, P.O. Box 70 02 65, D-70572 Stuttgart (Degerloch). Telephone: 0711-9764-0. Telefax: 0711-9764-900.

Berlin, Germany Office: Friedrichstrasse 130 a, 10117 Berlin. Telephone: 030-308792-0. Telefax: 030-238-5849.

Leipzig, Germany Office: August-Bebel-Strasse 38, 04275 Leipzig. Telephone: 0341-3912007. Fax: 0341-391-2085.

Chemnitz, Germany Office: Barbarossastraße 46, 09112 Chemnitz. Telephone: 0371-36974-0. Telefax: 0371-3697421.

Moscow, Russia Office: Sadovaja Samotjotschnaja, 103 051. Telephone: 007/095/258 50 55. Fax: 007/095/258 51 55.

Commerical, Corporation, Mergers and Acquisitions, Banking, Investment, Common Market, Antitrust, Unfair Competition, Copyright, Patent and Trademark, License Agreements, Press, Transportation, Insurance, Product Liability, Real Estate, Construction, Probate, Labor, Administrative, Tax, International, Litigation and Arbitration.

RESIDENT PARTNERS

DR. UDO SIMMAT, born Hannover, Germany, 1951; admitted, 1979, Stuttgart. *Education:* University of Augsburg (Doctor of Law, 1980). Co-Author: "Der Chef wird älter. Strategien zur Unternehmernachfolge," (Strategies for entrepreneurs's succession), 1987. Member of Supervisory Board: Klaus Autoparksysteme GmbH, Aitrach. *Member:* German Bar Association; International Bar Association; Chamber of Industry and Commerce in Tokyo; Japanese Chamber of Industry and Commerce, Düsseldorf; German-Korean Chamber Industry and Commerce, Seoul. *LANGUAGES:* German, English and French. *PRACTICE AREAS:* Mergers and Acquisitions.

DR. EVA ANNETT MASER, born Ratingen, Germany, 1961; admitted, 1990, Stuttgart. *Education:* Universities of Munich and Tübingen (Doctor of Law, 1992). Author: "Richterliche Alltagstheorien", (Rules of Thumb used by Judges), 1992. Assistant Lecturer, University of Konstanz "Praktikerforschungsgruppe Stuttgart," 1987-1988. *Member:* German Bar Association. *LANGUAGES:* German, English and French. *PRACTICE AREAS:* Corporate Law; Mergers and Acquisitions.

(This Listing Continued)

RESIDENT ASSOCIATES

DR. ANDREAS ZANNER, born Freiburg, Germany, 1962; admitted, 1991, Stuttgart. *Education:* Universities of Geneva and Mainz (Doctor of Law, 1989). *Member:* German Bar Association. *LANGUAGES:* German, English and French. *PRACTICE AREAS:* Corporate Law; Mergers and Acquisitions; Commercial Law.

SKADDEN, ARPS, SLATE, MEAGHER & FLOM

MESSETURM, 27TH FLOOR
60308 FRANKFURT am MAIN, GERMANY
Telephone: 011-49-69-9757-3000
Fax: 011-49-69-9757-3050

New York, New York Office: 919 Third Avenue, 10022. Telephone: 212-735-3000. Fax: 212-735-2000; 212-735-2001. Telex: 645899 Skarslaw.

Boston, Massachusetts Office: One Beacon Street, 02108. Telephone: 617-573-4800. Fax: 617-573-4822.

Washington, D.C. Office: 1440 New York Avenue, N.W., 20005. Telephone: 202-371-7000. Fax: 202-393-5760.

Wilmington, Delaware Office: One Rodney Square, 19899. Telephone: 302-651-3000. Fax: 302-651-3001.

Los Angeles, California Office: 300 South Grand Avenue, 90071. Telephone: 213-687-5000. Fax: 213-687-5600.

Chicago, Illinois Office: 333 West Wacker Drive, 60606. Telephone: 312-407-0700. Fax: 312-407-0411.

San Francisco, California Office: Four Embarcadero Center, 94111. Telephone: 415-984-6400. Fax: 415-984-2698.

Houston, Texas Office: 1600 Smith Street, Suite 4460, 77002. Telephone: 713-655-5100. Fax: 713-655-5181.

Newark, New Jersey Office: One Riverfront Plaza, 07102. Telephone: 201-596-4440. Fax: 201-596-4444.

Tokyo, Japan Office: 12th Floor, The Fukoku Seimei Building, 2-2-2, Uchisaiwaicho, Chiyoda-ku, 100. Telephone: 011-81-3-3595-3850. Fax: 011-81-3-3504-2780.

London, England Office: 25 Bucklersbury EC4N 8DA. Telephone: 011-44-171-248-9929. Fax: 011-44-171-489-8533.

Hong Kong Office: 30/F Peregrine Tower, Lippo Centre, 89 Queensway, Central. Telephone: 011-852-820-0700. Fax: 011-852-820-0727.

Sydney, New South Wales, Australia Office: Level 26-State Bank Centre, 52 Martin Place, 2000. Telephone: 011-61-2-224-6000. Fax: 011-61-2-224-6044.

Toronto, Ontario Office: Suite 1820, North Tower, P.O. Box 189, Royal Bank Plaza, M5J 2J4. Telephone: 416-777-4700. Fax: 416-777-4747.

Paris, France Office: 105 rue du Faubourg Saint-Honoré, 75008. Telephone: 011-33-1-40-75-44-44. Fax: 011-33-1-49-53-09-99.

Brussels, Belgium Office: 523 avenue Louise, Box 30, 1050. Telephone: 011-32-2-648-7666. Fax: 011-32-2-640-3032.

Beijing, China Office: 1605 Capital Mansion Tower, No. 6 Xin Yuan Nan Road, Chao Yang District, 100004. Telephone: 011-86-1-466-8800. Fax: 011-86-1-466-8822.

Budapest, Hungary Office: Mahart Building, H-1052 Apàczai Csere János u.11, Vl.em. Telephone: 011-36-1-266-2145. Fax:011-36-1-266-4033.

Prague, Czech Republic Office: Revolucni 16, 110 00. Telephone: 011-42-2-231-75-18. Fax: 011-42-2-231-47-33.

Moscow, Russia Office: Pleteshkovsky Pereulok 1, 107005. Telephone: 011-7-501-940-2304. Fax: 011-7-501-940-2511.

Firm engaged in general American and International law practice, but not authorized to appear before the German Courts.

ASSOCIATE

HILARY S. FOULKES, born Cincinnati, Ohio, 1961; admitted, 1987, New York (Not admitted in Germany). *Education:* University of Cincinnati (B.A., 1983); New York University (J.D., 1986).

(For Biographical data on other Personnel, see Professional Biographies at New York, New York).

SLAUGHTER AND MAY

WESTEND-CARREE
GRÜNEBURGWEG 16
D-60322 FRANKFURT/MAIN, GERMANY
Telephone: (69) 9551370
Fax: (69) 5 96 41 26

London, England Office: 35 Basinghall Street, EC2V 5DB. Telephone: (0171) 600 1200. Telex: 883486; 888926. Fax: (0171) 726 0038; (0171) 600 0289; (0171) 600 1455 (G-4).

Paris, France Office: 112 Avenue Kléber, 75116. Telephone: (1) 44.05.60.00. Telex: 642514. Fax: (1) 44.05.60.60; (1) 44 05 60 99 (G-4).

Brussels, Belgium Office: Rue D'Arlon 69/71, 1040. Telephone: (2) 230 5631. Fax: (2) 230 7699.

Hong Kong Office: 27th Floor, Two Exchange Square. Telephone: (852) 521 0551. Telex: HX 86230. Fax: (852) 845 2125; (852) 845 9079.

Tokyo, Japan Office: Mitsui Asahi Building, 1-1 Kanda Sudacho, Chiyoda-ku, 101. Telephone: (3) 3258 5700. Telex: 2227208. Fax: (3) 3258 5708.

New York, New York Office: 126 East 56th Street, 10022-3613. Telephone: (212) 888-1112. Fax: (212) 888-1170; (212) 832-2021; (212) 832 0075 (G-4).

English, EEC and General International Law Practice.

RESIDENT PARTNER

G.D. Child

DR. JUTTA STOLL, LL.M.

Established in 1990

HAINER WEG 50
60599 FRANKFURT/MAIN, GERMANY
Telephone: (069) 62 60 92
Telefax: (069) 603 12 87

International Business Transactions, Banking Law, Business Law, Corporate, Civil Litigation, Professional Responsibility, Wills.

DR. JUTTA STOLL, born Nuernberg, Germany, May 5, 1956; admitted, 1985, District of Columbia; 1986, Frankfurt. *Education:* Universities of Saarbrücken, Geneva and Heidelberg (Dr. jur., 1981); Georgetown University Law Center (LL.M., 1984). Assistant of the University of Heidelberg, 1981-1982. Author: "Vereinbarungen zwischen Staat und ausländischem Investor," (Agreements Between States and Foreign Investors), 1982. *Member:* German and American Bar Associations; German American Lawyers' Association. *LANGUAGES:* German, English, French and Spanish.

REPRESENTATIVE CLIENT: Arthur Andersen & Co. GmbH

JOHN C. STURGEON & ASSOCIATES, P.C.

FINKENWEG 4
67146 FRANKFURT/MAIN (DEIDESHEIM) GERMANY
Telephone: (49) 6326-7450
Telefax: (49) 6326-7450

London, England Office: 10 Greycoat Place, Suite 325, London SW1P 1SB, England.

Baltimore, Maryland Office: 111 South Calvert Street, Suite 2700, 21202.

General Practice, Corporate and Antitrust, Banking, Insurance Securities and Investments, U.S. Administrative and Tort Law, Immigration, U.S. Labor, Probate, Family and Property Law, Transportation.

JOHN C. STURGEON, admitted, 1986, Maryland; Germany as Rechtsbeistand. *Education:* U.S. Military Academy, West Point, NY (B.S., Engineering, 1972); University of Baltimore (M.S., International Business and Finance, 1982); University of Akron (J.D., 1985). General Counsel, Car Finance Bank GmbH and Car World Group, Kaiserslautern, Germany, 1987-1992. Lecturer: Business and Law, The University of Maryland, European Division; Schiller International University. *Member:* American Bar Association; Maryland Bar Association. *LANGUAGES:* English and German. *PRACTICE AREAS:* International Trade; Business; Financial Law; Insurance.

THÜMMEL, SCHÜTZE & PARTNER

Established in 1991

ESCHERSHEIMER LANDSHAβE 10
60322 FRANKFURT/MAIN, GERMANY
Telephone: (069) 9591350
Telefax: (069) 95913530

Stuttgart Office: Landhausstraße 90, 70190 Stuttgart. Telephone: (0711) 1667-0, Telefax: (0711) 286 44 66, 2 62 69 10.
Dresden Office: Friedrichstraße 33, 01067 Dresden. Telephone: (0351) 496 5302. Telefax: (0351) 496 5346.
Brussels Office: Avenue des Arts, 41 B-1040 Brussels. Telephone: (0032) 2-512 7846. Telefax: (0032) 2-512 7023.
Paris, France Office: 46, Rue de Bassano, F-75008 Paris. Telephone: (0033) 1-53 67 50 00. Telefax: (0033) 1-47 20 78 76.
Singapore Office: 9, Battery Road, #16-01 Straits Trading Building, Singapore 0104, Telephone: (00 65) 53 53 112. Telefax: (00 65) 53 43 100.
Berlin Office: Lützowstraße 33/36, 10785 Berlin. Telephone: (030) 2 61 11 31. Telefax: (030) 2 61 90 49. Telex: 3 01304.

Corporate, Commercial, Antitrust, Unfair Competition, Banking, Taxation, Trademark, Copyright, Media, Estate, Food Law, International, EEC Law, General Practice and Litigation.

DR. JUR. JOCHEN MITTAG, born Marl, Germany, December 4, 1964; admitted, 1994, Germany. *Education:* Universities of Würzburg, Geneva, Strasbourg, London (Referendar, 1991; Assessor, 1994; Doctor of Juris Prudence, 1995). *Member:* German-American Lawyers Association. *LANGUAGES:* German, English, French, Italian and Spanish.

GABRIELE FONTANE, born Frankfurt a/M., Germany, June 24, 1965; admitted, 1994, Germany. *Education:* Universities of Frankfurt and Luxemburg (Referendar, 1990; Assessor, 1993). Associated with U.S. Law firm, 1993-1994. *Member:* German Lawyers Association. *LANGUAGES:* German, English and French.

(For Complete Biographical Data on all Personnel, see Professional Biographies at Stuttgart, Germany).

FRIEDRICH U. TROCKELS

Rechtsanwalt

BOCKENHEIMER LANDSTRAβE 22
60323 FRANKFURT/MAIN, GERMANY
Telephone: (069) 71 93 147
Telefax: (069) 71 93 189

Mailing Address: P.O. Box 17 01 53, 60075 Frankfurt/Main, GERMANY

Banking, International Corporate, Business and Tax Law, National and Transnational Litigations, Establishing Subsidiaries and Branches, Labor Law, Estate Planning and Probate Law, Mergers and Acquisitions.

DR. IUR. FRIEDRICH U. TROCKELS, born Dortmund, Germany, November 24, 1954; admitted, 1986, Münster and Frankfurt/Main. *Education:* Städt. Gymnasium, Ahlen, Germany (B.A., 1973); Universities of Münster, Germany, Lausanne, Switzerland and Lille, France (J.D., 1. Staatsexamen, 1981; 2. Staatsexamen, 1984; S.J.D., Dr. iur., 1986). Clerk: Department of Justice, Dortmund, Germany, 1982-1984; Schürmann & Partner, Frankfurt and Paris Office, 1986-1989. Foreign Associate: G. Séguéla & Partner, St. Brieuc, France, 1984: Coudert Brothers, New York, 1988-1989. Lecturer, Tax Law. Author: "L'Indivision et la Répartition des Dettes et des Créances," Münster, 1987; "Der Konzern im französischen Internationalen Privatrecht," Recht der Internationalen Wirtschaft, 1988; "Take-over," Der Unternehmer, 1990; "Business Judgement Rule und Corporate Take-overs," Die Aktiengesellschaft, 1990; "Verteidigungsmaßnahmen gegen Corporate Take-overs in den USA," Zeitschrift für Vergleichende Rechtswissenschaft, 1990. *Member:* German Bar Association; Young Lawyers' International Association; German-French Lawyers' Association.

Languages: German, French and English

VOGEL & VOGEL

KETTENHOFWEG 29
D-60325 FRANKFURT/MAIN, GERMANY
Telephone: (49) 69.71.036.16
Fax: (49) 69.72.27.26

Paris, France Office: 6, Avenue Pierre 1 er de Serbie, 75116. Telephone: (33.1) 53.67.76.70. Fax: (33.1) 53.67.76.25.
Brussels, Belgium Office: Avenue du Diamant, 139, B-1040. Telephone: (32) 2.735.34.28. Fax: (32) 2.735.49.30.

Antitrust Law, European Community Law, International Business Law, International Investment Law, Mergers and Acquisitions, Product Distribution Law, Products Liability Law, Unfair Competition Law.

FIRM PROFILE: The firm offers a full range of legal services especially in the fields of Frendi and EEC, Antitrust Law, Distribution and General Business Law.

LOUIS VOGEL, born Saarbrücken, Germany, October 22, 1954; admitted, 1981, Paris; 1990, New York (Not admitted in Germany). *Education:* Institut d'Etudes Politiques de Paris (Diplômé, 1976); Yale Law School (LL.M., 1982); University of Paris I (Panthéon-Sorbonne) and Paris II Law School (Panthéon-Assas), Doctor of Law (1985); Agrégé des Facultés de Droit (1989). Author: "Droit commercial européen," with B. Goldman and A. Lyon-Caem, 835p., Dalloz, 1994; "Le droit européen des affaires," Dalloz, 128 p., 2nd ed., 1994; "Droit de la concurrence et concentration économique," 427 p., Economica, 1988; "Chronique du droit de la concurrence," Revue du Marché Commun, 1991—; "Chronique Concurrence," Revue Contrats Concurrence Consommation, 1991—; "Chronique de jurisprudence communautaire," Semaine juridique, 1990—; "French Merger Law," Fordham Corporate Law Institute, 1990. Professor of Law, University of Paris Law School. Director, Juris Classeurs de droit international et de droit comparé. Director, Encyclopédie Dalloz de Droit Commercial. *Member:* American Bar Association; Comité Français de Droit International Privé; International Law Association; Société de Législation Comparée; Union des Avocats Européens; Association des juristes franco-allemands, Deutscher Anwaltverein. (Also at Paris, France Office). *LANGUAGES:* French, English and German. *PRACTICE AREAS:* Antitrust Law; European Community Law; International Business Law.

(For Biographical Data on all Personnel, see Professional Biographies at Paris, France)

DR. VOLLER & PARTNER

EYSSENECKSTRAβE 10
60322 FRANKFURT/MAIN, GERMANY
Telephone: 069/594833
Telefax: 069/594840

General Practice, General Commercial Practice, Corporate Law, Contracts, Company Law, Litigation, International Debt Collection, Privatization, Tax Law, Construction Law, Matrimonial and Family Law, Wills, Trusts and Succession, Criminal Law, Real Estate, Unfair Competition, Notarial Practice.
Member of CONSULEGIS EEIG Attorneys at Law, a grouping of law firms with associated offices in Austria, Belgium, Bulgaria, Canada, Cyprus, Czech Republic, Denmark, England, Estonia, Finland, France, Germany, Greece, Italy, Israel, Norway, Russia, Spain, Sweden, Switzerland and U.S.A.

DR. THOMAS VOLLER, born Frankfurt/Main, August 14, 1953; admitted, 1982, Frankfurt/Main. *Education:* Universities of Tübingen (Dr. jur., 1983), Göttingen and Geneva. Member of the advisory board of Consulegis EEIG. *Member:* German Bar Association; German-British Attorneys' Association; German-American Lawyers Association; International Bar Association. *LANGUAGES:* German and English. *PRACTICE AREAS:* General Practice; Commercial Law; Labor Law; Litigation; Debt Collection; Construction Law.

THOMAS FIEDLER, born Lüneburg, August 30, 1949; admitted, 1981, Darmstadt, Fachanwalt für Steuerrecht. *Education:* University of Frankfurt (Law Degree, 1981). *Member:* German Bar Association. *LANGUAGES:* German, French and English. *PRACTICE AREAS:* General Practice; General Commercial Practice; Contracts; Company Law; Tax Law.

HANS-JOACHIM RICHNOW, born Schotten/Hessen, July 3, 1950; admitted, 1977, Darmstadt; 1979, Frankfurt; 1991, Notar. *Education:* University of Frankfurt and Tübingen. *Member:* German Bar Association; As-
(This Listing Continued)

sociation German Defense Counsels. *LANGUAGES:* German and English. *PRACTICE AREAS:* Matrimonial and Family Law; Criminal Law; Contracts; Wills; Real Estate; Unfair Competition.

VOMBERG & PARTNER

KURHESSENSTRAβE 94
60431 FRANKFURT/MAIN, GERMANY
Telephone: (069) 51 38 19
Telefax: (069) 51 38 17

General Practice, Commercial, Company, Corporations, Labor Law, Estate Planning, Wills, Succession, Insurance Law, Real Estate, National and International Matrimonial Law, Notary's Office.

FIRM PROFILE: *The firm was established in 1988 and provides qualified legal services on a personal basis including those of a notary public. Specialization in National and International Matrimonial Law since 1976. The client base is European and North American in scope.*

MEMBERS OF FIRM

WOLFGANG VOMBERG, born Duisburg, Germany, October 23, 1947; admitted, 1976, Frankfurt. *Education:* University of Frankfurt. Notary Public. *Member:* German Bar Association; International Bar Association; International Academy of Matrimonial Lawyers; Deutscher Familiengerichtstag e.V. *LANGUAGES:* German, English and French. *PRACTICE AREAS:* National and International Matrimonial Law; Real Estate; Estate Planning and Probate; Litigation.

JÖRG MANNEL, born Würzburg, Germany, February 25, 1960; admitted, 1990, Frankfurt. *Education:* University of Gießen. *Member:* German Bar Association. *LANGUAGES:* German and English. *PRACTICE AREAS:* National Matrimonial Law; Labor Law; Estate Law; Wills and Succession; Insurance Law; Litigation.

VON MAUR & PARTNERS

Counsellors and Attorneys

LIMES PARK
OTTO-VOLGER-STRASSE 5B
D-65843 FRANKFURT (SULZBACH), GERMANY
Telephone: (011) (49) 6196-750081
Local 06196-750081
Telefax: (011) (49) 6196-750088
Local 06196 750088

International Commercial Transactions, U.S. Government Contracts, Civil Litigation in U.S. Courts, U.S. Commercial and Tax Law, U.S. and Common Market Arbitration, Private Investments within the United States, Emphasizing Acquisition, Development, Financing and Restructuring, Trademark and Antitrust Law, U.S. Business and Corporate Law, Export and International Trade, including East European Business Establishment, Licensing and Distribution, U.S. Immigration Law, Personal injury claims involving tort liability under U.S. Laws.

MEMBERS OF FIRM

REED L. VON MAUR, born Davenport, Iowa, October 17, 1945; admitted, 1969, Iowa; 1977, District of Columbia (Not admitted in Germany). *Education:* De Pauw University; The University of Iowa (B.A., 1966; J.D., 1969). Clerk, the Hon. Bruce M. Snell, Supreme Court of Iowa, 1969-1970. United States Liaison to Justice Ministry in Germany for Legal Affairs under the NATO Status of Forces Agreement, including Procurement and Civil Claims Matters, 1973-1975. Military Judge: European Circuit, 1975-1976; Civil Litigation Division (Environmental and Commercial Law), Department of the Army, The Pentagon, Washington, D.C., 1976-1977. With Arent, Fox, Kintner, Plotkin and Kahn, Washington, D.C., 1977-1981. *Member:* Iowa State, Federal, American and International Bar Associations; Bar Association of American Lawyers in Germany (BAALG). *LANGUAGES:* English, German and Spanish.

MICHAEL J. MURPHY, born Glencoe, Minnesota, November 28, 1957; admitted, 1983, Colorado (Not admitted in Germany). *Education:* University of Notre Dame, Notre Dame, Ind. (B.B.A., B.A., German, 1980); University of Denver, Denver, Colorado (J.D. and M.B.A., 1983). With: Wegher & Fulton, Denver, Colorado, 1983; Irving Trust Company, Frankfurt, Germany 1983-1988; Norwest Bank, Minneapolis, Minnesota, 1989-1990. *Member:* American and International Bar Associations; Bar Association of American Lawyers in Germany (BAALG). *LANGUAGES:* English and German.

(This Listing Continued)

J. CASEY FOS, born New Orleans, Louisiana, March 14, 1963; admitted, 1992, Louisiana; 1994, U.S. District Court, Eastern District of Louisiana (Not admitted in Germany). *Education:* University of New Orleans (B.A., 1985); National Merit Scholar; Universität Innsbruck, Austria (1985-1988); Tulane University of Louisiana (J.D., 1991); Fulbright Scholar (1985). Internship with Greiter, Pegger, Kofler in Innsbruck, Austria, 1987-1988; with Müller-Horn & Soehring, Hamburg, Germany, 1989; Assistant City Attorney, City of Kenner, Louisiana, 1992-1994. Published Translations: "Federalism and Party Interaction in West Germany, Switzerland and Austria," 19 Publius, The Journal of Federalism 81 (Fall 1989). *LANGUAGES:* English and German.

WESSING BERENBERG-GOSSLER ZIMMERMANN LANGE

FREIHERR-VOM-STEIN-STRASSE 24-26
60323 FRANKFURT/MAIN, GERMANY
Telephone: (069) 971300
Telefax: (069) 97130100
Telex: 413926

Munich, Germany Office: Vilshofener Str. 8, D-81679 Munich, P.O. Box 86 08 67, D-81635 Munich. Telephone: 49-89-98 28 021. Telefax: 49-89-98 12 14.

Düsseldorf, Germany Office: Königsallee 92 A, D-40212 Düsseldorf, P.O. Box 10 53 61, D-40044 Düsseldorf. Telephone: 49-211-83 87-0. Telex: 858 19 14 wess d. Cable Address: "Wegolex". Telefax: 49-211-32 36 16.

Hamburg, Germany Office: Neuer Wall 46, D-20354 Hamburg. Telephone: 49-40-36 80 30. Cable Address: "Unilaw". Telex: 2-14111 Jura d. Teletex: 40 32 91 Unilaw. Telefax: 49-40-36 80 32 80.

Berlin, Germany Office: Spreeufer 5, D-10178 Berlin. Telephone: 49-30-238 45 45. Telefax: 49-30-238 45 34.

Leipzig, Germany Office: Ferdinand-Rhode-Strasse 16, D-04107 Leipzig. Telephone: 49-341-213 13 80. Fax: 49-341-213 13 88.

Dresden, Germany Office: Heinrichstrasse 16, D-01097 Dresden. Telephone: 49-351-567 12 12. Telefax: 49-351-567 12 13.

Brussels, Belgium Office: Avenue Louise 149, Box 42, B-1050 Brussels. Telephone: +32 (2) 537 01 86. Telefax: +32 (2) 534 25 31.

Commercial Law, Corporations, German and E.C. Antitrust, Trademark and Copyright, Computer Law, Labor, Administration, Environmental, Product Liability, Banking, Insurance, Real Property, Estate, Tax Law, Litigation, Conveyancing, General Practice. Civil Law Notaries.

DR. BERNHARD VON BRAUNSCHWEIG, born Frankfurt/Main, May 16, 1932; admitted, 1961. *Education:* Universities of Saarbrücken, Frankfurt/Main, Heidelberg and Marburg/Lahn (Dr. jur.). Tax Advisor, 1965. Civil Law Notary, 1968. Associate Judge, Frankfurt Superior Court Senate for Tax Advisors Affairs, 1971—. *Member:* German Lawyers Association; Hessen Institute of Tax Advisors; American Bar Association; International Fiscal Association; American Chamber of Commerce; French-German Chamber of Commerce (CCFA); International Bar Association; The International Academy of Trust and Estate Law (Member, Executive Council). *LANGUAGES:* German, English and French. *PRACTICE AREAS:* Tax Law; Inheritance and Estate Law; Corporate and General Commercial Law.

DR. GUSTAV-ADOLF LANGE, born Berlin, January 20, 1936; admitted, 1965; Notary 1971. *Education:* Universities of Frankfurt, Munich, Paris (Doctor of Law, 1962). *Member:* German Bar Association; International Bar Association. *LANGUAGES:* German, English and French. *PRACTICE AREAS:* Commercial Law; Corporate Law; Mergers and Acquisitions; Real Estate Transactions.

HEINRICH VON METTENHEIM, born Berlin, March 14, 1940; admitted, 1968. *Education:* Universities of Heidelberg and Frankfurt, Faculté de Droit, Paris. Notary, 1978. Fachanwalt für Steuerrecht (Tax Lawyer), 1978. *Member:* German Bar Association; International Bar Association; Asia-Pacific Lawyer Association; Gesellschaft für Umweltrecht e. V. *LANGUAGES:* German, English and French. *PRACTICE AREAS:* Tax Law; Insurance Law; Commercial Law; Mergers and Acquisitions; Real Estate Transactions.

DR. MICHAEL A. VELTINS, born Bochum, May 12, 1952; admitted, 1981. *Education:* Universities of Berlin, Bonn, Lausanne, Hamburg (Doctor of Law, 1981). Fachanwalt für Steuerrecht (Tax Lawyer). Assistant Professor of Civil Law, University of Hamburg. Adjunct Professor, Business Fac-

(This Listing Continued)

WESSING BERENBERG-GOSSLER ZIMMERMANN LANGE, *Frankfurt/Main—Continued*

ulty, University of Hamburg. With Coudert Brothers, New York, 1981-1982. Author: "Das Recht der U.S. Partnership und Limited Partnership einschliesslich ihrer Besteuerung," Herne 1984. Co-author of the Commentary of Kullmann/Pfister, "Produzentenhaftung," 1987. *Member:* British-German Lawyer Association; American-German Lawyer Association; International Bar Association. *LANGUAGES:* German and English. *PRACTICE AREAS:* Commercial and Business Law; Product Liability; Corporate Law; Tax Law; Arbitration; International Law.

THOMAS HEYMANN, born Bonn, November 19, 1952; admitted, 1985. *Education:* Universities of Frankfurt and Paris. *Member:* International Bar Association; German Bar Association; German Computer Law Association; (Vice Chairman, Co-Chairman, Software Protection Committee) American Computer Law Association; International Computer Lawyer (Advisory Board); Computer und Recht (Advisory Board). *LANGUAGES:* German, English and French. *PRACTICE AREAS:* Intellectual Property; Outsourcing; Strategic Alliances.

MICHAEL H. SPRING, born Frankfurt, July 10, 1946; admitted, 1976; Notary, 1983. *Education:* University of Frankfurt. *Member:* German Bar Association. *LANGUAGES:* German and English. *PRACTICE AREAS:* Construction Law; Real Estate Development; Law of Divorce; Inheritance and Estate Law.

HANS-WOLFGANG PFEIFER, born Frankfurt, May 18, 1931; admitted, 1960. *Education:* Universities of Marburg, Heidelberg, Frankfurt. President, Verband Freier Berufe in Hessen, 1977—. Chairman, Verband Hessischer Zeitungsverleger, 1963—. *Member:* German Bar Association. *LANGUAGES:* German, English and Italian.

JOACHIM SCHMIDT, born Mülheim/Ruhr, August 5, 1948; admitted, 1978. *Education:* University of Freiburg/Breisgau. Assistant Professor, University of Giessen/Hessen, 1975. *Member:* German Bar Association; Frankfurt Bar Association (Member of the Governing Board-Vorstand); Rhein/Main Real Property Managers Association (Executive Board Member); Club des Affaires de la Hesse. *LANGUAGES:* German, English and French.

DR. WALTER GREISNER, born Essen/Ruhr, August 23, 1928; admitted, 1959. *Education:* Universities of Koeln and Hamburg (Dr. jur.). Managing Director (Vorstand) of D. Stempel Aktiengesellschaft, Frankfurt/Main, 1967-1985. Chairman, Legal Committee of Association Typographique Internationale (A Typ I), Basel. *Member:* German Associations for the Protection of Industrial Property and Copyright, AIPPI. *LANGUAGES:* German and English.

DR. ALBRECHT MAGEN, born August 10, 1929; admitted, 1960. *Education:* Universities of Jena and Frankfurt/Main.

DR. ORTRUD SEIFERT-CRAMER, born Weilburg, December 12, 1954; admitted, 1987. *Education:* University of Giessen. *LANGUAGES:* German, English and French.

ALBRECHT VON EISENHART-ROTHE, born Bogota, Colombia, August 1, 1962; admitted, 1992. *Education:* Universities of Bonn and Munich. *LANGUAGES:* German, English and Spanish. *PRACTICE AREAS:* Corporate Law; Commercial Law.

JULIA WULF, born Frankfurt/Main, December 8, 1957; admitted, 1993. *Education:* Universities of Wurzburg, Bonn, Cologne. *Member:* Vereinigung für gewerblichen Rechtsschutz und Urheberrecht; International League for Competition Law. *LANGUAGES:* German, English and French. *PRACTICE AREAS:* Intellectual Property Law; Commercial Law; Mergers and Acquisitions.

DR. MICHAEL VON SAVIGNY, born Frankfurt am Main, February 5, 1959; admitted, 1989. *Education:* Universities of Göttingen, Bonn and Frankfurt am Main (Dr.jur.). *Member:* German Bar Association; Deutsche Geselischaft für Baurecht e.V. *LANGUAGES:* German and English. *PRACTICE AREAS:* General Practice; Construction Law; Insurance Law.

JÜRGEN HERRIEIN, born Regensburg, July 17, 1962; admitted, 1994. *Education:* University of Frankfurt. *Member:* German Bar Association. *LANGUAGES:* German and English. *PRACTICE AREAS:* Real Estate Law; Construction Law; Compulsory Auction Law.

DR. MARCUS HERRMANN, born April 1, 1964; admitted, 1994. *Education:* Universities of Freiburg, Munich and Münster (Dr.jur.). *Member:* German Bar Association. *LANGUAGES:* German and English. *PRAC-*

(This Listing Continued)

EU678B

TICE AREAS: Commercial Law; Corporate Law; Mergers and Acquisitions.

ALEXANDER H. STOPP, born Homburg/Saar, December 26, 1962; admitted, 1991, Germany; 1992, New York. *Education:* University of Augsburg (Referendar, 1987; Assessor, 1990; Dr. iur., 1993); University of Michigan, Ann Arbor (LL.M., 1988). Judicial Clerkship with the Hon. James M. Rosenbaum, U.S. District Court for the District of Minnesota, Minneapolis, March-May, 1989. *Member:* German-American Lawyers Association. *LANGUAGES:* German, English and French.

KAREN BETTINA KOMARNICKI, born Berlin, September 14, 1963; admitted, 1994. *Education:* University of Berlin, University of Kent at Canterbury, England (LL.M., International Commercial Law, 1990). Junior Barrister, Berlin, 1993. *Member:* DGRI. *LANGUAGES:* German, English and French.

MARTIN MEIBNER, born Flensburg, March 2, 1964. *Education:* University of Wuerzburg, Albany, New York. *LANGUAGES:* German and English. *PRACTICE AREAS:* Commercial Law; Mergers and Acquisitions.

WILKINSON, BARKER, KNAUER & QUINN

GOETHESTRASSE 23
60313 FRANKFURT/MAIN, GERMANY
Telephone: 011-49-69-20876
Telcopier: 011-49-69-297-8453

Washington, D.C. Office: 1734 New York Avenue, N.W. Telephone: 202-783-4141. Fax: 202-833-2360; 783-5851.

Administrative and Regulatory Practice before Federal Agencies, Legislative Practice before Congress, and Trial and Appellate Practice before Federal Courts. Practice sectors include Telecommunications, Broadcasting, Energy, Natural Resources, Financial Institutions, Tax, Health Insurance, Aviation, Domestic and International Corporate Transactions, Customs and International Trade.

FIRM PROFILE: The Firm specializes in regulatory, legislative, corporate and transactional matters. Our practice, which is centered in Washington, D.C, includes substantial involvement in proceedings before the Executive Branch, Congress, federal agencies, the federal courts, and financial institutions such as The Export-Import Bank and the World Bank.

Over the years, members of our firm have served in Congress and as Chairman of the Federal Communications Commission. Wilkinson, Barker attorneys have also clerked for distinguished jurists, counseled foreign governments, worked in executive positions at the Federal Energy Regulatory Commission and the Federal Communications Commission, and served as presidents of the Bar Associations.

Wilkinson, Barkers's domestic and international clients include Fortune 500 Companies, small and mid-sized corporations, utilities, municipalities, universities, trade associations, foreign governments and foundations.

DIPL. KFM. RICHARD LEITERMANN, born Munich, Germany, March 11, 1961; admitted, 1990, Germany. *Education:* Ludwig-Maximilians Univeritaet, Munich (Dipl. Kfm, 1985; Staatsexammen, 1987). Author, *Rechtsformwahl bei der Unternehmensgruendung in Unternehmensgruendung*, Verlag Vahlen. Member: American Chamber of Commerce in Germany, 1991—; Deutsher Anwaltsverein, 1993; Munich Bar Association, 1990-1993; Frankfurt Bar Association, 1993. *LANGUAGES:* German and English. *PRACTICE AREAS:* Telecommunications; Commercial Law.

(For Complete Biographical Data on all Personnel see Professional Biographies at Washington, D.C.)

ALBERT, WINKLER & PARTNER

Established in 1980

LUISENSTRAβE 3
79098 FREIBURG, GERMANY
Telephone: 0761/319000
Telefax: 0761/3190099

Administration, bankruptcy, commercial and corporate law, banking and finance, competition law, construction, estates, insurance, international trade law, labour, litigation and arbitration (including ADR), medical negligence, product liability, real estate, recovering restitutional claims, transport.

(This Listing Continued)

FIRM PROFILE: The firm was established in 1980. Acting mainly for commercial clients, particularly insurers, it offers a wide range of legal services within a network of European partners.

MEMBERS OF FIRM

MICHAEL ALBERT, born Bad Elster, Germany, August 1, 1948; admitted, 1978, Freiburg. *Education:* University of Freiburg. *Member:* Freiburg Bar Association; German Lawyers Association; Institute for the Law of Negligence and Traffic Law (President).

MICHAEL WINKLER, born Pirmasens, Germany, June 16, 1948; admitted, 1978, Freiburg. *Education:* University of Freiburg. *Member:* Freiburg Bar Association; German Lawyers Association; German Japanese Society (Board of Directors).

DIRK MEYER-HÖKE, born St. Tönis, Germany, October 31, 1960; admitted, 1991, Freiburg. *Education:* University of Munich and Freiburg. *Member:* American Trial Lawyers Association; German Institution of Arbitration; Association International des Jeunes Avocats; Freiburg Bar Association; Slowak Chamber of Commerce (Arbitrator).

HANS G. NISOLK, born Berlin, Germany, May 8, 1940; admitted, 1993, Freiburg. *Education:* University of Freiburg and Speyer. Managing Director, Freiburg Employer's Association, 1975-1992. Chairman, Board of Appeal AOK, 1980—. *Member:* Baden Arbitration Board of Labour Conflicts (1979—); Freiburg Bar Association.

Languages: German, English and French

BAPPERT, WITZ & SELBHERR

LEO-WOHLEB-STRASSE 6
D-79098 FREIBURG, GERMANY
Telephone: (0049) 761/218080
Telecopier: (0049) 761/2180821

Brussels, Belgium Office: 176, Avenue Louise, B-1050. Telephone: (0032) 2/6473300. Telecopier: (0032) 2/6476539.

Dresden, Germany Office: Berggartenstrasse 7, D-01309. Telephone: (0049) 351/4606131. Telecopier: (0049) 351/4655376.

General Practice and Litigation. Copyright, Trademarks, Patents, Unfair Competition, Antitrust, Corporation, Commercial, Tax, Real Estate, Labor, Wills, Administrative, Environmental Protection, EEC, International Law.

MEMBERS OF FIRM

PROF. DR. WALTER BAPPERT (1894-1985).

DR. PAUL WITZ, born Offenburg, Germany, May 2, 1911; admitted, 1946, Freiburg. (Retired).

DR. PAUL SELBHERR, born Saulgau, Germany, November 22, 1929; admitted, 1958, Stuttgart. *Education:* Universities of Tübingen and Cologne (Dr. jur., 1962). *Member:* Freiburg (President, 1989—) and German Bar Associations (Treasurer, 1991—); German Association for the Protection of Industrial Property and Copyright. *LANGUAGES:* German and English. *PRACTICE AREAS:* Corporate; Intellectual Property.

DR. EBERHARD FREIHERR VON RUMMEL, born Stuttgart, Germany, November 17, 1941; admitted, 1972, Freiburg. *Education:* Universities of Rome, Italy, Munich and Freiburg (Dr. jur., 1978); University of California at Berkeley (LL.M., 1968). *Member:* Freiburg, German and International Bar Associations; German-American Lawyers Association; German-Italian Legal Association; German Arbitration Committee. *LANGUAGES:* German, English, Italian, French, Spanish and Turkish. *PRACTICE AREAS:* International Commerce; Construction; Transportation.

DR. WOLFGANG SCHMID, born Radolfzell, Germany, October 1, 1943; admitted, 1973, Freiburg. *Education:* Universities of Freiburg, Munich and Bonn (Dr. jur., 1971). *Member:* Freiburg and German Bar Associations; German Association for the Protection of Industrial Property and Copyright. *LANGUAGES:* German, English and French. *PRACTICE AREAS:* Unfair Competition; Advertising; Trademarks.

GERHARD MANZ, born Stuttgart, Germany, April 23, 1952; admitted, 1978, Freiburg. *Education:* Universities of Berlin, Lausanne and Freiburg. *Member:* Freiburg, German and International Bar Associations; British-German Jurists' Association; Association Internationale des Jeunes Avocats. (Also Partner in Charge at Brussels, Belgium Office). *LANGUAGES:* German, English, French and Italian. *PRACTICE AREAS:* Companies; Antitrust; Copyright.

(This Listing Continued)

DR. KARL VON WOGAU, born Freiburg, Germany, July 18, 1941; admitted, 1984, Freiburg. *Education:* Universities of Freiburg, Munich and Bonn (Dr. jur., 1973); Diploma INSEAD for Business Administration, 1971 (Fontainebleau). *Member:* European Parliament (Member, Committee on Economic and Monetary Affairs); Freiburg and German Bar Associations. *LANGUAGES:* German, English, French, Italian, Dutch and Spanish. *PRACTICE AREAS:* European Community.

DR. JÜRGEN DRYWA, born Bad Kissingen, Germany, February 19, 1951; admitted, 1979, Freiburg. *Education:* Universities of Frankfurt, Marburg and Freiburg (Dr. jur., 1985). *Member:* Freiburg and German Bar Associations; Deutscher Familienrechtstag. *LANGUAGES:* German, English and Italian. *PRACTICE AREAS:* Taxation; Family.

DR. CHRISTIAN WOLF, born Hamburg, Germany, May 22, 1957; admitted, 1986, Freiburg. *Education:* Universities of Hamburg and Freiburg (Dr. jur., 1986). *Member:* Freiburg and German Bar Associations; German Association of Data Technics and Law. *LANGUAGES:* German and English. *PRACTICE AREAS:* Technology; Property; Inheritance.

DR. MICHAEL BENDER, born Cologne, Germany, September 16, 1956; admitted, 1988, Stuttgart. *Education:* Universities of Cologne and Freiburg (Dr. jur., 1989). *Member:* Freiburg and German Bar Associations; Association for Environmental Law; Administrative Law Committee of German Lawyers Association. *LANGUAGES:* German and English. *PRACTICE AREAS:* Administrative; Constitutional.

DR. CHRISTOPH FINGERLE, born Neu-Ulm, Germany, May 28, 1960; admitted, 1990, Freiburg. *Education:* Universities of Berlin and Freiburg (Dr. jur., 1991). *Member:* Freiburg and German Bar Associations. *LANGUAGES:* German and English. *PRACTICE AREAS:* Labor and Employment.

DR. ALBERT SCHRÖDER, born Düsseldorf, Germany, May 25, 1961; admitted, 1991, Freiburg. *Education:* University of Cologne (Dr. jur., 1989). *Member:* Freiburg and German Bar Associations. *LANGUAGES:* German and English. *PRACTICE AREAS:* Corporate; Taxation.

DR. BARBARA MAYER, born Heidelberg, Germany, September 5, 1964; admitted, 1993, Freiburg. *Education:* Universities of Berlin and Freiburg (Dr.jur., 1990). *Member:* Freiburg and German Bar Associations; German Association of Female Lawyers. *LANGUAGES:* German, French and English. *PRACTICE AREAS:* Contracts; Agency and Distributorship; Franchising.

TAX ADVISOR

GÜNTER MAIER, born Donaueschingen, Germany, April 1, 1950. Tax Advisor, 1981; Chartered Accountant, 1987. *Member:* Institute of Chartered Accountants. *LANGUAGES:* German and English.

ASSOCIATES

Eva-Maria Kuppe; Dr. Wendt Nassall.

Languages: German, English, French, Spanish, Italian, Dutch and Turkish

---

DR. MARTIN CLAUSNITZER, LL.M.

Member-Office of the IASW-EWIV (Frankfurt/M)

Established in 1984

MÖSLESTRASSE 1
D-79117 FREIBURG, GERMANY
Telephone: 49 (0) 761-703360
Fax: 49 (0) 761-7033636

General Practice, Contracts and Torts, Family, Real Estate, Wills, Tax and Administrative Law, Conflicts of Law, EC.

DR. MARTIN CLAUSNITZER, born 1951; admitted, 1984. *Education:* High School N.C. USA (Diploma, 1969); Abitur Ratsgymnasium Osnabrück (1970); Universities of Heidelberg, Geneva, Strasbourg (FIEDC), Freiburg. Assistant to Prof. W. Müller-Freienfels, Institute for Private, Int'l and Comp. Law.; Columbia University, LL.M., 1979, Doctor of Laws, Freiburg, 1985. Lecturer on Law at the Academy of Public Administration, Kehl, 1991-1992. Author: (e.g.): "Property Rights of Surviving Spouses and the Conflict of Laws", 18 J.Fam.L. 471-550, 1979-1980; "The Statute of Limitations for Murder in the FRG", 29 Int'l & Comp L.Q. 473-479, 1980; "Humanistic Education in Law", JURA 1981, 51-56;, "Die güter-und erbrechtliche Stellung des überlebenden Ehegatten nach den Kollisionsrechten der BRD und USA", 1986; "Die Durchsetzung europäischen Gemeinschaftsrechts im Steuerprozess", DStR 1987,641-643; "Europarech-

(This Listing Continued)

DR. MARTIN CLAUSNITZER, LL.M., Freiburg—
Continued

tliche Beschränkung der Eigenverbrauchsbesteuerung", EuZW 1990, 184-187; "Niederlassungs- und Dienstleistungsfreiheit der Selbständigen", in: EG-Handbuch, p. 183-234 , 1991; "Verjährung Vertraglicher Schadenersatzansprüche gegen Steuerberater", DStR 1991, 1362-1367; "Vorteilhafte Testamentsgestaltung," 1993; "EG-Recht in der Anwaltskanzlei," 1993. *Member:* German and Republican Bar Associations; American Field Service (AFS); German-American Lawyers Association (DAJV); Young Lawyers' International Association (AIJA).

Languages: German, English and French.

STELZER HOFFMANN SAUTER

Established in 1993

STADTSTRAßE 29

D-79104 FREIBURG, GERMANY

Telephone: 0761/3 87 79-0
Telefax: 0761/3 87 79-88

General Practice, Corporation, Commercial, National and International Tax, Accounting, Mergers and Acquisitions, National and EC Antitrust, Inheritance, Real Estate, Intellectual Property, Litigation.

DR. WOLF-DIETER HOFFMANN, born Freiburg, November 19, 1942; admitted, 1971, Tax Advisor; 1976, Certified Public Accountant. *Education:* University of Freiburg (Dipl.-Volkswirt, Dr. rer. pol.). *LANGUAGES:* German, English, French and Greek. *PRACTICE AREAS:* National and International Tax Law; Auditing and Valuation; Mergers and Acquisitions.

DR. WOLFGANG SAUTER, born Jagstzell, Germany, December 5, 1950; admitted, 1982, Freiburg; 1991, Certified Public Accountant. *Education:* University of Freiburg (Dr. jur., 1982). *LANGUAGES:* German, English and French. *PRACTICE AREAS:* General Practice; Corporation; Commercial; Mergers and Acquisitions; Antitrust; Inheritance; Real Estate; Intellectual Property; Litigation.

KLAUS STELZER, born Günthersdorf/Schlesien, November 18, 1938; admitted, 1972, Tax Advisor; 1979, Certified Public Accountant. *Education:* Universities of Munich and Freiburg (Dip.-Volkswirt, 1968). *LANGUAGES:* German, English and Russian. *PRACTICE AREAS:* Tax Law; Auditing and Valuation.

SCHAFFRATH & METZMACHER

BERLINER STR. 20

D-02826 GÖRLITZ, GERMANY

Telephone: (3581) 406396
Telecopier: (3581) 403750

Düsseldorf, Germany Office: Rosenstr. 11, D-40479. Telephone: (211) 49 222-0. Telecopier: (211) 49 82 408.

Dresden, Germany Office: Lortzingstraße 37, D-01307, Dresden. Telephone: 0351/4426234. Telecopier: 0351/4426238.

Administrative Law, Antitrust, Construction and Engineering Contracts, Corporate, Environmental Law, European Law, Family Law, Industrial and Intellectual Property, Labor Law, Litigation and Arbitration, Mergers and Acquisitions, Property Law of New German Member States, Trade Law, Transportation and Aviation, Unfair Competition.

MEMBERS OF FIRM

CHRISTIAN REICHARDT, born Mülheim, Germany, December 24, 1958; admitted, 1988, Germany. *Education:* Universities of Bochum and Münster (1979-1984). Legal Advisor, Free State of Saxonia, 1993—. *Member:* Task Force Program for Restitution of Property in Saxonia. *LANGUAGES:* German and English. *PRACTICE AREAS:* Administrative Law; Commercial Property Law; Litigation; Labor Law.

BRANDI DRÖGE PILTZ & HEUER

HOCHSTR. 19

33332 GÜTERSLOH, GERMANY

Telephone: 49 5241 5 88 86
Telecopier: 49 5241 5 88 81

Bielefeld, Germany Office: Elsa-Brändström-Str. 1 and 3, 33602. Telephone: 49 521 96535-0. Telecopier: 49 521 96535-99.

Detmold, Germany Office: Lindenweg 2, 32756. Telephone: 49 5231 9857-0. Telecopier: 49 5231 9857-50.

Berlin, Germany Office: Seelenbinderstr. 124, 12555. Telephone: 49 30 6509465. Telecopier: 49 30 6565679.

Leipzig, Germany Office: Katharinenstr. 1-3, 04109. Telephone: 49 341 287550. Telecopier: 49 341 289162.

Paris, France Office: 250 bis, Boulevard Saint-Germain, 75007. Telephone: 33-1 49 54 90 37. Telecopier: 33-1 49 54 90 02.

International Sales Law, International Agency, Distribution and Franchising Law, International Company Law and Joint Ventures, International Turnkey Projects, International Transactions, International Trademark Law, International Transfer of Technology and Licensing, International Transport Law, International Estate Planning, International Law of Succession, Business Immigration, EU Law.

MEMBERS OF FIRM

DR. BURGHARD PILTZ, born Gütersloh, Germany, January 4, 1947; admitted, 1977, Germany. *Education:* Universities of Münster and Munich (Erstes Juristisches Staatsexamen, 1973; Doctor of Jurisprudence, 1975). Author: "Internationales Scheidungsrecht," Munich, 1988; "UN-Kaufrecht," Bonn, 1991; "Internationales Kaufrecht", Munich, 1993; "Auslandsinvestitionen in Argentinien", 1981 DB 457; "Grundzüge des Argentinischen Technologie-Transfer-Rechts", IWB Nr. 19 Oct. 10, 1986. S. 27; Der Anwendungsbereich des UN-Kaufrechts," 1991 AnwBl 57; "(Spanisches) Kaufrecht," in: Löber/Peuster, Aktuelles Spanisches Handels- und Wirtschaftsrecht, 1991, S. 207. Lecturer: University of Hamburg, 1990-1992; University of Bielefeld, 1991—; German Attorneys Academy, 1984—. *Member:* German Bar Association; Argentine-German Lawyers Association (Vice President); Union International des Avocats; International Bar Association. *LANGUAGES:* German, English, Spanish and Italian. *PRACTICE AREAS:* International Sales Law (esp. 1980 UN Sales Convention); International Company Law; International Estate Planning; International Commercial Law.

HARTMUT SANDERING, born Diepholz, Germany, September 10, 1956; admitted, 1984, Germany. *Education:* University of Bielefeld (Examination, 1984). *Member:* German Bar Association; Gütersloh Lawyers Association; German-Belgian Lawyers Association; Union Internationale des Avocats. *LANGUAGES:* German, English and French. *PRACTICE AREAS:* National and International Transport Law; Commercial Agency Law; International and National Commercial Law; Litigation.

DR. FRANZ TEPPER, LL.M., born Lippstadt, Germany, March 24, 1960; admitted, 1990, Germany; 1991, New York. *Education:* Bankkaufmann (1981); University of Münster (Erstes Juristisches Staatsexamen, 1986; Doctor of Jurisprudence, 1989); University of Pennsylvania, Philadelphia (LL.M., 1987). Author: "Die Auswirkungen ausländischer Devisenembargos auf Bürgschaften im deutschen und Guaranties im USamerikanischen Recht," Dissertation, 1989; "Einige Bemerkungen zur Wirksamkeit von Haustürgeschäften im Kreditgewerbe," 1990 JR 356; "Anwaltshaftung und EuGVU," 1991 IPRax 98; "Immigration Law and Business in Europe," London, 1993, (Co-Editor and Co-Author). Lecturer: German Attorneys Academy, 1994—. *Member:* German Bar Association; New York State Bar Association; State Bar of California (International Law Section); American Bar Association; Canadian-German Lawyers-Association (Vice-President); Board German American Lawyers Association; German-British Jurists' Association; German Association for Intellectual Property and Copyright Law; Licensing Executives Society; American Chamber of Commerce, Germany; Association Internationale des Jeunes Avocats; European Immigration Lawyers Group. *LANGUAGES:* German and English. *PRACTICE AREAS:* International Transfer of Technology and Licensing; International Distribution/Agency/Franchising; Business Immigration; International Commercial and EEC Law.

MANFRED REINKEMEIER, born Rietberg, Germany, May 8, 1962; admitted, 1991, Germany. *Education:* Universities of Kaiserslautern and Bielefeld (Mathematics, 1982-1984); University of Bielefeld (Law, Examination, 1991). German-Venezuelan Chamber of Commerce, Caracas, 1990. *LANGUAGES:* German, English and Spanish. *PRACTICE AREAS:* International Commercial Law.

(This Listing Continued)

RAINER SCHACKMAR, born Rheda-Wiedenbrück, Germany, April 18, 1963; admitted, 1993, Germany. *Education:* Industriekaufmann 1984; Betriebswirt (VWA 1985); University of Münster (Erstes juristisches Staatsexamen 1990). *LANGUAGES:* German and English. *PRACTICE AREAS:* International Commercial Law.

BENKELBERG & VON STEIN-LAUSNITZ

Established in 1974

HANSERING 1
06108 HALLE, GERMANY
Telephone: 0345-388440
Telefax: 0345-3884430

Emmerich, Germany Office: Steinstraße 10, 46446 Emmerich. Telephone: 02822-92340. Telefax: 02822-923430.

Tallinn, Estonia Office: Livalaia 14, EE 0106 Tallinn. Telephone: 003722691766. Telefax: 003722682283.

Civil, Contract, Commercial, and Company Law; Family Law, Wills and Inheritance Law; Transport Law (including Freight-forwarders Law and Air Transportation), Banking and Finance, Insurance, Real Estate; Employment and Labour-Law; Unfair Competition, Trademark, and Copyright; Administrative Law (including Environmental, Planning, and Construction); EU-Law, International Private Law; Litigation and Arbitration.

FIRM PROFILE: *Founded in 1974 by Eckhard Benkelberg, this modern office has steadily grown to a firm of eight lawyers and a staff of 18 paralegal assistants. In November 1989 a branch office was established in the former German Democratic Republic, which soon succeeded to become the main office. In 1993, a partnership was created with an Estonian lawyer.*

The firm is a member of the EU-LEX International Practise Group, a Network of sixty firms of lawyers, accountants and tax advisers in 17 countries of Europe and residents in the USA, Australia, Far and Middle East. Languages: German, English, French, Russian, Estonian, Dutch.

MEMBERS OF FIRM

ECKHARD BENKELBERG, born Kirn, Germany, March 1947; admitted, 1973, Düsseldorf, 1990 for an official branch office in Halle. *Education:* Universitas Saraviensis, Saarbrücken. *Member:* German Society of Transportation Law; German Association of Inheritance Law; Dutch-German Chamber of Commerce; Chairman of the Board of EU-LEX/IPG. (Also at Emmerich, Germany Office).

DIETRICH VON STEIN-LAUSNITZ, born Leipzig, Germany, March 1958; admitted, 1987, Düsseldorf, 1990 for an official branch office in Halle. *Education:* University of Tübingen. (Also at Emmerich, Germany Office).

KNUD FRANZ, born Worms am Rhein, Germany, February 1960; admitted, 1993, Frankfurt am Main; 1994, Halle. *Education:* Universities of Marburg and Mainz. *Member:* German Association for Industrial Property Rights and Copyrights.

MARLIS LEHMANN, born Halle, Germany, February 1951; admitted, 1990, Halle. *Education:* University of Halle.

KURT KALTENBORN, born Kleingräfendorf, Germany, November 1949; admitted, 1990, Halle.

RESIDENTS IN EMMERICH

MONIKA DOLD, born Rheinberg, Germany, July 1965; admitted, 1993, Düsseldorf. *Education:* Universities of Freiburg and Bonn.

JOCHEN KÖSTER, born Emmerich, Germany, June 1965; admitted, 1994, Düsseldorf. *Education:* Universities of Giessen and Münster.

RESIDENTS IN TALLINN

MAIDO PAJO, born Jogeva, Estonia, October 1950. *Education:* University of Tartu; School of Agricultural Banking, Credit and Finance, Iowa/USA. Legal Counsellor since 1993, 1990-1992 Estonian Vice-Minister for Agriculture.

EIMER • HEUSCHMID • MEHLE

RUDOLF-BREITSCHEID-STR. 92
06108 HALLE, GERMANY
Telephone: 01149-345-29392
Fax: 01149-345-29392

Bonn, Germany Office: Friedrich-Breuer-Str. 104-112, 53225 Bonn. Telephone: 01149-228-466025. Fax: 01149-228-460708.
Cologne, Germany Office: Hohenstaufenring 44-46, 50674 Cologne. Telephone: 01149-221-235555. Fax:01149-221-236121.

Civil, Commercial and Company Law, Patents and Trade Marks, Family Law and Estate Administration, Labour Law, Private International and EC Law, Insurance and Medical Malpractice Law, Criminal Law, Serious Fraud, Tax and Environmental Offenses.

FIRM PROFILE: *The firm was established in 1973 and offers a full range of services including litigation in all judicial branches. It is well known for its wide-ranging commercial, family and specialized criminal law. Its client base is European. The firm is a member of a European Economic Interest Grouping (AVRIO), the partners of which are well-known firms throughout Europe; close cooperation and advice on European scale is offered.*

RESIDENT PARTNER

UWE MERTIN, born Siegen, November 14, 1962; admitted, 1993, Halle. *Education:* Bonn University. *Member:* German Bar Association. *LANGUAGES:* German and English. *PRACTICE AREAS:* Construction Law; Labour Law; Administration Law.

KRAMEYER, v. FALKENHAUSEN, HANKE & PARTNERS

Established in 1990

HANSERING 4
D-06108 HALLE, GERMANY
Telephone: 0345-28053; 0345-21669
Telefax: 0345-21669

Essen, Germany Office: Gildehofstraße 1, P.O. Box 102031, D-45020 Essen. Telephone: 0201-82015-0. Telefax: 0201-8201510.
Brussels, Belgium Office: 6, Drève des Renards, B-1180 Brussels. Telephone: 02/3749200. Telefax: 02/3754525.

General Practice, Contracts, Company, Commercial, Construction and Engineering, Corporation, Banking, Antitrust Law and Unfair Competition, Labor, Patent and Trademark, Intellectual Property, Law of the former GDR, Product Liability, Real Estate, Insurance, Family, Inheritance, Environment, Energy and Natural Resources, Taxes, European Community, Arbitration, Administration, Notaries.

FIRM PROFILE: *The firm was established in 1952 in Essen and offers the full range of legal services. It is well known for its practice in all fields of commercial law. The client base is European and North American. The firm has two branch offices in Halle (former GDR) and in Brussels (Belgium).*

MEMBERS OF FIRM

DR. EBERHARD BESCH, born Dessau, Germany, May 18, 1942; admitted, 1991, Halle. *Education:* Martin Luther Universitat, Halle-Wittenberg (Dr. jur.). *Member:* Halle and German Lawyers Association. *LANGUAGES:* German and Russian. *PRACTICE AREAS:* General Practice; Commercial; Law of the former GDR.

Languages: German, English, French, Italian and Russian.

SCHOLZ, KRAATZ, DITTMANN & PARTNER

BERNBURGER STRASSE 9
D-06108 HALLE, GERMANY
Telephone: +49-345-50 12 71
Telefax: +49-345 5 50 17 84

Düsseldorf, Germany Office: Königsallee 100, D-40215. Telephone: +49-211-3 88 00-0. Telefax: +49-211-37 36 78. Telex 8 58 72 46 skd d.

(This Listing Continued)

SCHOLZ, KRAATZ, DITTMANN & PARTNER, Halle—Continued

General Practice of Commercial Law, Corporate, Tax, Finance, Banking, Unfair Competition, German and EEC Antitrust, Labour, Bankruptcy, Commercial Litigation and Arbitration, Trademark, Licensing, Mergers, Acquisitions, International Construction Contracts.

RESIDENT LAWYERS

DR. MARKUS ROHNER, born Korschenbroich, October 12, 1961; admitted, 1991, Germany. *Education:* University of Bonn (Dr. of Law, 1991). *Member:* German-American Lawyer's Association; German (West)-German (East) Lawyers' Association. *LANGUAGES:* German, English and French. *PRACTICE AREAS:* International Private and Civil Procedure Law; Commercial Sales Law; Law of Warranties; Real Property Law; Corporate Law; Law of Associations; Tax Law.

ANDREAS VOGEL, born Ludwigsburg, April 3, 1964; admitted, 1994, Germany. *Education:* Universities of Tübingen and Bonn. *LANGUAGES:* German, English and French. *PRACTICE AREAS:* Business Law; General Contract Law; Commercial Law.

BERENBERG-GOSSLER & PARTNERS

HAMBURG, GERMANY

(See Wessing Berenberg-Gossler Zimmermann Lange)

BOLLMANN, KIESSELBACH & PARTNER

Established in 1895

NEUER WALL 42

P.O. BOX 300 549

20302 HAMBURG, GERMANY

Telephone: 040-362241

Cable Address: "Kiesselsie"

Telefax: 36 69 30

Admiralty, Antitrust, Appellate, Arbitration, Civil, Commercial, Copyright, Corporation, Insurance, International, International Trade, Labor Law, Litigation, Press, Real Estate, Transportation, Railroad, Unfair Competition, Wills, Trusts, Estates.

FIRM PROFILE: Established 1895. Mainly active in the area of Commercial Law.

MEMBERS OF FIRM

DR. HANS BOLLMANN (1920-1976).

DR. THEODOR KIESSELBACH (1926-1973).

DR. HANS-DIETRICH PREYER (1917-1990).

GERHARD MAEDER, born Koenigsberg, March 30, 1916; admitted, 1952, Hamburg. *Education:* University of Hamburg. Fachanwalt fuer Steuerrecht (Specialist for Tax Law). Former Chief Justice of Finance Court Hamburg. *Member:* Deutscher Juristentag e.V.; Deutsche Steuerjuristische Gesellschaft e.V. *LANGUAGES:* German. *PRACTICE AREAS:* Tax Law.

DR. KNUT SUHR, born Berlin, August 1, 1938; admitted, 1969, Hamburg. *Education:* University of Texas (LL.M., 1967); Universities of Lausanne/Switzerland, Gottingen and Hamburg (Dr. jur. [Max-Planck-Institute for Foreign and International Private Law] 1970). *Member:* Hamburg Bar Association; British-German Jurists' Association (Secretary General, 1989—); German-American Lawyers' Association; International Bar Association; Association of the Bar of the City of New York. *LANGUAGES:* German, English and French. *PRACTICE AREAS:* Company Law; International Sales Law; Agency; Arbitration; Maritime Law.

DR. F. MICHAEL BOEMKE, born Giessen, November 29, 1943; admitted, 1974, Hamburg. *Education:* Universities of Tuebingen and Hamburg (Dr. jur., 1977). *Member:* Hamburg Bar Association; British-German Jurists' Association. *LANGUAGES:* German and English. *PRACTICE AREAS:* Company Law; International Sales Law; Agency; Arbitration.

MICHAEL A. KUNERT, born Hamburg, October 30, 1946; admitted, 1974, Hamburg. *Education:* University of Hamburg. *Member:* Hamburg

(This Listing Continued)

Bar Association; British-German Jurists' Association; International Commission of Jurists (German Section). *LANGUAGES:* German and English. *PRACTICE AREAS:* Litigation; Labour Law; Transport Law; Administrative Law; Family Law.

JOBST-GUENTHER MAEDER, born Hamburg, March 6, 1957; admitted, 1986, Hamburg. *Education:* University of Hamburg. Fachanwalt fuer Steuerrecht (Specialist for Tax Law). *Member:* Hamburg Bar Association; British-German Jurists' Association. *LANGUAGES:* German. *PRACTICE AREAS:* Tax Law.

VERENA ZAHN, born Hamburg, November 1, 1948; admitted, 1978, Hamburg. *Education:* Universities of Hamburg and Freiburg. Fachanwältin fuer Arbeitsrecht (Specialist for Labor Law). *Member:* Hamburg Bar Association; German Women Jurists' Association; FIDA. *LANGUAGES:* German and English. *PRACTICE AREAS:* Litigation; Labour Law; Family Law.

Languages: German, English and French.

BRUCKHAUS WESTRICK STEGEMANN

ALSTERARKADEN 27

20354 HAMBURG, GERMANY

Telephone: (040) 36 90 60

Telefax: (040) 36 906-155

Telex: 212 522 EURO D

Düsseldorf Office: Freiligrathstrasse 1, 40479 Düsseldorf. Telephone: (02 11) 49 79-0. Telefax: (02 11) 49 79-1 03; 4 98 12 21. Telex: 858 7027 JUS D.

Frankfurt Office: Taunusanlage 11, 60329 Frankfurt am Main. Telephone: (069) 27308-0. Telefax: (069) 232664. Telex: 41 49 17 WEST C D.

Berlin Office: Friedrichstrasse 95 (IHZ), 10117 Berlin. Telephone: (030) 26 43-3303. Telefax: (030) 26 43-3366.

Leipzig Office: Grimmaische Strasse 25, 04109 Leipzig. Telephone: (0341) 127230. Telefax: (0341) 1272333.

Brussels, Belgium Office: Rue de la Loi 99/101, B-1040 Brussels. Telephone: (32-2) 2 87 26 11. Telefax: (32-2) 2 30 39 03.

Tokyo, Japan Office: Ark Mori Building, 22F, 12-32, Akasaka 1-chome, Minato-ku, Tokyo 107. Telephone: (81-3) 55610-236. Telefax: (81-3) 55610-238.

New York, New York Office: 767 Fifth Avenue, GM Building, New York 10153. Telephone: (212) 486-1100. Telefax: (212) 759-3151.

Moscow, Russia Office: Malyj Gnezdnikovskij per. 9 No. 2, 103009 Moscow. Telephone: (7-503) 9562300; (7-501) 9401200. Telefax: (7-503) 9562301; (7-501) 9401211.

Corporate Law, Commercial Law, Mergers, Acquisitions and Divestitures, Joint Ventures, Banks and Banking, Finance, Securities, Capital Markets, Leases and Leasing, Equipment Finance, Aircraft Finance and Leasing, Antitrust and Trade Regulation, German and EC Cartel Law, Competition, Unfair Trade, Intellectual Property (trademarks, patents, copyrights), Taxation, Property, Real Estate, Energy, Natural Resources, Environmental Law, Administrative Law, Computers and Software, Food and Drug, Biotechnology, Labour and Employment, Products Liability, Insurance, Litigation, Arbitration, Broadcasting, Telecommunications, Aviation, Subsidies and State Aids, Construction Law, Zoning, Planning and Land Use, Customs and Foreign Trade Law, European Community Law, German-French Investments, Russian and Post Soviet Commerce.

MEMBERS OF FIRM

DR. KLAUS REINHARDT WACHS, born Dillenburg, Germany, December 28, 1928; admitted, 1957, Germany. *Education:* Universities of Hamburg (Dr. jur., 1954); Cologne and Frankfurt am Main; New York University. Associate Judge, Hamburg Constitutional Court. *LANGUAGES:* German and English. *PRACTICE AREAS:* Commercial Law; Corporate Law; Company Law.

DR. WOLFGANG MUELLER-STÖFEN, born Hamburg, Germany, February 20, 1931; admitted, 1960, Hamburg, Germany. *Education:* Universities of Freiburg im Breisgau, Lausanne (Switzerland), Munich, Hamburg (Dr. jur., 1960); New York University (M.C.J., 1959). (Travelling Partner, Hamburg and Moscow Office). *LANGUAGES:* German and English. *PRACTICE AREAS:* Corporate Law; Commercial Law; Mergers, Acquisitions and Divestitures; Russian and Post Soviet Commerce.

DR. FRIEDRICH HEIBEY, born Stettin, Germany, February 6, 1938; admitted, 1964, Germany. *Education:* University of Hamburg (Dr. jur.,

(This Listing Continued)

1968). *LANGUAGES:* German and English. *PRACTICE AREAS:* Litigation; Arbitration; Labor Law; Commercial Law.

DR. MICHAEL LICHTENAUER, born Rostock, Germany, November 8, 1939; admitted, 1967, Germany. *Education:* Universities of Hamburg, Lausanne (Switzerland) and Munich (Dr. jur., 1966). *LANGUAGES:* German, English and French. *PRACTICE AREAS:* Commercial Law; Corporate Law; Tax Law; Banks and Banking; Finance.

DR. JAN-PETER DE WALL, born Leer, Germany, December 17, 1939; admitted, 1970, Germany. *Education:* Universities of Hamburg (Dr. jur., 1972), Munich and University of Chicago. *LANGUAGES:* German and English. *PRACTICE AREAS:* Intellectual Property; Competition; Unfair Trade.

DR. CHRISTIAN WILDE, born Düsseldorf, Germany, September 21, 1939; admitted, 1970, Germany. *Education:* Universities of Lausanne (Switzerland), Hamburg and Göttingen (Dr. jur., 1969); University of California, Berkeley (LL.M., 1966). *LANGUAGES:* German, English and French. *PRACTICE AREAS:* Corporate Law; Mergers, Acquisitions and Divestitures; Tax Law; Real Estate.

DR. HANS JOCHEN WAITZ, born Hamburg, Germany, February 6, 1944; admitted, 1973, Germany. *Education:* Universities of Freiburg im Breisgau, Lausanne (Switzerland) and Berlin (Dr. jur., 1973). *LANGUAGES:* German and English. *PRACTICE AREAS:* Corporate Law; Mergers, Acquisitions and Divestitures; Real Estate; Environmental Law.

DR. WINFRIED STEEGER, born Hamburg, Germany, November 30, 1949; admitted, 1977, Germany. *Education:* University of Hamburg (Dr. jur., 1980). *LANGUAGES:* German and English. *PRACTICE AREAS:* Corporate Law; Commercial Law; German and EC Cartel Law.

DR. ANDREAS RITTSTIEG, born Remscheid, Germany, April 6, 1956; admitted, 1984, Germany. *Education:* Universities of Bochum, Geneva (Switzerland) and Bonn (Dr. jur., 1982). *LANGUAGES:* German, English and French. *PRACTICE AREAS:* Corporate Law; Commercial Law; Mergers, Acquisitions and Divestitures; Cartel Law.

DR. HANS-WILHELM JENCKEL, born Lüneburg, Germany, October 9, 1955; admitted, 1986, Germany; 1990, New York. *Education:* Universities of Göttingen, Geneva, Switzerland, and Hamburg (Dr. jur., 1986). Author: "Gemeinschaftsunternehmen mit DDR-Betrieben, Der Betrieb," Cologne, Germany, 1990, p. 361. *LANGUAGES:* German, English and French. *PRACTICE AREAS:* Corporate Law; Mergers, Acquisitions and Divestitures; Commercial Law.

DR. DIETER G. ZWICKER, born Zwickau, Germany, September 5, 1952; admitted, 1984, New York; 1985, Germany. *Education:* University of Hamburg (Dr. jur., 1983); Harvard University (LL.M., 1980). *LANGUAGES:* German and English. *PRACTICE AREAS:* Corporate Law; Mergers, Acquisitions and Divestitures; Joint Ventures.

DR. ERWIN B. VON BRESSENSDORF, born Gräfelfing, Germany, August 28, 1957; admitted, 1989, Germany. *Education:* University of Hamburg (Dr. jur., 1990). *LANGUAGES:* German and English. *PRACTICE AREAS:* Real Estate; Corporate Law; Commercial Law; Company Law.

UWE MOMSEN, born Hamburg, Germany, November 23, 1933; admitted, 1984, Germany. *Education:* Universities of Hamburg and Munich. *LANGUAGES:* German. *PRACTICE AREAS:* Litigation; Arbitration; Commercial Law.

DR. MICHAEL HAIDINGER, born Karlsruhe, Germany, July 18, 1960; admitted, 1988, Germany. *Education:* Universities of Freiburg im Breisgau (Dr. jur., 1990) and Geneva (Switzerland). *LANGUAGES:* German, English and French. *PRACTICE AREAS:* Corporate Law; Commercial Law; Banking; Environmental Law.

DR. MARIUS B. BERENBROK, born Hamburg, Germany, September 15, 1959; admitted, 1991, Germany. *Education:* Universities of Hamburg (Dr. jur., 1988) and Geneva, Switzerland. Research Assistant, Max-Planck-Institut for Foreign and International Private Law, 1985-1988. *LANGUAGES:* German, English and French. *PRACTICE AREAS:* Corporate Law; Mergers, Acquisitions and Divestitures; Commercial Law.

HUBERTUS LEO, born Hamburg, Germany, May 16, 1962; admitted, 1991, Germany. *Education:* Universities of Munich and Paris, France. *LANGUAGES:* German, English and French. *PRACTICE AREAS:* Corporate Law; Cartel Law; Tax Law.

DR. RAINER LOGES, born Hamburg, Germany, February 3, 1963; admitted, 1992, Germany. *Education:* Universities of Freiburg im Breisgau and Göttingen (Dr. jur., 1990); Fernuniversität Hagen (Dipl.-Kfm., 1991).

(This Listing Continued)

LANGUAGES: German and English. *PRACTICE AREAS:* Corporate Law; Commercial Law.

DR. PETER VERSTEEGEN, born Kiel, Germany, April 30, 1963; admitted, 1992, Germany. *Education:* Universities of Kiel and Freiburg im Breisgau (Dr. jur., 1992). *LANGUAGES:* German, English, Italian and French. *PRACTICE AREAS:* Corporate Law; Commercial Law.

ROBERT P. WETHMAR, born Bremen, Germany, September 15, 1961; admitted, 1992, Germany; 1993, New York. *Education:* University of Hamburg; New York University (LL.M., 1992). *LANGUAGES:* German, Dutch, English and French. *PRACTICE AREAS:* Commercial Law; Corporate Law.

DR. KLAUS-STEFAN HOHENSTATT, born Stuttgart, Germany, June 11, 1961; admitted, 1992, Germany. *Education:* Universities of Freiburg and Hamburg (Dr. jur., 1993). *LANGUAGES:* German, English and French. *PRACTICE AREAS:* Labor Law; Commercial Law.

DR. JOHANNES CONRADI, born Hamburg, Germany, September 10, 1962; admitted, 1993, Germany. *Education:* Universities of Munich and Hamburg (Dr. jur., 1993). Milbank, Tweed, Hadley & McCloy, New York, 1992-1993. Research Assistant, Max-Planck-Institute for Foreign and International Private Law, 1988-1991. *LANGUAGES:* German and English. *PRACTICE AREAS:* Corporate Law; Mergers, Acquisitions and Divestitures; Tax Law; Real Estate.

DR. HARTWIG SCHMIDT-HOLLBURG, born Hamburg, Germany, December 19, 1963; admitted, 1993, Germany. *Education:* University of Hamburg (Dr. jur., 1991). *LANGUAGES:* German, English and French. *PRACTICE AREAS:* Intellectual Property; Trademark Patent; Copyright; Food and Drug; Cartel Law.

DR. GEZA MARTIN TOTH, born Bad Godesberg, Germany, October 25, 1965; admitted, 1994, Germany. *Education:* Universities of Cologne, Bonn and Passau (Dr. jur., 1992). *LANGUAGES:* German, English, Italian and Hungarian. *PRACTICE AREAS:* Commercial law; Corporate Law; Law of Succession; Insolvency Law; Arbitration and Litigation.

DR. DIRK HAMANN, born Ahrensburg/Hamburg, Germany, April 15, 1963; admitted, 1992, Germany. *Education:* Universities of Münster (Dr. jur., 1991) and Mainz. Faculty Assistant, Institute of Commercial and Economic Law, University of Münster, 1991-1992. *LANGUAGES:* German and English. *PRACTICE AREAS:* Corporate Law; Commercial Law; Real Estate.

DR. STEPHANIE HUNDERTMARK, born Hamburg, Germany, May 30, 1964; admitted, 1994, Germany. *Education:* Universities of Freiburg (Dr. Jur., 1994) and Lausanne, Switzerland. *LANGUAGES:* German, English, French and Spanish.

PETER NUSSBAUM, born Munich, Germany, January 18, 1963; admitted, 1991, New York; 1993, Germany. *Education:* University of Munich (First State Exam, 1989); C.I.F.E., Munich, Nice/France (Diploma of Studies in European Community Affairs, 1988); New York University School of Law, New York (M.C.J., 1990). *Member:* German Bar Association; German Association for International Maritime Law. *LANGUAGES:* German, English and French. *PRACTICE AREAS:* Corporate and Commercial Law; International Public Law; International Law of the Sea.

ANDREA PIRSCHER, born Herford, Germany, February 4, 1966; admitted, 1994, Germany. *Education:* Universities of Cologne and Bielefeld, Germany. *LANGUAGES:* German and English. *PRACTICE AREAS:* Employment Law.

ANDREAS F. BAUER, born Frankfurt, Germany, March 15, 1966; admitted, 1994, Germany. *Education:* University of Munich and the National Law Center, George Washington University, Washington, D.C. (LL.M., 1991). *LANGUAGES:* German, English, French and Italian. *PRACTICE AREAS:* Corporate Law; Commercial Law; Banking and Financing.

BRÜGMANN - HAGEN - LÜBCKE

Established in 1946

MÖNCKEBERGSTRAßE 13
20095 HAMBURG, GERMANY
Telephone: 49-40-33 77 55
Fax: 49-40-33 65 71

Construction Law, Real Estate, Commercial Law, Corporate, Tax Law, Unfair Competition, Law of the Press, Copyright, Wills, Environmental Law.

(This Listing Continued)

BRÜGMANN - HAGEN - LÜBCKE, Hamburg—
Continued

FIRM PROFILE: The firm has a reputation mainly for Construction Law and connected areas, i.e. Real Estate, Administrative Construction Law etc. Also the firm concentrates on special fields as shown below (concentration), at present by four partners and two assistants. The firm is member of EUROJURIS network of independent European-based law firms, thus providing support in all legal needs in relevant European places.

MEMBERS OF FIRM

DR. WALTER BRÜGMANN (1946-1984).

KLAUS BRÜGMANN, born Hamburg, June 7, 1938; admitted, 1971, Germany. *Education:* Universities of Hamburg and Freiburg/Br. *Member:* German Bar Association; Deutsche Ges. f. Baurecht; International Bar Association; International Construction Projects; IPBA. *LANGUAGES:* German and English. *PRACTICE AREAS:* Construction Law.

CHRISTIAN BRÜGMANN, born Hamburg, July 5, 1951; admitted, 1978, Germany. *Education:* Universities of Hamburg, Tübingen and Geneva. Research Assistant, University of Hamburg, 1975-1976. *Member:* German Bar Association; Deutsche Gesellschaft für Baurecht. *LANGUAGES:* German and English. *PRACTICE AREAS:* Construction Law; Commercial Law; Unfair Competition; Inheritance/Wills; Law of the Press; Copyright.

UWE HAGEN, born Hamburg, May 20, 1935; admitted, 1967, Germany. *Education:* Universities of Kiel, Freiburg and Hamburg. Special Education in Tax Law by Financial Office. *Member:* German Bar Association. *LANGUAGES:* German and English. *PRACTICE AREAS:* Construction Law; Trade Law; Corporate and Partnership Law; Franchise Law; Tax Law; Insolvency Law; Inheritance/Wills.

THOMAS LÜBCKE, born Hamburg, April 24, 1957; admitted, 1987, Germany. *Education:* University of Hamburg. With Office of the Public Defender, San Francisco. *Member:* German Bar Associations. *LANGUAGES:* German and English. *PRACTICE AREAS:* Construction Law; Administrative Construction Law; Environmental Law; Real Estate.

BUSE KOCH GORSLER NESSELHAUF MOERCHEN

Established in 1973

ABTEISTRASSE 55-57

20149 HAMBURG, GERMANY

Telephone: 49/40/41999-0

Telefax: 49/40/41999-269

Commercial, Corporate, Partnership, Antitrust, Banking, Unfair Competition, Trademark, Copyright, Entertainment, Licensing, Press, Personal Injury, Family, Labour, Real Estate, Inheritance, Tax, Shipping, Transport, International Trade, European Community Law, Arbitration and General Practice, Insurance, Reinsurance, Mergers and Acquisitions.

MEMBERS OF FIRM

DR. PHILIPP R. BUSE, born Hamburg, November 23, 1939; admitted, 1971, Hamburg. *Education:* University of Hamburg (Dr. jur., 1968). *Member:* Hamburg Bar Association. *LANGUAGES:* German and English.

BERND KOCH, born Hamburg, December 23, 1942; admitted, 1973, Hamburg. *Education:* Universities of Freiburg and Hamburg. *Member:* Hamburg Bar Association. *LANGUAGES:* German and English.

KAI GORSLER, born Lübeck, February 2, 1942; admitted, 1971, Hamburg; 1976, Tax Counsel. *Education:* Universities of Marburg, Berlin, Munich and Hamburg. Teaching Assignment, Industrial Relations Law, University Clausthal, 1975-1983. *Member:* Hamburg Bar Association; German-British Jurist Association; German-Japanese Lawyers Association; International Association of Entertainment Lawyers. *LANGUAGES:* German and English.

MICHAEL NESSELHAUF, born Berlin, October 15, 1939; admitted, 1972, Hamburg. *Education:* Universities of Munich, Vienna, Kiel and Freiburg. *Member:* Hamburg Bar Association. *LANGUAGES:* German and English.

FRANK MOERCHEN, born Wuppertal, November 29, 1944; admitted, 1975, Hamburg. *Education:* Universities of Heidelberg, Speyer and Lau-

(This Listing Continued)

---

sanne. *Member:* Hamburg Bar Association. *LANGUAGES:* German, English and French.

DR. DIETRICH H. MANKOWSKI, born Danzig, December 8, 1936; admitted, 1965, Hamburg. *Education:* Kiel, Stockholm, Hamburg (Dr.jur., 1964). Author: "Haftung nach dem Wasserhaushaltsgesetz und Haftpflichtversicherung," Liability under the water Protection act and its Insurance, Versicherungswissenschaft, 1964. Member: Royal Commercial Court Committee, London; Disciplinary Court of Lawyers, Hamburg. *Member:* Hamburg Bar Association; Hamburg Lawyer's Association; German Institute for Arbitration. *LANGUAGES:* German and English.

DETLEF DEICKE, born Kiel, May 1, 1940; admitted, 1970, Hamburg. *Education:* Universities of Hamburg and Berlin. *Member:* Hamburg Bar Association. *LANGUAGES:* German and English.

RAFAEL BARBER-LLORENTE, born Madrid, September 21, 1951; admitted, 1983, Hamburg; 1990, Balearic Islands, Spain. *Education:* University of Hamburg. *Member:* Hamburg Bar Association; Balearic Islands Bar Association; German-Spanish Lawyers Association. *LANGUAGES:* German, Spanish and English.

RAINER HOSIE, born Hamburg, October 12, 1952; admitted, 1982, Hamburg. *Education:* Universities of Freiburg and Kiel. *Member:* Hamburg Bar Association. *LANGUAGES:* German and English.

DR. PETER J. BLUMENTHAL, born Hamburg, September 15, 1944; admitted, 1973, Hamburg. *Education:* Universities of Lausanne, Munich and Hamburg (Dr. jur., 1975). *Member:* Hamburg Bar Association. *LANGUAGES:* German, English and French.

INES HYDASCH, born Hamburg, November 4, 1956; admitted, 1986, Hamburg. *Education:* Universities of Hamburg and Miami (LL.M., 1985). *Member:* Hamburg Bar Association; German-American Jurist Association (DAJV). *LANGUAGES:* German and English.

DR. SABINE ERHARDT-RENKEN, born Hamburg, June 28, 1957; admitted, 1983, Hamburg. *Education:* Universities of Munich, Geneva and Hamburg (Dr. jur., 1984). *Member:* Hamburg Bar Association. *LANGUAGES:* German, English and French.

DR. MICHAEL RAUDSZUS, born Wuppertal, April 9, 1954; admitted, 1981, Düsseldorf; 1985 Tax Adviser (Steuerberater); 1989, Hamburg, Chartered Accountant (Wirschaftsprüfer). *Education:* University of Freiburg (Dr. jur., 1980). *Member:* Institute of German Chartered Accountants (Institut der Wirtschaftsprüfer). *LANGUAGES:* German and English.

TORSTEN KÖHNHORN, born Hamburg, June 20, 1957; admitted, 1988, Hamburg. *Education:* University of Hamburg. *Member:* Hamburg Bar Association; German-Portuguese Jurists Association. *LANGUAGES:* German and English.

DR. CHRISTOPH STOECKER, born Düsseldorf, October 8, 1959; admitted, 1988, Düsseldorf. *Education:* Universities of Cologne, Lausanne, Sydney (LL.M., 1989) and Hamburg (Dr. jur., 1991). Author: "The Lex Mercatoria: To what extent does it exist?" 1990 Journal Int. Arbitration, p. 101. *Member:* Hamburg and International Bar Associations; German-British Jurists Association. *LANGUAGES:* German, English and French.

SIDONIE VON WEDEL, born Cologne, February 23, 1963; admitted, 1992, Hamburg. *Education:* Universities of Cologne and Munich. *Member:* Hamburg Bar Association. *LANGUAGES:* German, English and French.

CARLOS CLAUSSEN & PARTNER

Established in 1980

MÖNCKEBERGSTRAßE 31

20095 HAMBURG, GERMANY

Telephone: 0049-40-30 96 40-0

Fax: 0049-40-30 96 40-99

Potsdam, Germany Office: Benkertstraße 13, 14467 Potsdam. Telephone: 0049-331-28 46 90. Fax: 0049-331-280 48 31.

Berlin, Germany Office: Josef-Orlopp-Strasse 89-91, 10365 Berlin. Telephone: 0049 172 309 03 10. Fax: 0049 30 558 81 16.

General Commercial, Corporation, EC Law, Unfair Competition, Insurance, Trademark, Copyright, International Private Law, Litigation and Arbitration, Banking, Probate, East-European Law, Property Law (Restitution of Property Rights), Labour Law, Corporate Tax, Maritime, Transportation, Press.

(This Listing Continued)

FIRM PROFILE: The firm was established in 1980 in Hamburg, Germany and has now offices as well in Potsdam, Germany as in Berlin, Germany. It offers a full range of legal services and is a member of the EULEX-IPG Group, Europe with their professional service. The client base is European and North American in scope.

MEMBERS OF FIRM

CARLOS CLAUSSEN, born Hamburg, Germany, May 6, 1950; admitted, 1980, Germany. *Education:* Hamburg, Kiel, Freiburg, Lausanne (Switzerland), San Francisco. *Member:* Hamburg Bar Association; Hamburg and German Lawyers Association; American Society of International Law. *LANGUAGES:* German, English and French. *PRACTICE AREAS:* Commercial; Corporation; Unfair Competition; Press.

BARBARA FUHRHOP, born Hamburg, Germany, June 7, 1951; admitted, 1979, Germany. *Education:* Hamburg, Munich, Freiburg, Lausanne (Switzerland), Madrid (Spain). *Member:* Hamburg Bar Association; Hamburg and German Lawyers Association. *LANGUAGES:* German, English, French and Spanish. *PRACTICE AREAS:* Civil Litigation; Arbitration.

CARSTEN GLOMBIK, born Hamburg, Germany, October 7, 1952; admitted, 1983, Germany. *Education:* University of Hamburg. *Member:* Hamburg Bar Association. *LANGUAGES:* German, English and Spanish. *PRACTICE AREAS:* Civil Litigation; Arbitration.

JOACHIM H. GRANZOW, born Hamburg, Germany, August 27, 1956; admitted, 1987, Germany. *Education:* Universities of Hamburg (Dr. jur., Max-Planck-Institute for Foreign International Private Law, 1988), Tübingen and Geneva; Georgetown University Law Center (LL.M., 1983). Member, Georgetown Alumni Admissions Program. *Member:* Hamburg Bar Association; German-American Lawyers Association. *LANGUAGES:* German, English and French. *PRACTICE AREAS:* Maritime; Transportation; Press; Banking; Probate; Corporate Tax; General Commercial.

ARMIN GÖLLNER, born Wiesen, December 6, 1947; admitted, 1990, Germany. *Education:* Humboldt University, Berlin (Dr. iur, 1978, facultas docendi, 1979). Professor, Civil Law and Civil Procedure, Humbold University, Berlin, 1974-1978; Professor, Civil Procedure, Akademie für Staats- und Rechtswissenschaft, Berlin, 1984-1985. *LANGUAGES:* German, English, Russian. *PRACTICE AREAS:* East European Trade Law; Property Restitution Law.

ULLRICH JUNG-LINDEMANN, born Rheine, Germany, February 17, 1956; admitted, 1987, Germany. *Education:* Universities of Frankfurt, Münster (Westf.), Heidelberg, Paris and Brussels (Commission of the European Communities). *Member:* Hamburg Bar Association; German-American Lawyers Association. *LANGUAGES:* German, English and French. *PRACTICE AREAS:* Trademark; Copyright; Labour Law; Litigation.

KERSTIN MOCK, born Stendal, Germany, September 18, 1960; admitted, 1990, Germany. *Education:* Martin-Luther University, Halle/Wittenberg. *LANGUAGES:* German, English and Russian. *PRACTICE AREAS:* East European Trade Law; Property Restitution Law; Litigation.

HEIKO ORMANSCHICK, born Hamburg, Germany, July 21, 1958; admitted, 1990, Germany. *Education:* University of Hamburg. *Member:* Hamburg Bar Association. *LANGUAGES:* German and English. *PRACTICE AREAS:* Insurance; International Private Law; EC Law; Litigation and Arbitration.

TIM SCHNEEMILCH, born Hamburg, Germany, September 5, 1961; admitted, 1993, Germany. *Education:* University of Hamburg. *Member:* Hamburg Bar Association; Hamburg and German Lawyers Association; German-British Jurists Association. *LANGUAGES:* German, English and French. *PRACTICE AREAS:* Corporate Tax; General Commercial; Commercial Litigation.

DR. COELER & PARTNER

Established in 1953

ALSTERTERRASSE 2
D-20354 HAMBURG, GERMANY
Telephone: (+49 40) 41 46 45 - 0
Fax: (+49 40) 41 46 45 44

Sofia, Bulgaria Office: 4a Benkorski Str., BG-1000 Sofia, Telephone: +0359 2 - 818866 or 897024 or 806432. Fax: +0359 - 2 - 881727.

International Trade, Business, Commercial and Corporate Law, Transport Law, Marine and Marine Insurance Law, Foreign Investment, International Private, Family and Inheritance Law, Competition Law, Trade-

(This Listing Continued)

marks, Pharmacological and Medical Law, Product Liability, Software and Computer Law, Banking, Insurance, Press, Tax, General Practice, Litigation and Arbitration.

FIRM PROFILE: The firm offers a full range of legal services and is well known for its commercial and international private law. The firm is a member of Eurolink for Lawyers, a network of independent legal practices and has an office in Sofia, Bulgaria.

DR. GERD COELER, born Berlin, Germany, April 25, 1923; admitted, 1953, Hamburg. *Education:* Universities of Marburg, Göttingen and Hamburg (Referendar, 1949; Doctor of Law, magna cum laude, 1950; Assessor, 1952); City of London College; The Hague Academy of International Law. *Author:* "The Through Bill of Lading, Especially the Liability of the Concerned Carriers According to the German, French and Anglo-American Law, Taking Also in Consideration the International Private Law," University of Hamburg, 1950. Fellow, Institute of Arbitrators, London. *Member:* International Bar Association; International Law Association; International Maritime Committee (CMI); Court Arbitrale Europenne; Union International des Avocats International Association for the Protection of Industrial Property (AIPPI). *LANGUAGES:* German, English, French, Italian and Spanish. *PRACTICE AREAS:* International Trade and Business; Commercial and Corporate Law; Transport Law; Marine and Marine Insurance Law; Foreign Investment; Competition Law; Trademarks; Product Liability; Insurance; Banking.

MICHAEL RASCHENDORFER, born Schwabmünchen, Germany, November 8, 1948; admitted, 1978, Hamburg. *Education:* Universities of Hamburg, 1973 and Rome 1975. Member, German-Bolivian Chamber of Commerce, LaPaz, 1975. Interpreter for the Italian Language. *Member:* German Bar Association; Association for Exchange of thoughts between German and Italian Jurists; International Association of Young Lawyers (AIJA); Association of German and Spanish Lawyers. *LANGUAGES:* German, English, French, Italian and Spanish. *PRACTICE AREAS:* International Trade; Business; Commercial and Corporate Law; Transport Law; Foreign Investment; Trademarks; International Private; Family Law; Inheritance Law.

DR. FRANK SCHMITZ, born Dortmund, December 18, 1960; admitted, 1991, Hamburg. *Education:* University of Bochum (Sociology and History, 1978-1979); University of Heidelberg (Jurisprudence, 1980-1985); University of Montpellier, France (1984); Referendar, Hamburg (1987-1990). Doctor of Law, 1994. Guest Solicitor, Auckland, New Zealand, 1990. *Author:* 'The Bulgarian Privatization Act 1991"; "Investment in Bulgaria"; "Taxation of Foreigners in Bulgaria"; Co-editor: "Handbook of Business Law in Eastern Europe/Bulgaria". *Member:* German and Hamburg Bar Associations; Association of French and German Lawyers; Association for the Exchange of Thoughts between Italian and German Lawyers; International Association of Young Lawyers (AIJA); German-Bulgarian Lawyer's Association. *LANGUAGES:* German, English, French, Italian and Portuguese. *PRACTICE AREAS:* International Trade; Business; Commercial Law; Corporate Law; Transport Law; Marine and Marine Insurance Law; Foreign Investment; Software; Computer Law; Tax.

DR. STEPHAN HEES, born Wuppertal, June 7, 1960; admitted, 1991, Hamburg, Germany. *Education:* Universities of Marburg and Münster. *Author:* "Die vertragstypologische Bestimmung des Vorkaufsfalls und die Wirkungen einzelner Vereinbarungen und Störungen des Drittvertrages für das Vorkaufsverhältnis," Pfaffenweiler, 1991; "Zur persönlichen Reichweite der Verjährungsunterbrechung nach §78 c Abs. 1 Nr. 4 StGB," Wistra 1994, 81 f.; "Erstattung der Kosten des Eilverfahrens nach Obsiegen in der Hauptsache," MDR 1994, 438 f. Lecturer and Research Assistant, University of Kiel, 1986-1990. *Member:* Hamburg and German Bar Associations; Hamburg Lawyers Association (Committee of Lawyers Examination). *LANGUAGES:* German and English. *PRACTICE AREAS:* Commercial Law; Corporate Law; Competition Law; Pharmacological Law; Software Law; Computer Law; Press.

EDGAR SIEMUND, born Höxter, Germany, November 22, 1960; admitted, 1994, Hamburg, Germany. *Education:* University of Berlin (1981); University of Heidelberg (1984-1988); University of Hamburg (1988-1990). Referendar, 1991-1994. Legal Apprenticeship, Springfield, N.J., USA, 1993. *Member:* Hamburg and German Bar Associations; Association for the Exchange of Thoughts between Italian and German Lawyers. *LANGUAGES:* German, English, Italian. *PRACTICE AREAS:* International

(This Listing Continued)

DR. COELER & PARTNER, Hamburg—Continued

Trade; Business; Commerical Law; Corporate Law; Transport Law; Marine Law; Foreign Investment; International Private; Family Law; Inheritance Law; Product Liability; Software; Computer Law; Banking; Insurance.

Languages: German, English, French, Italian, Portuguese and Spanish.

CURSCHMANN, ROLLENHAGEN & PARTNER

Established in 1895

BAUMWALL 7 (20459 HAMBURG)

P.O. BOX 112 111

20421 HAMBURG, GERMANY

Telephone: 040 36 95 90

Telex: 211 630 jus d

Fax: 040 36 959 36

Associated German Offices:

Berlin, Germany Office: Hackenberger, Schmidt, Heberlein, Schwerdtner, Uhlandstraße 171/172, 10719 Berlin. Telephone: 30 881 40 49. Telecopier: 30 882 59 17.

Düsseldorf, Germany Office: Brockmann, Schreiner & Partner, Berliner Allee 34-36, 40212 Düsseldorf. Telephone: 211 32 30 121. Telex: 8584092. Telecopier: 2 11 13 25 30.

Dresden, Germany Office: Koch-Heintzeler, Widmann & Partner. Alberstraße 34, 01097 Dresden. Telephone: 03 51 502 23 11. Telecopier: 03 51 502 31 32.

Frankfurt/Main, Germany Office: Bauer, Heberer & Reinmüller, Myliusstraße 14, 60323 Frankfurt/Main. Telephone: 69 97 10 97-0. Telex: 4189790 BGHD. Telecopier: 69 72 35 99.

Munich, Germany Office: Zoglmann, Kainz & Partner, Maximilianplatz 18, 80333 Munich. Telephone: 89 22 66 51. Telex: 5 214 522 zkd. Telecopier: 89 22 44 68.

Stuttgart, Germany Office: Koch-Heintzeler, Widmann & Partner, Uhlandstraße 11, 70182 Stuttgart. Telephone: 07 11 210 46-0. Telex: 722 805 jus d. Telecopier: 07 11 210 46 47.

Associated European Offices/Stanbrook & Partners:

Brussels, Belgium Office: Stanbrook and Hooper S.C., European Community Lawyers. Rue du Taciturne 42, 1040 Brussels, Belgium. Telephone: 32 2 230 50 59. Telex: 61975 Stalaw b. Telecopier: 32 2 230 57 13

Copenhagen, Denmark Office: Qvist, Dahl & Partnere. Gutenberghus, Pilestraede 58, 4, 112 Copenhagen K, Denmark. Telephone: 45 33 12 45 22. Telex: 22449 hcalaw dk. Telecopier: 45 33 93 60 23.

Lisbon, Portugal Office: Noronha e Andrade, Cardoso Alves e Associados, Rua das Amoreiras, 23-2.°, 1200 Lisbon, Portugal. Telephone: (351.1) 387 59 48/387 59 69. Telecopier: (351.1) 387 59 80.

London, England Office: Stanbrook & Henderson, 2 Harcourt Building, Temple, London EC4Y 3DB, United Kingdom. Telephone: 071 353 0101. Telecopier: 071 404 5258.

Madrid, Spain Office: Sanchez-Bella & Aldama. Juan de Mena 14 4°D. 28014 Madrid, Spain. Telephone: 91 523 47 46. Telecopier: 91 532 70 94.

Paris, France Office: Cabinet Leva, Espi, Rochmann-Lochen, 109, Avenue Henri Martin, Paris XVIè, France. Telephone: (33.1) 45 04 51 00. Telecopier: (33.1) 45 04 22 79.

General Practice. Commercial, Corporate, Competition, Trademark, Common Market, Administration, Labor, Insurance, Real Estate, Inheritance, Tax and Duty Law, Latin American Law, Banking, Criminal and Family, European Community Law.

FIRM PROFILE: *Curschmann, Rollenhagen and Partner practices in virtually all areas of civil and commercial law and has an international clientele. It is the German partner of the European firm of Stanbrook and Partners and is associated with leading law firms throughout Germany. The firm also has particular experience regarding North and Latin America and investments in Eastern Europe.*

MEMBERS OF FIRM

DR. HEINRICH F. CURSCHMANN, born Greifswald, April 28, 1913; admitted, 1948, Hamburg. *Education:* Greifswald, Göttingen, Dresden (Economics; Dr. jur.). Author: "Lebensmittel-Rundschau," Victual Law. Leading Officer in the Ministry for Lodging of the City of Hamburg, 1945-

(This Listing Continued)

1948. *Member:* Hamburg University Society (Section on Company Law). *LANGUAGES:* English and German.

VOLKER E.H. ROLLENHAGEN, born Rathenow, Germany, February 13, 1930; admitted, 1957, Hamburg. *Education:* Universities of Erlangen and Hamburg. *Member:* Hamburg Bar Association (Member of Board, 1965-1990; President, 1984-1990); Hamburg Law Society. *LANGUAGES:* English and German.

DR. HANS-DIETRICH SCHUBEL, born Hamburg, February 4, 1924; admitted, 1954, Hamburg. *Education:* Hamburg (Dr. jur.). Co-Author: "Kommentar zum Arbeitnehmerüberlassungsgesetz," (Commentary on German Law of Temporary Work), Heidelberg, 1973. Chairman, Committee of the Charitable Institution for German Lawyers, 1973—. President, German Confederation of Temporary Work, 1976-1983 and 1987-1990. *LANGUAGES:* English and German.

DR. HAJO WANDSCHNEIDER, born Hamburg, Germany, December 21, 1925; admitted, 1955, Hamburg. *Education:* Universities of Hamburg (Dr. jur.) and Southampton. *Member:* Hamburg Bar Association (Member of Board, 1965-1970); Hamburg Court of Honour (1970-—). *LANGUAGES:* English and German.

DR. CHRISTOPH VON OPPELN-BRONIKOWSKI, born Dessau, February 25, 1938; admitted, 1967, Hamburg. *Education:* Hamburg, Tübingen, Strasbourg and Giessen (Dr. jur., 1974). *Author:* "Aspects of Law in the Public Opinion," 1974. Lecturer, Law of Succession, Deutsche Anwaltsakademie, German Lawyers Academy. *LANGUAGES:* English and German.

DR. GEORG ENGELBRECHT, born Heiligenbeil, December 3, 1940; admitted, 1969, Hamburg. *Education:* Freiburg, Paris and Hamburg (Dr. jur., 1980). Author: "Die Abgrenzung der Arbeitnehmerüberlassung von der Arbeitsvermittlung," 1980. Co-Author: "Kommentar zum Arbeitnehmerüberlassungsgesetz," (Commentary on German Law of Temporary Work), Heidelberg, 1973. *Member:* Union Internationale des Avocats; International Society for Labour Law; Ibero-Amerika Verein (Member of Board). *LANGUAGES:* French, English, German and Spanish.

DR. TORBEN TODSEN, born Bad Doberan, Germany, March 10, 1945; admitted, 1976, Hamburg. *Education:* Universities of Hamburg (Dr. jur.), Lausanne (Switzerland) and London School of Economics. *Member:* Hamburg Bar Association; Hamburg Law Society. *LANGUAGES:* English and German.

DR. KLAUS WILLENBRUCH, born Hamburg, June 16, 1949; admitted, 1977, Hamburg; 1988, Specialized attorney for Administrative Law. *Education:* Hamburg (Dr. jur.); Johannesburg, South Africa. Author: "Das Armenrecht der Juristischen Personen" (Legal Aid for Companies), Berlin, 1977. Research Associate, University of Hamburg, 1974-1975. *Member:* Deutsch-Britische Juristenvereinigung; Hamburg Bar Association (Member of Board). *LANGUAGES:* English and German.

DR. JAN CURSCHMANN, born Hamburg, April 14, 1952; admitted, 1982, Hamburg. *Education:* Hamburg (Dr.jur.), Lausanne, Grenoble and Rio de Janeiro, Brazil. Author: "Warenzeichenlizenzen in Brasilien," (Trademark licenses in Brazil), 1986. *Member:* Deutsch-Brasilianische Juristenvereinigung (Member of Board); Deutsch-Spanische Juristenvereinigung; Young Lawyers International Association. *LANGUAGES:* Portuguese, English, German, French and Spanish.

DR. KAI GREVE, born Hamburg, Germany, November 24, 1953; admitted, 1988, Hamburg. *Education:* Universities of Cologne and Hamburg (Dr.jur.). Author: *Haftung für Datenverarbeitung,* 1988. *Member:* Hamburg Bar Association; Hamburg Law Society. *LANGUAGES:* English, German and Danish.

DR. AXEL R. E. BOESCH, born Bremerhaven, Germany, November 16, 1955; admitted, 1984, Hamburg; 1987, New York. *Education:* Universities of Bielefeld and Hannover (Dr.jur., 1988); New York University Law School (M.C.J., 1985). Author: "Interim Relief in International Commercial Arbitration" (Einstweiliger Rechtsschutz in der Internationalen Handels-Schiedsgerichtsbarkeit), Diss., Hannover, 1988. *Member:* American Bar Association; Association Internationale des Jeunes Advocats (AIJA); Foreign Lawyer's Association Hamburg. *LANGUAGES:* German, French and English.

DR. MARTIN SCHIMKE, born Hagen, Germany, January 20, 1959; admitted, 1988, Hamburg. *Education:* Universities of Münster and Hamburg (Dr.jur., 1990); University of Leuven, Belgium (Master of European Law, LL.M., 1993). Author: "Die historische Entwicklung der Unterbeteiligungsgesellschaft" (The historical development of sub-partnerships), Diss. Hagen 1990. *Member:* Union International des Avocats (UIA); Ger-

(This Listing Continued)

man Association on national and international Sports Law; German-Japanese Law Association. *LANGUAGES:* English, Japanese (basic) and German.

TAX CONSULTANT

HERBERT WERNER, born Hamburg, November 28, 1944; admitted, 1973, Hamburg. *Education:* Lausanne; Hamburg. Tax Consultant, 1975. German Certified Public Accountant, 1978. *LANGUAGES:* French, English and German.

ASSOCIATES

SABINE MEYER, born Hamburg, June 21, 1961; admitted, 1993, Hamburg. *Education:* University of Hamburg. *LANGUAGES:* German and English.

MANUEL SACK, born Cologne, June 28, 1964; admitted, 1994, Hamburg. *Education:* Universities of Hamburg and Freiburg. *LANGUAGES:* German and English.

MARK SGARBOSSA, born Chicago, Illinois, November 24, 1967; admitted, 1993, Illinois (Not admitted in Germany). *Education:* Catholic University of Milan, Italy; University of Illinois (Bachelor of Science); Minnesota Law School (Dr. jur.); University of Kiel, Germany. *Member:* American Bar Association. *LANGUAGES:* Italian, French, Spanish, German and English.

COUNSEL

DR. JAN PETER WAEHLER, born Ranis, October 21, 1933; admitted, 1963, Hamburg. *Education:* Hamburg (Dr.jur.), Berlin (AOIB, Osteuropainstitut an der Fu), Leningrad (LGU). Research Associate, Max-Planck-Institute for Foreign Private and Private International Law, Hamburg, since 1963. Author: "Die Aussenhandels- und See-Schiedsgerichtsbarkeit in der UdSSR" (Foreign Trade and Maritime Arbitration in the USSR), 1974; "Deutsches und sowjetisches Wirtschaftsrecht" (German and Soviet Law of Economics) I - IV 1981-1989, Editor. *LANGUAGES:* English, Russian and German.

Languages: German, English, French, Spanish, Portuguese, Italian and Russian.

CYRUS, MAKOWSKI & PARTNER

Established in 1971

OST-WEST-STRAβE 61
20457 HAMBURG, GERMANY
Telephone: (040) 36 33 43
Telefax: (040) 374 37 91
Telex: 21 321 699 HS D

Berlin, Germany Office: Auguste-Viktoria-Allee 2, 13403. Telephone: 030/412 30 56. Telefax: 030/413 72 30.

Rostock, Germany Office: Grosse Wasserstrasse 2/3, 18055. Telephone: 0381/499 60 60. Telefax: 0381/499 63 51.

Member of CYRUS ROSS INTERNATIONAL (E.E.I.G.) Association of Law Firms: Alphen (NL), Athens, Berlin, Brussels, Copenhagen, Dublin, Hamburg, Limassol, London, Madrid, Nicosia, Oslo, Padua, Paris, Rostock, Sion, Vienna.

Commercial, International Trade, Maritime, Transport, Forwarding, Shipbuilding, Shipfinancing, Banking, Corporation, Mergers and Acquisitions, Antitrust, Unfair Competition, Industrial Property (Trademark, Patent, Copyright), Real Estate, Environment, Common Market, Insurance, Lease and Rent, Labour, Construction, Computer and Software, Bankruptcy, Product Liability, Administrative Law, Litigation and Arbitration, Building Construction Trade, Motor Vehicle Industry, Insurance, Companies in Beverage Industry, Mechanical Engineering, Hotel Business, Computer and Trade.

FIRM PROFILE: Each partner in CMP processes the general core area of business law and in addition specialises in certain specific fields.

PARTNERS OF FIRM

DR. JOACHIM CYRUS, born 1930; admitted, 1961, Hamburg. *Education:* University Hamburg (Dr.jur.). Member, Federal Ministry of Economics' Committee, Government Guarantees in Foreign Trade Operations, 1969-1972. *Member:* Hamburg Bar Association; German Bar Association; German Association for the Protection of Industrial Property. *PRACTICE AREAS:* Competition Law; Cartel Law; Copyright Law; Patent Law; Industrial Property; Company Law; Acquisition and Selling of Companies; Banking Law; Successions.

(This Listing Continued)

DR. BERND MAKOWSKI, born 1936; admitted, 1967, Hamburg. *Education:* University München (Dr.jur.). Principal Corporate Counsel, Shipping Companies of the Oetker Group, 1969—. *Member:* German Maritime Arbitration Association; German Association for Maritime International Law. *PRACTICE AREAS:* Shipping and Transport Law; Investment Law; Banking Law; Company Law; Acquisition and Selling of Companies; Financing Law; Mortgage Law; Ship Financing.

GÖTZ F. KAHLE, born 1941; admitted, 1970, Hamburg. *Education:* Universities München, Berlin and Kiel. Standing Counsel, Honda Deutschland, 1972—. *Member:* Legal Committee of the Federation of Importers of Motor Vehicles, "VDIK"; Hamburg Bar Association; German Bar Association; German-Japanese Lawyers' Association. *PRACTICE AREAS:* Contract Law; Breweries; Restaurant Business Law; Trade Law; Tenancy and Hire Law; Product Liability Law.

PETER-ALFRED SCHÜLER, born 1940; admitted, 1972, Hamburg. *Education:* Universities Hamburg and Tübingen. *Member:* Hamburg Bar Association; German Bar Association. *PRACTICE AREAS:* Construction Law; Labour Law; Insurance Law; Transport Law.

DR. ROLAND WACHS, born 1940; admitted, 1983, Hamburg. *Education:* Universities Marburg, Freiburg and Hamburg (Dr.jur.). Coudert Bros. New York, 1970-1971; United Nations, Geneva, 1977-1979; Delegate 3rd UNCLOS; Corporate Counsel Hamburg-Sud, 1979-1992. *Member:* Hamburg Bar Association; German Bar Association; German Maritime Arbitration Association; German Association for Maritime International Law. *PRACTICE AREAS:* Shipping and Transport Law; Ship Sales; International Law; Ship Financing; European Law; Competition Law; Environmental Law.

REINKE DUHME, born 1953; admitted, 1983, Hamburg. *Education:* Universities Hamburg and Geneva; Emory University, Atlanta (M.C.L.). Member, Round Table on Science and Economics of the BDI (National Federation of German Industries), BDA (National Federation of German Employer Associations) and DIHT (Federation of German Chambers of Industry and Commerce). (Resident, Berlin Office). *PRACTICE AREAS:* Foreign Trade; Mercantile Law; Transport Law; Banking Law; Insurance Law; Construction Law; Tenancy and Hire Law; Restitution Law.

THOMAS JASTER, born 1956; admitted, 1984, Berlin. *Education:* University of Berlin. *Member:* Berlin Bar Association; German Association for the Protection of Industrial Property; Berlin Retailers' Association (Adviser). (Resident, Berlin Office). *PRACTICE AREAS:* Competition Law; Copyright Law; Industrial Property; Company Law; Banking Law; Labour Law; Trade Law.

ANDREA GROSSMANN-KOCH, born 1953; admitted, 1988, Lübeck. *Education:* Universities Augsburg and Hamburg. *Member:* German Bar Association. (Resident, Rostock Office). *PRACTICE AREAS:* Company Law; Construction Law; Bankruptcy Law; German Democratic Republic Law; Restitution Law.

UWE BÖHRENSEN, born 1955; admitted, 1988, Lübeck. *Education:* University of Kiel. *Member:* German-Nordic Lawyers' Association. (Resident, Rostock Office). *PRACTICE AREAS:* Construction Law; Labour Law; Tenancy and Hire Law; Condominium Law; German Democratic Republic Law; Restitution Law.

LEGAL SUPPORT PERSONNEL

MONIKA SCHOLZ (Senior Clerk).

Languages: German, English, French and Spanish

DROSTE

The Merged Firms of Droste, Pietzcker, Sprick, Ohlgart & Klosterfelde; Triebel & Weil; Strobl, Killius & Vorbrugg

WARBURGSTRASSE 50
20354 HAMBURG, GERMANY
Telephone: (040) 4 1993-0
Telecopier: (040) 4 1993 200

Düsseldorf, Germany Office: Berliner Allee 48, 40212 Düsseldorf. Telephone: (0211) 13 680. Telecopier: (0211) 32 44 39.

Munich, Germany Office: Marstallstrasse 8, 80539 Munich. Telephone: (089) 290120. Telecopier: (089) 29012 222. Telex: 524 793 skv.

Frankfurt/Main, Germany Office: Schaumainkai 91, 60596 Frankfurt/Main. Telephone: (069) 63 00 89-0. Telecopier: (069) 630089-99.

(This Listing Continued)

DROSTE, Hamburg—Continued

Berlin, Germany Office: Kurfürstendamm 54-55, 10707 Berlin.
  Telephone: (030) 88 24 300. Telefax: (030) 88 24 393.
Brussels, Belgium Office: Avenue des Gaulois 9, B-1150 Brussels.
  Telephone: 02-7358945. Telefax: 02-7352251.

General and International Practice, Commercial Law, Corporate, Banking, Finance, Tax, Mergers and Acquisitions, EU Law, Antitrust, Unfair Competition, Trademarks, Copyright, Patents, Licensing, Food and Drug Law, Law of the Press, Products Liability, Environmental Law, Labor Law, Real Estate, Estate Planning, International Construction, Contracts, Commercial Litigation and Arbitration, Bankruptcy, Administrative Law.

FIRM PROFILE: Droste is engaged in the practice of corporate and commercial law. The firm is the result of the merger of Droste, Pietzcker, Sprick, Ohlgart& Klosterfelde in Hamburg (formed in 1887), Strobl, Killius & Vorbrugg in Munich (formed in 1961) and Triebel & Weil in Düsseldorf (formed in 1951). The firm's traditional areas of practice are: corporate law, including mergers and acquisitions; industrial property law, including copyright, unfair competition and anti-trust law; trademark law; tax law, both domestic and international; real estate law. Further areas of particular expertise include banking and finance, computer and software law, environmental law, labour law, EU law and commercial litigation and arbitration.

RESIDENT PARTNERS

DR. HELMUT DROSTE (1916-1979).

DR. ROLF R. PIETZCKER, born Hamburg, Germany, December 30, 1927; admitted, 1958, Germany. *Education:* Universities of Tübingen and Hamburg (Law Degree, 1956; Doctor of Laws, 1956). Lecturer, Culture-management. *Member:* International Association for the Protection of Industrial Property (Member, Executive Committee). *LANGUAGES:* German and English. *PRACTICE AREAS:* Patent and Utility Model Law; Plant Varieties Protection Law; Copyright Law; Competition and Trademark Law.

DR. DIETRICH C. OHLGART, LL.M., born Angerburg, Germany, October 26, 1934; admitted, 1965, Germany. *Education:* Universities of Munich and Hamburg (Law Degree, 1958; Doctor of Laws, 1963); Harvard Law School (LL.M., 1961). Lecturer, University of Hamburg. Research Assistant, Max-Planck-Institute for Foreign and Private International Law, 1958-1965. Lecturer, Law School of Hamburg. *Member:* Society for Comparative Law; European Community Trademark Practitioners' Association (Member of Council); Council of the Bars and Law Society of the European Community; International Bar Association; United States Trademark Association. German-American Law Association; German-British Jurists' Association. *LANGUAGES:* German and English. *PRACTICE AREAS:* Industrial Property Law; Copyright Law; EC and German Antitrust Laws, Licensing and Franchising; Mergers and Acquisitions.

DR. WOLFGANG GLOY, born Greifenhagen, Germany, December 22, 1933; admitted, 1964, Germany. *Education:* Universities of Marburg and Hamburg (Law Degree, 1959; Doctor of Laws, 1962). *Member:* German Association for Industrial Property and Copyright; International Association for the Protection of Industrial Property. *LANGUAGES:* German and English. *PRACTICE AREAS:* Trademark Law; Law of the Press; Unfair Competition Law; Food Law; Law on authors' societies and antitrust law.

DR. WALTER KLOSTERFELDE, born Hamburg, Germany, December 27, 1937; admitted, 1968, Hamburg. *Education:* Universities of Munich and Hamburg (Law Degree, 1962; Doctor of Laws, 1965). *Member:* Hamburg Bar Association (Member of Board); Council of the Bars and Law Societies of the European Community; International Association for the Protection of Industrial Property; International Bar Association. *LANGUAGES:* German, English and French. *PRACTICE AREAS:* Contract and Corporate Law; Mergers and Acquisitions; Antitrust; Unfair Competition and Media Law.

FRIEDRICH-WILHELM BUSCH, born Düsseldorf, Germany, May 3, 1925; admitted, 1963, Germany. *Education:* Universities of Bonn, Basle (Switzerland) and Cologne (Law Degree, 1960). *Member:* International Association for the Protection of Industrial Property Law. *LANGUAGES:* German and English. *PRACTICE AREAS:* Trademark Law.

REINER SCHMIDT, born Grünberg, Germany, July 26, 1941; admitted, 1969, Germany. *Education:* University of Hamburg (Law Degree, 1965). *Member:* International Association for the Protection of Industrial Property; European Community, Trademark Practitioners Association; German Association for Industrial Property and Copyright. *LAN-*

(This Listing Continued)

GUAGES: German and English. *PRACTICE AREAS:* Industrial Property Law; Antitrust Law; Food Law; Drug Law; Civil and Commercial including Litigation.

DR. HENNING HARTE-BAVENDAMM, born Hamburg, Germany, March 9, 1950; admitted, 1975, Germany. *Education:* University of Hamburg (Law Degree, 1973; Doctor of Laws, 1977). *Member:* German Association for Industrial Property and Copyright; INTA. *LANGUAGES:* German and English. *PRACTICE AREAS:* Unfair Competition Law; Antitrust Law; Industrial Property Law; Computer Law.

DIRK KEMPEN, born Hannover, Germany, October 12, 1939; admitted, 1971, Germany. *Education:* Universities of Berlin, Geneva (Switzerland) and Würzburg (Law Degree, 1964). *LANGUAGES:* German, English, French and Portuguese. *PRACTICE AREAS:* Trademark Law.

DR. CARSTEN C. ALBRECHT, born Hamburg, Germany, June 18, 1955; admitted, 1985, Germany. *Education:* University of Hamburg (Law Degree, 1981; Doctor of Laws, 1988). *Member:* International Trademark Association. *LANGUAGES:* German, English and French. *PRACTICE AREAS:* Trademark Law; Law of the Firm Name; Unfair Competition Law; Law of Associations.

DR. VOLKER MEINBERG, born Hamburg, Germany, March 6, 1953; admitted, 1989, Germany. *Education:* University of Hamburg (Law Degree, 1981; Doctor of Laws, 1985). Research fellow, Max-Planck Institute for Foreign and International Criminal Law, 1981-1990. *LANGUAGES:* German and English. *PRACTICE AREAS:* Environmental Law; Media (Press-) Law; Business Criminal Law; Unfair Competition Law; Administrative Law.

DR. EVA SCHELLER, born Munich, Germany, October 7, 1959; admitted, 1990, Germany. *Education:* University of Marburg (History and Political Science); University of Passau (Law Degree, 1986; Doctor of Laws, 1994). *Member:* German American Lawyers Association. *LANGUAGES:* German and English. *PRACTICE AREAS:* Unfair Competition Law; Industrial Property Law; Product Liability.

DR. ANDREAS MEYER-WEGNER, born Hamburg, Germany, October 13, 1959; admitted, 1990, Germany. *Education:* University of Hamburg (Law Degree, 1985; Doctor of Law, 1992); Indiana University, Bloomington, School of Law (LL.M., 1987). Research Assistant, 1987-1990. Lecturer, University of Hamburg, School of Law. *Member:* German American Lawyers Association. *LANGUAGES:* German and English. *PRACTICE AREAS:* Corporate and Commercial Law; Standard Contract Terms Law; Company Law.

ANDREAS BOTHE, born Stadtlohn, Germany, April 29, 1962; admitted, 1990, Germany. *Education:* University of Münster (Law Degree, 1987). *Member:* German Association for Industrial Property and Copyright. *LANGUAGES:* German and English. *PRACTICE AREAS:* Trademark Law; Unfair Competition Law; Design Patent Law.

DR. JÖRG PAURA, born Hamburg, Germany, June 12, 1961; admitted, 1991, Germany. *Education:* University of Hamburg (Law Degree, 1986; Doctor of Laws, 1995). Academic Assistant, Institute of Commercial, Corporate and Maritime Law, University of Hamburg, 1987-1991. *LANGUAGES:* German and English. *PRACTICE AREAS:* Corporate and Commercial Law.

DR. WALTER SCHEUERL, born 1961; admitted, 1991, Germany. *Education:* University of Hamburg (Law Degree; Doctor of Law, 1991). Trainee, German Patent Office, Munich, 1988/89. *LANGUAGES:* German and English. *PRACTICE AREAS:* Copyright Law; Press Law; Unfair Competition Law; Trade Mark Law.

CHRISTOPH SCHUMANN, born 1959; admitted, 1991, Germany. *Education:* University of Hamburg (Law Degree). *Member:* German Association for Industrial Property and Copyright. *LANGUAGES:* German and English. *PRACTICE AREAS:* Unfair Competition Law; Commercial Law; Civil Law.

SUSANNE KAROW, born Hamburg, January 17, 1962; admitted, 1991, Germany. *Education:* University of Hamburg (Law Degree). *LANGUAGES:* German and English. *PRACTICE AREAS:* Trademark Law; Unfair Competition Law.

DR. KARSTEN METZLAFF, born Bad Pyrmont, Germany, June 8, 1959; admitted, 1991, Germany. *Education:* Universities of Lausanne, Switzerland and Münster (Law Degree, 1986; Doctor of Laws, 1994). Trainee with GD IV (Competition) of the EU-Commission, 1987. *Member:* Studienvereinigung Kartellrecht. *LANGUAGES:* German, English, French and

(This Listing Continued)

Spanish. *PRACTICE AREAS:* German and EU-antitrust Law; Commercial Law; EU-Law.

ASSOCIATES

Thomas Salomon, LL.M.
Dr. Ralf Hackbarth, LL.M
Dr. Sönke Ahrens
Dr. Christoph Cordes
Gerd Jaekel
Dr. Martin Sura
Dr. Andreas Wehlau

Languages: German, English, French, Spanish, Russian, Italian, Portuguese, Latvian, Chinese and Japanese.

(For list of personnel at Berlin, Düsseldorf, Frankfurt/Main and Munich, see Professional Biographies at those locations)

DR. EHLERMANN & JESCHONNEK

Established in 1982

TROSTBRÜCKE 1

20457 HAMBURG, GERMANY

Telephone: 37 48 140
Telex: 17402037 ELAW D
Teletex: 402037 ELAW D
Fax: 37 48 1430

Ship Registration, Ship Mortgages, Banking, Corporate, Aircraft Financing.

MEMBERS OF FIRM

DR. PETER EHLERMANN, born Altona, February 8, 1936; admitted, 1973, Germany. *Education:* Dr. juris, 1965. Thesis: Shipowner's liability in case of passenger accidents under French and German Law. *Member:* Hamburg and International Bar Associations; German Maritime Law Association. *LANGUAGES:* German, English and French.

HANS JESCHONNEK, born Breslau, November 28, 1944; admitted, 1983, Germany. *Education:* Universities of Bonn and Hamburg. *Member:* Hamburg Bar Association. *LANGUAGES:* German, English and French.

HARTWIG C.M. GADOW, born Flensburg, December 28, 1950; admitted, 1988, Germany. *Education:* University of Kiel. *Member:* Hamburg Bar Association. *LANGUAGES:* German and English.

ASSOCIATES

DIRK ZOEPFFEL, born Bielefeld, April 14, 1959; admitted, 1991, Germany. *Education:* University of Hamburg (Law Degree, 1987). *Member:* Hamburg Bar Association. *LANGUAGES:* German and English.

JAN HÜTTMANN, born Hamburg, Germany, March 14, 1959; admitted, 1989, Germany. *Education:* University of Hamburg. *Member:* Hamburg Bar Association. *LANGUAGES:* German and English.

ESCHE SCHÜMANN COMMICHAU

Established in 1822

HERRENGRABEN 31

20459 HAMBURG, GERMANY

Telephone: (+49 40) 368050
Telex: 212 327 legal d
Telefax: (+49 40) 36 28 96; 36 28 97

Accounting and Auditing, Arbitration and Litigation, Banking, Commercial Real Estate, Company and Commercial, Competition, Construction, Engineering Contracts, Finance Leasing, Inheritance and Family, Insurance, Intellectual Property, Labour Law and Industrial Relations, Mergers and Acquisitions, Product Liability, Shipping and Ship Finance, Stock Exchange, Tax Consulting and Tax, Technology Transfer.

FIRM PROFILE: Established in 1822, the firm covers all aspects of commercial and corporate law. It is a multidisciplinary partnership of lawyers, tax advisers and chartered accountants. Auditing services are rendered by the affiliated auditing company HTU Hanseatische Treuhand-Union GmbH. In the European association ABLE - Associated Business Lawyers in Europe, the firm has established a constant working relationship with law firms in Brussels, London, Paris and Stockholm.

(This Listing Continued)

MEMBERS OF FIRM

DR. ERNST ESCHE, born Hamburg, Germany, April 17, 1913; admitted, 1947, Germany. *Education:* Universities of Freiburg and Leipzig (Dr. jur., 1936). Counsellor of Verein Deutscher Maschinenbauanstalten, 1950-1982. *Member:* Hamburg Bar Association.

JENS SCHÜMANN, born Hamburg, Germany, September 17, 1913; admitted, as Tax Adviser (Steuerberater). *Education:* Universities of Tübingen and Hamburg. President, Steuerberaterkammer Hamburg, 1972.

GÜNTER STERNBERG, born Hamburg, Germany, June 9, 1929; admitted, 1959, Germany. *Education:* University of Hamburg, Fachanwalt für Steuerrecht. *Member:* Hamburg Bar Association.

DR. GERHARD COMMICHAU, born Wittenberg, Germany, August 17, 1933; admitted, 1961, Hamburg. *Education:* Universities of Erlangen and Hamburg (Dr. jur.). Author: "Grundzüge des Kartellrechts," "Der Anwalt und seine Praxis," 2nd ed. 1985. Co-Author: "Münchener Rechts-Lexikon." Lecturer, Civil and Arbitration Law, University of Hamburg. *Member:* Hamburg, German and International Bar Associations; International Chamber of Commerce; German-American Lawyers Association; German Association for the Protection of Industrial Property and Copyright Law (GRUR).

REINHARD PREUSCHOFF, born Kiel, Germany, March 7, 1935; admitted, as Tax Adviser (Steuerberater). *Education:* Universities of Kiel and Hamburg (Dipl.-Kfm., Steuerberater - Tax Adviser). *Member:* Gesellschaft für Betriebswirtschaftslehre, Kiel.

DR. ROBERT MANN, born Rostock, Germany, April 30, 1937; admitted, 1965, Germany. *Education:* Universities of Kiel and Hamburg (Dr. jur., 1964); University of Lausanne. Member, Board of Directors, O&K Orenstein & Koppel AG, 1978-1986. Counsellor of Verein Deutscher Maschinenbauanstalten. *Member:* Hamburg Bar Association.

DR. HELMUT HUBER, born Hamburg, Germany, July 18, 1934; admitted, as Chartered Accountant (Wirtschaftsprüfer). *Education:* Universities of Berlin and Hamburg (Dipl.-Kfm., Dr. rer. pol. 1966).

GERD ERBUT, born Hamburg, Germany, September 15, 1941; admitted, 1970, Germany. *Education:* University of Hamburg. *Member:* Hamburg Bar Association; Judicial Committee Verband für Schiffbau and Meerestechnik e.V.

WOLFGANG KIRCH, born Danzig, January 15, 1930; admitted, as Chartered Accountant (Wirtschaftsprüfer). *Education:* University of Hamburg (Dipl.-Kfm). *Member:* Institut der Wirtschaftsprüfer in Deutschland e.V.

DR. JÜRGEN BRÜGGEMANN, born Hamburg, Germany, April 30, 1936; admitted, 1969, Germany. *Education:* Universities of Freiburg, Munich, Hamburg, Heidelberg (Dr. jur., 1970) and Ann Arbor, Michigan, (M.C.L., 1965). Judge, Hamburg Constitutional Court. *Member:* Hamburg Bar Association.

HANS DOMINIK, born Kiel, Germany, August 4, 1937; admitted, as Tax Adviser (Steuerberater). *Education:* Universities of Hamburg, Cologne, Saarbrücken and Vienna (Dipl.-Kfm.).

AXEL RIECKE, born Hamburg, Germany, April 26, 1947; admitted, 1975, Germany. *Education:* University of Hamburg. *Member:* German-Greek Lawyers Association; German-Swiss Chamber of Commerce; German Association for the Protection of Industrial Property and Copyright Law (GRUR).

PAUL-JUSTUS KOHL, born Goslar, Germany, August 25, 1942; admitted, 1977, Germany. *Education:* Norddeutsche Landesbank, Universities of Braunschweig, Göttingen, Hamburg and Paris. *Member:* Hamburg Bar Association.

DR. AXEL LOHR, born Hamburg, Germany, July 5, 1945; admitted, as Chartered Accountant (Wirtschaftsprüfer) and Tax Adviser (Steuerberater). *Education:* Universities of Hamburg, Freiburg and Bonn (Dipl.-Kfm., Dr. agr).

DR. JOACHIM UMLAUF, born Eutin, Germany, March 27, 1944; admitted, 1978, Germany. *Education:* Universities of Berlin and Kiel (Dr. jur., 1978). Assistant Professor, Kiel University, 1975-1978. *Member:* Hamburg Bar Association; German International Maritime Law Association; Judicial Committee Verband für Schiffbau and Meerestechnik e.V.; Association of West European Shipbuilders.

MARIANNE GÜNTHER, born Flaskeby, Germany, September 3, 1949; admitted, as Chartered Accountant (Wirschaftspüfer) and Tax Ad-

(This Listing Continued)

ESCHE SCHÜMANN COMMICHAU, Hamburg— Continued

viser (Steuerberater). *Education:* University of Hamburg (Dipl.-Kfm., 1976). *Member:* Institut der Wirschaftsprüfer in Deutschland e.V.

DR. HANS-W. KORTMANN, born Hamburg, Germany, June 7, 1950; admitted, as Chartered Accountant (Wirtschaftsprüfer) and Tax Adviser (Steuerberater). *Education:* Universities of Hamburg and Kiel (Dipl.-Kfm., Dr. sc.pol., 1989). *Member:* Institut der Wirtschaftsprüfer in Deutschland e.V., Gesellschaft für Betriebswirtschaftslehre, Kiel.

DR. WOLFGANG DEUCHLER, LL.M. (McGill); born August 7, 1952; admitted, 1982, Germany. *Education:* Universities Freiburg, Lausanne (Switzerland), Montreal (Canada). *Member:* Canadian-German Chamber of Commerce; German-American Lawyers Association; International Bar Association.

WALTER SCHÜSCHKE, born Wiesbaden, Germany, January 30, 1952; admitted, 1983, Germany. *Education:* Universities of Münster/-Westf., Geneva and Freiburg/Br.; New York University (M.C.J., 1980). Member, Corporate Legal Department, Philips International B.V., Eindhoven, The Netherlands, 1987-1990. *Member:* German-American Lawyers Association.

DR. BERND OHLENDORF, born Bonn, Germany, January 20, 1960; admitted, 1989, Germany. *Education:* University of Bonn (1980-1985; Dr.jur., 1986); New York; Taipeh, Taiwan. Lecturer, National Examen for Attorneys, Berlin, Hamburg, 1986-1989. *Member:* German-American Lawyers Association; AIJA.

FLORIAN DOBROSCHKE, born Munich, Germany, December 18, 1957; admitted, 1985, Germany; 1989, Tax Adviser; 1991, Chartered Accountant (Wirtschaftsprüfer). *Education:* University of Munich. *Member:* Institut der Wirtschaftsprüfer in Deutschland.

JAKOB KLEEFASS, born Karlsruhe, Germany, November 10, 1956; admitted, 1989, Germany; 1992, Tax Adviser. *Education:* University of Hamburg (Dipl.-Betriebswirt).

CLAUS SCHNITZERLING, born Kassel, Germany, September 22, 1955; admitted, 1987, Steuerberater (Certified Tax Advisor); 1989, Wirtschaftsprüfer (Chartered Accountant). *Education:* University of Göttingen.

SABINE SCHELLSCHEIDT, born Essen, Germany, January 16, 1961; admitted, 1992, Germany. *Education:* Foreign Office, Bonn; University of Münster and McGill University, Montreal (LL.M., 1989). *Member:* Canadian-German and German-American Lawyers Associations.

Languages: German, English, French and Dutch.

FEDDERSEN LAULE SCHERZBERG & OHLE HANSEN EWERWAHN

JUNGFERNSTIEG 51
(PRIEN-HAUS)
D-20354 HAMBURG, GERMANY
Telephone: 49-40-35005-0
Telex: 212 799 lawtd
Telefax: 49-40-35005-111

Frankfurt/Main, Germany Office: Stiftstraße 9-17, P.O. Box 100836, D-60313 Frankfurt am Main. Telephone: 49-69-29994-0. Telefax: 49-69-282615. Telex: 41 33 96 fls d.

Berlin, Germany Office: Kurfürstendamm 185, D-10707 Berlin. Telephone: 49-30-88 57 16 0. Telefax: 49-30-88 57 16 50.

Dresden, Germany Office: Königsbrücker Straße 17, D-01099 Dresden. Telephone: 49-03 51-567 02 77. Telefax: 49-03 51-567 02 79.

Brussels, Belgium Office: 118, Rue d'Arlon, B-1040 Brussels. Telephone: 32-2-280-1544. Telefax: 32-2-280-0703.

Prague, Czech Republic Office: Spanělská 2, CZ-120 00 Prague 2. Telephone: 42-2-268203; 268229. Telefax: 42-2-260310.

General Practice, Administrative Law, Admiralty, Antitrust, Arbitration, Aviation, Banking, Commercial and Corporate Law. Environmental Law, Insurance, Labor Law, License, Merger and Acquisition, Patent, Trade Mark and Copyright, Real Estate, Securities Law, Tax, Transportation, Unfair Competition, Litigation.

FIRM PROFILE: The firm offers a full range of legal services. It is well known for its commercial, corporate, banking and tax law and its practice in the field of merger and acquisitions, real estate and environmental law.

(This Listing Continued)

The firm has a broad national and international client base with a focus on Europe, the United States and Japan. The firm has 79 attorneys at law (8 of whom are notaries public) and 5 tax advisors.

MEMBERS OF FIRM

DR. HANS H. EWERWAHN, born Hamburg, Germany, December 16, 1917; admitted, 1951, Germany. *Education:* Universities of Hamburg (Dr. jur., 1942) and Freiburg. Author: "The Natur of English Prize Courts and the Solution of Conflicts of International Public Law and National Law in English Prizage." State Prosecutor, 1953-1954 and Judge, 1954-1955, Hamburg. *Member:* German and International Bar Associations. *LANGUAGES:* German and English.

DR. MAX SCHERZBERG, born Hamburg, Germany, March 12, 1922; admitted, 1951, Germany. *Education:* The Law Society School of Law, London (1948); Universities of Innsbruck, Freiburg and Hamburg (Dr. jur.). Honorary Legal Adviser to the British Consul-General. *Member:* Hamburg Bar Association; German - British Jurists' Association. *LANGUAGES:* German, English, French and Danish. *PRACTICE AREAS:* Company Law; Labour Law; Inheritance.

DR. ERIK A. UNDRITZ, born Hamburg, Germany, March 21, 1930; admitted, 1960, Germany. *Education:* University of Hamburg (Dr. jur.; B.Sc., Econ. - Dipl. rer. pol, Certified Public Accountant). *Member:* German and Hamburg Bar Associations; International Fiscal Association; The International Academy of Estate and Trust Law; German Institute of Certified Public Accountants; German Institute for Foreign and International Finance and Tax Matters Hamburg University (International Tax Institute Hamburg University). *LANGUAGES:* German, English and French. *PRACTICE AREAS:* Corporate Law; Anti-Trust and Trade Regulation; EC Law.

DR. MANFRED ANDRAE, born Chemnitz, Germany, March 24, 1933; admitted, 1964, Germany. *Education:* Universities of Göttingen and Kiel (Dr. jur., 1966). Author: "The Law of Inheritance in Schleswig-Holstein." *Member:* German Bar Association; Hamburg Bar Society; Union of German-Russian Economic Law. *LANGUAGES:* German, English and Spanish. *PRACTICE AREAS:* Inheritance; Company Law; Insurance; Construction Law; Real Estate; Law of the five New Laender (former GDR); Law of East European Countries.

JÜRGEN JANTZEN, born Lauban, Germany, June 23, 1936; admitted, 1966, Germany. *Education:* Universities of Hamburg, Freiburg and Berlin. *LANGUAGES:* German, English and French.

DR. DR. DEDO HUNDERTMARK, born Hamburg, Germany, July 30, 1936; admitted, 1963, Germany. *Education:* Universities of Hamburg, Freiburg, Graz, Madrid (Law grad., 1957; Dr. jur., 1961; Dr. rer. pol., 1966; Tax Counsel, 1968; Certified Public Accountant, 1969). Author: "Mutual Funds and Taxes," 1969; Articles: "Tax Fraud", "Escalator Clauses," "Income Tax", in: Management Enzyklopädie, 1985. Member, Advisory Committee on Corporation Tax and Foreign Tax Affairs at the German Institute of Certified Public Accountants. *Member:* International Fiscal Association. *LANGUAGES:* German, English and Spanish. *PRACTICE AREAS:* Merger and Acquisition; Tax Law; International Tax Law; Corporate Taxation.

DR. ERNST MECKLING, born Königsberg, Germany, July 20, 1933; admitted, 1969, Germany. *Education:* Universities of Tübingen, Freiburg and Hamburg (Dr. jur., 1970); London School of Economics and Political Science. Assistant, University Institute for Private International and Foreign Private Law, Hamburg, 1965-1969. Author: "Imputed Contributory Negligence: Comparison of English, American and German Law." Co-Author: "Business Transactions in Germany (FRG)," 1983, Chapter on Arbitration. *Member:* German Association of Comparative Law; International Bar Association. *LANGUAGES:* German and English. *PRACTICE AREAS:* Company Law; Agency and Distributorship; Franchising; Banks and Banking; Family Law; Labour Law.

DR. URS ASCHENBRENNER, born Bremen, Germany, March 2, 1940; admitted, 1969, Germany. *Education:* Universities of Freiburg, Hamburg (Dr. jur., 1969) and Michigan. Author: "The Rights of the Accused in the Pretrial Procedure in the U.S.A." Co-author, "Münchner Vertragshandbuch," Vol 2, Handels- und Wirtschaftsrecht, 1982, Section, Leasing of Enterprises. *Member:* Hamburg and International Bar Associations. *LANGUAGES:* German and English. *PRACTICE AREAS:* Company Law; Administration and Labour Organization.

DR. EBERHARD MEINCKE, born Hamburg, Germany, April 7, 1944; admitted, 1972, Germany. *Education:* Universities of Heidelberg, Freiburg and Hamburg (Dr. jur.). Author: "Integrierte Datenverarbeitung in der

(This Listing Continued)

öffentlichen Verwaltung," 1970; "Internationale Amtshilfe in Steuersachen," Festgabe für Werner Thieme, 1988; "Zur aktuellen rechtlichen Situation von Immobilien in den neuen Bundesländern," Falk, Gewerbe-Immobilien, 5. Aufl. 1992. *Member:* Hamburg and International Bar Associations; German Banking Law Associations; German-Scandinavian Lawyers Associations; German-Chinese Lawyers Associations; German-Japanese Lawyers Associations. *LANGUAGES:* German, English, French and Danish. *PRACTICE AREAS:* Company Law; Corporate Law; Banks and Banking; Construction Law; Real Estate.

DR. JÖRG G.-A. SCHMEDING, born Hamburg, Germany, May 14, 1945; admitted, 1975, Germany. *Education:* Universities of Freiburg, Bordeaux, Luigi Bocconi Milan, Hamburg (Law grad., 1970; Dr. jur., 1974) and Harvard (LL.M., 1975). Author: "The Prevention of Imports within the EEC by Means of the Exclusive Rights of the Producers of Phonographic Records in Germany, Italy and Great Britain," 1973; "Merger Control in Great Britain," WuW, 1973, 405 et seq.; "Advertising of Separate Products Sold Jointly as one Package," WRP, 1974, 304 et seq.; "Relevance of Parties' Stipulations for the Governing Law in the Functional Approach to Conflict of Laws," Rabels Z, 1977, 299 et seq.; "Application of the Unfair Competition Act to Selling Prospectuses for Securities," BB, 1978, 735. Co-Author: "Business Transactions in Germany (FRG)," 1983, Chapters on Agency and Distributorship and Competition, Unfair Practices and Advertising. Co-Author with G. Schohe: "Circumvention of Art. 177 EEC-Treaty by Non-Admission of the Final Appeal?" Festschrift für Gaedertz, 1992. *Member:* Hamburg, New York State and International Bar Associations; German American Lawyers Association; German Association for the Protection of Industrial Property and Copyright Law; AIPPI; Association for Food Law and Food Science; Studienvereinigung Kartellrecht. *LANGUAGES:* German, English and French. *PRACTICE AREAS:* Mergers and Acquisitions; Company Law; Antitrust; Advertising and Marketing.

DR. JÜRGEN STRÜWER, born Warchallen, Ostpreußen, April 12, 1942; admitted, 1976, Germany. *Education:* University of Hamburg (Dr. jur.). *Member:* Hamburg Bar Association. *LANGUAGES:* German and English. *PRACTICE AREAS:* Litigation; Labour and Employment Law.

DR. CORNELIUS FISCHER-ZERNIN, born Hamburg, Germany, March 14, 1950; admitted, 1978, Germany. *Education:* Universities of Freiburg and Hamburg (Dr. jur.). *Member:* Hamburg and International Bar Associations; German Arbitration Institute (DIS); German Maritime Arbitration Association (GMAA); Swiss Arbitration Association (ASA); German Banking Law Association. *LANGUAGES:* German, English, French and Spanish. *PRACTICE AREAS:* Arbitration and Mediation; Company Law; Corporate Law; Banking and Securities; Trusts and Estates.

KLAUS PANNEN, born Elmshorn, Germany, February 22, 1952; admitted, 1982, Germany. *Education:* University of Hamburg. *Member:* Hamburg and International Bar Associations; Arbeitskreis Insolvenzrecht im DAV. *LANGUAGES:* German and English. *PRACTICE AREAS:* Bankruptcy and Insolvency; Banks and Banking; Company Law; Law of the five New Laender (former GDR).

CORINNE HAUSS-LÖHDE, born Stuttgart, Germany, August 21, 1957; admitted, 1987, Hamburg. *Education:* Universities of Mainz, Dijon, Geneva, Strasbourg, Munich. Assistant, Max-Planck-Institute for Foreign and International Patent, Copyright and Unfair Competition Law, Munich, 1982-1983 and Max-Planck-Institute for Foreign and Private International Law, Hamburg, 1984-1985. *LANGUAGES:* German, French and English. *PRACTICE AREAS:* Intellectual Property; Trademarks; Copyrights; Entertainment.

SUSANNE WEISS-REICHELT, born Opperhausen, Germany, February 20, 1958; admitted, 1987, Germany. *Education:* Universities of Würzburg and Göttingen (Ass. jur.); London School of Economics and Political Science, Hague Academy of International Law. *LANGUAGES:* German, English and French. *PRACTICE AREAS:* Company Law; Banks and Banking; Real Estate; Litigation.

DR. FRANK EVERS, born Mannheim, Germany, April 24, 1958; admitted, 1987, Germany. *Education:* University of Oxford, University of Geneva, University of Bonn (Dr. jur., 1986). *Member:* Hamburg and International Bar Associations; Association Internationale des Jeunes Avocats; German Maritime Arbitration Association; Association des Anciens Stagiaires des Communautés Européennes. *LANGUAGES:* German, English, French and Spanish. *PRACTICE AREAS:* Company Law; EEC Law.

DR. GERRIT SCHOHE, born Göppingen, Germany, July 17, 1958; admitted, 1987, Germany; 1989, New York. *Education:* Universities of Frankfurt, Lausanne and Freiburg (Dr. jur., 1988). Author: "Die Haftung juristischer Personen für die Organe im internationalen Privatrecht," 1991.

(This Listing Continued)

Co-Author with J. Schmeding: "Circumvention of Art. 177 EEC-Treaty by Non-Admission of the Final Appeal?" Festschrift für Gaedertz, 1992. *Member:* German-American Lawyers' Association; German-French Lawyers' Association; European Lawyers' Union. *LANGUAGES:* German, French and English. *PRACTICE AREAS:* Corporate Law; Anti-Trust and Trade Regulations; EEC Law.

DR. CHRISTIAN ROHNKE, born Munich, Germany, October 30, 1958; admitted, 1985, New York; 1988, Germany. *Education:* Universities of Munich, Geneva (Dr. jur., 1986) and Texas at Austin (M.C.J., 1984). Lecturer at the Law Department of the University of Jena, 1993. Author: "Verhaltenskontrolle multinationaler Unternehmen," Munich, 1987; "Werbung mit Umweltschutz," GRUR 1988, 667; "U.S. Einfuhrbeschränkungen durch die "National Security Clause," §232 Trade Expansion Act: Strategien für deutsche Unternehmen," RIW 1988, 689; "Protection of External Product Features in West Germany," European Intellectual Property Review 1990, 41; "Product Placement and Sponsoring in TV Programs," Entertainment Law Review 1990, 145; "Neuerer, Arbeitnehmererfinder und Unternehmensgründer in den neuen Bundesländern," BB 1991, Beil, 9, 14; "Wieweit reicht 'Dimple'?" GRUR 1991, 284; "Firma und Kennzeichen bei der Veräußerung von Unternehmensteilen" WM 1991, 1405; "A Unified Intellectual Property Law for a Unified Germany, Patent World 1992, 16; "Rechtsverletzendes Anbieten durch Abbilden im Versandkatalog?" WRP 1992, 296; "Bewertung von Warenzeichen beim Unternehmenskauf," DB 1992, 1941; "Warenzeichen als Kreditsicherheit," NJW 1993, 561. Country correspondent for Germany, Entertainment Law Review. *Member:* German American Lawyer Association; German Association for Industrial Property and Copyright Law; German Japanese Lawyers Association; European Food Law Association; International Bar Association; Association Internationale pour le Protection de la Propriete Industrielle. *LANGUAGES:* German, English and French. *PRACTICE AREAS:* Intellectual Property; Media Law; Computer Law.

DR. SEBASTIAN G. KÜHL, born Hamburg, Germany, November 14, 1955; admitted, 1986, Germany. *Education:* University of Hamburg (Dr. jur., 1988). Author: "Das Gesetz zum deutschen Internationalen Schiffahrtsregister," Transportrecht, 1989; "Schiedsgerichtsbarkeit im Seehandel," Engel Verlag, 1990; "Die Nutzung deutscher Gewässer durch ausländische Schiffe," Transportrecht, 1993. *Member:* German International Maritime Law Association; German Maritime Arbitration Association; German Taiwanese Lawyers' Association; German and International Bar Associations; International Fiscal Association. *LANGUAGES:* German, English and French. *PRACTICE AREAS:* Arbitration and Mediation; Company Law; Corporate Law; Taxation.

DR. GERD LEMBKE, born Duisburg, Germany, December 2, 1956; admitted, 1987, Germany. *Education:* University of Cologne (Dr. jur., 1991). Author: "Vorhersehbarkeit und Geschäftsgrundlage - Eine Untersuchung über die Bedeutung der Vorhersehbarkeit und der Erkennbarkeit für den Rechtsbehelf des Fehlens oder Wegfalls der Geschäftsgrundlage," 1991. *Member:* Deutscher Juristentag. *LANGUAGES:* German and English. *PRACTICE AREAS:* Litigation; Real Estate.

DR. JAN-PETER KECKER, born Kiel, Germany, August 1, 1955; admitted, 1989, Germany. *Education:* University of Hamburg (Dr. jur., 1990). Author: "Die Fungibilisierung von GmbH-Geschäftsanteilen," Köln 1992. *Member:* Hamburg and International Bar Associations. *LANGUAGES:* German, English and French. *PRACTICE AREAS:* Real Estate; Construction Law; Corporate Law; Taxation; Law of the five New Laender (former GDR).

DR. HELGE SCHÄFER, born Kiel, Germany, September 23, 1959; admitted, 1989, Germany. *Education:* Universities of Freiburg and Munich. Assistant, Institute for Public Law, Munich University, 1983-1984. *Member:* Hamburg and International Bar Associations; Studienvereinigung Kartellrecht. *LANGUAGES:* German and English. *PRACTICE AREAS:* Company Law; Merger and Acquisition; Anti-Trust Law (Cartells); Agency and Distributorship.

DR. MARTIN HOFFMANN, born Meschede, Germany, December 9, 1957; admitted, 1987, Germany. *Education:* Universities of Würzburg and München (Dr. jur., 1988). Author: "Der grundrechtliche Schutz der marktwirtschaftlichen Unternehmertätigkeit und der gesellschaftsrechtlichen Unternehmerorganisation durch die Unternehmensfreiheit." Assistant, Institute for Politics and Public Law, Munich University, 1983-1987. *LANGUAGES:* German and English. *PRACTICE AREAS:* Environmental Law; Zoning, Planning and Land Use; Public Law.

(This Listing Continued)

FEDDERSEN LAULE SCHERZBERG & OHLE
HANSEN EWERWAHN, Hamburg—Continued

ASSOCIATES

DR. MARTIN MUNZ, born Bad Homburg, Germany, June 14, 1959; admitted, 1991, Germany. *Education:* University of Freiburg (1980-1986), University of Illinois at Urbana-Champaign (LL.M., 1988); University of Freiburg (Dr. iur., summa cum laude, 1991). Assistant, Institute of Foreign and International Private Law Freiburg, 1986-1987; Graduate Research Assistant, University of Illinois, 1987-1988. Author: "Allgemeine Geschäftsbedingungen in den USA und Deutschland im Handelsverkehr." Heidelberg, 1992. *Member:* German American Lawyers Association. *LANGUAGES:* German, English and French. *PRACTICE AREAS:* Commercial Law; Unfair Competition Law; Trademark; International Private Law.

BETTINA SCHMUDDE, born Hamburg, Germany, may 31, 1962; admitted, 1992, Germany. *Education:* University of Hamburg. *LANGUAGES:* German and English. *PRACTICE AREAS:* Bankruptcy; Insolvency; Labour Law.

DR. CAROLA E. STENGER, born Frankfurt, Germany, December 20, 1958; admitted, 1991, Germany. *Education:* Universities of Giessen (Dr. jur., 1991) and Wisconsin Law School (LL.M., 1990). Author: "Auswirkungen der EMRK auf bundesdeutsche Rechtsprechung," 1992. *LANGUAGES:* German and English. *PRACTICE AREAS:* Corporate Law; Commercial Law; Banking Law.

KERSTEN WAGNER, born Bielefeld, Germany, October 23, 1959; admitted, 1989, Germany. *Education:* University of Hamburg. Author: "Rechtliche Voraussetzungen für die Durchführung von Maßnahmen der Altlastensanierung," UPR 1990, 95; "Die rechtliche Zulässigkeit der Rohrleitungssanierung im Berstlining-Verfahren," TIS (Tiefbau-Ingenieurbau-Straßenbau), Heft 12, 1990; "Abfallverbrennung in Industrieanlagen," IUR, 1991, 31; "Anforderungen an die Bodenabdichtung beim Umgang mit Sonderabfällen," ENTSORGA Magazin Heft 10/91. Co-author: "Altlasten und Abfallproduzentenhaftung," 1988. *Member:* Hamburg Bar Association. *LANGUAGES:* German, English and Spanish. *PRACTICE AREAS:* Environmental Law; Planning Law; Technology Law; Law concerning the award of Contracts; Civil Building and Engineering Law; Project Assistance.

DR. MARTIN DIECKMANN, born Buchholz, Germany, November 15, 1963; admitted, 1990, Germany. *Education:* Universities of Hamburg, Bologna and Sheffield (LL.M., 1992). Author: "Das Abfallrecht der Europäischen Gemeinschaft," Baden-Baden 1994; "Der Abfallbegriff des EG-Rechts und seine Konsequenzen für das nationale Recht," Natur und Recht 1992, 407; "Das neue Abfallverbringungsrecht der europäischen Gemeinschaft," Zeitschrift für Umweltrecht 1993, 109; "Die europäischen Vorgaben für eine Neuorientierung in der Abfallwirtschaft," Sutter/Held (eds)., "stofökologische Perspektiven der Abfallwirtschaft," 1993, 125. Co-Author: "Altlasten und Abfallproduzentenhaftung," 1988. *LANGUAGES:* German, English and Italian. *PRACTICE AREAS:* Environmental Law; Zoning, Planning and Land Use; Administrative Law; EEC Law.

BRITTA HANNEMANN, born Hamburg, Germany, August 12, 1966; admitted, 1993, Germany. *Education:* University of Hamburg. *LANGUAGES:* German and English. *PRACTICE AREAS:* Litigation; Insurance Law.

DR. PHILIPP VON DIETZE, born Bremen, Germany, December 26, 1964; admitted, 1994, Germany. *Education:* University of Freiburg, Bonn and Munich (Dr. jur. 1994). *LANGUAGES:* German, English and French. *PRACTICE AREAS:* Corporate Law; EEC-Law.

JOACHIM SCHÄFER, born Mainz, Germany, June 19, 1948; admitted, 1994, Germany. *Education:* University of Mainz, Lausanne and Grenoble. Author: Thieme/Schäfer, "Niedersächsische Gemeindeordnung," Kommentar, 2. Aufl. 1994. Retired City Manager. *Member:* Internationales Institut für Verwaltungswissenschaften, Deutsche Sektion. *LANGUAGES:* German, English and French. *PRACTICE AREAS:* Public Law; Construction Planning and Public Works Planning Law; Local Government Law; International Law of Sea.

BIRGIT DANNHORN, born Coburg, Germany, February 12, 1967; admitted, 1994, Germany. *Education:* University of Bayreuth. *LANGUAGES:* German, English, French, Italian and Spanish. *PRACTICE AREAS:* Competition Law; Company Law; Labour Law; Private International Law; Criminal Law.

FISCHÖTTER, MICHELI & PARTNER
MITTELWEG 13
20148 HAMBURG, GERMANY
Telephone: 49/40/445081
Telex: 2-173356 fimi
Fax: 49/40/451435

General Practice. Antitrust, Trademarks, Unfair Competition, Patent Law, Copyright, Corporation and Commercial Law, Press and Publishing Law, Entertainment Law, Food and Drug Law, Labor Law.

FIRM PROFILE: Fischötter, Micheli & Partner is a 13 lawyer firm with 9 partners. The origin of the law firm goes back into the 1930ies. Most of the lawyers in the firm, in addition to their legal training, have worked as research associates at renowned universities where they received their special knowledge in the field on which they are working today and/or qualified themselves through a sophisticated doctorate degree. Some of the lawyers of the firm furthermore have received legal training with the EEC Commission in Brussels.

The firm's main activities and its special expertise refer to unfair competition law, antitrust law, intellectual property rights (trademarks, patents), food and drug law, press and media law and publishing and entertainment law. Some of the lawyers moreover work in the fields of corporate law, mergers and acquisitions, commercial law, distribution, labor relations, real estate and environment law. The firm corresponds with foreign law firms which are renowned in their respective jurisdictions.

MEMBERS OF FIRM

WERNER FISCHÖTTER, born Stuttgart, Germany, April 26, 1926; admitted, 1958, Germany. *Education:* University of Tübingen. Co-author of joint commentary, "Law against Restraints of Competition and European Antitrust Law," 1982. *Member:* German and International Bar Association; Studienvereinigung Kartellrecht (Member of the Board); German Society for The Protection of Industrial Property and Copyright Law (GRUR); International Association for the Protection of Industrial Property (AIPPI). *LANGUAGES:* German and English.

HANS-DIETRICH MICHELI, born Berlin, Germany, July 27, 1934; admitted, 1966, Germany. *Education:* Universities of Hamburg and Berlin. *Member:* German Bar Association; GRUR. *LANGUAGES:* German and English.

DR. ULRICH KÜLPER, born Hamburg, Germany, October 18, 1945; admitted, 1974, Germany. *Education:* University of Hamburg (Dr.jur., 1976); Research Associate Max-Planck-Institute for Private and International Law, 1970-1973. Lecturer, University of Hamburg, 1993-1994. *Member:* GRUR. *LANGUAGES:* German and English.

DR. HANS-DIETER LÜBBERT, born Hamburg, Germany, August 5, 1945; admitted, 1976, Germany. *Education:* Universities of Hamburg (Dr.jur., 1975); Freiburg. Author: "Concerted Actions in German and European Cartel Law (including Antitrust Law)." Research Associate, Institute for Trade and Company Law, Heidelberg, 1975-1976. *Member:* GRUR; Studienvereinigung Kartellrecht. *LANGUAGES:* German, English and French.

DR. BURKHARD RHEINECK, born Wuppertal, Germany, April 9, 1950; admitted, 1979, Germany. *Education:* Universities of Freiburg and Kiel (Dr.jur., 1978). Author: "Misappropriation and Proprietor's Interests," Treatise on Penal Law, NF Volume 33, 1979. Research Associate, Criminal Law, University of Kiel, 1974-1978. *Member:* German Bar Association; GRUR. *LANGUAGES:* German and English.

BERND ROOCK, born Hamburg, Germany, November 5, 1952; admitted, 1981, Germany. *Education:* University of Hamburg; Institute for Trade and Company Law, Hamburg (Research Associate, 1978); Institute for Civil Procedure Law and Labor Relations (1979-1980). *LANGUAGES:* German and English.

THOMAS MELCHERT, born Hamburg, Germany, May 5, 1951; admitted, 1982, Germany. *Education:* University of Hamburg; Institute for Trade and Company Law, Hamburg (Research Associate, 1980-1981). *Member:* German Bar Association; GRUR. *LANGUAGES:* German and English.

DR. HEIDI WRAGE-MOLKENTHIN, born Hamburg, Germany, September 22, 1953; admitted, 1983, Germany. *Education:* University of Hamburg (Dr.jur., 1983). Research Associate, Institute for Trade and Company Law, Hamburg, 1981-1983. Author: *Sanctions of Unfair Competition in case of Anti-Trust-Law Offences?* R.v. Decker's Heidelberg, 1984. Co-Author: Frankfurt Joint Commentary "Law Against Restraints of Competition,"

(This Listing Continued)

1989 ff; Encyclopedia on Commercial Law. Lecturer, University of Leipzig, 1994. *Member:* Studienvereinigung Kartellrecht; GRUR. *LANGUAGES:* German and English.

DR. THOMAS J. MEYER, born Gelsenkirchen, Germany, September 17, 1955; admitted, 1987, Germany. *Education:* University of Hamburg (Dr. jur., 1986). Research Associate, Institute for Trade, Shipping and Business Law, Hamburg, 1982-1986. Author: "The Request of Information by the Cartel Authority," Florentz, Munich, 1987. *Member:* GRUR. *LANGUAGES:* German and English.

Languages: German, English and French.

GAPPMAYER & PARTNER

Established in 1976

HERBERT-WEICHMANN-STR. 56
D-22085 HAMBURG, GERMANY
Telephone: 49 40 229 20 91
Fax: 49 40 220 79 12
Telex: 82202-227 gso d
E-Mail: GEOD: Gappmayer

Commercial, Corporate, Trade, Transport, Unfair Competition, Trademark, Labour, Real Estate, Construction Contracts and Medical Law, Commercial Litigation and Arbitration, Private International Law.

FIRM PROFILE: The firm was established in 1976. It offers a full range of legal services in the commercial field, The firm is well known for its expertise in Real Estate, Labour and Private International Law. The firm is a member of AdvoSelect EEIG, a European network of independent law firms being represented in 51 cities throughout Europe, pooling their resources in special fields and crossborder cases.

MEMBERS OF FIRM

CHRISTOPH GAPPMAYER, born Hamburg, Germany, October 28, 1947; admitted, 1976, Hamburg. *Education:* Universities of Freiburg and Hamburg. *Member:* German Bar Association; Hamburg Bar Association. *LANGUAGES:* German, English and Spanish. *PRACTICE AREAS:* Real Estate Law; Law of Construction Contracts and Labour Law.

HANS-JÜRGEN WULF, born Hamburg, Germany, November 21, 1947; admitted, 1976, Hamburg. *Education:* Universities of Freiburg and Hamburg. *Member:* German Bar Association; Hamburg Bar Association; German-British Jurists' Association. *LANGUAGES:* German and English. *PRACTICE AREAS:* Corporate, Trade and English Law.

BURKHARD STÜBEN, born Hamburg, Germany, May 6, 1954; admitted, 1988, Hamburg. *Education:* Universities of Geneva and Hamburg. *Member:* German Bar Association; Hamburg Bar Association; Association Internationale des Jeunes Advocats. *LANGUAGES:* German, English, French and Italian. *PRACTICE AREAS:* Private International Law; Transport Law; Unfair Competition; Trade law; Russian (Joint Venture) Law.

MARTIN OBERNESSER, born Hamburg, Germany, June 18, 1953; admitted, 1981, Hamburg. *Education:* University of Hamburg. *Member:* German Bar Association (Member of Labour Law Commission); Hamburg Bar Association; Deutscher Juristentag. *LANGUAGES:* German and English. *PRACTICE AREAS:* Labour Law; Medical Law; Law of Tenancy; Litigation.

GRAF von WESTPHALEN & MODEST

The Merged Firms of Modest-Gundisch-Landry, Hamburg, Graf von Westphalen-Ebel-Genzow, Cologne, Samuel & Partner, Hamburg

POSTSTRAßE 9 A
POSTFACH 30 36 10
20354 HAMBURG, GERMANY
Telephone: (040) 35922-0
Telex: 211 729 MOD D
Telefax: (040)344573

Cologne, Germany Office: Salierring 42, 50677. Telephone: (0221) 208 07 0. Fax: (0221) 239255.
Leipzig, Germany Office: Katharinenstraße 15, 04109. Telephone: (0341) 28 10 73. Fax: (0341) 281073.
Dresden, Germany Office: Winterbergstraße 2. 01277. Telephone and Fax: 0351-2516 024 or 2516032.

(This Listing Continued)

Brussels, Belgium Office: Avenue de la Joyeuse Entrée 1, Boîte 16, B-1040. Telephone: (32) (2) 230.46.69. Telefax: (32) (2) 231.00.35.
Paris, France Office: 198, Avenue Victor Hugo, 75116. Telephone: (01) 45.04.61.73. Telex: FUGELEX 614570. Telefax: (1) 45.04.41.43.

E.C. Law, Trade Regulations and Tariff, Tax, Food and Drug Regulations, Commercial, Corporation, Arbitration, Unfair Competition, Antitrust, Labor, Public, Administrative and Environmental Law. General Practice.

MEMBERS OF FIRM

DR. LEOPOLD KOENIGSBERG (1862-1929).

DR. WALTER SAMUEL 1878-1939).

DR. ALEXANDER BACHUR (1883-1941).

DR. WALTER POINTT (1893-1940).

DR. ALFRED WOLFF (1880-1941).

HERBERT W. SAMUEL (1901-1982).

DR. FRITZ MODEST (1905-1932).

DR. JÜRGEN GÜNDISCH, born Dresden, February 26, 1929; admitted, 1957, Hamburg. *Education:* Universities of Munich and Tübingen (Dr. iur., 1954); Harvard Law School (LL.M., 1953). Author, "General Principles of Law Recognized by Civilized Nations," Rabels Zeitschrift, 1962; "Grenzen der wirtschaftslenkenden Eingriffe der europäischen Organe," Recht der Internationalen Wirtschaft, 1978. Research Assistant, Max Planck-Institute for Foreign and International Private Law, 1953-1960. Ford Fellow, Cornell Law School, 1960-1961. Member: State Parliament of Hamburg, 1971-1974; Committee for the Election of Judges, Hamburg; Constitutional Court of the State of Hamburg. *Member:* German Association of Comparative Law. Fédération Internationale pour le Droit Européen; German-American Lawyer's Association; GRUR; Association for Antitrust Law. *LANGUAGES:* German, English, French and Hungarian.

DR. KLAUS LANDRY, born Zittau, November 1, 1938; admitted, 1968, Hamburg. *Education:* Universities of Munich, Heidelberg, London (University College), Frankfurt and Kiel (Dr. iur., 1966). *Member:* Hamburg (President) and International Bar Associations; GRUR; German Institute for Arbitration; German Association for Food Law; German Association of Comparative Law. (Also Of Counsel to Funck-Brentano & Partners, Paris, France). *LANGUAGES:* German, French and English.

GABRIELE RAUSCHNING, born Hamburg, May 18, 1936; admitted, 1965, Hamburg. *Education:* Universities Frankfurt, Freiburg and Hamburg. *Member:* German-Dutch Law Association; Hamburg Bar Association. *LANGUAGES:* German and English.

BARBARA FESTGE, born Hamburg, May 6, 1937; admitted, 1970, Hamburg. *Education:* Universities of Tübingen and Hamburg. *Member:* Hamburg Bar Association; German Association of Comparative Law; Fédération Internationale pour le Droit Européen; German-British Jurists' Association; European Lawyers' Union (Member, Executive Committee, UAE). *LANGUAGES:* German, English and French.

DR. HORST HEEMANN, born Lauenburg/Pommern, March 4, 1942; admitted, 1972, Hamburg, Tax Counsel. *Education:* Universities of Lausanne, Marburg and Hamburg (Dr. jur., 1972). *Member:* Hamburg Bar Association; German Association of Comparative Law. *LANGUAGES:* German and English.

ERNST-JUERGEN MELLIN, born Kiel, Germany, May 24, 1940; admitted, 1972, Germany. *Education:* University of Hamburg. *Member:* Hamburg Bar Association; German Association for Industrial Property and Copyright Law. *LANGUAGES:* German and English.

JOERG D. HISAM, born Mössingen, November 19, 1944; admitted, 1976, Bremen, Germany; 1977, Hamburg. *Education:* Kiel; Hamburg; Association Internationale de Droit Comparé, Strasbourg (Diplome, 1974). *Member:* Hamburg Bar Association; Hamburg Law Society. *LANGUAGES:* German, English and French.

DR. THOMAS VOLKMANN-SCHLUCK, born Leipzig, Germany, December 31, 1947; admitted, 1980, Hamburg. *Education:* Universities of Cologne, Lausanne and Freiburg (Dr. iur., 1979); Harvard Law School (LL.M., 1980). Author: "Continental European Criminal Procedures: True or Illusive Model," 9 American Journal of Criminal Law 1, 1981; "Der Spanische Strafprozess zwischen Inquisitions- und Parteiverfahren," Nomos, 1979. Co-author: Jescheck-Löffler, "Quellen und Schrifttum des Strafrechts," Vol. II, Latinamerica, Beck, 1980. Research Assistant, Max-Planck-Institute for Foreign and International Criminal Law, Freiburg, 1973-1979. *Member:* German American Lawyers Association; Hamburg

(This Listing Continued)

GRAF VON WESTPHALEN & MODEST, Hamburg—
Continued

Bar Association; GRUR; Committee for Lawyer's Examination, Hamburg.
LANGUAGES: German, English, Spanish and French.

DR. HORST GIESEKE, born Hannover, September 16, 1953; admitted, 1980, Hamburg. *Education:* University of Hamburg (1972-1978); Kammergericht Berlin (1978-1980); Institute for Business Law, University of Hamburg (Dr.jur., 1981). Author: "Die Ordnungsfunktion des Zivilrechts für die steuerliche Zurechnung," (Treaties on Principals of Tax Allocation) DSTR, 1982; "Besondere Probleme bei der Mittelbaren Beteilingung," (Special Problems in "Mediate Partnerships"), DB, 1984. *Member:* German-American Lawyer's Association; German-British Jurists' Association; Association International Des Jeunes Avocats. **LANGUAGES:** German and English.

DR. RONALD STEILING, born Lüneburg, Germany, January 12, 1957; admitted, 1988, Hamburg. *Education:* Universities of Berlin and Göttingen (Dr. jur., 1988). Author: "Das Seefischereirecht der Europäischen Gemeinschaften," Köln, 1988. Research Assistant, Institute for International Law, University of Göttingen, 1982-1988. Member, Committee for Lawyer's Examination. **LANGUAGES:** German, English and French.

JULIANE ZUTT, born Heidelberg, Germany, September 23, 1959; admitted, 1990, Hamburg. *Education:* Universities of Hamburg and Lausanne/Switzerland (Referendar, 1985; Assessor, 1989); New York University (M.C.J., 1991). *Member:* Hamburg Bar Association; German-American Lawyers Association. **LANGUAGES:** German, English and French.

FABIENNE BOULANGER, born Reunes, France, February 2, 1960; admitted, 1990, Hamburg. *Education:* Universities of Reunes (Maitríse en droit, 1983) and Hamburg. Research Assistant to Professor Dr. P. Behrens, Research Institut Europa - Koppeg Hamburg. *Member:* German-French Lawyers Association. **LANGUAGES:** French, German and English.

SUSANNE WITTHÖFT, born Lüneburg, Germany, May 4, 1964; admitted, 1993, Hamburg. *Education:* Universities of Hamburg, Geneva and Strasburg. Member, Commission of the European Community DG VI, Bruxelles. *Member:* Hamburg Bar Association; Europa Union; German-French Lawyers Association. **LANGUAGES:** German, English and French.

DR. LISE FUNCK-BRENTANO, born Saabrücken, Germany, August 21, 1929; admitted, 1954, Paris (Not admitted in Germany). *Education:* Paris University (Maître en droit); Frankfurt a.M., Germany (Docteur Juris). *Member:* Paris Bar; European Lawyers Association (Secretary General, 1978-1987; President, 1988—); German Bar; A.F.E.C. (French Association for Competition Study); International League Against Unfair Competition; GRNR (Germany). (Also Member, Funck-Brentano & Partners, Paris, France). **LANGUAGES:** French, German and English.

OF COUNSEL

PROFESSOR PIERRE MATHIJSEN, born Lilburg, Netherlands, March 7, 1924; (Not admitted in Germany). *Education:* University of Minnesota (M.A. Economics, 1952); University of Leyden (M.A., 1957; Ph.D., 1957). Assistant Professor, Law School, University of Michigan, 1961-1962. Professor: Law Faculty, University of Nijmegen, Netherlands, 1967-1985; Law Faculty, University of Brussels, Belgium, 1986—. Attaché, ECSe Court of Justice, 1953-1958. Legal Adviser, EAEC Commission, 1958-1967. Director, EEC Commission, 1968-1977. Director General for Regional Policy, EC Commission, 1977-1986. Member of the Board, European Investment Bank, 1977-1986. Delegate General, CIAA, Brussels, Belgium, 1986-1989. Author: "A Guide to European Community Law," London/New York, 1972, 5. Edition, 1990. Member, Editorial Staff, "Encyclopedia of European Community Law," and "European Law Review," 1973—. (Also Of Counsel, Funck-Brentano & Partners, Paris, France). **LANGUAGES:** Dutch, French, English and German.

PROFESSOR DR. PETER KIEL, born January 21, 1955; admitted, 1987, Hamburg. *Education:* Universities of Hamburg and Salzburg. Assistant to Professor Dr. K. Schmidt, 1982 and Professor Dr. H. Kötz, 1982-1985, Institute for International Private Law, University of Hamburg. Research Fellow, Max-Planck-Institute for Foreign and International Private Law, Hamburg, 1987-1990. **LANGUAGES:** German and English.

DR. GREBE, SCHLICHTING, MODES & PARTNER
JUNGFERNSTIEG 40
D-20354 HAMBURG, GERMANY
Telephone: 0049-40-34 66 53
Fax: 0049-40-34 52 79

General and International Practice, Commercial, Company, Tax, Customs, Bankruptcy, Transportation, Insurance, Real Estate, Unfair Competition, Trademarks, Copyright, Inheritance, Family, Labor, Immigration and Naturalization Law.

MEMBERS OF FIRM

DR. MICHAEL GREBE, born Hamburg, Germany, July 16, 1950; admitted, 1983, Germany. *Education:* Universities of Munich and Hamburg (graduate in Business Management; Dr. jur.). *Member:* German Lawyers Association; Inter-Pacific Bar Association; Vietnam Euro Trade Center, Hamburg (President).

STEPHAN SCHLICHTING, born Hamburg, Germany, October 16, 1953; admitted, 1983, Germany. *Education:* Universities of Freiburg and Hamburg. *Member:* Hamburg and German Bar Associations.

HANS-GERHARD MODES, born Hamburg, Germany, January 5, 1951; admitted, 1983, Germany. *Education:* University of Hamburg. Research Assistant, Institute of Commercial Law, Hamburg, 1979-1983. Lecturer, Commercial Law, University of Hamburg, since 1980. *Member:* Hamburg and German Bar Associations; German Society for the Protection of Industrial Property and Copyright Law (GRUR).

HANS-BERND GIESLER, born Berlin, Germany, February 9, 1929; admitted, 1958, Germany. *Education:* Universities of Erlangen, Göttingen and Paris. Representative, American Chamber of Commerce in Northern Germany, 1983-1986. *Member:* German-Japanese Society, Hamburg (Member of Board and Honorary President); German-Japanese Society, Bremen (President); German-Korean Society (Co-Founder and Vice-President); Taiwan Committee of the German Industry (Managing Director); East Asia Association and Australia-New Zealand-South Pacific Association (Executive Member of Board).

BEATRICE E. YBARRA, born Zürich, Switzerland, May 11, 1948; admitted, 1987, Germany. *Education:* Universities of Zürich and Hamburg. *Member:* Hamburg and German Bar Associations.

WERNER SCHWENN, born November 4, 1923; admitted, 1992, Germany. *Education:* University of Hamburg. Leading Government Director, Head of the Division of Constitutional and Administrative Law, Board of Justice, Hamburg, 1969-1989.

WALTHER SCHLICHTING, born Hamburg, Germany, April 19, 1920; admitted, 1991, Germany. *Education:* Universities of Leipzig and Hamburg. Government Official, Legal Board of the Senate and Leading Government Director, Board of Justice, Hamburg, 1949-1983.

HOLGER MORISSE, born Hamburg, Germany, February 26, 1954; admitted, 1989, Germany. *Education:* University of Hamburg. *Member:* Hamburg and German Bar Associations.

DR. KLAUS HORMANN, born Hamburg, Germany, March 9, 1957; admitted, 1988, Germany. *Education:* University of Hamburg (Dr. jur.). *Member:* German Asia-Pacific Business Association; German-Korean Society.

Languages: German, English, French, Spanish, Chinese and Vietnamese.

GRÜTZMACHER, GRAVERT & PARTNER
HERRENGRABEN 3
20459 HAMBURG, GERMANY
Telephone: 040/36 96 33-0
Fax: 040/36 96 3333

Frankfurt/Main, Germany Office: Brobstrabe 6, 60487. Telephone: 069/979 61-0. Fax: 069/979 61100.
Leipzig, Germany Office: Lessingstraße 17, 04109. Telephone: 0341-20 98 69/79. Fax: 0341-20 98 59.
Berlin, Germany Office: Kurfürstendamm 216, 10719. Telephone: 030-882 66 04. Fax: 030-882 17 63.

Law: Company Law, Business and Economic Legislation, Company Purchasing, LBO/MBO, Mergers and Acquisitions, Company Succession (Laws of Succession), Competition and Licensing Legislation, Anti-Trust

(This Listing Continued)

Law, Law of Commerce and Marketing, Franchising, Labor Legislation, EDP Law, Legislation governing Real Estate, Private Building Law.

Taxation: German and International Taxation Legislation (esp. US Tax Law), Fiscal Planning, Counselling on Taxation Concepts, Legislation regulating the Transformation of Companies in Fiscal and Commercial Terms, Balance Sheet Planning and Dividend Schedules, Taxation Counselling for New Enterprises, Representation at Financial Courts of Law, Tax Litigation, Legislation regarding Fiscal Offenses, Administration of Property.

Auditing: Annual Audits, Auditing Work such as required on the Banking Sector, support given in clarifying matters of Business Management particularly in the new German Länder, Counselling on Privatization, Company Reorganization, drawing up of expert opinions.

(For Biographical Data on all Personnel, see Professional Biographies at Frankfurt/Main, Germany)

HARMSEN & UTESCHER

Established in 1895

ADENAUERALLEE 28
20097 HAMBURG, GERMANY
Telephone: 0 40-24 97 57
Telex: 2162 830 apli
Telecopier: 040-280 3672 AUTOMATIC G II and G III

Dresden, Germany Office: Grunaer Str. 2, 01069 Dresden. Telephone: (51) 4 87 45 01. Telecopier: (51) 4 87 31 20.

General and International Practice, Commercial, Corporate, Banking, Finance, Mergers and Acquisitions, EEC Law, Antitrust, Unfair Competition, Trademarks, Copyrights, Patents, Licensing, Food and Drug Law, Law of the Press, Labor Law, Real Estate, Estate Planning, Litigation and Arbitration.

MEMBERS OF FIRM

DR. HEINZ HARMSEN, born Hamburg, Germany, November 8, 1901; admitted, 1927, Germany. Education: Universities of Munich, Göttingen and Hamburg (Doctor of Laws, 1924). President, Court of Appeals of High Court of Discipline, Hamburg, 1975—. Member: Hamburg and German Bar Associations; German Society for the Protection of Industrial Property and Copyright Law (President, North German Section, 1959—); International Association for the Protection of Industrial Property. **LANGUAGES:** German, English and French.

DR. WOLFGANG UTESCHER, born Hamburg, Germany, March 6, 1928; admitted, 1959, Hamburg. Education: Universities of Hamburg, Göttingen, Zurich and Paris (Dr.jur., 1959). Member: Hamburg Bar Association; German Society for the Protection of Industrial Property and Copyright Law; International Association for the Protection of Industrial Property; United States Trademark Association. **LANGUAGES:** English, German and French.

PETER HARMSEN, born Hamburg, Germany, April 21, 1931; admitted, 1966, Germany. Education: Braunschweig Technical University (Diploma in Chemistry, 1956); University of Hamburg. Member: Hamburg and German Bar Associations; German Society for the Protection of Industrial Property and Copyright Law; International Association for the Protection of Industrial Property. **LANGUAGES:** German, English and French. **PRACTICE AREAS:** Trademarks; Patents; Arbitration; Litigation; Competition.

DR. MICHAEL SCHAEFFER, born Hamburg, Germany, April 7, 1940; admitted, 1971, Germany. Education: University of Hamburg (Dr.jur., 1971). Member: Hamburg Bar Association; German Society for the Protection of Industrial Property and Copyright Law; International Association for the Protection of Industrial Property; United States Trademark Association. **LANGUAGES:** German, English and French. **PRACTICE AREAS:** Mergers and Acquisitions; Patents; Companies; Corporations; Anti-trust; European Law; Competition; Trademarks.

DR. FRIEDRICH W. FRICKE, born Wunstorf, Germany, August 5, 1947; admitted, 1976, Germany. Education: University of Hamburg (Dr.jur., 1976); University of Göttingen. Member: Hamburg Bar Association. **LANGUAGES:** English and German. **PRACTICE AREAS:** Labour; Arbitration; Litigation.

MATTHIAS WOLTER, born Hamburg, Germany, August 22, 1953; admitted, 1983, Germany. Education: University of Hamburg. Member: Hamburg Bar Association; German Society for the Protection of Industrial Property and Copyright Law. **LANGUAGES:** English and German.

(This Listing Continued)

PRACTICE AREAS: Competition; Anti-trust; European Law; Companies; Corporation; Commercial Law; Trademarks.

RAINER KAASE, LL.M., born Hannover, Germany, April 7, 1959; admitted, 1989, Germany. Education: University of Marburg; University of Geneva, Switzerland; University of Cambridge/England, Queen's College (Master of Law, 1985). Member: Hamburg Bar Association; German Society for the Protection of Industrial Property and Copyright Law; German-British Jurists Association; Food Law Association. **LANGUAGES:** German, English, French and Spanish. **PRACTICE AREAS:** Contracts and Arbitration; Pharmaceutical Law; Food Law; Commercial Law.

DR. GESCHA SIEWERS, born Rostock, Germany, September 23, 1941; admitted, 1974, Germany. Education: University of Neuchatel, Switzerland; University of Hamburg (Doctor of Natural Science). Member: Patent Attorneys Bar Association; FICPI; German Society for the Protection of Industrial Property and Copyright Law; International Association for the Protection of Industrial Property. **LANGUAGES:** German, English, French and Spanish. **PRACTICE AREAS:** Patents; Trademarks.

HASCHE ALBRECHT FISCHER

HAMBURG, GERMANY

(See Weiss & Hasche)

HEIMANN, HARDENBERG, BEŸN, DOSE, MÖLLER, TAPFER

Established in 1971

WARBURGSTRASSE 50
20354 HAMBURG, GERMANY
Telephone: 49-40-44 10 91
Facsimile: 49-40-44 10 98

Mailing Address: Postfach 30 24 99, 20308 Hamburg, Germany

Securities, Corporate, Tax, Trade, Bankruptcy, Banking, Investment, Estate and Public Law, Mutual Funds, Insurance, Mergers and Acquisitions, MBO and Litigation.

FIRM PROFILE: Dr. Klaus Heimann established the firm in 1971 as a partnership, and it presently consists of ten partners and several employees.

The partnership concentrates on all aspects of business law, with a particular focus on corporate, banking, tax, investment fund, and construction law. Two of the partners are qualified tax accountants. The firm also represents clients in litigation, while believing that litigation is only the final phase of what should be a comprehensive counselling service.

The investment fund department represents and advises major foreign fund companies that seek to participate in the enormous German capital market by registering their offerings in Germany.

The firm also acts as legal advisor to private and public real estate developers and to government authorities in Eastern Europe.

The firm is not involved in criminal law.

PARTNERS

DR. KLAUS B. HEIMANN, born Kaiserslautern, Germany, December 6, 1941; admitted, 1969, Germany. Education: University of Munich (Dr. jur.). **LANGUAGES:** German, English and French. **PRACTICE AREAS:** Banking; Corporate Law; Mergers and Acquisitions; Business Law; Privatisation.

DR. CARL GRAF HARDENBERG, born Berlin, Germany, January 10, 1939; admitted, 1972, Germany. Education: University of Munich (Dr.jur.); University of Sorbonne, Paris. Author: "Membership of Associations in Corporations," Schön Verlag, Munich, 1972. **LANGUAGES:** German, English and French. **PRACTICE AREAS:** Foreign Investments; Corporate Law; Estate Law; Litigation.

EDGAR N. BEŸN, born Hamburg, Germany, September 8, 1938; (Not admitted in Germany). Education: University of Munich (Dipl. Kfm., Steuerberater, 1974). **LANGUAGES:** German and English.

DR. STEFAN DOSE, born Hamburg, Germany, October 20, 1940; admitted, 1969, Hamburg. Education: Hamburg (Dr.jur., 1969). Author: "The

(This Listing Continued)

HEIMANN, HARDENBERG, BEŸN, DOSE, MÖLLER, TAPFER, Hamburg—Continued

Legal Position of Board Members in a Corporation," Dr. Otto Schmidt Verlag, Köln, 1975. **LANGUAGES:** German, English and French.

KAI J. B. MÖLLER, born Hamburg, Germany, April 23, 1941; admitted, 1971, Hamburg. *Education:* Universities of Marburg, Freiburg, Hamburg (Steuerberater, Tax Accountant, 1978). **LANGUAGES:** German and English.

GABRIELE LAKEBRINK, born Hamburg, Germany, October 6, 1954; admitted, 1982, Hamburg. *Education:* Hamburg. **LANGUAGES:** German and English. **PRACTICE AREAS:** Family Law; Tenant and Estate Law.

ROLAND TAPFER, born Handorf, Germany, April 4, 1944; admitted, 1972, Hamburg. *Education:* Munich, Hamburg. **LANGUAGES:** German and English. **PRACTICE AREAS:** Investments; Real Estate Law.

DR. HARALD BAUM, born Hamburg, Germany, May 13, 1952; admitted, 1981, Germany. *Education:* Universities of Hamburg and Freiburg (Dr.jur.). Numerous publications on Japanese law; editor of "Japanese Trade and Economic Law," Berlin, 1994. *Member:* German-Japanese Lawyers Association. **LANGUAGES:** German, English and Japanese. **PRACTICE AREAS:** German-Japanese Legal Matters; Private International Law; Law of International Procedure.

DR. GUNNAR THIES, born Hamburg, Germany, February 4, 1955; admitted, 1988, Hamburg. *Education:* University of Hamburg (Dr. jur.). Author: "Public Real Estate Companies," C.H. Beck Verlag, München, 1986; "Shopping Centers and Urban Construction Law," C.H. Beck Verlag, München, 1992. **LANGUAGES:** German, English and French. **PRACTICE AREAS:** Private and Public Real Estate Law; Labour Law.

ROLAND W. BAUM, born Grünstadt, Germany, August 31, 1960; admitted, 1991, Germany. *Education:* Universities of Göttingen and Lausanne (Switzerland). **LANGUAGES:** German, English and French. **PRACTICE AREAS:** Mutual Funds; Insurance; Computer and Software Contracts; Corporate Law.

Languages: German, English, French and Japanese

HEISSNER & STRUCK

HUDTWALCKERSTRASSE 11
22299 HAMBURG, GERMANY
Telephone: (040) 461 007
Telefax: (040) 480 23 32

General Practice, Commercial, Corporate, Transport, Labor, Real Estate, Construction, Banking, Tax, Unfair Competition, Computer, Copyright, Entertainment, Licensing, Litigation, Inheritance, Bankruptcy, Administrative Law.

MEMBERS OF FIRM

THOMAS HEISSNER, born Borna, Germany, September 8, 1946; admitted, 1977, Hamburg. *Education:* Universities of Cologne and Hamburg (Law Degree, 1973); College for Administrative Law, Speyer (1976). Research Assistant, Institute for Application of Data-Processing and Computer-Science to Law (Institut für Rechtsinformatik), University of Hannover, 1978-1980. *Member:* Hamburg Bar Association.

DR. DIETER STRUCK, born West-Bargum, Germany, June 17, 1952; admitted, 1982, Hamburg. *Education:* University of Hamburg (Law Degree, 1978; Doctor of Laws, 1981). Research Assistant, Institut for Commercial, Corporate and Maritime Law, University of Hamburg, 1979-1980. *Member:* Hamburg Bar Association.

DR. RAINALD COMMANDEUR, born Essen, Germany, August 21, 1960; admitted, 1990, Hamburg. *Education:* Universities of Freiburg and Kiel (Law Degree, 1986; Doctor of Laws, 1988); German Lawyers Institute, Detmold (Tax Law course, 1988). With, Blake Dawson Waldron, Sydney, 1990. *Member:* Hamburg Bar Association; German-German Lawyers Association.

STEFAN HABERT, born Düsseldorf, Germany, July 7, 1961; admitted, 1993, Hamburg. *Education:* University of Hamburg (Law Degree, 1988). *Member:* Hamburg Bar Association.

DR. CHRISTIAN LEMKE, born Hamburg, Germany, March 31, 1963; admitted, 1993, Hamburg. *Education:* University of Hamburg (Law Degree, 1988; Doctor of Laws, 1994). With, Federal Cartel Office (Bundeskartellamt), Berlin, 1990-1991; German-American Chamber of Commerce,

(This Listing Continued)

Chicago, 1992; Fehmel & Associates, Los Angeles, 1992. *Member:* Hamburg Bar Association; German Association for the Protection of Industrial Property; German-American Lawyers Association.

Languages: German, English and French

HEUKING KÜHN KUNZ WOJTEK

BLEICHENBRÜCKE 9
D-20354 HAMBURG, GERMANY
Telephone: 49 40 355 280 0
Telefax: 49 40355 280 80

Other Offices: Düsseldorf, Frankfurt, Berlin, Chemnitz (Germany); Paris (France).

Corporate, Banking, Tax, National and EC Antitrust, Mergers, Acquisitions, Intellectual Property, Unfair Competition and Trade Law, Commercial and International Law, EC Law, Maritime Law, Legislative Drafting Advice, Environmental Law, Administrative Law, Telecommunications and Media Law, Insurance Law, Product Liability, International Arbitration, Litigation, General Practice.

FIRM PROFILE: All Attorneys are Members of Denton International and of the Hamburg Bar Association. All Attorneys speak English and German, other languages include French and Italian.

MEMBERS OF FIRM

DR. RALF J. WOJTEK, born Bredstedt, Germany, May 29, 1945; admitted, 1974, Germany. *Education:* Universities of Freiburg and Hamburg (1964-1968); University of California at Berkeley (LL.M., 1970); University of Hamburg (Dr. jur., 1977). Author: "Insider Trading Under German and American Law," Berlin, 1978. Lecturer, University of Hamburg, 1971. Assistant, Max-Planck-Institute for Foreign and Private International Law, Hamburg, 1972-1974, Corporate Counsel and General Counsel, 1974-1980. Co-author: "Business Transactions in Germany (FRG)," 1983, Chapter, Government Incentives and Permit Requirements for Industrial Development. Co-author: "Münchener Vertragshandbuch," Vo. 2, Commercial and Business Law, Chapter on Energy Contracts, Munich 1982; "Transportmärkte, Kurier-, Express- und Paketdienste," Spiegel-Verlagsreihe Märkte im Wandel, Bd. 13, Hamburg, 1987. Member: German Environmental Law Association, Member of Consulting Board of European Business Law Journal (EWS). Chairman, German Express Catner Association (BIE K). **PRACTICE AREAS:** Environmental; Telecommunications and Media Law; Corporate Law.

DR. ULRICH H. WITTKOPP, born Hamburg, Germany, February 26, 1950; admitted, 1977, Germany. *Education:* Universities of Hamburg (Dr. jur., 1977) and Geneva (Assistant, 1974-1975); Institut Universitaire d'Etudes Européennes Geneva. Author: "EEC Liberty of Establishment and Sovereignty Clause," 1977; "Haftungsausschlüsse in Werftbedingungen," Versicherungsrecht 1987, 242-247. *Member:* International Bar Association; German Association for International Maritime Law. **PRACTICE AREAS:** Corporate; Insurance; Maritime Law; Arbitration; Mergers & Acquisitions.

DR. FRANK MITZKUS, born Hamburg, Germany, June 30, 1950; admitted, 1978, Germany. *Education:* University of Hamburg (1970-1974); University of Bayreuth (Dr. jur., 1982). Author: "Wohnraummodernisierung und Mieterhöhung," NJW 1981, 199 et seq.; "Zur Reichweite wohnraummietrechtlicher Schutzbestimmungen," ZMR 1982, 197 et seq.; "Internationale Zuständigkeit im Vormundschafts-, Pflegschafts- und Sorgerecht," Frankfurt, 1982. Lecturer, University of Bayreuth, 1980-1982. Corporate Counsel, 1982-1983. *Member:* Deutscher Juristentag. German Association for the Protection of Industrial Property and Copyright Law. **PRACTICE AREAS:** Litigation; Unfair Competition; Trade Law; Entertainment; Arbitration.

KAY JACOBSEN, born Hamburg, Germany, March 29, 1957; admitted, 1987, Germany; certified counsel for labour law. *Education:* University of Hamburg. *Member:* Deutscher Juristentag; Hamburg Bar Association. **PRACTICE AREAS:** Labour Law; Real Estate; Corporate and Commercial Law.

ASSOCIATES

MARINA TODTENHAUPT, born LesLau, July 7, 1944; admitted, 1974, Germany. *Education:* Universities of Berlin and Hamburg (Dr. jur. 1978). Research Associate Max-Planck-Institue for Foreign and Private International Law, Hamburg 1974; Collaborator preparing French Reservation of title act, 1976. Author: "Les factures protestables," 1978; Les habi-

(This Listing Continued)

tudes de paiement de la clientèle allemade, Revue Chamber of Commerce Reims, 1978; "Unterhaltsrecht in Frankreich," in: Unterhaltsrecht in Europa 1983, Hamburg; Rapport sur ll'obligation alimentaire en droit privéinternational allemaid pour le Service de Recherches Juridiques Comparatives du CNRS, Ivry, 1984. Co-Author: "La Responsabil ité du fabricant," in Vente en Allemagne, Paris, 1978. **PRACTICE AREAS:** Conflict of Laws; International Trade; International Divorce and Domestic Relations; Litigation.

DR. ANDREA M. PARTIKEL, born Hamburg, Germany, January 22, 1962; admitted, 1988, Germany. *Education:* University of Hamburg (1981-1988), German-French Chamber of Commerce, Paris (1988). Author: "Gesellschafter minderen Rechts im Recht der Personenhandelsgesellschaften," Hamburg, 1992. **PRACTICE AREAS:** Transportation; Computer Law; Contracts; Construction Law.

DR. CHRISTOPH FRONING, born Hannover, June 1, 1958; admitted, 1987, Germany. *Education:* University of Hamburg (1979-1984; Dr. jur., 1988-1990); University of Miami, Florida (LL.M., 1990). Author: "Gewinnverwendungsprobleme in der GmbH." Associate in intern Law Firm, Boden, Oppenhoff Rasor Raue, Cologne, 1990-1993. *Member:* German-American Lawyers Association. **PRACTICE AREAS:** Corporate and Commercial Law; Mergers and Acquisitions.

LUTZ GARBERS, born Lüneburg, Germany, February 24, 1963; admitted, 1993, Germany. *Education:* Free University of Berlin (1985-1990), Treuhandanstalt (1991-1992). Legal Department German Trade Office, Taipei, 1992-1993. *Member:* Hamburg Bar Association. *LANGUAGES:* German and English. **PRACTICE AREAS:** Commercial and Civil Law; Transportation and Media Law.

DR. MATHIAS J. MÜNCHAU, born Hamburg, Germany, May 22, 1961; admitted, 1994, Germany. *Education:* Universities of Kiel/Germany and Paris V/France (1983-1989). Research Assistant: Institute of Public International Law, Kiel (1989-1990). Author: "Terrorismus auf See aus Völkerrechtlicher Sicht," Kiel, 1993; "Ost-West-Beziehungen," Handbunch Vereinte Natioen, R. Wolfram ed, Munich, 1992. **PRACTICE AREAS:** Administrative; Environmental Law; EEC Law; Transport Law.

CHRISTIAN GUMMIG, born Hilden, Germany, May 27, 1964; admitted, 1994, Germany. *Education:* Universities of Passau and Munich (1984-1989). Research Assistant: Institute for Trade and Labour Law, Munich, 1986-1989. Editorial Assistant of ZUM, Journal for Copyright and Media Law, Munich, 1990-1993; Foreign Associate, New York Law Firm, 1993. **PRACTICE AREAS:** Copyright; Entertainment; Media Law; Unfair Competition; Litigation.

HOYER, WITTHUHN, WIECHMANN, CLAUSSEN, NAGEL, PÜTTER

EPPENDORFER LANDSTRASSE 61
20249 HAMBURG, GERMANY
Telephone: 040-4604026; 475051
Telefax: 040-474655

Mailing Address: P.O. Box 202555, 20218

General Practice, Commercial, Company, Contract, Joint Ventures, Mergers and Acquisitions, Tax, International Trade, Partnership, Competition, Trade Mark, Copyright, Licensing, Real Estate, Transport, Insurance, Product Liability, Constitutional, Administration, Environmental, Labor, Divorce, Inheritance, International Law and Arbitration.

MEMBERS OF FIRM

ASKO A. WITTHUHN, born Berlin, Germany, December 5, 1941; admitted, 1971, Hamburg, Germany. *Education:* Universities of Berlin, Marburg and Göttingen. Assistant, Institute for Corporate and Labour Law, Free University, Berlin, 1965-1968; Public Prosecutor, 1969-1971. Specialist for Tax Law ("Fachanwalt fur Steurrecht"). *Member:* Hamburg (Board Member, 1988—) and German Bar Associations; Hamburg and German Law Society; German-Scandinavic Jurist's Association; Committee of Lawyer's Examination. *LANGUAGES:* German, English and Finnish.

ANDREAS WIECHMANN, born Hamburg, Germany, October 9, 1952; admitted, 1983, Hamburg, Germany. *Education:* University of Hamburg. Specialist for Labor Law ("Fachanwalt fur Arbeitsrecht"). *Member:* Hamburg and German Bar Associations; Hamburg and German Law Society; Association of Self-Employed Entrepreneurs (ASU). *LANGUAGES:* German and English.

CHRISTIAN WOLFGANG CLAUSSEN, born Hamburg, Germany, October 23, 1951; admitted, 1984, Hamburg, Germany. *Education:* Univer-

(This Listing Continued)

sity of Hamburg. *Member:* Hamburg and German Bar Associations; Hamburg and German Law Society; German Society for Environmental Law. *LANGUAGES:* German and English.

DR. KLAUS ANDREAS NAGEL, born Hamburg, Germany, October 3, 1952; admitted, 1985, Hamburg, Germany. *Education:* University of Hamburg. Assistant, Institute for International Affairs, University of Hamburg, 1981-1984. (On Leave, United Nations, New York, Office of the Legal Counsel, 1983). Lecturer, University of Hamburg, 1982-1989. Author: "Werbeverbote," Baden-Baden, 1992. *Member:* Hamburg and German Bar Associations; Hamburg and German Law Society; Hamburg Society for International Law. *LANGUAGES:* German and English.

TAX CONSULTANT

BERND PÜTTER, born Hamburg, Germany, May 26, 1957. *Education:* University of Hamburg. Tax Consultant, 1987. *Member:* Hamburg and German Tax Consultants Associations; Hamburg and German Tax Consultants Society. *LANGUAGES:* German and English.

ASSOCIATES

DR. CARL ALBRECHT CLAUSSEN, born Hamburg, Germany, August 17, 1955; admitted, 1987, Hamburg, Germany. *Education:* Universities of Freiburg and Munich. *Member:* Hamburg and German Bar Associations. *LANGUAGES:* German and English.

JÜRGEN THIES, born Hamburg, Germany, December 20, 1952; admitted, 1987, Hamburg, Germany. *Education:* University of Hamburg. *Member:* Hamburg and German Bar Associations. *LANGUAGES:* German and English.

OF COUNSEL

DR. RUDOLF HOYER, born Hamburg, Germany, June 14, 1920; admitted, 1950, Hamburg, Germany. *Education:* Universities of Freiburg and Hamburg. *Member:* Hamburg and German Bar Associations; Hamburg and German Law Society. *LANGUAGES:* German, English and French.

HUTH DIETRICH HAHN

WARBURGSTRASSE 50
20354 HAMBURG, GERMANY
Telephone: (49-40) 41 52 50
Fax: (49-40) 41 52 51 11

Mergers and Acquisitions, Corporate Law, Real Estate Transactions, International Transactions, Tax Law, Anti-trust Law, Trust and Estate Planning, EC Law, Labour Law.

DR. KLAUS D. HUTH, born Hamburg, Germany, April 22, 1935; admitted, 1966. *Education:* Universities of Hamburg (Dr. jur., 1965), Munich, Oxford, Paris and Barcelona. Author: "The Position of Public Enterprise in the Common Market"; "Auffassungswandel beim Firmenzusatz 'deutsch'?" GRUR 1965, 290; "Öffentliche Wirtschaft und EWG-Vertrag," AWD 1965, 121; "Die Rechtspflichten der öffentlichen Unternehmen und Betriebe im Gemeinsamen Markt," DÖW 1965, 166. Co-Author: "Das Gesonderte Kanadische Vermächtnis-Testament von Deutschen mit Vermögen in Kanada," Zeitschrift fur Vergleichende Rechtswissenschaft 1987, 338-358. *Member:* German Association of Comparative Law; International Bar Association. *LANGUAGES:* German, English, French and Spanish. **PRACTICE AREAS:** Trust and Estate Planning; Corporate Law.

DR. HARTMUT DIETRICH, born Breslau, Germany, December 29, 1943; admitted, 1975, Germany. *Education:* Universities of Tuebingen, Berlin, Goettingen; University of California, School of Law at Berkeley (LL.M., 1971); University of Hamburg (Dr. jur., 1974). Author: "The Tender Offer in the Federal Law of the U.S.A.," 1975; "International Arbitration Clauses Before American Courts," Rabels Zeitschrift, 1976, 1 et seq. Co-Author: "Legal Politics and Comparative Law," Jogtudomanyi Koezloeny Budapest, 1977, 270 et seq.; "The Federal Constitutional Court—Institution with a Future?," 1979; "Business Transactions in Germany (FRG)," 1983, Chapters, Co-Determination and Conflict of Law. Associate, Max-Planck-Institute for Foreign and Private International Law, Hamburg, 1975-1979. Lecturer: University of California, School of Law, Berkeley, 1977-1978; University of Hamburg, 1978-1979. *Member:* Hamburg and International Bar Associations; German Association of Comparative Law; German-American Lawyers Association. *LANGUAGES:* German, English and French. **PRACTICE AREAS:** Mergers and Acquisitions; Corporate Law; Real Estate Transactions.

DR. KARL FRHR. VON HAHN, born Oldenburg, Germany, June 2, 1945; admitted, 1972, Hamburg, Germany. *Education:* Universities of Hei-

(This Listing Continued)

HUTH DIETRICH HAHN, Hamburg—Continued

delberg, Hamburg (Dr. jur., 1970), Paris and London; INSEAD Fontainebleau (Master of Business Administration, 1974). Co-Author: "Financial Times Handbook of European Employment Law," 1992, Chapter Federal Republic of Germany. *LANGUAGES:* German, English and French. *PRACTICE AREAS:* Corporate Law; Commercial Law; Mergers and Acquisition; Tax Law.

DR. WOLFGANG VON REINERSDORFF, born Kiel, Germany, October 6, 1954; admitted, 1984, Germany. *Education:* Universities of Munich, Geneva (Switzerland) and Bonn (Dr. jur., 1983); Trinity College, Cambridge, England (LL.B., 1981). Author: "Die Bestimmung der Anspruchsberechtigten bei der Leistungskondiktion," MDR 1981, 800 ff.; "Einwendungserhalt und Einwendungsdurchgriff im Dreipersonenverhältnis," NJW 1984, 961 f.; "Die Tätigkeit Deutscher Banken in den USA," RIW/AWD 1987, 909 ff.; "Der Preis des Übergabepunktes bei der Breitbandverkabelung," BB 1990, 936 ff.; "Die Gestaltung von Gesellschaftsverträgen," 1993. *LANGUAGES:* German, English and French. *PRACTICE AREAS:* Corporate Law; Media Law.

DR. MARTIN K. WOLFF, born Mettlach, Germany, November 1, 1952; admitted, 1983, Germany. *Education:* Universities of Hamburg (Dr. jur., 1985), Tuebingen, Geneva and Freiburg; University of Michigan, Ann Arbor (LL.M., 1982). *LANGUAGES:* German and English. *PRACTICE AREAS:* Corporate Law; Mergers and Acquisitions; Anti-trust Law; EC Law.

DR. GERNOT STENGER, born Ewersbach, Germany, March 29, 1957; admitted, 1988, Germany. *Education:* University of Wisconsin Law School (LL.M., 1987); University of Giessen (Dr. jur., 1988). Phi Alpha Delta. Author: "The Development of American Export Control Legislation after World War II," 6 Wisconsin International Law Journal 1, 1987; "Das Handelsembargo im Aussenwirtschaftsrecht - Praxis und Zulässigkeit," 1988. *Member:* German-American Lawyers Association; German-Taiwanese Lawyers Association. *LANGUAGES:* German, English and French. *PRACTICE AREAS:* Mergers and Acquisitions; Corporate Law; Joint Ventures; EC Law.

DR. GEORG A. WITTUHN, born Hamburg, Germany, August 26, 1958; admitted, 1987, Germany. *Education:* Universities of Hamburg, Geneva, Cambridge (England), Madison (Wisconsin), McGill (LL.M., 1988), Montreal (Dr. jur., Hamburg, 1987). Author: "Conflict of Laws of Trusts," Frankfurt/Bern/New York/Paris, 1987; "Pre-trial Discovery in Canada," Frankfurt/Bern/New York/Paris, 1989; "Pre-trial Discovery in Kanada," RIW 424, 1989, p. 424 et seq.; "Kleinwort Benson Ltd. v. Malaysia Mining Corporation Bhd - A Comparative Note on Comfort Letters," 35 (1990) McGill Law J. p. 488 et seq.; "Patronatserklärungen im Anglo-Amerikanischen Rechtskreis," RIW 1990, p. 495 et. seq.; "Liability of Corporate Directors," Chapter Germany, London, 1993. Co-Author: "Are Hostile Take-Overs Possible in The Federal Republic of Germany," 12 (1990) Comparative Law Yearbook of International Business, p. 227 et seq. *LANGUAGES:* German, English, French and Spanish. *PRACTICE AREAS:* Corporate Law; Commercial Law; Mergers and Acquisitions; Private International Law; Trusts and Estates; Banking Law.

DR. WOLFGANG ROETTGER, born Hamburg, Germany, January 27, 1958; admitted, 1990, Germany. *Education:* Certified apprentice (Tax Consultant and Chartered Accountant), 1976-1978; Universities of Freiburg and Hamburg (1976-1981; Dr. jur., Hamburg, 1991). Associate, Max-Planck-Institute for Foreign and Private International Law, Hamburg, 1982-1983. Lecturer, University of Hamburg, 1982-1985. In-House Counsel, Munich and Hannover, 1988-1989. *Member:* Hamburg Bar Association. *LANGUAGES:* German and English. *PRACTICE AREAS:* Corporate Law; Mergers and Acquisition; Software Law; Tax Law.

DR. RALF STUCKEN, born Hamburg, Germany, June 5, 1961; admitted, 1991, Germany. *Education:* University of Hamburg (Dr. jur., 1990). Author: "Einseitige Rechtskraftwirkung von Urteilen im deutschen Zivilprozeß" (1990). Co-Author: " Die Gestaltung von Gesellschaftsverträgen" (1993). *LANGUAGES:* German and English. *PRACTICE AREAS:* Corporate Law; Commercial Law; Litigation; Real Estate.

DR. JOHANNES JUSTUS BRINKSCHMIDT, born Bielefeld, Germany, April 9, 1959; admitted, 1988, Germany. *Education:* Universities of Tuebingen, Hamburg and Kiel (Dr. jur., 1992). *LANGUAGES:* German and English. *PRACTICE AREAS:* Corporate Law; Commercial Law; Environmental Law.

DIRK MICHELS, born Wuppertal, Germany, March 10, 1962; admitted, 1992, Germany. *Education:* University of Hamburg; University of Wis-

(This Listing Continued)

consin Law School. *Member:* Hamburg Bar Association; German-American Lawyers Association. *LANGUAGES:* German, English and French. *PRACTICE AREAS:* Labor Law; Litigation; Corporate Law; Commercial Law.

DR. ANNA HEIDELBACH, born Kassel, Germany, January 5, 1964; admitted, 1991, Germany. *Education:* Universities of Hamburg, Freiburg and London (LSE) (Dr. jur., 1993). *LANGUAGES:* German, English and French. *PRACTICE AREAS:* Probate Law; Corporate Law; Commercial Law.

FRANK SEIFERT, born Hamburg, Germany, January 28, 1943; admitted, 1972, Germany. *Education:* Universities of Lausanne, Geneva and Hamburg. Author: "Rahmenbedingungen für Gemeinschaftsunternehmen in Bulgarien" (DER BETRIEB, Köln 1992, 463). *Member:* Hamburg Bar Association; German Bulgarian Jurists' Association (Vice President). *LANGUAGES:* German and English. *PRACTICE AREAS:* Commercial and Corporate Law; Mergers and Acquisitions; Real Estate; East-European Corporate Law especially Hungarian and Bulgarian Law.

KANZLEI KAI KÄHLER

Established in 1975

THIELBEK 6
20355 HAMBURG, GERMANY
Telephone: +49-40-344 344
Telecopier: +49-40-345 345

International Mergers and Acquisition, International Trade, Energy Law, Futures and Commodities, Banking and Financing, Maritime, Aviation, Commercial, Contracts.

FIRM PROFILE: *The firm offers special legal services in international commercial transactions and is particularly active in national and international trade and acquisition.*

KAI KÄHLER, born Hamburg, Germany, May 19, 1946; admitted, 1975, Germany. *Education:* Universities of Hamburg and Göttingen. Co-author: "Effektivzinsangabe in der Werbung fur Realkredite," GRUR 1983, 357. *Member:* German Bar Association. *LANGUAGES:* German and English. *PRACTICE AREAS:* Oil and Energy; Futures.

KRETSCHMAR, VON TEUFFEL, LEVERKUS

Established in 1986

KLEINE JOHANNISSTRASSE 2-4
RATHAUSMARKTHOF
20457 HAMBURG, GERMANY
Telephone: 040/36 23 53
International: 0049/40/36 23 53
Telecopy/Telefax: 040/36 72 93
International: 0049/40/36 72 93
Telex: 2 166 20l ek d
Cable Address: "hansa lawyers"

General and International Practice. Arbitration, Commercial, Corporation, Antitrust, Unfair Competition, Maritime, Transport, Real Estate, Insurance, Product Liability, Administrative Law.

FIRM PROFILE: *The firm was established in 1986. Its senior partner was formerly partner of a big Hamburg law firm. The firm offers a full range of legal services, particular in National and International Business Law including Company, Maritime and Product Liability Law.*

MEMBERS OF FIRM

DR. EKKEHARD KRETSCHMAR, born Breslau, Germany, September 14, 1927; admitted, 1960, Germany. *Education:* Universities of Göttingen, Karlsruhe, Cambridge (Diploma in Comparative Legal Studies, 1957) and Hamburg (Dr. jur., 1961). Author: "The English Administration and the Rule of Law." Co-Author: "Länderbericht Produkthaftungsrecht der Vereinigten Staaten von Amerika in Produkthaftungshandbuch," C.H. Beck'sche Verlagsbuchhandlung, München, 1991. *Member:* German and International Bar Associations; German-British Jurists' Association; German Institution for Arbitration. *PRACTICE AREAS:* International Business Law; Corporation; Product Liability; Arbitration.

DR. NIKOLAI FRHR. VON TEUFFEL, born Düsseldorf, Germany, May 25, 1954; admitted, 1982, Germany. *Education:* Universities of Würzburg, Freiburg, Geneva, Munich (Dr. jur., 1985). Author: "The Effectiveness of Buying out Clauses in General and Limited Partnership Agree-

(This Listing Continued)

ments," published by Messrs. L ° B Verlagsdruck, Hamburg, 1985. *Member:* German Bar Association; German Society for Industrial Property and Copyright Law (GRUR). *PRACTICE AREAS:* Commercial; Maritime; Transport; Unfair Competition Law; Corporate Law.

JOACHIM LEVERKUS, born Stuttgart, Germany, August 31, 1956; admitted, 1987, Germany. *Education:* Universities of Bonn and Münster. *Member:* German Bar Association; German-French Jurists Association. *PRACTICE AREAS:* Commercial; Real Estate; Administrative Law.

Languages: German, English and French.

KREYE & KREYE

COLONNADEN 104
20354 HAMBURG, GERMANY
Telephone: (40) 3 58 99 14; 3 58 99 15
Telefax: (40) 3 58 99 17

General Practice, Antitrust, Trademarks, Unfair Competition, Patent, Copyright, Ornamental Plant Protection, Corporation, Commercial Law, Insurance.

MEMBERS OF FIRM

DR. PETER KREYE, born Hamburg, Germany, September 12, 1936; admitted, 1965, Germany. *Education:* Universities of Hamburg (Dr.jur., 1967); Freiburg. *Member:* German and International Bar Associations; GRUR; USTA; AIPPI; Institute of Trademark Agents; German American Lawyers Association; Bund für Lebensmittelrecht und Lebensmittelkunde e.V. *LANGUAGES:* German and English.

NIELS KREYE, born Hamburg, Germany, May 18, 1942; admitted, 1970, Germany. *Education:* Universities of Hamburg and Freiburg. *Member:* German and International Bar Associations; GRUR; AIPPI. *LANGUAGES:* German and English.

LEBUHN & PUCHTA

VORSETZEN 35
D-20459 HAMBURG, GERMANY
Telephone: 40-3747780
Telefax: 40-364650; 40-37 29 48

Rostock, Germany Office: Thomas-Mann-Strasse 25, D-18055. Telephone: 0381 45 40 09. Telefax: 0381 45 54 68.

Arbitration, Business Law, Commercial Law, Corporate Law, Insurance Coverage, International Trade, Labour, Litigation, Mergers and Acquisitions, Mortgages, Directors and Officers Liability, Real Estate Investment, Transportation.

FIRM PROFILE: The basic philosophy of the firm is to offer highly specialized but still personal legal services of outstanding quality to corporate clients. The firm's main areas with particular experience include International Trade Law, Maritime and Transport, Mergers and Acquisitions, Company Law, Real Estate, Banking Law, Labour Law, Arbitration and Litigation. The firm is engaged in Eastern Germany.

MEMBERS OF FIRM

PROFESSOR DR. JUERGEN LEBUHN, born Hamburg, Germany, May 22, 1922; admitted, 1950, Hamburg. *Education:* University of Königsberg (PR) and Hamburg (Dr. jur. utriusque, 1948); School of Law, London, England. Author: "Modern Bill of Lading-Questions," 1949; "The Liner Bill of Lading," 1958; "FOB and FOB-Customs," 1968, 3. Ed., 1971; "L'Assistence en Mer," Paris, 1962; "Container Problems under German Law," 1968. Honorary Professor on Marine Contract Law, University of Aachen. President, Hamburg Harbour-Association. *LANGUAGES:* German, English and French.

DR. KARL FERDINAND PUCHTA, born Hamburg, Germany, December 15, 1934; admitted, 1963, Hamburg. *Education:* Universities of Freiburg and Hamburg (Dr. jur. utriusque, 1967). Author: "The Gencon-Charter," 1968. *Member:* Association of Insurance Research; German International Maritime Law Association; International Bar Association; German Maritime Arbitration Association (Arbitrator). *LANGUAGES:* German, English and French. *PRACTICE AREAS:* Maritime Law; Commercial Law; Insurance Law; Arbitration; Litigation.

DR. CHRISTIAN BREITZKE, born Berlin, Germany, June 13, 1943; admitted, 1973, Hamburg. *Education:* University of Hamburg (Dr. jur., 1971). Author: "The Norwegian Saleform," 1970. Managing Director of German Duty Free Association (Deutscher Duty Free Verband e.V.) and of

(This Listing Continued)

Hamburg Free Port Association (Freihafenverband Hamburg e.V.). *Member:* German International Maritime Law Association; International Bar Association; German Maritime Arbitration Association (Arbitrator). *LANGUAGES:* German, English and French. *PRACTICE AREAS:* Maritime Law; Commercial Law; Transport Law; Real Estate; Labour Law.

DR. HEINRICH-WERNER GOLTZ, born Hamburg, Germany, February 16, 1952; admitted, 1981, Hamburg. *Education:* Universities of Mannheim, Heidelberg and Freiburg (Dr.oec., 1979); King's College, London, (1981). Author: "Legal Aspects of Rollover-Euro-Credits," 1979. Chairman of the Supervisory Board, VEMAG Maschinenbau GmbH and Begarat Anlagenbau GmbH. *Member:* International Bar Association. *LANGUAGES:* German, English and French. *PRACTICE AREAS:* Mergers and Acquisitions; Company Law; Business Law; Real Estate Investments; Directors and Officers Liability.

DR. ULRICH H. STAHL, born Neustadt, Germany, April 8, 1955; admitted, 1987, Hamburg. *Education:* Universities of Munich, Göttingen, London, Cambridge, U.K. (LL.B., 1981; Dr.jur. Hamburg, 1987). Author: "Timecharters under English Law". *Member:* Association Internationale des Jeunes Advocats; German Maritime Arbitration Association (Arbitrator); London Maritime Arbitration Association; German International Maritime Law Association. *LANGUAGES:* German, English and Spanish. *PRACTICE AREAS:* Maritime Law; Transport Law; Commercial; Litigation; Arbitration.

ASSOCIATES

VOLKER BEECKEN, born Hamburg, Germany, May 30, 1959; admitted, 1990, Hamburg; 1992, Rostock. (Resident, Rostock Office). *LANGUAGES:* German, English and Spanish. *PRACTICE AREAS:* Labour Law; Legal Problems related to East Germany.

DR. SABINE RITTMEISTER, born Hamburg, Germany, April 7, 1963; admitted, 1992, Hamburg. *LANGUAGES:* German, English and French. *PRACTICE AREAS:* Maritime Law; Transport Law.

DR. CLAUDIUS MANN, born Freiburg, Germany, May 16, 1964; admitted, 1992, Hamburg. *LANGUAGES:* German and English. *PRACTICE AREAS:* Commercial Law; Company Law; Business Law; Labour Law.

PETER KIPPHOFF, born Hamburg, Germany, October 27, 1959; admitted, 1991, Hamburg. *Education:* King's College, London (LL.M., 1992). *LANGUAGES:* German and English. *PRACTICE AREAS:* International Trade Law; Commercial Law.

DR. MICHAEL JANI, born Hamburg, Germany, July 11, 1964; admitted, 1995, Hamburg. *LANGUAGES:* German, English and French. *PRACTICE AREAS:* Public Law; Commercial Law.

IMKE WULFMEYER, born Celle, Germany, June 5, 1965; admitted, 1995, Hamburg. *LANGUAGES:* German, English and Dutch. *PRACTICE AREAS:* Transport Law; Commercial Law.

KLAUS RAMMING, born San Francisco, California, USA, September 28, 1959; admitted, 1983, Master Mariner; 1995, Hamburg. *LANGUAGES:* German, English and Norwegian. *PRACTICE AREAS:* Maritime Law; Commercial Law.

All Members of the Firm are Members of the Hamburg Bar Association.

DR. GERHARD LÜDERS

Established in 1967

KLEINE JOHANNISSTRASSE 6
20457 HAMBURG, GERMANY
Telephone: 49-40-36 66 36
Telefax: 49-40-36 63 89

Trusts and (international) Estates, Company, Business and Commercial Law, Contracts, Labor and Employment, Restitution Claims, General Practice.

DR. GERHARD LÜDERS, born Hamburg, Germany, March 10, 1934; admitted, 1967, Germany. *Education:* Universities of Bonn and Heidelberg (Economics and Law); University of Hamburg (Dr. jur., 1967). Corporate Counsel, 1967-1970. Lecturer in Law, Akademie Nord, Hamburg, 1973-1974. Member, Advisory Board of German Lawyers Insurance Corp., 1979—. Vice President, National Association of German Economists, 1980—. Regional Representative of European Consultants Unit (ECU),

(This Listing Continued)

DR. GERHARD LÜDERS, Hamburg—Continued

1992—. *Member:* Hamburg and German Bar Associations; German-American Lawyers Association; German-British Jurists Association. *LANGUAGES:* German and English.

LUTHER & PARTNER
HERMANNSTRASSE 46
D-20095 HAMBURG, GERMANY
Telephone: (040) 32 81 180
Cable Address: "Kapitel"
Telefax: (040) 32 73 57

Berlin, Germany Office: Hardenbergstrasse 12, D-10623 Berlin.
Telephone: (030) 315 956-0. Telefax: (030) 21 82 612.

German, EEC and International Practice: Corporate, Commercial, Mergers and Acquisitions, Joint Ventures, Banking and Financing, Foreign Investment, Securities and Capital Markets, Leasing, Antitrust, Unfair Competition, Anti-Dumping, Intellectual Property (Trademark, Patent and Copyright), Tax, Real Estate, Energy and Natural Resources, Environmental and Administrative Law, Computer and Software Law, Food and Drug, Labour, Product Liability, Insurance, Estate Planning, Probate, Transportation, Maritime, Entertainment, Litigation and Arbitration.

FIRM PROFILE: Luther & Partner is a steadily growing law firm with offices in Hamburg and Berlin. The origin of the firm goes back into the 1930's. Various lawyers of the firm, in addition to their legal training, have worked as research associates at renowned universities and have received legal training in the United States, other European countries and/or with the EEC-Commission in Brussels. Several lawyers of the firm have published books and articles on topics relating to their fields of expertise. All partners are members of specialized professional associations.

The firm's lawyers have broad experience in domestic and international business law including EEC law with a special emphasis on corporate and corporate-related matters. The firm handles corporate issues and, through various specialized departments, all business related areas of law.

In its major fields of practise, the firm represents and renders its services to well-known German and international companies.

MEMBERS OF FIRM

MARTIN LUTHER (1906-1985).

DR. ERHARD JAHN, born Leipzig, Germany, September 3, 1930; admitted, 1959, Germany. *Education:* Universities of Munich, Göttingen and Hamburg (Dr. jur., 1958). Presiding Judge, Hamburg Court of Legal Ethics, 1976. Author: Die Haftung der Gesellschafter einer offenen Handelsgesellschaft, 1957, (on liability of partners in a partnership). *Member:* Hamburg Bar Association; Hamburg Lawyers Association; Association Européenne d'Etudes Juridiques et Fiscales. *LANGUAGES:* German, English and Swedish.

WERNER HOFER, born Frankfurt, Germany, June 13, 1935; admitted, 1964, Germany. *Education:* Universities of Hamburg and Göttingen. *Member:* Hamburg Bar Association; Hamburg Lawyers Association; International Fiscal Association; League for Food Law and Science. *LANGUAGES:* German and English.

DR. JOHANN TILING, born Berlin, Germany, November 11, 1936; admitted, 1967, Germany. *Education:* Universities of Freiburg, Grenoble, Hamburg (Dr. jur. 1965), Paris (France) Referendar 1967. Author: Numerous articles including Vertragsgestaltung im Industrieanlagenexport, RIW 1986, 91-93, (on export of industrial plants); Software-Güteprüfung und Rechtsproblematik, CR 1987, 80-85, (on software quality control). Lecturer, Corporate Law, University of Hamburg, 1966-1969. *Member:* Hamburg and International Bar Associations; Hamburg Lawyers Association; The Law Society London. *LANGUAGES:* German, English and French.

DR. WILHELM HAPP, born Cologne, Germany, April 30, 1936; admitted, 1966, Germany. *Education:* University of Cologne (Dr. jur., 1966). Author and Co-Author: Numerous Books and Articles including Formular-Kommentar Aktienrecht (22nd ed.) 1988, (on stock corporation law); Münchener Handbuch des Gesellschaftsrechts, vol. 2, (on corporate law). *Member:* Hamburg Bar Association; Society of Hamburg Jurists; Deutscher Juristentag. *LANGUAGES:* German, English, French and Spanish.

HUBERTUS FREIHERR VON DER RECKE, born Berlin, Germany, July 9, 1942; admitted, 1977, Germany. *Education:* Universities of

(This Listing Continued)

Göttingen, Munich. Chartered Accountant, Hamburg, 1977. Tax Advisor, Hamburg, 1975. *LANGUAGES:* German and English.

DR. ULRICH THEUNE, born Helmstedt, Germany, September 1, 1942; admitted, 1975, Germany. *Education:* Universities of Bordeaux, Strasbourg and Hamburg (Dr. jur., 1977). Author: Die Beurteilung ausschliesslicher Patentlizenzverträge nach Art. 85 EWG-Vertrag, 1977, (on patent license agreements), also published in GRUR Int. 1977, 63-71 and 111-121. Lecturer, Corporate Law, University of Hamburg, School of Law, 1981. *Member:* Hamburg Bar Association; German and International Associations for Industrial Property and Copyright. *LANGUAGES:* German, English, French and Spanish.

DR. MARTIN LUTHER, born Tondern, Denmark, September 3, 1945; admitted, 1976, Germany. *Education:* Universities of Tübingen, Kiel and Münster (Dr. jur., 1978). Author: Die genossenschaftliche Aktiengesellschaft, 1978, (on corporate law). *Member:* Hamburg Bar Association; German and International Associations for Industrial Property and Copyright. *LANGUAGES:* German and English.

DR. KLAUS VON GIERKE, born Heidelberg, Germany, October 2, 1954; admitted, 1982, New York; 1984, Germany. *Education:* Universities of Freiburg (Dr.jur., 1983) and Geneva; Tulane University of Louisiana, School of Law, New Orleans (LL.M., 1980). Author: Die Dritthaftung des Rechtsanwalts, 1984, (on lawyer's Liability). *Member:* German-American Lawyers' Association. *LANGUAGES:* German, English and French.

AXEL LOEHDE, born Weilheim, Germany, April, 4, 1951; admitted, 1982, Germany. *Education:* University of Hamburg. Author: Recht für Werbetexter, 1988, (on advertising law). *Member:* Hamburg Bar Association; International Association for the Protection of Industrial Property; German Association for Industrial Property and Copyright Law. *LANGUAGES:* German and English.

VOLKER VON ALVENSLEBEN, born Aurich, November 6, 1955; admitted, 1984, Germany. *Education:* Universities of Kiel and Freiburg; Paris (France). Author: Europäische wirtschaftliche Interessenvereinigung (EWIV) (on European Economic Interest Groupings), Hamburger Unternehmer 1990 I, 16; Eigentumsformen in der DDR (on East German property law), Hamburger Unternehmer 1990 II, 18; Vorstellung der Verordnung über die Vermeidung vonVerpackungsabfällen (Verpackungsverordnung; on waste law), Hamburger Unternehmer 1991 III, 9. *Member:* German Society for the Protection of Industrial Property and Copyright Law; Association of Young Entrepreneur (BJU). *LANGUAGES:* German, French and English.

DR. DIRK KLEVEMAN, born Bederkesa, Germany, January 22, 1958; admitted, 1990, Germany. *Education:* Universities of Göttingen, Lausanne (Switzerland) and Freiburg (Dr. jur., 1989). Author: Gesetzliche Sicherungsrechte im Internationalen Privat-und Konkursrecht, 1990. *Member:* Hamburg Bar Association. *LANGUAGES:* German, English and French.

ASSOCIATES

PHILIP DOHSE, born Lübeck, Germany, April 17, 1961; admitted, 1992, Germany. *Education:* Universities of Munich, Hamburg and Bonn. *Member:* Hamburg Bar Association. *LANGUAGES:* German and English.

DR. ECKART J. BROEDERMANN, born Hamburg, Germany, July 13, 1958; admitted, 1984, New York; 1991, Germany. *Education:* University of Paris (France) (Licence en droit, 1980; Lauréat du Concours Général, 1980; Maîtrise en droit, 1981); Harvard Law School (LL.M., 1983); University of Hamburg (Dr. jur., 1994). Author: Numerous articles including Enforcement of American Arbitral Awards in Germany, International Litigation Quarterly (ILQ) 1, 219-239, 1985; Europäisches Gemeinschaftsrecht versus IPR: Einflüsse und Konformitätsgebot, MDR 1992, 89-95. Co-Author: Internationales Privatrecht, Hamburg, 1989, (conflicts of law hornbook). *Member:* Gesellschaft für Rechtsvergleichung; American Society of International Law; American Bar Association (Member, Sections of Business Law, International Law and Practice Litigation); Hamburg Bar Association. *LANGUAGES:* German, English, French and Italian.

ULF LIEBELT-WESTPHAL, born Neumünster, Germany, August 13, 1960; admitted, 1992, Germany. *Education:* University of Hamburg. *Member:* Hamburg Bar Association. *LANGUAGES:* German and English.

HEIKE BRUNKHORST, born Klein Kollmar, Germany, March 27, 1960; admitted, 1985, Germany. *Education:* University of Hamburg. Co-Author: "Formular-Kommentar Aktienrecht," 22nd ed., 1988 (on stock corporation law). *LANGUAGES:* German and English.

(This Listing Continued)

RÜDIGER LUDWIG, born Hamburg, Germany, January 27, 1961; admitted, 1993, Germany. *Education:* University of Hamburg. *Member:* Hamburg Bar Association. *LANGUAGES:* German and English.

DR. GUIDO CHRISTENSEN, born Hamburg, Germany, October 27, 1964; admitted, 1994, Germany. *Education:* University of Hamburg (Dipl. Kfm., 1990; Dr. jur., 1994). Author: "Gestörter Gesamtschuldnerausgleich bei familienrechtlichen Haftungsbeschränkungen," MDR, 1989, 948 (on tort law). *LANGUAGES:* German and English.

Languages: German, English, French, Spanish, Italian and Swedish.

DR. MARX & PARTNER

Founding Member of CONSULEGIS EEIG An Association of European Lawyers.

Associated Offices: Austria, Belgium, Bulgaria, Canada, Cyprus, Czech Republic, Denmark, England, Estonia, Finland, France, Germany, Greece, Hong Kong, Israel, Italy, Latvia, Monaco, Netherlands, Norway, Poland, Russia, Spain, Sweden, Switzerland and USA.

Established in 1973

AUGUSTSTRASSE 14
22085 HAMBURG, GERMANY
Telephone: 040/229 28-0
Telefax: 040/22928-200

General Practice, Corporation and Commercial Law, Unfair Competition, Mergers and Acquisitions, Antitrust, Trademarks, Copyright, Law of the Press, Tax Law, Labor Law, Environmental Law, Criminal Law, Public and Administrative Law, Litigation and Arbitration.

MEMBERS OF FIRM

DR. THOMAS MARX, born Grünberg, November 2, 1941; admitted, 1973, Germany. *Education:* Universities of Berlin and Hamburg. Author: "Die Beziehung der Wirtschaftstheorie zur Rechtsanwendung des Zivilrichters," Diss. jur. Hamburg 1973; "Kartell- und beweisrechtliche Fragen zu Marktinformationsverfahren," WuW 1975, S. 620-626; "Die gemeinsame Wahrnehmung von Sicherungsrechten im Konkurs (Poolvereinbarungen)," NJW 1978, S. 246-251; "Zum Nachweis aufeinander abgestimmten Verhaltens," BB 1978, S. 331-375; "Wettbewerbsrecht. Fälle und Materialien zum Kartellrecht, zum Gesetz gegen den unlauteren Wettbewerb und zu den Nebengesetzen," Berlin/Bielefeld/München 1977 (Verlag ESV); "Steuerstrafrecht-Hamburger Kompendium 1990," Haufe, Freiburg, 1990. Associate Professor, 1972-1984 and Lecturer in Law, 1971-1995, Competition Law, Company Law and International Tax Law, University of Hamburg. Visiting Scholar, International Tax Program, Harvard Law School, 1975. Member of Deutsche Institution Für Schiedsgerichtsbarkeit (DIS) and Deutsche Zolljuristische Vereinigung e.V. *Member:* Hamburg and German Bar Associations; Hamburg Lawyers Association; German Lawyers Association; German Society for the Protection of Industrial Property and Copyright Law (GRUR). *LANGUAGES:* German, English and Italian. *PRACTICE AREAS:* Tax Law; Competition Law; Antitrust Law; Criminal Law.

PETER E. SCHMIDT-EYCH, born Braunschweig, August 2, 1945; admitted, 1974, Berlin, Germany; 1984-1994, Notary Public, Berlin. *Education:* Universities of Göttingen and Freiburg. *Member:* Hamburg and German Bar Associations; Berlin Lawyers Association; German Lawyers Association. *LANGUAGES:* German and English. *PRACTICE AREAS:* Tax Law; Company Law; Competition Law; Real Estate Law.

DR. THOMAS JÜRGEN REMMERBACH, born Uetersen, Germany, November 29, 1956; admitted, 1988, Germany. *Education:* University of Münster (First State Exam, 1983); University of Hamburg (Second State Exam, 1987). Author: "Der Konkurs des Bankkunden im Überweisungs- und Lastschriftverkehr," Diss. jur., 1984. Lecturer, Commercial and Antitrust Law, University of Hamburg, 1993. *Member:* Hamburg Bar Association. *LANGUAGES:* German, English and French. *PRACTICE AREAS:* Unfair Competition; Commercial and Corporate.

PETER SCHMID, born Stuttgart, Germany, February 23, 1963; admitted, 1993, Hamburg, Germany. *Education:* University of Tübingen. *Member:* Hamburg and German Bar Associations. *LANGUAGES:* German, Dutch and English. *PRACTICE AREAS:* Commercial Law; Inheritance Law; Public and Administrative Law.

GUNTER KRAMPER, born Hamburg, Germany, April 17, 1963; admitted, 1993, Germany. *Education:* University of Hamburg. Recipient, Stu-

(This Listing Continued)

dienstiftung des Deutschen Volkes, 1982-1989. *LANGUAGES:* German and English. *PRACTICE AREAS:* Tax Law; Tax Crimes.

DR. BARBARA VON HYMMEN, born Stralsund, April 23, 1940; admitted, 1979, Germany. *Education:* Universities of Hamburg, Innsbruck and Munich (Dr. jur. 1989). Author: "Festsetzungsfrist und Strafverfolgungsverjährung nach der AO 1977," Peter Lang GmbH, 1989. Lecturer in Law: University of Hamburg, 1975-1990; Academy of Economics, Hamburg, 1988-1989; International Business School, Lippstadt/Malente, 1989-1990; University for Study by Correspondence, Hagen, 1988-1990. *Member:* Hamburg and German Bar Associations. *LANGUAGES:* German and English.

ANDREAS STRUTH, born Geldern, March 18, 1959; admitted, 1988, Germany. *Education:* University of Bonn. Referendarzeit at Court of Appeals, Hamburg, 1985-1988. Lecturer in Law, Unfair Competition, University of Hamburg, Institute of Commercial Law, 1990—. *Member:* Hamburg and German Bar Associations. *LANGUAGES:* German and English.

OF COUNSEL

DR. KLAUS ZIPPEL, born Hamburg, West Germany, April 22, 1940; admitted, 1971, Germany, Certified Auditor. *Education:* Universities of Freiburg, Berlin and Hamburg (Dr. jur., 1977). Member: Hamburg and German Bar Associations, Committee of Lawyer's Examination; Wirtschaftsprüferkammer (professional organization of all recognized certified auditors and sworn auditors in Germany). *LANGUAGES:* German and English. *PRACTICE AREAS:* Company Law; Commercial Law; Transportation Law; Insurance Law; Civil Liability.

DR. MITTELSTEIN & PARTNER

Established in 1848

NEUER WALL 10
D-20354 HAMBURG, GERMANY
Telephone: (040) 35 75 95-0
Telefax: (040) 35 75 95-15

Arbitration, Banking, Bankruptcy, Business and Commercial, Contract, Company and Corporate, Computer and Software, Copyright, Customs, EEC, Food and Drug, Insurance, Intellectual Property, International, Labour, Mergers and Acquisitions, Products Liability, Real Estate, Transport, Unfair Competition and Trademark Law.

FIRM PROFILE: The firm specialized traditionally and of extensive experience in business and international matters offers personal services of high-grade quality by its partners and their legal staff.

PARTNERS OF FIRM

GUNTER STOLTENBERG, born Hamburg, Germany, October 1, 1946; admitted, 1976, Germany. *Education:* Hamburg University. EEC Brussels and ICC Paris. *LANGUAGES:* German, English and French.

DR. NICOLAUS ROLTSCH, born Hamburg, Germany, August 19, 1951; admitted, 1982, Germany. *Education:* Hamburg University. Chamber of Commerce Hamburg and U.S. law firm in San Diego, Ca. *LANGUAGES:* German and English.

DR. REINHARD ARNDTS, born Hamburg, Germany, November 18, 1951; admitted, 1982, Germany. *Education:* Kiel and Hamburg Universities. Chamber of Commerce Hamburg and U.S. law firm in San Francisco, Ca. *LANGUAGES:* German and English.

All Partners of the firm are Members of the Hamburg and German Bar Associations.

Languages: German, English and French

MODEST, GUNDISCH, LANDRY

HAMBURG, GERMANY

(See Graf von Westphalen & Modest)

MÜLLER-HORN & MATZ

Rechtsanwälte

Established in 1972

ROTHENBAUMCHAUSSEE 20

20148 HAMBURG, GERMANY

Telephone: 49/40/450 10 80; 49/40/41 80 75; 49/40/44 46 57

Telefax: 49/40/449794

Commercial, Corporate, Partnership, Antitrust, Banking, Unfair Competition, Trademark, Copyright, Licensing, Press, Personal Injury, Family, Labor, Real Estate, Inheritance, Construction, Tax Law, International Contracts, Private International Law and General Practice.

MEMBERS OF FIRM

DR. HANS MÜLLER-HORN, born Freschluneberg, May 21, 1936; admitted, 1965, Hamburg. *Education:* University of Hamburg (Dr.jur., 1965). *Member:* Hamburg Bar Association; Hamburgischer Anwaltsverein; German Association for Construction Law. *LANGUAGES:* German. *PRACTICE AREAS:* Corporate; Construction; Banking.

WOLFGANG MATZ, born Hamburg, April 18, 1938; admitted, 1966, Hamburg. *Education:* University of Hamburg. *Member:* Hamburg Bar Association; German Association for the Protection of Industrial Property and Copyright; Studienvereinigung für Kartellrecht. *LANGUAGES:* German and English. *PRACTICE AREAS:* Corporate; Anti Trust; Unfair Competition; Industrial Property.

DR. PETER RINDFLEISCH, born Kiel, October 7, 1936; admitted, 1965, Hamburg. *Education:* Universities of Freiburg and Hamburg (Dr. jur. 1965). *Member:* Hamburg Bar Association; German-British Law Association; German-Italian Law Association. *LANGUAGES:* German and English. *PRACTICE AREAS:* Commercial; Corporate; Construction.

KARIN VOGES, born Stettin, March 19, 1934; admitted, 1962, Hamburg. *Education:* Universities of Marburg, Berlin and Hamburg. *Member:* Hamburg Bar Association. *LANGUAGES:* German. *PRACTICE AREAS:* Family.

DR. JÖRG PÜSCHEL, born Itzehoe, June 8, 1953; admitted, 1982, Hamburg. *Education:* University of Hamburg (Dr.jur., 1982). *Member:* Hamburg Bar Association. *LANGUAGES:* German and English. *PRACTICE AREAS:* Commercial; Real Estate; Banking.

UNNO LUTHER, born Hamburg, October 27, 1956; admitted, 1985, Hamburg. *Education:* Universities of Tübingen, Kiel and Hamburg. *Member:* Hamburg Bar Association. *LANGUAGES:* German and English. *PRACTICE AREAS:* Commercial; Construction; Real Estate; Press; Copyright; Shipping Law.

ASSOCIATES

JÜRGEN PALDER, born Hamburg, September 12, 1958; admitted, 1991, Hamburg. *Education:* University of Hamburg. *Member:* Hamburg Bar Association. *LANGUAGES:* German and English. *PRACTICE AREAS:* Commercial.

OHLE HANSEN EWERWAHN

HAMBURG, GERMANY

(See Feddersen Laule Scherzberg & Ohle Hansen Ewerwahn)

PRINZ, NEIDHARDT, ENGELSCHALL

Established in 1987

16 TESDORPFSTRASSE

20148 HAMBURG, GERMANY

Telephone: (040) 443066

Telex: (040) 214837 caphb

Telefax: (040) 4106714

Entertainment, Communication and Media, Advertising and Marketing, Copyrights, Intellectual Property, Libel and Defamation, General Practice, Corporate, Mergers and Acquisitions, Real Estate, Press and Publishing Law, Unfair Competition, Labor Law and Equipment Finance and Leasing.

(This Listing Continued)

FIRM PROFILE: *Established in 1987, PRINZ, NEIDHART, ENGELSCHALL has quickly become one of Germany's leading firms in all areas of communications and media law, including copyright, libel and defamation, intellectual property and press and publishing law. The firm offers a full range of legal services in business transactions and corporate law, and in commercial litigation and arbitration, to an international client base.*

MATTHIAS PRINZ, born Berlin, Germany, August 27, 1956; admitted, 1984, New York; 1985, Hamburg. *Education:* Harvard Law School (LL.M., 1983), New York, Rio de Janeiro, (Brazil); Hamburg (Assistant at the Institute for International and Foreign Private and Procedural Law (Dr. jur., 1985). *Member:* Hamburg and New York State Bar Associations; Cambridge Transnational Associates. *LANGUAGES:* German, English, French and Portuguese. *PRACTICE AREAS:* Communications; Entertainment and Media.

SABINE NEIDHARDT, born Hamburg, Germany, August 7, 1956; admitted, 1984, Hamburg. *Education:* Hamburg, Los Angeles, (California). *Member:* Hamburg Bar Association; Hamburg and German Lawyers Associations. *LANGUAGES:* German, English and French. *PRACTICE AREAS:* Copyrights; Unfair Competition; Equipment Finance and Leasing.

MANFRED ENGELSCHALL, born Hamburg, Germany, October 23, 1921; admitted, 1991, Hamburg. *Education:* Hamburg University Law School; Freiburg University Law School; London School of Economics. Judge in Hamburg, 1950-1986. Retired Presiding Judge, Court of Appeals, Vorsitzender Richter am Hanseatischen Oberlandesgericht. *LANGUAGES:* German, English and French. *PRACTICE AREAS:* Intellectual Property; Copyright; Press Law.

JENS FRÖMMING, born Hamburg, Germany, July 1, 1960; admitted, 1991, Hamburg. *Education:* Hamburg University Law School (Dr. jur., 1991), Paris. *LANGUAGES:* German, English and French. *PRACTICE AREAS:* Tax Law; Corporate Law; International Joint Ventures.

CHRISTOPH MEYER-BOHL, born Hamburg, May 28, 1958; admitted, 1993, Hamburg. *Education:* Hamburg University Law School (Dr. iur., 1992). *LANGUAGES:* German and English. *PRACTICE AREAS:* Insurance Law; Administrative Law; Law of the Government Committees of Inquiry.

COUNSEL

PATRICE F. THOMAS-BARRENECHEA, born Lima, Peru, October 1, 1958; admitted, 1983, Peru (Not admitted in Germany). *Education:* Pontificia Universidad, Lima, Peru (B.A., 1976; Bachiller en derecho, 1981; Abogado, 1982); Université Paul Valery, Montpellier, France (Certificat d'aptitude à L'eneseignement du Francais, 1978); Harvard Law School (LL.M., 1983). *Member:* Colegio de Abogados de Lima; Harvard Law School Association of Europe. *LANGUAGES:* Spanish, English, French, Italian and German. *PRACTICE AREAS:* International Business and Corporate Law.

REDEKER SCHÖN DAHS & SELLNER

Established in 1929

BÜSCHSTRASSE 12

20354 HAMBURG, GERMANY

Telephone: (040) 342737/8

Telefax: (040) 352144

Bonn, Germany Office: Oxfordstrasse 24, 53111 Bonn. Telephone: (0228) 72625-0. Telefax: (0228) 650479.

Cologne, Germany Office: Kaiser-Wilhelm-Ring 22, 50672 Cologne. Telephone: (0221) 912 8680. Telefax: (0221) 912 86838.

Leipzig, Germany Office: Mozartstr. 1, 04107 Leipzig. Telephone: (0341) 213780. Telefax: (0341) 2137830.

London, England Office: 43 Brook Street, London W1Y 2BL. Telephone: (0171) 3225823. Telefax (0171) 6292621.

Administrative, Anti-Trust, Aviation, City Planning, Civil, Corporate and Commercial, Constitutional and Parliamentary, Construction, Criminal, Environmental, European Community Law, Family, Health, Insurance, Labour, Media and Copyright, Medical Malpractice, Domestic and International Tax, Trade, Transportation Law, Litigation and Appeals.

(This Listing Continued)

PARTNERS

GERNOT LEHR, born Bonn, February 23, 1957; admitted, 1987, Bonn; 1989, Hamburg. *Education:* Universities of Bonn and Munich. *Member:* German-German Lawyers' Association. *LANGUAGES:* German and English.

YVONNE F. SÜCHTING, born Oberhausen, October 2, 1964; admitted, 1993, Hamburg. *Education:* Universities of Hamburg and Bonn. *Member:* German-German Lawyers Association; Lawyers Administrative Law Committee, Schleswig-Holstein-Section. *LANGUAGES:* German and English.

(For data on all firm personnel see Professional Biographies at Bonn)

ROLLENHAGEN, WANDSCHNEIDER & PARTNER

HAMBURG, GERMANY

(See Curschmann, Rollenhagen & Partner)

General Practice. Commercial, Corporate, Competition, Trademark, Common Market, Administration, Labor, Insurance, Real Estate, Inheritance, Tax and Duty Law, Latin American Law, Banking, Criminal and Family.

SAGAWE & KLAGES

RABOISEN 5
D-20095 HAMBURG, GERMANY
Telephone: +49 40 323020
Fax: +49 40 339327
CompuServe 100016, 1001

Corporate, Commercial, International Trade (esp. Scandinavian Countries), EEC Law, Mergers and Acquisitions, Real Estate, Tax Law and Computer Law.

MEMBERS OF FIRM

CHRISTIAN SAGAWE, born 1954; admitted, 1982, Germany. *Education:* University of Freiburg (Law Degree 1979), Bristol and Hamburg. Vereidigter Buchprüfer (Chartered Accountant). *Member:* German-Nordic Law Association. *LANGUAGES:* German, Danish and English.

DR. JOHANNES KLAGES, born 1957; admitted, 1989, Germany. *Education:* Universities of Regensburg, Oslo and Freiburg (Law Degree, 1983; Dr. jur., 1989). Research Assistant, Max-Planck-Institute for Foreign and International Law, 1983-1989. *Member:* German-Nordic Law Association. *LANGUAGES:* German, Norwegian and English.

MATTHIAS JAGENBERG, born 1963; admitted, 1994, Germany. *Education:* University of Bonn (Law Degree, 1990). *Member:* German-Nordic Law Association. *LANGUAGES:* German, Swedish, English and French.

Languages: German, English, Danish, Norwegian and Swedish

SAMUEL & PARTNER

HAMBURG, GERMANY

(See Graf von Westphalen & Modest)

SCHEUERMANN & PARTNER

NEUER WALL 26-28
D-20354 HAMBURG, GERMANY
Telephone: (040) 37 47 95-0
Telefax: (040) 37 47 95-33

International Banking and Business Law, Corporate Restructuring, Mergers and Acquisitions, Real Estate, Family Law, Iranian Law.

FIRM PROFILE: The firm combines Legal Practice with long-standing Banking Practice. The client basis is European, North American and Iranian in scope, with emphasis on corporations in the eastern parts of Germany.

(This Listing Continued)

MEMBERS OF FIRM

DR. THOMAS SCHEUERMANN, born Berlin, Germany, March 12, 1941; admitted, 1973, Germany. *Education:* Universities of Munich, Aix-en-Provence and Hamburg (Referendar, 1965; Dr. jur., 1968; Assessor, 1969). Assistant Lecturer, University of Munich, Institute for International Law, 1965-1968. Legal Department, Bayerische Hypotheken und Wechsel Bank, 1969-1972. Trainee: Kelley, Drye & Warren; Simpson Thatcher, New York, 1971; Bayerische Hypotheken und Wechsel Bank, International Department, 1972-1973. Chief Representative, ABECOR (Algemene Bank Netherlands N.V., Banque Bruxelles-Lambert S.A., Bayerische Hypotheken und Wechsel Bank AG, Dresdner Bank AG, Österreichische Länderbank AG). Teheran Representative Office, 1973-1976. Manager: Bayerische Hypotheken und Wechsel Bank, Hamburg Branch, 1976-1984; The Royal Bank of Canada AG, Hamburg Branch, 1984-1987; Attorneys Schwarz, Schniewind, Kelwing, Munich, 1988-1989. *Member:* International Bar Association; Hamburg Bar Association. *LANGUAGES:* German, English, French and Italian.

HELGA SPRINGENEER, born Dülmen, Germany November 8, 1961; admitted, 1993, Hamburg. *Education:* Universities of Münster Freiburg and London; volunteer in the law office Mollenbeck & Associates, Sydney/Australia; journalist-volunteer, 1992. *Member:* German-Israelite Law Association (Member, Executive Board); Hamburg Bar Association. *LANGUAGES:* German, English, French and Hebrew.

OF COUNSEL

BEHJAT MOAALI, born Maragheh, Iran, January 13, 1949; admitted, 1979, Iran (Not admitted in Germany). *Education:* Tabriz (Graduate in Teaching, 1967); Teheran University (1970-1975; Graduate in Law, 1977). Teacher, Shariati School, Teheran, 1967-1977. Law Office, Teheran, 1979-1989. Counsel to Bank Tejarat, 1981-1989. *LANGUAGES:* Persian, Azeri-Turkish, German and English.

SCHLUTIUS, ESPEY & PARTNER

Established in 1962

SPITALERSTRASSE 4/KURZE MÜHREN 2
20095 HAMBURG, GERMANY
Telephone: XX 49/40/33 40 10
Telefax: XX 49/40/33 68 69

Berlin, Germany Office: 10117 Berlin, Friedrichstrasse 105b. Telephone: XX 49/30/229 90 20; 282 35 58. Telefax: XX 49/30/283 41 17.

Commercial, Corporation, Labor, Unfair Competition, Trademarks, Copyright, German and EEC Antitrust Law, Tax and Duty, Antidumping, Customs, Arbitration, Environmental Law, Law of the former GDR, Privatization, Restitution, Family Law, Inheritance and General Practice.

FIRM PROFILE: Schlutius, Espey & Partner is a nation wide and international orientated lawyer's office concentrating on the advice needs of business clients with offices in Hamburg and Berlin.

The circle of clients consists mainly of medium-sized businesses from industry, trade and the service sector.

With their respective specialized fields the firm's partners cover the complete range of Commercial Law. The key focal points are Mercantile and Company Law, Competition and Unfair Trade Practices Law, Protection of Industrial Property Rights and Copyright, Labour and Industrial Relations Law, International Law of Contract, Family and Inheritance Law, Tariff Legislation and EC Law.

The firm acts chiefly in an advisory capacity.

RESIDENT PARTNERS

DR. WOLFGANG SCHLUTIUS, born Oberhausen, Germany, June 12, 1908; admitted, 1952, Hamburg. *Education:* Universities of Jena and Grenoble. *Member:* Hamburg Bar Association; Hamburg Bar Society. *LANGUAGES:* German, English and French.

DR. GÜNTHER ESPEY, born Hamburg, Germany, August 1, 1928; admitted, 1959, Hamburg. *Education:* University of Hamburg (Doctor jur., 1956). Author: "Acceptance Credit," (Der Akzeptkredit) Diss., Hamburg, 1956. Co-Author: "Liability of a Managing Director of a GmbH and Possible Safeguards," (Haftung des GmbH-Geschäftsführers und Absicherungsmöglichkeiten), 1990. *Member:* Hamburg Bar Association (Board Member, 1971—); Hamburg Bar Society. *LANGUAGES:* German and English. *PRACTICE AREAS:* Business Law; Administration of Property; Law of Succession; Executor.

(This Listing Continued)

SCHLUTIUS, ESPEY & PARTNER, Hamburg—Continued

HANS-ULRICH WILHELMI, born Lage/Lippe, Germany, May 8, 1932; admitted, 1967, Hamburg. *Education:* Universities of Marburg, Tübingen, Hamburg. Co-Author: "Value Added Tax and its Impact on Commerce," (Die Netto-Umsatzsteuer (Mehrwertsteuer) und Auswirkungen auf die Praxis des Handels), Hamburg, 1967. *Member:* Hamburg Bar Association; Hamburg Bar Society. *LANGUAGES:* German and English. *PRACTICE AREAS:* Mercantile Law; Law of Associations.

ULRICH FICHTEL, born Rebbol, Denmark, November 18, 1936; admitted, 1967, Hamburg. *Education:* Universities of Heidelberg, Berlin, Kiel. Author: "Annotation to Federal Basic Agreement on Tariffs for Pharmacies," (Kommentar zum Bundesrahmentarif für Apotheken), 1975—. *Member:* Hamburg and International Bar Associations; Hamburg Bar Society. *LANGUAGES:* German, English and French. *PRACTICE AREAS:* Mercantile Law; Company Law; Business Law; Labour Law; Law of Succession.

DR. CLAUS-DETLEV BROSE, born Breslau, Germany, May 7, 1936; admitted, 1967, Hamburg. *Education:* Universities of Freiburg i.Br. and Kiel (Doctor jur., 1965). Author: "The Problem of Product Liability re Brand Name Products," (Das Problem des Haftungsdurchgriffs bei Markenartikeln), Diss., Kiel, 1965. Co-Author: Handbook on the "Communication and Advertising Business," (Handbuch der Kommunikations und Werbewirtschaft), 1981, 1982; Marketing Journal, 1978—. *Member:* Hamburg Bar Association; Hamburg Bar Society; Association for Anti-Trust Law (Studienvereinigung Kartellrecht); German Society for the Protection of Industrial Property and Copyright Law (GRUR); International Association for the Protection of Industrial Property (AIPPI). *LANGUAGES:* German and English. *PRACTICE AREAS:* Industrial Property Law; Trade Mark Rights; Copyright; Law in the new Bundesländer (former GDR).

DR. HELMUTH BAUMEISTER, born Welschen Ennest, Germany, June 30, 1938; admitted, 1969, Hamburg. *Education:* Universities of Bonn, München, Köln (Doctor jur., 1967). Author: "Legal Nature, Exclusion, and Limitations of Recourse Claim of the Social Security Authorities acc. to Article 640 RVO (German Social Insurance Code)". Co-Author: "Handbook on China Trade," (Chinahandbuch für die Wirtschaft), 1985; "Handbook for Sales Representatives," (Verkaufsrechtsberater), 1987. *Member:* Hamburg Bar Association; Hamburg Bar Society; German Institute of Arbitration; Society of Comparative Law; British and German Chamber of Commerce. *LANGUAGES:* German, English and French. *PRACTICE AREAS:* Mercantile and Commercial Law; International Law of Contract; Product Liability.

CHRISTIAN VON BITTER, born Hannover, Germany, October 10, 1950; admitted, 1981, Hamburg, Fachanwalt für Arbeitsrecht. *Education:* University of Bielefeld. Co-Author: "Liabilities of a Manager of a GmbH," (Haftungsrisiken des GmbH-Geschäftsführers), 1990; "Forms of Agreements in Tax Law," Chapter on Usufructuary Enjoyment (Steuerlich anerkannte Nießbrauchsgestaltungen), 1982—; "Forms of Agreements for Tax Practice," (Musterverträge für die steuerberatende Praxis), 1984—. *Member:* Hamburg Bar Association; Hamburg Bar Society. *LANGUAGES:* German and English. *PRACTICE AREAS:* Labour and Industrial Relations Law; Company Law; Law of Succession.

CHRISTIAN KLAWITTER, born Lübeck, Germany, February 4, 1955; admitted, 1984, Hamburg. *Education:* University of Hamburg. Research Assistant, University of Hamburg, Institute for Commercial Law, 1981-1984. *Member:* Hamburg Bar Association; Hamburg Bar Society; German Society for the Protection of Industrial Property and Copyright Law (GRUR); Association for Antitrust Law (Studienvereinigung Kartellrecht); German Institute for the Protection of Geographic Indications of Origin on Goods (DIGH); Licensing Executives Society (L.E.S., German Group); German Association of Industrial Designer (VDID). *LANGUAGES:* German and English. *PRACTICE AREAS:* European and German Competition Law; Unfair Trade Practices Law; Trade Mark Rights; Design Rights; Copyright; Press Law.

DR. JÜRGEN SPARR, LL.M., born Hamburg, Germany, February 27, 1956; admitted, 1989, Hamburg. *Education:* Universities of Hamburg (Doctor jur., 1991) and London (Master of Laws 1985). Research Assistant University of Hamburg, Department of European Community Law 1985-1990. Author: "Cultural sovereignty and the EEC - Treaty," (Kulturhoheit and EWG-Vertrag), 1991. *Member:* Hamburg Bar Society; Hamburg Bar Association; Law Society, Solicitors' European Group (U.K.); German-Greek Lawyers Association; Scientific Association of European Law; Association

(This Listing Continued)

for Antitrust Law (Studienvereinigung Kartellrecht). *LANGUAGES:* German; English. *PRACTICE AREAS:* EC Law; European Competition Law; Tariff Legislation and Anti-Dumping Law; International Mercantile and Contract Law.

UWE PETZOLD, born München, Germany, July 14, 1935; admitted, 1990, Germany. *Education:* Universities of Munich and Hamburg. *Member:* Hamburg Bar Association and Deutscher Juristentag. *LANGUAGES:* German. *PRACTICE AREAS:* Collective Bargaining Law; Law of Retirement Pension Schemes.

ILSE ROHR, born Bad Schwalbach, Germany, August 4, 1958; admitted, 1988, Germany. *Education:* Universities of Mainz and Hamburg. *Member:* Hamburg Bar Association; Hamburg Bar Society. *LANGUAGES:* German, English and Spanish. *PRACTICE AREAS:* Unfair Trade Practices Law; Patent Law; Trade Mark Rights; Design Right; Copyright; Press Law.

CHRISTINE FLOTO, born Uetersen, Germany, November 30, 1962; admitted, 1991, Germany. *Education:* Universities of Hamburg; Tübingen; Fribourg (Switzerland); Freiburg i.Br. and London (Master of Laws, 1993). *Member:* Hamburg Bar Association; Hamburg Bar Society. *LANGUAGES:* German, English and French. *PRACTICE AREAS:* Mercantile and Commercial Law; International and National Transport Law.

UTE BALTEN, born Celle, Germany, April 2, 1950; admitted, 1982, Hamburg. *Education:* University of Hamburg. *Member:* Hamburg Bar Society (Board Member); Hamburg Bar Association; German Bar Association (Working Group, Family Law; Arbeitsgemeinschaft Familienrecht des Deutschen Anwaltvereins). *LANGUAGES:* German, English and French. *PRACTICE AREAS:* Family and Inheritance Law.

Languages: German, English, French, Italian and Spanish

SCHÖN NOLTE FINKELNBURG & CLEMM

WARBURGSTRASSE 50
D-20354 HAMBURG, GERMANY
Telephone: (40) 41 40 30
Telex: 2161611 clnt d
Telecopier: (40) 41 40 31 30

Other Offices: Berlin and Dresden, Germany; Brussels, Belgium.

General Corporate and Commercial Practice.

MEMBERS OF FIRM

DR. WERNER SCHÖN (1946-1991)(Retired).

DR. PETER NOLTE, born Hamburg, Germany, 1923; admitted, 1949, Hamburg. *Education:* Universities of Freiburg and Hamburg (Dr.jur., 1947). *LANGUAGES:* German and English. *PRACTICE AREAS:* Corporate Law; Estates.

DR. ERNST LÖWE, born Hamburg, Germany, 1931; admitted, 1959, Hamburg. *Education:* University of Hamburg (Dr.jur., 1957). Board Member, Hamburg Bar Association, 1971-1991. *LANGUAGES:* German and English. *PRACTICE AREAS:* Admiralty and Maritime Law; Business Law; Company Law.

PROF. DR. HANS-JÜRGEN RABE, born Hamburg, Germany, 1935; admitted, 1964, Hamburg. *Education:* Universities of Heidelberg, Berlin and Hamburg (Dr. jur., 1962). Editor, "Europarecht," (Periodical on European Law). Co-Editor, Neue Juristische Wochenschrift (NJW). Professor of EEC Law, University of Hamburg, 1992—. *Member:* German Bar Association (Member, Executive Committee, 1971; President, 1978-1983); International Bar Association (Member, Council, 1975-1993); State of Hamburg Constitutional Court; Deutscher Juristentag (President, 1993); Association of Food Law (Member, Council, 1978—); Association of the Bar of the City of New York; American Bar Association. (Also at Brussels, Belgium Office). *LANGUAGES:* German, English and French. *PRACTICE AREAS:* Antitrust and Trade Regulation; European Community Law; Food and Drug Regulation; International Arbitration.

KONRAD BENNECKE, born Berlin, Germany, 1940; admitted, 1968, Hamburg. *Education:* Universities of Göttingen and Bonn. *LANGUAGES:* German, English and French. *PRACTICE AREAS:* Agency and Distributorships; Antitrust and Trade Regulation; Contracts; Corporate Law.

DR. DIETER RABE, born Hamburg, Germany, 1937; admitted, 1966, Hamburg. *Education:* Universities of Heidelberg, Munich, Göttingen and Hamburg (Dr. jur., 1970). Author: "Prüssmann/Rabe Seehandelsrecht,"

(This Listing Continued)

German Maritime Law, 3rd ed. 1991. Contributor to the Journal "Transportrecht" (Transport Law). 1984—. Member, Commission of the Revision of the Law of Obligations with the Minister of Justice, 1984-1991. *Member:* Comité Maritime International (Member Titulaire). *LANGUAGES:* German and English. *PRACTICE AREAS:* Admiralty and Maritime Law; Maritime Arbitration; P and I Clubs; Commercial Law; Transportation.

JÜRGEN LIBBERT, born Berlin, Germany, 1942; admitted, 1971, Hamburg. *Education:* Universities of Hamburg, Munich and Bonn. *LANGUAGES:* German and English. *PRACTICE AREAS:* Commercial Law; Company Law; Mergers, Acquisitions and Divestitures.

DR. JÖRG SOEHRING, born Stettin, Germany, 1942; admitted, 1971, Hamburg. *Education:* Universities of Berlin and Freiburg (Dr.jur., 1970); Boalt Hall School of Law, University of California, Berkeley (Master of Laws, 1968). Teaching Assignments, Commercial, 1980-1985 and Press and Publishing Law, 1987-1992, Hamburg University. *LANGUAGES:* German and English. *PRACTICE AREAS:* Advertising and Marketing; Communications and Media; Intellectual Property; Hotels and Resorts; Mergers, Acquisitions and Divestitures.

DR. JÜRGEN HÜBNER, born Bremen, Germany, 1947; admitted, 1974, Hamburg. *Education:* Universities of Hamburg and Berlin (Dr.jur., 1973). Vice-Chairman, Committee on Real Estate Law, International Bar Association. *LANGUAGES:* German and English. *PRACTICE AREAS:* Bankruptcy; Construction Law; Property; Real Estate; Reinsurance.

CHRISTOPH VON TEICHMAN, born Magdeburg, Germany, 1947; admitted, 1976, Hamburg. *Education:* University of Hamburg. Secretary, Committee on Professional Development and Technology, International Bar Association. *LANGUAGES:* German and English. *PRACTICE AREAS:* Banks and Banking; Finance; Mergers, Acquisitions and Divestitures; Mutual Funds; Insurance Regulation.

EBERHARD MILLARG, born Stettin, Germany, 1938; admitted, 1969, Hamburg. *Education:* Universities of Freiburg and Hamburg. Assistant, Department Law of the European Communities, University of Hamburg, 1969-1977. *LANGUAGES:* German and English. *PRACTICE AREAS:* European Community Law; Food and Drug Regulation; Pharmaceutical Regulation; Antitrust and Trade Regulation; Environmental Law.

DR. ANTJE MATTFELD, born Hamburg, Germany, 1946; admitted, 1975, Hamburg. *Education:* Universities of Hamburg, Lausanne and Freiburg (Dr. jur., 1972; Diploma of Economics); Boalt Hall School of Law, University of California at Berkeley (LL.M.). Assistant Professor, Institute of Private International Law, University of Freiburg, 1973-1975. *LANGUAGES:* German, English, French, Italian and Russian. *PRACTICE AREAS:* Antitrust and Trade Regulation; Corporate Law; Agency and Distributorships; Computers and Software; Mergers, Acquisitions and Divestitures; Aviation and Aerospace.

DR. JOACHIM FREIHERR VON FALKENHAUSEN, born Kipfenberg, Germany, 1951; admitted, 1980, Hamburg. *Education:* Universities of Göttingen, Lausanne and Freiburg (Dr. jur., 1980); Boalt Hall School of Law, University of California, Berkeley (LL.M., 1976). Board Member, Hamburg Bar Association, 1991—. *LANGUAGES:* German, English and French. *PRACTICE AREAS:* Finance; Mergers, Acquisitions and Divestitures; Securities; Shipbuilding; Corporate Law.

PETER MARKL, born Preetz, Germany, 1951; admitted, 1981, Hamburg. *Education:* University of Hamburg. *LANGUAGES:* German and English. *PRACTICE AREAS:* Labour; Employment; Insurance Law.

DR. CHRISTIAN R. SCHARFF, born Lübeck, Germany, 1954; admitted, 1984, Hamburg. *Education:* University of Kiel (Dr. jur., 1982). *LANGUAGES:* German and English. *PRACTICE AREAS:* Mergers, Acquisitions and Divestitures; Company Law; Admiralty and Maritime Law; Contracts.

DR. CORD LÜBKE-DETRING, born Weener, Germany, 1957; admitted, 1987, Hamburg. *Education:* University of Hamburg (Dr.jur., 1988). *LANGUAGES:* German and English. *PRACTICE AREAS:* Construction Law; Leases and Leasing; Property; Zoning, Planning and Land Use.

DR. CHRISTIAN E. EDYE, born Hamburg, Germany, 1957; admitted, 1988, New York and Connecticut; 1989, Hamburg. *Education:* New York University (M.C.J., 1987) Universities of Hamburg and Salamanca, Spain. *LANGUAGES:* German, English, Spanish and French. *PRACTICE AREAS:* Corporate Law; International Law; Franchises and Franchising; Agency and Distributorship.

(This Listing Continued)

UTE LELGEMANN, born Essen, Germany, 1956; admitted, 1988, Hamburg. *Education:* University of Münster. *LANGUAGES:* German and English. *PRACTICE AREAS:* Administrative Law; Environmental Law; Communications and Media; Libel and Defamation.

JAN WÖLPER, born Bremen, Germany, 1958; admitted, 1988, Hamburg. *Education:* Universities of Hamburg, Guildford and Kiel. *LANGUAGES:* German, English and Norwegian. *PRACTICE AREAS:* Admiralty and Maritime Law; Transportation.

DR. NIKOLAUS LORENZ, born Dortmund, Germany, 1958; admitted, 1988, Hamburg. *Education:* Universities of Freiburg and Münster. *LANGUAGES:* German and English. *PRACTICE AREAS:* Banks and Banking; Company Law; Contracts; Mergers, Acquisitions and Divestitures.

SENIOR ASSOCIATE

RAINER WULF, born Lübeck, Germany, 1943; admitted, 1975, Hamburg. *Education:* Universities of Göttingen and Munich (Dipl., Chem., 1969). *LANGUAGES:* German and English. *PRACTICE AREAS:* Environmental Law; Food and Drug Regulation; Intellectual Property; Pharmaceutical Regulation.

Languages: German, English, French, Spanish, Italian, Norwegian and Russian

---

SCHULZ NOACK BÄRWINKEL

Established in 1959

MÖNCKEBERGSTRASSE 7
20095 HAMBURG, GERMANY
Telephone: 040/32 55 72-0
Fax: 040/32 63 02

Rostock, Germany Office: Alter Markt 15. Telephone: 0381/454860. Fax: 0381/4548614.

Shanghai, China Office: Apartment 1106, Galaxy Hotel, 888 Zhongshan Xi Lu 200051. Telephone and Fax: 8621/2196829.

Commercial, Corporations, Competition, Banking, Insurance, Labour, Media Law, Wills, International Law.

MEMBERS OF FIRM

PETER SCHULZ, born Rostock, April 25, 1930; admitted, 1959, Hamburg; 1992, Rostock. *Education:* Hamburg University. Author: "Der Einfluss der Amerikanischen und Französischen Revolution auf die deutschen Verfassungen," Hoffmann & Campe, 1989; "Parlamentsrecht der deutschen Stadtstaaten," De Gruyter, 1989. Minister of Justice, Hamburg, 1966-1970. Minister of Education, Hamburg, 1970-1971. Governor of the State of Hamburg, 1971-1974. Chairman, Hamburg State Assembly, 1978-1986. *Member:* German-Chinese Law Association; International Bar Association. *LANGUAGES:* German and English. *PRACTICE AREAS:* Corporations; Commercial Law; Labor Law; Media Law; Eastern-European Relations.

DR. ROLAND NOACK, born Hannover, June 13, 1936; admitted, 1964, Hamburg. *Education:* Cologne and Hamburg Universities. Author: "Tatverlauf und Vorsatz," 1964. *Member:* German-Norwegian Chamber of Commerce. *LANGUAGES:* German and Norwegian. *PRACTICE AREAS:* Commercial Law; Insurance Law; Tort.

DR. RICHARD BÄRWINKEL, born Kassel, July 18, 1939; admitted, 1969, Hamburg. *Education:* Marburg, Göttingen Universities. Author: "Zur Struktur der Garantieverhältnisse bei den unechten Unterlassungsdelikten," 1968. Lecturer on Law, University of Hamburg, 1964-1966. *Member:* Hamburg Bar Association. *LANGUAGES:* German and English. *PRACTICE AREAS:* Commercial Law; Corporations; Banking.

AXEL NEELMEIER, born Bremen, November 28, 1951; admitted, 1981, Hamburg. *Education:* Hamburg University. *Member:* Hamburg Bar Association; German-American Lawyers Association; German Chinese Law Association; German Society for the Protection of Industrial Property and Copyright Law. *LANGUAGES:* German and English. *PRACTICE AREAS:* Commercial; Competition; International Law; Intellectual Property.

DR. OLAF SCHULZ-GARDYAN, LL.M., born Hamburg, June 17, 1961; admitted, 1992, Hamburg. *Education:* University of Münster; University of Cambridge (LL.M., 1988). Traineeship with EEC-Commission, 1990. Author: "Die sogenannte Aktionärsklage," Duncker & Humblot, 1991. *Member:* Hamburg Bar Association; International Bar Association. *LANGUAGES:* German, English and French. *PRACTICE AREAS:* Commercial Law; Corporations; International Law; EEC Law.

(This Listing Continued)

SCHULZ NOACK BÄRWINKEL, Hamburg—Continued

NORBERT WENDT, born Kühlungsborn, January 5, 1953; admitted, 1990, Rostock. *Education:* Humboldt-Universität zu Berlin (Dipl. Jur., 1988). *LANGUAGES:* German, English and Russian. *PRACTICE AREAS:* Unification Law; Real Estate.

ASSOCIATES

DOROTHEA BÄRWINKEL, born Berlin, November 26, 1938; admitted, 1971, Hamburg. *Education:* Göttingen University, Free University of Berlin. *LANGUAGES:* German and English. *PRACTICE AREAS:* Banking; Tort; Real Estate.

THOMAS SCHIKORRA, born Lübeck, December 30, 1962; admitted, 1992, Hamburg. *Education:* University of Regensburg. *LANGUAGES:* German and English. *PRACTICE AREAS:* Commercial Law; Corporations; Banking.

ANKE STÜWE, born Hamburg, October 10, 1963; admitted, 1992, Hamburg. *Education:* University of Hamburg. Traineeship: Law firm, New York, 1991. *LANGUAGES:* German and English. *PRACTICE AREAS:* Civil Law; Commercial Law.

DR. DETLEV GEERDS, born Kiel, August 14, 1964; admitted, 1993, Rostock. *Education:* Universities of Kiel and Bayreuth. Author: "Wirtschaftsstrafrecht und Vermögensschutz," 1990. *Member:* Rostock Bar Association. *LANGUAGES:* German and English. *PRACTICE AREAS:* Tax Law; Unification Law.

DIETRICH DEHNEN, born Duisburg, March 23, 1963; admitted, 1993, Hamburg. *Education:* University of Hamburg. Practice in accounting firm. *LANGUAGES:* German and English. *PRACTICE AREAS:* Corporate; Labour; General Contract Law.

DR. DETLEF GOTTSCHALCK, born Hamburg, August 27, 1963; admitted, 1994, Hamburg. *Education:* University of Hamburg. Author: "Die Hamburgische Bürgerschaft" (The City-State Parliament), Duncker & Humblot, Berlin 1993. Member of the staff of the State Parliament of Mecklenburg-Vorpommern, 1991-1993. Lectures at the University of Rostock, 1993. *LANGUAGES:* German and English. *PRACTICE AREAS:* Constitutional Law; Administration Law; Tort Law.

CORD IMELMANN, born July 17, 1962; admitted, 1995, Rostock. *Education:* Hamburg University. *LANGUAGES:* German and English. *PRACTICE AREAS:* Corporate; Commercial; Litigation.

CHEN JUN, born Nanjing, October 10, 1966; (Not admitted in Germany). *Education:* Nanjing University; Göttingen University; Hamburg University. *LANGUAGES:* Chinese, German and English. *PRACTICE AREAS:* Chinese Relations.

DR. SCHWARZ VON SALDERN

DIEKMANN

RATHAUSMARKT 5
20095 HAMBURG, GERMANY
Telephone: (040) 32 70 40
Telefax: (040) 32 40 11

Corporate Counselling, Acquisition and Mergers, Tax, International Investment and Tax Planning, Joint Ventures, Trademark, Patent, Antitrust, Unfair Competition, Administrative and Common Market Law, Contract and Labour Law, Construction Law, Food Law, Commercial Licence and Real Estate, Family and Inheritance Law, Banking, Video, Copyright, Arbitration.

MEMBERS OF FIRM

DR. HUBERTUS SCHWARZ, born Rastorf, Germany, October 22, 1944; admitted, 1974, Germany. *Education:* Universities of Hamburg, Madrid, Aix-en-Provence, Lisbon (Law, Business Administration, Languages, Doctor of Law, 1975). Fachanwalt f. Steuerrecht (tax attorney), Assistant Max-Planck-Institute for Private and International Law, Hamburg, 1970-1975. Bank Trainee, 1974-1975, Corporate, Tax and General Counsel for Foreign Direct Investments and Banking at a Bank's subsidiary in São Paulo, 1975-1976. Managing Director of a major german construction company, 1976-1979. Author: "(Interalia) Portuguese Law of Real Estate," AWD/RIW 448 et seq., 1973; "Mistake and Fraudulent Misrepresentation at Conclusion of Contract by means of an Agent, Comparative Study and Proposal for Reform as Basis of Unification of Common Law and Civil Law," Hamburg, 1975; "Sale of Property in Spain," RIW/AWD 757 et seq.,

(This Listing Continued)

1977; "Tax Saving in Brazil with Export of Technology form Germany," RIW/AWD 105 etro seq.; "Foundation of Companies in Bahrain," IWBf Gr. 3, 1 et seq., 1978; "German Investor and the Reform of Corporate Law in Brazil," RIW/AWD 103 et seq., 1979; "French Law of Apparent Authority and Acting for Third Parties," IWB 3, 257 et seq., 1981; "Practice of Spanish Arbitration from German Point of View," RIW/AWD et seq., 1983; "Acquisition of Real Estate in Brazil," Haus- und Grundbesitz im Ausland, 1985-1986; "EEIG - An Euro - Dimensional Legal Form for the GDR - Market?" Handelsblatt 17.03.1990, 7; "The D-Mark should be followed by the Tax Law - Tax Problems with Inter-German Cooperation," Blick durch die Wirtschaft, 10.05.1990, 7; "Setting up of a Corporation or a Partnership in the former GDR —Tax planning issues after reunification," Blick durch die Wirtschaft 19.11.1990; "Foreign Subsidiaries or Branches: Special Assets from Shareholders of a "European Economic Interest Grouping," RIW 1990, 917 et seg., Taxation of European Activities of German Corporate Entities— Use of a European Subsidiary or Holding," IWB Nr. 1, 10.1.1991, Gr. 2, 557 et seg., "German European Tax Planning via Holding Companies in case of Operative Activities in Great Britain and the USA," Der Betrieb, 1991, 198 et seg., "Tax Aspects with Contribution of Parts of a Business Enterprise to a "European Economic Interest Grouping," RIW 1991, 135 et seg., "Portugal Dossier," Deutsch-Schweizerische Schutzgemeinschaft (1991), "Acquisition of Real Estate in Portugal," Haus- und Grundbesitz im Ausland, 1987-1991. Co-Author: "German Treaty Overriding-New Clauses in the German Foreign Tax Act," RIW 1991, p. 49; "Tax Questions on the Privatization of Enterprises in the new Bundeslaender," Blick durch die Wirtschaft, 1/9/92 and 1/16/92, p. 7; "Earthquakes," Video-Judgement, Der Betrieb, 1992, p. 1792; "Taxation of German Investors in Argentine," IWB 1992, p. 985; "Taxation of Foreign Companies with German Management," Blick durch die Wirtschaft 12/10/92, p.7; "Liberalization of the Investment Law in Spain," IStR 1994, p. 602. *Member:* Deutscher Juristentag; Society of Comparative Law; Deutsch-Französische, Deutsch-Spanische, Deutsch-Brasilianische and Deutsch Argentinische Juristenvereinigungen; Deutsch-Portugiesische Gesellschaft; Association of Entrepreneurs (ASU). *LANGUAGES:* English, French, Spanish, Portuguese and Italian. *PRACTICE AREAS:* International Business Law on Cross-Border Transactions; Company, Contract, Labour and Tax Law; International Tax Structures.

SIEGHARD VON SALDERN, born Wanfried, Germany, April 15, 1945; admitted, 1975, Germany. *Education:* University of Hamburg. *LANGUAGES:* German and English. *PRACTICE AREAS:* Construction Law; Real Estate Law; Family Law; Environmental Law; Inheritance Law; Rental Law.

THOMAS J. DIEKMANN, born Wuppertal, Germany, August 11, 1947; admitted, 1976, Germany. *Education:* Universities of Hamburg and Freiburg. *Member:* IBA; UAE; Union des Avocats Européens; DACH Deutsch-Östereichisch-Schweizerische Anwaltsvereinigung; ADVONET (President); Deutsch-Europäische-Anwaltsvereinigung; Deutscher Anwaltsverein; Arbeitsgemeinschaft für Internationalen Rechtsverkehr; ECTA European Communities Trademark Association; Deutsche Vereinigung für gewerblichen Rechtschutz und Urheberrecht e.V. *LANGUAGES:* German and English. *PRACTICE AREAS:* Unfair Competition; Trademark; Patent; Antitrust; Company; Contract; Labor; Licence; Joint Venture Law.

JOACHIM KNIES, born Rostock, Germany, January 13, 1946; admitted, 1985, Germany. *Education:* University of Hamburg. *LANGUAGES:* German and English. *PRACTICE AREAS:* Family; Real Estate; Construction; Rental; Commercial Law; Labor Law.

JUSTUS FISCHER-ZERNIN, Fachanwalt f. Steuerrecht (tax attorney), M. Int. Law/A.N.U., born Hamburg, Germany, February 5, 1956; admitted, 1988, Hamburg. *Education:* University of Hamburg (Law, Economic Geography, Economics); Australian National University/Canberra (Graduate International Law Program, International Economics) 1988 degree: Master of International Law. Assistant Professor, International Tax Institute/University of Hamburg, 1985-1987. Legal Counsel and Project Manager: (Foreign Subsidiaries) of a Germany Company, 1987-1989; Law and Tax Department of a German Auditing Company ("Big Eight"), 1989-1991. Author: DISC and FSC, The Troublesome Relationship Between US-Tax Law and GATT, Intertax 1986 p. 40; Taxation of German Labour according to the German-U.K. Tax Treaty, RIW 1986 p. 284; Taxation Problems under the so-called 183 days Rule of Tax Treaties, FR 1986, p. 375; Results of the Australian Tax Reform, IWB 1986 p 807; The General Agreement on Tariffs and Trade (GATT), IWB 1987 p 117; Basic Elements of the U.S. Tax Reform, Steuer und Studium 1987 p. 66; GATT vs. Tax Treaties? JWTL 1987 III p. 39; The South Korean Tax System, IWB 1987 p. 317; Abuse of Tax Treaties, RIW 1987 p. 362; Tax Treaties as Instruments of International Law and Domestic Law, RIW 1987 p. 785; The Ma-

(This Listing Continued)

laysian Tax System, IWB 1988 p. 286; Rules of International Tax Law in International Trade Agreements (FCN/GATT); RIW 1988 p. 286; Tax Treaties and International Jurisdiction, Institut für Finanz- und Steuerrecht, University of Osnabrück II 1988 p. 13; Tax Treaties "Farewell to a Myth," RIW 1988 p. 727; German Wealth Tax for Non-Residents, IWB 1989 p. 185; International Tax Authorities in Progress? RIW 1990 p . 305; The U.S . Branch-Profits for German Investors, DB 1990 p. 1940; Partners' Special Reimbursements and Tax Treaties, RIW 1991 p. 493. Co-Author: Tax Law for International Enterprises, Cologne 1991/1992; "German Treaty Overriding-New Clauses in the German Foreign Tax Act," RIW, 1991, p. 49; "Tax Questions on the Privatization of Enterprises in the new Bundeslaender," Blick Durch Die Wirtschaft, 1/9/92 and 1/16/92, p. 7; "Earthquakes," Video-Judgement, Der Betrieb, 1992, p. 1792; "Taxation of German Investors in Argentine," IWB 1992, p. 985; "Taxation of Foreign Companies with German Management," Blick durch die Wirtschaft 12/10/92, p. 7. *Member:* Deutsche Steuerjuristische Gesellschaft. *LANGUAGES:* English and French. *PRACTICE AREAS:* German, Foreign and International Tax and Company Law; Tax Planning; Public International Law.

RAFAEL VILLENA Y SCHEFFLER, born Neuss, Germany, November 9, 1961; admitted, 1992, Hamburg. *Education:* Universities of Regensburg, Münster/Germany, Barcelona/Spain. Author: "The Legal Framework for Investments in Poland," Deutsches Steuerrecht 1991, p. 392. Co-Author: "Liberalization of the Investment Law in Spain," IStR 1994, p. 602. *Member:* Deutsch-Spanische Juristenvereinigung. *LANGUAGES:* Spanish, English, Portuguese and Italian. *PRACTICE AREAS:* General Civil Law; Company, Commercial, Labour, Business and Construction Law; Private International law; Spanish and Latin American Law; East European Investments; Real Estate.

All Members of the Firm are Members of the Hamburg and German Bar Associations.

Languages: German, English, French, Spanish, Portuguese and Italian

---

LAW OFFICES
OF
HENNING SCHWARZKOPF, M.C.L.

ZIPPELHAUS 4
20457 HAMBURG, GERMANY
Telephone: (040) 32 43 33
Telefax: (040) 32 41 81

FIRM PROFILE: The firm was established in 1984 and offers the full range of legal services. It is well known for its specialized expertise on U.S. law, as well as its emphasis on issues relating to international investment funds and cross border leasing. The client base is European and American. The firm has associated offices in London, Miami, Nice, Philadelphia, San Francisco and St. Petersburg.

HENNING SCHWARZKOPF, born Hamburg, Germany, June 3, 1951; admitted, 1978, Hamburg and Supreme Court of Hamburg. *Education:* University of Hamburg; University of Leiden, The Netherlands (Post Graduate Studies, 1976); University of Miami, Florida (M.C.L., 1979). *Member:* German Bar Association; Florida Bar Association; International Bar Association; German-American Lawyers Association; German-Japanese Lawyers Association; European Managed Futures Association. *LANGUAGES:* German, English, French and Spanish. *PRACTICE AREAS:* International Business Law; Futures and Options; Aviation Law; Cross-Border Leasing; International Tax Structures.

SEELIG, EHLERS, ZIEHM, RICHTER & PARTNERS

Established in 1846

ADOLPHSBRUCKE 11
20457 HAMBURG, GERMANY
Telephone: +40.378901-0
Telex: 212451 aloma d
Telecopier: +40.366298
Cable Address: aloma

Member of The Delta Group of European Lawyers (E.E.I.G.)

(This Listing Continued)

Antitrust, Corporate, Energy and Natural Resources, Environment and Administration, Inheritance, Insurance, Intellectual Property, Labour, Litigation and Arbitration, Maritime, Mergers and Acquisition, Press and Publishing, Product Liability, Tax, Trade and Transport, Unfair Competition.

MEMBERS OF FIRM

DR. GEERT WOLFGANG SEELIG, born 1933; admitted, 1960. *Education:* Universities of Heidelberg and Hamburg (Dr. jur., 1958). Lecturer, CEIPI, Centre d'Etudes Internatioles de la Propriete Industrielle de l'Universite Strasbourg). Co-Author: "La Publicite et la Loi," Greffe, 1990; "Traite des Dessins et des Modeles," Greffe, 1988. *Member:* German Society for the Protection of Industrial Property and Copyright Law (GRUR); Association Internationale pour la Protection de la Propriete Industrielle (AIPPI); Association Francaise des Praticiens du Droit des Marques et Modeles (APRAM); European Community's Trademark Association (ECTA). *LANGUAGES:* German, French and English. *PRACTICE AREAS:* Intellectual Property; Unfair Competition; Inheritance and Real Estate.

DR. HOLGER ZIEHM, born 1936; admitted, 1965. *Education:* Universities of Tubingen and Hamburg (Dr. jur., 1966). *Member:* Hamburg Attorneys' Disciplinary Court. *LANGUAGES:* German, English and French. *PRACTICE AREAS:* Litigation and Arbitration; Civil, Commercial and Corporate Law; Electricity and Nuclear Energy; Third Party Liability; Medical and Attorney's Malpractice; Maritime.

DR. WOLFGANG RICHTER, born 1935; admitted, 1967. *Education:* University of Munster (Dr. jur., 1965). *Member:* German Society for the Protection of Industrial Property and Copyright Law (GRUR); International Trademark Association (INTA); Pharmaceutical Trademark Group; Association Francaise des Praticiens du Droit des Marques et Modeles (APRAM). *LANGUAGES:* German, French and English. *PRACTICE AREAS:* Intellectual Property; Unfair Competition.

DR. HOLGER EHLERS, born 1939; admitted, 1969. *Education:* Universities of Marburg and Hamburg (Dr. jur., 1969). *Member:* International Bar Association; German-Nordic Law Association; German Norwegian Chamber of Commerce; Board of Hamburg Bar Association. *LANGUAGES:* German, English, Norwegian and French. *PRACTICE AREAS:* Corporate and Tax Law; Third Party Liability; Attorney and Accountant Malpractice; Insurance; Environment.

CHRISTIAN HERTZ-EICHENRODE, born 1952; admitted, 1981. *Education:* Universities of Strasbourg, Geneva and Bonn; Ecole Nationale d'Administration (ENA) Paris. *Member:* German Society for the Protection of Industrial Property and Copyright Law (GRUR); Association Francaise des Praticiens du Droit des Marques et Modeles (APRAM); German-American Law Association. *LANGUAGES:* German, French and English. *PRACTICE AREAS:* Computer and Telecommunication; Intellectual Property; Unfair Competition; Antitrust Law; EEC Law.

DR. CARSTEN HARMS, born 1955; admitted, 1986. *Education:* Universities of Marburg, Geneva and Freiburg (Dr. jur., 1988). Assistant Lecturer, University of Freiburg, 1982-1983. *Member:* German Association of Transport Law; Deutscher Verein für Internationales Seerecht. *LANGUAGES:* German, French and English. *PRACTICE AREAS:* Insurance; Energy; Transport; Maritime Law.

ANNETTE HOYER-GLASMACHER, born 1953; admitted, 1980. *Education:* Universities of Freiburg and Lausanne. *LANGUAGES:* German and English.

DR. DETLEF VON SCHULTZ, born 1956; admitted, 1988. *Education:* Universities of Hamburg (Dr. jur., 1986) and Heidelberg. *Member:* German Society for the Protection of Industrial Property and Copyright Law (GRUR). *LANGUAGES:* German, Spanish, French and English. *PRACTICE AREAS:* Intellectual Property; Unfair Competition; EEC Antitrust Law.

ASSOCIATES

HILDE DRESSLER, born 1940; admitted, 1973. *Education:* University of Hamburg. *LANGUAGES:* German, French and English. *PRACTICE AREAS:* Labour; General Contract Conditions; Real Property.

MIRIAM B. JAHN, born 1962; admitted, 1992. *Education:* University of Hamburg. *LANGUAGES:* German and English.

STAFFAN WEGDELL, born 1962; admitted, 1992. *Education:* University of Hamburg. *Member:* German-Nordic Law Association. *LANGUAGES:* German, Swedish and English.

Languages: German, English, French, Spanish, Norwegian and Swedish

SEGELKEN & SUCHOPAR

Established in 1949

BAUMWALL 7, "UBERSEEHAUS"
20459 HAMBURG, GERMANY
Telephone: (040) 37 68 050
Telefax: (040) 36 20 71
Telex: 213 094 sesu d

Berlin, Germany Office: Zimmerstraße 86-91, 10117 Berlin. Telephone: (030) 229 41 81. Telefax: (030) 391 44 34.

General Practice, National and International Business Law, Insurance and Liability Law, Transportation including Admiralty Law, Aviation, Road and Rail, Corporate and Contract Law, Insolvency and Bankruptcy, Competition and Anti-Trust Law, Construction, E.C. Law, Litigation, Arbitration.

FIRM PROFILE: The firm was established in 1949 and offers a full range of legal service. It is well-known for its commercial and transportation/maritime law.

MEMBERS OF FIRM

HANS-HELMUT SEGELKEN, born Bremerhaven, May 6, 1930; admitted, 1957, Hamburg. *Education:* Universities of Freiburg i.Br., Innsbruck and Hamburg. *Member:* International Bar Association; German International Maritime Law Association; German Transport Law Association; Bejing-Hamburg Couciliation Cen tre. *LANGUAGES:* German and English. *PRACTICE AREAS:* Admiralty and Maritime Law; Insurance; Company and Business Law; Litigation.

DR. CHRISTIAN ANDREAE, born Berlin, August 26, 1942; admitted, 1973, Hamburg. *Education:* Universities of Freiburg i.Br., München and Hamburg. Author: "Zwangsvollstreckungsrecht in Miteigentumsanteile an Grundstücken." *Member:* Hamburg and International Bar Associations; Deutscher Anwaltsverein; German Transport Law Association; Ostasiatischer Verein e.V.; Ibero-America Verein e.V.; German Society for the Protection of Industrial Property and Copyright Law (GRUR); Beijing-Hamburg Conciliation Centre e.V., Hamburg; Hamburg Society for Insurance Law; Arbeitsgemeinschaft für Internationalen Rechtsverkehr im Deutschen Anwaltsverein. *LANGUAGES:* German and English. *PRACTICE AREAS:* Aviation and Aerospace; Transportation; Insurance; Company and Business Law; Mergers and Acquisitions; Bank; Bankruptcy.

DR. KLAUS HEUER, born Olpe/Westfalen, January 11, 1942; (Not admitted in Germany). *Education:* Universities of Marburg, Berlin and Hamburg. Author: "Die Haftung des Frachtführers nach der CMR"; "Verkehrshaftungsversicherungen"; "Der Spediteur als Frachtführer." *Member:* Hamburg Bar Association; Deutscher Anwaltsverein; German Transport Law Association. *LANGUAGES:* German and English. *PRACTICE AREAS:* Transportation; Insurance.

INGEBORG SUCHOPAR, born Berlin, February 2, 1938; admitted, 1972, Hamburg. *Education:* Universities of Frankfurt/M. and Kiel. *Member:* Hamburg Bar Association. *LANGUAGES:* German and English. *PRACTICE AREAS:* Admiralty and Maritime Law; Aviation and Aerospace; Transportation; Insurance.

ARMIN ROHDE, born Bonn, May 30, 1943; admitted, 1979, Hamburg. *Education:* University of Hamburg. Author: "Vertraglicher Abschluß des Versorgungsausgleiches." *Member:* Hamburg Bar Association. *LANGUAGES:* German and English. *PRACTICE AREAS:* Advertising and Marketing; Criminal Law; Labour and Employment; Medical Malpractice; Personal Injury; Property.

THOMAS WANCKEL, born Oldenburg, March 18, 1953; admitted, 1984, Hamburg. *Education:* University of Hamburg. Law Clerk, Public Defenders Office, Providence, Rhode Island, 1982. *Member:* German International Maritime Association; German Law Association; German Society for the Protection of Industrial Property and Copyright Law (GRUR). *LANGUAGES:* German and English. *PRACTICE AREAS:* Admiralty and Maritime Law; Advertising and Marketing; Insurance; Company and Business Law; Transportation; Bankruptcy.

DR. THOMAS REICHELT, born Frankfurt, September 17, 1959; admitted, 1987, Hamburg. *Education:* University of Gießen. Author: "Der Vorbescheid im Verwaltungsverfahren"; "Neuere Tendenzen im Wettbewerbsrecht der Apotheker." Lecturer in Law, Academy of Advertising, Hamburg. Research Assistant, University of Gießen, 1981-1984. *Member:* Hamburg Bar Associations; German Society for the Protection of Industrial Property and Copyright Law (GRUR). (Resident, Berlin Office). *LANGUAGES:* German, English and French. *PRACTICE AREAS:* Ad-

(This Listing Continued)

---

vertising and Marketing; Property; Intellectual Property; Professional Liability.

DR. WOLF-PETER GROẞ, born Stuttgart, November 15, 1961; admitted, 1993, Hamburg. *Education:* Universities of Bayreuth and Kiel. *Member:* Hamburg Bar Association; German Transportation Association. *LANGUAGES:* German and English. *PRACTICE AREAS:* Admiralty and Maritime Law; Antitrust and Trade Regulations; Insurance; Company and Business Law; Transportation; Bankruptcy.

FOLKERT BAARS, born Wilhelmshaven, December 16, 1960; admitted, 1993, Hamburg. *Education:* Universities of Nürnburg-Erlangen, Göttingen. *Member:* Hamburg Bar Association. *LANGUAGES:* German and English. *PRACTICE AREAS:* Contracts; Family Law; Leaser and Leases; Insurance; Property; Real Estate; Transportation.

SUSANNE KRAFT, born Hamburg, August 26, 1964; admitted, 1994, Hamburg. *Education:* University of Hamburg. *LANGUAGES:* German and English. *PRACTICE AREAS:* Bankruptcy; Company and Business Law; Contracts; Transportation; Labour and Employment; Litigation.

UEXKÜLL & STOLBERG

(Patent Agents and European Patent Attorneys Exclusively, Not

Attorneys at Law)

Established in 1958

BESELERSTRASSE 4
D-22607 HAMBURG, GERMANY
Telephone: (40) 899-6540
Telex: 214 204 UXPAT D
Facsimile: (40) 899-65488

Patent and Trademarks; Admitted as Patentanwälte and European Patent Attorneys but not Authorized to act as Rechtsanwälte.

FIRM PROFILE: The firm was established in 1958 and offers legal services in intellectual property matters. The client base is European, North American and East Asian in scope.

MEMBERS OF FIRM

ULRICH GRAF STOLBERG, born Munich, Germany, May 4, 1935; registered to practice before the German Patent and Trademark Office, 1967; European Patent Office, 1979. *Education:* University of Munich (Dr. in Chemistry, 1961); Industrial Property Study Program, organized by the German Patent Office (1967). *Member:* German Patent Attorney Bar Association; International Federation of Industrial Property Attorneys (FICPI); International Association for the Protection of Industrial Property (AIPPI); German Association for the Protection of Industrial Property and Copyright Law (GRUR); Gesellschaft Deutscher Chemiker (GDCh); Institute of Trademark Agents (ITMA; Associate Member); United States Trademark Association (USTA; Associate Member). *LANGUAGES:* German and English. *PRACTICE AREAS:* Patent and Trademark Law.

JÜRGEN SUCHANTKE, born Hamburg, Germany, December 14, 1936; registered to practice before the German Patent and Trademark Office, 1970; European Patent Office, 1979. *Education:* Technical University of Berlin (Diploma in Electrical Engineering, 1964); Industrial Property Study Program, organized by the German Patent Office (1968-1969). *Member:* German Patent Attorney Bar Association; International Federation of Industrial Property Attorneys (FICPI); International Association for the Protection of Industrial Property (AIPPI); German Association for the Protection of Industrial Property and Copyright Law (GRUR); American Intellectual Property Law Association (AIPLA). *LANGUAGES:* German and English. *PRACTICE AREAS:* Patent and Trademark Law.

ARNULF HUBER, born Hecklingen, Germany, April 13, 1943; registered to practice before the German Patent and Trademark Office, 1978; European Patent Office, 1979. *Education:* University of Vienna; University of California at Berkeley; University of Graz (Dipl. Ing., 1970); Industrial Property Study Program, organized by the German Patent Office (1977-1978). *Member:* German Patent Attorney Bar Association; International Federation of Industrial Property Attorneys (FICPI); German Association for the Protection of Industrial Property and Copyright Law (GRUR). *LANGUAGES:* German and English. *PRACTICE AREAS:* Patent and Trademark Law.

ALLARD VON KAMEKE, born Walsrode, Germany, December 12, 1946; registered to practice before the German Patent and Trademark Office, 1978; European Patent Office, 1979. *Education:* University of Hannover (Dr. in Chemistry, 1974); Stanford University (Post Doctorate, 1975);

(This Listing Continued)

Industrial Property Study Program, organized by the German Patent Office (1977-1978). *Member:* German Patent Attorney Bar Association; International Federation of Industrial Property Attorneys (FICPI); German Association for the Protection of Industrial Property and Copyright Law (GRUR); The Licensing Executives Society (LES). *LANGUAGES:* German and English. *PRACTICE AREAS:* Patent and Trademark Law.

INGEBORG VOELKER, born Hamburg, Germany, April 13, 1935; registered to practice before the German Patent and Trademark Office, 1985; European Patent Office, 1986. *Education:* University of Pretoria (Bachelor of Science, 1957); University of Hamburg (Diploma in Biology, 1981); Industrial Property Study Program, organized by the German Patent Office (1984-1985). *Member:* German Patent Attorney Bar Association; International Federation of Industrial Property Attorneys (FICPI); German Association for the Protection of Industrial Property and Copyright Law (GRUR). *LANGUAGES:* German and English. *PRACTICE AREAS:* Patent and Trademark Law.

PETER FRANCK, born Oberhausen/Rhld., Germany, July 24, 1953; registered to practice before the German Patent and Trademark Office, 1987; European Patent Office, 1988. *Education:* Technical University Clausthal; University Freiburg; ETH Zürich, Swiss Institute of Technology (Diploma in Chemistry, 1977; Dr. in Chemistry, 1984); Industrial Property Study Program, organized by the German Patent Office (1987). *Member:* German Patent Attorney Bar Association; International Federation of Industrial Property Attorneys (FICPI). *LANGUAGES:* German, English and French. *PRACTICE AREAS:* Patent and Trademark Law.

GEORG BOTH, born Cologne, Germany, December 30, 1954; registered to practice before the German Patent and Trademark Office, 1992. *Education:* University of Cologne (Dr. in Physics, 1982); Argonne National Laboratory (Post Doctorate, 1985-1986); Harvard Medical School (Post Doctorate, 1987-1988);Industrial Property Study Program, organized by the German Patent Office (1991-1992). *Member:* German Patent Attorney Bar Association; American Physical Society (APS); Deutsche Physikalische Gesellschaft (DPG). *LANGUAGES:* German and English. *PRACTICE AREAS:* Patent and Trademark Law.

HELMUT VAN HEESCH, born Rhede, Germany, April 13, 1957; registered to practice before the German Patent and Trademark Office, 1991. *Education:* University of Kiel (Dr. in Chemistry, 1985); Industrial Property Study Program, organized by the German Patent Office (1989-1990). *Member:* German Patent Attorney Bar Association; Gesellschaft Deutscher Chemiker (GDCh). *LANGUAGES:* German and English. *PRACTICE AREAS:* Patent and Trademark Law.

ULRICH-MARIA GROSS, born Hamburg, Germany, October 17, 1958; registered to practice before the German Patent and Trademark Office, 1993. *Education:* University of Hamburg (Diploma in Chemistry, 1985; Dr. in Chemistry, 1987); Industrial Property Study Program organized by the German Patent Office (1990-1991). *Member:* German Patent Attorney Bar Association. *LANGUAGES:* German and English. *PRACTICE AREAS:* Patent and Trademark Law.

JOACHIM STÜRKEN, born Hamburg, Germany, September 30, 1960; registered to practice before the German Patent and Trademark Office, 1993. *Education:* University of Hamburg (Diploma in Biology, 1989); Industrial Property Study Program organized by the German Patent Office (1992-1993). *Member:* German Patent Bar Association; Deutsche Genetische Gesellschaft (DGG). *LANGUAGES:* German, English and French. *PRACTICE AREAS:* Patent and Trademark Law.

JOHANNES AHME, born Hamburg, Germany, June 27, 1960; registered to practice before the German Patent and Trademark Office, 1993. *Education:* University of Hamburg (Dr. in Physics, 1988); Deutsches Elektronensynchrotron DESY (Post Doctorate, 1989-1990); Industrial Property Study Program, organized by the German Patent Office (1990-1993). *Member:* German Patent Attorney Bar Association; Deutsche Physikalische Gesellschaft (DPG). *LANGUAGES:* German and English. *PRACTICE AREAS:* Patent and Trademark Law.

Languages: German, English and French.

USSLAR, MORGEN, BORCKE

LURUPER CHAUSSEE 125
22761 HAMBURG, GERMANY
Telephone: 040-894023
Fax: 040-8992397

General Practice, Financial Services and Investment Law, License Agreements, Computer and Telecommunication Law.

(This Listing Continued)

DR. LEVIN VON USSLAR, born Hamburg, Germany, May 9, 1943; admitted, 1977, Germany. *Education:* University of Göttingen (1965-1968); University of California at Berkeley (LL.M., 1970). Co-Author: "Aktuelle Rechtsfragen der Kreditkartenpraxis," Hoppenstedt, 1989. *Member:* Hamburg Bar Association; German-American Lawyers Association; German-British Lawyers Association. *LANGUAGES:* German and English.

DR. ROBERT D. VON MORGEN, born Hamburg, Germany, June 29, 1959; admitted, 1986, Germany. *Education:* University of Hamburg (Dr. iur., 1989). Co-Author: "Aktuelle Rechtsfragen der Kreditkartenpraxis," Hoppenstedt, 1989. *Member:* European Lawyers Association (UAE). *LANGUAGES:* English and German.

SITTA VON BORCKE, born Hamburg, Germany, December 24, 1940; admitted, 1972, Germany. *Education:* University of München (1962-1964); University of Hamburg (1964-1966). *LANGUAGES:* German and English.

DAPHNE DE CHAPEAUROUGE-GEHRCKENS, born Vienna, Austria, May 5, 1942; admitted, 1971, Germany. *Education:* University of Hamburg; University of Paris, France. *LANGUAGES:* German, English, French and Italian.

WEISS & HASCHE

A merger of the law firms Hasche Albrecht Fischer, Hamburg, Ott Weiss Eschenlohr & Partner, Munich and Rosenberg, Berlin.

VALENTINSKAMP 88
20355 HAMBURG, GERMANY
Telephone: (040) 35 00 20
Cable Address: "Lawyers"
Telex: 215461 LAWY D
Teletex: 402276 LAWY D
Telefax: (040) 35 00 21 52

Munich, Germany Office: Brienner Strasse 11/V (Luitpoldblock), 80333 Munich. Telephone: (089) 23 80 70. Cable Address: "Interlaw", Munich. Telex: 5 22957 Law. Telefax: (089) 23 80 71 10.

Leipzig, Germany Office: Karl-Tauchnitz-Strasse 10 B, 04107 Leipzig. Telephone: (0341) 216 720. Telefax: (0341) 216 72 33.

Berlin, Germany Office: Meinekestrasse 13, 10719 Berlin. Telephone: (030) 881 97 83. Telefax: (030) 882 34 79.

Prague, Czech Republic Office: Dělnická 30, 170 00 Prague 7. Telephone: (2) 683 40 23. Telefax: (2) 683 40 23.

Commercial, International Trade, Maritime, Transport, Forwarding, Shipbuilding, Shipfinancing, Tax, Banking, Corporation, Mergers and Acquisitions, Antitrust, Unfair Competition, Industrial Property, Real Estate, Environment, Common Market, Insurance, Aviation, Arbitration, Media, Administrative, Labor, Computer, German Reunification, Litigation.

MEMBERS OF FIRM
(HAMBURG OFFICE)

DR. WALTER HASCHE, born Hamburg, Germany, December 23, 1909; admitted, 1946, Germany. *Education:* University of Tübingen and University of Hamburg (Dr. jur., 1937). Member, Hamburg Parliament, 1953-1957 and 1966-1970. Deputy to the Hamburg Department of Commerce, 1957-1961. Member, Advisory Board for Maritime Affairs with the Ministry of Transport and Traffic, 1964-1976. Vice-President, German International Maritime Law Association, 1967-1975. Retired President, Deutsche Schiffsbeleihungs-Bank AG, Hamburg, 1956-1976. *Member:* Hamburg Bar Association; Hamburg Society of Lawyers; Board of Flensburger Schiffsparten-Vereinigung AG; Membre Titulaire, Comité Maritime International. *LANGUAGES:* German and English.

DR. HANS-CHRISTIAN ALBRECHT, born Berlin, Germany, April 18, 1920; admitted, 1952, Germany. *Education:* University of Hamburg and University of Tübingen (Dr. jur., 1950). Member, Hamburg State Parliament, 1947-1948. *Member:* Hamburg Bar Association; International Bar Association (Business Section); Hamburg Society of Lawyers; German International Maritime Law Association (Vice President). *LANGUAGES:* German, English and French.

DR. BURKHARD VOGELER, born Berlin, Germany, March 19, 1925; admitted, 1959, Germany. *Education:* University of Kiel (Dr. jur., 1953). *Member:* Hamburg Bar Association; Hamburg Society of Lawyers; International Law Association; German International Maritime Law Association; London Maritime Arbitrators Association; German Maritime Arbitration

(This Listing Continued)

WEISS & HASCHE, Hamburg—Continued

Association; German-Greek Lawyers Association (Secretary General). *LANGUAGES:* German, English and French.

ISA DROBNIG, born Lueben, Germany, October 14, 1929; admitted, 1959, Germany. *Education:* University of Bonn and University of Ann Arbor, Michigan (LL.M., 1956). *Member:* Hamburg Bar Association; German International Maritime Law Association; Hamburg Society of Lawyers; German Maritime Arbitration Association (Member of the Board). *LANGUAGES:* German and English.

DR. JOST NEUBAUER, born Flensburg, Germany, March 3, 1935; admitted, 1963, Germany. *Education:* University of Köln, University of Hamburg (Dr. jur., 1962); University of Berlin. Assistant Professor at Frankfurt University, 1963-1964. *Member:* Hamburg Bar Association; Hamburg Society of Lawyers; President of the Hamburg Professional Disciplinary Court; Hamburg Legal Examination Commissions; German Industrial Property Law Association; International Bar Association (Business Section). *LANGUAGES:* German and English.

DR. MICHAEL STROBEL, born Hamburg, Germany, March 31, 1938; admitted, 1966, Germany. *Education:* Universities of Marburg, Köln, Bonn and Hamburg (Dr. jur., 1966). *Member:* International Bar Association (Business Section); Hamburg Bar Association. *LANGUAGES:* German and English.

DR. VOLKER LOOKS, born Oldenburg/Holst., Germany, November 28, 1942; admitted, 1970, Germany. *Education:* University of Kiel (Dr. jur., 1969); University of Tübingen. *Member:* Hamburg and International Bar Associations; Hamburg Society of Lawyers; German International Maritime Law Association; German Maritime Arbitration Association. *LANGUAGES:* German, English and French.

DR. THOMAS SEIFFERT, born Melsungen, Germany, September 12, 1944; admitted, 1974, Germany. *Education:* Universities of Freiburg and Hamburg (Dr. jur., 1973). *Member:* Hamburg Bar Association; International Bar Association (Business Section); Hamburg Society of Lawyers; Deutscher Juristentag; Society for Environmental Law. *LANGUAGES:* German, English and French.

HELMUT STANGE, born Kiel, Germany, March 28, 1943; admitted, 1974, Germany. *Education:* Universities of Tübingen, Berlin, Kiel; King's College, London. *Member:* Hamburg Bar Association; German International Maritime Law Association. *LANGUAGES:* German and English.

DR. LUDWIG LINDER, born Bad Waldsee, Germany, July 25, 1947; admitted, 1980, Germany. *Education:* Universities of Tübingen (Dr. jur., 1979); Aix-en-Provence/Marseille (Diplôme d'Etudes Juridiques Générales, 1969); Hamburg, Speyer, Berkeley (LL.M., 1976); Max-Planck-Institute for Foreign and Private International Law (Assistant, 1977-1980). *Member:* International Bar Association (Business Section); German-American Lawyers Association; International and U.S. Boalt Hall Alumni Association; International League for Competition Law. *LANGUAGES:* German, English and French.

FRIEDRICH GRAF VON LUCKNER, born Buxtehude, Germany, June 5, 1947; admitted, 1976, Germany. *Education:* Universities of Göttingen and Freiburg. *Member:* Hamburg Bar Association; German Industrial Property Law Association; International League for Competition Law. *LANGUAGES:* German, English, French and Italian.

CORNELIUS BRANDI, born Wanne-Eickel, Germany, January 30, 1955; admitted, 1983, Germany. *Education:* University of Bonn. *Member:* Hamburg Bar Association; German International Maritime Law Association; French Maritime Law Association (Correspondent Member); German-Greek Lawyers Association; Young Lawyers' International Association (AIJA). *LANGUAGES:* German, English and French.

JAN GRAF VON SPEE, born Bremen, Germany, December 15, 1956; admitted, 1985, Germany. *Education:* Universities of Berlin and Bonn. Trainee, Haight, Gardner, Poor & Havens, New York, 1984. *Member:* Hamburg Bar Association. *LANGUAGES:* German, English and French.

DR. CHRISTIAN VON LENTHE, born Lenthe, Germany, February 14, 1960; admitted, 1989, Germany. *Education:* Universities of Tübingen and Freiburg. *Member:* Hamburg Bar Association. *LANGUAGES:* German and English.

DR. FRITZ FRHR. VON HAMMERSTEIN, born Braunschweig, Germany, May 17, 1959; admitted, 1989, Germany. *Education:* Universities of Heidelberg (Dr. jur., 1984) and Freiburg im Breisgau. *Member:* International Bar Association (Business Section); Hamburg Bar Association; Ham-

(This Listing Continued)

burg Society of Lawyers; German Environmental Law Society; European Environmental Lawyers Association. *LANGUAGES:* German and English.

MARC RIEDE, born Hamburg, Germany, July 11, 1960; admitted, 1990, Germany. *Education:* University of Hamburg. *Member:* Hamburg Bar Association. *LANGUAGES:* German and English.

DR. JOST KIENZLE, born Stuttgart, Germany, November 16, 1958; admitted, 1989, Germany. *Education:* University of Hamburg (Dr. jur., 1992); Institute for International Maritime Law and Law of the Sea, Hamburg (Assistant, 1989-1991). *Member:* Hamburg Bar Association. *LANGUAGES:* German, English and Spanish.

Languages: German, English, French, Italian and Spanish

WEISS • WALTER • FISCHER-ZERNIN

Established in 1994

GLOCKENGIESSERWALL 2 (WALLHOF)

20095 HAMBURG, GERMANY

Telephone: +49-40-32 21 19

Fax: +49-40-32 25 90

Munich, Germany Office: Salvatorplatz 4/II, 80333. Telephone: +49-89-2 90 71 90. Fax: +49-89-29 07 19 17.

New York, New York Office: 90 Park Avenue, 10016. Telephone: 221-210 94 00. Fax: 212-210-94 44.

FIRM PROFILE: The firm was established by Dr. Karl Heinz Weiss, Prof. Dr. Dr. Otto L. Walter and Dr. Vincent Fischer-Zernin, former senior partners of leading international commercial law firms. They concentrate the synergetic use of their joint domestic and global experience and connections, to serve and render counsel to management, especially in the fields of long range strategy, financial planning, labor relations and the avoidance or solving of business and tax problems. The firm offers to its clients full service in all branches of commercial and corporate law for both the domestic and international area.

MEMBERS OF FIRM

DR. VINCENT FISCHER-ZERNIN, born Hamburg, October 7, 1925; admitted, 1952, Germany. *Education:* Universities of Hamburg and Frankfurt (First Law Degree, 1948; Dr. jur., 1950). Dissertation: "The Removal of Domicile of Companies from the Eastern Territories of Germany to the Territory of the Western Zones" ("Die Sitzverlegung von Handelsunternehmen aus den deutschen Ostgebieten in das Gebiet der Westzonen"). Former Member, Hamburg Constitutional Court. Chairman, Advisory Board, E.H. Worlée & Co., Hamburg; Theodor Willee, Hamburg. *Member:* Hamburg Bar Association; Hamburg Society of Lawyers; International Law Association of the Hague; German Arbitration Committee; German Arbitration Institute; German Maritime Arbitration Association (Founding Member of the Board); Bugsier-Reederei- und Bergungs GmbH, Hamburg (Advisory Board); Geyer-Werke GmbH, Hamburg; Rohde & Liesenfeld (GmbH & Co.), Hamburg; Objekt Pro-Markt Buxtehude, Hamburg; Zipperling, Kessler & Co., Ahrensburg; Robert Bornhold (GmbH & Co.), Hamburg; Blohm und TEREG Industriedienstleistungen GmbH, Hamburg. *LANGUAGES:* German, English and French. *PRACTICE AREAS:* Commercial Law; Company Law; Corporate Law; Banking; Finance; Investments; Merger and Acquisition; Real Estate; Taxation; Arbitration.

DR. AXEL MAY, born Hamburg, Germany, August 13, 1948; admitted, 1976, Germany. *Education:* University of Hamburg (Referendar, 1973; Assessor, 1976; Dr. jur., 1982). Author: "Die Schutzschrift im Arrest- und Einstweiligen Verfügungs-Verfahren." Co-Chairman: Haraldt Quandt Vermögensverwaltung GmbH, Bad Homburg. Board Member: Harrow Industries Corp., New York; Real Estate Capital Partners, L.P., New York; AUDA Management Inc., New York. *LANGUAGES:* German, English and French. *PRACTICE AREAS:* Business Law; Estate Law; Taxation; Finance and Investments.

WESSING BERENBERG-GOSSLER ZIMMERMANN LANGE

NEUER WALL 46
D-20354 HAMBURG, GERMANY
Telephone: 49 40 36 80 30
Cable Address: "Unilaw"
Telex: 2-14111 Jura d
Teletex: 40 32 91 UNILAW
Telefax: 49 40 36 80 32 80

Munich, Germany Office: Vilshofener Str. 8, D-81679 Munich, P.O. Box 86 08 67, D-81635 Munich. Telephone: 49-89-98 28 021. Telefax: 49-89-98 12 14.

Düsseldorf, Germany Office: Königsallee 92 A, D-40212 Düsseldorf, P.O. Box 10 53 61, D-40044 Düsseldorf. Telephone: 49-211-83 87-0. Telex: 858 19 14 wess d. Cable Address: "Wegolex". Telefax: 49-211-32 36 16.

Frankfurt, Germany Office: Freiherr-Vom-Stein-Strasse 24-26, D-60323 Frankfurt. Telephone: 49-69-971300. Telefax: 49-69-97130100.

Berlin, Germany Office: Spreeufer 5, D-10178 Berlin. Telephone: 49-30-238 45 45. Telefax: 49-30-238 45 34.

Leipzig, Germany Office: Ferdinand-Rhode-Strasse 16, D-04107 Leipzig. Telephone: 49-341-213 13 80. Fax: 49-341-213 13 88.

Dresden, Germany Office: Heinrichstrasse 16, D-01097 Dresden. Telephone: 49-351-567 12 12. Telefax: 49-351-567 12 13.

Brussels, Belgium Office: Avenue Louise 149, Box 42, B-1050 Brussels. Telephone: +32 (2) 537 01 86. Telefax: +32 (2) 534 25 31.

Commercial, Corporation, Mergers and Acquisition, Banking, Investment, Common Market, Antitrust, Unfair Competition, Copyright, Patent and Trademark, License Agreements, Press, Maritime, Transportation, Insurance, Product Liability, Real Estate, Construction, Probate, Labor, Administrative, Litigation and Arbitration, Environmental Law, German Reunification and Restitution Law.

MEMBERS OF FIRM

DR. GÜNTHER VON BERENBERG-GOSSLER, born Freiburg i. Breisgau, Germany, February 21, 1911; admitted, 1941, Germany.

DR. MAXIMILIAN FRHR. VON GLEICHENSTEIN, born Hamburg, Germany, January 5, 1926; admitted, 1955, Germany. *Education:* Universities of Kiel, Hamburg and Zurich; Academy for International Law, The Hague and The Graduate Institute of International Studies (University of Geneva) (Dr. jur., 1952). *Member:* German Bar Association; International Law Association; Hamburg Bar Association; Societies of Lawyers; British-German Jurists' Association. *LANGUAGES:* German and English. *PRACTICE AREAS:* Wills and Estate Law; Insolvency; Real Estate.

VOLKER SACHAU, born Berlin, Germany, March 12, 1933; admitted, 1963, Germany. *Education:* Universities of Hamburg and Freiburg. *Member:* Hamburg and International Bar Associations; Societies of Lawyers; British-German Jurists' Association. *LANGUAGES:* German and English. *PRACTICE AREAS:* Commercial; Insurance; Real Estate; Labour; Litigation.

DR. GISELA WILD, born Bad Warmbrunn, Germany, September 18, 1932; admitted, 1961, Germany. *Education:* University of Freiburg i. Breisgau (Dr. jur., 1960). *Member:* Hamburg Bar Association; Societies of Lawyers; British-German Jurists' Association; German Society for the Protection of Industrial Property and Copyright Law; International Association for the Protection of Industrial Property (AIPPI). *LANGUAGES:* German, English and French. *PRACTICE AREAS:* Antitrust; Unfair Competition; Copyright; Patent and Trademark; Press.

HARTWIG LÜBBE, born Hamburg, Germany, July 17, 1939; admitted, 1967, Germany. *Education:* Universities of Kiel, Copenhagen and Hamburg. Deputy of the Hamburg Ministry for Fine Arts and Culture. *Member:* Societies of Lawyers; British-German Jurists' Association; Hamburg and International Bar Associations; German-Scandinavian Lawyers Society. *LANGUAGES:* German, English and Danish. *PRACTICE AREAS:* Commercial; Corporation; Mergers and Acquisitions; Investment; Real Estate.

JÜRGEN REIP, born Hamburg, Germany, January 11, 1939; admitted, 1969, Germany. *Education:* Universities of Hamburg, Munich and Tübingen. *Member:* Hamburg Bar Association; Societies of Lawyers; British-German Jurists' Association. *LANGUAGES:* German and English. *PRACTICE AREAS:* Commercial; Transportation; Insurance; Product Liability; Real Estate; Probate; Labour; Litigation; Arbitration.

(This Listing Continued)

DR. JOHANNES TRAPPE, born Trier, Germany, June 13, 1930; admitted, 1964, Germany. *Education:* Universities of Mainz, Freiburg and Grenoble (Dr. jur., 1956). Advisor, Maritime Law, Egypt, 1959-1962. *Member:* German International Maritime Law Association; Hamburg International Bar Association; German Maritime Arbitration Association; London Maritime Arbitrators' Association; Chartered Institute of Arbitrators, London; Beijing-Hamburg Conciliation Center, Hamburg. *LANGUAGES:* German, English and French. *PRACTICE AREAS:* Commercial; Maritime; Transportation; Insurance; Litigation; Arbitration.

KLAUS VORWERK, born Hamburg, Germany, May 25, 1945; admitted, 1975, Germany. *Education:* Universities of Göttingen and Hamburg. *Member:* Hamburg Bar Association; Societies of Lawyers; German Society for the Protection of Industrial Property and Copyright Law; International Association for the Protection of Industrial Property (AIPPI). *LANGUAGES:* German and English. *PRACTICE AREAS:* Commercial; Corporate; Antitrust; Unfair Competition; License Agreement; Press; Copyright.

AXEL C. FILGES, born Hamburg, Germany, July 28, 1947; admitted, 1976, Germany. *Education:* Universities of Hamburg and Bonn. *Member:* Board of the Hamburg Bar Association; Societies of Lawyers. *LANGUAGES:* German and English. *PRACTICE AREAS:* Product Liability; Construction; Labour.

MAJA STADLER-EULER, born Berlin, Germany, August 13, 1941; admitted, 1978, Germany. *Education:* Universities of Lausanne (Switzerland), Berlin, Köln and Bonn. Judge of the Hamburg Constitutional Court. *Member:* Hamburg Bar Association; Societies of Lawyers. *LANGUAGES:* German, English and French. *PRACTICE AREAS:* Administrative; Protection of the Environment; Family.

DR. BERND LAUDIEN, born Neuwied, Germany, August 29, 1946; admitted, 1978, Germany. *Education:* Universities of Lausanne, Switzerland and Freiburg. With United Nations Office of Legal Affairs, 1976. *Member:* Hamburg and International Bar Associations; German International Maritime Law Association. *LANGUAGES:* German, English and French. *PRACTICE AREAS:* Commercial; Insurance; Maritime and Arbitration.

BERNHARD KLOFT, born Hadamar, Germany, September 10, 1953; admitted, 1980, Germany. *Education:* Universities of Bonn and Freiburg. *Member:* Hamburg Bar Association. *LANGUAGES:* German and English. *PRACTICE AREAS:* Corporate; Mergers and Acquisition; Banking.

DR. CHRISTOPH HASCHE, born Hamburg, Germany, May 4, 1953; admitted, 1982, Germany. *Education:* Universities of Tübingen, Munich and Hamburg (Dr.jur., 1986). *Member:* International Bar Association; German International Maritime Law Association; German Maritime Arbitration Association; Nautical Association Hamburg; German Travel Law Association. *LANGUAGES:* German and English. *PRACTICE AREAS:* Commercial; Maritime; Transportation; Insurance; Litigation; Arbitration.

DR. DAGMAR ENTHOLT-LAUDIEN, born Bonn, April 26, 1959; admitted, 1987, Germany. *Education:* University of Freiburg. *Member:* Hamburg Bar Association. *LANGUAGES:* German, English and French. *PRACTICE AREAS:* Corporate; Commercial; Maritime.

DR. ANDREAS MEISSNER, born Rendsburg, June 9, 1959; admitted, 1988, Germany. *Education:* University of Hamburg. law office at Jeddah. *Member:* Hamburg Bar Association; German Society for the Protection of Industrial Property and Copyright Law. *LANGUAGES:* German, English and French. *PRACTICE AREAS:* Commercial; Corporation; Antitrust; Unfair Competition; License Agreement; Litigation.

DR. THOMAS HÖRNER, born September 14, 1961; admitted, 1990, Germany. *Education:* University of Würzburg, Lausanne, Hamburg. *Member:* Hamburg Bar Association; German Society for the Protection of Industrial Property and Copyright Law. *LANGUAGES:* German, English and French. *PRACTICE AREAS:* Common Market; Unfair Competition; Copyright; Patent and Trademark; Press; Litigation.

WESTPHAL & VOGES

ESPLANADE 41
20354 HAMBURG, GERMANY
Telephone: 040-356100
Telecopier: 040-35610-180

Berlin Office: Kurfürstendamm 46, 10701. Telephone: 030/883 40 04/05. Telefax: 030/882 57 26.

(This Listing Continued)

WESTPHAL & VOGES, Hamburg—Continued

Rostock Office: Lange Strasse 1 A, 19055. Telephone: 0381/4 58 20 70. Telefax: 0381/4 58 20 71.

Banking, Stockmarkets and Securities, Commercial Law, Competition and Anti-Trust Law, Computer Law, Corporate Law, Environmental Law, European and International Private Law, General Contractual Terms and Conditions, Inheritance Law, Wills and Succession, Insolvency Law, Insurance and Re-Insurance, Intellectual Property, Labour Law, Media Law, Mergers and Acquisitions, Property and Construction law, Property Rights in the New Federal States, Public and Administrative Law, Shipping-/Maritime Law, Tax Law.

MEMBERS OF FIRM

DR. JÜRGEN WESTPHAL, born December 1, 1927. *Education:* University of Hamburg (Dr. jur., 1954); University of Nancy, France (Diplome des etudes superieures Europiennes). State Minister for Economic and Traffic Affairs of Schleswig-Holstein at Kiel, 1973-1986. *Member:* German and International Bar Associations; British-German Jurists Association; German International Maritime Law Association. *LANGUAGES:* German, English and French. *PRACTICE AREAS:* Corporate Law; Membership in Supervisory Boards; EC and Public Economic Law.

HANS H. VOGES (1929-1993).

DR. KAY SOEHRING, born Stettin, July 7, 1939; admitted, 1969, Hamburg. *Education:* Universities of Kiel and Saarbrücken (Dr. jur., 1967). *Member:* German and International Bar Associations; German International Maritime Law Association; British-German Jurists Association; German Association of Comparative Law. *LANGUAGES:* German, English and French. *PRACTICE AREAS:* Banking Law; Insolvency Law; Tax Law.

DR. HENNING VON WEDEL, born Wentorf, June 24, 1945; admitted, 1975, Hamburg. *Education:* Universities of Freiburg and Hamburg (Dr. jur.). Editor in Chief, Verfassung und Recht in Ubersee (a Quarterly on Law and Modernization), 1974-1975. Research Fellow, Institute of International Affairs of University of Hamburg, 1970-1975. *Member:* Hamburg Bar Association; German International Maritime Law Association; German Association for the Protection of Industrial Property and Copyright Law. *LANGUAGES:* German and English. *PRACTICE AREAS:* Unfair Competition Law; Trademark Law; Product Liability Law.

DR. PETER HERTEL, born Hamburg, Germany, April 3, 1950; admitted, 1978, Hamburg. *Education:* Universities of Hamburg, Geneva, Freiburg and Gottingen (Dr. iur.). *Member:* Hamburg Bar Association. *LANGUAGES:* German and English. *PRACTICE AREAS:* Labor Law; Transport Law; Environmental Law.

EBERHARD VON DEM HAGEN, born Berlin, October 19, 1928; admitted, 1991, Germany. *Education:* University of Hamburg. Experience: General Counsel, Hapag-Lloyd AG, Hamburg, 1965-1990. *Member:* German Maritime Law Association. *LANGUAGES:* German and English. *PRACTICE AREAS:* Shipping Law; Company Law; Antitrust Law.

EBERHARDT KÜHNE, born Lemgo, Germany, April 17, 1958; admitted, 1989, Germany. *Education:* Universities of Heidelberg, Geneva (Switzerland) and Bonn (1.Staatsexamen, 1985); New York University (M.C.J., 1992). *Member:* German-American Lawyers' Association; International Association of Young Lawyers (AIJA). *LANGUAGES:* German, English and French. *PRACTICE AREAS:* Antitrust Law; International Private and EEC Law; Real Property Investments and Construction Law.

KARL-L. GRAF VON BAUDISSIN, born Lütjenburg, January 8, 1952; admitted, 1983, Assessor; 1991, Germany. *Education:* University of Kiel. Experience: Credit Operation Department, Deutsche Bank, Lübeck, Frankfurt and London, 1983-1991. *Member:* German Bar Association. *LANGUAGES:* German and English.

ASSOCIATES

AXEL HENRIKSEN, born January 29, 1959; admitted, 1993, Hamburg. *Education:* Universities of Hamburg and Lausanne (Switzerland). *Member:* German Bar Association; German-South-African Lawyers' Association. *LANGUAGES:* German, English, French and Spanish.

(This Listing Continued)

DR. DAGMAR MÜLLER-COLLIN, born Hamburg, July 29, 1965; admitted, 1994, Hamburg. *Education:* Universities of Hamburg and Geneva (Dr. jur). *Member:* Hamburg Bar Association; British-German Jurists Association. *LANGUAGES:* German, English, French.

Languages: German, English and French.

WOEDTKE RESZEL & PARTNER
ZIPPELHAUS 4
20457 HAMBURG, GERMANY
Telephone: 040/321266
Telefax: 040/323037

Dresden, Germany Office: Königsbrücker Straße 62, 01099. Telephone: 0351/8011893. Telefax: 0361 53631.

Düsseldorf, Germany Office: Königsallee 12, 40212. Telephone: 0211/86477-0. Telefax: 0211/86477-30.

FIRM PROFILE: The firm was established in 1986 and offers a full range of legal and business services. It is well known for General Practice, Corporate, Company, Commercial Taxation, Customs, Unfair Competition, Antitrust, EEC, Trademark and Copyright Law. The client base is Europe, North America, Japan and Scandinavia. The firm has a legal support staff of 22 consisting of attorneys, paralegal assistants and an office administrator.

DR. ANDREAS F. SONNTAG, born July 16, 1960. *Education:* University of Hamburg. *LANGUAGES:* English. *PRACTICE AREAS:* Leasing Law; Trademark and Copyright Law; Banking Law.

STEFAN SCHULTE, born Hamburg, Germany, April 1, 1966; admitted, 1994, Germany. *Education:* University of Hamburg (J.D., 1991). *LANGUAGES:* English. *PRACTICE AREAS:* Labour Law; Insurance Law.

ZENK TIPPENHAUER OSMER SCHROETER SCHMIDT-DECKER BERGMANN
Established in 1973
HARTWICUSSTR. 5
22087 HAMBURG, GERMANY
Telephone: (040) 220 1061
Fax: (040) 220 18 05

Berlin, Germany Office: Panoramastr. 1/Alexanderplatz, 10178 Berlin. Telephone: (030) 2425698. Fax: (030) 2424555.

Commercial, Corporation, Mergers and Acquisitions, Joint Ventures, Antitrust, Unfair Competition, Intellectual Property (Trademark, Copyright), EC Law (including CAP), Admiralty, Customs, Transport, Food and Drug, Product Liability, Environmental and Administrative, Labour, Real Estate, Leasing, Probate, Property Law (Restitution of Property Rights in East Germany), Taxation, Banking and Financing, Arbitration, Litigation, General Practice.

FIRM PROFILE: Established as a general practice in 1973, the firm has since grown to offer the full range of legal services for commercial matters. The Berlin office particularly deals with investment and restructuring in the former GDR.

MEMBERS OF FIRM

JÜRGEN ZENK, born Hamburg, Germany, October 5, 1938; admitted, 1969, Germany. *Education:* Universities of Hamburg and Munich. Deutsche Bank, 1960-1962. *Member:* Hamburg and German Bar Associations; German Association for International Maritime Law. *LANGUAGES:* German and English. *PRACTICE AREAS:* Banking Law; Insurance Law; Transport Law; Litigation.

ERHARD TIPPENHAUER, born Hamburg, Germany, September 26, 1940; admitted, 1970, Germany. *Education:* University of Hamburg. Research Assistant: Max-Planck Institute of Foreign and International Private Law; University of Hamburg. *Member:* Hamburg, German and International Bar Associations. *LANGUAGES:* German and English. *PRACTICE AREAS:* Property/Real Estate; Conveyancing; Corporate Law; Tax Law.

DR. DIERK OSMER, born Berlin, Germany, September 2, 1939; admitted, 1968, Germany. *Education:* Universities of Berlin and Hamburg (Dr. iur., 1966). Research Assistant, University of Hamburg, 1964-1968. *Member:* Hamburg and German Bar Associations. *LANGUAGES:* German and

(This Listing Continued)

English. *PRACTICE AREAS:* Administrative Law; Construction Law; Conveyancing; Landlord and Tenant Law; Transport Law; Insurance Law.

DR. KLAUS ALFRED SCHROETER, born Ausker, Germany, September 23, 1935; admitted, 1966, Germany. *Education:* Universities of Bonn, Munich and Cologne (Dr. iur., 1968). Author: "The Rule of Law as reflected in the Publications of the International Commission of Jurists," 1968; Co-Author: "The Revised Food Act," 1974, "Food Additives," 1978 and 1983. Legal and Management Functions in Industry, 1966-1986. *Member:* Hamburg, German and International Bar Associations; Deutscher Juristentag; Association for Food Law and Food Science (Vice President, 1984—); European Food Law Association. *LANGUAGES:* German, English and French. *PRACTICE AREAS:* Antitrust Law; Arbitration; Corporate Law; Food & Drugs Law; Property/Real Estate; Cross-Border Transactions.

NILS-PETER SCHMIDT-DECKER, born Amberg, Germany, July 22, 1945; admitted, 1976, Germany. *Education:* University of Hamburg. Author: "Product Liability, EEC-Directive as compared to the German Law," SGLH 19 p. 79, 1986. Research Assistant, University of Hamburg. Director and Head of Legal Department, German Subsidiary of a multinational company. *Member:* Hamburg, German and International Bar Associations; Association for Food Law and Food Science. *LANGUAGES:* German and English. *PRACTICE AREAS:* Property/Real Estate; Product Liability; European Community Law; Foreign Investments; Entertainment Law.

JOACHIM BERGMANN, born Dortmund, Germany, January 12, 1948; admitted, 1980, Germany. *Education:* Universities of Göttingen and Hamburg. Research Assistant, University of Hamburg. *Member:* Hamburg, German and International Bar Associations; Association for Food Law and Food Science. *LANGUAGES:* German and English. *PRACTICE AREAS:* Competition Law; Advertising; Intellectual Property Law; Food & Drugs Law.

ASSOCIATES

DR. PETRA SCHAAFF, born Hamburg, Germany, July 29, 1957; admitted, 1985, Germany. *Education:* University of Cologne (Dr. iur., 1983). Author: "Discovery and Other Instruments of Fact-Finding in English Pre-Trial Procedure," 1983; "UK and USA Takeover Defence Strategies," RIW 1985, p. 273; "Pre-Trial Discovery in English Law," RIW 1988, p. 844. Research Assistant, Institute of International and Foreign Private Law, Cologne, 1979-1984. *Member:* Hamburg, German and International Bar Associations; German-British Jurists Association. *LANGUAGES:* German, English, French and Danish. *PRACTICE AREAS:* Cross-Border Transactions; International Corporate Law; International Sales Law; International Distribution/Agency Law; Inheritance Law; Litigation.

MARTIN GOGREWE, born Essen, Germany, April 22, 1961; admitted, 1991, Germany. *Education:* University of Hamburg. Co-Author: "The Acquisition of Corporations in the New German Lander - A Survey of the Latest Regulations," DtZ 1991, p. 353 (with J. Rodegra). *Member:* Hamburg and German Bar Associations. *LANGUAGES:* German, English and Spanish. *PRACTICE AREAS:* Distribution/Agency Law; Computer Law; Employment Law; Transport Law; Litigation.

ALEXANDER BADEN, born Hamburg, Germany, December 6, 1963; admitted, 1992, Germany. *Education:* Universities of Passau and Hamburg. Author, "Repayment of CAP Subsidies," ZfZ 1991, S. 310ff. *LANGUAGES:* German, English. *PRACTICE AREAS:* European Community Law; Customs Law; Agricultural Law; Tax Law.

DR. MICHAEL REHR-ZIMMERMANN, born Hamburg, Germany, June 22, 1961; admitted, 1993, Germany. *Education:* University of Hamburg (Dr. iur., 1994). Author: "The Structure of Injustice," 1994. Research Assistant, Institute of Legal Philosophy, Hamburg, 1989-1993. *Member:* Hamburg and German Bar Associations. *LANGUAGES:* German and English. *PRACTICE AREAS:* Administrative Law; Criminal Law; White Collar Crime; Litigation.

HEINZ-DIETHER BENDIG, born Berlin, Germany, January 1, 1925; admitted, 1991, Germany. *Education:* Free University of Berlin. Judge, Berlin, 1956-1990. Vice President, Berlin Labour Court, 1977. *LANGUAGES:* German. *PRACTICE AREAS:* Labour and Employment Law.

GÖHMANN, DIESELHORST & SCHERRER
Established in 1949

LANDSCHAFTSTRASSE 6
30159 HANNOVER, GERMANY
Telephone: 0511 302770
Fax: 0511 329216

Leipzig, Germany Office: Eisenbahnstraße 84, 04315. Telephone: 0341/6 31 52. Telecopier: 0341/6 31 52.

Notary Public, General Commercial Law, Trade, Banking and Insurance Law, Corporate and Competition Law, Civil Litigation, Labour Law, Mergers and Acquisitions, Tax Law, German Reunification.

FIRM PROFILE: The firm was established in 1949 and offers a full range of legal services. It is known for its Litigation, Corporate and all kinds of Competition Law. At the beginning of 1990 it has opened an office in Leipzig (former GDR) and provides comprehensive assistance in all questions after the German Reunification.

MEMBERS OF FIRM

RUDOLF GÖHMANN, born Hannover, April 16, 1921; admitted, 1950, Germany. *Education:* University of Göttingen (Dr. jur., 1947). Notary Public. Former Member, Constitutional Court of the State of Lower Saxony. *LANGUAGES:* English and French. *PRACTICE AREAS:* Notariate; Corporate Law; Property Law; Law of Succession.

JÜRGEN DIESELHORST, born Hannover, November 29, 1926; admitted, 1956, Germany. *Education:* University of Erlangen (Dr. jur., 1950). Notary Public. *Member:* German Society for Industrial Property Law. *LANGUAGES:* English. *PRACTICE AREAS:* Notariate; Competition Law; Proprietary Right and Publishing Law; Press Law; Intellectual Property.

BURKHARD SCHERRER, born Hannover, May 24, 1939; admitted, 1968, Germany. *Education:* Universities of Munich, Tübingen and Göttingen. Notary Public. Tax Lawyer. *Member:* Chamber of Notaries (Presiding Board). *LANGUAGES:* English. *PRACTICE AREAS:* Notariate; Company and Corporate Law; Property Law; Trade Law; Bank and Insurance Law.

WULF MEINECKE, born Hannover, May 25, 1947; admitted, 1978, Germany. *Education:* University of Göttingen. Notary Public. *Member:* Board of the Bar Association. *LANGUAGES:* English. *PRACTICE AREAS:* Litigation; Labour Law; Building Law; Law of the German Reunification; Company and Corporate Law.

ULRICH VON JEINSEN, born Hannover, June 21, 1952; admitted, 1979, Germany. *Education:* University of Göttingen (Dr. jur., 1980). Tax Lawyer. *Member:* Young Lawyers International Association; German Society for Agricultural Law. *LANGUAGES:* English and French. *PRACTICE AREAS:* Agricultural Law; International Private Law; Aviation Accidents; Banking and Insurance Law; Trade and Corporate Law; Litigation.

AXEL MÜLLER-EISING, born Hannover, May 1, 1957; admitted, 1986, Germany. *Education:* University of Bonn. *Member:* Young Lawyers International Association. *LANGUAGES:* English. *PRACTICE AREAS:* Contract Law; Building Law; Trade and Corporate Law; Corporate and Business Law; Construction Law; Litigation.

ANNETTE RETHEL, born Celle, May 8, 1945; admitted, 1975, Germany. *Education:* Universities of Tübingen, Berlin and Heidelberg. Notary Public. *LANGUAGES:* French. *PRACTICE AREAS:* Notariate; General Litigation; Family Law.

VOLKER MÜLLER, born Saarbrücken, December 12, 1955; admitted, 1985, Germany. *Education:* Universities of Saarbrücken and Tübingen (Dr. jur., 1985). *LANGUAGES:* English, French and Spanish. *PRACTICE AREAS:* Environmental Law; Media Law.

ULRICH HAUPT, born Düsseldorf, May 17, 1956; admitted, 1985, Germany. *Education:* Universities of Cologne and Bonn (Dr. jur., 1988). *Member:* Young Lawyers International Association; German Society for Industrial Property Law. *LANGUAGES:* English and Spanish. *PRACTICE AREAS:* Litigation; Contract Law; Competition Law; Proprietary Right and Publishing Law; Press Law.

BETTINA CARL, born Leipzig, March 12, 1947; admitted, 1971, Germany. *Education:* University of Leipzig. (Resident, Leipzig Office). *PRACTICE AREAS:* Family Law; Law of the German Reunification.

ANDREAS BRUSE, born Hamm, July, 1960; admitted, 1990, Germany. *Education:* University of Wuerzburg. (Resident, Leipzig Office).

(This Listing Continued)

GÖHMANN, DIESELHORST & SCHERRER,
Hannover—Continued

LANGUAGES: English. **PRACTICE AREAS:** Labor Law; Tax Law; Law of the German Reunification; Civil Litigation.

ANDRÉ PIETREK, born Hannover, October 12, 1959; admitted, 1991, Germany. *Education:* Universities of Lausanne (CH) and Hamburg (Dr. jur., 1988). **LANGUAGES:** French and English. **PRACTICE AREAS:** Litigation; Insurance Law; Law of the European Union.

KENNETH S. KILIMNIK

KÖBELINGERSTRAβE 1
30159 HANNOVER, GERMANY
Telephone: (49-511) 327-533
Fax: (49-511) 320-555

International Commercial Transactions and Litigation.

KENNETH S. KILIMNIK, born Philadelphia, Pennsylvania, July 24, 1953; admitted, 1981, District of Columbia; 1986, Pennsylvania; 1991, New York; 1993, Hannover, FRG as Rechtskundiger for US Law (Not admitted in Germany). *Education:* University of Pennsylvania (B.A.); Columbia University (LL.M.); University of Trier (M.Iur.); Northeastern University (J.D.). Clerk, June L. Green, Judge, US District Court, Washington, DC, 1981-1983. US Counsel, German Law Firm, Herfurth and Partner, Hannover and Leipzig. **LANGUAGES:** English, German and Russian.

LUDEWIG & SCHÄFER

GEORGSTRAβE 48
30159 HANNOVER, GERMANY
Telephone: 0511-327641
Fax: 0511-323234

Civil and Commercial Litigation, (Offshore) Mining, Banking, Real Estate, Building, Unfair Competition, Labour, Leasing, Corporation Law, Mergers and Acquisitions.

FIRM PROFILE: *Since its foundation in 1981, the firm has been largely involved with clients from US, Canada, England, Australia, and France. It especially provides all kinds of legal assistance related to business matters throughout Germany.*

MEMBERS OF FIRM

DR. GERD LUDEWIG, born October 14, 1943; admitted, 1971, Germany. *Education:* Universities of Göttingen (Dr. iur., 1968); Freiburg, OLG Celle. Notary, 1979. Partner, Dr. Bach & Partners, 1971-1981. Author: "Practical legal questions on exploration and production of gas and oil in the German continental shelf," 1976; "Abtretung von Gewährleistungsansprüchen an Bauwerken und Einrede nach § 320 BGB," 1972; "Pflichtteilskürzung durch Schenkung an den Pflichtteilsberechtigten beim Erbvertrag ?," 1985. *Member:* Hannover and German Bar Association; British-German Jurists Association; German Society for Building Law; German Institution for Arbitration.

ANDREAS SCHÄFER, born March 19, 1960; admitted, 1991, Germany. *Education:* State Examination as Banking Merchant, 1982; Universities of Würzburg and Freiburg, OLG Bamberg. Clerk, Rooth & Wessels, Pretoria, South Africa, 1985. *Member:* Hannover and German Bar Associations.

Languages: German, English, French and Latin

RÖMERMANN & SCHWAB

Established in 1962
SCHUHSTRASSE 40
31134 HANNOVER (HILDESHEIM), GERMANY
Telephone: +49-5121 31055
Fax: +49-5121 33999

Investment Law, Commercial Law, International Business Law, Corporate Law, Real Estate Law, Administration Law, Litigation.

FIRM PROFILE: *Römermann & Schwab is a well established law firm in the area of Hannover. Contact facilities are in the perspective of the world exposition in Hannover in the year 2000 with Investment Law in Eastern Germany*

(This Listing Continued)

CLAUS-DIETER SCHWAB, born Germany, 1955; admitted, 1983, Uelzen; 1988, Hildesheim. *Education:* Göttingen University Law School. *Member:* Celle Bar Association; Unternehmensgruppe Kindermann (Advisory Board). **LANGUAGES:** German and English.

COUNSEL

VOLKER RÖMERMANN, born Germany, 1968; (Not admitted in Germany). *Education:* University of Hagen (Economy); University of Paris Sorbonne; Institut d'Etudes Politiques (Political Science); University of Geneva; International Academy of Constitutional Law, Tunis (Diploma); Bayreuth University Law School (Dr.jur., 1995). **LANGUAGES:** German, English, French and Spanish.

BAU, MAISS, WIDMAYER, IMO

Established in 1987
POSTSTRASSE 2
6900 HEIDELBERG, GERMANY
Telephone: (06221) 161076
Telefax: (06221) 29401

Real Estate and Construction Law, Corporate and Commercial, European Community and International Law, Banking and Finance, National and International Tax, Probate and Trusts, Intellectual Property, Labor Law, Accident and Personal Injury Claims, Debt Collection, Housing Law, Domestic Relations.

FIRM PROFILE: *The four partner firm was established in 1987 by the current senior partners and is a general practice specializing in Real Estate and Construction Law. The client base in both national and international. The firm is a member of the European lawyers network "The Association".*

MEMBERS OF FIRM

MICHAEL BAU, born Chemnitz, Germany, October 10, 1952; admitted, 1984, Heidelberg and Mannheim. *Education:* University of Heidelberg Law School. Corporate Counsel, Westphal Treuhand GmbH, 1984-1986. Research Assistant, University of Heidelberg, Criminal Law Department, 1984-1985. Berater des Vorstandes der österreichischen Termin und Optionenbörse AG, Wien (ÖTOB), February 1991-June 1991. *Member:* Anwaltsverein Heidelberg, Rechtsanwaltskammer Karlsruhe, Bundesverband Mittelständische Wirtschaft, The Association. **LANGUAGES:** German and English. **PRACTICE AREAS:** Real Estate and Construction Law; Corporation and Commercial; Banking and Finance; Labor Law; Housing Law.

JOACHIM MAISS, born Offenburg, Germany, March 4, 1954; admitted, 1982, Heidelberg, Mannheim and Karlsruhe. *Education:* German School, Washington, D.C. (1968-1973); University of Heidelberg Law School (1973-1979); Max Planck Institute (International Law Studies). Research Assistant, Max-Planck Institute for Foreign and International Law, 1977-1979. Law Internship with the state of Baden-Württemberg, 1979-1982. Correspondent of the Journal, European Business Lawyer. *Member:* German Bar Association; Anwaltsverein Heidelberg Rechtsanwaltskammer Karlsruhe, Bundesverband mittelständische Wirtschaft, The Association. **LANGUAGES:** German, English and French. **PRACTICE AREAS:** Real Estate and Construction Law; Corporate and Commercial; European Community and International Law; Probate and Trusts; Intellectual Property; Accident and Personal Claims; Debt Collection; Domestic Relations.

DR. GERD WIDMAYER, born Freudenstadt, Germany, December 15, 1950; admitted, 1983, Heidelberg and Mannheim. *Education:* University of Tübingen Law School (1974-1978); University of Heidelberg Law School (1978-1980); Tax School Stuttgart (1982-1983); University of Zurich (Dr. Juris., 1988). Research Assistant, University of Heidelberg, 1983-1984. *Member:* Rechtsanwaltkammer Karlsruhe, Bundesverband Mittelständische Wirtschaft, The Association. **LANGUAGES:** German and English. **PRACTICE AREAS:** Corporate and Commercial; National and International Tax; Probate and Trusts; Intellectual Property; Labor Law; Accident and Personal Injury Claims; Debt Collection; Domestic Relations.

DR. CHRISTIAN IMO, born Mannheim, Germany, January 27, 1955; admitted, 1987, Heidelberg and Mannheim. *Education:* Universities of Tübingen and Heidelberg Law School (Dr. Jur., 1988); University of Paris. Author: "Bürsentermin und Börsenoptions Geschäpte (Futures and Options Trading)," Volume I & II, published by Gabler Verlag Wiesbagen, 1988; "Einführung in Den Options Handel (Introduction to Options Trading), Deutsche Terminbírse Hrsg., Gabler Verlag Wiesbaden, 1989. Assistant to Professor Dr. Wilfried Küper, Chair for Criminal Law, University of Heidelberg, 1982-1987. Chief Trading Officer of the German Futures and Op-

(This Listing Continued)

tions Exchange (Deutsche Terminbörse), 1989-1990. Since 1991 Vorstand der österreichischen Termin-und Optionenbörse AG, Wien (öTOB). *Member:* Bundesverband mittelständischer Wirtschaft, The Association. *LANGUAGES:* German, English and French. *PRACTICE AREAS:* Banking and Finance.

ASSOCIATES

INGRID MOLLINGER-MENGES, born Osthofen, Rheinland-Pfalz, Germany, May 13, 1954; admitted, 1981, Heidelberg and Mannheim, since 1987 OLG Karlsruhe. *Education:* University of Heidelberg (1974-1981). *Member:* Rechtsanwaltskammer Karlsruhe, recommended Solicitor of the Family Association (ISUV/VDU). *LANGUAGES:* German, English and French. *PRACTICE AREAS:* Domestic Relations.

OF COUNSEL

PATRICK J. CLIFFORD, born Chicago, Illinois, July 17, 1955; admitted, 1985, Washington and Colorado; Authorized to practice in Germany before all U.S. Army and Air Force Courts and Boards; admitted in Germany as Rechtsbeistand (Legal Counselor) on U.S. Law and authorized to practice Law in Germany on Criminal and Civil matters involving members of the U.S. Forces. *Education:* DePaul University (B.S. in Commerce, 1977); Gonzaga University of Maryland (J.D., 1982; M.B.A., 1984), Asian Division, 1982-1984 and European Division, 1984. Lecturer, Business and Law, The University of Maryland, Asian Division, 1982-1984 and European Division, 1984—. *Member:* Washington State, Colorado, American and International Bar Associations. *LANGUAGES:* English.

JOHN C. STURGEON, born January 20, 1950; admitted, 1986, Maryland; as Rechtsbeitstand in Germany. *Education:* United States Military Academy, West Point, NY (B.S. Engineering, 1972); University of Baltimore (M.S. International Business & Finance, 1982); University of Akron (J.D., 1985). Lecturer: Business and Law, The University of Maryland, European Division; Schiller International University, 1990-1992. General Counsel, CFB Bank and Car World Group, 1987-1992. *Member:* American Bar Association, International Bar Association (Business Law Section; Administrative Law Section; Taxation Section; Environmental and Natural Resources Section). *LANGUAGES:* English and German. *PRACTICE AREAS:* Business; International Trade; Banking and Finance; Immigration.

GORNIK-BRINGER-BOZUNG

NEUENHEIMER LANDSTRASSE 20
69120 HEIDELBERG, GERMANY
Telephone: (0 62 21) 4 59 40
Telefax: (0 62 21) 45 94 60

Moscow, Russia Associated Office: Gornik & Partner Ltd. Mjasnitskaja Street 24, Bldg. 3-4, 10100 Moscow.

General Practice, Commercial, Tax, Corporate, Construction, Real Estate, Administrative, Labour, Unfair Competition, Foreign Investments.

MEMBERS OF FIRM

GÜNTER GORNIK, born Heidelberg, March 17, 1948; admitted, 1978, German Tax Courts, Tax Advisor. *Education:* University of Mannheim (Diplom-Kaufmann). *LANGUAGES:* German and English. *PRACTICE AREAS:* Tax Law.

DR. PETER BRINGER, born Cologne, November 11, 1947; admitted, 1981, Germany. *Education:* Universities of Cologne, Lausanne (Switzerland), Freiburg (Dr. jur., 1980); Harvard (USA, LL.M., 1977). Research Assistant, Max-Planck-Institut für ausländisches und internationales Strafrecht, 1977-1980. Certified Accountant, 1988. Author: "Die Stellung des Richters in Kamerun," (Baden-Baden 1981). *Member:* German and International Bar Associations. *LANGUAGES:* German, English and French. *PRACTICE AREAS:* Commercial; Corporate; Construction Law.

WERNER BOZUNG, born Landau, February 23, 1939; admitted, 1978, German Tax Courts, Tax Advisor and Certified Public Accountant. *Education:* University of Mannheim (Diplom-Kaufmann). *LANGUAGES:* German and English. *PRACTICE AREAS:* Tax Law.

DR. UWE JÄGER, born Stuttgart, October 2, 1957; admitted, 1986, Germany. *Education:* Universities of Heidelberg (Dr. jur., 1989) and Lausanne (Switzerland). Author: "Die Verteilung des Fälschungsrisikos im Wechsel-und Scheckrecht," Heidelberg, 1989. *Member:* German Bar Association. *LANGUAGES:* German, English and French. *PRACTICE AREAS:* Administrative; Labour; Unfair Competition Law.

HEINZ, HEINZ, LANGER & LANGER

Established in 1974

KAISERSTRASSE 27
6900 HEIDELBERG 1, GERMANY
Telephone: 06221, 27032
Telecopier: 06221-10663

Family, Labor, Probate, Medical Malpractice and Criminal.

MEMBERS OF FIRM

WOLFGANG HEINZ, born Karlshafen, Germany, July 21, 1944; admitted, 1974, Germany; 1979, Oberlandesgericht Karlsruhe. *Education:* University of München (1965-1966); University of Heidelberg (1st Juristisches Staatsexamen, 1970; 2nd Juristisches Staatsexamen, 1973). *Member:* German Bar Association; Anwaltsverein Heidelberg; Rechtsanwaltskammer Karlsruhe. *LANGUAGES:* German, English, French and Spanish. *PRACTICE AREAS:* Family Law; Probate; Administration.

VERENA HEINZ, born Baden-Baden, Germany, January 8, 1952; admitted, 1979, Germany; 1984, Oberlandesgericht Karlsruhe. *Education:* University of Heidelberg (1st Juristisches Staatsexamen, 1976; 2nd Juristisches Staatsexamen, 1979). *Member:* German Bar Association; Anwaltsverein Heidelberg; Rechtsanwaltskammer Karlsruhe. *LANGUAGES:* German, English, French and Greek. *PRACTICE AREAS:* Family; Labor.

FRANK LANGER, born Dreilinden, Germany, April 20, 1951; admitted, 1979, Germany. *Education:* Universities of Bonn and Heidelberg (1st Juristisches Staatsexamen, 1975; 2nd Juristisches Staatsexamen, 1978). *Member:* German Bar Association; Anwaltsverein Heidelberg; Rechtsanwaltskammer Karlsruhe; Arbeitsgemeinschaft der Fachanwalte für Arbeitsrecht. *LANGUAGES:* English and French. *PRACTICE AREAS:* Insurance; Labor.

ASSOCIATE

KARIN LANGER, born Heidelberg, Germany, March 23, 1961; admitted, 1990, Germany. *Education:* University of Heidelberg (1st Juristisches Staatsexamen, 1986; 2nd Juristisches Staatsexamen, 1990). *Member:* German Bar Association; Rechtsanwaltskammer Karlsruhe. *LANGUAGES:* German, English, French and Italian. *PRACTICE AREAS:* Medical Malpractice; Personal Injury; Leases.

JAKOB SCHOMERUS, born Karlsruhe, Germany, June 12 1963; admitted, 1993, Germany. *Education:* University of Bonn and Heidelberg (1st. Juristisches Staatsexamen, 1990; 2nd. Juristisches Staatsexamen, 1993). *Member:* German Bar Association; Rechtsanwaltskammer Karlsruhe. *LANGUAGES:* German and English. *PRACTICE AREAS:* Criminal Law; Administrative Law.

OF COUNSEL

WOLF-RÜDIGER GRAMM, born Neuwerk, Germany, August 5, 1941; admitted, 1977, Germany as Legal Counsel; Consulting Actuary. *Education:* University of Heidelberg (Diploma in Physics, 1970). Lecturer on Mathematics and Physics, Paedagogische Hochschule, Heidelberg, 1970-1973. *Member:* Bundesverband der Rechtsbeistaende, Muenchen; Fachvereninigung Mathematischer Sachverständiger der Arbeitsgemeinschaft fuer Betriebliche Alterversorgung e.V., Heidelberg; International Association of Consulting Actuaries, Deutsche Sektion, Muenchen.

MELCHERS, SCHUBERT, STOCKER, STURIES

Established in 1973

SLEVOGTSTRASSE 6
D-69126 HEIDELBERG, GERMANY
Telephone: (49-6221) 39 91 01
Telefax: (49-6221) 39 91 00; 37 40 69

Mailing Address: P.O. Box 10 52 22, D-69042

Berlin, Germany Office: Schiffbauerdamm 17, D-10117 Berlin. Telephone: (49-30) 2252 2133. Telecopier: (49-30) 2252 2108.

Frankfurt/Main, Germany Office: Beethovenstrasse 29, D-60325 Frankfurt/Main. Telephone: (49-69) 9757 3227. Telecopier: (49-69) 9757 3220.

Zwickau, Germany Office: Kolpingstrasse28, D-08058 Zwickau. Telephone: (49-375) 294023/4/5. Telecopier: (49-375) 521629.

(This Listing Continued)

MELCHERS, SCHUBERT, STOCKER, STURIES,
Heidelberg—Continued

Administrative Law, Banking, Commercial, Contracts, Corporate, EC-Law, Environmental Law, General Practice, Inheritance, Intellectual Property and Trade Marks, Arbitration, International Private Law, Investment, Labour Law, Mergers and Acquisitions, National and EC Antitrust, National and International Tax Law, Real Estate, Trade and Trade Show Law, Unfair Competition.

FIRM PROFILE: The law firm was founded in 1973 as a multidisciplinary partnership of lawyers, certified public accountants and tax advisors. Today, 31 professionals, of which 24 are lawyers, offer services and advice in the firm's offices in Berlin, Frankfurt/Main, Heidelberg and Zwickau. The multidisciplinary combination of legal services provides clients with comprehensive advice in the fields of business law, tax law, business administration and auditing.

RESIDENT PARTNERS

DR. IUR. UTR. RAINER STURIES, born Erlangen, December 9, 1948; admitted, 1977, Germany. Certified Tax Attorney, 1982, Germany. *Education:* Universities of Frankfurt and Heidelberg, Geneva, Nice and London. Author: "Bezugsrechtsausschluß bei Kapitalerhöhung," in Die Wirtschaftsprüfung, 1982, p. 581; "European Civil Procedure," in: Common Market Law Review, 1986, p. 236; "Zur Nachlaßplanung bei Erbfällen mit Auslandsberührung," in: Probleme der Rechts- und Steuerberatung in mittelständischen Unternehmen, Köln 1988. *Member:* Committee of Certified Tax Attorneys: Max Planck Society; German and Heidelberg Bar Associations. *LANGUAGES:* German, English and French. *PRACTICE AREAS:* Corporate Law; Company Law; Estate Planing Law; Arbitration; International Law.

DR. IUR. UTR. BERNHARD WINTER, born Weinheim, May 9, 1951; admitted, 1979, Germany. *Education:* University of Heidelberg (Doctor of Laws). Author: "Die Entwicklung der Mittäterschaft im 19. Jahrhundert," Heidelberg, 1981. Co-Author: "Die Rücknahmepflicht von Transportverpackungen nach der Verpackungsverordnung." *Member:* German and Heidelberg Bar Association. *LANGUAGES:* German and English. *PRACTICE AREAS:* Corporate Law; Company Law; Conversion Law; Mergers and Acquisitions; Antitrust Law; Contracts; Commercial Law; Real Estate Law; Leasing.

URSULA BLEIMLING, born Heidelberg, June 14, 1955; admitted, 1982, Germany. *Education:* University of Heidelberg. *Member:* German Society of Construction Law; German and Heidelberg Bar Association. *LANGUAGES:* German, English and French. *PRACTICE AREAS:* General Conditions of Contracts; Construction Law; Real Estate Law; Litigation; Company Law.

DR. IUR. UTR. BRUNHILDE ACKERMANN, born Ulm, July 22, 1953; admitted, 1983, Germany. *Education:* University of Heidelberg (Doctor of Laws). Research and Teaching Assistant at the Law Faculty, University of Heidelberg (1981-1983). Author: "Die Strafbarkeit Juristischer Personen im Deutschen Recht und in Ausländischen Rechtsordnungen," Europäische Hochschulschriften, vol. 362, Frankfurt, 1984; "Jubiläumsveranstaltungen eines Fertighausunternehmens - Verkaufsveranstaltung im Einzelhandel?" in: Wettbewerb in Recht und Praxis 1987, p. 152; "Chancen und Risiken der Industriekooperation im Bereich der Biotechnologie - der Technologiepark Heidelberg als Beispiel," in: Probleme der Rechts- und Steuerberatung in mittelständischen Unternehmen, Köln 1988; Co-Author: "Urteilsanmerkung zu BGH "Katorit"," in: Wettbewerb in Recht und Praxis, 1993, 469; "Verpackungspraxis, Arzneimittelrecht," Hüthig Verlag GmbH, 1993. *Member:* German Association for the Protection of Industrial Property Rights (GRUR); German and Heidelberg Bar Associations. *LANGUAGES:* German, English and French. *PRACTICE AREAS:* Unfair Competition; Intellectual Property; Medical and Pharmaceutical Law; Labour Law.

DR. RER. POL. DIETER THÜNNESEN, born Weeze, Germany, April 13, 1952; admitted, 1982, Germany. *Education:* Universities of Heidelberg and Munich. Research and Teaching Assistant at the Institute of German and International Economic Law, University of Darmstadt; Research Assistant at the Institute of German and International Banking Law, University of Mainz (1985-1988). Author: "Probleme der Umsatzbesteuerung bei Reiseveranstaltern," Munich, 1972; "Genußscheine als Finanzierungsmittel in der deutschen Wirtschaftsgeschichte und heutigen Unternehmenspraxis," Frankfurt, 1987; "Gesetzliche und vertragliche Kündigungsbeschränkungen bei der GbR, OHG und KG," Darmstadt, 1988. *Member:* German Bar Association. *LANGUAGES:* German, English and

(This Listing Continued)

Dutch. *PRACTICE AREAS:* Insolvency Law; Banking; Estate Planing; Company Law; Commercial Law.

ASSOCIATES

DR. IUR. UTR. KARIN MAY, born Mannheim, September 29, 1955; admitted, 1982, Germany. *Education:* Universities of Freiburg and Heidelberg (Doctor of Laws). Author: "Grenzen des Arbeitskampfrechts im Staatsnotstand", Heidelberg, 1985. *Member:* Heidelberg and German Bar Associations. *LANGUAGES:* German, English and French. *PRACTICE AREAS:* Commercial Law; Litigation; Family Law; Leases; Leasing.

DR. IUR. UTR. FRITZ FLANDERKA, born Pressath, Germany, July 25, 1958; admitted, 1990, Germany. *Education:* Universities of Münster, Lausanne, Passau and Heidelberg. Author: "Der Bundesbeauftragte für den Datenschutz", Heidelberg, 1989; "Die Tücken der Transportverpackung," in: Neue Zeitschrift für Verwaltungsrecht 1992. p. 648. Co-Author: "Strafbarkeit des Vertriebs von Bauherren-, Bauträger- und Erwerbermodellen gemäß 264 a StGB", in: Zeitschrift für Wirtschaft, Steuer, Strafrecht, 1990. p. 256; "Die Rücknahmepflicht von Transportverpackungen nach der Verpackungsverordnung," in: Betriebs-Berater 1992, p. 149. Editor: Brück/Flanderka, Verpackungspraxis, 1993. *Member:* German and Heidelberg Bar Associations. *LANGUAGES:* German, English, French. *PRACTICE AREAS:* Administrative Law; Environmental Law; Commercial Law; Company Law.

DR. JUR. NORBERT STEGEMANN, born Gelsenkirchen, November 12, 1959; admitted, 1988, Germany. *Education:* Universities of Münster, Heidelberg, Mainz and Freiburg. Research and Teaching Assistant, Institute of International Law, University of Mainz. Lecturer on Law, Private Law School (Alpmann u. Schmidt). *Member:* German and Heidelberg Bar Associations. *LANGUAGES:* German, English and French. *PRACTICE AREAS:* Labour Law; Industrial Relations; Commercial Law; Litigation; Criminal Law.

DR. JUR. KERSTIN REISERER, born Berlin, April 25, 1962; admitted, 1992, Germany. *Education:* Universities of Regensburg and Munich. Research and Teaching Assistant, Law Faculty, Universities of Munich and Heidelberg. Author: "Das elterliche Erziehungsrecht und die Eigentscheidung des heranwachsenden Minderjährigen im deutschen und französischen Recht," 1990; "Ausschluß und Rückzahlungsklauseln fur Gratifikationen beibetriebsbedingter Kündigung," in Betriebs-Berater 1991, p. 2457; Co-Author: "Partnerschaftsvermittlung und Verbraucherkreditgesetz," 1991; "Der Umfang der Unterrichtung des Betriebsrats bei Einstellungen," in Betriebs-Berater 1992, p. 2499; "Allgemeiner Kündigungsschutz bel Arbeltsverhältnissen mit Auslandsbezug," in Neue Zeltschrift für Arbeitsrecht 1994, p. 673; "Die ordentliche Kündlgung des Dienstvertrages des GmbH-Geschäftsführers," in Der Betrieb 1994, p. 1822. *Member:* German and Heidelberg Bar Associations. *LANGUAGES:* German, French and English. *PRACTICE AREAS:* Labour Law; Industrial Relation; Pensions; Family Law; Contracts.

DR. IUR. UTR. KNUT P. SCHULTE, born Wuppertal, October 10, 1963; admitted, 1993, Germany. *Education:* University of Heidelberg (Doctor of Laws). Research Assistant Law Faculty, University of Heidelberg, 1988-1992. Author: "Das standesrechtliche Werbeverbot für Ärzte unter Berücksichtigungwettbewerbs- und kartellrechtlicher Bestimmungen," Recht & Medizin, vol. 25, Frankfurt, 1992; "Urteilsanmerkungen zum ärztlichen Wettbewerbsrecht" in: Medizinrecht 1991, p. 32; 1992, p. 162; 1992, p. 280; "Private Standesregeln imWettbewerbsrecht" in: Medizinrecht 1991, p. 323; Co-Author: "Urteilsanmerkung zu BGH "Katovit"," in: Wettbewerb in Recht und Praxis, 1993, 469; since January 1993: monthly jurisdictionreview in: Medizinrecht. *Member:* German and Heidelberg Bar Associations; German-American Lawyers Association (DAJV). *LANGUAGES:* German and English. *PRACTICE AREAS:* Corporate Law; Labour Law; Medical Law.

DR. IUR. UTR. JÖRG HOFMANN, born Lüdenscheid, June 20, 1961; admitted, 1993, Germany. *Education:* University of Heidelberg (Doctor of Laws); intern with German-Australian Chambers of Industry and Commerce, Sydney, 1992. Author: "Der Deutsche als Tatbestand von Grundrechten und Grundpflichten," Heidelberg, 1993. *Member:* German and Heidelberg Bar Associations. *LANGUAGES:* German, English and French. *PRACTICE AREAS:* Contracts; Commercial Law; Administrative Law.

DR. JUR. KARL BENEDIKT BIESINGER, born Wangen/Allgäu, January 8, 1961; admitted, 1993, Germany. *Education:* University of Tübingen (Doctor of Laws); University of Freiburg. Research and Teaching Assistant, University of Tübingen. Author: "Die Behandlung steuerlicher Mehr-und Mindergewinne aus steuerlicher und handelsrechtlicher Sicht,"

(This Listing Continued)

Tübingen, 1993. Co-Author: "Die Aktiengesellschaft im Streit mit ihren Aktionären," in: DWiR 1992, p. 15. *Member:* German Bar Association. *LANGUAGES:* German, English and French. *PRACTICE AREAS:* Corporate Law; Commercial Law; Tax Law.

DR. JUR. THORSTEN SEEKER, born Diepholz, October 4, 1961; admitted, 1994, Germany. *Education:* University of Münster (Doctor of Laws). Author: "Die Übersicherung des Geldkreditgebers bei Sicherungsübertragungen," 1994. *German and Heidelberg Bar Associations. LANGUAGES:* German and English. *PRACTICE AREAS:* Contracts; Banking Law; Company Law; Commercial Law; Real Estate Law.

COUNSEL

DR. IUR. CHRISTOPH ZAHRNT, born Posen, March 1, 1944; admitted, 1977, Germany. *Education:* Universities of Kiel, Munich, Heidelberg (Doctor of Law; Diplom-Volkswirt, Degree in Economics). Author: "Datenverarbeitungsverträge," 1979; "Verdingungsordnung für Computerleistungen," Vol. I, 1977, Vol. II, 1981; "DV-Verträge," 1985; "DV-Rechtsprechung," Vol. I, 1983, Vol. II, 1986 (all: edp contracts/decision). Member, Board of Examiners for Edp Expert Witnesses Chamber of Commerce Cologne. *Member:* German Bar Association. *LANGUAGES:* German and English. *PRACTICE AREAS:* Computer Law; Commercial Law.

DR.-ING. ULRICH NAUMANN, born Heidelberg, February 11, 1956; admitted, 1989 as Patent Attorney; Germany, and 1991 as European Patent Attorney. *Education:* University of Karlsruhe, Faculty for General Engineering and Electronics (Dipl. Ing., Dr.-Ing.). *Member:* German Association for the Protection of Industrial Property Rights (GRUR); German Patent Attorneys Association; Association Internationale pour la Protection de la Propriété Industrielle; European Patent Institute. *LANGUAGES:* German, English, French and Spanish. *PRACTICE AREAS:* Patent Law; Trade Mark Law; Litigation.

CERTIFIED PUBLIC ACCOUNTANTS AND TAX ADVISORS

DR. RER. POL. PETER MELCHERS, born Lodz, February 6, 1921; admitted, 1960, German Tax Courts. Tax Advisor, Germany, 1960. Certified Public Accountant, Germany, 1963. *Education:* Universities of Berlin und Mannheim (Dipl.-Kfm., Dr. rer. pol.). *Member:* Institute of C.P.A. in Germany (I.d.W.). *LANGUAGES:* German, English and French. *PRACTICE AREAS:* National and International Tax Law; Auditing and Valuation.

DIETER STOCKER, born Frankfurt, May 23, 1936; admitted, 1966, German Tax Courts. Tax Advisor, Germany, 1966. Certified Public Accountant, Germany, 1970. *Education:* Universities of Frankfurt and Berlin (Dipl.-Kfm.). *Member:* Institute of C.P.A. in Germany (I.d.W.). *LANGUAGES:* German, English and French. *PRACTICE AREAS:* National and International Tax Law; Auditing and Valuation.

HEINZ P. RIEGER, born Heidelberg, Germany, May 1, 1941; admitted, 1972, German Tax Courts. Tax Advisor, Germany, 1972. Certified Public Accountant, Germany, 1976. *Education:* Universities of Heidelberg and Mannheim (Dipl.-Kfm.). Author: "Kritische Stellungnahme zu den Wirkungen steuerlicher Begünstigungen," in: Probleme der Rechts- und Steuerberatung in mittelständischen Unternehmen, Köln 1988. Co-Author: "Praxis der Steuerberatung," 1980. *Member:* Institute of C.P.A. in Germany (I.d.W.). *LANGUAGES:* German, English and French. *PRACTICE AREAS:* National and International Tax Law; Auditing and Valuation.

DR. OEC. MANFRED SCHNEIDER, born Heidelberg, November 16, 1948; admitted, 1984, German Tax Courts, Tax Advisor, Germany, 1984; Certified Public Accountant, Germany, 1986. *Education:* University of Mannheim (Dipl.Kfm., Dr. oec.). Author: "Unternehmerische Rechenschaft anhand prospektiver Rechnungslegungsinstrumente, Heidelberg, 1981. Lecturer on Auditing at the Law Faculty, University of Heidelberg (1989-1990). *Member:* Institute of C.P.A. in Germany (I.d.W.). *LANGUAGES:* German, English and French. *PRACTICE AREAS:* National and International Tax Law; Auditing and Valuation.

(For complete biographical data on Personnel at Berlin, Frankfurt/Main and Zwickau offices see Professional Biographies at those locations).

DR. SCHLATTER & PARTNERS
KURFÜRSTEN-ANLAGE 59
69115 HEIDELBERG, GERMANY
Telephone: 06221/9812-0
Fax: 06221/183952; 182475

Acquisitions, Agency, Banking Law, Company Law, Competition Law, Construction Law, Civil Law, Copyright Law, Environmental Law, European Community Law, Family Law, Intellectual Property Law, Insurance Law, Labour Law, Medical Malpractice, Planning Law, Taxation, Succession, Transportation.

FIRM PROFILE: Established in 1946 Dr. Schlatter & Partners is one of the regions leading commercial and administrative law firms. It provides a wide range of competitive legal services including litigation to corporate clients and to a certain extent to private individuals. The firm has ten lawyers who are admitted at the District Courts of Heidelberg and Mannheim. Languages spoken: English and French.

MEMBERS OF FIRM

GÜNTER HEYM, born 1923; admitted, 1956, Germany. *Education:* Universities of Munich and Heidelberg (Dr. Jur., 1956). President, Lawyers Court of Baden-Württemberg. *PRACTICE AREAS:* Company, Commercial and Intellectual Property Law.

HENNING ALBRECHT, born 1931; admitted, 1959, Germany. *Education:* Universities of Hamburg and Heidelberg (Dr. Jur., 1959). *Member:* Law Society (Board Member, 1972-1992); Association for Construction Law; Environmental Law Society. *PRACTICE AREAS:* Property; Environmental Law; Construction Law; Administrative Law.

VOLKER STEINHILPER, born 1941; admitted, 1969, Germany. *Education:* University of Heidelberg (1966). *Member:* German Association of Tax Lawyers. *PRACTICE AREAS:* Tax and Commercial Law; Law of Succession.

WOLF HERZBERGER, born 1952; admitted, 1981, Germany. *Education:* University of Mannheim (1978). *PRACTICE AREAS:* Medical Malpractice; Computer Law; Commercial Law; Family Law (Matrimonial Property and Prenuptial Agreements).

THOMAS HEINZ, born 1962; admitted, 1991, Germany. *Education:* University of Heidelberg (1988). *Member:* Administrative Law Society. *PRACTICE AREAS:* Property Law; Construction Law; Planning and Administrative Law.

RUTH MUNDANJOHL, born 1963; admitted, 1992, Germany. *Education:* University of Heidelberg (1988). *PRACTICE AREAS:* Law of Competition and Unfair Trade Practices; Law of Succession and Estate Duty.

CHRISTIAN ALBRECHT, born 1960; admitted, 1993, Germany. *Education:* Universities of Berlin, Cambridge (England) and Heidelberg (Dr. Jur., 1989). Previously lawyer with the Tax Administration. Author: Article 24 of the Brussels Convention of 1968 and the German and British Interim Remedies, 1990; articles on international litigation and on VAT. *Member:* European Lawyers Association; German-British Lawyers Association. *PRACTICE AREAS:* Tax Law (including VAT); Commercial Law; Conflict of Laws.

ANNEMARIE BÖTTCHER, born 1963; admitted, 1993, Germany. *Education:* University of Heidelberg (1990). *PRACTICE AREAS:* Labour; Agency and Family Law.

WALTER & PARTNER
(German and American Attorneys and Counsellors at Law)

(former Klamroth & Walter)

Established in 1972

LESSINGSTRASSE 24
P.O. BOX 103466
69024 HEIDELBERG 1, GERMANY
Telephone: 06221/12002
Telefax: 06221/20378

Dessau, Germany (East) Office: Walter & Partner, Kavalierstr. 35-39, 06844. Telephone: 0340-2207285. Telefax: 0340-213280.
Berlin, Germany Office: Walter & Partner, Martin Luther Strasse 19, 10777. Telephone: 030-2119092. Telefax: 030-2119094.

(This Listing Continued)

WALTER & PARTNER, *Heidelberg—Continued*

General Business and Civil Practice, Antitrust and Trade Regulation, Bankruptcy, Business, Civil Law, Commercial Law, Company and Corporate Law, Computer and Software, Consumer Law, Contracts, Copyrights, European Competition Law, Family Law, Insurance, Intellectual Property, Investments, East Europe, Labour and Employment, Leasing, Professional and Product Liability, Property, Real Estate, Trademarks.

FIRM PROFILE: *Established in 1972 by Ms. Sabine Klamroth, a former manager in German industry, the firm has become as Klamroth & Walter a well known law firm with a reputation for offering a full range of practice-based quality legal services. Clients are especially national and international commercial enterprises. The firm publicates monthly reviews on competition law, food law and on European food law. The firm is a founding member of LAW EUROPE (E.W.I.V.) an association of law firms based in all EC - Memberstates. Because of the retiring of Ms. Klamroth, the law firm is now named Walter & Partner.*

MEMBERS OF FIRM

REINHARD WALTER, born Heidelberg, Germany, February 3, 1954; admitted, 1982, Germany. *Education:* Universities of Mannheim and Heidelberg. Co-Author: "Rechtskunde für Kaufleute". Member of the Board, Lions Club Mittlere Bergstraße, 1982—. *Member:* German and European Bar Association; German Association for the Protection of Industrial Property and Copyright; International Association for the Protection of Industrial Property (AIPPI); American Chamber of Commerce; German Industrial Commerce Association (Member, Legal Committee, 1986—). (Resident Partner, Berlin Office). *LANGUAGES:* English, French and German.

DR. BERND GRÜBER, born Ingelbach, Germany, September 28, 1959; admitted, 1988, Germany. *Education:* Finanz-Fachhochschule Rhineland-Palatinate (special tax-college); University of Mannheim (Doctor of Law, 1990). Training at the European Communities, Brussels. Author: "Die missbräuchliche Abmahnung und Verfahrenseinleitung im Wettbewerbsrecht (abuse of law in unfair competition)". *Member:* German Chamber of Commerce. (Resident Partner, Berlin Office). *LANGUAGES:* English and German.

CLAUDIA ZWILLING-PINNA, born Heidelberg, Germany, December 25, 1957; admitted, 1988, Germany. *Education:* University of Heidelberg. Co-Author: "Rechtskunde für Kaufleute," "Recht im Einkauf". Chief-Editor: "Recht und Praxis im Einkauf". Lecturer for Trade Law at various Chamber of Commerce. *Member:* German Bar Association; Board of Lions Club, Mannheim-Rosengarten; German Association for Computer Law and Technology. *LANGUAGES:* English, French, Spanish and German.

DR. HARTMUT SCHWARZKOPF, born July 7, 1940; admitted, 1966, Massachusetts; admitted in Germany as Rechtsbeistand. *Education:* Wagner College, New York (B.A. Business Administration); New England School of Law (J.D.); Hague Academy of International Studies and Research in International Law and International Relations of the Hague, Fall (Curatorium Testimonial, 1966); Heidelberg University (Doctor of Law, 1974). Law Lecturer, Maryland University, European Division, 1968—. Lecturer for International Law, Business Law, Criminal Law, Constitutional Law, Domestic Relations Law, Law of Business Environment, Terrorism and Human Rights, Heidelberg University Law School, 1987—. Lecturer for Public and Private Common Law. Advisor on American Law at the Institute for International Private and Economic Law, University of Heidelberg, 1968-1976. Private Practice of Law, Advising Both American and German Citizens and Companies in Germany and Defending Military Personnel in Military Courts. *Member:* Massachusetts Bar Association; Deutsch-Amerikanische Juristenvereinigung; Association of American Lawyers in Europe; American Society of International Law. *LANGUAGES:* English and German.

DORIS SCHNEIDER, born Bentzin, Germany, July 22, 1951; admitted, 1992, Germany. *Education:* University of Berlin. Former Judge at Civil Court. *LANGUAGES:* Russian and German.

GUNTER KARL, born Heidelberg, Germany, January 29, 1965; admitted, 1993, Germany. *Education:* University of Heidelberg; College in Speyer (Public Law). Co-Author: "Legal Comments on Competition Law.". *LANGUAGES:* English and German.

BERTHOLD BOCKAMP, born Dorsten, Germany, August 27, 1963; admitted, 1993, Germany. *Education:* University of Heidelberg, Trier and Bonn. *Member:* German-Brazilian Bar Association. *LANGUAGES:* English, Portuguese and German.

(This Listing Continued)

DIRK SCHAFFRIN, born Bremen, Germany, March 3, 1961; admitted, 1994, Germany. *Education:* University of Heidelberg. *LANGUAGES:* English, Spanish and German.

STEFAN HERMLE, born Stuttgart, Germany, October 2, 1961; admitted, 1994, Germany. *Education:* Universities of Heidelberg and Guildford, England. *LANGUAGES:* English, French and German.

Member of "Law Europe", an association of European Law Firms for International Business

MENZEL, ROSSKOPF, METZGER & PARTNER

Established in 1963

MOLTKESTR. 54
POSTFACH 1655
74076 HEILBRONN, GERMANY
Telephone: (07131) 1840
Telefax: (07131) 184-84

General Practise, Business, Company Law, Corporation, Tax, Labor, Criminal, Traffic, Family Law, Probate, Administrative and Constitutional Law, Medical Malpractice, Personal Injury, Insurance Law, Litigation.

FIRM PROFILE: *Established in 1963, Menzel, Roßkopf, Metzger and Partner is a broad-based general practice, offering a wide range of legal services. Of the ten partners within the firm, all are specialists in their own particular field of work.*

The firm is also a member of CONSULEGIS, an European economic interest group which comprises a network of professional firms, seeking to further promote their business reputation.

MEMBERS OF FIRM

EIKE WERNER MENZEL, born Treuen, Germany, 1944; admitted, 1975, Heilbronn; 1988, Fachanwalt für Arbeitsrecht. *Education:* Universities of Mainz and Heidelberg. *Member:* German Bar Association, Arbeitsgemeinschaft für Arbeitsrecht (Labor Law Association). *LANGUAGES:* German and English. *PRACTICE AREAS:* Labor Law; Building Law.

DIETER W. ROSSKOPF, born Darmstadt, Germany, 1950; admitted, 1978, Heilbronn. *Education:* Universities of Mainz and Frankfurt. Author: "Risiken des Berufskraftfahrers," "Die Regulierung von Haftpflichtschäden an Veteranen- u. Liebhaberfahrzeugen." *Member:* German Bar Association; Arbeitsgemeinschaft für Verkehrsrechtsanwälte (Traffic Law Association); Deutsche Akademie für Verkehrswissenschaften e.V. *LANGUAGES:* German and English. *PRACTICE AREAS:* Insurance and Traffic Law; Personal Injury.

ALFRED METZGER, born Kassel, Germany, 1952; admitted, 1981, Heilbronn. *Education:* Universities of Freiburg and Kiel. Lecturer in Administrative and Constitutional Law, Higher Technical College of Economia, Stuttgart. Author: "Das Recht der Werbegestaltung." *Member:* German Bar Association. *PRACTICE AREAS:* Administrative and Constitutional Law; Building Law.

REINHART HEYDEL, born Zwenkau nr. Leipzig, Germany, 1945; admitted, 1975, Heilbronn; 1981, Fachanwalt für Steuerrecht. *Education:* University of Heidelberg. Author: "Strafbarkeit des Vertriebes von Bauherren-Bauträger- und Erwerbermodellen gemaess, § 264 a StGB. *Member:* German Bar Association; Arbeitsgemeinschaft der Fachanwälte für Steuerrecht (Tax Law Association). *PRACTICE AREAS:* Tax Law.

ROSEL GÖTZ-HERMANN, born Eschollbrücken, Germany, 1950; admitted, 1976, Heilbronn. *Education:* Universities of Marburg and Heidelberg. *Member:* German Bar Association, pro familia, Heilbronn (board), Frauen helfen Frauen e.V. *LANGUAGES:* German and French. *PRACTICE AREAS:* Family Law.

REGINA M. GRAF, born Wilhelmshaven, Germany, 1955; admitted, 1982, Mannheim. *Education:* University of Mannheim. *Member:* German Bar Association. *LANGUAGES:* German and English. *PRACTICE AREAS:* Probate; General Practice; Litigation.

MONIKA M. BAUMHACKEL, born Heilbronn, Germany, 1960; admitted, 1987, Heilbronn. *Education:* University of Konstanz. *Member:* German Bar Association; Arbeitsgemeinschaft für Strafverteidiger (Defence Counsel Association); German-British Lawyers Association. *LANGUAGES:* German and English. *PRACTICE AREAS:* Criminal Law; Medical Malpractice; Personal Injury.

(This Listing Continued)

JOCHEN HORCH, born Bad Mergentheim, Germany, 1958; admitted, 1988, Heilbronn. *Education:* University of Heidelberg. *LANGUAGES:* German, English and French. *PRACTICE AREAS:* Business Law; Executor Law.

GÜNTHER HÄUSLER, born Stuttgart, 1949; admitted, 1979, Stuttgart. *Education:* Notariatsschule Stuttgart, Universities of Tübingen and Freiburg. *Member:* German Bar Association. *LANGUAGES:* German and English. *PRACTICE AREAS:* Probate Law; Corporate Law.

DIETRICH M. HAUSER, born Vaihingen/Enz, Germany, 1961; admitted, 1992, Heilbronn. *Education:* University of Tübingen. *LANGUAGES:* German and English. *PRACTICE AREAS:* Family Law.

RÖMERMANN & SCHWAB

HILDESHEIM, GERMANY

(See Hannover, Germany)

Investment Law, Commercial Law, International Business Law, Corporate Law, Real Estate Law, Administration Law, Litigation.

BEITEN BURKHARDT MITTL & WEGENER

Rechtsanwälte

OBERER TORPLATZ 1
D-95028 HOF, GERMANY
Telephone: (09281) 80 23
Telefax: (09281) 1 65 69

Munich, Germany Office: Leopoldstrasse 236, D-80807. Telephone: (089) 35065-00. Telefax: (089) 35065-123.

Berlin, Germany Office: Kurfürstenstrasse 72-74, D-10787 Berlin. Telephone: (0 30) 264 71-0. Telefax: (0 30) 264 71-123.

Frankfurt/Main, Germany Office: Arndtstrasse 28, D-60325 Frankfurt/Main. Telephone: (0 69) 75 60 95-0. Telefax: (0 69) 75 60 95-12.

Nürnberg, Germany Office: Obere Turnstrasse 8, D-90429 Nürnberg. Telephone: (09 11) 2 79 71-0. Telefax: (09 11) 2 79 71-99.

Leipzig, Germany Office: Käthe-Kollwitz-Strasse 54, D-04109 Leipzig. Telephone: (03 41) 4 77 25 97. Telefax: (03 41) 4 77 25 99.

Potsdam, Germany Office: Heinrich-Mann-Allee 105 B, D-14473 Potsdam. Telephone: (0331) 33 43 06. Telefax: (0331) 33 43 29.

Plauen, Germany Office: Lindenstrasse 5, D-08523 Plauen. Telephone: (03741) 22 35 11; 22 49 62. Telefax: (03741) 22 49 62.

New York, New York Office: 215 East 73rd Street, New York, NY 10021. Telephone: (212) 570-2141. Telefax: (212) 734-7011.

London, England Office: Swedenborg House, 21 Bloomsbury Way, London, WC1A 2TH. Telephone: (0171) 2 42 44 66. Telefax: (0171) 2 42 44 67.

Moscow, Russia Office: Ul. Alekseja Tolstovo D.30/1, 103001 Moscow. Telephone and Telefax: (095) 202 37 60; 290 05 56.

Prague, Czech Republic Office: Na Bojišti 24, 120 00 Prague 2. Telephone: (2) 24 91 5808. Telefax: (2) 24 91 5804.

Budapest, Hungary Office: József Nádor Tér 9, H-1051 Budapest. Telephone: (1) 2 66 18 10. Telefax: (1) 2 66 18 11.

Hong Kong Office: 605 B, Sixth Floor, Peregrine Tower, Lippo Centre, 89 Queensway. Telephone: (852) 2524 6468. Telefax: (852) 2524 7028.

Beijing, People's Republic of China Office: Unit 10, 29th Floor, Jing Guang Centre, Hu Jia Lou, Chao Yang Qu, 100020. Telephone: (86-1) 501 4569; 501 3388 Ext. 2910. Telefax: (86-1) 501 3034.

Commercial Law, Company Law, M & A, Joint Ventures, Finance, Banking, Leasing, Domestic and International Tax, Antitrust, EC Law, Real Property and Private Construction, Electronic Data Processing (Protection and Licensing), Media, Publishing, Unfair Competition, Trademarks, Copyright, Labour, General and Special Administrative Law Particularly Public Construction and Planning Regulations and Public International Law, Environmental Law, Agricultural Law, Privatization and Restitution (former GDR), Probate, Family and Estate Planning, Insolvency and Sports, Insurance, Automobile Accidents and Injuries.

(This Listing Continued)

FIRM PROFILE: BEITEN BURKHARDT MITTL & WEGENER is a nation-wide and international law firm with 108 lawyers. The firm's head office is in Munich. All the firm's offices provide a comprehensive range of services in the main areas of civil and commercial law.

HUBERTUS BENECKE, born Coburg, 1960; admitted, 1990, Germany. *Education:* University of Bonn (law degree, 1987). *Member:* Bavarian Association of Real Estate Owners (Advisory Board). *LANGUAGES:* German and English. *PRACTICE AREAS:* Probate and Family Law; Expropriation and Restitution; Agricultural Law; Insolvency; Liquidations.

KLAUS SELCH, born Nürnberg, 1959; admitted, 1988, Germany. *Education:* University of Erlangen (law degree, 1985). Research Assistant, University of Erlangen, Institute for Commercial and Labour Law, Department for Intellectual Property and Competition, 1985-1987. Staff Member, University of Erlangen, Institute for Civil Law and Civil Procedure, 1987-1988. Lecturer on Management Science and Controlling as well as Labour Law, Fachhochschule Heilbronn, 1993—. *LANGUAGES:* German and English. *PRACTICE AREAS:* Company Law; Acquisitions and Sales; Restructuring; Labour and Employment; Expropriation and Restitution; Insolvency; Liquidations.

ANKE MEYER, born Offenbach, 1964; admitted, 1994, Germany. *Education:* Universities of Frankfurt a.M. and Speyer (law degree, 1991). Lecturer, Institute for Public Law, University of Frankfurt a.M., 1992-1993. *LANGUAGES:* German, English and Spanish. *PRACTICE AREAS:* Unfair Competition; Copyrights; Advertising and Marketing; Real Estate; Construction Law; Probate and Family Law.

(For Complete Biographical Data on all Personnel, see Munich, Germany Professional Biographies)

LAW OFFICE
ROLF A. SCHAUMLOEFFEL

51, EISENBAHN ST.
D-67655 KAISERSLAUTERN, GERMANY
Telephone: (49) (631) 64061; 64062
Facsimile: (49) (631) 64063

International, EEG Law, Banking, Corporate, Mergers and Acquisitions, Tax, Commercial, Antitrust, Labour, General Practice, Arbitration, Litigation, Collection of Debts, Intellectual Property, Trademarks, Shipping Law, Criminal Law.

ROLF A. SCHAUMLOEFFEL, born Kaiserslautern, Germany, 1937; admitted, 1968, Germany. *Education:* Universities of Munich, Bonn and Mainz. Foreign Studies at Montpellier, France, and University of California at Berkeley, USA. Trusty, German Realty Corp. *Member:* Kaiserslautern Bar Association; E.W.I.V. Ars Legis.

Languages: German, English, French, Italian.

BARTSCH UND PARTNER

Established in 1952

BAHNHOFSTRASSE 10
D-76137 KARLSRUHE, GERMANY
Telephone: 0721-93175-0
Telecopier: 0721-9317588

General Practice and Litigation, Computers and Software, Real Estate and Construction, Products Liability, Corporate, Commercial, Copyrights, Unfair Competition, Labor, International, Leasing, Company, Contracts.

MEMBERS OF FIRM

ALFRED BARTSCH. *Education:* Universities of Rostock and Breslau. *LANGUAGES:* German, English and French. *PRACTICE AREAS:* General Practice; Litigation; Civil; Contracts.

MICHAEL BARTSCH. *Education:* Universities of Hamburg, Geneva and Freiburg. Lecturer, Corporate, Commercial and Computer Law, University Karlsruhe. Many publications in Computer and Commercial Law. *Member:* Dt. Gesellschaft für Recht u. Informatik (German Computer Law Association, Executive Committee). *LANGUAGES:* German, English and French. *PRACTICE AREAS:* Computers and Software; Information Technology; Construction; Products Liability; Arbitration.

CORNELIA BETZ. *Education:* University of Freiburg. Lecturer in Computer Law, FH Karlsruhe. *LANGUAGES:* German, English and

(This Listing Continued)

BARTSCH UND PARTNER, Karlsruhe—Continued

French. *PRACTICE AREAS:* Computers and Software; Communications; Commercial; Property.

ARNDT BRILLINGER. *Education:* Universities of Tübingen, Geneva and Lausanne. *Member:* Dt. Gesellschaft für Baurecht; Arbeitsgem f. privates Bau- u. Architektenrecht im dt. Anwaltsverein. *LANGUAGES:* German, French and English. *PRACTICE AREAS:* Construction; Real Estate; Insolvency; Labor.

MARTIN EICHLER. *Education:* University of Freiburg. *LANGUAGES:* German, English and French. *PRACTICE AREAS:* Unfair Competition; Copyrights; Trademarks; Antitrust.

DR. JÖRG MAURER. *Education:* Universities of Munich and Heidelberg. *LANGUAGES:* German, English and Italian. *PRACTICE AREAS:* Software; Leasing; Company; Commercial.

BIRGIT ROTH. *Education:* University of Heidelberg. Lecturer in Computer Law, FH Karlsruhe. *LANGUAGES:* German, French and English. *PRACTICE AREAS:* Computer Contracts; Corporate; Torts; Agency and Distributorship.

RUPERT VOGEL. *Education:* Universities of Heidelberg and Dijon. Assistant, University of Montpellier, 1989-1990. Lecturer in French Law, University Mannheim. *LANGUAGES:* German, French and English. *PRACTICE AREAS:* Software; Leasing; Advertising; International.

Languages: German, English, French and Italian

HILMAR RAESCHKE-KESSLER

RECHTSANWALT BEIM BGH

76133 KARLSRUHE, GERMANY
Telephone: 07243/17077
Telecopier: 07243/13144

Mailing Address: Bismarckstrasse 3, 76275 Ettlingen, Germany
Litigation before German Federal Supreme Court, Arbitration.

HILMAR RAESCHKE-KESSLER, LL.M., born Mühlhausen, Germany, December 29, 1943; admitted to bar, 1975, West Germany; 1985, Federal Supreme Court. *Education:* Universities of Göttingen, Bonn and University of Chicago Law School (LL.M., 1975). Co-Author: Raeschke-Kessler/Schendel/Schuster, "Umwelt und Betrieb," Erich Schmidt-Verlag, 2nd ed. 1991 (Environmental Law and Industry); Raeschke-Kessler/Bühler, " Aufsicht über den Schiedsrichter durch den ICC-Schiedsgerichtshof (Paris) und rechtliches Gehör der Parteien," ZIP 1987, 1157 et. seq. Author: "Die neuere Rechtsprechung zur Schiedsgerichtsbarkeit," in Jahrbuch für die Praxis der Schiedsgerichtsbarkeit I, II, III, IV, 1987, 1988, 1989, 1990; Raeschke-Kessler/Lehne, "Aktuelle Rechtsfragen und Praxis der Schiedsgerichtsbarkeit," RWS-Skript; "Neuere Entwicklungen im Bereich der Internationen Schiedsgerichtsbarkeit," NJW 1988, 3041 et seq; Binnenmarkt, Schiedsgerichtsbarkeit und ordre public, EuZw 1990, 145 et seq.; "Arbitration in the Changed East-West Relationship," International Business Lawyer, 1993, p. 15 et seq.; "Der Vergleich im Schiedsverfahren," Festschrift für O. Glossner, 1993, p. 255 et seq.; "Bankenhaftung bei der Anlageberatung über neue Finanzprodukte," WM 1993, 1830 et seq. *Member:* International Chamber of Commerce-Institute of International Business Law and Practice; London Court of International Arbitration European Council; Association Suisse d'Arbitrage; Deutsche Institution für das Schiedsgerichtswesen; International Bar Association; German-American Lawyers Association; Deutscher Juristentag. *LANGUAGES:* German, English and French.

REINERT, APPY & PARTNER

STEINHÄUSERSTRASSE 17
76135 KARLSRUHE, GERMANY
Telephone: 0721-812024
Telecopier: 0721-818738

Dresden, Germany Office: Selliner Strasse 1, 01109 Dresden/Saxony. Telephone: 0351/4604353. Telecopier: 0351/460352. Mobile Phone: (0049) 161-3719355.

Strasbourg, France Office: 66, Rue Marchè-Gare, F-67200. Telephone: 0033 88-261426. Telecopier: 00330 88-268840.

(This Listing Continued)

Washington, D.C. Office: Suite 1004, 1101 Seventeenth Street, N.W., 20036-4798. Telephone: (202) 293-5555. Telecopier: (202) 293-9035.

General Practice and Litigation. Corporate, Commercial, Banking, Business, Antitrust, Trademark, Computer, Copyright, Tax, Unfair Competition, Civil Aviation, International and EC Law, Administrative Law.

MEMBERS OF FIRM

HANNO REINERT, born Lahr, Germany, May 14, 1947; admitted, 1976, Germany. *Education:* Kepler-G. Freiburg (Abitur, 1966); Freiburg University Law School (Referendar, 1970); Karlsruhe University (Social Sciences, Dipl.-Volkswirt, 1974); LG Karlsruhe (Assessor, 1976). Lecturer, Commercial and Business Law, University of Karlsruhe, 1980-1990. Academy of Savings and Loan Association, Rastatt, 1978-1991. Managing Director, German Association of Textile Raw Material Suppliers Inc. (Fachverband Textilrohstoffe in der Bundesrepublik Deutschland e.V.), 1981—. *Member:* German Bar Association; German-American Lawyers Association; International Bar Association. *LANGUAGES:* German and English.

SABINE APPY-ROSENTHAL, born Stuttgart, Germany, July 1, 1954; admitted, 1981, Germany. *Education:* Lessing G. Frankfurt (Hum. Abitur, 1973); Tübingen University Law School (Referendar, 1979); LG Tübingen (Assessor, 1981). *Member:* German Bar Association; International Bar Association (Secretary General); German-Israeli Lawyers Association. *LANGUAGES:* German, English and Italian.

LEONHARD BAUR, born Ulm, Germany, October 15, 1949; admitted, 1986, Germany; 1991, Dresden/Saxony. *Education:* Ludwig-Wilhelm-Gymnasium Rastatt (1966); Hotel Management Training Baden-Baden and Berlin (1967-1969); College for Business Administration Heidelberg (Dipl. Betriebswirt FH, 1976); Freiburg University Law School (Referendar, 1982). Hotel Manager, 1969-1973. Developer, Holiday Center for Handicapped Persons near Rome, Italy, 1976-1978. Assessor, District Court, Baden-Baden, 1986. *Member:* German Bar Association. *LANGUAGES:* German, English and Italian.

ROBERT HAAS, born Aschaffenburg, Germany, August 8, 1962; admitted, 1992, Germany. *Education:* F.-M.-Schwerdt-Gymn. Speyer (Abitur, 1982); Heidelberg and Mannheim University Law Schools (Referendar, 1989); OLG Zweibrücken (Assessor, 1992). Lecturer, Alpmann/Schmidt Private Law School, Heidelberg, 1989-1992. Managing Director, Atlantis-Odeon Cinema Corporation, Mannheim, 1985-1991. *Member:* German Bar Association. *LANGUAGES:* German and English.

MARTIN HIRSCH Justice (1913-1992).

MARTINA KREBS-FORKEL, born Karlsruhe, Germany, November 25, 1962; admitted, 1991, Germany. *Education:* Markgrafen-G. Karlsruhe (Abitur, 1982); Heidelberg University Law School (Referendar, 1988); LG Karlsruhe (Assessor, 1991). *Member:* German Bar Association. *LANGUAGES:* German and English.

ERNST GOTTFRIED MAHRENHOLZ, born Göttingen, Germany, June 18, 1929; admitted, 1994, Germany. *Education:* Universities of Tübingen and Göttingen (Doctor of Law, 1957). Co-Author: "Altern"; Kommentar Grundgesetz (German Constitution), Handbuch des Verfassungsrechts and numerous publications about Public Law. Assistant to Prof. Dr.Dr. Rudolf Smend, 1959; Professor, Frankfurt Law School, 1991. Administration, State of Lower Saxony (Germany), 1960-1965; Head of Broadcasting Station of Hannover, 1965-1970; State Secretary, Minister of Culture and School Education, Lower Saxony, 1970-1976; Member of Parliament, 1976-1981; Justice, Bundesverfassungsgericht (Federal Supreme Constitutional Court), 1981-1994; Vice President, Bundesverfassungsgericht, 1987. *Member:* International Commission of Lawyers (German Section). *LANGUAGES:* German and English.

DAMIEN WEDRYCHOWSKI, born Orleans, France, 1947; admitted, 1978, France (Not admitted in Germany). *Education:* Universities Orleans and Strasbourg (Licence en Droit, 1969; Diplome Etudes Superieures, Private Law, 1972). Assistant, Universities of Heidelberg and Strasbourg, 1973-1977. Lecturer, University of Heidelberg, 1974—; University of Freiburg/Breisgau, 1989—. *Member:* French Bar Association; Club d'Affaires Franco-Allemand, Germany. *LANGUAGES:* German, English and French.

ANWALTSKANZLEI
DR. DR. ULFERT ENGELS
WILHELMSSTR. 11
D-34117 KASSEL, GERMANY
Telephone: 0561-709.83-0
Fax: 0561-71.10.71

Frankfurt/Main, Germany Office: Klingerstr. 24, D-60313. Telephone: 069-28.11.39. Fax: 069-28.35.12.

Rotterdam, The Netherlands Office: Engels & Jongeneel Advocaten, Westersingel 92, NL 3015 LC. Telephone: (31-10) 436.07. 88. Fax: (31-10) 436.78.44.

Foreign Attorneys' Assistance, Business Coaching and Contact Tuition, Fiduciary Transactions, Eastern Europe and European Union, Public Subsidies, Taxes and Customs, International Clearing, Investment, Import Regulations, Food and Drug, Government Contracts, Real Estate, Banking and Financing, Leasing, Product and Criminal Liability, Insurance, Copyright, Mass Media, Publishing, Energy, Environment, Corporate and Commercial, Antitrust, Fair Trade, Settlement, Arbitration.

DR. DR. ULFERT ENGELS, born Kitzbuhel, Austria, May 8, 1943; admitted, 1976, Germany and Court of Appeal of Frankfurt a.M. *Education:* University of Munich (Doctor Juris, 1973); University of Paris (Doctor of Public Finance, 1974); University of Salamanca, Spain; Chamber of Commerce of Frankfurt (Diploma of Publishing Merchant, 1983). Sworn Interpreter of Spanish-German and French-German, 1978. Statutory Manager, Court-Registered European Attorney's, Tax Counsel's and CPA's EEIG (IASW EWIV), 1990. Amtsgericht Frankfurt a.M. HRA 26625. *LANGUAGES:* German, English, French, Spanish, Dutch, Italian and Indonesian.

HANS-WERNER WEINGART, born Kassel, Germany, September 27, 1954; admitted, 1983, Germany. *LANGUAGES:* German, English, French and Portuguese.

DIPL.-KFM. MANFRED ECKERT, born Waidach, Germany, January, 1947; admitted, 1984, Germany as Vereidigter Buchprüfer. Legal Advisor for Commercial, Corporate and Tax Law. *LANGUAGES:* German and English.

HEILIG & PARTNER
SOPHIENBLATT 74-78
KIEL, GERMANY
Telephone: 0049 / (0) 431 / 66 40 70
Telefax: 0049 / (0) 431 / 66 40 730

Mailing Address: Postfach 33 07, D - 24032

Commercial, Corporate, Finance, Real Estate, Construction, Family, Insurance, Personal Injury, Products Liability, Trusts and Estates, Labour and Employment, Insurance - Automobile Insurance, Leaves and Leasing - Commercial.

MEMBERS OF FIRM

HEINZ-KARL HEILIG, born KIel, January 18, 1947; admitted, 1976, Kiel. *Education:* University of Kiel. Notary Public, 1979. *Member:* German Bar Association; Consulegis European Joined Consulting EWIV; German-Nordic Lawyers Association. *LANGUAGES:* German and English. *PRACTICE AREAS:* Commercial Law; Corporate Law; Finance; Real Estate; Trusts and Estates.

JURGEN F. HEIMBECK, born Bremen, Germany, August 22, 1955; admitted, 1984, Bielefeld; 1991, Kiel. *Education:* University of Kiel. *Member:* German Bar Association; Consulegis European Joined Consulting EESC; German-Nordic Lawyers Association. *LANGUAGES:* German and English. *PRACTICE AREAS:* Construction Law - Contracts; Family Law - Separation and Divorce; Personal Injury - Wrongful Death; Products Liability - Product Safety.

THORSTEN HOLZ, born April 30, 1962; admitted, 1994, Kiel. *Education:* University of Kiel. *LANGUAGES:* German and English. *PRACTICE AREAS:* Labour and Employment; Insurance - Automobile Insurance; Leases and Leasing - Commercial.

HOFFMANN-FÖLKERSAMB JOHANSSON
& PARTNER
ZIEGELTEICH 29
24103 KIEL, GERMANY
Telephone: +49-431-97 40 30
Fax: +49-431-97 40 320

Rostock, Germany Office: Kröpeliner Straße 19, 18055 Rostock. Telephone: +49-381-4923821. Fax: +49-381-45 26 07.

Copenhagen, Denmark Office: Vagtelvej 58, 2000 Frederiksberg C. Telephone: +45-38 88 44 04. Fax: +45-38 88 20 16.

Commercial, Company, Corporate, Mergers and Acquisitions, International Sales, European Community Law, Real Estate, Taxation, Construction, Agricultural, Administrative, Labor and Employment, Maritime, Arbitration, Advertising and Marketing, Trademarks.

MEMBERS OF FIRM

ERNST JOHANSSON, born Riga, Latvia, August 22, 1934; admitted, 1965, Germany; 1971, Notary Public. *Education:* Universities of Kiel, Berlin and Paris. Author: "Die Freizügigkeit der freien Berufe in der Europäischen Gemeinschaft," 1985; "Byggeeksport til Tyskland," 1992; "Das Recht der Schausteller des Markt- und Reisegewerbes," 1993. *Member:* German-Nordic Lawyers Association (President); International Commission of Jurists (German Section); German Bar Association. *LANGUAGES:* German, English, French and Swedish. *PRACTICE AREAS:* Corporate; Company; EC Law; Real Estate.

GEORG MATZ, born Königsberg, Germany, January 3, 1941; admitted, 1971, Germany; 1977, Notary Public. *Education:* Universities of Hamburg, Tübingen and Kiel. *Member:* German Bar Association. *LANGUAGES:* German. *PRACTICE AREAS:* Litigation; Family; Real Estate; Maritime.

KLAUS HANSEN-KOHLMORGEN, born Itzehoe, Germany, September 25, 1947; admitted, 1975, Germany; 1983, Notary Public. *Education:* Universities of Hamburg and Kiel. *Member:* German Bar Association; German-Nordic Lawyers Association. *LANGUAGES:* German and English. *PRACTICE AREAS:* Corporate; Company; Transportation; Advertising and Marketing.

DR. CLAUS CORNELIUS, born Nordenham, Germany, July 8, 1954; admitted, 1983, Germany. *Education:* Universities of Kiel (Dr. jur., 1984) and Oslo. Author: "Der Schutz des Forderungsinhabers gegenüber Dritten im nordischen und deutschen Recht," 1985; "Die GmbH im dänischen Recht," 1991; "Byggeeksport til Tyskland," 1992; "Das Recht der Schausteller des Markt- und Reisegewerbes," 1993. *Member:* German Bar Association; International Bar Association; German-Nordic Lawyers Association (Secretary). *LANGUAGES:* German, English and Norwegian. *PRACTICE AREAS:* Company; Corporate; Mergers and Acquisitions; Labor and Employment.

JOHANN F.C. LUND, born Hamburg, Germany, February 16, 1956; admitted, 1986, Germany. *Education:* University of Kiel. Author: "Byggeeksport til Tyskland," 1992. *Member:* German Bar Association; German-Nordic Lawyers Association. *LANGUAGES:* German, English and Danish. *PRACTICE AREAS:* Administrative (Fachanwalt für Verwaltungsrecht); Litigation; General Practice.

DR. CARSTEN KRAGE, born Bad Segeberg, Germany, January 29, 1959; admitted, 1992, Germany. *Education:* Universities of Kiel (Dr. jur., 1989), Hamburg, Lausanne and Uppsala. Law firm at Helsinki. Author: "Einführung in das schwedische Kommunairecht," 1990. *Member:* German-American Lawyers Association; German-Nordic Lawyers Association; International Association of Young Lawyers (AIJA); German Bar Association. *LANGUAGES:* German, English, Swedish and Finnish. *PRACTICE AREAS:* Construction; International Sales; Trademarks; Taxation.

ASSOCIATES

ROLF WEHNER, born Elmshorn, Germany, October 10, 1948; admitted, 1981, Germany. *Education:* University of Kiel. Author: "Ehe- und Familienrecht, Konsequenzen für die bäuerliche Familie," 1990. *LANGUAGES:* German and English. *PRACTICE AREAS:* Agricultural; Taxation (Fachanwalt für Steuerrecht); Successions.

JOACHIM FUNK, born Kiel, Germany, May 11, 1962; admitted, 1993, Germany. *Education:* Universities of Freiburg and Kiel. *Member:* German Bar Association. *LANGUAGES:* German and English. *PRACTICE AREAS:* Labour and Employment; Agricultural; Insurance.

(This Listing Continued)

HOFFMANN-FÖLKERSAMB JOHANSSON &
PARTNER, Kiel—Continued

STEPHEN FITSCH, born Kiel, Germany, April 19, 1963; admitted, 1994, Germany. *Education:* University of Kiel. *LANGUAGES:* German, English and French. *PRACTICE AREAS:* Family Law; Landlord and Tenant; Criminal Law; General Practice.

Languages: German, English, French, Spanish, Swedish, Danish, Norwegian and Finnish

---

DR. LAUPRECHT & PARTNER

LAURENTZENDAMM 36
D-24103 KIEL, GERMANY
Telephone: (0431) 5 90 09-0
Telex: 292 728 RECHT D
Telefax: (0431) 554887

Mailing Address: Postfach 3107, D-24030 Kiel, Germany

Commercial, Corporation, Unfair Competition, Real Estate, Maritime Law and Administrative Law.

MEMBERS OF FIRM

DR. IUR. GOTTFRIED LAUPRECHT, born Hamburg, Germany, 1915; admitted, 1949, Kiel. Notary Public, 1952. *Education:* University of Göttingen (Dr. iur., 1944); Universities of Munich, Freiburg and Hamburg. Examiner in the Exams for Lawyers and Chartered Accounts. *Member:* German Bar Association; International Fiscal Association.

MICHAEL KOHLHAAS, born Stuttgart, Germany, 1937; admitted, 1964, Kiel. Notary Public, 1971. *Education:* Universities of Munich and Kiel. *Member:* German Bar Association; German Society for the Protection of Industrial Property and Copyright; Deutscher Juristentag.

JOCHEM RIEMANN, born Speyer, Germany, 1943; admitted, 1971, Kiel. Notary Public, 1975. *Education:* Universities of Kiel and Berlin (West). *Member:* German Bar Association; Northern Germany Society of Administrative Law.

DR. RER. AGR. KARSTEN WITT, born Berlin, Germany, 1942; admitted, 1972, Kiel. Notary Public, 1976. *Education:* University of Kiel (Dr. rer. agr., 1971); Universities of Göttingen and Freiburg. *Member:* German Bar Association; German Society for Agricultural Law.

DR. IUR. DETLEV BEHRENS, born Neustadt-Holstein, Germany, 1952; admitted, 1979, Hamburg. Notary Public, 1989. *Education:* University of Kiel (Dr. iur., 1979). *Member:* German Bar Association; German Society for the Protection of Industrial Property and Copyright; AIJA.

ULRICH PRAGER, born Husum, Germany, 1954; admitted, 1986, Kiel. *Education:* University of Kiel. *Member:* German Bar Association.

PETRA AHLERS-HOOPS, born Varel, Germany, 1957; admitted, 1985, Kiel. *Education:* University of Kiel. *Member:* German Bar Association.

DR. IUR. ANDREAS PILTZ, born Gütersloh, Germany, 1953; admitted, 1982, Güttingen. *Education:* University of Güttingen (Dr. iur., 1987); University of Kiel. *Member:* German Bar Association; German Society for Agricultural Law.

GOEBELS, POKORNY, KÄHLER & PARTNER

Established in 1947

WILHELMSHOFALLEE 79-81
47800 KREFELD, GERMANY
Telephone: 02151/507-0
Telefax: 02151/599608

Berlin, Germany Office: 10117 Berlin, Lindenstr. 54a. Telephone: 030/2384128. Telefax: 030/2071890.

Administrative Law, Antitrust, Banking and Financial Services, Common Market Law, Construction and Engineering Contracts, Corporate Matters, Environmental Law, Industrial and Intellectual Property, Labor Law, Litigation and Arbitration, Mergers and Acquisitions, Procurement Contracts, Product Liability, Taxation, High Technology and Telecommunication, Trade Law, Unfair Competition.

(This Listing Continued)

RESIDENT PARTNERS

DR. WALTER GOEBELS, born Krefeld, Germany, August 28, 1908; admitted, 1947. *Education:* Universities of Tübingen, Berlin, Marburg, Bonn. *LANGUAGES:* German and French.

DR. PETER POKORNY, born Glatz, Germany, May 27, 1926; admitted, 1953. *Education:* Universities of Köln, Bonn. *LANGUAGES:* German and English.

KURT KÄHLER, born Langenfeld, Germany, August 13, 1928; admitted, 1959. *Education:* Universities of Mainz, Hamburg, Köln. *LANGUAGES:* German and English. *PRACTICE AREAS:* Tax Law.

DR. WILHELM HAASE, born Paderborn, Germany, February 7, 1935; admitted, 1968. *Education:* Universities of Freiburg, München, Bonn, Köln. *LANGUAGES:* German. *PRACTICE AREAS:* Labor Law; Tax Law.

KLAUS STEFFEN, born Krefeld, Germany, December 19, 1938; admitted, 1967. *Education:* University of Köln. *LANGUAGES:* German and English.

DR. H. DIETER GOBBERS, born Düsseldorf, Germany, July 20, 1951; admitted, 1980. *Education:* Universities of Marburg, Rennes. *LANGUAGES:* German, English and French.

HANS FRIEDRICH DICKEL, born Wuppertal, Germany, November 14, 1928; admitted, 1989. *Education:* Universities of Freiburg, Paris. *LANGUAGES:* German, English and French.

HERIBERT DIETZ, born Bonn, Germany, April 18, 1940; admitted, 1989. *Education:* Universities of Bonn, Lausanne, Köln, Manchester. *LANGUAGES:* German, English and French. *PRACTICE AREAS:* Administrative Law.

DR. CHRISTIAN SCHMIDT, born Hamburg, Germany, February 19, 1960; admitted, 1991. *Education:* Universities of München, Tübingen, Bonn. *LANGUAGES:* German and English.

GABRIELA CORNELIUS, born Koblenz, Germany, May 10, 1953; admitted, 1979. *Education:* University of Freiburg. *LANGUAGES:* German, English and French.

ASSOCIATES

KLAUS KALENBERG, born Mönchengladbach, Germany, June 10, 1959; admitted, 1993. *Education:* University of Bonn. *LANGUAGES:* German and English.

DR. ROLAND REINFELD, born Nettetal, Germany, July 7, 1964; admitted, 1993. *Education:* University of Köln. *LANGUAGES:* German and English.

(For biographical data on Berlin personnel, see Professional Biographies at that location)

HERZOG, MEYER, WILL

SOLLBRÜGGENSTRAβE 52
47800 KREFELD, GERMANY
Telephone: +49 2151 589501
Telefax: +49 2151 598110
Modem: +49 2151 501244

Berlin, Germany Office: Schlüterstraβe 54, 10629. Telephone: +49 30 8857040. Telefax: +49 30 8824821.

Moers, Germany Office: Haagstraβe 12, 47441. Telephone: +49 2841 25207. Telefax: +49 2841 28384.

General Practice, Commercial law, Corporate Law, Trial, Corporation, Banks and Banking, Securities, Mergers, Acquisitions and Divestitures, Property, Real Estate, Taxation, Administrative Law, Computer and Software, Construction Law, Unfair Competition and Antitrust Law, Labour Law, Family Law, Air Law, Litigation.

MEMBERS OF FIRM

DR. TILMAN HERZOG, born Dresden, Germany, November 10, 1942; admitted, 1971, Krefeld. *Education:* Universities of Freiburg and Münster, Qualified Tax Lawyer, (Doctor of Laws, 1969). Author: "Die Grundrechts-Subjektivität überindividueller privatrechtlicher und öffentlich-rechtlicher Funktionseinheiten." Director of the BPG Wirtschaftsprüfungs- und Steuerberatungsgesellschaft mbH, Krefeld/Düsseldorf/-Frankfurt/Berlin/Munich/Dresden/Leipzig/Basel. *Member:* German Bar Association; Institute of C.P.A. in West Germany (IdW). *LANGUAGES:* German, English and French.

(This Listing Continued)

JÖRG-HENNING MEYER, born Greiz, Germany, June 11, 1945; admitted, 1973, Krefeld. *Education:* Universities of Cologne and Innsbruck, Austria. Qualified Labour Lawyer. *Member:* German Bar Association. *LANGUAGES:* German, English, Dutch and French.

DR. CHRISTIAN WILL, born Königsberg, Germany, September 19, 1936; admitted, 1967, Düsseldorf. *Education:* Banking practice in London, Paris and Germany for 3 1/2 years, Universities; London School of Economics and Political Science, London; Universities of Freiburg and Münster, Qualified Tax Lawyer (Doctor of Laws, 1967). Author: "Das Äquivalenzprinzip bei den Gewerbesteuern". *Member:* German Bar Association. *LANGUAGES:* German, English and French.

ANDREAS SEIDEL, born Hannover, Germany, November 24, 1956; admitted, 1986, Krefeld. *Education:* University of Mainz. *Member:* German Bar Association. *LANGUAGES:* German and English. *PRACTICE AREAS:* Construction Law; Labour Law; Corporate Law; Litigation.

CLAUS EßERS, born Oberhausen, Germany, May 6, 1954; admitted, 1988, Krefeld. *Education:* University of Bochum. Qualified Tax Lawyer. *Member:* German Bar Association. *LANGUAGES:* German and English.

ANDREAS BÖNING, born Kiel, Germany, July 10, 1960; admitted, 1991, Krefeld. *Education:* University of Freiburg, (Banker). *Member:* German Bar Association. *LANGUAGES:* German and English.

ASSOCIATES

KONRAD FRÖHLICH, born Münster, Germany, May 27, 1963; admitted, 1993, Krefeld. *Education:* Universities of Münster and Freiburg. *LANGUAGES:* German and English.

CHRISTOPH SCHMITT, born Düsseldorf, Germany, June 2, 1963; admitted, 1993, Düsseldorf. *Education:* University of Cologne. *Member:* German Bar Association. *LANGUAGES:* German and English. *PRACTICE AREAS:* Labour Law; Company Law; Competition Law.

TOBIAS H. STRÖMER, born Rheydt, Germany, May 1, 1960; admitted, 1991, Frankfurt; 1994, Krefeld. *Education:* Universities of Passau, Bonn and Lille (France). Author: "Die kollisionsrechtliche Regelung des Schwangerschaftsabbruchs im Bundesgebiet," ROW 11 (1991); "Gesetzliche Zinsen in Frankreich," EuZW 210 (1992); "Der Vielflieger-Bonus-punkte fürs Finanzamt?", BB 705 (1993). *Member:* German Bar Association; Wirtschaftsjunioren, Frankfurt (Member, Executive Board); German-French Lawyers Association. *LANGUAGES:* German, French and English. *PRACTICE AREAS:* Mergers, Acquisition and Divestitures; Commercial Law; Computer Law.

INGRID BOHR, born Hamburg, Germany, October 29, 1949; admitted, 1978, Frankfurt. *Education:* Universities of Hamburg and Munich. *Member :* German Bar Association. *LANGUAGES:* German and English. *PRACTICE AREAS:* Company Law; Commercial Law; Distribution and Transportation Law.

JUTTA ALBERS, born Emsdetten, Germany, April 27, 1966; admitted, 1994, Krefeld. *Education:* University of Münster. *Member:* German Bar Association. *LANGUAGES:* German and English.

DR. GOTTFRIED TEIPEL UND PARTNER

KOENIGSTRASSE 137
47798 KREFELD, GERMANY
Telephone: (02151) 28028
Telefax: (02151) 631576

Mailing Address: P.O. Box 2950, 47729

General Practice and Litigation, Corporate, Commercial, Banking, Business, Trademark and Copyright, Tax, Unfair Competition, Labour, Administrative, Marital, Inheritance, International and EEC Law.

MEMBERS OF FIRM

DR. GOTTFRIED TEIPEL, born Betzdorf, Germany, March 2, 1929; admitted, 1955, Krefeld. *Education:* University of Kiel (Doctor of Law, 1954). Chairman of "the Einigungstelle zur Beilegung von Bürgerlichen Rechtsstreitigkeiten bei der Industrie- und Handelskammer (IHK) Mittlerer Niederrhein Mönchengladbach-Neuss-Krefeld." Fachanwalt für Steuerrecht. *Member:* German and Krefeld Bar Association; German-Spanish Lawyers Association. *LANGUAGES:* German, Spanish, English and French. *PRACTICE AREAS:* Tax Law; International Business Law; Business Law.

ULRICH STIRKEN, born Krefeld, Germany, April 13, 1952; admitted, 1977, Krefeld. *Education:* University of Cologne. Fachanwalt für Arbeits-

(This Listing Continued)

recht. *Member:* German and Krefeld Bar Association; German-French Lawyers Association. *LANGUAGES:* German, French and English. *PRACTICE AREAS:* Labour Law; Construction Law; Administrative Law.

MATTHIAS TEIPEL, born Krefeld, Germany, April 27, 1957; admitted, 1986, Krefeld. *Education:* University of Kiel. Legal Clerk, Washington, D.C. *Member:* German and Krefeld Bar Association; German-American Lawyers Association; Young Lawyers International Association. *LANGUAGES:* German, English and French. *PRACTICE AREAS:* Business Law; Trade Law; Commercial Law; Criminal law; Accidents; Personal Injury; Public Law.

ALBERT, FLAD & SCHLOSSHAN

GOTTSCHEDSTRASSE 41
D-04109 LEIPZIG, GERMANY
Telephone: 49-341-211 36 16; 49-341-211 42 52
Telecopier: 49-341-211 42 82

Frankfurt/Main, Germany Office: Cronstettenstrasse 66, D-60322.
   Telephone: 49-69-55 02 26. Telex: 416314 coun d. Telecopier: 49-69-55 46 99.

Commercial and Corporate Law with emphasis on Mergers and Acquisitions, Contracts, Corporate Taxation, Real Estate, Zoning, Planning and Land Use, Expropriations and Restitution, Unfair Competition and Antitrust, EC Law, Intellectual Property, Computer, Telecommunications, Product Liability, Labor and Social Security, Banking and Securities, Administrative Law, Private and Public Construction, Environmental Law, Food and Drug, Bankruptcy, Litigation and Arbitration, Investment in Eastern Germany.

FIRM PROFILE: The firm, whose roots can be traced back to Berlin and Dresden of the early 1930's, was founded under the present name in Frankfurt/Main in 1967; it was among the first to open a branch office in Leipzig in 1990 after the collapse of the Communist regime in East Germany. The firm provides comprehensive legal services covering all areas of modern business and public services. Most of the work is internationally related. The clientele ranges from large multinational industrial corporations and financial institutions to medium-sized trading companies and public law bodies.

MEMBERS OF FIRM

DR. WERNER BLAU, born Hildesheim, Germany, June 11, 1952; admitted, 1981, Germany. *Education:* Universities of Frankfurt/Main and Freiburg/Breisgau (Referendar, 1978; Dr. jur., 1984). Chairman, Arbitration Board for the Settlement of Unfair Competition Disputes, Leipzig Chamber of Commerce. *Member:* German Association for the Protection of Industrial Property and Copyright; Asia-Pacific Lawyers' Association; German-Korea Lawyers' Association. (Also at Frankfurt/Main Office). *PRACTICE AREAS:* Competition; Antitrust; EC Law; Intellectual Property; Expropriations and Restitution.

DR. JÖRG MICHAEL LANG, born Frankfurt/Main, Germany, July 10, 1957; admitted, 1988, Germany. *Education:* University of Frankfurt/Main (Referendar, 1984; Dr. jur., 1989). *Member:* German-American Lawyers' Association; Banking Law Association. (Also at Frankfurt/Main Office). *PRACTICE AREAS:* Commercial and Corporate Law; Banking; Commercial Real Estate; Expropriations and Restitution.

DR. BARBARA SCHMIDT, born Coburg, Germany, February 25, 1962; admitted, 1990, Germany. *Education:* University of Würzburg (Referendar, 1987; Dr. jur., 1989). *PRACTICE AREAS:* Commercial Real Estate; Commercial and Corporate Law; Expropriations and Restitution; Litigation.

ASSOCIATES

DR. KLAUS SCHAFFNER, born Berlin, Germany, March 28, 1962; admitted, 1991, Germany. *Education:* University of Tübingen (Referendar, 1988); University of St. Gallen, Switzerland (Dr. jur., 1993). *Member:* EUREV Association of the Alumni of the St. Galler Europarechtskurse (European Law Courses). *PRACTICE AREAS:* Commercial and Corporate Law; Commercial Real Estate; Zoning, Planning and Land Use; Expropriations and Restitution; EC Law; Investment in Eastern Germany.

DIERK SCHLOSSHAN, born New York, NY, April 20, 1961; admitted, 1990, Germany. *Education:* University of Frankfurt/Main (Referendar, 1986). Member, Marketing-Club Leipzig. *Member:* American-German Business Club (Executive Board, Leipzig Chapter); Club des Affaires de la Saxe; Marketing Club, Leipzig. *PRACTICE AREAS:* Commercial and

(This Listing Continued)

ALBERT, FLAD & SCHLOSSHAN, Leipzig—Continued

Corporate Law; Commercial Real Estate; Zoning, Planning and Land Use; Construction Law; Investment in Eastern Germany; Communications and Media.

DR. KLAUS BEHRENS, born Freiburg/Breisgau, Germany, October 12, 1955; admitted, 1987, Germany. *Education:* Universities of Freiburg, Heidelberg and Marburg (Referendar, 1984; Dr. jur., 1987); University of Illinois, Urbana Champaign, U.S.A. (M.C.L., 1984). *PRACTICE AREAS:* Commercial and Corporate Law; Commercial Real Estate; Expropriations and Restitution; Law of Succession; Investment in Eastern Germany.

KLAUS STEFAN SCHARLEMANN, born Stuttgart, Germany, July 8, 1962; admitted, 1994, Germany. *Education:* Universities of Bayreuth and Munich (Referendar, 1992). *Member:* German-Asia-Pacific Business Association in Mitteldeutschland. *PRACTICE AREAS:* Competition; Antitrust; EC Law; Expropriations and Restitution.

MATTHIAS ARNDT, born Mainz, Germany, April 28, 1964; admitted, 1994, Germany. *Education:* University of Mannheim (Referendar, 1991). *PRACTICE AREAS:* Environmental Law; Commercial Real Estate; Expropriations and Restitution.

Languages: German, English and French

AULINGER, BOTTKE, KNÄLMANN

GOETHESTRASSE 1
04109 LEIPZIG, GERMANY
Telephone: (0341) 9600910
Fax: (0341) 9601169

Bochum, Germany Office: ABC-Str. 5, D-44787 Bochum. Telephone: (0234) 68779-0. Teletex: 234 334 (Dufhues) (from Telex: 17234334). Fax: (0234) 68 06 42.
Dresden, Germany Office: St. Petersburger Str. 15, 01069 Dresden. Telephone: (0351) 4 87 24 19. Fax: (0351) 4 87 33 27.
Erfurt, Germany Office: Kleine Arche 1, 99084 Erfurt. Telephone: (0361) 5667808. Fax: (0361) 5667810.

General Practice. Corporate, Commercial, Banking, Antitrust, Unfair Competition, Real Estate, Merger and Acquisition, Products Liability, Labor, Co-Determination, Tax, Arbitration, Administrative and Public, Building and Planning. Reversion of nationalized enterprises and real estate to private ownership.

MEMBERS OF FIRM

GERALD BAUSCH, born Halle, Germany, January 10, 1953; admitted, 1980, Leipzig. *Education:* University of Berlin (Humboldt-University). *LANGUAGES:* German, Russian.

BENEDIKT GALLE, born Münster, Germany, January 4. 1958; admitted, 1990, Hamburg. *Education:* Universities of Bochum and Münster. *LANGUAGES:* German, English and French.

(For Complete Biographical data on all Personnel, see Professional Biographies at Bochum)

BEISSWINGERT & PARTNER

Established in 1990

JOHANNISALLEE 20
04317 LEIPZIG, GERMANY
Telephone: (0341) 2619902; 275438; 275444
Telex: 512176 eweka dd
Telefax: (0341) 275593

Munich, Germany Office: Widenmayerstrasse 28, 80538. Telephone: (089) 290816-0. Cable Address: "Nomosrecht München". Telex: 05-22557 recht d. Telefax: (089) 290816-60; 290816-61; 290816-62.

General Practice. International, Tax, Probate, Antitrust, Unfair Competition, Patent, Copyright, Trademark, Family and International Transport Law.

FIRM PROFILE: The firm was established in 1930 in Berlin by Oskar Möhring, who in the beginning practised law mainly as a trial lawyer, and later often became administrator in important bankruptcy and arrangement proceedings. In 1945, due to the post-war confusion, the firm moved to Munich and later on specialized in the main fields of business and commercial law. Möhring died in 1984. In July 1990, the firm opened its office in Leipzig, then East Germany. Today it consists of six partners and

(This Listing Continued)

---

four associates. Its symbol is the elephant, which stands for sensitivity and the power of knowledge.

DR. ANGELA MÜLLER, born Leipzig, Germany, September 11, 1954; admitted, 1990 Leipzig. *Education:* University of Leipzig (Doctor of Law). Author: "Die innerkombinatlichen Rechtsverhältnisse bei Übernahme von Krediten durch das Kombinat," (Syndication of Loans and Intra-Combine Relationships), Leipzig, 1982. *Member:* Chamber of Industry and Commerce. *LANGUAGES:* German, French and Russian.

HAGEN ALBUS, born Treuenbrietzen, Germany, February 21, 1964; admitted, 1993, Leipzig. *Education:* University of Leipzig (Diplom-Jurist). Assessor, Bamberg, 1993. Author: "Die Staats-und Rechtskonzeption des Bischofs Wilhelm Emmanuel Freiherr von Ketteler (1811-1877)" (The Conception of State and Law of MSGR Wilhelm Emmanuel Freiherr von Ketteler, Bishop), Leipzig, 1990. *LANGUAGES:* German, English and Russian.

(For Complete Biographical Data on all Personnel, see Professional Biographies at Munich, Germany)

BEITEN BURKHARDT MITTL & WEGENER

Rechtsanwälte

KÄTHE-KOLLWITZ-STRASSE 54
D-04109 LEIPZIG, GERMANY
Telephone: (03 41) 4 77 25 97
Telefax: (03 41) 4 77 25 99

Munich, Germany Office: Leopoldstrasse 236, D-80807. Telephone: (089) 35065-00. Telefax: (089) 35065-123.
Berlin, Germany Office: Kurfürstenstrasse 72-74, D-10787 Berlin. Telephone: (0 30) 264 71-0. Telefax: (0 30) 264 71-123.
Frankfurt/Main, Germany Office: Arndtstrasse 28, D-60325 Frankfurt/Main. Telephone: (0 69) 75 60 95-0. Telefax: (0 69) 75 60 95-12.
Nürnberg, Germany Office: Obere Turnstrasse 8, D-90429 Nürnberg. Telephone: (09 11) 2 79 71-0. Telefax: (09 11) 2 79 71-99.
Potsdam, Germany Office: Heinrich-Mann-Allee 105 B, D-14473 Potsdam. Telephone: (0331) 33 43 06. Telefax: (0331) 33 43 29.
Hof, Germany Office: Oberer Torplatz 1, D-95028 Hof. Telephone: (09281) 80 23. Telefax: (09281) 1 65 69.
Plauen, Germany Office: Lindenstrasse 5, D-08523 Plauen. Telephone: (03741) 22 35 11; 22 49 62. Telefax: (03741) 22 49 62.
New York, New York Office: 215 East 73rd Street, New York, NY 10021. Telephone: (212) 570-2141. Telefax: (212) 734-7011.
London, England Office: Swedenborg House, 21 Bloomsbury Way, London, WC1A 2TH. Telephone: (0171) 2 42 44 66. Telefax: (0171) 2 42 44 67.
Moscow, Russia Office: Ul. Alekseja Tolstovo D.30/1, 103001 Moscow. Telephone and Telefax: (095) 202 37 60; 290 05 56.
Prague, Czech Republic Office: Na Bojišti 24, 120 00 Prague 2. Telephone: (2) 24 91 5808. Telefax: (2) 24 91 5804.
Budapest, Hungary Office: József Nádor Tér 9, H-1051 Budapest. Telephone: (1) 2 66 18 10. Telefax: (1) 2 66 18 11.
Hong Kong Office: 605 B, Sixth Floor, Peregrine Tower, Lippo Centre, 89 Queensway. Telephone: (852) 2524 6468. Telefax: (852) 2524 7028.
Beijing, People's Republic of China Office: Unit 10, 29th Floor, Jing Guang Centre, Hu Jia Lou, Chao Yang Qu, 100020. Telephone: (86-1) 501 4569; 501 3388 Ext. 2910. Telefax: (86-1) 501 3034.

Commercial Law, Company Law, M & A, Joint Ventures, Finance, Banking, Leasing, Domestic and International Tax, Antitrust, EC Law, Real Property and Private Construction, Electronic Data Processing (Protection and Licensing), Media, Publishing, Unfair Competition, Trademarks, Copyright, Labour, General and Special Administrative Law Particularly Public Construction and Planning Regulations and Public International Law, Environmental Law, Agricultural Law, Privatization and Restitution (former GDR), Probate, Family and Estate Planning, Insolvency and Sports, Insurance, Automobile Accidents and Injuries.

FIRM PROFILE: BEITEN BURKHARDT MITTL & WEGENER is a nation-wide and international law firm with 108 lawyers. The firm's head office is in Munich. All the firm's offices provide a comprehensive range of services in the main areas of civil and commercial law.

RALPH SCHMIDKONZ, born Kempten, 1962; admitted, 1989, Germany. *Education:* University of Munich (law degree, 1986). Trainee, Mar-

(This Listing Continued)

tin, Cavan & Andersen, Atlanta, 1989. *LANGUAGES:* German, English and French. *PRACTICE AREAS:* Press Law; Publishing and Radio; Expropriation and Restitution.

BERNET, WEITNAUER & PARTNER

ROSCHERSTR. 17-21
04105 LEIPZIG, GERMANY
Telephone: 0341-564 67 66
Telecopier: 0341-566 09 81

Munich, Germany Office: Möhlstraße 10/I, 81675. Telephone: 089-470 90 14. Telecopier: 089-470 74 27.

Dresden, Germany Office: Anton-Graff-Strasse 15, 01309. Telephone: 0357/447 62 80. Telecopier: 0357/447 62 89.

Commercial, Corporation, Mergers and Acquisitions, Taxation, Antitrust, EEC, Corporate Finance, Banking and Securities, Unfair Competition, Trademarks, Patents, Copyright, Computer, Media, Press and Publishing, Labour, Real Estate, Environment, Litigation and Arbitration.

CHRISTIAN BERNET, born Berlin, Germany, May 4, 1943; admitted, 1972, Germany. *Education:* Universities of Tübingen, Geneva/Switzerland and Munich (Referendar, 1967; Assessor, 1972). Author: "Management Buy-out in den neuen Bundesländern," (MBO in East Germany) Dresden, 1992; "Rechtsverkehr mit Kunstwerken," (Legal relations concerning works of art) Cologne, 1988. *Member:* Leipzig Bar Association. *LANGUAGES:* German, English and French. *PRACTICE AREAS:* Corporate Law; Mergers and Acquisitions Law; Real Estate Law; Restitution of Property and Investment in East Germany; Art Law; Litigation; Arbitration.

DR. HORST BUCHALI, born Mittelsteina, Germany, September 4, 1934; admitted, 1991, Germany. *Education:* Universities of Berlin and Leipzig (Dr. jur., 1979). General Counsel, VEB GISAG, Leipzig, 1977-1987; VEB baukema/baukema AG, Leipzig, 1987-1992. *LANGUAGES:* German, English and Russian. *PRACTICE AREAS:* Litigation; Investment and Commercial Law in East Germany.

BODEN OPPENHOFF RASOR RAUE

LEIPZIG, GERMANY

(See Oppenhoff & Rädler)

BRANDI DRÖGE PILTZ & HEUER

KATHARINENSTR. 1-3
04109 LEIPZIG, GERMANY
Telephone: 49 341 287550
Telecopier: 49 341 289162

Bielefeld, Germany Office: Elsa-Brändström-Str. 1 and 3, 33602. Telephone: 49 521 96535-0. Telecopier: 49 521 96535-99.

Detmold, Germany Office: Lindenweg 2, 32756. Telephone: 49 5231 9857-0. Telecopier: 49 5231 9857-50.

Gütersloh, Germany Office: Hochstr. 19, 33332. Telephone: 49 5241 58886. Telecopier: 49 5241 58881.

Berlin, Germany Office: Seelenbinderstr. 124, 12555. Telephone: 49 30 6509465. Telecopier: 49 30 6565679.

Paris, France Office: 250 bis, Boulevard Saint-Germain, 75007. Telephone: 33-1 49549037. Telecopier: 33-1 49549002.

Commercial Law, Labor Law, Unfair Competition, Company Law, Banking Law, Litigation, General Practice.

MEMBER OF FIRM

DIETMAR GÖTZ, born Unna, Germany, 1956; admitted, 1991, Detmold; 1992, Leipzig. *Education:* University of Mainz (Erstes juristisches Staatsexamen, 1985). Commerzbank, Frankfurt a.M., 1989-1991. *LANGUAGES:* German and English. *PRACTICE AREAS:* Commercial Law; Banking Law; Unfair Competition; Litigation; General Practice.

BRUCKHAUS WESTRICK STEGEMANN

GRIMMAISCHE STRASSE 25
04109 LEIPZIG, GERMANY
Telephone: (0341) 127230
Fax: (0341) 1272333

Düsseldorf Office: Freiligrathstrasse 1, 40479 Düsseldorf. Telephone: (0211) 49 79-0. Telefax: (0211) 49 79-103. Telex: 858 7027 JUS D.

Frankfurt Office: Taunusanlage 11, 60329 Frankfurt am Main. Telephone: (069) 27308-0. Telefax: (069) 232664. Telex: 41 49 17 WEST CD.

Hamburg Office: Alsterarkaden 27, 20354 Hamburg. Telephone: (040) 36 90 60. Telefax: (040) 36 906-155. Telex: 212 522 EURO D.

Berlin Office: Friedrichstrasse 95 (IHZ), 10117 Berlin. Telephone: (030) 26 43-3303. Telefax: (030) 26 43-3366.

Brussels, Belgium Office: Rue de la Loi 99/101, B-1040 Brussels. Telephone: (32-2) 2 87 26 11. Telefax: (32-2) 2 30 39 03.

Tokyo, Japan Office: Ark Mori Building, 22F, 12-32, Akasaka 1-chome, Minato-ku, Tokyo 107. Telephone: (81-3) 55610-236. Telefax: (81-3) 55610-238.

New York, New York Office: 767 Fifth Avenue, GM Building, New York 10153. Telephone: (212) 486-1100. Telefax: (212) 759-3151.

Moscow, Russia Office: Malyj Gnezdnikovskij per. 9 No. 2, 103009 Moscow. Telephone: (7-503) 9562300; (7-501) 9401200. Telefax: (7-503) 9562301; (7-501) 9401211.

Corporate Law, Commercial Law, Mergers, Acquisitions and Divestitures, Joint Ventures, Banks and Banking, Finance, Securities, Capital Markets, Leases and Leasing, Equipment Finance, Aircraft Finance and Leasing, Antitrust and Trade Regulation, German and EC Cartel Law, Competition, Unfair Trade, Intellectual Property (trademarks, patents, copyrights), Taxation, Property, Real Estate, Energy, Natural Resources, Environmental Law, Administrative Law, Computers and Software, Food and Drug, Biotechnology, Labour and Employment, Products Liability, Insurance, Litigation, Arbitration, Broadcasting, Telecommunications, Aviation, Subsidies and State Aids, Construction Law, Zoning, Planning and Land Use, Customs and Foreign Trade Law, European Community Law, German-French Investments, Russian and Post Soviet Commerce.

MEMBERS OF FIRM

MANFRED FINKEN, born Jülich, Germany, January 15, 1950; admitted, 1977, Germany. *Education:* University of Bonn. *LANGUAGES:* German and English. *PRACTICE AREAS:* Corporate Law; Commercial Law; Tax Law; Mergers and Acquisitions.

HARRY SCHMIDT, born Sehnde/Hannover, Germany, May 27, 1952; admitted, 1985, Germany. *Education:* University of Heidelberg (Dr. jur., 1985). Faculty Assistant, Institute for Commercial and Economic Law, University of Heidelberg, 1980-1985. *LANGUAGES:* German and English. *PRACTICE AREAS:* Corporate Law; Commercial Law.

NIKOLAUS REINHUBER, born Frankfurt am Main, Germany, May 6, 1960; admitted, 1990, Germany. *Education:* Universities of Frankfurt am Main, Hamburg and London (LL.B., 1988). *LANGUAGES:* German and English. *PRACTICE AREAS:* Commercial Law; Corporate Law; Company Law.

NILS MATTHIAS KOFFKA, born Helmstedt, Germany, July 26, 1962; admitted, 1992, Germany. *Education:* Universities of Heidelberg (Dr. jur., 1992) and Lausanne (Switzerland). *LANGUAGES:* German and English. *PRACTICE AREAS:* Corporate Law; Real Estate.

DERINGER TESSIN HERRMANN & SEDEMUND

BURGPLATZ 2
D-04109 LEIPZIG, GERMANY
Telephone: 49-341-711590
Telefax: 49-341-7115999

Cologne, Germany Office: Heumarkt 14, D-50667 Cologne. Telephone: 49-221-205070. Telefax: 49-221-2050790. Telex: 8 881 356 ELAW D.

Frankfurt/Main Germany Office: Bockenheimer Landstraße 51-53, D-60325 Frankfurt a.M. Telephone 49-69-971090-0. Telefax: 49-69-971090-90.

Brussels, Belgium Office: Place des Barricades 13, B-1000 Brussels. Telephone: 32-2-219 82 50. Telefax: 32-2-219 88 32.

Moscow, Russia Office: Ul. Bolschaja Ordymka 21, RF-113035 Moscow. Telephone: 7-095-2332450, 2315403. Telefax: 7-095-2334355.

(This Listing Continued)

EU725B

DERINGER TESSIN HERRMANN & SEDEMUND,
Leipzig—Continued

General German and International Practice. Reprivatisation, Joint Ventures, Restructuring of Formerly State-Owned Businesses, Mergers and Acquisition, Environmental, Labor and Commercial Law.

PARTNERS

DR. GÜNTER KRÖBER, born Leipzig, Germany, January 12, 1928; admitted, 1953, Leipzig. *Education:* Leipzig University (Referendar, 1950; Dr. jur., 1970). Author: "Guarantee in Civil and Commercial Law," 1970. In-house Counsel of "Centrum" Department Stores, Leipzig, 1966-1990. Member, Parliament of Saxony, 1950-1990, President of the Liberal Parliamentary Group. Member of the Board of the liberal Friedrich-Naumann-Foundation. *Member:* German Bar Association; German-American Lawyers Association.

ASSOCIATES

DR. ULRICH KEßLER, born Völklingen, Germany, May 8, 1961; admitted, 1993, Leipzig. *Education:* University of Saarbrücken (Referendar, 1990; Dr. jur., 1994). Author: "Private Shareholding in Public Enterprises with special Consideration of Deutsche Lufthansa AG." Lecturer, Public Law, 1987-1993. *LANGUAGES:* German, Spanish, French and English.

FRANK B. VENNEMANN, born Greven, Germany, May 16, 1964; admitted, 1994, Leipzig. *Education:* Universities of Münster and Lausanne. Research Assistant, Institute for Commercial, Economic and Labor Law, University of Münster, 1989-1992. *LANGUAGES:* German, English and French.

(For complete biographical data on all personnel, see Professional Biographies at Cologne, Germany)

FIEDLER & FORSTER

GRIMMAISCHE STR. 25

04109 LEIPZIG, GERMANY

Telephone: (0049-341) 2115112

Fax: (0049-341) 9602530

Berlin, Germany Office: Oranienburger Stasse 69, D-10117. Telephone: (0049) (30) 283 2418. Fax: (0049) (30) 283 2420.

Cologne, Germany Office: Bonner Strasse 172-176, D-50968 Cologne. Telephone: (0049) (221) 937050-0. Telefax: (0049) (221) 937050-50.

Frankfurt/Main, Germany Office: Opernplatz 2, D-60313 Frankfurt/Main. Telephone: (0049) (69) 298930. Telefax: (0049) (69) 2398259.

Munich, Germany Office: Brienner Strasse 12/III, D-80333 Munich. Telephone:(0049) (89) 23980; Telefax: (0049) (89) 2398259.

Stuttgart, Germany Office: Gänsheidestr. 68, D-70184. Telephone: (0049) (711) 16455-0. Fax: (0049) (711) 16445-11.

Paris, France Office: Tour Fiat la Dèfense 6, F-92084 Paris. Telephone: 33-1-47 76 28 10. Fax: 33-1-47 96 63 63.

Commercial, Corporate, Mergers and Acquisitions, Leasing, Banking, European Community, International and Private, International Commercial Arbitration, Tax, Unfair Competition, Intellectual Property, Anti-Trust, Copyright, Press and Publishing, Licensing and Know-How, Franchising, Computer and Software, Data Protection, Construction, Law of Tenancy, Real Estate, Condominium, Brokerage, Labour, Insurance, Air Traffic and Travel, Family, Divorce, Succession, Sequestration and Foreclosure, Litigation and Collection, Insolvency, Law pertaining to property claims in the former GDR.

PARTNERS

DR. PETER FORSTER, born Baden-Baden, Germany, July 29, 1937; admitted, 1967, Frankfurt; 1977, Notary. *Education:* University of Frankfurt. Professorial Assistant, Institute for Public Law, University of Frankfurt, 1963-1966. *Member:* Frankfurt Bar Association. *LANGUAGES:* German and English.

BERND CHRISTIAN HAAGER, born Nürnberg, Germany, December 10, 1950; admitted, 1980, Frankfurt, Attorney at Law and Special Tax Counsel; 1988, Frankfurt Court of Appeal. *Education:* Universities of Frankfurt, Munich and Mainz. Assistant Professor, Civil Law, University of Mainz, 1975-1976. Former General Counsel of F & F Burda Holding, 1988-1990. *Member:* GRUR (German Association for Intellectual Property and Copyright); Studienvereinigung Kartellrecht (Association for Antitrust Law). *LANGUAGES:* German, English and Swedish.

(This Listing Continued)

DR. WERNER WELLHÖFER, born Wuerzburg, Germany, August 22, 1947; admitted, 1976, Munich. *Education:* Universities of Lausanne and Munich (Dr. jur., 1977). Co-Author: "Rechtshandbuch Vermögen und Investitionen in der ehemaligen DDR," C.H. Beck Publications ("Property and Investments in the former GDR: a legal reference book"). With Law Firm, Washington, D.C., 1974. *Member:* Union Internationale Des Avocats; Association for Comparative Law. *LANGUAGES:* German, English and French.

DR. BERNHARD KUEHN, born Munich, Germany, July 31, 1960; admitted, 1989, Munich. *Education:* University of Munich (Dr. jur., 1987). *LANGUAGES:* German, English and French.

ASSOCIATES

DR. PETER HÖFLER, born Zwickau, Germany, October 6, 1960; admitted, 1990, Leipzig. *Education:* University of Leipzig (Dr. jur., 1990). *Member:* Deutscher Anwaltverein, Verein der Fachanwälte für Arbeitsrecht. *LANGUAGES:* German, English and Russian.

PETER LENKITSCH, born Königsberg, Germany, January 5, 1927; admitted, 1958, Leipzig. *Education:* University of Erlangen. *LANGUAGES:* German, English.

STEFAN STALLBAUM, born Nürnberg, Germany, February 4, 1963; admitted, 1992, Leipzig. *Education:* Universities of Passau and Munich. *LANGUAGES:* German, English, French.

DR. FRIEDRICHS & PARTNER

PAUL-LIST-STR. 22

D-04103 LEIPZIG, GERMANY

Telephone: 0341-9600659

Fax: 0341-9600659

Düsseldorf, Germany Office: Steinstraße 27, D-40210 Düsseldorf. Telephone: 3230108-9. Telefax: 0211-326147.

Commercial, Corporate and Business Law, Unfair Competition, Intellectual Property, International and German Law of Contracts, Tax Law, Transportation, Planning Law, Reprivatization, Litigation, Arbitration, Medical Malpractice, Family Law, Criminal Defense, Commercial Property, Residential Property Law and Conveyancing.

RESIDENT PARTNERS

DR. CHRISTOPH FRIEDRICHS, born 1950; admitted, 1978, Germany. *Education:* Universities of Freiburg, Münster, Hamburg, UC Berkeley and London (Kings College, London School of Economics) (Dr. jur.). Author: "Chancen der Aktiengesellschaft und des Aktionärs," Tax Attorney (FA f.SteuerR). *Member:* German Bar Association; German-American Lawyers Association; German British Lawyers Association; Association International des Jeunes Advocats; AG Internationaler Rechtsverkehr im DAV. *LANGUAGES:* German and English.

DR. HELMUT NASE, born 1951; admitted, 1991, Germany. *Education:* University Leipzig. *Member:* German Bar Association. *LANGUAGES:* German, English and Russian.

(For Complete Biographical Data on all Personnel, see Professional Biographies at Düsseldorf, Germany)

GAEDERTZ VIEREGGE QUACK KREILE

Rechtsanwälte

AUGUST-BEBEL-STR. 38

D-04275 LEIPZIG, GERMANY

Telephone: (341) 477 83 81/83

Telefax: (341) 477 83 88

Berlin, Germany Office: Kurfürstendamm 157 D-10709 Berlin. Telephone: (30)890 05-0. Telefax: (30)892 26 06. Teletex: 30 88 15 qkp d. Telex: 17 30 88 15 qkp d.

Cologne, Germany Office: Theodor-Heuss-Ring 19-21, D-50668 Cologne. Telephone:(221)77 16-0. Telefax: (221)77 16-110. Teletex: 221 43 76 olga d. Telex: 88 85 143 olga d.

Frankfurt/Main, Germany Office: Airport Center, Hugo-Eckener-Ring, D-60549 Frankfurt/Main. Telephone: (69)69 48 52. Telefax: (69)69 48 60. Telex: 40 32 145 zibr d.

Munich, Germany Office: Widenmayerstrasse 32, D-80538 Munich. Telephone: (89)212147-0. Telefax: (89)228 55 62.

Wiesbaden, Germany Office: Kaiser-Friedrich-Ring 65, D-65185 Wiesbaden. Telephone: (611)88 05-0. Telefax: (611)81 03 09. Telex: 41 86 295 gaed d. Teletex: 61 21 986 gaed.

Brussels, Belgium Office: Avenue de Tervuren 35, B-1040 Brussels. Telephone: (2) 736 07 97. Telefax: (2) 732 69 12.

(This Listing Continued)

Prague, Czech Republic Office: Betlémska 1, CR-11000 Prague 1. Telephone: (2) 24 22 94 98. Telefax: (2) 232 12 29.

General Practice. Commercial, Corporate, Antitrust and Tax Law. Mergers and Acquisitions, Unfair Competition, Industrial Property Rights, Labor Law and Environmental Law. Real Estate. International Construction and Joint Venture Contracts. Arbitration and Litigation. Notaries (Berlin and Wiesbaden).

FIRM PROFILE: *The law firm Gaedertz Vieregge Quack Kreile is the result of a merger between 4 partnerships: Heydt Vieregge & Partner, Cologne; Gaedertz Henn & Partner, Wiesbaden; Quack Kühn & Partner, Berlin; Prof. Kreile & Partner, Munich.*

Gaedertz Vieregge Quack Kreile is one of the major German based law firms representing domestic and foreign clients in all fields of law that are relevant for national and international enterprises. An important part of the practice are the legal aspects of transnational transactions especially in EC. The firm advises not only German clients in international matters but also foreign enterprises about all implications of doing business in Germany. Thus many attorneys and also members of the support staff are fluent in English. Other languages such as French, Spanish, Portuguese, Italian, Russian, and Dutch are also spoken.

In addition, the offices in Cologne and Wiesbaden have the specialized capacity to administer large trademark portfolios worldwide including registration and litigation of trademarks and registered designs.

Clients of the firm include many well-known German and foreign companies active in a wide variety of businesses. Gaedertz Vieregge Quack Kreile also represents various trade associations as well as German federal, state and local governmental authorities.

In the Berlin, Wiesbaden and Frankfurt/Main offices, there are 10 attorneys qualified to act as "Notar," specially licensed to prepare and execute documents relating to incorporation of companies, real estate matters and other important commercial transactions where a special form of document is prescribed.

Gaedertz Vieregge Quack Kreile has more than 70 attorneys, including 42 partners, plus a support staff of approximately 150 people, working in the eight different offices.

The offices have for the most part city centre locations. The Frankfurt office is situated at the Airport-Centre of the Rhein-Main Airport.

MEMBERS OF FIRM

DR. PETER KRÜGER, born Waldbrol, 1943; admitted, 1973, Leipzig. *Education:* Universities of Bonn, Berlin and Cologne (Dr.jur.). *Member:* Leipzig Bar Association; German Lawyers' Association; German Association for Industrial Property Rights and Copyright. PRACTICE AREAS: Corporate; Commercial Law; Legal Problems of Reunification, especially restitution claims and unfair competition.

DR. JOHANN-CHRISTOPH GAEDERTZ, born Wiesbaden, Germany, 1959; admitted, 1987, Frankfurt/Main. *Education:* Universities of Freiburg and Mainz; McGeorge School of Law, Sacramento (LL.M.); University of Konstanz (Dr. jur.). With Chartier, Hourcade & Associates, Paris, 1986; Fulbright, Jaworski, Reavis,Mc Grath, New York, 1989. *Member:* Leipzig Bar Association; Association Internationale des Jeunes Avocats; German Lawyers Association; German Association for Industrial Property Rights and Copyright. LANGUAGES: English, French. PRACTICE AREAS: Corporate; Commercial Law; Real Estate Law; Legal Problems of German Reunification, in particular Restitution Claims.

ASSOCIATES

BERND BRINKMANN, born Cologne, 1962; admitted, 1993, Leipzig. *Education:* University of Cologne. *Member:* Leipzig Bar Association. LANGUAGES: English.

DR. ANDREAS FINK, born Aachen, 1961; admitted, 1994, Leipzig. *Education:* Universities of Bonn and Cologne (Dr. jur.). *Member:* Leipzig Bar Association; German-American Lawyers Association.

FRANZ ROBERT BÄRTELS, born Ibbenbüren, Germany, 1960; admitted, 1994, Leipzig. *Education:* University of Münster. *Member:* Leipzig Bar Association. LANGUAGES: English and French.

(For complete biographical data on personnel at Berlin, Cologne, Frankfurt/Main, Munich and Wiesbaden, Germany Offices as well as Brussels, Belgium and Prague, Czech Republic Offices, see Professional Biographies at those locations).

GÖHMANN, DIESELHORST & SCHERRER

Established in 1990

EISENBAHNSTRAßE 84
04315 LEIPZIG, GERMANY
Telephone: 0341/6 31 52
Telecopier: 0341/6 31 52

Hannover, Germany Office: Landschaftstrasse 6, 30159. Telephone: 0511 302770. Fax: 0511 329216.

General Commercial Law, Trade, Banking and Insurance Law, Corporate and Competition Law, Civil Litigation, Labour Law, Mergers and Acquisitions, Tax Law, German Reunification.

PARTNERS

Wulf Meinecke   **Bettina Carl** (Resident)
                    Andreas Bruse (Resident)

(For complete biographical data, see Professional Biographies at Hannover, Germany)

GRAF VON WESTPHALEN & MODEST

KATHARINENSTRAßE 15
04109 LEIPZIG, GERMANY
Telephone: (0341) 281073
Fax: (0341) 281073

Hamburg, Germany Office: Poststraße 9 A, Postfach 30 36 10, 20354. Telephone: (040) 35922-0. Telex: 211 729 mod d. Telefax: 040/34 45 73.
Cologne, Germany Office: Salierring 42. 50677. Telephone: (0221) 20807-0. Fax: (0221) 239255.
Dresden, Germany Office: Winterbergstraße 2. 01277. Telephone and Fax: 0351-2516 024 or 2516032.
Brussels, Belgium Office: Avenue de la Joyeuse Entrée 1, Boîte 16, B-1040. Telephone: (32) (2) 230.46.69. Telefax: (32) (2) 231.00.35.
Paris, France Office: 198, Avenue Victor Hugo, 75116. Telephone: (1) 45.04.61.73. Telex: FUGELEX 614570. Telefax: (1) 45.04.41.43.

EEC Law, German, French and International Law.

STEPHAN EICHHORN, born Leipzig, Germany, November 1, 1953; admitted, 1990, Leipzig. *Education:* University of Leipzig. LANGUAGES: German and Russian.

ALEXANDER SCHMIDT, born Tübingen, Germany, May 15, 1961; admitted, 1989, Karlsruhe. *Education:* University of Würzburg. LANGUAGES: German, English and French.

(For Complete Biographical Data on all Personnel, see Professional Biographies at Hamburg, Germany and Cologne, Germany)

GURLAND & LAMBSDORFF

HAINSTRASSE 17/19
D-04109 LEIPZIG, GERMANY
Telephone: 341-2114412
Telefax: 341-2114617

Also offices in Cologne, Frankfurt and Berlin.

General Business and International Practice, Corporate, Company, Commercial, Unfair Competition, Acquisitions and Mergers, especially GDR Property Law, Unsolved Property Questions, Restitution Law.

MEMBERS OF FIRM

DR. DIETHER HOFFMANN, born 1929; admitted, 1987, Germany. *Education:* University of Frankfurt (Dr. of Law, 1959). Previous activities: International Banking Work, 1959-1982. Chairman of Bank für Gemeinwirtschaft, Germany, 1977-1982. Chairman of Neue Heimat, 1982-1986. Town Counsellor, Frankfurt, 1964-1974. *Member:* German-Israeli Trade Association; German Association for Comparative Law. LANGUAGES: German, English and French.

WOLFGANG TIMA, born 1951; admitted, 1983, Germany. *Education:* University of Berlin. Author: "Wettbewerbssituation der Medien und Grundgesetzliche Medienverfassung," 1979. LANGUAGES: German and English.

(This Listing Continued)

EU727B

GURLAND & LAMBSDORFF, Leipzig—Continued

ASSOCIATES

CHRISTINE WILLSCHÜTZ, born 1944; admitted, 1991, Germany. *Education:* University of Leipzig. **LANGUAGES:** German and Russian.

Member of LEGALLIANCE EEIG (Association of European Law Firms): ADER, JOLIBOIS & ASSOCIES, Paris; BAILEYS, SHAW & GILLETT, London; SARDA, CALOMARDE, CASTELO Y ASOCIADOS, Barcelona/Valencia/Madrid; SCAMONI E ASSOCIATI, Milano/Bologna/Padova; WILLEMART & ASSOCIES, Brussels/Tongres/-Namur; BARENTS & KRANS, The Hague/Brussels; VERUM ADVOKATFIRMAN, Stockholm.

HAARMANN, HEMMELRATH & PARTNER

NEUMARKT 24
D-04109 LEIPZIG, GERMANY
Telephone: (0341) 12 63-0
Telefax: (0341) 12 63-133

Munich Office: Effnerstrasse 38, D-81925 München. Telephone: (089) 924 00-0. Telefax: (089) 92400-133. Telex: 523900 HUP D.
Düsseldorf Office: Martin-Luther-Platz 26, D-40212 Düsseldorf. Telephone: (0211) 8399-0. Telefax: (0211) 8399-133.
Berlin Office: Budapester Strasse 40a, D-10787 Berlin. Telephone: (030) 26473-0. Telefax: (030) 26473-133.
Frankfurt Office: Neue Mainzer Strasse 75, D-60311 Frankfurt. Telephone: (069) 92059-0. Telefax: (069) 92059-133.
Tokyo Office: Shiroyama JT Mori Building, 8F, 3-1 Toranomon 4-chome, Minato-ku, Tokyo 105. Telephone: 81-3-34 59 54 85. Fax: 81-3-35 78 89 56.
Prague Office: Cermàkova 7, CZ-1200 00 Prague 2, Czech Republic. Telephone: 42-2-24 23 90 36. Telefax: 42-2-24 23 88 42.

Corporate and Business Law, International and National Tax Law, Banking, Commercial Law, Labour Law, all Areas of Mergers and Acquisitions, Financial Transactions, International Law, Antitrust Law, Unfair Competition and Intellectual Property Rights Law, EEC Law, Real Estate Transactions, Management and Leveraged Buy-outs, National and Cross-border Leasing Transactions, Structuring of Funds, Accounting Services.

FIRM PROFILE: The firm, established in 1987, has strongly developed as a multi-disciplinary firm in Germany with seven offices. The firm is affiliated with Graham & James (US, Italy, Japan and China), Taylor Joynson Garrett (UK) and Deacons (Hong Kong and Southeast Asia) and is a member of the international tax and audit network RSM International.

RESIDENT MEMBERS OF FIRM

ULRICH SCHRÖDER, born Bad Oeynhausen, Germany, June 10, 1956; admitted, 1985, Steuerberater (Certified Tax Advisor); 1988, Wirtschaftsprüfer (Certified Public Accountant); 1990, Public Accountant. *Education:* University of Paderborn (Business Administration, 1981). *Member:* Institute of German Chartered Accountants (IDW); AICPA. **LANGUAGES:** German and English. **PRACTICE AREAS:** Tax; Accounting.

DR. CORNELIA KERMEL, born Kiel, Germany, October 11, 1961; admitted, 1991, Berlin. *Education:* University of Berlin (J.D., 1988, Doctor at Law, 1993). **LANGUAGES:** German, English and French. **PRACTICE AREAS:** Commercial Law; Corporate Law; Property; Labour Law; Privatisation.

Languages: German, English, French, Dutch, Spanish, Italian, Russian, Czech and Slovakian, Japanese and Mandarin.

(For Biographical Data on other Members of Firm, See Professional Biographies at Munich, Berlin, Düsseldorf and Frankfurt, Germany, Tokyo, Japan and Prague, Czech Republic).

HECKER, WERNER & HIMMELREICH

Rechtsanwälte

RICHARD-LEHMANN-STRAßE 31
D-04275 LEIPZIG, GERMANY
Telephone: (0341) 477 83 77-79
Telefax: (0341) 477 82 10

Cologne, Germany Office: Brabanter Strasse 53, D-50672. Telephone: (0221) 5 79 99-0. Telefax: (0221) 57 999-200.

(This Listing Continued)

Berlin, Germany Office: Kurfürstendamm 66, D-10707. Telephone: (030) 8 85 26 05. Telefax: (030) 8 86 07 91.

General Practice, Company, Commercial, Banking, Competition, Labor, Construction, Real Property, Road Traffic, Insurance, Medical Malpractice, and Administrative Law, Arbitration and Litigation, Mergers and Acquisitions.

MEMBERS OF FIRM

JÜRGEN W. SCHWAN, born Cologne, Germany, August 23, 1958; admitted, 1991, Cologne; 1993, Leipzig. *Education:* University of Cologne. **LANGUAGES:** German and English. **PRACTICE AREAS:** Company and Commercial; Banking; Mergers and Acquisitions.

DR. CHRISTOPH NIERING, born Cologne, Germany, December 16, 1962; admitted, 1991, Leipzig. *Education:* Universities of Cologne (Dr. jur., 1991), Heidelberg, Speyer. *Member:* German Bar Association; Junior Chamber International (JCI). **LANGUAGES:** German and English. **PRACTICE AREAS:** Mergers and Acquisitions; Insolvency.

KLAUS HEINZERLING, born Kassel, Germany, April 22, 1956; admitted, 1984, Kassel; 1992, Leipzig; 1993, Dresden Court of Appeal. *Education:* Universities of Göttingen and Hanover. *Member:* German Bar Association (Member, Building Law Committee). **LANGUAGES:** German and English. **PRACTICE AREAS:** Construction Law; Real Property.

(For Complete Biographical Data on all Personnel, see Professional Biographies at Cologne, Germany)

HÖLTERS & ELSING

Established in 1989

NORDSTRASSE 23
LEIPZIG 04105, GERMANY
Telephone: (0341) 98 24 60
Telecopier: (0341) 98 24 612

Düsselforf, Germany Office: Immermannstrasse 40, 40210. Telephone: (0211) 36 78 70. Telefax: (0211) 35 39 28.
Berlin, Germany Office: Wielandstrasse 23, 10707. Telephone: (030) 885 74 20. Telefax: (030) 885 742 20.

General and International Practice, Business Organizations, Commercial Law, Corporate Banking, Finance, Mergers and Acquisitions, Bankruptcy and Reorganization, Labor, Antitrust, Unfair Competition, National and International Commercial Litigation and Arbitration, Consumer Affairs, Advertising, Product Liability, Real Estate, Estate Planning, International Construction Contracts, Trademark, Licensing, Franchise and Distribution Law, International and National Tax Planning and Tax Counselling, Protection of Intellectual Property, Administrative and Company Law, European Community Law.

RESIDENT MEMBER

BERND P. SCHULTE, born Dortmund, Germany, 1958; admitted, 1990, Frankfurt. *Education:* Ruprecht-Karl-University, Heidelberg and Westfälische Wilhelms University, Münster. Author: "Manager-Arbeitgeber oder Arbeitnehmer," (Manager-Employer or Employee), 1992. Employee of the Association of Employers of the Hotel and Restaurants Industry in Baden-Württemberg, 1988-1990. **LANGUAGES:** German and English.

RESIDENT ASSOCIATES

JENS KLISCHE, born Leipzig, Germany, 1962; admitted, 1990, East Germany. *Education:* Martin Luther University, Halle-Wittenberg and Hochschule für Ökonomie in East Berlin. **LANGUAGES:** German, English and Russian.

(For biographical data on personnel, see Professional Biographies at Düsseldorf and Berlin, Germany)

KANZLEI
DR. KOPPE & PARTNER
RECHTSANWÄLTE

Leipzig - Munich

Established in 1970

GOTTSCHEDSTRASSE 12
04109 LEIPZIG, GERMANY
Telephone: 49/341/96413-0
Telefax: 49/341/96413-10

Munich, Germany Office: Leopoldstrasse 20 (Am Siegestor), 80802 Munich. Telephone: 49/89/381 581-0. Telefax: 49/89/381 581-10. BTX: 49/89/381 581-91.

General Practice. International Private Law. EEC, Antitrust, Arbitration, Industrial Relations, Labor and Tax Law. Litigation. Corporate Law and Reorganizations, International Contracts including Negotiations, Founding and Accompanying of German Subsidiaries. Consultant to overseas enterprises.

DR. JUR. PETER J. R. KOPPE, born Garmisch-Partenkirchen, Germany, February 27, 1937; admitted, 1970, Bavaria. *Education:* Ludwig-Maximilian-Universität, Munich; Herzog-Albrecht-Universität, Kiel (Philosophy, Economics, Law; First and Second Bavarian State's Examinations); Trinity College, Dublin. Author: "Contributory Negligence in English and Irish Law", Doctoral Thesis, 1970; "Erfahrungen mit neuen Außenhandelsrecht GiW", Article Handelsblatt, 06.05. 1976. *Member:* Rechtsanwaltskammer OLG Bezirk (Munich); Steuerberaterkammer (Munich); American Chamber of Commerce (Germany); British Chamber (Germany); Federal Bar Association (Germany); Arbeitsgemeinschaft Selbständiger Unternehmer (Independent entrepreneurs' Union), of ERWUS (European Association of Attorneys); Exportclub Bayern (Association of Exporting Enterprises in Bavaria); TII (European Association for the Transfer of Technologies, Innovation and Industrial Innovation). *LANGUAGES:* German and English.

ASSOCIATES

ELER VON BOCKELMANN, born Frankfurt/Main, Germany, August 1, 1962; admitted, 1991, Munich. *Education:* University of Passau (1987); Referendardienst. Scientific Assistant, University of Passau, 1987-1991. Member, Rechtsanwaltskammer OLG Bezirk (Munich). *LANGUAGES:* German, English and French.

ANTJE JUNGK, born Goettingen, Germany, October 19, 1964; admitted, 1993, Munich. *Education:* University of Passau; East China Institute of Politics and Law, Shanghai. Referendardienst. Scientific Assistant, University of Passau, 1989-1991. *Member:* German-Chinese Lawyers' Association. Member, Rechtsanwaltskammer OLG Bezirk (Munich). *LANGUAGES:* German, English, Spanish, French and Chinese.

ALEXANDER WÜRDINGER, born Munich, Germany, December 15, 1964; admitted, 1992, Munich; 1994, Leipzig. *Education:* Ludwig-Maximilian-Universität, Munich. Member, Rechtsanwaltskammer OLG Bezirk (Munich). *LANGUAGES:* German, English and French.

KARBOWSKI, MASLING, HEGER & PARTNERS

Attorneys-at-Law and Notaries Public

Established in 1974

GOHLISER STRASSE 7
04105 LEIPZIG, GERMANY
Telephone: 0049-341-5662860; 0049-341-5662861
Telefax: 0049-341-5662862

Essen, Germany Office: Huyssenallee 86-88, 45128 Essen. Telephone: 0049-201-17580. Telefax: 0049-201-1758400. Dusseldorf, Germany Office: Kaiser-Wilhelm-Ring 43, 40545. Telephone: 49-211-55-57-17. Telefax: 49-211-55-57-85.

Administrative Law. Advertising Law. Banking Law. Bankruptcy. Competition Law. Constitutional Law. Consumer Protection Law. Customs and Excise Law. Distributorship, Agency and Franchise Law. EEC Law. Employer's Liability. Environmental Law. Family Law. Foreign Investments. International Contracts. International Private Law. Product Liability Law. Property and Real Estate Law. Rent and Lease. General Legal Practice.

(This Listing Continued)

International Taxation. General Commercial and Corporate Law. Industrial Labor and Shop Constitution Law on behalf of Management. International Trade Law. Antitrust and Unfair Trade Practices.

FIRM PROFILE: The firm was established in 1974. It has a sophisticated and extensive commercial practice, with strong concentrations in general corporate, antitrust and unfair trade practices, labor law and business-related civil litigation.

MEMBERS OF FIRM

E. ALEXANDER KARBOWSKI, born Gotha, Germany, February 16, 1945; admitted, 1974, Essen. Notary Public, 1984. *Education:* University of Münster (LL.B., 1971). Author: Periodical articles on national and international trade and company law. Co-Author: "Die Europäische Wirtschaftliche Interessenvereinigung," (european company law), 44 Wertpapier Mitteilungen 1313-1356, 1990. *Member:* Essen Bar Association; American Chamber of Commerce in Germany and New York. *LANGUAGES:* German, English and French. *PRACTICE AREAS:* Corporate Law; Banks and Banking; International Law; Company Law; Mergers, Acquisitions and Divestitures.

JÜRGEN MASLING, born Warnemünde, Germany, March 10, 1945; admitted, 1977, Hamburg; 1978, Essen. Notary Public, 1989. *Education:* Universities of Freiburg and Münster (LL.B., 1974). *Member:* Essen Lawyers Association; American Chamber of Commerce in Germany. *LANGUAGES:* German and English. *PRACTICE AREAS:* Labor and Employment.

KLAUS G. HEGER, born October 19, 1934, Chemnitz, Germany; admitted, 1968, Essen; 1970, Düsseldorf. *Education:* Universities of Tübingen, Hamburg and Münster (LL.B., 1964). *Member:* German Bar Association; International Bar Association; Industrieclub Düsseldorf. *LANGUAGES:* German and English. *PRACTICE AREAS:* Company Law; Mergers, Acquisitions and Divestitures; International Commercial Contracts.

DR. MARTIN HAMM, born Bonn, Germany, May 5, 1948; admitted, 1976, Cologne; 1984, Essen. *Education:* Universities of Freiburg and Cologne (LL.B., 1976); Freiburg (LL.D., 1976). Notary Public, 1990. Author: "Vorteilsausgleichung und Schadensminderungspflicht im Rahmen des § 844 BGB," (compensation and duty to prevent further damage), 1976. *Member:* Essen Lawyers Association. *LANGUAGES:* German and English. *PRACTICE AREAS:* Property; Real Estate; Labor and Employment; Commercial Law.

KLAUS BECKMANN, born Ennigloh, Germany, August 11, 1944; admitted, 1977, Essen. *Education:* University of Cologne. Parliamentary State Secretary to Federal Minister for Economics, 1989—. *LANGUAGES:* German and English. *PRACTICE AREAS:* Commercial Law.

BEATRIX EICKHOFF, born Legden, Germany, February 3, 1958; admitted, 1985, Essen. *Education:* University of Bonn (LL.B., 1982). *Member:* Essen Lawyers Association. *LANGUAGES:* German and English. *PRACTICE AREAS:* Contracts; Civil Law; Rent and Lease.

DR. CHRISTIAN GLORIA, born Lünen, Germany, June 9, 1957; admitted, 1989, Essen. *Education:* University of Bochum (LL.B., 1982; LL.D., 1987) and London. Author: "Das steuerliche Verständigungsverfahren und das Recht auf diplomatischen Schutz - zugleich ein Beitrag zur Auslegung der Doppelbesteuerungsabkommen," (study on the competent authority procedure under tax treaties), 1988; "Der subjektive Faktor" bei der Frage des Vorliegens einer verschleierten Handelsbeschränkung i. S. des Art. 36 Satz 2 EWG-Vertrag," (study on trade restrictions under the EEC-Treaty), 29 Recht der Internationalen Wirtschaft 898 - 905, 1983; "Die Doppelbesteuerungsabkommen der Bundesrepublik Deutschland und die Bedeutung der Lex-Fori-Klausel für ihre Auslegung," (study on the interpretation of tax treaties), 32 Recht der Internationalen Wirtschaft 970 - 978, 1986; "Verfassungsrechtliche Anforderungen an die gerichtlichen Geschäftsverteilungspläne," (due process of law under the Basic Law), 41 Die Öffentliche Verwaltung 849 - 858, 1988; "Die Verwirklichung des Rechts auf den gesetzlichen Richter im Prozess," (due process of law), 42 Neue Juristische Wochenschrift 445 - 446, 1989; "Die Stellplatzpflicht nach den Landesbauordnungen," 9 Neue Zeitschrift für Verwaltungsrecht 305 - 314, 1990; "Der Anspruch auf Erschließung", 10 Neue Zeitschrift für Verwaltungsrecht 720-728, 1991. Co-Author: Der "finale Todesschuß" im Landesrecht Nordrhein-Westfalens," (legality of shooting to kill), 3 Nordrhein-Westfälische Verwaltungsblätter 37 - 45, 1989; "Die Europäische Wirtschaftliche Interessenvereinigung," (european company law), 44 Wertpapier Mitteilungen 1313 - 1356, 1990. Ipsen, Völkerrecht, 3rd ed. (treatise on public international law; inter alia chapters on international law of the sea and on international economic law, 1990. *Member:* German American Lawyers Association. *LANGUAGES:* German, English and French. *PRACTICE AREAS:*

(This Listing Continued)

KARBOWSKI, MASLING, HEGER & PARTNERS, Leipzig—Continued

Administrative Law; Antitrust and Trade Regulation; Competition; European Community Law; International Law; Commercial Law; Company Law; International Contracts; International Joint Ventures; International Business.

DR. PETER M. MOMBAUR, born December 12, 1938, Solingen, Germany; admitted, 1991, Düsseldorf. *Education:* Universities of Marburg, Bonn and Cologne (LL.B., 1963; LL.D., 1964). Editor of several legal journals. Author: Bundeszwang und Bundestreue, 1964. Member, Committee of Energy, Technology and Research of the European Parliament. Deputy Judge, Northrhine-Westfalian Constitutional Court. *LANGUAGES:* German, English and French. *PRACTICE AREAS:* Administrative Law; Energy Regulation.

PROF. DR. MANFRED MÜLLER, born Rattwitz, Germany, October 2, 1926; admitted, 1990, Leipzig, Saxonia. *Education:* University Halle (Saale); University of Leipzig (LL.D., 1959); Habilitation, 1969. Legal Adviser in Industry and Foreign Trade, 1952-1967. Member of the Institute for Foreign and Comparative Law, Potsdam, 1967-1990. Full Professor 1975—. Publications on legal questions of international cooperation in science and technology and in the field of protection of intellectual property. Consultant on World Intellectual Property Organization, Geneva. *LANGUAGES:* German, English and French. *PRACTICE AREAS:* Intellectual Property.

ECKHARD H. POTT, born Essen, Germany, February 22, 1959; admitted, 1991, Essen. *Education:* University of Bochum (LL.B., 1987). *LANGUAGES:* German and English. *PRACTICE AREAS:* Contracts; Civil Law.

CHRISTOPH PESCH, born Essen, Germany, December 24, 1964; admitted, 1994, Essen. *Education:* University of Bochum (LL.B., 1990). *LANGUAGES:* German and English. *PRACTICE AREAS:* Commercial Law; Civil Law.

MARCUS HELF, born Essen, Germany, April 10, 1965; admitted, 1994, Essen. *Education:* Universities of Bochum and Münster (LL.B., 1991). *LANGUAGES:* German and English. *PRACTICE AREAS:* Labor and Employment; Civil Litigation.

KASPER, KNACKE, SCHÄUBLE, WINTTERLIN AND PARTNERS

KÖNNERITZSTRAßE 43
04229 LEIPZIG, GERMANY
Telephone: 03 41/4918429
Telefax: 03 41/4918215

Stuttgart, Germany Office: Schützenstraße 13, 70182. Mailing Address: P.O. Box 10 26 54, 70022. Telephone: 711-2236-3. Telefax: 711-2236-410.

Denver, Colorado Affiliated Office: Popham, Haik, Schnobrich & Kaufman, Ltd. Suite 2400, 1200 17th Street, 80202. Telephone: 303-893-1200. Telefax: 303-893-2194.

Minneapolis, Minnesota Affiliated Office: Popham, Haik, Schnobrich & Kaufman, Ltd. 3300 Piper Jaffray Tower, 222 South 9th Street, 55402. Telephone: 612-333-4800.

Washington, D.C. Affiliated Office: Popham, Haik, Schnobrich & Kaufman, Ltd. 1300 I Street, N.W., Suite 500 East, 20005. Telephone: 202-962-8700.

Miami, Florida Affiliated Office: Popham, Haik, Schnobrich & Kaufman, Ltd. 4000 International Place, 100 Southeast 2nd Street, 33131. Telephone: 305-530-0050; 800-486-0140.

General Civil and Trial Practice. Probate, Administrative, Insurance, Corporation, Trademark and Copyrights, Franchise, Unfair Competition, Licensing, Common Market, Antitrust, Labor Law, International Trade, Environmental Law and International Arbitration, Product Liability, Banking, Construction Law.

RESIDENT PARTNERS

DR. JUR. FRIEDER SCHÄUBLE, born Tübingen, Germany, August 25, 1937; admitted, 1965, West Germany. *Education:* Universities of Munich and Freiburg (Doctor of Jurisprudence, 1965; Assessor, 1965). Assistant Professor, University of Freiburg, 1961-1963. *Member:* Stuttgart Lawyers Association; German Bar Association; French-German Chamber of

(This Listing Continued)

Commerce; German-Belgian Chamber of Commerce; German Association for the Protection of Industrial Property and Copyright; Union Internationale des Avocats. *LANGUAGES:* German, French and English.

ASSOCIATES

ARNDT MAAS, born Cologne, Germany, March 25, 1962; admitted, 1993, Germany. *Education:* Universities of Gießen, Münster, Lausanne (Switzerland) and Cologne. *LANGUAGES:* English and French.

PETER SCHMARSLI, born May 21, 1966; admitted, 1994. *Education:* University of Hanover (1986-1987); University of Freiburg (1987-1990); Referendar (1991); University of Konstanz (Labor Law, 1993); Assessor (1993). *LANGUAGES:* German and English.

LANGE & VON BRAUNSCHWEIG

LEIPZIG, GERMANY

(See Wessing Berenberg-Gossler Zimmermann Lange)

Commercial Law, Corporations, German and E.C. Antitrust, Trademark and Copyright, Computer Law, Labor, Administration, Environmental, Product Liability, Banking, Insurance, Real Property, Estate, Tax Law, Litigation, Conveyancing, General Practice.

OPPENHOFF & RÄDLER

KOMMANDANT-TRUFANOW-STR. 14
D-04105 LEIPZIG, GERMANY
Telephone: (0341) 56649-0
Fax: (0341) 56649-99

Munich, Germany Office: Prinzregentenplatz 10, D-81675. Telephone: (089) 41808-0. Telecopier: (089) 41808-100.

Berlin, Germany Office: Meinekestr. 13, D-10719. Telephone: (030) 88471-0. Telecopier: (030) 88471-200.

Berlin, Germany Office: Rankestr. 21, D-10789. Telephone: (030) 21496-0. Telecopier: (030) 21496-100.

Cologne, Germany Office: Hohenstaufenring 62, D-50674. Telephone (0221) 2091-0. Telecopier: (0221) 2091-435. Telex: 8 882 294 bos. Teletex: 2627 221 4054BOS.

Frankfurt/Main, Germany Office: Bockenheimer Landstr. 51-53, D-60325. Telephone: (069) 170003-0. Telecopier: (069) 170003-33.

Frankfurt/Main, Germany Office: Myliusstr. 33-37, D-60323. Telephone: (069) 17093-0. Telecopier: (069) 17093-444.

Brussels, Belgium Office: Rue Brederode 13A, B-1000. Telephone: (2) 5050211. Telecopier: (2) 5022644.

London, England Office: Royex House, Aldermanbury Square, GB-London EC2V 7HR. Telephone: (171) 600 3609. Telecopier: (171) 600 1718.

New York, New York Office: 712 Fifth Avenue, 30th Floor, 10019, USA. Telephone: (212) 801 3410. Telecopier: (212) 801 3415.

New York, New York Office: 712 Fifth Avenue, 29th Floor, New York 10019, USA. Telephone: (212) 397 7580/7546. Telecopier: (212) 397 4292.

Prague, Czech Republic Office: Alliance Prague, Jachymova 2, CZ-11000 Prague 1. Telephone: (2) 232 1130. Telecopier: (2) 232 6371.

FIRM PROFILE: Oppenhoff & Rädler has been created by a merger of two large German firms, Boden Oppenhoff Rasor Raue and Rädler Raupach Bezzenberger. The firm at present has more than 90 partners and comprises together some 200 lawyers and tax advisers.

Oppenhoff & Rädler acts for domestic and for international clients. The firm offers a comprehensive range of legal services, including: General Corporate and Commercial; Taxation; Banking, Finance and Securities; Mergers and Acquisitions; Real Estate; Litigation and Arbitration; Intellectual Property and Trademarks; Construction Law; Antitrust and European Community Law; Administrative and Environmental Law; Media, Communications and Entertainment Law; Technology and Computer Law; Food, Drug and Chemistry; Family Law; Wills.

Oppenhoff & Rädler is a member of the ALLIANCE OF EUROPEAN LAWYERS EEIG (members: Oppenhoff & Rädler, Germany; De Bandt, van Hecke & Lagae, Belgium; De Brauw Blackstone Westbroek, The Netherlands; Jeantet & Associés, France; Lagerlöf & Leman, Sweden; Uria & Menendez, Spain) and of the LLR EEIG (members: Loyens & Volkmaars, The Netherlands; Bureau Francis Lefebvre, France; Oppenhoff & Rädler, Germany).

(This Listing Continued)

RESIDENT PARTNERS AND JUNIOR PARTNERS

DR. BERND BÜRGLEN, born Stuttgart, Germany, April 18, 1938; admitted, 1966, Germany. *Education:* University of Tübingen (Dr.jur.); University of Bonn. *LANGUAGES:* German, English, French. *PRACTICE AREAS:* Advertising and Marketing; Antitrust and Trade Regulations; Appellate Practice; Civil Law; Consumer Law; Commercial Law; Intellectual Property; Medical Malpractice; Products Liability; Professional Liability; Trademarks.

NORBERT MOHNS, born Vluyn, Germany, March 19, 1951; admitted, 1976, Germany. *Education:* University of Cologne. *LANGUAGES:* German, English. *PRACTICE AREAS:* Administrative Law; Construction Law; Environmental Law; Zoning, Planning and Land Use.

DR. HEINRICH GEDDERT, born Isernhagen, Germany, February 1, 1949; admitted, 1982, Germany. *Education:* Universities of Hamburg and Frankfurt (Dr.jur.). *LANGUAGES:* German, English. *PRACTICE AREAS:* Business Law; Civil Law; Real Estate; Litigation.

DR. WOLF GAEDE, born Karlsruhe, Germany, August 8, 1956; admitted, 1987, Germany. *Education:* Universities of Hamburg and Heidelberg (Dr.jur.); Sacramento College of Law, California. *LANGUAGES:* German, English, French. *PRACTICE AREAS:* Corporate Law; Computer and Software; International Law; Mergers, Acquisitions and Divestitures.

STEFFEN PRUGGMAYER, born Berlin, Germany, February 23, 1957; admitted, 1992, Germany. *Education:* Universities of Marburg/Lahn, Lausanne and Göttingen. *LANGUAGES:* German, English. *PRACTICE AREAS:* Administrative Law; Communications and Media; Labour and Employment; Litigation.

PROF. DR. GÜNTHER BERG, born Koemmlitz, Germany, May 28, 1930. *Education:* Universities of Leipzig and Halle (Dr.jur.; Dr.jur. habil). *LANGUAGES:* German. *PRACTICE AREAS:* Construction Law; Intellectual Property; Property; Trademarks.

PELTZER & RIESENKAMPFF

GOTTSCHEDSTRASSE 44
04109 LEIPZIG, GERMANY
Telephone: 341-28 21 46; 341-28 21 68
Telecopier: 341-980 04 18

Frankfurt/Main, Germany Office: Niedenau 68, 60325 Frankfurt/Main. Telephone: 49-69-71 73 66. Cable Address: "Peljus, Frankfurt." Telecopier: 49-69-7 24 10 63; 72 48 64. Telex: 416 307 pejus d. Teletex: 6997628 pejus.
Brussels, Belgium Office: Avenue du Diamant 139, B-1040. Telephone" 32-2-735 34 28. Telecopier: 32-2-735 26 78.

German and General International Practice.

PARTNERS

Alexander von Reden   **Gunther Bülow, Diplom-Jurist**

(For Complete Biographical Data, see Professional Biographies at Frankfurt, Germany)

PLUTA & KNORR

WEIßENFELSER STR. 15
D-04229 LEIPZIG, GERMANY
Telephone: 0341-4903650
Facsimile: 0341-4903699

Ulm, Germany Office: Olgastr. 83-85, P.O. Box 2530, D-89015 Ulm. Telephone: 0731-1450 0. Facsimile: 0371-1450-180.
Munich, Germany Office: Thomas-Wimmer-Ring 1, D-80539 Munich. Telephone: 089-29 00 37 0. Facsimile: 089-29 00 37 56.

Receivership, Intellectual Property, Software Law, Company Law, International Private Law, Commercial Law, Tax Law, Antitrust Law, Labor Law, Construction Law, Law of Medical Malpractice, Banking Law.

(For complete list of Personnel, see Professional Biographies at Ulm, Germany)

PRACHT RIEGL MIKOREY

Established in 1986
KARL-LIEBKNECHT-STR. 38
04107 LEIPZIG, GERMANY
Telephone: 0341/2131471
Telefax: 0341/2131473

Munich, Germany Office: Steinsdorfstrasse 13, 80538 Munich. Telephone: 089/227061. Telecopier: 089/2 28 54 66.

CARMEN SCHRÖTER, born Breitenbrunn, August 11, 1957; admitted, 1991, Leipzig. *Education:* Humboldt University, Berlin. *LANGUAGES:* German, English and Russian.

(For Complete Biographical Data on all Personnel, see Professional Biographies at Munich, Germany)

PÜNDER, VOLHARD, WEBER & AXSTER

BURGPLATZ 7
04109 LEIPZIG, GERMANY
Telephone: (49)(341) 21 49-0
Fax: (49)(341) 21 49-600

Frankfurt/Main, Germany Office: Mainzer Landstrasse 46, 60325 Frankfurt/Main. Telephone: (49)(69) 71 99-01. Fax: (49)(69) 71 99-4000. Telex: 414 827.
Düsseldorf, Germany Office: Cecilienallee 6, 40474 Düsseldorf. Telephone: (49)(211) 43 55-0. Fax: (49)(211) 43 55-600.
Berlin, Germany Office: Katharina-Heinroth-Ufer, 10787 Berlin. Telephone: (49)(30) 2546 5800. Fax: (49)(30) 2546 5900.
Beijing, People's Republic of China Office: Suite C 603, Beijing Lufthansa Center, 50 Liangmaqiao Road, Beijing 100 016. Telephone: (86)(1) 465 15 68; (86)(1) 465 18 08; (86)(1) 465 13 45. Fax: (86)(1) 467 12 56.
Brussels, Belgium Office: Rue d'Arlon 92, 1040 Bruxelles. Telephone: (32)(2) 230 90 11. Fax: (32)(2) 231 19 55.
Budapest, Hungary Office: Endrödy Sandor utca 48, 1026 Budapest. Telephone: (36) 60 33 26 18 international; (6) 60 33 26 18 national. Fax: (36) 60 33 26 17 international; (6) 60 33 26 17 national.
Moscow, Russia Office: ul. Wolchonka, 18/2, 121 019 Moskwa. Telephone: (7)(095) 202 64 90; (7)(095) 202 65 12; (7)(543) 708 00 900 from Germany; (49)(7545) 893 42 from other countries. Fax: (7)(095) 202 65 14; (7)(543) 708 00 990 from Germany; (49)(7545) 893 43 from other countries.
New York, New York Office: 152 West 57th Street, Carnegie Hall Tower, New York, N.Y. 10019. Telephone: (1)(212) 582 28 28. Fax: (1)(212) 582 24 24.
Warsaw, Poland Office: ul. Jasna 1, 00-013 Warszawa. Telephone: (48) 39 12 21 41. Fax: (48)(22) 27 15 29.

Administrative Law; Antitrust Law; Arbitration; Auditing and Valuations; Banking, Securities and Finance; Bankruptcy; Building Law; Chinese Law; Commercial Crime; Computer Law; Construction Law; Corporate Law; EU Law; Energy Law; Environmental Law; Franchising; Industrial Property Law; Insolvency; Intellectual Property Law; International and German Business Law; Labor and Employment Law; Litigation; Media Law; Mergers and Acquisitions; Pharmaceutical Law; Privatizations; Product Law; Public Law; Real Estate; Reorganizations; Russian Law; Tax Law; Telecommunications; Unfair Trade Law.

FIRM PROFILE: Member of PÜNDER GROUP

Members:

- *BURUMA MARIS, The Hague, Rotterdam*

- *CERHA, HEMPEL & SPIEGELFELD, Wien*

- *COPPENS, VAN OMMESLAGHE, HORSMANS & FAURES, Bruxelles.*

- *DE PARDIEU-LACOURTE G.I.E., Paris*

- *PÜNDER, VOLHARD, WEBER & AXSTER, Frankfurt/Main, Düsseldorf, Berlin, Leipzig*

- *STOFFEL & PARTNER, Zürich, Genève.*

Joint Offices of PÜNDER GROUP:

Beijing - Bruxelles - Budapest - Moskwa - New York - Warszawa

(This Listing Continued)

PÜNDER, VOLHARD, WEBER & AXSTER, Leipzig—Continued

MEMBER OF FIRM

DR. WOLFGANG SAMMLER, born Wiesbaden, Germany, January 14, 1947; admitted, 1991, Frankfurt/Main. *Education:* Universities of Frankfurt/Main, Freiburg, Marburg. Assistant of the Institute of Public Law, University of Marburg, 1972-1973. Legal Advisor of Wiesbaden Community, 1976-1980. Department of Federal Politics, State Chancellery Wiesbaden, 1981-1985. Head of Prime Minister's Office of Federal State of Hessen, State Chancellery, Wiesbaden, 1985-1991. Author: "Eigentum und Währungsparität," 1974. *Member:* German Bar Association. *LANGUAGES:* German and English. *PRACTICE AREAS:* Public and Administrative Law; German Business Law.

DR. WOLFGANG DORN-ZACHERTZ, born Sagan, Germany, November 17, 1944; admitted, 1973, Darmstadt; 1986, Munich; 1993, Frankfurt/Main. *Education:* Universities of Frankfurt/Main, Freiburg/Breisgau and Mainz. Author: "Die Unabhängigkeit und die Unbefangenheit des Abschlußprüfers in der aktienrechtlichen Pflichtprüfung", Mainz, 1976. *Member:* German Bar Association. *LANGUAGES:* German and English. *PRACTICE AREAS:* Commercial Law; Corporate Law; Privatizations; Real Estate; Banking Law; Energy Law.

STEFAN LÖCHNER, born Frankfurt/Main, Germany January 28, 1958; admitted, 1986, Mainz. *Education:* Universities of Frankfurt, Lausanne, Straßburg and Coimbra. *Member:* German-French Lawyers' Association. *LANGUAGES:* German, French and English. *PRACTICE AREAS:* Real Estate; Building Law; Business Law; Corporate Law.

ASSOCIATES

CLAUS BERGGOLD, born Hamburg, Germany, May 1, 1961; admitted, 1993, Frankfurt/Main. *Education:* Universities of Hamburg and Geneva. *Member:* Deutsch-Deutsche Juristische Vereinigung. *LANGUAGES:* German, English and French. *PRACTICE AREAS:* Mergers and Acquisitions; Corporate Law.

TAX ADVISOR

ULRIKE BREN, born Mühlheim/Ruhr, Germany, November 6, 1959; 1987, Tax Advisor. *Education:* University of Duisburg (Master of Economics, 1982). *Member:* German Tax Advisors' Association. *LANGUAGES:* German, English. *PRACTICE AREAS:* Tax Law; Auditing and Valuations.

(For complete biographical data on personnel at Frankfurt/Main, Düsseldorf and Berlin, Germany, Brussels, Belgium, Moscow, Russia, Warsaw, Poland, New York, New York and Beijing, People's Republic of China, see Professional Biographies at those locations)

RÄDLER RAUPACH BEZZENBERGER

LEIPZIG, GERMANY

(See Oppenhoff & Rädler)

REDEKER SCHÖN DAHS & SELLNER

Established in 1929

MOZARTSTR. 1
04107 LEIPZIG, GERMANY
Telephone: (0341) 213780
Telefax: (0341) 2137830

Bonn, Germany Office: Oxfordstrasse 24, 53111 Bonn. Telephone: (0228) 72625-0. Telefax: (0228) 650479.

Cologne, Germany Office: Kaiser-Wilhelm-Ring 22, 50672 Cologne. Telephone: (0221) 912 8680. Telefax: (0221) 912 86838.

Hamburg, Germany Office: Büschstrasse 12, 20354 Hamburg. Telephone: (040) 342737/8. Telefax: (040) 352144.

London, England Office: 43 Brook Street, London W1Y 2Bl. Telephone: (0171) 3225823. Telefax: (0171) 6292621.

Administrative, Anti-Trust, Aviation, City Planning, Civil, Corporate and Commercial, Constitutional and Parliamentary, Construction, Criminal, Environmental, European Community Law, Family, Health, Insurance,

(This Listing Continued)

Labour, Media and Copyright, Medical Malpractice, Domestic and International Tax, Trade, Transportation Law, Litigation and Appeals.

PARTNERS

MARTINA KIESGEN-MILLGRAMM, born Velbert/Rhine, July 20, 1956; admitted, 1991, Münster; 1992, Leipzig. *Education:* Universities of Munich, Bonn and Bochum. *Member:* German-German Lawyers' Association.

MANUELA M. GERHARD, born Stuttgart, August 16, 1960; admitted, 1992, Bonn; 1993, Leipzig. *Education:* University of Passau. Attachée adjointe German Foreign Office, 1979-1983. *LANGUAGES:* German, English, French and Italian.

DR. THOMAS STICKLER, born Hanau, Germany, April 28, 1963; admitted, 1991, Frankfurt/Main; 1994, Leipzig. *Education:* Universities of Würzburg, Lausanne (Switzerland) and Regensburg (Dr. jur., 1992). *Member:* German-British Lawyers' Association. *LANGUAGES:* German and English.

(For data on all firm personnel see Professional Biographies at Bonn)

ROHDE & PARTNER

Rechtsanwaltskanzlei

NICOLAISTRASSE 12/14
04109 LEIPZIG, GERMANY
Telephone: 0341/21 60 60
Fax: 0341/21 60 620

Würzburg, Germany Office: Kaiserstrasse 13, W-8700. Telephone: 0931/50353. Fax: 0931/18159.

Commercial and Corporate, Real Estate, Private and Public Construction and Environmental Law.

DR.IUR. GERD ROHDE, born Leipzig, Germany, February 13, 1948; admitted, 1974, Germany. *Education:* University of Lausanne, Switzerland; University of Würzburg. Tax Law Specialist and Certified Public Accountant. *LANGUAGES:* German, English, French and Russian.

KATRIN WELZEL, born Halle, Germany, September 23, 1962; admitted, 1992, Germany. *Education:* University of Halle-Wittenberg.

RÜCKEL, TRENKNER & COLLEGEN

MARPERGER STRAßE 20
04229 LEIPZIG, GERMANY
Telephone: (03 41) 401 13 41
Fax: (03 41) 401 14 54

Atlanta, Georgia Office: Ten Piedmont Center, Suite 350, 3495 Piedmont Road, 30305. Telephone: (404) 266-1008. Fax: (404) 266-0205.

Berlin, Germany Office: Kurfürstendamm 132 A, 10711. Telephone: (030) 896 6920. Fax: (030) 8966 9244.

Dresden, Germany Office: Bautzner Straße 14, 01099. Telephone: (0351) 502 43 00. Fax: (0351) 502 43 02.

Frankfurt/Main, Germany Office: Bockenheimer Anlage 13, 60322. Telephone: (069) 55 07 31. Fax: (069) 596 39 94.

Munich, Germany Office: Karollnenstraße 4, 80538. Telephone: (089) 212 38 70. Fax: (089) 212 38 75 0.

General Practice, Litigation and Commercial Law, International Business Transactions, Real Estate (including restitution of property rights), Corporate.

FIRM PROFILE: *The firm is a member of LAWORLD. LAWORLD is an international organization of law firms who coordinate and share information with other member firms in Brussels, Budapest, Hong Kong, Jerusalem, Lausanne, London, Moscow, New York, Padova, Stockholm, Taipei, Tel Aviv, Vancouver, Warsaw, Zagreb and Zug.*

MEMBERS OF FIRM

CHRISTOPH VON BAUER, born Wiesbaden, Germany, September, 15, 1958; admitted, 1991, Germany. *Education:* Dartmouth College, New Hampshire, USA (1980); University of Dijon, France (1981); University of Mainz, Germany (1987). *LANGUAGES:* English and French. *PRACTICE AREAS:* Civil Law; Corporate Law; Economic Law; Property Law.

(This Listing Continued)

ASSOCIATES

SONJA SCHINNECK, born Mannheim, Germany, April 20, 1955; admitted, 1982, Germany. *Education:* University of Mannheim (1978); University of Heidelberg (1980). *LANGUAGES:* English. *PRACTICE AREAS:* Civil Law; Tax Law; Corporate Law; Economic Law.

(For biographical data on additional personnel, see Professional Biographies at Munich, Germany)

SCHULTZE & BRAUN

Established in 1994

BRAHESTR.8
D-04347 LEIPZIG, GERMANY
Telephone: 0341/244340
Telefax: 0314/2443439

Achern, Germany Office: Eisenbahnstr. 19-23, 77855. Telephone: 07841-7080. Telefax: 07841-708301.
Dresden, Germany Office: Boltenhagener Platz 9, 01109. Telephone: 0351/8808046. Telefax: 0351/8808040.

General International Practice, Restructuring and Bankruptcy, Finance and Banking International Transactions, Corporate, Investment, Settlement.

FIRM PROFILE: The firm is specialised in reorganisation and bankruptcy law and taxation.

DETLEF SCHNEIDER, born Achern, Germany. *Education:* Academy of Villingen-Schwenningen. (Accountant). *LANGUAGES:* English. *PRACTICE AREAS:* Taxation.

SCHÜRMANN & PARTNERS

Established in 1990

GUSTAV-ADOLF-STRASSE 30
04105 LEIPZIG, GERMANY
Telephone: 0341-211-0622
Telefax: 0341-211-0625

Frankfurt/Main, Germany Office: Friedrich-Ebert-Anlage 14, 60325, P.O. Box 11 16 33, 60051. Telephone: 069-7 54 90. Telefax: 7549 290.
Berlin, Germany Office: Karl-Liebknecht-Strasse 32, 10178. Telephone: 030-247-5960. Telefax: 030-238-6032.
Bonn, Germany Office: Philosophenring 94, 53177 Bonn. Telephone: 0228-328-055, Telefax: 0228-311-863.
Brussels, Belgium Office: Avenue de la Raquette 24, B-1150. Telephone: 02-770-0878. Telefax: 02-770-0878.
Dresden, Germany Office: Schnorrstrasse 70, 01069. Telephone: 0351-477-770. Telefax: 0351-477-7799.
Milan, Italy Office: Via Gabrio Casati, 1, I-20123. Telephone: 02-809131/32. Telefax: 02-809-133.
New York, New York Office: 250 Park Avenue, 10177. Telephone: 212-972-3300. Telefax: 212-972-9374.
Paris, France Office: 12, rue d'Astorg F-75008 Paris. Telephone: 01-4451-0570. Telefax: 01-4266-3368.

General Practice. Trade, Banking, International and German Tax Law. Labor Law. Law on Mergers, Acquisitions, Fair Trade, Antitrust and EU Law, Administrative Law. Notary Public. Litigation Department.

(For complete biographical data on all Personnel, see Biographical Card at Frankfurt/Main, Germany)

SEUFERT

Rechtsanwälte

SPRINGERSTRAβE 7
04105 LEIPZIG, GERMANY
Telephone: 0341/5900614
Telefax: 0341/5900613

Munich Office: Residenzstraβe 12, 80333. Telephone: 089/222611. Telefax: 089/291100.

General Practice, Corporate, Mergers and Acquisitions, Commercial, Administrative Law, Town and Country Planning, Construction Law, Environmental Law, Real Estate, Labor, EEC/International Law.

(This Listing Continued)

FIRM PROFILE: The firm has been established 45 years ago in Munich and offers a wide range of services in Civil and Administrative Law. The client base is German but also extends to Europe and the USA. The firm has a total of 15 Lawyers, supported by a staff of 20, practising in 2 offices in Munich and Leipzig. The firm is also a member of ADVOC - International Network of Independent Lawyers, represented all over Europe and the near East.

RESIDENT MEMBERS

DR. CHRISTOPH HELLER, born 1960; admitted, 1992, Germany. *Education:* Universities of Regensburg and Bonn. *LANGUAGES:* German and English. *PRACTICE AREAS:* Company Law; Construction Law; Hospitals; Labor and Employment; Mergers, Acquisitions and Divestitures.

HANS-JÖRG KREYES, born 1964; admitted, 1993, Germany. *Education:* Universities of Würzburg, Geneva and Munich; Speyer Academy of Science of Management and Administration. *LANGUAGES:* German and English. *PRACTICE AREAS:* Administrative Law; Construction Law; Commercial Law; Environmental Law.

ALEXANDER KLATT, born 1962; admitted, 1994, Germany. *Education:* University of Freiburg; London School of Economics. *LANGUAGES:* German and English. *PRACTICE AREAS:* Administrative Law; Environmental Law; Labour Law.

SIGLE, LOOSE, SCHMIDT-DIEMITZ & PARTNERS

AUGUST-BEBEL-STRASSE 38
04275 LEIPZIG, GERMANY
Telephone: 0341-3912007
Telefax: 0341-391-2085

Stuttgart, Germany Office: Schöttlestr. 8, P.O. Box 70 02 65, D-70572 Stuttgart (Degerloch). Telephone: 0711-9764-0. Telefax: 0711-9764-900.
Berlin, Germany Office: Friedrichstrasse 130 a, 10117 Berlin. Telephone: 030-308792-0. Telefax: 030-238-5849.
Frankfurt/Main, Germany Office: Schumannstrasse 62, 60325 Frankfurt/Main. Telephone: 069-975849-0. Telefax: 069-975849-97.
Chemnitz, Germany Office: Barbarossastraβe 46, 09112 Chemnitz. Telephone: 0371-36974-0. Telefax: 0371-3697421.
Moscow, Russia Office: Sadovaja Samotjotschnaja, 103 051. Telephone: 007/095/258 50 55. Fax: 007/095/258 51 55.

Commerical, Corporation, Mergers and Acquisitions, Banking, Investment, Common Market, Antitrust, Unfair Competition, Copyright, Patent and Trademark, License Agreements, Press, Transportation, Insurance, Product Liability, Real Estate, Construction, Probate, Labor, Administrative, Tax, International, Litigation and Arbitration.

RESIDENT PARTNER

DR. ROLF-PETER GEIDEL, born Leipzig, Germany, 1950; admitted, 1982, Stuttgart. *Education:* University of Tübingen, Lausanne and Würzburg (Doctor of Law, 1983). Author: "Der Sozial-Ükonomische Rat der Niederlande" (The Social Economic Council of the Netherlands), Jahrbuch des Üffentlichen Rechts, Vol. 32, 1983. *Member:* German Bar Association; German-Dutch Chamber of Commerce. *LANGUAGES:* German, English, French and Dutch. *PRACTICE AREAS:* Commercial Law; Copyright Law; Property and Real Estate Law.

RESIDENT ASSOCIATES

DR. GÜNTER KRONE, born Leipzig, Germany, 1927; admitted, 1969, Leipzig. *Education:* University of Leipzig (Doctor of Law, 1951). Member of Parliament of Saxony. *LANGUAGES:* German, English. *PRACTICE AREAS:* Property and Real Estate Law.

KAI MALTE LIPPKE, born Hamm, Germany, 1960; admitted, 1993, Leipzig. *Education:* University of Tübingen. *LANGUAGES:* German, English and French. *PRACTICE AREAS:* Private Construction Law; Commercial Law.

ECKHART BRAUN, born Kassel, Germany, 1965; admitted, 1994, Leipzig. *Education:* University of Göttingen. *Member:* German Bar Association. *LANGUAGES:* German and English. *PRACTICE AREAS:* Commercial Law; Labor Law; Competition Law.

VON *BOETTICHER HASSE KALTWASSER*

PHILIPP-ROSENTHAL-STRASSE 21
04103 LEIPZIG, GERMANY
Telephone: 0341-31 03 03
Telecopier: 0341-31 03·25

Munich, Germany Office: Widenmayerstrasse 4, 80538 Munich.
Telephone: 089-22 33 11. Telex: 05-239 37 JUS D. Telecopier: 089-22 47 28.

Brussels, Belgium Office: Boulevard de la Révision 50 B-1070. Telephone: 02-5219531. Telecopier: 02-5218711.

Commercial, Corporations, Mergers and Acquisitions, Taxation, Antitrust, EEC, Corporate Finance, Banking and Securities, Unfair Competition, Pharma, Trademarks, Patents, Copyright, Computer, Press and Publishing, Labor, Real Estate, Environment, Aviation, Litigation and Arbitration, General Practice.

FIRM PROFILE: The firm was established in 1972 and has been internationally oriented from its beginnings. Seven of its lawyers hold law degrees from United States law schools. The firm offers to its clients full-service in all areas of business law and special advice in the computer, electronics, pharmaceuticals, construction, banking, insurance, publishing and asset management sectors. Clients of the firm are based primarily in the European community, the United States, Canada, Switzerland, Austria, Scandinavia, Japan and Southeast Asia.

PETER SCHMIDT-FICHTNER, born Wuppertal, Germany, August 25, 1957; admitted, 1986, Germany. *Education:* University of Munich (Referendar, 1983; Assessor, 1986); New York University (M.C.J., 1989). *Member:* Leipzig Bar Association; German American Lawyers Association. *LANGUAGES:* German, English and French.

CHRISTIAN KÜHN, born Eisleben, Germany, August 29, 1964; admitted, 1993, Germany. *Education:* University of Berlin (Diplom-Jurist, 1990; Assessor, 1993). *Member:* Leipzig Bar Association. *LANGUAGES:* German, French and Russian.

INES HEROLD, born Zwickau, Germany, March 21, 1967; admitted, 1994, Germany. *Education:* University of Bev Ciu (Diplom-Juristin, 1991; Assessorin, 1994). *Member:* Leipzig Bar Association. *LANGUAGES:* German, Russian and English.

Languages: German, English, French, Italian, Spanish, Dutch and Russian.

(For Complete Biographical Data on all Personnel, see Professional Biographies at Munich, Germany)

VON *PANDER WILLFORT & PARTNER*

MOZART STRASSE 1
D-04107 LEIPZIG, GERMANY
Telephone: (0341) 21 376-0
Telefax: (0341) 21 376-10

Munich, Germany Office: Arnulfstrasse 25, D-80335. Telephone: (089) 55 14 84 50. Telefax: (089) 55 14 84 80.

Dresden, Germany Office: Berggarten 11, D-01277. Telephone: (0351) 33 607-12. Telefax: (0351) 33 607-14.

New York, New York Office: Two Park Avenue, 10016. Telephone: (212) 685-55 09. Telefax: (212) 685-88 62.

The present structure of the firm is the result of a merger in April 1993 between the two partners who work together with seven other associate lawyers in offices located in Munich, Leipzig, Dresden and New York. The firm offers highly specialized legal services tailored to the needs of the individual commercial clients of an international clientele in the following areas: General European and International Practice, European Community Law, Corporate, Commercial, Intellectual and Industrial Property Rights, Copyright, Unfair Competition, Antitrust, Computer Law, Press Law, Entertainment Law, Franchising, Licensing, Insurance, Product Liability, Real Estate and Construction Law, Labor Law, Bank Law, Trusts and Estates, International Private Law, Administrative Law, Litigation, Arbitration, Transport Law. The offices in Leipzig and Dresden allow cooperative legal services in matters of restitution and investments in the new federal states of Germany.

(This Listing Continued)

EU734B

ASSOCIATE

TOM HORNIG, born Leipzig, Germany, September 27, 1957; admitted, 1990, East Germany. *Education:* Humboldt University of Berlin (Dipl. Jur., 1986). Legal Counsel: Baukombinat Leipzig, 1986-1989; Sportclub Leipzig, 1989-1990. *Member:* German Bar Association. *LANGUAGES:* German, English and Russian. *PRACTICE AREAS:* Business Law; Construction Law; Sports Law; Advertising Law; Marketing Law; Contract Law.

WEISS & HASCHE

A Merger of the law firms Hasche Albrecht Fischer, Hamburg, Ott Weiss Eschenlohr & Partner, Munich and Rosenberg, Berlin.

KARL-TAUCHNITZ-STRASSE 10 B
04107 LEIPZIG, GERMANY
Telephone: (0341) 216 720
Telefax: (0341) 216 72 33

Hamburg, Germany Office: Valentinskamp 88, 20355 Hamburg. Telephone: (040) 35 00 20. Cable Address: "Lawyers" Telex: 215461 LAWY D. Teletex: 402276 LAWY D. Telefax: (040) 35 00 21 52.

Munich, Germany Office: Brienner Strasse 11/V (Luitpoldblock), 80333 Munich. Telephone: (089) 23 80 70. Cable Address: "Interlaw," Munich. Telex: 5 22957 LAW. Telefax: (089) 23 80 71 10.

Berlin, Germany Office: Meinekestrasse 13, 10719 Berlin. Telephone: (030) 881 97 83. Telefax: (030) 882 34 79.

Prague, Czech Republic Office: Dělnická 30, 170 00 Prague 7. Telephone: (2) 683 40 23. Telefax: (2) 683 40 23.

Commercial, International Trade, Maritime, Transport, Forwarding, Shipbuilding, Shipfinancing, Tax, Banking, Corporation, Mergers and Acquisitions, Antitrust, Unfair Competition, Industrial Property, Real Estate, Environment, Common Market, Insurance, Aviation, Arbitration, Media, Administrative, Labor, Computer, German Reunification, Litigation.

MEMBERS OF FIRM
(LEIPZIG OFFICE)

DR. CHRISTIAN VON LENTHE, born Lenthe, Germany, February 14, 1960; admitted, 1989, Germany. *Education:* Universities of Tübingen and Freiburg. *Member:* Hamburg Bar Association. *LANGUAGES:* German and English.

GERD SCHMIDT, born Hannover, Germany, April 20, 1961; admitted, 1991, Germany. *Education:* University of Freiburg/Breisgau. *Member:* Saxon Bar Association. *LANGUAGES:* German and English.

ASSOCIATES
(LEIPZIG OFFICE)

FRANK GRÜNEN, born Krefeld, Germany, July 14, 1959; admitted, 1990, Germany. *Education:* Universities of Freiburg/Breisgau, Bonn and Aix-en-Provence (Law Degree, 1986). *Member:* German Industrial Property Law Association; Freiburg Society of Lawyers; Freiburg Bar Association. *LANGUAGES:* German, English and French.

ERNST GROETZ, born Chliwitz, Bohemia, August 25, 1936; admitted, 1990, Germany. *Education:* University of Halle/Saale (Law Degree, 1959). In-house counsel, Filmfabrik Wolfen, 1959-1965; Leuna-Werke, 1965-1990. *Member:* Saxon Bar Association; Leipzig Society of Lawyers. *LANGUAGES:* German.

BERNHARD VON DER DECKEN, born Freiburg/Elbe, Germany, December 12, 1956; admitted, 1992, Germany. *Education:* Universities of Marburg/Lahn and Göttingen (Law Degree, 1988). *Member:* Saxon Bar Association. *LANGUAGES:* German and English.

MICHAEL C. FREGE, born Düsseldorf, Germany, February 24, 1959; admitted, 1990, Germany. *Education:* Universities of Berlin, Freiburg/Breisgau and Speyer (Law Degree, 1985). Assistant, Freiburg University Institute for Historical Jurisprudence, 1986-1988. Judge, Court of Discipline for Lawyers in Saxony. *Member:* German-Japanese Association of Lawyers; Wustrau Association for Bankruptcy Law; Saxon Bar Association; Düsseldorf Society of Lawyers. *LANGUAGES:* German and English.

MARC-CHRISTIAN KYEWSKI, born Duisburg, Germany, March 16, 1961; admitted, 1991, Germany. *Education:* Universities of Freiburg/Breisgau, Munich and Speyer (Law Degree, 1987). Staff, German Permanent Representation at the OECD, Paris, 1989. *Member:* German Bar Association; German-Russian Society. *LANGUAGES:* German and English.

(This Listing Continued)

THOMAS BURKHART, born Friedrichshafen, Germany, July 16, 1964; admitted, 1993, Germany. *Education:* University of Konstanz and American University (Law Degree, 1990; LL.M., 1992). Gardner, Carton & Douglas, Chicago, 1992-1993. *LANGUAGES:* German and English.

Languages: German, English and French

WERNER, LUGER & WERNER

Rechtsanwälte, Wirtschaftsprüfer, Steuerberater

(Attorneys at Law, Auditors and Tax Advisers)

Established in 1992

BEETHOVENSTRASSE 29
D-04107 LEIPZIG, GERMANY
Telephone: (0341) 213 19 79
Telefax: (0341) 213 17 46

Munich Office: Josephspitalstrasse 15/II, D-80331 Munich. Telephone: (089) 54 52 1-0. Telefax: (089) 54 52 1-109.

Stockholm Office: Strandvägen 5 B,S-11451 Stockholm. Telephone: (0046-8) 663 49 10. Telefax: (0046-8) 663 40 77.

Member of Deutsch Nordische Juristenvereinigung e.V., Schwedische Handelskammer, Deutsch-Schwedische Handelskammer and Nordlund Group.

General Practice, Commercial Law, Company Law, Real Estate, Trademarks, Industrial and Intellectual Property, Media/Entertainment, Unfair Competition, EEC, Tax Law, Investment Consulting, East German Law, Litigation.

FIRM PROFILE: The firm was established in Munich in 1977 and opened its Stockholm office in 1990 and its Leipzig office in 1992. The firm offers the full range of legal services for commercial matters. The Leipzig office concentrates on investments in the new federal states of Eastern Germany and on restitution matters. The firm also provides qualified legal services for Scandinavian companies establishing branches in Germany as well as for German companies establishing branches in Scandinavia.

For many years the firm has been engaged in international activities of foreign enterprises in connection with establishment and investment in Germany. The firm has a wide experience in this area and cooperates with law firms of high professional standard in and outside Europe. The offices are situated right in the centre of Munich.

RESIDENT MEMBERS

MARIKA BJICK, born Treuenbrietzen/Potsdam, April 15, 1965; admitted, 1988, Diplom Jurist; 1990, Attorney at Law. *Education:* University of Leipzig (Studies of law and economics, 1984-1988; Diplom Jurist, 1988). Legal Adviser, Commercial Academy, Leipzig, 1988-1990. *LANGUAGES:* German, Russian and English. *PRACTICE AREAS:* Property Law; Commercial Law; East German Law.

(For Complete Biographical Data on all Personnel, see Professional Biographies at Munich, Germany)

WESSING BERENBERG-GOSSLER ZIMMERMANN LANGE

FERDINAND-RHODE-STRASSE 16
D-04107 LEIPZIG, GERMANY
Telephone: 49-341-213 13 80
Fax: 49-341-213 13 88

Munich, Germany Office: Vilshofener Str. 8, D-81679 Munich, P.O. Box 86 08 67, D-81635 Munich. Telephone: 49-89-98 28 021. Telefax: 49-89-98 12 14.

Düsseldorf, Germany Office: Königsallee 92 A, D-40212 Düsseldorf, P.O. Box 10 53 61, D-40044 Düsseldorf. Telephone: 49-211-83 87-0. Telex: 858 19 14 wess d. Cable Address: "Wegolex". Telefax: 49-211-32 36 16.

Hamburg, Germany Office: Neuer Wall 46, D-20354 Hamburg. Telephone: 49-40-36 80 30. Cable Address: "Unilaw". Telex: 2-14111 Jura d. Teletex: 40 32 91 Unilaw. Telefax: 49-40-36 80 32 80.

Frankfurt, Germany Office: Freiherr-Vom-Stein-Strasse 24-26, D-60323 Frankfurt. Telephone: 49-69-971300. Telefax: 49-69-97130100.

Berlin, Germany Office: Spreeufer 5, D-10178 Berlin. Telephone: 49-30-238 45 45. Telefax: 49-30-238 45 34.

(This Listing Continued)

Dresden, Germany Office: Heinrichstrasse 16, D-01097 Dresden. Telephone: 49-351-567 12 12. Telefax: 49-351-567 12 13.

Brussels, Belgium Office: Avenue Louise 149, Box 42, B-1050 Brussels. Telephone: +32 (2) 537 01 86. Telefax: +32 (2) 534 25 31.

Commercial Law, Corporations, German and E.C. Antitrust, Trademark and Copyright, Computer Law, Labor, Administration, Environmental, Product Liability, Banking, Insurance, Real Property, Estate, Tax Law, Litigation, Conveyancing, General Practice.

DR. MICHAEL A. VELTINS, born Bochum, May 12, 1952; admitted, 1981. *Education:* Universities of Berlin, Bonn, Lausanne, Hamburg (Doctor of Law, 1981). Fachanwalt für Steuerrecht (Tax Lawyer). Assistant Professor of Civil Law, University of Hamburg. Adjunct Professor, Business Faculty, University of Hamburg. With Coudert Brothers, New York, 1981-1982. Author: "Das Recht der U.S. Partnership und Limited Partnership einschliesslich ihrer Besteuerung," Herne 1984. Co-author of the Commentary of Kullmann/Pfister, "Produzentenhaftung," 1987. *Member:* British-German Lawyer Association; American-German Lawyer Association; International Bar Association. *LANGUAGES:* German and English. *PRACTICE AREAS:* Commercial and Business Law; Product Liability; Corporate Law; Tax Law; Arbitration; International Law.

ALEXANDER PAPE, born Jena, September 15, 1962; admitted, 1990. *Education:* University of Leipzig. (Resident). *LANGUAGES:* German, Russian and French. *PRACTICE AREAS:* Commercial and Business Law; Law of the former GDR; Labour Law; Real Property Law.

DR. KLAUS BANDEKOW, born Graz, Austria, February 24, 1960; admitted, 1992. *Education:* Universities of Würzburg, Bonn, Frankfurt/Main (Doctor of Law, 1989). Assistant Professor of Criminal Law, University of Frankfurt/Main. *LANGUAGES:* German and English. *PRACTICE AREAS:* Real Property Law; Construction Law; Landlord and Tenant Law; Insurance Law; Commercial and Business Law.

NIELS HERMANN KÖTHE, born Bonn, October 15, 1960; admitted, 1992. *Education:* Universities of Bonn and Munich. *LANGUAGES:* German, English and Dutch. *PRACTICE AREAS:* Unfair Competition Law; Intellectual Property; Landlord and Tenant Law; Construction Law; Commercial and Business Law.

DR. KARSTEN ZORN, born Dresden, March 20, 1962; admitted, 1994. *Education:* University of Leipzig (Doctor of Law, 1993). *LANGUAGES:* German, Russian and English. *PRACTICE AREAS:* Real Property Law; Law of the former GDR; Administrative Law.

MICHAEL E. STRAUCH, born Bad Kreuznach, March 31, 1963; admitted, 1993. *Education:* Universities of Augsburg, Heidelberg and London. *LANGUAGES:* German and English. *PRACTICE AREAS:* Commercial and Business Law; Corporate Law; Air Law.

DR. SUSANNE POHLE, born Osnabrück, June 01, 1964; admitted, 1994. *Education:* Universities of Osnabrück, Freiburg, Münster (Doctor of Law, 1993). *LANGUAGES:* German, English and Russian. *PRACTICE AREAS:* Administrative Law; Environmental Law; Commercial and Business Law.

GOLLASCH LÖWE & PARTNER

HANSEKONTOR
HANSESTR. 14
P.O. BOX 11 12 36
23521 LÜBECK, GERMANY
Telephone: 49 451/57185-0
Fax: 49 451/5718544

Schwerin, Germany Office: Werkstr. 213, Europahaus, 19061. Telephone: (0385) 616225. Fax: (0385) 616228.

General Practice, Commercial Law, Company Law, International Contracts and Business Transactions, Unfair Competition, Banking and Finance, Tourism, Real Estate, Building and Construction Planning Law, Tax Law, Administrative Law, Environmental Law, Agricultural Law, Former East German Law. Notary Public.

MEMBERS OF FIRM

MARTIN M. GOLLASCH, born Lübeck, Germany, April 2, 1953; admitted, 1983, Lübeck; 1988, Notary Public. *Education:* Universities of Göttingen and Freiburg/Brasg., Germany (Referendar, 1979). Appointed Specialist for Tax Law. *Member:* International Bar Association; German Society for the Protection of Industrial Property and Copyright Law; German-American Lawyers Association; German Nordic Lawyers Association;

(This Listing Continued)

GOLLASCH LÖWE & PARTNER, Lübeck—Continued

German Hungarian Lawyers Association. *LANGUAGES:* German and English.

FRANK LÖWE, born Kiel, Germany, July 20, 1950; admitted, 1980, Lübeck. *Education:* University of Göttingen, Germany (Referendar, 1978). Author: "Investitionsüberlegungen eines spanishen Investors aus rechtlicher und steurrectlicher Sicht, in Ansehung des spanish-deutschen Abkommens zur Vermeidung der Doppelbelastung (DBA);" Boletin Informativo Camara Official Espanola de Commercio en Alemania. Appointed Specialist for TaxLaw. *Member:* German Polish Lawyers Association. *LANGUAGES:* German, English and French.

CHRISTIAN KROEGER, born Lübeck, Germany, December 16, 1956; admitted, 1991, Lübeck. *Education:* Universities Freiburg/Breisgau and Geneva/Switzerland (Referendar, 1982). Assistant Institute for Foreign and International Private Law Freiburg University 1982-1984, Judicial Service Baden-Württemberg. *Member:* Association International des Jeunes Avocates; German French Lawyers Association. *LANGUAGES:* German, English and French.

KLAUS-RAINER TIETMANN, born Bremen, Germany, June 26, 1954; admitted, 1989, Lübeck. *Education:* University of Kiel, Germany. *Member:* German Lawyers Association. (Resident, Schwerin Office). *LANGUAGES:* German, English and French.

PETER KRAMER, born Göttingen, Germany, November 19, 1962; admitted, 1994, Schwerin. *Education:* University of Göttingen, Germany. (Resident, Schwerin Office). *LANGUAGES:* German, English and French.

GÖTZ GRUB, DR. WOLFGANG FRANK, GERHARD BAHMANN, MATTHIAS WISSMANN, CHRISTOPH SCHICKHARDT, GEORG ENGLERT, PETER GROSSE

SOLITUDESTR. 20
71638 LUDWIGSBURG, GERMANY
Telephone: (07141) 96 30-0
Facsimile: (07141) 96 30-99

General Civil and Litigation Practice, Commercial, Corporation, Banking, Construction, Labor Law, Unfair Competition.

GÖTZ GRUB, born Ludwigsburg, Germany, September 3, 1934; admitted, 1963, Germany. *Education:* Universities of Tübingen, Freiburg and Hamburg (Staatsexamen, 1958 and 1963). *Member:* German Bar Association. *LANGUAGES:* German, English and French.

DR. WOLFGANG ROBERT FRANK, born Frankfurt/Oder, Germany, March 9, 1943; admitted, 1971, Germany. *Education:* Augustana College, Rock Island, Illinois, USA, 1964; University of Tübingen (Staatsexamen, 1968 and 1971); University of Munich (Doctorate, 1972). *Member:* German Bar Association. *LANGUAGES:* German, English, French and Spanish.

GERHARD BAHMANN, born Oberkochen, July 10, 1951; admitted, 1979, Germany. *Education:* University of Regensburg, 1970-1972; University of Tübingen. *Member:* German Bar Association. *LANGUAGES:* German and English.

MATTHIAS WISSMANN, born Ludwigsburg, Germany, April 15, 1949; admitted, 1980, Germany. *Education:* University of Tübingen (Staatsexamen, 1976 and 1978). Member, German Parliament (Bundestag, 1976—). (Inactive). *LANGUAGES:* German, English and French.

CHRISTOPH SCHICKHARDT, born Essen, Germany, March 14, 1955; admitted, 1983, Germany. *Education:* University of Tübingen (Staatsexamen, 1980 and 1982). *Member:* German Bar Association. *LANGUAGES:* German, English and French.

GEORG F. ENGLERT, born Stuttgart, Germany, February 7, 1957; admitted, 1987, Germany. *Education:* Columbia University; University of Freiburg (Staatsexamen, 1983 and 1986). *Member:* German Bar Association. *LANGUAGES:* German, English and French.

(This Listing Continued)

PETER MICHAEL GROSSE, born Stuttgart, Germany, September 28, 1961; admitted, 1991, Germany. *Education:* University of Tübingen, Germany (Staatsexamen, 1987 and 1990). *LANGUAGES:* German and English.

NEUMEISTER, MELL & WERLING

VAN LEYDEN STR. 22
D-67067 LUDWIGSHAFEN, GERMANY
Telephone: 0621/56 80 55
Telecopier: 0621/56 80 58; 0621/5296095

General Practice

MEMBERS OF FIRM

MAX NEUMEISTER, born Lobenstein, October 14, 1925; admitted, 1954, Mannheim; 1966, Frankenthal. *Education:* University of Heidelberg. Member: Disciplinary Court of Lawyers, 1978-1986; Examination Board for Judges, 1978-1987. *Member:* Law Society of Ludwigshafen (Board Member, 1972-1974). *LANGUAGES:* German and French.

KARL MELL, born Eschwege, March 11, 1948; admitted, 1976, Frankenthal/Pfalz; 1981, Tax Attorney. *Education:* University of Heidelberg; University of Mainz. Member: Board of Law Society, Ludwigshafen, 1978-1981; Executing Board of the Bar Council, 1986—. *LANGUAGES:* German, English and French.

KURT WERLING, born Laudau/Pfalz, July 26, 1954; admitted, 1982, Frankenthal/Pfalz; 1986, Tax Attorney. *Education:* University of Mainz (Doctorate of Law, 1983). *Member:* Pension Scheme for Lawyers (Member, Representative Body); German Associates of Lawyers. *LANGUAGES:* German and English.

ANWALTSKANZLEI DR. BETTE, DR. BRINK, GÖLZ

Established in 1963

RHEINALLEE 3 D
D-55116 MAINZ, GERMANY
Telephone: 06131/23 28 67-69
Fax: 06131/22 01 99

Erfurt, Germany Office: Eugen-Richter-Str. 44, D-99089 Erfurt. Telephone: 0361-57699-0. Fax: 0361-57699-99.
Berlin, Germany Office: Kantstr. 152, D-10623 Berlin. Telephone: 030-315 2956; 030-313 6049. Fax: 030-313 3845.
Member Juropartner EWIV European Economic Interest Grouping (EEIG).

Commercial Law. Contract, Corporate, Banking, Collateral, Bankruptcy, Competition, Copyright, Venture, Financing and Labour Issues.

MEMBERS OF FIRM

DR. JUR. KLAUS BETTE, born Berlin, September 23, 1931. Executive Manager of Deutscher Factoring-Verband e.V., Mainz. *Member:* German British Jurist Association; German Spanish Jurist Association; German Jurist Association. *LANGUAGES:* English, Spanish and German. *PRACTICE AREAS:* Economic Law; Finance Law.

DR. JUR. ULRICH BRINK, born Berlin, August 17, 1948. Executive Manager, Deutscher Factoring-Verband e.V., Mainz. Vice President, EUROPAFACTORING, Bruxelles, Belgium. *Member:* German British Jurist Association; German French Jurist Association. *LANGUAGES:* English, French and German. *PRACTICE AREAS:* Fiscal Law; Company Law.

HEINZ GÖLZ, born Kirchheim/Teck, October 11, 1950. *LANGUAGES:* English, French and German. *PRACTICE AREAS:* Liquidations; Construction Law.

CHRISTIAN VON DER LÜHE, born Neuwied/Rhine, July 20, 1956. *Member:* German-Irish Jurist Association. *LANGUAGES:* English, French and German. *PRACTICE AREAS:* Mergers and Acquisitions.

ASSOCIATES

BIRGIT ANUSCHEK, born Ingelheim, November 22, 1962. (Resident, Erfurt Office). *LANGUAGES:* English, French and German. *PRACTICE AREAS:* Labour Law; Litigation.

(This Listing Continued)

JULIA BETTE, born Greven/Munster, December 13, 1958. (Resident, Berlin Office). *LANGUAGES:* English, Spanish and German. *PRACTICE AREAS:* Litigation.

HESS WIENBERG FREUND & PARTNER

WILHELM-THEODOR-RÖMHELD-STR. 14
P.O. BOX 261 351
55130 MAINZ, GERMANY
Telephone: 49/6131/2850-0
Fax: 49/6131/285028

Dresden Office: Loschwitzer Straße 7, 01309. Telephone: 49/351/34085-0. Fax: 49/351/43085-5.
Berlin Office: Friedrichstraße 180, 10117. Telephone: 49/30/22073-133. Fax: 49/30/22073-150.
Chemnitz Office: Treffurthstraße 17, 09120. Telephone: 49/371/590450-0. Fax: 49/371/590450-5.
Alzey Office: Antoniterstraße 65, 55232. Telephone: 49/6731/3066. Fax: 49/6731/3104.
Wiesbaden Office: Abeggstraße 2, 65193. Telephone: 49/611/52303-1. Fax: 49/611/52303-3.

Bankruptcy, Liquidation, Banking, Business Law, Partnerships, Limited Partnerships, Civil Law, Company Law, Contracts, Debtor and Creditor, Labour and Employment, Mergers and Acquisitions.

DR.IUR. HARALD HESS, born Mainz, Germany, February 14, 1942; admitted, 1974, Germany. *Education:* University of Mainz (Referendar, 1972; Assessor, 1974; Doctor of Jurisprudence, 1974; Auditor, 1986). Author and Co-Author: "Commentary on the Industrial Constitution Law,"; "Commentary on the Insolvency Law,"; "Commentary on the Gesamtvollstreckungsordnung,"; "Labour Law in Case of Bankruptcy and Reorganization,"; "Handbook for Reorganization". *Member:* German Bar Association (Member, Insolvency Association). *LANGUAGES:* German and English. *PRACTICE AREAS:* Insolvency; Bankruptcy; Banking; Labour and Employment; Mergers and Acquisitions.

KLAUS KNÖRIG, born Recklinghausen, Germany, December 6, 1952; admitted, 1982, Germany. *Education:* University of Mainz (Referendar, 1979; Assessor, 1982). Co-Author: "Labour Law in Case of Bankruptcy and Reorganization." *Member:* German Bar Association. *LANGUAGES:* German and English. *PRACTICE AREAS:* Labour and Employment; Bankruptcy; Civil Law; Business Law; Corporate Law.

RÜDIGER WIENBERG, born Lübeck, Germany; admitted, 1990, Germany. *Education:* Universities of Trier and Mainz (Referendar, 1987; Assessor, 1990). Co-Author: "Commentary on the Gesamtvollstreckungsordnung." *Member:* German Bar Association. (Resident Partner, Dresden Office). *LANGUAGES:* German, English and French. *PRACTICE AREAS:* Insolvency; Liquidation; Partnerships and Limited Partnerships; Contracts; Labour and Employment; Debtors and Creditors.

HANS WILHELM GOETSCH, born Bad Nauheim, Germany, September 4, 1961; admitted, 1991, Germany. *Education:* Universities of Konstanz, Trier and Mainz (Referendar, 1988; Assessor, 1991); Hochschule Verwaltungswissenchaften (1990). Co-Author: Employer's Handbook. *Member:* German Bar Association; German Association for the Protection of Industrial Property and Copyright (GRUR). *LANGUAGES:* German and English. *PRACTICE AREAS:* Insolvency and Liquidation; Bankruptcy; Company Law; Competition and Fair Trade; Business Law.

HENNING SCHORISCH, born Helmstedt, Germany, October 12, 1959; admitted, 1990, Germany. *Education:* University of Bayreuth (Referendar, 1987; Assessor, 1990). *Member:* German Bar Association. (Resident Partner, Dresden Office). *LANGUAGES:* German and English. *PRACTICE AREAS:* Bankruptcy; Banking Law; Civil Law; Contracts; Mergers and Acquisitions.

DR.IUR. FRITZ BINZ, born February 25, 1941; admitted, 1970, Germany. *Education:* Universities of Mainz and Freiburg (Referendar, 1967; Doctor of Jurisprudence, 1968; Assessor, 1970). Co-Author: "Commentary on the Gesamtvollstreckungsordnung." *Member:* German Bar Association. *LANGUAGES:* German and English. *PRACTICE AREAS:* Bankruptcy; Liquidations; Business Law; Competition and Fair Trade; Civil Law.

DR.IUR. JÜRGEN BLERSCH, born Weingarten, Germany April 5, 1956; admitted, 1986, Germany. *Education:* University of Freiburg (Referendar, 1983; Assessor, 1986; Doctor of Law, 1992). Author: "Interpretation of East German Bankruptcy Act." *Member:* German Bar Association.

(This Listing Continued)

LANGUAGES: German, English and French. *PRACTICE AREAS:* Bankruptcy; Corporate Law; Business Law; Civil Law; Unfair Competition.

KONRAD FREUND, born Alzey, Germany, November 4, 1949. *Education:* University of Mainz (1977; Tax Consultant, 1981; Accountant, 1984.

HANS GEORG BEHNKE, born July 19, 1955. *Education:* University of Mainz (Dipl., 1982; Tax Consultant, 1987; Accountant, 1994).

ERNST-REINER HAUPT, born Flonheim, Germany, August 5, 1961. Tax Consultant, 1991.

DEPRÉ & COLL.

Anwaltskanzlei

0 4, 13 - 16
68161 MANNHEIM, GERMANY
Telephone: 49/621/153881
Telefax: 49/621/153800

Commercial, Corporation, Unfair Competition, Banking, Business, Bankruptcy, Labor Law, Divorce, Real Estate; Probate, Inheritance, Insolvency and Reorganization, General Civil Practice and Litigation.

PETER DEPRÉ, born Neustadt an der Weinstraße, January 16, 1951; admitted, 1982, Germany. *Education:* Universities of Heidelberg and Speyer. Assistant, University of Heidelberg. Junior Barrister, German-French Chamber of Commerce, Paris. *Member:* Examination Board of the civil Service Examination, German Bar Association; International Bar Association (Section on Business Law); German-British Jurists' Association. *PRACTICE AREAS:* Bankruptcy; Insolvency; Corporate Law; Commercial Law.

KARIN HASCHER-HUG, born Pforzheim, May 25, 1954; admitted, 1987, Germany. *Education:* University of Heidelberg. Legal Assistant, University of Heidelberg, 1983-1986. *Member:* German Bar Association; Deutscher Anwaltsverein. *PRACTICE AREAS:* Divorce.

HARALD HECK, born Durmersheim, January 10, 1959; admitted, 1989, Germany. *Education:* University of Mannheim. *Member:* German Bar Association; Deutscher Anwaltsverein. *PRACTICE AREAS:* Labor Law.

MARKUS DAHMANN, born Cologne, December 1, 1963; admitted, 1992, Germany. *Education:* University of Mannheim. *Member:* German Bar Association; Deutscher Anwaltsverein.

BERNHARD THOMA, born Mannheim, March 28, 1962; admitted, 1994, Germany. *Education:* University of Mannheim. *Member:* German Bar Association; Deutscher Anwaltsverein.

Languages: German, English and French

KOLLE & PARTNER

Established in 1967
N 5, 12
MANNHEIM, GERMANY
Telephone: (0621) 10 20 36
International: (49) 621 10 20 36
Fax: (0621) 15 42 00
International: (49) 621 15 42 00

General German and International Practice, Commercial Transactions, International Business Transactions, Computer and Copyright Law, Licensing Agreements, Insurance, Personal Injury, Domestic Relations, Labour, Litigation.

MEMBERS OF FIRM

GEROLD KOLLE, born Namslau, Germany, September 13, 1936; admitted, 1966, Mannheim and Heidelberg; 1971, Karlsrube (Court of Appeals). *Education:* Universities of Göttingen and Heidelberg (Referendar 1962, Assessor 1966). *LANGUAGES:* German, English and French.

THOMAS KUGLER, born Mannheim, Germany, Oktober 29, 1964; admitted, 1994, Mannheim and Heidelberg. *Education:* University of Mannheim (Referendar, 1989); University of Oslo, Norway (1987); University of Iowa, USA (M.C.L., 1990). Oberlandesgericht, Karlsrube (Assessor, 1993); Corporate Counsel for NUKEM GmbH (since 1993). *Member:* German American Lawyers Association. *LANGUAGES:* German, English and Norwegian.

(This Listing Continued)

KOLLE & PARTNER, Mannheim—Continued

OF COUNSEL

SUSANNE WEBER-KAESSER, admitted, 1992, Mannheim and Heidelberg.

RITTERSHAUS, WISSMANN & VON ROSENSTIEL

Established in 1969

THEODOR-HEUSS-ANLAGE 2
D-68165 MANNHEIM, GERMANY
Telephone: (0) 621/41 10 02
Fax: (0) 621/41 33 89

Frankfurt, Germany Office: Leerbachstrasse 58, D-60322. Telephone: (0) 69/17 41 91. Fax: (0) 69/17 43 51.

Commercial Law and Contracts, Corporate Law, Mergers and Acquisitions, Unfair Competition, Taxation, Arbitration, Banking, Transportation and Labor Law, General Practice, Real Estate, Construction Law, Administrative Law, Divorce, Wills, Estates and Trusts, Entertainment and Sports.

MEMBERS OF FIRM

DR. GERALD RITTERSHAUS, born Mannheim, January 31, 1938; admitted, 1969, Germany. *Education:* Universities of Heidelberg (Dr. jur., 1967), Hamburg and Sevilla. Assistant Lecturer on Law, University of Mannheim, 1962-1968. Author: "Die Ersatzansprüche des beauftragten und auftraglosen Geschäftsführers für beiderseits unverschuldete Schäden," 1967. Co-Author: "BasiswissenRecht, Bürgerliches Recht für Wirtschaftswissenschaftler," 1982. *Member:* German-Spanish Lawyers' Association. **LANGUAGES:** German, English and Spanish. **PRACTICE AREAS:** Corporations; Mergers and Acquisitions; Banking; Restructuring; Arbitration; Sports.

MANFRED WISSMANN, born Ludwigshafen/Rhein, March 9, 1950; admitted, 1976, Germany. *Education:* Universities of Mannheim and Heidelberg; London School of Economics. Fachanwalt für Steuerrecht (Special Tax Counsel). Author: "Die Steuerberater GmbH," 1993; "Der GmbH Gesellschaftsvertrag," 1987; "Die Haftung des GmbH-Geschäftsführers," 1990. Co-Author: "Jahrbuch für den GmbH-Geschäftsführer," 1984-1993; "Die Kapitalerhöhung der GmbH," 1990; "Das GmbH-Handbuch," 1991; "Handbuch des Gesellschafts-und Wirtschaftsrechts," 1991; "Die Gesellschafterversammlung," 1993. Lecturer on Law, Association of German Chartered Accountants. *Member:* German-American Law Association. **LANGUAGES:** German and English. **PRACTICE AREAS:** Company Law; Partnerships; Mergers and Acquisitions; Banking; Taxation; Entertainment.

DR. WERNER H. VON ROSENSTIEL, born Anklam, May 13, 1911; 1939, Gerichtsassessor; admitted, 1976, Germany; 1943, New York; 1948, New Jersey; 1971, Pennsylvania, U.S. District Courts of Pennsylvania and New Jersey, Third Circuit Cour t of Appeals. *Education:* Universities of Breslau (Dr.jur., 1935) and Berlin; Fordham University School of Law, New York (LL.B., 1943). Assistant Professor, Rutgers University School of Law, (Newark), 1948-1954. Author: "Comparative Law," Selected Case Materials, 1953. (Also Of Counsel, Harrell, Ostow, Higgins & Keane, P.A., St. Petersburg, Florida). **LANGUAGES:** German and English. **PRACTICE AREAS:** Residential Mortgage Foreclosure; Bankruptcy Law; Eminent Domain Law; Wills and Estates; American Estates; Corporations.

PROF. DR. WOLFGANG GAST, born Nürnberg, May 17, 1940; admitted, 1985, Germany. *Education:* University of Erlangen (Dr.jur., 1968). Professor, University of Mannheim. Fachanwalt für Arbeitsrecht (Special Labor Law Counsel). Author: "Arbeitsvertrag und Direktion," 1978; "Tarifautonomie und Normsetzung durch Betriebsvereinbarung," 1981; "Das Arbeitsrecht als Vertragsrecht," 1984; "Mitarbeiterbeteiligung durch Genußrechte," BB 1987, Beilage 17; "Das Arbeitsrecht und die Deutsche Vereinigung," AuA 1990, 131 ff. **LANGUAGES:** German, Italian and English. **PRACTICE AREAS:** Labor Law.

DR. REINHOLD REIS, born Heidelberg, December 27, 1956; admitted, 1984, Germany. *Education:* University of Heidelberg (Dr.jur., 1986). Author: "Deutsches Privatrecht in den Weistümern der Zenten von Schriesheim und Kirchheim," 1987. **LANGUAGES:** German, English and French. **PRACTICE AREAS:** Labor Law; Collective Bargaining; Employment Relations.

(This Listing Continued)

DR. VERA LIEBERWIRTH, born Duisburg, September 16, 1961; admitted, 1987, Germany. *Education:* Universities of Mannheim and Freiburg (Dr.jur., 1990). Author: "Die provozierte Tat-ein untauglicher Versuch?" 1990. **LANGUAGES:** German and English. **PRACTICE AREAS:** Capital Gains Tax; Tax Planning; Carriers and Transport; Divorce.

DR. CHRISTOF HETTICH, born Singen, November 5, 1959; admitted, 1990, Germany. *Education:* Universities of Freiburg, Würzburg and Mannheim (Dr.jur., 1989). Author: "Parteispenden und Verfassungsrecht," 1989. Co-Author: "Immobilien-Baurecht (IBR)," concerning Real Estate, Trusts and similar subject matters. Lecturer, Tax Law, Professional Academy Baden-Württemberg. **LANGUAGES:** German and English. **PRACTICE AREAS:** Corporations; Commercial Contracts; Commercial Real Estate; Investments; Land and Land Owners.

WOLFGANG FLECK, born Besigheim, June 3, 1957; admitted, 1990, Germany. *Education:* University of Mannheim. Co-Author: "Lexikon des Rechts," 1989, concerning special subject matters of Civil Law. Assistant Lecturer, Labor Law, Administrative and Business Academy Baden-Württemberg. **LANGUAGES:** German, English and Italian. **PRACTICE AREAS:** Labor Law; Management; Employment Relations; Commercial Contracts; Real Estate.

DR. WOLF-HENRIK FRIEDRICH, born Worms, May 5, 1959; admitted, 1991, Germany. *Education:* Universities of Regensburg, Heidelberg and Freiburg (Dr.jur., 1989). Author: "Die Haftung des endgültigen Erben und des 'Zwischenerben' bei Fortführung eines einzelkaufmännischen Unternehmens," 1990. **LANGUAGES:** German and English. **PRACTICE AREAS:** Unfair Competition; Inheritance Law; Estate Law; Construction Law.

DR. ANDREAS NOTZ, born Mannheim, May 27, 1960; admitted, 1992, Germany. *Education:* University of Mannheim (Dr. jur., 1990). Assistant Lecturer on Law, University of Mannheim, 1987-1989. Author: "Zulässigkeit und Grenzen ärztlicher Untersuchungen von Arbeitnehmern," 1990. **LANGUAGES:** German and English. **PRACTICE AREAS:** Labor Law; Commercial Real Estate; Litigation.

CHRISTIAN HERBERT, born Mannheim, June 19, 1964; admitted, 1994, Germany. *Education:* Universities of Mannheim and Heidelberg; University of Grenoble (licence en droit, 1992). **LANGUAGES:** German, French, English and Italian. **PRACTICE AREAS:** Public Law; Administrative Law; European Community Law; Common Market; Conflict of Laws.

BERND KLEINSTEUBER, born Erbach, March 20, 1966; admitted, 1994, Germany. *Education:* University of Mannheim. *Member:* German-British Junist's Association. **LANGUAGES:** German and English. **PRACTICE AREAS:** Conflict of Laws; International Sale of Goods; Litigation; Probate; Construction Law.

MICHAEL H. GHAFFAR, born Mannheim, June 30, 1964; admitted, 1994, Germany. *Education:* University of Mannheim; New York University (LL.M., 1992). **LANGUAGES:** German and English. **PRACTICE AREAS:** Corporate Law; Commercial Law.

Languages: German, English, French, Spanish and Italian.

(For Biographical Data of the Frankfurt Germany Personnel, see Professional Biographies at Frankfurt, Germany)

ROWEDDER, ZIMMERMANN, v. KNIERIEM & HASS

Rechtsanwälte

OTTO-BECK-STRAßE 46
P.O. BOX 102754
D-68027 MANNHEIM, GERMANY
Telephone: 0621-4 19 38-0
Telefax: 0621-4 19 38-80; 41 51 92

General and International Practice, Commercial, Corporate, Mergers and Acquisitions, EEC Law, Antitrust, Unfair Competition, Copyrights, Patents, Licensing, Law of the Press, Labor Law, Taxation.

MEMBERS OF FIRM

PROF. HEINZ ROWEDDER, born Hamburg, Germany, July 26, 1919; admitted, 1948, Mannheim, Heidelberg and OLG Karlsruhe. *Education:* University of Heidelberg. Author: Konrad Duden/Heinz Rowedder Kommentar zum Vertragshilfegesetz, Berlin/München, 1955; Editor and Co-Author: Commentary for the limited liability company, Die Aktien-

(This Listing Continued)

gesellschaft und ihre Satzung, 2. Auflage von Möhring-Schwartz: Satzungsgestaltung nach neuem Aktienrecht, neubearbeitet von Rowedder und Haberlandt, Berlin und Frankfurt, 1966; Rowedder, Gesetz betreffend die Gesellschaften mit beschränkter Haftung (GmbHG); Bestandsschutz im faktischen GmbH-Konzern, in: Hommelhoff/Semmler/Doralt/Roth: Entwicklungen im GmbH-Konzernrecht, ZGR Sonderheft Nr. 6, Berlin, New York, 1986, S. 20-38; Die Zulässigkeit der Testamentsvollstreckung bei Kommanditbeteiligungen, in: Havermann (Hrsg.): Bilanz-und Konzernrecht, Festschrift für Goerdeler, Düsseldorf, 1987, S. 445-468; Gedanken zur Lückenlosigkeit der Vertriebsbindungen als Voraussetzung ihrer Zulässigkeit, in: von Gamm/Raisch/Tiedemann: (Hrsg.): Strafrecht Unternehmensrecht, Anwaltsrecht, Festschrift für Pfeiffer, München, 1988, S. 751-764; Der gemeinsame Vertreter gem. § 306 Abs. 4 AktG - Rechtsstellung, Vertretungsmacht und Aufgabe, in: Löwisch/Schmidt-Leithoff/Schmiedel (Hrsg.), Beiträge zum Handels-und Wirtschaftsrecht, Festschrift für Rittner, München, 1991, S. 509-520; Die rechtliche Gestaltung der AG und der GmbH unter Berücksichtigung der Unternehmenspraxis, in: Lutter/Semler (Hrsg.), Rechtsgrundlagen freiheitlicher Unternehmenswirtschaft, Köln, 1991, S. 50-70; Rügenwalder Teewurst und andere Köstlichkeiten. Beiläufige Überlegungen zum Schutz geografi scher Herkunftsangaben, in: Wild/-Schulte-Franzheim/Lorenz/Wolf (Hrsg.): Festsc hrift für Gaedertz, München, 1992, S. 465-480; Zur Außenhaftung des GmbH-Geschäftsführers - Versuch einer Systematisierung, in: Bierich/Hommelhoff/Kropff (Hrsg.): Festschrift für Semler, Berlin, New York, 1993, S. 311-328. *Member:* Mannheim Bar Association; German Bar Association; Chairman, Company Law Committee, 1973-1994); Association of Industrial Property; U.I.A. (President, 1973-1975). *LANGUAGES:* German, English, French and Italian. *PRACTICE AREAS:* International Practice; Commercial; Corporate; Antitrust; Unfair Competition; Trademarks; Copyrights; Patents; Arbitration.

DR. KLAUS ZIMMERMANN, born Heidelberg, Germany, November 12, 1927; admitted, 1955, Mannheim, Heidelberg, OLG Karlsruhe. *Education:* University of Heidelberg (Dr. jur., 1953). Author: "Nachfolge in Anteile an Personenhandelsgesellschaften aufgrund Gesellschaftsvertrages oder Erbrechts," 1970; Rowedder, Gesetz betreffend die Gesellschaft mit beschränkter Haftung (GmbHG) 3. Auflage, 1995, (Co-Author: Commentary for the limited liability company). *Member:* President of the Rechtsanwaltskammer Karlsruhe; Mannheim Bar Association; German Society for the protection of industrial property and copyright law; Studienvereinigung Kartellrect. *LANGUAGES:* German English and French. *PRACTICE AREAS:* Company Law; Patents; Copyrights; Unfair Competition; Arbitration.

DR. JÜRGEN V. KNIERIEM, born Mannheim, Germany, November 27, 1925; admitted, 1973, Mannheim, Heidelberg and OLG Karlsruhe. *Education:* University of Heidelberg (Dr.jur., 1952). *Member:* Mannheim Bar Association; German Society for the Protection of Industrial Property and Copyright Law; Studienvereinigung Kartellrecht. *LANGUAGES:* German, English and French. *PRACTICE AREAS:* Company Law; Trust Law; International Law.

DR. PETER HASS, born Stuttgart, Germany, October 17, 1936; admitted, 1964, Mannheim, Heidelberg and OLG Karlsruhe. *Education:* University of Heidelberg; University of Kiel; University of Mainz (Dr.jur., 1963). Author: Sach-und Vermögensschaden im Zusammenhang mit dem haftpflichtversicherten Risiko; Gedanken zur sklavischen Nachahmung GRUR, 1979, 361 ff; Weinbezeichnungs-und Warenzeichenrecht GRUR, 1980, 87 ff; Persönliche Haftung des GmbH-Geschäftsführers bei Wettbewerbsverstößen und Verletzung gewerblicher Schutzrechte GmbHR, 1994, 666 ff. *Member:* Mannheim Bar Association; U.I.A.; German Society for the Protection of Industrial Property and Copyright Law. *LANGUAGES:* German, English and French. *PRACTICE AREAS:* Intellectual Property; Patents, Trademarks and Copyrights; Unfair Competition Law; EEC Law; Company Law; Commercial Law; Pharmaceutical Law.

GUSTAV DUDEN, born Heidelberg, Germany, February 14, 1947; admitted, 1978, Mannheim, Heidelberg and OLG Karlsruhe. *Education:* Free University of Berlin. Author: "Artikel 85 EWG-Vertrag," DACH-Schriftenreihe, Heft 1, Wien, 1994; "Die Gruppenfreistellungsverordnungen zu Know-how-Vereinbarungen," 7ACH-Schriftenreihe, Heft 1; "Das Europäische Übereinkommen vom 7. June, 1968 betreffend Auskünfte über ausländisches Recht," DACH-Schriftenreihe, Heft 3. *Member:* Mannheim Bar Association; German Bar Association (Study Group for International Law); German-Austria-Swiss-Liechtenstein Bar Association. *LANGUAGES:* German and English. *PRACTICE AREAS:* Commercial Law; Contract Law; Intellectual Property; Patents, Trademarks and Copyrights; Unfair Competition; European Law.

(This Listing Continued)

DR. RALPH LANDSITTEL, born Mannheim, Germany, July 24, 1956; admitted, 1987, Mannheim, Heidelberg and OLG Karlsruhe. *Education:* University of Munich; University of Mannheim (Dr.jur., 1986). Assistant, European Institute University of Mannheim. Author: Dumping im Außenhandels-und Wettbewerbsrecht (Dumping in foreign trade and competition law), Nomos Verlag Baden-Baden, 1987; Dumpingsachen vor dem EuGH; Dumping und Wettbewerbsrecht, RIW, 1987, 450; Antidumpingzölle auf in der Gemeinschaft hergestellte Waren, WRP, 1988, 21; Die EG-Antidumpingregelungen für "Schraubenzieherfabriken" nach der Entscheidung des GATT-Panel, Europäische Zeitschrift für Wirtschaftsrecht, 1990, 177; Die Zurechnungsklausel in der Fusionskontrolle, Betriebsberater, 1994, 799. *Member:* Mannheim Bar Association; German Society for the Protection of Industrial Property and Copyright Law; Studienvereinigung Kartellrecht. *LANGUAGES:* German, English and French. *PRACTICE AREAS:* Mergers and Acquisitions; Antitrust; Unfair Competition; Patents; Corporate Law; European Law; Competition.

DR. ANDREAS PENTZ, born Frankfurt/Main, Germany, July 10, 1962; admitted, 1992, Mannheim and Heidelberg. *Education:* University of Marburg; University of Heidelberg (Dr.jur., 1994). Author: "Legal Position of a granddaughter-plc in a group of companies," 1994; Die Rechtsstellung der Enkel-AG in einer mehrstufigen Unternehmensverbindung; Zum Umfang der Schadensersatzpflicht eines Rechtsanwalts wegen unzutreffender Prozeßkostenschätzung, Anwbl., 1992, 128; Mitteilungspflichten gem. §§ 20, 21 AktG gegenüber einer mehrstufig verbundenen Aktiengesellschaft, AG, 1992, 55. *Member:* Mannheim Bar Association. *LANGUAGES:* German and English. *PRACTICE AREAS:* Company Law; Corporate Law; Commercial Law; Antitrust Law.

SCHILLING, ZUTT & ANSCHÜTZ

Established in 1925

OTTO-BECK-STRAßE 42
D-68165 MANNHEIM, GERMANY
Telephone: 49-621 42 57-0
Int'l Dialing: (49-621) 42 57-0
Telecopier: 49-621 42 57 280
Cable Address: "Advocat"

Mailing Address: P.O. Box 10 27 50, D-68027

Dresden, Germany Office: Hohe Strasse 12, D-01069. Mailing Address: P.O. Box 579, D-01067. Telephone: 49-351 472 4761. Telecopier: 49-351 472 47 66.

Administrative Law, Antitrust Law, Arbitration, Banking and Finance, Commercial Law, Company Law, Computer Law, Employment and Labour Law, Environmental Law, European Community Law, Franchising, Industrial and Intellectual Property, Litigation, Mergers and Acquisitions, Product Liability, Real Estate, Taxation, Trademarks, Unfair Competition Law.

PARTNERS

PROF. DR. WOLFGANG SCHILLING (1908-1992).

DR. JÜRG ZUTT, born Mannheim, Germany, July 25, 1929; admitted, 1957, Germany. *Education:* Universities of Heidelberg and Munich (Dr. jur., 1954). Co-Author: "Hachenburg, Grosskommentar zum GmbH-Gesetz," (Commentary on the Act of Limited Liability Companies), 8th Edition, 1989; Grosskommentar zum Handelsgesetzbuch (Commentary on Commercial Act) 4th Ed. *Member:* Nordbaden Bar Association (Member of Board, 1970-1982); German Association for the Protection of Industrial Property and Copyright (Member of Board, 1980—); Studienvereinigung Kartellrecht; International Association for the Protection of Industrial Property (AIPPI); Handelsrechtsausschuss (Commission on Commercial Law), established by the German Lawyers Association. *LANGUAGES:* German, English and French.

DR. KLAUS ANSCHÜTZ, born Heidelberg, Germany, June 24, 1935; admitted, 1961, Germany. *Education:* Universities of Heidelberg and Munich (Dr. jur., 1959). Co-Author: "Beck'sches Formularbuch zum Bürgerlichen Handels—und Wirtschaftsrecht," 6th Edition, 1992; "Beck'sches Prozessformularbuch," 6th Edition, 1992. *Member:* German Association for the Protection of Industrial Property and Copyright; Studienvereinigung Kartellrecht. *LANGUAGES:* German and English.

TILMAN SCHILLING, born Mannheim, Germany, July 29, 1937; admitted, 1966, Germany. *Education:* Universities of Kiel, Berlin and Heidelberg. *Member:* German Association for the Protection of Industrial Prop-

(This Listing Continued)

SCHILLING, ZUTT & ANSCHÜTZ, Mannheim—
Continued

erty and Copyright; German-American Lawyers Association. **LAN-GUAGES:** German and English.

DR. ARNDT OVERLACK, born Baden-Baden, Germany, July 31, 1942; admitted, 1972, Germany. *Education:* Universities of Saarbrücken, Tübingen and Freiburg (Dr. jur., 1969). Author: "Einfluss der Gesellschafter auf die Geschäftsführung der mitbestimmten GmbH," (Influence of Shareholders on Management in GmbH Subject to Co-determination), ZHR 141 (1977) 125. Associate to the law firm of Davis Polk & Wardwell, New York and Paris, 1971-1972. *Member:* Union Internationale des Avocats; American Chamber of Commerce. **LANGUAGES:** German, English and French.

DR. DIETER BAAS, born Grossenhain, Germany, December 5, 1944; admitted, 1975, Germany. *Education:* Universities of Heidelberg and Munich (Dr. jur., 1976). Author: "Leitungsmacht und Gemeinwohlbindung der Aktiengesellschaft," Frankfurt u. München, 1976. *Member:* Board of Bar of Nordbaden, 1990— ; German Association for the Protection of Industrial Property and Copyright; Studienvereinigung Kartellrecht. **LANGUAGES:** German, English and French.

THOMAS PSCHERA, born Heidelberg, Germany, August 10, 1952; admitted, 1980, Germany. *Education:* University of Heidelberg; Fachanwalt für Verwaltungsrecht. *Member:* German Association for Environmental Law. **LANGUAGES:** German, English and French. **PRACTICE AREAS:** Administrative Law; Constitutional Law; Environmental Law.

DR. WOLFGANG WITZ, born Freiburg i. Breisgau, Germany, December 14, 1951; admitted, 1982, Germany. *Education:* Universities of Freiburg and Lausanne (Dr.jur., 1985); University of Chicago Law School (LL.M., 1980). Author: "Der Unbestimmte Kaufpreis," 1989. Assistant Lecturer on Law, University of Freiburg, 1980-1982. *Member:* German-American Lawyers Association; Gesellschaft für Rechtsvergleichung; Union International des Avocats; Studienvereinigung Kartellrecht. **LANGUAGES:** German, English and French.

DR. GEORG JAEGER, born Heidelberg, Germany, July 17, 1956; admitted, 1984, Germany. *Education:* Universities of München and Freiburg (Dr. jur., 1982). Author: "Der Auslandsbezug des Betriebsverfassungsgesetzes," 1983, Europäische Hochschulschriften II/324; "Die Betriebsaufspaltung durch Ausgliederung einzelner Betriebsteile," BB 1988, S. 1036; "Der Anstellungsvertrag des GmbH-Geschäftsführers," 2nd ed. 1992, Beck'sche Musterverträge Bd. 2; "Vertragsformen und rechtliche Grenzen der Vergütungsregelung," in Handbuch des Führungskräftemanagements, BeckVerlag 1993. *Member:* Association of Labor Law Attorneys. **LAN-GUAGES:** German, English and French. **PRACTICE AREAS:** Employment and Labour Law.

DR. JOCHEM REICHERT, born Worms, Germany, March 2, 1956; admitted, 1984, Germany. *Education:* Universities of Mannheim and Heidelberg (Dr. jur., 1983). Author: "Das Zustimmungserfordernis zur Abtretung von Geschäftsanteilen in der GmbH," Heidelberg, 1984; "Zulässigkeit der nachträglichen Einführung oder Aufhebung von Vinkulierungsklauseln in der Satzung der GmbH," BB 1985, S. 1496; "Der GmbH-Vertrag," 2nd ed. 1994, Beck'sche Mustervertraege Bd. 8. Co-Author: "Les Pratiques Discriminatoires en Allemagne d' Après, L'Article 26 GWB," in Cahiers de droit de L'entreprise 1982, S. 22 ff.; with Winter, "Die Abberufung des geschäftsführenden Gesellschafters der Publikums-Personengesellschaft," BB 1988, S. 981 with Winter, "Vinkuierungsklauseln und Gesellschafterliche Treupflicht," in Festschrift 100 Jahre GmbHG, 1992. Assistant Lecturer on Law, University of Heidelberg, 1980-1982. *Member:* Studienvereinigung Kartellrecht. **LANGUAGES:** German and English.

DR. MARTIN WINTER, born Heilbronn, Germany, June 18, 1956; admitted, 1986, Germany. *Education:* University of Heidelberg (Dr.jur., 1986). Author: "Mitgliedschaftliche Treubindungen im GmbH-Recht," München, 1987; "Haftung des Gesamthandsvermögens der Gesellschaft bürgerlichen Rechts für Gesellschafterschulden?," KTS 1983, S. 394; "Verdeckte Gewinnausschüttungen im GmbH-Recht," ZHR 148, S. 579, 1984; "Mehrheitliche Vertragsänderungen im Personengesellschaftsrecht," GesRZ 1986, 74; "Organisationsrechtl Sanktionen bei Verletzung von Gesellschaftervereinbarungen?" ZHR 154, 259, 1990. Assistant Lecturer on Law, University of Heidelberg, 1983-1986. **LANGUAGES:** German, English and French.

CARSTEN A. SALGER, born Karlsruhe, Germany, March 31, 1959; admitted, 1988, Germany; 1991, Dresden. *Education:* University of Freiburg (1982); University of Illinois (Master of Laws, 1984). Lecturer, Com-

(This Listing Continued)

mercial Law, Labor Law and Civil Procedure, Professional Academy Baden-Württemberg, 1983-1985. *Member:* German-American Lawyers' Association; German Association for the Protection of Industrial Property and Copyright; Studienvereinigung Kartellrecht. **LANGUAGES:** German and English.

DR. HANS-CHRISTOPH IHRIG, born Frankfurt, Germany, August 23, 1959; admitted, 1990, Germany. *Education:* University of Heidelberg (Dr. jur., 1990). Author: "Die endgültige freie Verfügung über die Einlage von Kapitalgesellschaftern," Heidelberg, 1991; "Die Verwertung von GmbH-Mänteln," BB 1988, 1197. Co-Author: "Ein neuer Anleihetyp: Zero-Bonds. Zivil- und bilanzrechtliche Probleme," ZIP 1985, 1169; "Die Rechtsnatur der Ein-Mann-Gründungsorganisation," GmbH-Rdsch., 1988, 373. Assistant Lecturer on Law, University of Heidelberg, 1985-1990. *Member:* German-American Lawyers Association. **LANGUAGES:** German and English.

ASSOCIATES

HANS-JOACHIM HELLMANN, LL.M., born Cologne, Germany, October 8, 1960; admitted, 1989, Germany. *Education:* Universities of Erlangen/Nürnberg and Cologne; University of Miami Law School (Master of Laws, 1990). *Member:* German-American Lawyers Association; Association Internationale des Jeunes Avocats; Studienvereinigung Kartellrecht. **LANGUAGES:** German, English and French.

BEATE JANKE, born Hildesheim, Germany, October 7, 1962; admitted, 1991, Germany. *Education:* University of Osnabrück. **LANGUAGES:** German, English and French.

HEINO RÜCK, born Stuttgart, Germany, August 9, 1960; admitted, 1993, Germany. *Education:* University of Heidelberg; University of Bristol (Diploma in English Legal Studies). **LANGUAGES:** German and English.

DR. STEPHAN SCHERER, born Wiesbaden, Germany, February 23, 1962; admitted, 1993, Germany. *Education:* University of Mainz (Dr. jur., 1991). Author: "Die Gläubigeranfechtung der Bezugsberechtigung und der Prämienzahlung beim Lebensversicherungsvertrag zu Rechten Dritter," Mainz, 1991. *Member:* German-Machine Tool and Tool Trade Association (Chairman, Junior Organization, 1986-1991). **LANGUAGES:** German and English.

DR. AXEL BERNINGER, born Baunatal, Germany, March 16, 1960; admitted, 1993, Germany. *Education:* University of Göttingen (Dr. jur., 1993). Author: "Die societas quoad sortem - Eine Einbringungsform im Personengesellschaftsrecht"; "Unterbeteiligung an einem GmbH-Anteil in zivilrechtlicher und steuerrechtlicher Sicht," together with Prof. Dr. Uwe Blaurock, GmbHR 1990, 11, 87; "Kapitalkonto und Sonderbetriebsvermögen des Kommanditisten bei der Anwendung von § 15 a EStG," together with Prof. Dr. Uwe Blaurock, JZ 1992, 614. Dipl.-FW. (Diploma in Tax Law, 1983), Assistant Lecturer on Law, University of Göttingen, 1989-1990. **LANGUAGES:** German and English.

DR. MARKUS R. KÖHLER, born Mannheim, Germany, October 27, 1965; admitted, 1994, Germany. *Education:* University of Mannheim (Dr.iur, 1991). Author: "Rechtsfragen des inländischen und grenzüberschreitenden Rundfunkwerberechts," Frankfurt/Main, 1992; "Rechtspflicht des Verbrauchers zur Nutzung des 'grünen Punkts.'" Co-Author with Prof. Dr. H.W. Arndt, NJW 1994, 1945 ff. Assistant Lecturer on Law, University of Mannheim, 1990-1993. *Member:* German Bar Association; German Association for the Protection of Industrial Property and Copyright Law. **LANGUAGES:** German, English, French and Italian.

CLAIRE BASQUE, born St. Cloud, France, May 23, 1962; admitted, 1992, France; 1994, Germany. *Education:* University of Paris (DESS, 1990). **LANGUAGES:** French and German.

Languages: German, English, Spanish and French

GERATS, HARTUNG & PARTNER

Established in 1906

HUMBOLDTSTRASSE 63-65
P.O. BOX 10 04 60
41004 MOENCHENGLADBACH
D-41061 MOENCHENGLADBACH, GERMANY
Telephone: 02161/13030
Telecopier: 02161/16052

General Practice. Civil Litigation, Commercial, Company, Corporate, National and International Banking and Securities Law, Antitrust and Unfair Competition, Criminal Law, Traffic Accidents, Divorce, Family and Labor Law.

MEMBERS OF FIRM

EGON GERATS, born Moenchengladbach, Germany, June 29, 1926; admitted, 1957, Germany. *Education:* Universities of Cologne and Bonn. **LANGUAGES:** German and English.

DR. WOLFGANG HARTUNG, born Magdeburg, Germany, September 6, 1933; admitted, 1964, Germany. *Education:* Universities of Cologne and Bonn (Doctor of Jurisprudence). Author: "Verfügungsbeschränkung bei ehelichem Hausrat," 1962; "Der Schutz des guten Glaubens bei den Verfügungsbeschränkungen des Gleichberechtigungsgesetzes," NJW 1959, 1020 f.; "Standesrecht quo vadis?" AnwBL. 1988, 37 f.; "Das anwaltliche Standesrecht - Eine Bestandsaufnahme -," AnwBL. 1988, 374 ff.; "Düsseldorfer Regeln - Ein Beitrag zum künftigen Berufsrecht der Rechtsanwälte -,"AnwBL. 1988, 516 ff. Member, Order of Merit of the Federal Republic of Germany, 1985—. *Member:* Rechtsanwaltskammer Düsseldorf (Member of the Presidency and Board). **LANGUAGES:** German and English.

DR. KLAUS JOACHIM HARTUNG, born Moenchengladbach, Germany, June 19, 1961; admitted, 1991, Germany. *Education:* University of Bonn (Doctor of Jurisprudence). Author: "Traded Security Options in the Federal Republic of Germany", Berlin, 1989; "Termin- und Differenzeinwand beim Optionsscheinhandel", BB 1989, 2411 ff.; "Termineinwand bei Warentermingeschäften an Auslandsbörsen", ZIP 1991, 1185 ff. With Bankhaus Hermann Lampe KG, 1990-1992. *Member:* German-American Lawyers' Association. **LANGUAGES:** German, English and French.

DR. GERRIT WOLFGANG HARTUNG, born Moenchengladbach, Germany, March 29, 1964; admitted, 1993, Germany. *Education:* University of Cologne (Doctor of Jurisprudence). Author: "Das anwaltliche Verbot des Versäumnisurteils," Bonn, Essen, 1991; "Die beamtenrechtliche Konkurrentenklage im Widerstreit der Meinungen," VR 1988, 45 f. **LANGUAGES:** German, English and French.

ASSOCIATE

HELGA HARTUNG, born Breslau, Germany, May 13, 1934; admitted, 1981, Germany. *Education:* Universities of Cologne and Bonn. **LANGUAGES:** German, English and French.

Languages: German, English and French.

HERZOG, MEYER, WILL

HAAGSTRAßE 12
47441 MOERS, GERMANY
Telephone: +49 2841 25207
Telefax: +49 2841 28384

Krefeld, Germany Office: Sollbrüggenstrasse 52, 47800 Krefeld. Telephone: +49 2151 589501. Telefax: +49 2151 598110.
Berlin, Germany Office: Schlüterstraße 54, 10629 Berlin. Telephone: +49 30 8857040. Telefax: +49 30 8824821.

General Practice, Commercial, Corporation, Securities, Property, Taxation, International and Unfair Law. Antitrust Law. Labour Law. Air Law.

MEMBERS OF FIRM

KLAUS KALL, born Rheinberg, Germany, January 29, 1947; admitted, 1981, Bonn. *Education:* University of Bonn (Qualification for Public Administration Law, 1981). Assistant Professor, Environmental Law, University of Essen, 1983. Corporate Counsel, B.A.D., Bonn, 1983. Attorney at Law, Moers, 1983. Member, Federal Committee of Environmental Affairs, Bonn, 1987. Treasurer, Institute of Environmental Auditors, Cologne, 1994. *Member:* German Bar Association. **LANGUAGES:** German, English

(This Listing Continued)

and French. **PRACTICE AREAS:** National and International Environmental Law including Awareness Training Cleanup; Audit Procedures.

(For Complete Biographical Data on all Personnel, see Professional Biographies at Krefeld, Germany)

BARDEHLE, PAGENBERG, DOST, ALTENBURG, FROHWITTER, GEISSLER & PARTNERS

GALILEIPLATZ 1
81679 MUNICH, GERMANY
Telephone: (89) 92 80 50
Telefax: (89) 98 97 63; 92 805 292

Mailing Address: P.O. Box 86 06 20, 81633

Paris, France Office: 7, Boulevard De Sébastopol, 75001. Telephone: (1) 40 28 07 25. Telefax: (1) 40 28 06 29.
Houston, Texas Office: Three Riverway, Suite 550, 77056. Telephone: (713) 621-07030. Fax: (713) 622-1624.
Düsseldorf, Germany Office: Xantener Str. 12, 40474 Düsseldorf. Telephone: (211) 47 81 30. Telefax: (211) 47 81 331.

Industrial and Intellectual Property Law, Patent, Trademark, Copyright, Design, Antitrust and Computer Law, Licensing and Unfair Competition.

FIRM PROFILE: The firm was established in 1978 as a combined partnership of attorneys and patent attorneys specialized exclusively in the field of industrial and intellectual property law and litigation before all German courts, licensing and prosecution before the European and the German Patent Office. Clients were primarily U.S., Japanese, French and German companies. In 1992, offices were founded in Paris, Düsseldorf and Houston with altogether 10 partners in the 4 offices and a total staff of approximately 90 legal and technical persons as well as office administrators.

PARTNERS

HEINZ BARDEHLE, born Berlin, Germany, October 4, 1920; admitted, 1956, Munich Patent Bar; 1978, European Patent Office. *Education:* Technical Universities of Stuttgart and Berlin (Dipl.-Ing., 1946). *Member:* German Bar of Patent Attorneys; FICPI; AIPPI; epi; GRUR. **LANGUAGES:** German, English and French. **PRACTICE AREAS:** German and International Industrial Property Law; Patent Prosecution; Electrical Engineering.

DR. JOCHEN PAGENBERG, born Bielefeld, Germany, May 27, 1941; admitted, 1973, Munich. *Education:* Universities of Hamburg and Lausanne; Harvard University (LL.M., 1973); University of Munich (Referendar, 1969; Assessor, 1972; Dr.jur., 1974). Executive Editor of the International Review of Industrial Property and Copyright Law Munich, 1973—. Author: "Nonobviousness in US and German Patent Law," Heymanns, 1975; "European Patent Convention," (Commentary Volume 5), Heymanns, 1984; "Licence Agreements," Heymanns, 9/1991. Co-Author: "Protection and Exploitation of Computer Programs," Otto Schmidt KG, 8/1993. *Member:* Max-Planck-Institute for International Patent Law Munich; German Society of Computer Law; AIPPI; LES; AIPLA; ALAI; USTA; ECTA; CLA; GALA; GRUR; German and American Chamber of Commerce. **LANGUAGES:** German, English and French. **PRACTICE AREAS:** German and International Industrial Property Law; Patent; Trade Mark; Copyright Litigation; Licensing; Antitrust and Unfair Competition Law; European Community Law; Computer Law.

DR. WOLFGANG A. DOST, born Altenburg, Germany, May 13, 1938; admitted, 1972, Munich Patent Bar; 1978, European Patent Office. *Education:* University of Mainz (Ph.D. Chemistry, 1967). Co-Author: "European Patent Law - EPC," Heymanns, 1979. *Member:* AIPPI; FICPI; GRUR; epi; Association of German Chemists. **LANGUAGES:** German, English and French. **PRACTICE AREAS:** German and International Industrial Property Law; Patent Prosecution; Patent Litigation; Licensing; Chemistry including Biochemistry and Gene Technology.

UDO W. ALTENBURG, born Bitterfeld, Germany, April 28, 1942; admitted, 1972, Munich Patent Bar; 1978, European Patent Office. *Education:* Technical Universities of Hannover and Stuttgart (Dipl.-Phys., 1967); Universities of Würzburg and Frankfurt. Member, Max-Planck-Institute for International Patent Law, 1972-1974. *Member:* AIPPI; LES; FICPI; epi; GRUR; PAK. **LANGUAGES:** German, English and French. **PRACTICE AREAS:** German and International Industrial Property Law; Patent Prosecution; Patent Litigation; Licensing; Physics; Mechanical Engineering; Electronics.

(This Listing Continued)

BARDEHLE, PAGENBERG, DOST, ALTENBURG, FROHWITTER, GEISSLER & PARTNERS, Munich—Continued

BERNHARD FROHWITTER, born Wuppertal, Germany, September 24, 1944; admitted, 1980, Munich and European Patent Office. *Education:* German Air Force University, Munich (Dipl.-Ing., 1968); University of Munich(Assessor, 1980). Licensing Consultant. *Member:* German Association of Patentingenieure and Patentassessoren (VPP); AIPLA, German Association for the Protection of Industrial and Copyright Law (GRUR); LES. *LANGUAGES:* German and English. *PRACTICE AREAS:* German and International Industrial Property Law; Patent Prosecution; Contracts; Licensing; Antitrust; Unfair Competition and Infringement Litigation; Arbitration and Mediation; Acquisition and Merger of Technology Producing Companies.

DR. BERNHARD H. GEISSLER, born Berlin, Germany, March 16, 1939; admitted, 1971, Wiesbaden; 1978, European Patent Office; 1981, District of Columbia, USA. *Education:* Technical University of Munich (Dipl.-Phys., 1963); University of Munich (Dr.jur., 1971); George Washington University (M.C.L., 1980). Author: "Scope of Protection for Chemical Products," Heymanns, 1972. Co-Author "Protection and Exploitation of Computer Programs," Otto Schmidt KG, 8/1993. Co-Author: "License Agreements," Heymanns, 9/1991. Member, Max-Planck-Institute for International Patent Law Munich, 1968-1971. *Member:* AIPPI; AIPLA; ABA; epi; LES; FICPI; GRUR. *LANGUAGES:* German, English and French. *PRACTICE AREAS:* German and International Industrial Property Law; Patent Prosecution and Litigation; Licensing; Computer Law; Physics; Mechanical Engineering; Computer Technology.

JÜRGEN ROST, born Stettin, Germany, May 12, 1936; admitted, 1968, Munich Patent Bar; 1978, European Patent Office. *Education:* Technical University Aachen (Dipl.-Ing., 1963). *Member:* FICPI; epi; GRUR. *LANGUAGES:* German, English and French. *PRACTICE AREAS:* German and International Industrial Property Law; Patent Prosecution and Litigation; Mechanical Engineering.

PETER MUNZINGER, born Munich, Germany, August 11, 1954; admitted, 1982, Munich. *Education:* Universities of Munich and Berlin (Referendar, 1978; Assessor, 1982). Puma, Head of Patent and Trademark Division,1985-1992. *Member:* Munich Bar; GRUR. *LANGUAGES:* German and English. *PRACTICE AREAS:* German and Industrial Property Law; Trademark Prosecution and Litigation; Licensing; Unfair Competition Law.

DR. PETER DOSTERSCHILL, born Hannover, Germany, January 14, 1948; admitted, 1986, European Patent Office; 1993, Munich Patent Bar. *Education:* Technical University of Munich (Dipl.-Ing., 1973; Dipl.-Wirtsch.-Ing., 1975; Dr.rer.pol., 1979). Author: "Principles and reform of the Spanish Patent Law," Heymanns, 1982; "Spanish Patent Law," edition für internationale Wirtschaft, Heymanns, 1989. Member, Max-Planck-Institute for International Patent Law, 1976-1980. *Member:* epi, German Association of Patent-Engineers. *LANGUAGES:* German, Spanish, English, Portuguese and French. *PRACTICE AREAS:* German and International Industrial Property Law; Patent Prosecution; Electronical Engineering.

ASSOCIATES

DR. TATJANA KOWAL-WOLK, born Mannheim, Germany January 29, 1951; admitted, 1982, Munich. *Education:* Universities of Munich (Referendar, 1975); Heidelberg (Assessor, 1979; Dr.jur., 1982). Author: "Soviet Citizenship - Acquisition and Loss," Europäische Hochschulschriften, Peter Lang GmbH Verlag, 1982. Research Assistant of the Office of Legal Affairs of the UN, New York, 1976. *Member:* American Society of International Law; ALAI; Max-Planck-Institute for International Patent Law, Munich; GRUR; Munich Bar. *LANGUAGES:* German, English, French and Russian. *PRACTICE AREAS:* German and International Industrial Property Law; Patent Litigation; Licensing; Antitrust and Unfair Competition Law; European Law; Computer Law.

CHRISTINE ESCHENBURG-SCHRICKER, born Berlin, Germany, October 3, 1939; admitted, 1982, Munich. *Education:* University of Munich (Referendar, 1964; Assessor, 1968). *LANGUAGES:* German, French, Italian and English. *PRACTICE AREAS:* German and International Trade Mark Law; Unfair Competition Law; Trade Mark and Unfair Competition Litigation.

WALTER HOFFMANN, born Giesshuebel, Germany, November 6, 1927; admitted, 1967, Munich Patent Bar; 1978, European Patent Office. *Education:* Technical University of Darmstadt (Dipl.-Phys., 1952). Director

(This Listing Continued)

IBM Germany, Head of Patent Operations, 1967-1984. *Member:* epi; AIPPI; GRUR; FICPI; German Association of Electrical Engineers; Information Technology Society. *LANGUAGES:* German and English. *PRACTICE AREAS:* German and International Industrial Property Law; Patent Prosecution; Litigation; Licensing; Electronics.

ANDREAS RAUBENHEIMER, born 1960; admitted, 1991, Munich. *Education:* Universities of Tübingen (Referendar, 1988); Aix-Marseille III; Stuttgart (Assessor, 1991). *Member:* Munich Bar. *LANGUAGES:* German, French and English. *PRACTICE AREAS:* Unfair Competition Law; Computer Law.

PETER K. HESS, born Bremen, Germany, May 13, 1962; admitted, 1992, Munich Patent Bar. *Education:* University of Hannover (Dipl.-Phys, 1987). *Member:* FICPI; AIPPI; epi. *LANGUAGES:* German, English and Hungarian. *PRACTICE AREAS:* European and German Patent Prosecution; Infringement Litigation; Licensing; Laser Physics; Optoelectronics; Semiconductor Physics.

DR. ALBRECHT DEHMEL, born Wolfenbüttel, Germany, September 24, 1957; admitted, 1994, Munich Patent Bar and European Patent Office. *Education:* Technical University of Munich (Dipl.-Chem.); University of Cologne (Dr.rer.nat.). *LANGUAGES:* German, English, Italian and Dutch. *PRACTICE AREAS:* Patent Prosecution; Patent Litigation; Chemistry including Biochemistry; Gene Technology and Immunology.

KLAUS KOHLMANN, born Eichstätt, Germany, July 13, 1961; admitted, 1993, Munich. *Education:* Legal studies University of Munich; Electrical Engineering Technical College of Munich (Dipl.-Ing. FH 1991). *LANGUAGES:* German and English. *PRACTICE AREAS:* German and International Property Law; Patent Prosecution and Litigation; Electrical Engineering.

KARSTEN BRANDT, born Marburg, Germany, July 26, 1963; admitted, 1993, Munich. *Education:* Universities of Erlangen-Nürnberg, Würzburg and Geneva (Referendar, 1990); Munich (Assessor, 1993). *Member:* Max-Planck-Institute for International Patent Law, Munich; Munich Bar; GRUR; AIPPI; LES. *LANGUAGES:* German, English and French. *PRACTICE AREAS:* German and International Industrial Property Law; Licensing.

JOHANNES HESELBERGER, born Neukirchen, Germany, August 6, 1964; admitted, 1994, Munich. *Education:* University of Regensburg (Dipl.-Phys., 1990). *LANGUAGES:* German and English. *PRACTICE AREAS:* German and International Industrial Property Law; German and European Patent Prosecution; Infringement Litigation; Licensing; Magnetism and Thin Films Physics.

(For Biographical Data of the Düsseldorf, Germany Personnel, see Professional Biographies at Düsseldorf, Germany and Paris, France Personnel, see Professional Biographies at Paris, France)

BEISSWINGERT & PARTNER

Established in 1930

WIDENMAYERSTRASSE 28
80538 MUNICH, GERMANY
Telephone: (089) 290816-0
Cable Address: "Nomosrecht München"
Telex: 05-22557 recht d
Fax: (089) 290816-60; 290816-61; 290816-62

Leipzig, Germany Office: Johannisallee 20, 04317. Telephone: (0341) 2619902; 275438; 275444. Telex: 512176 eweka dd. Telefax: (0341) 275593.

General Practice. International, Tax, Probate, Antitrust, Unfair Competition, Patent, Copyright, Trademark, Family and International Transport Law.

FIRM PROFILE: *The firm was established in 1930 in Berlin by Oskar Möhring, who in the beginning practised law mainly as a trial lawyer, and later often became administrator in important bankruptcy and arrangement proceedings. In 1945, due to the post-war confusion, the firm moved to Munich and later on specialized in the main fields of business and commercial law. Möhring died in 1984. In July 1990, the firm opened its office in Leipzig, then East Germany. Today it consists of six partners and four associates. Its symbol is the elephant, which stands for sensitivity and the power of knowledge.*

(This Listing Continued)

MEMBERS OF FIRM

DR. ROLF BEISSWINGERT, born Stuttgart, Germany, July 6, 1934; admitted, 1961, Munich. *Education:* Universities of Cologne, Geneva and Munich (Doctor of Law); Institut des Hautes Etudes Internationales, Geneva. *Author:* "Die Einwirkung bundesstaatlicher Kompetenzverschiebungen auf völkerrechtliche Verträge" (State Succession with Respect to Treaties in Federal States), Munich, 1960; "Entschädigungsansprüche für enteignende Eingriffe in Betriebsgrundstücke" (Claims for Compensation for Expropriation of Commercial Property), *Der Betriebsberater,* 1961; "Handelsgeschäfte mit Frankreich" (Commercial Transactions with France), Stuttgart, 1969. Co-Author: with Dr. Möhring and Dr. Klingelhöffer, "Vermögensverwaltung in Vormundschafts-und Nachlaβsachen" ("Administration in Family and Estate Law"), Verlag Recht und Wirtschaft, Heidelberg, 7th edition 1992. *Member:* German Bar Association; German-American Chamber of Commerce; Association for the Protection of Industrial Property and Copyright Law. *LANGUAGES:* German, English, French and Italian.

DR. SVEN ILLERT, born Hanau, Germany, April 2, 1935; admitted, 1969, Rheinland-Pfalz; 1970, Düsseldorf; 1973, Munich. *Education:* University of Munich; University of Mainz (Doctor of Law). *Author:* "Der Preisvergleich mit empfohlenen Endverbraucherpreisen" (Price Comparison with Recommended final Consumers Prices), published by Carl Heymanns-Verlag, Cologne, 1965. *Member:* German Bar Association; Association for the Protection of Industrial Property and Copyright Law. *LANGUAGES:* German, English and French.

DR. DIETRICH BERNSTORFF, born Selchow/Pommern, Germany, June 27, 1937; admitted, 1969, Hamburg; 1973, Munich. *Education:* University of Hamburg (Doctor of Law). *Author:* "Personengesellschaften auf mangelhafter Vertragsgrundlage im deutschen, italienischen und amerikanischen Recht" (Partnerships on Imperfect Contractual Basis in German, Italian and American Law), Hamburg, 1969. Co-Author with Professor Zweigert, "Probleme des Statuts fur Europäische Aktiengesellschaften," (Problems of the Statute Concerning European Stock Companies), Brussels, 1972. Executive Officer at the Superior Revenue Authorities in Hamburg, 1971-1973. Research Associate, Max-Planck-Institute of Foreign and International Private Law, 1969-1973. *Member:* Association for the Exchange of Ideas between German and Italian Lawyers; German Association of Transport Law. *LANGUAGES:* German, English and Italian.

DR. HANS KLINGELHÖFFER, born Darmstadt, Germany, December 18, 1942; admitted, 1972, Munich. *Education:* University of Munich (Doctor of Law); Institute of Foreign Languages in Munich. *Author:* "Erbverträge im deutsch-französischen Verhältnis" (Contractsof Inheritance in German-French Relations"), 1971; "Reform des französischen Kindschaftsrechts" (Reform of Filiation Law in France), 1972, Rabels Z; "Die Ehesoheidung des Unternehmers" (The Divorce of a Business Owner), Heidelberg, 1992. Co-Author: with Dr. Möhring and Dr. Beisswingert, "Vermögensverwaltung in Vormundschafts-und Nachlaβsachen" ("Administration in Family and Estate Law"), Heidelberg, 7th edition 1992. Research Associate, Max-Planck-Institute of Foreign and International Private Law, 1970-1972. *Member:* German-French Lawyers' Association; German-Italian Lawyers' Association. *LANGUAGES:* German, English, French and Italian.

DR. MICHAEL ZAPP, born Stuttgart, Germany, May 19, 1954; admitted, 1982, Munich. *Education:* Universities of Tübingen and Munich (Doctor of Law); Institute of Politics and Public Law, Munich. *Author:* "Privatrechtliche Voraussetzungen und Privatrechtliche Wirkungen der Baugenehmigung" ("Requirements and Effects of the Building Permit under Private Law"), Munich, 1983. Research Associate, Institute of Politics and Public Law, Munich, 1979-1981. *Member:* German Bar Association; German Association of Transport Law; Young Lawyers International Association. *LANGUAGES:* German, English and French.

MARTINA PRINZ-KLINGELHÖFFER, born Solingen, Germany, May 10, 1954; admitted, 1982, Munich. *Education:* Universities of Göttingen and Freiburg. Research Associate, Institute of Foreign and International Private Law, University of Freiburg. *LANGUAGES:* German and English.

DR. MARTIN MIEBACH, born Bochum, Germany, November 20, 1959; admitted, 1988, Munich. *Education:* Universities of Bochum, Geneva and Munich (Dr. of Law, 1989). *Author:* "Zur Willkür- und Abwägungskontrolle des Bundesverfassungsgerichts bei der Verfassungsbeschwerde gegen Gerichtsurteile," (Constitutional Complaints against Decrees - Arbitrary and Weighing Control of the Federal Constitutional Court"), Munich, 1989. *Member:* German Bar Association. *LANGUAGES:* German, English, French and Italian.

(This Listing Continued)

DR. HEIKO CARRIE, born Münster, Germany, May 21, 1962; admitted, 1994, Munich. *Education:* Universities of Bonn and Heidelberg (Doctor of Law); Institute of Public Law and Public International Law, Heidelberg. *Author:* "Das diplomatische Asyl im gegenwärtigen Völkerrecht" (Diplomatic Asylum in Current International Law), Baden-Baden, 1994. *Member:* German Bar Association. *LANGUAGES:* German, English and French.

Languages: German, English, French and Italian.

BEITEN BURKHARDT MITTL & WEGENER

Rechtsanwälte

LEOPOLDSTRASSE 236
D-80807 MUNICH, GERMANY
Telephone: (089) 35065-00
Telefax: (089) 35065-123

Berlin, Germany Office: Kurfürstenstrasse 72-74, D-10787 Berlin. Telephone: (0 30) 264 71-0. Telefax: (0 30) 264 71-123.
Frankfurt/Main, Germany Office: Arndtstrasse 28, D-60325 Frankfurt/Main. Telephone: (0 69) 75 60 95-0. Telefax: (0 69) 75 60 95-12.
Nürnberg, Germany Office: Obere Turnstrasse 8, D-90429 Nürnberg. Telephone: (09 11) 2 79 71-0. Telefax: (09 11) 2 79 71-99.
Leipzig, Germany Office: Käthe-Kollwitz-Strasse 54, D-04109 Leipzig. Telephone: (03 41) 4 77 25 97. Telefax: (03 41) 4 77 25 99.
Potsdam, Germany Office: Heinrich-Mann-Allee 105 B, D-14473 Potsdam. Telephone: (0331) 33 43 06. Telefax: (0331) 33 43 29.
Hof, Germany Office: Oberer Torplatz 1, D-95028 Hof. Telephone: (09281) 80 23. Telefax: (09281) 1 65 69.
Plauen, Germany Office: Lindenstrasse 5, D-08523 Plauen. Telephone: (03741) 22 35 11; 22 49 62. Telefax: (03741) 22 49 62.
New York, New York Office: 215 East 73rd Street, New York, NY 10021. Telephone: (212) 570-2141. Telefax: (212) 734-7011.
London, England Office: Swedenborg House, 21 Bloomsbury Way, London, WC1A 2TH. Telephone: (0171) 2 42 44 66. Telefax: (0171) 2 42 44 67.
Moscow, Russia Office: Ul. Alekseja Tolstovo D.30/1, 103001 Moscow. Telephone and Telefax: (095) 202 37 60; 290 05 56.
Prague, Czech Republic Office: Na Bojišti 24, 120 00 Prague 2. Telephone: (2) 24 91 5808. Telefax: (2) 24 91 5804.
Budapest, Hungary Office: József Nádor Tér 9, H-1051 Budapest. Telephone: (1) 2 66 18 10. Telefax: (1) 2 66 18 11.
Hong Kong Office: 605 B, Sixth Floor, Peregrine Tower, Lippo Centre, 89 Queensway. Telephone: (852) 2524 6468. Telefax: (852) 2524 7028.
Beijing, People's Republic of China Office: Unit 10, 29th Floor, Jing Guang Centre, Hu Jia Lou, Chao Yang Qu, 100020. Telephone: (86-1) 501 4569; 501 3388 Ext. 2910. Telefax: (86-1) 501 3034.

Commercial Law, Company Law, M & A, Joint Ventures, Finance, Banking, Leasing, Domestic and International Tax, Antitrust, EC Law, Real Property and Private Construction, Electronic Data Processing (Protection and Licensing), Media, Publishing, Unfair Competition, Trademarks, Copyright, Labour, General and Special Administrative Law Particularly Public Construction and Planning Regulations and Public International Law, Environmental Law, Agricultural Law, Privatization and Restitution (former GDR), Probate, Family and Estate Planning, Insolvency and Sports, Insurance, Automobile Accidents and Injuries.

FIRM PROFILE: BEITEN BURKHARDT MITTL & WEGENER is a nation-wide and international law firm with 108 lawyers. The firm's head office is in Munich. All the firm's offices provide a comprehensive range of services in the main areas of civil and commercial law.

MEMBERS OF FIRM

GÜNTHER MITTL, born Munich, 1931; admitted, 1965, Munich; 1991, Plauen. Licensed Specialist for Tax Law. *Education:* Universities of Munich and Würzburg (law degree, 1955). Various publications on Tax Law. General Counsel, Bayerische Landesbuchstelle (Auditors and Tax Advisors), 1960-1965. *Member:* Institute of Tax Advisors; German-American Chamber of Commerce. *LANGUAGES:* German and English. *PRACTICE AREAS:* Company Law; Acquisitions and Sales; Restructuring; Tax Planning; Pensions; Financial Services; Probate and Family Law.

JÜRGEN BURKHARDT, born Konstanz, 1940; admitted, 1967, Germany. *Education:* Universities of Munich (law degree, 1963) and Zurich (Swiss law degree, 1966; Dr. jur., 1966). With Axel Springer Verlag, 1965-

(This Listing Continued)

BEITEN BURKHARDT MITTL & WEGENER,
Munich—Continued

1968. In-house counsel with Gruner+Jahr, Munich, 1969-1971. Member: Advisory Board, Vogel Medien GmbH & Co. KG, Würzburg; Supervisory Board, rotring international, Hamburg; Legal Committee, German Association of Publishers (VDZ); German-American Chamber of Commerce. Lecturer, Cartel, Competition and Media Law, University of Erlangen-Nürnberg, 1990—. *LANGUAGES:* German, English and Italian. *PRACTICE AREAS:* Company Law; Acquisitions and Sales; Restructuring; Press Law; Publishing and Radio; Cartels; Probate and Family Law.

GERHARD BEITEN, born Wuppertal, 1939; admitted, 1968, Germany. *Education:* Universities of Cologne, Paris and Munich (law degree, 1963; Dr. jur., 1966). Lecturer on Tax Law, University of Cologne, 1963-1964. District Director, German Shareholders' Protective Association, 1971-1979. Member, Supervisory Board, Augsburger Kammgarn-Spinnerei, Linde, Industriewerke Karlsruhe-Augsburg. *LANGUAGES:* German, English and French. *PRACTICE AREAS:* Company Law; Acquisitions and Sales; Restructuring; International Tax Planning; Pensions; Media and Entertainment; Video and Television.

CHRISTIAN-MICHAEL STEVER, born Berlinchen, 1939; admitted, 1968, Germany. *Education:* Universities of Freiburg, Santo Domingo, Paris and Munich (law degree, 1963). Member of Trust Advisory Board, USIF Real Estate, 1972-1979 and 1991—; Global Natural Resources, Inc., 1983-1987; MidAmerican Technologies, Inc., 1987-1991. *LANGUAGES:* German, English, French and Spanish. *PRACTICE AREAS:* Company Law; Acquisitions and Sales; Restructuring; Financial Services.

DIRK-REINER MARTENS, born Berlin, 1942; admitted, 1969, Germany. *Education:* Universities of Paris, Munich (law degree, 1966) and Hamburg (Dr. jur., 1971). Author: "German Civil Procedure and the Implementation of the Hague Evidence Convention." *Member:* International Bar Association; FIBA International Basketball Federation (Deputy Secretary General); South Western Legal Foundation (Advisory Board); American Arbitration Association, Court of Arbitration for Sport, Lausanne; German-American Jurists' Association. *LANGUAGES:* German, English, French and Italian. *PRACTICE AREAS:* Company Law; Acquisitions and Sales; Restructuring; Sports.

FRANK-PETER REISSINGER, born Munich, 1944; admitted, 1973, Germany. *Education:* Universities of Munich, Kiel and Erlangen (law degree, 1969; Dr. jur., 1974). *LANGUAGES:* German and English. *PRACTICE AREAS:* Labour and Employment.

CHRISTIAN MELCHER, born Berlin, 1943; admitted, 1972, Germany. *Education:* Universities of Munich, Bonn, Cologne (law degree, 1967) and Regensburg (Dr. jur., 1970); Columbia University, New York (1968). Research Assistant, Institute of International Private Law, University of Bonn, 1968-1970. Author: "The Computer Leasing and Dealer Industry" (1989). *LANGUAGES:* German, English and French. *PRACTICE AREAS:* Computers and Software; Financial Services.

CHRISTOPH FRHR. VON HUTTEN, born Würzburg, 1946; admitted, 1977, Germany. *Education:* Universities of Heidelberg, Würzburg and Munich (law degree, 1972; Dr. jur., 1976). Author: "The Public Broadcasting Networks and the Audio-Visual Market," 1976. *LANGUAGES:* German and English. *PRACTICE AREAS:* Company Law; Acquisitions and Sales; Restructuring; Media and Entertainment; Video and Television; Press Law; Publishing and Radio; Unfair Competition; Copyrights; Advertising and Marketing.

HARTMUT SPINDLER, (—1993), born Bremen, 1940; admitted, 1971, Germany. *Education:* Universities of Geneva and Munich (law degree, 1967; Dr.jur., 1972); University of Chicago Law School (M.C.L., 1968). Staff Member: University of Munich, Institute for Comparative Law, 1966-1967; Max-Planck-Institute for Foreign and International Patent, Copyright and Competition Law, 1969-1972. *Member:* German-American Jurists' Association. *LANGUAGES:* German, English and French. *PRACTICE AREAS:* Company Law; Acquisitions and Sales; Restructuring; Media and Entertainment; Video and Television; Cartels.

WINFRIED KLÖPPER, born Hanover, 1942; admitted, 1974, Germany; 1988, Licensed also as Wirschaftsprüfer (Chartered Accountant). *Education:* Bankkaufmann (banking diploma, 1966); Universities of Göttingen and Munich (law degree, 1974; Dr. jur., 1978). Lecturer, Institute for European and International Commercial Law, University of Munich and Max-Planck-Institute for Foreign and International Patent, Copyright and Competition Law. Author: "Current Legal Advice to Enterprises" in: Handbook for Lawyers, 1989; "The New Hungarian Legislation," 1989 and various

(This Listing Continued)

ous publications. *Member:* British-German Jurists' Association; Indo-German Chamber of Commerce; Südosteuropa-Gesellschaft; Lehndorff United Properties, Canada (Advisory Board). *LANGUAGES:* German and English. *PRACTICE AREAS:* Company Law; Acquisitions and Sales; Restructuring; Tax Planning; Pensions; Financial Services; Insolvency Liquidations.

JACK SCHIFFER, born Munich, 1948; admitted, 1975, Germany. *Education:* Universities of Paris and Munich (law degree, 1973) and Berlin (Dr. jur., 1976). Licensed also as Steuerberater (Tax Advisor), 1979. With Deutsche Treuhand-Gesellschaft, Frankfurt, a.M., 1975-1977. *LANGUAGES:* German, English, French and Italian. *PRACTICE AREAS:* Company Law; Acquisitions and Sales; Restructuring; Computers and Software; Unfair Competition; Copyrights; Advertising and Marketing; Insolvency; Liquidations.

MAX JOSEF BÖCK, born Augsburg, 1950; admitted, 1977, Germany. *Education:* Universities of Salzburg and Munich (law degree, 1973; Dr. jur., 1980). Research Assistant, Technical University of Munich, Institute for Private and Patent Law, 1977-1980. *LANGUAGES:* German and English. *PRACTICE AREAS:* Real Estate; Construction Law; Expropriation and Restitution.

REINHARD GAERTNER, born Trier, 1954; admitted, 1984, Germany. *Education:* University of Mainz (law degree, 1980; Dr. jur., 1984). *Member:* Legal Committee, German Association of Publishers (VDZ); German Association for the Protection of Industrial Property and Copyright (GRUR); Association Littéraire et Artistique Internationale (ALAI); Deutsche Landesgruppe. *LANGUAGES:* German and English. *PRACTICE AREAS:* Press Law; Publishing and Radio; Computers and Software; Unfair Competition; Copyrights; Advertising and Marketing; Cartels.

ALEXIUS LEUCHTEN, born Düsseldorf, 1948; admitted, 1978, Germany. *Education:* Universities of Würzburg, Hamburg and Munich (law degree, 1972; Dr. jur., 1979). Licensed specialist for Labour Law, 1988. Assistant Lecturer, Institute for Civil Law, University of Augsburg, 1976-1978. General Counsel, Adidas Sportschuhfabriken Adi Dassler KG, Herzogenaurach, Germany, 1979-1981. Author: "Proviso of Cancellation and time limitation of employment conditions, particularly commission plans." *Member:* Association of Licensed Specialists for Labour Law (DAV); International Bar Association (IBA). *LANGUAGES:* German, English, French and Spanish. *PRACTICE AREAS:* Labour and Employment.

BERNHARD VON LINSTOW, born Schwarzenbach, 1944; admitted, 1971, Germany. *Education:* Universities of Marburg and Munich (law degree, 1968; Dr. jur., 1973). Licensed also as Steuerberater (Tax Advisor), 1976. Publications in the field of Unfair Competition and Taxation. Lectures on Licensing and Taxation, German Academy for Lawyers. *Member:* German Association for the Protection of Industrial Property and Copyright (GRUR); Licensing Executives Society (LES). *LANGUAGES:* German and English. *PRACTICE AREAS:* Press Law; Publishing and Radio; Unfair Competition; Copyrights; Advertising and Marketing; Trademarks; Computers and Software; Trademarks.

FRIEDERIKE BAHR, born Hachenburg, 1947; admitted, 1976, Germany. *Education:* Universities of Münster, Erlangen and Munich (law degree, 1972). *Member:* German Association for the Protection of Industrial Property and Copyright (GRUR); European Communities Trademark Association (ECTA). *LANGUAGES:* German, English and Italian. *PRACTICE AREAS:* Press Law; Publishing and Radio; Unfair Competition; Copyrights; Advertising and Marketing; Trademarks.

RAYMUND BREHMENKAMP, born Essen, 1956; admitted, 1985, Germany. *Education:* Universities of Freiburg/Breisgau, Munich and Bonn (law degree, 1981); Law studies at the University for Administrative Sciences, Speyer and training at the Korean-German Chamber of Commerce and Industry, Seoul. *LANGUAGES:* German and English. *PRACTICE AREAS:* Press Law; Publishing and Radio; Unfair Competition; Copyrights; Advertising and Marketing.

HOLGER PERES, born Koblenz, 1954; admitted, 1989, Germany. *Education:* University of Munich (law degree, 1979; Dr. jur., 1989). Research Assistant, Institute for Criminal Law, University of Munich, 1981-1982. Assistant Lecturer, 1982—, and Lecturer, Private Commercial and Corporate Law, 1989—, University of Munich. *LANGUAGES:* German, English and French. *PRACTICE AREAS:* Company Law; Acquisitions and Sales; Restructuring; Financial Services; Probate and Family Law; Sports.

MICHAEL HERTSLET, born Halle, 1946; admitted, 1976, Germany; 1986, as Avocat à la Cour de Paris. *Education:* Universities of Heidelberg, Paris and Munich (law degree, 1971; Dr.jur., 1976); Common Market Certificate, 1986. Author: "Frankfurt Commentary on French Cartel Law,"

(This Listing Continued)

1989. *Member:* Munich and Paris Bar Association. *LANGUAGES:* German, French and English.

HANS-JÜRGEN SCHROTH, born Wiesbaden, 1944; admitted, 1972, Germany. *Education:* Universities of Munich, Heidelberg, Cologne and Bonn (law degree, 1968; Dr. jur., 1971); University of Exeter, England (Ph.D., 1980). Lecturer, University of Exeter, England, 1974-1978; Institute for European Law, Saarbrücken, 1978-1986. Habilitation (University of Giessen, 1992). Author: "Economic Offenses in EEC Law," 1983; "Liability of Undertakings," 1992. *Member:* British-German Jurists' Association; German-French Jurists' Association. *LANGUAGES:* German, French and English. *PRACTICE AREAS:* Company Law; Acquisitions and Sales; Restructuring; Financial Services; Cartels; European Community Law.

ANGELICA VON DER DECKEN, born Hamburg, 1954; admitted, 1981, Germany. *Education:* Universities of Freiburg, Munich and Hamburg (law degree, 1978). *Member:* German Association for the Protection of Industrial Property and Copyright (GRUR); European Communities Trademark Association (ECTA). *LANGUAGES:* German and English. *PRACTICE AREAS:* Press Law; Publishing and Radio; Unfair Competition; Copyrights; Advertising and Marketing; Trademarks.

CHRISTOPH KUHMANN, born Düsseldorf, 1955; admitted, 1988, Germany. *Education:* Universities of Münster, Lausanne and Munich (law degree, 1980; Dr. jur., 1989); Columbia University School of Law, New York (LL.M., 1984). Staff Member, Max Planck Institute for Foreign and International Patent, Copyright and Competition Law, 1986-1988. Author: "The Protection of Applied Art under German and American Copyright Law," 1991. *Member:* German-American Jurists' Association. *LANGUAGES:* German, English and French. *PRACTICE AREAS:* Company Law; Acquisitions and Sales; Restructuring; Media and Entertainment; Video and Television.

GÜNTHER GREWE, born Straussdorf/Oberbayern, 1943; admitted, 1975, Germany; 1977, Steuerberater (Tax Advisor) in Germany; 1979, Certified Public Accountant in New York and California; 1981, Wirtschaftsprüfer (Chartered Accountant) in Germany. *Education:* Universities of Cologne (law degree, 1968), Frankfurt, a.M. (Dr. jur., 1978) and Berkeley, California (MBA, 1971; Dr., 1976). With major German and U.S. accounting firms in Munich, San Francisco and New York, 1976-1982. *Member:* German American Jurists' Association; Institute of Certified Public Auditors in Germany (IDW); American Institute of Certified Public Accountants; New York State Society of Certified Public Accountants; The California Society of Certified Public Accountants. *LANGUAGES:* German and English. *PRACTICE AREAS:* International Tax Planning; Pensions.

MICHAEL WALTHER, born Minden, 1959; admitted, 1987, Germany. *Education:* Universities of Erlangen and Munich (law degree, 1984). *Member:* Forschungsinstitut für Wirtschaftsverfassung und Wettbewerb e.V. *LANGUAGES:* German and English. *PRACTICE AREAS:* Company Law; Acquisitions and Sales; Restructuring; Financial Services; Cartels; Insolvency; Liquidations.

PETER WALTL, born Munich, 1957; admitted, 1986, Germany. *Education:* Universities of Munich and Berlin (law degree, 1983; Dr. jur., 1990). Licensed also as Steuerberater (Tax Advisor), 1994. Author: "Library and Know-How Collection," 1989; "Legal Aspects of Computer Purchase," 1991. Editorship NJW Computer Report, 1991—. *Member:* German Association for Information Technology and Law. *LANGUAGES:* German and English. *PRACTICE AREAS:* Computers and Software; Unfair Competition; Copyrights; Advertising and Marketing.

OTTO GASSNER, born Starnberg, 1952; admitted, 1988, Germany. *Education:* University of Munich (law degree, 1978; Dr.jur., 1981). Research Assistant, Institute for European and International Commercial Law, University of Munich and Max-Plank-Institute for Foreign and International Patent, Copyright and Competition Law, 1981-1987. Lecturer for Private Law, University of Munich, 1985. In-house Counsel, Legal Department, Merck, Finck & Co., Private Bankers, 1987-1989. Visiting Attorney with Wilmer, Cutler & Pickering, Washington, D.C.,1989. General Counsel, Merck, Finck & Co., Private Bankers, 1990-1993. *LANGUAGES:* German and English. *PRACTICE AREAS:* Company Law; Acquisitions and Sales; Restructuring; Financial Services; Real Estate; Construction Law.

WOLF-D. SCHOEPE, born Essen, 1956; admitted, 1986, Germany. *Education:* Bankkaufmann (banking diploma, 1977); Universities of Munich and Speyer (law degree, 1983). Trainee with Mershon, Sawyer, Johnston, Dunwody & Cole, Miami, 1985-1986. *Member:* German Association for the Protection of Industrial Property and Copyright (GRUR). *LANGUAGES:* German and English. *PRACTICE AREAS:* Media and Enter-

(This Listing Continued)

tainment; Video and Television; Press law; Publishing and Radio; Unfair Competition; Copyrights; Advertising and Marketing.

CHRISTIAN V. SYDOW, born Hamburg, 1960; admitted, 1991, Germany. *Education:* Universities of Heidelberg, Hamburg, Freiburg/Breisgau (law degree, 1986). Trainee, Nagashima & Ohno, Tokyo, 1989-1990. *LANGUAGES:* German and English. *PRACTICE AREAS:* Company Law; Acquisitions and Sales; Restructuring.

ERNST LINDL, born Munich, 1961; admitted, 1991, Germany. *Education:* Universities of Munich and Berlin (law degree, 1987; Dr. jur., 1992); University of Munich (MA, Political Science, German Literature, 1988). Author: "Labour Safety Law. The Council Directive on the Approximation of the Laws of the Member States relating to Machinery," 1992. *LANGUAGES:* German, English and French. *PRACTICE AREAS:* Company Law; Acquisitions and Sales; Restructuring; European Community Law; Insolvency; Liquidations.

KÁLMÁN LÁSZLÓ, born Hatvan, 1946; admitted, 1974, Hungary; 1990, Germany. *Education:* Universities of Budapest and Bonn (law degree, 1971 (Budapest), 1985 (Bonn); Dr. jur., 1972). Author: "Freedom of Contract between State Enterprises," 1974; "Paternity Suits," 1978. *LANGUAGES:* Hungarian and German. *PRACTICE AREAS:* Company Law; Acquisitions and Sales; Restructuring.

RALF BUSCH, born Ostbevern, 1957; admitted, 1992, Germany. *Education:* University of Freiburg (law degree, 1984; Dr. jur., 1993). Staff Member, University of Freiburg, Institute for Foreign and International Private Law, 1988-1991. *LANGUAGES:* German and English. *PRACTICE AREAS:* Labour and Employment.

JÖRG KRETSCHMER, born Stuttgart, 1958; admitted, 1992, Germany. *Education:* Universities of Freiburg (law degree, 1984; Dr. jur., 1992) and Illinois, College of Law, Champaign (LL.M., 1990). Research Assistant, University of Freiburg, Institute for Foreign and International Private Law, 1985-1989. Staff Member, University of Illinois, 1989-1990. *LANGUAGES:* German and English. *PRACTICE AREAS:* Company Law; Acquisitions and Sales; Restructuring; Probate and Family Law.

ANDREAS GEIGER, born Hasel, 1959; admitted, 1992, Germany. *Education:* University of Freiburg i. Br. (law degree, 1986; Dr. jur., 1993). Staff Member: University of Freiburg, Institute for Public Law, 1987-1989; Max-Planck-Institute for Foreign and International Criminal Law, Freiburg i. Br., 1989-1990. *LANGUAGES:* German and English. *PRACTICE AREAS:* Media and Entertainment; Video and Television; Public, Administrative and Environmental Law; Ecclesiastical Law; Zoning, Planning and Land Use; Expropriation and Restitution.

BENNO SCHWARZ, born Osnabrück, 1965; admitted, 1993, Germany. *Education:* Universities of Bonn and Munich (law degree, 1989; Dr. jur., 1992). *LANGUAGES:* German, English, French and Russian. *PRACTICE AREAS:* Company Law; Acquisitions and Sales; Restructuring; Expropriation and Restitution; European Community Law.

HANS PETER MECHLEM, born Leverkusen, 1960; admitted, 1990, Germany. *Education:* Bankkaufmann (banking diploma, 1979); University of Munich (law degree, 1986; Dr. jur., 1992). With Deutsche Aerospace AG, Munich, 1989-1992. Corporate Counsel, Dornier Medical Systems GmbH, Munich, 1992-1993. *LANGUAGES:* German and English. *PRACTICE AREAS:* Company Law; Acquisitions and Sales; Restructuring; Financial Services; Labour and Employment; Insolvency; Liquidations.

DIETRICH KRESSEL, born Hamburg, 1963; admitted, 1993, Germany. *Education:* University of Hamburg (law degree, 1989). Staff Member, University of Erlangen-Nürnberg, 1990-1993. *LANGUAGES:* German and English. *PRACTICE AREAS:* Press Law; Publishing and Radio; Unfair Competition; Copyrights; Advertising and Marketing; Cartels.

STEFAN WEINHEIMER, born Düsseldorf, 1963; admitted, 1992, Germany. *Education:* Universities of Heidelberg and Munich (law degree, 1987; Dr. jur., 1991). Author: "Retroactiveness in German Tax Law," 1991. *LANGUAGES:* German and English. *PRACTICE AREAS:* Company Law; Acquisitions and Sales; Restructuring; Media and Entertainment; Video and Television; Press Law; Publishing and Radio; Unfair Competition; Copyrights; Advertising and Marketing.

MARTIN KOCK, born Hameln, 1961; admitted, 1992, Germany; 1994, California. *Education:* Universities of Marburg (law degree, 1986; Dr.jur., 1991) and Berkeley. Author: "The Privity of Law in Broker Contracts," 1991. *Member:* German-American Jurists' Association. *LANGUAGES:* German and English. *PRACTICE AREAS:* Company Law; Acquisitions and Sales; Restructuring; Financial Services; European Community Law.

(This Listing Continued)

BEITEN BURKHARDT MITTL & WEGENER,
Munich—Continued

RALF ECKERT, born Ebstorf, Lower Saxony, 1960; admitted, 1992, Germany. *Education:* University of Bonn (law degree, 1987). Publications on Tax Law. *Member:* German Tax Association of Lawyers. *LANGUAGES:* German, English and Russian. *PRACTICE AREAS:* Company Law; Acquisitions and Sales; Restructuring; Tax Planning; Probate and Family Law.

MATTHIAS W. STECHER, born Heidelberg, 1958; admitted, 1987, Germany. *Education:* University of Tübingen (law degree, 1984); New York University (M.C.J., 1987-1988); Bar Exam, State of New York (Attorney-at-Law, 1988). Research Assistant, University of Tübingen, 1984-1985. With law firm, Brosio, Casati e Associati, Milan, 1991. *LANGUAGES:* German, English, Italian and French. *PRACTICE AREAS:* Media and Entertainment; Video and Television; Unfair Competition; Copyrights; Advertising and Marketing; Expropriation and Restitution.

HANS-WERNER MORITZ, born Braunsberg/East Prussia, 1941; admitted, 1971, Germany. *Education:* Universities of Freiburg/Breisgau (law degree, 1966) and Konstanz (Dr.jur., 1988). Various publications on Commercial, particularly Computer and Antitrust Law. In-house Counsel, DIT Deutscher Investment Trust, Frankfurt a.M., 1970. Managing positions in the legal department of IBM Deutschland GmbH, 1970-1986. General Counsel, IBM Areas Division, Paris, 1986-1987. Senior Counsel, IBM Europe, Paris, 1986-1994. *LANGUAGES:* German, English and French. *PRACTICE AREAS:* Commerical Law; Telecommunications; Computer Law; Antitrust Law.

CHRISTOPH HOEBBEL, born Idar-Oberstein, Germany, 1961; admitted, 1991, Germany. *Education:* Universities of Würzburg, Geneva and Munich (law degree, 1985; Dr. jur., 1992); Harvard Law School, Cambridge, Massachusetts (LL.M., 1989). Bar Exam, State of New York, Attorney-at-Law, 1989. Author: "The Protection of Compilations, Fact Works and Data Bases under German and American Copyright Law," 1992 and various publications on Copyright and International Law. With Debevoise & Plimpton, New York, 1989-1990. Staff Member, Max-Planck-Institute for Foreign and International Patent, Copyright and Competition Law, 1985-1988 and 1990-1991. *LANGUAGES:* German, English and French. *PRACTICE AREAS:* Company Law; Acquisitions and Sales; Restructuring; Financial Services; Computers and Software.

KLAUS WIGAND, born Saarbrücken, 1964; admitted, 1994, Germany. *Education:* Universities of Saarbrücken and Munich (law degree, 1990). Staff Member of Prof. Dr. Lerche, Institute for Political Science and Public Law, University of Munich, 1987-1990. Trainee, Legal Department of SEAT, Barcelona, 1990. With Soler Padró (Attorneys and Tax Advisors), Barcelona, 1990-1991. *Member:* German-Spanish Jurists' Association. *LANGUAGES:* German, Spanish, English and French. *PRACTICE AREAS:* Company Law; Acquisitions and Sales; Restructuring; Probate and Family Law.

GÜNTER KOLLER, born Munich, 1965; admitted, 1994, Germany. *Education:* Universities of Munich and Bonn (law degree, 1991). *LANGUAGES:* German, English and French. *PRACTICE AREAS:* Expropriation and Restitution; Real Estate; Construction Law.

ALEXANDRA STRASSER-LAUSCHKE, born Munich, 1965; admitted, 1994, Germany. *Education:* University of Munich (law degree, 1991). *PRACTICE AREAS:* Company Law; Acquisitions and Sales; Restructuring.

MARKUS KÜNZEL, born Stuttgart, 1962; admitted, 1994, Germany. *Education:* Universities of Erlangen-Nürnberg, Göttingen and Munich (law degree, 1991). *PRACTICE AREAS:* Labour Law; Company Law; Acquisitions and Sales; Restructuring.

KARINA LACEY MACMAHON, born Digswell/Hertfordshire, England, 1964; admitted, 1990 as Solicitor, England and Wales (Not admitted in Germany). *Education:* Cambridge University, Queen's College (BA, 1986; MA, 1991); College of Law, Guildford (Solicitors Finals, 1988). *Member:* Law Society of England and Wales. *LANGUAGES:* English, German and French. *PRACTICE AREAS:* Company Law; Acquisitions and Sales; Restructuring.

BERNET, WEITNAUER & PARTNER
MÖHLSTRAßE 10/I
81675 MUNICH, GERMANY
Telephone: 089-470 90 14
Telex: 5212 110 SCIO D
Telecopier: 089-470 74 27

Leipzig, Germany Office: Roscherstr. 17-21, 04105. Telephone: 0341-564 6766. Telecopier: 0341-566 0981.

Dresden, Germany Office: Anton-Graff-Strasse 15, 01309. Telephone: 0357/447 62 80. Telecopier: 0357/447 62 89.

Commercial, Corporation, Mergers and Acquisitions, Taxation, Antitrust, EEC, Corporate Finance, Banking and Securities, Unfair Competition, Trademarks, Patents, Copyright, Computer, Media, Press and Publishing, Labour, Real Estate, Environment, Litigation and Arbitration.

MEMBERS OF FIRM

DR. WOLFGANG WEITNAUER, born Bonn, Germany, June 29, 1954; admitted, 1982, Germany. *Education:* Universities of Heidelberg, Lausanne/Switzerland and Freiburg (Referendar, 1978; Dr. jur., 1980; Assessor, 1981); University of Illinois at Urbana-Champaign (M.C.L., 1979). Author: "Der Vertragsschwerpunkt," (The contractual center of gravity) Frankfurt, 1981; "Die europäische grenzüberschreitende Gesellschaft," (The European Transborder Company) EWS, 1992, P. 165-173. Research Assistant to Dean Peter Hay, University of Illinois, 1978-1979. Assistant to Professor Dr. Hans Stoll, Institute for International Private Law and Comparative Law, University of Freiburg, 1979-1982. *Member:* Munich Bar Association; German-American Lawyers Association (DAJV); Association Internationale des Jeunes Avocats (AIJA); German Association of Industrial Property and Copyright Law (GRUR). *LANGUAGES:* German, English, French and Italian. *PRACTICE AREAS:* Corporate and Commercial Law; Real Estate and Construction Law; EC Law; Mergers and Acquisitions; Litigation.

DR. PHILIPP GRAF WRANGEL, born Berlin, Germany, June 11, 1959; admitted, 1989, Germany. *Education:* Universities of Munich and Freiburg (Referendar, 1984; Assessor, 1989; Dr. jur., 1988). Trainee, Federal Cartel Office, Berlin, 1987. Research Staff, Max-Planck-Institute for Foreign and International Patent, Copyright and Competition Law, 1989-1990. Author: "Der Gerichtsstand des Erfüllungsortes im deutschen, italienischen und europäischen Recht," (The Forum Solutionis in German, Italian and European Law) Munich, 1988; "Die Fusionskontrolle des italienischen Rundfunkgesetzes," (Merger Control under the Italian Broadcasting Act) GRUR Int. 1991, p. 870-882. *Member:* Munich Bar Association; Italian Chamber of Commerce, Munich; German-Italian Chamber of Commerce, Milan; German-Italian Lawyers Association; Studienvereinigung Kartellrecht (Antitrust Law Association). *LANGUAGES:* German, Italian, English, French and Portuguese. *PRACTICE AREAS:* Antitrust Law; Commercial and Corporate Law; Communications and Media; Intellectual Property; Unfair Competition Law; International Contracts.

HEIKE LEIBBRAND-BECKERT, born Heilbronn, Germany, June 9, 1962; admitted, 1990, Germany. *Education:* University of Munich (Referendar, 1987; Assessor, 1990). Counsel, German Journalist Association, 1990-1994. *LANGUAGES:* German, English and French. *PRACTICE AREAS:* Press and Publishing Law; Labour Law; Copyright Law.

DR. HANS SCHAEFER, born Munich, Germany, October 21, 1963; admitted, 1993, Germany; 1994, New York. *Education:* Universities of Munich and Geneva (Dr. jur., 1993); Columbia University, New York (LL.M., 1993). Research Assistant, Institute of International and Comparative Law, University of Munich. Author: "Drittinteressen im Zivilprozeß," (Third party interests in civil procedure). *LANGUAGES:* German, English and French. *PRACTICE AREAS:* Corporate and Commercial Law; International Contracts; EC Law; Tax Law.

DR. WOLFGANG BAARE-SCHMIDT, born Ehrhorn, Germany, April 29, 1946; admitted, 1982, Germany. *Education:* Universities of Kiel, Lausanne/Geneva, London and Hamburg (Referendar, 1977; Assessor, 1982; Dr. jur., 1983); Tulane Law School, Louisiana (LL.M., 1978). Career Officer, German Army Aviation, 1966-1974. District Manager, Coca Cola GmbH, Essen, 1985-1986. Managing Partner, Matuschka Group, Munich, 1987-1992. Author: "The Status of the International Olympic Committee in International Law," 1983. *LANGUAGES:* German, English and French. *PRACTICE AREAS:* Investment Banking; Finance; Real Estate.

DR. STEFAN SÖHN, born Düsseldorf, Germany, June 18, 1954; admitted, 1979, Germany. *Education:* Universities of Augsburg (Referendar, 1976; Assessor, 1979; Dr. jur., 1983). In-House Counsel: Bavarian State

(This Listing Continued)

Ministry for Commerce and Trade; Bavarian Cartel Office; Agrob AG, Munich, 1983-1990. Author: "Allgemeinverbindlicherklärung von Wettbewerbsregeln," (Declaration of generally binding validity of competition rules) Munich, 1983; "Benzinpreis undKartellgesetz," (Gasoline price and Antitrust law) BB 1982, p. 589-592; "Änderung der Rechtsprechung zum Ladenschlußgesetz?" (Change of the case law with regard to the Shop Closing Act?) NJW 1982, p. 319. *Member:* International Bar Association. *LANGUAGES:* German and English. *PRACTICE AREAS:* Antitrust Law; Labour Law; Corporate Law.

DR. RAINER ESSER, born Wolfenbüttel, Germany, January 11, 1957; admitted, 1986, Germany. *Education:* Universities of Munich and Geneva/Switzerland (Referendar, 1982; Assessor, 1986; Dr. jur., 1989); University of Georgia (LL.M., 1983). Trainee, Deutsche Bank, Bankkaufmann, 1977. Research Assistant, Institute of Civil Law, University of Munich, 1983-1987. Associate, Wilmer, Cutler & Pickering, London, 1984. Editor-in-Chief, European Law Press. Author: "Zur Immunität rechtlich selbständiger Staatsunternehmen," (The immunity of legally independent state-owned enterprises) RIW 1984, p. 577-585; "Klagen gegen ausländische Staaten," (Actions against foreign states), 1989; "Beseitigung der Doppelbesteuerung von Kapitalgesellschaften," (The elimination of the double-taxation of corporations) EWS 1991, p. 17-22; "World Intellectual Property Guide Book," (Introd.) 1991; "Business Transactions in Germany," (Foreign Investment), 1991; "Quellensteuerbefreiung, Schachtelprivileg und Staatshaftung," (Exemption from withholding taxes, affiliation privilege and government liability) RIW 1992, p. 293-297. *Member:* German-American Lawyers Association (DAJV). *LANGUAGES:* German, English, French and Spanish. *PRACTICE AREAS:* EC Law; International Tax Law.

DR. GERD WALDENMAIER, born Villingen-Schwenningen, Germany, January 29, 1958; admitted, 1988, Germany. *Education:* University of Freiburg (Referendar, 1981; Assessor, 1984; Dr. jur., 1986). Trainee and Investment Banker, Deutsche Bank, Frankfurt, 1985-1988. Author: "Der Betriebsführer nach dem Gesetz zur Ordnung der nationalen Arbeit vom 20 Januar 1934," (The manager under the Act of January 20, 1934 pertaining to the regulation of national labour), 1986. *LANGUAGES:* German, English and French. *PRACTICE AREAS:* Corporate Law; Banking Law; Mergers and Acquisition Law; Publishing Law; Unfair Competition Law; Labour Law.

BÖCK OPPLER HERING

Established in 1975

POCCISTRAßE 7
80336 MUNICH, GERMANY
Telephone: 089/725 40 24
Telefax: 089/721 21 11
Telex: 523215 BOHL

General and International Practice, Corporate Law, Commercial Law, Construction and Real Estate, EEC Law, Mergers and Acquisitions, Unfair Competition and Antitrust Laws, Trademarks, Copyrights, Computer and Software Laws, Licensing Contracts, International Wills, Trusts and Estates, Real Estate, Private International Law, German and International Taxation.

DR. MANFRED BÖCK, born Munich, Germany, July 7, 1945; admitted, 1975, Germany. *Education:* University of Munich (Law Degree, 1972; Doctor of Law, 1984). *Member:* Munich Bar Association. *LANGUAGES:* German and English. *PRACTICE AREAS:* Corporate Law; Commercial Law; Unfair Competition.

PETER MICHAEL OPPLER, born Munich, Germany, May 26, 1954; admitted, 1983, Germany. *Education:* University of Munich (Law Degree, 1980). Lecturer at the Bank Academy of Banking Laws, Munich. Chairman, Committee on Construction Law, German Lawyers Association. *Member:* Munich Bar Association. *LANGUAGES:* German and English. *PRACTICE AREAS:* Construction and Real Estate.

DR. WOLFGANG HERING, born Rennerod, Germany, September 8, 1954; admitted, 1984, Germany; 1986, New York. *Education:* University of Munich (Law Degree, 1979; Doctor of Laws, 1983); Dalhousie University Law School, Canada (LL.M., 1981). Member, Board of Editors, Computer Law Journal "EDV & Recht". Author: "The Commercial Laws of the F.R. of Germany," looseleaf, Digest of Commercial Laws of the World, Oceania; "The Rights of the Surviving Spouse in German-Canadian Cases," Beck-Verlag, 1984; "Immobilieninvestitionen in Canada," looseleaf, Haufe Verlag, German Jurisprudence on Software Laws- a Current Overview EDV & Recht, 3/1989; "International Tax Aspects of Philantrophic and other Non-

(This Listing Continued)

profit Organizations," Bulletin for International Fiscal Documentation, 1989/12; "Results Oriented Software Maintenance Warranty and Liability," Computer & Recht 1991, 398 et seq. *Member:* Munich Bar Association; American Bar Association; International Bar Association. *LANGUAGES:* German, English and French. *PRACTICE AREAS:* Corporate Law; Licensing and Distribution; Software and Computers; International Trusts and Estates; Foreign Investments.

BRUNO LANG, born Munich, Germany, July 20, 1929; admitted, 1958, Germany. *Education:* University of Munich (Law Degree, 1954). Member of the Disciplinary Court for Professional Conduct of Lawyers for the District of the Higher Regional Court Munich. *Member:* Munich Bar Association. *LANGUAGES:* German. *PRACTICE AREAS:* Wills, Trusts and Estates.

KLAUS BACHMANN, born Grassau, Germany, April 14, 1952; admitted, 1981, Germany; 1984, Steuerberater (Certified Tax Advisor). *Education:* University of Munich (Law Degree, 1978). *Member:* Munich Bar Association; Chamber of Tax Advisors. *LANGUAGES:* German and English. *PRACTICE AREAS:* National and International Tax Law; Corporate Law; Inheritance Law.

ASSOCIATES

Thomas Schnitzlein
Manfred Galitzdoerfer

BUCHHOLTZ, KISLING, DR. HARMSEN & PARTNERS

Established in 1962

KAUFINGERSTRASSE 24
D-80331 MUNICH, GERMANY
Telephone: 089-29 00 58-0
Telecopier: (National) 089-294219; (International) 49-89-294219 and 49-89-2904606

General Practice, Litigation, Commercial, Corporate, Mergers and Acquisitions, Leasing, Banking, International and Private Law, International Commercial Arbitration, Tax, Unfair Competition, Intellectual Property, Copyright, Press and Publishing, Licensing and Knowhow, Construction, Law of Tenancy, Real Estate, Condominium, Labour, Insurance, Travel, Family, Divorce, Succession, Litigation and Collection, Law pertaining to property claims in the former GDR.

FIRM PROFILE: Established in 1962 (and practicing under the name of Jost-Thiel Hecker and Partners until 1991), the law firm offers a wide range of legal services and has mainly Germany-based clients, but also clients in the European countries and the U.S.A. The law firm has 9 attorneys-at-law and 2 chartered accountants, 1 tax advisor and a legal and tax support staff of 20 (paralegal personnel and administrators).

MEMBERS OF FIRM

JUERGEN BUCHHOLTZ, born Dortmund, January 27, 1935; admitted, 1967, Munich, Bavaria; 1973, Court of Appeals, Munich. *Education:* University of Cologne. *Member:* AIPPI. *LANGUAGES:* German and English. *PRACTICE AREAS:* Company Law; Product Liability Law; Public and Private Construction Law; Industrial Property; Copyright and Publication Laws; Succession Law; Commercial Agent Law (Independent Dealer/Manufacturer Relationships); Civil Law.

RAINER KISLING, born Teschen, August 21, 1942; admitted, 1971, Munich, Bavaria; 1976, Court of Appeals, Munich. *Education:* Universities of Heidelberg and Munich; New York University Law School (1968-1969). *LANGUAGES:* German, English and French. *PRACTICE AREAS:* Civil Law; Business Law (Bank and Leasing Law); Company Law; Labor Law; International Contracts; Litigation.

DR. JENS HARMSEN, born Hamburg, August 22, 1935; admitted, 1968, Düsseldorf, Northrhein-Westfalia. *Education:* Universities of Munich and Hamburg (Dr. jur.). Author: Paragraph 3 UWG und das Problem der Beweislast, 1968. *Member:* Deutsche Vereinigung für gewerblichen Rechtsschutz und Urheberrecht e.V.; ALAI. *LANGUAGES:* German and English. *PRACTICE AREAS:* Industrial Property Law; Trademark Law; Unfair Competition Law; Copyright Law; Civil Law.

(This Listing Continued)

*BUCHHOLTZ, KISLING, DR. HARMSEN &
PARTNERS, Munich—Continued*

TAX ADVISORS

REINHOLD KOENINGER, born Kappelrodeck, April 2, 1939. *Education:* Universities of Mannheim and Cologne (Bachelor of Commerce); Chartered Accountant and Tax Expert. *Member:* Institut der Wirtschaftsprüfer in Deutschland e.V., Duesseldorf. *LANGUAGES:* German and English. *PRACTICE AREAS:* Tax Law; Audits; Foundation of Enterprises; Mergers and Acquisitions.

DIETER K. REINAUER, born Augsburg, January 31, 1943. *Education:* University of Munich (Bachelor of Commerce); Chartered Accountant and Tax Expert. *Member:* Institut der Wirtschaftsprüfer in Deutschland e.V., Duesseldorf. *LANGUAGES:* German and English. *PRACTICE AREAS:* Tax Law; Audits; Foundation of Enterprises; Mergers and Acquisitions.

ASSOCIATES

ULRICH IRMER, born Bochum, January 19, 1939; admitted, 1973, Munich, Bavaria; 1979, Court of Appeals, Munich. *Education:* University of Munich. Public Offices: 1976-1984. Member of European Parliament, 1987. Member of Deutscher Bundestag, Bonn. *LANGUAGES:* English, French and Italian. *PRACTICE AREAS:* Civil Law; Public Administration; International Relations.

HERBERT HOLZBOCK, born Bad Windsheim, September 5, 1955; admitted, 1987, Munich; 1992, Court of Appeals, Munich. *Education:* University of Munich. *LANGUAGES:* German and English. *PRACTICE AREAS:* Bank and Leasing Law; Civil Law; Litigation.

DR. GERALD NEUFERT, born Naumburg/Saale, February 7, 1955; admitted, 1989, Munich, Bavaria. *Education:* University of Münster (Dr. jur., 1987). Author: "Revisibilität der Auslegung individueller VertragserKlärungen," 1987. *LANGUAGES:* German and English. *PRACTICE AREAS:* Civil Law; Labor Law; Bank and Leasing Law; Litigation.

PETRA TRUMP, born Roding, May 4, 1953; admitted, 1988, Munich, Bavaria. *Education:* Universities of Tübingen and Berlin. Judge, Berlin (Amtsgericht, Landgericht), 1982-1986. *LANGUAGES:* German, English and French. *PRACTICE AREAS:* Civil Law; Travel Law; Succession Law.

Languages: German, English, French, Italian and Spanish.

RECHTSANWÄLTE BURGER, BOHL, MEYER-GUTKNECHT & PARTNERS

GARMISCHER STRAβE 8
80339 MUNICH, GERMANY
Telephone: 089/5409490
Teletex: 089/54094933

International, Commercial Transactions, Agencies, Business, Unfair Competition, Computer. Construction, Product Liability, Real Estate, Business Organization, Corporate Law, International Sales and Transactions, Franchise and Family Law.

DIERK BURGER, born Munich, Germany, July 11, 1941; admitted, 1968, Munich. *Education:* Universities of Hamburg, Berlin and Munich (Referendar, 1965). *Member:* Munich and German Bar Associations; JBA-SBL (Chairman of Comm. M, 1980-1986); Vereinigung für gewerbl. Rechtschutz und Urheberrecht (grur); APLA; American Chamber of Commerce in Germany. *LANGUAGES:* German and English.

THOMAS BOHL, born Munich, Germany, March 15, 1947; admitted, 1976, Munich. *Education:* University of Munich (Referendar, 1972). Author: "Die Haftung der Ingenieure im Bauwesen," Vieweg, 1979. *Member:* Munich and German Bar Associations;. *LANGUAGES:* German and English.

HANS-JORG MEYER-GUTKNECHT, born Bad Wildungen, December 15, 1944; admitted, 1972, Munich. *Education:* Universities of Münster and Munich (Referendar, 1968). *Member:* Munich and German Bar Associations. *LANGUAGES:* German and English.

HANS-PETER LINDLBAUER, born Munich, Germany, June 11, 1955; admitted, 1984, Munich. *Education:* University of Munich (Referendar, 1981). *Member:* Munich and German Bar Associations. *LANGUAGES:* German and English.

CHRISTIAN HEIMERI, born Munich, Germany, January 18, 1964; admitted, 1990, Munich. *Education:* University of Munich (Referendar, *(This Listing Continued)*

1987). *Member:* Munich and German Bar Associations. *LANGUAGES:* German, English and French.

THOMAS SCHABEL, born Geislingen, Germany, July 5, 1946; admitted, 1976, Munich. *Education:* Universities of Fribourg and Munich (Referendar, 1973). *Member:* Munich and Germany Bar Associations; Society of Construction Law. *LANGUAGES:* German, English, French and Italian.

MARION BRANDL, born Schöningen, Germany, June 10, 1963; admitted, 1993, Munich. *Education:* Universities of Tübingen and Munich (Referendar, 1988). *Member:* Munich and German Bar Associations. *LANGUAGES:* German, English, Spanish and French.

WILHELM JORDAN, born Reutlingen, Germany, June 4, 1961; admitted, 1993, Munich. *Education:* Universities of Tübingen and Munich (Referender, 1990). *Member:* Munich and German Bar Associations. *LANGUAGES:* German, English and French.

DR. DONALD J. CRAMER

Rechtsanwalt

MAX-JOSEPH-STR. 7A
80333 MUNICH, GERMANY
Telephone: (049-89) 554030; 596059
Fax: (049-89) 595889

Family Law, International Family Law, Child Abduction, Business Law and Civil Law.

DONALD J. CRAMER, born Göttingen, Germany, August 25, 1944; admitted, 1979, Germany. *Education:* Indiana University Law School (1965); University of Freiburg (First State Exam, 1969; Dr.jur., 1972). Licensed Interpreter for English-German. German Jrs. Auditing Services, 1973-1979. Founding Member, KMS Mediation Agency, Munich. *LANGUAGES:* German, English, Italian, Spanish and French.

PETER CZIRNICH

Established in 1962

NÖRDLICHE AUFFAHRTSALLEE 65
80638 MUNICH, GERMANY
Telephone: 49-89: 175095/175096
Fax: G3: 49-89-175098
Fax: G4: (ISDN): 49-89-17862-222
Cable Address: "Lawint" Munich

Paris France Office: 81, Avenue Raymond Poincare, 75116. Telephone: 33-1: 47 04 73 25. Fax: 33-1: 47 04 50 96. Telex: 610650 LAWINT Paris.

Firm engaged in German, French, European and International Law practice. Entitled to plead before the European Union, French and Munich Courts.
General, European and International Practice. Corporate Law including International Mergers and Acquisitions, Tax, Antitrust, Unfair Competition, Commercial Law, Public and International Private Law, International Arbitration, Litigation, EC Law, French Law, German Law.

DR. PETER CZIRNICH, born Reichenberg, Czechoslovakia, August 30, 1933; admitted, 1962, Munich; 1967, Court of Appeal, Munich and High Court of Bavaria; 1988, Paris. *Education:* Universities of Erlangen, Innsbruck, Geneva and Munich (Basic Law Degree, 1958; Doctorate, 1962); University of Paris (Licence en Droit, 1973; Examen CFPP, 1988). Author: "Die Stellung des Executors im englischen Recht," Munich, 1962. President, Verband der Rechtsreferendare Bayerns e.V., Munich, 1961-1962. Member: The Goodman Library; French-German Chamber of Commerce, 1966. *Member:* German-American Law Association E.V.; Munich and Paris Bar Associations. *LANGUAGES:* German, English and French. *PRACTICE AREAS:* German and European Antitrust and Trade Regulation; Litigation; Unfair Competition; International Arbitration; Agency and Distributorships; Consumer Product Law; German and French Business Law; Commercial Law; Company Law; Contracts; Corporate Law; European Union Law; International Private Law; Mergers, Acquisitions and Divestitures; Taxation.

CHRISTIAN CZIRNICH, born Munich, Germany, July 18, 1964; admitted, 1994, Munich. *Education:* University of Munich (Basic Law Degree, *(This Listing Continued)*

1990). *Member:* Munich Bar Association. *LANGUAGES:* German and English. *PRACTICE AREAS:* Civil Law; Computers and Software Law; European Community Law; Taxation; Family Law; Wills.

WOLFGANG A. DASE, B.A., J.D.

Attorney at Law (New York)

Rechtsanwalt (Munich)

HERZOG-RUDOLF-STR. 3
80539 MUNICH, GERMANY
Telephone: (089) 29 00 380
Telephone (after 7 P.M.): (089) 201 4176
Telefax: (089) 29 92 02

General U.S. and German Practice. German Company (GmbH) Law, Construction, Estate Planning, Probate, Recognition and Enforcement of U.S. Judgments, Litigation.

WOLFGANG ARTHUR DASE, born Potsdam, Germany, June 7, 1950; admitted, 1978, New York; 1989, Germany, Rechtsanwalt. *Education:* Amherst College, Amherst, Mass. (B.A., 1972); Tulane University School of Law, New Orleans, La. (J.D., 1977); University of Munich (Law Degree, 1985). Assessor, Munich, 1989. *Member:* New York Bar; Munich Bar Association. (Also Partner, Law Firm Tepelmann & Partners, Munich).

Languages: English and German

DROSTE

The Merged Firms of Droste, Pietzcker, Sprick, Ohlgart & Klosterfelde; Triebel & Weil; Strobl, Killius & Vorbrugg

MARSTALLSTRASSE 8
80539 MUNICH, GERMANY
Telephone: (089) 290120
Telecopier: (089) 29012 222
Telex: 524 973 skv

Düsseldorf, Germany Office: Berliner Allee 48, 40212 Düsseldorf. Telephone: (0211) 13 680. Telecopier: (0211) 32 44 39.
Hamburg, Germany Office: Warburgstrasse 50, 20354 Hamburg. Telephone: (040) 4 1993-0. Telecopier: (040) 4 1993 200.
Frankfurt/Main, Germany Office: Schaumainkai 91, 60596 Frankfurt/Main. Telephone: (069) 63 00 89-0 Telecopier: (069) 630089-99.
Berlin, Germany Office: Kurfürstendamm 54-55, 10707 Berlin. Telephone: (030) 88 24 300. Telefax: (030) 88 24 393.
Brussels, Beligum Office: Avenue des Gaulois 9, B-1150 Brussels. Telephone: 02-7358945. Telefax: 02-7352251.

General and International Practice, Commercial Law, Corporate, Banking, Finance, Tax, Mergers and Acquisitions, EU Law, Antitrust, Unfair Competition, Trademarks, Copyright, Patents, Licensing, Food and Drug Law, Law of the Press, Products Liability, Environmental Law, Labor Law, Real Estate, Estate Planning, International Construction Contracts, Commercial Litigation and Arbitration, Bankruptcy, Administrative Law.

FIRM PROFILE: Droste is engaged in the practice of corporate and commercial law. The firm is the result of the merger of Droste, Pietzcker, Sprick, Ohlgart& Klosterfelde in Hamburg (formed in 1887), Strobl, Killius & Vorbrugg in Munich (formed in 1961) and Triebel & Weil in Düsseldorf (formed in 1951). The firm's traditional areas of practice are: corporate law, including mergers and acquisitions; industrial property law, including copyright, unfair competition and anti-trust law; trademark law; tax law, both domestic and international; real estate law. Further areas of particular expertise include banking and finance, computer and software law, environmental law, labour law, EU law and commercial litigation and arbitration.

RESIDENT PARTNERS

DR. JAKOB STROBL, born Munich, Germany, November 11, 1926; admitted, 1952, Germany; 1960 as Specialist (Fachanwalt) on Tax Law. *Education:* University of Munich (Law Degree, 1949; Business Administration Degree, 1950; Doctor of Laws, 1957). Counsel, German Tax Administration, 1952-1959. Member, Tax Committee of American Chamber of Commerce; International Fiscal Association. *LANGUAGES:* German and English. *PRACTICE AREAS:* German and International Law; Tax Law.

(This Listing Continued)

DR. GEORG VORBRUGG, LL.M., born Berlin, Germany, May 22, 1936; admitted, 1966, Germany. *Education:* Universities of Freiburg, Munich (Law Degree, 1961; Doctor of Laws, 1965) and Harvard Law School (LL.M., 1962). Lecturer, University of Munich. *Member:* International Bar Association; International Committee of the German Lawyers Association (Member, Board). *LANGUAGES:* German, English, French and Italian. *PRACTICE AREAS:* Business Law; Agency and Distributorships; Antitrust and Trade Regulations; Mergers, Acquisitions and Divestitures.

DR. THILO VON BODUNGEN, born Bremen, Germany, February 28, 1939; admitted, 1969, Germany. *Education:* Universities of Freiburg, Munich (Law Degree, 1964; Doctor of Laws, 1968) and University of Michigan Law School (M.C.L., 1965). *Member:* International Association for the Protection of Industrial Property; German-British Jurists's Association (Member, Board). *LANGUAGES:* German and English. *PRACTICE AREAS:* Mergers and Acquisitions; Contracts; Intellectual Property Rights; Arbitration.

DR. MICHAEL WITZEL, born Melle, Germany, November 22, 1944; admitted, 1975, Germany; 1988, as Specialist (Fachanwalt) on Labour Law. *Education:* Universities of Saarbruecken, Freiburg, Munich (Law Degree, 1972; Doctor of Laws, 1974) and University of Michigan Law School (LL.M., 1976). *Member:* International Bar Association. *LANGUAGES:* German and English. *PRACTICE AREAS:* Labor Relations and Commercial Intermediaries.

DR. WOLFGANG BÜCHNER, born Kaufbeuren, Germany, December 25, 1953; admitted, 1979, Germany. *Education:* University of Augsburg (Law Degree, 1977; Doctor of Laws, 1982). *LANGUAGES:* German and English. *PRACTICE AREAS:* Intellectual Property Rights; International Contracts; Computer Law; Product Liability.

DR. BERNHARD HEISS, born Frankfurt, Germany, February 8, 1955; admitted, 1986, Germany. *Education:* Universities of Mayence, Heidelberg (Law Degree, 1979) and Munich (Doctor of Laws, 1986). *LANGUAGES:* German and English. *PRACTICE AREAS:* Mergers, Acquisitions and Divestitures including Management Buy-Outs & Leveraged Buy-Outs; Electronic Media and Entertainment.

DR. INGRID OHMANN, born Munich, Germany, October 6, 1958; admitted, 1988, Germany. *Education:* University of Munich (Law Degree, 1983; Doctor of Laws, 1987); University of Geneva and University of California, Berkley. *LANGUAGES:* German, English and French. *PRACTICE AREAS:* Labor Law; Estate Law; Conflict of Laws.

DR. STEPHAN SALZMANN, born Munich, Germany, May 13, 1960; admitted, 1988, Germany. *Education:* University of Munich (Law Degree, 1983; Doctor of Laws, 1985; M.B.A., 1987). Admitted a tax advisor, 1990. Associate with Arthur Andersen, 1987-1988. *LANGUAGES:* German and English. *PRACTICE AREAS:* Taxation including International Tax; Company Law; Corporate Law; Customs Law.

RUTH ZEHETMEIER-MÜLLER, born Munich, Germany, May 15, 1948; admitted, 1976, Germany; 1981, tax advisor. *Education:* University of Munich (Law Degree, 1972). Admitted as Tax Advisor, 1981. Associate, International CBA firm, 1983-1986. *LANGUAGES:* German and English. *PRACTICE AREAS:* German and International Tax Law; Corporate Law.

DR. CHRISTOPH HILTL, born Gräfelfing, Germany, September 17, 1958; admitted, 1989, Germany; 1992, as Specialist (Fachanwalt) on Administrative Law. *Education:* University of Passau (Law Degree, 1985; Doctor of Laws, 1990) and London, King's College. *LANGUAGES:* German and English. *PRACTICE AREAS:* Real Estate; Food and Drug Law; Public and Private Construction Law; Public Media Law.

DR. STEFAN AUER, born Weilheim, Germany, June 21, 1960. *Education:* University of Munich (Law Degree, 1987); University of Passau (Doctor of Laws, 1993). *LANGUAGES:* German and English. *PRACTICE AREAS:* National and International Litigation; Bankruptcy Law; Product Liability.

DR. ROLF FÜGER, born Augsburg, Germany, January 21, 1963. *Education:* University of Augsburg (Law Degree, 1986; Doctor of Laws, 1993). *Member:* International Fiscal Association. *LANGUAGES:* German and English. *PRACTICE AREAS:* German and International Tax Law; Corporate Law.

DR. NOBERT RIEGER, born Munich, Germany, October 19, 1962. *Education:* Universities of Bayreuth, Augsburg (Law Degree, 1986; Doctor of Laws, 1992); University of Michigan Law School (LL.M., 1993). *Member:* International Fiscal Association; German-American Lawyers Association. *LANGUAGES:* German and English. *PRACTICE AREAS:* German and International Tax Law; Corporate Law; Reorganization.

(This Listing Continued)

DROSTE, Munich—Continued

DR. ANGELIKA RUPERTSEDER, born Munich, Germany, February 18, 1963; admitted, 1991, Germany. *Education:* University of Munich (Law Degree, 1987; Doctor of Law, 1992); University of Geneva and University of Edinburgh, Scotland. *LANGUAGES:* German, English and French. *PRACTICE AREAS:* Computer Law; Unfair Competition Law; Commercial Law with emphasis on General Terms and Conditions.

REINER HANSERT, born Schutterwald, Germany, July 4, 1961; admitted, 1991, Germany. *Education:* Universities of Freiburg and Munich (Law Degree, 1988); University of Speyer, Germany. *LANGUAGES:* German, English and Italian. *PRACTICE AREAS:* Intellectual Property Rights; Contracts.

ASSOCIATES

Christoph Filip
Detlef Haß
VERENA v. BOMHARD
Dr. Klaus Großmann, LL.M. (also Attorney-at-Law (New York))
Stefan Geibel
Ute Sybille Bartholomä
Jan-Hendrik Brünink
Dietrich Firnhaber
Anne Rowland

Languages: German, English, French, Spanish, Russian, Italian, Portuguese, Latvian, Chinese and Japanese.

(For list of personnel at Düsseldorf, Frankfurt/Main, Hamburg, Berlin and Brussels, see Professional Biographies at those locations)

EHLERS, EHLERS & HECKER

Rechtsanwaltssocietät

PARZIVALPLATZ 1
D-80804 MUNICH, GERMANY
Telephone: +49/ +89/ 3 65 06-1
Fax: +49/ +89/ 3 68 96 66

General Practice, International, Aviation, Business, Products Liability, Insurance, Corporate, Antitrust, Unfair Competition, Medical, Pharmaceutical, Family, Trusts, Wills and Estates, Entertainment, Litigation, Arbitration, ADR.

PARTNERS

DR. IUR. P. NIKOLAI EHLERS, LL.M., born Berlin, January 7, 1958; admitted, 1985, New York; 1987, Germany. *Education:* Universities of Heidelberg, Munich and Cologne (First State Examination, 1982; Doctor iur.,1985; Second State Examination, 1987); Institute of Air and Space Law, McGill University, Montreal (LL.M., 1988). Since 1990: Past President and Secretary General of the Association of European Alumnae and Alumni of the Institute of Air and Space Law of McGill University. Co-Author of Books: "Warsaw Convention," (Loose-leaf) Editors, Giemulla/Schmid/Ehlers; "Frankfurter Kommentar zum Luftverkehrsrecht, Warschauer Abkommen," (Loose-leaf annotated version of the Warsaw Convention) Editors, Giemulla and Schmid; "Der Internationale Rechtsverkehr," (Loose-leaf) Editors, Bülow/Böckstiegel/Geimer/Schütze. Author of Books: "Computerized Reservations Systems in the Air Transport Industry," 1987, "Montrealer Protokolle Nr. 3 und 4," 1985. *Member:* German-American Lawyers' Association (DAJV); Institute of Air and Space Law Association (McGill University); European Air Law Association; German Canadian Business Club (Munich); Canadian German Lawyers' Association. *LANGUAGES:* German, English and some Russian. *PRACTICE AREAS:* Aviation; International Business; Products Liability; Insurance.

DR. MED. DR. IUR. ALEXANDER P.F. EHLERS, born Berlin, August 2, 1955; admitted, 1987, Germany. *Education:* Universities of Düsseldorf, Heidelberg and Munich (Licence to practice Medicine, 1980; Dr. of Medicine, 1981; First State Examination, 1984; Dr. iur, 1986; Second State Examination, 1987). Assistant Professor, Institute of Criminology, University of Munich, 1984. Lecturer, Forensic Psychiatry, 1987. Consultant, Pharmaceutical Industry, 1987. Lecturer, Medical and Pharmaceutical Law, University of Munich, 1989—. *Member:* American Society of Law and Medicine; Arbeitsgemeinschaft Rechtsanwälte im Medizinschadensrecht e.V.; Institut für das gesamte Arztrecht e.V.; NAV-Virchowbund; German Society for Medical Law; Deutsche Gesellschaft für Recht und Politik im Gesundheitswesen. *LANGUAGES:* German, English, Spanish and some French. *PRACTICE AREAS:* Pharmaceutical; Medical.

(This Listing Continued)

MICHAEL G. HECKER, born Rottweil, April 2, 1956; admitted, 1988, Germany. *Education:* Universities of Tübingen, Munich and Geneva (First State Examination, 1982; Second State Examination, 1988). Lecturer, Competition Law, Bayerische Akademie der Werbung, 1990—. *Member:* Deutsch-Französische Juristenvereinigung. *LANGUAGES:* German, French and English. *PRACTICE AREAS:* International Business; Corporate Law; Antitrust; Competition; Media Law; Insurance; Mergers and Acquisitions.

ASSOCIATES

Karin Gräfin von Strachwitz-Helmstatt
Beate Schnurrer
Peter Schönberger

FAHR-BECKER, JAKUBOWICZ & PARTNER

PRINZEGENTENSTR. 79
81675 MUNICH, GERMANY
Telephone: 49-89-4707042
Telefax: 49-89-479011

Chemnitz, Germany Office: Reichenhainer Str. 34-36, D-09126. Telephone: 49-371-445281. Telefax: 49-371-445285.
London, England Associated Office: Curry, Ch. Hausmann, Popeck, Solicitors 17 A, Welbeck Way, GB-London W1M 7PD. Telephone: 44-71-2246633. Telefax: 44-71-9354042.

FIRM PROFILE: Firm established in 1990. The firm has a broadly-based practice concentrating on a full range of civil legal services. The firm has concentrated on European Commercial and Corporate Law, General Civil Law and advising Multinational Corporations in European and German activities. In addition the firm has a close association with Central Treuhand AG, a Tax Advising and Auditing company with numerous offices in Germany.

MEMBERS OF FIRM

RANI C. JAKUBOWICZ, born Munich, Germany, July 9, 1947; admitted, 1977. *Education:* University of Geneva; University of Munich. *Member:* German Bar Association; International Bar Association; German-Israeli Association of Lawyers and Jurists. *LANGUAGES:* German, English, French, Hebrew, Italian and Polish. *PRACTICE AREAS:* Corporate Law; Business Law; Licence Agreements; International Joint Ventures; Franchising; General Civil Law.

DR. CHRISTOPH WEISSENBORN, born Dresden, Germany, February 28, 1942. "Doktor Juris" 1970, admitted, 1985. *Education:* University of Marburg, Lausanne and Würzburg. *LANGUAGES:* German, English, French and Spanish. *PRACTICE AREAS:* National and International Business Law; Technology Transfer; Licence Agreements; International Joint Ventures.

ASSOCIATES

BODO BATTENBERG, born Münster, Germany, May 20, 1963; admitted, 1994. *Education:* Universities of Augsburg and Munich. *LANGUAGES:* German and English. *PRACTICE AREAS:* Business Law; Tax Law; General Civil Law.

FASSBENDER ● SCHMITT-WALTER ● NISSEN

Established in 1970

WIDENMAYERSTR. 48
D-80538 MUNICH, GERMANY
Telephone: 089-21 21 37-0
Telefax: (089) 21 21 37-12; 21 21 37-23; 21 21 37-77

Business, Civil, Commercial, Corporate, Family Law, Contracts, Bankruptcy, Unfair Competition, Commodities and Securities, Federal Tax, Taxation, Finance, General Practice, Litigation, Labor and Employment, Landlord and Tenant, Property, Real Estate, Trademarks, Inheritance.

FIRM PROFILE: The firm was established in 1970 and offers a full range of legal and tax consulting services. The client base is international. The 6 partner firm has a support staff of 12 employees consisting of paralegal personnel, accountants and office administrators.

(This Listing Continued)

MEMBERS OF FIRM

HERBERT FASSBENDER, born Cologne, Germany, December 21, 1938; admitted, 1968, West Germany. *Education:* Universities of Bonn and Cologne, Germany, Lausanne, Switzerland (Referendar, 1963; Assessor, 1967). German-Venezuelan, "Chamber of Commerce in Caracas," Venezuela, January-September, 1965. Author: "The Future Taxation of Income and Capital Gains Derived from Foreign Mutual Funds," DB, 1977, 1228; "Investment Act— Considerations, Proposals for Changes Concerning the Draft Act of the Federal Government of January 2nd, 1978," DB, 1978, 1869; "Legal and Tax Aspects Concerning Real Estate Investments in the US," RIW/AWD, 1979, 20; "US - Tax Reform Act 1986 and German Real Estate Investments in the US," RIW, 1986, 882; "Legal and Tax Aspects related to Investment in US Real Estate," Falk, Gewerbe-Immobilien-Handbuch, 6th Edition, 1994. *Member:* German Bar Association; Institute for Tax Law of the German Lawyers; Association of German and Spanish Lawyers. *LANGUAGES:* German, English, French and Spanish. *PRACTICE AREAS:* Business Law; Corporate Law; Property; Real Estate; Securities; Commodities; Bankruptcy; Finance.

MICHAEL SCHMITT-WALTER, born Berlin, Germany, April 24, 1940; admitted, 1969, West Germany. *Education:* Universities of Munich and Cologne, Germany (Referendar, 1965; Assessor, 1969). *Member:* German Bar Association; Association of Tax Advisors. *LANGUAGES:* German and English. *PRACTICE AREAS:* Commercial Law; Corporate Law; Business Law; Taxation.

GÖTZ NISSEN, born Munich, Germany, January 7, 1951; admitted, 1980, West Germany. *Education:* American Field Service Scholarship (1967-1968); University of Munich (Referendar, 1977; Assessor, 1980). *Member:* German Bar Association; German Association for the Protection of Industrial Property and Copyright Law (GRUR). *LANGUAGES:* German, English and French. *PRACTICE AREAS:* Commercial Law; Civil Law; Unfair Competition; Trademarks; Contracts; Labor and Employment; General Practice.

ASTRID NISSEN, born Kassel, Germany, March 9, 1954; admitted, 1981, West Germany. *Education:* University of Munich (Referendar, 1978; Assessor, 1981). *Member:* German Bar Association. *LANGUAGES:* German, English and French. *PRACTICE AREAS:* Family Law; Inheritance; Landlord and Tenant Law; Civil Law; Litigation; General Practice.

GERT HAUX, born Essen, Germany, August 9, 1940; appointed Tax Advisor, 1969 and Wirtschaftsprufer (Certified Public Accountant), 1972. *Education:* Universities of Tübingen and Munich (Diploma in Business Administration). *Member:* Association of Certified Public Accountants; Association of Tax Advisors; Institute of Certified Public Accountants. *LANGUAGES:* German and English. *PRACTICE AREAS:* Federal Tax; Taxation; Real Estate.

MICHAEL EICHBERGER, born Meran, Italy, September 19, 1945; appointed Tax Advisor, 1978. *Education:* Universities of Stuttgart and Munich (Diploma in Business Administration). *Member:* Association of Tax Advisors. *LANGUAGES:* German, English and Spanish. *PRACTICE AREAS:* Federal Tax; Taxation; Real Estate.

JOHANNES FIALA, M.B.A.

Established in 1990

DE-LA-PAZ STRASSE 37
D-80639 MUNICH, GERMANY
Telephone: +49-89 179090-0
Mailbox: CIS 100120, 2234
Telegram Address: FIALA MUENCHEN
Fax: +49-89 179090-70

Tax, Civil, EU, Employment, Commercial, Banking, Property, Liquidation, Reconstruction, Economic Affairs, Trusteeship, Contracts.

JOHANNES FIALA, born May 8, 1959; admitted, 1991, Germany. *Education:* Universities of Munich (Law Degree, 1988) and Wales (M.B.A., 1992); International Center for European Formation, C.I.F.E. (EEC Expert Degree, 1989); A.L.G. (Finance and Investment Counselor Degree, 1992). Aufhaeuser Bank (Banker, 1982). Russische Akademie für Staatliche Dienste beim Präsidenten der Russischen Föderation, RASD (Postgraduate). *Member:* Institute of Finance and Tax; Associations of Information Services; Chamber of Commerce. *LANGUAGES:* German, English and

(This Listing Continued)

French. *PRACTICE AREAS:* Heritage; Inheritance; Real Estate; Financial Services; Expert Opinions; Accounting; Investigations; Trusts; Estates; Company Business Consulting.

FIEDLER & FORSTER

BRIENNER STRASSE 12
80333 MUNICH, GERMANY
Telephone: (0049-89) 2398-0
Fax: (0049-89) 2398-259

Berlin, Germany Office: Oranienburger Strasse 69, D-10117 Berlin. Telephone: (0049) (30) 283 2418. Fax: (0049) (30) 283 2420.
Cologne, Germany Office: Bonner Strasse 172-176, D-50968 Cologne. Telephone: (0049) (221) 937050-0. Telefax: (0049) (221) 937050-50.
Frankfurt/Main, Germany Office: Opernplatz 2, D-60313 Frankfurt/Main. Telephone: (0049) (69) 298930. Telefax: (0049) (69) 2398259.
Leipzig, Germany Office: Grimmaische Str. 25, 04109 Leipzig. Telephone: (0049) (341) 2115112. Telefax: (0049) (341) 9602530.
Stuttgart, Germany Office: Gänsheidestr. 68, D-70184. Telephone: (0049) (711) 16455-0. Fax: (0049) (711) 16445-11.
Paris, France Office: Tour Fiat la Dèfense 6, F-92084 Paris. Telephone: 33-1-47 76 28 10. Fax: 33-1-47 96 63 63.

Commercial, Corporate, Mergers and Acquisitions, Leasing, Banking, European Community, International and Private, International Commercial Arbitration, Tax, Unfair Competition, Intellectual Property, Anti-Trust, Copyright, Press and Publishing, Licensing and Know-How, Franchising, Computer and Software, Data Protection, Construction, Law of Tenancy, Real Estate, Condominium, Brokerage, Labour, Insurance, Air Traffic and Travel, Family, Divorce, Succession, Sequestration and Foreclosure, Litigation and Collection, Insolvency, Law pertaining to property claims in the former GDR.

PARTNERS

DR. ROLF FIEDLER, born Munich, Germany, September 23, 1920; admitted, 1952, Munich. *Education:* University of Munich (Dr. jur., 1950). *Member:* German Bar Association; International Bar Association. *LANGUAGES:* German and Spanish.

DR. MANFRED GEGERLE, born Munich, August 1, 1933; admitted, 1961, Munich. *Education:* Universities of Munich and Tuebingen (Dr. jur., 1960). *Member:* International Bar Association. *LANGUAGES:* German and English.

DR. MANFRED MAISCHEIN, born Darmstadt, Germany, February 7, 1937; admitted, 1966, Munich. *Education:* Universities of Frankfurt and Munich (Referendar, 1962; Assessor, 1966). *Member:* International Bar Association. *LANGUAGES:* German, English and French.

DR. WERNER WELLHÖFER, born Wuerzburg, Germany, August 22, 1947; admitted, 1976, Munich. *Education:* Universities of Lausanne and Munich (Dr. jur., 1977). With Law Firm, Washington, D.C., 1974. Co-Author: "Rechtshandbuch Vermögen und Investitionen in der ehemaligen DDR," C.H. Beck Publications ("Property and Investments in the former GDR: a legal reference book"). *Member:* Union Internationale Des Avocats; Association for Comparative Law. *LANGUAGES:* German, English and French.

DR. GERD SEELIGER, born Bonn, Germany, January 3, 1954; admitted, 1982, Munich. *Education:* University of Regensburg. Tax Consultant. *LANGUAGES:* German and English.

DR. RALF DIERCK, born Munich, Germany, August 6, 1960; admitted, 1989, Munich. *Education:* University of Munich (Dr. jur., 1989). *LANGUAGES:* German and English.

DR. BERNHARD KUEHN, born Munich, Germany, July 31, 1960; admitted, 1989, Munich. *Education:* University of Munich (Dr. jur., 1987). *LANGUAGES:* German, English and French.

DR. ECKHARD SCHMID, born Heilbronn, Germany, April 23, 1958; admitted, 1989, Munich. *Education:* University of Constance; Banking Certificate Chamber of Commerce Heilbronn. *LANGUAGES:* German, English, Italian and Spanish.

ASSOCIATES

ELISABETH MARIA FIEDLER, born Munich, Germany, December 25, 1951; admitted, 1983, Munich. *Education:* University of Munich (Referendar, 1978; Assessor, 1982). *LANGUAGES:* German, English and French.

(This Listing Continued)

FIEDLER & FORSTER, Munich—Continued

DR. LOUIS HAGEN, born May 15, 1958; admitted, 1988, Munich. *Education:* University of Munich; Banking Certificate Chamber of Commerce Munich. *LANGUAGES:* German, English and French.

BIRGIT ROTHENBERGER, born Seeheim, Germany, September 7, 1957; admitted, 1985, Munich. *Education:* Universities of Regensburg and Mannheim. *LANGUAGES:* German and English.

DOROTHEA G. VOGES, born Rustenburg, South Africa; admitted, 1990, South Africa (Not admitted in Germany). *Education:* University of Johannesburg (B.A., LL.B., 1987). *LANGUAGES:* German, English, Dutch and Afrikaans.

CHRISTINE GREINER, born Spalt, Germany, November 25, 1963; admitted, 1992, Munich. *Education:* Universities of Bayreuth and Erlangen-Nurnberg. *LANGUAGES:* German, English and French.

ENRES PETER, born Munich, Germany, November 24, 1965; admitted, 1994, Munich. *Education:* University of Munich. *LANGUAGES:* German and English.

OF COUNSEL

DR. HERMANN CLEMM, born Frankfurt, Germany, November 13, 1926; admitted, 1959, Munich. *Education:* Universities of Munich and Frankfurt (Dr. jur., 1959). Co-Author: "Beck'scher Bilanzkommentar," C.H. Beck, 1986; "Rechtshandbuch Vermögen und Investitionen in der ehemaligen DDR," C.H. Beck Publications, ("Property and Investments in the former GDR: a legal reference book"). Tax Consultant (Steuerberater), 1961. C.P.A. (Wirtschaftspruefer), 1963. *Member:* Institute of Chartered Accountants of Germany. *LANGUAGES:* German and English.

FINGERHUT, KARG & PARTNERS

Established in 1949

POTSDAMER STRASSE 12
D-80802 MUNICH, GERMANY
Telephone: 089/360 800-0
Fax: 089/361 77 63

Dresden, Germany Office: Hueblerstrasse 3-5, D-01309. Telephone: 0351-33 01 19. Fax: 0351-3 55 71.

Administrative Law, Air Traffic, Antitrust, Banking, Commercial, Construction, Copyright, Corporate, European Union, Family Law, Foreclosure, General Practice, Insolvency, Insurance, Intellectual Property, Labour, Licensing, Litigation, Medical, Mergers and Acquisitions, National and International Arbitration, Pharmaceutical, Product Liability, Tax Law, Trademark, Transportation, Trust and Estate, Unfair Competition.

MEMBERS OF FIRM

DR. MICHAEL FINGERHUT, born Waldshut/Rhein, Germany, November 2, 1943; admitted, 1972, Germany. *Education:* Universities of Bonn, Freiburg, Heidelberg (Referendar, 1967; Assessor, 1971). Stages at the Anti-trust Office of the Fed. Rep. of Germany, 1968, and the Commission of the European Communities, 1971. Author: "Das Rabattkartell," 1970; "Privatrecht für Wirtschaftswissenschaftler;" "Privatrecht, Fälle and Musterlösungen," 1.- 4. Edition; "Mergercontrol," (Authors: Raisch,Sölter, Kartte), BB 1971, IV et. seq (Bookreview); "Exclusive Distribution Agreements under the European Coal and Steel Community (ECSC)," AWD-BB, 1972, 120 et. seq.; "The Different Treatment under § 26 II GWB," BB 1973, 455 et. seq. Co-Author: "Warranty and Product Liability," DBW 1976, 123 et. seq. and 138 et. seq.; "Reimbursement of Recallexpenses," BB 1990, 725 et. seq.; "German-German Law of Identical Firm Names in Expropriation Cases," BB 1993, 1382 et. seq. Editor and Author: Nath/Schilling/Fingerhut, "Formbook on Contracts," 8, Edition, Heymanns Verlag, Köln 1994. Lecturer, Chamber of Commerce (IHK) Munich. *Member:* Munich and International (IBA) Bar Associations. *LANGUAGES:* German, English and French.

STEFAN KARG, born Munich, Germany, March 2, 1954; admitted, 1981, Germany. *Education:* University of Munich (Referendar, 1977; Assessor, 1980). Co-Author: Nath/Schilling/Fingerhut, "Formbook on Contracts," 8, Edition, Heymanns Verlag, Köln, 1994. Lecturer, Co-operative Union of Volks-und Raiffeisenbank, Banking-Association - Scientific Society of Banking Law, Frankfurt. *Member:* Munich Bar Association; American Chamber of Commerce. *LANGUAGES:* German and English.

(This Listing Continued)

HERBERT NATH, born Berlin, Germany, October 17, 1938; admitted, 1969, Germany. *Education:* Universities of Freiburg, Grenoble, Würzburg, Munich (Referendar, 1965; Assessor, 1968). *Member:* Munich Bar Association. *LANGUAGES:* German, English and French.

ASSOCIATES

ROLF RITZINGER, born Munich, Germany, April 20, 1956; admitted, 1985, Germany. *Education:* University of Munich, Germany (Referendar, 1982; Assessor, 1985). Co-Author: Nath/Schilling/Fingerhut, "Formbook on Contracts," 8, Edition, Heymanns Verlag, Köln, 1994. *Member:* German Association for Industrial Property and Copyright Law; Munich Bar Association. *LANGUAGES:* German and English.

ULRICH SCHULTE-SPECHTEL, born Marl, Germany, June 4, 1956; admitted, 1989, Germany. *Education:* University of Munch, Germany (Referendar, 1986; Assessor, 1989). Co-Author: Nath/Schilling/Fingerhut "Formbook on Contracts," 8, Edition, Heymanns Verlag, Köln, 1994. *Member:* Munich Bar Association. *LANGUAGES:* German and English.

MICHAEL TARABOCHIA, born Bregenz, Austria, November 11, 1960; admitted, 1992, Germany. *Education:* University of Munich, Germany (Referendar, 1989; Assessor, 1992). Co-Author: Nath/Schilling/Fingerhut "Formbook on Contracts," 8, Edition, Heymanns Verlag Köln, 1994. *Member:* Munich Bar Association. *LANGUAGES:* German and English.

DR. HORST BARBER, LL.M., born Detmold, Germany, March 16, 1959; admitted, 1992, Germany. *Education:* Universities of Erlangen-Nürnberg, Münster and Hamburg (Referendar, 1988; Assessor, 1992); Internship with the EEC Commission, Bruxelles, 1989; Southern Methodist University, Dallas, Texas (LL.M., 1988). Author: "The Power of Attorney at the German Federal Appeal Board of Maritime Investigation," HANSA 1989, pp. 1598 et seq.; "Share Deal Mergers and the Duty of Notification under the EEC Merger Control Regulation 4064/89/EEC, EWS 1992, pp. 98 et seq. Co-Author: "Objective Arbitrability and Public Policy in International Commercial Arbitration, Frankfurt/Main, 1994. *Member:* Munich Bar Association; German-American Lawyers' Association, DAJV; Association Internationale Des Jeunes Avocats, AIJA. *LANGUAGES:* German and English.

FLORKA & JUKOWSKI, P.C.

A PROFESSIONAL CORPORATION

A Partnership including a Professional Corporation

REZIDENZSTRASSE 27
MUNICH 80333, GERMANY
Telephone: 089-22-0639; 089-22-0630
Fax: 089-228-5894

Pontiac, Michigan Office: 120 East Wide Track Drive, Suite 300, 48342-2240. Telephone: 810-335-5530. Facsimile: 810-335-5535.

Probate, Estate Planning, Tax, Corporate, Commercial Litigation, Securities, Aviation Law, Personal Injury, Criminal Law, Municipal Law, Legal Malpractice.

ROBERT R. FLORKA, born Detroit, Michigan, August 14, 1957; admitted, 1983, Michigan. *Education:* Yale University (A.B., 1979); University of Detroit (J.D., 1983). Wayne County Charter Commission, 1980-1982. *Member:* State Bar of Michigan; American Bar Association. *PRACTICE AREAS:* Estate and Tax Planning; Corporation and Business; Defense Litigation; Real Estate; Municipal Law; Legal Malpractice.

LEON BRONISLAW JUKOWSKI, born Pontiac, Michigan, May 4, 1957; admitted, 1987, Michigan. *Education:* Georgetown University (B.S.F.S., 1981); University of Detroit; Washington College of Law (of American University) (J.D., 1987). *Member:* State Bar of Michigan; Association of Trial Lawyers of America (Associate Member). *LANGUAGES:* Arabic, German. *PRACTICE AREAS:* Commercial Litigation; Personal Injury Litigation; Municipal Law.

REPRESENTATIVE CLIENTS: Korean Airlines Co., Ltd.; City of Pontiac; U.S.A. Hockey, Inc.; Openings, Inc.; St. John's Armenian Church; Flexible Technologies, Inc.; Kut-Rite Manufacturing, Inc.; AAA Moving Co., Inc.; Lake Forest Health Services, Inc.

GAEDERTZ VIEREGGE QUACK KREILE

Rechtsanwälte

WIDENMAYERSTRASSE 32
D-80538 MUNICH, GERMANY
Telephone: (89) 212147-0
Telefax: (89)228 55 62

Berlin, Germany Office: Kurfürstendamm 157, D-10709 Berlin.
  Telephone: (30) 890 05-0. Telefax: (30) 892 26 06. Teletex: 30 88 15
  qkp d. Telex: 17 30 88 15 qkp d.
Cologne, Germany Office: Theodor-Heuss-Ring 19-21, D-50668 Cologne.
  Telephone: (221) 77 16-0. Telefax: (221)77 16-110. Teletex: 221 43 76
  olga d. Telex: 88 85 143 olga d.
Frankfurt/Main, Germany Office: Airport Center, Hugo-Eckener-Ring,
  D-60549 Frankfurt/Main. Telephone: (69)69 48 52. Telefax: (69)69 48
  60. Telex: 40 32 145 zibr d.
Leipzig, Germany Office: August-Bebel-Str. 38, D-04275 Leipzig.
  Telephone: (341) 477 83 81/83. Telefax: (341) 477 83 88.
Wiesbaden, Germany Office: Kaiser-Friedrich-Ring 65, D-65185
  Wiesbaden. Telephone: (611) 88 05-0. Telex: 41 86 295 gaed d.
  Teletex: 61 21 986 gaed. Telefax: (611) 81 03 09.
Brussels, Belgium Office: Avenue de Tervuren 35, B-1040 Brussels.
  Telephone: (2) 736 07 97. Telefax: (2) 732 69 12.
Prague, Czech Republic Office: Betlémska 1, CR-11000 Prague 1.
  Telephone: (2) 24 22 94 98. Telefax: (2) 232 12 29.

General Practice. Commercial, Corporate, Antitrust, Unfair Competition, Distribution and Franchise, Food and Drug Law, Intellectual Property, Trademarks, Designs, Investment East Germany, EC Law. Notaries (Berlin and Wiesbaden).

FIRM PROFILE: The law firm Gaedertz Vieregge Quack Kreile is the result of a merger between 4 partnerships: Heydt Vieregge & Partner, Cologne; Gaedertz Henn & Partner, Wiesbaden; Quack Kühn & Partner, Berlin; Prof. Kreile & Partner, Munich.

Gaedertz Vieregge Quack Kreile is one of the major German based law firms representing domestic and foreign clients in all fields of law that are relevant for national and international enterprises. An important part of the practice are the legal aspects of transnational transactions especially in EC. The firm advises not only German clients in international matters but also foreign enterprises about all implications of doing business in Germany. Thus many attorneys and also members of the support staff are fluent in English. Other languages such as French, Spanish, Portuguese, Italian, Russian, and Dutch are also spoken.

In addition, the offices in Cologne and Wiesbaden have the specialised capacity to administer large trademark portfolios worldwide including registration and litigation of trademarks and registered designs.

Clients of the firm include many well-known German and foreign companies active in a wide variety of businesses. Gaedertz Vieregge Quack Kreile also represents various trade associations as well as German federal, state and local governmental authorities.

In the Berlin, Wiesbaden and Frankfurt/Main offices, there are 10 attorneys qualified to act as "Notar," specially licensed to prepare and execute documents relating to incorporation of companies, real estate matters and other important commercial transactions where a special form of document is prescribed.

Gaedertz Vieregge Quack Kreile has more than 70 attorneys, including 42 partners, plus a support staff of approximately 150 people, working in the eight different offices.

The offices have for the most part city centre locations. The Frankfurt office is situated at the Airport-Centre of the Rhein-Main Airport.

MEMBERS OF FIRM

PROFESSOR DR. REINHOLD KREILE, born Aschaffenburg, Germany, 1929; admitted, 1958, Munich. *Education:* University of Munich. Various Publications on Tax Law and Copyright Law. Co-editor of Deutsche Steuerrechtszeitung and of Zeitschrift für Urheber - und Medienrecht. *LANGUAGES:* English. *PRACTICE AREAS:* Company; Commercial Law; Tax Law; Copyright.

DR. JOHANNES KREILE, born Munich, Germany, 1958; admitted, 1987, Munich. *Education:* University of Munich. Various Publications on Copyright Law and Media Law. *LANGUAGES:* English. *PRACTICE AREAS:* Media Law and Copyright.

(This Listing Continued)

DR. MARTIN FEYOCK, born Munich, Germany, 1962; admitted, 1989, Germany. *Education:* University of Munich. *LANGUAGES:* English, French.

DIETMAR PRÖCHEL, born Friedland/Schlesien, Germany, 1943; admitted, 1975, Cologne; 1978, Munich. *Education:* Universities of Munich and Cologne (Dr.jur.). *Member:* German Jurists' Conference; German Construction Law; German Association for Industrial Property Rights and Copyright. *LANGUAGES:* English, French.

ASSOCIATES

PROFESSOR DR. GÜNTER SÖFFING, born February 16, 1927; admitted, 1992, Munich. *Education:* University of Munich. Publisher of leading commentaries regarding tax law. Professor of Tax Law, University of Munich. Former Judge, Federal Fiscal Court. *LANGUAGES:* English.

Languages: German, English, French and Italian.

(For complete biographical data on personnel at Berlin, Cologne, Frankfurt/Main, Leipzig and Wiesbaden, Germany Offices as well as Brussels, Belgium and Prague, Czech, Republic Offices, see Professional Biographies at those locations).

GROLL, GROSS U. STEINER

ROSENTAL 10
80331 MUNICH, GERMANY
Telephone: (089) 23 69 06-0
Telefax: (089) 23 69 06-66

Real Estate, Estate Planning, Tax Law, Press Law, Sports Law.

DR. KLAUS MICHAEL GROLL, born Nienburg a.d. Weser, Germany, June 22, 1945; admitted, 1974, Germany. *Education:* Universities of Tübingen and Kiel (Law Degree, 1969; Dr. jur., 1972). Assistant Lecturer on Law, University of Kiel, 1973-1974. Author: "In der Flut der Gesetze," Droste Verlag, 1985; "Noten, Recht und Paragraphen,", Florian Noetzel Verlag, Wilhelms-Hafen, 1993. Lecturer, University of Munich and Musikhochscmule of Munich. *PRACTICE AREAS:* Media Law; Sports Law; Music; Wills.

ANTON STEINER, born Munich, Germany, September 20, 1961; admitted, 1988, Germany. *Education:* University of Munich (Law Degree, 1985). Research Associate, Institute of International Law, Munich, 1983-1987. *Member:* International Bar Association (Member, SGP Committee 1 and 5); Deutsche Gesellschaft für Erbrechtskunde e.V. (Member of Council). *PRACTICE AREAS:* Real Estate; Estate Planning; Inheritance.

DR. MICHAEL W. LAUTERBACH, born Frankfurt a.M., Germany, June 11, 1963; admitted, 1993, Germany. *Education:* Universities of Tübingen and Munich (Law Degree, 1990; Dr. jur., 1994). *PRACTICE AREAS:* Civil Litigation; Press Law.

PHILIPP CREMER, born Kranenburg, Germany, November 25, 1966; admitted, 1994, Germany. *Education:* Universities of Bayreuth; Geneve; Munich (Law Degree, 1992). *PRACTICE AREAS:* Civil Litigation; Contracts.

TAX ADVISORS

CARL ALEXANDER GROSS, born Garmisch-Partenkirchen, Germany, October 26, 1950; admitted, 1981, Tax Advisor; 1983, Certified Public Accountant. *Education:* University of Regensburg (Business Administration and Legal Science; Business Administration Degree, 1976). Professional Assistant, University of Regensburg, 1976-1982. *Member:* German Chamber of Auditors; Institute of Auditors; Tax Consultants' Association.

UDO BACHMAIER, born Eggenfelden, Germany, February 2, 1956; admitted, 1989, Tax Advisor. *Education:* University of Regensburg (Business Administration Degree, 1983). McDonald's Deutschland, Tax Department, 1984-1989. *Member:* Bavarian Chamber of Tax Advisors.

ALFONS SCHUSTER, born Munich, Germany, April 26, 1961; admitted, 1993, Tax Advisor. *Education:* University of Munich (Business Administration Degree, 1989). *Member:* Bavarian Chamber of Tax Advisors.

Languages: German and English

HAARMANN, HEMMELRATH & PARTNER

Established in 1987

EFFNERSTRAβE 38
D-81925 MUNICH, GERMANY
Telephone: (089) 924 00-0
Telefax: (089) 92400-133
Telex: 5 23 900 HUP D

Düsseldorf Office: Martin-Luther-Platz 26, D-40212 Düsseldorf. Telephone: (0211) 8399-0. Telefax (0211) 8399-133.

Berlin Office: Budapester Strasse 40a, D-10787 Berlin. Telephone: (030) 264 73-0. Telefax: (030) 264 73-133.

Frankfurt/Main Office: Neue Mainzer Strasse 75, D-60311 Frankfurt/Main. Telephone: (069) 92059-0. Telefax: (069) 92059-133.

Leipzig Office: Neumarkt 24, D-04109 Leipzig. Telephone: (0341) 1263-0. Telefax: (0341) 1263-133.

Tokyo Office: Shiroyama JT Mori Building, 8F, 3-1 Toranomon 4-chome, Minato-ku, Tokyo 105. Telephone: 81-3-34 59 54 85. Telefax: 81-3-35 78 89 56.

Prague Office: Cermàkova 7, CZ-1200 00 Prague 2, Czech Republic. Telephone: 42-2-24 23 90 36. Telefax: 42-2-24 23 88 42.

Corporate and Business Law, International and National Tax Law, Banking, Commercial Law, Labour Law, all Areas of Mergers and Acquisitions, Financial Transactions, International Law, Antitrust Law, Unfair Competition and Intellectual Property Rights Law, EEC Law, Real Estate Transactions, Management and Leveraged Buy-outs, National and Cross-border Leasing Transactions, Structuring of Funds, Accounting Services.

FIRM PROFILE: The firm, established in 1987, has strongly developed as a multi-disciplinary firm in Germany with seven offices. The firm is affiliated with Graham & James (US, Italy, Japan and China), Taylor Joynson Garrett (UK), Deacons (Hong Kong and Southeast Asia) and is a member of the international tax and audit network RSM International.

MEMBERS OF FIRM

DR. ALEXANDER HEMMELRATH, born Aschaffenburg, Germany, March 8, 1953; admitted, 1984, Munich, Steuerberater (Certified Tax Advisor); 1986, Wirtschaftsprüfer (Certified Public Accountant). *Education:* Universities of Berlin and Munich (Business Administration, 1977; Doctor at Law, 1981). Author: "Die Ermittlung des Betriebstättengewinns im Internationalen Steuerrecht," Verlag Florentz, 1982. Co-Author: "Vogel, DBA," Verlag Beck, 1983; *Rechtsformularbuch für das Unternehmen,* Verlag Beck, 1987. Learned Assistant of Professor Dr. Klaus Vogel, Holder of the Chair for Public Law, University of Munich, 1979-1980. *Member:* Institute of German Chartered Accountants (IDW); Deutsche Steuerjuristische Gesellschaft. *LANGUAGES:* German and English. *PRACTICE AREAS:* Tax; Real Estate; Finance; Property; Banks and Banking.

BODO RICHARDT, born Hannover, Germany, June 13, 1953; admitted, 1984, Munich, Steuerberater (Certified Tax Advisor); 1986, Wirtschaftsprüfer (Certified Public Accountant). *Education:* Technical Universities of Hanover and Munich (Mathematics, Physics, Business Administration, Dipl.-Math., 1980). *Member:* Institute of German Chartered Accountants (IDW). *LANGUAGES:* German, English and French. *PRACTICE AREAS:* Audit; Tax; Mergers and Acquisitions.

DR. ANDREAS OLDENBOURG, born Munich, Germany, June 3, 1952; admitted, 1983, Munich; 1987, Steuerberater (Certified Tax Advisor); 1989 Certified Public Accountant. *Education:* Universities of Munich and Freiburg (J.D., 1977; Doctor at Law, 1983). Author: "The Immediate Effect of the Directives of the European Community," Verlag Florentz, 1984. *Member:* International Bar Association; German-Brasilian Lawyers Association. *LANGUAGES:* German and English. *PRACTICE AREAS:* Corporate; Real Estate; Tax; Banks and Banking; Equipment Finance and Leasing.

DORIS PFLIEGER-STEININGER, born Stuttgart, Germany, August 23, 1954; admitted, 1983, Munich; 1986, Steuerberater (Certified Tax Advisor). *Education:* University of Heidelberg (J.D., 1981). *Member:* German-Japanese Lawyers Association. *LANGUAGES:* German and English. *PRACTICE AREAS:* Tax; Corporate; Commercial; Company; Bankruptcy.

DR. CLAUS SCHILD, born Munich, Germany, July 14, 1952; admitted, 1984, Munich, Steuerberater (Certified Tax Advisor); 1986, Wirtschaftsprüfer (Certified Public Accountant). *Education:* University of Munich (Business Administration, 1976). Author: "Erbschaftsteuer bel der Unter-

(This Listing Continued)

EU754B

nehmensnachfolge," (Estate and Inheritance Taxes), Frankfurt, 1980. *Member:* International Fiscal Association. *LANGUAGES:* German and English. *PRACTICE AREAS:* Tax; Finance; Federal Tax; Leases and Leasing.

PAULUS SCHILLING, born Waging a. S., Germany, July 29, 1946; admitted, 1976, Munich; 1982, Steuerberater (Certified Tax Advisor). *Education:* University of Munich and Regensburg (J.D., 1971). *LANGUAGES:* German, English, French and Italian. *PRACTICE AREAS:* Tax; Corporate; Bankruptcy; Debtor and Creditor.

HANSJÖRG ZELGER, born Waldshut, Germany, April 5, 1956; admitted, 1985, Munich, Steuerberater (Certified Tax Advisor). *Education:* University of Augsburg (Business Administration, 1981). *Member:* Institute of German Chartered Accountants (IDW). *LANGUAGES:* German and English. *PRACTICE AREAS:* Audit; Tax; Finance.

DR. CHRISTOPH VON EINEM, born Bremen, Germany, April 6, 1955; admitted, 1986, Göttingen. *Education:* Universities of Freiburg i. Br., and Göttingen (J.D., 1982; Doctor at Law, 1988); Boalt Hall School of Law, University of California at Berkeley (LL.M., 1986). Faculty Assistant, University of Göttingen, 1982-1986. *Member:* Studienvereinigung Kartellrecht; German Association for the Protection of Industrial Property and Copyright; German-American Lawyers Association; German British Lawyers Association; International Bar Association; Union Internationale des Avocats. *LANGUAGES:* German and English. *PRACTICE AREAS:* Corporate; Antitrust and Trade Regulation; Intellectual Property; European Community Law.

THOMAS KREMPL, born Munich, Germany, November 15, 1959; admitted, 1989, Munich; 1991, Steuerberater (Certified Tax Advisor). *Education:* University of Munich (J.D., 1985; Business Administration, 1989). *LANGUAGES:* German and English. *PRACTICE AREAS:* Corporate; Labour Law; Tax; Commercial.

ARNULF WAGNER, born Nürnberg, Germany, May 15, 1959; admitted, 1990 Steuerberater (Certified Tax Advisor). *Education:* University of Munich (Business Administration, 1986). *LANGUAGES:* German and English. *PRACTICE AREAS:* Tax.

MICHAEL V. WALDTHAUSEN, born Nürnberg, Germany, November 2, 1956; admitted, 1988, Munich. *Education:* University of Munich (J.D., 1984). *Member:* American Chamber of Commerce (IBC Section, Munich). *LANGUAGES:* German, English and French. *PRACTICE AREAS:* Corporate; Commercial; Tax; Computers and Software; International Law.

CHRISTIAN MARKOWSKY, born Neustadt a.d. Weinstr., Germany, November 25, 1954; admitted, 1987, Germany. *Education:* Universities of Munich and Göttingen. *Member:* German Association for the Protection of Industrial Property and Copyright Law (GRUR); AJPPJ. *LANGUAGES:* German and English. *PRACTICE AREAS:* Corporate Law; Intellectual Property Rights; Unfair Competition; Copyright and Media Law; Antitrust and Trade Regulation.

OF COUNSEL

DR. KARL-HEINZ KNEPPER, born Ahlen, Germany, July 22, 1925; admitted, 1965, Freiburg. *Education:* University of Freiburg (J.D., 1952; Doctor at Law, 1965). Co-Author: Kirchhof/Söhn EStG, Verlag C.F. Müller. *Member:* Deutsche Steuerjuristische Gesellschaft. *LANGUAGES:* German and English. *PRACTICE AREAS:* Tax; Corporate; Federal Tax.

PROFESSOR DR.DR. RUDOLPH LUKES, born Munich, October 30, 1924; admitted, 1954, Munich. *Education:* University of Munich (Doctor at Law, 1950, Doctor occonomiae publicac, 1952, Assistant Professor, 1958). Ordentlicher Professor der Rechte 1959 University at Muenster W. emeritieri, 1990. Author of various books and articles dealing with Competition Law and European Communities' Law. *LANGUAGES:* German and English. *PRACTICE AREAS:* European Community Law; Environmental Law; Antitrust; Energy; Telecommunication.

Languages: German, English, French, Japanese, Dutch, Spanish, Italian, Russian, Slovakian, Czech and Mandarin.

(For Biographical Data on other Members of Firm, See Professional Biographies at Düsseldorf, Berlin, Leipzig, Frankfurt, Germany, Tokyo, Japan and Prague, Czech Republic).

HANTKE, HELMING & PARTNERS

PRINZREGENTENSTRASSE 79
81675 MUNICH, GERMANY
Telephone: 49 89 470 50 48
Telefax: 49 89 470 65 90

Berlin, Germany Office: Taubenstrasse 11-13, Büro 2048, 10117. Telephone: 49-030-229 40 36. Telefax: 49-030-229 14 35.

A Member of AdvoSelect EEIG, a network of law firms pooling their resources in special fields and crossborder cases, specializing in business law for middle sized companies. AdvoSelect is represented in 51 cities throughout Europe.

General and International Practice, Commercial and International Law, Corporate, Banking, Mergers, Acquisitions, Leasing, Trade Law, Real Estate, Construction Law, Labour Law, Tax, Accounting Services, National and EC Antitrust, Copyright, Patent, Trademark, Intellectual Property, Unfair Competition, EC Law, Drug Law, Computer Law, Product Liability, Commercial Litigation, International Arbitration.

MEMBERS OF FIRM

DR. DIETMAR HANTKE, born Carlsruhe, Upper Silesie, March 14, 1944; admitted, 1973, Germany. *Education:* Universities of Münster and Würzburg (Doctor of Laws, 1970; Law Degree, 1973). Stage in a Paris Law Firm. Author: "Product Liability," 1989. Co-Author: "Beschränkung auf den Urkunden-Beweis im Schiedsverfahren," 1981. Co-Editor: "Nationale und Internationale Warenzeichen-Tabelle," annually since 1986. *Member:* Munich and International Bar Associations; German Institution of Arbitration; German-French and German-English Jurists' Associations. *LANGUAGES:* German, English and French. *PRACTICE AREAS:* Commercial and International Law; Corporate; Banking; Mergers and Acquisitions; International Arbitration.

BERND HELMING, born Beckum, Germany, March 27, 1950; admitted, 1978, Germany. *Education:* University of Munich (Law Degree, Law and Economics, 1978). Co-Author: "Für meine Familie alles geordnet," 1981. *Member:* IDL Interessenverband Deutscher Leasing-Unternehman e.V. (Chairman, Law Commission); Munich Bar Association. *LANGUAGES:* German, English and French. *PRACTICE AREAS:* Leasing; Corporate; Mergers; Acquisitions; Trade Law.

ANDREAS JASPER, born Prien am Chiemsee, October 22, 1950; admitted, 1978, Germany. *Education:* Universities of Munich and Geneva, Switzerland (Law Degree, 1978). *Member:* International Association of Young Lawyers (AIJA); German Association for Construction Law; Munich Bar Association; German-Hungarian Jurists' Association. *LANGUAGES:* German, English and French. *PRACTICE AREAS:* Real Estate; Construction Law; Wills; General Legal Practice.

ASSOCIATES

THOMAS WOLF, born Munich, July 22, 1956; admitted, 1987, Germany. *Education:* University of Munich (Law Degree, 1987). *Member:* Munich Bar Association. *LANGUAGES:* German and English. *PRACTICE AREAS:* Individual and Collective Labour Law; Corporate; General Legal Practice.

TAX ADVISORS

THOMAS NEUMANN, born Rheydt, Germany, October 15, 1954; admitted, 1985, Germany, Steuerberater (Certified Tax Advisor); 1988, Wirtschaftsprüfer (Certified Public Accountant). *Education:* University of Freiburg (Bachelor of Science, Econ.). *Member:* Chamber of Certified Public Auditors; Chamber of Tax Advisors. *LANGUAGES:* German and English. *PRACTICE AREAS:* Tax; Accounting services; Audit.

OF COUNSEL

KONRAD HUCH-HALLWACHS, born Dresden, August 3, 1931; admitted, 1959, Germany. *Education:* Universities of Freiburg, Mayence and Köln (Law Degree, 1959). *Member:* Munich and International Bar Associations; Deutsche Vereinigung für gewerblichen Rechtsschutz und Urheberrecht e.V.; AIPPI. (Also practices individually). *LANGUAGES:* German, English and French. *PRACTICE AREAS:* National and EC Antitrust; Copyright; Patent; Trademark; Intellectual Property; Unfair Competition.

MARCUS EHRHART, born Stuttgart, July 9, 1947; admitted, 1980, Germany. *Education:* University of Munich (M.B.A., Economics and Law, 1973; Law Degree, 1978). Stages in Denmark, France and USA. Member, Export Club of Bavaria, Union of Merchants and Industrialists of Berlin.

(This Listing Continued)

Member: German-American Chamber of Commerce; Berlin Bar Association. *LANGUAGES:* German, English, French, Spanish and Italian. *PRACTICE AREAS:* Corporate; Drug and Computer Law.

HASELTINE LAKE PARTNERS

(European Patent Attorneys)

Established in 1980

MOTORAMA HAUS 502
ROSENHEIMER STRASSE 30
D-81669 MUNICH 80, GERMANY
Telephone: (089) 448 89 89
Cables: SCOPO MUENCHEN
Telex: 522936 HASMU
Fax: (089) 48 56 86

Associated British Practice:
Haseltine Lake & Co., Hazlitt House, 28 Southampton Buildings, Chancery Lane, London, WC2A 1AT, England. Telephone: +44 (0) 171 405 6093. Cables: SCOPO London WC 2. Telex: 21995 SCOPO. Fax: +44 (0) 171 405 0965

Haseltine Lake & Co., Temple Gate House, Temple Gate, Bristol, BS1 6PT, England. Telephone: +44 (0) 171 926 0197. Cables: SCOPO BRISTOL. Telex: 449559 LAKES. Fax: +44 (0) 171 929 0387.

Haseltine Lake & Co., Park House, Park Square, Leeds, LS1 2PS, England. Telephone: +44 (0) 113 244 4616. Cables: SCOPO LEEDS. Telex: 557723 HASEL. Fax: +44 (0) 113 244 4511.

Associated British Practice specializing in Trademarks and Service Marks:
Haseltine Lake Trademarks, Hazlitt House, 28 Southampton Buildings, Chancery Lane, London WCA 1AT, England. Telephone: +44 (0) 171 242 4176. Cables: SCOPO LONDON WC2. Telex: 21995 SCOPO. Fax: +44 (0) 171 405 0965 also available at Bristol and Leeds offices listed above.

Practice before the European Patent Office.
Registered as European Patent Attorneys.
Entitled to practice in relation to all aspects of Industrial Property Rights before the European Patent Office, the German Patent Office and the German Courts.

PARTNERS

Michael A. Bull	Michael J. Abrams
Christopher R. K. Fane	John R.A.M. Cheyne
John K. Godsill	James H. Sunderland (Resident)
Richard D. Overbury	Timothy C. Stebbing (Resident)
Ian R. Muir	David A. Nash
Michael R. Jones	Christine L. Fenlon
Guy S. Bedggood	David C. O'Connell
Warren Silverman	Christopher C. Gibbs
Dr. Ulrich M. Benedum (Resident)	

HEISS & PARTNERS

BRIENNER STRASSE 1
80333 MUNICH, GERMANY
Telephone: (89) 29 08 29-0
Telecopier: (89) 29 08 29-29
Telex: 5 24 600 HEISS D
Telegrams: Attorney

Mailing Address: Postfach 20 10 26, 80010 Munich, Germany

Business, Commercial, Construction, Copyright, Corporate, E.E.C., Eastern European and other Foreign Investments, Entertainment, Intellectual Property, Labor, Litigation, New Media, Mergers and Acquisitions, Real Property, Receivership and Bankruptcy, Taxation, International Tax Planning, Unfair Competition. General Practice.

MEMBERS OF FIRM

DR. FRANZ LUDWIG HEISS, LL.M., born Tegernsee, Germany, January 18, 1947; admitted, 1974, Germany; 1986, as Tax Lawyer (FAStR) and Tax Advisor (StB); 1992, as Certified Public Accountant (WP). *Education:* Universities of Heidelberg, Würzburg, München (Referendar, 1970; Dr.Jur., 1973; Assessor, 1974); Boalt Hall School of Law, University of California at Berkeley (LL.M., 1975). Lecturer, University of Augsburg, 1982-1983. Author: "Allocation of Deductions of Multinational Enterprises," RIW/AWD 1975, 332 et seq.; "Basic Problems Regarding the Con-

(This Listing Continued)

HEISS & PARTNERS, Munich—Continued

sent to Dedications of Streets," DVBl 1976, 93 et seq. (co-author); "The US Way of Allocating Deductions to Domestic and Other Income," RIW-/AWD 1977, 476 et seq.; "Real Property and Taxes," Commerce in Germany, 2/78, pp. XVII et seq.; "Comments Regarding the Classification of a German GmbH for US. Tax Purposes," RIW/AWD 1978, 280; "The Association as Vehicle for Investments in the US," DB 1978, 1505 et seq.; "Taxation in Canada," Wirtschaftsverkehr mit dem Ausland, VWV Verlag, 1979, Kanada, pp. 20 et seq.; "US Real Property and Taxes," Investments in the US, A Guide for German Enterprises, published by Dresdner Bank, 1979, pp. 76 et seq.; "The Taxation of German Investments in U.S. Real Property," Vorteilhafte Geldanlagen, R. Haufe Verlag, Freiburg, 1982-1983, Gruppe 4, pp. 287-346; "Acquiring and Holding Real Property in the US, Haus- und Grundbesitz im Ausland," R. Haufe Verlag, Freiburg, 1983, pp. 1-110; "Romanian Privatization Act of 1991," WiRO, 1992; " The Setting-Up Of, And The Participation In, Companies by Germans in Poland" (co-author), Handbook for Business and Law in Easter Europe, C.H. Beck Verlag, 1992; Co-Editor: Handbook for Business and Law in Eastern Europe, C.H. Beck Verlag, loose-leaf. *Member:* The Association of the Bar of the City of New York; German Bar Association; International Bar Association (IBA, Member, Section on Business Law); German Association for the Protection of Industrial Property and Copyright; Institute for Copyright and Media Law; International Fiscal Association, IFA; Munich Chamber of Tax Advisors; German Chamber of Certified Public Accountants; Institute for Certified Public Accountants, IDW; German Tax Law Society, DSTJG; Munich Juridical Society, MJG; German-American Lawyers' Association, DAJV; American German Chamber of Commerce; Association of Independent Entrepreneurs, ASU. *LANGUAGES:* German, English and French.

DR. JÜRGEN KARL WENTE, LL.M., born Hannover, Germany, June 18, 1957; admitted, 1988, Germany. *Education:* Universities of Göttingen, Freiburg (Referendar, 1982); University of Pennsylvania Law School (LL.M., 1985); Göttingen (Dr.Jur., 1986); Bonn (Assessor, 1988). Recipient, Scholarships: Konrad-Adenauer-Stiftung; DAAD; Rotary Foundation of Rotary International. Author: "Data Protection and Basic Human Rights," NJW 1984, pp. 1446 et seq.; "Basics of Broadcasting Law in the USA,"UFITA 103, pp. 131 et seq.; "Data Transfer no Publication of Data," RDV 1986, pp. 256 et seq.; "Journalists' Access to Private Areas," ZUM 1987, pp.167 et seq.; "Law of the Research by Journalists," Nomos Verlag, Baden-Baden, 1987; "Privacy in the Process of Prosecution," Der Strafverteidiger 1988, pp.216 et seq; "The Exploitation Of Information Unlawfully Researched," ZUM 1988, pp. 438 et seq.; "Judicial Relief Against Decisions Of The Agency For The Protection Of The Juvenile Against Prints Endangering Public Morals," ZUM 1991, pp. 561 et seq.; "The Relevanc Of The Term 'Verfugungsberechtigter' For The Application Of The Property Statute," VIZ 1992, pp. 125 et seq. *Member:* German Bar Association; German-American Lawyers' Association; DAJV; German Association for the Protection of Industrial Property and Copyright. *LANGUAGES:* German and English.

PAUL M. KÖSSLER, M.C.J., born Munich, Germany, March 3, 1951; admitted 1979, Germany. *Education:* Universities of Munich and Geneva (Switzerland) (Referendar, 1977; Assessor, 1979); University of Texas at Austin (M.C.J., 1980). Internship with law firm in Atlanta, Georgia, 1977. Lecturer for Public Law at the University of the German Armed Forces in Munich, 1977-1979. Author: "The Practising Lawyer in the Federal Republic of Germany," The International Lawyer, Summer, 1980; "The Matter With The Compulsory Licence," Neue Medien, 1984/I, p. 65, ff; "Compromise on the Allocation of the Copyrights on VCR," (Videocassetten-recorder), Medien und Recht 3/85. Vice Chairman and Legal Counsellor of GVU (Association to Prevent Copyright Infringements), 1985-1980. Vice Chairman of BKS (Federal Association of Cable and Satellite). Legal Counsellor of BKS and Chairman of the Radio Department of BKS, 1986-1988. Board Member, BAF (Bavarian Academy of Television), 1993—. *Member:* German Bar Association. *LANGUAGES:* German, English and French.

DR. CHRISTOPH M. KEIM, born Straubing, West Germany, July 15, 1958; admitted, 1990, Germany. *Education:* Universities of Munich and Berlin (Referendar, 1985; Assessor, 1988; Dr. jur., 1991). *Member:* German Bar Association. *LANGUAGES:* German, English and French.

ARNE JOHANNES REIF, born Balingen, Germany, December 14, 1954; admitted, 1988, Germany. *Education:* Universities of Tübingen und Berlin (Referendar, 1986; Assessor, 1988). *Member:* German Bar Association. *LANGUAGES:* German and English.

DR. REINHARD M. EHRL, born Neumarkt/Oberpfalz, Germany, June 22, 1960; admitted, 1991, Germany. *Education:* Universities of Er-

(This Listing Continued)

langen, Munich and Regensburg (Referendar, 1986; Assessor, 1990; Dr. iur., 1994). Author: "The Administrative Execution of a Will with Respect to a Limited Partnership Interest," 1994. *Member:* German Bar Association. *LANGUAGES:* German, English and French.

ASSOCIATES

DR. ERNST L. GANZERT, born Darmstadt, Germany, April 24, 1961; admitted, 1991, Germany. *Education:* Universities of Munich and Regensburg (Referendar, 1987; Assessor, 1990; Dr. jur., 1992). Author: "The International Employment Relationship under German and French International Private Law," Frankfurt/Main, 1992. *Member:* German Bar Association. *LANGUAGES:* German, English and French.

SUSANNE MERTEN-WENTE, born Bonn, Germany, December 6, 1960; admitted, 1990, Germany. *Education:* Universities of Bonn and Freiburg (Referendar, 1984; Assessor, 1988). *Member:* German Bar Association. *LANGUAGES:* German and English.

PETER W. KREMER, born Hagen, Germany, May 9, 1963; admitted, 1991, Germany. *Education:* Universities of Passau (Germany) and Angers (France) (Referendar, 1988; Assessor, 1991). Internship with law firm in San Diego, California, 1990. *Member:* German Bar Association; German-French Lawyers' Association (DFJV). *LANGUAGES:* German, English and French.

JÜRGEN E. KAMMERLOHR, M.C.L., born Freising, Germany, November 1, 1963; admitted, 1990, Germany. *Education:* University of Munich (Referendar, 1987; Assessor, 1990); University of San Diego, School of Law (M.C.L., 1992). *Member:* German Bar Association. *LANGUAGES:* German and English.

Languages: German, English and French

HEUSSEN BRAUN von KESSEL & PARTNER

BRIENNERSTRASSE 9
D-80333 MUNICH, GERMANY
Telephone: 089-290 97-0
Telex: 5-216 022 ADVO D
Telefax: 089-22 85 117

Berlin, Germany Office: Schlüterstr. 37, 10629 Berlin. Telephone: 030-88 57 68 - 0. Fax: 030-88 87 68 - 30.

General International Practice.

MEMBERS OF FIRM

DR. BENNO HEUSSEN, born Stuhlingen, Germany, May 18, 1944; admitted, 1973, Germany. *Education:* Free University of West Berlin, Freiburg, Munich (Dr.jur., 1972). *Member:* German-Japanese Association; German and American Lawyers Association; German-British Chamber of Commerce; German-Japanese Chamber of Commerce. *LANGUAGES:* German and English.

DR. GUNTHER BRAUN, born Plauen, Germany, July 28, 1943; admitted, 1973, Germany. *Education:* University of Munich (Dr.jur., 1972). Author: "Rechtsnatur des Automatenaufstellvertrages," Munich, 1972. *Member:* German-British Chamber of Commerce. *LANGUAGES:* German, English and French.

DR. JUSTIN VON KESSEL, born Breslau, Germany, July 1, 1943; admitted, 1973, Germany. *Education:* Universities of Heidelberg and Munich (Dr.jur., 1973). Author: "Die konsolidierte Konzernbesteuerung im Körperschaftsteverrecht der USA," 1973 (Consolidated Income Tax Return in the US Corporation Tax System). *Member:* German-British Chamber of Commerce; International Bar Association. *LANGUAGES:* German and English.

DR. REINER PONSCHAB, born Peking, China, September 5, 1943; admitted, 1973, Germany. *Education:* Universities of Munich and Freiburg (Dr.jur., 1975); Fachanwalt fur Steuerrecht (tax law Expert). Author: "Zur Haftung der Hersteller von Sicherheitsbindungen," 1970; "Berufsverbote durch nichtstaatliche Spruchgremien," Bonn, 1971; "Die Völkerrechtliche Repräsentation der Bundesrepublik Deutschland durch zentrale und dezentrale Bundesorgane", 1975. Lecturer on Law, Munich University, 1970-1971. *Member:* German Tax Law Association; Young Lawyers International Association. *LANGUAGES:* German and English.

DR. JUR. PETER DECKER, born Munich, March 15, 1955; admitted, 1983, Germany. *Education:* University of Munich (Dr. jur., 1984). Author: "Recognition and Execution of Foreign Judgement under Law of Civil Pro-

(This Listing Continued)

cedure," 1984. *Member:* German-Italian Chamber of Commerce. *LANGUAGES:* English, Italian and Spanish.

MATTHIAS WOHLFAHRT, born Menden, West Germany, July 17, 1955; admitted, 1989, Germany. *Education:* University of Munich, 1989. *LANGUAGES:* English and French.

TAX ADVISOR

PETER HEE, born May 5, 1952; Chartered Accountant, Tax Adviser, Managing Director EC-Aktiengesellschaft, Wirtschaftsprüfungsgesellschaft. *Education:* University of Augsburg. *Member:* Institut der Wirtschaftsprüfer in Deutschland. *LANGUAGES:* English.

ASSOCIATES

ERNST PETER SACHSE, born Bochum, West Germany, December 1, 1937; admitted, 1964, Germany. *Education:* University of Munich, 1964. *LANGUAGES:* English.

ALICE MALY, born April 7, 1946; admitted, 1974, Germany. *Education:* Universities of Munich and Innsbruck, 1974. *LANGUAGES:* English.

DR.JUR. RALPH R. STEINBRÜCK, born Mainz, Germany, August 26, 1954; admitted, 1982, Munich. *Education:* Universities of Mainz and Munich (Dr.Jur., 1981). *LANGUAGES:* German and English.

DR. PETRA SAUCKEL, born November 17, 1956; admitted, 1983, Germany. *Education:* University of Munich. *LANGUAGES:* German, English and French.

ULRICH FRAULOB, born Erlangen, June 28, 1957; admitted, 1985, Germany. *Education:* University of Munich. *LANGUAGES:* German, English and French.

DR. BORIS A. MARIACHER, born Augsburg, West Germany, October 17, 1960; admitted, 1990, Germany. *Education:* University of Munich (Dr.Jur., 1988). *LANGUAGES:* English and French.

MICHAEL KETTERL, born Dachau, March 4, 1961; admitted, 1990, Germany. *Education:* University of Munich, 1990. *LANGUAGES:* English and Italian.

DR. AXEL CZARNETZKI, born Saarbrücken; admitted, 1991, Germany. *Education:* Saarbrücken and Munich University. *LANGUAGES:* German and English.

MONIKA BOENKE, born Wolfsburg, July 22, 1961; admitted, 1989, Heidelberg; 1991, Munich. *Education:* University of Würzburg and Heidelberg. *LANGUAGES:* English and French. *PRACTICE AREAS:* Family Law.

PETER LENZ, born Wuerzburg, August 31, 1963; admitted, 1991, Germany. *Education:* University of Frankfurt; University of Munich. *LANGUAGES:* German and English. *PRACTICE AREAS:* General International Practice.

MATTHIAS SCHIEMANN, born Kassel, Germany, April 23, 1956; admitted, 1986, Frankfurt; 1990, Madrid. *Education:* Universities of Göttingen and Munich. *Member:* German and Spanish Lawyers Associations; German-Spanish Chamber of Commerce. *LANGUAGES:* German, Spanish and English. *PRACTICE AREAS:* Anglo-American Law of Contract; Spanish Law of Contract; Trust Law.

DR. ANDRÉ TURIAUX, born Aachen, August 4, 1962; admitted, 1993, Munich. *Education:* University of Passau (1984-1986); University of Munich (1987-1989). *LANGUAGES:* German and English. *PRACTICE AREAS:* Administrative Law; Environmental law.

ANDREA MARIA WESSELS, born Hamburg, Germany, October 8, 1963; admitted, 1991, Munich. *Education:* Universities of Hamburg and Munich (1989). Author: "Franchise-Vestsage im Vergleich," DFV, 1992. *Member:* German Franchise Association. *LANGUAGES:* German and English. *PRACTICE AREAS:* Franchise Law; License Agreements; Industrial Property Law.

MICHAEL SCHNEIDER, born Regensburg, October 9, 1956; admitted, Munich. *Education:* University of Regensburg. Chartered Accountant, Munich, 1994. *LANGUAGES:* German, English and French.

MARKUS SCHMIDT, born Köln, July 17, 1965; admitted, 1994, Munich. *Education:* University of Munich. *LANGUAGES:* German and English.

DR. GABRIELE FRUHMANN, born Hildesheim, May 23, 1961; admitted, 1989, Munich. *Education:* University of Munich. *LANGUAGES:* German, English and French.

(This Listing Continued)

DR. BIRGIT SCHOELLER, born Kiel, February 21, 1965; admitted, 1994, Munich. *Education:* University of Munich. *LANGUAGES:* English, French and German.

KONRAD HUCH-HALLWACHS

PRINZREGENTENSTRASSE 79
D-81675 MUNICH, GERMANY
Telephone: (089) 4 70-60 31 (-50 48)
Telefax: (089) 4 70-65 90

General Practice, Litigation, Commercial, Corporate, EEC, International Antitrust, Arbitration, Copyright, Estate, Family, Protection of Industrial Property, Patent, Trademark, Taxation and Unfair Competition.

KONRAD HUCH-HALLWACHS, born Dresden, August 3, 1931; admitted, 1959, Düsseldorf, Northrhein-Westfalia; 1962, Baden-Württemberg; 1964, Bavaria, Regional Court Munich I and II, Court of Appeals, Munich. *Education:* Universities of Freiburg, Mayence and Cologne. *Member:* International Bar Association; Deutsche Vereinigung für Gewerblichen Rechtsschutz und Urheberrecht e.V.; AIPPI.

KANZLEI
DR. KOPPE & PARTNER
RECHTSANWÄLTE

Munich - Leipzig

Established in 1970

LEOPOLDSTRASSE 20
(AM SIEGESTOR)
80802 MUNICH, GERMANY
Telephone: 49/89/381 581-0
Telefax: 49/89/381 581-10
BTX: 49/89/381 581-91

Leipzig, Germany Office: Gottschedstrasse 12, 04109. Telephone: 49/341/96413-0. Telefax: 49/341/96413-10.

General Practice. International Private Law, EEC, Antitrust, Arbitration, Industrial Relations, Labor and Tax Law. Litigation. Corporate Law and Reorganizations, International Contracts including Negotiations, Founding and Accompanying of German Subsidiaries. Consultant to overseas enterprises.

DR. JUR. PETER J. R. KOPPE, born Garmisch-Partenkirchen, Germany, February 27, 1937; admitted, 1970, Bavaria. *Education:* Ludwig-Maximilian-Universität, Munich; Herzog-Albrecht-Universität, Kiel (Philosophy, Economics, Law; First and Second Bavarian State's Examinations); Trinity College, Dublin. Author: "Contributory Negligence in English and Irish Law", Doctoral Thesis, 1970; "Erfahrungen mit neuen Außenhandelsrecht GiW", Article Handelsblatt, 06.05. 1976. *Member:* Rechtsanwaltskammer OLG Bezirk (Munich); Steuerberaterkammer (Munich); American Chamber of Commerce (Germany); British Chamber (Germany); Federal Bar Association (Germany); Arbeitsgemeinschaft Selbständiger Unternehmer (Independent entrepreneurs' Union), of ERWUS (European Association of Attorneys); Exportclub Bayern (Association of Exporting Enterprises in Bavaria); TII (European Association for the Transfer of Technologies, Innovation and Industrial Innovation). *LANGUAGES:* German and English.

ASSOCIATES

ELER VON BOCKELMANN, born Frankfurt/Main, Germany, August 1, 1962; admitted, 1991, Munich. *Education:* University of Passau (1987); Referendardienst. Scientific Assistant, University of Passau, 1987-1991. *Member:* Rechtsanwaltskammer OLG Bezirk (Munich). *LANGUAGES:* German, English and French.

ANTJE JUNGK, born Goettingen, Germany, October 19, 1964; admitted, 1993, Munich. *Education:* University of Passau; East China Institute of Politics and Law, Shanghai. Referendardienst. Scientific Assistant, University of Passau, 1989-1991. *Member:* German-Chinese Lawyers' Association. Member, Rechtsanwaltskammer OLG Bezirk (Munich). *LANGUAGES:* German, English, Spanish, French and Chinese.

(This Listing Continued)

KANZLEI DR. KOPPE & PARTNER
RECHTSANWÄLTE, Munich—Continued

ALEXANDER WÜRDINGER, born Munich, Germany, December 15, 1964; admitted, 1992, Munich; 1994, Leipzig. *Education:* Ludwig-Maximilain-Universität, Munich. Member, Rechtsanwaltskammer OLG Bezirk (Munich). *LANGUAGES:* German, English and French.

KLAKA & PARTNER

DELPSTRASSE 4
D-81679 MUNICH, GERMANY
Telephone: (089) 99 89 19 0
Fax: (089) 98 00 36

Patent, Trademark, Copyright, Unfair Competition, Antitrust, Company and Commercial Law. General Practice.

MEMBERS OF FIRM

RAINER KLAKA, born Breslau, February 11, 1927; admitted, 1953, Germany. *Education:* University of Munich. Author: "Vorbenutzung im Kennzeichnungsrecht," Festschrift für von Gamm, 1990; "Personal Liability of Corporate Officers for Acts of Unfair Competition or Infringement of Intellectual Property Rights," Festschrift Döllerer, 1988. Lecturer, Deutsche Anwaltsakademie. *Member:* German Association for the Protection of Industrial Property and Copyright Law (GRUR). *LANGUAGES:* German and English.

DR. MICHAEL NIEDER, born Braunschweig, Germany, May 2, 1941; admitted, 1972, Germany. *Education:* Universities of Göttingen and Frankfurt. Research Associate, Institute of Civil Procedure, University of Munich, 1968-1969. Author: "Die Parteien der Widerklage". Member, Legal Department, Carl Zeiss, West Germany, 1969-1972. *Member:* German Association for the Protection of Industrial Property and Copyright Law. *LANGUAGES:* German, English and French.

GUIDO DIEMER, born Munich, Germany, August 29, 1945; admitted, 1972, Germany. *Education:* University of Munich. Author: "Meinungs-freiheit und Wettbewerbsrecht", FS Klaka 1987. *Member:* German Association for the Protection of Industrial Property and Copyright Law. *LANGUAGES:* German and English.

DR. CHRISTOF KRÜGER, born Hamburg, Germany, October 28, 1946; admitted, 1977, Germany. *Education:* Universities of Heidelberg, Lausanne, Freiburg (Dr.jur., 1979). Research Associate, Institute of Comparative Law, Paris, 1975-1977. Author: "Die Haftung des Dienstherrn für Gelegenheitsdelikte seiner Hilfspersonen nach deutschem und französischem Recht". Subauthor commentary to the German copyright act (Co-author, § 73 ff Urheberrechtsgesetz) Author: "Das Buch zum Film," FS Schwarz 1988; "Zur Wahrnehmung des Filmherstellungsrechts durch die GEMA," FS Reichardt 1990. *Member:* German Association for the Protection of Industrial Property and Copyright Law; German-French Lawyers' Association. *LANGUAGES:* German, French and English.

DR. ANDREAS SCHULZ, born Hamburg, Germany, May 29, 1953; admitted, 1983, Germany. *Education:* Universities of Munich and Göttingen (Dr. jur., 1981); Visiting Scholar , Stanford Law School (1982-1983). Assistant, Institute for European and International Business Law, University of Munich, 1979-1980. Author: "Kostenerstattung bei erfolgloser Abmahnung," WRP 90, 658; "Warenzeichenbenutzung - Das Dilemma bei fehlender oder abgewandelter Benutzung eines Warenzeichens," Markenartikel 86, 146. *Member:* German-American Lawyers Association; GRUR; AIJA. *LANGUAGES:* German and English.

DR. WOLFGANG STRAUB, born Pforzheim, Germany, November 12, 1954; admitted, 1984, Germany. *Education:* Universities of Freiburg and Munich (Dr. jur., 1985). Assistant University of Munich, 1981-1984. Research Assistant at the Max-Planck-Institute for Foreign and International Patent, Copyright and Unfair Competition Law, Munich, 1981-1984. Author: "Section 15 of the German Antitrust Code as the General Clause of the Statutory Law Against Contractual Restraints of Competition". *Member Licensing Executive Society (LES); GRUR. LANGUAGES:* German and English.

OLAF GIEBE, born Hannover, February 6, 1956; admitted, 1987, Germany. *Education:* University of Göttingen. Author: "Grundzüge des Patentrechts, ZAP 1990, 1079. *Member:* GRUR. *LANGUAGES:* German and English.

(This Listing Continued)

ASSOCIATES

DR. ALFRED H. MEYER, born Ludwigsburg, Germany, December 30, 1961; admitted, 1991, Germany. *Education:* Universities of Berlin, Tübingen and München (Dr. jur., 1992). Author: "Kennzeichnung importierter Lebensmittel," Bayreuth 1992; "Verbraucherleitbild des Europäischen Gerichtshofes," WRP 92, 215. *Member:* GRUR; German-Italian Lawyers Association. *LANGUAGES:* German, English and Italian.

Languages: German, French, English and Italian

LADAS & PARRY

ALTHEIMER ECK 2
D-80331 MUNICH, GERMANY
Telephone: (089) 269077
Fax: (089) 269040
Telex: 5-28474 LAWLAN D
Cable Address: "LawlanMunich"

New York, New York Office: 26 West 61st Street, 10023. Telephone: 212-708-1800. Telex: 233288. Telecopy: 212-246-8959. Cable Address: "Lawlan New York".

Chicago, Illinois Office: 224 South Michigan Avenue, 60604. Telephone: 312-427-1300. Telex: 203649. Telecopy: 312-427-6663; 312-427-6668. Cable Address: "Lawlan Chicago".

Los Angeles, California Office: 5670 Wilshire Boulevard, 90036. Telephone: 213-934-2300. Telex: 240423. Cable Address: "Lawlan USA". Telecopier: 213-934-0202.

London, England Office: High Holborn House, 52-54 High Holborn, WC1V 6RR. Telephone: 44-171-242-5566. Telex: 264255. Telecopy: 44-171-405-1908 (Groups 2 & 3). Cable Address: "LawlanLondon".

Practice before European Patent Office.
This Branch Limited to practice before European Patent Office and not authorized to appear before German Courts.

PARTNER IN ATTENDANCE

IAIN C. BAILLIE, born Kenmore, Perthshire, Scotland, July 14, 1931; admitted, 1966, New York. Admitted to practice before the European Patent Office (Not admitted in Germany). *Education:* Glasgow University (B.Sc., 1953); Fordham University (J.D., 1965).

EUROPEAN PATENT ATTORNEY

PAUL R. MADGWICK, born Haslemere, England, March 24, 1952. Admitted to practice before the European Patent office and British Patent Office, British Chartered Patent Agent. *Education:* Southampton University (B.Sc., 1974; Cert. Ed. 1975); College of Law (Guildford) 1976-1980. *Member:* Institution of Electrical Engineers.

(For biographical data of the New York personnel, see Professional Biographies at New York, New York)
(For biographical data of the Chicago personnel, see Professional Biographies at Chicago, Illinois)
(For biographical data of the Los Angeles personnel, see Professional Biographies at Los Angeles, California)
(For biographical data of the London personnel, see Professional Biographies at London, England)

LORENZ SEIDLER GOSSEL

Established in 1962

WIDENMAYERSTRASSE 23
80538 MUNICH, GERMANY
Telephone: 089/2 90 10-0
Telefax: 089/2 90 10-100
Telex: 524 109 LAWP D

Patents, Trademarks, Unfair Competition, Copyright, Antitrust, Licensing, Litigation, Food and Drug Law, Pharma, Law of the Press, Advertising, Practice before the German and European Patent Offices, General Corporate Practice.

MEMBERS OF FIRM

EDUARD LORENZ, born Süchteln, Germany, February 18, 1923; admitted, 1956, Germany. *Education:* University of Cologne. *LANGUAGES:* German, English and French.

BERNHARD SEIDLER (1962-1986).

DIPL.-ING. HANS K. GOSSEL, born Berlin, Germany, May 15, 1935; admitted, 1969, Germany. *Education:* Universities (Law Schools) of Tübin-

(This Listing Continued)

gen, Freiburg and Kiel (1955-1959); Technical University of Hannover (1961-1963 and 1965-1967). Judge, 1964-1968. *LANGUAGES:* German and English.

DR. INA PHILIPPS, born Frankfurt/Main, Germany, February 26, 1939; admitted, 1975, Germany. *Education:* Universities of Saarbrücken and Kiel (Law Degree, 1963; Dr. jur., 1971). *LANGUAGES:* German and English.

DR. PAUL B. SCHÄUBLE, born Waldshut, Germany, October 6, 1949; admitted, 1980, Germany. *Education:* University of Augsburg (Law Degree, 1978; Dr. jur., 1983). *Member:* German Association for the Protection of Industrial Property and Copyright Law. *LANGUAGES:* German and English.

DR. SIEGFRIED JACKERMEIER, born Rohr, Germany, March 28, 1953; admitted, 1983, Germany. *Education:* University of Munich Law School (Dr. jur., 1981). Research Staff, Max-Planck-Institute for Foreign and International Patent, Copyright and Competition Law, 1978-1981; Bavarian Ministry for Economics, Antitrust and Trade Restrictions Division, 1981-1983. *Member:* German Association for the Protection of Industrial Property and Copyright Law; European Communities Trademark Association; International Trademark Association. *LANGUAGES:* German, English and French.

DIPL.-ING. ARMIN ZINNECKER, born Bad Tölz, Germany, April 19, 1954; admitted, 1986, Germany. *Education:* Technical University of Munich (Dipl.-Ing., 1978); University of Munich Law School (Law Degree, 1982). *Member:* German Association for the Protection of Industrial Property and Copyright Law. *LANGUAGES:* German and English.

DR.-ING. DIETER LAUFHÜTTE, born Quierschied, Germany, January 3, 1958; admitted, 1989, German Patent Bar; 1990, European Patent Office. *Education:* University of Karlsruhe (Dipl.-Ing., 1982); Technical University of Munich (Doctor of Engineering, 1986). Assistant, Technical University of Munich, 1983-1985. *Member:* German Association for the Protection of Industrial Property and Copyright Law; FICPI; Society of the German Engineers (VDI). *LANGUAGES:* German, English and French.

DR. REINHARD E. INGERL, born Munich, Germany, May 11, 1960; admitted, 1988, Germany. *Education:* University of Munich Law School (Dr. jur., 1988); University of Geneva Law School; Harvard Law School (LL.M., 1985). Munich Reinsurance Company, Finance Department, 1988-1989. Lecturer, University of Jena Law School, 1992—. *Member:* American Bar Association; German-American Lawyers Association; German Association for the Protection of Industrial Property and Copyright Law. *LANGUAGES:* German, English, Spanish and French.

MAIWALD & PARTNER

Patentanwälte

European Patent Attorneys

BALANSTRAβE 57

81541 MUNICH, GERMANY

Telephone: +49 89/40 50 71

Telefax: +49 89/49 66 27

Lörrach, Germany Associated Office: Schulze & Althoff. Brühlstraβe 11, 79540. Telephone: +49 7621/85 66. Telefax: +49 7621/14 541.

Intellectual Property Law, Patent, Trademark and Design Law, IP-related Copyright, Unfair Competition, Computer and Software Law, Business, Commercial and Antitrust Law, Licensing, Infringement and Litigation.

FIRM PROFILE: *Established in its present form in 1993, the firm deals with all aspects of Intellectual Property for a worldwide client base. The firm has three attorneys in its Munich head office and practices in close association with the general law firm of Schulze & Althoff in Lörrach, Germany, where it has a branch office (only European Patent Attorneys). The firm specializes in patent and trademark infringement matters but also handles application filing and prosecution work, contracts and other IP-related matters.*

MEMBERS OF FIRM

WALTER MAIWALD, Dipl.-Chem., Dr. rer. nat., born Hamburg, Germany, August 11, 1951; admitted, 1985, German Patent Bar; 1987, European Patent Office. *Education:* University of Hamburg, Germany (Dipl.-Chem., 1979; Dr. rer. nat., 1980). Research Assistant, Imperial College, London, 1980-1981. Tutor, epi for European Patent Attorney Trainees, 1988-1991. *Member:* GRUR; AIPPI; FICPI; INTA; German Patent Attorneys Professional Organization; Mitteilungen der deutschen Patentanwälte

(This Listing Continued)

(Editorial Board). *LANGUAGES:* German and English. *PRACTICE AREAS:* German and International Intellectual Property Law; Patent and Trademark Prosecution; Infringement; Trademark Infringement; Licensing; Chemicals and Chemistry; Pharmaceutical Sciences and Engineering.

AXEL H. CH. DRAUDT, Dipl.-Ing., born Bad Buchau, Germany, 1953; admitted, 1991, German Patent Bar; 1992, European Patent Office. *Education:* University of the German Armed Forces, Munich (Dipl.-Ing., 1976). Helicopter Pilot. Air Force Officer. Assistant, University of the German Armed Forces, 1982-1985. *Member:* German Patent Attorneys Professional Organization, epi, Helicopter Forùm. *LANGUAGES:* German and English. *PRACTICE AREAS:* German and International Intellectual Property Law; Patent and Trademark Prosecution; Infringement; Trademark Infringement; Licensing; Electrical and Aerospace; Engineering; Software.

JUTTA DRAUDT, Dipl.-Chem., Dr. rer. nat., born Solingen, Germany; admitted, 1989, German Patent Bar. *Education:* University of Cologne (Dipl.-Chem., 1982; Dr. rer. nat., 1985). *Member:* German Patent Attorneys Professional Organization; German Chemists' Society (GdCh). *LANGUAGES:* German, English and French. *PRACTICE AREAS:* German and International Intellectual Property Law; Patent and Trademark Prosecution; Infringement; Trademark Infringement; Licensing; Chemicals and Chemistry; Biotechnology; Biochemicals; Genetics.

MÜHLBAUER & PARTNERS

ELISABETHSTRAβE 29

80796 MUNICH, GERMANY

Telephone: (89) 271 19 17

Telefax: (89) 272 13 00

A member of AdvoSelect EEIG, a network of law firms pooling their resources in special fields and crossborder cases, specializing in business law for middlesized companies. AdvoSelect is represented in 51 cities throughout Europe.

General Corporate Practice, Corporate Law, Commercial Law, Mergers and Acquisitions, Tax Law, Banking, Industrial and Private Property, Labour Law, Litigation, Unfair Competition, Intellectual Property, Copyright, Trademark.

MEMBERS OF FIRM

DR. DIETER MÜHLBAUER, born Munich, Germany, May 9, 1943; admitted, 1970, Germany. *Education:* University of Munich, Law School 1970 (Dr. jur., 1969). Specialist in Tax Law, 1973. Sworn Auditor, 1989. *Member:* Bar Association, Chamber of Certified Public Auditors. *LANGUAGES:* German and English. *PRACTICE AREAS:* Corporate Law; Tax Law; Commercial Law; Real Estate Law.

HANS G. WAGNER, born Pfaffenhofen, Germany, March 24, 1957; admitted, 1988, Germany. *Education:* Apprentice of Banking Business; Universities of Regensburg and Speyer, Law School (1988). *LANGUAGES:* German and English. *PRACTICE AREAS:* Labour Law; Unfair Competition; Commercial Law.

DR. UWE HAHN, born Lahr, Germany, February 22, 1962; admitted, 1991, Germany. *Education:* University of Konstanz, Law School (1988). *LANGUAGES:* German and English. *PRACTICE AREAS:* Labour Law; Unfair Competition; Commercial Law; Mercantile Law; Law of Contract; Product Liability.

ASSOCIATES

GÜNTHER VOLPERS, born Idar-Oberstein, Germany, October 3, 1958; admitted, 1990, Germany. *Education:* University of Munich, Law School (1988). *LANGUAGES:* German and English. *PRACTICE AREAS:* Landlord and Tenant Law; Labour Law; Copyright; Law Relating to Aliens.

DANIELA ANDERS, born Munich, October 21, 1966; admitted, 1995, Germany. *Education:* University of Munich Law School (1992). *LANGUAGES:* German and English. *PRACTICE AREAS:* Law of Contract; Labour Law; Law of Obligations; Law of Torts.

PETER MICHAEL MÜLLER

Established in 1974

MONTGELAS STRASSE 2
81679 MUNICH, GERMANY
Telephone: 49 89 98 49 41
Cable Address: INLAW MUNICH
Fax: 49 89 981 01 99

Criminal Law, General Practice, Business and General Crimes, Criminal Aspects in Banking, Tax, Competition, Environmental, Cartels and Comparative Law. Transnational Crimes, Export Control, War Technology Transfer Crimes, Extradition, Mutual Assistance in Criminal Matters, Transfer of Proceedings in Criminal Matters. International Counselling in corresponding Criminal Cases abroad. Human Rights.

PETER MICHAEL MÜLLER, born December 28, 1944; admitted, 1974, Germany. *Education:* Law, Universities of Munich, Germany and Lausanne, Switzerland; Economics, University of Zurich, Switzerland. Expert Participant, International UN Meetings on the Role of Lawyers and Treatment of Offenders, International Cooperation with Criminal Defense Lawyers. *Member:* Munich Bar Association; International Bar Association (Chairman, Criminal Law Committee); INTERLAW Institute (Founding Member and President); German-Brazilian Chamber of Commerce; Munich Merchants Casino. *LANGUAGES:* English, French, German and Spanish. *PRACTICE AREAS:* Business and General Crimes.

NÖRR, STIEFENHOFER & LUTZ

Established in 1950

BRIENNER STR. 28
80333 MUNICH, GERMANY
Telephone: 49-89-280111
Telecopier: 49-89-280110

Mailing Address: P.O. Box 101121, 80085 Munich, Germany

Frankfurt/Main, Germany Office: Freiherr-vom-Stein-Straße 11, 60323 Frankfurt/Main. Telephone: 49-69-172917. Telecopier: 49-69-172916.

Berlin, Germany Office: Schlüterstraße 36, D-10629 Berlin. Telephone: 49-30-8836700. Telecopier: 49-30-8835052.

Dresden, Germany Office: Böhmertstraße 3, 01099 Dresden. Telephone: 49-351-5671188, 49-351-5671187. Telecopier: 49-351-5671186.

Prague, Czech Republic Office: Masarykovo nábřeži 30, 11000 Prague 1. Telephone: 42-2-24913396, 42-2-24913882. Telecopier: 42-2-24911836.

Budapest, Hungary Office: Becsi utca 5/I. 1-2, 1052 Budapest V. Telephone: 36-1-1174905; 36-1-1378293. Telecopier: 36-1-1184035.

Warsaw, Poland Office: Kancelaria Adwokacka SP. Z O. O. UL. Nowogrodzka 50. Telephone: 48-2-6 21 6232. Telecopier: 48-2-6 25 1976.

Brussels, Belgium EEC Office: 106 Avenue Louise, 1050 Brussels. Telephone: 32-2-6470650. Telecopier: 32-2-6464729.

Moscow, Russian Office: Ul. Levoberezhnaya, 32. 125475. Telephone: 7-095-4585822; 7-095-4585792. Telecopier: 7-095-4585782.

German and International Practice, Corporate, Commercial, Mergers and Acquisitions, Finance and Banking, Tax, EEC, Public and Constitutional Law, Antitrust, Real Estate, Construction, Labor, Insurance, Landlord-Tenant, Agency, Leasing, Product Liability, Family, Estate, Aviation, Energy, Health, Food and Drugs, Industrial Property, Copyright, Trademarks, Unfair Competition, Media, Telecommunications, Computer, Advertising, White Collar Crime, Administrative and Planning Law, Environmental and Waste Law, Litigation and Arbitration, Joint Ventures, Appellate, Civil, Federal, Legislative, Trial Practice, Advice to Legislative Institutions in Eastern Europe, Central and Eastern European Law, Law of Restitution Claims.

MEMBERS OF FIRM

DR. EDUARD OEHL (1900-1983).

DR. RUDOLF NÖRR, born Munich, Germany, January 18, 1929; admitted, 1957, Germany. *Education:* Universities of Erlangen, Munich and Hamburg. *Member:* German Bar Association. *LANGUAGES:* German and English. *PRACTICE AREAS:* Corporate; Estate/Family; Arbitration Law.

DR. ALFRED STIEFENHOFER, born Munich, Germany, March 31, 1931; admitted, 1959, Germany; as Tax Advisor 1964. *Education:* University of Munich. *Member:* German Bar Association; Verein der Steuerberater; German-American Chamber of Commerce. *LANGUAGES:* Ger-

(This Listing Continued)

man and English. *PRACTICE AREAS:* Corporate; Mergers and Acquisitions; Tax; Banking.

DR. FRIEDRICH ZIMMERMANN, born Munich, Germany, July 18, 1925; admitted, 1963, Germany. *Education:* University of Munich. Member, M.P. Deutscher Bundestag, 1957-1990. Minister of the Federal Government, 1982-1990. *Member:* Munich and German Bar Associations. *LANGUAGES:* German and English.

ULRICH LUTZ (1935-1987).

PETER VON SCHAABNER (1937-1988).

DR. ECKART RABICH, born Berlin, Germany, March 22, 1940; admitted, 1968, Germany. *Education:* Universities of Berlin, Tübingen and Cologne. *Member:* German Bar Association. (Partner in charge of Warsaw and Moscow Offices). *LANGUAGES:* German and English. *PRACTICE AREAS:* Corporate Law; Central and Eastern European Privatization Law; Joint Ventures; Litigation.

RÜDIGER VON PEZOLD, born Würzburg, Germany, July 11, 1941; admitted, 1969, Germany. *Education:* Universities of Erlangen and Munich. *LANGUAGES:* German and English.

DR. BERTOLD GAEDE, born Essen, Germany, December 29, 1942; admitted, 1971, Germany; as Tax Advisor 1976. *Education:* Universities of Munich, Freiburg, Bonn and Cologne. *Member:* American Bar Association; German Bar Association. (Partner in charge of Budapest Office). *LANGUAGES:* German, English and French. *PRACTICE AREAS:* Corporate Law; Mergers and Acquisitions Law; Energy and Health Law.

DR. STEFAN B. TOMICIC, born Vienna, Austria, October 29, 1947; admitted, 1975, Germany. *Education:* Universities of Munich, Lausanne and Geneva. Assistant Lecturer, University of Munich, Institute of Commercial and Labor Law, 1973-1975. *Member:* German Bar Association. (Partner in charge of Budapest Office). *LANGUAGES:* German, English, French and Spanish. *PRACTICE AREAS:* Real Estate and Construction; Leasing; Labor; Administrative Law.

DR. HANS-PETER ZIER, born Stuttgart, Germany, February 26, 1950; admitted, 1976, Germany. *Education:* Universities of Geneva, Munich and London (King's College). With Linklaters & Paines, London, 1977-1978. *Member:* International Bar Association; British-German Jurists' Association; German-American Lawyers' Association. (Partner in charge of Prague and Warsaw Offices). *LANGUAGES:* German, English, French and Italian. *PRACTICE AREAS:* Commercial Law; International Finance Law; Central and Eastern European Privatization Law.

UWE FREIHERR VON SAALFELD, born Lenggries, Germany, May 9, 1947; admitted, 1978, Germany. *Education:* University of Berlin; Technical University of Berlin; University of Munich. *Member:* German Bar Association; Deutsche Steuerjuristische Gesellschaft e. V. *LANGUAGES:* German and English. *PRACTICE AREAS:* White Collar Crime; Food and Drugs Law.

DR. DIETER SCHENK, born Munich, Germany, August 4, 1952; admitted, 1980, Germany; as Tax Advisor, 1985. *Education:* Universities of Munich, Geneva, Freiburg and Tuebingen. Assistant Lecturer, Institute of International Law, University of Munich, 1977-1980. (Partner in charge of Dresden Office). *LANGUAGES:* German, English and French. *PRACTICE AREAS:* Tax Law; Corporate Law; Aviation Law.

DR. EBERHARD SIMMLER, born Bad Frankenhausen, Germany, 1948; admitted, 1982, Germany. *Education:* University of Freiburg and University of Münster. Assistant Lecturer, University of Freiburg, 1975-1981. *Member:* Gesellschaft für Rechtsvergleichung. *LANGUAGES:* German, English and French. *PRACTICE AREAS:* Banking Law; White Collar Crime Law; Litigation.

GEORG A. JAHN, born Mannheim, Germany, September 12, 1950; admitted, 1980, Germany; 1984, New York. *Education:* Universities of Munich, Geneva, Freiburg and Bonn; University of Virginia, School of Law, Charlottesville (M.C.L., 1977). With Winthrop, Stimson, Putnam & Roberts, New York, 1981-1983. *Member:* German Society for the Protection of Industrial Property and Copyright Law; AIPPI. (Partner in charge of Prague Office). *LANGUAGES:* German and English. *PRACTICE AREAS:* Advertising/Unfair Competition; Copyright, Trademark Law and License.

RAIMUND VOLPERT, born Würzburg, Germany, April 28, 1958; admitted, 1986, Germany. *Education:* Universities of Würzburg and Speyer. *Member:* Society for Environmental Law. *LANGUAGES:* German, English and French. *PRACTICE AREAS:* Administrative Law; Town Planning Law; Environmental Law.

(This Listing Continued)

MICHAEL MOLITORIS, born Erlangen, Germany, May 5, 1959; admitted, 1988, Germany. *Education:* University of Würzburg. *Member:* Munich Bar Association. *LANGUAGES:* German and English. *PRACTICE AREAS:* Estate, Commercial and Product Liability Law; Litigation.

DR. WOLFRAM THEISS, born Munich, Germany, March 28, 1960; admitted, 1988, Germany. *Education:* Universities of Heidelberg and Munich. With Ughi & Nunziante, Milan and Rome, 1988. *LANGUAGES:* German, English and Italian. *PRACTICE AREAS:* Commercial Law; Corporate Law; Mergers and Acquisitions; Litigation.

DR. ALEXANDER LIEGL, born Munich, Germany, August 14, 1958; admitted, 1989, Germany. *Education:* Universities of Munich and Nice. Assistant Lecturer, University of Regensburg, 1985-1987. With Walter, Conston, Alexander & Green, New York, 1988. Lecturer, Higher Technical College of Dresden, 1990—. *LANGUAGES:* German, English and French. *PRACTICE AREAS:* Commercial Law; Corporate Law; Estate Law; East German Law.

ASSOCIATES

DR. STEFAN WEISE, born Offenbach am Main, Germany, April 8, 1959; admitted, 1988, Germany. *Education:* University of Munich. *Member:* German Bar Association. *LANGUAGES:* German and English. *PRACTICE AREAS:* Real Estate; Construction; Administrative.

DR. KARL TH. RAUSER, born Munich, Germany, August 19, 1959; admitted, 1990, Germany. *Education:* University of Munich. Lecturer on Law, Institute for International and European Economic Law, University of Munich, 1985-1990. *Member:* Munich Bar Association. *LANGUAGES:* German and English. *PRACTICE AREAS:* EEC Law; Constitutional Law; International Law; Corporate Law.

ALINA JOLANTA SZARLAK, born Munich, Germany, May 25, 1958; admitted, 1990, Germany. *Education:* University of Munich, Hague Academy of International Law. *LANGUAGES:* German, English, French, Polish and Russian. *PRACTICE AREAS:* Polish Law; Commercial Law; Corporate Law; Real Estate; Privatization Law.

DR. ZSOLT K. RADNÓCZY, born Munich, Germany, February 16, 1954; admitted, 1989, Germany. *Education:* Universities of Munich and Budapest. With Lion Features World Article Service, Munich, Germany, 1979-1983. With Lindner & Radnóczy, Management Consultants, 1989, 1990. Member, Board of Directors, Hypo-Bank Hungaria Rt. since March 1, 1993. *Member:* German Bar Association; International Association Language and Business. (Locally in Charge of Budapest Office). *LANGUAGES:* Hungarian, German, English and French. *PRACTICE AREAS:* Hungarian Law; Real Estate Law; Commercial Law; Corporate Law; Banking and Tax Law.

CHRISTINE OSTWALD, born Bremerhaven, Germany, July 26, 1962; admitted, 1990, Germany. *Education:* University of Munich. *LANGUAGES:* German and English. *PRACTICE AREAS:* Commercial Law; Labor Law.

IRIS NATALY KNOBLOCH, born Munich, Germany, February 13, 1963; admitted, 1990, Germany; 1992, New York; 1993, California. *Education:* University of Munich (M.C.L., 1992, New York). *LANGUAGES:* German, English and French. *PRACTICE AREAS:* Media Law; Advertising/Unfair Competition; Copyright Law.

NICOLA SUZAN ROSE-STRÄSSER, born Hamburg, Germany, October 5, 1963; admitted, 1991, Germany. *Education:* University of Munich. *LANGUAGES:* German, English and French. *PRACTICE AREAS:* Unfair Competition; Commercial Law; Family Law.

JAROSLAV MELZER, born Vitkov, former Czechoslovakia, November 8, 1957; admitted, 1988, Germany; 1993, Czech Republic. *Education:* University of Heidelberg. *LANGUAGES:* German, Czech and English. *PRACTICE AREAS:* Czech Law; Commercial Law; Banking; Joint Ventures; Tax Law.

TILLMANN GEORG HECHT, born Nuremberg, Germany, August 10, 1960; admitted, 1989, Germany. *Education:* Universities of Erlangen and Munich. *LANGUAGES:* German and English. *PRACTICE AREAS:* Labor Law; Copyright Law; Unfair Competition.

DR. TOBIAS MAXIMILIAN BÜRGERS, born Germany, May 9, 1962; admitted, 1991, Germany. *Education:* University of Munich. *LANGUAGES:* German and English. *PRACTICE AREAS:* Civil Law; Litigation.

SILVIA SPARFELD, born Weidenhausen, Germany, March 21, 1962; admitted, 1992, Germany. *Education:* Universities of Giessen, M.A. (slavic

(This Listing Continued)

languages). *LANGUAGES:* German, English, Russian, French, Spanish and Czech. *PRACTICE AREAS:* Czech and Russian Law; Commercial Law; Antitrust Law; Tax Law; Privatization Law.

DR. CHRISTIANE ZEDELIUS, born Wuppertal, Germany, September 29, 1961; admitted, 1990, Germany. *Education:* Universities of Freiburg and Munich. *LANGUAGES:* German, English. *PRACTICE AREAS:* Competition Law; Food and Drugs Law; Civil Law.

DR. THOMAS SCHULZ, born Seefeld, Germany, October 5, 1963; admitted, 1992, Germany. *Education:* University of Munich and Georgetown University, Washington, D.C. (LL.M., 1992). *LANGUAGES:* German, English. *PRACTICE AREAS:* Corporate Law; Finance and Banking; Litigation and Arbitration.

ASTRID WILMER, born Madrid, Spain, September 24, 1964; admitted, 1992, Germany. *Education:* University of Munich, University of London Law School (LL.M., 1992). *LANGUAGES:* German, English, Spanish and French. *PRACTICE AREAS:* Intellectual and Industrial Property Rights; EEC Competition and Antitrust Law.

DANIEL KRONEN, born Hamburg, February 11, 1963; admitted, 1993, Germany. *Education:* University of Freiburg; University of München. *LANGUAGES:* German, English, French. *PRACTICE AREAS:* Construction Law; Labor Law; Landlord-Tenant Law.

DR. GUNTHER ELBING, born Munich, Germany, February 3, 1965; admitted, 1993, Germany. *Education:* University of Munich. *LANGUAGES:* German and English. *PRACTICE AREAS:* Public Law.

DR. HANS JOACHIM RADAU, born Calw, Germany, May 30, 1963; admitted, 1993, Germany. *Education:* Universities of Regensburg and Munich. *Member:* Deutsch Amerikanische Juristenvereinigung. *LANGUAGES:* German, English and Swedish. *PRACTICE AREAS:* Corporate and Tax Law; Product Liability; Medical Malpractice.

PETER MÜNSTER, born Munich, January 19, 1966; admitted, 1993, Germany. *Education:* University of Munich. *LANGUAGES:* German, English and Italian. *PRACTICE AREAS:* Labor Law; Construction Law.

HANS PETER GRÜTTEMEIER, born Saarbrücken, April 17, 1964; admitted, 1993. *Education:* Universities of Saarbrücken and Heidelberg and Freiburg. *LANGUAGES:* German, English and French. *PRACTICE AREAS:* Labor Law; Real Estate Law; Public Law.

DR. PETRA KIRMER, born Munich, Germany, September 3, 1964; admitted, 1993, Germany. *Education:* Universities of Munich and Augsburg. *LANGUAGES:* German, English and French. *PRACTICE AREAS:* Administrative Law; Construction Law; Corporate Law and Commercial Law.

PETER WILHELM GORZAWSKI, born Hindenburg, Poland, August 1, 1957; admitted, 1993, Germany. *Education:* Universities of Katowice and Cologne. Certified translator and interpreter for the Polish language. *LANGUAGES:* German, Polish, Russian, English. *PRACTICE AREAS:* Polish Law; Commercial; Corporate; Labor and Real Estate Law.

STEPHAN KOPP, born Bonn, Germany, June 7, 1964; admitted, 1994, Germany. *Education:* Universities of Passau and Speyer. *LANGUAGES:* German, English and French. *PRACTICE AREAS:* Public Law; EEC Law.

DR. PETER BRÄUTIGAM, born Munich, November 18, 1964; admitted, 1994, Germany. *Education:* University of Munich. *LANGUAGES:* German, English and French. *PRACTICE AREAS:* Civil Law; Product Liability Law.

THOMAS RALPH WERNICKE, born Stuttgart, April 20, 1963; admitted, 1994, Germany. *Education:* University of Augsburg, Tübingen and Munich; University of Geneva. *LANGUAGES:* German, English and French. *PRACTICE AREAS:* Commercial Law; Banking Law; Civil Law.

CHRISTINE HÜPER, born Peine, Germany, June 10, 1961; admitted, 1994, Germany. *Education:* University of Berlin. *LANGUAGES:* German, Russian, English, Spanish. *PRACTICE AREAS:* Civil Law; Public Law; Russian Commercial Law.

Languages: German, English, French, Italian, Spanish, Swedish, Hungarian, Polish, Czech, Russian.

OPPENHOFF & RÄDLER

PRINZREGENTENPLATZ 10
D-81675 MUNICH, GERMANY
Telephone: (089) 41808-0
Telecopier: (089) 41808-100

Berlin, Germany Office: Meinekestr. 13, D-10719. Telephone: (030) 88471-0. Telecopier: (030) 88471-200.

Berlin, Germany Office: Rankestr. 21, D-10789. Telephone: (030) 21496-0. Telecopier: (030) 21496-100.

Cologne, Germany Office: Hohenstaufenring 62, D-50674. Telephone (0221) 2091-0. Telecopier: (0221) 2091-435. Telex: 8 882 294 bos. Teletex: 2627 221 4054BOS.

Frankfurt/Main, Germany Office: Bockenheimer Landstr. 51-53, D-60325. Telephone: (069) 170003-0. Telecopier: (069) 170003-33.

Frankfurt/Main, Germany Office: Myliusstr. 33-37, D-60323. Telephone: (069) 17093-0. Telecopier: (069) 17093-444.

Leipzig, Germany Office: Kommandant-Trufanow-Str. 14, D-04105. Telephone: (0341) 56649-0. Telecopier: (0341) 56649-99.

Brussels, Belgium Office: Rue Brederode 13A, B-1000. Telephone: (2) 5050211. Telecopier: (2) 5022644.

London, England Office: Royex House, Aldermanbury Square, GB-London EC2V 7HR. Telephone: (171) 600 3609. Telecopier: (171) 600 1718.

New York, New York Office: 712 Fifth Avenue, 30th Floor, 10019, USA. Telephone: (212) 801 3410. Telecopier: (212) 801 3415.

New York, New York Office: 712 Fifth Avenue, 29th Floor, 10019, USA. Telephone: (212) 397 7580/7546. Telecopier: (212) 397 4292.

Prague, Czech Republic Office: Alliance Prague, Jachymova 2, CZ-11000 Prague 1. Telephone: (2) 232 1130. Telecopier: (2) 232 6371.

FIRM PROFILE: Oppenhoff & Rädler has been created by a merger of two large German firms, Boden Oppenhoff Rasor Raue and Rädler Raupach Bezzenberger. The firm at present has more than 90 partners and comprises together some 200 lawyers and tax advisers.

Oppenhoff & Rädler acts for domestic and for international clients. The firm offers a comprehensive range of legal services, including: General Corporate and Commercial; Taxation; Banking, Finance and Securities; Mergers and Acquisitions; Real Estate; Litigation and Arbitration; Intellectual Property and Trademarks; Construction Law; Antitrust and European Community Law; Administrative and Environmental Law; Media, Communications and Entertainment Law; Technology and Computer Law; Food, Drug and Chemistry; Family Law; Wills.

Oppenhoff & Rädler is a member of the ALLIANCE OF EUROPEAN LAWYERS EEIG (members: Oppenhoff & Rädler, Germany; De Bandt, van Hecke & Lagae, Belgium; De Brauw Blackstone Westbroek, The Netherlands; Jeantet & Associés, France; Lagerlöf & Leman, Sweden; Uria & Menendez, Spain) and of the LLR EEIG (members: Loyens & Volkmaars, The Netherlands; Bureau Francis Lefebvre, France; Oppenhoff & Rädler, Germany).

RESIDENT PARTNERS AND JUNIOR PARTNERS

PROF. DR. ALBERT J. RÄDLER, born Munich, Germany, May 6, 1933; admitted, 1962, Germany, Tax Advisor (Steuerberater). *Education:* University of Munich (Dipl.-Kfm./M.B.A.); Council of Europe-Fellowship (Dr.rer.oec.). *Member:* Confédération Fiscale Européenne (President, Tax Committee, 1984-1990); German Chamber of Tax Advisors (Member, International Tax Committee). *LANGUAGES:* German, English, French. *PRACTICE AREAS:* European Community Law; Finance; Mergers, Acquisitions and Divestitures; Taxation; International Tax Law; Transfer Pricing.

PROF. DR. ARNDT RAUPACH, born Freiberg, Germany, June 14, 1936; admitted, 1968, Germany; 1970, Tax Lawyer (Fachanwalt für Steuerrecht). *Education:* Universities of Muenster and Munich (Dr.jur.). *Member:* German Bar Association (DAV; Member of Committee on Commercial Law); Scientific Board of Deutsche Steuerjuristische Gesellschaft. *LANGUAGES:* German, English. *PRACTICE AREAS:* Corporate Law; Company Law; Taxation.

PETER JECH, born Boehmisch-Kamnitz, CSSR, July 11, 1937; admitted, 1972, Germany, Tax Advisor (Steuerberater). *Education:* University of Munich (Dipl.-Kfm./M.B.A.). *LANGUAGES:* German, English. *PRACTICE AREAS:* Taxation; Taxation of Employee Benefits.

DR. UWE CLAUSEN, born Osnabrück, Germany, May 23, 1941; admitted, 1972, Germany; 1979, Tax Lawyer (Fachanwalt für Steuerrecht). *Education:* Universities of Muenster and Munich (Dr.jur.). *Member:* Mu-

(This Listing Continued)

nich Bar Association (Board Member, 1982—). *LANGUAGES:* German, English. *PRACTICE AREAS:* Leases and Leasing; Taxation; White Collar Crime.

DR. HANS-JOACHIM HOLZAPFEL, born Berlin, Germany, March 2, 1943; admitted, 1973, Germany. *Education:* University of Munich (Dr.jur.); Northwestern University (LL.M.). *LANGUAGES:* German, English. *PRACTICE AREAS:* Contracts; Corporate Law; Commercial Law; Mergers, Acquisitions and Divestitures.

DR. MARGOT GRÄFIN VON WESTERHOLT, born Cham, Germany, June 11, 1945; admitted, 1978, Germany. *Education:* Universities of Munich (Dr.jur.) and Tübingen; Faculté Internationale du Droit Comparé; Columbia Law School. *LANGUAGES:* German, English, French. *PRACTICE AREAS:* Agency and Distributorships; Copyrights; Corporate Law; Computer and Software; Communications and Media; Entertainment and the Arts; Intellectual Property; Mergers, Acquisitions and Divestitures.

DR. ELISABETH STROBL, born Bad Aibling, April 22, 1946; admitted, 1977, Germany, Tax Advisor (Steuerberater); 1979, Certified Public Accountant (Wirtschaftsprüfer). *Education:* University of Munich (Dipl.-Kfm./M.B.A.; Dr.rer.pol.). *LANGUAGES:* German, English. *PRACTICE AREAS:* Taxation.

RICHARD L. ENGL, born Burghausen, Germany, June 28, 1950; admitted, 1980, Germany, Tax Advisor (Steuerberater). *Education:* University of Regensburg (Dipl.-Kfm./M.B.A.). *LANGUAGES:* German, English. *PRACTICE AREAS:* Taxation; International Tax Law; Taxation of Mergers, Acquisitions and Divestitures; Taxation of Reorganizations.

DR. JÜRGEN KILLIUS, born Munich, Germany, May 31, 1936; admitted, 1965, Germany; 1974, as Tax Counsel. *Education:* Universities of Berlin and Munich (Dr.jur.); Columbia School of Law (M.C.L.). *LANGUAGES:* German, English. *PRACTICE AREAS:* Finance; Investments; Mergers, Acquisitions and Divestitures; Sports Law; Taxation; Trust and Estates.

GÜNTER GEISSEN, born Koblenz, Germany, May 23, 1944; admitted, 1975, Germany, Tax Advisor (Steuerberater); 1977, Certified Public Accountant (Wirtschaftsprüfer). *Education:* University of Cologne (Dipl.-Volksw./M.B.A.). *LANGUAGES:* German, English. *PRACTICE AREAS:* Taxation.

DR. KARL J.T. WACH, born Obergünzburg, Germany, September 3, 1955; admitted, 1983, Germany. *Education:* University of Munich (Dr.jur.). *LANGUAGES:* German, English. *PRACTICE AREAS:* Banks and Banking; Commercial Law; Commodities; Litigation; Professional Liability; Securities; White Collar Crime.

DR. MATTHIAS BRUSE, born Hamm, Germany, September 4, 1956; admitted, 1984, Germany. *Education:* Universities of Munich and Bonn (Dr.jur.); University of Miami (LL.M.). *LANGUAGES:* German, English. *PRACTICE AREAS:* Corporate Law; Joint Ventures; Mergers, Acquisitions and Divestitures; Taxation.

DR. ANDREA VON DRYGALSKI, born Munich, Germany, January 15, 1958; admitted, 1988, Germany. *Education:* Universities of Munich (Dr.jur.) and Passau. *LANGUAGES:* German, English, French, Italian. *PRACTICE AREAS:* Business Law; Contracts; Corporate Law; Commercial Law; Company Law; Mergers, Acquisitions and Divestitures; Property; Real Estate.

DR. GOTTFRIED E. BREUNINGER, born Stuttgart, Germany, September 17, 1958; admitted, 1989, Germany. *Education:* University of Tübingen (Dr.jur.). *LANGUAGES:* German, English. *PRACTICE AREAS:* Corporate Law; Joint Ventures; Mergers, Acquisitions and Divestitures; Taxation; Company Taxation; International Taxation.

DIETER HEIDEMANN, born Wels, Austria, December 21, 1957; admitted, 1988, Tax Adviser (Steuerberater); 1990, Certified Public Accountant (Wirtschaftsprüfer). *Education:* University of Munich (Dipl.-Kfm./M.B.A.). *LANGUAGES:* German, English. *PRACTICE AREAS:* Mergers, Acquisitions and Divestitures; Taxation.

DR. TINA-FIONA MÜLLER, born Wiesbaden, Germany, January 10, 1960; admitted, 1988, Germany. *Education:* University of Munich (Dr.jur.). *LANGUAGES:* German, English, French, Italian, Spanish. *PRACTICE AREAS:* Business Law; Contracts; Corporate Law; Mergers, Acquisitions and Divestitures.

KLAUS SAFFENREUTHER, born Lünen, Germany, March 15, 1959; admitted, 1986, Germany. *Education:* University of Mainz. *LANGUAGES:* German, English. *PRACTICE AREAS:* Banks and Banking; Commercial Law; Litigation; White Collar Crime.

(This Listing Continued)

DR. KARL SCHÄFER, born Köln, Germany, May 14, 1955; admitted, 1985, Germany. *Education:* University of Munich (Dr.jur.). *LANGUAGES:* German, English. *PRACTICE AREAS:* Contracts; Company Law; Leases and Leasing; Taxation.

FRANZ WILLIBALD, born Lenggries, Germany, May 2, 1957; admitted, 1989, Germany, Tax Adviser (Steuerberater). *Education:* University of Munich. *LANGUAGES:* German, English. *PRACTICE AREAS:* Taxation.

MARIANNE WALDENMAIER, born Schwäbisch-Gmünd, Germany, March 9, 1953; admitted, 1989, Germany. *Education:* University of Munich. *LANGUAGES:* German, English. *PRACTICE AREAS:* Copyrights; Employee Benefits; Intellectual Property; Labour and Employment; Social Law; Trademarks.

LAURENZ SCHMITT, born Würzburg, Germany, December 10, 1961; admitted, 1990, Germany. *Education:* University of Würzburg. *LANGUAGES:* German, English, French. *PRACTICE AREAS:* Bankruptcy; Banks and Banking; Litigation; White Collar Crime.

GEORG VON WALLIS, born Munich, Germany, February 5, 1961; admitted, 1989, Germany. *Education:* University of Munich. *LANGUAGES:* German, English. *PRACTICE AREAS:* Taxation.

THOMAS STEFAN WIELAND, born Stuttgart, Germany, June 23, 1961; admitted, 1989, Germany. *Education:* University of Munich. *LANGUAGES:* German, English. *PRACTICE AREAS:* Bankruptcy; Corporate Law; Commercial Law; Mergers, Acquisitions and Divestitures.

OTT, WEISS, ESCHENLOHR & PARTNER

MUNICH, GERMANY

(See Weiss & Hasche)

PETERS, FLESCHUTZ & HAHN

Established in 1977

WIDENMAYERSTRASSE 6
80538 MUNICH, GERMANY
Telephone: 089/22 36 14
Telefax: (089) 291889

Corporate, Commercial, Tax and Business Law, including Litigation International Private Law.

MEMBERS OF FIRM

DR. HARALD PETERS, born Wuppertal-Elberfeld, Germany, April 27, 1933; admitted, 1963, Bavaria and as Tax Lawyer; 1968, as Tax Advisor. *Education:* University of Munich (Referendar, 1957; Doctorate and Assessor, 1963); University of Marburg. *LANGUAGES:* German and English. *PRACTICE AREAS:* Tax; Corporate; Private Law.

DR. PETER W. FLESCHUTZ, born Munich, Germany, June 14, 1933; admitted, 1968, Bavaria. *Education:* University of Munich (Referendar, 1956; Doctorate, 1958; Assessor, 1960). *LANGUAGES:* German, English, French and Italian. *PRACTICE AREAS:* Corporate; Commercial; Private; Tax; International Law.

DR. HORST HAHN, born Immenstadt, Germany, September 2, 1937; admitted, 1968, Bavaria. *Education:* University of Munich (Referendar, 1963; Doctorate, 1965; Assessor, 1967). *LANGUAGES:* German, English and French. *PRACTICE AREAS:* Corporate Competition; Private; Commercial International Law.

THOMAS C. FLESCHUTZ, born Munich, Germany, March 6, 1962; admitted, 1991, Bavaria. *Education:* University of Munich and Münster (Referendar, 1988; Assessor, 1991). *LANGUAGES:* German and English. *PRACTICE AREAS:* Administrative Law; Construction Law; Zoning and Planning.

Languages: German, English, French and Italian.

PLUTA & KNORR

THOMAS-WIMMER-RING 1
D-80539 MUNICH, GERMANY
Telephone: 089-29 00 37 0
Facsimile: 089-29 00 37 56

Ulm, Germany Office: Olgastr. 83-85, P.O. Box 2530, D-89015 Ulm. Telephone: 0731-1450 0. Facsimile: 0731-1450-180.
Leipzig, Germany Office: Weißenfelser Str. 15, D-04229 Leipzig. Telephone: 0341-4903650. Facsimile: 0341-4903699.

Receivership, Intellectual Property, Software Law, Company Law, International Private Law, Commercial Law, Tax Law, Antitrust Law, Labor Law, Construction Law, Law of Medical Malpractice, Banking Law.

(For complete list of Personnel, see Professional Biographies at Ulm, Germany)

POLLZIEN, MARTENS & GRAF

OHMSTRASSE 7
P.O. BOX 440319
80752 MUNICH, GERMANY
Telephone: (0 89) 34 70 01
Telefax: (0 89) 34 86 07

General Practice, International Law, Litigation, Corporate Law, Family Law, Estates, Contracts, Licensing, Enforcement of Foreign Judgments.

MEMBERS OF FIRM

DR. GÖTZ M. POLLZIEN, born Leipzig, Germany, December 3, 1914. *Education:* University of Geneva and Munich (Referendar, 1938; Dr. jur., 1948; Assessor, 1950). Co-Editor and Co-Author, "International Licensing Agreements," 1973. *Member:* German Bar Association; American Bar Association; International Bar Association (Chairman, Comm. 5 on Wills, Trust and Successions, 1988-1990); A.T.L.A. *LANGUAGES:* German, English and French.

WERNER U. MARTENS, born Munich, September 18, 1944; admitted, 1975, Munich. *Education:* Universities of Munich and Freiburg; University of Wisconsin, Madison. *Member:* German Bar Association; Munich Bar Association; American Bar Association; International Bar Association (Family Law Division Chair, 1984-1986); A.T.L.A.; International Academy of Matrimonial Lawyers (President Elect, 1994; Vice President 1992-1994; European Chapter President, 1992-1994). *LANGUAGES:* German, English and French.

JÖRG P. GRAF, born Munich, January 12, 1940; admitted, 1970, Munich. *Education:* Universities of Würzburg and Munich (Referendar, 1964; Assessor, 1970). Legal Advisor, Teacher's Organizations. *LANGUAGES:* German and English. *PRACTICE AREAS:* Public Law.

PRACHT RIEGL MIKOREY

Established in 1986

STEINSDORFSTRASSE 13
80538 MUNICH, GERMANY
Telephone: 089/227061
Telecopier: 089/2 28 54 66

Leipzig, Germany Office: Karl-Liebknecht-Str. 38, 04107. Telephone: 0341/2131471. Telefax: 0341/2131473.

Commercial Practice, EEC Law, Corporate, Joint Ventures, Mergers and Acquisitions, Domestic and International Taxation, Real Estate, Investment, Industrial and Intellectual Property, Licensing, Trademark, Press and Publishing, Entertainment, Labor, Unfair Competition, Antitrust, General Civil and Business Practice, Litigation and Arbitration.

MEMBERS OF FIRM

DR. DIETER PRACHT, born Karlsruhe, Germany, September 22, 1943; admitted, 1971, Bavaria; 1976, Tax Advisor. *Education:* Universities of Heidelberg, Munich, Geneva/Switzerland (Referendar, 1967; Assessor, 1971; Doctor Juris, 1974). *Member:* Munich Bar Association; Munich Chamber of Tax Advisors. *LANGUAGES:* German, English and French.

DR. WERNER RIEGL, born Augsburg, Germany, January 17, 1954; admitted, 1986, Munich. *Education:* University of Augsburg (Referendar, 1980; Assessor, 1982; Doctor Juris, 1986). Co-Author: "Steuerlich unwirksame Ehegatten Arbeitsverträge wegen Auslandsberührung," Finanz-Rundschau, 417ff, 1983. Assistant at the Institute for Civil, International

(This Listing Continued)

PRACHT RIEGL MIKOREY, Munich—Continued

Private and EEC Law, University of Augsburg, 1982-1985. *Member:* Munich Bar Association. *LANGUAGES:* German and English.

DR. FRANZ MIKOREY, born Munich, Germany, March 16, 1943; admitted, 1971, Munich. *Education:* Universities of Munich, Lausanne/-Switzerland (Referendar, 1968; Assessor, 1970; Doctor Juris, 1970). Co-Author: "Spitzweg Prozesse," 1990. *LANGUAGES:* German and French.

ASSOCIATE

DR. HANS-PETER GEBHARDT, born Heidelberg, Germany, July 7, 1962; admitted, 1992, Munich. *Education:* Universities of Heidelberg, Munich (Referendar, 1989; Assessor, 1992; Doctor Juris, 1994). *LANGUAGES:* German and English.

PREU, BOHLIG & PARTNERS

SEESTRASSE 13
D-80802 MUNICH, GERMANY
Telephone: 89-381 59 60
Telex: 05 215 591
Telefax: 89-39 25 22

Berlin, Germany Office: Mauerstrasse 77, D-10117 Berlin. Telephone: 30-6 09 36 60. Telefax: 30-6 09 36 64.

General Commercial and Corporate Practice. Patents, Trademarks, Models, Copyright, Unfair Competition, Advertising, Press and Media Law, Entertainment Law, Food and Drug Law, Computer Law, R & D Law, Construction Law, Product Liability Law, Labor Law, Corporations, Taxation, Antitrust, Franchising, Mergers and Acquisitions, Banking and Securities, International Trade, EEC-Law, Licensing, Litigation, Transactions, Arbitration Proceedings, International, Agency and Distribution, Biotechnology, Business Law.

MEMBERS OF FIRM

DR. MANFRED BOHLIG (1963-1987).

PROFESSOR DR. ALBERT PREU, born Ingolstadt (Danube), Germany, May 16, 1918; admitted, 1953, Germany. *Education:* University of Erlangen Law School (Referendar; Dr. jur.). Professor on Patent, Trademark, Unfair Competition and Antitrust Law, University of Erlangen. Author: Preu, Brandi-Dohrn, Gruber: "European and International Patent Law," Munich 1991; "The Scope of Patents and its National and International Development," FS Merz 1992; "Doctrine of Equivalents under the New Patent Law," GRUR 1988, 14; "Adequate Protection of Inventions and Legal Certainty," GRUR 1985, 728, et al. Member, Advisory Committee on Industrial Property with Federal Minister of Justice. *Member:* German Bar Association; German Association for Intellectual Property and Copyright (GRUR); Association International pour la Protection de Propriété Industrielle (AIPPI).

DR. MATTHIAS BRANDI-DOHRN, born Vienna, Austria, November 21, 1936; admitted, 1966, Germany. *Education:* University of Munich Law School (Referendar; Dr.jur.). Author: "The Option Contract in Copyright Law," Munich, 1965; "Warranties for Hard and Software Deficiencies," Munich, 1988; "Software Warranty Litigation and its Preparation, in: Protection and Marketing of Computer Programs," edit. M. Lehmann, Cologne 1988; "European and International Patent Law," Munich 1991. Member, Advisory Board to the Editor of "Computer Law (CR)" *Member:* German Bar Association; German Association for Industrial Property and Copyright (GRUR); Association International pour la Protection de Propriété Industrielle (AIPPI); Licensing Executives Society; German Association for Computer Technology and Law; Association for Construction Law. *LANGUAGES:* German, English and French.

DR. LUTZ DONLE, born Berlin, Germany, October 28, 1935; admitted, 1968, Germany. *Education:* University of Munich (Referendar); University of Würzburg Law School (Dr.jur.). Assistant, University of Munich, 1958-1960. Public Service: Legal Department German Patent Office, 1961-1964; District Court Judge, 1965-1967 (Patents and Trademarks); Staff Member of UNIDO (Model Laws for Developing Countries), 1970-1973. *Member:* German Bar Association; German Association for Intellectual Property and Copyright (GRUR); Association International pour la Protection de Propriété Industrielle (AIPPI); German-Bulgarian Government Commission on Technology Transfer; German-Chinese Government Commission on Patent Infringement Litigation. *LANGUAGES:* German, English, French and Italian.

(This Listing Continued)

DR. MICHAEL BUDDEBERG, born Ravensburg, Germany, November 10, 1940; admitted, 1973, Germany; 1983, Tax Lawyers' Bar. *Education:* Universities of Munich and West-Berlin Law School (Referendar; Dr.jur.). Internal Revenue Service, 1971-1973. Author: "The Law of Illustrated Books," 1972; "Trademarks and Designs," Cologne, 1992. *Member:* German Bar Association; German Association for Intellectual Property and Copyright (GRUR); Tax Lawyers' Association. *LANGUAGES:* German and English.

DR. STEFAN SCHWEYER, born Munich, Germany, September 18, 1950; admitted, 1978, Germany. *Education:* University of Munich Law School (Referendar; Dr.jur.). Research Fellow, Max-Planck Institute for Foreign and International Patent, Copyright and Unfair Competition, 1978-1980. Author: "The Limited Transfer Doctrine in German Copyright Law, Munich," 1982; "Protection of Computer Programs by Trademarks in: Protection and Marketing of Computer Programs," edit. M. Lehmann, Cologne, 1988. *Member:* German Bar Association; German Association for Intellectual Property and Copyright (GRUR); Association International pour la Protection de Propriété Industrielle (AIPPI); German Association for Computer Technology and Law (DGIR). *LANGUAGES:* German, English and French.

DR. PETER KATHER, born Hannover, Germany, March 1, 1954; admitted, 1983, Germany. *Education:* University of Augsburg Law School (Referendar; Dr.jur.). Assistant, University of Augsburg, 1980-1983. Author: "The UN-Code on Restrictive Business Practices," Munich, 1985; "Patent Infringement Penalties in Germany," London, 1989; "Immigration and Nationality Law in Germany," Salzburg 1992. *Member:* German Bar Association; German Association for Intellectual Property and Copyright (GRUR); German Association for Computer Technology and Law (DGIR Chairman, Committee on Labor Law); German-British Lawyers Association; Licensing Executives Society (LES). *LANGUAGES:* German and English.

DR. STEPHAN GRUBER, born Munich, Germany, October 31, 1956; admitted, 1984, Germany. *Education:* University of Munich Law School (Referendar; Dr.jur.). Research Fellow, Max-Planck-Institute for Foreign and International Patent, Copyright and Unfair Competition Law, 1981-1986. Author: "Consumer Protection by Certification Marks," Cologne, 1986; "European and International Patent Law," Munich 1991. *Member:* German Association for Intellectual Property and Copyright (GRUR). *LANGUAGES:* German and English.

ASSOCIATES

DR. ANTON M. OSTLER, born Munich, Germany, April 20, 1962; admitted, 1991, Germany. *Education:* University of Munich Law School (Referendar; Dr.jur.); London School of Economics, 1984; University of Munich, Degree in Business Administration (Diplomkaufmann) 1989. Foreign Associate: Rosenmann & Colin, New York, N.Y., 1990. *Member:* German Bar Association; German-American Lawyers' Association (DAJV). *LANGUAGES:* German, English and Russian.

DR. CHRISTIAN DONLE, born Munich, Germany, January 25, 1964; admitted, 1991, Germany. *Education:* University of Munich Law School (Referendar; Dr.jur.). Research Fellow, Max-Planck-Institute for Foreign and International Patent, Copyright and Unfair Competition Law, 1988-1992. Foreign Associate, Reed Smith Shaw & McClay, Pittsburgh, Pa., 1990. Co-Author: "Franchising in Germany and Europe 1992", Franchising Legal Digest, 1990; "Immigration and Nationality Law in Germany," Salzburg 1992; "Sec. 31 Copyright Act and its consequences for copyright contracts," Munich 1993. *LANGUAGES:* German and English.

Languages: German, English, French, Italian and Russian

(For Complete Biographical Data on other Personnel, see Professional Biographies at Berlin, Germany)

RÄDLER RAUPACH BEZZENBERGER

MUNICH, GERMANY

(See Oppenhoff & Rädler)

RAU, VAN DORP & PARTNER

Established in 1985

WIDENMAYERSTRASSE 38
D-80538 MUNICH, GERMANY
Telephone: (089) 21 12 13-0
Telefax: (089) 21 12 13-40

Dresden, Germany Office: Niederwaldstr. 23, 01277 Dresden. Telephone: (0351) 44 11 207. Telefax (0351) 44 11 210.

Berlin, Germany Office: Lietzenseeufer 10, 14057 Berlin. Telephone: (030) 32 25 023. Telefax: (030) 32 21 018. Telex: 185607.

Leipzig, Germany Office: Gustav Adolf Str. 12, 04105 Leipzig. Telephone: (0341) 27 12 29. Telefax: (0341) 27 12 29.

Budapest Hungary Office: Békés-Németh-Vékás & Társai, Ügyvédi Iroda, Egyetem tér 1-3, H-1053 Budapest. Telephone: (01) 117-4930. Telefax: (01) 117-4930.

Trento, Italy Office: Via Grazloli 6, I-38100 Trento. Telephone: (0461) 98 00 51. Telefax: (0461) 98 52 57.

General European and International Practice, European Community Law. Corporate, Commercial, Intellectual and Industrial Property Rights, Patents. Trademarks, Copyright, Unfair Competition, Antitrust, Computer Law, Press Law, Entertainment Law, Franchising, Licensing, Insurance, Product Liability, Real Estate, Construction, Labor Law, Trusts and Estates, International Private Law, Administrative Law, Litigation, Arbitration.

MEMBERS OF FIRM

ANDREAS RAU, born Dresden, Germany, March 30, 1944; admitted, 1976, Munich, Germany. *Education:* Universities of Freiburg, Würzburg and Munich (Referendar, 1973; Assessor, 1976). Research Assistant, Max-Planck-Institute for Foreign and International Patent, Trademark, Copyright and Competition Law, Munich, 1974-1978; Assistant Lecturer, University of Munich, School of Law, 1975-1977; Lecturer on Civil Law and Copyright Law, Bavarian State Academy for Photography, Munich, 1976-1979; Faculty Member, University of the Pacific, McGeorge School of Law, International Programs, Salzburg, 1988—. Author: "Harmonization of Copyright Law in the EC," (IBA Publications, 1979); "Works of Architecture in Copyright Law" (1980). Co-Author: "Enforcement of Contractual Penalties," (WRP, 1990); "The International Franchise Option-Product Liability," (British Franchise Association, 1990). *Member:* German Bar Association; German Lawyers Association (DAV); International Bar Association (IBA) (Member, Section on Business Law); German Association for the Protection of Industrial Property and Copyright (GRUR); International Association for the Protection of Industrial Property (AIPPI); British German Chamber of Commerce; American German Chamber of Commerce, Licensing Executive Society (LES); Brussels Bar List B; Association of Independent Entrepreneurs (ASU); German Jurists Association; Association for Computer Technology; International Antitrust Forum; Society for International Law. *LANGUAGES:* German, English and French.

DR. TOMAS VAN DORP, born Bonn, Germany, July 27, 1957; admitted, 1989, Munich, Germany. *Education:* Universities of Bonn, Freiburg and Munich (Referendar, 1984; Assessor, 1988; Dr. jur., 1992). Research Assistant, Federal Association of German Newspaper Publishers, Bonn, 1984. Research Assistant, Institute of International Law and Civil Procedure, University of Munich, 1984. Author: "The Influence of Antitrust Law on Unfair Trade"; "The Continuation of the Contract Law of the GDR for Business Contracts Concluded Before the European Currency Union," DB 1990, 3183. *Member:* German Bar Association. *LANGUAGES:* German, English and French.

JACQUES WOLHÄNDLER, born Paris, France, February 6, 1956; admitted, 1982, Munich, Germany. *Education:* University of Munich, Germany (Referander, 1979; Assessor, 1982). Counsel: Siemens AG, 1982-1985; Dornier Medizintechnik, 1986. *Member:* German Bar Association; German Association for the Protection of Industrial Property and Copyright (GRUR); German French Lawyers Association. *LANGUAGES:* German, French and English.

DR. STEFAN WEBER, born Munich, Germany, October 18, 1951; admitted, 1981, Munich, Germany. *Education:* University of Munich (Referendar, 1976; Assessor, 1980; Dr. jur., 1983). Staff Member, Research Assistant Max-Planck Institute for Foreign and International Patent, Trademark, Copyright and Competition Law, Munich, 1977-1978. Author: "The Principles of Truth Governing Firm Names under the German Commercial Code and the Prohibition against Use of Misleading Names under the German Unfair Competition Act," (Munich, 1983). Managing Director of the Bavarian Pharmacists Association, 1983—. *Member:* German Bar Associa-

(This Listing Continued)

tion; German Lawyers Association (DAV). *LANGUAGES:* German and English.

DR. MONIKA PASETTI BOMBARDELLA, born Wuppertal, Germany, July 31, 1956; admitted, 1987, Munich, Germany. *Education:* University of Munich (Referendar, 1980; Assessor, 1984; Dr. jur., 1988); Columbia University, New York (LL.M., 1989). Research Assistant, Institute of Public Law and Political Science, University of Munich, 1980-1982. Research Assistant, Institute of Philosophy of Law, University of Law, Munich, 1982-1986. Attorney at Law, New York, 1990. Author: "Symbolic Legislation-Aspects of Rationality in Criminal Law Legislation." *Member:* German Bar Association; German Lawyers Association (DAV); German Association for the Protection of Industrial Property and Copyright (GRUR); International Association for the Protection of Industrial Property (AIPPI); International Association for Philosophy of Law and Social Philosophy (IVR); German Society for Legislation (DGG); Association Internationale des Jeunes Avocates (AIJA). *LANGUAGES:* German, English and French.

ASSOCIATES

DR. ROLAND BÖMER, born Dortmund, Germany, September 26, 1957; admitted, 1986, Munich, Germany. *Education:* Universities of Bochum and Munich, Germany (Referendar, 1982; Assessor, 1986; Dr. jur., 1987). Studies in International Comparative Law at the University of Strasbourg, 1980; International Private Law, University Urbino, Italy, 1981; International Comparative Law, University of Coimbra, Portugal, 1981; High School of Administrative Law in Speyer, Germany, 1984. Author: "The Duties of the Partiesto a Computer Software Contract," (Munich, 1988); "Liability for Unavoidable Computer Software Mistakes," (CR, 1989). *Member:* German Bar Association; German Lawyers Association (DAV); Federal Association of Young Entrepreneurs (BJU). *LANGUAGES:* German, English, French and Spanish.

DR. LUDWIG VOHLAND, born Burgellern (Bamberg), Germany, September 20, 1945; admitted, 1978, Bavaria. *Education:* University of Munich (Referendar, 1974; Assessor, 1978; Dr. jur., 1980). Author: "Zur Konzentration von Patentverletzungsstreitigkeiten in den Vertragsstaaten des Europäischen Patentübereinkommens," GRUR Int., 1982, 42; "Die Voraussetzungen der patentfähigen Erfindung in Italien im Vergleich zum Münchener Patentübereinkommen," Carl Heymanns Verlag, Köln, 1981; "The New Italian Patent Act," IIC - International Review of Industrial Property and Copyright Law, 441, 1980. Member of Staff, Max Planck Institute for Foreign and International Patent, Copyright and Competition Law, Munich, 1973—. *Member:* German Bar Association; German Association for the Protection of Industrial Property and Copyright (GRUR); German-Italian Jurist Association. *LANGUAGES:* German, English and Italian.

HEIJO E. RUIJSENAARS, born Amsterdam, the Netherlands, November 19, 1959; admitted, 1991, Amsterdam, the Netherlands. *Education:* University of Amsterdam (Meester in de Rechten, 1984). Graduate Studies in German Law, University of Tübingen, Germany, 1984-1985. Research Assistant, Max-Planck Institute for Foreign and International Patent-Trademark Copyright and Competition Law, Munich, 1986—. Internship, Walt Disney Company, Burbank, California, 1987-1988. Author: "Product Placement: Permissible Sponsoring or Unpermissable Subliminal Advertising?" (AMI, 1987); "Protection against Misappropriation of Athletes?" (GRUR Int., 1988); "The Licensing of the Publicity Value of Well-Know n Trademarks by the Trademark Proprietor, in Germany, USA and Benelux," (GRUR Int., 1988-1989); "Start of a New Competition: Sports, Events and Broadcasting Rights," (GRUR, 1990); "Design Protection by Trademark Law?" (GRUR Int., 1990). *Member:* International Association for the Protection of Industrial Property (AIPPI); Association for Copyright, Amsterdam, the Netherlands; Association for Unfair Competition, The Hague, The Netherlands. *LANGUAGES:* Dutch, German, English and French.

DR. GEORG PETER KRÄNZLIN, born Neumünster, Germany, November 5, 1954; admitted, 1981, Augsburg, Germany. *Education:* University of Augsburg, Germany; University of Pittsburgh School of Law, Pittsburgh, Pennsylvania (Referendar, 1978; Assessor, 1981; Dr. jur., 1983). Legal Advisor Digital Equipment GmbH, Munich, 1986-1989. Author: "The Law of Distributorship under German International Private Law," 1983; "The Private International Law of Agency and Distributorship in US-German Business Transactions," (ZVR, 1985). *Member:* German Bar Association; German Association for the Protection of Industrial Property and Copyright (GRUR); German American Lawyers Association (GALA); German Lawyers Association (DAV). *LANGUAGES:* German, English and French.

HANS JOACHIM HERZOG, born Dresden, Germany, December 23, 1957; admitted, 1990, Dresden, Germany. *Education:* University of Leipzig

(This Listing Continued)

RAU, VAN DORP & PARTNER, Munich—Continued

(Dipl. jur., 1983). General Counsel, Saxonian Office of Engineering for Above and Below Ground Construction, Dresden, Germany, 1985—. *Member:* German Bar Association (Dresden). (Dresden Office). *LANGUAGES:* German, English and Russian.

DR. AXEL SCHOBER, born Bayreuth, Germany, October 23, 1961; admitted, 1993, Dresden, Germany. *Education:* Universities of Würzburg, Bayreuth and Bordeaux/France (Referendar, 1986; Assessor, 1990; Dr. jur., 1990). Research Assistant, University of Bayreuth, Chair for Private, International Private and Private Comperative Law, 1986-1987. Activities: Solicitor in Paris, France, 1990-1991. Lecturer at Dresden University for Private Law, 1991-1992. Judge at the Civil Court (Kreisgericht) at Dresden, 1991-1992 and at the Landgericht Munich, Chamber for Private Construction Law, 1992-1993. Author: "Possibilities of Integrating Third Persons into the Course of a Current Procedure-Analysis of French, German and European Civil Procedural Law," Diss., 1990. *Member:* German Bar Association (Dresden). (Dresden Office). *LANGUAGES:* German, English and French.

DIP. ING. MICHAEL RAU, born Berlin, Germany, December 11, 1939; admitted, 1992, Berlin, Germany. *Education:* University (Fachhochschule) for Textile-Chemistry of Reutlingen (Dipl.-Ing., 1970); University of Berlin (Referendear, 1989; Assessor, 1992). Research Assistant, Institut for Textile-Technique of Reutlingen, 1970-1985. Faculty Member of Humboldt University, Berlin. *Member:* German Bar Association; German Lawyers Association (DAV); German Association for the Protection of Industrial Property and Copyright (GRUR); International Association for the Protection of Industrial Property Right (AIPPI). (Berlin Office). *LANGUAGES:* German and English.

DR. ANDREAS GRIMM, born Munich, Germany, November 19, 1963; admitted, 1990, Munich, Germany. *Education:* University of Munich (Referendar, 1987; Assessor, 1990; Dr. jur., 1992). Author: "The New Consumer Credit Act, a Consumer Political Contribution to the Transformation of the EC Regulation into National Law," Diss., 1992. *Member:* German Bar Association (Munich). *LANGUAGES:* German, English and French.

OF COUNSEL

PROF. DR. DR. DIETER PFAFF, Professor of Law, University of Munich, Germany, School of Law; Director, Institute for Industrial Property and Copyright Law of the University of Munich since 1974; born Berlin, Germany, January 24, 1936; admitted, 1967, Hamburg, Germany and 1972, Munich, Germany. *Education:* University of West-Berlin, Kiel and Freiburg, Germany (Referendar, 1960; Assessor, 1966; Dr. jur. utriusque, 1964, (Freiburg); Dr. phil., 1976, Budapest) Senior Researcher: Max-Planck-Institut for Foreign and International Private Law, Hamburg, 1967-1972; Max-Planck-Institut for Foreign and International Patent, Trademark, Copyright and Competition Law, Munich, 1972-1976. Author: eight books and more than 100 articles, contributions in periodicals and broadcasting. *Member:* 15 National and International Scientific Societies and member of the Boards of Licensing Executive Society (LES), of South-Eastern Europe-Society, of German Society for Eastern-Europe, of Scientific Society for International Procedures and Arbitration Law; Candidate for membership in the Hungarian Academy of Science (Budapest). Arbitrator: International Chamber of Commerce, Paris, France; German Committee for Arbitration, Cologne, Germany; International Arbitration Court in Warsaw, Poland; Arbitration Court of the Federal Chamber of Commerce of former Yugoslavia (Belgrad/Zagreb). *LANGUAGES:* German, English, French, Russian, Hungarian and Bulgarian.

ENRICO GIAMMARCO, born Trento, Italy, October 19, 1957; admitted, 1984, Italy. *Education:* University of Bologna Law School (J.D., cum laude, 1981); Max-Planck-Institut for Foreign and International Patent, Copyright and Competition Law, Munich (1982-1984). *Member:* Ordine Avvocati Trento; German-Italian Jurist Association. *LANGUAGES:* Italian, German and English.

RIEDEL, WAGNER & PARTNER

ARCOSTRAβE 3
80333 MUNICH, GERMANY
Telephone: 0049/89/558576
Fax: 0049/89/554195

General German and US-practice, International Law, Commercial Law, Corporate Law, Contract Law, European Community Law, Estate Planning, Probate, Family Law, Separation and Divorce, Recognition and Enforcement of US Judgements.

MEMBERS OF FIRM

DR. ERWIN RIEDEL, born Fulda, Germany, December 29, 1925; admitted, 1964, Germany. *Education:* Universities Frankfurt/Main, Fribourg, Switzerland (law degree, 1956; Doctor of Law, 1960). Syndikus with the German Commerzbank, 1961-1964. *Member:* German Bar. *LANGUAGES:* German and English. *PRACTICE AREAS:* Commercial Banks; International Banking.

STEPHEN RIEDEL, born Fulda, Germany, April 21, 1959; admitted, 1987, Germany. *Education:* University Regensburg (law degree, 1984). *Member:* German Bar. *LANGUAGES:* German, French and English. *PRACTICE AREAS:* Insurance; Computer Contracts; Construction Law.

GISELHER WAGNER, born Herne, Germany, August 29, 1954; admitted, 1987, Germany. *Education:* University Munich (law degree, 1984). *Member:* German Bar. *LANGUAGES:* German, English and French. *PRACTICE AREAS:* Unfair Competition; Unfair Trade; Product Liability; Trademarks; Copyrights; License Agreements.

RENÉ PLATZER VON FABRICIUS, born Munich, Germany, September 25, 1927; admitted, 1957, Germany; 1960, Oregon; 1963, District of Columbia. *Education:* University of Munich (Law Degree, 1951; Dr. of Jurisprudence, 1970); University of Oregon (Bachelor of Law, 1960; Doctor of Law, 1967). Alumni, Lewis and Clark College. *Member:* German Bar; Oregon State Bar; Bar of the Supreme Court of the United States; Association of American Lawyers in Europe. *LANGUAGES:* English, German and Italian. *PRACTICE AREAS:* Anglo-American Law; International Contracts.

MICHAEL CHRISTIAN RÖSSNER

HÖCHLSTR. 4
81675 MUNICH, GERMANY
Telephone: (011-49) 89-99 89 22-0
Telefax: (011-49) 89-99 89 22-33; (011-49) 89-99 89 22-66

General Practice, Banking Law, Bankruptcy Law (trustee for the Munich bankruptcy court Konkursgericht), General Business Law, Commercial Litigation, Bank Fraud Litigation, Foreign Investment, Securities, Options, Futures, Investment Securities and Commodities Fraud Litigation.

FIRM PROFILE: The firm was formed in 1976 and specializes in commercial litigation emphazising investor representation in securities and commodities fraud litigation and international asset tracing.

Our client base is mainly German, Austrian, Scandinavian and Swiss. The firm has seven lawyers.

MICHAEL CHRISTIAN RÖSSNER, born 1943; admitted, 1973, Germany. *Education:* University of Munich (Referendar, 1968; Assessor, 1972). Contributions to, *Handbuch des Kapitalanlagerechts,* (Handbook of Capital Investment Law), 1990. *Member:* Eurojuris Europe, Munich Bar Association. *LANGUAGES:* German and English.

OLIVER BUSCH, born 1962; admitted, 1992, Germany. *Education:* University of Munich. Banking Apprenticeship. *LANGUAGES:* German and English. *PRACTICE AREAS:* Corporate Law; Banking Law; Investment Law.

DR. BABETTE GÄBHARD, born 1963; admitted, 1990, Germany. *Education:* University of Munich, Freiburg i. Br. (Doctor of Jurisprudence, 1993). Dissertation on, Kapitalanlagebetrug (Investment Fraud), 1993. *LANGUAGES:* German and English. *PRACTICE AREAS:* Civil Law; Investment Law; Banking Law.

IRIS R. KLEIN, born 1959; admitted, 1991, Germany. *Education:* University of Munich (Referendar, 1986; Assessor, 1989). Research Assistant, *Radbruch,* . Legal Assistant, Consulate General of Germany, Montréal, Canada. *Member:* German Bar Association. *LANGUAGES:* German and English. *PRACTICE AREAS:* Bankruptcy Law; Investment Law.

(This Listing Continued)

ULRIKE MORGENSTERN, born 1951; admitted, 1984, Germany. *Education:* University of Münster. *LANGUAGES:* German and English. *PRACTICE AREAS:* Civil Law.

CURT MÜLLER, born 1962; admitted, 1992, Germany. *Education:* University of Augsburg; University of Munich; University of Lausanne. Banking Apprenticeship. *LANGUAGES:* German, English and French. *PRACTICE AREAS:* Corporate Law; Banking Law; Investment Law.

A. HARTMUT THIMM, born 1941; admitted, 1973, Germany. *Education:* University of Freiberg i. Br.; University of Munich. *LANGUAGES:* German and English. *PRACTICE AREAS:* Corporate Law; Investment Law.

DR. HEINZ ROTH, HANS ROTH, FRIEDER ROTH, DR. GERD WIEDEMANN

Established in 1897

GEWÜRZMÜHLSTRAβE 5
80538 MUNICH, GERMANY
Telephone: (089) 222383/84
Telecopier: (089) 226360
Cable Address: "COPYROTH"

General Practice. Civil and Commercial Litigation, Copyright, Unfair Competition, Probate, Labor, Liability, Real Estate and Foundation Law.

FIRM PROFILE: The firm was established in 1897 and offers a full range of services in Civil Law. The firm specializes in Publishing Law, Copyright Law, the Law of Unfair Competition and Labour Law. The client base is Europe and the USA.

MEMBERS OF FIRM

DR. HEINZ ROTH (1906-1994).

HANS ROTH, born Munich, Germany, September 8, 1934; admitted, 1961, Munich. *Education:* Universities of Erlangen and Munich. *LANGUAGES:* German and English. *PRACTICE AREAS:* Road Traffic Law; Inheritance Law; Family Law.

FRIEDER ROTH, born Irschenhausen, Germany, June 27, 1945; admitted, 1973, Munich. *Education:* Universities of Erlangen, Bonn and Munich. Internship with Murray, Gudeman & Hammer, American Law Firm, 1970. Lecturer on Law, Willi-Graf-Gymnasium, 1975 and Luitpold-Gymnasium, 1978. Alumnus of Salzburg Seminar in American Studies. Board Member, Augenklinik Herzog Carl Theodor Foundation, 1985—. Member, Board of Trustees, Studienseminar Albertinum Foundation, 1987—. *Member:* German-American Lawyers Association (DAJV); Association Internationale des Jeunes Avocats (AIJA); German Association for the Protection of Industrial Property and Copyright Law (GRUR). *LANGUAGES:* German, English and French. *PRACTICE AREAS:* Copyright Law; Law of Unfair Competition; Publishing Law.

DR. GERD WIEDEMANN, born Erlangen, Germany, August 29, 1958; admitted, 1988, Munich. *Education:* Universities of Erlangen-Nürnberg, Bonn (Referendar, 1984; Assessor, 1988);. Internship with Sedgwick, Detert, Moran & Arnold, San Francisco, 1987-1988. Assistant at University of Erlangen-Nürnberg, 1985-1986. *LANGUAGES:* German and English. *PRACTICE AREAS:* Labour Law; Law of Tenancy.

Languages: German, English and French.

ROTHE, SENNINGER & KOLLMAR

Established in 1948

PIENZENAUERSTRASSE 4
D-81679 MUNICH, GERMANY
Telephone: (49 0) 89-98 89 37
Telefax: (49 0) 89-98 51 04

Labor and Employment, Commercial Law, Arbitration, Media Law, Corporation Law, Family Law and Insurance.

PARTNERS

DR. GERHART F. ROTHE, born Berlin, Germany, November 26, 1903; admitted, 1932, Berlin. Member, German-American Chamber of Commerce. *Member:* German Association for the Protection of Industrial Property. *LANGUAGES:* German and English.

ERHARD SENNINGER, born August 5, 1933; admitted, 1963, Munich. *Education:* Dickinson Law School, University of Munich. Member,

(This Listing Continued)

Advisory Board of the Federal Ministry of Economics for Small and Middlesized Business. *Member:* German Bar Association (President, 1988-1991); German Association for the Promotion of Independent Law Practice in Middle and Eastern Europe. *LANGUAGES:* German and English.

DR. EBERHARD KOLLMAR, born July 8, 1938; admitted, 1966, Munich. *Education:* University of Munich (Dr.Jur., 1964). Author: "Das Verhältnis der Grundstücksgeschäfte zu den Handelsgeschäften in der Entwicklung des deutschen Handelsrechts." *Member:* German Bar Association. *LANGUAGES:* German, English and French.

JÜRGEN BUNTROCK, born March 29, 1943; admitted, 1972, Munich. *Education:* University of Munich. *Member:* German Bar Association. *LANGUAGES:* German and English.

THOMAS DEBY, born Munich, Germany, December 31, 1965; admitted, 1993, Munich. *Education:* University of Munich. *Member:* German Bar Association. *LANGUAGES:* German and English.

GABRIELE GODL, born Munich, Germany, June 25, 1967; admitted, 1994, Munich. *Education:* University of Munich. *Member:* German Bar Association; German-American Lawyers Association. *LANGUAGES:* German and English.

RÜCKEL, TRENKNER & COLLEGEN

KAROLLNENSTRAβE 4
80538 MUNICH, GERMANY
Telephone: (089) 212 38 70
Fax: (089) 212 38 75 0

Frankfurt/Main, Germany Office: Bockenheimer Anlage 13, 60322. Telephone: (069) 55 07 31. Fax: (069) 596 39 94.

Atlanta, Georgia Office: Ten Piedmont Center, Suite 350, 3495 Piedmont Road, 30305. Telephone: (404) 266-1008. Fax: (404) 266-0205.

Berlin, Germany Office: Kurfürstendamm 132 A, 10711. Telephone: (030) 896 6920. Fax: (030) 8966 9244.

Dresden, Germany Office: Bautzner Straβe 14, 01099. Telephone: (0351) 502 43 00. Fax: (0351) 502 43 02.

Leipzig, Germany Office: Marperger Straβe 20, 04229. Telephone: (0341) 401 13 41. Fax: (0341) 401 14 54.

General Practice, Litigation and Commercial Law, International Business Transactions, Real Estate, Corporate.

FIRM PROFILE: The firm is a member of LAWORLD. LAWORLD is an international organization of law firms who coordinate and share information with other member firms in Brussels, Budapest, Hong Kong, Jerusalem, Lausanne, London, Moscow, New York, Padova, Stockholm, Taipei, Tel Aviv, Vancouver, Warsaw, Zagreb and Zug.

MEMBERS OF FIRM

DR.JUR. CHRISTOPH RÜCKEL, born Bad Kreuznach, Germany, May 7, 1949; admitted, 1976, Germany. *Education:* University of Heidelberg Law School; University of Geneva Law School, Munich (1st State Exam, 1973). Author: "Evidence by Witness"; Co-Author: German Attorneys Handbook and various articles. Member: German American Chamber of Commerce; American Chamber of Commerce in Germany. *Member:* Federal Bar Association (Criminal Law Committee); German-American Lawyers Association; German-Israeli Lawyers Association; Laworld (President). *LANGUAGES:* German, English and French. *PRACTICE AREAS:* Commercial; Corporate; Real Estate Law; Banking Law; Tax; White Collar Crime; Investments.

STEFAN VON MOERS, born Marburg, Germany, July 22, 1954; admitted, 1981, Germany. *Education:* University of Tübingen. *Member:* Laworld; German Lawyers Association (DAV); Association for Copyright and Media Law, Gesellschaft Urheber und Medienrecht. *LANGUAGES:* German and English. *PRACTICE AREAS:* Corporate Law; Media Law; Copyright Law; Antitrust Law; Civil Law.

THILO PFORDTE, born Dusseldorf, Germany, June 10, 1958; admitted, 1988, Germany. *Education:* University of Bonn and Munich. Author: "Anwaltshonorar und Geldwaesche," Brak, 1994. *Member:* Laworld; AG Strafrecht im DAV. *LANGUAGES:* English and French. *PRACTICE AREAS:* Criminal Law.

ASSOCIATES

NAILE PAPILA-HUBERT, born Hamburg, Germany, September 24, 1962; admitted, 1993, Germany. *Education:* University of Hamburg (1985); Ludwig-Maximilians University (1990). *LANGUAGES:* English and French. *PRACTICE AREAS:* Civil Law.

(This Listing Continued)

RÜCKEL, TRENKNER & COLLEGEN, Munich—
Continued

KARL W. DEGENHARD, born Munich, Germany, June 27, 1964; admitted, 1993, Germany. *LANGUAGES:* English, French and German. *PRACTICE AREAS:* Criminal; Antitrust; Real Estate.

MARTIN RINGEL, born Lich, Germany, August 25, 1959; admitted, 1993, Germany. *Education:* Ludwig-Maximilian University (1st State Exam, 1989; 2nd State Exam, 1992). *LANGUAGES:* English and Italian. *PRACTICE AREAS:* Commercial Law; Contract Law; Banking Law; Association Law; Private International Law.

JAN ANDREJTSCHITSCH, born Prague, Czech Republic, August 22, 1963; admitted, 1993, Germany. *Education:* Klenze Gymnasium, Munich (Abitur, 1983); Ludwig-Maximilians University (1st State Exam, 1989; 2nd State Exam, 1993). *LANGUAGES:* German and Czech. *PRACTICE AREAS:* Corporate Law; Bankruptcy; Insolvency; Criminal Law.

GABRIELE WESTERBURG, born Marl, Germany, October 2, 1948; admitted, 1979, Germany. *Education:* University of Munich Law School (1st State Exam; 2nd State Exam); University of Heidelberg Law School; Würzburg Law School. *LANGUAGES:* English and French. *PRACTICE AREAS:* Real Estate; Criminal; Corporate; Economic Law.

SCHEELE, SCHWARTZ, ZIELCKE & PARTNER
PRINZREGENTENPLATZ 15
81675 MUNICH, GERMANY
Telephone: 089/470 10 02
Fax: 089/470 10 06

Tirana, Albania Office: P. Myzeqari 31/18. Telephone: 00355-42-22354. Fax: 00355-42-22354.
Zagreb, Croatia Office: Dordiceva 6, 41001. Telephone: 00385-41-421 106. Fax: 00385-41-428 350.
Prague, Czech Republic Office: Wenzelsplatz 56, 110 00 Prague 1. Telephone: 0042-2-24230523. Fax: 0042-2-24230523.
Berlin, Germany Office: Alt-Moabit 101a, 10559. Telephone: 030 3992750. Fax: 030 399275-303; 030 399275-404.
Vilnius, Lithuania Office: Architektu 194/22 Vilnius 2049. Fax: 00370 2 443720.
Poznan, Poland Office: Ul. Stowianski 28a, 60-651. Telephone: 0048-61-485 107. Fax: 0048-61-485 107.
Warsaw, Poland Office: Ul. Zurawia 47, 00-680. Telephone: 0048-22-6300670. Fax: 0048-22-6300670.
Bucharest, Romania Office: Aleea Negru Voda, Nr. 6, Bloc C3, Scara 2, Etaj 4, Apartment 33. Telephone: 0040 1 7899589. Fax: 0040 1 7899589.
Moscow, Russia Office: Nem. Dantchenko 3, 103808. Telephone: 007-095-292-8595.
St. Petersburg, Russia Office: Ul. Fuhrmannowa 6-A, III. 191187. Telephone: 007-812-2751071.
Kiev, Ukraine Office: Ul. Zoloti Vorota 2-A. 252034. Telephone: 007-044-2245208. Fax: 007-044-2292835.

German and International Practice, Antitrust and Trade Regulation, Banks and Banking, Communications and Media, Construction, Business, Company, Computer and Software, Corporate, Eastern European and C.I.S., Environmental, European Community, International, Investments, Labor and Employment, Professional Liability, Products Liability, Property, Real Estate, Securities and Trust and Estates Law.

FIRM PROFILE: Scheele, Schwartz, Zielcke & Partner is an international law firm advising business clients and public institutions on all domestic and overseas corporate and commercial matters. The Munich based lawyers are qualified in a total of sixteen foreign jurisdictions. The firm specializes in Eastern European and C.I.S. matters. Members of the firm have written 8 books and approximately 70 articles and essays on domestic and foreign law and have translated over twenty statutes in Russia, the Czech and Slovak Republics and the Ukraine. Six of the firm's attorneys are correspondents for Eastern European legal periodicals. Currently the firm is representing a broad variety of business clients in Europe, North America, South America, Asia and Africa.

(This Listing Continued)

EU768B

DR. MICHAEL SCHEELE, born Höxter, Germany, 1948; admitted, 1977, Germany; 1994, Russia. *Education:* University of Stetson, Florida, U.S.A.; University of Munich and Münster, Germany (Law Degree, 1977; Doctor of Laws, 1978). *Member:* German Bar Association; International Bar Association. *LANGUAGES:* German, English and French. *PRACTICE AREAS:* Commercial; Corporate; International; Antitrust and Trade Regulation; Computer and Software; Mergers, Acquisitions and Divestitures; Privatization; Contract; Securities; Communications and Media; Trust and Estate Law.

MICHAEL SCHWARTZ, born Gräfelfing, Germany, 1961; admitted, 1991, Germany; 1994, Russia. *Education:* University of Munich; University of St, Petersburg. Awarded, The German People's Student Scholarship, 1987. Executive Member, International Chamber of Lawyers, St. Petersburg. *Member:* German Bar Association. *LANGUAGES:* German, English and Russian. *PRACTICE AREAS:* Banks and Banking; Commercial; International; Investments; Property and Real Estate; Eastern European and C.I.S. Law.

ANDREAS ZIELCKE, born Kaliningrad, Russia, 1943; admitted, 1985, Germany. *Education:* University of Munich and University of Frankfurt (Law Degree, 1970; Doctor of Law, 1979). Publicist for the German Weekly Magazine, "Der Spiegel." *Member:* German Bar Association. *LANGUAGES:* German and English. *PRACTICE AREAS:* Communications and Media; Computer and Media; Products Liability; Professional Liability; Commercial Law.

SCHMIDT-SIBETH ZIRNGIBL LANGWIESER HEISSE
MAXIMILIANSPLATZ 5
80333 MUNICH, GERMANY
Telephone: 089/54 56 5-0
Fax: 089/54 56 5-201

Berlin, Germany Office: Leipziger Straße 63, 10117 Berlin. Telephone: 030/20 22 73. Telefax: 030/20 22 7426.
Erfurt, Germany Office: Anger 23, 99084 Erfurt (Thuringia). Telephone: 0361/6 42 12 36. Telefax: 0361/6 42 25 04.

General Practice, Corporate, Commercial, E.E.C., International Law, Trademarks, Copyright, Unfair Competition, Real Estate, Construction and Building Law, Labor Law, Legal Affairs in former East Germany, Tax Law.

DR. HANS SCHMIDT-SIBETH, born Donauwörth, Germany, February 7, 1937; admitted, 1967, Munich. *Education:* University of Munich and Freiburg (Dr. jur., 1965). *Member:* Munich Bar Association (Executive Officer, 1976-1982). *LANGUAGES:* German and English.

FRIEDRICH ZIRNGIBL, born Tübingen, Germany, January 8, 1939; admitted, 1969, Munich. *Education:* University of Munich. *LANGUAGES:* German and English.

DR. HANS LANGWIESER, born Munich, Germany, February 13, 1939; admitted, 1967, Munich; 1988, Auditor Certificate, Munich. *Education:* Universities of Munich and Cologne (Dr. jur., 1967). *LANGUAGES:* German and English.

DR. MATTHIAS HEISSE, born Frankfurt/Main, Germany, July 28, 1960; admitted, 1989, Munich. *Education:* University of Munich (Dr. jur., 1988). *LANGUAGES:* German and English.

DR. ALEXANDER VON BERGWELT, born Nürnberg, Germany, December 10, 1963; admitted, 1991, Munich. *Education:* University of Munich (Business Administration Degree, Dipl.-Kfm. 1987, Law Degree, 1988; Dr. jur., 1991). Research Assistant, Max-Planck Institut (Foreign and International Patent, Copyright and Unfair Competition Law, 1988-1991). *Member:* AIJA. *LANGUAGES:* German, Spanish, English, French, Italian and Portuguese.

DR. WOLFGANG WEISSKOPF, born Stuttgart, Germany, December 11, 1959; admitted, 1991, Munich. *Education:* Universities of Regensburg and Tübingen (Dr. jur., 1992). *LANGUAGES:* German and English.

DR. STEFAN KURSAWE, born Munich, Germany, September 23, 1962; admitted, 1992, Munich. *Education:* Universities of Munich and Regensburg (Dr. jur., 1987). *LANGUAGES:* German, Russian and English.

(This Listing Continued)

CARSTEN BRÜNINGHAUS, born Berlin, Germany, November 17, 1962; admitted, 1991, Munich. *Education:* Freie Universität Berlin. Research Assistant, Institute for Corporate Law, Freie Universität Berlin (1988-1990). *LANGUAGES:* German, English and French.

ASSOCIATES

BETTINA BICK, born Mühlheim/Ruhr, Germany, September 26, 1961; admitted, 1990, Munich. *Education:* University of Münster. *LANGUAGES:* German, English and French.

DR. ULRIKE HELKENBERG, born Burghausen, Germany, June 13, 1962; admitted, 1991, Munich. *Education:* University of Munich (Dr. jur., 1993). *LANGUAGES:* German and English.

DR. KATHRIN THIELE, born Magdeburg, Germany, November 13, 1959; admitted, 1991, Munich. *Education:* University of Magdeburg (Dr. jur., 1987). *LANGUAGES:* German, Russian and English.

DR. AXEL ANKER, born Munich, Germany, May 8, 1962; admitted, 1992, Munich. *Education:* University of Munich (Dr. jur., 1991). *LANGUAGES:* German, English and Spanish.

ECKART VON LOJEWSKI, born Hannover, Germany, February 24, 1962; admitted, 1993, Munich. *Education:* Universities of Munich and Freiburg. Assistant, Institute of Criminal Law, University of Konstanz. *LANGUAGES:* German, English and French.

DR. ANDREAS ZUMSCHLINGE, born Haiger, Germany, June 17, 1961; admitted, 1993, Munich. *Education:* Universities of Munich and Passau (Dr. jur., 1992). Research Assistant, Max-Planck-Institut (Foreign and International Patent, Copyright and Unfair Competition Law, 1988-1991. *LANGUAGES:* German, English and French.

AXEL ZIMMERMANN, born Munich, Germany, November 25, 1962; admitted, 1994, Munich. *Education:* University of Munich (Law Degree, 1990). *LANGUAGES:* German, English, French and Italian.

DR. GERHARD SINZ, born Heimenkirch, Germany, October 19, 1963; admitted, 1994, Munich. *Education:* Bavarian Civil Servants Academy; Universities of Kostanz and Munich (Administration Degree, Dipl.-Verwaltungswirt (FH), 1985, Law Degree, 1990; Dr. jur., 1992). *LANGUAGES:* German, English and French.

THOMAS RICHTER, born Rosenheim, Germany, November 20, 1962; admitted, 1993, Munich. *Education:* Universities of Munich, Mainz, Barcelona and Madrid. Assistant, Institutes of Civil and International Law, University of Munich, 1989-1993. *LANGUAGES:* German, English, French, Spanish and Catalan.

DR. VOLKER MARKO, born Cologne, Germany, December 20, 1964; admitted, 1994, Munich. *Education:* Universities of Tübingen, Munich (Law Degree, 1990); Regensburg (Dr. jur., 1992); Georgetown University, Washington, D.C. (LL.M., 1994). *LANGUAGES:* German, English and French.

AXEL METZNER, born Düsseldorf, Germany, October 3, 1964; admitted, 1994, Düsseldorf. *Education:* Universities of Freiburg and Münster. *LANGUAGES:* German and English.

DR. EBERHARD WITTHOFF, born Gladbeck, Germany, October 10, 1963; admitted, 1994, Munich. *Education:* Universities of Tübingen and Freiburg (Dr. jur., 1992). *LANGUAGES:* German and English.

JOHANN KURRECK, born Erding, Germany, October 9, 1965; admitted, 1993, Munich. *Education:* Universities of Munich and Regensburg. *LANGUAGES:* German, English and French.

EVA STENGER, born Aschaffenburg, Germany, October 3, 1965; admitted, 1994, Munich. *Education:* Universities of Würburg and Munich. *LANGUAGES:* German and English.

DR. HEIKE BRAUNHOFER, born Passau, Germany, February 15, 1965; admitted, 1994, Munich. *Education:* Universities of Passau, Hamburg and Munich (Dr. jur., 1995). *LANGUAGES:* German and English.

JÖRG ZEISE, born Essen, Germany, July 11, 1965; admitted, 1995, Berlin. *Education:* University of Bonn. *LANGUAGES:* German and English.

SCHWARZ KURTZE SCHNIEWIND KELWING WICKE RECHTSANWÄLTE

WITTELSBACHERPLATZ 1 (ARCO-PALAIS)
80333 MUNICH, GERMANY
Telephone: (89) 235 00 40
Telefax: (89) 280 94 32

Berlin, Germany Office: Kurfürstendamm 220, 10719 Berlin. Telephone: (030) 885 92 70. Telefax: (030) 882 22 60.

Dresden, Germany Office: Münzgasse 10, 01067 Dresden. Telephone: (0351) 498 91 66. Telefax: (0351) 498 91 68.

Potsdam, Germany Office: Gregor-Mendel-Straße 14, 14469. Potsdam. Telephone: (0331) 280 07 06. Telefax: (0331) 280 07 76.

Copyright, Intellectual and Industrial Property, Media and Entertainment, Financing (Media, Construction and Real Estate), Banking, Unfair Competition and Antitrust, Corporate, Labour, Mergers & Acquisitions, Trademarks, Securities, Privatization and Restitution (East Germany), International Investment and Trade Matters, International Contracts, Arbitration & Litigation.

MEMBERS OF FIRM

PROF. DR. WOLF SCHWARZ, born Hoesel, Germany, June 10, 1917; admitted, 1949, Germany. Professor, 1984, Academy for Film and Television, Munich, Germany. Honorary Consul, General People's Republic of Bangladesh, July, 1980. *Member:* German and International Bar Associations; German Association for Protection of Industrial Property (AIPPI). *LANGUAGES:* German and English. *PRACTICE AREAS:* Arbitration Law; Banking Law; Copyright Law; Corporate Law; Entertainment Law.

DR. FRIEDRICH W.J. SCHNIEWIND, born Köln, Germany, January 26, 1937; admitted, 1967, Germany. *Member:* German and International Bar Associations; Japan Chamber of Commerce and Industry (Düsseldorf); International Law Association. *LANGUAGES:* German, English and French. *PRACTICE AREAS:* Corporate Law; Commercial Law; E.C. Law; Mergers and Acquisitions Law; Foreign Investments Law; Financing Law; Construction Law; Real Estate Law.

KLAUS J. KELWING, born Oberhausen, Germany, January 3, 1940; admitted, 1970, Germany. *Member:* German and International Bar Associations; German-Swedish Chamber of Commerce. *LANGUAGES:* German and English. *PRACTICE AREAS:* Corporate Law; Unfair Competition Law; Contract Law; Commercial Law.

DR. JOSEPH ZELLER, born Immenstadt, Germany, June 5, 1949; admitted, 1979, Germany. *Member:* German and International Bar Associations; Canadian-German Chambers of Commerce, 1977. *LANGUAGES:* German, English and French. *PRACTICE AREAS:* Litigation; Unfair Competition Law; Antitrust Law; Franchise Law; Securities Law; Options Law; Futures Law; Consumer Protection Law.

DR. BERND JOCH, born Wolfen/Bitterfeld, Germany, April 14, 1952; admitted, 1983, Germany. *Member:* German and International Bar Associations; German Association for Lawyers specialized in Labour Law; German-Chinese Lawyers Association. *LANGUAGES:* German and English. *PRACTICE AREAS:* Industrial Relations Law; Labour Law; Intellectual Property Law; Entertainment Law; Copyright Law; Corporate Law.

J.P. MICHAEL SCHWARZ, born Munich, Germany, May 15, 1957; admitted, 1984, Germany. *LANGUAGES:* German and English. *PRACTICE AREAS:* Aviation Law; Banking Law; Financing Law; Real Estate Law; Construction Law; General Legal Practice.

DR. MATHIAS SCHWARZ, born Munich, Germany, July 9, 1952; admitted, 1979, Germany. Qualified Chartered Accountant. *Member:* German, American and International Bar Associations. *LANGUAGES:* German, English, French and Italian. *PRACTICE AREAS:* Corporate Law; Entertainment Law; Media Law; Publishing Law; Film Financing Law; Mergers and Acquisitions Law.

DR. CHRISTOPH HAESNER, born Speyer, Germany, May 8, 1952; admitted, 1983, Germany. Master of Comparative Law/University of Illinois, 1979. Seven years experience with Film Industry (three years Managing Director of Production Company; two years Head of Legal Department). *LANGUAGES:* German, English and French. *PRACTICE AREAS:* Media Law; Entertainment Law; Publishing Law; Corporate Law.

DR. MICHAEL BRAUCH, born Hamburg, Germany, September 8, 1947; admitted, 1975, Germany. *Member:* UIA; AIJA (Honorary Vice

(This Listing Continued)

SCHWARZ KURTZE SCHNIEWIND KELWING WICKE RECHTSANWÄLTE, Munich—Continued

President, formerly National Vice President for Germany and Chairman of Congress Committee); German Lawyers Association (International Division). *LANGUAGES:* German, French and English. *PRACTICE AREAS:* Unfair Competition Law; Corporate Law; International Trade Matters; Mergers & Acquisitions; Labour Law.

ASSOCIATES

THOMAS VON PETERSDORFF-CAMPEN, born Hannover, Germany, December 14, 1954; admitted, 1984, Germany. LL.M., Los Angeles. Nine years experience with Film Industry (four years Head of Legal Department). *LANGUAGES:* German, English and French. *PRACTICE AREAS:* Media & Entertainment Law; Copyright Law; Corporate Law; Film Financing Law.

DANIELA A. BERGDOLT, born Munich, Germany, April 10, 1959; admitted, 1987, Germany. Managing Director of the Bavarian Section of the German Shareholder Association (Deutsche Schutzvereinigung für Wertpapierbesitz). *PRACTICE AREAS:* Corporate Law; Banking Law; Mergers & Acquisitions; Family Law.

CLAUS DOPPELHAMER, born Munich, Germany, April 19, 1963; admitted, 1992, Germany. *LANGUAGES:* English and German. *PRACTICE AREAS:* General Legal Practice; Litigation.

DR. ULRICH MUTH, born Heidelberg, Germany, April 3, 1963; admitted, 1992, Germany. *LANGUAGES:* German and English. *PRACTICE AREAS:* Commercial Law; Corporate Law.

WOLFGANG SCHALLER, born Gräfelfing, Germany, May 8, 1959; admitted, 1993, Germany. *LANGUAGES:* German, English and French. *PRACTICE AREAS:* Insurance Law; Trade Law; Commercial Law.

ALEXANDER VON KUHLBERG, born Stuttgart, Germany, February 16, 1962; admitted, 1993, Germany. *Member:* AIJA; German-Mexican Lawyers Association. *LANGUAGES:* German, English, French and Spanish. *PRACTICE AREAS:* Corporate Law; International Trade Matters; Privatization and Restitution (East Germany); Labour Law; Succession Law.

DR. ARMIN SCHWERDTFEGER, born Mülheim an der Ruhr, Germany, August 12, 1963; admitted, 1993, Germany. *LANGUAGES:* German, English and French. *PRACTICE AREAS:* Commercial Law; Corporate Law.

ALFONS M. BRAUN, born Glonn, Germany, August 25, 1963; admitted, 1994, Germany. *LANGUAGES:* German, English and French. *PRACTICE AREAS:* General Legal Practice; Art Law; Copyright Law.

SEUFERT

Rechtsanwälte

RESIDENZSTRASSE 12
80333 MUNICH, GERMANY
Telephone: 089/22 26 11
Telefax: 089/29 11 00

Leipzig Office: Springerstraße 7, 04105. Telephone: 0341/5900614. Fax: 0341/5900613.

General Practice, Corporate, Mergers and Acquisitions, Commercial, Administrative Law, Town and Country Planning, Construction Law, Environmental Law, Real Estate, Labor, EEC/International Law.

FIRM PROFILE: The firm has been established 45 years ago and offers a wide range of services in Civil and Administrative Law. The client base is German but also extends to Europe and the USA. The firm has 15 Lawyers, supported by a staff of 20, practising in 2 offices in Munich and Leipzig. The firm is also a member of ADVOC - International Network of Independent Lawyers, represented all over Europe and the near East.

DR. CHRISTOPH VON HEIMENDAHL, born 1937; admitted, 1968, Germany. *Education:* Universities of Munich and Bonn. *Member:* Munich Bar Association. *LANGUAGES:* German, English and Italian. *PRACTICE AREAS:* Administrative Law; Civil Appeals; Commercial Law; Labor and Employment; Real Estate.

DR. FRIEDRICH-WILHELM GRAF VON RITTBERG, born 1940; admitted, 1972, Germany. *Education:* Universities of Munich, Berlin and Paris. *LANGUAGES:* German, English and French. *PRACTICE AREAS:*

(This Listing Continued)

Corporate Law; Government (Finance); Hospitals; Mergers, Acquisitions and Divestitures; Securities (Shares and Shareholders).

DR. HERWIG BACHELIN, born 1940; admitted, 1970, Germany. *Education:* Universities of Oxford, Bonn and Munich. *Member:* Chamber of Commerce, Munich (Environmental Committee); Fachanwalt für Verwaltungsrecht (Specialist for Administrative Law). *LANGUAGES:* German, English, French and Italian. *PRACTICE AREAS:* Chemicals and Chemistry; Energy; Environmental Law; Oil and Gas; Property.

DR. KARSTEN KÜPPERS, born 1945; admitted, 1975, Germany. *Education:* University of Freiburg. Assistant Professor, University of Freiburg. *LANGUAGES:* German, English and Portuguese. *PRACTICE AREAS:* Business Law; Real Estate; Land Development; Investment.

HARALD BARDENHAGEN, born 1952; admitted, 1982, Germany. *Education:* University of Göttingen; Speyer Academy of Science of Management and Administration. Lecturer on Land Evaluation, Technical University of Munich. *LANGUAGES:* German and English. *PRACTICE AREAS:* Construction Law (Contracts, Development, Engineering); Nuclear; Mining and Minerals; Zoning, Planning and Land Use.

DR. CHRISTOPH SEILER, born 1958; admitted, 1986, Germany. *Education:* University of Erlangen-Nürnberg. *LANGUAGES:* German, English and French. *PRACTICE AREAS:* Administrative Law; Hospitals; Labor and Employment; Property (Expropriation and Restitution); Zoning, Planning and Land Use.

DR. MONIKA F. HARTL, LL.M., born 1956; admitted, 1988, Germany. *Education:* Universities of Würzburg, Lausanne, Göttingen and Berkeley. Assistant Professor, University of Göttingen. *LANGUAGES:* German, English and French. *PRACTICE AREAS:* Business Law (Contracts and Family Business); Corporate Law; Leases and Leasing; Land and Landowners; Resorts and Leisure (Hotels and Restaurants).

DR. NORBERT DASCH, born 1959; admitted, 1988, Germany. *Education:* University of Munich. *LANGUAGES:* German and English. *PRACTICE AREAS:* Antitrust and Trade Regulation (Unfair Competition); Construction Law; Environmental Law; Leases and Leasing (Landlord and Tenant); Natural Resources (Water).

DR. STEFAN DIETLMEIER, born 1963; admitted, 1992, Germany. *Education:* Universities of Regensburg, Cologne and Munich; London School of Economics. *LANGUAGES:* German and English. *PRACTICE AREAS:* Environmental Law (Liability, Pollution); International Law (Cross-Border Transactions); Natural Resources (Oil, Water); Professional Liability; Commercial Law; Public Taxes.

DR. ERNST SCHWARZ, born 1960; admitted, 1994, Germany. *Education:* Bavarian Academy of Administration; University of Munich. *LANGUAGES:* German and English. *PRACTICE AREAS:* Administrative Law; Construction Law; Landlord and Tenant; Family Law.

DR. SUSANNE MÜHLHÜLZL, born 1967; admitted, 1994, Germany. *Education:* University of Munich. [German, English and French]. *PRACTICE AREAS:* Commercial Law; Property; Corporate Law.

SPITZWEG & PARTNER

GUSTAV-HEINEMANN-RING 212
81739 MUNICH, GERMANY
Telephone: (011-49) 89-678006-0
Telefax: (011-49) 89-678006-10

Potsdam, Germany Office: Telephone: (011-49) 24639; (011-49) 161-2321996. Telefax: (011-49) 24639.

European Community Law, International Banking, Company and Trade Law, Tax Law, Environmental Law, Competition Law, Mergers and Acquisitions, Construction Law, International Labor Law, Arbitration Law, Product Liability Law, Civil Litigation, Italian Law.

FIRM PROFILE: The firm, which was originally founded in 1971, is well known for International Company and Tax law. The firm makes part of the "International Lawyer's Network" with firms in Brussels (Belgium), Chicago (USA), Paris (France), Salzburg (Austria), Stockholm (Sweden), Istanbul (Turkey), Copenhagen (Denmark) and Milan (Italy).

HANS - JÜRGEN SPITZWEG, born Munich, Germany, May 23, 1946; admitted, 1975, Germany. *Education:* University of Munich (1971). Lecturer in Labor Law, Bavarian Chamber of Industry and Commerce. Lecturer for Management Education, EUROFORUM, Frankfurt, 1991—. *Member:* Association of German and Italian Lawyers. *LANGUAGES:*

(This Listing Continued)

German, French, Italian. *PRACTICE AREAS:* Management Labour and Employment; Product Liability; International Civil Litigation.

MICHAEL PINKER, born Vohenstrauß, Germany, January 27, 1949; admitted, 1977, Germany. *Education:* University of Munich (1977). Mayor of Haar/Munich, 1981-1990. Local Council of Haar/Munich, 1981—. *Member:* Lions Club. *LANGUAGES:* German, English. *PRACTICE AREAS:* Divorce, Family Mediation; Marital Property; Matrimonial Law; Separation Agreement; Successions.

DR. NORBERT HERIG, DIP. ING., born Dortmund, Germany, May 30, 1951; admitted, 1984, Germany. *Education:* Ruhr Universität Bochum; Technical University of Munich (Dipl.Ing. Construction Engineer, 1976); University of Munich (Dr.Iur., 1985). Author: "Order Placement of the Public Authorities for the Building Industry," 1985, Technical University Munich. Co-Author: "VOB for Praktiker," 1991, 2nd Edition. *Member:* German Association of Construction Law. *LANGUAGES:* German, English, French, Portuguese. *PRACTICE AREAS:* National and International Private and Public Construction Law.

UDO WISSWEDE, born Kassel, Germany, December 9, 1957; admitted, 1989, Germany. *Education:* University of Göttingen (law degree, 1984). Lecturer in Labor Law: University of Göttingen, 1984-1985. *LANGUAGES:* German, English. *PRACTICE AREAS:* National and International Labour Law; Civil Litigation; Product Liability.

DR. HANNSPETER RIEDEL, born Wiesbaden, Germany, February 21, 1959; admitted, 1990, Germany. *Education:* Universities of Mainz and Göttingen (Dr.iur., 1991). Author: "US-(Re)-Exportcontroll and High Technology"; "Innovations in the US-Inheritance Tax-Law." *Member:* Young Lawyer's International Association (AIJA); Family Business Network (FBN). *LANGUAGES:* German, English. *PRACTICE AREAS:* Company Acquisitions and Sales; Company Commercial Law; Company Contracts and Format; Company Trust; Successions.

DR. PETER M. HORST, born Munich, Germany, August 19, 1957; admitted, 1991, Germany. *Education:* Universities of Munich, Germany; Lausanne, Switzerland (Law degree, 1982); Munich Law School (Dr.iur., 1986). Lecturer in Environmental Management, University of Augsburg, 1990—. Author: "Investor's Protection: Liability for Emission and Trade of Investments," Munich/Florence, 1987. Co-Author: Handbook for Environmental Protection: "Marketing with Ecology and Environmental Protection," "Environmental Penalty Law: Protection against Criminal Liability for the Management." Köln, 1990, 1991. Bavarian Ministry for Environmental Protection, Munich, 1986-1990. *Member:* German Federation for Environmental Management (B.A.U.M.); German Society for Environmental Law. *LANGUAGES:* German, English, French, Italian. *PRACTICE AREAS:* Environmental Law; Environmental Management.

DR. ANDREAS HEITMANN, born Bremen, Germany, October 13, 1958; admitted, 1988, Germany. *Education:* University of Göttingen (Dr.iur., 1989). Lecturer in Civil Law, Göttingen, 1984. Author: "Structural Crisis Cartel -a workable Instrument for the Managing of a Crisis," Göttingen, 1989. Co-Author: "Handbook for Environmental Protection: Marketing with Ecology and Environmental Protection," Köln, 1990. Federal Cartel Authority at Berlin, 1985. (Resident at Potsdam Office). *LANGUAGES:* German, English, French. *PRACTICE AREAS:* Industrial Property Law; Investment Law.

HEIKE WIELAND, born Berlin, Germany, July 31, 1962; admitted, 1990, Germany. *Education:* University of Passau, Germany (law degree, 1990). Co-Editor of the law review "Diritto comunitario e degli scambi internazionali,." Co-Author: "European Challenge 1992," Institute for European Law, Florence, Commission of the EEC, 1991. Assistant at the Collegio Europeo di Parma, Italy, 1989-1990. *Member:* Association of German and Italian Lawyers. *LANGUAGES:* German, Italian, English. *PRACTICE AREAS:* International Law; Community Law; European; Corporation International Law.

BIRGIT STAUBER, born Frankfurt/Main, Germany, March 18, 1958; admitted, 1992, Germany. *Education:* Universities of Freiburg and Göttingen (Law Degree, 1987). *LANGUAGES:* German, English, French and Portuguese. *PRACTICE AREAS:* Law of Domestic Relations; Family Law.

OLIVER LÜCKE, born Garmisch-Partenkirchen, Germany, June 11, 1962; admitted, 1993, Germany. *Education:* University of Munich (Law Degree, 1993). Author: "Reduction of working hours - collective policy on the back of the unorganized employees"; "The hierarchy of the medical service between independent profession and instruction.". *LANGUAGES:* German and English. *PRACTICE AREAS:* Management Labour; Employment Computer Law.

PHILIPP SCHWOERER, born Waiblingen, Germany, October 12, 1962; admitted, 1993, Germany. *Education:* University of Freiburg (Law Degree, 1992). (Resident at Potsdam Office). *LANGUAGES:* German, English and French.

STOCK, STROHM, REINELT, RAHN, ADERS, RAMERSHOVEN

Established in 1980

EFFNERSTRASSE 44-46
81925 MUNICH, GERMANY
Telephone: (89) 99 831-0
Telex: 17 89 86 39 ADVOS D
Teletex: 89 86 39
Telefax: (89) 99 831 70

General German and International Practice, Commercial, Corporate, Capital Investment, Tax, Intellectual Property, Copyright, Unfair Competition, Product Liability, Real Estate, Building, Construction, Tenancy, Housing, Family, Labor, Pharmaceutical, Medical, Traffic, Administrative, E.E.C., Japanese Civil and Commercial Law, Litigation and Arbitration.

MEMBERS OF FIRM

DR. PAUL DIETER STOCK, born Cologne, Germany, April 19, 1936; admitted, 1966, Munich. *Education:* Universities of Freiburg and Cologne. *LANGUAGES:* German and English. *PRACTICE AREAS:* Corporate Law; Commercial Law; Capital Investment Law; International Tax Law.

DR. HANS GOTTFRIED STROHM, born Würzburg, Germany, May 12, 1940; admitted, 1969, Munich. *Education:* Universities of Munich and Pisa, Italy. Academic Assistant, Institute for Industrial Property and Copyright Law, University of Munich, and Member, Research Staff, Max Planck Institute for Foreign and International Patent, Copyright and Competition Law. *Member:* East-West Association of Economics. *LANGUAGES:* German, English, French and Italian. *PRACTICE AREAS:* Real Estate Law; Commercial Law; Industrial Property Law; Copyright Law.

DR. EKKEHART REINELT, born Belgrad, Yugoslavia, November 17, 1943; admitted, 1971, Munich. *Education:* Universities of Marburg and Regensburg. Academic Assistant to the Professor for Civil and Comparative Law, University of Regensburg, 1967-1971. Member, Examiner's Board at the Office of Judicial State Examinations. *LANGUAGES:* German and English. *PRACTICE AREAS:* Real Estate Law; Building Law; Construction Law; Product Liability Law; Family Law.

DR. GUNTRAM RAHN, born Wernigerode, Germany, November 13, 1943; admitted, 1975, Munich. *Education:* Universities of Hamburg and Tokyo, Japan. Head, Japan and East Asia Department, Max Planck Institute for Foreign and International Patent, Copyright and Competition Law, Munich, 1975-1990. *Member:* German-Japanese Jurists' Association; Japan Association of Industrial Property Law. *LANGUAGES:* German, Japanese and English. *PRACTICE AREAS:* Japanese Civil Law; Commercial Law; Intellectual Property Law; E.E.C. Law.

DETLEV ADERS, born Wiesbaden, Germany, June 6, 1949; admitted, 1980, Munich. *Education:* Universities of Munich and George Washington University, Washington, D.C., USA. Member, Research Staff, Max Planck Institute for Foreign and International Patent, Copyright and Competition Law, Munich, 1977-1980. *LANGUAGES:* German, English and French. *PRACTICE AREAS:* Commercial Law; Tax Law; Corporate Law; Intellectual Property Law.

KURT RAMERSHOVEN, born Bonn-Beuel, Germany, August 20, 1954; admitted, 1984, Munich. *Education:* University of Bonn, Administrative Studies in Speyer. *LANGUAGES:* German and English. *PRACTICE AREAS:* Public Building Law; Construction Law; Liability Law; Traffic Law.

JÖRG-MICHAEL OSSENFORTH, born Neubeckum, Germany, April 28, 1953; admitted, 1985, Munich. *Education:* Universities of Tübingen and Munich. *LANGUAGES:* German and English. *PRACTICE AREAS:* Tenancy Law; Housing Law; Labor Law.

KATHARINA HAPP, born Munich, Germany, November 27, 1960; admitted, 1990, Munich. *Education:* University of Munich. *LANGUAGES:* German, Italian, English and Modern Greek. *PRACTICE AREAS:* Administrative Law; Labor Law; Liability Law; Traffic Law.

ANDREA GERTH, born Munich, Germany, November 12, 1961; admitted, 1990, Munich. *Education:* University of Munich. Assistant to the

(This Listing Continued)

(This Listing Continued)

STOCK, STROHM, REINELT, RAHN, ADERS, RAMERSHOVEN, Munich—Continued

Professor for Administrative Law, University of Munich, 1987-1990. *LAN-GUAGES:* German and English. *PRACTICE AREAS:* Labor Law; Tenancy Law; Housing Law; Traffic Law.

NIKOLAUS KIEFER, born Saarbrücken, Germany, November 22, 1961; admitted, 1990, Munich. *Education:* Universities of Munich and Berlin. *LANGUAGES:* German, English and French. *PRACTICE AREAS:* Building Law; Real Estate Law; Tenancy Law; Traffic Law.

JOCHEN TIEMANN, born Marl, Germany, November 23, 1961; admitted, 1993, Munich. *Education:* Universities of Gießen, Frankfurt, Hamburg and Cologne. *LANGUAGES:* German and English. *PRACTICE AREAS:* Real Estate Law; Competition Law; Insurance Law.

STRASSE, VONNEMANN & PARTNER

Patentanwälte

European Patent Attorneys

Established in 1894

BALANSTR. 55

D-81541 MUNICH, GERMANY

Telephone: +49-89-450 09 18 (0)

Fax: +49-89-450 09 18 12

Voice: +49-89-450 09 18 20

Telex: 522 054 pat d

Hamburg, Germany Office: An der Alster 84, D-20 099. Telephone: +49-40-2808 13 (0). Fax: +49-40-28 08 13 31.

Patent, Trademark, Utility and Design Model, Licensing, Litigation.

FIRM PROFILE: *The roots of Strasse, Vonnemann & Partner reach back about one hundred years, to the founding of our Hamburg Office in 1894. Our Munich Office also bases on decades of professional practice and is located in the Building of the Federal Patent Court. Our law firm, however, took its present form by the association of our two basic offices in Hamburg and München.*

This alliance of tradition and progress is reflected in the partnership, combining professionals with more than 30 years of experience with a multiplicity of younger attorneys and trainees.

PARTNERS

JOACHIM STRASSE, born Guben, Germany, May 22, 1931; admitted, 1962, Germany. *Education:* Technical University, Darmstadt and Berlin (Diploma, 1957). Licensed for professional representation, European Patent Office, 1978. Senior, Munich Office. Lecturer, German Patent Attorneys Trainees, 1986-1989. *Member:* Patent Bar; epi; FICPI; GRUR; AIPPI and VDI.

DR. GERHARD VONNEMANN, born Dortmund, Germany, October 3, 1947; admitted, 1987, Germany. *Education:* University Karlsruhe, Technical University Hannover (Dipl.-Ing, 1970); University of Dortmund (Dr.-Ing, 1977); Industrial Experiences (1970-1986). Licensed before EPO, 1989. Senior, Hamburg Office, founded in 1894. *Member:* Patent Bar; EPI; FICPI; GRUR; AIPPI; VDI.

DR. PETER BITTNER, born Munich, Germany, June 22, 1934; admitted, 1959, Germany. *Education:* Munich University (Doctorate, 1959). With Bölkow Entwicklungen KG/Munich, 1962. Head of Assets and Insurance Department, Messerschmitt-Bölkow GmbH. Head of Business Department, Space Engineer Division, 1976. Managing Director, ERNO Raumfahrttechnik GmbH, Bremen, 1981. Head of Traffic Technology Department, Messerschmitt-Bölkow-Blohm, 1984-1988. Managing Director, Messerschmitt-Bölkow Blohm Wirtschaftsdienst GmbH and debis Assekuranz (the Insurance Division of Mercedes-Benz Group), 1988-1993. *Member:* German Lawyers' Professional Organisation; Rotarian.

DR. ALFONS HOFSTETTER, born Landshut, Germany, April 21, 1963; admitted, 1994, German Patent Office. *Education:* Ludwig-Maximilians-University of Munich (Diploma in Geology, 1988; Dr.rer.nat., Geochemistry, 1993). Partner, Munich Office. *Member:* Patent Bar; FICPI.

(This Listing Continued)

DR. ANJA EDELMANN, born Oldenburg, Germany, May 19, 1964; admitted, 1995, Germany; registered to practice before the German Patent Office. *Education:* University of Göttingen (Diploma in Chemistry, 1989; Dr.rer.nat. 1991). *Member:* Patent Bar; Gesellschaft Deutscher Chemiker.

Languages: German, English, French and Spanish.

TREMML, SCHOLZ, BIHLER & PARTNERS

Established in 1975

MARTIUSSTRASSE 5/II

80802 MUNICH, GERMANY

Telephone: 089/349070

Telex: 5213222

Facsimile: 089/337293

Frankfurt/Main, Germany Office: Abrell Wendler Nacke & Partner. Holzhausenstr. 22, D-60322. Telephone: 49-(0) 69-5 96 40 11. Telefax: 49-(0) 69-55 53 99.

Dusseldorf, Germany Office: Abrell Wendler Nacke & Partner. Graf-Recke-Straße 82, D-40239. Telephone: 0211/96 15 04. Telefax: 0211/96 15 674.

Dresden, Germany Office: Bautznerstr. 22, 01099. Telephone: 0351/55515. Facsimile: 0351/51639.

General Corporate Practice, International Law, Mergers and Acquisitions, Banking, Computer, Industrial Property and Administrative Law, Trademarks, Copyright and Unfair Competition, Computer and Software.

MEMBERS OF FIRM

DR. BERND TREMML, born Bad Wiessee, Germany, November 2, 1944; admitted, 1974, Germany. *Education:* University of Munich (Dr.jur., 1975); University of Texas, Law School (M.C.J., 1977). Author: "Acquisition of German Corporations," 2. Ed 1992; "Legal Protection of Computer Software in West-Germany," Tokyo, 1987; "Pitfalls in Computer Law," 2. Ed 1990; "Professional Service Contracts," 3. Ed., 1992. Co-Author: "International Mergers and Acquisitions," Tokyo 2. Ed 1990. Briefing Clerk, Court of Appeals, Munich, 1970-1974. *LANGUAGES:* German, English and French.

DR. DR. GEORG SCHOLZ, born Allenstein, Germany, February 13, 1929; admitted, 1959, Germany. *Education:* University of Würzburg, Law School (Ph.D. in Economics, 1957; Dr.jur., 1961). Author, books published by Vahlen-Verlag Munich: *Administrative Law,* Volume I, 6. Edition, 1987; *Administrative Law,* Volume II, 5. Ed., 1985; *Procedural Rules of Administrative Courts,* 5. Ed., 1987; *City and Community Law,* 5. Ed., 1985; *Public Security Laws,* 5. Ed., 1987; *Federal Anti-Pollution Laws,* 4. Ed., 1986; *Federal Urban Development Law,* 5. Ed., 1987; *Compensation under eminent domain,* 4. Ed., 1986; *Constitutional Law,* Volume 1, 5. Ed., 1985; *Constitutional Law,* Volume 2, 5. Ed., 1987; "City and Community Law," 6. Ed. 1992; "Public Security Laws," 6. Ed., 1992; "Federal Urban Development Law," 6. Ed., 1991. *LANGUAGES:* German and English.

DR. MICHAEL BIHLER, born Wangen, Germany, August 15, 1950; admitted, 1979, Germany. *Education:* University of Munich, Law School (Dr.jur., 1979). Author: "Psychology in Legal Decisions," 1979; "Radio-broadcasting Law in Bavaria," 1985; "Atomic Energy - Summary and Case Law," 1986. Briefing Clerk, Court of Appeals, Munich, 1976-1979. Lecturer on International Law, University of Munich, 1974-1979. *LANGUAGES:* German, English, French and Italian.

DR. LUDWIG SÖLDNER, born Munich, Germany, March 27, 1926; admitted, 1955, Germany. *Education:* University of Munich (Dr.jur., 1956). Legal Consultant to Austrian and Belgian General Consulates. *LANGUAGES:* German, French and English.

WOLF SCHENK, born Danzig, May 4, 1944; admitted, 1974, Germany. *Education:* University of Hamburg (1963-1965); University of Lausanne (1965); University of Munich (1966-1968); King's College, London (1973-1974). Author: "Competitive Advertising," 1986; "The Foreign Execution of German Judgements," 1986; "Business Libel," 1987. *LANGUAGES:* German, English and French.

DR. ULRICH WIEDEMANN, born Dortmund, Germany, April 5, 1958; admitted, 1990, Germany. *Education:* Universities of Heidelberg. Author: "The Yugoslavian Joint Venture Law," 1989; "The Yugoslavian Subsistence Law," 1990; "The Croatian Privatization Code of 1991," 1992; "The Legal Framework for Investment in Poland," 1993. Briefing Clerk, Court of Appeals, Berlin, 1983-1986. Lecturer, Eastern European Law,

(This Listing Continued)

Institut für Ostrecht, Munich, 1986-1990. *LANGUAGES:* German, English, French, Serbo-Croation, Russian and Polish.

MICHAEL R. KARGER, born Munich, Germany, September 17, 1961; admitted, 1992, Germany. *Education:* University of Munich (1983-1989); University of California, Berkeley (1993). Briefing Clerk, Court of Appeals, Munich, 1989-1992. Co-Author: "Professional Service Contracts", 3.Ed. 1992. *Member:* German-American Lawyers Association (DAJV). *LANGUAGES:* German, English, French and Italian.

DR. MATTHIAS ABRELL, born Germany, 1948; admitted, 1987, Germany. *Education:* University of Mannheim (M.B.A., 1973; Dr. jur., 1978). Special Tax Counsel. Lecturer, Business Administration Law, University of Mannheim, 1975-1977. *Member:* German Bar Association. (Also at Abrell Wendler Nacke & Partner, Frankfurt/Main, Germany). *LANGUAGES:* German, English and French. *PRACTICE AREAS:* Corporate; Mergers and Acquisitions; Taxation.

Languages: German, English, French, Spanish and Italian

VIERING & JENTSCHURA

Patentanwälte

European Patent Attorneys

Attorneys at Law

STEINSDORFSTRASSE 6
80538 MUNICH, GERMANY
Telephone: 089/29 34 13
Fax: 089/2 28 39 20
Telex: 17 898 454 +

Mailing Address: P.O. Box 221443, Munich, Germany 80504

Branch Office: Essener Str. 5, 46047 Oberhausen, Germany. Telephone: 0208/202627. Fax: 0208/202727.

Industrial Property Rights, Patents, Utility Models, Designs, Trademarks, Copyrights, Unfair Competition, Search and Watch, Contracts and Licence Agreements, Litigations and Infringement Cases.

FIRM PROFILE: *The office disposes of a network of good relations to selected colleagues from all over the world. Such good relations are not only maintained to Western countries (USA, Western Europe), but also to Eastern European countries and to Asia.*

HANS-MARTIN VIERING, born February 18, 1938; registered to practice before the German Patent Office, 1976 and before the European Patent Office, 1978. *Education:* Technical University of Munich (Diploma in Mechanical Engineering, 1969). *Member:* German Association for the Protection of Industrial Property and Copyright Law (GRUR); Industrial Association for the Protection of Industrial Property (AIPPI); International Federation of Industrial Property Attorneys (FICPI); German Patent Attorney Bar Association; European Patent Institute (EPI). *LANGUAGES:* German, English and French. *PRACTICE AREAS:* European, German and Foreign Patents; Unfair Competition; Infringement Cases; Licence Agreements.

ROLF JENTSCHURA, born July 26, 1939; registered to practice before the German Patent Office, 1976, and before the European Patent Office, 1978. *Education:* Technical University of Munich and Stuttgart (Diploma in Mechanical Engineering, 1970). *Member:* German Association for the Protection of Industrial Property and Copyright Law (GRUR); Industrial Association for the Protection of Industrial Property (AIPPI); Pharmaceutical Trademark Group (PTMG); International Federation of Industrial Property Attorneys (FICPI); International Trademark Association (INTA); European Community Trademark Association (ECTA); German Patent Attorney Bar Association; European Patent Institute (EPI). *LANGUAGES:* German and English. *PRACTICE AREAS:* European, German and Foreign Patents; Unfair Competition; Trademarks; Copyrights; Contracts; Licence Agreements; Litigation.

ALEXANDER SCHLEE, born January 23, 1961; registered to practice before the German Patent Office, 1990 and before the European Patent Office, 1993. *Education:* Technical University of Darmstadt (Diploma in Mechanical Engineering, 1987). *Member:* German Patent Attorney Bar Association; European Patent Institute (EPI); The Licensing Executives Society (LES); Intellectual Property Law Association (AIPLA); International Federation of Industrial Property Attorneys (FICPI); Verband Deutscher Patentingenieure und Patentassessoren (VPP); American Chamber of Commerce in Germany (AmCham). *LANGUAGES:* German, English and French. *PRACTICE AREAS:* Industrial Property Rights; European, Ger-

(This Listing Continued)

man and Foreign Patents; Utility Models, Trademarks and Industrial Designs.

MATTHIAS NOBBE, born June 9, 1956; registered to practice before the German Patent Office, 1991, and before the European Patent Office, 1992. *Education:* Ruhr University, Bochum (Diploma in Organic Chemistry, 1982; Ph.D., 1986). *Member:* International Federation of Industrial Property Attorneys (FICPI); German Patent Attorney Bar Association; European Patent Institute (EPI). (Resident Partner, Oberhausen Office). *LANGUAGES:* German and English. *PRACTICE AREAS:* Organic and Biochemistry; Biotechnology and Pharmaceutical Sciences; Industrial Property Rights; European and German Patents and Trademarks; Utility Models and Industrial Designs.

ADAM BOGSCH, born Budapest, Hungary, August 30, 1964; registered to practice before the Hungarian Patent Office, 1992 and before the German Patent Office, 1993. *Education:* Technical University of Budapest (Diploma in Electrical-Technical Engineering, 1987). *Member:* German Patent Attorney Bar Association; International Federation of Industrial Property Attorneys (FICPI). *LANGUAGES:* German, English and Hungarian. *PRACTICE AREAS:* Industrial Property Rights; European, German and Foreign Patents; Utility Models, Trademarks and Industrial Designs.

WOLFGANG FESTL-WIETEK, born May 2, 1959; admitted, 1993, Germany. *Education:* bank clerk, University of Hagen (Intermediate Diploma Business and Administration), Ludwig Maximilians University (Attorney at Law, 1989), LL.D., 1989. *Member:* German Bar Association; International Bar Association; International Trademark Association (INTA), European Community Trademark Association (ECTA). *LANGUAGES:* German, English and Italian. *PRACTICE AREAS:* Company and Tax Law; Competition Law; Contract Law; Infringement Cases; Trademarks; Copyrights; Unfair Competition.

VON **BOETTICHER HASSE KALTWASSER**

WIDENMAYERSTRASSE 4
80538 MUNICH, GERMANY
Telephone: 089-22 33 11
Cable Address: "Interjus"
Telex: 05-239 37 JUS D
Telecopier: 089-22 47 28

Leipzig, Germany Office: Philipp-Rosenthal-Strasse 21, 04103 Leipzig. Telephone: 0341-31 03 03. Telecopier: 0341-31 03 25.

Brussels, Belgium Office: Boulevard de la Révision 50 B-1070. Telephone: 02-5219531. Telecopier: 02-5218711.

Commercial, Corporations, Mergers and Acquisitions, Taxation, Antitrust, EEC, Corporate Finance, Banking and Securities, Unfair Competition, Pharma, Trademarks, Patents, Copyright, Computer, Press and Publishing, Labor, Real Estate, Environment, Aviation, Litigation and Arbitration, General Practice.

FIRM PROFILE: *The firm was established in 1972 and has been internationally oriented from its beginnings. Seven of its lawyers hold law degrees from United States law schools. The firm offers to its clients full-service in all areas of business law and special advice in the computer, electronics, pharmaceuticals, construction, banking, insurance, publishing and asset management sectors. Clients of the firm are based primarily in the European Community, the United States, Canada, Switzerland, Austria, Scandinavia, Japan and Southeast Asia.*

MEMBERS OF FIRM

DIETRICH VON BOETTICHER, born Posen, Poland, March 6, 1942; admitted, 1972, Germany; 1974, Michigan, U.S.A.; 1980, Washington D.C., U.S.A. *Education:* Universities of Göttingen, Freiburg, Geneva/-Switzerland and Munich (Referendar, 1967; Assessor, 1972); Wayne State University Law School, Detroit, Michigan (LL.M., 1969). Author: "A New Approach to Taxation of Investments in Less Developed Countries," The American Journal of Law, 1969. *Member:* Munich and American Bar Associations; State Bar of Michigan; The District of Columbia Bar. *LANGUAGES:* German, English, French and Spanish.

DR. JOACHIM KÖRNIG, born Lüdinghausen, Germany, March 16, 1947; admitted, 1974, Germany. *Education:* Universities of Münster and Munich (Referendar, 1970; Doctor juris, 1972; Assessor, 1974). Author: "Schriftformklauseln und mündliche Abreden," Munich, 1972. *Member:* Munich Bar Association. *LANGUAGES:* German, English and French.

(This Listing Continued)

VON BOETTICHER HASSE KALTWASSER, Munich—Continued

DR. WOLFGANG FELTEN, born Dortmund, Germany, February 14, 1947; admitted, 1974, Germany. *Education:* Universities of Münster and Munich (Referendar, 1970; Doctor juris, 1972; Assessor, 1974). Author: "Die fingierte Bodenverkehrsgenehmigung," Munich, 1972. *Member:* Munich Bar Association. *LANGUAGES:* German, English and French.

DR. FRANK N. WINKEL, born Burgellern, Germany, April 3, 1945; admitted, 1976, Germany. *Education:* Universities of Munich, Freiburg and Saarbrücken (Referendar, 1971; Assessor, 1974; Doctor juris, 1976); University of California at Berkeley (LL.M., 1973). Author: "Formalschutz dreidimensionaler Marken," Cologne, 1976; "Das Verhältnis von Markenschutz zu Musterschutz und Urheberschutz in den U.S.A.," GRUR Int., 1978. Research Fellow, Max-Planck-Institute for Foreign and International Patent, Copyright and Competition Law, 1971-1976. *Member:* Munich Bar Association. *LANGUAGES:* German, English and French.

DR. BODO HASSE, born Berlin, Germany, March 6, 1943; admitted, 1975, Germany. *Education:* University of Hamburg (Referendar, 1967; Assessor, 1973; Doctor juris, 1980); Indiana University at Bloomington (LL.M., 1974). Author: "Interessenkonflikte bei der Lebensversicherung zugunsten Dritter," Karlsruhe, 1981; "Silent Partnership," Business Transactions in Germany, Chapter 22, New York, 1995. *Member:* Munich Bar Association; German Jurists Association (Deutscher Juristentag e.V.); German American Lawyers Association. *LANGUAGES:* German, English and French.

DR. FRANK KALTWASSER, born Bad Reichenhall, Germany, April 18, 1948; admitted, 1978, Germany. *Education:* University of Munich (Referendar, 1975; Assessor, 1978; Doctor juris, 1980). Author: "Selektiver Vertrieb durch einseitige Auswahl ohne vertragliche Bindung und seine Kontrolle durch das Diskriminierungsverbot des GWB," Munich, 1980. *Member:* Munich Bar Association. *LANGUAGES:* German, French and English.

DR. ULRICH LOHMANN, born Düsseldorf, Germany, January 28, 1954; admitted, 1982, Germany. *Education:* Universities of Cologne, Lausanne/Switzerland and Freiburg (Referendar, 1977; Assessor, 1981; Doctor juris, 1984); University of California at Berkeley (LL.M., 1982). Author: "Einwendungen gegen den Zahlungsanspruch aus einer Bankgarantie," Cologne, 1984; "Banks' Liabilities as Insiders under German Law," International Financial Law Rev., 1984; "Public Procurement," Business Transactions in Germany, Chapter 41, New York, 1994; "Distribution Agreements European Style," The Los Angeles Lawyer, September, 1994. Co-Editor and Co-Author: "Commercial Agency and DIstribution Agreements-Law and Practice in Member States of the EC and the EFTA," 2nd Edition, London, 1993. Co-Author: "The European Economic Interest Grouping," Deventer, 1993; "How to Commit Qualified Dealers: The Concept of Selective Distribution in the EEC," International Law Practicum, New York, Autumn, 1992. Assistant to Professor Dr. Klemens Pleyer, Institute for Banking Law, University of Cologne, 1983. *Member:* Munich Bar Association; German American Lawyers Association; Association Internationale des Jeunes Avocats. *LANGUAGES:* German, English, French, Spanish and Dutch.

DR. ANGELIKA HOCHE, born Rosenheim, Germany, July 23, 1957; admitted, 1985, Germany. *Education:* University of Munich (Referendarin, 1981; Assessorin, 1984; Doctor juris, 1987); University of Texas at Austin (M.C.J., 1987). Author: "Verhältnis der Zivilhaftungskonventionen für Atom- und Ölverschmutzungsschäden zur völkerrechtlichen Haftung," Munich, 1988; "Haftung des Bundes für Verbindlichkeiten von DDR-Banken," EWS, 1992; "The Legal System," Business Transactions in Germany, Chapter 4, New York, 1993. Research Assistant to Professor Dr. Bruno Simma, Institute for International Law and European Community Law, University of Munich, 1983-1984. *Member:* Munich Bar Association; German American Lawyers Association; Association Internationale des Jeunes Avocats. *LANGUAGES:* German, English and French.

DR. DETLEV VON BREITENSTEIN, born Saarbrücken, Germany, October 21, 1937; admitted, 1974, Germany and France. *Education:* Universities of Tübingen, Bonn and Berlin (Referendar, 1961; Doctor juris, 1966; Assessor, 1967); University of Paris (D.E.S., 1963; C.P.A., 1974). Author: "Zum Grundsatz der Gleichbehandlung in der Stromversorgung," Bonn, 1968. Lecturer, Centre de Droit du Commerce International, Université de Tours, France, 1974—. *Member:* Munich Bar Association; Paris Bar. *LANGUAGES:* German, English and French.

(This Listing Continued)

ASSOCIATES

BERND SCHELLKOPF, born Neuhaus, Germany, January 16, 1948; admitted, 1988, Germany. *Education:* Universities of Regensburg and Munich (Referendar, 1975; Assessor, 1977). *Member:* Munich Bar Association. *LANGUAGES:* German, English, French, Italian and Spanish.

RAINER CORNET, born Geneva, Switzerland, May 28, 1961; admitted, 1990, Germany. *Education:* University of Munich (Referendar, 1987; Assessor, 1990). *Member:* Munich Bar Association. *LANGUAGES:* German, French, English, Italian, Spanish and Dutch.

DR. JOACHIM GÜNTZER, born Bad Kreuznach, Germany, January 14, 1961; admitted, 1991, Germany. *Education:* Universities of Regensburg, Lausanne/Switzerland, Munich and Trier (Referendar, 1986; Assessor, 1989; Doctor juris, 1991); Madrid (Licenciado en Derecho, 1989). Author: "Die Reform des spanischen Gesellschaftsrechts," RIW, 1989; "Die Rechtsstellung des Geschäftsführers im spanischen Aktienrecht," Frankfurt, 1991. *Member:* Munich Bar Association; German Spanish Lawyers Association. *LANGUAGES:* German, English, French and Spanish.

PETER SCHMIDT-FICHTNER, born Wuppertal, Germany, August 25, 1957; admitted, 1986, Germany. *Education:* University of Munich (Referendar, 1983; Assessor, 1986); New York University (M.C.J., 1989). *Member:* Leipzig Bar Association; German American Lawyers Association. *LANGUAGES:* German, English and French.

DR. STEPHAN RETTENBECK, born Garmisch-Partenkirchen, Germany, January 7, 1964; admitted, 1992, Germany. *Education:* University of Munich (Referendar, 1988; Assessor, 1992; Doctor juris, 1993). Author: "Die Rückrufpflicht in der Produkthaftung," Munich, 1993. *Member:* Munich Bar Association. *LANGUAGES:* German and English.

DR. CLAUDIA BÖHM, born Recklinghausen, Germany, October 4, 1963; admitted, 1993, Germany. *Education:* University of Münster (Referendarin, 1988; Doctor juris, 1992; Assessorin, 1993). Author: "Umtausch beim Kauf," Baden-Baden, 1992. Assistant to Professor Dr. Berthold Kupisch, Institute for Roman Law, University of Münster, 1988-1990. *Member:* Munich Bar Association. *LANGUAGES:* German, English and French.

DR. LUTZ WITTKOWSKI, born Buxtehude, March 29, 1961; admitted, 1993, Germany. *Education:* University of Hamburg (Referendar, 1987; Doctor juris, 1990; Assessor, 1992); University of Virginia at Charlottesville (LL.M., 1993). Author: "Die Lehre vom Verkehrsgeschäft," Berlin, 1990; "Haftung und Haftungsvermeidung beim Management Buy-Out einer GmbH,"GmbHR, 1990. Assistant to Professor Dr. Karsten Schmidt, Institute for Commercial, Marine and Business Law, University of Hamburg, 1988-1991. *Member:* Munich Bar Association. *LANGUAGES:* German, English and French.

CHRISTIAN KÜHN, born Eisleben, Germany, August 29, 1964; admitted, 1993, Germany. *Education:* University of Berlin (Diplom-Jurist, 1990; Assessor, 1993). *Member:* Leipzig Bar Association. *LANGUAGES:* German, French and Russian.

INES HEROLD, born Zwickau, Germany, March 21, 1967; admitted, 1994, Germany. *Education:* University of Bev Ciu (Diplom-Juristin, 1991; Assessorin, 1994). *Member:* Leipzig Bar Association. *LANGUAGES:* German, Russian and English.

CLAUDIA STAHL, born Munich, Germany, November 19, 1964; admitted, 1994, Germany. *Education:* University of Munich (Referender, 1989; Assessor, 1993). Assistant to Professor Dr. Hans Zacher, Max Plauck Institute for Foreign and International Social Law, 1989-1991. *Member:* Munich Bar Association. *LANGUAGES:* German, English, French and Spanish.

Languages: German, English, French, Italian, Spanish, Dutch and Russian.

VON PANDER WILLFORT & PARTNER

ARNULFSTRASSE 25
D-80335 MUNICH, GERMANY
Telephone: (089) 55 14 84 50
Telefax: (089) 55 14 84 80

Leipzig, Germany Office: Mozart Strasse 1, D-04107. Telephone: (0341) 21 376-0. Telefax: (0341) 21 376-10.
Dresden, Germany Office: Berggarten 11, D-01277. Telephone: (0351) 33 607-12. Telefax: (0351) 33 607-14.

(This Listing Continued)

New York, New York Office: Two Park Avenue, 10016. Telephone: (212) 685-55 09. Telefax: (212) 685-88 62.

The present structure of the firm is the result of a merger in April 1993 between the two partners who work together with seven other associate lawyers in offices located in Munich, Leipzig, Dresden and New York. The firm offers highly specialized legal services tailored to the needs of the individual commercial clients of an international clientele in the following areas: General European and International Practice, European Community Law, Corporate, Commercial, Intellectual and Industrial Property Rights, Copyright, Unfair Competition, Antitrust, Computer Law, Press Law, Entertainment Law, Franchising, Licensing, Insurance, Product Liability, Real Estate and Construction Law, Labor Law, Bank Law, Trusts and Estates, International Private Law, Administrative Law, Litigation, Arbitration, Transport Law. The offices in Leipzig and Dresden allow cooperative legal services in matters of restitution and investments in the new federal states of Germany.

MEMBERS OF FIRM

DR. JOACHIM VON PANDER, born Hameln, Germany, May 8, 1946; admitted, 1982, Wiesbaden; 1985, Munich. *Education:* Universities of Munich, Frankfurt and Göttingen (1968-1973); University of Geneva (1970); Faculté de l'Enseignement de Droit Comparé, University of Strasbourg (Referendar, 1973; Assessor, 1979; Dr.jur., 1976). Research Assistant: Institute of Public International Law, International Commercial Law, European Law, and Nuclear Law, University of Göttingen, 1973-1975. Legal Advisor, Commission of the European Communities, Luxemburg and Brussels, 1975-1979, 1981-1987. Counsel: Preussen-Elektra, 1979-1981; Degussa Group, Frankfurt, 1981-1982. Author: "International Safeguards in the Member States of the European Communities in the Application of the Verification Agreement," Cologne, 1978; "Possibilities of Technical Surveillance Procedures for Reprocessing Plants," E.T., 1980; "Member States Obligation According to Article 33 of the EC-Treaty," EEC Publication, 1982; "International Turnkey Projects, International Construction Law," IBA Publications, 1986; "Liability of Engineers and Architects According to German Law," IBA Publications, 1987; "Strategies for Making the Most of Europe's New Economy," Kluwer Publications, 1988; "New EEC Code and Liability Directive and its impact on German Liability Law," June 1989. Member: Bavarian Management Academy, Faculty Member, Munich, 1988—; University of the Pacific, McGeorge School of Law, International Law Programs, Faculty Member, Salzburg, 1988—. *Member:* German Bar Association; German Lawyers Association (DAV); German American Lawyers Association (DAJV); German British Jurists Association; Association of Independent Entrepreneurs (ASU); Licensing Executive Society (LES); German Bank Law Association, Frankfurt; International Bar Association (IBA) (Member, Section of Business Law). *LANGUAGES:* German, English and French. *PRACTICE AREAS:* Construction Law; Business Law; Banks and Banking Law; Arbitration; European Community Law.

PHILIPP WILLFORT, born Vienna, Austria, May 29, 1953; admitted, 1982, Munich. *Education:* University of Munich (Referendar, 1979; Assessor, 1982). Research Assistant, Max-Planck Institute for Foreign and International Labor and Social Security Law, 1980. *Member:* German Bar Association; German Lawyers Association (DAV); German Society for Transport Law; Institut de Droit International de Transport (IDIT); German Law Practices Network (ADVONET); European Lawyers for Land, Sea and Air (ELLSA); Association Internationale des Jeunes Advocates (AIJA). *LANGUAGES:* German, Spanish, English and French. *PRACTICE AREAS:* Business Law; Transportation Law; Insurance Law; Distribution; Unfair Competition Law.

ASSOCIATES

DR. DIRK VON DETTEN, born Höxter, Germany, December 17, 1957; admitted, 1991, Munich. *Education:* Universities of Berlin and Munich (Referendar, 1987; Assessor, 1991; Dr. jur., 1992). Daimler-Benz Foundation Fellowship, Stuttgart, 1979-1981. Research Assistant: Württemberg Academy of Business Administration, Stuttgart, 1981; Institute for Commercial, Business and Labor Law, University of Munich, 1988-1991. Legal Advisor, Commission of the European Communities, 1992-1993. Author: "Protection of the Family under German Labor Law," Munich, 1992. *Member:* German Bar Association. *LANGUAGES:* German and English. *PRACTICE AREAS:* Corporate Law; Labor Law; Business Law; Securities; European Community Law.

KLAUS-PETER KUGLER, born Reutlingen, Germany, 1958; admitted, 1988, Munich. *Education:* Universities of Karlsruhe and Munich (Referendar, 1985; Assessor, 1988). *LANGUAGES:* German and English.

(This Listing Continued)

PRACTICE AREAS: Business Law; Labor Law; Employment Law; Leases and Leasing Law; Litigation; Criminal Law.

SIEGFRIED MARTEN, born Toronto, Canada, September 15, 1961; admitted, 1993, Munich. *Education:* Universities of Passau, Bonn and Munich (Referendar, 1988; Assessor, 1992). *Member:* German Bar Association. *LANGUAGES:* German, English, French and Russian. *PRACTICE AREAS:* Taxation Law; Commercial Law; Corporate Law.

ULRIKE MAYER, born Ingolstadt, Germany, February 27, 1964; admitted, 1993, Munich. *Education:* University of Munich (Referendar, 1990; Assessor, 1993). Research Assistant: Legal Department Pro 7, 1992; Institute of Criminal Law and Criminal Procedural Law, 1992; Legal Department, Union Bank of Bavaria, New York, 1993. Author: "Report on Channel Allocation for Cable TV in Nordrhein-Westphaien," 1992. *Member:* German Bar Association. *LANGUAGES:* German, English and French. *PRACTICE AREAS:* Administrative Law; Business Law; Construction Law; Communications Law; Media Law.

VOSSIUS & PARTNER

(Patent Attorneys, European Patent Attorneys, Attorney-at-Law)

Established in 1961

SIEBERTSTRASSE 4
81675 MUNICH, GERMANY
Telephone: Int. + 49-89-474075
Natl. 089-474075
Telefax: Int. + 49-89-4706053
Natl. 089-4706053 Telex: 529 453 vopat d

Industrial and Intellectual Property Law, Patent, Trademark, Design, Licensing and Unfair Competition.

FIRM PROFILE: *The firm was established in 1961. It is a combined Patent Attorney/Attorney-at-Law partnership. It specializes in legal services in industrial and intellectual property matters including patent and trademark prosecution before the German and the European Patent Office, litigation in the above matters before all German courts. The clientele is predominantly international. The office staff of approximately 90 persons in total includes eleven partners, seven persons with technical or legal background, one U.S. Patent Attorney and a number of translators (English/German).*

PARTNERS

DR. PAUL TAUCHNER, born Lodz, Poland, November 14, 1945; registered to practice before the German Patent and Trademark Office, 1977; European Patent Office, 1978. *Education:* University of Munich (Ph.D., Chemistry, 1974). Attended: Industrial Property Study Program, German Patent Office, Federal Patent Court and the Regional Court, Munich, 1977. *Member:* German Patent Attorney Bar Association; Institute of Professional Representatives before the European Patent Office (EPI); FICPI; AIPPI; German Bar Association for the Protection of Industrial Property and Copyright Law (GRUR); LES; International Bar Association (IBA); International Trademark Association (INTA); MARQUES (Special Membership); Pharmaceutical Trademarks Group (PTMG- Associated Member); European Community Trademark Association (ECTA); German-Japanese Lawyer's Association. *LANGUAGES:* German, English and French. *PRACTICE AREAS:* Organic, Inorganic and Technical Chemistry; Pharmaceutical Chemistry; Patent; Design Patent and Trademark Prosecution; Advisory work; Litigation.

DR. DIETER HEUNEMANN, born Kiel, Germany, September 17, 1942; Registered to practice before the German Patent and Trademark Office, 1977; European Patent Office, 1978. *Education:* Technical University of Munich, Germany (Ph.D., Physics, 1972); University of California, Berkeley, California, Nuclear Chemistry Division (LBL., 1972-1973). Attendend: Industrial Property Study Program, German Patent Office, Federal Patent Court and the Regional Court, Munich, 1976-1977. *Member:* German Patent Attorney Bar Association; Institute of Professional Representatives before the European Patent Office (EPI); FICPI; AIPPI; German Association for the Protection of Industrial Property and Copyright Law (GRUR); European Community Trademark Association (ECTA). *LANGUAGES:* German and English. *PRACTICE AREAS:* Physics; Nuclear Technology; Electrical Engineering and Electronics; Computer Technology and Software; Mechanics; German and International Intellectual Property Law; Prosecution and Litigation; Patents, Design Patents and Trademark.

(This Listing Continued)

VOSSIUS & PARTNER, Munich—Continued

DR. PETER A. RAUH, born Hubreith, Germany, May 22, 1943; Registered to practice before the German Patent and Trademark Office, 1979; European Patent Office, 1979. *Education:* Universities of Munich and Paris (Ph.D., Chemistry, 1974). Attended: Industrial Property Study Progam, German Patent Office, Federal Patent Court and the Regional Court, Munich, 1978. *Member:* German Patent Attorney Bar Association; Institute of Professional Representatives before the European Patent Office (EPI); FICPI; AIPPI; German Association for the Protection of Industrial Property and Copyright Law (GRUR). *LANGUAGES:* German, English and Spanish. *PRACTICE AREAS:* Patent Law.

DR. GERHARD HERMANN, born Stuttgart, Germany, June 18, 1949; Registered to practice before the German Patent and Trademark Office, 1983; European Patent Office, 1985. *Education:* University of Stuttgart, Germany; Max-Planck Institute for Metals Research, Institute for Material Science, Stuttgart, Germany (Ph.D., Physics, 1980). Postdoctoral Fellowship, Max-Planck Society. Attended: Industrial Property Study Program, German Patent Office, Federal Patent Court and the Regional Court, Munich, 1982-1983. *Member:* German Patent Attorney Bar Association; Institute of Professional Representatives before the European Patent Office (EPI); FICPI; AIPPI; European Community Trademark Association (ECTA); International Trademark Association (INTA); MARQUES (Special Membership); German-Japanese Lawyers' Association. *LANGUAGES:* German and English. *PRACTICE AREAS:* Physics; Mechanical and Electrical Engineering; Electronics; Computer Technology and Software; Medical Technology; Patent, Design Patent and Trademark Prosecution; Litigation.

JOSEF SCHMIDT, born Breslau, Poland, March 19, 1956; Registered to practice before the German Patent and Trademark Office, 1987; European Patent Office, 1988. *Education:* University of Paderborn (Ing.-grad., Degree, Electrical Engineering, 1977); University of Bochum (Ruhr) (Dipl.-Ing., Degree, Electronic Engineering, 1982). Attended: Industrial Property Study Progran, German Patent Office, Federal Patent Court and the Regional Court, Munich, 1986-1987. *Member:* German Patent Attorney Bar Association; Institute of Professional Representatives before the European Patent Office (EPI); FICPI; AIPPI; German Association for the Protection of Industrial Property and Copyright Law (GRUR); Institute of Professional Representatives before the EPO (EPI); Deutsche Gesellschaft für Recht und Informatik (DGRI). *LANGUAGES:* German and English. *PRACTICE AREAS:* Patent Law; Trademark Law.

DR. HANS-RAINER JAENICHEN, born Seelow, Germany, June 23, 1955; Registered to practices before the German Patent and Trademark Office, 1987; European Patent Office, 1988. *Education:* University of Hohenheim (Dipl.-Biol., Genetics, Microbiology, Biochemistry, Cell Biology, Virology, 1980); University of Munich (Ph.D., Biology, Molecular Immunology, 1984). Attended: Industrial Property Study Program, German Patent Office, Federal Patent Court and the Regional Court, Munich, 1986-1987. Author, "The European Patent Office's Case Law on the Patentability of Biotechnology Inventions," Heymanns, 1993. Board of Editors, Biotechnology Law Report. *Member:* German Patent Attorney Bar Association; Institute of Professional Representatives before the European Patent Office (EPI); FICPI; AIPPI; German Association for the Protection of Industrial Property and Copyright Law (GRUR). *LANGUAGES:* German and English. *PRACTICE AREAS:* Patent Prosecution; Opposition Proceedings; Litigation; Biotechnology Inventions; Patents.

HELGA TREMMEL, born Wiener Neustadt, Austria, December 3, 1941; admitted, 1984, Munich, Amtsgericht München (local court), Landgericht München I and II (regional court), Oberlandesgericht (higher regional court), Bayerisches Oberstes Landesgericht (Bavarian higher court). *Education:* University of Munich (Referendar, 1981; Assessor, 1984). *Member:* German Bar Association; INTA; AIPLA; PTMG; DAJV; German Association for the Protection of Industrial Property and Copyright Law (GRUR). *LANGUAGES:* German and English. *PRACTICE AREAS:* German and International Trademark Law; Design Law; Unfair Competition Law; Trademark and Unfair Competition Litigation.

DR. RENATE BARTH, born Rieschweiler, Germany, August 11, 1949; Registered to practice before the European Patent Office, 1990. *Education:* Universities of Tübingen and Freiburg (Ph.D., Chemistry, 1978). Postdoctoral Research, Universities of Kingston, Canada and Göttingen 1978-1985. *Member:* Institute of Professional Representatives before the European Patent Office (EPI). *LANGUAGES:* German and English. *PRACTICE AREAS:* Patent Law.

(This Listing Continued)

EU776B

DR. ALEXA VON UEXKÜLL, born Hong Kong, May 21, 1960; Registered to practice before the German Patent and Trademark Office, 1991; European Patent Office, 1992. *Education:* University of London, Queen Mary College (B.Sc., Hon., Biochemistry, 1982); Chelsa College (M.Sc., Pharmacology, 1983); King's College (Ph.D., Pharmacology, 1987). Attended: Industrial Property Study Program, German Patent Office, Federal Patent Court and the Regional Court, Munich, 1990-1991. *Member:* German Patent Attorney Bar Association; Institute of Professional Representatives before the European Patent Office (EPI); FICPI; AIPPI; German Association for the Protection of Industrial Property and Copyright Law (GRUR). *LANGUAGES:* German and English. *PRACTICE AREAS:* Patent Law; Litigation; Organic Chemistry; Biochemistry; Pharmaceutics.

DR. RUDOLF WEINBERGER, born Munich, Germany, August 16, 1957; Registered to practice before the German Patent and Trademark Office and the European Patent Office, 1992. *Education:* University of Munich (Ph.D., Chemistry, 1989). Attended: Industrial Property Study Program, German Patent Office, Federal Patent Office and the Regional Court, Munich, 1991-1992. *Member:* German Patent Attorney Bar Association; Institute of Professional Representatives before the European Patent Office (EPI); FICPI. *LANGUAGES:* German and English. *PRACTICE AREAS:* Patent Law; Trademark Law.

DR. WOLFGANG BUBLAK, born Munich, Germany, August 26, 1959; Registered to practice before the German Patent and Trademark Office and the European Patent Office, 1992. *Education:* Technical University of Munich (Ph.D., Chemistry, 1987). Visiting Research Scientist, E.I. du Pont de Nemours & Co., Inc., 1987-1988. Attended: Industrial Property Study Program, German Patent Office, Federal Patent Court and the Regional Court, Munich 1991-1992. *Member:* German Patent Attorney Bar Association; Inistute of Professional Representatives before the European Patent Office (EPI); FICPI; Gesellschaft Deutscher Chemiker (GdCh); American Chemical Society (ACS). *LANGUAGES:* German, English and French. *PRACTICE AREAS:* Patent Prosecution; Litigation.

ASSOCIATES

AXEL STELLBRINK, born Bielefeld, Germany, May 13, 1962; Registered to practice before the German Patent and Trademark Office, 1993. *Education:* Technical University of Munich (Dipl.-Ing., Degree, Mechanical Engineering , 1990). Attended: Industrial Property Study Program, German Patent Office, Federal Patent Court and the Regional Court, Munich, 1992-1993. *Member:* German Patent Attorney Bar Association. *LANGUAGES:* German and English. *PRACTICE AREAS:* Patent Law; Trademark Law.

DR. JOACHIM WACHENFELD, born Arolsen, Germany, May 28, 1957; Registered to practice before the German Patent and Trademark Office, 1993. *Education:* University of Frankfurt; Eastern Illinois University, Charleston, Illinois; University of Freiburg (Ph.D., Biology, Molecular Immunology, 1990). Attended: Industrial Property Study Program, German Patent Office, Federal Patent Court and the Regional Court, Munich, 1992-1993. *Member:* German Patent Attorney Bar Association; German Association for Immunology; American Association for the Advancement of Science. *LANGUAGES:* German and English. *PRACTICE AREAS:* Patent Law; Litigation; Biotechnological Inventions.

DR. ROBERT LELKES, born Cleveland, Ohio, February 23, 1955; admitted, 1984, Ohio, 1986, Court of Appeals for the District of Columbia and Court of Appeals for the Federal Circuit; Registered to practice before the United States Patent and Trademark Office (Not admitted in Germany). *Education:* Cleveland State University (B.S., Chemistry, 1980); Cleveland-Marshall College of Law (Juris Doctor, 1983). Co-Author: "Patent Term Restoration in Europe: Taking Advantage of the Supplementary Protection Certificate," Patent World, December 1992-January 1993; "Amendments and Corrections of European Patent Applications," Patent World, June 1994. *Member:* American Bar Association (ABA); AIPLA. *LANGUAGES:* English and German. *PRACTICE AREAS:* Patent Law.

WALTER, CONSTON, ALEXANDER & GREEN, P.C.

BRIENNER STRASSE 11
80333 MUNICH, GERMANY
Telephone: (89) 238070
Facsimile: (89) 23807110
Telex: 522957

New York, N.Y. Office: 90 Park Avenue, 10016. Telephone: 212-210-9400. Facsimile: 212-210-9444. Telex: 234436.

(This Listing Continued)

Washington, D.C. Office: 1140 Connecticut Avenue, N.W., Suite 250, 20036. Telephone: 202-775-3955. Facsimile: 202-775-3956.

Darien, Connecticut Office: 30 Center Street, 06820. Telephone: 203-655-6046. Facsimile: 203-656-1407.

Affiliated Office: Walter, Conston, Alexander & Green, P.C., 721 Route 202-206, P.O. Box 1018, Somerville, New Jersey, 08876. Telephones: 908-429-1749; 429-1752.

International, Corporate, Commercial, Litigation, Arbitration, Tax, Real Estate, Antitrust, Securities, Banking, Bankruptcy, Estate Planning and Probate. Employee Benefits, Copyright, Trademark, Immigration and German Law.

RESIDENT COUNSEL

ELIZABETH A. VOIGHT, born Sapulpa, Oklahoma, August 6, 1944; admitted, 1979, New York and U.S. Tax Court; 1990, Federal Republic of Germany as "Rechtskundige fuer US-Amerikanisches Recht". *Education:* University of Arkansas (B.A., 1967; M.A., 1969); Georgetown University (J.D., 1978); Scholarship Deutscher Akademische Austauschdienst, University of Hamburg. Phi Beta Kappa. *Member:* The Association of the Bar of the City of New York; International Fiscal Association; International Bar Association; Deutsch-Amerikanischer Juristenverein; American Chamber of Commerce in Germany. *LANGUAGES:* German.

RECHTSANWALTE
WEINBERGER, SOTTUNG,
ULSENHEIMER, SCHLÜTER, BÖCKER,
BOCK UND PARTNER

Established in 1965

MAXIMILIANSPLATZ 12/IV
80333 MUNICH, GERMANY
Telephone: 089/ 22 55 46
Telefax: 089/ 22 71 52

General Practice, Corporate, Commercial, Stock Exchange, Transactions, Banking, Tax, International, EC, Intellectual Property, Unfair Competition, Trademarks, Antitrust, Real Estate, Labor, Product Liability, Medical Malpractice, White Collar Crime, Family, Wills, Administrative and Constitutional Law, Litigation.

MEMBERS OF FIRM

DIPL. RER. POL. DR. FRANZ WEINBERGER (1915-1993).

DR. RUDOLF SOTTUNG, born Munich, Germany, March 7, 1928; admitted, 1958, Munich. *Education:* Ludwig-Maximilians-University Munich (Dr. jur., 1955; Assessor, 1956). Author: "Die Pfändung der Eigentümergrundschuld," Carl Heymanns Verlag, 1957. Presiding Judge at the Court of Honours for the District of Munich (Disciplinary Court), 1973-1981. *Member:* Munich Bar Association; Anwaltsverein München; Münchner Anwaltsclub. *LANGUAGES:* English and German. *PRACTICE AREAS:* Real Estate; Wills; Litigation; Commercial; General Practice.

PROF. DR. DR. KLAUS ULSENHEIMER, born Duisburg, Germany, April 13, 1940; admitted, 1975, Munich. *Education:* Universities of Freiburg, Berlin and Bonn (Dr. jur., 1964; Dr. rer. pol., 1967; Assessor, 1970; Habilitation, 1974). Author: "Zum Verhältnis zwischen Pflichtwidrigkeit und Erfolg bei den Fahrlässigkeitsdelikten," Röhrscheid, Bonn, 1965; "Untersuchungen zum Begriff 'Finanzverfassung'," Fischer-Verlag, Stuttgart, 1969; "Untersuchungen zum Rücktritt zum Versuch," de Gruyter, Berlin, 1976; "Arztstrafrecht in der Praxis," C.F. Müller, Heidelberg, 1988; "Rechtliche Probleme in Geburtshilfe und Gynäkologie," Enke-Verlag, 1990; "Der Arzt im Strafrecht," Laufs/Uhlenbruck, Handbuch des Arztrechts, CH. Beck Verlag, München, 1992. *Member:* Münchner Anwaltsverein; Münchner Juristische Gesellschaft; Deutsche Gesellschaft für Medizinrecht. *LANGUAGES:* English and German. *PRACTICE AREAS:* Medical Malpractice; White Collar Crime; Commercial.

DR. UWE SCHLÜTER, born Wilster, Germany, June 23, 1943; admitted, 1973, Munich. *Education:* Ludwig-Maximilians-University, Munich (Dr. jur., 1971; Assessor, 1972). Author: "Schuldenhaftg. bei Geschäftsveräußerung," 1971, "Rechtsstellung des Börsenmaklers," Knapp Verlag, 1986; "Beteiligung am OTC-Handel," NStZ, 1987; "Anästhesiezwischenfall beim ambulanten Operieren," Anästhesiologie u. Intensivmedizin, 1987; "Postoperative Überwachung nach Neuroleptanalgesie," Anästhesiologie u. Intensivmedizin, 1988; Rechtliche Probleme in Geburtshilfe u. Gynakolo-

(This Listing Continued)

gie," Enke-Verlag, 1990. Managing Director of Bundesverband der Freien Börsenmakler e.v. *Member:* Munich Bar Association. *LANGUAGES:* English, French and German. *PRACTICE AREAS:* Corporate; Commercial; Stock Exchange Transactions; Banking; Tax; Medical Malpractice; White Collar Crime; Litigation.

DR. MICHAEL H. BÖCKER, born Kapfenberg, Austria, April 13, 1953; admitted, 1980, Munich. *Education:* University of Augsburg (Assessor, 1980; Dr. jur., 1984). Author: "Der betriebliche Vertrauensmann in der deutschen Industrie," 1984; "Ist die Abgabe von Bierkonzentrat nach § 64 BierStDB genehmigungsfähig?" Brauwelt, 1988; "Rechtliche Probleme in Geburtshilfe u. Gynakologie," Enke-Verlag, 1990; "German Practical Commercial Law," Longman, 1992. *Member:* Munich Bar Association. *LANGUAGES:* English, French and German. *PRACTICE AREAS:* Corporate; Commercial; Tax; Unfair Competition; Trademarks; Labor; Product Liability; Litigation; General Practice.

ROLF-WERNER BOCK, born Kaltenengers, Germany, January 15, 1957; admitted, 1988, Munich. *Education:* Ludwig-Maximilians-University Munich (Assessor, 1985). Co-Author: "Patientenaufklärung-mutmaβliche Einwilligung-Erweiterungsoperation," Geburtshilfte und Frauenheilkunde; Heft 11, 1991, S.948; die zivilrechtliche Haftung und stafrechtliche Verantwortlichkeit des Arztes, Chirurg, BDC, 31. Jg., Nr. 9/1992, 176. *Member:* Munich Bar Association. *LANGUAGES:* German and English. *PRACTICE AREAS:* Medical Malpractice; White Collar Crime; Administrative and Constitutional Law; Litigation.

WEISS & HASCHE

A Merger of the law firms Hasche Albrecht Fischer, Hamburg, Ott Weiss Eschenlohr & Partner, Munich and Rosenberg, Berlin.

BRIENNER STRASSE 11/V (LUITPOLDBLOCK)
80333 MUNICH, GERMANY
Telephone: (089) 23 80 70
Cable Address: "Interlaw", Munich
Telex: 5 22957 Law
Telefax: (089) 23 80 71 10

Hamburg, Germany Office: Valentinskamp 88, 20355 Hamburg. Telephone: (040) 35 00 20. Cable Address: "Lawyers" Telex: 215461 LAWY D. Teletex: 402276 LAWY D. Telefax: (040) 35 00 21 52.

Leipzig, Germany Office: Karl-Tauchnitz-Strasse 10 B, 04107 Leipzig. Telephone: (0341) 216 720. Telefax: (0341) 216 72 33.

Berlin, Germany Office: Meinekestrasse 13, 10719 Berlin. Telephone: (030) 881 97 83. Telefax: (030) 882 34 79.

Prague, Czech Republic Office: Dělnická 30, 170 00 Prague 7. Telephone: (2) 683 40 23. Telefax: (2) 683 40 23.

Commercial, International Trade, Maritime, Transport, Forwarding, Shipbuilding, Shipfinancing, Tax, Banking, Corporation, Mergers and Acquisitions, Antitrust, Unfair Competition, Industrial Property, Real Estate, Environment, Common Market, Insurance, Aviation, Arbitration, Media, Administrative, Labor, Computer, German Reunification, Litigation.

MEMBERS OF FIRM
(MUNICH OFFICE)

DR. BERNHARD OTT, born Sulzberg, Germany, October 19, 1926; admitted, 1956, Germany. *Education:* University of Munich (Referendar, 1953; Assessor, 1955; Dr. jur., 1956). Author: Die öffentlich-rechtliche Stellung der Religionsgemeinschaft im Staat. *Member:* Munich Bar Association. *LANGUAGES:* German and English.

HARALD ESCHENLOHR, born Bamberg, Germany, May 26, 1936; admitted, 1964, Germany. *Education:* Universities of Munich and Madrid. Member, Supervisory Board of: Loden-Frey Verkaufshaus KG; Derag Deutsche Realbesitz AG & Co.; Feinpappenwerk Gebr. Schuster GmbH & Co.; Atex KG; Firma Klöpfer & Königer GmbH & Co. KG; Bärlocher GmbH. *Member:* Munich Bar Association. *LANGUAGES:* German, English and Spanish.

ULRICH NEHM, born Munich, Germany, March 16, 1937; admitted, 1968, Germany. *Education:* University of Munich (Referendar, 1963; Assessor, 1967). *Member:* Munich Bar Association. *LANGUAGES:* German and English.

DR. PETER VON BORCH, born Rome, Italy, October 30, 1939; admitted, 1969, Germany. *Education:* Universities of Heidelberg and Munich (Referendar, 1964; Assessor, 1969; Dr. jur., 1970); Harvard Law School (LL.M.). Author: *The Right of Codetermination of Labour in Management Decisions.* Co-Author: *Legal Aspects of Alien Acquisition of Real Property,*

(This Listing Continued)

WEISS & HASCHE, Munich—Continued

Kluwer, Deventer/The Netherlands, Antwerp, Boston, London, Frankfurt, 1980. *Member:* Munich and German Bar Associations; International Fiscal Association. *LANGUAGES:* German, English and French.

DR. FLORIAN BAUER, born Bad Wiessee, Germany, June 3, 1944; admitted, 1973, Germany. *Education:* University of Munich (Referendar, 1968; Assessor, 1971; Dr. jur., 1971). Author: "Die Agentenmarke" (Trademarks in International Agency Relationships). Research Assistant at the Max-Planck-Institute for Foreign and International Patent, Copyright and Competition Law, Munich, 1968-1971. Regierungsrat at the Bavarian Department of Finance, 1971-1972. *Member:* Munich Bar Association. *LANGUAGES:* German and English.

DR. DIETER M.W. STRAUB, born Landau/Pfalz, Germany, May 1, 1950; admitted, 1977, Germany. *Education:* Universities of Munich and Mainz (Referendar, 1974; Assessor, 1977; Dr. jur., 1977). Author: "Gründe für die Beendigung von Arbeitsverträgen im sowjetischen Recht," (Legal Grounds for Termination of Labor Contracts under Soviet Law), 1977; "Neuregelung der gesetzlichen Vorschriften über Lohnpfändung und Gehaltsabtretung," (Rearrangement of the Legal Regulations Concerning Garnishment of Wages and Assignment of Wages), Weka Verlag, Kissingen, Germany, 1979. Co-Author: "Musterbeispiele für arbeitsgerichtlich durchsetzbare Kündigungen anhand neuester Urteile" (Models for termination of employment in compliance with German labor law regulations, based on the latest court rulings), Weka Verlag, Kissingen, Germany, 1987. *Member:* Munich Bar Association; Fachanwalt für Arbeitsrecht. *LANGUAGES:* German, English, French and Russian.

DR. RUPERT SCHREINER, born Munich, Germany, March 15, 1951; admitted, 1979, Germany. *Education:* IHK, Bankkaufmann (1973); University of Munich (Referendar, 1977; Diplom-Kaufmann, 1978; Assessor, 1979; Dr. jur., 1982). Author: "Die Dienstleistungsmarke" (The Service-Mark), 1983. Research Assistant at the Max-Planck-Institute for Foreign and International Patent, Copyright and Competition Law, Munich, 1979-1982. Member of Supervisory Board of Mitteldeutsche Industrieanlagen- und Stahlbau GmbH, Leipzig; Paul Isphording GmbH & Co., Attendorn. *Member:* Munich Bar Association; Deutscher Juristentag e.V.; Deutsche Vereinigung für gewerblichen Rechtsschutz und Urheberrecht; Vereinigung für den Gedankenaustausch zwischen Deutschen und Italienischen Juristen e.V. *LANGUAGES:* German, English, French and Italian.

ANDREAS OBERMEYER, born Tegernsee, Germany, May 24, 1950; admitted, 1984, Germany. *Education:* University of Regensburg (Referendar, 1980; Assessor, 1984). *Member:* Munich Bar Association. *LANGUAGES:* German and English.

DR. KLAUS M. SACHS, born Bad Godesberg, Germany, July 26, 1951; admitted, 1977, Germany. *Education:* Universities of Cologne and Heidelberg (Referendar, 1973; Assessor, 1976; Dr. jur., 1976); Legal Trainee, FAO, Rome (1975). Author: "EG Handelspolitik und Zwischenstaatliche Kooperationsabkommen," (EEC Trade Policy and Bilateral Cooperation Treaties), 1976, Nomos-Verlag; "Gemeinschaftsunternehmen in Algerien," (Joint Ventures in Algeria), RIW/AWD 1985, 201; "Das bilaterale französisch-algerische Schiedsabkommen vom 27. März 1983 - Ein Muster auch für andere Staaten?" (The bilateral French-Algerian Arbitration Agreement of March 27, 1983 - a Model for other Countries?), IPRax 1986, 309. Associate with Curtis, Mallet-Prévost, Colt & Mosle, Paris, 1980-1984. *Member:* German Arbitration Institute; French-German Chamber of Commerce (Paris); German-French Lawyers Association; Association Internationale des Jeunes Avocats (AIJA); International Bar Association. *LANGUAGES:* German, English, French and Italian.

DR. MARTIN ERKER, born Munich, Germany, June 12, 1956; admitted, 1986, Germany. *Education:* University of Munich (Referendar, 1981; Assessor, 1984; Dr. jur., 1986). Assistant, University of Munich, 1984-1986. *Member:* Munich Bar Association; Deutscher Juristentag e.V.; Deutsche Vereinigung für Gewerblichen Rechtsschutz und Urheberrecht. *LANGUAGES:* German and English.

FOREIGN COUNSEL AND ASSOCIATES
(MUNICH OFFICE)

ELIZABETH A. VOIGHT, born Sapulpa, Oklahoma, U.S.A., August 6, 1944; admitted, 1979, New York; 1990, Germany as "Rechtskundige für US-amerikanisches Recht". *Education:* University of Arkansas (B.A., 1967; M.A., 1969); Georgetown University (J.D., 1978). *Member:* The Association of the Bar of the City of New York; New York State Bar Association; International Bar Association; International Fiscal Association; German-American Law Association; American Chamber of Commerce in Germany.

(This Listing Continued)

(Also Resident Counsel to Walter, Conston, Alexander & Green, P.C., New York, N.Y.). *LANGUAGES:* English and German.

SYLVIA JACOB, born Duisburg, Germany, August 20, 1959; admitted, 1986, Ontario, Canada; 1991, England (Not admitted in Germany). *Education:* University of Toronto (B.A., 1981; B.L., 1984). *Member:* Law Society of Upper Canada; Canadian Bar Association; Canadian-German Chamber of Industry and Commerce (Canada); German-Canadian Economics Club (Munich). *LANGUAGES:* German, English, French and Spanish.

Languages: German, English, French, Italian, Russian and Spanish

---

WEISS • WALTER • FISCHER-ZERNIN

Established in 1994

SALVATORPLATZ 4/II
80333 MUNICH, GERMANY
Telephone: 49-89-2 90 71 90
Fax: 49-89-29 07 19 17

Hamburg, Germany Office: Glockengiesserwall 2 (Wallhof), 20095. Telephone: 49-40-32 21 19. Fax: 49-40-32 25 90.
New York, New York Office: 90 Park Avenue, 10016. Telephone: 212-210-94 00. Fax: 212-210-94 44.

FIRM PROFILE: The firm was established by Dr. Karl Heinz Weiss, Prof. Dr. Dr. Otto L. Walter and Dr. Vincent Fischer-Zernin, former senior partners of leading international commercial law firms. They concentrate the synergetic use of their joint domestic and global experience and connections, to serve and render counsel to management, especially in the fields of long range strategy, financial planning, labor relations and the avoidance or solving of business and tax problems. the firm offers to its clients full service in all branches of commercial and corporate law for both the domestic and international area.

MEMBERS OF FIRM

DR. KARL HEINZ WEISS, born Munich, Germany, April 26, 1929; admitted, 1958, Germany. *Education:* Universities of Munich and Göttingen (Referendar, 1951; Assessor, 1956; Dr. jur., 1955). Author: "Die Unterbeteiligung als Innengesellschaft mit Gesamthandsvermögen." Managing Director, Dr. Alexander Wacker Familiengesellschaft. Member of the Supervisory Board, Wacker-Chemie GmbH, Munich. Chairman of the Supervisory Board, Paul Hartmann AG, Heidenheim. Member of the Supervisory Board, Joh. A. Benckiser GmbH; Röhm GmbH, Darmstadt; Xaver Fendt & Co. Marktoberdorf. Member of the Advisory Board, Deutsche Bank AG, Munich. Chairman of the Advisory Board, Christophsbad Dr. Landerer Söhne, Göppingen. *Member:* Munich Bar Association. *LANGUAGES:* German, English and French. *PRACTICE AREAS:* Commercial Law; Banking; Aviation; Business Law; Civil Law; Company Law; Corporate Law; Finance; Investments; Mergers and Acquisitions; Real Estate; Taxation.

DR. OTTO L. WALTER, born Hof, Germany, December 7, 1907; admitted, 1932, Germany; 1955, New York; 1979, European Economic Community. *Education:* University of Munich (LL.B., 1929); University of Erlangen (Dr. iur., cum laude, 1930); New York Law School (J.D., 1954; LL.D. honoris causa, 1984). Member, Board of Editors: New York Law Review, 1952-1954; Steuer und Wirtschaft, 1980-1993. Member, Board of Advisors, Journal of International and Comparative Law, 1983—. Certified Public Accountant, New York, 1940—. Co-author: with Dr. H. Debatin, "Commentary to the German American Tax Convention," 4 vols. Amsterdam, 1959. Member, Commission of the German Ministry of Finance on Double Taxation Questions, 1956—. Vice President, Consular Law Society, 1983—. Director, American Foreign Law Association, 1989—. Honorary Member, Deutsch-Amerikanische Juristen Vereinigung. Adjunct Professor of Law, New York Law School, 1976—. Recipient: German Order of Merit 1st Class, 1960; Grand Cross Order of Merit, 1982. Member, National Panel of Arbitrators, American Arbitration Association, 1969—. Trustee, American Institute of Contemporary Studies, 1994—. (Also Senior Consultant, Walter, Conston, Alexander & Green, P.C., New York). *LANGUAGES:* German and English. *PRACTICE AREAS:* International Business Taxation; International Estate Taxation; Tax Treaties; International Estate; Trust Law.

DR. SUSANNE WEISS, born Bogen, Germany, April 15, 1961; admitted, 1989, Germany. *Education:* University of Regensburg (Referendar, 1986; Assessor, 1989; Dr. jur., 1994). Author: "Das Konzept der Gewinnbegrenzung für die Preishöhenkontrolle über marktbeherrschende Unternehmen." Assistant Lecturer, University of Regensburg, 1986-1989. *LANGUAGES:* German, English and French. *PRACTICE AREAS:* Commer-

(This Listing Continued)

cial Law; Corporate Law; Contracts; Distribution Agreements; International Distribution; Arbitration; International Arbitration; Antitrust and Trade Regulation; Appellate Practice; International Law; Asia-Pacific Investment; Mergers and Acquisitions; International Successions.

DR. WALTER EBERL, born Freyung, Germany, November 14, 1960; admitted, 1989, Germany; 1992, Ireland (Solicitor); 1994, England and Wales (Solicitor). *Education:* Universities of Regensburg, Paris and Beverly Hills (Assessor, 1989); Assistant Lecturer, University of Regensburg (1986-1987); Doctor Juris, EC Law, 1990. *Member:* AIJA; International Bar Association; Munich Institute of Copyright and Media Law. *LANGUAGES:* German, English and French. *PRACTICE AREAS:* Corporate Law; EC Law; Intellectual Property Law.

ANDREA RAFFLER, born Munich, Germany, August 14, 1961; admitted, 1993, Germany. *Education:* University of Munich (Referendar, 1987; Assessor, 1991). *LANGUAGES:* German and English. *PRACTICE AREAS:* Labor and Employment Law; Civil Law; Commercial Law.

DR. ELISABEHT FRFR. VON WEICHS, born Kaiserslautern, Germany, May 27, 1963; admitted, 1992, Germany. *Education:* Universities of Munich and Budapest (Referendar, 1988; Assessor, 1992; Dr. jur., 1991). Author: "Lizenzverträge im Technologietransfer nach ungarischem Recht.". *LANGUAGES:* German, English, French and Hungarian. *PRACTICE AREAS:* Commercial Law; Corporate Law; Advertising and Marketing; Agency and Distributorships; Arbitration; Antitrust and Trade Regulation; Communications and Media; Computers and Software; Contracts; Copyright; Entertainment and the Arts; European Community Law; Franchises and Franchising; Intellectual Property; International Law; Leases and Leasing; Mergers and Acquisitions; Patents and Trademarks; Licence; Unfair Competition; Hungarian Commercial Law.

WERNER, LUGER & WERNER

Rechtsanwälte, Wirtschaftsprüfer, Steuerberater

(Attorneys at Law, Auditors and Tax Advisers)

Established in 1977

JOSEPHSPITALSTRASSE 15/II
D-80331 MUNICH, GERMANY
Telephone: (089) 54 52 1-0
Telefax: (089) 54 52 1-109

Leipzig Office: Beethovenstrasse 29, D-04107 Leipzig. Telephone: (0341) 213 19 79. Telefax: (0341) 213 17 46.

Stockholm Office: Strandvägen 5 B, S-11451 Stockholm. Telephone: (0046-8) 663 49 10. Telefax: (0046-8) 663 40 77.

Member of Deutsch Nordische Juristenvereinigung e.V., Schwedische Handelskammer, Deutsch-Schwedische Handelskammer and Nordlund Group.

General Practice, Commercial Law, Company Law, Real Estate, Trademarks, Industrial and Intellectual Property, Media/Entertainment, Unfair Competition, EEC, Tax Law, Investment Consulting, East German Law, Litigation.

FIRM PROFILE: *The firm was established in Munich in 1977 and opened its Stockholm office in 1990 and its Leipzig office in 1992. The firm offers the full range of legal services for commercial matters. The Leipzig office concentrates on investments in the new federal states of Eastern Germany and on restitution matters. The firm also provides qualified legal services for Scandinavian companies establishing branches in Germany as well as for German companies establishing branches in Scandinavia.*

For many years the firm has been engaged in international activities of foreign enterprises in connection with establishment and investment in Germany. The firm has a wide experience in this area and cooperates with law firms of high professional standard in and outside Europe. The offices are situated right in the centre of Munich.

MEMBERS OF FIRM

DR. KLAUS WERNER, born Munich, September 4, 1946; admitted, 1975, Honorary Consul of Sweden. *Education:* University of Munich (Dr. jur., 1975). *Member:* LES-Licensing Executive Society; Deutsch-Nordische Juristenvereinigung; Swedish Chamber of Commerce; International Bar Association. *LANGUAGES:* German, Swedish and English. *PRACTICE AREAS:* Corporation Law; Foreign Investment; Swedish Commercial Law; Copyright; Intellectual Property; Publishing Law; Media/Entertainment.

(This Listing Continued)

PETER LUGER, born Haselbach, July 9, 1948; admitted, 1977. *Education:* Law Studies in Munich (1970-1974). *Member:* German Bar Association. *LANGUAGES:* German and English. *PRACTICE AREAS:* Industrial Rights; Commercial Law; Law on Competition; Real Estate Law; Law on Medical Practitioners; Law on Pharmacists.

RALPH G. WERNER, born Berlin, January 26, 1950; admitted, 1978. *Education:* Law Studies in Munich, Lausanne and Berlin. Assistant Lecturer, University of Augsburg. *Member:* German Bar Association. *LANGUAGES:* German, English and French. *PRACTICE AREAS:* Commercial Law; Company Law; Real Estate Law; Building Law; Investment Consulting.

DR. WERNER P. SACHON, born Mindelheim, November 19, 1948; admitted, 1981. *Education:* Universities of Munich and Regensburg (Degree, Business and Economic Law, 1974-1977); Max-Planck-Institute, Munich (Doctor's Degree). *Member:* German Bar Association. *LANGUAGES:* German and English. *PRACTICE AREAS:* Labour Law; Publishing Law; Media Law; Law on Press-Competition.

PETER PAULSMEIER, born Munich, October 21, 1956; admitted, 1987. *Education:* Law Studies in Munich, Geneva and Berlin. Tax Supervisor. *Member:* DAJV-German American Lawyers Association. *LANGUAGES:* German and English. *PRACTICE AREAS:* Commercial Law; Corporation Law; Tax Law.

ASSOCIATES

REINER WEBER, born Bad Mergentheim, May 3, 1951; admitted, 1990. *Education:* Law Studies in Freiburg/Breisgau (1980). Training in executive service by the finance authorities. Tax Supervisor, 1973-1978. Traineeship, Dr. Florence & Advogados, São Paulo, Brazil. *LANGUAGES:* German and English. *PRACTICE AREAS:* Tax Law.

KATARINA BENNET, born Stockholm, June 23, 1939; (Not admitted in Germany). *Education:* University of Stockholm (LL.B., Jur. kand., 1990); Swedish Law Examination (1990). *LANGUAGES:* Swedish, German, English and French. *PRACTICE AREAS:* Swedish Law.

DR. CHRISTOPHER KRUSCHE, born Nurnberg, March 20, 1960; admitted, 1991. *Education:* Law Studies in Munich. *LANGUAGES:* German and English. *PRACTICE AREAS:* Commercial Law; Unfair Competition; Building Law.

CHRISTOPH HOFSTETTER, born Munich, April 8, 1965; admitted, 1993. *Education:* Law Studies in Munich. *Member:* German Association for Protection of Industrial Property and Copyright. *LANGUAGES:* German and English. *PRACTICE AREAS:* Copyright; Media Law; Computer Law.

WESSING BERENBERG-GOSSLER ZIMMERMANN LANGE

VILSHOFENER STR. 8
D-81679 MUNICH, GERMANY
Telephone: 49-89-98 28 021
Telefax: 49-89-98 12 14

Mailing Address: P.O. Box 86 08 67, D-81635 Munich, Germany

Düsseldorf, Germany Office: Königsallee 92 A, D-40212 Düsseldorf, P.O. Box 10 53 61, D-40044 Düsseldorf. Telephone: 49-211-83 87-0. Telex: 858 19 14 wess d. Cable Address: "Wegolex". Telefax: 49-211-32 36 16.

Hamburg, Germany Office: Neuer Wall 46, D-20354 Hamburg. Telephone: 49-40-36 80 30. Cable Address: "Unilaw". Telex: 2-14111 Jura d. Teletex: 40 32 91 Unilaw. Telefax: 49-40-36 80 32 80.

Frankfurt, Germany Office: Freiherr-Vom-Stein-Strasse 24-26, D-60323 Frankfurt. Telephone: 49-69-971300. Telefax: 49-69-97130100.

Berlin, Germany Office: Spreeufer 5, D-10178 Berlin. Telephone: 49-30-238 45 45. Telefax: 49-30-238 45 34.

Leipzig, Germany Office: Ferdinand-Rhode-Strasse 16, D-04107 Leipzig. Telephone: 49-341-213 13 80. Fax: 49-341-213 13 88.

Dresden, Germany Office: Heinrichstrasse 16, D-01097 Dresden. Telephone: 49-351-567 12 12. Telefax: 49-351-567 12 13.

Brussels, Belgium Office: Avenue Louise 149, Box 42, B-1050 Brussels. Telephone: +32 (2) 537 01 86. Telefax: +32 (2) 534 25 31.

General Practice. Commercial, Corporation, International, Tax, Economic Criminality, Antitrust, Unfair Competition, Patent, Press, Copyright and Trademark Law. Foreign Investments in Brazil, Portugal and Mexico. Estate, EEC-Law, Bank Law, International Arbitration Proceedings, Environmental Law, German Reunification and Restitution Law.

(This Listing Continued)

WESSING BERENBERG-GOSSLER ZIMMERMANN LANGE, Munich—Continued

MEMBERS OF FIRM

DR. KLAUS ZIMMERMANN, born Duisburg, Germany, November 5, 1934; admitted, 1966, Germany. *Education:* Universities of Cologne, Munich and Freiburg (Doctor of Law; Academic Degree in Economics; Tax Lawyer). Judge, Landgericht München I, 1965-1966. *Member:* German Bar Association; German-French Association; German-Brazilian Chambers of Commerce; German-Spanish Association; German-Brazilian Association; International Association for the Protection of Industrial Property (IAPIP-AIPPI); International Literary and Artistic Association (ALAI). *LANGUAGES:* German, English, Spanish and Portuguese. *PRACTICE AREAS:* Corporation; Tax; Antitrust; International Arbitration Proceedings; German Reunification and Restitution Law.

PETER PRINZ ZU HOHENLOHE-OEHRINGEN, born Altenstadt-/Iller, Germany, October 1, 1945; admitted, 1974, Germany. *Education:* Universities of Munich and Cologne. *Member:* German Bar Association; Arbeitskreis für Insolvenzrecht im Deutschen Anwaltsverein (team specialized in insolvency law in the German Bar Association); Bankrechtliche Vereinigung - wissenschaftliche Gesellschaft für Bankrecht e.V. (scientific Association for bank law). *LANGUAGES:* German and English. *PRACTICE AREAS:* Civil Law; Commercial Law; Insolvency Law; Real Estate; East German Law; Restitution Claims Law.

DR. DIETRICH REIMER (1931-1982).

DR. MICHAEL SOMMER, born Forbach, France, March 31, 1944; admitted, 1975, Germany. *Education:* University of Erlangen/Nürnberg (Doctor of Law; Tax Consultant). Author: "Die Gesellscatsvertraege der GmbH & Co KG" (The Articles of Association of a limited partnership with a GmbH as partner). Co-Author: "Beck'sches Rechtshandbuch fuer Steuerberater 1991," (Beck'sches law manual for tax consultants 1991). *Member:* International Bar Association; German Bar Association; American Chamber of Commerce in Germany; German Tax Lawyers' Association; Regional Association of Tax Consultants in Bavaria; Association of Lawyers. *LANGUAGES:* German and English. *PRACTICE AREAS:* Corporate; Tax; Estate; International.

DR. GÜNTER BRÜGGEMANN, born Bremen, Germany, January 19, 1912; admitted, 1975, Germany. *Education:* Universities of Munich, Berlin and Bonn. *Member:* German Bar Association; German-Portuguese Chamber of Industry and Commerce. *LANGUAGES:* German, English, French, Portuguese and Italian. *PRACTICE AREAS:* Investments in Portugal; Corporation; General Practice.

DR. SABINE ROJAHN, born Remscheid, Germany, March 12, 1950; admitted, 1977, Germany. *Education:* University of Munich (Doctor of Law). Author: "Arbeitnehmerurheber in Presse, Funk und Fernsehen," (Employees in Press, Radio and Television), 1977. Co-Author: "Deutscher Urheberrechtskommentar," (German Copyright Commentary), Munich, 1986. Assistant at the Institute for European and International Business Law, University of Munich, 1974-1977. *Member:* International Trademark Association; German-Japanese Association; German Bar Association; International Association for the Protection of Industrial Property (AIPPI); International Literary and Artistic Association (ALAI); German Association for the Protection of Industrial Property and Copyright Law (GRUR); European Communities Trade Mark Practitioner' Association (ECTA). *LANGUAGES:* German, English and French. *PRACTICE AREAS:* Intellectual Property; Unfair Competition; Patent; Antitrust; EEC Law; Copyright.

DR. URSEL PAAL, born Geislingen, Germany, February 9, 1951; admitted, 1983, Germany. *Education:* Universities of Tübingen, Lausanne, Switzerland and Munich; University of Würzburg (Doctor of Law). Assistant, Institute for International Law, European Law and International Currency Law, University of Würzburg. *Member:* German Bar Association; International Association of Competition Law. *LANGUAGES:* German, English and French. *PRACTICE AREAS:* Press; EEC Law; Public Law; Environmental Law; German Reunification and Restitution Law.

DR. WOLFGANG A. REHMANN, born Essen, Germany, July 3, 1956; admitted, 1983, Germany. *Education:* University of Würzburg (Doctor of Law). *Member:* German Bar Association; German Association for the Protection of Industrial Property and Copyright Law (GRUR); International Association of Competition Law (L.I.D.C.); Association Internationale De Droit Economique (A.I.D.E.). *LANGUAGES:* German, English, French and Russian. *PRACTICE AREAS:* Intellectual Property; Unfair Competition; Antitrust; EEC Law; Pharmaceutical and Drugs.

(This Listing Continued)

RÜDIGER ROBERT RAU, born Eschwege/Werra, Germany, November 3, 1955; admitted, 1985, Germany and Attorney for Labour Law. *Education:* University of Cologne. *Member:* German Bar Association. *LANGUAGES:* German, English and French. *PRACTICE AREAS:* Labour Law; Real Estate; General Practice.

DR. HANS-FRIEDRICH LOTH, born Düsseldorf, Germany, February 16, 1954; admitted, 1986, Germany. *Education:* University of Bonn. Co-Author: "Handbuch des Ausstattungrechts", (Handbook of National and International Law of the Get-Up), Weinheim/Deerfield Beach Fl., 1986. Author: "Neuheit und Neuheitsschonfrist im Patentrecht - Eine rechtsvergleichende Untersuchung," (Novelty and Grace Period in Patent Law - A Comparative Study), Cologne-Berlin-Munich, 1988. Department Head, Max Planck Institute for Foreign and International Patent, Copyright and Trade Mark Law, Munich, 1983-1986. Mitverfasser: "Münchner Gemeinschaftskommentar zum Europäischen Patentübereinkommen," 1984 ff (Co-author of the "Munich Joint Commentary on the European Patent Convention"), Cologne-Berlin-Munich, 1984 et seq. *Member:* International Association for the Protection of Industrial Property (AIPPI); German Association for the Protection of Industrial Property and Copyright Law (GRUR); Licensing Executive Society (LES); European Food Law Association (EFLA); Bund für Lebensmittelrecht und Lebensmittelkunde (BLL) (Association for food law and food science); International Association of Trademark Law (Marques). *LANGUAGES:* German, English and French. *PRACTICE AREAS:* Intellectual Property; Patent; Unfair Competition; Trademark Law; Food Law.

THOMAS RAAB, born Bamberg, Germany, October 30, 1956; admitted, 1986, Germany. *Education:* University of Munich. *Member:* International Trademark Association (INTA); German Bar Association; German Association for the Protection of Industrial Property and Copyright Law (GRUR); European Community Trade Mark Association (ECTA). *LANGUAGES:* German, English and French. *PRACTICE AREAS:* Trademark Law; Unfair Competition; Intellectual Property; Copyright.

DR. CORNELIUS WEITBRECHT, born Erlangen, Germany, May 19, 1958; admitted, 1988, Germany. *Education:* Universities of Erlangen and Munich (Doctor of Law). Assistant, Institute for Labor and Business Law, University of Munich, 1989. *Member:* German Bar Association. *LANGUAGES:* German and English. *PRACTICE AREAS:* Tax; Corporation; International.

HANS FRHR.V. STEIN, born Berlin, Germany, November 2, 1928. *Education:* Universities of Marburg/Lahn and Durham, N.C. Author: "The European Economic Community and Africa," Federalism and the New Nations of Africa, University of Chicago Press, 1964. Member: German Federal Ministry of Economics, 1957; German Department for Foreign Affairs; German Embassies of Addis Abeba and London; Society for Foreign Policy. Assistant to General Director, EC Commission, Brussels, 1958-1963. Envoy, German Embassy of Djidda/Riad. Ambassador in Brussels, 1991-1993. Permanent Representative, Federal Republic of Germany to West European Union, 1933—. *LANGUAGES:* German, English, French and Dutch. *PRACTICE AREAS:* EC Law; General Practice.

DR. ANDREAS B. SCHRETTL, born Göttingen, Germany, January 21, 1962; admitted, 1990, Germany. *Education:* Universities of Bayreuth and Augsburg (Doctor of Law). *Member:* German Bar Association; Association of Tax Lawyers. *LANGUAGES:* German, English and French. *PRACTICE AREAS:* Tax; Corporation; German Reunification and Restitution Law.

CHRISTIANE SCHMITZ, born Oberhausen, Germany, August 27, 1965; admitted, 1993, Germany. *Education:* University of Munich. *LANGUAGES:* German, English and French. *PRACTICE AREAS:* Labour Law; General Practice.

DETLEF G. BARTHMES, born Romania, December 28, 1962; admitted, 1994, Germany. *Education:* Universities of Konstanz and Augsburg. Research Assistant, University of Augsburg, 1991-1992. *Member:* German Bar Association. *LANGUAGES:* German, Romanian, English and Spanish. *PRACTICE AREAS:* Commercial Law; General Practice.

DR. ANDREAS KLOYER, born Ingolstadt, Germany, March 23, 1963; admitted, 1992, Germany. *Education:* Universities of Passau, Munich and Kiel (Doctor of Law). *Member:* German Bar Association; Inter-Pacific Bar Association; German-Japanese Lawyers Association; German Society of Tax Law; Society of Antitrust Studies. *LANGUAGES:* German, English, French and Japanese. *PRACTICE AREAS:* Tax; Corporation; Antitrust; Commerce; International.

(This Listing Continued)

RICHARD SCHÖNWERTH, born Bad Tölz, Germany, October 19, 1962; admitted, 1993, Germany. *Education:* University of Munich. *LANGUAGES:* German and English. *PRACTICE AREAS:* Intellectual Property; Trademark; Copyright.

WIRSING, MEINHOLD, HASS

Established in 1932

RESIDENZSTRASSE 18/III
80333 MUNICH, GERMANY
Telephone: (089) 29 00 71-0
Telecopier: (089) 29 00 71-11

Commercial, Corporation, Tax, International, Mergers and Acquisitions, Antitrust, Unfair Competition, Trademark, Copyright, Estate, Family.

MEMBERS OF FIRM

DR. GEORG WIRSING, born Berlin, Germany, October 18, 1933; admitted, 1965, Munich. *Education:* Munich Technical University (Prediplome, 1956); University of Wuerzburg (Referendar, 1962; Dr. jur., 1964; Assessor, 1965). Author: "Rechtliche Probleme bei Bau und Betrieb von Mineralöl-Fernleitungen," Thesis, 1964. Judge, Special District Court for the Legal Profession (Ehrengericht), 1976—. Member, Supervisory Board of Schmidt-Bank, Hof. *Member:* Munich and German Bar Associations; German Association for the Protection of Industrial Property and Copyright Law (GRUR). *LANGUAGES:* German, English and French. *PRACTICE AREAS:* Commercial; Corporation; Tax; Mergers and Acquisitions; Family.

DR. WILKO MEINHOLD, born Bielefeld, Germany, December 31, 1943; admitted, 1975, Munich. *Education:* University of Kiel and Munich (Referendar, 1971; Assessor, 1975; Dr. jur., 1977). Author: "Diversification, Konglomerate Unternehmen und Gesetze gegen Wettbewerbsbeschränkungen," 1977. Research Assistant, University of Augsburg, 1972. With Federal Cartel Office, Berlin, 1978-1979. Member, Supervisory Board of Nessler GmbH, Lahr, 1978—. *Member:* Munich Bar Association; German Association for the Protection of Industrial Property and Copyright Law (GRUR); Studienvereinigung Kartellrecht. *LANGUAGES:* German, English and French. *PRACTICE AREAS:* Antitrust; Unfair Competition; Commercial; Labour.

DR. CLAUS SIEGHART HASS, born Munich, Germany, June 8, 1954; admitted, 1981, Munich. *Education:* University of Munich (Prediploma, Business Administration, 1975; Referendar, 1978; Assessor, 1981; Dr. jur., 1986). Author: "The Unconscionability Doctrine (§ 2-302 UCC) and its Influence on the New German International Private Law," VVF Munich, 1986. Research Assistant, University of Munich, 1978-1979. Member, Supervisory Board of Tele-Muenchen Fernseh-GmbH & Co., 1989—. *Member:* Munich and German Bar Associations; International Bar Association; German-American Lawyers Association (DAJV); A.I.J.A. *LANGUAGES:* German, English and Italian. *PRACTICE AREAS:* Corporate; Commercial; Mergers and Acquisitions.

Languages: German, English, French and Italian.

DR. WUNDERLICH & PARTNERS

EFFNERSTR. 48
81925 MUNICH, GERMANY
Telephone: 089/99 89 17-0
Telefax: 089/99 89 17-17

General Practice. Commercial, Estate, International, Tax, Antitrust, Unfair Competition, Patent, Copyright and Trademark Law.

MEMBERS OF FIRM

DR. DETLEF WUNDERLICH, born Berlin, Germany, April 24, 1935; admitted, 1963, Germany. *Education:* Universities of Munich and Erlangen (Doctor of Law). Author: "Die gemeinschaftliche Erfindung" (Joint Invention), Munich, 1962; "Die Warenzeichenlizenz Schweiz" (Trade Mark License Switzerland), Munich, 1963; "Das Recht des unlauteren Wettbewerbs in den Mitgliedstaaten der EWG, Luxemburg" (Law of Unfair Competition in the Member Countries of the Common Market, Luxembourg), Munich, 1967. Assistant Professor, Max-Planck Institute for International and National Patent Law. Member of Administrative Council Gerling Konzern, Köln. Joint Director of "Menschen Für Menschen" e.V. Foundation, Munich. Member of Board of Supervisors of German Private Finance Academy, Munich. *Member:* German-Swiss Chamber of Commerce. *LANGUAGES:* German, English and French. *PRACTICE AREAS:* Business

(This Listing Continued)

Law; Corporate Law; International Law; Mergers, Acquisitions and Divestitures; Trusts and Estates.

DR. ADAM DEINLEIN, born Hammelburg, Germany, December 27, 1909; admitted, 1975, Germany. *Education:* Member of Maximilianeum, Universities of Munich and Erlangen (Doctor at Law). Public Prosecutor and Judge, 1936-1947. Chief Counsellor at Law, Municipality of Munich. Department Head, Bavarian State Ministry of Interior (Constitution, Organization, Budget). Governor of Upper Bavaria, 1961-1974. President of Tourisme Association of Munich and Upper Bavaria. Vice-President of Rotary Club, Munich Centre. *LANGUAGES:* German and English. *PRACTICE AREAS:* Administration Law; Government; Government Contracts; Constitutional Law; Public Law.

DR. MARTIN HINTERMAYER, born Munich, Germany, February 11, 1955; admitted, 1982, Germany. *Education:* Universities of Würzburg and Munich (Doctor of Law). Author: "Beitrag der Deutschen Rechtsprechung zu Art. 85, 86 EWG-Vertrag," (European Antitrust Law), Munich, 1984. *LANGUAGES:* German and English. *PRACTICE AREAS:* Advertising and Marketing; Antitrust and Trade Regulation; Banks and Banking; Bank Finance; Real Estate.

JUTTA LUISE NIERMANN, born Herford, Germany, April 15, 1962; admitted, 1990, Germany. *Education:* Universities of Marburg and Göttingen. *LANGUAGES:* German, English and French. *PRACTICE AREAS:* Business Law; Family Law; Labor and Employment; Leases and Leasing; Personal Injury.

MARTINE DORNIER-TIEFENTHALER, born Munich, Germany, August 21, 1954; admitted, 1982, Germany. *Education:* University of Munich. Executor of the estate of Prof. Claudius Dornier and member of supervisory of Dornier GmbH until 1990. Member, supervisory board, Mercedes Benz AG. *LANGUAGES:* German, English and French. *PRACTICE AREAS:* Banks and Banking; Business Law; Company Law; Corporate Law; Real Estate.

ZIMMERMANN, HOHENLOHE, SOMMER, ROJAHN

MUNICH, GERMANY

(See Wessing Berenberg-Gossler Zimmermann Lange)

General Practice. Commercial, Corporation, International, Tax, Economic Criminality, Antitrust, Unfair Competition, Patent, Press, Copyright and Trademark Law. Foreign Investments in Brazil, Portugal and Mexico. Estate, EEC-Law, Bank Law, International Arbitration Proceedings.

ALPMANN, RADDATZ, MOHR UND PARTNER

Established in 1961

ANNETTE-ALLEE 35
P.O. BOX 11 69
D-48149 MÜNSTER, GERMANY
Telephone: (0251) 981 0914
Telecopier: (0251) 981 0960

Commercial, Corporation, Litigation and Arbitration, Unfair Competition, Product Liability, Building and Planning, Real Property and Environmental, Medical Malpractice, Labor Relations, Estates, Domestic Relations and Legal Education Law.

MEMBERS OF FIRM

JOSEF ALPMANN, born Paderborn, Germany, July 26, 1920; admitted, 1960, Münster; 1967, Notary Public. *Education:* University of Kiel (Referendar, 1951; Assessor, 1955). Author: "German Law of Obligation," A+S Verlag, 1987. *Member:* German Bar Association; Münster Association of Lawyers; Society for Legal Studies. *LANGUAGES:* German and English. *PRACTICE AREAS:* Estates; Legal Education.

GUENTER RADDATZ, born Herne, Germany, December 19, 1931; admitted, 1963, Münster; 1972, Notary Public. *Education:* Universities of Freiburg and Münster (Referendar, 1957; Assessor, 1961). Author: *Inheritance Law,* 1985, *Domestic Relations,* 1986 and *Torts,* 1987, all published by A+S Verlag. *Member:* German Bar Association; Münster Association of Lawyers; Society for Legal Studies. *LANGUAGES:* German, English and Dutch. *PRACTICE AREAS:* Real Property; Product Liability.

(This Listing Continued)

ALPMANN, RADDATZ, MOHR UND PARTNER,
Münster—Continued

FRIEDRICH MOHR, born Muelheim-Ruhr, Germany, April 3, 1936; admitted, 1966, Kleve; 1968, Münster; 1973, Notary Public. *Education:* Free University of Berlin (Law and Political Sciences, 1956-1957); Mercer Law School, Macon, Georgia (1958-1959); University of Münster (Referendar, 1962; Assessor, 1966). Author: "Procedural Problems in Social Security Cases," 1982 and "Law of German Corporations," 1988, published by A+S Verlag; "Control of Public Health Service," Verlag Chmielorz, 1987. *Member:* German Bar Association (Member, Board of Director and National Ethics Committee); Münster Association of Lawyers (President, 1975-1981). *LANGUAGES:* German and English. *PRACTICE AREAS:* Medical Malpractice; Commercial Law; Corporations.

UWE MARX, born Plauen, Germany, May 16, 1943; admitted, 1973, Münster; 1982, Notary Public. *Education:* Universities of Marburg and Münster (Referendar, 1969; Assessor, 1973). *Member:* German Bar Association; Münster Association of Lawyers; Institute for Studies on Lawyers' Profession, University of Cologne. *LANGUAGES:* German, English and French. *PRACTICE AREAS:* Building and Planning Litigation and Arbitration.

ANNEGERD ALPMANN-PIEPER, born Vechta, Germany, July 10, 1951; admitted, 1981, Münster. *Education:* Universities of Freiburg and Münster (First State Examination, 1977; Second State Examination, 1981). Author: "Unjust Enrichment," Metzner-Verlag, 1981; "General Rules of the Civil Code," A+S Verlag, 1988. *LANGUAGES:* German, English and French. *PRACTICE AREAS:* Domestic Relations.

DR. ROLF KRUGER, born Rheine, Germany, February 1, 1953; admitted, 1983, Münster. *Education:* University of Münster (First State Examination, 1981; Second State Examination, 1983; Doctor of Law, 1983). Author: "Offenses in Connection with Environmental Damages," Metzner Verlag, 1981; "Securities," 1985 and " Criminal Law," 1985/1988, published in A+S Verlag. *Member:* German Bar Association; Münster Association of Lawyers. *LANGUAGES:* German, English and French. *PRACTICE AREAS:* Labor Relation.

JOSEF A. ALPMANN, born Liemke, Germany, April 11, 1955; admitted, 1986, Münster. *Education:* University of Münster (Referendar, 1981; Assessor, 1985). Author: *Human Rights,* 1986 and *Real Property,* 1988, published by A+S Verlag. *Member:* German Bar Association. *LANGUAGES:* German and English. *PRACTICE AREAS:* Unfair Competition.

HORST WÜSTENBECKER, born Münster, West Germany, March 21, 1957; admitted, 1986, Münster. *Education:* University of Münster (First State Examination, 1983; Second State Examination, 1986). Author: "Commercial Law," 1985, "Constitutional Law," 1988 and "Local Government Law," 1989, A +S Verlag. *Member:* German Bar Association; Deutscher Juristentag. *LANGUAGES:* German and English. *PRACTICE AREAS:* Building and Planning Commercial Law.

HARTMUT BRANDT-HENNINGE, born Melle, Germany, September 23, 1961; admitted, 1993, Münster. *Education:* University of Bielefeld (Assessor, 1990). *Member:* German Bar Association. *LANGUAGES:* German, English, French and Spanish. *PRACTICE AREAS:* Labor Law.

DR. MARCUS GEUTING, born Wesel, Germany, March 19, 1963; admitted, 1994, Münster. *Education:* University of Münster (First State Examination, 1989; Second State Examination, 1992; Doctor of Law, 1993). Author: "Hidden Profit Distributions caused by Contracts between Corporations and Shareholder's Relatives," 1993. *LANGUAGES:* German and English. *PRACTICE AREAS:* Unfair Competition; Corporation.

Languages: German, English, Dutch and French

DR. DREISMANN, BEHRMANN & PARTNER

Established in 1952

PRINZIPALMARKT 20
48143 MÜNSTER, GERMANY
Telephone: 49/251/58088
Fax: 49/251/45196

General Practice, Labor Law, Commercial Law, Business Law, Family Law including Catholic Marriage Law, Company Law, Insurance Law, Tenancy Law.

(This Listing Continued)

FIRM PROFILE: *Established in 1952. Firm is mainly engaged in Civil Law. Offers the full range of legal services, except Criminal Law. Special emphasis is being laid on Labor Legislation including Collective Labor Legislation, all fields of Commercial Law and Family Law. A member of the German-Dutch Chamber of Commerce/Nederlands-Duitse Kammer van Koophandel. A member of AdvoSelect EEIG, a network of law firms pooling their resources in special fields and crossborder cases, specializing in Business Law for middlesized companies. AdvoSelect is represented in 51 cities throughout Europe.*

MEMBERS OF FIRM

DR. HEINZ DREISMANN, born Münster, April 16, 1921; admitted, 1952, Münster; 1953, Expert Lawyers for Law of Taxation; 1962, Notary Public. *Education:* University of Münster and Cologne. Junior Lawyer, 1948 (Hamm); Junior Barrister, 1952 (Düsseldorf). *Member:* German Bar Association; Münster Association of Lawyers. *LANGUAGES:* German and English. *PRACTICE AREAS:* Business Law; Family Law.

JÜRGEN BEHRMANN, born Düsseldorf, April 23, 1941; admitted, 1972, Münster; 1981, Notary Public; 1987, Expert Lawyer for Labor Legislation. *Education:* University of Münster. Junior Lawyer, 1968 (Hamm); Junior Barrister, 1972 (Düsseldorf). *Member:* German Bar Association; Münster Association of Lawyers; Working Association of Expert Lawyers for Labor Legislation in the Bar Union of Germany. *LANGUAGES:* German and Dutch. *PRACTICE AREAS:* Labor Law; Business Law; Family Law.

BEITEN BURKHARDT MITTL & WEGENER

Rechtsanwälte

OBERE TURNSTRASSE 8
D-90429 NÜRNBERG, GERMANY
Telephone: (09 11) 2 79 71-0
Telefax: (09 11) 2 79 71-99

Munich, Germany Office: Leopoldstrasse 236, D-80807. Telephone: (089) 35065-00. Telefax: (089) 35065-123.

Berlin, Germany Office: Kurfürstenstrasse 72-74, D-10787 Berlin. Telephone: (0 30) 264 71-0. Telefax: (0 30) 264 71-123.

Frankfurt/Main, Germany Office: Arndtstrasse 28, D-60325 Frankfurt/Main. Telephone: (0 69) 75 60 95-0. Telefax: (0 69) 75 60 95-12.

Leipzig, Germany Office: Käthe-Kollwitz-Strasse 54, D-04109 Leipzig. Telephone: (03 41) 4 77 25 97. Telefax: (03 41) 4 77 25 99.

Potsdam, Germany Office: Heinrich-Mann-Allee 105 B, D-14473 Potsdam. Telephone: (0331) 33 43 06. Telefax: (0331) 33 43 29.

Hof, Germany Office: Oberer Torplatz 1, D-95028 Hof. Telephone: (09281) 80 23. Telefax: (09281) 1 65 69.

Plauen, Germany Office: Lindenstrasse 5, D-08523 Plauen. Telephone: (03741) 22 35 11; 22 49 62. Telefax: (03741) 22 49 62.

New York, New York Office: 215 East 73rd Street, New York, NY 10021. Telephone: (212) 570-2141. Telefax: (212) 734-7011.

London, England Office: Swedenborg House, 21 Bloomsbury Way, London, WC1A 2TH. Telephone: (0171) 2 42 44 66. Telefax: (0171) 2 42 44 67.

Moscow, Russia Office: Ul. Alekseja Tolstovo D.30/1, 103001 Moscow. Telephone and Telefax: (095) 202 37 60; 290 05 56.

Prague, Czech Republic Office: Na Bojišti 24, 120 00 Prague 2. Telephone: (2) 24 91 5808. Telefax: (2) 24 91 5804.

Budapest, Hungary Office: József Nádor Tér 9, H-1051 Budapest. Telephone: (1) 2 66 18 10. Telefax: (1) 2 66 18 11.

Hong Kong Office: 605 B, Sixth Floor, Peregrine Tower, Lippo Centre, 89 Queensway. Telephone: (852) 2524 6468. Telefax: (852) 2524 7028.

Beijing, People's Republic of China Office: Unit 10, 29th Floor, Jing Guang Centre, Hu Jia Lou, Chao Yang Qu, 100020. Telephone: (86-1) 501 4569; 501 3388 Ext. 2910. Telefax: (86-1) 501 3034.

Commercial Law, Company Law, M & A, Joint Ventures, Finance, Banking, Leasing, Domestic and International Tax, Antitrust, EC Law, Real Property and Private Construction, Electronic Data Processing (Protection and Licensing), Media, Publishing, Unfair Competition, Trademarks, Copyright, Labour, General and Special Administrative Law Particularly Public Construction and Planning Regulations and Public International Law, Environmental Law, Agricultural Law, Privatization and Restitution (former GDR), Probate, Family and Estate Planning, Insolvency and Sports, Insurance, Automobile Accidents and Injuries.

(This Listing Continued)

FIRM PROFILE: BEITEN BURKHARDT MITTL & WEGENER is a nation-wide and international law firm with 108 lawyers. The firm's head office is in Munich. All the firm's offices provide a comprehensive range of services in the main areas of civil and commercial law.

JOCHEN M. SCHÄFER, born Ebersbach, 1950; admitted, 1983, Germany. *Education:* University of Erlangen-Nürnberg (law degree, 1980; Dr.jur., 1981). Co-Author: "Handbook for International Marketing," 1987 and publications in thefield of Competition, Trademark and Distribution Law. General Counsel, Adidas Sportschuhfabriken Adi Dassler KG, 1980-1983. Legal Counsel, World Federation of the Sporting Goods Industry (WFSGI). Counsel for Europe, National Sporting Goods Association (NSGA), USA. *LANGUAGES:* German, English and French. *PRACTICE AREAS:* Company Law; Acquisitions and Sales; Restructuring; Unfair Competition; Copyrights; Advertising and Marketing; Sports.

THOMAS J. SACHER, born Crailsheim, 1958; admitted, 1987, Germany. *Education:* Universities of Munich and Regensburg (law degree, 1983; Dr. jur., 1990). Visiting Lecturer at the Academy of the Bavarian Press and the Academy for Electronic Media. *Member:* Federal Association of Young Entrepreneurs; Economic Association of Northern Bavaria. *LANGUAGES:* German and English. *PRACTICE AREAS:* Company Law; Acquisitions and Sales; Restructuring; Media and Entertainment; Video and Television; Press Law; Publishing and Radio; Cartels.

BERTHOLD F. MITRENGA, born Hamburg, 1951; admitted, 1991, Germany. *Education:* University of Erlangen-Nürnberg (law degree, 1979). Lecturer, Management Academy of the Federal Post Office; University of Erlangen-Nürnberg. Government Employee, Federal Employment Office (Bundesanstalt für Arbeit), 1980-1986. Responsible for Contractual Agreements with the Public Sector: Nixdorf Computer AG, 1986-1990; ICL Computer GmbH, 1991-1994. Chair, Law and Technology, 1991—. *LANGUAGES:* German and English. *PRACTICE AREAS:* Computer Law; Telecommunication and Technology; Administrative Law; Public Law of Economic and Traffic Affairs.

GERHARD STÄUDLE, born Öhringen, 1949; admitted, 1977, Germany. *Education:* Universities of Heidelberg and Freiburg/Breisgau (law degree, 1974). Private practice at Offenburg, 1977-1991. In-house counsel with Burda Verlag, Offenburg, 1980-1991. *LANGUAGES:* German and English. *PRACTICE AREAS:* Press Law; Publishing and Radio; Unfair Competition; Copyrights; Advertising and Marketing; Real Estate; Construction Law; Labour and Employment.

CHRISTIAN SCHMIDT, born Erlangen, 1957; admitted, 1986, Germany. *Education:* University of Erlangen-Nürnberg (law degree, 1985). *Member:* German Parliament for the Electoral District Fürth/Bavaria, 1991—. *LANGUAGES:* German and English. *PRACTICE AREAS:* European Community Law; Labour and Employment; Unfair Competition; Copyrights; Advertising and Marketing.

MARTINA HÖFS, born Stadthagen, 1963; admitted, 1991, Germany. *Education:* University of Bielefeld (law degree, 1990). Licensed Specialist for Labour Law, 1994. In-house Counsel with an association of the power producing industry, 1980; Associate with a law firm specialized in Labour Law, 1991-1993. *LANGUAGES:* German, English and French. *PRACTICE AREAS:* Unfair Competition; Copyrights; Advertising and Marketing; Labour and Employment; Insolvency; Liquidations.

CORNELIA SCHMID, born Eschenbach/Neustadt, 1963; admitted, 1991, Germany. *Education:* University of Bayreuth (law degree, 1990). Research Assistant, University of Bamberg, 1991-1992. Chair, Law and Economic Affairs. *LANGUAGES:* German. *PRACTICE AREAS:* Labour and Employment; Commercial Law; Unfair Competition; Copyrights; Advertising and Marketing.

GERHARD LANGHANS, born Erlangen, 1953; admitted, 1983, Germany. *Education:* University of Erlangen-Nürnberg (law degree, 1983). Staff Member, University of Erlangen-Nürnberg, 1982-1983. Legal Counsel, Bavarian Association of the Construction Industry. *LANGUAGES:* German. *PRACTICE AREAS:* Real Estate; Construction Law; Probate and Family Law; Automobile Accidents and Injuries.

MATTHIAS F. ETZEL, born Frankfurt a.M., 1962; admitted, 1994, Germany. *Education:* Universities of Lausanne and Frankfurt a.M. (law degree, 1989; Dr.jur., 1991). Staff Member, Institute for History of Law, Frankfurt a.M., 1987-1988. J.W. Goethe University-Prize, Frankfurt a.M., 1991. Trainee with the Commission of the European Union, 1992. *LANGUAGES:* German, English, French and Italian. *PRACTICE AREAS:*

(This Listing Continued)

Company Law; Acquisitions and Sales; Restructuring; Press Law; Publishing and Radio; European Community Law.

(For Complete Biographical Data on all Personnel, see Munich, Germany Professional Biographies)

FRORIEP RENGGLI

FRIEDRICHSTRASSE 6
90762 FUERTH (NÜRNBERG), GERMANY
Telephone: (+49)-911 77 39 82
Telecopier: (+49)-911 749 84 51

Zürich, Switzerland Office: Bellerivestrasse 201, 8034. Telephone: (+41)1 386 60 00. Telecopier: (+41)1 383 60 50 (Address until April 30, 1995: General Wille-Strasse 10, 8027. Telephone: (+41) 12017420. Telex: 815596 frp ch. Telecopier: (+41) 12023666).

Geneva, Switzerland Office: 4, Rue Charles-Bonnet, 1206. Telephone: (+41)-22 347 18 18. Telex: 423651 frob ch. Telecopier: (+41)-22 347 71 59.

Zug, Switzerland Office: Baarerstrasse 75, 6300. Telephone: (+41)-42 21 33 71. Telecopier: (+41)-42 23 07 15.

London, England Office: 1 Knightrider Court, EC4V 5JP. Telephone: (+44)171 236 60 00. Telecopier: (+44)171 248 02 09.

Swiss and International Commercial, Corporate and Civil Practice, International Business Transactions, Commercial Litigation and International Commercial Arbitration, Private and Public International Law, Banking, Taxation, Immigration, Bankruptcy, International Judicial Assistance, Trademarks and Copyrights, Aviation, EEC and Computer Law, Joint-Venture East-West.

FIRM PROFILE: Established in 1966, Froriep Renggli has grown to be one of the leading and largest Swiss law firms with principal offices in Zurich, Geneva and Zug. The firm is engaged in a broad range of Swiss and International practice. Froriep Renggli currently has a total of thirty-two lawyers, twelve of whom are partners. Two of the associates are qualified German lawyers, four lawyers are also admitted in New York and one is an English solicitor. Most of the lawyers have had, in addition to their Swiss training, legal education in England or the United States and/or have practice as foreign consultants with law firms there or elsewhere abroad. The firm has a three lawyers strong London office, an office in Fürth/Nürnberg, Germany, and an associated office in Bratislava, Slovakia. These, combined with an extensive network of correspondent lawyers, enhance the firm's international advisory, transactional and litigation capabilities.

OF COUNSEL

DR. GUIDO M. RENGGLI, born Zug, Switzerland, April 27, 1931; admitted, 1959, Switzerland (Not admitted in Germany). *Education:* Universities of Fribourg and Barne (Dr.jur., 1955). *LANGUAGES:* German, Swedish, English, French and Italian. *PRACTICE AREAS:* Commercial Law; Corporate Law; International Contract Law; Arbitration.

VIKTOR FOERSTER, born Grassau, Germany, July 15, 1946; admitted, 1979, Germany. *Education:* University of Regensburg (1st Juristisches Staatsexamen, 1974; 2nd Juristisches Staatsexamen, 1976). *Member:* German Bar Association; Rechtsanwaltskammer Nuernberg-Fuerth; Deutsches Institut für Schiedsgerichtswesen; Deutsch-Oesterreichisch-Schweizerisch-Liechtensteinische Anwaltsvereinigung e. V. *LANGUAGES:* German and English. *PRACTICE AREAS:* International Arbitration; Cross-Border Transactions; Computer Contracts; European Community Law; Commercial Contracts; Joint-Ventures; Company Law (Acquisition and Sales); Antitrust and Trade Regulation.

KLAUS JÜRGEN RUTOW, born Cloppenburg, Germany, May 24, 1952; admitted, 1979, Germany. *Education:* Studies of law, economics and journalism at the University of Mainz (1st Juristisches Staatsexamen, 1977; 2nd Juristisches Staatsexamen, 1979). Post Graduate training at the University of Speyer. *Member:* German Bar Association; Rechtsanwaltskammer Nürnberg-Fürth; Deutsch-Deutsche Rechtsanwälte. *LANGUAGES:* German and English. *PRACTICE AREAS:* Antitrust and Trade Regulation; Commercial Contracts; European Community Law; Computer Contracts; Cross-Border Transactions; International Arbitration; Joint-Ventures; Company Law (Acquisition and Sales).

HELM & PARTNER

AM STADTPARK 99
P.O. BOX 210 224
90120 NÜRNBERG, GERMANY
Telephone: 0911/360100
Telex: 06-26373
Telefax: 0911/3601050

General Practice. Commercial, Company, Corporate, Taxation, Banking, Financing, Insurance, Domestic Relations, International, Antitrust, Unfair Competition, Patents and Trademark, Law of the Press and EEC Law.

MEMBERS OF FIRM

RICHARD SCHMIDT, born Nürnberg, Germany, May 17, 1929; admitted, 1958, Bavaria. *Education:* University of Erlangen-Nürnberg (J.D., 1953). *LANGUAGES:* German and English. *PRACTICE AREAS:* Insurance Law; Personal Injury Litigation.

PETER STÜBINGER, born Nürnberg, Germany, December 16, 1938; admitted, 1965, Bavaria. *Education:* Universities of Freiburg, Kiel and Erlangen-Nürnberg, Germany (J.D., 1960). *LANGUAGES:* German and English. *PRACTICE AREAS:* Labour Law; Commercial Law.

DR. ALBERT G. HELM, born Nürnberg, Germany, March 17, 1949; admitted, 1978, Bavaria. *Education:* City of London College (1970); University of Erlangen-Nürnberg, Germany (J.D., 1972; Doctor of Jurisprudence, 1980); University of Miami (M.C.L., 1978). Regierungsrat, German Internal Revenue Service, 1975-1978. *LANGUAGES:* German, English and French. *PRACTICE AREAS:* International Business Law; National and International Commercial Litigation; Debt Collections.

RAINER MUTZBAUER, born Nürnberg, Germany, June 12, 1949; admitted, 1979, Bavaria. *Education:* Erlangen-Nürnberg (J.D., 1975). *LANGUAGES:* German and English. *PRACTICE AREAS:* National and International Family Law.

All Partners and Associates of the Firm are Members of the Nürnberg Bar Association.

DR. KREUZER & COLL.

Anwaltskanzlei

LORENZER PLATZ 3A
90402 NÜRNBERG, GERMANY
Telephone: 0911/209103 (24h-Tel-Service)
Datex-P: 44/9110/40363
Telex: 047753/2633 Krpaa
Telefax: 0911/226781; 0911/2059879

Mailing Address: P.O. Box 26 33, 90012

Dresden, Germany Office: Hüblerstr. 2, 01309. Mailing Address: P.O. Box 53 01 10, 01291. Telephone: 0351/337413. Fax: 0351/337415.

Member of International Jurists EEIG
General Practice, Wills, Unfair Competition, Company, Commercial, Banking, Bankruptcy, Personal Injury, Insurance, Employment, Family, Criminal, Construction, Product Liability, Patent and Trademark Law, Environmental Law.

FIRM PROFILE: Since the firm's establishment in 1976 there has been broad expansion notably with the establishment of our second office in Dresden in 1990. The firm, as a whole, (nine lawyers) is able to offer a comprehensive range of legal services. Individually, each lawyer has his own legal field of specialization.

We have a particularly healthy interest in international matters and were able to formalise this by the formation of "International Jurists" a European Economic Interest Grouping (EEIG).

International co-operation also features heavily in our activities as we feel the need, in order to be able to offer the optimal service to our clients, to keep abreast of issues within the fast moving realm of international law.

MEMBERS OF FIRM

DR. GÜNTHER KREUZER. PRACTICE AREAS: Labor Law; Company and Commercial Law; Intellectual Property; Competition Law; International Relations.

FELIX MÜLLER. PRACTICE AREAS: Social Security Law; Criminal Law; Road and Traffic Law; Landlord and Tenant Law; General Practice.

(This Listing Continued)

ARMIN GOSSLER. PRACTICE AREAS: Labour Law; Service Contracts.

BERND KREUZER. PRACTICE AREAS: Family Law particularly Marriage/Divorce Law; Data-Protection Law; Intellectual Property.

ANITA WILTSCHKA. PRACTICE AREAS: The Law of Succession; Administrative Law; General Practice.

BETTINA MICHELT. PRACTICE AREAS: Labour Law; Company and Commercial Law; Intellectual Property; Competition Law; International Relations.

NEUHOF SCHMIDT LINDE & PARTNER

ÄUβERE SULZBACHER STR. 98
P.O. BOX 250 205
90491 NÜRNBERG, GERMANY
Telephone: 0911/959700
Telefax: 0911/9597050

General Practice, Commercial, Company, Corporate, Banking, Finance, Unfair Competition, Bankruptcy, Insolvency, Insurance, Transport, Construction and Building, Labor, Reprivatization, Restitution Claims, Environmental and Administrative Law, Law of Domestic Affairs, Law of Inheritance.

MEMBERS OF FIRM

DR. RUDOLF NEUHOF, born 1946; admitted, 1975, Germany. *Education:* Universities of Erlangen-Nürnberg, Würzburg and München (Doctor of Jurisprudence, 1975). Member of the Supervisory Board of Bäcker Bank Nürnberg. *LANGUAGES:* German and English. *PRACTICE AREAS:* Commercial Law; Corporate Law; Banking; Bankruptcy; Insolvency.

DIPL. ING. GERHARD SCHMIDT, born 1949; admitted, 1981, Germany. *Education:* Universities of Erlangen-Nürnberg, Nürnberg and Köln. Member of Supervisory Board of Raiffeisenbank Kalchreuth. *LANGUAGES:* German and English. *PRACTICE AREAS:* Commercial Law; Building Law; Construction Law; Engineering Law.

DR. REINHARD URBANCZYK, born 1949; admitted, 1984, Germany. *Education:* University of München (Doctor of Jurisprudence, 1981). Faculty Assistant, University of Erlangen-Nürnberg, 1977-1983. Professor of Jurisprudence, 1994 at the University of Lüneburg (FH). *LANGUAGES:* German and English. *PRACTICE AREAS:* Leasing; Terms and Conditions; Unfair Competition.

BRIGITTE KRAUSS, born 1946; admitted, 1976, Germany. *Education:* University of Erlangen-Nürnberg. Faculty Assistant, University of Erlangen-Nürnberg, 1976-1981. *LANGUAGES:* German, English and Italian. *PRACTICE AREAS:* Transport Law; Insurance Law; Law of Inheritance.

MARIA BARTSCH, born 1959; admitted, 1987, Germany. *Education:* University of Erlangen-Nürnberg. *LANGUAGES:* German and English. *PRACTICE AREAS:* Broker and Rental Law; Road Traffic Law; Law of Domestic Affairs.

OTFRIED MÄCHTEL, born 1938; admitted, 1986, Germany. *Education:* University of Heidelberg. Expert Counsel Member, BDI and DIHT. *LANGUAGES:* German and English. *PRACTICE AREAS:* Terms and Conditions; Commercial Law; Corporate Law.

DETLEF ULLMANN, born 1960; admitted, 1992, Germany. *Education:* University of Erlangen-Nürnberg. Internship, Legal Department, Hewlett-Packard and Office of the District Attorney, Del Norte County, California. *LANGUAGES:* German and English. *PRACTICE AREAS:* Building Law; Construction Law; Labor Law.

MARTIN SARNOWSKI, born 1962; admitted, 1993, Germany. *Education:* Universities of Regensburg and München. *LANGUAGES:* German and English. *PRACTICE AREAS:* Leasing; Commercial Law; Unfair Competition.

MARKUS PENTEK, born 1963; admitted, 1993, Germany. *Education:* University of Konstanz. *LANGUAGES:* English, French and Hungarian. *PRACTICE AREAS:* Restitution Claims; Reprivatization; Administrative Law.

TAX PARTNERS AND CONSULTANTS

VOLKMAR LINDE, born 1943; admitted, 1977, Tax Advisor, Germany. *Education:* University (FH) Nürnberg, Diplom-Betriebswirt. Member of the Supervisory Board of FARE-AG. Prag. *LANGUAGES:* German and English.

(This Listing Continued)

WALTER HARBAUER, born 1958; admitted, 1991, Tax Advisor, Germany. *Education:* University (FH) Herrsching Diplom-Finanzwirt. *LANGUAGES:* German and English.

All Partners and Associates of the Firm are Members of the Nürnberg Bar Association

---

DR. BERND RÖDL & PARTNER

Established in 1973

AUBERE SULZBACHER STRAßE 100
90491 NÜRNBERG, GERMANY
Telephone: 911/91 93-0
Telefax: 91 93-960

Munich, Germany Office: Kanzlei Dr. Rödl & Partner. Arabellastraße 15, 81925 München. Telephone: 89/91 50 96. Telefax: 89/91 46 38.
Bayreuth, Germany Office: Wittelsbacher Ring 3, 95444. Telephone: 9 21/51 13 32. Telefax: 51 13 35.
Hof, Germany Office: August-Mohl-Strasse 13, 95030. Telephone: 92 81/97 78-0. Telefax: 97 78 10.
Plauen (Vogtland), Germany Office: Neundorfer Straße 68, 08523. Telephone: 3 741 23 964. Fax: 3 741 23964.
Chemnitz, Germany Office: Strasse der Nationen 12/IV, 09111. Telephone: 3 71 6634 204. Fax: 3 71 6634 137.
Radebeul, Germany Office: Kanzlei Dr. Rödl & Partner. Kellereistrasse 1, 01445 Radebeul. Telephone: 3 51 75624. Fax: 3 51 77 1001.
Jena, Germany Office: Krautgasse 6, 07743. Telephone: 3 641 53 425. Fax: 3 641 53 423.
Prague, Czech Republic Office: Dr. Rödl spol. s.r.o., Platnérská 4, CSFR-110 00 Prague 1. Telephone: 42/2 2 31 15 13. Fax: 42/2 2 32 70 50.

General Practice, Corporations, Commercial, Unfair Competition, Mergers & Acquisitions, Labor, Employment, Probate, Family Law, Litigation, Arbitration, Antitrust, Tax Law, International Tax, International Arbitration, Computer Law, EC, EC Competition Law, Trademark, Banking, Building and Planning, Licensing, Legal Education, Environmental Law, Joint Ventures, Eastern German Law, Treuhand Matters.

DR. BERND RÖDL, born Karlsbad, Germany, June 25, 1943; admitted, 1973, Germany Tax Advisor (Steuerberater); 1976, C.P.A. (Wirtschaftsprüfer). *Education:* University of Erlangen-Nürnberg (Referendar, 1966; Doctor of Jurisprudence, 1968; Assessor, 1970). Co-Author: "Das neue Recht der GmbH nach dem Bilanzrichtliniengesetz," 1987. Research Assistant, Public and Tax Law, University of Erlangen, 1970-1973. *Member:* Senate for Tax Advisors at the Nürnberg Appellate Court; Board of Examiners for C.P.A.'s with the Bavarian Ministry of Economics and Traffic; Admission Committee for Tax Advisors with the Tax Authorities Nürnberg; Expert of Valuation of Companies Appointed by the Nürnberg Chamber of Commerce. *Member:* Nürnberg Bar Association. *LANGUAGES:* German and English.

DR. NIKOLAUS P. WEBER, born Berlin, Germany, January 13, 1945; admitted, 1974, Germany; 1977, New York, U.S.A. *Education:* Universities of Geneva and Hamburg (Referendar, 1979; Doctor of Jurisprudence, 1973; Assessor, 1974); Georgetown University; New York University (M.C.J., 1975). C.P.A., (Vereidigter Buchprüfer), 1990. Author: "Die Richtlinie im EWG-Vertrag," (The Directive in the EEC-Treaty), 1974. With Law Firm Herzfeld & Rubin, New York, 1975-1977. Head of Legal Departments of Faun AG, 1980-1986 and of Orenstein & Koppel AG, 1986-1987. *Member:* Nürnberg, New York State Bar; American Bar Associations. *LANGUAGES:* German, English and French.

HANNELORE I. PROHASKA, born Mainz, Germany, August 4, 1942; admitted, 1990, Germany. *Education:* Universities of Mainz/Rhein and Frankfurt/Main, Germany (Referendar, 1966; Assessor, 1970). Judge: Amtsgericht and Landgericht, Frankfurt/Main and Essen, Germany, 1971-1981; Oberlandesgericht (Court of Appeals), Düsseldorf, Germany, 1982-1990. With law firm, King & Spaulding, Atlanta, Georgia, U.S.A., 1984. *Member:* Nürnberg Bar Association. *LANGUAGES:* German and English.

MICHAEL WIEHL, born Rottweil, Germany, October 15, 1959; admitted, 1988, Germany. *Education:* University of Freiburg, Germany (Referendar, 1985; Assessor, 1988). With law firm, Herzfeld & Rubin, New York, U.S.A., 1990. *Member:* Nürnberg Bar Association. *LANGUAGES:* German and English.

KAY R. BADENHOOP, born Halle/Saale, Germany, September 16, 1948; admitted, 1984, Germany. *Education:* Universities of Munich and Lausanne (Referendar, 1974; Assessor, 1978). Märker Zementwerk GmbH,

(This Listing Continued)

1978-1982. Syndicus of Diener Steinhaus GmbH & Co. KG, 1983-1984. Syndicus/Head of Legal Department of Schöller Lebensmittel GmbH & Co. KG, 1985-1994. *LANGUAGES:* German.

DR. GÜNTHER NIETHAMMER, born Dresden, Germany, August 12, 1944; admitted, 1973, Germany. *Education:* University of Munich, Germany (Referendar, 1969; Assessor, 1973; Doctor of Jurisprudence, 1973). Author: "Vermogensfragen unter Ehegatten richtig regeln." Law firm Haas, Bacher, Scheuer, Munich, 1973-1977; Tax Syndicus with Baycrische Vereinsbank, Munich, 1977-1980. Vice-president Diehl Group, Nurnber, 1980-1993. *Member:* Nurnberg Bar Association. *LANGUAGES:* German and English.

DR. REINER R. GAY, born Auerbach, Germany, June 3, 1961; admitted, 1989, Germany. *Education:* University of Erlangen-Nürnberg, Germany (Referendar, 1985; Assessor, 1988; Doctor of Jurisprudence, 1989). Author: "Schadensersatzklagen wegen der Verletzung des Rechtes auf die eigene Nichtexistenz" ("Wrongful Life"). Research Assistant, University of Erlangen-Nürnberg, Germany, 1985-1988. *Member:* Nürnberg Bar Association. *LANGUAGES:* German and English.

MARTIN THUENCHER, born Selb, Germany, January 8, 1962; admitted, 1991, Germany. *Education:* University of Bayreuth, Germany (Referendar, 1987; Assessor, 1990). With law firm, Herzfeld & Rubin, New York, U.S.A., 1992. *Member:* Nürnberg Bar Association. *LANGUAGES:* German, English and Italian.

ARIBERT M. PANZER, born Mehlmeisel, Germany, November 23, 1961; admitted, 1992, Germany. *Education:* University of Bayreuth (Referendar, 1989; Assessor, 1992). *Member:* Nürnberg Bar Association. *LANGUAGES:* German, English and French.

DR. STEFAN PÜRNER, born Nürnberg, Germany, December 22, 1960; admitted, 1992, Germany. *Education:* University of Regensburg (Referendar, 1988; Assessor, 1992; Doctor of Jurisprudence, 1991). Author: "The limited liability company as new form of foreign investment in Yugoslavia." With law firm, Boesebeck Barz & Partner, 1992-1993. *Member:* Nürnberg Bar Association. *LANGUAGES:* English, Serbocroatian and Czech.

TAX PARTNERS AND CONSULTANTS

KURT REINHARDT, born Roth, Germany, April 9, 1952; admitted, 1980, Tax Advisor (Steuerberater); 1988, C.P.A. (Wirtschaftsprüfer). *Education:* University of Erlangen-Nürnberg (M.B.A., Dipl.-Kfm., 1978). Member, Board of Examiners for Tax Advisers with the Bavarian Ministry of Finance. (Tax Advisor and Certified Public Accountant). *LANGUAGES:* German and English.

FRANZ SCHREYER, born Nürnberg, Germany, April 8, 1940; admitted, 1973, Tax Advisor (Steuerberater); 1976, C.P.A. (Wirtschaftsprüfer). *Education:* University of Erlangen-Nürnberg (M.B.A., Dipl.-Kfm., 1968). With, Süddeutsche Treuhand-Gesellschaft AG, Wirtschaftsprüfungsgesellschaft-Steuerberatungsgesellschaft, München and its legal successor Wollert-Ellmendorff Deutsche Industrie-Treuhand GmbH, Wirtschaftsprüfungsgesellschaft, Düsseldorf-München, 1969-1988. (Tax Advisor and Certified Public Accountant). *LANGUAGES:* German and English.

HEINRICH HÜBSCHMANN, born Ebermannstadt, Germany, February 12, 1954; admitted, 1983, Tax Advisor; 1989, C.P.A. (Wirtschaftsprüfer). *Education:* University of Erlangen-Nürnberg (M.B.A., Dipl.-Kfm., 1979). (Tax Advisor and Certified Public Accountant). *LANGUAGES:* German and English.

VIERING & JENTSCHURA

Patentanwälte

European Patent Attorneys

Attorneys at Law

ESSENER STRASSE 5
46047 OBERHAUSEN, GERMANY
Telephone: 0208/202627
Fax: 0208/202727

Main Office: Steinsdorfstr. 6, 80538 Munich, Germany. Telephone: 089/293413. Fax: 089/2283920. Telex: 17 898 454 +.

Industrial Property Rights, Patents, Utility Models, Designs, Trademarks, Copyrights, Unfair Competition, Search and Watch, Contracts and Licence Agreements, Litigations and Infringement Cases.

(This Listing Continued)

VIERING & JENTSCHURA, Oberhausen—Continued

FIRM PROFILE: The office disposes of a network of good relations to selected colleagues from all over the world. Such good relations are not only maintained to Western countries (USA, Western Europe), but also to Eastern European countries and to Asia.

RESIDENT PARTNER

MATTHIAS NOBBE, born June 9, 1956; registered to practice before the German Patent Office, 1991 and before the European Patent Office, 1992. Education: Ruhr University (Diploma in Organic Chemistry, 1982; Ph.D., 1986). Member: International Federation of Industrial Property Attorneys (FICPI); German Patent Attorney Bar Association; European Patent Institute (EPI). LANGUAGES: German and English. PRACTICE AREAS: Organic and Biochemistry; Biotechnology and Pharmaceutical Sciences; Industrial Property Rights; European and German Patents and Trademarks.

KNOLLE BRÜCK & KIND

GELEITSSTRASSE 63
63067 OFFENBACH AM MAIN, GERMANY
Telephone: 069/801 37
Telecopier: 069/800 1076

General German and International Practice, EEC, Corporate, Commercial, Estate, Notarial Recording, Mergers and Acquisitions, Trademarks, Unfair Competition, Copyright, Product Liability, Tax, Labor Law, Landlord-Tenant, Reprivatisation of Assets in former GDR, Family, Litigation and Arbitration, Environmental Matters, Administrative and Planning Law.

MEMBERS OF FIRM

DR. ULRICH KNOLLE, born Offenbach am Main, Germany, March 10, 1935; admitted, 1965, Germany. Education: Universities of Frankfurt am Main, Freiburg (Doctor of Law, 1964); Tulane University, School of Law, New Orleans (LL.M., 1960).

MICHAEL BRÜCK, born Kusel, Germany, September 26, 1948; admitted, 1976, Germany. Education: University of Heidelberg. Assistant Lecturer, University of Heidelberg, 1972-1974.

MANFRED KIND, born Frankfurt am Main, Germany, August 25, 1953; admitted, 1982, Germany. Education: University of Frankfurt am Main. Member: Frankfurt Bar Association (Board Member).

OLAF MEISTER, born Frankfurt am Main, Germany, June 5, 1960; admitted, 1988, Germany. Education: University of Frankfurt am Main. Academic Tutor, University of Frankfurt am Main, 1985-1986.

ASSOCIATES

THORSTEN WOLF, born Offenbach am Main, Germany, May 12, 1962; admitted, 1990, Germany. Education: University of Frankfurt am Main (Course, Tax Law, Detmold, 1990).

DR. HANS J. LEONHARDT, born Offenbach am Main, Germany, June 28, 1958; admitted, 1989, Germany. Education: Universities of Frankfurt am Main and Lausanne, Switzerland (Doctor of Law, 1994).

Admitted to all Municipal Courts, the District Court in Darmstadt, including panels for commercial matters in Offenbach am Main and the Higher Regional Court (Oberlandesgericht) in Frankfurt am Main. All Lawyers are Members of the Frankfurt Bar Association. The firm maintains good connections with the municipality, the local chamber of industry and commerce and the relevant economic associations.

Languages: German and English

BEHRENDS & SCHWACKENBERG

Established in 1976

SCHLEUSENSTRASSE 25
26135 OLDENBURG, GERMANY
Telephone: (0) 441-92172-0
Telefax: (0) 441-92172-72

In Co-operation with Bout Advocaten, Herestraat 113, NL-9711 LG Groningen (Netherlands).

Administrative Law, Agriculture Law, Business Law, Commercial Law, Company Law, Unfair Competition, Consumer Law, Corporate Law, Family Law, Insurance, Intellectual Property, Labour and Employment, Leases (Landlord and Tenant), Medical Malpractice, Personal Injury, Probate, Products Liability, Professional Liability, Property, Public Law, Social

(This Listing Continued)

Welfare, Trade Regulation, Traffic Law, General Practice, Notarial Services.

BERND BEHRENDS, born Oldenburg, Germany, July 18, 1937; admitted, 1968, Niedersachsen, Notary Public. Education: Universities of Freiburg, Berlin, Bonn and Cologne. Member: Oldenburg Bar Association; German Bar Association. LANGUAGES: German, English and French. PRACTICE AREAS: Agriculture Law; Unfair Competition; Intellectual Property; Property; Products Liability; Notary Public.

WOLFGANG SCHWACKENBERG, born Neuenhaus, Grafschaft Bentheim, Germany, January 20, 1948; admitted, 1976, Niedersachsen, Notary Public. Education: University of Münster. Member: Oldenburg Bar Association; German Bar Association; International Bar Association. LANGUAGES: German, English and French. PRACTICE AREAS: Business Law; Company Law; Family Law; Probate; Professional Liability; Notary Public.

KLAUS-DIETER BIRKNER, born Leer, Germany, February 21, 1952; admitted, 1979, Niedersachsen. Education: University of Bochum. Member: Oldenburg Bar Association; German Bar Association. LANGUAGES: German and English. PRACTICE AREAS: Insurance; Leases; Landlord and Tenant; Medical Malpractice; Personal Injury; Traffic Law.

HARTMUT LAUSCH, born Oldenburg, Germany, January 30, 1950; admitted, 1981, Niedersachsen. Education: University of Münster. Member: Oldenburg Bar Association; German Bar Association. LANGUAGES: German and English. PRACTICE AREAS: Business Law; Commercial Law; Family Law; Labour and Employment; Trade Regulation.

HERMANN-JOSEF HOLLAH, born Quakenbrück, Germany, February 6, 1954; admitted, 1984, Niedersachsen. Education: University of Münster. Member: Oldenburg Bar Association; German Bar Association. LANGUAGES: German, English, French and Dutch. PRACTICE AREAS: Administrative Law; Consumer Law; Property; Public Law; Social Welfare.

BERND KLÖTZING, born Elmshorn, Germany, August 21, 1957; admitted, 1992, Niedersachsen. Education: Universities of Göttingen and Lausanne (Switzerland). Member: Oldenburg Bar Association; German Bar Association. LANGUAGES: German, English and French. PRACTICE AREAS: Commercial Law; Company Law; Unfair Competition; Corporate Law; Intellectual Property.

FEITSCH • KORTE • DIERKES ET COLL.

PETERSTRASSE 6
D-26121 OLDENBURG, GERMANY
Telephone: (0) 441-9 25 85-0
Telecopier: (0) 441-9 25 85-88

Corporate and Commercial Law, Tax Law and Tax Planning, Mergers and Acquisitions, Successions, Commercial Contracts, Marital Property, Estate Planning, Employment Relations.

MEMBERS OF FIRM

DIPL.-VOLKSW. PETER FEITSCH, born December 12, 1938; admitted, 1971, Germany. Education: University of Marburg. Certified Public Accountant, Tax Advisor and Chartered Expert in Tax Law. Lecturer in Tax Law, University of Oldenburg. Member: German Bar Association; Chamber of Chartered Accountants; Chamber of Tax Advisors. LANGUAGES: German. PRACTICE AREAS: Accounting; Auditing; Finance and Securities; Agreements on Restitution of Property in the former GDR.

OTTO KORTE, born October 4, 1951; admitted, 1985, Germany. Education: University of Göttingen. Tax Advisor and Chartered Expert in Tax Law. Member: German Bar Association; Chamber of Tax Advisors; International Bar Association. LANGUAGES: English and German. PRACTICE AREAS: International Tax Law; Law regarding Fiscal Offences; Trusts and Foundations.

DIPL.-FINANZW. JOSEF DIERKES, born June 8, 1939; admitted, 1988, Germany. Education: Institute for Administration and Judicature (FH), Rinteln. Tax Advisor. Member: Chamber of Tax Advisors; Parliament of Lower Saxony (Committee for Economy, Technology and Transport). LANGUAGES: German and English. PRACTICE AREAS: Income Tax; Transformations; Subsidies and Investment Finance.

(This Listing Continued)

ASSOCIATES

DR. IUR. GERNOT NEUMANN, born October 20, 1939; admitted, 1971, Germany. *Education:* University of Marburg (Dr. iur., 1970). Chartered Expert in Tax Law. *LANGUAGES:* German. *PRACTICE AREAS:* Contracts.

DR. IUR. THOMAS TÜXEN, born October 10, 1957; admitted, 1988, Germany. *Education:* Universities of Munich and Münster (Dr. iur., 1987). *Member:* German Bar Association. *LANGUAGES:* German and English. *PRACTICE AREAS:* Antitrust; Unfair Competition.

ANKE RÖBKE, born June 3, 1965; admitted, 1993, Germany. *Education:* Universities of Trier and Münster. *Member:* German Bar Association. *LANGUAGES:* German and English. *PRACTICE AREAS:* Company Contracts; Share and Asset Sales.

DR. IUR. GERNOT BLANKE, born April 9, 1962; admitted, 1991, Germany. *Education:* Universities of Marburg, Munich and Göttingen (Dr. iur., 1989). Chartered Expert in Tax Law. *Member:* German Bar Association; International Bar Association. *LANGUAGES:* German and English. *PRACTICE AREAS:* Reorganization Law.

HILLMANN LEMKE WILKEN

Established in 1947

GARTENSTRASSE 18
26122 OLDENBURG, GERMANY
Telephone: 0441/950980
Telefax: 0441/9509833
Teletex: 441288 RAHILE

Company, Commercial, Unfair Competition, Labor, Traffic, Building and Architecture, Family and Medical Law, General Practice, Notary Public.

MEMBERS OF FIRM

ERNST HILLMANN, born Oldenburg, Germany, April 21, 1915; admitted, 1947, Germany. Notary Public. *Education:* Universities of Marburg, Rostock and Göttingen. *Member:* Oldenburg Bar Association; German Bar Association. *LANGUAGES:* German and English. *PRACTICE AREAS:* Family Law; Traffic Law; Notary Public.

FRANK R. HILLMANN, III, born Oldenburg, Germany, February 20, 1951; admitted, 1979, Nordrhein-Westfalen. *Education:* University of Münster. Corporate Lawyer, Allgemeiner Deutscher Automobile Club (ADAC). *Member:* Oldenburg Bar Association; German Bar Association. *LANGUAGES:* German and English. *PRACTICE AREAS:* Traffic Law; Medical Law; General Practice; Alcoholic Beverages.

DIRK WILKEN, born Oldenburg, Germany, February 2, 1938; admitted, 1967, Niedersachsen. *Education:* University of Göttingen, Saabrücken and Lausanne (Switzerland). *Member:* Oldenburg Bar Association; German Bar Association. *LANGUAGES:* German, French and English. *PRACTICE AREAS:* Company Law; Contracts; Commercial Law; Insurance Law; Unfair Competition; Notary Public.

THOMAS LEMKE, born Bremen, Germany, September 19, 1948; admitted, 1981, Niedersachsen. *Education:* University of Freiburg and University of Göttingen. Chartered Expert in Labor Law. *Member:* Oldenburg Bar Association; German Bar Association. *LANGUAGES:* German and English. *PRACTICE AREAS:* Labour Law; Commercial Law; Company Law; General Practice.

JAN J. KRAMER, born Weener, Germany, August 18, 1958; admitted, 1988 Schleswig-Holstein. *Education:* University of Kiel. *Member:* Oldenburg Bar Association; German Bar Association. *LANGUAGES:* German and English. *PRACTICE AREAS:* Commercial Law; Company Law; Unfair Competition; Building Law; Architecture Law; Contracts.

ASSOCIATE

GÜNTER MÖHLENKAMP, born Bissendorf, Germany, March 14, 1959; admitted, 1989, Niedersachsen. *Education:* University of Göttingen. *Member:* Oldenburg Bar Association; German Bar Association. *LANGUAGES:* German and English. *PRACTICE AREAS:* Commercial Law; Labour Law; Contracts; Traffic Law; General Practice.

DR. DÄLKEN & HARTMANN

NIEDERSACHSENSTRABE 11 A
D-49074 OSNABRÜCK, GERMANY
Telephone: 0541-35866-0
Telefax: 0541-35866-20

A Member of AdvoSelect EEIG, a network of law firms pooling their resources in special fields and crossborder cases, specializing in business law for middle-sized companies. AdvoSelect is represented in 51 cities throughout Europe.
Corporation, Commercial, Constructions, Administrative and Labour Law.

MEMBERS OF FIRM

JOHANNES DÄLKEN, born Osnabrück, Germany, December 22, 1955; admitted, 1984. *Education:* University of Cologne and Münster (Doctor of Law, 1986). *Member:* Deutscher Anwaltsverein. *LANGUAGES:* German and English. *PRACTICE AREAS:* Company Law; Labour Law; Trade Law; Law of Construction Contracts.

DELIA HARTMANN, born Paderborn, Germany, January 15, 1965; admitted, 1993. *Education:* University of Osnabrück (Doctoral Thesis on a theme concerning Labour Law). *LANGUAGES:* German and English. *PRACTICE AREAS:* Labour Law; Trade Law; Administrative Law.

LADENBURGER, NEIFEIND & SCHMÜCKER

Established in 1948

BAHNHOFSTRASSE 3
75172 PFORZHEIM, GERMANY
Telephone: 07231/38030
Telefax: 07231/380317

General Practice. Advertising, Antitrust, Arbitration, Banking, Bankruptcy, Competition, Construction, Conveyancing, Corporate, Distributorship, Agency and Franchise, EEC, Employer's Liability, Family, Health, Hospital and Malpractice Law. Industrial Relations, Labor, Insurance, International Contracts, International Private, Litigation, Negligence, Personal Injury, Product Liability, Property and Real Estate, Rent and Lease, Trade Regulations, Transportation, Intellectual Property, Copyright, License Negotiation, Patent Litigation, Patent Prosecution Trademark Litigation and General Intellectual Property Practice.
Practice Before the Courts of Karlsruhe.

MEMBERS OF FIRM

DR. CLEMENS LADENBURGER, born Ellwangen, West Germany, May 27, 1938; admitted, 1965, West Germany. *Education:* Universities of Tübingen and Cologne. Member, Municipal Council in Birkenfeld, 1975—. *Member:* Karlsruhe Bar Association; Germany's Association of Lawyers; German Association for the Protection of Industrial Property and Copyright (Deutsche Vereinigun für gewerblichen Rechtschutz und Urheberrecht). *LANGUAGES:* German, English and French. *PRACTICE AREAS:* Company Law; Mergers and Acquisitions.

WOLFGANG NEIFEIND, born Karlsruhe, West Germany, February 7, 1943; admitted, 1971, West Germany. *Education:* Universities of Heidelberg, Bonn and Freiburg. *Member:* Germany's Association of Lawyers. *LANGUAGES:* German. *PRACTICE AREAS:* Banking Law; Real Estate; Law of Succession.

DR. JOCHEN SCHMÜCKER, born Niedernberg, West Germany, January 5, 1945; admitted, 1973, West Germany. *Education:* University of Heidelberg. *Member:* Germany's Association of Lawyers; German Association for the Protection of Industrial Property and Copyright (Deutsche Vereinigung für gewerblichen Rechtschutz un Urheberrecht); Asociación Hispanoalemana de Juristas. *LANGUAGES:* German, English, French and Spanish. *PRACTICE AREAS:* Intellectual Property; Unfair Competition; Company Law.

KARL LUDWIG HOMANN, born Göttingen, West Germany, February 15, 1953; admitted, 1984, West Germany. *Education:* University of Göttingen. Judge in Administrative Court of Oldenburg, 1979-1984, *Member:* Germany's Association of Lawyers. *LANGUAGES:* German and English. *PRACTICE AREAS:* Administrative Law; Environmental Law; Real Estate.

DR. HANS-BERND MAUTE, born Mühlacker, West Germany, May 19, 1957; admitted, 1989, West Germany. *Education:* Universities of Göt-

(This Listing Continued)

LADENBURGER, NEIFEIND & SCHMÜCKER,
Pforzheim—Continued

tingen and St. Louis. *LANGUAGES:* German, English and French. *PRACTICE AREAS:* Labour Law; Family Law; Litigation.

PETER FALK, born Verden/Aller, West Germany, September 1, 1953; admitted, 1985, West Germany. *Education:* University of Heidelberg. *Member:* Germany's Association of Lawyers. *LANGUAGES:* German and English. *PRACTICE AREAS:* Labour Law; Building Disputes; Litigation.

DR. ULRICH MEIER-KRENZ, born Pforzheim, West Germany, November 15, 1955; admitted, 1990, West Germany. *Education:* University of Heidelberg. *Member:* Germany's Association of Lawyers. *LANGUAGES:* German, English and French. *PRACTICE AREAS:* Banking Law; Real Estate; Labour Law; Litigation.

UWE BODAMER, born Birkenfeld, Germany, October 10, 1961; admitted, 1991, Germany. *Education:* University of Freiburg. *LANGUAGES:* German, English and French. *PRACTICE AREAS:* Administrative Law; Litigation.

DR. CHRISTOPH BÜHLER, born Tuttlingen, July 12, 1960; admitted, 1993, Germany. *Education:* Universities of Augsburg and Tübingen. *LANGUAGES:* German, French and English. *PRACTICE AREAS:* Criminal Law; Administrative Law.

FIRM PROFILE: BEITEN BURKHARDT MITTL & WEGENER is a nation-wide and international law firm with 108 lawyers. The firm's head office is in Munich. All the firm's offices provide a comprehensive range of services in the main areas of civil and commercial law.

BERND GERBER, born Plauen, 1949; admitted, 1990, Germany. *Education:* Humboldt University of Berlin (political science diploma, 1976; law degree, 1982); Martin-Luther-University of Halle (Dr. jur., 1989). In-house Counsel in enterprises of textile and metal industry, 1982-1989. *LANGUAGES:* German, English and Russian. *PRACTICE AREAS:* Real Estate; Construction Law; Labour and Employment; Expropriation and Restitution.

PETRA WENDT, born Hildesheim, 1960; admitted, 1991, Germany. *Education:* University of Munich (law degree, 1987). *LANGUAGES:* German, English and French. *PRACTICE AREAS:* Real Estate; Construction Law; Labour and Employment.

ELKE BITTMANN, born Lambrecht, 1962; admitted, 1994, Germany. *Education:* Universities of Mannheim, Munich and Freiburg i. Br. (law degree, 1991). *LANGUAGES:* German, English and French. *PRACTICE AREAS:* Real Estate; Construction Law; Labour and Employment; Probate and Family Law.

(For Complete Biographical Data on all Personnel, see Munich, Germany Professional Biographies)

BEITEN BURKHARDT MITTL & WEGENER

Rechtsanwälte

LINDENSTRASSE 5
D-08523 PLAUEN, GERMANY
Telephone: (03741) 22 35 11; 22 49 62
Telefax: (03741) 22 49 62

Munich, Germany Office: Leopoldstrasse 236, D-80807. Telephone: (089) 35065-00. Telefax: (089) 35065-123.
Berlin, Germany Office: Kurfürstenstrasse 72-74, D-10787 Berlin. Telephone: (0 30) 264 71-0. Telefax: (0 30) 264 71-123.
Frankfurt/Main, Germany Office: Arndtstrasse 28, D-60325 Frankfurt/Main. Telephone: (0 69) 75 60 95-0. Telefax: (0 69) 75 60 95-12.
Nürnberg, Germany Office: Obere Turnstrasse 8, D-90429 Nürnberg. Telephone: (09 11) 2 79 71-0. Telefax: (09 11) 2 79 71-99.
Leipzig, Germany Office: Käthe-Kollwitz-Strasse 54, D-04109 Leipzig. Telephone: (03 41) 4 77 25 97. Telefax: (03 41) 4 77 25 99.
Potsdam, Germany Office: Heinrich-Mann-Allee 105 B, D-14473 Potsdam. Telephone: (0331) 33 43 06. Telefax: (0331) 33 43 29.
Hof, Germany Office: Oberer Torplatz 1, D-95028 Hof. Telephone: (09281) 80 23. Telefax: (09281) 1 65 69.
New York, New York Office: 215 East 73rd Street, New York, NY 10021. Telephone: (212) 570-2141. Telefax: (212) 734-7011.
London, England Office: Swedenborg House, 21 Bloomsbury Way, London, WC1A 2TH. Telephone: (0171) 2 42 44 66. Telefax: (0171) 2 42 44 67.
Moscow, Russia Office: Ul. Alekseja Tolstovo D.30/1, 103001 Moscow. Telephone and Telefax: (095) 202 37 60; 290 05 56.
Prague, Czech Republic Office: Na Bojišti 24, 120 00 Prague 2. Telephone: (2) 24 91 5808. Telefax: (2) 24 91 5804.
Budapest, Hungary Office: József Nádor Tér 9, H-1051 Budapest. Telephone: (1) 2 66 18 10. Telefax: (1) 2 66 18 11.
Hong Kong Office: 605 B, Sixth Floor, Peregrine Tower, Lippo Centre, 89 Queensway. Telephone: (852) 2524 6468. Telefax: (852) 2524 7028.
Beijing, People's Republic of China Office: Unit 10, 29th Floor, Jing Guang Centre, Hu Jia Lou, Chao Yang Qu, 100020. Telephone: (86-1) 501 4569; 501 3388 Ext. 2910. Telefax: (86-1) 501 3034.

Commercial Law, Company Law, M & A, Joint Ventures, Finance, Banking, Leasing, Domestic and International Tax, Antitrust, EC Law, Real Property and Private Construction, Electronic Data Processing (Protection and Licensing), Media, Publishing, Unfair Competition, Trademarks, Copyright, Labour, General and Special Administrative Law Particularly Public Construction and Planning Regulations and Public International Law, Environmental Law, Agricultural Law, Privatization and Restitution (former GDR), Probate, Family and Estate Planning, Insolvency and Sports, Insurance, Automobile Accidents and Injuries.

(This Listing Continued)

BEITEN BURKHARDT MITTL & WEGENER

Rechtsanwälte

HEINRICH-MANN-ALLEE 105B
D-14473 POTSDAM, GERMANY
Telephone: (0331) 33 43 06
Telefax: (0331) 33 43 29

Munich, Germany Office: Leopoldstrasse 236, D-80807. Telephone: (089) 35065-00. Telefax: (089) 35065-123.
Berlin, Germany Office: Kurfürstenstrasse 72-74, D-10787 Berlin. Telephone: (0 30) 264 71-0. Telefax: (0 30) 264 71-123.
Frankfurt/Main, Germany Office: Arndtstrasse 28, D-60325 Frankfurt/Main. Telephone: (0 69) 75 60 95-0. Telefax: (0 69) 75 60 95-12.
Nürnberg, Germany Office: Obere Turnstrasse 8, D-90429 Nürnberg. Telephone: (09 11) 2 79 71-0. Telefax: (09 11) 2 79 71-99.
Leipzig, Germany Office: Käthe-Kollwitz-Strasse 54, D-04109 Leipzig. Telephone: (03 41) 4 77 25 97. Telefax: (03 41) 4 77 25 99.
Hof, Germany Office: Oberer Torplatz 1, D-95028 Hof. Telephone: (09281) 80 23. Telefax: (09281) 1 65 69.
Plauen, Germany Office: Lindenstrasse 5, D-08523 Plauen. Telephone: (03741) 22 35 11; 22 49 62. Telefax: (03741) 22 49 62.
New York, New York Office: 215 East 73rd Street, New York, NY 10021. Telephone: (212) 570-2141. Telefax: (212) 734-7011.
London, England Office: Swedenborg House, 21 Bloomsbury Way, London, WC1A 2TH. Telephone: (0171) 2 42 44 66. Telefax: (0171) 2 42 44 67.
Moscow, Russia Office: Ul. Alekseja Tolstovo D.30/1, 103001 Moscow. Telephone and Telefax: (095) 202 37 60; 290 05 56.
Prague, Czech Republic Office: Na Bojišti 24, 120 00 Prague 2. Telephone: (2) 24 91 5808. Telefax: (2) 24 91 5804.
Budapest, Hungary Office: József Nádor Tér 9, H-1051 Budapest. Telephone: (1) 2 66 18 10. Telefax: (1) 2 66 18 11.
Hong Kong Office: 605 B, Sixth Floor, Peregrine Tower, Lippo Centre, 89 Queensway. Telephone: (852) 2524 6468. Telefax: (852) 2524 7028.
Beijing, People's Republic of China Office: Unit 10, 29th Floor, Jing Guang Centre, Hu Jia Lou, Chao Yang Qu, 100020. Telephone: (86-1) 501 4569; 501 3388 Ext. 2910. Telefax: (86-1) 501 3034.

Commercial Law, Company Law, M & A, Joint Ventures, Finance, Banking, Leasing, Domestic and International Tax, Antitrust, EC Law, Real Property and Private Construction, Electronic Data Processing (Protection and Licensing), Media, Publishing, Unfair Competition, Trademarks, Copyright, Labour, General and Special Administrative Law Particularly Public Construction and Planning Regulations and Public International Law, Environmental Law, Agricultural Law, Privatization and Restitution (former GDR), Probate, Family and Estate Planning, Insolvency and Sports, Insurance, Automobile Accidents and Injuries.

(This Listing Continued)

FIRM PROFILE: *BEITEN BURKHARDT MITTL & WEGENER is a nation-wide and international law firm with 108 lawyers. The firm's head office is in Munich. All the firm's offices provide a comprehensive range of services in the main areas of civil and commercial law.*

FRANK R. WALTER, born Berlin, 1961; admitted, 1992, Germany. *Education:* University of Berlin (law degree, 1989). *LANGUAGES:* German. *PRACTICE AREAS:* Financial Services; Insurance; Automobile Accidents and Injuries.

TILL NEUMANN, born Munich, 1955; admitted, 1988, Germany. *Education:* Industriekaufmann (diploma in business and commerce, 1977); University of Munich (law degree, 1984; Dr.jur., 1993). Staff Member, Max-Planck-Institute for Foreign and International Patent, Copyright and Competition Law, 1990-1992. Author: "Copyright and Educational Use," 1994. *Member:* German Association for the Protection of Industrial Property and Copyright (GRUR); Association Littéraire et Artistique Internationale (ALAI). *LANGUAGES:* German, English and French. *PRACTICE AREAS:* Media and Entertainment; Video and Television; Press Law; Publishing and Radio; Unfair Competition; Copyrights; Advertising and Marketing.

CARLOS CLAUSSEN & PARTNER

Established in 1980

BENKERTSTRAßE 13

14467 POTSDAM, GERMANY

Telephone: 0049-331-28 46 90

Fax: 0049-331-280 48 31

Hamburg, Germany Office: Mönckebergstraße 31, 20095 Hamburg. Telephone: 0049-40-30 96 40-0. Fax: 0049-40-30 96 40-99.
Berlin, Germany Office: Josef-Orlopp-Strasse 89-91, 10365 Berlin. Telephone: 0049 172 309 03 10. Fax: 0049 30 558 81 16.

Commercial, Corporation, Common Market, Unfair Competition, Admiralty, Insurance, Trademark, Copyright, International Private Law, Litigation and Arbitration, Banking Law, Probate, East-European Law, Property Law (Restitution of Property Rights), Labour Law.

FIRM PROFILE: *The firm was established in 1980 in Hamburg, Germany and has now offices as well in Potsdam, Germany as in Berlin, Germany. It offers a full range of legal services and is a member of the EULEX-IPG Group, Europe with their professional service. The client base is European and North American in scope.*

(For Complete Biographical Data on all Personnel, see Professional Biographies at Hamburg, Germany)

ANWALTSKANZLEI PROFESSOR ENDERLEIN

ROSA-LUXEMBURG-STRASSE 37 A

D-14482 POTSDAM (BABELSBERG), GERMANY

Telephone: (49-331) 705400; 7482026

Telefax: (49-331) 7482028

International Private Law, International Commercial Law, International Trade Law, Company Law and Joint Venture, Litigation and Arbitration, Restitution of Property, Real Estate.

FRITZ ENDERLEIN, born Einsiedel, Germany, 1929; admitted, 1990, Germany. *Education:* University Leipzig; Humboldt University, Berlin (Dr. jur., 1960); Economic University, Berlin (Dr. sc. oec., 1967). Professor, International Trade Law, Institute for Foreign and Comparative Law, 1967. Editor, Manuel on Foreign Trade Contracts, Vol. 1-4. Co-Author: "Commentary UN Sales Law." Former Vice President, International Institute for the Unification of Private Law, Rome. Former Senior Legal Officer, United Nations, Office of Legal Affairs, New York and Vienna. Arbitrator, International Arbitral Centre, Federal Economic Chamber, Vienna. *Member:* International Bar Association; International Law Association; German-American Lawyers Association; German-British Lawyers Association; German-Israel Lawyers Association. *LANGUAGES:* German and English.

HORLITZ, VON MENGES u. PARTNER

BEHLERTSTRASSE 27A

D-14469 POTSDAM, GERMANY

Telephone: 0049-331-27 15 30

Telefax: 0049-331-271 53 39

Essen, Germany Office: Rüttenscheider Platz 4 (Am Markt), D-45130. Telephone: 0049-201-77 70 44. Telefax: 0049-201-77 08 68.

General and International Practice, Bankruptcy, Business Law, Commercial, Contracts, Construction, Corporate, Environmental, Mergers and Acquisitions, Privatization and Restitution Claims, Real Estate, Taxation, Litigation.

MEMBERS OF FIRM

DR. JOHANN PETER HEBEL, born Kaufbeuren, June 19, 1964; admitted, 1991, Potsdam. *Education:* University of Augsburg (Dr. jur., 1992). *Member:* Electoral Committee for Judges for the State of Brandenburg since 1993; Potsdam and German Lawyer's Associations. *LANGUAGES:* German and English. *PRACTICE AREAS:* Bankruptcy; Construction; Corporate; Environmental; Mergers and Acquisitions; Privatization and Restitution Claims; Real Estate; Taxation.

HEIKE ENGELMANN, born Gehrden, May 25, 1965; admitted, 1995, Potsdam. *Education:* University of Hanover. Research Assistant, University of Hanover, 1987-1993. Treuhandanstalt, Berlin, 1993-1995. *LANGUAGES:* German. *PRACTICE AREAS:* General Practice; Commercial; Business Law; Contracts.

Languages: German, English and French

(For Biographical Data on other Personnel, see Biographies at Essen, Germany)

DR. KNAUTHE & PARTNER

Rechtsanwälte

Established in 1969

EISENHART STR. 2

14469 POTSDAM, GERMANY

Telephone: 0331-2803590

Telefax: 0331-2803592

Berlin (Head), Germany Office: Kurfürstendamm 44, 10719 Berlin. Telephone: 030-880008-0. Telefax: 030-880008-65. Telex: 185803 KNAPA D.
Other Berlin Office: Clara-Zetkin-Strasse 80, 10117 Berlin. Telephone: 030-22086-0. Telefax: 030-2292026.
Dresden, Germany Office: Ostra-Allee 25, 01067 Dresden. Telephone: 0351-4860165. Telefax: 0351-4860166.

Corporation, Building and Planning, Real Estate and Zoning, Construction, Mergers and Acquisitions, Joint Ventures, Common Market, Investment, Banking, Company, Commercial, Insurance, Trademark and Copyright, Labor, Family, Housing, Estates, Wills, Trusts, Restitution, Communist Expropriation, Investment in East Germany and Eastern Europe, Litigation, Notaries.

MEMBER OF FIRM

DR. THOMAS JÜRGENS, born Bruckmühl, June 5, 1955; admitted, 1988, Berlin. *Education:* Free University of Berlin (Dr.jur., 1987). Author: "Women's Rights - Their International Protection," 1986; "Diplomatic Protection for Stateless Persons," Doctoral Thesis, 1987; "Legal Foundations of the Development, Structure and Competence of the World Bank," 1988; "World Bank and International Monetary Fund - Basic Documents," 1988. *Member:* Brandenburg Bar Association; German Chapter United Nations Association. *LANGUAGES:* German and English. *PRACTICE AREAS:* Mergers and Acquisitions; Investment in East Germany and Eastern Europe; Resorts and Leisure.

ASSOCIATES

CHRISTIAN BEHRENDT, born Berlin, June 26, 1964; admitted, 1994, Potsdam. *Education:* Free University of Berlin. *Member:* Brandenburg Bar Association. *LANGUAGES:* German and English. *PRACTICE AREAS:* Administrative Law; Zoning, Planning and Land Use; Construction Law.

(For Biographical Data at Berlin (Head), Germany Office, Other Berlin Office and Dresden Office, see Professional Biographies at Berlin and Dresden, Germany)

SPITZWEG & PARTNER

GROßE WEINMEISTERSTR. 32
14469 POTSDAM, GERMANY
Telephone: (011-49) 24639; (011-49) 161-2321996
Telefax: (011-49) 24639

Munich, Germany Main Office: Gustav-Heinemann-Ring 212, 81739.
Telephone: 089-6780060. Telefax: 089-67800610.

European Community Law, International Banking, Company and Trade Law, Tax Law, Environmental Law, Competition Law, Mergers and Acquisitions, Construction Law, International Labor Law, Arbitration Law, Product Liability Law, Civil Litigation, Italian Law.

FIRM PROFILE: *The office at Potsdam particularly deals with investment problems and unresolved problems of asset allocation in the former GDR.*

RESIDENT MEMBERS

DR. ANDREAS HEITMANN, born Bremen, Germany, October 13, 1958; admitted, 1988, Germany. *Education:* University of Göttingen (Dr.iur., 1989). Lecturer in Civil Law, Göttingen, 1984. Author: "Structural Crisis Cartel - A Workable Instrument for the Managing of a Crisis," Göttingen, 1989. Co-Author: "Handbook for Environmental Protection: Marketing with Ecology and Environmental Protection," Köln, 1990. Federal Cartel Authority at Berlin, 1985. *LANGUAGES:* German, English, French. *PRACTICE AREAS:* Industrial Property Law; Investment Law.

PHILIPP SCHWOERER, born Waiblingen, Germany, October 12, 1962; admitted, 1993, Germany. *Education:* University of Freiburg (Law Degree, 1992). *LANGUAGES:* German, English and French.

(For Biographical Data on all Members, see Professional Biographies at Munich/Germany)

WOLLMANN & PARTNER

Established in 1920

DORTUSTRAßE 73
14467 POTSDAM, GERMANY
Telephone: 0049 331 27 19 70
Fax: 0049 331 27 19 755

Berlin, Germany Office: Kurfürstendamm 237, 10719. Telephone: 0049 884 10 90. Fax: 0049 884 10 930/39.
Brandenburg, Germany Office: Neustädtische Wassertorstraße 13, 14776. Telephone: 0049 3381 52 770. Fax: 0049 3381 52 7777.

General Practice, Commercial, Corporate, Real Estate, Building and Planning, Construction, Mergers and Acquisitions, Joint Ventures, Investment, Insurance, Labor, Family, Housing, Estates, Restitution, Investment in East Germany and Eastern Europe, Trademark and Copyright, Unfair Competition, Litigation, Notary.

MICHAEL KIRCHHOFF, born Berlin, January 8, 1961; admitted, 1994, Potsdam. *Education:* Free University of Berlin. *LANGUAGES:* German and English. *PRACTICE AREAS:* Commercial Law; Tax Law; Corporate Law; Successions; Real Estate; Restitution Claims.

MEISKI & DÖRPER

BLUMENSTRASSE 41
D-42853 REMSCHEID, GERMANY
Telephone: (02191) 40028
Telefax: (02191) 28046

A Member of AdvoSelect EEIG, a network of law firms pooling their resources in special fields and crossborder cases, specializing in business law for middle-sized companies. AdvoSelect is represented in 51 cities throughout Europe.
Tax Law, Tax-offense Cases, Labour Law, Family Law, Banking Law, Law concerning Building, Litigation.

MEMBERS OF FIRM

BERNHARD B. MEISKI, born Remscheid, October 7, 1957; admitted, 1989, Wuppertal, Bar Approved Specialist in Tax Law (Fachanwalt für Steuerrecht). *Education:* University of Cologne. *Member:* Wirtschaftsvereinigung Remscheid. *LANGUAGES:* German and English. *PRACTICE AREAS:* Tax Law; Tax-offense Cases; Law Concerning Building; Civil Law; Commercial and Company Law.

(This Listing Continued)

FRANK DÖRPER, born Remscheid, May 23, 1957; admitted, 1989, Wuppertal. *Education:* University of Cologne. *Member:* Wirtschaftsvereinigung Remscheid. *LANGUAGES:* German and English. *PRACTICE AREAS:* Labour Law; Family Law; Marriage Contracts; Civil Law; Law of Tenancy.

HANS-OTTO HAGEMEISTER, born Wuppertal, June 25, 1952; admitted, 1993, Wuppertal. *Education:* University of Cologne. Author: "Leistungsverweigerungsrechte des ersten Nehmers gegenüber Wechsel-und Scheckforderungen," ZIP 1983, 1427; "Zur rechtlichen Einordnung der eurocheque-Karte der Deutschen Bundespost," Wertpapiermitteilungen 1984, 1625; "Grundfälle zu Bankgeschäften mit Minderjährigen," JuS 1992, 724 and 839. Research Assistant, Institute for Banking Law, University of Cologne. Teacher at the Bankakademie, Federal Banking Supervisory Board. *Member:* German-German Lawyers Association. *LANGUAGES:* German, English, Spanish and French. *PRACTICE AREAS:* Banking Law; Commercial and Company Law; Restitutions Proceedings (former GDR).

RECHTSANWÄLTE DR. KROLL & PARTNER

Established in 1953

EBERHARDSTR.1
D-72674 REUTLINGEN, GERMANY
Telephone: 07121/324-0
Fax: 07121/324-10

Stuttgart, Germany Office: Vaihinger Straße 24, 70567. Telephone: (07 11) 161770. Telefax: (07 11) 71 00 34.
Balingen, Germany Office: Friedrichstr.57, D-72336. Telephone: (07433) 90160. Fax: (07433) 901632.

All fields of law, except Maritime Law.

FIRM PROFILE: *The firm was established in 1953 and offers a full range of legal services and tax-advising, with offices in Reutlingen, Stuttgart and Balingen. In 1990 association with attorneys' offices Villingen-Schwenningen (Black Forest), Schmalkalden (Thuringia) and Saverne (France) under the name of C.A.P. EWIV Cooperation Anwaltspartner, legal domicile Stuttgart.*

The Reutlingen office consists of 10 attorneys and a staff of 20 employees.

MEMBERS OF FIRM

DR. HARRO KROLL (1925-1993).

ABELE HARTWIG, born Esslingen/Neckar, Germany, 1933; admitted, 1962, Germany. *Education:* Universities of Tübingen and Heidelberg. *Member:* C.A.P.- EWIV Cooperation Anwaltspartner (European Economic Interest Grouping); Chamber of Lawyers, Tübingen (Board Vice-President). *LANGUAGES:* German, English and French. *PRACTICE AREAS:* Civil Law; Construction Law; Property.

JOHANN FRÄNKEL, born Kiel, Germany, 1933; admitted, 1966, Germany. *Education:* University of Kiel. *Member:* German Lawyers Association; C.A.P.- EWIV Cooperation Anwaltspartner (European Economic Interest Grouping). *LANGUAGES:* German, English, French and Italian. *PRACTICE AREAS:* Criminal Law; Insurance; Transportation; Family Law.

HANS-GEORG FRHR. VON GÜLTLINGEN, born Freiburg, Germany, 1934; admitted, 1967, Germany. *Education:* University of Freiburg. *Member:* C.A.P.- EWIV Cooperation Anwaltspartner (European Economic Interest Grouping); Examining Board of Baden-Württemberg; Von Gültlingen Forest Foundation Altensteig/Black Forest (Chief Manager); German Lawyers Association. *LANGUAGES:* German and English. *PRACTICE AREAS:* Administrative Law.

WOLFGANG HARM, born Stuttgart, Germany, 1941; admitted, 1969, Germany. *Education:* Universities of Tübingen, Munich and Berlin. *Member:* German Lawyers Association; C.A.P.- EWIV Cooperation Anwaltspartner (European Economic Interest Grouping). *LANGUAGES:* German, English and French. *PRACTICE AREAS:* Agency and Distributorships; Antitrust and Trade Regulation; Intellectual Property; International Law; Labor and Employment; Trademarks.

BERNHARD KUNATH (Also at Stuttgart Office).

FRIEDRICH REISSER, born Geislingen, Germany, 1958; admitted, 1984, Germany. *Education:* University of Tübingen. *Member:* German Lawyers Association; C.A.P.- EWIV Cooperation Anwaltspartner (Euro-

(This Listing Continued)

pean Economic Interest Grouping). *LANGUAGES:* German, English and French. *PRACTICE AREAS:* Business Law; Commercial Law; Corporate Law; Banks and Banking.

JOCHEN KROLL, born Reutlingen, Germany, 1958; admitted, 1989, Germany. *Education:* Universities of Tübingen and Freiburg. *Member:* German Lawyers Association. *LANGUAGES:* German, English and French. *PRACTICE AREAS:* Business Law; Civil Law; Criminal Law.

DR. MATTHIAS KLEIN, born Karlsruhe, Germany, 1959; admitted, 1991, Germany. *Education:* University of Tübingen (Doctor of Jurisprudence, 1992). *LANGUAGES:* German and English. *PRACTICE AREAS:* Environmental Law; Government; Personal Injury; Property; Zoning.

DR. KARL FRICK, born Fleischwangen, Germany, 1959; admitted, 1993, Germany. *Education:* University of Tübingen; University of Lausanne (Switzerland). *LANGUAGES:* German, English and French. *PRACTICE AREAS:* Antitrust and Trade Regulation; Business Law; Company Law; European Community Law; Taxation.

VOLKER BETTIN, born Arnstadt, Germany, 1964; admitted, 1993, Germany. *Education:* University of Jena. *LANGUAGES:* German, English and Russian. *PRACTICE AREAS:* Immigration and Naturalization; Natural Resources; Public Law; Transportation (Roads); Planning and Land Use.

HARALD KREITLEIN, born Crailsheim, 1964; admitted, 1994, Germany. *Education:* Universities of Konstanz and Tübingen. *LANGUAGES:* German and English. *PRACTICE AREAS:* Company Law; Business Law; Labour and Employment; Social Law.

CYRUS, MAKOWSKI & PARTNER

GROSSE WASSERSTRASSE 2/3
18055 ROSTOCK, GERMANY
Telephone: 0381/499 60 60
Telefax: 0381/499 63 51

Hamburg, Germany Office: Ost-West-Straße 61, 20457. Telephone: 040/36 33 43. Telefax: 040/374 37 91. Telex: 21 321 699 HS D.
Berlin, Germany Office: Auguste-Viktoria-Allee 2, 13403. Telephone: 030/412 30 56. Telefax: 030/413 72 30.

Member of CYRUS ROSS INTERNATIONAL (E.E.I.G.) Association of Law Firms: Alphen (NL), Athens, Berlin, Brussels, Copenhagen, Dublin, Hamburg, Limassol, London, Madrid, Nicosia, Oslo, Padua, Paris, Rostock, Sion, Vienna.

RESIDENT PARTNERS

ANDREA GROSSMANN-KOCH, born 1953; admitted, 1988, Lübeck. *Education:* Universities Augsburg and Hamburg. *Member:* German Bar Association. *PRACTICE AREAS:* Company Law; Construction Law; Bankruptcy Law; German Democratic Republic Law; Restitution Law.

UWE BÖHRENSEN, born 1955; admitted, 1988, Lübeck. *Education:* University of Kiel. *Member:* German-Nordic Lawyers' Association. *PRACTICE AREAS:* Construction Law; Labour Law; Tenancy and Hire Law; Condominium Law; German Democratic Republic Law; Restitution Law.

Languages: German and English

(For Complete Biographical Data on all Personnel, see Professional Biographies at Hamburg, Germany)

HOFFMANN-FÖLKERSAMB JOHANSSON & PARTNER

KRÖPELINER STRASSE 19
18055 ROSTOCK, GERMANY
Telephone: +49-381-4923821
Fax: +49-381-45 26 07

Kiel, Germany Office: Ziegelteich 29, 24103 Kiel. Telephone: +49-431-97 40 30. Fax: +49-431-97 40 320.
Copenhagen, Denmark Office: Vagtelvej 58, 2000 Frederiksberg C. Telephone: +45-38 88 44 04. Fax: +45-38 88 20 16.

Commercial, Company, Corporate, Mergers and Acquisitions, International Sales, European Community Law, Real Estate, Taxation, Construction, Agricultural, Administrative, Labour and Employment, Maritime, Arbitration, Advertising and Marketing, Trademarks.

(This Listing Continued)

RESIDENT MEMBER OF FIRM

DR. DORIS GEIERSBERGER, born Munich, Germany, February 2, 1956; admitted, 1985, Germany. *Education:* Universities of Munich and Geneva (Dr. jur., 1988). Stagiaire at the German-Colombian Chamber of Industry and Commerce, Bogotá, 1981. Judge, Amtsgericht Starnberg, Amtsgericht Weilheim, 1983-1985. Author: "Die Diskriminierung der Frau im Arbeitsleben," Munich, 1988. *Member:* German Bar Association. *LANGUAGES:* German, English, French and Spanish. *PRACTICE AREAS:* Labour Law; Real Estate Law; Press and Publishing Law; Litigation; Construction Law; Investment in East Germany.

INGO GLAS, born Husum, Germany, July 22, 1960; admitted, 1989, Germany. *Education:* Universities of Bayreuth and Kiel. *Member:* German Bar Association. *LANGUAGES:* German. *PRACTICE AREAS:* Company; Taxation; Agricultural.

Languages: German, English, French, Spanish, Swedish, Danish, Norwegian and Finnish

KRAFT RASCH & PARTNER

SAARPLATZ
18057 ROSTOCK, GERMANY
Telephone: (0381) 45 93 422
Telefax: (0381) 45 93 422

Bremen, Germany Office: Kurfürstenallee 4, 28211 Bremen 1. Telephone: (0421) 32 52 25; 3 49 12 36. Telefax: (0421) 3 49 12 38.

General Practice, Litigation, Commercial, Corporate, Tax, Acquisitions, Mergers and Entertainment Law, Unfair Competition, Insurance, Arbitration, Transportation, Advertising, Real Estate, EEC and International Law, Industrial and Intellectual Property Rights.

(For Complete Biographical Data on all Personnel, see Professional Biographies at Bremen, Germany)

LEBUHN & PUCHTA

THOMAS-MANN-STRASSE 25
ROSTOCK D-18055, GERMANY
Telephone: 0381 45 40 09
Telefax: 0381 45 54 68

Hamburg, Germany Office: Vorsetzen 35, D-20459. Telephone: 40-37 477 80. Telefax: 40-37 29 48.

Admiralty and Maritime, Commercial, Corporate, Mergers and Acquisition, Real Estate, Bankruptcy, Transport, Insurance, Labor Law, Unfair Competition, Arbitration, Litigation.

RESIDENT PARTNER

VOLKER BEECKEN, born Hamburg, Germany, May 30, 1959; admitted, 1990, Hamburg; 1992, Rostock. *LANGUAGES:* German, English and Spanish.

All other Members of the Firm are Members of the Hamburg Bar Association.

(For Complete Biographical Data on all Personnel, see Professional Biographies at Hamburg, Germany)

DR. SCHACKOW & PARTNER

Established in 1991

STRANDSTRASSE 25
18055 ROSTOCK, GERMANY
Telephone: (0381) 49 23440; 49 23750
Telecopier: (0381) 49 23262
Telex: 398145 dresr d

Bremen, Germany Office: Domshof 17, 28195 Bremen 1. Telephone: (0421) 36990. Telecopier: (0421) 3699144. Telex: 174 212 248; 244412 dres d. Teletex: 4212248. Cable Address: "Doctores"

Maritime, Company, Tax, Commercial, Transport, Bank, Bankruptcy and Labor Law, Real Estate and General Practice.

(This Listing Continued)

DR. SCHACKOW & PARTNER, Rostock—Continued

RESIDENT PARTNERS

HUBERT JOCKSCH-BROERMANN, born Paderborn, Germany, January 7, 1955. *Education:* Universities of Bielefeld and Göttingen. *Member:* Mecklenburg-Vorpommern Bar Association. *LANGUAGES:* German and English. *PRACTICE AREAS:* Company Law; Tax Law; Commercial Law; Bank Law; Real Estate; Bankruptcy; General Practice.

DR. SUSANNA HOENISCH, born Parchim, Germany, May 5, 1963. *Education:* Universities of Leipzig and Rostock (Dr. jur.). *Member:* Mecklenburg-Vorpommern Bar Association. *LANGUAGES:* German, English and French. *PRACTICE AREAS:* Maritime Law; Commercial Law; Transport Law; Labor Law.

(For Complete Biographical Data on all Personnel, see Professional Biographies at Bremen, Germany)

SCHULZ NOACK BÄRWINKEL

Established in 1959

ALTER MARKT 15
18055 ROSTOCK, GERMANY
Telephone: 0381/454860
Fax: 0381/4548614

Hamburg, Germany Office: Mönckebergstrasse 7. Telephone: 040/32 55 72-0. Fax: 040/326302.

Shanghai, China Office: Apartment 1106, Galaxy Hotel, 888 Zhongshan Xi Lu 200051. Telephone and Fax: 8621/2196829.

Business Consultants, Commercial, Competition, Labour, Insurance, Banking, International Law.

MEMBERS OF FIRM

PETER SCHULZ, born Rostock, April 25, 1930; admitted, 1959, Hamburg; 1992, Rostock. *Education:* Hamburg University. Author: "Der Einfluss der Amerikanischen und Französischen Revolution auf die deutschen Verfassungen," Hoffmann & Campe, 1989; "Parlamentsrecht der deutschen Stadtstaaten," De Gruyter, 1989. Minister of Justice, Hamburg, 1966-1970. Minister of Education, Hamburg, 1970-1971. Governor of the State of Hamburg, 1971-1974. Chairman, Hamburg State Assembly, 1978-1986. *Member:* German-Chinese Law Association; International Bar Association. *LANGUAGES:* German and English. *PRACTICE AREAS:* Corporations; Commercial Law; Labor Law; Media Law; Eastern-European Relations.

DR. ROLAND NOACK, born Hannover, June 13, 1936; admitted, 1964, Hamburg. *Education:* Cologne and Hamburg Universities. Author: "Tatverlauf und Vorsatz," 1964. *Member:* German-Norwegian Chamber of Commerce. *LANGUAGES:* German and Norwegian. *PRACTICE AREAS:* Commercial Law; Insurance Law; Tort.

DR. RICHARD BÄRWINKEL, born Kassel, July 18, 1939; admitted, 1969, Hamburg. *Education:* Marburg, Göttingen Universities. Author: "Zur Struktur der Garantieverhältnisse bei den unechten Unterlassungsdelikten," 1968. Lecturer on Law, University of Hamburg, 1964-1966. *Member:* Hamburg Bar Association. *LANGUAGES:* German and English. *PRACTICE AREAS:* Commercial Law; Corporations; Banking.

AXEL NEELMEIER, born Bremen, November 28, 1951; admitted, 1981, Hamburg. *Education:* Hamburg University. *Member:* Hamburg Bar Association; German-American Lawyers Association; German Chinese Law Association; German Society for the Protection of Industrial Property and Copyright Law. *LANGUAGES:* German and English. *PRACTICE AREAS:* Commercial; Competition; International Law; Intellectual Property.

DR. OLAF SCHULZ-GARDYAN, LL.M., born Hamburg, June 17, 1961; admitted, 1992, Hamburg. *Education:* University of Münster; University of Cambridge (LL.M., 1988). Traineeship, EEC-Commission, 1990. Author: "Die sogenannte Aktionärsklage," Duncker & Humblot, 1991. *Member:* Hamburg Bar Association; International Bar Association. *LANGUAGES:* German, English and French. *PRACTICE AREAS:* Commercial Law; Corporations; International Law; EEC Law.

NORBERT WENDT, born Kühlungsborn, January 5, 1953; admitted, 1990, Rostock. *Education:* Humboldt-Universität zu Berlin (Dipl. Jur., 1988). *LANGUAGES:* German, English and Russian. *PRACTICE AREAS:* Unification Law; Real Estate.

(This Listing Continued)

ASSOCIATES

DOROTHEA BÄRWINKEL, born Berlin, November 26, 1938; admitted, 1971, Hamburg. *Education:* Göttingen University, Free University of Berlin. *LANGUAGES:* German and English. *PRACTICE AREAS:* Banking; Tort; Real Estate.

THOMAS SCHIKORRA, born Lübeck, December 30, 1962; admitted, 1992, Hamburg. *Education:* University of Regensburg. *LANGUAGES:* German and English. *PRACTICE AREAS:* Commercial Law; Corporations; Banking.

ANKE STÜWE, born Hamburg, October 10, 1963; admitted, 1992, Hamburg. *Education:* University of Hamburg. Traineeship: Law firm, New York, 1991. *LANGUAGES:* German and English. *PRACTICE AREAS:* Civil Law; Commercial Law.

DR. DETLEV GEERDS, born Kiel, August 14, 1964; admitted, 1993, Rostock. *Education:* Universities of Kiel and Bayreuth. Author: "Wirtschaftsstrafrecht und Vermögensschutz," 1990. *Member:* Rostock Bar Association. *LANGUAGES:* German and English. *PRACTICE AREAS:* Tax Law; Unification Law.

DIETRICH DEHNEN, born Duisburg, March 23, 1963; admitted, 1993, Hamburg. *Education:* University of Hamburg. Practice in accounting firm. *LANGUAGES:* German and English. *PRACTICE AREAS:* Corporate; Labour; General Contract Law.

DR. DETLEF GOTTSCHALCK, born Hamburg, August 27, 1963; admitted, 1994, Hamburg. *Education:* University of Hamburg. Author: "Die Hamburgische Bürgerschaft" (The City-State Parliament), Duncker & Humblot, Berlin 1993. Member of the staff of the State Parliament of Mecklenburg-Vorpommern, 1991-1993. Lectures at the University of Rostock, 1993. *LANGUAGES:* German and English. *PRACTICE AREAS:* Constitutional Law; Administration Law; Tort Law.

CORD IMELMANN, born July 17, 1962; admitted, 1995, Rostock. *Education:* Hamburg University. *LANGUAGES:* German and English. *PRACTICE AREAS:* Corporate; Commercial; Litigation.

CHEN JUN, born Nanjing, October 10, 1966; (Not admitted in Germany). *Education:* Nanjing University; Göttingen University; Hamburg University. *LANGUAGES:* Chinese, German and English. *PRACTICE AREAS:* Chinese Relations.

WESTPHAL & VOGES

LANGE STRASSE 1 A
18055 ROSTOCK, GERMANY
Telephone: 0381/4 58 20 70
Telefax: 0381/4 58 20 71

Berlin Office: Kurfürstendamm 46, 10701. Telephone: 030/883 40 04/05. Telefax: 030/882 57 26.

Hamburg Office: Esplanade 41. Telephone: 040-356100. Telecopier: 040-35610-180

Banking, Stockmarkets and Securities, Commercial Law, Competition and Anti-Trust Law, Computer Law, Corporate Law, Environmental Law, European and International Private Law, General Contractual Terms and Conditions, Inheritance Law, Wills and Succession, Insolvency Law, Insurance and Re-Insurance, Intellectual Property, Labour Law, Media Law, Mergers and Acquisitions, Property and Construction law, Property Rights in the New Federal States, Public and Administrative Law, Shipping-/Maritime Law, Tax Law.

RESIDENT PARTNER

UWE WITT, born Hamburg, December 28, 1958; admitted, 1991, Germany. *Education:* University of Hamburg. *Member:* German Bar Association. *LANGUAGES:* German and English. *PRACTICE AREAS:* Intellectual Property; Competition Law; Property Law; Corporate Law; Restitution and Compensation Law in the New Federal States.

Languages: German, English and French.

GOLLASCH LÖWE & PARTNER

WERKSTR. 213, EUROPAHAUS
19061 SCHWERIN, GERMANY
Telephone: (0385) 616225
Fax: (0385) 616228

Lübeck, Germany Office: Hansekontor, Hansestr. 14, P.O. Box 11 12 36, 23521. Telephone: 49 451/57185-0. Fax: 49 451/5718544.

General Practice, Commercial Law, Company Law, International Contracts and Business Transactions, Unfair Competition, Banking and Finance, Tourism, Real Estate, Building and Construction Planning Law, Tax Law, Administrative Law, Environmental Law, Agricultural Law, Former East German Law. Notary Public.

RESIDENT PARTNERS

KLAUS-RAINER TIETMANN, born Bremen, Germany, June 26, 1954; admitted, 1989, Lübeck. *Education:* University of Kiel, Germany. *Member:* German Lawyers Association. *LANGUAGES:* German, English and French.

PETER KRAMER, born Göttingen, Germany, November 19, 1962; admitted, 1994, Schwerin. *Education:* University of Göttingen, Germany. *LANGUAGES:* German, English and French.

BALZ & HANKE

Established in 1991

ALTE WEINSTEIGE 73
70597 STUTTGART, GERMANY
Telephone: 0711/607 11 77
Telex: 72 18 76 avo tx
Telefax: 0711/640 66 43 avo fx

Corporate and Company Law, Mergers and Acquisitions, Unfair Competition, Tax, Inheritance, International and EEC Law. Real Estate, General Practice and Litigation, Arbitration, Public and Administrative Law.

FIRM PROFILE: *Established in 1991, Balz & Hanke has grown to become a commercial law firm with a reputation for offering a broad range of quality legal services. The client base is southern and eastern Germany, Switzerland and Austria. The firm has 2 partners and 1 assistant practicing in the Stuttgart office.*

MEMBERS OF FIRM

DR. GERHARD K. BALZ, born Stuttgart, Germany, 1953; admitted, 1982, Stuttgart. *Education:* University of Tübingen (Doctor of Jurisprudence, 1983). Author: "Bestandschutz der Gesellschaft mit beschränkter Haftung," Juristenzeitung 241, 1983; "Rechtstatsachen zur Ausschließung und zum Austritt von Gesellschaftern der GmbH," GmbH-Rundschau, 185, 1983; "Die Beendigung der Mitgliedschaft in der GmbH," 1984; "Rechte und Pflichten des Gesellschafters nach Austritt aus der GmbH," Der Betrieb, 1865, 1984; "Entnahme fiktiver Steuern bei der Personenhandelsgesellschaft," Der Betrieb 1305, 1988. *Member:* German Bar Association; American Chamber of Commerce in Germany; Handelskammer Deutschland-Schweiz. *LANGUAGES:* German and English. *PRACTICE AREAS:* Corporate and Company Law; Mergers and Acquisitions; Tax; Inheritance Law; Real Estate.

REINHARD HANKE, born 1940; admitted, 1991, Stuttgart, Certified Administrative Law Attorney. *Education:* University of Freiburg/Br. Government Official; Administrative Court Judge; Mayor and City Manager. *Member:* German Bar Association. *LANGUAGES:* German and English. *PRACTICE AREAS:* Public and Administrative Law.

PETER MARKOWSKY, born Rotenfels, Germany, 1958; admitted, 1990, Germany. *Education:* University of Freiburg. Assistant, German-Arabic Chamber of Commerce, Cairo. *LANGUAGES:* German, English and French. *PRACTICE AREAS:* Civil Law; Company Law; Conflict of Laws.

DR. WOLFGANG BAYER, ELMAR FÜLLER & DR. OTTMAR WEBER

Established in 1921

GEROKSTRASSE 8
D-70188 STUTTGART, GERMANY
Telephone: (0/49) 711-2364325
Fax: (0/49) 711-235389

Sevilla, Spain Associated Office: Manuel Marin Torres & Asociados, Av. Reina Mercedes, 19 A- 4° B, E - 41012. Telephone: (9/34) 5-461 63 91. Fax: (9/34) 5-423 1596.

International Banking and Business Law, General International Trade Law, Corporate Law, Real Estate, Foreign Investment, General Civil Litigation.

FIRM PROFILE: *The firm was established by Dr. Hugo Weber in 1921 (General Practice) and in the actual configuration since 1982 and offers specially legal services to Spanish and Latin-American investors in Germany and vice-versa to German, Swiss and Austrian clients for investment in Spain, Portugal and Latin America. Also special legal services for Investment and Financing in China (P.R.C), Malaysia and Singapore. No practice in Criminal and Administrative Law. Firm is associated with Manuel Marin Torres and Asociados, Seville, Spain. Wolfgang Bayer is partner of said firm since 1974.*

MEMBERS OF FIRM

DR. WOLFGANG BAYER, born Bad Mergentheim, Germany, April 13, 1949; admitted, 1974, Seville; 1977, Stuttgart. *Education:* University of Tubingen (1967-1968; 1970-1971; Dr.Jur., 1975); University of Geneva and Institut des Etudes Européenes, Geneva (1969); University of Seville (1972-1974). *Member:* Union Internationale des Avocats; Federación Inter-Americana de Abogados; World Association of Lawyers of the World Peace Through Law Center; Deutsch-Spanische Juristenvereinigung e.V.; Eurojuris (Germany); Deutscher Anwaltverein. *LANGUAGES:* German, Spanish, Portuguese, English, French and Chinese. *PRACTICE AREAS:* International Trade and Banking Law.

ELMAR FÜLLER, born Ehingen, Germany, March 1, 1955; admitted, 1984, Stuttgart. *Education:* University of Tübingen (1976-1981). *Member:* Eurojuris; Deutscher Anwaltsverein. *LANGUAGES:* German and English. *PRACTICE AREAS:* International Trade and Company Law; Transportation Law; General Civil Practice.

DR. WEBER OTTMAR, born Stuttgart, Germany, September 13, 1923; admitted, 1942, Stuttgart. *Education:* Universities Tübingen, Berlin and Bonn (Dr.Jur., 1938). *Member:* Eurojuris. *LANGUAGES:* German, English and French. *PRACTICE AREAS:* Company Law; Succession Law.

DIEM & PARTNER

HÖLDERLINPLATZ 5
D-70193 STUTTGART, GERMANY
Telephone: (0711) 299561
Telefax: (0711) 2265570

A Member of AdvoSelect EEIG, a network of law firms pooling their resources in special fields and crossborder cases, specializing in business law for middle-sized companies. AdvoSelect is represented in 51 cities throughout Europe.

Corporation, Commercial, Mergers and Acquisitions, Unfair Competition, Labour Law, Trademark, Computers and Software, Bankruptcy, Family Law, Litigation and Arbitration.

MEMBERS OF FIRM

FRANK E.R. DIEM, born Ludwigsburg, Germany, 1955; admitted, 1985, Stuttgart. *Education:* University of Tübingen (1981). *Member:* Association des Jeunes Avocats (Business Law Commission); German Bar Association (Commission for International Legal Relations); Deutscher Anwalt-Verein. *LANGUAGES:* German, English and French. *PRACTICE AREAS:* Company Law; Trade Law; Computer and Software Law; Labour Law.

SABINE-SARA GOETHERT, born Pforzheim, Germany 1957; admitted, 1987, Nuremberg. *Education:* University of Regensburg. *Member:* German Bar Association; Deutscher AnwaltVerein; Süddt. Anwältinnenverein. *LANGUAGES:* German and English. *PRACTICE AREAS:* Family Law; Law of Succession; Wills.

(This Listing Continued)

DIEM & PARTNER, Stuttgart—Continued

VOLKER SCHWARZ, born Pforzheim, Germany, 1962; admitted, 1993, Stuttgart. *Education:* University of Tübingen. Assistant, University of Tübingen. Doctoral thesis on a theme concerning unfair competition. *Member:* German Bar Association; Deutscher AnwaltVerein. *LANGUAGES:* German and English. *PRACTICE AREAS:* Unfair Competition; Intellectual Property; Industrial Property; Corporate Law.

DR. ENSSLIN, BILGER, RECHTSANWÄLTE

HEILBRONNER STRAβE 190
70191 STUTTGART, GERMANY
Telephone: (49-711) 1652141
Fax: (49-711) 1652213

Local and international business law.
Corporate, Commercial and Tax Law, Mergers and Acquisitions, Reorganization, Employment, Real Estate and Related Litigation.

FIRM PROFILE: The regulated law firm (Societät) is a member of Correspondent Law Firms of Price Waterhouse EEIG and cooperates with member firms and Price Waterhouse firms to render legal services throughout Europe, where appropriate on a multidisciplinary basis.

MEMBERS OF FIRM

DR. DANKWART ENSSLIN, born Marbach, Germany, August 18, 1934. *Education:* Universities of Bonn, Berlin, Tübingen, Doctorat Dr. iur., Steuerberater. *Member:* German Bar Association; Union of International Tax Law Specialists. *LANGUAGES:* German and English.

UTE BILGER-JUNG, born Trossingen, Germany, June 5, 1951. *Education:* University of Tübingen. *Member:* German Bar Association; Deutsch-amerikanische Juristenvereinigung e.V. *LANGUAGES:* German, English and French.

ASSOCIATES

JAN-F. SCHUBERT, born Stuttgart, Germany, April 8, 1959. *Education:* University of Tübingen. *Member:* German Bar Association; German Association of United Nations. *LANGUAGES:* German, English and French.

ROBERT DORR, born Nürnberg, Germany, October 30, 1960. *Education:* Universities of Erlangen, Tübingen, Munich, Steuerberater. *Member:* German Bar Association. *LANGUAGES:* German and English.

FIEDLER & FORSTER

GÄNSHEIDESTRAβE 68
70184 STUTTGART, GERMANY
Telephone: 0711 16445-0
Telefax: 0711 16445-11

Berlin, Germany Offfice: Oranienburger Strasse 69, D-10117 Berlin. Telephone: (0049) (30) 283 2418. Telefax: (0049) (30) 283 2420.
Cologne, Germany Office: Bonner Strasse 172-176, D-50968 Cologne. Telephone: (0049) (221) 937050-0. Telefax: (0049) (221) 937050-50.
Frankfurt/Main, Germany Office: Opernplatz 2, D-60313 Frankfurt/Main. Telephone: (0049) (69) 298930. Telefax: (0049) (69) 2398259.
Leipzig, Germany Office: Grimmaische Str. 25, 04109 Leipzig. Telephone: (0049) (341) 2115112. Telefax: (0049) (341) 9602530.
Munich, Germany Office: Brienner Strasse 12/III, D-80333 Munich. Telephone:(0049) (89) 23980; Telefax: (0049) (89) 2398259.
Paris, France Office: Tour Fiat la Dèfense 6, F-92084 Paris. Telephone: 33-1-47 76 28 10. Fax: 33-1-47 96 63 63.

Administrative Law, Antitrust Law, Competition Law, Construction Law, Consumer Protection Law, Corporate Law, EEC Law, Family Law, Industrial Relations and Labor Law, International Contracts, Litigation, Product Liability Law, Property and Real Estate Law, Transportation Law. Intellectual Property: Copyright Law, Licence Negotiation, General Intellectual Property Practice.

(This Listing Continued)

MEMBERS OF FIRM

DR. WOLFGANG BONGEN, born Geislingen/Steige, Germany, October 18, 1946; admitted, 1975, Stuttgart; 1980, Upper Court Stuttgart. *Education:* Universities of Tübingen, Geneva and Freiburg (Referendar, 1970; Assessor, 1974; Doctor of Law, 1974; Hochschule für Verwaltungswissenschaften, Speyer; Tax Lawyer, 1986). Author: *Schranken der Freizügigkeit aus Gründen der öffentlichen Ordnung und Sicherheit im Recht der Europäischen Wirtschaftsgemeinschaft,* 1974. *Member:* German Bar Association. *LANGUAGES:* German and English.

DR. WERNER RENAUD, born December 14, 1944; admitted, 1973, Karlsruhe; 1975, Stuttgart; 1978, Upper Court Stuttgart. *Education:* Universities of Saarbrücken and Heidelberg (Referendar, 1969; Assessor, 1972; Doctor of Law, 1977). Author: *Die Abgeltung von Urlaubsansprüchen nach dem Mindesturlaubsgesetz für Arbeitnehmer,* 1977. Assistant, University of Heidelberg, 1970-1971. Lecturer on Law, High School for Technic and Economy, Reutlingen, 1984-1986. *Member:* German Bar Association; German Association for the Protection of Industrial Property and Copyright. *LANGUAGES:* German, English and French.

MARTINA BONGEN, born Gelsenkirchen, Germany, January 18, 1957; admitted, 1983, Stuttgart; 1988, Upper Court Stuttgart. *Education:* Universities of Mannheim, Hamburg and Tübingen (Referendar, 1980; Assessor, 1983). Certified, Administrative Law Attorney. *Member:* German Bar Association. *LANGUAGES:* German, English and French.

DR. RAINER LAUX, born Rheinböllen, Germany, June 8, 1960; admitted, 1989, Stuttgart; 1994, Upper Court Stuttgart. *Education:* University of Mainz, Nice (France), Würzburg, Freiburg (Referendar, 1986; Assessor, 1989; Doctor of Law, 1992); College of Europe, Nice; Hochschule für Verwaltungswissenschaften, Speyer. Author: *Betriebsveräußerungen im Konkurs,* 1993. *Member:* German Bar Association. *LANGUAGES:* German, English, French and Portuguese.

THOMAS JANSSEN, born Stuttgart, Germany, February 21, 1961; admitted, 1991, Stuttgart. *Education:* University of Tübingen (Referendar, 1988; Assessor, 1990). Internship, New York, 1990. *Member:* German Bar Association; German Association for the Protection of Industrial Property and Copyright. *LANGUAGES:* German, English and French.

RALF KREMER, born Kaldenkirchen/Viersen, Germany, June 9, 1959; admitted, 1991, Stuttgart. *Education:* University of Tübingen (Referendar, 1988; Assessor, 1991). *Member:* German Bar Association. *LANGUAGES:* German, French and English.

ASSOCIATES

BERNHARD RESEMANN, born Albstadt-Ebingen, Germany, January 29, 1947; admitted, 1981, Stuttgart. *Education:* Universities of Tübingen, Geneva and Freiburg (Referendar, 1971; Assessor, 1974). *LANGUAGES:* German, English, Italian and French.

DR. ERICH BÜLOW, born Stuttgart, Germany, September 14, 1925; admitted, 1990, Stuttgart. *Education:* Universities of Stuttgart and Tübingen (Referendar, 1952; Assessor, 1956; Doctor of Law, 1956). "Die Vertragsübernahme im deutschen und italienischen Recht."Judge: District Court, Stuttgart, 1956-1960; Federal Department of Justice, 1960-1990. Director of Section Law of the European Communities, 1968. Person Commissioner for Human Rights by the Federal Government - Representative of the Federal Republic of Germany to the Institutions of Human Rights, Strasbourg, 1972. Member, Board of Trustees, Max-Planck-Institute for Foreign Public Law and Law of Nations, 1974. Director of Section, Public Law of Federal Department of Justice, 1982. Board Chairman of Bonn Legal Policy Association, 1984. Adviser of Treuhandanstalt, Berlin, by order of the Federal Government, 1990. *Member:* German Bar Association. *LANGUAGES:* German, English and French.

DIETER ULRICH, born Stuttgart, Germany, April 29, 1945; admitted, 1974, Stuttgart; 1979, Upper Court Stuttgart. *Education:* University of Tübingen, Berlin und Munich; (Referendar, 1970; Assessor, 1974; Tax Lawyer, 1977); Hochschule für Verwaltungswissenschaften Speyer, Internship Mexico-City, London; Certificate of Modern English Law 1973. *LANGUAGES:* German and English.

DR. JOERG FECKER, born Stuttgart, Germany, April 4, 1961; admitted, 1989, Stuttgart. *Education:* University of Würzburg, Geneva and Freiburg, (Referendar, 1986; Assessor, 1989; Doctor of Law, 1992); Diplômes des Droit Compare (1 Cycle 1983, 2 Cyle 1984); Faculte International de Droit Compare (Strasbourg). Author: *Rechte, Pflichten und Regelungsmöglichkeiten des privaten Arbeitgebers im Hinblick auf Alkoholkonsum von Arbeitnehmern.* *LANGUAGES:* German, English and French.

(This Listing Continued)

TOBIAS SCHOLL, born Marbach/Neckar, Germany, May 7, 1957; admitted, 1990, Germany. *Education:* Universities of Tübingen and Hamburg (Referendar, 1985; Assessor, 1990). Assistant, University of Hamburg, 1985-1987. *Member:* German Bar Association. *LANGUAGES:* German and English.

PETRA BERNHARD, born Offenburg, Germany, November 8, 1964; admitted, 1993, Stuttgart. *Education:* Universities of Freiburg and Tübingen (Referendar, 1990; Assessor, 1993). *Member:* German Bar Association. *LANGUAGES:* German and English.

MARTIN WAGNER, born Illingen, Germany, March 10, 1961; admitted, 1993, Stuttgart. *Education:* University of Saarbrücken (Referendar, 1987; Assessor, 1989); Hochschule für Verwaltungswissenschaften, Speyer, 1989. Civil Servant with Legal Expertise, Ministry of Labor, Health and Social Services, Saarland, 1990-1991; Legal Department, Daimler Benz AG, Stuttgart, 1991-1993. *Member:* German Bar Association. *LANGUAGES:* German and English.

DR. HANSPETER BENZ, born Backnang, Germany, May 8, 1962; admitted, 1995, Stuttgart. *Education:* University of Tübingen (Refendar, 1992; Assessor, 1995; Doctor of Law, 1995). Author: "Die verfassungsrechtliche Zulassigkeit der Beleihung einer Aktlengesellschaft mit Dienstreirenbefugnissen," 1995. *LANGUAGES:* German and English.

Languages: German, English, French, Portugese and Italian

FRANK, TRINKL & PARTNER

REINSBURGSTR. 11
70178 STUTTGART, GERMANY
Telephone: 0711/627091
Fax: 0711/625793

Real Estate, Inheritance, Property, Resorts and Leisure, Corporate and Commercial Law, Antitrust, Industrial Property, Agency and Distributorship, Franchising, Transportation, General Practise and Litigation, Notary Public.

PARTNERS

DR. KOLOMAN TRINKL, born Budapest, Hungary, 1936; admitted, 1964, Germany; 1969, Upper Court Stuttgart. *Education:* University of Tübingen (Doctor of Jurisprudence, 1966). *Member:* Stuttgart Lawyers Association; German-Hungarian Lawyers Association; Deutscher Juristentag, Comm. Law League of America (International Member); IBA. *LANGUAGES:* German and English. *PRACTICE AREAS:* Real Estate; Inheritance and Probate; Corporate and Commercial Law; Notary Public.

RAINER FRANK, born Stuttgart, Germany, 1946; admitted, 1975, Germany; 1980, Upper Court Stuttgart. *Education:* University of Tübingen (State exams, 1972, 1975). *Member:* German Bar Association; German-Hungarian Lawyers Association; Deutscher Familiengerichtstag. *LANGUAGES:* German and English. *PRACTICE AREAS:* Agency and Distributorship; Franchising; Resorts and Leisure; Property; Transportation.

DR. ALEXANDER BÖCK, born Stuttgart, Germany, 1961; admitted, 1989, Germany. *Education:* Universities of Regensburg and Göttingen (Doctor of Jurisprudence, 1992). Author: "The Compulsory License in the Field of Tension between Antitrust and Industrial Property Law." *Member:* German Bar Association. *LANGUAGES:* German, English and French. *PRACTICE AREAS:* Antitrust; Intellectual and Industrial Property; Property Claims and Restitution in the Former GDR.

FUCHS & PARTNERS

Established in 1960

OLGASTR. 77
D-70182 STUTTGART, GERMANY
Telephone: 0049-711-24 2244; 23 25 25; 236 47 13
Fax: 0049-711-233 900

Paris France Office: 5, Rue Taylor, F-75010. Telephone: 0033-1-42.45.08.80. Fax: 0033-1-42.45.08.61.

FIRM PROFILE: *The basic philosophy of our Firm is to offer highly specialized but still personal legal services of outstanding quality in the following fields of law: Commercial, Corporate, Unfair Competition, Construction Law, Real Estate, Computer, Banking, Taxation, Family, Debt Collection, Insurance, Criminal, Labor, Administrative, Transportation Law, General Practice and Litigation.*

MEMBERS OF FIRM

ANDREAS FUCHS, born Hannover, Germany, September 27, 1954; admitted, 1982, Germany. *Education:* University of Tübingen. *Member:*

(This Listing Continued)

German Bar Association; Stuttgart Lawyers Association; Doutschösterreichisch-Schweizerische-Anwaltsvereinigung (German-Austrian-Swiss Lawyers Association), Deutsch-Britische-Juristenvereinigung (German-British Jurists Association), Gesellschaft für Erbrechtsplege (Association for Heritage). *LANGUAGES:* German, English and French. *PRACTICE AREAS:* Commercial; Corporate; Unfair Competition; Computer; Banking; Criminal; Family Law.

KLAUS STUFFT, born Pforzheim, Germany, April 22, 1929; admitted, 1960, Germany. *Education:* University of Freiburg. *Member:* German Bar Association; Stuttgart Lawyers Association. *LANGUAGES:* German and English. *PRACTICE AREAS:* Construction; Real Estate; Taxation; Labor Law.

MICHAEL WILD, born Stuttgart, Germany, November 20, 1951; admitted, 1983, Germany. *Education:* Universities of Tübingen and Lausanne, Switzerland. *Member:* German Bar Association; Stuttgart Lawyers Association; American Chamber of Commerce. *LANGUAGES:* German, French, English and Spanish. *PRACTICE AREAS:* Transportation; Business; Securities Law.

DOROTHEE BOKELMANN, born Hamburg, Germany, June 18, 1960; admitted, 1992, Germany. *Education:* University of Freiburg. *Member:* German Bar Association; Stuttgart Lawyers Association. *LANGUAGES:* German and French. *PRACTICE AREAS:* Insurance; Labor Law; Litigation.

SEAN SAKSON, born Stuttgart, Germany, November 30, 1963; admitted, 1994, Germany. *Education:* University of Tübingen. *Member:* German Bar Association. *LANGUAGES:* German and English. *PRACTICE AREAS:* Criminal; Labor; Administrative Law.

DR. PAUL KLEINKNECHT, born Stuttgart, Germany, July 22, 1923; admitted, 1986, Germany. *Education:* University of Tübingen. *Member:* German Bar Association; Stuttgart Lawyers Association; Deutscher Juristentag. *LANGUAGES:* German and English. *PRACTICE AREAS:* Social; Family; International Law; Trademarks.

LEONARD GOODENOUGH, born Clichy sous Bois, France, September 24, 1949; admitted, 1989, Cour d'Appel de Paris, France (Not admitted in Germany). *Education:* Universities of Paris and Strasbourg. *Member:* Assistant to the French and European Parliament (1979-1984); German-French Chamber of Commerce. *LANGUAGES:* French, German, English and Russian. *PRACTICE AREAS:* International and EEC Law; Corporate; Commercial; Mergers and Acquisitions; Transportation Law.

GLEISS LUTZ HOOTZ HIRSCH & PARTNERS

Established in 1949

MAYBACHSTRASSE 6
D-70469 STUTTGART, GERMANY
Telephone: (49) (711) 89 97-0
Telefax: (49) (711) 85 50 96
Telex: 722 439 jura d (Head Office)

Frankfurt/Main, Germany Office: Eschersheimer Landstr. 19-21, D-60322 Frankfurt/Main. Telephone: (49) (69) 955 14-0. Telefax: (49) (69) 955 14-198; 955 14-199. Telex: 414 292glhcc d.
Berlin, Germany Office: Clara-Zetkin-Strasse 16, D-10117 Berlin. Telephone: (49) (30) 20 17 14-0. Telefax: (49) (30) 207 12 06.
Brussels, Belgium Office: Avenue Louise, 475, Bte. 13, B-1050 Brussels. Telephone: (32) (2) 647 63 74. Telefax: (32) (2) 640 92 31. Telex: 65348 jura b.
Prague, Czech Republic Office: Jugoslávská 29, CR-120 00 Prague 2. Telephone: (42) (2) 24007-510. Telefax: (42) (2) 24007-555.

German, EC and International Practice, in particular Administrative, Anti-Dumping, Anti-Trust, Arbitration, Banking, Capital Markets, Competition, Commercial, Copyright, Corporate/Company, Corporate Finance, Environmental, Finance, Foreign Investment, Industrial Property Rights, Insurance, Labour, Litigation, Media, Mergers and Acquisitions, Real Property, Regulated Industries, Securities, Tax, Telecommunications, Trade, Trademark, Unfair Competition, Zoning.

FIRM PROFILE: *The firm was established in 1949 in Stuttgart and developed from a German and later EC competition and anti-trust law boutique to a corporate practice with a full range of corporate legal services. The firm opened its Brussels office in 1987, its Berlin and Frankfurt of-*

(This Listing Continued)

GLEISS LUTZ HOOTZ HIRSCH & PARTNERS,
Stuttgart—Continued

fices in 1990, and its Prague office in 1992. It employs in total 85 lawyers and expects to grow in Central Europe in particular.

MEMBERS OF FIRM

PROF. DR. ALFRED GLEISS, born Neumuenster, 1904; admitted, 1931, Germany. *Education:* Universities of Marburg, Munich, Kiel and London School of Economics/United Kingdom (State Exams, 1926, 1931; Dr. jur., 1926). Author: "Soll ich Rechtsanwalt werden?" (Should I Become a Lawyer? (A Plaidoyer for the Legal Profession), 2nd ed., 1988; "Common Market Cartel Law," 3rd ed., 1980. Co-author with Dr. Hirsch: "EWG-Kartellrecht" (EC Antitrust Law), 3rd ed., 1978. Co-author with Dr. Hootz: "Gesetz gegen Wettbewerbsbeschränkungen" (German Antitrust Law), 1966. Chairman, German Decartelization Agency in the Württemberg Ministry of Economics under the Directives of US Military Government, 1946-1949. (Retired). *LANGUAGES:* German, English, Norwegian, Danish, Swedish, French and Italian.

DR. HELMUTH LUTZ, born Stuttgart, 1927; admitted, 1957, Germany. *Education:* University of Tübingen (State Exams, 1951, 1956; Dr.jur., 1954); Duke University/USA (Cert. 1953). Co-author: "Handbuch des Wettbewerbsrechts" (Manual on Competition Law), 1986. Member: Supervisory Board of Procter & Gamble GmbH, 1980—. *Member:* German and International Bar Associations; Association for the Study of Antitrust Law; German Society of Intellectual Property and Copyright. *LANGUAGES:* German and English. *PRACTICE AREAS:* Commercial; Corporations; German and EC Antitrust; German and EC Merger Control; Mergers and Acquisitions.

DR. CHRISTIAN HOOTZ, born Stettin, 1928; admitted, 1959, Germany. *Education:* University of Hamburg (State Exams, 1953, 1958; Dr. jur., 1954). Editor and Co-Author: "Gemeinschaftskommentar zum Gesetz gegen Wettbewerbsbeschränkungen (Joint Commentary on the Acts against Restraints on Competition), 5th ed., 1993. Author: "Seeschiffahrt im Deutschen und im EG-Kartellrecht" (Shipping in German and EC Antitrust Law), 1988. Contributor to Prof. Dr. Gleiss and Dr. Hirsch: "EWG-Kartellrecht" (EC Antitrust Law), 3rd ed., 1978. Co-author with Prof. Dr. Gleiss: "Gesetz gegen Wettbewerbsbeschränkungen" (German Antitrust Law), 1966. Author: "Grenzen der Freizeichnung des Spediteurs, § 41 ADSp" (Scope of Limited Liability of the Forwarding Agent), 1955. *Member:* German Bar Association; German Society of Insurance Science; German Society of Intellectual Property and Copyright; Association for the Study of Antitrust Law; German Association for International Maritime Law; German Association for the Science of Insurance. *LANGUAGES:* German and English. *PRACTICE AREAS:* Antitrust; Insurance; Intellectual Property; Unfair Competition.

DR. MARTIN HIRSCH (Resident Partner in the Frankfurt Office; see CV and details listed under Frankfurt, Germany).

DR. WERNER KLEINMANN, born Stuttgart, 1937; admitted, 1965, Germany. *Education:* Universities of Munich and Tübingen (State Exams, 1961, 1965; Dr. jur., 1963). Co-author with Dr. Bechtold: "Kommentar zur Fusionskontrolle," (Commentary on Merger Control), 2nd ed., 1989. Author: "Warenzeichenrecht" (Trademark Law), 1968. Lecturer on Law, University of Hohenheim/Stuttgart, 1991—. Member, Board of Examiners, State of Baden-Württemberg, 1984—. *Member:* German Bar Association. *LANGUAGES:* German and English. *PRACTICE AREAS:* Antitrust; Commercial; Distribution; General EC Law; Licensing.

DR. HORST HELM, born Berlin, 1937; admitted, 1967, Germany. *Education:* Universities of Hamburg, Geneva/Switzerland and Heidelberg (State Exams, 1961, 1966; Dr. jur., 1966). Co-author: "Handbuch des Wettbewerbsrechts" (Manual on Competition Law), 1986. Author: "Kartellrecht in der Wirtschaftspraxis" (Practical Antitrust Law), 2nd ed., 1977; "Das Diskontgeschäft der Banken" (Discount of Negotiable Instruments by Banks), 1967. Lecturer on Law, University of Heidelberg, 1966-1967. *Member:* German Bar Association; German Society of Intellectual Property and Copyright. *LANGUAGES:* German, English and French. *PRACTICE AREAS:* Antitrust; Food; Intellectual Property; Trademark; Unfair Competition.

DR. WOLFGANG BLUMERS, born Berlin, 1939; admitted, 1969, Germany. *Education:* Universities of Freiburg, Lausanne/Switzerland, Bonn and Cologne (State Exams, 1965, 1968; Dr. jur., 1983). Co-editor with Dr. Frick: "Handbuch der Betriebsprüfung" (Tax Audit Manual), loose-leaf. Co-author: "Handbuch des Beraters und Verteidigers im Steuerstrafverfahren" (Manual on Defending in Criminal Tax Proceedings), 1984. Author: "Bilanzierungstatbestände und Bilanzierungsfristen" (Statutory Accounting

(This Listing Continued)

Principles and Deadlines), 1983. Co-author: "Praktiken der Steuerfahndung" (Tax Investigation Practice), 1982. Board Member, Breuninger Foundation, 1980—. *Member:* German and International Bar Associations; German Society of Tax Law. (Certified Tax Attorney). *LANGUAGES:* German, English and French. *PRACTICE AREAS:* Corporations; International Tax Planning; Limited Partnerships; Mergers and Acquisitions; Tax.

DR. RAINER BECHTOLD, born Munich, 1941; admitted, 1972, Germany. *Education:* Universities of Berlin, Besançon/France and Freiburg (State Exams, 1964, 1968; Dr. jur., 1969). Author: "Kartellgesetz - Gesetz gegen Wettbewerbsbeschränkungen" (Commentary on German Antitrust Law), 1993. Co-author with Dr. Kleinmann: "Kommentar zur Fusionskontrolle" (Commentary on Merger Control), 2nd ed., 1989. Author: "Das neue Kartellrecht" (Mondern Antitrust Law), 1981. Lecturer on Law, University of Freiburg, 1968-1970. *Member:* German Bar Association; Association for the Study of Antitrust Law (Member, Executive Committee). *LANGUAGES:* German, English and French. *PRACTICE AREAS:* Distribution; EC State Aid; General EC Law; German and EC Antitrust; German and EC Merger Control.

DR. JÖRG FRICK, born Heilbronn, 1941; admitted, 1973, Germany. *Education:* Universities of Tübingen and Hamburg (State Exams, 1967, 1970; Dr. oec., 1973). Co-editor with Dr. Blumers: "Handbuch der Betriebsprüfung" (Tax Audit Manual), loose-leaf. Senior Officer, Stuttgart Corporate Tax Office, 1970-1973. *Member:* German Bar Association, German Society of Tax Law. (Tax Advisor). *LANGUAGES:* German, English and French. *PRACTICE AREAS:* Antidumping; Criminal Tax; Customs; Tax; Tax Planning.

DR. JOBST-HUBERTUS BAUER, born Gera, 1945; admitted, 1975, Germany. *Education:* University of Freiburg (State Exams, 1971, 1974; Dr. jur., 1976). Author: "Arbeitsrechtliche Aufhebungsverträge" (The Agreed Termination of Employment Contracts), 3rd ed., 1993. Co-author: "Beck'sches Rechtsanwaltshandbuch" (Beck'sches Attorneys' Manual), 3rd ed., 1993; "Rechtsformularbuch" (Legal Forms Manual), 13th ed., 1993; "Handbuch des Unternehmens- und Beteiligungskaufs" (Acquisitions Manual), 3rd ed., 1992. Author: "Betriebsänderungen" (Change in Enterprises), 1992. Co-author with Dr. Röder: "Kündigungsfibel" (How to Terminate an Employment Contract), 2nd ed., 1991. Author: "Der Anwalt vor den Arbeitsgerichten" (Litigation before the Labor Courts), 3rd ed., 1991; "Sprecherausschußgesetz mit Wahlordnung" (Management Consultative Committee), 2nd ed., 1990. Co-author with Dr. Röder: "Krankheit im Arbeitsverhältnis" (Sickness in Labor Law), 1987. Author: "Aktuelle Probleme betriebsbedingter Kündigung unter besonderer Berücksichtigung des Betriebsübergangs" (Current Problems of Employment Termination, particularly in the Context of the Sale of a Business), 1986; "Unternehmensveräusserung und Arbeitsrecht" (Labor Law in the Sale of a Business), 1983. Co-editor: "Neue Zeitschrift für Arbeitsrecht" (New Journal on Labor Law). Lecturer on Law, University of Freiburg, 1974-1975. Managing Director, Employers' Association of German Publishing Houses, 1985—; Employers' Association of Energy Utilities, Baden-Württemberg, 1993—. *Member:* German Bar Association (Member, Labor Law Committee); Stuttgart Bar Association (Member, Board of Directors). (Certified Labor Attorney). *LANGUAGES:* German, English and French. *PRACTICE AREAS:* Co-Determination; Collective Bargaining; Industrial Relations; International Labor Law; Pension Law; Services Contracts.

DR. BODO RIEGGER, born Karlsruhe, 1943; admitted, 1970, Germany. *Education:* Universities of Tübingen, Cologne, Lausanne/Switzerland, Wirtschaftsakademie/West Berlin and Walbrook College, London/United Kingdom (State Exams, 19 65, 1970; Dr. jur., 1969). Co-editor and Co-author: "Münchener Handbuch des Gesellschaftsrechts" (Munich Manual of Corporate Law), Vol. 2, 1991. Co-author: "Münchener Vertragshandbuch" (Munich Contracts Manual), Vol. 1: Partnerships and Corporations, 1985. Author: "Die Rechtsfolgen des Ausscheidens eines Gesellschafters aus einer zweigliedrigen Personengesellschaft" (Legal Consequences of the Withdrawal of a Partner from a Two-Member Partnership), 1969. Member: Advisory Board, Horst Mosolf GmbH & Co. Internationale Spedition; Johann Grohman GmbH & Co.; Adelholzener Mineralbrunnen; Meissner & Wurst GmbH & Co. *Member:* German and International Bar Associations. *LANGUAGES:* German and English. *PRACTICE AREAS:* Corporations; Limited Partnerships; Mergers and Acquisitions; Privatizations; Securities.

DR. CHRISTOPH MOENCH, born Freiburg, 1948; admitted, 1976, Germany. *Education:* Universities of Bochum and Freiburg (State Exams, 1972, 1974; Dr. jur., 1975). Author: "Die Freiheit der Baugestaltung" (Freedom of Construction Design), 1989. Co-author: "Grundzüge des US-Umweltrechts" (Outline of US Environmental Law), 1986. Author: "Verfassungswidriges Gesetz und Normenkontrolle" (Unconstitutionality and the Powers of the Federal Constitutional Court), 1977. Lecturer on Law, Uni-

(This Listing Continued)

versities of Freiburg, 1980-1992 and Frankfurt, 1992—. *Member:* German Bar Association (Member, Administrative Law Committee); German Lawyers Association; German Society of Environmental Law; Union Internationale d'Avocats (Member, EEC Section); European Law Association. (Certified Administrative Law Attorney). *LANGUAGES:* German, English and French. *PRACTICE AREAS:* Constitutional; EC Law; EC State Aid; Environmental; Regulated Industries.

DR. GERHARD WIRTH, born Tübingen, 1944; admitted, 1972, Germany. *Education:* Universities of Tübingen and Hamburg, Academy of Administrative Science, Speyer (State Exams, 1968, 1972; Dr. jur., 1976). Co-author: "Münchener Handbuch des Gesellschaftsrechts" (Munich Manual of Corporate Law), Vol. 2, 1991. Author: "Die Klagebefugnis von Verbänden gemäß § 13 des Gesetzes über unlauteren Wettbewerb" (Standing of Associations under Article 13 of the Unfair Competition Law), 1976. *Member:* German Bar Association. *LANGUAGES:* German and English. *PRACTICE AREAS:* Commercial; Corporations; Limited Partnerships; Mergers and Acquisitions; Securities.

UTE STIHL, born Flensburg, 1945; admitted, 1976, Germany. *Education:* University of Hamburg (State Exams, 1973, 1976). *Member:* German Bar Association; German Society of Intellectual Property and Copyright; European Communities Trade Mark Practitioners' Association; United States Trademark Association. *LANGUAGES:* German and English. *PRACTICE AREAS:* Design Models; Intellectual Property; Trademark; Unfair Competition; Utility Models.

DR. HANS SCHLARMANN (Resident Partner in the Frankfurt Office; see CV and details listed under Frankfurt, Germany).

DR. MICHAEL UECHTRITZ, born Heidelberg, 1951; admitted, 1982, Germany. *Education:* University of Freiburg (State Exams, 1977, 1981; Dr. jur., 1983). Co-editor and Co-author: "Anwaltshandbuch des Verwaltungsverfahrens" (Lawyers' Handbook on Administrative Procedure), loose-leaf, 1992. Author: "Kooperationsverträge zwischen Hochschulen und Gesellschaftlichen Verbänden" (Cooperation Agreements between Universities and Social/Business Associations), 1983. Lecturer on Law, University of Freiburg, 1980-1982 and Stuttgart, 1992—. *Member:* German Bar Association; German Federal Bar Commission (Member, Constitutional Law Committee, 1985—); German Society of Environmental Law. (Certified Administrative Law Attorney). *LANGUAGES:* German, English and French. *PRACTICE AREAS:* Constitutional; Environmental; GDR-Restitution Law; Real Property; Zoning.

DR. GERHARD WEGEN, born Salem, 1950; admitted, 1981, Germany; 1983, New York; registered, 1987 as Foreign Attorney, Brussels. *Education:* Universities of Hamburg, Geneva/Switzerland, Strasbourg/France, Tübingen (State Exams, 1975, 1978; Diplôme de Droit Comparé, 1973-1975; Dr. jur., 1985); Harvard Law School/USA (LL.M., 1981). Co-editor: "Insider Trading in Western Europe - Current Status," 1994. Co-author with Prof. Dr. Glaesner: "Die anwaltliche Praxis im Gemeinschaftsrecht" (Practising Community Law), 1994. Co-author: "International Securities Regulation," 1992; "Takeovers and Mergers in Europe," 1992; "Business Transactions in Germany," 4 Vols. loose-leaf. Author: "Vergleich und Klagerücknahme im internationalen Prozeß" (Amicable Settlement and Discontinuance in International Litigation), 1987; "International Securities: Law and Practice," 1985. Co-author: "International Investment Disputes: Avoidance and Settlement," 1985. Corresponding Editor, International Legal Materials. Adjunct Professor of Law: Export Academy Baden-Württemberg, 1985—; University of Tübingen, 1987—. Member, Board of Examiners, State of Baden-Württemberg, 1987—. With Cleary, Gottlieb, Steen & Hamilton, New York, 1982. Banking Trainee, Deutsche Bank AG, 1968-1970. *Member:* German (Member, Working Group on International Business Transactions), New York State, American and International (Vice Chairman, Committee Q, "Issues and Trading in Securities," Section of Business Law; Executive Committee, Capital Markets Forum) Bar Associations; American Society of International Law; International Law Associations-American and German Branches (Member, International Securities Regulation Committee); Association of the Bar of the City of New York; German Arbitration Institution; Swiss Arbitration Association. *LANGUAGES:* German, English and French. *PRACTICE AREAS:* Arbitration and Litigation; Corporations; Financial Services; International Law; Mergers and Acquisitions.

DR. DETLEF SCHMIDT (Resident Partner in the Berlin Office; see CV and details listed under Berlin, Germany).

DR. GERHARD RÖDER, born Biberach, 1952; admitted, 1984, Germany. *Education:* Universities of Tübingen and Freiburg (State Exams, 1976, 1980; Dr. jur., 1983). Co-author with Dr. Baeck: "Interessenausgleich und Sozialplan" (Reconciliation of Interests and Social Plan), 1993. Co-

(This Listing Continued)

author with Dr. Bauer: "Krankheit im Arbeitsverhältnis," (Sickness in Labor Law), 1987. "Kündigungsfibel" (How to Terminate an Employment Contract), 1986. Author: "Das Betriebliche Wohnungswesen im Spannungsfeld zwischen Betriebsverfassungsrecht und Wohnungsmietrecht" (Company Housing at the Intersection between Corporate and Landlord-Tenant Law), 1983. Lecturer on Law, University of Freiburg, 1977-1983, 1987—. *Member:* German Bar Association (Member, Labor Law Committee); International Bar Association. (Certified Labor Attorney). *LANGUAGES:* German, English and French. *PRACTICE AREAS:* Co-Determination; Collective Bargaining; Industrial Relations; Labor; Pensions.

DR. HANS-JÖRG NIEMEYER (Resident Partner in the Brussels Office; see CV and details listed under Brussels, Belgium).

DR. CLEMENS WEIDEMANN, born Rhede, 1953; admitted, 1982, Germany. *Education:* University of Münster (State Exams, 1977, 1980; Dr. jur., 1982). Author: "Abfallrecht - insbesondere Verfahren der Anlagenzulassung" (Waste Disposal - Special Licensing of Sites), 1992. Co-author with Dr. Uechtritz: "Anwaltshandbuch für Verwaltungsverfahren" (Lawyers' Handbook on Administrative Procedure), loose-leaf. Author (of the introduction): "Abfallgesetz mit Verordnungen, Verwaltungsvorschriften und sonstigen einschlägigen Regelungen" (Waste Disposal Legislation and Statutory Materials), 1992. Co-author: "Abfallrecht" (Waste Disposal), 1991. Author: "Rechtsschutz der Gemeinden gegen regionale Raumordnungspläne," (Legal Redress of Municipalities against Regional Development Plans), 1983; "Die Staatsaufsicht im Städtebaurecht als Instrument zur Durchsetzung der Raumordnung und Landesplanung" (State Supervision in Urban Development Law as an Instrument for Enforcement of Regional and State Planning), 1982. *Member:* German Bar Association; German Society of Environmental Law. (Certified Administrative Law Attorney). *LANGUAGES:* German and English. *PRACTICE AREAS:* Administrative; Environmental; Regulated Industries; Waste Disposal; Zoning.

DR. ULRICH BAECK, born Rosenheim, 1956; admitted, 1987, Germany. *Education:* University of Würzburg (State Exams 1981, 1986; Dr. jur. utr., 1988). Co-author with Dr. Röder: "Interessenausgleich und Sozialplan" (Reconciliation of Interests and Social Plan), 1993. Author: "Das Scheingeschäft - ein fehlerhaftes Rechtsgeschäft" (The Sham Transaction - A Voidable Transaction), 1988. Lecturer on Law, University of Würzburg, 1982-1984, 1986. *Member:* German Bar Association (Member, Labor Law Committee); German Lawyers' Association. *LANGUAGES:* German and English. *PRACTICE AREAS:* Collective Bargaining; Co-Determination; Industrial Relations; Labor; Pensions.

DR. THOMAS BOPP, born Saarlouis, 1956; admitted, 1989, Germany. *Education:* Universities of Würzburg and Saarbrücken (State Exams, 1982, 1985; Dr. jur., 1990). Author: "Vertragsstrukturen internationaler Kompensationsgeschäfte" (Structure of International Countertrade Agreements), 1992. Co-editor: "Französisches Recht für deutsche Exporteure" (French Law for German Exporters), 1989. Lecturer on Law, University of Saarbrücken, 1985-1988. *Member:* German Bar Association. *LANGUAGES:* German, English and French. *PRACTICE AREAS:* Computer; Intellectual Property; Licensing; Media and Telecommunications; Unfair Competition.

DR. ECKART SCHWEYER, born Stuttgart, 1956; admitted, 1989, Germany. *Education:* University of Tübingen (State Exams, 1982, 1986; Dr. jur., 1990). Author: "Tatbegriff und Tatidentität im Steuerrecht" (Definition and Characteristics of Offenses under Tax Law), 1990. Senior Tax Officer, Ministry of Finance, 1986-1989. *Member:* German Bar Association; Association of German Tax Advisors. (Certified Tax Advisor). *LANGUAGES:* German, English and French. *PRACTICE AREAS:* Corporations; International Tax Planning; Mergers and Acquisitions; Tax.

DR. MARTIN SCHOCKENHOFF, born Stuttgart, 1955; admitted, 1986, Germany. *Education:* Universities of Tübingen and Lausanne/Switzerland (State Exams, 1982, 1985; Dr. jur., 1987). Co-author: "Deutsches Rechtshandbuch" (Handbook of German Law), 1990. Author: "Gesellschaftsinteresse und Gleichbehandlung beim Bezugsrechtsausschluß" (Exclusion of Subscription Rights in Public Companies), 1988. Head of the Legal Department of the Archbishop of Munich, 1991-1993. *Member:* German Bar Association. *LANGUAGES:* German, English and French. *PRACTICE AREAS:* Corporations; German and EC Antitrust; Intellectual Property; Trademark; Unfair Competition.

DR. WOLFGANG BOSCH, born Konstanz, 1961; admitted, 1990, Germany. *Education:* University of Konstanz (State Exams, 1984, 1987; Dr. jur., 1990); University of Bern (lic. jur., 1990). Co-author: "Die internationale Schiedsgerichtsbarkeit in der Schweiz" (International Arbitration in Switzerland), 1992. Author: "Rechtskraft und Rechtshängigkeit im Schiedsverfahren" (Res judicata and litispendence in arbitration), 1991. Lecturer on Law, University of Bern, 1987-1990. (Also Partner, Brussels Office). *LAN-*

(This Listing Continued)

GLEISS LUTZ HOOTZ HIRSCH & PARTNERS,
Stuttgart—Continued

GUAGES: German, English and French. *PRACTICE AREAS:* Arbitration and Litigation; Commercial; EC and German Antitrust; General EC Law; International Law.

DR. UWE EYLES (Resident Partner in the Frankfurt Office; see CV and details listed under Frankfurt, Germany).

DR. MARKUS DEUTSCH, born Kirschhausen, 1960; admitted, 1990, Germany. *Education:* University of Mannheim (State Exams, 1986, 1990; Dr. jur., 1991). Author: "Die heimliche Erhebung von Informationen und deren Aufbewahrung durch die Polizei" (Secret Gathering of Information and its Documentation by the Police), 1991. *Member:* German Society of Environmental Law. (Certified Administrative Law Attorney). *LANGUAGES:* German and English. *PRACTICE AREAS:* Administrative Law; Constitutional; Environmental; Regulated Industries; Zoning.

DR. STEFAN VÖLKER, born Stuttgart, 1960; admitted, 1989, Germany. *Education:* University of Tübingen (State Exams, 1985, 1988; Dr. jur., 1989). Co-Author: "Europa-Leitfaden. Ein Wegweiser zum Europäischen Binnenmarkt 1992," (European Manual. A Guide to the European Internal Market 1992), 2nd ed., 1990. Author: "Passive Dienstleistungsfreiheit im Europäischen Gemeinschaftsrecht" (The Freedom to Receive Services under European Community Law), 1990. Lecturer on Law, University of Tübingen, 1986-1989. *Member:* German Bar Association; German Lawyers' Association; German Society of Intellectual Property and Copyright; German Society for Food Law and Food Science; International Bar Association (Business Law Section, Committees L and S). *LANGUAGES:* German, English and French. *PRACTICE AREAS:* Intellectual Property; Unfair Competition; Media; Trademarks; Food.

DR. LILO SCHLARMANN, born Berge, 1952; admitted, 1988, Germany. *Education:* Universities of Münster and Geneva/Switzerland (State Exams, 1978 (Philosophy, Literature); 1985, 1988 (Law); Dr. jur., 1991). Author: "Die Alternativenprüfung im Planungsrecht" (Investigation of the Alternatives in Planning Law), 1991. *Member:* German Bar Association; German Society of Intellectual Property and Copyright; European Communities Trade Mark Practitioners' Association; United States Trademark Association. *LANGUAGES:* German, English and French. *PRACTICE AREAS:* Intellectual Property; Licensing; Trademark; Unfair Competition; Utility Models.

DR. HOIMAR VON DITFURTH, born Düsseldorf, 1962; admitted, 1991, Germany. *Education:* Universities of Bonn and Freiburg (State Exams, 1987, 1990; Dr. jur., 1993). Author: "Einbeziehung subjektivöffentlicher Berechtigungen, insbesondere von Sozialversicherungsansprüchen, unter die Eigentumsgarantie" (Inclusion of Subjective Public Rights, in particular the Rights to Social Security Benefits, within the Concept of Constitutional Rights), 1993. *Member:* German Bar Association; German-Polish Law Association (Vice President). *LANGUAGES:* German, English and French. *PRACTICE AREAS:* Commercial; Corporations; International Law; Mergers and Acquisitions; Privatizations.

DR. MARCUS DANNECKER, born Stuttgart, 1961; admitted, 1990, Germany. *Education:* Universities of Tübingen, Munich and Konstanz (State Exams, 1985, 1990; Dr. jur., 1992). Author: "Die richterliche Inhaltskontrolle der Gesellschaftsverträge von Personengesellschaften" (Judicial Control of Partnership Agreements), 1992. *Member:* German Bar Association; German Lawyers' Association; German Society of Environmental Law. *LANGUAGES:* German and English. *PRACTICE AREAS:* Administrative Law; Environmental; Real Property; Regulated Industries; Zoning.

DR. RALF THAETER (Resident Partner in the Prague Office; see CV and details listed under Prague, Czech Republic).

DR. MARTIN DILLER, born Basel, Switzerland, 1962; admitted, 1992, Germany. *Education:* University of Mainz (State Exams, 1988, 1992; Dr. jur., 1994). Author: "Gesellschafter und Gesellschaftsorgane als Arbeitnehmer" (Shareholders and Corporate Governance Bodies as Employees), 1995. Co-author: "Wettbewerbsverbote" (Contractual Prohibitions of Competition), 1994. *Member:* German Bar Association. *LANGUAGES:* German, English, French and Italian. *PRACTICE AREAS:* Co-Determination; Employment; Labor; Pensions.

COUNSEL

PROF. DR. THEODOR HEINSIUS (Resident Counsel in the Frankfurt Office; see CV and details listed under Frankfurt, Germany).

(This Listing Continued)

PROF. DR. HANS JOACHIM GLAESNER (Resident Counsel in the Brussels Office; see CV and details listed under Brussels, Belgium).

DIPL. JUR. SABINE QUARG (Resident Counsel in the Berlin Office; see CV and details listed under Berlin, Germany).

MICHAEL J. DELANY, J.D., born St. Louis, Missouri, 1960; admitted, 1986, Illinois; 1988, Missouri (Not admitted in Germany). *Education:* University of Notre Dame, Indiana (B.A. Econ., 1983); University of Illinois College of Law, Urbana-Champaign, Illinois (J.D., 1986). *Member:* American, International, Illinois State and Missouri Bar Associations. *LANGUAGES:* English and German. *PRACTICE AREAS:* U.S. Corporate and Commercial Law; Joint Ventures; Mergers and Acquisitions; Trade Law.

JUDR. TOMÁŠ LINHART (Resident Counsel in the Prague Office; see CV and details listed under Prague, Czech Republic).

DR. IVO NESROVNAL (Resident Counsel in the Prague Office; see CV and details listed under Prague, Czech Republic).

JEAN-GABRIEL RECQ, born Châtillon sur Seine, France, 1964; admitted, 1991, Paris (Not admitted in Germany). *Education:* Institut Supérieur de Gestion, Paris (1987); University of Paris X-Nanterre (Maîtrise in Private Law, 1988; D.E.A. - Specialisation in Corporate Law, 1989); CAPA (1990). Member, ISG-Alumni; Member of the Board, French-German Business Club of Baden-Württemberg. *LANGUAGES:* French, German and English. *PRACTICE AREAS:* French Corporate and Commercial Law; Mergers and Acquisitions; Trade Law.

JAMES SHERER, born Auckland, New Zealand, 1961; admitted, 1985, New Zealand; 1991, England and Wales (Not admitted in Germany). *Education:* University of Auckland (B.Com., 1983; LL.B., 1984). German Academic Exchange Scholar at Düsseldorf and University of Tübingen, 1991-1992. *Member:* English Law Society; British-German Jurists Association. *LANGUAGES:* English and German. *PRACTICE AREAS:* UK and New Zealand Commercial and Corporate Law; International Commercial Law; Joint Ventures; Mergers and Acquisitions.

DR. MARTIN KUBÁNEK (Resident Counsel in the Prague Office; see CV and details listed under Prague, Czech Republic).

HAAS & HALBGEWACHS

KÖNIG-KARL-STRAßE 49
70372 STUTTGART, GERMANY
Telephone: 0711/95559 - 0
Fax: 0711/95559 - 35

Corporate and Company Law, Tax, General Practice and Litigation.

FIRM PROFILE: *Through an intensive combination of tax and legal counseling, Haas & Halbgewachs try to achieve the highest possible level of service for their clients. At the same time, the number of collaborators are kept purposely small to ensure the control of professional quality and personal integrity often lacking in large law firms. The clientele consists mostly of medium-sized enterprises and free professionals, but also several insurance companies. The firm is made up of two partners and two salaried tax consultants.*

PARTNERS

LUDWIG HAAS, born Kirrlach, Germany, 1945. *Education:* University of Mannheim. Tax Consultant; Chartered Accountant; Legal Advisor. Member: European Consultants Unit; Institut of Auditors. *LANGUAGES:* German, English and French. *PRACTICE AREAS:* Tax; Tax Law.

REINHARD HALBGEWACHS, born Stuttgart, Germany, 1961; admitted, 1989, Stuttgart. *Education:* Universities of Würzburg and Speyer. With: Munich Reinsurance, Munich, 1988-1989; Sigle, Loose, Schmidt-Diemitz & Partner, Stuttgart, 1989-1992; Lieser, Rombach & Partner, Erfurt, 1992-1993. Author: "Die Haftung des Kfz. Sachverständigen" ("Liability of the motor vehicle appraiser"), 1992; "EG-Produkthaftungsrichtlinie," ("EC product liability directive"), 1993; "Zuschläge zum Wiederbeschaffungswert" ("Additions to replacement value") in Neue Zeitschrift für Verkehrsrecht, 1993, 380; "Product Liability: European Laws and Practice," 1993. *Member:* German Bar Association (Deputy Chairman, Working Group for Construction and Architectural Law); International Bar Association; German-Philippine Lawyers Association; German-Canadian Lawyers Association; Young Lawyers International Association. *LANGUAGES:* German,

(This Listing Continued)

English and French. *PRACTICE AREAS:* Corporate and Company Law; Insurance and Reinsurance; Third Party Liability; Construction Law; General Practice and Litigation.

HAVER & MAILAENDER

Established in 1965

LENZHALDE 83

D-70192 STUTTGART, GERMANY

Telephone: (0711) 227440
Cable Address: "Intertax", Stuttgart
Telex: 721738 advo d
Telecopier: (0711) 2991935

Frankfurt, Germany Office Beethovenstrasse 4, D-60325. Telephone: 069-740190. Telecopier: 069-740247.

Dresden, Germany Office: Bautzner Strasse 23-25, D-01099. Telephone: 0351-51955. Telecopier: 0351-53538.

Brussels, Belgium Office: Av. de la Renaissance 1, B-1040. Telephone: 02-7366375. Telecopier: 02-7360571.

Commercial, Corporation, Banking and Financial Services, Mergers and Acquisitions, High Technology and Telecommunication, Transportation and Aviation, Construction and Engineering Contracts, Antitrust, EEC-Law, Licensing, Patent, Trademark, Copyright, Trade Law and Product Liability, International and Tax Law, Litigation and Arbitration, Real Estate and Insolvency Law.

FIRM PROFILE: The firm was established in Stuttgart in 1965 and opened its Brussels Office in 1987, Frankfurt Office in 1990 and Dresden office in 1991. The firm offers the full range of legal services for commercial matters. The Brussels Office concentrates on Community Law issues. The Frankfurt Office concentrates on Banking and Securities Law, the Dresden Office concentrates on restitution matters and on investments in the new federal states of Eastern Germany.

MEMBERS OF FIRM

DR. FRIEDRICH HAVER (1905-1976).

RICHARD SCHIPPERT (1901-1975).

PROF. DR. K. PETER MAILAENDER, born Stuttgart, Germany, 1936; admitted, 1965, Stuttgart. *Education:* Universities of Munich and Tuebingen (Doctor of Law, 1963); New York University (Master of Comparative Jurisprudence, 1962). Author: "Export Trade Under the Impact of the Antitrust Laws in Germany and the U.S.A.," New York, 1962; *Privatrechtliche Folgen unerlaubter Kartellpraxis,* 1964; *Zustaendigkeit und Entscheidungsfreiheit nationaler Gerichte im EWG-Kartellrecht,* 1965; with Dr. Haver, *Lizenzvergabe durch deutsche Unternehmen in das Ausland,* 1967; "Gemeinschaftskommentar, EWG Kartellrecht," 1972. Assistant Professor at Tubingen and Munich Law Schools, 1962-1965. Professor of Law, University of Hohenheim, 1993. *Member:* International Bar Association (Member, Business Law Section); German Bar Association; German Association for the Protection of Industrial Property and Copyright; German Association of Comparative Law; International Federation of European Law (Member, Antitrust Committee, 1967-1974); American Chamber of Commerce in Germany (Member, Committee on Laws and Arbitration). *LANGUAGES:* German, English and French. *PRACTICE AREAS:* Antitrust Law; Banking Law; European Community Law; Arbitration; Mergers and Acquisitions.

DR. PETER W. ADOLFF, born Stuttgart, Germany, 1933; admitted, 1967, Stuttgart. *Education:* Universities of Munich, Paris, Hamburg and Tuebingen (Doctor of Law, 1961). Author: "Der Rechtsschutz des Kaeufers bei Lieferung einer fehlerhaften Sache in der arbeitsteiligen Wirtschaft nach amerikanischem, englischem, französischem und deutschem Recht," 1961; "Werbung in der Textilindustrie," 1966; "Textiles Marketing von der Faser bis zum Konsumenten," 1969; "Management in der Textilindustrie," 1970; "Unternehmensorganisation und Management in den 70er Jahren," 1970. Member, Executive Committee of Board of Managing Directors of Allianz Versicherungs AG. *Member:* Association of Donors for German Science (Stifterverband für die deutsche Wissenschaft). *LANGUAGES:* German, English and French. *PRACTICE AREAS:* Corporate Law; Industrial Relations; Labour Law; Insurance Law.

DR. ROLF M. WINKLER, born Krakau, Poland, 1942; admitted, 1974, Stuttgart. *Education:* Universities of Berlin, Frankfurt and Tuebingen (Doctor of Law, 1970); University of California at Berkeley (Master of Laws, 1973). Author: "Die Rechtsnatur der Geldbusse im Wettbewerbsrecht der Europaeischen Wirtschaftsgemeinschaft," 1971, "The New Joint Venture

(This Listing Continued)

Law of the European Community," 1994. Legal Assistant at the EEC Commission, Brussels, 1968-1969. Assistant at the University of Tubingen, 1969-1970. *Member:* German Bar Association; American Society of International Law; German-American Lawyers Association (Board Member); Canadian-German Lawyers Association (Board Member); International Bar Association (Member, Business Law Section). (Partner in Charge, Brussels Office). *LANGUAGES:* German, English and French. *PRACTICE AREAS:* Antitrust; Industrial Property Law; Franchising; European Union Law; Joint Ventures; Construction Contracts; Litigation; Arbitration.

DR. KLAUS-A. GERSTENMAIER, born Esslingen, Neckar, Germany, 1943; admitted, 1975, Stuttgart. *Education:* Universities of Tuebingen, Bonn and Göttingen (Doctor of Law, 1974); University of California at Berkeley. Author: "Justitiabilitaet und Justitiabilisierung der Sozialstaatsklausel des Grundgesetzes," 1974; "World Litigation Law & Practice-Germany," 1990; "Pre-emptive Remedies in Europe-Germany," 1992. Assistant at the University of Bonn, Law School, 1969-1973. *Member:* International Bar Association (Member, Business Law Section); Stuttgart and German Bar Associations; German-American Lawyers Association. *LANGUAGES:* German, English and French. *PRACTICE AREAS:* Corporation Law; Banking Law; Labour Law; Litigation; Foreign Investments; International Legal Relations; Arbitration.

DR. WERNER KARL KESSLER, born Neuenbuerg, Enzkreis, Germany, 1947; admitted, 1976, Cologne; 1979, Stuttgart. *Education:* Universities of Munich and Tuebingen (Doctor of Law, 1976); London University, King's College (1976). Author: "Die Filmwirtschaft im Gemeinsamen Markt. Rechtsfragen der Herstellung eines europaeischen Filmmarktes unter besonderer Beruecksichtigung der Dienstleistungs—und Niederlassungsfreiheit sowie der Filmfoerderung," 1976. Legal Assistant with the EEC Directorate for the Harmonization of Laws, EEC Commission, Brussels, 1972-1973. *Member:* Stuttgart and German Bar Associations; British-German Jurists' Association. *LANGUAGES:* German, English, French and Italian. *PRACTICE AREAS:* Intellectual Property; Unfair Trade; Licensing; Trademark; Litigation.

DR. GOETZ GABRIEL, born Stuttgart, Germany, 1939; admitted, 1967, Stuttgart. *Education:* Universities of Tuebingen, Berlin and Muenchen (Referendar, 1963; Assessor, 1967; Doctor of Law, 1969). *Member:* Stuttgart and German Bar Associations. *LANGUAGES:* German and English. *PRACTICE AREAS:* General Practice; Leases and Leasing; Commercial; Labour Law; Family; Inheritance Law.

DR. BERNT GRAF ZU DOHNA, born Lisbon, Portugal, 1944; admitted, 1987, Stuttgart. *Education:* Trinity College Dublin, Law School, Ireland; Universities of Bonn, Freiburg and Kiel (Doctor of Law, 1973). Author: "Die Grundprinzipien des Voelkerrechts ueber die Freundschaftlichen Beziehungen und die Zusammenarbeit zwischen Staaten," 1973. Assistant, University of Bonn, Law School, 1970-1974. Counsel with Babcock-Brown Boveri Reaktor GmbH, Mannheim, 1975-1977 and with Robert Bosch GmbH, Stuttgart, 1977—. *Member:* Stuttgart and German Bar Associations. *LANGUAGES:* German, English and French. *PRACTICE AREAS:* Product Liability; Corporate Law; Joint Ventures; Distributorship.

DR. FRIEDRICH BOZENHARDT, born Schwaebisch-Hall, Germany, 1958; admitted, 1990, Stuttgart. *Education:* University of Tuebingen (Doctor of Law, 1990). Author: "Freiwillige Übernahmeangebote (takeover bids) im Deutschon Recht," 1990. Co-author: "Internationale Handelsschieds-Gerichtsbarkeit," 1990. Assistant, University of Tubingen, 1986-1990. *Member:* Stuttgart and German Bar Associations; Young Lawyers International Association. *LANGUAGES:* German, English and French. *PRACTICE AREAS:* Securities Law; Corporate Law; Estates.

DR. GABRIELE SCHINLE, born Stuttgart, Germany, 1960; admitted, 1990, Stuttgart. *Education:* Universities of Tuebingen and Lausanne (Referendar, 1985; Assessor, 1988; Doctor of Law, 1993). *LANGUAGES:* German, English and French. *PRACTICE AREAS:* Private Law; Bankruptcy Law; Property Law; Copyright Litigation.

DR. PETER LADWIG, born Goeppingen, Germany, 1961; admitted, 1990, Stuttgart. *Education:* University of Freiburg/Breisgau and Freie Universitaet Berlin (Referendar, 1986; Assessor, 1990). *LANGUAGES:* German, English and French. *PRACTICE AREAS:* Tax Law; Licensing; Commercial Law.

DR. ULRICH SCHNELLE, born Essen, Germany, 1962; admitted, 1992, Stuttgart. *Education:* Universities of Passau, Genf, Freiburg, University of Illinois; Assistant, University of Freiburg, 1988-1990; Referendar, 1992 (Master of Laws, 1989; Doctor of Law, 1991). Author: "Die objektiv Anknüpfung von Dariehensverträgen im deutschen und amerikanischen

(This Listing Continued)

HAVER & MAILAENDER, Stuttgart—Continued

JPR," 1991. *Member:* Deutsch-Amerikanische Juristenvereinigung. *LAN-GUAGES:* German, English, French and Russian. *PRACTICE AREAS:* Corporate Law; Conflicts of Law; Litigation.

WALTER SIMON, born Landau/Pfalz, Germany; admitted, 1993, Stuttgart. *Education:* Universities Tuebingen, Lausanne, Freiburg/Breisgau (Referendar, 1990; Assessor, 1993). Assistant, University of Freiburg, 1990-1992. *LANGUAGES:* English and French. *PRACTICE AREAS:* Commercial Law; Real Estate; Insolvency Law.

JULIA ROEVER, born Oldenburg, Germany, 1963; admitted, 1993, Stuttgart. *Education:* Universities Tuebingen and Heidelberg (Referendar, 1989; Assessor, 1992). *LANGUAGES:* German, English, French and Spanish. *PRACTICE AREAS:* Personal Liability; Private Law; Health Law.

DR. GÜNTER KRUMSCHEID (Resident Partner, Frankfurt Office; For Biographical Data, see Professional Biographies at Frankfurt, Germany). *LANGUAGES:* German, English, French and Italian.

BERND HEILENZ (Resident Partner, Dresden Office. For Biographical Data, see Professional Biographies at Dresden, Germany).

Languages: German and English.

KASPER, KNACKE, SCHÄUBLE, WINTTERLIN AND PARTNERS

SCHÜTZENSTRAβE 13
70182 STUTTGART, GERMANY
Telephone: 711-2236-3
Telefax: 711-2236-410

Mailing Address: P.O. Box 10 26 54, 70022

Leipzig, Germany Office: Könneritzstraβe 43, 04229. Telephone: 03 41/4918429. Telefax: 03 41/4918215.

Denver, Colorado Affiliated Office: Popham, Haik, Schnobrich & Kaufman, Ltd. Suite 2400, 1200 17th Street, 80202. Telephone: 303-893-1200. Telefax: 303-893-2194.

Minneapolis, Minnesota Affiliated Office: Popham, Haik, Schnobrich & Kaufman, Ltd. 3300 Piper Jaffray Tower, 222 South 9th Street, 55402. Telephone: 612-333-4800.

Washington, D.C. Affiliated Office: Popham, Haik, Schnobrich & Kaufman, Ltd. 1300 I Street, N.W., Suite 500 East, 20005. Telephone: 202-962-8700.

Miami, Florida Affiliated Office: Popham, Haik, Schnobrich & Kaufman, Ltd. 4000 International Place, 100 Southeast 2nd Street, 33131. Telephone: 305-530-0050; 800-486-0140.

General Civil and Trial Practice. Probate, Administrative, Insurance, Corporation, Trademark and Copyrights, Franchise, Unfair Competition, Licensing, Common Market, Antitrust, Labor Law, International Trade, Environmental Law and International Arbitration, Product Liability, Banking, Construction Law.

MEMBERS OF FIRM

DR. JUR. HABIL. FRANZ KASPER, born Bad Schussenried, August 1, 1937; admitted, 1970, West Germany. *Education:* Universities of Munich, Vienna and Freiburg (Dr. of Jurisprudence, 1965; Assessor 1965; Dr. jur. habil., 1972). Author: *"Das Subjektive Recht - Begriffsbildung und Bedeutungsmehrheit,"* C.F. Muller-Verlag, Karlsruhe, 1967. Assistant Professor, University of Freiburg, 1962-1970. Lecturer, University of Freiburg for Civil Law, 1973—. *Member:* German Bar Association; Internationale Juristen Kommission. *LANGUAGES:* English and German.

DR. JUR. JÜRGEN KNACKE, born Wismar, Germany, January 1, 1938; admitted, 1967, West Germany. *Education:* Universities of Tübingen, Bonn and Kiel (Doctor of Jurisprudence, 1967; Assessor 1967). Author: "Die Vertragsstrafe im Baurecht," Werner Verlag, 1988. *Member:* Stuttgart Lawyers Association; German Bar Association; Deutsche Gesellschaft für Baurecht.

DR. JUR. FRIEDER SCHÄUBLE, born Tübingen, Germany, August 25, 1937; admitted, 1965, West Germany. *Education:* Universities of Munich and Freiburg (Doctor of Jurisprudence, 1965; Assessor, 1965). Assistant Professor, University of Freiburg, 1961-1963. *Member:* Stuttgart Lawyers Association; German Bar Association; French-German Chamber of Commerce; German-Belgian Chamber of Commerce; German Association for the Protection of Industrial Property and Copyright; Union Internatio-

(This Listing Continued)

nale des Avocats. (Resident, Leipzig Office). *LANGUAGES:* German, French and English.

DR. JUR. WERNER WINTTERLIN, born Berlin, Germany, May 11, 1941; admitted, 1969, West Germany. *Education:* Universities of Tübingen and Munich (Doctor of Jurisprudence, 1968; Assessor, 1968); Institute of Advanced Legal Studies, London. Author: "Die Haftung für fahrlässige Irreführung im englischen Delikts- und Vertragsrecht unter vergleichender Berücksichtigung des deutschen und nordamerikanischen Rechts," Alfred Metzner Verlag, Frankfurt/M.Berlin, 1968. Co-Author, "Franchising and Antitrust Law in West Germany," *International Franchising,* Continental Reports, Inc., Denver, 1970; "On some recent Federal German Developments in the Field of Copyright, Utility Patent, and Design patent," International Bar Journal, July, 1976; "Misrepresentation of Origins: Marketing Under False Colours," International Business Lawyer, February, 1983. *Member:* Stuttgart Lawyers Association; International Bar Association; German-English Lawyers Association. *LANGUAGES:* German and English.

KLAUS ULRICH BIRKHOLD, born Heidenheim, West Germany, September 6, 1953; admitted, 1981, West Germany. *Education:* University of Tübingen (Assessor, 1980).

JOSEF-WALTER KIRCHBERG, born Kassel, Germany, September 30, 1951; admitted, 1981, West Germany. *Education:* Universities of Giessen and Freiburg (Assessor, 1979). Judge, Administrative Court, Freiburg, 1979-1981.

DR. JUR. WOLFGANG HESSE, born Kemnath, Germany, July 1, 1952; admitted, 1983, West Germany. *Education:* University of Regensburg (Assessor, 1982; Doctor of Jurisprudence, 1984). *Member:* German Bar Association; German-American Lawyers Association. *LANGUAGES:* German and English.

DR. JUR. CHRISTIAN DÖRING, born Gütersloh, Germany, October 31, 1958; admitted, 1990, West Germany. *Education:* Universities of Bielefeld and Freiburg (Assessor, 1988); Graduate Fellowship, University of Freiburg, 1989. Assistant Professor, University of Freiburg, 1985-1988. Doctor of Jurisprudence, 1993. Author: "Die öffentlich-rechtliche Baulast und das nachbarrechtliche Grundverhältnis 1993.".

DR. JUR. FRANK HAHN, born Stuttgart, Germany, February 10, 1963; admitted, 1990, Germany. *Education:* University of Tuebingen (Doctor of Jurisprudence, 1987). Legal Training, Forum Management, Arbeitnehmerüberlassung, 1992. Author: "Union Activities in the Workplace," Die Personalvertretung, 1992; "Extraordinary Termination," WStH, 1991. *Member:* German Bar Association; Arbeitsgemeinschaft der Fachanwälte im Deutschen Anwaltsverein. *LANGUAGES:* German and English.

ASSOCIATES

DR. REGINA TZESCHLOCK, born Reichental, Germany, October 14, 1960; admitted, 1988, West Germany. *Education:* University of Konstanz (Assessor, 1987; Doctor of Jurisprudence, 1989. Co-Author: "Choice of Law in International Financial Transactions According to New York Law," IPRAX, 1988; "Reorganization of a Bank Realized by the Bank of England in Consideration of the 'Commercial Exception' of the US-Foreign Sovereign Immunity Act 1976," ZIP, 1988. Assistant Professor, University of Konstanz, 1987-1988. *Member:* Stuttgart Lawyers Association. *LANGUAGES:* German and English.

DR. OEC. THOMAS NICK, born Duisburg, Germany, May 23, 1955; admitted, 1991, Germany. *Education:* University of Muenster (Assessor, 1981-1991); Graduate Fellowship, University of Muenster, 1981. Assistant Professor, Institut fuer Rechtswissenschaft, University of Hohenheim, 1981-1991. Doctor of Economics, University of Stuttgart-Hohenheim, 1991. Author: "Legal Issues Relating to Environmental Protection and Agriculture," KTBL, 1983; "Central Works Council of Affiliated Companies and Social Compensation Plans," Duncker & Humblot, 1992; "The Permissibility of Establishing Blanket Liability Reserves for Product Liability," Der Betrieb, 1985; "Allocation of Burden of Proof in Civil Law Environmental Protection," Agrarrecht, 1985. *LANGUAGES:* German and English.

DR. JUR. FRANK JULIUS HOSPACH, born Stuttgart, Germany, January 15, 1962; admitted, 1992, Germany. *Education:* Universities of Tübingen, Munich and Paris (Assessor, 1991); University of Paris (Diplôme des Etudes Approfondies, 1988); London School of Economics (Summer Course, 1989). Doctor of Jurisprudence, 1992. Author: "Das Recht der franzoesischen Verwaltungsgerichtsbarkeit (The French Law of Administrative Jurisdiction)," NVwZ, 1990; Emoluments in Germany - a study in

(This Listing Continued)

constitutional history, 1992. *LANGUAGES:* German, English, French and Spanish.

DR. MARTIN WOLFRAM WESCH, born Waiblingen, Germany, May 10, 1964; admitted, 1993, Germany. *Education:* University of Tübingen (Referendar, 1989; Doctor of Jurisprudence, summa cum laude, 1992; Assessor, 1993). Author: "Neue Arbeitskampfmittel am Beispiel von Betriebsbesetzungen und Betriebsblockaden (New Methods of Labor Disputes)," Duncker & Humblot, Berlin, 1993. *LANGUAGES:* German and English.

KLEINER & KÜGEL

SILBERBURGSTRAßE 187
70178 STUTTGART, GERMANY
Telephone: 0711/640 20 66
Telefax: 0711/6 494 222

Berlin, Germany Office: Kleiststraße 35, 10787. Telephone: 030/217 64 91. Telefax: 030/217 69 47.

Patent, Trademark, Copyright, Unfair Competition, Corporation, Labour Law, Commercial, Antitrust, Private International Law, Administrative Law, Environmental and Pollution, Waste Disposal, Zoning and Construction Law, Food and Drugs, Litigation.

MEMBERS OF FIRM

DR. CHRISTOPH KLEINER, LL.M., born Pforzheim, Germany, January 17, 1954; admitted, 1983, Germany. *Education:* Universities of Freiburg im Breisgau, Geneva, Munich (Referendar, 1978; Assessor, 1981; Doctor of Jurisprudence, 1983); Harvard Law School (LL.M., 1982). Author: "Warenzeichen für Entwicklungsländer," (Trademarks for Developing Countries), Munich, 1985. Co-Author: "The Draft International Code of Conduct on the Transfer of Technology," Munich, 1980. Assistant at Max-Planck-Institut für ausländisches und internationales Patent, Urheber- und Wettbewerbsrecht, Munich, 1978-1983. Lecturer at Augsburg University, 1982-1985. *Member:* German Bar Association; German Association for the Protection of Industrial Property and Copyright; German American Lawyers' Association. *LANGUAGES:* German, English, French and Spanish. *PRACTICE AREAS:* Patent; Trademark; Copyright; Unfair Competition; Corporation; Commercial; Antitrust; Private International Law; Litigation.

DR. J. WILFRIED KÜGEL, born Forchheim, Germany, November 20, 1954; admitted, 1983, Germany. *Education:* University of Erlangen-Nürnberg (Referendar, 1980; Assessor, 1982; Doctor of Jurisprudence, 1985). Assistant, University of Erlangen-Nürnberg, 1977-1983. Author: "Der Planfeststellungsbeschluß und seine Anfechtbarkeit. Zugleich ein Beitrag zur Auslegung der §§ 74, 75 VwVfG," (The Environmental Impact Plan and Its Voidability through Legal Proceeding). Co-Author: Wirtschaftsrecht und Außenwirtschaftsrecht der Volksrepublik China (commercial law and foreign trade law of the People's Republic of China), 1987. *Member:* German Bar Association; Young Lawyers' International Association; Gesellschaft für Umweltrecht e.V. *LANGUAGES:* German, French and English. *PRACTICE AREAS:* Administrative Law; Environmental and Pollution; Waste Disposal; Zoning and Construction; Food and Drugs; Litigation.

DR. FRANK DEHN, born Heidelberg, Germany, September 19, 1960; admitted, 1990, Germany. *Education:* University of Heidelberg (Referendar, 1986; Assessor, 1989; Doctor of Jurisprudence, 1993). Tutor, University of Heidelberg. Foreign Intern Skadden, Arps, Slate, Meagher & Flom, New York, 1990. Author: "Verfahrenshindernis bei völkerrechtswidriger Entführung durch deutsche Strafverfolgungsorgane." (Terminating Criminal Proceedings due to Abduction by German Prosecution Institutions violating Public International Law). *Member:* German Bar Association; German-American Lawyers' Association; German Association for the Protection of Industrial Property and Copyright. *LANGUAGES:* German, French and English. *PRACTICE AREAS:* Patent; Trademark; Copyright; Unfair Competition; Corporation; Labour Law; Commercial; Antitrust; Private International Law; Litigation.

DR. PETER KOTHE, born Friedrichshafen, Germany, January 21, 1960; admitted, 1989, Germany; Fachanwalt für Verwaltungsrecht (Lawyer specializing in administrative law). *Education:* Universities of Bonn, Speyer (Referendar, 1985; Assessor, 1988; Doctor of Jurisprudence, 1990). Author: "Marktwirtschaftliche Instrumente in der Luftreinhaltung als Modell situationsgerechten Verwaltungshandelns. Ein Beitrag zur instrumentellen Erfassung des Kooperationsgedankens" (Economic Instruments of Air Pollution Control as a Model of Flexible Administration). *Member:* German Bar Association; Deutscher Juristentag; Gesellschaft für Umweltrecht e.V. (En-

(This Listing Continued)

vironmental Law Association). *LANGUAGES:* German and English. *PRACTICE AREAS:* Administrative Law; Environmental and Pollution; Waste Disposal; Zoning and Construction; Litigation.

RECHTSANWÄLTE DR. KROLL & PARTNER

Established in 1990

VAIHINGER STRAßE 24
D-70567 STUTTGART, GERMANY
Telephone: (07 11) 161770
Fax: (07 11) 71 00 34

Reutlingen, Germany Office: Eberhardstr.1, D-72764. Telephone: 07121/324-0. Fax: 07121/324-10.

Balingen, Germany Office: Friedrichstr.57, D-72336. Telephone: (07433) 90160. Fax: (07433) 901632.

All fields of law, except Maritime Law.

FIRM PROFILE: The firm was established in 1953 and offers a full range of legal services and tax-advising, with offices in Reutlingen, Stuttgart and Balingen. In 1990 association with attorneys' offices Villingen-Schwenningen (Black Forest), Schmalkalden (Thuringia) and Saverne (France) under the name of C.A.P. EWIV Cooperation Anwaltspartner, legal domicile Stuttgart.

The Reutlingen office consists of 10 attorneys and a staff of 20 employees.

MEMBER OF FIRM

BERNHARD KUNATH, born Freiburg, Germany, 1952; admitted, 1980, Germany. *Education:* University of Freiburg and Heidelberg. *Member:* German Lawyers Association; C.A.P.- EWIV Cooperation Anwaltspartner (Manager, European Economic Interest Grouping). (Also at Reutlingen Office). *LANGUAGES:* German and English. *PRACTICE AREAS:* Civil Law; Administrative Law; Environmental Law; Public Law.

LAHUSEN & CASPAR

CHEMNITZERSTRASSE 21
70597 STUTTGART, GERMANY
Telephone: 0711/7288171
Fax: 0711/7288777

Company, Commercial, Contracts, Computer, Wills, Labor, Mergers and Acquisitions, Commercial and Civil Litigation.

MEMBERS OF FIRM

DR. BRUNO CASPAR, born Hannover, Germany, January 16, 1950; admitted, 1978, Stuttgart. *Education:* Universities of Göttingen (Doctor of Jurispr., 1979); Edinburgh and Dundee (LL.M., 1979). *Member:* German and International Bar Associations. *LANGUAGES:* German, English and French.

DR. ANDREAS LAHUSEN, born Below, Germany, December 1, 1943; admitted, 1972, Stuttgart. *Education:* Universities of Tübingen (Doctor of Jurispr., 1971); Hamburg and Berlin. Author: "Restriktive Rechtsprechung bei Sparförderungsvergünstigungen," Der Betrieb, 1974, 892; " Residenzpflicht deutscher Anwälte und EWG-Vertrag," Außenwirtschaftsdienst, 1974, 491; "Berufsordnung für Journalisten," Zeitschrift für Rechtspolitik, 1976, 111; "Neue Formen der Gutschein-Werbung," Betriebs-Berater, 1985,-1233; "Die Anwendung des Betriebsrentengesetzes auf persönlich haftende Gesellschafter," NZA, 1986, 222; "Rechtsprechung zum nachvertraglichen Wettbewerbsverbot," NZA, 1985, 802; "Zur Durchsetzung vorläufiger personeller Einzelmaßnahmen," NZA, 1989, 869; "Streitigkeiten zwischen Unternehmer und Wirtschaftsausschuß," Betriebs-Berater, 1989, 1399. *LANGUAGES:* German, English and French.

LICHTENSTEIN, KÖRNER & PARTNERS

Established in 1949

HEIDEHOFSTRASSE 9
70184 STUTTGART, GERMANY
Telephone: 0711/4 89-79-0
Cable Address: "Interjus, Stuttgart"
Telex: 723251 ijus d
Telecopier: Group 3: 0711/4815 77; 0711/4873 65

Dresden, Germany Office: Leipziger Str. 1, 01097. Telephone: 0351-54040. Fax: 0351-54040.

Patent, Trademark, Copyright, Unfair Competition, Company, Commercial, Antitrust, Tax and Private International Law.

MEMBERS OF FIRM

PROF. DR. ERICH LICHTENSTEIN (1904-1976).

GÜNTHER JANSSEN (1927-1983).

DR. EBERHARD KÖRNER, born Berlin, Germany, July 25, 1935; admitted, 1964, West Germany. Education: University of Hamburg; University of Tübingen (Referendar, Doctor of Law, Assessor, 1958); New York University (Master of Comparative Jurisprudence, 1963); University of Paris (Doctorat, 1965). Author: Die Vertragsfreiheit im neuen Eheguterrecht, Tübingen, 1961; Trademark Protection in Foreign Countries, New York, 1963; Chapter, "Federal Republic of Germany," International Patent Litigation, Editor, Michael N. Meller, Washington, D.C., 1984. Assistant Professor at Tübingen University, 1959-1962. Member: Stuttgart Bar Association (Member of the Board, 1972-1990); German Association for the Protection of Industrial Property and Copyright (Member of the Board of Southwestern Section, 1976; President, 1986); AIPPI. LANGUAGES: German, English and French. PRACTICE AREAS: Patent Law; Antitrust Law.

CARMEN LICHTENSTEIN, born Prague, Czechoslovakia, February 5, 1944; admitted, 1974, Germany. Education: Universities of Tübingen and München (Referendar, 1969; Assessor, 1974). Member: Stuttgart Bar Association; German Association for the Protection of Industrial Property and Copyright. LANGUAGES: German and English. PRACTICE AREAS: Trademark Law.

KLAUS-ULRICH LINK, born Cuxhaven, Germany, August 22, 1948; admitted, 1980, West Germany. Education: University of Mannheim (Referendar, 1977; Assessor, 1979). Member: Stuttgart Bar Association; German Association for the Protection of Industrial Property and Copyright. LANGUAGES: German and English. PRACTICE AREAS: Corporate Law.

HELMUTH JORDAN, born New-Ulm, Germany, August 10, 1944; admitted, 1972, West Germany. Education: University of Tübingen and University of Geneva, Exchange year in California, 1962 (Scholarship of American Field Service). Author: "Incorporation in Nevada," Verlag Peter Lang AG., 1986. Member: Stuttgart Bar Association; International Bar Association; Registered Foreign Legal Consultant (German Law), California. LANGUAGES: German, English, French and Dutch. PRACTICE AREAS: Commercial Law.

DR. THOMAS SAMBUC, LL.M., born Berlin, Germany, January 16, 1951; admitted to bar, 1980, West Germany. Education: University of Berlin; University ot Tübingen; University of Konstanz (Referendar, 1974; Doctor of Law, 1976; Assessor, 1978); Yale Law School (Master of Laws, 1979). Author: "Folgenerwägungen im Richterrecht," Berlin, 1977. Teaching Assistant, University of Konstanz, 1974-1978. Lecturer on Law, University of Hamburg, 1979-1980. Member: Stuttgart Bar Association; German Association for Comparative Law; German Association for the Protection of Industrial Property and Copyright. LANGUAGES: German, English and French. PRACTICE AREAS: Trademark Law; Commercial Law.

DR. ERNST JACOB-WENDLER, born Reutlingen, Germany, May 25, 1954; admitted, 1984, Germany. Education: University of Freiburg (Referendar, 1979; Assessor, 1982); University of Tübingen (Doctor of Law, 1985). Author: "Reisevertragsrecht und Veranstalterreisen," Tübingen, 1985. Assistant at University of Tübingen, 1983-1984. LANGUAGES: German, English and French. PRACTICE AREAS: Commercial Law.

DR. ROLF DIEKMANN, born Essen, Germany, July 22, 1963; admitted, 1992, Germany. Education: University of Tübingen (Referendar, 1988; Assessor, 1991). Member: Stuttgart Bar Association; German Association for the Protection of Industrial Property and Copyright. LANGUAGES:

(This Listing Continued)

German and English. PRACTICE AREAS: Corporate Law; Commercial Law.

JUDITH ZSEMBERY, born Belgrade, Serbia, January 16, 1965; admitted, 1993, West Germany. Education: Universities of Konstanz and Tübingen. Member: Stuttgart Bar Association; German Association for the Protection of Industrial Property and Copyright. LANGUAGES: German and English. PRACTICE AREAS: Commercial Law.

TAX CONSULTANT

CHRISTIAN HEITMANN-LICHTENSTEIN, born Dresden, Germany, April 13, 1941; admitted, 1973, Munich. Education: Universities of Hamburg and Munich (Dipl. Kfm., 1968). LANGUAGES: German and English. PRACTICE AREAS: Tax Law.

Languages: German, English, French and Dutch

MENOLD HERRLINGER REINKING & PARTNER

MITTLERER PFAD 15
D-70499 STUTTGART, GERMANY
Telephone: 0049/711/13 86 800
Telefax: 0049/711/13 86 808

Berlin Office: Fraunhofer Straße 33-36 D-10587, Berlin. Telephone: (0049 30) 34 78 68 11. Telefax: (0049 30) 34 78 68 35.
Dresden Office: Uhlandstraße 39, 01069 Dresden. Telephone: (0049 351) 478 71-0. Telefax: (0049 351) 478 71 15.
Düsseldorf Office: Am Wehrhahn 50,40211 Düsseldorf. Telephone: (0049 211) 93 52 300. Telefax: (0049 211) 93 52 683.

Corporate, Commercial, Tax and Business Law Practice, including: Mergers and Acquisitions, Antitrust and Unfair Competition Law, Intellectual and Industrial Property Law, Reorganization and Bankruptcy, Labor Law and Redundancy Plans (Sozialpläne), Private Wealth Planning, Trusts, Foundations and Estate Law, Environmental, Waste and Administrative Law, The Laws of the East European Countries, Business Law for Japanese Clients (Düsseldorf), Restitution of Property in the East German Federal States (Dresden), General Civil Law and Civil Litigation, European Community Law.

FIRM PROFILE: The firm springs from a merger of the law firms Menold Herrlinger Maulbetsch Schick & Oltmanns (Stuttgart), Bezler & Partner (Stuttgart), Reith & Battke (Dresden) and Reinking, Frings & Drude (Düsseldorf).

MEMBERS OF FIRM

DR. DIETER MENOLD, born Stuttgart, Germany, 1939. Education: Universities of Munich and Tübingen (State Exams, 1961, 1967; Doctor of Law, 1966). Clerkship with German IRS (Ausbildung zum Finanzassessor), IRS-Officer (Finanzamts-Sachgebietsleiter), 1967-1969. Author: "Das materielle Prüfungsrecht des Handelsregisterrichters," 1967. Member: German Bar Association. LANGUAGES: German and English. PRACTICE AREAS: Corporate Law; Securities Law; Banking Law; Mergers and Acquisitions; Private Wealth Planning.

HARTMUT HERRLINGER, born Süßen, Germany, 1945. Education: Universities of Munich and Tübingen (State Exams, 1969, 1973). Member: German Bar Association. LANGUAGES: German and English. PRACTICE AREAS: Corporate Law; Tax Law; Mergers and Acquisitions.

DR. HANS-CHRISTOPH MAULBETSCH, born Stuttgart, Germany, 1951. Education: University of Tübingen (State Exams, 1977, 1981; Doctor of Law, 1983). Assistant Lecturer, University of Tübingen, 1978-1980. Author: "Beirat und Treuhand in der Publikumspersonengesellschaft," 1984; numerous articles on Corporate Law since 1983. Member: German Bar Association; German Lawyers Association. LANGUAGES: German and English. PRACTICE AREAS: Corporate Law; Tax Law; Securities Law; Banking Law; Mergers and Acquisitions.

RUDOLF BEZLER, born Heidenheim, Germany, 1954; admitted, 1983, Germany. Education: University of Tübingen (State Exams, 1980, 1983). Partner, Law Firm Bezler & Partner, 1990-1993. Author: Numerous articles and seminars on Corporate Law and Labor Law. Member: German Bar Association; German Lawyers Association. LANGUAGES: German and English. PRACTICE AREAS: Corporate Law; Mergers and Acquisitions; Business Law; Labor and Employment.

DR. MICHAEL J. OLTMANNS, born Nürnberg, Germany, 1956. Education: Universities of Erlangen, Freiburg im Breisgau and Geneva; Uni-

(This Listing Continued)

versity of Illinois (Master of Laws, 1987). Assistant, Institute for Foreign and International Private Law, Freiburg University, 1982-1984. Internship with Rogers & Wells, San Diego, CA, 1985. German Bar Exam 1986. Assistant of the Dean, University of Illinois Law School, 1986-1987. Certified Tax Adviser (Steuerberater), 1993. Author: Numerous articles on Corporate Law and Tax Law since 1988. *Member:* German Bar Association; German-American Lawyers Association; Illinois Law School Alumni Association (Germany); German Tax Advisers Association. *LANGUAGES:* German, English and French. *PRACTICE AREAS:* Corporate Law; Tax Law; Mergers and Acquisitions; Private Wealth Planning; Insurance Regulation.

DR. THOMAS REITH, born Sindelfingen, Germany, 1958; admitted, 1988, Germany. *Education:* University of Tübingen (State Exams, 1984, 1988; Doctor of Law, 1989); University of Warsaw (1984); City of London Polytechnic (Master of Arts Business Law, 1985). Author: "Das Phänomen Vorgesellschaft - ein Rechtsvergleich mit der Problematik der Pre-incorporation Contracts," 1990; "Wirtschaftspartner Polen," 3rd ed., 1993; numerous speeches and seminars on Eastern European Law and Investment Projects. *Member:* German Bar Association; German Lawyers Association; German-American Lawyers Association. *LANGUAGES:* German, English, Polish and French. *PRACTICE AREAS:* Corporate Law; Mergers and Acquisitions; International Law; Eastern European Law (Commerce and Investment).

ERICH SCHMID, Dipl.-Betriebswirt (BA), born Geislingen, Germany, 1956; admitted, 1988, Germany. *Education:* Berufsakademie für Betriebswirtschaft in Heidenheim (1977-1980). Trainee with Voith AG in Heidenheim; University of Tübingen, 1981-1984. Referendar, 1985-1988. Partner, Law Firm Bezler & Partner, 1991-1993. *Member:* German Bar Association; German Lawyers Association. *LANGUAGES:* German and English. *PRACTICE AREAS:* Business Law; Company Law; Unfair Competition.

JENS SCHMELT, born Dinslaken, Germany, 1960; admitted, 1988, Germany. *Education:* Universities of Freiburg and Lausanne (State Exams, 1985, 1988). Attorney, Pluta & Knorr, 1988-1990. *Member:* German Bar Association. *LANGUAGES:* German and English. *PRACTICE AREAS:* Corporate Law; Mergers and Acquisitions; Labor and Employment; Reorganization.

DR. BARBARA EBINGER, born Stuttgart, Germany 1961; admitted, 1991, Germany. *Education:* University of Bayreuth (State Exams, 1986, 1989; Doctor of Law, 1992). Assistant Lecturer, University of Bayreuth, 1989-1991. Author: "Der unbestimmte Rechtsbegriff im Recht der Technik." *Member:* German Bar Association. *LANGUAGES:* German, English and French. *PRACTICE AREAS:* Corporate Law; Business Law; Environmental Law; Administrative Law.

DR. KLAUS-DIETER ROSE, born Münster/Westfalen, Germany, 1962; admitted, 1992, Germany. *Education:* University of Passau; University College Cardiff/Wales, Law Department (1985-1986, State Exams, 1988, 1991; Doctor of Law, 1994). *Member:* German Bar Association. *LANGUAGES:* German, English and Russian. *PRACTICE AREAS:* Corporate Law; Mergers and Acquisitions; Business Law; Labor and Employment.

DR. BEATRICE FABRY, born Stuttgart, Germany, 1963; admitted, 1992, Germany. *Education:* Universities of Tübingen and Freiburg (State Exams, 1989, 1992; Doctor of Law, 1993). Assistant, University of Tübingen, 1989-1990. Author: "Private Unternehmen als Umwelt-Störer: Zur Polizeipflichtigkeit von Kapital- und Personengesellschaften," 1993. *Member:* German Bar Association. *LANGUAGES:* German and English. *PRACTICE AREAS:* Business Law; Corporate Law; Environmental Law (Waste Disposal); Charitable Organizations.

OPPENLÄNDER DOLDE OESTERLE & PARTNERS

ALTENBERGSTRASSE 3
70180 STUTTGART, GERMANY
Telephone: 0711/96730
Fax: 0711/9673222

FIRM PROFILE: *The basic philosophy of our Firm is to offer highly specialized but still personal legal services of outstanding quality in all major fields of law relevant to corporate clients. The Firm's traditional areas of practice are corporate law, industrial and intellectual property law, antitrust law and law of unfair competition, constitutional and administrative law, particularly urban development planning, public economic law and environmental law. Further areas of particular experience include mergers and acquisitions, arbitration and EEC law. The Firm is engaged in East-*

(This Listing Continued)

ern Germany. Clients include major blue chip corporations and state governments.

PARTNERS

DR. FRANK OPPENLÄNDER, born Stuttgart, Germany, 1942; admitted, 1971, Germany. *Education:* Universities of Tübingen, Berlin and Freiburg (Dr. iur., 1974). Author: "Enterprise Leasing," 1974 (in German) and various publications on Company Law and Antitrust Law. *Member:* German Association for Industrial Property Rights and Copyright; Association Internationale pour la Protection de la Propriété Industrielle (AIPPI); Association for the Study of Antitrust Law. *LANGUAGES:* German and English. *PRACTICE AREAS:* Company Law; Mergers and Acquisitions; Commercial; Intellectual Property.

PROF. DR. KLAUS-PETER DOLDE, born Schöntal, Germany 1944; admitted, 1972, Germany. *Education:* Universities of Tübingen and Berlin. Lecturer, Tübingen University Law School, 1977—. Honorary Professor, Tübingen University Law School, 1984—. Research Assistant: Prof. Bachof, 1970-1971; Dr. iur. Tübingen, 1972. Author: "The Political Rights of Aliens in the Federal Republic of Germany," 1972 (in German); "Urban Development Planning in Practice," 1981 (in German); "Official Warnings on non-marketable Foodstuffs," 1987 (in German) and numerous publications on Administrative Law, particularly Environmental Law and Zoning. Co-Editor: "New Administrative Law Review," (in German); Commercial and Business Law Review," (in German). Regular contributor to the "Review for the entire public and private construction law" (in German). *Member:* German Bar Association (Committee on Environmental Law); Society for Environmental Law (Board Member); Association for the Law and the Science of Foodstuffs (BLL) (Scientific Advisory Board, Section Law of Foodstuffs). *LANGUAGES:* German and English. *PRACTICE AREAS:* Environmental; Zoning; Real Property; State Aid.

DR. FRITZ OESTERLE, born Stuttgart, Germany, 1952; admitted, 1981, Germany. *Education:* Tübingen University (Dr. iur., 1980). Research Assistant, Department of Civil Law and Civil Procedure, 1976-1979. Author: "Concurrent Performance," 1980 (in German) and various publications on Unfair Competition and Antitrust Law. *Member:* German Association for Industrial Property Rights and Copyright; Association for the Study of Antitrust Law. *LANGUAGES:* German and English. *PRACTICE AREAS:* Antitrust; Merger Control; Unfair Competition; Pharmaceutical.

DR. RAINARD MENKE, born Fröndenberg, Germany, 1957; admitted, 1985, Germany. *Education:* Universities of Münster and Munich (Dr. iur., 1983). Scientific Assistant, Department of Regional Planning and Public Law, 1983-1985. Author: "Urban Development Planning in Mixed Zoning Area," 1984 (in German); "Federal Regional Planning and Regional Planning for the State of Rhineland Palatinate," 1986 (in German). *Member:* Society for Environmental Law. *LANGUAGES:* German and English. *PRACTICE AREAS:* Property Development; Environmental; Priority of Investment in Eastern Germany.

DR. MARC STUCKEL, born Neuilly, France, 1961; admitted, 1990, Germany. *Education:* Munich University (Dr. iur., 1991). Research Assistant, Max-Planck Institut für ausländisches und internationales Patent-, Urheber- und Wettbewerbsrecht, Munich, 1986-1990. Author: "Integrity of Trademark, Product and Packaging," 1991 (in German). *Member:* German Association for Industrial Property Rights and Copyright; Association for the Study of Antitrust Law. *LANGUAGES:* German, French and English. *PRACTICE AREAS:* Trademarks; Intellectual Property; Unfair Competition.

DR. ALBRECHT BACH, born Stuttgart, Germany, 1959; admitted, 1989, Germany. *Education:* Universities of Tübingen and Aix-en-Provence (Dr. iur., 1991). Research Assistant, Prof. Möschel, 1986-1990. Visiting Lawyer with Linklaters & Paines, London, 1988. Author: "Anticompetitive State Measures under EEC Law," 1991 (in German) and various publications on EC Law and Antitrust Law. *Member:* Association for the Study of Antitrust Law; International Bar Association SBL. *LANGUAGES:* German, English and French. *PRACTICE AREAS:* EC and German Competition Law; European Community Law; Company Law; International Transactions.

DR. ANDREA VETTER, born Stuttgart, Germany, 1962; admitted, 1992, Germany. *Education:* Universities of Tübingen and Freiburg i. Br. (Dr. iur., 1991). Research Assistant, Prof. Bullinger, 1986-1990. Author: "The Contractual Relations of the Service Companies of the Deutsche Bundespost," 1992 (in German). *Member:* Society for Environmental Law. *LANGUAGES:* German and English. *PRACTICE AREAS:* Environmental; Zoning; Media and Telecommunications.

(This Listing Continued)

OPPENLÄNDER DOLDE OESTERLE & PARTNERS,
Stuttgart—Continued

HEINZ-UWE DETTLING, born Horb a.N., Germany, 1963; admitted, 1993, Germany. *Education:* Tübingen University. Research Assistant, Research Department of International History of Civil Law, Prof. Nörr, 1988-1993. Visiting Scholar, University of California at Berkeley, 1993-1994. *LANGUAGES:* German, English and French. *PRACTICE AREAS:* Company Law; Commercial.

DR. THOMAS BAUMANN, born Cologne, Germany, 1963; admitted, 1994, Germany. *Education:* University of Cologne (Dr.iur., 1992). Research Assistant, Tübingen University, Prof. Oppermann, 1991-1992. *Author:* "Delegation of Authority to conclude Collective Agreements," 1992 (in German). *LANGUAGES:* German and English. *PRACTICE AREAS:* Labor and Employment; Co-Determination; Collective Bargaining; Industrial Relations; Pensions.

DR. EBERHARD OTT

GAISBURGSTRASSE 27
70182 STUTTGART, GERMANY
Telephone: 0711-235468; 235469
Telefax: 0711-244031

Corporate, Commercial, Antitrust, Unfair Competition, Drug Law, International and EEC Law, Probate, General Practice, Litigation and Arbitration.

DR. EBERHARD OTT, born Schwäbisch Hall, Germany, October 3, 1944; admitted, 1976, West Germany. *Education:* Universities of Tübingen, Munich and Kiel (Doctor of Jurisprudence, 1974, Kiel). *Author:* "Die Weltorganisation für Meteorologie (The World Meteorological Organization)," 1976. *Member:* Stuttgart Bar (Member of the Board); Stuttgart Lawyers Association (Member of the Board); German Lawyers Association (Member, International Legal Relations Committee); Deutsche Vereinigung für gewerblichen Rechtsschutz und Urheberrecht (Industrial and Copyright Association); International Bar Association; Union Internationale des Avocats; Association Internationale des Jeunes Avocats. *LANGUAGES:* German, English and French.

QUACK GUTTERER & PARTNER

Established in 1982

WILLY-BRANDT-STRASSE 50-54
70173 STUTTGART, GERMANY
Telephone: 0711-2238740
Telefax: 0711-2237954

Dresden, Germany Office: Melanchthonstr. 7,01099 Dresden. Telephone: 0351-5022418. Telefax: 0351-5022417.

Corporation, Commercial, Unfair Competition, Merger and Acquisition, Labour Law, Trusts, Foundations and Estate Law, International and EEC Law, Real Estate, General Practice and Litigation.

MEMBERS OF FIRM

NORBERT H. QUACK, born Mönchengladbach-Rheydt, Germany, 1947; admitted, 1975, Düsseldorf. *Education:* Universities of Munich and Bonn. Chairman of Supervisory Board: Helixor Heilmittel GmbH & Co., Rosenfeld; R.& A. Leibfarth GmbH, Pliezhausen; TPP Recycling GmbH, Ibbenbüren. Member of Supervisory Board: Index-Werke GmbH & Co. Hahn & Tessky, Esslingen; Vereinigte Motor-Verlage GmbH & Co., Stuttgart; Zinser Textilmaschinen GmbH, Ebersbach/Fils. *Author:* "Begrenzung der Nachhaftung für betriebliche Altersversorgung durch eine Verjährungsvereinbarung," Betriebsberater 1979, 1457 ff; "Die Testamentsvollstreckung an Kommanditanteilen, Betriebsberater," 1989, 2271 ff. *Member:* German Bar Association. *LANGUAGES:* German, English and French.

DR. BERNHARD K. GUTTERER, born Stuttgart, Germany, 1958; admitted, 1988, Stuttgart. *Education:* University of Tübingen (Doctor of Laws, 1991). *Author:* "Zur verbindlichen Zusage des Gerichts in der Hauptverhandlung, eine bestimmte verurteilung nach Geständnis des Angeklagten auszusprechen." *Member:* German Bar Association. *LANGUAGES:* German and English.

(This Listing Continued)

DR. CHRISTOPH HARTMANN, born Hannover, Germany, 1957; admitted, 1989. *Education:* University of Tübingen (Doctor of Laws, 1990). *Author:* "Der Begünstigtenanspruch im Dokumentenakkreditiv;" "Keine Fragen offenlassen, Vertragsrisiko begrenzen," Industrieanzeiger 43/94, 39 ff. *Member:* German Bar Association. *LANGUAGES:* German and English.

ACHIM E. ROTTNAUER, born Kaufbeuren, Germany, 1956; admitted, 1994. *Education:* Universities of Tübingen, Münster and Lausanne (Doctor of Laws, 1991). Assistant at the University of Tübingen, 1984-1988; Corporate Counsel, 1988-1994. *Author:* "Die Mobiliarkreditsicherheiten unter besonderer Berücksichtigung der besitzlosen Pfandrechte im deutschen und englischen Recht, 1992;" "Vertragsgestaltungsproblematik bei Mehrmütterorganschaft in GmbH-Konzernrecht," DB 1991, 27 ff; "Anmerkung zum LG Heilbronn, Beschluß vom 20.03.1991 - AZ 2 T 57/91 III," RdE 1991, 168 ff; "Publizität des Spaltungsplans und Gläubigerschutz," DB 1992, 1393 ff; "Reichweite der Anschlußklausel in § 24 Abs. 8 Satz 1 Nr. 2 GWB," WuW 1993, 369 ff; "Funktion der 500 Millionen-DM-Toleranzklause im geltenden Fusionsrecht," BB 1993, 2394 ff. *Member:* German Bar Association. *LANGUAGES:* German, English and French.

Languages: German, English and French

DR. SCHELLING & PARTNERS

Established in 1961

KOENIGSTR. 84
70173 STUTTGART, GERMANY
Telephone: 49-711-2079-0
Telecopier: 49-711-2079-290

Mailing Address: P.O. Box 104554, 70040

Antitrust, Banking, Commercial, Company, Corporation, Mergers and Acquisitions, Construction, Labor, Unfair Competition, Real Estate and Property, Litigation and Arbitration.

FIRM PROFILE: *Established in 1961 the firm has a broadly based practice offering specialized legal services in all commercial matters. The firm concentrates on corporate clients rendering personal legal services of top quality.*

MEMBERS OF FIRM

DR. ROLAND SCHELLING, born Stuttgart, 1930; admitted, 1956, Stuttgart. *Education:* University of Tübingen (Doctor of Law, 1953). Chairman of Supervisory Board: Carl Zeiss Jena GmbH, Jena; JENAer GLASWERK GmbH, Jena; Jenoptik GmbH, Jena; MITRAS Kunststoffe GmbH, Weiden. Member of Supervisory Board: Daimler-Benz AG, Stuttgart; Metallgessellschaft AG, Frankfurt; Badenwerk AG, Karlsruhe; Aesculap AG, Tuttlingen; Konrad Hornschuch AG, Weißbach; Traub AG, Reichenbach/Fils; Carl Zeiss, Oberkochen; Glaswerke Schott, Mainz. *LANGUAGES:* German and English. *PRACTICE AREAS:* Corporate Law; Mergers and Acquisitions.

DR. KLAUS KESSLER, born Flensburg, 1942; admitted, 1973, Stuttgart. *Education:* Universities of Heidelberg and Kiel (Doctor of Law, 1971). *Author:* "Übernahmeangebote (Take-over bids) im englischen Gesellschafts- und Börsenrecht," 1971. Certified Labor Attorney. Member of Supervisory Board: Kolbenschmidt AG, Neckarsulm; C.F. Braun GmbH, Stuttgart. *Member:* German Bar Association. *LANGUAGES:* German, English and French. *PRACTICE AREAS:* Industrial Relations; Labor; Mergers and Acquisitions.

DR. WOLFGANG HEEB, born Balingen, 1945; admitted, 1972, Germany. *Education:* Universities of Berlin (FU) and Tübingen (Doctor of Law, 1973). *Member:* German Bar Association; Society for Industrial Property and Copyright (GRUR). *LANGUAGES:* German and English. *PRACTICE AREAS:* Unfair Competition; Intellectual Property; Real Estate Law.

DR. WERNER FUTTER, born Reutlingen, 1946; admitted, 1975, Germany. *Education:* University of Tübingen (Doctor of Law, 1974). Assistant Lecturer, Tübingen Law School, 1973-1975. *Author:* "Die Subsidiarität der Amtshaftung - Instrument der Haftungslenkung," 1974; "Auf der Suche nach der Politik des Gesetzes," Festgabe für Josef Esser, S. 37 ff., 1975. Member of Supervisory Board: AEG, Frankfurt; Oberland Glas AG, Bad Wurzach; Stuttgarter Bank AG, Stuttgart; Verlagsgesellschaft "Das Wertpapier", Düsseldorf. *Member:* German Bar Association. *LANGUAGES:* German, English and French. *PRACTICE AREAS:* Corporate Law; Joint Ventures; Mergers and Acquisitions.

(This Listing Continued)

DR. ROLF BÜSCHER, born Cologne, 1953; admitted, 1982, Stuttgart. *Education:* University of Cologne and Tübingen (Doctor of Law, 1982; Diplom-Volkswirt, 1981). Author: "Conglomerate Mergers in U.S. and German Law," 1983. Member of Supervisory Board: GIVAG, Bad Mergentheim. Certified Administrative Law Attorney. *Member:* German Bar Association. *LANGUAGES:* German, English and French. *PRACTICE AREAS:* Administrative Law (Environmental, Zoning); Antitrust Law; Real Estate Law; Construction Law.

DR. HANS-ULRICH EPPINGER, born Münsingen, 1954; admitted, 1983, Stuttgart. *Education:* University of Tübingen (Doctor of Law, 1982). Assistant Lecturer, University of Tübingen, 1979-1982. Author: "Die gerichtliche Überprüfbarkeit strafprozessualer Zwangsmaßnahmen." *Member:* German Bar Association. *LANGUAGES:* German, English and French. *PRACTICE AREAS:* Banking Law; Family Law.

DR. JÜRGEN REIMER, born Heidelberg, Germany, 1958; admitted, 1987, Stuttgart. *Education:* University of Tübingen (Doctor of Law, 1989). Author: "Die aufgedrängte Bereicherung - Paradigma der 'negatorischen' Abschöpfung in Umkehrung zum Schadensersatz," 1990. *Member:* German Bar Association. *LANGUAGES:* German and English. *PRACTICE AREAS:* Corporate Law; Law of Succession.

DR. TOBIAS KÜBLER, born Stuttgart, Germany, 1960; admitted, 1989, Stuttgart. *Education:* University of Freiburg, München, Tübingen (Doctor of Law, 1989). Author: "Franchiseverträge in der deutschen Rechtspraxis," 1989. *Member:* German Bar Association. *LANGUAGES:* German and English. *PRACTICE AREAS:* Business and Real Estate Law.

SIGLE, LOOSE, SCHMIDT-DIEMITZ & PARTNERS

Established in 1962

SCHÖTTLESTR. 8

P.O. BOX 70 02 65

D-70572 STUTTGART (DEGERLOCH), GERMANY

Telephone: 0711-9764-0

Telefax: 0711-9764-900

Berlin, Germany Office: Friedrichstrasse 130 a, 10117 Berlin. Telephone: 030-308792-0. Telefax: 030-2385849.

Leipzig, Germany Office: August-Bebel-Strasse 38, 04275 Leipzig. Telephone: 0341-3912007. Telefax: 0341-391-2085.

Frankfurt/Main, Germany Office: Schumannstrasse 62, 60325 Frankfurt/Main. Telephone: 069-97 5841-0. Telefax: 069-97 584117.

Chemnitz, Germany Office: Barbarossastraße 46, 09112 Chemnitz. Telephone: 0371-36974-0. Telefax: 0371-3697421.

Moscow, Russia Office: Sadovaja Samotjotschnaja, 103 051 Moscow. Telephone: 007/095/528 50 55. Fax: 007/095/258 51 55.

Commerical Corporation, Mergers and Acquisitions, Banking Investment, Common Market, Antitrust, Unfair Competition, Copyright, Patent and Trademark, License Agreements, Press, Transportation, Insurance, Product Liability, Real Estate, Construction, Probate, Labor, Administrative, Tax, International, Litigation and Arbitration.

MEMBERS OF FIRM

DR. WALTER SIGLE, born Urach, Germany, 1930; admitted, 1958, Stuttgart. *Education:* University of Tübingen (Doctor of Law, 1955). Chairman of Supervisory Board: Fortuna-Werke Maschinenfabrik GmbH, Stuttgart; Friedrich Bilger GmbH & Co. KG, Ulm; LEGA Hotel - und Gaststättenbetriebs-Gesellschaft mbH, Stuttgart; Schwaben Bräu Rob. Leicht AG, Stuttgart; Karl Huber Verpackungswerke, Öhringen; Maschinenfabrik Müller-Weingarten AG, Weingarten; Württembergische Filztuchfabrik D. Geschmay GmbH, Göppingen. Member of Supervisory Board: Eckhardt AG, Stuttgart, Württembergische Lebensversicherung AG, Stuttgart; Württembergische Aktiengesellschaft Versicherungs—Beteiligungsgesellschaft, Stuttgart; Württembergische Versicherungs AG, Stuttgart; Leonberger Bausparkasse AG, Leonberg; Freudenberg & Co., Weinheim; Bankhaus Ellwanger & Geiger, Stuttgart; Koch & Mayer Bauunternehmung GmbH & Co. KG, Heilbronn; Mairs Geographischer Verlag, Kemnat; Procter & Gamble GmbH, Schwalbach; F. Kirchhoff Straßenbau GmbH, Stuttgart; Trumpf GmbH & Co., Ditzingen. *Member:* German Bar Association (Member, Legislative Committee for Commercial Law); International Bar Association. *LANGUAGES:* German and English. *PRACTICE AREAS:* Corporate Law; Mergers and Acquisitions.

(This Listing Continued)

JÖRG SCHNEIDER, born Stuttgart, Germany, 1936; admitted, 1964, Stuttgart. *Education:* Universities of Hamburg, Munich and Tübingen. *Member:* German Bar Association. *LANGUAGES:* German, English and French. *PRACTICE AREAS:* Construction Law; Trademark Law.

HANS-GERT LOOSE, born Aue, Germany, 1934; admitted, 1964, Stuttgart. *Education:* Universities of Halle, Münster and Basel (Bar Examen, 1956, DDR; Licentiatum juris utriusque, 1961, Basel, Switzerland). Judge Appellate Court of Professional Discipline (Baden-Wüerttemberg, 1979. *Member:* German Bar Association. *PRACTICE AREAS:* Construction Law; Negligence and Personal Injury Law.

DR. ROLF SCHMIDT-DIEMITZ, born Halle, Germany, 1939; admitted, 1968, Stuttgart. *Education:* Universities of Frankfurt, Munich and Freiburg (Doctor of Law, 1993). Co-Author: Munich Handbook of Contracts, Volume 1, Corporate Law, Section 10, "Changing the Corporate Form"; Handbook of Competition Law. Member, Supervisory Board: Aktivbank AG, Stuttgart. *Member:* German Bar Association; German Association for the Protection of Industrial Property and Copyright; Association International pour le Protection de la Propiete Industrielle; German Institution for Arbitration; International Bar Association. *LANGUAGES:* German and English. *PRACTICE AREAS:* Corporate Law; Mergers and Acquisitions.

DR. KLAUS KEMMLER (1936-1990).

DR. GOTTFRIED RAISER, born Stuttgart, Germany, 1936; admitted, 1966, Stuttgart. *Education:* Universities of Berlin, Munich and Tübingen (Doctor of Law, 1965); New York University. Author: "Die gerichtliche Kontrolle von Formularbedingungen im Amerikanischen und Deutschen Recht," (Judicial Control of Standard Form Contracts in American and German Law), 1966. *Member:* German Bar Association; German Association of Comparative Law; German-American Lawyers Association; International Bar Association. *LANGUAGES:* German and English. *PRACTICE AREAS:* Corporate Law; Construction Law; Insurance Law; International Contracts.

DR. FRANZ-JÖRG SEMLER, born Berlin, Germany, 1942; admitted, 1971, Frankfurt. *Education:* Universities of Tübingen and Munich (Doctor of Law, 1968); The European Institute of Business Administration, INSEAD, Fontainebleau, France (M.B.A., 1971). Co-Author i.a.: *Münchener Vertragshandbuch,* (Munich Contracts Handbook), Volume 1, Corporate Law, 1992, Volume 2, Commercial and Business Law, 1993, *Handbuch des Unternehmenskaufs,* (Handbook of Acquisitions of Enterprises), 1991; Handbuch des Aktienrechts (Handbook of Stock Corporation Law). Chairman of Advisory Board Hartmann & Laemmle GmbH & Co., Rutesheim. *Member:* German Bar Association; German Association for the Protection of Industrial Property and Copyright; Association Internationale pour la Protection de la Propriété Industrielle; International Bar Association. *LANGUAGES:* German, English and French. *PRACTICE AREAS:* Corporate Law; Mergers and Acquisitions; Distributorship Law; International Contracts; Arbitration.

DR. JÜRGEN SCHMID, born Stuttgart, Germany, 1948; admitted, 1977, Stuttgart. *Education:* University of Tübingen (Doctor of Law, 1979). Assistant Lecturer, Tübingen Law School, 1975-1976. Co-Author: Münchener Handbuch des Gesellschaftsrechts 1991 Beck'sches Rechtshandbuch für Steuerberater 1991. *Member:* German Bar Association; Deutsch-Polnische Juristenvereinigung. *LANGUAGES:* German and English. *PRACTICE AREAS:* Corporate Law; Property and Real Estate Law.

DR. GERHARD WILHELM, born Hülzweiler, Germany, 1952; admitted, 1981, Stuttgart. *Education:* University of Tübingen (Doctor of Law, 1980). Assistant Lecturer, Tübingen Law School, 1978-1980. Certified Labour Attorney. *Member:* German Bar Association. *LANGUAGES:* German and English. *PRACTICE AREAS:* Labor Law.

THOMAS HOENE, born Hann.-Münden, Germany, 1952; admitted, 1981, Stuttgart. *Education:* University of Münster. Assistant Lecturer, Münster Law School, 1978-1981. Member, Supervisory Board, Vortex Computersysteme GmbH, Flein; Maier & Partner AG, Stuttgart (Chairman); Albuch Fahrradfabrik GmbH, Boehmenkirch (Chairman); SUEDRAD GmbH, Ebersbach. *Member:* German Bar Association; German Association of Electronic Data Processing and Law (Chairman of the Board); German Australian Association; German-Australian Chamber of Commerce, Melbourne. *LANGUAGES:* German and English. *PRACTICE AREAS:* Corporate Law; Computer Law.

KARL-EDUARD VON DER HEYDT, born Kirchheim, Germany, 1949; admitted, 1978, Munich. *Education:* University of Munich. Tax Consultant, 1981. Co-Author: "The European Economic Interest Grouping," 1991. *Member:* German Bar Association; German Association of Tax Con-

(This Listing Continued)

SIGLE, LOOSE, SCHMIDT-DIEMITZ & PARTNERS,
Stuttgart—Continued

sultants. *LANGUAGES:* German, English and French. *PRACTICE AREAS:* Banking Law; Corporate Law; Tax Law.

ALBRECHT SCHULZ, born Liegnitz, Germany, 1941; admitted, 1973, Stuttgart. *Education:* Universities of Munich, Innsbruck, Kiel, Tübingen and Paris. Assistant, EEC Commission, Brussels, 1969-1970. With Kemmler & Rapp-Jung, Brussels, 1974-1975. Deputy Secretary General, European Insurance Committee, Paris, 1976-1982. *Member:* German Bar Association; International Bar Association (Vice-Chairman, Committee X International Franchising); French Bar Association; German Franchise Association; European Franchise Association (Chairman, Legal Committee); Licensing Executives Society. *LANGUAGES:* German, French and English. *PRACTICE AREAS:* Franchise; Distributorship and Agency Law; Licensing; Copyright Law; Competition Law; International Contracts.

DR. ANTON G. MAURER, born Schwäbisch Gmünd, Germany, 1950; admitted, 1982, Stuttgart. *Education:* University of Tübingen (Doctor of Jurisprudence, 1984). Assistant Lecturer, University of Tübingen, 1979-1984. With Johnson & Gibbs, Dallas, 1984-1985. Author: "Die staatsangehörigkeitsrechtlichen Beziehungen geteilter Staaten dargestellt am Beispiel von Irland, Nordirland und Grossbritannien," 1984 (The Relationship of Divided States in the Field of Nationality Law Exemplified by Ireland, Northern Ireland and Great Britain). Chairman of the Supervisory Board: E.A. Storz GmbH & Co. KG, Tuttlingen; Plischke GmbH & Co. KG, Tuttlingen. Member of Supervisory Board: Maschinenfabrik Ravensburg AG, Ravensburg; MTR Ravensburg, Inc., Rochester, N.Y., U.S.A.; Bettwaren Finanz Holding GmbH, Stuttgart; Nord Feder GmbH & Co. KG, Stuttgart; Blum-Novotest GmbH, Gullen. *Member:* German Bar Association; International Bar Association; American Bar Association (Country Coordinator for West Germany of the European Law Committee of the Section of International Law and Practice, 1986-1990); German-American Lawyers Association; German-American Chamber of Commerce, New York; The Southwestern Legal Foundation; German-Finnish Chamber of Commerce, Helsinki. *LANGUAGES:* German and English. *PRACTICE AREAS:* Foreign Investments; International Contracts; Mergers and Acquisitions.

DR. ANGELIKA SCHNELL, born Ludwigshafen/Rhein, Germany, 1958; admitted, 1986, Stuttgart. *Education:* Universities of Munich and Tübingen (Doctor of Law, 1986). Lecturer in Civil Law, Higher Technical College of Economica, Stuttgart, 1988—. *Member:* German Bar Association; German Association of Women Lawyers. *LANGUAGES:* German, English and French. *PRACTICE AREAS:* Family Law.

DR. DIRK RODEWOLDT, born Hannover, Germany, 1956; admitted, 1985, Hannover. *Education:* Universities of Göttingen and Geneva, Switzerland. Assistant Lecturer, Göttingen Law School, 1980, 1985. Certified Administrative Law Attorney. *Member:* German Bar Association; German Society of Environmental Law; International Bar Association. *LANGUAGES:* German, English and French. *PRACTICE AREAS:* Environmental Law; Planning Law; Construction Law.

DR. KARL-HEINZ KLETT, born Tuttlingen, Germany, 1958; admitted, 1988, Stuttgart. *Education:* University of Freiburg (Doctor of Law, 1988). Author: "Possessory Relationships within Partnerships," 1989. Assistant Lecturer, Freiburg Law School, 1985-1988. Lecturer in Civil Law at Higher Technical College of Economics, Stuttgart, 1989—. *Member:* German Bar Association. *LANGUAGES:* German, English and French. *PRACTICE AREAS:* Corporate Law; Commercial Law.

DR. ACHIM LINDEMANN, born Düsseldorf, Germany, 1958; admitted, 1987, Konstanz. *Education:* University of Konstanz (Doctor of Law, 1989). Author: "Die Durchbrechungen des Abstraktionsprinzips durch die Höchstrichterliche Rechtsprechung seit 1900," (Exceptions to the Abstraction Principle in Federal Court of Justice Decisions since 1900), 1989. Assistant Lecturer, Konstanz Law School, 1986-1988. Certified Labour Attorney. *Member:* German Bar Association. *LANGUAGES:* German and English. *PRACTICE AREAS:* Labor Law.

RALF KURNEY, born Duisburg, Germany, 1959; admitted, 1988, Stuttgart. *Education:* Universities of Münster, Hagen and Speyer. Seconded to McKenna & Co., London in 1991. *Member:* German Bar Association; German Association for the Protection of Industrial Property and Copyright. *LANGUAGES:* German and English. *PRACTICE AREAS:* Corporate Law; Mergers and Acquisitions; U.K. Related Matters.

DR. THOMAS MEYDING, born Hamburg, Germany, 1958; admitted, 1988, Stuttgart; 1992, England. *Education:* Universities of Tübingen, Frei-

(This Listing Continued)

burg, Konstanz (Doctor of Law, 1989) and Florida. With Mc Kenna & Co., London, 1991-1992. Author: "Die Mantel-GmbH im Gesellschafts- und Steuerrecht," (The GmbH-Shell in Corporate and Tax Law). Co-Author: "An Introduction to German Civil and Commercial Law," 1993; Europäische Integration und globaler Wettbewerb (European Integration and Global Competition), 1993. *Member:* German Bar Association. *LANGUAGES:* German and English. *PRACTICE AREAS:* Corporate Law; International Transactions Law.

DR. JOCHEN LAMB, born Ludwigshafen/Rhein, Germany, 1960; admitted, 1990, Stuttgart. *Education:* University of Heidelberg (Doctor of Law, 1991). With Gardner, Carton & Douglas, Chicago, 1992-1993. Author: "Die Vorfinanzierung von Kapitalerhöhungen durch Voreinzahlungen auf eine künftige Einlageverpflichtung ("Prefinancing of increases in capital by prepayment in respect of future subscription liabilities), 1991. Assistant Lecturer, Heidelberg Law School, 1983-1984, 1986. Lecturer in Corporate and Commercial Law: Higher Technical College of Economics, Stuttgart, 1991-1992. *Member:* German Bar Association. *LANGUAGES:* German, English and French. *PRACTICE AREAS:* Corporate Law; Mergers and Acquisitions; Foreign Investments; International Contracts Law.

DR. AXEL SIGLE, born Stuttgart, Germany, 1960; admitted, 1989, Stuttgart. *Education:* Universities of Tübingen, Salzburg (Doctor of Law, 1991) and Washington, D. C. at American (LL.M., 1990). Author: "Glaeubigerschutz in der Einmann-GmbH,"(Protection of Creditors in Corporation with only one shareholder), 1991. *Member:* German Bar Association; American Bar Association; German-American Lawyers Association; Foreign Lawyers Forum, Washington D.C. *LANGUAGES:* German, English and French. *PRACTICE AREAS:* Corporate Law; Commercial Law; International Contracts.

ASSOCIATES

DR. DOROTHEE RUCKTESCHLER, born Hamburg, Germany, 1955; admitted, 1983, Freiburg. *Education:* Universities of Grenoble, France, Freiburg (Doctor of Law, 1987), Boston, Mass., USA. Author: "Subunternehmer—Haftung" (Liability of Subcontractors), 1988. *Member:* German Bar Association; German Association of Comparative Law. *LANGUAGES:* German, English and French. *PRACTICE AREAS:* Corporate Law; Commercial Law; International Contracts.

MICHAEL BRENNER, born Schwäbisch Gmünd, 1961; admitted, 1991, Stuttgart. *Education:* University of Tübingen. Assistant Lecturer, Tübingen Law School, 1987-1991. Seconded to McKenna & Co., London, 1993-1994. *Member:* German Bar Association. *LANGUAGES:* German and English. *PRACTICE AREAS:* Corporate Law; Commercial Law.

DR. PETER BAISCH, born Reutlingen, Germany, 1961; admitted, 1991, Stuttgart. *Education:* Universities of Munich and Tübingen (Doctor of Law, 1992). Author: "Der Schutz des Opportunitätsprinzips im Ordnungswidrigkeitenrecht durch §336 StGB" (Protecting the principle according to which prosecution of an administrative offence is discretionary through §336 StGB), 1992. Seconded to McKenna & Co., London, 1994-1995. *Member:* German Bar Association. *LANGUAGES:* German, English and French. *PRACTICE AREAS:* Corporate Law; Commercial Law.

DR. THOMAS MUNDRY, born Berlin, Germany, 1962; admitted, 1990, Stuttgart. *Education:* Free University of Berlin (Doctor of Law, 1992). Author: "Darlehen und stille Einlagen im Recht der Kommanditgesellschaft" (Loans and Undisclosed Participations in a Limited Partnership), 1992. Assistant Lecturer in Company, Commercial and Civil Law, Free University of Berlin, 1987-1991, Center of National and International Cartel Law of the Free University of Berlin, 1987-1989. *Member:* German Bar Association. *LANGUAGES:* German, English and French. *PRACTICE AREAS:* Company Law; Commercial Law; Litigation.

DR. ANTJE-KATHRIN UHL, born Oldenburg, Germany, 1961; admitted, 1992, Stuttgart. *Education:* University of Konstanz and Tübingen (Doctor of Law, 1992). Judge, Regional Court, 1989-1992. Author: "Der Handel mit Kunstwerken im europaeischen Binnenmarkt - Freier Warenverkehr versus nationaler Kulturgutschutz," 1992 (Trading with works of art in the European internal market - Free trade versus national protection of cultural assets). Lecturer in labor law, Higher Technical College of Economics, Stuttgart, 1992—. *Member:* German Bar Association. *LANGUAGES:* German, English and French. *PRACTICE AREAS:* Labor Law.

DR. MATTHIAS ECK, born Bielefeld, Germany, 1959; admitted, 1991, Germany. *Education:* Universities of Munich and Tübingen (Doctor of Law, 1992). Assistant Lecturer, University of Tübingen, 1989-1991. Lecturer, Unfair Competition and Cartel Law, University of Chemnitz. Author: "New Approaches in Design and Pattern Protection," 1992 (in Ger-

(This Listing Continued)

man). Co-Author: "Handbook of Competition Law." *Member:* German Association for Industrial Property Rights and Copyright; Association for the study of Antitrust Law. *LANGUAGES:* German, English, French and Spanish. *PRACTICE AREAS:* Unfair Competition; Industrial and Intellectual Property Law; Licensing; Media; Copyright.

FRANK GUTSCHE, born Schwäbisch Gmünd, Germany, 1962; admitted, 1992, Stuttgart. *Education:* University of Tübingen. Assistant Lecturer, University of Tübingen, 1988-1992. *Member:* German Bar Association. *LANGUAGES:* German and English. *PRACTICE AREAS:* Corporate Law; Mergers and Acquisitions.

DR. HANS-GUNTHER NORDHUES, born Dortmund, Germany, 1962; admitted, 1991, Dortmund. *Education:* Universities of Bayreuth and Münster (Doctor of Law, 1993). Author: "Globalzession und Prioritätsprinzip," (Global Assignment of Receivables and the Principle of Priority), 1993. *Member:* German Bar Association; Deutscher Juristentag. *LANGUAGES:* German, English and French. *PRACTICE AREAS:* Foreign Investments; International Contracts; Private International Law.

DR. KLAUS IKAS, born Stuttgart, Germany, 1960; admitted, 1993, Stuttgart. *Education:* University of Tübingen (Doctor of Law, 1991). Author: "The Law of Electronic Payment with Debit Cards in Point of Sale Systems." *Member:* German Bar Association; German Association for Industrial Property Rights and Copyright. *LANGUAGES:* German and English. *PRACTICE AREAS:* Unfair Competition; Industrial and Intellectual Property; Licence Agreements; Press Law.

DR. KARSTEN HEIDER, born Stuttgart, Germany, 1963; admitted, 1993, Stuttgart. *Education:* University of Tübingen (Doctor of Law, 1994). Author: "Die Bedeutung der behördlichen Duldung im Unweltstrafrecht," (Meaning of an Official Toleration in Environmental Criminal Law). *LANGUAGES:* German and English. *PRACTICE AREAS:* Corporate Law; Commercial Law.

DR. MANFRED STUBER, born Bopfingen, Germany, 1961; admitted, 1992, Berlin. *Education:* Universities of Münster, Munich and Berlin (Doctor of Law, 1994). Assistant Lecturer, Center of National and International Cartel Law of the Freie Universität Berlin, 1989-1993. *Member:* German Bar Association. *LANGUAGES:* German and English. *PRACTICE AREAS:* Company Law; Commercial Law; Copyright Law; Cartel Law; Competition Law.

KLAUS-DIETER SCHICK, born Stuttgart, Germany, 1961; admitted, 1990, Stuttgart. *Education:* University of Tübingen. *Member:* German Bar Association. *LANGUAGES:* German and English. *PRACTICE AREAS:* Construction Law; Commercial Law; Insurance Law.

DR. FRANK MOSZKA, born Bottrop/Westfalen, Germany, 1961; admitted, 1993, Stuttgart. *Education:* University of Regensburg and Freiburg (Doctor of Law, 1992). Author: "Die Haftung des Nutzers und des Betreibers computergestützter Auskunftssysteme," (The Liability of the Users and Providers of Computer Based Information Systems), 1994. Assistant Lecturer, Civil Law, Computer Law and Legal History, University of Freiburg, 1988-1992. *Member:* German Bar Association; International Fiscal Association. *LANGUAGES:* German and English. *PRACTICE AREAS:* Corporate Law; International Tax Law; Tax Planning Law.

REGINE HAGEN-ECK, born Wipperfürth, Germany, 1962; admitted, 1993, Stuttgart. *Education:* Universities of Cologne and Tübingen. *Member:* German Bar Association. *LANGUAGES:* German and English. *PRACTICE AREAS:* Corporate Law; Mergers and Acquisitions Law.

DR. JÜRGEN KUNZ, born Tuttlingen, Germany, 1963; admitted, 1993, Stuttgart. *Education:* University of Freiburg (Doctor of Law, 1993). Author: "Die Vorgesellschaft im Prozeß und in der Zwangsvollstreckung," (The Pre-registration Limited Company in relation to Litigation and Compulsory Execution), 1994. Assistant Lecturer, Freiburg Law School, 1991-1992. *Member:* German Bar Association; German-Japanese Lawyers Association. *LANGUAGES:* German and English. *PRACTICE AREAS:* Corporate Law; Commercial Law; Probate Law; Transportation Law.

CATHERINE GOATES, born St. Albans, England, 1966; admitted, 1993, Solicitor. *Education:* Universities of East Anglia, England and Trier, Germany. *LANGUAGES:* English and German. *PRACTICE AREAS:* Company Law; Commercial Law.

DR. STROBEL & PARTNERS

HOHENZOLLERNSTR. 14
D-70178 STUTTGART, GERMANY
Telephone: (49) 711-60104-0
Telefax: (49) 711-6491545

General and International Civil Law Practice, Tax Law, Commercial Law, Corporate Law, Construction Law, Family Law, Licensing Law, Real Estate Law, Labour Law, Antitrust Law, Unfair Competition, Private International Law.

MEMBERS OF FIRM

DR. LOTHAR STROBEL, born Jungnau, Germany, January 23, 1928; admitted, 1958, Stuttgart. *Education:* University of Tübingen (Referendar, 1952; Assessor, 1957); University of Bochum (Doctor of Jurisprudence, 1972). Certified Tax Attorney, 1964. Chairman of Supervisory Board: Schwäbische Bank AG, Stuttgart. Member of Supervisory Board: Procter & Gamble GmbH, Schwalbach. *Member:* German-American Chamber of Commerce. *LANGUAGES:* German and English.

KARL FRIEDRICH HOHENSTEIN, born Winnenden, Germany, May 15, 1923; admitted, 1961, Stuttgart. *Education:* University of Tübingen (Referendar, 1957; Assessor, 1961). Notary, 1987. *LANGUAGES:* German and English.

GERHARD SIEGEL, born Ludwigsburg, Germany, October 15, 1937; admitted, 1968, Stuttgart. *Education:* Universities of Tübingen, Berlin and München (Referendar, 1964; Assessor, 1968). Certified Tax Attorney, 1975. *LANGUAGES:* German and English.

DR. HELLMUT MÜLLER, born Stuttgart, Germany, December 2, 1942; admitted, 1970, Stuttgart. *Education:* Universities of Tübingen, München, Würzburg; Academy of Administrative Science, Speyer (Referendar, 1967; Assessor, 1970; Doctor of Jurisprudence, 1971). Certified Tax Attorney, 1975. *Member:* German Society of Tax Law; Deutscher Juristentag. *LANGUAGES:* German and English.

HANS-JOACHIM REUTER, born Waiblingen, Germany, April 8, 1951; admitted, 1979, Stuttgart. *Education:* University of Tübingen (Referendar, 1976; Assessor, 1979). Chairman of Advisory Board: Hermann Stumpp Bauunternehmung GmbH & Co. KG, Stuttgart. Managing Director: Intercontinental Hotel Stuttgart GmbH & Co. KG, Stuttgart; HABET Handelsbeteiligungsgesellschaft mbH & Co. KG, Stuttgart. *LANGUAGES:* German, English and Italian.

DR. JÖRG RICHARDI, born Villingen, Germany, September 4, 1960; admitted, 1991, Stuttgart. *Education:* University of Konstanz (Referendar, 1986; Assessor, 1989; Doctor of Jurisprudence, 1991). *LANGUAGES:* German and English.

THÜMMEL, SCHÜTZE & PARTNER

Established in 1958

LANDHAUSSTRAßE 90
70190 STUTTGART, GERMANY
Telephone: (0711) 1667-0
Telefax: (0711) 286 44 66, 2 62 69 10

Berlin Office: Lützowstraße 33/36, 10785 Berlin. Telephone: (030) 2 61 11 31. Telefax: (030) 2 61 90 49. Telex: 3 01304.
Dresden Office: Friedrichstraße 33, 01067 Dresden. Telephone: (0351) 496 5302. Telefax: (0351)496 5346.
Frankfurt Office: Eschersheimer Landstraße, 10 60322 Frankfurt. Telephone: (069) 9591350. Telefax: (069) 95913530.
Brussels Office: Avenue des Arts, 41 B-1040 Brussels. Telephone: (0032) 2-512 7846. Telefax: (0032) 2-512 7023.
Paris, France Office: 46, Rue de Bassano, F-75008 Paris. Telephone: (0033) 1-53 67 50 00. Telefax: (0033) 1-47 20 78 76.
Singapore Office: 9, Battery Road, #16-01 Straits Trading Building, Singapore 0104, Telephone: (00 65) 53 53 112, Telefax: (00 65) 53 43 100.

Corporate, Commercial, Antitrust, Unfair Competition, Banking, Taxation, Trademark, Copyright, Media, Estate, Food Law, International, EEC Law, General Practice and Litigation.

PROF. DR. JUR. HANS THÜMMEL, born Luckenwalde, Germany, May 1, 1921; admitted, 1954, Germany; 1979, Notar. *Education:* Technische Hochschule of Stuttgart; University of Tübingen (Referendar, 1950; Doctor of Jurisprudence, 1952; Assessor, 1954); University of Virginia Law

(This Listing Continued)

THÜMMEL, SCHÜTZE & PARTNER, Stuttgart—Continued

School, U.S.A. Lecturer, Law on Unfair Competition and Media Law, University of Hohenheim(Honorary Professor, 1981). Author: "Franchising and Antitrust Law in West Germany," *International Franchising*, Continental Reports, Inc., Denver, 1970. *Member:* Stuttgart Lawyers Association; German Bar Association; Deutsche Vereinigung für gewerblichen Rechtsschutz und Urheberrecht (Industrial and Copyright Association); International Group Economics and Law (Member of the Board, 1967); Association for Food Law and Food Science; Landesanstalt für Kommunikation Baden-Württemberg (Member of Board, 1986); American Chamber of Commerce in Germany (Director, 1981—; Vice-President, 1985—); German-American Chamber of Commerce; International Bar Association; American Bar Association. *LANGUAGES:* German and English.

PROF. DR. JUR. ROLF A. SCHÜTZE, born Castrop-Rauxel, Germany, December 12, 1934; admitted, 1962, Germany. *Education:* Universities of Freiburg, Bonn, Geneva, Strasbourg, Doctor of Jurisprudence, 1960 (Bonn); Docteur en droît comparé, 1965 (Strasbourg); Assessor, 1962. Honorary Professor, International Civil Procedure, University of Tübingen. Author: "Vollstreckung ausländischer Urteile in Afrika," (Execution of Foreign Judgements in Africa), 1966; "Internationale Urteilsanerkennung," (Recognition of Foreign Judgments), Vol. I/1, 1983; I/2, 1984; II, 1971 (Co-author with Dr. Geimer); "Anerkennung und Vollstreckung deutscher Urteile im Ausland," (Recognition and Execution of German Judgments Abroad), 1973; Internationales Zivilprozessrecht (International Civil Procedure), 1980; Deutsches Internationales Zivilprozessrecht, 1985; Schütze-Tscherning-Wais, Handbuch des Schiedverfahrens, 1985 (Handbook on Arbitration); Rechtsverfolgung im Ausland, 1986 (Legal Proceedings in Foreign Countries, 1986); Wieczorek-Rössler - Schütze, "Zivilprozessrecht" (Commentary on Civil Procedure). Co-Editor: Münchener Vertragshandbuch, Bd. 2," Handels - und - Wirtschaftsrecht" (Munich Handbook for Contracts, Vol. 2, Trade and Commercial Law), 1982 and Vol. 3, 1984. *Member:* German Bar Association, Gesellschaft für Rechtsvergleichung (Comparative Law Association); Deutscher Juristentag; African Law Association. (Resident, Paris Office). *LANGUAGES:* German, English, French, and Spanish.

DR. JUR. TILO BODENDORF, born Breslau, Germany, May 10, 1942; admitted, 1970, Germany. *Education:* Universities of Munich, Tübingen, and Heidelberg (Referendar, 1967; Doctor of Jurisprudence and Assessor, 1970). Author: "Der Hausfriedensbruch, Rechtsgut und Tatbestand in neuerer Entwicklung," (Invasion of Privacy). *Member:* German Bar Association; Deutsche Vereinigung für gewerblichen Rechtsschutz und Urheberrecht (Industrial and Copyright Association); German-American Lawyers Association. *LANGUAGES:* German and English.

DR. JUR. WERNER OLDENBURG, born Stuttgart, Germany, March 6, 1945; admitted, 1973, Germany. *Education:* University of Tübingen (Referendar, 1969; Doctor of Jurisprudence, 1973; Assessor, 1973; Assistant, University of Tübingen, 1970-1973). Author: "Fremdgeschäftsführung und -vertretung in den Personengesellschaften," (Management of Partnership), 1973. Co-Author: "Münchener Vertragshandbuch, Bd. I, Gesellschaftsrecht" (Munich Handbook for Contracts, Vol. I, Corporate Law), 1982. *Member:* Stuttgart Lawyers Association; German Bar Association; Deutsche Vereinigung für gewerblichen Rechtsschutz und Urheberrecht (Industrial and Copyright Association); Bund für Lebensmittelrecht und Lebensmittelkunde (Association for Food Law and Food Science). *LANGUAGES:* German and English.

DR. JUR. HARRO WILDE, born Stuttgart, Germany, February 7, 1950; admitted, 1977, Germany. *Education:* Universities of Tübingen and Bonn (Referendar, 1973; Assessor, 1976; Doctor of Jurisprudence, 1977). Author: "Die Beziehungen des nichtehelichen Kindes zu seinem Vater in kollisionsrechtlicher Sicht," ("The Relations of the Illegitimate Child to his Father in Private International Law"). Co-Author: "Handbuch des Wettbewerbrechts," (Handbook on Competition Law). *Member:* German Bar Association; Deutsche Vereinigung für gewerblichen Rechtsschutz und Urheberrecht (Industrial and Copyright Association). *LANGUAGES:* German and English.

DR. JUR. GÜNTHER H. RAISER, born Stuttgart, Germany, May 16, 1947; admitted, 1976, Germany. *Education:* University of Tübingen (Referendar, 1973; Wissenschaftlicher Mitarbeiter, 1973-1974; Assessor, 1975); Doctor of Jurisprudence, 1978. Lecturer at Berufsakademie Baden-Württemberg for Commercial and Corporate Law. Author: "Einführung in das Zivilrecht" (Introduction to Civil Law), "Die Rechte des Scheinvaters in bezug auf geleistete Unterhaltszahiungen" (The Rights of the Quasi-Father

(This Listing Continued)

in Regard to Maintenance Paid), "Zur Frage hinreichender Bemühungen um angemessene Erwerbstätigkeit" (On the Question of Sufficient Efforts for an Appropriate Occupation). *Member:* German Bar Association; German Society for the Science of the Law of Succession; Committee on Succession in Firms and Drafting of Wills. *LANGUAGES:* German and English.

DR. JUR. WOLFGANG ADAM, born Plettenberg, Germany, May 21, 1945; admitted, 1980, Germany. *Education:* Universities of Marburg and Freiburg; University of Public Administration, Speyer (Referendar, 1969; Assessor, 1973; Doctor of Jurisprudence). Assistant, University of Regensburg, Department of Civil Law, Commercial Law and International Private Law, 1974-1980. Author: "Internationaler Versorgungsausgleich," 1985; "Zur Anwendbarkeit des Deutschen Versorgungsausgleichs aufgrund versteckter Rückverweisung durch das Englische Recht," (On the Applicability of the German Versorgungsausgleich by Disclosed Renvoi of the English Law), IPRax, 98, 1987. *Member:* German Bar Association; American Bar Association; Ancien Etudiant de l'Académie de Droit International à La Haye. *LANGUAGES:* German, English, French and Portuguese.

DR.JUR. DIRK PLAGEMANN, born Wuppertal, Germany, February 24, 1953; admitted, 1983, Germany. *Education:* University of Bonn and Freiburg i. Br. (Referendar, 1978; Assessor, 1981). Associate, Max-Planck-Institute for Foreign and International Criminal Law, Freiburg i. Br., 1979-1983, Doctor of Jurisprudence, 1984. *Member:* German Bar Association. (Resident, Dresden Office). *LANGUAGES:* German, English, French and Spanish.

DR.JUR. RODERICH C. THÜMMEL, born Stuttgart, West Germany, October 23, 1955; admitted, 1984, Germany; 1986, New York. *Education:* Universities of Munich and Tübingen (Referendar, 1979; Assessor, 1983; Doctor of Jurisprudence, 1982); Harvard University Law School (LL.M., 1984). Assistant, University of Tübingen, 1980-1981. Author: "Das Internationale Privatrecht der nichtehelichen Kindschaft - Eine rechtsvergleichende Untersuchung," (Conflict of Laws and Illegitimate Filiation - A Comparative Study), 1983; "Conflict of Laws and Unfair Competition - Comparative Reflections on American and German Legal Concepts, in: Campbell/Rohwer, Legal Aspects of International Business Transactions II, 1985, p.115-186". *Member:* German Bar Association; International Bar Association; German American Lawyers Association. *LANGUAGES:* German, English and French.

DR.JUR. HANS-JOCHEN OTTO, born Altena, West Germany, August 26, 1949; admitted, 1979, Germany. *Education:* Universities of Freiburg and Innsbruck (Referendar, 1977; Assessor, 1978; Doctor of Jurisprudence, 1980); Steuerberater (Tax Advisor), 1985. Author: "Übernahmeversuche bei Aktiengesellschaften und Strategien der Abwehr," (Take-over Attempts of German Stock Corporations and Strategies of Defence), 1988; "Fremdfinanzierte Übernahmen - Gessellschafts-und steuerrechtliche Kriterien des Leverged Buy-Out," (Debt-Financed Takeovers - Corporate Law and Tax Aspects of Leveraged Buy-Outs), 1989; "Management Buy-Out," in: Assmann/Schütze, Handbuch des Kapitalanlagerechts (Handbook for Capital Investment Law), 1989. *LANGUAGES:* German, English and Spanish.

DR. JUR. THOMAS R. KLÖTZEL, born Igersheim, West Germany, January 5, 1957; admitted, 1986, Germany. *Education:* Universities of Tübingen and Geneva (Referendar, 1982; Assessor, 1986; Doctor of Jurisprudence, 1987). Author: "Interzessionsformen in England und ihre kollisionsrechtliche Behandlung - Eine rechtsvergleichende Untersuchung" (Forms of Suretyship in England and Their Treatment in Private International Law - A Comparative Study), 1987. *Member:* German-British Jurists Association; International Bar Association. *LANGUAGES:* German, English and French.

DR. JUR. CHRISTINA MITSCH, born Fulda, West Germany, December 5, 1961; admitted, 1990, Germany. *Education:* Universities of Munich and Würzburg (Referendar 1986; Assessor 1990). Assistant, University of Würzburg, 1986-1987. (Resident, Berlin Office). *LANGUAGES:* German and English.

DR. JUR. SUSANNE WESCH, born Ulm/Donau, Germany, February 21, 1962; admitted, 1991, Germany. *Education:* University Tübingen (Referendar, 1986; Assessor, 1989; Doctor of Jurisprudence, 1993). *Member:* German Bar Association; German American Lawyers Association. *LANGUAGES:* German and English.

SEVERIN BIRKMANN, born Kiel, West Germany, February 2, 1962; admitted, 1991, Germany. *Education:* University of Würzburg and University of Public Administration in Speyer (Referendar, 1988; Assessor, 1991). Assistant, University Würzburg 1988-1989. *LANGUAGES:* German and English.

(This Listing Continued)

DR. JUR. RENÉ-ALEXANDER HIRTH, born Stuttgart, Germany, February 27, 1963; admitted, 1993, Germany. *Education:* University of Tübingen (Referendar 1989, Assessor 1993). Assistant, University of Tübingen, 1989-1991. Doctor of Jurisprudence, 1991. Author: "Die Entwicklung der Rechtsprechung zum Vertrag mit Schutzwirkung zugunsten Dritter in ihrer Bedeutung für den Ausgleich von Drittschäden im Zahlungsverkehr" (The Development of Case law in regard to the Contract with protective effect for the benefit of third parties in view of its importance for compensation of third parties' damages in payment transactions), 1991. *Member:* German Bar Association. (Resident, Singapore Office). *LANGUAGES:* German, English.

RALF FUHRMANN, born Bochum, Germany, October 25, 1959; admitted, 1993, Germany. *Education:* University of Bochum, Lausanne, Tübingen (Referendar, 1986, Assessor, 1989). Assistant, University of Tübingen, 1986-1993. Author: "Die Mitbestimmung des Personalrats bei Kündigungen" (The Co-determination of the staff-council in case of notices of termination), PersV 1990, 102 - 124. *LANGUAGES:* German, French, English.

DR. JUR. HERVÉ EDELMANN, born Beirut, Libanon, March 23, 1961; admitted, 1994, Germany. *Education:* University of Marburg (Referendar, 1991; Doctor of Jurisprudence, 1991; Assessor, 1994). *LANGUAGES:* German, English, French and Arabian.

CHRISTIAN ALTVATER, born Kiel, Germany, September 27, 1963; admitted, 1994, Germany. *Education:* University of Tübingen (Referendar, 1989; LL.M., 1990); University of Southampton (Assessor, 1993). *LANGUAGES:* German, English and French.

STEFAN WOLF, born Oberndorf a/N., Germany, September 12, 1961; admitted, 1993, Germany. *Education:* University of Tübingen (Assistant, 1986-1991; Referendar, 1990; Assessor, 1993). *Member:* German Bar Association. *LANGUAGES:* German, English, French and Spanish.

WACKENHUTH & UNTERRIKER

HAUßMANNSTR. 2
70188 STUTTGART, GERMANY
Telephone: 0711/23748-0
Telefax: 0711/23748-48

Corporation, International and EEC Law, International Arbitration, Merger and Acquisition, Real Estate, General Practice and Litigation.

MEMBERS OF FIRM

DR. MICHAEL WACKENHUTH, born Waiblingen, Germany, 1954; admitted, 1981, Stuttgart. *Education:* University of Tübingen (Doctor of Jurisprudence, 1980); European University of Florence (LL.M., 1985). Author: "Zur Behandlung der rügelosen Einlassung in Nationalen und Internationalen Schiedsverfahren," (The Voluntary Appearance of the Parties in National and International Arbitration Proceedings), Konkurs-, Treuhand- und Schiedsgerichtswesen 425 ff, 1984; "Ersetzbarkeit der Formerfordernisse des Artikel 2 des UN-Übereinkommens 1958 durch Klageerhebung und rügelose Einlassung vor dem Schiedsgericht?" (Are the Formal Requirements of Art. 2 Sec. 2 of the New York Arbitration Convention of 1958 replaceable by a Voluntary Appearance of the Parties?), Recht der Internationalen Wirtschaft 568 ff, 1985; "Die Schriftform für Schiedsvereinbarungen nach dem UN-Übereinkommen 1958 und Allgemeine Geschäftsbedingungen," (The in Writing of a Arbitration Clause According to the New York Arbitration Convention of 1958 and General Trade Terms), Zeitschrift für Zivilprozeßrecht 445 ff, 1986. *Member:* German Bar Association; Association Internationale des Jeunes Avocats; German American Lawyers Association; Deutsches Institut für Schiedsgerichtswesen e.V. *LANGUAGES:* German, English, French and Italian. *PRACTICE AREAS:* Commercial Mergers and Acquisitions; International Joint Ventures; International Arbitration.

STEFAN UNTERRIKER, born Esslingen, Germany; admitted, 1992. *Education:* University of Tübingen. *Member:* German Bar Association. *LANGUAGES:* German and English. *PRACTICE AREAS:* Company Formation; Distribution Agreements; Successions; Civil Litigation.

ANWALTSKANZLEI OELSCHIG

Established in 1971
HERZOG-FRIEDRICH-STRASSE 8
D-8220 TRAUNSTEIN, GERMANY
Telephone: 49 (0) 861-4346 or 7150
Fax: 49 (0) 861-8641

General Practice, Litigation and Arbitration, Family, Handicraft Regulations, (Int'l) Trade, Insurance, Building, Real Estate.

FIRM PROFILE: The firm was founded in 1930 by Dr. Bergtold, Traunstein, for General Practice.

KNUT OELSCHIG, born Mittweida, Germany, December 11, 1941; admitted, 1971, Germany. *Education:* University of Munich (1963-1968) (First State Exam, 1968; Second State Exam, 1970). *Member:* German Bar Association; IASW-EWIV. *LANGUAGES:* German, English, French and Russian. *PRACTICE AREAS:* General Practice; Marriage and Family; Automobile Insurance and Regulation; Labor (Compensation and Discrimination); Handicraft Regulations; Company and Trade Law; Civil Litigation; Arbitration; Real Estate; Traffic Violations.

PLUTA & KNORR

Established in 1985
OLGASTR. 83-85
P.O. BOX 2530
D-89015 ULM, GERMANY
Telephone: 0731-1450 0
Facsimile: 0731-1450-180

Munich, Germany Office: Thomas-Wimmer-Ring 1, D-80539. Telephone: 089-290037-0. Facsimile: 089-290037-56.

Leipzig, Germany Office: Weißenfelser Str. 15, D-04229. Telephone: 0341-4903650. Facsimile: 0341-4903699.

Receivership, Intellectual Property, Software Law, Company Law, International Private Law, Commercial Law, Tax Law, Antitrust Law, Labor Law, Construction Law, Law of Medical Malpractice, Banking Law.

MEMBERS OF FIRM

MICHAEL PLUTA, born Ulm, Germany, May 20, 1950; admitted, 1978, Hamburg; 1981, Ulm; 1986, Oberlandesgericht Stuttgart. *Education:* University of Hamburg (1971-1975); First State Exam, 1975, Second State Exam, 1978, Vereidigter Buchprüfer, 1990. *Member:* Deutscher Anwaltverein (Member, Marketing Committee); International Bar Association; AECCP; Anwaltsverein beim Landgericht Ulm (Member of Board). *LANGUAGES:* German, English, Italian.

DR. GÜNTER KNORR, born Ulm, Germany, May 8, 1949; admitted, 1975, Ulm; 1991, Munich. *Education:* University of Hamburg (1967-1969); Freie University of Berlin (1969-1971); First State Exam, 1971, Second State Exam, 1974 (Dr. 1981). Author: "Die Werkhöhe bei Software," IUR, 1986; "Softwareschutz in Frankreich," CUR, 1986; "Warranty for Software, an International Problem," Comparative Law Yearbook for International Business, 1990; "Know-How in the Common Market: Does the New Regime Helps," Comparative Law Yearbook of International Business, 1991; Lehrbeauftragter an der Universität Ulm, 1985-1986. *Member:* International Bar Association; UIA; APLA; GRUR. (Resident, Munich, Germany Office). *LANGUAGES:* English, German, French, Italian.

EBERHARD KNORR, born Ulm, Germany, November 13, 1936; admitted, 1965, Ulm; 1972, Oberlandesgericht Stuttgart. *Education:* Universities of Tübingen (1955), München (1956-1958), Freiburg (1959-1960); First State Exam, 1960, Second State Exam, 1964. *Member:* Anwaltverein beim Landgericht Ulm, Anwaltskammer für Nordwürttemberg (Member of the Board), Deutsche Gesellschaft für Baurecht. *LANGUAGES:* German, English.

LUISE WIDMAIER-MÜLLER, born Stuttgart, Germany, March 15, 1956; admitted, 1983, Ulm; 1988, Stuttgart. *Education:* Eberhard-Karls-Universität Tübingen (1975-1980). First State, 1980, Second State Exam, 1983. Author: "Die Aufgaben und Arbeiten der Schiedsstellen," 1991. *Member:* Deutscher Anwaltverein. *LANGUAGES:* German, English.

MICHAEL SCHOOR, born Cologne, Germany, November 6, 1955; admitted, 1983, Cologne; 1991, Leipzig. *Education:* Universities of Mainz and Cologne (1974-1980). First State Exam, 1980; Second State Exam, 1983; Steuerberater, 1991. *Member:* Deutscher Anwaltverein. (Resident, Leipzig, Germany Office). *LANGUAGES:* German, English, French.

(This Listing Continued)

PLUTA & KNORR, Ulm—Continued

DR. JOACHIM GESSLER, born Ulm, Germany, October 23, 1952; admitted, 1983, Ulm; 1988, Oberlandesgericht Stuttgart. *Education:* University of Tübingen, 1971-1976; First State Exam: 1976; Second State Exam: 1978 (Dr. 1983). 1975-1980, Trainee, Deutsche Bank; 1980-1982, Assistant, Institut für Bankrecht, Köln, Vereidigter Buchprüfer, 1990. Author: "Werbung der Banken," 1983. *LANGUAGES:* German, English.

FRITZ ZANKER, born Kirchheim/Teck, Germany, April 23, 1962; admitted, 1991, Ulm. *Education:* University of Tübingen (1982-1988); First State Exam: 1988; Second State Exam: 1991. *LANGUAGES:* German, English.

DOROTHÉE LANG-DANKOV, born Aschaffenburg, Germany, March 24, 1956; admitted, 1986, Ulm; 1991, Oberlandesgericht Stuttgart. *Education:* University of Würzburg (1975-1977); University of Lausanne (1977-1978); University of Tübingen (1978-1980); First State Exam: 1980; Second State Exam: 1986. *LANGUAGES:* German, English, French.

STEPHAN THIEMANN, born Oberhausen, Germany, May 23, 1963; admitted, 1994, Ulm and Leipzig. *Education:* University of Malaga, Spain (1983-1984); University of Münster (1984-1989); First State Exam, 1990, Second State Exam, 1994. Assistant, Institut für Wirtschaftsrecht, University of Münster. (Resident, Leipzig, Germany Office). *LANGUAGES:* German, English, Spanish.

MICHAEL WAHL, born Kirchheim/Teck, Germany, May 18, 1962; admitted, 1994, Ulm. *Education:* University of Tübingen (1982-1989); First State Exam, 1989; Second State Exam, 1994. *LANGUAGES:* German, English.

GERALD HAUSTEIN, born Bremerhaven, Germany, May 8, 1957; admitted, 1988, München; 1993, Oberlandesgericht München. *Education:* University of München (1978-1985); First State Exam, 1985, Second State Exam, 1988. (Resident, Munich, Germany Office). *LANGUAGES:* German.

TAX CONSULTANTS

DIETER MERATH, born Ulm, Germany, August 27, 1949. *Education:* University of Saarbrücken (Dipl. Kaufmann, 1975). *LANGUAGES:* German, English.

MARTINA HENGARTNER, born Ulm, Germany, February 22, 1957. *Education:* University of Nürnberg (Dipl. Kaufmann, 1980). *LANGUAGES:* German, English.

DE FARIA • BÜSSER • REISCHAUER

GUSTAV-FREYTAG-STRASSE 19
65189 WIESBADEN, GERMANY
Telephone: 0611/393-960
Fax: 0611/393-9611

General Practice. Company, Investment Law, Tax, Conflict of Laws, Real Estate, Labor, Wills, Unfair Competition, Soviet and Constitutional Law.

MEMBERS OF FIRM

DR. ALEXANDER DE FARIA E CASTRO, born Kovno, Lithuania, November 8, 1936; admitted, 1966, Germany. Notary Public. *Education:* Frankfurt and Mainz (Dr. of Jurisprudence). Author: "Conditions of Liability in Tort of the Soviet Union and its Historical Development," Studies of the Institute for Eastern Law, Volume 20, 1969. *Member:* Bar Association of Frankfurt; Lawyers Association of Wiesbaden; International Bar Association. *LANGUAGES:* English, Russian and French.

DR. KURT BÜSSER, born Berlin, Germany, May 16, 1939; admitted, 1969, Wiesbaden, Germany. Notary Public. *Education:* Berlin, Mainz and Frankfurt/Main (Dr. of Jurisprudence). Author: "The Challenge of the Constitutionality of Acts of Parliament," 1968. Legal Council of Wiesbaden Chamber of Commerce and Industry. Member of the Board of the Wiesbaden Public Health Insurance (AOK). *Member:* Lawyers Association of Wiesbaden. *LANGUAGES:* German and French.

DIRK REISCHAUER, born Prague, Czechoslovakia, March 24, 1943; admitted, 1972, Wiesbaden, Germany. Notary Public. *Education:* Universities of Göttingen, Berlin, Freiburg and Cambridge, England (LL.M., Cantab). Member, Legal Committee German Factoring Association. *Member:* International Bar Association (Chairman, Committee I, 1986-1990); Deutscher Juristentag; German-British Jurists Association. *LANGUAGES:* German, English, French and Italian.

(This Listing Continued)

ASSOCIATES

THOMAS RÖSKENS, admitted, 1992, Germany.

ANDREAS RIEDEL, admitted, 1993, Germany.

DR. STEPHAN PIEPER, admitted, 1994, Germany.

PETER H. FEUERSTEIN

RIEDERBERGSTRASSE 73
65195 WIESBADEN, GERMANY
Telephone: 49-611-52 1057; 49-611-52 7977
Facsimile: 49-611-59 0200

General Practice and Personal Practice, including Tax and Divorce.

DR. PETER H. FEUERSTEIN, born Worms, Germany, March 22, 1946; admitted, 1978, Wiesbaden. *Education:* University of Marburg, 1966-1976; University of Marburg, Institute of Comparative Law (Anglo-American Department, 1972-1973); University of Cambridge, England (Juris Doctorate, 1977). Author: Co-editor of Festschrift to Professor Dr. K. Lipstein, Cambridge, England, 1979. Umsatzsteuer bei Rechnungen an Mitglieder der Nato-Truppen, 1992. Einkommensteuerpflicht bei Nato-Beschäftigungsverhältnissen, 1993. Admittance as Tax Lawyer 1979. Dr. Blesinger, Schwelm 1978-1979. Berliner Handels-und Frankfurter Bank (BHF-Bank), Collateral Department, International Sector, 1979-1981. General Counsel to Haschtmann GmbH, Berlin, 1981-1982. Director, Mediation Service Germany (Alternative Dispute Resolution) 1990. Advisory Board Member, World Arbitration and Mediation Report (BNA). *Member:* German-American Lawyers Association (GALA), International Bar Association (Member, Section on Business Law), American Bar Association (Associate Member, 1993; Member, Section of Business Law). (Also Counsel to Cassidy & Associates, P.A. in Philadelphia, Pennsylvania). *LANGUAGES:* German, English and French.

GAEDERTZ VIEREGGE QUACK KREILE

Rechtsanwälte

KAISER-FRIEDRICH-RING 65
D-65185 WIESBADEN, GERMANY
Telephone: (611)88 05-0
Telex: 41 86 295 gaed d
Telefax: (611)81 03 09

Berlin, Germany Office: Kurfürstendamm 157, D-10709 Berlin. Telephone: (30)890 05 0. Telefax: (30)892 26 06. Teletex: 30 88 15 qkp d. Telex: 17 30 88 15 qkp d.
Cologne, Germany Office: Theodor-Heuss-Ring 19-21, D-50668 Cologne. Telephone:(221)77 16-0. Telefax: (221)77 16-110. Teletex: 221 43 76 olga d. Telex: 88 85 143 olga d.
Frankfurt/Main, Germany Office: Airport Center, Hugo-Eckener-Ring, D-60549 Frankfurt/Main. Telephone: (69)69 48 52. Telefax: (69)69 48 60. Telex: 4032 145 zibr d.
Leipzig, Germany Office: August-Bebel-Str. 38, D-04275 Leipzig. Telephone: (341) 477 83 81/83. Telefax: (341) 477 83 88.
Munich, Germany Office: Widenmayerstrasse 32, D-80538 Munich. Telephone: (89)212147-0. Telefax: (89)228 55 62.
Brussels, Belgium Office: Avenue de Tervuren 35, B-1040 Brussels. Telephone: (2) 736 07 97. Telefax: (2) 732 69 12.
Prague, Czech Republic Office: Betlémska 1, CR-11000 Prague 1. Telephone: (2) 24 22 94 98. Telefax: (2) 232 12 29.

General Practice. Commercial, Corporate, Antitrust, Unfair Competition, Real Estate and Conveyancing, Food and Drug Law, Labor Law, EC Law, Banking Law, Trademarks, Cartel Law, Insurance, Distribution. Notaries (Berlin and Wiesbaden).

FIRM PROFILE: The law firm Gaedertz Vieregge Quack Kreile is the result of a merger between 4 partnerships: Heydt Vieregge & Partner, Cologne; Gaedertz Henn & Partner, Wiesbaden; Quack Kühn & Partner, Berlin; Prof. Kreile & Partner, Munich.

Gaedertz Vieregge Quack Kreile is one of the major German based law firms representing domestic and foreign clients in all fields of law that are relevant for national and international enterprises. An important part of the practice are the legal aspects of transnational transactions especially in EC. The firm advises not only German clients in international matters but also foreign enterprises about all implications of doing business in Germany. Thus many attorneys and also members of the support staff are

(This Listing Continued)

fluent in English. Other languages such as French, Spanish, Portuguese, Italian, Russian, and Dutch are also spoken.

In addition, the offices in Cologne and Wiesbaden have the specialized capacity to administer large trademark portfolios worldwide including registration and litigation of trademarks and registered designs.

Clients of the firm include many well-known German and foreign companies active in a wide variety of businesses. Gaedertz Vieregge Quack Kreile also represents various trade associations as well as German federal, state and local governmental authorities.

In the Berlin, Wiesbaden and Frankfurt/Main offices, there are 10 attorneys qualified to act as "Notar," specially licensed to prepare and execute documents relating to incorporation of companies, real estate matters and other important commercial transactions where a special form of document is prescribed.

Gaedertz Vieregge Quack Kreile has more than 70 attorneys, including 42 partners, plus a support staff of approximately 150 people, working in the eight different offices.

The offices have for the most part city centre locations. The Frankfurt office is situated at the Airport-Centre of the Rhein-Main Airport.

MEMBERS OF FIRM

ALFRED-CARL GAERDERTZ, born Nürnberg, Germany, 1922; admitted, 1953, Wiesbaden. Notary Public. *Education:* University of Mainz; 1950, University of Chicago, School of Law. *Member:* German Bar Association; German Association for Industrial Property Rights and Copyright; Association for the Study of Cartel Law; German-American Lawyer's Association; International Bar Association. *LANGUAGES:* English. *PRACTICE AREAS:* Company Law; German and EEC Antitrust Law; Unfair Trade Practices and Trademarks.

KARLHANNS HENN, born Wiesbaden, Germany, 1927; admitted, 1959, Wiesbaden. Notary Public. *Education:* University of Mainz. *Member:* German Bar Association; German Lawyers' Association. *PRACTICE AREAS:* Company Law; Restructuring; Mergers and Acquisitions; Succession; Notarial Acts in connection with Commercial Transactions.

MICHAEL ORTH, born Goeppingen, Germany, 1956; admitted, 1986, Wiesbaden. *Education:* Universities of Marburg and Mainz. With Dresdner Bank (1978-1980). *Member:* German Bar Association; German Lawyers' Association. *PRACTICE AREAS:* Product Liability; Insurance Law; Banking; Real Estate.

REINHART LANGE, born Hannover, Germany, 1957; admitted, 1989, Wiesbaden. *Education:* University of Mainz. With Thuemmel, Schuetze & Partners, Singapore (1988). *Member:* German Bar Association; German Association for Industrial Property Rights and Copyright. *LANGUAGES:* English.

DR. CHRISTOFER EGGERS, born Frankfurt/Main, Germany, 1960; admitted, 1989, Wiesbaden. *Education:* University of Freiburg (Dr.jur.). With Bundeskartellamt 1988. *Member:* German Bar Association; German Lawyers' Association; Association for Industrial Property Rights and Copyright; Association for the Study of Cartel Law. *LANGUAGES:* English.

ASSOCIATES

DR. GEORG BÖNSCH, born Bonn, Germany, 1960; admitted, 1992, Cologne. *Education:* University of Bonn. Author: "Legal Possibilities of Private Economic Self Employment in Hungary," 1992. *Member:* Cologne Bar Association; Association for the Exchange of Views Between German and Hungarian Jurists; German Society of Eastern Europe Science. *LANGUAGES:* French, English, Hungarian.

Languages: German, English and French.

(For complete biographical data on personnel at Berlin, Cologne, Frankfurt/Main, Leipzig and Munich, Germany Offices as well as Brussels, Belgium and Prague, Czech, Republic Offices, see Professional Biographies at those locations).

VOLKER KEPPLER

Established in 1980

RHEINSTRASSE 30-32
D-65185 WIESBADEN, GERMANY
Telephone: 0611/371027
Telefax: 0611/373872

General Practice, Commercial, Corporate, Insolvency, Unfair Competition and Antitrust, Labour, Family, Torts, Product Liability and Professional Liability, Environmental Law.

FIRM PROFILE: The office is equipped with Germany's most modern legal software system, giving access to a network of numerable law firms all over Germany.

VOLKER KEPPLER, born Frankfurt, Germany, June 18, 1952; admitted, 1980, Wiesbaden. *Education:* Universities of Mainz and Frankfurt. *Member:* Bar Association of Frankfurt; Lawyers Association of Wiesbaden; Lawyers Association of Germany; Co-operative work team for private construction law; Wiesbaden Law Society. *LANGUAGES:* German and English.

GÜNTHER LIESEGANG TEMME & PARTNERS

DÖPPERSBERG 19
P.O. BOX 10 13 60
42103 WUPPERTAL, GERMANY
Telephone: 0202-45 03 51
Telecopier: 0202-45 56 76

Düsseldorf, Germany Office: Temme Visé Günther & Partners, Lindemannstraße 47, 40237. Telephone: 0211-66 60 31. Telecopier: 0211-66 69 97.

Corporate Law including cross-border Mergers and Acquisitions, Commercial Law, Banking and Business Law, General International Trade Law, General Tax and Corporate Taxation Law, Bankruptcy, ECL, Arbitration, Labour, Franchising, Unfair Competition and Trademark, Family Law.

MEMBERS OF FIRM

PAUL MICHAEL GÜNTHER, born Köthen, Germany, December 20, 1944; admitted, 1975, Germany; 1978, Tax Advisor; 1981, Certified Public Accountant. *Education:* Universities of Würzburg and Münster. *LANGUAGES:* German and English. *PRACTICE AREAS:* Corporate Law; Commercial Law; Business Law; General Tax and Corporate Taxation Law.

DR. HELMUTH LIESEGANG, born Frankfurt a.M., Germany, January 28, 1950; admitted, 1979, Chartered Expert in Tax Law. *Education:* University of Bochum (Dr. jur., 1976). Member of Supervising Boards of Public Companies; Official Receiver in Bankruptcy Proceedings. *LANGUAGES:* German and English. *PRACTICE AREAS:* Franchising and Company Law; Bankruptcy.

DR. BARBARA GÜNTHER, born Bielefeld, Germany, November 23, 1947; admitted, 1975, Germany. *Education:* Universities of Münster and Marburg (Dr. jur., 1980). Author: "Die Haftung für fehlerhafte, überbetriebliche, technische Normen." *Member:* IAML (International Academy of Matrimonial Lawyers, 1989—). *LANGUAGES:* German and English. *PRACTICE AREAS:* Family Law; Litigation; Business Law.

DR. STEFAN JANSEN, born Düsseldorf, Germany, April 23, 1958; admitted, 1989, Germany. *Education:* Universities of Cologne and Munich (Dr. jur., 1987). Author: "Widerruf freiwilliger Sozialleistungen unter Berücksichtigung betrieblicher Unterstützungskassen.". *LANGUAGES:* German and English. *PRACTICE AREAS:* Unfair Competition; Trademark; Arbitration; Labor.

ASSOCIATES

GERNOT A. WARMUTH, born Frankfurt a.M., Germany, June 5, 1955; admitted, 1984, Germany; 1990, California. *Education:* Universities of Frankfurt/Main and Pennsylvania (LL.M., 1986). *LANGUAGES:* German and English. *PRACTICE AREAS:* International Commercial Contracts; Commercial Leases; Business Litigation.

MEISKI & DÖRPER
WUPPERTAL, GERMANY
(see Remscheid)

A Member of AdvoSelect EEIG, a network of law firms pooling their resources in special fields and crossborder cases, specializing in business law for middle-sized companies. AdvoSelect is represented in 51 cities throughout Europe.

Tax Law, Tax-offense Cases, Labour Law, Family Law, Banking Law, Law concerning Building, Litigation.

DR. STEINHAUER & LUCKHAUS
HOFKAMP 138
D-42103 WUPPERTAL, GERMANY
Telephone: 49-202-450178/79
Fax: 49-202-4936774

Commercial, Corporate, Intellectual Property, Unfair Competition, Building Law, Civil Damages, Family Law, General Practice, Litigation.

DR. DIETER STEINHAUER, born 1928; admitted, 1958. *Education:* Universities of Mainz, Bonn, Cologne, Doctor of Laws, 1954. Author: "Der Streit um die Auslegung des 205 a AO," (The Dispute about Interpretation of 205 a AO + Taxation Law and Hushmoney), Dissertation, 1954; "Die Rechtsstellung des Ausübenden Künstlers" ("Artistic Copyright,") 1959. *Member:* German and International Bar Association; German Association of Building Law.

HANS PETER LUCKHAUS, born 1937; admitted, 1967. *Education:* Universities of Mainz and Göttingen.

Languages: German, English, French and Dutch

BORN, CALLAM, KLEIN, SCHNEIDER U. PARTNER
GUTENBERGSTRAßE 9
D-6660 ZWEIBRÜCKEN, GERMANY
Telephone: 49-(0) 6332/9214-0
Telefax: 49-(0) 6332/15152

Homburg, Germany Office: Eisenbahnstraße 2, D-6650. Telephone: 49-(0) 6841/15585. Telefax: 49-(0) 6841/15569.

Civil, Banking, Traffic, Insurance, Criminal and Domestic Relations Law.

MEMBERS OF FIRM

DR. HANS-PETER CALLAM, born Halle, December 19, 1942; admitted, 1971, Deutschland. *Education:* Universität Münster und Bonn (Staats-Examen, 1969).

HANS-JOACHIM KARL, born Pforzheim, January 3, 1931; admitted, 1959, Mannheim; 1981, Zweibrücken. *Education:* Universität Heidelberg, Hamburg (Staats-Examen, 1955).

JÖRG SCHNEIDER, born Homburg, December 30, 1949; admitted, 1977, Saarland. *Education:* Universität des Saarlandes (Staats-Examen, 1974).

RICHARD KLEIN, born Zweibrücken, December 18, 1949; admitted, 1979, Saarlandes; 1981, Rheinland-Pfalz. *Education:* Universität des Saarlandes; Universität Göttingen (Staats-Examen,1975).

ASSOCIATES

JOACHIM PICK, born Zweibrücken, March 10, 1955; admitted, 1981, Rheinland-Pfalz. *Education:* Universität des Saarlandes (Staats-Examen, 1978); Johannes-Gutenberg-Universität Mainz.

GERTRUD SCHILLER, born Mönchengladbach, March 23, 1948; admitted, 1982, Rheinland-Pfalz. *Education:* Universität des Saarlandes, Universität Kön (Staats-Examen, 1974).

MARLIS KERFIN, born Hannover, October 29, 1951; admitted, 1982, Hessen; 1987, Rheinland-Pfalz. *Education:* Universität Göttingen (Staats-Examen, 1975).

(This Listing Continued)

THOMAS BESENBRUCH, born Zweibrücken, December 3, 1964; admitted, 1994, Zweibrücken. *Education:* Universitat des Saarlandes (Staats-Examen, 1991).

Languages: German, English and French

MELCHERS, SCHUBERT, STOCKER, STURIES
Established in 1973
KOLPINGSTRASSE 28
D-08058 ZWICKAU, GERMANY
Telephone: (49-375) 294023/4/5
Telecopier: (49-375) 521629

Heidelberg, Germany Office: Slevogtstrasse 6, D-69126 Heidelberg. Mailing Address: P.O. Box 10 52 22, D-69042 Heidelberg. Telephone: (49-6221) 39 91 01. Telefax: (49-6221) 39 91 00; 37 40 69.

Berlin, Germany Office: Schiffbauerdamm 17, D-10117 Berlin. Telephone: (49-30) 2252 2133. Telecopier: (49-30) 2252 2108.

Frankfurt/Main, Germany Office: Beethovenstrasse 29, D-60325 Frankfurt/Main. Telephone: (49-69) 9757 3227. Telecopier: (49-69) 9757 3220.

Administrative Law, Banking, Commercial, Contracts, Corporate, EC-Law, Environmental Law, General Practice, Inheritance, Intellectual Property and Trade Marks, Arbitration, International Private Law, Investment, Labour Law, Mergers and Acquisitions, National and EC Antitrust, National and International Tax Law, Real Estate, Trade and Trade Show Law, Unfair Competition.

FIRM PROFILE: The law firm was founded in 1973 as a multidisciplinary partnership of lawyers, certified public accountants and tax advisors. Today, 31 professionals, of which 24 are lawyers, offer services and advice in the firm's offices in Berlin, Frankfurt/Main, Heidelberg and Zwickau. The multidisciplinary combination of legal services provides clients with comprehensive advice in the fields of business law, tax law, business administration and auditing.

RESIDENT PARTNERS

FRANK KÜHNERT, born Mü-St. Niclas, Germany, July 29, 1933; admitted, 1991, Germany. *Education:* University of Leipzig (Diploma in Law, 1956). Corporate Legal counsel with VEB Grubenlampen -und Akkumulatorenwerke Zwickau (1961 - 1988); with VEM Elektromotorenwerke Thurm, Zwickau (1988 - 1991). Lecturer on Comecon-Law at Technische Hochschule Zwickau (- 1990). Author: "Lieferungs- und Leistungsbedingungen im RGW", in: Wirtschaftsrecht 1977, p. 382. Former Member: Comecon Committee on Legal Affairs (East - German representative); Committees on Economic Relations between GDR/Hungary and GDR/Poland. *Member:* German Bar Association. **LANGUAGES:** German, Russian and English. **PRACTICE AREAS:** Former GDR-Law; Restitutional Law; Arbitration; Labour Law; Litigation.

DR. IUR. VALENTIN BOLL, born Pforzheim, Germany, July 31, 1957; admitted, 1990, Germany. *Education:* Universities of Bayreuth, Augsburg, Lausanne, Heidelberg and Innsbruck. Research and Teaching Assistant at the Institute of Foreign and International Private and Economic Law, University of Heidelberg (1986-1987). Author: "Ausländische AGB und der Schutz des inländischen Kaufmännischen Kunden", in: Praxis des Internationalen Privat- und Verfahrensrechts, 1987, p. 11; "Die Anerkennung des Auslandskonkurses", Vienna, 1990. Co-Author: "Das neue luxemburgische Gesetz vom 25.8.1983 zum Schutz des Konsumenten", Brussels, 1984 (German-Belgian-Luxembourg Chamber of Commerce). Intern with German-Belgian-Luxembourg Chamber of Commerce, Brussels, 1984 and with Berliner Commerzbank, Berlin, 1989. *Member:* German Bar Association, German-Italian Lawyers Association, (German) Banking Law Society. **LANGUAGES:** German, English and French. **PRACTICE AREAS:** Privatisation of State Owned Enterprises; Restitutional Law; Real Estate Law; Company Law; Commercial Law; International Law.

ASSOCIATES

TILL HEINZ, born Frankfurt/Main, Germany, December 29, 1958; admitted, 1992, Germany. *Education:* University of Frankfurt/Main. *Member:* German Bar Association. **LANGUAGES:** German, English and French. **PRACTICE AREAS:** Restitutional Law; Commercial Law; Real Estate Law; Product Liability; Litigation.

RONNY PÜHN, born Rodewisch, Germany, May 11, 1962; admitted, 1993, Germany. *Education:* University of Leipzig (Diploma in Law, 1984).

(This Listing Continued)

Corporate Legal Counsel: VEB Bekleidungswerke, Zwickau, 1984-1988; Sachsenbau GmbH, Zwickau, 1987-1992. *Member:* German Bar Association. *LANGUAGES:* German, English and Russian. *PRACTICE AREAS:* Former GDR Law; Restitutional Law; Labour Law; Litigation.

SIMONE MATTHEI, born Tettnang, Germany, November 24, 1964; admitted, 1994, Germany. *Education:* Universities of Regensburg and Freiburg. *Member:* German Bar Association. *LANGUAGES:* German and English. *PRACTICE AREAS:* Litigation; Commercial Law.

(For complete biographical data on Personnel at Berlin, Frankfürt/Main and Heidelberg offices see Professional Biographies at those locations).

GIBRALTAR

FOX & GIBBONS

Solicitors

Established in 1989

SUITE E, REGAL HOUSE
QUEENSWAY
P.O. BOX 246
GIBRALTAR, GIBRALTAR
Telephone: (350) 77750
Fax: (350) 77800

London, England Office: 2 Old Burlington Street, W1X 2QA. Telephone: (44-171) 439 8271. Fax: (44-171) 734 8843. Telex: 267108.

Dubai, United Arab Emirates Office: P.O. Box 1756. Telephone: (9714) 310220. Fax: (9714) 310201. Telex: 45614 GBLAW EM.

Abu Dhabi, United Arab Emirates Kudsi Fox & Gibbons Office: P.O. Box 46010. Telephone: (9712) 322858. Fax: (9712) 331586.

Cairo, Egypt Office: 126 Mohei El Din Abul Ezz Street, 9th Floor, Mohandiseen, Giza, Cairo, Egypt. Telephone: (202) 3485955. Fax: (202) 3492210.

Ruwi, Oman Office: P.O. Box 3552, Postal Code 112. Telephone: (968) 564346; Fax: (968) 564395. Telex: 5630 GIBLAW ON.

Kuwait Associated Office: P.O. Box 26473, Safat, 13125 Safat. Telephone: (965) 2462323/2462525/2462929. Fax: (965) 242 5830.

Fujairah, United Arab Emirates Office: P.O. Box 701. Telephone: (971 9) 229390. Fax: (971 9) 226470.

Yemen Associated Office: P.O. Box 148, Crater, Aden. Telephone: (9672) 255305/253824. Fax: (9672) 255305/255117.

Lebanon Associated Office: Saba K. Zreik Law Offices. Autostrade Dora, Cite Dora 3 Building, 10th Floor, P.O. Box 90-710, Beirut, Lebanon. Telephone: (961 1) 881387. Telex: 42949 MANAL LE.

FIRM PROFILE: Fox & Gibbons is an international law firm which provides a full range of legal services through its own network of offices and connections throughout the European Union and other parts of the world. The Firm is the only London based practice with an office in Gibraltar. A full range of offshore services is provided, including Company Formations, the establishment of Trusts (including asset protection trusts) and Tax Planning. The Firm specialises in Offshore Investment Funds and Collective Investment Schemes and advises upon Banking and Financial Transactions, Intellectual Property, Ship Registration and Maritime Law.

MANAGING PARTNER

Nicholas Keeling

LEGAL SUPPORT STAFF

Niall O'Toole (Solicitor)

(For a list of other Personnel, see Biographical Cards at London, England, Dubai, Abu Dhabi and Fujairah, United Arab Emirates, Cairo, Egypt, Ruwi, Sultanate of Oman, Kuwait, Lebanon and Yemen)

CHARLES A. GOMEZ & CO.

Barristers-at-Law

Established in 1988

2 HADFIELD HOUSE
LIBRARY STREET
P.O. BOX 659
GIBRALTAR, GIBRALTAR
Telephone: (350) 74998/73316
Telefax: (350) 73074

General Practice, Commercial Contracts, Corporation and Company, Insolvency and Debt Recovery, Litigation, Trial and Appellate practice. Opinions on matters of Gibraltar law (including E.U. law). Probate, Real Estate, Tax, Torts and Trust (Resident and offshore) Ship Registration.

CHARLES A. GOMEZ, LL.B. OF COUNSEL, born Gibraltar, April 23, 1959; admitted, 1982, Supreme Court of England and Wales and Supreme Court of Gibraltar. *Education:* Sacred Heart Grammar School, Gibraltar; University of London (Honours). Council of Legal Education (London); Commissioner for Oaths. *Member:* Honourable Society of the Inner Temple, London; Gibraltar Bar Association. *LANGUAGES:* English, Spanish and French.

STEPHEN V. CATANIA, LL.B. OF COUNSEL, born Gibraltar, November 16, 1963; admitted, 1987, Supreme Court of England and Wales and Supreme Court of Gibraltar. *Education:* Bayside School, Gibraltar; University of East Anglia (England). Council of Legal Education (London); Commissioner for Oaths. *Member:* Honourable Society of the Middle Temple, London; Gibraltar Bar Association. *LANGUAGES:* English and Spanish.

VIVIENNE ALCANTARA, B.A. Hons., born Gibraltar May 16, 1970; admitted, 1993, Supreme Court of England and Wales; 1994, Supreme Court of Gibraltar. *Education:* Westside School, Gibraltar; University of Kent (England); Complutense University of Madrid (Spain); Bar Finals Examinations (1993). *Member:* Honourable Society of the Middle Temple, London. *LANGUAGES:* English and Spanish.

KAREN LOUISE EVERETT, B.A. HONS., born Woking, Surrey, England, March 29, 1966. *Education:* Greenfield School, Woking, England; Lancashire Polytechnic; Law Society Finals Examinations 1991. *Member:* The Law Society, London. *LANGUAGES:* English and Spanish.

WILLIAM DAVID JONES, born Bangor, Gwynedd, United Kingdom, December 19, 1955. *Education:* Aberconwy School, Conwy, Gwynedd, United Kingdom. ILEX Associate, Institute of Legal Executives, 1980. *LANGUAGES:* English, Spanish and Welsh.

PRIVATE INTERNATIONAL LAW CONSULTANT

JOHN DE COTTA, M.A. (Oxon) called to the bar of England and Wales, 1955, Honourable Society of the Middle Temple, London Chambers 4 Essex Courts, Temple, London, Licenciate in law of the University of Alcala de Henares (Madrid) Abogado of the Colleges of Madrid, Granada and Malaga. *LANGUAGES:* English, Spanish, Portuguese and French.

CORPORATE AND TRUST EXECUTIVE

DESMOND R. REOCH, born Gibraltar, March 12, 1954. Management Consultant and Trust and Corporate Executive. *Education:* Durham University, England (Diploma in Business Administration (Dip.BA); Masters Degree of Business Administration (M.B.A.). *Member:* British Institute of Management (MIMgt). *LANGUAGES:* English and Spanish.

J.A. HASSAN & PARTNERS

Established in 1939

57/63 LINE WALL ROAD
P.O. BOX 199
GIBRALTAR, GIBRALTAR
Telephone: (350) 79000
Telefax: (350) 71966
Telex: 2280 HASBAR GK
Cable Address: JUDICIUM

Commercial, Corporate, Banking, Investment Funds, Commercial Litigation, Civil Litigation, Shipping, Property, Trust, Company Management. (Licensed by the Financial Service Commission Lincen No. FSC 219B).

(This Listing Continued)

J.A. HASSAN & PARTNERS, Gibraltar—Continued

FIRM PROFILE: General law firm departmentalized into Commercial, Litigation, Property and Company. Involved in most major developments in its jurisdiction. Instrumental in setting-up most of the international banks in the country and continues to act for many of these. Has strong links with major international legal and accountancy firms. Founding Member of TERRALEX. Firm Personnel fluent in English, Spanish, French, Hebrew, Hindu, Italian.

MEMBERS OF FIRM

SIR JOSHUA A. HASSAN, Q.C. *LANGUAGES:* English, Spanish and French. *PRACTICE AREAS:* Family; Probate; Nationality.

HAIM J.M. (JAMES) LEVY. *LANGUAGES:* English, Spanish, French and Hebrew. *PRACTICE AREAS:* Commercial; Corporate; Trust.

ANTHONY M. PROVASOLI. *LANGUAGES:* English and Spanish. *PRACTICE AREAS:* Banking; Privatisation.

DAVID J.V. DUMAS. *LANGUAGES:* English and Spanish. *PRACTICE AREAS:* Litigation.

PETER C. MONTEGRIFFO. *LANGUAGES:* English, Spanish and French. *PRACTICE AREAS:* Collective Investment Funds; Commercial; Trust and Asset Protection.

DICK J. AZOPARDI. *LANGUAGES:* English and Spanish. *PRACTICE AREAS:* Property Development.

LEWIS E.C. BAGLIETTO. *LANGUAGES:* English, Spanish, Italian and French. *PRACTICE AREAS:* Litigation; Admiralty.

ASSOCIATES

MARIO BALBAN. *LANGUAGES:* English and Spanish. *PRACTICE AREAS:* Property.

NITIN PALEKAR. *LANGUAGES:* English, Spanish and Hindu. *PRACTICE AREAS:* Commercial; Intellectual Property.

JAVIER CHINCOTTA. *LANGUAGES:* English and Spanish. *PRACTICE AREAS:* Commercial; Corporate.

LOUISE WARD. *LANGUAGES:* English. *PRACTICE AREAS:* Litigation.

JOHN VERRALL. *LANGUAGES:* English. *PRACTICE AREAS:* Commercial; Pensions.

GILBERT LICUDI. *LANGUAGES:* English and Spanish. *PRACTICE AREAS:* Litigation.

CHRISTOPHER RIDDEL. *LANGUAGES:* English and Spanish. *PRACTICE AREAS:* Commercial; Corporate.

NIGEL FEETHAM. *LANGUAGES:* English and Spanish. *PRACTICE AREAS:* Commercial.

MICHAEL CASTIEL. *LANGUAGES:* English and Spanish. *PRACTICE AREAS:* Commercial; Franchises.

FABIAN PILARDO. *LANGUAGES:* English and Spanish. *PRACTICE AREAS:* Litigation.

MOSES ANAHORY. *LANGUAGES:* English and Spanish. *PRACTICE AREAS:* Company; Commercial.

VALERIE HOLLIDAY. *LANGUAGES:* English and Spanish. *PRACTICE AREAS:* Company; Commercial.

JOHN RESTANO. *LANGUAGES:* English and Spanish. *PRACTICE AREAS:* Shipping/Admiralty.

ISABELLA LUGARO (Legal Executive). *LANGUAGES:* English and Spanish. *PRACTICE AREAS:* Property; Probate; Wills.

SANDRA SALMON (Legal Executive). *LANGUAGES:* English and Spanish. *PRACTICE AREAS:* Licensing; Debt Collection.

ISOLA & ISOLA

PORTLAND HOUSE
GLACIS ROAD
P.O. BOX 204
GIBRALTAR, GIBRALTAR
Telephone: (350) 78363
Fax: (350) 78990
Telex: 2255 ISOLA GK

International Company and Trust Law. Admiralty, Shipping and Commercial Law. Probate Law. Commercial Litigation.

FIRM PROFILE: A Leading firm within the jurisdiction.

Strong commercial law, commercial litigation and offshore corporate and trust practice specialising in advising High Net Worth Individuals companies alike on company and trust law, banking and financial services, admiralty and shipping.

Our corporate and trust service include the incorporation of offshore companies and trusts, tax planning advice and establishing discretionary and asset protection trusts within the jurisdiction.

One of our partners has spoken at international conferences including IBA and A B A conferences and has advised Government on joint ventures, property development and other commercial transactions.

A brochure on the firm and information on offshore companies and trusts, ship and yacht registration, banking, captive insurance, residency in Gibraltar for High Net Worth Individuals and financial services are readily available.

MEMBERS OF FIRM

THE HONOURABLE PETER J. ISOLA, OBE, MA (Oxon), born Gibraltar, March 20, 1929; admitted; 1952, Barrister-at-Law, England and Gibraltar. *Education:* Stonyhurst College, Lancashire; Pembroke College, Oxford University (Honours Degree in Jurisprudence); Council of Legal Education. Elected Member, Gibraltar Legislature Council, 1956-1969, Gibraltar House of Assembly, 1969-1983; Leader of Opposition, 1964-1967 and 1978-1983, Minister of Education, 1967-1968, Chairman, Public Accounts Committee, 1977. Order of British Empire, 1966. *Member:* Gibraltar Bar Association; Honourable Society of The Inner Temple; Royal Gibraltar Yacht Club. *LANGUAGES:* English and Spanish. *PRACTICE AREAS:* Admiralty; Maritime Law; Commercial Property Development; Commercial Property Finance; Banking Transactions.

PETER A. ISOLA, BA, born Gibraltar, December 27, 1958; admitted, 1982, Barrister-at-Law, England and Gibraltar; Notary Public, 1985. *Education:* Stonyhurst College, Lancashire; Kingston Polytechnic, Surrey (B.A. Honours Degree in Law); Council of Legal Education. *Member:* Gibraltar Bar Association; Honourable Society of The Inner Temple; International Fiscal Association; Royal Gibraltar Yacht Club. *LANGUAGES:* English and Spanish. *PRACTICE AREAS:* International Tax Planning; International Trusts; Corporate; Commercial Law; Notarial Service.

ALBERT J. ISOLA, BA, born Gibraltar, March 5, 1962; admitted, 1985, Barrister-at-Law, England and Gibraltar; Commissioner for Oaths. *Education:* Stonyhurst College, Lancashire; Kingston upon Thames, Surrey (B.A. Honours Degree in Law); Council of Legal Education. *Member:* Gibraltar Bar Association; Honourable Society of The Inner Temple; Royal Gibraltar Yacht Club. *LANGUAGES:* English and Spanish. *PRACTICE AREAS:* Financial Services; Estate Planning and Commercial Law.

LIONEL W.G.J. CULATTO, born Gibraltar, June 11, 1952; admitted, 1976, Barrister-at-Law, England, 1977, Gibraltar. *Education:* Stonyhurst College, Lancashire; College of Law, Chancery Lane, London; Council of Legal Education. *Member:* Gibraltar Bar Association; Honourable Society of The Middle Temple; Royal Gibraltar Yacht Club, Trustee of Gibraltar Heritage Trust; Committee Member Fortress Study Group. *LANGUAGES:* English. *PRACTICE AREAS:* Commercial Litigation; Commercial Advise.

NICHOLAS P. CRUZ, LLB, born Gibraltar, March 14, 1968; admitted, 1990, Barrister-at-Law, England and Gibraltar. *Education:* Worth Abbey, West Sussex; Kingston Polytechnic, Surrey; Council of Legal Education. *Member:* Gibraltar Bar Association; Honourable Society of The Middle Temple; Royal Gibraltar Yacht Club. *PRACTICE AREAS:* Conveyancing; Wills; Probate.

MAITE BENSADON, born Gibraltar, August 30, 1970; admitted, 1993, Barrister-at-Law, England and Gibraltar. *Education:* Westside Girls School, Gibraltar; University of Kent, Canterbury; La Complutense Madride (B.A., Honours Degree in English and Spanish Law); Council of Le-

(This Listing Continued)

gal Education. *Member:* Gibraltar Bar Association; Honourable Society of The Middle Temple; Royal Gibraltar Yacht Club. *LANGUAGES:* English, Spanish and French. *PRACTICE AREAS:* Intellectual Property; Patents and Trademarks; Copyright.

REFERENCES: Stuart Marks, Kaye, Scholer, Fierman, Hays & Handler, New York, N.Y.; Lars Forsberg, Burlingham, Underwood & Lord, New York, N.Y.; William A. Crump & Son, London, England.

MARRACHE & CO.

5 CANNON LANE
P.O. BOX 85
GIBRALTAR, GIBRALTAR
Telephone: (350) 79918/74901 (10 Lines)
Telefax: (350) 73315/74042
24 Hours Telephone: (350) 40730/40732

REVISERS OF THE GIBRALTAR LAW DIGEST FOR THIS DIRECTORY

International General Practice, Company, Administrative, Agency, Aviation, Banking, Bankruptcy, Construction, Conveyancing, Criminal, Debt Recovery, Defamation, EEC Law, Entertainment, Family, Franchising, Industrial Relations and Labour, Insurance and Reinsurance, International Contracts, International Private Law, Litigation, Maritime Shipping (Registration and Financing) and Admiralty, Media, Mortgages/Hypotecs, Negligence-Insolvency, Trademarks, Copyrights and Patents Registration, Personal Injury, Property and Real Estate Law, Privatizations, Assets Protection Trusts, Probate and Trusts, Investment and Financial Services, Tax and Offshore, Capital Taxation, Corporate Taxation, Estate and Gift Taxation, International Taxation, Personal Income, Taxation of Foreign Nationals, Taxation of Oil and Mining Companies, Investigations, General Tax Practice, Spanish and Portuguese Property Conveyancing.

FIRM PROFILE: Marache & Co have enjoyed sustained growth over the years and now ranks as one of the largest law firms in Gibraltar.

The firm pioneered in Gibraltar the concept of integrating in-house American, Spanish and Danish lawyers and thus at present the vast majority of work undertaken by the firm is of an international nature.

Marrache & Co. is a full service firm in general legal practice, however the areas of expertise for which the firm is renowned for is in the areas of Insolvency, Tax, Banking, Commercial Litigation and Corporate Law.

The firm also has recognized specialization in Financial Services Insurance, Shipping, Trusts and Probate and Labour Law.

Members of the firm are members of the Bar of Gibraltar, England and Wales, Republic of Ireland, Denmark, and Spain, and are also members of several associations including the International Tax Planning Association, the International Bar Association, American Bar Association and Pension Lawyers Association.

Significant Distinction: F Ashe Lincoln QC (Consultant) is a Master Bencher of the Honourable Society of the Inner Temple and K W Harris QC (Consultant) is the ex Attorney-General of Gibraltar.

MEMBERS OF FIRM

ISAAC S. MARRACHE, born Gibraltar, November 24, 1955; admitted, 1982, Supreme Court of England and Wales and Supreme Court of Gibraltar. *Education:* Brympton School, Gibraltar; Carmel College, Wallingford; Clifton College, B ristol; John Mackintosh Educational Trust Scholarship, Gibraltar; Government Scholarship, University of London, School of Oriental and African Studies (LL.B.); London School of Economics and Political Science (LL.M.). President of London University Law Students-London University Representative Council, Reported to the Royal Commission on Legal Services. Founder Member of the Editorial Board, Wig and Gavel. Council of Legal Education. Pupil 1 Crown Office Row, Temple, and 4 Essex Court, Temple, London. Tenant Robert Seabrook QC Chambers, 1 Crown Office Row, Temple. Freeman and Liveryman of the City of London, 1985. Elected Member Bar Council of Gibraltar. *Member:* Queens Commission Royal Naval Reserve; Society of Trusts Estate Practitioners; European Insolvency Practitioners Association; Association Europeanne des Procediens des Procedures Collectives; American Bar Association; International Bar Association; International Tax Planners Association; Notary Public of Gibraltar; Commissioner for Oaths; Honourable Society of the Inner Temple, London. *LANGUAGES:* English, Spanish, Portuguese and French. *PRACTICE AREAS:* Company; Commercial; Insolvency; Litigation and Tax.

(This Listing Continued)

ABRAHAM S. MARRACHE, born Gibraltar, June 14, 1950; (Not admitted in Gibraltar). *Education:* Clifton College; Queens College; Oxford (Master of Arts; Jurisprudence). *Member:* Honourable Society of the Inner Temple, London. (Consultant). *LANGUAGES:* English, Spanish, Italian, German and French. *PRACTICE AREAS:* Banking Law and Fund Management.

BENJAMIN J. S. MARRACHE, born Gibraltar, October 18, 1963; admitted, 1988, Supreme Court of England and Wales and Supreme Court of Gibraltar. *Education:* L'Ecole Francaise Malaga, Spain - UEL (LL.B.) London; London School of Economics (L.SE), University of London (LL.M.); Council of Legal Education. Commissioner for Oaths. Co-Author: "Asset Protection Trusts and Gibraltar's Legislation"; Co-Author: "International Bank Secrecy," Sweet & Maxwell, Gibraltar Section. Author: Law Digest on Gibraltar, Martindale-Hubbell Directory. Contributor to the New Law Journal. Contributor to the Journal of International Banking Law, Sweet & Maxwell, The Journal of Asset Protection and Financial Crime, Henry Stewart Publications, Offshore Investment Magazine, Offshore Financial Review. *Member:* International Tax Planning Association; Honourable Society of the Inner Temple; Society of Trusts and Estate Practitioners; Representative of the London School of Economics Alumni Association in Gibraltar. *LANGUAGES:* English, Spanish, French and Portuguese. *PRACTICE AREAS:* Company and Commercial; Banking; Trust; Tax and Funds.

MICHAEL PAUL MCDONNELL, born Ireland, October 15, 1963; admitted, 1986, Supreme Court of Ireland; 1989, Supreme Court of Gibraltar. *Education:* National University of Ireland BCL (NUI). *Member:* Honourable Society of King's Inn Dublin. *LANGUAGES:* English, Irish, Spanish and French. *PRACTICE AREAS:* Litigation; Insurance and Reinsurance.

ANTHONY E. DUDLEY, born Gibraltar, January 18, 1967; admitted, 1989, Supreme Court of Gibraltar. *Education:* Hull University (LL.B.). *Member:* Honourable Society of the Middle Temple. *LANGUAGES:* English and Spanish. *PRACTICE AREAS:* Property, Wills and Probate.

FREDMAN ASHE LINCOLN, QC, called to bar 1929, Inner Temple; (QC 1947) Northern Ireland, Gibraltar and Nigeria Bars Recorder. *Education:* Exeter College, Oxford (Master of Arts Jurisprudence); Bachelor of Civil Law, Oxford. (Consultant). *LANGUAGES:* English, French and Hebrew. *PRACTICE AREAS:* Commercial Litigation.

FRITZ VIDEBECH, born Denmark, September 27, 1933; admitted, 1963, Denmark. *Education:* Viborg State College, Denmark (1953); Oxford University (1953-1954); Copenhagen University (Cand. juris, 1960). Barrister at Appeal Court of Jutland, 1964; Deputy Judge Appeal Court, 1965-1966; Barrister at Supreme Court, 1969-1985; Public Defender and Q.C. at Supreme Court, 1985. President, urbanisation Cerros del Aguilla, 1986-1987. *Member:* Board of the Legal Association in Viborg; Tax Commission, 1965-1969; The Cultural Foundation, 1965-1970; Friends of Gambia, 1975-1977; The Commercial Council in Jutland; The Bank Council of Jyske Bank A/S, 1978-1985; Paul Hammerich Foundation; Hvidtfelt's Research Foundation; International Bar Association, the Danish Society for Insurance Law; Association of Tax Advisors. *LANGUAGES:* English, Spanish, Danish, German, French, Swedish, Norwegian. *PRACTICE AREAS:* General Practice; International Generation Change.

SHARON J. DAVIDSON, born Gibraltar, December 12, 1969; admitted, 1993, Supreme Court of England and Wales and Supreme Court of Gibraltar. *Education:* Westside School, Gibraltar; University of Kent, Canterbury, England (LL.B.). Inns of Court School of Law. *Member:* Honourable Society of the Inner Temple. *LANGUAGES:* English and Spanish. *PRACTICE AREAS:* Landlord and Tenant.

JANINE Y. BENSADON, born Gibraltar, June 27, 1969; admitted, 1984, Supreme Court of Gibraltar; 1993, Supreme Court of England and Wales. *Education:* Westside School, Gibraltar; Huddersfield University, England (LL.B., in Business and Finance). Inns of Court School of Law. *Member:* Honourable Society of Lincoln's Inn. *LANGUAGES:* English and Spanish. *PRACTICE AREAS:* Commercial and Taxation.

PAUL C.P. PERALTA, born Gibraltar, January 17, 1971; admitted, 1994, Supreme Court of England and Wales and Supreme Court of Gibraltar. *Education:* Bayside Comprehensive School, Gibraltar; St. Mary's College, Southhampton, England; University of East London, England; University of Utrecht, the Netherlands (LL.B. and National Diploma in Business and Finance), BPP Law School. *Member:* Honourable Society of the Middle Temple. *LANGUAGES:* English and Spanish. *PRACTICE AREAS:* Commercial and Litigation.

(This Listing Continued)

MARRACHE & CO., Gibraltar—Continued

GILLIAN M. GUZMAN, born Gibraltar, May 1, 1972; admitted, 1994, Supreme Court of England and Wales and Supreme Court of Gilbraltar. *Education:* Westside School, Gibraltar; Cardiff University, Wales (LL.B.). *Member:* Honourable Society of the Middle Temple. *LANGUAGES:* English and Spanish. *PRACTICE AREAS:* Family and Trust Law.

ASSOCIATES

CAROL S. HAW, born Peterborough, Cambridgeshire, England, July 15, 1957; (Not admitted in Gibraltar). *Education:* Stanford College, England; Associate Institute of Legal Executives (1989). *LANGUAGES:* English and Spanish. *PRACTICE AREAS:* Insolvency; Intellectual Property and Litigation.

GABRIEL GARCIA BENAVIDES, born San Roque (Cadiz) Spain, January 11, 1963; admitted, 1987 (Not admitted in Gibraltar). *Education:* Colegio Salesiano de Algeciras, Cadiz; Colegio Universitario San Juan Bosco Seville. Faculty of Law University of Seville. *Member:* Del Ilustre Colegio de Abogados de Cadiz, Spain. Spanish/Portuguese Dept. *LANGUAGES:* Spanish and English. *PRACTICE AREAS:* Property Purchase in Spain and Portugal.

HAYLEY ANN KING, born Gibraltar, August 20, 1969; (Not admitted in Gibraltar). *Education:* Westside Comprehensive School; University of London (LL.B.). *LANGUAGES:* Spanish and English. *PRACTICE AREAS:* Company Law.

ANTONIO LEON BOHORQUEZ, born Jerez de la Frontera (Cadiz), Spain, August 22, 1963; (Not admitted in Gibraltar). *Education:* Colegio el Pilar de Jerez de la Frontera (Cadiz), Spain; Yago School, Dublin, Ireland; Faculty of Law University Complutense of Madrid; I.C.A.D.E. (Master in Shipping Law). Spanish/Portuguese Dept. *LANGUAGES:* Spanish and English. *PRACTICE AREAS:* Property Purchase in Spain and Portugal.

REPRESENTATIVE CLIENTS: Agroman Emresa Constructora SA; Arthur Anderson; Banco de Santander S.A. Chemical Bank; Coopers & Lybrand; Cork Gully; Ernst & Young; John Laing International Construction Ltd.; K.P.M.G. Peat Marwick; Lehman Brokers; McDonalds Corp.; Moore Stephens; Wimpey Homes Holdings Ltd.; Riggs International Bank, Washington; The Peninsula and Oriental Steam Navigation Company; Al Rajhi Islamic International Bank; Royal Bank of Scotland PLC; Sydbank Schweiz A.G.; Bank International Luxembourg B L; Bank Continental du Luxembourg; Gotabanken A B; Robson Rhodes; Swiss Bank Corporation; Five Arrows Fund; Rothschild Inc. New York; Smith New Court Inc New York.

REVISERS OF THE GIBRALTAR LAW DIGEST FOR THIS DIRECTORY

MASSIAS & PARTNERS

117 MAIN STREET
P.O. BOX 213
GIBRALTAR, GIBRALTAR
Telephone: (350) 40888
Facsimile: (350) 40999

International General Practice including Company, Trusts, Banking, Conveyancing, Tax, Commercial, Shipping, Wills and Probate, etc.

MEMBERS OF FIRM

ISAAC C. MASSIAS, born London, England, March 4, 1962; admitted, 1986, Middle Temple, England and Gibraltar. *Education:* Liverpool Polytechnic (Bachelor of laws, Second Class, Upper Division with Hons.; LL.B., Hons.). Council of Legal Education (Part II Bar Finals). Commissioner for Oaths. *Member:* Committee Member, Gibraltar General Council of the Bar; The Honourable Society of the Middle Temple; The Bar Association for Commerce, Finance and Industry. *LANGUAGES:* English, Spanish and French.

VICTORIA E. MASSIAS, born London, England, February 8, 1966; admitted, 1989, Middle Temple, England; 1990, Gibraltar. *Education:* University of London, School of Oriental and African Studies (Bachelor of Law, Second Class, Lower Division with Hons; LL.B. Hons); University of London, University College London (Master of Laws; LL.M.). Council of Legal Education (Part II Bar Finals); Commissioner for Oaths. *Member:* Gibraltar General Council of the Bar; The Honourable Society of the Middle Temple. *LANGUAGES:* English, Spanish and French.

LOUIS W. TRIAY & PARTNERS

Barristers-at-Law, Acting Solicitors & Notary Public
Established in 1950
SUITE C, 2ND. FLOOR, REGAL HOUSE
QUEENSWAY
P.O. BOX 147
GIBRALTAR, GIBRALTAR
Telephone, 79423; 72712
Telex: 2243 TRIIEX GK
Fax: 71405

Admiralty, Banking Law, Commercial Law, Company Law, Company Formation, Financial Services, Insolvency, Joint Venture Capital, Litigation, Off-Shore Trusts & Investments, Ship Registration, International Tax.

PARTNERS

LOUIS W. TRIAY, Q.C., admitted, 1950, Gibraltar. *Education:* LL.B.

JAMES J. NEISH, admitted, 1979, Gibraltar. *Education:* LL.B.; Notary Public.

ASSOCIATES

CHARLES A. LAVARELLO, admitted, 1989, Gibraltar. *Education:* LL.B.

LOUIS B. TRIAY, admitted, 1989, Gibraltar. *Education:* LL.B.

Languages: English, Spanish and French.

TRIAY & TRIAY

(Incorporating Vasquez Benady)
Established in 1902
28 IRISH TOWN
GIBRALTAR, GIBRALTAR
Telephone: (350) 72020
Telex: 2219 TRIBAR GK
Telefax: (350) 72270

General Legal Practitioners , Commercial Banking, Conveyancing, Taxation, Trust, Company, Admiralty and Shipping (Registration and Finance), Litigation, Insolvency, Insurance, Private Client, Company (Formations and Administration), UCITS and Unit Trusts, Wills and Probate.

FIRM PROFILE: Triay and Triay is a firm presently constituted by 12 partners. It incorporates the firm of Vasquez Benady by a merger of the two firms which took place in 1991. The Firm continues the practice, first started by the late Arthur C. Carrara K.C. in 1902 and developed by the late S.P. Triay Q.C.; as well as the practice started by S. Benady Q.C. who later merged with Sir Alfred Vasquez Q.C.

The Style 'Triay and Triay' was first adopted after the death of Arthur C. Carrara in 1949, when J.J. Triay, the first son of S.P. Triay qualified and joined his father in partnership, to be joined three years later, by J.E. Triay Q.C. the present senior partner of the firm.

A number of clients to-day, can still trace the connection of their predecessors with the first origins of the firm. The firm's understanding of the requirements of clients in present times, has been built on a foundation of strong tradition and continuity.

The firm to-day prides itself in its breadth of experience as general practitioners who nevertheless shoulder habitually, the responsibility of their clients special needs in particular fields of law. The firm is engaged on a daily basis in both common law and chancery matters. It handles litigation as well as non-contentious matters. Its particular experience extends over the fields of banking, insurance and company law, shipping and admiralty, Conveyancing and property, trusts and fiscal matters and administrative law.

PARTNERS

J.E. Triay, Q.C., LL.B.	J.E. Triay, LL.B.
Sir A.J. Vasquez, C.B.E., Q.C., M.A.	A.A. Vasquez, M.A.
A.B. Serfaty, Q.C., LL.B.	F.J. Triay, LL.B.
P.R. Caruana, LL.B.	R.A. Triay, LL.B.
R.M. Vasquez, LL.B.	S.P. Triay, LL.B.
	M.W. Isola, LL.B.

(This Listing Continued)

J.R. Triay, LL.B. (Solicitor)

CONSULTANTS

S. Benady, C.B.E., Q.C., M.A.   *J.J. Triay, LL.B.*

Languages: English, Spanish and French

GREECE

ANAGNOSTOPOULOS & FIFIS

Established in 1990

ODOS SKOUFA 35

106.73 ATHENS, GREECE
Telephone: 0030-1-3633404, 3601442
Fax: 0030-1-3622246

Köln, Germany Office: Hohenstaufenring 17, D-50674 Köln. Telephone: 0221-2345156. Fax: 0221-248356.

FIRM PROFILE: *Our firm covers a broad area of Criminal, Civil and Commercial Law. We have built up close contacts with several European Embassies in Greece and we cooperate with renowned law firms in Europe and in the United States.*

MEMBERS OF FIRM

ILIAS G. ANAGNOSTOPOULOS, born Piraeus, Greece, January, 1956; admitted, 1981, Athens; 1993, Köln, Germany. *Education:* University of Athens (1978); University of Frankfurt am Main (Dr. juris., 1983). Recipient, Tsirimokos Prize awarded by the Greek Criminal Defence Lawyers Association. Lecturer at the University of Athens Faculty of Law in Criminal Law & Criminal Procedure. Author: "Haftgruende der Tatschwere und der Wiederholungsgefahr," Frankfurt/Bern/Las Vegas Lang, 1984; "Schwerpunkte neuerer Entwicklungen im griechischen Strafrecht," Zeitschrift fur die gesamte Strafrechtswissenschaft, vol. 98 (1986); "Criminal Law and Modern Biomedical Techniques" Révue International de Droit Pénal, vol. 59 (1988). *Member:* Athens Bar Association; Köln Bar Association; Criminal Law Experts Commission (Ministry of Justice); Board of Criminal Defence Lawyers Association; Association International de Droit Pénal; International Bar Association (Secretary, Criminal Law Committee). *LANGUAGES:* Greek, German, English and French. *PRACTICE AREAS:* Criminal Law; Criminal Litigation; Business Crimes; Drug Offenses; Extradition; Environment Crimes.

ANTONIOS N. FIFIS, born Athens, Greece, September 1955; admitted, 1980, Athens; 1993, Köln, Germany. *Education:* University of Thessaloniki (1978); University of Freiburg im Breisgau, Germany (1983). *Member:* Athens Bar Association; Köln Bar Association; European Studies Association; European Federalists Association; Greek Commercial Lawyers Association; International Bar Association. *LANGUAGES:* Greek, German and English. *PRACTICE AREAS:* Civil Law; Commercial and Company Law; Banking Law; Civil Litigation Law; Real Estate Law.

REPRESENTATIVE CLIENTS: National Mortage Bank of Greece, Macedonia-Thrace Bank; National Housing Bank; Interbank; Ethnos Editions S.A.

LAW OFFICES
ALEXANDER B. ATHANASSIADES

Established in 1963

5, STOURNARA STREET

ATHENS 10683, GREECE
Telephone: 01-3827779
Fax: 01-3843977

Civil and Criminal Trial Practice in all Courts, Real Estate, Corporate, Domestic Relations, Adoptions, Labor, Personal Injury, Commercial Law, Wills, Trademark, Patents Investment.

FIRM PROFILE: *The firm was established in 1963 and offers a full range of legal services. It is specialized in declaring executable by Greek Courts foreign judgements and the application of foreign law by Greek Courts. The firm has a legal support of 3 lawyers, 1 notary public and paralegal personnel.*

(This Listing Continued)

MEMBERS OF FIRM

ALEXANDER B. ATHANASSIADES, born Athens, Greece, September 26, 1931; admitted, 1963, Greece. *Education:* Law School of Athens University (Specialized in Conflicts of Law). Author: "Tax Study, a Summary of Penal Law and Criminal Procedures," Country Study into English. Legal Advisor for the U.S. Armed Forces in Greece, 1971-1991. *Member:* Athens Bar Association. *LANGUAGES:* Greek, English and French. *PRACTICE AREAS:* Application of Foreign Laws by Greek Courts.

STELLA N. SIARAVA, born Athens, Greece, 1948; admitted, 1973, Greece. *Education:* University of Athens Law School. Notary Public, 1977—. *Member:* Athens Bar Association. *LANGUAGES:* Greek. *PRACTICE AREAS:* Real Estate; Wills.

DINA G. PANORGIOU, born Sparta, Greece, 1960; admitted, 1985, Greece. *Member:* Athens Bar Association. *LANGUAGES:* Greek and English. *PRACTICE AREAS:* Family Law; Patents; Real Estate; General Practice.

KATERINA M. VALMA, born Athens, Greece, 1962; admitted, 1991, Greece. *Member:* Athens Bar Association. *LANGUAGES:* Greek, English and Italian. *PRACTICE AREAS:* Family Law; Inheritance Law.

ZETA E. GEORGIADIS, born Athens, Greece, 1968; admitted, 1991, Greece. Trainee. *Member:* Athens Bar Association. *LANGUAGES:* Greek, English, French and German. *PRACTICE AREAS:* International Law.

REPRESENTATIVE CLIENTS: Santa, SA Pharmaceutical Laboratories; Grafotechniki, SA, Computers and Office Machines; Poseidon SA, Fishfarms; Geofarm, SA, Agriculture and Pesticides.

AVRAMOPOULOS & PARTNERS
LAW FIRM

11, ALOPEKIS STREET
ATHENS 106 75, GREECE
Telephone: (01) 7250555
Fax: (01) 7253990

Corporate, Agency and Franchise, European Community Law, Foreign Investments, Mergers and Acquisitions, Privatizations, International Banking, Securities, Maritime, Labor, Tax, Real Estate, Trademarks and Patents, Liquidation, Telecommunications, Computer Law, Construction Law, Environment, Air and Space Law and Crisis Management.

MEMBERS OF THE FIRM

VASSILIS D. AVRAMOPOULOS, born Athens, Greece, January 30, 1955; admitted, 1981, Athens Court of Appeals. *Education:* University of Athens Law School (LL.B.); University of London (U.C.L.). Author: "Sex Discrimination Within E.E.C.," 1982; "The Application in Greece of E.E.C. Directive on Free Movement of Capital and the Investment Law 2687/55," 1985; "Foreign Companies in Greece," 1987; "Offshore Companies Under Law," 1989; "Setting Up a Greek Branch of a Foreign Corporation," 1989; "Doing Business in Greece," 1992. *Member:* Athens Bar Association; European Lawyer's Union; Association of European Studies. *LANGUAGES:* Greek and English. *PRACTICE AREAS:* Corporate Law; Investment Law; Privatizations; EEC Law; Crisis Management.

BASIL L. ANTONIOU, born Volos, Greece, July 27, 1950; admitted, 1976, Athens Court of Appeals. *Education:* University of Salonica Law School (LL.B.); New York University (LL.M., 1978). Associated With: Harbridge House, Boston, 1985; Crosby Associates, Florida, 1988; IMD, Lausanne, 1990. Vice Chairman, Board of Directors and Director, Legal and Government Affairs, Colgate-Palmolive, Hellas, S.A.I.C.; Vice Chairman, Greek Industry of Soaps and Detergents; Board Member: Federation of Industry Attica, Piraeus; Greek Cosmetics Association; Member, Greek Management Association; Administrative Committee Member, Greek Recycling and Recovery Association. *Member:* Athens Bar Association. *LANGUAGES:* Greek and English. *PRACTICE AREAS:* Corporate; Tax; Environment; Industrial Property; Investments; Public Affairs; Crisis Management.

MICHAEL K. POULAKOS, born Réthimnon, Greece, June 25, 1941; admitted, 1974, Athens Court of appeals. *Education:* University of Athens Law School (LL.B.). *Member:* Athens Bar Association. *LANGUAGES:* Greek. *PRACTICE AREAS:* Litigation; Labor Law.

EVAGGELOS J. APOSTOLOU, born Athens, Greece, March 5, 1956; admitted, 1981, Athens Court of Appeals and Supreme Court of Greece. *Education:* University of Athens Law School (LL.B.); University of Wales (LL.D.); University of London (LL.M.). Author: "The Institution of a Joint

(This Listing Continued)

AVRAMOPOULOS & PARTNERS LAW FIRM, Athens—Continued

Policy in Air Transport within the E.E.C.," 1983; "Five Freedoms of the Air," 1984; "E.E.C. and Power Politics in Air Transport," 1985; "The Position of the European Commission for Transparency in European Air Carriers," 1988; "Vat on Air Fares," 1989. *Member:* Athens Bar Association; Association of European Studies. *LANGUAGES:* Greek, English, French and Spanish. *PRACTICE AREAS:* Litigation; Air & Space Law; Shipping Law.

GEORGE M. VASSALAKIS, born Athens, Greece, March 2, 1962; admitted, 1986, Athens Court of First Instance. *Education:* University of Athens (LL.B., Hons, 1984) London School of Economics (LL.M., Hons, 1988); Secondment at Simmons & Simmons, London, (1989). Fraternity: British Graduates Society, LSE Alumni, Anglo-Hellenic Law Association. *Member:* Athens Bar Association; European Lawyers Association. *LANGUAGES:* English, German and Greek. *PRACTICE AREAS:* Commercial Law; Construction Law; International Banking.

FENY D. BOUZA, born Athens, Greece, February 3, 1966; admitted, 1991, Athens Court of First Instance. *Education:* Democritos University of Thrace Law School (LL.B, 1989). *Member:* Athens Bar Association. *LANGUAGES:* Greek and English. *PRACTICE AREAS:* Commercial Law.

ERASMIA G. SOTIROPOULOU, born Kalamata, Greece, February 21, 1966; admitted, 1990, Athens Court of First Instance. *Education:* University of Athens Law School (LL.B., 1988). *Member:* Athens Bar Association. *LANGUAGES:* Greek, English and French. *PRACTICE AREAS:* Litigation; Civil Law.

OF COUNSEL

PANAGIOTIS A. PAPANICOLAOU, born Nafpactos, Greece, November 1, 1949; admitted, 1977, Athens Court of Appeals and Supreme Court of Greece. *Education:* University of Athens Law School (LL.B.); University of Tubingen, West Germany (Ph.D., Dr.Jur). Author: "Schlechterfullung beim Vertrag zugunsten Dritter," 1977; "Interpretation of Articles 389-401 of the Greek Civil Code," 1979; "Interpretation of Articles 730-740 of the Greek Civil Code," 1980; "The Laesio Enormis in Article 388 of the Greek Civil Code and the Extent of the Judicial Intervention," 1985; "Abuse of the Freedom of Contracts," 1986. Professor, University of Athens Law School (Civil Law). *Member:* Athens Bar Association. *LANGUAGES:* Greek, German, English and French.

REPRESENTATIVE CLIENTS: AT&T; The Image Bank Inc.; TGI FRIDAY'S INC.; Bank Worms; First National Trustee Co. Ltd.; BABN Technologies Corp.; A. Moksel A.G.; Kemin Europa N.V.; RCI Europe Ltd.; Ladbroke Group Plc.; Brunswick G.M.B.H. (Sea Ray); Konings N.V.; American Airlines; Ideal Refractories S.A.; Ideal Telecommunications (Toshiba) S.A.; Eurocorp-Euroholdings S.A.; CIBAR Software Technologies; Europe S.A.; UNISOFT Software Applications S.A.; Inform-P. Lykos S.A.; Rhodes Chamber of Hoteliers; TRACTEBEL S.A.; Vianox-Franke; S.F. Systems; Sanitas; McCann-Errickson Hellas Ltd.

BAHAS, GRAMATIDIS & ASSOCIATES

Established in 1989

9 NAVARHOU NIKODIMOU

ATHENS 10558, GREECE

Telephone: 3229325; 3229328; 3243271; 3243272

Telex: 223769 LGMB-GR

Telefax: 01 3229329

London, England Associated Office: Xemophon Protopapas, Queens House, 180/182 Tottenham Court Road, London WLP 9LE.

Tirana, Albania Office: Albanian Legal Advisors Limited: Vaso Pasha Street, P.2, Sh.2, Ap.7. Telephone: +355 42 27 711. Fax: +355 42 23 383.

Commercial, Shipping, Banking, Corporate, Taxation, Foreign Investments in Greece, Admiralty, Aviation, Intellectual Property, Trademarks, Real Estate, Law of Succession, Family Law, Debit Collection, Insurance Law, Franchising, Telecommunications, Privatization, Arbitration, EC Law, Environmental Law.

FIRM PROFILE: Established in 1989 following the merger of the firms Macios Bahas Law Office (established in 1968) and Law Offices of Y. Gramatidis (established in 1988). Bahas Gramatidis & Associates is today one of the leading corporate and commercial law firms in Greece. The firm has a broadly-based practice with a recognized contribution to the development of the legal profession worldwide. The client base is Greek, European, Asian and North American in scope. The firm has 4 partners and 12 associates practicing in the Athens Office.

(This Listing Continued)

MEMBERS OF FIRM

YANOS GRAMATIDIS, born Larissa, Greece, May 12, 1952; admitted, 1977, and Supreme Court, Greece. *Education:* University of Athens Law School (LL.B.; Department of Political Sciences); The Hague Academy of International Law (D.O.A.); Institut International des Droits de l'Homme, Strasbourg (D.O.A.). Author: "The Protection of Human Rights in Europe," 1982; "La Nouvelle Loi qui concerne les Relations entre les Hommes et les Femmes," 1983; "Acquisition of Real Property in Greece by Aliens," 1985; "The New Law on Leasing in Greece, 1987; "Hotel Contracts in Greece," 1987; "Time sharing in Greece," 1987; "The establishment of Lawyers in the EEC," 1983; "Franchising: The Greek Legislation," 1988; "Investment Incentives in Greece," 1988; "Mergers and Acquisitions in the ECC," 1988; "Acquisitions of Greek Securities," 1988; "Mergers and Acquisitions in the EEC," 1988; "Bank Confidentiality in Greece," 1989; "International MOA Law," 1991; "Franchising - Greece," 1992; "Pre-emptive Remedies in Europe," 1992. Editor: "International Franchising," 1992. Special Representative in Greece of the International Franchise Association. *Member:* Athens, International (Member: Business Law Section; General Practice Section), American and Inter-American Bar Associations; Law Society of London; German-Hellenic Chamber of Commerce; Greek-Swedish Business Association; Greek-South African Business Club; Hellenic-American Chamber of Commerce; British-Hellenic Chamber of Commerce (Member of Board); Anglo-Hellenic Law Association, London (Chairman, 1988); Hellenic Hong-Kong Business Association (Member of Board); Institute of European Law, The University of Birmingham; Correspondent of Lexpress Ltd, Milwaukee, USA; EC Lawyers Society, London, England, World Jurist Association; International Litigation Practitioners Forum; Correspondent of the Centre of International Legal Studies, Salzburg, Austria; Correspondent of Butterworths Journal of International Banking and Financial Law; International Pension and Employees Benefits Lawyers Association; Solicitors European Group, London, England; Southwestern Legal Foundation (International and Comparative Law Center), Texas, USA (Member, Board of Advisors). (Managing Partner, Athens, Greece Office). *LANGUAGES:* Greek, English and French. *PRACTICE AREAS:* Corporate; Mergers and Acquisitions; Franchising; Telecommunications.

MARIOS BAHAS, born Athens, Greece, 1944; admitted, 1968, Athens Court of Appeals and Supreme Court of Greece. *Education:* University of Athens Law School (LL.B.); University of London Queen Mary College (LL.M.). Head of the Legal Department of the Bank of Central Greece, 1985—. Correspondent of Tax Letter Europe of European Law Press. *Member:* Athens Bar Association; International Bar Association. *LANGUAGES:* Greek, English and French. *PRACTICE AREAS:* Corporate; Mergers and Acquisitions; Commercial; Banking; Arbitration; Tax.

DIMITRIS EMVALOMENOS, born Athens, Greece, 1962; admitted, 1989, Piraeus Court of First Instance. *Education:* University of Athens Law School (LL.B.); University of London, Queen Mary and Westfield College (LL.M.). Author: " 'Legal entities in Greece," 1990; the Greek chapter in 'The Lawyer's Guide to Transnational Corporate Acquisitions," 1991; the Greek chapter in "International M&A Law," 1991; the Greek chapter in "European Companies Handbook," 1991 and 1992; "The financial incentives for investments in Greece," 1991; Investment portfolio companies and mutual funds in Greece," 1991; Personal Injury litigation in Greece," 1991; "The Greek Social Security System," IPEBLA 1991; "Country Updates-Greece," IBIS, 1991. *Member:* Piraeus Bar Association; European Federation for Retirement Provision. *LANGUAGES:* Greek, English. *PRACTICE AREAS:* Corporate; Mergers and Acquisitions; Commercial; Shipping; EC Law.

THEODOROS FILOTHEIDIS, born Thessaloniki, Greece, 1958; admitted, 1982, Athens Court of First Instance. *Education:* University of Athens Law School (LL.B.). Author: "Recent changes in the real Estate Law," 1990. *Member:* Athens Bar Association. *LANGUAGES:* Greek and English. *PRACTICE AREAS:* Real Estate; Family Law; Private and Commercial Litigation.

ASSOCIATES

GEORGE HADJIS, born Amfiklia, Greece, 1942; admitted, 1979, Athens Court of Appeals. *Education:* University of Athens Law School (LL.B.); Highest School of Economic and Commercial Studies of Athens (LL.B.). *Member:* Athens Bar Association. *LANGUAGES:* Greek and English. *PRACTICE AREAS:* Private and Commercial Litigation; Real Estate; Banking.

NICOLAOS HAIROPOULOS, born Athens, Greece, 1955; admitted, 1983, Athens Court of First Instance. *Education:* University of Athens Law School (LL.B.); Pantios Highest School of Political Sciences of Athens.

(This Listing Continued)

Member: Athens Bar Association. *LANGUAGES:* Greek and English. *PRACTICE AREAS:* Corporate; Banking; Commercial Litigation; Aviation.

PAPANIKOLAOU FOFI, born Athens, Greece, August 21, 1952; admitted, 1974, Athens Court of First Instance. *Education:* University of Athens Law School (LL.B.); School of Comparative Legal Studies, Strasbourg, France. *Member:* Athens Bar Association. *LANGUAGES:* Greek, English, French. *PRACTICE AREAS:* Family Law; Private and Commercial Litigation; Intellectual Property; Real Estate.

ATHANASIOS VAMVOUKOS, born Mithimna, Lesvos, Greece, July, 1946; admitted, 1973, Thessaloniki Court of First Instance, Greece. *Education:* Aristotelio University of Thessaloniki Law School (LL.B.); University of Santa Barbara (M.A.); George Washington University (LL.M.); Oxford University (Ph.D.). Author: The Modern Law of the Sea, 1986; Technology Transfer "The Legal Framework," 1988; Terrorism and International Law," 1992. Co-author: "The case of Greece in International Joint Ventures," Mathew Bender & Co., 1992; "EC Legal Systems, A Guide: Greece (Butterworths), 1992. Advisor to the Ministry of National Economy, Greece, 1982-1983. Special Scientific Advisor to the Ministry of Industry, Greece, 1984-1990. *Member:* Thessaloniki Bar Association; American Society of International Law; Greek Society for the study of European Law; British Universities Alumni Association. *LANGUAGES:* Greek, English, French. *PRACTICE AREAS:* Corporate; Commercial.

CHRISTINA STAMPOULTZI, born Thessaloniki, Greece, November 4, 1966; admitted, 1992, Greece and Thessaloniki Court of First Instance. *Education:* Aristotelion University of Thessaloniki Law School (LL.B.); University of Exeter (LL.M.). Author: "The Treatment of Television in European Competition Law," 1989. Attorney, European Commission, D.G. XV/B4 ("Stage"). *Member:* Thessaloniki Bar Association; E.C. Lawyers Society. *LANGUAGES:* Greek, English, Italian, French and Spanish. *PRACTICE AREAS:* E.U. Law; Corporate; Mergers and Acquisitions; Commercial.

PHILOTHEIDIS STAMATIA, born Athens, Greece, April 22, 1967; admitted, 1993, Athens Court of First Instance. *Education:* Democretion University of Thrace Law School (LL.B.); University of Newcastle Upon Tyne (LL.M.). *Member:* Athens Bar Association; Greek Association of European Jurists. *LANGUAGES:* Greek, English, French. *PRACTICE AREAS:* EC Law; Real Estate; Private and Commercial Litigation; Family Law; Law of Inheritance.

LAZARIDOU LENA, born Athens, Greece, September 7, 1966; admitted, 1992, Athens Court First Instance. *Education:* Athens University Law School (LL.B.); City of London Polytechnic (M.A., Business Law). *Member:* Athens Bar Association. *LANGUAGES:* Greek, English, French and German. *PRACTICE AREAS:* Private and Commercial Litigation; Labour Law; Employees Pensions and Benefits.

ALEXANDRA TSOUMBA-BIZOPOULOU, born Serres, Greece, 1953; admitted, 1978, Athens Court of Appeals, Greece. *Education:* Aristotelio University of Thessaloniki Law School (LL.B.). *Member:* Athens Bar Association. *LANGUAGES:* Greek, English. *PRACTICE AREAS:* Private and Commercial Litigation.

MICHAEL SARALEKOS, born Xanthi, Greece, February 12, 1965; admitted, 1987, Athens, Greece. *Education:* Demokritus University Law School (LL.B.). *Member:* Xanthi Bar Association. *LANGUAGES:* Greek and English. *PRACTICE AREAS:* Private and Commercial Litigation; Family Law; EEC Law.

BETTY SMYRNIOU, born Sidney, Australia, 1967; admitted, 1991, Athens, Greece. *Education:* University of Athens Law School (LL.B.); University of Bristol, England (non-degree within the EC Programee "ERASMUS"). *Member:* Athens Bar Association. *LANGUAGES:* Greek, English and German. *PRACTICE AREAS:* Labour Law; Insurance; Aviation; Corporate.

GEORGE FELLIDIS, born Athens, Greece, September 14, 1965; admitted, 1990, Athens, Greece. *Education:* Aristotelio University (LL.B., 1988); Kings College (LL.M., 1992). *LANGUAGES:* Greek, English. *PRACTICE AREAS:* Corporate Law; Insurance Law; EU Law.

OF COUNSEL

EUGENE TRIVIZAS, born Athens, Greece, 1946; admitted, 1972, Athens Court of Appeals. *Education:* University of Athens Law School (LL.B.); University of Athens School of Economic and Political Sciences (B.Sc.); University of London (LL.M.; Ph.D.). Lecturer in Criminology and Penology, University of Reading, 1985—. *Member:* Athens Bar Associa-

(This Listing Continued)

tion. *LANGUAGES:* Greek, English and French. *PRACTICE AREAS:* Criminology; Social Behaviour.

REPRESENTATIVE CLIENTS: The Greek General Consulate, London, England; The Times, London, England; Fisons plc, London, England; Balfour Beaty, London, England; The Bank of Central Greece, Athens, Greece; Allied Lyons plc, London, England; Hiram Walker-Allied Vintners International Ltd, London, England; A. Sulka & Co., Ltd, London, England; Investment Finance Ltd, London, England; Johnson & Higgins Ltd, London, England; Baltic Aviation, Sweden; Schwartzhaupt Gmbh, Germany; Paul Boskamp Gmbh, Germany; Valley View Packing Co., California, USA; Imperio Insurance Co., Athens, Greece; Societe Generale de Banques S.A., Brussels, Belgium; National Australian Bank, Australia; Thrifty Rent-A-Car System, Inc., Tulsa, Oklahoma, USA; Control Union Inspections Ltd, London, England; Motorola Inc., Chicago, Illinois, USA; BUPA, London, England; Prudential-Bache Securities (UK) Ltd., London, England; Sotheby's International Realty, London, England; Royale Energy, La Mesa, California, USA; Starkey Laboratories, Inc., Minneapolis, Minnesota, USA; Steinberg, Inc., Montreal, Canada; Bingo S.A., Athens, Greece; K.H.D. Manheim, Germany; M.W.M. Manheim, Germany; Texaco S.A., Athens, Greece; Bassatne Petroleum Group, Athens, Greece; The Trustees of the London Clinic Ltd, London, England; Dinners Club Hellas S.A., Athens, Greece; Dinners Club Ltd, London, England; Stoakes Systems Ltd., England; Swiss Bank Corporation, London, England; Campton (City) Ltd., London, England; Commercial Credit Co., London, England; American International Group, New York, USA; Arnold & Green Ltd, London, England; General Milk Products Ltd, London, England; International Pilot Training Course Pty Ltd, Sydney, Australia; The Royal Marsden Hospital, London, England; International Semi-tech Microelectronics Inc., Ontario, Canada; Mattey Securities Limited, London, England; Information Requirements Technology, Curacao, Netherlands Antilles; European Educational Organization, London, England; BBC Enterprises Ltd., London, England; MCI Inc., U.S.A.; Zivnostenska Banka, London, England; The Body Shop International, London, England; British Home Stores, London, England; Baskins Robbins, London, England; Eleftheros Typos Newspaper, Athens, Greece; High Point plc, London, England; Argo Tours Group, London, England; Virgin Airlines, London, England; United Airlines, Chicago, USA; Conde Nast Publications, USA; Commonwealth War Graves Commission, England; Ergon S.A., Athens, Greece; The Globe Group, Athens, Greece; Hambro Legal Protection Ltd, England; Allied Breweries Ltd, England; Allied Irish Bank, Ireland; Jardine Insurance Services Ltd, England; Kidder Peabody Inc, USA; Norwich Union, England; Polytechnic of Central London, England; World Leisure, London, England; Japan Travel Bureau (U.K.) Ltd, England; Bridgestone Corp, Japan; Berry Bros & Rudd, London, England; The National Tourist Organization of Greece, London, England; The Spanish Tourist Board, London, England; Dankin Donuts, USA; Egnatia Bank, Athens, Greece, Sun Microsystems Inc., California, USA; Health Care International (Scotland) Ltd. Scotland, U.K.; Browning Ferry Industries Inc., Texas, USA.; Curragh Inc.; Toronto Canada; Air Canada, Canada; GTG Telephone Corp, USA; Hyatt Corp, Chicago, USA; Regency Casinos Ltd, England; The Time Magazine, USA; Thames Water, England; ING Bank, The Netherlands; Hauwha Group, Korea; Whirlpool Inc. Michigan, USA.

BAILAS & PARTNERS

Established in 1972

1 VALAORITOU STREET
10671 ATHENS, GREECE
Telephone: +301-3602014
Telefax: +301-3625170
Telex: 216586 BAIL GR

Corporate, Commercial, Mergers and Acquisitions, Joint Ventures, Banking, Insurance, International Trade, Antitrust, Construction, Real Estate, Labor, Intellectual Property, Insolvency Law, Litigation (with emphasis on debt collection and the recognition and enforcement of foreign court judgments), Arbitration.

MEMBERS OF FIRM

DR. DIMITRIOS BAILAS, born Athens, Greece, February 28, 1927; admitted, 1952, Greece. *Education:* University of Athens, Greece (with honors, 1950); University of Göttingen, Germany (Dr. jur., 1960). Contributor in the Commentary of Civil Law in Greece and author of various publications in the fields of Corporate and Contract Law. *Member:* Athens Bar Association. *LANGUAGES:* Greek, German, English, French and Italian. *PRACTICE AREAS:* Banking; Mergers and Acquisitions; Joint Ventures; Insurance; International Trade Law; Arbitration.

DR. HABIL KLEANTHIS ROUSSOS, born Athens, Greece, October 12, 1956; admitted, 1980, Greece. *Education:* University of Athens, Greece (1978); University of Berlin, Germany (Dr. jur., 1982); University of Kiel, Germany (Habilitation, 1989). Lecturer in Law, University of Athens, 1990—. Professor of Law, University of Athens, 1995—. Contributor in the Commentary of Civil Law in Greece and author of various publications in the fields of Corporate, Contract and Compensation Law. *Member:* Athens Bar Association; International Bar Association; Hellenic Society for Construction and Technology Law. *LANGUAGES:* Greek, German and English. *PRACTICE AREAS:* Banking; Construction; Real Estate; Antitrust; Insolvency; Litigation; Arbitration.

(This Listing Continued)

BAILAS & PARTNERS, Athens—Continued

PANTELIS STATHATOS, born Athens, Greece, August 17, 1947; admitted, 1973, Greece. *Education:* University of Athens, Greece (1970). *Member:* Athens Bar Association; Institute of Professional Representatives before the European Patent Office. *LANGUAGES:* Greek, French, German and English. *PRACTICE AREAS:* Intellectual Property; Labor; Commercial Law; Litigation.

EFI KALOKOUVAROU, born Athens, Greece, September 29, 1948; admitted, 1974, Greece. *Education:* University of Athens, Greece (1971); University of Cambridge, UK (1973). *Member:* Athens Bar Association. *LANGUAGES:* Greek, English, German, French and Italian. *PRACTICE AREAS:* Corporate; Mergers and Acquisitions; Joint Ventures; International Trade Law; Litigation.

ELENA BAILAS, born Athens, Greece, June 24, 1963; admitted, 1991, Greece; 1992, Germany. *Education:* University of Munich, Germany (1988); Boston University, USA (LL.M., 1990). *Member:* Athens Bar Association; Hellenic Society for Construction and Technology Law. *LANGUAGES:* Greek, German, English and French. *PRACTICE AREAS:* Banking; Corporate; Mergers and Acquisitions; Joint Ventures; Construction Law.

BALLAS, PELECANOS & ASSOCIATES

Law Offices

Patent & Trade Mark Attorneys

European Patent Attorneys

Established in 1930

(Formerly "SIMITIS" Law Offices)

4, LYCABETTUS STREET, KOLONAKI
ATHENS 106 71, GREECE
Telephone: (01) 3625943; (01)3623721; (01) 3602506; (01) 3629229
Cable Address: ANWALTSIM, Athens
Telex: 225196 SIMI GR
Facsimile: (01) 3647925

Salonica, Greece Office: Souliadis, Haratsaris Law Offices. 17 Tsimiski Street, 54624. Telephone: (031) 224840; (031) 272232. Facsimile: (031) 284178.
Larissa, Greece Office: Zissis Bekos Law Offices. 4 M. Alexandrou Street, 41222. Telephone: (041) 255414.

International Practice, Patent Law, Trademark Law, Trade Name Law, Copyright Law, Technology Law, Computer Law, Antitrust Law, Unfair Competition Law, Unfair Trade Practices, Licensing Law, Advertising Law, Commercial Law, Company Law, Corporate Law, Contract Law, Investment Law, Acquisitions, Divestitures, Holding Companies, Franchise Law, Non-Profit Organizations, Association Law, Banking Law, Construction Contract Law, Real Estate Land Sales, Land Title Law, Lease Law, Mortgages Law, Securities, Property Management, Successions, Taxation Law, Debtor Creditor Law, Litigation, Civil Trial, Employment Law, Distribution & Development Agreements.

FIRM PROFILE: Established in 1930 as the "Simitis Law Offices" by Professor George Simitis, the firm enlarged its partnership in the 1960's and 1970's to include many leading Greek academics and practitioners. From the outset the firm has almost exclusively concentrated its services in the area of Business Law.

In the 1980's the firm was renamed and under its current partnership maintains its position amongst the top Greek Business Law firms. It also incorporates a most experienced special department for the protection of Intellectual and Industrial Property, headed by its two senior partners.

Traditionally, the firm has had and maintains a very strong international client base, representing many of the internationally most renowned corporations and its members offer legal advise and undertake litigation on all aspects of Greek and Common Market Business Law.

The firm has two partners, ten associates and five administrative support assistants.

MEMBERS OF FIRM

GEORGE A. BALLAS, born Athens, Greece, September 1, 1949; admitted, 1972, Athens. *Education:* University of Athens, Law School (LL.B., 1972) and University of Paris, Law School. Solicitor and Barrister at the Athens and Piraeus Court of Appeals, the Supreme Court of Greece and the

(This Listing Continued)

Council of State. European Patent Attorney. Secretary General of the Greek Parliament, 1981-1985. Chairman, Insurance Board, Public Power Corporation, 1985-1987. Chairman, Non profit Society for the establishment of Libraries. Member, Board of Directors: Public Power Corporation, 1985-1987; Fiat Auto Athens, S.A. *Member:* Athens Bar Association; Institute of Professional Representatives before the European Patent Office. (Managing Partner). *LANGUAGES:* Greek, English, French and Italian. *PRACTICE AREAS:* Corporate Law; Investment Law; Intellectual Property Law; Patents; Trademarks; Copyrights; Unfair Competition Law; Unfair Trade Practices; Debtor Creditor Law; Litigation.

GREGORY M. PELECANOS, born London, England, June 9, 1960; admitted, 1983, Athens. *Education:* University of Athens, Law School (LL.B., 1982) and University of London, Law School (LL.M., 1983). Solicitor and Barrister at the Athens and Piraeus Court of Appeals. Eighteenth Tax Law Seminar, Greek Productivity Center, 1991. Author: "Codes of Conduct for Transnational Corporations," Law and Politics, 1984; "Notorious Trademarks- Definition, Protection, Policy," Journal of Commercial Law, 1985; "Legal Protection of Computer Software," Technica, 1988; "New Technologies and Law," Economicos Tachydromos, 1988; Legal Editor (Greek edition), Doswel and Simons, "Fraud and abuse in I.T. Systems," 1990; "Commercial Agents and Dealers, The question of compensation under Greek and E.E.C. Law," Naftemboriki, 1992. Lecturer in Business Law and Business in the European Economic Community, American College of Greece, 1987—. Chairman, Computer Law Committee, Greek Computer Society, 1985-1990. *Member:* Athens Bar Association. *LANGUAGES:* Greek and English. *PRACTICE AREAS:* Competition Law; Antitrust Law; Unfair Competition Law; Contract Law; Intellectual Property Law; Licensing Law; Technology Law; Taxation Law; Corporate Law; Litigation.

PEPI H. TSIKLITIRAS, born Athens, Greece, August 16, 1959; admitted, 1982, Athens. *Education:* University of Athens, Law School (LL.B., 1982) and University of Paris II, Law School (D.E.A., 1984). Solicitor and Barrister at the Athens and Piraeus Court of Appeals. *Member:* Athens Bar Association. *LANGUAGES:* Greek, French and English. *PRACTICE AREAS:* Construction Contract Law; Real Estate Law; Land Sales; Lease Law; Land Title Law; Mortgage Law; Litigation.

GEORGIA J. CAMBILLI, born Athens, Greece, September 27, 1948; admitted, 1972, Athens. *Education:* University of Athens, Law School (LL.B., 1972). Solicitor and Barrister at the Athens and Piraeus Court of Appeals. Assistant in Taxation Legislation and Public Finance at the University of Athens, 1973-1980. *Member:* Athens Bar Association. *LANGUAGES:* Greek, English, French and Italian. *PRACTICE AREAS:* Non-Profit Organizations; Association Law.

MYROFORA A. PAPADOPOULOU, born Edessa, Greece, February 16, 1961; admitted, 1983, Athens. *Education:* University of Thrace, Law School (LL.B., 1983). Solicitor and Barrister at the Athens and Piraeus Court of Appeals. *Member:* Athens Bar Association. *LANGUAGES:* Greek, English and Spanish. *PRACTICE AREAS:* Employment Law; Contract Law; Litigation.

NATASHA A. GEORGIADOU, born Athens, Greece, January 11, 1966; admitted, 1987, Athens. *Education:* University of Salonica, Law School (LL.B., 1987) and University of Dijon, France, Law and Political Sciences School (D.E.S.S., 1990). Solicitor and Barrister at the Athens and Piraeus First Instance Court. *Member:* Athens Bar Association. *LANGUAGES:* Greek, French, English and German. *PRACTICE AREAS:* Commercial Law; Corporate Law; Contract Law; Litigation.

CATHERINE D. PAPAMANOLI, born Rhodes, Greece, October 21, 1964; admitted, 1987, Athens. *Education:* University of Salonica, Law School (LL.B., 1987). Solicitor and Barrister at the Athens and Piraeus First Instance Court. *Member:* Athens Bar Association. *LANGUAGES:* Greek, English and French. *PRACTICE AREAS:* Successions; Security; Property Management; Litigation.

SOPHOCLES M. STEFANIDES, born Athens, Greece, August 25, 1960; admitted, 1988, Athens. *Education:* Pantios University of Athens (LL.B., 1982); University of Thrace, Law School (LL.B., 1987); Pantios University of Athens, Institute of Regional Development (LL.M., 1986). Solicitor and Barrister at the Athens and Piraeus First Instance Court. *Member:* Athens Bar Association. *LANGUAGES:* Greek and English. *PRACTICE AREAS:* Commercial Law; Construction Contract Law; Real Estate Law; Land Sales; Litigation.

ANTONY G. MAVRIDES, born Athens, Greece, October 23, 1965; admitted, 1988, Athens. *Education:* University of Salonica, Law School (LL.B., 1988); University of Kent, Law School, Canterbury, U.K. (LL.M.,

(This Listing Continued)

1993). Solicitor and Barrister at the Athens and Piraeus First Instance Court. *Member:* Athens Bar Association. *LANGUAGES:* Greek, English and German. *PRACTICE AREAS:* Commercial Law; Corporate Law; Patent, Trademark and Copyright Law; Litigation.

HELEN C. MILLITSI, born Athens, Greece, June 1, 1965; admitted, 1990, Athens. *Education:* University of Athens, Law School (LL.B., 1989). Solicitor and Barrister at the Athens and Piraeus First Instance Court. *Member:* Athens Bar Association. *LANGUAGES:* Greek, English and French. *PRACTICE AREAS:* Banking Law; Securities.

GREGORIA CH. KATSOULI, born Athens, Greece, June 28, 1966; admitted, 1992, Athens. *Education:* University of Athens, Law School (LL.B., 1992). *Member:* Athens Bar Association. *LANGUAGES:* Greek, English and French. *PRACTICE AREAS:* Corporate Law; Unfair Competition Law; Unfair Trade Practices.

GEORGE C. MICHALOPOULOS, born Barquisimeto, Venezuela, June 20, 1966; admitted, 1993, Athens. *Education:* University of Athens, Law School (LL.B., 1993). *Member:* Athens Bar Association. *LANGUAGES:* Greek, Spanish and English. *PRACTICE AREAS:* Commercial Law; Corporate Law.

Languages: Greek, English, French, Italian, German and Spanish

REPRESENTATIVE CLIENTS: Fiat Auto S.p.A., Turin, Italy; Fiat Auto Hellas S.A., Athens, Greece; Alfa Romeo Hellas, S.A., Athens Greece; Philip Morris Products Inc., New York, N.Y., U.S.A.; Levi Strauss & Co., San Francisco, California, U.S.A.; Levi Strauss Hellas S.A., Athens, Greece; Levi Strauss Eximco Europe S.A., Brussels, Belgium; Telefonaktiebolaget LM Ericsson, Stockholm, Sweden; Microsoft Corporation, Redmond, Washington, U.S.A.; Microsoft Hellas S.A., Athens, Greece; Dell Computer Corporation, Inc., Austin, Texas, U.S.A.; Remington Arms Company, Inc., Wilmington, Delaware, U.S.A.; Mobil Oil Hellas S.A., Athens, Greece; Toyota Hellas S.A., Athens, Greece; Hoffmann la Roche and Co. A.G., Basel, Switzerland; Cinzano & Cia S.p.A., Turin, Italy; Playboy Enterprises Inc., Chicago, Illinois, U.S.A.; International Holiday on Ice Inc., Stamford, Connecticut, U.S.A.; Hungarian Embassy and Commercial Section, in Athens, Greece; Miller Brewing Company, Milwaukee, Wisconsin, U.S.A.; Fabriques de Tabac Reunies S.A., Neuchâtel, Switzerland; Papastratos Cigarettes Manufacturing Company S.A., Athens, Greece; Virgin Atlantic Airways Limited, Crawley, England; Virgin Enterprises Limited, London, England; Sega Europe Limited, London, England; Videoton A.G., Budapest, Hungary; Hungarotex A.G., Budapest, Hungary; Technoimpex A.G., Budapest, Hungary; Chemolimpex A.G., Budapest, Hungary; Schlumberger Foundation for Education and Research, Basel, Switzerland; Haifa Chemicals Ltd, Haifa, Israel; American Safety Razor Company, Verona, Virginia, U.S.A.; Dude Sportswear Inc., Long Beach, California, U.S.A.; Spectropharm Inc., Quebec, Canada; Conagra Inc., Omaha, Nebraska, U.S.A.; Magnetek Inc., Los Angeles, California, U.S.A.; Capcom Co. Ltd., Osaka, Japan; Clover Manufacturing Company Ltd., Osaka, Japan; Avery Dennison Corporation, Pasadena, California, U.S.A.; Bell Hotels S.A., Heraklion, Crete, Greece; Ergon S.A., Athens, Greece; Postipankki Ltd, Helsinki, Finland; BHF Bank, Frankfurt, Germany; Diesel S.p.A., Molvena, Italy; Diesel Hellas S.A., Athens, Greece.

M. AND P. BERNITSAS

Established in 1946

5 DIMOKRITOU STREET
ATHENS 106 71, GREECE
Telephone: 3615395; 3608496; 3605340; 3622305-6
Telex: 221631 BERN GR
Fax: 3640805; 3618789

Brussels, Belgium Office: 19-21 rue Capouillet, 1060.

European Community Law, Investment Law, Banking, Mergers, Acquisitions and Privatizations, Commercial and Company Law, Trademark and Patent, Antitrust and Competition Law, Human Rights, Council of Europe, Aviation, Arbitration (Local and International, ICC), Shipping Law, Inheritance, Tax and Real Estate, Civil Law.

FIRM PROFILE: *The firm was established in 1946 by Marinos Bernitsas and offers a wide range of legal services. It is well known for its expertise in European Community Law, International Business Law, Investment Law, Corporate and Banking Law.*

The client base is mainly European and North American. The firm has a branch office in Brussels. Experts' advice and documentation are made available to clients among others on Greek Investment Laws, Free Movement of Capital, Mergers and Acquisitions, Competition and Anti-Trust Law, Banking Law, Protection of Industrial Design and on the Establishment of Foreign Companies in Greece.

MARINOS P. BERNITSAS, born Athens, June 19, 1918; admitted, 1946, Athens, Athens Court of Appeals and Supreme Court of Greece. *Education:* University of Athens Law School. Counsel to Public Power Corpo-

(This Listing Continued)

---

ration, 1966-1979. *Member:* Athens Bar Association. *LANGUAGES:* Greek and German. *PRACTICE AREAS:* General Practice; Real Estate.

PROF. PANAYOTIS M. BERNITSAS, born Athens, October 16, 1948; admitted, 1974, Athens, Athens Court of Appeals and Supreme Court of Greece; Professional Representative before the European Patent Office. *Education:* University of Athens Law School; University of Paris (D.E.S. in Public Law, 1973); Hague International Law Academy (1973); Institute of Advanced Legal Studies, London (Research, 1975); University of Thessaloniki (Ph.D., 1979). Author: "Securities in International Transactions," Athens, 1978; "Transport Policy and Greece's Accession to the European Communities," Athens, 1980; "EEC Maritime Policy and its Application in Greece," 1981; "Exclusive Agency Agreements in European Community Law," Greek Review of European Law, 1981; "Transport Policy and Greece's Accession to the European Communities," 2nd ed. 1985; "Anti-dumping Law," 1987; "The 'Prinos 'Case: The International implications of the nationalization of companies," 1987; "European Community Law," 1988; "European Community Competition Law and its impact on the Enactment and Application of law 703/1977 on Monopolies and Oligopolies and on the protection of free competition," 1988; "Free movement of capital in European and Greek Law," 2nd ed. 1989. Associate Professor of International Economic Law and Law of International Business Transactions and European Community Law, University of Thrace, 1988. Counsel, Ministry of National Economy during Negotiations for Greece's Accession to European Communities (EEC), 1977-1982. Legal Counsel, Hellenic Banks Association, 1980-1990. Counsel to Greek Commissioner for Common Market Transport Policy, Brussels, 1983-1984. Special Secretary for Public Investments, Regional Policy and Integrated Mediterranean Programs, Ministry of National Economy, 1989. Counsel to Greek Prime Minister Zolotas on EEC matters, 1989-1990. Counsel to Minister of Foreign Affairs, 1989-1990. Counsel to the Minister of National Economy on illegal State Aids and privatization issues (1990-1991). Secretary General of the Hellenic Centre for European Studies, 1990-1993. Ad hoc counsel to the Minister of National Economy on EEC matters. Ad hoc counsel to the Ministry of National Economy on the Privitization of State-owned enterprises (National Telecommunications Organization [O.T.E.] and Refineries). 1991-1993. Prof. Bernitsas is or has been and active arbitrator in various ICC arbitrations. *Member:* Athens Bar Association; International Fiscal Association (IFA), Greek Section; Fédération Internationale de Droit Européen (F.I.D.E.), Greek Section; Greek Institute for International and Foreign Law (Athens); Hellenic Society for International Law and Relations; International Bar Association; Societé de Législation Comparée; International Law Association (I.L.A.); American-Hellenic Chamber of Commerce; British-Hellenic Chamber of Commerce. *LANGUAGES:* Greek, English, French, German and Italian. *PRACTICE AREAS:* EC Law; Banking; Investments; Mergers, Acquisitions and Privatisations; Arbitration; Aviation; Transport.

YANNIS G. CHRYSSOSPATHIS, born Athens, April 18, 1944; admitted, 1972, Athens, Athens Court of Appeals and Supreme Court. *Education:* University of Athens Law School (LL.B.); Faculty for Comparative Law Strasbourg (Diplôme, 1976). Representative of the Greek Association of Pharmaceutical Industries to the European Federation of Pharmaceutical Industries Associations. Representative for the Association of Greek Industries to the Standing Committee before the European Patent Office (SACEPO). *LANGUAGES:* Greek, English and French. *PRACTICE AREAS:* Legislation on Food and Beverages; Industrial Intellectual Property; Trademark and Patent Law.

CONSTANTINOS G. FLOROS, born Athens, September 13, 1945; admitted, 1974, Athens, Athens Court of Appeals and Supreme Court. *Education:* University of Thessaloniki Law School (LL.B.). *LANGUAGES:* English. *PRACTICE AREAS:* General Practice.

ANGELIKI D. VASAKA, born Athens, June 13, 1959; admitted, 1984, Athens; 1989, Athens Court of Appeals. *Education:* University of Athens Law School (LL.B.). *LANGUAGES:* Greek, English, French and Spanish. *PRACTICE AREAS:* Corporate Law; Commercial Contracts; Civil Law; Litigation; Trademark Law.

DOMNIKI D. MIRASYESI, born Athens, August 5, 1960; admitted, 1986, Athens. *Education:* University of Athens Law School (LL.B.); London School of Economics and Political Science (LL.M., in European Community Law, 1985). Collaborator at the Ministry of Foreign Affairs-European Communities, Legal Department, 1986-1987. Assistant at the Athens University. Collaborator at the Greek "Industrial Review.". *LANGUAGES:* Greek, French, German, English and Spanish. *PRACTICE AREAS:* EC Law; Human Rights; Competition and Anti-trust.

(This Listing Continued)

M. AND P. BERNITSAS, Athens—Continued

AUGUSTINE G. ALMIROUDI, born Athens, February 12, 1965; admitted, 1991, Athens. *Education:* University of Athens Law School (LL.B.); UniversitéLibre de Bruxelles (Licence Speciale, European Community Law). Trainee, Legal Service of the Commission of the European Community, Brussels, March-August 1991. *LANGUAGES:* Greek, English, French and Spanish. *PRACTICE AREAS:* EC Law; Competition and Anti-trust; Privatisations; Telecommunications; Tax and VAT.

TATIANA E. DERMATI, born Piraeus, November 20, 1967; admitted, 1992, Piraeus. *Education:* University of Athens Law School (LL.B.). *Member:* Piraeus Bar Association. *LANGUAGES:* Greek, English and French. *PRACTICE AREAS:* General Practice; Arbitration; Aviation; Banking; Mergers and Acquisitions.

ANGELIKA A. GOUSKOS, born Athens, October 9, 1965; admitted, 1991, Athens. *Education:* University of Athens Law School (LL.B.); University of Paris (LL.M., Banking and Financial Law); University of Lausanne-HEC (Advanced Certificate in the Management of International Banking and Financial Institutions); University of Athens (Ph.D., 1994). With Norton Rose and Watson Farley Williams, London, Shipping and Asset Finance Department, 1993. Author: "Letter of Guarantee on first demand," 1994; "Stand-by Letters of Credit," article in the Review, published by Hellenic Banks' Association, 1992. *Member:* Athens Bar Association; Greek Institute for International and Foreign Law; Piraeus Marine Club. *LANGUAGES:* Greek, English and French. *PRACTICE AREAS:* Banking and Finance; Shipping; Commercial Law.

REPRESENTATIVE CLIENTS: International Finance Corporation; European Investment Bank, C.S.; First Boston Limited; National Westminster Bank; Standard Chartered Bank; The Mitsubishi Bank Limited; Bankers Trust; Banque Nationale de Paris; Dresdner Bank A.G.; Credit Lyonnais/PK Airfinance; The Sumitomo Bank Limited; The Bank of New York Capital Markets Limited; The Agricultural Bank of Greece; The Association of Greek Pharmaceutical Industries; Johnson & Johnson - CILAG Division (Pharmaceutical section); Astra Pharmaceutical A.B.; Astra Hellas S.A.; Kabi Pharmaceutical International; Pharmacia S.A.; P.N. Gerolymatos S.A.; British Telecom; U.S. West International Inc.; BP Greece Ltd.; Rompetrol Company for Oil and Gas Cooperation; Chalkis Cement Company S.A.; Hydroaluminium Systems S.p.A.; Whirlpool Financial Corporation International; British American Tobacco; Browning Ferris International; Gillette Italy S.p.A.; Barilla G. e R. F.lli; Greek Bottling Company (3E); Société; Anonyme for Automobile Assistance Express Service S.A.; Association of Road Assistance Enterprises (EEOB); Goulandris Natural History Museum; Société Anonyme for the Protection of Intellectual Property (AEPI).

REFERENCES: Wilde Sapte, (London); Theodore Goddard, (London); C.S. First Boston, (London); Skadden, Arps Slate Meagher and Flom D.C. (U.S.A.); The Mitsubishi Bank Limited, London Branch, International Finance Department; Epstein, Becker & Green P.C.; Allen & Overy (London); Board of Directors of the Association of Greek Pharmaceutical Industries.

BLETAS & COSTAKIS

Barristers & Solicitors, Patent Attorneys, Business Consultants

Established in 1977

7 ASKLIPIOU STREET
ATHENS 10679, GREECE
Telephone: (1) 3616668, 3630830
Fax: (1) 3608724,
Telex: 222158 GSEP GR

European Economic Community, Foreign and Hotel Investments, Corporate, Real Estate, International Trade, Contracts, Trademarks, Industrial and Intellectual Property, Unfair Competition, Computer Law, Education, Taxation and Customs, Labour, Civil Litigations.

FIRM PROFILE: *Operates in Athens since 1977 and under its present form since 1990. Two partners. Offers a full range of services required by an enterprise in all fields of law.*

PARTNERS

APHRODITE A. BLETAS, born Athens, Greece, 1952; admitted, 1977, Athens; 1986, Supreme Court and Council of State. *Education:* University of Paris I (1974); University Center of Studies of the European Communities (1974); Institut of Political Sciences, Paris (1973-1975). Author: "Rules of Deontology," in the "Lawyer in the European Community," Sakkoulas, 1991. *Member:* European Lawyers' Union; Institut of Professional Representatives before the European Patents Office; Trustee of the Attica & Piraeus Federation of Industries. *Member:* Athens Bar Association. *LANGUAGES:* Greek, English, French, Italian and German. *PRACTICE AREAS:* International Trade Law; Business Law; Investment Law; Taxation Law; Labour Law.

(This Listing Continued)

EU822B

DIMITRI S. COSTAKIS, born Athens, Greece, April 15, 1958; admitted, 1983, Greece. *Education:* University of Athens (1981). Co-Author: "The Lawyer in the European Community," Sakkoulas, 1991. Member: European Lawyers' Union. *Member:* Athens Bar Association. *LANGUAGES:* Greek, English and French. *PRACTICE AREAS:* Corporate Law; Contract Law; Unfair Competition Law; Real Estate Law.

ASSOCIATES

MARY MIHELOYANNAKIS, admitted, 1982, Greece. LL.B. LL.M.

CHRIS MAHAIRAS, admitted, 1990, Greece. LL.B., DEA.

CHRISTY COZOMBOLIS, admitted, 1992, Greece. LL.B. M.C.L.

Languages: Greek, English, French, Italian, German, Spanish, Ethiopian

CALAVROS AND PARTNERS

Established in 1980

42, ASKLIPIOU STREET
114 71 ATHENS, GREECE
Telephone: 3645307; 3637407; 3613049
Telex: 224613 CAPA GR
Telefax: 0030/1/3639260

General and International Law Practice. Foreign Investments, International Transactions, Protection of Human Rights, Contracts, Industrial Property (Patents, Trademarks, Copyright, Performing and Publishing Rights), Unfair Competition, Banking and Finance, Air Transport, EEC Law, Real Estate, Civil Law (Property, Family, Inheritance, Personal Injury), Commercial, Corporate, Administrative, Tax, Criminal, Civil Litigation and Arbitration.

SENIOR PARTNER

PROF. CONSTANTIN CALAVROS, born Athens, Greece, April 8, 1951; admitted, 1975, Athens; 1984, Supreme Court of Greece. *Education:* University of Athens, Law School; University of Caen (France), Law School; University of Strassbourg (France) Law School; University of Würzburg, Law School (Ph.D., 1977). Author: "Res iudicata for third persons," 1978; "The meaning of the foreign arbitral award," 1982; "The object of civil litigation," 1983-1985; "Tape records in civil procedure, 1984; "Greek broadcasting law and community law," 1984; "The UNCITRAL Model Law for international commercial arbitration," 1988; "The jurisdiction of the arbitral tribunal," 1989; "The law of arbitration," 1990. Professor, Civil Procedure and International Commercial Arbitration, Law School, University of Thrace. President, Greek Institut for Arbitration. Director, "Arbitration," Greek magazine for arbitration. *Member:* International Association for Civil Procedure and International Arbitration; International Association for Comparative Law; International Federation for European Law; German Association for Jurists; Athens Bar Association; Greek Union for Civil Procedure; Greek Union for Arbitration; Hellenic Society for International Law and Relations.

PARTNERS

ATHANASIOS G. KARALEKAS, born Tripolis, Greece, September 27, 1953; admitted, 1979, Athens; 1989, Supreme Court of Greece. *Education:* University of Thessaloniki, Law School. Author: "Code of Civil Procedure." *Member:* Athens Bar Association; Greek Union of Civil Procedure; Greek Union for the Law of Social Security.

STYLIANOS G. STAMATOPOULOS, born Gargaliani, Greece, November 8, 1958; admitted, 1983, Athens; 1988, Athens Court of Appeals. *Education:* University of Athens, Law School. Author: "The procedural retrospection," 1989. *Member:* Greek Union of Civil Procedure.

THEMISTOKLIS TH. KLOUKINAS, born Tripolis, Greece, December 22, 1961; admitted, 1985, Athens; 1990, Athens Court of Appeals. *Education:* University of Thrace, Law School. Author: "Civil Procedure," vol. 1 (1987), vol. 2 (1989); "Arbitration - Case Law," 1986. *Member:* Athens Bar Association; Greek Union of Civil Procedure.

ARTEMIS G. TSILIKA, born Agrinion, Greece, February 14, 1964; admitted, 1988, Athens Court of First Instance. *Education:* University of Thrace, Law School. *Member:* Athens Bar Association.

STEFANOS TR. KALOGIROU, born Athens, Greece, September 20, 1963; admitted, 1989, Athens; 1994, Athens Court of Appeals. *Education:* University of Thrace, Law School. *Member:* Athens Bar Association.

NIKOLAOS E. MOSCHOS, born Athens, Greece, January 27, 1967; admitted, 1992, Athens Court of First Instance. *Education:* University of Thessaloniki, Law School. *Member:* Athens Bar Association.

(This Listing Continued)

GEORGIA A. PAPANTONOPOULOU, born Athens, Greece, May 9, 1967; admitted, 1992, Athens Court of First Instance. *Education:* University of Athens, Law School; University of Kent, Law School, England (LL.M.). *Member:* Athens Bar Association.

AGELOS MORFOPOULOS, born Athens, Greece, January 25, 1969; admitted, 1994, Athens Court of First Instance. *Education:* University of Thrace, Law School. *Member:* Athens Bar Association.

SPECIAL TAX COUNSEL

KONSTANTIN FINOKALIOTIS, Professor, Tax Law, University of Salonika, Law School.

Languages: English, French and German

CONSTANDINIDOU-PAPAIOANNOU LAW OFFICES

Established in 1977

62A SKOUFA ST.

ATHENS 106-80, GREECE

Telephone: 3636567; 3636088

Fax: 3636088

Paris, France Office: Maryan Green, Chillaz, Papaioannou. 205 Boulevard Saint Germain, 75007. Telephone: 1.44.39.29.19. Fax: 1.44.39.29.18.

Private International Law, Civil Law, Family and Inheritance Law, Commercial and Corporate Law, International Business Law, Public Works, Maritime Law, Employment Law, Real Estate Law, General Practice, E.E.C. Law, Trademarks and Personal Injury.

MEMBERS OF FIRM

HAROULA CONSTANDINIDOU, born Athens, Greece, September 6, 1947; admitted, 1973, Supreme Court of Greece; 1981, Greece. *Education:* University of Athens Law School (1971). Lecturer in Family Law: Athens American College, 1989; Foreign Women's Association, Athens, 1989. *Member:* Athens Bar Association; International Bar Association; International Academy of Matrimonial Lawyers. *LANGUAGES:* Greek, English, French and German. *PRACTICE AREAS:* Private International Law; Family Law; Corporate Law; International Corporate Law; Inheritance Law; Civil Law; Commercial Law; Trademark Law; Personal Injury Law; Real Estate Law.

VASSILIKI PAPAIOANNOU, born 1955; admitted, 1981, Greece; 1989, France. *Education:* Athens University (1977); Paris University (Masters Degree, Sociology, 1981; DEA, Employment Law, 1983). (Also Member, Maryan Green, Chillaz, Papaioannou, Paris, France). *LANGUAGES:* Greek, French and English. *PRACTICE AREAS:* Commercial Law; Employment Law; International Commercial Law; Public Works; E.E.C. Law; Maritime Law; Trademark Law; Personal Injury Law.

GEORGIA CONSTANDINIDOU, born Athens, Greece, October 10, 1969; admitted, 1994, Athens and Piraeus Courts of First Instance. *Education:* University of Athens Law School. *LANGUAGES:* Greek, English, French and German.

NICOLAOS E. VOGAS, born Athens, Greece, October 27, 1966; admitted, 1993, Athens and Piraeus Courts of First Instance. *Education:* University of Athens Law School (B.E.I., Computer Science Degree). *Member:* Athens Bar Association. *LANGUAGES:* Greek, English, French and Italian.

COUNSEL

NEVILLE A. MARYAN GREEN, born England, 1936; admitted, 1962, England; 1978, France (Not admitted in Greece). *Education:* Cambridge University, England (Master of Arts, 1960; Bachelor of Law, 1962); Hague Academy (Diploma, 1963); University of Paris (Law Degree, 1976). Author: "International Law," Batmans 3rd Edition, 1987. Lecturer: Law, University of Sheffield, 1963-1964; EEC Law, International Faculty of Comparative Law, Strasbourg, 1968-1970. Official in Legal Department of Council of Europe, Strasbourg, 1966-1973. *Member:* International Law Association; International Bar Association; Institut Français de Droit International. (Also Counsel, Constandinidou-Papaioannou Law Offices, Athens, Greece). *LANGUAGES:* English and French. *PRACTICE AREAS:* International Contract Law; International Business Law; European Law; Public and Private International Law; Family Law.

G. AND A. DIMOPOULOS AND ASSOCIATES

Established in 1928

3 KORAI STREET

ATHENS 105 64, GREECE

Telephone: (301) 3225985; 3222692

Fax: (301) 3228564

General Legal Practice. Civil and Commercial Law including Patent, Trademark, Unfair Competition Law. Corporate, Tax and Administrative Law. Real Estate, Foreign Investment, EEC and International Law.

ARISTIDES G. DIMOPOULOS, born 1933; admitted, 1959, Athens Supreme Courts. *Education:* University of Athens School of Law (1957; LL.D., 1964); Centre Europeen Universitaire de Nancy (D.E.S., 1961); Hague International Law Academy (1953). *LANGUAGES:* Greek, English, French and German.

ASSIMINA ANGELOPOULOU, born 1959; admitted, 1984, Athens Court of Appeals. *Education:* Democritos University of Northern Greece School of Law (1982). *LANGUAGES:* Greek and English.

ARTEMIS TOGOUSSIDOU, born 1963; admitted, 1987, Athens Court of Appeals. *Education:* University of Athens School of Law (1985). Scientific Assistant, International Law, University of Athens School of Law, 1986-1990. *LANGUAGES:* Greek, English, French and German.

PHAEDON DIMOPOULOS, born 1966; admitted, 1992, Athens Court of First Instance. *Education:* University of Athens, School of Law (1989); René Descartes-Paris V University/Paris (DESS of Jurist of International Business Law, 1991). *LANGUAGES:* Greek, English, French and German.

MARIA PANOUTSOPOULOU, born 1967; admitted, 1992, Athens Court of First Instance. *Education:* University of Athens School of Law (1990; Diploma, Postgraduate Studies in Civil Law, 1993). *LANGUAGES:* Greek, English, French and German.

ATHINA DIMOPOULOU, born 1968; admitted, 1993, Athens Court of First Instance. *Education:* University of Athens School of Law (1991); Pantheon-Assas University of Paris II (D.E.A. of History of Law, 1992). *LANGUAGES:* Greek, English, French, Italian and German.

Languages: Greek, English, French, German and Italian.

DOBSON & PINCI

6 YPERIDOU STREET

105 58 ATHENS, GREECE

Telephone: (30) (1) 324-3272

Telefax: (30) (1) 322-9329 E-Mail: 7252684@mcimail.com.

Milan, Italy Office: Via Santa Radegonda, 16, 20121. Telephone: (39) (2) 809816; 8056780. Telefax: (39) (2) 86464548; 86464601. E-Mail: 7232679@mcimail.com.

Rome, Italy Office: Via Panama 74, Int. 9, 00198. Telephone: (39) (6) 841-1611. Telefax: (39) (6) 841-1145. E-Mail: 7212680@mcimail.com.

Genoa, Italy Office: Via Garibaldi 7, 2nd Floor, 16124. Telephone: (39) (10) 206-851. Telefax: (39) (10) 202-738. E-Mail: 7222681@mcimail.com.

New York, New York Office: Manhattan Tower, 12th Floor, 600 Lexington Avenue, 10022-6018. Telephone: (212) 308-4440. Telefax: (212) 888-3839. E-Mail: 7262685@mcimail.com.

London, England Office: 1 Throgmorton Avenue, EC2N 2JJ. Telephone: (44) (171) 628-8163. Telefax: (44) (171) 920-0861. E-Mail: 7232682@mcimail.com.

Brussels, Belgium Office: Avenue Louise, 216, 1050. Telephone: (32) (2) 647-0700. Telefax: (32) (2) 647-6440. E-Mail: 7242683@mcimail.com.

Atlanta, Georgia Office: 1776 Resurgens Plaza, 945 East Paces Ferry Road, N.E., 30326. Telephone: (404) 262-5680. Telefax: (404) 262-5699. E-Mail: 7272686@mcimail.com.

San Diego, California Office: 1629 Columbia Street, 92101. Telephone: (619) 236-1310. Telefax: (619) 239-1208. E-Mail: 7282687@mcimail.com.

Miami, Florida Office: 701 Brickell Avenue, Suite 2000, 33131. Telephone: (305) 579-0012. Telefax: (305) 375-8075; 579-4722. E-Mail: 7292688@mcimail.com.

(This Listing Continued)

DOBSON & PINCI, Athens—Continued

Corporate, Banking and Securities Law with emphasis on Mergers and Acquisitions, Insurance, International Financial Transactions, Litigation, Arbitration, Employment Law, Debt Collection, Bankruptcy, Foreign Investments, Privatizations, Subsidiaries and Joint Ventures, Taxation, EU/-Common Market Law, Antitrust, Environmental Law, Transportation, Shipping, Licensing, Fashion and Textiles, Franchising, Commercial Real Estate (Investment, Structuring, Development, Retail), Project Finance, Computer, Software and Telecommunications Law, Agency and Distribution, Energy (Production, Operations, and Transmission), Food and Drug, Commodities, Visa/Immigration, Wills and Estates, Sports Law, Broadcasting, Motion Picture, TV, Video, Intellectual Property and General Entertainment Law.

FIRM PROFILE: Dobson & Pinci is an international law firm based in Europe and the United States that is staffed with both American and European attorneys. Of the small number of such firms, Dobson & Pinci holds a unique position because the firm's European offices are situated in Milan, Rome, Genoa, London, Brussels and Athens, thereby enabling the firm to serve clients conveniently and efficiently in both Northern and Southern Europe. The U.S. offices in New York, Atlanta, Miami and San Diego are placed in major U.S. cities to provide full support to the overall practice network. Each office is staffed by attorneys qualified to appear and litigate in the local courts.

MEMBERS OF FIRM

GIOVANNI LOMBARDO, born Rome, March 7, 1962; admitted, 1990, Italy. *Education:* La Sapienza University, Rome (J.D., 1985). Author: "A Practical Guide to Italian Rates - The New ICI," Belle Cose, Summer 1993; "Pension Reform in Italy," Belle Cose, June, 1993; "A New Cut in the VAT Rates on Maintenance Work in Italy," Belle Cose, Autumn 1994; "First Time Buyers in Italy," Belle Cose, Spring 1994; "Taxation of Foreign Companies in Italy," Belle Cose, Summer 1994. Conferences: State Bar of Georgia, "Doing Business in Southern Europe," Atlanta, May 1994; "Italy and Europe: The Economic Situation In the Current Political and Regulatory Climate," London, September 1994; "Italian Water Privatisation and the Galli Law," Birmingham, U.K., November 1994. *Member:* International Bar Association; Association of Personal Injury Lawyers. (Also at London Office).

COUNSEL

CHRISTINA STAMPOULTZI, born Athens, Greece, November 4, 1966; admitted, 1992, Greece. *Education:* Aristotelion University of Thessaloniki (J.D., 1989). Author: "The Treatment of Television in European Competition Law," 1989. Attorney, European Commission, DG XV/B/4 (Public Procurement). (Also with, Bahas, Gramatidis & Associates, Athens).

THEANO RADICOPOULOS, born Athens, Greece, October 11, 1969. *Education:* University of Kent (B.A., with honors, 1991); College of Law (J.D., 1992).

GEORGE KOMIS, born Athens, Greece; admitted, 1993, Athens. *Education:* University of Athens (J.D.). (Also with, Bahas, Gramatidis & Associates, Athens).

Languages: English, Italian, French, Greek, German, Spanish, Japanese and Russian

(For Complete Biographical Data on all Personnel and List of Representative Clients, see Professional Biographies at Milan, Italy)

DONTAS LAW OFFICES

Established in 1922

14, VOULIS STR.

ATHENS 105 63, GREECE

Telephone: 301-32 35 525; 32 36 526

Fax: 301-32 41 761

Antitrust Law and Trade Regulation, Banking and Finance, Commercial and Company Law, Employment Law, European Community Law, Intellectual Property Law, Investment Law, Litigation and Arbitration, Mergers and Acquisitions, Public Procurement, Real Estate, Shipping and Transport, Taxation.

FIRM PROFILE: Dontas Law Offices was established in 1922 by the late Nicholas A. Dontas and has a long standing experience in the practice of business and corporate law. Acting for a number of foreign corporations (mostly American and European multinationals) the firm has during the

(This Listing Continued)

last fifteen years developed a strong international practice. Accordingly, all the Firms resources are particularly well suited to meet the increasingly complex requirements of foreign investors and traders in Greece.

In addition to advisory work on business transactions and trading arrangements covering almost every area of commerce, industry and finance, Dontas Law Offices is particularly equipped to provide comprehensive legal services across the whole spectrum of Intellectual Property Law. The firm's Intellectual Property department assists clients in acquiring, protecting and exploiting their Patents, Trademarks/Servicemarks, Designs, Copyrights, Computer Software, Trade Secrets and Know-how.

At present the firm consists of eleven lawyers, four assistants and two practising lawyers, and can effectively advise clients in English, French, German, Italian and Greek. Members of the firm participate in the activities of professional associations both at the national and international level, and are authors of numerous legal articles spanning the entire area of business law.

MEMBERS OF FIRM

KYRIAKOS N. DONTAS, born Athens, Greece, 1934; admitted, 1958, Athens, Athens Court of Appeal and Supreme Court of Greece. *Education:* University of Athens Law School (1956); University of Athens School of Political and Economic Science (1959).

NICHOLAS K. DONTAS, born Athens, Greece, 1963; admitted, 1988, Athens. *Education:* University of Athens Law School (1986); University of London, London School of Economics and Political Science (LL.M., 1987).

THEODOROS FRANGOS, born Athens, Greece, 1927; admitted, 1950, Athens, Athens Court of Appeal and Supreme Court of Greece. *Education:* University of Thessaloniki Law School (1948).

SOTIRIS ANTONIOU, born Paphos, Cyprus, 1952; admitted, 1980, Athens, Athens Court of Appeal and Supreme Court of Greece. *Education:* University of Athens Law School (1979).

GEORGIOS AVGERINOS, born Athens, Greece, 1956; admitted, 1982, Athens, Athens Court of Appeal and Supreme Court of Greece. *Education:* University of Athens Law School (1980).

APHRODITE GOUGA, born Thessaloniki, Greece, 1962; admitted, 1988, Athens. *Education:* University of Athens Law School (1986); University of Munich, Max Planck Institute for Foreign and International Patent, Copyright and Competition Law (Ph.D., 1993).

NICHOLAS VOKAS, born Vitina, Greece, 1963; admitted, 1989, Athens. *Education:* University of Athens Law School (1986).

NICHOLAS KARAMANLIS, born Thessaloniki, Greece, 1964; admitted, 1988, Thessaloniki. *Education:* University of Thessaloniki Law School (1986); University of London, London School of Economics and Political Science (LL.M., 1990); Université Libre de Bruxelles (Licence Speciale, 1991).

KYRIAKI TSIKI, born Athens, Greece, 1964; admitted, 1988, Athens. *Education:* University of Thrace Law School (1986).

HELEN ECONOMIDES, born Athens, Greece, 1967; admitted, 1992, Athens. *Education:* University of Athens Law School (1989); College of Europe (Masters of advanced European Studies, 1992).

EVANGELIA CONTOUMAS, born Stuttgart, Germany, 1969; admitted, 1993, Athens. *Education:* University of Paris I Sorbonne Law School (1992); University of Paris II Assas, Institute of Comparative Law (Diplôme de Droit Comparé).

DRYLLERAKIS & ASSOCIATES

Established in 1970

25 VOUCOURESTIOU STR.

106 71 ATHENS, GREECE

Telephone: 01-3604735-3628159-3630108

Telefax: (01) 3644218

Business Law, Corporate, Offshore Companies, Competition Law, Trademarks, Administrative Law, Civil, Real Estate and Labor Law, Tax and Administrative Law, Mergers and Acquisitions, Banking Law, Law of the Air, Stock Exchange Legislation, Civil, Tax and Administrative Litigation.

FIRM PROFILE: Operates in Athens since 1970 and under this present form since 1978, 4 partners. Offers full range of legal and administrative services required by an enterprise. Long experience of senior partner and of special advisor from position as General Counsel and General Tax Counsel

(This Listing Continued)

of major multinationals and from participations in management teams and Board of Greek or international companies.

SENIOR MEMBERS OF FIRM

J.C. DRYLLERAKIS, born 1937; admitted, 1962, Athens. *Education:* Athens University Law School and Economics. Author: "Protection of Foreign Investment," L.D. 2687/53 (1975); "Protection of Foreign Capital Under New Constitution," 1976; "Investment Incentives," 1979; "Liberalization of Capital Movements," 1988; Contribution to "Introduction to the Greek Law by Kluwer," (1989, "Tax and Investment Incentives"); Contribution to "Limited Liability Companies," Balance Sheets and Other Financial Statements, 1994. Qualified to represent Clients before Supreme Courts. Member: Capital Market Commission; Competition Commission. *Member:* Athens Bar; IBA; IFA; Hellenic Association of Tax Law and Fiscal Studies (Director); Hellenic Association for European Law (Director). *LANGUAGES:* English. *PRACTICE AREAS:* Business Law; Civil Law; Competition Law; Mergers and Acquisitions Investment Incentives; Protection of Direct Investments; Tax Law.

J.G. DAMILAKIS, born 1950; admitted, 1975, Athens. *Education:* Athens University Law School. *Member:* Athens Bar. *LANGUAGES:* English. *PRACTICE AREAS:* Labor Law; Law of the Air; Stock Exchange; Litigation; Corporate; Commercial Law.

V.A. ANARGYROU, born 1949; admitted, 1973, Athens. *Education:* Athens University Law School. *Member:* Athens Bar. *LANGUAGES:* English. *PRACTICE AREAS:* Trademarks; Competition Law; Tax Law; Litigation.

A.J. DRYLLERAKIS, born 1939; admitted, 1975, Athens. *Education:* Athens University Law School and Economics. *Member:* Athens Bar. *LANGUAGES:* English. *PRACTICE AREAS:* Corporate Law; Offshore Companies; Foreign Investment Law.

VAYA C. TATSIDOU, born 1966; admitted, 1990, Athens. *Education:* Thrace University Law School. *Member:* Athens Bar. *LANGUAGES:* English and German. *PRACTICE AREAS:* Litigation; Corporate; Commercial Law.

J.A. APSOURIS, born 1967. *Education:* Athens University Law School (Diploma); University Aix-Marseille III (D.E.A.). *Member:* Stagiaire in Athens Bar. *LANGUAGES:* French, English, Spanish and Italian.

SPECIAL ADVISOR

E.B. THEOFANOPOULOS, born 1940; admitted, 1964, Athens. *Education:* Athens University Law School. Qualified to represent clients before Supreme Courts. *Member:* Athens Bar. *LANGUAGES:* English and French. *PRACTICE AREAS:* Tax Law; Business law; Banking Law; Mergers and Acquisitions; Arbitration.

REPRESENTATIVE CLIENTS: American National Can; Avis; Barilla; Beiersdorf A.G.; BSN Group; CITIBANK N.V.; Corman S.A.; Exxon Corporation; ITAS Reisebureau; Lauda Air; Lectra S.A.; Leo Burnett; Metsa Serla; Nobel; Obourg S.A.; Pechiney (Aluminium de Grece); Salomon Brothers; TVX Inc.; Weyerhauser.

PANAYOTIS J. ECONOMOU

Established in 1971

26, ASKLIPIOU STREET
ATHENS 106 79, GREECE
Telephone: 3603824; 6136797
Cable Address: "Lexecon" Athens
Telefax: 3639973

General Law Practice. Trade Collections, Banking, Royalties and Trademarks, Corporate, Industrial Property, Shipping. Tax, Greek Taxation, Foreign Investment, Real Estate, Europe Credit Card collections, Middle East and Africa. Specialist in Joint venture and management contracts in USSR. Resident Partner in Moscow, USSR.

FIRM PROFILE: *Established in 1971 in Athens the firm has grown ever since, to become one of Greece's leading commercial law firms. The firm has a trade collection practice in Europe, Middle East and Africa (Credit Card Collections).*

After the entry of Greece into the European Community in 1981 this one lawyer firm has developed a full range of high quality. Legal services which include consultation through resident partners in Fribourg Switzerland. The partners among whom European law professors are included, are experts in Swiss law and E.E.C. law.

(This Listing Continued)

PANAYOTIS J. ECONOMOU, born Istanbul, Turkey, January 3, 1941; admitted, 1965, Athens. *Education:* Athens University Law School (Bachelor Degree); Diplome D-Etude Superieures. *LANGUAGES:* Greek, English, French, German and Turkish. *PRACTICE AREAS:* Admiralty and Maritime Law; Banks and Banking; Computer and Software; Debtor and Creditor; Trade Marks.

REFERENCES AND REPRESENTATIVE CLIENTS: American Express; Diners Club International; The Bank of Nova Scotia; Canadian Imperial Bank of Commerce; The Bank of Montreal; Diners Club; IBM; Chevron; Coca Cola.

ONOUFRIOS FARMAKIDES
HELLENIC LAW
LAW OFFICES

Established in 1974

115 VASILISSIS SOFIAS AVENUE
11521 ATHENS, GREECE
Telephone: 0030-1-6424549; 6438584; 226676 Fron Gr.
Cable Address: FARMANWALT
Fax: 0030-1-6424549

International Law, Corporate Law, Commercial Law, Tax Law, Real Estate Law, Antitrust Law, Banking Law and Securities, Copyright Law, Trademark Law, Patent Law, Immigration Law, Administrative Law, Finance Law, Contracts Law, Consumer Law, Litigation and International Arbitration, Business Law.

FIRM PROFILE: *Firm engaged in Greek and International Law, with orientation to European and East European clients in Greece. Strong reputation in Procedural Litigation before the Courts (Prozessanwälte).*

PROF. DR. ONOUFRIOS FARMAKIDES, born Symi Island, Greece, 1949; admitted, 1974, Athens; 1976, Athens Court and Athens Court of Appeal; 1982, Supreme Court of Greece (Areios Pagos). *Education:* University of Athens, Law School; Universität Justus-Liebig, Germany Juris Doctor (PH.D.). Author: "Travel-Contracts and Consumer Protection" (German: Reisevertag und Verbraucherschutz), Frankfurt am Main 1978; "The Law of Economy and the Social Theory" (a critical analysis to Jurisprundenz), Athens 1985 (p. 211) Papazisis; "The Contract of Agency" (Real Estate and Commercial Agency) Athens 1989 (p. 261); "The Contract of Exclusive Distributor", Athens 1990 (p. 61); "Law of the Greek Export and Import Trade," Athens 1993 (p. 380); "The Codification of the American Commercial Law," Athens 1993 (p. 100). Associate Professor for Commercial and Economic Law, Panteios University of Athens, Law Department, Sygrou Ave. 166. Wissenschaftlicher Assistant, 1974-1976 (Germany). Member and Legal Counsel, National Drug Administration, 1982-1989. Counsel, Minster of Commerce, 1987-1989. Vice-Chairman, Greek Securities and Exchange Commission, 1994—. *Member:* Athens Bar Association; European Patent Attorney; Intellectual Property Association; Association of the Maritime Law; Trademark and Patent rights Association; Gesellschaft Für die Rechtsvergleichung (Germany). *LANGUAGES:* Greek, German and English. *PRACTICE AREAS:* International Commercial Transactions; Bankruptcy Law; Patents and Trademark Law; Copyright Law; Corporation Law; Partnership Law; Consumer Protection; Agency Distribution; Franchise Law; Securities Law.

DR. JUR. VASSILIOS GIKAS, born Aedipsos, Greece, 1964; admitted, 1990, Athens, Greece. *Education:* University of Hamburg (Ph.D.); University of Thessaloniki Law School (1987). Author: "Chancengleichheit der Politischen Parteien in Griechenland," Hamburg, 1993; "The Local Tax," Dodecanese, Athens, 1993. *Member:* Athens Bar Association; German Greek Board of Jurists. *LANGUAGES:* Greek, English and German. *PRACTICE AREAS:* Comparative International Law; Administrative Law; Constitutional Law; Public Supplies; Environmental Law.

ANNA KANTZIA, born Athens, Greece, 1963; admitted, 1990, Athens, Greece. *Education:* University of Athens Law School. *Member:* Athens Bar Association. *LANGUAGES:* Greek, English and German. *PRACTICE AREAS:* Civil Law; Commercial Litigation Law; Trademark Law.

NASOS BOTSOS, born Johannina, Greece, 1965; admitted, 1992, Athens, Greece. *Education:* University of Athens Law School. *Member:* Athens Bar Association. *LANGUAGES:* Greek, English and German. *PRACTICE AREAS:* Insurance; Torts; Civil Product Liability.

VICTORIA TZAMTZI, born Volos, Greece, 1963. *Education:* Queen Mary College, University of London (LL.M., 1993); Panteios University of Athens (Business Administration, 1990). *LANGUAGES:* Greek, English

(This Listing Continued)

ONOUFRIOS FARMAKIDES HELLENIC LAW LAW OFFICES, *Athens—Continued*

and Italian. *PRACTICE AREAS:* Contract Law; European Community Law; Tariffs and Taxation Law; Finance Law; Maritime Law.

ASSOCIATES

PAPANAGIOTOU MANOLIS, born Rodes, Greece, 1965; admitted, 1991, Volos Court of First Instance. *Education:* Law School Athens; Kent, England (LL.M.). *LANGUAGES:* Greek, English and French. *PRACTICE AREAS:* General Practice; Commercial Law; Transportation Law.

LEGAL SUPPORT PERSONNEL

ALKIVIADIS TRAPEZIOTIS, Ex Police Officer. Economic and General Investigation. *LANGUAGES:* Greek. *PRACTICE AREAS:* Administrative Law; Immigration Law.

REPRESENTATIVE CLIENTS: Hoffman La Roche; Philip Morris; B.H.F. Bank; Baltimore Air coil Co.; BFG AG; Marquint S.A.; Metalimpex; Medicor Hungarian; Techoimpex AG; Metallgesellschaft AG; Edwin International S.A., Frankfurt, Germany.

HADJIPRODROMOU-TRIANTAPHILLOU & PARTNERS

18 PARTRIARCHOU IOAKEIM
106 75 ATHENS, GREECE
Telephone: (301) 7242 306; 7242 307; 7228 957; 7238 563
Fax: (301) 7240 228

Business, Corporate Law, Investments, Banking Law, Funds and Trusts, Securities, Mergers and Acquisitions, Antitrust, Competition and Trade Law, Taxes, Intellectual Property, Patents/Trademarks, Advertising, Media, Tourism, International/Civil Litigation, Arbitration, Real Estate, International Construction Projects, E.C. Law.

FIRM PROFILE: The firm has a broadly-based practice with a wide range of quality legal services. The client base is European, North American and Asian in scope. The firm has been organized as a legal Partnership and has five Partners.

JOHN HADJIPRODROMOU, born Kos, Dodecanese, Greece, March 14, 1950; admitted, 1975, Athens, Athens Court of Appeals and Athens Supreme Court. *Education:* University of Athens Law School (LL.B.); London University (LL.M., 1978). Author: several articles on legal and tax issues. Contributor, Goldman Sachs Foreign Exchange Handbook. Board Member of numerous foreign and Greek companies. *Member:* Athens Bar Association; International Union of Lawyers (Paris). *LANGUAGES:* Greek, English and French.

EVANGELOS TRIANTAPHILLOU, born Corinth, Greece, April 18, 1954; admitted, 1977, Athens, Athens Court of Appeals and Athens Supreme Court. *Education:* University of Athens Law School (LL.B.); State's Council (One year training); Greek Association of Business Administration (Certificate of first and second courses in Business Administration). Contributor, Allen and Overy's Take/Over Bids edition, London. Author: "The Revocation of The Acts of Administration," State Council, Athens, 1978. Comparative Report on Force Majeure, Helsinki, 1982. Board Member of several foreign and Greek companies. *Member:* Greek Association of United Nations; Athens Bar Association; International Association of Lawyers (Paris). *LANGUAGES:* Greek, English and French.

ANGELIKI KARADIMA, born Athens, Greece, May 22, 1957; admitted, 1983, Athens, Athens Court of Appeals. *Education:* University of Thessaloniki, School of Law and Economics (LL.B.). *Member:* Athens Bar Association. *LANGUAGES:* Greek, English and French.

MARINA HADJIDAKI, born Rethymnon, Crete, Greece, September 13, 1962; admitted, 1987, Athens, Athens Court of Appeals. *Education:* University of Thessaloniki, School of Law and Economics (LL.B.). *Member:* Athens Bar Association; International Association of Young Lawyers. *LANGUAGES:* Greek and English.

JOHN BOBOS, born Agrinio, Greece, March 19, 1962; admitted, 1987, Athens and Athens Court of Appeals. *Education:* University of Athens Law School (LL.B.). Author: "Agency and Distribution Agreements in Greece," International Agency and Distribution Agreements, Butterworths, 1991. Various legal publications and papers. *Member:* Athens Bar Association; International Union of Lawyers (Paris). *LANGUAGES:* Greek, English and French.

(This Listing Continued)

EU826B

ANASTASIA DRITSA, born Athens, Greece, April 20, 1965; admitted, 1991, Athens and Athens Court of First Instance. *Education:* University of Thrace Law School (LL.B.); University of Exeter (LL.M., 1991). *Member:* Athens Bar Association; EC Lawyers Society, London; International Association of Young Lawyers. *LANGUAGES:* Greek, English, French and German.

HELENA CHRYSSANTHACOPOULOS, born Athens, Greece, November 20, 1967; admitted, 1992, Athens, Athens Court of First Instance. *Education:* Athens University Law School (LL.B. and LL.M., 1994). *Member:* Athens Bar Association; International Association of Young Lawyers. *LANGUAGES:* Greek, English and French.

IRENE CHRYSSOU, born Athens, Greece, December 22, 1966; admitted, 1992, Athens, Athens Court of First Instance. *Education:* Athens University Law School. *Member:* Athens Bar Association; International Association of Young Lawyers. *LANGUAGES:* Greek, English and French.

ALEXANDER KOSMOPOULOS, born Athens, Greece, July 15, 1969; admitted, 1993, Athens, Athens Court of First Instance. *Education:* Athens University Law School (LL.B.); University of London (Graduate Studies). *Member:* Athens Bar Association. *LANGUAGES:* Greek, English, French and German.

NICHOLAS CHRISTAKIS, born Athens, Greece, March 30, 1969; admitted, 1994, Athens, Athens Court of First Instance. *Education:* Athens University Law School (LL.B.; Post Graduate Studies, Public Law). *Member:* Athens Bar Association. *LANGUAGES:* Greek, English and French.

JOHN KYRNASSIOS, born Athens, Greece, November 5, 1969; admitted, 1994, Athens and Athens Court of First Instance. *Education:* University of Athens Law School (LL.B.); University of Kent (LL.M., 1994). *Member:* Athens Bar Association. *LANGUAGES:* Greek, English and French.

OF COUNSEL

GEORGE A. LEVENTIS, born Piraeus, Greece, December 17, 1945; admitted, 1970, Athens, Athens and Piraeus Court of Appeals and Athens Supreme Court. *Education:* Athens University Law School (LL.B., 1968); Munich University, Germany (J.D., 1973). Editor-in-Chief, "Labour Legislation," Review. Author, several monographs and articles on individual and collective labour law, Two-volume book on individual and collective labour law. Professor, Labor Law, Athens University Law School. *Member:* Athens Bar Association. *LANGUAGES:* Greek, German, English and French.

REPRESENTATIVE CLIENTS: Adam Opel AG; Akzo Nobel N.V.; Alko Ltd.; Bank of America NT and SA; Bank of New York; Best Foods S.A.; DHL Corporation; Europe Tax-Free Shopping AB; General Motors Corporation; Alamo Rent-a-Car, Inc.; Gerber Foods Holdings Ltd.; Initiative Media S.A.; Itochu Corporation; Kentucky Fried Chicken Corporation; Lambert Smith Hampton Hellas S.A.; Lintas Worldwide; McCann-Erickson Worldwide; Mamidakis Hotels of Greece; Marubeni Corporation; Mattel Inc.; New Japan Air Service Co.; Nintendo of America, Inc.; Pepsico Inc.; Pizza Hut Worldwide; Publicis FCB Communications; Reuters Ltd.; Seven Up Nederland BV; Snack Venture Europe SCA; Societe Bouygues; State Street Banque S.A.; Tasty Foods S.A.; The C & A Group of Companies; The Interpublic Group of Companies; Van Leer; Weight Watchers International, Inc.

HAHALIS, McKARSKI & KOUNOUPIS

GREEK LAW GROUP

VOUKOURESTIOU 29
ATHENS 10673, GREECE
Telephone: 301-360-5033; 301-360-2790
Fax: 301-364-4424

Bethlehem, Pennsylvania Office: Hahalis McKarski & Kounoupis, Suite 1000, 2045 City Line Road, 18017. Telephone: 215-865-2608. Fax: 215-691-8418.

Commercial and Corporate, Foreign Investments and Business Law. Firm engaged in American, Greek and General International Practice.

FIRM PROFILE: The Greek Law Group was formed by experienced, U.S. admitted corporate counsel in an effort to address real concerns of U.S. corporate counsel in dealing with and/or referring cases to foreign counsel in Greece. George S. Kounoupis, in addition to being a licensed attorney admitted both in the U.S. and Greece, practiced at a major Philadelphia corporate law firm and is a practicing U.S. corporate lawyer. The firm offers distinct advantages in communication and efficiency (over Greek firms with referring arrangements), whose attorneys are not admitted in the U.S. and who have a nominal knowledge of U.S. corporate practice. In addition, the firm's dual presence in Greece and the U.S. provides a solu-

(This Listing Continued)

tion to problems of accountability, professional responsibility, and confidentiality, which often arise in dealing with non-U.S. admitted attorneys who do not have an established presence in the U.S. In addition to George S. Kounoupis (admitted PA, NJ, and Athens, Greece Bars), the firm has attorneys admitted both in Greece and the U.S. together with legal support staff, notary publics and paralegal personnel.

MEMBERS OF FIRM

GEORGE S. KOUNOUPIS, born Sparta, Greece, June 12, 1962; admitted, 1987, Pennsylvania and New Jersey; 1989, Athens, Greece; U.S. District Court, Eastern District of Pennsylvania; U.S. District Court, District of New Jersey; U.S. Court of Appeals, Third Circuit; Athens Court of First Instance. *Education:* Lehigh University (B.A., with honors, 1984); Temple University School of Law (J.D., 1987); Athens University School of Law (Law Degree, 1989). Listed in: Hellenic Who's Who in Business and the Professions; Who's Who in Practicing Attorneys. Contributing Author: "A Survey of the Developing Pennsylvania Law of Attorney Malpractice," No. 4, 61 Temple Law Review, 1988. Lecturer: "Trade and Investment Opportunities in Greece," Lehigh University International Trade Development Program, 1990. Associate, Corporate Department, Fox, Rothschild, O'Brien and Frankel, Philadelphia, Pennsylvania, 1987-1990. Co-Chairman: "Doing Business in Greece - EEC 1992," I.B.F., 1990. Co-Author: "U.S.-Greece Trade and Investment Guide". Legal Consultant, Hellenic Restructuring Investment Development Group. President, Hellenic American Chamber of Commerce of Greater Philadelphia. *Member:* American Society of International Law; American-Hellenic Chamber of Commerce of Athens, Greece; AHEPA- Philadelphia Branch, Board of Governors; Union Internationale Des Avocats. *LANGUAGES:* English and Greek. *PRACTICE AREAS:* International Law; International Practice; International Business; International Sales; Greek Law.

JOHN TRIPIDAKIS, born Athens, Greece, April 1, 1958; admitted, 1983, Athens Court of Appeals. *Education:* University of Athens Law School (LL.B.); London University (LL.M.). *Member:* Athens Bar. *LANGUAGES:* English, Greek and French.

ARIS KEFALOGIANNIS, born Athens, Greece, 1960; admitted, 1985, Athens Court of First Instance. *Education:* University of Athens Law School (LL.B.); London University (LL.M.). *LANGUAGES:* English, Greek and French.

HURT, SINISI & PAPADAKIS

KANARI 7
106 71 ATHENS, GREECE
Telephone: (30) (1) 364-2320/30; 363-8876
Telefax: (30) (1) 364-2323

Piraeus, Greece Office: 1 Loudovikou, 5th Floor, 185 31. Telephone: (30) (1) 417-4998. Telefax: (30) (1) 413-4289.

Rome, Italy Office: Via Laurina, 40, 00187. Telephone: (39) (6) 322-1485; 322-1487. Telecopier: (39) (6) 361-3266.

Milan, Italy Office: Corso Italia 8, 20122. Telephone: (39) (2) 866 727. Telefax: (39) (2) 866 771.

Atlanta, Georgia, USA Office: 1050 Crown Pointe Parkway, Suite 310, 30338. Telephone: (404) 913-9999. Telecopier: (404) 671-8513.

Hartford, Connecticut, USA Office: 294, New London Turnpike, Glastonbury, 06033. Telephone: (203) 633-3903. Telefax: (203) 633-4599.

San Diego, California, USA Office: Suite 1400, One America Plaza, 600 West Broadway, 92101-3377. Telephone: (619) 234-1798. Telefax: (619) 234-8475.

New York, New York, USA Office: 375 Park Avenue, Suite 2904, 10152. Telephone: (212) 755-1550. Telefax: (212) 755-1575.

Corporate, Banking and Securities Law with emphasis on Mergers and Acquisitions, Insurance, International Financial Transactions, Litigation, Arbitration, Bankruptcy, Foreign Investments, Privatizations, Joint Ventures, Taxation, European Common Market Law, Antitrust, Environmental Law, Transportation, Shipping, Licensing, Financing, Distribution Law, Commercial Real Estate (Investment, Structuring and Development), Project and Trade Finance, Computer, Software, Trademark Law, Telecommunications Law, Agency and Distribution, Labor, Visa/Immigration, Wills and Estates, Sports Law, Broadcasting, Motion Pictures, Video, Intellectual Property and General Entertainment Law.

FIRM PROFILE: Hurt, Sinisi & Papadakis is an International Law Firm based in the United States and Europe. Fundamental to the firm is a commitment to provide a high quality of personalized service with an excellent standard of professionalism. The United States Offices are located in the

(This Listing Continued)

Northeast, Southeast and Western United States in order to service clients conveniently and efficiently, as well as provide full support to the firm's European Offices. The European Offices are staffed with both American and European attorneys. Each office, in Europe and the United States, has attorneys that are qualified to appear and litigate in the local courts. Hurt, Sinisi & Papadakis has a strong focus on the Southern European region. This gives this firm a unique strategic position for businesses seeking legal advice and representation in this area.

MEMBERS OF FIRM

JOHN R. HURT, born Los Angeles, California, August 20, 1940; admitted, 1970, California; 1971, U.S. District Court for the Southern District of California; 1975, U.S. Supreme Court. *Education:* University of California, Berkeley (B.S., 1962); Cornell University School of Law (J.D., 1969). International Legal Centre Fellow, San Jose, Costa Rica, 1969-1971. Co-author: "Country Handbook on Italy," Italian American Business, 1992; "Environmental Laws of Italy," International Environmental Law and Regulations, Butterworths, 1991; "Dobson & Sinisi, Rome and San Diego," 1084-1994"; "Joint Ventures - A European Perspective," Ninth Annual Southeastern Corporate Counsel Institute, Atlanta, December, 1990; "Film Production and Loan Subsidies in Italy," Rome, July, 1990; "The Need for Appropriate Legal Protection of Software in Italy," Rome, 1988. General Counsel, Intermaritime Group, Geneva, 1987-1988. Private Practice, Paris and Rome, 1982-1987. General Counsel and Corporate Secretary, Cinema International Corporation, N.V., Amsterdam, 1978-1982. Division Counsel, Sea-Land Service, Inc., Menlo Park, N.J., 1975-1978. Associate, Gray, Cary, Ames & Frye, San Diego, 1971-1974. *Member:* State Bar of California; American (Member, Section on International Law and Practice) and International Bar Associations. (At San Diego Office). *LANGUAGES:* English, Spanish, Italian and French.

VINCENZO SINISI, born Bari, Italy, January 10, 1960; admitted, 1983, Italy (Not admitted in Greece). *Education:* University of Bari, Italy (J.D., magna cum laude, 1983). Yale Law School Visiting Scholar, 1985-1986. National Research Council Scholar, 1985-1986. Arbitrator, AFMA Arbitration Committee. Note Editor, Il Foro Italiano, 1982-1985. Speaker: International Bar Association 25th Biennial Conference, "Agency Distribution, Licensing and Franchising Agreements in Italy," Sydney, October, 1994; The Study Group for International Commercial Contracts, "Choice of Law and Choice of Forum in International Contracts," London, April, 1993; International Bar Association "Joint Ventures - An Italian Perspective," Tel-Aviv, 1993; Post M&A Organization, Milan, 1992; "The New Italian S.I.M. Legislation," Conference on "The New Organization of the Italian Securities Markets," London, 1991; "Financial Engineering and Tax Planning," Paris, 1991; "Film Production in Italy: Corporate, Contractual, Fiscal and Copyright Considerations Including Government Incentives," Milan, 1989; "New Financial Law Developments - An Overview on Mutual Funds, Options, Futures, Indexed Bonds and Other Financing Instruments," Milan, 1989;; "European Co-productions in Film and Television," Symposium on Film and Media Law, Munich, 1988. Author: "Co-Producing with Italy: Legal and Regulatory Issues," Co-Production International, 1994. Co-Author: "Choice of Law and International Contracts: the EEC Convention on the Law Applicable to Contractual Obligations," Corporate Counsel's International Adviser; "Franchising in Italy," Corporate Counsel's International Adviser, September, 1994; "Italian Labor Law: Collective Dismissal," Corporate Counsel's International Adviser, April, 1993; "Privatization in Italy," Corporate Counsel's International Adviser, May, 1993; "Agency and Distribution Agreements in Italy," Corporate Counsel's International Adviser, July, 1993; "Commercial Aspects of Italian Law," Business America, October, 1992; "International Contract Manual: Italy," Kluwer Law and Taxation, 1992; "Legal Aspects of Corporate Reorganization Post M&A," and "Environmental Laws of Italy," International Environmental Law and Regulation, Butterworths, 1991; Legal Studies and Services, Ltd., Amsterdam, 1987. Researcher: Energy Law, Institute of Comparative Law, University of Bari, 1984-1985; Center for Studies in the Public Interest, 1983. *Member:* International Bar Association. (At Rome, and Milan Offices). *LANGUAGES:* Italian and English.

ALEC PAPADAKIS, born Athens, Greece, January 27, 1947; admitted, 1979, Georgia (Not admitted in Greece). *Education:* Hartwick College; Iberoamericana University, Mexico City, Mexico; University of Akron (J.D., 1976). Author: "Forms of Doing Business in Greece," International Corporate Counsel, Fall, 1992; "Immigration Considerations for Foreign Investors in U.S."; "Impact of the Tax Reform Act of 1984 on Resident and Non-Resident Aliens"; "Memorandum on United States Immigration Law - Immigrant and Non-Immigrant Visas"; Selected Memoranda for Foreign Investors, Immigration, Estate Planning, Taxation; "Foreign Investment in Georgia - Immigration Considerations." Co-Author: "A Synopsis of the

(This Listing Continued)

HURT, SINISI & PAPADAKIS, Athens—Continued

Greek Corporate Tax System," State of California EC Law Handbook, 1993; Franchise Handbook for Foreign Companies Doing Business in U.S., Federal & State Compliance; Franchise Handbook for U.S. Companies Doing Business in European Common Market; Country Handbook on Greece Business & Employment Visas under IMMACT '90. Board of Advisors, International Quarterly. *Member:* International Franchise Association; American Bar Association (Sections on International Law and Franchising); State Bar of Georgia (Sections on Franchise, International and Environmental Law); International Bar Association; American Hellenic Chamber of Commerce (Athens, Greece); American Immigration Lawyers Association; Hellenic American Institute, Washington, D.C. (Board of Directors); Hellenic American Chamber of Commerce of Atlanta (Founder, President); Italy-America Chamber of Commerce of Southeast, U.S. (Founder, Board of Directors); International Leadership Council of the Southeast (Founding Member, Board of Directors). (At Atlanta, USA, Athens and Piraeus Offices). *LANGUAGES:* Greek and English.

DIMITRIOS G. DIAKOPOULOS, SR., born Athens, Greece, May 31, 1960; admitted, 1986, Athens. *Education:* School of Law of the Kapodistrian University of Athens (LL.D., 1983); University College, London (LL.M., 1984). Co-Author: "Doing Business in Greece," Corporate Counsel's International Advisor, December, 1992; "A Synopsis of the Greek Corporate Tax System," State of California EC Law Handbook, 1993; "Contractual Provisions and Dispute Resolution for American Basketball Players in Greece," September, 1993; "Debt Recovery in Greece: Collection on a Judgement," Turnarounds & Workouts Europe, October, 1993; "Franchising in Greece," International Franchise Association Annual Conference, Las Vegas, 1994; "Doing Business through the licensing of Trademarks," International Trademark Association Conference on the "The Role of Brands in Market Economies," Budapest, Hungary, 1994. Private Practice, 1986-1992. *Member:* Athens Bar Association; Hellenic Maritime Law Association; Hellenic Arbitration Association; Franchise Association of Greece. (At Athens and Piraeus Offices).

STEVEN N. KOURTIS, born Sydney, New South Wales, Australia, December 6, 1961; admitted, 1991, Pennsylvania (Not admitted in Greece). *Education:* Duquesne University, Pittsburgh, Pennsylvania (B.A., 1984); American University, Washington, D.C. (Washington Semester in U.S. Foreign Policy, 1983); graduate work, International Affairs, George Washington University, Washington, D.C. (1984-1987); Catholic University of America, Columbus School of Law, Washington, D.C. (J.D., 1991). Author: "Liability for Petroleum Storage Tank Owners and Operations," National Shipbuilders Research Project, Environmental Symposium, Crystal City, Virginia, 1991; "How to Lobby Congress," Independent Lubricant Manufacturers Association Annual Government Affairs Committee Meeting, Washington, D.C., 1992. Co-Author: "A Synopsis of the Greek Corporate Tax System," State of California EC Law Handbook, 1993; "Doing Business in Greece," Corporate Counsel's International Advisor, December 1992; Associate, Collier, Shannon, Rill & Scott, Washington, D.C., 1991-1992. *Member:* American Society for International Law; American Hellenic Educational and Progressive Association (AHEPA); American Bar Association (Section of Natural Resources, Energy and Environmental Law). (At Atlanta, USA, Athens and Piraeus Offices).

GEORGE DIAKOPOULOS, born Volos, Greece, January 22, 1929; admitted, 1957, Athens, Greece; 1966, Supreme Court. *Education:* Highest School of Economic and Commercial Sciences of Athens (B.Sc. in Economics, 1951); School of Law of University of Athens (LL.B., 1955). Member, Greek Parliament, 1974-1981. Vice Chair, National Economy and Finance, Budget and Appropriations Committees of the Parliament of Greece, 1974-1981. Columnist, Financial Section, "Kyriakatiki (Sunday) Eleftherotypia," 1990. Main Columnist, "Euroeconomia." *Member:* Athens Bar Association; Hellenic Maritime Law Association. (Resident at Piraeus Office).

DIMITRIOS N. DIAKOPOULOS, JR., born Athens, Greece, September 21, 1964; admitted, 1992, Athens, Greece. *Education:* School of Law of the Kapodistrian University of Athens (LL.D., 1988); University of Paris IV (D.E.A., 1992). Author: "La copropriete maritime," 1990. *Member:* Athens Bar Association; Hellenic Maritime Law Association. (At Athens and Piraeus Offices).

GEORGE S. MYLONOYANNIS, born Athens, Greece, August 5, 1963; admitted, 1993, Athens. *Education:* School of Law of the Kapodistrian University of Athens (LL.D., 1991); Department of Economics of the Kapodistrian University of Athens (B.Sc Economics, 1987); Center for Economic Research of Athens School of Economics (Diploma in Marketing, 1987); University de Paris IV (Diploma in Marketing, 1985). Researcher

(This Listing Continued)

EU828B

Institute of Economic and Industrial Research (I.O.V.E.), Athens, 1987-1989; Consultant to the Greek Chamber of Shipping, Piraeus, 1989-1990; Economic Advisor to Director General of Greek Telecommunications Organization (O.T.E.), 1989-1990; Investment Advisor to Prime Minister of Greece, 1990-1993. Co-Author: "The Greek Labour Market and the Economic and Monetary Union," I.O.V.E., 1990; "The Continuation of the Sabotage for the Greek Coastal Shipping," Greek Chamber of Shipping, 1990. *Member:* Athens Bar Association. (At Athens Office).

NICOLAOS HLEPAS, born Athens, Greece, March 11, 1961; admitted, 1987, Athens, Greece. *Education:* School of Law of the Kapodistrian University of Athens (LL.D., 1983); University of Bremen, on the Scholarship of the Public Scholarships Institution (J.D., magna cum laude, 1989). Author: "Unterschiedliche rechtliche Behandlung von Gross-und Kleingemeinden," Peter Lang Editions, 1991; Ungleichbehandlung als Verfassungsproblem," Archiv für Kommunalwissenschaften, 1990; "Grundgesetz und Besirksverfassung," Deutsches Verwaltungsblatt, 1991. *Member:* Athens Bar Association; Deutsch-Griechische Juristenvereinigung (German-Greek Lawyers Association). (At Athens and Piraeus Offices).

CHRISTINA PANAGI, born Volos, Greece, October 7, 1965; admitted, 1990, Athens, Greece. *Education:* School of Law of the Kapodistrian University of Athens (LL.D., 1988). *Member:* Athens Bar Association. (At Athens Office).

KLEANTHI SEIMANIDOU, born Athens, Greece, August 19, 1964; admitted, 1989, Athens, Greece. *Education:* School of Law of the Kapodistrian University of Athens (LL.D., 1987). *Member:* Athens Bar Association.

OF COUNSEL

HARRIET TAMEN, born Yonkers, New York, May 17, 1947; admitted, 1974, New York. *Education:* Bryn Mawr College (A.B., 1969); National Law Center, George Washington University (J.D., 1973). Lecturer: American Women's Economic Development Corporation on International Business and Trade Finance (1992-1995); New York University School of Continuing Education on Credit Enhancement and Banking Law (1991-1995); Financial Services Volunteer Corps (Mongolia) on Commercial Banking (1993-1994); Conference on Black Sea Region and Central Asian Republics; Economic Development & Business Opportunities - Harriman Institute, Columbia University (1994). *Member:* Association of the Bar of the City of New York; Inter-American Affairs Subcommittee; New York State Bar Association; SABLAW-Soviet-American Banking Law Working Group (1990-1995); American Bar Association. (New York Office).

WILLIAM C. BRUCE, born Louisville, Kentucky, April 11, 1952; admitted, 1977, Connecticut; 1978, District of Columbia; 1982, Florida; U.S. District Court, District of Connecticut; U.S. District Court, Eastern and Western Districts of Arkansas; U.S. District Court, Southern District of New York; U.S. Court of Appeals, 2nd, 6th and 11th Circuits; U.S. Supreme Court (Not admitted in Greece). *Education:* University of New Haven (B.A. summa cum laude, 1974); Yale University (J.D., 1977). Author: "Employment Law in the 1990's," Conn. L. Trib, November, 1992; "Preventive Law in the Non-U.S. Owned Corporation," No. 2 Preventive Law Reporter 10, 1991; "Theft of Business Opportunity," Conn. Bar Journal, 1979. Adjunct Professor of Management, Rennselaer Polytechnic Institute (Hartford Graduate Center). Senior Consultant to AON Re-Engineering Corp. on Employment and Privitization Issues. Formerly Vice President, General Counsel and Corporate Secretary, Pirelli Tire Corporation. General Counsel and Secretary, University of New Haven. *Member:* Connecticut and American (Committees on International Business Law and Product Liability Law); The Corporate Bar Association (Past Chair of the Litigation and Insurance Committee, International Law Committee). (At Atlanta and Hartford, USA and at Sinisi, Ceschini, Mancini & Partners, Rome Offices).

CHRISTOS V. GORTSOS, born Athens, Greece, June 4, 1961; admitted, 1985, Athens. *Education:* Kapodistrian University of Athens, Law School (LL.D., 1983), Faculty of Economics (1987); University of Zurich, Law School (LL.D., 1985); Graduate Institute of International Studies, University of Geneva (D.E.S. in International Law, 1988; D.E.S. in International Economics, 1992; Ph.D. candidate in International Banking Law); The Wharton Business School, Finance Department, University of Pennsylvania (R.A., 1989-1990). Author: "The Greek Banking System," Hellenic Banks' Association, 1992; "Legal and Financial Aspects of International Banks' Capital Adequacy Regulation," Ph.D. Thesis (to be defended in 1993); "The Macroprudential Regulation of International Banks: Toward an International Regime," Graduate Institute of International Studies, 1992; "The New Greek Banking Legislation within the Perspective of an International and Community Developments," Bulletin of Hellenic Banks' Association (Bul HBA), 1991; "The Management and Regulation of Com-

(This Listing Continued)

mercial Banks' Interest Rate Risk," Bul HBA, 1992; "The Proposal for a Directive on Deposit-guarantee Schemes: An Assessment," Bul HBA, 1992; "The Restructuring of the U.S. Banking System," Bul HBA, 1991; "The Legal Foundations of the Economic and Monetary Union," Journal Epikentra, 1992; "Toward a Liberalized Greek Banking System," Journal Epikentra, 1991; "The Treatment of Foreign Banks in the U.S.A.," Bul HBA, 1991; "The Basle Agreement on the Capital Adequacy of International Banks," Bul HBA, 1991; "Tendencies in the Regime Concerning the Protection of Banking Secrecy," Bul HBA, 1992; "The GATT Agreement for the Liberalization of International Trade in Financial Services," Bul HBA, 1992; "Financial Portfolio Management," Bul HBA, 1992; "The Application of the Brady Plan," Bul HBA, 1991; "On the Development and Stability of the European Monetary System," Bul HBA, 1992; "The Economic and Monetary Unification of Europe," Journal Epilogi, 1991. Co-author: "On the Creation of a Market for Mortgage-backed Securities in Greece," Paper submitted to the Committee on the Restructuring of the Greek Banking System, Athens, 1992.

REPRESENTATIVE CLIENTS: Fieldcrest Cannon, Inc.; EDS Hellas S.A.; E.D.S. International S.A.; Arby's, Inc.; Benjamin Moore & Co.; Twentieth Century Fox Film Corporation; Citizens Fidelity Bank & Trust Company; Aegean Fish Export, Ltd.; Newcrest Mining International; Eurocom, S.A.; Integrated Payment Systems, Inc.; Biobrn International; Frank E. Basil, Inc.; SMLK, S.A.; Team Sports, Inc.; Wegal/Tricotel; Euro-RSCG, S.A.; World Zaharoff; Reginald Turner Management Group; Arthur E. Abrahams & Gross, Inc.; J.D. Von Wahlde and Sons, Inc.; The Litdis Group, Inc.; Oppenheimer Inc.; Swank Records; Heinemman Hellas - Reed International Brooks Ltd.; Broadsystems Limited, Vierex S.A.; Expert Hellas; Subway Greece; Europartners Ltd.; Uniflame S.A.; Amber S.A.; Technologiki S.A.; Datamedia S.A.; Offitech S.A.; Korona Pasta S.A.; Inform Lykos S.A.

ATHANASIUS TH. IATROU & ASSOCIATES

Established in 1966

38 DIDOTOU STREET
ATHENS 106 80, GREECE
Telephone: 3621363; 3628798
Telex: 214242 POLY GR.
Fax: 3635722

Civil, Commercial, Private International Law, EEC, Law of Succession, Patent and Trade Mark Law, Legal Problems of Doing Business Abroad, Notarial and Conveyances, Companies, Foreign Investments and Criminal Law.

FIRM PROFILE: The firm was established in 1966. It is well known for its Decedent Estate, Foreign Investment, Conveyances and International Law.

The client basis is English speaking and E.E.C. countries.

MEMBERS OF FIRM

ATHANASIUS THEMIS IATROU, born Tripolis, Greece, 1927; admitted, 1953, Supreme Court of Greece. *Education:* Athens Law School; Suffolk University, Boston (International Law). Author: In English: Civil and Criminal Proceeding in Greece (1981), An Outline of the Greek Civil Law (1985), Euthanasia in the Greek Law (1988), Property Investment in Greece (1990), Selections from the Greek Law of Succession (1991), In Greek: The Intestate and Testamentary Succession in U.S.A. (1965, 2nd ed. 1979), The Intestate and Testamentary Succession in England and British Commonwealth (1979), On Corporations in Great Britain, the Republic of Ireland and the U.S.A. (1980), The Form of Wills in English and American Law (1968), The Trust in English and American Law (1971). *LANGUAGES:* Greek and English. *PRACTICE AREAS:* Decedent Estate; Foreign Investment; International Law.

MARY A. IATROU-NIKA, born Athens, Greece, 1934; admitted, 1960, Athens. Notary Public, 1968. Author: (in French): Comparative Studies on Mortgage Federation (Federation Hypothequaire, 1980), The Notarial Profession in the Contemporary World (1984), Comparative Studies on Companies with Limited Liability in Europe (1979), Comparative Studies on the Notarial Profession in Europe (1990). *LANGUAGES:* Greek, English and French. *PRACTICE AREAS:* Notarial; Conveyances; European Community Law; Corporations.

ASSOCIATE

MARY HADJI, born Athens, Greece, 1948; admitted, 1994, Athens. *Education:* Athens Law School. *LANGUAGES:* Greek and English.

(This Listing Continued)

OF COUNSEL

EURIPIDES YAZOS, born Ioannina, Greece, 1955; admitted, 1983, Athens. *Education:* Athens Law School. Author: Intellectual Property (1979). *LANGUAGES:* Greek, English, French and Italian. *PRACTICE AREAS:* Patent and Trademark; Foreign Investment; Criminal Law.

LEGAL SUPPORT PERSONNEL

DIMITRIOS KIOULHATZIS, born Athens, Greece, 1958. *Education:* Athens Law School (1983); Athens University (Degree of Economics, 1991). *LANGUAGES:* Greek, English, French and Italian. *PRACTICE AREAS:* Banks and Banking Law.

GEORGIOS IATROU, born Athens, Greece, 1973. *Education:* Athens Law School. *LANGUAGES:* Greek, English and Japanese.

Languages: Greek, English, French, Italian and Japanese.

REFERENCES: Embassies of Australia, Canada, G.Britain, Ireland, N.Zealand and U.S.A. (in Athens).

IKONOMOPOULOS & PARTNERS

Established in 1993

4 KOUMBARI STREET
106 74 ATHENS, GREECE
Telephone: (01) 3613615; 3613543; 3613143
Fax: (01) 3641806

Telecommunications, Mass Media, Privatisations, Foreign Investment, Banking, Capital Markets, Corporate, Mergers and Acquisitions, Commercial, Contracts, Franchise, Real Estate, Succession, Litigation, Debt Collection, Administrative, Energy, Industrial and European Union Law.

MEMBERS OF FIRM

HARRIS A.D. IKONOMOPOULOS, admitted, 1991, Athens.

CHRISTOS V. GORTSOS, admitted, 1985, Athens.

DR. NICHOLAOS A. KOULOURIS, admitted, 1986, Athens.

ATHANASSIOS D. LOUKOPOULOS, admitted, 1988, Athens.

DIMOSTHENIS A. DIMOPOULOS, admitted, 1985, Athens.

OF COUNSEL

SPYROS NICOLAOU, admitted, 1989, Athens. *Education:* University of Athens, Law School (LL.B., 1956); Diplome d' Etudes Superieures en Droit Public (1955, 1966). Conseil d' Etat (Marseille's Prefecture) in service training. Chief of Staff, Legal Department, Greek Prime Minister's Office, 1974-1975. Chief Justice, Supreme Administrative Court, 1977-1988. Advisor, to the Minister: Agricultural Legislation and EEC Law, Ministry of Agriculture; Urban Planning Legislation, Ministry of the Environment, Public Works and Urban Planning. Author: several studies and commentaries on the jurisprudence of the Greek Supreme Administrative Court (council of State), "The French E.N.A.".

LEGAL SUPPORT PERSONNEL

KITTY VOULTSOU. *Education:* University of Essex, England (B.Sc., 1993; M.Sc., 1994). *LANGUAGES:* English and German. *PRACTICE AREAS:* European Community Law; International Trade and Finance Law; Banking Law; Company Law; Private International Law.

Languages: Greek, English, French, German and Italian.

LAW OFFICES
KARAGOUNIS AND PARTNERS

18 VALAORITOU STR.
10671 ATHENS, GREECE
Telephone: 01 3626821; 3621669
Fax: 01 3619617
Telex: 216801 DEPA GREECE

Paris, France Associated Office: 46 Avenue d'Ilena, 75116.

Commercial and Civil, International Private, Contracts, Litigation, Distribution, Corporate, Trademarks and Patents, Mergers and Acquisitions, Intellectual and Industrial Property, Transportation, Banking, Foreign Investments, Real Estate, Tax, Administrative.

(This Listing Continued)

LAW OFFICES KARAGOUNIS AND PARTNERS,
Athens—Continued

FIRM PROFILE: *Our firm was established in 1925 and offers a full range of legal services. It serves a varied clientele from most of the European countries, especially the European Union ones; and specializes in International Commercial and Civil Law.*

MEMBERS OF FIRM

THEODOROS KARAGOUNIS, born Karditsa, Greece, August 25, 1920; admitted, 1946, Supreme Court. *Education:* Athens Law School (LL.B., 1943). President, Rotary Club of Athens, 1983-1984 and 1991-1992; Governor, Greek District of Rotary, 1995. Member: French Chamber of Commerce; British Kellenic Chamber of Commerce; Rotary Club; Red Cross. *Member:* Athens Bar Association. **LANGUAGES:** Greek, Italian, English and French. **PRACTICE AREAS:** Civil; Real Estate; Commercial; Contracts; Construction.

CONSTANTINOS KARAGOUNIS, born Athens, Greece, November 14, 1961; admitted, 1985, Athens Court of Appeals. *Education:* Jean Moulin, Lyons, France (Licence, 1982; Maitrise, 1983); Strasbourg III, Strasbourg, France (Diploma, 1984). Presidential Delegate of AIJA in Greece. Author: "Mergers Under the Greek Law," Business Administration Bulletin; "Acquisitions Under the Greek Law," Cahiers Juridiques et Fiscaux; "International Arbitration Under the Greek Law," Chaiers Juridiques et Fiscaux; "Doing Business in France," Organization for the Promotion of Greek Exports; "Doing Business in Greece," Paris Chamber of Commerce. Member: French Chamber of Commerce; British Hellenic Chamber of Commerce; German Hellenic Chamber of Commerce; Rotary Club. *Member:* Athens Bar Association; AIJA; Institute of Professional Representatives before the E.P. (European Patent Office); Ligue Francohellenique. **LANGUAGES:** Greek, English, French and Italian. **PRACTICE AREAS:** Corporate; Distribution; Real Estate; Foreign Investments; Litigation.

ASSOCIATES

MARIA TSANTANI, born Athens, Greece, April 30, 1967; admitted, 1992, Athens Court of First Instance. *Education:* Erasmus Exchange Student Programme, Kiel, Germany (Certificate, 1990); Athens Law School, Athens, Greece (LL.B., 1990). *Member:* Athens Bar Association; A.E.G.E.E. (Association des Etats Generaux des Etudiants de L'Europe. **LANGUAGES:** Greek, English, French and Spanish. **PRACTICE AREAS:** Corporate; Trade Marks and Patents; Foreign Investments; Tax; Real Estate.

CHRISTINA AGOROGIANNI, born Athens, Greece, November 9, 1968; admitted, 1993, Athens Court of First Instance. *Education:* Thessaloniki Law School (LL.B., 1991); University of Kent at Canterbury (LL.M., 1993). President, Rotaract Club, 1994-1995. Author: "Shipowner's Liability for Loss of or Damage to the Goods," Kent's University Library. *Member:* Athens Bar Association. **LANGUAGES:** Greek, English and French. **PRACTICE AREAS:** International Commercial; Corporate; Transportation; Bankruptcy; Civil/Litigation.

VASSILIS PORTOKALIS, born Athens, Greece, September 15, 1969; admitted, 1994, Athens Court of First Instance. *Education:* Erasmus Exchange Student Programme, Essex, England (Certificate, 1991); Athens Law School, Athens, Greece (LL.B., 1992). Author, "Conventions of Lome I, II, III and Yaoude," Legal Review Periodical, 1990. *Member:* Athens Bar Association; ERGA OMNES (Organization of Legal Action). **LANGUAGES:** Greek, Italian, English and French. **PRACTICE AREAS:** Corporate; Labor; Civil; International Commercial; Tax.

KARATZAS & PERAKIS

Established in 1962

6 OMIROU STREET

ATHENS 10564, GREECE

Telephone: 32.29.141; 32.23.930; 32.17.676;
32.45.891; 32.31.142; 32.52.962

Cable: Advocati

Telex: 214664 KART GR

Facsimile: (01) 32.34.363

Banking, Corporate, Contracts, Foreign Investments, Shipping, Mergers and Acquisitions, Intellectual and Industrial Property, EEC Law, Taxation, Financial Services.

(This Listing Continued)

EU830B

MEMBERS OF FIRM

THEODORE B. KARATZAS, born Athens, Greece, 1930; admitted, 1955, Athens Supreme Court. *Education:* University of Athens Law School (LL.B.); Universite de Strasbourg Centre des Hautes Etudes Europeennes (1957). Co-Author: "The Greek Code of Private Maritime Law," Martinus Nijhoff Publishers, The Hague, 1982. Deputy Minister for National Economy, 1987-1988. General Secretary of the Ministry of National Economy, 1983-1987. Chairman of the Committee for the Reform of the Banking System, 1986-1987. Managing Director, National Investment Bank for Industrial Development, 1982-1985. Chairman, Banque Franco-Hellenique de Commerce International et Maritime, 1982-1985. Chairman, Hellenic Industrial and Mining Investment Company S.A., 1982-1985. Chairman of Aspis Mortgage Bank S.A. Member, Board of Directors: Dorian Bank S.A., Titan S.A. *Member:* Athens Bar Association; The American-Hellenic Chamber of Commerce; Hellenic Maritime Law Association. **LANGUAGES:** Greek, English and French. **PRACTICE AREAS:** Capital Markets; Banking Law; Finance Law; Foreign Investment Law.

EVANGHELOS E. PERAKIS, born Crete, Greece, 1946; admitted, 1971, Athens Supreme Court. *Education:* University of Athens Law School (LL.B.); Universite de Paris II (Diplome d'Etudes Superieures, 1973); Athens University, Faculty of Law (Doctorate, 1976). Associate Professor of Commercial Law, Athens University, 1991. Author: "Voting Agreements among Shareholders," Athens, 1976; "The Auditing of Limited Companies," Athens, 1984; "Introduction to the Law of the Reorganization of Companies," Athens, 1987; "International Bankruptcy Law," Athens, 1990. Co-Author: "Commentary to the Greek Civil Code," Athens, 1976-1978; "World Law of Competition," Greek Chapter, Matthew Bender, New York, N.Y., 1983; "Doing Business in Europe," Greek Chapter, CCH International, London, 1990. Member, Legal Council of Commercial Bank of Greece. *Member:* Athens Bar Association; Hellenic Maritime Law Association; Association Europeenne pour le Droit Bancaire et Financier. **LANGUAGES:** Greek, English and French. **PRACTICE AREAS:** Company Law; Foreign Investment Law.

OLGA MARIDAKIS-KARATZAS, born Athens, Greece, 1936; admitted, 1961, Athens Court of Appeals. *Education:* University of Athens Law School (LL.B.). Fellow, University of Athens. *Member:* Athens Bar Association. **LANGUAGES:** Greek, English and French. **PRACTICE AREAS:** Industrial and Intellectual Property Law; Trust Law; Estates.

ASSOCIATES

DIMITRIS G. TSIMBANOULIS, born Volos, Greece, 1957; admitted, 1983, Athens Court of Appeals. *Education:* University of Athens Law School (LL.B., 1980); University of Frankfurt (Doctorate in Law, DAAD Fellowship, 1986). Tutor for Methologie of Law, University of Frankfurt, 1983-1985; Assistant at the Institute for Transport Law, University of Frankfurt and at the Max-Planck-Institute, Department of History of Law, 1985-1987. Member, Legal Department of the Bank of Greece. "Die genossenschaftliche," Peter Lang Verlag, Frankfurt aus Hain, 1987; "Investment Services in Greek and EEC Law," Athens, 1989. *Member:* Athens Bar Association; European Lawyers' Union; European Society for Banking and Financial Law. **LANGUAGES:** Greek, German, French and English. **PRACTICE AREAS:** Banking Law; Finance Law; Capital Markets; Company Law.

CATHERINE M. KARATZA, born Athens, Greece, 1964; admitted, 1989, New York and Athens Court of First Instance. *Education:* University of Athens Law School (LL.B.); Columbia University School of Law (LL.M., 1988). Associate with, Shearman & Sterling, New York, New York, 1988-1992. *Member:* Athens, American and International Bar Associations. **LANGUAGES:** Greek, English, French, German and Spanish. **PRACTICE AREAS:** Capital Markets; Mergers and Acquisitions; Banking Law; Finance Law; Shipping Finance Law.

ATHANASSIOS C. VASSILAKIS, born Athens, Greece, 1963; admitted, 1990, Athens Court of First Instance. *Education:* University of Athens Law School (LL.B.). *Member:* Athens Bar Association. **LANGUAGES:** Greek and English. **PRACTICE AREAS:** Real Estate Law; Labor Law.

PADAZIS O. KARAMANOLIS, born Thessaloniki, Greece, 1960; admitted, 1992, Thessaloniki Court of First Instance. *Education:* Thessaloniki University School of Law (LL.B.); Queen Mary College, University of London (LL.M., 1984); Magdalene College, University of Cambridge (Ph.D., 1989); Fulbright Scholar (1990). Intern, Simmons & Simmons, London, England, 1987. Member: Fellow of Salzburg Seminar, Austria. Author: "Interest Rate Swaps: An Empirical Analysis," Bulletin of the Association of Greek Banks, Athens, 1990; "Sovereign Syndicated Euro-credits: Negotiating Techniques," Bulletin of the Association of Greek Banks, Athens,

(This Listing Continued)

1991; "The Legal Implications of Sovereign Lending Through Syndicated Loan Agreements," Oceana, New York, 1992; "Liability in Tort for Negligent Misrepresentations in Sovereign Loan Agreements and Placing Memoranda," Bulletin of the Association of Greek Banks, Athens, 1992. *LANGUAGES:* Greek and English. *PRACTICE AREAS:* Banking Law; Finance Law; Capital Markets.

EVANGELOS G. POLITIS, born Agrinio, Greece, 1967; admitted, 1992, Athens Court of First Instance. *Education:* University of Athens Law School (LL.B.); Duke University School of Law (LL.M., 1993). *Member:* Athens Bar Association. *LANGUAGES:* Greek, English and French. *PRACTICE AREAS:* Banking Law; Finance Law; Foreign Investment Law.

EMMANOUIL G. SEISSOGLOU, born Athens, Greece, 1967; admitted, 1994, Athens Court of First Instance. *Education:* University of Athens Law School (LL.B.); University College London University of London (LL.M., 1993). *LANGUAGES:* Greek, English, Spanish and French. *PRACTICE AREAS:* Banking Law; Finance Law; EC Law.

KALLIOPI SKOULARIKI, born Athens, Greece, 1969. *Education:* University of Athens Law School (LL.B.); University of Hannover, Germany. Trainee. *LANGUAGES:* Greek, English, German and French. *PRACTICE AREAS:* Intellectual and Industrial Property Law; Company Law.

Languages: Greek, English, French and German

REPRESENTATIVE CLIENTS: Aspis Mortgage Bank S.A.; Dorian Bank S.A.; The Chase Manhattan Bank, N.A.; Alpha Finance S.A.; Alpha Venture Capital, S.A.; Groupe Bruxelles Lambert; ANZ Grindlays Bank, PLC; Union Carbide; Ralston Energy Systems S.A.; The Coca-Cola Company; The Timberland Company; Upjohn; Allergan; Consolidated Contractors International Company; BSB; Cargill International S.A.; Petzetakis S.A.; Lavipharm S.A.; Chemical Industries of Northern Greece (SICNG) S.A.; Euroclear; Papastratos Tobacco Manufacturing Company; The Nikko Securities, Co.; J. Henry Schroder Wagg & Co. Ltd.; Nippon Telegraph and Telephone Corp.
REFERENCES: Allen & Overy, London, England; Shearman & Sterling, New York; Davis, Polk & Wardwell, New York; Darby & Darby, New York; Sinclair, Roche & Temperly, London, England.

CONSTANTINE S. KATSIGERAS

Established in 1973

8, PATRIARCH IOAKIM STR.
ATHENS 106 74, GREECE
Telephone: 7232580; 7222728
Telex: 21-8419 KATS GR.
Fax: 7249186

General Practice, Corporate, Foreign Investments, Maritime, Real Estate, Taxation, Banking, EEC Law, Patents and Trademark.

FIRM PROFILE: *It is an internationally oriented law firm which provides a full range of legal services and specializes in Foreign Investments, Corporate and Maritime Law.*

MEMBERS OF FIRM

DR. CONSTANTINE S. KATSIGERAS, born Athens, Greece, March 6, 1942; admitted, 1967, Athens; 1971, Athens Court of Appeals; 1977, Athens Supreme Court. *Education:* Athens University (Diploma, 1964); Paris University (D.E.S. Droit Privé, 1966; Doctorat d'Etat, 1969). Author: "Le Déroutement en Droit Maritime Comparé," Doctorial Thesis, Libraries Techniques, 1971. Professor, Business Law and Shipping Law, American College in Athens, 1975—. Represented the Ministry of Merchant Marine and the Creek Chamber of Shipping on various United Nations and OECD Conferences, 1975—. *Member:* Athens and International Bar Associations; International Fiscal Association; Greek Association of Maritime Law; Greek Chamber of Shipping (Arbitrator and Member of Legal Committee); American-Hellenic Chamber of Commerce; British-Hellenic Chamber of Commerce; French-Hellenic Chamber of Commerce. *LANGUAGES:* Greek, English, French, German and Italian. *PRACTICE AREAS:* International Transactions; Corporate Law; Maritime Law.

ASSOCIATES

ANDREW J. PANTELAKIS, born 1958; admitted, 1983, Athens. *Education:* University of Athens, Law School (LL.B.); University of London (LL.M.). *LANGUAGES:* Greek, English, French and German. *PRACTICE AREAS:* International Transactions; Corporate Law.

MARIA V. TSOURAPIS, born 1945; admitted, 1974, Athens. *Education:* University of Athens, Law School (LL.B.). *LANGUAGES:* Greek and English. *PRACTICE AREAS:* Litigation; Real Estate Law.

(This Listing Continued)

MARIA-CHRISTINA G. PARISSAKIS, born 1960; admitted, 1987, Athens. *Education:* University of Athens, Law School (LL.B.). *LANGUAGES:* Greek, English and French. *PRACTICE AREAS:* Corporate Law; Patents and Trademarks.

REPRESENTATIVE CLIENTS: Digital Equipment Corp; GTE Corp; Cray Research Inc.; Hearst Corp.; Fremantle International Inc. (USA); Peugeot-Citroën; Thomson CSF; Hachette; Wagons Lits; GEC Alsthom (France); Rizzoli (Italy); Solvay; UCB (Belgium); ISS Service Systems; ESS Food (Denmark); Kone B.V. (Finland).

KEFALEAS & MOUSSAS

Established in 1930

22 RAVINE STREET
ATHENS 115 21, GREECE
Telephone: (01) 723 7668; 724 8639
Telefax: (01) 724 3391

Corporate, Commercial, Patent and Trademark, Banking, Family, Inheritance, Tax and Real Estate Law, General Practice.

PARTNER MEMBERS

TASSOS N. KEFALEAS (SNR. PTNR), born Athens, Greece, 1933; admitted, 1959, Athens; 1969, Supreme Court of Greece. *Education:* University of Athens School of Law (LL.B., 1957). Author: "Negotiable Instruments," Athens, 1956. Lecturer on Law, Commercial Law Department, University of Athens School of Law, 1960-1979. Board Member, Hellenic Telecommunications Company (OTE SA). Judge, Supreme Disciplinary Court. Representative for Greece, Conference on the European Economic Interest Croup, Brussels, 1992. *Member:* Athens Bar Association (Board Member, 1976-1993); Hellenic Society on Commercial Law (Founding Member and Board Member, 1977—). *LANGUAGES:* Greek and German. *PRACTICE AREAS:* Commercial; Corporate; Telecommunications; Construction; Real Estate; Gaming (Casino) Licensing; Trademarks; Mergers.

NICHOLAS D. MOUSSAS (JNR. PTNR), born Athens, Greece, 1962; admitted, 1986, Athens, Athens Court of Appeals. *Education:* University of Athens School of Law (LL.B., 1984); Boalt Hall School of Law, University of California at Berkeley (LL.M., 1988). *LANGUAGES:* Greek, English, French and German. *PRACTICE AREAS:* Commercial; Corporate; Securities; Banking; Financial Services; International Business; Agency; Distributorships and Franchising; International Litigation; Gaming Licensing; Private International; Cross Border Mergers and Acquisitions; Aviation.

ASSOCIATES

MARIA A. KANELLAKOU, born 1966; admitted, 1991, Athens. *LANGUAGES:* Greek and English. *PRACTICE AREAS:* Civil; Commercial; Commercial Leases.

VASSILIOS D. MOUSSAS, born 1965; admitted, 1991, Athens. *LANGUAGES:* Greek, English and French. *PRACTICE AREAS:* Civil Litigation.

LOUKIA PAPAHATZI, born 1966; admitted, 1993, Athens. *LANGUAGES:* Greek, English and French. *PRACTICE AREAS:* Civil; Tax.

Languages: Greek, English, Franch, German

LAW OFFICE TRYFON J. KOUTALIDIS

Established in 1930

4, VALAORITOU STREET
ATHENS 106 71, GREECE
Telephone: (01) 3607.811; 3607.812; 3607.813; 3607.814
Telefax: (01) 3600.069
Telex: 214602 TJK GR

REVISERS OF THE GREECE LAW DIGEST FOR THIS DIRECTORY.

Commercial, Aviation, Shipping, Banking, Corporate, Taxation, Foreign Investments, Admiralty, Real Estate, Public and Private International Law, Mergers and Acquisitions, European Community Law, Administrative Law, Construction Law.

MEMBERS OF FIRM

TRYFON J. KOUTALIDIS, born Athens, Greece, October 25, 1934; admitted, 1959, Athens Court of Appeals and Supreme Court of Greece. *Education:* University of Athens Law School (LL.B.); London University and Athens Law School (Dr.Jur., 1965). Author: "The Commercial Laws of Greece," Oceana Pub. Inc., N.Y., 1966; "Patent Law-Trademark Law of

(This Listing Continued)

LAW OFFICE TRYFON J. KOUTALIDIS, Athens—
Continued

Greece," Oceana Pub. Inc., N.Y., 1968. *Member:* Athens Bar Association. *LANGUAGES:* Greek, English and French. *PRACTICE AREAS:* Mergers, Acquisitions and Divestitures; Aviation and Aerospace; Arbitration; Corporate Law; Company Law; Investments; Taxation; Banks and Banking; Commercial Law; Contracts; Trusts and Estates; Securities; International Law.

CONSTANTINE G. BONIFATSIS, born Athens, Greece, April 7, 1933; admitted, 1962, Greece. *Education:* University of Athens Law School (LL.B.). *Member:* Athens Bar Association. *LANGUAGES:* Greek, English and French. *PRACTICE AREAS:* Admiralty and Maritime Law; Banks and Banking Law; Business Law; International Loans; Copyrights; Debtor and Creditor; Insurance; Mortgages.

DIMITRIOS C. HADJIGRIGORIADIS, born Naoussa, Greece, August 26, 1937; admitted, 1963, Greece. *Education:* University of Athens Law School (LL.B.). Member, Board of the Capital Markets Committee. *Member:* Athens Bar Association; Chartered Insurance Institute (A.C.I.I.); International Bar Association (Member, Committee C, International Construction Contracts). *LANGUAGES:* Greek, English and French. *PRACTICE AREAS:* Construction Law; Company Law; Sports Law; Real Estate; Immigration and Naturalisation; Intellectual Property Leasing; Franchises; Family Law; Bankruptcy.

TIMOS E. SKOTIDAS, born Athens, Greece, May 30, 1936; admitted, 1964, Athens Court of Appeals and Supreme Court of Greece. *Education:* University of Athens, Law School (LL.B); University of Paris, Law School, Centre Universitaire des Communautes Europeennes. Director, Legal Department of Olympic Airways, 1977-1982. *Member:* Athens Bar Association. *LANGUAGES:* Greek, English and French. *PRACTICE AREAS:* Antitrust and Trade; Regulations; Aviation and Aerospace; Litigation; Transportation; Real Estate; Property; Arbitration; Corporate Law.

CONSTANTINE AL. KARAMANLIS, born Athens, Greece, September 24, 1956; admitted, 1983, Greece. *Education:* University of Athens, Law School (LL.B.); Tufts University-Fletcher School of Law and Diplomacy (M.A.L.D., Ph.D.). Instructor, Business Law, Deree College, Athens, Greece, 1983-1984. Member of the Parliament. *Member:* Athens Bar Association. *LANGUAGES:* Greek, English, German and French. *PRACTICE AREAS:* General Practice; Corporate Law; Government Energy.

HELEN K. TROVA, born Athens, Greece, May 10, 1963; admitted, 1989, Greece. *Education:* University of Athens Law School (LL.B.); University of Paris II, Pantheon-Sorbonne (D.E.A.; Doctorat d'Etat en Droit Public Interne; Dr.Jur.). Author: "Le Statut Juridique de l'Action Culturelle et Linguistique de la France à étranger," LGDJ, Paris; "The Concept of Cultural Environment Pursuant to Greek Constitution of 1975/86," Sakkoulas, Greece. *Member:* Athens Bar Association; Association of Greek Constitutionalists; Association of Greek Administrativistes. *LANGUAGES:* Greek, French and English. *PRACTICE AREAS:* Administrative Law; Art Law; Tax Law; Communications and Media; Constitutional Law; Gaming; Environmental Law; Investments; Trusts; Government Contracts.

PANAGIOTIS E. KOUTALIDIS, born Kalamata, Greece, June 12, 1952; admitted, 1975, Athens Court of Appeals and Supreme Court of Greece. *Education:* University of Athens Law School (LL.B.); London University (Diploma in Shipping Law, 1978). *Member:* Athens Bar Association. *LANGUAGES:* Greek and English. *PRACTICE AREAS:* Trademarks; Wills; Social Law; Property; Family Law; Patents Litigation; Health Care; Leases and Leasing; Franchising; Labour and Employment.

NIKOS C. KORITSAS, born Athens, Greece, February 10, 1965; admitted, 1990, Greece. *Education:* University of Athens School of Law (LL.B.); London University (LL.M. in International Business Law, 1989). *Member:* Athens Bar Association. *LANGUAGES:* Greek, English, French and German. *PRACTICE AREAS:* Mergers, Acquisitions and Divestitures; Banks and Banking; Investments; Taxation; Company Law; Business Law; Commercial Law; Corporate Law; Securities; Intellectual Property.

NIKITAS P. FORTSAKIS, born Athens, Greece, October 27, 1956; admitted, 1982, Greece. *Education:* University of Athens School of Law (LL.B.); University of Paris II, Panthéon-Sorbonne (D.E.A.) Cand. Doctorat d'Etat en Droit Constitutionel. *Member:* Athens Bar Association; Centre International de Formation Européenne (C.I.F.E.), Alumni Association of Athens College. *LANGUAGES:* Greek, English, French and Italian. *PRACTICE AREAS:* European Community Law-European Parliament (1983); Agency and Distributorships; Computers and Software Litigation; Telecommunications; Business Law.

(This Listing Continued)

MARIA C. MAKRIS, born Athens, Greece, May 19, 1962; admitted, 1989, Greece. *Education:* University of Athens Law School (LL.B.); University of Cambridge (LL.M., Ph.D.). *Member:* Athens Bar Association. *LANGUAGES:* Greek, English and French. *PRACTICE AREAS:* European Community Law; Administrative Law; Investments; International Law; Health Care; Products Liability; Technology and Science; Company Law; Antitrust and Trade Regulation; Environmental Law.

CHRISTIANA D. HADJIGRIGORIADOU, born Athens, Greece, September 25, 1965; admitted, 1994, Greece (Not admitted in Greece). *Education:* University of Athens, School of Law (LL.B.); University of Southampton (LL.M., 1993). Author: Articles on the Sociology of Law Subtitled "Legal Studies, Legal Professions in Greece", edit. Sakkoulas, 1987. Seconded to Slaughter and May, London, 1993-1994. *Member:* Athens Bar Association. *LANGUAGES:* Greek, English, French and German. *PRACTICE AREAS:* European Law; Information Technology Law; Intellectual Property Law; Commercial Law; Corporate Law; Family Law; Construction Law; Consumer Law; Transport Law.

CATHERINE CHR. LANARA, born Athens, Greece, July 4, 1965; admitted, 1993, Greece. *Education:* University of Grenoble II (Maîtrise); University of Paris I (D.E.A.). *Member:* Athens Bar Association. *LANGUAGES:* Greek, English and French. *PRACTICE AREAS:* Company Law; Trademarks; Family Law; General Practice.

Languages: Greek, English, French, German and Italian.

REPRESENTATIVE CLIENTS: Bankers Trust Co.; Manufacturers Hanover Trust Co.; Banque Nationale de Paris; Banque Française de Credit International Ltd.; Schiffshypothekenbank zu Lübeck A.G.; Banque Louis Dreyfus; Banque Bruxelles Lambert S.A.; A.C. Nielsen Co.; Cummins Engine Co. Inc.; Dassault International; Intercontinental Hotels Corporation; Noxell Corporation; Stena Lines; Credit Bank S.A.; Lambrakis Press S.A.; Jacobs Suchard A.G.; C.E. Heat Plc.; Guinnes Plc.; Baring Brothers; Timewarner International, Inc.; Bechtel; Hochtief A.G.; Credit Swisse.

REVISERS OF THE GREECE LAW DIGEST FOR THIS DIRECTORY.

KYRIAKIDES & PARTNERS
LAW FIRM

Established in 1933

6, QUEEN SOPHIAS AVENUE
ATHENS 10674, GREECE
Telephone: 724-3072 through 724-3076
Telex: 216075 KYRI GR
Telecopier: 7250670-1

General Law Practice. Corporate, Foreign Investment, Banking, Private International, Mergers and Acquisitions, Maritime, Mining, Oil and Gas, Tax, Labor, Real Estate, Trademarks and Patents and EEC Law.

FIRM PROFILE: The firm offers a full range of legal services. It is well known for its expertise on big and complex investment projects, mergers and acquisitions and legal assistance to foreign investors in Greece, as well as for handling complex cases before courts or arbitration panels, including patent and trademark infringements. The total staff of the firm is 25 consisting of partners, Junior Partners, associates, paralegal personnel and office clerks.

KYRIACOS S. KYRIAKIDES (1910-1993).

MEMBERS OF FIRM

CONSTANTINE K. KYRIAKIDES, born Athens, Greece, February 6, 1944; admitted, 1969, Athens Court of Appeals and Supreme Court of Greece. *Education:* University of Athens Law School (LL.B.); University of London (Diploma in Maritime Law); Southwestern Legal Foundation, Dallas, Texas. Author: "Legal Aspects of Doing Business in Western Europe-Greece," Kluwer-West Pub., 1983; "Transnational Legal Practice-Greece," Kluwer, 1982; "International Liability of Corporate Directors - Greece," Lloyd's of London PIESS, 1993. *Member:* American Bar Association; International Bar Association; Athens Bar Association; Academy of American and International Law; European Lawyers' Union; Association of European Studies. *LANGUAGES:* Greek and English. *PRACTICE AREAS:* Tax and Labour; Oil and Gas; Mining; Mergers and Acquisitions; Public Works; Arbitration; Business Law; Government Contracts.

LEONIDAS C. GEORGOPOULOS, born Athens, Greece, September 1, 1940; admitted, 1968, Athens Court of Appeals and Supreme Court of Greece. *Education:* University of Athens Law School (LL.B.); Political and Economical Science Athens University (LL.B.); University of London

(This Listing Continued)

(Maritime Law); University of Nancy (Public Law). *Member:* Athens Bar Association. *LANGUAGES:* Greek, English and French. *PRACTICE AREAS:* Banking; International Business Law; Foreign Investment; Maritime; Mergers and Acquisitions; Securities; Resorts and Leisure; Casinos.

ANTHONY B. HADJIOANNOU, born Corinth, Greece, December 18, 1947; admitted, 1976, Athens Court of Appeals. *Education:* University of Athens Law School (LL.B.). Author: "Transnational Legal Practice - Greece," Kluwer, 1982. *Member:* Athens Bar Association. *LANGUAGES:* Greek and English. *PRACTICE AREAS:* Estates; Private International Law; Trademarks and Patents; Litigation; Franchising; Shipping; Bankruptcy; Leases.

EFFIE G. MITSOPOULOU, born Athens, Greece, June 7, 1960; admitted, 1986, Athens Court of Appeals. *Education:* University of Aix-Marseille III (Maitrise en Droit); University of London, King's College (LL.M., 1983). Author: "The United Kingdom and the European Community's Fisheries Policy," University of Aix, 1982; "The Application of the EEC Competition Rules on Air Transportation," Legal Service-European Parliament, 1984. *Member:* Athens Bar Association. *LANGUAGES:* Greek, English and French. *PRACTICE AREAS:* Corporate; Trademarks and Patents; Litigation; Real Estate; Pharmaceutical Law; Mortgages; Labour Law.

CLAIRE A. PAVLOU, born Athens, Greece, December 20, 1963; admitted, 1989, Athens Court of First Instance. *Education:* University of Athens Law School (LL.B.). *Member:* Athens Bar Association. *LANGUAGES:* Greek and English. *PRACTICE AREAS:* Corporate; Foreign Investment; International Business Law; Franchising; Mergers and Acquisitions; Air Law; Leases.

KONSTANTINOS GR. VOUTERAKOS, born Athens, Greece, April 22, 1964; admitted, 1987, Athens Court of First Instance. *Education:* University of Athens Law School (LL.B., 1987) University of London (LL.M., 1988). *Member:* Athens Bar Association; Association of Greek Commercial Lawyers. *LANGUAGES:* English, French, Spanish and Greek. *PRACTICE AREAS:* EEC Law; Real Estate; Mining; International Trade Law; Telecommunications Law; Agency and Distributorships; Gaming.

KONSTANTINOS J. PAPAMICHALOPOULOS, born New York, N.Y., March 11, 1965; admitted, 1991, Athens and Athens Court of First Instance. *Education:* University of Thessaloniki Law School (LL.B., 1988). Author: "Protection of Industrial and Intellectual Property in Greece," Kluwer, 1993. *Member:* Athens Bar Association. *LANGUAGES:* Greek and English. *PRACTICE AREAS:* Corporate; Taxation Law; Public Works; Foreign Investment; Trademarks and Patents; Intellectual Property; Cable T.V.; Resorts and Leisure.

ELENI SOULIOTOU, born Athens, Greece, May 19, 1963; admitted, 1988, Athens. *Education:* University of Athens Law School (LL.B., 1986); University of Saarland, Germany, (LL.M., EEC Law with specialization in Competition Law, 1989). Trainee, Financial Institutions and Company Law, Commission of the European Communities, General Direction XV. *Member:* Athens Bar Association; ADEK (Association concerning the ex-Stragiaires of the Commission of the European Community). *LANGUAGES:* English, French, German, Spanish, Italian and Greek. *PRACTICE AREAS:* Corporate; Environmental Law; Mergers and Acquisitions; EEC Law; Real Estate.

ALEXANDRA A. NIKOLAIDOU, born Serres, Greece, September 6, 1965; admitted, 1991, Athens. *Education:* University of Thessaloniki, Law School (LL.B.); University of Brussels, European Studies Institut (LL.M., Law of the European Community). *LANGUAGES:* Greek, English and French. *PRACTICE AREAS:* Corporate; European Law; Competition Law.

GEORGE N. BAKAMITSOS, born Athens, Greece, October 8, 1966; admitted, 1991, Athens. *Education:* University of Athens Law School (LL.B., 1989); University of Hull, England (LL.M., International Business Law, 1990); University of Southampton, England (LL.M., Maritime Law, 1991). *LANGUAGES:* Greek, English, French and German. *PRACTICE AREAS:* Maritime Law; Real Estate; Litigation.

MARIANTHI PAPANI, born Athens, Greece, August 27, 1965; admitted, 1994, Athens. *Education:* University of Athens Law School (LL.B., 1992). *Member:* Athens Bar Association. *LANGUAGES:* Greek, English and French. *PRACTICE AREAS:* Trademarks; Immigration Law; Consumer Protection; Corporate Law.

(This Listing Continued)

OF COUNSEL

CONSTANTINE GEORGOPOULOS. *Education:* Schools of Law and Political Economical Sciences of the University of Athens (Ph.D.). Professor Emeritus of Constitutional Law and ex-Rector of the University of Athens, ex-legal advisor to the Prime Minister, Associate Member of the Supreme Council for Public Services. Author: The Collaboration of the Houses of Parliamentary (1935); La ratification des Traitees, Paris (1939); Parliamentary System of Governing (1947); Elements of Constitutional Law (1968); Greek Constitutional Law in 3 Volumes (1969-1978); La Democracie en Danger, Paris (1977); Contribution a la Classification des Regimes Politique Paris (1987); Principals of Constitutional Law, 4th edition (1992). *LANGUAGES:* Greek and French.

GEORGE MITSOPOULOS. *Education:* Law School of the University of Athens (Ph.D.); University of Tubingen (Doctor Juris Honoris Causa). Professor Emeritus of Civil Procedural Law and ex-Rector of the University of Athens, Member of the Athens Academy, President of the Association of the Greek Civil Procedural Law Professionals. *LANGUAGES:* Greek, French, German and Italian.

Languages: Greek, English, French and German.

C.B.E. & D. LAMBADARIOS

Established in 1863

STADIOU STR. 3

ATHENS 105 62, GREECE

Telephone: 3224.047; 3224.517; 3224.419; 3231.135; 3246.324

Cable Address: "Cebelaw"

Telex: 216902

Telefax: 3226.368

Private, Commercial, Corporate, Foreign Investments, Finance, Private International, Admiralty, Labor, Taxation, Banking, Copyright, Trademark and Patents, Common Market, Real Estate and General Practice, Mergers and Acquisitions.

FIRM PROFILE: The firm was established in 1863. It is the oldest legal firm in Greece and offers a full range of legal services. The client base is mainly European and North American in scope. It consists presently of 4 members of the same family and seven associates.

CONSTANTINE E. LAMBADARIOS, SR. (1863-1928).

EPAMINONDAS C. LAMBADARIOS, SR. (1896-1955).

MEMBERS OF FIRM

CONSTANTINE E. LAMBADARIOS, born Athens, Greece, July 19, 1915; admitted, 1937, Athens Supreme Court. *Education:* University of Athens Law School (LL.B.); Harvard Law School (1952-1953). Member, Board of Directors: Dow Hellenic Chemical SA.; Amstel Athenian Brewery SA.; Janssen Pharmaceutical SA.; Merzario; Grey Advertising. *Member:* Athens Bar Association; The Association of the Bar of the City of New York (Non resident Member); World Peace Through Law Center; International Law Association; American Arbitration Association. *LANGUAGES:* Greek, English and French. *PRACTICE AREAS:* Corporate; Commercial; Foreign Investments; Conflict of Laws; Government and Public Law Contracts.

BASIL E. LAMBADARIOS, born Athens, Greece, July 19, 1915; admitted, 1937, Athens Supreme Court. *Education:* University of Athens Law School (LL.B.); Freiburg in Breisgau Law School (1938); Berlin Law School (1939). Member, Board of Directors: Proctor & Gamble Hellas SA.; Ideal Standard SA. *Member:* Athens Bar Association; National Committee for Comparative Law (Secretary General); World Peace Through Law Center. *LANGUAGES:* Greek, English, French and German. *PRACTICE AREAS:* Civil Law; Corporate; Commercial.

EPAMINONDAS C. LAMBADARIOS, born Athens, Greece, August 10, 1944; admitted, 1970, Athens. *Education:* University of Athens Law School (LL.B., 1967); Harvard Law School (LL.M., 1969). Legal Training, Cleary, Gottlieb, Steen & Hamilton, New York, N.Y., 1969-1970. Member, Board of Directors: Sunwing Hotels S.A.; Phillip Morris Hellas, S.A.; Viamyl, S.A.; Levi Strauss and Co. *Member:* Athens Bar Association; World Peace Through Law Center. *LANGUAGES:* Greek, English and French. *PRACTICE AREAS:* Finance; Banking; Corporate; Foreign Investments; Government and Public Law Contracts.

DIMITRIOS C. LAMBADARIOS, born Athens, Greece, January 1, 1949. *Education:* University of Athens Law School (LL.B.); University College of London Law School (LL.M., 1976). Legal Training: Cleary, Gott-

(This Listing Continued)

C.B.E. & D. LAMBADARIOS, Athens—Continued

lieb, Steen & Hamilton, Brussels, 1977-1978. *Member:* Athens Bar Association; Association Europeenne d'Etudes Juridiques et Fiscales. *LANGUAGES:* Greek and English. *PRACTICE AREAS:* European Community Law; Corporate; Competition; Real Estate; Admiralty; Government and Public Law Contracts.

ASSOCIATES

STEFEN D. PAPADOUKAKIS, born Chania-Crete, Greece, April 6, 1932; admitted, 1967, Athens. *Education:* University of Athens Law School (LL.B.). *LANGUAGES:* Greek and English. *PRACTICE AREAS:* Civil Law.

JOHN FILIOTIS, born Zante, Greece, November 23, 1944; admitted, 1970, Athens Supreme Court. *Education:* University of Athens Law School (LL.B.). *Member:* Athens Bar Association; Greek Union for Arbitration; Greek Union of Civil Procedure. *LANGUAGES:* Greek and English. *PRACTICE AREAS:* Civil Law; Litigation; Commercial Law; Arbitration.

MARIA FRONISTA-KASSIMIDI, born Athens, Greece, February 17, 1950; admitted, 1974, Athens. *Education:* University of Athens Law School (LL.B.). *Member:* Athens Bar Association; Greek Union of Arbitration; Greek Union of Civil Procedure. *LANGUAGES:* Greek and English. *PRACTICE AREAS:* Civil Law; Real Estate; Commercial; Litigation.

NIKOS P. TRATAROS, born Athens, Greece, November 18, 1959; admitted, 1984, Athens. *Education:* University of Athens Law School (LL.B.); University College of London Law School (LL.M., 1985). *Member:* Athens Bar Association. *LANGUAGES:* Greek, English and German. *PRACTICE AREAS:* Shipping Law; Commercial; Litigation.

FOTINI J. KEFALIDOU, born Athens, Greece, July 8, 1968; admitted, 1992, Athens. *Education:* University of Thrace Law School (LL.M., 1993). *Member:* Athens Bar Association; Hellenic Association of Commercial Law. *LANGUAGES:* Greek, English and French. *PRACTICE AREAS:* Civil Law; Commercial; Taxation.

HELEN G. FOSCOLOU, born Athens, Greece, June 2, 1966; admitted, 1991, Athens. *Education:* University of Thrace Law School (LL.B.). *Member:* Athens Bar Association. *LANGUAGES:* Greek, English and French. *PRACTICE AREAS:* Criminal Law; Labor Law.

SOCRATES G. PARSANOS, born Athens, Greece, June 8, 1966; admitted, 1992, Athens. *Education:* University of Thessaloniki Law School (LL.B.). *Member:* Athens Bar Association. *LANGUAGES:* Greek, English and French. *PRACTICE AREAS:* Corporate; Commercial.

SPECIAL TAX COUNSEL

E.B. THEOFANOPOULOS, born 1940; admitted, 1964, Athens. *Education:* Athens University Law School. Qualified to represent clients before Supreme Courts. *Member:* Athens Bar. *LANGUAGES:* Greek, English and French.

REPRESENTATIVE CLIENTS: Dow Hellenic Chemical SA.; Boeing Corp.; Proctor and Gamble Hellas SA.; Ideal Standard SA.; Goodyear Hellas SA.; Amstel Athenian Brewery SA.; Caterpillar Overseas SA.; Stel Hellas SA; Vingressor Club/33AB; Johnson Wax International; Lockheed Aircraft International; Johnson & Johnson; USA Government; Levi Strauss & Co.; Philipp Morris International; Lafarge Coppee SA.; Foster Wheeler Italiana; Thomson Holidays; Makro Cash & Carry Wholesale S.A.; Grey Advertising. Technicas Reunidas; CAE.
REFERENCES: Cleary, Gottlieb, Steen and Hamilton, New York City (USA); De Bandt, Van Hecke and Lagae, Brussels; USA Embassy, Athens.

GEORGE LAZARIMOS & SONS

Established in 1875

24, OMIROU STREET

ATHENS 106 72, GREECE

Telephone: 3613-124; 3624-221

Fax: 3600536

Corporate, Banking, Commercial, Maritime, Labor, Investments and Taxation Law.

GEORGE A. GEORGIADES, born Piraeus, Greece, February 26, 1924; admitted, 1950, Athens; 1954, Athens Court of Appeals; 1962, Supreme Court of Greece. *Education:* Athens University. *Member:* Athens Bar Association. *LANGUAGES:* Greek and English.

GEORGE TSAROUCHAS, born Athens, Greece, June 18, 1926; admitted, 1953, Athens; 1958, Court of Appeals; 1965, Supreme Court of Greece.

(This Listing Continued)

Education: Athens University; Law School of Paris University. *Member:* Athens Bar Association. *LANGUAGES:* Greek, French and English.

ASSOCIATES

Z. AGGELIDOU, admitted, 1985, Athens.

A. GEORGIADES, admitted, 1990, Athens.

A. KASSIMATI-KEMOU, admitted, 1988, Athens.

L. STYLIANIDOU-DIMINAKI, admitted, 1976, Athens.

A. ROUSSOPOULOS, admitted, 1992, Athens.

Languages: Greek, French and English.

REPRESENTATIVE CLIENTS: Bank of America N.T. & S.A.; Société Général; Credit Lyonnais; Bank Franco-Hellenique; First National Bank of Chicago; The American Tobacco Company of the Orient; S. Livanos Shipbrokers S.A.; Wilbur Smith & Associates, Inc.; Norwich Eaton (Hellas) S.A.; American Bureau of Shipping.
REFERENCES: Bank of America N.T. & S.A.; First National Bank of Chicago; Maritime Brokers, Inc., New York.

DR. KIMON A. LEGAKIS

14 NIKITARAS STREET

ATHENS 10678, GREECE

Telephone: 3833.340, 6463.275, 3612.004, (02) 9927.111

Fax: 3820.838

Scarsdale, New York Office: 209 Garth Road, 10583. Telephone: (914) 725-4717. Fax: (914) 725-4936.

Other Athens, Greece Offices: 7 Koniaris Street and 73 Skoufa Street.

Civil Law (Property, Family, Inheritance, Personal Injury), Private International, Commercial and Corporate, Foreign Investments and Business Law, Common Market Law and Practice, Taxation, Banking, Labor, Real Estate.

DR. KIMON A. LEGAKIS, born Koronos, Naxos, Greece, August 7, 1923; admitted, 1949, Athens, Greece; 1965, Supreme Court of Athens. *Education:* University of Athens (Law Degree, 1949; graduate studies in Political and Economic Science, 1949-1951); Harvard Law School (LL.M. in International Law, 1961); Hague Academy of International Law (Certificate, 1970); University of Thessalonika (Doctor of Juridical Science in International Law, 1977). Author: "Settlement of Investment Disputes Between States and Nationals of Other States," Thessalonika, 1977, 413pp. Legal Consultant, Appellate Division, Second Supervisory District, State of New York, 1976. *Member:* Athens and International Bar Associations; International Law Association; American Society of International Law; British Institute of International and Comparative Law; Harvard Law School Association of Europe; Greek-American Chamber of Commerce; The Propeller Club of Port of Piraeus. *LANGUAGES:* Greek and English.

ANTHONY A. PAPADIMITRIOU, born Lumbashi, Zaire, May 21, 1956; admitted, 1981, Athens, Greece; 1986, Court of Appeals. *Education:* University of Athens (LL.B., 1979; LL.D., candidate, International Law); Temple University (Comparative Law, 1979); University of London U.C.L. (Public International and European Community Law, 1979-1980). Scientific Assistant, International Law, University of Athens Law School. Served Commission of the European Communities Legal and Social Affairs Department, Brussels, Belgium, 1983. Council of Europe, Human Rights Department, Strasbourg, France, 1984. Author: "The Substantive E.E.C. Law," Athens, 1981, 635 pp. *Member:* Athens Bar Association; European Studies Association of Greece (President, 1984); Foreign Press Association of Greece. *LANGUAGES:* Greek, English and French.

EVRIDIKI LEROU, born Athens, 1940; admitted, 1972, Athens, Greece; 1973, Court of Appeals; 1987, Supreme Court of Athens. *Education:* University of Athens (Law Degree, 1973); University of Thessalonika (Political and Economic Degree, 1975). *Member:* Union of Greek Jurists; League of Women Scientists. *LANGUAGES:* Greek.

COUNSEL

PETER BRASIDAS NICKLES, ATTORNEY-AT-LAW, admitted, 1964, New York. (Not admitted in Greece; Also Practicing Individually at 925 South Street, Peekskill, New York). *LANGUAGES:* English and Greek.

JANE S. LEVIEN, ATTORNEY-AT-LAW, admitted, 1975, New York. (Not admitted in Greece; Also Practicing individually at 6 West 77th Street, New York, NY1 0024). *LANGUAGES:* English and Greek.

LYKOUREZOS LAW OFFICES

Established in 1910

19 DIMOKRITOU STREET
ATHENS 106 73, GREECE
Telephone: 3607913-4; 3603943-4
Telex: 218175 ALYZ
Fax: 3607983

Criminal and General Civil Trial Practice.

ALEXANDER LYKOUREZOS, born Athens, Greece, February 4, 1934; admitted, 1960, Athens, Athens Court of Appeals and Supreme Court of Greece. *Education:* University of Athens Law School (LL.B.); University of Heidelberg; London University. *Member:* Athens Bar Association. *LANGUAGES:* English, French and German. *PRACTICE AREAS:* Criminal Law.

ASSOCIATES

ANGELOS PARSALIS, born Athens, Greece, January 5, 1960; admitted, 1984, Athens, Athens Court of Appeals and Supreme Court of Greece. *Education:* University of Thrace Law School (LL.B.). *Member:* Athens Bar Association. *PRACTICE AREAS:* Criminal Law.

NICHOLAS KALLIOURIS, born Athens, Greece, June 4, 1950; admitted, 1978, Athens and Athens Court of Appeals. *Education:* University of Salonika Law School (LL.B.). *Member:* Athens Bar Association. *PRACTICE AREAS:* Civil Law.

NANA MELETI, born Athens, Greece, December 8, 1948; admitted, 1984, Pireaus, Greece and Pireaus Court of Appeals. *Education:* University of Salonika Law School (LL.B.); Pantios School of Political Science (B.A.). *Member:* Pireaus Bar Association. *PRACTICE AREAS:* Criminal Litigation; Civil Law.

ANGELIKE NESTORIDES, born New York, New York, May 13, 1963; admitted, 1991, Maryland. *Education:* Tufts University (B.A., magna cum laude, 1985); National Law Center, George Washington University (J.D., honors, 1990). *Member:* Maryland Bar Association. *LANGUAGES:* English and French.

ATHANASIOS KEHAGIOGLOU, born Volos, Greece, December 16, 1961; admitted, 1990, Veria, Greece. *Education:* University of Salonika Law School (LL.B., 1985); American University (M.A., 1987). *LANGUAGES:* English. *PRACTICE AREAS:* Criminal Law.

VASSILIA SEITANIDOU, born Salonika, Greece, January 21, 1968; admitted, 1993, Athens. *Education:* University of Athens Law School (LL.B., 1990). *Member:* Athens Bar Association. *LANGUAGES:* English and French. *PRACTICE AREAS:* Civil Law.

IOANNA PAPAKONSTANTINOU, born Athens, Greece, June 16, 1966; admitted, 1993, Athens. *Education:* University of Athens Law School (LL.B., 1990). *Member:* Athens Bar Association. *LANGUAGES:* English, French, German and Spanish. *PRACTICE AREAS:* Criminal Law.

KATERINA DIMITRAKOPOULOU, born Athens, Greece, November 26, 1964; admitted, 1993, Athens. *Education:* University of Athens Law School (LL.B., 1990). *Member:* Athens Bar Association. *PRACTICE AREAS:* Criminal Law.

IRO KOKKOU, born Athens, Greece, December 28, 1949; admitted, 1976, Athens and Athens Court of Appeals. *Education:* University of Athens Law School (LL.B., 1974). *Member:* Athens Bar Association. *LANGUAGES:* English and French.

MARGELLOS & PARTNERS

Attorneys and Counsellors at Law

European Patent Attorneys

EM BENAKI 37
ATHENS GR-106 81, GREECE
Telephone: +30 (1) 363-9462; +30 (1) 361-1139
Facsimile: +30 (1) 360-5385

Brussels, Belgium Office: Boulevard de la Revision, 50. B-1070. Telephone: +32 (2) 732-5745. Fax: +32 (2) 732-5745.

Civil, Commercial, Litigation, E.E.C., Private International, Trade, Contracts, Winding-up, Patent, Mark, Copyright, Unfair Competition, Investments, Real Estate and Family Law, Eastern and Central European Business Law, Environmental Law.

(This Listing Continued)

FIRM PROFILE: Firm engaged in Greek, European and International Law practice. Entitled to plead before the European Commission and the European Court of Justice.

MEMBERS OF FIRM

MILTIADIS A. MARGELLOS, born Athens, Greece, 1912; admitted, 1939, Athens, Greece. *Education:* University of Athens Law School (1938); School of Economics (1940). Barrister and Solicitor at the Council of State and the Supreme Court of Greece. *LANGUAGES:* Greek.

THEOPHILE MILTIADIS MARGELLOS, born Athens, Greece, November 21, 1953; admitted, 1977, Athens, Greece and Supreme Court of Greece; European Patent Office, Münich, Germany. *Education:* University of Athens Law School (LL.B., 1975); Institute of High European Studies (Diploma, 1977); University of Strasbourg Law School (D.E.A., 1977; Ph.D., 1983); University of Athens Department of Political Science (B.Pol.Sc., 1978) University of Freiburg (Germany) Law School (1979-1980). Author: "La protection du vendeur á crédit d'objets mobiliers corporelsà travers la clause de réserve de propiété" Paris, L.G.D.J., 1989; "Free movement of Lawyers within the European Community," A. Sakkoulas, 1990, European Economic Interest Grouping," A. Sakkoulas, 1990. Lecturer on law, University of Picardie Law School, Amiens, France, 1988 —. Legal Service Commission of the European Communities, 1990-1993. *Member:* Société de législation comparée, Paris, France; Fédération Internationale de Droit Européen (Member Greek Section) (F.I.D.E.) European Lawyers Union (U.A.E.); Young Lawyers International Association (A.I.J.A.); European Patent Institute (Member, Standing Advisory Committee of the European Patent Office-SACEPO). *LANGUAGES:* Greek, French, English and German.

AIKATERINI MARGELLOU, born Athens, Greece, 1959; admitted, 1982, Athens, Greece and Athens Court of Appeal; 1985, European Patent Office, (Münich, Germany). *Education:* University of Athens Law School (LL.B., 1981); University of Strasbourg Law School, Center of International Studies in Industrial Property (CEIPI) (LL.M., 1983). *Member:* Athens Bar Association; European Patent Institute (Münich); Administrative Council of the European Patent Office (Münich); Hellenic European Studies Association. *LANGUAGES:* Greek, French and German.

GEORGIOS NIKOLAOS BOUKAOURIS, born Athens, Greece, 1953; admitted, 1981, Athens, Greece; 1986, European Patent Office, Münich, Germany. *Education:* University of Athens Law School (LL.B., 1976); McGill University Law School (LL.M., 1989). *Member:* Athens Bar Association; European Patent Institute (Münich); Administrative Council of the European Patent Office (Münich); Society of Comparative Legislation (Paris); Hellenic European Studies Association. *LANGUAGES:* Greek, English, French and Russian.

ASSOCIATES

MARIA BRA, born Athens, Greece, 1963; admitted, 1990, Brussels, Belgium. *Education:* Université Libre de Bruxelles (U.L.B.), Law School (L.L.B., 1989); Institute d'Etudes Européennes, U.L.B., Brussels (License spéciale, 1990). *Member:* Brussels Bar Association; Assossiazione di Giuristi di Lingua Italiana.

EMILIA LIASKA, born Arta, Greece, 1965; admitted, 1989, Athens, Greece. *Education:* University of Athens Law School (LL.B., 1987); Institut d'Etudes Européennes, ULB, Brussels (Licence Spéciale, 1991; LL.M., 1993, EAEME, European Association for Environmental Management Education, Commissions' Scholarship, Athens, Brussels, Varese). Experience: Commission of the European Communities, DG XVI (Regional Policy, DG XI (Environment)-European Environment Agency. *Member:* Athens Bar Association; Greek Environmental Law Association; Association Internationale de Jeunes Avocats (AIJA). *LANGUAGES:* Greek, French, English, German and Italian.

Member of Lawrope EEIG. A grouping of European Law firms.

Languages: Greek, English, French, German, Russian, Italian.

MASKALERIS & ASSOCIATES

STADIOU 28
FOURTH FLOOR
ATHENS, GREECE
Telephone: 322-6790

Morristown, New Jersey Office: 30 Court Street. Telephone: 201-267-0222.
New York, New York Office: 123 Bank Street. Telephone: 212-724-8669.
Newark, New Jersey Office: Federal Square Station, P.O. Box 20207. Telephone: 201-622-4300.

(This Listing Continued)

MASKALERIS & ASSOCIATES, Athens—Continued

Far Hills, New Jersey Office: Route 202 Station Plaza. Telephone: 201-234-0600.

General and International Law Practice.
Firm engaged in American and General International Practice, not authorized to appear before Greek Courts.

STEPHEN N. MASKALERIS, born Newark, New Jersey, June 23, 1927; admitted, 1953, New Jersey; 1980, New York. (Not admitted in Greece; Of Counsel on American and International Legal Matters).

GREEK LAW ADVISOR

MODESTOS PETRIDIS, born Agro Lemesou Cyprus, May 1930; admitted, 1956 Greece. *Education:* University of Athens. (Independent, unassociated law practitioner for Greek Matters, with Individual Practice at this address.).

*(For biographical data on New Jersey Personnel, see Biographical Section, Morristown, New Jersey)

Languages: Greek and English.

LAW OFFICES THANOS MASOULAS

SINA STREET, 11
ATHENS GR-106 80, GREECE
Telephone: (01) 362 7842
Telex: 210336 MAS GR
Telefax: (01) 3646477

General Legal Practice. Arbitration and Litigation. Advertising, Antitrust, Competition, Corporate, Distributorship, Agency and Franchise, EEC, Foreign Investments, Industrial Relations, Labour, International Contracts, Product Liability, Commercial, Banking, Common Market and Trade Regulations Law. Intellectual Property Practice. Patent, Trademark and Copyright Law.

MEMBERS OF FIRM

THANOS MASOULAS, born Kalavryta, Greece, December 1, 1935; admitted, 1963, Athens; 1967, Athens Court of Appeals; 1972, Supreme Court of Athens. *Education:* University of Athens, Law School (LL.B.); University of Cologne, Germany. Author: "Scheme and Gift Advertising," Athens, 1970. *Member:* AIPPI; Institute of Trade Mark Agents of London; Vereiningung für GRUR; Benelux M.M.; Greek Association for the Protection of Industrial Property. *LANGUAGES:* English, German and Greek.

ATHINA MASOULAS, born Agrinion, Greece, June 5, 1948; admitted, 1974, Athens. *Education:* University of Athens, Law School (LL.B.). *LANGUAGES:* English and Greek.

ASSOCIATES

JOHN KATRAS, born Athens, Greece, October 19, 1952; admitted, 1977, Athens. *Education:* University of Thessaloniki, Law School (LL.B.). Author: "Unions' Legislation.". *LANGUAGES:* English and Greek.

THEODOROU APOSTOLOS, born Agrinion, May 6, 1959; admitted, 1985, Athens. *Education:* University of Athens, Law School. *LANGUAGES:* English and Greek.

Languages: English, German and Greek

MASSOURIDIS - STAVROPOULOS & ASSOCIATES

39 PANEPISTIMIOU STREET
ATHENS 105 64, GREECE
Telephone: (01) 322.24.09; 322.09.02; 325.06.28
Telefax: (01) 322.09.02

Thessaloniki, Greece Office: 20 Komninon Street, 546 24 THES/KI.

Commercial, Banking and Corporate, Foreign Investment and Finance, Private International, Real Estate and Probate, Labor and Tax Law, EEC Law.

FIRM PROFILE: The origins of the law office under the name N.A. Massouridis go back to the 1920's. Our firm presently includes 3 partners and 6 associate lawyers and offers a broad range of legal services to private and corporate clients on a personalized basis. Over the years, it has specialized in the provision of advice to foreign enterprises on investment, contractual

(This Listing Continued)

and commercial matters and ensures legal support in their transactions with public sector authorities and agencies.

PARTNERS

ANTHONY N. MASSOURIDIS, born 1933; admitted, 1959, Athens Supreme Court. *Education:* University of Athens Law School; Munich University (Postgraduate Studies). Author: "Application in Greece of the Dispositions Concerning Restrictive Trading Agreements of the E.E.C. Treaty," Athens. Articles in various periodicals. *Member:* Athens Bar Association; British-Hellenic Chamber of Commerce. *LANGUAGES:* Greek, English and French. *PRACTICE AREAS:* Commercial Law; Foreign Investment Law; Corporate Law; EEC Law.

CONSTANTINE A. STAVROPOULOS, born 1946; admitted, 1971, Athens Supreme Court. *Education:* University of Athens Law School; Tuebingen University (Postgraduate Studies). *Member:* Athens Bar Association. *LANGUAGES:* Greek, English and German. *PRACTICE AREAS:* Civil Law; Commercial Law; Criminal Law.

ASSOCIATES

M. PARISSI-THOMAIDOU, born 1946; admitted, 1971, Athens Supreme Court. *Education:* University of Athens Law School. *Member:* Athens Bar Association. *LANGUAGES:* Greek, English, German and French. *PRACTICE AREAS:* Administrative Law; Fiscal Law.

THEOFANO PAPAZISI, born 1946; admitted, 1971, Thessaloniki Supreme Court. *Education:* University of Thessaloniki Law School, Faculty of Law; University of Cologne, Germany (Postgraduate Studies in Civil Law). Studies and articles concerning Civil Law. Associate Professor, Civil Law, University of Thessaloniki Law School. *Member:* Thessaloniki Bar Association. *LANGUAGES:* Greek, English, French and German. *PRACTICE AREAS:* Civil Law.

CONSTANTIN P. ECONOMIDES, born 1962; admitted, 1989, Athens Court of First Instance. *Education:* University of Athens Law School; University of Strasbourg III Law School; McGill University Institute of Air and Space Law (LL.M.). *Member:* Athens Bar Association. *LANGUAGES:* Greek, English and French. *PRACTICE AREAS:* European Community Law; Air and Space Law.

NICOLETTA BEHLIVANI, born 1964; admitted, 1990, Thessaloniki Court of Appeals. *Education:* University of Thessaloniki Law School, Faculty of Law; University of Thessaloniki Law School (Postgraduate Studies, Labour Law). *Member:* Thessaloniki Bar Association. *LANGUAGES:* Greek, English and French. *PRACTICE AREAS:* Civil Law; Labour Law.

VASSILIKI A. KALOPISSI, born 1965; admitted, 1993, Athens Court of Appeals. *Education:* University of Athens Law School. *Member:* Athens Bar Association. *LANGUAGES:* Greek, English and French. *PRACTICE AREAS:* Commercial Law; Corporate Law; Labour Law; Civil Law.

GEORGE N. MARINIDIS, born 1945; admitted, 1970, Athens Supreme Court. *Education:* University of Athens Law School. Legal Adviser, National Tourist Organization of Greece. *Member:* Athens Bar Association. *LANGUAGES:* Greek, English and French. *PRACTICE AREAS:* Civil Law; Labour Law; Real Estate Law; Administrative Law.

OF COUNSEL

ANDREW PH. ZAIMIS, born 1934; admitted, 1958, Athens Supreme Court. *Education:* University of Athens Law School. Minister, Undersecretary in various Administrations. *Member:* Athens Bar Association. *LANGUAGES:* Greek, English and French. *PRACTICE AREAS:* Real Estate Law; Probate Law; Administrative Law.

DIMITRIOS S. TSEMENTZIS, born 1946; admitted, 1980, Athens Court of Appeals. *Education:* University of Athens Law School. *Member:* Athens Bar Association. *LANGUAGES:* Greek, English, French and German. *PRACTICE AREAS:* Commercial Law; Corporate Law.

ATHANASIOS CHR. FELONIS, born 1953; admitted, 1975, Athens Supreme Court. *Education:* University of Thessaloniki Law School; New York University Law School (LL.M.; M.C.J.). *Member:* Athens Bar Association; American Bar Association (Corporation, Banking and Business Law and International Law and Practice Sections). *LANGUAGES:* Greek and English. *PRACTICE AREAS:* Commercial Law; Taxation Law; Foreign Investment Law.

Languages: Greek, English and French

(This Listing Continued)

Lavoro S.A., Rome; Trevi Spa., Cesena; Olmi Spa, Bergamo; Farsura Spa, Roma;
REFERENCES: Hambros Bank Limited, London; Rowe & Maw, London; Armand, Boedels & Associes, Paris; Porter & Dunham, Paris; Traverso e Associati, Milan; Luther & Partner, Hamburg; Buruma Maris Scheer Van Solkema, Rotterdam; Smith & Grette, Oslo; Advokatfirman Cederquist, Stockholm; Milbank, Tweed, Hadley & McCloy, New York.

LAW FIRM MAVRIDIS-MARINOS & PARTNERS

9 B VALAORITOU
ATHENS 106 71, GREECE
Telephone: (301) 3600 680; 3620 163; 3612 985
Fax: (301) 360 75 39
Telex: 21 90 49 Mavr

Commercial, Corporate and Labour Law, Debt Collections, Intellectual Property and Copyright, Computer Law, Banking, Competition Law, Administrative and EEC Law.

PARTNERS

VASSILI MAVRIDIS, born Athens, Greece, 1928; admitted, 1954, Athens Court of Appeals and Supreme Court of Greece. *Education:* University of Athens Law School (LL.B.); University of Cologne (Dr.jur., 1956). Counsellor: The Greek Embassy, Bonn, 1974-1975; The General Secretariat of Press of Greece, 1979-1980; The Ministry of Coordination of Greece, 1980-1981. Author: "Boundaries of Employment Contract and Contract of services," Cologne, 1956; "Employer's Compensation Rights," Review of Labour Law, 1958; "Authentic Interpretation of Collective Agreements," Review of Labour Law, 1959; "Notice of Termination of Employment Contract for Important Reasons," Review of Labour Law, 1961. *Member:* Athens Bar Association. *LANGUAGES:* Greek, German, English and French.

MICHAIL THEODOROS MARINOS, born Athens, Greece, 1954; admitted, 1979, Athens Court of Appeals and Supreme Court of Greece. *Education:* University of Athens Law School (LL.B.); University of Hamburg (Dr.jur., 1982). Representative: Greek Government in the EEC Software Directive, 1990-1991; negotiations for a Treaty about Microchips Protection in World Intellectual Property Organization, 1989-1990. Author: Publications: "The Unlawful Imitation of Commercial Signs," Munich, 1983; "Software Protection and Software Contracts," Athens Vol. I, 1989, Vol. II, 1992; "Protection of Semiconductor Products," Athens, 1991; "The Reform of the Uniform Rules and Usages concerning Letters of Credit and Standby Letters of Credit," Bulletin of the Hellenic Bank Association, 1987; "Selective Distribution Systems in: Protection of Free Competition," 1992. Various articles on Intellectual Property, Competition, Corporate and Banking Law. Assistant Professor, Commercial Law, University of Thrace, 1993. *Member:* Athens Bar Association. *LANGUAGES:* Greek, German and English.

PANAGIOTIS LAZARATOS, born Athens, Greece, 1961; admitted, 1989, Athens Court of Appeals and Supreme Court of Greece. *Education:* University of Athens Law School (LL.B.); University of Tübingen (Dr.jur., 1990). Author: "Legal Impacts of Computer Automatization on Public Administration," Berlin, 1990; "The Right of Hearing in the Administrative Procedure," Athens, 1993; "The Revocation of the Illegal Administrative Act according to EEC Law and the Law of EEC Member States," Diki, 1993; "The Efficiency of the Administration as legal Argument in the Public Law," The Constitution, 1991. Various articles on Administrative Law, Law of Administrative Procedure and EEC Law. Assistant Professor, Administrative Law, University of Athens, 1993. *Member:* Athens Bar Association. *LANGUAGES:* Greek, German, English and French.

DANAI MYLONAKI, born Athens, Greece, 1940; admitted, 1979, Athens Court of Appeals. *Education:* University of Athens Law School (LL.B.); School of Economics, Sorbonne, Pantheon (Ph.D., Economics, 1979). Counsellor: Directorate for Planning and Research, Agricultural Bank of Greece, Division of EEC Relations, Division Head, 1979—; Assistant Minister of National Economy, responsible for the Greek Memorandum, Integrated Mediterranean Programs and Social Fund, 1983-1985; responsible for the application of Common Market Law, Ministry of Labour and Manpower Employment Organization, 1982-1983. Division Head, Legal Department of the Agricultural Bank of Greece, 1985-1987. Author: Publications: "State Intervention and the Transfer of Agricultural Surplus to the Urban Sector," Athens, 1979; "The Application of Community Policy to the Agricultural Markets in Greece," European Commission, Agricultural Information, 1987; "Greek Public Markets Law and Commu-

(This Listing Continued)

nities Legislation," CEG, DG III, 1989-1990. *Member:* Athens Bar Association. *LANGUAGES:* Greek, English and French.

MARIA VOURNA, born Athens, Greece, 1963; admitted, 1989, Athens District Court. *Education:* University of Athens Law School (LL.B.); University of Tübingen (Postgraduate Studies, Administrative and EEC Law). *Member:* Athens Bar Association. *LANGUAGES:* Greek, German, English and French.

ASSOCIATES

CHRYSSA VELOPOULOU, born Patra, Greece, 1968; admitted, 1993, Athens District Court. *Education:* University of Athens Law School (LL.B.); University of Kent (LL.M., International Commercial Law). *Member:* Athens Bar Association. *LANGUAGES:* Greek, English and Italian.

ANGELA-ECKE MARINOS, born Giessen, Germany, 1956; admitted, 1990, Frankfurt District Court. *Education:* University of Göttingen and Hamburg, Germany. *Member:* Giessen Bar Association. *LANGUAGES:* Greek, German, French and English.

AGIS METAXOPOULOS LAW OFFICES

79, VAS. SOFIAS AVENUE
115 21 ATHENS, GREECE
Telephone: 01-7246 340; 01-7225 597; 01-7223 862
Fax: 01-7215 330

FIRM PROFILE: *Intellectual and Industrial Property, Commercial and Corporate, Unfair Competition, European Union Law, Foreign Investments, Civil, Banking, Taxation, Real Estate, Litigation, Labor, Penal Law.*

The office has the benefit of computerized word processing and data processing systems and is a member of TELFA (Trans European Law Firms Association) in association with Interlega (for more details see the TELFA-Interlega entry under Belgium, Brussels) and ALAI (Association Litteraire et Artistique Internationale).

AGIS METAXOPOULOS, admitted, 1955, Athens; Supreme Court of Athens. *Education:* University of Athens, Law School (Law Degree, 1953). Member: International Antipiracy Council of A.F.M.A. (American Film Market Association). Legal Counsel to EPOE (Greek Association for the Protection of Audiovisual Works). Special Counsel to the Minister of Cultural Affairs, 1979-1981.

KRITON METAXOPOULOS, admitted, 1986, Athens; 1991, Athens Court of Appeals. *Education:* University of Athens, Law School (LL.B., 1984); University of London, London School of Economics (LL.M., 1985). Served Commission of the European Communities (DGX from February 1986 until July 1986); Country correspondent for the Entertainment Law Review.

ANDROMACHI ELIANOU, admitted, 1986, Athens; 1991, Athens Court of Appeals. *Education:* University of Athens, Law School (LL.B., 1984); University of Strasbourg, Seminar on European Community Law, 1983; University of London, London School of Economics (LL.M., 1986).

DESPINA KOKKINOU, admitted, 1981, Athens; 1986, Athens Court of Appeals; 1994, Supreme Court of Athens. *Education:* Athens University, Italian Literature, 1976; Athens University Law School (LL.B., 1979).

NAFSIKA ADRAKTA, admitted, 1989, Athens. *Education:* Athens University, Law School (LL.B., 1987).

KONSTANTINOS KARAMBAMBAS, admitted, 1989, Athens. external associate.

CHRISTINE PIGAKI, admitted, 1992, Athens. external associate.

Languages: Greek, English, French, German and Italian

REPRESENTATIVE CLIENTS: Caterpillar Inc.; Motion Picture Export Association of America; Time-Warner Group; Avis Rent a Car; Abela Group; BMG-Ariola; Greek Association for the Protection of Audiovisual Works; Greek Association of Film and TV Producers; Greek Car Rental Association; CIC International N.V.; Walt Disney Company; Carolco International; New Line Cinema; Cannon International N.V.

MINOUDIS LAW OFFICES

Established in 1988

3, SEKERI STREET
ATHENS 10671, GREECE
Telephone: 01-3634430, 3602222
Fax: 01-3634326

Foreign Investment, Companies and Corporations, Hotel and Resort Developments, Banking and Finance, Mergers and Acquisitions, Arbitration, Litigation, Intellectual Property, European Community Law.

FIRM PROFILE: *The firm offers a wide range of legal services. Our clients include banks and other financial institutions, government agencies, public and private companies and other institutions. Our senior staff includes 3 university professors as well as Legal Counsellors in companies.*

MEMBERS OF FIRM

MICHAEL G. MINOUDIS, born Athens, Greece, 1942; admitted, 1967, Athens Court of Appeal and Supreme Court. *Education:* University of Athens Law School (LL.B.); Frei Universitaet, Berlin; University of Leiden; University of Lausanne; Athens Law School (Dr. Juris, 1972). Professor, Company Law, University of Athens. Author: "The Right of Minority Shareholders in Limited Companies to Demand Information under German and Greek Law"; "The Exclusion of a Partner in Partnerships," 1972; "Auditors in Limited Companies," 1978; "Patent Licence Agreements," 1987; "The Protection of Industrial Designs in Greece," 1991; "Commercial Law Code," Georgakopoulos & Minoudis, 1985. *Member:* Athens Bar Association; German Society of Comparative Law; AIPPI; Greek Association for the Protection of Industrial Property; EPI; Association of Insurance Law; Association of Maritime Law; Legal Council of Commercial Bank of Greece. *LANGUAGES:* Greek, German, English and French.

PANATIOTIS SOLDATOS, born Athens, Greece, 1941; admitted, 1967, Athens Court of Appeal and Supreme Court. *Education:* University of Athens Law School (LL.B.); University of Paris (LL.D.); University of Brussels (Ph.D. in Political Science). Author: "The New International Cities Era," Provo, University Press; "Le Systeme Institutionnel et Politique des Communautes Europeénes," Brussels, ed. Bruylant, 1989; "The European Communities in Action," Brussels, ed. Bruylant, 1981. Professor, University of Montreal. Vice President, Canadian Council for European Affairs. General Director, Institute for the Study of International Cities. *Member:* Athens Bar Association. *LANGUAGES:* Greek, French and English.

EVI A. SOUKOU, born Greece, 1943; admitted, 1972, Athens Court of Appeal and Supreme Court. *Education:* University of Athens Law School (LL.B.); University of Paris (Postgraduate Studies in Labour Law). Professor, Athens Institute for Technical Education. Author: "The Dissolution of Partnerships,"; "The Protection of Maternity in Greek Law,"; "The Situation of the Employee in Case of Illness in Greek Law,"; "The Protection of Children's Labour." *Member:* Athens Bar Association; EPI; Greek Women's Lawyers Association (Vice/President). *LANGUAGES:* Greek, French and English.

KONSTANTINOS S. KATSOUDAS, born Athens, Greece, 1942; admitted, 1967, Athens Court of Appeal and Supreme Court. *Education:* University of Athens Law School (1965, with honours). Assistant Professor, Civil Law, University of Athens Law School, 1970-1981. *Member:* Athens Bar Association. *LANGUAGES:* Greek, English and German.

KONSTANTINOS L. PAPAKONSTANTINOU, born Levadia, Greece, 1937; admitted, 1979, Athens Court of Appeal and Supreme Court. *Education:* School of Economics and Business Science (ASOE)(LL.B.); University of Thessaloniki Law School (LL.B.); City University, London (Postgraduate courses in Managerial Economics). *LANGUAGES:* Greek and English.

KONSTANTINOS A. TOMARAS, born Athens, Greece, 1957; admitted, 1984, Athens Court of First Instance. *Education:* University of Thessaloniki Law School (LL.B., 1981); University of Brussels (Postgraduate Studies in EEC Law, with honours, 1986). Author: "Some tax implications on the directive on capital movements," Intertax, November, 1988; "The Tetra Pak Case," International Business Lawyer, March, 1991; "New Commercial Policy Instrument: The Japanese Harbour Management Fund Case," Lawyer's Europe, Summer 1992. *Member:* Athens Bar Association; International Bar Association; Union of European Lawyers. *LANGUAGES:* Greek, English and French. *PRACTICE AREAS:* European Community Law; Company Law; Competition Law; Intellectual Property Law.

(This Listing Continued)

EU838B

MATINA I. DANAKA, born Athens, Greece, 1961; admitted, 1988, Athens Court of Appeal. *Education:* University of Athens Law School (LL.B. with honors). *Member:* Athens Bar Association. *LANGUAGES:* Greek, English and French. *PRACTICE AREAS:* Company and Commercial Law.

EVI I. MATTHEOU, born Athens, Greece, 1966; admitted, 1992, Athens Court of First Instance. *Education:* University of Thessaloniki, Faculty of Law (LL.B.); University of Athens (Postgraduate studies in Company and Corporate Law). *Member:* Athens Bar Association; Association of European Lawyers. *LANGUAGES:* Greek, French and English.

LABRINI K. KOLETTA, born Athens, Greece, 1969; admitted, 1992, Athens Court of First Instance. *Education:* University of Athens Law School (LL.B.); University of Athens (Postgraduate studies in Civil Law). *LANGUAGES:* Greek, French, English and Spanish. *PRACTICE AREAS:* Contracts; Product Liability; Litigation.

G. MOURGELAS - J. KOTRONAKIS - A. DAMASKINOS & ASSOCIATES

Established in 1975

67 VAS. SOFIAS AVENUE
115 21 ATHENS, GREECE
Telephone: (30-1) 7227.534 - 7224.227 - 7229.606 - 7249.327
Fax: (30-1) 7249.329

International, EEC (Competition Law), Investment, Corporations/Taxation, Banking and Finance, Contracts, International Trade, Industrial Property (Copyright, Performing, Publishing Rights), Property Law, Intellectual Property, Entertainment Business, Labor Relations, Litigation.

FIRM PROFILE: *The firm was established in 1975 and offers a full range of legal services. It is mainly occupied with the establishment of foreign companies in Greece, investments, business and corporate law, intellectual property and contracts.*

MEMBERS OF FIRM

GREGORY MOURGELAS, born Athens, Greece, August 8, 1939; admitted, 1967, Athens. *Education:* University of Athens (LL.M., 1964). *LANGUAGES:* Greek and English. *PRACTICE AREAS:* Investment Law; Business Law; Corporate Law; Competition Law; Advertising and Marketing Law.

JOHN KOTRONAKIS, born Athens, Greece, October 5, 1945; admitted, 1974, Athens. *Education:* University of Athens (LL.M., 1972). *LANGUAGES:* Greek and English. *PRACTICE AREAS:* Real Estate Law; Litigation.

ARISTOTELIS DAMASKINOS, born Athens, Greece, September 2, 1939; admitted, 1966, Athens. *Education:* University of Athens (LL.M., 1964). Lecturer, Constitutional Law, University of Athens, 1969-1975. *LANGUAGES:* Greek and English. *PRACTICE AREAS:* Intellectual Property Law; Corporate Law; Entertainment Business Law.

ASSOCIATES

FOTINI ARGYROPOULOU, admitted, 1988, Athens. *Education:* University of Athens (LL.M., 1987). *LANGUAGES:* Greek and English. *PRACTICE AREAS:* Litigation; Family Law; Business Law.

EVGENIA GAVREL, admitted, 1991, Athens. *Education:* University of Athens (LL.M., 1990). *LANGUAGES:* Greek and French. *PRACTICE AREAS:* Property Law; Lease Law; Trademark Law; Company Law.

ELENA CHRISSANTHAKOPOULOU, admitted, 1993, Athens. *Education:* University of Athens (LL.M., 1992; M.A.). *LANGUAGES:* Greek, English and French. *PRACTICE AREAS:* Trademark Law; Corporate Law; Business Law; Lease Law.

EVRIDIKI TOPALIDOU. *Education:* University of Salonica (LL.M., 1993). *LANGUAGES:* Greek and English (fluent) and French, Spanish, German, Italian, and Russian (fair). *PRACTICE AREAS:* General Practice; Corporate Law; Competition Law.

Languages: Greek, English, French, Spanish, German and Italian

REPRESENTATIVE CLIENTS: Pratt & Whitney Aircraft Group; United Technologies; Lee Cooper Group Ltd.; Stora Feldmuehle AG; Publicitas Holding S.A.; Canon Europa N. V.; Olympic DDB Needham Worldwide S.A.; Tupperware S.A.; Enco S.A.; Nutri-Metics International, Inc.; Greek American Chamber of Commerce; Alfred Karcher GmbH & Co.; Vinnell Corp.; Polygram Records S.A.; International Federation of Phonogram and Videogram Producers (IFPI); Greek Phonographic Industries S.A.; Gruppo Editoriale Sugar; Virgin Records.

(This Listing Continued)

REFERENCES: Walker Martineau, London; Mckenna & Cuneo, Brussels; Burlion, Bolle & Houben, Brussels; Coudert Brothers, New York City; Simmons & Simmons, London; Howe, Wilkinson & Lawry, Melbourne; Schnader, Harrison, Segal & Lewis, Philadelphia; Gordon & Rees, San Francisco.

DR. D.S. OEKONOMIDIS AND PARTNERS LAW OFFICES

Established in 1907

9, SINA STREET
ATHENS 10680, GREECE
Telephone: (301) 3610043; 3610049
Telefax: (301) 3634427
Telex: 219809 Koma GR/184

Transnational Business Law, Intellectual and Industrial Property, Information Technology Law, European Competition Law, Private International Law, Arbitration, Litigation, EEC Law, Foreign Investment and General Practice.

FIRM PROFILE: *The firm was established in 1907. It is an Athens based firm operating throughout Greece and offering a wide range of services.*

DIMITRIS OEKONOMIDIS, born Athens, 1938; admitted, 1963, Athens; 1975, Supreme Court of Greece. *Education:* University of Athens Law School (LLB, 1960); University of Munich (Doctor Juris, 1968); University of London (LL.M., Commercial, Copyright Law and Law of Unfair Competition, 1976). European Patent Agent. Member of Faculty, 1969-1972 and Assistant Professor, Juris Faculty, 1973, University of Munich. Member, Max Planck Institut für internationales und auslandisches Patent, Watenzeichen, Wettbewerbs und Urheberrecht, Munich, 1973. European Patent Agent, 1985. *Member:* Athens and International Bar Association; ALAI; AIPPI; FICPI; UNION; ECTA; CLA; ITMA; INTA (former USTA); UIA; UAE; IT LAW GROUP/EUROPE; International Society of Comparative Law. *LANGUAGES:* Greek, German, English, French and Italian. *PRACTICE AREAS:* Litigation; Contract Law; Investment Law; EEC Law; Intellectual Property Law; Industrial Property Law; ADR; Arbitration.

ASSOCIATES

ANGELIKI DELICOSTOPOULOU, born Athens, 1964; admitted, 1989, Athens; 1994, Athens Court of Appeal. *Education:* University of Athens School of Law (LL.B., 1987); University of Exeter, England (LL.M., in International Business Legal Studies, 1988). *Member:* Athens and International Bar Associations; UNION; ECTA; CLA; AIJA. *LANGUAGES:* Greek, English, French, Spanish and German. *PRACTICE AREAS:* Industrial Property Law; Transnational Business Law; Company Law; Civil Law.

ANDROMACHI DELICOSTOPOULOU, born Athens, 1966; admitted, 1991, Athens Court of First Instance. *Education:* University of Athens School of Law (LL.B., 1988); University of Exeter, England (LL.M. in International Business Legal Studies, 1990). Tutor, Faculty of Law, University of Exeter, England, 1990-1991. *Member:* Athens Bar Association; AIJA. *LANGUAGES:* Greek, English, French, German, Spanish. *PRACTICE AREAS:* Information Technology Law; Intellectual Property Law; EDI; Telecommunications; Competition Law; Civil Law.

CARSTEN NIEMER, born Hannover, Germany, 1957; admitted, 1990, Berlin First Instance Court; 1992, Athens First Instance Court. *Education:* Rheinische Friedrich-Wilhelms Universität Bonn (1985). *Member:* Athens and Berlin Bar Association. *LANGUAGES:* German, Greek, English. *PRACTICE AREAS:* International Civil Law.

REPRESENTATIVE CLIENTS: Dresdner Bank S.A. (Germany); Deutsche Bank S.A. (Germany); ABC Barkredit-Bank Berlin, Noris Bank (Germany); AEG Hellas S.A. (Greece); Giancarlo Ferre S.A. (Italy); Bauknecht S.A. (Germany); Spiegel KG (Germany); Unilever (Netherlands/USA); Bergo Montanus S.A. (Germany); Continental Tyres SA (Germany); Montanus Hellas SA. (Greece); Geestemunder Bank S.A. (Germany); Abigliamento Abruzzese (Italy); Agentur für Mitsegler (Switzerland); C & A S.A. (England & Germany); ENI SA (Italy); Albert Rene S.A.(France); Meggle Milch Union (Germany); Dargaüd S.A. (Paris); G. Plessl Editions (Germany); Gausepol S.A. (Netherlands); E.P.O., E.P.T./Peugeot (France); Fidia SPA (Italy); Helen Harper (USA/Germany/Italy); Inditex S.A. (Spain and Greece); Utong Holding; Austrotel.

LAW OFFICES OF MICHAEL G. PAPACONSTANTINOU

Established in 1955

10 LYCABETTUS STREET
106 71 ATHENS, GREECE
Telephone: (01) 3631535, 3619722, 3626368
Telex: 215356 EVMA GR
Telefax: (01) 3619168

Commercial, Company, Mergers and Acquisitions, Antitrust, European Community, Foreign Investments, Insurance, Real Estate, Banking, Finance, Labour, Taxation Law, Transport, Environment Law, Inheritance Law, Intellectual Property, Civil Litigation.

FIRM PROFILE: *The firm was established in 1955 in Thessaloniki, moved in 1970 to Athens and offers a full range of legal services. Over these years, it has serviced several international business concerns undertaking operations/envisaging ventures and/or involved in litigation in Greece. In recent years, it has focused on Mergers and Acquisitions, Company, Finance, Banking, Competition and European Community Law.*

MICHAEL G. PAPACONSTANTINOU, born Kozani, Greece, November 1, 1919; admitted, 1945, Thessaloniki; 1969, Athens. *Education:* Thessaloniki University Law School (LL.B.); Victoria University of Manchester; Cambridge University; Heidelberg University, West Germany. Author: "An Introduction to the Study of the Council of Europe"; "The Problem of Minorities"; "Aliens in International Law". *Member:* Thessaloniki and Athens Bar Associations; Parliament (Ex Minister of Foreign Affairs). *LANGUAGES:* English, French and German.

HELEN PAPACONSTANTINOU, born Thessaloniki, Greece, October 27, 1958; admitted, 1982, New York and Athens. *Education:* London School of Economics and Political Science (LL.B., 1979); Harvard Law School (LL.M., 1980); Université Libre de Bruxelles (Ph.D., 1986). Author: "The Extraterritorial Effects of EEC Antitrust Laws," Cambridge, Massachusetts, 1981; "Is the Greek State Monopoly of Petrol Consistent with EEC Laws?" Economicos Tahidromos, 11.8.83; "Is the Greek Policy on Public Supplies Consistent with EEC Laws?" Economicos Tahidromos, 12.1.84 English Translation in Greece's Weekly, 10.3.84; "Greek Foreign Exchange Controls and Community Law," Economicos Tahidromos, 14.-6.84; "Is the Campaign 'Insist Greek' Consistent with EEC Law?" Economicos Tahidromos, 9.8.84; "Is it Possible to Safeguard National Interests without Contravening EEC Law?" Economicos Tahidromos, 26.12.85; "Free Trade and Competition in the EEC: Law, Policy and Practice," published by Routledge, 1988; "Mergers and Acquisitions in Europe," Chapter on Greek Law, Professional Publishing Ltd., 1990; "European Franchising," Chapter on Greek Law, Waterlaw Publishers. *Member:* Athens, New York State and American Bar Associations. *LANGUAGES:* English, French and German. *PRACTICE AREAS:* Mergers and Acquisitions; Company; Antitrust; Finance; Insurance; Intellectual Property; European Community Law; Taxation; Banking.

DIMITRIOS N. PITTEROS, born Nafplio, Greece, February 25, 1958; admitted, 1983, Athens. *Education:* Athens University Law School (LL.B., 1981). *Member:* Athens Bar Association. *LANGUAGES:* English. *PRACTICE AREAS:* Company; Real Estate; Labor; Social Security; Taxation; Civil Litigation.

MARINA PAPACONSTANTINOU, born Thessaloniki, Greece, June 23, 1960; admitted, 1987, Athens. *Education:* Pantios School of Political Science (B.A., 1983); Thrace University Law School (LL.B., 1985). *Member:* Athens Bar Association. *LANGUAGES:* English and French. *PRACTICE AREAS:* Company; Labor; Real Estate; Civil Litigation; EEC Law.

GEORGE RISVAS, born Athens, Greece, May 5, 1966; admitted, 1990, Athens. *Education:* Athens University Law School (LL.B., 1987); Strasbourg University Law School (D.E.A., 1990). Author: "La libre circulation des activites bancaires a l'intérieur de la C.E.E." Strasbourg, 1989. *Member:* Athens Bar Association. *LANGUAGES:* French, English, German and Spanish. *PRACTICE AREAS:* Company; Banking; Insurance; Antitrust; Environment Law; EEC Law.

STATHIS BRAOUZIS, born Athens, Greece, May 12, 1966; admitted, 1992, Athens. *Education:* Athens University Law School (LL.B., 1989). *Member:* Athens Bar Association. *LANGUAGES:* English and German. *PRACTICE AREAS:* Company; Real Estate; Criminal; Taxation; Civil Litigation; Social Security.

Languages: English, French, German and Spanish.

(This Listing Continued)

LAW OFFICES OF MICHAEL G. PAPACONSTANTINOU, Athens—Continued

REPRESENTATIVE CLIENTS: Careal Holding S.A., Switzerland; Inchcape PLC, England; Swarovski International A.G., Switzerland; Spa, Italy; DSM Resins B.V., Netherlands; Elopak S.A., Norway; Banque de Paris et des Pays-Bas, Belgium; Antec International S.A., England; Toyota Hellas S.A.; Gellatly Morphy S.A.; Unicot S.A.; Avionic S.A.; Antec Hellas S.A.; Ellkat S.A.; Bain Clarkson SA.;

REFERENCES: Simmons & Simmons, London; Philips, Nizer, Benjamin, Krim & Ballon, N.Y.; George Ioannides, Attorney at Law, Washington, D.C.; American Embassy, Greece; International Chamber of Commerce, Paris; Athens Chamber of Commerce; Federation of Greek Industries; Piraeus Chamber of Commerce; Thessoloniki Chamber of Commerce; Office in Greece of the Commission of the European Communities.

PATRINOS & KILIMIRIS

Established in 1919

38, YPSILANTOU STREET
ATHENS 11521, GREECE
Telephone: 01-722.29.06; 01-724.83.47
Facsimile: 01-722.28.89
Telex: 22 23 01 ANTA GR

Commercial Law including Patent, Trademark, Unfair Competition Law, Corporate Law, Civil, Copyright, Private International, Labor and Tax Law.

FIRM PROFILE: Established in 1919 by E. Patrinos, the firm is one of the leading law firms in Greece. The firm actively practices in all sectors of Commercial Law, with a primary focus on Intellectual Property protection. More specifically the firm provides services on filing, prosecution and litigation of all kinds of Patents (Chemical, Pharmaceutical, Electronic, ect.) and Trademarks, Copyright Protection, Transfer of Technology, Plant Varieties, Licensing Negotiations and Arbitration.

The firm's lawyers have a great experience, both as litigators and legal consultants, in the field of Intellectual Property rights. The firm employs 14 technical assistants of very high level of expertise, covering all fields of science, all of which have a Ph.D. degree in their area of speciality, while many of them are professors at technical institutions and universities. Further fields of activity include Unfair Competition Law, Corporate Law, Civil, Copyright, Private International Law, Labor and Tax Law.

The firm's clients consist of both local and international companies and law firms. A substantial number of Patent and Trademark applications are filed annually both in Greece and abroad by Greek and foreign clients, e.g., General Electric Co., The Proctor and Gamble Co., 3M Co., Bristol-Myers Squibb Co., Mobil Oil Corp., The Gillette Co., ICI/Zeneca Ltd., Sumitomo Chemical Co. Ltd., Solvay SA, Aluminium Pechiney, L'Oréal SA, The Coca Cola Co., Nabisco Inc., Merck & Co Inc.

MEMBERS OF FIRM

TASSOS KILIMIRIS, born Andritsena Olympia, Greece, 1928; admitted, 1962, Athens Court of Appeals; 1970, Supreme Court of Greece and the Council of State. Education: University of Athens, Law School (LL.B.). Member: Athens Bar Association; European Patent Institute; ECTA; AIPPI; FICPI; AIPLA; PTI Canada; CPA London. LANGUAGES: Greek, English and Italian. PRACTICE AREAS: Intellectual Property; Acquisition and Distribution; Patent; Trademark; Licensing Negotiations; Arbitrations.

ANNA PATRINOS-KILIMIRIS, born Athens, Greece, 1934; admitted, 1968, Athens Court of Appeals; 1985, Supreme Court of Greece and the Council of State. Education: Supreme School of Political and Economic Sciences of Athens (Diploma); University of Thessaloniki, Law School (LL.B.). Member: Athens Bar Association; European Patent Institute; ECTA; AIPPI; FICPI; ITMA; UNION. LANGUAGES: Greek, English and French. PRACTICE AREAS: Intellectual Property; Licensing; Patent; Trademark.

ASSOCIATES

CONSTANTINOS KILIMIRIS, born Athens, Greece, 1967; admitted, 1992, Athens. Education: University of Athens, Law School (LL.B.); Université Libre de Bruxelles (M.Sc. in Environmental Studies). Member: Athens Bar Association; AIPPI. LANGUAGES: Greek, English, French and German. PRACTICE AREAS: Patents; Trademarks.

MARIA KILIMIRIS, born Athens, Greece, 1967; admitted, 1993, Athens. Education: University of Athens, Law School (LL.B.). Member:

(This Listing Continued)

Athens Bar Association; ECTA; AIPPI. LANGUAGES: Greek, English, French and Spanish. PRACTICE AREAS: Patent; Trademark.

DIMITRI SCHINAS, born Athens, Greece, 1933; admitted, 1966, Athens Court of Appeals and the Supreme Court of Greece. Education: University of Athens, Law School (LL.B.). Member: Athens Bar Association; European Patent Institute. LANGUAGES: Greek, English and French.

ANGELA SCHINAS-TSOKARI, born Athens, Greece, 1943; admitted, 1970, Athens Court of Appeals and Supreme Court of Greece. Education: University of Athens, Law School (LL.B.). Member: Athens Bar Association; European Patent Institute. LANGUAGES: Greek and French.

MARO GYZI, born Athens, Greece, 1949; admitted, 1975, Athens Court of Appeals and Supreme Court of Greece. Education: University of Athens, Law School (LL.B.). Member: Athens Bar Association; Greek Organization of Standardization; European Patent Institute. LANGUAGES: Greek, English and French.

JOHN CASSOUNIS, born Kalapodion Fthiotidos, Greece, 1927; admitted, 1965, Athens Court of Appeals and Supreme Court of Greece. Education: Supreme School of Political and Economic Sciences of Athens (Diploma); University of Thessaloniki, Law School (LL.B.). With, Ministry of Economics, Tax Office, 1955-1965. Member: Athens Bar Association. LANGUAGES: Greek and English.

COUNSEL

PROF. CONSTANTINOS ASPROGERAKAS-GRIVAS, born Athens, Greece, 1930; admitted, 1965, Athens Court of Appeals; 1972, Supreme Court of Greece and the Council of State. Education: University of Athens, Law School (LL.B.); University of Munich (J.D.). Lecturer, Law of Intellectual Property, University of Athens. Professor, Thrace University, Law School, 1980. LANGUAGES: Greek, French and German. PRACTICE AREAS: Intellectual Property; Licensing; Trademark.

REPRESENTATIVE CLIENTS: General Electric Co.; The Procter and Gamble Co.; 3M Co.; Bristol-Myers Squibb Co.; Mobil Oil Corp.; The Gillette Co.; Imperial Chemical Industries PLC; Aluminium Pechiney; Aluminium Suisse SA; Total SA; Nabisco Inc.; L'Oréal SA.; Glaxo Group Ltd.; The Coca Cola Co.; Fujisawa Pharmaceuticals Co., Ltd.; Toyota Motor Corp.; Rhome and Haas Co; The Clorox Co.; L'Air Liquide SA; ELF Atochem SA; Solvay SA; SANOFI; Dunlop Ltd.; Imperial Tobacco Ltd.; Sumitomo Chemical Co. Ltd.

DR. LEON D. PLEIONIS LAW OFFICE

Established in 1962

51 SOLONOS STREET
ATHENS 106 72, GREECE
Telephone: (01) 362-8521; 363-5756
Telefax: (01) 364-5807

Civil Litigation, Commercial, Commercial Property, Company, Debt Recovery, Bankruptcy and Insolvency, E.E.C., Family, Intellectual Property and Investments, Matrimonial, Mortgages, Notaries, Real Estate Purchase, Wills and Probate, Conflict of Laws.

FIRM PROFILE: The law office was established in 1962 and offers a full range of legal services. It is well known for its Civil, Commercial and Private International Law. This three persons law firm has a legal support staff of 4 consisting of paralegal personnel.

MEMBERS OF FIRM

DR. LEON D. PLEIONIS, born Lavrion, Greece, October 10, 1927; admitted, 1960, Greece. Education: Pantios University of Athens (B.Sc., 1951); Athens University (LL.B., 1954); London University College (LL.M., 1965); Athens University of Economics (Ph.D., 1969). Author: "The History of Greek Constitutions," 1963; "The Influence of the Rhodian Sea Law," 1968; "The Theory of Renvoi," 1969; "International Jurisdiction of the Greek Courts," 1971; "Adoption in Comparative and P.I. Law," 1979; "The European Lawyer," 1982. Member: Athens Bar Association; Commercial Law League of Athens; Greek Institute of International and Foreign Law; British Institute of International and Comparative Studies. PRACTICE AREAS: Conflict of Laws; EEC Law; Commercial Law; General Practice.

GEORGE RIGANIAS, born Athens, Greece, 1954; admitted, 1980, Greece. Education: Athens University (1978). PRACTICE AREAS: Family Law; Civil Litigation; General Practice.

GEORGE PAN. BARITIS, born Athens, Greece, September 23, 1961; admitted, 1991, Greece. Education: Athens University (1989). PRACTICE

(This Listing Continued)

AREAS: Debt Recovery; Investment Law; Mortgage Law; Wills; General Practice.

LEGAL SUPPORT PERSONNEL

KATERINA D. PLEIONIS, born Athens, Greece, November, 1967. *Education:* College of Economics (1989); American College of Greece (Degree, 1990). Financial Consultant.

Languages: Greek and English.

K. POLYZOGOPOULOS & PARTNER

Established in 1974

SKOUFA 60 A

106 80 ATHENS, GREECE

Telephone: 0030-1-3632 662

Fax: 0030-1-3645 757

Civil Law, Commercial Law, Intellectual Property Law, Banking Law, Trade Marks and Investment Law.

The firm is entitled to plead before the Greek Courts including the Greek Supreme Court.

FIRM PROFILE: The firm has two partners and two associates and provides a full range of legal services in civil law to its corporate and private, foreign and Greek clients.

It has also close cooperation with distinguished lawyers from the academic field in Athens and Thessaloniki, as well as with leading law firms in the main cities of Greece.

The firm is also a member of LOGOS, a group of law firms with associated offices throughout the EC.

KONSTANTINOS POLYZOGOPOULOS, born Athens, Greece, March 25, 1950; admitted, 1974, Athens. *Education:* University of Athens; University of Tuebingen, Germany, Post Graduate (Dr.iur., Civil Procedure); Max-Planck-Institut, Munich (Intellectual Property); Salzbug Seminar, American Law and Legal Institutions. Associate Professor of Law Faculty, University of Athens. Author: "Parteianhoerung und Parteivernehmung in ihrem gegenseitigen Verhaeltnis," thesis, Berlin, 1976; "Execution on Copyright," vol. I, Athens, 1987; "The Nationalisation of Companies," Epitheorissis Dimosiou Dikaiou 25 (1981), 309 ff.; "Copyright and Photocopy," NoB (Juridical Tribune) 1983, 1130 ff.; "The Protection of Software in Greece," ELKEPA 1987, 31 ff.; "Les mesures provisoires en procédure hellénique"; "Atti del colloquio internazionale tenuto a Milano," 1984, 55 ff. *Member:* Athens Bar Association; Association of Greek Proceduralists; ALAI (Greek sector); ELPA (Greek Automobile Club) President, National Appeal Court. *LANGUAGES:* German, French, English and Italian. *PRACTICE AREAS:* Civil Procedure; Intellectual Property; Commercial; Investment Law.

KATERINA PAPADOPOULOU, born Athens, Greece, March 10, 1955; admitted, 1981, Athens. *Education:* University of Athens; City Investment School of London; Athens College. Member, Chartered Institute of Bankers (London). *Member:* Athens Bar Association. *LANGUAGES:* English and Italian. *PRACTICE AREAS:* Civil Law; Banking Law.

SPYROS CATRAMIS, born Athens, Greece, August 13, 1960; admitted, 1990, Athens. *Education:* University of Athens; University of Grenoble II, France (Docteur en Droit, Trade Marks). Author: "Les Marques Notoires et de Haute Renommeé en Droit Grec et en Droit Francais," thesis, Grenoble, 1987. *LANGUAGES:* French and Italian. *PRACTICE AREAS:* Trade Mark; Civil Law.

ATHINA BALOMENOU-DIVARI, born Athens, Greece, February 10, 1966; admitted, 1990, Athens. *Education:* University of Athens. *Member:* Athens Bar Association. *LANGUAGES:* German and English. *PRACTICE AREAS:* Civil and Commercial Law.

I.K. ROKAS & PARTNERS LAW OFFICES

25 BOUKOURESTIOU ST. & SOUTSOU

ATHENS 106 71, GREECE

Telephone: (1) 3604618; 3612977; 3608116; 3605926; 3601878; 3609470; 3603992; 3619139; 3623343; 4121248; 4131734

Telefax: (1) 3604133; 4131734

Telex: 221983 IROK GR

Athens, Greece Office: 19 Boukourestiou st. & Valaoritou, 106 71.
Piraeus, Greece Office: 7-9 Akti Miaouli, 185 35.

(This Listing Continued)

FIRM PROFILE: Established in 1977, I. K. Rokas & Partners is one of the leading law firms in Greece. The founding partner, Professor Dr. I. K. Rokas, has been co-editor of the quarterly review entitled "Commercial Law Review" since 1981. The firm advises a wide range of both corporate and private clients, and has a broad network of connections throughout Greece and abroad. With a qualified staff of 17 attorneys and five legal support personnel, I. K. Rokas & Partners can conveniently and efficiently serve its clients.

The law firm, both as litigators and legal consultants, actively practices in all sectors of commercial law, with emphasis on insurance, corporate, maritime, industrial property, intellectual property, product liability, transport, international investments and transactions, telecommunications, and taxation law. It provides representation to its clients in major litigation cases, as well as in extra judicial settlement of disputes, and has a department which specializes in marine litigation. The firm also provides legal services for the establishment of enterprises, branch offices, and major mergers and acquisitions. Along with its associated offices in Thessaloniki and Eastern Europe, the firm is in the process of expanding its services to clients interested in investments in Eastern Europe, particularly the Balkans.

Further fields of activity involve criminal law, international commercial arbitration, labour, tax, patent, trademark and copyright, mining, product liability, environmental and real estate law.

MEMBERS OF FIRM

IOANNIS K. ROKAS, born Athens, Greece, December 1, 1945; admitted, 1971, Athens. *Education:* Athens University Law School (Diploma, 1968); University of Berlin (Dr. Jur., 1975). Author: "Summenver-sicherung und Schadensersatz," (Life Insurance and Indemnity); "Carriage of Goods by Road and Civil Liability"; "Introduction to Insurance Law," 3rd ed.; "Introduction to Maritime Law"; "Cases on Private Insurance Law"; "Introduction to Business Law"; "Greece: Insurance Law" (in English, entry for Kluwer Encyclopaedia of Insurance Law); "Greece: Practical Commercial Law" (in English); numerous articles. Associate Professor, Commercial and Business Law, Athens University for Economics and Business Sciences, 1990. Judge, Court of Appeal for Trademarks, 1987-1990. Editor and Publisher, Commercial Law Review (quarterly law review published in Athens since 1950). Correspondent for the German review "Versicherungsrecht," and the Belgian review, "European Transport Law." *Member:* Comité Maritime International (General Secretary, Greek Session); Association Internationale du droit des Assurances (Member, Board of Directors, Greek Session); Mediterranean Maritime Arbitration Association (Chairman, Legislation and Drafting Committees, Greek Commercial Code, Insurance Law, Patent Law). *LANGUAGES:* Greek, English, German and French. *PRACTICE AREAS:* General Commercial Law; Insurance Law; Environmental Law; Admiralty and Maritime Law.

ALKISTIS CHRISTOFILOU, born Athens, Greece, August 1, 1961; admitted, 1986, Athens. *Education:* University of Athens Law School (Diploma, 1984); London School of Economics and Political Science (LL.M., 1986). Author: "Remedies for foreign sellers of goods, Greece,Sweet & Maxwell," 1993; "Greek Insurance Law" (in Longman's International Insurance Law), 1994. Lecturer, Company and Business Law, Chartered Institute of Management Accountants. *Member:* International Bar Association. *LANGUAGES:* Greek, English, German and French. *PRACTICE AREAS:* Corporate Law; Business Law; Mergers and Acquisitions; Insurance Enterprise Law; Communications and Media Law.

ANASTASSIOS TSIRONIS, born Komotini, Greece, August 1, 1959; admitted, 1983, Athens. *Education:* University of Athens Law School (Diploma, 1981); University of Munich (Dr. Jur., 1988). Author: "Stoff-und Verfahrensschutz unter besonderer Berücksichtigung der Arzneimittelerfindung nach deutschem, griechischem und europäischem Patentrecht" (Product Protection or Process Protection for Chemical Inventions under German, Greek and European Patent Law) 1988; "Patents for Drugs," Commercial Law Review, 1990. *LANGUAGES:* Greek, English, German, French and Italian. *PRACTICE AREAS:* Intellectual Property Law; Patent Law; Transport Law.

MARIA DIMITROPOULOU, born Athens, Greece, December 3, 1963; admitted, 1988, Athens. *Education:* University of Athens Law School (Diploma, 1986). *LANGUAGES:* Greek, English and French. *PRACTICE AREAS:* Law of Transport by Land, Sea and Air.

STELIOS PAPAGEORGIOU-GONATAS, born Athens, Greece, October 21, 1958; admitted, 1985, Athens. *Education:* University of Athens Law School (Diploma, 1980); University of Munich (Dr. Jur., 1988). Author: "Wo liegt die Grenze zwischen Vorbereitungshandlung und Versuch?," (The distinction between preparatory act and attempt); "Should the unsuitable

(This Listing Continued)

I.K. ROKAS & PARTNERS LAW OFFICES, Athens— Continued

attempt be sanctioned?," Nomiko Vema, 1988; "Unlawful indirect means of proof in Penal Law," Nomiko Vema, 1989; "The Right of the Accused to remain silent," Poinika Chronika 3/1990. *LANGUAGES:* Greek, English, German, French and Italian. *PRACTICE AREAS:* Criminal Law.

ELIAS KONSTANTOPOULOS, born Athens, Greece, October 6, 1963; admitted, 1990, Athens. *Education:* University of Athens Law School (Diploma, 1987). *LANGUAGES:* Greek, English. *PRACTICE AREAS:* Litigation; Civil Law; Commercial Law.

CHRISTOS THEODOROU, admitted, 1987, Athens.

TEFTA KYRIAKOU, admitted, 1991, Athens.

CARLOTTA KOUTSOMITOPOULOU, admitted, 1986, Athens.

EPAMINONDAS TSANDIS, admitted, 1986, Athens.

EVANGELIA ATHANASSIOUR, admitted, 1992, Athens.

MICHALIS PANAGOPOULOS, admitted, 1990, Athens.

SOLOMONI PARALIDOU, admitted, 1992, Athens.

ELEFTHERIA KAMENOPOULOU, admitted, 1992, Athens.

PANTELIS PANTELIDAKIS, admitted, 1992, Athens.

PANAGIOTIS PANAGAKIS, admitted, 1989, Athens.

OF COUNSEL

STELIOS KOUSSOULIS, born Piraeus, Greece, July 27, 1959; admitted, 1984, Piraeus. *Education:* Athens University Law School (Diploma, 1982); University of Erlangen (Dr. Jur., 1986). Lecturer, Civil Procedure, University of Athens Law School. Author: "Beiträge zur modernen Rechtskraftlehre," (Doctoral thesis); "Intervention in Civil Procedure," 1987; "Legal nature of Res Judicata," 1988; "Modern Forms of written Communication - telefax-telex-electronic document," 1992; "Issues on the electronic Bill of Lading," 1992. Department Head, Legislative Support of the Scientific Service, Greek Parliament, 1988. *Member:* Greek Association for Civil Procedure; Greek Arbitration Association; German Arbitration Institute; German Association for Civil Procedure. *LANGUAGES:* Greek, German and English. *PRACTICE AREAS:* Civil Procedure; Alternative Dispute Resolution.

Languages: Greek, English, German, French, Italian and Spanish.

REPRESENTATIVE CLIENTS: General Construction S.A.; Stork PMT BV; Henninger S.A.; Fuji Film Hellas S.A.; Ciba Geigy Hellas S.A.; Roche Hellas S.A.; C. Rokas Industry of Transport & Lifting Equipment S.A.; Lamda Alfa Advertising S.A.; Ventouris Lines Ship Co.; Bodyline S.A.; Silhouette Ltd.; Miss Raxevsky (textile production and exports) S.A.; Holderbank Cement Industries; Aegean Terminals S.A.; Legion Telecommunications S.A.; G.A. Keranis Cigarettes S.A.; E.T.E.P. S.A.; Agrotiki Ins. Co.; Astir Ins. Co.; Eteva Ins. Co.; Commercial Ins. Co.; Phoenix Ins. Co.; The Yasuda Fire & Marine Ins. Co.; The Cigna Group; Nordstern Ins. Co.; VAG, Allianz Ins. Co.; Aachener & Münchener Group; Royal Ins. Co.; National Ins. Co.; National Capital Investment Co.; National Securities Brokers; Hellenic Bank for Industrial Development (Capital Markets Dept.).

ROMANOS & CHOIDAS

Established in 1973

3, ALEXANDROU SOUTSOU STREET
ATHENS 106 71, GREECE
Telephone: 362 0420; 361 7287; 362 3683
Telecopier: 362 9711

Civil, Commercial, Company, Banking, Shipping, Private International, Copyright, Trademark, Unfair Competition, Patent Law, Industrial Property, Administrative Law, Tax, Common Market and Family Law.

THEODORE CONSTANTINE CHOIDAS, born 1945; admitted, 1971, Athens. *Education:* University of Athens; University College, London. Barrister and Solicitor at the Supreme Court and the Council of State.

CATHERINA R. STAMOU, born 1945; admitted, 1971, Athens. *Education:* University of Athens; London School of Foreign Trade, London (Diploma in Maritime Law). Barrister and Solicitor at the Supreme Court and the Council of State. *Member:* Hellenic Union of Maritime Law.

THEOHARIS N. BLIATSOS, born 1962; admitted, 1986, Athens. *Education:* University of Athens; University College, London (LL.M., Commercial and Corporate Law). Barrister and Solicitor at the Court of Appeal.

(This Listing Continued)

JOANNA V. PETRAKAKI, born 1966; admitted, 1991, Athens. *Education:* University of Athens. Barrister and Solicitor.

COUNSEL

GEORGE ARISTIDES ROMANOS, born 1908; admitted, 1930, Athens. *Education:* Universities of Athens, Munich, Berlin, Paris and London. Barrister and Solicitor at the Supreme Court of Greece and the Council of State. Professor, Pantios School for Finance and Politics, 1938-1941. Member of Parliament, 1952-1956. Under Secretary of State in the Ministry of Coordination, 1954.

Languages: Greek, English and French.

SCANDAMIS c.s.

Established in 1975

8, AG. TRYFONOS STR.
145 10 KIFISSIA
P.O. BOX 51339
ATHENS, GREECE
Telephone: (30 1) 80.19.738; 80.19.649; 80.86.260
Telefax: (30 1) 80.83.508

EEC and Economic Law, Counselling and Litigation.

MEMBERS OF FIRM

NICOLAS SCANDAMIS, born Athens, Greece, 1943; admitted, 1970, Athens. *Education:* Athens University (LL.M., 1966); Columbia Law School (American Law, 1972); Paris University (Doctorat en Droit, 1973). Tax Counsel with ESSO Greece, 1973. Negotiator for Greece's accession to EEC, 1975. Director of the Commission of the European Communities, 1982-1988. Professor of EEC Law: Salonica University, 1982; Athens University, 1989.

ASSOCIATES

CONSTANTINE VRETTOS, born Athens, Greece, 1967; admitted, 1993, Athens. *Education:* Athens University (LL.B., 1991); University of Kent, Canterbury (LL.M., Int ernational Commercial Law, 1992).

TERINA RAPTI, born Athens, Greece, 1969; admitted, 1993, Athens. *Education:* Athens University (LL.B., 1991); University of Cambridge (LL.M., EEC Law, 1992).

ELENA YANNOPOULOU, born Patras, Greece, 1964; admitted, 1990, Athens. *Education:* Athens University (LL.B., 1987); Brussels ULB University (Licence Spéciale, EEC Law, 1989).

EVI ALIKANIOTOU, born Athens, 1963; admitted, 1988, Athens. *Education:* Athens University (LL.B., 1986); Brussels ULB University (Licence spéciale, EEC Law, 1987); Munich University (Magister, 1988).

DIONYSIA LAGIOU, born Athens, 1956; admitted, 1982, Athens. *Education:* Athens University (LL.B., 1979).

CHARIKLIA TZELLI, born Athens, 1962; admitted, 1989, Athens. *Education:* Salonica University (LL.B., 1986); Paris University (DEA, EEC Law, 1988).

Languages: Greek, English, French, German, Italian, Spanish, Portuguese and Russian.

REPRESENTATIVE CLIENTS: General Dynamics Corp.; Pratt & Whitney Aircraft Group; Siemens Allis Inc.; Lee Cooper Group Ltd.; Air Liquide International, Paris, Athens; Danish Dairy Board, Brussels; Sensormatic Electronics, Florida; MD Foods, Copenhagen.
REFERENCES: Coudert Brothers, Brussels, Paris; Bureau d'Etudes Fiscales et Juridiques Françis Lefebvre, Paris; Ackermann and Dr. D. Schultze Zeu, Berlin; De Smedt Dassesse & Akin, Gump, Strauss, Hauer Feld International, Brussels; Trèves International, Marseille; Cappelli e De Caterini, Rome.

SOURIADAKIS, FRANGAKIS & ASSOCIATES

Established in 1975

6, KRIEZOTOU STREET
ATHENS 106 71, GREECE
Telephone: 1-3626888; 1-3607320; 1-3613237
Telex: 219534 DAKO GR
Telefax: 1-3631631 SOFRALAW

Civil, Commercial, Corporate, Criminal, Administrative, Labor, Real Estate and Conveyancing, Inheritance, Banking and Finance, Insurance, Investments, Taxation, Shipping, Industrial Property, EEC Law, Conflict of Laws, Arbitration, General Practice and Litigation.

MEMBERS OF FIRM

JOHN SOURIADAKIS, born Ierapetra-Crete, August 5, 1927; admitted, 1955, Athens and Piraeus Court of Appeals and Supreme Court of Greece. *Education:* University of Athens Law School (Diploma, 1952); Institut des Hautes Etudes Internationales, University of Geneva (These). General Secretary, Ministry of Transport and Communication, 1974. Editor and President, Editorial Board of "The European Communities Review," 1980—. President, Board of Greek Center of European Studies and Research. *Member:* Athens Bar Association (Member of the Board, 1967, 1974 and 1976); Hellenic Society of International Law and Relations; Greek League on Human Rights (Vice-President). *LANGUAGES:* Greek, French and English. *PRACTICE AREAS:* Civil Law; Commercial Law; General Practice; Litigation; Investments.

NIKOS FRANGAKIS, born Athens, September 15, 1945; admitted, 1971, Athens and Piraeus Court of Appeals and Supreme Court of Greece. *Education:* University of Athens Law School (Diploma, 1968); Cambridge University (Extra-mural Studies on English Law); University of Amsterdam (Amsterdam-Leyden-Columbia Program of American Law). Head of Legal Service of the P.R. of Greece to the EEC, Brussels, 1986-1989. Author: "Elements of Labor Law," 1979, 3rd Edition, 1986; "Divorce Matters of Foreigners in Greece," 1973; "Internationally Protected Persons and Terrorism," 1974; "Enforcing Judgements of U.S. Courts in Greece," in *Enforcing Foreign Judgements in the U.S. and U.S. Judgements Abroad,* American Bar Association Section of International Law and Practice, Ronald A. Brand (Ed.) 1992; "Enlargement of the Community and the Consequences for the Implementation of Law," in *The European Union in the 1990's,* W. Wessels & C. Engel (Eds.), 1993; "Law Harmonization," in *Greece and EC Membership Evaluated,* Kazakos & Ioakimidis (Eds.), 1994; "The Court of First Instance of the E.C. and the Judicial Control after the Single European Act," 1990. Member of the Editorial Committee of the "European Communities Review," 1980—. *Member:* Athens Bar Association (Editor-in-Chief, "Legal Forum" official monthly Journal of the Athens Bar); European Commission against Racism and Intolerance (Strasbourg), Trans European Policy Studies Association (Brussels); Hellenic Society of Political Science; Hellenic Society of International Law and Relations (Treasurer, 1983-1987); Saltzbourg Seminar; European Lawyers Association; FIDE; Greek League on Human Rights (Secretary General); Greek Center of European Studies and Research (Director Gen., 1991—). *LANGUAGES:* Greek, English, French and Italian. *PRACTICE AREAS:* European Law; Corporate Law; Arbitration; International Business Law; Investments.

ASSOCIATES

POPI HITIROGLOU, born Athens, March 2, 1949; admitted, 1978, Athens Court of Appeals. *Education:* Athens University Law School (1976). *Member:* Athens Bar Association. *LANGUAGES:* Greek, English and Italian. *PRACTICE AREAS:* Criminal Law; Real Estate Law; Conveyancing; Inheritance.

MANOLIS SOURIADAKIS, born Athens, September 21, 1961; admitted, 1990, Athens Court of Appeals. *Education:* University of Athens Law School (Dpl). *Member:* Athens Bar Association. *LANGUAGES:* Greek, French and English. *PRACTICE AREAS:* Commercial Law; Banking Law; Finance; Insurance Law; Industrial Property Law.

NASSIA KAZANTZI, born Athens, June 29, 1967; admitted, 1993, Athens. *Education:* University of Athens Law School (Dpl., 1990); University of London (L.S.E., LL.M.). Author: "The Acquis parlementaire: On the Road to European Union." *Member:* Athens Bar Association. *LANGUAGES:* Greek, English and French. *PRACTICE AREAS:* European Community Law; Administrative Law; Taxation.

HARA SAOUNATSOU, born Athens, September 17, 1967; admitted, 1992, Athens. *Education:* University of Athens Law School (Dpl., 1990);

(This Listing Continued)

University of London (U.C.L., LL.M.). *Member:* Athens Bar Association. *LANGUAGES:* Greek, English and French. *PRACTICE AREAS:* European Community Law; Company Law.

STAVROPOULOS, TSIRI & PAPADOPOULOU, LAW OFFICE

7, VALAORITOU STR.
ATHENS 10671, GREECE
Telephone: 3634107; 3634262; 3610817
Fax: 3633204

Taxation, Company Law, Mergers and Acquisitions, Industrial and Intellectual Property, Anti-Trust, Banking, European Community Law, Computer Law, Civil Law, Administrative law, Real Estate, Foreign Investments.

MEMBERS OF FIRM

IOANNIS F. STAVROPOULOS, admitted, 1986, Athens. *Education:* University of Athens Law School (LL.B.); University of Kent, Canterbury, U.K. (LL.M., 1985); Greek Productivity Center (14th Taxation Seminar, 1987). *Member:* Athens Bar Association; AIJA; Greek Computer Society; Hellenic Association for European Studies; American Hellenic Chamber of Commerce. *LANGUAGES:* Greek and English. *PRACTICE AREAS:* Taxation Law; Mergers and Acquisitions; Company Law; Computer Law.

EVANTHIA V. TSIRI, admitted, 1981, Athens. *Education:* University of Athens Law School (LL.B.); College of Europe, Burges, Belgium (Certificat de Hautes Etudes Européenes, 1982); Free University of Brussels, Belgium (License Spéciale en Droit Européen, 1983). Stage with the Commission of the European Communities, Internal Market and Industrial Affairs, 1983. *Member:* Athens Bar Association; International Association of Lawyers; American Hellenic Chamber of Commerce; French Hellenic Chamber of Commerce; Hellenic Association for European Studies. *LANGUAGES:* Greek, English and French. *PRACTICE AREAS:* Banking Law; Mergers and Acquisitions; Company Law; Commercial Law.

MARIA D. PAPADOPOULOU, admitted, 1986, Athens. *Education:* University of Athens Law School (LL.B.); University of London, London School of Economics and Political Science, Law School (LL.M., 1985). *Member:* Athens Bar Association; American Hellenic Chamber of Commerce; French Hellenic Chamber of Commerce; German Hellenic Chamber of Commerce. *LANGUAGES:* Greek, English, French and German. *PRACTICE AREAS:* Company Law; Mergers and Acquisitions; Industrial and Intellectual Property Law; Anti-Trust Law; European Community Law.

ELENI D. SOULI, admitted, 1993, Athens. *Education:* University of Athens Law School (LL.B.). *Member:* Athens Bar Association. *LANGUAGES:* Greek, English and French. *PRACTICE AREAS:* Civil Law; Administrative Law; Taxation; Environmental Law; Real Estate; Corporate and Company Law.

ELISABETH F. RAZI, admitted, 1993, Athens. *Education:* University of Paris, Paris II-Assas (Maitrise); University of Paris, Paris I, Pantheon Sorbonne (DEA, 1990). *Member:* Athens Bar Association. *LANGUAGES:* Greek, French, English and Spanish. *PRACTICE AREAS:* International Economic Law; European Community Law; Corporate and Company Law; Foreign Investments; International Contracts.

REPRESENTATIVE CLIENTS: Lafarge Coppée S.A.; Du Pont De Nemours International S.A.; Heineken Technical Services B.V.; Thorn EMI Business Communication Ltd.; Amstel International B.V.; Louis Vuitton Hellas S.C.A.; Intergraph Hellas S.A.; Athenian Brewery S.A.; Metrobus S.A.; Sulzer Hellas S.A.; Black & Decker Hellas S.A.; Chaine & Trame Hellas S.A.; Cretabank S.A.; Mallinckrodt Veterinary S.A.
REFERENCES: Euro-American Lawyers Group; Administration Offices: Centurion House, Deansgate, Manchester, M3 3WT, England; Leboeuf, Lamb, Greene & Macrae, California, U.S.A.; Penningtons, London, U.K.

TSECOURAS, COCALIS & ASSOCIATES

Established in 1913

15 ACADEMIAS STREET
ATHENS 106 71, GREECE
Telephone: (01) 3613661, 3627190
Telex: 221915 BATS GR
Facsimile: (01) 3641258

Corporate, Contract, Commercial, Foreign Investment, Banking, Trademark, Fiscal, Patent, Insurance and Franchise Law.

(This Listing Continued)

TSECOURAS, COCALIS & ASSOCIATES, Athens—Continued

FIRM PROFILE: The firm has concentrated on corporate clients, since the early years of this century. The original driving force, the late Greek Minister of Foreign Affairs John Sofianopoulos, together with Nicholas Tsecouras, not only made the firm one of the most important ones in the early days of Greek industry, but also gave it an international scope. From the early 1960's the firm has been active in international trade, oil trading and the insurance business. From the mid 1970's, it has been active with foreign investment, mergers and acquisitions. Since the late 1980's, the firm has acquired considerable experience in dealing with the former Soviet Union and East European countries neighbouring to Greece. The firm has been retained by the public sector for several important projects, including the natural gas contracts between Greece-former Soviet Union and Greece-Algeria. The client base, besides local corporations, is mainly Western European, North American and Japanese.

JOHN A. SOFIANOPOULOS (1893-1953).

NICHOLAS B. TSECOURAS (1901-1963).

MEMBERS OF FIRM

BASIL N. TSECOURAS, born Athens, Greece, November 3, 1935; admitted, 1963, Court of First Instance; 1967, Court of Appeal; 1974, Supreme Court of Greece. Education: Athens University Law School (Law Degree). Consultant to the Minister of Commerce, 1985. Member: Athens Bar Association. LANGUAGES: Greek, English, French, German and Italian. PRACTICE AREAS: Oil, Natural Gas and Mining; Banking; Fiscal; Contract; Investments in Eastern Europe.

DIMITRI N. COCALIS, born Athens, Greece, February 1, 1951; admitted, 1977, Court of First Instance; 1981, Court of Appeal; 1988, Supreme Courts of Greece. Education: University of Thessaloniki, Law School (Law Degree). Consultant to the Minister of Commerce, 1985. Member: Athens Bar Association. LANGUAGES: Greek, English and French. PRACTICE AREAS: Corporate; Contract; Commercial; Foreign Investment; Mergers and Acquisitions; Securities; Fiscal; Competition; Trademark; Arbitration.

ASSOCIATES

ALKIVIADIS CONSTANTINOS PSARRAS, born Athens, Greece, January 25, 1964; admitted, 1989, Greece. Education: University of Athens, Law School (Law Degree, 1986); University of Kent, Canterbury, UK (LL.M, 1988; Ph.D., 1994). Author: "Towards the New Trade Marks Law," Liakopoulos Th. Sakoulas, Athens 1991; "The Protection of the Fame of Persons and Works of the Intellect," Character and Personality Merchandising, Commercial Law Review, p. 345, 1993. Member: Athens Bar Association. LANGUAGES: Greek and English. PRACTICE AREAS: Intellectual Property Law; Competition Law; Commercial Law.

NAYA C. RAXI, born Karditsa, Greece, June 29, 1963; admitted, 1988, Greece. Education: University of Athens, Law School (Law Degree, 1986). Member: Athens Bar Association. LANGUAGES: Greek, English, French and German. PRACTICE AREAS: Civil Law; Commercial Law; Company Law.

ANGELIKI IOANNIDOU, born Athens, Greece, April 11, 1968; admitted, 1994, Greece. Education: University of Athens, Law School (Law Degree, 1992); University College London (UCL), London, UK (LL.M., 1993). Member: Athens Bar Association. LANGUAGES: Greek and English. PRACTICE AREAS: Intellectual Property Law; EEC Competition Law; Commercial Law.

Languages: Greek, English, French, German, Italian and Spanish.

REPRESENTATIVE CLIENTS: Ionian Bank Group; SaraLee/DE; Akzo Pharma; Econ Industries Group; Bank of Crete; Fiat Auto Hellas; Artisti Italiani; Bergendhal & Son AB; Inco Hellas; Club Méditeranée; Intergross.

EU844B

LAW OFFICES
VAINANIDIS, SCHINA & ECONOMOU

Established in 1987

5 AKADIMIAS STREET
10671 ATHENS, GREECE
Telephone: 01.36.34.287, 36.43.846, 36.35.824
Fax: 01.36.04.611

European Community Law, Commercial Law, Corporate Law, Antitrust Law, Patent and Trademark Law, Banking and Insurance Law, Law of Succession.

FIRM PROFILE: The client base is European and North American in scope. The firm is a member of "The Association," a network of European law firms. It consists of four partners, four associates and supporting personnel.

MEMBERS OF FIRM

COSTAS VAINANIDIS, born Athens, 1950; admitted, 1976, Greece; 1984, Supreme Court. Education: University of Athens, Faculty of Laws (LL.B.), Faculty of Public Law & Political Sciences (B.Sc.), London University (LL.M.). Correspondent and Member Editorial Advisory Board of the European Competition Law Review (ESC Publishing Ltd). Co-Contributor with Dr. Schina and Dr. Economou to "Corporate Acquisitions and Mergers Greece" (Graham & Trotman, 1990). Contributor: "The Practitioners Guide to European Corporate Insolvency" (Westminster Management Consultant Ltd. 1992); Handbook of European Company Law" (on print, Sweet & Maxwell). Member: Athens Bar Association; International Bar Association. LANGUAGES: Greek and English. PRACTICE AREAS: Litigation; Antitrust Law; Franchise Law; Commercial Law; Corporate Law; Real Estate Law; Mergers and Acquisitions.

DR. DESPINA SCHINA, born Athens, 1955; admitted, 1980, Greece. Education: University of Athens, Faculty of Laws (LL.B. mark: excellent); London University (LL.M.), Ph.D. on "State Aids under EEC law"). Author: "State Aids under the EEC Treaty, Art. 92-94" (ESC Publishing Ltd. 1987). Member, Editorial Advisory Board and Contributor to the European Business Law Review (Graham & Trotman, 1990). Contributor: "The Second Banking Directive" (Butterworths, 1991); "Managing Capital Adequacy" (Woodhead Faulkner Ltd. 1991). Member, Legal Service of the Bank of Greece, 1984—. Member: Athens Bar Association; International Bar Association. LANGUAGES: Greek, English and French. PRACTICE AREAS: Foreign Investment Law; Banking Law; Commercial Law; Corporate Law.

DR. AIDA ECONOMOU, born Athens, 1960; admitted, 1984, Greece. Education: University of Athens, Faculty of Laws (LL.B. mark: excellent), London University (LL.M mark of distinction), (Ph.D on "The Common Market in Insurance Services"). Member: Athens Bar Association; International Bar Association. LANGUAGES: Greek, English and French. PRACTICE AREAS: Foreign Investment Law; Insurance Law; Litigation; Commercial Law; Corporate Law; Mergers and Acquisitions.

ANNITA VAINANIDIS, born Athens, 1951; admitted, 1975, Greece; 1983, Supreme Court. Education: University of Athens, Faculty of Law (LL.B.). LANGUAGES: Greek and English. PRACTICE AREAS: Litigation; Corporate Law; Labour Law; Commercial Law.

MENIA TSOUMAKI-KYRIAKOPOULOU, born Athens, 1939; admitted, 1965, Greece, 1975, Supreme Court. Education: University of Athens, Faculty of Laws (LL.B.). LANGUAGES: Greek and English. PRACTICE AREAS: Litigation; Corporate Law; Commercial Law.

GEORGE KYRIAKOPOULOS, born Athens, 1966; admitted, 1991, Greece. Education: University of Athens, Faculty of Laws (LL.B.); London University (LL.M.). LANGUAGES: Greek and English. PRACTICE AREAS: Trademark Law; Patent Law; Computer Law; Litigation; Commercial Law.

ANGELIKI POURNARA, born Athens, 1967; admitted, 1991, Greece. Education: University of Athens, Faculty of Laws (LL.B.); Bristol University (LL.M.). LANGUAGES: Greek, French and English. PRACTICE AREAS: Antitrust Law; Commercial Law; Customs Union; Insurance Law.

HELENA VARVAYANNIS, born Athens, 1966; admitted, 1992, Greece. Education: University of Athens, Faculty of Laws (LL.B.); Univer-

(This Listing Continued)

sity of Kent at Canterbury, U.K. (LL.M.). *LANGUAGES:* Greek and English. *PRACTICE AREAS:* EEC Law; Intellectual Property Law; International Business Transactions.

VARDIKOS & VARDIKOS

Attorneys and Counselors at Law, Tax Consultants

Established in 1888

(Formerly Varvoglis & Plantzas Law Offices)

3 MAVROMICHALI STREET
ATHENS 106 79, GREECE
Telephone: (01) 3627854; 3611505
Fax: (01) 3617848

Canada Representative Office: Michael Pandev & Ass. 84 Rue Notre-Dame O, Suite 600, Montreal H2Y 1S6, Quebec, Canada. Telephone: (514) 287-3557. Fax: (514) 285-8589.

Corporate, Commercial, Mergers and Acquisitions, Labor, Tax (Tax Planning, Accounting and Offshore Services), Banking, Finance, Shipping, E.E.C., Insurance, Civil (Inheritance, Family, Products Liability), Administrative, Public, Property and Real Estate Law, Foreign Investments in Greece, International and Public Sector Transactions, General Practice.

ANASTASSIOS P. VARVOGLIS, SR. (1853-1932).

IOANNIS A. PLANTZAS, SR. (1881-1950).

ATHANASSIOS I. PLANTZAS (1918-1944).

MEMBERS OF FIRM

THEODOROS CH. VARDIKOS, born 1926; admitted, 1958, Athens; 1966, Supreme Court of Athens. *Education:* University of Athens Law School (LL.B., 1956). Legal Counselor, Municipality of Taurus, Athens, 1964—. *Member:* Athens Bar Association. *LANGUAGES:* Greek and English. *PRACTICE AREAS:* Corporate Law; Commercial Law; Administrative Law; Public Law; Civil Law; Immigration and Naturalization.

MARIA PLANTZA-VARDIKOS, born 1926; admitted, 1955, Athens; 1966, Supreme Court of Athens. *Education:* University of Athens Law School (LL.B., 1953). *Member:* Athens Bar Association. *LANGUAGES:* Greek, English and French. *PRACTICE AREAS:* Property Law; Real Estate Law; Civil Practice; Inheritance Law; Family Law; Labour Law.

CHRISTOS TH. VARDIKOS, born 1966; admitted, 1991, Athens. *Education:* University of Rouen (Maitrise en Droit Prive avec mention); University of Paris I Panthéon-Sorbonne (D.E.A. Droit des Affaires; Specialized in North American and English Business Law). *Member:* Athens Bar Association. *LANGUAGES:* Greek, English and French. *PRACTICE AREAS:* Shipping Law; Finance Law; Taxation Law; Foreign Investment Law; EEC Law; Corporate Law; Securities; Debt Recovery.

FRANCOIS ANTOINE CADET, (Not admitted in Greece). *Education:* University of Saarbrucken, Germany (Maitrise en droit des affaires et droit international, DESS droit du commerce exterieur, 1991); University of Paris I Pantheon-Sorbonne. *LANGUAGES:* French, German, English and Italian. *PRACTICE AREAS:* International Trade Arbitration; Contracts; Franchising; Intellectual Property; Patents.

SPECIAL TAX COUNSEL

GEORGE CH. VARDIKOS, born 1932; (Not admitted in Greece). *Education:* University of Athens Highest School of Economic and Commercial Studies of Athens (LL.B.); University of Thessaloniki Law School (LL.B.). Ministry, National Economy, 1964-1988. Director, Corporate Tax Division, 1986. Specialist, Tax Law, Tax Practice and Accounting. Advisor, Corporate Tax, Finance and Investment. Former Member, Athens Bar Association. *PRACTICE AREAS:* Taxation Law; Corporate Tax Law; Tax Practice and Accounting; Estate Planning.

VAROTSOS & VAROTSOS

Established in 1932

45 SOLONOS STR.
GR 106 72 ATHENS, GREECE
Telephone: (01) 361.9429; 363.4989; 360.6855
Telex: 218876 VARO GR
Telefax: (01) 360.2679

Corporate, Commercial and Competition, Business, Mergers and Acquisitions, Shipping, Investments and Banking, Labour, Civil, Administrative, International Private Law, Transport, Insurance, Public Works, Law of Intellectual Property and Computers, Real Estate and Construction, Law of the European Communities, Tax, Gas and Oil Law, Criminal Law and Litigation.

ALEXIOS J. VAROTSOS (1932-1984).

YANNIS A. VAROTSOS, born Athens, Greece, 1945; admitted, 1970, Athens, Athens Court of Appeals, Supreme Court and Conseil d'Etat. *Education:* Athens University Law School (LL.B.); School of Political and Economic Sciences, Paris University II (Diplôme d'Etudes Supérieures, D.E.S.); Salzburg Seminar in American Studies (Fellow, 1984). *Member:* Athens Bar Association; Commercial Law Association; Labour and Social Security Law Association. *LANGUAGES:* Greek, English, German and French. *PRACTICE AREAS:* Corporate Law; Commercial Law; Competition Law; Business Law; Mergers and Acquisitions; Investment Law; Banking Law; Labour Law; Administrative Law; Private International Law; Public Works and Supplies; Intellectual Property; Computer Law; European Communities Law.

MICHAEL A. VAROTSOS, born Athens, Greece, 1953; admitted, 1978, Athens, Athens Court of Appeals, Supreme Court and Conseil d'Etat. *Education:* Athens University School of Law (LL.B.); London School of Economics and Political Science (LL.M.). President, Rotary Club of Athens-North. *Member:* Athens Bar Association; Hellenic Association of European Studies (President). *LANGUAGES:* Greek, English and French. *PRACTICE AREAS:* Commercial Law; Shipping Law; Corporate Law; European Law; Labour Law; Civil Law; Gas and Oil Law; Transport Law; Insurance Law; Mergers and Acquisitions; Real Estate Law; Construction Law; Criminal Law; Litigation.

IOANNA M. MORALI, born Athens, Greece, 1950; admitted, 1975, Athens, Athens Court of Appeals. *Education:* Athens University Law School (LL.B.). *Member:* Athens Bar Association. *LANGUAGES:* Greek, English and French. *PRACTICE AREAS:* Civil Law; Labour Law; Real Estate Law; Construction Law; Gas and Oil Law.

DIMITRIOS TSIKRIKAS, born 1961; admitted, 1987, Athens, Athens Court of Appeals. *Education:* Athens University Law School (LL.B.); Constance University Law School (F.R.G.; Doctor Juris). *Member:* Athens Bar Association; Procedure Law Association, Institute for Procedure Law Studies. *LANGUAGES:* Greek, German and French. *PRACTICE AREAS:* Civil Law; Private International Law; Insurance Law; European Community Law; Litigation; Arbitration; European Court Litigation.

PANAGIOTIS SOTIROPOULOS, born Athens, Greece, 1966; admitted, 1994, Athens, Athens Court of First Instance. *Education:* Athens University School of Law (LL.B.); Southampton University of Great Britain (LL.M.). *Member:* Athens Bar Association. *LANGUAGES:* Greek, English and Italian. *PRACTICE AREAS:* Shipping Law; Civil Law; Corporate Law; Commercial Law; Litigation.

ELENI KARIOFILLI, born Velos, Corinth, Greece, 1968; admitted, 1993, Athens, Athens Court of First Instance. *Education:* Athens University School of Law (LL.B.); McGill University of Canada (LL.M.). *Member:* Athens Bar Association. *LANGUAGES:* Greek, English and French. *PRACTICE AREAS:* Civil Law; Communications Law; Shipping Law; European Community Law; Commercial Law; Litigation.

GEORGE STAVRIDIS, born Paris, France, 1955; admitted, 1984, Athens, Athens Court of Appeals. *Education:* Athens University, School of Laws (LL.B.). *Member:* Athens Bar Association. *LANGUAGES:* Greek, English, French and German. *PRACTICE AREAS:* Civil Law; Commercial Law; Motor Insurance Law; Litigation.

(This Listing Continued)

VAROTSOS & VAROTSOS, Athens—Continued

OF COUNSEL

ANASTASIOS A. PANAGIOTOPOULOS, born Athens, Greece, 1940; admitted, 1967, Athens, Athens Court of Appeals, Supreme Court and Conseil d'Etat. *Education:* Athens University Law School (LL.B.). *LANGUAGES:* Greek, English and French. *PRACTICE AREAS:* Administrative Law; Tax Law; Gas and Oil Law; Corporate Law.

REPRESENTATIVE CLIENTS: Oracle Hellas S.A. (Subsidiary of ORACLE Corporation, Belmond, California, USA); Lummus International Inc.; Texaco Hellas S.A.; Texaco Fuel & Marine Marketing Inc.; Shell Company Hellas Ltd.; AEG Aktiengesellschaft; AEG Hellas S.A.; Friesland Hellas S.A.C.I. (Subsidiary of FRICO DOMO, Netherlands); C. Van Heezik B.V.; Militzer und Munch International Spedition; United Marine Services (London); Hanwa Engineering & Running Repair Co. Ltd. (Japan); Nippon Trading Co. Ltd. (Japan); Global Shipping S.p.A. (Treviso, Venice, Italy).
REFERENCES: Oracle Hellas S.A.; Lummus International Inc.; AEG Aktiengesellschaft; Texaco Hellas S.A.; Friesland Hellas S.A.C.I.; Shell Company Hellas Ltd.

VGENOPOULOS & PARTNERS

Established in 1983

15 KOLONAKI SQUARE
ATHENS 106 73, GREECE
Telephone: 01-7221 832; 7220 149
Fax: 01-7231 462
Telex: 217493 LOAV GR

Piraeus, Greece Office: 96-98 Filonos Street, Piraeus 185 36. Telephone: 01-4294 095-6; 4293 980-1. Telex: 241389 LOAV GR. Fax: 01-4294 045.
Thessaloniki, Greece Office: 3, Nikis Avenue, Thessaloniki 546 24. Telephone: 031-271 056. Telex: 419379 LOAV GR. Fax: 031-220 703.
London, England Office: 6, Minories (3rd floor), London EC3N 1BJ. Telephone: 071-4880 210. Telex: 269449 LOAV G. Fax: 071-4812 614.
Nicosia, Cyprus Office: Hawaii Nicosia Tower, 41 Th. Dervis Street, Flat No 807, Nicosia. Telephone: 02-458 244, 365 546. Telex: 5713 LOAV CY. Fax: 02-458 277.
Valletta, Malta Office: 18/2 South Street, Valletta. Telephone: 0356-236 206, 238 256. Telex: 1079 DINGCO MW. Fax: 0356-240 321.
Moscow, Russia Office: 9B, Dmitrovskoye chaussee, Moscow 127 434. Telephone: 095-976 8967; 095-976 4722. Fax: 095-976 2478.

Investment and Banking, Corporate Law, Mergers and Acquisitions, Aviation, Trade Marks, Intellectual Property, Commercial and Civil Law (general), EEC Law, Marine Law (Charter-Party Disputes, Marine Insurance, Salvage) Shipping Finance, Vessels' Sale and Purchase, Litigation.

FIRM PROFILE: The firm was established in 1983 and it now comprises 43 lawyers working in Athens, Piraeus and the other representative and associate offices. The firm is also supported by the appropriate administrative personnel. It offers a wide range of legal services domestically and internationally in the fields of Investment and Banking, Corporate, Commercial, Litigation and Shipping and Shipping Finance.

The firm has also established associate offices in Thessaloniki, Greece, Nicosia, Cyprus, Valletta, Malta and Moscow, Russia, which handle the cases of the firm's clients under their respective jurisdictions, and an office in London which functions mainly as a representative office.

ANDREAS E. VGENOPOULOS, admitted, 1981, Athens.

LOUKAS ROUFOS-KANAKARIS, admitted, 1976, Athens.

ELIANA PASCHALIDES, admitted, 1979, Athens.

ALEXANDRA TATAGIA, admitted, 1984, Athens.

ATHINA ZOULOU, admitted, 1984, Piraeus.

NIKOS DAMIGOS, admitted, 1981, Piraeus.

JOHN PAPAPETROS, admitted, 1984, Athens.

MILTO PAPANGELIS, admitted, 1986, Piraeus.

STEPHANOS KARAISKAKIS, admitted, 1982, Athens.

RANIA PAPANASTASIOU, admitted, 1977, Athens.

CALLIOPE METAXOTOU, admitted, 1973, Athens.

ALEXANDROS KALANTZIS, admitted, 1978, Athens.

IOANNA ANASTASSOPOULOU, admitted, 1981, Athens.

(This Listing Continued)

HELEN WARREN-KALAIDOPOULOS, admitted, 1981, Athens.

SOTIRIS KIPOUROPOULOS, admitted, 1985, Athens.

LAOURA LIMBEROPOULOU, admitted, 1985, Athens.

EFSTRATIOS PASCHALIDIS, admitted, 1990, Athens.

STERIOS ANASTASSIADIS, admitted, 1990, Athens.

GEORGE IATRIDIS, admitted, 1989, Piraeus.

MARIA LOUISA HIMARIOU, admitted, 1989, Athens.

ROSEMARY RONTIRI, admitted, 1985, Athens.

MARIA MALEVITI, admitted, 1992, Athens.

VICTORIA POSIOPOULOU, admitted, 1991, Athens and Solicitor of the Supreme Court of Judicature in England and Wales, 1991.

PANOS VENETIS, admitted, 1990, Piraeus.

DENISE NERI, admitted, 1991, Athens.

VASSILIOS CONSTANTES, admitted, 1992, Athens.

KYRIAKOS SPOULLOS, admitted, 1992, Athens.

MICHAEL SERGAKIS, admitted, 1990, Athens.

ALEXANDRA STAVROPOULOU, admitted, 1993, Piraeus.

ALEXIA KATSIAVOU, admitted, 1993, Athens.

Languages: Greek, English, French, German, Italian and Russian

VOSEMBERG-VRETOS

AEGIALIAS 30
PARADISOS AMAROUSIOU
ATHENS 151 25, GREECE
Telephone: (01) 685 8904; (01) 685 8905
Cable Address: "Bergpat"
Telex: 21-4645 Pat GR
Fax: (01) 681 9237

Commercial Law, Patent, Trademark, Unfair Competition, Copyright, Patent and Trademark Prosecution and Litigation and Corporate Law.

DR. THEODOROS VOSEMBERG-VRETOS, born Athens, Greece, December 22, 1922; admitted, 1955, Athens; 1961, Court of Appeals, Athens; 1970, Supreme Court of Greece. *Education:* University of Thessalonika (Diploma); University of Athens Law School (Doctor of Law). Author: "Conditions for Registrability of Trademarks," published in Athens, 1969, Greek language. With Foreign Press Department, Greek Diplomatic Service, 1947-1951. Member, Greek Delegation to the United Nations Special Committee on the Balkans, 1948-1950. Foreign News Editor, Greek Radio Institute, 1951-1954. Member of the Board, Schering-Plough S.A. (Greece). *Member:* Athens Bar Association; American Bar Association (Member, Section on Intellectual Property Law); Greek Association for the Protection of Industrial Property; International Association for the Protection of Industrial Property A.I.P.P.I.; European Community Trademark Practitioners' Association (E.C.T.A.); United States Trademark Association (U.S.T.A.); Institute of Professional Representatives before the European Patent Office (EPI). *LANGUAGES:* Greek, English, German and French.

NICHOLAS VOSEMBERG-VRETOS, born Athens, Greece, 1955; admitted, 1983, Greece. *Education:* Athens University, Law School (B.A.); Law School of Napoli, Italy. Member of the Board, Colgate Palmolive (Hellas) S.A. *Member:* Athens Bar Association; Greek and International Association for the Protection of Industrial Property (AIPPI; U.S. Trademark Association (USTA); European Communities Trademark Practitioners' Association (ECTA); Institute of Professional Representative before the European Patent Office (EPI). *LANGUAGES:* Greek, English and Italian.

ILEANA VOSEMBERG-VRETOS, born Athens, Greece, 1961; admitted, 1985, Greece. *Education:* Athens University, Law School (B.A.). *Member:* Athens Bar Association; Greek and International Association for the Protection of Industrial Property (AIPPI); U.S. Trademark Association (USTA); European Communities Trademark Practitioners' Association (ECTA); Institute of Professional Representatives before the European Patent Office (EPI). *LANGUAGES:* Greek, English, German and French.

ELISABETH ZOULAMOGLOU-VOSEMBERG, born Athens, Greece, 1957; admitted, 1985, Athens. *Education:* Athens University Law

(This Listing Continued)

School (Political Sciences and International Law Degree, B.Sc., 1980); Law Degree, LL.B., 1983); University of Wales (M.Sc., Shipping Law, 1982). *LANGUAGES:* Greek, English and French.

Languages: Greek, English, German, French and Italian

REPRESENTATIVE CLIENTS: Colgate Palmolive Co., N.Y.; Bristol-Myers Squibb Co., N.Y.; Pepsico, Inc., N.Y.; NBA Properties, Inc., N.Y.; Texaco Inc., N.Y.; Revlon, Inc., N.Y.; Wella AG, Germany; Time Warner Inc., N.Y.; Kraft General Foods, Inc., Illinois; MasterCard International, Inc., N.Y.; McDonald's Corp., Illinois; Monsanto Co., Missouri; R.J. Reynolds Tobacco Co., North Carolina.

C. YANNOPOULOS & ASSOCIATES

Tax Attorneys

62, ACADIMIAS STREET
ATHENS 106 79, GREECE
Telephone: (301) 361 0407; (301) 362 3473; (301) 361 0991
Fax: (301) 364 5059

Domestic & International Taxation, Investments & Tax Planning, Tax Litigation.

FIRM PROFILE: Based in central Athens, C. Yannopoulos & Associates has a strong reputation in advising Greek and International clients on tax matters arising in connection with trading and investments in Greece. The firm's attorneys are qualified to appear before all Greek courts.

CONSTANTINE Y. YANNOPOULOS, SR. (1870-1953).

YERASSIMOS C. YANNOPOULOS (1889-1949).

CONSTANTINE Y. YANNOPOULOS, born Athens, Greece, January 15, 1933; admitted, 1958, Athens Court of Appeals and Supreme Court of Greece. *Education:* University of Athens, Faculty of Law (Graduate, 1955). Author: "The General Principles of Law Theory," Athens 1957; "Interpretation of Tax Exemptions," Part I & II, Athens 1957 and 1958; "The Tax Aspects of Advertising," Athens 1959; "Transfer Tax on Immovable Property," Athens 1966; "Corporate Merger and Turn-Over Taxes," Athens 1968; "The Tax Aspects of Oil Refining," Athens 1977; "Mutual Agreement-Procedure and Practice," Cahiers de Droit Fiscal International, vol. LXVIa, Deventer 1981; "Introduction of VAT in Greece," Athens 1986; and numerous articels, book reviews and commentaries on Court decisions. Member, American-Hellenic Chamber of Commerce. *Member:* Athens Bar Association; International Fiscal Association, IFA (National Reporter, 1981 IFA Congress, Berlin); Greek Society of Tax Law and Public Finance (Secretary General, 1990-1992; Vice-President, 1992-1994).

PANAYOTIS YANNAKOURIS, born Athens, Greece. *Education:* Athens School of Economics; University of Athens, Faculty of Law. Author: "Turnover Tax in Greece," Athens 1984; "On Turn-over Tax," Athens 1982; "Value Added Tax in Combination with Stamp Duty," Athens 1988 and 1989; "Value Added Tax"; "Codification of the VAT Law, 1642/1986," Athens 1990 and 1992.Former Director, Greek Ministry of Finance, Department of Indirect Taxati on. Former President, Legislative Council that prepared and drafted the Value Added Tax Law, 1987. Honorary Director, Greek Ministry of Finance.

THEODORE G. GRIGORAKOS, born Mani, Greece, 1928. *Education:* Athens School of Economics (Graduate, 1956); University of Athens, Faculty of Law (Graduate, 1963). Author: "The S.A.'s Balance Draw Up," Athens 1964; "Annual Stock-Taking," Athens 1967; "The New Company Law Provisions According to the 4th EEC Directive," Athens 1989; "General Principles of Auditing," Athens 1989; "Greek Uniform Chart of Accounts: Analysis and Interpretation," Athens 1991. Co-Author: "Greek Company Law," with E. Levantis, Tome III, Athens 1989. Lecturer, Athens School of Economics; Greek Productivity Center. Former Member, Council that prepared and drafted the Greek Uniform Chart of Accounts. Member, Legislative Council that prepared and drafted law decrees 409/1986, 419/1986 and 498/1987 adjusting Greek Company Law to EEC Directives. *Member:* National Council of Accounting (Vice-President, 1989—); Institute of Certified Public Accountants of Greece-S.O.L.

PANAYOTIS REPPAS, born Patras, Greece, 1936. *Education:* University of Athens, Faculty of Political Science and Economics; University of Athens, Faculty of Law. Author: "Stamp Duty Code," Athens 1985; "Stamp Duty Code, Interpretation of its Provisions," Tome I and II, Athens 1991; "Tax on Movement of Funds and Special Tax on Bank Services, Interpretation of the Law 1676/1986," Athens 1989. Lecturer, Greek Productivity Center. Former Director, Greek Ministry of Finance, Department of Stamp Duty.

(This Listing Continued)

YERASSIMOS C. YANNOPOULOS, born Athens, Greece, October 12, 1965; admitted, 1991, Athens Court of First Instance. *Education:* Aristotle University of Thessaloniki, Faculty of Law (Graduate, 1988); University of Paris 2, Faculty of Law (D.E.A. in Public Finance and Taxation, 1990). Member, American-Hellenic Chamber of Commerce. *Member:* Athens Bar Association; International Fiscal Association, IFA. *LANGUAGES:* Greek, English and French.

OLGA D. MASSAS, born Karditsa, Greece, September 16, 1966; admitted, 1993, Greece. *Education:* Aristotle University of Thessaloniki, Faculty of Law (Graduate, 1992); University of Rouen, Faculty of Law, 1993. *Member:* Athens Bar Association. *LANGUAGES:* Greek, English, French and Spanish.

COUNSEL

ANNA DESPOTIDOU-ANTONIADOU, born Serres, Macedonia, Greece, November 23, 1966; admitted, 1991, Thessaloniki Court of First Instance. *Education:* Aristotle University of Thessaloniki (Graduate, 1988); University of California at Berkeley, School of Law, Boalt Hall (Master of Laws, LL.M., 1989). Master Thesis: "Abuse" under art. 86 of the E.E.C. Treaty and the conduct requirement in the offence of monopolization under section 2 of the Sherman Act-A comparative approach (Prof. L.A. Sullivan). Author: Publications: "The Moral Right of the Author to Reconsider," Art. 4, par.1-2 of the Law 2121/1993 on "Copyright Law and Neighbouring Rights". Co-Author, A. Papadopoulou, published Scientific Review of the Bar of Thessaloniki, No. 13, 1992. *Member:* Thessaloniki Bar Association; Macedonian Society of Commercial Law. *LANGUAGES:* Greek, English and German. *PRACTICE AREAS:* Anti-Trust Law; Unfair Competition Law; Copyright Law; Industrial Property Law; European Economic Law.

ZEPOS & ZEPOS

Established in 1893

120 VAS. SOPHIAS AVENUE
ATHENS 115 26, GREECE
Telephone: (30.1) 775.45.71; 775.33.41
Cable Address: "Dezepos"
Telex: 216703 LEX GR
Telefax: (30.1) 770.28.25; 771.12.50

Private, Corporate, Foreign Investment, Private International, Banking, Finance, Unfair Competition, Intellectual Property, Advertising, Insurance, Telecommunications, Air Law, Environmental Law, Joint Ventures, Mergers and Acquisitions, Privatizations, Secured Finance, Franchising, Public Works, Securities, Stock Exchange Regulations, Litigation and Arbitration, Administrative Law, EEC Law, Labor and Tax Law.

JOHN ZEPOS, SR. (1893-1933).

DIMITRIOS ZEPOS, SR. (1926-1970).

MEMBERS OF FIRM

JOHN ZEPOS, born Athens, Greece, July 5, 1929; admitted, 1956, Athens, Athens Court of Appeals and Athens Supreme Court. *Education:* University of Athens Law School (LL.B.); Southern Methodist University School of Law; Institute on Oil and Gas Law and Taxation, Southwestern Legal Foundation, 1958. Practical Legal Training: Kilgore & Kilgore, Dallas, Texas, 1958; Debevoise, Plimpton, Lyons & Gates, New York, N.Y., 1959-1960. Author: Statute 3948/59, "Greek Oil & Gas Law," Translation into English, published in *Revue Hellenique de Droit International*, 1959. Lecturer, "Investing in Greece," International and Comparative Law Center, Dallas, Texas, 1971. *Member:* Athens Bar Association; International Bar Association; Greek Institute for Foreign and International Law; American-Hellenic Chamber of Commerce; Hellenic-American Union. *LANGUAGES:* Greek, English and French.

THRASSYVOULOS MITSIDIS, born Athens, Greece, March 22, 1935; admitted, 1964, Athens, Athens Court of Appeals and Athens Supreme Court. *Education:* University of Athens Law School (LL.B.); London University (LL.M. in International Economic Law, International Law of the Sea, Maritime Law and Law of the European Institutions). Ex-General Counsel at Mobil Oil Hellas S.A. and Ex-Legal Counsel at Hellenic Industrial Development Bank (ETBA). Former Assistant in Private International Law at the University of Athens. Author: "The Treaty for the Settlement of Investment Disputes, Analysis and Comments," published in *Economicos Tachidromos*, 1969; "Consolato del Mare, The Medieval Maritime Code and its Contribution to the Development of International Law," published in *Revue Hellenique de Droit International*, 1969. *Member:*

(This Listing Continued)

ZEPOS & ZEPOS, Athens—Continued

Athens Bar Association; Greek Institute for Foreign and International Law. **LANGUAGES:** Greek, English and Italian.

ARIS STEFOPOULOS, born Piraeus, Greece, May 21, 1933; admitted, 1963, Athens, Athens Court of Appeals and Athens Supreme Court. *Education:* University of Athens Law School (LL.B.); University at Amsterdam (Leyden-Amsterdam-Columbia, Studies in American Law). Legal Counsel at the Hellenic Industrial Development Bank (ETBA). *Member:* Athens Bar Association. **LANGUAGES:** Greek, English and French.

ELLI SOUTSOU-VAROTSOU, born Alexandria, Egypt, August 9, 1944; admitted, 1971, Athens and Athens Court of Appeals. *Education:* University of Athens Law School (LL.B.). *Member:* Athens Bar Association. **LANGUAGES:** Greek, English, French and German.

PANAGIOTIS CHORTARAS, born Imbros, Turkey, August 26, 1938; admitted, 1972, Athens and Athens Court of Appeals and Athens Supreme Court. *Education:* Athens Highest School of Commercial and Economic Sciences, University of Thessaloniki Law School (LL.B.). *Member:* Athens Bar Association. **LANGUAGES:** Greek, English, German and Turkish.

MARGARET PAPADIMITRIOU, born Drama, Greece, November 4, 1938; admitted, 1970, Athens, Athens Court of Appeals and Athens Supreme Court. *Education:* University of Thessaloniki School of Law and Economics (LL.B.), School of Social Welfare (Diploma in Social Work); Louisiana State University, U.S.A. *Member:* Athens Bar Association. **LANGUAGES:** Greek, English and French.

CONSTANTIN KABILAFKAS, born Athens, Greece, 1933; admitted, 1965, Athens, Athens Court of Appeals and Athens Supreme Court. *Education:* Athens Supreme School of Commercial and Economic Sciences, University of Thessaloniki Law School (LL.B.); London University (LL.M. in International Economic Law, EEC Law, Marine Insurance, Carriage of Goods by Sea). Former Legal Counsel at the Hellenic Industrial Development Bank (ETBA). *Member:* Athens Bar Association. **LANGUAGES:** Greek, English and French.

ELEFTHERIOS YANNOPOULOS, born Athens, Greece, July 5, 1958; admitted, 1985, Athens, Athens Court of First Instance and Athens Court of Appeals. *Education:* University of Athens Law School (LL.B.). *Member:* Athens Bar Association. **LANGUAGES:** Greek, English and Spanish.

IRENE GRAMMATOPOULOU, born Alexandroupolis, Greece, November 10, 1964; admitted, 1989, Athens and Athens Court of First Instance. *Education:* University of Athens Law School (LL.B.); University of Strasbourg (D.E.A. in European Community Law, Law of Mergers and Acquisitions). *Member:* Athens Bar Association. **LANGUAGES:** Greek, English and French.

DIMITRIOS ZEPOS, born Athens, Greece, July 2, 1964; admitted, 1992, Athens and Athens Court of First Instance. *Education:* Connecticut College (B.A., Economics, Political Science); Universite de Lausanne (LL.B.). *Member:* Athens Bar Association. **LANGUAGES:** Greek, English, French and Italian.

KALLIOPI RAKIDJI, born Athens, Greece, April 30, 1968; admitted, 1992, Athens and Athens Court of First Instance. *Education:* University of Athens Law School (LL.B.). *Member:* Athens Bar Association. **LANGUAGES:** Greek and English.

NICHOLAS A. DESSYPRIS, born Larissa, Greece, February 1, 1962; admitted, 1988, Athens, Athens Court of Appeals. *Education:* University of Athens Law School (LL.B.). One year training at Council of State. *Member:* Athens Bar Association. **LANGUAGES:** Greek, English and French.

VASSILIOS P. DIGENOPOULOS, born Athens, Greece, October 10, 1943; admitted, 1969, Athens, Athens Court of Appeals and Athens Supreme Court. *Education:* University of Athens Law School (LL.B.); University of Hamburg, Germany (Dr.iur.). Former Assistant, Max-Planck-Institute for Foreign and International Private Law, Hamburg, Germany. Author: "New Developments in C.I.F. and F.O.B. Contracts," in German, published in Frankfurt, Germany, 1978; various publications in the fields of Corporate and Banking Law. Legal Counsel, National Investment Bank for Industrial Development (ETEBA). *Member:* Athens Bar Association; Hamburg Bar Association. **LANGUAGES:** Greek, German, English and French.

MICHAEL R. TSIBRIS, born Athens, Greece, May 6, 1962; admitted, 1987, Athens. *Education:* University of Athens Law School (Diploma, 1984); Harvard Law School (LL.M., 1986); University of Athens Law

(This Listing Continued)

EU848B

School (Doctorate, 1993). Dissertation on: "Takeover Bid in Greek Law." Author: "Economic Analysis of Law," Nomiko Vima, 1989, 574-586; "Buying a Listed Company in Greece," Oikonomikos Tachidromos, April 27, 1989; "Trading on Inside Information," Oikonomikos Tachidromos, December 28, 1989; "Employees as Shareholders," Oikonomikos Tachidromos, May 3, 1990; "Obligations of Listed Companies to Disclose Information to the Public," Oikonomikos Tachidromos, July 19, 1990; "Stock Loan and Short-selling," Kathimerini, August 28, 1990; "Underwriters' Liability in IPOs," Oikonomikos Tachidromos, November 15, 1990; "Underwriting Public Offers of Securities," Nomiko Vima, 1991, 1177-1192; "Developments in the Regulation of the Capital Market," Oikonomikos Tachidromos, August 6, 1992; "Privatisations in Greece, International Business Lawyer, March, 1993. *Member:* Athens Bar Association; International Bar Association. **LANGUAGES:** Greek, English, German, French and Italian.

JOSEPH S. AVRAMIDES, born Athens, Greece, November 30, 1965; admitted, 1991, Athens and Athens Court of First Instance. *Education:* University of Athens Law School (LL.B.); University of Leicester, England (Master of Arts in Mass Communication Research). *Member:* Athens Bar Association. **LANGUAGES:** Greek, English and German.

NIKOLAOS AL. ANDRIOPOULOS, born Athens, Greece, December 14, 1953; admitted, 1977, Athens, Athens Court of Appeals and Athens Supreme Court. *Education:* University at Gottingen, Germany (Studies in German Law); University of Dundee, Scotland (Course in UK Petroleum Law). Legal Counsel, Bank of Crete. *Member:* Athens Bar Association. **LANGUAGES:** Greek, German and French.

STEFANOS FETZIAN, born Athens, Greece, April 8, 1967; admitted, 1992, Athens, Athens Court of First Instance. *Education:* University of Athens Law School (LL.B.); London University (LL.M., in Commercial and Corporate Law). *Member:* Athens Bar Association. **LANGUAGES:** Greek, English and German.

REPRESENTATIVE CLIENTS: AT&T International, Basking Ridge, N.J.; Aer Lingus, Plc., Dublin, Ireland; Associated Aviation Underwriters, New York, N.Y.; Banque Indosuez Belgique, Bruxelles, Belgium; Banque Worms, Paris, France; B.A.T. Cigarettenfabriken GmbH, Hamburg, Germany; Baxter World Trade S.A., Brussels Belgium; Bear, Sterns & Co., Inc., New York, N.Y.; Benetton Group SpA, Ponzano Ven, Italy; Boeing Co., Seattle, Washington; Boeing Defense & Space Group, Philadelphia, Pennsylvania; Cadbury Schweppes Plc., Birmingham, England; Chevron Chemical Company, San Ramon, California; Chiquita Brands International, Cincinnati, Ohio; Compaq Computer Europe, Munchen, Germany; Computer Associates SpA, Milano, Italy; Delta Airlines, Inc., Atlanta, Georgia; FMC Corporation, Chicago, Illinois; Gambro Engstrom, Bromma, Sweden; Goldman, Sachs & Co., New York, N.Y.; Grundfos Management AG., Bjenringbro, Denmark; Halliburton Engineering and Services, Ltd., London, England; Hilton Hotels Corporation, Beverly Hills, California; Japan Tobacco, Inc., Tokyo, Japan; Kloster Cruise, Ltd., Coral Gables, Florida; Les Mutuelles du Mans Assurances, Le Mans, France; Lindner GmbH, Bamberg, Germany; Louis Vuitton Malletier, Paris, France; Merrill Lynch, Pierce, Fenner & Smith, Inc., New York, N.Y.; Mobil Petrochemicals International, Zaventem, Belgium; Nalco Italiana SpA, Roma, Italy; Ralli Brothers & Coney, Liverpool, England; Remy Associes S.A., Paris, France; Schiapparelli Benessere Pikenz, Milano, Italy; Sepia International Aquaculture S.A., Paris, France; Sharp Corporation, Osaka, Japan; Skandinavisca Enskilda Banken, Stockholm, Sweden; Sperry Rand Corporation, New York, N.Y.; Sterling Winthrop, Inc., New York, N.Y.; STET SpA, Rome, Italy; Sweda Italia SpA, Rome, Italy; The Olivetti Group, Ivrea, Italy; The Yokohama Rubber Co. Ltd., Tokyo, Japan; Young & Rubicam, Inc., New York, N.Y.; YKK Zipper (M.E.) SAL, Beirut, Lebanon; Waste Management International, Inc., Oak Brook, Illinois.
REFERENCES: Debevoise & Plimpton, New York, N.Y.; White & Case, New York, N.Y.; Jones, Day, Reavis & Pogue, New York, N.Y.; Mayer, Brown & Platt, New York, N.Y.; Allen & Overy, London, England; Clifford Chance, London, England; Herbert Smith, London, England; Slaughter and May, London, England; Bureau Francis Lefebvre, Paris, France; Gide Loyrette Nouel, Paris, France; Coudert Brothers, Brussels, Belgium; Lafili & Van Crombrugghe, Brussels, Belgium; Chiomenti e Associati, Rome, Italy; Studio Carnelutti, Milano, Italy; Nauta Dutilh, Rotterdam, The Netherlands; Loyens & Volkmaars, Amsterdam, The Netherlands; Boesebeck, Barz & Partner, Frankfurt/Main, Germany; Arthur Cox, Dublin, Ireland; McCann Fitzgerald, Dublin, Ireland; Naschitz, Brandes & Co., Tel Aviv, Israel; Yuasa and Hara, Tokyo, Japan; Kim & Chang, Seoul, Korea.

HILL TAYLOR DICKINSON O.E.

K. PALEOLOGOU 5
18535 PIRAEUS, GREECE
Telephone: (30) 1 4220330
Fax: (30) 1 4225458

London, England Office: Irongate House, 22-30 Duke's Place, EC3A 7LP. Telephone: 0171 283-9033; 071 895-0888. Telex: 888470 HILTAD G. Fax: 0171 283-1144.

FIRM PROFILE: London and the Greek Office are operated as a single entity, providing a full range of shipping litigation services, including disputes concerning charter parties, sales and purchase, marine insurance,

(This Listing Continued)

collisions, salvages, casualties and cargo claims, as well as general advice in relation to shipping legal matters.

RESIDENT PARTNER

Patrick Hawkins

ASSISTANT SOLICITOR

Ella Hagell

HOLMAN, FENWICK & WILLAN (CONSULTANTS) O.E.

6TH FLOOR
86 FILONOS STREET
185 35 PIRAEUS, GREECE
Telephone: 429-3978
Telefax: 429-3118

London, England Office: Marlow House, Lloyds Avenue. Telephone: 0171-488-2300. Telefax: 0171-481-0316.
Paris, France Office: 3 Rue la Boetie, 75008. Telephone: 44-94-40-50. Telex: 281699F HFWPA A. Telefax: 42-65-46-25.
Hong Kong Office: 1418 Two Pacific Place, 88 Queensway. Telephone: 2522 3006. Telex: 63536 HFWHK HX. Telefax: 2887 8110.
Singapore Office: 10 Collyer Quay, #08-02, Ocean Building, Singapore, 0104. Telephone: 534-0195. Telex: HFWSIN RS 26188. Telefax: 534-5864.
Rouen, France Office: 47 Avenue Gustave Flaubert, 76000. Telephone: 32.08.18.60. Telefax: 35.89.90.54.

Associated office of English solicitors, providing advice on admiralty, all aspects of maritime law, international trade, commodities, transportation, insurance and reinsurance, corporate litigation and insolvency, ship finance, company and commercial matters, commercial property, aviation and professional negligence.

CONSULTANTS

JOHN N. KRZYWKOWSKI. LANGUAGES: English and Italian. **PRACTICE AREAS:** International Trade; P and I Clubs; Maritime Law; Charter Parties and Bills of Lading; Marine Disasters.

HURT, SINISI & PAPADAKIS

1 LOUDOVIKOU, 5TH FLOOR
185 31 PIRAEUS, GREECE
Telephone: (30) (1) 417-4998
Telefax: (30) (1) 413-4289

Athens, Greece Office: Kanari 7, 106 71. Telephone: (30) (1) 364-2320/30; 363-8876. Telefax: (30) (1) 362-2323.
Rome, Italy Office: Via Laurina, 40, 00187. Telephone: (39) (6) 322-1485; 322-1487. Telecopier: (39) (6) 361-3266.
Milan, Italy Office: Corso Italia 8, 20122. Telephone: (39) (2) 866 727. Telefax: (39) (2) 866 771.
Atlanta, Georgia, USA Office: 1050 Crown Pointe Parkway, Suite 310, 30338. Telephone: (404) 913-9999. Telecopier: (404) 671-8513.
Hartford, Connecticut, USA Office: 294, New London Turnpike, Glastonbury, 06033. Telephone: (203) 633-3903. Telefax: (203) 633-4599.
San Diego, California, USA Office: Suite 1400, One America Plaza, 600 West Broadway, 92101-3377. Telephone: (619) 234-1798. Telefax: (619) 234-8475.
New York, New York, USA Office: 375 Park Avenue, Suite 2904, 10152. Telephone: (212) 755-1550. Telefax: (212) 755-1575.

Specialists in Shipping, Commercial, Insurance and Reinsurance Litigation, Ship Sale Purchase and Financing, Public Inquiries, Environmental Issues, Pollution and Maritime Disasters, Professional Indemnity Claims, Insurance Regulatory Issues, Corporate and Commercial Transactions.

FIRM PROFILE: Hurt, Sinisi & Papadakis is an International Law Firm based in the United States and Europe. Fundamental to the firm is a commitment to provide a high quality of personalized service with an excellent standard of professionalism. The United States Offices are located in the Northeast, Southeast and Western United States in order to service clients conveniently and efficiently, as well as provide full support to the firm's European Offices. The European Offices are staffed with both American and European attorneys. Each office, in Europe and the United States, has

(This Listing Continued)

attorneys that are qualified to appear and litigate in the local courts. Hurt, Sinisi & Papadakis has a strong focus on the Southern European region. This gives this firm a unique strategic position for businesses seeking legal advice and representation in this area.

RESIDENT ATTORNEYS

GEORGE DIAKOPOULOS, born Volos, Greece, January 22, 1929; admitted, 1957, Athens, Greece; 1966, Supreme Court. Education: Highest School of Economic and Commercial Sciences of Athens (B.Sc. in Economics, 1951); School of Law of University of Athens (LL.B., 1955). Member, Greek Parliament, 1974-1981. Vice Chair, National Economy and Finance, Budget and Appropriations Committees of the Parliament of Greece, 1974-1981. Columnist, Financial Section, "Kyriakatiki (Sunday) Eleftherotypia," 1990. Main Columnist, "Euroeconomia." Member: Athens Bar Association; Hellenic Maritime Law Association. (At Athens Office).

(For Complete Biographical Data on all Personnel, See Professional Biographies at Athens, Greece)

CONSTANTIN MATTHEOS LAW OFFICES

Established in 1966

155 KARAISKOU STREET
185 35 PIRAEUS, GREECE
Telephone: 429-6960; 429-7036; 429-6756
Fax: 429-6758

Athens, Greece Office: 6 Homer Street, 105 64. Telephones: 322-4135; 322-4155. Fax: 325-4049.

Shipping, Admiralty, Commercial, Corporate, Mergers and Acquisitions, Foreign Investments, Real Estate, Inheritance, European Community Law, Banking, Franchising, Taxation, Conflict of Laws, Arbitration and General Practice.

CONSTANTIN MATTHEOS, born Kos Dodecanese, November 30, 1937; admitted, 1966, Athens Court of Appeals, Supreme Court. Education: University of Thessaloniki, Law School (LL.B., 1961, Valedictorian); University of Nancy, France (LL.M. in European Community Law, 1962); University of Paris, School of Law (Doctorat de l'Université, Final Exams, 1963); University of Paris, Institut de Criminologie (Diploma, 1965); New York University, School of Law (M.C.J., 1967); Fordham University School of Law (studies in U.S. Law, 1970-1971); M.I.T. - Harvard Law School (Legal and Policy Aspects of Ocean Resources Management Certificate, 1978); World Trade Institute, New York (Certificates in: Marine Insurance: Cargo, Hull & P&I, 1975-1977; Chartering and Ship Brokerage, 1976; Ocean Shipping, 1976; Maritime Arbitration, 1976; Maritime Law, 1978). Author: "La Protection de la jeunesse par le censure cinematographique en France et a l'etranger," Librarie Gener. de Droit, Paris, 1966; "The origin of Modern Maritime Law," (in Greek and English), Athens 1989. New York University School of Law, Research Assistant, Comparative Criminal Law Project, 1967. Guest Lecturer, University of Bridgeport Law School, 1978. Member: Athens Bar Association; The American Society of International Law; Hellenic American Chamber of Commerce; Piraeus Marine Club. **LANGUAGES:** Greek, English, French and Italian. **PRACTICE AREAS:** Maritime; Foreign Investment; Arbitration; Contracts; Corporate.

ASSOCIATES

MICHAEL A. COTINIS, born Agrinion, May 6, 1935; admitted, 1961, Athens Court of Appeals, Supreme Court. Education: Athens University, Law School (LL.B., 1957); Paris University, School of Law (LL.D., 1964); London School of Economics (Diploma in Shipping Law, 1965). Author: "The Principle of Utmost Good Faith and Its Effects in Marine Insurance, a Comparative Study," 1965. Lecturer, Commercial Law, Athens School of Economics and Business, 1982—. Member: Athens Bar Association; Hellenic Maritime Law Association. **LANGUAGES:** Greek, English and French. **PRACTICE AREAS:** Commercial; Corporate; Bankruptcy.

COUNSEL

ACHILLEAS KOUTSOURADIS, born Athens, May 6, 1952; admitted, 1982, Athens Court of Appeals, Supreme Court. Education: University of Thessaloniki Law School (LL.B., 1974, Valedictorian); Wurzburg, Germany, Law School (Ph.D., summa cum laude, 1980); Faculté intern. de Droit, Strasbourg, France (Diplome de droit Comparé, 1979). Author: "Die Stellung der Nichtelelichen Kinder" (1980); "Family Law" (in Greek, 1985-1987); "Discovery of Lost Objects" (in Greek, 1987). Associate Professor of

(This Listing Continued)

CONSTANTIN MATTHEOS LAW OFFICES, Piraeus—
Continued

Civil Law, Thessaloniki University, 1987—. *Member:* Athens Bar Association; Zurich Institute of Civil Procedure; Greek Association of Commercial Arbitration; German Association of Civil Procedure, Comparative Law and Commercial Arbitration. *LANGUAGES:* Greek, German, English and French. *PRACTICE AREAS:* Civil; Taxation; Arbitration.

REPRESENTATIVE CLIENTS: Atlantic Bank of New York; Bank of New England N.A.; Israel Discount Bank of New York; United Bank of Denver N.A.; Irving Trust Company; Citibank N.A., (Shipping) N.Y.; Seagroup Inc. New York, N.Y.; Mobil Oil Corporation, New York, N.Y.; Scio Shipping Inc., New York, N.Y.; Chevron U.S.A. Inc., San Francisco, Calif.; Agro Company of Canada Limited, Montreal, Canada; The Sanwa Bank Limited (New York Agency); Mitsui Shipbuilding & Engineering Co. Ltd.; The Hakodate Dock Co., Ltd.; Namura Shipbuilding Co. Ltd., Osaka; Ceres Hellenic Shipping Enterprises Ltd., Piraeus, Greece; Banque de Paris et des Pays-Bas (Suisse) S.A., Geneve; Dornier GmdH, W. Germany; Aclon Finance S.A., Geneve.
REFERENCES: Burke & Parsons, New York; Grant, Hermann, Schwartz & Klinger, New York; Cadwalader, Wickersham & Taft, New York; Burlingham, Underwood & Lord, New York; Shearman & Sterling, New York; Holme Roberts & Owen, Denver, Colorado; Storme, Leroy, Gent; Granrut Chresteil, Paris; Salvatore Trifino & Associates, Milan; Pels Rijcken, Hague; Phillips, Nizer, Benjamin, Krim & Ballon, New York.

MITRAKOS & YANAKAKIS

109 ALKIVIADOU STREET
PIRAEUS 185 32, GREECE
Telephone: 411.22.42/76
Telecopier: 411.22.43

Commercial and Corporate Law, Admiralty and Maritime matters, Shipping and Aviation Financing, General Civil Law Practice.

MEMBERS OF FIRM

THEODORE G. MITRAKOS, born Athens, Greece, July 22, 1958; admitted, 1983, Athens; 1987, Court of Appeals. *Education:* University of Athens (LL.B., 1981); New York University (LL.M., International Legal Studies, 1985). *Member:* International Bar Association; American Foreign Law Association; Maritime Law Association of Greece.

SOTIRIS K. YANAKAKIS, born Athens, Greece, December 16, 1960; admitted, 1985, Piraeus; 1993, Court of Appeals. *Education:* University of Thrace (LL.B., Summa cum Laude, 1982); Harvard Law School (LL.M., Transnational Legal Problems, International Trade Law, Foreign Investments and Corporate Law, 1984). *Member:* Harvard Law Association; Maritime Law Association of Greece.

Languages: English, French and Greek.

NORTON ROSE

Norton Rose Consultants O.E.

126 KOLOKOTRONI STREET
185 35 PIRAEUS, GREECE
Telephone: +30 1 428 0202; +30 1 428 2429; +30 1 452 5360
Telex: 213851 JUST GR
Fax: +30 1 428 2427; +30 1 428 2428

Other Offices: London, Bahrain, Brussels, Hong Kong, Moscow, Paris, Prague and Singapore.

FIRM PROFILE: Norton Rose is a leading City and International law firm with its principal office in the City of London. The firm provides a wide range of legal services primarily to the business and financial communities as well as to a number of sovereign governments and state organizations. We are known particularly for our corporate and debt finance, banking, company and commercial law, natural resources, insurance, property development, aerospace and maritime practices and wide-ranging expertise on tax matters. Norton Rose has a major litigation department handling all forms of commercial dispute resolution.

In Piraeus the firm specializes in banking; EC matters; commercial law; insurance; privatizations; shipping finance; shipping litigation; commodities; asset/project finance.

(This Listing Continued)

RESIDENT PARTNER

TIMOTHY C.M. HOWARD, admitted, 1973. *PRACTICE AREAS:* Shipping; Commercial and Insurance Litigation; Arbitration; Commodities and EC Law.

(For Complete Biographical Data on all Personnel, see Professional Biographies at London, England).

ROUSSOS & HATZIDIMITRIOU
LAW OFFICES

Established in 1974

5-7 FILELLINON STREET
PIRAEUS 185 36, GREECE
Telephone: 42.94.200
Cable Address: "MARLAW"
Telex: 21-3295 PTPS GR
Telefax: 42.94.625

Resident Counsel for: Poles, Tublin, Patestides and Stratakis, 46 Trinity Place, New York, N.Y. 10006. Telephone: 212-943-0110.

General Practice, Litigation, Admiralty and Shipping, Commercial, Corporate, Marine Insurance, Banking and Investment Law.

FIRM PROFILE: The firm serves the local and international business community in Greece. All members have received postgraduate education in the U.S.A. or Great Britain. The two senior partners have had considerable legal experience in London and New York.

MEMBERS OF FIRM

COSTAS ROUSSOS, born Athens, Greece, January 1, 1941; admitted, 1966, Athens; 1980, Court of Appeals; 1988, Supreme Court of Greece. *Education:* University of Athens Law School (LL.B., 1964); University of London (Academic Postgraduate Diploma in Law, 1968; LL.M., 1969). Legal Training: Norton, Rose, Botterell and Roche, London, England, 1971; Poles, Tublin, Patestides and Stratakis, New York, N.Y., 1973-1974. *Member:* Athens Bar Association; Greek Maritime Law Association. *LANGUAGES:* Greek, English and French. *PRACTICE AREAS:* Admiralty and Maritime Law; Bankruptcy; Banks and Banking; Civil and Commercial Law; Company Law; Contracts; Entertainment and the Arts; Finance; Leases and Leasing; Litigation.

ZAFIRIS HATZIDIMITRIOU, born Paleon Faliron, Attica, Greece, December 9, 1952; admitted, 1978, New York; 1980, Athens; 1985, Court of Appeals. *Education:* University of Athens Law School (LL.B., summa cum laude, 1975); New York University (LL.M., 1976). Legal Training: Poles, Tublin, Patestides and Stratakis, New York, N.Y., 1976-1978. *Member:* New York Bar Association; Athens Bar Association; Maritime Law Association of the U.S.; Greek Maritime Law Association. *LANGUAGES:* Greek and English. *PRACTICE AREAS:* Admiralty and Maritime Law; Banks and Banking; Business and Corporate Law; Communications and Media; Gaming; Investments and Securities.

IO GREKOUSSI, born Alexandria, Egypt, November 26, 1946; admitted, 1973, Athens; 1980, Court of Appeals. *Education:* University of Athens Law School (LL.B., 1970); University of London (Diploma in Shipping Law, 1972). *Member:* Athens Bar Association; Greek Maritime Law Association. *LANGUAGES:* Greek, English and French. *PRACTICE AREAS:* Admiralty and Maritime Law; Company Law; Corporate Law; Finance; Family Law; Mortgages.

MICHAEL RAPSOMANIKIS, born Corfu, Greece, April 7, 1954; admitted, 1982, Athens; 1988, Court of Appeals. *Education:* University of Athens Law School (LL.B., summa cum laude, 1977); Harvard Law School (LL.M., 1979). Author: "Frustration of Contract in Comparative Law and International Trade Law," 18 Duquesne Law Review 551-605, 1980 (in English); Leasing Contract, in Georgiades-Stathopoulos, Civil Code Commentary, Articles 574-607, Athens 1980 (in Greek). *Member:* Athens Bar Association; Greek Maritime Law Association. *LANGUAGES:* Greek, English and German. *PRACTICE AREAS:* Admiralty and Maritime Law; Bankruptcy; Banks and Banking; Business Law; Gaming; Insurance; Litigation; Property; Real Estate; Trademarks.

COSTAS COTSIYANNIS, born Athens, Greece, December 31, 1958; admitted, 1989, Athens; 1994, Court of Appeals. *Education:* University of Athens Law School (LL.B., 1983); UWIST, Wales (Diploma in Port and Shipping Administration, 1985). *Member:* Athens Bar Association; Greek Maritime Law Association. *LANGUAGES:* Greek and English. *PRACTICE AREAS:* Admiralty and Maritime Law; Banks and Banking; Busi-

(This Listing Continued)

ness Law; Contracts; Corporate Law; Leases and Leasing; Property; Real Estate; Taxation; Trusts and Estates.

JOHN KAMPANIS, born Athens, Greece, November 14, 1963; admitted, 1992, Athens. *Education:* University of Athens Law School (LL.B., 1989); University of Southampton (LL.M., 1992). *Member:* Athens Bar Association. *LANGUAGES:* Greek, English and French. *PRACTICE AREAS:* Admiralty and Maritime Law; Banks and Banking; Civil Law; Company Law; Contracts; Finance; Insurance; Investments; Leases and Leasing; Mortgages.

TINA PAPATHANASSIOU, born Athens, Greece, December 22, 1968; admitted, 1993, Athens. *Education:* University of Athens Law School (LL.B., 1991); University of London (LL.M., Maritime Law, 1992). *Member:* Athens Bar Association. *LANGUAGES:* Greek, English, French and Spanish. *PRACTICE AREAS:* Admiralty and Maritime Law; Company Law; Corporate Law; Property; Trademarks; Transportation.

ALEXANDROS VASSILIOU, born Athens, Greece, July 27, 1967; admitted, 1993, New York; 1993, Athens. *Education:* University of Athens Law School (LL.B., magna cum laude, 1990); New York University (LL.M., 1992). With, Healy & Baillie, New York, N.Y., 1992-1993. *Member:* New York Bar Association; Athens Bar Association. *LANGUAGES:* Greek, English, French and German. *PRACTICE AREAS:* Admiralty and Maritime Law; Business Law; Commercial Law; Company Law; Contracts; Leases and Leasing; Transportation; Wills.

STELLA ALEXANDRI, born Athens, Greece, October 10, 1968; admitted, 1994, Athens. *Education:* University of Athens Law School (LL.B., 1992); University of Southampton (LL.M., 1994). *Member:* Athens Bar Association. *LANGUAGES:* Greek, English and German. *PRACTICE AREAS:* Admiralty and Maritime Law; Commercial Law; Transportation.

REPRESENTATIVE CLIENTS: Citibank N.A.; Credit Commercial de France, Paris (Shipping Department); National Shipping & Trading Corp., New York; Trade and Freight International Limited; Maritime Company of Lesvos S.A.; Hellenic Fuels and Lubricants Co. S.A.; SHELL Company (Hellas) Ltd.; CIGNA Insurance Company of Europe S.A.; N.V. Argonaut Enterprises Ltd.; Oceanic Financial Services Limited; BellSouth Europe; Astron Group of Companies.

THEO V. SIOUFAS
LAW OFFICES

Established in 1971

ALASSIA BUILDING
DEFTERAS MERARCHIAS 13
GR 185.35 PIRAEUS, GREECE
Telephone: (01) 422 1210 (10 lines)
Fax: (01) 422 5090/422 5146
Telex: 213951 LEX GR

Banking, Contracts, Investments, Admiralty, Shipping, Corporate, Commercial, Trading, Real Estate, Marine Insurance, Mergers and Acquisitions, General Practice, Labor Law, General Civil and Commercial Litigation, Enforcement of Securities, Judgements and Arbitration Awards.

MEMBERS OF FIRM

THEO V. SIOUFAS, born Hellinopyrgos, Karditsa, Greece, July 17, 1940; admitted, 1966, Athens and Piraeus Courts of Appeals and Supreme Courts of Greece. *Education:* University of Athens Law School (LL.B., 1963); London University (Diploma in Law, 1969). Private Secretary to the Minister of Industry, 1962-1963. Expert Witness, Greek Law in U.S., English and South African Courts. Legal Counsel: First National City Bank (Citibank), Piraeus, 1971-1973; Continental Illinois National Bank and Trust Company of Chicago, Piraeus, 1973-1986; ABN-ANRO Bank N.V., 1992—; Banque Indosuez, 1992—. *Member:* Athens and International Bar Associations; Greek Maritime Law Association; European Lawyer's Union; Yacht Club; Piraeus Marine Club. *LANGUAGES:* Greek and English.

CHARALAMBOS V. SIOUFAS, born Hellinopyrgos, Karditsa, Greece, February 17, 1946; admitted, 1974, Athens and Piraeus Courts of Appeals. *Education:* University of Athens Law School (LL.B., 1972). Legal Counsel, ABN-AMRO Bank N.V. *Member:* Athens Bar Association. *LANGUAGES:* Greek and English.

STYLIANOS G. PAPANDREOPOULOS, born Santorini, Greece, January 18, 1940; admitted, 1967, Athens and Piraeus Courts of Appeals and Supreme Court of Greece. *Education:* University of Athens Law School (LL.B., 1965). Legal Counsel of the Organization for the Rehabilitation of

(This Listing Continued)

Ailing Companies (O.A.E.). *Member:* Athens Bar Association. *LANGUAGES:* Greek.

PAUL V. SIOUFAS, born Hellinopyrgos, Karditsa, Greece, January 4, 1948; admitted, 1978, Athens and Piraeus Courts of Appeals and Supreme Court of Greece. *Education:* University of Thessaloniki, School of Political and Economic Science (B.Sc., 1974); University of Athens Law School (LL.B., 1976). *Member:* Athens Bar Association. *LANGUAGES:* Greek and English.

CONSTANTINOS G. EMMANUEL, born Athens, Greece, March 14, 1952; admitted, 1977, Athens and Piraeus Courts of Appeals and Supreme Court of Greece. *Education:* University of Athens Law School (LL.B., 1975). *Member:* Athens Bar Association. *LANGUAGES:* Greek, English and French.

PANAGOS G. ANAGNOSTOPOULOS, born Athens, Greece, September 21, 1950; admitted, 1977, Athens and Piraeus Courts of Appeals and Supreme Court of Greece. *Education:* Athens University, Law School (LL.B., 1974). *Member:* Athens Bar Association. *LANGUAGES:* Greek and English.

HELEN G. SIOUFAS, born Athens, Greece, February 6, 1964; admitted, 1988, Athens and Piraeus Courts. *Education:* University of Thessaloniki Law School (LL.B., 1987). *Member:* Athens Bar Association. *LANGUAGES:* Greek, English and Italian.

ANGELA C. ARCADIS, born Piraeus, Greece, June 22, 1963; admitted, 1989, Athens and Piraeus Courts of First Instance. *Education:* University of Athens Law School (LL.B., 1987); University of Strasbourg (LL.M. in European Community Law, 1989). Author: LL.B. Thesis, The European Convention on Human Rights; LL.M. Thesis, Freedom of Establishment and Provision of Services in Banking under European and Greek Law. *Member:* Athens Bar Association. *LANGUAGES:* Greek, English, French and German.

ARIS D. VOURDAS, born Larissa, Greece, February 8, 1963; admitted, 1990, Athens and Piraeus Courts. *Education:* University of Athens Law School (LL.B., 1987); London University (Diploma in International Commercial Arbitration, 1990). Legal Training, Watson, Farley & Williams, Solicitors, London, 1990. *Member:* Piraeus Bar Association; Greek Maritime Law Association. *LANGUAGES:* Greek, English and French.

ABBY V. KARLAFTI, born Athens, Greece, January 28, 1965; admitted, 1990, Athens and Piraeus Courts of First Instance. *Education:* University of Athens Law School (LL.B., 1988); Vrige Universiteit Brussel (V.U.B.) (LL.M. International and Comparative Law, 1991). Author: LL.B. Thesis, Free Movement of Information and the National Sovereignty; LL.M. Thesis, The Arrest of Ships; Greece, U.S.A., England & Wales: A Comparative Study. *Member:* Piraeus Bar Association. *LANGUAGES:* Greek, English, French and German.

APHRODITE P. ADAMAKOU, born Athens, Greece, February 10, 1967; admitted, 1992, Athens Court of First Instance. *Education:* University of Athens Law School (LL.B., 1990); Erasmus University of Rotterdam, The Netherlands; University of Ghent, Belgium; University of Paris IX, France (LL.M. in Economic Analysis of EEC Competition, Commercial and Civil Law, 1991). Author: LL.B Thesis: The Bankruptcy of Foreign Shipping Companies in Greece; LL.M. Thesis: Economic Analysis of the Franchising Contracts in EEC. *Member:* Athens Bar Association. *LANGUAGES:* Greek, English, French and German.

HARA A. MAMALI, born Karditsa, Greece, May 8, 1965; admitted, 1992, Athens and Piraeus Courts. *Education:* University of Athens Law School (LL.B., 1990). *Member:* Athens Bar Association. *LANGUAGES:* Greek and English.

EMMANUEL C. STAVRIANAKIS, born Athens, Greece, 1940; admitted, 1968, Athens and Piraeus Courts of First Instance. *Education:* University of Athens Law School (LL.B., 1966); London University (Diploma in Shipping Law, 1969). Legal Counsel, J.C. Carras (Shipbrokers) Ltd., London, 1972-1988. *Member:* Athens Bar Association; The Greek Trust (London). *LANGUAGES:* Greek, English, French and Spanish.

OF COUNSEL

STYLIANOS F. MAZARAKIS, Honorary President of the Court of Appeal; former Supervising Judge of Piraeus Court of Appeal.

REPRESENTATIVE CLIENTS: Morgan Guaranty Trust Company of New York; Continental Bank N.A. of Chicago; International Finance Corporation (World Bank); Racal Electronics Group; Vodafone Group; Banque Indosuez; Enterprises Shipping and Trading S.A.; Societe Generale, Paris; Banque de la Societe Financiere Europeenne; ABN-AMRO Bank N.V. (Piraeus Branch); American Express Bank Limited (Athens Branch); Barclays Bank Plc, Greece;

(This Listing Continued)

THEO V. SIOUFAS LAW OFFICES, Piraeus—Continued

Hill Samuel Bank Ltd., London; British Airports International Plc.; Safari Parks Ltd., London; Australian Trade Commission, Sydney; Export Finance and Insurance Corporation, Sydney; Deutsche Schiffsbank A.G. of Bremen and Hamburg; Schiffshypothekenbank zu Luebeck, A.G., Hamburg; International Bankers Incorporated S.A., Luxembourg; The Royal Bank of Scotland Plc. (Piraeus Branch); FAGE S.A., Athens; TGE (Porto Carras) S.A., Thessaloniki; Ermis Maritime Corporation, Athens.

VGENOPOULOS & PARTNERS

Established in 1983

96-98 FILONOS STREET
PIRAEUS 185 36, GREECE
Telephone: 01-4294 095-6, 4293 980-1
Fax: 01-4294 045
Telex: 241389 LOAV GR

(For biographical data on all personnel, see Professional Biographies at Athens, Greece)

WATSON, FARLEY & WILLIAMS

5TH FLOOR, ALASSIA BUILDING
DEFTERAS MERARCHIAS 13
185-35 PIRAEUS, GREECE
Telephone: (30-1) 422 3660
Telex: 24 1311 WFW GR
Fax: (30-1) 422 3664

London, England Office: 15 Appold Street, London EC2A 2HB. Telephone: (44 71) 814 8000. Telex: 8955707 WFW LON G. Fax: (44 71) 814 8141.
New York, New York Office: 380 Madison Avenue, 10017. Telephone: 212-922-2200. Telex: 6790626 WFW NY. Fax: 212-922-1512.
Paris, France Office: 19 Rue de Marignan, 75008 Paris. Telephone: (33 1) 45 63 15 15. Telex: WFW PAR 651096 F. Fax: (33 1) 45 61 09 01.
Oslo, Norway Office: Beddingen 8, Aker Brygge, 0250 Oslo. Telephone: (47 22) 83 83 08. Telex: 79209 WFW N. Fax: (47 22) 83 83 13.
Moscow, Russia Office: 36 Myaskovskovo Street, Moscow 121019. Telephone: (7 502) 224 1700 (international only); (7 095) 291 8046/5968. Fax: (7 502) 224 1701 (international only); (7 095) 202 9027.
Copenhagen, Denmark Office: Lille Kongensgade 20 DK-1074 Copenhagen K. Telephone: (45 33) 91 33 03. Fax: (45 33) 91 49 12.

Firm engaged in General International Practice, Corporate, Commercial and Financing, Shipping, Aviation, Banking, Taxation, Commercial Litigation and Arbitration, European Community Law. Not qualified to advise on Greek law.

RESIDENT PARTNERS

R. A. Rice

(For Biographical Data on additional partners, see Professional Biographies at Copenhagen, Denmark, London, England, Paris, France, Oslo, Norway and Moscow, Russia)

NOMOS
THESSALONIKI LAW FIRM

26 VASSILEOS HERAKLIOV STREET
54624 THESSALONIKI, GREECE
Telephone: (30 31) 263.665; 273.949; 273.484; 271.230; 278.723; 263.450
Fax: (30 31) 222.405; 230.483; 273.987

Civil and Criminal Law Practice in all Courts, Administrative and Tax Law, Agency, Antitrust, Unfair Competition, Advertising, Intellectual and Industrial Property, Franchise, Banking, Corporate Finance, Commercial Law, Company Law, Computer Law, Contracts, Criminal Law, EEC Law, Family and Inheritance Law, Foreign Investments, Labour Law, Real Estate, International Transactions and Disputes.

FIRM PROFILE: The firm was established in 1994 and offers a full range of legal services. The firm has 5 partners, 13 associates and the legal support of 1 notary public, paralegal personnel and a range of counsels throughout Greece and in Brussels.

(This Listing Continued)

EU852B

PARTNERS

CONSTANTINE G. HADJIYANNAKIS, born Thessaloniki, Greece, 1942; admitted, 1970, Thessaloniki. *Education:* University of Thessaloniki Law School (LL.B., 1965); University of Rennes, France Law School (Doctorat D'Etat, Honours, 1969). Former Assistant, University of Rennes, France Law School; University of Thessaloniki Law School; Professor of Penal Law, Pandios University of Political Sciences, 1973-1984. Supreme Court Attorney, Law Commission, Department of Justice regarding the Penal Code and the Code of Penal Procedure. *Member:* Thessaloniki Bar Association. *LANGUAGES:* Greek, English and French.. *PRACTICE AREAS:* Business; Banking Law.

VASSILIOS G. ANTONOPOULOS, born Aeghio, Greece; admitted, 1972, Thessaloniki. *Education:* University of Thessaloniki Law School (LL.B., Honours, 1968; Ph.D., Honours); University of Munich Law School (Postgraduate Studies). Associate Professor, University of Thessaloniki Law School. Author, Contributor to law periodicals. Court of Appeals Attorney. *Member:* Thessaloniki Bar Association; International and Greek Scientific Unions. *LANGUAGES:* Greek, German, English and French. *PRACTICE AREAS:* Company Law; Industrial Property Law; Commercial Law.

ATHANASSIOS G. GHEORGHIADIS, born Thessaloniki, Greece, 1954; admitted, 1978, Thessaloniki. *Education:* University of Thessaloniki Law School (LL.B., 1978). Supreme Court Attorney, 1988. Secretary-General of "Northern Greece Lawyers' Corporation." *Member:* Thessaloniki Bar Association (Member, Information Technology and Attorneys' Code Commissions); I.B.A.; A.I.J.A.; U.I.A. International Law Association. *LANGUAGES:* Greek, English and German. *PRACTICE AREAS:* Civil Law; Law of International Carriage by Road.

PERICLES AL. KALLIDOPOULOS, born Thessaloniki, Greece, 1959; admitted, 1986, Thessaloniki. *Education:* Pandios University of Political Sciences (LL.B., Honours, 1981); University of Thessaloniki Law School (LL.B., 1984; LL.M., Private International, Commercial and Labour Law, Honours, 1985). Court of Appeal Attorney. Member: Macedonia-Thrace European Club; Sport Society Heracles. *Member:* Thessaloniki Bar Asociation; Northern Greece Lawyers' Corporation. *LANGUAGES:* Greek, English and French. *PRACTICE AREAS:* Civil Law; Criminal Law.

IFIGENIA DIMITRIADOU-GHEORGHIADOU, born Thessaloniki, Greece, 1956; admitted, 1981, Thessaloniki. *Education:* University of Thessaloniki Law School (LL.B., 1979). Supreme Court Attorney, 1990. *Member:* Thessaloniki Bar Association; "Northern Greece Lawyers' Corporation.". *LANGUAGES:* Greek, English, Italian and French. *PRACTICE AREAS:* Civil Law; Commercial Law.

ASSOCIATES

MATINA KORDI-ANTONOPOULOU, born Chlos, Greece; admitted, 1972, Thessaloniki. *Education:* University of Thessaloniki Law School (LL.B., Honours, 1968; Ph.D., Honours); University of Munich Law (Postgraduate Studies). Lecturer, University of Thessaloniki Law School. *Member:* Thessaloniki Bar Association. *LANGUAGES:* Greek, German, English and French. *PRACTICE AREAS:* Company Law; Negotiable Instruments.

ANGELIKI IOANNIDOU, born Drama, Greece; admitted, 1976, Thessaloniki. *Education:* University of Thessaloniki Law School (LL.B., 1975). *Member:* Thessaloniki Bar Association. *PRACTICE AREAS:* Civil Law.

EFTIHIA PALTATZIDOU-TROHIDOU, born Thessaloniki, Greece, 1961; admitted, 1986, Thessaloniki. *Education:* University of Thessaloniki Law School (LL.B., 1984). *Member:* Thessaloniki Bar Association. *LANGUAGES:* Greek and English. *PRACTICE AREAS:* Civil Law; Commercial Law.

DESPINA KLAVANIDOU-KALLIDOPOULOU, born Thessaloniki, Greece, 1962. *Education:* University of Thessaloniki Law School (LL.B., Honours, 1984; Postgraduate Studies, Private Law; Ph.D., Honours, 1991); University of Heidelberg (Postgraduate Studies). Lecturer, University of Thessaloniki Law School. *Member:* Thessaloniki Bar Association. *LANGUAGES:* Greek, German, English and French. *PRACTICE AREAS:* Civil Law.

EFTIHIA MOUAMELETZI, born Thessaloniki, Greece, 1963; admitted, 1987, Thessaloniki. *Education:* University of Thessaloniki Law School (LL.B., Honours, 1985; Ph.D., Honours, 1994); University of Brussels-Institute of European Studies (Post Graduate Studies, 1987). Author, Summarised decisions of the E.C.J. Contributor to the periodical, "Greek Review of European Law." With Legal Department, E.C. Commission, Brussels. Associate, Centre of International and European Economic Law.

(This Listing Continued)

Member: Thessaloniki Bar Association. *LANGUAGES:* Greek, English, Italian and French. *PRACTICE AREAS:* European Community Law.

ELEFTHERIA MILA, born Halklda, Greece, 1962; admitted, 1987, Thessaloniki. *Education:* University of Thessaloniki Law School (LL.B., 1985; LL.M., Commercial and Economic Law, Honours, 1988). *Member:* Thessaloniki Bar Association. *LANGUAGES:* Greek, German and English. *PRACTICE AREAS:* Real Estate; Commercial Law.

BARBARA SPANOPOULOU, born Volos, Greece, 1963; admitted, 1989, Thessaloniki. *Education:* University of Thessaloniki Law School (LL.B., 1986). Court of Appeal Attorney, 1994. *Member:* Thessaloniki Bar Association. *LANGUAGES:* Greek, French and English. *PRACTICE AREAS:* Civil Law; Commercial Law.

ANASTASIOS TSILIMIGAKIS, born Thessaloniki, Greece, 1961; admitted, 1989, Thessaloniki. *Education:* University of Thessaloniki Law School (Ll.B., 1985; LL.M., Commercial and Economic Law, Honours). Lecturer, Administration Officers' School, 1991. Court of Appeal Attorney. *Member:* Thessaloniki Bar Association. *LANGUAGES:* Greek and French. *PRACTICE AREAS:* Civil Law; Labour Law.

ARISTOTELES PRIOVOLOS, born Athens, Greece, 1965; admitted, 1991, Thessaloniki. *Education:* University of Thessaloniki Law School (LL.B., 1988; LL.M., Public Law, 1990; Ph.D. student). *Member:* Thessaloniki Bar Association. *LANGUAGES:* Greek and English. *PRACTICE AREAS:* Administrative Law; Tax Law.

DEMETRIOS KAVALLARIS, born Goettingen, Germany, 1968; admitted, 1993, Thessaloniki. *Education:* University of Thessaloniki Law School (LL.B., 1991; Studies in Labour and Civil Law). *Member:* Thessaloniki Bar Association. *LANGUAGES:* Greek, German and English. *PRACTICE AREAS:* Labour Law.

ELENI PAPADOPOULOU, born Thessaloniki, Greece, 1971; admitted, 1994, Thessaloniki. *Education:* University of Thessaloniki Law School (LL.B., Honours, 1992); Queen Mary and Westfield College-University of London (LL.M., International Business Law). *Member:* Thessaloniki Bar Association. *LANGUAGES:* Greek, English, French, Russian, Italian and Spanish. *PRACTICE AREAS:* Industrial Property; Computer Law; International Transactions.

VASSILIKI PAPAYANNI, born Kozani, Greece, 1967; admitted, 1994, Thessaloniki. *Education:* University of Thessaloniki Law School (LL.B., 1992). *Member:* Thessaloniki Bar Association. *LANGUAGES:* Greek, French, German and English. *PRACTICE AREAS:* Civil Law.

CRISTINA KARIZONI, born Thessaloniki, Greece, 1968; admitted, 1995, Thessaloniki. *Education:* University of Thessaloniki Law School (LL.B., 1992). *Member:* Thessaloniki Bar Association. *LANGUAGES:* Greek, English and Italian.

REPRESENTATIVE CLIENTS: Porto Carras Casino S.A.; Marox GmbH; Car Center S.A.; Arhiteh A.T.E.; Aktina S.A.; Epilogi STI; Domisi Ltd.; Tsobanidi Bros. S.A.; Gianni Callisti S.A.; Trofeklect S.A. (Mars Representative in Greece); Thessaloniki Cultural Capital of Europe 1997 Organisation; SYNEL (Co-operative Company of Fertilizers) S.A.; Coplam S.A.; Karella Tobacco Industry; Nana S.A.; Perivallontiki Drasi S.A.; Minerva S.A.; K. Doulgeridis S.A.-Lana Moda; Orfanidis S.A.; Cotton Trust Ltd.; Keramourgia Sedes S.A.; MTC (Pretty Baby); Oro Vildiridis; Filina Ltd.; Penlidis-Plakontanakis S.A.; Atlantic Tours; Aluminco S.A.; Build Up (Construction Corporation); Zwettler GmbH; Ippokratis S.A.; Campas S.A.; Midas S.A.; Tania Moda Ltd.; Ellebi S.A.; Henninger Hellas S.A.; E.B.I. Kam. S.A.; Eurotrans Hellas Ltd.; Zeuxi S.A. (Olivetti SpA Representative in Greece); Kronen Brauerei GmbH; N. Kanellopoulos-X. Adamantiadis S.A. (National Union S.A. Representative in Greece); D. Matsos & Son S.A.

MICHAEL E. PANAYOTOPOULOS & ASSOCIATES

13 METROPOLEOS STREET
THESSALONIKI 546 24, GREECE
Telephone: 031/274-490, 274 491
Telefax: (031) 271 879

Local and International Practice. Commercial, Civil, Labor, Administrative, Tax, Immigration and Penal Law.

MICHAEL E. PANAYOTOPOULOS, born Thessaloniki, May 2, 1931; admitted, 1957, Greece, Thessaloniki Primary and Court of Appeals and Supreme Court (Ariopagus) Athens. *Education:* Faculty of Law, Aristotelian University of Thessaloniki (LL.B., 1954). *Member:* Thessaloniki Bar Association. *LANGUAGES:* English.

(This Listing Continued)

STERGIOS GEORGALIS, born Volos, Greece, 1956; admitted, 1981, Thessaloniki Primary Courts and Court of Appeals. *Education:* Faculty of Law, Aristotelian University of Thessaloniki (LL.B., 1978).

STATHIS M. PANAYOTOPOULOS, born Thessaloniki, 1962; admitted, 1987, Thessaloniki Primary Courts. *Education:* Faculty of Law, Aristotelian University of Thessaloniki (LL.B., 1985). *LANGUAGES:* English, French, German and Russian.

JENNY KOULOURI, born Thessaloniki, 1964; admitted, 1989, Thessaloniki Primary Courts. *Education:* Faculty of Law, Aristotelian University of Thessaloniki (LL.B., 1987). *LANGUAGES:* English.

VGENOPOULOS & PARTNERS

Established in 1983

3 NIKIS AVENUE
THESSALONIKI 546 24, GREECE
Telephone: 031-271 056
Telex: 419379 LOAV GR.
Fax: 031-220 703.

GEORGE GOULIELMOS, admitted, 1983, Thessaloniki.

DIMITRIS GOULIELMOS, admitted, 1991, Thessaloniki.

MARIA ECONOMOU, admitted, 1994, Thessaloniki.

Languages: Greek, English and French

(For biographical data on all personnel, see Professional Biographies at Athens, Greece)

HUNGARY

ALLEN & OVERY

MÁDACH TRADE CENTER
MÁDACH IMRE UTCA 13-14
H-1075 BUDAPEST, HUNGARY
Telephone: (361) 268 1511
Facsimile: (361) 268 1515

London, England Office: One New Change, EC4M 9QQ. Telephone: 0171 330 3000. Facsimile: 0171 330 9999.

Beijing, China Office: Suite 3204, Jing Guang Centre, Hu Jia Lou, Chaoyang District, 100020. Telephone: (86 1) 501 4681. Facsimile: (86 1) 501 4682.

Brussels, Belgium Office: Rue de la Loi 99, Box 8, 1040. Telephone: (32 2) 230 27 91. Facsimile (32 2) 230 66 13.

Dubai, United Arab Emirates Office: 501 Al Futtaim Tower,P.O. Box 3251, Deira. Telephone: (971 4) 282296. Facsimile: (971 4) 212860.

Frankfurt, Germany Office: Taunusanlage 11, 11th Floor, 60329. Telephone: (49 69) 242 6120. Facsimile: (49 69) 242 61220.

Hong Kong Office: 9th Floor, Three Exchange Square, 8 Connaught Place. Telephone: (852) 2840 1282. Telex: 68757. Facsimile: (852) 2840 0515.

Madrid, Spain Office: Antonio Maura 7, 6°, 28014. Telephone: (34 1) 521 2654. Facsimile: (34 1) 523 0458.

Moscow, Russia Office: 9 ul Tverskaya, Entrance No 5, 8th Floor, 103009. Telephone: (7 501) 940 4500. Facsimile: (7 501) 940 4501.

New York Office: Swiss Bank Tower, 10 East 50th Street, 10022. Telephone (1-212) 754 3340. Facsimile: (1-212) 754 7903.

Paris, France Office: 1 Avenue Franklin D. Roosevelt, 75008. Telephone (33-1) 49 53 06 37. Telex: 651079. Facsimile: (33-1) 49 53 91 52.

Prague, Czech Republic Office: Jindřišská 34, 110 00 Prague 1. Telephone: (42 2) 2410 3317. Facsimile: (42 2) 2410 3235.

Singapore Office: 20 Raffles Place #08-03, Ocean Towers, 0104. Telephone: (65) 533 0988. Facsimile: (65) 533 1322.

Tokyo, Japan Office: NSE Building, 5th Floor, 1-7-1 Kanda Jinbo-cho, Chiyoda-ku Tokyo 101. Telephone (81 3) 3259 9898. Facsimile (81 3) 3259 9888.

Warsaw, Poland Office: ul. Kopernika 17, IV Floor, 00-359. Telephone: (48 22) 262 226. Facsimile: (48 22) 262 360.

Firm engaged in English and International Practice.
(This Listing Continued)

ALLEN & OVERY, Budapest—Continued

CONTACT PARTNERS

Ian F. Elder (Also at Budapest, Hungary)

RESIDENT ASSOCIATES

Patrick Beringer

(For Complete List of Firm Personnel, see Professional Biographies at London, England).

ARENT FOX KINTNER PLOTKIN & KAHN

NAGYMEZO UTCA 44
H-1065 BUDAPEST, HUNGARY
Telephone: (36-1) 269 0596; 269 0597
Facsimile: (36-1) 269 0599

Washington, D.C. Office: Washington Square, 1050 Connecticut Avenue, N.W. Telephone: 202-857-6000. Fax: 202-857-6395. Telex: WU-892672. Telecopier: 202-857-6395.

Bethesda, Maryland Office: Suite 900, 7475 Wisconsin Avenue. Telephone: 202-857-6000. Fax: 202-857-6395.

Vienna, Virginia Office: Suite 700, 8000 Towers Crescent Drive. Telephone: 202-857-6000. Fax: 202-857-6395.

N.Y.C. Office: 1675 Broadway, 25th Floor. Telephone: 212-484-3900. Fax: 212-484-3990.

Kingdom of Saudi Arabia Office: Law Offices of His Royal Highness Prince Saad Al Faisal Bin Abdul Aziz, P.O. Box 15836, Jeddah, Kingdom of Saudi Arabi. Telephone: (966-2) 651-9373. Facsimile: (966-2) 651-9465.

MEMBERS OF FIRM

ANDRE H. FRIEDMAN, born Budapest, Hungary, March 4, 1928; admitted, 1985, New York and U.S. Court of International Trade (Not admitted in Hungary). *Education:* Hungarian State University; Bernard M. Baruch School of Business, City University of New York; Hebrew University, Jerusalem (LL.M., 1957); University of Nice, France (Diplome de Francais Juridique, Economique et Commercial, 1985). General Counsel, National Association of Export Companies, 1985—. *Member:* New York State (Member, International Law and Practice Section; Chairman, 1987-1989 and Co-Chair, 1989—, Committee on International Sales and Related Commercial Transactions) and American (Member: International Law and Practice Section; Litigation Section; Arbitration Committee, 1985—; Forum Committee on Communication Law/Construction/Franchising, 1985—) Bar Associations; Union International des Avocats; International Bar Association. (Also at New York, N.Y. Office). *LANGUAGES:* French, Hebrew and Hungarian.

JEFFREY B. NEWMAN, born Washington, D.C., December 27, 1954; admitted, 1979, Virginia; 1989, District of Columbia; formerly, Conseil Juridique in France. *Education:* Ohio University (B.A., summa cum laude, 1976); Ohio State University College of Law (J.D., 1979); University of Paris Law School (D.S.U., 1980). *LANGUAGES:* French. *PRACTICE AREAS:* International Business Law; International Law; International Practice.

ASSOCIATES

ATTILA BECZNER, (Not admitted in Hungary). *Education:* Budapest University School of Law (J.D., 1992); Centreal European University (LL.M., 1993). *LANGUAGES:* Hungarian. *PRACTICE AREAS:* International.

DAVID S. DEDERICK, born Point Pleasant, New Jersey; admitted, 1989, District of Columbia (Not admitted in Hungary). *Education:* Cornell University (B.S., 1985); George Washington University (J.D., 1988). Senior Articles Editor, The George Washington Law Review, 1987-1988. Co-author with R. Sczudlo: "Directors' and Officers' Liability After FIRREA," PLI No. 535 (1990). Author: Note, "Publicizing Labor Disputes," 55 Geo. Wash. L. Rev. 1012 (1987). Judicial Clerk to the Honorable Lawrence S. Margolis, United States Claims Court, 1988-1989. *Member:* American Bar Association (Member: Central and Eastern European Law Initiative) International Bar Association. *PRACTICE AREAS:* International Commercial Transactions in Central and Eastern Europe; Real Estate; Banking.

(For complete biographical data on all personnel, see Professional Biographies at Washington, D.C.)

ARNOLD & PORTER
REPRESENTATIVE OFFICE
RETEK UTCA 26
H-1024 BUDAPEST, HUNGARY
Telephone: 36-1-212-1110
Telefax: 36-1-135-7857

Washington, D.C. Office: Thurman Arnold Building, 1200 New Hampshire Avenue, N.W., 20036-6885. Telephone: 202-872-6700. Telecopy: 202-872-6720.

Los Angeles, California Office: 44th Floor, 777 Figueroa Street, 90017-2513. Telephone: 213-243-4000. Telecopy: 213-243-4199.

Denver, Colorado Office: 1700 Lincoln Street, 80203-4540. Telephone: 303-863-1000. Telecopy: 303-832-0428.

New York, New York Office: 399 Park Avenue, 10022-4690. Telephone: 212-715-1000. Telecopy: 212-715-1399.

Istanbul, Turkey Representative Office: Büyükdere Caddesi No. 118/10, Esentepe 80280. Telephone: 90-212-275-2160. Fax: 90-212-275-2079.

Moscow, Russia Representative Office: Ozerkovskaya NA. 50, 113532. Telephone: 7095-235-3774. Telefax: 7095-235-5181.

International, Corporate and Legislative Practice including Acquisitions of State Assets (Privatizations), Joint Ventures, Financial Institutions, Franchising and Tax.

ASSOCIATES

THEODORE S. BOONE, born Urbana, Illinois, January 7, 1961; admitted, 1988, New York; 1989, District of Columbia. *Education:* University of Illinois (B.A., 1983) Phi Beta Kappa ; Ludwig Maximilians University Munich, Munich, Germany (Fulbright Grantee and Bavarian State Grantee, 1983-1984); Columbia University (J.D., 1987) U.S. FLAS Fellowship for Hungary; Eötvös Loránd University School of Law, Budapest, Hungary (IREX Grantee, 1987-1988). President, American Chamber of Commerce, Hungary, 1991-1993 and Co-Chair, Political and Legislative Affairs Committee, 1989—. Author: "Joint Ventures in Hungary," Joint Ventures with International Partners, Butterworths, 1991. *Member:* American Bar Association (Co-Chair, Committee on Central European Law, International Law Section); American Society of International Law; Council on Foreign Relations (Term Member). *LANGUAGES:* German and Hungarian.

DAVID F. NOTEWARE, born Dallas, Texas, October 25, 1966; admitted, 1992, Texas; 1994, District of Columbia (Not admitted in Hungary). *Education:* Duke University (A.B., magna cum laude, 1989); University of Texas School of Law (J.D., with honors, 1992). National Merit Scholar; Order of the Coif. Member, 1990-1991, and Associate Editor, 1991-1992, Texas Law Review. *State Bar of Texas. PRACTICE AREAS:* International; Corporate.

HUNGARIAN COUNSEL

DR. ZOLTAN GRMELA, born Karcag, Hungary, June 18, 1966. *Education:* University of Miskolc School of Law, Miskolc, Hungary (J.D., with honors, 1990); New York University School of Law (Master of Laws, 1992). Soros Scholarship; Lasker Scholarship; Kenneson Fellowship. Member, Political and Legislative Affairs Committee, American Chamber of Commerce, Hungary. *LANGUAGES:* English, Hungarian and Russian.

BACHER, KÁLMÁN, KOLOSSVÁRY,
PINTÉR, SÁRKÖZY AND SZILASI
SZERB UTCA 17-19
H-1056 BUDAPEST, HUNGARY
Telephone: (36-1) 117 45 57
Fax: (36-1) 118 97 18
(36-1) 137 33 86

Antitrust, Arbitration, Banking and Securities, Business Law, Civil Law and Litigation, Commercial, Corporate and Real Estate, Intellectual Property and Trademarks, Foreign Investments and Joint Ventures, Privatization, Unfair Competition.

MEMBERS OF FIRM

DR. VILMOS BACHER, admitted, 1957, Hungary.

DR. JÁNOS KÁLMÁN, admitted, 1973, Hungary.

DR. ISTVÁN KOLOSSVÁRY, admitted, 1959, Hungary.

DR. ZOLTÁN PINTÉR, admitted, 1983, Hungary.

(This Listing Continued)

DR. TAMÁS SÁRKÖZY, admitted, 1993, Hungary.

DR. ANDRÁS SZILASI, admitted, 1985, Hungary.

DR. ALAJOS DORNBACH, admitted, 1964, Hungary.

DR. LÁSZLÓ PARTOS, admitted, 1993, Hungary.

DR. TAMÁS GÖDÖLLE, admitted, 1991, Hungary.

Hungarian, English, German, Italian, French.

BAKER & McKENZIE

ANDRÁSSY-ÚT 125
H-1062 BUDAPEST, HUNGARY
Telephone: (1) 251-5777; 268-0422
Intn'l Dialing: (36-1) 251-5777; 268-0422
Telex: 22 3554
Answer Back: BMCK H
Facsimile: (36-1) 342-0513

Associated Offices of Baker & McKenzie in: Almaty, Amsterdam, Bangkok, Barcelona, Beijing, Berlin, Bogotá, Brasília, Brussels, Buenos Aires, Cairo, Caracas, Chicago, Dallas, Frankfurt, Geneva, Hanoi, Ho Chi Minh City, Hong Kong, Juárez, Kiev, London, Madrid, Manila, Melbourne, México City, Miami, Milan, Monterrey, Moscow, New York, Palo Alto, Paris, Prague, Rio de Janeiro, Riyadh, Rome, St. Petersburg, San Diego, San Francisco, São Paulo, Singapore, Stockholm, Sydney, Taipei, Tijuana, Tokyo, Toronto, Valencia, Warsaw, Washington, D.C. and Zürich.
Correspondent Law Firm: Hadiputranto, Hadinoto & Partners, Jakarta.

Internationally Oriented Legal Matters including the Establishment of Hungarian Joint Venture Companies with Foreign Participation, Tax Advice Affecting Hungarian Joint Venture Companies, Establishment of Representative Offices and all Transnational Legal Advice.

PARTNERS

ROBERT C. KNUEPFER, JR., born Oak Park, Illinois, February 23, 1952; admitted, 1978, Illinois, U.S.A.; 1980, U.S. District Court, Northern District of Illinois and U.S. Court of Appeals, Seventh Circuit; 1983, Northern District, Illinois Trial Bar; 1988, U.S. Supreme Court (Not admitted in Hungary). *Education:* Denison University (B.A., magna cum laude, 1974); Northwestern University (M.B.A., 1978; J.D., 1978). Baker & McKenzie Chicago Office, 1983-1992; Budapest Office, 1992—. *LANGUAGES:* French and German.

PETER PÁSINT MAGYAR, born New Haven, Connecticut, December 9, 1962; admitted, 1988, England and Wales (Not admitted in Hungary). *Education:* The London School of Economics and Political Science (LL.B., 1983); St. Edmund Hall, Oxford University (B.C.L., 1984); City of London Polytechnic (Solicitors' Final Examination, 1985). *Member:* The Law Society of England and Wales. *LANGUAGES:* Hungarian and French.

DR. JÁNOS MARTONYI, born Kolozsvár, Rumania, April 5, 1944; admitted, 1970, Hungary. *Education:* Law School of University (Szeged, Hungary) (Law, 1967). *Member:* Budapest Chamber of Attorneys; Hungarian Lawyers' Society. *LANGUAGES:* Hungarian, English, German and French. *PRACTICE AREAS:* Mergers and Acquisitions; Trade (International); Arbitration and Dispute Resolution; Antitrust Law; EC Law.

LOCAL PARTNER

DR. GÉZA KAJTÁR, born Budapest, Hungary, September 29, 1950; admitted, 1978, Hungary. *Education:* Eötvös Loránd University (J.D., cum laude, 1975). *Member:* Hungarian Bar Association. *LANGUAGES:* English, French and German.

SENIOR COUNSEL

DR. KÁLMÁN GYÁRFÁS, born Budapest, Hungary, January 23, 1930; admitted, 1961, Hungary. *Education:* University Eötvös Lorand (LL.D., summa cum laude, 1959). Lecturer, Comparative Trade Law, Institute for Postgraduate Legal Studies, 1983—. Member: Hungarian and Polish Arbitration Courts. *LANGUAGES:* English and German.

ASSOCIATES

JOHN F. LANGAN, born Rotherham, Yorkshire, England, January 3, 1959; admitted, 1984, England and Wales (Not admitted in Hungary). *Education:* Corpus Christi College, Oxford (English, 1980); Nottingham Law School (Common Professional Examination, 1981; Law Society Finals, 1982). *Member:* Law Society of England and Wales. *LANGUAGES:* Ger-

(This Listing Continued)

man, French and Italian. *PRACTICE AREAS:* Corporate and Partnership Law; Mergers and Acquisitions; Securities and Financial Products.

NATHALIE PIGEON, born Lyon, France, February 6, 1962; admitted, 1990, France (Not admitted in Hungary). *Education:* Lyon University (J.D., 1986); Dijon University (Ph.D., Economics, 1990). *Member:* Lyon Bar Association. *LANGUAGES:* English, Hungarian, Italian and German.

INES K. RADMILOVIC, born Zagreb, Yugoslavia, January 5, 1964; admitted, 1988, Illinois, U.S.A. (Not admitted in Hungary). *Education:* Tufts University (B.A., magna cum laude, 1985); Georgetown University (J.D., cum laude, 1988). *LANGUAGES:* Croatian, English and French. *PRACTICE AREAS:* Mergers and Acquisitions; Trade (Hungary and Central Europe); Corporate and Partnership Law.

AFFILIATED HUNGARIAN ATTORNEYS

DR. ZITA FEKETE, born Debrecen, Hungary, May 27, 1966; admitted, 1993, Hungary. *Education:* Eötvös Lorand University Law School (J.D., 1990). *Member:* Hungarian Bar Association. *LANGUAGES:* English and German.

DR. ANNA HALUSTYIK, born Budapest, Hungary, April 7, 1953; admitted, 1987, Hungary. *Education:* Eötvos Lorand University Law School (J.D., 1977); Hungarian Academy of Science (Ph.D., Law, 1985); University of Illinois (M.C.L., 1985). *Member:* Hungarian Bar Association. *LANGUAGES:* English, French, Spanish, Russian and Portuguese.

DR. ÉVA HEGEDÜS, born Szeged, Hungary, February 10, 1962; admitted, 1992, Missouri and Illinois, U.S.A.; 1994, District of Columbia, U.S.A. and Hungary. *Education:* József Attila University, School of Law (J.D., 1985); Washington University School of Law (J.D., 1991). *Member:* Illinois State Bar Association; The Missouri Bar; District of Columbia Bar. *LANGUAGES:* English, German, French, Spanish and Russian.

DR. TÜNDE HEGYI, born Budapest, Hungary, September 30, 1962; admitted, 1991, Hungary. *Education:* Eötvös Loránd University (J.D., 1986). *Member:* Hungarian Bar Association; Hungarian-Canadian Law Society. *LANGUAGES:* English, German and Russian.

DR. KONRÁD SIEGLER, born Budapest, Hungary, October 1, 1966; admitted, 1994, Hungary. *Education:* Arany János High School (1981-1985); University Eötvös Lóránd (Dr. Jur., 1991). *Member:* Hungarian Bar Association. *LANGUAGES:* Hungarian, English.

BEITEN BURKHARDT MITTL & WEGENER

Rechtsanwälte

JÓZSEF NÁDOR TÉR 9
H-1051 BUDAPEST, HUNGARY
Telephone: (1) 2 66 18 10
Telefax: (1) 2 66 18 10

Munich, Germany Office: Leopoldstrasse 236, D-80807. Telephone: (089) 35065-00. Telefax: (089) 35065-123.
Berlin, Germany Office: Kurfürstenstrasse 72-74, D-10787 Berlin. Telephone: (0 30) 264 71-0. Telefax: (0 30) 264 71-123.
Frankfurt/Main, Germany Office: Arndtstrasse 28, D-60325 Frankfurt/Main. Telephone: (0 69) 75 60 95-0. Telefax: (0 69) 75 60 95-12.
Nürnberg, Germany Office: Obere Turnstrasse 8, D-90429 Nürnberg. Telephone: (09 11) 2 79 71-0. Telefax: (09 11) 2 79 71-99.
Leipzig, Germany Office: Käthe-Kollwitz-Strasse 54, D-04109 Leipzig. Telephone: (03 41) 4 77 25 97. Telefax: (03 41) 4 77 25 99.
Potsdam, Germany Office: Heinrich-Mann-Allee 105 B, D-14473 Potsdam. Telephone: (0331) 33 43 06. Telefax: (0331) 33 43 29.
Hof, Germany Office: Oberer Torplatz 1, D-95028 Hof. Telephone: (09281) 80 23. Telefax: (09281) 1 65 69.
Plauen, Germany Office: Lindenstrasse 5, D-08523 Plauen. Telephone: (03741) 22 35 11; 22 49 62. Telefax: (03741) 22 49 62.
New York, New York Office: 215 East 73rd Street, New York, NY 10021. Telephone: (212) 570-2141. Telefax: (212) 734-7011.
London, England Office: Swedenborg House, 21 Bloomsbury Way, London, WC1A 2TH. Telephone: (0171) 2 42 44 66. Telefax: (0171) 2 42 44 67.
Moscow, Russia Office: Ul. Alekseja Tolstovo D.30/1, 103001 Moscow. Telephone and Telefax: (095) 202 37 60; 290 05 56.
Prague, Czech Republic Office: Na Bojišti 24, 120 00 Prague 2. Telephone: (2) 24 91 5808. Telefax: (2) 24 91 5804.

(This Listing Continued)

BEITEN BURKHARDT MITTL & WEGENER, Budapest—Continued

Hong Kong Office: 605 B, Sixth Floor, Peregrine Tower, Lippo Centre, 89 Queensway. Telephone: (852) 2524 6468. Telefax: (852) 2524 7028.

Beijing, People's Republic of China Office: Unit 10, 29th Floor, Jing Guang Centre, Hu Jia Lou, Chao Yang Qu, 100020. Telephone: (86-1) 501 4569; 501 3388 Ext. 2910. Telefax: (86-1) 501 3034.

Commercial Law, Company Law, M & A, Joint Ventures, Finance, Banking, Leasing, Domestic and International Tax, Antitrust, EC Law, Real Property and Private Construction, Electronic Data Processing (Protection and Licensing), Media, Publishing, Unfair Competition, Trademarks, Copyright, Labour, General and Special Administrative Law Particularly Public Construction and Planning Regulations and Public International Law, Environmental Law, Agricultural Law, Privatization and Restitution (former GDR), Probate, Family and Estate Planning, Insolvency and Sports, Insurance, Automobile Accidents and Injuries.

FIRM PROFILE: BEITEN BURKHARDT MITTL & WEGENER is a nation-wide and international law firm with 108 lawyers. The firm's head office is in Munich. All the firm's offices provide a comprehensive range of services in the main areas of civil and commercial law.

KÁLMÁN LÁSZLÓ, born Hatvan, 1946; admitted, 1974, Hungary; 1990, Germany. *Education:* Universities of Budapest and Bonn (law degree, 1971 (Budapest), 1985 (Bonn); Dr. jur., 1972). Author: "Freedom of Contract between State Enterprises," 1974; "Paternity Suits," 1978. *LANGUAGES:* Hungarian and German. *PRACTICE AREAS:* Company Law; Acquisitions and Sales; Restructuring.

ERNST LINDL, born Munich, 1961; admitted, 1991, Germany (Not admitted in Hungary). *Education:* Universities of Munich and Berlin (law degree, 1987; Dr. jur., 1992); University of Munich (MA, Political Science, German Literature, 1988). Author: "Labour Safety Law. The Council Directive on the Approximation of the Laws of the Member States relating to Machinery," 1992. *LANGUAGES:* German, English and French. *PRACTICE AREAS:* Company Law; Acquisitions and Sales; Restructuring; European Community Law; Insolvency; Liquidations.

RALF KELLERWESSEL, born Amberg/Oberpfalz, 1957; admitted, 1995, Germany. *Education:* Universities of Cologne (law degree, 1988) and Pécs, Hungary. Author: "Hungary in Securities and other Credit Enhancement Methods," 1995. Bank Trainee with DG Bank, 1988-1990; Credit Executive with Deutsch-Ungarische Bank (affiliate of DG-Bank), 1990; Metallgesellslchaft, Central Planning Department (projects in Hungary), 1990-1993; Deputy Department Director, Bayerische Hypotheken-und Wechselbank AG, Munich (corporate accounts of the Bank's Budapest affiliate), 1993-1994. Certified Translator for Hungarian. *Member:* AIESEC Alumni International; German-Hungarian Jurists' Association. *LANGUAGES:* German, English, Hungarian and Portuguese. *PRACTICE AREAS:* Company Law; Acquisitions and Sales; Restructuring; Financial Services.

ÁGNES KALÓ, born Miskolc, 1967; admitted, 1994, Hungary (Not admitted in Hungary). *Education:* University of Miskolc (law degree, 1990; Dr.jur., 1990); Yale Law School, Connecticut (LL.M., 1992). Staff Member, University of Miskolc, Department of Civil Law, 1990-1994. *LANGUAGES:* Hungarian, German and English. *PRACTICE AREAS:* Company Law; Acquisitions and Sales; Restructuring; Unfair Competition; Copyrights; Advertising and Marketing; Cartels.

BOGSCH & PARTNERS

BAJCSY-ZSILINSZKY ÚT 16.
1051 BUDAPEST, HUNGARY
Telephone: 36-1-266-2245, 118-1111
FAX: 36-1-137-7828

Corporate Law, Company Law, Business Law, Industrial Property Law, Infringements, Purchase and Selling Contracts, Joint Ventures, Privatization, International Civil Law, Acquisitions and Sales, Real Estate, Banking.

DR. ATTILA BOGSCH, born Budapest, Hungary, March 21, 1929; admitted, 1962, Hungary. *Education:* Eötvös Lóránd University of Law, Budapest (Dr.Jur., summa cum laude, 1957). Attorney, Lawyers' Cooperatives, 1961-1991. Private practice, 1991—. Guest Professor, Eötvös Lóránd University of Law. Chairman of Hungarian Copyright Expert Body. *Member:* Budapest Bar; AIPPI; Hungarian Association for Protection of Industrial Property. (Also Of Counsel To Danubia). *LANGUAGES:* Hungarian,

(This Listing Continued)

German, English, Italian and French. *PRACTICE AREAS:* Industrial Property Rights; Corporate Law; Business Law.

DR. PETER S. SZABÓ, born Budapest, Hungary, December 8, 1956; admitted, 1983, Budapest. *Education:* Eötvös Loránd University, Faculty of Law, Budapest (Doctor of Law, summa cum laude, 1981). Member, Academy of American and International Law. Southwestern Legal Foundation, Dallas, Texas, 1992. Reporteur for the International Lawyer, quarterly publication of the American Bar Association. *Member:* Budapest Bar; AIJA Hungarian Presidential Delegate. *LANGUAGES:* Hungarian, English and German.

DR. ALICE DESSEWFFY, born Budapest, Hungary, November 9, 1946; admitted, 1972, Budapest. *Education:* Eötvös Loránd University, Faculty of Law (Doctor of Law). *Member:* Budapest Bar; German-Hungarian Chamber of Industry and Commerce. *LANGUAGES:* Hungarian, English and German.

ASSOCIATES

Dr. Gyula Gábriel
Dr. Hedvig Bozsonyik
Dr. Andrea Szabadkai

DR. KATALIN BREUER

I/A MARKÓ STREET
H-1055 BUDAPEST, HUNGARY
Telephone: (36-1) 112-5918
Fax: (36-1) 112-5918

Company and Trade Law, Commercial Law, Civil and Business Litigation, Arbitration, International Sales, Intellectual Property.

FIRM PROFILE: Established in 1992, it offers a full range of quality legal services for domestic and foreign investors and companies to set up businesses in Hungary. As a sole practitioner, the firm is able to serve its clients efficiently.

DR. KATALIN BREUER, born Budapest, Hungary, November 1, 1961; admitted, 1991, Hungary. *Education:* Eötuös Loránd University, Faculty of Law (LL.D., 1984). *Member:* Budapest Bar Association; International Bar Association (Section on Business Law). *LANGUAGES:* English and Hungarian.

DANUBIA

Patent & Trademark Attorneys
Established in 1949

BAJCSY-ZSILINSZKY ÚT 16
P.O. BOX 198
H-1368 BUDAPEST, HUNGARY
Telephone: (+361) 118-1111; (+361) 266-5760
Fax: (+361) 138-2304; (+361) 266-5770

Hungarian Industrial Property Practice, Prosecution, Litigation. Entitled to plead before the Hungarian Patent Office and Courts, including Supreme Court, in all IP matters.

FIRM PROFILE: Established in 1949 under the name of Patentbureau Danubia and has evolved into a professional corporation in 1989 with the new name of Danubia Patent and Trademark Attorneys. The firm has grown to be the largest IP firm in Hungary and probably in all of Central Europe. The activities can be grouped in three main branches: Representing Foreign Clients in Hungarian Proceedings, Foreign Clients in Proceedings in Foreign Countries (mainly in Central and Eastern Europe) and Acting for Hungarian Companies to Obtain, Defend and Maintain Rights in Foreign Countries. Major International companies use Danubia as their Hungarian agent and also numerous foreign companies as a satellite office for their operation in Central and Eastern Europe. The firm has the broadest IP enforcement practice before Hungarian authorities, with more than 30 patent attorneys covering all fields of technology, three trademark lawyers and a total staff of 130. There is a close cooperation between Danubia and the law firm of Bogsch & Partners. A four person management team including a managing partner and three deputies is elected every three years. The present team runs the firm until the end of 1996.

(This Listing Continued)

MANAGING PARTNER

MICHAEL LANTOS, born Budapest, Hungary, August 20, 1944; admitted, 1974, Hungary; Registered Patent Attorney. *Education:* Budapest Technical University (M.Sc., 1967; B.Sc., Economist, 1972). Danubia Patent & Trademark Attorneys, 1972—. *Member:* Hungarian Association of Patent Attorneys; Hungarian Association for Protection of Industrial Property (Member of Presidial Board); AIPPI (Member of Presidial Board); Hungarian Trademark Association (Vice President); LES Hungary; LIDC Hungary; UNION. *LANGUAGES:* Hungarian, English and German. *PRACTICE AREAS:* Industrial Property Rights; Patents; IP Litigation.

DEPUTY MANAGING PARTNERS

IMRE MOLNÁR, born Kecskemét, Hungary, April 21, 1946; admitted, 1980, Hungary; Registered Patent Attorney. *Education:* Eötvös Lóránd University of Science Budapest (M.Sc., 1979). Danubia Patent & Trademark Attorneys, 1972—. *Member:* Hungarian Association of Patent Attorneys; Hungarian Association for Protection of Industrial Property; AIPPI. *LANGUAGES:* Hungarian, English and German. *PRACTICE AREAS:* Industrial Property Rights; Patents; IP Litigation.

PÉTER ERDÉLY, born Kolozsvár, Hungary, September 10, 1943; admitted, 1974, Hungary; Registered Patent Attorney. *Education:* Budapest Technical University (M.Sc., 1967). Danubia Patent & Trademark Attorneys, 1971—. *Member:* Hungarian Association of Patent Attorneys; Hungarian Association for Protection of Industrial Property; AIPPI; FICPI; UNION. *LANGUAGES:* Hungarian, English and German. *PRACTICE AREAS:* Industrial Property Rights; Patents; IP Litigation; Valuation of IP Assets.

DR. ÉVA SZIGETI, born Pápa, Hungary, July 2, 1952; admitted, 1978, Hungary. *Education:* University of Law, Budapest (LL.D., 1975). Trademark Department Head, Danubia Patent & Trademark Attorneys, 1979—. *Member:* Hungarian Trademark Association (Board Member); Hungarian Association for Protection of Industrial Property (Board Member); AIPPI; MARQUES (Council Member); Institute of Trademark Agents (Overseas Member); International Trademark Association (Member, International Committee). *LANGUAGES:* Hungarian, English and German. *PRACTICE AREAS:* Industrial Property Rights; Trademarks; IP Litigation.

OF COUNSEL

DR. ATTILA BOGSCH, born Budapest, Hungary, March 21, 1929; admitted, 1962, Hungary. *Education:* Eötvös Lóránd University of Law, Budapest (Dr.Jur., summa cum laude, 1957). Attorney, Lawyers' Cooperatives, 1961-1991. Private practice, 1991—. Guest Professor, Eötvös Lóránd University of Law. *Member:* Budapest Bar; AIPPI; Hungarian Association for Protection of Industrial Property; Hungarian Copyright Experts' (Chairman). (Also Member Bogsch & Partners). *LANGUAGES:* Hungarian, German, English, Italian and French. *PRACTICE AREAS:* Intellectual Property Rights; Corporate Law; Business Law.

SENIOR PARTNERS

ANDRÁS WEICHINGER, born Budapest, Hungary, April 14, 1933; admitted, 1965, Hungary; Registered Patent Attorney. *Education:* Budapest Technical University (M.Sc., 1956). Patent Examiner, Hungarian Patent Office, 1956-1959. Danubia Patent & Trademark Attorneys, 1963—. *Member:* Hungarian Association of Patent Attorneys; Hungarian Association for Protection of Industrial Property; AIPPI. *LANGUAGES:* Hungarian, English and German. *PRACTICE AREAS:* Industrial Property Rights; Patents; IP Litigation.

HENRIETTE KALMÁR, born Budapest, Hungary, April 25, 1933; admitted, 1965, Hungary; Registered Patent Attorney. *Education:* Budapest Technical University (M.Sc., 1956). Danubia Patent & Trademark Attorneys, 1962—. *Member:* Hungarian Association of Patent Attorneys; Hungarian Association for Protection of Industrial Property; AIPPI. *LANGUAGES:* Hungarian, English, French and German. *PRACTICE AREAS:* Industrial Property Rights; Patents; Designs.

JUDIT KERÉNY, born Budapest, Hungary, May 28, 1946; admitted, 1977, Hungary; Registered Patent Attorney. *Education:* Technical University, Prague, Czech Republic (M.Sc., 1969). Danubia Patent & Trademark Attorneys, 1975—. *Member:* Hungarian Association of Patent Attorneys; Hungarian Association for Protection of Industrial Property; AIPPI; UNION. *LANGUAGES:* Hungarian, Czech, English, French, German and Russian. *PRACTICE AREAS:* Industrial Property Rights; Patents; IP Litigation.

KINGA KOVÁCS, (MS.), born Budapest, Hungary, January 29, 1942; admitted, 1980, Hungary; Registered Patent Attorney. *Education:* Buda-

(This Listing Continued)

pest Technical University (M.Sc., 1965). Danubia Patent & Trademark Attorneys, 1982—. *Member:* Hungarian Association of Patent Attorneys; Hungarian Association for Protection of Industrial Property; AIPPI. *LANGUAGES:* Hungarian, English and German. *PRACTICE AREAS:* Industrial Property Rights; Patents; Documentation; Search.

DR. JÓZSEF MARKÓ, born Jászberény, Hungary, July 20, 1943; admitted, 1975, Hungary; Registered Patent Attorney. *Education:* University for Agricultural Engineering, Budapest (M.Sc., 1966; Ph.D., 1984). Danubia Patent & Trademark Attorneys, 1975—. Lecturer, Official Qualification Course of Industrial Property, 1984—. *Member:* Hungarian Association of Patent Attorneys (Secretary); Hungarian Association for Protection of Industrial Property (Ex-Co. Member); AIPPI; LES Hungary; FICPI; UNION (President, Hungarian Group). *LANGUAGES:* Hungarian, English and German. *PRACTICE AREAS:* Industrial Property Rights; Patents; IP Litigation; Licensing.

ERNÖ NAGY, born Budapest, Hungary, June 16, 1944; admitted, 1980, Hungary; Registered Patent Attorney. *Education:* Poznan University, Poland (M.Sc., 1971). Danubia Patent & Trademark Attorneys, 1978—. Co-Author: "Physical Encyclopedia," Kandó Technical College, Budapest, 1977. *Member:* Hungarian Association of Patent Attorneys; Hungarian Association for Protection of Industrial Property; AIPPI; Hungarian Trademark Association; FICPI. *LANGUAGES:* Hungarian, English, French, German, Polish and Russian. *PRACTICE AREAS:* Industrial Property Rights; Patents.

DR. TIVADAR PALÁGYI, born Szár, Hungary, November 13, 1923; admitted, 1959, Hungary. *Education:* Budapest Technical University (M.Sc., 1950; Ph.D., 1959). Research Chemist, 1950-1963; Danubia Patent & Trademark Attorneys, 1959—. Lecturer in Foreign Patent Law: Law Faculty, Eötvös University, Budapest; Marx University of Economics, Budapest. Author: "Patentability of Chemical Inventions," 1967; "Foreign Patent and Utility Model Law," 1987 and 1989. Co-Author: "Foreign Patent and Trademark Law," 1972 and 1977; "Handbook of Industrial Property," 1986, 1989 and 1994. *Member:* AIPPI (President, Hungarian Group); UNION; Hungarian Association for the Protection of Industrial Property (Member of Presidium); Hungarian Chamber of Patent Attorneys (Member of Board). *LANGUAGES:* Hungarian, English, French, German, Italian and Spanish. *PRACTICE AREAS:* Industrial Property Rights; International Patent Law.

RÓBERT SIKOS, born Budapest, Hungary, April 12, 1927; admitted, 1972, Hungary; Registered Patent Attorney. *Education:* Budapest Technical University (M.Sc., 1950). Designer and Research Engineer, 1950-1961; Elektro-Apparate Werke Berlin, 1961-1963; Scientific Section Head, Research Institute for Electrical Instruments, 1963-1970; Danubia Patent & Trademark Attorneys, 1970—. Assistant, Budapest Technical University, 1963-1970. Guest Lecturer, Vienna Technical University, Austria, 1965. *Member:* Hungarian Association of Patent Attorneys; Hungarian Association for Protection of Industrial Property; AIPPI; FICPI. *LANGUAGES:* Hungarian, English and German. *PRACTICE AREAS:* Industrial Property Rights; Patents.

ÁGNES SZEMZÖ, born Sopron, Hungary, February 11, 1945; admitted, 1981, Hungary; Registered Patent Attorney. *Education:* Eötvös Lóránd University (M.Sc., 1963). Danubia Patent & Trademark Attorneys, 1978—. *Member:* Hungarian Association of Patent Attorneys; Hungarian Association for Protection of Industrial Property; AIPPI. *LANGUAGES:* Hungarian, English and German. *PRACTICE AREAS:* Industrial Property Rights; Patents.

ELEMÉR SZUHAI, born Szikszó, Hungary, February 25, 1936; admitted, 1974, Hungary; Registered Patent Attorney. *Education:* Budapest Technical University (M.Sc., 1961). Research Engineer, Chief Engineer of Technical Development, Works for Electronic Measuring Instruments. Danubia Patent & Trademark Attorneys, 1971—. *Member:* Hungarian Association of Patent Attorneys; Hungarian Association for Protection of Industrial Property; AIPPI. *LANGUAGES:* Hungarian, English and German. *PRACTICE AREAS:* Industrial Property Rights; Patents.

PARTNERS

ANDRÁS ANTALFFY-ZSIROS, born Budapest, Hungary, June 21, 1955. *Education:* Technical Academy for Electric Industry (B.Sc., 1977). Patent Attorney, Danubia Patent & Trademark Attorneys, 1982—. *Member:* Hungarian Association of Patent Attorneys; Hungarian Association for Protection of Industrial Property; AIPPI. *LANGUAGES:* Hungarian, English and German. *PRACTICE AREAS:* Industrial Property Rights; Patents.

(This Listing Continued)

DANUBIA, Budapest—Continued

ÉVA BARANYI, born Budapest, Hungary, April 19, 1946; admitted, 1989, Hungary; Registered Patent Attorney. *Education:* Budapest Technical University (M.Sc., 1969). Danubia Patent & Trademark Attorneys, 1987—. *Member:* Hungarian Association of Patent Attorneys; Hungarian Association for Protection of Industrial Property; AIPPI. *LANGUAGES:* Hungarian, English, French and German. *PRACTICE AREAS:* Industrial Property Rights; Patents.

DR. HANNA BOGSCH, born Budapest, Hungary, June 21, 1963. *Education:* University of Law, Budapest (Dr.Jur., 1986). Trademark Lawyer, Danubia Patent & Trademark Attorneys, 1993—. *LANGUAGES:* Hungarian, English and German. *PRACTICE AREAS:* Industrial Property Rights; Trademarks.

ILONA GÁRDONYI, (MS.), born Budapest, Hungary, February 15, 1947; admitted, 1983, Hungary; Registered Patent Attorney. *Education:* Budapest Technical University (M.Sc., 1971). Danubia Patent & Trademark Attorneys, 1979—. *Member:* Hungarian Association of Patent Attorneys; Hungarian Association for Protection of Industrial Property; AIPPI. *LANGUAGES:* Hungarian, English and German. *PRACTICE AREAS:* Industrial Property Rights; Patents.

ANNEMARIE KIS KOVÁCS, born Wriezen, Germany, January 31, 1949; admitted, 1986, Hungary; Registered Patent Attorney. *Education:* Technical University Kiew, U.S.S.R. (M.Sc., 1973). Danubia Patent & Trademark Attorneys, 1983—. *Member:* Hungarian Association of Patent Attorneys; Hungarian Association for Protection of Industrial Property; AIPPI; FICPI. *LANGUAGES:* Hungarian, English, German and Russian. *PRACTICE AREAS:* Industrial Property Rights; Patents.

DR. ILDIKÓ KISS, (MS.), born Csongrád, Hungary, April 11, 1947; admitted, 1985, Hungary. *Education:* University of Sciences, Szeged (M.Sc., 1970; Ph.D., 1981). Research Chemist, 1970-1982. Danubia Patent & Trademark Attorneys, 1982—. *Member:* Hungarian Association of Patent Attorneys; Hungarian Association for Protection of Industrial Property; AIPPI. *LANGUAGES:* Hungarian, English and German. *PRACTICE AREAS:* Industrial Property Rights; Patents.

JUDIT KOMÁROMI, born Budapest, Hungary, June 11, 1948; admitted, 1982, Hungary; Registered Patent Attorney. *Education:* Budapest Technical University (M.Sc., 1972). Danubia Patent & Trademark Attorneys, 1978—. *Member:* Hungarian Association of Patent Attorneys; Hungarian Association for Protection of Industrial Property; AIPPI. *LANGUAGES:* Hungarian, English, French and German. *PRACTICE AREAS:* Industrial Property Rights; Patents.

GÁBOR KOVÁCS, born Budapest, Hungary, November 24, 1946; admitted, 1986, Hungary; Registered Patent Attorney. *Education:* Budapest Technical University (M.Sc., 1971). Danubia Patent & Trademark Attorneys, 1982—. *Member:* Hungarian Association of Patent Attorneys; Hungarian Association for Protection of Industrial Property; AIPPI. *LANGUAGES:* Hungarian, English and German. *PRACTICE AREAS:* Industrial Property Rights; Patents; Licensing.

ERZSÉBET OLCHVÁRY, (MS.), born Budapest, Hungary, July 29, 1939; admitted, 1986, Hungary; Registered Patent Attorney. *Education:* Budapest Technical University (M.Sc., 1967). Danubia Patent & Trademark Attorneys, 1982—. *Member:* Hungarian Association of Patent Attorneys; Hungarian Association for Protection of Industrial Property; AIPPI. *LANGUAGES:* Hungarian, English and German. *PRACTICE AREAS:* Industrial Property Rights; Patents.

LÁSZLÓ SCHLÄFER, born Budapest, Hungary, August 10, 1953; admitted, 1983, Hungary; Registered Patent Attorney. *Education:* Budapest Technical University (M.Sc., 1976). Researcher, Chinoin Pharmacy Company, 1976-1980. Danubia Patent & Trademark Attorneys, 1980—. *Member:* Hungarian Association of Patent Attorneys; Hungarian Association for Protection of Industrial Property; AIPPI. *LANGUAGES:* Hungarian, English and German. *PRACTICE AREAS:* Industrial Property Rights; Patents.

JÓZSEF SIPOS, born Budapest, Hungary, October 30, 1951; admitted, 1981, Hungary; Registered Patent Attorney. *Education:* Bauakademie Freiberg, Germany (M.Sc., 1974). Danubia Patent & Trademark Attorneys, 1977—. *Member:* Hungarian Association of Patent Attorneys; Hungarian Association for Protection of Industrial Property; AIPPI; FICPI. *LANGUAGES:* Hungarian, English, French, Finnish and German. *PRACTICE AREAS:* Industrial Property Rights; Patents.

(This Listing Continued)

MIKLÓS SÓVÁRI, born Budapest, Hungary, April 21, 1958; admitted, 1988, Hungary; Registered Patent Attorney. *Education:* Budapest Technical University (M.Sc., 1982); Pannon University, Mosonmagyaróvár (Spec. Degree of Industrial Property, 1990). Danubia Patent & Trademark Attorneys, 1984—. *Member:* Hungarian Association of Patent Attorneys; Hungarian Association for Protection of Industrial Property; AIPPI; UNION. *LANGUAGES:* Hungarian, English and German. *PRACTICE AREAS:* Industrial Property Rights; Patents; Licensing.

ANNETTE TOPOR, born Berlin, Germany, August 15, 1939; admitted, 1981, Hungary; Registered Patent Attorney. *Education:* Engineers School Frederic Joliot Curie, Köthen, Germany (M.Sc., 1962). Danubia Patent & Trademark Attorneys, 1972—. *Member:* Hungarian Association of Patent Attorneys; Hungarian Association for Protection of Industrial Property; AIPPI. *LANGUAGES:* Hungarian and German. *PRACTICE AREAS:* Industrial Property Rights; Patents.

FERENC TÖRÖK, born Budapest, Hungary, March 4, 1961; admitted, 1988, Hungary; Registered Patent Attorney. *Education:* Eötvös Loránd University (M.Sc., 1985). Chemical Works of Gedeon Richter, 1985-1989; Danubia Patent & Trademark Attorneys, 1989—. *Member:* Hungarian Association of Patent Attorneys; Hungarian Association for Protection of Industrial Property; AIPPI; UNION. *LANGUAGES:* Hungarian and English. *PRACTICE AREAS:* Industrial Property Rights; Patents.

ELVIRA VALYON, born Budapest, Hungary, October 9, 1947; admitted, 1983, Hungary; Registered Patent Attorney. *Education:* Budapest Technical University (M.Sc., 1971). Researcher, Institute for Engineering in Organic Chemistry, Budapest, 1971-1983. Danubia Patent & Trademark Attorneys, 1983—. *Member:* Hungarian Association of Patent Attorneys; Hungarian Association for Protection of Industrial Property; AIPPI. *LANGUAGES:* Hungarian and English. *PRACTICE AREAS:* Industrial Property Rights; Patents.

DR. ÁGNES VÁLAS, born Budapest, Hungary, November 7, 1941; admitted, 1985, Hungary; Registered Patent Attorney. *Education:* Budapest Technical University (M.Sc., 1964; Ph.D., 1981). Researcher, Institute for Food and Nutrition, 1973-1982. Danubia Patent & Trademark Attorneys, 1982—. *Member:* Hungarian Association of Patent Attorneys; Hungarian Association for Protection of Industrial Property; AIPPI. *LANGUAGES:* Hungarian, English and German. *PRACTICE AREAS:* Industrial Property Rights; Patents.

DR. LÁSZLÓ VITÁLIS, born Kisvárda, Hungary, January 1, 1944; admitted, 1992, Hungary; Registered Patent Attorney. *Education:* Veszprém University of Chemistry (M.Sc., 1967; Ph.D., 1978). Researcher, Research Institut for Non-Ferrous Metals, 1967-1989. Danubia Patent & Trademark Attorneys, 1989—. *Member:* Hungarian Association of Patent Attorneys; Hungarian Association for Protection of Industrial Property; AIPPI. *LANGUAGES:* Hungarian, English and German. *PRACTICE AREAS:* Industrial Property Rights; Patents.

CONSULTANTS

DR. ERZSÉBET FARKAS, born Miskolc, Hungary, March 12, 1935; admitted, 1974, Hungary; Registered Patent Attorney. *Education:* University of Debrecen (M.Sc., 1957); Semmelweis University, Budapest (Ph.D., 1965). Danubia Patent & Trademark Attorneys, 1972—. *Member:* Hungarian Association of Patent Attorneys; Hungarian Association for Protection of Industrial Property; AIPPI. *LANGUAGES:* Hungarian, English and German. *PRACTICE AREAS:* Industrial Property Rights; Patents.

DR. ALEXANDER VIDA, born Budapest, Hungary, June 6, 1924; admitted, 1950, Hungary. *Education:* University of Law, Budapest (LL.D., 1946); University of Strasbourg, France (Professor Degree, 1983). Company Lawyer. Lecturer, Patent and Trademark Law, Technical University of Budapest; University of Strasbourg, France. Consultant, Danubia Patent & Trademark Attorneys, 1979—. *Member:* Hungarian Chamber of Commerce (Court of Arbitration, 1980—); AIPPI (Vice-President, 1977—). *LANGUAGES:* Hungarian, English, French and German. *PRACTICE AREAS:* Trademarks; Unfair Competition Law.

DEBEVOISE & PLIMPTON

Established in 1931

1065 BUDAPEST

RÉVAY KÖZ 2.III/2.

BUDAPEST, HUNGARY

Telephone: (36-1) 112-8067

Telecopier: (36-1) 132-7995

New York Office: 875 Third Avenue, 10022. Telephone: 212-909-6000. Telex: (Domestic) 148377 DEBSTEVE NYK. Telecopier: (212) 909-6836.

Washington, D.C. Office: 555 13th Street, N.W., 20004. Telephone: 202-383-8000. Telex: 405586 DPDC WUUD. Telecopier: (202) 383-8118.

Los Angeles, California Office: 601 South Figueroa Street, Suite 3700, 90017. Telephone: 213-680-8000. Telex: 401527 DPLA. Telecopier: 213-680-8100.

Paris, France Office: 21 Avenue George V 75008. Telephone: (33-1) 40 73 12 12. Telecopier: (33-1) 47 20 50 82. Telex: 648141F DPPAR.

London, England Office: 1 Creed Court, 5 Ludgate Hill. Telephone: (44-171) 329-0779. Telex: 884569 DPLON G. Telecopier: (44-171) 329-0860.

Hong Kong Office: 13/F Entertainment Building, 30 Queen's Road Central. Telephone: (852) 2810-7918. Fax: (852) 2810-9828.

American and General International Practice.

FIRM PROFILE: OFFICE PROFILE: Opened in 1991, the Budapest office is staffed with lawyers with experience in privatizations, joint ventures and international mergers and acquisitions; banking; telecommunications; equity placements; debt financings, including leveraged lease and project financings; general Hungarian and international corporate law. The Budapest office works closely with our other offices in Paris and London, our attorneys and affiliates based in Prague and Moscow and our U.S. offices.

RESIDENT COUNSEL

DAVID F. HICKOK, born May 18, 1959; admitted, 1985, N.Y.; 1991, Paris (Not admitted in Hungary). *Education:* Princeton (A.B., 1981); New York University School of Law (J.D., 1984). *Member:* The Association of the Bar of the City of New York. **PRACTICE AREAS:** Mergers and Acquisitions; Financings; Joint Ventures; General Corporate.

RESIDENT ATTORNEY

VERA LOSONCI, born Budapest, Hungary, July 5, 1967; admitted, 1993, New York (Not admitted in Hungary). *Education:* Hunter College (B.A., 1989); Cardozo Law School (J.D., 1992). Co-Author: "Rule by Law in East Central Europe: Is the Emperor's New Cloth a Strait Jacket?" Constitutionalism & Democracy in Eastern Europe-Transformation in the Modern World (1992), *Member:* The Association of the Bar of the City of New York. **PRACTICE AREAS:** Joint Ventures; Privatizations; Financings; International Corporate Transactions; Securities.

HUNGARIAN COUNSEL

DR. ZSUZSA KOVÁCS, born January 7, 1960; admitted, 1986, Budapest. *Education:* Eotvos Lorand University Faculty of Law (1983). **PRACTICE AREAS:** Privatizations; Hungarian and International Corporate Transactions; Banking; Telecommunications.

DR. ZSUZSANNA NAGY, born June 19, 1968; admitted, 1994, Hungary. *Education:* Eotvos Lorand University Faculty of Law (1991). **PRACTICE AREAS:** Privatizations; Hungarian and International Corporate Transactions.

(For Biographical Data of other Lawyers, see Professional Biographies at New York, N.Y.)

STUDIO LEGALE DE CAPOA - GUIDUCCI & ASSOCIATI

HONVED UT 38, IV/7

BUDAPEST 1027, HUNGARY

Telephone: 36-1-1121683

Telefax: 36-1-1121683

Bologna, Italy Office: Via Albertazzi 22, 40137. Telephone: (39-51) 34799; 346062; 348835. Telefax: (39-51) 344125.

(This Listing Continued)

International and Domestic Commercial Law, General and Civil Practice, Contracts, Litigation, Intellectual Property, EEC and Tax Law.

Antonio de Capoa	*Michele Draghetti*
Elena Baroni	*Sebastiano Negri di Montenegro*
Giorgio Caramori	*Andrea Csilla Csiby*
	Julianna Kovàcs

(For Complete Biographical Data on all Personnel, see Professional Biographies at Bologna, Italy)

DEWEY BALLANTINE THEODORE GODDARD

VADASZ UTCA 31

H-1054 BUDAPEST, HUNGARY

Telephone: (36-1) 111-9620

Fax: (36-1) 112-2272

Dewey Ballantine Offices:

New York, New York Office: 1301 Avenue of the Americas, 10019-6092. Telephone: 212-259-8000. Fax: 212-259-6333.

Washington, D.C. Office: 1775 Pennsylvania Avenue, N.W., 20006-4605. Telephone: 202-862-1000. Fax: 202-862-1093.

Los Angeles, California Office: 333 South Hope Street, 90071-1406. Telephone: 213-626-3399. Fax: 213-625-0562.

London, England Office: 150 Aldersgate Street, London EC1A 4EJ, England. Telephone: (44-71) 606-6121. Fax: (44-71) 600-3754.

Hong Kong Office: Asia Pacific Finance Tower, Suite 3907, Citibank Plaza, 3 Garden Road, Central, Hong Kong. Telephone: 852-2509-7000. Fax: 852-2509-7088.

Theodore Goddard Offices:

London, England Office: 150 Aldersgate Street, EC1A 4EJ. Telephone: (44-71) 606-8855. Fax: (44-71) 606-4390.

Paris, France Office: Klein Goddard, 44 Avenue des Champs Elysées, 75008. Telephone: (33-1) 4495-2000. Fax: (33-1) 4953-0397.

Brussels, Belgium Office: 79 avenue de Cortenberg/Kortenberglaan 79, B-1040. Telephone: (32-2) 732-2700. Fax: (32-2) 735-2352.

Other Dewey Ballantine Theodore Goddard Offices:

Prague, Czech Republic Office: Revolucni 13, 110 00 Prague 1. Telephone: (42-2) 2481-0283. Fax: (42-2) 231-0983.

Warsaw, Poland Office: ul. Klonowa 8, 00-591. Telephone: 48-22-49-32-88. Fax: 48-22-49-80-23.

Kraków, Poland Office: Pl. Axentowicza 6. 30-034 Kraków Poland. Telephone: 48-12-340-339. Fax: 48-12-333-624.

General Corporate and Commercial Practice.

FIRM PROFILE: Dewey Ballantine Theodore Goddard is a joint venture between the U.S.-based international law firm of Dewey Ballantine and the British-based international law firm of Theodore Goddard. Dewey Ballantine Theodore Goddard also has offices in Prague and Warsaw.

MANAGING LAWYER

JAMES D. SIMPSON, JR., born Arlington, Virginia, 1958; admitted, 1985, New York (Not admitted in Hungary). *Education:* Duke University (A.B., 1981); Washington & Lee University (J.D., 1984).

COUNSEL

DR. NORBERT CHRIST, born Kaposvar, Hungary, 1964. *Education:* Janus Pannonius University of Peos (1987). **LANGUAGES:** English, Hungarian.

DR. ISTVAN LEVENTE, born Debrecen, Hungary, 1965; admitted, 1994, Hungary. *Education:* Miskolc University (1990). **LANGUAGES:** English, Hungarian.

EASTEUROPELAW, LTD.

EAST-WEST BUSINESS CENTER PF. 300/25
RÁKÓCZI 1-3 ÚT
1088 BUDAPEST, HUNGARY
Telephone: (36-1) 266-4979
Telecopier: (36-1) 266-6360

Washington, D.C. Office: Brownstein Zeidman and Lore, A Professional Corporation: Suite 900, 1401 New York Avenue, N.W. Telephone: 202-879-5700. Telecopier: 202-879-5773. TWX: 710-8229772. Cable Address: "Caveat-Wsh".

PHILIP F. ZEIDMAN, born Birmingham, Alabama, May 2, 1934; admitted, 1958, Alabama; 1960, Florida; 1968, District of Columbia; 1981, New York (Not admitted in Hungary). *Education:* Yale University (B.A., cum laude, 1955); Harvard University (LL.B., 1958). Assistant General Counsel, 1963-1965 and General Counsel, 1965-1968, Small Business Administration. Special Assistant to the Vice-President of the United States, 1968. Government Relations Manager, National Alliance of Businessmen, 1968. Consulting Editor, *Global Franchising Alert,* Commerce Clearinghouse, 1993—. Co-Author: *Franchising: Regulation of Buying and Selling a Franchise,* Bureau of National Affairs/Corporate Practice Series, 1983. Editor: *Survey of Foreign Laws and Regulations Affecting International Franchising,* American Bar Association, 1982, 2nd Edition, 1989; *Legal Aspects of Selling and Buying,* Shepard's- McGraw-Hill, 1983, 2nd edition 1991. Author: "International Franchising," in *Business Franchise Guide,* Commerce Clearing House, 1987; Co-Author: "Franchising in Eastern Europe and the Soviet Union," *DePaul Business Law Journal,* Fall 1991. Associate Editor, *The Journal of International Franchising and Distribution Law,* 1986—. General Counsel, International Franchise Association. Special Counsel, Japanese Franchise Association, 1973—. Secretary and Counsel, American Business Conference, 1980—. *Member:* The District of Columbia Bar; Bar Association of the District of Columbia; New York State, Federal, American (First Chairman, Franchising Committee, Antitrust Section, 1977-1981; Forum on Franchising) and International (Vice Chairman, 1983-1986 and Chairman, 1986-1990, International Franchising Committee, Section of Business Law) Bar Associations; Alabama State Bar; The Florida Bar; American Intellectual Property Law Association (Chairman, Franchise Law Committee, 1987-1990); International Bar Association (Vice-Chairman, Asia-Pacific Forum). *PRACTICE AREAS:* Antitrust and Trade Regulation; International Franchising and Distribution Law.

MARTIN MENDELSOHN, (Not admitted in Hungary). Author: *The Guide to Franchising,* 5th edition; *How to Evaluate a Franchise,* 4th edition; The UK Department of Trade *Obtaining a Franchise,* "How to Franchise Internationally," "The Ethics of Franchising," "The Franchisers Manual," and *Comment Negocier une Franchise,* 2nd edition. Co-author: *How to Franchise Your Business,* 3rd edition. Contributor: United Kingdom and European Community sections of the American Bar Association's *Survey of Foreign Laws and Regulations Affecting Franchising,* 2nd edition. Editor: *International Franchising - An Overview.* General Editor: *The Journal of International Franchising and Distribution Law,* 1986—. Visiting Professor of Franchising and Director, Nat West Centre for Franchising, The City University Business School, London. Legal consultant to the British Franchise Association. First Chairman of the International Franchising Committee of the Section of Business Law of the International Bar Association. Member: American Bar Association Forum Committee on Franchising. *PRACTICE AREAS:* International Franchising and Distribution Law.

LEWIS G. RUDNICK, born May 31, 1935; admitted, 1964, Illinois and U.S. District Court, Northern District of Illinois (Not admitted in Hungary). *Education:* University of Illinois (A.B., with honors, 1957); Columbia University (M.B.A., 1960); Northwestern University (J.D., 1964). Co-Author: *Franchising, A Planning and Sales Compliance Guide,* Commerce Clearing House, 1987. Associate Editor, *Journal of International Franchising and Distribution Law,* 1987—. Counsel, International Franchise Association. Member: Illinois Franchise Advisory Board, 1974—; Governing Committee, 1977-1983 and Chairman, 1980-1982, Forum Committee on Franchising, American Bar Association. *PRACTICE AREAS:* International Franchising and Distribution Law.

EastEuropeLaw, Ltd., is an affiliation of independent law firms and attorneys in London, Washington, D.C. and Chicago, Illinois

EÖRSI AND PARTNERS

Established in 1987

BELGRÁD RAKPART 13-15
H-1056 BUDAPEST, HUNGARY
Telephone: (36-1) 266-5570
Fax: (36-1) 266-1444
Telex: 22-3677

Antitrust Law, Arbitration, Bankruptcy, Commercial Law, Competition Law, Construction Law, Corporate Law, Energy, Foreign Investments, Insurance Law, International Contracts, International Private Law, Labour Law, Litigation, Mergers and Acquisitions, Telecommunications, Privatization, Product Liability Law, Property and Real Estate Law, Transfer of Technology, General Intellectual Property Practice, Joint Ventures.

FIRM PROFILE: Founded in 1987 as the International Trade Law Office, Eörsi & Partners has extensive experience in commercial and foreign trade law being the first Hungarian firm to specialize in these areas. The firm provides a complete range of services in the commercial and related legal fields including advice on and management of foreign investments in Hungary and privatization. It therefore aims to satisfy the diverse needs of its client base, drawn largely from Europe and North America, which reinforces its international credentials. The active participation of its partners in various commercial fields of activity in Hungary and abroad has greatly enhanced the reputation of Eörsi & Partners, The firm is currently comprised of seven partners and seven associates which figure is expected to increase as the demands for its services grow.

DR. MÁTYÁS EÖRSI, born Budapest, Hungary, November 24, 1954; admitted, 1981, Hungary. *Education:* Eötvös Loránd University, Faculty of Law, Budapest (Doctor of Administration and Law, 1979). Member of Parliament. *Member:* Hungarian Lawyers' Association. *LANGUAGES:* Hungarian, English, German. *PRACTICE AREAS:* International Commercial Contracts; Company Law; Mergers and Acquisitions; Privatization; Arbitration.

DR. MIKLÓS BAUER, born Budapest, Hungary, January 20, 1921; admitted, 1956, Hungary. *Education:* Pázmány Péter University, Budapest (Doctor of Law and Political Science, 1943). Correspondent, International Construction Law Review, London. Member, Presidium of Legal Committee and of International Trade Law Section of Hungarian Chamber of Commerce. Member: Panel of Court of Arbitration at Hungarian Chamber of Commerce; Court of Arbitration at Austrian Federal Economic Chamber, Vienna. Nominated as Arbitrator before I.C.C., Paris. *Member:* Hungarian Lawyers' Association (Member, Private International Law Section). *LANGUAGES:* Hungarian, French, German, English, Italian. *PRACTICE AREAS:* Private International Law; Arbitration; Competition Law; Construction Law; Transfer of Technology; Joint Ventures.

DR. ÁGNES SZENT-IVÁNY, born Budapest, Hungary, July 28, 1955; admitted, 1982, Hungary. *Education:* Eötvös Loránd University, Faculty of Law, Budapest (Doctor of Administration and Law, 1979). *Member:* Hungarian Lawyers' Association; International Bar Association. *LANGUAGES:* Hungarian, English, German, Russian. *PRACTICE AREAS:* Commercial Law; Corporate Law; Competition Law; Joint Ventures; Mergers and Acquisitions; Privatization; Litigation.

DR. ILDIKÓ SZEGEDI, born Budapest, Hungary, March 8, 1951; admitted, 1976, Hungary. *Education:* Eötvös Loránd University, Faculty of Law, Budapest (Doctor of Administration and Law, 1974). *Member:* Hungarian Lawyers' Association. *LANGUAGES:* Hungarian, German, English. *PRACTICE AREAS:* International Trade; Corporate Law; Joint Venture; Mergers and Acquisitions; Privatization; Litigation.

DR. KÁROLY BÁRD, born Budapest, Hungary, November 25, 1924; admitted, 1957, Hungary. *Education:* Pázmány Péter University, Budapest (Doctor of Law and Political Science, 1948); Eötvös Loránd University, Budapest (Doctor in Social Sciences, 1957). Member, Panel of Court of Arbitration at Hungarian Chamber of Commerce; Deputy Chairman, International Association for Insurance Law; Editorial Board, Insurance Law Review (Budapest) and Assicurazioni (Rome); Presidium and Special Committee, Hungarian Motor Club. *Member:* Hungarian Lawyers' Association. *LANGUAGES:* Hungarian, German, English. *PRACTICE AREAS:* Private International Law; Litigation; Joint Ventures; Insurance; Damage Liability.

DR. TIBOR BIHARY, born Budapest, Hungary, February 20, 1959; admitted, 1986, Hungary. *Education:* Eötvös Loránd University, Faculty of Law, Budapest (Doctor of Administration and Law, 1983); Comparative Law Degree (Masters, Strasbourg, 1982); Courses Messina, 1983 and

(This Listing Continued)

Queen Mary and Westfield College, London, 1990. Secretary General of LIDC Hungarian Association of Competition Law. *Member:* Hungarian Lawyers' Association. *LANGUAGES:* Hungarian, German, French, English. *PRACTICE AREAS:* Commercial Law; Competition Law; Joint Ventures; Company Law; Mergers and Acquisitions.

DR. TAMÁS SÁNDOR, born Budapest, Hungary, September 9, 1946; admitted, 1984, Budapest. *Education:* Eötvös Loránd University, Faculty of Law, Budapest (Doctor of Administration and Law, 1971); Comparative Law Degree (Masters, Strasbourg, 1974); Doctor of Philosophy in Legal Science (Hungarian Academy of Sciences, 1984). Member, Panel of Court of Arbitration at Hungarian Chamber of Commerce; Institute of Administrative and Legal Sciences, Hungarian Academy of Sciences, 1972-1990. Assistant Professor, University of Budapest School of Economics, 1988—. Member, Government Committee on Legislation, drafting Companies Act, Act on Foreign Investments in Hungary; Acts on Transformation and on Protection of State-owned property. *LANGUAGES:* Hungarian, German, English. *PRACTICE AREAS:* International Trade Law; Comparative Contract Law; Company Law; Competition Law; Privatization; Mergers and Acquisitions; Transformation; Bankruptcy.

FOUCAUD, TCHÉKHOFF, POCHET & ASSOCIÉS

4 TARS UTCA
1118 BUDAPEST, HUNGARY
Telephone: (36-1) 267 11 66
Fax: (36-1) 267 11 70

Paris, France Office: 1 Bis Avenue Foch, 75116. Telephone: (1) 4500.86.20. Telex: 611221. Fax: (33-1) 44.17.41.65; 45.01.98.20; 45.00.08.19.

MEMBERS OF FIRM

GÉZA SIMONFAY. *Education:* Diplomatic Academy, Vienna (Legal and Interpreting Studies); Vienna University (Dr.iur.; Mag. Phil., 1976). *LANGUAGES:* English, French, German and Hungarian.

ZOLTAN JAKYES. *Education:* Eötvos Lorand University, Budapest (Dr.iur.).

ANDRÉA BAYER. *Education:* Vienna (Mag.iur.). (Resident Associate, Budapest Office).

DR. GELLÉRTHEGYI'S LAW OFFICE

Established in 1989

ALKOTMÁNY U. 29
H-1054 BUDAPEST, HUNGARY
Telephone: (361) 132-3929
Fax: (361) 111-5826

Corporate Commercial, Environmental and Civil Law.

DR. ISTVAN GELLÉRTHEGYI, born March 6, 1950; admitted, 1973, Hungary. *Education:* University of Budapest (Eötvös Lóránd; Dr., 1973). General Manager, Legal Ministry of Environment and Water Management 1978-1989. Legal Intern, Canadian Bar Association, Central European Program and Canadian Law Reform Commission, Shibley Righton, Toronto 1990. Author, "The Future of the Environment in Eastern Europe and Related Problems," Centre for International Environmental Law Conference, London, July 1991 - EBRD. *Member:* Hungarian Bar Association; International Bar Association; Canadian Hungarian Law Association. *LANGUAGES:* Hungarian, English and German. *PRACTICE AREAS:* Corporate and Commercial Law; Environmental Law; Civil Law.

GIDE LOYRETTE NOUEL

EMKE BUILDING
RÁKÓCZI ÚT 42, BP 409
BUDAPEST VII 1072, HUNGARY
Telephone: (36.1) 268.1236; 268.1237; 268.1238
Telecopier: (36.1) 268.1239

Paris, France Office: 26 Cours Albert 1er, 75008. Telephone: (1) 40.75.60.00. Cable Address: "3 Avocagidva Paris 86." Telex: 651261F GILOY. Telecopier: (1) 43.59.37.79.

(This Listing Continued)

New York, New York Office: Swiss Bank Tower, 10 East 50th Street, 10022. Telephone: (1-212) 644-1201. Telex: 424353 GIDE. Telecopier: (1-212) 644-1205.

Brussels, Belgium Office: Rue de la Loi 99.101, B-1040. Telephone: (32.2) 231.11.40. Telecopier: (32.2) 231.11.77.

Warsaw, Poland Office: Ul. Kopernika 17, 00-359. Telephone: (48.22) 26.22.21. Telecopier: (48.22) 26.03.02.

Riyadh, Saudi Arabia Office: P.O. Box 4615, 11412. Telephone: (966.1) 476.60.39. Telex: 401677 NASHWA. Telecopier: (966.1) 476.18.96.

Tokyo, Japan Office: Homei Building 3F, 3-19 Akasaka 1-Chome, Minato-Ku, 107. Telephone: (81.3) 55.62.03.01. Telecopier: (81.3) 55.62.03.06.

Beijing, People's Republic of China Office: Suite 3309 A, Jing Guang Centre, Hu Jia Lou, Chaoyang District, 100020. Telephone: (86.1) 501 4511. Telecopier: (86.1) 501 4551.

Prague, Czech Republic Office: 34 Jindrisska, 11207. Telephone: (42.2) 24.21.34.65;24.21.36.50. Telecopier: (42.2) 24.21.09.12;24.22.58.53.

St. Petersburg, Russia Office: 34 Souvorovsky Prospect, App 45, P.O. Box 172, 193015. Telephone by satellite: (7.812) 850.16.85. Telecopier by satellite: (7.812) 850.16.86.

Moscow, Russia Office: 9, Ulitsa Tverskaya - App 66, 103009. Telephone by satellite: (7.501) 940.45.00. Telecopier by satellite: (7.501) 940.45.01.

Madrid, Spain Office: Antonio Maura 7, 6°, 28014. Telephone: (34.1) 531.25.01. Telecopier: (34.1) 531.35.30.

Hanoi, Vietnam Office: Hanoi Business Centre, 51 Ly Thai To. Telephone: (84.42) 66.122.3. Telecopier: (84.42) 66.030.1.

French and International Law.

RESIDENT ASSOCIATES

Jacques de Servigny
Patrice Doat
Andréa Bayer

(For Biographical Data on Personnel, see Professional Biographies at Paris, France).

HELLER, LÖBER, BAHN & PARTNERS

Established in 1989

JÁNOS ZSIGMOND U. 7B
H-1121 BUDAPEST, HUNGARY
Telephone: (361) 2093370
Fax: (361) 1868481

Vienna, Austria Office: Seilergasse 16, A-1010. Telephone: (431) 515 15 0. Fax: (431) 512 63 94. Telex: 114874 lawco a.

Prague, Czech Republic Office: Italská 27, CZ-12000. Telephone: (422) 24231006. Fax: (422) 24218375.

Bratislava, Slovakia Office: Laurinská 12, SK-81101. Telephone: (427) 361439. Fax: (427) 361478. Brussels, Belgium Office: Rue de La Loi 99/101, B-1040. Telephone: (322) 237 26 55. Fax: (322) 280 09 83.

Advice and assistance in the preparation, negotiation and conclusion of international transactions, privatizations and tender procedures including advice on competition law, labor law, taxation and other commercial law aspects; telecommunication law, banking and finance, real estate acquisition and development as well as arbitration.

PARTNER

ULRIKE E. REIN, born Feldkirch, Austria, 1962; admitted, 1992, Austria. *Education:* University of Vienna Law School (Dr. iur.). *LANGUAGES:* German, English and French.

RESIDENT COUNSELS

KLÁRA OPPENHEIM, born Budapest, Hungary, 1950; admitted, 1976, Hungary. *Education:* Eötvös Lorand University of Budapest Law School (Dr. iur.); Sdanov University, St. Petersburg. *LANGUAGES:* Hungarian, English, German and Russian.

EVA FRIED-KALLÓS, born Budapest, Hungary, 1958; admitted, 1993, Hungary. *Education:* Eötvös Lorand University of Budapest Law School (Dr. iur.). *LANGUAGES:* Hungarian and German.

ASSOCIATES

ÁDÁM MÁTTYUS, born Budapest, Hungary, 1967; admitted, 1994, Hungary. *Education:* Eötvös Lorand University of Budapest Law School (Dr. iur.). *LANGUAGES:* Hungarian, English and German.

(This Listing Continued)

HELLER, LÖBER, BAHN & PARTNERS, Budapest—
Continued

LÁSZLÓ LEHMANN, born Devecser, Hungary, 1961; admitted, 1994, Hungary. *Education:* Janus Pannonius University of Pées Law School (Dr. iur.). *LANGUAGES:* Hungarian and English.

ÁKOS MESTER, born Jászberénny, Hungary, 1969. *Education:* József Attila University of Szeged Law School (Dr. iur.). *LANGUAGES:* Hungarian, English and German.

HENGELER MUELLER WEITZEL WIRTZ

Rechtsanwälte

TERÉZ KRT. 38

H-1066 BUDAPEST, HUNGARY

Telephone: (1) 1323121

Telefax: (1) 2690098

Frankfurt/Main, Germany Office: Bockenheimer Landstrasse 51, D-60325 Frankfurt/Main. Telephone: (069) 17095-0. Telefax: (069) 725773 & 723983. Telex: 41 45 95 Jura D.

Düsseldorf, Germany Office: Trinkausstrasse 7, D-40213 Düsseldorf. Telephone: (0211) 8304-0. Telefax: (02ll) 13 26 41 & 8 04 61. Telex: 85 87 300 whds d.

Berlin, Germany Office: Kurfürstendamm 54/55, D-10707 Berlin. Telephone: (030) 882 76 47. Telefax: (030) 882 7144.

Brussels, Belgium Office: Boulevard du Régent 50, Bte. 6, B-1000 Brussels. Telephone: (02) 511 41 15. Telefax: (02) 514 02 12.

New York Office: 712 Fifth Avenue, New York, New York, 10019. Telephone: (212) 586-4600. Telefax: (212) 586-4481.

Joint ventures and Foreign Investments in Hungary, Privatization, Banking and Insurance, General German Business Law practice, EEC Law.

RESIDENT PARTNER

DR. GERHARD LANG, born Straubing, Germany, 1956; admitted, 1984, Frankfurt/Main (Not admitted in Hungary). *Education:* Universities of Munich and Freiburg (Dr. jur.); London School of Economics. Foreign Associate, Washington Law Firm, 1986-1987. (Also at Frankfurt/Main, Germany Office).

Languages: German, English and French

(For Complete Biographical Data on all Personnel, see Professional Biographies at Berlin, Dusseldorf and Frankfurt/Main, Germany)

KÖVES & PARTNERS
CLIFFORD CHANCE

MADÁCH TRADE CENTER

MADÁCH IMRE ÚT 14

BUDAPEST 1075, HUNGARY

Telephone: (36 1) 268 1600

Fax: (36 1) 268 1610

Other Offices: Amsterdam, Bahrain, Barcelona, Brussels, Budapest, Dubai, Frankfurt, Hanoi, Hong Kong, London, Madrid, Milan, Moscow, New York, Paris, Riyadh, Rome, Shanghai, Singapore, Tokyo, Warsaw. (See Clifford Chance, London for full address details).

Corporate Law, Banking, Energy and Natural Resource, Media and Tele-communications, Regulatory and Legal Infrastructure Projects, Privatizations.

RESIDENT PARTNER

PÉTER KÖVES, admitted, 1986, Budapest. *Education:* University of Eötvös Lóránd, Budapest (Doctorate in Law). *LANGUAGES:* Hungarian, English, German, Spanish and French.

RESIDENT MANAGER

RICHARD LOCK, admitted, 1986, Solicitor.

DR. MÁRIA MÁRAI LAW OFFICES

DÁNIEL ÚT 15

H-1125 BUDAPEST, HUNGARY

Telephone: (36 1) 176 0192; 274 2123

Telefax: (36 1) 274 2124

General Practice; Commercial, Corporate Law; Real Estate; Mergers and Acquisitions; Joint Ventures; Foreign Investment.

DR. MÁRIA MÁRAI, born Szeged, Hungary, February 18, 1954; admitted, 1978, Hungary. *Education:* Jozsef Attila University, Szeged (J.D., cum laude, 1978); Eötvös Loránd University (Foreign Trade Law, cum laude, 1982). Counsel, Notary, 1981-1983. International Counsel, Budavox, 1985-1989; Counsel, Hunguard Float Glass Kft, 1989-1990; Associate, Baker & McKenzie, Budapest, 1990-1992. *Member:* Hungarian Bar Association. *LANGUAGES:* German, English and Russian.

McDOWELL, RICE & SMITH

A PROFESSIONAL PARTNERSHIP

H-1027 BUDAPEST

KAPÁS UTCA 11-15

BUDAPEST, HUNGARY

Telephone: 011-361-202-6044

Fax: 011-361-202-6790

Kansas City, Kansas Office: McDowell, Rice & Smith, A Professional Corporation, 600 Security Bank Building, Seventh & Minnesota. Telephones: 913-621-5400; 371-7750. Telecopier: 913-621-7238.

Kansas City, Missouri Office: McDowell, Rice & Smith, A Professional Corporation, 13th Floor, Twelve Wyandotte Plaza, 120 West 12th Street, 64105-1932. Telephone: 816-221-5400 Telecopier: 816-474-7304.

Overland Park, Kansas Office: McDowell, Rice & Smith, A Professional Corporation, 2nd Floor, Forty Executive Hills, 7101 College Boulevard. Telephone: 913-338-5400.

Banking and Financial Services, Commercial and Bankruptcy, Acquisitions and Mergers, Environmental, Real Estate, International, Transactions, Import-Export, Tax, Administrative/Regulatory.

KORNELIA NAGY-KOPPANY, born Budapest, Hungary, March 29, 1955; admitted, 1981, Hungary. *Education:* Eövös Lorant Budapest, Hungary (J.D., 1978); New York University School of Law (LL.M., 1989). *Member:* International Bar Association. *LANGUAGES:* Hungarian, French and English.

ELLEN C. WRIGHT, born Kansas City, Missouri, March 11, 1962; admitted, 1989, California (Not admitted in Hungary). *Education:* Georgetown University (A.B., 1984); Boston University (J.D., 1989). *Member:* State Bar of California (Member, International Law Section). *PRACTICE AREAS:* General Corporate and International.

GYÖRGYI VISZMEG, born Kiskunhalas, Hungary, January 6, 1970. *Education:* Attila Jozsef University, Szeged, Hungary (J.D., 1994). *LANGUAGES:* English and Hungarian.

LEGAL SUPPORT PERSONNEL

ANNA J. CSEH, born Budapest, Hungary, November 27, 1972. *Education:* St. Lawrence University (B.A., 1993). *LANGUAGES:* English, Hungarian, French and Spanish.

REPRESENTATIVE CLIENTS: *Banking/Financial Services:* Bannister Bank & Trust; Central Bank of Kansas City; Citizens Bank & Trust; Citizens Jackson County Bank; The Douglass Bank; Eastrich Multiple Investor Fund; The Hungarian Credit Bank; Industrial State Bank; Home State Bank; Mark Twain Bank; Midland Loan Services; The Mission Bank; Security Bank of Kansas City; Union Bank; United Kansas Bank & Trust; Valley View State Bank; Heller International. *Corporations:* A.E. West Petroleum Company, Inc.; ANR Freight System Inc.; Arrow Truck Sales, Inc.; Artex Manufacturing; Community Water Company, Inc.; Colgate-Palmolive Company; Correctional Services Group, Inc.; Faultless Starch/Bon Ami Company; Ferrellgas, Inc.; Fleming Companies; General Standard, Inc.; Golden Ox, Inc.; The Lockton Companies; Image-Mark Software Labs, Inc.; Mobilfone, Inc.; Topsy's International, Inc.; Toy's R Us; Valentine-McCormick-Ligebel, Inc. *Governmental Entities:* The Port Authority of Kansas City, Missouri. *Insurance and Surety:* Atlantic Casualty Company; Catholic Mutual Relief Society of America; Cigna Insurance Co.; Chubb Group of Companies; Crum & Forster; Great Westerrn Casualty Company; Medical Defense Associates; Nobel Insurance Company; Kansas Health Care Stabilization Fund; Integon Indemnity Corp.; PCM Intermediaries, Ltd.; St. Paul Fire & Marine Insurance Company; Unicare, Inc.; National Chiropractic Mutual Insurance Company; The Travelers Insurance Company; USF&G Insurance Company *Labor and Employment:* ABB Power T & D Company, Inc.; Helz-

(*This Listing Continued*)

berg Diamond Shops, Inc.; Silver Dollar City. *Real Estate:* River Market Redevelopment; Stratford Development Corporation; Block & Company; Balcor; Republic Real Estate. *Environmental:* Kingston Environmental Services, Inc.; C.C. EnviroKlean, Inc. *Health Care:* I.D. Russell Company Laboratories, Inc.; Kansas City Allergy & Asthma Associates, Inc.; Kansas University Surgery Associates; HealthNet; Midwest Neurosurgery Associates, Inc.; Providence Medical Center; Radiation Therapy Foundation. *Securities:* B.C. Christopher, a Division of Fahnstock & Company, Inc.; Central Life Assurance Co.; Security Investment Co. *Non-Profit:* KCMC Child Development Corporation; Professional Secretaries International; Corrections Research Institute; Women's Division of Kansas City Museum. *International:* Colgate-Palmolive Company; Data General Corporation, The Hungarian State Asset Holding Agency, Motion Picture Export Association of America; United Biscuits. *Telecommunications:* U.S. Sprint. *Employee Benefits:* Kimberly Quality Care, a division of The Olsten Corporation; Dean Machinery Co.

McKENNA & CO

in association with Veröci & Ormai & Co., Hungarian Lawyers

H-1122

MAROS UTCA 22, 1ST FLOOR

BUDAPEST, HUNGARY

Telephone: (361) 202 6527

(361) 202 6936

(361) 156 5353

Fax: (361) 156 5391

London, England Office: Mitre House, 160 Aldersgate Street, EC1A 4DD. Telephone: 0171 606 9000. Telex: 27251. Fax: 0171-606 9100. CDE Box 724.

London Lloyd's Office: 908 Lloyd's, One Lime Street, London EC3M 7DQ. Telephone: 0171-929 1250. Fax: 0171-626 5749 DX Box 724.

Brussels, Belgium Office: Avenue de Cortenberg 66, Box 10, B-1040. Telephone: (32)(2)735.38.36. Telex: 27122. Fax: (32)(2)735.77.43.

Budapest, Hungary Office: H-1122. Maros utca 22, 1st Floor. Telephone: (36)(1) 202 6527; (36)(1) 202 6936; (36)(1) 201 9199; (36)(1) 156 5354. Fax: (36)(1) 156 5391.

Moscow, Russia Office: McKenna & Co, International, MosenkáPlaza, 24/27 Sadovaya-Samotyochnaya Street, Russian Federation, Moscow, 103051. Telephone: (7 501) 258 5000. Fax: (7 501)258 5100.

Prague, Czech Republic Office: Betlémský palác, First Floor, Husova 5, 110 00 Prague 1. Telephone: (42)(2) 2424 8518-22. Fax: 42(2) 2424 8524.

Warsaw, Poland Office: McKenna & Co Sp. zo.o., ul. Kopernika 30, Suite 213, 00-950, Warsaw. Telephone: (48) 22 26 69 88. Fax: (48) 22 26 41 93.

Hong Kong Office: 5th Floor, Lippo Tower, 89 Queensway, Hong Kong. Telephone: (852) 846 9100. Fax: (852) 845 3575.

Associated Firms:

Sigle Loose Schmidt-Diemitz and Partners: Stuttgart, Berlin, Leipzig, Frankfurt/Main, Chemnitz and Moscow.

Minter Ellison: Sydney, Melbourne, Canberra, Brisbane and the Gold Coast.

Firm involved in all aspects of Hungarian privatization, corporate, competition and real estate Law and English commercial law

RESIDENT PARTNERS

Stephen J. Forster

RESIDENT SOLICITORS

David Stabb

ADMINISTRATIVE ASSISTANT

Andrea Kiss

Languages: English, French, German, Hungarian

MÉCS & PARTNERS KFT.
RADVÁNYI & PARTNERS

Established in 1991

BÁTHORI Ú 22, III/8

H-1054 BUDAPEST, HUNGARY

Telephone: (011-36-1) 131-9396 or 8932

Fax: (011-36-1) 131-9291

The Mécs/Radványi expertise covers most aspects of commercial activity and clients are regularly advised in Banking, Business and Commercial Law, Bankruptcy, Finance, Debtor and Creditor Matters, Real Estate, Commercial Litigation, Alternative Dispute Resolution.

FIRM PROFILE: Mécs/Radványi is a strategic alliance between Western trained Canadian lawyers, each with over 20 years of commercial practice in Canada and Hungary, and Hungarian-lawyers, with over 10 years of professional practice.

Mécs/Radvány presently consists of 7 professionals, all permanently based in Budapest. The Mécs/Radványi understanding of the industrial commercial manufacturing and financial conditions in Hungary enable them to provide expertise, guidance and business judgement to Hungarian and Western corporations and financial institutions in connection with their Hungarian transactions and business. Service is provided in Hungarian, English and French. The partners and associates of Radványi are authorized to appear before the courts in Hungary.

PARTNERS

ANDRÉ T. MÉCS, born Austria, 1947; admitted, 1971, Quebec, Canada (Not admitted in Hungary). *Education:* McGill University (Bachelor of Arts, 1967; Bachelor of Civil Law, 1970). *Member:* Quebec and Canadian Bar Associations; International Bar Association. **LANGUAGES:** Hungarian, French and English. **PRACTICE AREAS:** Workouts; Secured Lending; Construction Contracts; Corporate Finance; Real Estate Finance.

ANDREA FRANCOEUR MÉCS, born Montreal, Canada, 1949; admitted, 1974, Quebec, Canada (Not admitted in Hungary). *Education:* McGill University (Bachelor of Arts, 1970; Bachelor of Civil Law, 1973). *Member:* Quebec and Canadian Bar Associations; International Bar Association. **LANGUAGES:** English and French. **PRACTICE AREAS:** Joint Ventures; Venture Capital; Distribution; Commercial Leases; Equipment Finance and Leasing.

DR. ILDIKÓ RADVÁNYI, born Budapest, Hungary, 1961; admitted, 1985, Hungary. *Education:* Eötvös Lóránd University (J.D., 1985); Special Bar Exam (1988); Advanced Studies in Foreign Trade Law (1990-1992). *Member:* Hungarian Bar Association. **LANGUAGES:** Hungarian, English, Russian and Spanish (understood). **PRACTICE AREAS:** Company Acquisitions and Sales; Finance Restructuring; Power Projects; Privatization; Franchise and Franchising.

DR. MIKLOS ANDOR, born Budapest, Hungary, 1959; admitted, 1983, Hungary. *Education:* Eötvös Lóránd University (1983); Special Bar Exam (J.D., 1987). *Member:* Hungarian Bar Association. **LANGUAGES:** Hungarian and English. **PRACTICE AREAS:** Commercial Litigation; Debtor Creditor Remedies; Food and Agriculture; Receiverships; Real Estate Development.

MOQUET BORDE DIEUX GEENS & ASSOCIÉS

KOSSUTH TÉR 16-17. III/2/A.

(1245 BUDAPEST, P.O. BOX 1228)

H-1055 BUDAPEST, HUNGARY

Telephone: (36-1) 1531 255

Fax: (36-1) 1531 229

Paris, France Office: 30 avenue de Messine, 75008. Telephone: (33-1) 42.99.04.50. Fax: (33-1) 45.63.91.49.

Lyon, France Office: 11 Place Bellecour, 69002. Telephone: (33) 72.40.00.32. Fax: (33) 72.41.98.62.

Tallinn, Estonian Office: 10 Pärnu str., EE 0001 Tallinn, Estonia. Telephone: (372) 6405836. Fax: (372) 6405838.

Brussels, Belgium Office: Rue de la Bonté 5-7, B-1050. Telephone: (32-2) 538-6869. Fax: (32-2) 538-6867.

Hungarian, EEC, French and General International practice.

(This Listing Continued)

MOQUET BORDE DIEUX GEENS & ASSOCIÉS,
Budapest—Continued

RESIDENT COUNSEL

ANDRAS SZECSKAY, born Kecskemet, Hungary, December 3, 1948; admitted, 1975, Budapest. *Education:* University of Szeged (Master of Law, 1973). *Member:* Presidium of the Budapest Bar; Hungarian Association for the Protection of Industrial Property; Licensing Executives Society. *LANGUAGES:* Hungarian and English.

RESIDENT ASSOCIATES

JUDIT GULAS, born Budapest, Hungary, October 13, 1954; admitted, 1982, Budapest. *Education:* Eotvos Lorand Scientific University (J.D., 1978); Miskolc-Maastricht University (MBA, 1992). *LANGUAGES:* Hungarian and English.

MICHEL LEQUIEN, born Haiti, June 20, 1964; admitted, 1991, Paris (Not admitted in Hungary). *Education:* University of Paris II (Maîtrise en Droit Public, 1986); D.E.A. Droit communautaire, 1987; Maîtrise Carrières Judiciaires, 1988); German Academic Exchange Service, Program of Legal Studies, Tübingen and Düsseldorf (1988-1989). *LANGUAGES:* French, English and German.

JUDIT BUDAI, born Budapest, Hungary, December 11, 1967. *Education:* Eötvös Lorand Scientific University (J.D., 1991). *LANGUAGES:* Hungarian, English and German.

KATALIN GROSZ, born Zalaegerszeg, November 29, 1965. *Education:* Pecs Faculty of State and Legal Science (J.D., 1989); training program EEC Commission legal department (April-July 1992). *LANGUAGES:* Hungarian, English, French and German.

PATRICK TAUSZ, born Budapest, Hungary, September 15, 1969. *Education:* Eötvös Lorand Scientific University (J.D., 1992). *LANGUAGES:* Hungarian and English.

MICHAEL BURGESS, born Ft. Wayne, Indiana, U.S.A., April 28, 1964. *Education:* University of Oregon (B.A. in International Studies, magna cum laude, 1990; J.D., 1994). Recipient, Fulbright Scholar to Hungary, 1990-1991. Co-Author, "The Commercial Laws of Hungary," Commercial Law Digest of the World. *LANGUAGES:* English, Hungarian, German and Russian.

DR. GÁBOR NÁDAS AND ASSOCIATION

Attorney at Law

Established in 1991

WESSELÉNYI U. 4

H 1075 BUDAPEST VII, HUNGARY

Telephone: (36-1) 122-3591
Tel./Fax: (36-1) 117-5923

Corporate, Commercial, Private International Law, Contracts, Litigation, Arbitration, Products Liability, Construction and Taxation.

FIRM PROFILE: The office was founded in 1991 as a successor of the former 51st Legal Advisers' Partnership. It has a staff of five and associates besides Budapest in London and Sofia.

DR. GÁBOR NÁDAS, born Budapest, Hungary, February 2, 1954; admitted, 1979, Hungary. *Education:* Eötvös University, Budapest (Lawyer's Degree, 1983; International Private Commercial Law, 1989). *LANGUAGES:* Hungarian, English and German. *PRACTICE AREAS:* International Business; Commercial; Arbitration; Business Organizations; Establishment; Corporate Partnerships; General Practice.

NAGY ÉS TRÓCSÁNYI

PÁLYA UTCA 9

H-1012 BUDAPEST, HUNGARY

Telephone: (36) 1-212-0444
Telefax: (36) 1-212-0443

REVISERS OF THE HUNGARY LAW DIGEST FOR THIS DIRECTORY.

Basel, Switzerland Office: Birsigstrasse 2, CH-4054 Basel, Switzerland. Telephone: (41) 61-281-2170. Telefax: (41) 61-281-2001.
New York, New York Office: 1114 Avenue of the Americas, 10036-7794. Telephone: 1-212-626-4206. Telefax: 1-212-626-4208.

(This Listing Continued)

Administrative Law, Civil Law, Private and Public International Law, Company and Trade Law, Trade Disputes, Taxes, Banking and Financial Law, Antitrust and Competition Law, Securities, Media, Telecommunications, Energy, Corporations and Estate Matters, Government.

FIRM PROFILE: The Law Firm Nagy és Trócsányi is the first law firm in Hungary to have been founded after Hungarian Law had permitted. On October 1, 1991 the law firm was launched in part by lawyers returning home from acknowledged law firms abroad. The lawyers from fields of corporate, trade, banking, finance and litigation joined their knowledge and expertise in domestic and international legal practice together into one effort. They formed a law firm for the purpose of serving their clients efficiently. Today the Law Firm Nagy és Trócsányi with 20 lawyers and a 20 member staff is the largest and the most intensely growing law firm in Hungary. In 1993, the Law Firm opened up a branch office in Switzerland, the first foreign office ever to be established abroad by a Hungarian law firm, and in September of 1993 the Law Firm opened a branch office in New York.

PARTNERS

TIBOR BOGDÁN, admitted, 1993, Hungary. *Education:* Janus Pannonius University, Faculty of Law, Pécs (Doctor of Administration and Law). Former State Secretary of Ministry of Justice. *Member:* Hungarian Bar Association; Budapest Bar Association. *LANGUAGES:* Hungarian and Russian. *PRACTICE AREAS:* Administrative Law; Broadcasting; Business Law; Civil Law; Media; Government; Telecommunication Law.

JUDIT CSÁKI, admitted, 1991, Hungary. *Education:* Eötvös Loránd University, Faculty of Law, Budapest (Doctor of Administration and Law, 1979). *Member:* Budapest Bar Association. *LANGUAGES:* Hungarian and Italian. *PRACTICE AREAS:* Charitable Organizations; Child and Juvenile Law; Family Law.

LAJOS KISS, admitted, 1991, Hungary. *Education:* Eötvös Loránd University, Faculty of Law, Budapest (Doctor of Administration and Law, 1985). *Member:* Budapest Bar Association. *LANGUAGES:* Hungarian and English. *PRACTICE AREAS:* Business Law; Civil Law; Company Law; Contracts; Labor Law; Negligence; Property; Real Estate; Resorts and Leisure; Torts.

MIHÁLY KOBELA, admitted, 1990, Hungary. *Education:* University of Miskoc, Faculty of Law (Doctor of Administration and Law, 1988). *Member:* Budapest Bar Association. *LANGUAGES:* Hungarian, German and Russian. *PRACTICE AREAS:* Agricultural Law; Bankruptcy; Business Law; Debtor and Creditor Law; Finance; Litigation; Property; Real Estate; Torts.

FERENC KOHL. *Education:* Eötvös Loránd University, Faculty of Law, Budapest (Doctor of Administration and Law, 1980); Juristische Fakultät der Universität Basel (Lic.iur., 1983). (Resident Partner, New York Office). *LANGUAGES:* Hungarian, English, French and German. *PRACTICE AREAS:* Business Law; Commercial Law; Finance; Taxation.

PÉTER P. NAGY, admitted, 1983, Hungary; Legal Consultant, 1994, New York. *Education:* Eötvös Loránd University, Faculty of Law, Budapest (Doctor of Administration and Law, 1980); Université de Strasbourg, Faculté Internationale de Droit Comparé (Diplôme Superieure, 1985). Lawyers Exchange Program, American Bar Association, 1990-1991. *Member:* Budapest Bar Association; International Association of Students and Former Students in Comparative Law; Association of Attenders and Alumni of The Hague Academy of International Law. (Resident Partner, Switzerland Office). *LANGUAGES:* Hungarian, English, French and German. *PRACTICE AREAS:* Arbitration; Banks and Banking; Business Law; Commercial Law; Construction Law; Environmental Law; Finance; International Law; Litigation; Securities; Taxation; Media.

LÁSZLÓ TRÓCSÁNYI, admitted, 1985, Hungary. *Education:* Eötvös Loránd University, Faculty of Law, Budapest (Doctor of Administration and Law, 1980); Institut de Droit de la Faculté des Sciences Politique l'Université de Milan (Studies in public administration, 1987); Faculté de Droit de l'Université Catholique de Louvain, Louvain la Neuve (Studies in Public Administration, 1989). Candidate, Hungarian Academy of Sciences, 1991. *Member:* Budapest Bar Association; Association Internationale de la Fonction Publique, Avignon; Hungarian Inter-Church Aid; Foundation Interjustice. *LANGUAGES:* Hungarian, French and Russian. *PRACTICE AREAS:* Administrative Law; Agency and Distribution; Antitrust and Competition; Broadcasting; Business Law; Charitable Organizations; Entertainment; Environmental Law; Immigration; Real Estate; Telecommunications; Zoning, Planning and Land Use.

(This Listing Continued)

ILDIKÓ VARGA, admitted, 1991, New York; 1993, Hungary. *Education:* Eötvös Loránd University, Faculty of Arts, Faculty of Law, Budapest (Ph.D., 1984; Doctor of Administration and Law, 1988); New York University, Faculty of Arts and Law School (M.A., 1990); Universite de Strasbourg, Faculte Internationale de Droit Compare (1987). *Member:* Budapest Bar Association. (Resident Partner, Switzerland Office). *LANGUAGES:* Hungarian and English. *PRACTICE AREAS:* Agency and Distributorship; Business Law; Company Law; Construction Law; Energy; Corporate Law; Government; International Law.

PIROSKA VINCZE, admitted, 1992, Hungary. *Education:* Eötvös Loránd University, Faculty of Law, Budapest (Doctor of Administration and Law, 1980). *Member:* Budapest Bar Association. *LANGUAGES:* Hungarian and English. *PRACTICE AREAS:* Business Law; Civil Law; Labor and Employment; Libel and Defamation; Negligence; Personal Injury; Torts; Criminal Law.

ZSOLT ZAMOSTNY, admitted, 1991, Hungary. *Education:* Janus Pannonius University, Faculty of Law, Pécs (Doctor of Administration and Law, 1986); IATA Airline Contract Law, Geneva, Switzerland (1989). *Member:* Budapest Bar Association. *LANGUAGES:* Hungarian and English. *PRACTICE AREAS:* Business Law; Telecommunications; Company Law; Aircraft and Aviation.

OF COUNSEL

LÁSZLÓ DUDÁS, admitted, 1965, Hungary. *Education:* Eötvös Loránd University, Faculty of Law, Budapest (Doctor of Administration and Law). *Member:* Budapest Bar Association. *LANGUAGES:* Hungarian. *PRACTICE AREAS:* Real Estate; Mortgages.

GYÖRGY SZILÁGYI, admitted, 1958, Hungary. *Education:* Eötvös Loránd University, Faculty of Law, Budapest (Doctor of Administration and Law, 1954). *Member:* Budapest Bar Association (Former Vice President, 1975-1987). *LANGUAGES:* Hungarian, English and German. *PRACTICE AREAS:* Real Estate; Corporate Law; Litigation.

ASSOCIATES

ÉVA BORUZS, (admission pending). *Education:* School of Administrative Studies, Budapest (M.A., 1991). Paralegal, Ministry of Justice, Budapest, 1986-1991. *LANGUAGES:* Hungarian and English. *PRACTICE AREAS:* Labor Law; Social Welfare.

DÉNES GOMBAI, (admission pending). *Education:* Karl Ruschpecht University, Faculty of Law, Heidelberg (1992); Eötvös Loránd University, Faculty of Law (Doctor of Administration and Law, 1993); University of Basel (Magister Degree in Law, 1995). *LANGUAGES:* Hungarian and German. *PRACTICE AREAS:* Business Law; Real Estate Law; Labor Law.

ESZTER HÉJJA, admitted, 1994, Hungary. *Education:* Janus Pannonius University, Faculty of Law, Pécs (Doctor of Administration and Law). *LANGUAGES:* Hungarian and English. *PRACTICE AREAS:* Company Law; Business Transactions.

GABRIELLA HORVÁTH, (admission pending). *Education:* University of Paris I-Pantheon-Sorbonne; Eötvös Loránd University, Faculty of Law, Budapest (Doctor of Administration and Law, 1993). *LANGUAGES:* Hungarian, French and English. *PRACTICE AREAS:* Public Administration; Company Law.

KATALIN LEHNER, (admission pending). *Education:* Eötvös Loránd University, Faculty of Law, Budapest (Doctor of Administration and Law, 1992); University of Vienna, Institut für Rechtsvergleichung (1992). *LANGUAGES:* Hungarian, German and English. *PRACTICE AREAS:* Business Law; International Family Law.

ERIKA PAPP, admitted, 1994, Hungary. *Education:* József Attila University, Faculty of Law, Szeged (Doctor of Law, 1991); University of Birmingham, Faculty of Law (1992); Universite de Strasbourg, Faculte Internationale de Droit Compare (1993); Fordham University, Law School, New York (LL.M., 1995). (Resident Associate, New York Office). *LANGUAGES:* Hungarian, English, German, Russian and Spanish. *PRACTICE AREAS:* Business Law; Banks and Banking; Agency and Distributorship; Corporate Law; Intellectual Property.

KRISZTINA ROMHÁNYI, (admission pending). *Education:* University of Hamburg, Faculty of Law (1992); Universite Paris I-II, Faculty of Law (1993); Eötvös Loránd University, Faculty of Law, Budapest (Doctor of Administration and Law, 1993). *LANGUAGES:* Hungarian, French and German. *PRACTICE AREAS:* Company Law; Labor and Social Security; Corporate Law; Real Estate.

(This Listing Continued)

JÁNOS TAKÁCS, (admission pending). *Education:* Iuridicum, Vienna (1992); Eötvös Loránd University, Faculty of Law, Budapest (Doctor of Administration and Law, 1993); University of Basel (Magister Degree in Law, 1995). *LANGUAGES:* Hungarian and German. *PRACTICE AREAS:* Taxation; Company Law; Business Law.

ÁGNES TIGELMANN, (admission pending). *Education:* University of Saarlandes, Faculty of Law, Germany (1993); Janus Pannonius University, Faculty of Law, Pécs (Doctor of Administration and Law, 1986). *LANGUAGES:* Hungarian and German. *PRACTICE AREAS:* Company Law; Business Law.

ISTVÁN TÓTH, (admission pending). *Education:* University of Trier (1992); University of Miskolc, Faculty of Law (Doctor of Administration and Law, 1993). (Resident Associate, Basel Office). *LANGUAGES:* Hungarian, English and German. *PRACTICE AREAS:* Contracts; Business Law; Real Estate.

BASEL OFFICE
RESIDENT PARTNERS

PÉTER P. NAGY, admitted, 1983, Hungary; Legal Consultant, 1994, New York. *Education:* Eötvös Loránd University, Faculty of Law, Budapest (Doctor of Administration and Law, 1980); Université de Strasbourg, Faculté Internationale de Droit Comparé (Diplôme Superieure, 1985). Lawyers Exchange Program, American Bar Association, 1990-1991. *Member:* Budapest Bar Association; International Association of Students and Former Students in Comparative Law; Association of Attenders and Alumni of The Hague Academy of International Law. (Resident Partner, Switzerland Office). *LANGUAGES:* Hungarian, English, French and German. *PRACTICE AREAS:* Arbitration; Banks and Banking; Business Law; Commercial Law; Construction Law; Environmental Law; Finance; International Law; Litigation; Securities; Taxation; Media.

ILDIKÓ VARGA, admitted, 1991, New York; 1993, Hungary. *Education:* Eötvös Loránd University, Faculty of Arts, Faculty of Law, Budapest (Ph.D., 1984; Doctor of Administration and Law, 1988); New York University, Faculty of Arts and Law School (M.A., 1990); Universite de Strasbourg, Faculte Internationale de Droit Compare (1987). *Member:* Budapest Bar Association. (Resident Partner, Switzerland Office). *LANGUAGES:* Hungarian and English. *PRACTICE AREAS:* Agency and Distributorship; Business Law; Company Law; Construction Law; Energy; Corporate Law; Government; International Law.

RESIDENT ASSOCIATES

ISTVÁN TÓTH, (admission pending). *Education:* University of Trier (1992); University of Miskolc, Faculty of Law (Doctor of Administration and Law, 1993). *LANGUAGES:* Hungarian, English and German. *PRACTICE AREAS:* Contracts; Business Law; Real Estate.

NEW YORK OFFICE
RESIDENT PARTNER

FERENC KOHL. *Education:* Eötvös Loránd University, Faculty of Law, Budapest (Doctor of Administration and Law, 1980); Juristische Fakultät der Universität Basel (Lic.iur., 1983). *LANGUAGES:* Hungarian, English, French and German. *PRACTICE AREAS:* Business Law; Commercial Law; Finance; Taxation.

NEW YORK
RESIDENT ASSOCIATES

ERIKA PAPP, admitted, 1994, Hungary. *Education:* József Attila University, Faculty of Law, Szeged (Doctor of Law, 1991); University of Birmingham, Faculty of Law (1992); Universite de Strasbourg, Faculte Internationale de Droit Compare (1993); Fordham University, Law School, New York (LL.M., 1995). (Resident Associate, New York Office). *LANGUAGES:* Hungarian, English, German, Russian and Spanish. *PRACTICE AREAS:* Business Law; Banks and Banking; Agency and Distributorship; Corporate Law; Intellectual Property.

REPRESENTATIVE CLIENTS: Agroker Rt., (Getz Co.) Budapest; ALA Assicurazioni Insurance; Atomic Energy Plant, Paks; Bank of America; Bank Austria AG; British-Magyar International School; Budapesti & Pest megyei GMV, Budapest; Burger King, Budapest; CANA Corp., Paris; CWAG Kft., Budapest; Commerz Bank, Budapest; Consolidated, Inc.; Coopers & Lybrand; De La Roche; Denver & Ephrata; Walt Disney Co.; The European Bank for Reconstruction and Development, London; G.E.I. (Group International Engineering Italia, S.P.A.); Exportos India; Girozentrale Bank; Hamberger GmbH; Heti Világgazdaság Rt.,Budapest; Hungarian Inter-Church Aid, Budapest; Huntel Systems; ING Bank, Budapest; Internationale Nederlanden Bank; International Treuhand AG, Switzerland; Ipsos S.A., Budapest; IP Trading Ltd., Thailand; Kenetech Corporation; Kvantum Bank Rt.; LEROY SA.; Lyonnaise Des Eaux; MALÉv Hungarian Airlines; MATÁV Telecommunications, Rt.; Metalloglobus; Mező Bank, Ltd., Budapest; Ministry of Agriculture; Ministry of Transportation; National Tax Authority of Hungary; Nomura Bank, Ltd., Budapest;

(This Listing Continued)

NAGY ÉS TRÓCSÁNYI, Budapest—Continued

Okura & Co. Ltd.; Szerencsejáték Rt., Budapest; Philip Müller Gmbtt; Government Prefect of Budapest, Radio Juventus; Renault S.A., Paris; Portfolio Bank Rt.; Skala Department Store Rt.; Sprint International; The State Property Agency, Budapest; State Property Handling Co., Budapest; TOMEN (Toyo Menka Kaisha) Corporation, Budapest; Unilever Magyarország Kft.; Vitafort Rt., Dabas; Wossala és Társa Fkt., Budapest.
REFERENCE: Commercial Department of the Embassy of the United States of America in Budapest; Embassy of Belgium in Budapest; Embassy of France in Budapest; State Property Agency, Budapest; Ministry of Justice, Budapest; Ministry of Finance, Budapest.

REVISERS OF THE HUNGARY LAW DIGEST FOR THIS
DIRECTORY.

DR. PÉTER NÓGRÁDI
ATTORNEY AT LAW

FILLÉR ST. 25. GROUND FLOOR
1024 BUDAPEST, HUNGARY
Telephone: 36-1-1159777; 36-1-1174737; 36-1-1153882
Fax: 36-1-1174737

International Banking Law, International Trade Law, Franchising, Corporate Law, Competition Law, Contracts Law, Litigation, Mergers and Acquisitions, Bankruptcy and Insolvency.

DR. PÉTER NÓGRÁDI, born Hungary, October 20, 1959. *Education:* Eötvös Lóránd University Budapest (Dr.jur., 1984); Law Faculty, Cegla Institute of International Comparative Law (1987-1989). Researcher, Antidumping, Countervailing Duties and Trade Adjusting Charges, Tel-Aviv University. *Member:* Budapest Bar Association. *LANGUAGES:* Hebrew, English and Hungarian.

NÖRR, STIEFENHOFER & LUTZ

Established in 1990

BECSÍ UTCA 5/I. 1-2
1052 BUDAPEST, HUNGARY
Telephone: 36-1-1174905; 36-1-1378293
Telecopier: 36-1-1184035

Munich, Germany Office: Brienner Str. 28, 80333 Munich, Postfach 101121, 80085 Munich, Germany. Telephone: 49-89-280111. Telecopier: 49-89-280110.
Frankfurt/Main, Germany Office: Freiherr-vom-Stein-Straße 11, 60323 Frankfurt/Main. Telephone: 49-69-172917. Telecopier: 49-69-172916.
Berlin, Germany Office: Schlüterstraße 36, D-10629 Berlin. Telephone: 49-30-8836700. Telecopier: 49-30-8835052.
Dresden, Germany Office: Böhmertstraße 3, 01099 Dresden. Telephone: 49-351-5671188, 49-351-5671187. Telecopier: 49-351-5671186.
Prague, Czech Republic Office: Masarykovo nábřeži 30, 11000 Prague 1. Telephone: 42-2-24913396, 42-2-24913882. Telecopier: 42-2-24911836.
Warsaw, Poland Office: Kancelaria Adwokacka Sp. Z o. o. UL. Nowogrodzka 50, 00950 Warsaw. Telephone: 48-2-6216232. Telecopier: 48-2-6251976.
Brussels, Belgium EEC Office: 106 Avenue Louise, 1050 Brussels. Telephone: 32-2-6470650. Telecopier: 32-2-6464729.
Moscow, Russia Office: Ul. Levoberezhnaya, 32. 125475. Telephone: 7-095-4585822; 7-095-4585792. Telecopier: 7-095-4585782.

General and International Practice.

PARTNERS IN CHARGE

DR. BERTOLD GAEDE, born Essen, Germany, December 29, 1942; admitted, 1971, Germany; as Tax Advisor, 1976 (Not admitted in Hungary). *Education:* Universities of Munich, Freiburg, Bonn and Cologne. *Member:* American Bar Association; German Bar Association. *LANGUAGES:* German, English and French. *PRACTICE AREAS:* Corporate Law; Mergers and Acquisitions Law; Energy Law; Health Law.

DR. STEFAN B. TOMICIC, born Vienna, Austria, October 29, 1947; admitted, 1975, Germany (Not admitted in Hungary). *Education:* Universities of Munich, Lausanne and Geneva. Assistant Lecturer, Institute of Commercial and Labor Law, University of Munich, 1973-1975. *Member:* German Bar Association. *LANGUAGES:* German, English, French and Spanish. *PRACTICE AREAS:* Real Estate Law; Construction Law; Leasing Law; Labor Law; Administrative Law.

(This Listing Continued)

ASSOCIATES

DR. ZSOLT K. RADNÓCZY, born Munich, Germany, February 16, 1954; admitted, 1989, Germany (Not admitted in Hungary). *Education:* Universities of Munich and Budapest. With Lion Features World Article Service, Munich, Germany, 1979-1983. With Lindner & Radnóczy, Management Consultants, 1989, 1990. Member of the Board of Directors of the Hypo-Bank Hungaria Rt. since March 1, 1993. *Member:* German Bar Association; International Association Language and Business. *LANGUAGES:* Hungarian, German, English and French. *PRACTICE AREAS:* Real Estate Law; Commercial Law; Corporate Law; Banking Law; Tax Law.

LÁSZLO MÈZÁROS, born Budapest, Hungary, August 25, 1959; admitted, 1993, Munich (Not admitted in Hungary). *Education:* University of Budapest ELTE 1978-1980; University of Munich. *LANGUAGES:* German, Hungarian. *PRACTICE AREAS:* Construction and Real Estate Law; Banking and Commercial law.

DR. ANDREJ THOMAS SQUARRA, born Budapest, Hungary, February 15, 1967; admitted, 1994, Hungary. *Education:* University Eötrös Lorand Tudományegyetem, Budapest. *LANGUAGES:* Hungarian, German, English and Italian. *PRACTICE AREAS:* Media; Tax Law; Foreign Exchange Law.

OF COUNSEL

DR. JÓZSEF FARKAS, born Budapest, Hungary, May 2, 1926; admitted, 1967, Hungary. *Education:* University of Budapest. *Member:* Hungarian Bar Association; Hungarian Society for the Protection of Industrial Property and Copyright Law. *LANGUAGES:* Hungarian and German. *PRACTICE AREAS:* Commercial Law; Intellectual Property Law.

Languages: Hungarian, German, English, French and Spanish.

PÜNDER, VOLHARD, WEBER & AXSTER

ENDRÖDY SANDOR UTCA 48
1026 BUDAPEST, HUNGARY
Telephone: (36) 60 33 26 18 international; (6) 60 33 26 18 national
Fax: (36) 60 33 26 17 international; (6) 60 33 26 17 national

Frankfurt/Main, Germany Office: Mainzer Landstrasse 46, 60325 Frankfurt/Main. Telephone: (49)(69) 71 99-01. Fax: (49)(69) 71 99-4000. Telex: 414 827.
Düsseldorf, Germany Office: Cecilienallee 6, 40474 Düsseldorf. Telephone: (49)(211) 43 55-0. Fax: (49)(211) 43 55-600.
Berlin, Germany Office: Katharina-Heinroth-Ufer, 10787 Berlin. Telephone: (49)(30) 2546 5800. Fax: (49)(30) 2546 5900.
Leipzig, Germany Office: Burgplatz 7, 04109 Leipzig. Telephone: (49)(341) 21 49-0. Fax: (49)(341) 21 49-600.
Beijing, People's Republic of China Office: Suite C 603, Beijing Lufthansa Center, 50 Liangmaqiao Road, Beijing 100 016. Telephone: (86)(1) 465 15 68; (86)(1) 465 18 08; (86)(1) 465 13 45. Fax: (86)(1) 467 12 56.
Brussels, Belgium Office: Rue d'Arlon 92, 1040 Bruxelles. Telephone: (32)(2) 230 90 11. Fax: (32)(2) 231 19 55.
Moscow, Russia Office: ul. Wolchonka, 18/2, 121 019 Moskwa. Telephone: (7)(095) 202 64 90; (7) (095) 202 65 12; (7)(543) 708 00 900 from Germany; (49)(7545) 893 42 from other countries. Fax: (7)(095) 202 65 14; (7)(543) 708 00 990 from Germany; (49)(7545) 893 43 from other countries.
New York, New York Office: 152 West 57th Street, Carnegie Hall Tower, New York, N.Y. 10019. Telephone: (1)(212) 582 28 28. Fax: (1)(212) 582 24 24.
Warsaw, Poland Office: ul. Jasna 1, 00-013 Warszawa. Telephone: (48) 39 12 21 41. Fax: (48)(22) 27 15 29.

Administrative Law; Antitrust Law; Arbitration; Auditing and Valuations; Banking, Securities and Finance; Bankruptcy; Building Law; Chinese Law; Commercial Crime; Computer Law; Construction Law; Corporate Law; EU Law; Energy Law; Environmental Law; Franchising; Industrial Property Law; Insolvency; Intellectual Property Law; International and German Business Law; Labor and Employment Law; Litigation; Media Law; Mergers and Acquisitions; Pharmaceutical Law; Privatizations; Product Law; Public Law; Real Estate; Reorganizations; Russian Law; Tax Law; Telecommunications; Unfair Trade Law.

FIRM PROFILE: Member of PÜNDER GROUP

Members:

- *BURUMA MARIS, The Hague, Rotterdam*

(This Listing Continued)

- *CERHA, HEMPEL & SPIEGELFELD, Wien*
- *COPPENS, VAN OMMESLAGHE, HORSMANS & FAURES, Bruxelles*
- *DE PARDIEU-LACOURTE G.I.E., Paris*
- *PÜNDER, VOLHARD, WEBER & AXSTER, Frankfurt/Main, Düsseldorf, Berlin, Leipzig*
- *STOFFEL & PARTNER, Zürich, Genève.*

Joint Offices of PÜNDER GROUP:

Beijing - Bruxelles - Budapest - Moskwa - New York - Warszawa

MEMBER OF FIRM

DR. WOLFGANG DORN-ZACHERTZ, born Sagan, Germany, November 17, 1944; admitted, 1973, Darmstadt; 1986, Munich; 1993, Frankfurt/Main. *Education:* Universities of Frankfurt/Main, Freiburg/Breisgau and Mainz. Author: "Die Unabhängigkeit und die Unbefangenheit des Abschlußprüfers in der aktienrechtlichen Pflichtprüfung", Mainz, 1976. *Member:* German Bar Association. *LANGUAGES:* German and English. *PRACTICE AREAS:* Commercial Law; Corporate Law; Privatizations; Real Estate; Banking Law; Energy Law.

ASSOCIATE

GYÖRGY ARATÓ, born Györ, Hungary, March 4, 1968; admitted, 1994, Hungary. *Education:* University Janus Pannonius Pécs. *LANGUAGES:* Hungarian and German. *PRACTICE AREAS:* Commercial Law; Corporate Law; Civil Law; Family Law.

(For complete biographical data on personnel at Frankfurt/Main, Düsseldorf, Berlin and Leipzig, Germany, Brussels, Belgium, Moscow, Russia, Warsaw, Poland, New York, New York and Beijing, People's Republic of China, see Professional Biographies at those locations)

PUSCHNER & POIGNER

Established in 1993

FERENCZY ISTVAN UT. 14

H-1053 BUDAPEST, HUNGARY

Telephone: 361 137 84 91

Fax: 361 137 84 91

Vienna, Austria Office: Schubertring 8, A-1010 Wien I. Telephone: 222 513 80 91 series. Telefax: 43 1 513 86 66. Telex: 75 211358 ewla a.

Banking, Corporate, Commercial, Taxation, Property, Contract and Real Estate Law, International Transactions and Arbitration.

DR. JOHANN POIGNER, born Altmünster, Austria, September 26, 1953; admitted, 1990, Austria. *Education:* University of Vienna, Salzburg (1986). *Member:* East-West Lawyers Association; Austria Lawyers Association. *LANGUAGES:* German, English and Russian.

ASSOCIATES

KATALIN LEHNER, born Budapest, Hungary, July 15, 1968. *Education:* University of Budapest; University of Vienna; Professorial Assistant, Institute of Comparative Law. *LANGUAGES:* Hungarian, German and Russian.

Correspondence Language: German, English, Russian, Hungarian.

S.B.G. & K. PATENT AND LAW OFFICES

Partnership of Lawyers and Patent Attorneys Budapest

ANDRÁSSY-ÚT 113

H-1062 BUDAPEST, HUNGARY

Telephone: (36-1) 34-24-950

FAX: (36-1) 34-24-323

Telex: 22-4435

Mailing Address: P.O. Box 360, 1369 Budapest, Hungary

BOARD MEMBERS

Dr. Béla Kende
Dr. Katalin Szamosi
László Beliczay
Dr. Róbert Berczes
(This Listing Continued)

Adám Szentpeteri, Jr.

OF COUNSEL

Dr. Adam Szentpeteri

ATTORNEYS AT LAW

Dr. Róbert Berczes
Dr. László Kárpáti
Dr. László Kárpáti, Jr.
Dr. Béla Kende
Dr. Gabriella Sasvari
Dr. Éva Szalontay
Dr. Katalin Szamosi
Dr. Tamás Eless
Dr. István Bajkai
Dr. László Tokai

PATENT ATTORNEYS

László Beliczay
Tamás Bokor
Emilia Csanak
Dr. Bernadette Dalmy
Katalin Derzsi
Vilmos Klenk
Zerna Kováts
Dr. Zoltán Köteles
János Machytka
András Mák
Dr. Eva Parragh
Mária Somlai
Zoltán Ráthonyi
Adám Szentpeteri, Jr.

SEWARD & KISSEL

(Smith & Martin 1890)

NÁDOR UTCA 11.

1051 BUDAPEST, HUNGARY

Telephone: 361-132-7115

Facsimile: 361-132-7940

New York, N.Y., Office: One Battery Park Plaza. Telephone: 212-574-1200. Cable Address: "Sewkis New York." Telex: 23-9046; 62-0982. Facsimile: 212-480-8421.

Washington, D.C. Office: 1200 G Street, N.W., Suite 350. Telephone: 202-737-8833. Facsimile: 202-737-5184.

General Practice including Corporations, Securities, Banking, Taxes, Antitrust, Litigation, Real Estate, Municipal Financing, Maritime, Bankruptcy, Probate and Trusts.

COUNSEL

DR. PÉTER KOMÁROMI, born Budapest, Hungary, 1946; admitted, 1986, Hungary. *Education:* Janus Pannonius Law School (1969). Author: Lecture Books on International Private Law and International Trade Law, Foreign Trade College, Budapest. Associate Professor, College of Foreign Trade, Budapest, 1981—. Member of the Presidium of the Hungarian Chamber of Commerce Court of Arbitration, 1985—. Executive President, Hungarian Chamber of Commerce Court of Arbitration, 1975-1989. Member, Board of Professional Examination for Lawyers and Legal Advisors, 1981-1989. *Member:* Budapest (Member, Section of Law of Economy) and International (Member, East European Forum, 1992—) Bar Associations; Hungarian Chamber of Commerce (Member, Legal Section, 1981—. *LANGUAGES:* Hungarian, English, German. *PRACTICE AREAS:* General Corporate.

(For Biographical data on all Personnel, see Professional Biographies at New York, N.Y.)

SHEARMAN & STERLING

SZERB UTCA 17-19
1056 BUDAPEST, HUNGARY
Telephone: (36-1) 266-3522
Fax: (36-1) 266-3523

New York, N.Y. Office: 599 Lexington Avenue, New York, New York 10022-6069 and Citicorp Center, 153 East 53rd Street, New York, New York 10022-4676. Telephone: (212) 848-4000. Telex: 667290 Num Lau. Fax: 599 Lexington Avenue: (212) 848-7179. Citicorp Center: (212) 848-5252.

Abu Dhabi, United Arab Emirates Office: P.O. Box 2948. Telephone: (971-2) 324477. Fax: (971-2) 774533.

Beijing, People's Republic of China Office: Suite #2205, Capital Mansion, No. 6, Xin Yuan Nan Road. Chao Yang District Beijing, 100004. Telephone: (861) 465-4574. Fax: (861) 465-4578.

Düsseldorf, Federal Republic of Germany Office: Königsallee 46, D-40212 Düsseldorf. Telephone: (49-211) 13 62 80. Telex: 8 588 294 NYLO. Fax: (49-211) 13 33 09.

Frankfurt, Federal Republic of Germany Office: Bockenheimer Landstrasse 55, D-60325 Frankfurt am Main. Telephone: (49-69) 97-10-70. Fax: (49-69) 97-10-71-00.

Hong Kong, Hong Kong Office: Standard Chartered Bank Building, 4 Des Voeux Road Central, Hong Kong. Telephone: (852) 2978-8000. Fax: (852) 2978-8099.

London, England Office: 199 Bishopsgate, London EC2M 3TY. Telephone: (44-71) 920-9000. Fax: (44-71) 920-9020.

Los Angeles, California Office: 725 South Figueroa Street, 21st Floor, 90017-5421. Telephone: (213) 239-0300. Fax: (213) 239-0381, 614-0936.

Paris, France Office: 12 rue d'Astorg, 75008. Telephone: (33-1) 44-71-17-17. Telex: 282964 Royale. Fax: (33-1) 44-71-01-01.

San Francisco, California Office: 555 California Street, 94104-1522. Telephone: (415) 616-1100. Fax: (415) 616-1199.

Taipei, Taiwan Office: 7th Floor, Hung Kuo Building, 167 Tun Hwa North Road. Telephone: (886-2) 545-3300. Fax: (866-2) 545-3322.

Tokyo, Japan Office: Shearman & Sterling (Thomas Wilner Gaikokuho-Jimu-Bengoshi Jimusho), Fukoku Seimei Building, 5th Fl. 2-2-2, Uchisaiwaicho, Chiyoda-ku, Tokyo 100, Japan. Telephone: (81 3) 5251-1601. Fax: (81 3) 5251-1602.

Toronto, Ontario, Canada Office: Commerce Court West, Suite 4405, P.O. Box 247, M5L 1E8. Telephone: (416) 360-8484. Fax: (416) 360-2958.

Washington, D.C. Office: 801 Pennsylvania Avenue, N.W., Suite 900, 20004-2604. Telephone: (202) 508-8000. Fax: (202) 508-8100.

General and International Practice.

FIRM PROFILE: *Shearman & Sterling, founded in 1873, has more than 500 lawyers in 15 offices throughout the world. The firm's practice encompasses most major areas of business law, including: Antitrust and Trade Regulation; Banking; Bankruptcy and Corporate Reorganization; Compensation and Benefits; Environmental; Finance (including Corporate Finance, Domestic Private Finance, Financial Institutions, International Private Finance and Project Finance); Individual Clients, Trusts and Estates; Insurance; International Trade and Government Relations; Litigation and Arbitration; Mergers and Acquisitions; Oil and Gas; Privatizations; Real Estate; and Tax. The Firm is also engaged in the practice of French, German and Hungarian law through its offices in France, Germany and Hungary.*

MANAGING PARTNER

HUBERTUS V. SULKOWSKI, born Csikeszereda, Hungary, 1943; admitted, 1971, New York; 1981, U.S. Supreme Court; admitted in France (Not admitted in Hungary). *Education:* Trinity College (B.A., 1966); Boston College (J.D., 1969). *LANGUAGES:* English, French and Hungarian.

RESIDENT EUROPEAN COUNSEL

JOHN E. BALTAY, born Bicske, Hungary, 1933; admitted, 1960, New York (Not admitted in Hungary). *Education:* Union College (B.A., 1956); Harvard Law School (J.D., 1959). *LANGUAGES:* English, Hungarian, French and German.

RESIDENT ASSOCIATES

DR. CHRYSTA BÁN, born Budapest, Hungary, 1957; admitted, 1991, California; 1994, Hungary. *Education:* Eötovös Loránd University School of Law (J.D., 1980); Faculté Internationale de Droit Comparé, Strasbourg (DDC, 1981); Advanced Law Degree on International Commercial Law,

(This Listing Continued)

Institute of Advanced Legal Studies, Eötvös Lóránd University, Budapest (1987). *LANGUAGES:* Hungarian, English and German.

DR. ANDREA GYURÁCZ, born Sopron, Hungary, 1966; admitted, 1992, Hungary. *Education:* Eötvös Loránd University Law School (J.D., 1989); University of Illinois Law School (LL.M., 1992). *LANGUAGES:* Hungarian and English.

(For Biographical data of all Partners, see Professional Biographies at New York, New York).

SKADDEN, ARPS, SLATE, MEAGHER & FLOM

MAHART BUILDING, H-1052
APÁCZAI CSERE JÁNOS U.11, VL.EM.
BUDAPEST, HUNGARY
Telephone: 011-36-1-266-2145
Fax: 011-36-1-266-4033

New York, New York Office: 919 Third Avenue, 10022. Telephone: 212-735-3000. Fax: 212-735-2000; 212-735-2001. Telex: 645899 Skarslaw.

Boston, Massachusetts Office: One Beacon Street, 02108. Telephone: 617-573-4800. Fax: 617-573-4822.

Washington, D.C. Office: 1440 New York Avenue, N.W., 20005. Telephone: 202-371-7000. Fax: 202-393-5760.

Wilmington, Delaware Office: One Rodney Square, 19899. Telephone: 302-651-3000. Fax: 302-651-3001.

Los Angeles, California Office: 300 South Grand Avenue, 90071. Telephone: 213-687-5000. Fax: 213-687-5600.

Chicago, Illinois Office: 333 West Wacker Drive, 60606. Telephone: 312-407-0700. Fax: 312-407-0411.

San Francisco, California Office: Four Embarcadero Center, 94111. Telephone: 415-984-6400. Fax: 415-984-2698.

Houston, Texas Office: 1600 Smith Street, Suite 4460, 77002. Telephone: 713-655-5100. Fax: 713-655-5181.

Newark, New Jersey Office: One Riverfront Plaza, 07102. Telephone: 201-596-4440. Fax: 201-596-4444.

Tokyo, Japan Office: 12th Floor, The Fukoku Seimei Building, 2-2-2, Uchisaiwaicho, Chiyoda-ku, 100. Telephone: 011-81-3-3595-3850. Fax: 011-81-3-3504-2780.

London, England Office: 25 Bucklersbury EC4N 8DA. Telephone: 011-44-71-248-9929. Fax: 011-44-71-489-8533.

Hong Kong Office: 30/F Peregrine Tower, Lippo Centre, 89 Queensway, Central. Telephone: 011-852-820-0700. Fax: 011-852-820-0727.

Sydney, New South Wales, Australia Office: Level 26-State Bank Centre, 52 Martin Place, 2000. Telephone: 011-61-2-224-6000. Fax: 011-61-2-224-6044.

Toronto, Ontario Office: Suite 1820, North Tower, P.O. Box 189, Royal Bank Plaza, M5J 2J4. Telephone: 416-777-4700. Fax: 416-777-4747.

Paris, France Office: 105 rue du Faubourg Saint-Honoré, 75008. Telephone: 011-33-1-40-75-44-44. Fax: 011-33-1-49-53-09-99.

Brussels, Belgium Office: 523 avenue Louise, Box 30, 1050. Telephone: 011-32-2-648-7666. Fax: 011-32-2-640-3032.

Frankfurt, Germany Office: MesseTurm, 27th Floor, 60308. Telephone: 011-49-69-9757-3000. Fax: 011-49-69-9757-3050.

Beijing, China Office: 1605 Capital Mansion Tower, No. 6 Xin Yuan Nan Road, Chao Yang District, 100004. Telephone: 011-86-1-466-8800. Fax: 011-86-1-466-8822.

Prague, Czech Republic Office: Revolucni 16, 110 00. Telephone: 011-42-2-231-75-18. Fax: 011-42-2-231-47-33.

Moscow, Russia Office: Pleteshkovsky Pereulok 1, 107005. Telephone: 011-7-501-940-2304. Fax: 011-7-501-940-2511.

Firm engaged in general American and International law practice, but not authorized to appear before the Hungarian Courts.

PATRICK J. FOYE, born New York, N.Y., 1957; admitted, 1982, New York (Not admitted in Hungary). *Education:* Fordham College (B.A., cum laude, 1978; J.D., 1981). Associate Editor, Fordham Law Review, 1980-1981. (Also at New York, New York, Brussels, Belgium and Moscow Russia Offices).

(For Biographical data on other Personnel, see Professional Biographies at New York, New York).

SQUIRE, SANDERS & DEMPSEY

DEAK FERENC UT. 10
OFFICE 304
H-1052 BUDAPEST V., HUNGARY
Telephone: 011-36-1-266-2024
Fax: 011-36-1-266-2025

Cleveland, Ohio Office: 4900 Society Center, 127 Public Square, Cleveland, Ohio 44114-1304. Telephone: 216-479-8500. Fax's: 216-479-8780, 216-479-8781, 216-479-8787, 216-479-8795, 216-479-8777, 216-479-8783, 216-479-8776, 216-479-8788.

Columbus, Ohio Offices: 1300 Huntington Center, 41 South High Street, Columbus, Ohio 43215. Telephone: 614-365-2700. Fax: 614-365-2499.

Jacksonville, Florida Office: One Enterprise Center, Suite 2100, 225 Water Street, Jacksonville, Florida 32202. Telephone: 904-353-1264. Fax: 904-356-2986.

Miami, Florida Office: 201 South Biscayne Boulevard, Suite 2900 Miami Center, Miami, Florida 33131. Telephone: 305-577-8700. Fax: 305-358-1425.

New York, New York Office: 520 Madison Avenue, 32nd Floor, New York, New York 10022. Telephone: 212-872-9800. Fax: 212-872-9814.

Phoenix, Arizona Office: Two Renaissance Square, 40 North Central Avenue, Suite 2700, Phoenix, Arizona 85004-4441. Telephone: 602-528-4000. Fax: 602-253-8129.

Washington, D.C. Office: 1201 Pennsylvania Avenue, N.W., P.O. Box 407, Washington, D.C. 20044. Telephone: 202-626-6600. Fax: 202-626-6780.

London, England Office: 1 Gunpowder Square, Printer Street, London EC4A 3DE. Telephone: 011-44-71-830-0055. Fax: 011-44-71-830-0056.

Brussels, Belgium Office: Avenue Louise, 165, Box 15, 1050 Brussels, Belgium. Telephone: 011-32-2-648-1717. Fax: 011-32-2-648-1064.

Prague Office: Adria Palace, Jungmannova 31/36, 11000 Prague 1, Czech Republic. Telephone: 011-42-2-231-5661. Fax: 011-42-2-231-5482.

Bratislava Office: Mudronova 37, 811 01 Bratislava, Slovak Republic. Telephone: 011-42-7-313-362; 011-42-7-315-370. Fax: 011-42-7-313-918.

Kiev, Ukraine Office: vul. Prorizna 9, Suite 20, Kiev 252035, Ukraine. Telephones: 011-7-044-244-3452, 011-7-044-244-3453, 011-7-044-228-8687. Fax: 011-7-044-228-4938.

General and International Practice.

RESIDENT ASSOCIATES

ANDRAS I. HANAK, born Budapest, Hungary, 1951; admitted, 1987, Pennsylvania (Not admitted in Hungary). *Education:* Eotvos Lorand University (J.D., 1975); Columbia University (LL.M., 1982); University of Pennsylvania (J.D., 1987). Assistant Professor, Budapest University School of Economics, 1977-1981. **PRACTICE AREAS:** Corporate Finance and Privatization.

ANDREA KOZMA, born Hungary, 1962; admitted, 1991, Hungary. *Education:* Eotvos Lorand University Law School, Budapest (1985). *Member:* Hungarian Bar Association; Hungarian-Canadian Bar Association; Hungarian Journalists' Association. *LANGUAGES:* Hungarian (native), English. **PRACTICE AREAS:** International Law.

(For Biographical Data on Cleveland and Columbus, Ohio, Miami and Jacksonville, Florida, New York, New York, Phoenix, Arizona, Washington, D.C., Brussels, Belgium, Prague, Czech Republic, Bratislava, Slovak Republic, London, England and Kiev, Ukraine Personnel, see Professional Biographies at those Points Respectively).

STIKEMAN, ELLIOTT

ANDRÁSSY ÚT 100, II FLOOR
H-1062 BUDAPEST, HUNGARY
Telephone: 36-1-269-1790
Fax: 36-1-269-0655

Montreal, Quebec Office: 1155 René-Lévesque Boulevard West, 40th Floor, H3B 3V2. Telephone: 514-397-3000. Fax: 514-397-3222.

Toronto, Ontario Office: Commerce Court West, 53rd Floor, M5L 1B9. Telephone: 416-869-5500. Fax: 416-947-0866.

Ottawa, Ontario Office: 50 O'Connor Street, Suite 914, K1P 6L2. Telephone: 613-234-4555. Fax: 613-230-8877.

Calgary, Alberta Office: 855 - 2nd Street S.W., 1500 Bankers Hall, T2P 4J7. Telephone: 403-266-9000. Fax: 403-266-9034.

(This Listing Continued)

Vancouver, British Columbia Office: 666 Burrard Street, Suite 1700, Park Place, V6C 2X8. Telephone: 604-631-1300. Fax: 604-681-1825.

New York, New York Office: 126 East 56th Street, 11th Floor, Tower 56, 10022. Telephone: 212-371-8855. Fax: 212-371-7087.

Washington, D.C. Office: 1300 I Street, N.W., Suite 1210 West, 20005-3314. Telephone: 202-326-7555. Fax: 202-326-7557.

London, England Office: Cottons Centre, Cottons Lane, SE1 2QL. Telephone: 71-378-0880. Fax: 71-378-0344.

Paris, France Office: In Association with Société Juridique Internationale, 39, rue François Ier, 75008. Telephone: 33-1-40-73-82-00. Fax: 33-1-40-73-82-10.

Hong Kong Office: 29 Queen's Road Central, Suite 1506, China Building. Telephone: 852-2868-9903. Fax: 852-2868-9912.

Hong Kong: In Association with Shum & Co., 29 Queen's Road Central, Suite 1103, China Building. Telephone: 852-2526-5531. Fax: 852-2845-9076.

Taipei, Taiwan Office: 117 Sec. 3 Min Sheng East Road, 8th Floor. Telephone: 886-2-719-9573. Fax: 886-2-719-4540.

Taxation, Corporation, Tariff, Insurance, Freight Rates and Marine Law. Trials and General Practice. Labour Law.

PARTNERS AND ASSOCIATES

JEAN PHILIPPE EWART, born Montreal, Quebec, December 20, 1955; admitted, 1981, Quebec (Not admitted in Hungary). *Education:* College Jean de Brébeuf (D.E.C., 1975); University of Montreal (LL.L., 1980). *Member:* Quebec and Canadian Bar Associations.

ROBERT H. HAYHURST, born Jos, Nigeria, July 5, 1957; admitted, 1991, Quebec and New York (Not admitted in Hungary). *Education:* Laval University (B.A., 1981); McGill University (B.C.L., 1990; LL.B., 1990).

(For biographical data on other personnel, see Professional Biographies at Montreal, Quebec, Toronto, Ontario, Ottawa, Ontario, Calgary, Alberta, Vancouver, British Columbia, New York, New York, Washington, D.C., London, England, Paris, France, Hong Kong and Taipei, Taiwan)

STROOCK & STROOCK & LAVAN

EAST-WEST BUSINESS CENTER
RÁKÓCZI UT 1-3
H-1052 BUDAPEST H-1088, HUNGARY
Telephone: 011-361-266-9520; 011-361-266-7770
Telecopier: 011-361-266-9279

New York, New York Office: Seven Hanover Square, 10004-2696. Telephone: 212-806-5400. Telecopier: (212) 806-6006.

Washington, D.C. Office: 1150 Seventeenth Street, N.W., Suite 600, 20036-4652. Telephone: 202-452-9250. Telecopier: (202) 421-6234. Cable Address: "Plastroock, Washington." Telex: 89401 STROOCK DC.

Los Angeles, California Office: 2029 Century Park East, Floors 16 & 18, 90067-3086. Telephone: 310-556-5800. Telecopier: (310) 556-5959. Cable Address: "Plastroock L.A." Telex: Plastroock LSA 677190 (Domestic and International).

Miami, Florida Office: 200 South Biscayne Boulevard, Suite 3300, First Union Financial Center, 33131-2385. Telephone: 305-358-9900. Telecopier: (305) 789-9302. Telex: 803133 Stroock Mia (Domestic and International); Broward Line: 527-9900.

International and Corporate Law.

ROBERT C. BATA, born Budapest, Hungary, July 5, 1951; admitted, 1978, New York and U.S. District Court, Southern and Eastern Districts of New York; 1991, U.S. Court of Appeals, Second Circuit; 1992, U.S. Supreme Court (Not admitted in Hungary). *Education:* Yale University (B.A., 1973); University of Texas (J.D., 1977). Author: "Hungary Invites Privatization Bids," Parker School Bulletin on Soviet and East European Law, Vol. 2, No. 1 (1991). Co-author: "Stopping Payment on Letters of Credit," National Law Journal, October 9, 1989; "Can Commercial Bank's Participation in Acquisition Financing Make It a 'Bidder?'" New York Law Journal, June 5, 1989. *Member:* New York State (Member: Securities Committee, Commercial and Federal Litigation Section, 1989—; Bank, Corporation and Business Law Section, 1986—) and American (Member, Tort and Insurance Practice Section, 1988—) Bar Associations; Federal Bar Council; Securities Industry Association (Member, Compliance and Legal Division). (Also at New York, New York Office). *LANGUAGES:* Hungarian. **PRACTICE AREAS:** International Law; Corporate Law; Litigation.

(This Listing Continued)

STROOCK & STROOCK & LAVAN, Budapest— Continued

GEORGE G. LORINCZI, born Budapest, Hungary, 1929; admitted, 1953, Wisconsin; 1974, District of Columbia (Not admitted in Hungary). *Education:* University of Paris and University of Michigan (B.A., 1950); Marquette University (J.D., 1953). Associate Editor, Marquette Law Review, 1952-1953. Member, Legal Committee, U.S./USSR Trade and Economic Council, 1977—. Member, Hungarian-U.S. Business Council. Member, International Bar Association's Eastern European Forum Council 1991—. *Member:* The District of Columbia Bar; American Bar Association (Chairman, Committee on Unauthorized Practice of Law, 1968-1970; Vice-Chairman, Committee on International Law, 1977—); International Economic Organizations, Section of International Law, Association; American Society of International Law. (Also at Washington, D.C. Office). *LANGUAGES:* French, German, Hungarian and Italian. *PRACTICE AREAS:* International Law; Corporate Law.

RICHARD M. ORNITZ, born Annapolis, Maryland, July 4, 1945; admitted, 1971, New York; 1976, U.S. District Court, Eastern District of New York; 1984, U.S. Supreme Court (Not admitted in Hungary). *Education:* Cornell University (B.S., Met. Eng., 1967); New York University (J.D., 1970); M.I.T. Sloan School (Senior Executive Program, 1985). Associate Editor, Annual Survey, Law Journal of New York University School of Law. Speaker: Teamwork Between Inside/Outside Counsel, American Products Litigation, European Company Lawyers Association, Swiss Company Lawyers Association, Norwegian Company Lawyers Association. Member, Private Law Advisory Committee, U.S. Department of State, 1987—. Member, Advisory Board, National Institute for Preventive Maintenance, 1988—. Member and Co-Founder: European-American General Counsel's Group, 1982—; New Jersey General Counsel's Group, 1983-1989. Vice President, Secretary and General Counsel, and Member of the Management Committee, Degussa Corporation, 1977-1989. Member, Panel of Arbitrators, American Arbitration Association. *Member:* New York State, American (Member, Steering Committee, Counseling the Multinational Corporation, 1985-1987; Subcommittee Chairman, Employment and Labor Law, European Law Section, 1987-1991) and International Bar Associations; American Corporate Counsel Association (Vice Chairman, International Affairs Committee, 1985-1986; Chairman, 1987-1988); Cornell Society of Engineers. *PRACTICE AREAS:* Corporate Law; International Law; Project Finance Law.

GEORGE R. SHOCKEY, JR., born St. Louis, Missouri, April 10, 1947; admitted, 1977, New York (Not admitted in Hungary). *Education:* Washington University (A.B., magna cum laude, 1969); Yale University (M.Phil., 1972; J.D., 1976). Woodrow Wilson Fellow. *Member:* The Association of the Bar of the City of New York; American Bar Association. (Also at New York, New York Office). *PRACTICE AREAS:* Corporate Law; Securities Law; International Law.

DR. IVAN SZASZ, born Budapest, October 2, 1932; admitted, 1960, Hungary; 1994, District of Columbia. *Education:* University of Budapest (M.A., 1955). Honorary Professor, University of Budapest Law School. Professor, University of Economics, Budapest. Secretary General and Chief Legal Counsel, The Ministry of Trade, 1968-1985. Ambassador of Hungary to the European Communities, 1989-1992. Honorary Chairman, Legal Commission of Chamber of Commerce, Budapest, 1985—. *LANGUAGES:* Hungarian, French, German, Russian. *PRACTICE AREAS:* Company Law; Commercial Law; European Communities Law; International Trade.

ASSOCIATES

Krisztina L. Holtzman (Not admitted in Hungary); **Laszlo Tokai; György Udvardi.**

(For Information on New York, Washington, D.C., Los Angeles and Miami, Florida, see appropriate State professional Biographies)

SZEPESI & KASZÓ

Barristers & Solicitors, Patent & Trade Mark Agents

Established in 1992

39 ÁRPÁD FEJEDELEM ÚTJA

1023 BUDAPEST, HUNGARY

Telephone: 011 36-1 168 7372

Fax: 011 36-1 168 7372

(This Listing Continued)

MEMBERS OF FIRM

ISTVÁN SZEPESI, born Budapest, Hungary, June 25, 1959; admitted, 1994, Budapest. *Education:* University of Eötvös Loránd, Budapest (Dr.Jur., 1990). *Member:* Hungarian Bar Association; International Bar Association; British-Hungarian Law Association; Canadian Bar Association; American Chamber of Commerce; Canadian-Hungarian Chamber of Commerce. *LANGUAGES:* Hungarian and English. *PRACTICE AREAS:* Corporate Law; Civil Law; Business Law; Patent and Trademark Law.

KLÁRA KASZÓ, born Budapest, Hungary, January 8, 1962; admitted, 1990, Budapest. *Education:* University of Eötvös Loránd, Budapest (Dr. Jur., 1985). *Member:* Hungarian Bar Association; International Bar Association; British-Hungarian Law Association; Canadian Bar Association; American Chamber of Commerce; Canadian-Hungarian Chamber of Commerce. *LANGUAGES:* Hungarian, English and German. *PRACTICE AREAS:* Corporate Law; Banking Law; International Trade Law; Business Law; Patent and Trademark Law.

ÉVA KASZÓ, born Budapest, Hungary, February 9, 1957; admitted, 1985, Budapest. *Education:* University of Eötvös Loránd, Budapest (Dr. Jur., 1983). *Member:* Hungarian Bar Association. *LANGUAGES:* Hungarian and English. *PRACTICE AREAS:* International Trade Law; Civil Law.

RUDOLF NÉBALD, born Budapest, Hungary, September 17, 1952; admitted, 1988, Budapest. *Education:* University of Eötvös Loránd, Budapest (Dr. Jur., 1986). *Member:* Hungarian Bar Association. *LANGUAGES:* Hungarian, French and English. *PRACTICE AREAS:* International Trade Law; Civil Litigation.

ASSOCIATES

ZSUZSÁNNA SERES, born Budapest, Hungary, October 21, 1966; (Not admitted in Hungary). *Education:* University of Eötvös Loránd, Budapest (Dr. Jur., 1992). *Member:* Hungarian Bar Association. *LANGUAGES:* Hungarian, English, French, Italian and Russian.

ÁKOS KOZMA, born Budapest, Hungary, May 16, 1972; (Not admitted in Hungary). *Education:* University of Eötvös Lóránd, Budapest (Dr. Jur., 1995). *Member:* Hungarian Bar Association. *LANGUAGES:* Hungarian and German.

VEROCI, ORMAI & CO.

Established in 1989

MAROS U. 22

1122 BUDAPEST, HUNGARY

Telephone: (36-1) 201 9199; (36-1) 202 6244; (36-1) 156 5354

Fax: (36-1) 156 5391

FIRM PROFILE: Veroci, Ormai and Co., established in 1989, is engaged in all aspects of Hungarian corporate, commercial, property and construction law. A substantial part of its clients are foreign based entities. All partners and associates are admitted in Hungary and authorized to appear before Hungarian courts.

PARTNERS

DR. JUDIT VEROCI, born Budapest, Hungary; admitted, 1975, Hungary. *Education:* Eötvös Lóránd University, Budapest. *Member:* Bar of Budapest; Hungarian Law Society. *LANGUAGES:* Italian, Russian, French and English. *PRACTICE AREAS:* Corporate; Commercial Law; Foreign Trade Affairs; Litigation.

DR. GABRIELLA ORMAI, born Budapest, Hungary; admitted, 1975, Hungary. *Education:* Eötvös Lóránd University, Budapest. *Member:* Bar of Budapest; Hungarian Law Society; International Bar Association. *LANGUAGES:* German, English, Italian, Russian and French. *PRACTICE AREAS:* Corporate; Corporate Finance; Banking; Commercial; Construction; Property Law.

DR. ISTVÁN KOVÁRI, born Szombathely, Hungary; admitted, 1992, Hungary. *Education:* Eötvös Lóránd University, Budapest. *Member:* Bar of Budapest; International Bar Association. *LANGUAGES:* English. *PRACTICE AREAS:* Corporate; Commercial; Property Law.

The Firm is associated with McKenna & Co. Solicitors, London, U.K.

WEIL, GOTSHAL & MANGES

A Partnership including Professional Corporations

REVAY UTCA 10
BUDAPEST H-1065, HUNGARY
Telephone: 011-361-269-1144
Fax: 011-361-269-1233

New York, N.Y. Office: 767 Fifth Avenue. Telephone: 212-310-8000. Cable Address: "Wegoma". Telex: 424281; 423144. Telecopier: 212-310-8007.

Dallas, Texas Office: 100 Crescent Court, Suite 1300. Telephone: 214-746-7700. Fax: 214-746-7777.

Houston, Texas Office: Suite 1600, 700 Louisiana Street. Telephone: 713-546-5000. Telecopier: 713-224-9511.

Menlo Park, California Office: 2882 Sand Hill Road, Suite 280. Telephone: 415-926-6200. Telecopier: 415-854-3713.

Miami, Florida Office: Suite 2100, 701 Brickell Avenue. Telephone: 305-577-3100. Telecopier: 305-374-7159.

Washington, D.C. Office: Suite 700, 1615 L Street, N.W. Telephone: 202-682-7000. Telecopier: 202-857-0939; 857-0940. Telex: 440045.

Brussels, Belgium Office: 1 Place Madou, Box 34, 1030 Brussels. Telephone: 011-32-2-217-4003. Telecopier: 011-32-2-217-0215.

London, England Office: 50 Stratton Street, London W1X 5FL. Telephone: 011-44-71-493-9933. Telecopier: 011-44-71-629-7900.

Prague, Czechoslovakia Office: Charles Bridge Center, Krizovnicke nam. 1, 110 00 Prague 1, Czech Republic. Telephone: 011-42-2-24-09-73-00. Telecopier: 011-42-2-24-09-73-00.

Warsaw, Poland Office: ul Senatorska 12 00-082 Warsaw. Telephone: 011-48-22-27-61-44. Telecopier: 011-48-22-27-48-38.

General Practice.

RESIDENT PARTNERS

ARTHUR P. JACOBS, (P.C.), born New York City, January 15, 1934; admitted, 1961, New York (Not admitted in Hungary). *Education:* University of Pennsylvania (B.A., 1955); Yale University (LL.B., 1961). Editor, Yale Law Journal, 1960-1961.

GEORGE GLUCK, born Budapest, January 15, 1949; admitted, 1979, Ontario; 1981, New York (Not admitted in Hungary). *Education:* York University (B.A., (Hons - First Class), 1973); The Fletcher School of Law and Diplomacy, Tufts University (A.M., 1974); Osgoode Hall Law School (LL.B., 1977). Editorial Staff, Osgoode Hall Law Journal. *LANGUAGES:* English, Hungarian.

RESIDENT ASSOCIATES

MATTHEW D. BLOCH, born September 20, 1956; admitted, 1985, New York (Not admitted in Hungary). *Education:* Brandeis University (B.A., magna cum laude, 1977); Boston University School of Law (J.D., magna cum laude, 1984). Member, Boston University Law Review.

LASZLO I. KOPITS, born Baltimore, May 6, 1965; admitted, 1993, New York (Not admitted in Hungary). *Education:* Haverford College (A.B., 1987); Stanford Law School (J.D., 1992); Johns Hopkins School of Advanced International Studies (M.A., 1992). Recipient, Fulbright Scholarship at the Budapest University of Economics. *LANGUAGES:* English, Hungarian, Russian, Italian.

AGNES MAJOR, born Budapest, 1965; admitted, 1987, Budapest. *Education:* Law Faculty of Eotvos Lorand University (J.D., 1985). *LANGUAGES:* English, Hungarian.

(For complete biographical data on New York, New York, Dallas, Texas, Houston, Texas, Menlo Park, California, Miami, Florida, Washington, D.C., Brussels, Belgium, London, England, Prague, Czech Republic and Warsaw, Poland, see Professional Biographies at those locations)

WEISS-TESSBACH KFT.

Established in 1990

VÁRMEGYE U. 3-5
H-1052 BUDAPEST, HUNGARY
Telephone: 0036 1 2674227; 2674228; 2674229
Telecopier: 0036 1 2674241

Vienna, Austria Office: Weiss-Tessbach Rechtsanwälte OEG, Rotenturmstrasse 13, A- 1010. Telephone: 0043 1 5331651. Telecopier: 0043 1 5335252.

(This Listing Continued)

Prague, Czech Republic Representative Office: Weiss-Tessbach spol s.r.o., Celetna 11, 11000. Telephone: 0042 2 2318693; 2317237; 2319963. Telecopier: 0042 2 2317400.

Bratislava, Slovakia Representative Office: Weiss-Tessbach spol s.r.o., Panska 31, 81102. Telephone: 0042 7335769. Telecopier: 0042 7 331126.

Administrative Law, Advertising Law, Agricultural Law, Antitrust Law, Arbitration, Banking Law, Bankruptcy, Competition Law, Constitutional Law, Construction Law, Conveyancing, Corporate Law, Distributorship Agency and Franchise Law, EEC Law, Employer's Liability, Environmental Law, Foreign Investments, Immigration Law, Industrial Relations and Labor Law, Insurance Law, International Contracts, International Private Law, Litigation, Product Liability Law, Property and Real Estate Law, Rent and Lease, Trade Regulations, General Legal Practice, Copyright Law, Industrial Models, License Negotiation, Patent Litigation, Trademark Litigation, Trademark Prosecution, Transfer of Technology, General Intellectual Property Practice, Capital Taxation, Corporate Taxation, Indirect Taxation, Inheritance, Estate and Gift Taxation, International Taxation, Personal Income Taxation, Sales Turnover, Value Added Taxes, Taxation of Foreign Nationals, Exchange Control, East-West Relations (Countertrade, Joint Ventures), Hungarian Law, Czechoslovakian Law.

FIRM PROFILE: *Founded in 1878, Weiss-Tessbach offers the full range of Eastern European corporate legal services. The firm opened its Budapest office in 1990 and is currently composed of seven partners, one U.S. attorney and 23 associates and expects to grow in Eastern Europe in particular.*

PARTNERS IN CHARGE

DR. WIELAND SCHMID-SCHMIDSFELDEN, born St. Pölten, July 1, 1959; admitted, 1989, Austria. (Not admitted in Hungary). *LANGUAGES:* German and English. *PRACTICE AREAS:* Corporate Law; General Commercial Law; The Laws of Eastern European Countries; EEC Law; Banking Finance and Insurance Law; Industrial Installations; Environmental Law; Telecommunication Arbitration.

MAG. DR. STEFAN EDER, born Vienna, April 4, 1962; admitted, 1992, Austria. (Not admitted in Hungary). *LANGUAGES:* German and English. *PRACTICE AREAS:* Corporate Law; General Commercial Law; Computer Law; The Laws of Eastern European Countries; Banking Finance and Insurance Law; Capital Markets; Data Protection; Arbitration.

RESIDENT ASSOCIATES

DR. MONIKA HORVATH, born Budapest, October 26, 1966; admitted, 1992, Hungary. *LANGUAGES:* Hungarian, German and English. *PRACTICE AREAS:* Corporate Law; Banking and Financing; General Commercial Law.

DR. ANDREA OLTI, born Budapest, January, 1968. *Education:* Staats u. Rechtswissen-schafte Fakultät Universität; Heidelberg Juristische Fakultät (LL.M.; Dr.). *LANGUAGES:* Hungarian, English and German.

WHITE & CASE

SUBA CENTER
NAGYMEZO UTCA 44
1065 BUDAPEST, HUNGARY
Telephone: (36-1) 269-0550
Facsimile: (36-1) 269-1199

New York, New York: Telephone: 212-819-8200. Facsimile: 212-354-8113.

Washington, D.C.: Telephone: 202-872-0013. Facsimile: 202-872-0210.

Los Angeles, California: Telephone: 213-620-7700. Facsimile: 213-687-0758; 213-617-2205.

Miami, Florida: Telephone: 305-371-2700. Facsimile: 305-358-5744.

Mexico City, Mexico: Telephone: (52-5) 207-9717. Facsimile: (52-5) 208-3628.

Tokyo, Japan: Telephone: (81-3) 3239-4300. Facsimile: (81-3) 3239-4330.

Hong Kong: Telephone: (852) 2822-8700. Facsimile: (852) 2845-9070; Grice & Co., Solicitors, Telephone: (852) 2826-0333. Facsimile: (852) 2526-7166.

Singapore, Republic of Singapore: Telephone: (65) 225-6000. Facsimile: (65) 225-6009.

Bangkok, Thailand: Pacific Legal Group Ltd., In Association With White & Case, Telephone: (662) 236-6154/7. Facsimile: (662) 237-6771.

Hanoi, Viet Nam: Representative Office, Telephone: (84-4) 227-575/6/7. Facsimile: (84-4) 227-297.

Bombay, India: Telephone: (91-22) 282-6300. Facsimile: (91-22) 282-6305.

(This Listing Continued)

WHITE & CASE, Budapest—Continued

London, England: Telephone: (44-171) 726-6361. Facsimile: (44-171) 726-4314; (44-171) 726-8558.

Paris, France: Telephone: (33-1) 42-60-34-05. Facsimile: (33-1) 42-60-82-46.

Brussels, Belgium: Telephone: (32-2) 647-05-89. Facsimile: (32-2) 647-16-75.

Stockholm, Sweden: Telephone: (46-8) 679-80-30. Facsimile: (46-8) 611-21-22.

Helsinki, Finland: Telephone: (358-0) 631-100. Facsimile: (358-0) 179-477.

Moscow, Russia: Telephone: (7-095) 201-9292/3/4/5. Facsimile: (7-095) 201-9284.

Prague, Czech Republic: Telephone: (42-2) 2481-1796. Facsimile: (42-2) 232-5522.

Warsaw, Poland: Telephone/Facsimile: (48-22) 26-80-53; (48-22) 27-84-86. International Telephone/Facsimile: (48-39) 12-19-06.

Istanbul, Turkey: Telephone: (90-212) 275-68-98; (90-212) 275-75-33. Facsimile: (90-212) 275-75-43.

Ankara, Turkey: Telephone: (90-312) 446-2180. Facsimile: (90-312) 437-9677.

Jeddah, Saudi Arabia: Law Office of Hassan Mahassni, Telephone: (966-2) 651-3535. Facsimile: (966-2) 651-3636.

Riyadh, Saudi Arabia: Law Office of Hassan Mahassni, Telephone: (966-1) 476-7099. Facsimile: (966-1) 479-0110.

Almaty, Kazakhstan: Telephone: (7-3272) 50-7491/2. Facsimile: (7-3272) 61-0842.

General International Practice.

PARTNER

CARL H. AMON III, born Boston, Massachusetts, June 13, 1943; admitted, 1969, New York (Not admitted in Hungary). *Education:* Dartmouth College (A.B., 1965); University of Michigan (J.D., 1968).

RESIDENT ASSOCIATES

DAVID M. EISENBERG, born Port Chester, New York, August 23, 1956; admitted, 1988, New York (Not admitted in Hungary). *Education:* University of London (B.A., 1979); Princeton University (M.A., 1982); University of Virginia (J.D., 1987).

DR. KLARA HONTI, born Budapest, Hungary, August 4, 1965; admitted, 1992, Hungary. *Education:* Eotvos Lorand University (J.D., 1989).

EVA IMRIK, born Szeghalom, Hungary, September 8, 1955; admitted, 1986, Hungary. *Education:* Eotvos Lorand University (J.D., 1981); Institute of Foreign Trade Ministry (Foreign Trade Diploma, 1985); State Securities Supervision (Brokerage Diploma, 1991).

PHOEBE A. KORNFELD, born Huntington Station, New York, June 26, 1955. Admitted 1991, New York; (Not admitted in Hungary). *Education:* St. Lawrence University (B.A., 1977); Duke University (M.A., 1981; Ph.D., 1984; J.D., 1990).

MARIE THERESA O'CONNOR, born New York, New York, March 21, 1970; (Not admitted in Hungary). *Education:* Lehigh University (B.A., 1991); University of Chicago (J.D., 1994).

JESSICA GLASS POLLACK, born Bridgeport, Connecticut, June 29, 1964; admitted, 1990, New York; 1991, Connecticut (Not admitted in Hungary). *Education:* Barnard College (B.A., 1986); University of Chicago (J.D., 1990).

SZABOLCS POSTA, born Miskolc, Hungary, August 4, 1968. *Education:* Eotvos Lorand University (J.D., 1992).

(For biographical data as to other locations, see Professional Biographies at New York, New York; Washington, D.C.; Los Angeles, California; Miami, Florida; Mexico City, Mexico; Tokyo, Japan; Hong Kong; Singapore, Republic of Singapore; Bangkok, Thailand; Hanoi, Viet Nam; Bombay, India; London, England; Paris, France; Brussels, Belgium; Stockholm, Sweden; Helsinki, Finland; Moscow, Russia; Prague, Czech Republic; Warsaw, Poland; Istanbul and Ankara, Turkey; Jeddah and Riyadh, Saudi Arabia; Almaty Kazakhstan).

WINTER & PARTNER

Established in 1990

BENCZUR U, 13
H-1068 BUDAPEST, HUNGARY

Telephone: (1) 122 9840
Facsimile: (1) 1226267
Telex: 22 65 70

Zürich, Switzerland Office: Kirchgasse 40, 8024 Zürich. Telephone: (01) 251 81 00. Telex: 816981. Facsimile: (01) 251 81 28.

Zug, Switzerland Office: Bahnhofstrasse 16, 6300 Zug. Telephone: (042) 22 18 20. Facsimile: (042) 23 44 23.

International Trade and Commodities, Joint-Ventures, Foreign Investments, Commercial, Corporate and Civil Practice, Banking and Finance, Mergers and Acquisitions, Commercial Litigation and Arbitration.

RESIDENT MEMBER

DR. JANOS BURAI-KOVACS, born Budapest, Hungary, November 14, 1950; admitted, 1976, Budapest, Hungary. *Education:* University of Law in Budapest, postgraduate degree in International Corporate and Trade Law (Dr. iur., 1974). *Member:* Hungarian Bar Association. *LANGUAGES:* Hungarian, English and German.

(For Biographical Data on all Members, see Professional Biographies at Zurich, Switzerland)

ICELAND

ADALSTEINSSON & PARTNERS

BORGARTUN 24
P.O. BOX 399
121 REYKJAVIK, ICELAND

Telephone: 354-562-76-11
Telefax: 354-562-71-86

International Business Transactions, Aviation, Bankruptcy, Commercial, Construction, Corporation, Contracts, Maritime, Insurance, Torts, Trademark, Copyright, Real Estate, Family, Property and Labor Law. General Practice.

FIRM PROFILE: The law firm of Adalsteinsson & Partners has its roots in the law firm of Adalsteinsson which was founded in 1969. Ragnar Adalsteinsson was joined by new partners in 1985 and the existing law firm was founded. The firm has a broad range of clients including individuals, local business, governmental agencies, labour unions and multi-national corporations. The firm consists of five partners, four associates and a support staff of six persons. The firm is a member of the International Lawyers Network, which includes law firms in apprximately 50 countries.

MEMBERS OF FIRM

RAGNAR ADALSTEINSSON, born Reykjavík, Iceland, June 13, 1935; admitted, 1962, Iceland; 1966, Supreme Court of Iceland. *Education:* Reykjavík College (Exam, Art., 1955); Law Faculty, University of Iceland (Cand. Juris., 1962). Author: Several articles in Icelandic in learned journals in Iceland on criminal law procedure, human rights, copyright and damages. In English: A chapter on Iceland in "Legal Aspects of doing Business in Western Europe," Kluwer/West; "Enforcement of Money Judgements in Iceland" in "Enforcement of Money Judgements Abroad", Matthew Bender; "Copyright Law & Practice in Iceland" in "Digest of Intellectual Property Laws of the World", Oceana Publications Inc.; "Agency and Distribution Agreements in Iceland" in "International Agency and Distribution Agreements", Butterworth Legal Publishers; a chapter on Iceland in "EFTA Legal Systems: An Introductory Guide," Sheridan & Cameron, Butterworths 1993. Lecturer, Maritime Law, Law Faculty, University of Iceland, 1985. Instructor, Icelandic Technical Institution, 1971-1975. Member: Board of Insurance Supervision, 1974-1978; Council for Child Care, 1978-1982. *Member:* Icelandic Bar Association (President, 1992—); International Bar Association; Licensing Executive Society; Association of Icelandic Patent Agents. **LANGUAGES:** Icelandic, English and Scandinavian. **PRACTICE AREAS:** Admiralty Law; Maritime Law; Agency and Distributorships; Antitrust and Trade Regulation Law; Banking Law; Intellectual Property Law.

OTHAR ÖRN PETERSEN, born Reykjavík, Iceland, January 8, 1944; admitted, 1973, Iceland; 1981, Supreme Court of Iceland. *Education:* Reyk-

(This Listing Continued)

javík College (Exam. Art., 1965); Law Faculty, University of Iceland (Cand. Juris, 1972); post graduate studies in Contracts, Tort and International Law, Law Faculty of the University of Minnesota, St. Paul, Minnesota, U.S.A. (M.A, degree, 1974-1976). Lecturer, Construction Law, Faculties of Law and Engineering, University of Iceland, 1987—. Author: "Few words on Liquidated Damages in Construction Contracts," Úlfljótur, 1990. General Manager of the Icelandic Contractors Association, 1976-1985. *Member:* Icelandic Bar Association. *LANGUAGES:* Icelandic, English and Scandinavian. *PRACTICE AREAS:* Aviation Law; Aerospace Law; Construction Law; Trust Law; Estate Law; Taxation Law; Wills.

VIDAR MÁR MATTHÍASSON, born Reykjavík, Iceland, August 16, 1954; admitted, 1982, Iceland; 1988, Supreme Court of Iceland. *Education:* Tjörn College, Reykjavík (Exam. Art., 1974); Law Faculty, University of Iceland (Cand. Juris, 1979); studies in Law of Contracts and Obligation, Institute for Private Law, University of Oslo, Norway (1979-1981). Author: "New Remedies in Scandinavian Contract Law," Úlfljótur, 1984; "Changes in Chapter III in the Law of Contract no. 7/1936", Timarit Lögfraedinga, 1986; "Cancellation Clauses in the Bankruptcy Act," Timarit Lögfraedinga, 1988; Sections on the Legal Status of State Employees, Úlflj332 tur, 1993; "Employment Contracts," Úlfljótur, 1989: Icelandic Employment Law, a chapter on Iceland in "European Employment Law," A Handbook for managers, Financial Times/Pitman Publishing 1992. Lecturer, Sales Law and Law of Contract and Bankruptcy Law, Law Faculty, University of Iceland, 1984—. *Member:* Icelandic Bar Association. *LANGUAGES:* Icelandic, English and Scandinavian. *PRACTICE AREAS:* Contract Law; Finance Law; Labour Law; Employment Law; Probate Law; Real Estate Law.

TRYGGVI GUNNARSSON, born Reykjavík, Iceland, June 10, 1955; admitted, 1984, Iceland; 1990, Supreme Court of Iceland. *Education:* University College of Education (Exam. Art., 1975); Law Faculty, University of Iceland (Cand. Juris., 1982); studies of Real Property Law, Institute for Private Law, University of Oslo, Norway (1986-1987). Author: "The Constitution and Control of Fisheries and Agricultural Production," Tímarit Lögfraedinga, 1989. Lecturer, Real Property Law andLaw of Negotiable Instrument, Law Faculty, University of Iceland, 1988-1990. Head of Department in the Ministry of Agriculture, 1982-1984. Assistant to the Justices of the Supreme Court of Iceland, 1984-1986. Civil Court Judge at the Civil Law Court, Reykjavík, 1988. Assistant to the Parliamentary Ombudsman inIceland, 1989. *Member:* Icelandic Bar Association. *LANGUAGES:* Icelandic, English and Scandinavian. *PRACTICE AREAS:* Administrative Law; Agricultural Law; Natural Resources Law; Real Property Law; Zoning Law; Planning Law; Land Use Law.

JÓHANNES SIGURDSSON, born Reykjavík, Iceland, April 2, 1960; admitted, 1989, Iceland. *Education:* Sund College, 1980, Reykjaviik, (Exam. Art., 1980); Law Faculty, University of Iceland (Cand. Juris, 1986); studies in Corporate and Tort Law, Law School, University of Virginia (LL.M., 1987). Author: "Saga Orators," 1987; "The Legal System of Iceland," Modern Legal Systems Cyclopedia, 1989, Causation in Law of Torts, Úlfljótur, 1990; Sports Marketing Iceland" in "Sports Marketing Europe," The Legal and Tax Aspects, Kluwer Law and Taxation Publishers, 1993. Editor of Úlfljótur Law Review, 1983-1984. Lecturer, Corporation Law and Torts in Law and Economic Faculty, University of Iceland, 1987—. *Member:* Icelandic Bar Association. *LANGUAGES:* Icelandic, English and Scandinavian. *PRACTICE AREAS:* Bankruptcy Law; Commercial Law; Corporate Law; Insurance Law; Tort Law.

ASSOCIATES

HELGI BIRGISSON, born Reykjavík, Iceland, November 17, 1962; admitted, 1989, Iceland. *Education:* Hamrahlid College, Reykjavík (Exam Art., 1982); Law Faculty, University fo Iceland (Cand. Juris, 1988). *LANGUAGES:* Icelandic, English and Scandinavian.

HREFNA FRIDRIKSDÓTTIR, born Reykjavík, Iceland, April 25, 1965; admitted, 1990, Iceland. *Education:* Sund College, Reykjavík (Exam Art., 1984); Law Faculty, University of Iceland (Cand. Juris, 1989). *LANGUAGES:* Icelandic, English and Scandinavian.

ERLENDUR GÍSLASON, born Reykjavík, Iceland, December 11, 1966; admitted, 1992, Iceland. *Education:* Reykjavík College (Exam. Art., 1986); Law Faculty, University of Iceland (Cand. Juris, 1991). *LANGUAGES:* Icelandic, English, Spanish and Scandinavian.

ODDNÝ MJÖLL ARNARDÓTTIR, born Reykjavík, Iceland, January 16, 1970. *Education:* Laugarvatn College (Exam Art., 1989); Law Faculty, University of Iceland (Cand. Juris, 1994). *LANGUAGES:* Icelandic, English and Scandinavian.

T.S. GUNNARSSON INC.
LAW OFFICES

Established in 1981

ARMULA 17
P.O. BOX 8807
128 REYKJAVIK, ICELAND
Telephone: +354-1-681588
Cable Address: Odin
Fax: +354-1-681151

Agency, Distributorship and Franchise Agreements, Competition and Fair Trade, International Loans, Leasing and Securities, Intellectual Property, Collective Investment and Investment in Iceland, Litigation, Taxation and Debt Recovery.

FIRM PROFILE: The Firm which was established in 1981 is a member of EURO LINK for LAWYERS AND GLOBALAW.

THORDUR S. GUNNARSSON, born Reykjavik, Iceland, January 23, 1948; admitted, 1977, Iceland; 1982, Supreme Court of Iceland. *Education:* University of Iceland (c.j., 1975); Hague Academy of International Law (1973); Oslo University (1981). Author: "Depreciation," University of Iceland, 1975; "Mutual Funds, Unitholders rights to have units redeemed," Lawyers Gazette, 1990; "Franchising in Iceland," published by Mathew Bender, 1992, in the publication "Franchising in the International Marketplace"; "Agencies and Distributorships in Iceland," published by Prentice Hall, 1992, in the publication "Commercial Agencies and Distributorship: An International Guide." Lecturer on Law, 1977-1981 and External Examiner on General Jurisprudence and Legal History, 1984—, University of Iceland. Lecturer on Securities Regulations since 1991. *Member:* Icelandic Bar Association (Board Member, 1982-1984; Member, Law Committee, 1984-1988); International Bar Association; The Icelandic Law Society; The Association of Icelandic Patent Agents; International Union of Lawyers; International Trademark Association; American Collectors Association, Inc. *LANGUAGES:* English and Scandinavian.

ASSOCIATES

HELGA SIGTHORSDOTTIR, born January 22, 1943. *Education:* University of Iceland (Economist, 1982). *LANGUAGES:* English. *PRACTICE AREAS:* Tax Law; Debt Collection.

LÖGMANNASTOFAN

Member of the Parlex Group of European Lawyers

Established in 1956

ÁRMÚLA 26
108 REYKJAVIK, ICELAND
Telephone: (354) 1-685122
Fax: (354) 1-686503

Commercial, Corporation, Contracts, Insurance, Torts, Real Estate, Trade Marks, Family and Property Law.

MEMBERS OF FIRM

STEFÁN PÁLSSON, born Reykjavík, Iceland, July 3, 1945; admitted, 1974, Iceland; 1980, Supreme Court of Iceland. *Education:* University of Iceland (Cand.juris., 1973). *Member:* Icelandic Bar Association (Board Member, 1976-1980). *LANGUAGES:* Icelandic, English, Danish and Norwegian.

PÁLL ARNÓR PÁLSSON, born Reykjavík, Iceland, June 5, 1948; admitted, 1975, Iceland; 1981, Supreme court of Iceland. *Education:* University of Iceland (Cand.juris., 1974). Consul General for Israel in Iceland, 1993—. *Member:* Icelandic Bar Association (Vice-President, 1984-1986); American Bar Association (Honorary Member, 1984—). *LANGUAGES:* Icelandic, English and Danish.

SIGRÍDUR LOGADÓTTIR, born Reyujavík, Iceland, September 15, 1962; admitted, 1990, Iceland. *Education:* Law Faculty, University of Iceland (Cand.juris., 1988). Lecturer at the Icelandic College of Commerce, 1988—. *Member:* Icelandic Bar Association. *LANGUAGES:* Icelandic, English, Danish and Norwegian.

LAW OFFICE-SOLICITORS LÖGMENN

LAUGAVEGUR 97
IS-101 REYKJAVIK, ICELAND
Telephone: (354) 1 27166
Telefax: (354) 1 23356
Telex: (0501) 3147

Commercial Contracts, Company Law, Family and Property Law, Banking Law, Insurance and Torts, Labor Law and General Practice including Incasso-service.

ASGEIR THORODDSEN, born Reykjavik, Iceland, February 7, 1942; admitted, 1970, Iceland; 1990, Supreme Court of Iceland. *Education:* University of Iceland (Cand. Juris, 1967); New York University (1970-1972). *Member:* Icelandic Bar Association. *LANGUAGES:* Icelandic, English and Scandinavian.

BJARNI THOR OSKARSSON, born Reykjavik, Iceland, August 19, 1955; admitted, 1989, Iceland. *Education:* Law Faculty, University of Iceland (Cand. Juris, 1985); Law Faculty, The Tulane University of Louisiana (LL.M., 1986). Adjutant (Law): Faculty of Economics and Business Administration. *Member:* Icelandic Bar Association. *LANGUAGES:* Icelandic, English and Scandinavian.

TOMAS JONSSON, born Reykjavik, Iceland, April 9, 1962; admitted, 1991, Iceland. *Education:* University of Iceland (Cand. Juris, 1988); London University, University College, Law Faculty (LL.M., 1990). *Member:* Icelandic Bar Association. *LANGUAGES:* Icelandic, English and Scandinavian.

SVEINN ANDRI SVEINSSON, born Reykjavik, Iceland, August 12, 1963; admitted, 1993. *Education:* Law Faculty, University of Iceland (Cand. Juris, 1990). *Member:* Icelandic Bar Association. *LANGUAGES:* Icelandic, Dutch and Scandinavian.

EYJOLFUR AGUST KRISTJANSSON, born Reykjavik, Iceland, August 24, 1963. *Education:* Law Faculty, University of Iceland (Cand. Juris., 1991). *LANGUAGES:* Icelandic, English and Scandinavian.

GUNNAR THORODDSEN, born Reykjavik, Iceland, October 30, 1969. *Education:* Law Faculty, University of Iceland (Cand. Juris., 1994). *LANGUAGES:* Icelandic, English, German and Scandinavian.

PÉTURSSON, GUDMUNDARSON, ÁRNASON, MÖLLER

Established in 1907
SUDURLANDSBRAUT 4 A
P.O. BOX 127
121 REYKJAVIK, ICELAND
Telephone: (354) 5680900
Telefax: (354) 5680909

Maritime Law, Company Law, Banking Law, Insurance and Torts, Labor Law, Trademarks and other General Practice including Incasso-service.

FIRM PROFILE: Since its founding in 1907 the firm has offered comprehensive service to the Icelandic business community, and in later years also to international companies and institutions dealing with Icelandic institutions.

MEMBERS OF FIRM

GUÓMUNDUR PÉTURSSON, born 1917; admitted, 1947, Advocate to the Supreme Court of Iceland. *LANGUAGES:* Icelandic, Danish, Norwegian and English. *PRACTICE AREAS:* Maritime; Insurance; Litigation.

PÉTUR GUÓMUNDARSON, born 1950; admitted, 1978, Advocate to the Supreme Court of Iceland. *LANGUAGES:* Icelandic, English, Danish and Norwegian. *PRACTICE AREAS:* Corporate Law; Maritime Law; International Loan Agreements.

HÁKON ÁRNASON, born 1939; admitted, 1966, Advocate to the Supreme Court of Iceland. *LANGUAGES:* Icelandic, English, Danish and Norwegian. *PRACTICE AREAS:* Insurance; Commercial Law; Litigation.

JAKOB R. MÖLLER, born 1940; Law Degree, 1967; admitted, 1991, Advocate to the District Courts of Iceland. *LANGUAGES:* Icelandic, English, Danish and Norwegian. *PRACTICE AREAS:* Insurance; Maritime; Labor Law.

LAW OFFICE OF GUDJON STYRKARSSON

Established in 1964
ADALSTREET 9
101 REYKJAVIK, ICELAND
Telephone: 354 5518354
Cable Address: INKASS
Fax: 354 5628370

General Practice, Commercial and Insurance Law, Trade Marks and Patents.

GUDJON STYRKARSSON, born Iceland, December 12, 1931; admitted, 1965, Iceland and Supreme Court of Iceland. *Education:* University of Iceland (Cand. Jur., 1958); University of Bonn, Germany (1958-1959). *Member:* Icelandic Bar Association; International Bar Association; International Trademark Association; Association International for the Protection of Industrial Property. *LANGUAGES:* Icelandic, English, German, French, Spanish and Scandinavian.

IRELAND

G. J. MOLONEY AND COMPANY

Solicitors

COURTHOUSE CHAMBERS
27/29 WASHINGTON STREET
CORK, IRELAND
Telephone: 353-21-275261
Telefax: 353-21-271586

Dublin, Ireland Office: Hambleden House 19/26 Lower Pembroke Street. Telephone: 353-1-6785199. Fax: 353-1-6785-146.

Commerical and Litigation Practice including Corporate, Commercial, Competition, Insolvency, Environmental Law, EEC Law, Maritime Law, Commercial and General Litigation and General Practice including Property Law and Transactions.

MEMBERS OF FIRM

GERALD JOHN MOLONEY, born Cork, Ireland, August 15, 1928; admitted, 1951, Ireland. Trade Mark Agent. *Education:* National University of Ireland. *Member:* Incorporated Law Society of Ireland (First Law Society Representative, Consultative Committee of European Bars, 1972-1980); Southern Law Association; International Bar Association; Irish Maritime Law Association. *LANGUAGES:* English and French. *PRACTICE AREAS:* Corporate; Commercial; Maritime Law.

GERALD MOLONEY, born Cork, Ireland, July 23, 1957; admitted, 1981, Ireland. *Education:* National University of Ireland (B.C.L.). With, Legal Department of the Commission of the EEC, Brussels, 1982-1983. *Member:* Incorporated Law Society of Ireland; Southern Law Association; European Lawyers Union (Secretary General); International Bar Association; Irish Society of European Law; International Association of Young Lawyers. *LANGUAGES:* English and French. *PRACTICE AREAS:* Corporate; Commercial and Competition Law; Commercial Litigation; European Community Law.

DAVID J. PEARSON, born Cork, Ireland, July 7, 1958; admitted, 1982, Ireland. *Education:* National University of Ireland (B.C.L.; LL.B., Labor Law). *Member:* Incorporated Law Society of Ireland; Southern Law Association; International Bar Association (Irish Rapporteur of the Sub-Committee on European Environmental Law); Irish Environmental Law Society; Irish Society of Labor Law. *PRACTICE AREAS:* Environmental Law; Labour Law; Litigation.

BILL HOLOHAN, born Limerick, Ireland, January 28, 1960; admitted, 1983, Ireland. Trade Mark Agent. *Education:* National University of Ireland (B.C.L., LL.B., Maritime Law); A.C.I. ARB, London. Co-Author: "Bankruptcy Law and Practice in Ireland," May 1991. *Member:* Alumni of The Academy of International Law of the Hague; Incorporated Law Society of Ireland; Southern Law Association; Chartered Institute of Arbitrators; Irish Maritime Law Association (Council Member); Irish Society of Labor Law; Irish Centre for European Law; Irish Franchise Association (Legal Advisor); European Communities Trademark Practitioners Associa-

(This Listing Continued)

tion. (Resident, Dublin Office). *PRACTICE AREAS:* Insolvency; Franchising; Maritime Law; Litigation.

EDMUND PETER HOGAN, born Cork, Ireland, October 21, 1956; admitted, 1981, Ireland. *Education:* National University of Ireland (B.A.). Solicitor, Law Society. Notary Public and Commissioner for Oaths. *Member:* Incorporated Law Society of Ireland; Southern Law Association; Irish Society of European Law. *PRACTICE AREAS:* Litigation.

KATHLEEN COLLINS, born Cork, Ireland, September 23, 1959; admitted, 1984, Dublin. *Education:* University College, Cork (B.C.L.). *Member:* Incorporated Law Society of Ireland; Dublin Solicitors Bar Association. *PRACTICE AREAS:* Corporate and Commercial Law.

ASSOCIATES

DAPHNE BARR, born Cork, Ireland, May 21, 1966; admitted, 1990, Ireland. *Education:* National University of Ireland (B.C.L., LL.B., Adoption Law). *Member:* Incorporated Law Society of Ireland; Southern Law Association. *LANGUAGES:* English, French and German. *PRACTICE AREAS:* Litigation.

JEROME MAUME, born Cork, Ireland, November 19, 1967; admitted, 1992, Ireland. *Education:* National University of Ireland (B.C.L.). *Member:* Incorporated Law Society of Ireland; Southern Law Association. *LANGUAGES:* English and French. *PRACTICE AREAS:* Corporate; Commercial and Competition Law.

PATRICIA FURLONG, born Dublin, Ireland, March 12, 1964; admitted, 1992, Ireland. *Education:* National University of Ireland (B.C.L); Graduate of Institute of Chartered Secretaries and Administrators. *Member:* Incorporated Law Society of Ireland; Institute of Chartered Secretaries and Administrators. *PRACTICE AREAS:* Labour Law; Pensions and Health; Safety at Work.

NICOLA O'BRIEN, born Dublin, Ireland, March 1, 1967; admitted, 1992, Ireland. *Education:* National University of Ireland (B.C.L). *Member:* Incorporated Law Society of Ireland; Dublin Solicitors Bar Association. *LANGUAGES:* English, French and Spanish. *PRACTICE AREAS:* Litigation.

MARY WALSH, born Cork, Ireland, February 25, 1963; admitted, 1991, Ireland. *Education:* National University of Ireland (B.C.L). *Member:* Incorporated Law Society of Ireland; Southern Law Association. *PRACTICE AREAS:* Property Transactions and Probate.

NIAMH O'DRISCOLL, born Cork, Ireland, September 18, 1968; admitted, 1993, Ireland. *Education:* National University of Ireland (B.C.L.). *Member:* Incorporated Law Society of Ireland; Southern Law Association. *PRACTICE AREAS:* Litigation.

REFERENCE: Bank of Ireland, Cork.

(For Complete Biographical Data on all Personnel, see Professional Biographies at Dublin, Ireland)

RONAN DALY JERMYN

12 SOUTH MALL
CORK, IRELAND
Telephone: 352 (21) 272333
Fax: 353 (21) 273521
DX: 2 Cork

Corporate Law, Banking Law, Takeovers and Mergers, Maritime, Insolvency, Debt Recovery and Enforcement, EC Law, Arbitration, Insurance Law, Labour Law, Real Estate and General Practice.

FIRM PROFILE: *Established in 1982 Ronan Daly Jermyn can trace its roots back to 1730. The firm acts for a large number of Corporate clients including Government Bodies and Irish Based Foreign Companies and has forged valuable links with Associates in other jurisdictions. It has worked with the Industrial Development Authority over the years in establishing many Industries in this country and has excellent relationships with the major financial institutions. It is in a position to handle every facet of a client legal business, comprehensively, expertly and expeditiously. The firm has 5 Partners and 4 Associates with some 25 support staff.*

PARTNERS

FRANCIS D. DALY, born 1943; admitted, 1966. *Education:* University College Cork (BCL). Notary Public. Council Member, 1972-1994; Vice President 1991-1992;, Incorporated Law Society. Member, Executive Committee, Cork Chamber of Commerce. Chairman, Allied Metropole Hotel

(This Listing Continued)

Plc. Chairman, Solicitors Financial Services Limited. *PRACTICE AREAS:* Corporate Law; Mergers and Acquisitions; Banking.

NICHOLAS G. COMYN, born 1946; admitted, 1970. *Education:* Clongowes Wood College, University College Dublin (B.A., Honors in Economics, MCL). Commissioner for Oaths. Lecturer, Insolvency Law at Law School Incorporated Law Society of Ireland. Former President, Local Bar Association. Council Member, of Southern Law Association. *LANGUAGES:* English and French. *PRACTICE AREAS:* Corporate Law; Commercial and Insolvency; Environmental.

JOHN L. JERMYN, born 1948; admitted, 1970. *Education:* Portora Royal School, University College Cork. Commissioner for Oaths. Former President, Local Bar Association. Former Council Member of Incorporated Law Society of Ireland. Registrar Diocese of Cork, Cloyne and Ross. *PRACTICE AREAS:* Estate Planning and Administration; Trusts, Conveyancing and Land Use.

FERGUS LONG, born 1959; admitted, 1982. *Education:* University College Cork. *LANGUAGES:* English and French. *PRACTICE AREAS:* Employment Law; Personal and Commercial Litigation.

JOHN BUCKLEY, born 1960; admitted, 1985. *Education:* Newbridge College, University College Cork (BCL). *PRACTICE AREAS:* Insurance, Personal and Defence Litigation.

ASSOCIATES

TOM FOX, born 1965; admitted, 1988. *Education:* University College Cork (BCL; LL.B.; AITI). Member, Institute of Taxation of Ireland. *PRACTICE AREAS:* Commercial Lending, Company Law Taxation.

JOHN DWYER, born 1966; admitted, 1990. *Education:* University College Cork (BCL). Council Member, Society of Young Solicitors of Ireland. *LANGUAGES:* English and French. *PRACTICE AREAS:* Property Transactions, Property Litigation.

RICHARD L. MARTIN, born 1966; admitted, 1991. *Education:* Glenstal Abbey School; University College Cork; Dublin Institute of Technology (B.Comm. with Honours, DLS). *LANGUAGES:* English, French and Dutch. *PRACTICE AREAS:* Corporate, Commercial; Insolvency and Marine.

JAMES O' SULLIVAN, born 1957; admitted, 1993. *Education:* Dublin Institute of Technology (College of Commerce, DLS). *PRACTICE AREAS:* Insurance, Personal and Defence Litigation; Marine, Commercial Litigation; Consumer.

CONSULTANT

JOHN G. RONAN, admitted, 1948. *LANGUAGES:* French. *PRACTICE AREAS:* Consultancy, Tax and Trusts.

All Members of the Firm are Members of the Incorporated Law Society of Ireland, The Southern Law Association and Cork Chamber of Commerce.

Languages: French.

BEAUCHAMPS

Established in 1974

DOLLARD HOUSE
2/5 WELLINGTON QUAY
DUBLIN 2, IRELAND
Telephone: 01-6715522
Telefax: Group 2/3 01-6773783

Corporate, Commercial, European Community Law, Banking, Corporate Finance, Financial Services, Government Grant-Aided Projects; Arbitration, Litigation, Debt Collection, Insurance, Taxation, Real Estate, Planning and Project Management, Franchising, Telecommunications and Broadcasting, Energy, Computer Law and Intellectual Property, Probate, Trusts and Family Law.

MEMBERS OF FIRM

JOHN F. BUCKLEY, born 1931; admitted, 1956, Ireland. *Education:* University College, Dublin (B.A.; LL.B.). Associate, American Bar Association. Member of Council, Incorporated Law Society, 1973-1987, 1992-1994. Chairman, General Practice Section, International Bar Association, 1982—. Associate, Chartered Institute of Arbitrators. Commissioner, Law Reform Commission, 1987—. *LANGUAGES:* English, German and French. *PRACTICE AREAS:* Commercial Real Estate Law; Arbitration Law; Construction Law; Town Planning and Environmental Law; Libel and Defamation.

(This Listing Continued)

BEAUCHAMPS, Dublin—Continued

VALENTINE J.D. KIRWAN, born 1935; admitted, 1959, Ireland. (Silver Medal). *Education:* Trinity College, Dublin (M.A. in Legal Science; LL.B.). *LANGUAGES:* English. *PRACTICE AREAS:* Commercial Law; Commercial Real Estate Law; Sports; Town Planning and Environmental Law; Hotels and Leisure; Eminent Domain.

THOMAS J. O'REILLY, born 1942; admitted, 1965, Ireland. *Education:* University College, Dublin. *LANGUAGES:* English. *PRACTICE AREAS:* Grievance Defense Litigation; Medical Malpractice.

FRANKLIN J. O'SULLIVAN, born 1930; admitted, 1958, Ireland. *Education:* University College, Dublin; Michigan State University (B.C.L.; LL.B. Exhibition Award). Special Certificate of Merit. *LANGUAGES:* English. *PRACTICE AREAS:* Grievance Defense Litigation; Professional Liability.

W. JOHN CUNNINGHAM, born 1953; admitted, 1979, Ireland. *Education:* Trinity College, Dublin (B.A., Mod., Legal Science). *LANGUAGES:* English. *PRACTICE AREAS:* Real Estate Law; Probate Law; Trusts Law; Family Law.

JOSEPH M. BOWE, born 1958; admitted, 1983, Ireland. *Education:* University College, Dublin (B.C.L.). *LANGUAGES:* English. *PRACTICE AREAS:* Real Estate Law; Probate Law; Trusts Law.

NIALL G. COLEMAN, born 1958; admitted, 1985, Ireland. *Education:* University College, Dublin (B.A. Hons). *LANGUAGES:* English. *PRACTICE AREAS:* Commercial Real Estate Law; Project Management Law; Banking Law; Town Planning and Environmental Law.

MARK PERY-KNOX-GORE, born 1955; admitted, 1982, Ireland. *Education:* Oxford University (B.A.). *LANGUAGES:* English. *PRACTICE AREAS:* Corporate Law; Corporate Finance Law; Mergers Law; Acquisitions Law; Banking Law; Telecommunications and Broadcasting Law; Computer Law; Energy Law.

ROBERT A. RYAN, born 1960; admitted, 1986, Ireland; 1991, England and Wales. *Education:* University College, Dublin (B.C.L., Hons.). Formerly of Norton Rose, London. *LANGUAGES:* English. *PRACTICE AREAS:* Banking and International Finance Law; Capital Markets Law; Corporate Finance Law; Venture Capital Law; Asset Finance Law; Financial Services Law.

IMELDA M. REYNOLDS, born 1961; admitted, 1987, Ireland. *Education:* University College, Dublin (B.C.L.). *LANGUAGES:* English. *PRACTICE AREAS:* Commercial Real Estate Law; European Community Law; Franchising; Antitrust; Product Liability.

SOLICITORS

GABRIEL C. DALY, born 1959; admitted, 1983, Ireland. *Education:* University College, Dublin (B.C.L., Hons.). *LANGUAGES:* English and French. *PRACTICE AREAS:* Commercial Litigation; Corporate Restructuring; Corporate Insolvency; Insurance Regulation and Reinsurance; Insurance Brokerage Law; Anti-Trust/Competition Law.

ORLA O'NEILL, born 1967; admitted, 1992, Ireland. *Education:* Trinity College, Dublin (LL.B.). *LANGUAGES:* English and French. *PRACTICE AREAS:* Corporate Law; Mergers and Acquisitions; Immigration Law and Naturalization; European Community Law.

FRANKLIN O'SULLIVAN, born 1962; admitted, 1991, Ireland. *Education:* University College, Dublin (B.Comm.; Diploma in European Law). *LANGUAGES:* English. *PRACTICE AREAS:* Grievance Defence and Plaintiff Litigation; Debt Collection Law; Insolvency and Bankruptcy Law; Insurance Law; Arbitration.

VALENTINE ALAN KIRWAN, born 1965; admitted, 1991, Ireland. *Education:* Trinity College, Dublin (B.B.S.). *LANGUAGES:* English and German. *PRACTICE AREAS:* Commercial Law; Computer and Intellectual Property Law; Pensions and Retirement Benefit Schemes; Consumer Protection Law.

AIDAN MARSH, born 1970; admitted, 1994, Ireland. *Education:* University College, Dublin (BCL). *LANGUAGES:* English and French. *PRACTICE AREAS:* Commercial Real Estate Law; Town Planning and Environmental Law; Taxation of Real Estate; Construction Law.

All Members and Solicitors are Members of the Incorporated Law Society of Ireland and of the Dublin Solicitors Bar Association.

PATRICK J. BRADY & CO.

(in association with Mason Hayes & Curran)

7 FITZWILLIAM SQUARE
DUBLIN 2, IRELAND
Telephone: (353 1) 676 6961
Telex: 31073 MHC EI
Fax: (353 1) 676 3068

Debt Collections, Enforcement of Foreign Judgements, Insolvency and Corporate Bankruptcy including Corporate Reorganization, Restructuring and Creditors' Rights.

FIRM PROFILE: *Patrick J. Brady & Co. is the associated practice of Mason Hayes & Curran established to provide services in the area of debt recovery, insolvency and corporate bankruptcy only.*

MANAGING PARTNER

COLMAN P. CURRAN, born Dublin, Ireland, March 21, 1956; admitted, 1981, Ireland. *Education:* University College, Dublin (B.C.L.). Former Chairman, Technology Committee, Incorporated Law Society of Ireland. Co-author: "Solicitor's Technology Handbook," published by Irish Law Society. *Member:* Society for Computers and Law. (Also Member, Mason Hayes & Curran).

All Solicitors are Members of the Incorporated Law Society of Ireland and the Dublin Solicitors Bar Association.

Languages: French, Dutch, German and Spanish

REFERENCES: Chase Bank (Ireland) p.l.c.; St. Stephens Green, Dublin 2; Bank of Ireland, Head Office, Lower Baggot Street, Dublin 2.

(For Members of Firm, Associates, Consultant and other data, see Professional Biographies of Mason Hayes & Curran).

EUGENE F. COLLINS

61, FITZWILLIAM SQUARE
DUBLIN 2, IRELAND
Telephone: 6761924-5-6785766
Cable Address: "Sue, Dublin"
Telex: 33028
Fax: 6618906

Corporation, Commercial, Financial, EEC, Trademark Law, Insolvency, Labor, Antitrust, Real Estate and Probate Law. Litigation, Arbitration, Intellectual Property, Media and General Practice.
All Solicitors are Members of the Incorporated Law Society of Ireland and The Dublin Solicitors' Bar Association.

MEMBERS OF FIRM

ANTHONY E. COLLINS, born Dublin, Ireland, 1939; admitted, 1964, Ireland. *Education:* Trinity College, Dublin (B.A. and B.Comm., 1961). *Member:* Institute of Taxation; International Bar Association; Incorporated Law Society of Ireland (President, 1984-1985); Canadian Bar Association (Honorary Member).

EUGENE MURPHY, born 1947; admitted, 1970, Ireland. *Education:* University College, Dublin (B.C.L., 1968; LL.B., 1969). *Member:* International Bar Association.

MICHAEL W. CARRIGAN, born 1947; admitted, 1969, Ireland. *Education:* University College, Dublin (B.C.L., 1968; LL.B., 1969). *Member:* Association Internationale des Jeunes Avocats (President, 1985-1986).

GERARD COLL, born 1957; admitted, 1982, Ireland. *Education:* University College Dublin (B.C.L., 1978); Europa Institute University of Amsterdam (Dip. Eur. Integration). *Member:* International Bar Association.

MARGARET BURKE-STAUNTON, admitted, 1972, Ireland. *Member:* Institute of Taxation.

DAVID ENSOR, born 1948; admitted, 1973, Ireland. *Education:* University College, Dublin (B.A. (Econ.), 1970). *Member:* Association Internationale des Jeunes Avocats.

TERENCE LEGGETT, born 1954; admitted, 1978, Ireland. *Education:* University College, Dublin (B.C.L., 1975).

BARRY O'NEILL, born 1950; admitted, 1972, Ireland. *Education:* University College Dublin (B.C.L., 1971). *Member:* International Bar Association.

(This Listing Continued)

ASSOCIATES

SIMON MCCORMICK, born 1946; admitted, 1976, Ireland. *Education:* Trinity College, Dublin (B.B.S., 1969; M.A., 1974).

MARY BARRETT, admitted, 1978, Ireland. *Education:* University College, Dublin (B.C.L., 1975).

SUSAN RYAN, admitted, 1979, Ireland. *Education:* University College, Dublin (B.C.L., 1976).

LEONORA MALONE, admitted, 1989, Ireland. *Education:* University College, Dublin (B.A., 1985).

DAVID CANTRELL, born 1960; admitted, 1988, Ireland. *Education:* University College, Dublin (B.C.L., 1983).

RUTH FINLAY, admitted, 1987, Ireland. *Education:* University College, Dublin (B.C.L., 1983).

JOHN E. COSTELLO, born 1954; admitted, 1977, Ireland. *Education:* University College, Dublin (B.C.L., 1975).

LILIAN HALPIN, admitted, 1991, Ireland. *Education:* Trinity College Dublin (B.A., Mod Legal Science, 1986).

HILARY O'SULLIVAN, admitted, 1982, Ireland. *Education:* University College, Dublin (B.C.L., 1978).

ORLA O'DEA, admitted, 1992, Ireland. *Education:* University College, Dublin (B.C.L., 1987).

Languages: English, French and German

REFERENCE: Bank of Ireland 34, College Green, Dublin.

ARTHUR COX

Established in 1917

41/45 ST. STEPHEN'S GREEN
DUBLIN 2, IRELAND
Telephone: 353-1-676 4661
Telex: 93496
Telecopier: 353-1-668 8906/668 8893

New York, New York Office: 115 East 57th Street, Suite 1230, 10022. Telephone: (212) 759 0808. Fax: (212) 355 3594.

Corporate, Commercial, Mergers and Acquisitions, Foreign Investment, Stock Exchange/Public Listings, European Union, Competition, Banking and Financial Services, International Trade, Litigation and Arbitration, Corporate Defense, Communications, Taxation, Real Estate, Environmental, Probate, Labour, Insurance, Intellectual Property, Entertainment, Aviation, Energy and Natural Resources.

MEMBERS OF FIRM

JAMES O'DWYER, born 1947; admitted, 1969, Ireland; 1986, New York. *Education:* University College, Dublin (B.C.L., 1968; LL.B., 1971). *Member:* New York State and American Bar Associations. **PRACTICE AREAS:** Corporate; Commercial; Mergers and Acquisitions; International.

PAUL MCLAUGHLIN, born 1946; admitted, 1967, Ireland. *Education:* University College, Dublin (B.C.L., 1966). **PRACTICE AREAS:** Aviation Law; Tort; Defamation; Medical Negligence (Defendant).

IAN A. SCOTT, born 1943; admitted, 1965, Ireland. *Education:* University College, Dublin (B.C.L., 1963). **PRACTICE AREAS:** Property Development and Construction; Asset Based Lending.

JOHN G. FISH, born 1938; admitted, 1960, Ireland. *Education:* University of Dublin. Council Member of Incorporated Law Society and Head of Irish Delegation to the Counseil des Barreaux de la Communauté Européene. **PRACTICE AREAS:** Corporate; Commercial; Mergers and Acquisitions.

DANIEL E. O'CONNOR, born 1948; admitted, 1970, Ireland. *Education:* University College, Dublin (B.C.L., 1969). *Member:* Institute of Taxation in Ireland. **PRACTICE AREAS:** Property Development and Construction; Property Finance; Asset Based Lending; Environmental Law.

PETER MCLAUGHLIN, born 1952; admitted, 1974, Ireland. *Education:* University College, Dublin. **PRACTICE AREAS:** Property Development and Construction; Property Finance; Asset Based Lending; Environmental Law.

ROBERT BOLTON, born 1951; admitted, 1973, Ireland. *Education:* University of Dublin. **PRACTICE AREAS:** Property Development and Construction; Property Finance; Asset Based Lending; Charities.

(This Listing Continued)

JOHN V. O'DWYER, born 1950; admitted, 1975, Ireland. *Education:* University College, Dublin (B.C.L., 1973). **PRACTICE AREAS:** Employment and Employee Benefits; Public Sector; Corporate; Commercial.

RONAN WALSH, born 1952; admitted, 1975, Ireland. *Education:* University of Dublin (M.A.). *Member:* Institute of Taxation in Ireland; The Irish Society for European Law. **PRACTICE AREAS:** Banking and Finance; Corporate; Commercial.

EUGENE P. FANNING, born 1950; admitted, 1974, Ireland; 1978, California; 1981, New York; 1992, England and Wales. *Education:* University College, Dublin (LL.M., 1976); Harvard Law School (LL.M., 1977). *Member:* The Association of the Bar of the City of New York; New York State and American Bar Associations; State Bar of California; International Fiscal Association; Harvard Law School Association of Europe. **PRACTICE AREAS:** International; Foreign Investment; Corporate Tax; Commercial; Corporate; Media and Entertainment; Technology and Telecommunications.

DONOGH CROWLEY, born 1953; admitted, 1975, Ireland. *Education:* University College, Dublin (B.C.L., 1973). **PRACTICE AREAS:** Commercial Litigation; Defamation; Medical Negligence (Defendant); Maritime Law.

JOHN WALSH, born 1955; admitted, 1979, Ireland. *Education:* University College, Dublin (B.Comm., 1976). **PRACTICE AREAS:** Property Development and Construction; Property Finance; Asset Based Lending; Environmental Law.

MICHAEL MEGHEN, born 1954; admitted, 1980, Ireland. *Education:* University of Dublin (B.B.S., 1976; LL.B., 1978). **PRACTICE AREAS:** Corporate; Commercial; Mergers and Acquisitions; Information Technology.

JOSEPH LEYDEN, born 1954; admitted, 1976, Ireland. *Education:* University College, Dublin (B.C.L., 1975). **PRACTICE AREAS:** Commercial, Environmental and Insurance Litigation; Environmental Law; Intellectual Property; Product Liability.

WILLIAM F.R. JOHNSTON, born 1950; admitted, 1979, Ireland. *Education:* University of Dublin (M.A.). Author: Irish Section, Bankers' Liability : Risks and Remedies. Co-Author: Irish Section, Digest of the Commercial Laws of the World; Irish Section, Financial Services in the New Europe. *Member:* Incorporated Law Society of Ireland (Company and Commercial Law Committee); International Bar Association (Banking Law); Chartered Institute of Bankers. **PRACTICE AREAS:** Banking and Finance.

GERARD M. BOHAN, born 1958; admitted, 1982, Ireland. *Education:* University College, Dublin (B.C.L., 1978). *Member:* International Bar Association (European Environmental Law Sub Committee); Irish Environmental Law Association (Founder Member). **PRACTICE AREAS:** Environment; Corporate; Commercial.

EUGENE MCCAGUE, born 1958; admitted, 1982, Ireland. *Education:* University College, Dublin (B.C.L., 1978; Diploma in European Law, 1991). **PRACTICE AREAS:** Insolvency Law; Corporate Restructuring; Debt Recovery.

NICHOLAS G. MOORE, born 1957; admitted, 1980, Ireland. *Education:* Incorporated Law Society of Ireland. **PRACTICE AREAS:** Personal Injury; Public Sector Litigation; Sports Law; Health Law; Corporate Defense; White-Collar Fraud.

DECLAN HAYES, born 1957; admitted, 1984, Ireland. *Education:* University College, Dublin (B.Comm., 1978; M.B.S., 1979). *Member:* European Communities Trade Mark Practitioners Association; The Faculty of Notaries Public in Ireland. **PRACTICE AREAS:** Commercial; Corporate Reorganization; Foreign Investment; Trademarks; Pharmaceuticals; Food Drug and Cosmetic Law.

DAVID O'DONOHOE, born 1959; admitted, 1983, Ireland. *Education:* University College, Dublin (B.C.L.). **PRACTICE AREAS:** Aviation Law; Tort; Personal Injury; Maritime Law; Fraud; Alternative Dispute Resolution; Personal Injury (Defendant).

COLM DUGGAN, born 1960; admitted, 1985, Ireland. *Education:* University of Dublin (B.A. Mod.); London University (L.S.E.; LL.M.). Author: "Company and Partnership Law in Ireland.". **PRACTICE AREAS:** Corporate; Commercial; Mergers and Acquisitions; Energy and Natural Resources.

(This Listing Continued)

ARTHUR COX, Dublin—Continued

SIOBHAN DOWNEY, born 1959; admitted, 1984, Ireland. *Education:* University College, Dublin (B.A.). *PRACTICE AREAS:* Corporate; Commercial.

CARL O'SULLIVAN, born 1957; admitted, 1983, Ireland. *Education:* University of Dublin (B.A. Mod.); University College, Dublin (M.B.A.). *PRACTICE AREAS:* Financial Services; Securities; Corporate; Commercial.

ISABEL FOLEY, born 1961; admitted, 1985, Ireland. *Education:* University College, Dublin (B.C.L.). *PRACTICE AREAS:* Commercial Litigation; Tort; Property Litigation.

JOHN MEADE, born 1960; admitted, 1993. Northern Ireland and Ireland. *Education:* University of Dublin (B.A. (Mod.)); Cambridge University (LL.M.). *PRACTICE AREAS:* European Union; Competition Law.

RESIDENT NEW YORK COUNSEL

PÁDRAIG A. Ó RÍORDÁIN, born Cork, Ireland, 1965; admitted, 1988, Ireland; 1991, New York. *Education:* University College Cork (B.C.L., 1986; LL.M., 1989); the Honorable Society of King's Inns (B.L., 1988); Harvard Law School (LL.M., 1990). *Member:* Association of the Bar of the City of New York; American Bar Association; Union Internationale des Jeunes Avocats; Harvard Law School Association; International Bar Association. *PRACTICE AREAS:* Foreign Investment; International; Tax and Corporate.

ASSOCIATES

Grainne Ahern; Ciaran Bolger; Elizabeth Bothwell; Colin Byrne; William Day; Caroline Devlin; Deirdre Durcan; David Foley; Ailbhe Gallagher; Kathleen Garrett; Seamus Given; Gregory Glynn; Adrienne Grant; Stephen Hegarty; Grainne Henchy; Grainne Hennessy; Geraldine Hickey; Raymond Hurley; Conor McDonnell; Dermot McEvoy; Patrick McGovern; Justin McKenna; Patrick Murphy; Patrick O'Brien; Catríona O'-Mara; Henry Ong; Christine Scott; Mary Swords; Rory Williams.

BARRISTERS

DECLAN DRISLANE, born 1957; admitted, 1987, Ireland. *Education:* University of Dublin (B.B.S.); The Honorable Society of King's Inns (B.L.). *Member:* Association of Pension Lawyers (Republic of Ireland Regional Group). *PRACTICE AREAS:* Foreign Investment; Employee Benefits.

CONSULTANTS

Vincent Walsh   Niall McLaughlin (Litigation)
  (Foreign Investment)   David R. Pigot (Litigation)
Denis J. Bergin (Corporate)   Dr. Yvonne Scannell
Chetwode Hamilton (Corporate)   (Environmental)

Languages: French, German, Spanish, Russian and Chinese (Mandarin).

DILLON EUSTACE

Solicitors

GRAND CANAL HOUSE
1 UPPER GRAND CANAL STREET
DUBLIN 4, IRELAND
Telephone: +353-1-6670022
Fax: +353-1-6670042

Corporate, Commercial, Banking and Financial Services, Corporate Finance, Communications, Oil and Gas, Taxation Corporate Finance, Commercial Property, Environmental, Construction, Labour, Insurance, Intellectual Property, Entertainment and Defamation, Maritime, Aviation, Litigation and Arbitration.

MEMBERS OF FIRM

ANDREW BATES, born Dublin, Ireland, February 2, 1966; admitted, 1992, Ireland. *Education:* National University of Ireland (B.C.L.). *Member:* Incorporated Law Society of Ireland.

MARY A. CANNING, born Belfast County, Antrim, Northern Ireland, June 5, 1964; admitted, 1989, New York and Ireland; 1990, U.S. District Court, Southern and Eastern Districts. *Education:* National University of Ireland (B.C.L.). *Member:* Incorporated Law Society of Ireland.

KIERAN COWHEY, born Dublin, Ireland, December 26, 1954; admitted, 1979, Ireland. *Education:* National University of Ireland (B.C.L.).

(This Listing Continued)

Member: Incorporated Law Society of Ireland; Irish Maritime Law Association; International Bar Association.

DAVID DILLON, born Dublin, Ireland, October 22, 1955; admitted, 1978, Ireland. *Education:* National University of Ireland (B.C.L.); Dublin University (M.B.A.). *Member:* Incorporated Law Society of Ireland; Institute of Taxation in Ireland; International Bar Association (Trademark Agent).

JOHN DOYLE, born Dublin, Ireland, May 19, 1965; admitted, 1992, Ireland. *Education:* College of Commerce (B.Sc., Trinity College). *Member:* Incorporated Law Society of Ireland.

PAUL EUSTACE, born Dublin, Ireland, November 28, 1955; admitted, 1979, Ireland. *Education:* National University of Ireland (B.C.L.). *Member:* Incorporated Law Society of Ireland; International Bar Association.

PAUL A. GILL, born Dublin, Ireland, June 13, 1954; admitted, 1980, Ireland. *Education:* National University of Ireland (B.Sc.). *Member:* Incorporated Law Society of Ireland; Irish Maritime Law Association; International Bar Association.

BRIAN KELLIHER, born Kerry, Ireland, May 31, 1967; admitted, 1994, Ireland. *Education:* National University of Ireland (B.C.L.). *Member:* Incorporated Law Society of Ireland.

FIONA MULCAHY, born Dublin, Ireland, September 18, 1964; admitted, 1989, Ireland. *Education:* National University of Ireland (B.C.L.). *Member:* Incorporated Law Society of Ireland.

BRENDA O'HIGGINS, born Dublin, Ireland, November 30, 1955; admitted, 1978, Ireland. *Education:* National University of Ireland (B.C.L.). *Member:* Incorporated Law Society of Ireland.

KIMBERLEY HUGHES, born New Brunswick, Canada, August 13, 1965; admitted, 1989, British Columbia, Canada; 1991, England, Wales and Hong Kong; 1994, Ireland. *Education:* University of British Columbia (LL.B.). *Member:* Incorporated Law Society of Ireland; Incorporated Law Society of England and Wales; Incorporated Law Society of Hong Kong.

MARK L. HYLAND, born Waterford, Ireland, February 21, 1968; admitted, 1992, Ireland. *Education:* National University of Ireland (B.C.L DIP E.L.). *Member:* Incorporated Law Society of Ireland.

MARK THORNE, born Dublin, Ireland, March 13, 1970; admitted, 1995, Ireland. *Education:* National University of Ireland (B.C.L.). *Member:* Incorporated Law Society of Ireland, Trade Mark Agent.

DOCKRELL FARRELL

Established in 1977

51-52 FITZWILLIAM SQUARE
DUBLIN 2, IRELAND
Telephone: 353-1-6615866
Fax: 353-1-6789747

Corporate and Commercial Law, Commercial Litigation, Conveyancing/-Property, Defense of Insurance Claims, Insurance Law, Consumer Law, Defamation, Environmental Litigation, Probate, General Legal Practice.

MEMBERS OF FIRM

JOHN H. DOCKRELL, born August 23, 1943; admitted, 1966, Ireland; 1969, Barrister at Law, Ontario, Canada. *Education:* Dublin University (B.A., 1966). Member, EC Structural Funds Review Committee of Dublin. *Member:* Institute of Taxation in Ireland; Incorporated Law Society of Ireland; Dublin Solicitors Bar Association; Institute of Directors; Dun Laoghaire Rathdown County Council (Chairman). *PRACTICE AREAS:* Corporate; Commercial.

ERNEST B. FARRELL, born April 1, 1947; admitted, 1969, Ireland. *Education:* University College, Dublin (B.C.L.); Incorporated Law Society of Ireland. *Member:* Incorporated Law Society of Ireland; Dublin Solicitors Bar Association; Institute of Arbitrators; International Bar Association. *PRACTICE AREAS:* Property.

MARGARET M. CAREY, born January 24, 1955; admitted, 1977, Ireland. *Education:* University College, Dublin (B.C.L.). *Member:* Incorporated Law Society of Ireland; Dublin Solicitors Bar Association. *PRACTICE AREAS:* Litigation.

DAVID P. O'BEIRNE, born June 22, 1957; admitted, 1980, Ireland. *Education:* University College, Dublin (B.C.L. and Diploma in European Law). *Member:* Incorporated Law Society of Ireland; Dublin Solicitors Bar Association. *PRACTICE AREAS:* Corporate; Commercial.

(This Listing Continued)

BERNARD McEVOY, born August 24, 1958; admitted, 1982, Ireland. *Education:* University College, Dublin (B.C.L.). *Member:* Incorporated Law Society of Ireland; Dublin Solicitors Bar Association. *PRACTICE AREAS:* Corporate; Commercial.

BRENDAN O'DONOVAN, born December 7, 1959; admitted, 1982, Ireland. *Education:* University College, Cork (B.C.L.; LL.B.); University of Essex (LL.M.). *Member:* Incorporated Law Society of Ireland; Dublin Solicitors Bar Association. *PRACTICE AREAS:* Property.

ASSOCIATES

MARY ROSE McGOVERN, born December 24, 1965; admitted, 1991, Ireland. *Education:* Trinity College, Dublin (LL.B.). *Member:* Incorporated Law Society of Ireland; Dublin Solicitors Bar Association. *PRACTICE AREAS:* Litigation.

NICHOLAS PHEIFER, born March 16, 1965; admitted, 1993, Ireland. *Education:* Trinity College, Dublin (B.A., 1988). *Member:* Incorporated Law Society of Ireland; Dublin Solicitors Bar Association. *PRACTICE AREAS:* Corporate; Commercial.

STEPHEN WALKER, born June 25, 1963; admitted, 1990, Ireland. *Education:* Trinity College, Dublin (B.A.). *Member:* Incorporated Law Society of Ireland; Dublin Solicitors Bar Association. *PRACTICE AREAS:* Litigation.

WILLIAM FRY

Established in 1847

FITZWILTON HOUSE
WILTON PLACE
DUBLIN 2, IRELAND
Telephone: 01-668 1711
Telefax: 01-668 7016
Telex: 93469

London, England Office: Audrey House, 15-20 Ely Place, EC1N 6SN. Telephone: 0171 430 2738. Telefax: 0171 430 9982.

Corporate, Commercial, Banking/Financial Services, Investment Funds, EC, Competition, Insolvency, Taxation, Intellectual Property, Litigation and Real Estate.

FIRM PROFILE: *William Fry was founded in 1847 and is one of Ireland's leading law firms specializing in Corporate, Commercial and Banking/Financial Services Practice with specialities in Investment Funds, EC, Competition and Intellectual Property Law and with large Litigation and Real Estate departments, (also concerned principally with Corporate, Commercial and Banking Practice). The firm has 20 partners, 66 fee earners and a total staff of 120. One partner is based permanently in the firm's London office.*

MEMBERS OF FIRM

W.O. HOUGHTON FRY, born 1945; admitted, 1967, Ireland. *Education:* Trinity College, Dublin (B.A.; LL.B.). *Member:* Institute of Taxation in Ireland. *PRACTICE AREAS:* Corporate; Cross Border Mergers & Acquisitions.

FRANCIS EDWARD SOWMAN, born 1947; admitted, 1970, Ireland. *Education:* Trinity College, Dublin (B.A.; LL.B.). *PRACTICE AREAS:* Insolvency.

R. EDMUND FRY, born 1950; admitted, 1973, Ireland. *Education:* Trinity College, Dublin (B.A.; LL.B.); Fellow, Chartered Institute of Arbitrators. *PRACTICE AREAS:* Litigation.

NEVILLE RICHARD O'BYRNE, born 1945; admitted, 1971, Ireland. *Education:* Trinity College, Dublin (B.A., Mod.). *PRACTICE AREAS:* Banking; Financial Services.

ALVIN F.M. PRICE, born Dublin, 1950; admitted, 1973, Ireland. *Education:* University College, Dublin (B.C.L.). *PRACTICE AREAS:* Corporate Finance; Securities.

RICHARD A. EVANS, born 1953; admitted, 1978, Ireland. *Education:* Trinity College, Dublin (B.A.). *PRACTICE AREAS:* Property.

BRIAN H. O'DONNELL, born 1952; admitted, 1976, Ireland. *Education:* University College Galway (B.A., Legal Science; LL.B.; Diploma European Law). *Member:* Institute of Taxation in Ireland. *PRACTICE AREAS:* Corporate; Corporate Finance; Public Issues; Insurance.

DANIEL MORRISSEY, born 1955; admitted, 1977, Ireland. *Education:* University College, Dublin (B.C.L.; Diploma in European Law).

(This Listing Continued)

Member: Institute of Taxation in Ireland. *PRACTICE AREAS:* Mergers & Acquisitions; Joint Ventures; Mutual Funds.

OWEN O'CONNELL, born 1955; admitted, 1978, Ireland. *Education:* University College, Dublin (B.C.L.). Director, Irish Centre for Commercial Law Studies. *PRACTICE AREAS:* Corporate; Competition; Mergers and Acquisitions; Venture Capital.

MICHAEL O'CONNOR, born Dublin, 1948; admitted, 1971, Ireland. *Education:* National University of Ireland (B.C.L.). *PRACTICE AREAS:* Taxation.

MICHAEL WOLFE, born Dublin, 1954; admitted, 1979, Ireland. *Education:* Trinity College, Dublin (B.A., Mod; LL.B.). *PRACTICE AREAS:* Pensions.

H. JOHN ROUNDTREE, born 1946; admitted, 1976, Ireland. *Education:* Trinity College, Dublin (B.B.S.); London College of Music (ALCM). *Member:* Meath Solicitors Association; Incorporated Law Society of Ireland (Examiner in Real Property). *PRACTICE AREAS:* Property.

BOYCE C. SHUBOTHAM, born 1956; admitted, 1979, Ireland. *Education:* Incorporated Law Society of Ireland (Solicitor); Fellow Chartered Institute of Arbitrators. *PRACTICE AREAS:* Litigation.

GERARD HALPENNY, born 1957; admitted, 1981, Ireland. *Education:* University College Dublin (B.C.L.). *PRACTICE AREAS:* Corporate; Mergers & Acquisitions.

PATRICIA TAYLOR, born 1959; admitted, 1983, Ireland. *Education:* University College, Dublin (B.C.L.). *PRACTICE AREAS:* Corporate; Commercial; Mutual Funds.

BRENDAN PATRICK HENEGHAN, born 1960; admitted, 1986, Ireland. *Education:* Trinity College, Dublin (B.A., Mod; Legal Science). *PRACTICE AREAS:* Corporate; Securities.

AISLINN O'FARRELL, born 1960; admitted, 1986, Ireland. *Education:* Trinity College, Dublin (B.A., Mod.; Legal Science). *Member:* Law Society of England and Wales. *PRACTICE AREAS:* Corporate; Mergers & Acquisitions.

JOHN D. LARKIN, born 1960; admitted, 1984, Ireland. *Education:* University College, Dublin (B.C.L.). *PRACTICE AREAS:* Corporate Finance; Commercial.

MYRA GARRETT, born 1964; admitted, 1988, Ireland. *Education:* University College, Dublin (B.C.L.). *PRACTICE AREAS:* Corporate; Commercial.

ELAINE M. HANLY, born 1964; admitted, 1989, Ireland. *Education:* University College Dublin (B.C.L.). *PRACTICE AREAS:* Banking; Financial Services.

CONSULTANT

OLIVER G. FRY, born 1919; admitted, 1944, Ireland. *Education:* Trinity College, Dublin. *Member:* Institute of Taxation in Ireland.

ASSOCIATES

MICHAEL JOHN QUINN, born 1960; admitted, 1985, Ireland. *Education:* University College Dublin (B.C.L.).

KENNETH PETER MORGAN, born 1957; admitted, 1983, Ireland. *Education:* University College, Dublin (B.C.L.).

MARIA BRENNAN, born 1964; admitted, 1989, Ireland. *Education:* University College Dublin (B.C.L.).

FRANK KEANE, born 1959; admitted, 1984, Ireland. *Education:* Trinity College, Dublin (B.A. Mod., Legal Science). Associate, Chartered Institute of Arbitrators.

BRENDAN MARTIN CAHILL, born 1962; admitted, 1990, Ireland. *Education:* College of Commerce, Dublin (Diploma in Legal Studies).

PAULA M. WHELAN, born 1963; admitted, 1989, Ireland. *Education:* University College Dublin (B.C.L.).

NORA MARY WHITE, born 1959; admitted, 1983, Ireland. *Education:* University College, Cork (B.C.L.).

LOUISE CAREY, born 1960; admitted, 1985, Ireland. *Education:* University College, Cork (B.C.L.). Registered Trade Mark Agent. *Member:* Irish Association of Patent and Trade Mark Agents.

JOAN FRANCES FAGAN, born 1964; admitted, 1990, Ireland. *Education:* University College, Dublin (B.C.L., Diploma in European Law).

(This Listing Continued)

WILLIAM FRY, Dublin—Continued

WILLIAM JOSEPH PRASIFKA, born Los Angeles, California, 1958; admitted, 1985, New York (Not admitted in Ireland). *Education:* Columbia University (A.B., 1980; J.D., 1984). Associate, Townley & Updike, New York, 1984-1988.

SOLICITORS

ALICIA MARY COMPTON, born 1966; admitted, 1991, Ireland. *Education:* University College, Dublin (B.C.L.).

EDWARD NORMAN EVANS, born 1966; admitted, 1991, Ireland. *Education:* Trinity College (LL.B.).

DAVID EDWARD JOSEPH O'DONNELL, born 1966; admitted, 1992, Ireland. *Education:* Trinity College, Dublin (LL.B.).

JOSEPH O'SULLIVAN, born 1966; admitted, 1992, Ireland. *Education:* University College Dublin (B.C.L.).

DARAGH MCDONALD, born 1966; admitted, 1992, Ireland. *Education:* University College Dublin (B.C.L.).

JOHN FURLONG, born 1955; admitted, 1986, Ireland. *Education:* Trinity College, Dublin (B.Sc.); College of Commerce, Dublin.

BERNARD KEOGH, born 1967; admitted, 1993, Ireland. *Education:* University College, Dublin (B.Comm.; Diploma in Legal Studies).

FIONA HEALY, born 1966; admitted, 1992, Ireland. *Education:* Trinity College, Dublin (LL.B.).

JANET TARRANT, born 1963; admitted, 1988, Ireland. *Education:* University College Dublin (B.C.L.; AITI Diploma in Property Tax).

DARAGH BOHAN, born 1969; admitted, 1994, Ireland. *Education:* University College, Dublin (B.C.L.).

PAULINE LOUTH, born 1964; admitted, 1988, Ireland. *Education:* University of Limerick (B.A., European Studies).

CATERINA GARDINER, born 1968; admitted, 1994, Ireland. *Education:* Trinity College, Dublin (LL.B.).

FERGUS HEALY, born 1969; admitted, 1994, Ireland. *Education:* University College, Dublin (B.C.L.).

All Members of the Firm are Members of the Incorporated Law Society of Ireland and the Dublin Solicitors Bar Association.

Languages: English, French, German and Spanish

GERRARD, SCALLAN & O'BRIEN

Established in 1968

HAINAULT HOUSE
69/71 ST. STEPHEN'S GREEN
DUBLIN 2, IRELAND
Telephone: 01-4780699
Fax: (01) 4780324

REVISERS OF THE IRELAND LAW DIGEST FOR THIS DIRECTORY.

Banking and Financial Services, Corporate and Commercial, Aviation and Maritime, Acquisitions and Mergers, Property, Taxation, Litigation and Arbitration, Trusts and General Practice.

FIRM PROFILE: Gerrard, Scallan & O'Brien, an Irish firm of solicitors, offers a full range of legal services and operates through four principal departments; Corporate and Commercial, Property, Litigation, Probate and Trusts. Its offices are modern and situated in the heart of Dublin's commercial centre and are equipped with up-to-date computers, communications systems and an extensive library.

With roots reaching back into the early nineteenth century, Gerrard, Scallan & O'Brien resulted from the merger of three substantial law firms in the 1960's to meet the challenge of the significant economic and industrial development that commenced in Ireland at that time. Since then the firm has continued to develop and now acts for a wide range of Irish and international clients, both public and private, including banks, insurance companies, manufacturers, shipping companies, retailers, property developers and investors and insolvency practitioners.

(This Listing Continued)

MEMBERS OF FIRM

DAVID R. ANDERSON, born Dublin, Ireland, August 21, 1945; admitted, 1969, Ireland. *Education:* University College, Dublin. *Member:* Incorporated Law Society of Ireland; International Bar Association. **PRACTICE AREAS:** Environmental Law; Insolvency Law; Property Law.

CLAIRE M. CALLANAN, born Dublin, Ireland, September 28, 1957; admitted, 1979, Ireland. *Education:* University College, Dublin (B.C.L.). *Member:* Irish Society for Labour Law; Medical Legal Society; Incorporated Law Society of Ireland. **LANGUAGES:** French. **PRACTICE AREAS:** Litigation; Employment Law; Arbitration Law.

JAMES N. DUDLEY, born Dublin, Ireland, December 30, 1941; admitted, 1963, Ireland. *Education:* Trinity College, Dublin (B.A., 1963; M.A., LL.B., 1966). *Member:* International Bar Association; Associate of Institute of Taxation. **LANGUAGES:** French. **PRACTICE AREAS:** Banking Law; Commercial Law; Corporate Finance Law.

JOHN A. GLACKIN, (MANAGING PARTNER), born Dublin, Ireland, September 7, 1948; admitted, 1972, Ireland. *Education:* University College, Dublin (B.C.L.). *Member:* Incorporated Law Society of Ireland; International Bar Association; Institute of Taxation. **LANGUAGES:** French. **PRACTICE AREAS:** Mergers and Acquisitions; Corporate Finance; Insolvency Law.

EILEEN M. GRACE, born Dublin, Ireland, June 5, 1962; admitted, 1989, Ireland; 1991, England. *Education:* University College Dublin (B.Comm., 1983). Tutor, Business Law, Commerce Faculty in UCD, 1986-1987. *Member:* Incorporated Law Society of Ireland; Law Society of England and Wales. **LANGUAGES:** French. **PRACTICE AREAS:** International Capital Markets; Corporate Law; Mergers and Acquisitions.

LAURA MACDERMOTT, born Dublin, Ireland, July 18, 1956; admitted, 1980, Ireland; 1988, New York. *Education:* Trinity College, Dublin (B.A. Moderatorship). *Member:* Incorporated Law Society of Ireland; International Bar Association. **LANGUAGES:** French. **PRACTICE AREAS:** Competition; E.C. Law; Corporate Law; Insolvency Law; Banking.

HUGH B. O'DONNELL, born Dublin, Ireland, November 24, 1943; admitted, 1967, Ireland. *Education:* Trinity College, Dublin (B.A.; LL.B.); University College, Dublin (Dip.E.L.). *Member:* Incorporated Law Society of Ireland; Institute of Taxation. **LANGUAGES:** French, German. **PRACTICE AREAS:** Probate Law; Property Law; Landlord and Tenant Law.

BRYAN J. STRAHAN, born Dublin, Ireland, January 30, 1950; admitted, 1975, Ireland. *Education:* Trinity College, Dublin. *Member:* Incorporated Law Society of Ireland; International Bar Association; Irish Maritime Law Association. **PRACTICE AREAS:** Litigation; Insurance Law; Shipping Law.

CONSULTANT

FRANCIS J. PLUNKETT DILLON, born Dublin, Ireland, March 6, 1927; admitted, 1956, Ireland. *Education:* Trinity College. *Member:* Incorporated Law Society of Ireland. **PRACTICE AREAS:** Joint Ventures; Corporate Law; Securities Law.

ASSOCIATES

SHEENA BEALE, born Dublin, Ireland, July 24, 1953; admitted, 1977, Ireland. *Education:* University College, Dublin (B.C.L.). *Member:* Dublin Bar Association; Incorporated Law Society of Ireland. **LANGUAGES:** French, German. **PRACTICE AREAS:** Property Law; Building Contracts; Building and Construction.

LAURA B. BOOTH, born Dublin, Ireland, February 16, 1964; admitted, 1990, Ireland. *Education:* Trinity College, Dublin (B.A., Legal Science); Incorporated Law Society of Ireland. *Member:* Incorporated Law Society of Ireland. **PRACTICE AREAS:** Commercial Law; Contract Law; Corporate Law; Intellectual Property.

KENNETH M. CASEY, born Limerick, Ireland, May 6, 1965; admitted, 1990, Ireland. *Education:* University College Dublin, Dublin 4 (B.C.L., 1985; Diploma in European Law, 1990; C.Dip.A.F., Accounting). Tutor, Company Law, University College, Dublin, 1986-1988. *Member:* Incorporated Law Society of Ireland. **LANGUAGES:** French, Irish. **PRACTICE AREAS:** Banking Law; Competition Law; Mergers and Acquisitions.

EILEEN DOLAN, born Dublin, Ireland, May 11, 1952; admitted, 1988, Ireland. *Education:* Incorporated Law Society of Ireland. *Member:* Incorporated Law Society of Ireland. **PRACTICE AREAS:** General Litigation; Defamation; Intellectual Property.

(This Listing Continued)

CAROL M. DRURY, born Drogheda, Ireland, May 9, 1969; admitted, 1993, Ireland. *Education:* Trinity College, Dublin (LL.B., 1990); Incorporated Law Society of Ireland. *Member:* Incorporated Law Society of Ireland. **LANGUAGES:** French. **PRACTICE AREAS:** Company Law; Commercial Law; Commercial Banking; Charities.

JOANNE P. HYDE, born Cork City, Ireland, January 25, 1971; admitted, 1994, Ireland. *Education:* University College Cork (B.C.L., 1991). **LANGUAGES:** German and French. **PRACTICE AREAS:** Litigation; Arbitration.

ANNE MCHALE, born Belfast, Northern Ireland, June 6, 1961; admitted, 1987, Wales and England; 1991, Ireland. *Education:* Southampton University (LL.B., 1982); The College of Law, Guildford (1984). *Member:* Law Society of England and Wales; Incorporated Law Society of Ireland. **LANGUAGES:** French. **PRACTICE AREAS:** Aviation Finance; Banking Law; Commercial Law.

JANE E. MURNANE, born Dublin, Ireland, January 29, 1968; admitted, 1994, Ireland. *Education:* Trinity College, Dublin (LL.B., 1990); Incorporated Law Society of Ireland (Solicitor, 1994). *Member:* Incorporated Law Society of Ireland. **LANGUAGES:** French and German. **PRACTICE AREAS:** Taxation; Company Law; Corporate Law.

LINDA A. NICHOLSON, born Dublin, Ireland, November 10, 1959; admitted, 1994, Ireland. *Education:* Incorporated Law Society of Ireland. *Member:* Incorporated Law Society of Ireland. **PRACTICE AREAS:** Property Law; Insolvency Law.

JULIE O'CONNELL, born New York, New York, February 22, 1967; admitted, 1991, Ireland. *Education:* University College, Dublin (B.C.L., 1987). *Member:* Incorporated Law Society of Ireland. **LANGUAGES:** French. **PRACTICE AREAS:** Corporate Law; Insolvency Law; Taxation.

CÓMHNALL F. TUOHY, born Dublin, Ireland, March 22, 1971; admitted, 1994, Ireland. *Education:* University College Dublin (B.C.L., 1991; Dip. Euro. Law, 1993); Incorporated Law Society of Ireland (Solicitor, 1994). **LANGUAGES:** Irish and French. **PRACTICE AREAS:** Litigation.

MARTIN J. VARLEY, born County Mayo, Ireland, March 17, 1963; admitted, 1991, Ireland. *Education:* University College, Galway (B.A., 1984; LL.B., 1986). *Member:* Incorporated Law Society of Ireland. **LANGUAGES:** French. **PRACTICE AREAS:** Banking Law; Corporate Law; Pension Law.

CANICE M. WALSH, born Tralee, Ireland, November 1, 1968; admitted, 1992, Ireland. *Member:* Law Society of Ireland. [University College Dublin (B.C.L., 1989)]. **LANGUAGES:** Irish. **PRACTICE AREAS:** Residential and Commercial Property Law; Conveyancing Law.

Languages: English, Irish, French and German.
REVISERS OF THE IRELAND LAW DIGEST FOR THIS DIRECTORY.

A & L GOODBODY

1 EARLSFORT CENTRE
HATCH STREET
DUBLIN 2, IRELAND
Telephone: (353 1) 6613311
Fax: (353 1) 6613278
Telex: 30569 and 93296

New York, New York Office: 1 Rockefeller Plaza, Suite 1421, 10020. Telephone: 212-582-4499. Fax: 212-333-5126.
London, England Office: Pinnacle House, 23-26 St. Dunstan's Hill, EC3R 8HL. Telephone: 0171-929-2425. Fax: 0171-489-9677.
Brussels, Belgium Office: Rue des Deux Eglises 7, Boike 8, 1040. Telephone: 02-230-7512. Fax: 02-230-6422.

General Corporate and Business practice, Mergers and Acquisitions, Securities, Banking, Aircraft and Shipping Finance, Financial Services, Fund Management, Intellectual Property, European Union Law, Competition Law, Pensions, Litigation, Arbitration, Labour Law, Taxation, Property, Development and Building Contracts, Environmental Law, Debt Collection, Insolvency, Insurance, Inward Investment, Private Client Services.

MEMBERS OF FIRM

MARCUS T. BERESFORD, born Dublin, Ireland, August 5, 1948; admitted, 1977, Ireland.

ERIC BRUNKER, born Dublin, Ireland, May 18, 1942; admitted, 1967, Ireland.

(This Listing Continued)

RODERICK B. BUCKLEY, born Dublin, Ireland, June 11, 1947; admitted, 1976, Ireland.

PAUL J. CARROLL, born London, England, May 31, 1958; admitted, 1984, Ireland.

BARBARA M. COTTER, born Dublin, Ireland, June 1, 1960; admitted, 1986, Ireland.

MICHAEL G. DICKSON, born Dublin, Ireland, September 11, 1939; admitted, 1962, Ireland.

PAUL R. DOBBYN, born Dublin, Ireland, November 7, 1954; admitted, 1978, Ireland.

EITHNE M. FITZGERALD, born London, England, June 22, 1960; admitted, 1986, Ireland.

C. EAMON GILL, born Galway, Ireland, September, 16, 1957; admitted, 1982, Ireland.

MICHAEL A. GREENE, born Dublin, Ireland, January 14, 1954; admitted, 1977, Ireland.

JAMES G. GRENNAN, born Limerick, Ireland, November 14, 1962; admitted, 1988, Ireland. (Resident, London, England Office).

STEPHEN C. HAMILTON, born Dublin, Ireland, April 9, 1952; admitted, 1974, Ireland.

STEPHEN W. HAUGHEY, born Ireland, November 10, 1953; admitted, 1978, Ireland.

H. NATHANIEL HEALY, born Dublin, Ireland, September 2, 1949; admitted, 1975, Ireland.

JOHN H. HICKSON, born Bristol, England, September 9, 1955; admitted, 1980, Ireland; 1983, Turks and Caicos Islands.

PETER M. LAW, born Dublin, Ireland, July 3, 1954; admitted, 1979, Ireland.

SIOBHAN M. LOHAN, born Galway, Ireland, September 4, 1960; admitted, 1985, Ireland; 1986, New York.

NIGEL H. MARTIN, born Dublin, Ireland, November 28, 1947; admitted, 1971, Ireland.

J. DEIRDRE MORRIS, born Dublin, Ireland, May 5, 1951; admitted, 1975, Ireland.

THOMAS V. O'CONNOR, born Co. Sligo, Ireland, February 23, 1954; admitted, 1975, Ireland.

JOHN ANTHONY O'FARRELL, born Dublin, Ireland, November 28, 1958; admitted, 1985, Ireland.

MICHAEL F. O'GORMAN, born Dublin, Ireland, February 11, 1953; admitted, 1977, Ireland.

FRANCIS J. O'RIORDAN, born Dublin, Ireland, June 12, 1953; admitted, 1976, Ireland.

S. PETER POLDEN, born Dublin, Ireland, March 5, 1945; admitted, 1972, Ireland.

CAROLINE M. PRESTON, born London, England, April 12, 1955; admitted, 1980, Ireland.

DAVID J. SANFEY, born Athlone, Ireland, August 31, 1953; admitted, 1978, Ireland.

WILLIAM B. SOMERVILLE, born Dublin, Ireland, March 18, 1937; admitted, 1967, Ireland.

ASSOCIATES

JEAN BARRETT, born Dublin, Ireland, May 27, 1959; admitted, 1983, Ireland.

PAUL BINCHY, born Dublin, Ireland, December 19, 1963; admitted, 1989, Ireland.

BRYAN BOURKE, born Galway, Ireland, May 24, 1966; admitted, 1993, Ireland.

EAMON BRADY, born Dublin, Ireland, December 14, 1962; admitted, 1987, Ireland.

ORLA BRENNAN, born Dublin, Ireland, May 20, 1965; admitted, 1992, Ireland.

ADRIAN BURKE, born Galway, Ireland, October 29, 1968; admitted, 1995, Ireland.

(This Listing Continued)

A & L GOODBODY, Dublin—Continued

JULIA BURKE, born Tipperary, June 4, 1959; admitted, 1982, Ireland.

PATRICIA CARROLL, born Dublin, Ireland, December 20, 1952; admitted, 1976, Ireland.

SUSAN COFFEY, born Cork, Ireland, March 20, 1963; admitted, 1989, Dublin.

JOHN COMAN, born Dublin, Ireland, June 21, 1960; admitted, 1989, Ireland.

SARAH G. COX, born Grimsby, England, December 28, 1958; admitted, 1983, Dublin, Ireland.

EMER MORIARTY CROWLEY, born Dublin, Ireland, 1955; admitted, 1982, Ireland.

EMMA CROWLEY, born Dublin, Ireland, August 11, 1967; admitted, 1993, Ireland.

CAROLANNE CUNNINGHAM, born November 7, 1963; admitted, 1987, Ireland.

DEIRDRE CURTIS, born Dublin, Ireland, November 11, 1957; admitted, 1984, Ireland.

SHEENA DOGGETT, born Dublin, Ireland, February 9, 1965; admitted, 1990, Ireland.

PETER J. DONNELLY, born Belfast, Northern Ireland, March 18, 1964; admitted, 1989, Ireland.

ANDREW B. DOYLE, born Dublin, Ireland, November 15, 1962; admitted, 1988, Ireland.

CATHERINE DUFFY, born Belfast, North Ireland, March 22, 1962; admitted, 1988, Northern Ireland; 1991, Ireland.

ALISON V. FANAGAN, born Dublin, Ireland, February 3, 1967; admitted, 1991, Ireland.

PAT FLYNN, born Mayo, Ireland, May 31, 1963; admitted, 1987, Ireland.

NORA GALLAGHER, born Dublin, Ireland, October 20, 1968; admitted, 1995, Ireland.

DEIRDRE GIBLIN, born Cork, Ireland, March 4, 1962; admitted, 1988, Ireland.

S. PURUSHOTHAMAN GOVENDER, born Durban, Republic of South Africa, July 25, 1944; admitted, 1985, Ireland.

NOLLAIG K. GREENE, born Dublin, Ireland, December 25, 1960; admitted, 1985, Ireland.

CLIONA HICKEY, born Dublin, Ireland, November 12, 1963; admitted, 1987, Ireland.

DIANA B. JAMIESON, born London, England, November 4, 1947; admitted, 1987, Ireland.

AINE KEANE, born Clare, Ireland, February 9, 1966; admitted, 1990, Ireland.

EILEEN KELLEHER, born Killarney, Lo Kerry, Ireland, March 28, 1969; admitted, 1994, Ireland.

ANNE KELLY, born Cork, Ireland, October 6, 1966; admitted, 1994, Ireland.

JOSEPH KELLY, born Athlone, Ireland, December 29, 1961; admitted, 1992, Ireland.

EAMONN KENNEDY, born Leitrim, Ireland, April 7, 1966; admitted, 1991, Ireland.

LIAM KENNEDY, born Melbourne, Australia, December 17, 1962; admitted, 1985, New Zealand; 1990, England; 1994, Ireland.

AILEEN KEOGAN, born Dublin, Ireland, June 26, 1969; admitted, 1993, Ireland.

PAULA G. LYNCH, born Donegal, Ireland, March 17, 1963; admitted, 1987, Ireland.

DARA LYSAGHT, born October 2, 1963; admitted, 1988, Ireland; 1992, United Kingdom.

EOIN MACNEILL, born Dublin, Ireland, March 12, 1963; admitted, 1989, Ireland.

(This Listing Continued)

EU882B

DEBORAH MAGUIRE, born Galway, Ireland, September 6, 1969; admitted, 1993, Ireland.

PETER MAHER, born Dublin, Ireland, February 4, 1963; admitted, 1989, Ireland.

THOMAS MAHER, born Kilkenny, Ireland, July 31, 1966; admitted, 1992, Ireland.

ROBERT D. MARSHALL, born Dublin, Ireland, May 13, 1952; admitted, 1977, Ireland.

BRIAN W. MCDERMOTT, born Exeter, England, July 14, 1965; admitted, 1990, Ireland.

FIONNUALA MCGINLEY, born Dublin, Ireland, April 16, 1964; admitted, 1988, Ireland; 1990, New South Wales, Australia.

MARY P. MCKENNA, born Killarney, Ireland, January 9, 1959; admitted, 1991, Ireland.

IAN B. MOORE, born Dublin, Ireland, June 27, 1957; admitted, 1982, Ireland.

MARGARET M. MULDOWNEY, born Cheshire, England, August 19, 1960; admitted, 1985, Ireland.

MARJORIE MURPHY, born Drogheda, Co. Louth, Ireland, March 28, 1952; admitted, 1979, Ireland.

GRAINNE NI DHUBHCHAILL, born Limerick, Ireland, October 14, 1967; admitted, 1994, Ireland.

MAIRE ANNE NI GHALLCHOIR, born Donegal, Ireland, June 1, 1965; admitted, 1992, Ireland.

MUIRIS O'CEIDIGH, born Galway, Ireland, March 23, 1961; admitted, 1992, Ireland.

JOHN OLDEN, born Cork, Ireland, March 20, 1962; admitted, 1987, Ireland.

STEPHEN O'RIORDAN, born Dublin, Ireland, May 9, 1965; admitted, 1990, Ireland.

GER O'TOOLE, born Dublin, Ireland, September 4, 1967; admitted, 1991, Ireland.

CAROL L. PLUNKETT, born Dublin, Ireland, July 7, 1956; admitted, 1979, Ireland.

VINCENT POWER, born Cork, Ireland, July 23, 1963; admitted, 1987, Ireland.

NIAMH REEDY, born Dublin, Ireland, August 3, 1968; admitted, 1993, Ireland.

EILEEN A. ROBERTS, born Dublin, Ireland, July 26, 1965; admitted, 1991, Ireland.

FEENA ROBINSON, born Dublin, Ireland, August 13, 1969; admitted, 1995, Ireland.

JOHN B. ROCHE, born Limerick, Ireland, April 7, 1959; admitted, 1984, Ireland.

TIM SCANLON, born Dublin, Ireland, October 26, 1965; admitted, 1991, Ireland. (Resident, London, England Office).

DEBORAH H. SPENCE, born Dublin, Ireland, February 19, 1960; admitted, 1985, Ireland.

FIONA THORNTON, born Dublin, Ireland, June 12, 1957; admitted, 1979, Ireland.

JAMES TRUEICK, born Dublin, Ireland, January 2, 1959; admitted, 1988, Ireland.

MICHAEL J. TWOMEY, born Clonmel, Co. Tipperary, Ireland, March 8, 1967; admitted, 1990, Ireland.

MARK WARD, born Drogheda, Lo Louth, Ireland, March 26, 1970; admitted, 1994, Ireland.

PAUL WHITE, born Dublin, Ireland, August 15, 1965; admitted, 1990, Ireland.

CONSULTANTS

JAMES R. OSBORNE, born Dousland, Devon, England, April 28, 1949; admitted, 1973, Ireland.

(This Listing Continued)

JAMES J.C.W. WYLIE, born Belfast, North Ireland, June 7, 1943. *Education:* Harvard (LL.M.); Belfast (LL.D.). Professor of Law, University College Cardiff.

All Solicitors are members of the Incorporated Law Society of Ireland and the Dublin Solicitors' Bar Association.

Languages: English, French and German

HAYES & SONS

Established in 1840

15 ST. STEPHEN'S GREEN NORTH
DUBLIN 2, IRELAND
Telephone: 353-1-688399
Fax: 353-1-612163
Dx: Dublin 175

Litigation, Corporate and Commercial, Conveyancing, Probate and Trusts, Landlord and Tenant, Debt Collection.

PARTNERS

E.R. ADRIAN GLOVER, admitted, 1962, Ireland. *Education:* B.A., LL.B.

ROBERT E. BLAKENEY, admitted, 1960, Ireland. *Education:* B.A., LL.B.

PETER S. HARRISON, admitted, 1970, Ireland. *Education:* B.A., LL.B.

ANDREW G.M. O'RORKE, admitted, 1972, Ireland. *Education:* B.C.L.

ANDREW P. WALKER, admitted, 1978, Ireland. *Education:* M.A., LL.B.

ASSOCIATES

TERENCE C. MORAN, admitted, 1977, Ireland. *Education:* B.A.

CIARAN O'RORKE, admitted, 1982, Ireland. *Education:* B.C.L.

CAROLINE CROWLEY, admitted, 1988, Ireland. *Education:* B.A.

RUTH SHIPSEY, admitted, 1989, Ireland. *Education:* B.Comm.

FIONA HUNT, admitted, 1991, Ireland. *Education:* B.C.L., Dip. E.L.

MASON HAYES & CURRAN

(in association with Patrick J. Brady & Co.)

7 FITZWILLIAM SQUARE
DUBLIN 2, IRELAND
Telephone: (353 1) 676 6961
Telex: 31073 MHC EI
Fax: (353 1) 661 1431

Corporate, Commercial, Banking and Financial Services, European Community, Employment and Labor Law, Insurance, Insolvency, Antitrust, Intellectual Property, Litigation, Real Estate, Licensing, Agency and Distribution Contracts, Technology Transfer, Trusts and Estates, Taxation, Arbitration, Product Liability, Mergers and Acquisitions, Stock Exchange Funding, Venture Capital, Joint Ventures, Franchising, Computer Contracts, Entertainment and Media Law, Telecommunications, Medicine, Pharmaceuticals, Environmental Law, Pensions, Debt Collection, Enforcement of Foreign Judgements, Corporate Bankruptcy and Creditors Rights.

MEMBERS OF FIRM

MAURICE R. CURRAN, born Dublin, Ireland, November 5, 1938; admitted, 1961, Ireland. *Education:* National University of Ireland (B.C.L.; LL.B.). Council Member and Former President, 1988-1989. Incorporated Law Society of Ireland. *Member:* Institute of Taxation in Ireland; International Bar Association; Institute of Arbitrators; Faculty of Notaries Public. *PRACTICE AREAS:* Mergers, Acquisitions and Banking; Corporate.

CONAL J. CLANCY, born Longford, Ireland, July 11, 1936; admitted, 1959, Ireland. *Education:* University College Dublin Law School. *PRACTICE AREAS:* Litigation; Arbitration and Insurance.

MAEVE HAYES, born Cork, Ireland, January 27, 1947; admitted, 1969, Ireland. *Education:* University College, Cork (B.C.L.). Member, Conveyancing Committee, Incorporated Law Society of Ireland. *PRACTICE AREAS:* Real Estate; Environmental.

(This Listing Continued)

ANTHONY BURKE, born Dublin, Ireland, March 21, 1951; admitted, 1975, Ireland. *Education:* Trinity College, Dublin (B.A. Mod); Europa Institut University of Amsterdam, Netherlands (Dip. Eur. Integration). Member, International Law/EEC Committee, Incorporated Law Society of Ireland. *Member:* Irish Society for European Law; Irish Council of the European Movement; Irish Centre for European Law. *LANGUAGES:* French and Dutch. *PRACTICE AREAS:* European Community; Antitrust; Licensing; Agency and Distribution Contracts.

DECLAN MOYLAN, born Galway, Ireland, July 24, 1950; admitted, 1972, Ireland. *Education:* University College Dublin (B.C.L.). *Member:* International Bar Association; Irish Centre for European Law. *LANGUAGES:* French. *PRACTICE AREAS:* Commercial, International Practice, Administrative.

ROSALEEN FITZGERALD, born Dublin Ireland, January 22, 1948; admitted, 1975, Ireland. *Education:* University College Dublin Law School. *PRACTICE AREAS:* Real Estate; Trusts and Estates.

LORCAN BUCKLEY, born Dublin, Ireland, July 30, 1954; admitted, 1980, Ireland. *Education:* University College, Dublin (B.C.L.); Kings Inns, Dublin (B.L.); The Institute of Chartered Accountants in Ireland. *PRACTICE AREAS:* Litigation; Arbitration; Product Liability; Insurance.

EMER GILVARRY, born Killala, Ireland, August 12, 1957; admitted, 1979, Ireland. *Education:* University College, Dublin (B.C.L.). *Member:* Irish Society for Labour Law. *PRACTICE AREAS:* Litigation; Arbitration; Product Liability; Insurance; Employment and Labor Law.

PAUL J. G. EGAN, born Dublin, Ireland, March 24, 1956; admitted, 1981, Ireland. *Education:* Trinity College, Dublin (B.A. Mod); Université de Paris, Sorbonne (Dip. Lang. Fr.). Member, Company Law Committee, Incorporated Law Society of Ireland; Institute of Directors. *LANGUAGES:* French. *PRACTICE AREAS:* Corporate; Mergers and Acquisitions; Stock Exchange Funding; Venture Capital.

COLMAN P. CURRAN, born Dublin, Ireland, March 21, 1956; admitted, 1981, Ireland. *Education:* University College, Dublin (B.C.L.). Chairman, Technology Committee, Incorporated Law Society of Ireland. *Member:* Society for Computers and Law. (Also Member, Patrick J. Brady & Co.). *PRACTICE AREAS:* Debt Collection; Insolvency; Enforcement of Foreign Judgements; Creditors Rights.

RANDAL DOHERTY, born Dublin, Ireland, March 9, 1951; admitted, 1976, Ireland. *Education:* University College, Dublin (B.C.L.). *Member:* Incorporated Law Society of Ireland; Dublin Bar Association; Institute of Taxation. *PRACTICE AREAS:* Banking; Commercial Law; Venture Capital.

NORA LARKIN, born Tipperary, Ireland, November 6, 1953; admitted, 1981, Ireland. *Education:* Trinity College, Dublin (B.A.). Member, Tutorial Staff, Probate and Tax, Incorporated Law Society of Ireland. *PRACTICE AREAS:* Trusts and Estates.

DECLAN CURRAN, born Dublin, Ireland, October 27, 1957; admitted, 1982, Ireland. *Education:* University College, Dublin (B.C.L.). *Member:* Irish Association of Pension Funds. *PRACTICE AREAS:* Pensions; Commercial.

RICHARD A. WOULFE, born Limerick, Ireland, June 13, 1961; admitted, 1986, Ireland. *Education:* NIHE Limerick (B.A.). *PRACTICE AREAS:* Product Liability; Litigation; Arbitration.

KEVIN HOY, born Dublin, Ireland, June 8, 1964; admitted, 1987, Ireland. *Education:* University College, Dublin and Law Society. *Member:* International Law Association (Irish Branch). *PRACTICE AREAS:* Banking; Financial Services; Entertainment and Media Law.

CONSULTANT

A. DERMOT MASON, born Dublin, Ireland, July 10, 1917; admitted, 1940, Ireland. *Education:* Trinity College, Dublin (B.A.; LL.B.). *PRACTICE AREAS:* Trusts and Estates; Real Property.

All Solicitors are Members of the Incorporated Law Society of Ireland and the Dublin Solicitors Bar Association.

Languages: French, Dutch, German, Spanish.

REFERENCES: Chase Bank (Ireland) p.l.c.; St. Stephens Green, Dublin 2; Bank of Ireland, Head Office, Lower Baggot Street, Dublin 2.

(Mason Hayes & Curran practices in association with Patrick J. Brady & Co., see separate entry for Patrick J. Brady & Co.)

MATHESON ORMSBY PRENTICE

3 BURLINGTON ROAD
DUBLIN 4, IRELAND
Telephone: +353-1-6760981
Telex: 500-93310 MOP EI
Cable Address: "Matsack" Dublin
Fax: Group 3/Group +353-1-6760501

London, England Office: 1 Pemberton Row, Fetter Lane, EC4A 3BA.
Telephone: +44 71 404 0998. Fax: +44 71 583 5644.

Corporate and Commercial Law, Mergers and Acquisitions, Joint Ventures, Banking and Financial Services, Investment Fund Management, Aircraft and Ship Financing, Structured Finance, Corporate Insolvency and Rescues, Taxation, Intellectual Property and Information Technology Law, European Community Law, Competition Law, Trade Law, Pensions and Employment Law, Insurance and Reinsurance, Environmental Law, Real Estate, Construction Law, Commercial Litigation and Arbitration, Telecommunications, Oil and Gas and Mineral Exploration, Food and Drug Law, Consumer Law, Entertainment Law, Sports Law, Debt Recovery, Immigration Law and Probate, Trusts and Estate Planning.

FIRM PROFILE: *Matheson Ormsby Prentice was founded in 1825 and is one of Ireland's largest and leading law firms with a substantial domestic and international practice specializing in Corporate and Commercial Law, Mergers and Acquisitions, Banking and Financial Services, Corporate and Structural Finance, Investment Fund Management, European Community Law, Intellectual Property and Information Technology Law, Competition Law, Taxation and Environmental Law.*

MEMBERS OF FIRM

ERNEST J. MARGETSON, born 1929; admitted, 1951, Ireland. *Education:* University of Dublin (B.A.; LL.B.). Council Member, 1972-1975 and 1977-1988, Vice President, 1982-1983 and President, 1989-1990, Incorporated Law Society of Ireland. President, Dublin Solicitors Bar Association, 1965-1966. *Member:* Institute of Arbitrators and Insurance Ombudsman Council. *PRACTICE AREAS:* Commercial and Insurance related Litigation and Arbitration.

ANTHONY J. F. O'REILLY, born 1936; admitted, 1958, Ireland. *Education:* National University of Ireland (B.C.L.); University of Bradford, Yorkshire, England (Ph.D.). Chairman and C.E.O., H.J. Heinz Company; Chairman: American Ireland Fund; Waterford-Wedgewood plc., Fitzwilton Group plc.; Independent Newspaper plc.; Arcon plc.

MATTHEW P. DRUM, born 1933; admitted, 1956, Ireland. *Member:* International Bar Association. *PRACTICE AREAS:* Real Estate.

DAVID W. PRENTICE, born 1933; admitted, 1964, Ireland. *Education:* University of Dublin (B.A.; B.Comm.). *LANGUAGES:* Italian. *PRACTICE AREAS:* Banking and Financial Services; Aircraft and Ship Finance and Structured Finance.

GARRETT P. GILL, born 1945; admitted, 1968, Ireland. *Education:* University College Dublin (Dip. Eur. Jur.). Contributor, "A Guide for Business and Industry to Environmental Law in Ireland". Co-author: "The Impact of Planning, Licensing and Environmental Issues on Industrial Development in Ireland," (the Culliton Report). *Member:* UK Environmental Lawyers Association; Union Internationale des Avocats; Franco British Lawyers Association; Irish Environmental Law Association; UK Environmental Law Association; Dublin Chamber of Commerce; Ireland and France Chamber of Commerce; Ireland Canada Business Association. *LANGUAGES:* French. *PRACTICE AREAS:* Real Estate; Town Planning; Environmental Law.

MICHAEL G. IRVINE, born 1947; admitted, 1974, Ireland. *Education:* University of Dublin (B.B.S.; B.A.; LL.B.). *Member:* Incorporated Law Society of Ireland (Council Member and Member of the Company Law Committee); Asia Pacific Lawyers Association; Inter Pacific Bar Association; Institute of Taxation; International Bar Association. *PRACTICE AREAS:* Corporate; Commercial Law; Telecommunications.

ARTHUR D.S. MORAN, born 1949; admitted, 1975, Ireland. *Education:* University of Dublin (Moderatorship B.A.). *Member:* Union Internationale du Notariat Latin (Irish Representative); Institute of Taxation; German Irish Lawyers Association; British German Jurists Association; Franco British Lawyers Association. *LANGUAGES:* French, German and Spanish. *PRACTICE AREAS:* Corporate; Commercial Law.

GRAHAM C. RICHARDS, born 1951; admitted, 1975, Ireland. *Education:* University of Dublin (Moderatorship B.A.). *Member:* Institute of Tax-

(This Listing Continued)

EU884B

ation; Irish/Australian Business Association. *PRACTICE AREAS:* Estate Planning; Taxation.

ALAN G. GRAHAM, born 1952; admitted, 1976, Ireland. *Education:* University of Dublin (Moderatorship B.A.). *Member:* Association Internationale des Jeunes Avocats; Institute of Taxation. *PRACTICE AREAS:* Real Estate; Immigration Law.

MICHAEL W. TYRRELL, born 1953; admitted, 1976, Ireland. *Education:* University of Dublin (M.A.). *Member:* International Bar Association; Association Internationale des Jeunes Advocates; Institute of Taxation; Asia Pacific Bar Association; Irish Society of Labour Law; Litigation Committee of Incorporated Law Society of Ireland; International Association for the Protection of Industrial Property; Irish Maritime Law Association; Irish Danish Business Association; Irish Spanish Business Association. *PRACTICE AREAS:* Commercial Disputes Litigation; Intellectual Property; Product Liability; Admiralty; Labour Law.

FRANCIS B. NOWLAN, born 1954; admitted, 1978, Ireland. *Education:* University College Dublin (B.C.L.). *PRACTICE AREAS:* Litigation; Debt Recovery.

STUART P. MARGETSON, born 1956; admitted, 1979, Ireland. *Education:* University of Dublin (B.A.). Co-Author: "A Guide for Business and Industry to Environmental Law in Ireland"; "The Impact of Planning, Licensing and Environmental Issues on Industrial Development in Ireland," (the Culliton Report). *Member:* UK Environmental Lawyers Association; Union Internationale des Avocats; Irish Environmental Law Association; European Environmental Law Association; IBEC Environment Policy Committee. *PRACTICE AREAS:* Commercial Litigation; Employment Law; Environmental Law.

DONAL A. ROCHE, born 1954; admitted, 1980, Ireland. *Education:* University of Dublin (Moderatorship M.A.). Author: Articles on insider dealing and directors liability. *Member:* Institute of Directors; Dublin Chamber of Commerce. *PRACTICE AREAS:* Corporate; Commercial Law.

WILLIAM P.M. PRENTICE, born 1958; admitted, 1981, Ireland. *Education:* University of Dublin (Moderatorship B.A.). *PRACTICE AREAS:* Banking and Financial Services; Aircraft and Ship Finance; Structured Finance.

RODERIC J.S. ENSOR, born 1957; admitted, 1982, Ireland. *Education:* University College Dublin (B.A.). Author, Articles on insolvency and corporate rescues. *Member:* Ireland/France Chamber of Commerce. *PRACTICE AREAS:* Insolvency; Corporate Rescues.

JAMES J. HICKEY, born 1953; admitted, 1977, Ireland. *Education:* University of Dublin (M.A.; LL.B.). *Member:* Audio Visual Production Federation; Film Makers Ireland; Irish Music Copyright Reform Group. *PRACTICE AREAS:* Entertainment Law; Media Law; Telecommunications; Sports Law.

DAVID JAMES MCGEOUGH, born 1965; admitted, 1990, Ireland. *Education:* University College Dublin Law School (B.C.L., magna cum laude, 1986). Author: "Perils of Prepayment Premiums in Loan Documentation," Los Angeles Daily Journal, 1988; "Corporate Finance and Debt Securities," Irish Centre for Commercial Law Studies, 1993; "International Investment Funds and Fund Management in Ireland," International Financial Law Review, 1992; "Competition Issues in Mergers and Acquisitions," International Corporate Law, 1992. Tutor in the law of Torts, University College Dublin Law School, 1987-1988. *Member:* American Tax Institute; U.S. Chamber of Commerce; Ireland Canada Business Association; International Bar Association; American-Ireland Fund and Union Internationale des Avocats. *PRACTICE AREAS:* Corporate and Commercial Law; Corporate and Structured Finance; Mergers and Acquisitions; Joint Ventures and Investment Fund Management.

PAULINE O'DONOVAN, born 1947; admitted, 1985, Ireland. *Education:* Incorporated Law Society of Ireland. *PRACTICE AREAS:* Corporate and Commercial Law.

BRIAN D. BUGGY, born 1959; admitted, 1984, Ireland. *Education:* University College, Dublin (B.C.L.). *Member:* Association of Pension Lawyers in Ireland. *PRACTICE AREAS:* Corporate; Commercial Law; Pensions Law; Employment Law.

WILLIAM A. QUIRKE, born 1961; admitted, 1990, Ireland. *Education:* National University of Ireland (B.C.L). Associate of Institute of Taxation of Ireland. *Member:* American Tax Institute; Incorporated Law Society of Ireland (Corporate Tax Consultant and Examiner). *PRACTICE AREAS:* Taxation; International Financial Services; Inward Investment.

(This Listing Continued)

DON MCALEESE, born 1960; admitted, 1986, Ireland. *Education:* University of Dublin (B.A. Legal Science). Member, European Union Legal Advisory Board on the Information Market. Chairman, Legal Club Sub Committee, EDI Association of Ireland. Member, Editorial Board, EDI Law Review. *Member:* Association Internationale des Jeunes Advocates. *PRACTICE AREAS:* Information Technology Law; Commercial Law.

All Members of Firm and Associates are Members of the Incorporated Law Society of Ireland and Dublin Solicitors Bar Association.

Languages: English, French, German, Italian, Spanish, Russian and Japanese

REFERENCES: Citibank N.A., Dublin; Allied Irish Banks, Dublin; Bank of Ireland, Dublin.

McCANN FITZGERALD

2 HARBOURMASTER PLACE
CUSTOM HOUSE DOCK
DUBLIN 1, IRELAND
Telephone: +353-1-829 0000/670 1111
Fax: +353-1-829 0010

London, England Office: Imperial House, 15-19 Kingsway, London, WC2B 6UN. Telephone: +44-171-379 0914. Fax: +44-171-836 2759.

Brussels, Belgium Office: Rue de la Loi 99 Wetstraat, Brussels B-1040. Telephone: +32-2-230 3634. Fax: +32-2-230 2562.

New York, New York Office: Thirtieth Floor, 399 Park Avenue, NY 10022-4697. Telephone: +1-212-318 6700. Fax: +1-212-318 6710.

Corporate, Commercial, Banking and Financial Services, Foreign Investment, Mergers and Takeovers, Real Estate and Property Development, Litigation, Taxation, EU and Competition Law, Oil and Gas, Environmental Law, Aviation, Maritime and Shipping Law, Communications and Media, Insolvency, Labour Law, Pensions Law, Construction Contracts and Arbitration, Intellectual Property, Nationality, Probate, Trusts and General Practice.

MEMBERS OF FIRM

BRIAN J. O'CONNOR, born 1932; admitted, 1955, Ireland. *Education:* University College, Dublin (B.A.; M.A.; LL.B.). *PRACTICE AREAS:* Mergers, Acquisitions and Divestitures; Banking; Securities; Oil and Exploration.

WILLIAM GRANTHAM LEWIS FORWOOD, born 1927; admitted, 1954, England and Wales (Clement's Inn and Sheffield prizes); 1991, Ireland. *Education:* Eton College, Nr Windsor; Clare College, Cambridge (M.A.; LL.M.). *PRACTICE AREAS:* Retirement Benefits; Employee Stock Ownership Plan; Profit Sharing.

MICHAEL V. O'MAHONY, born 1941; admitted, 1964, Ireland. *Education:* University College, Dublin (B.C.L.; LL.B.); University of California (LL.M.). *PRACTICE AREAS:* Libel and Defamation; Litigation; Negligence; Products Liability.

RICHARD RICE, born 1946; admitted, 1968, Ireland. *Education:* University College, Dublin (B.A.). *PRACTICE AREAS:* Company Law; Corporate Law; Securities.

FERGUS ARMSTRONG, born 1944; admitted, 1967, Ireland. *Education:* University College, Dublin (B.C.L.; LL.B.); Harvard Law School (LL.M.). *PRACTICE AREAS:* Aviation and Aerospace; Company Law; Corporate Law; Insurance.

DAVID CLARKE, born 1947; admitted, 1970, Ireland. *Education:* University College, Dublin (B.C.L.). *PRACTICE AREAS:* Commercial Litigation; Administrative Law; Chancery and Equity; Constitutional Law.

GERALD FITZGERALD, born 1945; admitted, 1971, Ireland. *Education:* University College, Dublin (B.A.); Centre Europeen Universitaire de Nancy. *LANGUAGES:* French. *PRACTICE AREAS:* European Community Law; Anti-trust and Trade Regulation; Mergers, Acquisitions and Divestitures; Intellectual Property Licensing.

DAIRE HOGAN, born 1949; admitted, 1973, Ireland. *Education:* University College, Dublin (M.A.). *PRACTICE AREAS:* Collective Investments; Commercial Mergers and Acquisitions; Securities.

GUY FRENCH, born 1948; admitted, 1973, Ireland. *Education:* Trinity College, Dublin (B.A.). *PRACTICE AREAS:* International Joint Ventures/Partnerships; Company Acquisitions and Sales; Take-Overs; Secured Finance.

FIONNBAR F. CALLANAN, born 1930; admitted, 1952, Ireland. *Education:* University College, Dublin (B.A.; LL.B.). *PRACTICE AREAS:* Labour and Employment Law.

HENRY LAPPIN, born 1949; admitted, 1973, Ireland. *Education:* University College, Dublin (B.C.L.; LL.B.). *PRACTICE AREAS:* Personal Injury.

MICHAEL S. ROCHE, born 1948; admitted, 1971, Ireland. *Education:* University College, Dublin (B.C.L.; Diploma European Law). *LANGUAGES:* Spanish. *PRACTICE AREAS:* Commercial Property; Mortgages; Environmental Law; Resorts and Leisure.

J. VINCENT SHANNON, born 1943; admitted, 1975, Ireland. *Education:* University College, Dublin (B.C.L.). *PRACTICE AREAS:* Finance; Corporate Law; Aviation and Aerospace.

COLIN KEANE, born 1949; admitted, 1974, Ireland. *Education:* Trinity College, Dublin (B.A. Mod.). *PRACTICE AREAS:* Commercial Property; Retail Property and Shopping Centres; Zoning, Planning and Land Use; Mortgages.

WILLIAM EARLEY, born 1949; admitted, 1973, Ireland; 1991, England and Wales. *Education:* University College, Dublin (B.A.). *PRACTICE AREAS:* Corporate Law (International Corporate Finance); Computers and Software (Computer Contracts).

ROBERT BURKE, born 1946; admitted, 1981, Ireland. *Education:* University College, Dublin (B.A., B.C.L., LL.M.). *PRACTICE AREAS:* Commercial Taxation; International Business Taxation; Commercial Law.

PETRIA MCDONNELL, born 1952; admitted, 1974, Ireland. *Education:* University College, Dublin (B.C.L., Dip. European Law); Ancienne: College of Europe, Bruges. *PRACTICE AREAS:* Admiralty and Marine Law; Litigation; Transportation.

TIMOTHY BOUCHIER-HAYES, born 1953; admitted, 1974, Ireland. *Education:* University College, Dublin (B.C.L.). *PRACTICE AREAS:* Construction Law; Professional Liability; Arbitration.

HELEN COLLINS, born 1955; admitted, 1977, Ireland. *Education:* University College, Dublin (B.C.L.). *PRACTICE AREAS:* Commercial Litigation; International Arbitration; Intellectual Property (Infringement).

GERALD B. SHEEDY, born 1944; admitted, 1966, Ireland. *Education:* University College, Dublin (B.C.L.). *PRACTICE AREAS:* Trusts and Estates; Wills; Property.

RONAN MOLONY, born 1959; admitted, 1983, Ireland; 1991, England and Wales. *Education:* University College, Dublin (B.C.L.). *PRACTICE AREAS:* Finance; Banking; Taxation.

MARK PEARSON, born 1953; admitted, 1979, Ireland. *Education:* Trinity College, Dublin (B.A., Mod., LL.B.). *PRACTICE AREAS:* Business Law; Financing; Entertainment and the Arts.

MICHAEL J. O'REILLY, born 1952; admitted, 1979, Ireland. *Education:* University College, Dublin (B.C.L.). *PRACTICE AREAS:* Construction Law; Environmental Law; Professional Liability.

LONAN MCDOWELL, born 1957; admitted, 1980, Ireland. *Education:* University College, Dublin (B.C.L.). *PRACTICE AREAS:* Commercial Property; Landlord and Tenant Law; Agricultural Property; Mortgages.

PATRICIA RICKARD-CLARKE, born 1942; admitted, 1982, Ireland. *Education:* University College, Dublin (B.C.L.). *PRACTICE AREAS:* Probate; Taxation (Inheritance Tax/Trust Taxation/Capital Taxation/Estate and Gift Taxation); Wills (Successions); Immigration and Naturalization.

DAVID GLYNN, born 1947; admitted, 1986, Ireland. *Education:* National University of Ireland (B.Comm.). *PRACTICE AREAS:* Taxation; Insurance.

MICHAEL O'BRIEN, born 1947; admitted, 1988, Ireland. *Education:* Incorporated Law Society of Ireland. *PRACTICE AREAS:* Commercial Property; Mortgages; Residential Property Development; Zoning, Planning and Land Use.

JULIAN CONLON, born 1960; admitted, 1983, Ireland; 1992, England and Wales. *Education:* University College, Dublin (B.C.L.); London School of Economics (LL.M.). *PRACTICE AREAS:* Company Law; Corporate Law; Mergers, Acquisitions and Divestitures; Securities.

EDWINA DUNN, born 1956; admitted, 1981, Ireland. *Education:* Trinity College, Dublin (B.A., LL.B., M.A.); University of Amsterdam (Dip ICEI). *PRACTICE AREAS:* Agency and Distributorships; Franchises and Franchising; Sale of Goods.

(This Listing Continued)   *(This Listing Continued)*

McCANN FITZGERALD, Dublin—Continued

PATRICK J. FARRELL, born 1953; admitted, 1975, Ireland. *Education:* University College, Dublin (B.C.L., Dip European Law). *PRACTICE AREAS:* Corporate Insolvency; Corporate Recovery; Loan Workouts.

VIVIENNE BRADLEY, born 1953; admitted, 1977, Ireland. *Education:* University College, Dublin (B.A.). *PRACTICE AREAS:* Residential Property; Leases and Leasing.

CATHERINE DEANE, born 1961; admitted, 1987, Ireland. *Education:* Trinity College, Dublin (B.A. Mod.). *PRACTICE AREAS:* Aviation and Aerospace; Banks and Banking; Equipment Finance and Leasing.

PAUL HEFFERNAN, born 1964; admitted, 1988, Ireland. *Education:* University College, Dublin (B.C.L.). *PRACTICE AREAS:* Business Law; Mergers, Acquisitions and Divestitures; Contracts.

MICHAEL KEALEY, born 1958; admitted, 1986, Ireland. *Education:* University College, Dublin (B.A.); Cambridge University (LL.B.). *PRACTICE AREAS:* Libel and Defamation; Litigation; Communications and Media.

TERENCE MCCRANN, born 1961; admitted, 1986, Ireland. *Education:* University College, Dublin (B.C.L.). *PRACTICE AREAS:* Commercial Litigation; Banking Litigation; Chancery.

ULTAN STEPHENSON, born 1962; admitted, 1988, Ireland. *Education:* Trinity College, Dublin (B.A. Mod.). *PRACTICE AREAS:* Retirement Benefit/Employee Stock Ownership Plan/Profit Sharing.

MURIEL WALLS, born 1954; admitted, 1977, Ireland. *Education:* University College, Dublin (B.C.L.). *PRACTICE AREAS:* Family Law; Children; Wills.

RODERICK BOURKE, born 1959; admitted, 1985, Ireland; 1991, England and Wales. *Education:* University of Limerick (B.B.S.); Queen Mary College, London (LL.M). *PRACTICE AREAS:* Insurance; Products Liability; Medical Malpractice; Commercial Litigation.

GRACE SMITH, born 1961; admitted, 1989, Ireland and New York. *Education:* Trinity College, Dublin (B.A. Legal Science). *PRACTICE AREAS:* International Arbitration; Copyright; Trademarks; Torts.

AMBROSE LOUGHLIN, born 1961; admitted, 1992, Ireland. *Education:* University College, Dublin (B.C.L.). *PRACTICE AREAS:* Banks and Banking; Taxation; Finance; Collective Investment.

RESIDENT LONDON PARTNERS

JOHN A. CRONIN, born 1959; admitted, 1984, Ireland; 1991, England and Wales. *Education:* Trinity College, Dublin (B.A. Mod., Legal Science). *PRACTICE AREAS:* Banks and Banking; Asset Finance; Financial Services.

BARBARA JUDGE, born 1961; admitted, 1986, Ireland. *Education:* Trinity College, Dublin (B.A. Mod.). *PRACTICE AREAS:* Asset Finance; Banks and Banking; Corporate Law.

RESIDENT BRUSSELS PARTNERS

DAMIAN COLLINS, born 1960; admitted, 1984, Ireland. *Education:* Trinity College, Dublin (B.A. Mod); European University Institute, Florence (LL.M.). *PRACTICE AREAS:* Anti-Trust and Trade Regulation; International Law.

RESIDENT NEW YORK COUNSEL

JOHN A. MORAN, born 1966; admitted, 1988, New York; 1994, Ireland. *Education:* University College, Dublin (B.C.L.); University of Pennsylvania (LL.M.); Institute of Taxation in Ireland.

SEAN BARTON, born 1969; admitted, 1993, Ireland. *Education:* University College, Cork (B.C.L.); University College, Cork (LL.M.). (Resident, Brussels Office). *LANGUAGES:* French.

DAVID BYERS, born 1968; admitted, 1993, Ireland. *Education:* Trinity College, Dublin (LL.B.).

LIAM CARNEY, born 1965; admitted, 1992, Ireland. *Education:* Trinity College, Dublin (LL.B.). (Resident, London Office).

BRIAN COLLINS, born 1965; admitted, 1989, New York; 1994, Ireland. *Education:* University College, Dublin (B.C.L.); Associate of Institute of Taxation in Ireland.

(This Listing Continued)

MAURA CONNOLLY, born 1968; admitted, 1993, Ireland. *Education:* Trinity College, Dublin (LL.B.); Public Relations Institute of Ireland-Certificate. (Resident, London Office). *LANGUAGES:* French.

PADRAIG CRONIN, born 1969; admitted, 1994, Ireland. *Education:* University College, Cork (B.C.L.).

MARY ROSE CURTIS, born 1962; admitted, 1990, Ireland. *Education:* University College, Dublin (B.A., Hons.); College of Commerce, Rathmines (Dip. Legal Studies); College of Europe, Bruges, Brussels (Dip Advanced European (Legal Studies).

MAUREEN P. DOLAN, born 1957; admitted, 1990, Ireland. *Education:* University College, Dublin (B.A.).

MAJELLA EGAN, born 1966; admitted, 1993, Ireland. *Education:* University College, Dublin (B.A.); College of Commerce, Rathmines (Diploma in Legal Studies).

BERNICE EVOY, born 1970; admitted, 1993, Ireland. *Education:* University College, Dublin (B.C.L.). *LANGUAGES:* French.

PETER FAHY, born 1967; admitted, 1992, Ireland. *Education:* University College, Dublin (B.C.L.).

COLM FANNING, born 1970; admitted, 1995, Ireland. *Education:* University College, Dublin (B.Comm.); College of Commerce, Rathmines (Dip.L.S.).

GARRETT FENNELL, born 1965; admitted, 1992, Ireland. *Education:* University College, Dublin (B.A. Hons).

VANESSA FITZGERALD, born 1966; admitted, 1992, Ireland. *Education:* University College, Dublin (B.C.L.).

JOSEPH GAVIN, born 1958; admitted, 1988, Massachusetts. *Education:* University College, Dublin (B.C.L.); University College, Dublin (M.B.A.); New England School of Law (J.D.).

FRANCIS HACKETT, born 1963; admitted, 1988, Ireland. *Education:* University College, Dublin (B.C.L.).

JAMES HANGLOW, born 1967; admitted, 1994, Ireland. *Education:* University College, Dublin (B.C.L.).

DONAL HANLEY, born 1964; admitted, 1990, Ireland; 1991, England and Wales. *Education:* Trinity College, Dublin (B.A. Mod.).

DAVID F.J. HURLEY, born 1962; admitted, 1990, Ireland. *Education:* University College, Dublin (B.Comm.).

RACHEL HUSSEY, born 1965; admitted, 1991, New York (Not admitted in Ireland). *Education:* Trinity College, Dublin (LL.B.); King's Inns, Dublin (Barrister at Law); Harvard Law School (LL.M.).

PAUL KEARNEY, born 1962; admitted, 1988, Ireland; 1991, England and Wales. *Education:* Trinity College, Dublin (B.A. Mod.). (Resident, London Office).

NEIL E. KEENAN, born 1971; admitted, 1994, Ireland. *Education:* University College, Dublin (B.C.L.).

KEVIN KELLY, born 1964; admitted, 1989, Ireland. *Education:* University College, Dublin (B.C.L.).

HELEN KILROY, born 1966; admitted, 1991, Ireland. *Education:* University College, Dublin (B.C.L.).

CHRISTINE LAVELLE, born 1962; admitted, 1987, Ireland. *Education:* University College, Dublin (B.C.L.).

JUDITH LAWLESS, born 1967; admitted, 1992, Ireland. *Education:* Trinity College, Dublin (LL.B.).

PATRICIA LAWLESS, born 1965; admitted, 1991, Ireland. *Education:* Trinity College, Dublin (B.A. Mod.).

DAVID LYDON, born 1966; admitted, 1992, Ireland. *Education:* University College, Dublin (B.C.L.).

FINOLA MCCARTHY, born 1964; admitted, 1993, Ireland. *Education:* University College, Cork (B.C.L.); University of Dundee (Diploma in Petroleum and Mineral Law Studies); University College, Dublin (Diploma in European Studies). *LANGUAGES:* French.

SIONA MACCINNA, born 1967; admitted, 1992, Ireland. *Education:* University College, Dublin (B.C.L.).

CLAIRE MCWALTER, born 1969; admitted, 1994, Ireland. *Education:* University College, Galway (B.A.; LL.B.).

(This Listing Continued)

BARBARA MAGUIRE, born 1967; admitted, 1992, Ireland. *Education:* Trinity College, Dublin (LL.B.); University of Cambridge (LL.M.).

HILARY MARREN, born 1965; admitted, 1990, Ireland. *Education:* Trinity College, Dublin (B.A. Mod. Legal Science).

PAULA MULLOOLY, born 1969; admitted, 1993, Ireland. *Education:* Trinity College, Dublin (LL.B.); Institute of Taxation in Ireland. *LANGUAGES:* French.

JAMES MURPHY, born 1966; admitted, 1992, Ireland. *Education:* University College, Dublin (B.C.L.).

SEAN NOLAN, born 1960; admitted, 1986, England; 1991, Ireland. *Education:* University College, London (LL.B.); City of London Polytechnic (M.A.).

FIONA O'BEIRNE, born 1965; admitted, 1991, Ireland. *Education:* University College, Dublin (B.C.L.).

BENEDICTE O'CONNOR, born 1968; admitted, 1992, Ireland. *Education:* University College, Dublin (B.C.L.).

DENISE O'CONNOR, born 1962; admitted, 1990, Ireland. *Education:* Trinity College, Dublin (B.A.).

BRIDIN O'DONOGHUE, born 1966; admitted, 1993, Ireland. *Education:* Trinity College, Dublin (LL.B.); College of Europe, Bruges (Diploma in European Legal Studies). *LANGUAGES:* French.

EAMONN O'HANRAHAN, born 1965; admitted, 1990, Ireland; 1991, England and Wales. *Education:* Trinity College, Dublin (B.A. Mod.).

SARAH O'KEEFFE, born 1965; admitted, 1992, Ireland. *Education:* University College, Cork (B.A.).

OWEN O'SULLIVAN, born 1962; admitted, 1989, Ireland. *Education:* University College, Dublin (B.Comm.; Dip. L.S.).

ROY PARKER, born 1963; admitted, 1990, Ireland. *Education:* Trinity College, Dublin (B.A. Mod. Legal Science).

NIALL POWDERLY, born 1961; admitted, 1988, Ireland. *Education:* University College, Dublin (B.A.); College of Commerce, Rathmines (Diploma in Legal Science).

MICHAEL J. WALSHE, born 1964; admitted, 1988, Ireland. *Education:* University College, Dublin (B.C.L.).

CONSULTANTS

MAX W. ABRAHAMSON, born 1932; admitted, 1957, Ireland; 1973, Jamaica. *Education:* Trinity College, Dublin (LL.B.). *PRACTICE AREAS:* Construction Law; Arbitration.

BRIAN MCLOGHLIN, admitted, 1978, Ireland. *Education:* University College, Dublin (M.A., LL.M.).

JANE MARSHALL, born 1953; admitted, 1977, Ireland. *Education:* University College, Dublin (B.A.). *LANGUAGES:* German. *PRACTICE AREAS:* Corporate Insolvency; Corporate Restructuring; Banking Litigation; Mortgage Enforcement.

OF COUNSEL

WILLIAM P. CLARKE, JR., born 1931; admitted, 1958, California and U.S. District Court, Central District of California (Not admitted in Ireland). *Education:* University of Santa Clara; Loyola Law School of Los Angeles. *Member:* State Bar of California.

All Solicitors are Members of the Incorporated Law Society of Ireland. All Partners are Members of the Dublin Solicitors' Bar Association.

Languages: English, French, German and Spanish

G. J. MOLONEY AND COMPANY

Solicitors

HAMBLEDEN HOUSE
19/26 LOWER PEMBROKE STREET
DUBLIN 2, IRELAND
Telephone: 353-1-6785199
Fax: 353-1-6785-146

Cork, Ireland Office: Courthouse Chambers, 27/29 Washington Street. Telephone: 353-21-275261. Telefax: 353-21-271586.

(This Listing Continued)

Commerical and Litigation Practice including Corporate, Commercial, Competition, Insolvency, Environmental Law, EEC Law, Maritime Law, Commercial and General Litigation and General Practice including Property Law and Transactions.

BILL HOLOHAN, born Limerick, Ireland, January 28, 1960; admitted, 1983, Ireland. Trade Mark Agent. *Education:* National University of Ireland (B.C.L., LL.B., Maritime Law); A.C.I. ARB, London. Co-Author: "Bankruptcy Law and Practice in Ireland," May 1991. *Member:* Alumni of The Academy of International Law of the Hague; Incorporated Law Society of Ireland; Southern Law Association; Chartered Institute of Arbitrators; Irish Maritime Law Association (Council Member); Irish Society of Labor Law; Irish Centre for European Law; Irish Franchise Association (Legal Advisor); European Communities Trademark Practitioners Association. *PRACTICE AREAS:* Insolvency; Franchising; Maritime Law; Litigation.

KATHLEEN COLLINS, born Cork, Ireland, September 23, 1959; admitted, 1984, Dublin. *Education:* University College, Cork (B.C.L.). *Member:* Incorporated Law Society of Ireland; Dublin Solicitors Bar Association. *PRACTICE AREAS:* Corporate and Commercial Law.

ASSOCIATE

NICOLA O'BRIEN, born Dublin, Ireland, March 1, 1967; admitted, 1992, Ireland. *Education:* National University of Ireland (B.C.L). *Member:* Incorporated Law Society of Ireland; Dublin Solicitors Bar Association. *LANGUAGES:* English, French and Spanish. *PRACTICE AREAS:* Litigation.

REFERENCE: Bank of Ireland, Cork.

(For Complete Biographical Data on all Personnel, see Professional Biographies at Cork, Ireland)

RORY O'DONNELL & COMPANY

15/16 FITZWILLIAM PLACE
DUBLIN 2, IRELAND
Telephone: 353-1-6687622
Facsimile: 353-1-6619671
Telex: 33250

Corporate, Commercial, Banking and Financial Services, Stock Exchange, European Community, Franchising, Information Technology, Aviation, Anti-trust, Commercial Real Estate, Construction, Joint Ventures, Commercial Litigation, Insurance and Labour.
All Solicitors are Members of the Incorporated Law Society of Ireland and the Dublin Solicitors Bar Association.

MEMBERS OF FIRM

RORY O'DONNELL, born 1938; admitted, 1961, Ireland. *Education:* University College Dublin. *Member:* Dublin Solicitors Bar Association (Former President); Incorporated Law Society of Ireland (Former Vice President); International Bar Association. *PRACTICE AREAS:* Corporate; Construction; Arbitration.

HUGH O'DONNELL, born 1947; admitted, 1972, Ireland. *PRACTICE AREAS:* Commercial Litigation; Insurance.

PATRICIA HEFFERNAN, admitted, 1978, Ireland. *Member:* Institute of Taxation. *PRACTICE AREAS:* Commercial Real Estate.

DAVID BEATTIE, born 1953; admitted, 1981, Ireland. *Education:* Trinity College Dublin (B.A., 1975). *Member:* Association Internationale des Jeunes Avocats; Law Society Technology Committee (Vice Chairman, 1988—); Law Society Company Law Committee. *PRACTICE AREAS:* Corporate; Finance; Antitrust.

ASSOCIATES

ANNETTE CROWLEY, born 1949; admitted, 1972, Ireland. *Education:* University College Dublin (B.C.L., 1970).

FEDELMA BUTLER, born 1958; admitted, 1981, Ireland. *Education:* University College Dublin (B.C.L., 1978).

JILL CROWLEY, born 1949; admitted, 1982, Ireland. *Education:* University College Cork (B.A., 1970).

KIERAN KELLY, born 1961; admitted, 1986, Ireland. *Education:* University College Dublin (B.C.L., 1982).

EILEEN PRENDERGAST, born 1963; admitted, 1989, Ireland. *Education:* University College Dublin (B.C.L., 1985).

(This Listing Continued)

RORY O'DONNELL & COMPANY, Dublin—Continued

GAVIN BUCKLEY, born 1961; admitted, 1990, Ireland. *Education:* Trinity College Dublin (B.A. (Mod) Hons., 1983).

BREDA SWEENEY, born 1963; admitted, 1990, Ireland. *Education:* Trinity College Dublin (B.A. (Mod) Legal Science, 1986).

DEIRDRE KENNY, born 1964; admitted, 1990, Ireland. *Education:* University College Dublin (B.Comm., 1985).

TONY MCGOVERN, born 1962; admitted, 1992, Ireland. *Education:* University College Dublin (B.C.L., 1983); Dublin City University (Diploma in Accounting, 1984).

NORMAN FITZGERALD, born 1968; admitted, 1993, Ireland. *Education:* University College Dublin (B.C.L., 1983).

SEAN GREENE, born 1971; admitted, 1995, Ireland. *Education:* University College Dublin (B.C.L., 1991; LL.M., 1992).

Languages: English, French, Spanish and German.

REFERENCES: Allied Irish Bank

ORPEN FRANKS

Incorporating Montgomery & Chaytor

28/30 BURLINGTON ROAD
DUBLIN 4, IRELAND
Telephone: 353-1-6689622
Telecopier: 353-1-6689004

General Practice, including Corporate, Commercial, Real Estate, Litigation, Bankruptcy, European Community Law, Banking, Mergers and Acquisitions, Labour, Financial Services, Intellectual Property, Energy and Natural Resources, Aviation, Insurance, Environmental Law, Probate, Estates and Trusts.
Member of MacIntyre Sträter International Group of Professional Service Providers.

MEMBERS OF FIRM

JOHN O'DONOVAN, born Limerick, Ireland, 1952; admitted, 1975, Ireland. *Education:* University College, Dublin (B.C.L.). Contributor: "Doing Business in Europe," CCH International, 1993. *Member:* Incorporated Law Society of Ireland; Dublin Solicitors Bar Association; Dublin Chamber of Commerce.

FREDERICK JACKSON, born Dublin, Ireland, 1939; admitted, 1972, Ireland. *Education:* Cambridge University, Corpus Christi College (M.A., Natural Sciences); International Marketing Institute, Boston (1967). *Member:* Incorporated Law Society of Ireland; Irish Society of European Law; Dublin Solicitors Bar Association; Association of Pension Lawyers in Ireland; Institute of Directors in Ireland.

JOHN HANNON, born Castlebar, Ireland, 1948; admitted, 1970, Ireland. *Education:* University College, Dublin (B.C.L.). *Member:* Incorporated Law Society of Ireland; Dublin Solicitors Bar Association; Institute of Taxation in Ireland.

ALAN WOODS, born Dublin, Ireland, 1947; admitted, 1972, Ireland. *Education:* Trinity College, Dublin (B.A., Legal Science). *Member:* Incorporated Law Society of Ireland; Dublin Solicitors Bar Association; Medical Legal Society of Ireland (Council Member and Treasurer, 1979-1983).

JOSEPH STANLEY, born Boston, Massachusetts, 1964; admitted, 1988, Ireland and New York. *Education:* University College, Dublin (B.C.L.). Contributor: "Doing Business in Europe," CCH International, 1993. *Member:* Incorporated Law Society of Ireland; Dublin Solicitors Bar Association; Irish Society for European Law.

CHRISTIAN CARROLL, born Waterford, Ireland, 1957; admitted, 1979, Ireland. *Education:* University College, Dublin (B.C.L.). *Member:* Incorporated Law Society of Ireland; Dublin Solicitors Bar Association; Irish Society for European Law; Association of Pension Lawyers in Ireland.

JOHN LAWSON, born Dublin, Ireland, 1932; admitted, 1957, Ireland. *Education:* University of Dublin (B.A., LL.B.). *Member:* Incorporated Law Society of Ireland; The Institute of Taxation in Ireland.

KENNETH CLEAR, born Dublin, Ireland, 1928; admitted, 1950, Ireland. *Education:* Castleknock College and University College, Dublin (B.A. Legal and Political Science). *Member:* Incorporated Law Society of Ireland; Dublin Solicitors Bar Association.

(This Listing Continued)

ASSOCIATES

EDEL HARGADEN, born Carlow, Ireland, 1967; admitted, 1991, Ireland. *Education:* University College, Dublin (B.C.L.A.I.T.I.). *Member:* Incorporated Law Society of Ireland; Dublin Solicitors Bar Association; Institute of Taxation in Ireland; Association of Pension Lawyers of Ireland.

CONSULTANTS

LESLIE MELLON, born Dublin, Ireland, 1923; admitted, 1946, Ireland. *Education:* Avoca School, Dublin. Contributor: "Doing Business in Europe," CCH International, 1991. *Member:* Incorporated Law Society of Ireland.

RAYMOND WALKER, born Dublin, Ireland, 1931; admitted, 1954, Ireland. *Education:* Trinity College, Dublin (B.A., Legal Science; LL.B.). *Member:* Incorporated Law Society of Ireland; Dublin Solicitors Bar Association.

L. K. SHIELDS & PARTNERS

31 MERRION SQUARE
DUBLIN 2, IRELAND
Telephone: 353 1 661 0866
Facsimile: 353 1 661 0883

General Corporate and Business Practice, Mergers and Acquisitions, Financial Services, Litigation, EU Law, Property, Energy and Natural Resources, Insurance, Intellectual Property, Banking, Insolvency, Arbitration, Pensions, Competition Law and Private Client Service.

MEMBERS OF FIRM

LAURENCE K. SHIELDS, born 1950; admitted, 1971, Ireland. *Education:* University College, Dublin (B.C.L.; 1970). Lecturer and Examiner in Company Law and Partnership, The Incorporated Law Society of Ireland, 1972-1978. Contributor of Chapter on Irish Law to Kelly & Attree: European Product Liability. *Member:* Council Member of the Incorporated Law Society of Ireland (1978—), Former Chairman of Company Law, Education and Compensation Fund Committee. President, Dublin Solicitors Bar Association, 1983-1984. Institute of Taxation in Ireland (Associate Member); Irish Society for European Law; Institute of Arbitrators (Fellow, Irish Branch). **PRACTICE AREAS:** Company and Commercial Law; Mergers and Acquisitions; Management Buyouts; Shareholders Agreements; Building Society Law; Employment Law; Computer Software Law.

EDMUND BUTLER, born 1959; admitted, 1984, Ireland. *Education:* University College, Dublin (B.C.L., 1980). *Member:* Institute of Arbitrators (Fellow, Irish Branch). **PRACTICE AREAS:** Commercial Litigation; General Litigation; Defamation; Insurance Law; Competition Law; Employment Law; Domestic Banking; Debt Recovery; Personal Injury; Product Liability.

PATRICIA MCGOVERN, born 1961; admitted, 1987, Ireland. *Education:* Trinity College, Dublin (B.A. (Mod) Legal Science, 1983). Recipient, Guinness and Mahon Taxation Prize, 1984. *Member:* Institute of Taxation in Ireland; International Trade Mark Association; The Irish Association of Pension Funds and The Association of Pension Lawyers in Ireland. **PRACTICE AREAS:** Mergers and Acquisitions; Management Buyouts; Share Purchase Agreements; Asset Purchase and Shareholders Agreements; Rights Issues; Placings; Intellectual Property; Pensions Law; Listings; Film Financing; Entertainment Law; General Commercial Law.

ASSOCIATES

JOHN R. TARPEY, born 1963; admitted, 1989, Ireland. *Education:* Trinity College, Dublin (B.A., (Mod) Legal Science, 1985). **PRACTICE AREAS:** Commercial Leasing; Property Law; Building Contracts; Landlord and Tenant Law; Planning; Conveyancing.

PAT MORRISSEY, born 1965; admitted, 1990, Ireland. *Education:* University College Dublin (B.C.L., 1986). **PRACTICE AREAS:** Corporate and Commercial Law; Management Buyouts; Competition Law; Employment Law; Mergers and Acquisitions.

HUGH GARVEY, born 1966; admitted, 1992, Ireland. *Education:* University College Galway (B.A., LL.B., 1989). **PRACTICE AREAS:** Commercial Litigation; Tort Law; Property Litigation; General Litigation; Defamation; Mortgage Reinforcements; Personal Injury; Product Liability.

NORA RICE, born 1967; admitted, 1990, Ireland. *Education:* University College Cork (B.C.L., 1987; LL.M., 1989). Recipient: Guinness and Mahon Taxation Prize, 1989. **PRACTICE AREAS:** General Litigation; Personal

(This Listing Continued)

Injury; Landlord and Tenant Law; Residential and Commercial Property; Wills and Probate.

EMMET SCULLY, born 1970; admitted, 1994, Ireland. *Education:* Trinity College, Dublin (LL.B., 1991). *PRACTICE AREAS:* Corporate and Commercial Law; Competition Law; Mergers and Acquisitions.

CONSULTANT

THOMAS JACKSON, born 1922; admitted, 1960, Ireland. *Education:* Trinity College, Dublin. *Member:* Council Member, Incorporated Law Society of Ireland, 1967-1978; President, Dublin Solicitors Bar Association, 1977-1978. *PRACTICE AREAS:* General Practice.

All Members of the Firm are Members of the Incorporated Law Society of Ireland and the Dublin Solicitors Bar Association.

Languages: English and French.

MURRAY SWEENEY, SOLICITORS

Established in 1970

86/87 O'CONNELL STREET
LIMERICK, IRELAND
Telephone: (061) 317533
Facsimile: (061) 319496
Intl. Code. 353 61

Associated Office Dublin: 35 Molesworth Street, Dublin 2, Ireland.

Corporate, Commercial, Banking, EU Law, Probate, Real Estate, Litigation and General Practice.

MEMBERS OF FIRM

JOSEPH R. SWEENEY, born Galway, Ireland, November 20, 1951; admitted, 1975, Ireland. *Education:* University College Galway. Notary Public. Author: "Technology Handbook," published by the Law Society, 1985-1986. *Member:* Incorporated Law Society of Ireland (Council Member, 1981-1987). *LANGUAGES:* English. *PRACTICE AREAS:* Corporate; Commercial and Industrial Development.

MICHAEL D. MURRAY, born Limerick, Ireland, May 10, 1947; admitted, 1970, Ireland. *Education:* University College Dublin. *Member:* Incorporated Law Society of Ireland. *LANGUAGES:* English. *PRACTICE AREAS:* Litigation and Employment.

DAVID J. SWEENEY, born Galway, Ireland, April 28, 1953; admitted, 1975, Ireland. *Education:* University College Galway. *Member:* Incorporated Law Society of Ireland. *LANGUAGES:* English. *PRACTICE AREAS:* Real Estate.

ASSOCIATES

THERESA O'DONOGHUE, born Limerick, Ireland, July 20, 1961; admitted, 1985, Ireland. *Education:* University College Dublin (Bachelor of Civil Law, Honours Degree, 1981). *Member:* Incorporated Law Society of Ireland. *LANGUAGES:* English and French. *PRACTICE AREAS:* Litigation.

JOHN MCDERMOTT, born Dublin, Ireland, July 13, 1965; admitted, 1994, Ireland. *Education:* Trinity College Dublin (LL.B., 1988); University College Dublin (Dip. B.S., 1989; M.B.S., 1990). *Member:* Incorporated Law Society of Ireland. *LANGUAGES:* English. *PRACTICE AREAS:* Corporate and Banking.

JACQUELINE T. KEOHANE, born Cork, Ireland, November 30, 1965; admitted, 1990, Ireland. *Education:* University College Cork (Bachelor of Civil Law, Honours Degree, 1986). *Member:* Incorporated Law Society of Ireland. *LANGUAGES:* English and French. *PRACTICE AREAS:* Real Estate.

FINOLA FREEHILL, born London, England, March 22, 1968; admitted, 1992, Ireland. *Education:* University College Dublin (Bachelor of Civil Law, Hons.). *Member:* Incorporated Law Society of Ireland. *LANGUAGES:* English and French. *PRACTICE AREAS:* Litigation.

MAIREAD DANAHER, born Limerick, Ireland, July 14, 1964; admitted, 1993, Ireland. *Education:* University College Cork (Bachelor of Civil Law, Honours). *Member:* Incorporated Law Society of Ireland. *LANGUAGES:* English. *PRACTICE AREAS:* Real Estate.

GRACE CURTIS, born Wexford, Ireland, September 16, 1968; admitted, 1994, Ireland. *Education:* University College Dublin (Bachelor of Commerce, Honours). *Member:* Incorporated Law Society of Ireland. *LANGUAGES:* English, French and Italian. *PRACTICE AREAS:* Litigation.

(This Listing Continued)

DENIS BRODERICK, born Galway, Ireland, November 16, 1968; admitted, 1994, Ireland. *Education:* University College Galway (B.A.; LL.B.). *Member:* Incorporated Law Society of Ireland. *LANGUAGES:* English, French and Italian. *PRACTICE AREAS:* Commercial and Corporate Litigation.

CONSULTANT

PROFESSOR JOSEPH M. G. SWEENEY, born Galway, Ireland, December 9, 1922; admitted, 1947, Ireland. *Education:* University College Galway (B.A., and B. Comm., 1943); Hutchinson Stewart Scholar in French and Spanish; University College Dublin (LL.B., 1947). Author: Legal Articles in the Gazette of the Law Society, IrishLaw Times, Dii. Professor of Common Law, National University of Ireland, (Galway) 1966-1987. *Member:* Incorporated Law Society 0f Ireland. *LANGUAGES:* English, French and Spanish. *PRACTICE AREAS:* Real Estate and Administrative Law.

ISLE OF MAN

APPLEBY, SPURLING & KEMPE
FINCH CHAMBERS

FINCH ROAD
DOUGLAS IM1 2PS, ISLE OF MAN
Telephone: (44) 1624 629401
Facsimile: (44) 1624 673566

Geneva, Switzerland Office: ICC, Cointrin 20 Route de Pré-Bois; P.O. Box 1908, CH 1215 Geneva 15, Switzerland. Telephone: (41) 22 788 2453. Facsimile: (41) 22 788 2476.

Hamilton, Bermuda Office: Cedar House, 41 Cedar Avenue, P.O. Box HM1179, Hamilton HM EX. Telephone: (809) 295-2244. Facsimile: (809) 292-8666.

Hong Kong Office: 2217 Jardine House, 1 ConnaughtPlace, Central, Hong Kong. Telephone: (852) 523 8123. Facsimile: (852) 524 5548.

Banking, Insurance, Re-insurance, Unit Trust, Mutual Fund, Syndicated Loans, Aviation, Insurance Treaties, Trusts, Offshore Companies, Foreign Investment, Overseas Property, Immigration and Nationality, Shipping, Common Law, Taxation, Pensions, Investment, Personal Business.

JOHN D. CAMPBELL, Q.C. (Senior Partner). *PRACTICE AREAS:* Insurance.

DIANNA P. KEMPE, Q.C. (Managing Partner). *PRACTICE AREAS:* Litigation; Liquidations.

GERARD F.B. MACQUILLAN. *PRACTICE AREAS:* Company, Finance, Trusts, Settlements.

DAVID J. DOYLE

RICHARD D. SPURLING, M.P.

KENNETH E.T. ROBINSON

F. CHESLEY WHITE

JAY W. KEMPE

MICHAEL J. SPURLING (Resident, Hong Kong Office).

ALAN W. DUNCH. *PRACTICE AREAS:* Litigation.

PETER BUBENZER. *PRACTICE AREAS:* Company Finance.

MONICA J. JONES. *PRACTICE AREAS:* Trusts, Settlements.

JOHN BARRITT, M.P.

JUDITH COLLIS

THE HON. C. JEROME DILL, J.P., M.P.

WARREN CABRAL. *PRACTICE AREAS:* Captive Insurance.

SENIOR COUNSEL

GEOFFREY R. BELL, Q.C.

(This Listing Continued)

APPLEBY, SPURLING & KEMPE FINCH CHAMBERS,
Douglas—Continued

ASSISTANT SOLICITOR

JAMES CUNNINGHAM-DAVIS. PRACTICE AREAS: Intellectual
Property.

Languages: English, French and German

CAINS

Advocates, Solicitors and Notaries

Established in 1830

15 ATHOL STREET

DOUGLAS, ISLE OF MAN

Telephone: (01624) 628575

Fax: (01624) 672510

Douglas, Isle of Man Office: 15 Athol Street.
Peel, Isle of Man Office: Atholl Court, Atholl Street.
Ramsey, Isle of Man Office: 4 Auckland Terrace.

*Conveyancing, International Litigation, Commerce, Banking, Taxation,
Trusts, Insurance, Financial Services.*

PARTNERS

J. E. CRELLIN, Notary Public. **PRACTICE AREAS:** Trusts; Estates.

P. G. CRELLIN. *Education:* B.A. Notary Public. **LANGUAGES:**
French. **PRACTICE AREAS:** Insurance; Estates; Trusts.

J. KARRAN. *Education:* LL.B. Notary Public. **PRACTICE AREAS:**
Property; Private Client.

P. M. SAUNDERS. *Education:* LL.B. Notary Public. **PRACTICE
AREAS:** Personal Injuries Litigation; Contract Disputes.

A. J. CORLETT. *Education:* LL.B. **PRACTICE AREAS:** Financial Services; Commercial.

A. D. WEBB. *Education:* B.A. **LANGUAGES:** French. **PRACTICE
AREAS:** Insolvency; Commercial; Banking.

R. V. VANDERPLANK. *Education:* LL.B. **PRACTICE AREAS:** Collective Investment Schemes; Banking; Commercial.

J. R. G. WALTON. *Education:* LL.B. **PRACTICE AREAS:** Property;
Trusts.

S. F. CAINE. *Education:* LL.B. **PRACTICE AREAS:** Commercial Litigation; Contentious Insolvency.

W.H. WANNENBURGH. *Education:* B.A., LL.B. **PRACTICE
AREAS:** Criminal and Matrimonial Litigation.

ASSOCIATES

G. KIRKPATRICK. *Education:* LL.B. Advocate. **PRACTICE AREAS:**
Property.

C. J. ARROWSMITH. *Education:* LL.B. **PRACTICE AREAS:** Criminal Litigation; Commercial Litigation.

P.B. CLUCAS. *Education:* B.A. **PRACTICE AREAS:** Building Disputes; Litigation.

A.J. BAKER. *Education:* LL.B. Solicitor. **PRACTICE AREAS:** Corporate Acquisitions; Securities.

DAVID CAPPS & CO.

Established in 1987

CAPCO HOUSE

31/37 NORTH QUAY

DOUGLAS 1M1 4LB, ISLE OF MAN

Telephone: 01624 662977

Fax: 01624 662988

Telex: 626109 Capco G

St. Helier, Jersey, Channel Islands Office: Sir Walter Raleigh House,
48-50 The Esplanade. Telephone: 01534 89123. Fax: 01534 80522.
Telex: 4193259 Capco G.

(This Listing Continued)

Associated Trust Company: Capco Trust (Nevis) Limited, Springates
Building, Government Road, Charlestown, Nevis, West Indies.
Telephone: 0101 809 469 1558. Fax: 0101 809 469 1559. Telex:
397680 Capco KC.

*International Company and Trust Formation and Management, Shipping,
Commercial and Property Matters.*

FIRM PROFILE: *David Capps & Co. was founded in the Isle of Man in
1987 with one qualified and three unqualified staff, and now employs
fourteen people including two qualfied lawyers, and three paralegals. The
firm specializes in international company and trust formation, and administration, based on international commercial transactions, with particular
emphasis on shipping, though other commercial transactions are also handled. The firm prides itself on its speed of response, and acts for many of
the leading City of London firms of lawyers as well as firms in other jurisdictions. The firm has offices in Jersey, Channel Islands, and Nevis, West
Indies. The firm is a member of the following groups: European Maritime
Law Organization; British Nordic Lawyers Association; British Maritime
Law Association; Lawyers Associated World Wide (LAW). The partners
are members of the International Bar Association.*

MEMBERS OF FIRM

PHILIP J. HOBSON, admitted, 1959, English Solicitor. *Education:*
Oxford University (M.A.); Brussels University. *Member:* The Law Society,
International Bar Association. **LANGUAGES:** French and English.
PRACTICE AREAS: International Commercial Transactions; Companies
and Trusts; Shipping; Tax; Ship Management.

HAYDN E. BRICKELL, admitted, 1971, English Solicitor. *Education:*
Palmers Grammar School. *Member:* The Law Society. **LANGUAGES:**
French and English. **PRACTICE AREAS:** International Commercial
Transactions; Companies and Trusts; Shipping; Tax.

LEGAL SUPPORT PERSONNEL
PARALEGALS

DAVID F. J. COOIL. *Education:* Durham University (M.B.A., Arabic
Languages). **LANGUAGES:** English and Arabic. **PRACTICE AREAS:**
Insurance; Company Administration.

RUTH HELEN VONDY, born Isle of Man, August 27, 1960. Educated
at Ramsey Grammar School; worked in the Isle of Man Companies Registry for eleven years, and coordinated the computerization of the Companies
Registry. Joined David Capps & Co. in 1990. **LANGUAGES:** English.
PRACTICE AREAS: Manx Company Formation; Administration.

CONTI

Advocate & Commissioner for Oaths

17 CIRCULAR ROAD

DOUGLAS IM1 1AF, ISLE OF MAN

Telephone: 01624 670003

Fax: 01624 612281

Intl Code: +44 1624

*Civil and Commercial Litigation, Corporate and Trusts, Banking, Ship-
ping, Insurance and Financial Services, Property, Offshore Companies and
Tax Planning.*

JOHN PATRICK CONTI, born Sliema, Malta, April 1, 1966; admitted,
1988, England; 1991, Isle of Man. *Education:* University of Wales (LL.B.,
1987); Inns of Court School (1988). *Member:* English Bar (Inner Temple);
Isle of Man Law Society; International Bar Association. **LANGUAGES:**
English. **PRACTICE AREAS:** Litigation; Commercial Law; Mergers, Acquisitions and Divestitures; Trusts and Estates; Taxation.

FIDUCIAIRE TYRRELL HIGHAM

Established in 1976

BOURNE HOUSE

97 WOODBOURNE ROAD

DOUGLAS, ISLE OF MAN

Telephone: 44-1624-629615

Fax: 44-1624-626976

*Nationality and Citizenship worldwide, Offshore Company Formation and
Management, Captive Insurance Company Management, Fiduciary services
worldwide and International Tax Planning.*

(This Listing Continued)

TOM K.H. TYRRELL, born London, September 9, 1936; admitted, 1962, Barrister at Law England. *Education:* Trinity College, Cambridge, (B.A., 1960; M.A., 1965); London University (LL.B., 1962). Partner, Lauterpacht Sanne & Tyrrell of Geneva; Director, Fiduciaire Tyrrell Higham, The Belbond Co. Ltd. *Member:* International Bar Association (Committee on Immigration and Nationality); American Bar Association (International Associate); American Society of International Law; International Tax Planning Association; International Fiscal Association; Irish Genealogical Research Society; Genealogical Society (London). Fellow, National Genealogical Society (Washington, D.C). *LANGUAGES:* English, French, Spanish and Italian. *PRACTICE AREAS:* Immigration and Naturalization Law; Citizenship Law.

JANET KATZ, born Leicester, June 20, 1943. *Education:* University of Warwick (M.B.A.). Managing Director, Fiduciaire Tyrrell Higham Ltd. Director: InFid International Fiduciary Services Ltd.; ICD Corporate Managers Ltd.; Interisk Management Ltd.; Claremont Insurance Management Ltd.; Nordic Star Management. *Member:* Institute of Directors (Fellow); International Tax Planning Association; International Fiscal Association; Society of Trust and Estate Planners. *LANGUAGES:* English. *PRACTICE AREAS:* Offshore Company Formation and Management; International Estate and Business Planning; Captive Insurance Formation and Management.

MANN & CO.

20 FINCH ROAD
DOUGLAS IM1 2PS, ISLE OF MAN
Telephone: 44 1624 622221
Fax: 44 1624 627222

Trust Law, Corporate and Commercial Law, Commercial Litigation, Private Client, Probate, Conveyancing.
Number of Lawyers: 3.

PARTNERS

TIMOTHY A. MANN, admitted, 1982, Isle of Man, Notary Public. Co-Author: "Trusts Tax and Estate Planning through the Isle of Man.".

CHRISTOPHER J. MURPHY, LL.B., admitted, 1994, Isle of Man; 1990, England.

ASSOCIATES

JOHANNA M. COWMAN, B.C.L., admitted, 1988, Ireland.

SIMCOCKS

Established in 1919

50 ATHOL STREET
P.O. BOX 181
DOUGLAS IM99 1PY, ISLE OF MAN
Telephone: 01624 620821
Telex: 628675 SIMCO G
Fax: 01624 620994

Castletown, Isle of Man Office: Compton House, Parliament Square, IM9 1LA. Telephone: 0624 824321. Fax: 0624 824311.

FIRM PROFILE: Simcocks has its origin in the early years of the 20th Century and members of the firm and its predecessors have occupied high judicial office as the Isle of Man Attorneys General, Stipendiary Magistrates and Deemsters. The Isle of Man's present Attorney General J.M. Kerruish was formerly a partner in the firm.

Simcocks now has five Partners, two Manx Advocate Associates and a number of associates qualified in other jurisdictions. Simcocks is well known for its expertise in corporate and commercial, trust and estates, banking and insurance, litigation commercial, preemptive, construction and personal injury, family and matrimonial law as well as its involvement with large scale public inquiries in planning and other related matters.

PARTNERS

PHILIP B. GAMES, born 1959; admitted, 1986, Isle of Man. *Member:* Isle of Man Law Society. *PRACTICE AREAS:* Corporate and Commercial; Banking.

JOHN WRIGHT, born 1956; admitted, 1982, Isle of Man. *Education:* Universities of Staffordshire (B.A., Law, 1977) and Hull (M.A., Criminology, 1978). *Member:* Isle of Man Law Society; International Bar Association; Family Law Bar Association; Solicitors Family Law Association.

(This Listing Continued)

PRACTICE AREAS: Litigation; Commercial; Medical Negligence; Local Authority Child Care.

PAUL J.V. DOUGHERTY, born 1947; admitted, 1989, Isle of Man; 1975, Northern Ireland; 1976, Cayman Islands. *Education:* Queens University, Belfast (LL.B., 1972). *Member:* International Bar Association; Isle of Man Law Society; Law Society Northern Ireland; Society of Trust and Estate Practitioners. *PRACTICE AREAS:* Trusts; Corporate and Commercial; Mergers and Take Overs.

WILLIAM J.C. KELLY, born 1953; admitted, 1979, Isle of Man. *Education:* University of Cambridge (M.A., 1976). *Member:* Isle of Man Law Society. *PRACTICE AREAS:* Conveyancing; Commercial; Domestic Conveyancing; Leasing.

STEPHEN M. HARDING, born 1961; admitted, 1991, Isle of Man. *Education:* University of Lancaster (B.A., 1983). *Member:* Isle of Man Law Society. (Resident Partner, Castletown Office). *PRACTICE AREAS:* Matrimonial and Common Law; Litigation and Crime; Liquor Licensing; General Practice; Conveyancing; Leases.

ASSOCIATES

ANGELA M. CRAPPER, born 1967; admitted, 1993, Isle of Man. *Education:* University of Sheffield (B.A., 1989). *Member:* Isle of Man Law Society. *PRACTICE AREAS:* Common Law Litigation; Family and Matrimonial Matters; Criminal Law.

DAVID M. SPENCER, born 1946; admitted, 1993, Isle of Man; 1975, England. *Education:* University of Bristol (LL.B., 1972). *Member:* Isle of Man Law Society; Law Society of England and Wales. *PRACTICE AREAS:* Corporate and Commercial; Banking; Shipping; Insurance.

ITA M. MCARDLE, born 1964; admitted, 1989, Northern Ireland. *Education:* Queens University, Belfast (LL.B., 1987). *Member:* Law Society Northern Ireland; Law Society of England and Wales. *PRACTICE AREAS:* Corporate and Commercial; Trusts; Commercial Litigation.

PAULINE MCCRORIE, born 1951; admitted, 1976, England as Solicitor. *Education:* University of London (LL.B., 1973). *Member:* English Law Society. *PRACTICE AREAS:* General Practice; Wills; Probate; Domestic Leases.

FRANK DWYER, born 1923; called to Irish Bar, 1951; English Bar, 1958. *Education:* Trinity, Dublin (M.A., 1951). *PRACTICE AREAS:* Litigation; Drafting of Pleadings; Provisions of Opinions.

NIGEL CORDWELL, born 1961; admitted, 1989, England, Solicitor-Notary. *Education:* University of Liverpool (B.A., 1983). *Member:* English Law Society. *PRACTICE AREAS:* Personal Injury Litigation; Medical Negligence; Defence Litigation; Mental Health.

WENDY MONTGOMERIE, born 1953; admitted, 1979, England. *Education:* Newcastle Polytechnic (B.A., 1974). *Member:* English Law Society. (Resident Associate, Castletown Office). *PRACTICE AREAS:* Matrimonial; Conveyancing; Common Law Litigation; General Practice.

Simcocks is a member of the Terralex Association World Wide. Simcocks are associate members of the British Academy of Experts.

TRAVERS SMITH BRAITHWAITE

4 UPPER CHURCH STREET
DOUGLAS, ISLE OF MAN
Telephone: 1624 625515
Fax: 1624 624625
Telex: 887117 TRAVER G

London, England Office: 10 Snow Hill, EC1A 2AL. Telephone: 0171-248 9133. Fax: 0171-236 3728. Telex: 887117.

English Solicitors and Registered Legal Practitioners in the Isle of Man where they handle principally company and commercial and regulatory matters.

(This Listing Continued)

TRAVERS SMITH BRAITHWAITE, Douglas—Continued

RESIDENT PARTNERS

M.J. PINSON. PRACTICE AREAS: Company.

RESIDENT CONSULTANTS

R.B.M. Quayle

ITALY

CAPPELLO & ASSOCIATI

VIALE MICHELANGELO, 8
62100 AREZZO, ITALY
Telephone: 39-575-25818
Fax: 39-575-300443

Rome, Italy Office: 47, Piazza Barberini, 00187. Telephone:
39-6-4824781; 39-6-4820650. Fax: 39-6-4881327.

Administrative Law, Anti-Trust Law, Arbitration, Competition Law, Consumer Protection Law, Copyright Law, Criminal Law, Distributorship, Agency, Franchise, Know How Law, EEC Law, Family Law, General Commercial and Company Law, General Tax Practice, Intellectual Property, International Taxation, Joint Ventures, Labour Law, Litigation, Merger and Acquisitions, Transportation Law. General Legal Practice.

ROSSELLA ANGIOLINI, born Arezzo, December 25, 1965; admitted, 1985, Italy. Education: University of Florence (Jurisprudence Doctor, 1985).

GIUSI CASCIANO, born Roggio Calabria, November 7, 1962; admitted, 1990, Italy. Education: University of Moessina (Jurisprudence Doctor, 1987).

Languages: Italian and English

(For complete biographical data on other personnel, see Professional Biographies at Rome, Italy)

STUDIO LEGALE PATRONI GRIFFI

Founder: Antonio Patroni Griffi (1871-1940)

PIAZZA L. DI SAVOIA 41/A
70121 BARI, ITALY
Telephone: (39-80) 5246122
Telefax: (39-80) 5247329

Rome, Italy Office: Via Delle Carrozze 55, 00185. Telephone:
39-6-6798580. Telefax: 39-6-6790178.

International Business and Investments, Banking, Shipping, Labor, Intellectual Property, Contract, Litigation, Arbitration, Mergers and Acquisitions, Corporate, International Trade, EEC, Bankruptcy, Insurance.

MEMBERS OF FIRM

ANTONIO PATRONI GRIFFI, born Manduria, Italy, September 3, 1932; admitted, 1958, Italy. Education: University of Bari (J.D., cum Laude, 1956). Professor, Commercial and Corporate Law by Contractual Appointment, University of Cagliari, 1969-1974. Professor, Commercial and Corporate Law, University of Bari, 1976-1990. Professor, Commercial and Corporate Law, Luiss of Rome. Professor, Maritime Law by Contractual Appointment, University of Bari. Dean, Luiss of Rome, Faculty of Economics. President Parfin s.p.a., 1993-1994. Director, I R I s.p.a., 1993-1994. Author: Il controllo giudiziario sulle società per azioni, 1971; La concorrenza nel sistema bancario, 1974; Lezioni sull'impresa artigiana, 1993. Co-Author: La seconda direttiva CEE in materia societaria, 1984; Banche in crisi 1960-1985, 1987; Il fenomeno delle concentrazioni d'imprese nel diritto interno ed internazionale, 1989. Le attività finanziarie. I controlli, 1990. Editor: Giurisprudenza commerciale; Diritto della banca e del mercato finanziario ; La nuova giurisprudenza civile commentata. Member: Centro studi di diritto e legislazione bancaria. **PRACTICE AREAS:** Banking; Shipping; Mergers and Acquisitions; Corporate.

GIOACCHINO BÁRBERA, born Trani, Italy, February 25, 1947; admitted, 1976, Italy. Education: University of Bari (J.D., cum laude, 1972). Assistant Professor, Corporate and Commercial Law, University of Bari. **PRACTICE AREAS:** Labor; Contract; Litigation; Corporate.

(This Listing Continued)

ASSOCIATES

GIOVANNA CICCARELLA, born Rome, Italy, April 23, 1961; admitted, 1988, Italy. Education: University of Bari (J.D., cum laude, 1985). **PRACTICE AREAS:** Banking; Contract; Litigation; Corporate.

ANNA MARIA GRILLETTI, born Bari, Italy, March 23, 1962; admitted, 1989, Italy. Education: University of Bari (J.D., cum laude, 1986). **PRACTICE AREAS:** Labor; Litigation; General; Bankruptcy.

UGO PATRONI GRIFFI, born Bari, Italy, July 28, 1966; admitted, 1994, Italy. Education: University of Bari (J.D., cum laude, 1990); Katholieke University of Louvain (LL.M., magna cum laude, 1992); Academy of American and International Law, Dallas (1993). Assistant Professor, Corporate, Banking and Insurance Law, University of Bari. Member: American-Italian Law Association; International Bar Association. **PRACTICE AREAS:** Bankruptcy; Corporate; International Trade; EEC.

MARIA TERESA TAMBORRA, born Bari, Italy, April 3, 1965; admitted, 1993, Italy. Education: University of Bari (J.D., cum laude, 1989); ISTUD, Novara (1987). **PRACTICE AREAS:** Contract; Litigation; Arbitration; Corporate.

LEONARDO PATRONI GRIFFI, born Bari, Italy, October 10, 1967; (Not admitted in Italy). Education: University of Bari (J.D., cum laude, 1967); University College of Dublin (LL.M., 1993). Member: International Bar Association. **PRACTICE AREAS:** Contracts; Torts; International Trade; EEC.

VITTORIA METTEO, born Bari, March 2, 1966; admitted, 1994, Italy. Education: University of Bari (J.D., cum laude, 1990); Georgetown University (Orientation in U.S. Legal System, 1990); University of Rome (EC Law and Economics Master's Degree, 1993). **PRACTICE AREAS:** Corporate; Banking; Bankruptcy.

Languages: Italian, English and French.

REPRESENTATIVE CLIENTS: Italgrani s.p.a. Neaples; Italsilos s.p.a., Neaples; Mediocredito s.p.a., Bari; Parfin s.p.a., Bari: Sava s.p.a., Turin; Savafactoring, Turin; Savaleasing, Turin; Altecna s.p.a., Turin; Banca popolare della Murgia, Altamura; I.M.I., Rome; Banca di Italia, Rome; Credito Commerciale, Tirreno, Salerno; Bendix s.p.a.; Weber s.p.a.-Gruppo Magneti Marelli, Turin; Consorzio del SAO caffe, Modena; Municipality of Bari, Bari; Ferrovie del Gargano, Bari; EFIM, Rome; Saicaf s.p.a., Bari; Agusta, Cascina Costa di Samarate; Studi Finanziari s.p.a., Roma; Wella Italiana Labocos s.a.s., Castiglione delle Stiviere; Arch Renzo Piano, Genova.

STUDIO BERNINI E ASSOCIATI

Established in 1920

VIA MASCARELLA 94-96
40126 BOLOGNA, ITALY
Telephone: (39-51) 240788 (Multiple Line)
Cable Address: "Unalex" Bologna
Telex: 521554 BERLAW I
Telefax: (39-51) 240131

Arbitration, Litigation, General Practice, International Private Law, Corporate Law, Contracts, Antitrust, Unfair Competition, Industrial Property Law, International Tax Planning, Exchange Control Laws, EEC Law and International Trade Law, Family Law.

FIRM PROFILE: Studio Bernini e Associati is a family office founded by AVV. Sergio Bernini and presently headed by Prof. AVV. Giorgio Bernini, with two partners and associates. The office is engaged in the legal assistance of Italian as well as foreign clients in domestic, EEC and international commercial matters, specializing inter alia in arbitration, antitrust, corporate and international contracts.

PARTNERS

PROF.AVV. GIORGIO BERNINI, born Bologna, Italy, November 9, 1928; admitted, 1951, Italy; 1965, Supreme Court of Cassation (temporarily cancelled, at his own request, from the rolls and from the special rolls of attorneys admitted to the Italian Supreme Court and other higher jurisdictions, following his election to Parliament and appointment to the position of Minister for Foreign Trade). Education: University of Bologna (J.D. summa cum laude, 1950); University of Michigan Law School (LL.M., 1953; S.J.D., summa cum laude, 1958). Author of Numerous Texts and Monographs, Among Which "Un Secolo Di Filosofia Antitrust" (1991) and "L'Arbitrato" (1992). Contributor to Legal Periodicals on: Anti-trust Legislation in the U.S. and in the E.E.C.; Anti-trust in Italy, Mistake and Misrepresentation; Business Associations; International Arbitration; Product Liability; Consumer Protection; Trade Regulations; Corporate Reorganization; Multinational Corporations; International Contracts; International

(This Listing Continued)

Taxation; Customs and Tariff Problems; Oil and Gas Regulation. Member: Editorial Board of Il Foro Padano, Rassegna Dell' Arbitrato (Chief Editor), The Journal of World Trade Law. Professor of Commercial Law, University of Bologna (1970-1994). Professor of Arbitration Law, University of Bologna. President: International Council for Commercial Arbitration (ICCA), (1986-1994) presently Honorary President; Association for the Teaching and Study of Arbitration (AISA). Formerly: Professor, Universities of Ferrara, 1954-1966 and Padova, 1966-1970; Visiting Professor at Michigan Law School; The Johns Hopkins University, Bologna, Center; The International Faculty of Comparative Law, Strasbourg; The Ohio Legal Center Institute, Columbus, 1974. Adviser to: Italian Parliamentary Commission on Trade Restrictions, 1965; EEC Commission, 1965-1971; EEC Economic and Social Council, 1972; Italian Representative to Uncitral, 1968-1970; Council of Europe, 1971; G.A.T.T., 1973. The Italian Ministry for the European Communities, 1987—. The Italian Ministry of Industry (Anti-trust Bill), 1988. The Arbitral Chamber of the Chamber of Commerce of Milano. Testified before U.S. Senate Sub-Committee on Antitrust and Monopoly, 1968. President, European Michigan Law School Alumni Association. *Public Tasks:* Member of the Italian Chamber of Deputies (XIIth Legislature); Minister of Foreign Trade (1994-1995). *Member:* The Association of The Bar of the City of New York; American Bar Association; Special Committee for the Application of Geneva Convention on International Commercial Arbitration (Alternate President); American Arbitration Association; Italian Association for Arbitration (A.I.A.) (Executive Committee); Arbitral Chamber of the Chamber of Commerce of Bologna (Vice-President); London Court Panel of International Arbitrators; Legal Committees of the International Chamber of Commerce; American Chamber of Commerce for Italy (Legal Committee); Panel of Presiding Arbitrators; Stockholm Chamber of Commerce; International Bar Association; Ministry of Industry Commission for the Study of Competition in the Italian Economic System. Fellow: Institute of Arbitrators, London. *LANGUAGES:* Italian, English, French, Spanish and German. *PRACTICE AREAS:* Arbitration; Contracts; Antitrust; EEC Law; International Trade Law.

AVV. TIZIANA TAMPIERI, born Ravenna, Italy, July 28, 1956; admitted, 1984, Italy. *Education:* University of Bologna (J.D., summa cum laude, 1981). Author: Articles on "Interim Measures and Provisional Remedies with Particular Reference to Bank Guarantees." *Member:* Italian Association for Arbitration (AIA). *LANGUAGES:* Italian and English. *PRACTICE AREAS:* Arbitration; Contracts; Corporate Law; Litigation; Antitrust; Family Law.

DOTT. ANNA MARIA BERNINI, born Bologna, Italy, August 17, 1965. *Education:* University of Bologna (J.D., summa cum laude, 1991). *LANGUAGES:* Italian, English and French. *PRACTICE AREAS:* Arbitration; General Practice; Antitrust; EEC Law.

ASSOCIATES

DOTT. PROC. ANTONIO FRATICELLI, born Bologna, Italy, July 15, 1963; admitted, 1991, Italy. *Education:* Libera Università Internazionale Studi Sociali (L.U.I.S.S.), Roma (J.D., summa cum laude, 1988). *LANGUAGES:* Italian, English French and Spanish. *PRACTICE AREAS:* Arbitration; Litigation; Contracts; Antitrust; International Trade Law; Family Law.

DOTT.PROC. ALESSANDRO BARIOLA, born Modena, Italy, July 19, 1954; admitted, 1993, Italy. *Education:* University of Modena (J.D., summa cum laude, 1978). *LANGUAGES:* Italian, English. *PRACTICE AREAS:* General Practice; Contracts; Arbitration.

DOTT. PROC. PAOLO ZAMPIGA, born Terni, Italy, October 23, 1967; admitted, 1994, Italy. *Education:* University of Rome "La Sapienza" (J.D., summa cum laude, 1991); University of London (LL.M., 1994). *LANGUAGES:* Italian, English and French. *PRACTICE AREAS:* Arbitration; Contracts; Antitrust; International Trade Law; Family Law.

DOTT. INNOCENZO M. GENNA, born Ponte dell'Olio, Italy, June 21, 1966. *Education:* University of Macerata (J.D., summa cum laude, 1991); College of Europe, Bruges (LL.M., 1992); University of Trier (LL.M., 1993); The International Faculty of Comparative Law, Strasbourg (1993). *LANGUAGES:* Italian, English, French, German. *PRACTICE AREAS:* General Practice; EEC Law; Antitrust.

Languages: Italian, English, French, Spanish and German.

(This Listing Continued)

STUDIO LEGALE BORGHESI E ASSOCIATI

VIA DANTE 19
40125 BOLOGNA, ITALY
Telephone: int+39+(0)51+346524
Telefax: int+39+(0)51+346553

Modena, Italy Office: Via Emilia Centro, 211. Telephone: int+39+(0)59+216495. Telefax: int+39+(0)59+214962.
Ravenna, Italy Office: Via Rasponi, 8. Telephone: int+39+(0)544+212463.

Arbitration, General Civil Practice, Corporate Law, Contracts, Unfair Competition, Industrial Property Law, Domestic and International Taxation, Domestic and International Financing and Banking Law, European Union Market Law, Labour Law, Counselling in International Commercial Transaction.

PROF. AVV. DOMENICO BORGHESI, born Castel S. Pietro (Bo), Italy, September 26, 1944; admitted, 1976, Bologna, Italy; 1983, Supreme Court of Cassation. *Education:* University of Bologna (J.D.). Co-Editor, "Rivista Trimestrale di Diritto e Procedura Civile." Assistant Professor: University of Macorata, 1974; University of Ferrara, 1979. Professor of Law: Procedure Law, University of Bologna, 1980; Civil Procedure Law, University of Modena, 1990; Italian Association for the Study of Arbitration; Civil Procedure, Istituto di Applicazione Forense; Scuola di Specializzazione in Diritto Amministrativo. *Member:* Italian Arbitration Association (AIA); Italian-American Law Association; Associazione fra gli Studiosi del Processo Civile; Swiss Arbitration Association (ASA). *PRACTICE AREAS:* General Civil Practice; Corporate Law; Commercial Law; Commercial Arbitration.

AVV. PIER LUIGI MORARA, born Bologna, Italy, February 28, 1955; admitted, 1983, Bologna, Italy. *Education:* University of Bologna (J.D.). Former Counsel, AICA, (Alleanza Italian Cooperative-Agricole). *PRACTICE AREAS:* Corporate Law; Corporation Law; General Civil Practice; Mergers and Acquisitions.

AVV. CRISTINA VENTUROLI, born Bologna, Italy, September 9, 1954; admitted, 1981, Bologna, Italy. *Education:* University of Bologna (J.D.). Author: "La Transazione: quale contribuzione," 1993; "Una nuova figura contrattuale: i contratti senza formazione," 1986; "Contratti a termine e punte stagionali: una soluzione per il passato, un problema per il futuro," 1984. *PRACTICE AREAS:* Labour Law.

DOTT. PROC. FEDERICO DETTORI, born Milan, Italy, May 26, 1965; admitted, 1992, Bologna, Italy. *Education:* University of Bologna (J.D.). Seminar in European Internal Market Law, University of Bologna. *PRACTICE AREAS:* Corporate Law; Commercial Law; General Civil Practice; Family Law.

DOTT. PROC. PIETRO S. BUCCARELLI, born Vibo Valentia, Italy, August 4, 1964; admitted, 1993, Bologna, Italy. *Education:* University of Bologna (J.D.); School of International Arbitration, London, England (1993-1994). Co-Teacher: International Alternative Dispute Resolution (ADR), Golden Gate University of San Francisco, California, U.S.A., 1994; "Cultore della Materia," in Intellectual Property Law, University of Bologna; "Cultore della Materia," in Civil Procedure, University of Bologna. *Member:* Italian-American Law Association; Chartered Institute of Arbitrators; Italian Arbitration Association (AIA); London Court of International Arbitration (LCIA); Swiss Arbitration Association (ASA). *PRACTICE AREAS:* Commercial Arbitration; Corporate Law; Finance; Intellectual Property.

DOTT. PROC. ANTONIO FORMARO, born Botricello (Cz), Italy, July 8, 1964; admitted, 1993, Bologna, Italy. *Education:* University of Bologna (J.D.). "Cultore della Materia," in Civil Law, University of Bologna. Specalizations: Tax Law and Banking Law, University of Bologna. *Member:* Association of Young Lawyers. *PRACTICE AREAS:* Banking Law; General Civil Practice.

Italian, English, French and Swedish.

STUDIO CAGLI - ALESSANDRI

19 VIALE GOZZADINI
40124 BOLOGNA, ITALY
Telephone: 39-51-331401
Fax: 39-51-331510

Commercial Law, Intellectual Property, International Law.

MEMBERS OF FIRM

AVV. NICOLA ALESSANDRI, born Florence, Italy, November 10, 1955; admitted, 1978, Italy. *Education:* University of Florence (J.D., summa cum laude, 1978); IFOA - Reggio Emilia (International Law and Contracts, 1981); Harvard Law School (1985). Author: "Art. 17 of the Bruxelles Convention on Jurisdiction of Judgments in Civil and Commercial Matters and Enforcement and Art. 413 C.P.C.," Riv. Trim. Dir. E Proc. Civ. 1984; "Contracts and Legal Problems in the Music Business," Strum. Mus., 1986; "Copyright Protection and the Photocopy Problem in 'Contratto e Impresa'," Cedam, 1990; "Il Contratto di Agenzia nel Commercio Internazionale, UTET, 1991; "Copyright and sample copies," Il Diritto di Autore, Giuffré, 1994; "First Comments on the New Law on Photocopy," Il Diritto d i Autore, 1994; "Seizure and Injuctions against Directors of a Bankrupt Company in the Bankruptcy Proceeding and the new Civil Procedure Code," Riv. Trim, Proc. Civ in print." Voluntary Assistant, Civil Procedure, University of Bologna Faculty of Law, 1979-1982. *Member:* Bologna and International Bar Associations; Associazione Italiana per Gli Studiosi del Processo Civile. *LANGUAGES:* English, French and Italian. *PRACTICE AREAS:* Copyright; Trademark; Unfair Competition; Corporate and Commercial Law; Contracts; Private International Law; Antitrust.

AVV. BARBARA LAZIOSI, born Forli', Italy, January 24, 1955; admitted, 1980, Italy. *Education:* University of Bologna (J.D., summa cum laude, 1979). *LANGUAGES:* Italian and English. *PRACTICE AREAS:* Civil Law; Litigation.

DR. PROC. GIANLUCA UGHI, born Bologna, July 17, 1961; admitted, 1986, Italy. *Education:* University of Bologna (J.D., summa cum laude, 1985). Author: La difesa del marchio, 1991"; "Dir., CEE 86/653 la nuova normativa sugh agenti," 1993. *Member:* Bologna Bar Association; European Association of Lawyers; International Bar Association. *LANGUAGES:* English and Italian. *PRACTICE AREAS:* Commercial Law; Contracts; Private International Law.

GIULIA RONZANI, born Bologna, Italy, April 2, 1965; admitted, 1993, Italy. *Education:* University of Bologna (summa cum laude, 1990). *LANGUAGES:* Italian and English. *PRACTICE AREAS:* Copyright; Bankruptcy Law; Civil Law; Family Law.

ANNALISA LANZARINI, born Bologna, Italy, August 29, 1967; (admission pending). *Education:* University of Bologna (summa cum laude, 1991). *LANGUAGES:* Italian and English. *PRACTICE AREAS:* Corporate Law; Civil Law; Bankruptcy Law.

LUCA ENRIQUES, born Bologna, Italy, February 17, 1970; (admission pending). *Education:* University of Bologna, Faculty of Law (summa cum laude, 1993). Author: Il pegno di patrimonio oggetto di gestione mobiliare in 'Giurisprudenza commerciale', 1993. Voluntary Assistant, Commercial Law and Banking Law, University of Bologna, Faculty of Law. *LANGUAGES:* Italian, English, French and German. *PRACTICE AREAS:* Private International Law; Corporate Law; Antitrust; Copyright.

REPRESENTATIVE CLIENTS: Zanichelli Editore S.p.A.; Cedam S.p.A.; McGraw Hill Libri Italia S.r.l.; Giuffre's S.p.A.; Loescher S.p.A.; Piccin Nuova Libraria; Gazzoni 1909 S.p.A.; Tecnoform S.p.A.; Gaspare Segafredo S.p.A.; P.A.C.S. di Francesco Segafredo S.p.A.; Cariplo S.P.A.; Banco di Roma S.p.A.; Ansaloni di Edo Ansaloni; Paoloni Macchine S.p.A.; Kaeser Compressori S.r.L.

STUDIO DALLA VERITÀ

Established in 1953

Founder: Pietro Dalla Verità (1924-1982)

5, PIAZZA CALDERINI
40124 BOLOGNA, ITALY
Telephone: 51-264918; 51-264865
Telefax: 51-238788
Cable Address: "Daverlaw Bologna"
Telex: DAVE RL I 511238

Rome, Italy Office: Studio Dalla Verità-Tartaglia. 7, Via Vittorio Veneto, 00187. Telephone: 6-4883525. Telefax: 6-4740547. Telex: DAVERL I 626210. Cable Address: "Daverlaw Rome".

(This Listing Continued)

General and International Practice, Contract, Corporation, Patent, Trademark, Banking, Taxation, Litigation, Arbitration.

MEMBERS OF FIRM

FRANCO DALLA VERITÀ, born Faenza, Italy, February 10, 1935; admitted, 1960, Italy; 1975, Supreme Court of Cassation. *Education:* University of Bologna (J.D., 1959). *PRACTICE AREAS:* Contract; Corporation; Civil Litigation.

PIERGERARDO TRAMBAJOLO, born Este, Italy, September 2, 1927; admitted, 1959, Italy; 1974, Supreme Court of Cassation. *Education:* University of Bologna (J.D., 1952). *PRACTICE AREAS:* Criminal Law.

VITTORIO ZUCCONI, born Arcola, Italy, July 12, 1949; admitted, 1978, Italy. *Education:* University of Pisa (J.D., 1975). *PRACTICE AREAS:* Corporation; Patent; Trademark; Civil Litigation.

MARCO DALLA VERITÀ, born Bologna, Italy, September 11, 1957; admitted, 1984, Italy. *Education:* University of Bologna (J.D., cum laude, 1979). *PRACTICE AREAS:* Contract; Corporation; Banking; Taxation.

FEDERICO DALLA VERITÀ, born Bologna, Italy, June 6, 1961; admitted, 1989, Italy. *Education:* University of Bologna (J.D., cum laude, 1986). Assistant, Procedure Law, University of Bologna. *Member:* Italian Association for Arbitration. *PRACTICE AREAS:* Contract; International Law; Arbitration.

STEFANO DALLA VERITÀ, born Bologna, Italy, September 30, 1961; admitted, 1989, Italy. *Education:* University of Bologna (J.D., cum laude, 1986). Assistant, Trademarks and Copyrights Law, University of Bologna. *PRACTICE AREAS:* Patent; Trademark; Corporation.

TAX ADVISORS

GIORGIO DI GIORGI, born Ravenna, Italy, April 21, 1941; admitted, 1966, Italy. *Education:* University of Bologna (Doctor of Economics, 1964).

MARCO NANNI, born Bologna, Italy, September 18, 1949; admitted, 1976, Italy. *Education:* University of Bologna (Doctor of Economics, 1975).

LORENZO SALMON CINOTTI, born Pesaro, Italy, December 13, 1953; admitted, 1978, Italy. *Education:* University of Bologna (Doctor of Economics, 1977).

Languages: English, French and German.

REFERENCES: Savings Bank Association, New York; Barclays Bank International Ltd., London; Banque de La Société Financière Europeenne, Paris; Banque Paribas, Paris; Banca Nazionale Del Lavoro, Rome; Banca Commerciale Italiana, Milan; Banco di Roma, Rome; Istituto Centrale Delle Casse di Risparmio, Rome; Banco di S. Spirito, Rome; Credito Romagnolo, Bologna; G.E.P.I. - Gestioni e Partecipazioni Industriali, Rome; E.F.I.M. - Ente Partecipazioni e Finanziamenti Industriali e Manufatturieri, Rome; Finam S.p.A. - Finanziaria Agricla Del Mezzogiorno, Rome; Massey Ferguson Italia, Fabrico; Les Copains, Bologna.

STUDIO LEGALE DE CAPOA - GUIDUCCI & ASSOCIATI

VIA ALBERTAZZI 22
40137 BOLOGNA, ITALY
Telephone: (39-51) 343799; 346062; 348835
Telefax: (39-51) 344125

Brussels, Belgium Office: Square Ambirix 32, 1140. Telephone: 32-2-2308246.

Budapest, Hungary Office: Honved UT 38, 1065. Telephone: 36-1-1121683.

Milan, Italy Office: Corso Venezia 61. Telephone: 39-2-29510822. Telefax: 39-2-29510835.

Nice, France Office: 23, Rue de la Terrasse 6. Telephone: 33-9-38009232. Telexfax: 33-93806372.

Warsaw, Poland Office: Ul. Belwederska 14. Telephone: 48-22-412475. Telefax: 48-22-412475.

G.E.I.E. with the firm Spitzweg & Partners, Munchen, Germany.

Los Angeles, California Associated Office: Forward & Dix, 2049 Century Park East, Suite 1200, 90067. Telephone: 310-785-2150. Telecopier: 310-785-2099.

International and Domestic Commercial Law, General and Civil Practice, Contracts, Litigation, Arbitration, Intellectual Property, Labor, Product Liability, EEC and Tax Law, Foreign Investment,

ANTONIO DE CAPOA, born Bologna, Italy, January 18, 1955; admitted, 1982, Italy. *Education:* University of Bologna (J.D., 1980); University

(This Listing Continued)

of Barcelona (1979-1980); Advanced Course in Arbitration, College of Commerce and Tourism Milan, Italy (1989-1990); Courses in Foreign Commerce, IPSOA. Founder and Director, Promeuropa-Association for the Promotion and Development of European Culture. Former Member, Associazione Italiana Valutaristi. *Member:* European Consultants Unit; UIA; European Association of Lawyers (AEA); Giuristi Italo-Britannico; British-Italian Law Association. *LANGUAGES:* English and Spanish.

ELENA BARONI, born Ferrara, Italy, July 9, 1965; admitted, 1992, Italy. *Education:* University of Bologna (J.D., 1988); Course in Private International Law, The Hague Academy of International Law (1989); Business English for Lawyers, University of Edinburgh (1990); Course in German Law, University of Ferrara, (1990); European Young Lawyers Course, King's College, London (1991). Recipient, British Council Scholarship. Legal Assistant, Frere Cholmeley, London, 1991. *Member:* EC Lawyers' Society; European Lawyers Association. *LANGUAGES:* English, Spanish, French.

VIVIANA BONFIGLIOLI, born Bologna, Italy, October 17, 1954; admitted, 1983. *Education:* University of Bologna (J.D., 1979).

GIORGIO CARAMORI, born Castelmassa, Rovigo, Italy, February 25, 1958; admitted, 1989, Italy. *Education:* University of Ferrara (J.D., 1983); Advanced Course in Arbitration, College for Commerce and Tourism, Milan, Italy, (1989-1990).

CARLA DEGLI ESPOSTI, born Bologna, Italy, May 19, 1965. *Education:* University of Bologna (J.D., 1991).

SIMON DIX, born London, England, October 3, 1950; admitted, 1978, England; 1986, California. *Education:* Trinity College, Cambridge (B.A., 1972; M.A., 1975); University of Southern California (M.A., 1983). *Member:* Beverly Hills, Los Angeles County and American (Member, International Law Section) Bar Associations; State Bar of California. *LANGUAGES:* English, Italian and French. *PRACTICE AREAS:* International Business; Business; Entertainment.

MICHELE DRAGHETTI, born Bologna, Italy, February 24, 1961; admitted, 1990, Italy. *Education:* University of Bologna (J.D., 1985); Course in Business English, University of Edinburgh, UK (1990). Author: "Bankruptcy and the Claims of Minor Creditors," Dir. Fall., 1990-1991. *LANGUAGES:* English.

ALESSANDRA FRANCHI, born Bologna, Italy, May 16, 1966; admitted, 1993, Italy. *Education:* University of Bologna (J.D., 1990); New York University (LL.M., International Legal Studies, 1992). Recipient, Erasmus Scholarship, University of Paris, Paris II, 1989. *LANGUAGES:* English and French.

SEBASTIANO NEGRI DI MONTENEGRO, born Bologna, Italy, April 20, 1968. *Education:* University of Bologna (J.D., 1992). Assistant Lecturer, Bologna University. *LANGUAGES:* English, Spanish and Hungarian.

MICHEL ORTS, born Rouen, France, May 5, 1963; admitted, 1991, France (Not admitted in Italy). *Education:* University of Nice, France (J.D., 1987); University of Amiens (Lawyer's Aptitude Certificate, 1990). *LANGUAGES:* French, English.

DONATELLA PIZZI, born Bolzano, Italy, May 15, 1964. *Education:* University of Bologna (J.D., 1990); University of Freiburg (1985-1986); Course on Legal aspects regarding the establishment of the European Community Market, University of Bologna, 1989. *LANGUAGES:* German, English.

PIER PAOLO ZAMBONI, born Bologna, Italy, June 4, 1961; admitted, 1990, Italy. *Education:* University of Bologna (J.D., 1986; Advanced Course in Civil Law, 1988; Advance Course in Fiscal Law, 1993). *Member:* European Association of Lawyers.

Languages: Italian, English, French, German, Spanish and Hungarian.

FAZIO FRANCIA SERAFINI SOLAZZI TROMBETTI

Established in 1980

VIA DELLA ZECCA 1
BOLOGNA, ITALY
Telephone: (051) 23-69-91; Intn'l (39-51) 23-69-91
Telecopier: (Gr. III, II) (051) 22-24-86
Intn'l: (39-51) 22-24-86

Milan, Italy Associated Office: Scamoni e Associati, Via Mario Pagano 65. Telephone (02) 48-011-171. Telecopier: (02) 48-012-914.
Padua, Italy Associated Office: Rizzeri e Associati. Passeggiata del Carmine 2. Telephone: (049) 87-619-13. Telecopier: (049) 87-528-79.

General Practice, Corporation, Foreign Investments, Commercial Law, Contractual Assistance, Joint Ventures and all forms of Distribution and Franchising Agreements, Banking, EEC Law, Patent, Copyright and Intellectual Property, Bankruptcy and Labor Law, Family Law, Criminal Law, Litigation, including National and International Arbitration.

FIRM PROFILE: The firm is a member of LEGALLIANCE (EEIG), an alliance of law firms established in Paris, London, Madrid, Brussels, The Hague, Cologne, Frankfurt, Leipzig and Berlin, which offers European coordination and cooperation through a single point of contact.

MEMBERS OF FIRM

DOMENICO FAZIO, born Pergola, Italy, May 28, 1944; admitted, 1973, Italy. *Education:* University of Bologna (Doctor of Jurisprudence, 1969). *LANGUAGES:* Italian and French.

MARIO FRANCIA, born Bologna, Italy, August 19, 1943; admitted, 1973, Italy. *Education:* University of Bologna (Doctor of Jurisprudence, 1969). *LANGUAGES:* Italian and French.

GIANLUIGI SERAFINI, born Ravenna, Italy, December 9, 1957; admitted, 1984, Italy. *Education:* University of Bologna (Doctor of Jurisprudence, magna cum laude, 1980). *LANGUAGES:* Italian and English.

LUCIO SOLAZZI, born Fano, Italy, March 7, 1946; admitted, 1972, Italy. *Education:* University of Bologna (Doctor of Jurisprudence, 1969). *LANGUAGES:* Italian and French.

PAOLO TROMBETTI, born Bologna, Italy, August 20, 1945; admitted, 1974, Italy. *Education:* University of Bologna (Doctor of Jurisprudence, 1971). *LANGUAGES:* Italian, English and German.

ANNA RITA RONCUZZI, born Forlí, Italy, August 3, 1961; admitted, 1990, Italy. *Education:* University of Bologna (Doctor of Jurisprudence, magna cum laude, 1985). *LANGUAGES:* Italian and English.

ASSOCIATES

FRANCESCA CAPODIFERRO, born Bologna, Italy, September 15, 1959; admitted, 1990, Italy. *Education:* University of Bologna (Doctor of Jurisprudence, 1985). *LANGUAGES:* Italian.

MARIA FULVIA CASTELLI, born Bologna, Italy, June 18, 1963; admitted, 1991, Italy. *Education:* University of Bologna (Doctor of Jurisprudence, 1988). *LANGUAGES:* Italian, English, French and Spanish.

CARLA GALLETTI, born Ferrara, Italy, December 22, 1961; admitted, 1992, Italy. *Education:* University of Bologna (Doctor of Jurisprudence, 1989). *LANGUAGES:* Italian, English and French.

RICCARDO FRESA, born Faenza, Italy, April 19, 1964; admitted, 1993, Italy. *Education:* University of Bologna (Doctor of Jurisprudence, magna cum laude, 1989). *LANGUAGES:* Italian and English.

SILVIA FRATTESI, born Bologna, Italy, October 5, 1967; admitted, 1994, Italy. *Education:* University of Bologna (Doctor in Jurisprudence, magna cum laude, 1991). *LANGUAGES:* Italian, French, English and German.

ANTONELLA MICELE, born Bologna, Italy, February 16, 1970. *Education:* University of Bologna (Doctor of Jurisprudence, magna cum laude, 1994). *LANGUAGES:* Italian, German, French and English.

PARTNERS MILAN OFFICE

Mario Scamoni	Elena Granatello
Giovanni Ercoli	Francesco Milanese
Piero Fedi	Leila Piscopo
Marco Frazzica	

(This Listing Continued)

FAZIO FRANCIA SERAFINI SOLAZZI TROMBETTI,
Bologna—Continued

Gianluigi Puccioni

PARTNERS PADUA OFFICE

Giancarlo Rizzieri   Gianandrea Rizzieri
                Susanna Rizzieri

JACOBACCI & PERANI

VIA AURELIO SAFFI, 73/2
40131 BOLOGNA, ITALY
Telephone: 521081
Telex: 520613 Japebo I
Fax: 521038

Turin, Italy Office: Corso Regio Parco 27, 10152, P.O. Box 321, 10100
   Torino Centro. Telephone: 244031. Cable Address: "Casettaro-Torino."
   Telex: 221494 Patent I. Fax: 286300; 286676.
Milan, Italy Office: Via Visconti de Modrone 7, 20122. Telephone:
   76006884; 76020043. Telex: 335441 Japemi I. Fax: 794925.
Padua, Italy Office: Via Berchet 9, 35131. Telephone: 65.19.31; 65.01.46.
   Telex: 432321 Jacpad I. Fax: 65.16.31.

Patent, Design, Trademark and Copyright Law, Licensing, Franchising,
Unfair Competition and Contracts, EEC Law.

RESIDENT ASSOCIATES

FABIO ROVERATI. LANGUAGES: Italian, English and French.
PRACTICE AREAS: Trademark and Copyright Law; Litigation; Law of
Contracts.

PAOLO PROVVISIONATO. LANGUAGES: Italian, English and
French. **PRACTICE AREAS:** Patent and Design Law.

MARIA ELENA PIRETTI. LANGUAGES: Italian and English.
PRACTICE AREAS: Trademark and Copyright Law.

(For Complete Biographical Data and Personnel, See Professional
Biographies at Turin, Italy)

STUDIO LEGALE MORRESI

Established in 1985

VIA DANTE 19
40125 BOLOGNA, ITALY
Telephone: (051) 399 822
Telefax: (051) 393 271

Brussels, Belgium Office: The Morresi Law Office. Avenue Des Nerviens
   77, 1040. Telephone: (02) 7353410. Telefax: (02) 7354125.

FIRM PROFILE: *The firm offers a full range of legal services in the
areas of international trade and investments, European community and
intellectual property, litigation.*

Languages: *English, French and Italian.*

AVV. RENZO MARIA MORRESI, born Modigliana (FO) Italy, January 25, 1952; admitted, 1981, Italy. Education: University of Bologna (J.D.
summa cum laude, 1976); School of Advanced International Studies, The
Johns Hopkins University (M.A., International Affairs, 1977). Former
Counsel, Fiat Legal Services. Advisor, International Trade Center of the
Chamber of Commerce: Piemonte, Turin, Emilia, Romagna, Bologna, Tuscany, Florence. Author of Monographs on International Joint Ventures and
on Franchising in the EEC. (Also at Brussels Office). **LANGUAGES:** English, French and Italian. **PRACTICE AREAS:** European Community
Law; International Trade Law.

AVV. ALBERTO DAL FERRO, born Vicenza, Italy, March 9, 1955;
admitted, 1984, Italy. Education: University of Padua (J.D., 1982; Doctor
of Political Science, 1985). Formerly with Research and Documentation
Department, European Court of Justice, Luxembourg. (Resident, Brussels
Office). **LANGUAGES:** English, French and Italian. **PRACTICE AREAS:**
EEC Law.

ANDREA GATTAMORTA, born Ravenna, Italy, September 12, 1961;
admitted, 1990, Italy. Education: University of Bologna (J.D., 1987). Advisor, International Trade Center of the Chamber of Commerce: Tuscany;
Florence. **LANGUAGES:** English and Italian. **PRACTICE AREAS:** International Trade Law and Litigation.

(This Listing Continued)

MONICA MEDICI, born Rovigo, Italy, December 21, 1962; admitted,
1991, Italy. Education: University of Modena (J.D., 1988); College of Europe, Parma, Italy (Certificate of Advanced Studies in the Law, Economics
and Policy of the EEC).

MARIA LISA CRISERA, born Evanston, Illinois, October 4, 1965;
admitted, 1991, California. Education: Harvard University (A.B., magna
cum laude, 1987); University of California, Boalt Hall School of Law (J.D.,
1991). Phi Beta Kappa; Order of the Coif. **LANGUAGES:** English and
Italian. **PRACTICE AREAS:** International Business Transactions.

MASSIMILIANO BOVESI, born Imola (BO), Italy, September 21,
1967. Education: University of Bologna (J.D., magna cum laude, 1992);
Post Graduate Course of Advanced Studies in European Community Law
(1993). **LANGUAGES:** English and Italian. **PRACTICE AREAS:** Banking
and Securities Law.

   REPRESENTATIVE CLIENTS: Fiat Hitachi; Fiat New Holland; Credito Italiano;
   Montedison; Enron; Groupe Schneider; Nestlé; Ferrero; Alfa Wasserman;
   Schiapparelli; FAAC; Dolomite; Simint; La Perla Group.

BELVEDERI
ATTORNEYS AT LAW

71, VIA PALESTRO
FERRARA 44100, ITALY
Telephone: 39 532 202603-210750
Telefax: 39 532 200062

Milan Office: 5 Via Fontana, 20122 Milano. Telephone: 02-59901649.
   Telefax: 02-5462347.
Bologna Office: 6 Via degli Agresti, 40123 Bologna. Telephone:
   051-260620. Telefax: 051-221619.

*International Litigation, Commercial and Company Law, Serious Fraud,
Anti-Counterfeiting, Asset Recovery, Taxation and Comparative Conflict of
Laws.*

LUIGI BELVEDERI, born 1950; admitted, 1978. Education: University
of Ferrara, Italy (1973); University College, University of London, England
(LL.M., 1975). Professor of EEC Company Law, Universities of Cagliari
and Parma (1984-1988). Hor. Consul for South Africa in Bologna.

RITA REALI, born 1959; admitted, 1989.

RAFFAELLA PRENDIN, born 1963; admitted, 1994.

RICCARDO ZIOSI, born 1962; admitted, 1994.

OF COUNSEL

DR. K.V.S.K. NATHAN, (Not admitted in Italy). PhD., born, 1928,
Barrister at Law, England (1971).

ANDREA ALBERGHINI, born 1958. Certified Public Accountant
(1983). (Resident, Bologna Office).

STUDIO CONTRI

Chambers of Attorneys and Counsellors at Law

Established in 1902

VIA G. PICO DELLA MIRANDOLA, 9
50132 FLORENCE, ITALY
Telephone: (055) 579259; 578005
Cable Address: Studiolex Firenze
Telefax: (055) 578605

*General Civil Practice, International Trade and Contracts, Corporation
and Real Estate Law, Mergers and Acquisitions.*

FIRM PROFILE: *Studio Contri consists of a group of Italian lawyers as
well as a U.S. Attorney practicing both individually and jointly in various
areas of law, inclusive of international transactions.*

GIUSEPPE CONTRI, born Florence, Italy, December 12, 1913; admitted, 1947, Italy; 1955, Italian Supreme Court. Education: University of
Florence (LL.D.). O.B.E. Member: International Association of Jurists It-
aly-U.S.A.; Union Internationale Des Avocats. **LANGUAGES:** Italian,
English and French. **PRACTICE AREAS:** Real Estate Law.

LAPO PUCCINI, born Florence, Italy, June 10, 1921; admitted, 1948,
Italy; 1953 Italian Supreme Court. Education: University of Florence (De-
gree in Law). Author: "Contributo allo studio dell'accertamento privato,"
Milan, 1958; "Studi sulla nullità relativa," Milan, 1967; "Il dolo civile," Mi-

(This Listing Continued)

lan, 1970; "Contributo allo studio della simulazione nel matrimonio civile ," (art. 123 c.c.) Milan, 1980. Professor of Law, University of Florence, 1950-1994. *LANGUAGES:* Italian. *PRACTICE AREAS:* Supreme Court Litigation.

LORENZO CONTRI, born Florence, Italy, January 27, 1948; admitted, 1975, Italy; 1993, Italian Supreme Court. *Education:* University of Florence (LL.D.). Certificate of Achievement: Colombia Summer Program in American Law, Leyden, Amsterdam. *LANGUAGES:* Italian and English. *PRACTICE AREAS:* Commercial and Corporate Law; Mergers and Acquisitions.

BEATRICE PAZZAGLIA, born Genova, Italy, August 4, 1953; admitted, 1978, Italy. *Education:* University of Florence (LL.D.). *LANGUAGES:* Italian. *PRACTICE AREAS:* Family Law.

ANDREA L. DAVIS, born Boston, Massachusetts, October 25, 1954; admitted, 1979, Massachusetts (Not admitted in Italy). *Education:* Wellesley College (B.A., summa cum laude, 1976); Harvard Law School (J.D., 1979). Phi Beta Kappa. *Member:* American and International Bar Associations. *LANGUAGES:* English and Italian. *PRACTICE AREAS:* Mergers and Acquisitions; International Contracts.

SONJA KOFLER, born Bolzano, Italy, July 24, 1964. *Education:* University of Florence (LL.B., 1990). *LANGUAGES:* German, Italian, English and French.

Honorary Legal Adviser to H. M. British Consulate.

REPRESENTATIVE CLIENTS: Super Rifle S.p.A., Florence, Italy; Editoriale Olimpia S.p.A., Florence, Italy; Sta-Rite Industries, Inc., Milwaukee, Wisconsin; Peter Black International Ltd., London, England; Minet Group, London, England.

INTERNATIONAL LAW STUDIO
AVV. VINCENT E. LUALDI

Established in 1985

PIAZZA INDIPENDENZA, 21
50129 FLORENCE, ITALY
Telephone: +39 55 480055
Telefax: +39 55 471242

European Consultants:
Germany:
Berlin: Susanne Schaeff, Treskowallee 108, 10318. Telephone +49 5 080251. Fax: +49 5 080253.
International Consultants:
U.S.A.:
Atlanta, Georgia: Alston & Bird, 1201 West Peachtree Street, 30309-3424. TelephoneL +1 404 881 7000. Fax: +1 404 881 7777.
New York, N.Y.: Esterman & Reich, Counsellors at Law, 595 Madison Avenue., 10022. Telephone: +1 212 755 4152. Fax: +1 212 751 2532.
Chicago, Illinois: Hopkins & Sutter, Three First National Plaza, 60602. Telephone: +1 312 558 6600. Fax: +1 312 558 6538.
Brazil:
Rio de Janeiro-RJ: Luiz Bernardo Rocha Gomide, Av. Marechal Camara, 271-9° Andar, 20020-080-Centro. Telephone: +55 21 532 1311. Fax: +55 21 262 8765.
Venezuela:
Caracas: D'Empaire Reyna Bermudez y Asociados, 1ra. Transversal Los Palos Grandes, Centro Plaza, Torre D Nivel 19, Apartado Postal 60973, 1062-A.

Arbitration and Mediation, At Law, Bankruptcy, Biotechnology, Business Law, Civil Law, Company Law, Consumer Law, Contracts, Copyrights, Corporate Law, Criminal Law, Entertainment and the Arts, Environmental Law, European Community Law, Family Law, Medical Malpractice, Mergers, Acquisitions and Divestitures, Patents, Personal Injury, Probate, Products Liability, Property, Real Estate, Trusts and Estate, White Collar Crime, Wills.

FIRM PROFILE: *The Studio was established in 1985 following the experience gathered in the legal offices of Italian multinational operating Italian companies. Joint ventures in the Ukraine and Russia; inheritance, liability refunds and family law in the U.S.A.; industrial product liability in Australia; a Florence based foundation in association with the most important photography manufacturer in the world, and contracts for the construction of a major amusement park in Paris, France, are some of the major projects dealt with.*

(This Listing Continued)

Specialized legal support of colleagues, engineers, accountants, etc. cooperating in the same premises add to the professional standing of all operations.

AVV. VINCENT E. LUALDI, born Haverhill, Massachusetts, December 8, 1949; admitted, 1982, Florence. *Education:* University of Florence, Faculty of Law (Doctor of Jurisprudence, 1981). With, Recordati S.p.a. in Milano, 1982-1983 and S.I.E.T.T.E. in Florence, 1983-1984. *Member:* Florence Bar Association. *LANGUAGES:* English, Italian, French and German. *PRACTICE AREAS:* Arbitration and Mediation; Art Law; Bankruptcy; Biotechnology; Business Law; Civil Law; Company Law; Computers and Software; Consumer Law; Contracts; Copyrights; Corporate Law; Criminal Law; Entertainment and the Arts; Environmental Law; Family Law; Medical Malpractice; Mergers, Acquisitions and Divestitures; Patents; Personal Injury; Probate; Products Liability; Property; Real Estate; Trusts and Estates; White Collar Crime; Wills.

LEGAL SUPPORT PERSONNEL

DR. CARLOTTA BARBETTI, born Florence, Italy, June 22, 1964. *Education:* University of Florence, Faculty of Law (Doctor of Jurisprudence, 1991). Company Legal Consultant. *LANGUAGES:* Italian, English and French. *PRACTICE AREAS:* Civil Law; Consumer Law; Family Law,; Insurance; International Law; Liquidations and Workouts; Medical Malpractice; Personal Injury; Probate; Professional Liability; Property; Real Estate; Trusts and Estates; White Collar Crime.

DR. GIOVANNI DEL BENE, born Pistoia, Italy, April 13, 1964. *Education:* University of Pisa, Faculty of Law (Doctor of Jurisprudence, 1990); European College of Parma (Master in European Community Law, 1991); European Community Commission (Stage, 1991). *LANGUAGES:* Italian, French, English and German. *PRACTICE AREAS:* Civil Law; Common Market Law; Consumer Law; European Community Law; International Law; Products Liabilty.

BEATRICE GAGGIOLI, born Florence, Italy, October 19, 1971. *Education:* Perito per il Turismo, 1990. *LANGUAGES:* Italian, English and French. *PRACTICE AREAS:* General Contacts with Courts; Translations.

PATRICIA BAILEYS, born Atlanta, Georgia, August 19, 1962; admitted, 1989, California (Not admitted in Italy). *Education:* George Institute of Technology (B.A., Management, cum laude, 1984); University of San Diego School of Law (J.D., 1988); Europa Institute of the University of Amsterdam (LL.M., European Business Law, 1993); European University Institute (Ph.D. candidate, Fulbright Scholar). *Member:* American Bar Association. *LANGUAGES:* English and French.

STUDIO LEGALE MASTELLONE & ASSOCIATES

Established in 1983

VIA DELL'ORIUOLO, 45
50122 FLORENCE, ITALY
Telephone: (055) 282074-282518
Fax: (055) 282718 (G. 2 & 3)

Milan, Italy Associated Office: Studio Legale Pellegrini-Cislaghi. Via Nerino 8, 20121.

General Practice. Civil, Corporate and Commercial Law, Contracts, Real Estate, and Family Law, International Business Law, Insurance, Transportation.

CARLO H. MASTELLONE, born London, England, March 2, 1955; admitted, 1983, Italy. *Education:* University of Florence, Italy (Degree in Laws, Hons., 1978); Queen Mary College, University of London, England (LL.M., 1979). Research Fellow, European University Institute, Florence, 1983-1986. Author: "Prime Sentenze della Corte Comunitaria in Materia di Ambiente", Rivista di diritto Internazionale Privato e Processuale, p. 364 et seq., 1980; "The External Relations of the EEC in the Field of Environmental Protection", International & Comparative Law Quarterly, p. 104 et seq., 1981; "The Judicial Application of Community Law in Italy: 1976-1980" Common Market Law Review, p. 163 et seq., 1982; "Sul Principio Comunitario della Libera Circolazione dei Capitali", Rivista di Diritto Internazionale, p. 851 et seq., 1982; "Annotation to European Court of Justice Cases 266/81 and Joined Cases 267-269/81", Common Market Law Review, p. 559 et seq., 1983; "Know-how e Contratti di Know-how: Uno Studio Comparato", Rivista Valutaria e di Economia Internazionale, p. 407 et seq., 1986; "Short Outline of the New Italian Anti-trust Statute," European

(This Listing Continued)

STUDIO LEGALE MASTELLONE & ASSOCIATES,
Florence—Continued

Business Law Review, February 1991; "The New Italian Act on the Taxation of Capital Gains," European Business Law Review, July 1991; "Representative Offices: Direct Presence of Foreign Companies in Italy," Comparative Law Yearbook of International Business, p. 13 et seq., Vol 13, 1991. "New Italian Anti-Avoidance Measures: Tax Havens Black listed," European Business Law Review, July 1992; "Protections and Remedies in Italy for Foreign Sellers of Goods," (Sweet & Maxwell) 1993. *Member:* Florence Bar Association; British Institute of International and Comparative Law, London; Young Lawyers' International Association (A.I.J.A.); Licensing Executives Society (L.E.S. Italia); International Bar Association; EU-LEX International Practice Group. *LANGUAGES:* English, Italian and French.

Languages: Italian, English and French.

STUDIO LEGALE
AVV. F. OLIVIERI & PARTNERS

Established in 1980

Attorneys and Counsellors at Law

VIA FERDINANDO BARTOLOMMEI, 4
50129 FLORENCE, ITALY
Telephone: (055) 47 30 06
Telefax: (055) 47 30 49

General Civil Practice, International Trade and Contracts, Corporation and Real Estate Law, Mergers and Acquisitions, International Fiscal Law, Contracts and Foreign Investments, Arbitrations.

FIRM PROFILE: Studio Olivieri consist of a group of Italian and European Lawyers practicing both individually and jointly in various aspects of law, inclusive of international transactions.

Specialized legal support of colleagues, engineers, accountants, etc. cooperating in the same premises add to the professional standing of all operations. The firm is also the Legal Adviser to the French Consulate.

FRANCESCO OLIVIERI, born Milan, Italy, August 22, 1951; admitted, 1980, Italy. *Education:* University of Florence (J.D.). Member, Camera Arbitrale di Carrara. Legal Adviser: French Consulate of Florence; Consul of Grand Duchy of Luxembourg. *Member:* A.I.J.A.; U.A.E. Avocat au Barreau de Bruxelles. *LANGUAGES:* Italian, French and English. *PRACTICE AREAS:* International Fiscal Law; Arbitrations.

PAOLO ROSINI, born Carrara, Italy, January 13, 1962. *Education:* University of Florence, Faculty of Law (J.D.). *LANGUAGES:* Italian and English. *PRACTICE AREAS:* Commercial and Corporate Law; Litigation; International Contracts.

MANUELA TRALDI, born Rome, Italy, July 22, 1967. *Education:* University of Rome La Sapienza, Faculty of Law (J.D.); City of London Polytechnic (English Law). *Member:* British Italian Law Association. *LANGUAGES:* Italian, English, Portuguese and French. *PRACTICE AREAS:* Civil Law; Company and Commercial Law; Litigation.

CONSULTANTS

NURIA CALAFELL-GARRIGOSA, admitted, 1985, Barcelona; 1990, Malaró. *Member:* Barcelona Bar Association; Malaró Bar Association. *LANGUAGES:* Spanish, French, Italian and English. *PRACTICE AREAS:* Civil and Commercial Law.

THOMAS FRITZ, admitted, 1982, Münich. *LANGUAGES:* German, French, English and Italian. *PRACTICE AREAS:* Economic Law.

LAURENT MOSAR, admitted, 1983, Luxembourg. *LANGUAGES:* French, English and German. *PRACTICE AREAS:* Fiscal and Commercial International Law.

Languages: Italian, French, English, German, Spanish and Portuguese

STUDIO LEGALE BONELLI E ASSOCIATI

VIALE PADRE SANTO, 5/8
16122 GENOA, ITALY
Telephone: (10) 831-8341
Telefax: (10) 813-849; 831-0953
Telex: 271583 FRABO I

Milan, Italy Office: Via Borgonuovo, 12, 20121. Telephone: (2) 655-4499. Telefax: (2) 655-4554. Telex: 271583 FRABO I.

General Practice, International and Commercial Practice, Corporate Law, Commercial Law, Mergers and Acquisitions, Contracts, Construction Law, Banking, Antitrust, Securities Regulation, Trademark and Patent, Bankruptcy, Admiralty and Arbitration.

RESIDENT PERSONNEL

Franco Bonelli	Andrea Pericu
Giovanni Domenichini	(Not admitted in Italy)
Marco Arato	Riccardo Pontremoli
Silvia Porta	(Not admitted in Italy)
Giambattista D'Aste	Francesco Stella
Andrea Bettini	(Not admitted in Italy)
Ernesto Pugliese	Marcello Luly
Lucia Radicioni	(Not admitted in Italy)
Giuseppe Marvulli	Fulvio Marvulli
Vittorio Allavena	(Not admitted in Italy)
Vittorio Lupoli	Enrico Bazzano
Mario Olivieri	(Not admitted in Italy)
Amerigo Perasso	Paolo Bertoni
	(Not admitted in Italy)

Languages: Italian, English, French, German and Spanish.

(For Biographical Data on all Personnel, see Professional Biographies at Milan, Italy).

STUDIO AVV. ALBERTO CASTAGNOLI

CORSO ANDREA PODESTÁ, 11/8
16128 GENOA, ITALY
Telephone: 590.700
Cable Address: "Interlawoffice"
Telex (public): 270060 PPGE N. 871 INTERLAWOFFICE
Telefax: 5533113

Milan, Italy Office: Via Guastalla, 15. Telephone: 5456755 (Studio Danovi). Cable Address: "Interlawoffice".

General International Law Practice. Civil, Commercial, Corporation, Admiralty. Foreign Investments, Foreign Loans and Financings. Oil Law. Antitrust and Common Market Law.

ALBERTO CASTAGNOLI, born Rimini, Italy, May 29, 1929; admitted, 1955, Italy, all Courts. *Education:* University of Genoa (Doctor of Law, 1954); London University, University College, England (Academic Postgraduate Diploma in Law, 1959); City of London College, England (Certificate of English and Comparative Law, first class distinction, 1959); University of Milan (Certificate of Nuclear Law, 1962); University of Paris, France (1962). Author: Thesis, "The Excepted Perils under the Carriage of Goods by Sea Act, 1924," London, University College, 1959. *Member:* Genoa Bar Association; International Law Association; International Nuclear Law Association; London Institute of World Affairs; American Association of International Law; The Association of the Bar of the City of New York; The British Institute of International and Comparative Law; World Peace Through Law Center; International Bar Association. Honorary Legal Adviser to the British Chamber of Commerce for Italy-Genoa. *LANGUAGES:* Italian, English and French. *PRACTICE AREAS:* General International Practice; Conflict of Laws; European Community Law; Project Financing; Maritime Law; Investment Law.

ASSOCIATE

Giacomo Bonavera

DOBSON & PINCI

VIA GARIBALDI 7, 2ND FLOOR
16124 GENOA, ITALY
Telephone: (39) (10) 206-851
Telefax: (39) (10) 202-738 E-Mail: 7222681@mcimail.com.

Milan, Italy Office: Via Santa Radegonda, 16, 20121. Telephone: (39) (2) 809816; 8056780. Telefax: (39) (2) 86464548; 86464601. E-Mail: 7232679@mcimail.com.

Rome, Italy Office: Via Panama 74, Int. 9, 00198. Telephone: (39) (6) 841-1611. Telefax: (39) (6) 841-1145. E-Mail: 7212680@mcimail.com

New York, New York Office: Manhattan Tower, 12th Floor, 600 Lexington Avenue, 10022-6018. Telephone: (212) 308-4440. Telefax: (212) 888-3839. E-Mail: 7262685@mcimail.com.

London, England Office: 1 Throgmorton Avenue, EC2N 2JJ. Telephone: (44) (171) 628-8163. Telefax: (44) (171) 920-0861. E-Mail: 7232682@mcimail.com.

Brussels, Belgium Office: Avenue Louise, 216, 1050. Telephone: (32) (2) 647-0700. Telefax: (32) (2) 647-6440. E-Mail: 7242683@mcimail.com.

Athens, Greece Office: 6 Yperidou Street, 105 58. Telephone: (30) (1) 324-3272. Telefax: (30) (1) 322-9329. E-Mail: 7252684@mcimail.com.

Atlanta, Georgia Office: 1776 Resurgens Plaza, 945 East Paces Ferry Road, N.E., 30326. Telephone: (404) 262-5680. Telefax: (404) 262-5699. E-Mail: 7272686@mcimail.com.

San Diego, California Office: 1629 Columbia Street, 92101. Telephone: (619) 236-1310. Telefax: (619) 239-1208. E-Mail: 7282687@mcimail.com.

Miami, Florida Office: 701 Brickell Avenue, Suite 2000, 33131. Telephone: (305) 579-0012. Telefax: (305) 375-8075; 579-4722. E-Mail: 7292688@mcimail.com.

Corporate, Banking and Securities Law with emphasis on Mergers and Acquisitions, Insurance, International Financial Transactions, Litigation, Arbitration, Employment Law, Debt Collection, Bankruptcy, Foreign Investments, Privatizations, Subsidiaries and Joint Ventures, Taxation, EU/-Common Market Law, Antitrust, Environmental Law, Transportation, Shipping, Licensing, Fashion and Textiles, Franchising, Commercial Real Estate (Investment, Structuring, Development, Retail), Project Finance, Computer, Software and Telecommunications Law, Agency and Distribution, Energy (Production, Operations, and Transmission), Food and Drug, Commodities, Visa/Immigration, Wills and Estates, Sports Law, Broadcasting, Motion Picture, TV, Video, Intellectual Property and General Entertainment Law.

FIRM PROFILE: Dobson & Pinci is an international law firm based in Europe and the United States that is staffed with both American and European attorneys. Of the small number of such firms, Dobson & Pinci holds a unique position because the firm's European offices are situated in Milan, Rome, Genoa, London, Brussels and Athens, thereby enabling the firm to serve clients conveniently and efficiently in both Northern and Southern Europe. The U.S. offices in New York, Atlanta, Miami and San Diego are placed in major U.S. cities to provide full support to the overall practice network. Each office is staffed by attorneys qualified to appear and litigate in the local courts.

MEMBERS OF FIRM

FABIO G. MONTIN, born Paderno Dugnano, Italy, July 29, 1964; admitted, 1990, Italy. *Education:* Università Cattolica del S.Cuore, Milan (J.D., 1989). General Counsel, Recordati (Pharmaceuticals) S.p.A., 1992-1993. Author: "Chiarimenti sulla Rielaborazione dell'Etichettatura dei Prodotti in Conformità con le Nuove Regolamentazione dell'FDA" (Food and Drug Administration), Milan, 1994; "Uso del Computer e Tutela Penale: i Computer Crimes e la Tutela del Software," (Università Cattolica, 1989); "Development and Investment Opportunities for Commercial Centers in Italy," NACORE Conference (December, 1994). Conference: MIAD - "Prodotti Dolciari Italiana: Avere Successo nel Mercato U.S.A., "Milan, May 1994. *Member:* International Bar Association. (Also at Milan Office).

ASSOCIATES

SANDRA MORI, born Pisa, Italy, June 2, 1964; admitted, 1993, Italy. *Education:* Università degli Studi, Pisa (J.D., 1988). Visiting Scholar, Yale Law School, 1993-1994. Co-Author: "General Procedures for an Employee Transferred from the United States to Obtain Permission to Work in Italy," October, 1994; "Franchising in Italy," September, 1994. *Member:* International Bar Association. (Also at Milan Office).

(This Listing Continued)

COUNSEL

FRANCO DI LEO, born Bergamo, Italy, March 4, 1933; admitted, 1961, Genoa. *Education:* University of Genoa (LL.D., 1956). Assistant Professor, International Law, University of Genoa, 1968—.

ALESSANDRO MORINI, born San Paolo, Brazil, April 30, 1963; admitted, 1991, Genoa. *Education:* University of Genoa (LL.D., 1987). Professor, Securities Regulation, University of Bergamo, 1994—.

CLAUDIO MOLISANI, born Genoa, Italy, March 18, 1949; admitted, 1978, Genoa. *Education:* University of Genoa (LL.D., 1974).

Languages: English, Italian, French, Greek, German, Spanish, Japanese and Russian

(For Complete Biographical Data on all Personnel and List of Representative Clients, see Biographical card at Milan, Italy)

STUDIO LEGALE MEDINA-BOSIO-SIDERI

VIA S. SEBASTIANO 15
16123 GENOA, ITALY
Telephone: 010 / 561331; 581017
Fax: 5531302

General Practice, Conflicts, Corporation, Labor Relations, International and Admiralty Law.

MEMBERS OF FIRM

MASSIMO MEDINA, born Genoa, Italy, November 18, 1906; admitted, 1933, Italy. *Education:* University of Genoa (Doctor of Jurisprudence, 1928). *Member:* International Law Association. **LANGUAGES:** Italian, English, German and French. **PRACTICE AREAS:** General Practice.

CORRADO MEDINA, born Genoa, Italy, October 1, 1935; admitted, 1961, Italy. *Education:* University of Genoa (Doctor of Jurisprudence, 1958). Associate Professor in Admiralty and Air Law, University of Genoa, 1981—. *LANGUAGES:* Italian, English, French and Swedish. **PRACTICE AREAS:** International and Maritime-Air Law.

GUIDO SIDERI, born Genoa, Italy, September 5, 1940; admitted, 1967, Italy. *Education:* University of Genoa (Doctor of Jurisprudence, 1964). Assistant Professor in Industrial Law, University of Genoa, 1965—. *LANGUAGES:* Italian and German. **PRACTICE AREAS:** Corporation Law.

CESARE BOSIO, born Genoa, Italy, January 16, 1946; admitted, 1972, Italy. *Education:* University of Genoa (Doctor of Jurisprudence, 1969). *LANGUAGES:* Italian, French and English. **PRACTICE AREAS:** Labour Law.

CARLA PARODI, born Genova, November 26, 1945; admitted, 1972, Italy. *Education:* Genova University (Doctor of Jurisprudence, 1969). *LANGUAGES:* French.

Languages: Italian, English, German, French and Swedish.

LAW FIRM NAVARRA

VIA ASSAROTTI 13/8
16122 GENOA, ITALY
Telephone: (+39-10) 88 93 96
Telefax: (+39-10) 831 82 39
Telex: PP GENOVA 270060 I FOR NAVARLAW Telegraph: NAVARLAW GENOVA

Offices also in New York, Miami, Nice.

International Practice, Conflict of Laws, General International Trade Law, Civil Litigation, Corporate, Capital Investments, European Community and Anti-Trust Law, International Banking and Business Law, Bankruptcy Law, Family Law, Joint Ventures, Arbitration, Admiralty Law (Civil, Customs Probate Surrogate and Criminal procedures), Customs Law, Real Estate, Surrogate, Probate.

MEMBERS OF FIRM

MARINA NAVARRA, born Pesaro, Italy, October 7, 1946; admitted, 1972, Italy, all Courts, Supreme Court. *Education:* Baccalaureat Lycee Francais Bruxelles (1963); Baccalaureat de Philosophie (1964); University of Genoa (Doctor of Law, 1969). Cleary, Gottlieb, Steen & Hamilton Alummni, 1974. Legal Adviser, American Consulate General, Genoa and Milan, Italy. *Member:* Genoa Bar Association; Association of the Bar of the City of New York (Non resident member, 1974); CCBE Europeen Avocats, 1980; Cavaliere Italian Republic, 1983; International Bar Association;

(This Listing Continued)

LAW FIRM NAVARRA, Genoa—Continued

Union Internationale Avocats; International Association of Women Jurists Italy; Union des Avocats Euopéens; International Secretary Columbus Committee Italy of International Association of Jurists Italy-U.S.A.; Association Internationale des Droits de l'Homme; International Association Italy-Israel; International Association Ligurians in the Worlds (Italian Board Director); Propeller International Club (Italian Board of Directors); Association Italy-China.

ASSOCIATES

Marco Iurilli (Legal Adviser,   **Stefano De Marco**
   German Consulate, Genoa)   **Alessandro Turco**
Maria Mellano   **Samanta Librio**

LEGAL SUPPORT PERSONNEL

Piera Castelli Roberi (Paralegal)

Languages: Italian, English, French, German and Spanish, knowledge of Dutch.

REPRESENTATIVE CLIENTS: Banca Carige S.p.a. - B.N.A.- Banca Popolare di Bergamo-Compagnie De Navigation U.I.M.-Groupe Worms.
FOREIGN CORPORATIONS: ex. China Venturetech Investment Corp.; Swedish Oxelosunds Hamn AB; Sterling Services - Cannes (France).

STUDIO LEGALE RICCOMAGNO

Established in 1983

VIA ASSAROTTI, 4
16122 GENOA, ITALY
Telephone: (10) 8392385 / 8391095
Telex: 282860 MARIUS I.
Fax: (10) 873146

International and General Practice including: Shipping and Transportation Law, Conflicts, Finance, Corporations, Commerce, International Sales, Litigations, Arbitrations, Counselling in International Commercial Transactions.

FIRM PROFILE: Studio Legale Riccomagno has had since the beginning a strong orientation towards International Practice, Transportation and Commercial law. The firm has preferred relation with other firms in the countries of the Western World and it is member of the cross border network IAG International.

MARIO RICCOMAGNO, born Genoa, Italy, July 13, 1948; admitted, 1974, Italy; 1989, Supreme Court. *Education:* Catholic University of Milan (J.D., 1972); State University of Milan, Department of Private International Law (Post Graduate Research Fellow, 1972-1976); City of London Polytechnic (diplome in London, 1972); Parker School, Columbia University (diplome in New York, 1980). Co-Author: "Code of International Conventions," Milan, 1977. Author: "The Taxation of the Royalties of Foreign Enterprises in Italy," published in Gazzettino Tributario, 1979; Articles regarding transportation law, published monthly in "Trasporti Internazionali," February, 1982 - September, 1984; "Recognition and Enforcement of Foreign Arbitral Awards in Italy under the New York Convention of 1958," published in the Year Book Maritime Law, 1984; "Leading Italian Maritime Cases from 1980 to 1987," published in European Transport Law, 1988; "Note sulla Straight Bill of Lading," published in Il Diritto Marittimo, 1989; "Force Majeure and Supervening Circumstances - Italy," published in IAG International Newsletter, 1990; "Recenti modifiche in USA alla legislazione sul Non Vessel Operating Common Carrier," and " Il Cabotaggio nel Mediterraneo e la politica comunitaria," both published in Il Diritto Marittimo, 1991; "La Corte di Giustiziá CEE e la Disciplina Italiana del Lavoro Portuale," published in iL Foro Padano, 1992; "Cabotage andthe Liberalization in the E.C. of the Maritime Service Sector," published in European Transport Law, 1993. Arbitrator: Camera Arbitrale Maritime di Genova; Chambre Arbitrale Maritime de Monaco; European International Constructors (Wiesbaden); Wipo Arbitration Center. *Member:* Italian Bar Association; International Bar Association (Council Member of SBL); International Law Association; American Foreign Law Association; Associazione Italiana di Diritto Marittimo; A.C.I. Arb; London Maritime Arbitration Association (Supporting Member); The Mediterranean and Middle East Institute of Arbitration; The Mediterranean Maritime Arbitration Association (Secretary General); European Maritime Law Organization (Director); Columbia Law School Alumni Association. *LANGUAGES:* English and French.

(This Listing Continued)

FRANCA GALANTI RICCOMAGNO, born Milan, Italy, July 31, 1950; admitted, 1976, Italy; 1991, Supreme Court. *Education:* University of Milan (J.D., 1973). *LANGUAGES:* French and English. *PRACTICE AREAS:* Litigation; Administrative Law; Probate; Wills; Real Estate Law.

ENRICO SALA, born Milan, Italy, April 28, 1964; admitted, 1993. *Education:* University of Genoa (1989). *LANGUAGES:* English. *PRACTICE AREAS:* Litigation; Commercial Law.

ANDREA SALESI, born Genoa, Italy, January 7, 1969. *Education:* University of Genoa (J.D., summa cum laude, 1992). *LANGUAGES:* English. *PRACTICE AREAS:* Commercial Law; Litigation.

STUDIO LEGALE VINCENZINI

52 SCALI D'AZEGLIO
57100 LEGHORN, ITALY
Telephone: 586-897121
Telex: 501825 Vinlex I
Telecopier: 586-894474/893494

Milan, Italy Office: Via Borgonuovo, N° 5, 20121. Telephone: 02-86461426. Telefax: 02-86461426.
Rome, Italy Office: Via Sant'Andrea delle Fratte, 00187. Telephone: 06-6990490 Telefax: 06-6793517

Admiralty, Commercial, International and Common Market Law.

AVV. ENRICO VINCENZINI, born Livorno, Italy, August 23, 1934; admitted, 1959, Italy; 1974, Italian Supreme Court. *Education:* University of Pisa Law School, 1956. Assistant Professor of Admiralty Law, University of Pisa, 1958-1968. *Member:* Italian Bar Association; Italian Association of Admiralty Law; International Maritime Committee (Titular Member).

AVV. GIORGIO VINCENZINI, born Livorno, Italy, January 25, 1939; admitted, 1967, Italy. *Education:* University of Pisa Law School, 1964; University College of London, 1966. *Member:* Italian Bar Association; Italian Association of Admiralty Law.

AVV. LUCIANO CANEPA, born Zara, Italy, May 5, 1942; admitted, 1969, Italy. *Education:* University of Pisa Law School, 1966. *Member:* Italian Bar Association; Italian Association of Admiralty Law.

AVV. NINO SACCA, born Livorno, October 29, 1951; admitted, 1985, Italy. *Education:* University of Pisa Law School (1977). Honorary Assistant Professor of Admiralty Law, University of Pisa, 1988. *Member:* Italian Bar Association; Italian Association of Admiralty Law.

DOTT. UGO VINCENZINI, born Livorno, October 31, 1961; admitted, 1991, Italy. *Education:* University of Camerino Law School (1990). *Member:* Italian Association of Admiralty Law.

Languages: English, French and Spanish.

REPRESENTATIVE CLIENTS AND REFERENCE: *U.K.:* The United Kingdom Mutual Steamship Assurance Assn.; The Steamship Mutual Underwriting Assn. Ltd.; The Standard Steamship Owners P. and I. Assn. Ltd.; The Britannia Steamship Insurance Assn. Ltd.; The North of England P. and I. Assn. Ltd.; The Sunderland Steamship P. and I. Association; The West of England Shipowners Mutual Insurance Assn. Ltd. *France:* Fra huil SA Marseille; Comitè Des Assureurs Maritime Paris; Societè Navale Chargeurs Delmas Vieljeux Marseille. *Algerie:* Companie Navigation Algerienme. *W. Germany:* Verein Hamburger Assecuradeure Hamburg. *Bulgary:* Navibulgar Sofia. *Italy:* Soc. F.lli Neri Salvataggi S.p.A. Livorno; G. D'Alesio s.a.s. Livorno; Augustea Salvage S.p.A.; S.G.S. Livorno; Gruppo Ferruzzi Ravenna; Rimorchiatori Spezzini La Spezia; Rimorchiatori Laziali Civitavecchia; Societa Esercizio Rimorchi e Salvataggi; Ravenna. *Switzerland:* Keller Shipping Co. Basel; Banca della Svizzera Italiana Lugano; Banca del Gottardo, NL; Smit Tak BV Rotterdam; Nedlloyd's Rotterdam. *U.S.A.:* Haight Gardner Poor and Havens New York; Phelps, Dunbar, Marks, Claverie and Sims New Orleans; De Orchis & Partners, New York.

STUDIO Dell'AVVOCATO ERNESTO FIORILLO

VIA CAVOUR 143
98100 MESSINA (SICILY), ITALY
Telephone: (090) 362 548
Telecopier: (90) 362.602

Palermo (Sicily), Italy Office: Viale Campania 25. Telephone: (91) 520.230.

(This Listing Continued)

Rome, Italy Office: Via Piemonte, 32. Telephone: (06) 462.827. (06) 47. 58. 216. Fax: (06) 4820970.

Milan, Italy Office: Piazza Duomo-Passaggio Duomo, 2, 2 0123. Telephone: (02) 720 047 58. Telecopier: (02) 864 654 65.

General Civil Practice. Corporate, Family, Insurance, Foreign Investment and Banking Law. Import-Export. Maritime Law.

AVV. ERNESTO W. FIORILLO, born July 22, 1951; admitted, 1976, Italy; 1982, Superior Court. *Education:* Liceo "G. Seguenza", Messina (A.B., 1969); University of Messina, School of Jurisprudence (LL.D., 1974). Assistant, Messina University, 1974-1976. Research Assistant in International, Sociological, Penal and Penitentiary Research and Study Center, Messina, 1977-1978. Trustee, Bankruptcy, named by Messina's Court, 1979-1985. Member: International Sociological Penal and Penitentiary Research and Study Centre of Messina; Centro Studi di Dirit to del Lavoro di Messina; Rotaract International Club (Rotary's Junior) Chapter of Messina; Jaycees International, Chapter of Messina; Centro Studi Diritto Del Lavoro, Reggio Calabria. *Member:* Bar Association of Messina; A.I.J.A.

Languages: Italian, English, French and Spanish.

REFERENCES: Banca Agricola Etnea, Piazza Nettuno, 40, Catania; Banca Popolare Sicilinana, Cia XXVII Luglio, Messina; Cassa Mutua per gli Artigiani; Via dei Mille, 101; Messina Montedison USA (Vice-President), 1142 Avenue of Americas, New York, N.Y.; Sclavo Co. (President), Wayne, New Jersey.

STUDIO LEGALE ABBATESCIANNI

Associazione Professionale

CORSO DI PORTA VITTORIA 28
20122 MILAN, ITALY
Telephone: (39-2) 55.18.31.48
Fax: (39-2) 55.01.48.30
Telex: 335170 MILEX I

International General Practice, Corporate, Mergers and Acquisitions, Distribution, Banking and Finance, E.E.C. and Antitrust Law, Litigation, Arbitration, Copyright, Entertainment and Music Law.

MEMBERS OF FIRM

GIROLAMO ABBATESCIANNI, born Bari, Italy, April 17, 1955; admitted, 1983, Milan. *Education:* State University of Milan (Doctor in Political Sciences, magna cum laude, 1977; J.D., magna cum laude, 1980); King's College, London (1984). Lecturer: Private International Law, University of Milan (1977-1980); International Business Law (Faculty of Engineering, University of Milan), 1992. Author: "Service of Process in Italy,' London, 1985; "Enforcement of English judgements in Italy," London, 1985. Co-Author: "World Litigation Law and Practice," New York, 1986; French Courts and Lex Mercatoria, "1993. *Member:* AIJA (Former Chairman od International Business Law Commission; IBA: ELA. *LANGUAGES:* Italian, English and French.

FEDERICO M. FERRARA, born Foggia, Italy, August 24, 1961; admitted, 1990, Milan. *Education:* Fellow, Council of Europe, Strasbourg (1982); University of Perugia (J.D., 1985). *Member:* AIJA. *LANGUAGES:* Italian, Spanish, English and French.

ASSOCIATES

ODILE SICARD, born Nancy, France, May 17, 1963; admitted, 1989, France. *Education:* University of Nancy (J.D., 1986). *Member:* AIJA. *LANGUAGES:* French, Italian and German.

ALESSANDRO CUROTTI, born Florence, Italy, December 7, 1959; admitted, 1993. *Education:* University of Siena (J.D., 1985); City of London Polytechnic, London (1985); Bocconi University, Milan (Postgraduate Courses, Corporate Law, 1990). Assistant: Former in-house Counsel for Foster Wheeler Italiana, 1987-1988; Sony Music Entertainment Italy (1989-1991). *LANGUAGES:* Italian, English, French and Spanish.

MARA DE LA VEGA, born Sevilla, Spain, September 4, 1963; admitted, 1992, Spain; 1994, Italy. *Education:* Universidad Autonoma de Madrid (J.D., 1986); University of Milan (J.D., 1991). *LANGUAGES:* Spanish, Italian and English.

DONATELLA D'AMICO, born Milan, Italy, May 8, 1966. *Education:* State University of Milan (J.D., 1992). *LANGUAGES:* Italian and English.

MARIA LAURA BONI, born Milan, Italy, January 30, 1970. *Education:* State University of Milan (J.D., 1993). Staff Member of Patent and

(This Listing Continued)

Trade Mark Law Research Group. *LANGUAGES:* Italian, English and French.

RICCARDO ROVERSI, born Ancona, August 18, 1968. *Education:* State University of Milan (J.D., 1992). *LANGUAGES:* Italian and English.

Languages: English, French, Spanish, German and Italian

ACERBI & MAZZONI

Studio Legale Associato

Established in 1981

5, VIA BORGONUOVO
20121 MILAN, ITALY
Telephone: (2) 86460162
Telex: 312540 THEMISI
Facsimile: (2) 8690759-72003482

International and General Practice, Foreign Investments, Corporate, Bankruptcy, Banking, Securities, Structured Finance, Tax, Labor, Estate, Patent, Energy and Environmental Law.

MEMBERS OF FIRM

GIUSEPPE ACERBI, born Milan, Italy, February 29, 1944; admitted, 1971, Italy. *Education:* Catholic University of Milan Law School (J.D., summa cum laude, 1968). Assistant Professor, Commercial Law, Catholic University, 1968-1971. *LANGUAGES:* English and German.

ALBERTO MAZZONI, born Livorno, Italy, October 28, 1942; admitted, 1974, Italy. *Education:* University of Pisa Law School (J.D., summa cum laude, 1965); University of Chicago Law School (M.C.L., 1966). Research Fellow, University of Michigan Law School, 1970. Visiting Foreign Lawyer: Cohen-Meyohas, Paris, 1969-1970; White & Case, New York, 1972-1973. Professor, Commercial Law and International Trade Law, Catholic University of Milan. *LANGUAGES:* English, French, Swedish and German.

ADO CRISTOFOLI, born San Giorgio di Nogaro, Italy, August 1, 1944; admitted, 1972, Italy. *Education:* Catholic University of Milan Law School (J.D., 1969). *LANGUAGES:* French and German.

DARIO LOIACONO, born Milan, Italy, January 21, 1960; admitted, 1987, Italy; 1991, New York. *Education:* Catholic University of Milan Law School (J.D., 1984); Columbia University School of Law (LL.M., 1989); Bocconi University (LL.M., Corporate Tax, 1993). Associate: J.P. Morgan & Company, Inc., 1987-1988; Cleary, Gottlieb, Steen & Hamilton, New York, 1989-1991. *LANGUAGES:* German, English and French.

ASSOCIATES

DUCCIO REGOLI, born Lucca, Italy, July 8, 1961. *Education:* University of Pisa Law School (J.D., summa cum laude, 1986); Orientation Program in the U.S. Legal System, Georgetown University, D.C. (1987); University of Chicago Law School (LL.M., 1989). Recipient, Bank of Italy's Scholarship, D. Menchinella. Research Fellow, Commercial Law, University of Pisa. Visiting Foreign Lawyer, Paul, Weiss, Rifkind, Wharton & Garrison, New York, 1989-1990. *LANGUAGES:* English and French.

MARIA CHIARA MALAGUTI, born Bologna, Italy, February 26, 1964; admitted, 1991, New York; 1992, Italy. *Education:* University of Bologna Law School (J.D., summa cum laude, 1987); Harvard University (LL.M., 1989). Recipient, Rotary International Scholarship. Associate, Cleary, Gottlieb, Steen & Hamilton, Brussels, 1991-1994. *LANGUAGES:* English, French, Spanish and German.

SILVIA VANONI, born Milan, Italy, March 11, 1963; admitted, 1992, Italy. *Education:* Catholic University of Milan Law School (J.D., summa cum laude, 1988); City of London Polytechnic (Course of Introduction to English Law, 1985; Course of English Business Law, 1989). Recipient, British Council, European Lawyers Association Scholarship, 1991. Member, Editorial Staff, Banca, Borsa e Titoli di Credito. *LANGUAGES:* English and French.

NICOLA FERRINI, born Luino, Italy, March 30, 1966; admitted, 1994, Italy. *Education:* Catholic University of Milan Law School (1990); City of London Polytechnic (Course in European Business Law, 1992). *LANGUAGES:* English and French.

GIOVANNA PATANE', born August 5, 1966. *Education:* Catholic University of Milan Law School (J.D., summa cum laude, 1990). Research Fellow of Corporate and Commercial Law and International Trade Law, Catholic University of Milan.

(This Listing Continued)

ACERBI & MAZZONI, Milan—Continued

PAOLA DEL FAVERO, born June 26, 1969. *Education:* Bocconi University Business School (summa cum laude, 1992); Bocconi University (LL.M., Corporate Tax, 1993); University of Milan Law School (J.D., 1995). CPA, 1992, Italy. Research Fellow of Corporate Tax Law, Bocconi University. Member, Editorial Staff of Diritto e pratica tributaria and Tax Planning International Review.

FEDERICA GIOIA, born Seregno, Italy, April 25, 1968; admitted, 1994, Italy. *Education:* Catholic University of Milan Law School (J.D., summa cum laude, 1991). Research Fellow, Patent, Trademark and Intellectual Property Law, University of Ferrara. Member, Editorial Staff, Giurisprudenza annotata di diritto industriale, 1991-1992. *LANGUAGES:* English, French and German.

OF COUNSEL

MAURO POLITI, born Fabrica di Roma, Italy, September 13, 1944; admitted, 1967, Italy. *Education:* University of Florence Law School (J.D., 1966). Research Fellow: Columbia University, School of International Affairs, 1968; Yale Law School, 1979-1980. Judge, Court of Milan, 1975-1983. Professor, International Law, University of Trento. *LANGUAGES:* English and French.

STUDIO LEGALE ALBISINNI

Established in 1988

VIA ZENALE 3

20123 MILAN, ITALY

Telephone: (39) (2) 480.21655

Facsimile: (39) (2) 481.6725

Rome, Italy Office: Via Ciro Menotti N.4, 00195. Telephone: 06-3216171, 3210986. Facsimile: 06-3217034.

General Civil Practice, Business Law, Commercial Law, Corporate Law, Contracts, International Business Transactions, Documentary Credits, Property, Real Estate, Trusts and Estates, International Estate Planning, Agricultural Law, Resorts and Leisure, Copyrights, Intellectual Property, Patents, Bankruptcy, Civil Litigation.

AVV. FERDINANDO ALBISINNI, born Cosenza, Italy, August 28, 1948; admitted, 1974, Italy. *Education:* University of Rome (J.D., cum laude, 1971). Fellow Seminar in American Law, Salzburg, 1975. Researcher, Institute of Comparative Law, University of Rome, 1971-1977. Member of the Committee on "Agritourism," of the Ministry of Agriculture, 1980-1990; "Italian Contribution in Glosson International Trust Law" (1994). *Member:* Italian Association of Comparative Law; Italian Arbitration Association; European Lawyers' Union. *LANGUAGES:* English, German, Italian. *PRACTICE AREAS:* Business Law; Contracts; Resorts and Leisure; Real Estate; Litigation; Trusts and Estate; Agricultural Law.

AVV. MILENKA SALDARELLI, born Naples, Italy, January 2, 1954; admitted, 1985, Italy. *Education:* University of Naples (J.D., 1979); Confederation of Agriculture (scholarship, 1980-1981); University of Milan, postgraduate studies in arbitration (1989-1990). *Member:* Milan Bar. *LANGUAGES:* Italian, Spanish. *PRACTICE AREAS:* Litigation; Family Law; Commercial Law.

AMENTA, BIOLATO, CORRAO, LONGO, RIDOLA

Established in 1984

VIA BRERA, 6

20121 MILAN, ITALY

Telephone: (02) 86461365

Fax: (02) 72002140

Rome, Italy Office: Via del Babuino, 51, 00187. Telephone: (06) 3233001. Fax: (06) 3234238.

General Civil Law.

(This Listing Continued)

FLAVIA C. RAFFAELLI, born Milan, Italy, July 10, 1954; admitted, 1982, Milan. *Education:* Milan University (LL.D., 1978). *LANGUAGES:* Italian, English, French, Spanish.

Languages: Italian, English, French, Spanish.

(For biographical data on attorneys not resident in Milan, see Professional Biographies at Rome, Italy)

AMHURST BROWN COLOMBOTTI

VIA SETTEMBRINI 17

20124 MILAN, ITALY

Telephone: (02) 6698 4270

Fax: (02) 6698 4252

London, England Office: 2 Duke Street, St. James's, SW1Y 6BJ. Telephone: (071) 930-2366. Telex: 261857 AMBRON. Fax: (071) 930-2250.

Warsaw, Poland Office: ul. Koszykowa 59 m.6, 00-660. Telephone: 48 (22) 29 16 84; 48 (2) 625 30 51; 48 (2) 625 31 25. Satellite: 48 (39) 12 06 02. Fax: 48 (2) 6213289. Telex: 816370 AMPOL.

Madrid, Spain Office: Paseo del General Martinez Campos 41 8-B, 28010. Telephone: (91) 410 72 24. Fax: (91) 410 55 92.

General Commercial Practice specializing in Joint Ventures, Tax, Employment, Property and Finance, Privatizations.

PARTNERS

C.E.P. COLOMBOTTI (Also at London, England Office).

A.F.L. AMHURST (Also at London, England).

A.G. FACEY (Also at London, England Office).

(For complete list of Personnel see Professional Biographies at London, England)

ANTONELLI & COCUZZA

Studio Legale Associato

VIA FREGUGLIA, 8

20122 MILAN, ITALY

Telephone: 0039-2-55 19 04 09

Telex: 0039-2-55 19 07 71

General Commercial Practice, Corporate Law, Mergers and Acquisitions, Italian and EEC Antitrust, Banking and Securities Regulation, Labor, Domestic and International Taxation, Patents and Trademarks, Litigation and Arbitration.

PIERCARLO ANTONELLI, born Livorno, Italy, March 11, 1959; admitted, 1989, Milan. *Education:* University of Milan (J.D., maxima cum laude, 1984). Associate Training Program, Baker & McKenzie, London, 1989-1990. *Member:* Milan Bar Association; IDE; American Italian Legal Association. *LANGUAGES:* Italian and English. *PRACTICE AREAS:* Commercial Law; Mergers and Acquisitions; Labor; Domestic and International Taxation.

CLAUDIO COCUZZA, born Rome, Italy, March 30, 1963; admitted, 1990, Milan. *Education:* University of Siena (J.D., maxima cum laude, 1985); University of Pennsylvania Law School (LL.M., 1988); Bocconi University (C.E.R.T.I., Master Course in Corporate Taxation, 1993). Visiting Foreign Lawyer, Thompson, Hine & Flory, Washington, D.C. and Cleveland, 1988-1989. Author: "State Supporting International Terrorism and Economic Sanction: The Lybian Case," The Italian Yearbook of International Law, 1986-1987; "The Omnibus Trade and Competitiveness Act of 1988: An Overview," The Review of International Business Law, 1989. *Member:* Milan Bar Association; Italian Fulbright Association; Foreign Lawyers Forum, Washington, D.C. (Member, Steering Committee); AIJA. *LANGUAGES:* Italian, English and French. *PRACTICE AREAS:* Commercial Law; EEC Law; Mergers and Acquisitions; Antitrust; Arbitration and Private International Law; Tax.

ANDREA FORABOSCO, born Udine, Italy, March 9, 1966; admitted, 1995, Milan. *Education:* University of Modena, Italy (J.D., maxima cum laude, 1990); University of Kingston upon Hull Law Department, England (1989-1990; Erasmus Scholar); Italian Internal Revenue Service Academy, Bergamo, Italy (Advanced Studies in Taxation, 1991). Visiting Foreign Lawyer with: Payne, Hicks, Beach, Solicitors, London, 1991; Howard Kennedy, London, 1994. Officer with the Law Department of the General Headquarter, Internal Revenue Service, Rome, 1992-1993. Lecturer, Pri-

(This Listing Continued)

vate International Law, Hague Academy of International Law, 1993. *LANGUAGES:* Italian and English. *PRACTICE AREAS:* Commercial Law; Tax.

ELENA MAGNI, born Milano, Italy, December 13, 1969. *Education:* University of Milan, (J.D., 1994); Monmouth College, West Long Branch, N.J (1990); Pitzer College, Claremont, CA. (1990). *LANGUAGES:* Italian, English and German. *PRACTICE AREAS:* General Commercial Practice; EEC Law.

ARDITO E MAGRONE

VIA BORGONUOVO, 20
20121 MILAN, ITALY
Telephone: (02) 6575181
Telecopier: (Gr. 2-3): (02) 6570013

Rome, Italy Office: Via del Banco di S. Spirito, 42. Telephone: (06) 6879962. Telex: 611416 ITALAW. Telecopier (Gr. 2-3): (06) 6751240.
Turin, Italy Office: Via Bruno Buozzi, 10. Telephone: (011) 5623801. Telecopier (Gr. 2-3): (011) 3101043.
Brussels, Belgium Office: 13, Av. De Tervuren. Telephone: (02) 7359442. Telecopier (Gr. 2-3): (02) 7359622.

General, International and Domestic Practice.

MARIO ARDITO, born Castelfranco di Sotto, Pisa, Italy, October 16, 1919; admitted, 1946, Italy; 1950, Supreme Court. *Education:* University of Genoa Law School (J.D., 1941).

CESARE LANCIANI, born Civitavecchia, Rome, Italy, April 30, 1936; admitted, 1978, Italy; 1993, Supreme Court. *Education:* University of Rome Law School (J.D., 1959); Centre Universitaire Européen de Nancy (Diplôme, 1960). *Member:* International Fiscal Association. *LANGUAGES:* Italian and French. *PRACTICE AREAS:* Corporate and Commercial; Taxation; Antitrust; M & A.

OSCAR PODDA, born Milan, Italy, August 2, 1957; admitted, 1983, Italy. *Education:* University of Milan (J.D., 1980); University of Pennsylvania Law School (LL.M., 1985). Adjunct Member, Journal of Comparative Business and Capital Market Law, 1984-1985. *Member:* IBA. *LANGUAGES:* Italian and English. *PRACTICE AREAS:* Corporate and Commercial; Taxation.

FRANCESCO ABBOZZO FRANZI, born Milan, Italy, May 13, 1957; admitted, 1986, Italy. *Education:* University of Milan Law School (J.D., 1985). Visiting Foreign Lawyer, Hughes Hubbard & Reed, New York, 1985. *Member:* AIJA. *LANGUAGES:* Italian and English. *PRACTICE AREAS:* Corporate and Commercial; Litigation; Labour Law.

LUCA MINOLI, born Naples, Italy, January 29, 1961; admitted, 1988, Italy. *Education:* University of Milan Law School (J.D., 1985). Visiting Foreign Lawyer, Hughes Hubbard & Reed, New York, 1986. *Member IBA.* *LANGUAGES:* Italian and English. *PRACTICE AREAS:* Corporate and Commercial; M & A; Insurance Law.

PAOLA FAZZALARI, born Milan, Italy, June 11, 1964; admitted, 1994, Italy. *Education:* University of Milan Law School (J.D., 1989). *LANGUAGES:* Italian and English. *PRACTICE AREAS:* Civil Law; Litigation.

ROBERTO NICASTRO, born Palermo, Italy, May 27, 1959. *Education:* University of Milan Law School (J.D., 1992). *LANGUAGES:* Italian and English. *PRACTICE AREAS:* Corporate.

SILVIA CALARESU, born Milan, Italy, December 8, 1969. *Education:* University of Milan Law School (J.D., 1994). *LANGUAGES:* Italian, French and English.

ANTONIO ZANGARA, born Catania, Italy, January 1, 1969. *Education:* Catholic University of Milan Law School (J.D., 1993). *LANGUAGES:* Italian and English.

DUCCIO NEY, born Milan, Italy, May 23, 1969. *Education:* University of Milan Law School (J.D., 1994). *LANGUAGES:* Italian and English.

RESIDENTS AT ROME OFFICE

Giandomenico Magrone	**Margherita Bianchini**
(Also at Turin Office)	**Stefano Sacchetto**
Livia Magrone Furlotti	**Andrea Valli**
G. Massimiliano Danusso	**Riccardo Sallustio**
Cristoforo Osti	**Walter Vasselli**
Roberto Donnini	**Maria Carla de Giovanni**

(This Listing Continued)

Priscilla Pettiti	*Isabella Toth*

COUNSEL

Laura Rainaldi

Languages: Italian, English, French, Spanish and German

(For Biographical Data on Attorneys resident in Rome, see Professional Biographies at Magrone e Ardito, Rome, Italy)

STUDIO LEGALE ASSOCIATO
&
FRERE CHOLMELEY BISCHOFF

PIAZZA CASTELLO, 24
20121 MILAN, ITALY
Telephone: (39) (2) 72003457
Fax: (39) (2) 72003469

Rome Office: Viale Bruno Buozzi, 47, 00197 Rome. Telephone: (39) (6) 8080133. Fax: (39) (6) 8080134.
Frère Cholmeley Bischoff 4 John Carpenter Street, London EC4Y 0NH, England. Telephone: 0171/6158000. Fax: 0171/6158080. Offices in Paris, Milan, Monte Carlo, Berlin, Moscow, Dubai (For Biographical Listing, see London Office).

International and General Practice, Corporate, Mergers and Acquisitions, Aviation, Banking, Commercial and Private Real Estate, Privatizations, Foreign Investments, Computer and Software, EEC, Energy, Eastern European, Insurance, Joint Ventures, Licensing, Litigation, Education, Environmental, Bankruptcy, Labor, Patent, Trademark, Copyright, Entertainment, Media and Telecommunications, Public International Law, Visa and Immigration, Family, Taxation, Will and Estates.

FIRM PROFILE: The five partners, four Italian and one American, have practiced together and served the international community since 1982. The firm has built a strong reputation among corporations, private clients and other law firms as being experienced in assisting the foreign client with Italian and multi-jurisdicitional legal matters.

MEMBERS OF FIRM

ANTONELLO CORRADO, born Frosinone, Italy, August 8, 1952; admitted, 1979, Italy. *Education:* Institute of Comparative Law (1976); University of Rome (Doctor in Jurisprudence, LL.D., maxima cum laude, 1979); Seminar in American Legal Studies, Salzburg (1985). Faculty: Seminar "Judicial Business Practice-Joint Ventures." Tirana, Albania, 1992, sponsored by Idli and Ministry of Justice of Albania; Workshop "Legal Issues Raised by International Joint Ventures in Macedonia." Ohrid, Macedonia, 1994, sponsored by American Bar Association (CEELI) and The Economic Chamber of Macedonia. Contributing Editor, "Foro Italiano," 1980 to present. *Member:* Italian (Rome) and International Bar Associations (Member, East European Forum); Chairman, Association of Investigators and Experts for Air Safety; Member, Board of Directors, International Scientific Network Society - ISN; Member, Board of Directors, Keats-Shelly Memorial Association. *PRACTICE AREAS:* Corporate; Insurance; Trademark, Copyright and Patent; Entertainment and Media; East European.

ASSOCIATES

MARCO CONSONNI, born Milan, Italy, October 23, 1964; admitted, 1990, Italy. *Education:* University of Milan (Doctor in Jurisprudence, LL.D., 1989). *Member:* Italian (Milan) Bar Association. *PRACTICE AREAS:* Competition; Patent and Trademark; Civil Litigation; Entertainment and Media.

DAVIDE CONTINI, born Milan, Italy, August 11, 1963; admitted, 1989, Italy. *Education:* University of Milan (Doctor of Jurisprudence, LL.D., 1988). *Member:* Italian (Milan) Bar Association. *PRACTICE AREAS:* Finance and Banking; Corporate; Commercial and Civil Litigation.

STEFANIA CASORATI BICECCI, born Portoferraio, Italy, March 27, 1965; admitted, 1991, Italy. *Education:* University of Pisa (Doctor of Jurisprudence, LL.D., maxima cum laude, 1991). *Member:* Italian (Milan) Bar Association. *PRACTICE AREAS:* Company; Commercial; Intellectual Property; Copyright and Entertainment; Civil Litigation.

SARA MODENA, born Milan, Italy, July 20, 1966; admitted, 1990, Israel. *Education:* Hebrew University of Jerusalem (Doctor of Jurisprudence, LL.B., 1989); University of Milan (Master in ECC Law and Econ-

(This Listing Continued)

STUDIO LEGALE ASSOCIATO & FRERE CHOLMELEY BISCHOFF, Milan—Continued

omy, 1993). *Member:* Israel Bar Association. **PRACTICE AREAS:** Commercial; Competition; ECC.

ENRICO FADANI, born Heidelberg, Germany, September 25, 1967; admitted, 1993, Germany. *Education:* Universities of Bologna and Heidelberg (1993). *Member:* German and Italian Lawyers Association. **PRACTICE AREAS:** Industrial; Competition and Company.

Languages: Italian, English, French, German, Spanish and Hebrew

(For Biographical Data on all other Personnel and List of Representative Clients, See Professional Listing for Rome Office)

BAKER & McKENZIE

3 PIAZZA MEDA
20121 MILAN, ITALY
Telephone: (02) 76 01 39 21
Intn'l. Dialing: (39-2) 76 01 39 21
Cable Address: ABOGADO MILANO
Telex: 311655
Answer Back: 311655 ABOMIL I
Facsimiles: (39-2) 76 00 83 22; 76 00 81 65; 76 00 70 74; 76 00 75 17;
78 42 57

Associated Offices of Baker & McKenzie in: Almaty, Amsterdam, Bangkok, Barcelona, Beijing, Berlin, Bogotá, Brasília, Brussels, Budapest, Buenos Aires, Cairo, Caracas, Chicago, Dallas, Frankfurt, Geneva, Hanoi, Ho Chi Minh City, Hong Kong, Juárez, Kiev, London, Madrid, Manila, Melbourne, México City, Miami, Monterrey, Moscow, New York, Palo Alto, Paris, Prague, Rio de Janeiro, Riyadh, Rome, St. Petersburg, San Diego, San Francisco, São Paulo, Singapore, Stockholm, Sydney, Taipei, Tijuana, Tokyo, Toronto, Valencia, Warsaw, Washington, D.C. and Zürich.

Correspondent Law Firm: Hadiputranto, Hadinoto & Partners, Jakarta.

International and General Practice. Corporation, Commercial, Tax and Labor Law.

PARTNERS

CORRADO BARTOLI, born Naples, Italy, April 10, 1946; admitted, 1974, Italy. *Education:* University of Naples Law School (J.D., 1970). *Member:* Milan Bar. **LANGUAGES:** Italian and English.

GERARDO M. BONIELLO, born Muro Lucano, Italy, March 7, 1941; admitted, 1967, Italy. *Education:* Catholic University of Milan Law School (J.D., 1964); Institut Universitaire d'Etudes Européennes, Turin (Certificat Supérieur d'Etudes Européennes, 1965); Faculté Internationale pour l'Etude du Droit Comparé de Strasbourg (Diplôme d'Etudes Superieures de Droit Comparé, 1967); University of Chicago Law School (M.C.L., 1970). *Member:* Milan Bar. **LANGUAGES:** Italian, English and French.

CLAUDIO CAMILLI, born Pescara, Italy, October 9, 1935; admitted, 1959, Italy. *Education:* University of Naples Law School (J.D., 1957). Instructor in Commercial Law, Milan Catholic University, 1961-1966. *Member:* Milan Bar. **LANGUAGES:** Italian, English and French.

ALBERTO DE LIBERO, born Gorizia, Italy, September 8, 1931; admitted, 1957, Italy. *Education:* University of Rome Law School (J.D., 1954); University of Texas (LL.M., 1959). Fulbright Scholar. Panelist, American Arbitration Association. *Member:* Milan Bar. **LANGUAGES:** Italian, English and French.

GIANFRANCO DI GARBO, born Frignano, Italy, May 30, 1951; admitted, 1977, Italy. *Education:* University of Genoa Law School (J.D., 1972); The British Institute of International and Comparative Law, London (Certificate in Modern English Law, 1979); University of Texas at Dallas (Academy of American and International Law, Southwestern Legal Foundation, 1980). *Member:* Milan Bar. **LANGUAGES:** Italian, English and French.

PIERFRANCESCO FEDERICI, born Genoa, Italy, January 18, 1954; admitted, 1984, Italy. *Education:* University of Genoa (J.D., 1979). Traineeship, EEC Commission, Brussels, 1979-1980. *Member:* Milan Bar. **LANGUAGES:** Italian, English and French.

ALBERTO SEMERIA, born Turin, Italy, October 7, 1959; admitted, 1985, Italy; 1991, New York. *Education:* University of Turin Law School (J.D., 1983); New York University (M.C.J., 1990). *Member:* Milan Bar;

(This Listing Continued)

New York State Bar Association. **LANGUAGES:** Italian, English, French and Spanish.

ASSOCIATES

FRANCESCO ADAMI, born Milan, Italy, January 2, 1963; admitted, 1991, Italy. *Education:* University of Padua Law School (J.D., 1987); Europa Institut des Universitaet des Saarlandes. Recipient, University L. Bocconi, Milan, C. Manzoni Award. Academy Researcher at Keio University in Tokyo. *Member:* Milan Bar; International Fiscal Association; Italian-German Law Association. **LANGUAGES:** Italian, German, English and French.

PIETRO BERNASCONI, born Como, Italy, October 25, 1960; admitted, 1986, Italy. *Education:* Catholic University of Milan Law School (J.D., 1986). *Member:* Milan Bar; British-Italian Law Association; American-Italian Law Association. **LANGUAGES:** Italian, English and Spanish.

GIOVANNI BUCCIROSSI, born Naples, Italy, March 6, 1960; admitted, 1984, Italy. *Education:* University of Urbino Law School (J.D., 1984); Georgetown University (Orientation to the U.S. Legal System, July-August, 1986); George Washington University (M.C.L., 1987). *Member:* Milan Bar. **LANGUAGES:** Italian and English.

ROBERTO CAMILLI, born Naples, Italy, January 31, 1966; admitted, 1993, Italy. *Education:* Universitá Degli Studi Di Milano (Laurea, 1992). **LANGUAGES:** English and French.

RAFFAELE CAVANI, born Modena, Italy, October 17, 1964; admitted, 1991, Italy. *Education:* University of Modena (J.D., cum laude, 1988); University of Amsterdam-Europa Institute (Graduate Course in European Integration, 1988-1989); University of Chicago (LL.M., 1993). Member, Editorial Staff, "Diritto Dei Trasporti". *Member:* Milan Bar. **LANGUAGES:** Italian, English, Spanish.

ANDREA CICALA, born Bolzano, Italy, December 26, 1960; admitted, 1986, Italy. *Education:* University of Palermo Law School (J.D., 1985); City of London Polytechnic, Orientation to International Law; Institute of European Studies (ULB), Brussels (Certificate in European Law, 1987). Member, Southwestern Legal Foundation, UTD, Dallas, Texas (Academy of American and International Law), 1991. *Member:* Milan Bar. **LANGUAGES:** Italian, English, Spanish and French.

GIULIA COMPARINI, born Siena, Italy, February 28, 1962; admitted, 1990, Italy. *Education:* University of Siena Law School (J.D., 1985); University of Bridgeport, Visiting Student (1985-1986). Assistant to Professor F. Francioni, International Law, University of Siena Law School, 1986-1988. *Member:* Milan Bar. **LANGUAGES:** Italian, English and French.

ANNA DEIANA, born Cagliari, Italy, October 22, 1966; admitted, 1991, Italy. *Education:* University of Cagliari (Degree in Commercial Economics, First, 1990). *Member:* Dottori Commercialisti Association. **LANGUAGES:** Italian.

LORENZO DE MARTINIS, born Torino, Italy, April 25, 1961; admitted, 1989, Italy. *Education:* University of Pisa Law School (J.D., 1989). *Member:* Milan Bar. **LANGUAGES:** Italian, English and French.

ALBERTO MARIA FORNARI, born Parma, Italy, March 8, 1962; admitted, 1989, Italy. *Education:* University of Parma (J.D., 1985); New York University (LL.M., in International Legal Studies). *Member:* Milan Bar. **LANGUAGES:** Italian, English and German.

ELISE EDITH LEHOCZKY, born Paris, France, March 11, 1960; admitted, 1986, Italy; 1993, France. *Education:* University of Paris Law School (J.D., 1983); University of Milan Law School (J.D., 1986). *Member:* Milan Bar. **LANGUAGES:** Italian, French, Hungarian, English and German.

MARCO MAZZESCHI, born Siena, Italy, June 23, 1961; admitted, 1988, Italy. *Education:* University of Siena Law School (J.D., 1985). *Member:* Milan Bar. **LANGUAGES:** Italian, English and French.

TIZIANO MEMBRI, born Lodi (Milan), Italy, May 25, 1964; admitted, 1992, Italy. *Education:* Catholic University of Milan Law School (J.D., 1989); University of California at Berkeley, School of Business Administration. *Member:* Milan Bar. **LANGUAGES:** Italian, English and French.

GIOVANNI MARCO MILENI MUNARI, born Bergamo, Italy, August 11, 1963; admitted, 1991, Italy. *Education:* University of Parma Law School (J.D., 1987); McGeorge School of Law, The University of Edinburgh, Faculty of Law (Certificate in International Business Transactions, 1987); Georgetown University, Washington, D.C. (Orientation Program in the U.S. Legal System, 1990); University of Pennsylvania Law School (LL.M., 1991). Recipient, Bank of Italy's Scholarship, P. Andreini.

(This Listing Continued)

Member: Milan Bar. *LANGUAGES:* Italian, English and French.

UBERTO PERCIVALLE, born Vercelli, Italy, March 22, 1964; admitted, 1990, Italy. *Education:* University of Oregon Law School, Visiting Student (1987-1988); University of Pavia Law School (J.D., 1990); Alumnus of Collegio Ghislieri, Pavia, Italy. *Member:* Milan Bar. *LANGUAGES:* Italian and English.

SILVIA PICCHETTI, born Pisa, Italy, December 22, 1958; admitted, 1987, Italy. *Education:* University of Pisa (J.D., 1985); Yale University, Corporate Law Studies (1989). *Member:* Milan Bar. *LANGUAGES:* Italian, English and French.

GAETANO PIZZITOLA, born Castelvetrano (Trapani), Italy, April 20, 1961; admitted, 1991, Italy. *Education:* University of Palermo Law School (J.D., 1985); IPSOA Master in Tax Law. *Member:* Milan Bar. *LANGUAGES:* Italian and English.

GIULIANA POLACCO, born Venice, Italy, May 13, 1965; admitted, 1994, Italy. *Education:* Universitá Statale di Milano (1989). *LANGUAGES:* English and French.

DOMENICO VACCA, born Andria, Italy, July 22, 1962; admitted, 1987, Italy. *Education:* University of Bari, Italy (J.D., 1986); Accademia della Guardia di Finanza, Italy (Italian Internal Revenue Service Academy, Advanced Studies in Taxation, March-July, 1987); Georgetown University (Studies in U.S. Legal System, July-August, 1991); New York University (M.C.J., Master of Comparative Jurisprudence, 1992). Adjunct Professor, Scuola della Guardia di Finanza, Cuneo, Italy, 1987. *Member:* Italian Bar; American Foreign Law Association. *LANGUAGES:* Italian and English.

STUDIO LEGALE AVV. ROBERTO BALDI

Established in 1955

VIA VISCONTI DI MODRONE 8/1
20122 MILAN, ITALY
Telephone: 0039-2-76008711 (several Lines)
Telefax: 0039-2-76014033
Commercial and International Law.

FIRM PROFILE: *The firm was established in 1955 and offers a full range of legal services, it operates particularly in commercial law, international law, EC law, distributorship, agency and franchising areas.*

AVV. ROBERTO BALDI, born Milan, Italy, June 1, 1922; admitted, 1949, Italy. *Education:* University of Milan (Doctor of Law, 1946). Contributor to Books: La représentation et l'implantation des firmes étrangeres dans les pays de l'Europe (Chapter on Italy), Publisher, Frantec Paris, 1968; La représentation Commerciale Internationale (Chapter on Italy), Publisher, Etablissement Bruylant Bruxelles, 1971; "European Franchising-Law and Practice in the European Community (Chapter on Italy)," Publisher, Waterlow, London, 1991. Author: Treaties: 1) " Il contratto di agenzia La concessione di vendita Il Franchising," Commercial Agency Contract, Distributorship Franchising, 5th Ed., Publisher, Giuffré, Milano, 1992, 2nd ed., 1977, Translated into French: L'agent commercial, Publisher, Editions Jupiter, Paris, 1981; 2) "Il diritto della distribuzione commerciale nell'Europa comunitaria," (Distributorship inside the European Community), Publisher, Cedam Padova, 1984; Updated Translated: 1) into English, *Distributorship, Franchising, Agency, Community and National Laws and Practice in the E.E.C.*, Publisher, Kluwer, Deventer, 1987; 2) into Spanish, *El Derecho de la Distribución Comercial en la Europa Comunitaria*, Publisher Edersa, Madrid, 1987; 3) into French, *Le Droit de la Distribution Commerciale dans l'Europe Communautaire*, Publisher Bruylant, Bruxelles, 1988; 4) into German, *Das Recht des Warenvertriebs in der Europäischen Gemeinschaft*, Publisher, Müller, Heidelberg, 1988. Visiting Professor: in the Milan University, 1981-1982, 1984-1985; in the Milan I.U.L.M. (Instituto universitario lingue moderne, 1984-1988) University of modern languages. President of the international Association "Associazione Internazionale giuristi di lingua italiana" (International Association of italian speaking Lawyers). President, Club International du droit de la distribution commerciale (C.I.D.D.). *Member:* Milan Bar Association (Member of the Council, 1972-1982); Commission Consultative des Barreaux de La Communauté Européenne (CCBE), (Member and Head of the Italian Delegation, 1972-1982); International Bar Association (Member of the Council, Delegate of the Milan Bar Association, 1976-1986). *LANGUAGES:* Italian, French, English, German and Spanish. *PRACTICE AREAS:* Commercial Law; International Law; EC Law; Distributorship, Agency and Franchising.

(This Listing Continued)

ALBERTO VENEZIA, born Genova, Italy, November 12, 1963. *Education:* University of Milan (Doctor of Law, 1989, with thesis on franchising). *LANGUAGES:* Italian, English and French. *PRACTICE AREAS:* Commercial Law; International Law; EC Law; Distributorship; Agency and Franchising.

Languages: Italian, English, French, German and Spanish.

AVV. TITO BALLARINO

PIAZZA CASTELLO, 24
20121 MILAN, ITALY
Telephone: 2-72.02.38.2
Fax: 2-86.90.901

TITO BALLARINO, born Milan, Italy, June 13, 1934; admitted, 1959, Italy and Italian Supreme Court. *Education:* University of Pavia (J.D., magna cum laude, 1956). Author: *Dritto Internazionale Privato*, Padova, 1932; *Lineamenti di diritto comunitario*, 4th ed., Patova, 1993. Lecturer: "Questions of Private International Law and Catastrophic Damages"; The Hague Academy of International Law (1990), published in *Recueil des Cours*, Martinus Nijhoff Publisher. Member of U.I.A (Union Internationale des Avocats); Chairman, Committee on Private International Law. *LANGUAGES:* French, German, English, Italian. *PRACTICE AREAS:* Corporations; Private International Law; Aviation and Aerospace Law; EEC Law.

BARZANÕ & ZANARDO

Established in 1887

VIA BORGONUOVO 10
20121 MILAN, ITALY
Telephone: (39-2) 655 4287
Telecopier: (39-2) 659 8859
Telex: 320034-Zanard I

Rome, Italy Office: Via Piemonte 26, 00187. Telephone: (39-6) 474 3241. Telecopier: (39-6) 487 0273. Telex: 625579-Zanard I.
Turin, Italy Office: Corso Vittorio Emanuele II 61, 10128. Telephone: (39-11) 56 11172. Telecopier: (39-11) 548 050. Telex: 320034 Zanard I.

Patents, Designs, Trademarks, Copyright, Licensing and Transfer of Technology.

MEMBERS OF FIRM

GIOVANNI ZANARDO, born Lausanne, Switzerland, August 1, 1953; admitted to practice before the Italian Patent Office and Board of Appeal. *Education:* Geneva-French Baccalaureat in Economics. European Patent Attorney. (Also at Rome and Turin Offices). *LANGUAGES:* Italian, English and French.

DR. DOMENICO DE SIMONE, born Rome, March 26, 1949; admitted to practice before the Italian Patent Office and Board of Appeal. *Education:* Rome University (Doctor of Law). European Patent Attorney. (Also at Rome and Turin Offices). *LANGUAGES:* Italian, English and French.

DR.ING. RAIMONDO COLETTI, born Rome, March 25, 1957; admitted to practice before the Italian Patent Office and Board of Appeal. *Education:* Rome University (Mining-Mechanical Engineer). *LANGUAGES:* Italian, English and French.

DR.ING. GIORGIO LOTTI, born Turin, February 12, 1950; admitted to practice before the Italian Patent Office and Board of Appeal. *Education:* Polytechnic Institute University of Turin (Mechanical Engineer). European Patent Attorney. (Resident, Turin Office). *LANGUAGES:* Italian, English, German and French.

DR. ROMANO APPOLONI, born Milan, August 28, 1952; admitted to practice before the Italian Patent Office and Board of Appeal. *Education:* University of Milan (Industrial Chemistry). *LANGUAGES:* Italian and English.

DR.ING. MARINA BANCHETTI, born Rome, March 27, 1958; admitted to practice before the Italian Patent Office and Board of Appeal. *Education:* Rome University (Chemical Engineer). European Patent Attorney. (Resident, Rome Office). *LANGUAGES:* Italian, English and French.

MR. GIANNI DI FRANCESCO, born Luserna S. Giovanni, Turin, October 1, 1945; admitted to practice before the Italian Patent Office and Board of Appeal. European Patent Attorney. Specializes in automotive

(This Listing Continued)

BARZANÕ & ZANARDO, Milan—Continued

industry in general. (Resident, Turin Office). *LANGUAGES:* English, German and French.

DR.ING. MARIA AUGUSTA FIORUZZI, born Milan, December 14, 1958; admitted to practice before the Italian Patent Office and Board of Appeal. *Education:* Polytechnic Institute University of Milan (Civil Engineer). (Resident, Rome Office). *LANGUAGES:* Italian, English, German and French.

DR.ING. GEROLAMO FUSINA, born Turin, May 14, 1936. admitted to practice before the Italian Patent and Trademark Office and Board of Appeal. European Patent Attorney. Court official technical expert for patent litigations. *Education:* Polytechnic Institute University of Turin (Chemical Engineer). (Resident Milan Office). *LANGUAGES:* English and French.

DR. RINA GARAVAGLIA, born Cuggiono, February 6, 1924; admitted to practice before the Italian Patent Office and Board of Appeal. *Education:* University of Milan (Industrial Chemistry). (Counsel). *LANGUAGES:* Italian, English, German and French.

DR.ING. MAURIZIO GIULI, born Milan, January 3, 1949; admitted to practice before the Italian Patent Office and Board of Appeal. *Education:* Polytechnic Institute University of Milan (Mechanical Engineer). *LANGUAGES:* Italian, English and French.

ING. ERWIN HENKE, born Wien, Austria, September 8, 1922; Registered European Patent Attorney. *Education:* Foreign University Degree (Electrotechnical Engineer). (Counsel). *LANGUAGES:* German, Italian, English and French.

DR.ING. CARLO LUIGI IANNONE, born Rome, June 22, 1957; admitted to practice before the Italian Patent Office and Board of Appeal. *Education:* Rome University (Mechanical Engineer). European Patent Attorney. (Resident, Rome Office). *LANGUAGES:* Italian, English and German.

ANTONIO TALIERCIO, born Taranto, June 2, 1939; admitted to practice before the Italian Patent Office and Board of Appeal. *Education:* Rome University (Electronics). European Patent Attorney. (Resident, Rome Office). *LANGUAGES:* Italian, English, French and German.

DR.ING. ANGELO ZAPPELLA, born Bergamo, January 28, 1955; admitted to practice before the Italian Patent Office and Board of Appeal. *Education:* Polytechnic Institute University of Milan (Mechanical Engineer). *LANGUAGES:* Italian, English and French.

DR.ING. GIANLUCA BORTOLINI, born Milan, October 30, 1967. *Education:* Polytechnic Institute, University of Milan (Chemical Engineer). Resident Milan Office). *LANGUAGES:* German and English.

DR. OLGA CAPASSO, born Naples, May 11, 1956. *Education:* Naples University (Doctor in Molecular Biology, 1980); Postdoctoral training in Molecular Biology, Rockefeller Center University, New York, NY. (Resident, Rome Office). *LANGUAGES:* Italian, English and French.

DR. ANTONELLA DE GREGORI, born Milan, March 24, 1962. *Education:* University of Milan (Organic Chemistry). *LANGUAGES:* Italian and English.

DR.ING. CORRADO FIORAVANTI, born Turin, January 17, 1961. *Education:* Polytechnic Institute University of Turin (Civil Engineer). (Resident, Turin Office). *LANGUAGES:* Italian and English.

DOMESTIC AND FOREIGN TRADEMARK PROSECUTION, LITIGATION LICENSING AND TRANSFER

DR. MAURA ALIOTTI, born Rome, November 1, 1952. *Education:* Rome University (Doctor of Languages). (Resident, Rome Office) (Counsel). *LANGUAGES:* Italian, English and French.

DR. SOFIA CATALUCCI, born Rome, May 28, 1962. *Education:* Rome University (Doctor of Languages). (Resident, Rome Office). *LANGUAGES:* Italian, English, German and French.

DR. MARIA GRAZIA CAVALLO, born Amantea, April 15, 1959. *Education:* Rome University (Doctor of Political Sciences). (Resident, Rome Office). *LANGUAGES:* Italian, English and French.

DR. MASSIMO CIMOLI, born S. Stefano Magra (La Spezia), September 20, 1960. *Education:* University of Parma (Doctor of Law). (Resident Rome Office). *LANGUAGES:* English and French.

(This Listing Continued)

DR. ELISABETTA CONTA, born Monza, November 4, 1962. *Education:* University of Turin (Doctor of Law). (Resident, Turin Office). *LANGUAGES:* Italian and English.

DR. GIUSEPPE P. CUCCIA, born Brescia, September 22, 1954. *Education:* University of Parma (Doctor of Law). *LANGUAGES:* Italian, English and French.

DR. GIOVANNI DESIANTE, born Gravina di Puglia, July 31, 1949. *Education:* Bari University (Doctor of Economics). (Resident, Rome Office). *LANGUAGES:* Italian, English and German.

CARLA GIVA, born Ivrea, May 1, 1943. *LANGUAGES:* Italian, English, French, German and Russian.

DR. ALESSANDRO MASETTI ZANNINI DE CONCINA, born Rome, May 30, 1961. *Education:* Rome University (Doctor of Law). (Resident, Rome Office). *LANGUAGES:* Italian, English, French and Spanish.

DR. FABIO PASQUETTO, born Rome, April 19, 1962. *Education:* Rome University (Doctor of Law). (Resident, Rome Office). *LANGUAGES:* Italian, English, German and French.

PAOLA RUGGIERO, born Milan, September 6, 1964. *Education:* University of Milan (Law). *LANGUAGES:* Italian, English and French.

DR. LUISELLA TASSAN, born Turin, March 10, 1963. *Education:* University of Milan (Doctor of Law). *LANGUAGES:* Italian, English, German and French.

DR. ALESSANDRA TEDESCO, born Milan, July 19, 1963. *Education:* University of Milan (Doctor of Law). *LANGUAGES:* Italian and English.

Memberships: International Association for the Protection of Industrial Property (AIPPI); Federation Internationale des Conseils en Propiete Industrielle (FICPI); Licensing Executives Society (LES); The United States Trademark Association (USTA); American Intellectual Property Law Association (AIPLA); European Communities Trade Mark Practitioners Association (ECTA); UNION.

BESANA-STUDIO LEGALE ASSOCIATO

Established in 1969

8, VIA PASSIONE

20122 MILAN, ITALY

Telephone: 0039/2/76013993

Telex: 340425 AVUCAT I

Fax: 0039/2/76013547

General International Practice.

FIRM PROFILE: The firm specializes in assisting foreign corporate clients, both as advisor and litigator for their local operations and for acquisitions, mergers and commercial transactions. The majority of the clients are based in the United States, France, Great Britain and the Scandinavian countries. The members of the firm share a common experience on a wide range of areas, and individual concentration on specific areas as shown is, therefore, not particularly significant.

MARIO G. BESANA, born Breno, Italy, 1934; admitted, 1957, Italy. *Education:* University of Milan (J.D., 1957); University of Chicago. Commonwealth Fund Fellow, 1959-1961. Registered Comptroller of Accounts, 1971—. Secretary General, Italian Federation of Lawyers' Guilds, 1977-1983. *LANGUAGES:* Italian, English and French. *PRACTICE AREAS:* Taxation; Corporate Restructuring.

LAURA SPREAFICO, born Como, Italy, 1936; admitted, 1961, Italy. *Education:* University of Geneva, Switzerland; The City of London College, England; Università degli Studi di Milano (1961). Registered Controller of Accounts. *LANGUAGES:* Italian, English and French. *PRACTICE AREAS:* Litigation; Labour Law.

MARIA GRAZIA VASSALLO, born Rome, Italy, 1952; admitted, 1979, Italy. *Education:* University of Milan (J.D., 1976); University of Bologna (1977). *LANGUAGES:* Italian, English and French. *PRACTICE AREAS:* Company Law; Contracts.

ASSOCIATES

ISIDORO CAMPISI, born Milan, Italy, March 11, 1963; admitted, 1988, Italy. *Education:* Università degli Studi di Milano (Dottore in Giurisprudenza, 1987). *LANGUAGES:* Italian, English and French. *PRACTICE AREAS:* Litigation.

(This Listing Continued)

MICHELA BOTTAZZI, born Milan, Italy, September 23, 1963; admitted, 1987, Italy. *Education:* Universita La Sapienza di Roma (1986). *LANGUAGES:* Italian, English and French. *PRACTICE AREAS:* Company Law.

Languages: Italian, English and French.

STUDIO LEGALE BIANCHI E ASSOCIATI

Established in 1960

VIA VISCONTI DI MODRONE, 18
20122 MILAN, ITALY
Telephone: (02) 76.01.35.56
Cable Address: "Febius-Milano"
Telex: 333482 Febius I
Telefax: (02) 76.00.93.74

Corporate Law, Mergers and Acquisitions, Banking and Financing, Joint Ventures, Italian and European Antitrust and Competition Law, Agencies and Distributorships, Bankruptcy and Insolvency Law, Labor and Employment Law, Litigation and Arbitration, International Trade Regulations, European Communities Law, Product Liability, Food, Chemical and Pharmaceutical Law.

FIRM PROFILE: *The firm was established in 1960 and traditionally is mainly involved in assisting foreign corporations, including banks operating in Italy through subsidiaries or otherwise and in providing general counseling therefor.*

AVV. FEDERICO BIANCHI, born Como, Italy, November 19, 1920; admitted, 1948, Italy; 1960, Court of Cassation and other Supreme Courts of Italy. *Education:* Catholic University of Milan (Doctor of Law, cum laude, 1946); University of Geneva, Switzerland; Harvard University Law School, Cambridge, Massachusetts, U.S.A. (LL.M., 1954). Contributor to Law Reviews and Year Book of Institute of International and Foreign Law, University of Milan. President, Fulbright Association of Milan and Member of Board, Italian Fulbright Association, 1958-1961. Member: Legal Committee, American Chamber of Commerce for Italy; Panel of Arbitrators, American Arbitration Association and Associazione Italiana Arbitrato; Board of Examiners, Court of Appeal of Milan, 1971 Session of Examinations for Entrance to the Bar. *LANGUAGES:* English, French and German. *PRACTICE AREAS:* Commercial; Corporate; Private International Law; Arbitration.

AVV. FEDERICO MACCONE, born Piacenza, Italy, May 3, 1928; admitted, 1951, Italy; 1963, Court of Cassation and other Supreme Courts of Italy. *Education:* State University of Milan (Doctor of Law, cum laude, 1949). *LANGUAGES:* English, French and German. *PRACTICE AREAS:* Litigation; Civil and Commercial Law; Advertising.

AVV. PAOLO SORTENI, born Monza, Italy, July 10, 1933; admitted, 1968, Italy. *Education:* State University of Milan (Doctor of Law, 1957); SAIS Johns Hopkins University (1959); Insead France (M.B.A., 1960). National Roll of Official Examiner of Corporate Accounts, Admitted, 1980. President, Italian Insead Alumni Association, 1964-1968. *Member:* International Association for the Protection of Industrial Property (AIPPI); Licensing Executive Society (L.E.S.). *LANGUAGES:* English and French. *PRACTICE AREAS:* Commercial; Corporate; Industrial Property; EEC Law; Food; Chemical and Pharmaceutical Law.

AVV. MARIO PAOLO GINELLI, born Milan, Italy, December 25, 1936; admitted, 1963, Italy. *Education:* State University of Milan (Doctor of Law, cum laude, 1960). Fellow at Salzburg Seminar in American Studies, 1966. Former Assistant at the Università Commerciale Bocconi, Milano. *LANGUAGES:* English and French. *PRACTICE AREAS:* Commercial; Corporate Law; Foreign Investment; Mergers and Acquisitions; Joint Ventures.

AVV. CLAUDIO BONORA, born Inzago, Italy, June 19, 1952; admitted, 1980, Italy. *Education:* State University of Milan (Doctor of Law, 1977). *LANGUAGES:* German and French. *PRACTICE AREAS:* Commercial; Banking; Financial; Labor and Bankruptcy.

ROBERT RUDEK RECHTSANWALT, born Heilbronn, Germany, June 28, 1958; admitted, 1986, Federal Republic of Germany (Not admitted in Italy). *Education:* University of Munich (Referendar, 1982; Assessor, 1986). *Member:* Munich Bar Association; Vereinigung für Gedankenaustausch zwischen Deutschen und Italienischen Juristen e.V. *LANGUAGES:* German, English and French. *PRACTICE AREAS:* Commercial; Private International and Corporate Law.

(This Listing Continued)

AVV. ATTILIA FRACCHIA, born Alessandria, Italy, December 18, 1955; admitted, 1981, Italy. *Education:* University of Turin (Doctor of Law, 1980). International Functionary with the E.C. Court of Justice in Luxembourg, 1981-1984. *LANGUAGES:* English, French and German. *PRACTICE AREAS:* Litigation; Civil and Commercial Law; Private International Law.

DOTT. PROC. MARINA ISENBURG, born Milan, Italy, April 28, 1938; admitted, 1966, Italy. *Education:* State University of Milan (Doctor of Law, cum laude, 1962); University of Paris, Sorbonne (D.E.A., 1980). *LANGUAGES:* French and English. *PRACTICE AREAS:* Corporate Law; Bankruptcy; Foreign Investment; Financing.

DOTT. PROC. PAOLO BENAZZO, born Pavia, Italy, September 26, 1964; admitted, 1992, Italy. *Education:* State University of Pavia (Doctor of Law, cum laude, 1988). Assistant Professor, Commercial Law, State University of Pavia. *LANGUAGES:* English and French. *PRACTICE AREAS:* Commercial; Corporate; Financial; Bankruptcy Law.

REFERENCES: *USA:* Digital Equipment Corp.; Fischer & Porter Co.; Kraft General Foods Corp.; W.R. Grace & Co.; Mobil Chemical Co.-Mobil Oil Corp.; Sterling Winthrop Inc.; Sybron Corp. *England:* WPP Group plc. *France:* Caisse Nationale de Credit Agricole; Spie-Capag S.A.; Total Compagnie Francaise des Petroles. *Germany:* Deutsche Bank A.G. Dresdner Bank A.G. *Japan:* Nichimen & Co. *Netherlands:* Hendrix Int.; Yamaha Motor Europe N.V. *Norway:* Elopak S/A. *Sweden:* Beijer Invest; Frigoscandia AB; Promotion; Stiga AB (Industri AB Kuben Group). *Italy:* American Chamber of Commerce for Italy; Banca Commerciale Italiana; Banca di Roma; Credito Italiano; DHL International ; Elopak; Banco Ambroveneto; J. Walter Thompson; Leo Burnett; Sterling-Midy S.p.A.; Morgan Guaranty Trust; Mc Cann Erickson Italiana S.p.A.

BIRINDELLI CASTELLANI & ASSOCIATI

Established in 1988

26 VIA DURINI
20122 MILAN, ITALY
Telephone: (39.2) 76013442
Telefax: (39.2) 76013435

International and Domestic General Civil Practice, Corporate, Banking and Taxation Law, Sports and Entertainment Law.

FIRM PROFILE: *The Firm was established in 1988 under the name of Studio dell'Avvocato Birindelli. A complete range of services is available to both domestic clients in their Italian and International activities, with particular expertise in dealing with the Pacific Region, as well as to the International clients doing business in Italy.*

LUCA BIRINDELLI, born La Spezia, Italy, April 9, 1956; admitted, 1982, Italy. *Education:* Rome University (Doctor in Law, 1979); New York University, School of Law (M.C.J., 1980). *Member:* Milan Bar. *LANGUAGES:* Italian, English and French. *PRACTICE AREAS:* International Trade and Contracts; Foreign Investment Advising; Sports and Entertainment Law.

ENRICO CASTELLANI, born Bologna, Italy, June 18, 1960; admitted, 1989, Italy. *Education:* Trieste University (Doctor in Law, Magna cum laude, 1984). *Member:* Milan Bar. *LANGUAGES:* Italian and English. *PRACTICE AREAS:* Foreign Investment Advising; Corporate Banking and Taxation Law.

EMANUELA ROMOLI, born Viareggio, Italy, August 11, 1962; admitted, 1991, Italy. *Education:* Milan University (Doctor in Law, 1986). Trainee, General Directoraté of Competition, EEC Commission, 1990. *Member:* Milan Bar. *LANGUAGES:* Italian, English and French. *PRACTICE AREAS:* General Civil Practice; Competition Law.

CARLO EDOARDO PATELLANI, born Milan, Italy, April 26, 1958; admitted, 1986, Italy. *Education:* Milan University (Doctor in Law, 1984). *Member:* Milan Bar. *LANGUAGES:* Italian, English and German. *PRACTICE AREAS:* General Civil Practice; Corporate Banking and Taxation Law.

LIA VOZZA, born Modena, Italy, January 25, 1966; admitted, 1992, Italy. *Education:* Bologna University (Doctor in Law, 1989). *Member:* Milan Bar. *LANGUAGES:* Italian and English. *PRACTICE AREAS:* General Civil Practice.

RICCARDO CIAMPELLA, born Milan, Italy, May 5, 1965; admitted, 1994, Italy. *Education:* Milan University (Doctor in Law, 1990). *LANGUAGES:* Italian and English. *PRACTICE AREAS:* General Civil Practice.

(This Listing Continued)

BIRINDELLI CASTELLANI & ASSOCIATI, Milan—
Continued

STEFANO SONZINI, born Milan, Italy, January 14, 1969. *Education:* Milan University (Doctor in Law, 1994). *LANGUAGES:* Italian, English and French. *PRACTICE AREAS:* General Civil Practice.

STUDIO LEGALE BISCONTI

VIA SANTO SPIRITO, 14
20121 MILAN, ITALY
Telephone: (39-2) 782641
Telex: 335009 BRACTO I
Fax: (39-2) 781188

Rome, Italy Office: Via Bissolati, 76, 00187. Telephone: (39-6) 479881. Telex: 610409 BRACTO I. Fax: (39-6) 4872070.
New York, New York Office: 730 Fifth Avenue, 10019. Telephone: (212) 956-9400. Telex: 225120 BRACTON UR. Fax: (212) 956-9405.
London, England Office: 1 College Hill, EC4R 4RA. Telephone: (44-0171) 4899924. Telex: 893544 BRACTO G. Fax: (44-0171) 4898740.

Corporate Practice. Mergers and Acquisitions, Securities, International Finance and Banking, International Law, Domestic and International Taxation, EEC Law, Corporation Law, Labor, Bankruptcy, Environmental Law, Energy, Antitrust, Unfair Competition, Telecommunications, Patents, Trademarks, Alternative Dispute Resolution, Counselling in International Commercial Transactions.

GIUSEPPE BISCONTI, born Palmi, Italy, April 22, 1931; admitted to practice, 1953; admitted, 1954, Italy; 1968, Supreme Court, Italy. *Education:* Italy, University of Rome (Doctor of Jurisprudence, maxima cum laude), 1953; Austria, University of Graz, 1951; Germany, University of Münster, 1955; U.S.A., Louisiana State University Law School (LL.M., 1956; Post-doctoral Fellow, 1955-1956) and University of Michigan Law School (doctoral candidate and Research Associate, 1956-1958). Professorial Assistant of Comparative Law, University of Rome, 1958-1960. Scientific Collaborator, International Institute for the Unification of Private Law, 1958-1959; Guest Lecturer on Private International Law, Institut Universitaire d'Etudes Européennes, Turin, 1959 and 1960. Visiting Scholar, Columbia University Law School, 1979. *Member:* Italian Bar Association (Rome); American Bar Association (Honorary Member); Canadian Bar Association (Honorary Member); Mexican Bar Association (Honorary Member); American Bar Foundation (Fellow); The Association of the Bar of the City of New York; New York County Lawyers' Association; American Foreign Law Association; Southwestern Legal Foundation (Trustee; Vice-Chairman and Member of the Advisory Board); American Society of International Law; British Institute of International and Comparative Law; International Bar Association (President, 1990-1992); International Fiscal Association; International Law Association; Union Internationale des Avocats. (At Rome and Milan Offices). *LANGUAGES:* Italian, English, French, German, Spanish and Russian.

CARLO GARBARINO, born Genoa, Italy, September 23, 1959; admitted to practice, 1984; admitted, 1987, Italy. *Education:* Italy, University of Genoa (Doctor of Jurisprudence, maxima cum laude, 1983); University of Michigan Law School (Master of Laws, 1986); University of Genoa (Ph.D. in International Taxation, 1989). Visiting Scholar, Yale Law School, 1986-1987. Associate Professor, University of Siena, 1988. IBM Italia S.p.A., Office of the Legal Counsel, 1987-1988. Member, Editorial Board of Diritto e Pratica Tributaria; Contributing Editor of EC Tax Review. *Member:* Italian Bar Association (Genoa); International Bar Association; International Fiscal Association. *LANGUAGES:* Italian and English.

FABIO MARELLI, born Alessandria, Italy, July 11, 1963; admitted to practice, 1988; admitted, 1991, Italy. *Education:* Italy, University of Pavia (Doctor of Jurisprudence, 1987); University of Miami School of Law (LL.M., 1990). Research Associate, C.N.R.-Consiglio Nazionale delle Ricerche, Pavia, Italy, 1988. *Member:* Italian Bar Association (Milan). *LANGUAGES:* Italian and English.

GAUDIANA GIUSTI, born Livorno, Italy, July 14, 1962; admitted to practice, 1988, Italy; admitted, 1993, Italy (Not admitted in Italy). *Education:* University of Pisa, Italy (Doctor of Jurisprudence, maxima cum laude, 1987); Universite' Libre de Bruxelles (Licence Speciale en Droit Européen, 1989). *Member:* Italian Bar Association (Pisa); European Lawyers Association. (Resident). *LANGUAGES:* Italian and English.

STUDIO LEGALE BONELLI E ASSOCIATI

VIA BORGONUOVO, 12
20121 MILAN, ITALY
Telephone: (2) 655-4499
Telefax: (2) 655-4554
Telex: 271583 FRABO I

Genoa, Italy Office: Viale Padre Santo, 5/8, 16122. Telephone: (10) 831-8341 Telefax: (10) 813-849; 831-0953. Telex: 271583 FRABO I.

General Practice, International and Commercial Practice, Corporate Law, Commercial Law, Mergers and Acquisitions, Contracts, Construction Law, Banking, Antitrust, Securities Regulation, Trademark and Patent, Bankruptcy, Admiralty and Arbitration.

MEMBERS OF FIRM

FRANCO BONELLI, born Genoa, Italy, January 28, 1938; admitted, 1963, Italy. *Education:* University of Genoa (J.D., magna cum laude, 1960). Author: several books and articles on Contract Law and Corporate Law. Co-Editor, "Giurisprudenza Commerciale Società e Fallimento," Milan, 1974—. Editor-in-Chief, "Diritto del Commercio Internazionale," Milan, 1987—. Visiting Professor, Stanford University, 1970. Professor, Commercial Law, University of Genoa, 1976—. *Member:* Italian Bar Association (Genoa); Italian Maritime Law Association.

ANTONIO CRIVELLARO, born Padua, Italy, November 21, 1942; (Not admitted in Italy). *Education:* University of Padua (B.A., Pol. Sc., magna cum laude, 1967). Author: several articles on International Law, International Trade Law, International Construction Law and International Arbitration. Co-Editor, "Diritto del Commercio Internazionale," Milan, 1987. Assistant Professor, International Law, 1968-1978. Visiting Professor, Harvard Law School, 1974-1975. Professor: International Organization, University of Padua, 1976-1983; International Trade Law, University of Milan, 1987-1989, 1990-1991.

GIOVANNI DOMENICHINI, born Rome, Italy, January 5, 1948; admitted, 1973, Italy. *Education:* University of Pisa (J.D., magna cum laude, 1970); Scuola Superiore di Studi Universitari S. Anna (magna cum laude, 1973). Author: a book and several articles on Corporate Law. Professor, Commercial Law, University of Genoa, 1980—. Member, "Giurisprudenza Commerciale Società e Fallimento," Editorial Board, Milan, 1974—. *Member:* Italian Bar Association (Genoa); Italian Association of Comparative Law; Scuola Superiore di Studi Universitari S. Anna Alumni Association.

ROBERTO PISTORELLI, born Padua, Italy, September 5, 1953; admitted, 1983, Italy. *Education:* University of Padua (J.D., magna cum laude, 1977); Cambridge University (LL.M., 1979). Author: articles on Conflict of Laws and Contract Law. Visiting Fellow, European University, Florence, 1988. *Member:* Italian Bar Association (Milan).

GIULIO PONZANELLI, born Carrara, Italy, September 25, 1953; admitted, 1979, Italy. *Education:* University of Pisa (J.D., Magna cum laude, 1976); Scuola Superiore S. Anna Pisa (Magna cum laude, 1979). Author: three books and several articles and essays on Corporations, Tort, Contract Law and Civil Rights. Visiting Professor, Yale Law School, 1987-1990. Professor, Comparative Law, University of Pisa, 1990-1994; Civil Law University of Brescia, 1994—. *Member:* Italian Bar Association (Massa Carrara); Italian Association of Comparative Law; Association Henri Capitant.

MARCO ARATO, born Genoa, Italy, July 13, 1955; admitted, 1981, Italy. *Education:* University of Genoa (J.D., magna cum laude, 1977). Author: a book and several articles on Bankruptcy and Corporate Law. Professor: EEC Competition Law, University of Genoa, 1985-1988, 1990-1992; Commercial Law, University of Messina, 1992—. *Member:* Italian Bar Association (Genoa).

GIAMBATTISTA D'ASTE, born Genoa, Italy, April 30, 1956; admitted, 1984, Italy. *Education:* University of Genoa (J.D., magna cum laude, 1981). *Member:* Italian Bar Association (Genoa).

ALBERTO SARAVALLE, born Milan, Italy, November 13, 1956; admitted, 1984, Italy; 1986, New York. *Education:* University of Padua (J.D., 1981); Cambridge University (LL.B., 1982); Yale Law School (LL.M., 1985). Author: a book and several articles on Private International Law. Foreign Associate, Shearman & Sterling, New York, 1985-1986. Associate, Shearman & Sterling, Paris, 1990-1992. *Member:* Italian Bar Association (Milan); American Bar Association; Association of the Bar of the City of New York; International Bar Association; American Society of International Law; Association Henri Capitant.

(This Listing Continued)

SILVIA PORTA, born Genoa, Italy, June 3, 1958; admitted, 1984, Italy. *Education:* University of Genoa (J.D., 1982). *Member:* Italian Bar Association (Genoa); Italian Maritime Law Association.

ANDREA BETTINI, born Genoa, Italy, October 4, 1959; admitted, 1986, Italy. *Education:* University of Genoa (J.D., magna cum laude, 1983). *Member:* Italian Bar Association (Genoa).

ERNESTO PUGLIESE, born Turin, Italy, February 17, 1963; admitted, 1990, Italy. *Education:* University of Genoa (J.D., 1986). *Member:* Italian Bar Association (Genoa).

MARCO BAGNOLI, born Forli, Italy, March 24, 1964; admitted, 1993, Italy. *Education:* University of Bologna (J.D., magna cum laude, 1989); The London School of Economics and Political Science (LL.M., 1991); University Institute of European Studies, Turin (International Trade Law, 1992). Visiting Lawyer, Wragge and Co., Birmingham, United Kingdom, 1990. *Member:* Italian Bar Association (Milan); EC Lawyers Society (London).

LUCIA RADICIONI, born Genoa, Italy, December 16, 1964; admitted, 1991, Italy. *Education:* University of Genoa (J.D., magna cum laude, 1988). *Member:* Italian Bar Association (Genoa).

GIUSEPPE MARVULLI, born Genoa, Italy, April 1, 1966; admitted, 1992, Italy. *Education:* University of Genoa (J.D., magna cum laude, 1988).

VITTORIO ALLAVENA, born Genoa, Italy, April 30, 1965; admitted, 1992, Italy. *Education:* University of Genoa (J.D., magna cum laude, 1988).

VITTORIO LUPOLI, born La Spezia, Italy, June 22, 1965; admitted, 1993, Italy. *Education:* University of Genoa (J.D., 1990).

MARIO OLIVIERI, born Genoa, Italy, October 3, 1965; admitted, 1993, Italy. *Education:* University of Genoa (J.D., magna cum laude, 1990).

MICAELA MAGRI, born Bari, Italy, July 3, 1965; (Not admitted in Italy). *Education:* University of Milan (J.D., 1991); Institut d'Etudes Européens de l'Université Libre de Bruxelles (Licence spéciale en Droit européen, 1 992). Trainee at the European Community Commission-DG X (1993). Visiting Lawyer, Studio Legale Tizzano-Pappalardo, Brussels, 1994. *Member:* Italian Young Lawyers in Europe Association (AGAIE), Brussels.

AMERIGO PERASSO, born Genoa, Italy, October 19, 1965; admitted, 1994, Italy. *Education:* University of Genoa (J.D., magna cum laude, 1990).

MARCELLO LULY, born Cassano, Italy, April 26, 1967; (Not admitted in Italy). *Education:* University of Parma (J.D., 1992).

ANDREA PERICU, born Genoa, Italy, June 6, 1967; (Not admitted in Italy). *Education:* University of Genoa (J.D., magna cum laude, 1990); University College of London (LL.M., 1993).

RICCARDO PONTREMOLI, born Genoa, Italy, March 3, 1968; (Not admitted in Italy). *Education:* University of Genoa (J.D., 1994).

FRANCESCO STELLA, born La Spezia, Italy, July 26, 1968; (Not admitted in Italy). *Education:* Catholic University of Milan (J.D., magna cum laude, 1993).

FULVIO MARVULLI, born Genoa, Italy, January 18, 1969; (Not admitted in Italy). *Education:* University of Genoa (J.D. magna cum laude, 1991).

MATTEO BONELLI, born Genoa, Italy, January 25, 1969; (Not admitted in Italy). *Education:* University of Milan (J.D., magna cum laude, 1992).

ENRICO BAZZANO, born Savona, Italy, May 7, 1969; (Not admitted in Italy). *Education:* University of Genoa (J.D., magna cum laude, 1993).

PAOLO BERTONI, born Genoa, Italy, January 7, 1970; (Not admitted in Italy). *Education:* University of Genoa (J.D., magna cum laude, 1993).

ALESSANDRA DACCO, born Milan, Italy, September 10, 1970; (Not admitted in Italy). *Education:* University of Milan (J.D., magna cum laude, 1993).

Languages: Italian, English, French, German and Spanish.

STUDIO LEGALE BOSSI & GRONDONA

Established in 1991

VIA L. MANARA 15
20122 MILAN, ITALY
Telephone: 02/55181582-55181911
Fax: 02/59901941

International and General Practice, Corporate, Currency, EEC, Energy, Banking, Insurance, Investment, Family, Arbitration, Bankruptcy, Labor, Patent, Trademark, Copyright, Probate, Taxation, Real Estate, Estates, Civil and Commercial Litigation.

FIRM PROFILE: *The firm was established in 1991 and soon after it became a member of a network of other Italian firms, established in Modena, Rome and the Venice area. All firms of the network specialize in the Corporate and Commercial practice.*

MEMBERS OF FIRM

ALESSANDRO BOSSI, born Milan, Italy, July 24, 1956; admitted, 1983, Italy. *Education:* State University of Milan (J.D., magna cum laude, 1980); British Council Fellow (Law), King's College, London (1984). Lecturer, Legal Italian, The University of the Pacific, Mc George School of Law, Salzburg, 1984. *Member:* European Lawyers Association. *LANGUAGES:* Italian, English and French. *PRACTICE AREAS:* Competition Law; Commercial Agency; Litigation; Product Liability; Distribution.

PAOLO A. GRONDONA, born Milan, Italy, June 23, 1955; admitted, 1980, Italy. *Education:* University of Pavia (J.D., 1978); British Council Fellow (Law), King's College, London (1981); Parker School of Foreign and Comparative Law, Columbia University, New York, (1983). Seminar in American Law, Salzburg Seminars at Schloss Leopoldskron, Salzburg, (1985); Academy of American and International Law, The Southwestern Legal Foundation, Dallas, (1987). *Member:* Association Internationale des Jeunes Avocats; International Bar Association; British-Italian Law Association; European Lawyers Association. *LANGUAGES:* Italian, English and French. *PRACTICE AREAS:* Arbitration; Bankruptcy; Insurance; Labor Law; Company Law.

ASSOCIATE

IRINA PIAZZOLI, born Lecco, Italy, January 19, 1966; admitted, 1994, Italy. *Education:* University of Milan (J.D., magna cum laude, 1990). *LANGUAGES:* Italian, English and French. *PRACTICE AREAS:* Corporate Estates; Family; Labor Law.

REPRESENTATIVE CLIENTS: The Harris Group; The Cremonini Group; Iritech S.p.A.; MTV; Puritan Bennett Italia s.r.l.; Banco S. Gemignano e S. Prospero S.p.A.; ICI Plc; ICI Italia S.p.A.; TSB Plc; Digital Equipment S.p.A.; Boselli Sistemi S.p.A. Bachmann Co. Ltd.

STUDIO BROGGINI

VIA SAN VITTORE 45
20123 MILAN, ITALY
Telephone: 02-4988061
Telecopier: 02-463306

General Civil Practice.

GERARDO BROGGINI, born Locarno, Switzerland, November 16, 1926; admitted, 1952, Switzerland; 1968, Italy. *Education:* University of Fribourg, Rome and Heidelberg (Dr.iur.). Professor of Roman Law and Private International Law, University of Fribourg, Switzerland, 1956-1961, Heidelberg, Germany, 1961-1968 and Catholic University of Milan, 1968—.

ASSOCIATES

Eleonora Loiacono
Eva Lenski
Alfredo Tocchi
Jutta Welz
Alessandro Veralli

Languages: Italian, English, German and French.

BROSIO, CASATI E ASSOCIATI

VIA MANZONI, 41
20121 MILAN, ITALY
Telephone: (39) (2) 29010200
Telecopier: (39) (2) 29010278

Turin, Italy Office: Corso Vittorio Emanuele II, 68, 10121. Telephone: (39) (11) 5612005. Telecopier: (39) (11) 541018.

Rome, Italy Office: Via Valadier, 36, 00193. Telephone: (39) (6) 3230328. Telecopier: (39) (6) 3216107.

Brussels, Belgium Office: 99, Rue de la Loi, 1040. Telephone: (32) (2) 2300004. Telecopier: (32) (2) 2307473.

General Practice and Litigation. Corporation, Taxation, Foreign Investment, Mergers and Acquisitions, Banking, Administrative, Antitrust, Environmental, Labor, Real Estate and EEC Law.

MEMBERS OF FIRM

GUIDO BROSIO, born Moncalieri (Turin), Italy, February 1, 1943; admitted, 1972, Italy; 1988, Supreme Court. *Education:* University of Turin (J.D., 1967); Harvard University (LL.M., 1969). Visiting Foreign Lawyer: Sullivan & Cromwell, New York and Paris Offices, 1969-1971; Stegemann, Sieveking & Lutteroth, Hamburg, 1971. *Member:* A.B.A.; I.B.A.; U.I.A. (Resident, Turin Office).

ROBERTO CASATI, born Milan, Italy, April 26, 1948; admitted, 1973, Italy; 1979, New York. *Education:* University of Milan (J.D., 1970); University of Michigan Law School (LL.M., 1974); Columbia Law School (J.D., 1978). Visiting Foreign Lawyer: Sullivan & Cromwell, New York, 1975-1976. Member of Staff, Columbia Journal of Transnational Law, 1977-1978. Associate, Sullivan & Cromwell, New York, 1978-1981. Member, Advisory Board, The International and Comparative Law Center, Southwestern Legal Foundation, 1987—. *Member:* A.B.A.; I.B.A.; American Foreign Law Association.

CARLO PAVESIO, born Turin, Italy, February 1, 1956; admitted, 1983, Italy. *Education:* University of Turin (J.D., 1979); London School of Economics (LL.M., 1980). Trainee, Legal Service of the EEC Commission, 1980-1981. Visiting Foreign Lawyer: Gibson, Dunn & Crutcher, New York, 1985-1986. *Member:* I.B.A.; U.I.A.; European Lawyers Association. (Resident, Turin Office).

MARIO COLOMBATTO, born Turin, Italy, August 23, 1956; admitted, 1983, Italy. *Education:* University of Turin (J.D., 1979); London School of Economics (LL.M., 1980). Visiting Foreign Lawyer: Westrick & Eckholdt, Frankfurt, 1981-1982. Lecturer in: Comparative Private Law, University of Trento, 1984-1986; Fundamentals of Civil Law, Bocconi University, Milan, 1986-1991. *Member:* I.B.A.; U.I.A. (Resident, Turin Office).

DAVIDE D'ANGELO, born Catania, Italy, March 30, 1954; admitted, 1979, Italy. *Education:* University of Pisa (J.D., 1976); Scuola Superiore di Studi Universitari e di Perfezionamento, University of Pisa (J.D., 1977); Academy of American and International Law, Southwestern Legal Foundation, Dallas, 1987.

ALBERTO NANNI, born Milan, Italy, April 28, 1955; admitted, 1981, Italy. *Education:* Catholic University of Milan (J.D., 1979).

GIOVANNI MARIA MARINI, born Milan, Italy, July 9, 1958; admitted, 1984, Italy; 1991, New York. *Education:* University of Pavia (J.D., 1981); Seminar in American Legal Studies, Salzburg (1988); Georgetown University Law Center (LL.M., 1990). Visiting Foreign Lawyer: Wilmer, Cutler & Pickering, Washington D.C., 1990-1991; Cleary, Gottlieb, Steen & Hamilton, Brussels, 1991. *Member:* A.B.A.; Foreign Lawyers Forum, Washington D.C.

FILIPPO CESARIS, born Milan, Italy, December 20, 1960; admitted, 1991, Italy. *Education:* Catholic University of Milan (J.D., 1985). Assistant Professor, Department of Bankruptcy Law, Catholic University of Milan, 1985-1992. *Member:* I.B.A.; S.I.S.CO. (Società Italiana di Studi Concorsuali).

ASSOCIATES

MARCO TOSETTO BRICCO, born Turin, Italy, May 5, 1954; admitted, 1985, Italy. *Education:* University of Turin (J.D., 1980). (Resident, Turin Office).

MASSIMO GRECO, born Milan, Italy, October 11, 1959; admitted, 1985, Italy. *Education:* University of Milan (J.D., 1983).

(This Listing Continued)

FRANCESCO CANTONI, born Milan, Italy, October 21, 1959; admitted, 1986, Italy. *Education:* Milan University (Doctor in Law, 1984). *Member:* Milan Bar.

DANIELA JOUVENAL LONG, born Turin, Italy, October 10, 1958; admitted, 1985, Italy. *Education:* University of Turin (J.D., 1982). (Resident, Rome Office).

PAOLO ESPOSITO, born Rome, Italy, March 25, 1960; admitted, 1989, Italy. *Education:* University of Milan (J.D., 1985); Catholic University of Milan (Diploma in Company Law, 1988-1989); City of London Polytechnic (Summer School, 1989). Visiting Foreign Lawyer: Linklaters & Paines, London, 1993.

GIANCARLO CASTORINO, born Casagiove (Caserta), Italy, January 19, 1962; admitted, 1989, Italy. *Education:* University of Messina (J.D., 1985). Visiting Foreign Lawyer: Brobeck, Phleger & Harrison, San Francisco, 1994.

CRISTINA MANASSE, born Montevideo, Uruguay, July 15, 1961; admitted, 1990, Italy. *Education:* University of Milan (J.D., 1985; postgraduate qualification in EC Law, 1991); King's College, London, 1993. Visiting Foreign Lawyer: Lovell White Durrant, London, 1993. Teaching Assistant, Civil Law, University of Milan. Research Associate, C.N.R., Milan, 1991. *Member:* E.L.A.: B.I.L.A.: EC Lawyers Society.

DANIELA STELÉ, born Genoa, Italy, March 22, 1963; admitted, 1991, Nice, France (Not admitted in Italy). *Education:* University of Aix-en-Provence, France (J.D., 1985).

CLAUDIA CRESCENZI, born Rome, Italy, November 23, 1963; admitted, 1990, Italy. *Education:* University of Rome (J.D., 1987); College of Europe, Bruges, Belgium (Diploma in Advanced European Legal Studies, 1989). Visiting Foreign Lawyer: De Smedt & Dessesse-Akin, Gump, Strauss, Hauer & Feld International, Brussels, 1989-1991. (Resident, Brussels Office).

FRANCESCO SIMONESCHI, born Siena, Italy, June 11, 1961; admitted, 1991, Italy. *Education:* University of Bologna (J.D., 1988).

NICOLA CERAOLO, born Messina, Italy, January 4, 1964; admitted, 1992, Italy. *Education:* University of Messina (J.D., 1986); College of Europe, Bruges, Belgium (Diploma in Advanced European Legal Studies, 1988); Leiden-Amsterdam-Columbia Summer Program in American Law, 1994. *Member:* I.B.A. (Resident, Turin Office).

PAOLO CERINA, born Novara, Italy, June 27, 1963; admitted, 1992, Italy. *Education:* University of Milan (J.D., 1989); City of London Polytechnic (Certificate in Banking and Finance, 1990); Leiden-Amsterdam-Columbia Summer Program in American Law, 1991; Columbia Law School (LL.M., 1993). Visiting Foreign Lawyer: Pennie & Edmonds, New York, 1994. Lecturer in Private International Law, University of Milan, 1993. *Member:* American Foreign Law Association.

RICCARDO VENTURA, born Parma, Italy, April 7, 1964; admitted, 1992, Italy. *Education:* University of Parma (J.D., 1987); Georgetown University Law Center (LL.M., 1993). (Resident, Turin Office).

DONATELLA DE ROSA, born Turin, Italy, October 24, 1966; admitted, 1992, Italy. *Education:* University of Turin (J.D., 1989); University Institute for European Studies, Turin, Fall Program, 1989; Academy of American and International Law, Southwestern Legal Foundation, Dallas, 1994. (Resident, Turin Office).

CECILIA BURESTI, born Bologna, Italy, February 15, 1966; admitted, 1992, Italy. *Education:* University of Bologna (J.D., 1988).

GIOVANNI LUPPI, born Turin, Italy, January 6, 1965; admitted, 1993, Italy. *Education:* University of Turin (J.D., 1990). (Resident, Turin Office).

ALESSANDRA PERRAZZELLI, born Genoa, Italy, August 13, 1961; admitted, 1993, New York. *Education:* University of Genoa (J.D., 1986); New York University (LL.M., 1988). Associate, Winthrop, Stimson, Putnam & Roberts, New York and Brussels Offices, 1988-1993. *Member:* A.B.A.

SARA PANELLI, born Turin, Italy, November 19, 1967; admitted, 1994, Italy. *Education:* University of Turin (J.D., 1990). (Resident, Turin Office).

VITTORIO TORAZZI, born Turin, Italy, June 5, 1966; admitted, 1994, Italy. *Education:* University of Turin (J.D., 1990). (Resident, Turin Office).

MICHELE DELFINI, born Milan, Italy, May 17, 1967; admitted, 1994, Italy. *Education:* State University of Milan (J.D., 1991). Assistant Professor, Department of Commercial Law, University of Milan.

(This Listing Continued)

LAURA LAMERA, born Milan, Italy, January 9, 1966; admitted, 1994, Italy. *Education:* State University of Milan (J.D., 1991).

FABRIZIO FASANO, born Settimo Torinese (Turin), Italy, July 22, 1964; admitted, 1994, Italy. *Education:* University of Turin (J.D., 1990). (Resident, Turin Office).

MASSIMO TRENTINO, born Rome, Italy, December 12, 1966. *Education:* University of Rome (J.D., 1990). *Member:* U.A.E.

SILVIA D'AMARIO, born Turin, Italy, May 26, 1966. admitted to practice before the Lower Courts, 1994. *Education:* University of Turin (J.D., 1992). (Resident, Turin Office).

ANDREA AROSIO, born Turin, Italy, December 9, 1969. *Education:* University of Milan (J.D., 1994).

OF COUNSEL

RENATO CLARIZIA, born Salerno, Italy, October 10, 1950; admitted, 1975, Italy. *Education:* University of Rome (J.D., 1972); Columbia University School of Law, Visiting Scholar, 1977. Lecturer, Fundamentals of Civil Law, University of Rome, 1972-1977. Professor, Banking Law, 1979-1981 and Civil Law, 1981—, University of Urbino. Professor, Banking Law, Tax Inspectors Superior School, Rome, 1980—. Secretary General, ASSILEA (Italian Leasing Companies' Association), 1983-1990. (Resident, Rome Office).

ANTONELLA CAPRIA, born Rome, Italy, October 5, 1954; admitted, 1982, Italy. *Education:* University of Rome (J.D., 1977); Scuola in Governo dell'Ambiente e del Territorio, University of Pavia (1982). Instituto di Studi e Documentazione per il Territorio, Milan, Director; Institute for European Environmental Policy, Bonn, Italian correspondent; Instituto per l'Ambiente, Milan, law department, scientific coordination.

GUIDO ALVIGINI, born Biella, Italy, June 30, 1955; admitted, 1981, Italy. *Education:* Catholic University of Milan (J.D., 1978). Specializing in Far Eastern practice.

Languages: English, French and German.

STUDIO LEGALE
BRUNI GRAMELLINI & ASSOCIATI

CORSO DI PORTA VITTORIA 28
20122 MILAN, ITALY
Telephone: 02 - 55.19.03.78 / 54.54.149
Fax: 02 - 54.57.495

International General Practice, Corporate, Acquisitions, Business and Investments, Agency, Distribution, Banking, E.E.C., Labour, Insurance, Litigation, Arbitration, Patents and Trademarks, Copyright, Advertising, Entertainment Law, Real Estates,

GIAN BRUNO BRUNI, born Bolzano, Italy, March 15, 1950; admitted, 1979, Milan. *Education:* State University of Milan (J.D., magna cum laude, 1976); King's College, London (1984); Southwestern Legal Foundation, Dallas (1986). Author: "The floating charge in the English and Italian Experience," Milan, 1986; "New regulations for commercial agents under EEC Directive No. 88/653," Milan, 1991; "Protection of minority shareholders: comparative aspects Italy-U.K.", Milan 1993 "Nature and effects of the Retention of Title Clause under Italian Law" - B.J.I.B.F.L., London, 1994. Co-Author: "Pre-Trial and Pre-Hearing Procedures," I.B.A., London, 1990; "Trial and Court Procedures Worldwide," I.B.A., London, 1991; "International Corporate Insolvency Law," London, 1992; "International Liability of Corporate Directors," London, 1993. Lecturer: "International Transactions," Modena, 1988; "International bankruptcy law," Milan, 1988; "New Financial Products UK-Italy," Milan, 1990; "Contract Law, a comparison between Common and Civil Law," Milan, 1990-1991; "The regulation of financial market in Italy and in the U.K.," Milan, 1991. *Member:* I.B.A. (Committees E. G. O.; Country Chair, Committee J); E.L.A.; A.G.L.I.; A.E.D.B.F. *LANGUAGES:* Italian, English and French.

STEFANO GRAMELLINI, born Milan, Italy, December 12, 1948; admitted, 1980, Milan. *Education:* State University of Milan (J.D., 1974). Former In-House Counsel for ANIA (National Association of Insurance Companies, 1976-1981) and Daf Trucks S.p.A., 1982-1986. *LANGUAGES:* Italian, French.

SOFIA BOTTARO, born Novi Ligure, Italy, February 27, 1964; admitted, 1992, Milan. *Education:* State University of Milan (J.D., 1989); Sussex College, Cambridge (Postgraduate course). *Member:* AIJA. *LANGUAGES:* Italian, English, French.

(This Listing Continued)

FRANCESCO ROMOLI, born Milan, Italy, May 14, 1961; admitted, 1994, Milan. *Education:* State University of Milan (J.D., 1991). *Member:* ELSA. *LANGUAGES:* Italian, English, French.

NICCOLÓ ZANCHINI, born Milan, August 29, 1965. *Education:* Catholic University of Milan (J.D., 1993). *LANGUAGES:* Italian, English.

JOSEPH MOYERSOEN, born Milan, Italy, April 17, 1965. *Education:* State University of Milan (J.D., 1992); Postgraduate course: Juvenile Court (1993-1994); Magistracy courses (Court of Milan, 1993, Catholic University of Milan, 1994). *LANGUAGES:* Italian, French, Spanish, English.

PAOLA PIZZIGHINI, born Parma, Italy, September 17, 1964; admitted, 1992, Bologna. *Education:* University of Parma 9J.D., 1988); Postgraduate course: Institute of Labour Law (University of Bologna). *LANGUAGES:* Italian, English.

STEFANO DELL'ORTO, born Milan, Italy, August 1, 1968. *Education:* State University of Milan (J.D., 1993); Droste Rechtsanwaelte Frankfurt (Post-graduate, 1994). *LANGUAGES:* Italian, German, English.

Languages: English, French, German and Italian

GENERAL COUNSEL IN ITALY FOR: AVL Medical Instruments; Costar Nuclepore; Daf Trucks, Grolier Hachette International; Haemonetics; Helvetia General Branch for Italy; Hong Kong Trade Development Council; Micro Technology; Pitney Bowes; Royal International Insurance; Sociét é Auxiliaire d'Entreprises; The Continental Insurance Company; The Upper Deck Company; Xerox Engineering; Royal Insurance Global; Verbatim.

AVVOCATI BRUNO & ASSOCIATI

Established in 1953

10, VIA P. VERRI
20121 MILAN, ITALY
Telephone: (2) 76006996; (2) 798823; (2) 76008084
Fax: (2) 76001473

Chicago, Illinois Associated Office: Bowles, Keating, Hering & Lowe. 135 South LaSalle Street, Suite 1040, 60603-4295. Telephone: (312) 263-6300. Telefax: (312) 263-0415. Telex: 6504632942 MCI UW.

Civil and Commercial, Corporate, Foreign Investments. Common Market, Environmental Law. Assistance to Foreign Corporations, Establishment of Subsidiaries and Branches. Mergers and Acquisitions. Fiscal Matters.

FIRM PROFILE: The firm was formed by Mr. Mario Bruno in 1953, upon his return from the United States of America for a period of practice and study. Since the establishment, the firm developed in the area of assistance to foreign corporations, foreign investments, acquisitions, royalty and licence agreements. Through the strict collaboration with US and European similar firms, the firm has enlarged its practice to other specializations of the legal profession. The firm operates in the field of national and international corporate business, acquisition and mergers, corporate taxation. The partners from a well trained, expert team working in strict contact, covering the entire area of the firm's national and international practice.

PARTNERS

MARIO BRUNO, born Ascoli Piceno, Italy, August 25, 1921; admitted, 1949, Milan. *Education:* State University of Milan (LL.B., 1944). Author: "How to Invest Private Capital in Italy," 1953; "The Italian Atomic Law," 1956. *Member:* Milan and International Bar Associations; The Association of the Bar of the City of New York (Associate Member). (Also Member, Bowles, Keating, Hering & Lowe, Milan, Italy).

ROBERTO N. BRUNO, born Milan, Italy, April 8, 1950; admitted, 1974, Milan. *Education:* State University of Milan (LL.B., 1974). *Member:* International Bar Association (Member, Business Law Section); Aija (Young Lawyer's International Association); International Law Association; International Fiscal Association (IFA); American Chamber of Commerce in Italy (Member, Legal and Tax Committee). (Also Member, Bowles, Keating, Hering & Lowe).

ASSOCIATE

DR. PIERLUIGI MARAZZI, born Sanremo, Italy, June 3, 1935; admitted, 1967, Milan. *Education:* State University, Parma (B.A., 1967).

Languages: Italian, French and English.

STUDIO AVV. CAJOLA

Established in 1966

VIA G. ROSSINI, N. 5
20122 MILAN, ITALY
Telephone: (02) 76003305, 796720, 76001035
Fax: (02) 780177

General International Practice. International Agreements. Corporation, Taxation and Commercial Law. Mergers and Acquisitions. Patent and Trademark Litigation. Transport and Insurance. Arbitration, Publicity and Advertising cases.

AVV. ALBERTO CAJOLA, born Venice, Italy, October 13, 1940; admitted, 1966, Italy, Supreme Court. *Education:* University of Milan (Doctor of Law, 1963). Honorary Legal Adviser: British Chamber of Commerce for Italy; Sir James Henderson School of Milan. Consultant: Commercial Section of the British Consulate General; Australian Trade Commission in Milan. *LANGUAGES:* Italian, English and French.

ASSOCIATES

AVV. ROBERTO CORDINI, born Milan, Italy, January 2, 1954; admitted, 1981, Italy. *Education:* University of Milan (Doctor of Law, 1978). *LANGUAGES:* Italian and French.

DR. CRISTINA TACCONI, born Lucca, Italy, December 2, 1960; admitted, 1990, Italy. *Education:* University of Milan (Doctor in Law, 1984). *LANGUAGES:* Italian and English.

DR. FRANCESCA TALAMINI, born Venice, Italy, June 6, 1963; admitted, 1988, Italy. *Education:* University of Bologna (Doctor of Law, cum laude, 1988). *LANGUAGES:* Italian, English and French.

TAX ADVISOR

DR. GIANLUCA BOLELLI, born Castelmaggiore (BO), September 18, 1959. *Education:* University L. Bocconi of Milan (Doctor in Business and Economics, 1983). *LANGUAGES:* Italian, English and French.

REPRESENTATIVE CLIENTS: *Japan:* Matsushita Electric; Seiko-Epson Corporation; Hitachi Metals. *U.K.:* Sun Alliance Ins. Co.; National Transit Ins. Co.; Pilkington Brothers Plc; APV Baker Ltd; Penguin Books Ltd; Longman Group; Addison-Wesley Ltd.; Desoutter Brothers Ltd; G.K.N. International Trading Ltd; GEC Plessey Telecommunications Ltd; Saatchi & Saatchi Plc; Bunzl Merchanting Group Ltd.; Meteror Paper Holdings Ltd. *U.S.A.:* Hay Group Inc.; MacDermid Inc.; Georgia Bonded Fibers Inc.; Spencer Stuart & Associates; Gartner Group Inc; Avon Products Inc. *France:* Groupe Gamma S.A. *Germany:* Continental AG. *Australia:* Sola International Holdings Ltd. *Hong Kong:* Yangtzekiang Garment Manufacturing Ltd. *Netherlands:* Institute for International Research B.V.; Addison Wesley-Publishers B.V. *Sweden:* Seco Tools A.B. *Italy:* Rover Italia S.p.A.; Prodotti Roche S.p.A.; Reconta Ernst & Young; Zanella S.p.A.; Contitech Ages S.p.A.

CALABI & FRIGESSI DI RATTALMA

Established in 1909

VIA MONTENAPOLEONE 20
20121 MILAN, ITALY
Telephone: 39-2-76022178
Telecopier: 39-2-782743

General Civil and Corporate Practice, Securities, Insurance and Banking Law, International and EEC Law, Intellectual Property Law.

GIUSEPPE CALABI (1909-1955).

ENZO CALABI (1946-1990).

GIUSEPPE CALABI, born Milan, Italy, December 18, 1960; admitted, 1989, Italy. *Education:* University of Milan (J.D., 1984); Harvard Law School (LL.M., 1990). Author: "Conduct of Business Rules in Securities Law," 1987; "The Case Société Générale de Bélgique," 1988; "Freedom to provide financial services: Italian law v. EEC Law," 1992; "Serial Rights: from Copyright to Trademark Law Protection," 1993. *Member:* Harvard Law School Alumni Association. (Also Of Counsel to B.C. Toms & Co., London, England). *LANGUAGES:* Italian, English and French.

MARCO FRIGESSI DI RATTALMA, born Milan, Italy, October 13, 1960; admitted, 1990, Italy. *Education:* University of Milan (J.D., 1984; S.J.D., International Law, 1990). Research Professor: International Law, 1991. Author: "Foreign exchange regulations and international contracts," 1986 ; "The international contract of insurance," 1990; "Mutual recognition and minimum harmonization in EEC financial services law," 1991; "Freedom to provide financial services: Italian law v. EEC Law," 1992; "First

(This Listing Continued)

---

judgements applying the Rome convention of June 19, 1980," 1993. *Member:* International Association for Insurance Law. *LANGUAGES:* Italian, German, English and French.

STUDIO LEGALE CALESELLA & ASSOCIATI

Established in 1957

VIA M. CAMPERIO N. 14
20123 MILAN, ITALY
Telephone: 02/8051147 - 02/8051133 - 02/86465455
Facsimile: 02/8051067

Commercial, Corporate, Foreign Investments, Joint Ventures, Litigation and Arbitration, Mergers and Acquisitions, Labour and Trade Legislation, Trusts and Estates Law, Bankruptcy, Family and Property Law, Environmental Law, Banking Law.

MEMBERS OF FIRM

FRANCO CALESELLA, born Como, Italy, October 19, 1925; admitted, 1958, Milan, Italy. *Education:* University of Pavia (Doctor of Jurisprudence, 1950). Member, Board of Directors, Collegio Chislieri, Pavia. Chairman, Collegio Chislieri's Alumni League. *LANGUAGES:* French. *PRACTICE AREAS:* Commercial; Corporate; Litigation and Arbitration; Labour and Trade Legislation; Family and Property Law.

GIORGIO CALESELLA, born Milan, Italy, June 4, 1955; admitted, 1987, Milan, Italy. *Education:* University of Milan (Doctor of Jurisprudence, 1981). *Member:* Eurolegal. *LANGUAGES:* English and French. *PRACTICE AREAS:* Bankruptcy; Commercial; Corporate; Foreign Investment; Joint Ventures; Mergers and Acquisitions; Banking Law; Real Estate; Criminal/Bribery Cases.

DARIO TREVISAN, born Milan, Italy, May 4, 1964; admitted, 1988, Milan, Italy. *Education:* University of Milan (J.D., maxima cum laude, 1988). *Member:* EC Lawyers' Society; British-Italian Law Association. *LANGUAGES:* English and French. *PRACTICE AREAS:* Commercial; Corporate; Foreign Investments; Joint Ventures; Mergers and Acquisitions; Banking Law.

ASSOCIATE

EMANUELA BOTTONI, born Milan, Italy, March 13, 1965; admitted, 1993, Milan, Italy (Not admitted in Italy). *Education:* University of Milan, 1990. *LANGUAGES:* French and Spanish. *PRACTICE AREAS:* Commercial; Corporate; Foreign Investments; Litigation and Arbitration; Trade Legislation and Trusts; Bankruptcy; Family and Probate Law.

ANDREA POGLIANI, born Milan, Italy, May 22, 1963 (Swiss citizen); admitted, 1992, Milan, Italy. *Education:* University of Milan (1988). Attorney agreed at Swiss Consulate of Milan. *LANGUAGES:* French and English. *PRACTICE AREAS:* International Business and Commercial; Labour; Environmental Law; Litigation.

MARINA LEVI, born Milan, Italy, February 9, 1967; (admission pending). *Education:* University of Milan, 1992. *LANGUAGES:* French and English. *PRACTICE AREAS:* Foreign Investments; Commercial; Corporate; Foreign Investments; Litigation and Arbitration; Trade Legislation and Trusts; Bankruptcy; Family and Property Law.

CAMOZZI & BONISSONI

VIALE MAJNO, 17
MILAN, ITALY
Telephone: (02) 760-21542; Intn'l (39-2) 760-21542
Telecopier: (02) 760-21861; Intn'l (39-2) 760-21816

Mailing Address: Via Visconti di Modrone 33, Milan, Italy 20122

Rome, Italy Office: Via Tevere, 44, 00198. Telephone: (06) 841-3244; 841-2864; Intnl.: (39-6) 841-3244; 841-2864. Telecopier: (06) 841-3679; Intnl.: (39-6) 841-3679.

International and Domestic Practice, Mergers and Acquisitions, Taxation, Banking, Bankruptcy, Contracts, Corporate, Securities, European Common Market, Antitrust, Foreign Investment, Insurance, International Trade, Patents and Trademarks, Licensing, Labor, Product Liability, Litigation and Arbitration.

(This Listing Continued)

MEMBERS OF FIRM

MARIO CAMOZZI, born Ferrara, Italy, August 24, 1955; admitted, 1985, Italy. *Education:* University Bocconi of Milan (Doctor of Economics). Auditor and Tax Auditor, KPMG Peat Marwick, 1982-1985. Associate, Berchet, 1985-1986. *LANGUAGES:* Italian and English.

ANGELO BONISSONI, born Milan, Italy, April 13, 1959; admitted, 1986, Italy. *Education:* University Cattolica of Milan (Doctor of Economics). Auditor, RIA, 1979. Auditor and Tax Auditor, KPMG Peat Marwick, 1979-1983. Associate, Cassinis, 1983-1986. *LANGUAGES:* Italian, English and French.

ROBERTO BRUSTIA, born Novara, Italy, June 17, 1956; admitted, 1988, Italy. *Education:* University Bocconi of Milan (Doctor of Economics). Auditor and Tax Auditor, Price Waterhouse Associates, 1982-1985. Associate, Minoli e Associati, 1986-1988. *LANGUAGES:* Italian and English.

ALESSANDRO PINCI, born Rome, Italy, January 16, 1954; admitted, 1978, Italy. Auditor, Ernst & Whinney, 1976-1979. Chief Accountant, BP, British Petroleum, 1979-1980. Associate, Spagnolo Napolitano, 1980-1986. Senior Tax Manager, Ernst & Young, 1986-1990. *LANGUAGES:* Italian, English and French.

PAOLO BAROZZI, born Novara, Italy, March 14, 1958; admitted, 1988, Italy. *Education:* University of Milan (Doctor of Jurisprudence). Associate: Erede, Stefani e Associati, 1984-1985; Pavia, Ansaldo e Verusio, 1989-1991 (Visiting Associate, Pavia & Harcourt, New York, 1990). Attorney, Fininvest Group, 1986-1988. Director, Legal Department, OTIS ITALIA SpA, 1991. *LANGUAGES:* Italian and English.

PAOLO MANZATO, born Milan, Italy, December 6, 1955; admitted, 1981, Italy. *Education:* University of Milan (Doctor of Jurisprudence). *Member:* UAE (European Lawyers Union); AIJA (International Association of Young Lawyers). *LANGUAGES:* Italian, English, German, French and Spanish.

GIANCARLO TABEGNA, born Rome, Italy, September 13, 1968; admitted, 1984, Italy. *Education:* University of Rome (Doctor of Jurisprudence); London School of Economics (LL.M., Master of Laws, 1985). *Member:* International Bar Association. *LANGUAGES:* Italian and English.

ASSOCIATES

ANDREA BATAZZI, born Milan, Italy, June 6, 1963; admitted, 1994, Italy. *Education:* University of Milan (Doctor of Jurisprudence). *LANGUAGES:* Italian and French.

ROBERTA DE CECCO, born Milan, Italy, June 20, 1963; admitted, 1988, Italy. *Education:* University Cattolica of Milan (Doctor of Economics). *LANGUAGES:* Italian, English and French.

FAUSTO GALLAZZI, born Busto Arsizio (VA), Italy, November 5, 1960; admitted, 1988, Italy. *Education:* University Bocconi of Milan (Doctor of Economics). *LANGUAGES:* Italian, English and Spanish.

LAURA GIUSTINIANI, born Milan, Italy, January 28, 1961; admitted, 1990, Italy. *Education:* University Cattolica of Milan (Doctor of Economics). *LANGUAGES:* Italian, English and German.

ROSSELLA MARIANI, born Como, Italy, June 6, 1962; admitted, 1992, Italy. *Education:* University of Cattolica of Milan (Doctor of Jurisprudence). *LANGUAGES:* Italian, English and French.

GIORGIO PESTARINO, born Busto Arsizio (VA), Italy, September 9, 1961. *Education:* University of Torino (Doctor of Economics). *LANGUAGES:* Italian and English.

GIAN MARCO ANTONIO RUBINO, born Milan, Italy, August 13, 1968. *Education:* University of Milan (Doctor of Jurisprudence). *LANGUAGES:* Italian, English and Spanish.

PIETRO TERENZIO, born Milan, Italy, July 3, 1964; admitted, 1992, Italy. *Education:* University Bocconi of Milan (Doctor of Economics). *LANGUAGES:* Italian, English and French.

FRANCESCA AIMONE, born Milan, Italy, January 1, 1967; admitted, 1993, Italy. *Education:* University of Bocconi of Milan (Doctor of Economics). *LANGUAGES:* Italian, English and French.

LUIGI GLAREY, born Milan, Italy, May 29, 1967. *Education:* University of Bocconi of Milan (Doctor of Economics). *LANGUAGES:* Italian, English and German.

(This Listing Continued)

GIOVANNI BANDERA, born Legnano, Italy, July 25, 1968; admitted, 1994, Italy. *Education:* University Bocconi of Milan (Doctor of Economics). *LANGUAGES:* Italian, English and French.

MICHELE CITARELLA, born Salerno, Italy, July 2, 1968; admitted, 1993, Italy. *Education:* University Bocconi of Milan (Doctor of Economics). *LANGUAGES:* Italian, English and French.

SILVIA CURCI, born Milan, Italy, January 12, 1965; admitted, 1994, Italy. *Education:* University of Milan (Doctor of Jurisprudence). *LANGUAGES:* Italian, English and German.

MARCO GAREGANI, born Milan, Italy, March 13, 1962; admitted, 1991, Italy. *Education:* University of Cattolica of Milan (Doctor of Economics). *LANGUAGES:* Italian and English.

TIZIANA TRIPEPI, born Salerno, Italy, June 3, 1967. *Education:* University Bocconi of Milan (Doctor of Economics). *LANGUAGES:* Italian, English and French.

ALESSANDRA SIMETA, born Genova, Italy, July 11, 1969. *Education:* University of Genova (Doctor of Economics). *LANGUAGES:* Italian and English.

LUCA ZITIELLO, born Florence, Italy, July 21, 1963; admitted, 1992, Italy. *Education:* University of Florence (Doctor of Jurisprudence). *LANGUAGES:* Italian and English.

ALESSANDRA PEDOTTI, born Genoa, May 22, 1964; admitted, 1991, Italy. *Education:* University Cattolica of Milan (Doctor of Jurisprudence). *LANGUAGES:* Italian, English and French.

REPRESENTATIVE CLIENTS: Abbey National; Imprefin Imprese Finanziarie S.p.A.; DeGremont Italia S.p.A.; Cobarr S.p.A. Cogeb S.p.A. (Gruppo Coca Cola); DDB, Needham (Gruppo Omnicom); Coop Lombardia A R.L.; ABC Finanziaria S.p.A. (Gruppo Arab Banking); Finagel S.p.A. (Gruppo Sopaf); Gruppo Alfagomma; Gruppo Montedison; Gruppo Mittel; Olly's Int.; Elf Italiana; Efibanca S.p.A.; Monte dei Paschi di Siena S.p.A Sim; ROMA S.p.A. Sim; McQuay Italia S.p.A. (Gruppo Snyder General); Instant-Upright Int.; UCB Credicasa S.p.A.; Associated Press Italia S.r.l.; Egon Zehnder International S.r.l.; Toyota Italia S.p.A.; 3M S.p.A.; Gruppo Need; Lasmo Oil Development; Ideal Standard S.p.A.; Coin S.p.A.; Sci-Costruzioni e Insediamenti Edilizi S.p.A.

CAPURRO, MARCHINI, MICHETTI, ROJ & TOMASSINI

Established in 1983

1, PIAZZA CAVOUR
20121 MILAN, ITALY
Telephone: (02) 65 92 741 (Aut. Res.)
Telex: 325210 LEGAS I
Telefax: (02) 65 95 822

Corporation, Foreign Investments, EEC Law, International Commercial Law, Taxation, Banking Law, General Practice, Antitrust, Patents and Trademarks, Products Liability

ROBERTO CAPURRO, born Genoa, Italy, November 8, 1942; admitted, 1965, Italy. *Education:* University of Genoa (J.D.); John Marshall Law School of Chicago (1966-1967). *Member:* International Bar Association. *LANGUAGES:* Italian, English and French.

ORESTE MARCHINI, born Genoa, Italy, June 13, 1946; admitted, 1977, Italy. *Education:* University of Genoa (J.D.). *Member:* International Bar Association. *LANGUAGES:* Italian, English and French.

VALERIO MICHETTI, born Rome, Italy, March 1, 1944; admitted, 1970, Italy. *Education:* University of Genoa (J.D.). *LANGUAGES:* Italian, English and French.

GIANNI ROJ, born Genoa, Italy, May 27, 1947; admitted, 1975, Italy. *Education:* University of Genoa (J.D.); Royal Academy of International Law, The Hague (1967-1968); South Western Legal Foundation, Dallas (1980). *Member:* International Bar Association. *LANGUAGES:* Italian, English and French.

ERMANNO TOMASSINI, born Milan, Italy, March 31, 1941; admitted, 1967, Italy. *Education:* University of Milan (J.D.). *LANGUAGES:* Italian and French.

GIANLUCA BRIVIO SFORZA, born Milan, Italy, August 7, 1961; admitted, 1991, Italy. *Education:* University of Milan (J.D.). *LANGUAGES:* Italian and English.

(This Listing Continued)

CAPURRO, MARCHINI, MICHETTI, ROJ & TOMASSINI, Milan—Continued

MIRELLA MARCHINI, born Genoa, Italy, May 14, 1966. *Education:* University of Genoa (J.D.). *LANGUAGES:* Italian, English and French.

ANDREA NICODEMI, born Milan, Italy, February 2, 1968. *Education:* University of Milan (J.D.). *LANGUAGES:* Italian and English.

STUDIO CARNELUTTI

Established in 1900

CORSO MATTEOTTI 10
20121 MILAN, ITALY
Telephone: 02-7600.2042
Telefax: 02 -78.47.79

Rome, Italy Office: Via Parigi 11, 00185. Telephone: 06-473.901. Telex: 611325 UNILAW I. Telefax: 06-48.19.833.
London, England Office: Carnelutti. 76 Shoe Lane, EC4A 3BQ. Telephone: 171-242.2268. Telefax: 0171-3533352.
New York, New York Office: Werbel, Mc Millin and Carnelutti. 711 Fifth Avenue, 10022. Telephone: 212-832-8300. Telefax: 212-832-3353.

General Practice.

FRANCESCO CARNELUTTI Founder (1879-1965).

MARINO BASTIANINI, born Rome, Italy, November 26, 1936; admitted, 1962, Italy. *Education:* Milan University (LL.D., 1957).

LUIGI VITA SAMORY, born Rome, Italy, June 1, 1943; admitted, 1969, Italy. *Education:* Milan University (LL.D., 1967).

LUIGI COZZA, born Cosenza, Italy, November 16, 1941; admitted, 1971, Italy. *Education:* Milan University (LL.D., 1967).

ALBERTO RITTATORE VONWILLER, born Milan, Italy, October 23, 1949; admitted, 1974, Italy. *Education:* Milan University (LL.D., 1972).

LUCA FABBRINI BOCCETTI, born Florence, Italy, November 30, 1949; admitted, 1976, Italy. *Education:* Florence University (LL.D., 1973).

GIUSEPPE CATTANEO, born Luino (VA), Italy, September 8, 1947; admitted, 1973, Italy. *Education:* Milan University (LL.D., 1970).

FRANCO GALIANO, born Milan, Italy, October 10, 1955; admitted, 1981, Italy. *Education:* Milan University (LL.D., 1979).

ANDREA RITTATORE VONWILLER, born Milan, Italy, April 3, 1953; (Not admitted in Italy). *Education:* Milan Bocconi University (Economics, 1977). (Tax Adviser).

GIAN GIACOMO ATTOLICO TRIVULZIO, born Paris, France, February 5, 1951; admitted, 1990, Italy. *Education:* Milan University (LL.D., 1975); Columbia University, New York (LL.M., 1978).

NICOLO BASTIANINI, born Milan, Italy, September 13, 1954; admitted, 1983, Italy. *Education:* Turin University (LL.D., 1979).

FRANCESCO TABONE, born Monza, Italy, February 2, 1956; admitted, 1986, Italy. *Education:* Milan Catholic University (LL.D., 1979).

GUIDO TESTA, born Gallarate, Italy, October 13, 1957; admitted, 1989, Italy. *Education:* Milan University (LL.D., 1983).

ASSOCIATES

Vittorio Valcasara	*Luca Arnaboldi* (Resident)
Margherita Barié	*Paolo Carrière*
Renata Ricotti	*Gilberto Comi*
Giorgio Grandi	*Nicola Asti*
Francesco Seassaro	*Cristina Proto*
Giovanni N. Carcaterra	*Anna Gerometta*
Renato Fiumalbi	*Paolo Scarduelli*
Paolo Baruffi	*Nicola J. Chapman*

OF COUNSEL

Antonio V. Gambaro

Languages: Italian, French and English.

REFERENCES: Abbey National; Alcatel; Amstrad Plc.; BSN Group; Charterhouse Fund; Chubb Insurance; Chase Manhattan Bank N.A.; Dayco Inc.; Dollond International; Eaton Group; Friends Provident; Fininvest Group; Ferrari Cars; Gallaher Limited; Goldman Sachs (London); Groupama (Insurance); Hewlett Packard; Merryl Lynch Ltd.; Mattel; Nokia; ELF Atokem; Pilkington

(This Listing Continued)

Plc.; Pharmacia A.B. (formerly Procordia A.B.); Panasonic; Severn Trent Water Int.; Saatchi & Saatchi Ltd.; Standard Chartered Bank; Société Generale; Sony; Tunstall Ltd.; Valentino Group; Wilkinson Sword; Wiggins Teape (British American Tobacco Group); Warner Lambert Co.; Young & Rubicam.

STUDIO LEGALE AVV. PROF. MARIO CASELLA E ASSOCIATI

VIA GUASTALLA 15
20122 MILAN, ITALY
Telephone: (02) 5512066, 5512141, 5466180
Telefax: (02) 5400304

General Civil and International Practice. Commercial, Corporation, Contractual Assistance, Arbitration, Patent, Banking, Bankruptcy and Labor Law.

MEMBERS OF FIRM

AVV. PROF. MARIO CASELLA, born Fiorenzuola D'Arda (Piacenza), August 21, 1923; admitted, 1947, Milan. *Education:* University of Parma (J.D., magna cum laude, 1946). Author: "Il Contratto e l'Interpretazione Automatica di Clausole," Milano, 1974;"Impresa e Societâ," 1983. Professor: Labor Law, University of Pavia, 1967-1986; Private Law, University L. Bocconi, Milan, 1981—.

AVV. PROF. PAOLO CASELLA, born Milano, Italy, March 26, 1952; admitted, 1978, Milan. *Education:* University of Milan (J.D., magna cum laude, 1975); Harvard Law School (LL.M., 1979). Author: "Le Obbligazioni Convertibili in Azioni," Milano, 1983. Professor, Commercial Law, University Della Calabria, Cosenza, 1988-1990. Full Professor, Commercial Law, Messina University, 1990—. *LANGUAGES:* Italian, English and French.

AVV. ALDO MAUGERI, born Milan, Italy, July 8, 1946; admitted, 1971, Pavia; 1981, Milan. *Education:* University of Pavia (J.D., 1968); City of London College (Diploma in English and International Law, 1969). Assistant Professor, Commercial Law, University of Pavia, 1972—. *LANGUAGES:* Italian, English and French.

AVV. MARIA CRISTINA PAGNI, born Pisa, Italy, March 22, 1955; admitted, 1981, Pisa; 1983, Milan. *Education:* Pisa University (J.D., magna cum laude, 1978); British Council Fellow, London (Law, 1981-1982). *Member:* British-Italian Law Association. *LANGUAGES:* Italian, English and French.

ASSOCIATES

AVV. GIOVANNI FRAU, born Suelli (Cagliari), Italy, June 29, 1947; admitted, 1978, Brescia. *Education:* University of Pavia (J.D., magna cum laude, 1971). Assistant Professor, Commercial Law, University of Pavia, 1975. *LANGUAGES:* Italian, French and English.

DOTT. PROC. UGO MOLINARI, born Brescia, Italy, June 20, 1964; admitted, 1992, Milan. *Education:* University of Milan (J.D., 1988). Assistant, Private Law, University L. Bocconi, Milan, 1993. *LANGUAGES:* Italian, English and French.

DOTT. PROC. FRANCESCO RUFFINO, born Palermo, Italy, September 28, 1965; admitted, 1992, Palermo. *Education:* University of Palermo (J.D., magna cum laude, 1989). *LANGUAGES:* Italian and English.

LORITA GUARINO, born Castelluccio Inferiore, Italy, June 15, 1957; admitted, 1984, Milan. *Education:* University Sapienza of Rome (J.D., 1980). *Member:* Milan Bar. *LANGUAGES:* Italian, English and French.

EUGENIA CROCE, born Genova, Italy, March 2, 1965; admitted, 1994, Genova. *Education:* University of Genova (J.D., 1990). *LANGUAGES:* Italian, English and French.

CHIOMENTI E ASSOCIATI
STUDIO LEGALE

VIA A. BOITO 8
20121 MILAN, ITALY
Telephone: 02-721571
Cable Address: "Legal"
Telex: Milan: 340184 LEGAL I
Telecopier: 02-72157224/5

Rome, Italy Office: Via Bertoloni 44/46 and Piazza di Monte Savello, 30
Telephone: 06-809701. Telex: 622603 LEGAL I. Telecopier:
06-809706.
London, England, Office: 20 Berkeley Square. Telephone:
+44-171-4956430. Telecopier: +44-171-4956431.
Bruxelles, Belgium Office: 73 Av. R. Vendendriessche, B. 1150.
Telephone: +32-2-7728750. Telecopier: +32-2-7728736.

General Practice, Corporation, Commercial Law, Taxation, Foreign Investments, Banking, Securities, Investment Funds, E.C. Law, Antitrust, Litigation, Bankruptcy, Maritime and Labor Law.

RESIDENT LAWYERS

Michele Carpinelli
Michele G. Soldati
Emanuele Gamna
Carlo Croff
Franco Vigliano
Luca Radicati di Brozolo
Francesca Paletto
Laura Salvaneschi
Edoardo Andreoli
Roberto Ghio
Marzio Longo
Massimo V. Benedettelli
Renato Paternollo
Luca Bonetti (Resident, Milan Office)
Gabriella Opromolla (Resident, Milan Office)
Bruno Castellini (Resident, Milan Office)

(For Personnel, Biographical and other data, see Rome, Italy
Professional Biographies).

COLESANTI E GILIBERTI
STUDIO LEGALE

Established in 1988

VIA VISCONTI DI MODRONE 21
20122 MILAN, ITALY
Telephone: (02) 76.00.15.85
Telefax: (02) 78.08.58

General Practice, Litigation and Arbitration, Mergers and Acquisitions, Corporation Law, Labor, Bankruptcy, Antitrust, Real Estate, EEC, International Finance and Banking, Counselling in International Transactions.

MEMBERS OF FIRM

AVV. PROF. VITTORIO COLESANTI, born Rho, Milan, August 21, 1934; admitted, 1960, Italian Supreme Court. *Education:* University of Milan (cum laude). Professor: Civil Procedure, Università Cattolica of Milan, 1984—; Bankruptcy Law, Università Bocconi of Milan, 1975—.

AVV. ENRICO GILIBERTI, born Naples, June 29, 1945; admitted, 1969, Italian Supreme Court. *Education:* University of Naples (cum laude); New York University (Master of Comparative Jurisprudence). Formerly with Cahill, Gordon & Ohl, New York.

AVV. PAOLO MOROTTI, born Modena, April 6, 1957; admitted, 1984, Italy. *Education:* University of Modena (cum laude).

DR. PROC. ALESSANDRO TRISCORNIA, born Piacenza, November 26, 1961; admitted, 1990, Italy. *Education:* University of Parma (cum laude).

DR. PROC. CARLO PAPPALETTERA, born Milan, February 27, 1963; admitted, 1991, Italy. *Education:* University of Milan (cum laude); New York University (LL.M.). Formerly with Freshfields, London.

GIUSEPPE DE FRANCISCIS, born Caserta, July 23, 1965; admitted, 1992, Italy. *Education:* Luiss University of Rome (cum laude).

(This Listing Continued)

Languages: Italian, English, French and German.

REPRESENTATIVE CLIENTS: KPMG Klynveld Peat Marwick Goerderler; Goldman Sachs & Co.; Computer Associates International, Inc.; Citibank; Strafor Facom; C.I.C.H. Compagnie Internationale du Chauffage; Compagnie Generale De s Eaux; NAF NAF; AGA; Banque Bruxelles Lambert; Mitsui O.S.K. Lines; Edwin Company; Roche S.p.A.; KSB Italia S.p.A.; Mediobanca; Italmobiliare; SME Societa Finanziaria Meridionale; A.F.L. Falk; SAFFA S.p.A.; Fondiaria S.p.A.; Autogrill S.p.A.; Montedison S.p.A.; Ferruzzi Finanziaria S.p.A.; Banca Commerciale Italiana S.p.A.; Credito Italiano S.p.A.

CONTE-MAIENZA-VASILE

Studio Legale Associato

VIA FREGUGLIA 8/A
20122 MILAN, ITALY
Telephone: (39-2) 55011592 (5 lines)
Fax: (39-2) 5513884

Civil, Corporate, Labour, Commercial, Bankruptcy and International Practice, Criminal Law, Bankruptcy Criminal Law.

PARTNERS

RAFFAELE CONTE, born Pozzuoli, Italy, September 26, 1926; admitted, 1954, Italy. *Education:* University of Naples (J.D., 1952). *Member:* Bar Association of Milan. **LANGUAGES:** Italian and French. **PRACTICE AREAS:** Criminal and Bankruptcy Law; General Civil Law; Litigation.

RICCARDO CONTE, born Naples, Italy, June 15, 1955; admitted, 1982, Italy. *Education:* University of Milan (J.D., 1978). Author: "Principio costituzionale di eguaglianza ed impignorabilita delle retribuzioni dei pubblici dipendenti," in Resp. Civ. Prev. 1985; "Appunti sul risarcimento del danno alla persona nel trasporto aereo dopo la sentenza n.132/85 della Corte Costituzionale," in Resp. Civ. Prev. 1985; "Appunti in tema di legittimazione attiva del mittente nell'azione di responsabilita contro il vettore," in Resp. Civ. Prev. 1986; "La pignorabilita degli stipendi dei pubblici dipendenti nei piu recenti orientamenti della Corte Costituzionale," in Giur. It. 1988; "Profili costituzionale della rimessione in termini nel processo civile," in Riv. Dir. Proc. 1990. Voluntary Assistant Professor, Civil Procedure, University of Milan. *Member:* First Instance Tax Commission of Milan; Bar Association of Milan. **LANGUAGES:** Italian, English, Spanish and French. **PRACTICE AREAS:** Litigation; General Civil Law; Tax Law; Real Estate Law.

FABRIZIO CONTE, born Naples, Italy, February 22, 1960; admitted, 1989, Italy. *Education:* University of Milan (J.D., 1986). Author: "Sugli interessi tutelati dall'art. 2409 c.c.," Giur. Comm. 1986; "Partecipazione del consulente tecnico di parte all'ispezione ex art. 2409 c.c., intervento nel procedimento e diritto di controllo del socio," Giur. Comm. 1990. Voluntary Assistant Professor, Commercial and Corporate Law, University of Milan. *Member:* Bar Association of Milan. **LANGUAGES:** Italian and English. **PRACTICE AREAS:** Civil Law; Corporate Law; Commercial Law; Labour Law; Litigation.

MARGHERITA CONTE, born Naples, Italy, June 15, 1961; admitted, 1991, Italy. *Education:* University of Milan (J.D., 1986). Voluntary Assistant Professor, Comparative Criminal Procedure, University of Milan, 1986-1991. *Member:* Bar Association of Milan; Criminal Lawyers Chamber of Milan. **LANGUAGES:** Italian, English and French. **PRACTICE AREAS:** Criminal Law; Family Law.

MARIO MAIENZA, born Caserta, Italy, August 21, 1960; admitted, 1987, Italy. *Education:* University of Milan (J.D., 1982). Author: "Tempestivita nella denuncia dei vizi ex art. 1495 c.c. ed onere probatorio," Corr. Giur. 1991; "Sull'efficacia enderoprocessuale delle sentenze che regolano la giurisdizione," Corr. Giur. 1991; "Conversione del pignoramento e sospensione della procedura esecutiva," Corr. Giur. 1991; "Provvedimenti d'urgenza, impugnazioni e questioni di giurisdizione," Corr. Giur. 1990; "I contratti atipici," special issue of Summa, 1992. Voluntary Assistant Professor, Roman Law, University of Milan, 1983-1988. *Member:* Bar Association of Milan. **LANGUAGES:** Italian and English. **PRACTICE AREAS:** Civil Law; Contract Law; Corporate Law; Bankruptcy; Commercial Law.

NICOLA VASILE, born Palermo, Italy, April 1, 1960; admitted, 1990, Italy. *Education:* University of Milan (J.D., 1986); Columbia University (Summer Program in American Law, Leyden Session, 1982); Hague Academy of International Law (International Private Law Session, 1983). Voluntary Assistant Professor, Commercial and Corporate Law, University of Milan. *Member:* Bar Association of Milan. **LANGUAGES:** Italian, English and French. **PRACTICE AREAS:** Civil Law; Corporate Law; Commercial Law; Contract Law; International Practice; Litigation.

(This Listing Continued)

CONTE-MAIENZA-VASILE, Milan—Continued

LATTUILLE STEFANIA, born Rome, September 30, 1963; admitted, 1991, Italy. *Education:* University of Milan (J.D., 1987). Voluntary Assistant Professor, Commercial and Corporate Law, University of Milan, 1988-1992. *Member:* Bar Association of Milan. *LANGUAGES:* Italian and English. *PRACTICE AREAS:* Civil Law; Labour Law; Contracts; Commercial Law; Company Law; Litigation.

CROZE, RADICE ED ASSOCIATI
STUDIO LEGALE

Established in 1990

PIAZZA SAN BABILA, 5
20122 MILAN, ITALY
Telephone: 02-76008104 (four lines)
Fax: 02-76007196

International and Commercial Practice, Contract, Corporate Law, Foreign Investment, Mergers and Acquisitions, Antitrust and EEC Law, Patent and Copyright Law, Litigation and Arbitration.

ALBERTO CROZE, born Venice, Italy, June 3, 1946; admitted, 1972, Milan. *Education:* University of Padua (LL.D., 1969). *LANGUAGES:* Italian, English, French, Spanish and German.

RODOLFO RADICE, born Pavia, Italy, September 22, 1956; admitted, 1986, Milan. *Education:* University of Pavia (LL.M., 1983). *LANGUAGES:* Italian, English and French.

CRISTINA RAVELLI, born Milan, Italy, August 14, 1965; admitted, 1994, Milan. *Education:* Statale University of Milan (Law Degree, 1990). *LANGUAGES:* Italian, English and French.

MARZIA SUSAN ZAMBON, born Milan, Italy, March 21, 1970; admitted, to Lower Courts. *Education:* University of Milan (Law Degree, 1993). *LANGUAGES:* Italian and English.

DALLA VEDOVA

Studio Legale

11, VIA DEL PIATTI
20123 MILAN, ITALY
Telephone: 02/86757161
Fax: 02/80753836

Rome, Italy Office: 12, Via Vittorio Bachelet, 00185. Telephone: 06/4440821 (5 l.). Fax: 06/4452165 (24 h.).

International and General Practice, Corporate, EU Law, Energy, Banking, Insurance, Foreign Investment, Mergers and Acquisitions, Securities, Investments Funds, Antitrust, Aeronautical, Arbitration, Bankruptcy, Labor, Patent, Trademark, Real Estate, Estates, Taxation, Civil and Criminal Litigation.

FIRM PROFILE: Dalla Vedova studio legale is one of the oldest Italian law firms Engaged in Private and Public international law. Our lawyers have received legal education and training abroad and we are able to correspond in different languages.

MEMBERS OF FIRM

RICCARDO DALLA VEDOVA, born Naples, Italy, February 6, 1932; admitted, 1959, Italy; 1973, Supreme Court, Italy. *Education:* Fulbright Scholar, Wesleyan University (1952); University of Naples (J.D. maxima cum laude, 1954). Assistant Professor, Naples University, 1955 and University of Rome, 1956-1958. Lecturer, Temple University, Rome, 1980. *Member:* Italian Currency Law Association (President); Italian Trust Association (President); Union Internationale des Avocats, Italian (Rome), International and American Bar Associations. *LANGUAGES:* English. *PRACTICE AREAS:* Corporate Law.

MARCO DALLA VEDOVA, born Rome, Italy, July 17, 1961; admitted, 1987, Italy. *Education:* University of Rome (J.D., 1987). Lecturer, Civil Law, Rome University La Sapienza. Visiting Foreign Counsel, EUTELSAT (Paris, 1993). *Member:* I.B.A. Committees E, CH; A.I.J.A.; Computer Law Association; American Bar Association; Italian Arbitration Association. *LANGUAGES:* English and French. *PRACTICE AREAS:* Commercial Law; Corporate Law; Patents; EV Law; Telecommunication Law; Arbitration.

(This Listing Continued)

CARLO DALLA VEDOVA, born Rome, Italy, June 10, 1963; admitted, 1988, Italy. *Education:* University of Rome (J.D.); Harvard Summer School (1983); Seminar in American Legal Studies, Salzburg (1989). Seminar European Community Law (Associazione Italiana Giuristi Europei) Ispes Rome. Advisoe to EU-PHARE Project, Bucharest, Romania, 1994. *Member:* I.B.A.; A.I.J.A.; The Foreign Lawyers Forum of Washington, D.C.; British-Italiana Lawyers Association; Associazione Italiana Giuristi Europei; Associazione Italiana Giuristi dell' Est, Associazione Italiana dell' Arbitrato (AIA). *LANGUAGES:* English, French, German. *PRACTICE AREAS:* Commercial Law; Corporate Law; EV Law; Trademarks; Immigration; Criminal Law.

BENEDETTA ROSSI, born Rome, Italy, March 27, 1965; admitted, 1990, Italy. *Education:* University of Rome (J.D., maxima cum laude, 1990). Seminar, English Commercial Law, Cambridge, 1991. *Member:* I.B.A. *LANGUAGES:* English. *PRACTICE AREAS:* Real Estate; Family Law; International Transactions; EV Law.

ALESSANDRO PICCIOLI, born Rome, Italy, April 1, 1963; admitted, 1989, Italy. *Education:* University of Rome (J.D., 1988). Seminar Government Contracts, Rome 1991. *Member:* I.B.A. *LANGUAGES:* English. *PRACTICE AREAS:* Commercial Law; Corporate Law; Contracts; Computer Law; European Community Law.

FABIO QUOJANI, born Rome, Italy, October 5, 1967; admitted, 1993, Italy. *Education:* University of Rome (J.D., maxima cum laude, 1991). *LANGUAGES:* English and French. *PRACTICE AREAS:* Civil Law; Commercial Law; Corporate Law; Bankruptcy; Real Estate Law.

GIOVANNI IZZO, born Rome. Italy, August 2, 1969; admitted, 1994, Italy. *Education:* University of Rome (J.D., 1993); Corpus Christi College, Oxford University (1990-1991). *Member:* I.B.A. (Committees R, T); Italian Trust Association (Secretary). *LANGUAGES:* English and French. *PRACTICE AREAS:* Company Law; Commercial Law; Computer Law; Technology Law; Family Law.

PAOLA LA LICATA, born Palermo, Italy, July 31, 1969. *Education:* University of Rome "La Sapienza" (J.D.), maxima cum laude. Publication: "Modalities of Compensation," article in "Giurisprudenza del Lavoro nel Lazio" 1994. *LANGUAGES:* English. *PRACTICE AREAS:* Corporate Law; Labour Law; Bankruptcy; European Community Law; Family Law.

Languages: Italian, English, French, German and Spanish.

STUDIO LEGALE AVV. DANOVI

Established in 1936

VIA GUASTALLA 15
20122 MILAN, ITALY
Telephone: (39.2) 54.56.755
Fax: (39.2) 55.19.19.26

Banking, Civil Practice, Commercial Law, Contracts, Family Law, International Law, Legal Ethics and Professional Responsibility, Real Estate and Real Property.

MEMBERS OF FIRM

AVV. REMO DANOVI, born Milan, February 6, 1939; admitted, 1963, Milan. *Education:* University of Milan (J.D., magna cum laude, 1961). Visiting Professor, Bar organization and lawyers deontology, Milan University. Member, Italian delegation , CCBE Committee, 1990—. Author: several essays on Bankruptcy and Bank law, and on Legal ethics and Professional Responsibility; *Books:* Codice deontologico forense, I - Le norme deontologiche, Milano, 1984 (1993, n. ed.) and II - Il procedimiento disciplinare, Milano, 1985 (1993, n. ed.); Saggi sulla deontologia e professione forense, Milano, 1987; Codice delle professioni intellettuali, Milano, 1989; Corso di ordinamento forense e deontologia, Milano, 1989 (1992, 3° ed.); L'indipendenza dell'avvocato, Milano, 1990; La toga e l'avvocato, Milano, 1993. Contributor to Book: The legal professions in the New Europe, Oxford, Blackwell, 1993. Rotary Professionality Award 1987 for books on deontology. *Member:* Milan Bar (Member of the Council, 1982-1996 and Secretary, 1982-1987); Member of the Consiglio Nazionale Forense (1996—). *LANGUAGES:* Italian, English and French. *PRACTICE AREAS:* Civil Law; Commercial Law.

AVV. DINO DANOVI, born Mede, July 30, 1944; admitted, 1971, Milan. *Education:* University of Milan (J.D., 1965). *Member:* Milan Bar. *LANGUAGES:* Italian and French. *PRACTICE AREAS:* Civil Law; Commercial Law.

(This Listing Continued)

AVV. ANNA GALIZIA DANOVI, born Trento, November 18, 1941; admitted, 1968, Milan. *Education:* University of Milan (J.D., magna cum laude, 1964). Vice-President, Reformation Family Law Center. Teacher in Family Law, University of Milan for the attorney exams preparation, 1988—. Author of several essays on Family Law. *Member:* Milan Bar Association. *LANGUAGES:* Italian, English and French. *PRACTICE AREAS:* Family Law.

ASSOCIATES

AVV. ALESSANDRA DANTI, born S. Giovanni in Fiore (CS), March 17, 1956; admitted, 1983, Milan. *Education:* University of Milan (J.D., 1980).

AVV. ELISABETTA CROTTI, born Milan, December 25, 1954; admitted, 1984, Milan. *Education:* University of Milan (J.D., 1978).

DOTT. PROC. GUIDO BARTALINI, born Milan, May 7, 1964; admitted, 1991, Milan. *Education:* University of Milan (J.D., magna cum laude, 1987). Assistant Professor, Commercial Law, University of Milan, 1987.

DOTT. PROC. DONATA PIANTANIDA, born Novara, January 22, 1956; admitted, 1992, Milan. *Education:* University of Milan (J.D., magna cum laude, 1989).

DOTT. PROC. DANILA VALLI, born Lezzeno, November 6, 1963; admitted, 1991, Milan. *Education:* University of Milan (J.D., 1987).

DOTT. PROC. AGOSTINA DELLE FAVE, born Milan, April 5, 1964; admitted, 1991, Milan. *Education:* University of Milan (J.D., magna cum laude, 1988); Specialization School on European Community Law (1989-1992).

DOTT. PROC. ALBERTO MANFREDI, born Cremona, November 20, 1964; admitted, 1993, Milan. *Education:* Catholic University of Milan (J.D., 1989).

DOTT. PROC. MARIO BATTAGLIA, born Alessandria, July 16, 1965. *Education:* Catholic University of Milan (J.D., magna cum laude, 1990).

DOTT. LAURA SITZIA, born Milano, July 7, 1965. *Education:* University of Milan (J.D., 1990).

DOTT. PROC. ROSSELLA POL, born Milano, July 12, 1966. *Education:* University of Milan (J.D., 1990).

DOTT. PAOLA PIRODDI, born S. Gavino Monreale, June 27, 1964. *Education:* University of Milan (J.D., magna cum laude, 1991). Assistant Professor, International Law, University of Milan.

DOTT. SILVIA ANDREOLI, born Verona, October 18, 1970. *Education:* University of Milan (J.D., magna cum laude, 1993).

DOTT. PROC. FILIPPO DANOVI, born Milan, February 29, 1968. *Education:* University of Milan (J.D., magna cum laude, 1991). Assistant Professor, Civil Procedure Law, University of Milan, 1991.

DOTT. COMM. ALESSANDRO DANOVI, born Milan, Mat 21, 1966. *Education:* Commercial University of Milan, Luigi Bocconi (J.D., 1989).

STUDIO LEGALE DE BERTI & JACCHIA

Established in 1975

FORO BUONAPARTE, 20
I-20121 MILAN, ITALY
Telephone: 39-2-809486
Telex: 310295 Dejalx I
Facsimile: 39-2-8900391/864088

Rome, Italy Office: Lungotevere dei Mellini, 10, I-00193. Telephone: 39-6-3613489/322 7419. Facsimile: 39-6-3200824.
Brussels, Belgium Office: 139 Avenue du Diamant, B-1040. Telephone: 32-2-7353520. Facsimile: 32-2-7321985.

General, International and European Community Practice, with special emphasis on Corporate, Contracts, Mergers and Acquisitions, Securities and Financial Services, Banking and Finance, Shipping, Aviation and Insurance, Intellectual Property, Pharmaceuticals, Taxation, Competition, Antitrust and Environmental Law, Litigation and Arbitration connected with any of the preceding areas.

(This Listing Continued)

MEMBERS OF FIRM

GIOVANNI DE BERTI, born Milan, Italy, December 20, 1939; admitted, 1965, Italy; called to English Bar (Gray's Inn), 1970; 1979, Italian Supreme Court. *Education:* Milan State University (LL.D., 1962); Council of Legal Education, London (1967-1969). *Member:* Association Internationale des Jeunes Avocats (President, 1983-1984); Union Internationale des Avocats (President, Commission on Financial Services).

ROBERTO A. JACCHIA, born Genoa, Italy, July 22, 1946; admitted, 1971, Italy; 1985, Italian Supreme Court. *Education:* Genoa University (LL.D., 1968). Member, Editorial Board, European Business Law Review. Legal Practice Gymnasium, Lecturer, Commercial Cases, Milan State University.

MARIA CRISTINA FRANCHINI, born Genoa, Italy, July 22, 1945; admitted, 1974, Italy; 1988, Italian Supreme Court. *Education:* Genoa University (LL.D., 1968).

GIANNI FORLANI, born Albenga, Italy, January 22, 1946; admitted, 1976, Italy; 1990, Italian Supreme Court. *Education:* Genoa University (LL.D., 1969). Italian Correspondent, Word Tax Report.

RAFFAELLA ORSINI, born Rome, Italy, August 30, 1952; admitted, 1981, Italy; 1995, Italian Supreme Court. *Education:* Milan State University (LL.D., 1977). (Resident, Rome Office).

FEDERICA CASTIONI, born Milan, Italy, June 25, 1950; admitted, 1980, Italy; 1995, Italian Supreme Court. *Education:* Milan State University (LL.D., 1974).

ARRIGO GIACOMELLI, born Vicenza, Italy, July 11, 1956; admitted, 1983, Italy. *Education:* Padua University (LL.D., 1980).

BRIDGET M. ELLISON, born Amersham, England, June 4, 1951. London Notary Public; admitted 1978 (Not admitted in Italy). *Education:* Liverpool University (B.A., Hons., 1973).

FLAVIA SCARPELLINI, born Milan, Italy, May 19, 1963; admitted, 1990, Italy. *Education:* Milan State University (LL.D., 1987).

ASSOCIATES

SILVIA CONTESTABILE, born Rome, Italy, December 20, 1963; admitted, 1991, Italy. *Education:* Rome State University (LL.D., 1988). (Resident, Rome Office).

MASSIMO MORETTO, born Chioggia (Venice), Italy, July 29, 1961; admitted, 1991, Italy. *Education:* Ferrara University (LL.D., 1986). (Resident, Brussels Office).

GUIDO CALLEGARI, born Pavia, Italy, December 25, 1957; admitted, 1989, Italy. *Education:* Pavia University (LL.D., 1985).

MARCO FRANZINI, born Milan, Italy, July 18, 1961; admitted, 1990, Italy. *Education:* Milan Catholic University (LL.D., 1985).

PAOLA BIRESSI, born Milan, Italy, October 10, 1965; admitted, 1990, Milan. *Education:* Milan State University (LL.D., 1990).

MARIA CORRADO, born Milan, Italy, June 17, 1967. *Education:* Milan Catholic University (LL.D., 1991).

ANDREA CEVESE, born Vicenza, Italy, May 22,1965; admitted, 1994, Italy. *Education:* Milan State University (LL.D., 1991).

BARBARA CALZA, born Milan, Italy, April 10, 1967. *Education:* Milan Catholic University (LL.D., 1993).

SIMONE MONESI, born La Spezia, Italy, March 22, 1969. *Education:* Milan State University (LL.D., 1993).

FRANCESCO TORELLI, born Bari, Italy, December 20, 1969. *Education:* Bari State University (LL.D., 1993). (Resident, Brussels Office).

COUNSEL

BRUNO ROSSINI, born Perugia, Italy, October 21, 1941; admitted, 1968, Italy; 1982, Italian Supreme Court. *Education:* Milan State University (LL.D., 1965).

ETTORE DRAGO, born Genoa, Italy, May 14, 1939; admitted, 1976, Tax Courts, Italy. *Education:* Milan L. Bocconi University (Oec.D., 1963).

VADIM A. AVDYUNIN, born Irkutsk, Russian Federation, February 27, 1963. *Education:* Moscow State University (LL.D., 1985). (Resident, Milan Office).

Languages: Italian, English, French, German, Dutch, Russian, Ukrainian and Spanish.

STUDIO LEGALE F. DE LUCA

Associazione Professionale

Established in 1974

12 PIAZZA BORROMEO
20123 MILAN, ITALY
Telephone: 39-2 72 02 11 62
Telefax: 39-2 805 25 65
Telex: 340081 delaw
Cable Address: FRADELAW, Milan

Antitrust Law, Arbitration, Bankruptcy, Competition Law, Construction Law, Corporate Law, Distributorship, Agency and Franchise Law, EEC Law, Foreign Investments, Industrial Relations, Labour Law, International Contracts, Litigation, Oil and Mining Law, Intellectual Property, Industrial Models, License Negotiation, Transfer of Technology.

FIRM PROFILE: The firm was established in 1974. It offers a full range of legal services and is well-known in Italy and Europe for its Commercial and European Community Law experience. The firm's clients are mainly Italian, Japanese, South Korean, South African, French, and German.

PARTNERS

FRANCESCO DE LUCA, born 1935. Education: University of Naples (J.D.); Fordham Law School, New York (J.D.). Author: "Doing Business in Italy," 1990. Member: Milan Bar Association; International Bar Association. LANGUAGES: Italian, English and French. PRACTICE AREAS: Foreign Investments; Arbitration; Corporate Law; Distributorship, Agency and Franchise Law.

SERGIO COSTA, born 1943. Education: University of Milan (J.D.). Member: Milan Bar Association. LANGUAGES: Italian, English and French. PRACTICE AREAS: Foreign Investment; Arbitration; Corporate Law; Distributorship, Agency and Franchise Law; Family Law.

CARLA CORONELLI, born 1947. Education: University of Milan (J.D.). LANGUAGES: Italian, English and French. PRACTICE AREAS: Foreign Investment; Arbitration; Corporate Law; Distributorship, Agency and Franchise Law.

ASSOCIATES

ANTONELLA RATTELLINI, born 1962. Education: University of Milan (J.D.). LANGUAGES: Italian and English. PRACTICE AREAS: Civil Litigation.

FRANCESCA LIGABUE, born 1965. Education: University of Milan (J.D.). LANGUAGES: Italian, French and English. PRACTICE AREAS: Civil Litigation.

PATIMO FRANCESCO, born 1965. Education: University of Bari (J.D.). LANGUAGES: Italian, English and French. PRACTICE AREAS: Civil Litigation.

CATTANI GIUSEPPE, born 1967. Education: University of Milan (J.D.,). LANGUAGES: Italian, English and French. PRACTICE AREAS: Commercial and Antitrust Law.

OF COUNSEL

MARIO GULOTTA, born 1934. Education: University of Naples (J.D.). Member: Milan Bar Association. LANGUAGES: Italian and English. PRACTICE AREAS: Labour Law.

LAURA POLITI, born 1938. Education: University of Milan (J.D.). LANGUAGES: Italian and French. PRACTICE AREAS: Industrial Relations.

CARMINE DE LUCA, born 1945. Education: Queens College, New York (B.A.); University of Milan (M.B.A.). LANGUAGES: Italian, English and French. PRACTICE AREAS: Corporate and Tax Law.

PERNA SABATINO, born 1962. Education: University of Naples (J.D.). LANGUAGES: Italian and English. PRACTICE AREAS: Civil and Labour Law Litigation.

ARENA BRUNO, born 1962. Education: University of Naples (J.D.). LANGUAGES: Italian and English. PRACTICE AREAS: Commercial; Antitrust and Bankruptcy Law.

Languages: Italian, English and French

REPRESENTATIVE CLIENTS: Ajinomoto Co., Inc.; Allia S.A.; BSI-Banca della Svizzera Italiana; Banca Popolare di Lodi; Comit Factoring S.p.A.; Daewoo Corporation; Daihatsu Motor Co., Ltd.; Groupe Lafarge Coppée; Healey & Baker; Hitachi Construction Machinery Co., Ltd.; Hyundai Engineering Co.,

(This Listing Continued)

Ltd.; Matsushita Electric Works Co.; Metra A.G.; Nippondenso; Reconta Ernst & Young; Samsung Corporation; Sanyo Securities Co., Ltd.; SBS-Société de Banque Suisse; Seika Sangyo Co., Ltd.; Seiko Instruments Inc.; Sharp Corporation; SMH-Société Suisse de Micro-électronique et d'Horlogerie The Bank of Tokyo, Ltd.; Swissair Schweizerische Luftverkehr A.G.; The Nikko Securities Co., Ltd.; Wilkinson Sword Ltd.; Yamaichi Electronics Co.; Ltd.; Yamazaki Mazak; Yuasa Corporation; Ziegler & Cie S.a.r.l.

DE MEO & ASSOCIATI STUDIO LEGALE

PIAZZA SAN CAMILLO DE LELLIS, 1
20124 MILAN, ITALY
Telephone: (++39 2) 66988125
Fax: (++39 2) 66988179

Rome, Italy Office: Corso Vittorio Emanuele II, 287, 00186. Telephone: (++39 6) 6892623; 6740256 (++39336) 743496, 743497. Telefax: (++39 6) 6867594.

Naples, Italy Office: Piazza San Pasquale, 10, 80121. Telephone: (++39 81) 7642295; 7643402. Fax: (++39 81) 7646262.

General Practice, Admiralty, Aviation, Commercial Law, Business and Tax Consultants.

MEMBERS OF FIRM

*Michele de Meo   **Gianfranco Antonini**
*Rome, Milan and Naples

STUDIO LEGALE
DI PALMA E PIGNATTI

Established in 1952

VIA S. MARIA ALLA PORTA 9
20123 MILAN, ITALY
Telephone: +39 2 867946
Telecopier: +39 2 8054586

Firm engaged in Italian and International Law practice. The members of the firm are entitled to appear before the Italian Courts.
Corporate Law, Foreign Investments, Currency Regulations, Taxation, Agency and Distribution Agreements, European and Italian Antitrust Regulations, International Arbitration, Italian Bankruptcy Rules, International Commercial Law.

FIRM PROFILE: STUDIO LEGALE DI PALMA E PIGNATTI has always had as principal Clients U.S. Corporations, English, German and Japanese Companies in their dealings in Italy. A complete assistance is given from incorporation throughout the life of the Italian subsidiary or branch, including assistance on contracts, mergers and acquisitions, taxes, accounting and eventually winding up. Clients are based in Italy, Europe or the U.S.

The firm has four partners. The firm is a member of the British Chamber of Commerce for Italy and of the American Chamber of Commerce in Italy. The firm is also an Associate of the European network of independent lawyers called THE ASSOCIATION of European Lawyers.

MEMBERS OF FIRM

RUGGERO DI PALMA CASTIGLIONE, born Avignon, France, May 16, 1918; admitted, 1947, Italy and Supreme Court. Education: University of Pisa (Degree in Law; Degree in Political Sciences). Councillor and Honorary Legal Advisor of British Chamber of Commerce for Italy. Councillor and Member of Legal and Tax Committee, American Chamber of Commerce in Italy. Member: International Chamber of Commerce, Italian Section (Member, Committee on International Commercial Practices). LANGUAGES: Italian, English, French and German. PRACTICE AREAS: Corporate Law; Foreign Investment; Taxation; International Commercial Law; Arbitration; Mergers, Acquisitions and Divestitures.

TOMASO PIGNATTI MORANO, born Bern, Switzerland, March 31, 1928; admitted, 1971, Italy. Education: University of Rome (Degree in Law, 1951). LANGUAGES: Italian, English and French. PRACTICE AREAS: Corporate Law; Foreign Investments; International Contracts; European and Italian Antitrust Law; Mergers, Acquisitions and Divestitures; Taxation.

ALVISE DONA' DALLE ROSE, born Gaiole in Chianti (Siena), Italy, September 11, 1954; admitted, 1990, Italy. Education: University of Ferrara (Degree in Law). LANGUAGES: Italian, English and French. PRACTICE AREAS: Corporate Law; Distribution and Agency Agreements; Environmental Laws; Civil Litigation.

(This Listing Continued)

ROBERTO COCIANCICH, born Milan, Italy, June 26, 1961; admitted, 1992, Italy. *Education:* Milan University (Degree in Law). *LANGUAGES:* Italian, English and French. *PRACTICE AREAS:* Corporate Law; Contracts; European and Italian Antitrust Law; Mergers and Acquisitions.

DOBSON & PINCI

VIA SANTA RADEGONDA, 16
20121 MILAN, ITALY
Telephone: (39) (2) 809816; 8056780
Telefax: (39) (2) 86464548; 86464601 E-Mail: 7232679@mcimail.com.

Rome, Italy Office: Via Panama 74, Int. 9, 00198. Telephone: (39) (6) 841-1611. Telefax: (39) (6) 841-1145. E-Mail: 7212680@mcimail.com.
Genoa, Italy Office: Via Garibaldi 7, 2nd Floor, 16124. Telephone: (39) (10) 206-851. Telefax: (39) (10) 202-738. E-Mail: 7222681@mcimail.com.
New York, New York Office: Manhattan Tower, 12th Floor, 600 Lexington Avenue, 10022-6018. Telephone: (212) 308-4440. Telefax: (212) 888-3839. E-Mail: 7262685@mcimail.com.
London, England Office: 1 Throgmorton Avenue, EC2N 2JJ. Telephone: (44) (171) 628-8163. Telefax: (44) (171) 920-0861. E-Mail: 7232682@mcimail.com.
Brussels, Belgium Office: Avenue Louise, 216, 1050. Telephone: (32) (2) 647-0700. Telefax: (32) (2) 647-6440. E-Mail: 7242683@mcimail.com.
Athens, Greece Office: 6 Yperidou Street, 105 58. Telephone: (30) (1) 324-3272. Telefax: (30) (1) 322-9329. E-Mail: 7252684@mcimail.com.
Atlanta, Georgia Office: 1776 Resurgens Plaza, 945 East Paces Ferry Road, N.E., 30326. Telephone: (404) 262-5680. Telefax: (404) 262-5699. E-Mail: 7272686@mcimail.com.
San Diego, California Office: 1629 Columbia Street, 92101. Telephone: (619) 236-1310. Telefax: (619) 239-1208. E-Mail: 7282687@mcimail.com.
Miami, Florida Office: 701 Brickell Avenue, Suite 2000, 33131. Telephone: (305) 579-0012. Telefax: (305) 375-8075; 579-4722. E-Mail: 7292688@mcimail.com.

Corporate, Banking and Securities Law with emphasis on Mergers and Acquisitions, Insurance, International Financial Transactions, Litigation, Arbitration, Employment Law, Debt Collection, Bankruptcy, Foreign Investments, Privatizations, Subsidiaries and Joint Ventures, Taxation, EU/-Common Market Law, Antitrust, Environmental Law, Transportation, Shipping, Licensing, Fashion and Textiles, Franchising, Commercial Real Estate (Investment, Structuring, Development, Retail), Project Finance, Computer, Software and Telecommunications Law, Agency and Distribution, Energy (Production, Operations, and Transmission), Food and Drug, Commodities, Visa/Immigration, Wills and Estates, Sports Law, Broadcasting, Motion Picture, TV, Video, Intellectual Property and General Entertainment Law.

FIRM PROFILE: Dobson & Pinci is an international law firm based in Europe and the United States that is staffed with both American and European attorneys. Of the small number of such firms, Dobson & Pinci holds a unique position because the firm's European offices are situated in Milan, Rome, Genoa, London, Brussels and Athens, thereby enabling the firm to serve clients conveniently and efficiently in both Northern and Southern Europe. The U.S. offices in New York, Atlanta, Miami and San Diego are placed in major U.S. cities to provide full support to the overall practice network. Each office is staffed by attorneys qualified to appear and litigate in the local courts.

MEMBERS OF FIRM

DAVID M. DOBSON, born Belleville, Illinois, October 24, 1952; admitted, 1979, Georgia. *Education:* Harvard University (A.B., cum laude, 1974); Yale University Law School (J.D., 1978). Phi Beta Kappa. President, Yale Law School Alumni Association, European Division, 1987-1992; Executive Committee, Yale Law School Association, 1988—. Board of Advisers, Corporate Counsel's International Adviser (Business Laws, Inc.), 1987—; Intellectual Property Committee, American Chamber of Commerce, Italy. Author: NACORE Seminar at MIPIM 94: European Real Estate - "How U.S. - Based Multinational End-Users Do Business in Europe," Cannes, March, 1994; "The Negotiating Phase - U.K. Acquisitions in Italy." Conference: Mergers and Acquisitions in Italy, London, February, 1992; "Privatisation in Italy," Corporate Counsel's International Advisor, May, 1993; "Entering the Southern European Markets," State Bar of Georgia, Conference on Doing Business in Southern Europe, May, 1994; "Italy: Legal and Operational Issues," Conference on Doing Business with Italy, Houston, April, 1994; "Forms of Investment in the U.S.A.," The U.S. Market - Op-

(This Listing Continued)

portunities for Trade and Investment, Milan Chamber of Commerce, February 1992; "In Step With Europe: New Legislation Means Italian Property Is No Longer a Law Unto Itself," EuroProperty, October 1991. Co-Author: "Country Handbook on Italy," Italian American Business, 1992; "International Contract Manual: Italy," Kluwer Law and Taxation, 1992; "Incorporation of an Italian Company: An Overview of Italian Law," Corporate Counsel's International Adviser, February, 1993; "Structuring Italian Shopping Center Investments for German Open-Ended Property Funds," September, 1994; "A Synopsis of the Greek Corporate Tax System," State of California EC Law Handbook, 1993; "Coal Gasification Projects in Italy," December, 1994; "Legal Aspects of Property Investment in Europe," Corporate Real Estate Executive, International Association of Corporate Real Estate Executives (NACORE), July/August 1992; "La Cooperazione Imprenditoriale Fra Italia e Stati Uniti: la Via Della Joint-Venture," Iniziativa Italia - Joint-Ventures, Milan, June 1992; "Italian Real Estate - Tax and Legal Aspects," Immobilier & Property, February 1992; "The New Italian S.I.M./M&A Legislation," Communication and Strategy - The New Organization of the Italian Securities Markets, London, 1991; "New Italian Legislation Regulating Buying and Selling on the Italian Securities Markets, Real Estate and M & A Transactions," Conference on Mergers and Acquisitions in Italy, Paris, 1991; "Franchising Agreements and Competition Rules in Italy," Corporate Counsel's International Advisor, November, 1991; "The Negotiating Phase - French Acquisitions in Italy," Communication and Strategy - International Mergers and Acquisitions In Italy, Paris, November 1991; "Legal Aspects of Property Investment in Italy," New York State Bar Association International Law Practicum, 1991; "Key Legal Issues," Communication and Strategy International - Commercial Property Development, Investment and Finance in Italy, Paris, 1991; "Joint Ventures - A European Perspective," Ninth Annual Southeastern Corporate Counsel Institute, Atlanta, 1990; "Acquisition and Management of Real Property in Italy by Non-Residents," Conference on "International Tax Strategy," Milan, 1990; "Responsabilità Civile Prodotti (Products Liability Litigation): Commenti e Interpretazioni," American Chamber of Commerce in Italy, June 1986; "Legal Aspects of Doing Business in the EEC," State Bar of Georgia, Continuing Legal Education Conference, 1986; "Venture Capital: Il Capitale a Rischio Statunitense per l'Investitore Istituzionale Italiano," Italian American Business, December 1985; "Opportunities for Tax Relief Under the New U.S.-Italian Income Tax Treaty," ABA Section on International Law and Practice, European Bulletin, November 1985. Associate, Alston, Miller & Gaines (Alston & Bird), Atlanta and Washington, D.C., 1978-1982. Member, Legal and Tax Committee, American Chamber of Commerce in Italy, 1984—; Member, Board of Governors, Sir James Henderson School, Milan, 1987-1989. *Member:* State Bar of Georgia (Member, Sections on International, Corporate and Banking Law; Chair, International Law Task Force, 1980-1982); American Bar Association (Charter Member, Committee on the International Aspects of Litigation, 1983; Chair, Subcommittee on European Broadcasting Laws, European Law Committee, 1985-1986; Member, Subcommittee on International Financing, Section of Corporation, Banking and Business Law, 1983—); State Bar of Texas (International Trade Committee, Section on International Law); International Bar Association. (Also at Rome Office).

MARCANTONIO PINCI, born Vicenza, Italy, October 27, 1963; admitted, 1990, Italy; 1990, New York. *Education:* University of Milan (J.D., 1988); Georgetown University Law Center (LL.M., 1989); Bocconi University, Milan (Master in Business Tax Law, Certificate, 1991). Author: "Milan Real Estate - Tax and Legal Aspects," Immobilier & Property, February, 1992; "Italy, Legal Tax and Financing Aspects of Italian Property Transactions for Foreign Investors and Developers," Sunbelt Conference on Real Estate Opportunities in Southern France, Northern Spain and Northern Italy, Cannes, December, 1991; "The Negotiating Phase - French Acquisitions in Italy," C&S Conference on Mergers and Acquisitions in Italy, Paris, November, 1991; "Acquisizione, Fusione e Partecipazione di Società Italiane ed Imprese Estere nel Quadro delle Direttive CEE in Materia di Imposizione Diretta," Seminar on International Tax Strategy, Turin, October, 1991; MIPIM 94 Conference: Italia: Nuove Opportunità per Investimenti Promozione e Finanziamenti Immobiliari - "Aspetti Legali e Fiscali degli Investimenti Immobiliari in Italia alla Luce dei Più Recenti Sviluppi Normativi," Cannes, March, 1994; "Enforcement of Judgments in Italy," Corporate Counsel's International Adviser, October, 1991; Seminar: "Enforcement of Judgments in Europe-Italy," New York State Bar Association, International Practice Section, New York, June 1991; "Dematerialization of Investment Securities," Georgetown University Law Center, 1989; "Insider Trading Regulations in the U.S., U.K., France and the E.E.C.: An Analysis from the Standpoint of the Italian Legal System," University of Milan, 1988; "Unico Azionista: Responsabilità ex Articolo 2362," University of Milan, 1986. Co-Author: "La Cooperazione Imprenditoriale Fra Italia e

(This Listing Continued)

DOBSON & PINCI, Milan—Continued

Stati Uniti: la Via Della Joint-Venture," Conference on Joint-Ventures, Milan, June 1992; "La Direttiva CEE 434/90 sul Regime delle Riorganizzazioni Societarie," Acquisizioni, April 1992; "Coal Gasification Projects in Italy," December 1994; "Il Nuovo Contratto d'Agenzia-D.L. 10.09.91 N° 303," published in France-Italie no. 6, November/December, 1993 and continued in same publication, no. 1, January/February, 1994; "Deregulation of Retail Licenses in Italy," April, 1994; "Structuring Italian Shopping Center, Investments for German Open-Ended Property Funds," September, 1994; Conference, Agenti di Commercio - "Lo Scioglimento del Rapporto di Agenzia nella Nuova Normative Italiana di Recepimento della Direttiva CEE 86/653," Milan, April 1993; "Incorporation of an Italian Company: An Overview of Italian Law," Corporate Counsel's International Adviser, February, 1993; "Legal Aspects of Property Investment in Europe," Corporate Real Estate Executive, International Association of Corporate Real Estate Executives (NACORE) July/August 1992; "Country Handbook on Italy," Italian American Business, 1992; "Italy, Financial Engineering and Tax Planning," C&S Conference: Property Investment in Italy, Paris, April 1991 and IBC Conference: European Commercial Property Development Opportunities, London, June 1991; "Acquisition and Management of Real Property in Italy by Non-Residents," Conference on "International Tax Strategy," Milan, November 1990. Advisor, Real Estate Masters Program (Shopping Center Development), Politecnico University of Turin, 1992—; Assistant to the General Counsel, Pirelli-Armstrong Tire Corp., New Haven, CT, 1990; Foreign Associate (Corporate Area), Foley, Hoag & Eliot, Boston, MA, 1989. *Member:* The Foreign Lawyers Forum of Washington, D.C.; International Bar Association. (Also at Rome Office).

FABIO G. MONTIN, born Paderno Dugnano, Italy, July 29, 1964; admitted, 1990, Italy. *Education:* Università Cattolica del S.Cuore, Milan (J.D., 1989). General Counsel, Recordati (Pharmaceuticals) S.p.A., 1992-1993. Author: "Chiarimenti sulla Rielaborazione dell'Etichettatura dei Prodotti in Conformità con le Nuove Regolamentazione dell'FDA" (Food and Drug Administration), Milan, 1994; "Uso del Computer e Tutela Penale: i Computer Crimes e la Tutela del Software," (Università Cattolica, 1989); "Development and Investment Opportunities for Commercial Centers in Italy," NACORE Conference (December, 1994). Conference: MIAD - "Prodotti Dolciari Italiana: Avere Successo nel Mercato U.S.A.," Milan, May 1994. *Member:* International Bar Association. (Also at Genoa Office).

GIOVANNI LOMBARDO, born Rome, March 7, 1962; admitted, 1990, Italy. *Education:* La Sapienza University, Rome (J.D., 1985). Author: "A Practical Guide to Italian Rates - The New ICI," Belle Cose, Summer 1993; "Pension Reform in Italy," Belle Cose, June, 1993; "A New Cut in the VAT Rates on Maintenance Work in Italy," Belle Cose, Autumn 1994; "First Time Buyers in Italy," Belle Cose, Spring 1994; "Taxation of Foreign Companies in Italy," Belle Cose, Summer 1994. Conferences: State Bar of Georgia, "Doing Business in Southern Europe," Atlanta, May 1994; "Italy and Europe: The Economic Situation In the Current Political and Regulatory Climate," London, September 1994; "Italian Water Privatisation and the Galli Law," Birmingham, U.K., November 1994. *Member:* International Bar Association; Association of Personal Injury Lawyers. (At London and Athens Offices).

MARIA-CLAUDIA PICCARRETA, born Rome, Italy, April 2, 1963; admitted, 1992, Luxembourg; 1994, Italy. *Education:* La Sapienza University, Rome (J.D., 1990); University of Luxembourg (LL.M., 1992). Publications and Seminars: "European Community Environment Law: Problems in National Implementation," Association Européenne de Droit de l'Environnement (AEDE), Luxembourg, 1994; "La Suisse face à la TVA (VAT)," conference, Fiduciaire Price Waterhouse SA, Genève, 1993; "La lutte contre le blanchiment des capitaux," Institut Européen d'Administration Publique (IEAP), Luxembourg, 1993; "La droit de la concurrence dans le cadre des relations AELF/CEE," Institut Européen d'Administration Publique (IEAP), Luxembourg, 1993; "The Brussels and Lugano Conventions: Judicial Competence Regarding Civil and Commercial Matters," Institut Européen d'Administration Publique (IEAP), Luxembourg, 1993; "Le cautionnement bancaire: protéction juridique de l'acaution," Association Luxembourgeoise des Juristes de Banque (AJBL), Luxembourg, 1992; "Les accords de Schengen: politique migratoire à l'intérieur de la C.E.E." sessione estiva dell'Institut Universitaire de Luxembourg (IUIL), Luxembourg, 1992. *Member:* International Bar Association; International Association of Young Lawyers; Association Luxembourgeiose des Juristes Européens (ALJE). (At Rome Office).

(This Listing Continued)

ASSOCIATES

PETER F. MCLAUGHLIN, born Boston, Massachusetts, July 7, 1963; admitted, 1993, New York. *Education:* Columbia University (A.B., 1986); Georgetown University Law Center (J.D., 1993). Senior Articles Editor, Law & Policy in International Business, 1992-1993. Board of Advisors, Corporate Counsel's Importing Under the U.S. Customs Laws (Business Laws, Inc.), 1995—. Author: "Mexico's Antidumping and Countervailing Duty Laws: Amenable to a Free Trade Agreement?" 23 Law and Poly Int'l. Bus. 1009 (1992); "The European Community's Proposed Bioengineering Directive: A Potential Non-Tariff Barrier to U.S. Food Products," Washington Legal Foundation, 1992. Co-Author: "General Procedures for an Employee Transferred from the United States to Obtain Permission to Work in Italy," October 1994; "Multilateral Trade Negotiations (MTNs)" Chapter of "The GATT Uruguay Round Negotiations: 1986-1993," Kluwer Law and Taxation Publishers, 1993. Conferences and Seminars: "Agency and Distribution Law in Italy," (SMAU-Milan, October 1994). Chairman, American Citizens Abroad (Milan, Italy Chapter); Director, American Citizens Abroad-Italy. *Member:* American Bar Association (Sections on International and Business Law); International Bar Association; New York State Bar Association (International Law Section); Foreign Lawyers Association, Italy; Italian-Irish Business Association. (Also at New York, USA Office).

SANDRA MORI, born Pisa, Italy, June 2, 1964; admitted, 1993, Italy. *Education:* Università degli Studi, Pisa (J.D., 1988). Visiting Scholar, Yale Law School, 1993-1994. Co-Author: "General Procedures for an Employee Transferred from the United States to Obtain Permission to Work in Italy," October, 1994; "Franchising in Italy," September, 1994. *Member:* International Bar Association. (Also at Genoa Office).

ANTHONY A. SISTILLI, born Steubenville, Ohio, May 19, 1966; admitted, 1992, Pennsylvania. *Education:* West Virginia University (B.A., magna cum laude, 1988); Temple University School of Law, International Studies, Rome (1990); West Virginia University College of Law (J.D., 1992); McGeorge School of Law, Sacramento, California (Diploma in Advanced International Legal Studies, Salzburg, Austria, 1992). Publications, Business Law Europe, European Law Press, European Correspondent, Rome (1993). Author: "New Rules on Domestic and International Arbitration," April 1994; "Protection of Computer Programs," English Edition 5/93, March 1993; "Mutual Fund Investments in Italy," English Edition 7/93, April 1993; "Security Interests in Receivables in Italy," English Edition 13/93, June 1993. Co-author: "Coal Gasification Projects in Italy," December 1994; "Franchising in Italy," Corporate Counsel's International Adviser, September 1994; "Progressing From National to European Structures," European Market Law Report, March 1994; "Taxation of Foreign Companies in Italy," Belle Cose, Summer 1994; Conference: "Cutting Through the Red Tape: U.S. Customs, F.D.A., U.S.D.A., and Other Legal Issues Facing Foreign Food and Beverage Manufacturers Entering the U.S. Market," New York, June, 1993. Approaching 2000 - The Corporation in Transition, "EEC Driven Changes in Italian Corporate Law," Salzburg, June 1993. *Member:* International Bar Association. (At Brussels and Rome Offices).

FRANK FERRANTE, JR., born Canton, Ohio, May 20, 1968; admitted, 1994, New York. *Education:* The American University, School of International Service, Washington D.C. (B.A., Economics, cum laude, 1991); Milan University (Private Comparative Law and European Community Law, 1993); Case Western Reserve University School of Law (J.D., 1994). Associate, Case Western Reserve Law Review, 1992-1993; Associate, 1992-1993; Publisher, 1993-1994. Conference: "Cutting Through the Red Tape: U.S. Customs, F.D.A., U.S.D.A., and Other Legal Issues Facing Foreign Food and Beverage Manufacturers Entering the U.S. Market," New York, June, 1993. (At New York, USA Office).

ARMANDO AMBROSIO, born Naples, Italy, August 8, 1965; admitted, 1994, Italy. *Education:* University of Naples (J.D., 1991); City of London Polytechnic (Certificate in Export and Maritime Law, 1991); King's College London (LL.M., 1993). Seminar in Economies Transition, Salsburg, 1994. Visiting Foreign Lawyer: Theodore Goddard, London, 1992; Zeyen Beghin Feider, Luxembourg, 1994.

MASSIMO GALLI, born Ferrara, Italy, September 4, 1968; admitted, 1994, New York. *Education:* Georgetown University (B.S., cum laude, 1991); Columbia University (J.D., 1994). Note Editor, Columbia Business Law Review. Author: "Sue or Lose: An Agenda for US Corporations Seeking Compensation from Iraq," 2 Columbia Business Law Review 241, 1993. *Member:* International Bar Association. (Also at New York, USA Office).

CARLO SALA, born Milan, Italy, April 11, 1966; admitted, 1994, Italy. *Education:* Catholic University of Milan (J.D., 1991). Author: "EEC and

(This Listing Continued)

the Exhaustion of Intellectual Property Rights," 1992; "L'Evoluzione del Mutuo," su Milano Finanza, Mercato Immobiliare, July, 1993.

FRANK JORG GEFFERS, born Hofgeismar, Germany, June 4, 1963. admitted to practice, 1993, Italy. *Education:* La Sapienza University, Rome (J.D., 1993). Co-Author: "Structuring Italian Shopping Center Investments for German Open-Ended Property Funds," September 1994; "Procedures for Opening a Restaurant or Fast Food Operation in Italy," April 1994; "Debt Recovery in Italy," November 1993; "How to Obtain Retail Licenses in Italy," September 1994. President, Rotaract Club of Roma Ovest, 1991-1992. *Member:* International Bar Association. (At Rome Office).

ANDREA VOGHERA, born Alba, Italy, February 23, 1969. admitted to practice, 1993, Italy. *Education:* Catholic University, Milan (J.D., 1993); Schiller International University of London. Seminars: "European Community Law: An Introduction for Lawyers," Otzenhausen, Germany, 1994. *Member:* International Bar Association. (At London Office).

GIORGIO COGLIATI, born Rome, Italy, February 20, 1963. admitted to practice, 1992, Italy. *Education:* University of Milan (J.D., 1992); University of Paris (Certificate of EU Law, 1994). "Commercial Leases in Belgium," January 1993. *Member:* International Bar Association. (Also at Brussels Office).

MARIA CRISTINA VERDURA CABOT, born Cagliari, Italy, August 10, 1955. admitted to practice, 1979, Italy. *Education:* Università degli Studi di Cagliari (J.D., 1979). Author: "Nuclear Energy and Public International Law," Cagliari, 1979. Conference: "Introduction and Overview of the Italian Judicial System," Italian-American Lawyers Association, 1984.

ROGER O'BRIEN, born Yorkshire, England, August 1, 1964. *Education:* College of Law, Chancery Lane (B.A., Law, 1988); Manchester University (B.A., Hons., 1985). (At London Office).

FLAVIA UBERTI, born Milan, Italy, November 15, 1971. admitted to practice, 1994, Italy. *Education:* State University of Milan (J.D., 1994). Author: "The Interpretation of Conventions of Uniform Law: the Geneva Convention of June 7, 1930," Milan, 1994. (At London Office).

GIUSEPPE AMATO, born Catania, Italy, August 9, 1968. admitted to practice, 1994, Italy. *Education:* University of Pavia (J.D., 1994). Author: "Enforcement Policy in the E.E.C. and in the U.S.A.," Ireland, 1994; "Franchising e concorrenza nell'ordinamento comunitario e in quello interno," Pavia, 1994. (At London Office).

COUNSEL

GIORGIO VALENTI, born Milan, Italy, November 26, 1927; admitted, 1952, Italy. *Education:* University of Milan (J.D., 1952). General Counsel, Legal Department, Euromobiliare S.p.A. (Investment Bank), 1986-1987. Manager, Commercial Trade and Exchange Controls Office, Banca Commerciale Italiana/COMIT, 1975-1986. In-House Counsel, Legal Department (Litigation, Banking and Tax Sections), Banca Commerciale Italiana/COMIT, 1959-1972. *Member:* International Bar Association. (Also at Rome Office).

PIERLUIGI VALENTINO, born Naples, Italy, August 25, 1962; admitted, 1990, Italy. *Education:* La Sapienza University, Rome (J.D., 1985); Sraffa Institute, Bocconi University, Milan (Specialized courses on Giuristi di Impresa, 1987). Consob (National Committee for Companies and the Stock Exchange), Rome, 1985-1989. Professor: Institutions of Public Law, and Economy and Finance of Financial Intermediaries, LUISS University, Rome; Banking and Real Estate Politics and Regulations, La Sapienza University, Rome. Author: "Ordine di Borsa, Attività di Intermediazione Mobiliare e Contratti di Borsa"; "Fallimento di una SIM: Ruolo e Funzioni del Commissario Governativo e Limiti alla Restituzione dei Patrimoni alla Clientela"; "Liquidazione a Contante delle Operazioni di Borsa"; "SIM: La Legge 2 gennaio 1991"; "Nel d.d.l. sulla Borsa "Golden Share" e Autonomia Finanziaria della Consob"; "Gli Obblighi Informativi per gli Emittenti e le Società Quotate"; "Rassegna Normativa dei Provvedimenti della Consob (dal 1990)"; "La Quotazione di Diritto in Borsa delle Azioni di Risparmio ed il Nuovo Regolamento di Ammissione a Quotazione"; "Diritti di Quotazione ed Ammissione di Diritto alla Quotazione nelle Borse Valori"; "La Potestà Regolamentare della Consob e le Società Commissionarie di Borsa"; "Rilievo Costituzionale e Destinazione dei Diritti Inerenti ai Servizi delle Borse Valori"; "Tipicità Fiscale dei Titoli Atipici"; "Commentario al Testo Unico delle Leggi in Materia Creditizia e Bancaria"; "Codice Civile Commentato Diretto da Pietro Rescigno"; "Anagrafe degli Intermediari Mobiliari, Cedim"; "Strutture e Regolamentazione del Mercato Mobiliare"; "Consob L'Instituzione e la Legge Penale, AA.VV." Co-Author: "L'Instituzione Consob Funzione e Struttura.". (At Rome Office).

(This Listing Continued)

FRANCO DI LEO, born Bergamo, Italy, March 4, 1933; admitted, 1961, Genoa. *Education:* University of Genoa (LL.D., 1956). Assistant Professor, International Law, University of Genoa, 1968—. (At Genoa Office).

ALESSANDRO MORINI, born San Paolo, Brazil, April 30, 1963; admitted, 1991, Genoa. *Education:* University of Genoa (LL.D., 1987). Professor, Securities Regulation, University of Bergamo, 1994—. (At Genoa Office).

CLAUDIO MOLISANI, born Genoa, Italy, March 18, 1949; admitted, 1978, Genoa. *Education:* University of Genoa (LL.D., 1974). (At Genoa Office).

GIOVANNI ACERBI, born Milan, Italy, July 17, 1947; admitted, 1978, Italy. *Education:* University of Milan (J.D., 1972); University of Georgia at Athens (LL.M., 1974). Rotary International Scholarship. Comparative Law Council Scholar. General Counsel, Impresa Lodigiani S.p.A., 1978-1981. In-House Counsel, AGIP S.p.A. and AGIP Legal Representative to Joint Venture Operating Agreements with Oman, Brazil and Sudan, 1976-1978. Member, Committee on International Construction Contracts, Italian Industry Association, 1978-1981. *Member:* International Bar Association. (Also at Rome Office).

GIOVANNI PAOLO ACCINNI, born Milan, Italy, July 13, 1963; admitted, 1991, Milan. *Education:* University of Milan (J.D., summa cum laude, 1988). Author: "Criminal Law Aspects of Conflict of Interests for Groups of Companies," Rivista Società, 1991; "Is Art. 135 of the Code of Civil Procedure Constitutionally Valid?" Rivista di Diritto Processuale, 1992; "Aspects of Criminal Liability for Groups of Companies," Le Società, 1993; "Instances of Bankruptcy and Aspects of Criminal Liability for Managing Directors," Le Società 1993; "Grants of Loans or Guarantees for the Purchase of Stocks," Rivista delle Società, 1994; "Factoring Operations and Related Criminal Liability," Rivista di Diritto Penale dell'Economia, 1994; "Withholding of Interest Received from Foreign Non-Resident Banks as a Substitute Tax," Rivista di Diritto Penale dell'Economica, 1994. Teaching Assistant, Criminal Liability in Commercial Law, University of Milan.

DOMENICO SCOPELLITI, born Rome, Italy, July 1, 1967; admitted, 1993, Italy. *Education:* LUISS University, Rome (J.D., 1990). (At Rome Office).

DOMENICO NASO, born Rome, Italy, August 3, 1965. *Education:* La Sapienza University, Rome (J.D., 1993). Counsel: Secretary of the President of the Chamber of Deputies, Rome, 1989-1991; Centro Studi U.I.L. - Finanze, Rome, 1992-1993. (At Rome Office).

FRANCESCO FABBRI, born Rome, Italy, November 5, 1966. *Education:* La Sapienza University, Rome (J.D., 1993). (At Rome Office).

PAOLO BORGHI, born Saronno, Italy, November 13, 1952; admitted, 1981, Italy. *Education:* University of Pavia (J.D., 1980). *Member:* International Bar Association. (Also at Rome Office).

GIOVANNI LOMBARDO, born San Salvatore Monferrato, Italy, September 22, 1953; admitted, 1981, Italy. *Education:* University of Pavia (J.D., 1980). *Member:* International Bar Association. (Also at Rome Office).

ANDREW DUNCAN ROBSON COLVIN, born Berlin, Germany, July 13, 1948; admitted, 1972, London; 1987, Paris. *Education:* University of Kent (B.A., 1970), Inns of Court School of Law; Institut d'Etudes Europeennes, Université Libre de Bruxelles, Fondazione Giorgio Cini, Venice, Italy; University of Siena, Italy (J.D., 1994). Author: "Italian Competition Law," Corporate Lawyer, 1991; "The Control of Broadcasting in Italy: A Commentary on the New MAMMI Law," World Competition, December, 1990. Co-Author: "Round-up of New Laws in Italy," April, 1994; "Privatisation in Italy," Corporate Counsel's International Advisor, May, 1993. "Pension Reform in Italy," Belle Cose, June, 1993; "Agency and Distribution Agreements in Italy," Corporate Counsel's International Advisor, June, 1993; Legal Advisor and Company Secretary, Monsanto Oil Company of the U.K., Inc., 1982-1985; Fluor Corporation Subsidiaries, 1977-1982. (At London and Rome Offices).

R. SCOTT TOBIN, born High Point, North Carolina, April 29, 1954; admitted, 1981, Georgia. *Education:* Tulane University; University of North Carolina (B.A., 1975; J.D., with honors, 1981). Recipient, American Jurisprudence Award in Remedies. Assistant Attorney General, State of Georgia, 1983-1985. *Member:* Atlanta Bar Association; State Bar of Georgia. (At Atlanta, Georgia USA Office; Also Member, Weinstein, Rosenthal & Tobin, P.C., Atlanta, Georgia).

MICHAEL S. ROSENTHAL, born Chicago, Illinois, May 7, 1957; admitted, 1980, Georgia. *Education:* University of Florida (B.A., with honors,

(This Listing Continued)

DOBSON & PINCI, Milan—Continued

1977; J.D., 1980). Assistant Attorney General, State of Georgia, 1980-1984. Special Projects Coordinator, Governor's Office of Consumer Affairs, 1984-1985. Special Assistant Attorney General, State of Georgia, 1985-1990. *Member:* Atlanta and American Bar Associations; State Bar of Georgia. (At Atlanta, Georgia, USA Office; Also Member, Weinstein, Rosenthal & Tobin, P.C., Atlanta, Georgia).

MELVIN E. WEINSTEIN, (P.C.), born Athens, Georgia, July 17, 1941; admitted, 1968, District of Columbia; 1970, California; 1974, Florida and U.S. Tax Court; 1984, Georgia. *Education:* Emory University (A.B., 1963; J.D., 1967); New York University (LL.M. in Taxation, 1969). Phi Beta Kappa; Order of the Coif. Attorney-Advisor: National Office of the Chief Counsel, Internal Revenue Service, 1970-1972; Clerk to Honorable William M. Fay, U.S. Tax Court, 1972-1974. *Member:* The Florida Bar; District of Columbia Bar; State Bar of California; State Bar of Georgia; American Bar Association. (At Atlanta, Georgia, USA Office; Also Member, Weinstein, Rosenthal & Tobin, P.C., Atlanta, Georgia).

SATURNINO E. LUCIO, II, born Havana, Cuba, December 16, 1954; admitted, 1979, Florida and U.S. District Court, Southern District of Florida; 1987, U.S. Court of International Trade; 1988, U.S. Supreme Court. *Education:* Harvard University (B.A., magna cum laude, 1976; J.D., cum laude, 1979). Developments Editor, Harvard International Law Journal, 1978-1979. Chairman, International Countertrade and Currency Exchange, 1984—. Member, City of Miami International Trade Board, 1988—. Vice President, Miami World Trade Center, 1984-1990. Chairman, International Commercial Dispute Resolution Center of Florida, 1985-1987. Author: "Structuring Foreign Ownership Interests in Latin American Companies," The Florida Bar, Doing Business in Latin America: Free Trade - The Door Opens, February 6-7, 1992; "Debt-Equity Swaps and U.S. Banks: Alternatives to Regulation K," The Florida Bar, Legal Aspects of Doing Business in Latin America, February 2-3, 1989; "International Financial Transactions," in the Florida Bar International Transactions Manual (1988); "Twelve Tips on Countertrade Contracts," 2 Export Today 33, Fall, 1986. *Member:* American, Inter-American and Cuban American Bar Associations; The Florida Bar (Co-Editor, Florida Bar International Transaction Manual, 1988; Chairman, International Business Committee, 1986-1992). (At Miami, Florida, USA Office; Also Member, Weil, Lucio, Mandler, Croland & Steele, Miami, Florida).

JEFFREY L. MANDLER, born Miami, Florida, August 25, 1955; admitted, 1980, Florida. *Education:* Trinity College (B.A., 1977); University of Miami (J.D., 1980). Pi Gamma Mu. Member Advisory Board, Attorneys Title Insurance Fund, 1987. *Member:* Miami Beach (Member, Board of Directors, 1982-1983); Dade County and American Bar Associations; The Florida Bar (Member, Real Property, Probate and Trust Law Section and Tax Aspects of Real Property Law Committee). (At Miami, Florida, USA Office; Also Member, Weil, Lucio, Mandler, Croland & Steele, Miami, Florida).

THEANO RADICOPOULOS, born Athens, Greece, October 11, 1969. *Education:* University of Kent (B.A., with honors, 1991); College of Law (J.D., 1992). (At Athens Office).

GEORGE KOMIS, born Athens, Greece; admitted, 1993, Athens. *Education:* University of Athens (J.D.). (At Athens Office; also with, Bahas, Gramatidis & Associates, Athens).

RICHARD I. SINGER, born White Plains, New York, June 5, 1931; admitted, 1959, California. *Education:* Massachusetts Institute of Technology (B.S., 1953); University of Michigan (J.D., 1958). (At San Diego, California, USA Office).

SILVIA RAVIOLA, born Milan, Italy, October 5, 1963; admitted, 1992, California. *Education:* West Valley Community College (A.A., 1984); Monterey Institute of International Studies (M.A., 1987); Golden Gate University School of Law (J.D., 1991). Honorary Vice-Consul, Italy. Legal Consultant, Olivetti Advanced Technology Center, 1992. *Member:* American Bar Association; Italian American Bar Association; American Immigration Lawyers' Association. (At San Diego, USA Office).

YANOS GRAMATIDIS, born Larissa, Greece, May 12, 1952; admitted, 1977, Greece and Supreme Court of Greece. *Education:* University of Athens Law School (LL.B.; Political Science); The Hague Academy of International Law (D.O.A.); Institut International des Droits de l'Homme, Strasbourg (D.O.A.). Author: "Mergers and Acquisitions in the EEC," 1988; "Acquisition of Greek Securities," 1988; "Acquisition of Real Property in Greece by Aliens," 1985; "The New Law on Leasing in Greece," 1987; "Hotel Contracts in Greece," 1987; "Time sharing in Greece," 1987; "Fran-

(This Listing Continued)

chising: The Greek Legislation," 1988; "Investment Incentives in Greece," 1988; "Bank Confidentiality in Greece," 1989; "International MOA Law," 1991; "Franchising - Greece," 1992; "Preemptive Remedies in Europe," 1992. Editor: "International Franchising," 1992. Special Representative in Greece of the International Franchise Association. Correspondent: Lexpress Ltd., Milwaukee, USA; Centre of International Legal Studies, Salzburg, Austria; Butterworths Journal of International Banking and Financial Law. *Member:* Athens, International (Member: Business Law Section; General Practice Section), American and Inter-American Bar Associations; Hellenic-American Chamber of Commerce; British-Hellenic Chamber of Commerce; Institute of European Law, The University of Birmingham; EC Lawyers Society, London, England; International Pension and Employees Benefits Lawyers Association; Solicitors European Group, London, England. (At Athens Office; also Member, Bahas, Gramatidis & Associates).

CHRISTINA STAMPOULTZI, born Athens, Greece, November 4, 1966; admitted, 1992, Greece. *Education:* Aristotelion University of Thessaloniki (J.D., 1989). Author: "The Treatment of Television in European Competition Law," 1989. Attorney, European Commission, DG XV/B/4 (Public Procurement). (At Athens Office; also with, Bahas, Gramatidis & Associates, Athens).

Languages: English, Italian, French, Greek, German, Spanish, Japanese and Russian

REPRESENTATIVE CLIENTS: Blockbuster International Corporation; Matsushita Investment & Development (MID) U.K., Ltd.; Marriott Corporation; Marriott Ownership Resorts, Inc.; Electronic Data Systems Corporation (EDS); CCN Systems Limited (Financial and Credit Systems); Electricité de France (EdF); Ugine S.A. (Usinor-Sacilor); Occidental Petroleum Corporation; OXY Oil and Gas USA, Inc.; Midas International Corporation; Towers, Perrin, Forster & Crosby, Inc. (TPFC)/Tillinghast; Teledyne, Inc./Water Pik; Gerber Products Company; Kubota Europe S.A.; Komatsu Ltd.; Hong Kong Trade Development Council; P&O Ferrymasters (Transportation) B.V.; Fidelity Management & Research Company; Fidelity Investments; C.S. Immobilien-Fonds GmbH; Oppenheimer & Co., Inc.; Oppenheimer International Horizon Fund, Ltd.; Salomon Brothers International, Ltd.; County Natwest Securities, Ltd.; Close Asset Finance, Ltd.; The Carlyle Group, Inc.; Fieldstone Private Capital Group, Ltd.; Parc Securities Limited; Belga Factors N.V.; Citicorp Finanziaria S.p.A.; Barclays Bank PLC; Halifax Building Society; Pierson, Heldring & Pierson N.V.; The Bank of Tokyo, Ltd.; Comerica Incorporated; CoreStates-Philadelphia National Bank; First City, Texas-Houston, N.A.; National City Corporation; PNC Financial Corporation; Citizens Fidelity Bank & Trust Company; Worthen National Bank; Hailman Capital Partners; American Finance Group; Integrated Payment Systems, Inc. (IPS); Chubb Insurance Company; Hartford International Insurance Company; American International Group, Inc. (AIG); UNAT S.A.; Federal Insurance Co.; The Equitable Life Assurance Society (U.K.); Reliance National; General Reinsurance Corporation; Sedgwick James S.p.A.; BBC/British Broadcasting Corporation; MCI International; Hughes Communications DIRECTV; CNN/Cable News Network, Inc.; Twentieth Century Fox; World Films; Capella International, Inc.; Vision International; TBS/Turner Broadcasting System, Inc.; Weintraub Screen Entertainment, Ltd.; ICM/International Creative Management, Inc.; Tams-Witmark Music Library, Inc.; Gere Productions, Inc.; Summit (Film) Export Group, Inc.; Harold Fielding, Ltd.; Malcolm McLaren, Ltd.; Guinness Mahon & Co., Ltd.; Movie Acquisition Corporation Limited; Gilbert Doyle Advertising; Bain & Company, Inc.; Citicorp Real Estate/Europe; Marks & Spencer; Nationale-Nederlanden/ING Real Estate; Norwich Union Real Estate Managers, Ltd.; Le Meridien (Hotels) S.A.; MANG Property Services Italia S.r.l.; Shaftesbury (Property) Group; Prosim S.r.l.; GBB GmbH; CONAD (Supermarkets) Nordest; Mellon Stuart Company; The Donna Karan Company; Thor-Lo Sports Socks; Figgie International, Inc./Fred Perry Sportswear; Dockers Europe B.V. (Levi Strauss & Company); Itochu Fashion System Co., Ltd.; Hanil Synthetic Fiber Co., Ltd.; Foot Locker Europe B.V.; Fieldcrest Cannon, Inc.; Daniela Textiles S.r.l.; Tultex International; Edison Brothers Stores International, Inc. (J. Riggins/Outriggers); Dell Computer Corp.; Dun & Bradstreet Software Services, Inc.; International Data Corporation; Micro Technology, Inc.; Pilot Software; Mantech International Corp.; National Data Corporation International, Ltd. (NDC); Bachman Information Systems; Goal Systems International, Inc.; IDT/Integrated Device Technology Europe; Internet Systems Corp.; Meteor Communications Corporation; Scientific-Atlanta, Inc.; Southern Electric International; CAE-Link Corporation; Kockumation A.B.; Crompton & Knowles; Central National-Gottesman, Inc.; Constar International; Textainer Equipment Management (U.S.), Ltd.; Scholle Corporation; Circle Freight International; Mul-T-Lock Ltd.; Nordic Laboratories, Inc.; Industrie Chimiche Farmaceutiche Italiana S.p.A. (ICFI); Ing. Enea Mattei S.p.A.; Delle Vedove Levigatrici S.p.A.; Scaglia S.p.A.; Agnati, S.p.A.; Alpi S.p.A.; Lecce Pen Company S.p.A.; Simonelli S.p.A.; Valdarno S.p.A.; Vega S.p.A.; Risocomex Trading S.p.A.; Globtrade Italiana S.p.A.; Bindi/Società Italiana Prodotto Alimentari (SIPA) S.p.A.; STAR/Stabilimento Alimentare S.p.A.; Sapori S.p.A.; San Daniele S.p.A.; Armando Testa S.p.A.

EREDE E ASSOCIATI

Established in 1969

VIA SERBELLONI, 12
20122 MILAN, ITALY
Telephone: (02) 76-020-346; Intn'l. (39-2) 76-020-346
Telecopier: (Gr. III, II) (02) 780-687; Intn'l. (39-2) 780-687

International and Domestic Practice, Mergers and Acquisitions, Taxation, Litigation and Arbitration, Banking, Bankruptcy, Contracts, Corporate, Securities, Exchange Controls, UE Law, Antitrust, Foreign Investment, Insurance, International Trade, Patents and Trademarks, Licensing, Labor, Product Liability.

PARTNERS

SERGIO EREDE, born Florence, Italy, August 14, 1940; admitted, 1967, Italy. *Education:* University of Milan (Doctor of Jurisprudence, magna cum laude, 1962); Harvard Law School (LL.M., 1964). With Hale & Door, Boston, 1963-1964 and Sullivan & Cromwell, New York, 1964-1965. Manager, Legal Department, IBM Italia S.p.A., 1965-1969. Member: Harvard Law School Alumni Association; Fulbright - Hays Alumni Association. *LANGUAGES:* Italian, English and French.

AUGUSTO BIANCHI, born Milan, Italy, October 19, 1940; admitted, 1966, Italy; 1981, Italian Supreme Court. *Education:* University of Milan (Doctor of Jurisprudence, magna cum laude, 1963). *LANGUAGES:* Italian and English.

STEFANO BIANCHI, born Milan, Italy, February 7, 1954; admitted, 1982, Italy. *Education:* University of Milan (Doctor of Jurisprudence, 1979). *LANGUAGES:* Italian, English and French.

FABIO CAPPELLETTI, born Milan, Italy, November 13, 1956; admitted, 1982, Italy. *Education:* University of Milan (Doctor of Jurisprudence, magna cum laude, 1979). Comptroller of Accounts, 1988. *LANGUAGES:* Italian and English.

ROBERTO CERA, born Milan, Italy, June 24, 1955; admitted, 1981, Italy. *Education:* University of Milan (Doctor of Jurisprudence, magna cum laude, 1978). *LANGUAGES:* Italian and English.

CESARE DEGLI OCCHI, born Milan, Italy, July 14, 1951; admitted, 1979, Italy. *Education:* University of Milan (Doctor of Jurisprudence, magna cum laude, 1974). *LANGUAGES:* Italian and English.

UMBERTO NICODANO, born Milan, Italy, April 2, 1952; admitted, 1978, Italy. *Education:* University of Milan (Doctor of Jurisprudence, magna cum laude, 1974). Attorney, Sperry Univac Division of Sperry Corporation, 1976-1982. *LANGUAGES:* Italian, English and French.

ASSOCIATES

LAURA MARIA ARNOLETTI, born Milan, Italy, September 6, 1960; admitted, 1986, Italy. *Education:* University of Milan (Doctor of Jurisprudence, magna cum laude, 1984). *Member:* Milan Bar Association. *LANGUAGES:* Italian, French and English.

MICHELE BIGNAMI, born Milan, Italy, June 24, 1962; admitted, 1992, Italy. *Education:* University of Milan (Doctor of Jurisprudence, 1986); London University, Queen Mary College (I.P.LL.M., 1987). Legal Assistant, Foster Wheeler Energy Ltd., London, U.K., 1986-1988. *LANGUAGES:* Italian and English.

MARCELLO MARCANTONIO, born Chieti, Italy, July 7, 1960; admitted, 1990, Italy. *Education:* University of Rome (Doctor of Jurisprudence, 1986); London University, King's College (LL.M., 1993). With Constant & Constant, London, 1990-1992. *LANGUAGES:* Italian and English.

GIAN CARLO SESSA, born Milan, Italy, February 20, 1963; admitted, 1993, Italy. *Education:* University of Milan (Doctor of Jurisprudence, magna cum laude, 1988). *LANGUAGES:* Italian, English and French.

MARIA CRISTINA STORCHI, born Milan, Italy, September 26, 1964; admitted, 1993, Italy. *Education:* University of Milan (Doctor of Jurisprudence, magna cum laude, 1988). *LANGUAGES:* Italian, English and French.

STUDIO LEGALE FERRARI

39, VIA SAN BARNABA
20122 MILAN, ITALY
Telephone: (02) 55185886
Telex: 320547 FERARI
Telefax: (KONICA 285): 5459266

Rome, Italy Office: Via Porpora n. 9. Telephone: (06) 8558841. Telex: 612231.

PAOLO FERRARI, born Reggio Emilia, Italy, December 16, 1929; admitted, 1956, Milan; 1962, Italy. *Education:* Modena University (Doctor of Jurisprudence, 1953). Author: Commentator on Monitore dei Tribunali and Temi, Law Reviews. *Member:* Milan Bar. *LANGUAGES:* English and French. *PRACTICE AREAS:* Corporate Law; Banking Law; Foreign Investment Law; International Transaction Law.

ANNA F. BARBACCIA, born Milan, Italy, November 2, 1952; admitted, 1979, Milan. *Education:* Milan University (Doctor of Jurisprudence, 1977); Georgetown University, Washington, D.C. (1980). Visiting Foreign Lawyer: Elborne Mitchell, London, 1978; Milgrim, New York, 1981. *Member:* Milan Bar. *LANGUAGES:* Italian and English. *PRACTICE AREAS:* General Civil Practice Law; Patents and Trademarks Law; Estate Law.

GIORGIO R. BOJARDI, born Milan, Italy, March 10, 1947; admitted, 1977, Milan; 1983, Italy. *Education:* Milan University (Doctor of Jurisprudence, 1972). *Member:* Milan Bar. *LANGUAGES:* Italian and English. *PRACTICE AREAS:* General Civil Practice Law; Corporate Law; Banking Law; Foreign Investment Law; Estate Law.

GIANMARCO BRENELLI, born Milan, Italy, September 10, 1951; admitted, 1982, Milan. *Education:* Milan University (Doctor of Jurisprudence, 1977). *Member:* Milan Bar. *LANGUAGES:* Italian and English. *PRACTICE AREAS:* General Civil Practice Law; Corporate Law; Foreign Investment Law.

SUSANNA ZIMMARO, born Milan, Italy, February 28, 1962; admitted, 1989, Milan. *Education:* Milan University (Doctor of Jurisprudence, 1986). *LANGUAGES:* Italian, English and French. *PRACTICE AREAS:* General Practice Law; Estate Law.

Languages: Italian, English and French.

REFERENCES: Philip Morris EEC; Morgan Guaranty Trust Company, of New York; Nestlé; Stein; Heurtey-Bergeon; Lloyds Underwriters; Miller Brewing Company; Credit Lyonnaise; Fabriques de Tabac Reunies; Shandwick Company; Crediolease; Credito Emiliano S.p.A.; Credito Romagnolo S.p.A.; Instituto Italiano di Credito Fondiario S.p.A.; Sidercomit S.p.A. (Finsider Group); Toro Assicurazioni S.p.A.

DENNIS A. FOSTER AND ASSOCIATES

VIALE CORSICA, 3
20133 MILAN, ITALY
Telephone: (02) 70103440
Fax: (02) 70125078

MEMBER OF FIRM

DENNIS A. FOSTER, born Iron Station, North Carolina, August 24, 1949; admitted, 1988, Maryland (Not admitted in Italy). *Education:* University of North Carolina, Chapel Hill (B.A., summa cum laude, French, 1971); University of Florence, Institute of Comparative Law (externship, 1976); Stanford University (J.D., 1977); University of London (School of Oriental and African Studies; M.A. in Development Economics/Middle East Studies, 1981). With, Morrison and Foerster, San Francisco, California, 1975; Coudert Brothers, London, 1978-1979; Chambers, Stein, Ferguson and Becton, Charlotte, North Carolina, 1980; United States Diplomatic Corps (Foreign Service), 1981-1991. Specialist, political and economic/commercial affairs. Postings included Beirut, Genoa, Washington, D.C. and Abu Dhabi. Instructor, Comparative Law, University of Genoa, 1985-1986. Member, board of editors of the "Stanford International Law Journal." *Member:* Maryland Bar Association. [United States Army, 1971-1974; Russian Linguist/Intelligence specialist; One year at the National Defense Language Institute in Monterey, California; Two years in Stuttgart, West Germany]. *LANGUAGES:* English, French, Italian, Arabic, Russian, German and Spanish. *PRACTICE AREAS:* International Business Transactions.

(This Listing Continued)

DENNIS A. FOSTER AND ASSOCIATES, Milan—Continued

ASSOCIATES

GIANFRANCO BENVENUTO, born Firenze, Italy, March 26, 1957; admitted, 1986, Milan, Italy. *Education:* State University of Milan (Doctorate of Law, 1982). Court appointed executor, bankruptcy proceedings in the judicial district of Milan. Author: publications, "The Liability of Company officials for Tax Evasion," in Tax Law and Practice, 1986; "Sale and Leaseback," IPSOA, 1982; "Publicity and Information: How to Distinguish Them for Fiscal Purposes," Milan Lawyers' Union Journal, 1992. *Member:* Milan Bar Association. *LANGUAGES:* Italian and English. *PRACTICE AREAS:* Commercial Law; Civil Law; Litigation.

CRISTINA SCHIATTI, born Milan, Italy, May 14, 1964; admitted, 1992, Milan, Italy. *Education:* State University of Milan (J.D., 1988). *LANGUAGES:* Italian. *PRACTICE AREAS:* Commercial Law; General Practice.

STUDIO LEGALE FRANCESCHELLI

Established in 1939

VIA FESTA DEL PERDONO 14
20122 MILAN, ITALY
Telephone: (02) 58.30.70.58
Telecopier: (02) 58.30.72.40

Corporation, Contracts, Competition, Patent and Trademark Law.

AVV. PROF. REMO FRANCESCHELLI (1910-1992).

AVV. PROF. VINCENZO FRANCESCHELLI, born Milan, Italy, October 11, 1947; admitted, 1975, Milan. *Education:* University of Milan (LL.B., magna cum laude). Fulbright Scholar. Professor of Law, University of Milan. Visiting Professor of Law: Seton Hall School of Law, 1985; Temple University, Rome Program, 1984, 1987. Member, Academy of American and International Law, The Southwestern Legal Foundation, Dallas, Texas, 1978. *LANGUAGES:* English, French and Spanish.

AVV. MARIA ROSA BARBIERI, born Casteggio, Italy, October 17, 1947; admitted, 1975, Milan. *Education:* University of Pavia. *LANGUAGES:* Spanish and French.

GIAMPIETRO BOZZOLA, born Montichiari (Brescia), Italy, June 3, 1967; admitted, 1993, Milan. *Education:* University of Parma.

Languages: Italian, French and English

FRAU & PARTNERS
STUDIO LEGALE ASSOCIATO

VIA CARLO POERIO, 15
20129 MILAN, ITALY
Telephone: (02) 76003199 (r.a.)
Telefax: (02) 76003311

Verona Office: Piazza San Nicold, 3. Telephone (045) 597530-597449. Telefax: (045) 8003115.

Roma Office: Via Barberini, 29. Telephone (06) 4871151-4820666. Telefax: (06) 4827513.

Kiev Office: Kibalchicha, 12. Telephone: (044) 5127292-5128109. Telefax: (044) 5143305.

International Business Law, Corporate, Banking, Financing, Syndicated Loans, Eurobonds, Commodities, Asset Finance, Bond Issues, Aircraft Finance, Leasing, Merger and Acquisitions, Project Finance. Letters of Credit, Commercial Property, Securitization, Foreign Investments, Contracts, EEC, Antitrust and Competition, Real Estate, Building and Construction, International and Domestic Arbitration, International and Domestic Arbitration Litigation, International and Domestic Taxation, Aviation, Transportation, Tort and Intellectual Property, Licensing, Patent and Trademark, Distributorship, Agency and Franchising, Environmental and Media, Sport, Mining and Mineral.

MEMBERS OF FIRM

AVENTINO FRAU, born Piovene, Italy, March 3, 1939; admitted, 1965 Italy; Supreme Court of Cassation. *Education:* State University of Parma (J.D., 1963). Assistant Lecturer of International Law, 1966-1968. Law and Economics Lecturer , Secretary and President, ICEPS (International Economics Corporation Institute), 1967-1978. Former President of Italian Trade Missions to Tunisia, Kenya, Somalia, Jordan, Rumania. Member of the Board, Companies involved in International Trade. Reporter at Law Conventions. Former Rapporteur for the Italian Financial Law. Member, Italian Parliament, 1972-1976. Parliament Deputy: Member, of Parliamentary Committee of Finance and Treasury; Member of Parliamentary Committee of Defence; Member of Parliamentary Committee of Finance Reform. Former Mayor of the City of Gardone Riviera, Italy. Former President of the "Comunità del Garda" (Association of the Regional areas around the Lake of Garda). Former President of ANIT (Italian Association of Tourist Cities). Vice President of "Fondazione del Vittoriale degli Italiani" (Vittoriale National Foundation). *Member:* I.B.A. (International Bar Association; U.I.A. (Union Internationale des Avocats). *LANGUAGES:* Italian, English and French.

MAURIZIO CODURRI, born Brescia, Italy, March 7, 1961; admitted, 1988, Italy. *Education:* State University of Pavia (J.D., cum laude, 1987). Author: Articles, "Com'è la deregulation vista dal passeggero. Aspetti giuridici, economici e sociali della liberalizzazione" (Deregulation Seen by the Passenger. Legal, Economic and Social Aspects), Areavolo, Rome, No. 26, 1988; "Difesa del passeggero come consumatore aereo. Spunti di discussione in vista della deregulation del 1992" (Defense of the Passenger as Airline Services Consumer. Outlines for a Discussion in View of the 1992 Deregulation), Turismo d'affari, Milan, 8, No. 11, 1988-1989; "Investment Trusts in Italy: A System of Controls," Butterworths Journal of International Banking and Financial Law, London, Vol. 6, No. 2, February 1991 ((1991) 2 JIBFL 63); "La réglementation et les contrôles des fonds communs d' investissement en Italie - I p." (Regulation and Control of the Investment Trusts in Italy - 1st), Revue Fiscalité Européenne et Droit International des Affaires, Nice-Bruxelles, 1991; "La réglementation et les contrôles des fonds communs d' investissement en Italie -II p." (Regulation and Control of the Investment Trusts in Italy - 2nd), Revue Fiscalité Européenne et Droit International des Affaires, Nice-Bruxelles, 1991. Guest Lecturer: BIT International Tourism Exchange), Milan, 1989, Seminar: "Le aspettative degli utenti di fronte all'offerta delle compagnie aeree e del sistema aereoportuale" (Users' Expectations in Relation to the Services Offered by Airlines and by the Airport System); Congress of I.R.I - Instituto di Ricerca Internazionale on "I Contratti Internazionali" (International Contracts), Milan, May 1991. Congress of I.R.I. - Instituto di Ricerca Internazionale on "L'Arbitrato Internazionale" International Arbitration, Milan, March 1992. Congress of I,R.I. - Instituto di Ricerca Internazional on "Investmenti immobiliari. Aspetti strategici, giuridici e tributari" (Real Estates Investments: Strategical, Legal and Fiscal Aspects), Milan, March 1992. Moderator at the Conference of the University of the Pacific, McGeorge School of Law on "Bankers' Liability: Risks and Remedies," Waidring, March-April 1992. Seminar of the Office de Formation et de Documentation Internationales on "Les Arbitrages Internationaux" (International Arbitration), Paris, April 1992. Seminar of the Institut de formation post-universitaire pour Cadres Dirigeants on "Les Aspects Nouveaux des Contrats Internationaux" (International Contracts: New Aspects), Paris, May 1992. XXXVI Congress of U.I.A. (Union Internationale des Avocats), Berlin, August 1992. Seminar of the European Air Law Association - E.A.L.A. on "International Insolvency in the Aviation Industry," Paris, October 1992. Congress of I.R.I. - Instituto di Ricerca Internazionale on "La Pianificazone Fiscale Internazionale" (International Tax Planning), Milan, November 1992. Congress of I.R.I. - Instituto di Ricerca Internazionale on Appalti " Internazionali" (International Contracts), Milan February 1993. XXXVII Congress of U.I.A. (Union Internationale des Avocats), San Francisco, August-September 1993. Formal representative for Italy of IFAPA (International Foundation of Airline Passengers Association, Geneva). *Member:* E.A.L.A. (European Air Law Association); I.B.A. (International Bar Association; U.I.A. (Union International des Avocats); A.I.J.A. Association International des Jenunes Avocats; I.T.P.A. (International Tax Planning Association); A.B.A. (American Bar Association); N.Y.S.B.A. (New York State Bar Association). *LANGUAGES:* Italian, English and French.

GIAN LUCA PEDRAZZINI, born Padua, February 6, 1965; admitted, 1991, Italy. *Education:* State University of Milan (J.D., cum laude, 1989). Legal coordinator of the newsletter "Focus". Co-author: "Overheidsmaatregelen in Italië" (Governmental Regulations in Italy), Export Magazine, no. 24, 1990; "G.R.I.E.: le oportunità da cogliere" (E.E.I.G.: opportunities to be taken advantage of), Amministrazione & Finanza, no. 4, 1992. Guest speaker: Seminar organized by the Italiensk-Norske Handelskammer on "Norwegian/Italian Trade and Investments," Oslo, November 1992. Assistant Lecturer to the State University of Milan, Law Faculty, 1989-1990. *Member:* Association Internationale des Jeunes Avocats (A.I.J.A.); The European Law Students' Association (E.L.S.A.). *LANGUAGES:* Italian, English and French.

(This Listing Continued)

PIERO PORCIANI, born Torino, Italy, June 9, 1961. *Education:* Catholic University of Milan (J.D., 1989); University of Florida (Introduction to American Law, 1991). Author: "The Procedural and Philosophical Aspects of the Nuremberg Trial," 1989. *LANGUAGES:* Italian, German, English and French.

GIANLUCA MAININO, born Milan, Italy, January 28, 1966; admitted, 1993, Italy. *Education:* State University of Milan (J.D., cum laude, 1990). Assistant Lecturer to the Catholic University of Milan and to the State University of Pavia, Faculty of Law. *LANGUAGES:* Italian, English and French.

PAOLA TOMMASOLI, born San Pietro Incariano, Italy, September 2, 1943; admitted, 1980, Italy. *Education:* State University of Milan (J.D., 1978). *LANGUAGES:* Italian and French.

MICHELE PARISE, born Naples, Italy, November 7, 1960; admitted, 1990, Italy. *Education:* State University of Naples "Federico II" (J.D., 1989). Author: "Articolo 9 UCC; un sistema di garanzie a tutela dei fornitori che operano nel mercato USA" (Article 9 UCC; a Warranty System to Protect Suppliers Operating within the US Market), Commercio Estero, No. 18, 1992. Assistant Lecturer to the State University of Naples, Faculty of Political Science. *LANGUAGES:* Italian, English and Spanish.

IVANA MAFFEI, born La Spezia, Italy, April 1, 1962; admitted, 1990, Italy. *Education:* Catholic University of Milan (J.D., 1989). *LANGUAGES:* Italian, English and French.

FRANCESCA CHIARELLO, born Castelnovo Monti RE, Italy, November 18, 1964; admitted, 1991, Italy. *Education:* State University of Milan (J.D., 1989); Bocconi University of Milan (School for in-house Lawyers, 1993). *Member:* I.D.F. (Istituto di Diritto di Famiglia). *LANGUAGES:* Italian, German and English.

CORRADO VIAZZO, born Milan, Italy, November 5, 1963; admitted, 1993, Italy. *Education:* State University of Milan (J.D. cum laude, 1990). Author: "L' obbligo di tenuta delle scritture contabili nella legge Penale tributaria" (Duty To Keep Account Books in Criminal Financial Law), Rivista Italiana di Diritto e Procedural Italiana, 1991; "Profili di responsabilitá penale tributaria nelle imprese di grandi dimensioni" (Criminal Financial Responsibility of a Big Company), Rivista Italiana di Diritto e Procedura Italiana, 1992. *LANGUAGES:* Italian.

FRANCESCO B. CESATI, born Milan, Italy June 18, 1964; admitted, 1993, Italy. *Education:* State University of Milan (J.D., 1991). Author: "La tutela internazionale del diritto d'autore" (The International Protection of Copyright), Milan, 1993. *Member:* Italian Association of Journalists. *LANGUAGES:* Italian, French, English, German and Spanish.

PIETRO ADAMI, born Verone, Italy, November 6, 1966; admitted, 1993, Italy. *Education:* State University of Modena (J.D., 1991); University College Cork (Erasmus Scholarship, 1989-1990); University of Leicester (LL,M European and International Trade Law, 1992). *LANGUAGES:* Italian and English.

ALBERTO BELTRAMI, born Milan, Italy, October 24, 1963. *Education:* State University of Milan (J.D., 1990). *LANGUAGES:* Italian, English and Spanish.

CLAUDIO SACCHETTO, born Vigevano, Italy, February 16, 1944; admitted, 1970, Italy; Supreme Court of Cassation. *Education:* State University of Pavia (J.D., 1968). Professor of Financial Law at the State University of Bergamo, Italy, 1986-1993. Former Assistant Lecturer of Financial Law at the State University of Pavia, Italy. Former Assistant Professor of Administrative Law at the State of Bergamo, Italy, 1983-1985. Former Professor of Financial Law at the Guardia di Finanza Academy in Bergamo, 1984-1986. Teacher in various Post-University Master Degrees: Bergamo; IPSOA; Polytechnic Institute of Milan. Director of the Law Department at the State University of Bergamo. Fellow of seminars about "American Law and Legal Institutions" at Salzburg Seminar, 1973. Member, Comité Directeur de l'Association Europeene des Jeunes Enseignants et Cherheurs, at the European Communities, 1969-1971. Since 1987 Trustee of Scientific and Steering Committee of the Associazione Italiana per lo Studio dei Problemi Fiscali (Italian Association for Fiscal Matters) and of IFA - International Fiscal Association. Since 1987 Member of National Counsel of ANTI (Italian Association of Experts in Tax Law). Representative of Italy at the 1988 International Fiscal Association in Amsterdam, introducing "Recognition of Foreign Enterprises as Taxable Etities." Representative of Italy at 1993 IFA Convention in Florence introducing "NON Discrimination Rules in International Taxation." Presently Member of Scientific Committee of the following Italian Law Magazines: Rassegna Tributaria; Rivista di Diritto Tributario; Rivista di Diritto Pubblico Comunitario; Bol-

(This Listing Continued)

lettino Tributario di Informazione; Società e Dititto; La Finanza Locale. Contributor to : Corriere Tributario, La Gazzetta del Commercio Internazionale. Author: "La tutela all' estero della prestesa tributatis" (International Protection of Financial Claim), 1978; "La nozione tributaria di reddito di lavoro autonomo" (Financial Concept in Independent Work Income), 1984; "L' imposizione fisclae e l' attività artigiana" (Taxation & Craftwork), 1989. Author of encyclopedia items: Principio di Territorialità in materia tributaria (Principle of Territoriality in Financial Law), Item, Enciclopedia Diritto; Tassa (Tax) Item, Enciclopedia del Diritto; Armonizzazione Fiscale Europea (European Fiscal Harmonization) Item, Treccani Law-Encyclopedia; Politica fiscale europea (European Fiscal Politics) Item, Treccani Law-Encyclopedia; Rendita Fiscale (Fiscal Income) Item, Treccani Law-Encyclopedia. Editor of the Italian version of the European Tax Handbook, 1991-1993. *LANGUAGES:* Italian and English.

STUDIO LEGALE ASSOCIATO
&
FRERE CHOLMELEY BISCHOFF

Established in 1988

PIAZZA CASTELLO 24
20121 MILAN, ITALY
Telephone: (39) (2) 720 03 457
Fax: (39) (2) 720 03 469

London, England Office: 4 John Carpenter Street, London EC4Y 0NH. Telephone: 0171-615 8000. Fax: 0171-615 8080. Telex: 27623. LDE: DX 140.

Paris, France Office: 42 Avenue du Président Wilson, 75116. Telephone: (33) (1) 44 34 71 00. Telex: 645944. Fax: (33) (1) 44 34 71 11.

Rome, Italy Office: and Studio Legale Associato, 47, Viale Bruno Buozzi, 00197. Telephone: (39) (6) 808 0133. Fax: (39) (6) 808 0134.

Monte Carlo, Monaco Office: "Est Ouest", 24 Boulevard Princesse Charlotte, MC 98000. Telephone: (33) (39) 508 570 Fax: (33) (93) 502 210.

Berlin, Germany Office: im Internationalen Handelszentrum, Friedrichstrasse 95, 10117. Telephone: (49) (30) 26 43 2000. Telex: 305996 Kbihzd. Fax: (49) (30) 2643 1900.

Moscow, Russia Office: ul. Sadovaya-Samotyochnaya 24/27, 103051 Moscow. Telephone: (7) 095 258 5058. Fax: (7) 095 258 5060. Telex: 412348 ALM SU.

Dubai, United Arab Emirates Office: Suite 802, EBIL Building, PO Box 2510, Deira, Dubai. Telephone: (9714) 267085/268336. Fax: (9714) 260206. Telex: 45493 LAWMC EM.

General and International Practice.

FIRM PROFILE: *This office is involved primarily in providing advice on the acquisition of Italian investments by foreign clients and the setting up of joining ventures between foreign and Italian clients. Areas of specialization include banking and securities law, patent, trademark and copyright law, bankruptcy law and civil litigation.*

(For Biographical Data, see Professional Biographies for Studio Legale Associato & Frere Cholmeley Bischoff, Rome)

GIANNI, ORIGONI & PARTNERS

PIAZZA BELGIOIOSO, 2
20121 MILAN, ITALY
Telephone: (02) 76009756
Telefax: (02) 76009628

Rome, Italy Office: Via delle Quattro Fontane 20, 00184. Telephone: (06) 4871100. Telefax: (06) 4871101.

New York, New York Office: 885 Third Avenue, Suite 3000, 10022. Telephone: 212-826-2515. Telefax: 212-826-2519.

General Practice, Counselling in International Transactions, Mergers and Acquisitions, Finance and Banking, International, Taxation, European Economic Community Law, Corporate, Securities, Insurance, Labor, Antitrust, Unfair Competition, Industrial Property, Product Liability, Environmental, Mutual Funds, Sports, Administrative Law, Arbitration and Litigation.

GIAN BATTISTA ORIGONI DELLA CROCE, born Milan, Italy, September 6, 1946; admitted to practice, 1970; admitted to bar, 1972, Italy; 1986, Supreme Court of Italy. *Education:* Catholic University of Milan

(This Listing Continued)

GIANNI, ORIGONI & PARTNERS, Milan—Continued

(J.D., maxima cum laude, 1969); Academy of International Law, The Hague, 1972 and 1973; Seminar in American Law, Salzburg, 1975; Parker School of Foreign and Comparative Law, Columbia University, New York, 1979. Research Professor of Private International Law, Law School, University of Milan-1992. Visiting Foreign Lawyer: Dechert, Price & Rhoads, Philadelphia and Washington, D.C., 1980. *Member:* American and International Bar Associations; Associazione per gli Scambi Culturali tra Giuristi Italiani e Tedeschi; Associazione Giuristi Di Lingua Italiana; Associazione Italiana per l'Arbitrato.

FRANCESCO GIANNI, born Ravenna, Italy, February 9, 1951; admitted to practice, 1973; admitted to bar, 1975, Italy; 1979, New York. *Education:* University of Rome (J.D., maxima cum laude, 1973); Academy of International Law, The Hague (1975); University of London, King's College (LL.M., 1976); University of Michigan Law School (LL.M., 1977). Research Assistant, E.E.C. Law, University of Michigan Law School, 1977. Visiting Foreign Lawyer: Sidley & Austin, Chicago, 1977-1978; Rogers & Wells, New York, 1978-1979. Honorary Member, Association of Fellows and Legal Studies of the Center for International Legal Studies. Honorary Member, Association of Fellows and Legal Scholars of the Center for International Legal Studies. *Member:* New York State, American and International Bar Associations; The Southwestern Legal Foundation (Member, Advisory Board); American Foreign Law Association (Vice-President, 1988-1993); American Society of International Law; Honorary Member, Association of Fellows and Legal Scholars of the Center for International Legal Studies.

NICOLETTA PORTALUPI, born Milan, Italy, September 29, 1952; admitted to practice, 1976; admitted to bar, 1981, Italy. *Education:* University of Milan (J.D., maxima cum laude, 1976); Cambridge University, 1972, 1973 and 1974; Academy of International Law, The Hague, 1975; University of Mannheim, 1976; Leyden-Amsterdam-Columbia Summer Program in American Law, 1977; Parker School of Foreign and Comparative Law, Columbia University, New York, 1982. Researcher in International Law, University of Milan. *Member:* International Bar Association; Associazione per gli Scambi Culturali tra Giuristi Italiani e Tedeschi; Associazione Giuristi di Lingua Italiana.

CESARE VENTO, born Rome, Italy, September 16, 1954; admitted to practice, 1979; admitted to bar, 1984, Italy. *Education:* University of Rome (J.D., 1979); Leyden-Amsterdam-Columbia Summer Program in American Law, 1978; University of Michigan Law School (LL.M., 1980). Visiting Foreign Lawyer, Jones, Day, Reavis & Pogue, Cleveland, Ohio, 1980-1981. Special Advisor to the Ad Hoc Committee on Italian Securities Regulations of the Securities Industry Association (SIA)-1991. *Member:* New York State and American Bar Associations; International Bar Association; American Foreign Law Association; European Society for Banking and Financial Law (Director, 1988—); The Corporate Bar Association of Westchester and Fairfield.

TIZIANO PASINETTI, born Milan, Italy, December 8, 1930; admitted to practice, 1953; admitted to bar, 1956, Italy; 1970, Supreme Court of Italy. *Education:* University of Milan (J.D., 1953); City of London College.

MATTEO FUSILLO, born Barletta, Italy, May 7, 1958; admitted to practice, 1981; admitted to bar, 1983, Italy. *Education:* University of Rome (J.D., maxima cum laude, 1980); City of London Polytechnic, Summer Law School, 1989; English Advanced Business Law, 1990). *Member:* International Bar Association.

ENZO SCHIAVELLO, born Naples, Italy, August 28, 1957; admitted to practice, 1982; admitted to bar, 1987, Italy. *Education:* University of Milan (J.D., maxima cum laude, 1982); Advanced Course in Business Tax Law, CERTI, Bocconi University of Milan, 1990-1991). *Member:* International Bar Association.

GIOVANNI NARDULLI, born Bari, Italy, January 1, 1961; admitted to practice, 1984; admitted to bar, 1987, Italy; Licensed Legal Consultant, 1992, New York. *Education:* University of Rome (J.D., maxima cum laude, 1983); City of London Polytechnic, 1987; Parker School of Foreign and Comparative Law, Columbia University, 1988. Visiting Foreign Lawyer, Morrison & Foerster, San Francisco, 1990-1991. *Member:* International and American Bar Associations; Chair, Western European Law Committee, International Law and Practice Section, New York State Bar Association; Honorary Member, Center for International Legal Studies, Salzburg; European Society for Banking and Financial Law. (Resident, New York, New York Office).

(This Listing Continued)

ADRIANA DE ALBERTIS, born Como, Italy, May 9, 1943; admitted to practice, 1966; admitted to bar, 1968, Italy; Supreme Court of Italy. *Education:* University of Milan (J.D., 1966).

ALESSANDRO GIULIANI, born Lecce, Italy, November 7, 1961; admitted to practice, 1985; admitted to bar, 1988, Italy. *Education:* University of Pavia (J.D., 1984); City of London Polytechnic, 1988; Academy of American and International Law, The Southwestern Legal Foundation, University of Texas, Dallas, 1989. Visiting Foreign Lawyer, Simpson, Thacher & Bartlett, London and New York Offices, 1993-1994. *Member:* New York State and American Bar Associations; International Bar Association. (Resident, New York, New York Office).

AULO COSSU, born Rome, Italy, July 2, 1960; admitted to practice, 1985; admitted to bar, 1989, Italy. *Education:* University of Rome (J.D., 1984).

ANTONINO DI BELLA, born Catania, Italy, April 27, 1960; admitted to practice, 1985; admitted to bar, 1988, Italy. *Education:* University of Catania (J.D., maxima cum laude, 1985); City of London Polytechnic, 1985. *Member:* Young Lawyers International Association.

ANTONIO AURICCHIO, born Torre Del Greco, Italy, July 6, 1962; admitted to practice, 1985; admitted to bar, 1988, Italy. *Education:* University of Naples (J.D., maxima cum laude, 1984). Research Assistant of Civil Law, Law School, University of Naples, 1985-1988.

ALBERTO GIAMPIERI, born Rome, Italy, December 6, 1963; admitted to practice, 1987; admitted to bar, 1990, Italy. *Education:* University of Rome (J.D., maxima cum laude, 1986); City of London Polytechnic, 1990. Visiting Scholar and Special Student Yale Law School (1991-1992). Visiting Foreign Lawyer: Skadden, Arps, Slate, Meagher & Flom, New York, 1992-1993. *Member:* Tax Commission of Rome; Young Lawyers Association.

MASSIMO AGOSTINI, born Cortona, Italy, August 6, 1960; admitted to practice, 1986; admitted to bar, 1990, Italy. *Education:* University of Florence (J.D., 1986); The Dickinson School of Law, Pennsylvania (M.C.L., 1989). *Member:* International Bar Association; International Fiscal Association.

ALBERTO MAGGI, born Pavia, Italy, June 23, 1961; admitted to practice, 1985; admitted to bar, 1990, Italy. *Education:* University of Pavia (J.D., maxima cum laude, 1985).

CRISTINA FANARA, born Messina, Italy, April 18, 1964; admitted to practice, 1988; admitted to bar, 1991, Italy. *Education:* University of Messina, Italy (J.D., maxima cum laude, 1987); Advanced Business Administration Course, Bocconi University, Milan, 1987-1988; Business Law Advanced Course, University of Milan, 1990; Orientation in American Law Program, University of California, Davis, 1992; Advanced Course in Business Tax Law, Bocconi University, Milan, 1992-1993.

PAOLO CASSINIS, born Rome, Italy, October 9, 1964; admitted to practice, 1988, Italy; admitted to bar, 1991, Italy. *Education:* University of Rome (J.D., maxima cum laude, 1988). Research Assistant, Institute of Private Law, Law School, University of Rome, 1987-1989. EEC Commission, Directorate General for Telecommunications, Trainee 1993. Visiting Foreign Lawyer, Pavia & Harcourt, New York, 1988-1989.

STEFANO MARIA ZAPPALÀ, born Rome, Italy, July 9, 1963; admitted to practice 1987; admitted to bar, 1990, Italy. *Education:* University of Rome (J.D., maxima cum laude, 1987); Fordham University School of Law (Continuing Legal Education Program, 1991). Academy of American and International Law, The Southwestern Legal Foundation, University of Texas at Dallas, 1992. *Member:* Alumni Association, Academy of American and International Law.

STEFANO BUCCI, born Rome, Italy, July 11, 1961; admitted to practice, 1985; admitted to bar, 1990, Italy. *Education:* University of Rome (J.D., 1985). Research Assistant, Institute of Criminal Law, University of Rome, 1986—. Master of Tax and Corporate Practice, LUISS University, Rome, 1987-1988.

UGO BASSI, born Naples, Italy, August 3, 1966; admitted to practice, 1989, Italy; admitted to bar, 1992, Italy. *Education:* University of Naples (J.D., maxima cum laude, 1989); Graduate Students Intern Program, United Nations Headquarters, New York, 1989; Diploma of Advanced European Legal Studies, College of Europe, Bruges, 1990; City of London Polytechnic, 1990. Administrator, Research and Documentation, Department and Information Service, European Court of Justice, Luxembourg, 1990-1993. Member, Board of Editors, *Revue du marché unique europeen.* Research Assistant to the European Court of Justice, Luxembourg, 1990-1993.

(This Listing Continued)

PAOLO CRISCIONE, born Milan, Italy, May 9, 1961; admitted to practice, 1985; admitted to bar, 1990, Italy. *Education:* Catholic University of Milan (J.D., 1985); Bocconi University of Milan (corporate tax law, 1988-1989); King's College, London (LL.M. in EEC law, 1990-1992). Visiting Foreign Lawyer: Titmuss Sainer & Webb, London, 1990-1993. Italian correspondent and member, Editorial Advisory Board of European Competition Law Review. *Member:* British-Italian Law Association; Associazione Giuristi di Lingua Italiana.

RAFFAELLA BETTI BERUTTO, born Rome, Italy, November 20, 1965; admitted to practice, 1989; admitted to bar, 1992, Italy. *Education:* University of Rome (J.D., maxima cum laude, 1989); City of London Polytechnic, 1989. Academy of American and International Law; The Southwestern Legal Foundation, University of Texas, Dallas, 1993. Visiting Foreign Lawyer: Clifford Chance, Paris, 1993. (Resident, New York, New York Office).

FILIPPO TROISI, born Naples, Italy, April 28, 1965; admitted to practice 1988, Italy; admitted to bar, 1992 Italy and New York. *Education:* University of Naples (J.D., maxima cum laude, 1988); New York University School of Law (M.C.J., 1991). *Member:* New York State Bar Association; New York County Lawyers Association (Member, Foreign and International Law Committee).

BRUNO BARTOCCI, born Naples, Italy, July 8, 1962; admitted to practice, 1987, Italy; admitted to bar, 1991, Italy; admitted, 1994, New York. *Education:* Luiss University, Rome (J.D., maxima cum laude, 1987); Academy of American and International Law, Dallas, 1988; Georgetown University Law Center (LL.M. , 1992). Summer Foreign Associate, Lewis, D'Amato, Bribois & Brisgaard, Los Angeles, 1988. Visiting Foreign Lawyer: Vinson & Elkins, L.L.P., Washington, D.C., 1992-1993. Research Assistant of Communications Law, LUISS University. Member, Alumni Association Academy of American and International Law.

GIAN PAOLO TAGARIELLO, born Rome, Italy, May 2, 1967; admitted to practice, 1989, Italy; admitted to bar, 1992, Italy. *Education:* LUISS University of Rome (J.D., maxima cum laude, 1989). Diploma of Advanced European Legal Studies, College of Europe, Bruges, 1992. Research Assistant, Institute of International Law, Law Faculty, LUISS University.

LUIGI PAVANELLO, born Rome, Italy, April 25, 1960; admitted to practice, 1989, Italy; admitted to bar, 1991, New York; 1994, Italy. *Education:* University of Rome (J.D., 1985); New York University School of Law (LL.M., 1988). *Member:* American, International and New York State Bar Associations; Association of the Bar of the City of New York.

GIULIA FUSCO, born Venosa, Italy, September 21, 1960; admitted to practice, 1988, Italy; admitted to bar, 1992, Italy. *Education:* University of Bari (J.D., maxima cum laude, 1988). European University Institute, San Domenico di Fiesole, Florence, 1989-1992. Council of Europe, Strasburg (Research Assistant, 1990); Academy of European Law, Florence, 1991.

MARCELLO MARANI, born Bologna, Italy, March 3, 1961; admitted to practice, 1988, Italy; admitted to bar, 1992, Italy. *Education:* Bologna University (J.D., 1988; Master in Company Law, 1990); City of London Polytechnic (1991).

GIULIO RIVERA, born Milan, Italy, June 30 1963; admitted to practice, 1989, admitted to bar, 1992. *Education:* Catholic University of Milan (J.D., maxima cum laude, 1989). Research Assistant, Institute of International Law, Catholic University of Milan (1989-1990).

EMANUELA BERTOLLI, born Milan, Italy, March 25, 1961; admitted to practice, 1985; admitted to bar, 1993, Italy. *Education:* University of Milan (J.D., maxima cum laude, 1985).

ANTONIO SEGNI, born Genova, Italy, May 11, 1965; admitted to practice, 1988; admitted to bar, 1993, Italy; 1993, New York. *Education:* University of Rome (J.D., maxima cum laude, 1988); Harvard Law School (LL.M., 1992). Member: Legal Staff CONSOB, 1989-1994.

PAOLO RONCELLI, born Bergamo, Italy, September 26, 1963; admitted to practice, 1988, Italy. *Education:* University of Pavia (J.D., 1988); University of Texas School of law (M.C.J., 1991).

GIANLUCA GHERSINI, born Milan, Italy, September 29, 1965; admitted to practice, 1991. *Education:* University of Milan, Italy (J.D., 1990). *Member:* British-Italian Law Association; Anglo-Italian Business Association; Young Lawyers' International Association.

RENATO GIALLOMBARDO, born Rome, Italy, February 17, 1966; admitted to practice, 1990, Italy. *Education:* University of Rome (J.D., 1990). Diploma of Advanced Legal Studies, International Private Law, The Hague Academy of International Law, 1991; Diploma on Eu-

(This Listing Continued)

ropean Legal Studies, Institute Alcide De Gasperi, Rome, 1992; University of London, Commercial and Corporate Law (LL.M., 1994).

DANIEL VONRUFS, born Bergamo, Italy, February 26, 1965; admitted to practice, 1991, Italy. *Education:* University of Milan (J.D., 1991). Academy of International Law, The Hague, 1990.

ANDREA LORENZO CAPUSSELA, born Genova, Italy, September 11, 1969; admitted to practice, 1993, Italy. *Education:* University of Milan (J.D., maxima cum laude, 1993); University of London, Queen Mary and Westfield, 1992. Member, European Law Students Association.

ENRICO GARGALE, born Torino, Italy, April 19, 1966; admitted to practice, 1992. *Education:* University of Bologna (J.D., maxima cum laude, 1992); Advanced Course in Business Tax Law, Certi, Bocconi University of Milan (1993-1994).

PAOLO MARNATI, born Magenta, Italy, April 5, 1966; admitted to practice, 1992, Italy. *Education:* University of Milan (J.D., maxima cum laude, 1992).

OF COUNSEL

GUIDO ALPA, born Ovada (AL), November 26, 1947; admitted to practice, 1972; admitted to bar, 1974, Italy; 1984, Supreme Court of Italy. *Education:* University of Genoa (J.D. maxima cum laude, 1972). Visiting Foreign Professor: University of Oregon (at Eugene) 1977 and 1985; University of California (at Berkeley) 1979; University of London, 1982; University of Mannheim, 1984. Professor of Private Law and Private Comparative Law, at the University of Genoa (1983—); Director of the Private Law Institute of the Faculty of Law in Genoa (1981-1989); Full Professor at the University of Rome (1991—).*Member:* Commission Giannini to wind up useless public bodies, 1977; Commission Mirabelli; Commission Paladin to reform the Judiciary body, 1989; Commission INAIL for workers rights; European Research Association for Consumer Affairs; State Dept. Commission of Data Bank Protection; Vice-President of Consultant Commission for the protection of TV users, 1991; President of local section of AIDA (International Association of Insurance Laws); President of the CONSOB local commission. Member of the EEC Economic and Social Committee.

STUDIO LEGALE GILIOLI

Established in 1926

PIAZZALE PRINCIPESSA CLOTILDE, 8
20121 MILAN, ITALY
Telephone: (02) 29.00.29.32 International (39 2) 29.00.29.32
Telefax: (02) 65.75.969 International (39 2) 65.75.969.

Florence, Italy Associated Office: Studio Fortini. Via Santa Reparata, 40. Telephone: (39-55) 483.230.
New York, New York Associated Office: Marks & Murase. 399 Park Avenue, 10022. Telephone: 212-318-7700.

International and Domestic Practice, Antitrust, Bankruptcy, Contract, Corporate, Environmental, European Community, Foreign Investment, Intellectual Property, International Estate, International Trade, Labor, Licensing, Litigation and Arbitration, Mergers and Acquisitions, Products Liability, Tax.

ENRICO S. GILIOLI, born Milan, Italy, March 1, 1930; admitted, 1977, Italy. *Education:* Liceo Classico Beccaria, Milan (B.A., 1948); Guilford College, N.C. (B.A., 1953); New York University (1955); University of Milan (Doctor of Jurisprudence, 1973). Author: "Italy," Jordans' International Corporate Procedures, 1992. Executive, Olivetti Corporation of America, 1957-1961. Executive and Director, Roberts Italia S.p.A., 1961-1973. *Member:* American Italian Law Association. **LANGUAGES:** Italian and English.

(This Listing Continued)

STUDIO LEGALE GILIOLI, Milan—Continued

DANIEL E. GILIOLI, born Milan, Italy, June 27, 1933; admitted, 1957, Ohio; 1966, District of Columbia (Not admitted in Italy). *Education:* University of Cincinnati (B.A., 1955; J.D., 1957). President, American Chamber of Commerce in Italy, 1988-1992; Chairman, Legal and Tax Committee of the American Chamber of Commerce in Italy, 1993-1994; Director and Treasurer, Union of Foreign Chambers of Commerce in Italy, 1988-1992; Director, Norwegian Chamber of Commerce in Italy, 1984—; Founder and Director, American School of Milan, 1963-1980. *Member:* The Council for the United States and Italy; American Italian Law Association; American Arbitration Association (Panel of Arbitrators). *LANGUAGES:* English, Italian and French.

ERIC L. GILIOLI, born Cincinnati, Ohio, September 9, 1957; admitted, 1984, New York and U.S. Court of International Trade; 1985, District of Columbia (Not admitted in Italy). *Education:* Harvard University (A.B., magna cum laude, 1979); Fordham University (J.D., 1983); University of Milan (Doctor of Jurisprudence, 1995 exp.). Editor-in-Chief, Fordham International Law Journal, 1982-1983. Author: "Defining Jurisdictional Limits in International Antitrust: Should the E.C.C. Adopt the *Timberlane* Approach?" 5 Fordham International Law Journal 469,1982. *Member:* The Council for the United States and Italy; American Italian Law Association; American Society of International Law. *LANGUAGES:* English, Italian and French.

OF COUNSEL

SILVANO STEFANI, born Milan, Italy, April 15, 1940; admitted, 1965, Italy; 1978, Illinois; 1985, Supreme Court of the United States; 1987, New York. *Education:* University of Milan (Doctor of Jurisprudence, cum laude, 1962); Illinois Institute of Technology, Chicago-Kent College of Law (J.D., 1978). With Studio Scalfi, Milan, Italy, 1964-1971. With Baker & McKenzie, Milan, Italy, 1971-1976 and Chicago, Illinois, 1976-1988. Partner, Baker & McKenzie International Partnership, 1974-1988. Lecturer of Private Law, University of Parma, Parma, Italy, 1966-1968 and University L. Bocconi, Milan, Italy, 1969-1971. Member: Panel of Arbitrators, American Arbitration Association, 1986—; Legal and Tax Committee, American Chamber of Commerce in Italy, 1991—. *LANGUAGES:* Italian, English and French.

ASSOCIATES

ALESSANDRO ATZENI, born Milan, Italy, November 13, 1960; admitted, 1987, Certified Public Accountant, Italy. *Education:* University L. Bocconi, Milan, Italy (B.E.D., 1986). Member, Committee for International Relations, Milan Association of Certified Public Accountants, 1988—. *LANGUAGES:* Italian and English.

MIRELLA DEL PANTA, born Rome, Italy, April 20, 1963; admitted, 1993, Certified Public Accountant, Italy. *Education:* University L. Bocconi, Milan, Italy (B.E.D., 1991). *LANGUAGES:* Italian, English and French.

IVANO C. MAZZOLENI, born Bergamo, Italy, May 24, 1961; admitted, 1989, Italy. *Education:* University of Milan (Doctor of Jurisprudence, cum laude, 1985). Lecturer, Comparative Penal Procedure, University of Milan, 1985-1988. *LANGUAGES:* Italian and English.

LAURA NARDI, born Macerata, Italy, November 14, 1966. *Education:* Catholic University of Milan (Doctor of Jurisprudence, 1991). *LANGUAGES:* Italian and English.

GRAHAM & JAMES

12, MONTENAPOLEONE
20121 MILAN, ITALY
Telephone: (02) 76006839, (02) 76006484
Telex: 843-314157 GJ MIL I
Telecopier: (02) 783091

Other offices located in: San Francisco, Los Angeles, Newport Beach, Palo Alto, Sacramento and Fresno, California; Washington, D.C.; New York, New York; Beijing, China; Tokyo, Japan; London, England; Dusseldorf, Germany; Taipei, Taiwan.

Associated Offices: Deacons in Association with Graham & James, Hong Kong; Sly and Weigall, Sydney, Melbourne, Brisbane, Perth and Canberra, Australia.

(This Listing Continued)

Affiliated Offices: Graham & James in Affiliation with Taylor Joynson Garrett, London, England, Bucharest, Romania and Brussels, Belgium; Hanafiah Soeharto Ponggawa, Jakarta, Indonesia; Deacons and Graham & James, Bangkok, Thailand; Haarmann, Hemmelrath & Partner, Berlin, Munich, Leipzig, Frankfurt and Dusseldorf, Germany; Mishare M. Al-Ghazali & Partners, Kuwait; Sly & Weigall Deacons in Association with Graham & James, Hanoi, Vietnam and Guangzhou, China; Gallastegui y Lozano, S.C., Mexico City, Mexico; Law Firm of Salah Al-Hejailan, Jeddah and Riyadh, Saudi Arabia.

General Practice.

RESIDENT PARTNERS

GABRIELE BERNASCONE, born Greggio, Italy, 1948; admitted to practice, 1972, Italy; admitted, 1977, Italy. *Education:* Catholic University, Milan, Italy (LL.D., 1971). *LANGUAGES:* Italian, English and French. *PRACTICE AREAS:* Corporate Law; Commercial Law.

FILIPPO DISERTORI, born Trento, Italy, 1953; admitted to practice, 1978, Italy; admitted, 1981, Italy. *Education:* Catholic University of Milan, Italy (LL.D., 1978). *LANGUAGES:* Italian, English, French and German. *PRACTICE AREAS:* Commercial Law; Import and Export Law.

GIANFRANCO NEGRI CLEMENTI, born Rome, Italy, 1931; admitted, 1955, Italy. *Education:* State University of Milan (LL.B., 1953). *LANGUAGES:* Italian, English, French and German.

GABRIELLA AGLIATI, born Milan, Italy, 1956; admitted, 1985, Italy. *Education:* State University of Milan (LL.D., 1982). *LANGUAGES:* Italian, English, French and German.

PAOLO MONTIRONI, born Senigallia, Italy, 1962; admitted, 1991, Italy. *Education:* Catholic University, Milan (LL.D., 1987). *LANGUAGES:* Italian, English, French and German.

ROSSELLA ADAMO, born Bobbio, Italy, 1954; admitted, 1981, Italy. *Education:* State University of Milan (LL.D., 1978). *LANGUAGES:* Italian, English, French and German.

BARNABA RICCI, born Milan, Italy, 1950; admitted, 1982, Italy. *Education:* State University of Milan (LL.D., 1977). *LANGUAGES:* Italian, English and French.

RESIDENT ASSOCIATES

David Donald (Not admitted in Italy); **Massimo Mantovani; Fabrizia Maurici; Silvia Re; Priscilla Serena.**

STUDIO LEGALE GRIECO - VINTI

PIAZZETTA GIORDANO, 4
20122 MILAN, ITALY
Telephone: (39-2) 784583
Fax: (39-2) 784762

Rome, Italy Office: Via Bernardo Blumenstihl No. 40, 00135. Telephone: (39-6) 35502058. Fax: (39-6) 35501863.

General Civil Practice. Administrative Law, EEC Construction Law, International Business Practice, Corporate, Mergers and Acquisitions, Antitrust, Taxation, Environmental, Banking and Financing, Securities, Labor, Industrial Property, Oil and Gas, Telecommunications, EEC Law, Litigation and Arbitration.

FIRM PROFILE: Established in 1992, GRIECO-VINTI Has a broadly - based practice with a reputation for offering a full range of quality legal services. The firm has two partners who have been practising for more than ten years and seven associates. The firm has two offices, one in Rome and the other in Milan.

ANTONIO GRIECO, born Rome, Italy, April 2, 1960; admitted to practice, 1982; admitted to bar, 1985, Italy. *Education:* Italy, University of Rome (Doctor of Jurisprudence, maxima cum laude, 1982); Professoral Assistant of Civil Law, University of Rome Law School (1989—) ; U.S.A., University of Illinois Law School (M.C.L., 1984); New York University, Exchange Visiting Scholar (1985); Harvard University Law School, P.I.L. 1989. *Member:* Italian Bar Association (Rome); Italian Arbitration Association (International Associate); American Bar Association (International Associate); International Bar Association; London Court of International Arbitration; International Litigation Practitioners Forum. *LANGUAGES:* Italian and English. *PRACTICE AREAS:* Corporate; Competition; International Trade and Arbitration.

(This Listing Continued)

STEFANO VINTI, born Palermo, Italy, December 27, 1960; admitted to bar, 1986, Italy. *Education:* Italy, University of Rome (Doctor of Jurisprudence, maxima cum laude, 1984). Professor, Administrative Law, University of L'Aquila, 1992. Researcher, University of Perugia for Administrative and Construction Law. *LANGUAGES:* Italian and English. *PRACTICE AREAS:* Construction Law; Administrative Law.

CINO RAFFA UGOLINI, born Milan, Italy, March 8, 1960; admitted, 1986, Italy; 1990, New York. *Education:* University of Milan (J.D., summa cum laude, 1984); New York University of School of Law (M.C.J., 1989). Recipient, Scholarship from the Fulbright Foundation. Foreign Associate, O'Melveny & Myers, New York Office, 1989-1990. *LANGUAGES:* English and French.

PAOLA CHIRULLI, born Rome, Italy, October 30, 1965; admitted to bar, Italy, 1992. *Education:* University of Rome (Doctor of Jurisprudence, 1989). Professorial Assistant at L.U.I.S.S. University of Rome in Administrative Law. *LANGUAGES:* Italian and English. *PRACTICE AREAS:* Administrative Law.

FABRIZIO POLLARI MAGLIETTA, born Milano, Italy, October 1, 1963; admitted, 1994, Italy. *Education:* University of Rome (Doctor of Jurisprudence, maxima cum laude, 1990). *LANGUAGES:* Italian and English. *PRACTICE AREAS:* Corporate Law; Business Law.

VINCENZO MORICONI, born Rome, Italy, July 25, 1959. admitted to bar, 1991, Italy. *Education:* University of Rome (Doctor of Jurisprudence, 1983). *LANGUAGES:* Italian. *PRACTICE AREAS:* General Practice.

FEDERICA CORSINI, born Rome, Italy, February 24, 1967. admitted to practice, 1993, Italy. *Education:* L.U.I.S.S. University of Rome (J.D., 1993). *LANGUAGES:* Italian and English. *PRACTICE AREAS:* General Practice.

LUCA MARIANI, born Rome, Italy, September 16, 1968; admitted to practice, 1993, Italy. *Education:* University of Rome, Italy (Doctor of Jurisprudence, maxima cum laude, 1993). Professorial Assistant of European Community Law at the University of Rome (1993). *LANGUAGES:* English and French. *PRACTICE AREAS:* European Community Law.

LORENZO PARRONI, born Pesaro, Italy, October 2, 1968; Admitted to Practice, 1993. *Education:* University of Rome (Doctor of Jurisprudence, maxima cum laude, 1993). Practice at "Avvocatura dello Stato," January 1994—. *LANGUAGES:* Italian and English. *PRACTICE AREAS:* Administrative Law.

GRIMALDI E CLIFFORD CHANCE

In Association with Clifford Chance

VIA GESÚ, 3
20121 MILAN, ITALY
Telephone: (39 2) 7600 8040
Fax: (39 2) 7600 4950

Other Offices: Amsterdam, Bahrain, Barcelona, Brussels, Budapest, Dubai, Frankfurt, Hanoi, Hong Kong, London, Madrid, Moscow, New York, Paris, Riyadh, Rome, Shanghai, Singapore, Tokyo, Warsaw. (See Clifford Chance, London for full address details).

International and General Practice including Banking, Corporate Finance, Capital Markets, Stock Exchange Listings, Taxation, EEC, Arbitration, Bankruptcy, Patent, Trademark, Entertainment and Media, Securitization, Project and Asset Financing, Real Estate, Civil Litigation.

(See Studio Legale Grimaldi e Associati, Rome, Italy for details of Partners and Associates.)

STUDIO AVV. EUGENIO GRIPPO
E
SIMMONS & SIMMONS

Associazione Internazionale di Studi Legali

Established in 1985

VIA DEI BOSCHETTI, 1
20121 MILAN, ITALY
Telephone: 39-2-76003012
Fax: 39-2-782770

Rome, Italy Office: Piazza Sallustio, 9, 00187. Telephone: 39-6-4870920. Fax: 39-6-4828562.

(This Listing Continued)

London, England Office: Simmons & Simmons, 21 Wilson Street, London, EC2M 2TQ. Telephone: 44-171-628 2020. Facsimile: 44-171-588 4129.

Paris, France Office: Simmons & Simmons, 2 Avenue Bugeaud, 75116. Telephone: 33-1-45016767. Facsimile: 33-1-45012232. Telex: TRANSAV 649381F.

Brussels, Belgium Office: Simmons & Simmons, Rue d' Arlon 118, 1040 Brussels. Telephone: 32-2-2801670. Fax: 32-2-2800484.

Lisbon, Portugal Office, Grupo Legal Portugues E.E.I.G. in association with F. Castelo Branco, Nobre Guedes & P. Rebelo de Sousa, J & A Garrigues and Pinheiro Neto & Co: Rua Castilho, n° 32-9°, 1200 Lisbon. Telephone: 351-1-3521318. Fax: 351-1-3521418.

Hong Kong Office: Simmons & Simmons, 24th Floor, Jardine House, One Connaught Place, Central. Telephone: 852-28681131. Facsimile: 852-28105040. Telex: 75888 SANDS HX.

Abu Dhabi Office: Simmons & Simmons, The Blue Tower, Khalifa Street, P.O. Box 5931, Abu Dhabi, United Arab Emirates. Telephone: 971-2-347882. Facsimile: 971-2-347832.

New York Office: Simmons & Simmons, 115 East 57th Street, New York, NY 10022. Telephone: 1-212-6886620. Facsimile: 1-212-3553594. Telex: 149543.

Mergers and Acquisitions, Banking and Finance, Projects and Construction, Public Offerings, Company and Commercial Law, Investment Funds, Joint Ventures, Advertising and Sport, Labor Law, EC Law, International Tax, Anti-Trust and Competition, Intellectual Property Rights, Environmental Law, Litigation.

FIRM PROFILE: *Founded by Avv. Grippo since May 1993 the firm has operated as a joint legal practice with the international law firm, Simmons & Simmons.*

EUGENIO GRIPPO, born Rome, Italy, January 14, 1946; admitted, 1972, Rome, qualified to act before the Supreme Court (Corte di Cassazione). *Education:* Rome University (Doctor in Law, 1969); Institute of Comparative Law. Author: *"Dizionario Amministrativo,* Voce Commercio Estero - Cambi Giuffré, 1978; Comparative Studies on Education (Italy, England, Sweden)," Foro Amministrativo, 1974. *Member:* Milan Bar. (Resident, Milan Office). *LANGUAGES:* Italian, English and French.

BRUNO GATTAI, born Milan, Italy, January 18, 1959; admitted, 1990, Italy. *Education:* Milan University (J.D., maxima cum laude, 1983). *Member:* Milan Bar. (Resident, Milan Office). *LANGUAGES:* Italian, French and English.

FILIPPO PINGUE, born Benevento, Italy, June 24, 1961; admitted, 1988, Italy. *Education:* Naples University (J.D., maxima cum laude, 1983). *Member:* Rome Bar. (Resident, Rome Office). *LANGUAGES:* Italian and English.

STEFANO SPERONI, born Milan, Italy, June 8, 1962; admitted, 1990, Italy. *Education:* Milan University (Civil and Procedural International Law). *Member:* Milan Bar. (Resident, Milan Office). *LANGUAGES:* Italian and English.

JULIAN Z. BERGER, born London, England, January 5, 1960; admitted, 1984, England and Wales. *Education:* Sheffield University (LL.B., Hons). Author: Contributing author in the section on Italy in the European M&A Handbook, Euromoney 1991. *Member:* The Law Society; International Bar Association. (Resident, Milan Office). *LANGUAGES:* English and Italian.

MARTA FUSCO, born Milan, Italy, May 4, 1967. *Education:* Universitá di Bari (J.D., Maxima Cum Laude, 1990). (Resident, Milan Office). *LANGUAGES:* Italian and English.

OF COUNSEL

PROF. LUIGI A. BIANCHI, born Milan, Italy, June 3, 1958; admitted, 1994, Italy. *Education:* Universitá degli Studi di Milano (Doctor of Law cum laude, 1982). Associate Professor, Commercial Law, "L. Bocconi" University of Milan. Visiting Professor, Commercial Law, "Politecnico" University of Milan. Author: "Consolidated Balance Sheet and Disclosure," 1990; "Legal Problems in a Merger Process," 1993 and other contributions on commercial and corporate law. *Member:* Italian Bar Association (Milan). *LANGUAGES:* Italian, English, French and German.

Languages: Italian, English and French.

(This Listing Continued)

STUDIO AVV. EUGENIO GRIPPO E SIMMONS & SIMMONS, Milan—Continued

Export Limited, UK; Ernest Rubenstein and James Purcell of Paul Weiss, Rifkind, Wharton and Garrison, New York, USA; Lennart Hagberg, Mannheimer & Zetterlof, Sweden; Debevoise and Plimpton, Paris, France; Carnival Cruise Lines Inc., Miami, Florida, USA; AES Transpower, USA.

HURT, SINISI & PAPADAKIS

In Association with

Sinisi, Ceschini, Mancini & Partners

CORSO ITALIA 8

20122 MILAN, ITALY

Telephone: (39) (2) 866 727

Telefax: (39) (2) 866 771

Rome, Italy Office: Via Laurina 40, 00187. Telephone: (39) (6) 322-1485; 322-1487. Telefax: (39) (6) 361-3266.

Athens, Greece Office: Kanari 7, 106 71. Telephone: (30) (1) 364-2320/30; 363-8876. Telefax: (30) (1) 364-2323.

Piraeus, Greece Office: 1 Loudovikou, 5th Floor, 185 31 Piraeus. Telephone: (30) (1) 417-4998. Telefax: (30) (1) 413-4289.

Atlanta, Georgia, USA Office: 1050 Crown Pointe Parkway, Suite 310, 30338. Telephone: (404) 913-9999. Telecopier: (404) 671-8513.

Hartford, Connecticut, USA Office: 294, New London Turnpike, Glastonbury, 06033. Telephone: (203) 633-3903. Telefax: (203) 633-4599.

San Diego, California, USA Office: Suite 1400, One America Plaza, 600 West Broadway, 92101-3377. Telephone: (619) 234-1798. Telefax: (619) 234-8475.

New York, New York, USA Office: 375 Park Avenue, Suite 2904, 10152. Telephone: (212) 755-1550. Telefax: (212) 755-1575.

Corporate, Banking and Securities Law with emphasis on Mergers and Acquisitions, Insurance, International Financial Transactions, Litigation, Arbitration, Bankruptcy, Foreign Investments, Privatizations, Joint Ventures, Taxation, European Common Market Law, Antitrust, Environmental Law, Transportation, Shipping, Licensing, Financing, Distribution Law, Commercial Real Estate (Investment, Structuring and Development), Project and Trade Finance, Computer, Software, Trademark Law, Telecommunications Law, Agency and Distribution, Labor, Visa/Immigration, Wills and Estates, Sports Law, Broadcasting, Motion Pictures, Video, Intellectual Property and General Entertainment Law.

FIRM PROFILE: *Hurt, Sinisi & Papadakis is an International Law Firm based in the United States and Europe. Fundamental to the firm is a committment to provide a high quality of personalized service with an excellent standard of professionalism. The United States Offices are located in the Northeast, Southeast and Western United States in order to service clients conveniently and efficiently, as well as provide full support to the firm's European Offices. The European Offices are staffed with both American and European attorneys. Each office, in Europe and the United States, has attorneys that are qualified to appear and litigate in the local courts. Hurt, Sinisi & Papadakis has a strong focus on the Southern European region. This gives this firm a unique strategic position for businesses seeking legal advice and representation in this area.*

(For Complete Biographical Data on all Personnel, See Professional Biographies of Sinisi, Ceschini, Mancini & Partners, Rome & Milan, Italy)

STUDIO LEGALE INTERNAZIONALE

VIA MELEGARI 4

20122 MILAN, ITALY

Telephone: (02) 760.080.78

Fax: (02) 780.482

Rome, Italy Office: Via Vittorio Veneto, 96 - 00187. Telephone: (06) 4881119. (06) 4827601. (06) 4819105. (06) 483807. ne Fax: (06) 4873402. (06) 4825877.

Padua Office: Via del Santo, 30, 35123. Telephone: (049) 8750672. Fax: (049) 8753675.

Banking, Securities, Corporate Finance, Air-Financing, Investment Funds, EC Law, Anti-trust, Litigation, Bankruptcy, Maritime and Labour Law.

(This Listing Continued)

FIRM PROFILE: *Studio Legale Internazionale is one of the Italian leading international law firms in the banking and corporate finance fields, with an organization of 12 partners and other fees earners - consultants and an aggregate skilled staff of 50 persons.*

SENIOR PARTNERS

NICOLA TROILO, born Rome, Italy, May 4, 1930; admitted, 1955, Italy. *Education:* Milan University (LL.D., 1954). (Former Senior Partner of Studio Graziadei).

ALESSANDRO DI SAN BONIFACIO, born Padova, Italy, February 12, 1950; admitted, 1978, Italy. *Education:* Padova University (LL.D., 1976). (Resident, Padua Office) (Former Senior Partner of Studio Graziadei).

CARLO GALDO, born Naples, Italy, March 26, 1954; admitted, 1980, Italy. *Education:* Naples University (LL.D., 1977). (Former Senior Partner of Studio Graziadei).

VITTORIO VALIERI, born Rome, Italy, June 8, 1955; admitted, 1985, Italy. *Education:* Rome University (LL.D., 1980). Visiting Foreign Lawyer, University of Edinburgh. *Member:* International Bar Association. (Former Senior Partner of Studio Graziadei).

Languages: English, German, French

REFERENCES: Swiss Bank Corporation; WestDeutsche Landesbank Girozentrale; Merril Lynch & Co., Inc.; J.P. Morgan; Bank of Nova Scotia; Lehman Brothers; Banca di Roma; Mediocredito Centrale; Irfis-Mediocredito della Sicilia S.p.A.; Credito Industriale Sardo S.p.A.; Medicredito Piemontese; Johnson & JohnsonTwenieth Century Fox; Rockwell International; USX Corp.; Abbott Laboratories; Uniroyal Chemical Company, Inc.; Stone Webster Engineering; The J. Paul Getty Trust; British Aerospace; Christie's; Canadian Airlines; Meridiana S.P.A.; TPL S.p.A.

(A list of fee earners names is open for inspection in the above address).

STUDIO LEGALE PROF. AVV. BRUNO INZITARI

VIA VISCONTI DI MODRONE, 36

20122 MILAN, ITALY

Telephone: 39-2-76020902

Telefax: 39-2-76021025

Contract and Commercial Law, Companies and Corporations, Banking Law, Bankruptcy and Insolvency, Insurance, Securities, Mergers and Acquisitions, Establishment of Subsidiaries and Branches, Arbitration and Litigation, International and General Practice.

PROF. AVV. BRUNO INZITARI, born Cagliari, Italy, July 24, 1948; admitted, 1983, Italy. *Education:* State University of Rome (Dr. iur.). Professor of Civil Law, State University of Milan, 1994—. Professor of Civil Law, Law School of University of Pavia, 1987-1994. Professor of Civil Law, University of Bologna, 1980-1987. Research Fellow, University of Hamburg, 1978. Research Fellow, Max-Plank-Institut fuer auslaendisches und internationales Privatrecht, Hamburg, 1979-1981. Research Fellow, University of Michigan Law School, 1982. *Member:* Bar Association of Milan. **LANGUAGES:** German and English.

ASSOCIATES

DR. PROC. PATRIZIA PARENTI, born Reggio Emilia, Italy, September 8, 1952; admitted, 1976, Italy. *Education:* University of Bologna (Dr. iur.). *Member:* Bar Association of Monza. **LANGUAGES:** French and English.

DR. ANDREA SPARANO, born Mede, Italy, August 5, 1965; admitted, 1991, Italy. *Education:* State University of Pavia (Dr. iur.). **LANGUAGES:** English.

DR. CRISTINA BARUZZI, born Pavia, Italy, April 8, 1964; admitted, 1991, Italy. *Education:* State University of Pavia (Dr. iur.). **LANGUAGES:** French.

JACOBACCI & PERANI

VIA VISCONTI DI MODRONE 7
20122 MILAN, ITALY
Telephone: 76006884; 76020043
Telex: 335441 Japemi I
Fax: 794925

Turin, Italy Office: Corso Regio Parco 27, 10152, P.O. Box 321, 10100 Torino Centro. Telephone: 2440311. Cable Address: "Casettaro-Torino". Telex: 221494 Patent I. Fax: 286300; 286676.
Padua, Italy Office: Via Berchet 9, 35131. Telephone: 65.19.31; 65.01.46. Telex: 432321 Jacpad I. Fax: 65.16.31.
Bologna, Italy Office: Via Aurelio Saffi, 73/2, 40131. Telephone: 521081. Telex: 520613 Japebo I. Fax: 521038.

Patent, Design, Trademark and Copyright Law, Licensing, Franchising, Unfair Competition and Contracts, EEC Law.

RESIDENT PARTNERS

DR. ING. AURELIO PERANI. LANGUAGES: Italian, English, French and German. **PRACTICE AREAS:** Patent and Design Law.

DR. PAOLO PERANI. LANGUAGES: Italian, English and French. **PRACTICE AREAS:** Trademark; Copyright; Unfair Competition Law; EEC Law; Litigation; Law of Contracts.

DR. ING. TORQUATO VANNINI. LANGUAGES: Italian and English. **PRACTICE AREAS:** Patent and Design Law.

DR. CARLO MEZZANOTTE. LANGUAGES: Italian, English and French. **PRACTICE AREAS:** Trademark; Copyright; Unfair Competition Law.

DR. ING. ROBERTO DE NOVA. LANGUAGES: Italian, English, German and French. **PRACTICE AREAS:** Patent and Design Law.

DR. SERGIO MULDER. LANGUAGES: Italian, English and French. **PRACTICE AREAS:** Trademark and Copyright Law.

DR. CLAUDIO MAGGIONI. LANGUAGES: Italian, English, German, French and Spanish. **PRACTICE AREAS:** Patent and Design Law.

DR. ING. CARLO FALCETTI. LANGUAGES: Italian, English, German and French. **PRACTICE AREAS:** Patent and Design Law.

RESIDENT ASSOCIATES

MARCO FRANCETTI. LANGUAGES: Italian, English and French. **PRACTICE AREAS:** Trademark; Patent; Copyright; Unfair Competition Law; EEC Law; Litigation; Contracts.

FABIO SINISCALCO. LANGUAGES: Italian, English, German and French. **PRACTICE AREAS:** Patent and Design Law.

GABRIELE BORASI. LANGUAGES: Italian, English and French. **PRACTICE AREAS:** Trademark and Copyright Law.

LUCA MASSIMO GEONI. LANGUAGES: Italian, English and French. **PRACTICE AREAS:** Trademark and Copyright Law.

FILIPPO FERRONI. LANGUAGES: Italian, English and French. **PRACTICE AREAS:** Patent and Design Law.

GIULIA CAROLINA RUMI. LANGUAGES: Italian, English and French. **PRACTICE AREAS:** Trademark and Copyright Law.

RINALDO FERRECCIO. LANGUAGES: Italian, English, German and French. **PRACTICE AREAS:** Patent and Design Law.

MARIO LEONE. LANGUAGES: Italian, English and French. **PRACTICE AREAS:** Patent and Design Law.

(For Complete Biographical Data and Personnel, See Professional Biographies at Turin, Italy)

JENNY, PARMA & POZZI

Established in 1991

6 VIA COSIMO DEL FANTE
20122 MILAN, ITALY
Telephone: 39-2-58310113
Telefax: 39-2-58310377

International and General Practice, Corporation, Commercial, Tax, Securities, Industrial Property, Labor and Litigation.

(This Listing Continued)

FIRM PROFILE: Jenny, Parma & Pozzi was founded in 1991 and offers a full range of legal services, mainly in the fields of civil and commercial law. The firm's main area of practice include business and corporate law, tax planning, international law, finance and banking, bankruptcy and creditor's rights, securities laws, intellectual property, estate planning and administration, labor law and employees relations law. Jenny, Parma & Pozzi's litigation practice covers commercial litigation, intellectual property, product liability, worker's compensation, employment relations, collection and foreclosure actions, and corporate disputes.

Jenny, Parma & Pozzi represents clients on both a national and international level. The firm is comprised of a full staff of legal support personnel. All members of the staff are fluent in the English language and most of the staff are fluent in at least one other foreign language.

PARTNERS

CHRISTOPH JENNY, born Bolzano, Italy, October 20, 1959; admitted, 1984, Bolzano; 1989, Italy. Education: University of Bologna Law School (J.D., 1984); University of Chicago Law School (LL.M., 1988); Bocconi University (Master in Taxation, 1989). Clerkship, Commercial Court of Vienna, 1985-1986. Editor, Brendl - Produkt und Produzentenhaftung, 1989-1992. Member: Milan Bar; Italian-German Lawyers Association. **LANGUAGES:** Italian, German and English. **PRACTICE AREAS:** International Business Law; Corporate Law; Real Estate and Tax Law; Estate Planning.

PAOLA PARMA SFORZA, born Este, (Padua, Italy), March 31, 1960; admitted, 1984, Bologna; 1987, Italy. Education: University of Bologna Law School (J.D., 1984); Georgetown University, Law School, Washington, D.C. (Orientation in the US Legal System, 1986); University of California, Berkeley, Boalt Hall School of Law (LL.M., 1987); Fulbright Scholar; Bocconi University (Master in Taxation, 1988). Assistant to Professor G. Santini, Commercial Law, University of Bologna Law School, 1984-1986. Editor, Giurisprudenza Italiana, 1984-1986. Member: Milan Bar. **LANGUAGES:** Italian and English. **PRACTICE AREAS:** Commercial Law; Corporate Law; Intellectual Property; Banking Law and Securities Law.

MAURIZIO POZZI, born Milan (Italy), June 1, 1960; admitted, 1983, Milan; 1987, Italy. Education: Catholic University (1979-1982); University of Parma (1982-1983; J.D., 1983). Co-Editor, Trattato di Diritto Civile Commerciale, "Giuoco, Scommessa e Transazione," 1986; "Licenciements collectifs," International Bar Association, 1989. Member: Milan Bar. **LANGUAGES:** Italian, French and English. **PRACTICE AREAS:** Civil Litigation; Labor Law and Employment Relations.

ASSOCIATE

MARCO LONGO, born Milan (Italy), August 30, 1965; admitted, 1990, Milan; 1993, Italy. Education: Milan University (J.D., 1990). **LANGUAGES:** Italian and English. **PRACTICE AREAS:** Commercial Law; Civil Litigation; Collection and Foreclosure Actions.

LEGA, COLUCCI, ALBERTAZZI & ASSOCIATI
STUDIO LEGALE ASSOCIATO

Established in 1988

PIAZZA BORROMEO, 12
20123 MILAN, ITALY
Telephone: (02) 72021678 (r.a.)
Fax: (02) 72022031
Telex: 520526 TELEBO I CA 0208

Corporate, Banking, Bankruptcy, Mergers and Acquisitions, Securities, Antitrust, Tax, EEC, Construction, Administrative and Regulatory, Environmental, Intellectual Property, Insurance, Real Estate, Litigation, Foreign Investment in Developing Countries and in Central and Eastern Europe, General Practice.

FIRM PROFILE: This young and fast-growing firm was founded in 1988 and provides a full range of legal services, with a focus on mergers and acquisitions and international business transactions. In addition to a strong domestic practice and a traditional assistance of foreign businesses in Italy, a peculiarity of the firm is its extensive representation of companies doing business abroad and in particular in newly industrialized, developing or Socialist countries and in new democracies. The firm's client base is European, Asian and North American.

(This Listing Continued)

LEGA, COLUCCI, ALBERTAZZI & ASSOCIATI, STUDIO LEGALE ASSOCIATO, Milan—Continued

MEMBERS OF FIRM

GIOVANNI LEGA, born Milan, Italy, February 18, 1957; admitted, 1986, Italy. *Education:* Catholic University of Sacred Heart, Milan (J.D., 1981); Harvard Law School (LL.M., 1985). Justice Paul Garity, Superior Court of Massachusetts, 1983. Visiting Foreign Lawyer: Sullivan & Worcester, Boston, 1986. Windels, Marx, Davies & Ives, New York, 1986. Assistant Professor, Catholic University of Sacred Heart, Milan, 1988. *Member:* International Bar Association (Recipient, Honorary Award). *LANGUAGES:* Italian, English and French. *PRACTICE AREAS:* Corporate; International Business Transactions; Property Development; Foreign Investment in Developing Countries.

PAOLO A. COLUCCI, born Naples, Italy, February 27, 1959; admitted, 1986, Italy. *Education:* University of Naples School of Law (J.D., summa cum laude, 1981); Harvard Law School (LL.M., 1984). Visiting Foreign Lawyer: Chadbourne & Parke, New York, 1985. Author: "Mutuo-Diritto Tributario," Legal Encyclopedia Treccani, 1987. Lecturer: Tax Law, University of Naples School of Law, 1981-1983; International Tax Program, Harvard Law School, 1984. *Member:* International Bar Association. *LANGUAGES:* Italian, English and Spanish. *PRACTICE AREAS:* Mergers and Acquisitions; Leveraged Buyouts; Tax Law; Financial and Commercial Transactions.

ROBERTO ALBERTAZZI, born Pavia, Italy, March 10, 1955; admitted, 1986, Italy. *Education:* University of Pavia School of Law (J.D., 1979); Bocconi University, Milan (Master in Business Administration, 1981). Lecturer, Economics, University of Pavia, 1980-1981. *Member:* Associazione Giuristi D'Impresa. *LANGUAGES:* Italian, English. *PRACTICE AREAS:* Commercial Litigation; Banking; Bankruptcy; Securities.

FABRIZIO F. AROSSA, born Turin, Italy, October 11, 1959; admitted, 1987, Italy. *Education:* University of Turin School of Law (J.D., summa cum laude, 1985); Faculté Internationale de Droit Comparé, Strasbourg (Diplome Supérieur, 1985); Harvard Law School (LL.M., 1987). Visiting Foreign Lawyer: Thelen, Marrin, Johnson & Bridges, San Francisco, 1987; Siméon, Moquet, Borde & Associés, Paris, 1988. Adjunct Professor, International Business Transactions, University of Trento School of Law, 1991-1994. Co-Author: "International M&A Law - Italy", London, 1991. *Member:* International Bar Association; Italian Association of Comparative Law. *LANGUAGES:* Italian, English, French and German. *PRACTICE AREAS:* Corporate; Mergers and Acquisitions; Antitrust; Environmental and Foreign Investment in Eastern Europe.

ASSOCIATES

SANDRA PERILLI, born Palermo, Italy, April 17, 1959; admitted, 1989, Italy. *Education:* University of Milan School of Law (J.D., 1983). Author: "Un caso di impiego anomalo del leasing," in the Italian Journal of Leasing and Financial Brokerage, 1988. Visiting Foreign Lawyer: Morgan, Lewis & Bockius, Philadelphia, 1992. *LANGUAGES:* Italian, English, French and Spanish. *PRACTICE AREAS:* Corporate; Commercial; Construction.

LUIGI IMPERLINO, born Naples, Italy, September 20, 1955; admitted, 1986, Italy. *Education:* University of Naples School of Law (J.D., 1979). *LANGUAGES:* Italian, English. *PRACTICE AREAS:* Administrative Law.

CRISTINA CABELLA, born Milan, Italy, June 28, 1963; admitted, 1992, Italy. *Education:* University of Milan School of Law (J.D., 1988); University of London Queen Mary and Westfield College (LL.M., 1990; Associate Researcher in Intellectual Property, 1991). Visiting Foreign Lawyer: Lovell White Durrant, London, 1991. *LANGUAGES:* Italian, English and French. *PRACTICE AREAS:* Intellectual Property; Commercial; Environmental.

ANDREA CARRERI, born Mantova, Italy, May 8, 1964; admitted, 1993, Italy. *Education:* University of Milan School of Law (J.D., 1989). *LANGUAGES:* Italian and English. *PRACTICE AREAS:* Corporate and Bankruptcy.

ELISABETTA PAGNINI, born Naples, Italy, April 2, 1968; admitted, 1994, New York. *Education:* Federico II University of Naples School of Law (J.D., summa cum laude, 1991); Harvard Law School (LL.M., 1993). *LANGUAGES:* Italian, English and German. *PRACTICE AREAS:* Corporate; International Business Law.

(This Listing Continued)

MASSIMILIANO ANSELMI, born Ingolstadr, Germany, July 29, 1967. *Education:* University of Milan School of Law (J.D., 1992). *LANGUAGES:* Italian, German and English. *PRACTICE AREAS:* Commercial and Corporate Law.

GIUSEPPE CIOFFI, born Milan, July 23, 1963; admitted, 1992, Italy. *Education:* University of Scared Heart (J.D., 1986); University of Scared Heart, Milan (Master in Corporate Law, 1990); University of London Queen Mary and Westfield College (LL.M., 1992). *LANGUAGES:* Italian, English and Spanish. *PRACTICE AREAS:* Commercial and Corporate; Litigation.

EEC COUNSEL

DINO RINOLDI, born Sacile (Pordenone), Italy, November 11, 1951. *Education:* Catholic University of Sacred Heart, Milan (J.D., 1975). Professor: E.C. Law, Catholic University, Milan, 1988; University of Genoa, 1991.

TAX AND ACCOUNTING COUNSEL

DARIO GARBARINO, born Genoa, Italy, January 12, 1948. *Education:* University of Genoa School of Business and Economics (B.A., 1971). *LANGUAGES:* Italian and English. *PRACTICE AREAS:* Corporate Tax Compliance and Fiscal Planning.

FEDERICO CALISSANO, born Genoa, Italy, July 23, 1957. *Education:* University of Genoa School of Business and Economics (B.A., 1983). *LANGUAGES:* Italian and English. *PRACTICE AREAS:* Accounting and Financial Reports; Corporate Taxation.

GIOVANNI CIURLO, born Genoa, Italy, August 14, 1960. *Education:* University of Genoa School of Business and Economics (B.A., 1983). *LANGUAGES:* Italian and English. *PRACTICE AREAS:* Corporate Taxation; Accounting; Corporate Finance; Financial Evaluation.

LORENZO PASSADORE, born Genoa, Italy, May 12, 1949. *Education:* University of Genoa School of Business and Economics (B.A., 1972). *LANGUAGES:* Italian and English. *PRACTICE AREAS:* Corporate Taxation; Corporate Finance; Financial Evaluation.

CARLO BROCKHAUS, born Origgio (Milan), Italy, February 5, 1943. *Education:* University of Genoa School of Business and Economics (B.A., 1981). *LANGUAGES:* Italian and English. *PRACTICE AREAS:* Corporate Taxation and Tax Litigation.

ROBERTO LAZZARONE, born Turin, Italy, April 29, 1958. *Education:* University of Genoa School of Business and Economics (B.A., 1983). Formerly at KPMG. *LANGUAGES:* Italian and English. *PRACTICE AREAS:* Corporate Taxation; International Taxation; Fiscal Planning.

NOCOLETTA GARBINI, born Bolzano, Italy, April 19, 1942. *Education:* Padua University School of Political Sciences (B.A., 1965). Formerly In-House Counsel at Pirelli S.p.A., responsible for corporate and securities compliance for the Pirelli Group. *LANGUAGES:* Italian and English. *PRACTICE AREAS:* Corporate and Securities; Compliance and Formalities.

Languages: English, French, Spanish and German.

STUDIO AVVOCATO LEVI

Established in 1983

36 VIA GIOVANNI DA PROCIDA
20149 MILAN, ITALY
Telephone: 347282 - 3319669
Fax: 341838

Mergers and Acquisitions, Corporations, Contracts, Commercial Law, International Practice, Trademarks, Real Estate.

FIRM PROFILE: Established in 1983 the firm is counselling companies mainly in commercial and corporate law; it is a founding member of the Association of Independent European Lawyers' specialized in commercial law.

AVV. ALDO LEVI, born Milan, Italy, November 16, 1948; admitted, 1974, Milan. *Education:* State University of Milan (J.D. magna cum laude, 1971); New York University (Fulbright Grant, M.C.J., 1972). Author: "Use and Registration of a Trademark in the USA," 1972; Distinctiveness and Secondary Meaning of a Trademark," 1975; "Joint Ownership of the Invention," 1977; "Clauses of License Agreements of Patents, Know-How and Trade Marks and EEC Competition Law," 1977; "Trademark and EEC Laws," 1978; "Circulation of Trademark within Companies of Same Group,"

(This Listing Continued)

1978; "Trade Mark and Dominant Position," 1979; "Derogations to Legal Principles of Evaluation in Balance Sheet," 1981; "OCSE Code on Multinational Companies," 1982; "Protection of Software with Particular Regard to Foreign Legal Systems," 1984; "The John Player Special Trademark," 1985; "Software and Copyright," 1986. Assistant of Commercial Law, State University of Milan, 1973-1983. Board Member, Association of Young Attorneys of Milan, 1978-1979. President, Italian Fulbright Association of Milan, 1976-1979. Member of the Board of the National Association, 1978-1979. *LANGUAGES:* Italian, English and French. *PRACTICE AREAS:* Mergers and Acquisitions; Corporations; Contracts; International Practice; Trademarks.

ASSOCIATES

DR. REDAELLI FEDERICO, born Milan, Italy, July 10, 1961; admitted, 1992, Milan. *Education:* State University of Milan (J.D., 1987). *LANGUAGES:* Italian, English and French. *PRACTICE AREAS:* Commercial Law; Real Estate.

DR. CRISTINA PERACCHI, born Milan, Italy, June 13, 1959. *Education:* Catholic University of Milan (J.D., 1988). *LANGUAGES:* Italian, English and French. *PRACTICE AREAS:* Commercial Law.

DR. CINZIA FUMAGALLI, born Milan, Italy, April 21, 1968. *Education:* State University of Milan (J.D., 1993). *LANGUAGES:* Italian and English. *PRACTICE AREAS:* Commercial Law.

CESARE LOMBRASSA

Established in 1991

VIA TORINO 48
20123 MILAN, ITALY
Telephone: 02 72000548; 72000582
Facsimile: 72021281

Civil, Commercial and International Law.

CESARE LOMBRASSA, born Pesaro, Italy, June, 20, 1940; admitted, 1983, Milan. *Education:* University of Rome Faculty of Law (Law, 1964). Appointed: 1967, Uditore Giudiziario, Bolzano High Court and High Court Judge and Master for the Interlocutory Stage; 1970, High Court Judge, Como Court; 1976, Pretore of Como; 1979, Master for the Interlocutory Stage, Rome High Court; 1981, Appeal Court Judge; 1983, Magistrato di Cassazione. Board of Directors: Publicitas, Sipra S.p.A.; Ausimont S.p.A. (Ferruzzi Holdings); Galassia Viaggi S.p.A. (Ferruzzi Holding). Legal Counsellor, Telespazio S.p.A. (IRI Holding); Agusta S.p.A. (Efim Holding). *LANGUAGES:* English, French, German, Spanish and Portuguese.

LUPI & ASSOCIATI

VIA LARGA 9
20122 MILAN, ITALY
Telephone: 2-5830 3650
Fax: (02) 58304072

General Practice.

MASSIMO LUPI, born Volterra, Italy, November 12, 1950; admitted, 1977, Italy. *Education:* State University of Milan (Doctor, 1976). *LANGUAGES:* Italian, English, French. *PRACTICE AREAS:* Leasing & Factoring; Labour Law; Building & Construction Law; Agency & Distribution; Bankruptcy.

GIANANDREA CIPRIANI, born Milano, Italy, April 21, 1964; admitted, 1990, Italy. *Education:* State University of Milan (Doctor). *LANGUAGES:* Italian, English. *PRACTICE AREAS:* General Practice in Civil Law; Tort Law; Environmental Law; Labour Law.

RENATO SGROI SANTAGATI, born Sanremo, Italy, January 18, 1945; admitted, 1973, Italy. *Education:* State University of Catania (Dr., 1970). *LANGUAGES:* Italian, French. *PRACTICE AREAS:* Bankruptcy; Corporate; Tax Law.

FRANCESCO ARGENZIO, born Potenza, Italy, October 15, 1937; admitted, 1966, Italy. *Education:* Universita' La Sapienza, Rome (Doctor, 1963). *LANGUAGES:* Italian, English. *PRACTICE AREAS:* Administrative Law; Commercial Law.

STUDIO Dell'AVV. PROF. RICCARDO LUZZATTO

Established in 1989

GALLERIA S. BABILA, 4/D
20122 MILAN, ITALY
Telephone: (2) 76006765 (3 lines)
Fax: (2) 784158

General International Practice, including Acquisitions, Company Law, Competition, License Agreements, Patents and Trademarks, Taxation, Finance, Arbitration and Litigation, EEC Law.

FIRM PROFILE: The firm was established in its present form in 1989 and offers a wide range of legal services. It is particularly known for its practice in the field of International Business Law (including EEC Law), Competition and Intellectual Property Law. The Client base is European and North American in scope.

MEMBERS OF FIRM

RICCARDO LUZZATTO, born Milan, Italy, 1935; admitted, 1958, Italy; 1976, Italian Supreme Court. *Education:* University of Milan (Doctor of Jurisprudence). Professor of International and EEC Law, since 1968 (Universities of Urbino, Messina, Modena, Genoa, Milan 1980—). *Member:* International Association for the Protection of Industrial Property; Italian Arbitration Association (A.I.A.); International Law Association (I.L.A.). *LANGUAGES:* Italian, English, French and German. *PRACTICE AREAS:* International Commercial Law; EEC Law; Competition and Industrial Property Law; Arbitration.

BIANCA MARIA COZZI, born Milan, Italy, 1940; admitted, 1964, Italy. *Education:* University of Milan (Doctor of Jurisprudence). Registered Comptroller of Accounts, 1976—. *LANGUAGES:* Italian, English and French. *PRACTICE AREAS:* Company Law.

ASSOCIATES

RICCARDO FERRANTE, born Milan, Italy, 1957; admitted, 1987, Italy. *Education:* University of Milan (Doctor of Jurisprudence). *LANGUAGES:* Italian, French and English.

ELENA MONTALTO, born Milan, Italy, 1964; admitted, 1992, Italy. *Education:* University of Milan (Doctor of Jurisprudence). *LANGUAGES:* Italian, French and English.

PAOLO CAPE', born Milan, Italy, 1967; admitted, 1991, Milan. *Education:* University of Milan (Doctor of Jurisprudence). *LANGUAGES:* Italian, English and French.

Languages: Italian, English, French and German.

MACCHI di CELLERE e GANGEMI

VIA G. SERBELLONI, 4
20122 MILAN, ITALY
Telephone: (39-2) 76001616
Fax: (39-2) 76001618

Rome, Italy Office: Via G. Cuboni, 12, 00197, Rome. Telephone: (39-6) 3214238; 3221565. Fax: (39-6) 3222159.

International Business Practice, Corporate, Mergers and Acquisitions, Antitrust, Taxation, Environmental, Telecommunications, Commercial Transactions, Banking and Financing, Securities, Labor, Oil and Gas, International and EEC Law, Litigation and Arbitration.

Luigi Macchi di Cellere	*Ettore Scandale*
Bruno Gangemi	*Francesco Cerasi*
Claudio Visco	*Marco Lombardi*
Teodosio Luciano Monaco	*Corrado Angelelli*
Simona Bellettini	*Bernadette Accili*
Fabrizio Maria Romano	*Frederico Torzo*
Stefano Macchi di Cellere	*Micaela Di Benedetti*
Luca Simonetti	*Paolo Valenti*

Languages: Italian, English, French, German and Spanish

(For Biographical data, see Professional Biographies of Macchi di Cellere e Gangemi, Rome, Italy).

STUDIO MAISTO E MISCALI

PIAZZA MEDA, 5
20121 MILAN, ITALY
Telephone: 39.2.7602.3630
Telefax: 39.2.7602.3650-3750

International Business Practice, Corporate, Mergers and Acquisitions, Taxation, Commercial Transactions, Custom Law and Procedure, Banking and Finance, Securities, Administrative Law and Litigation.

GUGLIELMO MAISTO, born Genoa, Italy, September 13, 1952; admitted, 1977, Italy. *Education:* University of Genoa (J.D., cum laude, 1976); EEC Commission, Directorate General IV (Training, 1977); University of Amsterdam (Master Degree, European Integration). Co-Author: "Business Law Guide to Italy," CCH, 1992. Publications: National Reporter, XXXIV, Congresses of the International Fiscal Association, Buenos Aires, 1984; National Reporter, XXXVII, Congresses of the International Fiscal Association, Amsterdam, 1988. Editor and General Reporter, "Tax Treatment of Cost Contribution Arrangements," Kluwer, Deventer, 1988. Editorial Board, various Italian and Foreign Tax and Legal Journals. General Reporter, "Transfer Pricing in the Absence of Comparable Market Prices," International Fiscal Association Congress, 1992. Professor, Tax Law, Bocconi University, 1986-1991. Lecturer, International Corporate Tax Policy, Postgraduate Master Course in International Management, Business School, Bocconi University. Member: Business Industry Advisory Committee (Tax Committee); International Bureau of Fiscal Documentation (Advisory Board, Amsterdam); American Chamber of Commerce (Legal and Tax Committee); International Chamber of Commerce (Tax Committee). *Member:* International Bar Association; International Fiscal Association. *LANGUAGES:* Italian, English and French. *PRACTICE AREAS:* International and Domestic Tax and Business Law; Mergers and Acquisitions; Corporate Restructuring.

MARIO MISCALI, born Alessandria, Italy, April 28, 1954; admitted, 1981, Italy. *Education:* University of Florence (J.D., cum laude, 1977). Professor of Tax Law, LIUC University, Milan. Co-Author: "Business Law Guide to Italy," CCH, 1992. Publications: "Imposizione tributaria e territorio," Padoa, Cedam, 1984; "Il silenzio nel diritto tributario," Padoa, Cedam, 1990; "Il regime fscale della casa nella legge 22 aprile," n. 168, Milan, Giuffré, 1982; "Project financing" in Trattato dei contralli d'affari, by F. Galgano, Torino, 1994; "La tassazione delle plusvalenze speculative derivanti da cessioni azionarie" in Diritto e pratica tributaria, volume LII, 1981; " Pena pecuniaria, in Digesto IV, Torino, 1994. *LANGUAGES:* Italian and French. *PRACTICE AREAS:* Domestic Tax Law; Tax and Administrative Litigation; Real Estate Law; Custom Law; Project Finance Law.

ANDREA MANZITTI, born Genoa, Italy, June 24, 1961; admitted, 1989, Italy. *Education:* University of Genoa (J.D., cum laude, 1985); Bocconi University (Master, Business Tax Law, 1986); King's College, Post Graduate School (Diploma, International Contracts, 1987). Co-Author: "Business Law Guide to Italy," CCH, 1992. Publications: "Taxation of Individuals in Europe," section of Italy, Guide VI, loose-leaf, International Bureau of Fiscal Documentation. Lecturer, International Corporate Tax Policy, Postgraduate Master Course in International Management, Business School, Bocconi University. *Member:* International Bar Association; International Fiscal Association. *LANGUAGES:* Italian, English and French. *PRACTICE AREAS:* International and Domestic Tax and Business Law; Mergers and Acquisitions; Financial Products.

FABIO PACE, born Palermo, Italy, January 18, 1965; admitted, 1991, Milan. *Education:* University of Palermo (J.D., cum laude, 1987); Bocconi University (Master, Business and Corporate Law, 1988; Master, Corporate Tax Law, 1989); University of Amsterdam (Master, European Community Law, 1989). Co-Author: "Business Law Guide to Italy," CCH, 1992. *LANGUAGES:* Italian and French. *PRACTICE AREAS:* Domestic Tax Law; Tax and Administrative Litigation; Real Estate Law.

PAOLO LUDOVICI, born Rome, Italy, July 9, 1965. *Education:* Bocconi University (Doctor in Economics, cum laude, 1989; Master, Corporate Tax Law, 1990);. Co-Author: "Business Law Guide to Italy," CCH, 1992. *LANGUAGES:* Italian and English. *PRACTICE AREAS:* International and Domestic Tax and Business Law; Mergers and Acquisitions; Financial Products.

VITTORIO EMANUELE FALSITTA, born Milan, Italy, June 7, 1966. *Education:* University of Milan (J.D., 1991); Bocconi University (Master, Corporate Tax Law, 1991). Co-Author: "Business Law Guide to Italy," CCH, 1992. *LANGUAGES:* Italian and English. *PRACTICE AREAS:* Domestic Tax and Business Law; Mergers and Acquisitions; Financial Products.

(This Listing Continued)

EU934B

MASSIMO GIACONIA, born Caltagirone, Italy, July 22, 1959. *Education:* Bocconi University (Doctor in Economics, 1983). Author: "Tassazione dei capital gains per i non residenti' (Commercio Internazionale n. 8/1991); "Rimborso della ritenuta sui titoli di Stato ai non residenti" (Commercio Inernazionale n. 21/1991); "Paradisi fiscali: quando c'è di mezzo la convenzione (Commercio Internazionale n. 24/1992). Auditor Assistant, Peat Marwick & Mitchell, Milan, 1984-1985. Tax Consultant, KPMG, Milan, 1985-1989. Tax Manager: Agusta Group, Milan, 1989-1990; Banca d'America e d'Ilalia, Milan, 1990-1991; R.C.S. Editori, Milan, 1991-1994. *Member:* American Italian Law Association. *LANGUAGES:* Italian and English. *PRACTICE AREAS:* Mergers and Acquisitions; Banking; Financial Products; International and Domestic Tax and Business Law.

OF COUNSEL

CLAUDIA MOLINARI, born Genoa, Italy, January 10, 1953; admitted, 1978, Italy. *Education:* University of Genoa (J.D., cum laude, 1976). *LANGUAGES:* Italian and English. *PRACTICE AREAS:* Corporate Law; Contracts and Business Law.

TOMASO ROCCATAGLIATA, born Turin, Italy, September 2, 1949; admitted, 1993, Italy. *Education:* University of Pavia (J.D., 1976); London School of Economics (Course on English Law, 1974). Training, EEC Directorate General IV, 1976-1977. Co-Author: "Business Law Guide to Italy," CCH, 1992. Attorney: Industrie Zanussi S.p.a., Pordenone, 1978 -1980; General Electric Const. Group, Milan, 1980-1983. Legal Counsel: General Electric Information Services, Milan, 1983-1984; Hewlett Packard Italiana, Milan, 1984-1988; R.C.S. Editori, Milan, 1988-1991. Vice-President, Associazione Italiana Giuristi d'Impresa AIGI, 1990-1993. . *Member:* International Bar Association; AIGI. *LANGUAGES:* Italian, French and English. *PRACTICE AREAS:* Corporate Law; Real Estate Law; Contracts; International Business; Mergers and Acquisitions; Acquisitions.

MALCHIODI & BERNARDI

Established in 1962

VIA VISCONTI DI MODRONE 19
20122 MILAN, ITALY
Telephone: 78.22.01-76020931
Telecopier: 784448

Commercial and Corporation Law.

FIRM PROFILE: *The firm was established in 1862, originally as Pozzi & Malchmiodi. It offers a full range of legal services in the areas of commercial and corporation law and is associated with other firms in areas of tax and administrative law.*

MEMBERS OF FIRM

LUIGI MALCHIODI, born Turin, Italy, February 8, 1933; admitted, 1962, Italy. *Education:* Turin University (Dottore in Legge, 1956); Harvard Law School (LL.M., 1957). *LANGUAGES:* Italian and English.

PAOLO BERNARDI, born Trieste, Italy, August 17, 1932; admitted, 1970, Italy. *Education:* University of Pavia (Dottore in Legge, 1955); Harvard Law School (LL.M., 1957). *LANGUAGES:* Italian and English.

GIANNI MASSA

Established in 1988

13, VIALE BIANCA MARIA
20122 MILAN, ITALY
Telephone: (2) 76020726 - 76020776
Telecopier: (2) 782548

Civil, Commercial and Corporate Law, Domestic Taxation, Unfair Competition, Advertising Law.

GIANNI MASSA, born Gallarate, Italy, March 17, 1950; admitted, 1982, Milan. *Education:* State University of Milano (LL.D., 1975); Bocconi University (Taxation Course of Corporations, 1985-1986). *Member:* Milan Bar; International Bar Association. *LANGUAGES:* Italian and English.

ECONOMIC CONSULTANT

ROBERTO OGGIONI, born Monza, Italy, June 29, 1949. *Education:* Catholic University of Milan (LL.D., 1973).

STUDIO LEGALE
AVV. FRANCO M. MASTRACCHIO

VIALE VITTORIO VENETO, 24
20124 MILAN, ITALY
Telephone: 02/29001583
Telecopier: 02/6575509

Mergers and Acquisitions, Company Law, Commercial Law, Bank Law, Real Estate, Private International Law.

FRANCO M. MASTRACCHIO, born 1947; admitted, 1974, Italy. *Education:* University of Naples (Degree in Law, 1970). *LANGUAGES:* Italian, English, French and German.

LORENZO PINTUS, born 1958; admitted, 1988, Italy. *Education:* University of Milan (Degree in Law, 1985). *LANGUAGES:* Italian and English.

CLELIA LETO, born 1961; admitted, 1987, Italy. *Education:* University of Messina (Degree in Law, 1985). *LANGUAGES:* Italian and English.

RICCARDO RUSCONI, born 1963; admitted, 1991, Italy. *Education:* Catholic University of Milan (Degree in Law, 1988). *LANGUAGES:* Italian and English.

CINZIA BRAVIN, born 1960; admitted, 1991, Italy. *Education:* University of Bologna (Degree in Law, 1988). *LANGUAGES:* Italian, English and French.

INTERNATIONAL LAW FIRM MIZZAU

Established in 1979

VIA DONIZETTI, 37
20122 MILAN, ITALY
Telephone: 02-781057/781857/76000556/76002948
Fax: 76009444

Rome, Italy Office: 3, Via Bocca Di Leone, 00187 . Telephone: (39 6) 6797266. Telefax: (39 6) 6793779.
Trieste, Italy Office: 5, Via Conti, 34141. Telephone: (39 337) 271085. Telefax: (39 337) 271085.
Salzburg, Austria Office: 16, Getreidegasse, A-5020. Telephone: (43 662) 842742. Telefax: (43 662) 844142.
Amsterdam, Holland Office: Keizersgraght, 216, 1016-DZ. Telephone: (31 20) 6390043. Telefax: (31 20) 6254115.
Spezia, Italy Office: 25, via N. Tommaseo, 19121. Telephone: (39 167) 730709. Telefax: (39 187) 730709.
Curacao, Netherlands Antilles Office: 21-A, Van Engeleweg. Telephone: (599 9) 371677. Telefax: (599 9) 371765.

FIRM PROFILE: *The firm was established in Italy in 1979, originally specialized in currency law. During the last ten years, the firm has expanded its activities in other European countries, and has associated with other firms, in order to meet its clients requirements. It is well known for international business transactions, taxation, International Tax Planning, banking and finance, litigation and commercial disputes, environmental law. Moreover, it promotes and organizes international congresses and meetings in the legal-economic and environmental field. The firm's clients base is European and Australian.*

MEMBERS OF FIRM

ENNIO ALESSIO MIZZAU, born Enna, Italy, September 25, 1937; admitted, 1970, Italy. *Education:* State University of Milan (Degree in Law, 1967); Pro-Deo University of Rome (Master in Business Administration, 1967); Rome (Master in Currency Law at Bank of Italy, 1976); School of Fiscal and Economic Policy in Rome (Master in Domestic Taxation, 1972). Editor Director, Review of Currency Law and International Economics of Science, Law and Economy of the Environment. *Member:* Milan Bar Association; International Bar Association; Professional Association of Journalists. *LANGUAGES:* Italian, English and French. *PRACTICE AREAS:* International Transaction and Trade; Banking, Finance and Currency Regulations; Domestic and International Transactions; Foreign Investments; International Tax Planning; Business Law; International Joint Ventures; International Partnerships.

PATRIZIA SALVAGNO, born Venice, Italy, December 10, 1959; admitted, 1990, Italy. *Education:* State University of Padua (Degree in Law, 1987). *Member:* Venice Bar Association. *LANGUAGES:* Italian, French and English. *PRACTICE AREAS:* Litigation and Commercial Disputes; Environmental Law; Foreign Investment.

(This Listing Continued)

ALDO MILETIC, born Rasa, Yugoslavia, July 20, 1945. *Education:* State University of Rome (Degree in Political Sciences, 1969). *LANGUAGES:* Croatian, Slovenian, Serbian, German, Italian, English and French. *PRACTICE AREAS:* Banking; Finance and Currency Regulations; International Transactions and Trade.

PHILIP JOHANNES JACOB DROST, born Utrecht, Netherlands, April 11, 1967. *Education:* State University of Leiden (Degree in Civil Dutch Law, 1992). *LANGUAGES:* Dutch, English, Italian, German and French. *PRACTICE AREAS:* Civil Law; Copyright Law; Employment Law; Product Liability.

PATRIZIA GRIMALDI, born Napoli, Italy, June 29, 1957. *Education:* Diploma in Accountancy. *LANGUAGES:* Italian. *PRACTICE AREAS:* Economic and Financial Consultant; International Tax Planning.

RAFFAELE ALESSANDRO MIZZAU, born Turin, September 26, 1969; admitted, 1994, Italy. *Education:* State University, Turin (Law, 1994). *LANGUAGES:* English, Italian. *PRACTICE AREAS:* Civil Litigation; Company Commercial Law; Company Taxation.

MIKAELA VALAN, born Pordenone, 1968; admitted, 1993, Italy. *Education:* State University, Trieste (Law, 1993). *LANGUAGES:* Italian, English. *PRACTICE AREAS:* Offshore Companies; International Corporate Taxation; Company Commercial Law; Company Taxation.

ANDREA AMATI, born Savona, May 15, 1958; admitted, 1993, Italy. *Education:* State University, Parma (Law, 1984). *LANGUAGES:* English, French, Italian. *PRACTICE AREAS:* Construction Contracts; Construction Arbitration; Company Commercial Law; International Civil Law.

MODIANO & ASSOCIATI S.R.L.

Established in 1951

VIA MERAVIGLI, 16
20123 MILAN, ITALY
Telephone: 02-8692442
Fax: 02-863860

Munich, Germany Office: Baaderstrasse 3, D-8000. Telephone: 89-221216. Fax: 89-225809.

Italian and European Industrial Property Law, Competition Law, Transfer of Technology, Antitrust Law, assistance in Civil and Criminal Suits relating to Patents, Designs, Trademarks and Copyright.

FIRM PROFILE: *The firm was established in 1951 as Industrial Property Patent Attorneys in Italy and in 1979 as European Patent Attorneys with 12 European Patent Attorneys in Munich, Germany. The firm comprises a staff consisting of more than 115 persons, some with up to 35 years with the firm. The members are assisted by other 25 patent and trademark attorneys.*

MEMBERS OF FIRM

GUIDO MODIANO. *Education:* University of Milan (Ph.D., Electrochemical Engineering). Italian Patent Attorney, 1953. European Patent Attorney, 1978. Registered U.S. Patent Agent, Reg. No. 19,928 of 1960. Foreign Member, Chartered Patent Institute of London, 1960. Member, Government appointed Committee which drafted the new Italian Patent Law, 1979. *Member:* Board of the European Patent Institute; (AssoCIPI) Association of Italian Patent Attorneys (President); International Association for the Protection of Industrial Property; LES. *LANGUAGES:* English, German, French, Spanish and Italian.

ALBERT JOSIF. *Education:* (Ph.D., Mechanical and Aeronautical Engineering). Italian Patent Attorney, 1958. European Patent Attorney, 1978. Registered U.S. Patent Agent, Reg. No. 22,917 of 1966. *Member:* (AssoCIPI) Association of Italian Patent Attorneys; International Association for the Protection of Industrial Property; EPPC. *LANGUAGES:* English, German, French, Italian and Slavic.

MAURIZIO PISANTY. *Education:* (Ph.D., Electrotechnical Engineering). Italian Patent Attorney, 1966. European Patent Attorney, 1978. Former Member: Council of European Patent Institute; Board of (AssoCIPI) Association of Italian Patent Attorneys. *Member:* International Association for the Protection of Industrial Property. *LANGUAGES:* English, French, Spanish and Italian.

GABRIELLA STAUB. *Education:* (Ph.D., Chemical Engineering). Italian Patent Attorney, 1971. European Patent Attorney, 1978. *Member:* European Patent Institute (Member, Council); International Association for

(This Listing Continued)

MODIANO & ASSOCIATI S.R.L., Milan—Continued

the Protection of Industrial Property; (AssoCIPI) Association of Italian Patent Attorneys. *LANGUAGES:* English, German, French and Italian.

NEMO ZANOTTI. *Education:* Hannover University (Master, Electronic Engineering; B.S.c.). European Patent Attorney, 1978. Italian Patent Attorney, 1966. *LANGUAGES:* English, German, French and Italian.

MICHAEL L. SAND. *Education:* Pennsylvania State University (Ph.D., Chemical Engineering); Berkeley University (B.S.c., Chemical Engineering). *LANGUAGES:* English, German and Italian.

DANIEL O'BYRNE. *Education:* Berkeley University (B.S.c., Mechanical Engineering). U.S. Patent Agent. *LANGUAGES:* English and Italian.

PHILIP ANDREW BALL. *Education:* Sheffield Polytechnic (Higher Technicians Certificate). *LANGUAGES:* English and Italian.

ALBERTO TORNATO. *Education:* Law University, Milan. Attorney-at-Law. *Member:* United States Trademark Association. *LANGUAGES:* English, German and Italian.

STUDIO LEGALE MONDINI-RUSCONI

Established in 1969

VIA VISCONTI DI MODRONE, 2
20122 MILAN, ITALY
Telephone: 76004838
Facsimile: 76014053

General International Practice, including Company Law, Intellectual Property, Media and Telecommunications, EEC Law, Arbitration and Litigation.

FIRM PROFILE: *The firm was established in 1969 and offers a full range of legal services especially in conjunction with international practice. Over the years it has concentrated in some areas, namely International and EEC Law, Company Law and in Intellectual Property and Media Law where it has acquired an outstanding reputation both in Italy and abroad. The firm represents some of the largest companies in the Communications area and recently, in co-operation with various major foreign law firms, it has been dealing extensively in the field of Telecommunications. The client base is European and North American in scope. In addition to the lawyers listed below, the firm has a legal support staff of 6 consisting of paralegal and administrative personnel.*

MEMBERS OF FIRM

GIORGIO MONDINI, born Reggio Emilia, Italy, June 22, 1941; admitted, 1968, Milan; 1980, Italian Supreme Court. *Education:* State University of Milan (J.D. magna cum laude, 1965); Academy of American and International Law, Southwestern Legal Foundation, Dallas, Texas, U.S.A. (Fullbright Scholar, 1971). Author: *Planning Operations in Italy,* Prentice-Hall, 1972. Contributor to: L'Europa della CEE (Monthly Magazine), Pirola Ed., 1988-1991. Assistant Professor, International Law, University of Milan, 1967-1982. *Member:* International Bar Association; Association Europeenne des Avocats (European Lawyers Association); International Association of Entertainment Lawyers; International Association for the Protection of Industrial Property (AIPPI). (Also Member, Tomasetti & Partners, Milan, Italy). *LANGUAGES:* Italian, English and French. *PRACTICE AREAS:* Company Law; EEC Law; Arbitration; Media and Telecommunications Law; Intellectual Property.

GIUSEPPE RUSCONI, born Como, Italy, August 19, 1941; admitted, 1971, Milan. *Education:* State University of Milan (J.D. magna cum laude, 1965). Contributor to: L'Europa della CEE (Monthly Magazine), Pirola Ed., 1988-1991. (Also Member, Tomasetti & Partners, Milan, Italy). *LANGUAGES:* Italian and French. *PRACTICE AREAS:* Company Law; Arbitration; Litigation.

GIACOMO BONELLI, born Milan, Italy, October 21, 1956; admitted, 1985, Milan. *Education:* State University of Milan (J.D. magna cum laude, 1982). Contributor to: L'Europa della CEE (Monthly Magazine), Pirola Ed., 1988-1991. (Also Member, Tomasetti & Partners, Milan, Italy). *LANGUAGES:* Italian and English. *PRACTICE AREAS:* Intellectual Property; Labour Law; Competition Law; Litigation.

ANNA CARABELLI, born Como, Italy, August 27, 1958; admitted, 1985, Milan. *Education:* State University of Milan (J.D. magna cum laude, 1982); City of London Polytechnic (Summer Course in International Law, 1983); University of the Pacific McGeorge School of Law, Salzburg University (International Legal Studies, 1989). Contributor to: L'Europa della

(This Listing Continued)

CEE (Monthly Magazine), Pirola Ed., 1988-1991. *Member:* International Young Lawyers Association (AIJA). (Also Member, Tomasetti & Partners, Milan, Italy). *LANGUAGES:* Italian, English and French. *PRACTICE AREAS:* Intellectual Property; EEC Law; Media and Telecommunications Law; Litigation.

ASSOCIATES

GIUSEPPINA DALESSANDRI, born Milan, Italy, February 21, 1967; (Not admitted in Italy). *Education:* State University of Milan (J.D., magna cum laude, 1992). *LANGUAGES:* Italian, English and German.

ALESSANDRO FANO, born Milan, Italy, March 30, 1963; admitted, 1994, Italy. *Education:* Catholic University of Milan (J.D., 1987). *LANGUAGES:* Italian and English.

SIMONA GALANTI, born Milan, Italy, April 20, 1968; (Not admitted in Italy). *Education:* State University of Milan (J.D., magna cum laude, 1993). *LANGUAGES:* Italian, English and German.

LUCA TIBERI, born Pesaro, Italy, December 30, 1962; admitted, 1993, Italy. *Education:* Catholic University of Milan (J.D., 1987). *LANGUAGES:* Italian, English and French.

MARIAGRAZIA CALLORI, born Milan, Italy, August 16, 1967; (Not admitted in Italy). *Education:* State University of Milan (J.D., magna cum laude, 1994). *LANGUAGES:* Italian, English, French and German.

ALESSANDRA PIERSIMONI, born Milan, Italy, January 11, 1970; (Not admitted in Italy). *Education:* State University of Milan (J.D., magna cum laude, 1994). *LANGUAGES:* Italian, English and German.

Languages: Italian, English and French

STUDIO LEGALE
MONTANARI E RINALDI

VIALE MONTE SANTO, 1/3
20124 MILAN, ITALY
Telephone: (39-2) 29 00 56 55
Cable Address: "Responsa"
Telex: 333881 RESPON I
Fax: (39-2) 29 00 57 07/ 29 00 58 06

International Business Practice. Corporate, Mergers and Acquisitions, Taxation, Commercial Transactions, Banking and Financing, Securities, Labor, Oil and Gas, International and EEC Law, Litigation and Arbitration.

ALBERTO MONTANARI, born Milan, Italy, July 22, 1941; admitted to practice, 1965; admitted to bar, 1967, Italy. *Education:* University of Pavia (Doctor of Jurisprudence, maxima cum laude, 1964); Faculté Internationale pour l'Enseignement du Droit Comparé, Strasbourg and Coimbra (1965); University of Rome, Institute of Compartive Law (1966); Harvard University Law School (LL.M., 1967). Lecturer of Advanced Civil Law, University of Pavia, 1982-1983, 1984-1985. *Member:* Italian Bar Association (Milan); Italian Association of Comparative Law.

EGIDIO RINALDI, born Catania, Italy, April 1, 1937; admitted to practice, 1962; admitted to bar, 1964, Italy. *Education:* University of Catania, Italy (Doctor of Jurisprudence, maxima cum laude, 1961). Fellow, Seminar in American Law, Salzburg, 1968. *Member:* Italian Bar Association (Milan); International Bar Association.

LAURA BALDELLI, born Milan, Italy, July 16, 1938; admitted to practice, 1964; admitted to bar, 1965, Italy. *Education:* University of Milan (Doctor of Jurisprudence, maxima cum laude, 1963). *Member:* Italian Bar Association (Milan).

PASQUALFRANCO GROPPI, born Pavia, Italy, July 19, 1949; admitted to practice, 1973; admitted to bar, 1975, Italy. *Education:* University of Turin (Doctor of Jurisprudence, 1973); Columbia University, Parker Law School, New York (1984). *Member:* Italian Bar Association (Milan); International Association for the Protection of the Industrial Property, AIPPI; International Bar Association.

MARIA ROSA GALLETTI, born Pavia, Italy, July 25, 1962; admitted to practice, 1986, Italy; admitted, 1991. *Education:* University of Pavia (Doctor of Jurisprudence, maxima cum laude, 1986). Fellow, City of London Politechnic, English Law Introductory Course, 1986. Collaborator to the University of Pavia, Law Faculty, 1986; Academy of American and International Law, The Southwestern Legal Foundation, Dallas, 1991. *Member:* International Bar Association.

(This Listing Continued)

LAURA GRINGERI, born Milan, Italy, November 29, 1963; admitted to practice, 1987, Italy; admitted, 1992. *Education:* University of Milan (Doctor of Jurisprudence, 1986). Collaborator to the University of Milan, Law Faculty.

FEDERICO FONTANA, born Turin, Italy, June 1, 1967; admitted, 1993. *Education:* University of Turin (J.D., maxima, 1993); Harvard University (1990); Postgraduate Master in Corporate, Finance and Tax Law, Bocconi University. Traineeship International Legal Affairs Department IVECO S.p.A. (1991). Visiting Foreign Lawyers: De Bandt; Van Hecke & Lagae, Brussels (1991). *Member:* European Law Students Association (National President, 1991-1993).

Languages: Italian, English, French, German and Spanish.

NOTARBARTOLO & GERVASI

VIALE BIANCA MARIA, 33
I-20122 MILAN, ITALY
Telephone: 39-2-76009105 (5 lines)
Telefax: 39-2-799530
Telex: 330819 NOTAGE I

Florence Office: Lungarno A. Vespucci, 24 - 50123 Florence. Telephone-(39)(55)264467-264468. Telefax-(39)(55)289662.
Rome Office: Via Savoia, 82 - 00198 Rome. Telephone-(39)(6)8841698-8841697. Telefax-(39)(6)8841697.

European Patent Attorneys, Patent and Trade Mark Agents, Patent, Design, Trademark and Copyright Law, Licensing and Technology Transfer, Patent and Trademark Litigation, International Contracts, Unfair Competition, General Intellectual Property Practice.

MEMBERS OF FIRM

GEMMA GERVASI, born Milan, July 14, 1929. 1979, European Patent Attorney; 1983, Registered to practice before the Italian Patent and Trademark Office. *Education:* University of Palermo (Doctor in Chemistry, 1951). *Member:* Italian Patents Attorneys' Association; International Association for the Protection of Industrial Property (AIPPI); International Trademark Association (INTA); European Patent Institute (EPI); Licensing Executive Society (LES); European Community Trademark Association (ECTA); American Chemical Society (ACS); Società di Chimica Italiana (SCI). *LANGUAGES:* Italian, English, French and German.

DIEGO PALLINI GERVASI, born Milan, January 18, 1958. 1989, Registered to practice before the Italian Patent and Trademark office. *Education:* University of Milan (Doctor in Pharmacy, 1985). *Member:* Italian Patent Attorneys' Association; International Association for the Protection of Industrial Property (AIPPI); International Trademark Association (INTA); Licensing Executive Society (LES); European Community Trademark Association (ECTA); American Chemical Society (ACS). *LANGUAGES:* Italian, English, French and German.

ANDREINA PALLINI GERVASI, born Novara, March 27, 1955. *Education:* University of Milan (Doctor in Chemistry, 1984). Practiced in IP field since 1980. *LANGUAGES:* Italian, English and French.

ASSOCIATES

EMMA CASAGRANDE, born Padua, August 1, 1940. 1983, Registered to practice before the Italian Patent and Trademark Office. *Education:* University of Milan (Doctor in Law, 1964). *Member:* Italian Patent Attorneys' Association; International Trademark Association (INTA); Licensing Executive Society (LES); European Community Trademark Association (ECTA). *LANGUAGES:* Italian, English and French.

ANGELO PASSINI, born Milan, April 9. 1927. 1979, European Patent Attorney; 1983, Registered to practice before the Italian Patent and Trademark Office. *Education:* University of Milan (Industrial Chemistry, 1952). *Member:* Italian Patent Attorneys' Association; International Association for the Protection of Industrial Property (AIPPI); European Patent Institute (EPI); Licensing Executive Society (LES). *LANGUAGES:* Italian, English, French and German.

LUIGI PICCOLO, born Venice, February 26, 1928. *Education:* University fo Trieste (Doctor in Chemistry, 1952); University of Milan (Doctor in Medicine, 1992). Practice in IP field since 1975. *LANGUAGES:* Italian, English and French.

GIORGIO MORETTI, born Vicenza, August 6, 1924. 1979, European Patent Attorney; 1983, Registered to practice before the Italian Patent and Trademark Office. *Education:* University of Padua (Doctor in Industrial Chemistry, 1952). *Member:* Italian Patent Attorneys' Association; Interna-

(This Listing Continued)

---

tional Association for the Protection of Industrial Property (AIPPI); European Patent Institute (EPI). *LANGUAGES:* Italian, English, French and German.

DARIO LINARES, born Rovereto, December 27, 1922. *Education:* University of Milan (Doctor in Chemistry, 1946). *Member:* Italian Institute of Chemists; American Chemical Society (ASC): Royal Society of Chemistry; Society of Chemical Industry; Gesellschaft Deutscher Chemiker; Società di Chimica Italiana (SCI). *LANGUAGES:* Italian, English, French and German.

CESARE RENI, born Empoli (Florence), July 14, 1935. *Education:* University of Padua (Doctor in Industrial Chemistry, 1958). Practice in IP field since 1961. *Member:* American Chemical Society (ACS). *LANGUAGES:* Italian, English and French.

RAFFAELLA ASENSIO, born Milan, June 11, 1958. 1992, Registered to practice before the Italian Patent and Trademark Office. *Education:* University of Milan (Doctor in Industrial Chemistry, 1984). *Member:* Italian Patent Attorneys' Association. *LANGUAGES:* Italian, English, Spanish, German and French.

MARIA VITTORIA PRIMICERI, born Rome, March 8, 1954. 1988, Registered to practice before the Italian Patent and Trademark Office. *Education:* University of Rome (Doctor in Chemistry, 1979). *Member:* Italian Patent Attorneys' Association. (Rome Office). *LANGUAGES:* Italian and English.

LIVIO BRIGHENTI, born Milan, February 12, 1954. 1989, Registered to practice before the Italian Patent and Trademark Office. *Education:* University of Florence (Doctor in Chemistry, 1978). Former Patent Examiner for 10 years by European Patent Office (The Hague and Munich). *Member:* Italian Patent Attorneys' Association. (Florence Office). *LANGUAGES:* Italian, English, French, German and Spanish.

MARINA PALLINI, born Rome, January 10, 1962. *Education:* University of Rome (Doctor in Pharmacy, 1986). Practiced in IP field since 1989. (Rome Office). *LANGUAGES:* Italian and English.

CRISTINA CAZZETTA, born Milan, February 8, 1963. *Education:* University of Milan (Doctor in Law, 1989). Practice in IP field since 1990. *Member:* International Trademark Association(INTA); European Community Trademark Association (ECTA). *LANGUAGES:* Italian and English.

GIORGIO COGGI, born Trieste, August 1, 1941. 1980, European Patent Attorney; 1983, Registered to practice before the Italian Patent and Trademark Office. *Education:* University of Trieste (Doctor in Electronical Engineering, 1968). *Member:* Italian Patent Attorneys' Association; International Association for the Protection of Industrial Property (AIPPI); European Patent Institute (EPI). *LANGUAGES:* Italian, English, French and German.

SILVIA CAVICCHIOLI, born Milan, December 22, 1956. *Education:* University of Bologna (Doctor in Pharmaceutical Chemistry, 1981). Former Researcher in the organic chemistry field for 7 years. Practiced in IP field since 1990. *Member:* Italian Chemists Institute. *LANGUAGES:* Italian and English.

RAFFAELE BORRELLI, born Molochio (RC), November 26, 1953. *Education:* University of Rome (Doctor in Mechanical Engineering, 1981). Former Patent Examiner for 4 years by European Patent Office (The Hague). Practiced in IP field since 1985. (Florence Office). *LANGUAGES:* Italian, English, French, German, Dutch and Hungarian.

GIULIO MARIANI, born Vasto (CH), November 11, 1941. 1979, European Patent Attorney; 1983, Registered to practice before the Italian Patent and Trademark Office. *Education:* University of Rome (Doctor in Industrial Chemistry, 1967). *Member:* Italian Patent Attorneys' Association; International Association for the Protection of Industrial Property (AIPPI); European Patent Institute (EPI). (Rome Office). *LANGUAGES:* Italian, English and French.

GIANFRANCO MATTEUCCI, born Aprilia (LT), April 8, 1961. *Education:* University of Rome (Doctor in Biology, 1988). Stage by the Health Division of the Council of Europe (1990), Strasbourg. Practiced in IP field since 1990. (Florence Office). *LANGUAGES:* Italian, English, French, Spanish and German.

GIANCARLO AMBROSIONI, born Milan, July 20, 1930. *Education:* University of Pavia (Doctor in Pharmacy, 1954). *LANGUAGES:* Italian, English and French.

(This Listing Continued)

NOTARBARTOLO & GERVASI, Milan—Continued

ADAMIRA MOSCHETTINI, born Siracusa, April 22, 1967. *Education:* Catholic University of Milan (Doctor in Foreign Languages). (Florence Office). *LANGUAGES:* Italian, German, English and French.

COUNSELS

FRANCO PIRANI, born Pisa, April 6, 1927. 1979, European Patent Attorney; 1983, Registered to practice before the Italian Patent and Trademark Office. *Education University of Milan (Doctor in Chemical Engineering, 1951). Member:* Italian Patent Attorneys' Association; International Association for the Protection of Industrial Property (AIPPI); European Patent Institute (EPI); Licensing Executive Society (LES). *LANGUAGES:* Italian, English, French and German.

RENATO D'ANDREA, born Messina, July 21, 1958; admitted, 1991, Italy. *Education:* University of Milan (Doctor in Law, 1983). *LANGUAGES:* Italian and English.

FILIPPO BARBARINO, born Piazza Armerina (EN), April 29, 1944. *Education:* University of Turin (Doctor in Mechanical Engineering, 1971). *LANGUAGES:* Italian, French and English.

STUDIO LEGALE PAOLETTI

20 PIAZZA CASTELLO
20121 MILAN, ITALY
Telephone: (02) 878789, 878570
Facsimile: (02) 878643

Rome, Italy Office: 9 Via Sant Alberto Magno 00183. Telephone: (06) 5744021. 2. 3. 2 Telex: 622077 AVELAW I. Facsimile: (06) 5746021.

General Civil Practice, Admiralty, Litigation and Arbitration, International and Commercial Practice, Corporate Law, Patents, Trademarks and Foreign Investments, Family Law, Law of New Technologies (Genetic Engineering, Computer Law), Oil and Gas Law.

MEMBERS OF FIRM

CARLO PAOLETTI (1909-1980).

FABRIZIO PAOLETTI, born Rome, Italy, June 20, 1935; admitted, 1961, Rome; 1979, Italian Supreme Courts. *Education:* University of Rome (J.D., 1958). *Member:* Albo Avvocati e Procuratori di Roma. *LANGUAGES:* Italian and English.

GAETANO SEVERINI, born Cetraro, Italy, January 23, 1948; admitted, 1975, Rome; 1993, Italian Supreme Court. *Education:* University of Rome (J.D., 1971). *Member:* Albo Avvocati e Procuratori di Roma. *LANGUAGES:* Italian and English.

FABRIZIO PIETROSANTI, born Rome, Italy, May 11, 1951; admitted, 1979, Italy. *Education:* University of Rome, Institute of Comparative Law (J.D., magna cum laude, 1976). Note Editor, Foro Italiano, 1977-1990. Author: "Espropriazione in Favore del Proprietario," 1983, "Espropriabilità del Diritto del Conduttore?," 1984 and "Indennità di Esproprio e Criteri di Determinazione," 1985, all published in Foro Italiano. *Member:* Albo Avvocati e Procuratori di Roma. . *LANGUAGES:* Italian and English.

ASSOCIATES

MAURIZIO PAGANELLI, born Bari, Italy, August 14, 1959; admitted, 1988, Bari. *Education:* University of Bari (J.D., magna cum laude, 1984); Yale Law School (Visiting Scholar, 1988-1989). Note Editor, Foro Italiano, 1982-1990. Author: "Pagamento di Premio Assicurativo e Principio di Buona Fede," I, 2051, 1985, "La Vicenda 'Cattenom' e la Disciplina 'Esagonale' Degli Effluenti Radioattivi," IV 484, 1987, " I Parenti Poveri dell 'Etere," I, 347, 1989 and "Alla volta di Frankenstein: le Biotecnologie e la Proprietà(di parti) del Corpo," IV, 417, 1989, all published in Foro Italiano. Researcher, Energy Law, Institute of Comparative Law, University of Bari, 1985-1987. *Member:* Albo Procuratori di Bari. *LANGUAGES:* Italian, English and French.

OF COUNSEL

ERIK J. WATTEN, born Oslo, Norway, March 3, 1939; admitted, 1965, Oslo, Norway (Not admitted in Italy). *Education:* RIIS, Oslo (1957); Oslo University (1964). Norwegian Foreign Service, V. Consul Milan, Italy, 1965-1968. Norwegian Foreign Service, Attachee, Lagos, 1968. (Resident, Milan, Italy Office). *LANGUAGES:* Scandinavian, German, English, Italian and French.

(This Listing Continued)

REPRESENTATIVE CLIENTS: International Golf Corporation, Djarkata, Indonesia; Dyno Industrier A/S, Oslo, Norway, Norges Rederforbund (Norway Shipowners' Association) Oslo, Norway; NFT (ex Kongsberg), Kongsberg, Norway; Sysscan SpA, Rome, Italy; ELF Italia SpA, Rome, Italy; ACI (Automobile Association of Italy), Rome, Italy; Toro Insurance Co., Turin, Italy; Auselda AED Group SpA, Rome, Italy; Cantiere Navale Ferrari SpA, La Spezia, Italy.
REFERENCES: The Royal Norwegian Embassy in Italy; D.S.C. Srl, Milan, Italy; Mr. Robert K. Stevens, Department of State, Washington D.C. USA; Nuovi Cantieri Apuania SpA (GEPI Group), Massa Carrara, Italy; Fiduciaria Antonini SA, Lugano, Switzerland; Aeronavale Spa; Smosarski & Partner (London); Instituto Bancario San Paolo Di Torino.

PAVIA ANSALDO e VERUSIO

Established in 1961

VIA DELL'ANNUNCIATA 7
20121 MILAN, ITALY
Telephone: 2-63381
Cable Address: "Pavialaw"
Telecopier: 2-653306 or 2-281 00308.

Rome, Italy Office: Foro Traiano 1/A, 00187. Telephone 6-6780052. Telex: 611322. Telecopier: 6-6790005.
Padua, Italy Office: Corso Milano 26, 35139. Telephone: 49-8756070. Telecopier: 49-8756077.
Turin, Italy Office: Via Vittorio Amedeo II, 19, 10121. Telephone: 11-5359.22; 11-5359.21. Telecopier: 11-530.504.
New York, N.Y. Office: 600 Madison Avenue, 10022. Telephone: (212) 980-1633. Telecopier: (212) 980-1453.

General Practice. Industrial, Commercial, Corporate, Mergers and Acquisitions, Banking, Capital Markets, Corporate Restructuring, EC, Environment, Entertainment, Proprietory Rights, Commercial Arbitration and Litigation.

MEMBERS OF FIRM

ENRICO L. PAVIA (1899-1979).

GIUSEPPE ANSALDO, born Genoa, March 9, 1928; admitted, 1952, Italy. *Education:* University of Genoa (J.D.).

PIER LUIGI RAYMONDI, born Genoa, March 6, 1931; admitted, 1955, Italy. *Education:* University of Genoa (J.D.).

MICHELE CAPODANNO, born Naples, December 23, 1934; admitted, 1961, Italy. *Education:* University of Naples (J.D.).

MARCELLO AGNOLI, born Genoa, October 19, 1940; admitted, 1966, Italy. *Education:* University of Genoa (J.D.).

MAURIZIO BERNARDI, born Milan, July 9, 1950; admitted, 1976, Italy. *Education:* University of Milan (J.D.). (Also at Turin Office).

AGOSTINO MIGONE DE AMICIS, born Rosignano Marittimo, May 18, 1951; admitted, 1977, Italy. *Education:* University of Milan (J.D.).

GIAN PAOLO DI SANTO, born Bologna, July 10, 1955; admitted, 1981, Italy. *Education:* University of Bologna (J.D.). (Also at Padua Office).

MARINA SANTARELLI, born Rome, December 12, 1956; admitted, 1982, Italy. *Education:* Catholic University of Milan (J.D.).

ROBERTO ZANCHI, born Cremona, July 8, 1957; admitted, 1983, Italy. *Education:* University of Parma (J.D.).

GIAN PAOLO ZINI, born Reggio Emilia, August 18, 1958; admitted, 1984, Italy. *Education:* University of Modena (J.D.).

DANIELE RAYNAUD, born Milan, March 6, 1959; admitted, 1986, Italy. *Education:* University of Milano (J.D.).

MARIO ORTU, born Bolzano, August 8, 1960; admitted, 1989, Italy. *Education:* University of Padua (J.D.). (Also at Padua Office).

FRANCESCO OROMBELLI, born Milan, February 19, 1958; admitted, 1986, Italy. *Education:* University of Milan (J.D.).

GIACOMO SARTOR, born Castelfranco Veneto, November 3, 1958; admitted, 1989, Italy. *Education:* University of Padua (J.D.). (Padua Office).

PAOLO CANAL, born Milan, June 25, 1959; admitted, 1988, Italy. *Education:* Modena University (LL.D., 1983). (Padua Office).

PAOLO BIANCO, born Turin, September 7, 1959; admitted, 1989, Italy. *Education:* University of Turin (J.D.). (Turin Office).

(This Listing Continued)

GIUSEPPE DELL'ACQUA, born Genoa, November 18, 1959; admitted, 1988, Italy. *Education:* University of Genoa (J.D.); London School of Economics and Political Science (LL.M.).

GIORGIO SPANIO, born Rome, April 8, 1960; admitted, 1990, Italy. *Education:* Bologna University (J.D.). (Padua Office).

EZIO BISATTI, born Mogadiscio (Somalia), January 15, 1961; admitted, 1992, Italy. *Education:* University of Padua (J.D.). (Padua Office).

MONICA ZOCCA, born Milan, May 15, 1961; admitted, 1991, Italy. *Education:* University of Milan (J.D.).

ENRICO DEL GUERRA, born Milan, August 30, 1961; admitted, 1991, Italy. *Education:* University of Milan (J.D.).

PAOLO BRUGNERA, born Venice, November 17, 1961; admitted, 1990, Italy. *Education:* University of Padua (J.D.).

CARLO DEL CONTE, born Milan, April 14, 1962; admitted, 1991, Italy. *Education:* University of Milan (J.D.).

MATTEO ORSINGHER, born Trento, June 20, 1962; admitted, 1990, Italy. *Education:* University of Bologna (J.D.).

ILARIA BIANCHI, born Milan, October 3, 1962; admitted, 1993, Italy. *Education:* University of Florence (J.D.).

FRANCA DUTTO, born Cuneo, June 12, 1963; admitted, 1993, Italy. *Education:* University of Turin (J.D.). (Turin Office).

ANTONELLA ANDRIOLI, born Padua, June 13, 1963; admitted, 1991, Italy. *Education:* University of Padua (J.D., 1988).

ELENA FELICI, born Cuneo, November 4, 1963; admitted, 1991, Italy. *Education:* University of Milan (J.D.).

FRANCESCO MANARA, born Castellanza, August 4, 1964; admitted, 1993, Italy. *Education:* University of Milan (J.D.,).

OLIVIERO PESSI, born Padua, May 7, 1964; admitted, 1991, Italy. *Education:* University of Padua (J.D.).

DANIELA PIANEZZOLA, born Padua, January 4, 1965; admitted, 1994, Italy. *Education:* University of Padua (J.D.). (Padua Office).

BARBARA COVA, born Milan, February 25, 1965; admitted, 1994, Italy. *Education:* University of Milan (J.D.).

MARCO CASTAGNETTA, born Palermo, July 8, 1965; admitted, 1992, Italy. *Education:* University of Palermo (J.D.).

STEFANO BIANCHI, born Savona, October 16, 1965; admitted, 1993, Italy. *Education:* University of Milan (J.D.).

MARCO E. CUTORE, born Cantania, March 15, 1966; admitted, 1993, Italy. *Education:* University of Catania (J.D.).

ELISABETTA MINA, born Milan, June 24, 1966; admitted, 1994, Milan. *Education:* University of Milan (J.D.).

ELENA A. BERLUCCHI, born Brescia, July 20, 1966; admitted, 1993, Italy. *Education:* Catholic University of Milan (J.D.).

STEFANO M. GRASSANI, born Bologna, July 29, 1966; admitted, 1993, Italy; 1991, New York. *Education:* University of Bologna (J.D.): University of Michigan (LL.M.).

FRANCESCA DE FRAJA FRANGIPANE, born Milan, October 1, 1966; admitted, 1994, Italy. *Education:* University of Milan (J.D.).

RICCARDO AGOSTINELLI, born Genoa, May 22, 1967; admitted, 1992, Italy. *Education:* University of Genoa (J.D.).

NICOLA ROSSI, born Naples, April 3, 1968; admitted, 1993, Italy. *Education:* University of Naples (J.D.).

OF COUNSEL

PIERO SCHLESINGER, born Naples, May 19, 1930; admitted, 1955, Italy. *Education:* University of Turin (J.D.). Professor of Law, Università Cattolica, Milan.

PAOLO AGOSTONI, born Bressanone, June 4, 1936; admitted, 1962, Italy. *Education:* University of Padua (J.D.). (Padua Office).

GABRIELE CRESPI REGHIZZI, born Milan, April 3, 1941; admitted, 1966, Italy. *Education:* University of Milan (J.D.); Harvard Law School (LL.M.); S.J.D. Comparative Law and Legal and Social Institutions of USSR and Eastern Europe. Professor of Comparative Law and Director of the Development Cooperation Center, University of Pavia.

(This Listing Continued)

SERGIO M. CARBONE, born Genoa, July 1, 1941; admitted, 1966, Italy. *Education:* University of Genoa (J.D.). Professor of Law, University of Genoa.

FOREIGN CONSULTANTS

BRUNO R. PAVIA, born Genoa, July 9, 1931; admitted, 1959, New York; 1960, U.S. District Court, Southern and Eastern Districts of New York; 1962, U.S. Court of Appeals, 2nd Circuit; 1963, U.S. Supreme Court (Not admitted in Italy). *Education:* Hobart College (B.A., 1953); New York University (J.D., 1958).

FRANK DIEMER, born Düren, Germany, December 10, 1960; admitted, 1992, Cologne, Germany as Rechtsanwalt (Not admitted in Italy). *Education:* University of Bonn.

MARIO ABATE, born New York, N.Y., July 30, 1960; admitted, 1990, New Jersey; 1992, New York (Not admitted in Italy). *Education:* Temple University (J.D.); Georgetown University (LL.M.).

IVANA STJEPOVIC, born Vancouver, B.C., Canada, February 23, 1965; admitted, 1991, British Columbia. *Education:* University of British Columbia (LL.B., 1990); University of Cambridge (LL.M., 1992).

HOLGER BACKU, born Hermannstadt/Sibiu, Romania, March 30, 1965; admitted, 1994, Munich, Germany, as Rechtsanwalt (Not admitted in Italy). *Education:* Universities of Freiburg/Br. and Munich.

Languages: Italian, English, French, German and Russian.

STUDIO AVV. ALESSANDRO PEDERSOLI

VIA GESÙ, 2/A
20121 MILAN, ITALY
Telephone: 02-76033.1
Telecopier: 02-78.37.46

Civil, Corporate, Commercial Law. Contracts, Litigation, Mergers and Acquisitions, Antitrust. Arbitration.

AVV. ALESSANDRO PEDERSOLI, born Naples, Italy, April 24, 1929; admitted, 1952, Italy. *Education:* Catholic University of Milan (Doctor of Jurisprudence, 1950). *Member:* Italian Bar Association (Milan). **LANGUAGES:** Italian, English and French. **PRACTICE AREAS:** Corporate; Mergers and Acquisitions; Contracts; Banks and Banking; Arbitration.

AVV. CARLO PEDERSOLI, born Milan, Italy, December 5, 1953; admitted, 1980, Italy. *Education:* University of Milan Law School. **LANGUAGES:** Italian and English. **PRACTICE AREAS:** Contracts; Mergers and Acquisitions; Litigation; Arbitration.

AVV. STEFANO VERZONI, born Pavia, Italy, March 13, 1961; admitted, 1988, Italy. *Education:* University of Pavia Law School. **LANGUAGES:** Italian, English and French. **PRACTICE AREAS:** Litigation; Commercial Law; Contracts.

DR. PROC. ANTONIO PEDERSOLI, born Milan, Italy, June 12, 1959; admitted, 1991, Italy. *Education:* University of Milan Law School. **LANGUAGES:** Italian and English. **PRACTICE AREAS:** Litigation; Commercial Law; Corporate; Contracts.

DR. PROC. CARLO PAVESI, born Verona, Italy, June 19, 1963; admitted, 1991, Italy. *Education:* University of Milan Law School. **LANGUAGES:** Italian and English. **PRACTICE AREAS:** Litigation; Commercial Law; Corporate; Contracts.

DR. PROC. ENRICO ZATTONI, born Bergamo, Italy, February 27, 1965; admitted, 1993, New York; 1994, Italy. *Education:* University of Milan Law School; Harvard Law School (LL.M., 1992). *Member:* New York State Bar Association. **LANGUAGES:** Italian and English.

DR. GIANNI VETTORELLO, born Mestre, Italy, May 22, 1968. *Education:* University of Bologna Law School. **LANGUAGES:** Italian and English.

DR. GIOVANNI GHIRARDI, born Milan, Italy, June 24, 1969. *Education:* University of Milan Law School. **LANGUAGES:** Italian and English.

STUDIO LEGALE PELLEGRINI-CISLAGHI

VIA NERINO, 8
20123 MILAN, ITALY
Telephone: (02) 801031/2/3/4
Fax: (02) 801034

General Practice. Corporate, Business, Contracts, Foreign Investments, Labor, Patents and Copyright Law.

GIORGIO PELLEGRINI CISLAGHI, born Milan, Italy, July 21, 1934; admitted, 1967, Italy. *Education:* University of Milan (Degree in Law, 1962). Judge (Giudice Conciliatore), Campione d'Italia, 1985—. Legal Consultant to the Comune di Campione d'Italia, 1984—. *Member:* Milan Bar Association; International Rules Commission I.Y.R.U., London, England. *LANGUAGES:* Italian, French and English.

RAFFAELE DE FALCO, born Bergamo, Italy, August 29, 1945; admitted, 1973, Italy. *Education:* University of Milan (Degree in Law [Hons.], 1970). *Member:* Milan Bar Association. *LANGUAGES:* Italian, French, English and Spanish.

HORST GROMPE, born Darmstadt, Germany, February 6, 1955; admitted, 1983, Federal Republic of Germany (Not admitted in Italy). *Education:* University of Wuerzburg, Germany (Degree in Law, 1983). *Member:* Munich Bar Association; A.I.J.A.; Deutsch Italienische Juristen vereinigung. *LANGUAGES:* German, French, Italian and English.

CARLO H. MASTELLONE, born London, England, March 2, 1955; admitted, 1983, Italy. *Education:* University of Florence (Degree in Laws [Hons.], 1978); Queen Mary College, University of London, England (LL.M., 1979). Research Fellow, European University Institute, Florence, 1983-1986. *Member:* Florence Bar Association; International & Comparative Law Association; A.I.J.A. (Also practicing individually in Florence). *LANGUAGES:* English, Italian and French.

GIANANTONIO PELLEGRINI-CISLAGHI, born Milan, Italy, July 27, 1959; admitted, 1987, Italy. *Education:* University of Milan (Degree in Law). *Member:* Milan Bar Association. *LANGUAGES:* Italian, English and Portuguese.

GIORGIO GUERRA, born Milan, Italy, June 22, 1962; admitted, 1994, Italy. *Education:* Catholic University of Milan (J.D., 1989). *Member:* Milan Bar Association. *LANGUAGES:* Italian and English.

Languages: Italian, English, French, Spanish and German.

PESCE, FRIGNANI, PASTORE & RUBEN LAW FIRM

Established in 1947

VIA DEI GIARDINI, 4
I-20121 MILAN, ITALY
Telephone: 39-2-29003140 / 6575143
Fax: 39-2-6554886

Turin Office: via Argonne, 1, I-10133. Telephone: 39-11-6602302/6602151. Fax: 39-11-6601884.
Vienna Office: Kohlmarkt, 4/19, A-1010. Telephone: 43-1-5338437-5335856. Fax: 43-1-533585675.

General Legal Practice, International Contracts, Corporations, Banking Law, Acquisitions, Patent Trademark and Unfair Competition Law, Copyright Law, EEC Law, Antitrust Regulations, Transportation, Insurance and Reinsurance, International Private and Commercial Law, Family Law, Suretyships and Credit Protection, Product Liability.

FIRM PROFILE: The present Firm is the result of a merger, occured in 1990, of a Milan firm established in 1947 and a Turin firm established in 1982. It offers a full range of legal services and includes law professors and highly specialized lawyers, particularly skilled in commercial law, EEC law and international trade law. The client base is world-wide, mostly rooted in Western and Eastern Europe and the Americas.

MEMBERS OF FIRM IN MILAN

ANGELO PESCE, born Florence, December 30, 1925; admitted, 1947, Italy; 1959, Supreme Court. *Education:* University of Milan (J.D., 1945). Author: "Foreign Banks and the Italian Currency Law," 1968; "The Directors of the Corporation," 1969; "The Balance Sheet," 1980; "The Bank Guarantee," 1982; "International Contracts of Carriage by Road," 1984; "International Contracts of Carriage," 1994; "Products Liability," 1995. *Member:* International and American Bar Associations; Licensing Executive Society;

(This Listing Continued)

Association Internationale pour la Protection de la Propriété Industrielle. *LANGUAGES:* German, English, French. *PRACTICE AREAS:* International Commercial Law; Company Law; EEC Law; Transportation.

PAOLA PASTORE, born Sanremo, Italy, September 27, 1943; admitted, 1982, Italy. *Education:* University of Milan (J.D., 1967). *Member:* International Bar Association. *LANGUAGES:* English. *PRACTICE AREAS:* Family Law; Credit Collection.

MAURIZIO RUBEN, born Alexandria, Egypt, October 30, 1954; admitted, 1981, Italy. *Education:* University of Milan (J.D., 1979); McGeorge School of Law, University of the Pacific, Sacramento, CA (Diploma of Advanced International Legal Studies, 1988). *Member:* International Bar Association; Licensing Executive Society; International Association for the Protection of Industrial Property. *LANGUAGES:* English, French. *PRACTICE AREAS:* Patent, Trademark and Unfair Competition Law; Commercial Law; Corporations; Antitrust Regulations.

MYRIAM V. PESCE, born Milan, Italy, February 25, 1957; admitted, 1987, Milan. *Education:* University of Milan (J.D., 1983). *LANGUAGES:* English. *PRACTICE AREAS:* Commercial Law; International Private Law.

EMANUELA PESCE, born Milan, Italy, February 24, 1959; admitted, 1990, Milan. *Education:* University of Milan (J.D., 1985). *LANGUAGES:* English. *PRACTICE AREAS:* Labour Law.

ALESSANDRO PESCE, born Lugano, Switzerland, July 18, 1962. *Education:* University of Milan (J.D., 1991). *LANGUAGES:* German, French, English.

RICCARDO PRETI, born Monza, Italy, March 9, 1966. *Education:* University of Milan (J.D., 1992). *LANGUAGES:* English.

GIOVANNA IANNI, born Naples, Italy, February 24, 1967. *Education:* University of Milan (J.D., 1993). *LANGUAGES:* English, German , French and Spanish.

Languages: Italian, German, English, French and Spanish.

PIERGROSSI VILLA MANCA GRAZIADEI

VIA FESTA DEL PERDONO 10
20122 MILAN, ITALY
Telephone: +39-2-58.303.657 (multiple)
Telefax: +39-2-58.303.818
Telex: 333379 PERVIL I
Cable Address: PIERVILLA MILANO

Rome, Italy Office: Via dei Gracchi 320, 00192 Rome. Telephone: +39-6-3215901. Fax: +39-6-3213218.
Edinburgh, Scotland Office: 3 Walker Street, Edinburgh, EH3 7JY. Telephone: +44-131-2267722. Fax: +44-131-2267887.

General Civil and Commercial Practice. Acquisitions, Corporate, Licensing, Patents and Trademarks, International Law. Litigation. Arbitration. Environmental Law.

MEMBERS OF FIRM

GIANNI MANCA, born Genoa, Italy, July 21, 1924; admitted, 1952, Italy. *Education:* Rome University (J.D., 1948).

ALBERTO PIERGROSSI, born Milan, Italy, August 8, 1941; admitted, 1966, Italy. *Education:* University of Milan Law School, Italy (J.D., 1963); Harvard Law School (LL.M., 1967). Professor of Law, University of Milan Law School.

FRANCO P. VILLA, born Legnano, Italy, March 3, 1941; admitted, 1968, Italy. *Education:* University of Milan Law School, Italy (J.D., 1965); Reading University, England (M.A., 1967).

STEFANO M. CIMA, born Milan, Italy, April 4, 1954; admitted, 1980, Italy. *Education:* University of Milan Law School, Italy (J.D., 1977); University of Milan School of Political Science, Italy (1987).

FRANCESCO AMICUCCI, born Rome, Italy, February 25, 1955; admitted, 1985, Italy. *Education:* University of Rome Law School, Italy (J.D., 1980) University of Charleston, West Virginia (Diploma of Business Law, 1986).

ANTONIO J. MANCA GRAZIADEI, born Rome, Italy, April 5, 1958; admitted, 1989, Italy. *Education:* University of Rome Law School (J.D., 1985).

(This Listing Continued)

FABIO WEILBACHER, born Genoa, Italy, November 3, 1960; admitted, 1992, Italy. *Education:* Catholic University of Milan Law School, Italy (J.D., 1984).

RICCARDO BUIZZA, born Varese, Italy, February 26, 1962; admitted, 1991, Italy. *Education:* University of Milan Law School, Italy (J.D., 1985).

ASSOCIATES

ANTONIO F. LOMBARDO, born Trapani, Italy, August 17, 1965; admitted, 1992, Italy. *Education:* Luiss University of Rome Law School, Italy (J.D., 1989).

FRANCESCO M. ALEANDRI, born Rome, Italy, February 14, 1965; admitted, 1992, Italy. *Education:* University of Rome Law School, Italy (J.D., 1989).

MASSIMILIANO PINNA, born Sassari, October 14, 1964; admitted, 1992, Italy. *Education:* University of Sassari Law School, Italy (J.D., 1989).

LORENZO DA PRA GALANTI, born Milan, Italy, June 16, 1963; admitted, 1994, Italy. *Education:* University of Milan Law School, Italy (J.D., 1991).

OF COUNSEL

ARMANDO PIERGROSSI, born Milan, Italy, June 14, 1914; admitted, 1946, Italy. *Education:* University of Milan Law School, Italy (J.D., 1937).

Languages: Italian, English, French, German and Spanish.

STUDIO AVV. GIOVANNI M. PIRAS

Established in 1980

VIA CORRIDONI, 37
20122 MILAN, ITALY
Telephone: (02) 76.01.31.53/63/73
Telex: 332230 PIRAS I
Telefax: (02) 78.13.19

General Civil and Corporate Practice, Litigation, International Business Law, Bankruptcy, Factoring Banking and Foreign Investments. Mergers and Acquisitions.

GIOVANNI M. PIRAS, born Rimini, Italy, July 25, 1946; admitted, 1972, Milan; 1974, Italy; 1988, Supreme Court. *Education:* Milan University (LL.D., 1971); New York University (LL.M., Corporate Law, 1975). *Member:* Italian Bar Association; International Bar Association. *LANGUAGES:* Italian, English and French. *PRACTICE AREAS:* Civil; Corporate Litigation; International and Foreign Investments; Banking and Factoring Practice.

GIOVANNI BREGANI, born Milan, Italy, May 11, 1958; admitted, 1987, Milan. *Education:* Catholic University of Milan Law School (LL.D., 1986). *LANGUAGES:* Italian, English and French. *PRACTICE AREAS:* Factoring Litigation and Bankruptcy.

GAETANO G. FEDELI, born Genua, Italy, August 3, 1964; admitted, 1989, Milan. *Education:* Catholic University of Milan Law School (LL.D., 1988). *LANGUAGES:* Italian, German and English. *PRACTICE AREAS:* Civil and International Transactions.

CRISTINA J. DE HAAG, born New York, U.S.A., February 2, 1968; admitted, 1992, Milan. *Education:* University of Milan Law School (LL.D., 1992); Harvard Summer School (1992). *LANGUAGES:* Italian and English. *PRACTICE AREAS:* Civil and International Litigation.

FRANCESCO MARUFFI, born Milan, Italy, October 23, 1970; admitted, 1994, Milan. *Education:* University of Milan Law School (LL.D., 1994). *LANGUAGES:* Italian, English, German and Spanish. *PRACTICE AREAS:* Civil and International Litigation.

OF COUNSEL

BRUNO NASCIMBENE, born Gallarate (Varese), Italy, April 4, 1946; admitted, 1976, Italy; 1986, Supreme Court. *Education:* University of Milan Law School (1969) and Political Sciences School (1974). Professor: International EEC Law, University of Genoa, 1982; EEC Law, University of Milan, 1990. Visiting Scholar Harvard School, 1977-1978. *PRACTICE AREAS:* EEC and International Law.

Languages: Italian, English, French, German and Spanish

PIROLA PENNUTO ZEI & ASSOCIATI

Established in 1980

Studio di Consulenza Tributaria e Legale
VIA VITTOR PISANI, 16
20124 MILAN, ITALY
Telephone: (39)(2)669.951
Telefax: (39)(2)669.1800

Rome Office: Via del Quirinale, 26-00187. Telephone: (39)(6)487.1395. Fax: (39)(6)482.7133.
Turin Office: Corso V. Emanuele, 95-10128. Telephone: (39)(11)562.6226. Fax: (39)(11)562.7062.
Padua Office: Largo Europa, 16-35137. Telephone (39)(48)875.6022. Fax: (39)(49)662.703.
Bologna Office: Via S. Stefano, 97-40125. Telephone: (39)(51)341.501. Fax: (39)(51)341.833.
Brescia Office: Via Cefalonia, 55-25125. Telephone: (39)(30)242.2407. Fax: (39)(30)242.2408.

General Taxation and Corporate Practice, Domestic and International Contracts, Mergers and Acquisitions, Domestic and European Antitrust Law and Compliance, Private and Commercial Law, International Tax Planning, Bankruptcy and Special Receivership Procedures, Labor and Social Security Law and Practice, Banking and Financial Law; Securities Regulations, Domestic and International Arbitration and Litigation, Intellectual Property Law, White Collar Crimes.

MEMBERS OF FIRM

GIUSEPPE PIROLA, born Cernusco sul Naviglio, Italy, August 16, 1947. admitted to practice before Taxation Courts, 1970. *Education:* Tax and Business Consultant, Milan (1969). (Resident, Milan Office). *LANGUAGES:* Italian and French.

MARIO MORETTINI, born Montefano, Italy, November 17, 1943. admitted to practice before Taxation Courts, 1980. *Education:* Catholic University of Milan (Degree in Economics, 1970). (Resident, Rome and Milan Offices). *LANGUAGES:* Italian, English and French.

MASSIMO CREMONA, born Busto Arsizio, Italy, April 3, 1959. admitted to practice before Taxation Courts, 1986. *Education:* Catholic University of Milan (Degree in Economics, 1983). Author: Articles on Transfer Pricing and other International Taxation Issues. (Resident, Milan Office). *LANGUAGES:* Italian and English.

FULVIO PASTORE ALINANTE, born Naples, Italy, April 27, 1959; admitted, 1985, Rome; 1991, Italy. *Education:* University of Naples (J.D., magna cum laude, 1982); Seminar in American Legal Studies, Salzburg (1985); Fulbright Scholar, Columbia University School of Law, New York (LL.M., 1988). Contributing Editor: "La Giurisprudenza Italiana," National Law Review, 1985-1987. Foreign Associate, Bryan Cave, Washington, D.C., Saint Louis and Los Angeles, 1988-1989. *Member:* Fulbright Alumni Association, Italy. (Resident, Milan Office). *LANGUAGES:* Italian and English.

ANDREA GOTTARDO, born Venice, Italy, March 24, 1960; admitted, 1989, Padua. *Education:* University of Padua (J.D., magna cum laude, 1985). (Resident, Padua and Milan Offices). *LANGUAGES:* Italian, English and French.

MATTEO CANESTRINI, born Turin, Italy, September 19, 1959; admitted, 1990, Milan. *Education:* State University of Milan (J.D., magna cum laude, 1985). Visiting Foreign Lawyer, McDermott, Will & Emery, Chicago, 1990. *Member:* American-Italian Law Association, Milan. (Resident, Milan Office). *LANGUAGES:* Italian, English and French.

DONATELLA CUNGI, born Petropolis, Brazil, March 9, 1961; admitted, 1990, Milan. *Education:* State University of Milan (J.D., 1985). Research Assistant in Comparative Criminal Procedure, State University of Milan, 1985-1990. Research Assistant in Comparative Law, Creighton University School of Law, Omaha, 1992-1993. Co-Author: "The Great Reform of Italian Criminal Procedure: What Remains Today, After Three Years of Enforcement, of Its 'Accusatorial Soul'?", U.S.A., 1993. Visiting Foreign Lawyer, Dorsey & Whitney, Minneapolis, 1989. *Member:* American Chamber of Commerce in Italy; Professional Women Association, Milan. (Resident, Milan Office). *LANGUAGES:* Italian, English, French and Portuguese.

MARZIA BARBARA REGINATO, born Genoa, Italy, August 17, 1959; admitted, 1993, Treviso. *Education:* University of Trieste (J.D., 1990). (Resident, Padua Office). *LANGUAGES:* Italian and English.

(This Listing Continued)

PIROLA PENNUTO ZEI & ASSOCIATI, Milan—
Continued

COLIN ROBERT JAMIESON, born Edinburgh, U.K., August 29, 1962; admitted, 1987, as Solicitor of the Supreme Court of England and Wales (Not admitted in Italy). *Education:* University of Kent at Canterbury (B.A., Hons., 1983). Co-Author: "Taxation of Joint Ventures in Land," KeyHaven Publications, U.K., 1992. (Resident, Milan Office). *LANGUAGES:* English, Italian and French.

EDOARDO BARATELLA, born Venice-Mestre, Italy, October 29, 1965; admitted, 1994, Venice. *Education:* University of Padua (J.D., 1991). Summer Trainee, Clifford Chance, London, 1993. (Resident, MIlan Office). *LANGUAGES:* Italian and English.

PISANO, DE VITO, MAIANO & CATUCCI

Established in 1961

PIAZZA DEL DUOMO, 20
20122 MILAN, ITALY
Telephone: (02) 878281
Telex: 321289 PDMCMI
Telefax: (02) 861375

Rome, Italy Office: Via Giosue Borsi, 3. Telephone: (06) 8079087 Telex: 626448. Telefax: (06) 8078407

General Domestic and International Business Practice, including Commercial, Corporate, Securities and Corporate Finance, Venture Capital, Commercial Litigation, Arbitration, EEC Law, Taxation, Intellectual Property, Maritime and Aviation Law.

MEMBERS OF FIRM

PAOLO G. PISANO, born Chicago, Illinois, September 16, 1915; admitted, 1945, Italy; 1948, Italian Supreme Court. *Education:* Liceo Umberto, Palermo (A.B., 1933); University of Rome, School of Jurisprudence (J.S.D., 1937); University of Florence, School of Political Science (P.S .D., 1938). Assistant Professor of International Law, University of Rome, 1938-1945. *Member:* Rome and International Bar Associations. (Also at Rome Office). *LANGUAGES:* English, Italian, French and Spanish.

PAOLO V. DE VITO, born Rome, Italy, July 10, 1953. admitted to practice, 1977, Italy; admitted to the bar, 1980, Italy. *Education:* University of Rome, Faculty of Law (Doctor Juridical Science, Maxima, 1977); University of California Dans-Berkeley (Orientation in American Law Program, 1993). *Member:* Rome Bar Association. (Also at Rome Office). *LANGUAGES:* Italian and English.

MAURIZIO M. A. MAIANO, born Sanremo, Italy, December 20, 1956. admitted to practice, 1979, Italy; admitted to the bar, 1983, Italy. *Education:* University of London, Exeter College (Advanced Certificate of Education in Economics and British Constitutional Law, 1975); University of Milan, Faculty of Law (Doctor Juridical Science, Maxima, 1979); McGeorge School of Law, Salzburg, Austria (Diploma in Advanced International Legal Studies, 1987); University of the Pacific, McGeorge School of Law, Sacramento, California (LL.M., in Business and Taxation - Transnational Practice, 1989); Bocconi University, Milan (Master in Corporate Taxation, 1990). Visiting Attorney, Attia, Bartel, Eng & Torngren, Sacramento, California, 1988. *Member:* State Bar of California (Member, International Section); Milan and American Bar Associations; A.I.J.A. *LANGUAGES:* English, Italian and French.

ANTONIO CATUCCI, born Palagianello, Italy, June 14, 1956. admitted to practice, 1979, Italy; admitted to the bar 1983, Italy. *Education:* University of Rome, Faculty of Law (Doctor Juridical Science, 1979); Harvard Law School (P.I.L., 1991 and 1992). *Member:* Milan Bar Association; International Bar Association. *LANGUAGES:* Italian, English and Spanish..

COUNSELS

MASSIMO DE CAROLIS, born Milan, Italy, August 15, 1940; admitted, 1965, Italy. *Education:* Catholic University of Milan, Faculty of Law (Doctor Juridical Science, 1962). Member of Italian Parliament, 1976-1983. Secretary of Parliamentary Investigating Committee on Misconduct of Ministers, 1976-1979. Member, Foreign Affairs Committee of the Italian Parliament, 1979-1983. Member, North Atlantic Treaty Organization Assembly, 1980-1983. Municipal Councillor, City of Milan, 1970-1980 and 1990-1993. Member, Board of Advisors, Montedison Spa, 1971-1978. Member, Board of Directors, Montedison U.S.A., Inc., N.Y., 1978-1982. Member, Board of Directors, Navamont, Inc., N.Y., 1978-1980. Member,

(This Listing Continued)

Board of Directors, Chemstar International, Inc., N.Y., 1980-1984. Managing Director, Fidinvest Spa, Milan, 1967—. (Also at Rome Office). *LANGUAGES:* Italian and English.

CATHERINE C. PALO, born Rochester, New York, August 11, 1959; admitted, 1986, New York. *Education:* Niagara University (B.A. cum laude, 1981); Syracuse University (J.D., 1985); University of the Pacific, McGeorge School of Law (LL.M., Business and Taxation-Transnational Practice, 1988).

MARINA TAGER, Special Legal Counsel for Eastern European Countries. (Also at Rome Office). *LANGUAGES:* Russian, Italian, German, French and English.

ASSOCIATES

LAURA CAVALLARI, admitted to the bar, 1993, Italy. University of Milan, Tutor of Civil Law.

MARCO VINCIGUERRA

GIOVANNI IMBERGAMO, admitted to the bar, 1993, Italy. (Also at Rome Office).

STEFANO BOTTARO (Also at Rome Office).

MARIA ELENA LORETI (Also at Rome Office).

ROBERTA LEZZI (Also at Rome Office).

TAX AND BUSINESS CONSULTANT

Wilson Gomitoni

Languages: Italian, English, French, Portuguese, Spanish, German and Russian.

STUDIO LEGALE POJAGHI

Established in 1964

2, VIA VISCONTI DI MODRONE
I-20122 MILAN, ITALY
Telephone: (02) 7600 8947/7600 2655
Facsimile: (02) 7601 3950

Contract and Commercial Law, Copyright, Trademark and Intellectual Property, Arbitration and Litigation, Bankruptcy and Insolvency, Companies and Corporations, Competition and Anti-Trust, Computer, Communication and Information Law, Employment and Labour Law, Entertainment, Family and Matrimonial.

FIRM PROFILE: Avv. Alberto Pojaghi, senior partner of the firm, began practicing law in 1964. Since its foundation, the Firm has gradually and continuously expanded its practice, so that, in its present configuration, it covers all the main areas in civil and commercial law (including company acquisitions and labour law), arbitration and litigation, copyright (including entertainment and software protection) and competition law.

The Firm operates through its series of professional links in every major Italian city, in addition to its associated Offices in Brussels, Paris and Rome.

The Firm took part in the creation of the Italian law magazine "L'Europa dell CEE", whose main subjects are legislative and judicial EEC activities, and cooperated for many years in its publication.

MEMBERS OF FIRM

AVV. ALBERTO POJAGHI, born Milan, December 2, 1938; admitted, 1964, Milan; 1970, Italy. *Education:* University of Milan (J.D., Jurisprudence, 1962). Member of the Permanent Advisory Committee for Copyright established at the Italian Prime Ministership. *Member:* International Literary and Artistic Association (ALAI); International Association for the Advancement of Teaching and Research in Intellectual Property (ATRIP); International Association of Entertainment Lawyers (IAEL); International Bar Association (IBA); Union Internationale des Avocats (UIA); European Association of Lawyers (AEA). *LANGUAGES:* Italian, French and English.

AVV. GIULIANA PAGANUZZI, born Verona, July 7, 1955; admitted, 1983, Milan; 1992, Italy. *Education:* University of Milan. *LANGUAGES:* Italian French and English.

DR. PROC. ANTONELLA RIZZI, born Varese, July 1, 1961; admitted, 1986, Milan. *Education:* University of Milan. *LANGUAGES:* Italian, English, Spanish and French.

(This Listing Continued)

DR. GIANLUCA POJAGHI, born Milan, November 15, 1964. *Education:* University of Milan. *LANGUAGES:* Italian, English and French.

DR. FRANCESCA POJAGHI, born Milan, December 13, 1965. *Education:* University of Milan. *LANGUAGES:* Italian and French.

ASSOCIATES

DR. PROC. GIULIANA DURAND, born Milan, December 11, 1966; admitted, 1995, Milan. *Education:* University of Milan. *LANGUAGES:* Italian, German and French.

DR. PROC. FRANCESCA LAURINI, born Naples, December 17, 1966; admitted, 1993, Milan. *Education:* University of Naples. *LANGUAGES:* Italian, English and French.

DR. PROC. ANDREA RUDELLI, born Milan, August 7, 1964; admitted, 1995, Milan. *Education:* University of Milan. *LANGUAGES:* Italian, German, English and French.

STUDIO LEGALE
PORTALE VISCONTI

VIA SANTA VALERIA 3
20123 MILAN, ITALY
Telephone: (02) 72000227
Telefax: (02) 72000789

International and General Practice, Corporation and Commercial Law, Mergers and Acquisitions, Establishment of Subsidiaries and Branches, Construction Law, Banking Law, Bankruptcy Law, Arbitration.

MEMBERS OF FIRM

GIUSEPPE B. PORTALE, born Biancavilla, Italy, May 16, 1938; admitted, 1963, Italy. *Education:* Catholic University of Milan (Dr. iur.). Professor of Commercial Law, Catholic University of Milan, 1976—. *Member:* Bar Association of Milan. *LANGUAGES:* Italian and German.

GIUSEPPE VISCONTI, born Iseo, Italy, November 12, 1944; admitted, 1971, Italy. *Education:* State University of Florence (Dr. iur.); Columbia University (Special Student). Professional Training in New York, 1974. *Member:* Bar Association of Milan; International Bar Association. *LANGUAGES:* Italian, German, English and French.

ASSOCIATES

ALDO A. DOLMETTA, born Milan, Italy, March 24, 1951; admitted, 1978, Italy. *Education:* Catholic University of Milan (Dr. iur.). Temporary Professor of Private Law, Catholic University of Milan, 1993—. *Member:* Bar Association of Milan. *LANGUAGES:* Italian and French.

ROBERTO MORONI, born Milan, Italy, July 15, 1956; admitted, 1982, Italy. *Education:* State University of Pavia (Dr. iur.). *Member:* Bar Association of Voghera. *LANGUAGES:* Italian and English.

NICOLETTA SERSALE, born Torino, Italy, March 20, 1961; admitted, 1986, Italy. *Education:* State University of Pavia (Dr. iur.). *Member:* Bar Association of Pavia. *LANGUAGES:* Italian, French and English.

NICOLA RIVA, born Thiene, Italy, November 29, 1965; admitted, 1990, Italy. *Education:* State University of Milan (Dr. iur.); University of Wisconsin (Introduction to American Law). Professional Training in Hamburg and Paris. *LANGUAGES:* Italian, German, French and English.

Languages: Italian, German, English and French.

QUATTRONE CUCCHI LAZZATI &
SCURIATTI
STUDIO LEGALE E TRIBUTARISTA

VIA FONTANA 16
20122 MILAN, ITALY
Telephone: (2) 5460991
Fax: (2) 5460970

Rome, Italy Office: Via Filippo Civinini 111, 00197. Telephone: (6) 8085460-8081148. Fax: (6) 8072793.

(This Listing Continued)

Corporate, Banking and Securities Law, Tax Law, Subsidiaries and Joint Ventures, Litigation.

PARTNER

Avv. Marcello Lazzati

ASSOCIATES

Dott. Stefano Dell'Acqua
Dott. Raffaella Balestrieri

Languages: Italian, English and French.

STUDIO RICCI

Established in 1946

1, VIA PRIVATA C. BATTISTI
20122 MILAN, ITALY
Telephone: 0039-2-59901030
Fax: 0039-2-59901260

Civil Litigation, Corporate and Commercial Law, Labour, Family Law, Inheritance and Real Property.

MEMBERS OF FIRM

CARLO ALBERTO RICCI, *Member:* Milan Law Association. *LANGUAGES:* Italian, English and French. *PRACTICE AREAS:* General Civil Practice and Litigation; Corporate and Commercial Law; Contracts; Inheritance; Real Property; Arbitration; Bankruptcy; Agency and Distributorship.

BETTINA THIERRY, *Member:* Milan Law Association. *LANGUAGES:* Italian, English, French and German. *PRACTICE AREAS:* Civil Practice and Litigation; Family Law; Real Property; Medical Malpractice; Personal Injury; Insurance.

PAOLO BRUNO PULZE, *Member:* Milan Bar Association. *PRACTICE AREAS:* Civil Practice and Litigation; Labour.

STUDIO RUBINO-SAMMARTANO
E ASSOCIATI

Established in 1969

VIALE CASSIODORO 1
20145 MILAN, ITALY
Telephone: 4819041; 4984729; 4980554
Telex: 324257 DEFEND I
Fax: 48008277
Cable Address: "Defensor"

International Litigation Law, Arbitration, Trade Law. Construction Law. Sale of Goods and Acquisitions.

MAURO RUBINO-SAMMARTANO, born Milan, Italy, January 16, 1937; admitted, 1961, Italy; 1986, Paris. *Education:* Catholic University of Milan (J.D., 1958). *Author:* "Bibliographical Dictionary of the Library of the Bar," Milan, Giuffre', 1970; "Commercial Agency in Italy," in "Rights and Liabilities in Commercial Agency," Kluwer 1984; Commentary, "Defects, Delay, Prices and Subcontracting in Civil Law," in "Selected Problems of Construction Law: International Approach," University Press, Fribourg, 1983; The part on Civil Procedure in Italy of World Litigation Law and Practice, ed. Myrick, Matthew Bender, New York, 1985; The Lack of Conformity, in "A Survey of the International Sale of Goods," ed. Campbell, Lafili and Gevurtz, Kluwer, 1985; "Drafting and Enforcing Contracts in Civil and Common Law Jurisdictions," (Gen. Ed. K. Yelpaala, M. Rubino-Sammartano, D. Campbell, Kluwer, 1986); "International Arbitration Law," (Kluwer, 1990); "Public Policy in Transnational Relationships, co-gen ed (Kluwer, 1991); Il diritto dell'arbitrato (interno) (Domestic Arbitration Law) Cedam, 1991; "Warranties in Cross Border Acquisitions," (Gen. ed.) Erahaus & Trotterman, London, 1994. *Articles;* "The Channel Tunnel and the Tronc Commun Doctrine," J. Intl Arb. Vol. No 3 (1993); "Amiable Compositeur (Joint Mandate to Settle) and Ex Bono et Aequo (Discretional Authority to Mitigate Strict Law) Apparent Synonyms Revisited," J.Intl. Arb. Vol. 9 No. 1 (1992); "Is Arbitration to be just a Luxury Clinic?" 7 J.Intl Arb. 3, 25. "An International Arbitral Court of Appeal as an Alternative to Long attacks and Recognition Proceedings," Journal of International Arbitration, 181 (1989); "International and Foreign Arbitration," Journal of International Arbitration, 84 (1988); "Le Tronc Commun des Lois Nationales en Présence," Revue de l'Arbitrage, 2, 133 (1987); "Third Generation Arbitration," Journal

(This Listing Continued)

STUDIO RUBINO-SAMMARTANO E ASSOCIATI, Milan—Continued

of International Arbitration Vol. 4, no. 1 (1987); "The Role of the Engineer, Myth and Reality," International Business Lawyer, 81 (1986); "Rules of Evidence in International Arbitration," Journal of International Arbitration, 1986 (1987); "Supplies by order of the Court," (It) Il Foro Padano, I 165 (1984); "Examination of Witnesses and Articles of proof," (It) Il Foro Padano II, 61 (1983); "Telex, Telecopier and Computer Messages," (It) Il Foro Padano, I, 87 (1983); "Localization of Credits, Effects of Foreign Nationalizations on Them, Law Applicable to Guarantees," (It) Il Foro Padano, I, 139 (1983); "The Civil Law Approach to Evidence," The Arbitration Journal, 331 (1983); "International Construction Agreements - Employer's Breach and Consequent Right of the Contractor to Withhold Delivery of Site," Intl. Bus. Law, 1943 (1983); "The Arbitral Referee," (It) Il Foro Padano, II, 35, 1982; "International Construction Agreements; Extent of the Owner's Interference and Cases Where the Agreement Becomes Null and Void," Intl. Bus. Lawyer, 457 (1981) and Il Foro Padano, 457 (1980); "Multi-Party Arbitration," Intl. Bus. Lawyer, 436 (1981); "Performance Bonds and Injunctions," The Law Society Gazette, February 4, 1981; "Injunctions in International Contracts," (It) Il Foro Padano, I, 245 (1979); "The Keban Arbitration," The Arbitration Journal, 241 (1980). Offices: President, Union Internationale des Avocats; Secretary-General Emeritus of the Federation of European Bars; Co-Chairman, The Mediterranean and Middle East Institute of Arbitration; Chairman, Italian Section of Cour Européenne d'Arbitrage. Chairman Emeritus, Committee on International Construction Contracts and Immediate Past Chairman, International Sales and Related Commercial Transactions Committee of the International Bar Association. Former Council Member, International Bar Association. Fellow, Chartered Institute of Arbitrators. Member, Arbitration Committee of the International Chamber of Commerce. Chairman Emeritus, International Committee of the Milan Bar. Member, Advisory Board, Journal of International Arbitration. Member, Advisory Board, International Programme, McGeorge School of Law, University of Sacramento, California. Co-editor of Il Foro Padano and of Mediterranean and Middle East Arbitration Quarterly. Past Recorder of Desio, 1964-1969. Past President, European Society of Construction Law. Past President, Italian Society for Construction Law. Lecturer, International Arbitration, University of Padua, 1987-1989. Past Directeur des Travaux of Union Internationale des Avocats. LANGUAGES: English, French, Italian. PRACTICE AREAS: Contract Law; Arbitration; International Litigation; Construction; Acquisitions; Sale of Goods.

ENRICO CARUSO, born Agrigento, Italy, February 19, 1959; admitted, 1990, Italy. Education: University of Palermo (J.D., summa cum laude, 1982); Voluntary Assistant in Private Law (Catholic University, Milan, from 1989). LANGUAGES: French, Italian. PRACTICE AREAS: Contract Law; Company Law.

LUISA ZANFRAMUNDO, born Torino, Italy, December 23, 1965; admitted, 1994, Italy. Education: University of Milan (Universite Statale) (1989). LANGUAGES: English, French and Italian. PRACTICE AREAS: Conflict of Laws.

OF COUNSEL

RICCARDO VILLATA, born Parma, Italy, August 17, 1941; admitted, 1967, Italy. Education: Universita' Statale Milan (J.D., 1964). Full Professor of Administrative Law. LANGUAGES: French and Italian. PRACTICE AREAS: Administrative Law.

RICCARDO MUSATTI, born Padua, April 19, 1933; admitted, 1959, Italy. Education: Universita' Statale, Milan (J.D., 1957). LANGUAGES: French, Italian. PRACTICE AREAS: Labour Law.

AMALIA PARDO, born Milan, Italy, October 29, 1934; admitted, 1962, Italy. Education: Universita' Statale (J.D., 1960). LANGUAGES: French, Italian. PRACTICE AREAS: Landlord and Tenant; Real Estate.

ANNA DANOVI GALIZIA, born Trento, November 18, 1941; admitted, 1968, Italy. Education: Universita Statale di Milano (J.D., 1964). LANGUAGES: French, Italian. PRACTICE AREAS: Family Law.

MASSIMO L. FANTECHI, born Florence, Italy, December 26, 1957; admitted, 1988, New York. Education: University of Urbino (J.D., summa cum laude, 1983); Columbia University, Visiting Student (1984); University of Pennsylvania (LL.M., 1986) University of Pennsylvania Law School (presently enrolled in S.J.D. Program). Lecturer: International Arbitration Continuing Professional Development program, The Chartered Institute of Arbitrators; Arbitration Law, University of Bologna, 1993. Fellow, The Chartered Institute of Arbitrators, Member, Professional Development Committee, The Chartered Institute of Arbitrators. Member: Institut du

(This Listing Continued)

Droit et des Pratiques des Affaires Internationales de la Chamber de Commerce Internationale; American Arbitration Association (AAA); Italian Association for Arbitrato (AIA); International Bar Association; American Bar Association. LANGUAGES: Italian, English and French.

Languages: Italian, English and French.

RUCELLAI & RAFFAELLI

VIA MONTE NAPOLEONE, 18
20121 MILAN, ITALY
Telephone: 78.33.41; 79.49.51
Telex: 313413 ACTIO I
Telefax: 783524

Rome, Italy Office: Via del Poggio, Laurentino, 66, 00144 Roma. Telephone: 5914351. Telefax: 5914350.

General Civil, Corporate and International Practice.

MEMBERS OF FIRM

COSIMO RUCELLAI, born Florence, Italy, September 29, 1933; admitted to bar, 1957, Italy. Education: Florence University (LL.D., 1955); Harvard Law School (LL.M., 1959). LANGUAGES: Italian, English, French and German.

ENRICO ADRIANO RAFFAELLI, born Asolo, Italy, August 15, 1949; admitted to bar, 1976, Italy. Education: Milan University (LL.D., 1973). Chairman, Commission on Antitrust Law-UAE (European Lawyers' Union). LANGUAGES: Italian, English and French.

ASSOCIATES

ANDREA VISCHI, born Milan, Italy, July 18, 1959; admitted to bar, 1989, Italy. Education: Milan University. LANGUAGES: Italian and English.

FRANCESCA ROMANA TURITTO, born Rome, Italy, December 10, 1958. admitted to bar, 1985, Italy. Education: Rome University. LANGUAGES: Italian, English and French.

MADDALENA PALLADINO, born Milan, Italy, September 30, 1963. admitted to bar, 1992, Italy. Education: Milan University. LANGUAGES: Italian and English.

GERARDO PIRATONI, born Bari, Italy, January 28, 1958. admitted to bar, 1991, Italy. Education: Bari University. LANGUAGES: Italian and English.

CATALDO PALUMBO, born Monza, Italy, March 22, 1965; admitted to bar, 1995. Education: Milan University. LANGUAGES: Italian, English and French.

ENRICO SISTI, born Parma, Italy, July 5, 1966; admitted to practice, 1992. Education: Parma University. LANGUAGES: Italian, English and French.

GILBERTO NAVA, born Milan, Italy, January 3, 1965; admitted to practice, 1992. Education: Milan University. LANGUAGES: Italian and English.

EMANUELA TARDELLA, born Recanati, Italy, October 26, 1967. admitted to practice, 1992. Education: Milan University. LANGUAGES: Italian, English, French and German.

FRANCESCO ROCHLITZER, born Pavia, Italy, January 8, 1966. admitted to practice, 1990; admitted to New York Bar, 1992. Education: Pavia University; Fordham Law School (LL.M., 1992). LANGUAGES: Italian and English.

CECILIA VICEDOMINI, born Rome, Italy, July 26, 1965. admitted to bar, 1995. Education: Rome University; George Washington University (LL.M., 1991-1992). LANGUAGES: Italian, English and French.

ALESSANDRO TEODORO BELLOFIORE BRIOTTONE, born Brescia, Italy, July 7, 1967; admitted to practice, 1993. Education: Parma University. LANGUAGES: Italian, English and French.

MONICA ZANCAN, born Verona, Italy, May 28, 1966; admitted to practice, 1994. Education: Milan University. LANGUAGES: Italian, English, French and Spanish.

Languages: Italian, English, French, German and Spanish

STUDIO LEGALE SABELLI

VIA S. MAURILIO, 20
20123 MILAN, ITALY
Telephone: 02-8056042
Telefax: 02-8692571

Rome, Italy Office: Via Parigi, 11, 00185. Telephone: 06-4817141. Cable Address: "Eulaw Roma". Telex: 622641 EULAW I. Telefax: (06) 4884566.

General and Civil Practice. Corporation, Commercial, Tax, Industrial Property, Common Market Real Estate, Financial and Economic Consulting.

Aldo Sabelli   **Salvatore Luise**
         Andrea Sabelli

(For Complete Personnel and Biographical Data, see Professional Biographies at Rome, Italy)

STUDIO DEGLI AVVOCATI
SANTA MARIA-TRISTANO

GALLERIA SAN BABILA, 4/B
20122 MILAN, ITALY
Telephone: 76005365 (five lines)
Telex: SANLEX 315102
Telecopier: 76015360; 780924

General International Practice including Acquisitions, Company Law, Banking, License Agreements, Patents and Trademarks, Conflict of Laws, Exchange Control Regulations, Taxation, Finance, Arbitration and Litigation.

MEMBERS OF FIRM

ALBERTO SANTA MARIA, born Rome, Italy, 1940; admitted, 1966, Italy; 1980, Italian Supreme Court. *Education:* University of Milan (Doctor of Jurisprudence). Professor of Conflict of Laws, International Law and EEC Law: 1971, Bocconi University and Universities of Palermo, Trieste, Genoa and 1984, Milan. Author of several publications in Italian, English and French among which; Diritto Commerciale comunitario, Milan, Giuffré (1990); Le dumping et les subventions dans le cadre du droit international et du droit des Communautés Européennes, Etudes Ago, Giuffré (1987). *Member:* American Arbitration Association (A.A.A.); International Law Association (I.L.A.); Milan Bar Association. *LANGUAGES:* Italian, English and French.

FRANCESCO SANTA MARIA, born Rome, Italy, 1943; admitted, 1971, Italy; 1985, Italian Supreme Court. *Education:* University of Milan (Doctor of Jurisprudence). *Member:* Milan Bar Association. *LANGUAGES:* Italian, English and French.

GIUSEPPE TRISTANO, born Rome, Italy, 1934; admitted, 1959, Italy; 1973, Italian Supreme Court. *Education:* University of Palermo (Doctor of Jurisprudence). *Member:* Milan Bar Association. *LANGUAGES:* Italian, English and French.

CLAUDIO BISCARETTI DI RUFFIA, born Rome, Italy, 1950; admitted, 1979, Italy. *Education:* University of Milan (Doctor of Jurisprudence). Associate Professor of EEC Law, University of Pavia, 1985. *Member:* Milan Bar Association. *LANGUAGES:* Italian, English and French.

LIDIA GRIGIONI, born Milan, Italy, 1958; admitted, 1987, Italy. *Education:* Catholic University of Milan (Doctor of Jurisprudence magna cum laude). *Member:* Milan Bar Association. *LANGUAGES:* Italian, English and French.

LUIGI SANTA MARIA, born Milan, Italy, 1966; admitted, 1991, before the lower Courts. *Education:* University of Milan (Doctor of Jurisprudence magna cum laude); Fordham University, School of Law, New York, N.Y. (LL.M. International Business and Trade Law). *LANGUAGES:* Italian and English.

SCAMONI E ASSOCIATI

Established in 1922
VIA MARIO PAGANO 65
20145 MILAN, ITALY
Telephone: (02) 48-011-171; Intn'l (39-2) 48-011-171
Telecopier: (Gr. III, II) (02) 48-012-914; Intn'l (39-2) 48-012-914

Bologna, Italy Associated Office: Fazio, Francia, Serafini, Solazzi, Trombetti. Via della Zecca 1. Telephone: (051) 23 69 91. Telecopier: (051) 22-24-86.

Padua, Italy Associated Office: Studio Rizzieri e Associati. Passeggiata del Carmine 2. Telephone: (049) 87-619-13. Telecopier: (049) 87-528-79.

General Practice, Corporation, Foreign Investments, Commercial Law, Contractual Assistance, Joint Venture and all forms of Distribution and Franchising Agreements, Banking, EEC Law, Patent, Copyright and Intellectual Property, Bankruptcy and Labor Law, Family Law, Criminal Law, Litigation, including National and International Arbitration, Advertising Law.

FIRM PROFILE: The firm is a member of LEGALLIANCE (EEIG), an alliance of law firms established in Paris, London, Madrid, Brussels, The Hague, Cologne, Frankfurt, Leipzig and Berlin, which offers European coordination and cooperation through a single point of contact.

MEMBERS OF FIRM

MARIO SCAMONI, born Milan, Italy, January 2, 1929; admitted, 1954, Italy. *Education:* University of Milan (Doctor of Jurisprudence, 1953). Former Assistant of Civil Law at the University of Milan *Member:* A.I.J.A.-International Association of Young Lawyers (President, 1972-1973); A.E.A.-European Association of Lawyers (President, 1989-1990); U.I.A.-International Union of Lawyers (Secretary General, 1976-1981). *LANGUAGES:* Italian, French, English and Spanish.

GIOVANNI ERCOLI, born Lodi, Italy, January 20, 1937; admitted, 1962, Italy. *Education:* University of Milan (Doctor of Jurisprudence, magna cum laude, 1959). Honorary Judge at the Court of Milan. *LANGUAGES:* Italian, English, German and Spanish.

PIERO FEDI, born Montecatini, Italy, June 6, 1943; admitted, 1974, Italy. *Education:* University of Milan (Doctor of Jurisprudence, 1971). Former Member of the A.I.J.A.-International Association of Young Lawyers. *LANGUAGES:* Italian and French.

MARCO FRAZZICA, born Ancona, Italy, February 13, 1959; admitted, 1988, Italy. *Education:* University of Bologna (Doctor of Jurisprudence, magna cum laude, 1984). Visiting Foreign Lawyer, Baileys, Shaw & Gillett, London, 1990. *Member:* A.I.JA.-International Young Lawyers Association (Member of the Executive Committee). *LANGUAGES:* Italian, English, Swedish and French.

ELENA GRANATELLO, born Milan, Italy, December 30, 1961; admitted, 1990, Italy. *Education:* University of Milan (Doctor of Jurisprudence, magna cum laude, 1985). Visiting Foreign Lawyer, Ader, Jolibois & Associes, Paris, 1992. *Member:* A.I.J.A.-International Young Lawyers Association. *LANGUAGES:* Italian, French and English.

FRANCESCO MILANESE, born Milan, Italy, September 22, 1941; admitted, 1967, Italy. *Education:* University of Milan (Doctor of Jurisprudence, 1964). *LANGUAGES:* Italian and French.

LEILA PISCOPO, born Taurasi, Italy, June 23, 1950; admitted, 1980, Italy. *Education:* University of Naples (Doctor of Jurisprudence, 1975); University of Urbino (Diploma in Italian-French Comparative Law, 1977). *LANGUAGES:* Italian and French.

GIANLUIGI PUCCIONI, born Florence, Italy, April 30, 1949; admitted, 1976, Italy. *Education:* University of Milan (Doctor of Jurisprudence, 1974). Lecturer of Criminal Law at the Institute for University Student Rights of the University of Milan, 1989-1990. *LANGUAGES:* Italian and English.

ASSOCIATES

MICHELA DE GIULI, born Busto Arsizio, Italy, July 19, 1964. *Education:* University of Milan (Doctor of Jurisprudence, 1989). Assistant to the Stock Exchange Study Institute "A. Lorenzetti," Bocconi University, Milan. *LANGUAGES:* Italian and German.

SILVIA SCAMONI, born Milan, Italy, December 14, 1965; admitted, 1993, Italy. *Education:* University of Milan (Doctor of Jurisprudence, 1990). Assistant ot the Department of Private International Law of the
(This Listing Continued)

SCAMONI E ASSOCIATI, Milan—Continued

University of Milan. *Member:* A.I.J.A.-International Association of Young Lawyers. *LANGUAGES:* Italian and French.

LORENZA ZANNINI, born Milan, Italy, February 13, 1967; admitted, 1994, Italy. *Education:* University of Milan (Doctor of Jurisprudence, 1990). *LANGUAGES:* Italian, French and English.

KORNELIA YOUROUKOVA, born Simitli, Bulgaria, February 9, 1958; admitted, 1980, Bulgaria (Not admitted in Italy). *Education:* University of Sofia (J.D., magna cum laude, 1980). Judge of First Instance, Tribunal of Sofia, 1980-1983. President of the First Instance Tribunal of Sofia, 1983-1988. Magistrate of the Appellate Court of Sofia, 1989-1990. *LANGUAGES:* Bulgarian, Russian, Serbo-Croatian, Italian, French and English.

PARTNERS PADUA OFFICE

Giancarlo Rizzieri   Gianandrea Rizzieri
                  Susanna Rizzieri

PARTNERS BOLOGNA OFFICE

Domenico Fazio   Paolo Trombetti
Lucio Solazzi   Gianluigi Serafini
Mario Francia   Anna Rita Roncuzzi

SCHÜRMANN & PARTNERS

VIA GABRIO CASATI, 1
I-20123 MILAN, ITALY
Telephone: 02-809131/32
Telefax: 02-809-133

Frankfurt/Main, Germany Office: Friedrich-Ebert-Anlage 14, 60325, P.O. Box 11 16 33, 60051. Telephone: 069-7 54 90. Telefax: 7549 290.

Berlin, Germany Office: Karl-Liebknecht-Strasse 32, 10178. Telephone: 030-247-5960. Telefax: 030-238-6032.

Bonn, Germany Office: Philosophenring 94, 53177 Bonn. Telephone: 0228-328-055, Telefax: 0228-311-863.

Brussels, Belgium Office: Avenue de la Raquette 24, B-1150. Telephone: 02-770-0878. Telefax: 02-770-0878.

Dresden, Germany Office: Schnorrstrasse 70, 01069. Telephone: 0351-477-770. Telefax: 0351-477-7799.

Leipzig, Germany Office: Gustav-Adolf-Strasse 30. Telephone: 0341-211-0622. Telefax: 0341-211-0625.

New York, New York Office: 250 Park Avenue, 10177. Telephone: 212-972-3300. Telefax: 212-972-9374.

Paris, France Office: 12, rue d'Astorg F-75008 Paris. Telephone: 01-4451-0570. Telefax: 01-4266-3368.

General Practice, Corporation, Trade, Banking, Labor Law, Law on Mergers, Acquisitions, Fair Trade, Antitrust and EU Law, Administrative Law, Litigation.

WOLF MICHAEL KÜHNE, born Kassel, Germany, November 29, 1963; admitted, 1991, Germany (Not admitted in Italy). *Education:* Universities of Würzburg and Padua. *LANGUAGES:* German, Italian and English.

FEDERICO SUTTI, born Milan, Italy, January 6, 1965; admitted, 1992, Italy. *Education:* University of Milan. *LANGUAGES:* Italian, English and French.

PETER SCHIMMANN, born Essen/Kettwig, Germany, June 26, 1965; admitted, 1993, Germany (Not admitted in Italy). *Education:* Universities of Freiburg and Munich. *LANGUAGES:* German, Italian, English and French.

FRANCO RINDONE, born Milan, Italy, April 12, 1965; admitted, 1993, Italy. *Education:* University of Milan. *LANGUAGES:* Italian and English.

(For complete biographical data on all Personnel, see Professional Biographies at Frankfurt/Main, Germany)

STUDIO LEGALE SENA E TARCHINI

Established in 1983
2 CORSO VENEZIA (S. BABILA)
20121 MILAN, ITALY
Telephone: 76000579
Telefax: 782097
Telex: 334663 GESMI I

Antitrust, Contract, Corporate and Commercial Law, Unfair Competition, Trademark and Patent Law.

MEMBERS OF FIRM

AVV. PROF. GIUSEPPE SENA, born Milan, Italy, November 7, 1930; admitted, 1954, Milan; 1965, Supreme Court. *Education:* University of Milan (J.D., 1952). Author: "L'Interpretazione del Brevetto," Milan, 1955; "Il Voto nell' Assemblea delle Societá per Azioni," Milan, 1961; "Il Boicottaggio-Un Aspetto della Disciplina della Concorrenza," Milan, 1970; "I Diritti sulle Invenzioni e sui Modelli Industriali," Milan, 1990; "Codice dei Brevetti-Invenzioni e Modelli," Milan, 1989; "Codice dei Marchi," Milan, 1988; "Il nuovo diritto dei marchi-Marchio nazionale e marchio comunitario," Milan, 1994. Full Professor of Industrial Property, University of Milan, 1970—. *Member:* Association Internationale pour la Protection de la Propriété Industrielle- A.I.P.P.I.; Ligue Internationale pour le Droit de la Concurrence L.I.D.C. (President of Italian Group, 1982—); Licensing Executives Society L.E.S.; Union des Avocats Europeens U.A.E. *LANGUAGES:* Italian, French and English.

AVV. PAOLA TARCHINI, born Milan, Italy, December 11, 1950; admitted, 1976, Milan. *Education:* University of Milan (J.D., 1973). *Member:* Association Internationale pour la Protection de la Propriété Industrielle-A.I.P.P.I.; Ligue Internationale pour le Droit de la Concurrence L.I.C.D.; Licensing Executives Society L.E.S.; Union des Avocats Europeens U.A.E. *LANGUAGES:* Italian and French.

ASSOCIATES

AVV. FULVIO MELLUCCI, born Milan, Italy, January 31, 1957; admitted, 1982, Milan. *Education:* University of Pavia (J.D., 1980). *Member:* Ligue Internationale pour le Droit de la Concurrence L.I.D.C. *LANGUAGES:* Italian and English.

DOTT. PROC. ELISABETTA BERTI ARNOALDI VELI, born Bologna, Italy, February 18, 1960; admitted, 1990, Bologna. *Education:* University of Milan (J.D., 1984). *Member:* Ligue Internationale pour le Droit de la Concurrence L.I.D.C.; Union des Avocats Europeens U.A.E. *LANGUAGES:* Italian, English and French.

DOTT. PROC. GIANCARLO DEL CORNO, born Como, Italy, August 7, 1960; admitted, 1990, Milan. *Education:* University of Milan (J.D., 1985). *Member:* Ligue Internationale pour le Droit de la Concurrence L.I.D.C.; Union des Avocats Europeens U.A.E. *LANGUAGES:* Italian and English.

SHOOK, HARDY & BACON ITALIA S.R.L.

VIA MERAVIGLI 3
3RD FLOOR
20123 MILAN, ITALY
Telephone: 011-392-723-371
Fax: 011-392-7200-3637

Kansas City, Missouri, Shook, Hardy & Bacon P.C. Office: 1200 Main, One Kansas City Place.

Overland Park, Kansas, Shook, Hardy & Bacon P.C. Office: 40 Corporate Woods.

London, England, Shook, Hardy & Bacon Office: Manning House, 22 Carlisle Place, SW1P 1JA. Telephone: 011-44-171-821-5595. Facsimile: 011-44-171-834-5918.

Zurich, Switzerland, Shook, Hardy & Bacon Office: Bahnhofstrassee 20, CH-8800 Thalwil. Telephone: 011-41-1-721-0038. Facsimile: 011-41-1-721-2384.

Practice in all major areas of U.S. and International Commercial Practice. Product Liability, Litigation and Arbitration.

SHAREHOLDER

T. ANDREW RAGUSIN, born Trieste, Italy, 1957; admitted, 1984, California; 1988, New York (Not admitted in Italy). *Education:* Free University of Brussels, Belgium (LL.B., 1980); Southern Methodist University (M.C.L., 1981; J.D., 1983). Author: "Brother-Sister Corporate Guaranties:
(This Listing Continued)

Increased Legal Acknowledgement of Business World Realities," Journal of Corporation Law, 1986. Co-Author: "Belgium: defensive tricks under attack," International Financial Law Review, October, 1991; "Accor's Takeover of Wagons-Lits: an abrupt end to the honeymoon," International Financial Law Review, June, 1992. *Member:* Union Internationale Des Avocats, Chamber of Commerce; Belgian-Italian Chamber of Commerce; Luxembourg Italian Chamber of Commerce; U.S. Chamber of Commerce in Brussels. *LANGUAGES:* French, Italian, German. *PRACTICE AREAS:* International Law.

MARK D. OVINGTON, born Bethesda, MD., 1958; admitted, 1987, Missouri; 1988, Illinois (Not admitted in Italy). *Education:* Washington University (A.B., magna cum laude, 1981); Vanderbilt University (J.D., 1987). *PRACTICE AREAS:* International Law.

HEIMO SCHEUCH, born Villach, Austria, 1966. *Education:* University of Economics (B.A., 1990); Ecole Superieure de Commerce de, Paris, France (M.B.A., 1992); University of Vienna (J.D., 1993; Master of Law, 1990). *PRACTICE AREAS:* International Law.

GINO R. SERRA, born Pittsburg, KS., 1968; admitted, 1993, Kansas (Not admitted in Italy). *Education:* Rockhurst College (B.S.B.A., 1990); University of Kansas (J.D., 1993). *PRACTICE AREAS:* International Law.

(For complete biographical data on all personnel and list of Representative Clients, see Professional Biographies at Kansas City, Missouri)

SINISI, CESCHINI, MANCINI & PARTNERS

Law Offices

CORSO ITALIA 8
20122 MILAN, ITALY
Telephone: (39) (2) 866 727
Telefax: (39) (2) 866 771

Other Offices in: Milan, New York, Atlanta, Athens, Hartford and San Diego.

International and General Practice, Corporate, Mergers & Acquisitions, Joint Ventures. Taxation, Antitrust, Privatizations, Labor, Bankruptcy, Banking and Securities, Agency and Distribution, Licensing, Environmental Law, Franchising, Insurance, Shipping, Real Estates, Entertainment, Intellectual Property, Software and Telecommunications, Sports, Family Law, Wills and Estate and Litigation.

FIRM PROFILE: Sinisi, Ceschini, Mancini & Partners is an International Law Firm based in the United States and Europe. The offices outside of Italy are known under the name of Hurt, Sinisi & Papadakis. Fundamental to the firm is a committment to provide a high quality of personalized service with an excellent standard of professionalism. The United States Offices are located in the Northeast, Southeast and Western United States in order to service clients conveniently and efficiently, as well as provide full support to the firm's European Offices. The European Offices are staffed with both American and European attorneys. Each office, in Europe and the United States, has attorneys that are qualified to appear and litigate in the local courts.

MEMBERS OF FIRM

VINCENZO SINISI, born Bari, Italy, January 10, 1960; admitted, 1983, Italy. *Education:* University of Bari, Italy (J.D., magna cum laude, 1983). Yale Law School Visiting Scholar, 1985-1986. National Research Council Scholar, 1985-1986. Arbitrator, AFMA Arbitration Committee. Note Editor, Il Foro Italiano, 1982-1985. Speaker: International Bar Association 25th Biennial Conference, "Agency Distribution, Licensing and Franchising Agreements in Italy," Sydney, October, 1994; The Study Group for International Commercial Contracts, "Choice of Law and Choice of Forum in International Contracts," London, April, 1993; International Bar Association "Joint Ventures - An Italian Perspective," Tel-Aviv, 1993; Post M&A Organization, Milan, 1992; "The New Italian S.I.M. Legislation," Conference on "The New Organization of the Italian Securities Markets," London, 1991; "Financial Engineering and Tax Planning," Paris, 1991; "Film Production in Italy: Corporate, Contractual, Fiscal and Copyright Considerations Including Government Incentives," Milan, 1989; "New Financial Law Developments - An Overview on Mutual Funds, Options, Futures, Indexed Bonds and Other Financing Instruments," Milan, 1989;; "Eu-

(This Listing Continued)

ropean Co-productions in Film and Television," Symposium on Film and Media Law, Munich, 1988. Author: "Co-Producing with Italy: Legal and Regulatory Issues," Co-Production International, 1994. Co-Author: "Choice of Law and International Contracts: the EEC Convention on the Law Applicable to Contractual Obligations," Corporate Counsel's International Adviser; "Franchising in Italy," Corporate Counsel's International Adviser, September, 1994; "Italian Labor Law: Collective Dismissal,", Corporate Counsel's International Adviser, April, 1993; "Privatisation in Italy," Corporate Counsel's International Adviser, May, 1993; "Agency and Distribution Agreements in Italy," Corporate Counsel's International Adviser, July, 1993; "Commercial Aspects of Italian Law," Business America, October, 1992; "International Contract Manual: Italy," Kluwer Law and Taxation, 1992; "Legal Aspects of Corporate Reorganization Post M&A," and "Environmental Laws of Italy," International Environmental Law and Regulation, Butterworths, 1991; Legal Studies and Services, Ltd., Amsterdam, 1987. Researcher: Energy Law, Institute of Comparative Law, University of Bari, 1984-1985; Center for Studies in the Public Interest, 1983. *Member:* International Bar Association. (Also at Hurt, Sinisi & Papadakis, Rome, Athens and Atlanta, USA Offices). *LANGUAGES:* Italian and English.

ROBERTA CESCHINI, born Reggio Calabria, Italy, July 25, 1965; admitted, 1988, Italy. *Education:* La Sapienza University, Rome (J.D., 1988). Note Editor: Il Foro Italiano, 1988-1989. Consultant, "Rendezvous of Euroaim" (Media project) Munich, 1992. Speaker: "Death in a Rigid System," Conference on "Death and Taxes," Amsterdam, February, 1994; "The Legal Guarantees," Conference on "The different forms of public and private, cinematographic financing," Vercorin, Switzerland, July, 1993. Author: "Consulting Agreements under Italian Law, Corporate Counsel's International Adviser, October, 1994; "New Italian Cinema Law," International Association of Entertainment Lawyers, Newsletter, Summer, 1994; "Divorce Proceedings in Italy: Domestic and International Procedures," Family Law Quarterly - ABA Spring, 1994; "Registering a Trademark," Business Guide to Italy, U.S. & Foreign Commercial Service, 1994; "Image is All," and "Insync," Summer, 1993; "Opening Retail Shops in Rome," Guide to Doing Business in Rome, U.S. & Foreign Commercial Service, 1992. Co-Author: "Italian Labor Law: Collective Dismissal," Corporate Counsel's International Advisor, April 1993; "Franchising in Italy," Corporate Counsel's International Adviser, September, 1994; "Film Industry Law," Conference on Financing and Film Production, London, 1992; "Environmental Laws of Italy," International Environmental Law and Regulation, Butterworths, 1991. *Member:* International Bar Association; Women in Films and Television. (Also at Hurt, Sinisi & Papadakis, Atlanta, USA Office). *LANGUAGES:* Italian and English.

QUIRINO MANCINI, born Formia, Italy, November 8, 1961; admitted, 1987, Italy. *Education:* La Sapienza University, Rome (J.D., 1986). Speaker: Seminar on Italian/Canadian Film and Television Co-Production Deals, Cannes, May 1993. "Case Study: How to Enforce a Foreign Judgment in Italy," International Litigation Conference, Nice, February 1992. Author: "Bankruptcy of Brokerage Houses under Italian Securities Legislation," Turnarounds & Workouts Europe, March 1995; "Players as Assets of Clubs and Professional Sports - An Outlook of the Italian Situation," Sports Marketing Law & Finance, February/March 1995; "Debt Collection and Bankruptcy Issues," Turnarounds & Workouts Europe, July, 1993; Co-Author: "Privatization in Italy," Corporate Counsel's International Advisor, May, 1993; "The New Italian Legislation on Public Tender Offers (Law. No. 149 of February 19, 1992: Disciplina delle offerte Pubbliche di Vendita, Sottoscrizione, Acquisto e Scambio di titoli)," Acquiring in Europe Conference, London, February 1992; "Aspetti Contrattuali nell'ambito delle Sponsorizzazioni," Speaker: NBPA (National Basketball Players Association): Eight Agent Seminar, "New Developments in Italian Sports Law," New York, 1994; "Fisco, Spese di Pubblicità, Propaganda e Rappresentanza," Milan, May 1991; "The Italian Insolvency Situation," London, October, 1990. Italian Counsel to Hambro Legal Protection Ltd.; Lecturer, Sermoneta Seminar, International Development Law Institute (I.D.L.I.), 1988-1990. Member, National Basketball Players Association. *Member:* British-Italian Lawyers Association; British Chamber of Commerce of Italy; Italian-American Law Association; International Bar Association (Country Chair for Italy of the IBA Sub-Committee J6); European Insolvency Practitioners Association; Sports Lawyers Association. (Also at Hurt, Sinisi & Papadakis, Atlanta, USA Office). *LANGUAGES:* Italian, English and French.

GIANFRANCO PUOPOLO, born Naples, Italy, February 12, 1964; admitted, 1991, Italy. *Education:* Università di Napoli, Naples (J.D., 1988); SIOI (Italian Society for the International Organization), Naples, 1989; E.N.A. (Ecole Nationale d'Administration), Paris, France (June 1989-December 1989); L.S.E. (London School of Economics), London, United

(This Listing Continued)

SINISI, CESCHINI, MANCINI & PARTNERS, Milan—
Continued

Kingdom (1990). Legal Counsel, International Juridical Organization for Environment and Development, Rome, Italy, 1990-1991. Assistant Researcher, International Law, University of Naples; Chairman of Advisory Board of European Law Students Association. Speaker: NBPA (National Basketball Players Association): Eight Agent Seminar, "New Development in Italian Sports Law," Los Angeles, 1994; "Commercial Centers: Contractual Issues," Milan, 1993; "Commercial Agents: Termination of the Agency Contract," Milan, 1993; Publicity in Times of Crisis: " Analysis of Community and Italian Legislation on the Sponsorship of Radio and Television Programming," Milan, February, 1993; "An International Environmental Court within the United Nations' System," Florence, 1991. Author: "Italy greets Franchising as effective tool for expanding business," Global Franchising Alert, 1994; "Constitution d'une Société Italienne," Contract Franco-Italiens, Chambre Française de Commerce en Italie," 1993; "Privatisation en Italie," Contacts Franco-Italiens, Chambre Française de Commerce en Italie, 1993; "Il Nuovo Contratto di Agenzia," France-Italie, Chambre de Commerce Italienne pour la France, 1993; "Workers Protection in Italy," International Business Lawyer, 1992. Co-Author: "Agency and Distribution," Corporate Counsel's International Advisor, 1994; "Mutual Fund Investments in Italy," International Business Lawyer, 1993; "Legal Aspects of Corporate Reorganization Post M&A, Conference on Post M&A Organization, Milan, 1992. Member: Chambre de Commerce Italienne pour la France; Chambre de Commerce Française pour l'Italie; National Basketball Players Association. *Member:* International Bar Association. *LANGUAGES:* Italian, English and French.

NINO MATASSA, born San Giovanni Rotundo (FG), Italy, May 17, 1959; admitted, 1987, Italy. *Education:* University of Bari, Italy (J.D., magna cum laude, 1984). Yale Law School Visiting Scholar. Note Editor, Il Foro Italiano, 1982-1994. Researcher: Energy Law, Institute of Comparative Law, University of Bari, Italy, 1984-1985; Energy Law, Institute of Legal Advanced Studies, London and Dundee, 1984. Professor of Environmental Law, Puglia Region. Author: "Product Liability," Le Nuove Leggi Civili Commentate, 1989. *LANGUAGES:* Italian and English.

RENATO MOCCIA, born Bari, Italy, February 6, 1960; admitted, 1987, Italy. *Education:* University of Bari, Italy (J.D., magna cum laude, 1984). Note Editor, Il Foro Italiano, 1982-1994. Researcher, Energy Law, Institute of Comparative Law, University of Bari, Italy, 1984-1985. *LANGUAGES:* Italian and English.

ALEC PAPADAKIS, born Athens, Greece, January 27, 1947; admitted, 1979, Georgia (Not admitted in Italy). *Education:* Hartwick College, Oneonta N.Y. Ibero-Americana University, Mexico City, Mexico (1972); University of Akron, Ohio (J.D., 1976). Author: "Forms of Doing Business in Greece," International Corporate Counsel, Fall, 1992; "Immigration Considerations for Foreign Investors in U.S."; "Impact of the Tax Reform Act of 1984 on Resident and Non-Resident Aliens"; "Memorandum on United States Immigration Law - Immigrant and Non-Immigrant Visas"; Selected Memoranda for Foreign Investors, Immigration, Estate Planning, Taxation; "Foreign Investment in Georgia - Immigration Considerations." Co-Author: "A Synopsis of the Greek Corporate Tax System," State of California EC Law Handbook, 1993; Franchise Handbook for Foreign Companies Doing Business in U.S., Federal & State Compliance; Franchise Handbook for U.S. Companies Doing Business in European Common Market; Country Handbook on Greece Business & Employment Visas under IMMACT '90. Board of Advisors, International Quarterly. *Member:* International Franchise Association; American Bar Association (Sections on International Law and Franchising); State Bar of Georgia (Sections on Franchise, International and Environmental Law); International Bar Association; American Hellenic Chamber of Commerce (Athens, Greece); American Immigration Lawyers Association; Hellenic American Institute, Washington, D.C. (Board of Directors); Hellenic American Chamber of Commerce of Atlanta (Founder, President); Italy-America Chamber of Commerce of Southeast, U.S. (Founder, Board of Directors); International Leadership Council of the Southeast (Founding Member, Board of Directors). (Also at Hurt, Sinisi & Papadakis, Athens, Atlanta and Hartford, USA Offices). *LANGUAGES:* English and Greek.

JOHN R. HURT, born Los Angeles, California, August 20, 1940; admitted, 1970, California; 1971, U.S. District Court for the Southern District of California; 1975, U.S. Supreme Court (Not admitted in Italy). *Education:* University of California, Berkeley (B.S., 1962); Cornell University School of Law (J.D., 1969). International Legal Centre Fellow, San Jose, Costa Rica, 1969-1971. Co-author: "Country Handbook on Italy," Italian American Business, 1992; "Environmental Laws of Italy," International Environmen-

(This Listing Continued)

tal Law and Regulations, Butterworths, 1991; "Dobson & Sinisi, Rome and San Diego," 1084-1994"; "Joint Ventures - A European Perspective," Ninth Annual Southeastern Corporate Counsel Institute, Atlanta, December, 1990; "Film Production and Loan Subsidies in Italy," Rome, July, 1990; "The Need for Appropriate Legal Protection of Software in Italy," Rome, 1988. General Counsel, Intermaritime Group, Geneva, 1987-1988. Private Practice, Paris and Rome, 1982-1987. General Counsel and Corporate Secretary, Cinema International Corporation, N.V., Amsterdam, 1978-1982. Division Counsel, Sea-Land Service, Inc., Menlo Park, N.J., 1975-1978. Associate, Gray, Cary, Ames & Frye, San Diego, 1971-1974. *Member:* State Bar of California; American (Member, Section on International Law and Practice) and International Bar Associations. (Also at Hurt, Sinisi & Papadakis, Atlanta and Hartford, USA Offices). *LANGUAGES:* English, Spanish, Italian and French.

STEVEN N. KOURTIS, born Sydney, New South Wales, Australia, December 6, 1961; admitted, 1991, Pennsylvania (Not admitted in Italy). *Education:* Duquesne University, Pittsburgh, Pennsylvania (B.A., 1984); American University, Washington, D.C. (Washington Semester in U.S. Foreign Policy, 1983); graduate work, International Affairs, George Washington University, Washington, D.C. (1984-1987); Catholic University of America, Columbus School of Law, Washington, D.C. (J.D., 1991). Member, Journal of Contemporary Health Law and Policy; Testimony before the U.S. Environmental Protection Agency on oil recycling issues, American Car Rental Association and the National Association of Convenience Stores, Washington, D.C., November 1991. Author: "Liability for Petroleum Storage Tank Owners and Operations," National Shipbuilders Research Project, Environmental Symposium, Crystal City, Virginia, 1991; "How to Lobby Congress," Independent Lubricant Manufacturers Association Annual Government Affairs Committee Meeting, Washington, D.C., 1992. Co-Author: "A Synopsis of the Greek Corporate Tax System," State of California EC Law Handbook, 1993; "Doing Business in Greece," Corporate Counsel's International Advisor, December 1992; Associate, Collier, Shannon, Rill & Scott, Washington, D.C., 1991-1992. *Member:* American Society for International Law; American Hellenic Educational and Progressive Association (AHEPA); American Bar Association (Section of Natural Resources, Energy and Environmental Law). (Athens and Atlanta, USA Offices). *LANGUAGES:* English and Greek.

OF COUNSEL

HARRIET TAMEN, born Yonkers, New York, May 17, 1947; admitted, 1974, New York. *Education:* Bryn Mawr College (A.B., 1969); National Law Center, George Washington University (J.D., 1973). Lecturer: American Women's Economic Development Corporation on International Business and Trade Finance (1992-1995); New York University School of Continuing Education on Credit Enhancement and Banking Law (1991-1995); Financial Services Volunteer Corps (Mongolia) on Commercial Banking (1993-1994); Conference on Black Sea Region and Central Asian Republics; Economic Development & Business Opportunities - Harriman Institute, Columbia University (1994). *Member:* Association of the Bar of the City of New York; Inter-American Affairs Subcommittee; New York State Bar Association; SABLAW-Soviet-American Banking Law Working Group (1990-1995); American Bar Association. (New York Office).

WILLIAM C. BRUCE, born Louisville, Kentucky, April 11, 1952; admitted, 1977, Connecticut; 1978, District of Columbia; 1982, Florida; U.S. District Court, District of Connecticut; U.S. District Court, Eastern and Western Districts of Arkansas; U.S. District Court, Southern District of New York; U.S. Court of Appeals, 2nd, 6th and 11th Circuits; U.S. Supreme Court (Not admitted in Italy). *Education:* University of New Haven (B.A. summa cum laude, 1974); Yale University (J.D., 1977). Author: "Employment Law in the 1990's," Conn. L. Trib, November, 1992; "Preventive Law in the Non-U.S. Owned Corporation," No. 2 Preventive Law Reporter 10, 1991; "Theft of Business Opportunity," Conn. Bar Journal, 1979. Adjunct Professor of Management, Rennselaer Polytechnic Institute (Hartford Graduate Center). Senior Consultant to AON Re-Engineering Corp. on Employment and Privitization Issues. Formerly Vice President, General Counsel and Corporate Secretary, Pirelli Tire Corporation. General Counsel and Secretary, University of New Haven. *Member:* Connecticut and American (Committees on International Business Law and Product Liability Law); The Corporate Bar Association (Past Chair of the Litigation and Insurance Committee, International Law Committee).

(This Listing Continued)

ance Corporation; Hartford International Insurance Company; Pricoa Vita S.p.A. - Prudential Group; Wright Investors Service; Deutsche Factoring; Bank Belgo-Factors N.V.; Export-Import Bank of India; Guinness Mahon & Co. Limited; Comerica Bank; Imperial Bank; MeesPierson N.V.; Bachman Information Systems; Cognos Incorporated; Conner Peripherals; Dun & Bradstreet Software Services Limited; Mantech International Corp.; Pilot Software; Armando Testa Advertising; Capella International Inc.; Curzon Films Distributors Ltd.; Film Master Srl.; Merchant Ivory Productions Ltd.; Shadow Hill Entertainment; Wonderland Entertainment Ltd.; GNB Incorporated; Mucafer Construction; Si.A.C. Construction; Dan El Construction.

STUDIO LEGALE SPADARO E CASSOTTA

Established in 1979

PIAZZA CINQUE GIORNATE 10
20129 MILAN, ITALY
Telephone: 02/5510602 - 59902104 - 55180840-55184302
Cable Address: Spadaro
Telefax: 02/55018061

Private International Law, EEC Law, Commercial and Company Law.

FIRM PROFILE: *The firm was established in 1979 and offers legal services to multinational corporations doing business in Italy.*

MEMBERS OF FIRM

AVV. DOMENICO R. SPADARO, born Milan, Italy, March 2, 1945; admitted, 1973, Italy. *Education:* University of Milan (Law, 1969); University of Texas (M.C.L., 1976). *Member:* Milan Bar Association, American Bar Association and American Society of International Law. **LANGUAGES:** English, French and Italian. **PRACTICE AREAS:** International Trade Law; European Community Law.

DR. PROC. CHIARA CASSOTTA, born Bari, Italy, February 23, 1960; admitted, 1991, Italy. *Education:* Catholic University of Milan (J.D., 1984). **LANGUAGES:** French, Spanish, English and Italian. **PRACTICE AREAS:** European Community Law.

ASSOCIATES

AVV. PAOLA BOLIS, born Milan, Italy, April 8, 1949; admitted, 1977, Italy. *Education:* University of Milan (J.D., 1972). **LANGUAGES:** English and Italian. **PRACTICE AREAS:** Civil; Commercial Law.

AVV. MICHELANGELO ABRATE, born Turin, Italy, September 1, 1937; admitted, 1987, Italy. *Education:* University of Milan (J.D., 1968). **LANGUAGES:** French and Italian. **PRACTICE AREAS:** Media Law; Advertising.

REPRESENTATIVE CLIENTS: Guinness Italia; Mannesmann Demag; Landis & Gyr; Symbol Technologies; Harry Winston of New York S.A.; Bass Export Ltd.; Hartek GMBH; Mammoet Transport N.V.; Banque National de Paris (BNP) Leasing S.A.; UFB Leasing (Italia) S.p.a.

STUDIO AVVOCATO SPOLIDORO

PROFESSIONAL ASSOCIATION

2 VIA MOZART
20122 MILAN, ITALY
Telephone: 76.005.395; 780.830
Telecopier: 780.036

Corporate Practice, Contracts, Foreign Investments, Mergers and Acquisitions, Antitrust, Taxation, Patents and Trademarks.

PARTNERS

AVV. YORICK SPOLIDORO, born Piombino, Italy, July 8, 1918; admitted, 1944, Italy; 1949, admitted to plead before the Supreme Court. *Education:* University of Pisa (LL.D., magna cum laude, 1940); University of Genoa (Dr. of Political Sciences, 1942). Chairman, Legal and Tax Committee of the American Chamber of Commerce for Italy, 1986—. Member, National Academy of the Mercantile Navy. **LANGUAGES:** Italian, English, French and German.

AVV. SERGIO SPOLIDORO, born Milan, Italy, May 28, 1955; admitted, 1982, Italy. *Education:* Catholic University of Milan (LL.D., 1978); University of Virginia, U.S.A. (M.C.L., 1980). **LANGUAGES:** Italian, English and French.

PROF. AVV. MARCO S. SPOLIDORO, born Milan, Italy, July 4, 1957; admitted, 1982, Italy; 1992 admitted to plead before the Supreme Court. *Education:* Catholic University of Milan (LL.D., cum laude, 1979).

(This Listing Continued)

Professor of Commercial Law, University of Macerata, 1990—and Bocconi University, Milan, 1983— and Industrial Law, University of Trento, 1985-1987. Member, Editorial Board, Giurisprudenza Annotata di Diritto Industriale, Milan, 1979— and Editorial Board, Rivista delle Società, Milan, 1984—. *LANGUAGES:* Italian, English, French and German.

ASSOCIATES

DR. PROC. DANIELA D'AMORE DI UGENTO, born Bari, Italy, April 27, 1964; admitted, 1991, Italy. *Education:* University of Bari (LL.D., cum laude, 1988). **LANGUAGES:** Italian and English.

DR. LAURA D'AMBROSIO, born Rome, Italy, June 5, 1968; (Not admitted in Italy). *Education:* University of Rome "La Sapienza" (LL.D., cum laude, 1992). **LANGUAGES:** Italian and English.

STUDIO AVVOCATO SILVANO STEFANI

PIAZZALE PRINCIPESSA CLOTILDE, 8
20121 MILAN, ITALY
Telephone: (02) 29.00.29.32 International (39 2) 29.00.29.32
Telefax: (02) 65.75.969 International (39 2) 65.75.969

International and Domestic Practice, Antitrust, Bankruptcy, Contract, Corporate, E.E.C., Environmental, Foreign Investment, Intellectual Property, International Estate, International Trade, Labor, Licensing, Litigation and Arbitration, Mergers and Acquisitions, Product Liability, Tax.

SILVANO STEFANI, born Milan, Italy, April 15, 1940; admitted, 1965, Italy; 1978, Illinois; 1985, Supreme Court of the United States; 1987, New York. *Education:* University of Milan (Doctor of Jurisprudence, cum laude, 1962); Illinois Institute of Technology, Chicago-Kent College of Law (J.D., 1978). With Studio Scalfi, Milan, Italy, 1964-1971. With Baker & McKenzie, Milan, Italy, 1971-1976 and Chicago, Illinois, 1976-1988. Partner, Baker & McKenzie International Partnership, 1974-1988. Lecturer of Private Law, University of Parma, Parma, Italy, 1966-1968 and University L. Bocconi, Milan, Italy, 1969-1971. Member: Panel of Arbitrators, American Arbitration Association, 1986—; Legal and Tax Committee, American Chamber of Commerce in Italy, 1991-1994. **LANGUAGES:** Italian, English and French.

OF COUNSEL

ENRICO S. GILIOLI, born Milan, Italy, March 1, 1930; admitted, 1977, Italy. *Education:* Liceo Classico Beccaria, Milan (B.A., 1948); Guilford College, N.C. (B.A., 1953); New York University (1955); University of Milan (Doctor of Law, 1973). **LANGUAGES:** Italian and English.

DANIEL E. GILIOLI, born Milan, Italy, June 27, 1933; admitted, 1957, Ohio; 1966, District of Columbia (Not admitted in Italy). *Education:* University of Cincinnati (B.A., 1955; J.D., 1957). President, American Chamber of Commerce in Italy, 1988-1992. Director: Norwegian Chamber of Commerce in Italy, 1984—; American School of Milan, 1963-1980. Director and Treasurer, Union of Foreign Chambers of Commerce in Italy, 1988-1992. *Member:* American Arbitration Association (Panel of Arbitrators); American Society of International Law. **LANGUAGES:** English, Italian and French.

ERIC L. GILIOLI, born Cincinnati, Ohio, September 9, 1957; admitted, 1984, New York and U.S. Court of International Trade; 1985, District of Columbia (Not admitted in Italy). *Education:* Harvard University (A.B., magna cum laude, 1979); Fordham University (J.D., 1983). Editor-in-Chief, Fordham International Law Journal, 1982-1983. Author: "Defining Jurisdictional Limits of International Antitrust: Should the E.C.C. Adopt the Timberlane Approach?" 5 Fordham International Law Journal 469, 1982. *Member:* American Society of International Law. **LANGUAGES:** English, Italian and French.

ASSOCIATES

ALESSANDRO ATZENI, born Milan, Italy, November 13, 1960; admitted, 1987, Certified Public Accountant, Italy. *Education:* University L. Bocconi, Milan, Italy (B.E.D., 1986). Member, Committee for International Relations, Milan Association of Certified Public Accountants, 1988—. **LANGUAGES:** Italian and English.

MIRELLA DEL PANTA, born Rome, Italy, April 20, 1963; admitted, 1993, Certified Public Accountant, Italy. *Education:* University L. Bocconi, Milan, Italy (B.E.D., 1991). **LANGUAGES:** Italian, English and French.

IVANO C. MAZZOLENI, born Bergamo, Italy, May 24, 1961; admitted, 1989, Italy. *Education:* University of Milan (Doctor of Jurisprudence,

(This Listing Continued)

STUDIO AVVOCATO SILVANO STEFANI, Milan—
Continued

cum laude, 1985). Lecturer, Comparative Penal Procedure, University of Milan, 1985-1988. *LANGUAGES:* Italian and English.

LAURA NARDI, born Macerata, Italy, November 14, 1966. *Education:* Catholic University of Milan (Doctor of Jurisprudence, 1991). *LANGUAGES:* Italian and English.

STUDIO ASSOCIATO LEGALE
TRIBUTARIO

Established in 1990

Associated with ERNST & YOUNG INTERNATIONAL

VIA CORNAGGIA, 10
20123 MILAN, ITALY
Telephone: (02) 8514.1
Fax: (02) 89010199
Telex: 321599

Rome, Italy Office: Via del Pozzetto, 105, 00187. Telephone: (06) 6783296. Fax: (06) 6784877.
Bologna, Italy Office: Via M. D'Azeglio, 34, 40123. Telephone: (051) 260003. Fax: (051) 235538.
Verona, Italy Office: Via Manin, 6, 37122. Telephone: (045) 8007630. Fax: (045) 8003993.

FIRM PROFILE: *The firm that is associated with Ernst & Young International, was established in 1990 and offers a full range of tax and legal services. The firm was originally specialized in Domestic and International Tax Practice and during the last two years, has expanded its activities in Commercial and Corporate Law, Competition Law, Labour Law, as well as in Mergers & Acquisitions. The client base is European, North American and Japanese in scope, This 14 partner firm comprises 40 professionals and a support staff of 45 persons, including paralegal personnel.*

MEMBERS OF FIRM

FABIO GRECO, born Rome, Italy, September 30, 1941; admitted, 1973. *Education:* University of Rome (Degree in Law). *Member:* Italian Bar Association. *LANGUAGES:* Italian and English. *PRACTICE AREAS:* International Taxation; Mergers and Acquisitions.

JOHN A. STEWART, born Irvine, Scotland, January 14, 1947. *Education:* Kings Norton Grammar School. *Member:* England and Wales Chartered Accountants' Association (since November 1969 and Fellow since January 1979). *LANGUAGES:* English and Italian. *PRACTICE AREAS:* Mergers and Acquisitions.

FOSCO RONDININI, born Milan, Italy, March 31, 1946. *Education:* Bocconi University of Milan (Degree in Business Administration). Authorized Statutory Auditor since 1989. *Member:* Italian Chartered Accountants' Association (since 1981). *LANGUAGES:* Italian and English. *PRACTICE AREAS:* Domestic and International Taxation.

PIERA VITALI, born Mede, Italy, June 8, 1949. *Education:* Bocconi University of Milan (Degree in Business Administration). Authorized Statutory Auditor since 1989. *Member:* Italian Chartered Accountants' Association (since 1976). *LANGUAGES:* Italian and English. *PRACTICE AREAS:* Banking and Insurance Tax Practice.

MARIA CRISTINA CIARCHI, born Milan, Italy, July 10, 1952. *Education:* Institute G. Schiapparelli. Business evaluation expert appointed by the Court of Milan. *Member:* Italian Chartered Accountants' Association (since 1991). *LANGUAGES:* Italian, French and English. *PRACTICE AREAS:* Mergers and Acquisitions.

FRANCESCO GUIDI, born Rome, Italy, August 30, 1953. *Education:* LUISS University of Rome (Degree in Business Administration, 1976). *Member:* Italian Chartered Accountants' Association; ANTI-Italian Tax Advisors Association. *LANGUAGES:* Italian, English and French. *PRACTICE AREAS:* Mergers and Acquisitions.

ALESSANDRO DE NICOLA, born Milan, Italy, October 23, 1961; admitted, 1990. *Education:* Catholic University of Milan (Degree in Law 1985); Cambridge (UK) University (Master of Law LL.M., 1989). Lecturer in Anglo-American Law, University of Milan. *Member:* Milan Bar Association; American-Italian Law Association (General Secretary); Adam Smith Society (President); Oxford and Cambridge Alumni Association (Vice President); Professional Association of Journalists. *LANGUAGES:* Italian,

(This Listing Continued)

English and French. *PRACTICE AREAS:* Corporate and Commercial Law; M&A; Antitrust; Securities and Financial Law.

GIORGIO DE PACE, born Soverato, Italy, April 2, 1958. *Education:* La Sapienza University of Rome (Degree in Business Administration). Authorized Statutory Auditor since 1992. *Member:* Italian Chartered Accountant's Association (since 1985). *LANGUAGES:* Italian and English. *PRACTICE AREAS:* Domestic and International Banking Taxation.

MARCO DA RE, born Bergamo, Italy, June 30, 1958. *Education:* State University of Bergamo (Degree in Business Administration 1981). *Member:* Italian Chartered Accountants' Association. *LANGUAGES:* Italian and English. *PRACTICE AREAS:* Domestic and International Taxation and Mergers and Acquisitions.

GIANPAOLO GIANNINI, born Montefiorino, Italy, June 9, 1955. *Education:* Institute G. Schiapparelli. *Member:* Italian Chartered Accountants' Association. *LANGUAGES:* Italian, French and English. *PRACTICE AREAS:* Domestic and International Taxation.

FILIPPO DI CAROEGNA BRIVIO, born Meda, Italy, September 5, 1950. *Education:* Catholic University of Milan (Degree in Business Administration). Authorized Statutory Auditor since 1990. *Member:* Italian Chartered Accountants' Association (since 1981). *LANGUAGES:* Italian, English and French. *PRACTICE AREAS:* Tax and Corporate Advice; Banks and Financial Institutions.

LUCIANO OLIVIERI, born Milan, Italy, June 23, 1955. *Education:* Bocconi University of Milan (Degree in Business Administration). *Member:* Italian Chartered Accountants' Association (since 1989). *LANGUAGES:* Italian, English and French. *PRACTICE AREAS:* Domestic and International Taxation.

PIERGIORGIO VALENTE, born Turin, Italy, February 5, 1963. *Education:* University of Turin (Degree in Business Administration). *Member:* Turin Chartered Accountants' Association (since 1988); IFA; Junior Accountants' Association. *LANGUAGES:* Italian, English and French. *PRACTICE AREAS:* International Taxation.

GIUSI LAMICELA, born Bülach, Switzerland, October 3, 1963; admitted, 1991. *Education:* University of Catania (Degree in Law, 1986). *Member:* Milan Bar Association. *LANGUAGES:* Italian and English. *PRACTICE AREAS:* Tax Law; Company Law; Tax Litigation.

LEE OSTER, born Port Huron, Michigan (USA), September 23, 1956. *Education:* University of Illinois (Degree in Law and in Business Administration). Licensed Attorney and CPA in the State of Illinois. Responsible of the US Tax Desk at Milan's Office. *LANGUAGES:* English and Italian. *PRACTICE AREAS:* International Taxation.

JEROEN DAVIDSON, born Amsterdam, Netherlands, October 17, 1963. *Education:* University of Amsterdam (Degree in Law, 1988). Responsible of the Dutch Desk at Milan's Office. *Member:* NOB (Netherlands Order of Tax Advisors). *LANGUAGES:* Netherlands, English, Italian, German, French and Russian. *PRACTICE AREAS:* International Taxation.

MARCO GOLDA PERINI, born Milan, Italy, April 13, 1966; admitted, 1993. *Education:* Catholic University of Milan (Degree in Law, 1990). *Member:* Milan Bar Association. *LANGUAGES:* Italian and English. *PRACTICE AREAS:* Commercial and Competition Law.

STUDIO TOMASETTI

VIA VISCONTI DI MODRONE, 2
20122 MILAN, ITALY
Telephone: (39)(2) 76002022
Fax: (39)(2) 76002050

Rome, Italy Office: Viale Mazzini 11 4/B. Telephone: (39)(6) 372114.
Correspondent Offices: New York; Chicago; Washington; Los Angeles.

FIRM PROFILE: *The Italian part of the firm was established in 1971 and its practice has grown to include American counsel and tax counseling and services. The practice is concentrated in commercial and international law, tax consulting, intellectual property (copyright and trademarks, franchising, licensing and media), telecommunications, energy, transportation and health care law.*

Regarding commercial and corporate law, the services provided by the firm include the following:

•*Formation of companies, drafting of shareholders' agreements, as well as administrative and legal services in connection with their functioning, including labour law;*

(This Listing Continued)

•Commercial arrangements of all kinds including leasing, agency, and distribution agreements, service contracts;

•Bankruptcy, debt collections and workouts of trouble companies;

•All aspects of real estate law including financing and lease arrangements;

•Litigation before all courts, as well as arbitration; and,

•Accounting consultation and fulfillment of various tax obligations (tax returns, V.A.T., balance sheets, tax audits, etc.).

The client base is equally divided between corporations from English speaking countries, and Italian corporation doing business in common law countries.

U.S. PARTNERS

GIUSEPPE "JOE" TOMASETTI, born Parma, Italy, November 13, 1946; admitted, 1972, District of Columbia; 1974, Wisconsin (Not admitted in Italy). *Education:* Marquette University (B.A., 1968); The National Law Center, The George Washington University (D.C.) 1971; University of Wisconsin (Graduate Ph.D. Studies). Lecturer, The University of Wisconsin, Law School Legislative/Administrative Law Process (1976-1980). Administrative Assistant, U.S. Congressman John Culver. Legislative Director, U.S. Senator John Culver (1973-1975). Chief of Staff, Wi. Governor Martin J. Schreiber. "Doing Business in Italy, European Community and Europe: A Legal Guide to Business Development," California Chamber of Commerce and California Trade Commerce Agency, 1993; "Italy: A Paradoxical Opportunity," The Journal of European Business, March/April, 1992. Numerous public presentations on legal, regulatory and business aspects of regulated industries, including lobbying and international business transactions between Italy and English speaking countries. President, Board of Trustees, The American School of Milan (1993—). Appointed U.S. Counsel General of Milan, Special Mental Health Committee (1992-1994). Democrats Abroad (1989—); Italian-American Chamber of Commerce, Legal Tax Committee, Chair, U.S. Civil Law (1990—); Chicago/Milan Sister City Committee (1990—). (Also of Counsel, Studio Legale Mondini-Rusconi, Milan, Rome, Italy). *LANGUAGES:* English, Italian and Spanish. *PRACTICE AREAS:* Corporate and Administrative Law.

ITALIAN OF COUNSEL

GIORGIO MONDINI, born Reggio Emilia, Italy, June 22, 1941; admitted, 1968, Milan; 1980, Italian Supreme Court. *Education:* State University of Milan (J.D. magna cum laude, 1965); Academy of American and International Law, Southwestern Legal Foundation, Dallas, Texas, U.S.A. (Fullbright Scholar, 1971). Assistant Professor: International Law, University of Milan, 1967-1982; Commercial Law, Universitá degli Studi, Milan (1993—). Contributor to: L'Europa della CEE (Monthly Magazine), Pirola Ed., 1988-1991. (Also Member, Studio Legale Mondini-Rusconi, Milan, Italy). *LANGUAGES:* Italian, English and French. *PRACTICE AREAS:* Company Law; EEC Law; Arbitration; Media and Telecommunications Law; Intellectual Property.

GIUSEPPE RUSCONI, born Como, Italy, August 19, 1941; admitted, 1971, Milan. *Education:* State University of Milan (J.D. magna cum laude, 1965). Contributor to: L'Europa della CEE (Monthly Magazine), Pirola Ed., 1988-1991. (Also Member, Studio Legale Mondini-Rusconi, Milan, Italy). *LANGUAGES:* Italian and French. *PRACTICE AREAS:* Company Law; Arbitration; Litigation.

GIACOMO BONELLI, born Milan, Italy, October 21, 1956; admitted, 1985, Milan. *Education:* State University of Milan (J.D. magna cum laude, 1982). Contributor to: L'Europa della CEE (Monthly Magazine), Pirola Ed., 1988-1991. (Also Member, Studio Legale, Mondini-Rusconi, Milan, Italy). *LANGUAGES:* Italian and English. *PRACTICE AREAS:* Intellectual Property; Labour Law; Competition Law; Litigation.

ANNA CARABELLI, born Como, Italy, August 27, 1958; admitted, 1985, Milan. *Education:* State University of Milan (J.D. magna cum laude, 1982); City of London Polytechnic (Summer Course in International Law, 1983); University of the Pacific McGeorge School of Law, Salzburg University (International Legal Studies, 1989). Contributor to: L'Europa della CEE (Monthly Magazine), Pirola Ed., 1988-1991. (Also Member, Studio Legale Mondini-Rusconi, Milan, Italy). *LANGUAGES:* Italian, French and English. *PRACTICE AREAS:* Intellectual Property; EEC Law; Media and Telecommunications Law; Litigation.

(This Listing Continued)

ACCOUNTING/TAX COUNSEL

DOTT. GIULIO BOSELLI, (not admitted as a lawyer). born Bellano, Italy. 1974, Certified Accountant (Commercialista); 1981, Commercial Appraiser for the Milan Court. *Education:* University Bocconi (B.A. in Economics and Business Administration, 1970). *LANGUAGES:* Italian, English and French.

Representative Clients Upon Reguest, Associates upon request.

STUDIO LEGALE SUTTI

Established in 1952

VIA MOLINO DELLE ARMI 4
I 20123 MILAN, ITALY

Telephone: +39 2 8052982; 862340; 8693239; 862335; 72022126
Telefax: +39 2 8900732 *Telex:* 353063 WAY I
Electronic Mail Addresses: Internet: sutti@ibm.net *Compuserve:* 100524,3014
Mastermail 65: PGE17259; *Videotel* 013210401
Pcfax: +39 2 862340, *ISDN & Videoconference:* +39 2 86457021

Industrial Property Department: Via Molino delle Armi 4, I 20123 Milan. Telephone: +39 2 862340; 862335. Fax: +39 2 8900732.

Labour and Industrial Relations Department: Via Arcivescovado 1, I 20122 Milan. Telephone:+39 2 8633020. Fax: +39 2 86 10 71.

Accounting, Tax and Auditing Consultants: Studio Falcioni, via Montenapoleone, 8, 1 20122 Milan. Telephone: +39 2 796407. Fax: +39 2 796407.

Local Addresses:

Trescore Balneario (BG) Office: Piazza Cavour, I 24069 Trescore Balneario. Telephone: +39 35 940166.

Abbiategrasso (MI) Office: Corso Matteotti 56, I 20081 Abbiategrasso. Telephone: +39 2 94963208. Fax: +39 2 94969643.

Overseas Offices:

London Office: 19 Princes Street, London W1R 7RE, United Kingdom. Telephone: +44 171 4091384. Telefax: +44 171 4091384. ISDN & Videoconference: +44 171 4933395.

Tokyo Office: Nihonbashi-Honcho 4-chome, Chuo-ku, Tokyo 103, Japan. Telephone: +81 3 56404571. Fax: +81 356404575.

International Contracts, Foreign Investments, Mergers and Acquisition, Distributorship, Agency and Franchise Law, EEC Law, Competition Law, Antitrust Law, Corporate Law, Banking Law, Bankruptcy, Product Liability Law, Entertainment Law. Industrial Property Dept.: Patent Litigation and Prosecution, Trademark Litigation and Prosecution, Copyright Law, Industrial Models, License Negotiation, Technology Transfer, General Patent and Intellectual Property Practice, Advertising Law. Labour and Industrial Relations Dept.: Labour Law, Employer's Liability, Pension Law, Industrial Relations.

FIRM PROFILE: The firm is a member of LEGIT (Specialists in Legal Information Technology), INDICAM (Institute for the Protection of Trademarks), the Ligue pour l'Étude de la Concurrence, the British-Italian Chamber of Commerce, the American Chamber of Commerce in Italy, the French Chamber of Commerce and Industry in Italy and the Italian Chamber of Commerce for Great Britain. The firm's resources include networked, state-of-the-art groupware, word-processing, OCR, CAD, accounting systems which can communicate directly with clients via ISDN and modem (standard CCITT V21, 22, 22bis, 23, 32, 32bis, V.32terbo, V.fast, V.34, 42bis, MNP 5 and Videotex), and access to most known on-line data banks, including case law, commercial and industrial property information services.

The firm publishes a quarterly newsletter, which contains general information and news. Since June, 1991 the firm has published an international quarterly edition in English, addressed specifically to foreign clients and correspondents.

The firm's typical clients include: medium-sized companies, multinational corporations, financial institutions and investors. With regard to international matters, the firm specializes in, inter alia, providing consultative, litigation and representational services to foreign law firms and their clients within the Italian jurisdiction.

In 1993, the firm merged with Monti & Partners, a well-known Milan-based law firm which was established in 1927.

(This Listing Continued)

STUDIO LEGALE SUTTI, Milan—Continued

PARTNERS

ANGELO SUTTI, (1928-1993); admitted, Supreme Court. *Education:* University of Milan (J.D., 1951). Author: "The Contract of Commercial Agency," 1952. Cavaliere al merito della Repubblica Italiana, 1964. Diploma d'Onore of the Rose-Blue Cross, 1970. *Member:* Bar Association of Milan; Rose-Blue Cross (former Vice-President); Touring Club of Italy; Board of Arbitrators of the League of Professional Cyclists (CONI-FCI). (Founder of the Firm).

MARCO MONTI, born Milan, Italy, September 13, 1952. *Education:* State University of Milan (J.D. summa cum laude, 1980). Author: " International Sale: Applicable Law on International Sale," (1981);"International Sale: Uniform Law on International Sale," (1981); " International Sale: ECE-ONU General Conditions of Sale," (1981); "Incorporation of a Limited Liability Company in Italy," (1985); "InternationalContracts in Italo-Dutch Commerce," (1986). Legal Adviser: Italo-Dutch Chamber of Commerce, 1986; Italo-Mexican Chamber of Commerce. Director of the Italo-Dutch Chamber of Commerce. Representative in Italy of the Netherlands Foreign Investments Agency. *Member:* Milan Bar Association; International Bar Association (IBA); Union Internationale des Avocats (UIA). *LANGUAGES:* Italian, English, French and German. *PRACTICE AREAS:* Foreign Investments; Mergers and Acquisitions; Banking and Finance Law; Joint Ventures.

STEFANO SUTTI, born Milan, Italy, June 16, 1960. *Education:* Catholic University of Milan (J.D., summa cum laude, 1983; LL.M., 1987); Law School of the Bar of Milan (1985); XIX Course on Case Books Electronic Data Banks Inquiry (1986); AIJA, Dusseldorf (German Business Law, 1988); AIJA, Warsaw (Introduction to Polish Business Law, 1991); AIJA, Florence (Seminar on Cross-border Leasing Contracts, 1992). Author: "The Laws of Ethology," 1982; "The Indoeuropean Juridical Heritage," 1983; "The Lost Jurisdiction, The Crisis of Italian Justice," 1984; "The Man, The Technology and the Future," 1985; "Against the Human Rights Ideology," 1985; "Europe as a Destiny," 1985; "Information Technology and Law Firms," 1989; "Vertical Software for Lawyers: the State of the Art," 1989; "Operating Environments and Office Automation," 1991. Journalist, 1980—, Writer. Former Editor, 1982-1989, L'Uomo libero. Editor of the firm's Newsletter. Contributing Editor of PC Magazine. Contributing Editor of II Foro Padan, Quarterly Law Review. *Member:* Bar Association of Milan; AIJA; International Bar Association; Association of European Economic Lawyers (Member of Board and Secretary); Union Internationale des Avocats (UIA); Italian Exchange Control Lawyers Association; Press Association of Lombardy; Association of Italian Sommeliers; Club of Clubs; Rose-Blue Cross; Miyamoto Musashi Kendo Club; Ga-ryu-an laido Dojo. OS/2 Team Italy (Managing Partner). *LANGUAGES:* Italian, French, English, German and Latin. *PRACTICE AREAS:* Antitrust; Competition and EEC Law; Banking Law; Corporate Law; Distributorship; Agency and Franchise Law; Foreign Investments; Construction Law; International Contracts; Mergers and Acquisition.

SIMONA CAZZANIGA, born Abbiategrasso, Italy, April 29, 1962. *Education:* University of Milan (J.D.,1985); Law School of the Bar of Milan (1987); AIJA, Amsterdam (Seminar on Industrial Property Protection in Europe, 1988); AIJA, Florence (Seminar on Cross-Border Leasing Contracts, 1992). Author: "Introduction to the EEC Patent," Lecture, 1987; "The Conversion of Void Industrial Patents," 1988; "General Terms and Conditions of Trade Under Italian Law," 1988; "The Juridical Protection of Design," 1989; "Antitrust, A collection of Antitrust Statutes in Industrialized Countries and EEC," Ed., 1990; "Interior Design and Architectural Works, Copyright," 1991; "The Protection of Industrial Design in Italy," Italian Report at the XXX AIJA Congress, 1992. Assistant Professor, University of Milan, Industrial Property Department. Full Professor, Centro Europeo del Toscolano Master Course, Intellectual Property. *Member:* Bar Association of Milan; Association Internationale des Jeunes Avocats (AIJA-Member Executive Committee); Italian Exchange Control Lawyers Association (Lecturer); International Bar Association (IBA); Union Internationale des Avocats (UIA); Italian Association for the Protection of Design. (Head of Industrial Property Department). *LANGUAGES:* Italian, English and Spanish. *PRACTICE AREAS:* Patent Litigation and Prosecution; Trademark Litigation and Prosecution; License Negotiations; Antitrust; Competition Law; Industrial Models; Advertising Law; Copyright Law; Entertainment Law.

LUISA ZAMBON, born Milan, Italy, November 17, 1959. *Education:* University of Milan (J.D., 1982). Author: "A Survey on Contributory Infringements," 1985; "Problems Related to Managers Acquittance," 1985.

(This Listing Continued)

Assistant Professor, University of Milan. *Member:* Bar Association of Milan; AIJA (Associations Internationale des Jeunes Acocats); AIGA (Italian Association of Young Lawyers); UAE (Union des Avocats Européens). (Head of Labour Department). *LANGUAGES:* Italian, English, French and Dutch. *PRACTICE AREAS:* Labour Law; Employers Liability; Pension Law; Industrial Relations; Bankruptcy; Union Law.

ASSOCIATES

SEBASTIANO MASSIMO TINÉ, born Biella, Italy, August 18, 1963. *Education:* Sprachinstitut Tübingen (Sprachzeugnis, 1982); University of Minnesota (LL.B., 1983); University of Milan (J.D., cum laude, 1990); XXII Course on CaseBooks Electronic Data Banks Inquiry (1991). Author: "Jurisdiction and Conflict of Laws in Unfair Competition Trials," 1990. Former Technology Transfer Consultant in EEC-sponsored networks. *Member:* Association Internationale des Jeunes Avocats (AIJA); International Institute of Licensing Practitioners (IILP); Technology Innovation and Information (TII); Italian Federation of Traditional Karate Associations (FIKTA); Italian Association of Goshin Karatedo (AIGK). (Senior Associate). *LANGUAGES:* Italian, English, German and French. *PRACTICE AREAS:* Distributorship; Agency and Franchise Law; International Contracts; License Negotiations; Transfer of Technology; Pharmaceutical Patents; EEC Law; Product Liability Law.

DANIELA LANTICINA, born Magenta, Italy, August 15,1966. *Education:* University of Milan (J.D., cum laude, 1991); AIJA, Warsaw (Introduction to Polish Business Law, 1991); XXIII Course on Case Books Electronic Data Banks Inquiry (1992). Author: "The African Charter on Human and Peoples' Rights." Assistant Professor, International Law Department, University of Milan. *Member:* International Bar Association (IBA); Union Internationale des Avocats (UIA); AIJA; Rotaract Club; Italian Macrobiotic Association. (Senior Associate). *LANGUAGES:* Italian, English and French. *PRACTICE AREAS:* EEC Law; Bankruptcy; Litigation; International Private Law.

JULIA WILLIAMS, born London, England, May 10, 1964; admitted, Solicitor of the Supreme Court of England and Wales. *Education:* University College, Cardiff (B.A. Hons., Law and Italian, 1986). *Member:* Association Internationale des Jeunes Avocats (AIJA); The Law Society of England and Wales; Association of Women Solicitors; Association of Foreign Lawyers in Italy. *LANGUAGES:* English, Italian and German. *PRACTICE AREAS:* UK Law; International Contracts; Intellectual Property; Entertainment Law.

MARIA CARLA GIORGETTI, born Milan, Italy, October 19, 1969. *Education:* University of Milan (J.D., magna cum laude, 1992; LL.D. in Civil Procedure, 1994); XXVIII Course on Case Books Electronic Data Banks Inquiry, Milan (1993). Author: "The Order for Disclosure of Documents in Civil Proceedings in Italy and France;" "The Attorney's Right of Appeal with regard to Legal Costs." Assistant Professor, Civil Procedure Department, University of Milan. *Member:* Association Internationale des Jeunes Avocats (AIJA). *LANGUAGES:* Italian, English and French. *PRACTICE AREAS:* Litigation; Arbitration; EEC Law.

DAVIDE BRAGHINI, born Somma Lombardo, Italy, August 14, 1969. *Education:* University of Milan (J.D., magna cum laude, 1992). Co-Author: "Competition Laws of Europe - Italy," 1994. Author: "Abuse of a Dominant Position in Performing Handling Services in Italian Airports (1995)". *Member:* Association Internationale des Jeunes Avocats (AIJA); International Bar Association; British Italian Law Association. *LANGUAGES:* Italian, English and French. *PRACTICE AREAS:* Antitrust Law; Company Law; Commercial and International Contracts; Construction Law; Mergers and Acquisition; EEC Law.

LIVIA OGLIO, born Vigevano, Italy, October 25, 1969. *Education:* Catholic University of Milan (J.D., magna cum laude, 1992), XXVIII Course on Case Books Electronic Data Banks Inquiry, Milan (1993); School of the Chamber of Commerce of Milan (Specialisation in Arbitration Law, Milan, 1994); College of Europe, Brugges (LL.M., 1995). Author: Provisional Measures in International Commercial Arbitration (ICC Pre-Arbitral Referee). Assistant Professor, International Trade Law Department, Catholic University of Milan. *Member:* Association Internationale des Jeunes Avocats (AIJA); International Bar Association (IBA). *LANGUAGES:* Italian, French and English. *PRACTICE AREAS:* EEC Law; International Commercial Law; Arbitration; International Private Law.

HANNES LARCHER, born Bozen, Italy, January 27, 1968. *Education:* Catholic University of Milan (J.D., 1992), XVIII Course on Casé Books Electronic Data Banks Inquiry, Milan (1993). Author: "The Legal Protection of Software in Developed Countries, A Comparative Survey." *Member:* Association Internationale des Jeunes Avocats (AIJA); Kiwanis Club.

(This Listing Continued)

LANGUAGES: German, Italian and English. PRACTICE AREAS: Industrial and Intellectual Property; Legal IT; Corporate Law; Commercial Contracts; German Law.

MATTEO DE AGOSTINI, born Milan, Italy, October 2, 1965. Education: University of Milan (J.D., 1990). Author: "Trademarks and Product Imitation," 1990. LANGUAGES: Italian, English and French. PRACTICE AREAS: Labour Law; Employers Liability; Pension Law; Industrial Relations.

CLAUDIA BRAMBILLA, born Milan, Italy, April 30, 1965. Education: University of Milan (J.D., 1992). Author: "Settlement and Arbitration in the Law no. 108/90.". LANGUAGES: Italian, English and French. PRACTICE AREAS: Labour and Social Security Litigation; Labour Law.

CARLO PIANA, born Omegna, Italy, September 25, 1968. Education: University of Milan (J.D., 1992). Author: "The Contract of Franchising." Assistant Professor, Civil Law Department, University of Milan. LANGUAGES: Italian, English, French. PRACTICE AREAS: Distribution Agreements; Franchising; Commercial Law; Industrial Property; EEC Law.

LAURA PANCIROLI, born Milan, Italy, December 23, 1967. Education: Milan State University (J.D., 1993). Author: "The Treatment of EEC Citizens in Italy." Assistant Professor, International Law Department, University of Milan. LANGUAGES: Italian, English and French. PRACTICE AREAS: International Employment Contracts; Immigration Law.

FABIO DI PALMA, born Varese, Italy, September 14, 1963. Education: University of Milan (J.D., 1988). LANGUAGES: Italian, English. PRACTICE AREAS: Labour Law; Industrial Relations; Union Law.

STEFANIA SOPRANO, born Milan, Italy, January 21, 1967. Education: Milan University (J.D., magna cum laude, 1993). Author: "The Objects Clauses of Limited Companies' (1994). Assistant Professor, Company Law Department, University of Milan. Member: Association Internationale des Jeunes Avocats (AIJA). LANGUAGES: Italian and English. PRACTICE AREAS: Company Law; Mergers and Acquisitions; Banking Law; Finance Law; Joint Ventures.

OF COUNSEL

GUIDO MONTI, born Milan, Italy, November 4, 1903; admitted, Supreme Court. Education: Milan University (J.D. summa cum laude, 1926). Senior Partner, Monti & Partners, 1927-1983. Member: Bar of Milan (Director of the Council, 1954-1969); Italian Bar Association (Director, 1970-1976); The Bar National Insurance Fund (Director, 1970-1974). LANGUAGES: Italian, French. PRACTICE AREAS: Commercial Contracts; Litigation; Company Law; Construction Law; Real Estate.

ROBERTO DINI, born Turin, Italy, March 8, 1946. Education: University of Turin (Ph.D. in Electronic Engineering, 1970) Engineer (Italian State Examination, 1970). Registered Patent Attorney with the European Patent Office, Registered Industrial Property Consultant in Italy. Author: "Industrial Innovation: its Importance and its Implications within a Company," (1985); "Patent enforcement," (1990); "Strategical Importance of Patents and the Italian Situation," (1992). Teacher and Scientific Director of the Convey course for Intellectual Property Experts. Teacher of the course for neograduate engineers on "Industrial Property and Databases" held by ISVOR-Fiat. Member: Italian Association of Industrial Property Consultants of Business and Public Agencies (AICIPI) (Member, Directive Committee and Secretary); Italian Administrative Committee of Licensing Executive Society (LES); European Communities Trademark Practitioners' Association (ECTA); Italian Association of Advanced Documentation (AIDA); Italian Electro-Technical Association (AEI); Confindustria's working group on Intellectual Property. LANGUAGES: Italian, English, French and German. PRACTICE AREAS: Patents and Trademarks; Intellectual Property Corporate Policies; Licensing Contracts; Know-how Transfer; Technical Joint-Ventures; Technical Documentation and Data Retrieval.

LUDOVICO DELLA PENNA, born Nairobi, Kenya, October 10, 1961. Education: University of Milan (J.D., magna cum laude, 1985); Law School of the Bar of Milan (1988). Author: "Manslaughter in Italian Law." Former Referee of the Italian Rugby League. Member: Bar of Milan; Association of Criminal Lawyers of Milan; State Police Ex-Officers Association; Italian Basketball Federation. LANGUAGES: Italian and English. PRACTICE AREAS: Criminal Law; White Collar Crime; Insider Trading; Patent Prosecution; Trademark Prosecution; Counterfeiting.

(This Listing Continued)

CLERKS

GIOVANNI MAIOLI, born Milan, Italy, February 17, 1962. Education: GE.DA. (Computer Science Degree, 1986); XXIII Course on Case Books Electronic Data Bases Inquiry (1992). (EDP, Office Automation and Communications Manager). LANGUAGES: Italian and English. PRACTICE AREAS: Network Administration; Communications and Data Transfer Supervision; Office Automation Management; Audit of EDP Systems.

ELENA ALBINI, born Abbiategrasso, Italy, June 12, 1968. Education: Abbiategrasso Accounting School (Accounting Diploma, 1988); University of Milan (Law Student). (Head of Credit Collection Operations). LANGUAGES: Italian, French and English. PRACTICE AREAS: Debt Recovery and Bankruptcy Procedures.

LOREDANA FALCO, born Abbiategrasso, Italy, September 19, 1963. Education: Abbiategrasso Accounting School (Accounting Diploma, 1984). LANGUAGES: Italian, English and French. PRACTICE AREAS: Internal Accounting and Auditing.

Languages: Italian, English, French, German, Spanish, Japanese and Dutch.

REFERENCES: A list of typical clients is available upon request.

STUDIO LEGALE TAGLIORETTI FARESE CICERCHIA

VIA VINCENZO MONTI, 15
20123 MILAN, ITALY
Telephone: (2) 480.21.811
Telefax: (2) 481.93.877

Rome, Italy Office: Studio Legale Farese Cicerchia Taglioretti, Via Giovanni Nicotera, 24, 00195. Telephone: (6) 360.00.398 - 360.00.389. Telefax: (6) 360.00.397.

General Practice and Litigation, Corporation, Banking, Foreign Investment, EEC Law, Patent and Trademark, Intellectual Property, Labour, Distribution and Licensing.

FORTUNATO TAGLIORETTI, born Busto Arsizio, Varese, Italy, November 6, 1951; admitted, 1976, Italy. Education: University of Milan (J.D., 1973); Academy of American and International Law, Southwestern Legal Foundation, Dallas, Texas (1983). Member: International Bar Association. LANGUAGES: Italian and English. PRACTICE AREAS: Corporate Law; Banking Law; Foreign Investment Law; International Transaction Law.

PAOLO FARESE, born Rome, Italy, March 28, 1948; admitted, 1980, Italy. Education: University of Rome (J.D., 1973); University of Illinois College of Law (M.C.L., 1983). Rome Bar Association Award, 1976. Seminars; Institute of Comparative Law, University of Rome, 1976; American Legal Studies, Salzburg, 1977. Member: International Bar Association; American Bar Association. LANGUAGES: Italian and English. PRACTICE AREAS: Corporate Law; International Private Law; Labour Law.

PIETRO CICERCHIA, born Rome, Italy, January 8, 1955; admitted, 1983, Italy. Education: University of Rome (J.D., 1980). Seminar on EEC Law, Institute of European Community, Rome, 1984. LANGUAGES: Italian and English. PRACTICE AREAS: Corporate Law; Real Estate.

MASSIMO ZACCONI, born Milan, Italy, December 18, 1961; admitted, 1992, Italy. Education: Catholic University of the Sacred Heart (J.D., Magna cum laude, 1987); Freiburg University, Erasmus Program, (1991). Assistant Professor, History of Roman Law, Catholic University of the Sacred Heart, 1987-1992. LANGUAGES: Italian, English and German. PRACTICE AREAS: Labour Law.

MARCO GANDINI, born Milan, Italy, December 12, 1963. Education: Catholic University of the Sacred Heart of Milan (J.D., 1988); Bocconi University, Milan (Tax Law Master, 1992-1993); Cambridge Summer Programme (English Legal Method, 1992). LANGUAGES: Italian and English. PRACTICE AREAS: Company Law; Tax Law.

GIOVANNI LEONE, born Taranto, Italy, February 1, 1966. Education: Catholic University of the Sacred Heart (J.D., 1992); Hague Academy of International Law, Summer Program-Private International Law (1993). Assistant Professor, Private International Law, Catholic University of the Sacred Heart, 1992. LANGUAGES: Italian and English. PRACTICE AREAS: EEC Law; Patent and Trademark Law.

(This Listing Continued)

**STUDIO LEGALE TAGLIORETTI FARESE
CICERCHIA, Milan—Continued**

FRANCESCO TOMASSINI, born Rome, Italy, February 6, 1968; admitted, 1993, Rome. *Education:* University of Rome (J.D., 1992). *LAN-GUAGES:* Italian and English.

Languages: Italian, English and German.

TOFFOLETTO E ASSOCIATI

Studio Legale

Established in 1925

VIA EUGENIO CHIESA, 4
20122 MILAN, ITALY
Telephone: 0039 2 55187722
Telefax: 0039 2 55194527

Labour Law, Civil Law, Company Law, Commercial Law, Antitrust Law, Contracts, Mergers and Acquisitions, Litigation and Arbitration.

FIRM PROFILE: *Established in 1925 by Avv. Angelo Toffoletto. The firm has a wide knowledge of Legal services and it is specialized in Labour Law, Company Law, Commercial Law, Antitrust Law (Italian and EEC), Litigation and Arbitration. The firm is also linked with other firms in London, Paris, Amsterdam and Dusseldorf.*

MEMBERS OF FIRM

AVV. UMBERTO S. TOFFOLETTO, born Milan, Italy, July 3, 1929; admitted, 1953, Milan; 1965 Supreme Court. *Education:* University of Milan (J.D., 1951). Author of several articles in Labour Law area. Commentary Collective Labour Agreements: "Dirigenti di Aziende Industriali," 1956-1992; "Agenti e Rappresentanti di Commercio," 1956-1990; "Dirigenti di Aziende Commerciali," 1957-1992; "Viaggiatori e Piazzisti di Aziende Industriali," 1958-1975; "Viaggiatori e Piazzisti di Aziende Commerciali," 1958-1975; Codice Del Rapporto Di Lavoro Privato, 1989-1991. Assistant Professor, Labor Law, University of Milan, 1953-1963. *Member:* Associazione Italiana di Diritto del Lavoro. *LANGUAGES:* Italian. *PRACTICE AREAS:* Labour Law; Civil Law; Agency and Distributorship; Contracts; Litigation; Arbitration.

AVV. FRANCO TOFFOLETTO, born Milan, Italy, May 13, 1957; admitted, 1982, Milan. *Education:* University of Milan (J.D., 1980). Author of several articles in Labour Law area. Commentary, Collective Labor Agreement: "Dirigenti Aziende Industriali," 1982-1988; "Dirigenti Aziende Commerciali," 1983-1992; "Agenti e Rappresentanti di Commercio," 1982-1989; "I Licenziamenti individuali," Pirola, 1990 Codice. Contributor, legal columns, ie Il Sole 24 ore. *Member:* Associazione Italiana di Diritto del Lavoro; Associazione Internazionale Giuristi di Lingua Italiana. *LANGUAGES:* Italian and English. *PRACTICE AREAS:* Labour Law; Civil Law; Agency and Distributorship; Contracts; Litigation; Arbitration.

AVV. ALBERTO TOFFOLETTO, born Milan, Italy, May 6, 1960; admitted, 1988, Milan. *Education:* University of Milan (J.D., magna cum laude, 1983); University of London (LL.M., 1987). Author of several articles of Company Law and Antitrust Law. Assistant Professor, Company Law, University of Milan, 1990—. Lecturer, Company and Commercial Law, LIUC (Varese), 1992—. *LANGUAGES:* Italian and English. *PRACTICE AREAS:* Company Law; Commercial Law; Antitrust Law; EEC Law; Contracts; Merger and Acquisition; Litigation; Arbitration.

DOTT. PROC. PAOLA TRADATI, born Milan, Italy, February 5, 1961; admitted, 1991, Milan. *Education:* University of Milan (J.D., 1986). *LANGUAGES:* Italian and English. *PRACTICE AREAS:* Labour Law; Agency and Distributorship; Litigation.

DOTT. PROC. ANGELO ZAMBELLI, born Milan, Italy, October 27, 1962; admitted, 1992, Milan. *Education:* University of Milan (J.D., magna cum laude, 1987). *LANGUAGES:* Italian, French and English. *PRACTICE AREAS:* Labour Law; Litigation.

DOTT. PROC. MARCELLO GIUSTINIANI, born Milan, Italy, March 26, 1963; admitted, 1992, Milan. *Education:* University of Milan (J.D. magna cum laude, 1988). *LANGUAGES:* Italian and French. *PRACTICE AREAS:* Labour Law; Litigation.

(This Listing Continued)

ASSOCIATES

DOTT. PROC. ANTONELLA NEGRI, born Tradate, Italy, June 18, 1964; admitted, 1992, Milan. *Education:* University of Milan (magna cum laude, 1988). *LANGUAGES:* Italian, French and English. *PRACTICE AREAS:* Labour Law; Litigation.

DOTT. PROC. PAOLA PUCCI, born Milan, Italy, May 28, 1964. *Education:* University of Milan (J.D., 1990). *LANGUAGES:* Italian, French and English. *PRACTICE AREAS:* Labour Law; Litigation.

DOTT. PROC. LUISA MIAN, born Uboldo, Italy, December 20, 1964; admitted, 1993, Milan. *Education:* University of Milan (J.D., 1988). *LANGUAGES:* Italian, French and English. *PRACTICE AREAS:* Labour Law; Litigation.

DOTT. PROC. DIEGO PISELLI, born Bergamo, Italy, March 12, 1967; admitted, 1994, Milan. *Education:* University of Milan (J.D., magna cum laude, 1991). *LANGUAGES:* Italian, French and English. *PRACTICE AREAS:* Bankruptcy; Company Law; Commercial Law; Contracts; Torts; Litigation.

DOTT. PROC. LUCA TOFFOLETTI, born Milan, Italy, March 7, 1966. *Education:* University of Milan (J.D., magna cum laude, 1991); Yale Law School (visiting scholar, 1993-1994). Author of several articles on Antitrust Law. *LANGUAGES:* Italian and English. *PRACTICE AREAS:* Commercial Law; Antitrust Law; Company Law; Contracts.

DOTT. PAOLA BERTINELLI, born Milan, Italy, December 28, 1966. *Education:* University of Milan (J.D., 1991). *LANGUAGES:* Italian and English. *PRACTICE AREAS:* Commercial Law.

DOTT. PIERFRANCESCO GIUSTINIANI, born Milan, Italy, September 20, 1966. *Education:* University of Milan (J.D., magna cum laude, 1992). *LANGUAGES:* Italian, English and Spanish. *PRACTICE AREAS:* Labour Law.

DOTT. BARBARA MANGIACAVALLI, born Busto Arsizio, Italy, January 17, 1970. *Education:* University of Milan (J.D., magna cum laude, 1993). *LANGUAGES:* Italian and English. *PRACTICE AREAS:* Labour Law.

DOTT. LAURA MIANI, born Milan, Italy, August 24, 1970. *Education:* University of Milan (J.D., 1994). *LANGUAGES:* Italian and English. *PRACTICE AREAS:* Labour Law.

DOTT. EMANUELA NESPOLI, born Mariano C., Italy, June 3, 1969. *Education:* University Cattolica del Sacro Cuore of Milan (J.D., magna cum laude, 1992). *LANGUAGES:* Italian and English. *PRACTICE AREAS:* Labour Law.

DOTT. ALESSANDRA PAMPALONI, born Genoa, Italy, April 9, 1961. *Education:* University of Milan (J.D., 1992). *LANGUAGES:* Italian and English. *PRACTICE AREAS:* Labour Law.

Languages: Italian, French, Spanish and English.

TOSI & BONTEMPO

Established in 1979

VIA PAOLO DA CANNOBIO 10
20122 MILAN, ITALY
Telephone: 02/ 8052890
Fax: 02/ 72021655

Piacenza, Italy Office: Via F. Frasi 3, 29100. Telephone: 0523/335749; 384666. Fax: 0523/ 384475.

Civil Law, Real Estate Law, Company Law, Bankruptcy Law, Business Contracts (National & International), International Civil Procedure, Criminal Law, Administrative Law, Planning Law, Arbitration (National & International), Computer Law, Industrial Property Law, Labour Law, Family Law, Food Products Law and Russian Business Law.

FIRM PROFILE: *The firm is the Italian Legal Counselling Office Referee of important companies based in Moscow.*

PARTNERS

GIOVANNI TOSI, born Piacenza, Italy, June 21, 1938; admitted, 1969, Italy. *Education:* University of Ferrara (Dr.jur). Legal Adviser: ASTRA Veicoli Industriali SpA; RDB Edilizia SpA; RDB Hebel SpA; Camillo Corvi-Roussel SpA; CARIPLO, SpA; Cassa Di Risparmio di Parma e Piacenza SpA. Member: Special Rolls of the Legal Offices of Piacenza Court, 1969-1975; Rolls of Lawyer of Piacenza Court, 1976; Special Rolls of the High Courts, 1984; Rolls of Auditor, 1993; "Commendatore," of the Papal Order

(This Listing Continued)

of S. Gregorio Magno, 1985; Diocesan Association for the Support of Piacenza's Priesthood (I.D.S.C.); Lyons Club International. *LANGUAGES:* Italian, French and English. *PRACTICE AREAS:* Real Estate Law; Company Law; Bankruptcy Law; Business Contracts; Russian Business Law.

STEFANO BONTEMPO, born Piacenza, Italy, June 25, 1954; admitted, 1980, Italy. *Education:* University of Pavia (Dr.jur). Legal Adviser, ABB Group SpA: Pulimat SpA; Banca di Roma. Barrister, U.S.A. Consulate, Piacenza. Board of Audit: Cassa di Risparmio di Parma e Piacenza SpA, Parma, Gemofin SpA, Milano. Member: Rolls of Lawyer, Piacenza Court, 1986, Milan Court, 1990; Rolls of Auditor, 1988. Special Rolls of the High Courts, 1994. *LANGUAGES:* Italian, English and French. *PRACTICE AREAS:* Criminal Law; Banking Law; Insurance Law; National and International Arbitration; Russian Business Law.

ASSOCIATES

EMILIO TOSI, born Piacenza, Italy, July 16, 1968. *Education:* University of Parma (Dr.jur., summa cum laude). Junior Lecturer, Civil Law, University of Milan. Author: "I Contratti di Informatica," Pirola, 1993; "Il controllo giudiziario delle societa," Giuffré, 1994. *Member:* I.B.A.; AIGA; Rotaract Club International. *LANGUAGES:* Italian, English, French and German. *PRACTICE AREAS:* Company Law; National and International Business Contracts; Computer Law; International and National Arbitration; Industrial Property Law.

STUDIO LEGALE TRAVERSO E ASSOCIATI

VIA SANT'ANDREA 19
20121 MILAN, ITALY
Telephone: 39 (2) 76020566
Telefax: 39 (2) 76020430

International and Domestic Practice, Mergers and Acquisitions, Joint Ventures, Corporations, Contracts, Arbitration and Litigation, Banking, Foreign Investments, Patents and Trademarks, Advertising, Labor, Agency and Distributorship, Franchising, Competition, EC Law, Insolvency, Insurance, Real Estate, Administrative.

PARTNERS

MAURIZIO TRAVERSO, born Naples, Italy, October 16, 1945; admitted, 1971, Milan; 1977, Italy; 1985, Supreme Court. *Education:* University of Milan (Doctor of Jurisprudence, magna cum laude, 1969). *Member:* International Bar Association.

MARIO E. TRAVERSO, born Milan, Italy, August 28, 1954; admitted, 1982, Milan; 1988, Italy. *Education:* University of Milan (Doctor of Jurisprudence, 1980). Assistant of Industrial Property Law, University of Pavia, 1987-1988. Seminar in English Commercial Law, University of Cambridge (Great Britain) 1988. *Member:* International Bar Association.

EMANUELA FERRO, born Muggia, Italy, November 28, 1955; admitted, 1981, Milan; 1987, Italy. *Education:* University of Trieste (Doctor of Jurisprudence, 1978). Seminar in American Legal Studies, Salzburg, 1985. *Member:* International Bar Association.

BRUNO GIUFFRÈ, born Milan, Italy, January 11, 1962; admitted, 1988, Milan; 1994, Italy. *Education:* Catholic University of the Sacred Heart Milan (Doctor of Jurisprudence, magna cum laude, 1985). *Member:* International Bar Association.

ROCCO ROSA, born Bari, Italy, March 19, 1959; admitted, 1988, New York; 1989, Milan. *Education:* University of Bari (Doctor of Jurisprudence, magna cum laude, 1984); Columbia University, New York (LL.M., 1986). Associate, Willkie, Farr & Gallagher, New York, 1986-1987. *Member:* International Bar Association.

ASSOCIATES

RENATO OSCAR SCORCELLI, born Castronno, Italy, March 8, 1962; admitted, 1991, Milan. *Education:* University of Pisa (Doctor of Jurisprudence, 1986).

FRANCESCA ROLLA, born Milan, Italy, June 9, 1965; admitted, 1993, Milan. *Education:* University of Milan (Doctor of Jurisprudence, magna cum laude, 1988). Assistant of International and EEC law at University of Milan, 1988—. *Member:* Società Italiana per l'Organizzazione Internazionale.

(This Listing Continued)

SILVIA MIGIARRA, born Milan, Italy, October 22, 1966; admitted, 1993, Milan. *Education:* University of Milan (Doctor of Jurisprudence, 1990).

ANTHONY PEROTTO, born London, England, January 7, 1966; admitted, 1995, Milan. *Education:* University of Milan (Doctor of Jurisprudence, 1991). Assistant of Commercial Law, University of Milan.

MIRTA VINCI, born Messina, Italy, July 14, 1969. *Education:* European School, Luxembourgh (Baccalaureat, 1987); University of Milan (Doctor of Jurisprudence, 1994).

OF COUNSEL

MARCO MAZZARELLI, born Milan, Italy, October 27, 1953; admitted, 1983, Milan; 1989, Italy. *Education:* University of Milan (Doctor of Jurisprudence, 1980).

Languages: Italian, English, French and German

TREVISAN & CUONZO

AVVOCATI
VIA BRERA 6
20121 MILAN, ITALY
Telephone: 02/86463313
Telefax: 02/86463892

Intellectual Property, Patent, Trademark, Copyright and related Civil and Criminal Litigation, EEC and Italian Antitrust, Unfair Competition, General International Practice, Corporate and Commercial Contracts, Franchising, Licensing, Technology transfer, Merchandising, Agency and Distribution, Software, Joint Ventures, Entertainment and Media Law, Product Liability, Advertising.

LUCA TREVISAN, born Milan, Italy, November 25, 1956; admitted, 1982, Italy. *Education:* Parma University (J.D., 1980); Osnabrueck University (LL.M., 1992). Visiting Researcher, Osnabrueck University, Germany, 1988-1990. Editorial Staff, Il Foro Padano. Author: "Slavish Imitation," 1983; "Use of Another's Name for Commercial Purpose," 1986; "Use of Other's Trademarks in Advertising, The Rolls-Royce Case," 1988; Commentary on the Krizia case (in German) 1992; "Discovery in Italian Patent Litigation" (in German) 1992. *Member:* AIPPI; LIGUE; GRUR; INTA. *LANGUAGES:* German, English and French. *PRACTICE AREAS:* Industrial Property; Patent, Trademark and Copyright; Unfair Competition; Antitrust; Civil and Commercial Law; Distribution Agreements; Advertising; Litigation; Product Liability.

GABRIEL CUONZO, born Teramo, Italy, July 22, 1957; admitted, 1984, Italy. *Education:* Bari University (J.D., 1982). Research Assistant, Max-Planck-Institute, Munich, Germany, 1983-1987. Author: "Control of Advertising in Germany," 1987; "Protection of Famous Trademarks and Unfair Competition Law," 1988 (in German); "Trademark Piracy in Italy," 1988; "The Total Imitation of Products as an Act of Unfair Competition," 1989; "On Slavish Imitation of Perishable Products," 1990; "Evaluation of Damages in the Italian Patent Litigation," 1993 (Co-author, Julia Holden); "Design Protection for Motor Car Spare Parts?" 1994; "Criminal Law Approach to Trade Mark Protection in Italy," 1994. *Member:* AIPPI; IBA; GRUR; INTA. *LANGUAGES:* German, English and French. *PRACTICE AREAS:* Intellectual Property; Patents and Trademarks and related Criminal Law; Unfair Competition; Copyright; Antitrust; General Corporate Law; Product Liability.

JULIA HOLDEN, born Birkenhead, England, January 8, 1963; admitted, 1990, Solicitor of the Supreme Court of England and Wales. *Education:* University of Sussex (B.A., Hons. Law & German, 1986); Law School, London (1987); University of Constance, Germany (1984). Author: "Design & Development of Products & Services: Italy" (Co-author Gabriel Cuonzo); "Italian Position on IP and IT," 1993; "Report on the New Trade Mark Law in Italy," 1993; Intellectual Property Laws of Europe (Italy)," 1994. *Member:* INTA; AIPPI; IBA; GRUR. *LANGUAGES:* English, Italian, German and Japanese. *PRACTICE AREAS:* Intellectual Property; Copyright; Trademark and Patent; Company and Commercial; Employment Law; International Contracts; Product Liability.

MICHAELA MADNER, born Vienna, Austria, October 30, 1966. *Education:* Vienna University (1985-1990); Salzburg (Mag.jur, 1993). *Member:* GRUR. *LANGUAGES:* German, Italian, English and French.

SIMONA LAVAGNINI, born Bergamo, Italy, November 28, 1968. *Education:* Pavia University (J.D., 1993); University of Bristol, England

(This Listing Continued)

TREVISAN & CUONZO, AVVOCATI, Milan—Continued

(1992). *LANGUAGES:* Italian, English and German. *PRACTICE AREAS:* Intellectual Property; Copyright; Trademarks and Patents.

OF COUNSEL

RAFFAELLO NEMNI, born Tripoli, January 1, 1954; admitted, 1991, Italy. *Education:* University of Milan Law School. Counsel Member of Marques. *Member:* AIPPI. *LANGUAGES:* Italian and English. *PRACTICE AREAS:* Intellectual Property; Criminal Law.

STUDIO LEGALE TRUCILLO-DE ZIGNO

VIA MONTE DI PIETA, 1/A
20121 MILAN, ITALY
Telephone: (02) 87.81.88; 86.46.20.63
Telecopier: (02) 72.02.00.20
Telex: 332325 SLPT I

General Practice, Corporate, Commercial, Labor and Insurance Law.

AVV. PIERLUIGI TRUCILLO, born Montoro Superiore, Italy, January 28, 1943; admitted, 1972, Italy; 1988, Court of Cassation. *Education:* University of Milan Law School, (1966). ISPI, Milan, Research Institute of Foreign Affairs, 1967-1968.

AVV. FLAVIA DE ZIGNO, born Florence, Italy, March 31, 1955; admitted, 1981, Italy. *Education:* University of Florence Law School, (1977).

DOTT. PROC. EMANUELE MARTINOLI, born Milan, Italy, April 14, 1962; admitted, 1993, Italy. *Education:* University of Milan Law School (1988).

Languages: English and French.

UGHI & NUNZIANTE

Established in 1969

VIA SANT'ANDREA, 19
20121 MILAN, ITALY
Telephone: 76013368
Cable Address: "Novalex"
Telex: 311634 "UNALEX"
Fax: 784140

Rome, Italy Office: Via Venti Settembre 1. Telephone: 476841. Cable Address: "Novalex". Telex: 611459 NURLAW. Fax: h870397.

General and International Practice, Corporation, Foreign Investments, Patent, Trademark, Admiralty, Aviation, Taxation, Labor, Oil and Gas, Financing and Banking, EEC Law, Insolvency and Administrative Law.

PARTNERS

GIOVANNI M. UGHI, born Parma, Italy, January 26, 1924; admitted, 1948, Milan; 1951, Italy. *Education:* Parma University Law School (Doctor of Jurisprudence, magna cum laude, 1946); Harvard Law School (LL.M., 1953); Seminar in American Legal Studies, Salzburg, 1953. President, Harvard Law School Association of Europe, 1968-1971. Member: Committee on Restrictive Business Practices of International Chamber of Commerce, 1960—; Legal Committee of American Chamber of Commerce for Italy, 1962—. Honorary Legal Adviser to the British Chamber of Commerce for Italy, 1962. *Member:* International Bar Association (Committee on Business Organizations); The Association of the Bar of the City of New York; Associazione Italiana Giuristi Europei; Associazione-Italiana per L'Arbitrato. *LANGUAGES:* Italian, English.

GIORGIO DELBUE, born Mantova, Italy, July 16, 1936; admitted, 1972, Milan; 1978, Italy. *Education:* University of Milan (Doctor of Jurisprudence, 1960). *Member:* International Bar Association. *LANGUAGES:* Italian, English, French.

MARCO G. BRESCIA, born Lavagna, Genoa, Italy, November 29, 1938; admitted, 1968, Milan; 1974, Italy. *Education:* University of Genoa (Doctor of Jurisprudence, 1962); Institute of Comparative Law at New York University School of Law (M.C.J., 1976). *Member:* American Association of International Law; International Bar Association (Member, Committee on Business Organizations). *LANGUAGES:* Italian, English.

MICHAEL C. KIRKHAM, born Bournemouth, England, August 26, 1946; admitted, as Solicitor of the Supreme Court of England and Wales,

(This Listing Continued)

1975 (Not admitted in Italy). *Education:* University of Oxford (B.A., 1968). *LANGUAGES:* English, Italian.

FIORELLA F. ALVINO, born Milan, Italy, February 3, 1954; admitted, 1980, Milan. *Education:* University of Milan (Doctor of Jurisprudence, magna cum laude, 1977); Harvard Law School (LL.M., 1984); Orientation Program in U.S. Legal System, Georgetown University, D.C. (1983). Seminar in American Legal Studies, Salzburg, 1982. *Member:* International Bar Association (Committee on Business Organizations); Harvard Law School Association of Europe; Associazione Valutaristi Italiani. *LANGUAGES:* Italian, English, French.

OF COUNSEL

Pietro Rescigno   *Guido Nori*
Piero Bernardini   (Not admitted in Italy)

ASSOCIATES

ANNA MARIA FULGONI, born Pontypridd, S. Wales, March 19, 1952; admitted, 1978 as Solicitor of the Supreme Court of England and Wales and the College of Law (Not admitted in Italy). *Education:* University of Southampton (LL.B., 1974). *Member:* Young Lawyer's International Association (AIJA) (Member, Executive Committee). *LANGUAGES:* English, Italian.

MAURIZIO FRASCHINI, born Milan, Italy, November 2, 1958; admitted, 1989, Milan. *Education:* Catholic University of Milan (Doctor of Jurisprudence, magna cum laude, 1982).

STEFANO PADOVANI, born Ferrara, Italy, April 14, 1961; admitted, 1989, Italy. *Education:* University of Ferrara (Doctor of Jurisprudence, magna cum laude, 1985); University of Ferrara (Diploma of German Law Specialization, 1987; 1988; Diploma of Banking Law Specialization, 1988-1990); Diploma of Arbitration (Bologna, 1990); City of London Polytechnic (Summer School, Banking and Finance, 1991). Assistant Professor, Industrial Law, University of Pavia, 1990.

GIANVINCENZO LUCCHINI, born Bologna, Italy, January 3, 1960; admitted, 1990, Italy. *Education:* University of Bologna (Doctor of Jurisprudence, magna cum laude, 1987); St. John's University, New York (Certificate, 1986); Academy of American and International Law; Southwestern Legal Foundation, University of Texas at Dallas (Certificate, 1988).

VITTORIO NOSEDA, born Como, Italy, November 27, 1962; admitted, 1991, Milan. *Education:* University of Milan (Doctor of Jurisprudence, magna cum laude, 1987); Diploma of Advanced International Studies, Salzburg, 1988; McGeorge School of Law, University of the Pacific (LL.M., 1989).

GUIDO FAUDA, born Varese, Italy, April 4, 1962; admitted, 1991, Milan. *Education:* University of Milan (Doctor of Jurisprudence, 1986).

ALESSANDRO ORSUCCI, born Pisa, Italy, July 13, 1964; admitted, '992, Florence. *Education:* University of Pisa (Doctor of Jurisprudence, magna cum laude, 1988).

LEONARDO FEDRINI, born Sorengo, Switzerland, December 9, 1964; (Not admitted in Italy). *Education:* Bocconi University of Milan (Doctor of Economics and Commerce, 1989).

PIETRO CALICETI, born Ascoli Piceno, Italy, July 11, 1965; admitted, 1992, Milan. *Education:* University of Milan (Doctor of Jurisprudence, 1989).

ANDREA RESCIGNO, born Naples, Italy, January 2, 1965; admitted, 1992, Milan. *Education:* Catholic University of Milan (Doctor of Jurisprudence, 1989).

FABIO SCARAVILLI, born Lecco, Italy, August 6, 1963; admitted, 1991, Milan. *Education:* Catholic University of Milan (Doctor of Jurisprudence, 1988); Chamber of Arbitration of Milan (Diplome, 1992).

ALESSANDRA AZZOLINI, born Parma, Italy, February 8, 1965; admitted, 1993, Milan. *Education:* University of Parma (Doctor of Jurisprudence, magna cum laude, 1989).

LUCA PICONE, born Milan, Italy, July 12, 1963; (Not admitted in Italy). *Education:* University of Milan (Doctor of Jurisprudence, magna cum laude, 1992).

(This Listing Continued)

ADALBERTO CASTORO, born Milan, Italy, July 12, 1969; (Not admitted in Italy). *Education:* University of Milan (Doctor of Jurisprudence, 1993).

PARTNERS ROME OFFICE

Gianni Nunziante	Maurizio M. Delfino
Carlo Capua	Alessandro Varrenti
Marcello Gioscia	Rino Caiazzo

Languages: Italian, English, French and German

FOREIGN REFERENCES: Alfred Dunhill Ltd., London, U.K.; Amoco Corp., Chicago, U.S.A.; Asarco Inc., New York, U.S.A.; Akzo, Arnhem, The Netherlands; Bell & Howell Co., Wilmington, U.S.A.; Banque National de Paris, Paris, France; Bausch & Lomb Inc., Rochester, U.S.A.; Bayer; Caterpillar Overseas S.A., Geneva, Switzerland; Chanel, Paris, France; Columbia Pictures Industries, Inc., New York, U.S.A.; Chloride Group PLC, London, U.K.; The Coca Cola Corp., Atlanta, U.S.A.; Degussa AG, Frankfurt, West Germany; Dow Chemicals, Midland, U.S.A.; Dun & Bradstreet Corp., New York, U.S.A.; EEC International Ltd., St. Austell, U.K.; Firestone Co., Akron, U.S.A.; Ford Motor Co., Detroit, U.S.A.; The Gillette Company, Boston, U.S.A.; GPA Group, Shannon, Eize; Guinness P.L.C.; Harvard University, Cambridge, U.S.A.; Hercules Inc., Wilmington, U.S.A.; Holiday Co., Memphis, U.S.A.; ITALSTAT Spa, I.T.T., Inc.; Litton Industries, Beverly Hills, U.S.A.; Nomura Securities, Tokyo; Occidental Petroleum Corp., Los Angeles, U.S.A.; Omron Tateisi Electronics Co., Tokyo, Japan; Pitney Bowes Inc., Stamford, U.S.A.; Rochas S.A.; Rothschild, London; Rowntree Mackintosh Ltd., York, U.K.; Sogo Co. Ltd., Tokyo; Texas Instruments, Inc., Dallas, U.S.A.

(For Biographical Data, see Professional Biographies at Rome, Italy).

VILLA, GUISO, BROGLIO & MAMELI

CORSO DI PORTA VITTORIA 28
20122 MILAN, ITALY
Telephone: (39) (2) 55017889
Fax: (39) (2) 55188994
Telex: (0) (023) 192756

Corporate, International Business and Financial Transactions, Domestic and International Taxation, Estate Planning, Mergers and Acquisitions, Foreign Investments, Commercial Litigation, Bankruptcy, Banking, Securities, Environmental Law, Labor Law, Arbitration, Intellectual Property, Entertainment Law, Real Estate and Antitrust.

MEMBERS OF FIRM

ADRIANO VILLA, born Melzo (Milan), Italy, February 3, 1958; admitted to practice 1983; admitted to bar 1988. *Education:* University of Milan School of Law (Doctor of Jurisprudence, 1982). European Community Commission's Executive Training Programme in Japan, Tokyo (1986-1987). In-house Trainee Sumitomo Corporation, Tokyo, 1987. Visiting Foreign Lawyer, Nagashima & Ohno, Tokyo, 1987. Foreign Associate, Masuda & Ejiri (now Asahi Law Offices), Tokyo, 1988-1991. Visiting Researcher (Japanese Ministry of Education's Scholarship), Sophia University, Tokyo, Japan (1989-1991). *Member:* International Bar Association; Inter-Pacific Bar Association; Italian Chamber of Commerce in Japan; Italian Bar Association. *LANGUAGES:* Italian, English, Japanese, French.

STEFANO GUISO-GALLISAY, Born Rome, Italy, July 15, 1959; admitted to practice 1983; admitted to bar 1985; California 1989; U.S. Court of Appeals, Ninth Circuit 1989; U.S. District Court, Central District of California 1989; U.S. Tax Court 1989; U.S. Court of Claims 1989. *Education:* University of Rome School of Law (Doctor of Jurisprudence, cum laude, 1983); Arbitration Law Review; University of California, Berkeley, Boalt Hall School of Law (LL.M., 1987). Visiting Foreign Lawyer, Hale and Dorr, Boston (1987). Associate, Loeb and Loeb, Los Angeles (1988-1990). *Member:* California State Bar; International Fiscal Association; American Bar Association; Italian Bar Association. *LANGUAGES:* Italian, English.

GUIDO BROGLIO, born Bagnolo Cremasco (Cremona), Italy, January 26, 1958; admitted to practice 1983; admitted to bar 1987. *Education:* University of Milan School of Law (Doctor of Jurisprudence, 1982); University of California, San Diego Law School, Institute on International and Comparative Law (1990). *Member:* International Bar Association; Italian Bar Association. *LANGUAGES:* Italian, English, French.

ANTONELLA MAMELI, born Busto Arsizio (Varese), Italy, June 9, 1958; admitted to practice 1983; admitted to bar, Italy and New York 1989. *Education:* University of Cagliari School of Law (Doctor of Jurisprudence, summa cum laude, 1983); Yale Law School (LL.M., 1985, J.S.D., 1988). *Member:* Italian Bar Association; American Bar Association; New York State Bar Association; International Bar Association. *LANGUAGES:* Italian, English, French.

(This Listing Continued)

UMBERTO FANTINI, born Milan, Italy, June 22, 1958; admitted to practice 1982; admitted to bar 1985. *Education:* University of Milan School of Law (Doctor of Jurisprudence, summa cum laude, 1982). *Member:* Italian Bar Association. *LANGUAGES:* Italian, German.

JUDITH PAINE, born Tripoli, Libya, September 4, 1964; admitted 1990 Solicitor, Supreme Court of England and Wales (not admitted in Italy). *Education:* University of Warwick School of Law (LL.B. Hons, 1986). Allen & Overy, London (1988-1991). *Member:* Law Society of England and Wales; British-Italian Law Association. *LANGUAGES:* English, Italian.

SILVIA VILLA, born Melzo (Milan), Italy, September 29, 1963; admitted to practice 1988. *Education:* University of Milan School of Law (Doctor of Jurisprudence, 1988). *Member:* Italian Bar Association. *LANGUAGES:* Italian, English, French, German.

OF COUNSEL

ANGELO VILLA, born Pandino (Cremona), Italy, September 17, 1924; admitted to practice 1951; admitted to bar 1954. *Education:* University of Milan School of Law (Doctor of Jurisprudence, 1950). *Member:* Italian Bar Association. *LANGUAGES:* Italian.

STUDIO LEGALE VUOLI LANZA E ASSOCIATI

VIALE MAJNO, 17/A
20122 MILAN, ITALY
Telephone: 02-76.01.37.91
Telecopier: 02-76.00.87.67

General Domestic and International Practice, Litigation, Corporation, Labor, Foreign Investment, Patent and Trademark, Trusts and Estates, Bankruptcy, Real Estate and Family Law, Arbitration.

MEMBERS OF FIRM

PIER LUIGI LANZA, born Palermo, Italy, October 2, 1937; admitted, 1966, Milan. *Education:* University of Milan Law School (J.D., magna cum laude, 1962); Stage Academie du Droit International, The Hague, The Netherlands; Direction Générale Acier, CECA, Stage, 1964. *Member:* American Italian Law Association. *LANGUAGES:* Italian, French and English. *PRACTICE AREAS:* Corporate Law; Arbitration; Litigation; Financial and Commercial Transactions.

FEDERICA VUOLI, born Rapallo (GE), Italy, August 24, 1950; admitted, 1977, Milan. *Education:* University of Milan Law School (J.D., magna cum laude, 1974). *Member:* Milan Bar Association (Milan Bar Committee, 1992—); Istitueto Per Il Diretto Chi Famiglia (IDF). *LANGUAGES:* Italian, French and English. *PRACTICE AREAS:* Real Estate Law; General Civil Litigation; Family Law.

FRANCO DE GREGORIO, born Milan, Italy, January 2, 1949; admitted, 1979, Milan. *Education:* University of Milan Law School (J.D., 1974). Assistant Professor, Industrial Law, Patent, Trademark and Intellectual Property Law, University of Milan, 1982—. Chairman, Commission on Corporate Law, U.A.E. (Union des Avocats Europénnes, Luxembourg). Member, Tax Commission, 1980—. *Member:* Ligue International Real Du Droit De La Concurrence. *LANGUAGES:* Italian, French and English. *PRACTICE AREAS:* Intellectual Property Law; General Civil Practice; Corporate Law; Tax Law.

ASSOCIATES

FRANCO F. MACCABRUNI, born Milan, Italy, February 21, 1964; admitted, 1991, Milan. *Education:* University of Milan Law School (J.D., magna cum laude, 1987). Assistant Professor, Commercial Law, University of Milan, 1987—. Author: "Clausole statutarie di prelazione," in Giurisprudenza commerciale, 1986; "Considerazioni in tema di impugnativa della delibera di approvazione del bilancio certificato," in Giurisprudenza commerciale, 1992; "Questioni in tema di assemblea totalitaria," in Giurisprudenza commerciale, 1993; "Alcune questioni in tema di recesso dalle societá di capitali," in Societá & Diritto, 1993. *Member:* American Italian Law Association; U.A.E. *LANGUAGES:* Italian, French, English and German.

ELISABETTA MOTZO, born Como, Italy, August 8, 1966; admitted, 1992, Monza, Lower Courts. *Education:* University of Milan Law School (J.D., 1991). Assistant Professor, Commercial Law, University of Milan, 1991—. *Member:* U.A.E. *LANGUAGES:* Italian and English.

STUDIO LEGALE
ZAMBELLI-LUZZATI-MEREGALLI

in association with Camilotti-Ceccon-Polettini and with Studio Legale
Beltramo

5, VIA BORROMEI
20123 MILAN, ITALY
Telephone: 39-2-86451933
Fax: 39-2-86451997

General Civil Practice, International Practice, Mergers and Acquisitions, Corporate Laws, Foreign Investments, Tax, Employment, Labour, EEC Laws, Contracts, Arbitration and Litigation, Administrative Law, Commercial Law, Bankruptcy Law, Intellectual Property, Patents, Trademarks, Copyright.

PARTNERS

PAOLO ZAMBELLI, born Varese, Italy, July 4, 1952; admitted, 1979, Italy. *Education:* Milan University (LL.D., cum laude, 1975). *Member:* Milan Bar.

ANGIOLO LUZZATI, born Savona, Italy, February 6, 1922; admitted, 1980, Italy. *Education:* (LL.D., 1972). "Mandataire Agree" at the European Patent Office. Member of the Licensing Executive Society. Registered in the roll of the Industrial Property Consultants. Registered in the roll of the Official Translators of the Milan Court. *Member:* Milan Bar.

DANIELA MEREGALLI, born Milan, Italy, June 13, 1957; admitted, 1984, Italy. *Education:* Sacro Cuore University of Milan (LL.D., cum laude, 1981). *Member:* Milan Bar.

ASSOCIATES

GIULIA COCCHETTI, born Milan, Italy, September 22, 1962; admitted, 1989, Italy. *Education:* Milan University (LL.D., cum laude, 1986).

MATTEO ZAPELLI, born Pavia, Italy, December 29, 1964; admitted, 1992, Italy. *Education:* Sacro Cuore University of Milan (LL.D., cum laude, 1988).

ESTER GAMMIERI, born Manfredonia (Foggia), Italy, August 5, 1963; admitted, 1991, Italy. *Education:* University of Milan (LL.D., cum laude, 1987).

CESARA FIRPO, born Vigevano (Pavia), Italy, March 13, 1963; admitted, 1994, Italy. *Education:* University of Milan (LL.D., 1990).

RAFFAELLA MACCHI, born Varese, Italy, November 11, 1967. *Education:* University of Milan (LL.D., 1992).

FABRIZIO VERSÉ, born Pavia, Italy, November 23, 1963. *Education:* University of Pavia (LL.D., 1991).

LUCA GALEANDRO, born Milan, Italy, September 29, 1966. *Education:* Milan University (LL.D., 1991).

ASSOCIATED OFFICE (PADUA)
PARTNERS

FRANCESCO CAMILOTTI, born Padua, Italy, October 6, 1949; admitted, 1977, Italy. *Education:* University of Padua (LL.D., 1974). *Member:* Padua Bar.

ROBERTO CECCON, born Venice, Italy, February 24, 1954; admitted, 1983, Italy. *Education:* University of Padua (LL.D., 1979). Arbitrator, American Arbitration Association and Swiss Chamber of Commerce in Italy. *Member:* International Association of Young Lawyers; Padua Bar.

ALESSANDRO POLETTINI, born Modena, Italy, May 29, 1956; admitted, 1984, Italy. *Education:* University of Padua (LL.D., 1982). *Member:* Padua Bar.

ASSOCIATES

ILARIA BARTOLUCCI, born Rome, Italy, May 13, 1958; admitted, 1989, Italy. *Education:* University of Padua (LL.D., 1985).

ROBERTO SANTORO, born Padua, Italy, June 6, 1966; admitted, 1994, Italy. *Education:* University of Padua (LL.D., 1991).

ANTONIO GRAVA, born Udine, Italy, December 31, 1966. *Education:* University of Bologna (LL.D., 1989).

ALESSIO VIANELLO, born Venice, Italy, April 17, 1967; admitted, 1994, Italy. *Education:* University of Padua (LL.D., 1991).

(This Listing Continued)

EU958B

SILVIA FRIGO, born Lonigo, (Vicenza), Italy, May 3, 1967. *Education:* University of Padua (LL.D., 1992).

MATTIA DALLA COSTA, born Padua, Italy, June 19, 1968. *Education:* University of Ferrara (LL.D., 1992).

ALESSANDRA ROLANDI GIOI, born Padua, Italy, July 13, 1964; admitted, 1994, Italy. *Education:* University of Padua (LL.D., 1990).

ASSOCIATED OFFICE (ROME)
PARTNERS

MARIO BELTRAMO, born Rome, Italy, February 23, 1919; admitted, 1945, Italy. *Education:* Rome University (LL.D., 1942).

LUCIO FRANCARIO, born Campobasso, Italy, November 27, 1952; admitted, 1979, Italy. *Education:* Rome University (J.D., 1977). Extraordinary Professor, Private Law, Macerata University, 1990—.

SUSANNA BELTRAMO, born Rome, Italy, October 30, 1955; admitted, 1985, Italy. *Education:* L.U.I.S.S. University, Rome (Doctor of Political Science, 1977); Rome University (J.D., 1979); Stanford University, California (Post Graduate Courses, 1979-1980).

ASSOCIATES

GIUSEPPE SCHIAVELLO, born Vibo Valentia, Italy, May 1, 1966; admitted, 1993, Italy. *Education:* L.U.I.S.S. University, Rome (J.D., 1989).

SABRINA BRUNO, born Cosenza, Italy, January 30, 1965; admitted, 1992, Italy. *Education:* L.U.I.S.S. University, Rome (J.D., 1987); Oxford University, U.K. (M.Litt., 1994). Researcher, Corporate Law, Calabria University, 1993—.

OLGA SESSO, born Cosenza, Italy, March 12, 1965; admitted, 1992, Italy. *Education:* L.U.I.S.S. University, Rome (J.D., 1988).

GIULIO TOGNAZZI, born Rome, Italy, July 27, 1967. *Education:* Rome University (J.D., 1992).

MARINA SAVASTANO, born Copenhagen, Denmark, November 19, 1969. *Education:* Rome University (J.D., 1994).

STEFANO AGNOLI, born Rome, Italy, November 15, 1968. *Education:* Rome University (J.D., 1994).

Languages: Italian, English and French

REPRESENTATIVE CLIENTS: General Electric Plastics B.V.; Microsoft Corporation; Minnesota Mining Manufacturing (3M); Hydro Aluminium A.S.; Federal Express Corporation; JIB Group Plc. Creditanstalt Bankverein; Chaffoteaux et Maury; Cabot Corporation; Panasonic; Belleli SpA.; Goodyear Chemicals Europe; Silicon Graphics World Trade Corporation; Anz Grindlays Bank Plc.; B.S.F.E. - Banque de la Société Financiére Européenne; The Sumitomo Bank Ltd.; The Long-Term Credit Bank of Japan Ltd.; The Sanwa Bank Ltd.; The Mitsubishi Bank Ltd.; Hotel Investment Corporation; ABN AMRO Bank; Crédit Commercial de France; Mitsubishi Corporation; Emerson Radio Corporation; Compagnie de Distribution de Matériel Electrique S.A.

DE MEO & ASSOCIATI STUDIO LEGALE

PIAZZA SAN PASQUALE, 10
80121 NAPLES, ITALY
Telephone: (+ +39 81) 7642295; 7643402
Fax: (+ +39 81) 7646262

Rome, Italy Office: Corso Vittorio Emanuele II, 287, 80121. Telephone: (+ +39 6) 6892623; 6740256 (+ +39336) 743496, 743497. Telefax: (+ +39 6) 6867594.

Milan, Italy Office: Piazza San Camillo de Lellis, 1, 20124. Telephone: (+ +39 2) 66988125. Fax: (+ +39 2) 66988179.

General Practice, Admiralty, Aviation, Commercial Law, Business and Tax Consultants.

MEMBERS OF FIRM

*Michele de Meo	Roberto De Cristofaro
Martino Cilento	Claudio Mancini

*Rome, Milan and Naples

STUDIO LEGALE LAURO

19 VIA DEPRETIS
80133 NAPLES, ITALY
Telephone: 081 5800199
Fax: 5800195
Telex: 720338 LAURO I

Associated Offices in Gioia Tauro (Palmi), Italy and Crotone, Italy.

Commercial, Shipping, Aviation, International Trade, Corporate, including Cross border Mergers and Acquisitions, Insurance, Banking, Investment, EEC, Energy, Bankruptcy, Trademark, Patents, Copyright, Competition, Real Estate, Personal Injury, Product Liability, Distribution, Constitutional and Administrative, Public and Private International Law, National and International Arbitration and Civil Litigation.

FIRM PROFILE: The firm offers its Italian and Overseas clients assistance in the south and central Italy.

MEMBERS OF FIRM

FRANCESCO LAURO, born Naples, Italy, December 17, 1955. *Education:* University of Naples (Law Degree, with first class Hons.); University College London. *Member:* Naples Bar Association; London Maritime Arbitrators Association; Propellar Club; International Bar Association.

ERNESTO ARDIA. *Education:* University of Naples (Law).

ALFREDO DE FILIPPIS. *Education:* University of Naples (Law).

CLARA RUGGIERO. *Education:* University of Naples (Law).

VICTOR SOTUNDE. *Education:* Thames Valley University, England (LL.B.).

English, French, German, Italian and Spanish.

STUDIO LEGALE TESAURO

Established in 1958

VIA TOLEDO, 156
80134 NAPLES, ITALY
Telephone: 551 52 76
Fax: 552 39 35

Rome, Italy Office: Largo Messico 7, 00198. Telephone: 854 78 92. Fax: 855 44 38.

General and International Practice. Commercial and Corporation Law. Foreign Investment, Taxation, Unfair Competition, Bankruptcy and Administrative Law.

FIRM PROFILE: The firm was established in 1958 and offers a full range of legal services. It is well known for its General and International practice, especially European Community Law. The client base is European and North American in scope.

PAOLO TESAURO, born Naples, Italy, October 11, 1934; admitted, 1956. *Education:* University of Naples (Doctor of Jurisprudence. maxima cum laude, 1956). Full Professor of Law, University of Naples, 1967. Director, European-United States Legal Center, 1967-1977. Vice President, Arbitration Court of Naples, 1975-1983. Panel Arbitrator of American Arbitration Association, Associazione Italiana per l'Arbitrato. Author (Main Publications): "Le Indipendent Regolatory Commissions," 1966; "Espropriazione, indennizzo, tutela del cittadino nel sistema americano," 1968; "Stati Uniti d'America (ordinamento politico e giuridico)," in Novissimo Digesto Italiano, 1972. *LANGUAGES:* Italian and English. *PRACTICE AREAS:* General and International Practice; European Community Law; Administrative Law.

ASSOCIATES

PAOLA FERRARA, born Naples, Italy, November 13, 1961; admitted, 1990, Italy. *Education:* University of Naples (Doctor of Jurisprudence, maxima cum laude). Specialization in Administrative Law, University of Naples; PHD in Public Law 1992. *LANGUAGES:* Italian and English. *PRACTICE AREAS:* Bankruptcy; Administrative Law.

CLAUDIO TESAURO, born Naples, Italy, October 13, 1965; admitted, 1990, Italy. *Education:* University of Naples (Doctor of Jurisprudence, maxima cum laude); New York University (M.C.J., 1988). Commission of European Communities, Legal Service (Stage March, 1989). *LANGUAGES:* Italian, English, French and Spanish. *PRACTICE AREAS:* Foreign Investment; European Community Law.

(This Listing Continued)

ELISA SALDUTTI, born Naples, Italy, January 2, 1964; admitted, 1988, Italy. *Education:* University of Naples (Doctor of Jurisprudence, maxima cum laude, 1988). *LANGUAGES:* Italian and English. *PRACTICE AREAS:* Administrative Law; Unfair Competition.

BRUNO DE MARIA, born Naples, Italy, March 10, 1968; admitted, 1994, Italy. *Education:* University of Naples "Federico II" (Doctor of Jurisprudence, maxima cum laude, 1991). Specialization in European Community Law, Maxima cum laude, University of Naples 1993. *LANGUAGES:* Italian, English and French. *PRACTICE AREAS:* General and International Practice; Commercial and Corporation Law; European Community Law.

FRANCESCO TESAURO, born Naples, Italy, April 30, 1971; admitted, 1994, Italy. *Education:* University of Naples"Federico II" (Doctor of Jurisprudence, maxima cum laude, 1994). *LANGUAGES:* Italian and English. *PRACTICE AREAS:* General and International Practice; Commercial and Corporation Law.

Languages: English, French and Italian.

REPRESENTATIVE CLIENTS: Alfa Romeo-Alfasud; Alitalia; Aero Transporti Italiani (A.T.I.); E.L.I.V.I.E.; FINCANTIERI; Societa Esercizi Bacini Napoletani (S.E.B.N.); Banco di Napoli; Banca della Provincia; Banca Popolare di Napoli; I.S.V.E.I.M.E.R.; CIA. (Compagnia Italiana Alberghi); 3M-Minnesota, Mining & Manufacturing Co.; National Council of Stockbrokers; ENI; Italgas; Metano Citta'; Sidigas; Cementir; Deutsche Bank; CRAI (Consorzio Ricerche Applicazioni di Informatica).

STUDIO LEGALE CAMILOTTI-CECCON-POLETTINI

in association with Zambelli-Luzzati-Meregalli

and

Studio Legale Beltramo

Established in 1986

GALLERIA BORROMEO 3
35137 PADUA, ITALY
Telephone: (39-49) 8763200
Teletex: 418463 LEXFOR I
Telefax: 39-49-666086

Milan, Italy Associated Office: Via Borromei, 5, 20123. Telephone: (02) 86451933. Telefax: (02) 86451997.

Pordenone, Italy Office: Via Gorizia 2. 33170. Telephone: (0434) 524304. Telefax: (0434) 27595.

Rome, Italy Associated Office: Studio Legale Beltramo, Via Lazio 20/A. Telephone: (06) 4817747. Telefax: (06) 4820281.

Associated Office London: Howard Kennedy Solicitors, 23 Harcourt House, 19 Cavendish Square, London W1A 2AW. Telephone: (0171) 6361616. Fax: (0171) 4996871.

Associated Office Paris: Jalenques, Boyer Chammard et Associes, 47 Avenue Hoch, 75008 Paris. Telephone: (14) 7634563. Fax: (14) 3803159.

Associated Offices Munich: Klaka & Partners, Delpstrasse 4, 81679 Munchen. Telephone: (89) 9989190. Fax (89) 980036.

Business Law, Civil Law, International and Commercial Practice, Franchising, Corporate, Anti-trust and ECC Law, International Finance, Intellectual Property, Product Liability, Arbitration, Mergers and Acquisitions.

PARTNERS

FRANCESCO CAMILOTTI, born Padua, Italy, October 6, 1949; admitted, 1977, Italy. *Education:* University of Padua (LL.D., 1974). *Member:* Padua Bar. *LANGUAGES:* Italian and English.

ROBERTO CECCON, born Venice, Italy, February 24, 1954; admitted, 1983, Padua. *Education:* University of Padua (LL.D., 1979). Arbitrator, American Arbitration Association and Swiss Chamber of Commerce in Italy. *Member:* International Association of Young Lawyers; Padua Bar. *LANGUAGES:* Italian, English and French.

ALESSANDRO POLETTINI, born Modena, Italy, May 29, 1956; admitted, 1984, Padua. *Education:* University of Padua (LL.D., 1982). *Member:* Padua Bar. *LANGUAGES:* Italian, English and French.

ASSOCIATES

ILARIA BARTOLUCCI, born Rome, Italy, May 13, 1958; admitted, 1989, Padua. *Education:* University of Padua (LL.D., 1985). *LANGUAGES:* Italian and French.

(This Listing Continued)

STUDIO LEGALE CAMILOTTI-CECCON-POLETTINI,
Padua—Continued

ROBERTO SANTORO, born Padua, Italy, June 6, 1966; admitted, 1994, Padua. *Education:* University of Padua (LL.D., 1991). *LANGUAGES:* Italian, English and French.

ANTONIO GRAVA, born Udine, Italy, December 31, 1966. *Education:* University of Bologna (LL.D., 1989). *LANGUAGES:* Italian and English.

ALESSIO VIANELLO, born Venice, Italy, April 17, 1967; admitted, 1994, Venice. *Education:* University of Padua (LL.D., 1991). *Member:* Venice Bar. *LANGUAGES:* Italian and English.

SILVIA FRIGO, born Lonigo, Vicenza, Italy, May 3, 1967. *Education:* University of Padua (LL.D., 1992). *LANGUAGES:* Italian, English and German.

MATTIA DALLA COSTA, born Padua, Italy, June 19, 1968. *Education:* University of Ferrara (LL.D., 1992). *LANGUAGES:* Italian, English, French, German and Spanish.

ALESSANDRA ROLANDI GIOI, born Padua, Italy, July 13, 1964. *Education:* University of Padua (LL.D., cum laude, 1990). *LANGUAGES:* Italian and English.

ASSOCIATED OFFICE (MILAN)
PARTNERS

PAOLO ZAMBELLI, born Varese, Italy, July 4, 1952; admitted, 1979, Italy. *Education:* Milan University (LL.D., cum laude, 1975). *Member:* Milan Bar.

ANGIOLO LUZZATI, born Savona, Italy, February 6, 1922; admitted, 1980, Italy. *Education:* (LL.D., 1972). " Mandataire Agree" at the European Patent Office. Member of the Licensing Executive Society. Registered in the roll of the Industrial Property Consultants. Registered in the roll of the Official Translators of the Milan Court. *Member:* Milan Bar.

DANIELA MEREGALLI, born Milan, Italy, June 13, 1957; admitted, 1984, Italy. *Education:* Sacro Cuore University of Milan (LL.D., cum laude, 1981). *Member:* Milan Bar.

ASSOCIATES

GIULIA COCCHETTI, born Milan, Italy, September 22, 1962; admitted, 1989, Italy. *Education:* Milan University (LL.D., cum laude, 1986).

MATTEO ZAPELLI, born Pavia, Italy, December 29, 1964; admitted, 1992, Italy. *Education:* Sacro Cuore University of Milan (LL.D., cum laude, 1988).

ESTER GAMMIERI, born Manfredonia, (Foggia), Italy, August 5, 1963; admitted, 1991, Italy. *Education:* University of Milan (LL.D., cum laude, 1987).

CESARA FIRPO, born Vigevano (Pavia), Italy, March 13, 1963. *Education:* University of Milan (LL.D., 1990).

RAFFAELLA MACCHI, born Varese, Italy, November 11, 1967. *Education:* University of Milan (LL.D., 1992).

FABRIZIO VERSÉ, born Pavia, Italy, November 23, 1963. *Education:* University of Pavia (LL.D., 1991).

ASSOCIATED OFFICE (ROME)
PARTNERS

MARIO BELTRAMO, born Rome, Italy, February 23, 1919; admitted, 1945, Italy. *Education:* Rome University (LL.D., 1942).

LUCIO FRANCARIO, born Campobasso, Italy, November 27, 1952; admitted, 1979, Italy. *Education:* Rome University (J.D., 1977). Extraordinary Professor, Private Law, Macerala University, 1990—.

SUSANNA BELTRAMO, born Rome, Italy, October 30, 1955; admitted, 1985, Italy. *Education:* L.U.I.S.S. University, Rome (Doctor of Political Science, 1977); Rome University (J.D., 1979); Stanford University, California (Post Graduate Courses, 1979-1980).

ASSOCIATES

GIUSEPPE SCHIAVELLO, born Vibo Valentia, Italy, May 1, 1966; admitted, 1993, Italy. *Education:* L.U.I.S.S. University, Rome (J.D., 1989).

SABRINA BRUNO, born Cosenza, Italy, January 30, 1965; admitted, 1992, Italy. *Education:* L.U.I.S.S. University, Rome (J.D., 1987). Researcher, Corporate Law, Calabria University, 1993—.

(This Listing Continued)

OLGA SESSO, born Cosenza, Italy, March 12, 1965; admitted, 1992, Italy. *Education:* L.U.I.S.S. University, Rome (J.D., 1988).

GIULIO TOGNAZZI, born Rome, Italy, July 27, 1967. *Education:* Rome University (J.D., 1992).

MARINA SAVASTANO, born Copenhagen, Denmark, November 19, 1969. *Education:* Rome University (J.D., 1994).

The Legal Firm has been Admitted to Associazione Italiana del Franchising a Member of the International Franchise Association and European Franchising Federation.
For the Complete Biographical Data of the Rome Office see Studio Legale Beltramo, Rome.

STUDIO LEGALE GIORDANO
ASSOCIAZIONE PROFESSIONALE
PIAZZA SALVEMINI, 2
35131 PADUA, ITALY
Telephone: 39-49-8753575
Telefax: 39-49-8752304

Bassano del Grappa (Vicenza) Italian Office: Via Marinali, 63. Telephone and Telefax: (0424) 527931.
London Associated Office: Mackenzie Mills, Solicitors, 76 Shoe Lane, London EC4A 3JB. Telephone: 0171-583 4884. Telefax: 0171-242-4190.

General Civil Practice, International and Commercial Practice, Corporate, Anti-trust and ECC Law, International Finance, Trademarks and Copyright, Arbitration, Merger and Acquisition.

PARTNERS

CLAUDIO GIORDANO, born San Remo (Im), Italy, August 5, 1951; admitted, 1978. *Education:* University of Ferrara (LL.D., 1975). *Member:* Italian Bar Association (Padua); Italian-British Law Association.

FRANCO FABRIS, born Padua, Italy, February 26, 1959; admitted, 1990. *Education:* University of Ferrara (LL.D., 1985). *Member:* Italian Bar Association (Padua).

GIAN FRANCO FARINA BUSETTO, born Campo San Martino (Pd), Italy, July 7, 1957; admitted, 1989. *Education:* University of Bologna (LL.D., 1985). *Member:* Italian Bar Association (Padua).

SABINA RUBINI, born Padua, Italy, September 4, 1963; admitted, 1992. *Education:* University of Padua (LL.D., 1989). *Member:* Italian Bar Association (Padua).

ROBERTA CRIVELLARO, born Padua, Italy, January 15, 1966; admitted, 1994. *Education:* University of Padua)LL.D., 1991). *Member:* Italian Bar Association (Padua); EC Lawyers Society; Italian-British Law Association.

ASSOCIATES

GABRIELE CECCATO, born Bassano del Grappa (Vicenza), Italy, August 14, 1958; admitted, 1990. *Education:* University of Bologna (LL.D., 1986). *Member:* Italian Bar Association (Vicenza).

COSETTA BARINA, born Padua, Italy, March 27, 1967. *Education:* University of Padua (LL.D., 1992).

NICOLETTA GIACOMELLI, born Padua, Italy, November 10, 1967. *Education:* University of Padua (LL.D., 1993).

Languages: Italian, English, French, German and Spanish

JACOBACCI & PERANI
VIA BERCHET 9
35131 PADUA, ITALY
Telephone: 65.19.31; 65.01.46
Telex: 432321 Jacpad I
Fax: 65.16.31

Turin, Italy Office: Corso Regio Parco 27, 10152, P.O. Box 321, 10100 Torino Centro. Telephone: 2440311. Cable Address: "Casettaro-Torino". Telex: 221494 Patent I. Fax: 286300; 286676.
Milan, Italy Office: Via Visconti di Modrone 7, 20122. Telephone: 76006884; 76020043. Telex: 335441 Japemi I. Fax: 794925.
Bologna, Italy Office: Via Aurelio Saffi, 73/2, 40131. Telephone: 521081. Telex: 520613 Japebo I. Fax: 521038.

Patent, Design, Trademark and Copyright Law, Licensing, Franchising, Unfair Competition and Contracts, EEC Law.

(This Listing Continued)

RESIDENT PARTNER

DR. ING. STEFANO CANTALUPPI. LANGUAGES: Italian, English, French and German. **PRACTICE AREAS:** Patent and Design Law.

RESIDENT ASSOCIATE

BIANCA MARIA TESTA. LANGUAGES: Italian, English and French. **PRACTICE AREAS:** Trademark and Copyright Law.

(For Complete Biographical Data and Personnel, See Professional Biographies at Turin, Italy)

RIZZIERI E ASSOCIATI

Established in 1960

PASSEGGIATA DEL CARMINE 2
35 100 PADUA, ITALY
Telephone: (049) 87-619-13; Intn'l (34-49) 87-619-13
Telecopier: (Gr. III, II) (049) 87-528-79; Intn'l (39-49) 87-528-79

Milan, Italy Associated Office: Scamoni e Associati. Via Mario Pagano 65. Telephone: (02) 48-011-171. Telecopier: (02) 48-012-914.

Bologna, Italy Associated Office: Fazio, Francia, Serafini, Solazzi, Trombetti, Via della Zecca 1. Telephone: (051) 23-69-91. Telecopier (051) 22-24-86.

General Practice, Corporation, Foreign Investments, Commercial Law, Contractual Assistance, Joint Ventures and all forms of Distribution and Franchising Agreements, Banking, EEC Law, Patent, Copyright and Intellectual Property, Bankruptcy and Labor Law, Family Law, Criminal Law, Litigation, including National and International Arbitration.

FIRM PROFILE: The firm is a member of LEGALLIANCE (EEIG), an alliance of law firms established in Paris, London, Madrid, Brussels, The Hague, Cologne, Frankfurt, Leipzig and Berlin, which offers European coordination and cooperation through a single point of contact.

MEMBERS OF FIRM

GIANCARLO RIZZIERI, born Rovigo, Italy, March 12, 1931; admitted, 1959, Italy. *Education:* University of Ferrara (Doctor of Jurisprudence, 1957). Vice President of Banca del Monte. **LANGUAGES:** Italian and French.

GIANANDREA RIZZIERI, born Rovigo, Italy, July 30, 1959; admitted, 1987, Italy. *Education:* University of Ferrara (Doctor of Jurisprudence, 1984). Assistant at the Department of Civil Law of the University of Ferrara. **LANGUAGES:** Italian and English.

SUSANNA RIZZIERI, born Rovigo, Italy, August 25, 1964; admitted, 1992, Italy. *Education:* University of Bologna (Doctor of Jurisprudence). **LANGUAGES:** Italian and English.

ASSOCIATES

FEDERICA GREGGIO, born Padua, Italy, March 24, 1964. *Education:* University of Bologna (Doctor of Jurisprudence, 1991). **LANGUAGES:** Italian, English and Spanish.

PARTNERS MILAN OFFICE

Mario Scamoni	Elena Granatello
Giovanni Ercoli	Francesco Milanese
Piero Fedi	Leila Piscopo
Marco Frazzica	Gianluigi Puccioni

PARTNERS BOLOGNA OFFICE

Domenico Fazio	Paolo Trombetti
Lucio Solazzi	Gianluigi Serafini
Mario Francia	Anna Rita Roncuzzi

STUDIO LEGALE ASSOCIATO
SCASSELLATI-SFORZOLINI

Established in 1949

PIAZZA PICCININO N. 13
06122 PERÚGIA, ITALY
Telephone: (00)39 - (0)75-5725244,5,6: 5731580
Fax: (00)39 - (0)75-5728398

Milan Associate Law Firm: Studio Legale Delitala, Via Durini, 27, 20121. Telephone: 39.2.76008298. Fax: 39.2.784014.

(This Listing Continued)

Mergers and Acquisitions, International Commercial Contracts, Administrative Law, Corporate, Labor, Bankruptcy, Unfair Competition, Trademarks, Civil Litigation, Arbitration.

FIRM PROFILE: The Firm was established in 1949 and the Association founded in 1992.

LUIGI GIACOMO SCASSELLATI-SFORZOLINI, born March 19, 1926; admitted, 1949, Perúgia; 1963, Italian Supreme Court. *Education:* University of Perúgia (Doctor of Jurisprudence, maxima cum laude, 1947). *Member:* National Bar Council; Italian Delegation by Council of the Bars and Law Societies of the European Community; Union International des Avocats (Vice President for Italy); International Bar Association (Member of Council); International Lawyers Association; Inter-American Bar Association; inter-Pacific Bar Association. **LANGUAGES:** Italian, French and English.

PARTNERS

ANNALISA SEGOLONI, born January 14, 1955; admitted, 1983, Perúgia. *Education:* University of Perúgia (Degree in Laws, cum laude, 1980). **LANGUAGES:** Italian, French and English.

URBANO BARELLI, born August 18, 1956; admitted, 1988, Perúgia. *Education:* University of Perúgia (Degree in Laws, 1985). **LANGUAGES:** Italian and English.

STEFANO MAZZI, born July 19, 1962; admitted, 1989, Perúgia. *Education:* University of Perúgia (Degree in Laws, 1986). **LANGUAGES:** Italian and English.

ASSOCIATE

MARCO ANGELINI, born July 10, 1961; admitted, 1989, Perúgia. *Education:* University of Perúgia (Degree in Laws, 1986). **LANGUAGES:** Italian and English.

The Law Office Scassellati-Sforzolini is partner of the G.E.I.E.-LIBRALEX, a European Lawyers Group with seat in Paris (51, Av. Raymond Poincaré) and with law offices in Rome, Athens, Barcelona, Brussels, Copenhagen, Dublin, Edinburg, Hamburg, Lille, Lisbon, London, Luxemburg, Madrid, Munich, Paris, Rotterdam.

STUDIO LEGALE
CAMILOTTI-CECCON-POLETTINI

in association with Zambelli-Luzzati-Meregalli

and

Studio Legale Beltramo

Established in 1986

VIA GORIZIA 2
33170 PORDENONE, ITALY
Telephone: 39-434-524304
Telefax: 39-434-27595

Padua, Italy Office: Galleria Borromeo 3, 35137. Telephone: (049) 8763200. Telelex: 328641. LEXFOR I. Telefax: 049/666086.

Milan, Italy Associated Office: Via Borromei, 5, 20123. Telephone: (02) 86451933. Telefax: (02) 86451997.

Rome, Italy Associated Office: Via Lazio 20/A. Telephone: (06) 4817747. Telefax: (06) 4820281.

Associated Offices London: Howard Kennedy Solicitors, 23 Harcourt House, 19 Cavendish Square, London W1A 2AW. Telephone: (0171) 6361616. Fax: (0171) 4996871.

Associated Offices Paris: Jalenques, Boyer Chammard et Associes, 47 Avenue Hoch, 75008 Paris. Telephone: (14) 7634563. Fax: (14) 3803159.

Associated Offices Munich: Klaka & Partners, Delpstrasse 4, 81679 Munchen. Telephone: (89) 9989190. Fax: (89) 980036.

General Civil Practice, International and Commercial Practice, Franchising, Corporate, Anti-trust and ECC Law, International Finance, Patents, Trademarks and Copyright, Transport, Arbitration, Mergers and Acquisition.

PARTNERS

FRANCESCO CAMILOTTI, born Padua, Italy, October 6, 1949; admitted, 1977, Padua. *Education:* University of Padua (LL.D., 1974). *Member:* Padua Bar. **LANGUAGES:** Italian and English.

ROBERTO CECCON, born Venice, Italy, February 24, 1954; admitted, 1983, Padua. *Education:* University of Padua (LL.D., 1979). Arbitrator,

(This Listing Continued)

STUDIO LEGALE CAMILOTTI-CECCON-POLETTINI,
Pordenone—Continued

American Arbitration Association and Swiss Chamber of Commerce in Italy. *Member:* International Association of Young Lawyers; Padua Bar. *LANGUAGES:* Italian, English and French.

ALESSANDRO POLETTINI, born Modena, Italy, May 29, 1956; admitted, 1984, Padua. *Education:* University of Padua (LL.D., 1982). *Member:* Padua Bar. *LANGUAGES:* Italian, English and French.

RESIDENT ASSOCIATES

ANTONIO GRAVA, born Udine, Italy, December 31, 1966. *Education:* University of Bologna (LL.D., 1989). *LANGUAGES:* Italian and English.

For Complete Biographical Data of the Rome Office see Studio Legale Beltramo, Rome.

Languages: Italian and English

STUDIO LEGALE ALBISINNI

Established in 1978

VIA CIRO MENOTTI N.4
00195 ROME, ITALY
Telephone: 3216171 - 3210986
Facsimile: 3217034

Milan, Italy Office: Via Zenale no. 3, 20123. Telephone: 02-48021655. Telefax: 02-4816725.

General Civil Practice, Business Law, Commercial Law, Corporate Law, Contracts, International Business Transactions, Documentary Credits, Property, Real Estate, Trusts and Estates, International Estate Planning, Agricultural Law, Resorts and Leisure, Copyrights, Intellectual Property, Patents, Bankruptcy, Civil Litigation.

AVV. FERDINANDO ALBISINNI, born Cosenza, Italy, August 28, 1948; admitted, 1974, Italy. *Education:* University of Rome (J.D. cum laude, 1971). Fellow Seminar in American Law, Salzburg, 1975. Researcher, Institute of Comparative Law, University of Rome, 1971-1977. Author: "Trusts from the Italian Perspective," Trusts for Europe Conference, Legal Studies and Services, Amsterdam, 1987; "Trust and Fiduciary Relationships-Similarities and Differences," The Future for Trusts in Italy, Conference Milano, 1990; "Italian Law regarding Spousal Assets and Family Enterprise," Conference Venezia, 1990; "Italy as a Potential Trust Jurisdiction," Eurotrusts, The New Estate Planning Vehicles, Conference Geneva, 1991; "Capital Taxes and Estate Planning in Europe - Chapter on Italy," Longman Law Tax and Finance, 1991, "Giudici e Agriturismo," 1993; "Italian Contribution in Glosson International Trust Law," 1994. Member of the Committee on "Agritourism," of the Ministry of Agriculture, 1980-1990. *Member:* Italian Association of Comparative Law; Italian Arbitration Association; Union des Avocats Europeens. *LANGUAGES:* English, German and Italian. *PRACTICE AREAS:* Business Law; Contracts; Resorts and Leisure; Real Estate; Litigation; Trusts and Estate; Agricultural Law.

DOTT. PROC. VINCENZO PENTELLA, born Naples, Italy, February 15, 1960. *Education:* University of Rome (J.D., cum laude, 1989). *LANGUAGES:* English and Italian. *PRACTICE AREAS:* Labor and Employment; Intellectual Property; Copyright; Communications; Computers and Software.

DOTT. PROC. EMMA LOMBARDI, born Palermo, Italy, October 25, 1960; admitted, 1990, Rome. *Education:* University of Rome (J.D., 1985); Post Graduate Course, Criminal Procedure. Author: "Revisione del Giudicato" (1985). *LANGUAGES:* English, German and Italian. *PRACTICE AREAS:* Family Law; Wills; Entertainment Law; Criminal Law; Litigation.

DOTT. PROC. PAOLA CAPUANO, born Rome, Italy, March 3, 1966; admitted, 1994, Rome. *Education:* University of Rome (J.D., 1989); Post Graduate Course, Tax Law (1992). Author: "Employee Share Offerings" (1989). *LANGUAGES:* English and Italian. *PRACTICE AREAS:* Intellectual Property; Labor and Employment; Bankruptcy; Criminal Law; Taxation.

DOTT. DONATELLA CASTELLUCCI, born Rome, Italy, February 27, 1966. *Education:* L.U.I.S.S., Rome (J.D., 1990); Post Graduate Course, EEC Law (1991); Orientation in American Law, Davis University, Davis, California (1992). Author "Legal Characteristics of Agritourism," 1990. *LANGUAGES:* English, Italian. *PRACTICE AREAS:* Wills; Patents; Family Law; Real Estate; Agricultural Law.

(This Listing Continued)

DOTT. ANDREA DEL VECCHIO, born Rome, Italy, June 25, 1968. *Education:* University of Rome (J.D., 1991); Post Graduate course in Bankruptcy Law, University of Rome (1991-1992). Author "Defense Rights in Bankruptcy," 1991. *LANGUAGES:* Italian and English. *PRACTICE AREAS:* Business Law; Litigation; Bankruptcy.

DOTT. ANDREA RICCIO, born Rome, Italy, February 14, 1970. *Education:* University of Rome (J.D., cum laude, 1993). Author: "Liability of Directors, Trustee in Bankruptcy and Shareholder for Company Income Tax," (1993); "Tax Treatment of Compensation for Directors" (1993). *LANGUAGES:* English and Italian. *PRACTICE AREAS:* Taxation; Commercial Law; Real Estate Administration; Leases and Leasing.

ALEGI & ASSOCIATES

VIA VENTI SETTEMBRE 1
00187 ROME, ITALY
Telephone: (39) (6) 482.0147
Facsimile: (39) (6) 4871149

International Business Transactions and Taxation. General Practice, Computer and Software Law, Banking and Investment Law. Aviation Law. Industrial Property Law, European Community Law, Foreign Investments, Environmental Law.

FIRM PROFILE: The Firm is comprised of Italian lawyers admitted to practice before the courts of Italy and foreign lawyers specializing in international transactions and has extensive experience in mergers and acquisitions, joint ventures, international and Italian taxation and corporate law. It is active in a wide area of traditional commercial law, as well as the more recently developed areas of computer and software law, aviation law, industrial property law, sports and entertainment law. Our business is conducted in Italian, English, French and Spanish.

PETER C. ALEGI, born New Haven, Connecticut, July 26, 1935; admitted, 1959, Connecticut; 1962, Rhode Island; 1965, Illinois (Not admitted in Italy). *Education:* Yale University (B.A. cum laude, 1956); Yale Law School (LL.B., 1959). Visiting Lecturer in Law: Yale Law School, 1981—; Temple University Law School, 1980. Author: "Italian Income Taxes, Consolidated Text" (Translation), 1994; "Doing Business in Italy," CCH, 1991. Author: "Business Opportunities in Italy," Portfolio 84, Tax Management (BNA), 1989; "Nigeria: A Legal and Tax Primer for the U.S. Investor," 1978; "Proposed Changes in Italian Company Law," CCH, 1966; "Taxation of the Foreign Licensor in Italy," Idea, The Patent, Trademark & Copyright Journal, 1968; "U.S. Foreign Investment Restrictions: A Preliminary Outline," Italian-American Business, February 1968; "Italian Income Taxation/Le Imposte Dirette in Italia," 1974; "Italy Tries Tax Reform-Again," 52 Taxes-The Tax Magazine 216, 1974. Rapporteur, "Legal Aspects of Investing in Nigeria," American Management Association, New York, 1976-1979, Chairman, 1978-1979. Fulbright Scholar, University of Rome Law School, 1959-1960. Member, Commission for Educational and Cultural Exchange between Italy and the U.S., 1978-1990. Member, Executive Committee, Yale Law School Association, 1985-1992. *Member:* American and International Bar Associations; American Society of International Law. National Association of Italian Tax Consultants; Italian Order of Journalists. *LANGUAGES:* English, Italian and French. *PRACTICE AREAS:* International Business Transactions and Taxation; General Practice; Computer and Software Law; Banking and Investment Law; Aviation Law; Industrial Property Law; European Community Law; Foreign Investments; Environmental Law.

ASSOCIATES

EDVIGE ANNA MAGDA ALVINO, born Novoli, Italy, July 8, 1951; admitted, 1977, Italy. *Education:* University of Perugia Law School (J.D., with high distinction). Assistant Professor, University of Perugia, 1976-1979 and University of Rome, 1979—. Author: "Soviet Civil Procedure," (translation), Maggioli, 1977; "Polish Civil Procedure" (translation and commentary), Maggioli, 1979; "Bankruptcy and Pending Cases," Rivista di Diritto Commerciale. *LANGUAGES:* Italian, English, French, Polish and German. *PRACTICE AREAS:* International Law; Commercial Law; Litigation.

JEFFREY P. GREENBAUM, born Philadelphia, Pennsylvania, July 13, 1959; admitted, 1985, Pennsylvania (Not admitted in Italy). *Education:* Brown University (A.B., magna cum laude, 1981); University of Michigan (J.D., cum laude, 1984); European University Institute, Florence, Italy (LL.M., International and Comparative Law, 1985). Phi Beta Kappa. Law Clerk. President, Italian Constitutional Court, 1985-1987. Author: "Tender Offers in the European Community: The Playing Field Shrinks," 22 Vander-

(This Listing Continued)

bilt Journal of Transnational Law 923 (1989); "An American Perspective on the European Commission's Amended Proposal for a Council Regulation on the Control of Concentrations Between Undertakings and its Impact on Hostile Tender Offers," 7 Dickinson Journal of International Law 195 (1989). Editor, Giustizia costituzionale e diritti dell'uomo negli Stati Uniti, Giuffrè, 1992. Consultant, to Italian Constitutional Court on Dissenting Opinions, 1993. Co-Chairman, International Law Committee of Philadelphia Bar Association, 1990. Regional Coordinator, Export Legal Assistance Network, 1990. Adjunct Professor, Boston University M.S.M. Program, 1993—. *Member:* American and Pennsylvania Bar Associations. *LANGUAGES:* English and Italian. *PRACTICE AREAS:* International Law; Corporate Law; Commercial Law; Sports Law.

CHRISTINE MARCIASINI, born Stockton, California, October 6, 1962; admitted, 1989, California (Not admitted in Italy). *Education:* University of the Pacific (B.A., with high distinction, 1984); University of California Hastings College of the Law (J.D., 1987). Adjunct Professor, American University of Rome, 1992—. *Member:* American Bar Association; State Bar of California. *LANGUAGES:* English, Italian, Spanish and French. *PRACTICE AREAS:* International Law; Corporate Law; Commercial Law.

SILVIA FALCO, born Pescara, Italy, September 25, 1968. *Education:* L.U.I.S.S., Rome (J.D., 1992). *LANGUAGES:* Italian, English and French.

AMENTA, BIOLATO, CORRAO, LONGO, RIDOLA

Established in 1984

VIA DEL BABUINO, 51
00187 ROME, ITALY
Telephone: (06) 3233001
Fax: (06) 3234238

Milan, Italy Office: Via Brera 6, 20121. Telephone: (02) 86461365. Fax: (02)72002140.

General Civil Practice.

MEMBERS OF FIRM

ANTONIO CORRAO, born Genoa, Italy, September 23, 1924; admitted, 1951, Italy; 1965, to plead before Supreme Court of Italy. *Education:* Rome University (LL.D,, 1947).

FILIPPO AMENTA, born Rome, Italy, November 3, 1933; admitted, 1965, Italy. *Education:* Rome University (LL.D., 1962).

GIUSEPPE V. BIOLATO, born Savigliano, Cuneo, Italy, April 29, 1943; admitted, 1969, Italy; 1987, to plead before Supreme Court of Italy. *Education:* Perugia University (LL.D., 1965).

MARIO G. RIDOLA, born Taranto, Italy, January 4, 1954; admitted, 1981, Italy. *Education:* Rome University (LL.D., 1979).

LINDA LONGO, born Rome, Italy, September 13, 1957; admitted, 1984, Italy. *Education:* Rome University (LL.D., 1979).

LUIGI MORI, born Rome, Italy, February 2, 1965; admitted, 1992, Italy. *Education:* LUISS University, Rome (LL.D., 1989).

ANDREA ZINCONE, born Rome, Italy, January 1, 1964; admitted, 1992, Italy. *Education:* Rome University (LL.D. 1989).

GIUSEPPE CELLI, born Sora, Italy, September 26, 1963; admitted, 1994, Italy. *Education:* Rome University (LL.D., 1988).

MARCO UMBERTO MORICCA, born Rome, Italy, December 25, 1964; 1989, admitted to practice before the Lower Courts. *Education:* LUISS University Rome (LL.D., 1989).

RAFFAELLA CUGINI, born Rome, Italy, February 8, 1968. admitted to practice before the Lower Courts. *Education:* Rome University (LL.D., 1992). *LANGUAGES:* English.

PAOLA ASTORRI, born Luxembourg, January 31, 1970; admitted, 1994, Italy. *Education:* University La Sapienza, Rome Italy (LL.D., 1994). *LANGUAGES:* English, French and German.

Languages: Italian, English, French and German

STUDIO LEGALE ASSOCIATO
&
FRERE CHOLMELEY BISCHOFF

VIALE BRUNO BUOZZI 47
00197 ROME, ITALY
Telephone: (39) (6) 8080133
Fax: (39) (6) 8080134

Milan Office: Piazza Castello, 24, 20121 Milan. Telephone: (39) (2) 72003457. Fax: (39) (2) 72003469.

Frère Cholmeley Bischoff. 4 John Carpenter Street, London EC4Y 0NH, England. Telephone: 0171-615 8000. Fax: 0171-615 8080. Offices in Paris, Milan, Monte Carlo, Berlin, Moscow, Dubai (For Biographical Listing, see London Office).

International and General Practice, Corporate, Mergers and Acquisitions, Aviation, Banking, Commercial and Private Real Estate, Privatizations, Foreign Investments, Computer and Software, EEC, Energy, East European, Insurance, Joint Ventures, Licensing, Litigation, Education, Environmental, Bankruptcy, Labor, Patent, Trademark, Copyright, Entertainment, Media and Telecommunications, Public International Law, Visa and Immigration, Family, Taxation, Will and Estates.

FIRM PROFILE: The five partners, four Italian and one American, have practiced together and served the international community since 1982. The firm has built a strong reputation among corporations, private clients and other law firms as being experienced in assisting the foreign client with Italian and mult-jurisdicitional legal matters.

MEMBERS OF FIRM

ANDREA RUSSO, born Rome, July 15, 1955; admitted, 1978, Italy. *Education:* University of Rome (Doctor in Jurisprudence, LL.D., 1978). Author: "Guide to Family Law in Europe," Section on Italian Law, Solicitors Family Law Association, 1992. *Member:* Italian (Rome) and International Bar Associations (Secretary, Family Law Committee; Member, Aviation Committee); European Air Law Association; International Academy of Matrimonial Lawyers. *PRACTICE AREAS:* Aviation; Corporate; Family; Estates; Litigation.

ROBERTO PADOVA, born Rome, Italy, December 4, 1956; admitted, 1982, Italy. *Education:* University of Rome (Doctor in Jurisprudence, LL.D., maxima cum laude, 1981); Post Graduate School in European Studies (Diplome, maxima cum laude, 1982). *Member:* Italian (Rome) and International Bar Associations; European Air Law Association. *PRACTICE AREAS:* Acquisitions; Aviation; Corporate; Computer; Telecommunication.

GIORGIO CHERUBINI, born Rome, Italy, June 30, 1960; admitted, 1985, Italy. *Education:* University of Rome (Doctor in Jurisprudence, LL.D., 1984). Co-Author: "International Product Liability," The Center for International Legal Studies, 1993; "Current Issues in Cross-Border Insolvency and Reorganization," IBA, 1994. Co-Chair, Subcommittee on Publications and Current Developments, IBA Committee J. *Member:* Rotaract Roma Tevere (President, 1985-1987); Italian (Rome) and International Bar Associations; British-Italian Law Association; Associazione degli Investigatori ed Esperti della Sicurezza del Volo - ASV (Association Among Investigators and Experts for Air Safety). *PRACTICE AREAS:* Insurance; Personal Injury; Corporate; EEC.

ASSOCIATES

ANDREA MARANI, born Rome, Italy, July 3, 1962; admitted, 1987, Italy. *Education:* University of Rome (Doctor of Jurisprudence, LL.D., maxima cum laude, 1986); Notary School of Rome (1987-1988); IPSOA (Special course in Auditing and Balance Sheet Analysis, 1990). *Member:* Italian (Rome) Bar Association; American-Italian Law Association; International Tax Planning Association. *PRACTICE AREAS:* Corporate and Commercial Estates; Tax.

MARIA CLELIA CHINAPPI, born Rome, Italy, January 16, 1965; admitted, 1989, Italy. *Education:* University of Rome (Doctor in Jurisprudence, LL.D., maxima cum laude, 1988). *Member:* Italian (Rome) Bar Association. *PRACTICE AREAS:* Labor; Commercial Litigation; EEC.

IMMACOLATA GREGNI, born Rome, Italy, May 31, 1963. *Education:* University of Rome (Doctor of Jurisprudence, LL.D., 1989). *PRACTICE AREAS:* Collections; Personal Injury; Commercial Litigation.

(This Listing Continued)

STUDIO LEGALE ASSOCIATO & FRERE CHOLMELEY BISCHOFF, Rome—Continued

MARIA CHIARA MINERVA, born Altamura (BA), Italy, June 6, 1966. *Education:* University of Rome (Doctor of Jurisprudence LL.D., maxima cum laude, 1989). *PRACTICE AREAS:* Corporate; Commercial.

FRANCESCA AMICI, born Rome Italy, April 9, 1970. *Education:* University L.U.I.S.S. of Rome (Doctor of Jurisprudence (LL.D., maxima cum laude, 1994). *PRACTICE AREAS:* Corporate; Insurance.

PATRIZIO MESSINA, born Siracusa, Italy, November 25, 1969; admitted, 1993, Italy. *Education:* University of Catania (Doctor of Jurisprudence, LL.D., 1993). Seminar in Civil and Commercial law, Naples (1993-1994). Assistant Professor at the University of Rome. Contributing Editor, "Le Societa and "Nuova Giurisprudenza civile e commentata," 1993—. *PRACTICE AREAS:* Acquisitions; Corporate; Banking.

RESIDENT COUNSEL

DONALD J. CARROLL, born New York, N.Y., May 6, 1947; admitted, 1982, Rhode Island and U.S. District Court, Massachusetts (Not admitted in Italy). *Education:* University of Michigan (B.A., 1969); Columbia University (M.B.A., 1975); Franklin Pierce Law Center (J.D., 1982). Author: "Visas, Permits and Fiscal Code," Doing Business in Italy, U.S. & Foreign Commercial Service, American Embassy, Rome and Connect, 1993; "Leasing and Purchasing Real Estate in Italy,' Connect 1992. *Member:* Rhode Island, International Bar Association; International Tax Planning Association; International Association of Jewish Lawyers and Jurists. *PRACTICE AREAS:* Estate Planning and Administration; U.S. Colleges and Universities; Real Estate; Tax.

Languages: Italian, English, French, German, Spanish, Hebrew

REPRESENTATIVE CLIENTS: *Italy:* Assicurazioni Generali; Banca Brignone; Unione Fiduciaria (Banche Popolari Italiane); FIAMM; Safilo Group S.p.A.; Raggio di Sole (Rds) S.p.A. *USA:* Revlon; Gulf Oil International; Grapic Control; Boston University; Cornell University, Temple University; Washington University. *Ireland:* Aer Lingus; Ryan Air. *UK:* Legal & General Assurance Society; Henry Moore Foundation; Costain Engineering & Construction Ltd.; Christian & Nielsen; London Bottle; Liquor Bottle Int'l; Lloyds Bank; Midland Bank; Orbit Valve Olc.; Wace Computer Group; Clerical Medical Investment Group. *Asia:* Air India; Neil Pryde. *Swiss:* Jet Aviation. *AS:* Aerolineas Argentinas; Banco de la Nacion Argentina. *Int'l:* Food & Agricultural Organization of the UN; Multinational Forces and Observers of the UN; International Development Law Institute; Marymount International School; African Medical Research Association.

BAKER & McKENZIE

VIA DEGLI SCIPIONI, 288
00192 ROME, ITALY
Telephone: (06) 3225162
Intn'l. Dialing: (39-6) 3225162
Cable Address: ABOGADO ROMA
Telex: 611087
Answer Back: 611087 ABOROM I
Facsimile: (39-6) 3203502

Associated Offices of Baker & McKenzie in: Almaty, Amsterdam, Bangkok, Barcelona, Beijing, Berlin, Bogotá, Brasília, Brussels, Budapest, Buenos Aires, Cairo, Caracas, Chicago, Dallas, Frankfurt, Geneva, Hanoi, Ho Chi Minh City, Hong Kong, Juárez, Kiev, London, Madrid, Manila, Melbourne, México City, Miami, Milan, Monterrey, Moscow, New York, Palo Alto, Paris, Prague, Rio de Janeiro, Riyadh, St. Petersburg, San Diego, San Francisco, São Paulo, Singapore, Stockholm, Sydney, Taipei, Tijuana, Tokyo, Toronto, Valencia, Warsaw, Washington, D.C. and Zürich.

Correspondent Law Firm: Hadiputranto, Hadinoto & Partners, Jakarta.

International and General Practice. Corporation, Commercial, Tax and Labor Law.

RESIDENT PARTNERS

FABIO M. BREMBATI, born Paris, France, August 21, 1957; admitted, 1985, Italy. *Education:* Rome University (J.D.); Boalt Hall School of Law, University of California at Berkeley (LL.M.); Georgetown University. Professor of Contract Law, Ponteficia Universitas Lateranensis, 1987. *Member:* Rome Bar Association; Association Des Ancient Stagiaires of EEC. *LANGUAGES:* Italian, English, French and Spanish. *PRACTICE AREAS:* Banking and Finance; Mergers and Acquisitions; Securities and Financial Products; Communications and Media Law; Computers and Technology Law.

(This Listing Continued)

AURELIO GIOVANNELLI, born Viterbo, Italy, November 16, 1955; admitted, 1982, Italy. *Education:* University of Rome (J.D., 1979); Georgetown University-International Law Institute (Summer, 1983); Columbia University, N.Y. (LL.M., 1987). *Member:* Rome Bar Association; Italian Association of Exchange Control and Foreign Trade Experts. *LANGUAGES:* Italian and English. *PRACTICE AREAS:* Taxation; Securities and Financial Products; Mergers and Acquisitions; Antitrust Law; Commercial Litigation.

G. FRANCO MACCONI, born Milan, Italy, June 13, 1940; admitted, 1965, Italy. *Education:* University of Florence (J.D., 1963); Columbia University (LL.M., 1964). Fulbright Scholar. Assistant Professor, Institute of Comparative Law, University of Florence, 1964-1974. *Member:* Rome Bar Association; International Bar Association; Italian Association of Comparative Law; Italian Arbitration Association; Italian Fulbright Association; Columbia Law School Alumni Association. *LANGUAGES:* Italian, English and French. *PRACTICE AREAS:* Communications and Media Law; Mergers and Acquisitions; Corporate and Partnership Law; Banking and Finance; E.C. Competition and Trade.

ASSOCIATES

CLAUDIA BARSOTTI, born Terni, Italy, September 16, 1966; admitted, 1992, Italy. *Education:* University of Rome (J.D., 1991). *Member:* Rome Bar Association. *LANGUAGES:* Italian, English. *PRACTICE AREAS:* Taxation; Mergers and Acquisitions; Banking and Finance; Antitrust Law; Commercial Litigation.

GUIDO BROCCHIERI, born Rome, Italy, October 19, 1959; admitted, 1986, Italy. *Education:* University of Rome (J.D., 1983). *Member:* Rome Bar Association. *LANGUAGES:* Italian and English. *PRACTICE AREAS:* Commercial Litigation; Civil Litigation; Labor and Employment Law; Arbitration and Dispute Resolution; Bankruptcy, Insolvency and Reorganization.

GIULIO BRUNELLI, born Rome, Italy, May 10, 1966; admitted, 1991, Italy. *Education:* University of Rome (J.D., 1991). *Member:* Rome Bar Association. *LANGUAGES:* Italian, English and French. *PRACTICE AREAS:* Communications and Media Law; Mergers and Acquisitions; EC Competition and Trade; Antitrust Law.

ANTONELLA CENTRA, born Rome, Italy, September 20, 1969; admitted, 1994, Italy. *Education:* La Sapienza University (J.D., 1994). *Member:* Rome Bar Association. *LANGUAGES:* Italian, English and French.

STEFANO CIULLO, born Perugia, Italy, March 2, 1968; admitted, 1991, Italy. *Education:* University of Perugia (J.D., 1991). *Member:* Perugia Bar Association. *LANGUAGES:* Italian, English and French. *PRACTICE AREAS:* Corporate and Partnership Law; Communications and Media Law; EC Competition and Trade; Antitrust Law; Administrative Law.

GIADA CORTESI, born Como, Italy, March 18, 1969; admitted, 1993, Italy. *Education:* University of Rome (J.D., 1993). *Member:* Rome Bar Association. *LANGUAGES:* Italian, English and French. *PRACTICE AREAS:* Environmental Law; Intellectual Property Law; Regulatory Law; Corporate and Partnership Law.

GIORGIO GALLENZI, born Rome, Italy, May 31, 1963; admitted, 1988, Italy. *Education:* II University of Rome (J.D., 1988). *Member:* Rome Bar Association. *LANGUAGES:* Italian and English.

RAFFAELE GIARDA, born Rome, Italy, July 6, 1966; admitted, 1990, Italy. *Education:* University of Rome (J.D., 1989); New York University (M.C.J., 1994). *Member:* Rome Bar Association. *LANGUAGES:* Italian and English. *PRACTICE AREAS:* Corporate and Partnership Law; Communications and Media Law; Taxation; Banking and Finance; Mergers and Acquisitions.

FEDERICO LIMITI, born Rome, Italy, December 27, 1969; admitted, 1994, Italy. *Education:* University of Rome (J.D., 1993). *Member:* Rome Bar Association. *LANGUAGES:* Italian.

ANGELICA LODIGIANI, born Milan, Italy, November 1, 1966; admitted, 1992, Italy. *Education:* University of Rome (J.D., 1990). *Member:* Rome Bar Association. *LANGUAGES:* Italian, English, French, Spanish. *PRACTICE AREAS:* Computers and Technology Law; Mergers and Acquisitions; Corporate and Partnership Law; Commercial Litigation.

ALFREDO LUCENTE, born Cuneo, Italy, February 22, 1960; admitted, 1982, Italy. *Education:* University of Bologna (J.D., 1982). *Member:* Rome Bar Association. *LANGUAGES:* Italian, English and French. *PRACTICE AREAS:* Construction and Property Development; Environmental Law; Arbitration and Dispute Resolution; Communications and Media Law; Entertainment, the Arts and Sports Law.

(This Listing Continued)

ANNA SOFIA N. MAURO, born Rome, Italy, September 6, 1955; admitted, 1979, Italy. *Education:* University of Rome (J.D., 1979). *Member:* Rome Bar Association. *LANGUAGES:* Italian and French. *PRACTICE AREAS:* Corporate and Partnership Law; Commercial Litigation; Civil Litigation; Mergers and Acquisitions.

FRANCESCO PORTOLANO, born Naples, Italy, August 3, 1969; admitted, 1992, Italy. *Education:* L.U.I.S.S. (J.D., 1991). *Member:* Rome Bar Association. *LANGUAGES:* Italian, English and Spanish. *PRACTICE AREAS:* Corporate and Partnership Law; Commercial Litigation; Civil Litigation; Labor and Employment Law.

RAFFAELE G. RIZZI, born Bari, Italy, April 10, 1967; admitted, 1992, Italy. *Education:* L.U.I.S.S. (J.D., 1989); George Washington University (LL.M., 1993). *Member:* Rome Bar Association. *LANGUAGES:* Italian, English. *PRACTICE AREAS:* Banking and Finance; Securities and Financial Products; Mergers and Acquisitions; Corporate and Partnership Law; Antitrust Law.

BARZANÕ & ZANARDO

Established in 1887

VIA PIEMONTE 26
00187 ROME, ITALY
Telephone: (39-6) 474 32 41
Telecopier: (39-6) 487 0273
Telex: 625579-Zanard I

Milan, Italy Office: Via Borgonuovo 10.20121. Telephone: (39-2) 6554287. Telecopier: (39-2) 659 8859. Telex: 320034-Zanard I.
Turin, Italy Office: Corso Vittorio Emanuele II 61, 10128. Telephone: (39-11) 548 050. Telex: 32004-Zanard I.

Patents, Designs, Trademarks, Copyrights, Licensing and Transfer of Technology.

(For Complete Biographical Data, see Professional Biographies at Milan, Italy)

STUDIO LEGALE BELTRAMO

Associazione Professionale

in association with Zambelli-Luzzati-Meregalli and

Camilotti-Ceccon-Polettini

20/C, VIA LAZIO
00187 ROME, ITALY
Telephone: 39-6-4817747
Fax: 39-6-4820281

REVISERS OF THE ITALY LAW DIGEST FOR THIS DIRECTORY

Corporate Finance, Mergers and Acquisitions, Securities and Banking Law, Domestic and International Transactions, Labor and Employment Law, Antitrust and Unfair Competition, Industrial and Intellectual Property, Bankruptcy, Arbitration and Litigation.

MARIO BELTRAMO, born Rome, Italy, February 23, 1919; admitted, 1945, Italy. *Education:* Rome University (J.D., 1942).

LUCIO FRANCARIO, born Campobasso, Italy, November 27, 1952; admitted, 1979, Italy. *Education:* Rome University (J.D., 1977). Extraordinary Professor, Private Law, Macerata University, 1990—.

SUSANNA BELTRAMO, born Rome, Italy, October 30, 1955; admitted, 1985, Italy. *Education:* L.U.I.S.S. University, Rome (Doctor of Political Science, 1977); Rome University (J.D., 1979); Stanford University, California (Post Graduate Courses, 1979-1980).

GIUSEPPE SCHIAVELLO, born Vibo Valentia, Italy, May 1, 1966; admitted, 1993, Italy. *Education:* L.U.I.S.S. University, Rome (J.D., 1989).

SABRINA BRUNO, born Cosenza, Italy, January 30, 1965; admitted, 1992, Italy. *Education:* L.U.I.S.S. University, Rome (J.D., 1987); Oxon (M. Litt., 1994). Researcher, Corporate Law, Calabria University, 1993—.

OLGA SESSO, born Cosenza, Italy, March 12, 1965; admitted, 1992, Italy. *Education:* L.U.I.S.S. University, Rome (J.D., 1988).

GIULIO TOGNAZZI, born Rome, Italy, July 27, 1967. *Education:* Rome University (J.D., 1992).

MARINA SAVASTANO, born Copenhagen, Denmark, November 19, 1969. *Education:* Rome University (J.D., 1994).

(This Listing Continued)

STEFANO AGNOLI, born Rome, Italy, November 15, 1968. *Education:* Rome University (J.D., 1994).

ASSOCIATED OFFICE (MILAN)

PAOLO ZAMBELLI, born Varese, Italy, July 4, 1952; admitted, 1979, Italy. *Education:* Milan University (LL.D., cum laude, 1975). *Member:* Milan Bar.

ANGIOLO LUZZATI, born Savona, Italy, February 6, 1922; admitted, 1980, Italy. *Education:* (LL.D., 1972). " Mandataire Agree" at the European Patent Office. Member of the Licensing Executive Society. Registered in the roll of the Industrial Property Consultants. Registered in the roll of the Official Translators of the Milan Court. *Member:* Milan Bar.

DANIELA MEREGALLI, born Milan, Italy, June 13, 1957; admitted, 1984, Italy. *Education:* Sacro Cuore University of Milan (LL.D., cum laude, 1981). *Member:* Milan Bar.

GIULIA COCCHETTI, born Milan, Italy, September 22, 1962; admitted, 1989, Italy. *Education:* Milan University (LL.D., cum laude, 1986).

MATTEO ZAPELLI, born Pavia, Italy, December 29, 1964; admitted, 1992, Italy. *Education:* Sacro Cuore University of Milan (LL.D., cum laude, 1988).

ESTER GAMMIERI, born Manfredonia (Foggia), Italy, August 5, 1963; admitted, 1991, Italy. *Education:* University of Milan (LL.D., cum laude, 1987).

CESARA FIRPO, born Vigevano (Pavia), Italy, March 13, 1963; admitted, 1994, Italy. *Education:* University of Milan (LL.D., 1990).

RAFFAELLA MACCHI, born Varese, Italy, November 11, 1967. *Education:* University of Milan (LL.D., 1992).

FABRIZIO VERSÉ, born Pavia, Italy, November 23, 1963. *Education:* University of Pavia (LL.D., 1991).

LUCA GALEANDRO, born Milan, Italy, September 29, 1966. *Education:* Milan University (LL.D., 1991).

ASSOCIATED OFFICE (PADUA)

FRANCESCO CAMILOTTI, born Padua, Italy, October 6, 1949; admitted, 1977, Italy. *Education:* University of Padua (LL.D., 1974). *Member:* Padua Bar.

ROBERTO CECCON, born Venice, Italy, February 24, 1954; admitted, 1983, Italy. *Education:* University of Padua (LL.D., 1979). Arbitrator, American Arbitration Association and Swiss Chamber of Commerce in Italy. *Member:* International Association of Young Lawyers; Padua Bar.

ALESSANDRO POLETTINI, born Modena, Italy, May 29, 1956; admitted, 1984, Italy. *Education:* University of Padua (LL.D., 1982). *Member:* Padua Bar.

ILARIA BARTOLUCCI, born Rome, Italy, May 13, 1958; admitted, 1989, Italy. *Education:* University of Padua (LL.D., 1985).

ROBERTO SANTORO, born Padua, Italy, June 6, 1966; admitted, 1994, Italy. *Education:* University of Padua (LL.D., 1991).

ANTONIO GRAVA, born Udine, Italy, December 31, 1966. *Education:* University of Bologna (LL.D., 1989).

ALESSIO VIANELLO, born Venice, Italy, April 17, 1967; admitted, 1994, Italy. *Education:* University of Padua (LL.D., 1991).

SILVIA FRIGO, born Lonigo, (Vicenza), Italy, May 3, 1967. *Education:* University of Padua (LL.D., 1992).

MATTIA DALLA COSTA, born Padua, Italy, June 19, 1968. *Education:* University of Ferrara (LL.D., 1992).

ALESSANDRA ROLANDI GIOI, born Padua, Italy, July 13, 1964. *Education:* University of Padua (LL.D., 1990).

Languages: Italian, English, French and Danish

(This Listing Continued)

STUDIO LEGALE BELTRAMO, Rome—Continued

tional S.r.l.;Lamaro Appalti S.p.A.; Meliorconsorzio S.p.A.; Meridiana Finanza S.p.A.; Monte dei Paschi di Siena. LUXEMBOURG: IMI Bank (Lux); SPAIN: Caja de Madrid. SWEDEN: Elekta Instruments A.B. SWITZERLAND: Union Banks of Switzerland; UNITED KINGDOM: Bankers Trust International PLC.; Bank of Tokyo International Ltd.; Baring Brothers; The Chase Manhattan Bank N.A.; Chemical Bank Ltd.; Credit Suisse Financial Products; Cs First Boston Ltd.; The Dai-Ichi Kangyo Bank; Hill Samuel Bank Limited; The Industrial Bank of Japan Ltd.; Lehman Brothers International Inc.; The Mitsubishi Bank Ltd.; Mitsubishi Finance International Plc.; Nomura International plc.; Samuel Montagu; The Sumitomo Bank Ltd.

REVISERS OF THE ITALY LAW DIGEST FOR THIS DIRECTORY

STUDIO LEGALE BIAMONTI

Established in 1938

LUNGOTEVERE MICHELANGELO, 9
00192 ROME, ITALY
Telephone: 6-3212608, 6-3212609, 6-3225993
Cable Address: BIAVIDIR ROMA
Facsimile: 6-3236940; 6-3211959

General Civil Practice, Corporate, Tax, Contracts, Banking, Industrial Property, EEC Antitrust, Labor Law, Marine Law, Arbitration; Distributorships and Franchising, Mergers and Acquisitions.

MEMBERS OF FIRM

AVV. ENRICO BIAMONTI, born Rome, Italy, March 26, 1914; admitted, 1939, Italy. *Education:* University of Rome (Doctor in Law, 1935 and in Economics, 1939). President, Commission Speciale "Droit des Societes" of the Commission Consultative des Barreaux de la Communaute Europeenne, CCBE, 1973-1977. *Member:* Rome Bar Council (Member of the Board, 1966-1972); Union Internationale des Avocats.

AVV. FILIPPO BIAMONTI, born January 7, 1922; admitted, 1946, Italy. *Education:* University of Rome (1945).

AVV. LUIGI BIAMONTI, born Rome, Italy, February 15, 1943; admitted, 1969, Italy; 1983, Italian Supreme Court. *Education:* University of Rome (1966); University of Cambridge, Trinity Hall College (1966-1967); City of London College (1967); Columbia University, New York, Parker School of Private and Comparative Law (1974); Salzburg Seminars in American Studies (1978). Member of the Italian Delegation, Commission Special "Droit des Sociétés of the Conseil Consultatif des Barreaux de la Communaute Europeenne, CCBE, 1977-1987. *Member:* International Bar Association; International Fiscal Association; Institute of International Law and Practice of the ICC; Licensing Executive Society; Association of European Jurists.

ASSOCIATES

DR. PROC. ALBERTO IMPRODA, born Rome, Italy, January 14, 1964; admitted, 1992, Italy. *Education:* University of Rome (1989).

DR. PROC. FRANCESCO DE BIASI, born Rome, Italy, April 18, 1966; admitted, 1993, Italy. *Education:* University of Rome (1990).

DR. ANDREA LO GAGLIO, born Rome, Italy, December 28, 1966. *Education:* Institut d'Études Politiques, Paris, France (Maîtrise, 1987); University of Rome (1993).

Languages: Italian, English, French and Spanish

STUDIO LEGALE BISCONTI

Established in 1960

VIA BISSOLATI, 76
00187 ROME, ITALY
Telephone: (39-6) 479881
Telex: 610409 BRACTO I
Fax: (39-6) 487-2070

Milan, Italy Office: Via Santo Spirito, 14, 20121. Telephone: (39-2) 782641. Telex: 335009 BRACTO I. Fax: (39-2) 781188.
New York, New York Office: 730 Fifth Avenue, 10019. Telephone: (212) 956-9400. Telex: 225120 BRACTON UR. Fax: (212) 956-9405.
London, England Office: 1 College Hill, EC4R 4RA. Telephone: (44-0171) 4899924. Telex: 893544 BRACTO G. Fax: (44-0171) 4898740.

(This Listing Continued)

Corporate Practice. Mergers and Acquisitions, Securities, International Finance and Banking, International Law, Domestic and International Taxation, EEC Law, Corporation Law, Labor, Bankruptcy, Environmental Law, Energy, Antitrust, Unfair Competition, Telecommunications, Patents, Trademarks, Alternative Dispute Resolution, Counselling in International Commercial Transactions.

GIUSEPPE BISCONTI, born Palmi, Italy, April 22, 1931; admitted to practice, 1953; admitted, 1954, Italy; 1968, Supreme Court, Italy. *Education:* Italy, University of Rome (Doctor of Jurisprudence, maxima cum laude, 1953); Austria, University of Graz, 1951; Germany, University of Münster, 1955; U.S.A., Louisiana State University Law School (LL.M., 1956; Post-doctoral Fellow, 1955-1956) and University of Michigan Law School (doctoral candidate and Research Associate, 1956-1958). Professorial Assistant of Comparative Law, University of Rome, 1958-1960. Scientific Collaborator, International Institute for the Unification of Private Law, 1958-1959; Guest Lecturer on Private International· Law, Institut Universitaire d'Etudes Européennes, Turin, 1959 and 1960. Visiting Scholar, Columbia University Law School, 1979. *Member:* Italian Bar Association (Rome); American Bar Association (Honorary Member); Canadian Bar Association (Honorary Member); Mexican Bar Association (Honorary Member); American Bar Foundation (Fellow); The Association of the Bar of the City of New York; New York County Lawyers Association; American Foreign Law Association; Southwestern Legal Foundation (Trustee; Vice-Chairman and Member of the Advisory Board); American Society of International Law; British Institute of International and Comparative Law; International Bar Association (President, 1990-1992); International Fiscal Association; International Law Association; Union Internationale des Avocats. (At Rome and Milan Offices). *LANGUAGES:* Italian, English, French, German, Spanish and Russian.

NICCOLÒ PASOLINI DALL'ONDA, born Rome, Italy, February 9, 1931; admitted to practice, 1957; admitted, 1959, Italy. *Education:* Italy, University of Rome (Doctor of Jurisprudence, 1955). *Member:* Italian Bar Association (Rome); International Bar Association. *LANGUAGES:* Italian, English, French and German.

NICOLA STERBINI, born Rome, Italy, September 6, 1952; admitted to practice, 1978; admitted, 1981, Italy. *Education:* Italy, University of Rome (Doctor of Jurisprudence, maxima cum laude, 1978); Leyden-Amsterdam-Columbia Summer Program in American Law, 1981; U.S.A. Columbia University (LL.M., 1982). *Member:* Italian Bar Association (Rome); International Bar Association. *LANGUAGES:* Italian, English and French.

GIUSEPPE BARRECA, born Rome, Italy, March 22, 1960; admitted to practice, 1984; admitted, 1986, Italy. *Education:* Italy, University of Rome (Doctor of Jurisprudence, maxima cum laude, 1984). Academy of American and International Law, Southwestern Legal Foundation, Dallas, 1988; L.U.I.S.S. Libera Universita' Internazionale degli Studi Sociali, Rome (Professorial Assistant, 1985-1987). *Member:* Italian Bar Association (Rome); International Bar Association. (Resident at London Office). *LANGUAGES:* Italian and English.

FABIO DELORENZI, born Alessandria, Italy, January 1, 1961; admitted to practice, 1985; admitted, 1987, Italy. *Education:* Italy, University of Turin (Doctor of Jurisprudence, maxima cum laude, 1984); U.S.A., Columbia University, 1986; UK, London, City of London Polytechnic School of Law (Diploma, Antitrust and Intellectual Property, 1989); U.S.A., Dallas, Academy of American and International Law, Southwestern Legal Foundation, 1990; U.S.A., New York University (LL.M., 1993). *Member:* Italian Bar Association (Milan); International Bar Association; American Bar Association; New York State Bar Association; Association of the Bar of The City of New York. (Resident at New York Office). *LANGUAGES:* Italian and English.

SILVANA DE VINCOLIS, born Bolzano, Italy, October 5, 1946; admitted to practice, 1972; admitted, 1975, Italy. *Education:* University of Rome (Doctor of Jurisprudence, 1971). Professorial Assistant, Law of Admiralty, University of Rome, 1971-1973. Special Student, Yale Law School, 1986-1987. Lecturer, Private International Law, L.U.I.S.S., Libera Universita' Internazionale degli Studi Sociali, Rome, 1987. Member: E.N.I. Law Department, 1973-1980; I.R.I. Law Department, 1980-1988; Law and Competition Committee, CEEP, 1985-1988; Committee on Competition, International Chamber of Commerce, 1985-1988. *Member:* Italian Bar Association (Rome). *LANGUAGES:* Italian and English.

CARLO GARBARINO, born Genoa, Italy, September 23, 1959; admitted to practice, 1984; admitted, 1987, Italy. *Education:* Italy, University of Genoa (Doctor of Jurisprudence, maxima cum laude, 1983); University of Michigan Law School (Master of Laws, 1986); University of Genoa (Ph.D.

(This Listing Continued)

in International Taxation, 1989). Visiting Scholar, Yale Law School, 1986-1987. Associate Professor, University of Siena, 1988—. IBM Italia S.p.A., Office of the Legal Counsel, 1987-1988. Member, Editorial Board of Diritto e Pratica Tributaria; Contributing Editor of EC Tax Review. *Member:* Italian Bar Association (Genoa); International Bar Association; International Fiscal Association. (Resident at Milan Office). *LANGUAGES:* Italian and English.

GAUDIANA GIUSTI, born Livorno, Italy, July 14, 1962; admitted to practice, 1988; admitted, 1993, Italy. *Education:* University of Pisa, Italy (Doctor of Jurisprudence, maxima cum laude, 1987); Universite' Libre de Bruxelles, Belgium (Licence Speciale en Droit Européen, 1989). *Member:* Italian Bar Association (Pisa); European Lawyers Association. (Resident at Milan Office). *LANGUAGES:* Italian and English.

FABIO MARELLI, born Alessandria, Italy, July 11, 1963; admitted to practice, 1988; admitted, 1991, Italy. *Education:* Italy, University of Pavia (Doctor of Jurisprudence, 1987); University of Miami School of Law (LL.M., 1990). Research Associate, C.N.R.-Consiglio Nazionale delle Ricerche, Pavia, Italy, 1988. *Member:* Italian Bar Association (Milan). (Resident at Milan Office). *LANGUAGES:* Italian and English.

COSTANZO RAPONE, born Rome, Italy, January 17, 1964; admitted to practice, 1988; admitted, 1990, Italy. *Education:* Italy, University of Rome (Doctor of Jurisprudence, 1987); UK, London, City of London Polytechnic School of Law (Diploma, International Law, 1987); London, King's College, Young European Lawyers Scholarship, 1990; The Netherlands, University of Amsterdam, Columbia Summer Program in American Law, 1988. *Member:* Italian Bar Association (Rome); International Bar Association; ELA (European Lawyers Association). *LANGUAGES:* Italian and English.

ANDREA BISCONTI, born Rome, Italy, September 4, 1963; admitted to practice, 1989, Italy. *Education:* University of Rome, Italy (Doctor of Jurisprudence, 1989); Academy of International Law, The Hague, 1993; Academy of American and International Law, Southwestern Legal Foundation, Dallas, 1992; University of Amsterdam (Course on European Integration, 1992). *Member:* International Bar Association. *LANGUAGES:* Italian, English, French, German and Spanish.

FRANCESCO PAOLO CROCENZI, born Rome, Italy, September 6, 1963; admitted to practice, 1987; admitted, 1990, Italy. *Education:* Italy, L.U.I.S.S., Libera Universita' Internazionale degli Studi Sociali, Rome (Doctor of Jurisprudence, Maxima cum Laude, 1987); Universite' Libre de Bruxelles, Belgium (Licence Speciale en Droit Europeen, 1990). Professorial Assistant of EC Law, L.U.I.S.S., Libera Universita' Internazionale degli Studi Sociali, Rome, 1992—. *Member:* Italian Bar Association (Rome). *LANGUAGES:* Italian, English and French.

PAOLO CIERI, born Rome, Italy, June 20, 1966; admitted to practice, 1989; admitted, 1993, Italy; 1994, New York. *Education:* Italy, University of Rome (Doctor of Jurisprudence, maxima cum laude, 1989); U.S.A. University of Houston Law School (LL.M., 1993). Professorial Assistant, University of Rome Law School, 1990-1992. *Member:* Italian Bar Association (Rome). *LANGUAGES:* Italian, English and French.

MARIA SERENA LAPERGOLA, born Rome, Italy, July 30, 1970; admitted, 1994, Italy. *Education:* Italy, University of Rome (Doctor of Jurisprudence, maxima cum laude, 1993); U.S.A. Harvard Law School (LL.M., 1994). *LANGUAGES:* Italian, English and French.

BROSIO, CASATI E ASSOCIATI

VIA VALADIER, 36
00193 ROME, ITALY
Telephone: (39) (6) 3230328
Telecopier: (39) (6) 3216107

Milan, Italy Office: Via Manzoni, 41, 20121. Telephone: (39) (2) 29010200. Telecopier: (39) (2) 29010278.
Turin, Italy Office: Corso Vittorio Emanuele II, 68, 10121. Telephone: (39) (11) 5612005. Telecopier: (39) (11) 541018.
Brussels, Belgium Office: 99, Rue de la Loi, 1040. Telephone: (32) (2) 2300004. Telecopier: (32) (2) 2307473.

General Practice and Litigation, Corporation, Taxation, Foreign Investment, Mergers and Acquisitions, Banking, Administrative, Antitrust, Environmental, Labor, Real Estate and EEC Law.

(This Listing Continued)

OF COUNSEL

RENATO CLARIZIA, born Salerno, Italy, October 10, 1950; admitted, 1975, Italy. *Education:* University of Rome (J.D., 1972); Columbia University School of Law, Visiting Scholar, 1977. Lecturer, Fundamentals of Civil Law, University of Rome, 1972-1977. Professor, Banking Law, 1979-1981 and Civil Law, 1981—, University of Urbino. Professor, Banking Law, Tax Inspectors Superior School, Rome, 1980—. Secretary General, ASSILEA (Italian Leasing Companies' Association), 1983-1990.

ASSOCIATE

DANIELA JOUVENAL LONG, born Turin, Italy, October 10, 1958; admitted, 1985, Italy. *Education:* University of Turin (J.D., 1982).

RESIDENTS AT MILAN OFFICE

Roberto Casati	*Alberto Nanni*
Davide D'Angelo	*Giovanni Maria Marini*
	Filippo Cesaris

Massimo Greco	*Paolo Cerina*
Francesco Cantoni	*Cecilia Buresti*
Paolo Esposito	*Alessandra Perrazzelli*
Giancarlo Castorino	*Michele Delfini*
Cristina Manasse	*Laura Lamera*
Daniela Stelé	*Massimo Trentino*
Francesco Simoneschi	*Andrea Arosio*

Antonella Capria	*Guido Alvigini*

RESIDENTS AT TURIN OFFICE

Guido Brosio	*Carlo Pavesio*
	Mario Colombatto

Marco Tosetto Bricco	*Sara Panelli*
Nicola Ceraolo	*Vittorio Torazzi*
Riccardo Ventura	*Fabrizio Fasano*
Donatella De Rosa	*Silvia D'Amario*
Giovanni Luppi	
(Resident, Turin Office)	

RESIDENT AT BRUSSELS OFFICE

Claudia Crescenzi

Languages: English, French and German.

(For biographical data on attorneys not resident at Rome, see Professional Biographies at Milan, Italy)

CAMOZZI & BONISSONI

VIA TEVERE, 44
00198 ROME, ITALY
Telephone: (06) 841-3244; 841-2864; Intn'l (39-6) 841-3244; 841-2864
Telcopier: (06) 841-3679; Intn'l: (39-6) 841-3679

Milan, Italy Office: Viale Majno, 17. Telephone: (02) 760-21542; Intnl.: (39-2) 760-21542. Telecopier: (02) 760-21861; Intnl.: (39-2) 760-21816.

International and Domestic Practice, Mergers and Acquisitions, Taxation, Banking, Bankruptcy, Contracts, Corporate, Securities, European Common Market, Antitrust, Foreign Investment, Insurance, International Trade, Patents and Trademarks, Licensing, Labor, Product Liability, Litigation and Arbitration.

MEMBERS OF FIRM

MARIO CAMOZZI, born Ferrara, Italy, August 24, 1955; admitted, 1985, Italy. *Education:* University Bocconi of Milan (Doctor of Economics). Auditor and Tax Auditor, KPMG Peat Marwick, 1982-1985. Associate, Berchet, 1985-1986. *LANGUAGES:* Italian and English.

ANGELO BONISSONI, born Milan, Italy, April 13, 1959; admitted, 1986, Italy. *Education:* University Cattolica of Milan (Doctor of Economics). Auditor, RIA, 1979. Auditor and Tax Auditor, KPMG Peat Marwick, 1979-1983. Associate, Cassinis, 1983-1986. *LANGUAGES:* Italian, English and French.

(This Listing Continued)

CAMOZZI & BONISSONI, Rome—Continued

ROBERTO BRUSTIA, born Novara, Italy, June 17, 1956; admitted, 1988, Italy. *Education:* University Bocconi of Milan (Doctor of Economics). Auditor and Tax Auditor, Price Waterhouse Associates, 1982-1985. Associate, Minoli e Associati, 1986-1988. *LANGUAGES:* Italian and English.

ALESSANDRO PINCI, born Rome, Italy, January 16, 1954; admitted, 1978, Italy. Auditor, Ernst & Whinney, 1976-1979. Chief Accountant, BP, British Petroleum, 1979-1980. Associate, Spagnolo Napolitano, 1980-1986. Senior Tax Manager, Ernst & Young, 1986-1990. *LANGUAGES:* Italian, English and French.

PAOLO BAROZZI, born Novara, Italy, March 14, 1958; admitted, 1988, Italy. *Education:* University of Milan (Doctor of Jurisprudence). Associate: Erede, Stefani e Associati, 1984-1985; Pavia, Ansaldo e Verusio, 1989-1991 (Visiting Associate, Pavia & Harcourt, New York, 1990). Attorney, Fininvest Group, 1986-1988. Director, Legal Department, OTIS ITALIA SpA, 1991. *LANGUAGES:* Italian and English.

PAOLO MANZATO, born Milan, Italy, December 6, 1955; admitted, 1981, Italy. *Education:* University of Milan (Doctor of Jurisprudence). *Member:* UAE (European Lawyers Union); AIJA (International Association of Young Lawyers). *LANGUAGES:* Italian, English, German, French and Spanish.

GIANCARLO TABEGNA, born Rome, Italy, September 13, 1968; admitted, 1984, Italy. *Education:* University of Rome (Doctor of Jurisprudence); London School of Economics (LL.M., Master of Laws, 1985). *Member:* International Bar Association. *LANGUAGES:* Italian and English.

ASSOCIATES

FRANCESCO DE LEVA, born Rome, Italy, November 28, 1959; admitted, 1985, Italy. *Education:* University of Rome (Doctor of Economics). *LANGUAGES:* Italian, English and German.

MASSIMO GENTILE, born Rome, Italy, November 28, 1963; admitted, 1989, Italy. *Education:* University of Rome (Doctor of Economics). *LANGUAGES:* Italian and English.

LUCA MARCHETTI, born Rome, Italy, November 17, 1959; admitted, 1985, Italy. *LANGUAGES:* Italian, English and German.

PASQUALE PASTORE, born Messina, Italy, February , 1962; admitted, 1990,. *Education:* University of Rome (Doctor of Economics). *LANGUAGES:* Italian and English.

ALBERTO ZOPPINI, born Rome, Italy, July 13, 1967. *Education:* University of Rome (Doctor of Economics). *LANGUAGES:* Italian, English and French.

CLAUDIO CASTELLANI, born Rome, Italy, April 19, 1965; admitted, 1991, Italy. *Education:* University Sapienza of Rome (Doctor of Economics). *LANGUAGES:* English and Italian.

MASSIMO CECCHI, born Bari, Italy, October 2, 1967; admitted, 1990, Italy. *Education:* University of Bari (Doctor of Economics). *LANGUAGES:* Italian, English and French.

ENRICO MARTINO, born Rome, Italy, January 30, 1966; admitted, 1990, Italy. *Education:* University Sapienza of Rome (Doctor of Economics). *LANGUAGES:* Italian and English.

STEFANO CELA, born Foggia, Italy, May 25, 1965; admitted, 1992, Italy. *Education:* LUISS University of Rome (Doctor of Jurisprudence); City of London Polytechnic (Advanced Business Law, 1991); Columbia University Program in American Law (Columbia and Leyden Universities, 1994). *Member:* International Bar Association. *LANGUAGES:* Italian and English.

REPRESENTATIVE CLIENTS: Abbey National; Imprefin Imprese Finanziarie S.p.A.; DeGremont Italia S.p.A; Cobarr S.p.A. Cogeb S.p.A. (Gruppo Coca Cola); DDB, Needham (Gruppo Omnicom); Coop Lombardia A R.L.; ABC Finanziaria S.p.A. (Gruppo Arab Banking); Finagel S.p.A. (Gruppo Sopaf); Gruppo Alfagomma; Gruppo Montedison; Gruppo Mittel; Olly's Int.; Elf Italiana; Efibanca S.p.A.; Monte dei Paschi di Siena S.p.A Sim; ROMA S.p.A. Sim; McQuay Italia S.p.A. (Gruppo Snyder General); Instant-Upright Int.; UCB Credicasa S.p.A.; Associated Press Italia S.r.l.; Egon Zehnder International S.r.l.; Toyota Italia S.p.A.; 3M S.p.A.; Gruppo Need; Lasmo Oil Development; Ideal Standard S.p.A.; Coin S.p.A.; Sci-Costruzioni e Insediamenti Edilizi S.p.A.; Fujitsu Personal System Italia S.r.l.; Gruppo MAA; Giubergia Warburg; Gruppo Belleli.

(For Complete Biographical Data on all Rome, Italy Personnel, see Professional Biographies at Milan, Italy).

CAPPELLO & ASSOCIATI

47, PIAZZA BARBERINI
00187 ROME, ITALY
Telephone: 39-6-4824781; 39-6-4820650
Fax: 39-6-4881327

Arezzo, Italy Office: Viale Michelangelo, 8, 62100. Telephone: 39-575-25818. Fax: 39-575-300443.

Administrative Law, Anti-Trust Law, Arbitration, Competition Law, Consumer Protection Law, Copyright Law, Criminal Law, Distributorship, Agency, Franchise, Know How Law, EEC Law, Family Law, General Commercial and Company Law, General Tax Practice, Intellectual Property, International Taxation, Joint Ventures, Labour Law, Litigation, Merger and Acquisitions, Transportation Law. General Legal Practice.

RICCARDO CAPPELLO, born Reggio Calabria, February 13, 1944. *Education:* University of Rome, Law School (Jurisprudence Doctor, 1969).

FRANCESCA BOCCHESE, born Vicenza, December 19, 1954. *Education:* University of Padova, Law School (Jurisprudence Doctor, 1978).

CONSULTANTS

TULLIO GALIANI, born Naples, May 6, 1939. *Education:* University of Naples (Jurisprudence Doctor, 1969). Professor in Criminal Law at Camerino University.

STELIO GICCA-PALLI, born Roma, October 29, 1946. *Education:* University of Rome, Law School (Jurisprudence Doctor, 1971).

LUIGI GROSSI, born Roma, March 12, 1939. *Education:* University of Perugia, Law School (Jurisprudence Doctor, 1966).

MARIO MARCHETTI, born Roma, October 9, 1930. *Education:* University of Rome Law School (Jurisprudence Doctor, 1954). *LANGUAGES:* Italian, English, French and German.

Languages: Italian, English, French and German

STUDIO CARNELUTTI

Established in 1900

VIA PARIGI 11
00185 ROME, ITALY
Telephone: 06-473.901
Telex: 611325 UNILAW
Telefax: 06-4 8.19.833

Milan: Corso Matteotti 10, 20121. Telephone: 02-7600.2042. Cable Address: "Unilaw Milano". Telex: 321094 UNILAW I. Telefax: 02-784.779.
London: Carnelutti. 76 Shoe Lane, EC4A 3BQ. Telephone: 0171-242.2268. Telex: 298389 CARMAC G. Telefax: 0171-242.4190.
New York: Werbel, McMillin and Carnelutti. 711 Fifth Avenue, 10022-3194. Telephone: (212) 832-8300. Telefax: (212) 832-3353.
Paris: Cabinet Carnelutti, 3, Avenue George V, 75008 Paris. Telephone: (1) 4723-3181. Telefax: (1) 4720-2509.

General Practice with a particular concentration in the following areas: Agency and Distributorship, Antitrust and Trade Regulations, Arbitration, Litigation and Mediation, Business Law, Company and Corporate Law, Construction Law, Mergers and Acquisitions, European Community Law, Finance, Project Financing and Developments Projects, Franchising, Immigration and Naturalization, International Law, Labour Law, Real Estate, Estates Planning, Inheritance, Taxation, Foreign Investments, International Commercial Transactions.

FRANCESCO CARNELUTTI Founder (1879-1965).

TITO CARNELUTTI (1904-1983).

LEONE FRANCO INCUTTI, born Salerno, Italy, February ll, 1935; admitted, 1962, Italy. *Education:* Naples University (J.D., 1957). Fulbright Scholar. Seminar on Comparative Law, American University, Washington, D.C., 1957-1958. *Member:* Rome Bar Association.

ANTONIO PERNO, born Rome, Italy, March 28, 1942; admitted, 1969, Italy. *Education:* Rome University (J.D., 1966). *Member:* Rome Bar Association.

(This Listing Continued)

FERDINANDO CARABBA TETTAMANTI, born Rome, Italy, January 5, 1944; admitted, 1970, Italy. *Education:* Rome University (J.D., 1967). *Member:* Rome Bar Association.

VINCENZO FIGUS, born Rome, Italy, June 6, 1944; admitted, 1968, Italy. *Education:* Rome University (Doctor of Economics, 1967).

GIANFRANCO GRANDONI, born Rome, Italy, November 28, 1943; admitted, 1968, Italy. *Education:* Rome University (Doctor of Economics, 1967).

ANGELO CREMONESE, born Rome, Italy, January 7, 1958; admitted, 1983, Italy. *Education:* Rome University (Doctor of Economics, 1981). Tax Department coordinator, Postgraduate School of Economics, L.U-.I.S.S. University, Rome (1988-1990). Lecturer on Taxation Theory (Scienza delle Finanze), Faculty of Economics, L.U.I.S.S. University, Rome.

CARLO DI GIULIO, born Brindisi, Italy, June 11, 1954; admitted, 1985, Italy. *Education:* Bologna University (J.D., 1979); International Comparative Law School, Strasbourg (1980); Post Graduate Specialization School in European Studies, Rome (1981-1982). *Member:* International Bar Association; Rome Bar Association; Association of Legal Scholars of the Center for International Legal Studies, Salzburg.

PIER ANDREA FRÉ TORELLI MASSINI, born Rome, Italy, February 6, 1961; admitted, 1986, Italy. *Education:* L.U.I.S.S. University, Rome (Doctor of Economics, 1986).

PIERGIACOMO JUCCI, born Rome, Italy, September 10, 1964; admitted, 1988, Italy. *Education:* L.U.I.S.S. University, Rome (Doctor of Economics, 1986).

STEFANO CRISCI, born Rome, Italy, October 2, 1962; admitted, 1989, Italy. *Education:* Rome University (J.D., 1985); New York University, New York, NY (LL.M., 1988). Lecturer on Administrative Law, Rome University. *Member:* Rome Bar Association.

NICOLETTA CIMBOLLI SPAGNESI, born Rome, Italy, April 19, 1962; admitted, 1988, Italy. *Education:* L.U.I.S.S. University (Doctor of Economics, 1986).

FRANCESCA CAPORALE, born Rome, Italy, February 28, 1966; admitted, 1992, Italy. *Education:* Rome University (J.D., 1989). *Member:* Rome Bar Association.

LUCA ALBANESE, born Rome, Italy, April 28, 1965; admitted, 1992, Italy. *Education:* L.U.I.S.S. University, Rome (J.D., 1989). *Member:* Rome Bar Association.

OF COUNSEL

CARLO SANTAGATA, Professor of Insurance Law, University of Rome, Rome, Italy.

ALEXANDRE CARNELUTTI, Professor of EEC Law, University of Paris, France.

Languages: Italian, English, French and Spanish

STUDIO LEGALE CAVASOLA

Established in 1901

VIA AGOSTINO DEPRETIS, 86
00184 ROME, ITALY
Telephone: 39.6.488 1516
Fax: 39.6.48 3755

Milan Office: Via Mario Pagano, 65, 20145, Milano. Telephone: 39.2.48011171. Fax: 39.2.48012914.

General Civil Practice, Business and Corporate Law, Labour Law, European Community Law, Conflict of Laws, Civil Litigation and Arbitration. Member, International Grouping of Lawyers.

MEMBERS OF FIRM

GIANNETTO CAVASOLA, born Rome, Italy, January 2, 1919; admitted, 1945, Italy; 1949, Supreme Court. *Education:* University of Rome (J.D.). Certified Public Auditor, 1966. Associate Judge, Supreme Court during the Lockheed trial, 1978. *LANGUAGES:* Italian and French.

NICOLA CAVASOLA, born Rome, Italy, April 10, 1925; admitted, 1952, Italy; 1960, Supreme Court. *Education:* University of Rome (J.D.). *LANGUAGES:* Italian and French.

(This Listing Continued)

PIETRO CAVASOLA, born Rome, Italy, February 18, 1952; admitted, 1977, Italy; 1991, Supreme Court. *Education:* University of Rome (J.D., maxima cum laude). Co-Author: "European Economic Interest Grouping," Amsterdam, 1990; "Translation German-Italian East German Civil Code," Rome, 1976. Past Secretary, Conference of Young Lawyers, Rome. EEC Juridical Services, Bruxelles, 1975. Certified Public Auditor, 1992. Secretary of I.G.L. International Grouping of Lawyers, 1994. *Member:* International Young Lawyers Association (Vice-President); American Bar Association (Honorary Member, Young Lawyers Division). *LANGUAGES:* Italian, English, French and German.

CLAUDIO COGGIATTI, born Rome, Italy, August 19, 1956; admitted, 1983, Italy. *Education:* University of Rome (J.D., maxima cum laude). *Member:* International Young Lawyers Association (Executive Committee); Italian Young Lawyers Association (President, Rome Section); British American Law Association (BILA). *LANGUAGES:* Italian, English and French.

LAURA OPILIO, born Rome, Italy, October 2, 1962; admitted, 1989, Italy. *Education:* University of Rome (J.D., maxima cum laude, 1985). *Member:* International Young Lawyers Association. *LANGUAGES:* Italian, French and English.

FABRIZIO SPAGNOLO, born Rome, Italy, February 24, 1964; admitted, 1991, Italy. *Education:* University of Rome (J.D., 1988). Past Secretary, Conference of Young Lawyers, Rome. *Member:* International Young Lawyers Association; The British Institute of International and Comparative Law. *LANGUAGES:* Italian and English.

FEDERICO VECCHIO, born Mazara del Vallo, Trapani, Italy, November 11, 1962; admitted, 1992, Italy. *Education:* University of Rome (J.D., maxima cum laude, 1988). Judge, Federal Football League. *Member:* International Young Lawyers Association. *LANGUAGES:* Italian and English.

ASSOCIATES

MASSIMO F. DOTTO, born Rome, Italy, February 3, 1963; admitted, 1991, Rome, Italy. *Education:* University of Rome (J.D., maxima cum laude, 1988). *Member:* International Young Lawyers Association. *LANGUAGES:* Italian, English and French.

FRANCESCO FERRINI, born Padova, Italy, September 24, 1968; admitted, 1993, Rome, Italy. *Education:* University of Ferrara (J.D., 1993). ERASMUS, University of Leeds, England, 1991-1992. *LANGUAGES:* Italian and English.

VALERIA PANZIRONI, born Rome, Italy, November 10, 1969. *Education:* L.U.I.S.S. University, Rome (J.D., maxima cum laude, 1993). ERASMUS, University of Lyon, France, 1991-1992. *LANGUAGES:* Italian, French and English.

ASSOCIATE SOLICITOR

ANDREW G. PATON, born Sydney, Australia, October 31, 1955; admitted, 1981, New South Wales, Australia; 1990, England and Wales; Registered European Lawyers, Rome Bar Council. *Education:* University of Sydney (B.A., 1977; LL.B., 1980). Professor, Law Faculty, L.U.I.S.S. University, Rome, 1988—. Fellow, Chartered Institute of Arbitrators, London. *Member:* Law Society of England and Wales; Law Council of Australia; International Bar Association. *LANGUAGES:* English and Italian.

CHIOMENTI E ASSOCIATI
STUDIO LEGALE

VIA BERTOLONI 44/46
00197 ROME, ITALY
Telephone: 06-809701
Cable Address: "Legal"
Telex: 622603 LEGAL I
Telecopier: 06-809706

Other Rome, Italy Office: Piazza di Monte Savello, 30.

Milan, Italy Office: Via A. Boito 8. Telephone: 02-721571. Telex: 340184 LEGAL I. Telecopier: 02-72157224/5.

London, England Office: 20 Berkeley Square. Telephone: +44-171-4956430. Telecopier: +44-171-4956431.

Bruxelles, Belgium Office: 73 Av. R. Vendendriessche, B. 1150. Telephone: +32-2-7728750. Telecopier: +32-2-7728736.

(This Listing Continued)

CHIOMENTI E ASSOCIATI STUDIO LEGALE, Rome— Continued

General Practice, Corporation, Commercial Law, Taxation, Foreign Investments, Banking, Securities, Investment Funds, E.C. Law, Antitrust, Litigation, Bankruptcy, Maritime and Labor Law.

PIER CARLO BRUNA, born Bergamo, Italy, May 27, 1924; admitted, 1949, Italy; 1965, Supreme Court. *Education:* University of Turin (J.D., 1946).

CARLO CHIOMENTI, born Rome, Italy, May 23, 1943; admitted, 1969, Italy. *Education:* University of Rome (J.D., 1966); Barrister, Lincoln's Inn, London (1970).

FILIPPO D. VASSALLI, born Turin, Italy, August 27, 1941; admitted, 1967, Italy. *Education:* University of Rome (J.D., 1965); Institute of Advanced Legal Studies, London. *Member:* The Association of the Bar of the City of New York; International Bar Association. (Resident, London Office).

FILIPPO CHIOMENTI, born Rome, Italy, April 4, 1940; admitted, 1977, Italy; 1979, Supreme Court. *Education:* University of Rome (J.D., 1963). Professor of Commercial Law, University of Rome.

MICHELE CARPINELLI, born Milan, Italy, November 22, 1948; admitted, 1986, Italy; admitted to practice before Taxation Courts, 1972. *Education:* University of Rome (Doctor in Economics, 1971; J.D., 1980). *Member:* International Fiscal Association. (Resident, Milan Office).

FRANCESCO AGO, born Turin, Italy, September 30, 1951; admitted, 1977, Italy. *Education:* University of Rome (J.D., 1973); Georgetown University (M.C.L., 1978). Visiting Foreign Lawyer, Covington and Burling, 1978. *Member:* International Bar Association; International Association of Young Lawyers.

MICHELE G. SOLDATI, born Rome, Italy, October 14, 1949; admitted, 1979, Italy. *Education:* University of Milan (J.D., 1971); University of California, Berkeley (LL.M., 1974). Assistant Researcher, International Taxation, Berkeley, 1975. (Resident, Milan Office).

LUIGI BENDI, born Milan, Italy, June 29, 1951; admitted to practice before Taxation Courts, 1982. *Education:* Catholic University of Milan (Doctor in Economics, 1976). (Resident, London Office).

EMANUELE GAMNA, born Turin, December 7, 1952; admitted, 1979, Italy. *Education:* University of Turin (J.D., 1976). Visiting Foreign Lawyer, White & Case, New York Office, 1980-1981. (Resident, Milan Office).

CARLO CROFF, born Auronzo di Cadore, (Belluno), Italy, August 24, 1955; admitted, 1982, Italy; 1985, New York. *Education:* University of Padova (J.D., 1979); University of Cambridge, U.K. (LL.B., 1980); Harvard University (LL.M., 1981). Foreign Associate: Crowell & Moring, Washington, D.C., 1982; Debevoise & Plimpton, New York, 1982-1984. (Resident, Milan Office).

ALBERTO DEL DIN, born Campobasso, Italy, October 27, 1955; admitted, 1984, Italy. *Education:* University of Rome (J.D., 1980). Fellow of the Salzburg Seminar, American Law and Legal Institutions, 1982. Visiting Foreign Lawyer, De Paul University, Chicago, Summer, 1986. (Resident, London Office).

FRANCO VIGLIANO, born Livorno, Italy, January 29, 1956; admitted, 1983, Italy. *Education:* University of Rome (J.D., 1979); Columbia University, New York (LL.M., 1986). *Member:* International Bar Association; Young Lawyers' International Association. (Resident, Milan Office).

LUCA RADICATI DI BROZOLO, born Birmingham, U.K., June 27, 1952; admitted, 1988, Italy. *Education:* University of Florence (M.A. in Political Sciences, 1974). Legal Service, Bank of International Settlements, Basel, Switzerland, 1978-1984. Professor of International Law, University of Turin. (Resident, Milan Office).

MASSIMO G.G. COLOZZA, born Milan, Italy, April 16, 1954; admitted, 1982, Italy. *Education:* University of Rome (J.D., 1978). Visiting Foreign Lawyer, Coward Chance, London, 1983.

ANDREA F. CECCHETTI, born Rome, Italy, July 18, 1947; admitted, 1973, Italy; 1988, Supreme Court, Italy. *Education:* University of Rome (J.D., 1971).

CARLO F. CARNACINI, born Bologna, Italy, December 12, 1949; admitted, 1976, Italy. *Education:* University of Bologna (J.D., 1973).

VITTORIO TADEI, born Ancona, Italy, May 26, 1956; admitted, 1988, Italy. *Education:* University of Rome (J.D., 1980); University of Michigan

(This Listing Continued)

(M.C.L., 1983). Visiting Foreign Lawyer, Gibson, Dunn and Crutcher, Los Angeles, 1983-1984.

UGO TRIBULATO, born Rome, Italy, February 25, 1956; admitted to practice before Taxation Courts, 1983. *Education:* University of Rome (Doctor in Economics, 1982).

FRANCESCA PALETTO, born September 4, 1959; admitted, 1988, Italy. *Education:* University of Milan (J.D., 1984). (Resident, Milan Office).

LAURA SALVANESCHI, born Milan, Italy, June 5, 1958; admitted, 1985, Italy. *Education:* University of Milan (J.D., 1981). Professor of Civil Procedure, University of Sassari. (Resident, Milan Office).

EDOARDO ANDREOLI, born Turin, Italy, October 13, 1958; admitted, 1986, Italy. *Education:* University of Turin (J.D., 1983); University of California, Los Angeles (LL.M., 1985). (Resident, Milan Office).

ROBERTO GHIO, born Naples, Italy, April 21, 1961; admitted, 1986, Italy. *Education:* Milan University (J.D., 1983). Visiting Foreign Lawyer, Debevoise & Plimpton, New York, 1988. (Resident, Milan Office).

MARZIO LONGO, born Vittorio Veneto (Treviso), Italy, April 27, 1959; admitted, 1986, Italy. *Education:* University of Trieste (J.D., 1984). (Resident, Milan Office).

MASSIMO V. BENEDETTELLI, born Bari, Italy, May 30, 1957; admitted, 1987, Italy. *Education:* University of Bari (M.A. in Political Sciences, 1979; J.D., 1984); University of Pennsylvania (LL.M., 1983); European University Institute, San Domenico di Fiesole (Florence) (Ph.D., 1987). Fellow of the Salzburg Seminar, American Law and Legal Institutions, 1981. (Resident, Milan Office).

ENNIO CICCONI, born Rome, December 28, 1962; admitted, 1988, Italy. *Education:* University of Rome (J.D., 1985).

FRANCESCO TEDESCHINI, born Perugia, Italy, March 18, 1961; admitted, 1989, Italy. *Education:* University of Perugia (J.D., 1984). Foreign Intern, Skadden, Arps, Slate, Meagher & Flom, New York, 1990.

ANDREA BERNAVA, born Rome, December 3, 1958; admitted, 1990, Italy. *Education:* University of Rome (J.D., 1987).

PAOLA ADRIANI, born Rome, Italy, July 19, 1960; admitted, 1989, Italy. *Education:* University of Rome (J.D., 1985); American University, Washington College of Law, Washington, D.C. (LL.M., 1989).

RENATO PATERNOLLO, born Thiene (Vicenza), December 15, 1962, admitted to practice before Taxation Courts, 1990. *Education:* University of Milan (Doctor in Economics, 1987). (Resident, Milan Office).

RICCARDO GENTILI, born Terni, Italy, April 9, 1963; admitted to practice before Taxation Courts, 1989. *Education:* University of Rome (Doctor in Economics, 1987).

LUCA BONETTI, born Rovereto (Trento), September 8, 1965; admitted, 1992, Italy. *Education:* Catholic University of Milan (J.D., 1989); Oxford, Wadham College, Summer School for International Financial Law (1993). Visiting Foreign Lawyer, Pritchard Inglefield & Tobin, London, 1991. (Resident, Milan Office).

EMANUELA DA RIN, born Rome, July 14, 1967; admitted, 1992, Italy. *Education:* University of Rome (J.D., 1989). Visiting Foreign Lawyer, Freshfields, London Office, 1992.

ENRICO GIORDANO, born Rome, January 13, 1965; admitted, 1992, Italy. *Education:* University of Rome (J.D., 1989; Ph.D., 1995). Research Assistant, Linacre College, Oxford, 1991.

GABRIELLA OPROMOLLA, born Naples, Italy, March 25, 1964; admitted, 1992, Italy. *Education:* University of Milan (J.D., 1988). (Resident, Milan Office).

BRUNO CASTELLINI, born Genoa, Italy, February 20, 1959; admitted, 1992, Italy. *Education:* University of Genoa (J.D., 1984); University of London, Queen Mary College (LL.M., 1988). Foreign Associate: Linklaters & Paines, London, 1990-1992. *Member:* International Bar Association. (Resident, Milan Office).

GIULIA BATTAGLIA, born Milan, Italy, June 4, 1968; admitted, 1991, Italy. *Education:* University of Rome "La Sapienza" (Doctor in Economics, 1991). (Resident, London Office).

MONICA CURCURUTO, born Naples, Italy, April 11, 1964; admitted, 1993, Italy. *Education:* University of Rome (J.D., 1989).

GIULIA DI TOMMASO, born Rome, Italy, April 1, 1964; admitted, 1993, Italy. *Education:* University of Rome (J.D., 1988). Fellow of Interna-

(This Listing Continued)

tional Court of Justice (1989). Directorate General Internal Market, EC Commission, 1990-1993. (Resident, Brussels Office).

LEE UNTERHALTER, born Johannesburg, South Africa, April 17, 1961; admitted, 1986, New York (Not admitted in Italy). *Education:* Stanford Law School (J.D., 1985).

Languages: English, French and German.

REFERENCES: *U.S.A.:* American Airlines; Citibank N.A.; EDS Electronic Data Systems Corp.; Exxon Corp.; General Motors; Gillette; McDonald's International; R.J. Reynolds; Sara Lee; United International Pictures; Morgan Stanley; General Electric. *UNITED KINGDOM:* British American Tobacco; British Petroleum Co., Ltd.; Credit Suisse First Boston; Goldman Sachs; Royal Insurance; S.G. Warburg & Co., Ltd. *FRANCE:* Crédit Commercial de France; Credit Lyonnais; Elf-ERAP; Axa. *GERMANY:* Deutsche Bank; Siemens A.G. *JAPAN:* Bank of Tokyo; Honda; Industrial Bank of Japan; Nomura. *SWITZERLAND:* La Baloise, Compagnie d'Assurances; Swiss Bank Corporation; Union des Banques Suisses. *BAHREIN:* Arab Banking Corporation. *ITALY:* Alitalia; Banca Commerciale Italiana; Banca di Roma; Barilla; Fiat; IFI; IRI; Istituto Bancario San Paolo di Torino; Mediobanca; Montedison; STET.

COLLODEL, LEONE, LIGI, QUEIROLO

Studio Legale

Established in 1990

VIA EMANUELE GIANTURCO, 11
00196 ROME, ITALY
Telephone: 3224262
Fax: 3224282

Milan, Italy Office: Via Eustachi, 12. 20129. Telephone: 29400399-29400041. Fax: 29400041.

Civil Law in General, Commercial, Corporate, Industrial Property, E.U. and Labor Law, Counselling on Contracts in General, including Mergers and Acquisitions, Licensing, Distribution, Joint Venture Agreements, Civil (including Labor) and Criminal Litigation.

PARTNERS

ROBERTO COLLODEL, born Milan, Italy, December 14, 1949; admitted, 1974, Italy. *Education:* University of Rome (J.D., 1973). Foreign Associate, Hughes, Hubbard & Reed, New York, N.Y., 1975-1976. *Member:* Italian Bar Association; International Bar Association. *LANGUAGES:* Italian and English.

ARTURO MARIA LEONE, born Caltanissetta, Italy, August 22, 1955; admitted, 1980, Italy. *Education:* University of Rome (J.D., 1980). Former Assistant Professor, Civil Law, University of Rome. *Member:* Italian Bar Association; Licensing Executives Society (LES), Italy. *LANGUAGES:* Italian and English.

ANDREA GHERARDO LIGI, born Rome, Italy, April 10, 1953; admitted, 1978, Italy. *Education:* University of Rome (J.D., 1978); University of Illinois, U.S.A. (M.C.L., 1979). *Member:* Italian Bar Association; International Bar Association. *LANGUAGES:* Italian and English.

STEFANO QUEIROLO, born Bern, Switzerland, August 25, 1956; admitted, 1978, Italy. *Education:* University of Rome (J.D., 1978). Legal Consultant of the Embassy of the United States of America, Rome, 1983-1985. *Member:* Italian Bar Association; International Bar Association. *LANGUAGES:* Italian and English.

ASSOCIATES

ANTONIO COLAVINCENZO, born Como, Italy, December 25, 1966. *Education:* University of Rome (J.D., 1990). *LANGUAGES:* Italian and English.

PIERLUIGI DE PALMA, born Bari, Italy, November 30, 1964. *Education:* University of Rome (J.D., 1989). *LANGUAGES:* Italian and English.

RAFFAELLA GAMBARDELLA, born San Severo (Foggia), Italy, August 6, 1965. *Education:* LUISS University of Rome (J.D., 1988). *LANGUAGES:* Italian and English.

ALESSANDRO SPINELLA, born Rome, Italy, August 17, 1966. *Education:* University of Rome (J.D., 1991). *LANGUAGES:* Italian, German and English.

SILVIA VENTURINI, born Rome, Italy, November 22, 1965. *Education:* University of Rome (J.D., 1990). *LANGUAGES:* Italian, French, English and German.

MASSIMO SERRA, born Rome, Italy, August 24, 1966. *Education:* University of Rome (J.D., 1991). *LANGUAGES:* Italian and English.

DALLA VEDOVA

Studio Legale

12, VIA VITTORIO BACHELET
00185 ROME, ITALY
Telephone: 06/4440821 (5 l.)
Fax: 06/4462165

Milan, Italy: 11, Via del Piatti, 20123. Telephone: 02/86757161 Fax: 02/86753936.

International and General Practice, Corporate, EU Law, Energy, Banking, Insurance, Foreign Investment, Mergers and Acquisitions, Securities, Investment Funds, Antitrust, Aeronautical, Arbitration, Bankruptcy, Labor, Patent, Trademark, Real Estate, Estates, Taxation, Civil and Criminal Litigation.

FIRM PROFILE: *Dalla Vedova studio legale is one of the oldest Italian law firms engaged in Private and Public international law. Our lawyers have received legal education and training abroad and we are able to correspond in different languages.*

MEMBERS OF FIRM

RICCARDO DALLA VEDOVA, born Naples, Italy, February 6, 1932; admitted, 1959, Italy; 1973, Supreme Court, Italy. *Education:* Fulbright Scholar, Wesleyan University (1952); University of Naples (J.D. maxima cum laude, 1954). Assistant Professor, Naples University, 1955 and University of Rome, 1956-1958. Lecturer, Temple University, Rome, 1980. *Member:* Italian Currency Law Association (President); Italian Trust Association (President); Union Internationale des Avocats, Italian (Rome), International and American Bar Associations. *LANGUAGES:* English. *PRACTICE AREAS:* Commercial Law.

MARCO DALLA VEDOVA, born Rome, Italy, July 17, 1961; admitted, 1987, Italy. *Education:* University of Rome (J.D., 1987). Lecturer, Civil Law, Rome University "La-Sapienza". Visiting Foreign Counsel, EUTELSAT (Paris), 1993. *Member:* I.B.A Committees E, CM; A.I.J.A; Computer Law Association; American Bar Association; Italian Arbitration Association. *LANGUAGES:* English and French. *PRACTICE AREAS:* Commercial Law; Corporate Law; Patents; EV Law; Telecommunication; Arbitration.

CARLO DALLA VEDOVA, born Rome, Italy, June 10, 1963; admitted, 1988, Italy. *Education:* University of Rome (J.D.); Harvard Summer School (1983); Seminar in American Legal Studies, Salzburg (1989). Seminar European Community Law (Associazione Italiana Giuristi Europei) Ispes Rome. Advisor to EU-PHARE Project, Bucharest, Romania, 1994. *Member:* I.B.A.; A.I.J.A; The Foreign Lawyers Forum of Washington, D.C.; British-Italian Lawyers Association; Associazione Italiana Giuristi Europei; Associazione Italiana Giuristi delle' Est, Associazione Italiana dell' Arbitrato (AIA). *LANGUAGES:* English, French, German. *PRACTICE AREAS:* Commercial Law; Corporate Law; EV Law; Trademarks; Immigration; Criminal Law.

BENEDETTA ROSSI, born Rome, Italy, March 27, 1965; admitted, 1990, Italy. *Education:* University of Rome (J.D., maxima cum laude, 1990). Seminar, English Commercial Law, Cambridge, 1991. *Member:* I.B.A. *LANGUAGES:* English. *PRACTICE AREAS:* Real Estate; Family Law; International Transactions; EEC Law.

ALESSANDRO PICCIOLI, born Rome, Italy, April 1, 1963; admitted, 1990, Italy. *Education:* University of Rome (J.D., 1988). Seminar Government Contracts, Rome 1991. *Member:* I.B.A. *LANGUAGES:* English. *PRACTICE AREAS:* Commercial Law; Corporate Law; Contracts; Company Law; European Community Law.

FABIO QUOJANI, born Rome, Italy, October 5, 1967; admitted, 1993, Italy. *Education:* University of Rome (J.D., maxima cum laude, 1991). *LANGUAGES:* English and French. *PRACTICE AREAS:* Civil Law; Commercial Law; Corporate Law; Bankruptcy; Family Law; Real Estate Law.

GIOVANNI IZZO, born Rome. Italy, August 2, 1969; admitted, 1994, Italy. *Education:* University of Rome (J.D., 1993); Corpus Christi College, Oxford University (1990-1991). *Member:* I.B.A. (Committees R, T); Italian Trust Association (Secretary). *LANGUAGES:* English and French. *PRACTICE AREAS:* Company Law; Commercial Law; Computer Law; Technology Law; Family Law.

PAOLA LA LICATA, born Palermo, Italy, July 31, 1969. *Education:* University of Rome "La Sapienza" (J.D.), maxima cum laude. Publication: "Modalities of Compensation" in "Giurisprudenza del Lavoro nel Lazio"

(This Listing Continued)

DALLA VEDOVA, Rome—Continued

1994. *LANGUAGES:* English. *PRACTICE AREAS:* Corporate Law; Labour Law; Bankruptcy; European Community Law; Family Law.

COUNSEL

CRAIG M. J. ALLELY, born Greeley, Colorado, July 25, 1961; admitted, 1987, New York; 1988, Colorado and U.S. District Court, Southern District of New York (Not admitted in Italy). *Education:* Colorado College (B.A., 1983); Georgetown University Law Center (J.D., magna cum laude, 1986). Author: Comity and Conflict, Laker Airways v. Sabena; 17 Law & Policy in International Business 157 (1985). *Member:* American Bar Association. *LANGUAGES:* English and Italian. *PRACTICE AREAS:* Commercial Law; Sports Law; Contracts; Litigation; Tax; Estates.

Languages: Italian, English, French, German and Spanish.

STUDIO DALLA VERITÀ-TARTAGLIA

Founder: Piero Dalla Verità (1924-1982)

7, VIA VITTORIO VENETO
00187 ROME, ITALY
Telephone: 4883525 (multiple); 4740547
Cable Address: "Daverlaw Rome"
Telecopier: 4740547

Bologna, Italy Office: Studio Dalla Verità. 5, Piazza Calderini, 40124. Telephone: 051-264918; 031-264865 Telefax: 051-238788 Cable Address: "Daverlaw Bolonga" Telex: DAVERL I 511238.

General Practice.

MEMBERS OF FIRM

FRANCO DALLA VERITÀ, born Faenza, Italy, February 10, 1935; admitted, 1960, Italy; 1975, Supreme Court. *Education:* Bologna University (LL.D., 1959). (Also at Bologna Office).

PAOLO TARTAGLIA, born Rome, Italy, August 12, 1951; admitted, 1976, Italy; 1986, Supreme Court. *Education:* Rome University (LL.D., 1973). Assistant Professor of Civil Law, Rome University, 1979-1985; Associate Professor of Civil Law, Cagliari University, 1985—.

GIOVANNI SERGES, born Catania, Italy, July 21, 1951; admitted, 1977, Italy. *Education:* Catania University (LL.D., 1974). Assistant Researcher, Public Law, Rome University, 1981—.

MARCO VINCENTI, born Rome, Italy, July 24, 1960; admitted, 1987, Italy. *Education:* Rome University (LL.D., 1984).

CLAUDIO MAGNANTI, born Caserta, Italy, December 28, 1968; admitted, 1993, Italy. *Education:* Rome University (L.D., 1992).

TAX ADVISOR

MAURIZIO BARONI, born Alexandria, Egypt, July 3, 1920; admitted, 1950, Italy. Started activity as Tax Advisor, 1945. President, Certified Public Accountants of Bologna, 1975.

COUNSEL

ANGELO FALZEA, born Messina, Italy, August 26, 1914; admitted, 1944, Italy; 1948, Supreme Court. *Education:* Messina University (LL.D., 1936). Full Professor, Civil Law, Messina University, 1944—. Academician of the LINCEI. Editor, Italian Law Encyclopedia.

DELFINO SIRACUSANO, born Catania, Italy, December 16, 1929; admitted, 1955, Italy. *Education:* Catania University (LL.D., 1952). Full Professor of Criminal Procedure, Rome University, 1979—.

STUDIO LEGALE DE BERTI & JACCHIA

Established in 1983

LUNGOTEVERE DEI MELLINI, 10
I-00193 ROME, ITALY
Telephone: 39-6-3227491
Facsimile: 39-6-3200824

Milan, Italy Office: Foro Buonaparte, 20, 1-20121. Telephone: 39-2-809486. Facsimile: 39-2-8900391 / 864088. Telex: 310295 Dejalx l.

Brussels, Belgium Office: 139 Avenue du Diamant, B-1040. Telephone: 32-2-7353520. Facsimile: 32-2 -7321985.

General Civil and Commercial Practice, Securities and Financial Services, Telecommunications, Pharmaceuticals, Competition, Antitrust, Administrative Law.

RESIDENT PARTNER

RAFFAELLA ORSINI

RESIDENT ASSOCIATE

SILVIA CONTESTABILE

(For Complete List of Firm Personnel, see Professional Biographies at Milan, Italy)

DE MEO & ASSOCIATI STUDIO LEGALE

CORSO VITTORIO EMANUELE II, 287
00186 ROME, ITALY
Telephone: (+ +39 6) 6892623; 6740256(+ +39336) 743496, 743497
Telefax: (+ +39 6) 6867594

Milan, Italy Office: Piazza San Camillo de Lellis, 1, 20124. Telephone: (+ +39 2) 66988125. Fax: (+ +39 2) 66988179.

Naples, Italy Office: Piazza San Pasquale, 10, 80121. Telephone: (+ +39 81) 7642295; 7643402. Fax: (+ +39 81) 7646262.

General Practice, Admiralty, Aviation, Commerical Law, Business and Tax Consultants.

MEMBERS OF FIRM

MICHELE DE MEO, born Naples, Italy, May 20, 1941; admitted, 1967, Rome; 1974, Italy; 1983, Supreme Court. *Education:* University of Rome (Doctor of Jurisprudence, cum laude, 1965); University College, London, England, 1967-1968; Seminar in American Legal Studies, Salzburg, 1970; Academy of American and International Law, Southwestern Legal Foundation, Dallas, Texas, 1971. Author: Italian Section of "Encyclopedia of International Commercial Litigation," Graham & Trotman, 1992. Professor and Assistant Professor, Admiralty and Aviation Law. Founder of the Association of Friends of the International Development Law Institute (IDLI) of Rome and of the Association of Roman Transportation Lawyers. Member of the Advisory Board of the Southwestern Legal Foundation, Dallas, Texas. *Member:* International Bar Association; International Law Society. (Milan, Rome and Naples).

SILVANA MARCOTULLI, born Rome, Italy, November 6, 1960; admitted, 1987, Rome; 1991, Italy. *Education:* University of Rome (Doctor of Jurisprudence, 1986); City of London, Polytechnic Summer School (Diploma, International Law, 1992); Academy of American and International Law, South Western Legal Foundation, Dallas, Texas, U.S.A., 1994. *Member:* Rome and International Bar Associations; Association of Friends of the International Development Law Institute. (Rome).

JOSEPH LOURDESAMY, born Kuala Lumpur, Malaysia, 1960; admitted, 1988, England and Wales. *Education:* University of London (LL.B., 1986); Council of Legal Education, London (Bar, 1987). *Member:* Middle Temple; Euroadvocaten. (Rome).

MASSIMILIANO NICODEMO, born Naples, Italy, December 28, 1963. *Education:* University of Naples (Doctor of Jurisprudence, 1989); Master's Degree in Fiscal Law, IPSOA, Milan. (Milan).

JOHN HAWITT, born Calgary, Canada, 1963; admitted, 1993, England and Wales. *Education:* Queen's University, Canada (B.A., 1985); University of Wales, Cardiff (LL.B., 1989). *Member:* Law Society of England and Wales. (London).

HELEN ABBOTT, born Cardiff, Wales, 1965; admitted, 1988, England and Wales. *Education:* University of London (LL.B., 1987); Council of Legal Education, London (Bar, 1988). *Member:* Gray's Inn; Bar Association of England and Wales; International Bar Association. (Rome).

(This Listing Continued)

FABIO DEL BENE, born Lecce, Italy, 1965. *Education:* University of Rome (Doctor of Jurisprudence, 1989). *Member:* Rome Bar Association. (Rome).

EMANUELA ERCOLE, born Rome, Italy, June 18, 1966; admitted, 1991, Rome. *Education:* University of Rome, L.U.I.S.S. (Doctor of Jurisprudence, magna cum laude, 1991); City of London Polytechnic Summer School (Diploma, International Law, 1992). (Rome).

CONSULTANTS

ITALO TUCCI, born Caserta, Italy, 1932; admitted, 1959, Italy. *Education:* University of Naples (Doctor of Jurisprudence, 1954). Former Head of Legal and General Affairs Office at: Alfa Romeo (motor cars); Aeritalia (aircrafts); Aeroporti di Roma (handling agent); Agusta (helicopters). Justice of the Peace. *Member:* Rome Bar Association. (Rome).

GABRIELE CATERINA, born Rome, Italy, November 19, 1936. *Education:* University of Rome, Faculty of Economy and Commerce. Author: "Transfer Pricing in International Transactions". Member: Rome Association of Accountants and Auditors, 1962—; Public Chartered Accountant, 1967. (Rome).

MARTINO CILENTO, born Naples, Italy, January 12, 1940. *Education:* University of Naples, Faculty of Economy and Commerce (1968). Member: Naples Association of Accountants and Auditors, 1972—; Public Chartered Accountant, 1979—. (Naples).

DOMENICO REPETTO, born Catania, Italy, 1963; admitted, 1989. *Education:* University of Catania (Doctor of Jurisprudence, 1989). *Member:* AWR Association for War Refugees; Italian Council for War Refugees. (Rome).

ALESSANDRO CATERINA, born Rome, Italy, April 14, 1964. *Education:* Istituto Tecnico Commerciale Gioberti (1984). (Rome).

Languages: Italian and English.

REPRESENTATIVE CLIENTS: Schweder (Austria); Intercounsel Limited (Canada); Lonrho (England); Compagnie Generale de Chauffe (France); Compagnie Generale des Eaux (France); Montenay (France); Storck International A.G. (Germany); Hegenscheidt (Germany); Assos International Shipping (Greece); Alitcalia (Italy); Banca di Roma (Italy);Ecolmare (Italy); Finenergia (Italy); Insud-Nuove Iniziative per il Sud (Italy); Mistral (Italy); Enichem S.p.A. (Italy); Sipra (Italy); Valtur (Italy); Anstalt fur Industrie-Anlagen (Liechtenstein); PLV Management Pte-Ltd (Singapore); Mitsubishi Bank (Switzerland) Ltd. (Switzerland); Italovenezolana de Inversiones (Venezuela); Editorial Economia Hoy (Venezuela); Banco Construction (Venezuela); Britannica de Seguros (Venezuela).

DOBSON & PINCI

VIA PANAMA 74, INT. 9

00198 ROME, ITALY

Telephone: (39) (6) 841-1611

Telefax: (39) (6) 841-1145 E-Mail: 7212680@mcimail.com.

Milan, Italy Office: 16 Via Santa Radegonda, 20121. Telephone: (39) (2) 809816; 8056780. Telefax: (39) (2) 86464548; 86464601. E-Mail: 7232679@mcimail.com.

Genoa, Italy Office: Via Garibaldi 7, 2nd Floor, 16124. Telephone: (39) (10) 206-851. Telefax: (39) (10) 202-738. E-Mail: 7222681@mcimail.com.

New York, New York Office: Manhattan Tower, 12th Floor, 600 Lexington Avenue, 10022-6018. Telephone: (212) 308-4440. Telefax: (212) 888-3839. E-Mail: 7262685@mcimail.com.

London, England Office: 1 Throgmorton Avenue, EC2N 2JJ. Telephone: (44) (171) 628-8163. Telefax: (44) (171) 920-0861. E-Mail: 7232682@mcimail.com.

Brussels, Belgium Office: Avenue Louise, 216, 1050. Telephone: (32) (2) 647-0700. Telefax: (32) (2) 647-6440. E-Mail: 7242683@mcimail.com.

Athens, Greece Office: 6 Yperidou Street, 105 58. Telephone: (30) (1) 324-3272. Telefax: (30) (1) 322-9329. E-Mail: 7252684@mcimail.com.

Atlanta, Georgia Office: 1776 Resurgens Plaza, 945 East Paces Ferry Road, N.E., 30326. Telephone: (404) 262-5680. Telefax: (404) 262-5699. E-Mail: 7272686@mcimail.com.

San Diego, California Office: 1629 Columbia Street, 92101. Telephone: (619) 236-1310. Telefax: (619) 239-1208. E-Mail: 7282687@mcimail.com.

Miami, Florida Office: 701 Brickell Avenue, Suite 2000, 33131. Telephone: (305) 579-0012. Telefax: (305) 375-8075; 579-4722. E-Mail: 7292688@mcimail.com.

(This Listing Continued)

Corporate, Banking and Securities Law with emphasis on Mergers and Acquisitions, Insurance, International Financial Transactions, Litigation, Arbitration, Employment Law, Debt Collection, Bankruptcy, Foreign Investments, Privatizations, Subsidiaries and Joint Ventures, Taxation, EU/-Common Market Law, Antitrust, Environmental Law, Transportation, Shipping, Licensing, Fashion and Textiles, Franchising, Commercial Real Estate (Investment, Structuring, Development, Retail), Project Finance, Computer, Software and Telecommunications Law, Agency and Distribution, Energy (Production, Operations, and Transmission), Food and Drug, Commodities, Visa/Immigration, Wills and Estates, Sports Law, Broadcasting, Motion Picture, TV, Video, Intellectual Property and General Entertainment Law.

FIRM PROFILE: Dobson & Pinci is an international law firm based in Europe and the United States that is staffed with both American and European attorneys. Of the small number of such firms, Dobson & Pinci holds a unique position because the firm's European offices are situated in Milan, Rome, Genoa, London, Brussels and Athens, thereby enabling the firm to serve clients conveniently and efficiently in both Northern and Southern Europe. The U.S. offices in New York, Atlanta, Miami and San Diego are placed in major U.S. cities to provide full support to the overall practice network. Each office is staffed by attorneys qualified to appear and litigate in the local courts.

MEMBERS OF FIRM

DAVID M. DOBSON, born Belleville, Illinois, October 24, 1952; admitted, 1979, Georgia. *Education:* Harvard University (A.B., cum laude, 1974); Yale University Law School (J.D., 1978). Phi Beta Kappa. President, Yale Law School Alumni Association, European Division, 1987-1992; Executive Committee, Yale Law School Association, 1988—. Board of Advisers, Corporate Counsel's International Adviser (Business Laws, Inc.), 1987—; Intellectual Property Committee, American Chamber of Commerce, Italy. Author: NACORE Seminar at MIPIM 94: European Real Estate - "How U.S. - Based Multinational End-Users Do Business in Europe," Cannes, March, 1994; "The Negotiating Phase - U.K. Acquisitions in Italy." Conference: Mergers and Acquisitions in Italy, London, February, 1992; "Privatisation in Italy," Corporate Counsel's International Advisor, May, 1993; "Entering the Southern European Markets," State Bar of Georgia, Conference on Doing Business in Southern Europe, May, 1994; "Italy: Legal and Operational Issues," Conference on Doing Business with Italy, Houston, April, 1994; "Forms of Investment in the U.S.A.," The U.S. Market - Opportunities for Trade and Investment, Milan Chamber of Commerce, February 1992; "In Step With Europe: New Legislation Means Italian Property Is No Longer a Law Unto Itself," EuroProperty, October 1991. Co-Author: "Country Handbook on Italy," Italian American Business, 1992; "International Contract Manual: Italy," Kluwer Law and Taxation, 1992; "Incorporation of an Italian Company: An Overview of Italian Law," Corporate Counsel's International Adviser, February, 1993; "Structuring Italian Shopping Center Investments for German Open-Ended Property Funds," September, 1994; "A Synopsis of the Greek Corporate Tax System," State of California EC Law Handbook, 1993; "Coal Gasification Projects in Italy," December, 1994; "Legal Aspects of Property Investment in Europe," Corporate Real Estate Executive, International Association of Corporate Real Estate Executives (NACORE), July/August 1992; "La Cooperazione Imprenditoriale Fra Italia e Stati Uniti: la Via Della Joint-Venture," Iniziativa Italia - Joint-Ventures, Milan, June 1992; "Italian Real Estate - Tax and Legal Aspects," Immobilier & Property, February 1992; "The New Italian S.I.M./M&A Legislation," Communication and Strategy - The New Organization of the Italian Securities Markets, London, 1991; "New Italian Legislation Regulating Buying and Selling on the Italian Securities Markets, Real Estate and M & A Transactions," Conference on Mergers and Acquisitions in Italy, Paris, 1991; "Franchising Agreements and Competition Rules in Italy," Corporate Counsel's International Advisor, November, 1991; "The Negotiating Phase - French Acquisitions in Italy," Communication and Strategy - International Mergers and Acquisitions In Italy, Paris, November 1991; "Legal Aspects of Property Investment in Italy," New York State Bar Association International Law Practicum, 1991; "Key Legal Issues," Communication and Strategy International - Commercial Property Development, Investment and Finance in Italy, Paris, 1991; "Joint Ventures - A European Perspective," Ninth Annual Southeastern Corporate Counsel Institute, Atlanta, 1990; "Acquisition and Management of Real Property in Italy by Non-Residents," Conference on "International Tax Strategy," Milan, 1990; "Responsabilità Civile Prodotti (Products Liability Litigation): Commenti e Interpretazioni," American Chamber of Commerce in Italy, June 1986; "Legal Aspects of Doing Business in the EEC," State Bar of Georgia, Continuing Legal Education Conference, 1986; "Venture Capital: Il Capitale a Rischio Statunitense per l'Investitore Istituzionale Italiano," Italian American Business, December 1985; "Opportunities for Tax Relief

(This Listing Continued)

DOBSON & PINCI, Rome—Continued

Under the New U.S.-Italian Income Tax Treaty," ABA Section on International Law and Practice, European Bulletin, November 1985. Associate, Alston, Miller & Gaines (Alston & Bird), Atlanta and Washington, D.C., 1978-1982. Member, Legal and Tax Committee, American Chamber of Commerce in Italy, 1984—; Member, Board of Governors, Sir James Henderson School, Milan, 1987-1989. *Member:* State Bar of Georgia (Member, Sections on International, Corporate and Banking Law; Chair, International Law Task Force, 1980-1982); American Bar Association (Charter Member, Committee on the International Aspects of Litigation, 1983; Chair, Subcommittee on European Broadcasting Laws, European Law Committee, 1985-1986; Member, Subcommittee on International Financing, Section of Corporation, Banking and Business Law, 1983—); State Bar of Texas (International Trade Committee, Section on International Law); International Bar Association. (Also at Milan Office).

MARCANTONIO PINCI, born Vicenza, Italy, October 27, 1963; admitted, 1990, Italy; 1990, New York. *Education:* University of Milan (J.D., 1988); Georgetown University Law Center (LL.M., 1989); Bocconi University, Milan (Master in Business Tax Law, Certificate, 1991). Author: "Milan Real Estate - Tax and Legal Aspects," Immobilier & Property, February, 1992; "Italy, Legal Tax and Financing Aspects of Italian Property Transactions for Foreign Investors and Developers," Sunbelt Conference on Real Estate Opportunities in Southern France, Northern Spain and Northern Italy, Cannes, December, 1991; "The Negotiating Phase - French Acquisitions in Italy," C&S Conference on Mergers and Acquisitions in Italy, Paris, November, 1991; "Acquisizione, Fusione e Partecipazione di Società Italiane ed Imprese Estere nel Quadro delle Direttive CEE in Materia di Imposizione Diretta," Seminar on International Tax Strategy, Turin, October, 1991; MIPIM 94 Conference: Italia: Nuove Opportunità per Investimenti Promozione e Finanziamenti Immobiliari - "Aspetti Legali e Fiscali degli Investimenti Immobiliari in Italia alla Luce dei Più Recenti Sviluppi Normativi," Cannes, March, 1994; "Enforcement of Judgments in Italy," Corporate Counsel's International Adviser, October, 1991; Seminar: "Enforcement of Judgments in Europe-Italy," New York State Bar Association, International Practice Section, New York, June 1991; "Dematerialization of Investment Securities," Georgetown University Law Center, 1989; "Insider Trading Regulations in the U.S., U.K., France and the E.E.C.: An Analysis from the Standpoint of the Italian Legal System," University of Milan, 1988; "Unico Azionista: Responsabilità ex Articolo 2362," University of Milan, 1986. Co-Author: "La Cooperazione Imprenditoriale Fra Italia e Stati Uniti: la Via Della Joint-Venture," Conference on Joint-Ventures, Milan, June 1992; "La Direttiva CEE 434/90 sul Regime delle Riorganizzazioni Societarie," Acquisizioni, April 1992; "Coal Gasification Projects in Italy," December 1994; "Il Nuovo Contratto d'Agenzia-D.L. 10.09.91 N° 303," published in France-Italie no. 6, November/December, 1993 and continued in same publication, no. 1, January/February, 1994; "Deregulation of Retail Licenses in Italy," April, 1994; "Structuring Italian Shopping Center, Investments for German Open-Ended Property Funds," September, 1994; Conference, Agenti di Commercio - "Lo Scioglimento del Rapporto di Agenzia nella Nuova Normative Italiana di Recepimento della Direttiva CEE 86/653," Milan, April 1993; "Incorporation of an Italian Company: An Overview of Italian Law," Corporate Counsel's International Adviser, February, 1993; "Legal Aspects of Property Investment in Europe," Corporate Real Estate Executive, International Association of Corporate Real Estate Executives (NACORE) July/August 1992; "Country Handbook on Italy," Italian American Business, 1992; "Italy, Financial Engineering and Tax Planning," C&S Conference: Property Investment in Italy, Paris, April 1991 and IBC Conference: European Commercial Property Development Opportunities, London, June 1991; "Acquisition and Management of Real Property in Italy by Non-Residents," Conference on "International Tax Strategy," Milan, November 1990. Advisor, Real Estate Masters Program (Shopping Center Development), Politecnico University of Turin, 1992—; Assistant to the General Counsel, Pirelli-Armstrong Tire Corp., New Haven, CT, 1990; Foreign Associate (Corporate Area), Foley, Hoag & Eliot, Boston, MA, 1989. *Member:* The Foreign Lawyers Forum of Washington, D.C.; International Bar Association. (Also at Milan Office).

MARIA-CLAUDIA PICCARRETA, born Rome, Italy, April 2, 1963; admitted, 1992, Luxembourg; 1994, Italy. *Education:* La Sapienza University, Rome (J.D., 1990); University of Luxembourg (LL.M., 1992). Publications and Seminars: "European Community Environment Law: Problems in National Implementation," Association Européenne de Droit de l'Environnement (AEDE), Luxembourg, 1994; "La Suisse face à la TVA (VAT)," conference, Fiduciaire Price Waterhouse SA, Genève, 1993; "La lutte contre le blanchiment des capitaux," Institut Européen d'Administration Publique (IEAP), Luxembourg, 1993; "La droit de la concurrence dans

le cadre des relations AELF/CEE," Institut Européen d'Administration Publique (IEAP), Luxembourg, 1993; "The Brussels and Lugano Conventions: Judicial Competence Regarding Civil and Commercial Matters," Institut Européen d'Administration Publique (IEAP), Luxembourg, 1993; "Le cautionnement bancaire: protéction juridique de l'acaution," Association Luxembourgeoise des Juristes de Banque (AJBL), Luxembourg, 1992; "Les accords de Schengen: politique migratoire à l'intérieur de la C.E.E." sessione estiva dell'Institut Universitaire de Luxembourg (IUIL), Luxembourg, 1992. *Member:* International Bar Association; International Association of Young Lawyers; Association Luxembourgeiose des Juristes Européens (ALJE).

ANTHONY A. SISTILLI, born Steubenville, Ohio, May 19, 1966; admitted, 1992, Pennsylvania. *Education:* West Virginia University (B.A., magna cum laude, 1988); Temple University School of Law, International Studies, Rome (1990); West Virginia University College of Law (J.D., 1992); McGeorge School of Law, Sacramento, California (Diploma in Advanced International Legal Studies, Salzburg, Austria, 1992). Publications, Business Law Europe, European Law Press, European Correspondent, Rome (1993). Author: "New Rules on Domestic and International Arbitration," April 1994; "Protection of Computer Programs," English Edition 5/93, March 1993; "Mutual Fund Investments in Italy," English Edition 7/93, April 1993, "Security Interests in Receivables in Italy," English Edition 13/93, June 1993. Co-author: "Coal Gasification Projects in Italy," December 1994; "Franchising in Italy," Corporate Counsel's International Adviser, September 1994; "Progressing From National to European Structures," European Market Law Report, March 1994; "Taxation of Foreign Companies in Italy," Belle Cose, Summer 1994; Conference: "Cutting Through the Red Tape: U.S. Customs, F.D.A., U.S.D.A., and Other Legal Issues Facing Foreign Food and Beverage Manufacturers Entering the U.S. Market," New York, June, 1993. Approaching 2000 - The Corporation in Transition, "EEC Driven Changes in Italian Corporate Law," Salzburg, June 1993. *Member:* International Bar Association. (Also at Brussels Office).

FRANK JORG GEFFERS, born Hofgeismar, Germany, June 4, 1963. admitted to practice, 1993, Italy. *Education:* La Sapienza University, Rome (J.D., 1993). Co-Author: "Structuring Italian Shopping Center Investments for German Open-Ended Property Funds," September 1994; "Procedures for Opening a Restaurant or Fast Food Operation in Italy," April 1994; "Debt Recovery in Italy," November 1993; "How to Obtain Retail Licenses in Italy," September 1994. President, Rotaract Club of Roma Ovest, 1991-1992. *Member:* International Bar Association.

COUNSEL

PIERLUIGI VALENTINO, born Naples, Italy, August 25, 1962; admitted, 1990, Italy. *Education:* La Sapienza University, Rome (J.D., 1985); Sraffa Institute, Bocconi University, Milan (Specialized courses su Giuristi di Impresa, 1987). Consob (National Committee for Companies and the Stock Exchange), Rome, 1985-1989. Professor: Institutions of Public Law, and Economy and Finance of Financial Intermediaries, LUISS University, Rome; Banking and Real Estate Politics and Regulations, La Sapienza University, Rome. Author: "Ordine di Borsa, Attività di Intermediazione Mobiliare e Contratti di Borsa"; "Fallimento di una SIM: Ruolo e Funzioni del Commissario Governativo e Limiti alla Restituzione dei Patrimoni alla Clientela"; "Liquidazione a Contante delle Operazioni di Borsa"; "SIM: La Legge 2 gennaio 1991"; "Nel d.d.l. sulla Borsa "Golden Share" e Autonomia Finanziaria della Consob"; "Gli Obblighi Informativi per gli Emittenti e le Società Quotate"; "Rassegna Normativa dei Provvedimenti della Consob (dal 1990)"; "La Quotazione di Diritto in Borsa delle Azioni di Risparmio ed il Nuovo Regolamento di Ammissione a Quotazione"; "Diritti di Quotazione ed Ammissione di Diritto alla Quotazione nelle Borse Valori"; "La Potestà Regolamentare della Consob e le Società Commissionarie di Borsa"; "Rilievo Costituzionale e Destinazione dei Diritti Inerenti ai Servizi delle Borse Valori"; "Tipicità Fiscale dei Titoli Atipici"; "Commentario al Testo Unico delle Leggi in Materia Creditizia e Bancaria"; "Codice Civile Commentato Diretto da Pietro Rescigno"; "Anagrafe degli Intermediari Mobiliari, Cedim"; "Strutture e Regolamentazione del Mercato Mobiliare"; "Consob L'Instituzione e la Legge Penale, AA.VV." Co-Author: "L'Instituzione Consob Funzione e Struttura.".

GIORGIO VALENTI, born Milan, Italy, November 26, 1927; admitted, 1952, Italy. *Education:* University of Milan (J.D., 1952). General Counsel, Legal Department, Euromobiliare S.p.A. (Investment Bank), 1986-1987. Manager, Commercial Trade and Exchange Controls Office, Banca Commerciale Italiana/COMIT, 1975-1986. In-House Counsel, Legal Department (Litigation, Banking and Tax Sections), Banca Commerciale Italia-

(This Listing Continued)

na/COMIT, 1959-1972. *Member:* International Bar Association. (Also at Milan Office).

DOMENICO SCOPELLITI, born Rome, Italy, July 1, 1967; admitted, 1993, Italy. *Education:* LUISS University, Rome (J.D., 1990).

DOMENICO NASO, born Rome, Italy, August 3, 1965. *Education:* La Sapienza University, Rome (J.D., 1993). Counsel: Secretary of the President of the Chamber of Deputies, Rome, 1989-1991; Centro Studi U.I.L. - Finanze, Rome, 1992-1993.

FRANCESCO FABBRI, born Rome, Italy, November 5, 1966. *Education:* La Sapienza University, Rome (J.D., 1993).

ANDREW DUNCAN ROBSON COLVIN, born Berlin, Germany, July 13, 1948; admitted, 1972, London; 1987, Paris. *Education:* University of Kent (B.A., 1970), Inns of Court School of Law; Institut d'Etudes Euro-peennes, Université Libre de Bruxelles, Fondazione Giorgio Cini, Venice, Italy; University of Siena, Italy (J.D., 1994). Author: "Italian Competition Law," Corporate Lawyer, 1991; "The Control of Broadcasting in Italy: A Commentary on the New MAMMI Law," World Competition, December, 1990. Co-Author: "Round-up of New Laws in Italy," April, 1994; "Privati-sation in Italy," Corporate Counsel's International Advisor, May, 1993. "Pension Reform in Italy," Belle Cose, June, 1993; "Agency and Distribution Agreements in Italy," Corporate Counsel's International Advisor, June, 1993; Legal Advisor and Company Secretary, Monsanto Oil Company of the U.K., Inc., 1982-1985; Fluor Corporation Subsidiaries, 1977-1982. (Also at London Office).

GIOVANNI ACERBI, born Milan, Italy, July 17, 1947; admitted, 1978, Italy. *Education:* University of Milan (J.D., 1972); University of Georgia at Athens (LL.M., 1974). Rotary International Scholarship. Comparative Law Council Scholar. General Counsel, Impresa Lodigiani S.p.A., 1978-1981. In-House Counsel, AGIP S.p.A. and AGIP Legal Representative to Joint Venture Operating Agreements with Oman, Brazil and Sudan, 1976-1978. Member, Committee on International Construction Contracts, Italian Industry Association, 1978-1981. *Member:* International Bar Association. (Also at Milan Office).

PAOLO BORGHI, born Saronno, Italy, November 13, 1952; admitted, 1981, Italy. *Education:* University of Pavia (J.D., 1980). *Member:* International Bar Association. (Also at Milan Office).

GIOVANNI LOMBARDO, born San Salvatore Monferrato, Italy, September 22, 1953; admitted, 1981, Italy. *Education:* University of Pavia (J.D., 1980). *Member:* International Bar Association. (Also at Milan Office).

Languages: English, Italian, French, Greek, German, Spanish, Japanese and Russian

(For Complete Biographical Data on all Personnel and List of Representative Clients, see Biographical card at Milan, Italy)

STUDIO LEGALE
FARESE CICERCHIA TAGLIORETTI

VIA GIOVANNI NICOTERA, 24
00195 ROME, ITALY
Telephone: (6) 360.00.398 - 360.00.389
Telefax: (6) 360.00.397

Milan, Italy Office: Studio Legale Taglioretti Farese Cicerchia, Via Vincenzo Monti, 15, 20123. Telephone: (2) 480.21.811. Telefax: (2) 481.93.877.

General Practice and Litigation, Corporation, Banking, Foreign Investment, EEC Law, Patent and Trademark, Intellectual Property, Labour, Distribution and Licensing.

PAOLO FARESE, born Rome, Italy, March 28, 1948; admitted, 1980, Italy. *Education:* University of Rome (J.D., 1973); University of Illinois College of Law (M.C.L., 1983). Rome Bar Association Award, 1976. Seminars; Institute of Comparative Law, University of Rome, 1976; American Legal Studies, Salzburg, 1977. *Member:* International Bar Association; American Bar Association. *LANGUAGES:* Italian and English. *PRAC-TICE AREAS:* Corporate Law; International Private Law; Labour Law.

PIETRO CICERCHIA, born Rome, Italy, January 8, 1955; admitted, 1983, Italy. *Education:* University of Rome (J.D., 1980). Seminar on EEC Law, Institute of European Community, Rome, 1984. *LANGUAGES:* Italian and English. *PRACTICE AREAS:* Corporate Law; Real Estate.

(This Listing Continued)

FORTUNATO TAGLIORETTI, born Busto Arsizio, Varese, Italy, November 6, 1951; admitted, 1976, Italy. *Education:* University of Milan (J.D., 1973); Academy of American and International Law, Southwestern Legal Foundation, Dallas, Texas (1983). *Member:* International Bar Association. *LANGUAGES:* Italian and English. *PRACTICE AREAS:* Corporate Law; Banking Law; Foreign Investment Law; International Transaction Law.

MASSIMO ZACCONI, born Milan, Italy, December 18, 1961; admitted, 1992, Italy. *Education:* Catholic University of the Sacred Heart (J.D., Magna cum laude, 1987); Freiburg University, Erasmus Program, (1991). Assistant Professor, History of Roman Law, Catholic University of the Sacred Heart, 1987-1992. *LANGUAGES:* Italian, English and German. *PRACTICE AREAS:* Labour Law.

MARCO GANDINI, born Milan, Italy, December 17, 1963. *Education:* Catholic University of the Sacred Heart of Milan (J.D., 1988); Bocconi University, Milan (Tax Law Master, 1992-1993); Cambridge Summer Programme (English Legal Method, 1992). *LANGUAGES:* Italian and English. *PRACTICE AREAS:* Company Law; Tax Law.

GIOVANNI LEONE, born Taranto, Italy, February 1, 1966. *Education:* Catholic University of the Sacred Heart (J.D., 1992); Hague Academy of International Law, Summer Program-Private International Law (1993). Assistant Professor, Private International Law, Catholic University of the Sacred Heart, 1992. *LANGUAGES:* Italian and English. *PRACTICE AREAS:* EEC Law; Patent and Trademark Law.

FRANCESCO TOMASSINI, born Rome, Italy, February 6, 1968; admitted, 1993, Rome. *Education:* University of Rome (J.D., 1992). *LANGUAGES:* Italian and English.

Languages: Italian, English and German

FRAU & PARTNERS
STUDIO LEGALE ASSOCIATO

VIA BARBERINI, 29
00187 ROME, ITALY
Telephone: (06) 4871151; 4820666
Telefax: (06) 4827513

Milan Office: Via Carlo Poerio, 15, 20129. Telephone: (02) 76003199 (r.a.). Telefax: (02) 7600331.
Verona Office: Piazza San Nicolõ, 3, 37121. Telephone: (045) 8001533. Telefax: (045) 8003115.
Kiev Office: Kibalchicha 12, 253125. Telephone (044) 5127292 - 5128109. Telefax: (044) 5143305.

International Business Law, Corporate, Banking, Financing, Syndicated Loans, Eurobonds, Commodities, Asset Finance, Bond Issues, Aircraft Finance, Leasing, Merger and Acquisitions, Project Finance. Letters of Credit, Commercial Property, Securitization, Foreign Investments, Contracts, EEC, Antitrust and Competition, Real Estate, Building and Construction, International and Domestic Arbitration, International and Domestic Arbitration Litigation, International and Domestic Taxation, Aviation, Transportation, Tort and Intellectual Property, Licensing, Patent and Trademark, Distributorship, Agency and Franchising, Environmental and Media, Sport, Mining and Mineral.

(For Complete Biographical Data on all Personnel, see Professional Biographies at Milan, Italy).

STUDIO LEGALE ASSOCIATO
&
FRERE CHOLMELEY BISCHOFF

Established in 1991

47 VIALE BRUNO BUOZZI
00197 ROME, ITALY
Telephone: (39 (6) 808 0133
Fax: (39) (6) 808 0134

London, England Office: 4 John Carpenter Street, London EC4Y ONH. Telephone: 0171-615 8000. Fax: 0171-615 8080. Telex: 27623. LDE: DX 140.
Paris, France Office: 42 Avenue de Président Wilson, 75116 Paris. Telephone: (33) (1) 44 34 71 00. Fax: (33) (1) 44 34 71 11.
Milan, Italy Office: and Studio Legale Associato, Piazza Castello 24, 20121 Milan. Telephone: (39) (2) 720 03457. Fax: (39) (2) 720 03469.

(This Listing Continued)

STUDIO LEGALE ASSOCIATO & FRERE CHOLMELEY BISCHOFF, Rome—Continued

Monte Carlo, Monaco Office: "Est Ouest", 24 Boulevard Princesse Charlotte, MC 98000. Telephone: (33) (39) 508 570. Fax: (33) (93) 502 210.

Berlin, Germany Office: im Internationalen Handelszentrum, Friedrichstrasse 95, 10117 Berlin. Telephone: (49) (26) 43 2000. Fax: (49) (30) 2643 1900. Telex: 305966 Kbohzd.

Moscow, Russia Office: ul. Sadovaya-Samotychnaya 24/27, 103051 Moscow. Telephone: (7) 095 258 5058. Fax: (7) 095 258-5060. Telex: 412348 ALM SU.

Dubai, United Arab Emirates Office: Suite 802, EBIL Building, PO Box 2510, Deira, Dubai. Telephone: (9714) 267085/268336. Fax: (9714) 260206. Telex: 45493 LAWMC EM.

FIRM PROFILE: This office is involved primarily in providing advice on the acquisition of Italian investments by foreign clients and the setting up of joining ventures between foreign and Italian clients. Areas of specialization include banking and securities law, patent, trademark and copyright law, bankruptcy law and civil litigation.

(For Biographical Data, see Professional Biographies for Studio Legale Associato & Frere Cholmeley Bischoff, Rome)

STUDIO LEGALE
GALLAVOTTI HONORATI & PASCOTTO

VIA PO, 9
00198 ROME, ITALY
Telephone: (39-6) 85301100
Telecopier: (39-6) 8541323

Los Angeles, California Associated Office: Pascotto & Gallavotti. 1800 Avenue of the Stars, 90067-4276. Telephone: 310-273-7515. Telecopier: 310-284-3021.

General Civil Practice, Entertainment Law, Tax Law.

MARIO GALLAVOTTI, born Naples, Italy, July 25, 1948; admitted, 1973, Italy; 1987, Supreme Court of Italy. *Education:* Universities of Rome and of Perugia (J.D.). Secretary of the Conference of Young Lawyers of Rome Bar, 1975. A.I.J.A., Member.

CLAUDIO HONORATI, born Rome, Italy, September 7, 1948; admitted, 1974, Italy. *Education:* University of Rome (J.D.).

ALVARO PASCOTTO, born Rome, Italy, March 8, 1949; admitted, 1976, Italy; 1987, California. *Education:* University of Rome (J.D., 1973). Member, Italy-America Chamber of Commerce, Inc., 1987. *Member:* Los Angeles County and American Bar Associations; State Bar of California; National Italian American Bar Association; Italian American Lawyers Association.

MARIA ASSUNTA ZUCCO, born Rome, Italy, August 15, 1963; admitted, 1991, Italy. *Education:* University of Rome (J.D.).

SABRINA PIZZICARIA, born Rome, Italy, May 3, 1963; admitted, 1992, Italy. *Education:* University of Rome LUISS (J.D.). Secretary of the Conference of young Lawyers of Rome Bar, 1991.

ANTONIO BERNARDINI, born Rome, Italy, August 12, 1966; admitted, 1992, Italy. *Education:* University of Rome LUISS (J.D.).

LORENZO DE ROSSI, born Rome, Italy. August 4, 1965; admitted, 1994, Italy. *Education:* University of Rome (J.D.).

OF COUNSEL

ROBERTO G. ALOISIO, born Crotone, Italy, June 24, 1949; admitted, 1977, Italy; 1981, Supreme Court of Italy. *Education:* University og Rome (J.D.).

BENIAMINO CARAVITA DI TORITTO, born Rome, Italy, April 19, 1954; admitted, 987. Italy; 1992, Supreme Court of Italy. *Education:* University of Rome (J.D.). Full Professor, Constitutional Law, University of Perugia.

FRANCESCO NAPOLITANO, born Rome, Italy, November 11, 1947; admitted, 1974, Italy; 1988, Supreme Court of Italy. *Education:* University of Rome (J.D.). Editor, La Giustizia Tributaria e le Imposte Dirette.

Languages: Italian, English and French

STUDIO LEGALE
GHIRON

VIA ARCHIMEDE NR. 164
00197 ROME, ITALY
Telephone: (06) 8085062-8070877
Telecopier: 06-8088934

Naples Office: Via N. Tommaseo nr. 9, Telephone: (081) 7643878. Telecopier: (081) 7644305.

London Office: 2 Duke Street, St. James's London SW1. Telephone: (0171) 9302366. Telecopier: (0171) 9302250.

New York Office: 32 East 57th Street, 10022. Telephone: (212) 2230022. Telecopier: (212) 8889830.

General Practice and Litigation, Estate Law, Foreign Investments, Conflict of Law, Banking, Labor, EEC Law, Arbitration, Corporate Law, International Law.

GIORGIO GHIRON, born Rome, January 14, 1933; admitted, 1967, Rome; 1980, Supreme Court. *Education:* University of Rome (J.D., 1961).

ANDREA BADANAI, born Rome, April 8, 1959; admitted, 1982, Rome. *Education:* University of Rome (J.D., 1982); Master Bocconi University, Milan (M.B.A., 1988).

PAOLO DE SANCTIS MANGELLI, born Rome, August 20, 1961; admitted, 1986, Rome. *Education:* University of Rome (J.D., cum laude, 1986).

ROBERTO BONGIANNI, born Rome, July 1, 1966; admitted, 1993, Rome. *Education:* University of Rome (J.D., 1993). Judge in the Lower Court of Rome.

COUNSELS

PROF. ENZO GAITO, born S. Maria Capuavetere, June 19, 1925; admitted, 1967, Supreme Court. *Education:* University of Rome (J.D., 1949). Professor, Criminal Law, Rome University.

AVV. CARLO DE GIORGIO, born Naples, September 17, 1943; admitted, 1975, Supreme Court. *Education:* University of Naples (J.D., 1967). **PRACTICE AREAS:** Commercial Law.

DOTT. FRANCO TERRACINA, born Rome, April 27, 1932; (Not admitted in Italy). CPA, 1958. Auditor, 1971. Professor, Accounting, Banking and Maritime Law, University of Rome, 1979. **PRACTICE AREAS:** Tax Law; Corporate Law.

DOTT. SAVERIO SIGNORI, born Rome, December 27, 1961; (Not admitted in Italy). *Education:* University of Rome (Doctor in Economics and Trade Law, 1986). Assistant to the Professor, Banking Law, University of Rome.

Languages: English, French, Spanish.

GIANNI, ORIGONI & PARTNERS

VIA DELLE QUATTRO FONTANE, 20
00184 ROME, ITALY
Telephone: (06) 4871100
Telefax: (06) 4871101

Milan, Italy Office: Piazza Belgioioso, 2, 20121. Telephone: (02) 76009756. Telefax: (02) 76009628.

New York, New York Office: 885 Third Avenue, Suite 3000, 10022. Telephone: 212-826-2515. Telefax: 212-826-2519.

General Practice, Counselling in International Transactions, Mergers and Acquisitions, Finance and Banking, International Taxation, European Economic Community Law, Corporate, Securities, Insurance, Labor, Antitrust, Unfair Competition, Industrial Property, Product Liability, Environmental, Mutual Funds, Sports, Administrative Law, Arbitration and Litigation.

GIAN BATTISTA ORIGONI DELLA CROCE, born Milan, Italy, September 6, 1946; admitted to practice, 1970; admitted to bar, 1972, Italy; 1986, Supreme Court of Italy. *Education:* Catholic University of Milan (J.D., maxima cum laude, 1969); Academy of International Law, The Hague, 1972 and 1973; Seminar in American Law, Salzburg, 1975; Parker School of Foreign and Comparative Law, Columbia University, New York, 1979. Research Professor of Private International Law, Law School, University of Milan. Visiting Foreign Lawyer, Dechert, Price & Rhoads, Philadelphia and Washington, D.C., 1980. *Member:* American and International Bar Associations; Associazione per gli Scambi Culturali tra Guiristi

(This Listing Continued)

Italiani e Tedeschi; Associazione Giuristi di Lingua Italiana; Associazione Italiana per l'Arbitrato.

FRANCESCO GIANNI, born Ravenna, Italy, February 9, 1951; admitted to practice, 1973; admitted to bar, 1975, Italy; 1979, New York. *Education:* University of Rome (J.D., maxima cum laude, 1973); Academy of International Law, The Hague (1975); University of London, King's College (LL.M., 1976); University of Michigan Law School (LL.M., 1977). Research Assistant, E.E.C. Law, University of Michigan Law School, 1977. Visiting Foreign Lawyer: Sidley & Austin, Chicago, 1977-1978; Rogers & Wells, New York, 1978-1979. *Member:* New York State, American and International Bar Associations; The Southwestern Legal Foundation (Member, Advisory Board); American Foreign Law Association (Vice-President, 1988-1993); American Society of International Law; Honorary member, Association of Fellows and Legal Scholars of the Center for International Legal Studies.

NICOLETTA PORTALUPI, born Milan, Italy, September 29, 1952; admitted to practice, 1976; admitted to bar, 1981, Italy. *Education:* University of Milan (J.D., maxima cum laude, 1976); Cambridge University, England, 1972, 1973 and 1974; Academy of International Law, The Hague, 1975; University of Mannheim, 1976; Leyden-Amsterdam-Columbia Summer Program in American Law, 1977; Parker School of Foreign and Comparative Law, Columbia University, New York, 1982. Researcher in International Law, University of Milan. *Member:* International Bar Association; Associazione per gli Scambi Culturali tra Giuristi Italiani e Tedeschi; Associazione Guiristi di Lingua Italiana.

CESARE VENTO, born Rome, Italy, September 16, 1954; admitted to practice, 1979; admitted to bar, 1984, Italy. *Education:* University of Rome (J.D., 1979); Leyden-Amsterdam-Columbia Summer Program in American Law, 1978; University of Michigan Law School (LL.M., 1980). Visiting Foreign Lawyer, Jones, Day, Reavis & Pogue, Cleveland, Ohio, 1980-1981. Special Advisor to the Ad Hoc Committee on Italian Securities Regulations of the Securities Industry Association (SIA)-1991. *Member:* New York State and American Bar Associations; International Bar Association; American Foreign Law Association; European Society for Banking and Financial Law (Director, 1988—); The Corporate Bar Association of Westchester and Fairfield.

TIZIANO PASINETTI, born Milan, Italy, December 8, 1930; admitted to practice, 1953; admitted to bar, 1956, Italy; 1970, Supreme Court of Italy. *Education:* University of Milan (J.D., 1953); City of London College.

MATTEO FUSILLO, born Barletta, Italy, May 7, 1958; admitted to practice, 1981; admitted to bar, 1983, Italy. *Education:* University of Rome (J.D., maxima cum laude, 1980); City of London Polytechnic Summer Law School, 1989; English Advanced Business Law, 1990. *Member:* International Bar Association.

ENZO SCHIAVELLO, born Naples, Italy, August 28, 1957; admitted to practice, 1982; admitted to bar, 1987, Italy. *Education:* University of Milan (J.D., maxima cum laude, 1982); Advanced Course in Business Tax Law, CERTI, Bocconi University of Milan, 1990-1991). *Member:* International Bar Association.

GIOVANNI NARDULLI, born Bari, Italy, January 1, 1961; admitted to practice, 1984; admitted to bar, 1987, Italy; Licensed Legal Consultant, 1992, New York. *Education:* University of Rome (J.D., maxima cum laude, 1983); City of London Polytechnic (1987); Parker School of Foreign and Comparative Law, Columbia University (1988). Visiting Foreign Lawyer, Morrison & Foerster, San Francisco, 1990-1991. *Member:* International and American Bar Associations, Chair, Western European Law Committee, International Law and Practice Section, New York State Bar Association; Honorary Member, Center for International Legal Studies, Salzburg; European Society for Banking and Financial Law. (Resident, New York, New York Office).

ADRIANA DE ALBERTIS, born Como, Italy, May 9, 1943; admitted to practice, 1966; admitted to bar, 1968, Italy; Supreme Court of Italy. *Education:* University of Milan (J.D., 1966).

ALESSANDRO GIULIANI, born Lecce, Italy, November 7, 1961; admitted to practice, 1985; admitted to bar, 1988, Italy. *Education:* University of Pavia (J.D., 1984); City of London Polytechnic, 1988; Academy of American and International Law, The Southwestern Legal Foundation, University of Texas, Dallas, 1989. Visiting Foreign Lawyer, Simpson, Thacher & Bartlett, London and New York Offices, 1993-1994. *Member:* New York State and American Bar Associations; International Bar Association. (Resident, New York, New York Office).

(This Listing Continued)

AULO COSSU, born Rome, Italy, July 2, 1960; admitted to practice, 1985; admitted to bar, 1989, Italy. *Education:* University of Rome (J.D., 1984).

ANTONINO DI BELLA, born Catania, Italy, April 27, 1960; admitted to practice, 1985; admitted to bar, 1988, Italy. *Education:* University of Catania (J.D., maxima cum laude, 1985); City of London Polytechnic, 1985. *Member:* Young Lawyers International Association.

ANTONIO AURICCHIO, born Torre Del Greco, Italy, July 6, 1962; admitted to practice, 1985; admitted to bar, 1988, Italy. *Education:* University of Naples (J.D., maxima cum laude, 1984). Research Assistant of Civil Law, Law School, University of Naples, 1985-1988.

ALBERTO GIAMPIERI, born Rome, Italy, December 6, 1963; admitted to practice, 1987; admitted to bar, 1990, Italy. *Education:* University of Rome (J.D., maxima cum laude, 1986); City of London Polytechnic (1990). Visiting Scholar and Special Student Yale Law School (1991-1992). Visiting Foreign Lawyer: Skadden, Arps, Slate, Meagher & Flom, New York, 1992-1993. *Member:* Tax Commission of Rome; Young Lawyers Association.

MASSIMO AGOSTINI, born Cortona, Italy, August 6, 1960; admitted to practice, 1986; admitted to bar, 1990, Italy. *Education:* University of Florence (J.D., 1986); The Dickinson School of Law, Pennsylvania (M.C.L., 1989). *Member:* International Bar Association; International Fiscal Association.

ALBERTO MAGGI, born Pavia, Italy, June 23, 1961; admitted to practice, 1985; admitted to bar, 1990, Italy. *Education:* University of Pavia (J.D., maxima cum laude, 1985).

CRISTINA FANARA, born Messina, Italy, April 18, 1964; admitted to practice, 1988; admitted to bar, 1991, Italy. *Education:* University of Messina, Italy (J.D., maxima cum laude, 1987); Advanced Business Administration Course, Bocconi University, Milan, 1987-1988; Business Law Advanced Course, University of Milan, 1990; Orientation in American Law Program, University of California, Davis, 1992; Advanced Course in Business Tax Law, Bocconi University, Milan, 1992-1993.

PAOLO CASSINIS, born Rome, Italy, October 9, 1964; admitted to practice, 1988, admitted to bar, 1991, Italy. *Education:* University of Rome (J.D., maxima cum laude, 1988). Research Assistant, Institute of Private Law, Law School, University of Rome, 1987-1989. EEC Commission, Directorate General for Telecommunications, Trainee, 1993. Visiting Foreign Lawyer, Pavia & Harcourt, New York, 1988-1989.

STEFANO MARIA ZAPPALÀ, born Rome, Italy, July 9, 1963; admitted to practice 1987; admitted to bar, 1990, Italy. *Education:* University of Rome (J.D., maxima cum laude, 1987); Fordham University School of Law (Continuing Legal Education Program, 1991). Academy of American and International Law, The Southwestern Legal Foundation, University of Texas at Dallas, 1992. *Member:* American Foreign Law Association; Alumni Association, Academy of American and International Law.

STEFANO BUCCI, born Rome, Italy, July 11, 1961; admitted to practice, 1985; admitted to bar, 1990, Italy. *Education:* University of Rome (J.D., 1985). Research Assistant, Institute of Criminal Law, University of Rome, 1986—. Master of Tax and Corporate Practice, LUISS University, Rome, 1987-1988.

UGO BASSI, born Naples, Italy, August 3, 1966; admitted to practice, 1989, Italy; admitted to bar, 1992, Italy. *Education:* University of Naples (J.D., maxima cum laude, 1989); Graduate Students Intern Program, United Nations Headquarters, New York, 1989; Diploma of Advanced European Legal Studies, College of Europe, Bruges, 1990; City of London Polytechnic, 1990. Administrator, Research and Documentation, Department and Information Service, European Court of Justice, Luxembourg, 1990-1993. Member, Board of Editors, *Revue du marché unique europeen* . Research Assistant to the European Court of Justice, Luxembourg, 1990-1993.

PAOLO CRISCIONE, born Milan, Italy, May 9, 1961; admitted to practice, 1985; admitted to bar, 1990, Italy. *Education:* Catholic University of Milan (J.D., 1985); Bocconi University of Milan (corporate tax law, 1988-1989); King's College, London (LL.M. in EEC law, 1990-1992). Visiting Foreign Lawyer: Titmuss Sainer & Webb, London, 1990-1993. Italian correspondent and member, Editorial Advisory Board of European Competition Law Review. *Member:* British-Italian Law Association; Associazione Giuristi di Lingua Italiana.

RAFFAELLA BETTI BERUTTO, born Rome, Italy, November 20, 1965; admitted to practice, 1989; admitted to bar, 1992, Italy. *Education:* University of Rome (J.D., maxima cum laude, 1989); City of London Poly-

(This Listing Continued)

GIANNI, ORIGONI & PARTNERS, Rome—Continued

technic, 1989. Visiting Foreign Lawyer: Clifford Chance, Paris, 1993. *Member:* Academy of American and International Law; The Southwestern Legal Foundation, University of Texas, Dallas, 1993. (Resident, New York, New York Office).

FILIPPO TROISI, born Naples, Italy, April 28, 1965; admitted to practice 1988, Italy; admitted to bar, 1992, Italy and New York. *Education:* University of Naples (J.D., maxima cum laude, 1988); New York University School of Law (M.C.J., 1991). *Member:* New York State Bar Association; New York County Lawyers Association (Foreign and International Law Committee).

BRUNO BARTOCCI, born Naples, Italy, July 8, 1962; admitted to practice, 1987, Italy; admitted to bar, 1991, Italy; admitted, 1994, New York. *Education:* Luiss University, Rome (J.D., maxima cum laude, 1987); Academy of American and International Law, Dallas, 1988; Georgetown University Law Center (LL.M. , 1992). Summer Foreign Associate, Lewis, D'Amato, Brisbois & Brisgaard, Los Angeles, 1988. Visiting Foreign Lawyer: Vinson & Elkins, L.L.P., Washington, D.C., 1992-1993. Research Assistant of Communications Law, LUISS University. Member, Alumni Association Academy of American and International Law.

GIAN PAOLO TAGARIELLO, born Rome, Italy, May 2, 1967; admitted to practice, 1989, Italy; admitted to bar, 1992, Italy. *Education:* LUISS University of Rome (J.D., maxima cum laude, 1989). Diploma of Advanced European Legal Studies, College of Europe, Bruges, 1992. Research Assistant, Institute of International Law, Law Faculty, LUISS University.

LUIGI PAVANELLO, born Rome, Italy, April 25, 1960; admitted to practice, 1989, Italy; admitted to bar, 1991, New York; 1994, Italy. *Education:* University of Rome (J.D., 1985); New York University School of Law (LL.M., 1988). *Member:* American, International and New York State Bar Associations; Association of the Bar of the City of New York.

GIULIA FUSCO, born Venosa, Italy, September 21, 1960; admitted to practice, 1988, Italy; admitted to bar, 1992, Italy. *Education:* University of Bari (J.D., maxima cum laude, 1988). European University Institute, San Domenico di Fiesole, Florence, 1989-1992. Council of Europe, Strasburg (Research Assistant, 1990); Academy of European Law, Florence, 1991.

MARCELLO MARANI, born Bologna, Italy, March 3, 1961; admitted to practice, 1988; admitted to bar, 1992, Italy. *Education:* Bologna University (J.D., 1988; Master in Company Law, 1990); City of London Polytechnic (1991).

GIULIO RIVERA, born Milan, Italy, June 30 1963; admitted to practice, 1989, admitted to bar, 1992. *Education:* Catholic University of Milan (J.D., maxima cum laude, 1989). Research Assistant, Institute of International Law, Catholic University of Milan (1989-1990).

EMANUELA BERTOLLI, born Milan, Italy, March 25, 1961; admitted to practice, 1985; admitted to bar, 1993, Italy. *Education:* University of Milan (J.D., maxima cum laude, 1985).

ANTONIO SEGNI, born Genova, Italy, May 11, 1965; admitted to practice, 1988; admitted to bar, 1993, Italy; 1993, New York. *Education:* University of Rome (J.D., maxima cum laude, 1988); Harvard Law School (LL.M., 1992). *Member:* Legal Staff CONSOB, 1989-1994.

PAOLO RONCELLI, born Bergamo, Italy, September 26, 1963; admitted to practice, 1988, Italy. *Education:* University of Pavia (J.D., 1988); University of Texas School of Law (M.C.J., 1991).

GIANLUCA GHERSINI, born Milan, Italy, September 29, 1965; admitted to practice, 1991. *Education:* University of Milan, Italy (J.D., 1990). *Member:* British-Italian Law Association; Anglo-Italian Business Association; Young Lawyers' International Association.

RENATO GIALLOMBARDO, born Rome, Italy, February 17, 1966; admitted to practice, 1990, Italy. *Education:* University of Rome (J.D., 1990). Diploma of Advanced Legal Studies, International Private Law, The Hague Academy of International Law, The Hague, 1991; Diploma on European Legal Studies, Institute Alcide De Gasperi, Rome, 1992; University of London, Commercial and Corporate Law (LL.M., 1994).

DANIEL VONRUFS, born Bergamo, Italy, February 26, 1965; admitted to practice, 1991, Italy. *Education:* University of Milan (J.D., 1991). Academy of International Law, The Hague, 1990.

ANDREA LORENZO CAPUSSELA, born Genova, Italy, September 11, 1969; admitted to practice, 1993, Italy. *Education:* University of Milan

(This Listing Continued)

(J.D., maxima cum laude, 1993); University of London, Queen Mary and Westfield, 1992. Member, European Law Students Association.

ENRICO GARGALE, born Torino, Italy, April 19, 1966; admitted to practice, 1992. *Education:* University of Bologna (J.D., maxima cum laude, 1992); Advanced Course in Business Tax Law, Certi, Bocconi University of Milan (1993-1994).

PAOLO MARNATI, born Magenta, Italy, April 5, 1966; admitted to practice, 1992, Italy. *Education:* University of Milan (J.D., maxima cum laude, 1992).

OF COUNSEL

GUIDO ALPA, born Ovada (AL), November 26, 1947; admitted to practice, 1972; admitted to bar, 1974, Italy; 1984, Supreme Court of Italy. *Education:* University of Genoa (J.D. maxima cum laude, 1972). Visiting Foreign Professor: University of Oregon (at Eugene) 1977 and 1985; University of California (at Berkeley) 1979; University of London, 1982; University of Mannheim, 1984. Professor of Private Law and Private Comparative Law, at the University of Genoa (1983—); Director of the Private Law Institute of the Faculty of Law in Genoa (1981-1989); Full Professor at the University of Rome (1991—).*Member:* Commission Giannini to wind up useless public bodies, 1977; Commission Mirabelli; Commission Paladin to reform the Judiciary body, 1989; Commission INAIL for workers rights; European Research Association for Consumer Affairs; State Dept. Commission of Data Bank Protection; Vice-President of Consultant Commission for the protection of TV users, 1991; President of local section of AIDA (International Association of Insurance Laws); President of the CONSOB local commission. Member of the EEC Economic and Social Committee.

REFERENCES: AGIP Petroli S.p.A.; Armstrong World Industries, Inc.; Associated Press; Automatic Data Processing; Banca Commerciale Italiana; Bausch & Lomb, Inc.; Bear Stearns & Co., Inc.; CH Werfen S.A.; Credito Italiano; Danieli Ecologia, S.p.A.; Data General Corp.; Dean Witter Reynolds Inc.; Dresser Industries Inc.; Duracell Holdings International Corp.; Europcar Italia S.p.A.; Hitachi, LTD.; Ingersoll-Rand Company; Istituto Bancario San Paolo di Torino; ITT Sheraton Corporation; Kelsey-Hayes Co.; Kidder Peabody & Co., Inc.; Maytag Corporation; Merrill Lynch International; McKesson Corp.; Monte dei Paschi di Siena; Nissho-Iway; Oppenheimer & Co., Inc.; Phoenix Mutual Life Insurance Company; Playtex Apparel, Inc.; Prudential Securities, Inc.; Rentokil Group Plc; Sea Containers, Ltd.; The New York Times, Co.; The Pullman-Peabody Co.; Sara Lee Corporation; Takeda Chemical Industries, Ltd.; The Sumitomo Bank; The Walt Disney Company; TLC-Beatrice International, Inc.; UniRoyal Chemical Company, Inc.

STUDIO AVV. ERCOLE GRAZIADEI

ROME, ITALY

Due to a strict interpretation of the Italian Professional law made by the Italian Supreme Civil Court preventing a law firm from using the name of its deceased founder. Studio Avv. Ercole Graziadei was compelled to abandon its name (see the entry of Studio Legale Internazionale).

STUDIO LEGALE GRIECO - VINTI

VIA BERNARDO BLUMENSTIHL N. 40
00135 ROME, ITALY
Telephone: (39-6) 35502058
Fax: (39-6) 35501863

Milan Office: Piazzetta Giordano, 4, 20122 Milan, Italy. Telephone: (39-2) 784583. Fax: (39-2) 784762.

General Civil Practice. Administrative Law, EEC Construction Law, International Business Practice, Corporate, Mergers and Acquisitions, Antitrust, Taxation, Environmental, Banking and Financing, Securities, Labor, Industrial Property, Oil and Gas, Telecommunications, EEC Law, Litigation and Arbitration.

FIRM PROFILE: *Established in 1992, GRIECO-VINTI Has a broadly - based practice with a reputation for offering a full range of quality legal services. The firm has two partners who have been practising for more than ten years and seven associates. The firm has two offices, one in Rome and the other in Milan.*

ANTONIO GRIECO, born Rome, Italy, April 2, 1960; admitted to practice, 1982; admitted to bar, 1985, Italy. *Education:* Italy, University of Rome (Doctor of Jurisprudence, maxima cum laude, 1982); Professorial Assistant of Civil Law, University of Rome Law School (1989—) ; U.S.A., University of Illinois Law School (M.C.L., 1984); New York University, Exchange Visiting Scholar (1985); Harvard University Law School, P.I.L.

(This Listing Continued)

1989. *Member:* Italian Bar Association (Rome); Italian Arbitration Association (International Associate); American Bar Association (International Associate); International Bar Association; London Court of International Arbitration; International Litigation Practitioners Forum. *LANGUAGES:* Italian and English. *PRACTICE AREAS:* Corporate; Competition; International Trade and Arbitration.

STEFANO VINTI, born Palermo, Italy, December 27, 1960; admitted to bar, 1986, Italy. *Education:* Italy, University of Rome (Doctor of Jurisprudence, maxima cum laude, 1984). Professor, Administrative Law, University of L'Aquila, 1992. Researcher, University of Perugia for Administrative and Construction Law. *LANGUAGES:* Italian and English. *PRACTICE AREAS:* Construction Law; Administrative Law.

CINO RAFFA UGOLINI, born Milan, Italy, March 8, 1960; admitted, 1986, Italy; 1990, New York. *Education:* University of Milan (J.D., summa cum laude, 1984); New York University of School of Law (M.C.J., 1989). Recipient, Scholarship from the Fulbright Foundation. Foreign Associate, O'Melveny & Myers, New York Office, 1989-1990. *LANGUAGES:* English and French.

PAOLA CHIRULLI, born Rome, Italy, October 30, 1965; admitted to bar, Italy, 1992. *Education:* University of Rome (Doctor of Jurisprudence, 1989). Professorial Assistant at L.U.I.S.S. University of Rome in Administrative Law. *LANGUAGES:* Italian and English. *PRACTICE AREAS:* Administrative Law.

FABRIZIO POLLARI MAGLIETTA, born Milano, Italy, October 1, 1963; admitted, 1994, Italy. *Education:* University of Rome (Doctor of Jurisprudence, maxima cum laude, 1990). *LANGUAGES:* Italian and English. *PRACTICE AREAS:* Corporate Law; Business Law.

VINCENZO MORICONI, born Rome, Italy, July 25, 1959. admitted to bar, 1991, Italy. *Education:* University of Rome (Doctor of Jurisprudence, 1983). *LANGUAGES:* Italian. *PRACTICE AREAS:* General Practice.

FEDERICA CORSINI, born Rome, Italy, February 24, 1967. admitted to practice, 1993, Italy. *Education:* L.U.I.S.S. University of Rome (J.D., 1993). *LANGUAGES:* Italian and English. *PRACTICE AREAS:* General Practice.

LUCA MARIANI, born Rome, Italy, September 16, 1968; admitted to practice, 1993, Italy. *Education:* University of Rome, Italy (Doctor of Jurisprudence, maxima cum laude, 1993). Professorial Assistant of European Community Law at the University of Rome (1993). *LANGUAGES:* English and French. *PRACTICE AREAS:* European Community Law.

LORENZO PARRONI, born Pesaro, Italy, October 2, 1968; Admitted to Practice, 1993, Italy. *Education:* University of Rome (Doctor of Jurisprudence, maxima cum laude, 1993). Practice at "Avvocatura dello Stato," January 1994—. *LANGUAGES:* Italian and English. *PRACTICE AREAS:* Administrative Law.

GRIMALDI E CLIFFORD CHANCE

In Association with Clifford Chance

VIALE GIOACCHINO ROSSINI, 7
00198 ROME, ITALY
Telephone: (39 6) 807 2251
Fax: (39 6) 807 8201

Other Offices: Amsterdam, Bahrain, Barcelona, Brussels, Budapest, Dubai, Frankfurt, Hanoi, Hong Kong, London, Madrid, Milan, Moscow, New York, Paris, Riyadh, Shanghai, Singapore, Tokyo, Warsaw. (See Clifford Chance, London for full address details).

International and General Practice including Banking, Corporate, Corporate Finance, Capital Markets, Stock Exchange Listings, Taxation, Investment, EEC, Arbitration, Bankruptcy, Patent, Trademark, Entertainment and Media, Securitization, Project and Asset Financing, Real Estate, Civil Litigation.

VITTORIO GRIMALDI, born Rome, Italy, February 20, 1941; admitted, 1968, Italy. *Education:* Rome University (LL.D., 1968).

MICHAEL BRAY, born London, March 27, 1947; admitted, 1972, London. *Education:* Liverpool University (LL.B., 1970). (Milan).

FRANCESCO NOVELLI, born Rome, Italy, June 16, 1958; admitted, 1984, Italy. *Education:* Rome University (LL.D., 1982).

DANIELA TROILO, born Rome, Italy, December 18, 1957; admitted, 1986, Italy. *Education:* Rome University (LL.D., 1982).

(This Listing Continued)

ROBERTO CAPPELLI, born Rome, Italy, March 19, 1959; admitted, 1986, Italy. *Education:* Rome University (LL.D., 1982).

NICHOLAS WRIGLEY, born Ulverston, England, October 25, 1961; admitted, 1987, London. *Education:* Sussex University (B.A., 1984).

ANDREW WOOLMER, born Ottawa, Canada, November 13, 1955; admitted, 1980, London. *Education:* Oxford University (B.A., 1977).

FRANCESCO MACARIO, born Bari, Italy, January 19, 1960; admitted, 1985, Italy. *Education:* Bari University (LL.D., 1983).

PAOLO RULLI, born Rome, Italy, July 21, 1965; admitted, 1992, Italy. *Education:* Rome University (LL.D., 1989).

FILIPPO EMANUELE, born Newcastle-upon-Tyne, England, July 20, 1964; admitted, 1991, London. *Education:* Leeds University (LL.B., 1987). (Milan).

SILVIO RIOLO, born Pisa, Italy, October 7, 1965; admitted, 1992, Italy. *Education:* Milan University (LL.D., 1989). (Milan).

LUIGI CHESSA, born Rome, March 5, 1964; admitted, 1992, Rome. *Education:* Rome University (J.D., 1986).

GREGORIO DONA' DALLE ROSE, born Venice, Italy, June 22, 1962; admitted, 1994, Italy. *Education:* Padua University (LL.D., 1990). (Milan).

FILIPPO MURATORI, born Morciano di Romagna, Italy, February 12, 1963; admitted, 1993, Italy. *Education:* Bologna University (LL.D., 1990); University of London (LL.M.).

CHARLES ADAMS, born Paris, France, November 18, 1968; admitted, 1994, London. *Education:* Oxford University (B.A., Hons., 1990).

FRANCO GRILLI CICILIONI, born Penne, Italy, March 7, 1964; admitted, 1993, Italy. *Education:* Bologna University (LL.B., 1988); Boston University (LL.M.).

MASSIMO NOVO, born Pinerolo, Italy, April 9, 1962. *Education:* Turin University (LL.B., 1985). (Milan).

SAMANTHA PANDOLFI, born Rome, Italy, March 14, 1969; admitted, 1993, Italy as trainee. *Education:* Rome University (LL.D., 1993).

PAOLO CALDERARO, born Pompei (Naples), Italy, June 25, 1966; admitted, 1991, Italy as trainee. *Education:* Rome University (LL.D., 1991).

TANJA SVETINA, born Trieste, Italy, March 26, 1969; admitted, 1992, Italy as trainee. *Education:* Trieste University (LL.D., 1992).

ANDREA GRANZOTTO, born Rome, Italy, March 8, 1969; admitted, 1993, Italy as trainee. *Education:* Rome University (LL.D., 1992).

ALBERTO DUBINI, born Milan, Italy, September 22, 1968; admitted, 1992, Milan as trainee. *Education:* Milan State University (LL.D., 1992). (Milan).

MARIA CHIARA CALDART, born Valdobbiadene, Italy, October 7, 1969; admitted, 1994, Milan as trainee. *Education:* Bologna State University (LL.D., 1994). (Milan).

ALESSANDRO BOZZA, born Rome, Italy, August 25, 1968; admitted, 1993, Rome as trainee. *Education:* Rome State University (LL.D., 1993).

ALBERTA FIGARI, born Milan, Italy, January 1, 1964. *Education:* Milan University (LL.B., 1988); Kings College, London (LL.M., 1994). (Milan).

PAUL MATTHEWS, born London, England, May 1, 1969; admitted, 1993, London as trainee. *Education:* Warwick University (LL.B., 1991); Aberdeen University (LL.M., 1993).

Languages: Italian, English, French, Spanish, German and Slovenian

STUDIO AVV. EUGENIO GRIPPO
E
SIMMONS & SIMMONS

Associazione Internazionale di Studi Legali

Established in 1985

PIAZZA SALLUSTIO, 9
00187 ROME, ITALY
Telephone: 39-6-4870920
Fax: 39-6-4828562

Milan, Italy Office: Via dei Boschetti, 1, 20121. Telephone:
39-2-76003012. Fax: 39-2-782770.
London, England Office: Simmons & Simmons, 21 Wilson Street,
London EC2M 2TQ. Telephone: 44-171-628 2020. Fx: 44-171-588
4129.
Offices in Paris, Brussels, Lisbon, Hong Kong, Abu Dhabi and New
York (for listing for addresses, see entry under Milan, Italy).

Mergers and Acquisitions, Banking and Finance, Projects and Construction, Public Offerings, Company and Commercial Law, Investment Funds, Joint Ventures, Advertising and Sport, Labor Law, EC Law, International Tax, Anti-Trust and Competition, Intellectual Property Rights, Environmental Law, Litigation.

FIRM PROFILE: Founded by Avv. Grippo since May 1993 the firm has operated as a joint legal practice with the international law firm, Simmons & Simmons.

FILIPPO PINGUE, born Benevento, Italy, June 24, 1961; admitted,
1988, Italy. *Education:* Naples University (J.D., maxima cum laude, 1983).
Member: Rome Bar. *LANGUAGES:* Italian and English.

CLAUDIA VOLPI, born Neuilly-Sur-Seine, France, April 29, 1965;
admitted, 1994, Italy. *Education:* La Sapienza University, Rome (J.D.,
1991). *LANGUAGES:* Italian, English and French.

ANGELA MANNAERTS, born Tilburg, The Netherlands, June 16,
1963; admitted, 1992, New York (Not admitted in Italy). *Education:* University of Amsterdam, The Netherlands (J.D., 1989); University of Nebraska-Lincoln, U.S.A. (J.D., High Distinction, 1991). Nebraska Law Review,
1990-1991. Nebraska Chapter of the Order of the Coif. Clerk, Supreme
Court of Nebraska, U.S.A., 1991-1992. Associate, Paul, Weiss, Rifkind,
Wharton & Garrison, New York, 1992-1994. *Member:* New York Bar Association. *LANGUAGES:* Dutch, English, French, German and Italian.

MANFREDI VIANINI TOLOMEI, born Rome, Italy, February 22,
1966. *Education:* La Sapienza University, Rome (J.D. Maxima Cum Laude,
1990). *LANGUAGES:* Italian, English and French.

(For Complete Biographical Data of All Members of Firm and Listing
of All International Offices, see entry under Milan, Italy)

STUDIO LEGALE GUERRERI

Established in 1955

15, VIA DELLE QUATTRO FONTANE
00184 ROME, ITALY
Telephone: (39) (6) 488-3979; 488-0981
Telex: 616313 GUEATT I
Telecopier: (3 9) (6) 482.0686

General Practice, Corporate and Commercial, Aviation and Admiralty Law, Insurance, Oil and Gas, Immunities of States and International Organizations, International Trade, Litigation.

MEMBERS OF FIRM

GIUSEPPE GUERRERI, born Parma, 1932; admitted, 1955, Italy.
Education: Rome University (LL.D.); McGill University, Montreal
(LL.M., 1961).

FRANCESCO CANEPA, born Cagliari, 1948; admitted, 1974, Italy.
Education: Rome University (LL.D.).

GABRIELE BRICCHI, born Pisa, 1963; admitted, 1989. *Education:*
Rome University (LL.D.); King College, London (EYL., 1993).

(This Listing Continued)

ROSSELLA GALANTE, born Milan, 1960; admitted, 1984. *Education:*
Rome University (LL.D.); Columbia University, Leyden (Summer Course
1994).

Languages: Italian, English and French.

HURT, SINISI & PAPADAKIS

In Association with

Sinisi, Ceschini, Mancini & Partners

VIA LAURINA 40
00187 ROME, ITALY
Telephone: (39) (6) 322-1485; 322-1487
Telefax: (39) (6) 361-3266

Milan, Italy Office: Corso Italia 8, 20122. Telephone: (39) (2) 866 727.
Telefax: (39) (2) 866 771.
Athens, Greece Office: Kanari 7, 106 71. Telephone: (30) (1)
364-2320/30; 363-8876. Telecopier: (30) (1) 364-2323.
Piraeus, Greece Office: 1 Loudovikou, 5th Floor, 185 31 Piraeus.
Telephone: (30) (1) 417-4998. Telefax: (30) (1) 413-4289.
Atlanta, Georgia, USA Office: 1050 Crown Pointe Parkway, Suite 310,
30338. Telephone: (404) 913-9999. Telecopier: (404) 671-8513.
Hartford, Connecticut, USA Office: 294, New London Turnpike,
Glastonbury, 06033. Telephone: (203) 633-3903. Telefax: (203)
633-4599.
San Diego, California, USA Office: Suite 1400, One America Plaza, 600
West Broadway, 92101-3377. Telephone: (619) 234-1798. Telefax:
(619) 234-8475.
New York, New York, USA Office: 375 Park Avenue, Suite 2904, 10152.
Telephone: (212) 755-1550. Telefax: (212) 755-1575.

Corporate, Banking and Securities Law with emphasis on Mergers and Acquisitions, Insurance, International Financial Transactions, Litigation, Arbitration, Bankruptcy, Foreign Investments, Privatizations, Joint Ventures, Taxation, European Common Market Law, Antitrust, Environmental Law, Transportation, Shipping, Licensing, Financing, Distribution Law, Commercial Real Estate (Investment, Structuring and Development), Project and Trade Finance, Computer, Software, Trademark Law, Telecommunications Law, Agency and Distribution, Labor, Visa/Immigration, Wills and Estates, Sports Law, Broadcasting, Motion Pictures, Video, Intellectual Property and General Entertainment Law.

FIRM PROFILE: Hurt, Sinisi & Papadakis is an International Law Firm based in the United States and Europe. Fundamental to the firm is a committment to provide a high quality of personalized service with an excellent standard of professionalism. The United States Offices are located in the Northeast, Southeast and Western United States in order to service clients conveniently and efficiently, as well as provide full support to the firm's European Offices. The European Offices are staffed with both American and European attorneys. Each office, in Europe and the United States, has attorneys that are qualified to appear and litigate in the local courts. Hurt, Sinisi & Papadakis has a strong focus on the Southern European region. This gives this firm a unique strategic position for businesses seeking legal advice and representation in this area.

(For Complete Biographical Data on all Personnel, See Professional
Biographies of Sinisi, Ceschini, Mancini & Partners, Rome & Milan,
Italy)

STUDIO LEGALE INTERNAZIONALE

96, VIA VITTORIO VENETO
00187 ROME, ITALY
Telephone: (06) 47.98.01 (multiple line); (06) 488.11.19; (06) 482.76.01;
(06) 481.91.05; (06) 483.807
Fax: (06) 487.34.02; (06) 482.58.77

Milan, Italy Office: Via Melegari, 4, 20122. Telephone: (02) 76008078.
Fax: (02) 780482.
Padua Office: Via del Santo, 30, 35123. Telephone: (049) 8750672. Fax:
(049) 8753675.

Banking, Securities, Corporate Finance, Air-Financing, Investment Funds, EC Law, Anti-trust, Litigation, Bankruptcy, Maritime and Labour Law.

FIRM PROFILE: Studio Legale Internazionale is one of the Italian leading international law firms in the banking and corporate finance fields, with an organization of 12 partners and other fees earners - consultants and an aggregate skilled staff of 50 persons.

(This Listing Continued)

SENIOR PARTNERS

NICOLA TROILO, born Rome, Italy, May 4, 1930; admitted, 1955, Italy. *Education:* Milan University (LL.D., 1954). (Former Senior Partner of Studio Graziadei).

ALESSANDRO DI SAN BONIFACIO, born Padova, Italy, February 12, 1950; admitted, 1978, Italy. *Education:* Padova University (LL.D., 1976). (Resident, Padua Office) (Former Senior Partner of Studio Graziadei).

CARLO GALDO, born Naples, Italy, March 26, 1954; admitted, 1980, Italy. *Education:* Naples University (LL.D., 1977). (Former Senior Partner of Studio Graziadei).

VITTORIO VALIERI, born Rome, Italy, June 8, 1955; admitted, 1985, Italy. *Education:* Rome University (LL.D., 1980). Visiting Foreign Lawyer, University of Edinburgh. *Member:* International Bar Association. (Former Senior Partner of Studio Graziadei).

Languages: English, German, French.

REFERENCES: Swiss Bank Corporation; WestDeutsche Landesbank Girozentrale; Merril Lynch & Co., Inc.; J.P. Morgan; Bank of Nova Scotia; Lehman Brothers; Banca di Roma; Mediocredito Centrale; Irfis-Mediocredito della Sicilia S.p.A.; Credito Industriale Sardo S.p.A.; Medicredito Piemontese; Johnson & Johnson Twentieth Century Fox; Rockwell International; USX Corp.; Abbott Laboratories; Uniroyal Chemical Company, Inc.; Stone Webster Engineering; The J. Paul Getty Trust; British Aerospace; Christie's; Canadian Airlines; Meridiana S.P.A.; TPL S.p.A.

(A list of fee earners names is open for inspection in the above address).

STUDIO LEGALE ITALIA

28 VIA SAN TEODORO
00186 ROME, ITALY
Telephone: 06-6781438 /6784744 /6790822
Fax: 06-6784285

General Practice, Commercial and Company Law, Labor and Pension Law, Litigation, Insolvency, Intellectual Property.

MEMBERS OF FIRM

SEBASTIANO ITALIA, born Rome, Italy, October 6, 1930; admitted, 1955; 1971, Supreme Court. *Education:* University of Rome (Doctor of Jurisprudence 1952). *Member:* Rome Bar. *LANGUAGES:* Italian. *PRACTICE AREAS:* Labor and Pension Law.

SALVATORE ITALIA, born Rome, Italy, December 24, 1955; admitted, 1983. *Education:* University of Rome (Doctor of Jurisprudence 1979); University of Cambridge, U.K; St. John's College (LL.M., 1981); City of London Polytechnic (Diploma in European Business Law 1979). Salzburg Seminar on American Law and Legal Institutions (1986). Visiting Foreign Lawyer, Linklaters & Paines London Office (1987-1988). *Rome Bar; International Bar Association; British Italian Law Association; A.I.J.A.; U.I.A. LANGUAGES:* Italian, English and French. *PRACTICE AREAS:* Commercial and Company Law; Labour Law.

ROBERTO BARALDINI, born Ferrara, April 3, 1960; admitted, 1990. *Education:* University of Rome (Doctor of Jurisprudence 1987). *Member:* Rome Bar. *LANGUAGES:* Italian and French.

GASPARE DORI, born Pontecorvo (Frosinone), October 31, 1967. *Education:* L.U.I.S.S. University of Rome (Doctor of Jurisprudence, magna cum laude, 1992); London School of Economics (Diploma Law Summer Course, 1994). *LANGUAGES:* Italian and English.

PIERPAOLO MAIO, born Forlí, April 16, 1968. *Education:* L.U.I.S.S. University of Rome (Doctor of Jurisprudence 1993). *LANGUAGES:* Italian and English.

STUDIO LEGALE LEONE

Established in 1905

VIA PRINCIPESSA CLOTILDE 2
00196 ROME, ITALY
Telephone: (+ +-6) 3611429-3611460
Telefax: (+ +-6) 3216334

Naples Office: Telephone: (39-81) 5527879. Fax: (39-81) 5527855.

General Practice, Litigation and Arbitration, Criminal Law, Administrative Law.

(This Listing Continued)

PAOLO LEONE, born Naples, October 23, 1954; admitted, 1981, Italy. *Education:* University of Naples (Doctor of Jurisprudence, cum laude, 1977). Trainee, Chase Manhattan Bank, 1977-1979. *Member:* Rome and International Bar Associations. (Resident Rome Office). *LANGUAGES:* Italian, English and French.

FRANCESCA R. NATALE, born Castrovillari, Italy, September 3, 1942; admitted, 1969, Italy; 1987, Supreme Court. *Education:* University of Rome (Doctor of Jurisprudence, 1967); Catholic University "Pro Deo" Rome (Journalist, 1975). Researcher, Penal Procedure Law, University of Rome. *Member:* Rome Bar Association. (Resident Rome Office).

GIOVANNI LEONE, born Naples, Italy, August 14, 1951; admitted, 1975, Italy, Supreme Court. *Education:* University of Naples (Doctor of Jurisprudence, cum laude, 1973). Professor of Administrative Law since 1985. *Member:* Naples Bar Association. (Resident Naples Office). *LANGUAGES:* Italian and French.

LOEB AND LOEB

A Partnership including Professional Corporations

Established in 1909

PIAZZA DIGIONE 1
ROME 00197, ITALY
Telephone: 011-396-808-8456
Telecopier: 011-396-674-8223

Los Angeles, California Office: Suite 1800, 1000 Wilshire Boulevard, 90017-2475. Telephone: 213-688-3400. Cable Address: "Loband LSA". Telecopier: 213-688-3460; 688-3461.

Century City (Los Angeles), California Office: Suite 2200, 10100 Santa Monica Boulevard, Los Angeles, 90067-4164. Telephone: 310-282-2000. Telecopier: 310-282-2191; 282-2192.

New York, N.Y. Office: 345 Park Avenue, 10154-0037. Telephone: 212-407-4000. Facsimile: 212-407-4990.

Nashville, Tennessee Office: 45 Music Square West, 37203-3205. Telephone: 615-749-8300. Facsimile: 615-749-8308.

General Civil Trial and Appellate Practice in all Courts. Banking and Finance, Institutional Lending, Corporate and Transactional Matters, International Business, Real Estate, Securities, Private Placements, Franchising, Intellectual Property, Motion Picture, Television, Music Industry, Sports, Entertainment, Advertising, Constitutional and Civil Rights, Federal Income, Gift and Estate Taxation, State and Local Taxation, Estate Planning, Pension and Employee Benefits, Antitrust, Bankruptcy and Insolvency, White Collar Criminal Investigation, Environmental, Labor and Employment, Trust and Probate Law.

FIRM PROFILE: Loeb and Loeb is a full-service law firm representing business organizations and individuals in the business community. The firm was established in Los Angeles in 1909 and now maintains offices in the Central Business District and Century City areas of Los Angeles, in New York City, in Nashville, Tennessee and in Rome, Italy. Its principal practice areas include civil litigation in all federal and state courts, general corporate and corporate securities law, banking, insurance company, pension fund and other institutional lending, real estate law, real estate financing, real estate securities, leveraged leasing, franchising, intellectual property, entertainment law (including motion pictures, television, sports, music and dramatic and literary arts), advertising, health care, international, federal, state and local taxation, estate planning, pension and employee benefits, insolvency and workout matters, environmental law, labor and employment, white collar criminal investigation law matters, and probate and trust law. Although the firm has been identified historically with both the entertainment industry and institutional lending, its client base throughout its history has encompassed individuals and entities engaged in most types of domestic and international businesses.

MEMBERS OF FIRM

JOHN J. DELLAVERSON, born New Castle, Pennsylvania, July 5, 1946; admitted, 1978, New York; 1980, California (Not admitted in Italy). *Education:* University of Pittsburgh (B.S., 1968); Cornell University; Fordham University School of Law (J.D., 1977). Member: National Labor Relations Board, Region 2, New York, N.Y., 1977-1979; Region 32, Oakland, California, 1979. *Member:* The State Bar of California (Member, Labor Relations Law Section); American Bar Association (Member, Labor and Employment Law Section). *LANGUAGES:* English, Italian. *PRACTICE AREAS:* Labor Law; Entertainment Law.

(This Listing Continued)

LOEB AND LOEB, Rome—Continued

LORENZO DE SANCTIS, born Rome, Italy, June 4, 1947; admitted, 1975, Rome, Italy; 1982 Albo Degli Avvocati of Rome. *Education:* University of Rome (Dr. in Jurisprudence, 1970; European Studies, 1970-1972). Author: "Industrial right problems in jurisprudence of the Court of Justice of ECC," Rivista del Diritto D'Autore (Copyright Revue), 1972 - n. 2; "Reprography and copyright," Rivista Diritto D'Autore, 1974 n.1; "Short notes about the protection of critical editions," Rivista Diritto D'Autore 1976 n. 4; "Short notes about videogames protection," Rivista Diritto D'Autore 1984 - n. 2; "Territorial competence in urgent proceedings," Temia Romana 1987 - n.3; "Some remarks about immaterial works in contractual activity," Rivista Diritto D'Autore 1987 n. 2; "Again about computer programs," Rivista Diritto D'Autore 1988, N.3. *Member:* American Film Market Association; Italian Association of European Council of Jurists. [With Italian Air Force, 1970-1972]. *LANGUAGES:* English, French and Italian. *PRACTICE AREAS:* Litigation.

GUENDALINA PONTI, born Rome Italy, December 5, 1948; admitted, 1979, Rome, Italy; 1985, Albo Degli Avvocati of Rome. *Education:* University of Rome (Dr. of Jurisprudence, magna cum laude, 1972). Guest Professor, "Commercial Navigation Law," University of Rome, 1972-1975. *Member:* American Film Market Association; Italian Association of European Council Jurists. *LANGUAGES:* English, French and Italian. *PRACTICE AREAS:* Corporate Law; Entertainment Law.

ASSOCIATES

Giovanni A. Pedde   Paola Amelia Massardi
(Not admitted in Italy)   Riccardo Siciliani

STUDIO LEGALE LUPOI

Established in 1934

VIA BERTOLONI 55
00197 ROME, ITALY
Telephone: 010-39 6 8070851
Telefax: 8080919

New York, New York Associated Office: Epstein Becker & Green, 250 Park Avenue, 10177. Telephone: 212-351-4500. Telex: 5101008171.

General Practice. Commercial Law, Company Law, Foreign Investments, Arbitration, Distributorship, Agency and Franchising, International Contracts, International Private Law, Intellectual Property Law, Copyright Law and International Taxation.

AVV. PROF. MAURIZIO LUPOI, born Rome, Italy, May 11, 1942; admitted, 1966, Italy; Licensed as Legal Consultant; 1980, New York. *Education:* University of Rome (Doctor of Jurisprudence, 1964); University of Oxford (Diploma in Law, 1966). Professor of Comparative Law, 1975-1984.

ASSOCIATES

DOTT. PROC. FRANCESCA ROMANA LUPOI, born Oxford, England, November 30, 1964; admitted, 1992, Italy. *Education:* University of Rome (Doctor of Jurisprudence, 1988).

DOTT. ALBERTO LUPOI, born Rome, Italy, March 29, 1970. *Education:* University of Rome (Doctor of Jurisprudence, 1993).

DOTT. DONATELLA CARUSO, born Rome, Italy, May 7, 1967. *Education:* University of Rome (Doctor of Jurisprudence, 1993).

DOTT. WANDA COSTA, born Rome, Italy, January 23, 1969. *Education:* University of Rome (Doctor of Jurisprudence, 1994).

DOTT. EMANUELA MARÉ, born Rome, Italy, June 26, 1969. *Education:* University of Rome (Doctor of Jurisprudence, 1994).

MACCHI di CELLERE e GANGEMI

VIA G. CUBONI, 12
00197 ROME, ITALY
Telephone: (39-6) 3214238; 3221565
Fax: (39-6) 3222 159

Milan, Italy Office: Via G. Serbelloni, 4, 20122, Milan. Telephone: (39-2) 76001616. Fax: (39-2) 76001618.

(This Listing Continued)

International Business Practice. Corporate, Mergers and Acquisitions, Antitrust, Taxation, Environmental, Telecommunications, Commercial Transactions, Banking and Financing, Securities, Labor, Oil and Gas, International and EEC Law, Litigation and Arbitration.

LUIGI MACCHI DI CELLERE, born Tokyo, Japan, November 11, 1937; admitted to practice, 1961; admitted to bar, 1964, Italy; Licensed in New York as Legal Consultant, 1980. *Education:* Italy, University of Rome, Doctor of Jurisprudence, maxima cum laude (1961) and Institute of Comparative Law (1963-1964); U.S.A., University of Michigan Law School (M.C.L., 1965). *Member:* Italian Bar Association (Rome); Italian Arbitration Association (Rome); American Bar Association (International Associate); American Arbitration Association (International Panelist); The Association of the Bar of the City of New York; American Foreign Law Association; International Law Association; American Society of International Law; The Southwestern Legal Foundation (Member, Advisory Board, International and Comparative Law Center); Institute of International Business Law and Practice of the ICC; International Bar Association; Union Internationale des Avocats.

BRUNO GANGEMI, born Messina, Italy, November 8, 1938; admitted to practice, 1963; admitted to bar, 1971, Italy. *Education:* Italy, University of Rome (Doctor of Jurisprudence, 1962); Professorial Assistant of Finance and Taxation, University of Rome Law School, 1963-1966; Germany, University of Cologne (1965). Austria, Fellow, Seminar in American Law, Salzburg, 1971. *Member:* Italian Bar Association (Rome); American Bar Association (International Associate); International Bar Association (Co-Chairman, Committee on Taxes, Section on Business Law); Italian Delegate to the Confederation Fiscale Europeene; International Fiscal Association (Member of the General Council; Secretary of the Italian Branch; General Reporter, Stockholm, 1990).

CLAUDIO VISCO, born Rome, Italy, March 26, 1957; admitted to practice, 1981; admitted to bar, 1983, Italy. *Education:* Italy, University of Rome (Doctor of Jurisprudence, maxima cum laude, 1981); Public Administration School, Rome (1981-1982); U.S.A. Georgetown University Law School, Summer Program in American Law (1982); University of Michigan Law School (LL.M., 1983). *Member:* Italian Bar Association (Rome); International Bar Association; International Fiscal Association; State Bar of Michigan (International Law Section).

TEODOSIO LUCIANO MONACO, born Laufenburg, Switzerland, June 15, 1955; admitted to practice, 1979; admitted to bar, 1984, Italy. *Education:* Italy, University of Salerno (Doctor of Jurisprudence, maxima cum laude, 1978). Fellow, Seminar in European Community Law, Faculté Internationale de Droit Comparé de Strasbourg, Turin, 1978; Germany, University of Hamburg, Institut für Integrationsforschung, Scientific Collaborator, 1980-1982 and Max Planck Institut, Hamburg, Scientific Collaborator, 1982-1983. *Member:* Italian Bar Association (Rome); American Bar Association (International Associate); International Bar Association; American Foreign Law Association.

SIMONA BELLETTINI, born Bologna, Italy, December 25, 1960; admitted to practice, 1985; admitted to bar, 1987, Italy. *Education:* Italy, University of Bologna (Doctor of Jurisprudence, maxima cum laude, 1985). Belgium, Trainee with the EEC Commission, 1987; England, University of London, King's College (LL.M., 1989). *Member:* Italian Bar Association (Rome); International Fiscal Association; International Bar Association.

FABRIZIO MARIA ROMANO, born Rome, Italy, October 18, 1959; admitted to practice, 1987, admitted to bar, 1991, Italy. *Education:* Italy, University of Rome, Italy (Doctor of Jurisprudence, 1987). *Member:* Italian Bar Association (Rome); International Bar Association; Young Lawyers International Association.

STEFANO MACCHI DI CELLERE, born Rome, Italy, April 4, 1963; admitted to practice, 1990; admitted to bar, 1993, Italy. *Education:* Italy University of Rome (Doctor of Jurisprudence, 1990); Italian Association of European Jurists, Rome (Seminar in EC Law, 1992); U.S.A., Academy of American and International Law, The Southwestern Legal Foundation, Dallas, 1990; Georgetown University Law School, Summer Program in American Law, 1991. *Member:* Italian Bar Association (Rome); International Bar Association; American-Italian Law Association; The Institute for Lawyers in Europe; Alumni Association Academy of American and International Law (Deputy Secretary General, 1990-1991).

LUCA SIMONETTI, born Rome, Italy, September 19, 1964; admitted to practice 1990; admitted to bar, 1993, Italy. *Education:* Italy, University of Rome (Doctor of Jurisprudence, maxima cum laude, 1988); Ph.D. in Comparative Law, University of Florence, (1993); U.S.A., Academy of American and International Law, The Southwestern Legal Foundation,

(This Listing Continued)

Dallas , 1992. Professorial Assistant of Comparative Law, University of Rome (1988-1994); Scientific Collaborator, Center for Comparative and Foreign Law Studies, Unidroit, Rome (1991-1994). *Member:* Italian Bar Association (Rome); Alumni Association Academy of American and International Law.

ETTORE SCANDALE, born Rome, Italy, April 8, 1964; admitted to practice 1990, Italy. *Education:* University of Rome (Doctor of Jurisprudence, 1989). Professorial Assistant, Roman Law, 1989-1991; U.S.A. Academy of American and International Law, The Southwestern Legal Foundation, Dallas, 1993. *Member:* International Bar Association; International Fiscal Association; Alumni Association Academy of American and International Law (Deputy Secretary General, 1993-1994).

FRANCESCO CERASI, born Rome, Italy, February 21, 1966; admitted to practice, 1989; admitted to bar, 1992, Italy. *Education:* Italy, University of Rome (Doctor of Jurisprudence, maxima cum laude, 1989); Notarial School T. Anselmi of Rome (1990); School of Catholic Jurists of Rome (1991); England, Polytechnic of London (1992). *Member:* Italian Bar Association (Rome).

MARCO LOMBARDI, born Forli, Italy, December 27, 1965; admitted to practice, 1991. *Education:* Italy, University of Bologna (Doctor of Jurisprudence, maxima cum laude, 1990); England, University of London, Queen Mary and Westfield College (LL.M., 1992).

CORRADO ANGELELLI, born Milan, Italy, August 21, 1967: admitted to practice, 1992, Italy. *Education:* Italy, University of Milan (Doctor of Jurisprudence, 1992). Professorial Assistant of Civil Law, University of Milan (1993-1994).

BERNADETTE ACCILI, born L'Aquila, Italy, April 16, 1968; admitted to practice, 1991, Italy. *Education:* Italy, University of Rome (Doctor of Jurisprudence, 1991); Italian Association of European Jurists, Rome (Seminar in EC Law, 1992); Belgium, College of Europe, Bruges (LL.M. in EC Law, 1993).

FREDERICO TORZO, born Venice, Italy, November 5, 1966; admitted to practice, 1990; admitted to bar, 1993, Italy. *Education:* Italy, University of Bologna, Doctor of Jurisprudence, maxima cum laude (1990), and Seminar in International Relations (1990). *Member:* Italian Bar Association (Milan).

MICAELA DI BENEDETTI, born Rome, Italy, June 20, 1966; admitted to practice, 1993, Italy. *Education:* Italy, University of Rome (Doctor of Jurisprudence, 1993); England, University of East Anglia in Norwich (1990-1991); Professorial Assistant of Comparative Law, University of Rome (1993-1994); Scientific Collaborator, Center of Comparative and Foreign Law Studies, Unidroit, Rome (1991-1994).

PAOLO VALENTI, born Milan, Italy, August 27, 1968; admitted to practice, 1993, Italy. *Education:* Italy, University of Rome (Doctor of Jurisprudence, 1993); U.S.A., Academy of American and International Law, The Southwestern Legal Foundation, Dallas, 1994.

Languages: Italian, English, French, German and Spanish.

MAGRONE E ARDITO

VIA DEL BANCO DI S. SPIRITO, 42
00186 ROME, ITALY
Telephone: (06) 6879962
Telex: 611416 ITALAW
Telecopier (Gr. 2-3): (06) 6751240

Milan, Italy Office: Via Borgonuovo, 20. Telephone: (02) 6575181. Telecopier (Gr. 2-3): (02) 6570013.
Turin, Italy Office: Via Bruno Buozzi, 10. Telephone: (011) 5623801. Telecopier (Gr. 2-3): (011) 3101043.
Brussels, Belgium Office: 13 Av. De Tervuren. Telephone: (02) 7359442. Telecopier (Gr. 2-3): (02) 7359622.

General, International and Domestic Practice.

GIANDOMENICO MAGRONE, born Rome, Italy, December 25, 1929; admitted, 1954, Italy; 1968, Supreme Court. *Education:* University of Rome (J.D., 1951). (Also at Turin Office). *LANGUAGES:* Italian and English. *PRACTICE AREAS:* Corporate; Litigation; Arbitration; Bankruptcy; Antitrust.

LIVIA MAGRONE FURLOTTI, born Catania, Italy, September 11, 1933; admitted, 1961, Italy; 1982, Supreme Court. *Education:* University of Rome (J.D., 1957). *Member:* U.I.A. *LANGUAGES:* Italian, English and

(This Listing Continued)

French. *PRACTICE AREAS:* Corporate; Patent and Trademark; Antitrust; EC; Aviation; Telecommunication.

G. MASSIMILIANO DANUSSO, born Rome, Italy, December 14, 1958; admitted, 1984, Italy. *Education:* University of Rome (J.D., 1981; S.J.D., 1988); City of London Polytechnic (Advanced Certificate, Private English Law, 1983); Seminar in American Legal Studies, Salzburg, 1984; University of Michigan Law School (LL.M., 1988). Visiting Foreign Lawyer: Steptoe & Johnson, Washington, D.C., 1988-1989; Reed Smith Shaw & McClay, Pittsburgh, 1989. *LANGUAGES:* Italian, English and French. *PRACTICE AREAS:* Corporate; Oil and Gas; Banking and Project Financing.

CRISTOFORO OSTI, born Genoa, Italy, April 18, 1959; admitted, 1986, Italy; 1987, New York. *Education:* University of Rome (J.D., 1981); University of Michigan Law School (LL.M., 1985). Trainee, General Directorate of Competition of the EEC Commission, 1981-1982. Visiting Foreign Lawyer: Olwine, Connelly, Chase, O'Donnell & Weyher, New York, 1985-1986; Feddersen Laule Scherzberg & Ohle Hansen Ewerwahn, Berlin, 1992. Lecturer, Economic Analysis of Law and Antitrust Law, L.U.I.S.S. University, Rome, 1994—. *Member:* The Association of the Bar of The City of New York; American Bar Association. *LANGUAGES:* Italian, English, German and French. *PRACTICE AREAS:* Antitrust; Corporate.

ROBERTO DONNINI, born Rome, Italy, July 29, 1960; admitted, 1988, Italy. *Education:* University of Rome (J.D., 1985); Tulane Law School (M.C.L., 1986). Seminars on International Law at The Hague Academy, 1987. Visiting Foreign Lawyer: Coudert Brothers, New York (1990-1991). *LANGUAGES:* Italian, English, French and German. *PRACTICE AREAS:* Corporate; Labour; Arbitration.

PRISCILLA PETTITI, born Rome, Italy, June 28, 1963; admitted, 1990, Italy. *Education:* University of Rome, Italy (J.D., 1987); Duke University Summer Institute in Transnational Law, Copenhagen, 1987-1988. Trainee, Legal Service of the EEC Commission, 1989. *LANGUAGES:* Italian, English and Danish. *PRACTICE AREAS:* Corporate; Industrial Property.

MARGHERITA BIANCHINI, born Macerata, Italy, July 7, 1963; admitted, 1990, Italy. *Education:* University of Macerata (J.D., 1987); University of Rome (Civil Law, Scholarship, 1991); University of Heidelberg (1993). *LANGUAGES:* Italian, German and English. *PRACTICE AREAS:* Civil Law; Corporate.

STEFANO SACCHETTO, born Bossano del Grappa, Italy, May 23, 1960; admitted, 1991, Italy. *Education:* University of Bologna (J.D., 1985). *LANGUAGES:* Italian and English. *PRACTICE AREAS:* Administrative Law; Public Works; Environmental.

ANDREA VALLI, born Rome, Italy, February 27, 1964; admitted, 1992, Italy. *Education:* Libera Universita' Internazionale degli Studi Sociali, Rome (J.D., 1989); EC Law Courses, Universite' Libre de Bruxelles (1990); University of London, Queen Mary and Westfield College (LL.M., 1991); Georgetown University Law Center, Washington, D.C. (1994). Trainee, General Directorate of Competition of the EEC Commission (1989-1990). Visiting Foreign Lawyer: Wilkinson, Barker, Knauer & Quinn, Washington, D.C. (1994). *LANGUAGES:* Italian, English and French. *PRACTICE AREAS:* Antitrust; Telecommunications; Arbitration.

RICCARDO SALLUSTIO, born Naples, Italy, May 3, 1966; admitted, 1993, Italy. *Education:* University of Naples (J.D., 1990); Queen Mary and Westfield College, University of London (LL.M., 1991); International Trade Law Diploma (Turin) 1993. Visiting Foreign Lawyer: Clyde & Co. Solicitors, London, 1991; Withers Solicitors, London, 1991-1993. *LANGUAGES:* Italian and English. *PRACTICE AREAS:* Corporate; Insurance; Project Financing.

WALTER VASSELLI, born Rome, Italy, October 14, 1966; admitted, 1994, Italy. *Education:* University of Perugia (J.D., 1993). *LANGUAGES:* Italian and English. *PRACTICE AREAS:* Oil and Gas Law; Environmental Law.

MARIA CARLA DE GIOVANNI, born Cagliari, Italy, September 4, 1967. *Education:* University of Rome, Italy (J.D., 1994). *LANGUAGES:* Italian, English, French and Spanish. *PRACTICE AREAS:* Corporate; Antitrust; Administrative Law.

ISABELLA TOTH, born Modena, Italy, October 3, 1968. *Education:* University of Bologna (J.D., 1992); University of California at Berkeley (LL.M., 1994). *LANGUAGES:* Italian, English and French. *PRACTICE AREAS:* Corporate; Antitrust Law.

(This Listing Continued)

MAGRONE E ARDITO, Rome—Continued

COUNSEL

LAURA RAINALDI, born L'Aquila, Italy, September 9, 1947; admitted, 1974, Italy; 1990, Supreme Court. *Education:* University of Rome (J.D., 1971). Appointments, Assistant Professor of Administrative Law, University of Rome, 1980—. *LANGUAGES:* Italian and French. *PRACTICE AREAS:* Administrative Law; Environmental.

RESIDENTS AT MILAN OFFICE

Mario Ardito	Paola Fazzalari
Cesare Lanciani	Roberto Nicastro
Oscar Podda	Silvia Calaresu
Francesco Abbozzo Franzi	Antonio Zangara
Luca Minoli	Duccio Ney

Languages: Italian, English, German, French and Spanish.

(For Biographical Data on Attorneys resident in Milan, see Professional Biographies at Ardito e Magrone, Milan, Italy)

MAZZETTI ROSSI E ASSOCIATI

VIA DI MONTE GIORDANO 36
00186 ROME, ITALY
Telephone: 6-68803543
Telefax: 6-68805144

Milan, Italy Office: Via Manzoni 9, 20121. Telephone: 2-72023958 or 2-878891. Telefax: 2-865877. Resident: Claudio Migliorisi, LL.M.

General Practice, Industrial, Commercial, Corporate, Mergers and Acquisitions, Banking, Labor, EC, Environment, Publishing, Proprietory Rights, Entertainment, Commercial Arbitration and Litigation, Cultural Property.

LEOPOLDO MAZZETTI, born Siena, February 15, 1931; admitted, 1962. *Education:* University of Florence (J.D.); Fellow, Salzburg Seminar in American Studies.

MAURIZIO ROSSI, born Rome, Italy, March 8, 1956; admitted, 1983. *Education:* University of Rome (J.D.).

ENRICO PAMPHILI, born Rome, Italy, August 16, 1955; admitted, 1983. *Education:* University of Rome (J.D.). *Member:* International Association of Entertainment Lawyers.

FABIO MASSIMO MISSORI, born Rome, Italy, September 17, 1958; admitted, 1986. *Education:* University of Rome (J.D.); Salzburg Seminar in American Studies (1989); Orientation Program in The U.S. Legal System, International Law Institute, Washington, D.C. (1990); Georgetown University School of Law (LL.M., 1991).

MASSIMILIANO MARINOZZI, born Rome, Italy, April 23, 1966. *Education:* University of Rome (J.D.).

VITTORIANA MEGNA, born Lecce, Italy, August 21, 1966; admitted, 1993. *Education:* University of Rome (J.D.).

ANNA MARCANTONIO, born Chieti, Italy, July 26, 1965; admitted, 1993. *Education:* University of Rome (J.D.).

GIUSEPPINA MARCANTONI, born Rozzano (Milan), Italy, August 14, 1965. *Education:* University of Rome (J.D.).

CARLA VECCHINI, born Rome, Italy, May 24, 1970. *Education:* University of Rome (J.D.).

GABRIELE TRAVAGLINI, born Rome, Italy, May 5, 1967. *Education:* University of Rome (J.D.).

Languages: Italian, English, French, German and Spanish.

STUDIO LEGALE MOTTOLA & CONTE

Established in 1961

VIA MARZIALE, 36
00136 ROME, ITALY
Telephone: (06) 39735265; (06) 39736905
Fax: (06) 39735265

General Practice. Commercial Law, Arbitration, Contracts, International Private Law, Family, Succession, Will and Testament, Bankruptcy, Insurance and Third Party Liability, Property and Real Estate, Recovery of Debts, Child Abduction and Custody.

(This Listing Continued)

FIRM PROFILE: The Firm was established in 1961. The Clients are Italian, British, Swedish, Australian, Maltese, Canadian and U.S. citizens.

MEMBERS OF FIRM

MARIA RAFFAELLA MOTTOLA, born Barletta, Italy, December 7, 1931; admitted, 1961, Italy; 1975, Italian Supreme Courts. *Education:* University of Rome, Law School, Italy (Doctor of Jurisprudence, maxima cum laude, 1955). Legal Adviser to the British Ambassador. On the list of Lawyers of: British, Swedish, Canadian, Maltese, U.S.A. Consulates. *LANGUAGES:* Italian, English and French. *PRACTICE AREAS:* General Practice; Commercial Law; Contracts; Family; Succession; Property; Real Estate; Civil Arbitration; Child Abduction and Custody.

FRANCESCO CONTE, born Montemilone, Potenza, Italy, March 26, 1925; admitted, 1949, Italy; 1958, Italian Supreme Courts. *Education:* University of Bari, Italy (Doctor of Jurisprudence). *LANGUAGES:* Italian and English. *PRACTICE AREAS:* Bankruptcy; Insurance and Third Party Liability; Recovery of Debts.

ASSOCIATE

ALESSANDRA PASSERINI, born Rome, Italy, September 23, 1962; admitted, 1992, Italy. *Education:* University of Rome (Doctor of Jurisprudence, maxima cum laude, 1987); Academy of International Law, The Hague, 1989. *LANGUAGES:* Italian, English and German. *PRACTICE AREAS:* General Practice; Family; Succession; Recovery of Debts; Contracts.

Languages: Italian, English, French and German

REPRESENTATIVE CLIENTS: Australian Embassy; British Embassy; British Embassy to the Holy See; British Tourist Authority; British Council; British School at Rome; Malta Embassy; Swedish Embassy; Swedish Embassy to the Holy See; Swedish Byggnadsstrylesen; Eli Lilly Italia, S.p.A.; Nobel Foundation; Wellcome Italia S.p.A.; Liechtenstein Anstalts; Università Cattolica del Sacro Cuore; Assitalia; Le Assicurazioni d'Italia S.p.A., Roma; Riunione Adriatica di Sicurtà S.p.A., Roma; L'Italica S.p.A., Roma; Lavoro & Sicurtà S.p.A., Roma.
REFERENCE: Mr. Roemer McPhee, Hamel & Park, Washington, D.C.

STUDIO LEGALE PAOLETTI

9 VIA SANT' ALBERTO MAGNO
00153 ROME, ITALY
Telephone: (06) 5744021, 2, 3, 4
Telex: 622077 AVELAW I
Facsimile: (06) 5746021

Milan, Italy Office: 20 Piazza Castello, 20121. Telephone: (02) 878789, 878570. Facsimile: (02) 878643.

General Civil Practice, Admiralty, Litigation and Arbitration, International and Commercial Practice, Corporate Law, Patents, Trademarks and Foreign Investments, Family Law, Law of New Technologies (Genetic Engineering, Computer Law), Oil and Gas Law.

MEMBERS OF FIRM

CARLO PAOLETTI (1909-1980).

FABRIZIO PAOLETTI, born Rome, Italy, June 20, 1935; admitted, 1961, Rome; 1979, Italian Supreme Courts. *Education:* University of Rome (J.D., 1958). *Member:* Albo Avvocati e Procuratori di Roma. *LANGUAGES:* Italian and English.

GAETANO SEVERINI, born Cetraro, Italy, January 23, 1948; admitted, 1975, Rome; 1993, Italian Supreme Court. *Education:* University of Rome (J.D., 1971). *Member:* Albo Avvocati e Procuratori di Roma. *LANGUAGES:* Italian and English.

FABRIZIO PIETROSANTI, born Rome, Italy, May 11, 1951; admitted, 1979, Italy. *Education:* University of Rome, Institute of Comparative Law (J.D., magna cum laude, 1976). Note Editor, Foro Italiano, 1977-1990. Author: "Espropriazione in Favore del Proprietario," 1983, "Espropriabilità del Diritto del Conduttore?," 1984 and "Indennità di Esproprio e Criteri di Determinazione," 1985, all published in Foro Italiano. *Member:* Albo Avvocati e Procuratori di Roma. . *LANGUAGES:* Italian and English.

ASSOCIATES

MAURIZIO PAGANELLI, born Bari, Italy, August 14, 1959; admitted, 1988, Bari. *Education:* University of Bari (J.D., magna cum laude, 1984); Yale Law School (Visiting Scholar, 1988-1989). Note Editor, Foro Italiano, 1982-1990. Author: "Pagamento di Premio Assicurativo e Principio di Buona Fede," I, 2051, 1985, "La Vicenda 'Cattenom' e la Disciplina 'Esagonale' Degli Effluenti Radioattivi," IV 484, 1987, " I Parenti Poveri

(This Listing Continued)

dell 'Etere," I, 347, 1989 and "Alla volta di Frankenstein: le Biotecnologie e la Proprietà (di parti) del Corpo," IV, 417, 1989, all published in Foro Italiano. Researcher, Energy Law, Institute of Comparative Law, University of Bari, 1985-1987. *Member:* Albo Procuratori di Roma. *LANGUAGES:* Italian, English and French.

OF COUNSEL

ERIK J. WATTEN, born Oslo, Norway, March 3, 1939; admitted, 1965, Oslo, Norway (Not admitted in Italy). *Education:* RIIS, Oslo (1957); Oslo University (1964). Norwegian Foreign Service, V. Consul Milan, Italy, 1965-1968. Norwegian Foreign Service, Attachee, Lagos, 1968. *LANGUAGES:* Scandinavian, German, English, Italian and French.

REPRESENTATIVE CLIENTS: International Golf Corporation, Djarkata, Indonesia; Dyno Industrier A/S, Oslo, Norway, Norges Rederforbund (Norway Shipowners' Association) Oslo, Norway; NFT (ex Kongsberg), Kongsberg, Norway; Sysscan SpA, Rome, Italy; ELF Italia SpA, Rome, Italy; ACI (Automobil Association of Italy), Rome, Italy; Toro Insurance Co., Turin, Italy; Auselda AED Group SpA, Rome, Italy; Norapp A/S, Oslo, Norway; Alumix S.p.A. (Gruppo Efim); Simrad Albatroes A/S, Kongsberg, Norway; Skandia AB, Sweden; Global Petrochemical, N.Y.C.; DNB Finans A/S, Norway; N.C.T., Norway; City of Stavanger, Norway.
REFERENCES: The Royal Norwegian Embassy in Italy; D.S.C. Srl, Milan, Italy; Mr. Robert K. Stevens, Department of State, Washington D.C. USA; Nuovi Cantieri Apuania SpA (GEPI Group), Massa Carrara, Italy; Fiduciaria Antonini SAn Lugano, Switzerland; Aeronavale Spa; Smosarski & Partner (London); Istituto Bancario San Paolo Di Torino.

PAVIA ANSALDO e VERUSIO

Established in 1961

FORO TRAIANO 1/A
00187 ROME, ITALY
Telephone: 6-6780052
Cable Address: "Counsel"
Telex: 611322
Telecopier: 6-6790005

Milan, Italy Office: Via dell'Annunciata 7, 20121. Telephone 2-63381. Cable Address: "Pavialaw". Telex: 320386. Telecopier 2-653306 or 2-28100308.
Padua, Italy Office: Corso Milano 26, 35139. Telephone: 49-8756070. Telecopier: 49-8756077.
Turin, Italy Office: Via Vittorio Amedeo II, 19, 10121. Telephone: 11-5359.22; 11-5359.21. Telecopier: 11-530.504.
New York, N.Y. Office: 600 Madison Avenue, 10022. Telephone: (212) 980-1633. Telex: 66146. Telecopier: (212) 980-1453.

General Practice. Industrial, Commercial, Corporate, Mergers and Acquisitions, Banking, Capital Markets, Corporate Restructuring, EC, Environment, Entertainment, Proprietary Rights, Commercial Arbitration and Litigation.

GIOVANNI VERUSIO, born Florence, October 27, 1932; admitted, 1957, Italy. *Education:* University of Florence (J.D); Harvard University Law School (LL.M ., 1956).

GIAN PAOLO ZANCHINI, born Rome, August 26, 1939; admitted, 1964, Italy. *Education:* University of Rome (J.D., 1962).

ALBERTO FELICIANI, born Terni, May 27, 1942; admitted, 1970, Italy. *Education:* University of Perugia (J.D., 1966).

GIORGIO COSMELLI, born Rome, December 22, 1942; admitted, 1972, Italy. *Education:* University of Palermo Law School (J.D.).

ERNESTO IRACE, born Naples, November 11, 1949; admitted, 1974, Italy. *Education:* University of Naples (J.D).

MARIO AMOROSO, born Naples, August 28, 1950; admitted, 1975, Italy. *Education:* University of Naples (J.D); New York University (M.C.J., 1975). Assistant Professor, University of Naples.

GIULIANO BERRUTI, born Rome, June 15, 1956; admitted, 1980, Italy. *Education:* University of Rome (J.D.).

PAOLO BERRUTI, born Rome, June 15, 1956; admitted, 1982, Italy. *Education:* University of Rome (J.D.).

MAURIZIO VASCIMINNI, born Rome, April 4, 1959; admitted, 1986, Italy. *Education:* University of Rome (J.D.).

DOMENICO TULLI, born Pescara, September 27, 1959; admitted, 1986, Italy. *Education:* University of Bologna, Italy (J.D.); Southwestern Legal Foundation, Dallas (1989).

(This Listing Continued)

PAOLO PONTECORVI, born Sezze, April 26, 1960; admitted, 1990, Italy. *Education:* University of Rome (J.D.).

GIOVANNA GIANSANTE, born Rome, July 22, 1961; admitted, 1990, Italy. *Education:* University of Rome (J.D.).

RODOLFO MANCINI, born Rome, December 24, 1961; admitted, 1990, Italy. *Education:* University of Rome (J.D.).

ALESSANDRO MAURIZI, born Perugia, February 23, 1962; admitted, 1989, Italy. *Education:* University of Rome (J.D.).

FULVIA ASTOLFI, born Rome, July 12, 1963; admitted, 1990, Italy. *Education:* University of Rome (J.D.).

FRANCESCA MASTROIANNI, born Rome, July 10, 1964; admitted, 1993, Italy. *Education:* University of Rome (J.D.).

GIANDOMENICO CIARAMELLA, born Naples, June 17, 1965; admitted, 1990, Italy. *Education:* University of Rome (J.D.).

EMMA ALESII, born l'Aquila, September 21, 1966; admitted, 1993, Italy. *Education:* LUISS University, Rome (J.D.).

ANDREA MAZZIOTTI DI CELSO, born Rome, December 31, 1966; admitted, 1990, Italy. *Education:* L.U.I.S.S., Rome (J.D.).

OF COUNSEL

ENRICO BUGLIELLI, born Rome, November 30, 1921; admitted, 1948, Italy. *Education:* University of Rome (J.D.).

Languages: English, French, German, Spanish and Russian.

PIERGROSSI VILLA MANCA GRAZIADEI

VIA DEI GRACCHI 320
00192 ROME, ITALY
Telephone: +39-6-321.5901
Telefax: +39-6-321.3218

Milan, Italy Office: Via Festa del Perdono 10, 20122 Milano. Telephone: +39-2-58303657 (multiple). Fax: +39-2-58303818.
Edinburgh, Scotland Office: 3 Walker Street, Edinburgh, EH3 7JY. Telephone: +44-131-2267722. Fax:+44-131-2267887.

General Civil and Commercial Practice. Acquisitions, Corporate, Licensing, Patents and Trademarks, International Law. Litigation. Arbitration. Environmental Law, EEC Law.

MEMBERS OF FIRM

GIANNI MANCA, born Genoa, Italy, July 21, 1924; admitted, 1952, Italy. *Education:* University of Rome Law School, Italy (J.D., 1948).

ALBERTO PIERGROSSI, born Milan, Italy, August 8, 1941; admitted, 1966, Italy. *Education:* University of Milan Law School, Italy (J.D., 1963); Harvard Law School (LL.M., 1967). Professor of Law, University of Milan Law School.

FRANCO P. VILLA, born Legnano, Italy, March 3, 1941; admitted, 1968, Italy. *Education:* University of Milan Law School, Italy (J.D., 1965); Reading University, England (M.A., 1967).

STEFANO M. CIMA, born Milan, Italy, April 4, 1954; admitted, 1980, Italy. *Education:* University of Milan Law School, Italy (J.D., 1977); University of Milan School of Political Science, Italy (1987).

FRANCESCO AMICUCCI, born Rome, Italy, February 25, 1955; admitted, 1985, Italy. *Education:* University of Rome Law School, Italy (J.D., 1980) University of Charleston, West Virginia (Diploma of Business Law, 1986).

ANTONIO JACOPO MANCA GRAZIADEI, born Rome, Italy, April 5, 1958; admitted, 1989, Italy. *Education:* University of Rome Law School (J.D., 1985).

FABIO WEILBACHER, born Genoa, Italy, November 3, 1960; admitted, 1992, Italy. *Education:* Catholic University of Milan Law School, Italy (J.D., 1984).

RICCARDO BUIZZA, born Varese, Italy, February 26, 1962; admitted, 1991, Italy. *Education:* University of Milan Law School, Italy (J.D., 1985).

ASSOCIATES

ANTONIO F. LOMBARDO, born Trapani, Italy, August 17, 1965; admitted, 1992, Italy. *Education:* Luiss University of Rome Law School, Italy (J.D., 1989).

(This Listing Continued)

PIERGROSSI VILLA MANCA GRAZIADEI, Rome—
Continued

FRANCESCO M. ALEANDRI, born Rome, Italy, February 14, 1965; admitted, 1992, Italy. *Education:* University of Rome Law School, Italy (J.D., 1989).

MASSIMILIANO PINNA, born Sassari, October 14, 1964; admitted, 1992, Italy. *Education:* University of Sassari Law School, Italy, (J.D., 1989).

LORENZO DA PRA GALANTI, born Milan, Italy, June 16, 1963; admitted, 1994, Italy. *Education:* University of Milan Law School, Italy (J.D., 1991).

OF COUNSEL

ARMANDO PIERGROSSI, born Milan, Italy, June 14, 1914; admitted, 1946, Italy. *Education:* University of Milan Law School, Italy (J.D., 1937).

Languages: Italian, English, French, German and Spanish.

PISANO, DE VITO, MAIANO & CATUCCI

Established in 1961

VIA G. BORSI, 3
00197 ROME, ITALY
Telephone: (06) 8079087
Telex: 626448 PDMCRM
Telefax: (06) 8078407

Milan, Italy Office: Piazza del Duomo, 20. Telephone: (02) 878281. Telex: 321289. Telefax: (02) 861375.

General Domestic and International Business Practice, including Commercial, Corporate, Securities and Corporate Finance, Venture Capital, Commercial Litigation, Arbitration, EEC Law, Taxation, Intellectual Property, Maritime and Aviation Law.

MEMBERS OF FIRM

PAOLO G. PISANO, born Chicago, Illinois, September 16, 1915; admitted, 1945, Italy; 1948, Italian Supreme Court. *Education:* Liceo Umberto, Palermo (A.B., 1933); University of Rome, School of Jurisprudence (J.S.D., 1937); University of Florence, School of Political Science (P.S.D., 1938). Assistant Professor of International Law, University of Rome, 1938-1945. *Member:* Rome and International Bar Associations. (Also at Milan Office). *LANGUAGES:* English, Italian, French and Spanish.

PAOLO V. DE VITO, born Rome, Italy, July 10, 1953. admitted to practice, 1979; admitted to the bar, 1980, Italy. *Education:* University of Rome, Faculty of Law (Doctor Juridical Science, Maxima, 1977); University of California, Dans-Berkeley (Orientation in American Law Program, 1993). *Member:* Rome Bar Association. (Also at Milan Office). *LANGUAGES:* Italian and English.

MAURIZIO M. A. MAIANO, born Sanremo, Italy, December 20, 1956. admitted to practice, 1979, Italy; admitted to the bar, 1983, Italy. *Education:* University of London, Exeter College (Advanced Certificate of Education in Economics and British Constitutional Law, 1975); University of Milan, Faculty of Law (Doctor Juridical Science, Maxima, 1979); McGeorge School of Law, Salzburg, Austria (Diploma in Advanced International Legal Studies, 1987); University of the Pacific, McGeorge School of Law, Sacramento, California (LL.M., Business and Taxation - Transnational Pracice, 1989); Bocconi University, Milan (Master in Corporate Taxation, 1990). Visiting Attorney, Attia, Bartel, Eng & Torngren, Sacramento, California, 1988. *Member:* State Bar of California (Member, International Section); Milan and American Bar Associations; A.I.J.A. (Also at Milan Office). *LANGUAGES:* English, Italian and French.

ANTONIO CATUCCI, born Palagianello, Italy, June 14, 1956. admitted to practice, 1979, Italy; admitted to bar, 1983, Italy. *Education:* University of Rome, Faculty of Law (Doctor Juridical Science, 1979); Harvard Law School (P.I.L., 1991 and 1992). *Member:* Milan Bar Association; International Bar Association. (Also at Milan Office). *LANGUAGES:* Italian, English and Spanish..

COUNSELS

MASSIMO DE CAROLIS, born Milan, Italy, August 15, 1940; admitted, 1965, Italy. *Education:* Catholic University of Milan, Faculty of Law (Doctor Juridical Science, 1962). Member of Italian Parliament, 1976-1983. Secretary of Parliamentary Investigating Committee on Misconduct of
(This Listing Continued)

Ministers, 1976-1979. Member, Foreign Affairs Committee of the Italian Parliament, 1979-1983. Member, North Atlantic Treaty Organization Assembly, 1980-1983. Municipal Councillor, City of Milan, 1970-1980 and 1990-1993. Member, Board of Advisors, Montedison Spa, 1971-1978. Member, Board of Directors, Montedison U.S.A., Inc., N.Y., 1978-1982. Member, Board of Directors, Navamont, Inc., N.Y., 1978-1980. Member, Board of Directors, Chemstar International, Inc., N.Y., 1980-1984. Managing Director, Fidinvest Spa, Milan, 1967—. (Also at Milan Office). *LANGUAGES:* Italian and English.

MARINA TAGER, Special Legal Counsel for Eastern European Countries. (Also at Milan Office). *LANGUAGES:* Russian, Italian, German and English.

ASSOCIATES

LAURA CAVALLARI, admitted to the bar, 1993, Italy. University of Milan, Tutor of Civil Law. (Also at Milan Office).

MARCO VINCIGUERRA (Also at Milan Office).

GIOVANNI IMBERGAMO, admitted to the bar, 1993, Italy. (Also at Milan Office).

STEFANO BOTTARO (Also at Rome Office).

MARIA ELENA LORETI (Also at Rome Office).

TAX AND BUSINESS CONSULTANT

Wilson Gomitoni (C.P.A.) (Also at Milan Office)

Languages: Italian, English, French, Portuguese, Spanish, German and Russian.

QUATTRONE CUCCHI LAZZATI & SCURIATTI
STUDIO LEGALE E TRIBUTARISTA

VIA FILIPPO CIVININI 111
00197 ROME, ITALY
Telephone: (6) 8085460-8081148
Fax: (6) 8072793

Milan, Italy Office: Via Fontana 16, 20122. Telephone: (2) 5460991. Fax: (2) 5460970.

Corporate, International Financial Transaction, Banking and Securities Law, Foreign Investments, Subsidiaries and Joint Ventures, Tax Law, EEC Law, Antitrust Law, Software and Telecommunications Law, Labour Law and Litigation.

PARTNERS

Avv. Antonio Diego Quattrone
Avv. Frederick Cucchi, MA (Oxon).
Dott. Proc. Maurizio Campolo
Dott. Lorenzo Faustini
Dott. Claudio Scuriatti

ASSOCIATES

Dott. Proc. Anna Maria Manifredi
Dott. Proc. Alessandro di Napoli
Dott. Francesco Venditti
Dott. Edoardo Sansoni
Dott. Luca Scuriatti

Languages: Italian, English, German, French and Dutch.

STUDIO Dell'AVV. GIULIO ROSAUER

Established in 1976

VIA UMBRIA, 7
00187 ROME, ITALY
Telephone: 4818321
Cable Address: "Rosalex Roma"
Telecopier: 4871242

General Civil and International Business Practice, Corporate, European Economic Community and Domestic Antitrust Law, Arbitration.

GIULIO ROSAUER, born Rome, Italy, April 9, 1935; admitted, 1960, Rome; 1976, Italian Supreme Court. *Education:* Rome University (LL.D.,
(This Listing Continued)

1958). Author: "Le regole di concorrenza nel sistema giuridico delle Comunità Europee: raffronto tra le norme stabilite al riguardo dal Trattato C.E.C.A. e dal Trattato C.E.E.," Rivista di Diritto Europeo, 1964; "L'orientamento della Commissione della Comunità Economica Europea in materia di contratti di esclusiva," Annuario di Diritto Comparato e di Studi Legislativi, 1966; "La giurisprudenza della Corte di Giustizia delle Comunità Europee in tema di contratti di esclusiva," Rivista di Diritto Industriale, 1966; "The proposed reform of the Italian Tax System," Italian American Business, 1968; "An outline of the new Italian Tax System," Italian American Business, 1974; "Le limitazioni della concorrenza nei c.d.: contratti di licenza," Rivista di Diritto Industriale, 1976; "L'accertamento delle infrazioni alle norme comunitarie sulla concorrenza," Rivista di Diritto Industriale, 1982. Lecturer, Corporate Law, Trusts and Cartels, American Universities Field Staff, Center for Mediterranean Studies, 1974. Assistant to the U.S. Representative on the Italian U.S. Conciliation Commission, 1960.

ASSOCIATES

FRANCESCA LODIGIANI, born S. Margherita Ligure, Italy, June 24, 1954; admitted, 1981, Genoa, Italy. *Education:* Genoa University (LL.D., 1978).

SERGIO LA VIA, born Rome, Italy, July 18, 1963; admitted, 1993, Rome, Italy. *Education:* Rome University (LL.D., 1989).

Languages: Italian, English, French and German.

REPRESENTATIVE CLIENTS: Agency for International Development; American Broadcasting Co.; Chicago Bridge & Iron Co.; Chrysler Corporation - Marine Products; Charles of the Ritz Group Ltd.; Dunfey Family Corp.; Getty Oil Co.; Kaiser Engineers, Inc.; Marriott Corp.; McQuay Inc.; Modtronio, Inc.; Northwestern National Bank of Minneapolis; Olin Corp.; Thomson McKinnon Securities, Inc.; U.S. Feed Grains Council; Warner Bros. International Television Distribution. *Belgium:* Banque Bruxelles Lambert; Pneu Uniroyal Englebert S.A. *Canada:* Northern Telecom Limited; Scarboro Resources Limited. *France:* Clarins S.A.; Préservatrice Foncière TIARD Compagnies d'Assurances; Union Laitiere Normande; Yves Saint Laurent Parfums S.A. *Holland:* Ceteco Trading and Industrial Corp.; Diepvries Breskens B.V. *Japan:* Kawasho Corp. *Luxembourg:* Société Européenne de Banque. *Sweden:* Sala International AB. *United Kingdom:* Associated Container Transportation (Australia) Limited; Bunzl Pulp & Paper Ltd.; Dan-Air Services Limited; Filtrona International Limited; H.P. Bulmer Ltd.; Mountleigh Group plc.; The Rank Organization Ltd.

STUDIO LEGALE SABELLI

VIA PARIGI, 11
00185 ROME, ITALY
Telephone: 06-4817141
Telefax: (06) 4884566

Milan, Italy Office: Via S. Maurilio, 20, 20123. Telephone: 02-8056042. Telefax: (02) 8692571.

General and Civil Practice. Corporation, Commercial, Tax, Industrial Property, Europen Economic Community, Real Estate, Financial and Economic Consulting.

MEMBERS OF FIRM

ALDO SABELLI, born Campobasso, Italy, May 10, 1929; admitted, 1952, Italy; 1979, admitted as Legal Consultant, State of New York. *Education:* Rome University. Author: "How to Form a Company in Italy—A Guide for Foreign Investors," 1977. *Member:* Italian Bar Association. *LANGUAGES:* Italian and English.

LEONARDO CAPPUCCILLI, born Ripabottoni, Italy, June 2, 1927; admitted, 1956, Italy. *Education:* Rome University. *Member:* Italian Bar Association. *LANGUAGES:* Italian and English.

ADRIANO GIUFFRE', born Nocera Inferiore, Italy, October 28, 1938; admitted, 1981, Supreme Court of Cassation. *Education:* Rome and Sassari Universities. Assistant Professor, Universities Sassari, Modena and Rome. *Member:* Italian Bar Association. *LANGUAGES:* Italian, English and French.

GAETANO IACONO, born Gela, Italy, March 26, 1939; admitted, 1985, Supreme Court of Cassation. *Education:* Rome University. Stage CEE, Bruxelles, 1964. Secretary, Young Lawyers Conference, 1969. *Member:* Italian Bar Association. *LANGUAGES:* Italian, English and French.

SALVATORE LUISE, born Naples, Italy, February 25, 1961; admitted, 1988, Italy. *Education:* Naples University (J.D., 1984); London Polytechnic Certificate in International Law, 1989; Summer Program in American Law, Leyden, Amsterdam, 1990. *Member:* Italian Bar Association. *LANGUAGES:* Italian and English.

(This Listing Continued)

ROBERTO MUSELLA, born Sora (FR), Italy, August 20, 1962; admitted, 1991, Italy. *Education:* Rome University (J.D., 1985). *Member:* Italian Bar Association. *LANGUAGES:* Italian and English.

ANDREA SABELLI, born Rome, Italy, February 18, 1958. *LANGUAGES:* Italian, Spanish and English.

LUCA SABELLI, born Rome, Italy, May 15, 1960. *Education:* Rome University, University of Illinois (Master in Comparative Law). Co-author: "International Franchising Law," 1992. *LANGUAGES:* Italian and English.

DANIELA SABELLI, born Campobasso, Italy, June 8, 1966. *Education:* Rome III University (J.D., 1992). *LANGUAGES:* Italian and English.

STUDIO LEGALE SANGIORGI

Established in 1960

PIAZZA CAMPITELLI 16
00186 ROME, ITALY
Telephone: (6) 6865469
Cable Address: SANLAW
Telecopier: (6) 6865256

General Civil Practice, Corporate, Contracts, International Business Transactions and Civil Litigation, Telecommunications Law.

GIORGIO SANGIORGI, born Rome, Italy, May 23, 1930; admitted, 1958, Rome; 1964, Italy; 1972, Supreme Court. *Education:* University of Siena (J.D., 1954). Author: "The Engineer in Italy and Abroad." Lecturer: Salzburg, American Law, 1969; Harvard Law School, American Law, 1972. Contributor, Temi Romana, Rivista delle Società, Il Fallimento, Giurisprudenza Commerciale (Reorganization). *Member:* Italian Bar Association (Board of Editors Rassegna Forense); Rome Bar Association (Committee for International Law and Practice). *LANGUAGES:* Italian, English and French.

MUZIO CENTI COLELLA, born Aquila, Italy, March 22, 1932; admitted, 1958, Rome; 1975, Italy. *Education:* University of Rome (J.D., 1956). *LANGUAGES:* Italian and English.

MARINA VALENTINETTI, born Rome, February 1, 1949; admitted, 1978, Rome. *Education:* University of Rome. *LANGUAGES:* Italian and English.

Languages: English, French and Italian.

REFERENCES: ESSO Italiana; Credito Fondiario; Winterthur; The Medical Defence Union; Illinois State Bar Association; Foster Wheeler Italiana; V.A.P.

SINISI, CESCHINI, MANCINI & PARTNERS

Law Offices

VIA LAURINA, 40
00187 ROME, ITALY
Telephone: (39) (6) 322-1485
Telefax: (39) (6) 361-3266

Other Offices in: Milan, New York, Atlanta, Athens, Hartford and San Diego.

International and General Practice, Corporate, Mergers & Acquisitions, Joint Ventures, Taxation, Antitrust, Privatizations, Labor, Bankruptcy, Banking and Securities, Agency and Distribution, Licensing, Environmental Law, Franchising, Insurance, Shipping, Real Estates, Entertainment, Intellectual Property, Software and Telecommunications, Sports, Family Law, Wills and Estate and Litigation.

FIRM PROFILE: Sinisi, Ceschini, Mancini & Partners is an International Law Firm based in the United States and Europe. The offices outside of Italy are known under the name of Hurt, Sinisi & Papadakis. Fundamental to the firm is a committment to provide a high quality of personalized service with an excellent standard of professionalism. The United States Offices are located in the Northeast, Southeast and Western United States in order to service clients conveniently and efficiently, as well as provide full support to the firm's European Offices. The European Offices are staffed with both American and European attorneys. Each office, in Europe and the United States, has attorneys that are qualified to appear and litigate in the local courts.

(This Listing Continued)

SINISI, CESCHINI, MANCINI & PARTNERS, Rome—
Continued

MEMBERS OF FIRM

VINCENZO SINISI, born Bari, Italy, January 10, 1960; admitted, 1983, Italy. *Education:* University of Bari, Italy (J.D., magna cum laude, 1983). Yale Law School Visiting Scholar, 1985-1986. National Research Council Scholar, 1985-1986. Arbitrator, AFMA Arbitration Committee. Note Editor, Il Foro Italiano, 1982-1985. Speaker: International Bar Association 25th Biennial Conference, "Agency Distribution, Licensing and Franchising Agreements in Italy," Sydney, October, 1994; The Study Group for International Commercial Contracts, "Choice of Law and Choice of Forum in International Contracts," London, April, 1993; International Bar Association "Joint Ventures - An Italian Perspective," Tel-Aviv, 1993; Post M&A Organization, Milan, 1992; "The New Italian S.I.M. Legislation," Conference on "The New Organization of the Italian Securities Markets," London, 1991; "Financial Engineering and Tax Planning," Paris, 1991; "Film Production in Italy: Corporate, Contractual, Fiscal and Copyright Considerations Including Government Incentives," Milan, 1989; "New Financial Law Developments - An Overview on Mutual Funds, Options, Futures, Indexed Bonds and Other Financing Instruments," Milan, 1989;; "European Co-productions in Film and Television," Symposium on Film and Media Law, Munich, 1988. Author: "Co-Producing with Italy: Legal and Regulatory Issues," Co-Production International, 1994. Co-Author: "Choice of Law and International Contracts: the EEC Convention on the Law Applicable to Contractual Obligations," Corporate Counsel's International Adviser; "Franchising in Italy," Corporate Counsel's International Adviser, September, 1994; "Italian Labor Law: Collective Dismissal," Corporate Counsel's International Adviser, April, 1993; "Privatisation in Italy," Corporate Counsel's International Adviser, May, 1993; "Agency and Distribution Agreements in Italy," Corporate Counsel's International Adviser, July, 1993; "Commercial Aspects of Italian Law," Business America, October, 1992; "International Contract Manual: Italy," Kluwer Law and Taxation, 1992; "Legal Aspects of Corporate Reorganization Post M&A," and "Environmental Laws of Italy," International Environmental Law and Regulation, Butterworths, 1991; Legal Studies and Services, Ltd., Amsterdam, 1987. Researcher: Energy Law, Institute of Comparative Law, University of Bari, 1984-1985; Center for Studies in the Public Interest, 1983. *Member:* International Bar Association. (Also at Hurt, Sinisi & Papadakis, Rome, Athens and Atlanta, USA Offices). *LANGUAGES:* Italian and English.

ROBERTA CESCHINI, born Reggio Calabria, Italy, July 25, 1965; admitted, 1988, Italy. *Education:* La Sapienza University, Rome (J.D., 1988). Note Editor: Il Foro Italiano, 1988-1989. Consultant, "Rendezvous of Euroaim" (Media project) Munich, 1992. Speaker: "Death in a Rigid System," Conference on "Death and Taxes," Amsterdam, February, 1994; "The Legal Guarantees," Conference on "The different forms of public and private, cinematographic financing," Vercorin, Switzerland, July, 1993. Author: "Consulting Agreements under Italian Law, Corporate Counsel's International Adviser, October, 1994; "New Italian Cinema Law," International Association of Entertainment Lawyers, Newsletter, Summer, 1994; "Divorce Proceedings in Italy: Domestic and International Procedures," Family Law Quarterly - ABA Spring, 1994; "Registering a Trademark," Business Guide to Italy, U.S. & Foreign Commercial Service, 1994; "Image is All," and "Insync," Summer, 1993; "Opening Retail Shops in Rome," Guide to Doing Business in Rome, U.S. & Foreign Commercial Service, 1992. Co-Author: "Italian Labor Law: Collective Dismissal," Corporate Counsel's International Advisor, April 1993; "Franchising in Italy," Corporate Counsel's International Adviser, September, 1994; "Film Industry Law," Conference on Financing and Film Production, London, 1992; "Environmental Laws of Italy," International Environmental Law and Regulation, Butterworths, 1991. *Member:* International Bar Association; Women in Films and Television. (Also at Hurt, Sinisi & Papadakis, Atlanta, USA Office). *LANGUAGES:* Italian and English.

QUIRINO MANCINI, born Formia, Italy, November 8, 1961; admitted, 1987, Italy. *Education:* La Sapienza University, Rome (J.D., 1986). Speaker: Seminar on Italian/Canadian Film and Television Co-Production Deals, Cannes, May 1993. "Case Study: How to Enforce a Foreign Judgment in Italy," International Litigation Conference, Nice, February 1992. Author: "Bankruptcy of Brokerage Houses under Italian Securities Legislation," Turnarounds & Workouts Europe, March 1995; "Players as Assets of Clubs and Professional Sports - An Outlook of the Italian Situation," Sports Marketing Law & Finance, February/March 1995; "Debt Collection and Bankruptcy Issues," Turnarounds & Workouts Europe, July, 1993; Co-Author: "Privatization in Italy," Corporate Counsel's International Advisor, May, 1993; "The New Italian Legislation on Public Tender Offers (Law.

(This Listing Continued)

No. 149 of February 19, 1992: Disciplina delle offerte Pubbliche di Vendita, Sottoscrizione, Acquisto e Scambio di titoli)," Acquiring in Europe Conference, London, February 1992; "Aspetti Contrattuali nell'ambito delle Sponsorizzazioni," Speaker: NBPA (National Basketball Players Association): Eight Agent Seminar, "New Developments in Italian Sports Law," New York, 1994; "Fisco, Spese di Pubblicità, Propaganda e Rappresentanza," Milan, May 1991; "The Italian Insolvency Situation," London, October, 1990. Italian Counsel to Hambro Legal Protection Ltd.; Lecturer, Sermoneta Seminar, International Development Law Institute (I.D.L.I.), 1988-1990. Member, National Basketball Players Association. *Member:* British-Italian Lawyers Association; British Chamber of Commerce of Italy; Italian-American Law Association; International Bar Association (Country Chair for Italy of the IBA Sub-Committee J6); European Insolvency Practitioners Association; Sports Lawyers Association. (Also at Hurt, Sinisi & Papadakis, Atlanta, USA Office). *LANGUAGES:* Italian, English and French.

GIANFRANCO PUOPOLO, born Naples, Italy, February 12, 1964; admitted, 1991, Italy. *Education:* Università di Napoli, Naples (J.D., 1988); SIOI (Italian Society for the International Organization), Naples, 1989; E.N.A. (Ecole Nationale d'Administration), Paris, France (June 1989-December 1989); L.S.E. (London School of Economics), London, United Kingdom (1990). Legal Counsel, International Juridical Organization for Environment and Development, Rome, Italy, 1990-1991. Assistant Researcher, International Law, University of Naples; Chairman of Advisory Board of European Law Students Association. Speaker: NBPA (National Basketball Players Association): Eight Agent Seminar, "New Development in Italian Sports Law," Los Angeles, 1994; "Commercial Centers: Contractual Issues," Milan, 1993; "Commercial Agents: Termination of the Agency Contract," Milan, 1993; Publicity in Times of Crisis: " Analysis of Community and Italian Legislation on the Sponsorship of Radio and Television Programming," Milan, February, 1993; "An International Environmental Court within the United Nations' System," Florence, 1991. Author: "Italy greets Franchising as effective tool for expanding business," Global Franchising Alert, 1994; "Constitution d'une Société Italienne," Contract Franco-Italiens, Chambre Française de Commerce en Italie," 1993; "Privatisation en Italie," Contacts Franco-Italiens, Chambre Française de Commerce en Italie, 1993; "Il Nuovo Contratto di Agenzia," France-Italie, Chambre de Commerce Italienne pour la France, 1993; "Workers Protection in Italy," International Business Lawyer, 1992. Co-Author: "Agency and Distribution," Corporate Counsel's International Advisor, 1994; "Mutual Fund Investments in Italy," International Business Lawyer, 1993; "Legal Aspects of Corporate Reorganization Post M&A, Conference on Post M&A Organization, Milan, 1992. Member: Chambre de Commerce Italienne pour la France; Chambre de Commerce Française pour l'Italie; National Basketball Players Association. *Member:* International Bar Association. *LANGUAGES:* Italian, English and French.

NINO MATASSA, born San Giovanni Rotundo (FG), Italy, May 17, 1959; admitted, 1987, Italy. *Education:* University of Bari, Italy (J.D., magna cum laude, 1984). Yale Law School Visiting Scholar. Note Editor, Il Foro Italiano, 1982-1994. Researcher: Energy Law, Institute of Comparative Law, University of Bari, Italy, 1984-1985; Energy Law, Institute of Legal Advanced Studies, London and Dundee, 1984. Professor of Environmental Law, Puglia Region. Author: "Product Liability," Le Nuove Leggi Civili Commentate, 1989. *LANGUAGES:* Italian and English.

RENATO MOCCIA, born Bari, Italy, February 6, 1960; admitted, 1987, Italy. *Education:* University of Bari, Italy (J.D., magna cum laude, 1984). Note Editor, Il Foro Italiano, 1982-1994. Researcher, Energy Law, Institute of Comparative Law, University of Bari, Italy, 1984-1985. *LANGUAGES:* Italian and English.

ALEC PAPADAKIS, born Athens, Greece, January 27, 1947; admitted, 1979, Georgia (Not admitted in Italy). *Education:* Hartwick College, Oneonta N.Y. Ibero-Americana University, Mexico City, Mexico (1972); University of Akron, Ohio (J.D., 1976). Author: "Forms of Doing Business in Greece," International Corporate Counsel, Fall, 1992; "Immigration Considerations for Foreign Investors in U.S."; "Impact of the Tax Reform Act of 1984 on Resident and Non-Resident Aliens"; "Memorandum on United States Immigration Law - Immigrant and Non-Immigrant Visas"; Selected Memoranda for Foreign Investors, Immigration, Estate Planning, Taxation; "Foreign Investment in Georgia - Immigration Considerations." Co-Author: "A Synopsis of the Greek Corporate Tax System," State of California EC Law Handbook, 1993; Franchise Handbook for Foreign Companies Doing Business in U.S., Federal & State Compliance; Franchise Handbook for U.S. Companies Doing Business in European Common Market; Country Handbook on Greece Business & Employment Visas under IMMACT '90. Board of Advisors, International Quarterly. *Member:* International

(This Listing Continued)

Franchise Association; American Bar Association (Sections on International Law and Franchising); State Bar of Georgia (Sections on Franchise, International and Environmental Law); International Bar Association; American Hellenic Chamber of Commerce (Athens, Greece); American Immigration Lawyers Association; Hellenic American Institute, Washington, D.C. (Board of Directors); Hellenic American Chamber of Commerce of Atlanta (Founder, President); Italy-America Chamber of Commerce of Southeast, U.S. (Founder, Board of Directors); International Leadership Council of the Southeast (Founding Member, Board of Directors). (Also at Hurt, Sinisi & Papadakis, Athens, Atlanta and Hartford, USA Offices). *LANGUAGES:* English and Greek.

JOHN R. HURT, born Los Angeles, California, August 20, 1940; admitted, 1970, California; 1971, U.S. District Court for the Southern District of California; 1975, U.S. Supreme Court (Not admitted in Italy). *Education:* University of California, Berkeley (B.S., 1962); Cornell University School of Law (J.D., 1969). International Legal Centre Fellow, San Jose, Costa Rica, 1969-1971. Co-author: "Country Handbook on Italy," Italian American Business, 1992; "Environmental Laws of Italy," International Environmental Law and Regulations, Butterworths, 1991; "Dobson & Sinisi, Rome and San Diego," 1084-1994"; "Joint Ventures - A European Perspective," Ninth Annual Southeastern Corporate Counsel Institute, Atlanta, December, 1990; "Film Production and Loan Subsidies in Italy," Rome, July, 1990; "The Need for Appropriate Legal Protection of Software in Italy," Rome, 1988. General Counsel, Intermaritime Group, Geneva, 1987-1988. Private Practice, Paris and Rome, 1982-1987. General Counsel and Corporate Secretary, Cinema International Corporation, N.V., Amsterdam, 1978-1982. Division Counsel, Sea-Land Service, Inc., Menlo Park, N.J., 1975-1978. Associate, Gray, Cary, Ames & Frye, San Diego, 1971-1974. *Member:* State Bar of California; American (Member, Section on International Law and Practice) and International Bar Associations. (Also at Hurt, Sinisi & Papadakis, Atlanta and Hartford, USA Offices). *LANGUAGES:* English, Spanish, Italian and French.

STEVEN N. KOURTIS, born Sydney, New South Wales, Australia, December 6, 1961; admitted, 1991, Pennsylvania (Not admitted in Italy). *Education:* Duquesne University, Pittsburgh, Pennsylvania (B.A., 1984); American University, Washington, D.C. (Washington Semester in U.S. Foreign Policy, 1983); graduate work, International Affairs, George Washington University, Washington, D.C. (1984-1987); Catholic University of America, Columbus School of Law, Washington, D.C. (J.D., 1991). Member, Journal of Contemporary Health Law and Policy; Testimony before the U.S. Environmental Protection Agency on oil recycling issues, American Car Rental Association and the National Association of Convenience Stores, Washington, D.C., November 1991. Author: "Liability for Petroleum Storage Tank Owners and Operations," National Shipbuilders Research Project, Environmental Symposium, Crystal City, Virginia, 1991; "How to Lobby Congress," Independent Lubricant Manufacturers Association Annual Government Affairs Committee Meeting, Washington, D.C., 1992. Co-Author: "A Synopsis of the Greek Corporate Tax System," State of California EC Law Handbook, 1993; "Doing Business in Greece," Corporate Counsel's International Advisor, December 1992; Associate, Collier, Shannon, Rill & Scott, Washington, D.C., 1991-1992. *Member:* American Society for International Law; American Hellenic Educational and Progressive Association (AHEPA); American Bar Association (Section of Natural Resources, Energy and Environmental Law). (Athens and Atlanta, USA Offices). *LANGUAGES:* English and Greek.

OF COUNSEL

HARRIET TAMEN, born Yonkers, New York, May 17, 1947; admitted, 1974, New York. *Education:* Bryn Mawr College (A.B., 1969); National Law Center, George Washington University (J.D., 1973). Lecturer: American Women's Economic Development Corporation on International Business and Trade Finance (1992-1995); New York University School of Continuing Education on Credit Enhancement and Banking Law (1991-1995); Financial Services Volunteer Corps (Mongolia) on Commercial Banking (1993-1994); Conference on Black Sea Region and Central Asian Republics; Economic Development & Business Opportunities - Harriman Institute, Columbia University (1994). *Member:* Association of the Bar of the City of New York; Inter-American Affairs Subcommittee; New York State Bar Association; SABLAW-Soviet-American Banking Law Working Group (1990-1995); American Bar Association. (New York Office).

WILLIAM C. BRUCE, born Louisville, Kentucky, April 11, 1952; admitted, 1977, Connecticut; 1978, District of Columbia; 1982, Florida; U.S. District Court, District of Connecticut; U.S. District Court, Eastern and Western Districts of Arkansas; U.S. District Court, Southern District of New York; U.S. Court of Appeals, 2nd, 6th and 11th Circuits; U.S. Su-

(This Listing Continued)

preme Court (Not admitted in Italy). *Education:* University of New Haven (B.A. summa cum laude, 1974); Yale University (J.D., 1977). Author: "Employment Law in the 1990's," Conn. L. Trib, November, 1992; "Preventive Law in the Non-U.S. Owned Corporation," No. 2 Preventive Law Reporter 10, 1991; "Theft of Business Opportunity," Conn. Bar Journal, 1979. Adjunct Professor of Management, Rennselaer Polytechnic Institute (Hartford Graduate Center). Senior Consultant to AON Re-Engineering Corp. on Employment and Privitization Issues. Formerly Vice President, General Counsel and Corporate Secretary, Pirelli Tire Corporation. General Counsel and Secretary, University of New Haven. *Member:* Connecticut and American (Committees on International Business Law and Product Liability Law); The Corporate Bar Association (Past Chair of the Litigation and Insurance Committee, International Law Committee).

REPRESENTATIVE CLIENTS: Baxter Healthcare Corporation; Blockbuster International Corporation; Cafè Do Brasil; Consoltex Group Inc.; Delta Air Lines; Hard Rock Cafe; Laurent Perrier & Co.; Levi Strauss Europe; Marriott Management Services Corporation; ITT Sheraton; Mary Kay Cosmetics (U.K.) Limited; L'Oréal; National Services Industries; Oil & Natural Gas Commission of India; Petrolite Corporation; Scientific Atlanta; Teledyne Industries International; Ugine S.A.; American Finance Group; AIG Europe; General Reinsurance Corporation; Hartford International Insurance Company; Pricoa Vita S.p.A. - Prudential Group; Wright Investors Service; Deutsche Factoring; Bank Belgo-Factors N.V.; Export-Import Bank of India; Guinness Mahon & Co. Limited; Comerica Bank; Imperial Bank; MeesPierson N.V.; Bachman Information Systems; Cognos Incorporated; Conner Peripherals; Dun & Bradstreet Software Services Limited; Mantech International Corp.; Pilot Software; Armando Testa Advertising; Capella International Inc.; Curzon Films Distributors Ltd.; Film Master Srl.; Merchant Ivory Productions Ltd.; Shadow Hill Entertainment; Wonderland Entertainment Ltd.; GNB Incorporated; Mucafer Construction; Si.A.C. Construction; Dan El Construction.

STUDIO LEGALE TESAURO

Established in 1958

LARGO MESSICO 7
ROME, ITALY
Telephone: 854 78 92; 855 94 83
Fax: 855 44 38

Naples, Italy Office: Via Toledo, 156, 80134. Telephone: 551 52 76. Fax: 552 39 35.

General and International Practice. Commercial and Corporation Law. Foreign Investments, Taxation, Bankruptcy, and Administrative Law.

FIRM PROFILE: The firm was established in 1958 and offers a full range of legal services. It is well known for its General and International practice, especially European Community Law. The client base is European and North American in scope.

RESIDENT PARTNER

VALENTINO BENEDETTI, born Naples, Italy, June 2, 1941; admitted to practice, 1964; admitted, 1967, Italy; 1981, Italian Supreme Court of Cassation. *Education:* University of Rome (Doctor of Jurisprudence, maxima cum laude, 1964). *LANGUAGES:* Italian and English. *PRACTICE AREAS:* Constitutional Law; Bankruptcy.

ASSOCIATES

CLAUDIO TESAURO, born Naples, Italy, October 13, 1965; admitted, 1990, Italy. *Education:* University of Naples (Doctor of Jurisprudence, maxima cum laude); New York University (M.C.J., 1988). Commission of European Communities, Legal Service (Stage March, 1989). *LANGUAGES:* Italian, English, French and Spanish. *PRACTICE AREAS:* Foreign Investments; European Community Law.

BRUNO DE MARIA, born Naples, Italy, March 10, 1968; admitted, 1994, Italy. *Education:* University of Naples "Federico II" (Doctor of Jurisprudence, maxima cum laude, 1991). Specialization in European Community Law, Maxima cum laude, University of Naples 1993. *LANGUAGES:* Italian, English and French. *PRACTICE AREAS:* General and International Practice; Commercial and Corporation Law; European Community Law.

Languages: English, French and Italian.

(For Complete Personnel and Biographical Data, see Professional Biographies at Naples, Italy)

STUDIO LEGALE TONUCCI

VIA PRINCIPESSA CLOTILDE, 7
00196 ROME, ITALY
Telephone: 39-6-3212215
Facsimile: 39-6-3235161

Corporate, Antitrust, Securities Regulation, Privatization, Investment Funds, Banking and Finance, Telecommunications, Insurance, Sports and Gambling, Taxation, Labor, Environmental, Litigation, Arbitration and EU Laws.

FIRM PROFILE: Studio Legale Tonucci is an Italian law firm with a significant background in international law. The firm has its main office in Rome with corresponding offices in Milan, Turin and Brussels.

MARIO TONUCCI, born Rome, Italy, June 25, 1947; admitted to practice, 1971; admitted to bar, 1974, Italy; 1988, Supreme Court of Italy. *Education:* University of Rome (J.D., 1971); Cambridge University, England (1990); Seminar in American Law, Salzburg, 1991. Research Assistant of Labor Law, University of Rome, 1972-1975. Certified Public Auditor, 1976. *Member:* International Bar Association. *LANGUAGES:* Italian, English and French.

MARCO NICOLINI, born Terni, Italy, June 12, 1962; admitted to practice, 1986; admitted to bar, 1989, Italy; 1993, New York. *Education:* Catholic University of Milan (J.D., 1986); Leyden-Amsterdam-Columbia Summer Program in American Law, 1989; Harvard Law School (LL.M., 1992). Associate Instructor, Private and Corporative Law, LUISS University of Rome, 1990. Member, Harvard International Law Journal (Editorial Consultant). *Member:* New York State and American Bar Associations; International Bar Association. *LANGUAGES:* Italian, English and Spanish.

RICCARDO TROIANO, born Avellino, Italy, November 8, 1961; admitted to bar, 1989, Italy. *Education:* University of Rome (J.D., maxima cum laude, 1985). Assistant to the Professor of Civil Procedure, Rome University. *LANGUAGES:* Italian and English.

ROBERTO GIUFFRIDA, born Catania, Italy, September 12, 1951; admitted to bar, 1979, Italy. *Education:* University of Rome (J.D., 1974); Seminar, American Corporate Law, Salzburg, 1978. Awarded, Research Scholarship for the relationship between EEC and Italian Law, National Research Council, 1976. Assistant Professor, Public and Private International Law, University of Rome, 1984—. Appointed reviewer of Eastern Europe contracts by EEC Phare Program, 1993. *LANGUAGES:* Italian, English and French.

MARIA SOFIA TONOLO, born Rome, Italy, December 14, 1960; admitted to bar, 1987, Italy. *Education:* University of Rome (J.D., 1985); Georgetown University, Orientation in the U.S. Legal System, 1985; European Lawyer Association Seminar, Litigations before the EEC Court, 1987; King's College, London, European Young Lawyers Course, 1990. *LANGUAGES:* Italian, French and English.

OLSEN-TOMAS ODUSANYA, born London, England, September 28, 1961; admitted, England and Wales, 1986. *Education:* King's College, London University (LL.B., 1985). *LANGUAGES:* English and Italian.

MICHELE CARRELLI PALOMBI, born Rome, Italy, September 17, 1965; admitted to practice, 1991, Italy; admitted to bar, 1994, Italy. *Education:* University of Rome, Italy (J.D., 1991); King's College, London (LL.M., 1994). Awarded Scholarship, University of Padua. *LANGUAGES:* Italian and English.

FABRIZIO LAURIAN CUGIA DI S. ORSOLA, born Rome, Italy, March 14, 1963; admitted to practice, 1989, Italy; admitted to Bar, 1992, Italy. *Education:* University of Rome (J.D., 1988). Awarded, ISDA M.B.A. Scholarship, 1991. Former Parliament Legislative Assistant. Contracts Manager, British Telecommunications, Italy, 1991-1993. *LANGUAGES:* Italian, English and French.

ANTERO OVOLI, born Civitella del Tronto, Italy, March 18, 1943; admitted to practice, 1993, Italy. *Education:* University of Teramo (J.D.). *LANGUAGES:* Italian and English.

PIER MARIO TELMON, born Turin, Italy, June 3, 1965; admitted to practice, 1991, Italy. *Education:* University of Rome (J.D., 1990). *LANGUAGES:* Italian, English and French.

ANTONIO DONNANGELO, born Cassano allo Ionio, CS, January 6, 1969; admitted to practice, 1991, Italy; admitted to bar, 1994, Italy. *Education:* University of Rome (J.D., 1991). *LANGUAGES:* Italian and English.

CRISTINA PETRUCCI, born Rome, Italy, December 12, 1963; admitted to practice, 1988, Italy. *Education:* University of Rome (J.D., 1988).

(This Listing Continued)

Researcher, Civil Law, University of Rome, 1990—. *LANGUAGES:* Italian and English.

MURIELLE VINCENTI, born Montreuil s/Bois, France, March 27, 1964; admitted to practice, 1993, Italy. *Education:* University of Paris, La Sorbonne, France (Deug LEA, 1985); University of Catanzaro, Italy (J.D., 1993); San José State University, U.S.A., 1991. *LANGUAGES:* Italian, French and English.

DOMENICO FRISINI, born Rome, Italy, October 27, 1952; admitted to practice, 1979, Italy. *Education:* University of Rome (J.D., 1979). *LANGUAGES:* Italian and French.

ANDREA PATRIZI MONTORO, born Rome, Italy, April 17, 1965; admitted to practice, 1992, Italy. *Education:* University of Rome (J.D., 1992). *LANGUAGES:* Italian and English.

ANDREA ROSI PIERMARTINI, born Rome, Italy, January 26, 1960. *Education:* University of Rome (Business School, 1984; J.D., 1990). Researcher, Corporate Business, University of Rome. *LANGUAGES:* Italian and English.

ALESSANDRO BENEDETTI, born Taranto, Italy, November 15, 1966; admitted to practice, 1993, Italy. *Education:* University of Rome (J.D., 1993). *LANGUAGES:* Italian and English.

GOFFREDO GUERRA, born Rome, Italy, August 4, 1966; admitted to practice, 1991; admitted to bar, 1994, Italy. *Education:* Eton College, U.K. (A-levels, 1985); University of Rome (J.D., 1991). *LANGUAGES:* Italian and English.

CRISTINA CABELLO GONZALEZ, born Seville, Spain, November 26, 1971; admitted to bar, 1994, Spain. *Education:* University of Barcelona (J.D., 1993); LUISS University of Rome (EC Erasmus Program, 1994). *LANGUAGES:* Spanish, English and Italian.

ANTONIO CUPPONE, born Nardo (LE), Italy, April 30, 1970; admitted to practice, 1993, Italy. *Education:* LUISS University of Rome, Italy (J.D., 1993). *LANGUAGES:* Italian and English.

REPRESENTATIVE CLIENTS: Telecom Italia; Agip Petroli; Kuwait Petroleum; Jefferson Smurfit; Europcar; Stanhome; Deutsche Bank; Banque Indosuez; La Fondiaria; Ilva; Association of Pharmaceutical Distributors (ADF); Difarma; Società Autostrade; Telematic Service Center (CST); Ria Mazars; Italian Olympic Committee (CONI); SIAC; Recognition Equipment; Terre Armee Int.; De Beers Industrial Diamond Division, Ltd.; Credito Industriale Sardo; Aziende Chimiche Riunite Angelini Francesco; Macchine Automezzi Industriali Agricoli (MAIA).

STUDIO LEGALE TOSATO

Established in 1980

VIA SALLUSTIANA, 26
00187 ROME, ITALY
Telephone: (06) 481.94.19
Telefax: (06) 488.53.30
Telex: 616208

Milan, Italy Office: Via Santa Sofia, 12, 20122. Telephone: (02) 58307511/874996. Telefax: (02) 805.65.07.

General Practice, Commercial, Corporate, Banking, Italian and EEC Antitrust, Trade Protection, Arbitration, Telecommunications, Antidumping, Sports, Industrial Property, EEC, Public and Private International Law.

GIAN LUIGI TOSATO, born Milan, Italy, May 13, 1940; admitted, 1976, Italy. *Education:* University of Rome (J.D., 1962). Visiting Scholar, Michigan University, 1973 and Stanford University, 1974, 1975. Professor of International and EEC Law, Scuola di Polizia Tributaria Guardia di Finanza, Rome, 1973—. Professor of International Law, University of Perugia, 1975-1978. Professor of Private and Public International Law, University of Rome, 1979—. Professor of EEC Laws, Luiss, Rome. Chairman, Commission on Computing, Telecommunications and Information Policies, ICC, Paris. *Member:* American Society of International Law; The Japanese American Society for Legal Studies; International Law Association; International Fiscal Association; Inter Pacific Bar Association. *LANGUAGES:* Italian, English, French, Spanish and German.

GIULIO RAFFAELE IPPOLITO, born Rome, Italy, August 31, 1953; admitted, 1980, Italy. *Education:* Rome University (J.D., 1976); College of Europe, Bruges, Belgium (Certificate of Advanced European Studies, 1977-1978); Seminar in American Legal Studies, Salzburg, Austria (1980); Academy of American and International Law, Southwestern Legal Foundation, Dallas, Texas (1984). Coordinator of a Post-Graduate Course of International Law, Faculty of Law, University of Costa Rica, 1984-1987. Foreign

(This Listing Continued)

Lawyer, Covington & Burling, Washington, D.C., 1987. Member: Advisory Board, The International and Comparative Law Center, Dallas, Texas, 1986—. *LANGUAGES:* Italian, English, French and Spanish.

MASSIMO COCCIA, born Rome, Italy, September 12, 1957; admitted, 1988, Italy. *Education:* University of Rome (J.D., 1981); University of Michigan (LL.M., 1984). Fulbright Fellow, 1983-1984. Researching Professor, Institute of International Law, University of Rome, 1991—. Assistant Professor, International Law, LUISS, Rome, 1984-1992. Visiting Professor, International Economic Organization, University of Perugia, 1988-1990. Visiting Scholar, University of Michigan, 1986. *Member:* American Society of International Law; Inter Pacific Bar Association. *LANGUAGES:* Italian, English, French and Spanish.

MARIA ALESSANDRA LIVI, born Florence, Italy, April 5, 1964; admitted, 1991, Italy. *Education:* University of Rome (J.D., 1988); City of London Polytechnic (Seminar in English Law, 1989); Academy of American and International Law, Southwestern Legal Foundation, Dallas, Texas (1990). *LANGUAGES:* Italian and English.

FRANCESCA TROILO, born Rome, Italy, October 11, 1965; admitted, 1994, Italy. *Education:* EEC Commission (Traineeship, 1989); University of Rome (J.D., 1990). Traineeship, Pritchard, Englefield & Tobin Solicitors, London, 1991. *LANGUAGES:* Italian, English and French.

GIUSEPPE CHINÉ, born Locri, Italy, August 16, 1968. *Education:* Foreign Trade Institute, Rome (Traineeship 1990); University of Rome L.U.I.S.S. (J.D., 1991); University of California "La Jolla", San Diego (Seminar in American Law, 1993). *LANGUAGES:* Italian and English.

SALLY M. SILVERS, born Philadelphia, Pennsylvania, July 27, 1959; admitted, 1985, New York (Not admitted in Italy). *Education:* New York University (B.F.A., 1980); Fordham University (J.D., 1984). *LANGUAGES:* English and Italian.

Languages: Italian, English, French, Spanish and German.

STUDIO LEGALE EMANUELE TURCO

Established in 1988

VIALE G. ROSSINI 9
00198 ROME, ITALY
Telephone: (0039-6) 8088244/6/7
Fax: (0039-6) 8088980

Corporate, Contracts, Natural Resources, Taxation, Privatization, Admiralty and Aviation.

FIRM PROFILE: The firm specializes in international corporate, contracts, taxation and in natural resources law and is expanding in the area's of privatization and financial law. The Firm is a Sponsor of the European Law Research Center at Harvard Law School.

MEMBERS

EMANUELE TURCO, born Naples, Italy, January 3, 1940; admitted, 1966, Rome; 1972, Italy. *Education:* University of Rome (Doctor of Jurisprudence, 1964); Salzburg Seminar on American Law and Legal Institutions, 1965; Seminar at the Institute of Comparative Law, University of Rome, 1965-1966; Orientation Program in American Law, Princeton University, 1966; Harvard Law School (LL.M., 1967). Author: "The Bilateral Treaties in Force Between the U.S.A. and Italy," 2 Vols., 1975. President, Harvard Law School Association of Europe, 1980-1983. Council Member, Harvard Law School Association, 1992-1994. Director, Harvard Alumni Association, 1995. *Member:* International Bar Association (Rapporteur for Italy, Section on Energy and Natural Resources Law, 1983-1984); International Law Association. *LANGUAGES:* Italian and English. *PRACTICE AREAS:* Corporate; Contracts; Natural Resources; Privatization and International Taxation.

ELDA TURCO BULGHERINI, born Rome, Italy, April 13, 1946; admitted, 1972, Rome; 1983, Italy. *Education:* University of Rome (Doctor of Jurisprudence, 1969); Hague Academy of International Law, 1969; Salzburg Seminar on American Law and Legal Institutions, 1976; Academy of American and International Law, The Southwestern Legal Foundation, Dallas, 1978. Professor of Navigation Law, University of Rome. Author:

(This Listing Continued)

"La disciplina giuridica degli accordi aerei bilaterali," 1 Vol., 1984; "Impresa di navigazione e servizi aerei di linea," 1 Vol. 1988. *Member:* International Law Association; A.L.A.D.A. Latin American Association of Air Law; Italian Association of Admiralty Law. *LANGUAGES:* Italian and English. *PRACTICE AREAS:* Corporate; Admiralty and Aviation.

GIOVANNI TRADARDI, born Ivrea, Italy, October 31, 1963; admitted, 1991, Rome. *Education:* University of Rome (Doctor of Jurisprudence, 1988); Leyden-Amsterdam-Columbia, Summer Program in American Law, Leyden, 1990; University of California, Orientation in American Law, 1993. *LANGUAGES:* Italian and English. *PRACTICE AREAS:* Corporate and Natural Resources.

CARLO RICCI, born Florence, Italy, March 29, 1961; admitted, 1994, Matera. *Education:* University of Florence (Doctor of Jurisprudence 1990); Harvard Law School (LL.M., 1993); International Law Institute of Georgetown Law Center; Orientation in The U.S. Legal System, 1992. *Member:* International Bar Association; Harvard Law School Association of Europe. *LANGUAGES:* Italian and English. *PRACTICE AREAS:* Corporate; Contracts and EU.

GREGORY VALENTI, born New York, October 10, 1966; admitted, 1994, New York and Pennsylvania (Not admitted in Italy). *Education:* Trinity College, Hartford, CT (B.A. in Political Science, 1988); The American University, Washington College of Law and School of International Service, Washington, D.C. (J.D., magna cum laude and M.A. in Law and International Affairs, 1993). Author: "Digital Audio Broadcasting: An International Perspective on Compact-Disc Quality Radio," in American University Journal of International Law and Policy (Winter 1992). *Member:* International Bar Association; Association of Foreign Lawyers in Italy; New York State and American Bar Associations. *LANGUAGES:* English and Italian. *PRACTICE AREAS:* Contracts; Privatization and Natural Resources.

ANTONELLA BARBIERI, born Vasto, Italy, June 18, 1967; admitted, 1994, Vasto. *Education:* LUISS (Free International University for Social Studies) (Doctor of Jurisprudence, 1991; (ICE) Institute for Foreign Trade; Diploma of Specialization in Foreign Trade, 1993). Author: "Le Societa Di Capitali e Le Societá Miste Nella Legislazione Russa," Le Societá (August 1994). *LANGUAGES:* Italian, English and Spanish. *PRACTICE AREAS:* Corporate; Natural Resources.

Languages: Italian and English.

UGHI & NUNZIANTE

Established in 1969

VIA VENTI SETTEMBRE 1
00187 ROME, ITALY
Telephone: 476841
Cable Address: "Novalex"
Telex: 611459 "Nurlaw"
FAX: 487 03 97

Milan, Italy Office: Via Sant' Andrea 19. Telephone: 76013368. Cable Address: "Novalex". Telex: 311634 UNALEX. Fax: 784140.

General and International Practice, Corporation, Foreign Investments, Patent, Trademark, Admiralty, Aviation, Taxation, Labor, Oil and Gas, Financing and Banking, EEC Law, Insolvency and Administrative Law.

PARTNERS

GIANNI NUNZIANTE, born Salerno, Italy, April 25, 1930; admitted, 1954, Naples; 1960, Italy; 1971, Supreme Court. *Education:* University of Naples (Doctor of Jurisprudence, 1952); Columbia University School of Law, New York (M.C.L., 1962); Seminar in American Legal Studies, Salzburg, 1960, Commonwealth Fund Fellow, 1961-1962. Member, Advisory Board, The Southwestern Legal Foundation, Dallas, Texas. *Member:* International Bar Association; The Association of the Bar of the City of New York. *LANGUAGES:* Italian, English.

(This Listing Continued)

UGHI & NUNZIANTE, Rome—Continued

CARLO CAPUA, born Naples, Italy, August 21, 1934; admitted, 1959, Naples; 1967, Italy; 1980, Supreme Court. *Education:* University of Naples Law School (Doctor of Jurisprudence, 1959); Seminar in American Legal Studies, Salzburg, 1966; New York University School of Law, 1967-1968, (M.C.J., 1969). *Member:* The Association of the Bar of the City of New York; International Bar Association (Committee: Labour Law); American Bar Association. *LANGUAGES:* Italian, English.

MARCELLO GIOSCIA, born Genoa, Italy, May 31, 1937; admitted, 1964, Genoa; 1971, Italy. *Education:* Grenoble University (1955-1956); University of Genoa (Doctor of Jurisprudence, 1961); Seminar in American Legal Studies, Salzburg, 1969; Orientation Program in American Law, Brown University, 1970; Columbia University School of Law, New York (LL.M., 1971). Member, Panel of Arbitrators, American Arbitration Association. *Member:* International Bar Association (Co-Chairman, Banking Committee). *LANGUAGES:* Italian, English, French.

MAURIZIO DELFINO, born Rome, Italy, May 4, 1955; admitted, 1979, Rome; 1985, Italy. *Education:* University of Rome (Doctor of Jurisprudence, magna cum laude, 1976; Master's Degree in Administrative Sciences, 1977; Fulbright Scholar, Stanford Law School (Doctor of the Science of Law, J.S.D., 1983). Legal Service, Competition Equipe, EEC Commission, 1981. *Member:* Young Lawyers' International Association (AIJA); Italian Association of European Lawyers; Italian Association of Administrative Lawyers; American Bar Association; International Bar Association. *LANGUAGES:* Italian, English, French.

ALESSANDRO VARRENTI, born Rome, Italy, September 26, 1956; admitted, 1981, Rome; 1987, Italy. *Education:* University of Rome (Doctor of Jurisprudence, magna cum laude, 1979); Columbia University, New York (LL.M., 1982). Master, Tax Law, Institute of Management Studies, Rome, 1988. *Member:* The Association of the Bar of the City of New York; International Bar Association. *LANGUAGES:* Italian, French, English.

RINO CAIAZZO, born Rome, Italy, April 7, 1958; admitted, 1985, Rome; 1991, Italy. *Education:* University of Rome (Doctor of Jurisprudence, 1981); University of London, London School of Economics and Political Sciences (LL.M., 1986). Recipient, Rome Bar Association Award, 1982. *Member:* International Bar Association (Committee: Banking Law). *LANGUAGES:* Italian, English.

OF COUNSEL

PIETRO RESCIGNO, born Salerno, Italy, January 15, 1928; admitted, 1951, Naples; 1959, Italy. *Education:* Naples University Law School (Doctor of Jurisprudence, magna cum laude, 1948). Professor of Private Law at the Universities of: Macerata, 1954-1958; Pavia, 1958-1960; Bologna, 1960-1970; Luxemburg Faculte Internationale de Droit Comparè, 1958-1964; Rome, 1970—. *Member:* Accademia Nazionale dei Lincei; Accademia Pontaniana; Istituto dell' Accademia delle Scienze; Istituto dell'Enciclopedia Italiana; International Encyclopedia of Comparative Law; Istituto di Ricerche sui problemi dello Stato e delle Istituzioni. *LANGUAGES:* Italian, German, English.

PIERO BERNARDINI, born Rome, Italy, December 24, 1937; admitted, 1965, Rome; 1971, Italy; 1978, Supreme Court. *Education:* Rome University Law School (Doctor of Jurisprudence, magna cum laude, 1961). Member: Academic Council of the Institute of Internationale Business Law and Practices of the International Chamber of Commerce, Paris; Academic Council of the Institute for the Promotion of International Arbitration, Milan. Vice-President: Italian Arbitration Association; Euro-Arab Forum for Arbitration and Business Law, Paris. Section Arbitration, International Law Association. *Member:* International Bar Association (Committee: Procedures for Settling Disputes). *LANGUAGES:* Italian, English, French.

ASSOCIATES

ANNE VINCENT, born Paris, France, November 1, 1947; admitted, 1976, Paris, France; 1987, New York (Not admitted in Italy). *Education:* University of Paris (License en droit, with honors, 1971); New York University School of Law (LL.M., 1987). *Member:* American Bar Association; International Bar Association. *LANGUAGES:* French, Italian, English.

FABRIZIO PAVAROTTI, born Lucca, Italy, July 7, 1955; admitted, 1986, Rome. *Education:* University of Rome (Doctor of Jurisprudence, 1981). Researcher, Private Law, University of Rome, 1982-1986.

TOMASO CENCI, born Rome, Italy, April 29, 1963; admitted, 1990, Rome. *Education:* University of Rome (Doctor of Jurisprudence, magna cum laude, 1987). Seminar in American Law, University of Amsterdam,

(This Listing Continued)

1989. Seminar in English Law, City of London Polytechnic U.K., 1988. *LANGUAGES:* Italian, English.

RODOLFO MAZZEI, born Cosenza, Italy, April 16, 1964; admitted, 1991, Rome. *Education:* University of Rome (Doctor of Jurisprudence, magna cum laude, 1987).

LISA CURRAN, born Toronto, Ontario, May 18, 1963; admitted, 1988, Ontario (Not admitted in Italy). *Education:* Queen's University (LL.B., 1986). *LANGUAGES:* English, Italian, French.

ANGELO ANGLANI, born Brindisi, Italy, August 5, 1963; admitted, 1990, Lecce. *Education:* University of Bari (Doctor of Jurisprudence, 1986).

SILVIO TERSILLA, born Verona, Italy, May 1, 1968; (Not admitted in Italy). *Education:* Libera Universitá Internazionale degli Studi Sociali (LUISS), Rome (Doctor of Jurisprudence, cum laude, 1992).

PARTNERS MILAN OFFICE

Giovanni M. Ughi	Michael C. Kirkham
Giorgio Delbue	(Not admitted in Italy)
Marco G. Brescia	Fiorella F. Alvino

Languages: Italian, English, French and German

FOREIGN REFERENCES: Alfred Dunhill Ltd., London, U.K.; Amoco Corp., Chicago, U.S.A.; Asarco Inc., New York, U.S.A.; Akzo, Arnhem, The Netherlands; Wilmington, U.S.A.; Banco Nazionale del Lavosa, Rome, Italy; Banque National de Paris, Paris, France; Bausch & Lomb Inc., Rochester, U.S.A. Bayer; Caterpillar Overseas S.A., Geneva, Switzerland; Chanel, Paris, France; Columbia Pictures Industries, Inc., New York, U.S.A.; Chloride Group PLC, London, U.K.; The Coca Cola Corp., Atlanta, U.S.A.; Credit Lyonnais, Paris, France; Degussa AG, Frankfurt, West Germany; Dow Chemicals, Midland, U.S.A.; Dun & Bradstreet Corp., New York, U.S.A.; EEC International Ltd., St. Austell, U.K.; Firestone Co., Akron, U.S.A.; Ford Motor Co., Detroit, U.S.A.; The Gillette Company, Boston, U.S.A.; GPA Group, Shannon, Eize; Guinness P.L.C.; Harvard University, Cambridge, U.S.A.; Hercules Inc., Wilmington, U.S.A.; Holiday Co., Memphis, U.S.A.; ITALSTAT Spa; I.T.T., Inc.; Litton Industries, Beverly Hills, U.S.A.; Nomura Securities, Tokyo; Occidental Petroleum Corp., Los Angeles, U.S.A.; Omron Tateisi Electronics Co., Tokyo, Japan; Pitney Bowes Inc., Stamford, U.S.A.; Rochas S.A.; Rothschild, London; Rowntree Mackintosh Ltd., York, U.K.; Sogo Co. Ltd., Tokyo; Texas Instruments, Inc., Dallas, U.S.A.; Ytong AG, Munich, Germany.

STUDIO LEGALE VASSALLI

VIA ELEONORA DUSE, 35
VIA DI VILLA EMILIANI, 46
00197 ROME, ITALY
Telephone: (0039 6) 808 58 05
Telefax: (0039 6) 808 00 15

General Practice. Corporate, Foreign Investments, Banking Law, Securities Regulation, International Finance, Arbitration, Taxation, Bankruptcy, EC Law, Competition and Antitrust, Labor Law, Criminal Law, Criminal Bankruptcy Law, White Collar Crime, Criminal Tax Law, Civil and Criminal Litigation.

MEMBERS OF FIRM

PROF. AVV. FRANCESCO VASSALLI, born Rome, Italy, March 3, 1943; admitted, 1968, Italy. *Education:* University of Rome (J.D., 1966). Professor, Commercial Law, University of Perugia, 1971-1981; Professor, Bankruptcy Law, University of Rome "La Sapienza," 1982—. Member, Editorial Board of "Rivista di giurisprudenza commerciale" and "Rivista del diritto commerciale"; Associate Editor, "Rivista di legislazione economica". Author: "Composizione della lite e tutela dei crediti: I la transazione" (1980); "Responsabilita d'impresa e potere di amministrazione nelle societa personali" (1973); "La condotta del debitore nella conversione delle procedure concorsuali" (1994); "Diritto fallimentare I" (1994). *LANGUAGES:* Italian, English, French. *PRACTICE AREAS:* Banking; Corporate; Bankruptcy; Finance and Criminal Law.

PROF. AVV. ANTONIO FIORELLA, born Veroli (FR), Italy, January 17, 1948; admitted, 1977, Italy. *Education:* University of Rome (J.D., 1971). Professor of White Collar Crime, University of Teramo. Author: "Il Transfimento di funzioni nel diritto penale dell'impresa" (1985); "Reato in generale" in "Enciclopedia del diritto" 1987; "Responsabilita penale" in "Enciclopedia del diritto" 1998. *LANGUAGES:* Italian, German, English. *PRACTICE AREAS:* Criminal Business Law.

AVV. RICCARDO OLIVO, born Rome, Italy, October 10, 1951; admitted, 1982, Italy. *Education:* University of Rome (J.D., 1976). *LANGUAGES:* Italian, English, Portuguese. *PRACTICE AREAS:* White Collar Crime; Criminal Tax Law; Criminal Litigation.

(This Listing Continued)

AVV. FRANCO PASQUALE D'URBANO, born Bomba (CH), Italy, February 24, 1944; admitted, 1972, Italy. *Education:* University of Rome (J.D., 1968). Research Assistant, Criminal Law, University of Rome. *LANGUAGES:* Italian, French. *PRACTICE AREAS:* Criminal Law.

AVV. ALBERTO GOMMELLINI, born Roma, Italy, January 30, 1958; admitted, 1984, Italy. *Education:* University of Rome (J.D. magna cum laude, 1981). Visiting Lawyer, Clifford Chance, London, September 1990 - March 1991; Assistant, Commercial Law (1982-1983), Bankruptcy Law and Civil Procedure Law (1983-1993), University of Rome. Author: "Prestiti dei soci, societa sottocapitalizzata e causa del contratto di mutuo" in Rivista di diritto commerciale e del diritto generale delle obbligazioni" 1990; "Le operazioni di leveraged buy-out di fronte al diritto italiano delle societa", in "Rivista del diritto commercials e del diritto generale delle obbligazioni", 1989; Co-Author: "Buyouts in Europe", edited by Clifford Chance, London, 1991. *LANGUAGES:* Italian, English. *PRACTICE AREAS:* Banking Law; Corporate; Bankruptcy and Finance Law.

DOTT. PROC. GIORGIO PERRONI, born Rome, Italy, January 13, 1962; admitted, 1989, Italy. *Education:* University of Rome (J.D., 1985). *LANGUAGES:* Italian, English. *PRACTICE AREAS:* Criminal Tax Law; White Collar Crime; Criminal Litigation.

AVV. FRANCESCO PAPPALARDO, born Catania, Italy, November 23, 1961; admitted, 1989, Italy. *Education:* University of Catania (J.D., 1984). Assistant, Bankruptcy Law, University of Rome; Consultant: Minister of the Treasury and Banca d'Italia. *LANGUAGES:* Italian, English. *PRACTICE AREAS:* Banking Law; Commercial Law; Corporate.

DOTT. PROC. MICHELE CAROSONE, born Rome, Italy, October 24, 1963; admitted, 1991, Italy. *Education:* University of Rome (J.D., 1988). *LANGUAGES:* Italian, English. *PRACTICE AREAS:* Criminal Law.

DOTT. PROC. STEFANO PANTALANI, born Rome, Italy, May 18, 1964; admitted, 1991, Italy. *Education:* University of Rome (J.D., 1988). *LANGUAGES:* Italian, English, French, Spanish. *PRACTICE AREAS:* Commercial Law.

DOTT. LAURA DI PIETROPAOLO, born Rome, Italy, March 25, 1963; admitted, 1993, Italy. *Education:* University of Rome (J.D., 1988). Author: "Domino sull'impresa e c.d. amministrazione di fatto" in "Rivista trimestrale di Diritto Penale", 1992. *LANGUAGES:* Italian, French. *PRACTICE AREAS:* Criminal Law.

DOTT. FABIO ROSCIOLI, born Rome, Italy, March 16, 1966; admitted to practice before lower courts. *Education:* University of Rome (J.D., 1993). Voluntary Assistant, Banking Law, University of Rome. Author: "Commento sub art. 139, Testo Unico delle leggi in materia bancaria e Creditizia," "Commentario" (1994). *LANGUAGES:* Italian. *PRACTICE AREAS:* Commercial Law; White Collar Crime.

DOTT. FRANCESCA ROMANA OLIVO, born Rome, Italy, January 16, 1966; admitted to practice before lower courts. *Education:* University of Rome (J.D., 1992). *LANGUAGES:* Italian, English, French. *PRACTICE AREAS:* Criminal Litigation.

DOTT. ROBERTO PERA, born Rome, Italy, May 3, 1964; admitted to practice before lower courts. *Education:* University of Rome (J.D., 1992); University of Hamburg (1990-1991). Visiting Lecturer, University of Hannover, Germany (1994); Assistant Comparative Law, University of Rome; Research Assistant, Comparative Antitrust Law, University of Rome. Author: "Das neue italienische Kartellgesetz - Darstellung und Problemstellung," (1992). Co-author of "Collection of cases on the Vienna Sales Convention" in "Rivista di diritto del commercio internazionale" 1993-1994. *Member:* German Association between German and Italian Lawyers. *LANGUAGES:* Italian, German, English. *PRACTICE AREAS:* EC and Italian Antitrust Law; EC Law; International Commercial Law.

DOTT. ELISABETTA BUSUITO, born Rome, Italy, April 1, 1966; admitted to practice before lower courts. *Education:* University of Rome (Doctor in Economics, 1990; J.D., 1993). Voluntary Assistant, Criminal Law, Libera Universita Internazionale per gli Studi Sociali (LUISS), Rome. *LANGUAGES:* Italian, English. *PRACTICE AREAS:* White Collar Crime.

ANTONIO GRILLO, born Foggia, Italy, November 9, 1964; admitted, 1990, Italy. *Education:* University of Bari (Doctor of Jurisprudence, magna cum laude, 1986); University College of London (1988). Co-Author: "Pensions in the European Community," edited by Clifford Chance, London, 1991. *Member:* International Bar Association. *LANGUAGES:* Italian and English. *PRACTICE AREAS:* EC Law; Antitrust; Corporate; Contracts.

FRANCESCO MAZZEI

CORSO VITTORIO EMANUELE, 35
I-84123 SALERNO, ITALY
Telephone: (0) 89-237 573; 241 189
Fax: (0) 89-241 189

Legal Consultancy and Litigation, General Civil International and Domestic Practice.

FRANCESCO MAZZEI, born Naples, Italy, October 8, 1963; admitted, 1992, Italy. *Education:* University of Naples (J.D., 1988); University Institute of European Studies, Turin (Post graduate course on International Trade Law, 1992); L.U.I.S.S., Rome, Scholarship, (Post graduate course on Tax Company and Accounting, 1990). Author, Review: " A.M. Valenti, Il problema della circolazione dei capitali nella prospettiva dell'Unione Europea," European Law Review, January, 1991; "L.C. Urertazzi, L'armonizzazione dei servizi bancari nazionali," European Law Review, February, 1990; "S. Ferlito, L'attività , internazionale della Santa Sede," La Comunita Internazionale S.I.O.I. Review, March, 1989. Auditor: XXV European Studies meeting on, "The European in Community after the Treaty of Maastricht," S.I.O.I. Piemonte, 1992; Academy of International Law, The Hague, 1985 and 1986. Co-Author: Article, "Elements of EEC Institutional Law," University Institute of European Studies, Turin, 1992; "Legal Aspects of Contractual Negotiation in International Contracts," University Institute of European Studies, Turin, 1992. Lecturer Assistant, Chair of International Law Faculty of Law, University of Salerno. Instructor: 15th. Professional Course for Accounters, Academic Year, 1991-1992; Course CO.R.CE., Preparation of officers in the foreign trade area, Genovesi Foundation/S.-D.O.A., Academic Year, 1992-1993; European Study Meeting, "Cristo Re" Institute, 1992; 2nd course of preparation for the Bar Examination, International and E.E.C. Law Area, Academic Year, 1992-1993. Foreign Speaker, "Ethics and Law, the Problem of the Economic Democracy," International Congress, Budapest University, 1994. Speaker, "The Carbon Tax," Congress on Energy Conservation, L.U.I.S.S. University, 1991. Licensed to plead before the Courts of Merits in Italy. *Member:* Italian Bar Association. *LANGUAGES:* Italian and English.

BARZANÕ & ZANARDO

Established in 1887

CORSO VITTORIO EMANUELE II, 61
10128 TURIN, ITALY
Telephone: (39-11) 56 11172
Telecopier: (39-11) 548050
Telex: 320034-Zanard I.

Milan, Italy Office; Via Borgonuovo 10.20121. Telephone (39-2) 655 4287. Telecopier: (39-2) 659 8859. Telex: 320034-Zanard I.
Rome, Italy Office: Via Piemonte 26, 00187. Telephone: (39-6) 487 0273. Telex: 625579-Zanard I.

Patents, Designs, Trademarks, Copyright, Licensing and Transfer of Technology.

(For Complete Biographical Data, see Professional Biographies at Milan, Italy)

STUDIO LEGALE
BORTOLOTTI MATHIS & ASSOCIATI

Established in 1980

VIA SAN DALMAZZO, 24
10121 TURIN, ITALY
Telephone: (011) 562.46.46./562.40.36
Telefax: (011) 562.31.70

Milan, Italy Office: Via De Grassi, 3. Telephone: (02) 866698. Telefax: (02) 866704.
Treviso, Italy Office: via A. Diaz, 26. Telephone: (0422) 412716. Telefax: (0422) 56673.

General Civil Practice. Arbitration, Antitrust and Common Market Law, Licensing, Joint Ventures, Corporation and Foreign Investments. Counselling in International Commercial Transactions.

(This Listing Continued)

STUDIO LEGALE BORTOLOTTI MATHIS & ASSOCIATI, Turin—Continued

MEMBERS OF FIRM

FABIO BORTOLOTTI, born Innsbruck, Austria, November 15, 1939; admitted, 1981, Italy. *Education:* University of Turin (J.D., 1966). Author: "Introduzione al diritto dei contratti internazionali" (Introduction to the Law of International Contracts), 1986; "Modelli di contratto e condizioni generali per il commercio estero" (Forms of Contract and General Conditions for International Trade), 1985; "Il Contratto di concessione di vendita nel diritto italiano e comunitario" (Distributorship Contract under Italian and EEC Law), 1983; "Guida alla stipulazione di contratti con agenti e concessionari all'estero" (Guide for Drawing up Contracts with Agents and Distributors Abroad), 1985. Co-Author: "Le regole di concorrenza nei trattati della CEE e della CECA" (Rules of Competition in the EEC and ECSC Treaties), 1971; "Guide pour la conclusion de contrats d'agence et de la concession à l'etranger", 1980; "Contratti internazionali di trasferimento di tecnologia: legislazioni" (International Contracts of Transfer of Technology: Legislations), 1986. Professor, International Commercial Law, University of Turin. ICC Observer at Vienna Convention on the International Sale of Goods, 1980—. Advisor to the Milan and Venice Export Centres of Chambers of Commerce. Vice Chairman of the Committee on International Commercial Practices of the International Chamber of Commerce. *Member:* International Chamber of Commerce (Committees on: Restrictive Practices and International Commercial Practices); Organisme de Liaision des Industries Métalliques Européennes (ORGALIME, Member, Legal Committee); Associazione Italiana per l'Arbitrato; International Bar Association; Licensing Executives Society. *LANGUAGES:* Italian, English, French, German and Dutch. *PRACTICE AREAS:* Agency and Distributorship; Antitrust; Arbitration; Business Law; European Community Law.

MAURO MATHIS, born Trieste, Italy, May 16, 1942; admitted, 1977, Italy. *Education:* University of Trieste (J.D., 1964). Author: "Condizioni Generali di Vendita" (General Condition of Sales), 1986. Assistant Professor, Civil Law, University of Turin, 1969-1982. Advisor to the Milan and Venice Export Centres of Chambers of Commerce, 1979-1992. *LANGUAGES:* Italian, English and German. *PRACTICE AREAS:* General Practice; Taxation; Business Law.

GUIDO CRAVETTO, born Torino, Italy, September 14, 1950; admitted, 1980, Italy. *Education:* University of Turin (J.D., 1977). Co-Chairman of Committee O of the International Bar Association. *LANGUAGES:* Italian, English and French. *PRACTICE AREAS:* Litigation; Mergers and Acquisitions.

ASSOCIATES

CLAUDIO COSTA, born La Spezia, Italy, January, 1, 1955; admitted, 1993. *Education:* University of Turin (P.S., 1984; J.D., 1990). Co-Author: "Contratti internazionali di trasferimento di tecnologia: legislazioni" (International Contracts of Transfer of Technology: Legislations), 1986; "Contratto di Licenza D'uso del Marchio e di Know-How" (Trademark and Know-How Licensing), 1991. Author: Contratto Internazionale di Licenza di Know-How: Modello e Commento (International Know-How License Agreement: Comment to a Model Form), 1992. Advisor: Turin Export Centre of Chamber of Commerce, 1984-1987; Milan Export Centre of Chamber of Commerce, 1987-1992. *LANGUAGES:* Italian and English. *PRACTICE AREAS:* Intellectual Property; Licensing; Trademarks.

CARLO MOSCA, born Treviso, Italy, April 10, 1957; admitted, 1986, Italy. *Education:* University of Bologna (J.D., 1983). *LANGUAGES:* Italian, English and French. *PRACTICE AREAS:* Agency and Distributorship; Aviation; Business Law; Trademarks.

Languages: Italian, English, French, German and Dutch.

BROSIO, CASATI E ASSOCIATI

CORSO VITTORIO EMANUELE II, 68
10121 TURIN, ITALY
Telephone: (39) (11) 5612005
Telecopier: (39) (11) 541018

Milan, Italy Office: Via Manzoni, 41, 20121. Telephone: (39) (2) 29010200. Telecopier: (39) (2) 29010278.
Rome, Italy Office: Via Valadier, 36, 00193. Telephone: (39) (6) 3230328. Telecopier: (39) (6) 3216107.
Brussels, Belgium Office: 99, Rue de la Loi, 1040. Telephone: (32) (2) 2300004. Telecopier: (32) (2) 2307473.

(This Listing Continued)

EU994B

General Practice and Litigation, Corporation, Taxation, Foreign Investment, Mergers and Acquisitions, Banking, Administrative, Antitrust, Environmental, Labor, Real Estate and EEC Law.

GUIDO BROSIO, born Moncalieri (Turin), Italy, February 1, 1943; admitted, 1972, Italy; 1988, Supreme Court. *Education:* University of Turin (J.D., 1967); Harvard University (LL.M., 1969). Visiting Foreign Lawyer: Sullivan & Cromwell, New York and Paris Offices, 1969-1971; Stegemann, Sieveking & Lutteroth, Hamburg, 1971. *Member:* A.B.A.; I.B.A.; U.I.A.

CARLO PAVESIO, born Turin, Italy, February 1, 1956; admitted, 1983, Italy. *Education:* University of Turin (J.D., 1979); London School of Economics (LL.M., 1980). Trainee, Legal Service of the EEC Commission, 1980-1981. Visiting Foreign Lawyer: Gibson, Dunn & Crutcher, New York, 1985-1986. *Member:* I.B.A.; U.I.A.; European Lawyers Association.

MARIO COLOMBATTO, born Turin, Italy, August 23, 1956; admitted, 1983, Italy. *Education:* University of Turin (J.D., 1979); London School of Economics (LL.M., 1980). Visiting Foreign Lawyer: Westrick & Eckholdt, Frankfurt, 1981-1982. Lecturer in: Comparative Private Law, University of Trento, 1984-1986; Fundamentals of Civil Law, Bocconi University, Milan, 1986-1991. *Member:* I.B.A.; U.I.A.

ASSOCIATES

MARCO TOSETTO BRICCO, born Turin, Italy, May 5, 1954; admitted, 1985, Italy. *Education:* University of Turin (J.D., 1980).

NICOLA CERAOLO, born Messina, Italy, January 4, 1964; admitted, 1992, Italy. *Education:* University of Messina (J.D., 1986); College of Europe, Bruges, Belgium (Diploma in Advanced European Legal Studies, 1988); Leiden-Amsterdam-Columbia Summer Program in American Law, 1994. *Member:* I.B.A.

RICCARDO VENTURA, born Parma, Italy, April 7, 1964; admitted, 1992, Italy. *Education:* University of Parma (J.D., 1987); Georgetown University Law Center (LL.M., 1993).

DONATELLA DE ROSA, born Turin, Italy, October 24, 1966; admitted, 1992, Italy. *Education:* University of Turin (J.D., 1989); University Institute for European Studies, Turin, Fall Program, 1989; Academy of American and International Law, Southwestern Legal Foundation, Dallas, 1994.

GIOVANNI LUPPI, born Turin, Italy, January 6, 1965; admitted, 1993, Italy. *Education:* University of Turin (J.D., 1990).

SARA PANELLI, born Turin, Italy, November 19, 1967; admitted, 1994, Italy. *Education:* University of Turin (J.D., 1990).

VITTORIO TORAZZI, born Turin, Italy, June 5, 1966; admitted, 1994, Italy. *Education:* University of Turin (J.D., 1990).

FABRIZIO FASANO, born Settimo Torinese (Turin), Italy, July 22, 1964; admitted, 1994, Italy. *Education:* University of Turin (J.D., 1990).

SILVIA D'AMARIO, born Turin, Italy, May 26, 1966;. admitted to practice before the Lower Courts, 1994. *Education:* University of Turin (J.D., 1992).

RESIDENTS AT MILAN OFFICE

Roberto Casati	Alberto Nanni
Davide D'Angelo	Giovanni Maria Marini
	Filippo Cesaris

Massimo Greco	Paolo Cerina
Francesco Cantoni	Cecilia Buresti
Paolo Esposito	Alessandra Perrazzelli
Giancarlo Castorino	Michele Delfini
Cristina Manasse	Laura Lamera
Daniela Stelé	Massimo Trentino
Francesco Simoneschi	Andrea Arosio

(This Listing Continued)

Antonella Capria   Guido Alvigini

RESIDENTS AT ROME OFFICE

Renato Clarizia

Daniela Jouvenal Long

RESIDENT AT BRUSSELS OFFICE

Claudia Crescenzi

Languages: English, French and German.

(For biographical data of attorneys not resident at Turin, see Professional Biographies at Milan, Italy)

STUDIO AVV. COLONNA

Established in 1982

CORSO SICCARDI 11
10122 TURIN, ITALY
Telephone: 0039-11-5621423/5619272
Fax: 0039-11-537.521

General Practice. Corporation, Foreign Investments in Italy, Probate, Real Estate, Labor, Patent Law and International Contracts.

MEMBERS OF FIRM

AVV. DR. GUIDO COLONNA, born Turin, Italy, October 1, 1930; admitted, 1955, Italy. Education: University of Pavia (LL.D., 1955). Member: Bar Association of Turin; The American Chamber of Commerce in Italy (Vice President). LANGUAGES: Italian, English and French. PRACTICE AREAS: International Contracts; Corporation; Civil Litigation.

DOTT. PROC. CLAUDIO OLIVETTI, born Turin, May 23, 1959; admitted, 1987, Italy. Education: University of Turin (LL.D., 1985). Member: Bar Association of Turin. LANGUAGES: Italian and English. PRACTICE AREAS: Civil Litigation; Commercial; Company.

AVV. GABRIELLA CHIERA DI VASCO, born Turin, July 29, 1949; admitted, 1978, Italy. Education: University of Turin (LL.D). LANGUAGES: French and Italian. PRACTICE AREAS: Family; Matrimonial; Civil Litigation.

Languages: Italian, French and English.

GAMNA E ASSOCIATI
STUDIO LEGALE

Established in 1980

39, VIA LAMARMORA
10128 TURIN, ITALY
Telephone: 011-597.733-597.616-599.652
Telecopier: 011-505.742

Milan, Italy Office: 8, Via Boito. Telephone: 02-72.15.71.

General Practice. Corporation, Taxation, Patent, Labor Law, Banking, Estate and Foreign Investments, Bankruptcy, Commercial Law, Administrative, Mergers and Acquisitions.

MEMBERS OF FIRM

FEDERICO GAMNA, born Turin, Italy, February 11, 1924; admitted, 1948, Italy; 1962, Supreme Court. Education: University of Turin (J.D., 1946). Lecturer on Commercial Law, Turin University, 1947-1953. LANGUAGES: Italian, French, English and German. PRACTICE AREAS: Corporation; Banking; Estate and Foreign Investments; Mergers and Acquisitions; Taxation.

CARLO GAMNA, born Turin, Italy, November 20, 1951; admitted, 1978, Italy; 1992, Supreme Court. Education: University of Turin (J.D., 1975). Member: Young Lawyers Association of Turin; A.I.J.A. (Young Lawyers' International Association); German-Italian Jurists' Association; UIA; Associazione Internazionale Giuristi di Lingua Italiana. LANGUAGES: Italian, French and English. PRACTICE AREAS: Corporation; Banking; Patent; Commercial Law; Estate and Foreign Investments; Mergers and Acquisitions.

(This Listing Continued)

GUIDO CANALE, born Turin, Italy, July 18, 1958; admitted, 1984, Italy. Education: University of Turin (J.D., 1981). Professor of Bankruptcy Law, Urbino University. Member: Società Italiana Studi Concorsuali; Associazione Italiana Studiosi Del Processo Civile; Young Lawyers Association of Turin. LANGUAGES: Italian, French and English. PRACTICE AREAS: General Practice; Commercial Law; Corporation; Labor Law; Bankruptcy.

ALESSANDRA SPAGNOL, born Turin, Italy, August 13, 1960; admitted, 1991, Italy. Education: University of Turin (J.D., 1985). Member: Young Lawyers Association of Turin. LANGUAGES: Italian and English. PRACTICE AREAS: General Practice; Commercial Law.

GIANCARLO ASTEGIANO, born Bra (Cuneo), Italy, February 22, 1964; admitted, 1992, Italy. Education: University of Turin (J.D., 1989). Member: Young Lawyers Association of Turin. LANGUAGES: Italian and English. PRACTICE AREAS: Corporation; Commercial Law; Administrative; Banking; Estate and Foreign Investments; Labor Law; Taxation.

ASSOCIATES

FRANCESCA PAMPARARO, born Asmara, Ethiopia, February 27, 1965; admitted, 1993, Italy. Education: University of Turin (J.D., 1990). Member: Young Lawyers Association of Turin. LANGUAGES: Italian and French. PRACTICE AREAS: General Practice; Commercial Law.

BARBARA PELISSERO, born Roma, Italy, July 29, 1968; admitted before the Lower Courts, 1994, Italy; Education: University of Turin (J.D., 1993). LANGUAGES: Italian, English and French. PRACTICE AREAS: General Practice; Commercial Law; Corporation.

ALBERTO MURATORE, born San Remo (Imperia), Italy, May 3, 1970; admitted before Lower Courts, 1995, Italy; Education: University of Turin (J.D., 1994). LANGUAGES: Italian, English and French. PRACTICE AREAS: General Practice; Commercial Law; Corporation.

ALBERTO CORTASSA, born Pinerolo (Torino), Italy, April 23, 1967; admitted before Lower Courts, 1994, Italy; Education: University of Turin (J.D., 1993). Member: ADEK (Association des Anciens Stagiaires de l'Union Europeenne). LANGUAGES: Italian, French and English. PRACTICE AREAS: General Practice; Commercial Law.

COUNSEL

MARIA TERESA ARMOSINO, born Turin, Italy, July 20, 1955; admitted, 1982, Italy. Education: University of Turin (J.D., 1978). LANGUAGES: Italian and English. PRACTICE AREAS: General Practice; Commercial Law.

VINCENZO M. CARENA, born Turin, Italy, September 12, 1956; admitted, 1987, Italy. Education: University of Turin (J.D., cum laude, 1983). Member: A.I.J.A. (Young Lawyers' International Association); Young Lawyers Association of Turin. LANGUAGES: Italian and French. PRACTICE AREAS: General Practice; Commercial Law; Patent.

PAOLO TOSI, born Carrara, Italy, March 25, 1943; admitted, 1979, Italy. Education: University of Pavia (J.D., 1965). Professor of Labor Law, University of Turin and Catholic University of Sacro Cuore of Milan. Member: Associazione Italiana del Diritto del Lavoro e della Sicurezza Sociale. LANGUAGES: Italian and French. PRACTICE AREAS: General Practice; Labor Law.

JACOBACCI & PERANI

Established in 1872

CORSO REGIO PARCO 27
10152 TURIN, ITALY
Telephone: 2440311
Cable Address: "Casettaro-Torino"
Telex: 221494 Patent I
Fax: 286300; 286676 (automatic reception, group II and III)

Mailing Address: P.O. Box 321, 10100 Torino Centro, Italy

Milan, Italy Office: Via Visconti di Modrone 7, 20122. Telephone: 76006884; 76020043. Telex: 335441 Japemi I. Fax: 794925.
Padua, Italy Office: Via Berchet 9, 35131. Telephone: 65.19.31; 65.01.46. Telex: 432321 Jacpad I. Fax: 65.16.31.
Bologna, Italy Office: Via Aurelio Saffi, 73/2, 40131. Telephone: 521081. Telex: 520613 Japebo I. Fax: 521038.

Patent, Design, Trademark and Copyright Law, Licensing, Franchising, Unfair Competition and Contracts, EEC Law.

(This Listing Continued)

JACOBACCI & PERANI, Turin—Continued

MEMBERS OF FIRM

DR. ING. FILIPPO JACOBACCI, born Turin, Italy, September 4, 1918. Admitted to practice before the Patent Office and the Commission of Appeals of the Patent Office; European Patent Attorney. *Education:* Polytechnic Institute, University of Turin (Mechanical Engineer, 1942). *Member:* AIPPI; International Federation of Patent Agents; LES-Italy. *LANGUAGES:* Italian, English, French and German. *PRACTICE AREAS:* Patent and Design Law.

DR. GUIDO JACOBACCI, born Turin, Italy, December 28, 1926. Admitted to practice before the Patent Office and the Commission of Appeals of the Patent Office; European Patent Attorney. *Education:* Law School, University of Turin (Doctor of Law, 1952). *Member:* AIPPI; International Federation of Patent Agents; LES-Italy (President, 1980-1986). *LANGUAGES:* Italian, English, French and German. *PRACTICE AREAS:* Trademark; Patent; Design; Copyright; Unfair Competition Law.

DR. ING. AURELIO PERANI, born Milan, Italy, March 29, 1933. Admitted to practice before the Patent Office and the Commission of Appeals; European Patent Attorney. *Education:* Polytechnic Institute, University of Milan (Electrotechnical Engineer, 1958). *Member:* AIPPI; LES-Italy. (Resident, Milan Office). *LANGUAGES:* Italian, English, French and German. *PRACTICE AREAS:* Patent and Design Law.

DR. ING. PIERRE SACONNEY, born Turin, Italy, March 5, 1933. Admitted to practice before the Italian Patent Office and the Commission of Appeals; European Patent Attorney. *Education:* Polytechnic Institute University of Turin (Electrical Engineer, 1958; Aeronautical Engineer, 1960). *Member:* AIPPI; LES-Italy. *LANGUAGES:* Italian, English, French, German and Spanish. *PRACTICE AREAS:* Patent and Design Law.

DR. FABRIZIO JACOBACCI, born Turin, Italy, March 7, 1963; Trademark Attorney *Education:* Law School, University of Turin (Doctor of Law, 1988). *Member:* AIPPI; LES Italy. *LANGUAGES:* Italian, English, French and German. *PRACTICE AREAS:* Trademark; Copyright; Unfair Competition Law; EEC Law; Litigation; Law of Contracts.

DR. PAOLO PERANI, born Milan, Italy, March 14, 1964; Trademark Attorney. *Education:* Law School, University of Milan (Doctor of Law, 1988). *Member:* AIPPI; LES Italy. (Resident, Milan Office). *LANGUAGES:* Italian, English and French. *PRACTICE AREAS:* Trademark; Copyright; Unfair Competition Law; EEC Law; Litigation; Law of Contracts.

DR. ING. TORQUATO VANNINI, born Milan, Italy, January 28, 1934. Admitted to practice before the Italian Patent Office and the Commission of Appeals; European Patent Attorney. *Education:* Polytechnic Institute, University of Milan (Chemical Engineer). (Resident, Milan Office). *LANGUAGES:* Italian and English. *PRACTICE AREAS:* Patent and Design Law.

DR. CARLO MEZZANOTTE, born Modena, Italy, January 26, 1941. Admitted to practice before the Italian Patent Office and the Commission of Appeals. *Education:* Law School, University of Milan (Doctor of Law, 1972). *Member:* LES-Italy; AIPPI. (Resident, Milan Office). *LANGUAGES:* Italian, English and French. *PRACTICE AREAS:* Trademark; Copyright; Unfair Competition Law.

DR. ING. GIUSEPPE QUINTERNO, born Moncalieri (Turin), Italy, March 18, 1952. Admitted to practice before the Italian Patent Office and the Commission of Appeals; European Patent Attorney. *Education:* Polytechnic Institute, University of Turin (Electronic Engineer, 1977). *Member:* AIPPI. *LANGUAGES:* Italian, English, French and German. *PRACTICE AREAS:* Patent and Design Law.

DR. MASSIMO INTROVIGNE, born Rome, Italy, June 14, 1955. Admitted to practice before Italian Patent Office and the Commission of Appeals. *Education:* Law School, University of Turin (Doctor of Law, 1979). Assistant Lecturer, Law Institute, University of Turin. *Member:* LES-Italy; AIPPI. *LANGUAGES:* Italian, English and French. *PRACTICE AREAS:* Trademark; Copyright; Patent; Unfair Competition Law; EEC Law; Litigation; Law of Contracts.

DR. ING. LUCIANO BOSOTTI, born Turin, Italy, December 29, 1952. Admitted to practice before the Italian Patent Office and the Commission of Appeals; European Patent Attorney. *Education:* Polytechnic Institute, University of Turin (Electronic Engineer, 1976). *Member:* AIPPI. *LANGUAGES:* Italian, English, French and German. *PRACTICE AREAS:* Patent and Design Law; Contracts.

(This Listing Continued)

DR. ING. PAOLO RAMBELLI, born Turin, Italy, December 9, 1951. Admitted to practice before the Italian Patent Office and the Commission of Appeals, European Patent Attorney, Chemical Engineer. *Education:* Polytechnic Institute (1976); University of Turin; Worcester Polytechnic Institute, Massachusetts. *Member:* AIPPI. *LANGUAGES:* Italian, English, German and French. *PRACTICE AREAS:* Patent and Design Law.

DR. ING. STEFANO CANTALUPPI, born Milan, Italy, December 3, 1954. Admitted to practice before the Patent Office and the Commission of Appeals of the Patent Office; European Patent Attorney. *Education:* Polytechnic Institute, University of Milan (Mechanical Engineer, 1980). *Member:* AIPPI. (Resident, Padua Office). *LANGUAGES:* Italian, English, French and German. *PRACTICE AREAS:* Patent and Design Law.

DR. PATRIZIA FRANCESCHINA, born Turin, Italy, April 18, 1957; Trademark Attorney. *Education:* Law School, Political Sciences School (Doctor of Law, 1980). *LANGUAGES:* Italian, English, German and French. *PRACTICE AREAS:* Trademark; Copyright; Unfair Competition Law; EEC Law; Law of Contracts.

DR. ING. ROBERTO DE NOVA, born Messina, Italy, April 29, 1938; Admitted to practice before the Patent Office and the Commission of Appeals of the Patent Office; European Patent Attorney. *Education:* Polytechnic Institute, University of Milan (Mechanical Engineer, 1963). (Resident, Milan Office). *LANGUAGES:* Italian, English, German and French. *PRACTICE AREAS:* Patent and Design Law.

DR. CLAUDIO MAGGIONI, born Rome, Italy, September 9, 1940; Admitted to practice before the Patent Office and the Commission of Appeals of the Patent Office; European Patent Attorney. *Education:* University of Catania (Degree in Physics). (Resident, Milan Office). *LANGUAGES:* Italian, English, German, French and Spanish. *PRACTICE AREAS:* Patent and Design Law.

DR. SERGIO MULDER, born Milan, Italy, March 3, 1951; Trademark Attorney *Education:* University of Milan (Degree in Philosophy, 1977). *Member:* AIPPI. (Resident, Milan Office). *LANGUAGES:* Italian, English and French. *PRACTICE AREAS:* Trademark and Copyright Law.

DR. ING. CARLO FALCETTI, born Milan, Italy, April 23, 1937; Admitted to practice before the Patent Office and the Commission of Appeals of the Patent Office; European Patent Attorney. *Education:* Polytechnic Institute University of Milan (Electronic Engineer, 1963). *Member:* AIPPI. (Resident, Milan Office). *LANGUAGES:* Italian, English, German and French. *PRACTICE AREAS:* Patent and Design Law.

DR. ENRICO RICCARDINO, born Turin, Italy, January 3, 1962; Trademark Attorney. *Education:* Law School, University of Turin (Doctor of Law, 1985). *LANGUAGES:* Italian, English and French. *PRACTICE AREAS:* Trademark and Copyright Law.

ASSOCIATES

GIOVANNI SERTOLI. *LANGUAGES:* Italian, English, French, German and Russian. *PRACTICE AREAS:* Trademark and Copyright Law.

MARCO FRANCETTI (Resident, Milan Office). *LANGUAGES:* Italian, English and French. *PRACTICE AREAS:* Trademark; Patent; Copyright; Unfair Competition Law; EEC Law; Litigation; Contracts.

FABIO SINISCALCO European Patent Attorney (Resident, Milan Office). *LANGUAGES:* Italian, English, German and French. *PRACTICE AREAS:* Patent and Design Law.

MAURO MARCHITELLI, European Patent Attorney. *LANGUAGES:* Italian, English and French. *PRACTICE AREAS:* Patent and Design Law.

ANGELO GERBINO, European Patent Attorney. *LANGUAGES:* Italian, English and French. *PRACTICE AREAS:* Patent and Design Law.

PAOLA GELATO. *LANGUAGES:* Italian, English, German, French, Russian and Spanish. *PRACTICE AREAS:* Trademark; Unfair Competition and Copyright Law.

BIANCA MARIA TESTA (Resident, Padua Office). *LANGUAGES:* Italian, English and French. *PRACTICE AREAS:* Trademark and Copyright Law.

LUCA MASSIMO GEONI (Resident, Milan Office). *LANGUAGES:* Italian, English and French. *PRACTICE AREAS:* Trademark and Copyright Law.

GABRIELE BORASI (Resident, Milan Office). *LANGUAGES:* Italian, English and French. *PRACTICE AREAS:* Trademark and Copyright Law.

(This Listing Continued)

PAOLO CIAN. *LANGUAGES:* Italian, English and French. *PRACTICE AREAS:* Patent and Design Law.

FABIO ROVERATI (Resident, Bologna Office). *LANGUAGES:* Italian, English and French. *PRACTICE AREAS:* Trademark and Patent Law; Litigation; Law of Contracts and Copyright Law.

FILIPPO FERRONI (Resident, Milan Office). *LANGUAGES:* Italian, English and French. *PRACTICE AREAS:* Patent and Design Law.

MASSIMO STERPI. *LANGUAGES:* Italian, English and French. *PRACTICE AREAS:* Trademark, Copyright and Unfair Competition Law; EEC Law; Litigation; Law of Contracts.

PAOLO PROVVISIONATO (Resident, Bologna Office). *LANGUAGES:* Italian, English and French. *PRACTICE AREAS:* Patent and Design Law.

SILVIA LAZZAROTTO. *LANGUAGES:* Italian, English and French. *PRACTICE AREAS:* Trademark and Copyright Law.

MARCO BALDAN. *LANGUAGES:* Italian, English and French. *PRACTICE AREAS:* Patent and Design Law.

FRANCESCO SERRA, European Patent Attorney. *LANGUAGES:* Italian, English and French. *PRACTICE AREAS:* Patent and Design Law.

GIULIA CAROLINA RUMI (Resident, Milan Office). *LANGUAGES:* Italian, English and French. *PRACTICE AREAS:* Trademark and Copyright Law.

CARLO ALBERTO DEMICHELIS. *LANGUAGES:* Italian, English and French. *PRACTICE AREAS:* Trademark and Copyright Law.

RINALDO FERRECCIO (Resident, Milan Office). *LANGUAGES:* Italian, English, German and French. *PRACTICE AREAS:* Patent and Design Law.

MARIO LEONE (Resident, Milan Office). *LANGUAGES:* Italian, English and French. *PRACTICE AREAS:* Patent and Design Law.

MARIA ELENA PIRETTI (Resident, Bologna Office). *LANGUAGES:* Italian and English. *PRACTICE AREAS:* Trademark and Copyright Law.

Languages: Italian, English, French, German, Spanish and Russian

---

MAGRONE E ARDITO

VIA BRUNO BUOZZI, 10
10123 TURIN, ITALY
Telephone: (011) 5623801
Telecopier (Gr 2-3): (011) 3101043

Rome, Italy Office: Via del Banco di S. Spirito, 42. Telephone: (06) 6879962. Telex: 611416 ITALAW. Telecopier (Gr.2-3): (06) 6751240.
Milan, Italy Office: Via Borgonuovo, 20. Telephone: (02) 6575181. Telecopier (Gr. 2-3): (02) 6570013.
Brussels, Belgium Office: 13, Av. De Tervuren. Telephone: (02) 7359442. Telecopier (Gr. 2-3): (02) 7359622.

General, International and Domestic Practice.

(For Complete Biographical Data on all Personnel, see Professional Biographies at Rome, and Milan, Italy)

PESCE, FRIGNANI, PASTORE & RUBEN
LAW FIRM

VIA ARGONNE, 1
I-10133 TURIN, ITALY
Telephone: 39-11-6602302/6602151/6604257
Telex: 325065 LEXMIL I
Telecopier: 39-11-6601884

Milan, Italy Office: via dei Giardini, 4, I-20121. Telephone: 39-2-29003140/6575143. Telex: 325065 LEXMIL I. Telecopier: 39-2-6554886.
Vienna, Austria Office: Kohlmarkt, 4/19,A-1010. Telephone: 43-1-5338437-5335856. Fax: 43-1-533585675-533843775.

General Legal Practice, International Contracts, Corporations, Banking Law, Acquisitions, Patent, Trademark and Unfair Competition Law, Copyright Law, EEC Law, Antitrust Regulations, Transportation, Insurance and Reinsurance, International Private and Commercial Law, Family Law, Suretyships and Credit Protection, Product Liability.

(This Listing Continued)

MEMBERS OF FIRM

ALDO FRIGNANI, born Modena, Italy, November 23, 1937; admitted, 1965, Italy. *Education:* University of Modena (J.D., 1962); Johns Hopkins University (1963); Faculté Internationale de Droit Comparé, Strasbourg (1965); New York University Law School (1971); Academy of American and International Law, Dallas (1975). Author: "L'injunction nella common law e l'inibitoria in diritto italiano," 1974; "Disciplina della concorrenza nella CEE," 4th ed., 1995 (in cooperation with Waelbroock; 2nd ed. in French, 1995); "Factoring, Leasing, Franchising, Venture Capital Hardship Clause, Leveraged Buy-Out, Countertrade, Merchandising Know-how," 5th ed., 1993; "Il diritto del commercio internazionale," 2nd ed., 1992; "Il contratto internazionalc," 1990; "Il franchising," 1990; "Italian Company Law," 1992, (in cooperation with Elia); "Commentary on Italian Antitrust Law" (in cooperation with others), 1993. Professor of Comparative Law, University of Turin. Professor of USA and EEC Antitrust Law. Visiting Professor: Paris (Sorbonne); Gand; Louvain; Varsaw; Cracow; Lublin Fordham University, New York; Salzburg-McGeorge School of Law; Lyon; Istanbul. *LANGUAGES:* Italian, English, French, German, Spanish, Portuguese. *PRACTICE AREAS:* Industrial Property; Antitrust; Acquisitions; International Contracts; EEC Law; Arbitration.

PAOLA PIVANO, born Turin, July 13, 1954; admitted, 1982, Italy. *Education:* University of Turin (J.D., cum laude, 1979). *LANGUAGES:* Italian, English. *PRACTICE AREAS:* Commercial Law; Contracts; Banking; Bankruptcy Law.

PATRIZIA GROSSO, born Ancona, April 30, 1947. *Education:* University of Bologna (B.A., 1970); University of Ferrara (J.D., 1973). Faculté Internationale de Droit Comparé , Strasbourg (1981). Author: "I controlli interni nelle società cooperative," 1990; "La metamorfosi delle società cooperative," Giurisprudenza ital, 1993; "Osservazioui in tema di categorie di azioui e Assemblee speciali," in Giur. it, 1991,I,2,59l. Assistant Professor, Commercial Law, University of Turin. *LANGUAGES:* Italian, French, English. *PRACTICE AREAS:* Company Law; Commercial Law.

ROBERTO GANDIN, born Turin, February 21, 1962; admitted, 1992, Turin. *Education:* University of Turin (J.D., cum laude, 1988). Author: "Appunti in tema di attività inventiva," Foro Padano, 1988, I, 494; "La disciplina CEE del franchising," Giur.comm., 1991,I,495; "La comunione di brevetti," Contratto e impresa, 1992. *LANGUAGES:* Italian, French, English. *PRACTICE AREAS:* Industrial Property; Copyright.

NADIA TECCHIATI, born Turin, May 22, 1962; admitted, 1993, Turin. *Education:* University of Turin (J.D., 1989). *LANGUAGES:* French. *PRACTICE AREAS:* Contracts.

ROBERTA DI GREGORIO, born Turin, October 21, 1967. *Education:* University of Turin (J.D., maxima cum laude, 1991). Faculté Internationale de Droit Comparé , Strasbourg (license 1991). *LANGUAGES:* Italian, French, English. *PRACTICE AREAS:* Credit Collecting; Contracts.

ENRICO BELLA, born New York, December 5, 1967. *Education:* University of Turin (J.D., cum laude, 1991). *LANGUAGES:* Italian, English. *PRACTICE AREAS:* Factoring; Leasing.

ALBERTO RITUCCI, born Turin, November 4, 1963. *Education:* University of Turin (J.D., cum laude, 1993). *LANGUAGES:* English and French. *PRACTICE AREAS:* Credit Collecting.

Languages: Italian, German, English, French, Spanish and Portuguese.

STUDIO LEGALE FORLATI - MINELLI -
RIZZI

SAN MARCO 3830
30124 VENICE, ITALY
Telephone: (3941)-523-5354
Fax: (3941)-5221-032

General Practice, International Law, Maritime Law, Commercial Law, Family Law, Administrative Law, Bankruptcy Law and Civil Law.

PARTNERS

ZENO FORLATI, born Trieste, August 1, 1935; admitted, 1960, Italy. *Education:* University of Padua (J.D., 1958); Southern Methodist University, Dallas Texas (M. C. L., 1961). Member, Eurojuris Italia (E.E.I.Q.). *Member:* American Society International Law. *LANGUAGES:* English, French, German and Italian.

GIOVANNI MINELLI, born Venice, Italy, February 13, 1952; admitted, 1978, Italy. *Education:* University of Padua, (Doctor of Jurisprudence,

(This Listing Continued)

STUDIO LEGALE FORLATI - MINELLI - RIZZI,
Venice—Continued

1976). *Member:* Eurojuris Italia (E.E.I.Q.). *LANGUAGES:* English, French and Italian.

GIUSEPPE RIZZI, born Mantua, November 12, 1957; admitted, 1990, Italy. *Education:* University of Padua, Italy (Doctor of Jurisprudence). *Member:* (E.E.I.Q.). *LANGUAGES:* English and Italian.

FRANCESCO IADEROSA, born Venice, Italy, July 17, 1966; admitted, 1994, Italy. *Education:* University of Padua (Doctor of Jurisprudence, 1991). *Member:* Eurojuris, Italy (E.E.I.Q.). *LANGUAGES:* English and Italian.

FRAU & PARTNERS
STUDIO LEGALE ASSOCIATO

PIAZZA SAN NICOLÒ, 3
37121 VERONA, ITALY
Telephone: (045) 8001533
Telefax: (045) 8003115

Milan Office: Via Carlo Poerio, 15, 20129. Telephone: (02) 76003199 (r.a.). Telefax: (02) 7600331.
Rome Office: Via Barberini, 29, 00187. Telephone: (06) 4871151. Telefax: (06) 4827513.
Kiev Office: Kibalchicha 12, 253125. Telephone (044) 5127292 - 5128109. Telefax: (044) 5143305.

International Business Law, Corporate, Banking, Financing, Syndicated Loans, Eurobonds, Commodities, Asset Finance, Bond Issues, Aircraft Finance, Leasing, Merger and Acquisitions, Project Finance. Letters of Credit, Commercial Property, Securitization, Foreign Investments, Contracts, EEC, Antitrust and Competition, Real Estate, Building and Construction, International and Domestic Arbitration, International and Domestic Arbitration Litigation, International and Domestic Taxation, Aviation, Transportation, Tort and Intellectual Property, Licensing, Patent and Trademark, Distributorship, Agency and Franchising, Environmental and Media, Sport, Mining and Mineral.

(For Complete Biographical Data on all Personnel, see Professional Biographies at Milan, Italy).

AVV. DR. SILVIO MARZARI E COLLEGHI

VIA AMATORE SCIESA 8
37122 VERONA, ITALY
Telephone: 045/8034343; 045/942446; 045/8009958
Telex: 481806
Telefax: 045/8032641; 045/942423
Office Hours: Monday to Friday 8:30-12:30 15:30-19:00

Commercial, Corporate, Civil and Administrative Law. Insurance. Conflict of Laws. International and General Practice. Litigation.

AVV. DR. SILVIO MARZARI (1886-1967).

AVV. DR. SILVIO MARZARI, born Venice, December 24, 1943; admitted, 1972, Venice; 1978, Italy; 1986, Supreme Court, Italy. *Education:* Universities of Trieste and Padua (Doctor of Jurisprudence, 1969); University of Erlangen, Germany (1970). Research Associate, Universities of Padua and Verona, 1970-1984. Professor of Public Law, University of Verona, 1985-1986. *Member:* British Institute of International and Comparative Law, London; American Chamber of Commerce in Milan, Italy; Swiss Chamber of Commerce, Milan, Italy; Italian Chamber of Commerce, Munich, Germany; German Italian Law Society. *LANGUAGES:* Italian, English and German. *PRACTICE AREAS:* International Trade; Commercial Law.

AVV. DR. FAUSTO MAESTRONI, born Brescia, April 6, 1951; admitted, 1980, Venice; 1986, Italy. *Education:* University of Modena (Doctor of Jurisprudence, 1979). *Member:* German Italian Law Society. *LANGUAGES:* Italian, English and German.

AVV. DR. GABRIELLA MAGGIORA, born Nocera Inferiore, March 19, 1957; admitted, 1986, Venice. *Education:* University of Bologna (Doctor of Jurisprudence, 1985). *LANGUAGES:* Italian and English.

(This Listing Continued)

DR. PROC. ROBERTO NICOLINI, born Verona, February 23, 1964; admitted, 1991, Venice. *Education:* University of Bologna (Doctor of Jurisprudence, 1988). *LANGUAGES:* Italian, English and German.

DR. STEFANIA GIOCO, born Verona, March 20, 1965. *Education:* University of Padua (Doctor of Jurisprudence, 1991). *LANGUAGES:* Italian, English and German.

DR. MAURO MAZZONE, born Verona, August 8, 1967. *Education:* University of Bologna (Doctor of Jurisprudence, 1991). *LANGUAGES:* Italian, English and German.

DR. GIANFRANCO GALLO, born Cremona, December 4, 1967. *Education:* University of Bologna (Doctor of Jurisprudence, 1992). *LANGUAGES:* Italian and English.

DR. ELENA MUTTI, born Feltre, October 2, 1969. *Education:* University of Milan (Doctor of Jurisprudence, 1994). *LANGUAGES:* Italian, English and German.

COUNSEL

AVV. DR. SERGIO MAZZONE, born Senerchia, June 6, 1935; admitted, 1964, Italy.

AVV. DR. ANTONIO LIUZZI, born Lecce, May 30, 1934; admitted, 1961, Italy. (Rme Office).

REFERENCES: Volkswagen Werke AG, Wolfsburg, Germany; Allianz Versicherungs-AG, Munich and Berlin, Germany; Gerling Konzern AG, Cologne, Germany; AA, The Automobile Association, England; ADAC, German Automobile Club, Munich, Germany; ANWB, Royal Dutch Touring Club, The Hague, Netherlands; Automobile Club Verona, Italy; Shultz Steel Co., South Gate, California; Sparkasse München, Munich, Germany; Grossversandhaus Quelle Gustav Schickedanz KG, Fürth, Germany; Jil Sander AG, Hamburg, Germany; Tiroler Sparkasse, Innsbruck, Austria; Bolla Wines, Verona, Italy; MAN Veicoli Industriali Spa, Verona, Italy; The Council of Verona, Italy; Gerolsteiner Brunnen GmbH & Co., Gerolstein, Germany; Lidl Italia Srl, Verona, Italy.

REPUBLIC OF LATVIA

MAIJA SIBILLA BLAUBERGA,
ZVERINATU ADVOKATU BIROJS

Established in 1993

KR. BARONA IELA 31
RIGA LV-1011, REPUBLIC OF LATVIA
Telephone: (371) 9-348670; 2-283856
Telefax: (371) 9-348670; 2-283856

General Corporate and Business Law, Joint Ventures and General International Trade Law, Copyright, Trademarks and Intellectual Property Law, Entertainment Law, Real Estate and Property Development, Banking Law, International Arbitration, International Adoptions.

MAIJA SIBILLA BLAUBERGA, born Oldenburg, Germany, February 20, 1947. *Education:* University of Toronto (B.A., 1968); University of California, Santa Barbara (M.A., 1970; Ph.D., 1972); University of Georgia (Juris Doctor, magna cum laude, 1983, Order of the Coif). Articles Editor, Ga. J. Int'l & Comp. L., 1982-1983. Law Clerk, Honorable Robert Madden Hill, United States Court of Appeals, Fifth Circuit, Dallas, Texas, U.S.A., 1984-1985. Staff Attorney, Staff Counsel's Office, United States Court of Appeals, Fifth Circuit, New Orleans, Louisiana, U.S.A., 1983-1984. Legal Advisor: Ministry of Foreign Trade, Republic of Latvia, 1992; Council of Ministers, Department of Foreign Economic Relations, Republic of Latvia, 1991. Associate, Steptoe & Johnson, Attorneys at Law, Washington, D.C., U.S.A., 1985-1992. Of Counsel, Carroll, Burdick & McDonough, San Francisco, California, U.S.A., and Riga, Latvia, 1992-1993. Author: "Jurisdiction Over Imports Controversies After the Customs Courts Act of 1980," 12 Ga. J. Int'l & Comp L 232, 1982; "Residence of Foreign Sovereign Diplomatic and Consular Staff is Immune from Taxation under A Bilateral Agreement and the Foreign Sovereign Immunities Act," 12 Ga. J. Int'l & Comp. L 429, 1982; "Gaps in Latvian Copyright Legislation," The Latvian Lawyer, 1992. *Member:* Latvian Bar Association; District of Columbia Bar and State of Georgia Bar; Latvian Lawyers' Society (Member, Board of Directors); Latvian Film Producers Association (Vice President); Legal Translators Association (Member, Board of Directors). *LANGUAGES:* English and Latvian.

BLUEGER & PLAUDE

8/10 L. PILS STREET
RIGA LV-1050, REPUBLIC OF LATVIA
Telephone: (3712) 225231
Facsimile: (3719) 348201

FIRM PROFILE: *The Law Firm offers a wide range of legal services; drafting the foundation documents of the companies with different types of property; drafting the legal documents such as contracts, agreements, etc.; legal assistance in privatization, financial and tax problems; consulting on the issues of copyrights and intellectual property; entertainment law practice; representing clients in courts, in the Latvian court of arbitration; real estate law.*

VALENTIN BLUEGER, born Riga, December 23, 1959; admitted, 1981, Latvia. *Education:* Lativan University, Riga (1982); Vanderbilt University, Nashville, Tennessee (1989-1990). Associate: Farris, Warfield & Kanaday, Nashville, Tennessee (1989-1990); Carro, Spanbock, Kaster & Cuiffo, New York, N.Y. (1989). *LANGUAGES:* Latvian, Russian and English.

BAIBA PLAUDE, born Riga, July 17, 1956; admitted, 1979, Latvia. *Education:* Latvian University (1979); American Bar Association Internship Program for Lawyers. Law Firm, Jenner & Block, Chicago, Il. USA (1989). Lecturer: Latvian University Law Faculty on "Legal Regulations on Foreign Investments in Latvia." *Member:* Latvian Lawyer's Association; Examination Committee of the Latvian Collegium of Advocats. *LANGUAGES:* Latvian, Russian and English.

VAIRIS REINHOLDS, born Plavinas, Latvia, 1940; admitted, 1966, Latvia. *Education:* Latvian University Law Faculty (1963). *LANGUAGES:* Latvian and Russian.

EUGENE MANENKOV, born Ivanovo, Russia, August 19, 1959; admitted, 1987, Latvia. *Education:* Latvian University Law Faculty (1981). *LANGUAGES:* Latvian, Russian and English.

ASSOCIATES

JĀNIS ZELMENIS, born Riga, Latvia, September 24, 1971. *Education:* Moscow State Institute of International Relations, Faculty of International Law (M.A. in Law, 1993). Author: "The legal aspects of electronic documents in international maritime transport.". *LANGUAGES:* Latvian, Russian, English, Swedish and Portuguese.

BLUKIS & ELKSNE

BRIVIBAS STREET 40-24
RIGA LV-1050, REPUBLIC OF LATVIA
Telephone: (+371-2) 288-264; (+371-9) 348-185
Fax: (+371-9) 348-185

Foreign Investment Law, Corporate Law, Tax Laws, Privatization Law, Labour Law, Litigation.

FIRM PROFILE: *The firm has a wide practice with a reputation for offering a full range of quality legal services to the foreign investor. The client base is European and North American. The firm has specialized experience in EC PHARE, EBRD and British Know-How Fund projects relating to privatization and provides a wide variety of legal services to the Latvian and foreign governmental organizations.*

MEMBERS OF FIRM

RAIMONDS BLUKIS, born Latvia, March 2, 1956; admitted, 1979. *Education:* University of Latvia Law School. *Member:* Latvian Bar Association; International Bar Association; Eastern European Forum. *LANGUAGES:* Latvian, English and Russian.

VALENTINA ELKSNE, born Latvia, February 23, 1947; admitted, 1973. *Education:* University of Latvia Law School. *Member:* Latvian Bar Association; Latvian Lawyers' Association. *LANGUAGES:* Latvian, Russian and English.

ASSOCIATES

IVO ALEHNO, born Latvia, December 25, 1967; admitted, 1993. *Education:* University of Latvia Law School. *LANGUAGES:* Latvian, Russian, French and English.

CARROLL, BURDICK & McDONOUGH

TERBATAS IELA 4
LV 1011 RIGA, REPUBLIC OF LATVIA
Telephone: +371-782-8181 (International);
Local Telephone: 228022
International Fax: +371-782-8171
Local Fax: 283615

San Francisco, California Office: 44 Montgomery Street, Suite 400. Telephone: 415-989-5900.
Walnut Creek, California Office: 1676 North California Boulevard, Suite 620. Telephone: 510-945-8579.
Sacramento, California Office: Wells Fargo Center, 400 Capitol Mall, Suite 1400. Telephone: 916-446-2222.

Latvian Practice.

FIRM PROFILE: *Carroll, Burdick & McDonough was established in 1948 and is an international business and commercial law firm serving clients throughout the United States and around the world in a wide scope of business and litigation matters. The firm has grown dramatically in recent years to its present size of over 80 lawyers located in offices in San Francisco, Sacramento, Walnut Creek, California as well as Riga, Latvia.*

JUSTS N. KARLSONS, born Riga, Latvia, September 22, 1943; admitted, 1969, California and Washington; 1993, Latvia. *Education:* Yale University (A.B., cum laude, 1965); University of Munich, Germany; Stanford University (LL.B., 1968). Recipient, American Jurisprudence Book Award for Tort Law. Member, Product Liability Advisory Council. Guest Lecturer, Legal Reforms for a New Latvia, University of Riga. *Member:* Bar Association of San Francisco; Washington State and American (Member, International Law Section) Bar Associations; State Bar of California; American-Latvian Bar Association; Defense Research Institute; Northern California Defense Association; Latvian Advocate College; Union International des Avocats. [Lt., J.A.G.C., USNR, 1969-1972]. (Also at San Francisco, California Office). *LANGUAGES:* German, Latvian, Russian and English.

IVARS J. BARS, born Toronto, Canada, 1954; admitted, 1981, Ontario, Canada and California; 1988, District of Columbia; 1993, Republic of Latvia. *Education:* University of Toronto (B.A., 1976); Osgoode Hall Law School (LL.B., 1979). Guest Lecturer, International Contract Law, University of Latvia. Who's Who in American Law. International Legal Counsel, Bell Canada International, (Ottawa, Canada, 1982-1984, Riyadh, Saudi Arabia, 1984-1987). *Member:* Bar Association of San Francisco; American and Latvian Bar Associations. (Also at San Francisco, California Office). *LANGUAGES:* English and Latvian.

WALTER E. KRONBERGS, born Toronto, Canada, August 8, 1960; admitted, 1992, Ontario. *Education:* University of Toronto, University College (B.A., with honors, 1984); Queen's University Faculty of Law (LL.B., 1990). *Member:* Law Society of Upper Canada; Canadian Bar Association; Latvian Canadian Business Council (Secretary, International Commission of Jurists, Latvia Section). *LANGUAGES:* Latvian; English.

INETA KRODEGE, born Riga, Latvia, March 25, 1962; admitted, 1985, Latvia. *Education:* Latvian University, Law Faculty (1981). Internship program with the Law Firm of Lang Michener, Toronto, Canada (1993). *Member:* Latvian Bar Association; International Bar Association. *LANGUAGES:* Latvian, Russian and English.

ILZE BUKANE, born Jekabpils, Latvia, February 1, 1965; admitted, 1988, Latvia. *Education:* Latvian University, Law Faculty (1988); Institute of International Studies of Latvia, (1992); Capital University Law School, Ohio, U.S.A. (LL.M., 1993). *Member:* Latvian Lawyers Association; International Bar Association; International Association of Young Lawyers. *LANGUAGES:* Latvian, Russian and English.

ARMANDS SKUDRA, born Riga, Latvia, November 19, 1963; admitted, 1993, Latvia. *Education:* Latvian University, Law Faculty (1993); New York University Law School, New York, U.S.A. (LL.M., 1994). *LANGUAGES:* Latvian, Russian and English.

ZIEDONIS UDRIS, born Riga, Latvia, February 27, 1963; admitted, 1986, Latvia. *Education:* Latvian University, Law Faculty (1986); Case Western Reserve University School of Law (LL.M., 1994). Internship programs with American Arbitration Association, Cleveland, Ohio, U.S.A., and the International Arbitration in Milan, Italy. *Member:* Latvian Lawyers Association. *LANGUAGES:* Latvian, Russian, English and French.

PETERIS JURJANS

In Association with Ludins and Eglitis

RAINA BLVD. NR 25 SUITE 409
RIGA LV-1050, REPUBLIC OF LATVIA
Telephone: +371-2-210971
International Fax: +371-9-342568

Cleveland Ohio, U.S.A. Office: 38201 Euclid Avenue, Cleveland (Willoughby), Ohio, 44094. Telephone: 216-951-6665. Fax: 216-951-4797.

International Business and Commercial Practice, Foreign Investments in the Republic of Latvia, Contract Law, Real Estate Law, Privatization Projects.

PETERIS JURJANS, born Wurzburg, Germany, March 22, 1947; admitted, 1972, Ohio; 1977, U.S. Supreme Court. *Education:* The Ohio State University (B.S.B.A., International Trade & Marketing, 1969); Cleveland State University (J.D., 1972). Legal Advisor to Latvian Parliament and sub-committee witness for draft legislation, 1991—. Partner, Greene, Tulley & Jurjans, 1977-1991. U.S. Department of Justice, Immigration and Naturalization Service, 1971-1972. Honorary Consul (Cleveland), Republic of Latvia, 1994—. *Member:* Lake County, Ohio State (Member, International Law Committee, 1988—) and Latvian Bar Associations. *LANGUAGES:* Latvian. *PRACTICE AREAS:* International Law; Real Estate; Probate Law.

INDULIS LUDINS, born Ainazi, Republic of Latvia, July 23, 1960; admitted, 1983, Latvia. *Education:* University of Latvia, Law Faculty, 1983. *Member:* Latvian Bar Association. *LANGUAGES:* English, Latvian, Russian.

JURIS EGLITIS, born Riga, Republic of Latvia, January 21, 1959; admitted, 1983, Latvia. *Education:* University of Latvia, Law Faculty, 1983. *Member:* Latvian Bar Association. *LANGUAGES:* English, Latvian, Russian.

RAYMONDS KRASTINS, born Riga, Republic of Latvia, November 17, 1966. *Education:* University of Latvia, Law Faculty, 1993, Magistracy. *LANGUAGES:* English, Latvian, Russian.

KLAVINS & SLAIDINS

KR. VALDEMARA 31
RIGA LV-1010, REPUBLIC OF LATVIA
Telephone: 328820
Direct International: +371-783-0000
Facsimile: +371-783-0001

General and International Practice, Foreign Investments in the Republic of Latvia, Industrial and Agricultural Privatization Projects, Corporate and Real Estate Law, Patent and Trademark Registrations.

FILIP K. KLAVINS, born Durham, North Carolina, January 10, 1961; admitted, 1986, Connecticut; 1988, New York; 1992, Republic of Latvia. *Education:* Tufts University, Medford, Ma. (B.A., cum laude, History and English, 1983); Duke University, Durham, NC (J.D., 1986). Legal Advisor: Supreme Council Standing Committee on Legislation; Ministry of Foreign Affairs of the Republic of Latvia, 1990-1991. Lecturer, American Contracts Law, University of Latvia Law School, 1990-1991. Guest Lecturer in Law, Stockholm School of Economics, Riga. Member: American Chamber of Commerce in Latvia (Board of Directors); Senator A. Leber Legal Scholarship Foundation (Board of Directors); American Bar Association Dictionary of Legal Synonyms Latvian/English (Board of Advisors). Associate: Baker & McKenzie, New York, NY, 1988-1990; Finley, Kumble, Wagner, Heine, Underberg, Manley, Myerson & Casey, New York, NY, 1986-1988. *Member:* Connecticut, American and Latvian-American (Vice-President, 1989-1991) Bar Associations (USA); Latvian Lawyers' Association, Latvian Bar Association (Latvia). *LANGUAGES:* English and Latvian.

RAYMOND L. SLAIDINS, born Omaha, Nebraska, May 30, 1958; admitted, 1985, California; 1992, Republic of Latvia. *Education:* University of California, Berkeley, CA (B.A., Political Science, 1980); Santa Clara University, Santa Clara, CA (J.D., 1984). Honorary Legal Advisor to the British Ambassador, Latvia. Guest Lecturer in Law, Stockholm School of Economics, Riga. American Bar Association Dictionary of Legal Synonyms Latvian/English (Board of Advisors); Board of Directors, Latvian Volleyball Federation. Counsellor to the Foreign Minister, Ministry of Foreign

(This Listing Continued)

Affairs of the Republic of Latvia, 1991-1992. Senior Corporate Counsel, Ingres Corporation, Alameda, CA, 1990-1991. Senior Associate, Carroll, Burdick & McDonough, San Francisco, CA, 1986-1990. *Member:* California and Latvian-American Bar Associations (USA); Latvian Lawyers' Association, Latvian Bar Association (Latvia). Registered Trademark Agent, Latvia. *LANGUAGES:* English and Latvian.

JANIS LOZE, born Riga, Republic of Latvia, July 6, 1966. *Education:* University of Latvia, Law Faculty (Bakalaurs, 1992). Magistrants. Legislative Assistant to the Deputy Chairman of the Latvian Supreme Council Standing Committee on Legislation and to the Deputy Chairman of the Supreme Council, 1991-1992. Riga Yacht Club (Board of Directors). *Member:* Latvian Bar Association (Latvia); Latvian Lawyers' Association. Registered Patent and Trademark Agent, Latvia. *LANGUAGES:* Latvian, Russian and English.

ANITA TAMBERGA, born Riga, Republic of Latvia, October 20, 1969. *Education:* University of Latvia, Law Faculty (Bakalaurs, 1992); Magistrants; Baltic Education Program, Denmark (1993); Latvian Institute of International Law (1994). *Member:* Latvian Lawyers' Association. *LANGUAGES:* Latvian, Russian and English.

EGONS PIKELIS, born Birmingham, England, June 3, 1962. *Education:* University of Wales (B.A., Hons., Russian and Russian Studies, 1988); Nottingham Polytechnic, Faculty of Law (L.S.F., 1992). Assistant Solicitor, Simmons & Simmons, 1992-1995. *Member:* British Law Association with Estonia, Latvia and Lithuania (Committee Member, 1994). *LANGUAGES:* English, Latvian, Russian, French and German.

LINDA I. PRIEDE, born Philadelphia, Pennsylvania, May 16, 1963; admitted, 1991, New York. *Education:* Sarah Lawrence College, Bronxville, New York; New York University, New York, New York (B.A., Journalism, 1986); Hofstra University, Hempstead, New York (J.D., 1991). Public Defender, Legal Aid Society of Nassau County, New York, 1991-1994. Associate, Caleca & Towner, East Hampton, New York, 1991. Law Intern, Mag. David E. Jordon, E.D.N.Y., 1990. Supervising Judge, Hon. Marie G. Santagata, Nassau County Court, 1990. *Member:* New York and Latvian-American Bar Associations (USA). *LANGUAGES:* English and Latvian.

GUNTARS GRINVALDS, born Riga, Republic of Latvia, June 1, 1973. *Education:* University of Latvia, Law Faculty (Bakalaurs, 1995). Legal Counsel, Latvian Copyright Agency, 1993. *Member:* Latvian Lawyers' Association. *LANGUAGES:* Latvian, Russian and English.

LIECHTENSTEIN

DR. DR. BATLINER & PARTNERS

Established in 1954

AEULESTRASSE 74
P.O. BOX 86
9490 VADUZ, LIECHTENSTEIN
Telephone: 41-75-231 1166
Telex: 889 370 drba fl
Cable Address: "Dorbat Vaduz"
Telecopier: 41-75-232 4343

General Practice, Litigation, Corporate and Commercial Law, Contracts, Intellectual Property, Banks and Banking, Bankruptcy, Taxation, Trusts and Estate Planning, Offshore Trusts and Companies.

PARTNERS

PROF. DR. DR. HERBERT BATLINER, born 1928; admitted, 1955, Principality of Liechtenstein. *Education:* Universities of Bern, Innsbruck and Lyon (Dr.iur., 1952; Dr.rer.oec., 1953). Author: "The Trust under Liechtenstein Law," 1968; "The Participating Share for Employees," 1970; "Introduction to the Liechtenstein Company Law," 1968; "The Foundation in the Principality of Liechtenstein," 1971; "The Private Establishment under Liechtenstein Law," 1968; "The Limited Company under Liechtenstein Law," 1972; "Liability of the Company Executives in Special Consideration of the Trustee's Responsibility," 1975; "Introduction to Liechtenstein Company Law," 1987. President, High Court of Administration, 1965-1970. President, Constitutional Court of Liechtenstein, 1975-1980. Appointed to the post of Consul of the Republic of Austria in Liechtenstein, 1966. Appointed to the post of Consul General of the Republic of Austria in Liechtenstein, 1974, resigned, 1980. Honorary Senator of the University of Innsbruck, 1969. Fürstlicher Kommerzienrat, 1988. Honorary Professor by

(This Listing Continued)

Decree of the President of the Republic of Austria, 1989. Grosskreuz des Fürstlich Liechtensteinischen Verdienstordens, 1993. *Member:* Liechtenstein Bar Association. *LANGUAGES:* German, English and French. *PRACTICE AREAS:* Corporate Law; Trusts and Estate Planning.

LIC. IUR., LIC. OEC. ANDREAS BATLINER, born 1959; admitted, 1989, Principality of Liechtenstein. *Education:* University of St. Gallen, Switzerland (lic.oec., 1982; lic.iur., 1984). Author: "International Bank Secrecy—Liechtenstein," 1992. *Member:* Liechtenstein Bar Association; Association International des Jeunes Avocats. *LANGUAGES:* German and English. *PRACTICE AREAS:* Litigation; Commercial Law; Banks and Banking; Bankruptcy.

DR. IUR. MATTHIAS DONHAUSER, LL.M., born 1958; admitted, 1989, Principality of Liechtenstein. *Education:* University of Vienna (Dr.iur., 1983); London School of Economics and Political Science (LL.M., 1987). *Member:* Liechtenstein Bar Association. *LANGUAGES:* German, English and French. *PRACTICE AREAS:* European Community Law; Competition; Product Liability Law; Intellectual Property Law.

ASSOCIATES

DR. IUR. PETER MONAUNI, born 1938. *Education:* University of Innsbruck (Dr.iur., 1961). *LANGUAGES:* German and English. *PRACTICE AREAS:* Litigation; International Commercial Law; Trusts; Taxation.

MAG. IUR. KARLHEINZ KONRAD, born 1961; admitted, 1992, Principality of Liechtenstein. *Education:* University of Innsbruck (Mag.iur., 1989). *Member:* Liechtenstein Bar Association. *LANGUAGES:* German and English. *PRACTICE AREAS:* Litigation; Civil Law; Contract Law; Criminal Law.

LAW OFFICE GSTÖHL

BÜROHAUS GSTÖHL
AUSTRASSE 42
P.O. BOX 239
FL-9490 VADUZ, LIECHTENSTEIN
Telephone: +4175/23 257 02; 23 223 51; 23 262 82
Telex: 889 381; 889 378
Facsimile: +4175/23 232 11

Administrative Law, Arbitration, Bankruptcy, Corporate Law, Entertainment Law, Family Law, International Contracts, International Private Law, Local and International Tax Law.

LIC. IUR. HARRY GSTÖHL, born September 13, 1948; admitted, 1977, Liechtenstein. *Education:* University of Geneva, Faculty of Law (Diplôme de Licencié en Droit, 1971; D.E.S., Diplôme d'Etudes Supérieurs en Droit, 1976). President: High Court of Administration, 1982-1986, 1986-1989, 1989-1992; National Board of Examination for Trustees, 1984-1988, 1988-1992; President, National Board of Examination for Lawyers, 1993—; Supreme Constitutional Court, 1992—. *Member:* Liechtenstein and International Bar Associations; International Fiscal Association; Union Internationale des Avocats; Swiss Arbitration Association; International Chamber of Commerce, Paris; International Lawyers Network. *LANGUAGES:* German, English, French, Italian and Spanish.

ASSOCIATES

DR. IUR. ARTHUR GASSNER. *Education:* University of Innsbruck, Faculty of Law (Doktor der Rechte, 1985); London School of Economics and Political Science (Master of Laws, LL.M., 1986). *LANGUAGES:* German, English and French.

DR. IUR. CORNELIA GASSNER. *Education:* University of Innsbruck, Faculty of Law (Doktor der Rechte, 1985); London School of Economics and Political Science (Master of Laws, LL.M., 1986). Member, Liechtenstein Government, Minister of Construction. *LANGUAGES:* German, English and French.

LAW OFFICE HOOP

MEIERHOFSTRASSE 2
P.O. BOX 1221
FL-9490 VADUZ, LIECHTENSTEIN
Telephone: +4175/235 51 55
Telefax: +4175/235 51 64

General Practice, Administration, Financial, Tax, Corporate and Business Law, Trusts and Estate Planning, Trademarks and Copyright, Domiciling and Management of Offshore Companies and Trusts, International Law, Insolvency Law, Inheritance, Litigation.

LIC.IUR. WILFRIED HOOP, born Liechtenstein, February 16, 1961; admitted, 1992, Liechtenstein. *Education:* University of Fribourg, Faculty of Law and Economics, Switzerland (lic.iur., 1988). *Member:* Liechtenstein Bar Association; Association International des Jeunes Avocats; DACH Deutsch-Oesterreichisch-Schweizerisch-Liechtensteinische Anwaltsvereinigung e.v. *LANGUAGES:* German, English and French. *PRACTICE AREAS:* Litigation; Business Law; Insolvency Law; Private Law; Contract Law.

ASSOCIATES

DR.IUR. ALFRED STEINBRUGGER born Austria, September 2, 1944. *Education:* University of Graz, Faculty of Law, Austria (Dr.iur., 1970). Department Manager, Austrian Textile Factory, 1969-1971; Department Manager, Liechtenstein Industrial Chenstry, 1971-1974. Associate, Liechtenstein Law Firm, 1975-1986. Partner, Liechtenstein Trust Company, 1986—. *Member:* International Advisory Group (IAG, Foundation Member). *LANGUAGES:* German and English. *PRACTICE AREAS:* Trusts and Estate Planning; International Law; Financial and Tax Law.

GABRIEL MARXER

MEIERHOFSTRASSE 5
9490 VADUZ, LIECHTENSTEIN
Telephone: 0041-75-236-00-11
Fax: 0041-75-233-30-69

General Litigation, Corporation and Trust Law.

DR. GABRIEL MARXER, born 1960; admitted, 1985, Liechtenstein. *Education:* University of Innsbruck (Dr.jur., 1984). Vice-President of the "Staatsgerichtshof" (Supreme Court of Liechtenstein in constitutional matters), 1989—. *Member:* Verein Liechtensteiner Rechtsanwälte. *LANGUAGES:* German and English.

ADVOKATURBÜRO DR. MARXER & PARTNER

Established in 1925
HEILIGKREUZ 6
P.O. BOX 484
9490 VADUZ, LIECHTENSTEIN
Telephone: (075) 235 81 81
Telex: 889 333 Doma
Fax: (075) 235 82 82

General Practice, Corporate, Commercial, Tax, Trust, Estate Planning, Patent, Trademark and Copyright Law, Litigation.

PARTNERS

DR. IUR. PETER MARXER, born Vaduz, Liechtenstein, May 11, 1933; admitted, 1959, Liechtenstein. *Education:* University of Innsbruck (Dr.iur., 1957). Co-Author: "Companies and Taxes in Liechtenstein," Liechtenstein Verlag, 1991. Member of Parliament, 1966-1982. Speaker of the Minority resp. Majority in Liechtenstein Parliament, 1967-1982. *Member:* Liechtenstein Bar Association. *LANGUAGES:* German, English and French.

DR. IUR. WALTER KIEBER, born Feldkirch, Austria, February 20, 1931; admitted, 1955, Liechtenstein. *Education:* University of Innsbruck (Dr.iur., 1954). Co-Author: "Companies and Taxes in Liechtenstein," Liechtenstein Verlag, 1991. Deputy Head, 1970-1974 and Head, 1974-1978, of the Liechtenstein Government. Minister of Justice, 1970-1980. *Member:* Liechtenstein Bar Association. *LANGUAGES:* German and English.

DR. IUR. PETER GOOP, born Vaduz, Liechtenstein, June 18, 1949; admitted, 1982, Vaduz. *Education:* University of Bern, Switzerland (lic.iur.,

(This Listing Continued)

ADVOKATURBÜRO DR. MARXER & PARTNER,
Vaduz—Continued

1975); University of Vienna, Austria (Dr.iur., 1978). Co-Author: "Companies and Taxes in Liechtenstein," Liechtenstein Verlag, 1991. *Member:* Liechtenstein and International Bar Associations; Association Internationale de Jeunes Avocats. *LANGUAGES:* German, English, French and Italian.

ASSOCIATES

DR. IUR. WOLFGANG MÜLLER, born Feldkirch, Austria, October 28, 1937; admitted, 1961, Feldkirch, Austria; 1967, Liechtenstein. *Education:* University of Innsbruck, Austria (Dr. iur., 1959). *Member:* Vorarlberger Juristische Gesellschaft, Austria. *LANGUAGES:* German, English and Italian.

DR. IUR. HERBERT OBERHUBER, born Dornbirn, Austria, November 30, 1946; admitted, 1971, Liechtenstein. *Education:* University of Vienna (Dr.iur., 1971). *LANGUAGES:* German and English.

DR. IUR. ROLF SANTO-PASSO, born Fohnsdorf, Austria, April 16, 1933. *Education:* University of Innsbruck, Austria (Dr.iur., 1957). *LANGUAGES:* German, English and French.

DR. IUR. HERMANN BOECKLE, born Hohenems, Austria, March 26, 1941; admitted, 1987, Liechtenstein; 1983, Austria (Attorney of Defense). *Education:* University of Innsbruck, Austria (Dr.iur., 1982). Assistant at the Institute of Commercial Law of the University of Innsbruck, 1982-1983. Lecturer: University of Klagenfurt 1983-1992; University of Lienz, 1992—. *Member:* Vorarlberger Juristische Gesellschaft, Austria. *LANGUAGES:* German and English.

DR.IUR. KARL JOSEF HIER, born Rottenmann, Austria, November 16, 1957; admitted, 1990, Austria. *Education:* University of Graz, Austria (Dr.iur., 1982). Assistant at the Institute of Public Law, Political Science and Administrative Theory of the University of Graz, 1982-1983. *Member:* Bar Association of Vienna. *LANGUAGES:* German and English.

DR.JUR. JOHANNES MICHAEL BURGER, born Bregenz, Austria, August 30, 1960; admitted, 1991, Austria. *Education:* University of Innsbruck, Austria (Dr.iur., 1982). Assistant at the Institute of Commercial Law of the University of Innsbruck, 1982-1984. *LANGUAGES:* German and English.

LIC. IUR. ISABELLA BADER-MARXER, born Vaduz, Liechtenstein, February 18, 1960; admitted, 1990, Liechtenstein. *Education:* University of Fribourg, Switzerland (lic.iur., 1986). *LANGUAGES:* German, French and English.

DR. DANIEL KIEBER, born Vaduz, Liechtenstein, August 15, 1960; admitted, 1990, Liechtenstein. *Education:* University of Innsbruck, Austria (Dr.iur, 1985); New York University (M.C.J., 1987). *LANGUAGES:* German, English and French.

DR. IUR. HEINZ GRABHER, born Lustenau, Austria, January 11, 1958; admitted, 1991, Austria. *Education:* University of Innsbruck, Austria (Dr.iur., 1982). *LANGUAGES:* German and English.

DR.IUR. PETRA JULIA VETERE-MATT, born Mauren, Liechtenstein, May 9, 1962; admitted, 1993, Liechtenstein. *Education:* University of Zürich, Switzerland (Dr.iur., 1990). *LANGUAGES:* German, Italian, English and French.

Languages: German, English, French and Italian

LIC. JUR. WALTER MATT

Attorney at Law

Established in 1958

WERDENBERGERWEG 11

P.O. BOX 483

9490 VADUZ, LIECHTENSTEIN

Telephone: 075/ 232 55 66

Fax: 075/ 232 44 80

Company Law, International Company Law, Trust Services, International Banking, Business Law, Tax Law, Private International Law, Civil Law, Criminal Law and Civil Litigation.

FIRM PROFILE: *The Law office lic. jur. Walter Matt and his trust companies are working with trust structures on an international basis and high quality personal service by an experienced and professional team.*

(This Listing Continued)

LIC. JUR. WALTER MATT, born 1934; admitted, 1958, Liechtenstein. *Education:* University Fribourg, Swiss. *Member:* International Bar Association; Union Internationale des Avocats, World Jurist Association; International Federation of Agencies; European Conferences; Law Associations of Liechtenstein, Swiss, Austria and Germany. *LANGUAGES:* German, English, French, Spanish, Italian and Russian. *PRACTICE AREAS:* International Company Law; Trust Services; International Banking Law; Business Law; Business Law; Tax Law.

LEGAL SUPPORT PERSONNEL

DR. BIRGIT-MERCEDES AMANN, born 1961. *LANGUAGES:* German and English. *PRACTICE AREAS:* Private International Law; Civil Law; Criminal Law; Litigation.

Languages: German, English, French, Spanish, Italian and Russian

LAW OFFICE
MEIER & WOLF

Established in 1979

LETTSTRASSE 8

P.O. BOX 656

FL-9490 VADUZ, LIECHTENSTEIN

Telephone: (075) 237 36 00

Telefax: (075) 237 36 60

Telex: 889270 miur fl

Tax, Business, Corporate and Trust Law, International Law, Inheritance Law, General and Litigation Practice.

GUIDO MEIER, DR. IUR., born Vaduz, Liechtenstein, 1948; admitted, 1979, Liechtenstein. *Education:* University of Tampa, U.S.A.; University of Basel, Switzerland (Doctor of Law, 1977). Justice, Constitutional Court of the State of Liechtenstein, 1984-1993; President, Liechtenstein Bar Examination Board 1987-1993; President, Liechtenstein Institute 1986—; Member, Liechtenstein Parliament, 1993—. Author: "Basic Personal Law and Specific Legal Issue in Liechtenstein Conflicts Law of Companies"; "The Trust in the Liechtenstein Law on Persons and Companies". *Member:* Liechtenstein Bar Association. *LANGUAGES:* German, English and French. *PRACTICE AREAS:* Tax; Corporate and Trust Law; Business Law; Conflicts Law; Constitutional Law.

GUNTRAM WOLF, LIC. OEC. HSG, LIC. IUR., born Vaduz, Liechtenstein, 1950; admitted, 1983, Liechtenstein. *Education:* St. Gall Graduate School of Economics, Switzerland; University of Berne, Switzerland. *Member:* Liechtenstein Bar Association. *LANGUAGES:* German, English, French and Spanish. *PRACTICE AREAS:* Corporate and Business Law; Civil Litigation; Insolvency.

HILMAR HOCH, DR. IUR., born Triesen, Liechtenstein, 1958; admitted, 1991, Liechtenstein; 1993, New York. *Education:* University of Berne, Switzerland (Lic.iur., 1983; Dr.iur., 1991); Harvard Law School (LL.M., 1992). Author: (Dissertation) "History of Liechtenstein Social Security Law.". *LANGUAGES:* German, French and English. *PRACTICE AREAS:* Civil Litigation; Business Law; Constitutional Law; International Law.

GERHARD HOLZHACKER, DR. IUR., born Vienna, 1956; admitted, 1981, Austria. *Education:* University of Vienna (Dr.iur., 1980). *LANGUAGES:* German and English. *PRACTICE AREAS:* Corporate and Business Law; Civil Litigation; EC Regulations; Insolvency.

FRIEDRICH WOHLMACHER, DR. IUR., born Austria, 1947; admitted, 1974, Austria. *Education:* University of Innsbruck, Austria (Dr.iur., 1971). *LANGUAGES:* German, English and French. *PRACTICE AREAS:* Corporate and Business Law; Civil Litigation.

REFERENCE: Private Trust Bank Corporation, Vaduz.

DDR. PROKSCH & PARTNER

International Lawyers
ITA P&A BÜROTEL BUILDING
LANDSTRASSE 161-163
FL-9494 SCHAAN
VADUZ, LIECHTENSTEIN
Telephone: 41 75 2332303, 2322614, 2324121
Fax: 41 75 2323562, 2324133, 2329181
Telex: 899520 ita fl E-Mail: 100415,1733@compuserve.com

Associated Office, Vienna, Austria: Erich Proksch, Auhofgasse 1, A-1130
Associated Office, London, England/UK: Joseph Kanann, 33 Jermyne Street, SW1
Associated Office, Beverley Hills, CA/USA: Dana B. Taschner, 9545 Wilshire Boulevard, Suite 550, 90212 (offices also in Pasadena, California and Dallas, Texas)

International (Onshore/Offshore) Corporate Law, Trusts, and Asset Management and Control. Trustees and Directors Responsibility. Private Client. Media Law and Licensing. Movie and Entertainment Financing. Sports and Sponsoring. Arbitration. International Litigation.

MEMBERS OF FIRM

REINHARD J. PROKSCH, born Salzburg, Austria, April 11, 1962; admitted, 1990, New York. *Education:* Universities of Salzburg and Vienna (Dr.Mag.iur.; 1984, Dr.phil., sub auspiciis praesidentis rei publicae, in Communication/Mass Media and International Business Law, 1986); McGeorge School of Law (LL.M. in Business and Taxation, 1988). Fulbright Scholar. Co-Editor: "International Business Transactions," Deventer (Kluwer), 1988—. Author: "Trusts and Foundations in Liechtenstein," Vaduz 1993; "The Austrian Private Foundation," Feldkirch 1993; "International Estate Planning: The European Perspective," in Campbell/Carlisle, The Transactional Person, Deventer (Kluwer), p. 185-204, 1991; "International Banking: Liechtenstein," in International Banking - A Legal Guide, International Financial Law Review, Supplement 1991; and various articles on European Media Law and Telecommunications. Faculty Member, Golden Gate University, San Francisco/USA. Associate Attorney with law firms in Los Angeles and New York, 1988-1990. Director and Corporate Counsel, Liechtenstein Trust Operations of leading Swiss and International banks, 1990-1994. Director, Center of International Studies CILS, Salzburg/Austria. Former Assistant Professor and Lecturer: Salzburg University Law School, Salzburg, Austria; McGeorge School of Law, Sacramento/CA USA and Edinburgh/Scotland. Board Member, EWI European Economic Institute, Liechtenstein and Brussels/Belgium. *Member:* New York State and International Bar Associations; Swiss-American Chamber of Commerce (Member, Business and Tax Committees); Austrian Chamber of Commerce. Fellow, Salzburg Seminar, Schloss Leopoldskron. *LANGUAGES:* German and English. *PRACTICE AREAS:* International Corporate; Media Law; Entertainment Law; Tax and Estate Planning; Arbitration.

WERNER WALSER, born Bludenz, Austria, September 14, 1925. admitted as legal agent and trustee 1954, Liechtenstein. *Education:* Innsbruck University (Dr. phil., 1953); Academia Mexicana de Derecho Internatinal (Dr.h.c., 1972). President, EWI European Economic Institute, Brussels, Foerdererkreis Prof. H. Oberth and Wernherr von Braun, Academia Mexicana de Derecho International, Mexico and Liechtenstein. Recipient, various national and international honors: Mexican Order of Culture and Peace, 1976; Ercolo d'Oro and Leader dell'Opinione, Italy, 1974; Ordre de la Reconnaissance au Grade de Commandeur, 1978. Consul of the Republic of Chad, Liechtenstein, 1972—. Ambassadeur Itinérant of Central Africa, 1978—.*Member:* Liechtenstein Trustee Association; Association of the Diplomatic Corps (Board Member); European Confederation of Associations of Small and Medium-sized Enterprises, Brussels (Board Member). *LANGUAGES:* German, English and French. *PRACTICE AREAS:* Liechtenstein and International Corporate; Private Client; Residency and Nationality Matters.

OF COUNSEL

CHRISTIAN HOPP, born Feldkirch, Austria, September 13, 1956; admitted, 1991, Austria. *Education:* Innsbruck University Law School (Dr.iur., 1980); Court Practices with Austrian Law Courts (1980); Schloss Hofen/Innsbruck University (Postgraduate studies, "Expert in European Law," 1994). Trainee and Associate with international law firms in Vaduz/Liechtenstein, Salzburg/Austria, and Sydney/Australia, 1981-1986. *Member:* Austrian Bar Association; Association of Attorneys in Austria, Germany, Liechtenstein and Switzerland.

(This Listing Continued)

ERICH PROKSCH, born Bad Goisern, Austria, October 21, 1945; admitted, 1973, Austria. *Education:* Vienna University (Dr.Mag.iur., 1967); Court Practice with Vienna Law Courts and the Constitutional Court of Austria. Lecturer: Hernstein Institute, Austria and Austrian Bar Academy. Professor, Krems Academy, Postgraduate Studies. *Member:* Austrian Bar Association. (International Counsel; Not Resident in Liechtenstein).

DANA B. TASCHNER, born Long Beach, California/USA, October 12, 1960; admitted, 1988, California, U.S. District Court, District of Hawaii, U.S . District Court, Central District of California and U.S. Court of Appeals, Ninth Circuit; 1989, U.S. District Court, Southern, Eastern and Northern Districts of California; 1990, U.S. Court of International Trade, U.S. Court of Federal Claims and U.S. Claims Court; 1991, U.S. Court of Appeals for the Federal Circuit; 1992, U.S. District Court, District of Arizona and U.S. Temporary Emergency Court of Appeals; 1994, U.S. District Court, Northern District of Texas (Not admitted in Liechtenstein). *Education:* University of Southern California (B.A., 1983); William S. Richardson School of Law, University of Hawaii (J.D., 1987). Judicial Extern, Honorable Justice Yoshima Hayashi, Associate Justice, Supreme Court of Hawaii, 1987. *Member:* Federal Bar Association (National Co-Chair, Trial and Appellate Practice Committee, 1991-1993); American Bar Association (Co-Chair, Subcommittee on Asia-Pacific Law, International Committee, Section on Business Law, 1991-1992; Liaison with the Judiciary Committee). (International Counsel, Not Resident in Liechtenstein).

INTERNATIONAL TAX COUNSEL

JOSEPH N. KANAAN, born Brummana, Lebanon, May 23, 1938. (Not Resident in Liechtenstein).

LAW OFFICE
DR.IUR. KARLHEINZ RITTER
LIC.IUR. CORNELIA RITTER

STÄDTLE 36
P.O. BOX 685
FL-9490 VADUZ, LIECHTENSTEIN
Telephone: 075-233 2822
Telefax: 075-232 8079
Telex: 88 95 88 iurit fl

General Practice, Corporate and Commercial Law, Financial, Tax, Trust, Trademark and Copyright Law, Litigation.

PARTNERS

DR.IUR. KARLHEINZ RITTER, born Vaduz, Liechtenstein, July 1, 1929; admitted, 1958, Liechtenstein. *Education:* University of Bern, Switzerland (Dr.iur., 1958). Author: "The Functioning of the Administrative Jurisdiction in the Principality of Liechtenstein." Member: Court of Administration 1962-1969; Parliament, 1966-1992. President, 1970-1974, 1978-1992. Fürstlicher Justizrat, 1981. *Member:* Liechtenstein Bar Association: International Fiscal Association. *LANGUAGES:* German, English and French.

LIC.IUR. CORNELIA RITTER, born Chur, Switzerland, January 20, 1952; admitted, 1987, Liechtenstein. *Education:* University of Bern, Switzerland (Lic.iur., 1981). *Member:* Liechtenstein Bar Association. *LANGUAGES:* German, English and French.

ASSOCIATES

DR.IUR. ALEXANDER FITZ, born Hohenems, Austria, November 15, 1943; admitted, 1970, Austria; 1973, Liechtenstein. *Education:* University of Vienna (Dr.iur., 1970). *LANGUAGES:* German and English.

LIC.IUR. MARZELL BECK, born Triesenberg, Liechtenstein, June 11, 1952; admitted, 1986, Liechtenstein. *Education:* University of Fribourg, Switzerland (lic. iur., 1977). Graduate Assistant, Constitutional, Administrative and International Law, University of Basle, 1977-1980. Departmental Secretary of the Liechtenstein Government, Ministry of Justice, 1986-1993. *Member:* Liechtenstein Bar Association; Swiss Society of International Law. *LANGUAGES:* German, English and French.

DR.IUR. ANGELIKA GREBER, born Feldkirch, Austria, August 5, 1960. *Education:* University of Innsbruck, Austria (Dr. iur., 1990). Author: "The problem of languages in international conventions and treaties with special reference to the European Convention on Human Rights.". *LANGUAGES:* German, English, French and Spanish.

RITTER, WOHLWEND, WOLFF

Established in 1978

PFLUGSTRASSE 10 (KASTANIENHOF)
P.O. BOX 731
VADUZ, LIECHTENSTEIN
Telephone: (41-75) 236 55 33
Telex: 889266 iur fl
Telefax: (41-75) 236 56 11
Cable Address: "Triur 9490 Vaduz"

REVISER OF THE LIECHTENSTEIN LAW DIGEST FOR THIS DIRECTORY.

Company and Commercial, Patent, Trademark and Copyright Law, Trust and Revenue Law, General Litigation, International Legal Transactions, International Private Law, Trust Law.

MEMBERS OF FIRM

DR. IUR. P. RITTER, born 1938; admitted, 1961, Fürstentum Liechtenstein. *Education:* University of Innsbruck (Dr. jur., 1961). Secretary, 1966-1970, Vice President, 1970-1974, President of the Board of Directors of Liechtensteinische Landesbank, 1974-1978. Judge in the Court of Administration, 1970-1974, President of the Court of Administration, 1974-1978. *Member:* Liechtensteinische Rechtsanwaltskammer. *LANGUAGES:* English, French and German.

DR. IUR. HELMUT WOHLWEND, born Vaduz, Liechtenstein, September 24, 1945; admitted, 1977, Fürstentum Liechtenstein. *Education:* University of Innsbruck (Dr. iur.). Vice President of the Court of Administration, 1978-1989. *Member:* Liechtensteinische Rechtsanwaltskammer. *LANGUAGES:* German and English.

DR. IUR. PETER WOLFF, born Milano, Italy, May 10, 1946; admitted, 1974, Fürstentum Liechtenstein. *Education:* University of Vienna (Dr. iur.). *Member:* Liechtensteinische Rechtsanwaltskammer (Vice President, 1978-1980, President, 1980-1982). *LANGUAGES:* German and English.

ASSOCIATES

DR. IUR. SIGRID LAUNOIS-MAYER, born Austria, January 24, 1941; admitted, 1967, Vienna, Austria; 1973, Fürstentum Liechtenstein. *Education:* University of Vienna (Dr. iur. 1963). *LANGUAGES:* German and English.

DR. IUR. CHRISTOPH EBERSBERG, born Austria, July 11, 1947; admitted, 1979, Liechtenstein. *Education:* University of Innsbruck (Dr. iur., 1974; private law, public law and economics); studies at the John Hopkins University of Bologna; Institut Européen des Hautes Etudes Internationales at Nice. *LANGUAGES:* German, English, French, Italian and Spanish.

Languages: English, French, German, Italian and Spanish

REFERENCE: National Bank of Liechtenstein, Vaduz.

REVISER OF THE LIECHTENSTEIN LAW DIGEST FOR THIS DIRECTORY.

ADVOKATURBURO DR. IUR. NORBERT SEEGER

POSTFACH 1618
AM SCHRÄGEN WEG 14
9490 VADUZ, LIECHTENSTEIN
Telephone: +41 75 232 08 08
Fax: +41 75 232 06 30

Corporate, Commercial and Taxation Law, Trusts and Estate Planning, Domiciling and Management of Offshore Companies and Trusts, Investment Counselling, Portfolio Management, Law of the European Communities, International Law, International Business Transactions, Trademarks and Copyright, Litigation, General Practice.

FIRM PROFILE: Dr. Seeger practices law with two associates, both of whom have been admitted to foreign bars.

DR. IUR., LIC. OEC. NORBERT SEEGER, born Liechtenstein, 1953; admitted, 1984, Liechtenstein. *Education:* St. Gallen School of Economics (lic. oec., 1978); University of Berne (lic. iur., 1980; Dr. iur., 1986). Author: Dissertation, "The Doctrine of Responsibility as defined in sections 218 to 228 of the Liechtenstein Persons and Companies Law," Nr. 504 of "Abhandlungen zum Schweizerischen Recht," ASR, Essays on Swiss Law,

(This Listing Continued)

EU1004B

published by Stämpfli & Cie AG Berne; Regular Correspondent, Principality of Liechtenstein, Bulletin for International Fiscal Documentation, official journal of the International Fiscal Association. Part-time Judge, Liechtenstein Administrative Court of Justice, 1986-1989; Deputy Chairman, Liechtenstein Administrative Court of Justice, 1989-1993; Chairman, Commission Responsible for the Admission of Professional Trustees, 1992—. President of the Council, National Library Foundation of Liechtenstein, 1987—. *Member:* Liechtenstein Bar Association (Board of Directors, 1986—); German-Austrian-Swiss-Liechtenstein Bar Association, DACH (Board of Directors); Swiss-Czech Bar Association; Union Internationale des Avocats; Association Internationale des Jeunes Avocats; International Tax Planning Association; Offshore Institute; Swiss Association for Copyright and Media Law. *LANGUAGES:* German, English and French.

SELE & FROMMELT

MEIERHOFSTRASSE 5
P.O. BOX 1617
FL-9490 VADUZ, LIECHTENSTEIN
Telephone: +41-75-237 11 55
Fax: +41-75-232 00 06

General Practice, Arbitration, Tax, Business and Corporate Law, Trusts and Estate Planning, Trademarks and Copyright Law, Insolvency Law, Litigation.

MEMBERS OF FIRM

HUGO J. SELE, Lic. Oec. Hsg, Lic. Iur., born Vaduz, Liechenstein, 1949; admitted, 1980, Liechtenstein. *Education:* St. Gall Graduate School of Economics, Switzerland; University of Southampton, England; University of Zurich (Law School) Switzerland. *Member:* Liechtenstein Bar Association (Board of Directors); UIA, Union Internationale des Avocats; DACH, Deutsch-Oesterreichische-Schweizerische-Liechtensteinische Anwaltsvereinigung e.V. *LANGUAGES:* German, English, French and Spanish.

DR. IUR. VEIT E. FROMMELT, born Vaduz, Liechtenstein, 1957; admitted, 1985, Liechtenstein. *Education:* University of Innsbruck (Law School), Austria (Dr.iur., 1982); Legal internships, Geneva, 1983; Pittsburgh, USA, 1984. *Member:* Liechtenstein Bar Association; DACH, Deutsch-Oesterreichische-Schweizerische-Liechtensteinische Anwaltsvereinigung e.V. *LANGUAGES:* German, English and French.

DR. IUR. HEINZ J. FROMMELT, born Vaduz, Liechtenstein, 1960; admitted, 1989, Liechtenstein. *Education:* University of Zurich (Law School), Switzerland, (Dr.iur., 1988); Legal internships, Richmond, Washington, D.C., New York, USA, 1989. Author: "The Liechtenstein Banking Secrecy." *Member:* Liechtenstein Bar Association; AIJA, Association International des Jeunes Avocats; DACH, Deutsch-Oesterreichische-Schweizerische-Liechtensteinische Anwaltsvereinigung e.V. *LANGUAGES:* German, English and French.

REFERENCE: Bank in Liechtenstein, Vaduz; National Bank of Liechtenstein, Vaduz; Private Trust Bank Corporation, Vaduz.

DR. IUR. URSULA WACHTER-MAHLKNECHT

LANDSTRASSE 107
P.O. BOX 954
9490 VADUZ, LIECHTENSTEIN
Telephone: 075-233-18-03
Telefax: 075-233-18-61

Litigation, Business and Corporation Law, International Law, General Practice, Arbitration.

DR. IUR. URSULA WACHTER-MAHLKNECHT, born Liechtenstein, March 12, 1957; admitted, 1989, Principality of Liechtenstein. *Education:* University of Innsbruck, Austria (Dr.iur., 1985). *Member:* Liechtenstein Bar Association. *LANGUAGES:* German, English, French and Spanish.

WALCH & SCHURTI

ZOLLSTRASSE 9
P.O. BOX 1611
9490 VADUZ, LIECHTENSTEIN
Telephone: +41 75 237 2000
Telefax: +41 75 232 21 23

General Practice, Corporate, Commercial and Financial Law, Trusts and Estate Planning, Private International Law, Law of the European Communities, Litigation, Administrative Law, Family Law, Bankruptcy, Banking Law, Company Law (Formation, Taxation, Administration), Intellectual Property, White Collar Crime, International Judicial Assistance.

DR. IUR. ERNST J. WALCH, born Liechtenstein, 1956; admitted, 1984, Fürstentum Liechtenstein; 1983, New York. *Education:* University of Innsbruck (Dr.iur., 1980); New York University (Master of Comparative Jurisprudence, 1981). Author: Section on Liechtenstein, in Digest of Commercial Laws of the World, by Lester Nelson, Oceana Publications, Inc., Dobbs Ferry, New York, January 1986. Generally Licensed and Sworn Interpreter and Translator for the Principality of Liechtenstein. President of Parliament, 1993. *Member:* Liechtenstein Bar Association; Association Internationale des Jeunes Avocats; New York State Bar Association; DACH Deutsch-Oesterreichisch-Schweizerisch-Liechtensteinische Anwaltsvereinigung e.V.; The International Academy of Estate and Trust Law. *LANGUAGES:* English, German and French. *PRACTICE AREAS:* Corporate Law; Trusts and Estate Planning; Litigation.

DR. IUR. HSG ANDREAS SCHURTI, born Liechtenstein, 1960; admitted, 1989, Fürstentum Liechtenstein; 1991, New York. *Education:* Universities of Constance and St. Gallen (Dr.iur. HSG, 1989); University of San Diego, School of Law (Master of Comparative Law, 1990); College of Europe, Bruges (Diploma of Advanced European Legal Studies, 1991). Author: Das Verordnungsrecht der Regierung des Fürstentums Liechtenstein (The Power of the Government of Liechtenstein to Promulgate Regulations), St. Gallen, 1989. Generally Licensed and Sworn Interpreter and Translator for the Principality of Liechtenstein. *Member:* Liechtenstein Bar Association; New York State Bar Association; International Bar Association. *LANGUAGES:* English, German and French. *PRACTICE AREAS:* Commercial, Corporate, Banking and Financial Law; Law of European Communities; Litigation.

ASSOCIATES

DR. IUR. HELGAR GEORG SCHNEIDER, born Dornbirn, Austria, 1964. *Education:* University of Innsbruck (Mag.iur., 1987); University of Virginia (LL.M., 1988); University of Graz (Dr.iur., 1992). Fulbright Scholar. Generally Licensed and Sworn Interpreter and Translator, English and German. *LANGUAGES:* German and English. *PRACTICE AREAS:* Corporate, Commercial, Banking and Contracts Law; Intellectual Property; International Judicial Assistance; Litigation.

BETTINA PETRA ALEXANDRA KAISER, born Chur, Switzerland, 1967. *Education:* University of Fribourg (Lic.iur., 1992). *LANGUAGES:* German, French and English. *PRACTICE AREAS:* Family Law; Litigation; Bankruptcy Law.

JASON CONRAD LOFTS, born Christchurch, New Zealand, 1959; admitted, 1982, New Zealand; 1990, England and Wales (Not admitted in Liechtenstein). *Education:* University of Canterbury, New Zealand (LL.B., Hons., 1982); McGeorge School of Law Internship Program, Salzburg, Austria (Diploma in Advanced International Legal Studies, 1986). *Member:* Law Society of England and Wales; Solicitors' European Group; British-German Jurists' Association. *LANGUAGES:* English, German and French. *PRACTICE AREAS:* Corporate and Financial Law; Trusts and Estate Planning.

CONSULTANTS

URS HANSELMANN, born Liechtenstein, 1960; (Not admitted in Liechtenstein). Certified Accountant. Licensed Trustee. *LANGUAGES:* German, English, French and Italian. *PRACTICE AREAS:* Trusts and Estate Planning; Asset Protection; Auditing.

LAW OFFICES
DR. IUR. MARKUS WANGER

LANDSTRASSE 36
P.O. BOX 1608
FL-9490 VADUZ, LIECHTENSTEIN
Telephone: (075) 232 0062, 232 0063
Telefax: (075) 232 0064
Telex: 889594 iurt fl
Cable Address: IURTEL

General Practice including Arbitration and Mediation, Administration, Banking and Finance, Bankruptcy and Insolvency, Central and Eastern European Projects, Commercial Litigation, Company and Commercial Work (including off-shore), Contracts, Corporate Finance and Tax, European Community, Financial Services, Inheritance, International Law, Insurance and Reinsurance, Investment, Intellectual Property, Joint Ventures, Litigation, Media and Entertainment, Mergers, Acquisitions and Disposals, Patent, Private Client, Property and Construction, Trade-Mark and Copyright, Products Liability, Real Estate and Taxation.

DR. IUR. MARKUS WANGER, born Austria, August 28, 1955; admitted, 1982, Principality of Liechtenstein. *Education:* University of Innsbruck, Austria (Dr. iur., 1981); University of Salzburg. Judge in the Court of Administration, 1989-1993. Author: The Stifung in Liechtenstein Law, 1990; "Liechtensteinisches Wirtschafts-und Gesellschaftsrecht mit einer Darstellung des liechtensteinischen Schiedsgerichtsverfahrens, 1992." Co-Author: "International Execution Against Judgment Debtors," London, 1993; Paper: "Liechtenstein Companies - A Brief Survey," 1992; "Arbitration in Liechtenstein," 1994; Recognition and Enforcement of Foreign Judgment in Liechtenstein; Taxation in Liechtenstein, 1994. Member: Board of Examination of Liechtenstein Lawyers, (1989-1993); Board of Examination of Liechtenstein Trustees, (1992—); Panel of Arbitrators of Court of Arbitration at Polish Chamber of Commerce, Warsaw. *Member:* Liechtensteinische Rechtsanwaltskammer; Vereinigung liechtensteinischer Richter; ABA, American Bar Association (International Associate); American Intellectual Property Law Association, AIPLA; ASA, Association Suisse de l'Arbitrage; Deutscher Anwalt Verein; IBA, International Bar Association; UIA, Union International des Advocats; The International Tax Planning Association, ITPA; ICC, Institute of International Business Law and Practice, Paris; Association of Fellows and scholars of the Center for International Studies, Salzburg, Austria (Honorary Member). Fellow of the Chartered Institute of Arbitration, London.

DR. IUR. MARKUS MAYER, born Austria, December 9, 1956; admitted, 1990. *Education:* University of Innsbruck, Austria (Dr. iur. 1982). Austrian Revenue Office, 1984-1990.

DR. IUR. JOHANNES DÖTZER, born Germany, November 23, 1931; admitted, 1966, European Patent Attorney. *Education:* University of Regensburg, Innsbruck, Graz, Würzburg (Dr. Chem., 1962, Basel). Ciba-Geigy AG, 1966-1991.

DR. IUR. PAUL MEIER, born Liechtenstein, February 8, 1966; admitted, 1993. *Education:* University of Innsbruck, Austria (Dr. iur. 1993). Author: "Die Kontrollstelle im liechtensteinischen Gesellschaftsrecht," 1993.

MAG. MANUEL TOMMASI, born Austria, April 30, 1963; admitted, 1994. *Education:* University of Innsbruck, Austria (Mag.iur., 1993).

LIC. IUR. PHILIPP SCHNYDER, born Switzerland, July 19, 1953; admitted, 1983, Notar; 1985, Advokat. *Education:* University of Bern. Swiss Revenue Office, 1986-1990. *LANGUAGES:* English, German and French.

(This Listing Continued)

EU1005B

LAW OFFICES DR. IUR. MARKUS WANGER, Vaduz—
Continued

VALÉRIA HORÁCICAVÁ , born Slovak, Republic, March 12, 1958;
admitted, 1991, Commercial Lawyer. *Education:* J.A. Kommensky University, Bratislava, Slovak Republic. *LANGUAGES:* Slovak, Czech, Hungarian, Russian and German.

Languages: English, German and French

LITHUANIA

BALLARD SPAHR ANDREWS & INGERSOLL

Established in 1885 in Philadelphia, Pennsylvania, USA.

DONELAIČIO 71-2
3000 KAUNAS, LITHUANIA
Telephone: (370-7) 20 56 66
Fax: (370-7) 20 56 91

*REVISERS OF THE PENNSYLVANIA LAW DIGEST FOR THIS
DIRECTORY*

Baltimore, Maryland Office: 300 East Lombard Street, 19th Floor.
Telephone: 410-528-5600. Fax: 410-528-5650.
Camden, New Jersey Office: 800 Hudson Square, 5th Floor. Telephone:
609-541-5577. Fax: 609-541-8272.
Denver, Colorado Office: Seventeenth Street Plaza Building, Suite 2300,
1225 17th Street. Telephone: 303-292-2400. Fax: 303-296-3956.
Kaunas, Lithuania Office: Donelaičio Street 71-2, Kaunas 3000.
Telephone: (370-7) 20 56 66. Fax: (370-7) 20 56 91.
Philadelphia, Pennsylvania Office: 1735 Market Street, 51st Floor.
Telephone: 215-665-8500. Fax: 215-864-8999.
Salt Lake City, Utah Office: One Utah Center, Suite 1200, 201 South
Main Street. Telephone: 801-531-3000. Fax: 801-531-3001.
Washington, D.C. Office: Suite 900 East, 555 13th Street, N.W.
Telephone: 202-383-8800. Fax: 202-383-8877; 383-8893.

GENERAL PRACTICE
*Ballard Spahr Andrews & Ingersoll was founded in Philadelphia in the
1880 's and has been engaged in the general practice of law since then.
The firm now has over 260 lawyers who practice in Philadelphia,
Baltimore, Camden (NJ), Denver, Salt Lake City and Washington, D.C.
Ballard's lawyers practice in seven departments: Business and Finance,
Litigation, Taxation, Real Estate, Employee Benefits, Public Finance and
Estates.*
INTERNATIONAL PRACTICE
*Ballard Spahr's international practice principally includes representation of
domestic clients in the acquisition of foreign businesses or the formation of
joint ventures with such businesses. The transactions are usually structured
from an American perspective, but undertaken in consultation with experienced attorneys practicing in the jurisdiction of the foreign business. During the past few years, we have represented clients in German, Dutch, English, French, Chilean and other Latin American, Japanese, Lithuanian,
Latvian and Russian business ventures. The transactions have involved
manufacturing, service and distribution businesses, educational institutions,
political organizations, cable, insurance brokerage, mining and energy companies.*
*Transactions involving acquisition of foreign businesses have included both
asset and stock acquisitions, In acquisitions involving less than all of the
outstanding stock, we have advised clients with respect to and drafted
shareholders agreements and buy-sell agreements to provide for management of the target company and exit strategies.*
*Foreign joint venture transactions have involved licensing agreements for
transfers of technology and joint ventures to establish and operate partnerships between domestic and foreign businesses. Such transactions have also
been structured through the formation of a holding company and sister
subsidiaries into which existing domestic and foreign corporations merged
to establish foreign and domestic subsidiaries. Joint ventures have occasionally involved local government participation. Ballard Spahr lawyers have
advised clients of investment opportunities in the Baltic states involving
both privatization of state owned enterprises and joint ventures with private
enterprises. In order to support our clients' business and investment activi-*

(This Listing Continued)

*ties in the Baltic states, we have opened an office in Kaunas, Lithuania
and have affiliated with local firms in both Lithuania and Latvia.*
*Ballard Spahr lawyers have also advised domestic and foreign clients who
have entered into international distribution agreements, sales representative
agreements and international sales contracts.*
*We have assisted clients in obtaining co-financing and commercial and
political risk insurance for their ventures through a number of U.S. agencies and international organizations.*

BRIAN T. KEIM, born West Chester, Pennsylvania, March 22, 1943;
admitted, 1969, District of Columbia; 1970, Pennsylvania (Not admitted in
Lithuania). *Education:* Yale University (B.A., 1965); University of Pennsylvania (LL.B., 1968). *Member:* Philadelphia, Pennsylvania and American
Bar Associations.

REVISERS OF THE PENNSYLVANIA LAW DIGEST FOR THIS
DIRECTORY

(For Complete Biographical Data on Other Personnel, See Professional
Biographies at Philadelphia, Pennsylvania, Denver, Colorado,
Washington, D.C., Baltimore, Maryland, Camden, New Jersey and Salt
Lake City, Utah)

A.A.A. BALTIC SERVICE COMPANY

Established in 1992

RUDNINKU 18/2
2001 VILNIUS, LITHUANIA
Telephone: +(370 2) 61 32 32
Fax: +(370 2) 22 04 22

Tallinn, Estonia Office: A.A.A. Baltic Service Company. Regati pst.
1-329A, EE0019. Telephone: (372 2) 237 321. Fax: (372 6) 398 542.

General Practice.

FIRM PROFILE: *A general practice law firm employing local attorneys, a
financial tax advisor and an attorney who practiced in the West for 20
years.*

MARIUS JAKULIS JASON, born February 15, 1946; admitted, 1974,
Ohio; 1976, New York; 1977, Connecticut; 1992, Lithuania. *Education:*
Case Western Reserve University (B.A., 1968); Cleveland State University
College of Law (J.D., 1974); New York University School of Law (Master
of Law in Trade Regulation, 1975). Formerly a partner of a New York Law
Firm. Registered, Number 27,805, before the U.S. Patent and Trademark
Office; Registered, Number 3, before the Lithuanian Patent and Trademark
Office. Recipient of 1st Prize in Nathan Burkan Memorial Copyright Competition. Consultant to the Lithuanian Patent and Trademark Office. *Member:* Lithuanian AIPPI Group (President); International Bar Association;
Association of Lithuanian Patent Attorneys (former President); Copyright
Society of the U.S.A.; Licensing Executives Society; International Trademark Association. *LANGUAGES:* English, Lithuanian and Russian.
PRACTICE AREAS: Trademarks; Patents; Copyrights; Intellectual Property; Banking; Business Law; Commercial Law; Contracts; Investments.

LIDEIKA, PETRAUSKAS, VALIUNAS & PARTNERS

Established in 1992

VILNIAUS 25
2001 VILNIUS, LITHUANIA
Telephone: +370 6706382 (International); +370 2226681; +370 2617009
Fax: +370 6706381; +370 2225591

Mailing Address: P.O. Box 1247, 2001, Vilnius, Lithuania

*Firm engaged in Lithuanian and International law practice. Entitled to
plead before Lithuanian Courts.*
*International Business Law, International Trade Law, Corporate Law,
Foreign Investment Law, Banking Law, Intellectual Property, Labour
Law, Litigation.*

FIRM PROFILE: *Established in 1992, within 1 year "Lideika, Petrauskas,
Valiunas & Partners," has grown to become one of the leading commercial
law firms in Lithuania and the biggest law partnership in the state. The
firm is broadly based with a reputation for offering a full range of quality
legal services. The firm represents both foreign and domestic clients. The
firm has 6 partners, 2 consultants, 6 associates. The lawyers of the firm
act as members of working groups of law drafts.*

(This Listing Continued)

MEMBERS OF FIRM

ROLANDAS VALIŪNAS, born Vilkaviskis, Lithuania, January 13, 1965; admitted, 1989, Lithuania. *Education:* Law Faculty, Vilnius University (1989). Scholarship in Commerical Law, International Development Law Institute, Rome, Italy, 1993. Seminar for Polish and Baltic Lawyers, Copenhagen, Denmark, 1993; Queen Mary & Westfield College, London University, 1994. *Member:* IBA; UIA (Vice President); Lithuanian Young Bar Association (President). *LANGUAGES:* Lithuanian, Russian, English and Polish. *PRACTICE AREAS:* Foreign Investment Law; International Business Law; International Financing Law.

GINTAUTAS BARTKUS, born Vilnius, Lithuania, June 13, 1966; admitted, 1989, Lithuania. *Education:* Law Faculty, Vilnius University (1989); The John Marshall Law School, Chicago, Illinois, USA, (1993). Law Faculty, University of Helsinki, Finland (1991). Commercial Law, Raising Rights Consciousness, Democracy after Communism Foundation & Law Center, Columbia University, Budapest, Hungary, 1992; Commercial Law, CEELI, American Bar Association, Lodz, Poland, 1992. *LANGUAGES:* Lithuanian, English and Russian. *PRACTICE AREAS:* International Business Law; Company Law; International Sales of Goods.

EGLE MICKEVICIUTE, born Prienai, Lithuania, June 2, 1966; admitted, 1989, Lithuania. *Education:* Law Faculty, Vilnius University (1989); Suffolk University Law School Boston, USA (1990); Northeastern University, Boston, USA (1992); Academy of European Law, Italy (1993). *LANGUAGES:* Lithuanian, English and Russian. *PRACTICE AREAS:* Copyright Law; Patent Law; Intellectual Property Law; Foreign Investment Law; International Business Law.

VIKTORAS TIAŽKIJ, born Vilnius, Lithuania, November 27, 1957; admitted, 1983, Lithuania. *Education:* Law Faculty, Vilnius University (1983); Moscow University (Ph.D., 1988). *LANGUAGES:* Lithuanian and Russian. *PRACTICE AREAS:* Labour Law; Civil Law.

RAIMUNDAS JUREVIĆIUS, born Vilnius, Lithuania, April 8, 1964; admitted, 1989, Lithuania. *Education:* Law Faculty, Vilnius University (1989); The John Marshall Law School, Chicago, Illinois, USA (LL.M., 1993). *LANGUAGES:* Lithuanian, English and Russian. *PRACTICE AREAS:* International Business Law; Foreign Investment Law; Corporations Law.

GIEDRIUS STASEVIĆIUS, born Siauliai, Lithuania, March 25, 1960; admitted, 1982, Lithuania. *Education:* Law Faculty, Vilnius University (1982); University of Houston Law Center, Houston, U.S.A. (LL.M., 1994). *LANGUAGES:* Lithuanian, English and Russian. *PRACTICE AREAS:* International Business Law; Foreign Investment Law; Corporate Law.

McDERMOTT, WILL & EMERY

A Partnership including Professional Corporations

Established in 1934

SMETONOS 6

2600 VILNIUS, LITHUANIA

Telephone: 370 2 61-43-08
Facsimile: 370 2 22-79-55

Boston, Massachusetts Office: 75 State Street, Suite 1700, 02109-1807. Telephone: 617-345-5000. Telex: 951324 MILAM BSN. Facsimile: 617-345-5077.
Chicago, Illinois Office: 227 West Monroe Street, 60606-5096. Telephone: 312-372-2000. Telex: 253565 MILAM CGO. Facsimile: 312-984-7700.
Los Angeles, California Office: 2049 Century Park East, 90067-3208. Telephone: 310-277-4110. Facsimile: 310-277-4730.
Miami, Florida Office: 201 South Biscayne Boulevard, 33131-4336. Telephone: 305-358-3500. Telex: 441777 LEYES. Facsimile: 305-347-6500.
Newport Beach, California Office: 1301 Dove Street, Suite 500, 92660-2444. Telephone: 714-851-0633. Facsimile: 714-851-9348.
New York, N.Y. Office: 1211 Avenue of the Americas, 10036-8701. Telephone: 212-768-5400. Facsimile: 212-768-5444.
Washington, D.C. Office: 1850 K Street, N.W., 20006-2296. Telephone: 202-887-8000. Telex: 253565 MILAM CGO. Facsimile: 202-778-8087.
St. Petersburg, Russia Office: 2/2 Tchaikovsky Street, #517, 191187 St. Petersburg, Russia. Telephone: (7) (812) 273- 9831. Facsimile (7) (812) 273-9831.

(This Listing Continued)

Associated (Independent) Offices:
Brussels, Belgium: Uettwiller Grelon Lippens Dekeyser, 73 avenue Vandendriessche, 1150 Brussels, Belgium. Telephone: (32) (2) 772-87-50. Facsimile (32) (2) 772-87-52.
London, England: Paisner & Co, Bouverie House, 154 Fleet Street, London EC4A 2DQ, England. Telephone: (44) (171) 353-0299. Facsimile: (44) (171) 583-8621.
Paris, France: Uettwiller Grelon Gout Canat & Associes, 68, boulevard de Courcelles, 75017 Paris, France. Telephone: (33) (1) 48 88 89 00. Facsimile: (33) (1) 48 88 05 50.

General Practice (including Corporate, Employee Benefits, Estate Planning, Health, Litigation and Tax Law).

FIRM PROFILE: Founded in Chicago in 1934, the firm originally focused on federal taxation matters. Over the years it has grown to become a leading international law firm with a diversified business practice. We represent a wide range of industrial, financial, and commercial enterprises, both publicly and privately held. Our clientele includes some of the world's largest corporations as well as individuals and small and medium-sized businesses.

The firm is organized along lines of functional specialization—most attorneys focus on a particular aspect of the law from the outset of their career. The firm's 500 attorneys practice in corporate, employee benefits, estate planning, health, litigation, and tax law. Many attorneys also practice in interdepartmental groups. This structure distinguishes us from many other national law firms of our size and experience and permits maximum flexibility and efficiency in handling client matters.

MEMBERS OF FIRM

EGIDIJUS BERNOTAS, born Vilnius, Lithuania, April 10, 1971; admitted, 1993, Lithuania. *Education:* University of Vilnius (J.D., 1993). Attorney, Legal and International Treaties Department, Ministry of Foreign Affairs. *LANGUAGES:* Lithuanian and English.

KESTUTIS JASKUTELIS, born Inkutzk, Russia, May 30, 1965; admitted, 1992, Lithuania. *Education:* Oslo University, Hague Academy; Vilnius University (J.D., 1992). First Secretary, International Treaties Department, Ministry of Foreign Affairs, 1990-1992. *LANGUAGES:* Lithuanian and English.

EUGENIJA SUTKIENE, born Vilnius, Lithuania, February 3, 1956; admitted, 1984, Lithuania. *Education:* Vilnius University (J.D., 1984). *LANGUAGES:* Lithuanian, Russian, Polish and English.

(For Biographical data on all firm personnel, see Professional Biographies listings at other office locations)

SCHEELE, SCHWARTZ, ZIELCKE & PARTNER

ARCHITEKTU 194/22

2049 VILNIUS, LITHUANIA

Telephone: 00370 2 443720
Fax: 00370 2 443720

Munich, Germany Office: Prinzregentenplatz 15, 81675. Telephone: 089/470 10 02. Fax: 089/470 10 06.

FIRM PROFILE: Scheele, Schwartz, Zielcke & Partner is an international law firm advising business clients and public institutions on all domestic and overseas corporate and commercial matters. The firm specializes in Eastern European and C.I.S. matters. Currently the firm is representing a broad range of clients in Europe, North America, South America, Asia and Africa.

(For biographical data and areas of practice see listing at Munich, Germany)

LUXEMBOURG

ARENDT & MEDERNACH

8-10, RUE MATHIAS HARDT
BOITE POSTALE 39
LUXEMBOURG L-2010, LUXEMBOURG
Telephone: (352) 40 78 78
Telefax: (352) 40 78 04
Telex: 1302

Administrative, Aeronautical, Arbitration, Banking, Competition, Corporate, EEC, Tax, Industrial Relations and Labor and Insurance Law, Litigation, Intellectual Property, Entertainment and Communications.

PARTNERS AND ASSOCIATES

ERNEST ARENDT, born Luxembourg, August 6, 1916; admitted, 1940, Luxembourg. *Education:* University of Paris, Ecole Libre de Sciences Politiques (Docteur en Droit, 1940). Chairman, Luxembourg Bar Council, 1976-1978. President, International Union of Lawyers, 1981-1983. Honorary President, Conseil d'Etat, 1988—.

JACQUES MERSCH, born Luxembourg, September 18, 1921; admitted, 1949, Luxembourg. *Education:* University of Lausanne (Docteur en Droit).

JEAN MEDERNACH, born Luxembourg, September 24, 1938; admitted, 1963, Luxembourg. *Education:* Universities of Paris and Aix-en-Provence, France (Docteur en Droit).

PAUL MOUSEL, born Luxembourg, October 15, 1953; admitted, 1978, Luxembourg and Brussels. *Education:* Free University of Brussels (Licencié en Droit, 1976; Licencié en Droit économique, 1977). Professor, General Jurisprudence, University Center of Luxembourg, 1982—.

GUY HARLES, born Luxembourg, May 4, 1955; admitted, 1980, Luxembourg; 1993, Paris. *Education:* University of Strasbourg (Maître en Droit, 1978; Diplômé en Techniques Bancaires et Financiéres, 1979). Lecturer, Banking Law, (1981—), Business Law (1993—), University of Strasbourg, Faculty of Economic Sciences. . Professor, Business Law, 1982-1994. General Jurisprudence (1994), University Center of Luxembourg. *Member:* President, Luxembourg Young Bar Association, 1990-1991. President-Elect (1994), International Association of Young Lawyers.

CLAUDE KREMER, born Luxembourg, July 27, 1956; admitted, 1982, Luxembourg. *Education:* University of Grenoble (Maître en droit); London School of Economics (Master in Accounting and Finance). Lecturer in International Tax Law, University Center of Luxembourg, 1984—. *Member:* Luxembourg Young Bar Association (President, 1993-1994).

PHILIPPE DUPONT, born Luxembourg, January 8, 1961; admitted, 1986, Luxembourg. *Education:* Universities of Paris and Aix-en-Provence (Maître en Droit, 1984); London School of Economics (LL.M., 1985).

LOUIS BERNS, born Luxembourg, March 2, 1961; admitted, 1987, Luxembourg. *Education:* University of Strasbourg (Maître en Droit, 1985); Diplômé de l'Institut d'Administration des Entreprises, Strasbourg (1986).

PATRICK KINSCH, born Luxembourg, October 6, 1962; admitted, 1988, Luxembourg. *Education:* University of Strasbourg (Maître en Droit, 1986; Docteur en droit, 1992); Lauréat de la Faculté. Lecturer, University Center of Luxembourg, 1994—. *Member:* French Committee of Private International Law.

FRANÇOIS KREMER, born Luxembourg, May 14, 1963; admitted, 1988, Luxembourg. *Education:* Universities of Strasbourg and Paris (Maître en Droit 1986); London School of Economics (LL.M., 1987).

JOËLLE BADEN, born Luxembourg, June 22, 1965; admitted, 1989. *Education:* University of Nancy.

CHRISTIAN KREMER, born Belgium, February 25, 1965; admitted, 1990, Luxembourg and Brussels. *Education:* Free University of Brussels (Licence en Droit, 1989).

(This Listing Continued)

JOBST-JOACHIM NEUSS, born Germany, May 27, 1958; admitted, 1992, Bonn; 1994, Luxembourg. *Education:* Universities of Munich and Bayreuth (2. Staatsexamen, 1985; Dr.iur., 1989). *LANGUAGES:* Italian, Spanish and Portuguese.

Languages: French, German, English and Dutch

GEORGES BADEN

7, PLACE DU THEATRE
L-2613 LUXEMBOURG, LUXEMBOURG
Telephone: 47 50 61
Telecopier: 46 25 17

General and International Corporate Law Practice.

GEORGES BADEN, born Luxembourg, October 26, 1937; admitted, 1961, Luxembourg (Avocat-Avoué). *Education:* Universities of Nancy, France and Bruxelles, Belgium (Doctor en droit, 1961); UniversitéLibre de Bruxelles (Certificat Finances Publiques). *Member:* Luxembourg and International Bar Associations. *LANGUAGES:* English, French and German.

NICOLAS BANNASCH, born Wuppertal, October 17, 1964; admitted, 1990, Luxembourg (Avocat). *LANGUAGES:* English, French and German.

JOHAN BAKEROOT, born Kortrijk, October 18, 1966; admitted, 1991, Luxembourg (Avocat). *LANGUAGES:* English, French, German and Dutch.

MARC THILL, born Luxembourg, March 6, 1965; admitted, 1993, Luxembourg (Avocat). *LANGUAGES:* English, French and German.

MARC BADEN

Established in 1960

24 RUE MARIE-ADELAIDE
2128 LUXEMBOURG, LUXEMBOURG
Telephone: 44 41 41
Telefax: 44 41 66

General and International Law Practice.

MEMBERS OF FIRM

MARC BADEN, born Luxembourg, August 21, 1936; admitted, 1960, Luxembourg. *Education:* Universities of Paris, Grenoble, Aix-en-Provence and Strasbourg.

ROBERT LOOS, born Luxembourg, February 3, 1966; admitted, 1989, Luxembourg. *Education:* Universities of Paris, Louvain and London (L.S.E.).

NADINE GLESENER, born Luxembourg, July 26, 1962; admitted, 1990, Luxembourg. *Education:* University of Montpellier.

ERIC BOISSAUX, born Luxembourg, January 17, 1965; admitted, 1992, Luxembourg. *Education:* University of Paris.

Languages: French, German and English.

BONN & SCHMITT

62, AVENUE GUILLAUME
L-1650 LUXEMBOURG, LUXEMBOURG
Telephone: (352) 45 58 58
Telex: 60 392
Telefax: (352) 45 58 59; (352) 45 01 82

REVISERS OF THE LUXEMBOURG LAW DIGEST FOR THIS DIRECTORY.

Brussels, Belgium Office: 13, rue Bréderode, B-1000. Telephone: (32-2) 517 91 86. Telefax: (32-2) 517 94 94.

General Luxembourg and International Practice with emphasis on Financial and Corporate Law.

MEMBERS OF FIRM

ALEX SCHMITT, born Luxembourg, March 24, 1953; admitted, 1979, Brussels, Belgium; 1983, Luxembourg. *Education:* University of Brussels, Belgium (Lic. Jur., 1979); Institute of European Studies, Brussels (Lic. Droit Européen, 1980); Harvard Law School, USA (LL.M., 1981. Lecturer, University of Brussels Law School. *LANGUAGES:* English, French, German and Italian. *PRACTICE AREAS:* Financial Law; Corporate Law.

(This Listing Continued)

GUY ARENDT, born Luxembourg, April 13, 1954; admitted, 1980, Luxembourg. *Education:* University of Nancy, France (Maître en droit, 1979). Justice of the Peace. *LANGUAGES:* English, French and German. *PRACTICE AREAS:* Litigation; Computer Law.

LUC FRIEDEN, born Luxembourg, September 16, 1963; admitted, 1989, Luxembourg. *Education:* University of Paris, France (Maîtrise en Droit des Affaires, 1986); University of Cambridge, UK (LL.M., 1987); Harvard Law School, USA (LL.M., 1988). Lecturer, University Center of Luxembourg. *LANGUAGES:* English, French, German and Dutch. *PRACTICE AREAS:* Media Law; Banking Law.

JEAN STEFFEN, born Luxembourg, April 11, 1966; admitted, 1991, Luxembourg. *Education:* University of Paris, France (Maîtrise en Droit des Affaires, 1989; DEA, 1992); London School of Economics, UK (LL.M., 1990). *LANGUAGES:* English, French and German. *PRACTICE AREAS:* Financial Law; Tax Law.

LAURENT LAZARD, born Luxembourg, January 28, 1965; admitted, 1990, Luxembourg. *Education:* University of Paris, France (Maîtrise en Droit, 1989; DEA, 1990); University of Chicago Law School, USA (LL.M., 1993). *LANGUAGES:* English, French and German. *PRACTICE AREAS:* Corporate Law; Financial Law; Tax Law.

OF COUNSEL

ALEX BONN, born Luxembourg, June 18, 1908; admitted, 1932, Luxembourg. *Education:* Docteur en Droit, 1931. Former Chairman of the Luxembourg Bar Association; Former Chairman of the Luxembourg Council of State.

ASSOCIATES

CORINNE PHILIPPE, born Belgium, October 9, 1955; admitted, 1979, Tournai, Belgium (Not admitted in Luxembourg). *Education:* University of Louvain, Belgium (Lic. Jur., 1978). *LANGUAGES:* English, French and Dutch.

CHANTAL KEEREMAN, born Belgium, November 26, 1960; (Not admitted in Luxembourg). *Education:* University of Louvain, Belgium (Lic. Jur., 1983); University of Brussels, Belgium (Insurance Law, 1984; Notarial Law, 1988). *LANGUAGES:* English, French and Dutch.

ANNE SCHOLLEN, born Belgium, October 21, 1966; (Not admitted in Luxembourg). *Education:* University of Brussels, Belgium (Lic. Jur., 1991); Duke University Law School, USA (LL.M., 1992). *LANGUAGES:* English, French and Dutch.

FABIO TREVISAN, born Luxembourg, February 24, 1966; admitted, 1992, New York; 1993, Luxembourg. *Education:* University of Milan, Italy (Laurea in Giurisprudenza, 1991); New York University School of Law, USA (LL.M., 1992). *LANGUAGES:* English, French and Italian.

FRANCOISE THOMA, born Luxembourg, August 25, 1969; admitted, 1994, Luxembourg. *Education:* Centre Universitaire de Luxembourg, Grand-Duchy of Luxembourg (Certificate d'Etudes Juridiques et Economiques, 1989); University of Paris I (Maîtrise en Droit Privé et Certificat du Centre des CE, 1992); University of Paris II (DEA de Droit Communautaire, 1993); London Chamber of Commerce (Certificate, Level 4). *LANGUAGES:* English, French, German and Italian.

LUC COURTOIS, born Belgium, August 21, 1970; admitted, 1994, Luxembourg. *Education:* Université Catholique de Louvain, Belgium (Deuxième Licence en Droit et Première Licence en Affaires Publiques et Internationales, 1992). *LANGUAGES:* English, French and Dutch.

REVISERS OF THE LUXEMBOURG LAW DIGEST FOR THIS DIRECTORY.

BRUCHER & TABERY

RUE PIERRE D'ASPELT 10

P.O. BOX 619

LUXEMBOURG L-2016, LUXEMBOURG

Telephone: (+352) 45 62 62

Fax: (+352) 45 94 65

Company and Commercial Law, National and International Tax Law, Banking and Financial Law, Private International Law, Litigation (Civil, Commercial and Labour Law), Corporate Insolvency, Intellectual Property.

JEAN BRUCHER, born Luxembourg, December 4, 1949; admitted, 1975, Luxembourg. *Education:* Universities of Aix-en-Provence and Paris

(This Listing Continued)

(Licencié en droit, des affa ires); Institut d'Etudes Politiques de Paris (Diplômé Eco-Fi). *LANGUAGES:* French, English, German.

SERGE TABERY, born Brussels, Belgium, September 13, 1951; admitted, 1992, Luxembourg. *Education:* Universities of Brussels and Louvain (Lic. Jur.-Economy and Finance). *LANGUAGES:* French, English, Dutch, Italian, German.

FRANCOIS LATOUR, born Marseille, France, February 27, 1964; admitted, 1991, Luxembourg. *Education:* University of Aix-en-Provence (Maître en droit des affaires, Lauréde la Faculté de Droit 1987-1988). *LANGUAGES:* French, English.

MARC SEIMETZ, born Esch/Alzette, Luxembourg, October 15, 1966; admitted, 1990, Luxembourg. *Education:* Universities of Luxembourg, Paris and London (Maître en droit des affaires); Université Paris I-Panthéon-Sorbonne; University of London (LL.M., Certificate in Luxembourg Tax Laws). *LANGUAGES:* French, English, German.

VERONIQUE WAUTHIER, born Arlon, Belgium, March 11, 1965; admitted, 1992, Luxembourg. *Education:* Universities of Namur and Louvain (Licenciée en droit), Diplômée en droit fiscal luxembourgeois. *LANGUAGES:* French, English, German.

OLIVIER BOONEN, born Ixelles, Belgium, December 13, 1964; admitted, 1993, Luxembourg. *Education:* Universities of Louvain (Droit, 1987 et Administration des Affaires, 1988); Brussels (Master in European Law, 1990); South Carolina (MBA, 1992). *LANGUAGES:* French, English.

JEROME AUSS, born Uccle, Belgium, October 7, 1963; admitted, 1993, Luxembourg. *Education:* Universities of Louvain and Leiden (Licencié en droit), Licence en droit international. *LANGUAGES:* French, English, Dutch.

SOPHIE MATHOT, born Bastogne, Belgium, June 18, 1964; admitted, 1994, Luxembourg. *Education:* Universities of Namur and Louvain (Licenciée en droit). *LANGUAGES:* French, English.

MARC SUNNEN, born Luxembourg, June 10, 1969; admitted, 1994, Luxembourg. *Education:* University of Louvain (Licencié en droit)Licence spéciale en droi t économique. *LANGUAGES:* French. English.

Languages: French, English, Dutch, Italian and German

DENNEMEYER & ASSOCIATES

S.A.R.L.

Conseils en Propriete Industrielle

Established in 1962

55, RUE DES BRUYÈRES

L-1274 HOWALD/LUXEMBOURG, LUXEMBOURG

Telephone: 49 98 41-1

Telex: 2769 DENPAT LU

Cable Address: "Denpat"

Fax: Gr. III & II, 49 98 41-222; 49 98 41-237

Mailing Address: P.O. Box 1502, Luxembourg L-1015

Brussels, Belgium Office: 40, Square Marie-Louise, Bte. 19, B-1040. Telephone: 2 230 79 63. Fax: 2 231 11 29.

Munich, Germany Office: Balanstrasse 55, D-81541. Telephone: 89 40 50 88. Fax: 89 49 36 10.

Zug, Switzerland Office: Gartenstrasse 3, CH-4754. Telephone: 41 42 212 396. Fax: 41 42 218 843.

Firm engaged in International Intellectual Property Law Practice. Registration and maintenance of Patents, Trademarks, Copyrights, Licensing, Unfair Competition. Trademark database searching.

FIRM PROFILE: Established in 1959 in Washington, D.C. by U.S. Patent Attorney, John J. Dennemeyer and transferred to Luxembourg in 1962, it is one of the leading Intellectual Property law firms in Europe. The client base is North American and European in scope. The firm has seven patent attorneys and 18 assistants in their Luxembourg office.

JOHN J. DENNEMEYER, born Los Angeles, California, February 17, 1921; admitted, 1949, District of Columbia; Registered U.S., Luxembourg and European Patent Attorney. *Education:* University of Munich (1941-1942); George Washington University, Washington, D.C. (J.D.). Instructor, Foreign Languages, George Washington University, 1947-1948. *Member:* American Patent Law Association; U.S. Trademark Association; Licensing Executives Society; International Federation of Patent Counsels; Union of Patent Counsels; International Association for the Protection of

(This Listing Continued)

DENNEMEYER & ASSOCIATES, Luxembourg—
Continued

Industrial Property. *LANGUAGES:* English, French, German, Italian and Spanish.

LEGAL SUPPORT PERSONNEL

John Bleyer (European Patent Attorney; Chemical Engineer)

Jean Schmitz (European Patent Attorney; Chemical Engineer)

Jean Waxweiller (European Patent Attorney; Electrical **Engineer)**

Robert Weydert (European Patent Attorney; Mechanical Engineer)

Manuel Schockmel (Electrical Engineer)

Muriel Mathieu (Biochemical Engineer)

DOERNER, LAPLUME, LUDOVISSY, OOSTVOGELS

Avocats à la Cour

13, RUE ALDRINGEN

P.O. BOX 221

L-2012 LUXEMBOURG, LUXEMBOURG

Telephone: (352) 46.40.01

Telefax: (352) 46.40.47

Banking and Finance Law, Corporate Finance Law, Taxation Law, Competition Law, Real Estate Law, Industrial Relations and Labor Law, Insurance and Reinsurance Law, Litigation, Media, Entertainment and Communications Law, Pharmaceutical Law, General Business Law, Contracts, Bankruptcy Law, Foreign Investments, Investment Funds, Holding and Off-Shore Companies, International Private Law.

PARTNERS

JEAN DOERNER, born Luxembourg, October 1, 1954; admitted, 1981, Luxembourg. *Education:* University of Aix-en Provence III, France (Maîtrise en Droit). *Member:* Luxembourg Bar; Association Luxembourgeoise des Juristes de Banque; GEIE. *LANGUAGES:* Luxembourgish, English, French and German. *PRACTICE AREAS:* Civil Law; Commercial Law; Criminal Law.

FELIX LAPLUME, born Dudelange, Luxembourg, February 2, 1961; admitted, 1987, Luxembourg. *Education:* University of Strasbourg, France (Maîtrise en Droit). *Member:* Luxembourg Bar; Association Internationale des Jeunes Avocats (AIJA); International Bar Association (IBA). *LANGUAGES:* Luxembourgish, English, French and German. *PRACTICE AREAS:* Corporate Finance; Business; Media; Real Estate; Competition Law.

GUY LUDOVISSY, born Luxembourg, July 9, 1964; admitted, 1989, Luxembourg. *Education:* University of Montpellier, France (Maîtrise en Droit); London School of Economics (Master, International Business Law). Lector, Institut de Formation Bancaire Luxembourg. Member, Chamber of Commerce of Spain. *Member:* Luxembourg Bar; Association Luxembourgeoise de Juristes de Banque. *LANGUAGES:* Luxembourgish, English, French and German. *PRACTICE AREAS:* Corporate Finance; Banking and Finance; Taxation Law.

STEF OOSTVOGELS, born Brussels, Belgium, April 21, 1962; admitted, 1987, Brussels; 1990, Luxembourg. *Education:* UFSAL University, Brussels, Belgium; Katholieke Universiteit Leuven KUL, Belgium (Licentiaat in de Rechten). Author: "Participation Companies in the Grand-Duchy of Luxembourg," in collaboration with René Faltz, International Business Lawyer, 1991; "Luxembourg Banking Secrecy," International Business Lawyer, 1993; "Les Activités Professionnelles Non Bancaires du Secteur Financier," Droit Bancaire et Financier au Grand-Duché de Luxembourg, 1994. Lector, Institut de Formation Bancaire Luxembourg. Member: Chamber of Commerce of the Netherlands for Belgium and Luxembourg. *Member:* Luxembourg Bar; Brussels Bar; International Bar Association (IBA); American Bar Association (ABA); Association Luxembourgeoise de Juristes de Banque; Association Luxembourgeoise d'Etudes Fiscales. *LANGUAGES:* Dutch, English, French and German. *PRACTICE AREAS:* Corporate Finance; Banking and Finance; Taxation; Real Estate; Business Law.

(This Listing Continued)

ASSOCIATES

CLAUDIA PICCARRETA, born Rome, Italy, April 2, 1963; admitted, 1991, Rome; 1992, Luxembourg. *Education:* University of Rome, La Sapiencia, Italy (Laurea in Giurisprudenza). *Member:* Luxembourg Bar; Rome Bar; Association Luxembourgeoise Juristes Européens; Association Internationale des Jeunes Avocats (AIJA). *LANGUAGES:* Italian, English and French.

CHRISTIAN SCHULLER, born Luxembourg, April 7, 1968; admitted, 1992, Luxembourg. *Education:* University of Aix-en-Provence, France (Maîtrise en Droit; DEA Diplôme d'Etudes Approfondies). *Member:* Luxembourg Bar. *LANGUAGES:* Luxembourgish, French, English and German.

MICHELE KRIER, born Luxembourg, May 19, 1968; admitted, 1992, Luxembourg. *Education:* University of Nancy II, France (Maîtrise en Droit). *Member:* Luxembourg Bar. *LANGUAGES:* Luxembourgish, French, English, German and Italian.

KARIN WEIRICH, born Calcutta, India, August 7, 1968; admitted, 1992, Luxembourg. *Education:* Centre Universitaire Luxembourg; University Louvain la Neuve, Belgium (Licence en Droit). *Member:* Luxembourg Bar. *LANGUAGES:* Luxembourgish, French, English and German.

LAURENCE JACOBS, born Bourg-la-Reine, France, February 26, 1967; admitted, 1994, Luxembourg. *Education:* University of Nancy II, France (Maîtrise en Droit; DESS Diplôme d'Etudes Supérieures Spécialisées); University of Metz, France. *Member:* Luxembourg Bar. *LANGUAGES:* French.

STEPHANE HADET, born Nancy, France, May 25, 1968; admitted, 1994, Luxembourg. *Education:* Université de Nancy II, France (Maîtrise en droit). *Member:* Luxembourg Bar. *LANGUAGES:* French, English, Italian and Spanish.

Languages: Luxembourgish, English, French, German, Dutch and Italian

---

DUPONG & ASSOCIES

Established in 1947

14A, RUE DES BAINS

P.O. BOX 472

L-2014 LUXEMBOURG, LUXEMBOURG

Telephone: 352-46 18 38

Telex: 2221 duas lu

Telefax: 352-46 19 09 (GP 2/3)

Administrative, Aeronautical, Arbitration, Banking, Commercial, Construction, Corporate, Industrial Relations and Labour, Insurance, Intellectual Property, International Contracts, Litigation, Tax, Transportation, General Legal Practice.

PARTNERS

LAMBERT H. DUPONG, born Luxembourg, September 23, 1917; admitted, 1947, Luxembourg. *Education:* University of Grenoble, University of Louvain, Harvard University (Docteur en Droit). Past Chairman, Luxembourg Bar Council. *PRACTICE AREAS:* Aeronautical; Arbitration; Banking; Corporate; Insurance.

JEAN DUPONG, born Luxembourg, May 18, 1922; admitted, 1948, Luxembourg. *Education:* University of Paris; University of Lausanne (Docteur en Droit). Past President, Council of State. *PRACTICE AREAS:* Administrative; Banking; Corporate Tax.

LUCY DUPONG, born Luxembourg, June 30, 1952; admitted, 1977, Luxembourg. *Education:* University of Aix-en-Provence (Maître en Droit). *PRACTICE AREAS:* Commercial; Corporate; International Contracts; Transportation.

MICHEL MOLITOR, born Luxembourg, January 31, 1961; admitted, 1985, Luxembourg. *Education:* University of Strasbourg (Maître en Droit; Maître en Sciences Politiques); University of Vienna (Ph.D.). *PRACTICE AREAS:* Banking; Commercial; Corporate; Industrial Relations and Labour.

ANDRE HARPES, born Luxembourg, March 17, 1960; admitted, 1988, Luxembourg. *Education:* University of Strasbourg (Maître en Droit); University of Metz (Licencié en Gestion d'entreprises). *PRACTICE AREAS:* Commercial; Construction; Insurance; Transportation.

(This Listing Continued)

PIERRE FELTGEN, born Luxembourg, October 27, 1966; admitted, 1991, Luxembourg. *Education:* University of Strasbourg (Maître en Droit, DESS Accords et Propriété Industrielle). *PRACTICE AREAS:* Bankruptcy; Corporate; Intellectual Property; International Contracts.

Languages: English, French, German, Italian and Spanish

FALTZ & ASSOCIES

Established in 1982

6 RUE HEINE

L-1720 LUXEMBOURG, LUXEMBOURG

Telephone: (352) 48 50 50

Facsimile: (352) 48 13 85

Mailing Address: P.O. Box 1147, L-1011 Luxembourg, Luxembourg

The Practice of the firm is wide-ranging, encompassing both the domestic and international spheres. The Main areas of activity are General Practice, Banking and Finance Law, Corporate Law, Tax Law, Holding Company Law, Administrative Law, Real Estate, International Arbitration, Competition Law, Intellectual Property, Labor Law, Collective Investment Fund Law, Insurance and Reinsurance law.

MEMBERS OF FIRM

RENÉ FALTZ, born Luxembourg, Grand-Duchy of Luxembourg, August, 1953; admitted, 1977, Luxembourg. *Education:* University of Nancy, France, "Prix du meilleur étudiant", (1974-1975). Former partner of the Law Office Schaeffer, Hengel & Faltz; Former consultant to Morret Gudde Brinkman, Luxembourg S.A., (actually Ernst and Young). *Member:* Luxembourg Bar Association, I.F.A.; I.B.A.; U.I.A. (President of the Tax Commission). *LANGUAGES:* Luxemburgish, English, French and German. *PRACTICE AREAS:* Tax Law; Banking; Finance Law.

LYDIE LORANG, born Luxembourg, Grand-Duchy of Luxembourg, March, 1954; admitted, 1980, Luxembourg. *Education:* University of Liege, Belgium. Former Associate of the Law Office Schaeffer, Hengel & Faltz; Former Professor at the "Institut de Formation Administrative". *Member:* Luxembourg Bar Association; I.B.A.; Union Internationale des Avocats. *LANGUAGES:* Luxemburgish, English, French, German and Italian. *PRACTICE AREAS:* Family law; Banking Law; Litigation; Criminal Law; Labour Law.

PATRICK WEINACHT, born Neuilly-sur-Seine, France, December, 1953; admitted, 1982, Luxembourg. *Education:* University of Aix-en-Provence, France, University of Strasbourg (Specialisation in International Private and Public law), France. *Member:* The Bar Association of Luxembourg. *LANGUAGES:* Luxemburgish, English, French and German. *PRACTICE AREAS:* Agency and Distributorships; Bankruptcy; Children; Commercial Law; Construction Law; Consumer Law.

CHARLES DURO, born Luxembourg, Grand-Duchy of Luxembourg, June, 1958; admitted, 1984, Luxembourg. *Education:* University of Nancy, France; University of Liège, Belgium (Specialization in European Legislation). Correspondent member for Luxembourg at the "Institut de Droit International des Transports". *Member:* The International Fiscal Association; The Association Internationale des Jeunes Avocats; The Luxembourg Bar Association. *LANGUAGES:* French, Luxemburgish, German and English. *PRACTICE AREAS:* Company Law; Corporate Law.

JACQUES SCHROEDER, born Luxembourg, Grand-Duchy of Luxembourg, June, 1959; admitted, 1986, Luxembourg. *Education:* University of Strasbourg, France (Specialization in Political Sciences). *Member:* The Bar Association of Luxembourg. *LANGUAGES:* Luxemburgish, English, French and German. *PRACTICE AREAS:* Securities Law; Banking Law; Corporate Law; Investment Funds Law.

ASSOCIATES

SILVIA LOPEZ-GARCIA, born Avila, Spain, September, 1964; admitted, 1989, Luxembourg. *Education:* University of Salamanca, Licenciatura de Derecho, Faculté Internationale de Droit comparé de Strasbourg. *Member:* Luxembourg Bar Association. *LANGUAGES:* Spanish, French and English. *PRACTICE AREAS:* Bankruptcy; Children; Civil Law; Consumer Law; Debtor and Creditor; Family Law.

KOEN DE VLEESCHAUWER, born Lubbeek, Belgium, May, 1963; admitted, 1990, Brussels; 1992, Luxembourg. *Education:* Katholieke Universiteit Leuven; Université Libre de Bruxelles (Licence Spéciale en Droit Economique. Former associate of the law office Lafili & Van Crombrugghe. *Member:* Luxembourg Bar Association. *LANGUAGES:* Dutch, English and French. *PRACTICE AREAS:* Company Law; Corporate Law.

(This Listing Continued)

ALBERT MORO, born Bettembourg, Grand-Duchy of Luxembourg, August, 1967; admitted, 1992, Luxembourg. *Education:* University of Strasbourg, Law School (Maîtrise en Droit, Private Law, 1991); "Prix du meilleur étudiant" year 1990-1991; "Prix du meilleur étudiant en droit civil" (1990-1991). *LANGUAGES:* Luxemburgish, French, German, English and Italian. *PRACTICE AREAS:* Business Law; Civil Law; Construction Law; Contracts; Labour and Employment; Litigation.

JEAN DAMIEN VICQ, born Epinal, France, October, 1967; admitted, 1993, Luxembourg. *Education:* University of Nancy, Law School (Maîtrise en Droit, Business Law, 1991); "Prix du meilleur éetudiant en droit Communautaire," 1990-1991, Specialization in Business Law (DESS) 1992. *LANGUAGES:* French, English. *PRACTICE AREAS:* Business Law; Civil Law; Commercial Law; Contracts; Criminal Law; Labour and Employment.

ANICK WOLFF, born Ettelbruck, Grand-Duchy of Luxembourg, August, 1968; admitted, 1993, Luxembourg. *Education:* University of Paris I Panthéon-Sorbonne: Maîtrise en Droit, Business Law, 1991, Specialization in Environmental Law, 1992. *LANGUAGES:* Luxembourgish, German, French, English. *PRACTICE AREAS:* Civil Law; Environmental Law; Divorce; General Practice; Labour and Employment; Litigation.

PHILIPPE MORALES, born Savigny, France, February, 1968; admitted, 1994, Luxembourg. *Education:* University of Aix en Provence; Law School (Maîtrise en Droit, 1991); Specialization in Business Law (DESS, Magistere, DJCE, 1992); "Prix du meilleur étudiant en droit public," 1988-1991; Prix du meilleur étudiant en droit commercial," 1990. *LANGUAGES:* French, English and Spanish. *PRACTICE AREAS:* Company Law; Corporate Law.

LEGAL CONSULTANTS

LARS JENSEN, born Copenhagen, Denmark, January, 1966. *Education:* University of Aarkus, Denmark. Former associate of Bech-Bruun and Trolle (DK). *LANGUAGES:* Danish, Swedish, Norwegian, French, German and English. *PRACTICE AREAS:* Company Law; Corporate Law; Intellectual Property; Investments; Patents.

HELDENSTEIN

5 BOULEVARD ROYAL

L-2449 LUXEMBOURG, LUXEMBOURG

Telephone: 352-22 05 82

Fax: 352-22 05 83

Paris, France Office: 7, Rue Royale, 75008. Telephone: 33-1-42 65 03 71. Fax: 33-1-42 65 03 88.

The firm handles both matters in Luxembourg and French law, mainly in the financial area.

Securities and Negotiable Instruments, Financial Futures and other Derivative Products, Banking, Stock Market Regulation, Tax Planning, Formation of Investment Funds, Investment Trusts and Holding Companies, International Trade and Financial Litigation.

GEORGES HELDENSTEIN, born Luxembourg, Luxembourg, December 22, 1951; admitted, 1976, Luxembourg; 1986, Paris. *Education:* Faculté de Droit de l'Université Paris II (Maîtrise, 1975); Institut d'Etudes Politiques de Paris (Diplôme, 1975); Harvard Business School (M.B.A., 1978). *Member:* Belgium-Luxembourg Chamber of Commerce in France (Director). *LANGUAGES:* English, French and German. *PRACTICE AREAS:* Securities; Commodities Futures Law; Brokerage Law; Banking Law; Taxation of Individuals and Business Entities.

KLEYR COLLARINI KERGER & GRASSO

17 RUE LOUVIGNY

L-1946 LUXEMBOURG, LUXEMBOURG

Telephone: 352 22 73 30

Telefax: 352 22 73 32

Mailing Address: P.O. Box 1753, L-1017 Luxembourg

Civil and Commercial Law, Competition Law, Corporate Law, Intellectual Property Law, Labor Law, Real Estate, Banking and Finance Law, Litigation and Criminal Law.

(This Listing Continued)

KLEYR COLLARINI KERGER & GRASSO,
Luxembourg—Continued

MEMBERS OF FIRM

MARC KLEYR, born Luxembourg, September, 1963; admitted, 1991, Luxembourg. *Education:* University of Saarbruecken and University of Strasbourg, Law School(Maîtise en droit privé, Private Law). *Member:* Luxembourg Bar Association; Union Internationale des Avocats (UIA). *LANGUAGES:* Luxemburgish, French, German and English.

CLAUDE COLLARINI, born Luxembourg, November 1962; admitted, 1991, Luxembourg. *Education:* University of Montpellier, Law School (Maîtrise en droit de l'entreprise, Maîtrise en droit, optionétudes comptables). *Member:* Luxembourg Bar Association; Union Européenne des Avocats (UEA). *LANGUAGES:* Luxemburgish, French, German, English and Italian.

MARC KERGER, born Luxembourg, August 1967; admitted, 1991, Luxembourg. *Education:* University of Strasbourg, Law School (Maîtrise en droit privé, Private Law). *Member:* Luxembourg Bar Association; Association Internationale des Jeunes Avocats (AIJA).

ROSARIO GRASSO, born Luxembourg, July 1961; admitted, 1991, Luxembourg. *Education:* University of Catania, Law School (Maîtrise en droit). *Member:* Luxembourg Bar Association. *LANGUAGES:* Luxemburgish, French, German, English and Italian.

CABINET D'AVOCATS KRONSHAGEN

12, BOULEVARD DE LA FOIRE
LUXEMBOURG L-1528, LUXEMBOURG
Telephone: 45.44.04 / 45.44.05
Fax: 45.44.25

ARSENE KRONSHAGEN, born Esch/Azette, July 16, 1955; admitted, 1979, Luxembourg. *Education:* Luxembourg Strasbourg III (Licence en Droit); Paris II (Maitrise en Droit). *Member:* Luxembourg Bar Association; I.B.A. *PRACTICE AREAS:* Corporate Law; Administrative Law; Telecommunication.

LOESCH & WOLTER

11 RUE GOETHE
L-1637 LUXEMBOURG, LUXEMBOURG
Telephone: 352-48 11 48-1
Telefax: 352-49 49 44

Mailing Address: P.O. Box 1107, L-1011 Luxembourg

General Civil and Commercial Practice, Banking, Corporate, Construction, Commercial, EEC, Finance, Intellectual Property, International Private Law, Labor Law, Media, Taxation, Insurance and Reinsurance Law, Litigation.

PARTNERS

JACQUES LOESCH, born Luxembourg, April 9, 1928; admitted, 1952, Luxembourg. *Education:* University of Paris Law School (Dr. Jur. 1952). Chairman, Luxembourg Bar Council, 1988. Honorary Chamberlain to H.R.H. The Grand Duke of Luxembourg. Vice-President for Luxembourg, International Union of Lawyers. *Member:* Luxembourg Bar Association; Association Européennes d'Etudes Juridiques et Fiscales; International Union of Lawyers. *LANGUAGES:* French, German and English. *PRACTICE AREAS:* Company Law; Civil and Commercial Law; Banking and Finance; International Contracts; Tax Law; Litigation.

JANINE BIVER, born Luxembourg, August 5, 1944; admitted, 1968, Luxembourg. *Education:* University of Paris Law School (Dr. Jur., 1967). Former Secretary General of the Young Bar, Luxembourg. *Member:* Luxembourg Bar Association; International Bar Association. *LANGUAGES:* French, German and English. *PRACTICE AREAS:* Banking and Finance; Securities Law; Civil and Commercial Law; International Contracts; Labor Law; Construction Law.

RENÉ DIEDERICH, born Luxembourg, December 12, 1954; admitted, 1980, Luxembourg. *Education:* University of Grenoble Law School (Master of Laws, 1978); Institute of Political Sciences (Lic. Pol. Sc., 1979). Former Secretary General of the Young Bar, Luxembourg. *Member:* Luxembourg Bar Association; International Union of Young Lawyers; International Bar Association. *LANGUAGES:* French, German and English. *PRACTICE*
(This Listing Continued)

AREAS: Civil and Commercial Law; Litigation; International Contracts; Labor Law; Construction Law.

TOM LOESCH, born Luxembourg, April 26, 1956; admitted, 1982, Luxembourg. *Education:* University of Aix-en-Provence Law School (Master of Laws, 1979); University of Paris Law School (DESS, Finance and Banking, 1980); University of London, London School of Economics (LL.M., 1981). *Member:* Luxembourg Bar Association; Association Européennes d'Etudes Juristiques et Fiscales; International Bar Association; International Fiscal Association. *LANGUAGES:* French, German and English. *PRACTICE AREAS:* Corporate and Commercial Law; Investment Funds; Banking and Finance; International Contracts; Tax Law.

ALFRED (FREDDY) BRAUSCH, born Luxembourg, February 20, 1955; admitted, 1983, Luxembourg. *Education:* University of Aix-en-Provence Law School (Master of Laws, 1979); University of London, London School of Economics (LL.M., 1980). *Member:* Luxembourg Bar Association; International Bar Association; International Union of Lawyers. *LANGUAGES:* French, German and English. *PRACTICE AREAS:* Banking and Finance; Investment Funds; Securities Law; Corporate and Commercial Law; International Contracts; EEC Law.

MARC LOESCH, born Luxembourg, April 24, 1957; admitted, 1983, Luxembourg. *Education:* University of Aix-en-Provence Law School (Master of Laws, 1981); University of London, London School of Economics (LL.M., 1982). *Member:* Luxembourg Bar Association; International Bar Association. *LANGUAGES:* French, German and English. *PRACTICE AREAS:* Corporate and Commercial Law; Holding Companies; Insurance and Re-Insurance Law; Shipping Law.

JEAN-FRANÇOIS HEIN, born Luxembourg, July 24, 1960; admitted, 1986, Luxembourg. *Education:* University of Paris Law School (Master of Laws, 1985; DEA, Business Law, 1986). *Member:* Luxembourg Bar Association; International Association of Young Lawyers. *LANGUAGES:* French, German and English. *PRACTICE AREAS:* Banking and Finance; Securities Law; Commercial Law; Tax Law.

COUNSEL

JEAN-CLAUDE WOLTER, born 1937; admitted, 1962, Luxembourg. *Education:* University of Paris Law School (Dr. Jur., 1962); Institute of Political Sciences, Paris (Lic. Pol. & Econ. Sc., 1961). *Member:* Luxembourg Bar Association. *LANGUAGES:* French, German and English. *PRACTICE AREAS:* Investment Funds; Banking and Finance; International Contracts.

ASSOCIATES

ANDRÉ SEREBRIAKOFF, born Luxembourg, August, 6, 1959; admitted, 1984, Luxembourg. *Education:* University of Nancy Law School (Master of Laws, 1982; DEA Private Law, 1983). *Member:* Luxembourg Bar Association; International Association of Young Lawyers. *LANGUAGES:* French, English, German and Russian. *PRACTICE AREAS:* Civil and Commercial Law; Company Law; Litigation.

GUY LOESCH, born Luxembourg, September 13, 1962; admitted, 1987, Luxembourg. *Education:* University of Strasbourg Law School (Master of Laws, 1986). *LANGUAGES:* French, German and English. *PRACTICE AREAS:* Civil and Commercial Law; Labor Law; Litigation.

PIERRE JAEGER, born Luxembourg, May 18, 1961; admitted, 1988, Luxembourg. *Education:* University of Strasbourg Law School (Master of Laws, 1987). *LANGUAGES:* French, German and English. *PRACTICE AREAS:* Civil and Commercial Law; Litigation.

FRANCINE KEISER, born Luxembourg, December 20, 1964; admitted, 1989, Luxembourg. *Education:* University of Paris Law School (Master of Laws, 1987); University of London, University College London (LL.M., 1988). *LANGUAGES:* French, German and English. *PRACTICE AREAS:* Commercial Law; Investment Funds; Banking Law.

DANIEL RUPPERT, born Luxembourg, June 18, 1965; admitted, 1991, Luxembourg. *Education:* University of Strasbourg Law School (Master of Laws, 1990). *LANGUAGES:* French, German and English. *PRACTICE AREAS:* Civil and Commercial Law; Banking and Securities Law.

HERMANN BEYTHAN, born 1963; admitted, 1992, Luxembourg. *Education:* University of Nancy Law School (Master of Laws, 1989); University of Saarbrücken Law School (First Legal State Exam, 1991); International Christian University, Tokyo, Japan (1985). *LANGUAGES:* French, German and English. *PRACTICE AREAS:* Commercial and Corporate Law; Banking and Securities Law; EEC Law.
(This Listing Continued)

JEAN-PAUL SPANG, born 1967; admitted, 1992, Luxembourg. *Education:* University of Paris Law School (Master of Laws, 1990; DEA, International Law, 1991). *LANGUAGES:* French, German and English. *PRACTICE AREAS:* Civil and Commercial Law; Corporate Law.

Languages: French, German and English

REDING & FELTEN

99, GRAND-RUE
L-1661 LUXEMBOURG, LUXEMBOURG
Telephone: (352) 46 91 86
Fax: (352) 46 91 85

Commercial and Civil Law, Contract Law, Company and Corporate Law, EC Law, Mergers and Acquisitions, Tax, Banking and Finance Law, Insolvency and Bankruptcy and Debt Collection Law.

ROY REDING, born Luxembourg, 1965; admitted, 1990, Luxembourg, Avocat-Avoué. *Education:* Universities of Aix-en-Provence and Strasbourg, France (Master in Business Law). Auxiliary Judge, Luxembourg District Court.

BERNARD FELTEN, born Belgium, 1964; admitted, 1992, Luxembourg, Avocat-Avoué. *Education:* University of Louvain, Belgium (Law Degree; Diploma in European Studies).

ISABELLE GIRAULT, born France, 1969; admitted, 1992, Luxembourg, Avocat. *Education:* Universities of Nancy, France and Saarbrücken, Germany (Master in Law; Diploma in Advanced Studies of EC Law).

CHRISTIANE GOERENS, born Luxembourg, 1943; admitted, 1968, Luxembourg, Avocat-Avoué. *Education:* University of Caen, France (Dr.jur., 1967).

CHRISTEL DUMONT, born France, 1969; admitted, 1994, Luxembourg, Avocat. *Education:* Universities of Lyon and Dijon, France (Master in Business Law; Superior Degree in International Commercial Law).

Members of Union Internationale des Avocats, UIA and the International Bar Association, IBA.

Languages: French, English, German, Dutch and Luxembourgish

SCHILTZ ET DELAPORTE

Established in 1932

2 RUE DU FORT RHEINSHEIM
LUXEMBOURG L-2419, LUXEMBOURG
Telephone: (352) 45 64 80
Fax: (352) 45 64 44

Administrative, Arbitration, Banking, Competition, Corporate, EEC, Industrial Relations and Labour, Insurance, Intellectual Property, Litigation, Real Estate, Tax, Transportation, General Legal Practice.

MEMBERS OF FIRM

LOUIS SCHILTZ, born Luxembourg, August, 1934; admitted, 1959, Luxembourg. *Education:* Universities of Strasbourg and Paris (Docteur en Droit, 1959). Past Chairman: Luxembourg Bar Council; Council of European Bars and Law Societies (CCBE). *Member:* International Bar Association (Council Member); Union Internationale des Avocats.

JEAN-LOUIS SCHILTZ, born Luxembourg, August, 1964; admitted, 1989, Luxembourg. *Education:* University of Paris (Maîtrise en Droit des Affaires, 1987; Diplôme d'Etudes Approfondies en Droit des Affaires et de l'Economie, 1988). Former Lecturer, Commercial Law, Paris University. Lecturer, General Jurisprudence, University Center of Luxembourg, 1991—.

Languages: French, German, English and Italian

THIELEN & KRIEGER

Established in 1991

10, RUE WILLY GOERGEN
P.O. BOX 679
L-2016 LUXEMBOURG, LUXEMBOURG
Telephone: (352) 22 29 69
Fax: (352) 22 29 75

International Banking and Business Law, Corporate Law, Tax Law, Economic Fraud Law, Criminal Law, Administrative Law.

(This Listing Continued)

FIRM PROFILE: Firm engaged in Luxembourg and International Law practice. Entitled to plead before Luxembourg courts.

MEMBERS OF FIRM

LEX THIELEN, born Luxembourg, July 21, 1962; admitted, 1987, Luxembourg. *Education:* University of Paris/Panthéon-Sorbonne, France (Master of Laws, 1985; Diplôme d'Etudes Approfondies, 1986). Lecturer, University of Paris/Panthéon-Sorbonne, 1986-1988. *Member:* Luxembourg Bar Association; International Bar Association. *LANGUAGES:* French, English, German and Spanish. *PRACTICE AREAS:* Banking Law; Business Law; Taxation Law; Economic Fraud Law; Criminal Law; Corporate Law; Civil Law.

GEORGES KRIEGER, born Grevenmacher, Luxembourg, July 7, 1960; admitted, 1988, Luxembourg. *Education:* Catholic University of Louvain-la-Neuve, Belgium (Master of Laws, 1987; Master of Economics, 1987). *Member:* Luxembourg Bar Association. *LANGUAGES:* French, English and German. *PRACTICE AREAS:* Banking Law; Business Law; Corporate Law; Administrative Law; Taxation Law.

PHILIPPE STROESSER, born Barr, France, October 30, 1969; admitted, 1992, Luxembourg. *Education:* University of Strasbourg (Master, 1992). *Member:* Luxembourg Bar Association. *LANGUAGES:* French and English. *PRACTICE AREAS:* Commercial Law; Civil Law.

CHRISTEL HENON, born Verdun, France, April 29, 1968; admitted, 1993, Luxembourg. *Education:* University of Metz (Master of Laws, 1990); University of Lille (Diplôme d'Etudes Supérieures en Droit Notarial, 1991). *Member:* Luxembourg Bar Association. *LANGUAGES:* French and English. *PRACTICE AREAS:* Business Law; Taxation Law.

LAURENT GEBELIN, born Woippy, France, July 19, 1965; admitted, 1994, Luxembourg. *Education:* University of Metz (Master of Laws, 1986); University of Strasbourg (Diplôme d'Etudes Approfondies en Droit International, International Private Law and E.C. Law, 1987). *Member:* Luxembourg Bar Association. *LANGUAGES:* French and English. *PRACTICE AREAS:* Business Law; Civil Law; International Private Law.

PIERRE LAMMAR, born Esch/Alzette, Luxembourg, July 2, 1967; admitted, 1994, Luxembourg. *Education:* University of Strasbourg (Master of Laws, 1993). *LANGUAGES:* French, German, English and Italian. *PRACTICE AREAS:* Commercial Law; Civil Law.

WAGENER & RUKAVINA

Established in 1970

10 A, BOULEVARD DE LA FOIRE
L-1528 LUXEMBOURG, LUXEMBOURG
Telephone: 45 31 13
Telex: 1250
Fax: 45 32 52

Mailing Address: P.O. Box 660, L-2016

Commercial, Corporate, Bankruptcy, Labor, Intellectual Property, Insurance, Mortgage, Real Estate, Arbitration, Litigation, Environment, Administrative Labor, Entertainment and Communications, General Legal Practice and Banking Law.

FIRM PROFILE: The firm was established in 1970 and offers a full range of legal services. Its activity concentrates on Corporate, Commercial and Business Law, including Litigation. The client base is international with strong links in Europe, the US and the Middle East.

MEMBERS OF FIRM

JEAN WAGENER, born 1938; admitted, 1963, Luxembourg; Licensed as a Legal Consultant, 1983, New York. *Education:* University of Nancy, Law School (Grand Duchy of Luxembourg: Doctor of Law, 1962). *Member:* Luxembourg Bar Association. *LANGUAGES:* French, English and German.

PAULE KETTENMEYER, born 1955; admitted, 1978, Luxembourg. *Education:* University of Grenoble, Law School (Licencié en droit, 1976); University of Nancy, Law School (Maître en Droit, 1977). *Member:* Luxembourg Bar Association. *LANGUAGES:* French, English, German and Italian.

ALAIN RUKAVINA, born 1956; admitted, 1981, Luxembourg. *Education:* University of Strasbourg, Law School (Maître en droit). *Member:* Luxembourg Bar Association. *LANGUAGES:* French, English and German.

(This Listing Continued)

WAGENER & RUKAVINA, Luxembourg—Continued

PATRICIA THILL, born 1962; admitted, 1987, Luxembourg. *Education:* University of Strasbourg, France (Maître en Droit privé, 1985; DESS Gestion d'entreprises, 1986). *Member:* Luxembourg Bar Association. *LANGUAGES:* French, English and German.

ARTHUR SCHUSTER, born 1928; admitted, 1990, Luxembourg. *Education:* University of Liège (Belgium), Applied Sciences School (Civil Mining Engineer, 1954); University of Nancy (France) Law School (Licencié en Droit, 1974). Director of the Luxembourg Labour and Mines Inspection, Ministry of Labour, 1962-1989. *Member:* Luxembourg Bar Association. *LANGUAGES:* French, English and German.

Languages: French, English and German

ZEYEN BEGHIN FEIDER

In Association with Loeff Claeys Verbeke

Established in 1990

67, RUE ERMESINDE
L-1469 LUXEMBOURG, LUXEMBOURG
Telephone: 46 89 46
Telefax: 46 89 47

Offices:

Rotterdam, The Netherlands Office: Loeff Claeys Verbeke, 70 Weena, P.O. Box 74, 3000 AB. Telephone: 31-10-4034777. Telex: 23395 LEX NL. Telecopier: 31-10-41493 88.

Amsterdam, The Netherlands Office: Loeff Claeys Verbeke, 15 Apollolaan, P.O. Box 75088, 1070 AB. Telephone: 31-20-5741200. Telex:14291 (LEX NL). Telecopier: 31-20-6718775.

New York, New York Office: Loeff Claeys Verbeke, Swiss Bank Tower, 10 East 50th Street, 10022. Telephone: 212-759-9000. Telecopier: 212-759-9018.

Brussels, Belgium Office: Loeff Claeys Verbeke, 168 Avenue de Tervueren, 1150 Bruxelles. Telephone: 32-2-778 22 11. Telecopier: 32-2-762 68 89.

Antwerp, Belgium Office: Loeff Claeys Verbeke, 92 Desguinlei, B8, 2078 Antwerp. Telephone: 32-3-2385656. Telecopier: 32-3-2387877.

Paris, France Office: Loeff Claeys Verbeke, 1 Avenue Franklin D. Roosevelt, 75008. Telephone: 33-1-49539125. Telecopier: 33-1-45610664.

Barcelona, Spain Office: Balana & Eguia, Avenida Diagonal 550, 4° la, 08021. Telephone: 34-3-20071777. Telecopier: 34-3-2023098.

General Practice, Corporate, Mergers and Acquisitions, Commercial, Banking, Financial Services, Capital Markets, Investment Funds, Insurance and Reinsurance, Taxation, Labor, Civil and Criminal Law, International Private Law, Litigation, Media Law, Economic Fraud Law, Insolvency Law.

MEMBERS OF FIRM

CARLOS ZEYEN, born Luxembourg, March 30, 1955; admitted, 1979, Luxembourg; Avocat-Avoué, High Court of Justice. *Education:* University of Grenoble, France (Master of Laws, 1978); Advanced Course of Law, Luxembourg. Lecturer, Institut de Formation Administrative, 1983—. Speaker at the United Nations 25th UNCITRAL Congress (New York) on Uniform Commercial Law in the 21st Century, 1992. Justice of the Peace, 1984—. Member, Advisory Commission to the Minister of Justice on Foreigner Police, 1987—. *Member:* Luxembourg Bar Association; European Society for Banking and Financial Law (Founding Member); Association Luxembourgeoise des Juristes de Banque; International Fiscal Association. *LANGUAGES:* English, French and German. *PRACTICE AREAS:* Banking and International Finance; Corporate Law.

PAUL BEGHIN, born Luxembourg, June 28, 1929; admitted, 1954, Luxembourg; Avocat-Avoué, High Court of Justice. *Education:* University of Lausanne, Switzerland (Doctor of Laws, 1954), Economic Studies. Member of the Luxembourg State Council, 1974—; First Vice-Chairman, Luxembourg State Council (Premier Vice Président du Conseil d'Etat, 1990—). Member of Parliament, 1971-1974. Deputy Mayor of the City of Luxembourg, 1978-1985. Auxiliary Judge with the BENELUX Court of Justice, 1989—. *Member:* Luxembourg Bar Association. *LANGUAGES:* English, French and German. *PRACTICE AREAS:* Commercial Law; Administrative Law; Intellectual Property Law.

MARC FEIDER, born Luxembourg, October 5, 1958; admitted, 1985, Luxembourg; Avocat-Avoué, High Court of Justice. *Education:* University of Strasbourg, France (Master of Laws, 1984); Advanced Course of Law,

(This Listing Continued)

Luxembourg. Contributing Author: "Tax Letter Europe," Matthew-Bender/Bertelsmann. Secretary, Luxembourg Young Bar Association, 1985-1986. *Member:* Luxembourg Bar Association; Young Lawyers International Association; International Fiscal Association; International Tax Planning Association; Association Luxembourgeoise des Juristes de Banque. *LANGUAGES:* English, French and German. *PRACTICE AREAS:* Corporate Law; Mergers and Acquisitions; Tax and Investment Funds; Off-Shore Structuring.

ANDRE MARC, born Luxembourg, January 3, 1963; admitted, 1988, Luxembourg; Avocat-Avoué, High Court of Justice. *Education:* University of Paris, Panthéon-Sorbonne, France (Master of Laws, 1986); Postgraduate Studies at the London School of Economics, (Master of Laws, LL.M. in International Business Law, European Comparative Law, International Economic Law and Politics of Money, 1987); Advanced course of Law, Luxembourg. Lecturer at the "Institut de Formation Administrative," 1992—. *Member:* Luxembourg Bar Association. *LANGUAGES:* English, French and German. *PRACTICE AREAS:* Banking; Capital Markets; Insurance and Reinsurance.

ROMAIN ADAM, born Luxembourg, January 3, 1963; admitted, 1989, Luxembourg; Avocat-Avoué, High Court of Justice. *Education:* University of Aix-Marseille, France (Master of Laws, 1988); Advanced Course of Law, Luxembourg. Director, Institut Européen des Juristes en Droit Social, 1991—. *Member:* Luxembourg Bar Association. *LANGUAGES:* French, German and English. *PRACTICE AREAS:* Investment Funds; Labour Law; Litigation.

OF COUNSEL

GASTON THORN, born Luxembourg, September 3, 1928; admitted, 1956, Luxembourg; Avocat-Avoué, High Court of Justice. *Education:* Universities of Montpellier, Lausanne and Paris (Doctor of Laws); Universities of Aix, France; Louvain, Belgium; Miami and Texas Wesleyan College, USA; London, United Kingdom; Torino and Urbino, Italy; Dublin, Ireland and Saarbrucken, Germany (Honorary Doctorates). Awarded, Grand Prix of the Academy of Ethics and Political Sciences, 1988. President, Commission of the European Communities, 1981-1985; Prime Minister and Minister of Foreign Affairs, 1974-1979; Deputy Prime Minister, Minister of Foreign Affairs, Foreign Trade and Cooperation, Minister of Economic Affairs, Minister of Justice, 1979-1980; President of the 30th Session of the General Assembly of the United Nations, 1975-1976; Member of Parliament, 1959-1974; Member of the European Parliament, Chairman of the Committee on Developing Countries, Chairman of the EEC-AASM Joint Committee, 1959-1969; Town Counsellor of the City of Luxembourg, 1957-1969; Deputy Mayor of the City of Luxembourg, 1961-1963; President of the Liberal International, 1970-1982; President, Compagnie Luxembourgeoise de Télédiffusion, CLT-RTL, 1987—; Chairman, Banque Internationale à Luxembourg, 1985—. Member, Jean Monnet Committee, 1985; Member, Comité d'Action pour l'Union Monétaire de l'Europe, 1985. *LANGUAGES:* French, English, German, Spanish and Catalan. *PRACTICE AREAS:* International Relations; International Trade Law; International Public Law; Arbitration; Banking and Monetary Law.

REAGAN WYLIE, admitted, 1978, Barrister, England and Wales (Not admitted in Luxembourg). *Education:* University of St. Andrews (M.A., 1969); University of Illinois (LL.M., 1980). Barrister - Member, Middle Temple. In-house Counsel, British Petroleum, Standard Telephone Cables and Gerling Konzem. *LANGUAGES:* English, French and German.

FLORENCE COMANZO, born France, April 12, 1968. *Education:* University of Bourgogne, France (Master of Laws, 1990; Master in Fiscal Law, 1990; DJCE, Diplôme de Juriste Conseil d'Entreprise, 1991); University of Lyon, France (D.F.S.S., 1991; Master in Business Law, 1991). *LANGUAGES:* French and English.

ASSOCIATES

HENRI WAGNER, born Luxembourg, June 5, 1965; admitted, 1990, Luxembourg, Avocat, Court of Appeal of Paris. *Education:* University of Strasbourg, France (Master of Laws, 1989); Institute for Comparative Law; Advanced course of Law, Luxembourg; University of Paris - Panthéon Sorbonne, France (DESS in Banking and Financial Law). Author: Bancassurance et Assurbanque: un grand dessein pour l'Europe bancaire et financiére?," Cahiers Economiques - Banque Internationale á Luxembourg, 1992. Internship with Gide Loyrette Nouel, Paris, 1990-1991; Internship with Allen & Overy, London, 1992-1993. *Member:* Luxembourg Bar Association. *LANGUAGES:* English, French and German. *PRACTICE AREAS:* Banking; Financial Services; Capital Markets.

JEAN SCHAFFNER, admitted, 1994. France (Hauts-de-Seine). *Education:* University of Strasbourg (Master of Law, 1989); Master of Political

(This Listing Continued)

Science, 1989; HEC, Paris (1991); Université of Paris, Sceaux (DESS in International Tax Law, 1991). Lecturer, International Tax Law, the Institut Supérieur du Commerce, Paris. *LANGUAGES:* French and English. *PRACTICE AREAS:* International; French and Luxembourg Tax Law; Corporate Law.

PATRICE CIPRE, born France, June 9, 1965; admitted, 1991, Luxembourg - Avocat. *Education:* University of Nice, School of Law (Master of Laws, private and commercial law, 1988); University of the Pacific, McGeorge School of Law (LL.M., Business and Taxation, Transnational Practice, 1990); Advanced Course of Law, Luxembourg (Certificate, 1991). *Member:* Luxembourg Bar Association; American Society of International Law; Pacific International Law Society. *LANGUAGES:* English and French. *PRACTICE AREAS:* Civil Law; Commercial Law; Intellectual Property Law.

MICHÉLE RAUS, born Luxembourg, November 25, 1968; admitted, 1991, Luxembourg - Avocat. *Education:* University of Strasbourg, France (Master of Laws, 1991). *Member:* Luxembourg Bar Association. *LANGUAGES:* English, French and German. *PRACTICE AREAS:* Litigation; Civil Law.

KATIA MANHAEVE, born Belgium, May 26, 1968; admitted, 1993, Luxembourg-Advocat. *Education:* University of Namur and Leuven, Belgium; University de Salamanca, Spain (Licence en Droit, 1991). *Member:* Brussels Bar Association; Luxembourg Bar Association. *LANGUAGES:* Dutch, English and French. *PRACTICE AREAS:* Civil Law; Commercial Law.

DANIEL SCHWARZ, born France, November 27, 1965; admitted, 1993, Luxembourg-Advocat. *Education:* University of Paris II (Assas) -(Master of Laws in Corporate & Tax Law, 1988)- Diplôme d'Etudes Approfondies (D.E.A. in Private Law, 1989)- Master o f Laws (LL.M., Cantab., 1990). *Member:* Anglo-French Lawyers Society. *LANGUAGES:* French and English.

PIERRE SCHLEIMER, born Luxembourg, May 15, 1968; admitted, 1994, Luxembourg. *Education:* University of Brussels, Belgium (Masters of Law, 1992); Institut d'Etudes Européenes, Belgium (Masters Degree in Community Law, 1993). *LANGUAGES:* French, German and English. *PRACTICE AREAS:* Commercial Law; Contract Law; Corporate Law; Insolvency Law.

CAROLE WINTERSDORFF, born Luxembourg, September 15, 1970. *Education:* University of Paris, Panthéon-Sorbonne, France (Master of Private Laws, 1992; D.E.A. in Private Law, 1993). Thesis: "The Legal Nature of Negotiable Certificates of Deposit in France," Advanced Course of Law, Luxembourg. Traineeships with a Paris based law firm and the National Environmental Law Center, New York, USA. *LANGUAGES:* French, German and English.

ERIC ROUSSEAUX, born France, May 1, 1966; admitted, 1994, Luxenbourg. *Education:* University of Nancy, France (Master of Laws, 1988; D.E.A. in Public Law, 1989); University of Strasbourg, France, Institut d'Etudes Politiques (Degree, 1991). Lecturer: Centre National de la Ponction Publique, France, 1990-1992; Law Faculty, University of Nancy, France, 1989-1994. Officer and Legal Advisor with the General Staff of the French Army, Ministry of Defense Paris, France, 1993. *LANGUAGES:* French, German and English.

NADIA ERPELDING, born Luxembourg, February 8, 1971; admitted, 1995, Luxembourg. *Education:* University of Strasbourg, France (Master of Laws, 1994). *LANGUAGES:* French, German and English.

MICHEL SCHAUS, born Luxembourg, August 30, 1968; admitted, 1995, Luxembourg. *Education:* University of Aix-Marseille, France (Master of Laws, International and European Law, 1993); University of London, London School of Economics (LL.M., Commercial and Corporate Law, 1994). *LANGUAGES:* French, German and English.

MARIE HELEN PICHLER, born Vienna, December 6, 1959; admitted, 1995, Luxembourg. *Education:* University of Vienna (Master of Law and Doctorate of Law, 1983); McGill University, Montreal, Canada (Master of Law, Institute of Air and Space Law, 1986. Publication, "Copyright Problems of Satellite and Cable Television in Europr," 1987. Board Member, European Center for Space Law. *LANGUAGES:* German, English, French and Spanish. *PRACTICE AREAS:* European Community Law; Commercial; Competition; Company Law; Media and Entertainment; Telecommunications; Copyright; Advertising; Film Acquisition; Space Law.

CLAUDE WERER, born Luxembourg, November 10, 1968; admitted, 1995, Luxembourg. *Education:* University of Strasbourg, France (Master of Laws, 1994). *LANGUAGES:* French, German and English.

(This Listing Continued)

ANDREE DICHTER, born Luxembourg, March 20, 1967; admitted, 1995, Luxembourg. *Education:* University of Air-Marseille, France (Master of Law, 1994). *LANGUAGES:* French, German and English.

LAURA MOLENKAMP, born The Netherlands, June 10, 1966; admitted, 1995, Luxembourg. *Education:* Business School of the Hague, The Netherlands (Bachelor of Economics, 1990); Université de Savoie, Annecy, France (Diplôme d'Études Françaises, 2ème degré, 1991); University of Leiden, The Netherlands (Master of Law, 1994). Assistant Director, Legal and Internal Affairs, Dutch Information Office, Rijksvoorlichtingsdienst, 1991-1993. Student Trainee, Loeff Claeys Verbeke, Rotterdam, The Netherlands, 1994. *LANGUAGES:* Dutch, French and English.

MADEIRA

TEIXEIRA DE FREITAS & JARDIM FERNANDES

FUNCHAL, MADEIRA

(See Funchal (Madeira), Portugal)

MALTA

BUSUTTIL & BUSUTTIL

12 TAGLIAFERRO MANSIONS
PRINCESS MARGARET STREET
TA'XBIEX, MALTA
Telephone: 371640; 344115
Fax: 345450
Telex: 1569 Olytel MW

General Practice. Offshore, Commercial, Company, Insurance, Taxation, Admiralty, Shipping and Arbitration Law and Offshore Law . Registration of Foreign Judgements. Trademarks and Patents.

CLARENCE BUSUTTIL, LL.D., University of Malta.

GRAHAM BUSUTTIL, LL.D., University of Malta.

VERONICA ROSSIGNAUD, L.P., University of Malta.

J.H. SAYDON, B.A., LL.D., University of Malta.

ASSOCIATE

PROF. EDWIN BUSUTTIL, B.A., LL.D., University of Malta; M.A., B.LITT, Oxford University.

Languages: Maltese, English, Italian, French and Spanish.

REPRESENTATIVE CLIENTS: Philip Morris Inc.; The Seven-Up Co.; Budget Rent-A-Car International, Inc.; Heublien Inc.; Hollister Inc.; J. I. Case Co.; United Vintners Inc.; Fabriques de Tabac Reunies S.A.; Jordache Enterprises Inc.; Dresser Industries, Inc.; Gray Laboratories International Ltd.; Miller Brewing Co.; Oregon Freeze Dry Foods Inc.; English & American Insurance Co. Ltd.; Sociedad Espanola De Automobiles Turismo, (SEAT) S.A.; STP Corporation; Prentice-Hall, Inc.; Institut Francais du Petrole; Ritz Hotel Ltd; Kentucky Fried Chicken International Corp.; Hamleys; American Express Europe Ltd.; Bulova; Pepsico; Scotiabank; Guinness PLC; Harley Davidson Inc.; Mattel Toys; Thrifty Rent-a-car; Cigna Europe; Quaker Chiari & Forte srl; British Telecommunications Plc; Pan American World Airways Inc.; United States Shoe Corporation; Contributors to the World Tax Thesaurus; Merill Lynch Europe Ltd.; Estee Lauder; N.J. Heinz Co. Ltd.; Chase Manhattan Corp.

ADVOCATES MICALLEF & CO.

191 MERCHANTS STREET, SUITE 2
VALLETTA VLT 10, MALTA
Telephone: (356) 246034; (356) 246027
Fax: (356) 244652

Company Law, Bankruptcy Law, Intellectual Property Law, Copyright Law, Maritime Law, Banking Law, Trusts, Offshore Companies, Property Law, Conflict of Laws and Public International Law.

FIRM PROFILE: Established in 1949 as the Law Offices of Prof J.A. Micallef LL.D., Dr. Jur. (E.U.R.). The Firm has established itself as a leading international and commercial law practice. A substantial majority

(This Listing Continued)

ADVOCATES MICALLEF & CO., Valletta—Continued

of its client base is corporate and foreign owned. For more than three decades the Firm has advised banks, international institutions and public companies of international repute. The Firm has a track record for settling disputes out of court in jurisdiction where litigation, though not prohibitive, may be lengthy and protracted.

An "in-house" accountant and office manager complement the Firm's staff and ensure that clients' needs are served promptly and thoroughly.

PROFESSOR JOSEPH A. MICALLEF, born 1922. admitted as an Advocate to the Malta Bar, 1945. *Education:* Faculty of Law, Royal University of Malta (LL.D., 1945); London School of Economics, University of London (followed LL.M. degree, 1947); Erasmus University Rotterdam (Dr. Jur., 1972). Appointed to the Chair of Commercial Law, Faculty of Law, University of Malta, 1974. Current Professor Emeritus of Commercial Law. *Member:* UNIDROIT, Institute of Private Law, Rome, Italy (Local Correspondent); Malta Chamber of Advocates; Malta Society of Arts, Manufacture and Commerce (Vice-President); Malta Agrarian Society (President). *LANGUAGES:* English and Italian. *PRACTICE AREAS:* Company Law; Shareholders' Rights; Mergers and Acquisitions; Winding Up and Bankruptcies; Copyright Law; Maritime Law; Broadcasting and Media Law; Commercial and Civil Litigation.

ANTON MICALLEF, born 1961. admitted as Advocate to the Malta Bar, 1984. *Member:* Faculty of Law, University of Malta (LL.D., 1984); London School of Economics, University of London (Ph.D., 1992). Senior Lecturer and Member of the Board, Law Faculty, University of Malta. *Member:* Malta Chamber of Advocates (Member, Executive Committee); American Society of International Law. *PRACTICE AREAS:* Registration and Management of Foreign Corporations in Malta; Trusts; Tax Advice; Commercial Contracts; Probate; Conflicts of Laws; Human Rights; Public International Law; Offshore Companies.

CEFAI & ASSOCIATES

Advocates, Notaries and Tax Consultants

Established in 1976

5/2 MERCHANTS STREET
VALLETTA VLT 10, MALTA
Telephone: (356) 222097; 230428; 234495
Telefax: (356) 234941; 448273
Telex: 1806 MW
Cellular: (356) 99 2479

General Legal Advice: Formation of Companies, Acquisition and Sale of Companies, Commercial Agreements, Taxation, Debt Collection, Registration of Maltese Offshore Companies, Registration of Ships/Yachts under Maltese Flag, Acquisition of Maltese Resident Permits, Purchase, Sale and Leasing of Domestic and Commercial Properties; Banking.

FIRM PROFILE: This law firm is adequately sized and geared for international practice. We have correspondents in most European countries as well as in Hong Kong, U.S.A., Australia.

Over the years we have established ourselves as one of the leading law and tax firms in Malta and our modern offices are centrally located in Valletta where most of the Government Departments and the Law Courts are found.

MEMBERS OF FIRM

DR. RENATO CEFAI, LL.D. - born, 1951; LL.D. 1976.

DR. JOHN GAMBIN, LL.D. - born 1958; LL.D. 1980.

MR. EDGAR MONTANARO, L.P. - born 1951; L.P. 1978.

Languages: Maltese, English, Italian, French and German

PROFESSOR J.M. GANADO & ASSOCIATES

171 OLD BAKERY STREET
VALLETTA VLT 09, MALTA
Telephone: 242096; 235406/7/8; 243882; 233886
Cable Address: "Attorney Malta"
Telex: 1707 PHAX MW
Fax: 225908

General Civil and Commercial Practice with specialization in Shipping, Registration of Ships and Aircraft and Related Mortgages and Arrest of Ships, Company Law and Banking (including Offshore Companies), Industrial Establishments and Hotels, Trademarks, Franchising.

MEMBERS OF FIRM

PROFESSOR J.M. GANADO, born 1925; B.A., LL.D., 1947, Malta; Ph.D., 1950, London. *LANGUAGES:* English and Italian. *PRACTICE AREAS:* Business Law; Company Law; Touristic Projects.

DR. PHILIP BIANCHI, born 1949; LL.D., 1974, Malta. *LANGUAGES:* English and Italian. *PRACTICE AREAS:* Ship Mortgage; Estate and Property Law.

DR. MAX GANADO, born 1959; LL.D., 1981, Malta; LL.M., 1983, Dalhousie. *LANGUAGES:* English and Italian. *PRACTICE AREAS:* Maritime Law; Touristic Projects; Aviation Mortgages; Offshore Companies including Banking.

DR. ADRIAN M. GABARRETTA, born 1961; LL.D., 1984, Malta. *LANGUAGES:* English and Italian. *PRACTICE AREAS:* Ship Mortgages; Intellectual Property; Franchising.

DR. ADRIAN BORG CARDONA, born 1953; LL.D., 1979, Malta; LL.M., 1980, London. *LANGUAGES:* English and Italian. *PRACTICE AREAS:* Maritime Law; Ship Registration.

DR. STEFAN FRENDO, born 1958; LL.D., 1984, Malta. *LANGUAGES:* English and Italian. *PRACTICE AREAS:* Estates and Property Law; Litigation; General Civil and Commercial Law Practice.

DR. LOUIS CASSAR PULLICINO, born 1961; LL.D., 1986, Malta. *LANGUAGES:* English and Italian. *PRACTICE AREAS:* Litigation; General Civil and Commercial Law Practice.

DR. KARL GRECH ORR, born 1964; LL.D., 1988, Malta; LL.M., 1989, (Lond.). *LANGUAGES:* English and Italian. *PRACTICE AREAS:* Company Law; Ship Registration.

DR. STEPHEN ATTARD, born 1967; LL.D., 1991, Malta; D.E.J.E. (Bruges) 1992. *LANGUAGES:* English, Italian and French. *PRACTICE AREAS:* Offshore Companies including Banking; Ship Registration and Mortgages.

DR. JOTHAM SCERRI-DIACONO, born 1969; LL.D., 1993; LL.M. (I.M.L.I.), Malta, 1994. *LANGUAGES:* English and Italian.

LEGAL PROCURATOR

VERA LUNGARO MIFSUD, born 1952; B.A., L.P., 1990, Malta. *LANGUAGES:* English and Italian. *PRACTICE AREAS:* Legal Procurator; General Litigation.

CHARLES GRECH ORR, born 1927; L.P., 1950, Malta. *LANGUAGES:* English, Italian and French. *PRACTICE AREAS:* Legal Procurator; Company Administration Services.

RUTTER GIAPPONE & ASSOCIATES

166, OLD BAKERY STREET
VALLETTA, MALTA
Telephone: 236767; 225929; 240219
Facsimile: 244153

REVISORS OF THE MALTA LAW DIGEST FOR THIS DIRECTORY.

Civil and Commercial Practice with Specialization in Corporate Matters, Offshore Companies Incorporation and Administration, Trust Incorporation and Administration, Tax Planning Consultancy, Project Consultants, Developers and Coordinators, Maritime Matters Including Registration of Vessels, Ship Mortgages and Shipping Transactions.

ADVOCATES

DR. ANTHONY RUTTER GIAPPONE, born 1954; LL.D., 1977, Malta.

(This Listing Continued)

DR. ROBERT MANGION, born 1961; LL.D., 1986, Malta.

DR. ENRICO CORTIS, born 1927; LL.D., 1952, Malta.

REVISORS OF THE MALTA LAW DIGEST FOR THIS DIRECTORY.

HUGH PERALTA & CO.

Established in 1984

3 INDEPENDENCE SQUARE
VALLETTA, MALTA
Telephone: 248025; 241507
Telex: 1536 LEXMAR
Facsimile: (00356-Malta) 220222

Maritime, Registration of Vessels and Mortgages; Arrest of Vessels; Claims (and Cargo Claims) Against Vessels; Offshore Business; Industrial (Company Formation-Industrial Matters-Hotels); Debt Recovery; Trademark and Patent Registration; Insurance and Banking; Litigation (Superior Courts); Conveyancing.

MEMBERS OF FIRM

HUGH J. PERALTA, born Malta, January 20, 1945; admitted, 1971, Valletta. *LANGUAGES:* Maltese, English and Italian. *PRACTICE AREAS:* Insurance; Banking; Company.

MARTHESE FELICE, born 1955; admitted, 1979, Valletta, Notary Public. *LANGUAGES:* Maltese, English and French. *PRACTICE AREAS:* Conveyancing; Estates.

DAVID GRECH, born Malta, April 19, 1957; admitted, 1982, Valletta. *LANGUAGES:* Maltese, English and French. *PRACTICE AREAS:* Offshore Business; Debt Collecting; Trade Mark Patent Registration.

CARMEL CHIRCOP, born Malta, December 28, 1963; admitted, 1993, Valleta. *LANGUAGES:* English, Italian, French and Maltese. *PRACTICE AREAS:* Admiralty and Maritime.

Languages: Maltese, English, Italian and French.

TONNA, CAMILLERI, VASSALLO & CO.

Established in 1988

52 OLD THEATRE STR.
VALLETTA, MALTA
Telephone: 232271; 225385; 223316
Telex: 1886 TOCAVO MW
Fax: 244291

General International Practice, Corporate, Commercial, Financing, Banking, Securities, Insurance, Tax (Offshore companies and Trusts), Trademark, Patents and Designs (Registration and Litigation), Copyright Agency, Distribution, Franchise, Licensing, Intellectual Property, Hotel and Resort Development, Creditors' Rights, Industrial Establishments, Shipping and Ship and Mortgage registration and Arrest of Ships.

FIRM PROFILE: One of Malta's leading Commercial law Firms. The client base is European, North American and Maltese. The firm has three partners and five associates. The firm has close association with leading London and North American Law firms. The firm is also founder member of the Malta Maritime Law Association.

MEMBERS OF FIRM

DR. DAVID TONNA, born 1956. *Education:* (LL.D., 1981 Malta). *LANGUAGES:* Maltese, English, Italian and French. *PRACTICE AREAS:* Maritime Law and Offshore companies; Finance; Banking Securities.

DR. RICHARD CAMILLERI, born 1956. *Education:* (LL.D., 1979 Malta; LL.M., 1980 London). *LANGUAGES:* Maltese, English and Italian. *PRACTICE AREAS:* Insurance and Company Law; Intellectual Property; Hotels and Resort Development.

DR. FRANCO B. VASSALLO, born 1961. *Education:* (LL.D., 1984 Malta). *LANGUAGES:* Maltese, English and Italian. *PRACTICE AREAS:* Litigation; Civil Law; Agency Distribution; Franchise; Corporate; Industrial Development.

DR. NOEL BUTTIGIEG SCICLUNA, born 1951. *Education:* (LL.D., 1975 Malta). *LANGUAGES:* Maltese, English, Italian, French and Dutch. *PRACTICE AREAS:* Banking; Offshore Companies and Industry.

(This Listing Continued)

ASSOCIATES

DR. RUDOLPH RAGONESI, born 1963. *Education:* (LL.D., 1988 Malta). *LANGUAGES:* Maltese, English and Italian. *PRACTICE AREAS:* Commercial and Civil Litigation.

DR. TANYA SCIBERRAS CAMILLERI, born 1967. *Education:* (LL.D., 1994 Malta). *LANGUAGES:* Maltese, English and Italian. *PRACTICE AREAS:* Commercial Litigation; Civil Litigation.

DR. EMILY CAMILLERI, born 1967. *Education:* (LL.D., 1993 Malta; LL.M., 1994 Southampton). *LANGUAGES:* Maltese, English and Italian. *PRACTICE AREAS:* Company Law; Intellectual Property; Software Protection; Industrial Business Law.

DAVINA CACHIA, born 1970. *Education:* (B.A. Socio-Legal Studies/L.P. 1992). *LANGUAGES:* Maltese, English and Italian. *PRACTICE AREAS:* Civil Litigation; Commercial Litigation; Creditors' Rights.

MONACO

GORDON S. BLAIR LAW OFFICES

Established in 1920

3 RUE LOUIS AUREGLIA
BOITE POSTALE 449
MC 98011 MONACO CEDEX
MONACO
Telephone: 93.25.85.25
Fax: (33) 93.25.79.58

General Practice. Real Estate, Taxation, Wills, Trusts and Estate Planning, Successions, Immigration, Corporate and Commercial Law.
Engaged in English, French, Monégasque and General International Practice but not admitted to the Monégasque Bar.

PARTNER

JEAN CLAUDE SERVIGNAT, born Paris, France, January 29, 1951; Ecole Supérieure de Commerce de Paris, 1973; Lawyer.

ASSOCIATES

FLORENCE S. PECHERAL, born Antibes, France, July 8, 1947; Lawyer (Maîtrise de Droit, Nice, 1969; D.E.S. Droit Privé, 1970).

DOMINIQUE L. LUCAS, born Le Puy, France, July 23, 1943; Lawyer (Maîtrise de Droit, Montpellier, 1966).

JAMES W. HILL, born Salisbury, England, September 4, 1961; admitted, 1987, Solicitor, Supreme Court of England and Wales; (LL.B. with French, Leicester 1984; Diplôme d'Etudes Juridiques Françaises, Strasbourg, 1983).

CONSULTANT

ROLLA EDWARDES-KER, born Wye, England, July 4, 1913. Solicitor, Supreme Court of England and Wales; former French Avocat; Advocate and Solicitor, Singapore; Advocate, Cyprus.

Languages: English, French, German, Spanish and Italian

JAMES P. DUFFY, III

GILDO PASTOR CENTER
7, RUE DU GABIAN
MC 98000, MONACO
Telephone: 92.05.79.99
Telecopier: 92.05.77.22

New York, New York Office: 333 East 14th Street, 10017. Telephone: (212) 466-6966.

Mineola, New York Office: 200 Willis Avenue, 11501. Telephone: (516) 877-0070, extension 146. Cable Address: "Profcorp." Telecopier: (516) 877-1188.

General Civil Practice, Corporate, Securities, Corporate Financing, Federal Taxation, International, Probate and Estate Planning Law.

JAMES P. DUFFY, III, born Jamaica Estates, New York, July 14, 1942; admitted, 1968, New York, U.S. Tax Court and U.S. Court of Appeals, Second Circuit; 1969, U.S. District Court, Southern and Eastern Districts of New York; 1973, U.S. Supreme Court; 1975, New Jersey and U.S.

(This Listing Continued)

JAMES P. DUFFY, III, Monte Carlo—Continued

District Court, District of New Jersey; 1989, U.S. Court of Appeals for the Federal Circuit (Not admitted in Monaco). *Education:* Webb Institute of Naval Architecture (B.S., 1964); Fordham University (J.D., 1967); New York University. Gamma Eta Gamma (Quaestor, Chapter XI, 1966-1967). Minority Counsel, United States Senate Select Committee on Small Business, 91st Congress, 1969-1970. President, 1977-1978, Nassau-Suffolk Chapter, Fordham Law Alumni Association. *Member:* Nassau County (Member, Tax Committee), New York State (Member, Sections on Taxation and International Law and Practice) and American (Member, Sections on Taxation and International Law and Practice) Bar Associations.

INTERNATIONAL COUNSEL

LUCIEN R. LELIEVRE, born Vitry, France, April 21, 1914; (Not admitted in Monaco). admitted to bar, 1946, New York and Massachusetts; 1957, U.S. Supreme Court and U.S. Claims Court. *Education:* University of Paris; University of Paris Law School (LL.B., 1935; LL.D., 1939); Harvard Law School (LL.M., 1938; LL.B., 1943). Chevalier de la Legion d'Honneur. Professor of Comparative Law, New York Law School, 1955-1958. Member, Bar of the Court of Appeal of Paris, France, 1935-1937. Associate General Counsel, French Supply Council, Washington, D.C., 1944-1946. U.S. Correspondent, Journal du Droit International, 1950-1981. Director General, America-European Community Association, Belgium, 1982—. *Member:* The Association of the Bar of the City of New York; The Federal Bar Council (Chairman, Committee on International Law, 1966); American Bar Association; Consular Law Society. *LANGUAGES:* English and French.

ASSOCIATE

MICHAEL REA JACKSON, born Philadelphia, Pennsylvania, January 26, 1952; admitted, 1979, Louisiana (Not admitted in Monaco). *Education:* Paris I, Paris, France (DEUJ., 1974); Dijon, Dijon, France (Maitrise Droit Privé, 1976); Tulane University (J.D., 1979). *Member:* Louisiana State Bar Association.

FRERE CHOLMELEY BISCHOFF

Established in 1979

"EST OUEST"

24 BOULEVARD PRINCESSE CHARLOTTE
MONTE CARLO 98000, MONACO
Telephone: (33) (93) 50 85 70
Fax: (33) (93) 50 22 10

London, England Office: 4 John Carpenter Street, London EC4Y 0NH. Telephone: 0171-615 8000. Fax: 0171-615 8080. Telex: 27623. LDE: DX 140.

Paris, France Office: 42 Avenue du Président Wilson, 75116. Telephone: (33) (1) 44 34 71 00. Fax: (33) (1) 44 34 71 11.

Rome, Italy Office: and Studio Legale Associato, 47, Viale Bruno Buozzi, 00197. Telephone: (39) (6) 808 0133. Fax: (39) (6) 808 0134.

Milan, Italy Office: and Studio Legale Associato, Piazza Castello 24, 20121, Milan. Telephone: (39) (2) 720 03 457. Fax: (39) (2) 720 03 469.

Berlin, Germany Office: im Internationalen Handelszentrum, Friedrichstrasse 95, 10117 Berlin. Telephone: (49) (30) 26 43 2000. Telex: 305996 Kbihzd. Fax: (49) (30) 26 43 1900.

Moscow, Russia Office: ul. Sadovaya-Samotyochnaya 24/27, 103051. Telephone: (7) 095 258 5058. Fax: (7) 095 258 5060. Telex: 412348 ALM SU.

Dubai, United Arab Emirates Office: Suite 802, EBIL Building, PO Box 2510, Deira, Dubai. Telephone: (9714) 267085/268336. Fax: (9714) 260206. Telex: 45493 LAWMC EM.

FIRM PROFILE: Frere Cholmeley Bischoff is the only English based law firm authorized to practise private International Law in the Principality of Monaco. The office undertakes a wide range of International Corporate, Commercial and Real Estate Matters with special emphasis on Taxation and the use of Offshore Jurisdictions and Trusts.

RESIDENT PARTNERS

WILLIAM EASUN, born Epsom, England, 1955; admitted, 1979, Solicitor. Partner, 1983. *Education:* Haileybury College; Guildford College of Law; University of Aix-En-Provence. *PRACTICE AREAS:* Art Law; Auction Conditions; Tax and Estate Planning; Wills and Trusts; Property; VAT; Importation; Protection of Wealth; Family Law.

(This Listing Continued)

PETER V. WALFORD, born Stockton-on-Tees, UK, 1953; admitted, 1979, Solicitor. Partner, 1989. *Education:* Trinity College, Oxford (M.A.; B.A. Hons. Modern History and Modern Languages). *PRACTICE AREAS:* International Trust; Tax Planning; Wills and Estates; Corporate Law.

ASSOCIATES

IRENE LUKE, born Paisley, UK, 1964; admitted, 1989, Solicitor. *Education:* St. Hilda's College, Oxford (M.A.). *PRACTICE AREAS:* Property Law; Taxation; Art Law; VAT; Visas and Residence.

SIMON BECK, born London, UK, 1965; admitted, 1990, Solicitor. *Education:* Bristol University (LL.B., Hons); Lancaster Gate College of Law. *PRACTICE AREAS:* Commercial Law; Intellectual Property; Entertainment Law; Family Law.

(For a full list of the Partners see Professional Biographies, London, England Office)

JEAN-CHARLES S. GARDETTO

Avocat prés la Cour d'Appel de MONACO

Admitted to appear before Monegasque Courts

LE SUFFREN

7, RUE SUFFREN REYMOND

MC 98000, MONACO
Telephone: 92.16.16.17
Telefax: 93.50.42.41; 93.25.46.46

General and International Practice, Business Law, Contracts, Company Law, Business Litigation, Construction Law, Real Estate, Commercial Law, Foreign Investments, International Law.

JEAN-CHARLES S. GARDETTO, born Monaco, November 1, 1961; admitted, 1988, Monaco. *Education:* Cornell Law School (LL.M., 1987); University of Aix-Marseille III, Institute of Business Law, France (Diplôme d'Etudes Supérieures Spécialisées de Juriste d'Affaires Internationales-Commerce Extérieur, 1985; Diplôme de Juriste Conseil d'Entreprises-option Internationale, 1985, Honors); Nice University Law School, France (Maîtrise en Droit Privé, 1984, Honors; Licence en Droit, 1983, Honors). *Member:* City Council of Monaco; Ordre des Avocats et Avocats-Defenseurs de Monaco; American Bar Association; Union Internationale des Avocats; International Bar Association; European Lawyers Union. *LANGUAGES:* French and English.

DONALD M. MANASSE

Established in 1989

4, BOULEVARD DES MOULINS

MONTE CARLO 98000, MONACO
Telephone: 93.50.29.21
Fax: 93.50.82.08

Nice, France Office: 2, Rue Du Congres, 06000. Telephone: 93.16.36.80. Telefax: 93.16.36.81.

Engaged in General and International Law Practice.

DONALD M. MANASSE, born Milan, Italy, November 29, 1951; admitted, 1978, New York; 1979, Connecticut; 1986, Avocat, Nice.

(For Complete Biographical data, see Professional Biographies at Nice, France).

THE NETHERLANDS

BOEKEL DE NERÉE

Advocaten/Solicitor

Notarissen Tax Advisers

Established in 1990

ATRIUM BUILDING
STRAWINSKYLAAN 3037
NL-1077 ZX AMSTERDAM, THE NETHERLANDS
Telephone: 020-541 52 52
Telex: 10156 asnot nl
Telecopier: 020-644 69 48

Mailing Address: P.O. Box 2508, 1000 CM Amsterdam, The Netherlands

Associate Offices: Platteeuw, De Witte & Grisar, advocaten. J. Jacobsplein 5, 1000 Brussel. Telephone: (32.2) 514 54 00. Telefax: (32.2) 514 29 32. Huybrechts, Engels, Craen & vennoten, advocaten. Amerikalei 73, 2000 Antwerpen. Telephone: (32.2) 248 15 00. Telefax: (32.2) 238 41 40.

Administrative, Advertising, Aeronautical, Antitrust, Arbitration, Banking, Bankruptcy, Competition, Computer, Construction, Corporate, Distributorship, Agency, Franchise, EEC, Employer's Liability, Entertainment, Environmental, Family, Foreign Investments, Health, Hospital, Malpractice, Immigration, Industrial Relations, Labor, Insurance, International Contracts, International Private Law, Litigation, Maritime, Admiralty, Mergers and Acquisitions, Negligence, Pension, Personal Injury, Products Liability, Property, Real Estate, Rent, Lease, Social Security, Tax Law, Tax Planning, International Taxation, Trade Regulations and Transportation Law. General Legal Practice. Copyright, Industrial Models, License Negotiation, Trademark Litigation, Trademark Prosecution, Intellectual Property.

MEMBERS OF FIRM/ADVOCATEN

F. Salomonson	F.G. Vreede
J.I. van Praag Sigaar	Hester Uhlenbroek
M.E. Jonker	P.H. Ariëns Kappers
H.P.C. Reinhold	J.G. ter Meer
G.F. Scheltema	Yvonne E. Kastein
A.J. van der Marel	H.J. Sachse
H.J. Bunjes	C.A.M.J. Raymakers
P.H. Paterson, Solicitor	W.J.P. Jongepier
J.W. Knipscheer	J.K. Brandse
R.J. Graaf Schimmelpenninck	H. van Son
A.D. Flesseman	H. Nicaise
Els. H. Swaab	J. Pel
	J.A. Schaap

ASSOCIATES

J.K. Six-Hummel	R.J.G. Mengelberg
Hildegard J. Weidinger,	M. van Empel
Rechtsanwältin	E.A.S. Loudon
E.M. Coosen	J.J. Roos
J.Th. van Wees	F.F.F. de Beaufort
P.L. Visser	K.H. Heenk
J.C. Banz	F. Sickinghe
A.M. Klijn	A.T.P. Haitsma
M.T. Grutterink	A.E. Hol
J.C. Toorman	A. de Heij
S.N.S.M. Mak	J.J. Dijk
J. Cox	L.M. Graal
T.S. Pieters	I. Huinck
T.S. Deckers	J.B.J.M. Boelrijk
E.D.G. Kiersch	F.J. Leeflang
T.H.G. Steenmetser	B.A.M. van Bennekom
W. van Heest	B. Linnartz
	M. Van Hasselt

MEMBERS OF FIRM/NOTARIES

W.A.J.M. de Nerée tot	W.J. Poldermans
Babberich	J.C.R. van Reedt Dortland
A.A. van Velten	A.L.M. Schulte

(This Listing Continued)

CANDIDATE-NOTARIES

H. Mannheim	M.J.M.M. van Wynhoven
A. Buma	W.M. Ketwaru
Akke de Haan	A.A. Velten, Jr.
A.K. Polhuis	Ph.A. Ledeboer
J.W. Stouthart	M. Vandersmissen

TAX ADVISERS

J.Th. Krebbers	J.A. de Jong

Languages: Dutch, English, French, German, Russian, Chinese and Spanish

BOS, OOSTERBAAN & VAN EEGHEN

KONINGSLAAN 35
1075 AB AMSTERDAM, THE NETHERLANDS
Telephone: +31.20.6716756
Fax: +31.20.6718669; 6717446

Corporate, Commercial, Computers and Software, Telecommunications, Real Estate, Banking, Trust, Labor, Agency, Distribution, International Contracts, Copyright, Trademarks, Unfair Competition.

MEMBERS OF FIRM

DINANT T.L. OOSTERBAAN, born 1944; admitted, 1981, Amsterdam. *Education:* Erasmus University, Rotterdam (1968); New York University, Institute of Comparative Law (M.C.J., 1972). Legal Counsel, IBM, 1971-1980. President, International Federation of Computer Law Associations, 1992-1994. Director, Computer Law Association Inc. (USA), 1988—. President, Netherlands Association for Computers and Law, 1986—. Co-Editor-In-Chief, International Computer Law Adviser, 1986-1992. Member, Editorial Board Computerrecht, 1984—. Member, Editorial Advisory Board, The International Computer Lawyer, 1992—. *Member:* International Bar Association; US Computer Law Association. **PRACTICE AREAS:** Corporate Law; Computers and Software; Telecommunications Law.

ROELOF H. BOS, born 1942; admitted, 1986, Amsterdam. *Education:* Universities of Groningen, Amsterdam and Tilburg (J.D. and LL.M., Taxation). Tax Advisor, 1971—. Tax Partner, H.J. Vooren and Price Waterhouse, Europe, 1978-1983. *Member:* International Fiscal Association. **PRACTICE AREAS:** Tax Law; Corporate Law.

CHRIS P. VAN EEGHEN, born 1951; admitted, 1978, Amsterdam. *Education:* University of Amsterdam (1978; Columbia Summer Program in American Law, 1977). Associate, Van Doorne & Warendorf and Clifford-Turner, 1978-1988. Substitute Judge, District Court, Haarlem. **PRACTICE AREAS:** Real Estate Law; Banking Law; Litigation.

EDZARD A.R.M. VAN DEN CLOOSTER BARON SLOET TOT EVERLO, born 1951; admitted, 1982, Amsterdam. *Education:* Nijmegen University (1982). Managing Director, Benelux Trust BV. **PRACTICE AREAS:** Trust Law; Corporate Law; Commercial Law; Litigation.

MARIE-ANNE P. SCHOUTEN, born 1944; admitted, 1986, Amsterdam. *Education:* Vrije University, Amsterdam (1984; Salzburg Seminar in American Studies, 1991). Account Manager, Investment Bank, 1971-1975. Researcher, Vrije University, Amsterdam, 1983-1986. *Member:* US Computer Law Association; International Bar Association. **PRACTICE AREAS:** Computer Law; Labor Law; Commercial Law; Trademark Law.

ASSOCIATES

ANJA E. DEKHUIJZEN, born 1966; admitted, 1991, Amsterdam. *Education:* University of Amsterdam (1990; Law and Legal Public Administration); New York University, Institute of Comparative Law (M.C.J., 1991). **PRACTICE AREAS:** Commercial Law; Computers and Software.

ELISABETH P.M. THOLE, born 1964; admitted, 1991, Amsterdam. *Education:* University of Utrecht (1986; Ph.D., 1991). Author: "Software, a new item in Netherlands law"; over 30 publications on software, copyright and escrow. *Member:* Union Internationale des Avocats. **PRACTICE AREAS:** Computers and Software; Copyright Law.

ANDRE T.A. TILLEMAN, born 1964; admitted, 1993, Amsterdam. *Education:* University of Hull, England (LL.M., International Business, 1988); University of Utrecht (1989). Lecturer, EC Law, University of Hertfordshire, 1991-1992. Contracts Officer, British Aerospace, 1991-1993. **PRACTICE AREAS:** Commercial Law; EC Law; Air Law.

(This Listing Continued)

BOS, OOSTERBAAN & VAN EEGHEN, Amsterdam—Continued

ALLARD A.H.J. HUIZING, born 1967; admitted, 1993, Amsterdam. *Education:* University of Amsterdam (1993; Law and Philosophy). **PRACTICE AREAS:** Trust Law; Commercial Law; Corporate Law; Litigation.

Languages: Dutch, English, French and German

CARON & STEVENS

(Associated Office of Baker & McKenzie)

LEIDSEPLEIN 29

1017 PS AMSTERDAM, THE NETHERLANDS
Telephone: (020) 5517555
Intn'l. Dialing: (31-20) 5517555
Cable Address: ABOGADO
Telex: 16474
Answer Back: 16474 ABOG NL
Facsimiles: (31-20) 6267949; 6232884

Mailing Address: P.O. Box 19720, 1000, GS Amsterdam

JACOBUS J. J. BLOCKS, born Amsterdam, The Netherlands, 1946; admitted, 1973, The Netherlands. *Education:* University of Amsterdam (LL.B., 1970; Master of Taxation, 1975).

MARK P. BONGARD, born Hengelo, The Netherlands, 1949; Civil Law Notary, 1987. *Education:* Utrecht University (LL.B.); Leyden University (Master of Taxation).

M. H. FRANK VAN BUUREN, born Utrecht, The Netherlands, 1947; admitted, 1981, The Netherlands. *Education:* Erasmus University, Rotterdam (LL.B).

PETER DEKKER, born The Hague, The Netherlands, 1948; admitted, 1981, The Netherlands. *Education:* Leyden University (LL.B., 1975); Tilburgh University (Master in Taxation, 1974).

EDUARD J. FERMAN, born Woodford, England, 1948; admitted, 1977, The Netherlands. *Education:* Utrecht University (LL.B., 1975).

CARLA HAMBURGER, born Amsterdam, The Netherlands, 1952; admitted, 1977, The Netherlands. *Education:* University of Amsterdam (LL.B., 1976).

ALBERT VAN HERK, born The Hague, The Netherlands, 1943; admitted, 1969, The Netherlands. *Education:* University of Amsterdam (LL.B., 1968; Master of Taxation, 1975); University of Montpellier (Diploma Private Law, 1969).

FREDERICUS C. DE HOSSON, born Lareyden, The Netherlands, 1948; admitted, 1989, The Netherlands. *Education:* Leyden University (LL.B., Master of Taxation, 1975).

NORBERT R. JANSEN, born Alkmaar, The Netherlands, 1956; admitted, 1991, The Netherlands. *Education:* University of Amsterdam (LL.B., Master of Taxation, 1983).

MAARTEN L. B. VAN DER LANDE, born Eindhoven, The Netherlands, 1950; admitted, 1987, The Netherlands. *Education:* Leyden University (LL.B., 1974); Master of Taxation, 1974); University of Miami (M.C.L., 1980). **LANGUAGES:** Dutch, English, German and French.

GIJSBERT LOOS, born Workum, The Netherlands, 1942; admitted, 1969, The Netherlands. *Education:* Groningen University (LL.B., 1965); New York University (LL.M., Taxation, 1965); Columbia University (LL.M., 1966).

HENDRIKUS M. N. SCHONIS, born Middelburg, The Netherlands, 1943; admitted, 1989, The Netherlands. *Education:* Tax Academy Rotterdam (Master of Taxation, 1966); Tilburg University (LL.B., 1975; Ph.D., 1985).

PIET L. A. M. SCHROEDER, born Heerlen, The Netherlands, 1947; admitted, 1976, The Netherlands. *Education:* Groningen University (LL.B., 1970); City of London Polytechnic (M.A. in Business Law, 1971).

WILLEM F. C. STEVENS, born The Hague, The Netherlands, 1938; admitted, 1965, The Netherlands. *Education:* Leyden University (LL.D., 1961); Academy of Rotterdam (Master of Taxation, 1962); Harvard Law School (LL.M., 1963).

(This Listing Continued)

JOSEPH F. VAN VLIJMEN, born Rotterdam, The Netherlands, 1949; admitted, 1975, The Netherlands. *Education:* University of Utrecht (LL.B., 1974). **LANGUAGES:** Dutch, English, German and French.

WILLEM C. B. VAN WETTUM, born Maarssen, The Netherlands, 1953; admitted, 1990, The Netherlands. *Education:* Groningen University (M.B.A., 1978); Leyden University (Master of Taxation, 1989).

A. JURRIAAN ZOETMULDER, born Eindhoven, The Netherlands, 1944; admitted, 1976, The Netherlands. *Education:* Leyden University (LL.B., 1967); University of Amsterdam (Master of Taxation, 1970).

LOCAL PARTNERS

THEO L. VAN MAAREN, born Breda, The Netherlands, 1946; admitted, 1975, The Netherlands. *Education:* University of Utrecht (LL.B., 1974); University of Amsterdam (Masfer of Taxation, 1984).

HÉLÈNE A. M. STUIJT, born Amsterdam, The Netherlands, 1953; admitted, 1978, The Netherlands; Civil Law Notary, 1990. *Education:* Amsterdam University (LL.B.).

WIL VAN WILLIGEN, born Kampen, The Netherlands, 1932; admitted, 1965, The Netherlands. *Education:* Free University, Amsterdam (LL.B., 1956); University of Amsterdam (Master of Taxation, 1969).

HENK VAN WILSUM, born Texel, the Netherlands, 1960; 1983, Civil Law Notary. *Education:* Leyden University (LL.B.).

BORIS M. VAN BEEK, born Arnhem, The Netherlands, 1967; admitted, 1993, The Netherlands. *Education:* Nijmegen University (LL.B., 1991).

MIRJAM A. DE BLÉCOURT-WOUTERSE, born Zeist, The Netherlands, 1964; admitted, 1990, The Netherlands. *Education:* Leyden University (LL.B., 1988; Master of Taxation, 1990).

KARIN W. M. BODEWES, born Arnhem, The Netherlands, 1960; admitted, 1986, The Netherlands. *Education:* Nijmegen University (LL.B., 1983).

J. ARNAUD BOOIJ, born Utrecht, The Netherlands, 1963; admitted, 1989, The Netherlands. *Education:* Leyden University (LL.B., 1988; Master of Taxation, 1988). **LANGUAGES:** Dutch, English, German and French.

CAROLINE A. BUN, born Breda, The Netherlands, 1967; admitted, 1992, The Netherlands. *Education:* Rijksuniversiteit Groningen (LL.M., 1992).

JAN LOUIS BURGGRAAF, born Rotterdam, The Netherlands, 1964; admitted, 1992, The Netherlands. *Education:* University of Utrecht; University of Edinburgh; London School of Economics; Harvard Law School.

PAUL W. J. COENEN, born Groesbeek, The Netherlands, 1964; admitted, 1993, The Netherlands. *Education:* University of Nijmegen; University of Münster; University of Hamburg; University of Leiden.

ERNST W. J. FERDINANDUSSE, born Rotterdam, The Netherlands, 1964; admitted, 1992, The Netherlands. *Education:* Erasmus University Rotterdam (J.D., 1988); University of Leyden (J.D., 1989); University of Exeter, UK; College of Europe, Bruges Belgium (LL.M., 1991). **LANGUAGES:** Dutch, French, English and German.

JAN-WILLEM GERRITSEN, born Bussum, The Netherlands, May 17, 1965; admitted, 1991, The Netherlands. *Education:* Utrecht University (LL.B., 1989); Amsterdam University (Master of Taxation, 1990).

LUCAS P. L. HABETS, born Breda, The Netherlands, 1965; admitted, 1989, The Netherlands. *Education:* University of Utrecht (LL.B., 1988); Temple University, Philadelphia (LL.M., 1989).

RENÉ M. M. HAERKENS, born Amsterdam, The Netherlands, 1969; admitted, 1994, The Netherlands. *Education:* Titus Brandsma Lyceum (V.W.O., 1988); University of NPmegen (LL.B., 1994).

ANNE C. J. G. VAN DER HENST, born Naarden, The Netherlands, 1968; admitted, 1993, The Netherlands. *Education:* Rijksuniversity Groningen (Master of Law, 1992); University, Rouen, France.

PETER C. HILDERS, born Gravenhage, The Netherlands, 1963; admitted, 1990, The Netherlands. *Education:* Rijksuniversiteit Leiden (Masters in Tax Law, 1988); Erasmus University of Rotterdam (Masters in Economics, 1989).

CAREL R. F. HILFERINK, born Nymegen, The Netherlands, 1965; admitted, 1993, The Netherlands. *Education:* Vrije Universiteit.

(This Listing Continued)

JEROEN O. HOEKSTRA, born Den Haag, 1967; admitted, 1991, The Netherlands. *Education:* Leiden University (Civil Law, 1990).

ROELOF O. N. VAN HOLTHE TOT ECHTEN, born Arnhem, The Netherlands, 1960; admitted, 1984, The Netherlands. *Education:* University of Utrecht (LL.M., 1984).

ANITA A. DE JONG, born Spijk, The Netherlands, 1959; admitted, 1985, The Netherlands. *Education:* University of Utrecht (LL.B., 1985). **LANGUAGES:** Dutch, English and German.

BART LB. H. J. JONKMAN, born Eindhoven, The Netherlands, 1967; admitted, 1992, The Netherlands. *Education:* Tilburg University Rotterdam (Economics, 1986; LL.M., 1990); Notre Dame Law School, U.S.A. (LL.M., cum laude, International Law, 1992).

G. CHRISTINE KOELMAN, born Zwolle, The Netherlands, 1965; admitted, 1990, The Netherlands. *Education:* Groningen University (LL.B., 1989; Social Legal Studies, 1989).

ANTAL STEVEN VAN DER LAKEN, born Breda, The Netherlands, 1964; admitted, 1992, The Netherlands. *Education:* State University of Utrecht (M.A., 1991).

LENET T. LEUSINK, born Nunspect, The Netherlands, 1966; admitted, 1992, The Netherlands. *Education:* University of Utrecht (Master of Law, 1990); Queen Mary University and Vestfield College (LL.M.).

ROBERTUS M. VAN MEERWIJK, born St. Michiels Gestel, The Netherlands, 1961; admitted, 1993, The Netherlands. *Education:* University of Amsterdam (Tax Law, 1988); Superior Hotel Management School; University of Amsterdam (Dutch Civil Law, 1989).

LOES M. DE MOOR, born Vlaardingen, The Netherlands, 1966; admitted, 1991, The Netherlands. *Education:* Erasmus University, Rotterdam (LL.B., 1990).

ARNOUD J. NOORDAM, born Amsterdam, May 23, 1965; admitted, 1991, The Netherlands. *Education:* Amsterdam University (Civil Law, 1990).

WENDELA P. VAN OOSTEROM, born Leiden, The Netherlands, 1966; admitted, 1991, The Netherlands. *Education:* Leiden State University (Master in Law, 1991); Bologna Università degli studi.

HANS V. VAN OPHEM, born Noordwijk, The Netherlands, 1963; admitted, 1987, The Netherlands. *Education:* University of Amsterdam (LL.B., 1986).

TJEERD F. W. OVERDIJK, born Heerlen, The Netherlands, 1959; admitted, 1984, The Netherlands. *Education:* Leyden University (LL.B., 1984). **LANGUAGES:** Dutch, English, German and French.

WOUTER A. PAARDEKOOPER, born Valkenswaard, The Netherlands, 1965; admitted, 1992, The Netherlands. *Education:* Tilburg University; Fiscal Institute Tilburg (1990).

LEONIE C. V. PELS RIJCKEN, born The Hague, The Netherlands, 1967; admitted, 1994, The Netherlands. *Education:* State University Leiden (Masters, 1993).

CHARLES G. A. VAN RIJCKEVORSEL, born Middelburg, The Netherlands, 1965; admitted, 1994, The Netherlands.

CARLO P. M. ROELOFS, born 1963; admitted, 1992, The Netherlands. *Education:* University of NPmegen (Civil Law, 1991).

PETER ROOS, born Eindhoven, The Netherlands, 1965; admitted, 1990, The Netherlands. *Education:* Maastricht University (LL.B., 1989).

FRANÇOISE A. ROOSENBOOM-DE VRIES, born Rotterdam, The Netherlands, 1961; admitted, 1990, The Netherlands. *Education:* University of Amsterdam (LL.B., 1988); University of San Diego (M.C.L., 1990).

ERIC T. SCHEER, born Sneek, The Netherlands, 1963; admitted, 1991, The Netherlands. *Education:* Leyden University (Master of Taxation, 1988; LL.B., 1991).

KARIN J. T. SMIT, born Hengelo, The Netherlands, 1958; admitted, 1988, The Netherlands. *Education:* Utrecht University (M.D., History, 1986; LL.B., 1987).

JUSTINE A. TAKX, born Haarlem, The Netherlands, 1965; admitted, 1993, The Netherlands. *Education:* University of Amsterdam (J.D., 1991).

KLAAS-JAN VISSER, born Arnhem, The Netherlands, 1964; admitted, 1992, The Netherlands. *Education:* Erasmus University Rotterdam (Economics, 1990).

(This Listing Continued)

PATRICK H. DE WAAL, born Amsterdam, The Netherlands, 1965; admitted, 1994, The Netherlands.

MARCO WALLART, born Amsterdam, The Netherlands, 1967; admitted, 1993, The Netherlands. *Education:* Vrije Universiteit Amsterdam (Mr, 1992).

REDMAR A. WOLF, born Zwolle, The Netherlands, 1966; admitted, 1992, The Netherlands. *Education:* University of Utrecht (LL.M., 1988).

GERARD D. J. ZAALBERG, born Utrecht, The Netherlands, 1964; admitted, 1993, The Netherlands. *Education:* State University Leiden (Master, 1990).

BAREND W. J. M. DE ROY VAN ZUIDEWIJN, born 's-Hertogenbosch, The Netherlands, 1959; admitted, 1984, The Netherlands. *Education:* University of Utrecht (LL.B., 1983).

(For offices in other countries, see Chicago, Illinois, U.S.A. listing for Baker & McKenzie)

CLIFFORD CHANCE

Established in 1972

APOLLOLAAN 171

1077 AS AMSTERDAM, THE NETHERLANDS

Telephone: (31 20) 577 71 11

Fax: (31 20) 676 93 26

Mailing Address: P.O. Box 7301, 1007 JH Amsterdam, Netherlands

Bahrain, Manama Associated Office: Law Office of Shaikh Isa bin Mohammed Al Khalifa. P.O. Box 20717. Telephone: (973) 531535; 531073. Fax: (973) 536272; 530608.

Barcelona, Spain Office: Pau Claris 102, 08009. Telephone: (34 3) 318 68 64. Fax: (34 3) 317 73 23.

Brussels, Belgium Office: Avenue Louise 65, Box 2, 1050. Telephone: (32 2) 533 59 11. Fax: (32 2) 533 59 59.

Budapest, Hungary Office: Köves & Partners, Clifford Chance. Madách Trade Center, Madách Imre Út 14, 1075. Telephone: (36 1) 268 1600. Fax: (36 1) 268 1610.

Dubai, United Arab Emirates Office: 18th Floor, Dubai World Trade Centre, P.O. Box 9380. Telephone: (971 4) 314333. Fax: (971 4) 313990; 314565.

Frankfurt/Main, Germany Office: Friedrichstraße 2-6, 60323. Telephone: (49 69) 971 4090. Fax: (49 69) 971 40977.

Hanoi, Vietnam Office: 52 Nguyen Binh Khiem. Telephone: (844) 229 182/3/4/5/6. Fax: (844) 229 190.

Hong Kong Office: 30th Floor, Jardine House, One Connaught Place. Telephone: (852) 2810 0229. Fax: (852) 2810 4708; 2810 4858; 2810 4743.

London, England Office: 200 Aldersgate Street, EC1A 4JJ. Telephone: (44 171) 600 1000. Fax: (44 171) 600 5555.

Madrid, Spain Office: Paseo de la Castellana 110, 28046. Telephone: (34 1) 562 7674. Fax: (34 1) 562 49 93.

Milan, Italy Associated Office: Grimaldi e Clifford Chance. Via Gesú, 3, 20121. Telephone: (39 2) 7600 8040. Fax: (39 2) 7600 4950.

Moscow, Russia Office: Ul. Sadovaya - Samotechnaya 24/27, 2nd Floor, 103051. Telephone: (7 501) 258 50 50. Fax: (7 501) 258 50 51.

New York, New York Office: Swiss Bank Tower, 10 East 50th Street, 10022. Telephone: (1 212) 750 1440. Fax: (1 212) 758 6625.

Paris, France Office: 112 avenue Kléber, BP 163 Trocadéro, 75770 Paris Cedex 16. Telephone: (33 1) 44 05 52 52. Fax: (33 1) 44 05 52 00.

Riyadh, Saudi Arabia Associated Office: The Law Firm of Salah Al-Hejailan. P.O. Box 1454, 11431. Telephone: (966 1) 479 2200. Fax: (966 1) 479 1717.

Rome, Italy Associated Office: Grimaldi e Clifford Chance. Viale G. Rossini 7, 00198. Telephone: (39 6) 807 2251. Fax: (39 6) 807 8201.

Shanghai, People's Republic of China Office: Suite 898, Shanghai Centre, 1376 Nanjing Xi Lu, 200040. Telephone: (86 21) 279 8461. Fax: (86 21) 279 8462.

Singapore Office: 16 Collyer Quay #31-00, 0104. Telephone: (65) 535 1855. Fax: (65) 535 6855.

Tokyo, Japan Office: 6th Floor, South Hill Nagatacho Building, 11-30 Nagatacho 1-chome, Chiyoda-ku, 100. Telephone: (81 3) 3581 4311. Fax: (81 3) 3593 0651.

Warsaw, Poland Office: Warsaw Corporate Centre, ul. Emilii Plater 28, 00-688. Telephone: (48 2) 630 3344. Fax: (48 2) 630 3355.

Banking, Securities and Finance, Commercial, Company, Mergers and Acquisitions, Entertainment, Litigation, Tax.

(This Listing Continued)

CLIFFORD CHANCE, Amsterdam—Continued

Firm engaged in Dutch, English and General International Practice.

RESIDENT PARTNERS

CONSTANT T. BARBAS, Advocaat. *LANGUAGES:* Dutch, English and French. *PRACTICE AREAS:* Securities; Venture Capital; Corporate Law; Mergers and Acquisitions.

PETER S. BAYLIFF, (Not admitted in The Netherlands). Solicitor. *LANGUAGES:* Dutch, English, French and German. *PRACTICE AREAS:* Motion Picture Finance; Acquisitions, Divestitures, Mergers; Entertainment Industry Transactions; Media Law; Joint Ventures.

RENÉ CITROEN, Advocaat. *LANGUAGES:* Dutch and English. *PRACTICE AREAS:* Capital Markets; Structured Finance; Leases and Leasing; Project Finance.

JHR. JOOST E. VAN DER DOES DE WILLEBOIS, Advocaat. *LANGUAGES:* Dutch and English. *PRACTICE AREAS:* Corporate Law; Arbitration; Joint Ventures; Mergers and Acquisitions.

JOACHIM FLEURY, Advocaat. *LANGUAGES:* Dutch and English. *PRACTICE AREAS:* Media Law; Joint Ventures; Telecommunications Law; Mergers and Acquisitions.

FRANK G.B. GRAAF, Advocaat. *LANGUAGES:* Dutch and English. *PRACTICE AREAS:* Securities Offerings; Financial Services; Securities Regulation; Banking Law; Securities.

JOOST J.B.M. HENGST, Advocaat. *LANGUAGES:* Dutch, English, French and German. *PRACTICE AREAS:* Mergers and Acquisitions; Commercial Law; Property; Environmental Law.

THEO A.L. KLIEBISCH, Advocaat. *LANGUAGES:* Dutch, English, French and German. *PRACTICE AREAS:* Banking Law; Finance Law; Securities; Asset Based Lending; Project Financing; Equipment Leasing; Aircraft Financing.

WEPKO P. SCHELTEMA, Advocaat. *LANGUAGES:* Dutch, English, French and German. *PRACTICE AREAS:* Litigation; Corporate Law; Arbitration.

WILLEM H.A. SPECKEN, Advocaat, belastingadviseur. *LANGUAGES:* Dutch, English, French and German. *PRACTICE AREAS:* Taxation; International Tax Planning.

FRANK DE VOS, Advocaat, belastingadviseur. *LANGUAGES:* Dutch and English. *PRACTICE AREAS:* International Tax Planning; Taxation.

ASSOCIATES

RUTH D. VAN ANDEL, Advocaat.

MONIQUE BEKKERING, Advocaat.

ROELAND I.V.F. BERTRAMS, Advocaat.

LOUIS C. BOUCHEZ, Advocaat.

KEN BREKEN, Advocaat.

GENEVIEVE DECKERS, Advocaat.

JEREMY L. EVANS, Solicitor.

MARK S. HUDDLESTONE, Solicitor.

EDWIN M. VAN KASTEREN, Advocaat Belastingadviseur.

A. ADRIAAN KOCH, Advocaat.

JEROEN D. KOSTER, Advocaat.

TINEKE J. KOTHE, Advocaat.

JULIETTE M. LUYCKS, Advocaat.

MIRJAM K. MANN, Advocaat.

EVELINE J.D. MUTSAERS, Advocaat.

ALBERT NIJENHUIS, Advocaat.

JUDY D. OPPEDIJK, Advocaat.

DUCO J. ORANJE, Advocaat.

JEROEN OUWEHAND, Advocaat.

P. TIMON REIJN, Belastingadviseur.

LISA ROUTER, Solicitor.

MICHAEL B. SWINDEN, Solicitor.

(This Listing Continued)

ATE R.T. VAN IJLZINGA VEENSTRA, Advocaat Belastingadviseur.

RICK L.E. VERHAGEN, Advocaat.

MARIKE VERMEER, Advocaat.

TJEPCO H. VAN VOORST VADER, Advocaat.

PIETER N.J. VAN WELZEN, Advocaat.

KEES WESTERMANN, Advocaat.

MAURITS B.M. WIJFFELS, Advocaat.

ELS DE WIND, Advocaat.

RENE C. VAN ZELST, Advocaat, belastingadviseur.

CAROLINE H. VAN DER ZWET, Advocaat.

Languages: Arabic, Dutch, English, French, German, Spanish and Italian

(All Partners and Associates are Members of the Amsterdam Bar Except where Otherwise Stated).
(For the Names of Partners Resident in other Offices, see the Professional Biographies for those Offices).

DE BRAUW BLACKSTONE WESTBROEK

Attorneys and Civil Law Notaries
ATRIUM
7TH FLOOR, STRAWINSKYLAAN 3115
1077 ZX AMSTERDAM, THE NETHERLANDS
Telephone: (20) 5 481 481
Telex: 10227
Telecopier: (20) 5 481 485

REVISERS OF THE NETHERLANDS LAW DIGEST FOR THIS DIRECTORY.

The Hague, The Netherlands Office: Zuid Hollandlaan 7, 2596 AL. Telephone: (70) 328 5 328. Telex: 32321. Telecopier: (70) 328 5 325.

Rotterdam, The Netherlands Office: 10th Floor, Coolsingel 139, 3012 AG. Telephone: (10) 401 88 99. Telex: 24676. Telecopier: (10) 411 35 48.

Eindhoven, The Netherlands Office: Parklaan 42a, 5613 BG. Telephone: (40) 464442. Telecopier: (40) 466288.

Brussels, Belgium Office: Brederodestraat 13A, B-1000. Telephone: (2) 505 0211. Telecopier: (2) 502 2644.

London, England Office: Royex House, Aldermanbury Square, EC2V 7HR. Telephone: (171) 600 1719. Fax: (171) 600 1718.

New York, New York Office: 712 Fifth Avenue, 30th Floor, 10019-4102. Telephone: (212) 801-3430. Fax: (212) 801-3435; (212) 801-3436.

Dutch Attorneys may represent clients before all Dutch Courts, before the European Court of Justice and the Benelux Court of Justice, and are admitted to plead before all Courts of the member states of the Common Market (EEC).

Member of Alliance of European Lawyers (EEIG) which regroups six law firms from Continental Europe. The Alliance consists of Oppenhoff & Rädler at Munich, Berlin, Cologne, Frankfurt am Main and Leipzig; De Bandt, van Hecke & Lagae at Brussels and Antwerp; DeBrauw Blackstone Westbroek at Amsterdam, The Hague, Rotterdam, Brussels, London and New York; Jeantet & Associés at Paris and Warsaw; Lagerlöf & Leman at Stockholm, Gothenburg and Malmö; Uria & Menendez at Madrid and Barcelona.

The Alliance member firms have joint offices at Brussels, London, New York and Prague.

ATTORNEYS AT LAW
MEMBERS OF FIRM

BERNHARD SLUYTERS, born 1938; admitted, 1963, Netherlands. *Education:* Utrecht University; University of Amsterdam (Fiscal Law, 1970); Harvard Law School (LL.M., 1964). Professor of Health Care Law, Leyden University. *LANGUAGES:* English and French. *PRACTICE AREAS:* General Practice; Health Care Law.

JAN R. SCHAAFSMA, born 1938; admitted, 1966, The Hague. *Education:* Leyden University. Professor of Banking Law, Leyden University. *Member:* International Bar Association. *LANGUAGES:* English, French and German. *PRACTICE AREAS:* Corporate Law; Business and Banking Law; Financial Law.

(This Listing Continued)

PAUL C. DE GRAAUW, born 1943; admitted, 1967, The Hague. *Education:* Nijmegen University. *Member:* International Bar Association. *LANGUAGES:* English and French. *PRACTICE AREAS:* Corporate and Business Law; Intellectual Property Law; Advertising Law.

DIRK C. MEERBURG, born 1949; admitted, 1977, The Hague. *Education:* Utrecht University. *LANGUAGES:* English and German. *PRACTICE AREAS:* Corporate Law; Financial Law; Business Law; Banking Law.

BEREND J.H. CRANS, born 1952; admitted, 1977, The Hague. *Education:* Leyden University. *Member:* European Air Law Association; Netherlands Maritime- and Transport Law Association; Netherlands Association for EEC Law. *LANGUAGES:* English, French and German. *PRACTICE AREAS:* Aircraft and Asset Financing; Aviation Law; Corporate Law; Financial Law.

EDUARD C. DE BOUTER, born 1949; admitted, 1977, The Hague. *Education:* Utrecht University; Harvard Law School (LL.M., 1973; S.J.D., 1978). *Member:* International Bar Association; Union Internationale des Avocats; International Young Lawyers Association. *LANGUAGES:* English and Spanish. *PRACTICE AREAS:* Corporate Law; Financial Law; Business and Banking Law.

EVERT JAN HENRICHS, born 1958; admitted, 1983, Netherlands. *Education:* University of Amsterdam. *LANGUAGES:* English and German. *PRACTICE AREAS:* Corporate Law; Labour Law; Real Estate Law.

PAUL CRONHEIM, born 1957; admitted, 1983, Netherlands and New York; 1987, California. *Education:* Leyden University; Columbia University School of Law (LL.M., 1982). *Member:* American and International Bar Associations. *LANGUAGES:* English, German and French. *PRACTICE AREAS:* Corporate Law; Financial Law; American Law and Practice.

ELISABETH TH.M. SNEEK, born 1959; admitted, 1984, Amsterdam. *Education:* Rotterdam University. *LANGUAGES:* English and French. *PRACTICE AREAS:* Corporate Law; Labour Law; Business and Banking Law.

LODEWIJK J. HIJMANS VAN DEN BERGH, born 1963; admitted, 1988, The Hague. *Education:* Utrecht University. (Resident, London Office). *LANGUAGES:* English. *PRACTICE AREAS:* Corporate Law; Financial Law; Securities Law.

ASSOCIATES

MARK E.J. SALOMONS, born 1961; admitted, 1987, Amsterdam. *Education:* University of Amsterdam. *LANGUAGES:* English and German. *PRACTICE AREAS:* Corporate Law; Financial Law.

ROB W. POLAK, born 1960; admitted, 1988, The Hague. *Education:* University of Amsterdam; Columbia Law School (LL.M., 1987). *LANGUAGES:* English and French. *PRACTICE AREAS:* General Practice; Labour Law.

FRANCYNA M. SCHLINGMANN, born 1966; admitted, 1988, The Hague. *Education:* Utrecht University. *LANGUAGES:* English, French and German. *PRACTICE AREAS:* Financial Law; Securities and Banking.

JOHANNA M.E. FEIJE, born 1964; admitted, 1988, The Hague. *Education:* Leyden University. *LANGUAGES:* English, French and German. *PRACTICE AREAS:* General Practice; EC Law.

H. RUTGER DE WITT WIJNEN, born 1962; admitted, 1989, Amsterdam. *Education:* Leyden University. *LANGUAGES:* English and French. *PRACTICE AREAS:* Corporate Law; Asset Leasing and Financing.

PAUL P.J. JONGEN, born 1960; admitted, 1989, Amsterdam. *Education:* University of Amsterdam. *LANGUAGES:* English, French and German. *PRACTICE AREAS:* Corporate Law; Financial Law; Labour Law.

MERIJNEN T. KREEK, born 1960; admitted, 1989, The Hague. *Education:* Groningen University; New York University. *LANGUAGES:* English, French and German. *PRACTICE AREAS:* Corporate Law; Labour Law.

E.M. LOKKE MOEREL, born 1965; admitted, 1989, The Hague. *Education:* Leyden University. *LANGUAGES:* English. *PRACTICE AREAS:* Corporate Law; Intellectual Property Law.

MARCELLE SPIEGEL, born 1961; admitted, 1990, Amsterdam. *Education:* University of Amsterdam. *LANGUAGES:* English. *PRACTICE AREAS:* Corporate Law.

NICO A.J. BEL, born 1963; admitted, 1990, Amsterdam. *Education:* Leyden University. (Resident, Brussels Office).

(This Listing Continued)

NIEK K. BIEGMAN, born Cairo, Egypt, September 23, 1964; admitted, 1990, The Hague. *Education:* University of Amsterdam (J.D., 1987; New York University (LL.M. 1988). (Resident, New York Office). *LANGUAGES:* English, Dutch. *PRACTICE AREAS:* Corporate Law; Business Law; Banking Law.

A. HENRIETTE VAN ZUTPHEN, born 1962; admitted, 1990, The Hague. *Education:* University of Amsterdam.

N. BERNARD SPOOR, born 1963; admitted, 1991, Amsterdam. *Education:* Groningen University. (Resident, London Office).

GEORG C. VAN DAAL, born 1964; admitted, 1991, The Hague. *Education:* Leyden University.

TILL KRESSIN, born 1963; admitted, 1991, Amsterdam. *Education:* Utrecht University.

ANTHONIE SCHUTTE, born 1966; admitted, 1991, Amsterdam. *Education:* Utrecht University.

ONNO RŸSDIJK, born 1965; admitted, 1991, Amsterdam. *Education:* Utrecht University.

WILLEM KOKKEDEE, born 1963; admitted, 1992, Amsterdam. *Education:* Leyden University (Ph.D., 1992, thesis on Health Care Law).

JAAP M. VAN SLOOTEN, born 1966; admitted, 1992, Amsterdam. *Education:* University of Amsterdam.

SIMON A. REININK, born 1966; admitted, 1992, Amsterdam. *Education:* Utrecht University.

RENATE DE BOER, born 1963; admitted, 1992, The Hague. *Education:* Groningen University.

RENÉ R. BROUWER, born 1966; admitted, 1993, The Hague. *Education:* University of Amsterdam.

HELEEN E.M. VELTHUYSE, born 1966; admitted, 1993, Amsterdam. *Education:* University of Amsterdam.

ISA BOEZER, born 1968; admitted, 1933, Amsterdam. *Education:* Leyden University.

M. ANNETTE MAK, born 1964; admitted, 1993, Amsterdam. *Education:* Utrecht University.

ROB P. VAN BEEK, born 1965; admitted, 1993, Amsterdam. *Education:* Free University of Amsterdam.

JANET L. STUYT, born 1969; admitted, 1993, Amsterdam. *Education:* Leyden University.

GERARD VAN SOLINGE, born 1962; admitted, 1993, Amsterdam. *Education:* Free University of Amsterdam.

ANNICK M.T. JANSSEN, born 1966; admitted, 1994, Amsterdam. *Education:* Catholic University of Brabant.

CATRIEN W. NOORDA, born 1969; admitted, 1994, Amsterdam. *Education:* University of Amsterdam.

MARLIES STEK, born 1966; admitted, 1994, Amsterdam. *Education:* University of Amsterdam.

PIM W.J. HORSTEN, born 1963; admitted, 1994, Amsterdam. *Education:* Leyden University.

MURIEL L. BLACKSTONE, born 1967; admitted, 1994, Amsterdam. *Education:* Leyden University.

SŸA M. VAN MOURIK, born 1954; admitted, 1994, Amsterdam. *Education:* Groningen University; University of Pennsylvania Law School (LL.M., 1980).

ANNEKE S.M. GALAMA, born 1967; admitted, 1994, Amsterdam. *Education:* University of Amsterdam.

MICHAEL TH. HOOGEBOOM, born 1966; admitted, 1994, Amsterdam. *Education:* Free University of Amsterdam.

CIVIL LAW NOTARIES
MEMBERS OF FIRM

GERRIT J. DE JONGH, born 1946; appointed Civil Law Notary, 1987, Amsterdam. *Education:* Leyden University. *LANGUAGES:* English and German. *PRACTICE AREAS:* Corporate Law; Construction/Real Estate Law; Notarial Law.

(This Listing Continued)

DE BRAUW BLACKSTONE WESTBROEK,
Amsterdam—Continued

RENÉ W. CLUMPKENS, born 1954; appointed Civil Law Notary, 1991, Amsterdam. *Education:* Leyden University. **LANGUAGES:** English. **PRACTICE AREAS:** Corporate Law; Financial Law; Notarial Law.

MARTIN VAN OLFFEN, born 1961. *Education:* Leyden University (Ph.D., 1989). Appointed, Civil Law Notary, 1994, Amsterdam. **LANGUAGES:** English and German. **PRACTICE AREAS:** Corporate Law; Financial Law; Notarial Law.

ASSOCIATES

JULIËTTE NIJENHUIS-WILDERVANCK, born 1957. *Education:* Groningen University. **LANGUAGES:** English, French and German. **PRACTICE AREAS:** Corporate Law; Construction/Real Estate Law; Notarial Law; Family Law.

BART S. VELDKAMP, born 1958. *Education:* Leyden University. **LANGUAGES:** English and Russian. **PRACTICE AREAS:** Corporate Law; Notarial Law.

MARINA H. VAN GOOR, born 1966. *Education:* University of Amsterdam.

PAULINE J. CAHEN, born 1967. *Education:* University of Amsterdam.

DANIËLLE R.J. LOOY, born 1966. *Education:* Nijmegen University.

CYNTHIA S. GUMAN, born 1969. *Education:* Free University of Amsterdam.

MARCEL D.P. ANKER, born 1965. *Education:* Leyden University.

MARIËTTE L.E. PLAGGEMARS, born 1969. *Education:* Groningen University.

SASKIA E. VAN DEN BERG, born 1971. *Education:* Utrecht University.

REVISERS OF THE NETHERLANDS LAW DIGEST FOR THIS DIRECTORY.

(For list of Partners and Counsel of the respective Member Firms see Professional Biographies at: Oppenhoff & Rädler at Munich, Cologne, Frankfurt am Main, Berlin and Leipzig, Germany; De Bandt van Hecke & Lagae at Brussels and Antwerp, Belgium; De Brauw Blackstone Westbroek at The Hague, Rotterdam, Amsterdam and Eindhoven, The Netherlands; Jeantet & Associés, at Paris, France and Warsaw, Poland; Lagerlöf & Leman at Stockholm, Gothenburg and Malmö, Sweden; Uria & Menendez at Madrid and Barcelona, Spain)

DOLK-VERBURG-DIAMAND

Established in 1950

CRONENBURG 75
1081 GM AMSTERDAM, THE NETHERLANDS
Telephone: 020-6464146
Telex: 11666 (alaw)
Telefax: 020-6464716
Cable Address: "Solicitor"

Mailing Address: P.O. Box 7911, Amsterdam, 1008 AC

General Practice. Corporate, Agency Contracts, Air Law, Collection Accounts, Maritime, Industrial Property, Insurance (Transport, Hull, Fire, Constructions), International Trade, Labor Contracts, Naval Architecture, Real Estate and Take-Overs Law. Litigation

MEMBERS OF FIRM

W. DIAMAND (1949-1982).

H.J.P. DOLK (1948-1985).

GERH VERBURG, admitted, 1945, The Netherlands. *Education:* University of Amsterdam.

E.H. SERVATIUS, admitted, 1971, The Netherlands. *Education:* University of Amsterdam.

H. HAMPE, admitted, 1971, The Netherlands. *Education:* University of Amsterdam.

H. POSTHUMUS MEYJES, admitted, 1978, The Netherlands. *Education:* Erasmus University of Rotterdam. Master Mariner.

(This Listing Continued)

A.J. DOLK, admitted, 1979, The Netherlands. *Education:* University of Leyden.

F.J.H. MULDER, admitted, 1982, The Netherlands. *Education:* Erasmus University of Rotterdam.

P.M.G.W. BRINGMANN, admitted, 1984, The Netherlands. *Education:* University of Amsterdam.

R.P.M. VAN LEEUWEN, admitted, 1986, The Netherlands. *Education:* University of Leyden.

B.O. ESCHWEILER, admitted, 1987, The Netherlands. *Education:* University of Amsterdam.

P.W. SNOEKER, admitted, 1988, The Netherlands. *Education:* University of Leyden.

ASSOCIATES

P. OSCHATZ, admitted, 1991, The Netherlands. *Education:* University of Leyden.

C. DE KONING, admitted, 1991, The Netherlands. *Education:* University of Utrecht.

J. FREYER, admitted, 1992, The Netherlands. *Education:* University of Amsterdam.

V.L. VIERGEVER, admitted, 1993, The Netherlands. *Education:* University of Leyden.

N.M. SLUMP, admitted, 1993, The Netherlands. *Education:* University of Utrecht.

R. VAN DER POL, admitted, 1994, The Netherlands. *Education:* University of Leyden.

Languages: Dutch, English, French, German and Russian

EKELMANS DEN HOLLANDER

Attorneys at Law - Civil Law Notary

FREDERIKSPLEIN 42
POSTBUS 545 (1000 AM)
1017 XN AMSTERDAM, THE NETHERLANDS
Telephone: (020) 553 3600
Telefax: (020) 553 3777

Corporate, Securities Law, Banking and Finance, Merger and Acquisitions, Construction and Real Estate, Title Transfer, Mortgages, Leaseholds, Intellectual Property, Litigation, Labour Law, Environmental Law, Anti-Trust and Competition, EEC Law, Tourism, Information Technology and Telecommunications Law.

MEMBERS OF FIRM

JAN EKELMANS, born Utrecht, The Netherlands, January 24, 1951; admitted, 1974, Amsterdam. *Education:* University of Utrecht. **PRACTICE AREAS:** Mergers and Acquisitions; Securities; Finance; Leasing; Insolvency; General Corporate; Business Law.

HENRI C. DEN HOLLANDER, born Middelharnis, The Netherlands, January 6, 1949; admitted, 1975, Amsterdam. *Education:* University of Leiden. **PRACTICE AREAS:** Employment Matters; Reorganization; Redundancy; General Finance; Business Law.

RONALD J. VLES, born Rotterdam, The Netherlands, April 14, 1947; admitted, 1973, Amsterdam. *Education:* University of Groningen. **PRACTICE AREAS:** Intellectual Property; Trademark Infringement; Copyright; Licensing; Entertainment; Telecommunications; General Corporate and Business Law.

LUUD J.M. PIJNENBURG, born Valkenswaard, The Netherlands, December 9, 1939; admitted, 1967, The Netherlands. *Education:* University of Utrecht. **PRACTICE AREAS:** Mergers and Acquisitions; Public Finance; Restructuring; General Corporate; Business Law.

PAUL M.J. SCHOENMAECKERS, born Maastricht, The Netherlands, March 6, 1946; admitted, 1974, The Netherlands. *Education:* University of Amsterdam. **PRACTICE AREAS:** Labour Law; Reorganization; Litigation.

PETER A.W. VAN BUREN, born Haarlem, The Netherlands, July 30, 1942; admitted, 1974, Amsterdam; 1989, Appointed by the Crown. *Education:* University of Amsterdam. Civil Law Notary. **PRACTICE AREAS:** Property Law; Corporate Law; Family Law.

(This Listing Continued)

MARINUS J.M. VROMANS, born Oudenbosch, The Netherlands, September 3, 1950; admitted, 1978, Amsterdam. *Education:* University of Utrecht. *PRACTICE AREAS:* European Law; Tourism and Travel; Agency; Franchising and Distribution; Litigation.

GERRIT JAN G. BOLDERMAN, born Rotterdam, The Netherlands, September 18, 1960; admitted, 1983, Amsterdam. *Education:* University of Leiden. *PRACTICE AREAS:* Mergers and Acquisitions; Securities; Public and Private Finance; General Corporate; Business Law.

HELEEN C. HOOGEVEEN, born Portugal, The Netherlands, November 6, 1957; admitted, 1984, Amsterdam. *Education:* University of Utrecht. *PRACTICE AREAS:* Information Technology; Intellectual Property; General Business Law.

GUUS N.H. KEMPERINK, born Amsterdam, The Netherlands, August 17, 1958; admitted, 1984, Amsterdam. *Education:* University of Amsterdam (Master of Law). *PRACTICE AREAS:* European Law; Telecommunication; General Corporate; Business Law.

JAN B. DE SNAYER, born Dirksland, The Netherlands, May 21, 1960; admitted, 1984, Amsterdam. *Education:* University of Leiden. Civil Law Notary. *PRACTICE AREAS:* Corporate; Finance; Business Organization; Joint Venture; Structuring and Restructuring.

GIJS H.J. HEUTINK, born Almelo, The Netherlands, January 24, 1959; admitted, 1985, Utrecht; 1991, Amsterdam. *Education:* University of Utrecht. *PRACTICE AREAS:* Real Estate; Property Development; General Finance; Trade Law.

HENRIËTTE J. BRONSGEEST, born Leiden, The Netherlands, July 22, 1961; admitted, 1986, Amsterdam. *Education:* University of Leiden. *PRACTICE AREAS:* Labour Law; Litigation; General Business; Trade Law.

ASSOCIATES

BAS B. VAN VLIET, born Amsterdam, The Netherlands, March 30, 1960; admitted, 1986, Amsterdam. *Education:* University of Amsterdam. *PRACTICE AREAS:* Construction Law; Environmental; Property Development; Litigation.

K. BERNARD BLIJLEVEN, born Overschie, The Netherlands, December 28, 1959; admitted, 1987, Amsterdam. *Education:* University of Amsterdam. Associate Civil Law Notary. *PRACTICE AREAS:* Property; Finance; Environmental; General Business; Trade Law.

HENRI F. LANTSHEER, born Rotterdam, The Netherlands, April 5, 1958; admitted, 1988, Amsterdam. *Education:* University of Utrecht. *PRACTICE AREAS:* Insolvency; Reorganization; Restructuring; Moratorium; Bankruptcy; General Business; Trade Law.

EP W.J. HANNEMA, born Amsterdam, The Netherlands, September 5, 1961; admitted, 1988, Rotterdam. *Education:* Leyden University. *PRACTICE AREAS:* Insolvency; Reorganization; Restructuring; Moratorium; Bankruptcy; East European Trade.

ERIK H. DEUR, born Amsterdam, The Netherlands, February 20, 1963; admitted, 1989, Dordrecht. *Education:* University of Leiden. *PRACTICE AREAS:* Employment Law; Litigation; General Business; Trade Law.

ANNERIE M.J.M. PLOUMEN, born Eys-Wittem, The Netherlands, July 28, 1964; admitted, 1988, Amsterdam. *Education:* University of Leiden. Associate Civil Law Notary. *PRACTICE AREAS:* Property; Corporate; Finance Law.

JOOST E.W. HOUTMAN, born Breda, The Netherlands, August 19, 1962; admitted, 1990, Amsterdam. *Education:* University of Groningen. *PRACTICE AREAS:* Information Technology; Licensing; Litigation; General Business; Trade Law.

MARC C.S. DE BOER, born The Hague, The Netherlands, September 10, 1964; admitted, 1990, Amsterdam. *Education:* University of Amsterdam. *PRACTICE AREAS:* Intellectual Property; Trademark Infringement; Copyright; Entertainment; Licensing; Litigation.

CAROLINE P. BLEEKER, born Dordrecht, The Netherlands, August 1, 1965; admitted, 1990, Amsterdam. *Education:* University of Leiden. *PRACTICE AREAS:* Agency; Franchising; Distribution; General Business; Trade Law.

ARIE C. DE GROOT, born Haarlem, The Netherlands, February 6, 1964; admitted, 1991, Amsterdam. *Education:* University of Amsterdam. *PRACTICE AREAS:* Consumer Right; General Terms and Conditions; Warranty Protection; Disclaimers; General Business; Trade Law.

(This Listing Continued)

NINE J. VAN HOEK, born Oegstgeest, The Netherlands, November 2, 1965; admitted, 1991, Amsterdam. *Education:* University of Leiden. *PRACTICE AREAS:* Corporate; Business Organization; General Business; Trade Law.

PETER B. HEMMES, born Groningen, The Netherlands, April 18, 1964; admitted, 1991, Amsterdam. *Education:* University of Leiden. *PRACTICE AREAS:* Litigation; Contracting; General Trade.

GEORGE F.J.M VAN ZINNICQ BERGMANN, born Berlicum, The Netherlands, July 10, 1964; admitted, 1992, The Netherlands. *Education:* University of Utrecht. *PRACTICE AREAS:* Labour Law; Litigation; General Business; Trade Law.

DAPHNE C. KOENE, born Amsterdam, The Netherlands, January 18, 1967; admitted, 1992, Amsterdam. *Education:* University of Amsterdam. *PRACTICE AREAS:* Intellectual Property; General Business; Trade Law.

PETER L.F. FELIX, born Amersfoort, The Netherlands, January 6, 1966; admitted, 1993, The Netherlands. *Education:* University of Amsterdam; Dickinson School of Law. *PRACTICE AREAS:* Employment Law; General Business; Trade Law.

CEES VAN DE VEGT, born Utrecht, The Netherlands, January 23, 1965; admitted, 1993, The Netherlands. *Education:* University of Utrecht. *PRACTICE AREAS:* Business Organization; Contracting; Trade Law.

ROSE MARIE C. APPEL, born Delft, The Netherlands, January 11, 1968; admitted, 1993, Amsterdam. *Education:* University of Leiden. Associate Civil Law Notary. *PRACTICE AREAS:* General Corporate; Property and Family Law.

HANNA M. ISKE-MEESTER, born Leidschendam, The Netherlands, October 18, 1966; admitted, 1993, Amsterdam. *Education:* University of Leiden. *PRACTICE AREAS:* Business Organization; General Business; Trade Law.

JOHANNES BUNTJER, born Schiedam, The Netherlands, November 11, 1967; admitted, 1994, Amsterdam. *Education:* University of Leiden. *PRACTICE AREAS:* Business Organization; General Business; Trade Law.

ANNE MARIE DIJKHUIZEN, born Veenendaal, The Netherlands, May 12, 1970; admitted, 1994, Amsterdam. *Education:* University of Utrecht. *PRACTICE AREAS:* Business Organization; General Business; Trade Law.

Individual Lawyers of Ekelmans Den Hollander are Members of: the International Bar Association, Union International des Avocats, Association International des Jeune Avocats, the Interlex Group, Club Oasis, Network 92.

Languages: Dutch, English, French, German and Spanish

EVERAERT ADVOKATEN

Immigration Lawyers

WETERINGSCHANS 28

1017 SG AMSTERDAM, THE NETHERLANDS
Telephone: (31) 20-6271181
Fax: (31) 20-6273231

FIRM PROFILE: Established in 1982, Everaert Immigration Lawyers provides a knowledgeable experienced team of eight solicitors to assist clients in following the step-by-step procedures now mandatory for obtaining visas, work and residence permits in The Netherlands. In this field Everaert Advokaten is the largest and best known firm in The Netherlands. Everaert Immigration Lawyers has built up a considerable reputation throughout The Netherlands for providing expert advice and assistance to business firms and private individuals for all matters related to relocation to The Netherlands, whether it be for temporary stay or for the establishment of residency or citizenship. The firm is a member of the Europea Immigration Lawyers Group, a network which provides immigration services by specialized law firms in all EC countries and in Sweden.

PARTNERS

PIETER BOELES, born Rotterdam, The Netherlands, August 1, 1942; admitted, 1975, The Netherlands. Lecturer, European Migration Law, Catholic University of Nijmegen. Member, Standing Committee of Experts on International Immigration, Refugee and Criminal Law. *LANGUAGES:* English, French and German. *PRACTICE AREAS:* Immigration Law.

(This Listing Continued)

EVERAERT ADVOKATEN, Amsterdam—Continued

MICHIEL TJEBBES, born Naarden, The Netherlands, December 16, 1942; admitted, 1971, The Netherlands. *LANGUAGES:* English, French, German, Spanish and Swedish. *PRACTICE AREAS:* Immigration Law.

CARL EVERAERT, born Surabaja, Indonesia, June 27, 1946; admitted, 1975, The Netherlands. Lecturer, Immigration Law, Post Graduate Courses, University of Rotterdam. *LANGUAGES:* English and German. *PRACTICE AREAS:* Immigration Law.

HANS HELSPER, born Amsterdam, The Netherlands, July 16, 1947; admitted, 1987, The Netherlands. *LANGUAGES:* English and German. *PRACTICE AREAS:* Immigration Law.

TED BADOUX, born Aalsmeer, The Netherlands, March 30, 1948; admitted, 1977, The Netherlands. *Member:* European Immigration Lawyers Group (Vice-President). *LANGUAGES:* English, French and German. *PRACTICE AREAS:* Immigration Law.

HANS JAGER, born Amsterdam, The Netherlands, October 2, 1954; admitted, 1980, The Netherlands. *LANGUAGES:* English. *PRACTICE AREAS:* Immigration Law.

GERT JAN VAN ANDEL, born Renkum, The Netherlands, September 14, 1943; admitted, 1987, The Netherlands. *LANGUAGES:* English, French, German and Russian. *PRACTICE AREAS:* Immigration Law.

ASSOCIATES

ALDO KUIJER, born Rotterdam, The Netherlands, June 13, 1960; admitted, 1986, The Netherlands. Lecturer, Immigration Law, State University of Utrecht. *LANGUAGES:* English and German. *PRACTICE AREAS:* Immigration Law.

JEANINE VERHOEF, born Sittard, The Netherlands, December 15, 1958; admitted, 1991, The Netherlands. *LANGUAGES:* English, German and Spanish. *PRACTICE AREAS:* Immigration Law.

GOUDSMIT & BRANBERGEN

Advocaten

J.J. VIOTTASTRAAT 46
1071 JT AMSTERDAM, THE NETHERLANDS
Telephone: (31) (20) 662 30 31
Telefax: (31) (20) 673 65 58

Mailing Address: P.O. Box 75458, 1070 AL Amsterdam, The Netherlands

Insurance and Liability Law, Corporate and Commercial Law, EC and Competition Law, Intellectual and Industrial Property Law (Copyright/Trademarks/Designs and Models/Tradenames), Labor Law, Real Estate and Construction Law, Computer Law, Administrative and Environmental Law, Expropriation Law, Civil Litigation, Mergers and Acquisitions, Leasing.

FIRM PROFILE: The firm, with a history dating back to 1884, has a large commercial and litigation practice with numerous Dutch and foreign clients. It has many personal contacts with lawyers throughout the world through various networks, such as the International Lawyers' Group and its Strategic Alliance with the international law firm of Oppenheimer Wolff & Donnelly (offices in Brussels, specialized in EC-law, international corporate and tax law and Chicago, London, Minneapolis, New York, Paris, St. Paul and Washington DC).

MEMBERS OF FIRM

FREDERIK CASPAR SAMWEL, born Java, Indonesia, September 19, 1933; admitted, 1964, Amsterdam. *Education:* Amsterdam University (Medicine, 1957; Private Law, 1963). *PRACTICE AREAS:* Insurance Law; Product Liability; Environmental Aspects; Torts; Compensation and Litigation.

MAARTEN MUNT FLESSEMAN, born New York, N.Y., November 28, 1942; admitted, 1967, Amsterdam. *Education:* Amsterdam University (Private Law, 1966). *Member:* International Lawyer's Group. *PRACTICE AREAS:* Corporate and Commercial Law; Bankruptcy; Competition Law and Litigation; Mergers and Acquisitions.

EDUARD ARMAND PETER ENGELS, born Velsen, The Netherlands, March 21, 1946; admitted, 1972, Amsterdam. *Education:* Amsterdam University (Private Law, 1970). Alternate Member, International Lawyers' Group. Teacher, Institute on Information Law, Amsterdam Uni-

versity. *PRACTICE AREAS:* Intellectual and Industrial Property; Media Law; Telecommunications and Broadcasting Law; Competition Law and EC Law.

JOHANNES JAN DE BACK, born Goes, The Netherlands, June 20, 1946; admitted, 1973, Amsterdam. *Education:* Free University of Amsterdam (Private Law, 1969; Dissertation, 1971). Teacher, Free University of Amsterdam, 1970-1971. *PRACTICE AREAS:* Labor Law; Real Estate Law.

NELLEKE VAN 'T HOOGERHUIJS, born Rotterdam, The Netherlands, February 3, 1946; admitted, 1978, Amsterdam. *Education:* Amsterdam University (Private Law, 1978). *PRACTICE AREAS:* Family and Matrimonial Law; Labor Law; Rental Law.

PIETER VAN DER NAT, born Zoetermeer, The Netherlands, April 25, 1947; admitted, 1983, Amsterdam. *Education:* Certificate Insurance Broker (1976); Free University of Amsterdam (Private Law, 1983). Editor: Section Insurance and Tort, Bedrijfsjuridische Berichten; Product Liability Handbook and Insurance Courses, Stichting Vakontwikkeling Verzekeringsbedrijf. Teacher: Post-Graduate Courses, Law of Evidence, since 1985 and Compensation on Personal Injury, 1988; Traffic Law, Nijmegen University, 1988. Guest Teacher: Litigation, Leiden University since 1988. *Member:* Dutch Association Personal Injury Lawyers (LSA). *PRACTICE AREAS:* Insurance Law; Product Liability; Environmental Aspects; Torts; Compensation and Litigation.

WILLEM ALEXANDER ROOS, born Haarlem, The Netherlands, August 11, 1954; admitted, 1981, Amsterdam. *Education:* Amsterdam University (Private Law, 1978). *Member:* International Association of Entertainment Lawyers. *PRACTICE AREAS:* Intellectual and Industrial Property Law; Entertainment Law; Computer Law; Labor Law.

SALOMON LAMBERT SCHRAM, born Oosterend, The Netherlands, April 30, 1949; admitted, 1982, Amsterdam. *Education:* Dutch Scientific Institute for Tourism and Recreation (1972); Amsterdam University (Public Law, 1981). Administrative Policy Consultant to Provincial and Municipal Governments, 1976-1982. *Member:* Association of Expropriation Lawyers. *PRACTICE AREAS:* Administrative Law; Expropriation Law; Real Estate Law.

ELIAS JOHANNES RUITENBERG, born Westmaas, The Netherlands, December 24, 1953; admitted, 1982, Amsterdam. *Education:* Leiden University (Chemistry, 1976; Private Law, cum laude, 1982). *PRACTICE AREAS:* Corporate and Commercial Law; Bankruptcy; Real Estate Law; Litigation.

CHARLES YVES MARIE MOONS, born Roermond, The Netherlands, May 30, 1957; admitted, 1983, Amsterdam. *Education:* Leiden University (Private Law, Constitutional and Administrative Law, 1981); Bayler Law School, Texas (Environmental Law, Constitutional and Administrative Law, 1980). *PRACTICE AREAS:* Constitutional and Administrative Law; Real Estate and Environmental Law; Labor Relations; Commercial Law and Litigation.

PETRUS MARIA KLINCKHAMERS, born Terneuzen, The Netherlands, June 24, 1961; admitted, 1985, Maastricht; 1987, Amsterdam. *Education:* Amsterdam University (Private and Administrative Law, 1985). Teacher: Post-Graduate Courses, Labor Law, 1990, Free University of Amsterdam. Co-Editor, "Schikken en Onderhandelen," 1990. *Member:* International Labor Lawyer's Group. *PRACTICE AREAS:* (International) Labor Law; Labor Relations; Social Security; Litigation.

MARGOT BAKHUIS, born Breda, The Netherlands, January 17, 1964; admitted, 1988, Amsterdam. *Education:* Institut d'Etudes Françaises pour Etudiants Etrangers connected to the University Aix-Marseille, France (1983); Amsterdam University (Private Law, 1987). *PRACTICE AREAS:* Corporate and Commercial Law; Litigation; Leasing.

ASSOCIATES

MARINUS MATTHEUS MACLEAN, born Rotterdam, The Netherlands, May 25, 1955; admitted, 1988, Amsterdam. *Education:* Free University of Amsterdam (Private Law, 1983). Lecturer, Free University of Amsterdam, 1983-1988. Teacher, Post-Graduate Courses, Free University of Amsterdam, 1986-1991. Guest Lecturer, EEC-Directive, Nissan Motorcompany, 1988. *PRACTICE AREAS:* Insurance; Liability Law.

MARTIJN ROBERT LAUXTERMANN, born Amsterdam, The Netherlands, December 17, 1965; admitted, 1990, Amsterdam. *Education:* Amsterdam University (Private and Notarial Law, 1990). *PRACTICE AREAS:* Insurance; Liability Law.

(This Listing Continued)

GERARD CHRISTIAAN ENDEDIJK, born Arnhem, The Netherlands, November 9, 1964; admitted, 1991, Amsterdam. *Education:* Utrecht University (History, Private and Criminal Law, 1990). *PRACTICE AREAS:* Insurance; Liability Law; Criminal Law.

GRAHAM, SMITH & PARTNERS

Established in 1988

KONINGSLAAN 34
1075 AD AMSTERDAM, THE NETHERLANDS
Telephone: +31 20 5712500
Fax: +31 20 6733656

Rotterdam, The Netherlands Office: Parklaan 1. Telephone: +31 10 436 5144. Telefax: +31 10 436 2162.

Dutch and International Tax Law including Value Added Taxation, Inheritance Taxes, Social Security and Tax Litigation.

PARTNERS

JOHN GRAHAM, born 1954. *Education:* University of Birmingham (UK); University of Amsterdam. *Member:* Dutch Association of Tax Advisors; IBA; IFA; ITPA. *LANGUAGES:* English, Dutch, French, German and Italian. *PRACTICE AREAS:* International Tax Law.

FRED BOOTSMA, born 1959. *Education:* University of Amsterdam (Master in Civil and Tax Law). *Member:* Dutch Association of Tax Advisors; IBA; IFA; ITPA. *LANGUAGES:* Dutch, English and German. *PRACTICE AREAS:* International Tax Law; Family Owned Business.

ASSOCIATES

ROELOF VOS, born 1965. *Education:* University of Groningen (Master of Law). *Member:* Dutch Association of Tax Advisors; Dutch Bar Association, IBA. *LANGUAGES:* Dutch, English, French, German and Spanish. *PRACTICE AREAS:* Value Added Tax; Customs and Excise Duties.

RUTGER HAFKENSCHEID, born 1964. *Education:* University of Groningen (Master of Tax Law). Assistant Professor, International Tax Law, Erasmus University Rotterdam. *Member:* IBA; ITPA. *LANGUAGES:* Dutch, English and German. *PRACTICE AREAS:* International Reorganizations; Mergers and Acquisitions; Financing Instruments and International Financing Structures.

GERDIE RECHTUIJT, born 1966. *Education:* University of Amsterdam (Master in Tax Law, 1991). *Member:* Dutch Association of Tax Advisors. *LANGUAGES:* Dutch, English, French and German. *PRACTICE AREAS:* Wage Tax and International Social Security; Income Tax; Corporate Income Tax; Inheritance and Estate Tax.

HÖCKER, RUEB & DOELEMAN

Established in 1987

VAN EEGHENSTRAAT 80
1071 GK AMSTERDAM, THE NETHERLANDS
Telephone: 020-6711301
Fax: 020-6719710

International Grouping:
Associated with Compton, Carr, Solicitors, 6 Dyers Buildings, Holborn, London EC 1 N2 Jt.

Firm engaged in the The Netherlands, European and International Law Practice. Entitled to plead before The Netherlands Courts.

FIRM PROFILE: *Höcker, Rueb & Doeleman is a middle size Amsterdam law firm with a history dating back to 1967. The present structure is the result of a merger in 1987. The firm consists of several lawyers who have consciously left "large" firms in search for direct client relationships and high quality against acceptable rates. The know-how within the firm is not only the result of wide experience but is also achieved by means of lawyers who are/were (part-time) attached to universities and who publish regularly. Höcker, Rueb & Doeleman works closely together with civil law notaries and tax advisors and has formal and informal ties with law firms outside the Netherlands. The firm seeks to render tailored services to its wide range of clients from individuals to multinationals.*

Höcker, Rueb and Doeleman handles all main areas of commercial Netherlands, European and International Law, which, apart from general commercial and contract law, includes a.o. corporate law (acquisitions, mergers, restructuring, joint ventures and establishing of new companies), employment and labour law, housing/rental/real estate, intellectual property

(This Listing Continued)

(trade mark, copyright, computer law), media/entertainment/advertising/-promotion, bankruptcy/insolvency, litigation/arbitration, EC and competition, distribution/agency/franchise, code of ethics (Dutch bar), administrative law.

PARTNERS

ADOLF S. RUEB, admitted, 1974, Amsterdam. *PRACTICE AREAS:* Housing; Rental Law and Real Estate; Litigation/Arbitration.

FREDERIK W. GROSHEIDE, admitted, 1967, Amsterdam. *PRACTICE AREAS:* Intellectual Property; Copyright, Media and Entertainment.

ANTONIUS M. HÖCKER, admitted, 1973, Amsterdam. *PRACTICE AREAS:* Mergers and Acquisitions; Bankruptcy and Insolvency; Litigation/Arbitration.

HERMAN F. DOELEMAN, admitted, 1974, Amsterdam. *PRACTICE AREAS:* Intellectual Property; Employment and Labour Law.

GERM J. KEMPER, admitted, 1975, Amsterdam. *PRACTICE AREAS:* Mergers and Acquisitions; Copyright, Media and Entertainment.

LEO A.M. SAPIR, admitted, 1977, Amsterdam. *PRACTICE AREAS:* Employment and Labour Law; General Commercial and Contract Law.

OTTO ALBERS, admitted, 1986, Amsterdam. *PRACTICE AREAS:* Employment and Labour Law.

LUCAS J. VAN EEGHEN, admitted, 1979, Amsterdam. *PRACTICE AREAS:* General Commercial and Contract Law.

GERDA J. DRIESSEN, admitted, 1982, Amsterdam. *PRACTICE AREAS:* Family Law and Labor Law.

J. ANTOINE ENDTZ, admitted, 1984, Amsterdam. *PRACTICE AREAS:* Corporate and Business; EC and Competition.

GIJSBERT BRUNT, admitted, 1985, Amsterdam. *PRACTICE AREAS:* Employment Law; Computer Law; Intellectual Property.

MARC WOLTERS, admitted, 1989, Amsterdam. *PRACTICE AREAS:* Mergers and Acquisitions; Bankruptcy and Insolvency; Litigation/Arbitration.

FROTHO K.A. DE HAAN, admitted, 1991, Amsterdam. *PRACTICE AREAS:* Corporate and Business.

All Members are Members of the Amsterdam Bar.

HOEGEN DIJKHOF & VAN BRAKEL

Established in 1976

EMMASTRAAT 40
1075 HW AMSTERDAM, THE NETHERLANDS
Telephone: (31)-20-6791801
FAX: (31)-20-6769081

Utrecht, The Netherlands Office: Wilhelminapark 24, P.O. Box 14215, 3508 SH Utrecht, 3581 NE Utrecht. Telephone: (31) 30-520220. Fax: (31) 30-516885.

Mergers Law, International Tax Law, Business Law, Labour Law, Intellectual and Industrial Property, Computer Law, EC Law, Commercial Litigation and Arbitration.

MEMBERS OF FIRM

HANS J. HOEGEN DIJKHOF, born Doetinchem, Netherlands, June 5, 1947; admitted, 1973, Rotterdam; 1976, Utrecht; 1990, Amsterdam. *Education:* Baarns Lyceum, Baarn; Gymnasium A; Utrecht University Law School (Cand. with Honors, 1970; Doct. with Honors, 1972), specializing in Company Law and Law of International Organizations, especially EEC Law, Post Doctoral Exams in Administrative Law, Tax Law, Dutch Economic Law, International Law. Chairman, Integrated Advisory Group IAG International, 1989—, an Association of Independent Professional Firms with 80 offices throughout Europe and the U.S.; Honorary President, 1993—. *Member:* Amsterdam, Dutch and International Bar Associations. *LANGUAGES:* Dutch, English, German, French and Italian. *PRACTICE AREAS:* Mergers Law; International Tax Law; Business Law.

HANS C. VAN BRAKEL, born Beesd (Gld), Netherlands, February 28, 1950; admitted, 1974, Maastricht; 1976, Utrecht. *Education:* Utrecht University Law School (Cand. 1970; Doct., 1973); Economic University at Tilburg, Post Doctoral Examination in Analyzing Financial Statements. *Member:* Utrecht, Dutch and International Bar Associations. *LANGUAGES:*

(This Listing Continued)

HOEGEN DIJKHOF & VAN BRAKEL, Amsterdam—
Continued

Dutch, English, German and French. **PRACTICE AREAS:** Business Law; Intellectual Property Law; Computer Law; Litigation.

ASSOCIATES

LOUISE G. DE GIER, born Bunnik, Netherlands, October 15, 1960; admitted, 1987, Utrecht. *Education:* Utrecht University Law School (Cand., 1982; Doct., 1985); Free University of Brussels (Master, International Comparative Law, LL.M., 1986)). *Member:* Utrecht and Dutch Bar Associations. **LANGUAGES:** Dutch, English, French, German and Italian. **PRACTICE AREAS:** EC Law; International Law; Intellectual Property Law.

RICHARD H.M. RUIJGROK, born Delft, Netherlands, June 27, 1957; admitted, 1990, Amsterdam. *Education:* Leyden University Law School (Doct., 1984). Candidate Notary, Post-doctoral exams in Administrative Law and Criminal Law, 1980-1987. Honorary Consul, 1987— and Honorary Consul-General, 1984—, Thailand in Amsterdam. Business Advisor, specialized in South-East Asia. Member, Order of Notaries. *Member:* Amsterdam and Dutch Bar Associations. **LANGUAGES:** Dutch, English, German, French and Thai. **PRACTICE AREAS:** Business Law; International Taxation Law.

RENATE J.E. REIDINGA, born Loenen, Netherlands, April 20, 1966; admitted, 1992, Utrecht. *Education:* Utrecht University of Law School (Doct., 1991). *Member:* Utrecht and Dutch Bar Associations. **LANGUAGES:** Dutch, English, French and German. **PRACTICE AREAS:** Litigation; Administrative Law; Insurance Law.

J. EDGAR STAM, born Utrecht, Netherlands, February 26, 1965; admitted, 1993, Utrecht. *Education:* Utrecht University of Law School (Cand., 1985; Doct., 1990). Johns Hopkins University School of Advanced International Studies, Bologna, Italy (Bologna Center Diploma, 1990). *Member:* Utrecht and Dutch Bar Associations. **LANGUAGES:** Dutch, English, German, Italian, French and Russian. **PRACTICE AREAS:** Business Law; International Contracts; Labour Law.

AAD DE BRUIJN, born Abidjan, Ivory Coast, April 13, 1967; admitted, 1994, Utrecht. *Education:* University of Amsterdam Law School (Cand., 1990; Doct., 1993); School of Advanced Economic Studies of Amsterdam (International Management, Diploma, 1989); University of Bordeaux, Diplome d'Etudes Francaises, June 1986. *Member:* Utrecht and Dutch Bar Associations. **LANGUAGES:** Dutch, English, German and French. **PRACTICE AREAS:** Insurance Law; Transport Law; Contracts.

HOUTHOFF

Advocaten

PARNASSUSWEG 126
1076 AT AMSTERDAM, THE NETHERLANDS
Telephone: (31) (20) 57 00 200
Facsimile: (31) (20) 57 00 280

Mailing Address: P.O. Box 75505, 1070 AM Amsterdam

Rotterdam, The Netherlands Office: WEENATOREN, Weena 355, 3013 AL ROTTERDAM, The Netherlands. Mailing Address: P.O. Box 1507, 3000 BM ROTTERDAM, The Netherlands. Telephone: (31) (10) 2244666. Fax: (31) (10) 2244668.

Houthoff is one of the Netherlands' leading law firms. It was formed in 1970 by merging three long established Amsterdam commercial prctice law firms. our history goes back to the year 1815. In 1991 Houthoff reinforced its presence in Rotterdam through the merger with a prominent Rotterdam firm.

Firm consisting of attorneys at law, civil law notaries and tax advisors engaged in the Law regarding Mergers and Acquisitions, Joint Ventures, Corporations, Incorporation of Legal Entities, Business Transactions, Venture Capital, Antitrust, Real Estate and Construction, Banking, International Finance, Reorganisations, Bankruptcy and Insolvency, Insurance and Reinsurance, Employment and Labor, National and International Taxation, Computers and Software, Telecommunications, Media and Entertainment, Trade Marks, Copyright, Patents, Designs and Models, Advertising, Medical and Professional Liability, Government Regulations, Environmental Issues, Immigration, Litigation and Arbitration, Trust Services, European Community Law, Government and Utilities Procurement, Energy Law.

(This Listing Continued)

EU1028B

LEO J. BOUCHEZ, born Eindhoven, The Netherlands, 1932; admitted, 1979, Amsterdam. *Education:* Utrecht University (Master of Laws, 1957; LL.D. cum laude, 1963); Cambridge University, United Kingdom (Diploma in International Law, 1961); Research Certificate, The Hague Academy of International Law (1961). Recipient, Kluwer Prize 1966 for "The Legal Régime of Bays in International Law", 1964. Assistant and Lecturer at the Law School of the University of Utrecht, 1958-1969. Professor in International Law at the University of Utrecht and Legal Counsel to several companies. Rapporteur of the Deep Sea Mining Committee of the International Law Association, 1967-1975. Rapporteur of the Symposium on the International Regime of the Sea Bed, organized by l'Instituto di Affari Internazionali, Rome. Rapporteur of the Legal Committee of the Technical Conference of the F.A.O. on Maritime Pollution and the Living Resources of the Sea, Rome, 1970. Counsel to the Conference Pacem in Maribus, Malta, 1970. Member of a group of Experts of the OECD dealing with the legal aspects of transfrontier pollution, 1975. Member of the Consultative Committee of the Ministry of Justice on the reform of the Netherlands Penal Code concerning public morality legislation, 1970-1973. Chairman, Committee established by a group of industries dealing with the legal aspects of the construction of Artificial Islands in the North Sea, 1973-1974. Legal Counsel of Alaska and Louisiana with respect to their claims to adjacent waters, 1969-1970. President, Committee on Environmental Law of the Netherlands Association of International Law, 1975-1978. Member of several consultative committees of the Netherlands Government dealing with legal questions on the Law of the Sea, 1975-1979. President, Committee dealing with the Reform of Legal Education in the Law Faculty of the University of Utrecht, 1978-1979. Professor of International Business Law, Utrecht University, 1985-1988. Member, Advisory Board on matters of International Law of the Netherlands Ministry of Foreign Affairs. Member, Netherlands Council on Maritime Scientific Research. Member, Board of Editors, The Netherlands Yearbook of International Law. Member, Advisory Board of the Journal of Maritime Law and Commerce (New York). Corresponding Member of the Associacion Argentina del Derecho Internacional. **LANGUAGES:** Dutch and English. **PRACTICE AREAS:** Energy; International; Arbitration.

FRITZ H.A. ARISZ, born Groningen, The Netherlands, 1933; admitted, 1958, Amsterdam. *Education:* Groningen University (Master of Laws, 1956). Substitute Judge Amsterdam Court of Appeal, 1977—. **LANGUAGES:** Dutch, English and French. **PRACTICE AREAS:** Litigation; Arbitration; Insurance Law; Professional Liability Law.

ERICK W. VAN SLOOTEN, born Haarlem, The Netherlands, 1935; admitted, 1960, Amsterdam. *Education:* University of Amsterdam (Master of Laws, 1959). *Member:* Netherlands Association for Insurance Studies. **LANGUAGES:** Dutch and English.

RUUD H.L. POST, born Utrecht, The Netherlands, 1938; admitted, 1965, Amsterdam. *Education:* Utrecht University (Master of Laws, 1965). Substitute Cantonal Judge. **LANGUAGES:** Dutch and English.

BERT NIEMAN, born Hoogeveen, The Netherlands, 1938; Appointed Civil Law Notary, 1981. *Education:* Groningen University (Master of Laws, 1963). In-house Legal Counsel C&A, 1968-1979. Chairman, Ring Amsterdam Koninklijke Notariële Broederschap, 1989-1991. **LANGUAGES:** Dutch and English.

ANTOON KASDORP, born Roermond, The Netherlands, 1940; admitted, 1981, Amsterdam. *Education:* University of Amsterdam (Master of Laws, 1966). Assistant Tax Law Department, University of Amsterdam, 1963-1968. Associate, Van Keulen International Tax Law, 1969-1971. Senior Partner, Van Brunschot & Kasdorp, 1971-1973. Senior Partner, Moret Gudde Brinkman International, 1973-1979. Senior Partner, Kasdorp c.s., 1979-1981. Chairman, The Netherlands Bar Association's Committee for Tax Law. **LANGUAGES:** Dutch and English.

JAN A.M. NEIJZEN, born Monnickendam, The Netherlands, 1943; appointed Civil Law Notary, 1981. *Education:* University of Amsterdam (Master of Laws, 1970). **LANGUAGES:** Dutch and English.

HANS J. VAN ES, born Hilversum, The Netherlands, 1944; admitted, 1970, Amsterdam. *Education:* University of Leyden (Master of Laws, 1968). Member, The Amsterdam Bar Disciplinary Council. Substitute Cantonal Judge. **LANGUAGES:** Dutch, English and German. **PRACTICE AREAS:** Commercial Law; Insolvency; Employment.

ENNO VAN DER SCHANS, born The Hague, The Netherlands, 1945; admitted, 1970, Amsterdam. *Education:* Free University of Amsterdam (Master of Laws, 1968). Substitute Judge, Amsterdam District Court. Substitute Cantonal Judge, Amsterdam. *Member:* The Netherlands Bar Associ-

(This Listing Continued)

ation; International Bar Association (Committees F and 7). *LAN-GUAGES:* Dutch, English, German and French. *PRACTICE AREAS:* Administrative Law; Government; Environmental Law.

MARTEN MEES, born Rotterdam, The Netherlands, 1946; admitted, 1973, Amsterdam; 1976, Supreme Court The Hague, readmitted 1989, Amsterdam. *Education:* University of Leyden (Master of Laws, 1973; Master of Tax Law, 1973). Attorney and Tax Advisors, The Hague and New York Offices, Loyens & Volkmaars, 1973-1980 and 1984-1989; Tax Litigation before Tax Courts, Supreme Court and Court of Justice of the European Communities and litigation on Oil and Gas Taxation before Council of State, 1983-1989. Senior Staff Attorney to tax chamber of the Supreme Court, 1980-1983. Substitute Judge, Tax Court of Appeals, 1993. Publications: Netherlands report for International Fiscal Association Congress, 1977. *LANGUAGES:* Dutch, English, German and French. *PRACTICE AREAS:* International Taxation; Tax Litigation.

ERIC R.S.M. MARRES, born Maastricht, The Netherlands, 1946; admitted, 1974, Amsterdam. *Education:* Free University of Amsterdam (Master of Laws, 1974). Substitute Cantonal Judge. Member, Netherlands Association for Insurance Studies. Member, Association of Attorneys for Personal Injury claims. *LANGUAGES:* Dutch and English.

HANS C. SCHREUDER, born Amsterdam, The Netherlands, 1946; admitted, 1973, Amsterdam. *Education:* Free University of Amsterdam (Master of Laws, 1970); University of Virginia (LL.M., 1971). Substitute Judge, Amsterdam District Court. *LANGUAGES:* Dutch, English, French and German. *PRACTICE AREAS:* Banking; Financing; Securities; Mergers and Acquisitions.

PETER L.M. HUSTINX, born 's-Hertogenbosch, The Netherlands, 1947; admitted, 1972, Rotterdam; 1974, Amsterdam. *Education:* Utrecht University (Master of Laws, 1972). Reporter, Risk Aggravation in Insurance Law. *Member:* Netherlands Association for Insurance Studies. *LANGUAGES:* Dutch and English.

JANKEES A.C. HOUTHOFF, born Amsterdam, The Netherlands, 1947; admitted, 1976, Zutphen; 1991, Rotterdam; 1994, Amsterdam. *Education:* Advanced School for Economics and Business Administration, Amsterdam (1971); University of Leyden (Master of Laws, 1976). Founder and Chairman, Young Lawyers Association, Zutphen, 1977. *LANGUAGES:* Dutch and English.

LAURENCE W. GORMLEY, born Macclesfield, United Kingdom, 1953; called to the Bar of England and Wales (Middle Temple), 1978; (Not admitted in The Netherlands). *Education:* Oxford University (M.A., Hons. in Modern History & Modern Languages (German), 1975); London School of Economics (M.Sc., European Studies, 1978); Inns of Court School of Law (Barrister, Middle Temple, 1978); Utrecht University (LL.D., 1985); Salzburg Seminar, 1988. Recipient, Hon. Sir Peter Bristow Award, Middle Temple, 1978; Rotary Foundation Graduate Fellowship (at Utrecht University), 1978. Professor of European Law and Head of the Department of European and Economic Law, Groningen University; Visiting Professor of EC Law, University College, London, United Kingdom. Professor at the College of Europe, Bruges & Warsaw. Previously: an Official of the Commission of the European Communities, Brussels, Belgium, 1983-1990; Hon. Visiting Lecturer then Senior Lecturer, University College, London, 1988-1990; Lecturer in Law (Assistant then Associate Professor), Liverpool University, United Kingdom, 1980-1984. Consulting Editor, European Business Law Review. Member, Editorial Board, Public Procurement Law Review and European Business Law Review. Correspondent, European Law Review. Myriad publications on European Community Law, including: Prohibiting Restrictions on Trade within the EEC (North Holland, 1985); Kapteyn & VerLoren van Themaat: Introduction to the Law of the European Communities (Kluwer Law & Taxation. 2nd ed., 1983), and contributions to Halsbury's Laws of England (Butterworths, 4th. ed., Vol. 52, 1986). *LANGUAGES:* Dutch and English.

REINOUT DE WAAL, born Blovstrød, Denmark, 1950; admitted, 1981, Amsterdam. *Education:* Erasmus University Rotterdam (Master of Laws, 1975); Legal Researcher, Institut de Droit Comparé, University of Paris, II (1976). International Tax Advisor: Moret Gudde Brinkman International, 1976-1979; Kasdorp c.s., 1979-1981. Co-Author: "Forme et Preuve du Contrat" and "Les Vices du Consentement dans la Contrat," published by Professor René Rodière, Paris, Ed. Pedone, 1977. *LANGUAGES:* Dutch, English, French and German. *PRACTICE AREAS:* Corporate and Commercial Law; Mergers and Acquisitions; Industry; Venture Capital.

MAARTEN A.J.M. SCHOLTENS, born Deventer, The Netherlands, 1950; (Not admitted in The Netherlands). *Education:* Groningen University (Master of Laws, 1978). Appointed Civil Law Notary, 1993. Member, In-

(This Listing Continued)

ternational Fiscal Association. Lecturer, University of Nijmegen (professional training). *LANGUAGES:* Dutch and English. *PRACTICE AREAS:* Corporate Law.

JACOB F.A. DOELEMAN, born Utrecht, The Netherlands, 1952; admitted, 1980, Amsterdam. *Education:* Groningen University (Master of Laws, 1979). Assistant Groningen University Dept. of International Relations, 1975-1977. Officer, United Nations Forces in Lebanon, 1979. Resident Lawyer, Nutter McClennen & Fish, Boston, Mass., 1987. Member: IBA, Media and Communications Law, Copyright Law and Commercial Law. *LANGUAGES:* Dutch and English. *PRACTICE AREAS:* Corporate; Competition and Telecommunication Law.

MARJAN A. GOSLINGS, born Leiden, The Netherlands, 1951; admitted, 1980, Amsterdam. *Education:* University of Leyden (Bachelor of Social Science, 1972; Master of Laws, 1979). Publication: "Medical Experiments With Healthy Volunteers, Liability: Fault or No Fault?" in "Report on the VIIIth Congress of the World Association for Medical Law, Prague, 1988, Report II, page 190-198"; "Incorrect Evaluation of Cytological Material: Aspects of Law," (Lecturer for the Dutch Association for Pathologist, held in October 1991). Appointments: Former Assistant Secretary of One of the Regional Disciplinary Counsels of the Netherlands Institute for Psychologists, 1980-1984. Former Assistant Secretary, College of Medical Disciplinary Law, Amsterdam, 1984-1992. Secretary to a threesome Regional Disciplinary Counsels of the Dutch Dental Association, 1990—. Member of the Counsel of the Amsterdam Bar, 1992—. *LANGUAGES:* Dutch, English and German. *PRACTICE AREAS:* Litigation; Arbitration; Insurance Law; Professional Liability Law.

TJAKKO A. KNOOP PATHUIS, born Hengelo, The Netherlands, 1951; admitted, 1982, Amsterdam. *Education:* University of Leyden (M.A. Faculty of Political Science and International Public Law, 1977; Master of Laws, 1978). Junior Lecturer, Public and Constitutional Law, Leyden University, 1977-1978. *LANGUAGES:* Dutch and English.

R. SEBASTIAAN LE POOLE, born Rotterdam, The Netherlands, 1956; admitted, 1982, Amsterdam. *Education:* University of Leyden (Master of Laws, 1981). *Member:* The Netherlands Association for Computers and Law; The Netherlands Association for Media and Communication Law; The Netherlands Association for Copyright Law. Publications: "Protection of T.V.-formats," Mediaforum, 1992. *LANGUAGES:* Dutch, English and German. *PRACTICE AREAS:* Media and Entertainment Law; Intellectual Property Law; Information Technology Law.

ARENT G.J. VAN WASSENAER, born Den Helder, The Netherlands, 1956; admitted, 1983, Amsterdam. *Education:* Groningen University (Master of Laws, 1983). Worked at Nutter McClennen & Fish, Boston, U.S.A., January through September, 1988. Publications: "How Procurement is regulated," (Dutch), Kluwer, 1990; "Claiming Reclamation - Six years of arbitration in public procurement disputes in the Netherlands," International Construction Law Review, January 1993; "The Day after the Battle of Britain - Towards an alternative competition system in construction?" (Dutch), Dutch Journal for Construction Law (Bouwrecht), January 1993; "The developing government after the EC-Directives Works (71/305/EEC) and Services (92/50/EEC)" (Dutch), Dutch Journal for Construction Law (Bouwrecht), August 1993; "Art. 7.17.7 New Civil Code, a clause with an interesting defect" (Dutch), in "In volle verzakerdheid" (Dutch), Kluwer 1993; "Standard regulations in construction: a useful option?" (Dutch), Publication Dutch Society for Construction Law, 1993; Member of Dutch Society for Construction law, 1993; Member of Dutch Society for Construction Law, International Bar Association, Committee. Lecturer at Grotius Academy. *LANGUAGES:* Dutch, English and German. *PRACTICE AREAS:* Construction Law; Bankruptcy.

GIJSBERT C.L. VAN LEEUWEN, born Amsterdam, The Netherlands, 1956; admitted, 1983, Amsterdam. *Education:* Free University of Amsterdam (Master of Laws, 1980). Directorate of General Policy Affairs Ministry of Defense, 1981-1982. Assistant to the Secretary General of Defense, 1982-1983. Worked at Nutter McClennen & Fish, Boston, U.S.A., February through November 1989. Author of Chapter 13 - The Netherlands, International Corporate Governance, Euromoney Publications PLC, London (1990). *LANGUAGES:* Dutch and English. *PRACTICE AREAS:* Banking and (Corporate) Finance; Corporate Law and Securities; Trade and Transport.

RINSKE C. VAN RAMSHORST-CNOSSEN, born Utrecht, The Netherlands, 1946; admitted, 1979, Amsterdam. *Education:* Free University of Amsterdam (1975). *Member:* Netherlands Litigation Association. *LANGUAGES:* Dutch, English and German. *PRACTICE AREAS:* Professional Negligence Civil Law Notaries; Employment.

(This Listing Continued)

HOUTHOFF, Amsterdam—Continued

JAAP HOEKSTRA, born Rotterdam, The Netherlands, 1958; admitted, 1984, Amsterdam. *Education:* University of Leyden (Master of Law, 1983). Legal Advisor to National Territorial Commander, Royal Dutch Army, 1983-1984. Publications: Report for the Netherlands Society for construction law; Enforcement of planning law, 1991. Editor, Environmental Law-letter. *LANGUAGES:* Dutch and English.

JAAP H.W. KOSTER, born Utrecht, The Netherlands, 1958; admitted, 1985, Amsterdam. *Education:* University of Leyden (Master of Laws, 1983). Secretary of the Military Court of Justice, Arnhem, The Netherlands, 1983-1985. Publications: co-author of a reference book on Dutch environmental liability. *LANGUAGES:* Dutch, English and French. *PRACTICE AREAS:* Environmental Law; Administrative Law; Real Estate; Privatisation; Public-Private Partnership; Public Transport; Liability of Public Bodies; Zoning Law.

ARIE BOUMAN, born Strijen, The Netherlands, 1952; admitted, 1993, Amsterdam. *Education:* Groningen University (Master of Tax Law, 1979). Inspector of Income Revenue Tax, 1980-1986. Inspector of Corporate Revenue Tax, 1986-1989. Partner, Berkleef & Bouman, Tax Advisors, 1989-1990. *LANGUAGES:* Dutch and English. *PRACTICE AREAS:* Tax; Corporate Law.

MICHIEL VAN BREMEN, born Curaçao, The Netherlands Antilles, 1959; admitted, 1985, Amsterdam. *Education:* University of Amsterdam (Master of Laws, 1984); City of London Polytechnic, United Kingdom (Certificate English Law, 1982); King's College London and London School of Economics, United Kingdom (1984-1985). Co-Author: "How and Why the U.S. finally joined the Berne International Copyright Convention," Leiden Journal of International Law, Volume 2 Nr. 1 (May 1989, p. 83-90). *LANGUAGES:* Dutch and English. *PRACTICE AREAS:* Venture Capital; General Commercial.

H. WOLTER WEFERS BETTINK, born Deventer, The Netherlands, 1953; admitted, 1987, Amsterdam. *Education:* University of Utrecht (Master of Laws, 1979). Ministry of Transport, Shipping Department, 1980-1984. Adviser on shipping legislation to the Ministry of Communications, Indonesia (1984-1987). Trademark Attorney, Member of the Benelux Trade Mark and Model Right Association. Rapporteur to the ALAI-conference on the protection of ideas, Barcelona, October 1992. Co-author of various reports of the Netherlands Association on copyright. *LANGUAGES:* Dutch, English, German and French. *PRACTICE AREAS:* Copyright, Trademarks; Patents; Information Technology.

LOUIS C. M. KUYPERS, born 1954; admitted, 1987, Amsterdam. *Education:* Free University of Amsterdam (1977); University of Amsterdam (1981) Tax Consultancy. *LANGUAGES:* Dutch, English, German and French. *PRACTICE AREAS:* Business Law; Tax Law; Pension Law.

ASSOCIATES

ANNETTE VOLDERS, born Bussum, The Netherlands, 1945; admitted, 1982, Amsterdam. *Education:* Free University of Amsterdam (Master of Laws, 1980). *Member:* Netherlands Bar Association (Member: Committee for Family Law). *LANGUAGES:* Dutch, English and German. *PRACTICE AREAS:* Liability; Family Law.

GIENEKE J. VAN WULFFTEN PALTHE-SCHOLTEN, born Ermelo, The Netherlands, 1957; admitted, 1982, Amsterdam. *Education:* University of Leyden (Master of Laws, 1982). *LANGUAGES:* Dutch and English.

A. PATRICIA PRENT, born Enschede, The Netherlands, 1959; admitted, 1987, Amsterdam. *Education:* Free University of Amsterdam (M.A. French Language and Literature, 1983); Utrecht University (Master of Laws, 1986). *LANGUAGES:* Dutch, English, French and German. *PRACTICE AREAS:* Employment; Housing.

E.M. NOOR VAN GILS, born Wageningen, The Netherlands, 1961; admitted, 1987, Amsterdam. *Education:* University of Amsterdam (Master of Laws, 1986). *LANGUAGES:* Dutch, English, German and Spanish. *PRACTICE AREAS:* Insurance Law; Liability Litigation; Labour Law.

ANDREW E.L. TUCKER, born Canberra, Australia, 1963; admitted, 1988, Victoria, Australia; 1991, England and Wales. *Education:* University of Melbourne (Bachelor of Arts; Bachelor of Laws, with honours, 1987); University of Oxford (Bachelor of Civil Laws, 1992). Solicitor at Corrs Chambers Westgarth, Melbourne, 1987-1989. Senior Research Officer at High Court of Australia, Canberra, Australia, 1989-1990. Solicitor at Herbert Smith, London, 1990-1991. *LANGUAGES:* Dutch and English. *PRACTICE AREAS:* EC Law; Energy Law; Central and Eastern Europe.

(This Listing Continued)

L.J. ELSBETH VAN RHIJN, born The Hague, The Netherlands, 1963; admitted, 1988, Amsterdam. *Education:* Groningen University (Master of Laws, 1987). Law Clerk, Wilmer, Cutler & Pickering, Washington, D.C., 1987. *LANGUAGES:* Dutch, English and French. *PRACTICE AREAS:* Mergers and Acquisitions; Telecommunications; Automotive Industry.

MARRY T.H. DE GAAY FORTMAN, born Amsterdam, The Netherlands, 1965; admitted, 1988, Amsterdam. *Education:* Free University of Amsterdam (Master of Laws, 1988). Marshall to Justice C. Schiemann, London, U.K., 1987. *LANGUAGES:* Dutch and English.

PHILIPPE N.M. CREIJGHTON, born Linschoten, The Netherlands, 1963; admitted, 1988, Amsterdam. *Education:* University of Leyden (Master of Laws, 1987). *LANGUAGES:* Dutch and English.

MIGNON H. DE LANGE, born Voorburg, The Netherlands, 1963; admitted, 1988, Amsterdam. *Education:* University of Leyden (Master of Laws, 1988). *LANGUAGES:* Dutch, English and German. *PRACTICE AREAS:* Trade and Transport; Secured Transactions.

MARTINE BIJKERK, born Harderwijk, The Netherlands, 1964; admitted, 1989, candidate civil law notary. *Education:* Free University Amsterdam (Master of Laws, 1989). *LANGUAGES:* Dutch and English. *PRACTICE AREAS:* Corporate Law.

MICHIEL R. VAN SCHOOTEN, born Bussum, The Netherlands, 1964; admitted, 1989, Amsterdam. *Education:* University of Amsterdam (Master of Laws, 1989). *LANGUAGES:* Dutch and English. *PRACTICE AREAS:* General Commercial; Venture Capital.

JUDITH E. POLAK-VAN PRAAG, born Schiedam, The Netherlands, 1964; admitted, 1989, Amsterdam. *Education:* University of Leyden (Master of Laws, 1989). *LANGUAGES:* Dutch and English.

MICHIEL F. LAMERS, born Rotterdam, The Netherlands, 1963; admitted, 1989, Amsterdam. *Education:* Utrecht University (Master of Laws, 1988). Recruiting Officer, Royal Dutch Navy, 1988-1989. *LANGUAGES:* Dutch and English.

JAN BLOKLAND, born 1963; admitted, 1989, The Hague; 1992, Amsterdam. *Education:* Leyden University (Master of Laws, 1988). *LANGUAGES:* Dutch and English. *PRACTICE AREAS:* Intellectual Property; Insurance Law.

I. WEYER VERLOREN VAN THEMAAT, born Brussels, Belgium, 1962; admitted, 1990, Amsterdam. *Education:* University of Amsterdam (Master of Laws, 1988); City of London Polytechnic (Certificate English Law, 1986). Trainee European Commission, 1988-1989. *Member:* Netherlands Federation for European Law; Netherlands Anti-Trust Law Association. *LANGUAGES:* Dutch and English. *PRACTICE AREAS:* European Law; Anti-trust Law; Competition Law.

RONALD H.C. BIEMANS, born Steenwijk, The Netherlands, 1961; admitted, 1990, Hertogenbosch; 1993, Amsterdam. *Education:* Tilburg University (Master of Laws, 1989; Master of International Law, 1990); University of Leuven, Belgium (1989-1990). Teacher European Law Tilburg University, 1989-1990. *LANGUAGES:* Dutch, English and German. *PRACTICE AREAS:* Insolvency Law.

BEREND J. SCHOLTEN, born The Hague, The Netherlands, 1964; admitted, 1990, Rotterdam; 1992, Amsterdam. *Education:* University of Groningen (Master of Laws, 1988). *LANGUAGES:* Dutch and English. *PRACTICE AREAS:* Construction Law.

MARCEL R. DE ZWAAN, born Appingedam, The Netherlands, 1962; admitted, 1990, Amsterdam. *Education:* Groningen University (Master of Laws, 1986). Legal Affairs, Staff, 1986-1989 and Assistant Managing Director, 1989-1990, Holland Festival. *LANGUAGES:* Dutch and English.

LUYKE T. VENEMA, born Hellevoetsluis, The Netherlands, 1964; admitted, 1990, Amsterdam. *Education:* Free University of Amsterdam (Master of Laws, 1988). Recruiting Officer, Royal Dutch Navy, 1989-1990. *LANGUAGES:* Dutch and English.

EDWARD S. DE BOCK, born Amsterdam, The Netherlands, 1965; admitted, 1990, Amsterdam. *Education:* Free University of Amsterdam (Master of Laws, 1988; Master of Notarial Law, 1990). *LANGUAGES:* Dutch and English. *PRACTICE AREAS:* General Commercial; Corporate Law.

ELIZABETH VAN SCHILFGAARDE, born Rotterdam, The Netherlands, 1965; admitted, 1991, Amsterdam; 1992, New York. *Education:* University of Utrecht (Master of Laws, cum laude, 1989); Harvard Law School (LL.M., 1990). Author: "Negligence under the Netherlands Civil Code - an

(This Listing Continued)

economic analysis," 21 Cal. W. Intl. L. J. 265 (1990). *LANGUAGES:* Dutch and English. *PRACTICE AREAS:* Commercial Litigation; General Commercial.

REMMERT M. SLUIJTER, born Haarlem, The Netherlands, 1965; admitted, 1991, Amsterdam. *Education:* Bates College, Lewiston ME, USA (1983-1984); University of Amsterdam (Master of Laws, 1990); Catholic University of Nijmegen (Tax Law, 1989-1990). Associate in the Mergers and Acquisitions Department of Amsterdam-Rotterdam Bank in Sydney, Australia, 1988-1989 and in Amsterdam, The Netherlands, 1989-1990. *LANGUAGES:* Dutch, English and French. *PRACTICE AREAS:* Financial Law; Mergers and Acquisitions.

ROBERT R. CRINCE LE ROY, born Utrecht, The Netherlands, 1964; admitted, 1991, Amsterdam. *Education:* University of Utrecht (Master of Public Administration, 1989; Master of Laws, 1989). *LANGUAGES:* Dutch and English.

ALEXANDER E.H. VAN DER VOORT MAARSCHALK, born The Hague, The Netherlands, 1965; admitted, 1991, Amsterdam. *Education:* University of Groningen (Master of Tax Law, Master of Laws, 1989). *LANGUAGES:* Dutch and English. *PRACTICE AREAS:* Tax.

RUTGER M. PRAKKE, born Amsterdam, The Netherlands, 1966; admitted, 1991, Amsterdam. *Education:* University of Amsterdam (Master of Laws, 1991). *LANGUAGES:* Dutch and English. *PRACTICE AREAS:* Venture Capital; General Commercial.

MYRIAM H.J. JANSEN, born Doetinchem, The Netherlands, 1965; admitted, 1991, Amsterdam. *Education:* University of Utrecht (Master of Laws, 1990). *LANGUAGES:* Dutch and English.

GEERTJE E. SLUIJK, born Amsterdam, The Netherlands, 1966; admitted, 1992, Amsterdam. *Education:* University of Leyden (Master of Laws, 1990); University of London, England (LL.M., 1991). *LANGUAGES:* Dutch and English. *PRACTICE AREAS:* Administrative Law; Immigration Law.

ANNETTE M. VAN KALMTHOUT, born De Bilt, The Netherlands, 1966; admitted, 1992, Amsterdam. *Education:* University of Leyden (Master of Laws, 1991). *LANGUAGES:* Dutch and English.

J.A. COOSJE R.W. VAN DER HOEVEN, born Leyden, The Netherlands, 1963; admitted, 1991, Rotterdam. *Education:* University of Leyden (Master of Laws, 1988). *LANGUAGES:* Dutch and English.

PIETER G. VAN DRUTEN, born Vriezenveen, The Netherlands, 1962; Candidate Civil Law Notary, 1992. *Education:* University of Leyden (Master of Laws, 1992). *LANGUAGES:* Dutch and English. *PRACTICE AREAS:* Corporate Law.

WAPKE VELDHUIJZEN VAN ZANTEN, born Amsterdam, The Netherlands, 1964; admitted, 1992, Amsterdam. *Education:* University of Amsterdam (Master of Laws, 1991). *LANGUAGES:* Dutch and English.

EDO R. ANKUM, born Aerdenhout, The Netherlands, 1965; admitted, 1992, Amsterdam. *Education:* University of Amsterdam (Master of Laws, 1990). *LANGUAGES:* Dutch and English.

SUSAN C. LAMBRECHTSEN, born Brielle, The Netherlands, 1966; admitted, 1992, Amsterdam. *Education:* University of Leyden (Master of Laws, 1991). *LANGUAGES:* Dutch and English.

J. DOUWE UDING, born The Hague, The Netherlands, 1964; admitted, 1992, Amsterdam. *Education:* University of Leyden (Master of Laws, 1992). *LANGUAGES:* Dutch and English.

MONIQUE FAVEREY, born Groningen, The Netherlands, 1964; admitted, 1992, Amsterdam. *Education:* University of Utrecht (Master of Laws, 1991; Bachelor of Laws in International Law, 1991). Winner (Utrecht Team) of the National Rounds of the Philip C. Jessup International Law Moot Court Competition, 1988-1989 and winner of the Elona E. Evans Award, 1988-1989, Chicago. *LANGUAGES:* Dutch and English. *PRACTICE AREAS:* General Commercial.

MARTINE C. PIJNAPPELS, born Abcoude, The Netherlands, 1966; admitted, 1992, Amsterdam. *Education:* University of Utrecht (Master of Laws, cum laude, 1989); University of Georgia, U.S.A. (LL.M., 1991); Düsseldorf, Germany (Certificate German Law, 1992). *LANGUAGES:* Dutch and English. *PRACTICE AREAS:* General Commercial.

HANS LONDONCK SLUIJK, born Amstelveen, The Netherlands, 1968; admitted, 1993, Amsterdam. *Education:* University of Amsterdam (Master of Laws, 1992; Master of Communication Science, 1992). *LANGUAGES:* Dutch and English.

(This Listing Continued)

DIRK JAN RUTGERS, born Heemstede, The Netherlands, 1966; admitted, 1993, Amsterdam. *Education:* University of Leyden (Master of Laws, 1991). *LANGUAGES:* Dutch, English and German. *PRACTICE AREAS:* Labour Law.

MACHTELD I.M. GEERTSEMA, born Haarlemmermeer, The Netherlands, 1966; admitted, 1993, Amsterdam. *Education:* University of Leyden (Master of Laws, 1992). *LANGUAGES:* Dutch and English.

CASPAR O. WENKEBACH, born The Hague, The Netherlands, 1968; admitted, 1993, Amsterdam. *Education:* University of Leyden (Master of Laws, 1991); University of London (LL.M., 1992). *LANGUAGES:* Dutch and English.

CHARLES A.C.G. DE LOË, born Mheer, The Netherlands, 1967; admitted, 1993, Amsterdam. *Education:* University of Utrecht (Master of Laws, 1992). European Commission D9 VII, International Shipping Politics, 1992-1993. *LANGUAGES:* Dutch and English.

MARTIEN PELINCK, born Apeldoorn, The Netherlands, 1967; admitted, 1993, Amsterdam. *Education:* University of Groningen (Master of Laws, 1993). *LANGUAGES:* Dutch, English, German and French. *PRACTICE AREAS:* Tax.

HERMAN L. KAEMINGK, born Hoogeveen, The Netherlands, 1967; admitted, 1993, Amsterdam. *Education:* Free University of Amsterdam (Master of Laws, 1993). Editor of Students' Law Review Ars Aequi, 1989-1993. *LANGUAGES:* Dutch, English and German. *PRACTICE AREAS:* General Commercial.

PIETER L. VAN DELDEN, born Utrecht, The Netherlands, 1968; admitted, 1993, Amsterdam. *Education:* University of Leyden (Master of Laws, 1993). *LANGUAGES:* Dutch, English, French and German.

REIN M. EVERARD, born Bloemendaal, The Netherlands, 1963; admitted, 1993, Amsterdam. *Education:* University of Amsterdam (Master of Laws, 1993). *LANGUAGES:* Dutch, English and German. *PRACTICE AREAS:* Administrative Law; Environmental Law.

MARC J.L. VAN CAMPEN, born Venlo, The Netherlands, 1969; admitted, 1994, Amsterdam. *Education:* University of Amsterdam (Masters of Laws, 1992); London School of Economics (Masters of Laws of Taxation, 1993). *LANGUAGES:* Dutch and English.

ANNETTE C. OLLAND, born De Bilt, The Netherlands, 1968; admitted, 1993, Amsterdam. *Education:* University of Leyden (Masters of Laws, 1992; Bachelor of Arts (French), 1993). *LANGUAGES:* Dutch and English. *PRACTICE AREAS:* Employment.

PATRICK L.G. HACCOU, born Groningen, The Netherlands, 1967; admitted, 1993, Amsterdam. *Education:* University of Leyden (Master of Laws, 1992). *LANGUAGES:* Dutch and English.

JAN J.H. JOOSTEN, born The Hague, The Netherlands, 1967; admitted, 1994, Amsterdam. *Education:* University of Leyden (Master of Laws, Master of Law, 1989); Harvard Law School (LL.M., 1992). Foreign Associate Hughes, Hubbard & Reed, Washington, D.C., 1992. *Member:* American Bar Association. *LANGUAGES:* Dutch and English. *PRACTICE AREAS:* General Commercial.

B.E. ELODIE VAN SYTZAMA, born Zuidelijke Ijsselmeerpolders, The Netherlands, 1967; admitted, 1993, Amsterdam. *Education:* University of Leyden (Master of Laws, 1993). *LANGUAGES:* Dutch and English.

Languages: Dutch, English, German, French, Spanish.

KENNEDY VAN DER LAAN

Established in 1992

HERENGRACHT 466

P.O. BOX 15744

1001 NE AMSTERDAM, THE NETHERLANDS

Telephone: 31-20-550.6666

Fax: 31-20-550.6777

Information Technology Law, International Commercial Transactions and Arbitrations, Tort Law and Litigation, Real Estate Law, Labor and Employment Law, Intellectual Property Law, Construction Law, Administrative Law, Insolvency, Business Law.

(This Listing Continued)

KENNEDY VAN DER LAAN, Amsterdam—Continued

MEMBERS OF THE FIRM

MARIAN KENNEDY, born 1948; admitted, 1974, California and U.S. District Court, Northern District of California, USA; 1982, New York, USA; 1988, Amsterdam. *Education:* University of Connecticut (B.A., 1970); University of Santa Clara Law School (J.D., summa cum laude, 1974); Harvard Law School (LL.M., 1980); University of Leiden (J.D., Dutch Law, 1989). *Member:* New York State and American Bar Associations; State Bar of California (Member, Sections on: International Law; Business Law) U.S. Computer Law Association; Netherlands Association for Computers and Law. Fellow: The Chartered Institute of Arbitrators (London). *LANGUAGES:* English and Dutch. *PRACTICE AREAS:* Information Technology Law; International Arbitrations.

PETER C.M. BRANDJES, born 1951; admitted, 1977, Amsterdam. *Education:* University of Amsterdam (1976). *LANGUAGES:* English. *PRACTICE AREAS:* Real Estate Law; Administrative Law; Litigation.

EBERHARD E. VAN DER LAAN, born 1955; admitted, 1984, Amsterdam. *Education:* Vrije Universiteit Amsterdam (1983). Council Member, City of Amsterdam, 1990—. *Member:* Netherlands Association for Personal Injury Lawyers. *LANGUAGES:* English and German. *PRACTICE AREAS:* Torts; Insurance and Real Estate Law; Litigation; Criminal Law.

HENK L. VREEMAN, born 1953; admitted, 1980-1983, Rotterdam, The Netherlands; 1982, New York, USA; 1983, California and U.S. District Court, Southern District of California, USA; 1993, Amsterdam. *Education:* University of Groningen (1979); Harvard Law School (LL.M., 1980). Fulbright Scholar. In-house Counsel and Executive Vice-President, industrial group, Corpeq B.V., 1986-1993. *Member:* New York State and American Bar Associations; State Bar of California. *LANGUAGES:* English. *PRACTICE AREAS:* Business Law; International Commercial Transactions.

RICHARD H.G. KLATTEN, born 1964; admitted, 1988, Utrecht; 1992, Amsterdam. *Education:* University of Rotterdam (1988). Author: The Works Council: Requirements & Procedures, 1981. *Member:* Netherlands Association for Labor Law. *LANGUAGES:* English. *PRACTICE AREAS:* Labor and Employment Law; Business Law; Litigation.

COEN E. DRION, born 1956; admitted, 1988, Rotterdam; 1991, Amsterdam. *Education:* University of Groningen (1988). *Member:* Netherlands Association for Computers and Law; Netherlands Society for Computer Science; Netherlands Society for Civil Law; Benelux Study Group on Industrial Property. *LANGUAGES:* English, French and German. *PRACTICE AREAS:* Information Technology Law; International Commercial Transaction; International Arbitrations.

MARCEL A.L.M. WILLEMS, born 1962; admitted, 1989, Amsterdam. *Education:* Catholic University of Nijmegen (1981-1983); University of Leiden (1983-1985); Freie Universität Berlin (1985-1986); Universität Osnabrück (1986); University of Leiden (1987). *Member:* Association for Construction Law; Association for Insolvency Law. *LANGUAGES:* English and German. *PRACTICE AREAS:* Insolvency Law; Commercial Transactions; Business Law; Real Estate Law; Litigation.

KEES STUURMAN, born 1956; admitted, 1989, Amsterdam. *Education:* Vrije Universiteit Amsterdam (Physics, 1981; Law, 1985). Assistant Professor of Computer Law, Vrije Universiteit, Amsterdam, 1987-1989. Research Associate, Computer Law Institute, Vrije Universiteit Amsterdam, 1985-1987, 1989—. *Member:* Netherlands Association for Computers and Law (Board Member, 1986-1994); International Bar Association; Union International des Avocats; U.S. Computer Law Association; Netherlands Society for Computer Science. *LANGUAGES:* English. *PRACTICE AREAS:* Information Technology Law; Commercial Transactions; Litigation.

TOM A. NIEUWENHUIJSEN, born 1955; admitted, 1990, Amsterdam. *Education:* University of Amsterdam (1985). Corporate Lawyer, National Housing Board, 1983-1990. *LANGUAGES:* English and German. *PRACTICE AREAS:* Real Estate Law; Construction Law; Insolvency Law; Administrative Law.

CHRIS H. VAN DIJK, born 1961; admitted, 1990, Amsterdam. *Education:* Vrije Universiteit Amsterdam (1984). Professional Training for Judicial Appointment, 1986-1992. Author, Computer Crimes, 1994. *Member:* Netherlands Association for Personal Injury Lawyers. *LANGUAGES:* English. *PRACTICE AREAS:* Insurance Law; Criminal Law; Information Technology Law.

ALFRED P. MEIJBOOM, born 1960; admitted, 1990, Amsterdam. *Education:* Vrije Universiteit Amsterdam (1985). Co-Editor: Software Protection in the European Community, 1993; The Law of Information Technology in Europe 1992, 1992. Research Fellow, Computer Law Institute, Vrije Universiteit Amsterdam, 1985-1992. *Member:* International Bar Association; Netherlands Copyright Association; Netherlands Society for Computer Science; U.S. Computer Law Association; Benelux Study Group on Industrial Property; Netherlands Association for Computers and Law. *LANGUAGES:* English and German. *PRACTICE AREAS:* Intellectual Property Law; Litigation; Information Technology Law; Commercial Transactions.

OF COUNSEL

LOEK J. MALMBERG, born 1942; admitted, 1980-1991, Rotterdam. *Education:* University of Leiden (1967). General Counsel and Chief Financial Officer, Group 4 Securitas. Frequent Arbitrator: International Chamber of Commerce; Netherlands Arbitration Institute. *LANGUAGES:* Arabic, English, French and German. *PRACTICE AREAS:* International Arbitrations; Business Law; Corporate Law.

ASSOCIATES

ERWIN VAN DER WIEL, born 1958; admitted, 1986, Rotterdam. *Education:* Erasmus University Rotterdam (1985). Teacher of General Principles of Law at University of Rotterdam. *LANGUAGES:* English and German. *PRACTICE AREAS:* Real Estate Law; Construction and Project Development Law; Facility Management (Outsourcing) Law; Litigation.

CAROLINE E.M. MALMBERG, born 1963; admitted, 1988, Rotterdam. *Education:* Erasmus University Rotterdam (1988). *LANGUAGES:* English. *PRACTICE AREAS:* Business Law; Banking Law; Corporate Finance Law.

DIEDERIK WACHTER, born 1963; admitted, 1989, The Hague; 1990, Amsterdam. *Education:* University of Amsterdam (1988). *Member:* Netherlands Association for Personal Injury Lawyers. *LANGUAGES:* English. *PRACTICE AREAS:* Insurance Law; Torts; Litigation.

MADELEINE W. VAN ROON, born 1962; admitted, 1990, Amsterdam. *Education:* University of Amsterdam (1990). *Member:* International Bar Association; Netherlands Association for Computers and Law; Netherlands Copyright Association. *LANGUAGES:* English and German. *PRACTICE AREAS:* Information Technology Law; Intellectual Property Law; International Contracting; Litigation.

GERRARD C. BOOT, born 1961; admitted, 1990, Amsterdam. *Education:* University of Amsterdam (B.L., cum laude, 1986). *Member:* Netherlands Association for Labor Law (Study Group Dismissal Law). *PRACTICE AREAS:* Labor Law.

ESMÉ M. KALSHOVEN, born 1968; admitted, 1993, Amsterdam. *Education:* University of Leiden (1986-1992); University of Salamanca, Spain (1990). *LANGUAGES:* Spanish and English. *PRACTICE AREAS:* Torts; Insurance Law.

JOOST J. LINNEMANN, born 1964; admitted, 1993, Amsterdam. *Education:* University of Amsterdam (1992). Information Technology Consultant, 1990-1992. *Member:* Netherlands Society for Computer Science; Netherlands Association for Computers and Law; Netherlands Copyright Association. *LANGUAGES:* English, French and German. *PRACTICE AREAS:* Information Technology Law; Intellectual Property Law.

MARLIES S.A. VEGTER, born 1965; admitted, 1993, Amsterdam. *Education:* University of Amsterdam (1991). *LANGUAGES:* English. *PRACTICE AREAS:* Labor and Employment Law; Social Security Law.

OTTO M.B.J. VOLGENANT, born 1969; admitted, 1993, Amsterdam. *Education:* Vrije Universiteit Amsterdam (1993). *Member:* Netherlands Association for Computers and Law; Netherlands Society for Computer Science; Netherlands Copyright Association; Netherlands Association of Media and Communications Law. *PRACTICE AREAS:* Information Technology Law; Intellectual Property Law.

EVELIEN MENTINK, born 1969; admitted, 1994, Amsterdam. *Education:* University of Leiden (1988-1994); University of Salamanca, Spain, (1992). *LANGUAGES:* English and Spanish. *PRACTICE AREAS:* Real Estate Law; Insurance Law; Torts.

REINOUD J.J. WESTERDIJK, born 1968; admitted, 1994, Amsterdam. *Education:* University of Leiden (1986-1990). Author, Thesis, "Products Liability for Software," 1995. Research Fellow, Computer Law Institute and Private Law Department, Vrije Universiteit Amsterdam, 1990-1994. *Member:* Netherlands Association for Computers and Law. *LAN-*

(This Listing Continued)

(This Listing Continued)

GUAGES: English and German. PRACTICE AREAS: Information Technology Law; Torts.

THERA F. HESSELINK, born 1966; admitted, 1995, Amsterdam. Education: University of Groningen (1989). Professional training for judicial appointment, 1990—. LANGUAGES: English. PRACTICE AREAS: Insurance Law; Real Estate Law; Criminal Law.

FROUKE VLASKAMP, born 1966; admitted, 1995, Amsterdam. Education: University of Groningen (1990). Department of Social Affairs, international labor relations, staff advisor, 1991-1995. PRACTICE AREAS: Labor and Employment Law.

KORTELAND & PARTNERS

HAAKSBERGWEG 49
1101 BR AMSTERDAM, THE NETHERLANDS
Telephone: +31 20 691 08 56
Fax: +31 20 691 07 26

Dutch and International Tax Law.

FIRM PROFILE: Korteland & Partners is an independent firm with offices in Amsterdam and The Hague. The firm's services include: Advice on all matters of Netherlands tax and company law, advice on all matters of EC, Netherlands Antilles and international taxation, negotiation of tax rulings, filing of tax returns, filing of appeals in tax procedures, planning, structuring and coordination of investments and projects for international clients, guiding of national and international mergers and acquisitions, management buy-ins and management buy-outs.

Korteland & Partners works closely together with Netherlands solicitors, civil law notaries and accountants and has informal ties with numerous law offices outside of the Netherlands. This enables Korteland & Partners to offer its clients ready access to legal specialists in and outside the Netherlands.

CEES G.J. KORTELAND, born 1951. Education: University of Leyden (Master in Tax and Civil Law). LANGUAGES: Dutch, English and French. PRACTICE AREAS: Dutch, Netherlands Antilles and International Tax Law; Dutch Contract and Company Law; International Tax Planning; Death Duty and Gift Tax; Litigation in Tax Cases.

CAMIEL J.L. ENGELEN, born 1965. Education: University of Tilburg (Master in Tax Law). LANGUAGES: Dutch, English, Spanish and French. PRACTICE AREAS: Tax Planning; Criminal Law in Tax Cases; Dutch Contract and Company Law.

ERIK HULSKER, born 1967. Education: University of Leyden (Tax Law). LANGUAGES: Dutch and English. PRACTICE AREAS: Preparation and Filing of Tax Returns.

FRANK M.J. VAN NIEUWBURG, born 1960. Education: University of Leyden (Master in Tax Law); University of Rotterdam (Master in Business Administration). LANGUAGES: Dutch, English and German. PRACTICE AREAS: Dutch, International and Netherlands Antilles Tax Law; Preparation and Negotiation of Tax Rulings; Mergers and Acquisitions.

PETER M.H. VAN NIEUWBURG, born 1963. Education: University of Leyden (Master in Tax Law). LANGUAGES: Dutch, English and German. PRACTICE AREAS: Dutch and International Tax Law; International Tax Planning; Death Duty and Gift Tax; Litigation in Tax Cases.

KLAAS VAN DER VALK, born 1949. Education: University of Leyden (Master in Tax Law). LANGUAGES: Dutch and English. PRACTICE AREAS: Dutch and Netherlands Antilles Tax Law; Preparation and Negotiation of Tax Rulings; Studies upon Tax Incentives in Europe; Pension and Stock Option Schemes.

ELLEN VAN DER VALK-CLAASSEN, born 1952. Education: University of Leyden (Master in Civil Law). LANGUAGES: Dutch and English. PRACTICE AREAS: Dutch Contract and Company Law; Mergers and Acquisitions.

BARBARA C. VAN WELSEM, born 1970. Education: University of Leyden (Master in Tax Law). LANGUAGES: Dutch and English. PRACTICE AREAS: Dutch Tax Law; Preparation and Filing of Tax Returns.

LOEFF CLAEYS VERBEKE

15 APOLLOLAAN
P.O. BOX 75088
1070 AB AMSTERDAM, THE NETHERLANDS
Telephone: 31-20-5741200
Telex: 14292 LEX NL
Telecopier: 31-20-6718775

Brussels, Belgium Office: 268 A Avenue de Tervueren, A-1150. Telephone: 02-778.22.11. Fax: 02-763.21.85.

Liege, Belgium Office: 13, Rue Simonon, (Place de Bronckart), B-4000. Telephone: 32-41-527722. Telecopier: 32-41-527511.

Antwerp, Belgium Office: "De Hertoghe," 8th Floor, 92 Desguinlei, B.8, B-2018. Telephone: 32.3.2385656. Telex: 72748 (EURLAWB). Telecopier: 32.3.2387877.

New York, New York Office: Swiss Bank Tower, 23rd Floor, 10 East 50th Street, 10022. Telephone: 212-759-9000. Fax: 212-759-9018.

Paris, France Office: 1, Avenue Franklin D. Roosevelt, 75008. Telephone: 33-1-49539125. Telecopier: 33-1-42891460.

Rotterdam, The Netherlands Office: 70 Weena, P.O. Box 74, 3000 AB. Telephone: 31-10-4034777. Telex: 23395 (LEX NL). Telecopier: 31-10-4149388.

Singapore Office: 20 Raffles Place, #08-03, Ocean Towers, Singapore 0104. Telephone: 65-5335332. Fax: 65-5330313.

Tokyo, Japan Office: NSE Building, 5th Floor, 1-7-1 Kanda Jinbo-Cho. Telephone: 81-3-32599831. Telecopier: 81-3-32599888.

Barcelona, Spain Office: 550, 4° 1A, Av. Diagonal, 08021. Telephone: 34-3-2007117. Telecopier: 34-3-2023098.

Madrid, Spain Office: Balañá Eguía, Antonio Mauro 7, 5°, 28014. Telephone: 34-1-5312501. Telecopier: 34-1-5313530.

Jakarta, Indonesia Associated Office: Ali Budiardjo, Nugroho, Reksodiputro, Niaga Tower, 24th floor, Jalan Jenderal Sudirman Kav. 58, 12920. Telephone: 62.21.2505125/2505136, Telecopier: 62.32.2505121/2505001.

Luxembourg, Luxembourg Office: Zeyen Beghin Feider. 67, Rue Ermesinde, P.O. Box 5017, 1050. Telephone: 352.468946. Telex: 60736 (zflaw lu). Telecopier: 352.468947.

Dutch attorneys may represent clients before all Dutch Courts, before the European Court of Justice and the Benelux Court of Justice, and are admitted to plead before all Courts of the Memberstates of the Common Market (EEC).

MEMBERS OF FIRM

CAREL A. ADRIAANSENS, born 1947; admitted, 1989, Amsterdam. Education: Tilburg University (1973); Delft University (Doctor Juris, 1990). Professor of Law, Limburg University, 1984—. Member: Netherlands Association for Construction Law.

JOHAN L.F. BAKKER, born 1947; appointed Civil Law Notary, 1984. Education: Vrije Universiteit Amsterdam (1972). Member: International Fiscal Association.

WILLEM H. VAN BAREN, born 1956; admitted, 1988, Amsterdam. Education: Amsterdam University (1984); Harvard School of Public Health (M.P.H., 1985). Member: Netherlands Association of Medical Law; American Society for Law and Medicine; Harvard Club of the Netherlands (Member, Governing Board).

MICHAEL W. DEN BOOGERT, born 1943; admitted, 1973, Amsterdam. Education: Nijmegen University (1969, 1973). Editor, "Takeovers and Asset Protections," 1988 (Dutch language). Member: International Bar Association; Netherlands Commercial Law Association.

MAARTEN DAS, born 1948; admitted, 1975, Amsterdam. Education: Vrije Universiteit Amsterdam (1973). Member: International Bar Association.

PETER V. EIJSVOOGEL, born 1958; admitted, 1984, New York and Amsterdam. Education: University of Amsterdam (1982); New York University (M.C.J., 1983). Member: Association Internationale des Jeunes Avocats; American Bar Association.

JAAP W. HAMMING, born 1946; admitted, 1972, Utrecht; 1986, Amsterdam. Education: Utrecht University (1972). Member: Netherlands Institute for Planning and Environmental Law; Netherlands Association for Construction Law.

HUBERT J.M. HARMELING, born 1955; admitted, 1983, Amsterdam. Education: Nijmegen University (1983). Paris Office, 1987-1989. Con-

(This Listing Continued)

LOEFF CLAEYS VERBEKE, Amsterdam—Continued

tributor/Member, Advisory Bar, "World Intellectual Property Report". *Member:* Association Internationale des Jeunes Avocats (Commercial Law Section); Netherlands Copyright Association; Ligne Internationale du Droit de la Concurrence; United States Trademark Association; Marques.

AART D.G. HEERING, born 1941; appointed Civil Law Notary, 1976. *Education:* Vrije Universiteit Amsterdam (1969). *Member:* Union Internationale du Notariat Latin U.I.N.L. (Chairman, Netherlands Delegation EEC-section); International Fiscal Association.

ERIC P.A. KEYZER, born 1953; admitted, 1979, Amsterdam. *Education:* Leyden University (1976). *Member:* Association Internationale des Jeunes Avocats (Member, Committee on Arbitration and Committee on Execution of Foreign Judgments); Association Internationale pour la Protection de la Propriété Industrielle; Association Littéraire et Artistique Internationale.

JOHAN D. KLEYN, born 1949; admitted, 1976, Utrecht; 1980, Amsterdam. *Education:* Utrecht University (1976); University of London (1978); New York University (LL.M., 1980). New York Office, 1984-1989. *Member:* International Fiscal Association; International Bar Association; New York State Bar Association; The Association of the Bar of the City of New York; Union International des Avocats; American Arbitration Association (Panel Member).

J. ANDRÉ VAN DER KOLK, born 1953; admitted, 1977, The Hague; 1982, Rotterdam; 1992, Amsterdam. *Education:* Utrecht University (1976); Northwestern University, Chicago (LL.M., 1977). *Member:* Netherlands Association for Construction Law; Netherlands Association for Environmental Law; Netherlands Maritime Law Association.

ELISABETH KOOIJ, born 1947; admitted, 1977, Amsterdam. *Education:* Leyden University (1972). New York Office, 1981-1984. *Member:* The New York State Bar Association; Netherlands Commercial Law Association.

A.P. (TED) VAN LIDTH DE JEUDE, born 1942; appointed Civil Law Notary, 1979. *Education:* Utrecht University (1967).

PIETER A. MACKAAIJ, born 1945; acting tax lawyer, 1971. *Education:* Leyden University (Tax Law, 1971).

EBEL MAGNIN, born 1952; acting tax lawyer, 1980. *Education:* University of Delft (Analytical Chemistry, 1973); University of Leyden (Tax Law, 1980). *Member:* Netherlands Association for Tax Law; Dutch Association of Tax Lawyers.

BART J.M.A. MEESTERS, born 1954; admitted, 1982, Amsterdam. *Education:* University of Amsterdam (Law School, 1981; Business School, 1981); Columbia University, New York (LL.M., 1982). New York Office, 1989-1990. *Member:* American Bar Association; The Association of the Bar of the City of New York.

MAARTEN H. MULLER, born 1954; admitted, 1984, Amsterdam. *Education:* Leyden University (1979); Columbia University, New York (M.I.A., 1980). *Member:* American Society of International Law; Netherlands International Law Association.

STEVEN PERRICK, born 1949; admitted, 1973, Rotterdam; 1984, Amsterdam; appointed Civil Law Notary, 1983. *Education:* Nijmegen University (1972; Doctor Juris, 1976). Co-Editor, Asser Series Wills and Estate Laws. Professor, Securities Regulation and Commercial Paper, Erasmus University Rotterdam, 1988. Netherlands Correspondent for the Letters of Credit Report, 1988—. *Member:* International Bar Association; Netherlands Association for International Law.

PIETER W. VAN DER PLOEG, born 1935; appointed Civil Law Notary, 1973. *Education:* Vrije Universiteit Amsterdam (1963). *Member:* Netherlands Commercial Law Association.

JAN C. POSCH, born 1935; appointed Civil Law Notary, 1977. *Education:* University of Amsterdam (1964). *Member:* Netherlands Commercial Law Association.

STEVEN R. SCHUIT, born 1942; admitted, 1970, Groningen; 1972, Rotterdam; 1974, Amsterdam; Licensed Legal Consultant in New York. *Education:* Groningen University (1969). General Editor, "Dutch Business Law". New York Office, 1980-1989. *Member:* International Bar Association; International Fiscal Association; Union Internationale des Avocats; American Bar Association; The Association of the Bar of the City of New York; New York State Bar Association; Netherlands Association for Inter-

(This Listing Continued)

national Law Association; Netherlands Association for European Law; Netherlands-US Chamber of Commerce (Member, Executive Committee).

VICTOR P.G. DE SERIÈRE, born 1949; admitted, 1977, Amsterdam. *Education:* Leyden University (1972); Cambridge University, England (LL.B., 1974). Jakarta Correspondent Office, 1980-1986. New York Office, 1986-1987. Corresponding Editor of: (i) Commercial Arbitration in Asia and the Pacific, 1987; (ii) Tax Treatment of Cost-contribution Arrangements, 1988. *Member:* International Bar Association; Asia-Pacific Law Association; Lawasia; American Bar Association; The Association of the Bar of the City of New York.

ALBERT G. VAN SOLINGE, born 1932; appointed Civil Law Notary, 1969. *Education:* Vrije Universiteit Amsterdam (1957). *Member:* Advisory Committee on Corporate Law of Justice Department of the Netherlands; Joint-Committee on Corporate Law of the Netherlands Bar Association and the Netherlands Association of Civil Law Notaries; Netherlands Commercial Law Association.

LEO J.C.M. SPIGT, born 1948; admitted, 1975, Amsterdam. *Education:* University of Amsterdam (1975). *Member:* International Bar Association.

JAN WILLEM VAN DER STAAY, born 1957; admitted, 1985, Amsterdam. *Education:* Utrecht University (1982). *Member:* Netherlands Association for European Law; Netherlands Commercial Law Association.

LEONARD G. VERBURG, born 1955; admitted, 1980, Rotterdam; 1988, Amsterdam. *Education:* Leyden University (1979). *Member:* Association Internationale des Jeunes Avocats; International Pension and Employee Benefit Law Association (IPEBLA); International Society for Labor Law and Security; Netherlands Association for Labor Law; Netherlands Association for Litigation Law; Commercial Law Association.

NIELS VAN DE VIJVER, born 1961; admitted, 1986, Amsterdam. *Education:* University of Amsterdam (Civil Law, 1985; Tax law, 1991).

ROBERT VAN DE VIJVER, born 1934; admitted, 1960 and 1991, Amsterdam. *Education:* University of Amsterdam (1957).

GERBRAND W.CH. VISSER, born 1955; Deputy Civil Law Notary, 1983. *Education:* Groningen University (Notarial Law, 1982; Fiscal Law, 1984). *Member:* Netherlands Commercial Law Association.

ANTON A. VOORNEMAN, born 1947; Deputy Civil Law Notary, 1980. *Education:* University of Amsterdam (1980).

ALLARD VOÛTE, born 1941; admitted, 1969, Amsterdam. *Education:* Utrecht University (1967). *Member:* International Bar Association; Netherlands Commercial Law Association.

ASSOCIATES

J. ALEXANDER ALFERINK, born 1957; Deputy Civil Law Notary, 1984. *Education:* Nijmegen University (1984). *LANGUAGES:* English, French and German.

FRANK W.G. AMBAGTSHEER, born 1951; admitted, 1990, Amsterdam. *Education:* Amsterdam University (1982).

J. CASPER BANZ, born 1963; admitted, 1990, Amsterdam. *Education:* Leyden University (Law School, 1988; School of Economics, 1988).

INE H.P.A. BASTIAENS, born 1969; admitted, 1994, Amsterdam. *Education:* Leyden University (1993).

MAURITS S. BERGER, born 1964; admitted, 1992, Amsterdam. *Education:* University of Utrecht (Law School, 1990; Arabic, 1991).

PATRICK C.T. BERNHART, born 1968; admitted, 1993, Amsterdam. *Education:* Leyden University (1992).

E.H.M. (LISETTE) BIELEVELD, born 1967; admitted, 1992, Amsterdam. *Education:* University of Nijmegen (1991).

BRITTA BÖHLER, born 1960; acting tax lawyer, 1989. *Education:* University of Freiburg, Germany (1984).

RUDOLF VAN BORK, born 1961; Deputy Civil Law Notary, 1990. *Education:* Vrije Universiteit Amsterdam (1989).

CORINE J. BOSCH, born 1966; Deputy Civil Law Notary, 1992. *Education:* University of Leyden (1991).

MONICA L. BREMER, born 1964; admitted, 1992, Amsterdam. *Education:* University of Amsterdam (1988).

(This Listing Continued)

JOHANNES C. BROUWER, born 1962; admitted, 1994, Amsterdam. *Education:* Groningen University (Law School, 1987; Tax Law, 1988); University of New York, U.S.A. (LL.M., 1990).

DICK R. BUTER, born 1960; admitted, 1985, Rotterdam; 1989, Amsterdam. *Education:* Rotterdam University (1984).

ERIK A. BUYS, born 1970; admitted, 1994, Amsterdam. *Education:* Leyden University (1994).

M.J. (THIJS) CLEMENT, born 1959; acting tax lawyer, 1987. *Education:* Amsterdam University (1987).

JACOB K.M.P. CORNEGOOR, born 1968; admitted, 1993, Amsterdam. *Education:* Erasmus University Rotterdam (1993).

ARNOLD R.J. CROISET VAN UCHELEN, born 1961; admitted, 1989, Amsterdam. *Education:* Groningen University (1988).

AREANE A.E. DORSMAN, born 1959; admitted, 1986, Amsterdam. *Education:* University of Amsterdam (1986).

MARIE-ANNE V.E. DREESMANN-BEERKENS, born 1965; admitted, 1990, Amsterdam. *Education:* University of Amsterdam (1990).

DINA A. DUIJM, born 1948; admitted, 1994. *Education:* Utrecht University (1973); New University School of Law (M.C.J., 1992).

RICHARD J. FENS, born 1966; admitted, 1990, Amsterdam. *Education:* Nijmegen University (1988).

CHANTAL B.J.M. GEENEN-TIMMERMANS, born 1951; Deputy Civil Law Notary. *Education:* University of Amsterdam (1975, 1980).

ROBERT D. GEERLINGS, born 1965. *Education:* Amsterdam University (Law School, 1990; International Law, 1992).

JAN MAARTEN GERRETSEN, born 1965; admitted, 1990, Amsterdam. *Education:* Groningen University (1989); Duke University (LL.M., 1990).

WILFRED A. GROEN, born 1966; Deputy Civil Law Notary, 1994. *Education:* Leyden University (1992).

NICK F. HESSELS, born 1969; admitted, 1993, Amsterdam. *Education:* Leyden University (1993).

G.T.J. (JERRY) HOFF, born 1962; admitted, 1990, Amsterdam. *Education:* Leyden University (1985).

ANNEMARIEKE TEN HOONTE, born 1966; admitted, 1991, Amsterdam. *Education:* Nijmegen University (1990). New York Office, 1992-1993.

GEERT H.H.J. JANSSEN, born 1966. Deputy Civil Law Notary, 1992. *Education:* Leyden University (1992).

JAN-ERIK JANSSEN, born 1969; admitted, 1994, Amsterdam. *Education:* Utrecht University (1993).

JEROEN J.M. JANSSEN, born 1968; admitted, 1994, Amsterdam. *Education:* Vrije Universiteit Amsterdam (1994).

MATTHIJS CH. KAAKS, born 1967; admitted, 1992, Amsterdam. *Education:* Leyden University (1991).

J. ONNO VAN KLINKEN, born 1969; admitted, 1993, Amsterdam. *Education:* Leyden University (1993).

GEERT W. VAN DER KLIS, born 1965; admitted, 1990, Amsterdam. *Education:* Vrije Universiteit Amsterdam (1989). *Member:* Netherlands Association for European Law. Brussels Office, 1990-1992.

BRUNO F.G. KOREN, born 1963; admitted, 1992, Maastricht; 1993, Amsterdam. *Education:* Limburg University (1991).

WEERO KOSTER, born 1959; admitted, 1993, Amsterdam. *Education:* Utrecht University (1985). *Member:* International Bar Association; Netherlands Association of Company Lawyers; Netherlands Commercial Law Association; Netherlands Association for Environmental Law.

TINEKE E. LAMBOOY, born 1961; admitted, 1988, Amsterdam. *Education:* Leyden University (1985); Baylor University, Waco, Texas (1986-1987); Grotius Academy, Amsterdam (1988).

JOKE M.M. LAUMANS-VAN DER WIJST, born 1946; Deputy Civil Law Notary, 1990. *Education:* Nijmegen University (1972, Civil Law; 1989, Notarial Law). Lecturer, Conflicts of Law, Nijmegen University.

STEPHANIE E.L. LEIJTEN, born 1966; admitted, 1991, Amsterdam. *Education:* Utrecht University (1991).

(This Listing Continued)

GUY R.P. LOYSON, born 1963; Deputy Civil Law Notary, 1992. *Education:* Leyden University (1991).

JACOLINE DE MAA, born 1967; admitted, 1992, Amsterdam. *Education:* Utrecht University (1992).

CLAUDINE G.H. MAEIJER, born 1965; admitted, 1992, Amsterdam. *Education:* Leyden University (1991).

MANUEL J.W.M. MANDERS, born 1960; Deputy Civil Law Notary, 1989. *Education:* Tilburg University (Fiscal Law, 1987); University of Amsterdam (Notarial Law, 1988).

RIEN H. MEPPELINK, born 1959; Deputy Civil Law Notary, 1985. *Education:* Groningen University (1984).

ALEX TH. MEIJER, born 1969; admitted, 1994, Amsterdam. *Education:* Nijmegen University (1993).

JUDITH C.M. MONTIJN-SWINKELS, born 1961; admitted, 1985, The Hague; 1992, Amsterdam. *Education:* Leyden University (1984). *Member:* Netherlands Association for European Law.

JOHANN H. MULLER, born 1964; acting tax lawyer, 1990. *Education:* Amsterdam University (Tax Law, 1989).

LEENDERT VAN DER NIET, born 1961. Deputy Civil Law Notary, 1989. *Education:* Vrije Universiteit Amsterdam (1989).

MARCO P. NIEUW WEME, born 1965; admitted, 1993, Amsterdam. *Education:* Amsterdam University (1991, 1992).

MARION TH. NIJHUIS, born 1961; admitted, 1987, Amsterdam. *Education:* University of Amsterdam (1986).

EUGENIE NUNES, born 1963; admitted, 1992, Amsterdam. *Education:* Utrecht University (1989).

HENK OTTEN, born 1967; admitted, 1993, Amsterdam. *Education:* Groningen University (School of Economics, 1991; Law School, 1992).

MARIJKE OVERMARS, born 1963; admitted, 1989, Amsterdam. *Education:* Groningen University (1987); University of New York (1988).

HEMMO M. PARSON, born 1968; admitted, 1994, Amsterdam. *Education:* Utrecht University (1993).

ANNELIES E. VAN DER PAUW, born 1960; admitted, 1987, Amsterdam. *Education:* Utrecht University (1984); (1987); University of Florida (1983); Leyden University (1987). New York Office, 1991-1992.

R.L.S.M. PESSERS, born 1967; admitted, 1992, Amsterdam. *Education:* Leyden University (1991).

SUZANNE J.C. REEMERS, born 1967; admitted, 1992, Amsterdam. *Education:* Nijmegen University (1992).

ISABELLE S.T.A. VAN RIET, born 1968; Deputy Civil Law Notary, 1994. *Education:* Amsterdam University (1993).

C.F. (KEES) DE RU, born 1968; admitted, 1994, Amsterdam. *Education:* Utrecht University (1994).

MARION E. RICHHEIMER-DE VRIES, born 1951; Deputy Civil Law Notary. *Education:* University of Amsterdam (1977).

WERNER F.L. RUNGE, born 1967; admitted, 1994, Amsterdam. *Education:* Leyden University (1993).

SIMONE M. SCHIMMER, born 1969; acting tax lawyer, 1994. *Education:* Amsterdam University (Law School, 1993; Tax Law, 1994).

PENELOPE J. SIMMERS, born 1967; admitted, 1992, Amsterdam. *Education:* Vrije Universiteit Amsterdam (1992).

JAN MAARTEN SLAGTER, born 1969; admitted, 1993, Amsterdam. *Education:* Leyden University (1993).

ARNOLD J. VAN DER SMEEDE, born 1965; acting tax lawyer, 1989. *Education:* Leyden University (1989). *Member:* Dutch Association of Tax Lawyers.

CHRISTIAAN M. STOKKERMANS, born 1963; Deputy Civil Law Notary, 1990. *Education:* Vrije Universiteit Amsterdam (1988); Centre Européen Universitaire de Nancy (1989).

ARNOUT C. STROEVE, born 1966; Deputy Civil Law Notary, 1993, Amsterdam. *Education:* Vrije Universiteit Amsterdam (1990).

BAS J. VAN SUSANTE, born 1964; admitted, 1991, Amsterdam. *Education:* Nijmegen University (1990).

(This Listing Continued)

LOEFF CLAEYS VERBEKE, Amsterdam—Continued

NICOLAAS JOHAN VISSER, born 1960; Deputy Civil Law Notary, 1986. *Education:* Groningen University (1983).

PAUL WANDERS, born 1961; admitted, 1989, Amsterdam. *Education:* University of Amsterdam (1988).

GERJANNE TE WINKEL, born 1964; admitted, 1988, Amsterdam. *Education:* Utrecht University (1988).

MATHIJS H. TEN WOLDE, born 1963; Deputy Civil Law Notary, 1990. *Education:* Groningen University (1988).

ARJEN C. VAN DER ZIEL, born 1967; admitted, 1994, Amsterdam. *Education:* Leyden University (1992).

Languages: Dutch, English, French, German, Italian, Japanese, Russian and Spanish.

(For Personnel and other data, see Professional Biographies at Antwerp, Barcelona, Brussels, Liège, New York, Paris, Rotterdam, Singapore and Tokyo)

LOYENS & VOLKMAARS

Tax Lawyers

Member of Loyens Lefebvre Rädler-European Tax Network

GROEN VAN PRINSTERERLAAN 114
1181 TW AMSTELVEEN
P.O. BOX 71170
1008 BD AMSTERDAM, THE NETHERLANDS
Telephone: 20-6564-600
Fax: 20-6435-396

Offices in the Netherlands:
Arnhem : Utrechtseweg 163, P.O. Box 170, 6860 AD Oosterbeek. Telephone: 85-337700. Fax: 85-337342.
Breda : Claudius Prinsenlaan 130, P.O. Box 2223 4800 CE. Telephone: 76-237700. Fax: 76-203950.
Eindhoven : Parklaan 34, P.O. Box 2186, 5600 CD. Telephone: 40-451355. Fax: 40-440789.
Enschede : Nijverheidstraat 5, P.O. Box, 2002, 7500 CA. Telephone: 53-308585. Fax: 53-308335.
Haarlem : Zuiderhoutlaan 12, P.O. Box 4325, 2003 EH. Telephone: 23-292060. Fax: 23-281779.
The Hague : Scheveningseweg 60, P.O. Box 29717, 2502 LS. Telephone: 70-3580-101. Fax: 70-3580-158.
Rotterdam : Weena 325, P.O. Box 2888, 3000 CW. Telephone: 10-2246-224. Fax: 10-4125-839.
Offices Abroad:
Antwerp, Belgium Office: Jan van Rijswijcklaan 128, B-2018. Telephone: 3-2370-822. Fax: 3-2379-636.
Oranjestad, Aruba Office: Eagle Town Center N.V., Sun Plaza, 160 L.G. Smith Boulevard. Telephone: 8-24837. Fax: 8-35214.
Brussels, Belgium Office: Tervurenlaan 270/272, Box 12, B-1150. Telephone: 2-7720-510. Fax: 2-7723-217.
Curacao, Netherlands Antilles Office: Kaya Flamboyan 22, P.O. Box 507, Willemstad. Telephone: 9-372544. Fax: 9-372290.
Frankfurt/Main, Germany Office: Bockenheimer Landstrasse 51-53, P.O. Box 17011, 60075. Telephone: 69-172364. Fax: 69-174506.
Geneva, Switzerland Office: 4, rue Petitot, CH-1204. Telephone: 22-8188000. Fax: 22-3120203.
Hong Kong Office: Baskerville House, 6th Floor, 22 Ice House Street. Telephone: 25257-246. Telex: 60260 lvtax hx. Fax: 28459-048.
London, England Office: Royex House, 14th Floor, Aldermanbury Square, P.O. Box 576, EC2V 7LX. Telephone: 171-6060-200. Fax: 171-6060-206.
Luxemburg Office: Royal Rome I, 3, Boulevard Royal, L-2449. Telephone: 352-466233. Fax: 352-466234.
New York, U.S.A. Office: 712 Fifth Avenue, 10019. Telephone: 212-489-0620. Fax: 212-489-0710.
Paris, France Office: 16, rue d'Orléans, 92200 Neuilly. Telephone: 1-4738-2099. Fax: 1-4738-2095.
Singapore Office: 80 Anson Road, 31-01B IBM Towers, 0207. Telephone: 65-2225-748. Fax: 65-2246-462.
Tokyo, Japan Office: 5f, Maeda Building, 12-3, Uchi-Kanda, 1-chome Chiyoda-ku, 101. Telephone: 3-3233-3141. Fax: 3-3233-3100.

(This Listing Continued)

FIRM PROFILE: Loyens & Volkmaars, a partnership of Netherlands, Netherlands Antilles and Belgian tax lawyers based in the Netherlands has, in the past seventy-five years, built up a leading position in the profession. The firm has specialized in tax law, a field to which it has deliberately restricted itself, offering a full range of services across the entire tax spectrum.

Loyens & Volkmaars employs approximately 600 people. It works for a large variety of clients, including multinationals, large and medium-sized businesses, individuals, government agencies and institutional investors, which are based in the Netherlands and elsewhere. To provide such a wide range of clients with the best possible service, Loyens & Volkmaars has offices in Europe, the U.S.A., the Caribbean and the Far East. Outside the Netherlands, the offices in Belgium, the Netherlands Antilles and Aruba have developed domestic tax law practices of high repute.

Loyens & Volkmaars, together with Bureau Francis Lefebvre and Oppenhoff Rädler, forms Loyens Lefebvre Rädler-European Tax Network, combining the expertise of three firms whose tax law practices rank among the top of the profession in Europe.

MEMBERS OF FIRM

R. BATEMA, born 1946, Arnhem Office.

C.B. BAVINCK, born 1946, Amsterdam Office.

H.R. BEHRENS, born 1945, Amsterdam Office.

W.P. VAN BERKEL, born 1951, Haarlem Office.

S.P. BERTELS, born 1953, Rotterdam Office.

R.H. BOON, born 1945, Amsterdam Office.

J.P.G.M. BROEKMAN, born 1933, Eindhoven Office.

J.M BUIT, born 1948, Amsterdam Office.

A. COOIMAN, born 1940, Rotterdam Office.

W.M. VAN DALEN, born 1947, Rotterdam Office.

H.G.M. DIJSTELBLOEM, born 1945, Enschede Office.

H.A. DOEK, born 1947, Arnhem Office.

M.J.W.M. ELLIS, born 1941, Rotterdam Office.

A. EIJSSEN, born 1955, Eindhoven Office.

J.I.H.M. GALAVAZI, born 1955, Frankfurt Office.

H.C. DE GROOT, born 1949, London Office.

J.F.T. VAN HAAREN, born 1942, Brussels Office.

W.J.G. HAGENS, born 1960, Rotterdam Office.

S.H. HARKEMA, born 1942, Breda Office.

A. HARTMAN, born 1933, The Hague Office.

J.M. HELLMAN, born 1943, Rotterdam Office.

M. VAN DEN HEUVEL, born 1953, Amsterdam Office.

J.P. VAN HILTEN, born 1952, The Hague Office.

D. A. HOFLAND, born 1954, Amsterdam Office.

A.H.M. JANSSEN, born 1941, Breda Office.

E.J. JONKER, born 1948, Rotterdam Office.

D. JUCH, born 1940, Breda Office.

L.F. VAN KALMTHOUT, born 1955, Rotterdam Office.

W. KAPOEN, born 1961, The Hague Office.

J.M. VAN KEMPEN, born 1942, Amsterdam Office.

H.N. VAN DER KOLK, born 1947, Amsterdam Office.

J. KOOI, born 1955, Tokyo Office.

H.J. KRUISINGA, born 1942, Rotterdam Office.

M.V. LAMBOOIJ, born 1962, Amsterdam Office.

M.W.M. VAN DE LEUR, born 1954, Amsterdam Office.

H.T. VAN DER MEER, born 1949, Amsterdam Office.

G. MELCHING, born 1960, Rotterdam Office.

W.R.M. NAN, born 1958, The Hague Office.

E.J.O. PICAVET, born 1949, Brussels Office.

(This Listing Continued)

A.H.A.M. RENS, born 1951, The Hague Office.

A.K.J. SCHALEKAMP, born 1946, Breda Office.

P.H.M. SIMONIS, born 1954, Rotterdam Office.

P.H. SLEURINK, born 1957, New York Office.

R.M.R.M. VAN THIEL, born 1947, Eindhoven Office.

MARIËTTE A.TH. TURKENBURG, born 1960, Rotterdam Office.

M.A.C. VALKS, born 1958, Breda Office.

M. VANDENDIJK, born 1958, Brussels Office.

P.A.A. VANHAUTE, born 1954, Antwerp Office.

R.M. VERMEULEN, born 1955, Amstelveen Office.

J.G. VERSEPUT, born 1942, Rotterdam Office.

A.C.J. VIERSEN, born 1949, The Hague Office.

P.G. VOS, born 1942, Haarlem Office.

B. WESTENDORP, born 1952, Rotterdam Office.

J. WISSE, born 1945, Amsterdam Office.

J.P.M. VAN DE WOLFSHAAR, born 1952, Enschede Office.

R.J.B. WIJS, born 1961, Paris Office.

MORET ERNST & YOUNG TAX ADVISERS

CORPORATE LAW ADVISORY GROUP

20, DRENTESTRAAT
P.O. BOX 7925
1008 AC AMSTERDAM, THE NETHERLANDS
Telephone: 31-20-5497333
Fax: 31-20-6462553

Rotterdam Office: 51, Marten Meesweg, P.O. Box 2295, 3000 CG.
Telephone: 31-10-4072627. Fax: 31-10-4072612.
The Hague Office: 80, Wassenaarseweg, P.O. Box 90636, 2509 LP.
Telephone: 31 70-3286542. Fax: 31 70-3244003.
Groningen Office: 17, Leonard Springerlaan, P.O. Box 997, 9700 AZ.
Telephone: 31-50-994444. Fax: 31-50-270852.
Arnhem Office: Kronenburgsingel 12, P.O. Box 30116, 6803 AC.
Telephone: 31-85-209500. Fax: 31-85-235151.

Civil Law (general). Computer Law, Insolvency Law, (International) Contracts, Corporate Law, Environmental Law, EC Law, Intellectual Property, Labour Law and Workers Participation, Mergers and Acquisitions, Taxation.

FIRM PROFILE: The Corporate Law Advisory Group of Moret Ernst & Young Tax Advisers was established on January 1, 1990. The Group operates as a specialized unit within the Moret Ernst & Young Accountants, Moret Ernst & Young Tax Advisers and Moret Ernst & Young Management Consultants organization and offers a full range of quality legal services. The Group consists of four partners and 34 lawyers, practicing in four offices.

PARTNERS

HIDDE HOEKSTRA, born Amsterdam, 1947. *Education:* Groningen University (1971). (Amsterdam Office).

JOOST KEMPERINK, born 1948. *Education:* Nijmegen University (1973 and 1974). (Groningen Office).

HANS VAN GIJZEN, born 1951. *Education:* Leyden University. (Rotterdam, The Hague and Arnhem Office).

BOB WESSELS, born 1949. *Education:* Amsterdam University (1974 and 1977; Ph.D., 1988). (Amsterdam Office).

SENIOR-ADVISORS

AMSTERDAM OFFICE

ANDRE WIEDIJK, born 1959. *Education:* Amsterdam University(1984).

ANNEMIEK TUBBING, born 1957. *Education:* Utrecht University (1982); Amsterdam University (1986).

(This Listing Continued)

ELS VAN DIEPEN-SALET, born 1951. *Education:* Nijmegen University (1974).

REYN BARON SNOUCKAERT-VAN SCHAUBURG, born 1957. *Education:* Leyden University (1986).

SHIREEN MOUS-VAN CASSEL, born 1961. *Education:* Leyden University (1986).

BERENT BLIJDENSTEIN, born 1957. *Education:* Amsterdam University (1984).

ROTTERDAM OFFICE

DENIS WILLEMARS, born 1956. *Education:* Groningen University (1986).

RUUD HARINCK, born 1957. *Education:* Groningen University (1985).

BERT GRAVENDEEL, born 1961. *Education:* Leyden University (1987).

STEFANO FRANCOVICH, born 1965. *Education:* Utrecht University (1990).

RUTGER ALSBACH, born 1963. *Education:* Utrecht University (1990).

THE HAGUE OFFICE

DORIEN ALEMAN, born 1958. *Education:* Rotterdam University(1981).

HUUB PLEIJSIER, born 1961. *Education:* Leyden University (1986).

GRONINGEN OFFICE

FRÉDÉRIQUE HUUSSEN-DE GROOT, born 1942. *Education:* Leyden University (1976).

ARNHEM OFFICE

DENIS WILLEMARS, born 1956. *Education:* Groningen University (1986).

NAUTA DUTILH

Attorneys, Civil Law Notaries, Tax Advisers
PRINSES IRENESTRAAT 59
NL-1077 WV AMSTERDAM, THE NETHERLANDS
Telephone: (31-20) 5414646
Telecopier: (31-20) 6612827
Telex: 13411 NDA NL

Mailing Address: P.O. Box 7113, NL-1007 JC Amsterdam, The Netherlands

MEMBERS OF FIRM ATTORNEYS AT LAW

JOHN WERNER, born 1932; admitted, 1960, The Netherlands. *Education:* Amsterdam University.

WILLEM C. VAN MANEN, born 1934; admitted, 1960, The Netherlands. *Education:* Leyden University.

P. J. PETER VERLOOP, born 1932; admitted, 1962, The Netherlands. *Education:* Leyden University.

FLORIS A. W. BANNIER, born 1941; admitted, 1966, The Netherlands. *Education:* Utrecht University.

G. WOUTER KERNKAMP, born 1941; admitted, 1968, The Netherlands. *Education:* Utrecht University.

CEES CH. MOUT, born 1942; admitted, 1968, The Netherlands. *Education:* Amsterdam University.

CEES A. J. CRUL, born 1941; admitted, 1968, The Netherlands. *Education:* Leyden University.

JAN WILLEM SODDERLAND, born 1942; admitted, 1969, The Netherlands. *Education:* Leyden University.

GERLOF J. S. POSTMA, born 1944; admitted, 1971, The Netherlands. *Education:* Groningen University.

WILLEM D. T. D. WIARDA, born 1943; admitted, 1971, The Netherlands. *Education:* Amsterdam University.

PROF. CHARLES GIELEN, born 1947; admitted, 1971, The Netherlands. *Education:* Tilburg University.

E. (NOOR) A. MOUT-BOUWMAN, born 1943; admitted, 1968, The Netherlands. *Education:* Amsterdam University.

(This Listing Continued)

NAUTA DUTILH, Amsterdam—Continued

HUIB G. VAN EVERDINGEN, born 1946; admitted, 1973, The Netherlands. *Education:* Leyden University.

STEFAN F. SCHÜTZ, born 1947; admitted, 1974, The Netherlands. *Education:* Leyden University.

JAN J.M. BLESS, born 1946; admitted, 1974, The Netherlands. *Education:* Nijmegen University.

R. HEIN HOOGHOUDT, born 1950; admitted, 1975, The Netherlands. *Education:* Leyden and Cambridge Universities.

DICK A. VAN DER STELT, born 1951; admitted, 1975, The Netherlands. *Education:* Rotterdam University.

HARMEN M. DE MOL VAN OTTERLOO, born 1949; admitted, 1975, The Netherlands. *Education:* Leyden University.

JAN C. VAN APELDOORN, born 1946; admitted, 1978, The Netherlands. *Education:* Leyden University.

JEROEN M.T.THIJSSEN, born 1953; admitted, 1978, The Netherlands. *Education:* Leyden University.

C. REINOUD BREDIUS, born 1959; admitted, 1988, The Netherlands. *Education:* Amsterdam University.

MARC A. BLOM, born 1956; admitted, 1981, The Netherlands. *Education:* Leyden University.

WILLEM RUYS, born 1955; admitted, 1981, The Netherlands. *Education:* Leyden and Columbia Universities.

G. WARNER ROETERS VAN LENNEP, born 1954; admitted, 1981, The Netherlands. *Education:* Leyden University.

BERNARD R. TER HAAR, born 1957; admitted, 1982, The Netherlands. *Education:* Leyden University.

ERIK A. MINDERHOUD, born 1958; admitted, 1982, The Netherlands. *Education:* Leyden University.

JOOST ITALIANER, born 1957; admitted, 1983, The Netherlands. *Education:* Groningen University.

RUPRECHT HERMANS, born 1955; admitted, 1983, The Netherlands. *Education:* Groningen University.

RICHARD EBBINK, born 1957; admitted, 1984, The Netherlands. *Education:* Amsterdam University.

GIJS P. GERRETSEN, born 1959; admitted, 1984, The Netherlands. *Education:* Utrecht University.

A. JOANNE KELLERMANN, born 1960; admitted, 1984, The Netherlands. *Education:* Leyden University.

CHRISTIAAN A. BAARDMAN, born 1958; admitted, 1985, The Netherlands. *Education:* Leyden University.

MEMBERS OF FIRM CIVIL LAW NOTARIES

PIETER M. VAN DER LAAN, born 1935; notary since, 1966. *Education:* Amsterdam University.

LEO J.W.M. SCHROEDER, born 1943; notary since, 1974. *Education:* Amsterdam University.

PIET HEIN M. GERVER, born 1942; notary since, 1980. *Education:* Amsterdam University.

CEES P. BOODT, born 1946; notary since, 1985. *Education:* Amsterdam University.

MEMBERS OF FIRM TAX ADVISERS

ARNOLD F. LINNEWIEL, born 1946. *Education:* Amsterdam University.

W. EWOUT BARON VAN ASBECK, born 1956. *Education:* Rotterdam University.

ASSOCIATES ATTORNEYS AT LAW

ELSBETH M. POLAK, born 1954; admitted, 1981, The Netherlands. *Education:* Amsterdam University.

J. (HANS) R.E. KIELSTRA, born 1955; admitted, 1982, The Netherlands. *Education:* Leyden and Amsterdam Universities.

(This Listing Continued)

E. (GENIA) E.H.M. OTTENHOFF, born 1960; admitted, 1985, The Netherlands. *Education:* Utrecht University.

J.C.M. (ANNEMIEKE) VAN DER BEEK, born 1958; admitted, 1986, The Netherlands. *Education:* Leyden University.

ELZELINE K.E. VAN HERK, born 1947; admitted, 1986, The Netherlands. *Education:* Utrecht and Rotterdam Universities.

MARC A. PINCKAERS, born 1959; admitted, 1986, The Netherlands. *Education:* Utrecht University and NYU School of Law, New York.

ELIANE I.M.C. DE VILDER, born 1961; admitted, 1987, The Netherlands. *Education:* Leyden University.

JAAP W. ROTGANS, born 1960; admitted, 1988, The Netherlands. *Education:* Utrecht University.

JAN W. VAN RIJSWIJK, born 1952; admitted, 1988, The Netherlands. *Education:* Utrecht University.

J. PETER H. VISSER, born 1963; admitted, 1988, The Netherlands. *Education:* Leyden University.

MATTHIEU PH. VAN SINT TRUIDEN, born 1961; admitted, 1988, The Netherlands. *Education:* Nijmegen University.

TACO C. WIERSMA, born 1963; admitted, 1989, The Netherlands. *Education:* Utrecht University.

GABY CRINCE LE ROY, born 1962; admitted, 1989, The Netherlands. *Education:* Amsterdam University.

TRUDEKE G. SILLEVIS SMITT, born 1963; admitted, 1989, The Netherlands. *Education:* Amsterdam University.

SVEN A. KLOS, born 1963; admitted, 1989, The Netherlands. *Education:* Amsterdam University.

DIRK WILLEM BLAISSE, born 1960; admitted, 1989, The Netherlands. *Education:* Leyden University.

MARJOLEIN N.J. VAN DER LINDEN, born 1963; admitted, 1990, The Netherlands. *Education:* Amsterdam University.

FROUKJE J. RESIUS, born 1963; admitted, 1990, The Netherlands. *Education:* Amsterdam University.

PIETER A. DE JONG, born 1966; admitted, 1991, The Netherlands. *Education:* Groningen University.

W.A.K. (PIM) RANK, born 1958; admitted, 1991, The Netherlands. *Education:* Leyden University.

BART M. MENDEL, born 1965; admitted, 1991, The Netherlands. *Education:* Leyden University.

REINOUT G. PRAKKE, born 1966; admitted, 1991, The Netherlands. *Education:* Amsterdam University.

JASPER H. STEK, born 1964; admitted, 1991, The Netherlands. *Education:* Amsterdam University.

LIESBETH A.M. MARIJNISSEN, born 1967; admitted, 1991, The Netherlands. *Education:* Utrecht University.

ASSOCIATES CANDIDATE CIVIL LAW NOTARIES

FERDINAND A. HECK, born 1944; admitted, 1975, The Netherlands. *Education:* Utrecht University.

JANNETTE BLOM, born 1949; admitted, 1984, The Netherlands. *Education:* Amsterdam University.

MARNIX C. AARTS, born 1961; admitted, 1991, The Netherlands. *Education:* Utrecht University.

J. (HANS) R.E. KIELSTRA, born 1955; admitted, 1992, The Netherlands. *Education:* Leyden and Amsterdam Universities.

STEVEN VAN DER WAAL, born 1962; admitted, 1992, The Netherlands. *Education:* Leyden University.

Languages: English, French, German, Indonesian, Italian, Japanese, Russian, Spanish and Swedish.

(For Complete Biographical Data on all Personnel, see Professional Biographies at Rotterdam, The Netherlands)

PARRAMORE ADVOCATEN AMSTERDAM

Established in 1981

International Business-and Tax Lawyers

BURG. STRAMANWEG 102
1101 AA AMSTERDAM, THE NETHERLANDS
Telephone: + 31 20 6963211
Fax: + 31 20 6968581

Mailing Address: P.O. Box 22871, 1100 DJ Amsterdam, The Netherlands

Correspondence offices:
Brussels, Belgium: Mr. Ph. Schreinemacher, Goghenlaan 208, 1180 Brussels. Telephone (2) 346 2203. Fax: (2) 346 2467.
Paris, France: Cabinet L.G. Laisney, Avocats à la Cour, 87, Avenue Mozart, 75016 Paris. Telephone (1) 4525 4433. Fax: (1) 4520 1937.
Willemstad, Curaçao, Netherlands Antilles: Mr. A. Huizing, Pietermaai 1-7, Curaçao, N.A. Telephone: (599-9) 611 711. Fax: (599-9) 616 766.
Bangkok, Thailand: Prof. Dr. Bhokin Bhalakula, 3rd Floor 942/6-7, Rama 4 Rd., Suriyawongse, Bangrak, Bangkok, 10500, Thailand. Telephone (2) 372 598/9. Fax: (2) 376 278.

Parramore Advocaten Amsterdam is engaged in Dutch, European and International law practice. The lawyers are entitled to plead in European Community-courts and the Dutch courts and, through correspondences, in courts in residing countries. Apart from the above mentioned correspondences Parramore Advocaten Amsterdam is part of a worldwide network of specialized advisors. Parramore Advocaten Amsterdam is engaged in an agreement with a large Taxation-office.
International Business Law, General International Trade Law, Corporate Law, International Tax Law, Agricultural Law, Intellectual Property- / Copyright- / Patent- / Trademark- and Computer Law, Health Care- / Personal Injury- and Insurance Law, Criminal Law, Collections and Litigation.

FIRM PROFILE: Parramore Lawyers constitutes of lawyers and a tax lawyer, who all have had their training in large firms. From this experience the members of Parramore Advocaten realise that clients are in need of quick service, practical and creative solutions, the best results and easy and direct contact with their lawyers.

Parramore Advocaten Amsterdam enjoys a wide range of major domestic and foreign clients, mainly national and international companies.

MEMBERS OF FIRM

MICHAEL E.F. PARRAMORE, born Amsterdam, 1950; admitted, 1978, The Netherlands. *Member:* Dutch Bar Association; A.I.J.A.-Brussels. *LANGUAGES:* Dutch, English, German and French. *PRACTICE AREAS:* International Business; Transport and Trade Law; Contracts; Trusts.

ROBERT VAN LIER, born Rotterdam, 1954. *Member:* Dutch Association of Tax-consultants; International Fiscal Association. *LANGUAGES:* Dutch, English, French and German. *PRACTICE AREAS:* National and International Tax Law; Trusts.

PETER W.M. STEENBERGEN, born Utrecht, 1961; admitted, 1990, The Netherlands. *Member:* Dutch Bar Association. *LANGUAGES:* Dutch, English, German and French. *PRACTICE AREAS:* Intellectual Property Law; Agricultural Law; Business Law; Contracts; Product Liability; Criminal Law.

HANS BOS, born Haarlem, 1965; admitted, 1992, The Netherlands. *Member:* Dutch Bar Association. *LANGUAGES:* Dutch, English, French and German. *PRACTICE AREAS:* Contracts; Employment Law and Social Securities; Business Law; Landlord and Tenant Law; Collections.

ASSOCIATES

CORNELIS M. VISSER, born Bergen op Zoom, 1962; admitted, 1990, The Netherlands. *Member:* Dutch Bar Association; Dutch Association Personal Injury Lawyers (LSA); Dutch Association Collection Lawyers (VIA). *LANGUAGES:* Dutch, English, German and French. *PRACTICE AREAS:* General Business Law; Computer Law; Contracts; Bankruptcy Law; Personal Injuries.

PRICE WATERHOUSE

STRAWINSKYLAAN 3127
1077 ZX AMSTERDAM, THE NETHERLANDS
Telephone: (31-20) 54982000
Fax: (31-20) 5498250

Deventer, The Netherlands Office: Hanzeweg 70, 7418AT. Telephone: (31-5700) 87700. Telecopier: (31-5700) 87777.
Eindhoven, The Netherlands Office: Fellenoord 310, 5611 ZD. Telephone (31-40) 652352. Telecopier: (31-40) 652375.
The Hague, The Netherlands Office: Koninginnegracht 8, 2514 AA. Telephone: (31-70) 3108308. Telecopier: (31-70) 3108305.
Rotterdam, The Netherlands Office: Hofplein 19, 3032 AC. Telephone: (31-10) 4008600. Telecopier: (31-10) 4008670.

Local and International Taxation and Dutch Corporate and Business Law. Corporate and Individual Taxation, International Taxation, Transfer Pricing, International Assignments Taxation.
Corporate and Business Law, M&A, Employment Law.

FIRM PROFILE: The firm offers tax and legal services to both national and international clients. It cooperates with member firms of Correspondent Law Firms of Price Waterhouse EEIG and Price Waterhouse firms to render legal services throughout Europe where appropriate on a multidisciplinary basis.

MEMBERS OF FIRM

TOINE PA BINDELS. *Education:* Leiden University (Civil Law Degree, 1980; Tax Law Degree, 1982). *Member:* Dutch Association of Tax Consultants; International Fiscal Association. *LANGUAGES:* Dutch, English and German. *PRACTICE AREAS:* Corporate Taxation; International Tax.

FRANS M. CLAESSEN. *Education:* Leiden University (Tax Law Degree, 1978). *Member:* Dutch Association of Tax Consultants; International Fiscal Association. *LANGUAGES:* Dutch, English and German. *PRACTICE AREAS:* Corporate Taxation; Real Property Taxation.

IMAN DAMSTE. *Education:* Amsterdam University (Civil Law Degree, 1976; Tax Law Degree, 1985). *Member:* Dutch Association of Tax Consultants (Treasurer); International Fiscal Association; International Bar Association. *LANGUAGES:* Dutch, English and German. *PRACTICE AREAS:* Corporate Taxation; International Tax; Oil & Gas Taxation.

GUDO OR DOEVE. *Education:* Groningen University (Tax Law Degree, 1978). *Member:* Dutch Association of Tax Consultants; International Fiscal Association. *LANGUAGES:* Dutch, English and German. *PRACTICE AREAS:* Corporate Taxation; International Tax; Oil & Gas Taxation.

NIEK AJM VAN DOEVEREN. *Education:* Utrecht University (Civil Law Degree, 1978); Amsterdam University (Tax Law Degree, 1984). *Member:* Dutch Association of Tax Consultants; International Fiscal Association. *LANGUAGES:* Dutch, English and German. *PRACTICE AREAS:* Corporate Taxation; Value Added Tax; Corporate Law.

JAN CAREL VAN DORP. *Education:* Rotterdam University (Civil Law Degree, 1976); Tilburg University (Post Graduate Tax Courses, 1978-1980). *Member:* Dutch Association of Tax Consultants; International Bar Association; International Fiscal Association. *LANGUAGES:* Dutch, English and German. *PRACTICE AREAS:* International Tax and Turnkey Projects Planning.

DAVID J. FAIRHEAD. *Education:* Exter University (Bachelor of Arts Economics). Fellow, Institute of Chartered Accountants in England and Wales. *Member:* Dutch Association of Tax Consultants; International Fiscal Association. *LANGUAGES:* English and Dutch. *PRACTICE AREAS:* International Tax Planning and Restructuring.

WIM VAN GELDER. *Education:* Leiden University (Tax Law Degree). *Member:* Dutch Association of Tax Consultants; International Fiscal Association. *LANGUAGES:* Dutch, English and German. *PRACTICE AREAS:* Corporate Taxation.

WIM HOGEWEG. *Education:* Nijmegen University (Civil Law Degree, 1964); Tilburg University (Tax Law Degree, 1973). *Member:* Dutch Association of Tax Consultants; Dutch and International Bar Associations; International Fiscal Association. *LANGUAGES:* Dutch, English and German. *PRACTICE AREAS:* Corporate Taxation; Company Law.

FRED AH KLAASSEN. *Education:* Amsterdam University (Tax Law Degree, 1975). *Member:* Dutch Association of Tax Consultants; International Fiscal Association. *LANGUAGES:* Dutch, English and German.

(This Listing Continued)

PRICE WATERHOUSE, Amsterdam—Continued

PRACTICE AREAS: US/Europe Cross-Border Tax Planning; Transfer Pricing.

PAUL JM VAN LEENT. *Education:* Civil and Tax Law. *Member:* Dutch Association of Tax Consultants; The Netherlands International Fiscal Association (Member, Disciplinary Council, Accountancy Body). *LANGUAGES:* Dutch, English and German. *PRACTICE AREAS:* Corporate Taxation; Corporate Law; M&A.

COR FJ LOOMAN. *Education:* Rotterdam University (Civil and Business Law Degree). *Member:* Dutch Association of Tax Consultants; International Fiscal Association. *LANGUAGES:* Dutch, English and German. *PRACTICE AREAS:* Corporate Taxation; International Tax.

JAN W. SAVELBERGH. *Education:* Nijmegen University (Civil Law Degree, 1971). *Member:* Dutch Association of Tax Consultants; (Member, Disciplinary Court); Dutch and International Bar Associations; International Fiscal Association. *LANGUAGES:* Dutch, English and German. *PRACTICE AREAS:* Corporate Taxation; Insurance Taxation; Corporate and Business Law.

THEUN Y. STEENSMA. *Education:* Leiden University (Tax Law Degree, 1973). *Member:* Dutch Association of Tax Consultants; International Fiscal Association. *LANGUAGES:* Dutch, English and German. *PRACTICE AREAS:* Cross Border Tax Planning; Corporate Taxation.

BERNARD H. STUIVINGA. *Education:* Groningen University (Tax Law Degree, 1980). *Member:* Dutch Association of Tax Consultants; International Bar Association; International Fiscal Association. *LANGUAGES:* Dutch, English and German. *PRACTICE AREAS:* Corporate Taxation; Insurance Taxation.

PETER D. VEERMAN. *Education:* Rotterdam University (Tax and Economics Degree, 1979). *Member:* Dutch Association of Tax Consultants; International Fiscal Association. *LANGUAGES:* Dutch, English and German. *PRACTICE AREAS:* Corporate Taxation; International Tax.

HUGO A. VOLLEBREGT. *Education:* Rotterdam University (Economics, 1980); Geneva University (Tax Law, 1985). *Member:* Dutch Association of Tax Consultants; International Fiscal Association. *LANGUAGES:* Dutch, English, German and French. *PRACTICE AREAS:* Corporate Taxation; Income Tax Planning.

ASSOCIATES

MARIEKE VAN DEN BOUT. *Education:* Utrecht University (Dutch Law Degree, 1985). *LANGUAGES:* Dutch, English and French. *PRACTICE AREAS:* Corporate and Business Law.

MARGA CTM GERICHHAUSEN. *Education:* Utrecht University (Dutch Law Degree, 1988). *LANGUAGES:* Dutch, English and German. *PRACTICE AREAS:* Corporate and Business Law.

FRED HAAK. *Education:* Rotterdam University (Dutch Law Degree, 1986). *LANGUAGES:* Dutch, English and German. *PRACTICE AREAS:* Employment and Business Law.

AIKE GH VAN DER STAAY. *Education:* Utrecht University (Dutch Law Degree, 1987). *LANGUAGES:* Dutch, English and German. *PRACTICE AREAS:* Corporate and Business Law.

RUSSELL ADVOCATEN

Established in 1942

REIMERSBEEK 2
1082 AG AMSTERDAM, THE NETHERLANDS
Telephone: (20) 3015555
Telecopier: (20) 3015678;
Telex: 18698;
Cable Address: RULAW

The Hague, The Netherlands Office: Nassauplein 1B, 2585 EA Den Haag, The Netherlands. Telephone: (70) 3654822. Telecopier: (70) 3624144.

Attorneys may represent clients before all Dutch Courts. Member of Alliance of International Lawyers (EEIG). General Practice, Corporate Law, Administrative Law, Environmental Law, EEC Law, Labor Law, Intellectual Property, Family Law, Travel/Tourism Insurance, Art, Real Estate Property, Mergers and Take-over, Commercial Contracts, Banking, Bankruptcy and Insolvency, Arbitration and Litigation, Agency and Distributorships, Business Law, Civil Law, Company Law, Consumer Law, Criminal

(This Listing Continued)

Law, Debtor and Creditor, International Law, Personal Injury, Property Law, Copyrights and Trademark Law.

MEMBERS OF FIRM

WILLEM O. RUSSELL, born 1952; admitted, 1975, Amsterdam. *Education:* Free University of Amsterdam (1974); Amsterdam University (1975).

PAUL W.L. RUSSELL, born 1954; admitted, 1976, Amsterdam. *Education:* Free University of Amsterdam (1976).

ASSOCIATES

ALBERDINA MENKMAN, born 1918; admitted, 1941, Amsterdam. *Education:* University of Amsterdam (1941). Clerk to the President of the District Court Amsterdam, 1969-1973.

HARRY MANUEL, born 1960; admitted, 1984, Amsterdam. *Education:* Free University of Amsterdam (1983). Secretary of IFTTA (International Forum of Travel and Tourism Advocates), European and worldwide.

KAREL FRIELINK, born 1964; admitted, 1989, Amsterdam. *Education:* Free University of Amsterdam (1989).

RUUD VOS, born 1958; admitted, 1989, Amsterdam. *Education:* University of Amsterdam (1986).

AUKE BAAS, born 1965; admitted, 1990, Amsterdam. *Education:* Free University of Amsterdam (1988); Université de Nancy (1989).

SUZE M.G. WEITJENS, born 1964; admitted, 1990, Amsterdam. *Education:* University of Amsterdam (1989).

REINIER W.L. RUSSELL, born 1965; admitted, 1990, Amsterdam. *Education:* Free University of Amsterdam (1990). (Resident Associate at The Hague, The Netherlands Office).

SUZAN L. HAASDIJK, born 1965; admitted, 1991, Amsterdam. *Education:* University of Amsterdam (1990).

RON G.J. LAAN, born 1966; admitted, 1992, Amsterdam. *Education:* Free University of Amsterdam (1992).

JET MEELKER, born 1968; admitted, 1992, Amsterdam. *Education:* Free University of Amsterdam (1992).

CAROLINE OBENHUYSEN, born 1967; admitted, 1993, Amsterdam. *Education:* Catholic University of Nijmegen (1992).

Languages: English, German, French, Spanish and Italian

SCHUT & GROSHEIDE

VAN BOSHUIZENSTRAAT 12
1083 BA AMSTERDAM, THE NETHERLANDS
Telephone: (+31) (20) 5419888
Telefax: (+31) (20) 6464966
Telex: 17099 ADVOC

Mailing Address: P.O. Box 75258, 1070 AG Amsterdam, The Netherlands

FIRM PROFILE: Schut & Grosheide is a law firm founded in 1916 and based in Amsterdam (The Netherlands). It offers a full range of legal services to its Dutch and foreign clients. The firm has strategic alliances with foreign law-firms of simular reputation. Presently, the firm consists of 37 lawyers admitted to the Amsterdam Bar, of which 14 partners and 23 associates. Dutch lawyers may represent clients before all Dutch Courts.

Schut & Grosheide offers services in the following areas of practice:

Administrative law, including environmental law, town planning and zoning; Banking, finance and leasing; Bankruptcy and insolvency; Commercial law, including distribution, agency, franchising, sales and related commercial transactions; Company law and business organizations; Competition, both European and national; Computer law and technology; Contracts; Criminal law, including tax fraud and business crime; Employment and labour relations; Entertainment, broadcasting and media; European community law; Insurance, transportation and maritime law; Intellectual property, including trademarks, patents and copyright protection, merchandising, unfair competition; Litigation, including civil litigation, administrative procedure, commercial arbitration and international litigation; Mergers and acquisitions, both domestic and cross-border; Negligence and personal injury; Product liability, advertising and consumer law; Professional liability, malpractice and professional indemnity; Real estate and construction law; Trust related services.

(This Listing Continued)

MEMBERS OF FIRM

JAN HEERES, born Bolsward, The Netherlands, June 15, 1939; admitted, 1966, The Netherlands. *Education:* University of Amsterdam (LL.M., 1966). *LANGUAGES:* Dutch, English, French and German. *PRACTICE AREAS:* Commercial Law; Business Law; Business Practice; Mergers and Acquisitions; Company Law; Arbitration.

DAVID J.S. VOORHOEVE, born The Hague, The Netherlands, June 2, 1947; admitted, 1974, The Netherlands. *Education:* University of Groningen (LL.M., 1972). *LANGUAGES:* Dutch, English, French and German. *PRACTICE AREAS:* Banking; Finance.

MARINUS PANNEVIS, born Rotterdam, The Netherlands, July 30, 1949; admitted, 1976, The Netherlands. *Education:* University of Utrecht (LL.M., 1974). Permanent Secretary, BVA (Dutch Association of Advertisers). Member, Board of the Stichting Reclame Code (Board for Observance of the Advertising Code). *LANGUAGES:* Dutch and English. *PRACTICE AREAS:* Commercial Law; Business Law; Computer Law; Directors and Professional Liability; Bankruptcy and Insolvency.

W.G. BART NEERVOORT, born Lagos, Nigeria, October 1, 1953; admitted, 1978, The Netherlands. *Education:* University of Leyden (LL.M., 1977). *LANGUAGES:* Dutch, English, French and German. *PRACTICE AREAS:* Transportation; Insurance; Maritime Law.

SIEBE C. DE LANGE, born Zuid-Laren, The Netherlands, June 26, 1951; admitted, 1979, The Netherlands. *Education:* Free University Amsterdam (LL.M., 1978). *LANGUAGES:* Dutch and English. *PRACTICE AREAS:* Commercial Law; Business Law; Criminal Law; Tax Fraud; Business Crime.

T. DIEDERIK DE GROOT, born Zwolle, The Netherlands, December 12, 1952; admitted, 1981, The Netherlands. *Education:* Free University Amsterdam (LL.M., 1980; M.A. in Philosophy, 1982). *Member:* Association of Dutch Lawyers for International Trade (Member of the Board). *LANGUAGES:* Dutch, English and French. *PRACTICE AREAS:* Commercial Law; Business Law; International Law; Entertainment Law; Broadcasting Law; Arbitration; Mergers and Acquisitions.

HUIB J. BLAISSE, born Amsterdam, The Netherlands, March 31, 1953; admitted, 1982, The Netherlands. *Education:* University of Amsterdam (LL.M., 1982). Vice-Chairman, Dispute Resolution Committee, NIVRA (Netherlands Institute of Chartered Accounts). *LANGUAGES:* Dutch and English. *PRACTICE AREAS:* Commercial Law; Business Law; Directors and Professional Liability; Insurance Law.

M. RUTGER ORANJE, born Rijswijk, The Netherlands, April 6, 1958; admitted, 1982, The Netherlands. *Education:* Free University Amsterdam (LL.M., 1982). Chairman, Board of Appeal, ANVR (Professional Association of Dutch Tour Operators). *Member:* Association of Dutch Lawyers for Environmental Law. *LANGUAGES:* Dutch and English. *PRACTICE AREAS:* Commercial Law; Business Law; Administrative Law; Environmental Law.

FERDINAND B.J. GRAPPERHAUS, born Amsterdam, The Netherlands, November 8, 1959; admitted, 1984, The Netherlands. *Education:* University of Amsterdam (LL.M., 1984). *LANGUAGES:* Dutch, Italian, German, English and French. *PRACTICE AREAS:* Commercial Law; Business Law; Mergers and Acquisitions; Company Law.

SASKIA R. REULING, born 's-Hertogenbosch, The Netherlands, December 3, 1956; admitted, 1984, The Netherlands. *Education:* University of Amsterdam (LL.M., 1982); New York University School of Law (Master of Comparative Jurisprudence). *LANGUAGES:* Dutch, English, French and German. *PRACTICE AREAS:* Commercial Law; Business Law; Intellectual Property; Copyrights.

FRANS D. STIBBE, born Arnhem, The Netherlands, September 22, 1959; admitted, 1985, The Netherlands. *Education:* University of Groningen (LL.M., 1985). *LANGUAGES:* Dutch and English. *PRACTICE AREAS:* Commercial Law; Business Law; Mergers and Acquisitions; Company Law; Employment.

MARC A.R.C. PADBERG, born Warmond, The Netherlands, September 4, 1959; admitted, 1986, The Netherlands. *Education:* University of Leyden (LL.M., 1986). *LANGUAGES:* Dutch, English and German. *PRACTICE AREAS:* Transporation; Insurance; Maritime Law.

LÉON E.J. KORSTEN, born Veghel, The Netherlands, August 31, 1961; admitted, 1987, The Netherlands. *Education:* University of Utrecht (LL.M., 1985). *LANGUAGES:* Dutch, English and German. *PRACTICE AREAS:* Commercial Law; Business Law; Contracts; Competition Law; European Community Law.

(This Listing Continued)

PIETER J. VAN DER KORST, born Nijmegen, The Netherlands, February 25, 1962; admitted, 1988, The Netherlands. *Education:* University of Utrecht (LL.M., 1985). *LANGUAGES:* Dutch, English, German and French. *PRACTICE AREAS:* Commercial Law; Business Law; Mergers and Acquisitions; Company Law.

ASSOCIATES

INGE M. GROOTENHUIS, born New Guinea, January 2, 1962; admitted, 1986, The Netherlands. *Education:* University of Amsterdam (LL.M., 1985; LL.M. in International Law, 1990); Columbia University, New York (LL.M., 1986). *LANGUAGES:* Dutch, English and French. *PRACTICE AREAS:* Commercial Law; Business Law; International Contracts; Mergers and Acquisitions; Computer Law; Employment.

GEA DIETZ-KALSBEEK, born Assen, The Netherlands, July 18, 1958; admitted, 1988, The Netherlands. *Education:* University of Groningen (LL.M., 1988). *LANGUAGES:* Dutch and English. *PRACTICE AREAS:* Commercial Law; Business Law; Insurance; Family Law.

SIMONE M.T. BLOMMESTIJN, born Amsterdam, The Netherlands, October 22, 1963; admitted, 1990, The Netherlands. *Education:* Free University Amsterdam (M.A. in Dutch Language and Literature, 1986; LL.M., 1989). *LANGUAGES:* Dutch and English. *PRACTICE AREAS:* Commercial Law; Business Law; Insurance; Negligence; Liability; Employment.

ALEXANDER MACLEAN, born Nieuwer-Amstel, The Netherlands, August 7, 1962; admitted, 1990, The Netherlands. *Education:* Free University Amsterdam (M.Sc. in Medicine, 1986; LL.M., 1990). *LANGUAGES:* Dutch, English and German. *PRACTICE AREAS:* Commercial Law; Business Law; Employment; Health Care; Medical Malpractice.

CORINA L. VALKENBURG, born Beverwijk, The Netherlands, January 24, 1958; admitted, 1990, The Netherlands. *Education:* University of Amsterdam (LL.M., 1990). *LANGUAGES:* Dutch, English and French. *PRACTICE AREAS:* Commercial Law; Business Law; Employment.

MASCHA E.F. BOTS, born Nijmegen, The Netherlands, April 17, 1965; admitted, 1991, The Netherlands. *Education:* Catholic University of Nijmegen (LL.M., 1989) Free University Brussels (Special Licence in International and European Law, 1990). *LANGUAGES:* Dutch, English, French and German. *PRACTICE AREAS:* Commercial Law; Business Law; Intellectual Property; Copyrights; Administrative Law; Environmental Law.

JAN-JAAP VAN DEVENTER, born Oldenzaal, The Netherlands, December 10, 1964; admitted, 1991, The Netherlands. *Education:* Leyden University (LL.M., 1989). *LANGUAGES:* Dutch and English. *PRACTICE AREAS:* Commercial Law; Business Law; Insurance; Bankruptcy; Insolvency; Criminal Law.

JAN E.T.F. VAN DER BEEK, born Bloemendaal, The Netherlands, May 23, 1966; admitted, 1991, The Netherlands. *Education:* University of Groningen (LL.M., 1991). *LANGUAGES:* Dutch, English and Spanish. *PRACTICE AREAS:* Commercial Law; Business Law; Bankruptcy; Insolvency.

CLEMENT A.P. WERRE, born Marseille, France, November 28, 1960; admitted, 1991, The Netherlands. *Education:* University of Amsterdam (M.A. in Philosophy, 1987; LL.M., 1990). *LANGUAGES:* Dutch, English and German. *PRACTICE AREAS:* Commercial Law; Business Law; Employment; Litigation.

FEMKE C. WEIJTENS, born Utrecht, The Netherlands, July 22, 1967; admitted, 1992, The Netherlands. *Education:* University of Utrecht (LL.M., 1991). Certified, Anglo/American Company Law and European Community Law, University of East London. *LANGUAGES:* Dutch, English and German. *PRACTICE AREAS:* Commercial Law; Business law; Employment; European Community Law.

MARIANNE D. RUIZEVELD, born Amstelveen, The Netherlands, July 8, 1968; admitted, 1992, The Netherlands. *Education:* Free University Amsterdam (LL.M., 1992). *LANGUAGES:* Dutch, English, French, German, Danish and Italian. *PRACTICE AREAS:* Commercial Law; Business Law; Employment; Criminal Law.

AREND C. LAGEMAAT, born Leusden, The Netherlands, January 17, 1966; admitted, 1992, The Netherlands. *Education:* Erasmus University Rotterdam (LL.M., 1992). *LANGUAGES:* Dutch, English and German. *PRACTICE AREAS:* Commercial Law; Business Law; Employment Law; Litigation; Criminal Law.

CHARLOTTE E. DINGEMANS, born Amsterdam, The Netherlands, December 21, 1966; admitted, 1992, The Netherlands. *Education:* Univer-

(This Listing Continued)

SCHUT & GROSHEIDE, Amsterdam—Continued

sity of Amsterdam (LL.M., 1992). *LANGUAGES:* Dutch and English. *PRACTICE AREAS:* Commercial Law; Business Law; Bankruptcy; Insolvency.

ANNE-MARIE MICHELS, born Utrecht, The Netherlands, June 8, 1967; admitted, 1993, The Netherlands. *Education:* University of Leyden (LL.M., 1992). *LANGUAGES:* Dutch, English and German. *PRACTICE AREAS:* Commercial Law; Business Law.

ALEXANDER C.G. GOLDMAN, born Veldhoven, The Netherlands, May 6, 1967; admitted, 1993, The Netherlands. *Education:* University of Amsterdam (LL.M., 1991). *LANGUAGES:* Dutch, English, German and French. *PRACTICE AREAS:* Commercial Law; Business Law; Employment.

DAVID F. BLACKMON, born The Hague, The Netherlands, October 3, 1968; admitted, 1993, The Netherlands. *Education:* University of Leyden (LL.M., 1993). *LANGUAGES:* Dutch, English and French. *PRACTICE AREAS:* Commercial Law; Business Law; Criminal Law; Broadcasting Law.

PAUL C.H. BEENDERS, born Utrecht, The Netherlands, October 12, 1968; admitted, 1993, The Netherlands. *Education:* University of Utrecht (LL.M., 1993). *LANGUAGES:* Dutch, English and German. *PRACTICE AREAS:* Commercial Law; Business Law; Employment.

ELLEN M. SOERJATIN, born The Hague, The Netherlands, January 25, 1966; admitted, 1993, The Netherlands. *Education:* University of Utecht (LL.M., 1993; M.A. in French, 1994). *LANGUAGES:* Dutch, English and French. *PRACTICE AREAS:* Commercial Law; Business Law; Employment.

FROUKJE J. LOURENS, born Vleuten-De Meern, The Netherlands, January 11, 1969; admitted, 1994, Netherlands. *Education:* Free University Amsterdam (LL.M., 1994). *LANGUAGES:* Dutch, English and French. *PRACTICE AREAS:* Commercial Law; Business Law; Employment; Intellectual Property.

CARLA M. ZILLI, born Arnhem, The Netherlands, July 18, 1968; admitted, 1994, The Netherlands. *Education:* Free University Amsterdam (LL.M., 1994). *LANGUAGES:* Dutch, English, Italian, French and German. *PRACTICE AREAS:* Commercial Law; Business Law.

ALLARD J.D. BEKIUS, born Schiedam, The Netherlands, February 20, 1969; admitted, 1994, The Netherlands. *Education:* University of Utrecht (LL.M., 1994). *LANGUAGES:* Dutch and English. *PRACTICE AREAS:* Commercial Law; Business Law.

NIELS C. VAN VEEN, born Amsterdam, The Netherlands, February 17, 1969; admitted, 1994, The Netherlands. *Education:* University of Amsterdam (LL.M., 1994). *LANGUAGES:* Dutch, English, French and German. *PRACTICE AREAS:* Commercial Law; Business Law; Employment.

ASTRID J.M. BARKMANS, born Etten-Leur, The Netherlands, August 27, 1968; admitted, 1995, The Netherlands. *Education:* University of Utrecht (LL.M., 1993). *LANGUAGES:* Dutch, German and English. *PRACTICE AREAS:* Commercial Law; Business Law.

Languages: Dutch, English, German, French, Italian, Spanish, Danish

---

SHUTTS & BOWEN, B.V.

EUROPA BOULEVARD 59
AMSTERDAM 1083 AD, THE NETHERLANDS
Telephone: (31 20) 661-0969
Telefax: (31 20) 642-1475

Key Largo, Florida Office: Suite A206, 31 Ocean Reef Drive. Telephone: 305-367-2881.
Miami, Florida Office: 1500 Miami Center, 201 South Biscayne Boulevard. Telephone: 305-358-6300. Cable Address: "Shuttsbo." Telefax: 305-381-9982.
Orlando, Florida Office: 20 North Orange Avenue, Suite 1000. Telephone: 407-423-3200. Fax: 407-425-8316.
West Palm Beach, Florida Office: One Clearlake Centre. 250 Australian Avenue, Suite 500. Telephone: 407-835-8500. Fax: 407-650-8530.
London, England Office: 48 Mount Street, London W1Y 5RE. Telephone: 4471493-4840. Telefax: 4471493-4299.

Firm engaged in American and International Law Practice but not allowed to appear in the Netherlands Court.

(This Listing Continued)

ROSEMARIE N. SANDERSON SCHADÈ, (P.A.), born Buffalo, New York, April 6, 1952; admitted, 1978, Florida; 1980, U.S. Tax Court, U.S. Court of Appeals, Fifth Circuit and U.S. District Court, Southern District of Florida (Not admitted in The Netherlands). *Education:* Florida State University (B.A., summa cum laude, 1974); University of Miami (J.D., cum laude, 1978; LL.M., 1979). Author: "The Florida Probate Code," University of Miami Law Review, Volume 32 October, 1978. *Member:* Dade County and American Bar Associations; The Florida Bar; International Bar Association; International Fiscal Association; International Tax Planning Association. *LANGUAGES:* English and Dutch.

(For complete biographical data on all personnel, see Professional Biographies at Miami, Florida)

SJÖCRONA VAN STIGT DE ROOS & PEN

Lawyers
Established in 1992
KEIZERSGRACHT 332
1016 EZ AMSTERDAM, THE NETHERLANDS
Telephone: +31 (0) 20/6275411
Telefax: +31 (0) 20/6226577

Rotterdam, The Netherlands Office: Zeemansstraat 11, 3016 CN. Telephone: +31 (0) 10/4364311. Telefax: +31 (0) 10/4366700.
The Hague, The Netherlands Office: Oranjestraat 7, 2514 JB. Telephone: +31 (0) 70/3467472. Telefax: +31 (0) 70/3924378.

Commercial Criminal Law and Criminal Procedures.
Firm engaged in Dutch, European and International Criminal Law practise. All lawyers are entitled to plead before the European Commission in Brussels, the European Court of Human Rights in Strassbourg and the Supreme Court of the Netherlands.

FIRM PROFILE: Established in 1992, Sjöcrona Van Stigt De Roos & Pen is the largest Commercial Criminal Law Firm in the Netherlands. The firm has a broadly based practise with a reputation for offering a full range of quality legal services in the field. The client base is worldwide. The firm has eight partners and four associates practising in three offices. Two members of the firm hold professorships in Criminal Law and Criminal Procedure at Dutch Universities.

MEMBERS OF FIRM

Prof. Dr. Theo A. de Roos	**Prof. Dr. Jan M. Sjöcrona**
Jurjen S. Pen	**Boudewijn C.W. van Eijck**
Arthur J.N. van Stigt	**Marlies van Strien**
Lian A.M. Mannheims	**Annelies E.M. Röttgering**

ASSOCIATES

Chantal P.E. Meewisse	**Jetty A. Bult**
Peter W.J. van der Spek	**Dr. Stijn A. Franken**

(For Complete Biographical Data on all Personnel, see Professional Biographies at The Hague, The Netherlands)

STIBBE SIMONT MONAHAN DUHOT

STRAWINSKYLAAN 2001
P.O. BOX 75640
1070 AP AMSTERDAM, THE NETHERLANDS
Telephone: (20) 546 06 06
Cable Address: "Mandatum"
Telex: 16414 (Stib NL)
Telecopier: (20) 546 01 23

Brussels, Belgium Office: Henri Wafelaerts 47-51 (box 1), B-1060. Telephone: 533.52.11. Telex: 24.519. Telefax: 533.52.12.
Paris, France Office: 154, Rue de l'Université, 75007. Telephone: (1) 40 62 20 00. Telecopier: (1) 40 62 20 62.
London, England Office: 66 Gresham Street, EC2V 7NH. Telephone: (44 171) 600-4400. Telecopier: (44 171) 600-4411.
New York, New York Office: 335 Madison Avenue, 10017. Telephone: (1-212) 972-4000. Telecopier: (1-212) 972-4929.

Administrative Law (Environmental Law), Corporate Law, Corporate Reorganization and Insolvency, Tax Law, Banking and Financial Law, Competition Law (Dutch, Belgium, French and EC), Computer Law, Construction Law, Law of the European Communities, Distributorships and Agencies, Energy Law, Food Law, Industrial and Intellectual Property Law (Trademarks, Patents, Know How, Copyrights, Models and Designs, Pi-

(This Listing Continued)

racy), Merger and Acquisitions, Labor Law, Litigation and Arbitration, Press and Media Law (Protection of Information, Telecommunications), Real Property (Leases, Conveyances).

Dutch attorneys may represent clients before all Dutch Courts, before the European Court of Justice and the Benelux Court of Justice, and are admitted to plead before all Courts of the member states of the Common Market (EEC).

MEMBERS OF FIRM
ATTORNEYS AT LAW

GERT MOSLER, born 1930; admitted, 1956, Amsterdam. *Education:* Leyden University (1955). Substitute Justice, County Court of Amsterdam. *Member:* International Bar Association/SBL. *PRACTICE AREAS:* Banking; Contracts; Corporations; Investment; Companies; Funds and Trusts; Litigation (all areas of practice); Real Estate; Mergers and Acquisitions.

THEO R. BREMER, born 1934; admitted, 1960, Amsterdam. *Education:* University of Utrecht (1958). Substitute Justice, Court of Appeals, Amsterdam. President of the Amsterdam Bar (1988-1992). President, Dutch Group, AIPPI. *Member:* Union Internationale des Avocats; Association Littéraire et Artistique Internationale (ALAI); Association Industrielle (AIPPI); Association Benelux des Conseils en Marques et Modèles (BMM). *PRACTICE AREAS:* Intellectual and Industrial Property; Entertainment and Media; Agency and Distribution.

PAUL C. VAN DEN HOEK, born 1939; admitted, 1965, Amsterdam. *Education:* University of Amsterdam (1964). Professor of Law, University of Amsterdam. President, The Netherlands Order of Advocates, 1981-1984. Member of the Board, The Netherlands Arbitration Institute. *PRACTICE AREAS:* Arbitration; Corporations; Mergers and Acquisitions.

RONALD W. DE RUUK, born 1941; admitted, 1967, Amsterdam. *Education:* University of Amsterdam (1967). *Member:* International Bar Association (Former Chairman and Co-Chairman, Committee on Creditor's Rights, Insolvency, Liquidation and Reorganization of the Section on Business Law); European Association of Insolvency Practitioners (AEPPC). *PRACTICE AREAS:* General Commercial; Bankruptcy, Insolvency and Reorganization; Industrial Relations and Labor; Litigation.

ROBERT SAMKALDEN, born 1939; admitted, 1969, Amsterdam. *Education:* Leyden University. President, Amsterdam Society of Practitioners. Substitute Justice, Court of Amsterdam. President, Architecture Centre, Amsterdam (ARCAM). Member, International Federation for Housing and Planning. *PRACTICE AREAS:* Administrative Law; Environment; Government Regulatory Matters; Real Estate; Public-Private Partnership.

HANS M. VAN VEGGEL, born 1941; admitted, 1969, Amsterdam. *Education:* University of Amsterdam. Substitute Justice, County Court, Amsterdam. Member, Council of the Bar of Amsterdam, 1979-1987. *PRACTICE AREAS:* Entertainment and Media; Litigation; Real Estate; Sports.

TOM DE WAARD, born 1946; admitted, 1971, Amsterdam. *Education:* Leyden University (1971). *Member:* Dutch Bar Association (President); International Bar Association (Council member); American Chamber of Commerce (Legal Committee). *PRACTICE AREAS:* Corporations; Corporate Finance; Mergers and Acquisitions; Securities; Arbitration.

MARIUS W. JOSEPHUS JITTA, born 1946; admitted, 1973, Amsterdam. *Education:* Bowdoin College, Maine (USA); University of Paris II; Leyden University. *PRACTICE AREAS:* Mergers and Acquisitions; Financing Venture Capital; Bankruptcy.

NIELS S. J. KOEMAN, born 1949; admitted, 1974, Amsterdam. *Education:* University of Utrecht (1972). Professor of Law, University of Amsterdam. *PRACTICE AREAS:* Administrative Law; Environment; Regulatory Matters; Litigation.

W. FRANS TH. CORPELEIJN, born 1948; admitted, 1975, Amsterdam. *Education:* University of Utrecht (1973); Business School, Cornell University (M.B.A., 1975). *Member:* International Bar Association. *PRACTICE AREAS:* Corporations; Mergers and Acquisitions.

D. W. FEER VERKADE, born 1944; admitted, 1978, Amsterdam. *Education:* Leyden University (1968). Substitute Justice, Court of Appeals, Arnhem. Professor of Law, University of Leiden. Member, Committee on Consumer Affairs of the Social-Economic Council (SER). *Member:* Association Littéraire et Artistique Internationale (ALAI); Association Internationale pour la Protection de la Propriété Industrielle (AIPPI); Ligue Internationale du Droit de la Concurrence; Association Benelux des Conseils en Marques et Modèles (BMM). *PRACTICE AREAS:* Industrial and Intellectual Property; Advertising and Press Law; Product Liability; Computers.

(This Listing Continued)

FRANK W. G. M. VAN BRUNSCHOT, born 1940; admitted, 1979, Amsterdam. *Education:* University of Amsterdam. Professor of Tax Law, University of Amsterdam. Substitute Justice, Court of Appeals, Amsterdam. *Member:* International Fiscal Association; American Tax Institute; International Bar Association. *PRACTICE AREAS:* Taxation; Mergers and Acquisitions; Corporations.

JOOP G. J. JANSSEN, born 1948; admitted, 1974, Amsterdam. *Education:* University of Tilburg (1974). *Member:* International Bar Association; Construction Law Society (Member, European Section). *PRACTICE AREAS:* Building and Construction; Computers; General Practice; Real Estate.

PETER A. M. HENDRICK, born 1947; admitted, 1976, Amsterdam. *Education:* University of Nijmegen. Substitute Justice, District Court Arnhem. *Member:* Association Internationale pour la Protection de la Propriété Industrielle (AIPPI); Lique Internationale du Droit de la Concurrence; European Trademark Practitioner's Association (ECTA); Association Benelux des Conseils en Marques et Modèles (BMM); United States Trademark Association (USTA). *PRACTICE AREAS:* Industrial and Intellectual Property; International Business; Transactions; Agency and Distribution; Antitrust and Competition.

MARTIJN VAN EMPEL, born 1941; admitted, 1983, Amsterdam. *Education:* Leyden University (1965); University of Paris (1966). Professor of Law, University of Amsterdam. *Member:* International Bar Association; Union Internationale des Avocats; Ligue Internationale de Droit de la Concurrence; Netherlands Association for European Law (Member of the Board). *PRACTICE AREAS:* European Community; Product Liability.

CHARLES J. LANGEREIS, born 1948; admitted, 1984, Amsterdam. *Education:* Leyden University, 1971; University of Tilburg (Doctor of Laws, 1986). Substitute Justice, Court of Appeals, The Hague. Professor of Tax Law, Leyden University. *Member:* International Fiscal Association; Association of Administrative Law (Member of the Board). *PRACTICE AREAS:* Taxation.

J. MAURITS VAN DEN WALL BAKE, born 1950; admitted, 1976, Amsterdam. *Education:* Leyden University (1974). *Member:* Union Internationale des Avocats; International Bar Association. *PRACTICE AREAS:* Banking; Contracts; Corporations; Mergers and Acquisitions.

BOUDEWIJN A. VAN HEUVELN, born 1946; admitted, 1977, Amsterdam. *Education:* University of Amsterdam (1974). *Member:* International Bar Association. *PRACTICE AREAS:* International Business Transactions; Corporations; Mergers and Acquisitions; Corporate Finance; Industrial Relations and Labor; Litigation; Real Estate.

JAN J. TRAP, born 1946; admitted, 1977, Amsterdam. *Education:* University of Utrecht (1971). Substitute Justice, County Court, Amsterdam. *Member:* International Bar Association. *PRACTICE AREAS:* Industrial Relations and Labor.

JAAP WILLEUMIER, born 1953; admitted, 1979, Amsterdam. *Education:* University of Amsterdam (1979). *Member:* Union Internationale des Avocats; The Association of the Bar of The City of New York; American Bar Association (Member, Section on Business Law). (Resident, London Office). *PRACTICE AREAS:* Corporations; Corporate and Structured Finance; International Business Transactions; Mergers and Acquisitions; Securities.

JAAP E. M. POLAK, born 1955; admitted, 1979, Amsterdam. *Education:* Leyden University (1979). Member, Legislation Committee of Public Water-Works. *PRACTICE AREAS:* Administrative Law; Building and Construction; Environment; Health Care; Government Regulatory Matters; Real Estate.

PETER ROORDA, born 1952; admitted, 1980, Amsterdam; 1990, New York. *Education:* University of Groningen (1978); University of Pennsylvania (LL.M., 1979). Greenfield Fellowship for Human Rights, 1978-1979. Editor, National Law Review Ars Aequi, 1974-1977. Acting Secretary, Board of Editors, 1978. Member, Panel of Sworn Arbitrators, American Arbitration Association, 1989—. *Member:* The Association of the Bar of The City of New York; New York State and American (Member, Section of International Law and Practice, Task Force, 1990—). *PRACTICE AREAS:* Arbitration; Bankruptcy, Insolvency and Reorganization; Contracts; Corporations; International Business; Transactions; Real Estate; Litigation.

ALBERT JAN VAN DEN BERG, born 1949; admitted, 1980, Rotterdam; 1988, Amsterdam. *Education:* University of Amsterdam (1973); University of Aix-en-Provence (European and International Law, 1974); New York University (Comparative Jurisprudence, 1975); University of Aix-en-

(This Listing Continued)

STIBBE SIMONT MONAHAN DUHOT, Amsterdam—Continued

Provence (Docteur en Droit, 1977); University of Rotterdam (Doctor of Law, 1981). Professor of Tax Law, University of Rotterdam, 1989—. Secretary General, Netherlands Arbitration Institute, 1980-1988. Editor, Dutch Journal on Arbitration, 1980—. General Editor, Yearbook Commercial Arbitration, 1986—. General Editor, The International Handbook on Commercial Arbitration, 1989—. *Member:* Chartered Institute of Arbitrators, London (Member, Arbitration Committee); Court of Arbitration of the London Court of International Arbitration; Commission of International Arbitration of the ICC, Paris; Chartered Institute of Arbitrators (Fellows); Institute of International Business Law and Practice of the ICC, Paris; International Bar Association; International Council for Commercial Arbitration; Court of Arbitration of the Hong Kong International Arbitration Center; Euro Arab Forum for Arbitration and Business Law, Paris. *PRACTICE AREAS:* Agency and Distribution; Arbitration; Building and Construction; East-West Trade; Electricity, Oil and Gas; International Business Transactions; Litigation.

PAUL P.M. WIJNANDS, born 1954; admitted, 1978, Utrecht; 1990, Amsterdam. *Education:* University of Utrecht (M.L., Private Law, 1977); University of Amsterdam (Tax Law, 1977-1980). Substitute Judge, Cantonal Court of Hilversem, 1989. *Member International Bar Association.* *PRACTICE AREAS:* Industrial Relations and Labor; Contracts; Agency and Distribution.

JOOST J. J. VAN LANSCHOT, born 1955; admitted, 1982, Amsterdam; 1992, Paris. *Education:* University of Utrecht (1981); University of Pennsylvania (LL.M., 1981). *Member:* Union Internationale des Advocats. *LANGUAGES:* Dutch, English and French. *PRACTICE AREAS:* Mergers and Acquisitions; Corporations; International Business Transactions.

ONNO W. BROUWER, born 1954; admitted, 1980, Amsterdam; 1989, Brussels. *Education:* University of Amsterdam; London School of Economics (1978). Legal Secretary Court of Justice of the European Communities, 1985-1989. *Member:* Amsterdam and Brussels Bar Associations. *PRACTICE AREAS:* European Community.

HANS MARSEILLE, born 1941; admitted, 1989, Amsterdam. *Education:* Leyden University (Tax Law Degree, 1966); University of Amsterdam (1969). *Member:* International Fiscal Association. *PRACTICE AREAS:* Corporate Tax; International Tax.

HANS BECKMAN, born 1944. *Education:* University of Rotterdam (Business Economics, 1966; Fiscal Degree, 1968; Law Degree, 1971; Auditors' Degree, 1972). Professor, Business Economics and Financial Accounting Law, Law Faculty Erasmus Universitat, 1981—. *Member:* Dutch Institute of Auditors (NIVRA). *PRACTICE AREAS:* Corporations; Corporate Finance; Financial Accounting and Reporting; Mergers and Acquisitions.

ALLARD C. METZELAAR, born 1957; admitted, 1982, Amsterdam. *Education:* Leyden University (1981). *Member:* International Bar Association. *LANGUAGES:* Dutch, English, German and Norwegian. *PRACTICE AREAS:* Banking and Financial Services; Corporations; Mergers and Acquisitions; Bankruptcy and Reorganization; Litigation.

HECTOR W. L. DE BEAUFORT, born 1956; admitted, 1984, Amsterdam and New York. *Education:* University of Utrecht (1981); University of Pennsylvania (LL.M., 1983). *Member:* Association of the Bar of the City of New York; American Bar Association; Association Internationale des Jeunes Avocats; International Bar Association. *PRACTICE AREAS:* Corporations; International Business Transactions; Mergers and Acquisitions; Securities.

DICK C. J. A. VAN ENGELEN, born 1958; admitted, 1984, Amsterdam. *Education:* University of Nijmegen (1984). *Member:* Association Littéraire et Artistique Internationale (ALAI); Association Internationale pour la Protection de la Propriété Industrielle (AIPPI); Association Benelux des Conseils en Marques et Modèles (BMM); Ligue Internationale du Droit de la Concurrence; European Food Law Association. *PRACTICE AREAS:* Intellectual and Industrial Property; Antitrust and Competition; Agency and Distribution; Entertainment and Media; Litigation; Advertising and Press Law; Product Liability.

ALFONS F. J. A. LEIJTEN, born 1959; admitted, 1984, Amsterdam. *Education:* University of Amsterdam (1983); University of California at Los Angeles (LL.M., 1984). *Member:* International Bar Association. *LANGUAGES:* Dutch and English. *PRACTICE AREAS:* Mergers and Acquisitions; Corporate Finance; Agency and Distribution; Computers; Contracts; International Business Transactions; Litigation.

(This Listing Continued)

ANTONIE VAN HEES, born 1959; admitted, 1989, Amsterdam. *Education:* University of Nijmegen (1982). *PRACTICE AREAS:* Banking; Bankruptcy, Insolvency and Reorganization; Contracts; Litigation.

REIN JAN PRINS, born 1960; admitted, 1985, Amsterdam. *Education:* Leyden University (1984). *Member:* Association Internationale pour la Protection de la Propriété Industrielle (AIPPI); Ligue Internationale Du Droit De la Concurrence; Association Litteraire et Artistique Internationale (ALAI); European Communities Trade Mark Associations (ECTA); Association Bénélux pour le Droit des Marques et Modéles (BMM); Dutch Association of European Law (NVER). *LANGUAGES:* Dutch, French and English. *PRACTICE AREAS:* Intellectual Property; Agency and Distribution; Antitrust and Competition; Contracts; Entertainment and Media; Litigation.

ARNOLD J. H. W. M. VERSTEEG, born 1959; admitted, 1986, Amsterdam. *Education:* Nijmegen University (1982). *LANGUAGES:* Dutch, English and German. *PRACTICE AREAS:* Administrative Law; Media; Environment; Government Regulatory Matters; Health Care; European Community; Litigation.

ELLA C. B. ADRIAANSE, born 1961; admitted, 1986, Amsterdam. *Education:* Leyden University (1985). *LANGUAGES:* Dutch, English and German. *PRACTICE AREAS:* Contracts; Investment Companies; Funds and Trust; Litigation (all areas of practice); Mergers and Acquisitions; Real Estate; Sports (Players, Clubs and Sponsors).

STEF VAN WEEGHEL, born 1960; admitted, 1987, Amsterdam. *Education:* University of Leiden (Dutch Law, 1983; Tax Law, 1987); New York University (LL.M. in Taxation, 1990). (Resident, New York Office). *PRACTICE AREAS:* Taxation.

DIANA C. C. VAN EVERDINGEN, born 1957; admitted, 1987, Amsterdam. *Education:* University of Amsterdam (1987). *PRACTICE AREAS:* Contracts; Corporations; Corporate Finance; International Business Transactions; Investments; Companies; Funds and Trusts; Mergers and Acquisitions; Securities.

MAARTEN P. H. SANDERS, born 1959; admitted, 1987, Amsterdam. *Education:* University of Amsterdam (1987). Member of firm effective July 1, 1995. *PRACTICE AREAS:* Corporations; Mergers and Acquisitions; Litigation; Corporate Finance; Bankruptcy; Securities.

MARTIN J.F. IN DE BRAEKT, born 1962; admitted, 1988, Amsterdam. *Education:* Leiden University (Dutch Law, 1985; Tax Law, 1988). (Member of Firm effective July 1, 1995). (Resident, Paris Office). *PRACTICE AREAS:* Taxation; Mergers and Acquisitions; International Business Transactions.

MEMBERS OF FIRM
CIVIL LAW NOTARIES

NELSON M. J. DAMEN, born 1935; appointed Civil Law Notary, 1975. *Education:* University of Amsterdam (1961). *PRACTICE AREAS:* Company Law; Real Estate; Family Relations.

J. HANS M. CARLIER, born 1942; appointed Civil Law Notary, 1980. *Education:* University of Nijmegen (1969). *PRACTICE AREAS:* Banking; Corporations; Corporation Finance; Family Relations.

LAURA C. KLEIN, born 1950; appointed Civil Law Notary, 1988. *Education:* University of Groningen (1972). *PRACTICE AREAS:* Real Estate; Securities; Family Relations; Foundations and Associations.

H. BART H. KRAAK, born 1950; admitted, 1977, The Netherlands. *Education:* Leyden University (1977). *Member:* Koninklijke Notariële Broederschap; De Notarieele Vereniging; International Fiscal Association. *PRACTICE AREAS:* Company Law; Mergers and Acquisitions; Contracts.

ASSOCIATES
ATTORNEYS AT LAW

MARIAN WIGLEVEN, born 1946; admitted, 1970, Amsterdam. *Education:* University of Amsterdam (1970). *PRACTICE AREAS:* Family Relations.

MICHAEL HERSCHDORFER, born 1950; admitted, 1976, Amsterdam. *Education:* University of Amsterdam (Law, 1975; Chemistry, 1976). *Member:* European Association of Insolvency Practitioners (AEPPC). *PRACTICE AREAS:* Agency and Distribution; Bankruptcy, Insolvency and Reorganization; Contracts; Entertainment and Media; Industrial and Intellectual Property; Litigation; Real Estate.

(This Listing Continued)

ELLIS P. STOLP, born 1949; admitted, 1980, Amsterdam. *Education:* Leiden University (1980). *PRACTICE AREAS:* Real Estate; Litigation; Contracts; Agency and Distribution.

JENNY S. A. M. SCHOKKENBROEK, born 1957; admitted, 1982, Amsterdam. *Education:* University of Groningen (1982). *PRACTICE AREAS:* Industrial Relations and Labor.

YOLANDA A. A. G. DE VRIES, born 1956; admitted, 1984, Amsterdam. *Education:* University of Amsterdam (1984). *LANGUAGES:* Dutch, French and Spanish (certified translator). *PRACTICE AREAS:* Administrative Law; Environment.

W. F. REINOUT RINZEMA, born 1959; admitted, 1983, Amsterdam. *Education:* University of Utrecht. *PRACTICE AREAS:* Computers; Real Estate.

MONETTA V. ULRICI, born 1960; admitted, 1985, Amsterdam. *Education:* University of Amsterdam (1984). *Member:* International Law Association. *PRACTICE AREAS:* Industrial Relations and Labor.

MIRIAM J. J. DE BONTRIDDER, born 1957; admitted, 1985, Amsterdam. *Education:* University of Ghent (Philosophy, 1980; Introduction to Belgium Law, 1982); University of Amsterdam (Dutch Law, 1984; International Law, 1985).

RIENK VAN DER WOUDE, born 1946; admitted, 1989, Amsterdam. *Education:* University of Amsterdam (1973).

PETRA A. CHARBON, born 1958; admitted, 1982, Groningen; 1989, Alkmaar; 1994, Amsterdam. *Education:* Rijks Universiteit, Groningen (1982). *PRACTICE AREAS:* Industrial Relations; Labor.

P. BERNT HUGENHOLTZ, born 1955; admitted, 1990, Amsterdam. *Education:* University of Groningen (Masters, 1980); University of Amsterdam (Doctor, 1989). *Member:* Dutch Media and Communications Law Society; Dutch Copyright Law Society; ALAI; Dutch Group AIPPI.

KURT TH. M. STÖPETIE, born 1961; admitted, 1988, Amsterdam. *Education:* University of Utrecht (1986); Grotius-Academy (1987).

FRANS JOZEF A. CROUSEN, born 1962; admitted, 1988, Amsterdam. *Education:* University of Utrecht (Law, 1986).

MARIËTTE LAFARRE, born 1960; admitted, 1988, Amsterdam. *Education:* Amsterdam University (1987). *Member:* Construction Law Society (European Section).

ANTOIN D.R. VAN HOREN, born 1960; admitted, 1991, Amsterdam. *Education:* University of Tilburg (1986); Leiden University (1989). Inspector, Direct and Corporate Taxes, 1986-1989. Ministry of Finance, Legislative Office, 1989-1991. *Member:* American Tax Institute in Europe.

CARLA J. M. KLAASSEN, born 1961. *Education:* University of Nymson (1985; Doctor's Degree, 1991).

MAARTEN B. KOETSER, born 1949; admitted, 1991, Amsterdam. *Education:* University of Amsterdam (Master in law, 1973).

ANNEMIEK LOUWRIER, born 1961; admitted, 1989, Amsterdam. *Education:* Leiden University (Philosophy, 1983; Law, 1988).

MARC P. VOGEL, born 1962; admitted, 1989, Amsterdam. *Education:* University of Amsterdam (1987).

JOOST J. VETTER, born 1964; admitted, 1989, Amsterdam. *Education:* University of Amsterdam (Tax Law, 1987). (Resident, London Office).

MAARTEN DE BRUIN, born 1964; admitted, 1989, Amsterdam. *Education:* University of Tilburg (1989). (Resident, New York Office).

RUDOLF J. DE VRIES, born 1962; admitted, 1991, Amsterdam. *Education:* University of Groningen (Master of Law, 1981). Author: Cursus Belastingrecht (Vennootschapsbelasting), Gonda Quist. Lecturer, Fiscal Law, University of Leiden. *Member:* Nederlandse Orde van Advocaten.

HELEEN H. KERSTEN, born 1965; admitted, 1989, Amsterdam. *Education:* Leiden University (1987 and 1989); University of Florida (1988). *Member:* International Law Association.

LAMBERT OOSTING, born 1959; admitted, 1989, Amsterdam. *Education:* University of Utrecht (1985; Doctoral, 1986; Law, 1989).

BRIGITTE L. RUŸS, born 1963; admitted, 1989, Amsterdam. *Education:* University of Utrecht (LL.M., 1988); Université de Paris II (1989). Lecturer on Roman Law, 1985-1986.

CATHERINE M. VAN DEN BRINK, born 1964; admitted, 1990, Amsterdam. *Education:* Rijks Universiteit Groningen Medical Faculty

(This Listing Continued)

(Doctoral, 1987); University of Amsterdam (Masters, 1989). *Member:* Dutch Law Society (NYV).

BART F. DE JONG, born 1961; admitted, 1990, Amsterdam. *Education:* Katholieke Universiteit Nijmegen (Masters, 1985).

MARC A.I.M. ZANDHUIS, born 1960; admitted, 1989, Amsterdam. *Education:* University of Amsterdam (Master of Law). *LANGUAGES:* Dutch, English, German and French. *PRACTICE AREAS:* Industrial Relations and Labor; Litigation (General); Company Law.

FRITS SCHNEIDER, born 1954; admitted, 1991, Amsterdam. *Education:* Vrye Universiteit, Amsterdam (Master of Law, 1990). *Member:* Nederlandse Orde van Advocaten.

E.D. MILDRED KNEGT, born 1954; admitted, 1991, Amsterdam. *Education:* University of Amsterdam (1981); University of Utrecht (1991). Advisor of the Council of State, 1984-1991. Member, Society for Construction Law, 1982-1985 and 1991.

JAAP GOEMANS, born 1963; admitted, 1990, Amsterdam. *Education:* Rijks Universiteit Utrecht (Master of Law, 1988). Officer for Legal Affairs and Deputy to Head of Civil Military Co-operation, First Dutch Corps., 1989-1990. *Member:* Dutch and Local Bar Associations.

PETER VAN DER VLIS, born 1966; admitted, 1990, Amsterdam. *Education:* University of Utrecht (Master of Law, 1990). *Member:* Dutch Bar Association.

HELEEN S.R. WEEBER, admitted, 1990, Amsterdam. *Education:* University of Groningen (LL.M., 1987); University Sorbonne (1989).

TOM VAN WIJNGAARDEN, born 1963; admitted, 1990, Amsterdam. *Education:* Academy for Physical Education (1981-1985); University of Utrecht (1986-1987); University of Groningen (Master of Law, 1990). *Member:* Dutch Bar Association.

JEROEN FLEMING, born 1966; admitted, 1991, Amsterdam. *Education:* University of Groningen (Master of Law, 1990).

RIAN KALDEN, born 1966; admitted, 1991, Amsterdam. *Education:* Leiden University (LL.B., 1989); University of London, Queen Mary College (LL.M., 1990).

YOLA E. J. GERADTS, born 1967; admitted, 1991, Amsterdam. *Education:* Rijks Universiteit, Leiden (1990).

GERT-JAN T. M. VAN DEN BERGH, born 1962; admitted, 1991, Amsterdam. *LANGUAGES:* Dutch, English, French, German.

MATHILDE BOOTSMA, born 1969; admitted, 1991, Amsterdam. *Education:* Rijks Universiteit, Groningen (Masters, 1991). *LANGUAGES:* English, French, German.

FRANK M. A. 'T HART, born 1967; admitted, 1992, Amsterdam. *Education:* Amsterdam University School of Law; Cologne University School of Law. *LANGUAGES:* Italian.

DERK J. R. LEMSTRA, born 1965; admitted, 1992, Amsterdam. *Education:* Leiden University Law School (J.D., 1989); Columbia University School of Law (LL.M., 1990). (Resident, New York Office).

JANNA G. VAN OLST, born 1964; admitted, 1992, Amsterdam. *Education:* University of Groningen (Law, 1989); University of London (LL.M., 1990).

OSCAR A. H. VAN DALSUM, born 1968; admitted, 1992, Amsterdam. *Education:* Catholic University of Nijmegen (Mr., 1990). *LANGUAGES:* Dutch, English, French, German.

AALDERT TEN VEEN, born 1966; admitted, 1992, Amsterdam. *Education:* University of Groningen (1991). *Member:* Dutch Environmental Law Association. *LANGUAGES:* Dutch, German and English. *PRACTICE AREAS:* Administrative Law; Environment; Health Care.

ERICA L.S. VERKERK, born 1967; admitted, 1992, Amsterdam. *Education:* University of Groningen (1992).

PETER S. BAKKER, born 1967; admitted, 1992, Amsterdam. *Education:* University of Utrecht (1991, Master). *LANGUAGES:* Dutch, English, French and German. *PRACTICE AREAS:* Industrial Relations and Labor Law.

MICHAEL L. MOLENAARS, born 1968. *Education:* University of Amsterdam (Taxation Law, 1992; Dutch/Civil Law , 1992). *PRACTICE AREAS:* Taxation.

(This Listing Continued)

STIBBE SIMONT MONAHAN DUHOT, *Amsterdam—Continued*

WILLEMIEKE M.E. VAN GORKUM, born 1968; admitted, 1992, Amsterdam. *Education:* University of Leiden (1990, Dutch Law; 1992, Tax Law).

LIESBETH KOOMEN, born 1967; admitted, 1992, Amsterdam. *Education:* University of Leiden (1992). *Member:* A.D.E.K. *LANGUAGES:* Dutch, English, French, German.

CARMEN F. BAKAS, born 1968; admitted, 1992, Amsterdam. *Education:* University of Leiden (1991;1992). *LANGUAGES:* Dutch, English, German, French, Hindi. *PRACTICE AREAS:* Intellectual Property; General Practice.

WOUTER M. HES, born 1965; admitted, 1992, Amsterdam. *Education:* University of Amsterdam (LL.M., 1992).

MARTIGUE F. HARTSTRA, born 1964; admitted, 1992, Amsterdam. *Education:* University of Leiden (1992; Spanish, 1993). *LANGUAGES:* Dutch, English, French, German, Spanish, Portuguese.

A.J.G. TAZELAAR, born 1960; admitted, 1991, Amsterdam. *Education:* University of Amsterdam (LL.M., 1991). *PRACTICE AREAS:* Industrial Relations and Labor.

MARLEEN P. DE BRUYN, born 1966. *Education:* University of Amsterdam (1992). *LANGUAGES:* Dutch, English, German, French. *PRACTICE AREAS:* Real Estate; Litigation (all areas of practice); Corporations; Contracts; Labour Law.

CHARLES E. HONÉE, born 1967; admitted, 1992, Amsterdam. *Education:* Katholieke University Nijmegen (1992). *LANGUAGES:* Dutch, English, German. *PRACTICE AREAS:* Company and Commercial.

BAREND R. POST, born 1967; admitted, 1993, Amsterdam. *Education:* University of Amsterdam (1985). *LANGUAGES:* Dutch, French, English, German.

GERHARDT J. VELS, born 1966; admitted, 1993, Amsterdam. *Education:* University of Amsterdam (1992). *Member:* Environmental Law Association; Administrative Law Association; Trade Law Association. *LANGUAGES:* Dutch, English, German, French. *PRACTICE AREAS:* Corporate Law; Contracts; Administrative Law; Environmental Law; Mergers and Acquisitions.

JOANNE L. ANKUM-BRINKMAN, born 1966; admitted, 1993, Amsterdam. *Education:* University of Amsterdam (1992). Member, "RIMO" Association for the Study of Islamic Law and Laws of the Middle East. *LANGUAGES:* Dutch, English, French, German, Italian, Egyptian, Arabic.

ROBERT JAN DE CLERCQ ZUBLI, born 1967; admitted, 1993, Amsterdam. *Education:* University of Amsterdam (LL.M., 1992). *PRACTICE AREAS:* Taxation.

JAN D. ROELAND, born 1966; admitted, 1993. *PRACTICE AREAS:* Taxation.

SHEILA C. HAGEDOORN, born 1966; admitted, 1993, Amsterdam. *Education:* University of Amsterdam (1990; Doctorate, 1991); Exeter University, Great Britain (LL.M., 1992). Member, ADEK, 1993. *LANGUAGES:* Dutch, English, French, German. *PRACTICE AREAS:* Company Law; Commercial Law.

PAUL BAVELAAR, born 1962; admitted, 1993, Amsterdam. *Education:* University of Amsterdam (1990); University of Kiel, Germany (LL.M., 1993). *LANGUAGES:* Dutch, German. *PRACTICE AREAS:* Contract Law; Company; Groups of Company; German Law.

GABRIËLLA C. DE ROOIJ, born 1966; admitted, 1993, The Netherlands. *Education:* Rijks Universiteit Groningen (1993). *LANGUAGES:* French, German and English. *PRACTICE AREAS:* General Practice.

LENNAERT J. POSCH, born 1967; admitted, 1993, The Netherlands; 1994, New York, U.S.A. *Education:* University of Amsterdam (J.D., 1992); Duke University (LL.M., 1993). *LANGUAGES:* English, French, German. *PRACTICE AREAS:* Corporate Law; International Arbitration; Commercial Law.

J. (ANNET) J. DRAAIJER, born 1967; admitted, 1994, The Netherlands. *Education:* Rijks Universiteit, Groningen (Doctorate, 1989); University of Amsterdam (Mr., 1990). *PRACTICE AREAS:* Administrative Law.

(This Listing Continued)

FRANCISCUS W.E. EIJSVOGELS, born 1967; admitted, 1994, The Netherlands. *Education:* University of Utrecht (Mr., 1992); University of Hull (LL.M., 1992). *PRACTICE AREAS:* Intellectual Property.

HANS P. WITTEVEEN, born 1969; admitted, 1994, The Netherlands. *Education:* University of Amsterdam (LL.M., 1993). *LANGUAGES:* Dutch, English, French and German. *PRACTICE AREAS:* Company Law; Commercial Law.

MICHIEL DE WIT, born 1967; admitted, 1994, The Netherlands. *Education:* University of Amsterdam (Mr., 1994). *LANGUAGES:* Dutch, German and English. *PRACTICE AREAS:* Taxation; Company Law; Commercial Law.

GENEVIÈVE J. SCHOLMAN, born 1966; admitted, 1994, The Netherlands. *Education:* University of Nijmegen (LL.M., 1994). *LANGUAGES:* Dutch and English. *PRACTICE AREAS:* General Practice; Insolvency and Bankruptcy; Litigation; Contracts.

ANNEMARIE C. MULDER, born 1965; admitted, 1994, The Netherlands. *Education:* Rijks Universiteit, Utrecht (Civil Law, 1989) ; University of Amsterdam (Taxation, 1993). *LANGUAGES:* English. *PRACTICE AREAS:* Taxation.

LARISSA R. MOERMAN, born 1969; admitted, 1994, The Netherlands. *Education:* Leiden University (LL.M., 1993). *LANGUAGES:* Dutch, English, German and French. *PRACTICE AREAS:* General Practice; Real Estate Law; Building Law; Construction Law.

ASSOCIATES
CIVIL LAW NOTARIES

LEO A. GALMAN, born 1957; admitted to practice as Civil Law Notary, 1985. *Education:* University of Utrecht.

CORNELIS BINNENKADE, born 1959; admitted, 1983, The Netherlands. *Education:* Rijks Universiteit, Leiden (Mr., 1983). *LANGUAGES:* English. *PRACTICE AREAS:* Real Estate Law; Securities; Family Relations.

ERNST H. ROZELAAR, born 1961. *Education:* Leiden University.

BIANCA NAGTEGAAL, born 1966. *Education:* Leiden University.

NEELTJE JANSEN, born 1965; admitted, 1989. Rotterdam; 1992, Amsterdam. *Education:* University of Groningen (Mr. 1989). *LANGUAGES:* Dutch, English, German.

ROBERT H. J. SCHREUDER, born 1965; admitted, 1991, Amsterdam. *Education:* Università Di Bologna (1989); Rijks Universiteit, Leiden (Master at Law, 1990). *LANGUAGES:* French, Italian.

FRANÇOISE C.E. SCHOORDIJK, born 1966; admitted, 1991, Amsterdam. *Education:* University of Amsterdam (LL.M., 1991). *Member:* Koninklijke Notariële Broederschap.

RUDOLF CREMERS, born 1964; admitted, 1991, Amsterdam. *Education:* Free University Amsterdam (Ph.D., 1989); Leiden University (Ph.D., 1990). Member, Amsterdam's Juridisch Genootschap, 1992. *LANGUAGES:* Dutch, English, German.

SARAH RADEMA, born 1968; admitted, 1992, Amsterdam. *Education:* Rijks Universiteit Leiden (Candidate Civil Law Notary, Mr., 1992). Member, Koninklijke Broederschap (at The Hague). *LANGUAGES:* French, English, German.

PAUL A.J. WESTHOFF, born 1965; admitted, 1993, The Netherlands. *Education:* Rijks Universiteit, Leiden (Mr., 1992). Civil Law Notary. *LANGUAGES:* Dutch, English and French.

ANNE J. VAN DER KUYL, born 1968; admitted, 1992, Amsterdam. *Education:* University of Amsterdam (1992). Member, Koninklijke Notariële Broederschap, 1992—.

BIANCA E.J. VAN DEN BERG, born 1966; admitted, 1993, Amsterdam. *Education:* University of Utrecht (1992). Member, Koninklijke Notariële Broederschap, 1993—.

Languages: English, French, Dutch and German

(For a List of other Partners and Associates, see Professional Biographies at Brussels, Belgium, Paris, France, London, England and New York, New York)

TRENITÉ VAN DOORNE

Established in 1888

DE LAIRESSESTRAAT 133
1075 HJ AMSTERDAM, THE NETHERLANDS
Telephone: 31 (0) 20-6789 123
Telex: 16144 tvda nl
Telefax: 31 (0) 20-6789 589

Mailing Address: P.O. Box 75265, 1070 AG Amsterdam

Rotterdam, Netherlands Office: Weena 666. Mailing Address: P.O. Box 190, 3000 AD ROTTERDAM. Telephone: 31 (0) 10-404 2111. Telefax: 31 (0) 10-404 2333.

Rijswijk, Netherlands Office: Haagweg 175. Mailing address: P.O. Box 1073, 2280 CB RIJSWIJK. Telephone: 31 (0) 70-390 10 15. Telefax: 31 (0) 70-399 68 44.

The Hague, Netherlands Office: Churchillplein 5. Mailing address: P.O. Box 17207, 2502 CE THE HAGUE. Telephone: 31 (0) 70-338 3131. Telefax: 31 (0) 70-358 4798.

Brussels, Belgium Office: Avenue Louise 149, 1050 BRUSSELS. Telephone: 32-2-537 5159. Telefax: 32-2-537 6961.

Willemstad, Curaçao, Netherlands Antilles Office: Promes, Trenité Van Doorne, Julianaplein 22, P.O. Box 504. Telephone: 599-9-613400. Telefax: 599-9-612023.

Tokyo, Japan Office: Akasaka Wing Building 5 F, 6-6-15 Akasaka, Minato-ku, 107. Telephone: 813-5563-2911. Telefax: 813-5563-2912.

Corporate Law, Mergers and Acquisitions, Banking and Financing, Joint Ventures, Dutch and European Antitrust and Competition Law, Agencies and Distributorships, Transportation and Maritime Law, Insurance Law, Bankruptcy and Insolvency Law, Administrative Law, Construction, Engineering and Real Estate Law, Environmental Law, Press and Media Law, Industrial and Intellectual Property Law, Computer and Telecommunications Law, Labor and Employment Law, Litigation and Arbitration, International Trade Regulations, European Communities Laws and other International Law.

Dutch attorneys represent clients before all courts in the Netherlands, the European Court of Justice and the Benelux Court of Justice.

FIRM PROFILE: Trenité Van Doorne, first established in 1888, is one of the largest law firms in The Netherlands and on the European continent, with offices in Amsterdam, Rotterdam, The Hague, Brussels and Curaçao. The firm consists of over 240 advocates and civil notaries.

Trenité Van Doorne's main activities consist of providing legal advice and services in the fields of corporate, securities, banking, energy, maritime, and other areas of commercial law. Major industries, both in The Netherlands and abroad, served by Trenité Van Doorne include manufacturing, oil and gas, transport, trade, distribution, finance, insurance, food and chemical industries, construction, real estate and governmental (including public-private) relationships.

MEMBERS OF FIRM
ATTORNEYS AT LAW

HESSEL A. BOUMAN, born 1933; admitted, 1957, Rotterdam; 1961, Amsterdam. *Education:* University of Leiden (1957). Judge Pro Tem, Amsterdam Court of Appeal, 1993—. Editor of "Verkeersrecht", a Monthly Journal Specializing in Insurance and Liability, 1975—. *LANGUAGES:* English, German and French. *PRACTICE AREAS:* Insurance Law; Personal Injury Law; Malpractice.

HANS C.S. WARENDORF, born 1934; admitted, 1960, Amsterdam. *Education:* University of Amsterdam (1958); Institute of Comparative Law, New York University School of Law (1959-1960). Legal Translator. Co-Author: "Companies and Other Legal Persons under Netherlands and Netherlands Antilles Law," Kluwer, 1988; "Guide to the Regulation of Securities Markets in The Netherlands," Kluwer, 1993. Board Member of the Institute of Court interpreters and translators. *Member:* International Bar Association; International Fiscal Association. *LANGUAGES:* English and French. *PRACTICE AREAS:* Corporation Law; Commercial Law.

JAAP R. GLASZ, born 1935; admitted, 1962, Amsterdam. *Education:* Vrije Universiteit Amsterdam (1958). Chief Editor, Handbook for Non-Executive Directors, 1984. Author: "Recommended Rules of Conduct for Non-Executive Directors," 1986. Chairman of the Netherlands Delegation at the Council of the Law Societies and Bars of the EEC, 1983-1987. Holder of the Mark of Honor of the German Bar Association. Member, Senate of the Netherlands Parliament, 1987—. *Member:* Netherlands Bar Association (President, 1984-1986); International Bar Association (Council Member, 1982-1986). *LANGUAGES:* English, French and German. *PRACTICE*

(This Listing Continued)

AREAS: Corporate Law; Commercial Law; Mergers and Acquisitions Law.

HANS MEIJER, born 1935; admitted, 1964, Rotterdam; 1973, Amsterdam. *Education:* University of Amsterdam (1964). Author: "Commercial Leases in Holland," Property Law Bulletin, June 1980. Judge Pro Tem, Alkmaar District Court, 1974—. *LANGUAGES:* English and German. *PRACTICE AREAS:* Commercial Real Estate Law; Corporate Law; Commercial Law.

H. LEONARD DE HAAS, born 1939; admitted, 1966, Amsterdam. *Education:* University of Leiden (1966). Board Member of Social Insurance Bank, 1979-1989. President of the Dutch Foundation for liberal professions. Member, Amsterdam Bar, 1984-1988 and President, 1992-1993. l'Union Internationale des Avocats (President; President, Employment Committee, 1987-1990). *LANGUAGES:* English, French and German. *PRACTICE AREAS:* Corporate Law; Employment Law.

L. PETER BROEKVELDT, born 1944; admitted, 1970, Amsterdam. *Education:* Universities of Leiden and Amsterdam (1970). Treasury Counsel, 1975—. *LANGUAGES:* French, English and German. *PRACTICE AREAS:* Litigation; Insolvency Law; Credit Insurance Law.

JANHEIN BERKVENS, born 1945; admitted, 1973, Amsterdam; 1977, Netherlands Antilles. *Education:* University of Amsterdam (1971). Judge Pro Tem, The Hague District Court, 1993—. *LANGUAGES:* English, French and German. *PRACTICE AREAS:* Dutch and Netherlands Antilles Corporate Law; Contract Law; Real Estate Law.

L.D.G. BERT REESER CUPERUS, born 1947; admitted, 1975, Amsterdam. *Education:* University of Amsterdam (1974). General Legal Counsel, Netherlands Jaycees, 1979-1981. *Member:* Dutch Association for Construction Law; IBA; SBL; SGP. *LANGUAGES:* English, French and German. *PRACTICE AREAS:* Corporate Law; Commercial Law; Real Estate Law.

DOOK TH. MOERKOERT, born 1945; admitted, 1976, Rotterdam. *Education:* University of Groningen (1972). Judge Pro Tem, Rotterdam District Court, 1992—. *LANGUAGES:* English, French and German. *PRACTICE AREAS:* Insurance Law; Environmental Law; Litigation.

ALEXANDER M. BRENNINKMEIJER, born 1941; admitted, 1979, Amsterdam. *Education:* University of Nijmegen (1966; LL.D., 1973). Author: "Shareholders Agreements," Kluwer, 1973. Co-Author: "Handbook for Non-Executive Directors," 1984. Lecturer, Corporate Law, University of Nijmegen, 1966-1971. Corporate Legal Counsel, 1971-1980. *Member:* Trade Law Association. *LANGUAGES:* English, French and German. *PRACTICE AREAS:* Corporate Law; Commercial Law.

PAUL A.M. WITTEVEEN, born 1953; admitted, 1977, Amsterdam. *Education:* University of Groningen (1977); Traineeship European Commission, City of London Polytechnics (English Law). *LANGUAGES:* English, French and German. *PRACTICE AREAS:* Employment Law; Workers' Participation Law.

DRIES S. FRANSEN VAN DE PUTTE, born 1949; admitted, 1981, Amsterdam. *Education:* University of Leiden (1974). Judge Pro Tem, Amsterdam, District Court, 1987—. *LANGUAGES:* English. *PRACTICE AREAS:* Litigation; Insurance Law; Computer Law.

EMILE D. UYLDERT, born 1950; admitted, 1976, Amsterdam. *Education:* University of Leiden (Civil Law, 1973; Notarial Law, 1976). *LANGUAGES:* English and German. *PRACTICE AREAS:* Corporate Law; Commercial Law; Aircraft Leasing Law.

EDO TH. GROENEWALD, born 1946; admitted, 1978, Rotterdam, 1982, Amsterdam. *Education:* University of Leiden (1977). Judge Pro Tem, Utrecht District Court, 1994. *Member:* Association Internationale des Jeunes Avocats (AIJA; President, 1987-1988); International Bar Association (IBA). *LANGUAGES:* English, French and German. *PRACTICE AREAS:* Corporate Law; Commercial Law.

EVERT WIGGERS, born 1951; admitted, 1978, Amsterdam. *Education:* University of Amsterdam (1978). *LANGUAGES:* English and German. *PRACTICE AREAS:* Commercial Litigation; Corporate Finance; Leasing; Banking; Deputy Treasury Counsel.

PIETER N. VAN REGTEREN ALTENA, born 1953; admitted, 1980, Amsterdam. *Education:* University of Groningen (1980). *Member:* International Bar Association (Insurance Law and International Litigation). *LANGUAGES:* English and German. *PRACTICE AREAS:* Insurance Law; Tort Law.

(This Listing Continued)

EU1047B

TRENITÉ VAN DOORNE, Amsterdam—Continued

JOHN C. JAAKKE, born 1954; admitted, 1984, Amsterdam. *Education:* Vrije Universiteit Amsterdam (1981). Manager, Steenkolen Handels Vereniging (Coal Trade Company) 1982-1984. *Member:* International Bar Association (Member, Section on Energy and Natural Resources); Association Internationale des Jeunes Avocats (AIJA). *LANGUAGES:* English and German. *PRACTICE AREAS:* Corporate Law; Commercial Law; Energy Law.

MARC E. WALLHEIMER, born 1960; admitted, 1984, Amsterdam. *Education:* University of Amsterdam (1983). *Member:* International Trademark Association; Deutsche Vereinigung für Gewerblichen Rechtsschutz und Urheberrecht; Benelux Trademark Practitioners; Licensing Executives Society-Benelux (Board Member, 1987-1990; Secretary, 1987); Lex Mundi Intellectual Property Committee (Chairman). *LANGUAGES:* English and German. *PRACTICE AREAS:* Intellectual Property Law; Unfair Competition Law; Media Law.

JOS A.M. BOS, born 1951; admitted, 1977, Dordrecht; 1988, Amsterdam. *Education:* University of Utrecht (1977). *LANGUAGES:* English and French. *PRACTICE AREAS:* Corporate Law; Commercial Law; Energy Law; Insolvency Law.

WALTER F. HENDRIKSEN, born 1958; admitted, 1983, Amsterdam. *Education:* University of Utrecht (1982). Deputy Treasury Counsel. *LANGUAGES:* English and German. *PRACTICE AREAS:* Commercial Litigation; Professional Malpractice Claims.

EVA SCHUTTE, born 1959; admitted, 1984, Amsterdam. *Education:* University of Amsterdam (1984). Deputy Treasury Counsel. *LANGUAGES:* English and German. *PRACTICE AREAS:* Professional Malpractice Claims; Litigation.

ALBERT G. VAN MARWIJK KOOY, born 1958; admitted, 1986, Amsterdam. *Education:* University of Groningen (1983); Duke University (LL.M., 1985). *Member:* Association Internationale des Jeunes Avocats (AIJA). *LANGUAGES:* English, French and German. *PRACTICE AREAS:* Labor and Employment Law; Commercial Law.

ECKHARD W. MEHRING, born 1947; admitted, 1977, Muenster, Germany, 1994, Amsterdam. *Education:* Universities of Bonn, Kiel, Mainz, Cologne, Munich and Leiden. Legal Counsel, Dutch-German Chamber of Commerce, 1980-1990. *LANGUAGES:* Dutch, English and German. *PRACTICE AREAS:* Corporate Law; Commercial Law; Distributorship and Commercial Agency Law; Fiscal Law.

CHARLES J.R. EIJSBOUTS, born 1959; admitted, 1986, Amsterdam. *Education:* University of Groningen (1985); New York University (M.C.J., 1986). *LANGUAGES:* English, French and German. *PRACTICE AREAS:* Corporate Law; Acquisitions; Mergers; Joint Ventures; Venture Capital Investment; Divestitures.

MEMBERS OF FIRM
PATENT ATTORNEYS

ARJEN J.W. HOOIVELD, born 1959; Patent Attorney at the Dutch Patent Office, 1990; Professional Representative before the European Patent Office, 1990. *Education:* University of Amsterdam (M.Sc., Physics, 1984). *Member:* Dutch Institute of Patent Agents; E.P.I. (Institute of Professional Representatives Before the European Patent Office); Union of Patent Attorneys; Benelux Association of Trademark Agents; International Association for the Protection of Industrial Property. *LANGUAGES:* English. *PRACTICE AREAS:* Patent Law and Patent Procedures.

ARNOLD LOUËT FEISSER, born 1945; Patent Attorney at the Dutch Patent Office, 1975; Professional Representative before the European Patent Office, 1978. *Education:* Technical University of Twente (Mechanical Engineering, 1972); University of Leiden (J.D., Civil Law, 1979). Senior Lecturer, University of Twente, 1984—. *Member:* Dutch Institute of Patent Agents; International Association for the Protection of Industrial Property. *LANGUAGES:* English and German. *PRACTICE AREAS:* Intellectual Property; Licensing; Patent Procedures.

MEMBERS OF FIRM
CIVIL LAW NOTARIES

RICKERT J.F. BLOKHUIS, born 1946; appointed Civil Law Notary 1988 by Her Majesty The Queen. *Education:* University of Amsterdam (Notarial Law, 1970); Vrije Universiteit Amsterdam (J.D., 1971). Judge Pro Tem, District Court of Amsterdam, 1985-1988. *Member:* International Fiscal Association; Royal Netherlands Association of Civil Law Notaries; Netherlands Commercial Law Association. *LANGUAGES:* English, Ger-

man and French. *PRACTICE AREAS:* Family Law; Real Estate Law; Corporate Law; Foundations and Associations.

ASSOCIATES
ATTORNEYS AT LAW

EVERT A.G. BRAUTIGAM, born 1922; admitted, 1952 and 1987, Amsterdam. *Education:* University of Amsterdam and Copenhagen (1952). Judge Pro Tem in the Court of Appeal of Amsterdam, 1987-1992. Alderman, Amsterdam, 1970-1974. Burgomaster, Uithoorn, 1975-1987. Government Commissioner with the Netherlands Performing Rights Society (BUMA), 1976—. *LANGUAGES:* Danish, English, French and German. *PRACTICE AREAS:* Municipal Law; Criminal Law.

PAUL R.W. SCHAINK, born 1950; admitted, 1977, Amsterdam. *Education:* Vrije Universiteit Amsterdam (1974). *LANGUAGES:* English and French. *PRACTICE AREAS:* Labor Law; Immigration Law; Commercial Law.

HERMINE M. TEN HAAFT, born 1953; admitted, 1977, Amsterdam. *Education:* University of Leiden (1977). *LANGUAGES:* English and French. *PRACTICE AREAS:* Insurance Law; Litigation.

RICHARD A.C.G. MARTENS, born 1955; admitted, 1982, Amsterdam. *Education:* University of Amsterdam (1982); London Polytechnic (Summer course, 1981). *Member:* Association for Labour Law; Association for Labour Law Lawyers; Dutch Association of Lawyers for Human Rights (NJCM). *LANGUAGES:* English and German. *PRACTICE AREAS:* Labor and Employment Law; Family Law.

JORIS LENSINK, born 1958; admitted, 1985, Amsterdam. *Education:* University of Amsterdam (1984). Young Bar Association (Vice-President, 1987-1988). Board Member of the Dutch Reproduction Rights Organization, 1992—and of the Lending Retribution Society (section documents, 1991—). *Member:* International Trademark Association; European Association of Insolvency Practitioners. *LANGUAGES:* English and French. *PRACTICE AREAS:* Intellectual Property Law; Media Law; Entertainment Law; Bankruptcy Law.

ARNOUT L. VAN DEN BERGH, born 1953; admitted, 1986, Roermond; 1987, Maastricht; 1992, Amsterdam. *Education:* University of Amsterdam (International Law, 1980); University of Utrecht (Dutch Civil Law, 1986); University of South Africa (Master in Laws, 1990). *LANGUAGES:* English, French and German. *PRACTICE AREAS:* Labour Law; Public International Law.

MECHELINE A. WABEKE, born 1961; admitted, 1988, Amsterdam. *Education:* University of Groningen (1986); University of Cambridge (LL.M., 1987). *LANGUAGES:* English. *PRACTICE AREAS:* Litigation; Intellectual Property Law.

JAN VAN OVEREEM, born 1962; admitted, 1988, Amsterdam. *Education:* University of Amsterdam (Civil Law; M.A. History, 1988). *LANGUAGES:* English and German. *PRACTICE AREAS:* Corporate Law; Commercial Law; Insolvency Law.

ROEL J. BOTTER, born 1962; admitted, 1988, Amsterdam. *Education:* Erasmus University Rotterdam (1986); University of Leiden (Tax Law, 1987). *LANGUAGES:* English. *PRACTICE AREAS:* Corporate Law; Commercial Law; Banking Law; Insolvency Law; Capital Markets and Financial Institutions.

CORNELIS M. SLANGEN, born 1960; admitted, 1988, Utrecht; 1992, Amsterdam. *Education:* Utrecht University Law School (1987). *Member:* Utrecht and Dutch Bar Associations. *LANGUAGES:* English. *PRACTICE AREAS:* Real Estate Law; Construction Law; Environmental Law.

LEO J. VERHOEFF, born 1963; admitted, 1988, Amsterdam. *Education:* University of Utrecht (1987). *LANGUAGES:* English and German. *PRACTICE AREAS:* Commercial Law; Corporate Law; Litigation; Banking Law.

MONIQUE P.H.J. NILLESSEN, born 1964; admitted, 1989, Amsterdam. *Education:* University of Nijmegen (1987); Grotius Academy (1988). *LANGUAGES:* English and German. *PRACTICE AREAS:* Corporate Law; Law of the European Communities; Labor Law; Employment Law; Public Procurement Law.

JOSÉE M. VAN DE LAAR, born 1952; admitted, 1989, Amsterdam. *Education:* University of Amsterdam (1988). *LANGUAGES:* English, German and French. *PRACTICE AREAS:* Insurance Law; Litigation; Wrongful Death and Injury; Tort Law.

PIETER SIPPENS GROENEWEGEN, born 1962; admitted, 1989, Rotterdam; 1991, Amsterdam. *Education:* University of Amsterdam

(This Listing Continued)

(This Listing Continued)

(1988). *LANGUAGES:* English, Spanish and German. *PRACTICE AREAS:* Commercial Law; Insurance Law; Litigation; Computer and Tele-communications Law.

ANJA J. P. SMITS, born 1966; admitted, 1989, Amsterdam. *Education:* University of Amsterdam (1989). *LANGUAGES:* English and German. *PRACTICE AREAS:* Labor and Employment Law; Litigation.

SERGE J.H. GIJRATH, born 1964; admitted, 1990, Amsterdam. *Education:* University of Amsterdam (Civil Law, 1988; International Law and International Relations, 1988); European University Institute, Florence, Italy (LL.M., 1989); Salzburg Seminar Fellow (1989). *Member:* Netherlands Association for Computers and Law; Computer Law Association; Netherlands Copyright Association. *LANGUAGES:* English, French, Italian, German and Spanish. *PRACTICE AREAS:* Computer and Telecommunication Law; Intellectual Property Law; Law of the European Communities.

ELISABETH H.M. VAN DER VOORT, born 1963; admitted, 1990, Amsterdam. *Education:* Vrije Universiteit Amsterdam (1987). *Member:* Association Internationale des Jeunes Avocats. *LANGUAGES:* English, French and German. *PRACTICE AREAS:* Notarial Law; Corporate Law; Commercial Law; Litigation.

ALEXANDER R.T. ODLE, born 1963; admitted, 1990, Rotterdam; 1992, Amsterdam. *Education:* University of Leiden (1989). *LANGUAGES:* English and French. *PRACTICE AREAS:* Law of the European Communities; Commercial Law; Intellectual Property Law; Unfair Competition; Litigation.

GONNE H.A. POTT HOFSTEDE, born 1964; admitted, 1990, Amsterdam. *Education:* University of Amsterdam (1990). *LANGUAGES:* English. *PRACTICE AREAS:* Labor Law; Litigation.

DAVID M. DE KNIJFF, born 1963; admitted, 1990, Amsterdam. *Education:* University of Utrecht (1987); European University Institute Florence, Italy (1988). *LANGUAGES:* English, French, German, Italian and Russian. *PRACTICE AREAS:* Company Law; Employment Law; Litigation.

RICHARD G.J. NOWAK, born 1960; admitted, 1990, The Hague; 1992, Amsterdam. *Education:* Nijmegen University (1989). Researcher at the Slavonic Department of the University of Amsterdam, 1992—. Contributor to the East European Business Law of the Financial Times, 1992—. Sworn Translator in Russian, Polish and Bulgarian, 1986. Lawyer, Dutch Supreme Court, The Hague, 1990-1992. *LANGUAGES:* English, German, Russian, Polish, Bulgarian, French and Italian. *PRACTICE AREAS:* Russian Commercial Law; Polish Commercial Law.

LISA M. BROWNLEE, born 1961; admitted, 1990, Washington. *Education:* Pennsylvania State University (B.A., 1983); University of Washington (M.A., 1986); University of Puget Sound, School of Law (J.D., 1990). Lead Articles Editor, University of Puget Sound Law Review, 1990. Fellowship Recipient, Max Planck Institute for Foreign and International Patent, Copyright and Competition Law. Author: "Mead Data Central v. Toyota and other Contemporary Dilution Cases," 79 Trademark Reporter 471, 1989; "Trade Secret Use of Patentable Inventions, Prior User Rights and Patent Law Harmonization," Journal of the Patent and Trademark Office Society 523, 1990; "Trademark Rights and Registration," West's Washington Practice Vol. 22A, 1993. *PRACTICE AREAS:* Intellectual Property Law; Computer Law.

WILLEMIEN K. BISCHOT, born 1966; admitted, 1991, Amsterdam. *Education:* University of Amsterdam (1991). *LANGUAGES:* English. *PRACTICE AREAS:* Labor Law; Litigation.

ASTRID E. MERKUS, born 1966; admitted, 1991, Amsterdam. *Education:* University of Utrecht; University of Coimbra, Portugal (Erasmus Program, 1990; B.A., Portuguese Language and Literature, 1991). *LANGUAGES:* English, German, Portuguese. *PRACTICE AREAS:* Company Law; Intellectual Property.

H.A.J.M. (BERTIL) VAN KAAM, born 1963; admitted, 1991, Amsterdam. *Education:* University of Antwerp, Institute for Interpreters and Translators (1987); Erasmus University, Rotterdam (1991). *LANGUAGES:* English, French, German and Portuguese. *PRACTICE AREAS:* Intellectual Property; Unfair Competition.

BEATRIJS J. SLOT, born 1961; admitted, 1992, Amsterdam. *Education:* Vrije Universiteit Amsterdam (Adult Educational Theory, 1985); University of Amsterdam, Civil Law (1990). *LANGUAGES:* English and German. *PRACTICE AREAS:* Litigation; Labor Law.

(This Listing Continued)

NIELS VAN GELDER, born 1966; admitted, 1992, Amsterdam. *Education:* University of Amsterdam (1990); University of Cambridge (LL.M., 1991). *LANGUAGES:* English and German. *PRACTICE AREAS:* Litigation; Labor Law.

HENDRIK JAN WALRAVE, born 1964; admitted, 1992, Amsterdam. *Education:* University of Leiden (1991). *LANGUAGES:* English. *PRACTICE AREAS:* Corporate Law; Insurance Law.

JAN HENDRIK B. CRUCQ, born 1965; admitted, 1992, Amsterdam. *Education:* University of Leiden (1991). *LANGUAGES:* English. *PRACTICE AREAS:* Corporate Law; Civil Law.

SANDRA Z. WIARDA, born 1965; admitted, 1992, Amsterdam. *Education:* University of Amsterdam (1992). *LANGUAGES:* English and French. *PRACTICE AREAS:* Labor Law; Corporate Law.

JETSKE A.J. HEIKENS, born 1963; admitted, 1992, Amsterdam. *Education:* University of Groningen (1988). *LANGUAGES:* English and German. *PRACTICE AREAS:* Real Estate Law; Administrative Law.

OTTOKAR J. INGWERSEN, born 1962; admitted, 1992, Amsterdam. *Education:* University of Utrecht (1986). *LANGUAGES:* English. *PRACTICE AREAS:* Corporate Law.

W.B.G. (MINOUCHE) VAN DE VEN, born 1965; admitted, 1992, Amsterdam. *Education:* State University Limburg (1990). *Member:* Society of Environmental Law. *LANGUAGES:* English. *PRACTICE AREAS:* Environmental Law; Administrative Law.

MAARTEN J. DROP, born 1968; admitted, 1992, Amsterdam. *Education:* University of Amsterdam (1992). *Member:* Associazione Giuristi di Lingua Italiana. *LANGUAGES:* English, Italian, German, French and Spanish. *PRACTICE AREAS:* Corporate Law; Litigation.

LISETTE L.M. HESLENFELD, born 1965; admitted, 1992, Amsterdam. *Education:* University of Amsterdam (1991). *LANGUAGES:* English and French. *PRACTICE AREAS:* Intellectual Property Law.

ROELIEN VOSSERS, born 1969; admitted, 1993, Amsterdam. *Education:* University of Amsterdam (1992). *LANGUAGES:* German and English. *PRACTICE AREAS:* Computer Law; Telecommunications Law.

HESTER W. INSINGER, born 1967; admitted, 1993, Amsterdam. *Education:* University of Leiden (1992). *LANGUAGES:* German and English. *PRACTICE AREAS:* Insurance Law; Real Estate Law; Administrative Law.

JOP POLLMANN, born 1967; admitted, 1993, Amsterdam. *Education:* Erasmus University Rotterdam, Bachelor Modern Japanese Studies (1988); University of Amsterdam (1992). *LANGUAGES:* English and French. *PRACTICE AREAS:* Corporate Law.

JUDITH M.J. LANGELAAR, born 1968; admitted, 1993, Amsterdam. *Education:* University of Leiden (1992). *LANGUAGES:* English. *PRACTICE AREAS:* Insurance Law.

WIJNAND H.J.M. NUYTS, born 1967; admitted, 1993, Amsterdam. *Education:* University of Leiden (1992). *LANGUAGES:* English, German and French. *PRACTICE AREAS:* European Law; Litigation.

ARTHUR G.J. KNIPPING, born 1967; admitted, 1993, Amsterdam. *Education:* University of Amsterdam (1993). *LANGUAGES:* German and English. *PRACTICE AREAS:* Labor Law.

CLAUDIA D.S. LANTOS, born 1967; admitted, 1993, Amsterdam. *Education:* Erasmus University, Rotterdam (1993). *LANGUAGES:* English. *PRACTICE AREAS:* Labor Law.

STEFAN A.J. VAN ROSSUM, born 1970; admitted, 1993, Rotterdam. *Education:* Free University of Amsterdam (1993). *LANGUAGES:* English and Italian. *PRACTICE AREAS:* Banking Law; Corporate Law.

GEERT H. DRESE, born 1966; admitted, 1994, Amsterdam. *Education:* Delft Agricultural College (Business Economics, 1989); University of Groningen (1993). *LANGUAGES:* English. *PRACTICE AREAS:* Corporate Law; Civil Law.

HATTIE M.E. DE LEEUW, born 1965; admitted, 1994, Amsterdam. *Education:* University of Utrecht (1992). *LANGUAGES:* English and French. *PRACTICE AREAS:* Real Estate Law; Environmental Law; Construction Law.

ANNELIES E. VAN ZOEST, born 1968; admitted, 1994, Amsterdam. *Education:* University of Amsterdam (1993). *LANGUAGES:* English and French. *PRACTICE AREAS:* Intellectual Property Law; Computer Law.

(This Listing Continued)

TRENITÉ VAN DOORNE, Amsterdam—Continued

SILVIA S. BRENS, born 1970; admitted, 1994, Amsterdam. *Education:* University of Leiden (1994). *LANGUAGES:* English, French and German. *PRACTICE AREAS:* Litigation.

ASSOCIATE
PATENT ATTORNEY

KEES W.A.M. KLAVERS, born 1951; admitted, Patent Attorney at the Dutch Patent Office, 1988. *Education:* Technical University of Eindhoven (Electro Technical Engineering, 1983). *Member:* Dutch Institute of Patent Agents; Benelux Association of Trademark and Design Agents. *LANGUAGES:* English and German. *PRACTICE AREAS:* Intellectual Property; Licensing; Patent Procedures.

ASSOCIATES
CIVIL LAW NOTARIES

SERVÉ J.A.M. SONDEIJKER, born 1966; admitted as Civil Law Notary, 1990. *Education:* University of Nijmegen (1990). *LANGUAGES:* English and German. *PRACTICE AREAS:* Corporate Law; Real Estate Law; Family Law.

JELLE D. VAN DER BEEK, born 1965; admitted as Civil Law Notary, 1990. *Education:* University of Amsterdam (1990). *LANGUAGES:* English and German. *PRACTICE AREAS:* Real Estate Law.

MICK D. VAN WAATERINGE, born 1958; admitted, as Civil Law Notary, 1988, Amsterdam. *Education:* University of Amsterdam (1985). *LANGUAGES:* English, French and German. *PRACTICE AREAS:* Corporate Law; Tax Law; Real Estate Law; Family Law.

INGRID BLEEKER, born 1960; admitted, as Civil Law Notary, 1989. *Education:* Free University of Amsterdam (Civil Law, Notarial Law, 1985). *LANGUAGES:* English, French and German. *PRACTICE AREAS:* Corporate Law; Tax Law; Real Estate Law.

OF COUNSEL

LOWIK G. EYKMAN, born 1931; admitted, 1955, Rotterdam; 1984, Amsterdam. *Education:* University of Utrecht (1955). *LANGUAGES:* English. *PRACTICE AREAS:* Insurance Law.

PROFESSOR WILLEM M. KLEIJN, born 1927. *Education:* University of Leiden (Civil Law, 1951; Notarial Law, 1953). Professor of Civil and Notarial Law, University of Leiden, 1970-1992. Supervisory Director of the RaboBank, 1980-1992, Chairman of the Subcommittee on Publication of Public Information of the Commission on Real Estate Information, 1988. Member of the Board of Directors, 1980— and Chairman, 1980-1988 of the Building Trade Law Association. *LANGUAGES:* English, French and German. *PRACTICE AREAS:* Real Property Law; Personal Property Law; Marital Property Law; Inheritance Law; Real Property Pollution Law.

PROF. DR. JAAP H. SPOOR, born 1942; admitted, 1982, Amsterdam. *Education:* Vrije Universiteit Amsterdam (1966); University of Utrecht (LL.D., 1976). Professor, Intellectual Property Law, Vrije Universiteit Amsterdam 1976—. *Member:* Netherlands Copyright Association (Board Member); Computer Law Association; International Copyright Association ALAI (Member, Executive Committee); International Association for the Protection of Industrial Property; Ligue Contre la Concurrence Déloyale; Licensing Executives Society. *LANGUAGES:* English, French and German. *PRACTICE AREAS:* Computer Law; Intellectual Property Law.

Trenité Van Doorne forms together with Wessing Berenberg-Gossler Zimmermann a European Economic interest grouping. Wessing has offices in Berlin, Brussels, Düsseldorf, Hamburg, Leipzig and Munich. Trenité Van Doorne is a member of Lex Mundi.

Languages: Dutch, English, French, German, Italian and Swedish

VAN SCHOONHOVEN IN 'T VELD

Advocaten & Notaris
119 APOLLOLAAN
P.O. BOX 75999
1070 AB AMSTERDAM, THE NETHERLANDS
Telephone: (31) 20 6796969
Fax: (31) 20 6764339

Mergers, Acquisitions and Joint Ventures, Corporate Reorganizations, Insolvency and Restructuring, Financing Arrangements, Real Estate, Construction and Leasing Law, Administrative and Environmental Law, European Law, Labour Law, Litigation, Arbitration and Notarial Services.

PARTNERS

FERRY H.J. VAN SCHOONHOVEN, born 1959; admitted, 1985, Amsterdam. *Education:* Free University of Amsterdam (Master of Law, 1983); University of Illinois (Master of Comparative Law, 1984).

SANDRA A. IN 'T VELD, born 1949; admitted, 1982, Amsterdam. *Education:* Leyden University (Master of Law, 1977).

ARTHUR KASPERS, born 1958; admitted, 1987, Amsterdam. *Education:* University of Amsterdam (Master of Law, 1986; Public Administration, 1987).

EDO SMID, born 1962; admitted, 1988, Amsterdam. *Education:* Free University of Amsterdam (Master of Law, Notarial Degree, 1986).

CHRISTIAAN J. DEN HARTOG, born 1933; admitted, 1963, Amsterdam. *Education:* State Examination (Notarial Degree, 1959); University of Amsterdam (1961). Civil Law Notary.

CAROLIEN J. BOSCH, born 1961; admitted, 1985, Amsterdam. *Education:* Free University of Amsterdam (Master of Law, Notarial Degree, 1985). Candidate Notary.

Languages: Dutch, English, German and French

ADVOCATENKANTOOR MR W.J.K. VONK

HERENGRACHT 254
1016 BV AMSTERDAM, THE NETHERLANDS
Telephone: (31-20) - 622.3344
Telefax: (31-20) - 627.2272

International Real Estate Transactions.

WYBE JOHAN KRISTIAN VONK, born Amsterdam, The Netherlands, July 17, 1958; admitted, 1987, The Netherlands. *Education:* University of Amsterdam; Harvard Law School (LL.M., 1986). *Member:* Amsterdam Bar.

Languages: Dutch, English, French, German and Japanese

WIERINGA ADVOCATEN

Established in 1953
HERENGRACHT 425-429
1017 BR AMSTERDAM, THE NETHERLANDS
Telephone: +31 (0) 20 624 68 11
Telefax: +31 (0) 20 627 22 78

Company and Commercial Law, Mergers and Acquisitions, European Competition Law, Labor Law, Property Law, Agency, Distributorship and Franchising, Banking and Finance, Administrative Law, Intellectual Property, Bankruptcy/Insolvency, Environment, Travel/Tourism, Medical Law, Insurance, Tax Law, Litigation.

FIRM PROFILE: Wieringa Advocaten is a middle sized internationally oriented law firm, established in 1953. All members are fluent in English, several in German, Italian, French and Spanish.

PARTNERS

HENK C. BITTER, born 1935; admitted, 1963, Amsterdam. *Education:* Free University of Amsterdam. *PRACTICE AREAS:* Insurance.

GEORGE A. OFFERHAUS, born 1944; admitted, 1969, Amsterdam. *Education:* University of Groningen. *PRACTICE AREAS:* Company and Commercial; Agency; Distributorship.

JAAP A.L. REHBOCK, born 1943; admitted, 1974, Amsterdam. *Education:* University of Leyden. *PRACTICE AREAS:* Real Estate; Construction.

(This Listing Continued)

ROB H. WOLTJER, born 1941; admitted, 1966, Rotterdam. *Education:* University of Groningen. *PRACTICE AREAS:* Commercial and Company; Contracts.

WIM TH. SNOEK, born 1947; admitted, 1975, Amsterdam. *Education:* Free University of Amsterdam. *PRACTICE AREAS:* Labour; Computers.

M. BART KASTELEIJN, born 1950; admitted, 1977, Amsterdam. *Education:* University of Utrecht. *PRACTICE AREAS:* Company and Commercial; Mergers and Acquisitions; Banking and Finance.

CAREL N.A.M. CLAASSEN, born 1948; admitted, 1977, Amsterdam. *Education:* Free University of Amsterdam. *PRACTICE AREAS:* Labour; Administrative Law; Zoning; Environmental.

ERIK J. BINK, born 1958; admitted, 1984, Amsterdam. *Education:* University of Leyden. *PRACTICE AREAS:* Insolvency and Liquidations; Contracts.

ASSOCIATES

PIA J.Y. BORINGA, born 1960; admitted, 1984, Groningen. *Education:* Free University of Amsterdam. *PRACTICE AREAS:* Tax; Family Law.

BARBARA C. PENDERS, born 1957; admitted, 1987, Amsterdam. *Education:* University of Utrecht. *PRACTICE AREAS:* Labour; Debt Collection.

ARCO C. SIEMONS, born 1963; admitted, 1989, Amsterdam. *Education:* University of Leyden. *PRACTICE AREAS:* Litigation; Labour.

DRIES DUYNSTEE, born 1963; admitted, 1990, Amsterdam. *Education:* University of Amsterdam. *PRACTICE AREAS:* Competition; Mergers and Acquisitions; Franchising.

SEBASTIAAN LEVELT, born 1962; admitted, 1990, Amsterdam. *Education:* University of Utrecht. *PRACTICE AREAS:* Real Estate; Construction; Environmental; Zoning.

ALEXANDER A.H. BRUINHOF, born 1961; admitted, 1990, Amsterdam. *Education:* University of Amsterdam. *PRACTICE AREAS:* Intellectual Property; Entertainment.

OLIVIER SUEUR, born 1965; admitted, 1991, Amsterdam. *Education:* University of Amsterdam. *PRACTICE AREAS:* Insolvency; Bankruptcy; Insurance.

DOMINIQUE H.M. PLAISIER, born 1966; admitted, 1991, Amsterdam. *Education:* University of Leyden.

KENNETH J. DEFARES, born 1967; admitted, 1992, Amsterdam. *Education:* University of Amsterdam.

H. DÉSIRÉE VAN DEN BERG, born 1968; admitted, 1992, Amsterdam. *Education:* University of Leyden.

WIKKE D. KOOTSTRA, born 1967; admitted, 1992, Amsterdam. *Education:* University of Utrecht.

ANTON PIETER VAN LOGTESTIJN, born 1967; admitted, 1994, Amsterdam. *Education:* Erasmus University of Rotterdam.

Languages: Dutch, English, German, French, Italian and Spanish

---

VAN DIJK & VAN ARNHEM

SOERENSEWEG 146A
7313 EM APELDOORN, THE NETHERLANDS
Telephone: +31 55 55 98 99
Fax: +31 55 55 98 18

Firm engaged in Netherlands and International law practice. Entitled to plead before The Netherlands courts.
International Sale of Goods, Netherlands Contract Law and Conflict of Laws, International Trade Law, Netherlands Corporate Law, Netherlands Commercial Law, Netherlands Employment Law, Litigation in The Netherlands.

FIRM PROFILE: Established in 1988, Van Dijk & Van Arnhem has now specialized in advising foreign small and middle sized companies, trading with The Netherlands, as well as Netherlands companies connected with foreign companies. The firm has many clients from Germany and Scandinavia, as well as good professional contacts with these countries.

(This Listing Continued)

MEMBERS OF FIRM

SIPKE W. VAN DIJK, admitted, 1984, The Netherlands. *Education:* Leyden University (LL.M., 1984). *Member:* Netherlands Bar Association. *LANGUAGES:* Dutch, German and English. *PRACTICE AREAS:* Agency and Distributorships; Business Law; Civil Law; Commercial Law; Contracts; Debtor and Creditor; Debt Recovery; Labour and Employment; Litigation.

MARGARETHA M. VAN ARNHEM, admitted, 1984, The Netherlands. *Education:* Utrecht University (LL.M., 1983); Leyden University (LL.M., 1989). *Member:* Netherlands Bar Association.

DSH DERKS • STAR BUSMANN

Attorneys at Law
OFFICE BUILDING "DE GROENVESTE"
35-I VELPERWEG
6824 BE ARNHEM, THE NETHERLANDS
Telephone: 085-511910
Telefax: 085-458169

Mailing Address: P.O. Box 3042, 6802 DA

Utrecht, Netherlands Office: 2 Pythagoraslaan, 3584 BB, P.O. Box 85250, 3508 AG. Telephone: 030-562611. Telefax: 030-562626.
Amersfoort, Netherlands Office: Office Building "De Runmolen", 98 Zonnehof, 7th and 8th Floor, 3811 ND, P.O. Box 506, 3800 AM. Telephone: 033-698698. Telefax: 033-698600.
Hilversum, Netherlands Office: 37 Borneolaan, 1217 GX, P.O. Box 710, 1200 AS. Telephone: 035-218547. Telefax: 035-215039.
Hilversum, Netherlands Office: 4 Oude Enghweg, 1217 JC, P.O. Box 272, 1200 AG. Telephone: 035-244853. Telefax: 035-284216.
Brussels, Belgium Office: 391 Avenue Louise, B 11, 1050. Telephone: 02-6403525. Telex: 64880 DSHBRU. Telefax: 02-6406904.
Berlin, Germany Office: 66, Bernadottestrasse, 14195 Berlin. Telephone: 30-8316300, 8324431, 8325715. Telefax: 30-8316528.

General Practice and Administrative Law.

MEMBERS OF FIRM

F.P. Lomans   C.M.A. Delissen-Buijnsters
I.P.A. van Heijst

ASSOCIATES

H.L.J.M. Kersten   G.F. van den Berg
Drs. I.E. Nauta   M.A. Zon
C.A. Segaar   H. Bijl

TAX LAWYER

J.H. SASSEN

(For Complete Biographical data on all Personnel see Professional Biographies at Utrecht, Netherlands).

DIRKZWAGER

Attorneys At Law - Civil Law Notaries
"VELPERBEEK"
VELPERWEG 26
P.O. BOX 6802 DA ARNHEM
ARNHEM, THE NETHERLANDS
Telephone: 85 53 83 00
Telefax: 85 51 07 93

Nijmegen, The Netherlands Office: "Stella Maris," S Mathonsingel 4, P.O. Box 55 6500 AB Nijmegen. Telephone: 80 22 66 41. Telefax: 80 22 20 74.

Contract, General Commercial, Companies, Corporations, Insurance, Damages, Personal Injury, Product Liability, Mergers and Acquisitions, Competition, Anti-Trust, Bankruptcy, Insolvency, Dutch-German Legal Relationships, Trademarks, Intellectual Property, Employment, Labour, Construction, Building, Environmental Law, Planning, Commercial Property, Family Law, Public Health Law, Law of Mineral Extractions.

FIRM PROFILE: Dirkzwager in its present form was founded in 1990 as a result of a merger between well respected firms of lawyers and notaries in Arnhem and Nijmegen of which the origins go back to the early nineteenth century. The firm is very much active in the commercial and indus-

(This Listing Continued)

DIRKZWAGER, Arnhem—Continued

trial field; our clients are spread out nationwide. We maintain good relations with other law firms abroad. Being a medium-sized firm Dirkzwager is able to build up a good personal relationship with its clients, taking care of their specific interests. All matters can be dealt with in an efficient and quick manner. The internal communication is direct and fully automated. We have a fruitful and productive teamwork amongst all lawyers and notaries so that our clients can benefit from everyone's specific know-how and expertise in the various legal subject matters.

Members of Interlega in association with TELFA (Trans European Law Firms Association).

TELFA-Interlega is an association of European Law Firms, whose members have offices in Athens, Arnhem, Barcelona, Basel, Bologna, Brussels, Budapest, Düsseldorf, Edinburg, Geneva, Glasgow, Guernsey, Halle, Kopenhagen, Lisboa, London, Luxembourg, Madrid, Milan, Nijmegen and Paris. For more details see the TELFA-Interlega entry under Brussels.

The firm has a total number of 20 partners and 25 associates. The total number of all staff is 110.

Languages: Dutch, English, German, French and Spanish.

PARTNERS

FREDERIK J. BOOM, born Zwolle, The Netherlands, July 11, 1945; admitted, 1969, The Netherlands. Education: University of Croningen (M.R., 1968).

ROBERT PH. ELZAS, born Zeist, The Netherlands, March 17, 1948; admitted, 1973, The Netherlands. Education: University of Leiden (M.R., 1973).

JAN TH.M. PALSTRA, born The Hague, The Netherlands, December 19, 1943; admitted, 1977, The Netherlands. Education: University of Nijmegen (M.R., 1967).

FRANCISCUS A.M. KNÜPPE, born Dordrecht, The Netherlands, June 5, 1955; admitted, 1978, The Netherlands. Education: University of Utrecht (M.R., 1978).

MAARTEN R.J. BANEKE, born Amsterdam, The Netherlands, October 23, 1957; admitted, 1982, Rotterdam. Education: University of Leiden (M.R., 1982).

J. MARIUS W. WERKER, born Nijmegen, The Netherlands, April 21, 1957; admitted, 1983, The Netherlands. Education: University of Leiden (M.R., 1983).

ASSOCIATES

JOSEPHINA M.A. FELDHUSEN-WAGEMAKERS, born Oss, The Netherlands, May 3, 1934; admitted, 1968, The Netherlands. Education: Universit0 of Amsterdam (M.R., 1966).

ALBERTUS J. KRONENBERG, born Den Haag, The Netherlands, October 27, 1958; admitted, 1986, The Netherlands. Education: University of Utrecht (M.R., 1985).

JEANINE A.M. VAN DEN BERK, born Breda, The Netherlands, July 9, 1961; admitted, 1991, The Netherlands. Education: University of Groningen (M.R., 1986).

GEERTRUID M. TILANUS-VAN WASSENAER, born Den Haag, The Netherlands, May 19, 1962; admitted, 1986, Utrecht. Education: University of Leiden (M.R., 1986).

NANCY A. VIELLEVOYE-GEERS, born Heerlen, The Netherlands, May 10, 1963; admitted, 1990, The Netherlands. Education: University of Nijmegen (M.R., 1987).

IVO M. TRIJBITS, born Arnhem, The Netherlands, March 13, 1964; admitted, 1990, The Netherlands. Education: University of Leiden (M.R., 1990).

ERIC BOERMA, born Arnhem, The Netherlands, October 19, 1965; admitted, 1991, The Netherlands. Education: Rijksuniversiteit Groningen (M.R., 1991).

OF COUNSEL

O. FREDERIK J. MOORMAN VAN KAPPEN, born Utrecht, The Netherlands, June 14, 1964; admitted, The Netherlands, 1991. Education: University of Leyden (M.R., 1991).

(This Listing Continued)

EU1052B

BERT H. BAKKER, born Vriescheloo, The Netherlands, April 9, 1966; admitted, 1993, The Netherlands. Education: University of Leiden (M.R., 1993).

LAMBERTUS B.A. VAN LOGTESTIJN, born Utrecht, The Netherlands, April 2, 1969; admitted, 1993, The Netherlands. Education: University of Utrecht (M.R., 1993).

ANTHONIE O.J. VERKUIJL, born Purmerend, The Netherlands, July 1, 1967; admitted, 1994, The Netherlands. Education: Rijksuniversiteit Leiden (Masters, 1993).

JOANNES M.P. LEFERINK, born Haaksbergen, The Netherlands, May 24, 1969; admitted, 1994, The Netherlands. Education: University of Nijmegen (M.R., 1994).

CHRISTINE E. HEMRICA, born Grootegast, The Netherlands, September 22, 1963; admitted, 1994, The Netherlands. Education: University of Nijmegen (M.R., 1994).

PARTNERS
CIVIL LAW NOTARIES

CORNELIS VENEMANS, born Achtkarspelen, The Netherlands, December 15, 1937; admitted, 1965, The Netherlands. Education: Free University of Amsterdam (Doct.Ex, 1965).

BERT E. RIBBERS, born Amsterdam, The Netherlands, October 7, 1942; admitted, 1969, The Netherlands. Education: University of Amsterdam (M.R., 1969).

A. WALTER O. JANSEN, born Rotterdam, The Netherlands, January 21, 1950; admitted, 1979, The Netherlands. Education: University of Utrecht (M.R., 1979).

MAARTEN S. SCHELLINGERHOUT, born Markelo, The Netherlands, June 1, 1959; admitted, 1984, The Netherlands. Education: University of Leiden (M.R., 1984).

ASSOCIATES
CIVIL LAW NOTARIES

KAREN A. VERKERK, born Hillegom, The Netherlands, June 2, 1965; admitted, 1988, The Netherlands. Education: University of Nijmegen (M.R., 1987).

MAUD A.O.J. PHIJFFER-LAUMANS, born Nijmegen, The Netherlands, July 18, 1964; admitted, 1990, The Netherlands. Education: University of Nijmegen (M.R., 1990).

TON K. LEKKERKERKER, born Leiden, The Netherlands, October 12, 1958; admitted, 1995, The Netherlands. Education: University of Groningen (M.R., 1982).

HANNEKE W.R. TRUSCHEL, born Holten, The Netherlands, November 30, 1964; admitted, 1991, The Netherlands. Education: University of Leiden (M.R., 1991).

JUNIOR NOTARIES

CHRISTEL A.M. SAMSON, born Nijmegen, The Netherlands, August 17, 1967; admitted, 1991, The Netherlands. Education: University of Nijmegen (M.R., 1991).

JAN A. JANSSENS, born Eindoven, The Netherlands, July 6, 1970; admitted, 1994, The Netherlands. Education: University of Groningen (M.R., 1994).

MORET ERNST & YOUNG TAX ADVISERS
CORPORATE LAW ADVISORY GROUP

12, KRONENBURGSINGEL
P.O. BOX 30116
6803 AC ARNHEM, THE NETHERLANDS
Telephone: 31-85-209500
Fax: 31-85-235151

Amsterdam Office: 20, Drentestraat, P.O. Box 7925, 1008 AC. Telephone: 31-20-5497333. Fax: 31-20-6462553.
Rotterdam Office: 51, Marten Meesweg, P.O. Box 2295, 3000 CG. Telephone: 31-10-4072627. Fax: 31-10-4072612.
The Hague Office: 80, Wassenaarseweg, P.O. Box 90636, 2509 LP. Telephone: 31 70-3286542. Fax: 31 70-3244003.

(This Listing Continued)

Groningen Office: 17, Leonard Springerlaan, P.O. Box 997, 9700 AZ. Telephone: 31-50-994444. Fax: 31-50-270852.

Civil Law (general). Computer Law, Insolvency Law, (International) Contracts, Corporate Law, Environmental Law, EC Law, Intellectual Property, Labour Law and Workers Participation, Mergers and Acquisitions, Taxation.

PARTNERS

HANS VAN GIJZEN, born 1951. *Education:* Leyden University. (Resident).

SENIOR-ADVISORS

DENIS WILLEMARS, born 1956. *Education:* Groningen University (1986).

(For complete data see at Amsterdam, The Netherlands)

WINTERS & BOSNAK

Winters & Bosnak are members of Netlaw, a network consisting of 11 independent law firms in the Netherlands and of Interlaw, an international association of independent law firms in major world centers.

30, JANSBUITENSINGEL
P.O. BOX 560
6800 AN ARNHEM, THE NETHERLANDS
Telephone: +31.85.538211
Fax: +31.85.538292

Düsseldorf Office: Postbox 110735, D-40507 Düsseldorf, Burggrafenstraße 5, D-40545 Düsseldorf. Telephone: +49.211.559430. Telefax: +49.211.5594310.

General Civil and Commercial Law Practice and Litigation, Administrative, Agency, Agricultural, Anti-Trust, Arbitration, Bankruptcy and Insolvency, Computer, Construction, Copyright, Corporate, Criminal, Distribution, General EEC, Environmental, Family, Injury, Insurance, International Litigation, Labor, Mergers and Acquisitions, Sports, Rent and Lease, Trademark, Torts, Medical.

FIRM PROFILE: The firm was formed in 1987 by a merger between two firms with a longstanding reputation. It now offers a varied range of legal services to the business community. All lawyers of Winters & Bosnak practice general commercial law, general civil law, contract and litigation in civil cases. More specialized topics are listed below per lawyer.

MEMBERS OF FIRM

COEN H.B. WINTERS. LANGUAGES: Dutch, English, German and French. **PRACTICE AREAS:** Corporate; Bankruptcy and Insolvency.

JOHN M. BOSNAK (Also Member of the Düsseldorf Rechtsanwaltskammer (Bar of the Federal Republic of Germany)). **LANGUAGES:** Dutch, English, German, French and Russian (passive). **PRACTICE AREAS:** Construction; Private International; Agency; Distribution.

MICHIEL P.H. WINTERS. LANGUAGES: Dutch, English, German and French. **PRACTICE AREAS:** Corporate; Rent and Lease; Computer.

CEES B.J.M. SAMSON. LANGUAGES: Dutch, English, German, French and Russian (passive). **PRACTICE AREAS:** Corporate; Mergers and Acquisitions; Bankruptcy and Insolvency.

DIRK-JAN BENDER. LANGUAGES: Dutch, English, German and French. **PRACTICE AREAS:** Labor; Arbitration; Tort; Medical; Sports.

MARK H.M. BOEKHORST. LANGUAGES: Dutch, English, German and French. **PRACTICE AREAS:** Criminal.

EUGENE PH.R. SUTORIUS. LANGUAGES: Dutch, English, German and French. **PRACTICE AREAS:** Medical; Labor; Arbitration; Criminal.

PIET M. GUNNING. LANGUAGES: Dutch, English, French and German. **PRACTICE AREAS:** Tort; Anti-Trust; Insurance; Copyright; Trademark; Bankruptcy and Insolvency.

SIMON S. VAN STEENBERGEN. LANGUAGES: Dutch, English and German. **PRACTICE AREAS:** Corporate; Mergers and Acquisitions; Joint Ventures; (International) Contracts; Anti-Trust.

(This Listing Continued)

ROBERT JAN A. DIL. LANGUAGES: Dutch, French, English and German. **PRACTICE AREAS:** Tort; Labor; Arbitration; Bankruptcy and Insolvency; Sports.

DOMINIQUE M.H.M. VAN DIJK. LANGUAGES: Dutch, English, French and German. **PRACTICE AREAS:** Rent and Lease; Agricultural; Administrative; Environmental; Bankruptcy and Insolvency.

BART J.M. VAN MEER. LANGUAGES: Dutch, English, German and French. **PRACTICE AREAS:** Administrative; Agricultural; Environmental; Bankruptcy and Insolvency.

ASSOCIATES

REINA P. DE VALK. LANGUAGES: Dutch, English and German. **PRACTICE AREAS:** Medical; Labor.

HENK WIM LIJFTOGT. LANGUAGES: Dutch, English and German. **PRACTICE AREAS:** Administrative; Medical; Tort.

SANDER J.B. DRIJBER. LANGUAGES: Dutch, English and German. **PRACTICE AREAS:** General Practice; Securities.

MIKE JANSEN. LANGUAGES: Dutch, English and German. **PRACTICE AREAS:** General Practice; Labor.

DIRK VON ROSENSTIEL (Also Member of the Düsseldorf Rechtsanwaltskammer (Bar of the Federal Republic of Germany). **LANGUAGES:** Dutch and German. **PRACTICE AREAS:** General Practice.

ELSE LOES PASMA. LANGUAGES: Dutch, English, French, Spanish and German. **PRACTICE AREAS:** General Practice; Trademark.

ELS H.M. HARBERS. LANGUAGES: Dutch, English and German. **PRACTICE AREAS:** Agricultural; Administrative.

JAN-PAUL VAN NES. LANGUAGES: Dutch, English and German. **PRACTICE AREAS:** General Practice.

REINIER A. OSKAMP. LANGUAGES: Dutch, English and German. **PRACTICE AREAS:** General Practice.

ANDRÉ G. COUMANS. LANGUAGES: Dutch, English, French and German. **PRACTICE AREAS:** General Practice; Public; Criminal.

MARJOLEINE R. DE BOORDER. LANGUAGES: Dutch, English and German. **PRACTICE AREAS:** Family.

Languages: Dutch, English, French, German and Russian.

NAUTA DUTILH

Attorneys, Civil Law Notaries, Tax Advisers

HEERBAAN 46-48
NL-4817 NL BREDA, THE NETHERLANDS
Telephone: (31-76) 224410
Telecopier: (31-76) 220106

Mailing Address: P.O. Box 2118, NL-4800 CC, Breda, The Netherlands

MEMBERS OF FIRM ATTORNEYS AT LAW

ERIK C.G. KLINKHAMER, born 1944; admitted, 1971, The Netherlands. *Education:* Leyden University.

PIETER DE BOORDER, born 1946; admitted, 1974, The Netherlands. *Education:* Rotterdam University.

ED C.M. WAGEMAKERS, born 1947; admitted, 1976, The Netherlands. *Education:* Nijmegen University.

JOB A. VAN DER HAVE, born 1953; admitted, 1981, The Netherlands. *Education:* Leyden University.

GER J.M. CARTIGNY, born 1947; admitted, 1982, The Netherlands. *Education:* Nijmegen University.

JAN PAUL FRANX, born 1959; admitted, 1986, The Netherlands. *Education:* Amsterdam University.

ASSOCIATES ATTORNEYS AT LAW

TINEKE M. VAN DE PEPPEL-MOLEMA, born 1935; admitted, 1981, The Netherlands. *Education:* Utrecht University.

WOUTER W. KORTEWEG, born 1957; admitted, 1983, The Netherlands. *Education:* Leyden University.

ARENT G.J. WESSELMAN VAN HELMOND, born 1953; admitted, 1983, The Netherlands. *Education:* Leyden University.

(This Listing Continued)

NAUTA DUTILH, Breda—Continued

JOHN VAN BAAREN, born 1965; admitted, 1989, The Netherlands. *Education:* Rotterdam University.

JASPER A. BOVENBERG, born 1964; admitted, 1994, The Netherlands. *Education:* Leyden and Michigan Universities.

MARJOLEIN C.J. PALLANDT, born 1968; admitted, 1991, The Netherlands. *Education:* Tilburg University.

(For Complete Biographical Data on all Personnel, see Professional Biographies at Rotterdam, The Netherlands)

VAN WIJMEN & KOEDAM

Established in 1922

"QUADRIUM"

CLAUDIUS PRINSENLAAN 126

P.O. BOX 4714

4803 ES BREDA, THE NETHERLANDS

Telephone: (31) (76) 223100

Telefax: (31) (76) 142575

Rotterdam, The Netherlands Office: Westzeedijk 140, P.O. Box 23070, 3001 KB Rotterdam. Telephone: (31) (10) 4364066. Telefax: (31) (10) 4360582.

(For Complete Data on the firm and all Personnel, See Professional Biographies at Rotterdam, The Netherlands)

TEN HOLTER VAN NISPEN HOOGENBOOM

Advocaten

Established in 1926

ORANJEPARK 9

3311 LP DORDRECHT, THE NETHERLANDS

Telephone: 31-78 13 71 77

Fax: 31-78 13 01 71

Telex: 29408 nomos nl

Vevey, Switzerland Office: 7 Tour Carrée, CH-1800. Telephone: 41-21 922 67 67. Fax: 41-21 944 91 17. Telex: 851356 nati ch.

Company and Commercial Law, Company Take-Overs, Management Buy-Outs, Mergers, Acquisitions, Joint Ventures, Partnerships, Company Formations, Bankruptcy, Winding-Up and Dissolution of Companies, Construction Law, Contracting, Litigation, Arbitration, Off-Shore Constructions, Cranes and other Steel Constructions, Landlord and Tenant and Property Development, International Private Law, Conventions and Treaties, Employment and Labour Management Law, General Criminal Law, Commercial Crimes, Tax Fraud, Domestic Law, Administrative Tribunal Work.

FIRM PROFILE: The firm has 7 partners and 10 associates. The clientèle of the firm is varied, consisting of small, medium and large national and international companies, professional practitioners, non profit institutions, governmental institutions and private persons.

PARTNERS

HARRY W. TEN HOLTER, born 1930; admitted, 1960. *LANGUAGES:* English, French, German and Spanish. *PRACTICE AREAS:* Contracts; Company; Construction; Arbitration.

OCCI J.L. VAN NISPEN TOT SEVENAER, born 1932; admitted, 1964. *LANGUAGES:* English and French. *PRACTICE AREAS:* Contracts; Company; Construction.

MARI I. HOOGENBOOM, born 1944; admitted, 1974. *LANGUAGES:* English and German. *PRACTICE AREAS:* Contracts; Company.

PETER J.G.M. VAN GOOL, born 1951; admitted, 1978. *LANGUAGES:* English. *PRACTICE AREAS:* Computers and Software; Labour; Social.

LEON R.T. PEETERS, born 1955; admitted, 1980. *LANGUAGES:* English. *PRACTICE AREAS:* Labour; Social; Construction.

(This Listing Continued)

VINCENT J. GROOT, born 1955; admitted, 1982. *LANGUAGES:* English and German. *PRACTICE AREAS:* Bankruptcy; Debtor and Creditor.

HUGO A.H.W. MEIJER, born 1957; admitted, 1986. *LANGUAGES:* English. *PRACTICE AREAS:* Real Estate; Contracts; Agency and Distributorships.

ASSOCIATES

HENRI STODEL, born 1921; admitted, 1973. *LANGUAGES:* English, French and German. *PRACTICE AREAS:* International Trade; Agency and Distributorships; Insurance.

NIA MULLER-VAN DER SLIKKE, born 1946; admitted, 1972. *LANGUAGES:* English, French and German. *PRACTICE AREAS:* Family; Agriculture.

ADRIANA A. BOULOGNE, born 1939; admitted, 1983. *LANGUAGES:* English, French and German. *PRACTICE AREAS:* Family; Inheritance.

BERT A.W. TEN HOLTER, born 1956; admitted, 1985. *LANGUAGES:* English. *PRACTICE AREAS:* Administrative; Construction; Antitrust and Trade Regulation.

ANNE KIM VAN ECK, born 1962; admitted, 1985. *LANGUAGES:* English and German. *PRACTICE AREAS:* Family; Children.

MARCEL J. SMIT, born 1961; admitted, 1988. *LANGUAGES:* English and German. *PRACTICE AREAS:* Criminal; White Collar Crime.

FREDERIK W. VAN HOGENDORP, born 1946; admitted, 1973, Rotterdam; 1993, Dordrecht. *LANGUAGES:* English, French and German. *PRACTICE AREAS:* Transportation; Agency and Distributorships.

ARAM VAN BUNGE, born 1967; admitted, 1991. *LANGUAGES:* English. *PRACTICE AREAS:* General Practice; Labour.

FRED M.N. JANSSEN, born 1962; admitted, 1992. *LANGUAGES:* English, German and Italian. *PRACTICE AREAS:* General Practice; Commercial.

EMMA D.A. GELEIJNS, born 1969; admitted, 1993,. *LANGUAGES:* English and German. *PRACTICE AREAS:* General Practice; Family.

Languages: Dutch, English, German, French, Italian and Spanish

---

VELDHUIJZEN & SCHEP

Established in 1978

HOUTTUINEN 36

P.O. BOX 1080

3300 BB DORDRECHT, THE NETHERLANDS

Telephone: 31-78-133966

Fax: 31-78-310938

General Practice, Administrative, Arbitration, Litigation, Negligence, Injury, Property and Real Estate, Rent and Lease, Transportation, Insurance, International Private Law, Maritime Law and Company Law.
All Offices are affiliated with the International ICC (Inter Continental Consultants) group of lawyers and accountants.

MEMBERS OF FIRM

Maarten L. Veldhuijzen	Jaap van Drongelen
Aart Schep	Pim Nuiten

ASSOCIATES

Hans Pijnacker	Gert Jan Hoyting
Job Van Breevoort	Frank Schmitz
Arno Quispel	Maurice Bol
Zsiga Gyömörei	Anita Wohler
Gellian Krol	

Languages: Dutch, English, French, German and Spanish (written only)

DE BRAUW BLACKSTONE WESTBROEK

Attorneys and Civil Law Notaries

PARKLAAN 42A

5613 BG EINDHOVEN, THE NETHERLANDS
Telephone: (40) 464442
Telecopier: (40) 466288

REVISERS OF THE NETHERLANDS LAW DIGEST FOR THIS DIRECTORY.

The Hague, The Netherlands Office: Zuid Hollandlaan 7, 2596 AL.
Telephone: (70)328 5 328. Telex: 32321. Telecopier: (70) 328 5 325.

Amsterdam, The Netherlands Office: Atrium - 7th Floor, Strawinskylaan 3115, 1077 ZX. Telephone: (20) 5 481 481. Telex: 10227. Telecopier: (20) 5 481 485.

Rotterdam, The Netherlands Office: 10th Floor, Coolsingel 139, 3012 AG. Telephone: (10) 401 88 99. Telex: 24676. Telecopier: (10) 411 35 48.

Brussels, Belgium Office: Brederodestraat 13A, B-1000. Telephone: (2) 505 0211. Telecopier: (2) 502 2644.

London, England Office: Royex House, Aldermanbury Square, EC2V 7HR. Telephone: (171) 600 1719. Fax: (171) 600 1718.

New York, New York Office: 712 Fifth Avenue, 30th Floor, 10019-4102. Telephone: (212) 801-3430. Fax: (212) 801-3435; (212) 801-3436.

Dutch Attorneys may represent clients before all Dutch Courts, before the European Court of Justice and the Benelux Court of Justice, and are admitted to plead before all Courts of the member states of the Common Market (EEC).

Member of Alliance of European Lawyers (EEIG) which regroups six law firms from Continental Europe. The Alliance consists of Oppenhoff & Rädler at Munich, Berlin, Cologne, Frankfurt am Main and Leipzig; De Bandt, van Hecke & Lagae at Brussels and Antwerp; DeBrauw Blackstone Westbroek at Amsterdam, The Hague, Rotterdam, Brussels, London and New York; Jeantet & Associés at Paris and Warsaw; Lagerlöf & Leman at Stockholm, Gothenburg and Malmö; Uria & Menendez at Madrid and Barcelona.

The Alliance member firms have joint offices at Brussels, London, New York and Prague.

MEMBERS OF FIRM

WILLEM A. HOYNG, born 1946; admitted, 1973, The Hague. *Education:* Leyden University; Kings College London (1976); University of California at Los Angeles (1982). Professor of Civil Law especially Intellectual Property Law, University of Tilburg. *Member:* Association Internationale pour la Protection de la Propriété Industrielle (AIPPI); LICP; LES; USTA; PTG. (Also at The Hague Office). *LANGUAGES:* English, French and German. *PRACTICE AREAS:* EC Law; Intellectual Property Law.

ASSOCIATES

ERNEST MEYER SWANTEE, born 1964; admitted, 1989, The Hague. *Education:* Leyden University. *LANGUAGES:* English. *PRACTICE AREAS:* Corporate Law; Computer Law; Bankruptcy Law.

MONICA F.M.T. FRANKE, born 1967; admitted, 1990, The Hague. *Education:* Nijmegen University; D.E.A. de droit privé Université de Poitiers. (Also at The Hague Office).

PAULINE H.M. KESER, born 1964; admitted, 1992, Amsterdam. *Education:* University of Amsterdam. (Also at The Hague Office).

REVISERS OF THE NETHERLANDS LAW DIGEST FOR THIS DIRECTORY.

(For list of Partners and Counsel of the respective Member Firms see Professional Biographies at: Oppenhoff & Rädler at Munich, Cologne, Frankfurt am Main, Berlin and Leipzig, Germany; De Bandt van Hecke & Lagae at Brussels and Antwerp, Belgium; De Brauw Blackstone Westbroek at The Hague, Rotterdam and Amsterdam, The Netherlands; Jeantet & Associés, at Paris, France and Warsaw, Poland; Lagerlöf & Leman at Stockholm, Gothenburg and Malmö, Sweden; Uria & Menendez at Madrid and Barcelona, Spain)

NAUTA DUTILH

Attorneys, Civil Law Notaries, Tax Advisers

GEBOUW VIERLANDER
FELLENOORD 19
NL-5612 AA EINDHOVEN, THE NETHERLANDS
Telephone: (31-40) 656500
Telecopier: (31-40) 461375

Mailing Address: P.O. Box 6019, NL-5600 HA Eindhoven, The Netherlands

MEMBERS OF FIRM ATTORNEYS AT LAW

ANTHONY E. DRIESSEN, born 1937; admitted, 1964, The Netherlands. *Education:* Leyden University.

JEROEN N.D.M. KAGER, born 1945; admitted, 1969, The Netherlands. *Education:* Amsterdam University.

PAUL F.M. KAGER, born 1948; admitted, 1973, The Netherlands. *Education:* Leyden University.

MEMBERS OF FIRM CIVIL LAW NOTARIES

MICHEL E.A. BESNARD, born 1939; notary since, 1978. *Education:* Utrecht University.

HARRIE A. VAN IERSEL, born 1944; notary since, 1988. *Education:* Nijmegen University.

JEROEN A.M. TEN BERG, born 1952; notary since, 1988. *Education:* Leyden and Tilburg Universities.

ASSOCIATES ATTORNEYS AT LAW

ERNST R. SCHAEDTLER, born 1957; admitted, 1984, The Netherlands. *Education:* Leyden University.

WENDY TH.M. RAAB, born 1963; admitted, 1987, The Netherlands. *Education:* Utrecht University.

ANITA P.J.M. VERBEEK, born 1962; admitted, 1988, The Netherlands. *Education:* Rotterdam University.

MARC A. WINTGENS, born 1961; admitted, 1989, The Netherlands. *Education:* Leyden University.

LUDO J. MEES, born 1960; admitted, 1991, The Netherlands. *Education:* Groningen and Washington Universities.

NATHALIE A.M.E. FANOY, born 1956; admitted, 1992, The Netherlands. *Education:* Leyden University.

LIESBETH A.M. ZWITSERLOOD, born 1968; admitted, 1992, The Netherlands. *Education:* Maastricht University.

ASSOCIATES CANDIDATE CIVIL LAW NOTARIES

J. FRANS VERLINDEN, born 1956; admitted, 1988, The Netherlands. *Education:* Utrecht University.

HANNEKE I. DRIESSEN-KLEIJN, born 1961; admitted, 1990, The Netherlands. *Education:* Leyden University.

MARJOLEIN VAN DER HEIJDEN, born 1965; admitted, 1994, The Netherlands. *Education:* Groningen University.

KATHERINE M. IGNACZEWSKI, born 1967; (admission pending). *Education:* Utrecht University.

(For Complete Biographical Data on all Personnel, see Professional Biographies at Rotterdam, The Netherlands)

PRINSEN VAN DER PUTT

BOSCHDIJK 15
P.O. BOX 666
NL 5600 AR EINDHOVEN, THE NETHERLANDS
Telephone: 040-433 433
Fax: 040-433 033

General Civil and Commercial Law Practice, Mergers and Acquisitions, Re-Organization, MBO, Joint Ventures, Banking and Finance, Intellectual and Industrial Property, Real Estate and Construction, Lease, Bankruptcy and Insolvency, Employment and Labour, Insurance, Administrative Law, Environmental Issues, Agency, Distribution, Family Law, Health Law, Punitive Law, European Law, Antitrust, Private International Law, Wills and Estates, Litigation and Arbitration.

(This Listing Continued)

PRINSEN VAN DER PUTT, Eindhoven—Continued

MEMBERS OF FIRM
ATTORNEYS AT LAW

HUIBERT J.M. VAN DER PUTT, born 1939; admitted, 1965. *Education:* University of Amsterdam.

JAN HEIN W.M. OP DE COUL, born 1940; admitted, 1967. *Education:* Utrecht University.

JAN B. KIN, born 1946; admitted, 1972. *Education:* Tilburg University.

ADRIAAN P.P.M. VAN BEURDEN, born 1948; admitted, 1973. *Education:* Utrecht University.

SERVAAS A.J.M. MUNNICHS, born 1948; admitted, 1974. *Education:* Utrecht University.

G. ELISABETH MULLER, born 1950; admitted, 1975. *Education:* Utrecht University.

ALBERT HEIKENS, born 1952; admitted, 1978. *Education:* Utrecht University.

NICO J.M. BROERS, born 1954; admitted, 1978. *Education:* University of Amsterdam.

JAN E. STADIG, born 1957; admitted, 1982. *Education:* Utrecht University.

VINCENT H.M. WIBAUT, born 1957; admitted, 1984. *Education:* Groningen University.

MARIEKE A.J. BURGERS-THOMASSEN, born 1955; admitted, 1982. *Education:* Rotterdam University.

C.B. ERIK GRAMBERG, born 1957; admitted, 1986. *Education:* Groningen University.

MEMBERS OF FIRM
CIVIL LAW NOTARY

JOS. P.A.M. LOMBARTS, born 1937; admitted, 1979. *Education:* Utrecht University.

ASSOCIATES
ATTORNEYS AT LAW

TOM M. OVERBOOM, born 1962; admitted, 1986. *Education:* Tilburg University.

MARK J. KEUSS, born 1962; admitted, 1989. *Education:* Utrecht University.

RENATE H. STAM, born 1967; admitted, 1990. *Education:* Nijmegen University.

MARC A.J.G. JANSSEN, born 1966; admitted, 1990. *Education:* Nijmegen University.

MARGRET E. DEKKER, born 1967; admitted, 1991. *Education:* Groningen University.

MARC VAN DEN BERG, born 1965; admitted, 1991. *Education:* Utrecht University.

ANN GILES-CREUTZBERG, born 1951; admitted, 1992. *Education:* Utrecht University.

BARBARA DU FOSSÉ, born 1967; admitted, 1992. *Education:* Tilburg University.

PHILIPPE J.M. PETIT, born 1967; admitted, 1993. *Education:* Rotterdam University.

RUUD KEUKEN, born 1965; admitted, 1993. *Education:* Tilburg University.

BRIGITTE J.E.M. ABBENHUIS, born 1966; admitted, 1993. *Education:* Nijmegen University.

MARIËLLE C.J. SLUITER, born 1967; admitted, 1994. *Education:* Leiden University.

ERIK J. KARS, born 1966; admitted, 1994. *Education:* Tilburg University.

A. MARIE-JOSÉ A. VAN DE KERKHOF, born 1969; admitted, 1994. *Education:* Rotterdam University.

ASSOCIATES
(This Listing Continued)

CIVIL LAW NOTARY

HANS F.M. VERHAGEN, born 1957. *Education:* Amsterdam University.

OF COUNSEL

HENDRIK I. PRINSEN, born 1934; admitted, 1962. *Education:* Nijmegen University.

Prinsen van der Putt is a member of ACL International, an International Association of commercial lawyers with associated offices in over 20 countries around the world.

Languages: Dutch, English, French, German and Italian

QUARLES & JURGENS
ADVOCATEN

Established in 1976

F. DEN HOLLANDERLAAN 10A
4461 HN GOES, THE NETHERLANDS
Telephone: (31) (1100) 11640
Facsimile: (31) (1100) 32559

Effective 10/10/95 - Telephone: (0113) 211640 and Facsimile: (0113) 232559

Mailing Address: P.O. Box 130, Goes, 4460 AC

Firm engaged in the Law regarding Mergers and Acquisitions, Joint Ventures and Corporations, Business Transactions, Real Estate and Construction, Banking, Bankruptcy and Insolvency, Employment and Labor, Landlord and Tenants, Government Regulations, Environmental Issues, Litigation and Arbitration, Debt-collection, Intellectual Property Law, Tort, Personal Injuries, Oyster and Mussel Culture.
The Firm's 18 Attorneys in Goes, Breda, Tilburg, Dordrecht, Luxembourg and Geneva (Interjurist) may represent clients before all Dutch courts, before the European Court of Justice and the Benelux Court of Justice, and are admitted to plead before all Courts of the Member-States of the Common Market (EC). Member of Branson E.E.S.V. with offices in France, Belgium, The Netherlands and Norway (Associated Member).

CONTACTING PARTNER

STEPHEN D. SPRUIJT, born Woking, Great Britain, 1945; admitted, 1973. *Education:* Utrecht University, The Netherlands (Master of Law, 1973). *Member:* Netherlands Bar Association; International Bar Association.

Languages: Dutch, English, German and French.

MORET ERNST & YOUNG TAX
ADVISERS
CORPORATE LAW ADVISORY GROUP

17, LEONARD SPRINGERLAAN
P.O. BOX 997
9700 AZ GRONINGEN, THE NETHERLANDS
Telephone: 31-50-994444
Fax: 31-50-270852

Amsterdam Office: 20, Drentestraat, P.O. Box 7925, 1008 AC.
Telephone: 31-20-5497333. Fax: 31-20-6462553.
Rotterdam Office: 51, Marten Meesweg, P.O. Box 2295, 3000 CG.
Telephone: 31-10-4072627. Fax: 31-10-4072612.
The Hague Office: 80, Wassenaarseweg, P.O. Box 90636, 2509 LP.
Telephone: 31 70-3286542. Fax: 31 70-3244003.
Arnhem Office: Kronenburgsingel 12, P.O. Box 30116, 6803 AC.
Telephone: 31-85-209500. Fax: 31-85-235151.

Civil Law (general), Computer Law, Insolvency Law, (International) Contracts, Corporate Law, Environmental Law, EC Law, Intellectual Property, Labour Law and Workers Participation, Mergers and Acquisitions, Taxation.

PARTNERS

JOOST KEMPERINK, born 1948. *Education:* Nijmegen University (1973 and 1974). (Resident).

(This Listing Continued)

SENIOR-ADVISORS

FRÉDÉRIQUE HUUSSEN-DE GROOT, born 1942. *Education:* Leyden University (1976).

(For complete data see at Amsterdam, The Netherlands)

TEEKENS ADVOKATEN

KAROLUSGULDEN 32-38
2353 TA LEIDERDORP, THE NETHERLANDS
Telephone: 0031-71413021
Fax: 0031-71410684

Mailing Address: P.O. Box 118, NL-2350 AC Leiderdorp

Leiden, Netherlands Office: Haagse Schouwweg 8e. Telephone: 0031-71322738. Fax: 0031-71321421.

Administrative Law, Arbitration, Bankruptcy, Building and Construction Law, Business Law, Corporate Law, Civil Law, Company Takeovers, Acquisitions and Mergers, Commercial Law, Competition, Contracts, Debt Recovery, Enforcements of Foreign Judgements, Environmental Law, European Union Law, Family Law, Intellectual Property, Labour Law, Litigation, Personal Injury, Property, Tenancy Law, Transport Law.

FIRM PROFILE: *Teekens Advocaten has a broadly based practice with a reputation for offering a full range of quality legal services in the area of commercial law. Teekens law firm was founded in Leiden in 1950. In 1983, the firm moved to a suburb of Leiden, named Leiderdorp. In 1992 a branch office was founded on the West side of Leiden. At the end of 1995, the firm will move to a new location in Leiden, in a modern building. The present offices and the future office are located near the main highways connecting The Netherlands' main cities, Amsterdam, The Hague, Rotterdam and Utrecht. The firm now has two partners, six associates and one paralegal employee. The latter will become an associate in April 1995.*

The partners and associates are admitted to all Dutch Courts, including the Supreme Court of the Netherlands. The Supreme Court of the Netherlands has its seat in The Hague.

Teekens Advocaten has had international professional contacts since the early nineteen sixties. Now, the firm has a close association with law firms throughout Europe, working closely together in the E.E.I.G. Law Span International, an international association of law firms throughout the European Union. Teekens Advocaten will be pleased to act as a contact firm for referral to quality law firms throughout Europe.

The correspondence languages of the firm are Dutch, English, German and French.

MEMBERS OF THE FIRM

MICHAEL TEEKENS, born 1916; admitted, 1939, The Hague. *Education:* Leiden University (Law Degree), Promoted to LL.D., 1954. Author, "De Deurwaarder" (The Bailiff), Leiden, 1954. (Founder). *LANGUAGES:* Dutch, English, German and French. *PRACTICE AREAS:* Litigation; Arbitration; Contract Law; Matters Concerning Bailiff.

MICHAEL TEEKENS, JR., born 1950; admitted, 1975, The Hague. *Education:* Leiden University (Law Degree). *LANGUAGES:* Dutch, English, German and French. *PRACTICE AREAS:* Litigation; Corporate Law; Labour Law; Contracts; Property; Administrative Law; Bankruptcy; Insolvency; Building Law; Construction Law; Debt Collection; Arbitration.

JOHAN FREDERIK LANGELAAR, born 1952; admitted, 1981, Rotterdam; 1985, The Hague. *Education:* Leiden University (Law Degree). *LANGUAGES:* Dutch, English and German. *PRACTICE AREAS:* Corporate Law; Litigation; Transport Law; Contracts; Business Law; Bankruptcy; Labour Law; Company Take-overs; Mergers; Acquisitions; Tenancy Law; Debt Collection.

ASSOCIATES

EDITH SCHENKIUS, born 1944; admitted, 1971, Amsterdam; 1987, The Hague. *Education:* Leiden University (Law Degree). *LANGUAGES:* Dutch, English and French. *PRACTICE AREAS:* Litigation; Contracts; Labour Law; Tenancy Law; Debt Collections; Family Law; Criminal Law.

ROBERT JAN H. VAN DER WART, born 1965; admitted, 1992, The Hague. *Education:* Leiden University (Law Degree). *LANGUAGES:* Dutch, English and French. *PRACTICE AREAS:* Litigation; Contracts; Tenancy Law; Labour Law; Administrative Law; Environmental Law.

CORNELIS VAN OOSTEN, born 1967; admitted, 1992, The Hague. *Education:* Leiden University (Law Degree). *LANGUAGES:* Dutch, En-

(This Listing Continued)

glish and German. *PRACTICE AREAS:* Litigation; Contracts; Tenancy Law; Labour Law; Bankruptcy; Debt Collection; Intellectual Property.

JOSEPHINE ANNE INES VAN GOOL, born 1968; admitted, 1993, The Hague. *Education:* Leiden University (Law Degree). *LANGUAGES:* Dutch, English and German. *PRACTICE AREAS:* Litigation; Labour Law; Tenancy Law; Family Law.

MARTIJN SNOEK, born 1969; admitted, 1993, The Hague. *Education:* Leiden University (Law Degree). *LANGUAGES:* Dutch, English and French. *PRACTICE AREAS:* Litigation; Labour Law; Tenancy Law; Corporate Law.

PARALEGALS

FRANK ERADUS, born 1959. *Education:* Leiden University. *LANGUAGES:* Dutch, English and German. *PRACTICE AREAS:* Litigation; Corporate Law; Tenancy Law; Labour Law; Contracts.

Dutch, English, German and French.

ADRIAANSE & VAN DER WEEL

35, ROUAANSEKAAI
P.O. BOX 240
NL-4330 AE MIDDELBURG, THE NETHERLANDS
Telephone: (31) 01180-35365
FAX: (31) 01180-36178

(Middelburg is near River Scheldt)

Associated Office: P.O. Box 25, NL-4530 AA Terneuzen. Telephone: 31-1150-13 1 75. Telephone Copier: 31-1150-17 7 64.

Administrative Law, Advertising Law, Agricultural Law, Arbitration, Competition Law, Construction Law, Corporate Law, Criminal Law, Employer's Liability, Environmental Law, Family Law, Food and Drug Regulations, Health, Hospital and Malpractice Law, Immigration Law, Industrial Relations and Labour Law, Insurance Law, International Private Law, Litigation, Maritime and Admiralty Law, Negligence Law, Personal Injury Law, Property and Real Estate Law, Rent and Lease, Social Security, Transportation Law, General Legal Practice.

MEMBERS OF FIRM

F.K. Adriaanse	**A. Minderhoud**
C.H. Brinkman	**U.T. Hoekstra**
C.F.E.P. Galama	**N.H. Van Everdingen**
	I.P. de Groot

ASSOCIATES

A. Van Werkum-Hoekstra	**A.P.M. Corstjens**
J.M. Van Koeveringe-Dekker	**J.C.M. Bol**
M. van der Bent	**D.W. Boer**
H.A.J. Krijger	**C.J. Ijdema**

Languages: Dutch, English, French, German and Swedish

DIRKZWAGER

Attorneys At Law - Civil Law Notaries

"STELLA MARIS"
S. MATHONSINGEL 4
P.O. BOX 55 6500 AB NIJMEGEN
NIJMEGEN, THE NETHERLANDS
Telephone: 80 22 66 41
Telefax: 80 22 20 74

Arnhem, The Netherlands Office: "Velperbeek," Velperweg 26, P.O. Box 6802 DA Arnhem. Telephone: 85 53 83 00. Telefax: 85 51 07 93.

Contract, General Commercial, Companies, Corporations, Insurance, Damages, Personal Injury, Product Liability, Mergers and Acquisitions, Competition, Anti-Trust, Bankruptcy, Insolvency, Dutch-German Legal Relationships, Trademarks, Intellectual Property, Employment, Labour, Construction, Building, Environmental Law, Planning, Commercial Property, Family Law, Public Health Law, Law of Mineral Extractions.

FIRM PROFILE: *Dirkzwager in its present form was founded in 1990 as a result of a merger between well respected firms of lawyers and notaries in Arnhem and Nijmegen of which the origins go back to the early nineteenth century. The firm is very much active in the commercial and industrial field; our clients are spread out nationwide. We maintain good relations with other law firms abroad. Being a medium-sized firm Dirkzwager*

(This Listing Continued)

DIRKZWAGER, Nijmegen—Continued

is able to build up a good personal relationship with its clients, taking care of their specific interests. All matters can be dealt with in an efficient and quick manner. The internal communication is direct and fully automated. We have a fruitful and productive teamwork amongst all lawyers and notaries so that our clients can benefit from everyone's specific know-how and expertise in the various legal subject matters.

Members of Interlega in association with TELFA (Trans European Law Firms Association).

TELFA-Interlega is an association of European Law Firms, whose members have offices in Athens, Arnhem, Barcelona, Basel, Bologna, Brussels, Budapest, Düsseldorf, Edinburg, Geneva, Glasgow, Guernsey, Halle, Kopenhagen, Lisboa, London, Luxembourg, Madrid, Milan, Nijmegen and Paris. For more details see the TELFA-Interlega entry under Brussels.

The firm has a total number of 20 partners and 25 associates. The total number of all staff is 110.

Languages: Dutch, English, German, French and Spanish.

PARTNERS

FONS W.T.TH. MARRES, born Heiloo, The Netherlands, May 23, 1938; admitted, 1966, The Netherlands. *Education:* University of Utrecht (M.R., 1964).

CAS P. AUBEL, born Arnhem, The Netherlands, March 17, 1936; admitted, 1968, The Netherlands. *Education:* University of Nijmegen (M.R., 1964).

FRANS J. PERQUIN, born Breda, The Netherlands, December 30, 1946; admitted, 1972, The Netherlands. *Education:* University of Nijmege (M.R., 1972).

DR. PAUL J.M. VAN WERSCH, born Kerkrade, The Netherlands, July 2, 1946; admitted, 1979, The Netherlands. *Education:* University of Leiden (M.R., 1970).

WILBERT J.M. GITMANS, born Tegelen, The Netherlands, December 8, 1948; admitted, 1980, The Netherlands. *Education:* University of Nijmegen (M.R., 1973).

HENK A. HOVING, born Drachten, The Netherlands, May 2, 1959; admitted, 1983, The Netherlands. *Education:* University of Groningen (M.R., 1983).

FRANK J.P. DELISSEN, born Roermond, The Netherlands, December 20, 1956; admitted, 1984, The Netherlands. *Education:* University of Nijmegen (M.R., 1984).

PIETER BERGKAMP, born Den Bosch, The Netherlands, September 9, 1959; admitted, 1986, The Netherlands. *Education:* University of Nijmegen (M.R., 1986).

ASSOCIATES

HANNA ZEILMAKER, born Haarlem, The Netherlands, April 4, 1963; admitted, 1987, Amsterdam. *Education:* University of Amsterdam (M.R., 1987).

LIESBETH HEMRICA, born Groote Gast, The Netherlands, September 1, 1959; admitted, 1989, The Netherlands. *Education:* University of Utrecht (M.R., 1989).

OF COUNSEL

LOUIS G.H.J. HOUWEN, born Horst, The Netherlands, September 25, 1960; admitted, 1993, The Netherlands. *Education:* University of Nijmegen (M.R., 1986).

TOM BERNARD VANDEGINSTE, born Kortrijk, Belgium, March 2, 1967; admitted, 1994, The Netherlands. *Education:* Katholieke Universiteit Nijmegen (M.R., 1994).

MAAIKE L.J. BOMERS, born Nijimegen July 9, 1970; admitted, 1994, The Netherlands. *Education:* University of Nijmegen (M.R., 1994).

CIVIL LAW NOTARIES

Jos M.J.L.S. Schuijren   Fons H.N. Stollenwerck

TRENITÉ VAN DOORNE

HAAGWEG 175
2281 AJ RIJSWIJK, THE NETHERLANDS
Telephone: 31 (0) 70-390 10 15
Telefax: 31 (0) 70-399 68 44

Mailing Address: P.O. Box 1073, 2280 CB RIJSWIJK

Amsterdam, Netherlands Office: De Lairessestraat 133. Mailing Address: P.O. Box 75265, 1070 AG AMSTERDAM. Telephone: 31 (0) 20-6789 123. Telex: 16144 tvda nl. Telefax: 31 (0) 20-6789 589.

Rotterdam, Netherlands Office: Weena 666. Mailing Address: P.O. Box 190, 3000 AD ROTTERDAM. Telephone: 31 (0) 10-404 2111. Telefax: 31 (0) 10-404 2333.

The Hague, Netherlands Office: Churchillplein 5. Mailing Address: P.O. Box 17207, 2502 CE THE HAGUE. Telephone: 31 (0) 70-338 3131. Telefax: 31 (0) 70-358 4798.

Brussels, Belgium Office: Avenue Louise 149, 1050 BRUSSELS. Telephone: 32-2-537 5159. Telefax: 32-2-537 6961.

Willemstad, Curaçao, Netherlands Antilles Office: Promes, Trenité Van Doorne. Julianaplein 22, P.O. Box 504. Telephone: 599-9-613400. Telefax: 599-9-612023.

Tokyo, Japan: Akasaka Wing Building 5 F, 6-6-15 Akasaka, Minato-ku, 107. Telephone: 813-5563-2911. Telefax: 813-5563-2912.

MEMBERS OF FIRM
CIVIL LAW NOTARIES

DICK CAMINADA, born 1938; appointed Civil Law Notary by her Majesty the Queen, 1977. *Education:* University of Leiden (1961). *LANGUAGES:* English and German. *PRACTICE AREAS:* Family Law; Real Estate.

WILLIAM R. AVENARIUS, born 1938; appointed Civil Law Notary by Her Majesty the Queen, 1977. *Education:* University of Leiden (1967). *LANGUAGES:* English and German. *PRACTICE AREAS:* Real Estate Law; Family Law.

CORNELIS E.M. VAN STEENDEREN, born 1943; appointed Civil Law Notary by Her Majesty the Queen, 1991. *Education:* University of Utrecht (J.D., 1967) and Leiden (Notarial Law, 1974). *LANGUAGES:* English and German. *PRACTICE AREAS:* Corporate Law.

ASSOCIATES
CIVIL LAW NOTARIES

THEO F.H. REIJNEN, born 1963; admitted as Civil Law Notary, 1991. *Education:* Universities of Tilburg (Tax Law, 1987) and Leiden (Notarial Law, 1991). *LANGUAGES:* English and German. *PRACTICE AREAS:* Family Law; Corporate Law.

ALEX Q. BLOMAARD, born 1964; admitted as Civil Law Notary, 1989, Rijswijk. *Education:* University of Leiden (J.D. and Notarial Law, 1989). *LANGUAGES:* English and German. *PRACTICE AREAS:* Corporate Law; Family Law; Real Estate Law.

MARION C.M. VULLINGHS-KNIJNENBURG, born 1946; admitted as Civil Law Notary, 1992, Rijswijk. *Education:* University of Leiden (J.D., 1989), Notarial Law (1992). *LANGUAGES:* English, French, German and Spanish. *PRACTICE AREAS:* Family Law; Real Estate Law.

MICHIEL H. KOUWENHOVEN, born 1966; admitted as Civil Notary, 1993. *Education:* University of Amsterdam (1992). *LANGUAGES:* English and German. *PRACTICE AREAS:* Family Law.

A. GEA VAN GASTEL, born 1967; admitted as Civil Notary, 1993. *Education:* University of Groningen (1991). *LANGUAGES:* English and German. *PRACTICE AREAS:* Real Estate Law; Corporate Law.

PETER H.M. VAN DER WAAIJ, born 1965; admitted as Civil Law Notary, 1990, Harmelen, 1993, Rijswijk. *Education:* University of Nijmegen (J.D. and Notarial Law, 1990). *LANGUAGES:* English and German. *PRACTICE AREAS:* Family Law; Corporate Law.

MELANIE E.C. FRANTZEN, born 1968; admitted as Civil Law Notary, 1993, Rijswijk. *Education:* University of Leiden (Notarial Law, 1993). *LANGUAGES:* English and German. *PRACTICE AREAS:* Real Estate Law.

Trenité Van Doorne forms together with Wessing Berenberg-Gossler Zimmermann a European Economic interest grouping. Wessing has offices in Berlin, Brussels, Düsseldorf, Hamburg, Leipzig and Munich. Trenité Van Doorne is a member of Lex Mundi.

Languages: English, French and German

DE BRAUW BLACKSTONE WESTBROEK

Attorneys and Civil Law Notaries

10TH FLOOR, COOLSINGEL 139
3012 AG ROTTERDAM, THE NETHERLANDS
Telephone: (10) 401 88 99
Telex: 24676
Telecopier: (10) 411 35 48

REVISERS OF THE NETHERLANDS LAW DIGEST FOR THIS
DIRECTORY.

The Hague, The Netherlands Office: Zuid Hollandlaan 7, 2596 AL.
Telephone: (70) 328 5 328. Telex: 32321. Telecopier: (70) 328 5 325.
Amsterdam, The Netherlands Office: Atrium - 7th Floor, Strawinskylaan
3115, 1077 ZX. Telephone: (20) 5 481 481. Telex: 10227. Telecopier:
(20) 5 481 485.
Eindhoven, The Netherlands Office: Parklaan 42a, 5613 BG. Telephone:
(40) 464442. Telecopier (40) 46628.
Brussels, Belgium Office: Brederodestraat 13A, B-1000. Telephone: (2)
505 0211. Telecopier: (2) 502 2644.
London, England Office: Royex House, Aldermanbury Square, EC2V
7HR. Telephone: (171) 600 1719. Fax: (171) 600 1718.
New York, New York Office: 712 Fifth Avenue, 30th Floor, 10019-4102.
Telephone: (212) 801-3430. Fax: (212) 801-3435; (212) 801-3436.

Dutch Attorneys may represent clients before all Dutch Courts, before the
European Court of Justice and the Benelux Court of Justice, and are ad-
mitted to plead before all Courts of the member states of the Common
Market (EEC).
Member of Alliance of European Lawyers (EEIG) which regroups six law
firms from Continental Europe. The Alliance consists of Oppenhoff & Rä-
dler at Munich, Berlin, Cologne, Frankfurt am Main and Leipzig; De
Bandt, van Hecke & Lagae at Brussels and Antwerp; DeBrauw Blackstone
Westbroek at Amsterdam, The Hague, Rotterdam, Brussels, London and
New York; Jeantet & Associés at Paris and Warsaw; Lagerlöf & Leman at
Stockholm, Gothenburg and Malmö; Uria & Menendez at Madrid and
Barcelona.
The Alliance member firms have joint offices at Brussels, London, New
York and Prague.

CIVIL LAW NOTARIES
MEMBERS OF FIRM

WILLEM EDUARD DE VIN, born 1935; appointed Civil Law Notary,
1971, Rotterdam. *Education:* Utrecht University. *LANGUAGES:* English.
PRACTICE AREAS: Corporate Law; Notarial Law; Family Tax Planning.

HUBERTUS RICHARD OKKENS, born 1941; appointed Civil Law
Notary, 1974, Rotterdam. *Education:* Utrecht University. *LANGUAGES:*
English and German. *PRACTICE AREAS:* Construction/Real Estate
Law; Notarial Law.

WILLEM A. KOUDIJS, born 1938; appointed Civil Law Notary, 1975,
Rotterdam. *Education:* Utrecht University. *LANGUAGES:* English and
German. *PRACTICE AREAS:* Corporate Law; Notarial Law; Privatisa-
tions.

PETER J. DORTMOND, born 1944; appointed Civil Law Notary,
1976, Rotterdam. *Education:* Utrecht University. Professor, Corporate
Law, Nijmegen University, 1989. *LANGUAGES:* English and German.
PRACTICE AREAS: Corporate Law; Notarial Law.

KASPER M.F.J. HOUBEN, born 1941; appointed Civil Law Notary,
1979, Rotterdam. *Education:* Nijmegen University. *LANGUAGES:* English, French and German. *PRACTICE AREAS:* Estate Law; Estate Tax
Law; Matrimonial Property Law; Notarial Law.

ALBERT A. SCHULTING, born 1945; appointed Civil Law Notary,
1981, Rotterdam. *Education:* Leyden University. *LANGUAGES:* English.
PRACTICE AREAS: Notarial Law; Corporate Law.

FREDERIK K. BUIJN, born 1950; appointed Civil Law Notary, 1981,
Rotterdam. *Education:* Leyden University; Rotterdam University (Ph.D.,
1983). *LANGUAGES:* English. *PRACTICE AREAS:* Corporate Law;
Notarial Law.

CORNELIS WILLEM DE MONCHY, born 1950; appointed Civil Law
Notary, 1989, Rotterdam. *Education:* Leyden University. *LANGUAGES:*
English and French. *PRACTICE AREAS:* Corporate Law; Notarial Law.

FRANS D. ROSENDAAL, born 1952; appointed Civil Law Notary,
1985, Rotterdam. *Education:* Rotterdam University; Leyden University.
Member: International Bar Association; International Fiscal Association.

(This Listing Continued)

LANGUAGES: English. *PRACTICE AREAS:* Corporate Law; Financial
Law; Notarial Law.

HERMAN M.I.TH. BREEDVELD, born 1953; appointed Civil Law
Notary, 1987, Rotterdam. *Education:* Rotterdam University; Leyden Uni-
versity. *LANGUAGES:* English. *PRACTICE AREAS:* Corporate Law;
Financial Law; Construction/Real Estate Law.

PAUL KLEMANN, born 1958; appointed Civil Law Notary, 1991, Rotterdam. *Education:* Groningen University. *LANGUAGES:* English and
German. *PRACTICE AREAS:* Corporate Law; Notarial Law.

PAUL A.E. KERCKHOFFS, born 1959. *Education:* Leyden University.
Appointed, Civil Law Notary, 1994, Rotterdam. *LANGUAGES:* English.
PRACTICE AREAS: Real Estate Law; Notarial Law.

ASSOCIATES

ROELOF H. MAATHUIS, born 1932. *Education:* Leyden University.
LANGUAGES: English. *PRACTICE AREAS:* General Practice.

WILLEM E. JANSEN, born 1943. *LANGUAGES:* English. *PRAC-
TICE AREAS:* Admiralty; Maritime/Transportation Law.

HETTY J. KUIPER, born 1950. *Education:* University of Amsterdam.
LANGUAGES: English. *PRACTICE AREAS:* Real Estate Law.

EDITH K.W.J. REVET, born 1955. *Education:* Leyden University;
Duke University School of Law, Durham, North Carolina (LL.M.). *LAN-
GUAGES:* English and German. *PRACTICE AREAS:* Corporate Law;
Maritime/Transportation Law.

CAROLINA J.M. VAN BEEK, born 1958. *Education:* Free University
of Amsterdam. *LANGUAGES:* English. *PRACTICE AREAS:* Notarial
Law.

C.J. KRAAIVELD, born 1960. *Education:* Nijmegen University. *LAN-
GUAGES:* English. *PRACTICE AREAS:* Corporate Law; Notarial Law.

HELEN M. KOLSTER, born 1960. *Education:* Leyden University.
LANGUAGES: English. *PRACTICE AREAS:* Corporate Law; Construc-
tion/Real Estate Law.

JEAN D.M. SCHOONBROOD, born 1960. *Education:* Nijmegen University. *LANGUAGES:* English and German. *PRACTICE AREAS:* Corporate Law; Tax Law; Notarial Law.

ELINE H.A. SANDBERG, born 1960. *Education:* Utrecht University.
LANGUAGES: English, French and German. *PRACTICE AREAS:* Construction Law; Real Estate Law; Notarial Law.

CHERYL J. CONIJN-BARTELINGS, born 1960. *Education:* Leyden
University. *LANGUAGES:* English. *PRACTICE AREAS:* Corporate Law;
Notarial Law.

PIETER A. VAN ONZENOORT, born 1963. *Education:* Leyden University. *LANGUAGES:* English. *PRACTICE AREAS:* General Practice;
Notarial Law.

BARBARA BIER, born 1964. *Education:* Leyden University. *LAN-
GUAGES:* English, German and Spanish. *PRACTICE AREAS:* Corporate
Law; Financial Law; Notarial Law.

JELLE TEN HAVE, born 1960. *Education:* Utrecht University. *LAN-
GUAGES:* English. *PRACTICE AREAS:* Real Estate Law; Notarial Law.

PHILIP J. SIMONS, born 1962. *Education:* Leyden University. *LAN-
GUAGES:* English, German and French. *PRACTICE AREAS:* Corporate
Law; Notarial Law.

JAN W.A. HOCKX, born 1966. *Education:* Leyden University. *LAN-
GUAGES:* English. *PRACTICE AREAS:* Real Estate; Notarial Law.

NICOLE C. VAN SMAALEN, born 1962. *Education:* Leyden University.

MANON Y.H.J. DEN BOER, born 1964. *Education:* Leyden University.

CORRINE HOLDINGA, born 1965. *Education:* Free University of Amsterdam.

MENNO VAN GRONINGEN, born 1964. *Education:* Free University
of Amsterdam.

PETER A. NOORT, born 1964. *Education:* Leyden University.

LIEKE E. HOGE, born 1965. *Education:* Nijmegen University.

JET G.M. NABER, born 1964. *Education:* Groningen University.

(This Listing Continued)

DE BRAUW BLACKSTONE WESTBROEK, Rotterdam— Continued

JEROEN A. VAN DER WEIDE, born 1966. *Education:* Free University of Amsterdam.

ROBERT J.P. KONING, born 1966. *Education:* Leyden University.

MONIQUE M. RENS, born 1967. *Education:* Leyden University.

HUBERT-JAN M.M. VAN BOXEL, born 1968. *Education:* Leyden University.

MAURITS M. HES, born 1965. *Education:* Leyden University.

EELKO D. SMIT, born 1968. *Education:* Leyden University.

ANNEMIEKE J.W. WESSELS, born 1967. *Education:* Groningen University.

DANIËLLE A. TH. VAN GASSELT, born 1964. *Education:* Utrecht University.

JEROEN H.M. SWEENS, born 1964. *Education:* Groningen University.

PETRA M. DE JONG, born 1970. *Education:* Groningen University.

PATRICIA J.M. DE BRUYCKERE, born 1968. *Education:* Utrecht University.

ALEID B.A. DOODEHEEFVER, born 1966. *Education:* University of Amsterdam.

CEES A. DE ZEEUW, born 1965. *Education:* Leyden University.

STAN C.J.M. COMMISSARIS, born 1968. *Education:* Leyden University.

MILENA E. ASSELBERGS, born 1970. *Education:* Utrecht University.

ATTORNEYS AT LAW
MEMBERS OF FIRM

JAN A. VAN ARKEL, born 1933; admitted, 1960, The Hague. *Education:* Leyden University. *Member:* International Bar Association; Association Internationale pour la Protection de la Propriété Industrielle (AIPPI); ALAI. *LANGUAGES:* English. *PRACTICE AREAS:* Intellectual Property Law; Computer Law.

FLORIS O.W. VOGELAAR, born 1944; admitted, 1969, The Hague. *Education:* University of Amsterdam. Chairman, Legal Committee, AmCham Netherlands. *Member:* International Bar Association. *LANGUAGES:* English, German, French and Italian. *PRACTICE AREAS:* EC Law; Competition Law; Arbitration.

FOLKERT WAARDENBURG, born 1944; admitted, 1972, The Hague. *Education:* University of Amsterdam. *Member:* International Council of Environmental Law. *LANGUAGES:* English. *PRACTICE AREAS:* Administrative Law; Environmental Law; Health Care Law.

PETER N. WAKKIE, born 1948; admitted, 1972, The Hague. *Education:* Utrecht University. *Member:* International Bar Association. *LANGUAGES:* English. *PRACTICE AREAS:* Corporate Law; Business and Banking Law.

SIJMEN H. DE RANITZ, born 1951; admitted, 1976, Netherlands. *Education:* Leyden University. *Member:* European Association of Insolvency Practitioners (AEPPC). *LANGUAGES:* English, French and German. *PRACTICE AREAS:* Corporate Law; Bankruptcy Law.

CORNELIS N. PEIJSTER, born 1956; admitted, 1984, The Hague. *Education:* Leyden University. *Member:* Association of Internationale des Jeunes Advocates. *LANGUAGES:* English and German. *PRACTICE AREAS:* Corporate Law; Financial Law; Bankruptcy Law.

KOOS N. DE BLÉCOURT, born 1956; admitted, 1982, Netherlands. *Education:* Groningen University. *LANGUAGES:* English. *PRACTICE AREAS:* Corporate Law; Labour Law; Retail/Lease Contracts for Oil Companies.

MAARTEN C. SCHEPEL, born 1961; admitted, 1985, The Hague. *Education:* Leyden University; London University (LL.M., 1985). (Resident Partner, New York Office). *LANGUAGES:* English. *PRACTICE AREAS:* Corporate Law; Financial Law.

AAI SCHABERG, born 1958; admitted, 1984, The Hague. *Education:* Leyden University. *LANGUAGES:* English. *PRACTICE AREAS:* Corporate Law; Labour Law; Bankruptcy Law.

(This Listing Continued)

ASSOCIATES

BART L.P. VAN REEKEN, born 1963; admitted, 1988, The Hague. *Education:* Rotterdam University. *LANGUAGES:* English. *PRACTICE AREAS:* Corporate Law; Competition Law; EC Law.

BERNARD W. ROELVINK, born 1962; admitted, 1989, Rotterdam. *Education:* Leyden University. (Resident, London Office). *LANGUAGES:* English and German. *PRACTICE AREAS:* Corporate Law.

OLGA J. DE VRIES, born 1964; admitted, 1989, Rotterdam. *Education:* Rotterdam University. *LANGUAGES:* English and German. *PRACTICE AREAS:* Labour Law; Rent Law.

JOHAN T. JOL, born 1963; admitted, 1989, The Hague. *Education:* Utrecht University. *LANGUAGES:* English and French. *PRACTICE AREAS:* Corporate Law; Labour law; Bankruptcy Law.

ANNETJE T. OTTOW, born 1965; admitted, 1990, The Hague. *Education:* Leyden University. (Resident, Brussels Office). *LANGUAGES:* English, French and German. *PRACTICE AREAS:* EC Law.

BART P. VAN DER BŸLL, born 1953; admitted, 1990, Rotterdam. *Education:* Utrecht University.

JOOST K.F. MAASSEN, born 1963; admitted, 1990, Rotterdam. *Education:* Rotterdam University. *LANGUAGES:* English, German and Spanish. *PRACTICE AREAS:* General Practice; Labour Law.

BERT WINTERS, born 1962; admitted, 1992, The Hague. *Education:* Rotterdam University.

MONIQUE C. WESKI, born 1966; admitted, 1992, Rotterdam. *Education:* Rotterdam University.

T. MARTŸN SNOEP, born 1968; admitted, 1992, Rotterdam. *Education:* Rotterdam University.

PAULINE H.M. KESER, born 1964; admitted, 1992, Amsterdam. *Education:* University of Amsterdam. (Also at Eindhoven Office).

JOOST J.J. SCHUTTE, born 1966; admitted, 1993, Rotterdam. *Education:* Leyden University.

MARC V.M. SLUYTERS, born 1969; admitted, 1993, Rotterdam. *Education:* Catholic University of Brabant.

MENNO STOFFER, born 1965; admitted, 1993, Rotterdam. *Education:* Leyden University.

MARIUS O. KRAAMWINKEL, born 1965; admitted, 1994, Rotterdam. *Education:* Leyden University.

TATJANA PAVIĆEVIC, born 1967; admitted, 1994, Rotterdam. *Education:* Utrecht University.

JAN JOB DE VRIES ROBBÉ, born 1967; admitted, 1994, Rotterdam. *Education:* Leyden University.

ANNE-MARIE VAN DEN BOS, born 1968; admitted, 1994, Rotterdam. *Education:* Rotterdam University.

REVISERS OF THE NETHERLANDS LAW DIGEST FOR THIS DIRECTORY.

(For list of Partners and Counsel of the respective Member Firms see Professional Biographies at: Oppenhoff & Rädler at Munich, Cologne, Frankfurt am Main, Berlin and Leipzig, Germany; De Bandt van Hecke & Lagae at Brussels and Antwerp, Belgium; De Brauw Blackstone Westbroek at The Hague, Rotterdam, Amsterdam and Eindhoven, The Netherlands; Jeantet & Associés, at Paris, France and Warsaw, Poland; Lagerlöf & Leman at Stockholm, Gothenburg and Malmö, Sweden; Uria & Menendez at Madrid and Barcelona, Spain)

ENGELS & JONGENEEL ADVOCATEN

WESTERSINGEL 92
NL 3015 LC ROTTERDAM, THE NETHERLANDS

Telephone: (31-10) 436.07.88

Fax: (31-10) 436.78.44

Kassel, Germany Office: Anwaltskanzlei Dr. Dr. Ulfert Engels, Wilhelmsstr. 11, D-34117. Telephone: 0561-709.83-0. Fax: 0561-71.10.71.

Frankfurt/Main, Germany Office: Anwaltskanzlei Dr. Dr. Ulfert Engels, Klingerstr. 24, D-60313. Telephone: 069-28.11.39. Fax: 069-28.35.12.

(This Listing Continued)

Gerrit P. Jongeneel   *Ulfert Engels*

(Also see Biographical Sections at Kassel and Frankfurt/Main, Germany)

GRAHAM, SMITH & PARTNERS

Established in 1988

PARKLAAN 1
3016 BA ROTTERDAM, THE NETHERLANDS
Telephone: (+31) 10 436 5144
Fax: (+31) 10 436 2162

Amsterdam, The Netherlands Office: Koningslaan 34. Telephone: +31 20 5712500. Fax: +31 20 6733656.

Dutch and International Tax Law including Value Added Taxation, Inheritance Taxes, Social Security and Tax Litigation.

(For complete biographical data on all personnel, see Professional Biographies at Amsterdam)

HOUTHOFF

WEENATOREN, WEENA 355
3013 AL ROTTERDAM, THE NETHERLANDS
Telephone: (31) (10) 22 44 666
Telefax: (31) (10) 22 44 668

Mailing Address: P.O. Box 1507, 3000 BM Rotterdam

Amsterdam, The Netherlands Office: Parnassusweg 126, 1076 AT Amsterdam, The Netherlands. Mailing Address: P.O. Box 75505, 1070 AM Amsterdam, The Netherlands. Telephone: (31) (20) 57 00 200. Telefax: (31) (20) 57 00 280.

Houthoff is one of the Netherlands' leading law firms. It was formed in 1970 by merging three long established Amsterdam commercial prctice law firms. our history goes back to the year 1815. In 1991 Houthoff reinforced its presence in Rotterdam through the merger with a prominent Rotterdam firm.
Firm consisting of attorneys at law, civil law notaries and tax advisors engaged in the Law regarding Mergers and Acquisitions, Joint Ventures, Corporations, Incorporation of Legal Entities, Business Transactions, Venture Capital, Antitrust, Real Estate and Construction, Banking, International Finance, Reorganisations, Bankruptcy and Insolvency, Insurance and Reinsurance, Employment and Labor, National and International Taxation, Computers and Software, Telecommunications, Media and Entertainment, Trade Marks, Copyright, Patents, Designs and Models, Advertising, Medical and Professional Liability, Government Regulations, Environmental Issues, Immigration, Litigation and Arbitration, Trust Services, European Community Law, Government and Utilities Procurement, Energy Law.

MEMBERS OF FIRM

WILLEM J. HENGEVELD, born Haarlem, The Netherlands, 1946; admitted, 1972, Rotterdam. *Education:* Utrecht University (Master of Laws, 1972). *LANGUAGES:* Dutch and English.

J. GERARD C. KAMPHUISEN, born Goudo, The Netherlands, 1938; admitted, 1967, readmitted 1993, Rotterdam. *Education:* University of Leyden (Masters of Laws, 1967). Director, Hudig Langeveldt, Director, Bain Clarkson 1990-1992. Publications, Secretary Insurance Law Association. *LANGUAGES:* Dutch and English.

JANMARK M.F. DINGEMANS, born Gorinchem, The Netherlands, 1944; admitted, 1972, Amsterdam; 1991, Rotterdam. *Education:* University of Leyden (Master of Laws, 1970). Chairman, International Dutch Student Travel Organization, 1970; Publications; Commissions. *LANGUAGES:* Dutch and English.

PETER J.M. DRION, born Breda, The Netherlands, 1947; admitted, 1972, Rotterdam. *Education:* Catholic University of Nijmegen (Master of Laws, 1972). Member, Committee on Insurance Law. *LANGUAGES:* Dutch and English.

CHRIS M.F.M. GOUMANS, born Venray, The Netherlands, 1948; admitted, 1993, Rotterdam. *Education:* Catholic University of Nijmegen (Master of Laws, 1972). Legal Counsel Laura Group, 1973-1980. Head Legal Department Wilma Group, 1980-1983. *LANGUAGES:* Dutch and English.

(This Listing Continued)

HUGOLINE M.A. DE GROOT, born The Hague, The Netherlands, 1954; admitted, 1977, The Hague; 1986, Rotterdam. *Education:* University of Leyden (Master of Laws, 1977). Substitute District Court Judge, The Hague. *LANGUAGES:* Dutch and English.

MICHIEL C.D. WESSELING, born Eindhoven, The Netherlands, 1956; admitted, 1983, Rotterdam. *Education:* University of Leyden (Master of Laws, 1983). Associate: Van Heycop ten Ham, lawyers, 1983-1987; Loeff, Claeys Verbeke, 1987-1992. *LANGUAGES:* Dutch and English.

PETER J. CHARPENTIER, born Rotterdam, The Netherlands, 1960; admitted, 1986, Rotterdam. *Education:* Erasmus University of Rotterdam (Master of Laws, 1986). *LANGUAGES:* Dutch and English. *PRACTICE AREAS:* International Trade and Transport.

DERK-JAN VAN DER KOLK, born Wierden, The Netherlands, 1960; admitted, 1986, Rotterdam. *Education:* University of Utrecht (Master of Laws, 1986). *LANGUAGES:* Dutch and English.

JAN H.N.M. VAN DER HORST, born Sint Oedenrode, The Netherlands, 1958; admitted, 1987, Amsterdam. *Education:* Utrecht University (Master of Laws, 1982); City of London Polytechnic, United Kingdom (Certificate English Law, 1981). Legal Staff Member of the Food and Agriculture Organization of the U.N., Brasilia, Brazil, 1982-1986. *LANGUAGES:* Dutch and English.

ASSOCIATES

JACQUELINE MEYST-MICHELS, born Raalte, The Netherlands, 1953; admitted, 1978, Rotterdam; 1981, The Hague; 1984, Rotterdam. *Education:* University of Leyden (Master of Laws, 1977). *LANGUAGES:* Dutch and English.

ERNST N. NEUERBURG, born The Hague, The Netherlands, 1949; admitted, 1993, Rotterdam. *Education:* University of Leyden (Master of Laws, 1974). Legal advisor, Roosendaal (municipality), 1974-1978. Legal adviser and head of department, Central Environmental Control Agency Rijnmond-Rotterdam, 1978-1993. *LANGUAGES:* Dutch and English.

HANNEKE W.J. ROOS-VAN TOOR, born Vlaardingen, The Netherlands, 1955; admitted, 1980, Amsterdam; 1986, Rotterdam. *Education:* University of Leyden (Master of Laws, 1980). *LANGUAGES:* Dutch and English.

THOMA J. SLEESWIJK VISSER-DE BOER, born The Hague, The Netherlands, 1964; admitted, 1988, Amsterdam; 1992, Rotterdam. *Education:* University of Utrecht (Master of Laws, 1988). *LANGUAGES:* Dutch and English.

ALEXANDRA A. BOOT, born The Netherlands, 1964; admitted, 1989, Rotterdam. *Education:* University of Leyden (Master of Laws, 1987), Grotius Academy, 1987-1988, Internship with Graham & James, Law Firm in San Francisco, 1988. *LANGUAGES:* Dutch and English.

PETER J.R. HABRAKEN, born Veghel, The Netherlands, 1962; admitted, 1989, Amsterdam; 1991, Rotterdam. *Education:* University of Leyden (Master of Laws, 1989). Interpreter/Translator, Russian, Royal Dutch Army, 1986-1987. *LANGUAGES:* Dutch and English.

PETRA DAHM, born Duisburg, Germany, 1963; admitted, 1989, Rotterdam. *Education:* University of Leyden (Master of Laws, 1988), Grotius Academie, 1989. *LANGUAGES:* Dutch and English.

SIJBOLT VAN SOLKEMA, born The Hague, The Netherlands, 1962; admitted, 1989, Rotterdam. *Education:* University of Leyden (Master of Laws, 1988; Master of Tax Law, 1992). *LANGUAGES:* Dutch and English.

MARCEL WINDT, born Dinslaken, Germany, 1965; admitted, 1991, Rotterdam. *Education:* University of Leyden (Master of Laws, 1990). *LANGUAGES:* Dutch and English.

RUTGER J. SARK, born Amsterdam, The Netherlands, 1965; admitted, 1992, Rotterdam. *Education:* Erasmus University of Rotterdam (Master of Laws, 1992). *LANGUAGES:* Dutch and Englsih.

JACQUELINE J. MOS, born Alkemade, The Netherlands, 1967; admitted, 1992, Rotterdam. *Education:* University of Leyden (Master of Laws, 1992). *LANGUAGES:* Dutch and English.

JAN C.W. DE SAUVAGE NOLTING, born Amsterdam, The Netherlands, 1964; admitted, 1992, Rotterdam. *Education:* University of Amsterdam (Master of Laws, 1990; Master of International Law, 1992); Duke University, North Carolina, U.S.A. (LL.M., 1992). *LANGUAGES:* Dutch and English.

(This Listing Continued)

HOUTHOFF, Rotterdam—Continued

MARGREET EIJKELENBOOM, born Rotterdam, The Netherlands; admitted, 1993, Rotterdam. *Education:* University of Leyden (Master English Language and Literature, 1988); Erasmus University of Rotterdam (Master of Laws, 1992). *LANGUAGES:* Dutch and English.

MICHIEL H. VAN STRAATEN, born Diepenveen, The Netherlands, 1965; admitted, 1993, Rotterdam. *Education:* University of Leyden (Master of Laws, 1991). *LANGUAGES:* Dutch and English.

JOHN M. WOLFS, born Maastricht, The Netherlands, 1968; admitted, 1993, Rotterdam. *Education:* University of Limburg (Master of Laws, 1991). Legal Adviser to Personnel Staff, Royal Dutch Army, 1991-1993. Internship with Venable Baetjer Howard and Civiletti, Law firm in Washington DC, 1993. *LANGUAGES:* Dutch and English.

HENRIËT TH. VOS, born Spijkenisse, The Netherlands, 1966; admitted, 1993, Rotterdam. *Education:* Erasmus University of Rotterdam (Master of Laws, 1993). *LANGUAGES:* Dutch and English.

MARIJKE S. BOGTSTRA, born Sneek, The Netherlands, 1968; admitted, 1994, Rotterdam. *Education:* University of Leyden (Master of Laws, 1993). *LANGUAGES:* Dutch and English.

ANDREAS J. VAN ROOIJEN, born Eindhoven, The Netherlands, 1970; admitted, 1994, Rotterdam. *Education:* University of Tilburg (Master of Laws, 1994). *LANGUAGES:* Dutch and English.

SIMON M. VAN DER SCHENK, born Bergum, The Netherlands, 1965; admitted, 1994, Rotterdam. *Education:* University of Leyden (Master of Laws, 1991). *LANGUAGES:* Dutch and English.

KERNKAMP ADVOCATEN

in cooperation with the joint venture Kernkamp & Buzek

VEERKADE 5D
3016 DE ROTTERDAM, THE NETHERLANDS
Telephone: +31 10 411-6471
Telex: 24318 KERN NL
Fax: +31 10 413-6923

Middleburg (Scheldt) Office: Balans 13, 4331 BL Middleburg. Telephone: +31 1180 33888. Fax: +31 1180 26750.

FIRM PROFILE: *A boutique-size shipping, maritime and commercial law firm. Areas of practice include International Trade, Shipping, Transportation, Collision, Salvage, Forwarding, Shipbroking, Storage, etc., Commercial law and litigation. Company Law, Air Transport Licensing, Anti-trust Law, Environmental Law, Insurance, Insolvency, Property, Building and Construction.*

PARTNERS

FRITS H. KERNKAMP. *Education:* University of Amsterdam (1955). Res. Captain Royal Marine Corps. *Member:* Rotterdam Bar; Dutch Association for Maritime and Transportation Law; titular member Association Internationale de Dispacheurs Européens.

CAPTAIN FRANÇOIS J. BUZEK. *Education:* University of Leyden (1958). Naval Academy Rotterdam, 1950. Author: "Collision Cases," London, 2nd edition, 1990. *Member:* Rotterdam Bar; Dutch Association for Maritime and Transportation Law; Dutch Association of Master Mariners.

HANS WIND. *Education:* University of Groningen (1983). Licensed Aircraft Pilot. Lecturer, Insolvency Law - Dutch Bar Association. *Member:* Middleburg Bar; European Insolvency Practitioners Association (EIPA).

ROELAND B. GOLTERMAN. *Education:* University of Leyden (1984). *Member:* Rotterdam Bar; Dutch Association for Maritime and Transportation Law.

ASSOCIATES

DORINE A. CLETON. *Education:* University of Leyden (1984). *Member:* Rotterdam Bar; Civil Law Association; Construction Law Association.

HARRY J. BODIFÉE. *Education:* University of Nijmegen (1984). Deputy Judge. *Member:* Rotterdam Bar; Dutch Association of European Law; International Law Association.

CAJA J. OLDENBURGER. *Education:* University of Groningen (1984). Practice Teacher - Dutch Bar Association. *Member:* Middleburg Bar.

(This Listing Continued)

HEIN T. KERNKAMP. *Education:* University of Utrecht (1988). *Member:* Rotterdam Bar; Dutch Association for Maritime and Transportation Law; Dutch Association of Environmental Law.

ANNEMARIKE NELEMAN. *Education:* University of Leyden (1989); University of San Diego (MCL, 1990). *Member:* Rotterdam Bar.

MARK H.L. WESTSTRATE. *Education:* University of Rotterdam (1989). *Member:* Rotterdam Bar.

Languages: English, German French and Dutch

KOSTER, CLAASSEN & SMALLEGANGE

BOOMPJES 550
P.O. BOX 408
3011 XZ ROTTERDAM, THE NETHERLANDS
Telephone: 31-10-4132180
Telecopier: 31-10-4122125
Telex: 23773 kova nl.

Transport Law, Maritime Law, Insurance Law, Commercial Law, International Trade Law, Arbitration Law, General Practice, Litigation.

MEMBERS OF FIRM

JEF M.G.C. KOSTER, born Heerlen, The Netherlands, 1943; admitted, 1969, Rotterdam. *Education:* Amsterdam University (1969). *PRACTICE AREAS:* Transport Law; Maritime Law; Commercial Law; International Trade Law; Insurance Law; Arbitration Law.

WILLEM H. CLAASSEN, born Hapert, The Netherlands, 1948; admitted, 1976, Rotterdam. *Education:* Hannover College, Ind. USA (1966/1967); Leyden University (1967/1972); College of Europe, Bruges, Belgium (1972/1973). *PRACTICE AREAS:* Transport Law; Maritime Law; Commercial Law.

GOVERT J.W. SMALLEGANGE, born Tegelen, The Netherlands, 1941; admitted, 1980, Rotterdam. *Education:* Nautical Academy, Amsterdam (1958-1960; at sea 1960-1972, Master, 1971-1972); Rotterdam University (1972-1975). Staff- and Management Positions, Multinational Shipping and Trading Co (1975-1979). *PRACTICE AREAS:* Maritime Law; Transport Law; Insurance Law; Commercial Law.

JOHAN (HANS) VAN NOORT, born Rotterdam, The Netherlands, 1956; admitted, 1984, Amsterdam; 1987, Rotterdam. *Education:* Utrecht University. *PRACTICE AREAS:* Maritime Law; Transport Law; Insurance Law; Commercial Law.

PIETER FRANK W.A. VAN DAM, born Breda, The Netherlands, 1955; admitted, 1983, Amsterdam; 1988, Rotterdam. *Education:* Royal Netherlands Naval College (1976); Tilburg University (1983). *PRACTICE AREAS:* Maritime Law; Transport Law; Inland Navigation Law; Insurance Law; Personal Injury Law.

ASSOCIATES

PETER VAN DER VELDEN, born Rotterdam, The Netherlands, 1960; admitted, 1986, Breda; 1990, Rotterdam. *Education:* Rotterdam University. *PRACTICE AREAS:* Maritime Law; Transport Law; Commercial Law.

J. (JAN) F. VAN DER STELT, born Haaksbergen, The Netherlands, 1953; admitted, 1990, Rotterdam. *Education:* Maritime Academy Vlissingen (Masters, 1982); Rotterdam University (1990). *PRACTICE AREAS:* Maritime Law; Transport Law; Insurance Law; Commercial Law.

WILHELMINA M. (HELMA) VAN DIJK, born Nootdorp, The Netherlands, 1965; admitted, 1990, Rotterdam. *Education:* Rotterdam University. *PRACTICE AREAS:* Maritime Law; Transport Law; Insurance Law; Commercial Law.

ALBERT-JAN (ALBERT) DE HEER, born Rotterdam, The Netherlands, 1962; admitted, 1991, Rotterdam. *Education:* Rotterdam University. *PRACTICE AREAS:* Maritime Law; Transport Law; Insurance Law; Commercial Law.

RICHARD L. LATTEN, born Utrecht, The Netherlands, 1965; admitted, 1991, Rotterdam. *Education:* Leyden University. *PRACTICE AREAS:* Maritime Law; Transport Law; Insurance Law; Commercial Law.

(This Listing Continued)

LAURA C. BARONESSE VAN PALLANDT, born Rossum, The Netherlands, 1970; admitted, 1994, Rotterdam. *Education:* Utrecht University. *PRACTICE AREAS:* General Law; Commercial Law.

Languages: Dutch, English, German and French

LOEFF CLAEYS VERBEKE

70 WEENA
P.O. BOX 74
3000 AB ROTTERDAM, THE NETHERLANDS
Telephone: 31-10-4034777
Telex: 23395 LEX NL
Telecopier: 31-10-4149388

Amsterdam, The Netherlands Office: 15 Apollolaan, P.O. Box 75088, 1070 AB. Telephone: 31-20-5741200. Telex: 14291 (LEX NL). Telecopier: 31-20-6718775.

New York, New York Office: Swiss Bank Tower, 23rd Floor, 10 East 50th Street, 10022. Telephone: 212-759-9000. Fax: 212-759-9018.

Brussels, Belgium Office: 268 A Avenue de Tervueren, A-1150. Telephone: 02-778.22.11. Fax: 02-763.21.85.

Antwerp, Belgium Office: "De Hertoghe," 8th Floor, 92 Desguinlei, B.8, B-2018. Telephone: 32.3.2385656. Telex: 72748 (EURLAWB). Telecopier: 32.3.2387877.

Liege, Belgium Office: 13, Rue Simonon, (Place de Bronckart), B-4000. Telephone: 32-41-527722. Telecopier: 32-41-527511.

Paris, France Office: 1, Avenue Franklin D. Roosevelt, 75008. Telephone: 33-1-49539125. Telecopier: 33-1-42891460.

Singapore, Singapore Office: 20 Raffles Place, #08-03, Ocean Towers, Singapore 0104. Telephone: 65.5335332. Fax: 65.5330313.

Tokyo, Japan Office: NSE Building, 5th Floor, 1-7-1 Kanda Jinbo-cho, Chiyoda-ku, Tokyo 101, Japan. Telephone: 81-3-32599831. Fax: 81-3-32599888.

Barcelona, Spain Office: 550, 4° 1A, Av. Diagonal, 08021. Telephone: 34-3-2007117. Telecopier: 34-3-2023098.

Madrid, Spain Office: Balañá Eguía, Antonio Mauro 7, 5°, 28014. Telephone: 34-1-5312501. Telecopier: 34-1-5313530.

Jakarta, Indonesia Associated Office: Ali Budiardjo, Nugroho, Reksodiputro, Niaga Tower, 24th floor, Jalan Jenderal Sudirman Kav. 58, 12920. Telephone: 62.21.2505125/2505136. Telecopier: 62.21.2505121/2505001.

Luxembourg, Luxembourg Office: Zeyen Beghin Feider. 67, Rue Ermesinde, P.O. Box 5017, 1050. Telephone: 352.468946. Telex: 60736 (zflaw lu). Telecopier: 352.468947.

Dutch attorneys may represent clients before all Dutch Courts, before the European Court of Justice and the Benelux Court of Justice, and are admitted to plead before all Courts of the Memberstates of the Common Market (EEC).

MEMBERS OF FIRM

ROB J. ABENDROTH, born 1959; admitted, 1984, Rotterdam. *Education:* Rotterdam University (1983).

MICHEL A.J.C.M. VAN AGT, born 1953; admitted, 1982, Amsterdam; appointed Civil Law Notary, 1988. *Education:* University of Amsterdam (1979).

KAREL F.M. BERGER, born 1939; appointed Civil Law Notary, 1978. *Education:* University of Amsterdam (1967). Dean, Rotterdam District of the Netherlands Association of Civil Law Notaries, 1987-1989.

HENK J. BREEMAN, born 1957; admitted, 1988, Rotterdam. *Education:* Utrecht University (1980). *Member:* Netherlands Association for Construction Law.

KAREL W. BREVET, born 1932; admitted, 1958, Rotterdam. *Education:* Leyden University (1955). Contributor: "Products Liability, an International Manual of Practice," 1987. Member, Board of Trustees, Netherland Association for Insurance Law. *Member:* Netherlands Bar Association (Chairman, Committee on Professional Liability Insurance); Union Internationale des Avocats; Association Internationale de Droit des Assurances.

JAN C.P. EKERING, born 1942; admitted, 1968, Rotterdam. *Education:* Groningen University (1966). *Member:* Netherlands Association for Insurance Law; International Bar Association.

HENRY C. VAN GEEN, born 1960; admitted, 1986, Rotterdam. *Education:* Leyden University (1985).

(This Listing Continued)

SIETZE HEPKEMA, born 1953; admitted, 1981, California; 1987, Rotterdam. *Education:* Erasmus University Rotterdam (1975); Harvard University (LL.M., 1977). *Member:* State Bar of California; American Bar Association; Netherlands International Law Association; Netherlands Commercial Law Association; International Bar Association (Chairman, Committee on Computers, Electronics, Technology and Data Flows, 1987—).

LEONARD H. VAN HOUTEN, born 1947; admitted, 1975, Rotterdam. *Education:* Leyden University (1974). *Member:* Netherlands Maritime Law Association.

ERNST P. JANSEN, born 1944; admitted, 1970, Rotterdam. *Education:* Leyden University (1969, 1975). *Member:* Netherlands Commercial Law Association; Netherlands Labor Law Association.

HERALD D.J. JONGEN, born 1961; admitted, 1985, Rotterdam. *Education:* Vrije Universiteit Amsterdam (1985). *Member:* Netherlands Commercial Law Association; Netherlands Society for Information Technology (Computer Law Section); Netherlands Association for Information and Telecommunication Technology and the Law; Computer Law Association.

HUUB F.J. JOOSTEN, born 1937; admitted, 1989, Rotterdam. *Education:* Netherlands Fiscal Academy Rotterdam (1961); Leyden University (1961). Vice President, 1985-1988 and Chairman of the Enterprise Division, 1985-1988, Amsterdam Court of Appeal. Panel Member, Netherlands Arbitration Institute.

L. RENÉ KIERS, born 1957; admitted, 1981, Rotterdam. *Education:* Leyden University (1981). *Member:* Netherlands Maritime Law Association; Netherlands Commercial Law Association.

ROBERT JAN J. LIJDSMAN, born 1952; appointed Civil Law Notary, 1986. *Education:* Amsterdam University (1978). *Member:* International Fiscal Association; Netherlands Commercial Law Association.

FRISO MEETER, born 1936; admitted, 1962, Rotterdam. *Education:* University of Amsterdam (1960). Dean of the Bar of the District of Rotterdam, 1987-1989. *Member:* Association Européene des Practiciens des Procureurs Collectives.

WINFRIED H.A.M. VAN DEN MUIJSENBERGH, born 1954; admitted, 1980, Rotterdam. *Education:* Leyden University (1977). Visiting Professor McGeorge School of Law, Salzburg, Austria. *Member:* International Bar Association; Union Internationale des Avocats; Netherlands Commercial Law Association; Netherlands Association for European Law.

JAN A.A. OOMENS, born 1946; admitted, 1970, Rotterdam. *Education:* University of Amsterdam (1969); Columbia University, New York (LL.M., 1972). *Member:* Association Internationale pour la Protection de la Propriété Industrielle; European Communities Trade Mark Practitioners' Association; Association Benelux des Conseils en Marques et Modèles; Association Littéraire et Artistique International; Ligue Internationale du Droit de la Concurrence.

LEONARD H.W. VAN SANDICK, born 1933; admitted, 1957, Rotterdam. *Education:* Leyden University (1956). Member: Advisory Board, International and Comparative Law Center, University of Texas, Dallas; Corresponding Editor of: (i) Droit et Affaires, 1982; (ii) International Banking Law, 1982; (iii) Oil and Gas Law and Taxation Review, 1982; (iv) Journal of Energy and National Resources Law, 1982; (v) International Legal Materials, 1985. *Member:* International Bar Association (Chairman, Banking Committee, 1984-1988; Council Member, 1988—); Netherlands Association for International Law; American Society of International Law; American Arbitration Association (Panel Member); London Maritime Arbitration Association; Netherlands Maritime Law Association; Netherlands Commercial Law Association; American Bar Association.

HANS A. DE SAVORNIN LOHMAN, born 1955; admitted, 1983, The Hague and New York; 1990, Rotterdam. *Education:* Leyden University (1979); Columbia University (LL.M., 1980). *Member:* The Association of the Bar of the City of New York.

JOSSIE H.A.M. SCHEIFFERS, born 1956; admitted, 1980, Rotterdam. *Education:* Leyden University (1980). *Member:* Netherlands Association for Construction Law; Netherlands Association for Administrative Law.

RENÉ STOKMAN, born 1949; admitted, 1979, Rotterdam. *Education:* Leyden University (1974). *Member:* International Bar Association; Netherlands Bar Association (Council Member).

WILLEM VERHOEVEN, born 1947; admitted, 1973, Rotterdam. *Education:* Leyden University (1971). *Member:* International Bar Association; Netherlands Maritime Law Association.

(This Listing Continued)

EU1063B

LOEFF CLAEYS VERBEKE, *Rotterdam—Continued*

BAS W.S. VLETTER, born 1960; admitted, 1984, Rotterdam. *Education:* Leyden University (1984). *Member:* Netherlands Maritime Law Association.

JOOST WILDEBOER, born 1956; admitted, 1981, Rotterdam. *Education:* Leyden University (1980). Co-Editor, Consumer Law Review. *Member:* Netherlands Association for Insurance Law.

NIEK D.F.M.M. ZAMAN, born 1955; admitted, 1977, Rotterdam; appointed Civil Law Notary, 1987. *Education:* Leyden University (1977). Co-Editor, Elseviers Almanak on Corporation Law. *Member:* Netherlands Commercial Law Association (Member, Board of Governors); Netherlands-German Chamber of Commerce.

ASSOCIATES

GERT-JAN ANTVELINK, born 1967; admitted, 1993, Rotterdam. *Education:* Leyden University (1992).

MARIE-LOUISE C. VAN BASTEN BATENBURG, born 1964; admitted, 1990, Rotterdam. *Education:* Leyden University (1988).

META E.M. BEELAERTS VAN BLOKLAND, born 1962; admitted, 1990, Rotterdam. *Education:* Groningen University (School of Arts, 1987; Law School, 1988).

PIETER H. BOLLAND, born 1961; appointed Deputy Civil Law Notary, 1994. *Education:* Leyden University (1984).

P.G.M.J. (ELLEN) BONGAERTS, born, 1967. Deputy Civil Law Notary, 1992. *Education:* Limburg University (1990); Leyden University (1992).

JEROEN VAN DEN BRANDE, born 1966; admitted, 1991, Rotterdam. *Education:* Rotterdam University (1989).

PETER L. DE BROCK, born 1956; acting tax lawyer, 1987. *Education:* University of Rotterdam.

TOM L. CLAASSENS, born 1967; admitted, 1992, Rotterdam. *Education:* Leyden University (1991).

A. SOFIE DERSJANT, born 1969; admitted, 1993, Rotterdam. *Education:* Utrecht University (1992).

ALBERT DREESE, born 1957; admitted, 1984, Rotterdam. *Education:* Leyden University (1984).

MARGOT J. DUSSEL, born 1963; Deputy Civil Law Notary, 1990. *Education:* Leyden University (1989).

RAGNA M. VAN DER DUSSEN, born 1963; admitted, 1992, Rotterdam. *Education:* Erasmus University, Rotterdam (1989); Institut Universitare d'Etudes Européennes, Genève, Switzerland (1992); Institut Universitaire de Hautes Etudes Internationales Genève, Switzerland (1992).

ANS VAN DUIJVENDIJK-BRAND, born 1956; admitted, 1990, Rotterdam. *Education:* Leyden University (1980; Doctor Juris, 1990).

PAUL ELION, born 1960; admitted, 1987, Rotterdam. *Education:* Leyden University (1984); Baylor University (J.D., 1986). New York Office, 1989-1992. *Member:* International Law Association; Netherlands Association for International Law; International Young Lawyers Association.

JEAN-PIERRE F.W. VAN EIJCK, born 1964; admitted, 1991, Rotterdam. *Education:* Rotterdam University (1991).

RENÉ DE GRAAF, born 1966; admitted, 1991, Rotterdam. *Education:* Leyden University (1990).

ELISE M. FOKKENS, born 1968; admitted, 1993, Rotterdam. *Education:* Leyden University (1993).

F.A. CONSTANTIJN FUCHS, born 1964; admitted, 1993, Rotterdam. *Education:* Leyden University (1990).

MARIJA C.M. DE HAAS, born 1966; admitted, 1990, Rotterdam. *Education:* Utrecht University (1990).

JACOMIJN J. VAN HAERSHOLTE-VAN HOF, born 1963; admitted, 1992, Rotterdam. *Education:* Leyden University (1991).

PHILIP A. HARTMAN, born 1964; admitted, 1990, Rotterdam. *Education:* Leyden University (1990).

BRAM H.P. VAN HEEL, born 1963; admitted, 1991, Rotterdam. *Education:* Leyden University (1989).

(This Listing Continued)

ESTHER M. HOVENIER, born 1963; admitted, 1993, Rotterdam. *Education:* Leyden University (1993).

LINDA JANSEN, born 1963; acting lawyer, 1988. *Education:* University of Rotterdam (1988).

RUDOLF L.M.C. JANSSEN, born 1964; Deputy Civil Law Notary, 1988. *Education:* Leyden University (1987; 1988).

R. WILLEM JARIGSMA, born 1967; admitted, 1993, Rotterdam. *Education:* Groningen University (1992).

HENRY J. KEETELL, born 1966; appointed Deputy Civil Law Notary, 1994. *Education:* Utrecht University (1994).

MARTIN W.A.M. VAN KEMPEN, born 1968; admitted, 1994, Rotterdam. *Education:* Erasmus University, Rotterdam (1993).

A. KARINE KODDE, born 1968; admitted, 1993, Rotterdam. *Education:* Erasmus University Rotterdam (1993).

A NELLEKE KROL, born 1966; admitted, 1992, Rotterdam. *Education:* Erasmus University Rotterdam (School of Economics, 1990; Law School, 1992).

BART C. KUIL, born 1969; admitted, 1994, Rotterdam. *Education:* Leyden University (1993).

HELENE H. LAMMERS, born 1968; admitted, 1992, Rotterdam. *Education:* Utrecht University (1992).

RISTO H.C. LARSSON, born 1963; admitted, 1990, Rotterdam. *Education:* Leyden University (1987).

J.T.H. (HANS) LEIJSER, born 1961. Deputy Civil Law Notary, 1986. *Education:* Leyden University (1986).

KITTY W.M. LIEVERSE, born 1966; admitted, 1989, Rotterdam. *Education:* Leyden University (1988).

HERMAN L.A.M. LOHMAN, born 1967; Deputy Civil Law Notary, 1991. *Education:* Leyden University (1989).

J.M. (HANS) LOTH, born 1968; admitted, 1992, Rotterdam. *Education:* Leyden University (1992).

PAUL W. MENDEL, born 1968; admitted, 1993, Rotterdam. *Education:* Leyden University (1992).

G. MARC MENON, born 1966; admitted, 1993, Rotterdam. *Education:* Leyden University (1990); University of London (QMW; LL.M., 1991).

BOWINE MEIJER, born 1964; admitted, 1989, Rotterdam. *Education:* Leyden University (1988).

JAN-HEIN MEIJER, born 1968; admitted, 1993, Rotterdam. *Education:* Leyden University (1992).

JAN A. MEIJERMAN, born 1963; admitted, 1987, Rotterdam. *Education:* Rotterdam University (1986). Paris Office, 1989-1990.

ERNO P. OLIE, born 1964; admitted, 1993, Rotterdam. *Education:* Leyden University (1991).

MAX WILLEM F. OOSTERHUIS, born 1960; admitted, 1988, Rotterdam. *Education:* Leyden University (1986).

INA M. PANNEKOEK-DUBOIS, born 1942; admitted, 1984, Rotterdam. *Education:* Utrecht University (1967).

HENDRIK-JAN PORTENGEN, born 1969; Deputy Civil Law Notary, 1993. *Education:* Utrecht University (1993).

ESTER ROOD, born 1965; admitted, 1993, Rotterdam. *Education:* Utrecht University (1991).

ESTHER H.M. ROSENBERG, born 1967; admitted, 1994, Rotterdam. *Education:* Limburg University (1993).

MONIQUE RUS-VAN DER VELDE, born 1961; admitted, 1987, Rotterdam. *Education:* Leyden University (1983). *Member:* Netherlands Association for Environmental Law.

PETER J. SCHOONES, born 1961; admitted, 1994, Rotterdam. *Education:* Leyden University (1994).

PATRICK F.F. RIDDER DE VAN DER SCHUEREN, born 1963; admitted, 1990, Rotterdam. *Education:* Utrecht University (1989).

A. HELEEN A. SPRENGER, born 1964; admitted, 1990, Rotterdam. *Education:* Groningen University (Law School, 1989; School of Economics, 1989).

(This Listing Continued)

HELENA J. UNGER, born 1967; admitted, 1993, Rotterdam. *Education:* Leyden University (1987).

G. ONNO VAN VELDHUIZEN, born 1962; admitted, 1991, Rotterdam. *Education:* Leyden University (1988); Osnabrück, Germany University (Doctor Juris, 1993).

MARTINE VAN DER VLUGT, born 1963; admitted, 1992, Rotterdam. *Education:* Leyden University (Spanish Linguistics, 1987, Law School, 1992); University of Southern California, Los Angeles, U.S.A. (M.A., Spanish Linguistics, 1989).

PETER T. VOLWERK, born 1968; appointed Deputy Civil Law Notary. *Education:* Utrecht University (1993).

HENK TEN VOORDE, born 1965; Deputy Civil Law Notary, 1991. *Education:* Leyden University (Civil Law, 1990; Notarial Law, 1991).

SANDER J. VAN DER VOORDE, born 1967; admitted, 1994, Rotterdam. *Education:* Groningen University (1993).

GIJS J. VOÛTE, born 1962; admitted, 1988, Rotterdam. *Education:* Leyden University (1987).

P. HERMINE E. VOÛTE, born 1964; admitted, 1988, Rotterdam. *Education:* Leyden University (1987).

GAIUS VOÛTE, born 1968; admitted, 1994, Rotterdam. *Education:* Utrecht University (1993).

JOOST F.L.P.M. VRANCKEN PEETERS, born 1965; admitted, 1992, Rotterdam. *Education:* Nijmegen University (1989).

GERRIT A. VRIEZEN, born 1963; admitted, 1989, Rotterdam. *Education:* Leyden University (1987); Collège d'Europe, Bruges (1989).

RICHARD M. WALESON, born 1945; admitted, 1971, Rotterdam. *Education:* Leyden University (1971). *Member:* Netherlands Maritime Law Association.

GUUS G.M. WARRINGA, born 1969; admitted, 1994, Rotterdam. *Education:* Leyden University (1993).

TJEERD G. WASSENAAR, born 1969; admitted, 1994, Rotterdam. *Education:* Leyden University (1993).

MARGO P.A.J. WEUSTEN, born 1967; Deputy Civil Law Notary, 1993, Rotterdam. *Education:* Leyden University (1993).

WIEGER J. WIELINGA, born 1967; admitted, 1992, Rotterdam. *Education:* Leyden University (1991).

JACOBIJN W. ZEVENBERGEN, born 1964; admitted, 1991, Rotterdam. *Education:* University of Rotterdam (1991).

SERGE P.J.F. ZWANEN, born 1968; admitted, 1994, Rotterdam. *Education:* Limburg University (1994).

Languages: Dutch, English, French, German, Italian, Japanese, Russian and Spanish.

(For personnel and other data, see Professional Biographics at Amsterdam, Antwerp, Barcelona, Brussels, Liège, New York, Paris, Singapore and Tokyo).

MORET ERNST & YOUNG TAX ADVISERS
CORPORATE LAW ADVISORY GROUP

51, MARTEN MEESWEG
P.O. BOX 2295
3000 CG ROTTERDAM, THE NETHERLANDS
Telephone: 31-10-4072627
Fax: 31-10-4072612

Amsterdam Office: 20, Drentestraat, P.O. Box 7925, 1008 AC. Telephone: 31-20-5497333. Fax: 31-20-6462553.
The Hague Office: 80, Wassenaarseweg, P.O. Box 90636, 2509 LP. Telephone: 31 70-3286542. Fax: 31 70-3244003.
Groningen Office: 17, Leonard Springerlaan, P.O. Box 997, 9700 AZ. Telephone: 31-50-994444. Fax: 31-50-270852.
Arnhem Office: Kronenburgsingel 12, P.O. Box 30116, 6803 AC. Telephone: 31-85-209500. Fax: 31-85-235151.

(This Listing Continued)

Civil Law (general). Computer Law, Insolvency Law, (International) Contracts, Corporate Law, Environmental Law, EC Law, Intellectual Property, Labour Law and Workers Participation, Mergers and Acquisitions, Taxation.

PARTNERS

HANS VAN GIJZEN, born 1951. *Education:* Leyden University. (Resident).

SENIOR-ADVISORS

DENIS WILLEMARS, born 1956. *Education:* Groningen University (1986).

RUUD HARINCK, born 1957. *Education:* Groningen University (1985).

BERT GRAVENDEEL, born 1961. *Education:* Leyden University (1987).

STEFANO FRANCOVICH, born 1965. *Education:* Utrecht University (1990).

RUTGER ALSBACH, born 1963. *Education:* Utrecht University (1990).

(For complete data see at Amsterdam, The Netherlands)

NAUTA DUTILH

Attorneys, Civil Law Notaries, Tax Advisers

WEENA 750
NL-3014 DA ROTTERDAM, THE NETHERLANDS
Telephone: (31-10) 2240000
Telecopier: (31-10) 4148444
Telex: 22410 NDR

Mailing Address: P.O. Box 1110, NL-3000 BC Rotterdam, The Netherlands

Amsterdam, The Netherlands Office: Prinses Irenestraat 59, NL-1077 WV, P.O. Box 7113, NL-1007 JC. Telephone: (31-20) 5414646. Telecopier: (31-20) 6612827. Telex: 13411 NDA NL.
Breda, The Netherlands Office: Heerbaan 46-48, NL-4817 NL, P.O. Box 2118, NL-4800 CC. Telephone: (31-76) 224410. Telecopier: (31-76) 220106.
Eindhoven, The Netherlands Office: Gebouw Vierlander, Fellenoord 19, NL-5612 AA, P.O. Box 6019, NL-5600 HA. Telephone: (31-40) 656500. Telecopier: (31-40) 461375.
Brussels, Belgium Office: Terhulpsesteenweg 177/6, (Chaussée de la Hulpe, 177/6), B-1170. Telephone: (32-2) 6730007. Telecopier: (32-2) 6722854.
Paris, France Office: 77, Avenue Raymond Poincaré, F-75116. Telephone: (33-1) 44344747. Telecopier: (33-1) 44344748; 44344749.
Madrid, Spain Office: Hermosilla 29-1°, E-28001. Telephone: (34-1) 4359764. Telecopier: (34-1) 4359815.
New York, New York Office: 101 Park Avenue, N.Y. 10178. Telephone: (1-212) 922-0022. Telecopier: (1-212) 922-1407.
Singapore, Singapore Office: City House # 07-06, 36, Robinson Road, S-0106. Telephone: (65) 2241932. Telecopier: (65) 2224724.
Jakarta, Indonesia Correspondent Office: Soemadipradja & Taher, Bank BNI Building, Level 22, Jl. Jenderal Sudirman Kav. 1, 10220. Telephone: (62) 215702588. Telecopier (62) 215702598.

Accountancy and Financial Statements; Administrative Law; Agency, Distribution, Licensing; Air Law (incl. Aviation Finance); Arbitration; Banking and Financial Law; Collective Labour Disputes; Commodities Trade; Competition and Anti-Trust Law (Netherlands); Computer and Telecommunications Law; Construction Law, Project Development; Corporate Finance; Corporate Law - Advice and Disputes; Corporate Law - Incorporation, Reorganization, Advice; Criminal Litigation; Energy Law; Engineering; Entertainment; Environment, Planning and Zoning; Environmental Liability; European Law; Family Law, Pensions; Franchising; Health Care; Holding and Financing Companies; Immigration and Naturalization Law; Insolvency and Bankruptcy; Insurance Practice; Intellectual Property Law (Trademarks, Patents, Copyrights, Models and Designs, Unfair Competition); International Public Law; Labour Law; Letters of Credit; Liability; Litigation; Management (legal and organization) of Large Projects; Maritime Law (All Aspects); Medical Negligence; Merchandising; Mergers and Acquisitions, Joint Ventures, Reorganizations; Pharmaceutical Industry; Press and Media Law, Libel and Slander (incl. Protection of Information); Private International Law; Product Liability; Real Property - Compulsory Acquisitions; Real Property - Conveyancing, Mortgages, Leasing; Real Property - Leases and Other Matters; Securities Law (incl. Stock Exchange

(This Listing Continued)

NAUTA DUTILH, Rotterdam—Continued

Quotation); Shipbuilding; Ship Financing; Social Security Law; Taxation; Transportation by Rail and Road; Trust Matters; Wills and Estates.

MEMBERS OF FIRM ATTORNEYS AT LAW

JAN A. VAN DE VEN, born 1930; admitted, 1956, The Netherlands. *Education:* Utrecht University.

JOOP A. NAGTEGAAL, born 1931; admitted, 1957, The Netherlands. *Education:* Leyden University.

FRITS KORTHALS ALTES, born 1931; admitted, 1958, The Netherlands. *Education:* Leyden University.

MICHIEL A. VAN PESKI, born 1933; admitted, 1958, The Netherlands. *Education:* Leyden University.

OTTO L.O. DE WITT WIJNEN, born 1935; admitted, 1961, The Netherlands. *Education:* Leyden University.

JACQUES SCHUIJERS, born 1934; admitted, 1962, The Netherlands. *Education:* Nijmegen and Leyden Universities.

EDUARD W.J.H. DE LIAGRE BÖHL, born 1936; admitted, 1963, The Netherlands. *Education:* Leyden University.

PROF. PAUL M. STORM, born 1937; admitted, 1963, The Netherlands. *Education:* Leyden University.

WALTER DOMMERING, born 1940; admitted, 1965, The Netherlands. *Education:* Utrecht University.

JENS N. JACOBSEN JENSEN, born 1939; admitted, 1966, The Netherlands. *Education:* Utrecht University.

PIETER BLUSSÉ VAN OUD ALBLAS, born 1939; admitted, 1966, The Netherlands. *Education:* Leyden University.

FEIKE A. TROMP, born 1938; admitted, 1966, The Netherlands. *Education:* Utrecht University.

RUDY P. VOOGD, born 1941; admitted, 1967, The Netherlands. *Education:* Leyden and Amsterdam Universities.

JEAN-PIERRE ESCHAUZIER, born 1941; admitted, 1969, The Netherlands. *Education:* Utrecht University.

C. GIJS SCHOLTENS, born 1946; admitted, 1970, The Netherlands. *Education:* Leyden University.

W. LAURENT NOUWEN, born 1944; admitted, 1970, The Netherlands. *Education:* Nijmegen and Michigan Universities.

ROLOF H.A.M. BARON VAN HÖVELL TOT WESTERFLIER, born 1940; admitted, 1971, The Netherlands. *Education:* Leyden and Columbia Universities.

PROF. HENRI P. J. OPHOF, born 1939; admitted, 1971, The Netherlands. *Education:* Rotterdam University.

JAN D. LOORBACH, born 1947; admitted, 1971, The Netherlands. *Education:* Groningen University.

WILLEM J.L. CALKOEN, born 1946; admitted, 1972, The Netherlands. *Education:* Utrecht University.

HEN E.M. VROLIJK, born 1946; admitted, 1972, The Netherlands. *Education:* Utrecht University.

JAN KIST, born 1945; admitted, 1973, The Netherlands. *Education:* Leyden University.

WILLEM DEGELINK, born 1945; admitted, 1975, The Netherlands. *Education:* Rotterdam University.

RONALD PFEIFFER, born 1945; admitted, 1975, The Netherlands. *Education:* Leyden University.

HUUG H. LUIGIES, born 1949; admitted, 1975, The Netherlands. *Education:* Utrecht University.

JHR VINCENT M. DE BRAUW, born 1947; admitted, 1975, The Netherlands. *Education:* Leyden University.

ERIC G. HEILBRON, born 1950; admitted, 1976, The Netherlands. *Education:* Amsterdam University.

ARNOLD J. VAN STEENDEREN, born 1953; admitted, 1976, The Netherlands. *Education:* Rotterdam University.

FRANS DE VRIES LENTSCH, born 1948; admitted, 1976, The Netherlands. *Education:* Amsterdam University.

GERARD F. CARRIÈRE, born 1951; admitted, 1976, The Netherlands. *Education:* Amsterdam University and Columbia Law School.

HUUG E. SCHWEERS, born 1950; admitted, 1977, The Netherlands. *Education:* Groningen University.

WILLEM P. SPRENGER, born 1953; admitted, 1978, The Netherlands. *Education:* Utrecht University.

A. (GUUS) J. BRAAKMAN, born 1948; admitted, 1978, The Netherlands. *Education:* Groningen University.

LOES J.H. GIJBELS, born 1954; admitted, 1979, The Netherlands. *Education:* Leyden University.

R. BART GERRETSEN, born 1953; admitted, 1979, The Netherlands. *Education:* Rotterdam University and King's College, London.

CHRIS A. FONTEIJN, born 1955; admitted, 1980, The Netherlands. *Education:* Leyden University.

GIJS NOORDAM, born 1954; admitted, 1980, The Netherlands. *Education:* Leyden University.

LIEUWE DE BOER, born 1957; admitted, 1981, The Netherlands. *Education:* Rotterdam University.

RICHARD C.K. VAN OERLE, born 1954; admitted, 1981, The Netherlands. *Education:* Nijmegen University.

J. FREEK K. JONKHART, born 1956; admitted, 1981, The Netherlands. *Education:* Rotterdam University.

NORBERT J.M. DE MUNNIK, born 1953; admitted, 1982, The Netherlands. *Education:* Leyden University.

LOES DOMMERING-VAN RONGEN, born 1946; admitted, 1982, The Netherlands. *Education:* Leyden University.

EDDIE T. MEIJER, born 1952; admitted, 1982, The Netherlands. *Education:* Rotterdam University.

CH. PETER BANNIER, born 1958; admitted, 1985, The Netherlands. *Education:* Rotterdam University.

ERIC J.W.M. VAN NIEKERK, born 1959; admitted, 1983, The Netherlands. *Education:* Leyden University.

MARIANNE F.A. EVERS, born 1960; admitted, 1983, The Netherlands. *Education:* Groningen University.

JAAP J. FEENSTRA, born 1956; admitted, 1987, The Netherlands. *Education:* Groningen University.

HILLE P. CH. VAN DIJK, born 1953; admitted, 1988, The Netherlands. *Education:* Rotterdam and Leyden Universities.

R. (BERT) A. FIBBE, born 1948; admitted, 1977, The Netherlands. *Education:* Amsterdam University.

ROBERT J. VAN GALEN, born 1957; admitted, 1985, The Netherlands. *Education:* Amsterdam University.

JOAN B. VAN MARWIJK KOOY, born 1958; admitted, 1985, The Netherlands. *Education:* Leyden University.

PETER W.A. GOES, born 1959; admitted, 1985, The Netherlands. *Education:* Groningen University.

ALBERT VAN DER KOLK, born 1958; admitted, 1987, The Netherlands. *Education:* Amsterdam University.

MEMBERS OF FIRM CIVIL LAW NOTARIES

DIRK M. DRAGT, born 1936; notary since, 1971. *Education:* Leyden University.

RUDY P. VOOGD, born 1941; notary since, 1977. *Education:* Leyden and Amsterdam Universities.

J. (HANS) P. VAN DER STAP, born 1943; notary since, 1977. *Education:* Nijmegen University.

PROF. HANS W. HEYMAN, born 1941; notary since, 1978. *Education:* Amsterdam University.

ROLF P. KROES, born 1938; notary since, 1978. *Education:* Utrecht University.

BART TH. DÉROGÉE, born 1941; notary since, 1979. *Education:* Leyden University.

(This Listing Continued)

FRANS X. OLMER, born 1941; notary since, 1974. *Education:* Utrecht University.

HANS OUDENAARDEN, born 1948; notary since, 1983. *Education:* Utrecht and Leyden Universities.

RONALD PFEIFFER, born 1945; notary since, 1988. *Education:* Leyden University.

HILLE P. CH. VAN DIJK, born 1953; notary since, 1990. *Education:* Rotterdam and Leyden Universities.

LUUTZEN F. TAMMINGA, born 1955; notary since, 1991. *Education:* Groningen University.

MARIANNE F.E. DE WAARD-PRELLER, born 1960; notary since, 1994. *Education:* Utrecht University.

MEMBERS OF FIRM CANDIDATE CIVIL LAW NOTARIES

JOOP A. NAGTEGAAL, born 1931; admitted, 1957, The Netherlands. *Education:* Leyden University.

JACQUES SCHUIJERS, born 1934; admitted, 1962, The Netherlands. *Education:* Nijmegen University.

JEROEN H.J. PRELLER, born 1961; admitted, 1988, The Netherlands. *Education:* Utrecht University.

FRITS W. OLDENBURG, born 1961; admitted, 1987, The Netherlands. *Education:* Leyden University.

MEMBERS OF FIRM TAX ADVISERS

EDGAR A. BROOD, born 1956. *Education:* Rotterdam and Tilburg Universities.

RODERIK A.L.H.M. BOUWMAN, born 1957. *Education:* Rotterdam University.

ASSOCIATES ATTORNEYS AT LAW

MIEK E. VAN HAGEN-HOYNG, born 1942; admitted, 1969, The Netherlands. *Education:* Utrecht University.

MARTHE M.A. GERRITZEN-GUNST, born 1945; admitted, 1986, The Netherlands. *Education:* Leyden University.

PROF. MAARTEN H. CLARINGBOULD, born 1949; admitted, 1975, The Netherlands. *Education:* Utrecht University.

MARGRIET P. BLEES-SLUIS, born 1951; admitted, 1976, The Netherlands. *Education:* Groningen University.

JOHANNA KABEL, born 1945; admitted, 1977, The Netherlands. *Education:* Amsterdam University.

BAS J. CAMMELBEECK, born 1950; admitted, 1977, The Netherlands. *Education:* Groningen University.

SYLVIA I. WITKAMP, born 1956; admitted, 1980, The Netherlands. *Education:* Rotterdam University.

EMILY DÉROGÉE-VAN ROOSMALEN, born 1951; admitted, 1985, The Netherlands. *Education:* Rotterdam University.

PIET C. VOÛTE, born 1959; admitted, 1986, The Netherlands. *Education:* Leyden and Amsterdam Universities.

CARLA L.M. SMEETS, born 1963; admitted, 1987, The Netherlands. *Education:* Leyden University.

ELISABETH N. SCHAAP, born 1959; admitted, 1987, The Netherlands. *Education:* Leyden University.

JOHAN G.F. RIJLAARSDAM, born 1960; admitted, 1987, The Netherlands. *Education:* Leyden University.

WALTER A.M. SCHELLEKENS, born 1962; admitted, 1987, The Netherlands. *Education:* Leyden University.

TESSA M. MOOK, born 1961; admitted, 1987, The Netherlands. *Education:* Leyden University.

ROB W. ELGERS, born 1961; admitted, 1987, The Netherlands. *Education:* Rotterdam University.

MARGREET J. BLAISSE, born 1962; admitted, 1987, The Netherlands. *Education:* Amsterdam University.

SIMON A. TAN, born 1963; admitted, 1987, The Netherlands. *Education:* Rotterdam University.

(This Listing Continued)

MICHAEL BOUMA, born 1960; admitted, 1988, The Netherlands. *Education:* Rotterdam University.

PETER J. DE WAAL, born 1961; admitted, 1988, The Netherlands. *Education:* Utrecht University.

MARIKE L. NIEMÖLLER, born 1964; admitted, 1988, The Netherlands. *Education:* Leyden University.

IRENE A.M. KROFT, born 1962; admitted, 1988, The Netherlands. *Education:* Amsterdam University.

HENDRIK WALING, born 1959; admitted, 1988, The Netherlands. *Education:* Amsterdam University.

PATRICIA M. JANSON, born 1963; admitted, 1989, The Netherlands. *Education:* Leyden University.

RUTGER E.N. PLOUM, born 1964; admitted, 1989, The Netherlands. *Education:* Leyden University.

J. MAARTEN TROMP, born 1963; admitted, 1989, The Netherlands. *Education:* Leyden University.

PETRA G. LANSER, born 1964; admitted, 1989, The Netherlands. *Education:* Leyden University.

BART J.R. VAN TONGEREN, born 1963; admitted, 1990, The Netherlands. *Education:* Leyden University.

ANTOINETTE M. VAN CAPPELLE, born 1965; admitted, 1990, The Netherlands. *Education:* Leyden University.

KARIN TH. SCHOUWENBURG, born 1960; admitted, 1990, The Netherlands. *Education:* Groningen University.

DUCO H. LODDER, born 1965; admitted, 1990, The Netherlands. *Education:* Leyden University.

WENDELA J.N. VAN UCHELEN, born 1966; admitted, 1990, The Netherlands. *Education:* Amsterdam and Cambridge Universities.

TACO VAN DER VALK, born 1965; admitted, 1990, The Netherlands. *Education:* Leyden University.

DORINE P. TEN BRINK, born 1968; admitted, 1991, The Netherlands. *Education:* Rotterdam University.

MARC A.W. VAN MAANEN, born 1964; admitted, 1991, The Netherlands. *Education:* Utrecht University.

TJITSKE L. CIEREMANS, born 1964; admitted, 1991, The Netherlands. *Education:* Leyden University.

TOM ENSINK, born 1967; admitted, 1991, The Netherlands. *Education:* Maastricht University and Tulane Law School, New Orleans.

MARJA GORTER, born 1957; admitted, 1991, The Netherlands. *Education:* Curaçao and Nijmegen Universities.

DIRK KNOTTENBELT, born 1965; admitted, 1991, The Netherlands. *Education:* Leyden University.

GERARD-JAN SPREY, born 1966; admitted, 1991, The Netherlands. *Education:* Leyden University.

ANNEMARIEKE VERHOEFF, born 1967; admitted, 1992, The Netherlands. *Education:* Leyden University.

ASSOCIATES CANDIDATE CIVIL LAW NOTARIES

ERIK H. GEERLING, born 1962; admitted, 1991, The Netherlands. *Education:* Groningen University.

CÉCILE M.A.A. DE WERT, born 1967; admitted, 1994, The Netherlands. *Education:* Leyden University.

JOLANDE P. VAN LOON, born 1966; (admission pending). *Education:* Rotterdam University.

NANCY E.W.M. SIMONS, born 1966; admitted, 1994, The Netherlands. *Education:* Maastricht and Nijmegen Universities.

ASSOCIATES TAX ADVISERS

LOTTY VAN DER GIESSEN-BOERSMA, born 1951. *Education:* Rotterdam University.

PAULA M.E. KAGER, born 1956. *Education:* Amsterdam University.

Languages: Arabic, Danish, English, French, German, Greek, Hungarian, Italian, Papiamento, Polish, Russian and Spanish.

POT & STOOP ADVOCATEN

Attorneys at Law

VEERKADE 2

3016 DE ROTTERDAM, THE NETHERLANDS

Telephone: (+31-10)-4116222

Fax: (+31-10) 4117676

FIRM PROFILE: *General and international commercial practice. Firm is involved in all legal aspects of doing business in the Netherlands. The firm has longstanding working relationships with other professional advisors for tax/fiscal, notarial, accounting, trustee and company management services and not being bound by any particular interprofessional association is free to introduce each client to the professional advisor most suited to his individual needs. The areas of concentration within the firm are Corporate and Company, EEC-customs and Levies, Litigation, Business Law, International Law, General Commercial Law, Labour and Employment, Resorts and Leisure, Family Law, Bankruptcy, Administrative Law, Banking, Intellectual Property, Construction Law and Transportation. The firm is a member of an Europe-wide association of independent law firms through which it is able to provide cross-border legal services. The firms attorneys may represent clients before all Dutch Courts, the European Court of Justice and the Benelux Court of Justice.*

PARTNERS

B. JOOST POT, born Rijswijk, 1923; admitted, 1952, Rotterdam. *Education:* Leyden University (1948). **LANGUAGES:** French, English, German, Spanish and Dutch. **PRACTICE AREAS:** Corporate Law; Business Law.

JHR. ADRIAN E. STOOP, born The Hague, 1938; admitted, 1965, Rotterdam. *Education:* Leyden University (1964). *Member:* Multinational Fiscal Associates; International Tax Planning Association; Union Internationale des Avocats; Association Internationale des Jeunes Avocats. **LANGUAGES:** French, English, German and Dutch. **PRACTICE AREAS:** Business Law; Corporate Law.

PETER A. MASTENBROEK, born Haarlem, 1955; admitted, 1980, Rotterdam. *Education:* Leyden University (1979). **LANGUAGES:** English, French, Spanish, German and Dutch. **PRACTICE AREAS:** International Law; Commercial Law; Litigation; Corporate Law.

GERARD W. PEN, born Caracas, 1959; admitted, 1988, Rotterdam. *Education:* Leyden University (International Law, 1987; Civil Law, 1988). *Member:* Association Internationale des Jeunes Avocats. **LANGUAGES:** German, English, French and Dutch. **PRACTICE AREAS:** Company Law; Agency and Distributorship; Contracts; Business Law.

ASSOCIATES

HENRIËTTE A.H. HOLM, born Groningen, 1961; admitted, 1987, Groningen; 1989, Rotterdam. *Education:* Groningen University (1986). **LANGUAGES:** English, French, German and Dutch. **PRACTICE AREAS:** Family Law; Resorts and Leisure; Company Law.

AART M. SCHOTTE, born Amsterdam, 1961; admitted, 1989, Rotterdam. *Education:* Amsterdam University (1988). *Member:* Insolvency Lawyers Association (INSOLAD). **LANGUAGES:** English, French, German and Dutch. **PRACTICE AREAS:** Bankruptcy; Debtor and Creditor; Commercial Law.

BERNADETTE J.W.M. RAAIJMAAKERS, born Vught, 1966; admitted, 1991, Rotterdam. *Education:* Leyden University (1990); Siena (1990). *Member:* Association Internationale des Jeunes Avocats; French Chamber of Commerce. **LANGUAGES:** Italian, French, English and Dutch. **PRACTICE AREAS:** Labour and Employment; Family Law; Business Law.

ANNE B. SCHELL, born Leyden, 1967; admitted, 1992, Rotterdam. *Education:* Leyden University (Corporate Law, Civil Law, 1991). **LANGUAGES:** English, French, German and Dutch. **PRACTICE AREAS:** Administrative Law; Intellectual Property; Transportation; Construction Law.

All attorneys are members of the Netherlands Bar Association and of the Rotterdam Bar Association.

SCHAAP & PARTNERS

PARKLAAN 17

P.O. BOX 23052

3001 KB ROTTERDAM, THE NETHERLANDS

Telephone: (31) 10-4405600

Fax: (31) 10-4364977

Gouda, Netherlands Office: Bleulandweg 1d. P.O. Box 182. Telephone: (31) 1820-35577. Fax: (31) 1820-39726.

Company Law/Mergers and Acquisitions, Employment Law, Trade Disputes and Employee Benefits, Property, Project Development, Construction Law, Public Sector, Environmental Law, Shipping, Commercial Transaction, Product Liability and Intellectual Property, Private and Matrimonial Law, Litigation, Arbitration, General Practice.

PARTNERS

FONS VAN DER WOUDE, born 1936; admitted, 1961, The Netherlands. Partner since 1967. (Advocate). **LANGUAGES:** Dutch, English and German.

BÖRRE VAN NIEVELT, born 1935; admitted, 1960, The Netherlands. Partner since 1971. (Notary). **LANGUAGES:** Dutch, French, English, German and Norwegian.

DICK VAN EIJCK, born 1939; admitted, 1960, The Netherlands. Partner since 1974. (Notary). **LANGUAGES:** Dutch, French, English and German.

JAN KLINKENBERG, born 1947; admitted, 1972, The Netherlands. Partner since 1979. (Notary). **LANGUAGES:** Dutch, English and German.

HUGO SMIT, born 1947; admitted, 1974, The Netherlands. Partner since 1979. (Advocate). **LANGUAGES:** Dutch, English and German.

ONNO OKKINGA, born 1946; admitted, 1975, The Netherlands. Partner since 1984. (Notary and Advocate). **LANGUAGES:** Dutch, English, French and German.

JACK LEEMAN, born 1948; admitted, 1978, The Netherlands. Partner since, 1984. (Advocate). **LANGUAGES:** Dutch, English and German.

PETER VOLLEBREGT, born 1952; admitted, 1978, The Netherlands. Partner since 1985. (Advocate). **LANGUAGES:** Dutch, English and French.

LUPO WESTERHUIS, born 1948; admitted, 1976, The Netherlands. Partner since 1986. (Notary). **LANGUAGES:** Dutch, English and German.

PIM WITHOLT, born 1947; admitted, 1977, The Netherlands. Partner since 1990. (Advocat). **LANGUAGES:** Dutch, English and German.

ARNOUT GEERLING, born 1950; admitted, 1976, The Netherlands. Partner since 1992. (Notary). **LANGUAGES:** Dutch, English and German.

JOHAN BOEREN, born 1961; admitted, 1985, The Netherlands. Partner since 1992. (Advocate). **LANGUAGES:** Dutch, English and German.

JAN ANEMA, born 1944; admitted, 1971, The Netherlands. Partner since 1993. (Notary and Advocate). **LANGUAGES:** Dutch, French, English, German and Spanish.

FRAN MOEREL, born 1932; admitted, 1960, The Netherlands. Partner since 1994. (Notary). **LANGUAGES:** Dutch, English and German.

HANS KEMPER, born 1960; admitted, 1985, The Netherlands. Partner since 1993. (Notary). **LANGUAGES:** Dutch, English and German.

OF COUNSEL

PROFESSOR W.J. SLAGTER, Professor Emeritus of Law, Rotterdam Erasmus University (Civil Law, Commercial and Business Law and Private International Law). (Permanent Adviser). **LANGUAGES:** Dutch, French, German and English.

SJÖCRONA VAN STIGT DE ROOS & PEN

Lawyers

Established in 1992

ZEEMANSSTRAAT 11

3016 CN ROTTERDAM, THE NETHERLANDS

Telephone: +31 (0) 10/4364311

Telefax: +31 (0) 10/4366700

Amsterdam, The Netherlands Office: Keizersgracht 332, 1016 EZ. Telephone: +31 (0) 20/6275411. Telefax: +31 (0) 20/6226577.

(This Listing Continued)

The Hague, The Netherlands Office: Oranjestraat 7, 2514 JB. Telephone: +31 (0) 70/3467472. Telefax: +31 (0) 70/3924378.

Commercial Criminal Law and Criminal Procedures.
Firm engaged in Dutch, European and International Criminal Law practise. All lawyers are entitled to plead before the European Commission in Brussels, the European Court of Human Rights in Strassbourg and the Supreme Court of the Netherlands.

FIRM PROFILE: *Established in 1992, Sjöcrona Van Stigt De Roos & Pen is the largest Commercial Criminal Law Firm in the Netherlands. The firm has a broadly based practise with a reputation for offering a full range of quality legal services in the field. The client base is worldwide. The firm has eight partners and four associates practising in three offices. Two members of the firm hold professorships in Criminal Law and Criminal Procedure at Dutch Universities.*

MEMBERS OF FIRM

Prof. Dr. Theo A. de Roos	*Prof. Dr. Jan M. Sjöcrona*
Jurjen S. Pen	*Boudewijn C.W. van Eijck*
Arthur J.N. van Stigt	*Marlies van Strien*
Lian A.M. Mannheims	*Annelies E.M. Röttgering*

ASSOCIATES

Chantal P.E. Meewisse	*Jetty A. Bult*
Peter W.J. van der Spek	*Dr. Stijn A. Franken*

(For Complete Biographical Data on all Personnel, see Professional Biographies at The Hague, The Netherlands)

TRENITÉ VAN DOORNE
WEENA 666
ROTTERDAM, THE NETHERLANDS
Telephone: 31 (0) 10-4042111
Telefax: 31 (0) 10-4042333

Mailing Address: P.O. Box 190, 3000 AD Rotterdam

Amsterdam, Netherlands Office: De Lairessestraat 133. Mailing Address: P.O. Box 75265, 1070 AG AMSTERDAM. Telephone: 31 (0) 20-6789 123. Telex: 16144 tvda nl. Telefax: 31 (0) 20-6789 589.
Rijswijk, Netherlands Office: Haagweg 175. Mailing Address: P.O. Box 1073, 2280 CB RIJSWIJK. Telephone: 31 (0) 70-390 10 15. Telefax: 31 (0) 70-399 68 44.
The Hague, Netherlands Office: Churchillplein 5. Mailing Address: P.O. Box 17207, 2502 CE THE HAGUE. Telephone: 31 (0) 70-338 3131. Telefax: 31 (0) 70-358 4798.
Brussels, Belgium Office: Avenue Louise 149, 1050 BRUSSELS. Telephone: 32-2-537 5159. Telefax: 32-2-537 6961.
Willemstad, Curaçao, Netherlands Antilles Office: Promes, Trenité Van Doorne. Julianaplein 22,P.O. Box 504. Telephone: 599-9-613400. Telefax: 599-9-612023.
Tokyo, Japan Office: Akasaka Wing Building 5 F, 6-6-15 Akasaka, Minato-ku, 107. Telephone: 813-5563-2911. Telefax: 813-5563-2912.

Corporate Law, Mergers and Acquisitions, Banking and Financing, Joint Ventures, Dutch and European Antitrust and Competition Law, Agencies and Distributorships, Transportation and Maritime Law, Insurance Law, Bankruptcy and Insolvency Law, Administrative Law, Construction, Engineering and Real Estate Law, Environmental Law, Press and Media Law, Industrial and Intellectual Property Law, Computer and Telecommunications Law, Labour Law, Litigation and Arbitration, Family Law, International and Economic Criminal Law, International Trade Regulations, European Communities Laws and other International Law.
Dutch attorneys represent clients before all courts in the Netherlands, the European Court of Justice and the Benelux Court of Justice.

MEMBERS OF FIRM
ATTORNEYS AT LAW

JAN G. HOOGENRAAD, born 1932; admitted, 1958, Rotterdam. *Education:* University of Leiden (1955); University of Utrecht (1958). *LANGUAGES:* German and English. *PRACTICE AREAS:* Real Estate Law; Arbitration Law; Litigation.

HANS MENTINK, born 1934; admitted, 1958, Rotterdam. *Education:* University of Utrecht (1958). *LANGUAGES:* English and German. *PRACTICE AREAS:* General Contract Law; Litigation; Administrative Law; Insolvency Law; Land Planning Law.

(This Listing Continued)

JAN SCHEPEL, born 1933; admitted, 1958, The Hague. *Education:* University of Utrecht (1956). *LANGUAGES:* English, French and German. *PRACTICE AREAS:* Corporate Law.

HANS L.F. VAN MOORSEL, born 1932; admitted, 1964, Rotterdam. *Education:* University of Leiden (1959). *LANGUAGES:* English, French and German. *PRACTICE AREAS:* Corporate Law; Finance Law; Mergers and Acquisitions Law.

PETER HOUTMAN, born 1937; admitted, 1964, Rotterdam. *Education:* University of Utrecht (1962). *LANGUAGES:* English, French and German. *PRACTICE AREAS:* Finance Law; Corporate Law.

FRANS L.J. VAN WERSCH, born 1943; admitted, 1967, Rotterdam. *Education:* University of Leiden (1967). *LANGUAGES:* English and German. *PRACTICE AREAS:* Inland Navigation Law; Transport Law; Customs Law; Insurance Law; Insolvency Law.

LODEWIJK W.H. VAN DIJK, born 1942; admitted, 1969, Dordrecht; 1973, Rotterdam. *Education:* University of Leiden (1967). *LANGUAGES:* English. *PRACTICE AREAS:* Insurance Law; Contracting Law; Litigation; Arbitration Law.

GERARD M.C.C. BRUYNINCKX, born 1944; admitted, 1969, Rotterdam. *Education:* University of Leiden (1969). *LANGUAGES:* English, French and German. *PRACTICE AREAS:* Maritime Law; Transport Law; Commodities Law.

FRED J. RUTGERS, born 1944; admitted, 1971, Rotterdam. *Education:* University of Leiden (1969). *LANGUAGES:* English, French and German. *PRACTICE AREAS:* Maritime Law; Insurance Law; Litigation.

WILLEM G. VAN HASSEL, born 1946; admitted, 1971, Rotterdam. *Education:* Erasmus University of Rotterdam (1969). Substitute Justice, District Court of Rotterdam. *Member:* The Netherlands Bar Association (President, 1991-1993); International Bar Association (Council Member). *LANGUAGES:* English, French and German. *PRACTICE AREAS:* Corporate Law; Insolvency Law; Public-Private Partnerships; Arbitration Law.

D. CEES BUIJS, born 1942; admitted, 1988, Rotterdam. *Education:* Erasmus University Rotterdam (1974). *LANGUAGES:* English, French and German. *PRACTICE AREAS:* Corporate Law; Securities Law; Law of the European Communities.

P. ROBERT SCHIPPERS, born 1945; admitted, 1973, Rotterdam. *Education:* University of Leiden (1972). *LANGUAGES:* English. *PRACTICE AREAS:* Maritime Law; Transport Law.

FRANK STADERMANN, born 1949; admitted, 1973, Rotterdam. *Education:* University of Leiden (1972). *LANGUAGES:* English. *PRACTICE AREAS:* Insurance Law; Tort; Contractual Liability Law.

HERMAN BOONK, born 1945; admitted, 1974, Rotterdam. *Education:* University of Groningen (1969). *LANGUAGES:* English. *PRACTICE AREAS:* Commercial Law; Maritime Law.

PIETER W. VAN BAAL, born 1949; admitted, 1975, Rotterdam. *Education:* University of Utrecht (1974). *LANGUAGES:* English, French and German. *PRACTICE AREAS:* International Sale of Goods Law; Arbitration Law.

ANTON DE VRIES, born 1944; admitted, 1976, Rotterdam. *Education:* University of Groningen (1975). *LANGUAGES:* English and German. *PRACTICE AREAS:* Real Estate Law; Labor Law; Litigation; Medical Law.

ADRIAN H. BOS, born 1949; admitted, 1976, Rotterdam. *Education:* University of Leiden (1975). *LANGUAGES:* English and German. *PRACTICE AREAS:* Corporate Law; Insolvency Law.

HANS A. VAN RAMSHORST, born 1949; admitted, 1976, Rotterdam. *Education:* University of Leiden (1976). *LANGUAGES:* English and German. *PRACTICE AREAS:* Banking Law; Corporate Law.

HARM D.M. MULDER, born 1946; admitted, 1977, Rotterdam. *Education:* Vrije Universiteit Amsterdam (1970). *LANGUAGES:* English, French, German and Italian. *PRACTICE AREAS:* Commercial Law; Maritime Law; Insurance Law.

JAN G.A. VAN ZUUREN, born 1952; admitted, 1979, Rotterdam. *Education:* University of Leiden (1978). *LANGUAGES:* English and German. *PRACTICE AREAS:* Commercial Law; Commodity Trade Law; Maritime Law; Insurance Law.

VINCENT DISSELKOEN, born 1948; admitted, 1976, Amsterdam; 1982, Rotterdam. *Education:* University of Amsterdam (1975). *LANGUAGES:* English. *PRACTICE AREAS:* Labor Law.

(This Listing Continued)

TRENITÉ VAN DOORNE, Rotterdam—Continued

RALPH P. KRÖNER, born 1950; admitted, 1976, Rotterdam. *Education:* Lugdunum Batavorum (1975). *Member:* International Bar Association (Country Representative, 1989—); International Bar Association (Chairman, Committee on Insurance, 1987—); European Center for Space Law (Board Member, 1989—). *LANGUAGES:* English, French, German and Luxemburgish. *PRACTICE AREAS:* Litigation; Trade Law; Insurance Law; Space Law; Banking.

WILLEM M.P.M. WEERDESTEIJN, born 1950; admitted, 1980, Rotterdam. *Education:* Erasmus University Rotterdam (1975). *LANGUAGES:* English. *PRACTICE AREAS:* Computer Law; Environmental Law; Real Estate Law; Administrative Law.

JAN WILLEM BRUIDEGOM, born 1954; admitted, 1980, Rotterdam. *Education:* University of Leiden (1980). *LANGUAGES:* English and German. *PRACTICE AREAS:* Maritime Law; Transport Law; Commercial Law.

LINDA J. SARLEMIJN, born 1952; admitted, 1979, Rotterdam. *Education:* Erasmus University Rotterdam (1979). *LANGUAGES:* English. *PRACTICE AREAS:* Labor Law.

JEAN-PIERRE W.M. VAN LEEUWE, born 1957; admitted, 1982, Rotterdam. *Education:* University of Leiden (1980 and 1982). *LANGUAGES:* English and German. *PRACTICE AREAS:* Corporate Law; Mergers and Acquisitions; International Corporate Finance; Banking Law.

ALAN R. STEELE-NICHOLSON, born 1945; admitted, 1982, District of Columbia (USA) (Not admitted in The Netherlands). *Education:* Northwestern University (B.S., 1967); University of Iowa (M.A., 1969); Catholic University (J.D., 1982). *LANGUAGES:* Dutch and English. *PRACTICE AREAS:* Commercial Transactions; Law of the European Communities and Lobbing; Arbitrations.

WIM A. LUITEN, born 1946; admitted, 1984, Rotterdam. *Education:* Erasmus University Rotterdam (1974). *LANGUAGES:* English, French and German. *PRACTICE AREAS:* Insurance Law.

MICHIEL J. FARO, born 1952; admitted, 1983, Rotterdam. *Education:* University of Rotterdam (1975). *LANGUAGES:* English and German. *PRACTICE AREAS:* Real Estate Law; Government Law; Environmental Law.

JAN WILLEM BITTER, born 1952; admitted, 1983, Rotterdam. *Education:* University of Leiden (J.D., 1977); European University Institute, Florence, Italy (S.J.D., 1989). *LANGUAGES:* English, French, German, Italian and Spanish. *PRACTICE AREAS:* Commodity Contracts Law; Labor Law; Agency; Distributorship; Franchising; Arbitration Law; Litigation.

GÉRARD J.M. MOUSSAULT, born 1955; admitted, 1984, Rotterdam. *Education:* University of Utrecht (1983). *LANGUAGES:* English, French and German. *PRACTICE AREAS:* International Finance; Corporate and Maritime Law.

SHAWN C. CONWAY, born 1956; admitted, 1983, District of Columbia (USA); 1984, Illinois (USA) (Not admitted in The Netherlands). *Education:* Northern Illinois University (B.A., 1979); University of Notre Dame (J.D., 1982). Instructor, International Business Law, Webster University Leiden, 1990-1993. *Member:* District of Columbia Bar; Illinois State, American and International Bar Associations. *LANGUAGES:* Dutch, English, French and Spanish. *PRACTICE AREAS:* International Commercial Transactions; Construction Projects; East European Investment; International Arbitration.

ED A. BIK, born 1945; admitted, 1984, Rotterdam. *Education:* Erasmus University Rotterdam (1979). *LANGUAGES:* English and German. *PRACTICE AREAS:* Maritime Law.

JENNEKE VIJLBRIEF-VAN DER SCHAFT, born 1945; admitted, 1976, Rotterdam. *Education:* University of Utrecht (1972). *LANGUAGES:* English and German. *PRACTICE AREAS:* Real Estate Law; Physical Planning Law; Environmental Law; Administrative Law.

LYKE IN 'T VELD-MARREE, born 1946; admitted, 1971, Rotterdam. *Education:* University of Utrecht (1970). *LANGUAGES:* English. *PRACTICE AREAS:* Family Law.

ONNO G. BOERSTRA, born 1958; admitted, 1984, Rotterdam. *Education:* Vrije Universiteit Amsterdam (1982); Cornell Law School (LL.M., 1983). *LANGUAGES:* English and German. *PRACTICE AREAS:* Corporate Law; Commercial Law.

JOHAN SMIT, born 1959; admitted, 1985, Rotterdam. *Education:* University of Utrecht (1985). *LANGUAGES:* English and German. *PRACTICE AREAS:* Commercial Law; Transport Law; Maritime Law.

MICHIEL M. VAN LEEUWEN, born 1958; admitted, 1985, Rotterdam. *Education:* University of Amsterdam (1983). *LANGUAGES:* English, French and German. *PRACTICE AREAS:* Maritime Law.

ED VAN LIERE, born 1959; admitted, 1986, Rotterdam. *Education:* University of Leiden (1985). Member, Advisory Committee on Criminal Law of Dutch Bar Association. Teacher, Criminal Law and Examiner for Dutch Bar Exam. *LANGUAGES:* English. *PRACTICE AREAS:* International Criminal Law; Economic Criminal Law.

GERHARD H. GISPEN, born 1960; admitted, 1986, Rotterdam. *Education:* University of Leiden (1985). *Member:* Dutch Association of Insolvency Lawyers (Insolad), INSOL. *LANGUAGES:* English and German. *PRACTICE AREAS:* Banking Law; Asset Finance; Insolvency Law.

PAUL CH.J.M. BERGER, born 1956; admitted, 1982, Rotterdam, The Netherlands; 1990, Netherlands Antilles. *Education:* University of Groningen; Vrije Universiteit Amsterdam (1982). Curaçao, Netherlands Antilles Office (1990-1992). *Member:* International Bar Association (Country Representative Netherlands Antilles, 1990-1992). *LANGUAGES:* English, French and German. *PRACTICE AREAS:* Company Law; Restructurings.

MEMBERS OF FIRM
CIVIL LAW NOTARIES

VICTOR J.A.J.C. VAN HEESWIJK, born 1947; appointed Civil Law Notary by Her Majesty the Queen, 1981. *Education:* University of Nijmegen (1972). *LANGUAGES:* English, French and German. *PRACTICE AREAS:* Real Estate Law; Corporate Law.

GEORGE G.B. WORTELBOER, born 1952; appointed Civil Law Notary by Her Majesty the Queen, 1990. *Education:* University of Leiden (1976). *LANGUAGES:* English, French and German. *PRACTICE AREAS:* Corporate Law; Maritime Law; Real Estate Law.

RICHARD G.M.C. VAN RAPPARD, born 1948; appointed Civil Law Notary by Her Majesty the Queen, 1991. *Education:* University of Utrecht (1974 and 1976). *LANGUAGES:* English, French and German. *PRACTICE AREAS:* Corporate Law.

FRANK E. ROOS, born 1957; admitted, 1984, Rotterdam; appointed Civil Law Notary by Her Majesty The Queen, 1993. *Education:* University of Utrecht, Civil Law and Notarial Law (1982). *LANGUAGES:* English and German. *PRACTICE AREAS:* Corporate Law.

ASSOCIATES
ATTORNEYS AT LAW

A. BARTJE SCHABERG, born 1955; admitted, 1980, Rotterdam. *Education:* University of Leiden (1979). *LANGUAGES:* English. *PRACTICE AREAS:* Labor Law.

JAN MICHIEL HEBLY, born 1955; admitted, 1982, Rotterdam; 1993, Netherland Antilles. *Education:* University of Leiden (1982). Author: "Netherlands Civil Evidence Act, 1988," Kluwer Law & Taxation, 1992. Lecturer, Civil Procedural Law, University of Leiden, 1990—. *Member:* IBA; SBL; SGP; ILS; Netherlands Health Law Association; Netherlands Competition Law Association; Netherlands Association Civil Procedure. *LANGUAGES:* English. *PRACTICE AREAS:* Commercial Law; Health and Hospital Law; Litigation.

ALIDA JEULINK, born 1957; admitted, 1983, Almelo; 1987, Rotterdam. *Education:* University of Groningen (1982). *LANGUAGES:* English and German. *PRACTICE AREAS:* Family Law.

HENRIËTTE E. MEERMAN, born 1957; admitted, 1983, Rotterdam. *Education:* University of Utrecht (1982). *LANGUAGES:* English. *PRACTICE AREAS:* Labor Law.

C. JACQUELINE HERMAN DE GROOT, born 1961; admitted, 1985, Rotterdam. *Education:* University of Leiden (1984). *LANGUAGES:* English. *PRACTICE AREAS:* Labor Law.

ARNOLD STENDAHL, born 1953; admitted, 1987, Rotterdam. *Education:* Erasmus University Rotterdam (1985). *LANGUAGES:* English and Norwegian. *PRACTICE AREAS:* Transport Law; Insurance Law; Insolvency Law; Litigation.

EVELINE T. SILLEVIS SMITT, born 1961; admitted, 1987, Rotterdam. *Education:* University of Leiden (1986); College of Europe (1987),

(This Listing Continued)

Rotterdam. *LANGUAGES:* English. *PRACTICE AREAS:* Litigation; Administrative Law; Environmental Law; Land Planning Law.

DIRK J. POST, born 1962; admitted, 1987, Rotterdam. *Education:* Erasmus University Rotterdam (1987). *LANGUAGES:* English. *PRACTICE AREAS:* Administrative Law; Environmental Law; Land Planning Law.

TON NEDERVEEN, born 1959; admitted, 1988, Rotterdam. *Education:* University of Utrecht (1986); Grotius Academy (1987). *LANGUAGES:* English. *PRACTICE AREAS:* Corporate and Securities Law.

ALEXANDER C. STEENSMA, born 1961; admitted, 1988, Rotterdam. *Education:* University of Utrecht (1986); Law School of Paris (1987). *LANGUAGES:* English and French. *PRACTICE AREAS:* Corporate Law; Labor Law.

MIK BREEK, born 1963; admitted, 1988, Rotterdam. *Education:* University of Amsterdam (1988). *LANGUAGES:* English. *PRACTICE AREAS:* Employment Law.

BERNADETTE E.M. STATIUS VAN EPS, born 1962; admitted, 1988, Netherlands Antilles; 1992, Rotterdam. *Education:* University of Leiden, The Netherlands (1988). *LANGUAGES:* English and Spanish. *PRACTICE AREAS:* Maritime Law.

PIETER W.G. RIEMER, born 1961; admitted, 1989, Rotterdam. *Education:* University of Nijmegen (1988). *LANGUAGES:* Arabic and English. *PRACTICE AREAS:* Corporate Law; Mergers and Acquisitions; Commercial Law.

ROELANT A. KLAASSEN, born 1962; admitted, 1987, Rotterdam. *Education:* University of Leiden (1987). *LANGUAGES:* English and German. *PRACTICE AREAS:* Maritime Law; Commercial Law.

WILLEM W. DE NIJS BIK, born 1963; admitted, 1989, Rotterdam. *Education:* University of Utrecht (1987). *LANGUAGES:* English and French. *PRACTICE AREAS:* Corporate Law; Maritime Law; Commercial Law.

DORIANNE T.J.C.M. BROEKMAN, born 1965; admitted, 1989, Rotterdam. *Education:* University of Utrecht (1988). *LANGUAGES:* English. *PRACTICE AREAS:* Corporate Law; Corporate Finance; Banking.

NICOLE M. EDELENBOS, born 1962; admitted, 1990, Rotterdam. *Education:* Erasmus University Rotterdam (1987). *LANGUAGES:* English and German. *PRACTICE AREAS:* Insurance Litigation; Insolvency Law.

DORINE M. FERNHOUT, born 1965; admitted, 1989, Haarlem; 1993, Rotterdam. *Education:* University of Leiden (1989). *LANGUAGES:* English. *PRACTICE AREAS:* Employment Law.

JAN JAAP SCHELLING, born 1964; admitted, 1990, Rotterdam. *Education:* Erasmus University Rotterdam (1989). *LANGUAGES:* English. *PRACTICE AREAS:* Maritime Law; Commercial Law.

RIMMERTIEN A. VAN DAM, born 1961; admitted, 1990, Rotterdam. *Education:* University of Leiden (1989). *LANGUAGES:* English. *PRACTICE AREAS:* Labor Law.

MARTIJN A. KOOPAL, born 1964; admitted, 1990, Rotterdam. *Education:* University of Groningen (1990). *LANGUAGES:* English. *PRACTICE AREAS:* Corporate Law; Commercial Law.

MARC V. VAN DER STORM, born 1963; admitted, 1990, Rotterdam. *Education:* University of Leiden (1989). *LANGUAGES:* English. *PRACTICE AREAS:* Labor Law; Commercial Law.

ELIZABETH C. KOLSHORN, born 1963; admitted, 1990, District of Columbia (USA); 1991, Ohio (USA); 1992, Colorado (USA) (Not admitted in The Netherlands). *Education:* Miami University, Ohio (B.A., B.S., 1986); Columbia University, New York (J.D., 1989). *LANGUAGES:* English. *PRACTICE AREAS:* International Commercial Transactions; Arbitration Law.

LUDMILLA A. VITANOVA, born 1960; admitted, 1990, Rotterdam. *Education:* University of Tárnovo, Bulgaria (Slavonic Languages, 1982); University of Amsterdam (International Law, 1989); University of Leiden (Dutch Law, 1990). *LANGUAGES:* Dutch, Bulgarian, Russian, English, German, Serbo-Croation and Slovakian. *PRACTICE AREAS:* Maritime Law; Corporate Law; Central and Eastern European Law.

A. BÉNINE VAN KARNEBEEK, born 1966; admitted, 1991, Rotterdam. *Education:* University of Utrecht (1990). *LANGUAGES:* English, French and German. *PRACTICE AREAS:* Insurance Law; Tort; Contractual Liability; Maritime Law.

(This Listing Continued)

GUY H.M. VAN ASTEN, born 1965; admitted, 1991, Rotterdam. *Education:* University of Leiden (1991). *LANGUAGES:* English. *PRACTICE AREAS:* Maritime Law.

SJOERD J.H. RUTTEN, born 1962; admitted, 1991, Rotterdam. *Education:* Erasmus University, Rotterdam (1991). *LANGUAGES:* Dutch and English. *PRACTICE AREAS:* Construction Law.

FRANS C. VAN SPENGLER, born 1965; admitted, 1991, Rotterdam. *Education:* University of Groningen (1991). *LANGUAGES:* English. *PRACTICE AREAS:* Corporate Law.

BERNA J. VAN WIJNGAARDEN, born 1962; admitted, 1991, Rotterdam. *Education:* Erasmus University, Rotterdam (1991). *LANGUAGES:* English and German. *PRACTICE AREAS:* Family Law; Insurance Law.

SEBASTIAAN A.C. BERGER, born 1964; admitted, 1992, Rotterdam. *Education:* University of Leiden (1990). *LANGUAGES:* English, German and French. *PRACTICE AREAS:* Civil Law; Corporate Law.

LIESBETH W. SEGAAR, born 1965; admitted, 1992, Rotterdam. *Education:* University of Amsterdam (1992). *LANGUAGES:* English and French. *PRACTICE AREAS:* Insurance Law; Labor Law.

EVELIEN VAN HOUWENINGE GRAFTDIJK, born 1965; admitted, 1992, Rotterdam. *Education:* University of Leiden (1991). *LANGUAGES:* English and German. *PRACTICE AREAS:* Maritime Law.

N.JASPER HELDER, born 1968; admitted, 1992, Rotterdam. *Education:* Erasmus University of Rotterdam. *LANGUAGES:* English, German and French. *PRACTICE AREAS:* Customs Law; Construction Law.

MARISKA N. BENSCHOP, born 1964; admitted, 1992, Rotterdam. *Education:* University of Utrecht (1991). *LANGUAGES:* French and English. *PRACTICE AREAS:* Criminal Law.

NILS E.W. VAN DIJKMAN, born 1965; admitted, 1992, Rotterdam. *Education:* University of Leiden (1990). *LANGUAGES:* English and Swedish. *PRACTICE AREAS:* Employment Law.

RICHARD-JAN ROKS, born 1966; admitted, 1992, Amsterdam. *Education:* University of Amsterdam (1991). *LANGUAGES:* German and English. *PRACTICE AREAS:* Construction Law; Real Estate Law.

MARCEL H. VAN DE VORST, born 1967; admitted, 1992, Rotterdam. *Education:* Erasmus University Rotterdam (1992). *LANGUAGES:* English and French. *PRACTICE AREAS:* Corporate Law.

LUCIEN PH. DEFAIX, born 1966; admitted, 1992, Rotterdam. *Education:* University of Utrecht (B.B.A., 1987); Erasmus University Rotterdam (1991). *LANGUAGES:* French, English and German. *PRACTICE AREAS:* Company Law.

MARCO M. SLOTBOOM, born 1965; admitted, 1992, The Hague. *Education:* University of Leiden (1989); College of Europe, Bruges (1990). *LANGUAGES:* English, French and German. *PRACTICE AREAS:* Law of the European Communities; Labor Law; Employment Law; Commercial Law.

EVELINE A.M. VAN OUDENHOVEN, born 1965; admitted, 1993, Rotterdam. *Education:* University of Leiden (1990). *LANGUAGES:* English and German. *PRACTICE AREAS:* Insurance Law; Maritime Law.

THÉRÈSE A.G. PRISSE, born 1968; admitted, 1993, Rotterdam. *Education:* Groningen University (1992). *LANGUAGES:* English. *PRACTICE AREAS:* Corporate Law; Maritime Law; International Sale of Goods.

MEIKE E. TERHORST, born 1967; admitted, 1993, Rotterdam. *Education:* University of Leiden (1992). *LANGUAGES:* English and German. *PRACTICE AREAS:* Construction Law; Real Estate Law; Corporate Law; Distribution and EEC Competition Law.

E. HUGO WIJDICKS, born 1964; admitted, 1993, Rotterdam. *Education:* University of Utrecht (1992). *LANGUAGES:* German and English. *PRACTICE AREAS:* Insurance Law; Corporate Law.

KOEN J.T.M. HEHENKAMP, born 1967; admitted, 1993, Rotterdam. *Education:* University of Leiden (1992). *LANGUAGES:* English and German. *PRACTICE AREAS:* Commercial Contracting; Litigation.

DIANA N.H.M. SPRUIT, born 1963; admitted, 1993, Rotterdam. *Education:* Erasmus University Rotterdam (1992). *LANGUAGES:* English and German. *PRACTICE AREAS:* Family Law.

IRENE D. JACOBS, born 1962; admitted, 1993, Rotterdam. *Education:* University of Leiden (1989). *LANGUAGES:* English, French, German and Italian. *PRACTICE AREAS:* Maritime Law.

(This Listing Continued)

TRENITÉ VAN DOORNE, Rotterdam—Continued

VINCENT P.J. MEIJER, born 1963; admitted, 1993, Rotterdam. *Education:* University of Leiden (1988). *LANGUAGES:* English and French. *PRACTICE AREAS:* Construction Law; Real Estate Law.

O.G. (MENNOLT) BUNJES, born 1967; admitted, 1993, Rotterdam. *Education:* University of Utrecht (1991). *LANGUAGES:* English and German. *PRACTICE AREAS:* Insurance Law.

JOHAN F.G. DE FLINES, born 1965; admitted, 1993, Rotterdam. *Education:* Erasmus University Rotterdam (1990). *LANGUAGES:* English and Italian. *PRACTICE AREAS:* Corporate Law.

HESTER M. VAN DER SLUIS, born 1968; admitted, 1993, Rotterdam. *Education:* University of Amsterdam (1993). *LANGUAGES:* English. *PRACTICE AREAS:* Real Estate Law; Government Law; Environmental Law.

CAROLINE M.T. NIJS, born 1964; admitted, 1993, Rotterdam. *Education:* University of Leiden (1992). *LANGUAGES:* German and English. *PRACTICE AREAS:* Corporate Law.

A.T.G.M. (LOET) VENROOY, born 1966; admitted, 1993, Rotterdam. *Education:* University of Nijenrode (1988); University of Leiden (1993). *LANGUAGES:* English and German. *PRACTICE AREAS:* Insolvency Law; Corporate Law.

JACOB BECK, born 1967; admitted, 1994, Rotterdam. *Education:* University of Groningen (1993). *LANGUAGES:* English and German. *PRACTICE AREAS:* Maritime Law.

MARTIJN W.A. VAN GILS, born 1967; admitted, 1994, Rotterdam. *Education:* Erasmus University Rotterdam (1993). *LANGUAGES:* English and French. *PRACTICE AREAS:* Labor Law.

MARK A. MOOLHUIZEN, born 1968; admitted, 1994, Rotterdam. *Education:* University of Leiden (1993). *LANGUAGES:* English. *PRACTICE AREAS:* Administrative Law; Environmental Law; Land Planning Law.

BAS BORIS VISSER, born 1967; admitted, 1994, Rotterdam. *Education:* University of Groningen (1993). *LANGUAGES:* English. *PRACTICE AREAS:* Corporate Law.

SASKIA D. BORSBOOM, born 1967; admitted, 1994, Rotterdam. *Education:* University of Leiden (1993). *LANGUAGES:* English, French and German. *PRACTICE AREAS:* Labor Law.

JULIAN A. OGGEL, born 1968; admitted, 1994, Rotterdam. *Education:* University of Leiden (1993). *LANGUAGES:* English, French and German. *PRACTICE AREAS:* Maritime Law.

SUSANNE C. VAN PUTTEN, born 1965; admitted, 1994, Rotterdam. *Education:* University of Amsterdam (1991). *LANGUAGES:* English, French, German and Spanish. *PRACTICE AREAS:* Criminal Law.

ASSOCIATES
CIVIL LAW NOTARIES

ALBERT J. STEL, born 1946; admitted as a Civil Law Notary, 1974, Rotterdam. *Education:* University of Leiden (1973 and 1974). *LANGUAGES:* English and French. *PRACTICE AREAS:* Corporate Law; Real Estate Law.

JACOBUS C.G. TEN BRINK, born 1956; admitted as Civil Law Notary, 1982, Rotterdam, 1990, Apeldoorn, 1992, Rijswijk. *Education:* Vrije Universiteit, Amsterdam, Notarial Law (1981). *LANGUAGES:* English and French. *PRACTICE AREAS:* Mergers and Takeovers; Law on Corporate Accounts; Law on Associations and Foundations (Trusts).

DIRK W.M. VAN NIEKERK, born 1956; admitted, as a Civil Law Notary, 1986, Rotterdam. *Education:* University of Leiden (1982). *LANGUAGES:* English. *PRACTICE AREAS:* Real Estate Law; Corporate Law.

HENDRINE PLANTEN, born 1962; admitted as a Civil Law Notary, 1988, Rotterdam. *Education:* University of Leiden (1987 and 1988). *LANGUAGES:* English. *PRACTICE AREAS:* Corporate Law; Real Estate Law.

EDWIN STOLK, born 1964; admitted as Civil Law Notary, 1992, Rijswijk. *Education:* Vrije Universiteit, Amsterdam (1991). *LANGUAGES:* English and French. *PRACTICE AREAS:* Real Estate; Family Law; Corporate Law.

(This Listing Continued)

STEVEN J.P. KOENEN, born 1967. *Education:* Erasmus University Rotterdam (1990); Vrije Universiteit Amsterdam (1994). *LANGUAGES:* English. *PRACTICE AREAS:* Corporate Law.

BEATRIJS M. VERHOEVEN, born 1967; admitted, as Civil Law Notary, 1990, Rotterdam. *Education:* University of Leiden (1990). *LANGUAGES:* English. *PRACTICE AREAS:* Family Law.

ELSBETH E. GERRITSE, born 1967. *Education:* University of Amsterdam (1992; Political Science, 1993). *LANGUAGES:* English. *PRACTICE AREAS:* Corporate Law.

BRUNO A.E.A. BERGER, born 1966; admitted, as Civil Law Notary, 1994, Rotterdam. *Education:* University of Leiden (1994). *LANGUAGES:* English, French and German. *PRACTICE AREAS:* Corporate Law.

OF COUNSEL

BERNARD C.J. SJOLLEMA, born 1929; admitted, 1954, Amsterdam; 1956, Rotterdam. *Education:* University of Leiden (1952). *LANGUAGES:* English, French and German. *PRACTICE AREAS:* Banking Law; Corporate Law.

Trenité Van Doorne forms together with Wessing Berenberg-Gossler Zimmermann a European Economic interest grouping. Wessing has offices in Berlin, Brussels, Düsseldorf, Hamburg, Leipzig and Munich. Trenité Van Doorne is a member of Lex Mundi.

Languages: Arabic, Chinese, Dutch, English, French, German, Italian, Norwegian, Russian and Spanish

---

VAN DONGEN ISRAELS SCHOT

International Corporate Lawyers

WORLD TRADE CENTER
BEURSPLEIN 37
P.O. BOX 30220
3001 DE ROTTERDAM, THE NETHERLANDS
Telephone: (31-10) 405 32 65
Fax: (31-10) 405 51 49

Corporate Finance, International Corporate Restructuring, Corporate Trusts, International Finance, Entertainment Law, Intellectual Property and Licensing, Foreign Investments, International Leasing, International and Offshore Taxation, Loans, Shipping and Aircraft, International Trust and Estate Planning.

FIRM PROFILE: Established in 1992, Van Dongen Israels Schot is an independent small sized international law firm. The firm has a specialized corporate law practise with a reputation for offering a selected range of quality international legal services in the field. The client base is worldwide.

MEMBERS OF FIRM

DR. YVONNE C. VAN DONGEN, born 1959. *Education:* University of Leyden (1984; Diploma of International Law, 1990); Erasmus University of Rotterdam (1987); University of Notre Dame (1990); University of Groningen (Ph.D., International Law, 1991). *Member:* Dutch Association for Corporate Lawyers (NeVOA); International Bar Association; International Fiscal Association; International Tax Planning Association; American Tax Institute in Europe; The Offshore Institute; Society for Trust and Estate Practitioners; American Society of International Law. *PRACTICE AREAS:* International Corporate Law; Cross-Border Finance; International and Offshore Taxation; Investments; Trust and Estate Planning.

VAN WIJMEN & KOEDAM

Established in 1922

WESTZEEDIJK 140
P.O. BOX 23070
3001 KB ROTTERDAM, THE NETHERLANDS
Telephone: (31) (10) 4364066
Telefax: (31) (10) 4360582

Breda, The Netherlands Office: Claudius Prinsenlaan 126. P.O. Box 4714, 4803 ES Breda. Telephone: (31) (76) 223100. Telefax: (31) (76) 142575.

Administrative, Agricultural, Arbitration, Bankruptcy, Building Permits, Competition, Compulsory Expropriation, Computer, Construction, Contracts, Corporate, Distribution, EEC, Environmental, Financing, Franchising, Insolvency, Intellectual Property, Insurance, International Trade and Commodities, Joint Ventures, Know How, Labour, Lease of Real Property,

(This Listing Continued)

Licensing, Litigation, Maritime, Matrimonial, Medical Malpractice, Mergers & Acquisitions, Pensions, Personal Injury, Real Estate, Software, Tort, Transport, Trust.

FIRM PROFILE: At present Van Wijmen & Koedam consists of 51 lawyers of whom 21 are members of firm. The present size of the partnership was established in the beginning of the eighties. The origin of the Breda and Rotterdam offices, however, dates back respectively to the twenties and thirties of this century.

The firm is associated with Schuermans & Schuermans at Turnhout, Belgium.

Van Wijmen & Koedam is a member of the JCS Group which comprises Van Wijmen & Koedam in Rotterdam and Breda, Jacques & Lewis in London, Brussels, the Isle of Man and Jersey, Chaintrier Caillard in Paris and Schmidt von der Osten & Huber in Essen and Berlin.

The JCS Group is an integrated association of law firms providing a comprehensive range of legal services to international clients.

PARTNERS

DR. PETER C.E. VAN WIJMEN, born 1938; admitted, 1962, Breda. *Education:* Nijmegen University. (Resident, BREDA Office). *PRACTICE AREAS:* Administrative; Compulsory Expropriation; Building Permits; Energy and Water Boards.

JAN P. SCHOUTEN, born 1934; admitted, 1962, Breda. *Education:* Amsterdam University (VU). (Resident, BREDA Office). *PRACTICE AREAS:* General Insurance; Labour.

LEX PH. VAN GELDER, born 1931; admitted, 1959, Rotterdam. *Education:* Leyden University. *PRACTICE AREAS:* Compulsory Expropriation; Real Estate.

GEERT C. VAN SPAENDONCK, born 1934; admitted, 1964, Breda. *Education:* Nijmegen University. (Resident, BREDA Office). *PRACTICE AREAS:* Corporate; Arbitration; Insolvency; Bankruptcy.

VIC W.L.M. VAN DIJK, born 1936; admitted, 1964, Breda. *Education:* Nijmegen University. (Resident, BREDA Office). *PRACTICE AREAS:* Construction.

KOOS L.M. ARTS, born 1943; admitted, 1968, Breda. *Education:* Nijmegen University. (Resident, BREDA Office). *PRACTICE AREAS:* General Commercial; Labour; Bankruptcy.

ROB O.E. MEIJER, born 1949; admitted, 1973, Rotterdam. *Education:* Rotterdam University. *PRACTICE AREAS:* General Commercial; Construction; Arbitration; Corporate.

LEO A.S. BOERSEN, born 1948; admitted, 1976, Rotterdam. *Education:* Nijmegen and Leyden Universities; OS Goode Hall, Toronto, Canada. *PRACTICE AREAS:* General Commercial; Transport; Maritime; Trade.

HERMAN J.M. VAN MIERLO, born 1948; admitted, 1976, Breda. *Education:* Nijmegen University. (Resident, BREDA Office). *PRACTICE AREAS:* Administrative; Compulsory Expropriation; Real Estate; Building Permits.

IGNO J.M. WOLTRING, born 1946; admitted, 1978, Breda. *Education:* Nijmegen University. *PRACTICE AREAS:* Labour; Public Servants; Social Security; Criminal.

CEES M. DE REGT, born 1950; admitted, 1976, Breda. *Education:* Groningen University. (Resident, BREDA Office). *PRACTICE AREAS:* General Commercial; Corporate; Environmental.

TON A.B. GAALMAN, born 1950; admitted, 1976, Breda. *Education:* Tilburg University. (Resident, BREDA Office). *PRACTICE AREAS:* Labour; Works Council; Bankruptcy.

PETER S.A. OVERWATER, born 1956; admitted, 1982, Breda; 1993, Rotterdam. *Education:* Leyden University. *PRACTICE AREAS:* Real Estate; Agricultural; Corporate; Environmental; Administrative.

JAN D. DE ROOIJ, born 1956; admitted, 1981, Rotterdam. *Education:* Rotterdam University. *PRACTICE AREAS:* Corporate; Labour; General Commercial.

PAUL J.W.M. SLIEPENBEEK, born 1955; admitted, 1983, Rotterdam. *Education:* Tilburg University. *PRACTICE AREAS:* Labour; Matrimonial; Trade.

VINCENT E.W.M. VAN WIJMEN, born 1954; admitted, 1981, Breda. *Education:* Nijmegen University. (Resident, BREDA Office). *PRACTICE AREAS:* Construction; Lease.

(This Listing Continued)

PETER N.A.M. CLAASSEN, born 1957; admitted, 1985, Breda. *Education:* Nijmegen University; Miami University (US). LL.M. (Resident, BREDA Office). *PRACTICE AREAS:* Intellectual Property; Computer; EEC; Corporate.

DRS. BRUNO P.M. VAN RAVELS, born 1958; admitted, 1986, Breda. *Education:* Nijmegen University (Law and Dutch Language Studies). (Resident, BREDA, Office). *PRACTICE AREAS:* Administrative; Environmental; Government Liability.

ERNST J. LOUWERS, born 1959; admitted, 1986, Rotterdam. *Education:* Leyden and Amsterdam Universities. *PRACTICE AREAS:* Intellectual Property; Franchising; Advertising; Publishing; Computer; EEC; Corporate.

MARY-LOU L. SIMONS-VINCKX, born 1944; admitted, 1987, Breda. *Education:* Leyden University (Certificate Biochemical Analyst). (Resident, BREDA Office). *PRACTICE AREAS:* Environmental; Pesticides; Soil Polution; Administrative.

PAUL J. PETERS, born 1960; admitted, 1986, The Hague; 1993, Rotterdam. *Education:* Nijmegen University. *PRACTICE AREAS:* Insolvency; Bankruptcy; Personal Injury.

SENIOR ASSOCIATES

HEIN W.P.B. TAMINIAU, born 1952; admitted, 1980, Maastricht. *Education:* Tilburg and Utrecht Universities. (Resident, BREDA Office). *PRACTICE AREAS:* Medical, Hospital and Personal Injury.

JOOST M.A. LOEVENDIE, born 1954; admitted, 1982, Breda. *Education:* Amsterdam University (VU). (Resident, BREDA Office). *PRACTICE AREAS:* Criminal; Economic Offenses.

MARJON H.G. HABETS, born 1960; admitted, 1985, Breda. *Education:* Tilburg University. (Resident, BREDA Office). *PRACTICE AREAS:* Labour; Lease; Matrimonial.

KOEN DE BRUIN, born 1961; admitted, 1987, Amsterdam; 1993, Breda. *Education:* Tilburg University. (Resident, BREDA Office). *PRACTICE AREAS:* Taxation.

JURGEN R. VERMEULEN, born 1964; admitted, 1988, Rotterdam. *Education:* Rotterdam University. *PRACTICE AREAS:* Administrative; Construction; Compulsory Expropriation; Real Estate.

JOS. A.M. VAN DER VELDEN, born 1963; admitted, 1988, Breda; 1993, Rotterdam. *Education:* Nijmegen University. *PRACTICE AREAS:* Administrative; Environmental; Planning.

JOOST J.M. VAN MIERLO, born 1962; admitted, 1989, Breda. *Education:* Nijmegen University. (Resident, BREDA Office). *PRACTICE AREAS:* General Commercial; Labour; Works Council; Corporate.

PIETER H.L.M. KUIJPERS, born 1964; admitted, 1989, Breda. *Education:* Utrecht University; Faculté Internationale de Droit Comparé, Strasbourg. (Resident, BREDA Office). *PRACTICE AREAS:* General Commercial; Private International Law; EEC; Corporate.

SABINE M. MULDER, born 1965; admitted, 1990, Rotterdam. *Education:* Leyden University; University of Florida. *PRACTICE AREAS:* Labour; Works Council.

JAN WILLEM KAMP, born 1964; admitted, 1991, Dordrecht. *Education:* Tilburg University. *PRACTICE AREAS:* Insolvency; Bankruptcy; General Practice.

CONSULTANT

PROF. DR. D.A. LUBACH, Professor, Groningen University.

Lawyers admitted to the Dutch Bar may represent clients and plead cases before the Courts of all EEC Member States, the European Courts of Justice and the Benelux Court of Justice.

Languages: English, French, German and Dutch

BARENTS & KRANS

Advocates and Notaries

(Attorneys and Civil Law Notaries)

PARKSTRAAT 107

P.O. BOX 30457

2500 GL THE HAGUE, THE NETHERLANDS

Telephone: +31-70-376.06.06

Telecopier: +31-70-365.18.56

Brussels, Belgium Office: Avenue de la Toison d'Or 55, bte 10-11 B-1060. Telephone: +32 2 534 9739. Telefax: +32 2 534 9740.

Agricultural Law, Administrative Law, Agency, Franchising and Distributorships, Antitrust and Trade Regulations, Arbitration, Bankruptcy, Corporate Law, (International) Commercial Law, Environmental Law, EC Law, Family Law, Intellectual and Industrial Property Law, Industrial Relations and Employment Law, Liability and Insurance Law, Mergers and Acquisitions, Real Estate (including Transfer of Property), Securities and Investment, Supreme Court Litigation, Trusts and Estates, Wills.

FIRM PROFILE: *Dutch Attorneys may represent clients before all Dutch Courts, before the European Court of Justice and the Benelux Court of Justice and are permitted to plead before all Courts of the Member States of the Common Market (EC). Only attorneys admitted to The Hague Bar may plead before the Supreme Court of the Netherlands.*

Barents & Krans' commercial clients are drawn from a cross-section of local, national and international business, ranging from one-man enterprises to multinational corporations.

PROF. WILLY ALEXANDER, Advocate of Counsel. *LANGUAGES:* English, French, German and Italian. *PRACTICE AREAS:* EC Law.

ADVOCATES/PARTNERS

ROB LARET. *LANGUAGES:* English, French and German. *PRACTICE AREAS:* Industrial and Intellectual Property.

LEONARD F. PELS RIJCKEN. *LANGUAGES:* English and French. *PRACTICE AREAS:* Real Estate; Leasing; Dealer Contracts; Licensing.

GILLES HOOFT GRAAFLAND. *LANGUAGES:* English and French. *PRACTICE AREAS:* Investment Law.

CLEMENS E.M. VAN NISPEN TOT SEVENAER. *LANGUAGES:* English and French. *PRACTICE AREAS:* International, Commercial and Corporate Law; EC Law (Competition).

HARCO J.J. DE BOSCH KEMPER. *LANGUAGES:* English and German. *PRACTICE AREAS:* Insurance Law.

HERMAN G.T.J. JANSEN. *LANGUAGES:* English, French, German and Italian. *PRACTICE AREAS:* Intellectual Property; International Competition Law; Corporate and Commercial Law.

MAARTEN P.A.M. FRUYTIER. *LANGUAGES:* English, French and German. *PRACTICE AREAS:* Labour Law.

PETER C. VAS NUNES. *LANGUAGES:* English, French and German. *PRACTICE AREAS:* Labour Law; Industrial Relations.

ANTON H.J. WOLF. *LANGUAGES:* English and German. *PRACTICE AREAS:* Plant Breeders Rights.

GERARD VAN DER WAL (Resident, Brussels, Belgium Office). *LANGUAGES:* English, French and German. *PRACTICE AREAS:* EC Law; Franchising and Distribution; Commercial Cooperation Agreements; Counterfeiting.

PETER J.L.J. DUIJSENS. *LANGUAGES:* German. *PRACTICE AREAS:* General Commercial Law; Agricultural and Environmental Law.

ERIC GRABANDT. *LANGUAGES:* English and French. *PRACTICE AREAS:* EC Law; Supreme Court Litigation.

ALEXANDER W. BEELAERTS VAN BLOKLAND. *LANGUAGES:* English. *PRACTICE AREAS:* Industrial Relations; Bankruptcy.

HARRY FERMENT. *LANGUAGES:* English and German. *PRACTICE AREAS:* Industrial and Intellectual Property; Commercial Law; Leasing.

(This Listing Continued)

MAX J.M.T. KEULAERDS. *LANGUAGES:* English. *PRACTICE AREAS:* Commercial Law; Labour Law.

ASSOCIATES

Johan A. Verhage	Laurent P.A. Zwijnenberg
Saskia E. Marseille	Pieter B. Kamminga
Dineke Duthler	Dirk J.A. van den Berg
Marleen H.J. van den Horst	Ingrid van Berkel
Dick Th.J. van der Klei	Govert M. Kerpestein
Caroline I. van Gent	Koen M. van Holten
Joost A. Huijgen	Tjeerd E. Monasch
Wietje P. de Muinck Keizer	Sander J. Kaarls
Walter B.J. van Overbeek	Katinka Huges
(Resident, Brussels, Belgium Office)	

NOTARIES/PARTNERS

H. MICHIEL KRANS. *LANGUAGES:* English and German. *PRACTICE AREAS:* Family Law; Foundations; Associations.

ALBIN A. VAN GASTEL. *LANGUAGES:* English, French and Spanish. *PRACTICE AREAS:* Family Law; Real Estate.

EDO A. MULDER. *LANGUAGES:* English, French, German and Portuguese. *PRACTICE AREAS:* Family Law; Real Estate.

JAN WILLEM MEUTER. *LANGUAGES:* English. *PRACTICE AREAS:* Corporate Law.

HENK J.W.M. BRESSERS. *LANGUAGES:* English. *PRACTICE AREAS:* Corporate Law.

J. AART BORGHUIS, Notarial Lawyer. *LANGUAGES:* English and German. *PRACTICE AREAS:* Industrial Real Estate.

OTTO W. DE JONG, Junior Notary. *LANGUAGES:* English and German. *PRACTICE AREAS:* Corporate Law; Industrial Real Estate.

ASSOCIATES

Marja Schimmel	Jacques P. Buiteman
Frank W.M. Roes	Pieter H. Hendrikse
Frans J.M.I. van Rijckevorsel van Kessel	Paul M. Eversdijk
	Nini E. Schot
L. Nicolette de Groot	Annemarie Th. Heymen
Patricia J.M. Burgemeester	

BURUMA MARIS

Civil Lawyers, Tax Lawyers and Civil Law Notaries

Established in 1968

SCHEVENINGSEWEG 66

2517 KX THE HAGUE, THE NETHERLANDS

Telephone: 070-3529500

Telefax: 070-3503014

Mailing Address: P.O. Box 84046, 2508 AA The Hague

Rotterdam, The Netherlands Office: Schouwburgplein 32, 3012 CL. Mailing Address: P.O. Box 1174, 3000 BD. Telephone: 010-4333755. Telefax: 010-4141503; 010-4045908.

All cases before The Supreme Court of The Netherlands, International Law, Product Liability, Civil and Business related Criminal Litigation, Corporate Law, Banking Law, EEC Law (Antitrust Competition and Trade Matters), Tort, Intellectual Property Law (Trademark, Patent, Know How, Copyright, Model and Designs, Piracy), Employment Law, Medical Law, Insurance Law, National and International Tax Law, International Arbitration, Press and Media Law (Protection of Information), Computer Law, Telecommunication Law, Real Estate and Lease Law, Construction Law, Administrative Law, Conveyance of Real Estate, Environmental Issues, Mortgages, Incorporation of Public and Private Limited Liability Companies.

Associations and Foundations, Wills, Marriage Settlements, Distributorship, Agency, Franchise, Foreign Investment, International Contracts, Mergers and Acquisitions, Joint Ventures, Reorganizations, Securities Law and International Finance.

Dutch attorneys may represent clients before all Dutch courts, before the European Court of Justice and the Benelux Court of Justice and are admitted to plead before all courts of the member States of the Common Market (EC). Only attorneys admitted to The Hague Bar may plead before the Supreme Court of the Netherlands.

(This Listing Continued)

PARTNERS CIVIL LAWYERS

S. LEONARD BURUMA (Retired, 1993).

AUGUST G. MARIS (Retired, 1992).

JAN WILLEM MEIJER, born 1932; admitted, 1957, The Hague. *Education:* Leyden University (1955). Deputy Judge, Court of Appeal, The Hague, 1985—. *Member:* Netherlands Bar Association. *LANGUAGES:* Dutch, English, French and German. *PRACTICE AREAS:* Property; Planning Law; Expropriation; Environmental Law.

JAN Y. GROENEVELD, born 1934; admitted, 1959, The Hague. *Education:* Leyden University (1956); Harvard Law School (LL.M., 1957). *Member:* Netherlands Bar Association. *LANGUAGES:* Dutch, English, French and German. *PRACTICE AREAS:* Insurance Law; Pension Law; Medical Law; Employment Law; Administrative Law; Litigation.

SICCO V. LANGEVELD, born 1935; admitted, 1962, The Hague. *Education:* Leyden University (1958). Arbitrator, International Chamber of Commerce and Netherlands Arbitration Institute. Member, Appeal Court of Ethics, Netherlands Tax Lawyers Organization. *Member:* Netherlands Bar Association; International Law Association; Netherlands Comparative Law Association. *LANGUAGES:* Dutch, English, French and German. *PRACTICE AREAS:* Corporate Law; Arbitration; Civil and Business related Criminal Litigation.

ERNST M. ENSCHEDÉ, born 1938; admitted, 1965, The Hague. *Education:* Leyden University (1962). Member: Board of Supervisory, Director of John Brown Engineers & Construction B.V.; De Weger Architecten - en Ingenieursbureau B.V.; 3M Nederland B.V.; Netherlands Refining Company (BP/Texaco Joint Venture) B.V.; Texaco Raffinaderij Pernis B.V.; Texaco Investment Netherlands Inc.; Texaco Petroleum Maatschappij B.V.; Director of Netherlands Association of Enterprises listed on the Amsterdam Stock Exchange. *Member:* Netherlands Bar Association. *LANGUAGES:* Dutch, English, French and German. *PRACTICE AREAS:* Corporate Law; Commercial Arbitration and Litigation.

PROF. EGBERT J. DOMMERING, born 1943; admitted, 1968, The Hague. *Education:* Amsterdam University (1968). Professor, Media and Telecommunication, Intellectual Property and Computer Law, Amsterdam University, 1988—. Editor, "Computer Law." Member, Editorial Board of AMI (Law on Information and Copyright), 1985—. Annotator of the Judgements of the European Court of Human Rights in the Dutch Official Legal Report, 1991—. Deputy Judge, District Court, The Hague. *Member:* Netherlands Bar Association; AIPPA; ALAI. *LANGUAGES:* Dutch, English, French and German. *PRACTICE AREAS:* Media; Telecommunications; Computers; Data Protection; Intellectual Property; Civil Rights.

ABRAHAM L. ASSCHER, born 1943; admitted, 1969, The Hague. *Education:* Amsterdam University (1967). Member, Supervisory Board of Directors, Beleggingsmaatschappij De Bron, 1985—. Deputy Cantonal Judge, The Hague, 1984—. *Member:* International (SBL) and Netherlands Bar Associations. *LANGUAGES:* Dutch, English, French and German. *PRACTICE AREAS:* Labour Law; Collective Labour Law; Arbitration.

FRANK H.A.M. THUNNISSEN, born 1943; admitted, 1971, The Hague. *Education:* Leyden University (1967); University of Grenoble, France (1964); Kings College, London, England (1973). Member, Supervisory Board of Starke Diekstra. Member of the Board of the Association for Construction Law. Member of the Board, Netherlands Arbitration Institute. *LANGUAGES:* Dutch, English, French and German. *PRACTICE AREAS:* Property; Planning Law; Construction; Environmental Law.

JUSTUS VOÛTE, born 1948; admitted, 1973, The Hague; 1990, Rotterdam. *Education:* Amsterdam University (1973). Arbitrator, Netherlands Arbitration Institute. Co-Author: "Due Diligence, Disclosures and Warranties in the Corporate Acquisitions Practice and Remedies for International Sellers of goods." Member, Board of Directors, Administratiekantoor Weweler N.V. *Member:* International (SBL) and Netherlands Bar Associations. *LANGUAGES:* Dutch and English. *PRACTICE AREAS:* Corporate Law; Foreign Investment; Joint Ventures; Mergers and Acquisitions; International Contracts; Distributorship; Agencies.

PETER J.M. VON SCHMIDT AUF ALTENSTADT, born 1947; admitted, 1975, The Hague. *Education:* Leyden University (1973). *Member:* Netherlands Bar Association. *LANGUAGES:* Dutch, English, French and German. *PRACTICE AREAS:* Litigation; Lease; Labour Law.

CEES JAN HAGEN, born 1954; admitted, 1980, The Hague. *Education:* Free University of Amsterdam (1978). *Member:* Netherlands Bar Association. *LANGUAGES:* Dutch, English, French and German. *PRACTICE AREAS:* Labour Law; Collective Labour Law.

(This Listing Continued)

ROBERT S. MEIJER, born 1948; admitted, 1984, The Hague. *Education:* Amsterdam University (1972); London University (LL.M., 1973). Former Assistant Professor: Amsterdam University; Netherlands Bar Association. Former Member, New Civil Code Division of the Ministry of Justice, 1979-1984. Co-Editor, Handbook on Administrative Law. *Member:* Netherlands Bar Association (Chairman of it's Committee on Civil Law and tutor of it's Civil Procedure Course). *LANGUAGES:* Dutch, English, French and German. *PRACTICE AREAS:* Litigation; Insurance Law; General Practice.

SEVERIN DE WIT, born 1952; admitted, 1978, Rotterdam; 1980, Amsterdam; 1989, The Hague. *Education:* Amsterdam University (Political Sciences); Free University of Amsterdam (Civil Law). Member, Board of Editors, IER (Intellectual Property and Advertisement Law), 1984—. Deputy Judge, District Court, The Hague, 1988—. *Member:* ABA; USTA; AIPLA; AIPPI. *LANGUAGES:* Dutch, English, French and German. *PRACTICE AREAS:* Intellectual Property; Pharmaceutical Law.

INNE G.F. CATH, born 1952; admitted, 1979, Amsterdam; 1989, The Hague. *Education:* Erasmus University, Rotterdam; Cambridge University Board of Extramural Studies (English Legal Method). Member, Strassbourg University (EEC and Comparative Law); Extramural Advisory Board on Post Graduate Studies. Lecturer, EEC Law, Limburg University, 1987—. Contributor, EC Law Practice Book. *Member:* Netherlands and International Bar Associations; League Internationale contre la Concurrence Déloyale; Fédération Internationale de Droit Européen (Dutch Section); Netherlands Association of International Law; European Movement (Dutch Section). *LANGUAGES:* Dutch, English, French, German and Russian. *PRACTICE AREAS:* EEC Law (Competition, Free Movement, Anti-Dumping).

SEBASTIAAN A. BOELE, born 1957; admitted, 1983, The Hague. *Education:* Leyden University (1983). *Member:* Netherlands and International Bar Associations. *LANGUAGES:* Dutch, English, French and German. *PRACTICE AREAS:* Corporate and Banking Law.

MONIQUE A.J. VREEBURG, born 1963; admitted, 1986, The Hague. *Education:* Leyden University (1985). *Member:* Netherlands Bar Association. *LANGUAGES:* Dutch, English, French and German. *PRACTICE AREAS:* Corporate Law; Mergers and Acquisitions; Franchise Law; Employment Law.

MARJOLEIN J. GEUS, born 1962; admitted, 1986, The Hague. *Education:* Utrecht University (1986). *Member:* International Bar Association; European Air Law Association; AIPPI; LES. *LANGUAGES:* Dutch, English, French and German.

OF COUNSEL

AUGUST G. MARIS, born 1924; admitted, 1946, The Hague. *Education:* Utrecht University (1946). Member, Board of Supervisory Directors, ABN AMRO Holding N.V., Heineken N.V. *Member:* Netherlands Bar Association. (Retired). *LANGUAGES:* Dutch, English, French and German.

DAAN SCHEER, born 1932. *Education:* State Tax Academy (RBA), 1955). Tax Inspector, 1957-1964. *Member:* NOB (Dutch Association of Tax Lawyers); International Fiscal Association. (Retired). *LANGUAGES:* Dutch, English, French and German. *PRACTICE AREAS:* Capital Taxation; Corporate Taxation; Inheritance; Estate and Gift Taxation; Personal Income Taxation; General Tax Practice.

PARTNERS TAX LAWYERS

DAAN SCHEER (Retired, 1993).

JAN J.J.H. DANIËLS, born 1944. *Education:* State Tax Academy, Rotterdam (1966); Tilburg University (1969). Tax Inspector, 1966-1969. Assistant Professor Tilburg University, 1969-1977. Member of the Board, Tilburg University, 1974-1976. Tax Lawyer, 1976—. *Member:* NOB (Dutch Association of Tax Lawyers); International Bar Association; International Fiscal Association. *LANGUAGES:* Dutch, English, French and German. *PRACTICE AREAS:* Corporate Income Tax; Mergers and Acquisitions; EC Tax Legislation; International Investments Tax.

RENE N.G. VAN DER PAARDT, born 1952. *Education:* Erasmus University, Rotterdam (Economics, 1975); Leyden University (Tax Law, 1977). Tax Inspector 1978-1984. *Member:* NOB (Dutch Association of Tax Lawyers); International Bar Association. *LANGUAGES:* Dutch, English, French and German. *PRACTICE AREAS:* Indirect Taxation; Value Added Taxation; Customs and Excise Legislation; Real Estate Investment.

MARC L.M. DE BRUIJN, born 1947. *Education:* Leyden University (Tax Law, 1974). Tax Inspector, 1974-1978. *Member:* NOB (Dutch Associ-

(This Listing Continued)

BURUMA MARIS, The Hague—Continued

ation of Tax Lawyers); International Fiscal Association; International Bar Association. *LANGUAGES:* Dutch, English, French and German. *PRACTICE AREAS:* Corporate Taxation; Financial Instruments; Venture Capital; Taxation of Foreign Nationals; General Tax Practice; Mergers and Acquisitions.

PETER H.M. FLIPSEN, born 1954. *Education:* Tilburg University (1980). *Member:* NOB (Dutch Association of Tax Lawyers); International Fiscal Association; International Bar Association. *LANGUAGES:* Dutch, English, French and German. *PRACTICE AREAS:* International Tax Law; Corporate Taxation; General Tax Practice.

HANS C. BOL, born 1956. *Education:* Leyden University (1981 and 1983). *Member:* NOB (Dutch Association of Tax Lawyers); International Fiscal Association; International Bar Association. *LANGUAGES:* Dutch, English, French and German. *PRACTICE AREAS:* International Taxation; Trusts.

PETER C.P. PRIESTER, born 1955. *Education:* Erasmus University Rotterdam (1980); Leyden University (1983). *LANGUAGES:* Dutch and English.

PARTNERS CIVIL LAW NOTARIES

LAMBERTUS VAN SOLKEMA, born 1929. *Education:* Leyden University (1952). Member: Board of Supervisory Directors, VSB Groep N.V.; Onderlinge Levensverzekeringmaatschappij's-Gravenhage H. Wesselius & Co B.V. (Effectenbank). *Member:* Koninklijke Notariële Broederschap. *LANGUAGES:* Dutch, English, French and German.

ONNO J.M. DE BRUIJN, born 1949. *Education:* Leyden University (1973). *Member:* Koninklijke Notariële Broederschap; International Fiscal Association; Association of Construction Law. *LANGUAGES:* Dutch and English.

WILLEM F.O. STRICKER, born 1947. *Education:* Leyden University (1972). *Member:* Koninklijke Notariële Broederschap; International Fiscal Association; Board of Supervisory Directors Vendue Huis der Notarissen; Internationaal Juridisch Instituut. *LANGUAGES:* Dutch, English, French and German.

GERDA KLEYKAMP-VAN DER BEN, born 1954. *Education:* Leyden University (Civil Law, 1980; Notarial, 1989). *Member:* Koninklijke Notariële Broederschap; International Fiscal Association. *LANGUAGES:* Dutch, English, French and German.

ASSOCIATES CIVIL LAWYERS

HENRIETTE M. SLAGHEKKE, born 1958; admitted, 1983, The Hague. *Education:* Utrecht University (1982). *Member:* Netherlands Bar Association. *LANGUAGES:* Dutch, English and German. *PRACTICE AREAS:* Construction; Property; Planning Law.

HARRY L.M. REK, born 1961; admitted, 1985, Rotterdam. *Education:* Erasmus University, Rotterdam (1985); Columbia Law School (Summer Program, 1986). *Member:* Netherlands and International Bar Associations; Netherlands Securities Law Association. *LANGUAGES:* Dutch and English. *PRACTICE AREAS:* Corporate Law; Securities Law; Mergers and Acquisitions; International Finance; Joint Ventures.

MARTIN E. GELPKE, born 1958; admitted, 1987, The Hague. *Education:* Free University of Amsterdam (1986). *Member:* Netherlands Bar Association. *LANGUAGES:* Dutch, English, French and German. *PRACTICE AREAS:* Environmental Law; Zoning Law; Administrative Law.

TANJA H. TANJA-VAN DEN BROEK, born 1964; admitted, 1987, The Hague. *Education:* Leyden University (1987). *Member:* Netherlands Bar Association. *LANGUAGES:* Dutch, English, French and German. *PRACTICE AREAS:* Civil Law; Labour Law.

ERIC J.J.M. LIMPENS, born 1960; (admission pending); admitted, 1987, The Hague. *Education:* Nijmegen University (1987). *Member:* Netherlands Bar Association. *LANGUAGES:* Dutch, English, French and German. *PRACTICE AREAS:* Corporate Law; Security Law; General Business Law.

FRANCISCA C. BOEL, born 1960; admitted, 1989, The Hague. *Education:* Amsterdam University (International Law, 1987; Civil Law, 1988); Grotius Academy, Amsterdam. *Member:* Netherlands Bar Association. *LANGUAGES:* Dutch, English, French and German. *PRACTICE AREAS:* Labour Law.

(This Listing Continued)

MAYA A. KUYT-FOKKENS, born 1961; admitted, 1990, The Hague. *Education:* Leyden University (Literature, 1985); Utrecht University (Civil Law, 1990). *Member:* Netherlands Bar Association. *LANGUAGES:* Dutch, English, French and German.

JAN PETER VAN DEN BERG, born 1962; admitted, 1991, The Hague. *Education:* Leyden University (1988). *Member:* Netherlands Bar Association. *LANGUAGES:* Dutch, English and German.

ROEL W.J. KERCKHOFFS, born 1965; admitted, 1990, The Hague. *Education:* Tilburg University (1988). *LANGUAGES:* Dutch, English, French and German. *PRACTICE AREAS:* Tax Law; Corporate Law.

LEONIE M. EBBEKINK, born 1967; admitted, 1991, The Hague. *Education:* Leyden University (1989); Edinburgh University (LL.M., 1990). *Member:* Netherlands Bar Association. *LANGUAGES:* Dutch, English, French and German.

JANET M. VAN ZOEST-KRIJGER, born 1966; admitted, 1991, The Hague. *Education:* Leyden University (1988 and 1991). *Member:* Netherlands Bar Association. *LANGUAGES:* Dutch, English, French and Spanish.

INGRID W.A. PUTKER-OOSTENBRINK, born 1964; admitted, 1991, The Hague. *Education:* Free University of Amsterdam (1989); University of London (LL.M., 1990). *Member:* Netherlands Bar Association. *LANGUAGES:* Dutch, English, French and German.

BERNARD E.L.J.C. VERBUNT, born 1966; admitted, 1991, The Hague. *Education:* Leyden University (1991). *Member:* Netherlands Bar Association. *LANGUAGES:* Dutch, English, French and German.

DOROTHÉ T.M.J. SMITS, born 1966; admitted, 1992, The Hague. *Education:* Erasmus University, Rotterdam (1991). *Member:* Netherlands Bar Association. *LANGUAGES:* Dutch, English, French and German.

JEANETTE C. MINGAARS, born 1969; admitted, 1992, The Hague. *Education:* Erasmus University, Rotterdam (1992). *Member:* Netherlands Bar Association. *LANGUAGES:* Dutch, English, French and German.

KLEIS W.H. BROEKHUIZEN, born 1967; admitted, 1992, The Hague. *Education:* Erasmus University, Rotterdam (1992). *Member:* Netherlands Bar Association. *LANGUAGES:* Dutch, English and German.

JANINE W.C. VERSCHOOR, born 1967; admitted, 1992, The Hague. *Education:* Leyden University (1992). *Member:* Netherlands Bar Association. *LANGUAGES:* Dutch, English, French and German.

ROEL J.G. VEUGELERS, born 1968; admitted, 1992, The Hague. *Education:* Erasmus University, Rotterdam (1991); College of Europe Bruges, Belgium (EC Law, 1992). *Member:* Netherlands Bar Association. *LANGUAGES:* Dutch, English, French and German.

LIANNE J. VAN POORTVLIET, born 1968; admitted, 1992, The Hague. *Education:* Leyden University (1992). *Member:* Netherlands Bar Association. *LANGUAGES:* Dutch, English and German.

JOLANDA M. BOSSINK, born 1969; admitted, 1993, The Hague. *Education:* Utrecht University (1992). *Member:* Netherlands Bar Association. *LANGUAGES:* Dutch, English, French, German and Spanish.

WILLEM WILLE, born 1967; admitted, 1993, Rotterdam. *Education:* Leyden University (1991); University of Chicago (LL.M., 1992). *Member:* Netherlands Bar Association. *LANGUAGES:* Dutch, English, French and German.

HESTER H. DE KROON-BIEWENGA, born 1967; admitted, 1993, The Hague. *Education:* Leyden University (1992). *Member:* Netherlands Bar Association. *LANGUAGES:* Dutch, English and German.

EUGÈNE J.M. ROSIER, born 1961; admitted, 1993, Rotterdam. *Education:* Amsterdam University (1986); Maastricht University (1992). *Member:* Netherlands Bar Association. *LANGUAGES:* Dutch, English and German. *PRACTICE AREAS:* Tax Law; Business related Criminal Litigation.

DESIREE T.G.F.M. MERKX, born 1967; admitted, 1993, The Hague. *Education:* Leyden University (1992). *Member:* Netherlands Bar Association. *LANGUAGES:* Dutch, English and German.

FERRY E. KERKVLIET, born 1966; admitted, 1993, The Hague. *Education:* Utrecht University (1993). *Member:* Netherlands Bar Association. *LANGUAGES:* Dutch, English and German.

PIETER BAS SISSING, born 1964; admitted, 1993, The Hague. *Education:* Groningen University (1991). *Member:* Netherlands Bar Association. *LANGUAGES:* Dutch, English, French, and German.

(This Listing Continued)

MAARTJE J. HAMER, born 1956; admitted, 1993, The Hague. *Education:* Groningen University (1983); Amsterdam University (1986). *Member:* Netherlands Bar Association. *LANGUAGES:* Dutch and English.

NATHALIE VAN WOERKOM, born 1970; admitted, 1993, The Hague. *Education:* Erasmus University, Rotterdam (1993). *Member:* Netherlands Bar Association. *LANGUAGES:* Dutch, English and French.

IRMA C. VAN EENDENBURG, born 1965; admitted, 1993, Rotterdam. *Education:* Leyden University (1993). *Member:* Netherlands Bar Association. *LANGUAGES:* Dutch and English.

DIANA G.A. VAN DER AREND, born 1969; admitted, 1994, Rotterdam. *Education:* Erasmus University, Rotterdam (1994). *Member:* Netherlands Bar Association. *LANGUAGES:* Dutch, English, French and German.

KATINKA J. TATTERSALL, born 1968; admitted, 1994, The Hague. *Education:* Leyden University (1992); University of London (LL.M., 1993). *Member:* Netherlands Bar Association. *LANGUAGES:* Dutch and English.

GREGOR S.P. VOS, born 1967; admitted, 1994, The Hague. *Education:* Amsterdam University (1992); London University (1993). *Member:* Netherlands Bar Association. *LANGUAGES:* Dutch, English and German.

ARTHUR M.B. HOLTGREFE, born 1968; admitted, 1994, The Hague. *Education:* Leyden University (1993). *Member:* Netherlands Bar Association. *LANGUAGES:* Dutch, English and German.

MARCEL G.C.M. PEETERS, born 1957; admitted, 1994, The Hague. *Education:* Erasmus University, Rotterdam (1977 and 1982); Cambridge University (1981 and 1984); Leyden University (1994). *Member:* Netherlands Bar Association. *LANGUAGES:* Dutch, English, French, German and Italian.

EDITH C. VAN DUUREN, born 1968; admitted, 1994, The Hague. *Education:* Leyden University (1993). *Member:* Netherlands Bar Association. *LANGUAGES:* Dutch, English and German.

ASSOCIATES TAX LAWYERS

LEO F. DELFGAAUW, born 1954. *Education:* Leyden University (1981). *LANGUAGES:* Dutch, English and German. *PRACTICE AREAS:* National Tax Law.

MAARTJE J. HAMER, born 1956. *Education:* Amsterdam University (1986). *LANGUAGES:* Dutch and English.

EUGÈNE J.M. ROSIER, born 1961; admitted, 1993, Rotterdam. *Education:* Amsterdam University (1986); Maastricht University (1992). *Member:* Netherlands Bar Association. *LANGUAGES:* Dutch, English and German. *PRACTICE AREAS:* Tax Law; Civil and Business related Criminal Litigation.

RENÉ E.P.J. VAN ELDONK, born 1962. *Education:* Tilburg University (1987). *LANGUAGES:* Dutch and English.

ROEL W.J. KERCKHOFFS, born 1965. *Education:* Tilburg University (1988). *LANGUAGES:* Dutch and English.

FRISO J.H. VAN DE PAVOORDT, born 1951. *Member:* Dutch Federation of Tax Consultants. *LANGUAGES:* Dutch and English. *PRACTICE AREAS:* Tax Law.

THEO OSTERMANN, born 1964. *Education:* Leyden University (1994). *Member:* Dutch Federation of Tax Consultants. *LANGUAGES:* Dutch, English and German. *PRACTICE AREAS:* National Tax Law.

ERIK H.J. KAMPHUIS, born 1964. *Education:* Groningen University (1990); Erasmus University, Rotterdam (1994). *LANGUAGES:* Dutch, English and German.

FRANK P.G. PÖTGENS, born 1964. *Education:* Tilburg University (1989); Brussels University (1991). *LANGUAGES:* Dutch and English.

JOHN WILLEKES MACDONALD, born 1966. *Education:* Leyden University (1993). *LANGUAGES:* Dutch and English.

HANS R. VERSTAPPEN, born 1971. *Education:* Maastricht University (1993). *LANGUAGES:* Dutch, English and German.

LUC A. VAN DIJK, born 1966. *Education:* Neijenrode University (1988); Leyden University (1993). *LANGUAGES:* Dutch, English and German.

(This Listing Continued)

ASSOCIATES CIVIL LAW NOTARIES

BOUDEWIJN WAAIJER, born 1959. *Education:* Leyden University (1982); Tilburg University (1986). *LANGUAGES:* Dutch and English.

JAN W.T. THOMASSEN, born 1962. *Education:* Utrecht University (1986); Amsterdam University (1988). *LANGUAGES:* Dutch and English.

MARLEEN U.M.A. LINDERS, born 1968. *Education:* Leyden University (1993). *LANGUAGES:* Dutch and English.

KLAS INE J. VISSER, born 1969. *Education:* Leyden University (1993). *LANGUAGES:* Dutch and English.

MARIKE F. VISSER, born 1970. *Education:* Utrecht University (1993-1994). *LANGUAGES:* Dutch, English and German.

JÖRGEN L.E. HUYBEN, born 1968. *Education:* Leyden University (1993). *LANGUAGES:* Dutch, English, French and German.

DE BRAUW BLACKSTONE WESTBROEK

Attorneys and Civil Law Notaries

ZUID HOLLANDLAAN 7
2596 AL THE HAGUE, THE NETHERLANDS
Telephone: (70) 328 5 328
Telex: 32321
Telecopier: (70) 328 5 325

REVISERS OF THE NETHERLANDS LAW DIGEST FOR THIS DIRECTORY.

Amsterdam, The Netherlands Office: Atrium - 7th Floor, Strawinskylaan 3115, 1077 ZX. Telephone: (20) 5 481 481. Telex: 10227. Telecopier: (20) 5 481 485.

Rotterdam, The Netherlands Office: 10th Floor, Coolsingel 139, 3012 AG. Telephone: (10) 401 88 99. Telex: 24676. Telecopier: (10) 411 35 48.

Eindhoven, The Netherlands Office: Parklaan 42a, 5613 BG. Telephone: (40) 464442. Telecopier: (40) 466288.

Brussels, Belgium Office: Brederodestraat 13A, B-1000. Telephone: (2) 505 0211. Telecopier: (2) 502 2644.

London, England Office: Royex House, Aldermanbury Square, EC2V 7HR. Telephone: (171) 600 1719. Fax: (171) 600 1718.

New York, New York Office: 712 Fifth Avenue, 30th Floor, 10019-4102. Telephone: (212) 801-3430. Fax: (212) 801-3435; (212) 801-3436.

Dutch Attorneys may represent clients before all Dutch Courts, before the European Court of Justice and the Benelux Court of Justice, and are admitted to plead before all Courts of the member states of the Common Market (EEC).

Member of Alliance of European Lawyers (EEIG) which regroups six law firms from Continental Europe. The Alliance consists of Oppenhoff & Rädler at Munich, Berlin, Cologne, Frankfurt am Main and Leipzig; De Bandt, van Hecke & Lagae at Brussels and Antwerp; DeBrauw Blackstone Westbroek at Amsterdam, The Hague, Rotterdam, Brussels, London and New York; Jeantet & Associés at Paris and Warsaw; Lagerlöf & Leman at Stockholm, Gothenburg and Malmö; Uria & Menendez at Madrid and Barcelona.

The Alliance member firms have joint offices at Brussels, London, New York and Prague.

ATTORNEYS AT LAW
MEMBERS OF FIRM

HAN COLLOT D'ESCURY, born 1924; admitted, 1953, Netherlands. *Education:* University of Amsterdam. *Member:* International Bar Association. *LANGUAGES:* English, German and French. *PRACTICE AREAS:* Corporate Law; Arbitration.

JAN K. FRANX, born 1929; admitted, 1990, Netherlands. *Education:* University of Amsterdam, Ph.D. University of Amsterdam Private International Law. *LANGUAGES:* English and French. *PRACTICE AREAS:* Competition Law; Maritime/Transportation Law; Private International Law.

TEARTSE SCHAPER, born 1931; admitted, 1958, Netherlands. *Education:* Leyden University; Columbia University, New York; University of Madrid. *Member:* AIPPI (Chairman of the Netherlands Group; Past Executive President and Member of the Board); ALAI; USTA; ECTA; PTMG; LES; FIDE; LIDS. *LANGUAGES:* English, French and German. *PRACTICE AREAS:* Intellectual Property.

(This Listing Continued)

DE BRAUW BLACKSTONE WESTBROEK, The Hague—Continued

J. LODEWIJK W. SILLEVIS SMITT, born 1932; admitted, 1961, The Hague. *Education:* University of Amsterdam. President, Standing Advisory Commission of the Dutch Bar on Dutch Civil Law. President, Netherlands Arbitration Institute. *LANGUAGES:* English, French and German. *PRACTICE AREAS:* Arbitration.

BENNO H. TER KUILE, born 1931; admitted, 1962, Netherlands. *Education:* Leiden University. Professor of European Law, Rotterdam University. *LANGUAGES:* English and French. *PRACTICE AREAS:* EC Law.

PETER VAN SCHILFGAARDE, born 1936; admitted, 1962, Netherlands. *Education:* Leyden University (Ph.D., 1969). Professor of Corporate Law: Groningen University, 1970; Utrecht University, 1989. Member, Supervisory Board, Dutch Central Bank. *LANGUAGES:* English, French and German. *PRACTICE AREAS:* Corporate Law; Bankruptcy Law; Arbitration.

HUGO P. UTERMARK, born 1937; admitted, 1963, The Hague. *Education:* Leyden University. *LANGUAGES:* English. *PRACTICE AREAS:* Labour Law; Health Care Law.

H.D. ONNO BLAUW, born 1941; admitted, 1966, The Hague. *Education:* Utrecht University. *LANGUAGES:* English and German. *PRACTICE AREAS:* Labour Law.

WYBE TAEKEMA, born 1939; admitted, 1966, The Hague. *Education:* Free University of Amsterdam. Substitute Contonnal Judge, The Hague, 1980. *LANGUAGES:* English. *PRACTICE AREAS:* Litigation; Arbitration; Construction/Real Estate Law.

ENNO D. WIERSMA, born 1941; admitted, 1966, Netherlands. *Education:* Leyden University. *LANGUAGES:* English, French and German. *PRACTICE AREAS:* Corporate Law; Labour Law; Arbitration.

OSCAR DE SAVORNIN LOHMAN, born 1940; admitted, 1967, The Hague. *Education:* Leyden University; Harvard Law School (LL.M.). *Member:* U.J.A.; Union Internationale des Avocats; Harvard Law School Association of Europe. *LANGUAGES:* English. *PRACTICE AREAS:* Administrative Law; Environmental Law.

JAN G. DE VRIES ROBBÉ, born 1941; admitted, 1967, The Hague. *Education:* Groningen University. *LANGUAGES:* English. *PRACTICE AREAS:* Administrative Law; Environmental Law.

PIET A. WACKIE EYSTEN, born 1939; admitted, 1967, The Hague. *Education:* Leyden University; Bell School of Languages, Cambridge (1958). Member, 1984-1986 and Head, 1986—, Netherlands Delegation at the Council of the Bars and Law Societies of the European Community (CCBE). *Member:* Netherlands Order of Advocates (Council Member, 1984-1986; President, 1986-1989). *LANGUAGES:* English, French and German. *PRACTICE AREAS:* EC Law; Arbitration; Civil Procedure.

RUUD M. SCHUTTE, born 1943; admitted, 1969, Netherlands. *Education:* Free University of Amsterdam. *LANGUAGES:* English. *PRACTICE AREAS:* General Practice; Landlord Tenant; Construction Law.

J.L.R. ANTHONY HUYDECOPER, born 1945; admitted, 1970, The Hague. *Education:* Utrecht University. *LANGUAGES:* English and German. *PRACTICE AREAS:* Intellectual Property Law; Computer Law; Construction/Real Estate Law.

ROGIER A.A. DUK, born 1947; admitted, 1972, The Hague. *Education:* University of Amsterdam; Columbia University School of Law (LL.M., 1970). *LANGUAGES:* English, French and German. *PRACTICE AREAS:* Labour Law; EC Law; Arbitration.

SJOERD E. EISMA, born 1949; admitted, 1972, Netherlands. *Education:* Leyden University. *LANGUAGES:* English. *PRACTICE AREAS:* Corporate Law; Financial Law; Arbitration.

SJEF WUISMAN, born 1947; admitted, 1973, The Hague. *Education:* Leyden University. *LANGUAGES:* English and German. *PRACTICE AREAS:* General Practice; Product Liability Law.

LOUIS H. VAN LENNEP, born 1948; admitted, 1973, The Hague. *Education:* Leyden University. Member, Board of Directors of Netherlands Institute of International Relations 'Clingendael'. (Resident, Brussels Office). *LANGUAGES:* English, French and German. *PRACTICE AREAS:* EC Law.

(This Listing Continued)

WILLEM A. HOYNG, born 1946; admitted, 1973, The Hague. *Education:* Leyden University; Kings College London (1976); University of California at Los Angeles (1982). Professor of Civil Law especially Intellectual Property Law, University of Tilburg. *Member:* Association Internationale pour la Protection de la Propriété Industrielle (AIPPI); LICP; LES; USTA; PTG. (Also at Eindhoven Office). *LANGUAGES:* English, French and German. *PRACTICE AREAS:* EC Law; Intellectual Property Law.

JULES C. VAN OVEN, born 1948; admitted, 1975, Netherlands. *Education:* Groningen University. *LANGUAGES:* English. *PRACTICE AREAS:* General Practice including Litigation before the Dutch Supreme Court.

HARRO J.A. KNIJFF, born 1951; admitted, 1975, The Hague. *Education:* Rotterdam University. *LANGUAGES:* English. *PRACTICE AREAS:* Labour Law; Construction/Real Estate Law; Arbitration; Employment Law.

CONSTANT J.J.C. VAN NISPEN, born 1950; admitted, 1977, The Hague. *Education:* Leyden University (Ph.D., 1978). Professor, Civil Procedure, Free University of Amsterdam, 1993. *Member:* International Bar Association; Association Internationale pour la Protection de la Propriété Industrielle (AIPPI). *LANGUAGES:* English. *PRACTICE AREAS:* Competition Law; Intellectual Property Law; Supreme Court Litigation.

HAJO J. BRONKHORST, born 1944; admitted, 1981, The Hague. *Education:* University of Amsterdam. *LANGUAGES:* English, French and German. *PRACTICE AREAS:* EC Law.

PIERRE J.A.M. NIJNENS, born 1953; admitted, 1977, The Hague. *Education:* Utrecht University. *Member:* Association of the Bar of the City of New York; American and International Bar Associations; American Foreign Law Association; Association for the International Commission of Jurists. *LANGUAGES:* English. *PRACTICE AREAS:* Corporate Law; Business Law; Banking Law.

KOEN LIMPERG, born 1954; admitted, 1981, The Hague. *Education:* University of Amsterdam. Researcher, Max-Planck-Institute, Munich, 1981. *Member:* Association Internationale pour la Protection de la Propriété Industrielle (AIPPI); ALAI. *LANGUAGES:* English, French and German. *PRACTICE AREAS:* Intellectual Property Law; Media Law; Advertising and Labelling Law.

MARJA DE LEEUW, born 1955; admitted, 1979, Netherlands. *Education:* Rotterdam University. *LANGUAGES:* English and French. *PRACTICE AREAS:* General Practice; Construction/Real Estate Law; Bankruptcy Law.

J. MAURITS BARENDRECHT, born 1956; admitted, 1982, Netherlands. *Education:* Leyden University. *LANGUAGES:* English. *PRACTICE AREAS:* Labour Law; General Practice; Litigation; Constitutional Law.

MARK B.W. BIESHEUVEL, born 1953; admitted, 1987, The Hague. *Education:* Leyden University. Editor of the Dutch Law Review. *Member:* European Air Law Association; International Association of European Law. *LANGUAGES:* English and French. *PRACTICE AREAS:* Competition Law; EC Law; Distribution/Franchising; Air Transport; Administrative Law.

ERIK H. PIJNACKER HORDIJK, born 1958; admitted, 1983, Amsterdam. *Education:* Utrecht University. *Member:* International Bar Association; Dutch Association for European Law. (Resident, Brussels Office). *LANGUAGES:* English, French and German. *PRACTICE AREAS:* EC Law.

RUUD M. HERMANS, born 1959; admitted, 1984, The Hague. *Education:* Leyden University. *LANGUAGES:* English. *PRACTICE AREAS:* General Practice; Labour Law; Bankruptcy Law.

GODERT C.W. VAN DER FELTZ, born 1955; admitted, 1982, The Hague. *Education:* Utrecht University; University of Michigan Law School, Ann Arbor (LL.M., 11981); Centre de Philosophie du Droit, Universitité de Paris II. *LANGUAGES:* English, French and Ki Swahili. *PRACTICE AREAS:* Environmental Law; Administrative Law; Rural Law.

MAARTEN J. SCHENCK, born 1959; admitted, 1985, The Hague. *Education:* Leyden University. *LANGUAGES:* English. *PRACTICE AREAS:* Litigation especially Supreme Court Litigation.

MARINA S. DE KORT-DE WOLDE, born 1962; admitted, 1985, The Hague. *Education:* Groningen University. *LANGUAGES:* English and German. *PRACTICE AREAS:* General Practice; Labour Law.

KAARINA A. ZIMMER, born 1952; admitted, 1988, The Hague. *Education:* Indiana University Chinese (1972); Leyden University. (Resident,

(This Listing Continued)

New York Office). *LANGUAGES:* English, French, German and Chinese. *PRACTICE AREAS:* Corporate Law; Labour Law; International Private Law; Public International Law.

ASSOCIATES

DYMPHNA M. SCHUURMANS, born 1947; admitted, 1973, The Hague. *Education:* Leyden University. *LANGUAGES:* English. *PRACTICE AREAS:* Environmental Law; Administrative Law.

MARTINE H. VAN DER WOUDE, born 1958; admitted, 1985, The Hague. *Education:* University of Amsterdam; Harvard Law School (LL.M., 1984). *LANGUAGES:* English and French. *PRACTICE AREAS:* General Practice.

ALEXANDRA J. SWELHEIM, born 1962; admitted, 1986, The Hague. *Education:* Leyden University. *LANGUAGES:* English. *PRACTICE AREAS:* General Practice; Labour Law.

MARISKA F. BAAIJ, born 1962; admitted, 1987, The Hague. *Education:* Leyden University (1986). *LANGUAGES:* English and German. *PRACTICE AREAS:* General Practice; Labour Law.

WILLEMIEN J.M. DIEKMAN, born 1960; admitted, 1988, Amsterdam. *Education:* University of Amsterdam. *LANGUAGES:* English and French. *PRACTICE AREAS:* Intellectual Property Law; Insurance Law.

PAUL L. REESKAMP, born 1961; admitted, 1988, The Hague. *Education:* University of Amsterdam. *LANGUAGES:* English. *PRACTICE AREAS:* Intellectual Property Law; Computer Law.

SÉBASTIEN W.A.M. VISÉE, born 1963; admitted, 1988, The Hague. *Education:* Leyden University. *LANGUAGES:* English and German. *PRACTICE AREAS:* Corporate Law; Financial Law; Labour Law.

ADRIAAN P. KRANENBURG, born 1964; admitted, 1988, Rotterdam. *Education:* Rotterdam University. *LANGUAGES:* English, French and German. *PRACTICE AREAS:* General Practice.

HANS M.M. STEENBERGHE, born 1959; admitted, 1988, Eindhoven. *Education:* Utrecht University. *LANGUAGES:* English. *PRACTICE AREAS:* Labour Law; Construction/Real Estate Law; Contract Law.

GUIDO F. KEULEN, born 1964; admitted, 1993, The Hague. *Education:* Leyden University. *LANGUAGES:* English and German. *PRACTICE AREAS:* Corporate Law.

JACQUELINE SPIERDIJK, born 1962; admitted, 1988, Amsterdam. *Education:* Groningen University; University of Pennsylvania (LL.M., 1987). *LANGUAGES:* English, French and Spanish. *PRACTICE AREAS:* Intellectual Property Law; Copyright Law.

UCO W. JOUSTRA, born 1963; admitted, 1989, The Hague. *Education:* Groningen University. *LANGUAGES:* English, French and German. *PRACTICE AREAS:* Labour Law; General Practice.

NEILL ANDRÉ DE LA PORTE, born 1961. *Education:* Leyden University; Southern Methodist University, Dallas (LL.M., 1988). *LANGUAGES:* English, French and German. *PRACTICE AREAS:* Corporate Law; Financial Law.

JOHAN T. JOL, born 1963; admitted, 1989, The Hague. *Education:* Utrecht University. *LANGUAGES:* English and French. *PRACTICE AREAS:* Corporate Law; Labour law; Bankruptcy Law.

ROLINE REPELAER VAN DRIEL, born 1964; admitted, 1989, The Hague. *Education:* Utrecht University. *LANGUAGES:* English and German. *PRACTICE AREAS:* General Practice; Criminal Law; Family Law.

WOUTER E. PORS, born 1959; admitted, 1989, The Hague. *Education:* Catholic University of Brabant. *LANGUAGES:* English, French and German. *PRACTICE AREAS:* General Practice; Intellectual Property Law; Education Law.

JAAP TH.A. DE KEIJZER, born 1962; admitted, 1989, The Hague. *Education:* Utrecht University. (Resident, Prague Office). *LANGUAGES:* English. *PRACTICE AREAS:* Corporate Law; Financial Law; Energy Law.

REMMINE A. DUDOK VAN HEEL, born 1965; admitted, 1989, Amsterdam. *Education:* Utrecht University. (Resident, London Office). *LANGUAGES:* English and French. *PRACTICE AREAS:* Corporate Law; Labour Law.

G. ROBERT B. VAN PEURSEM, born 1962; admitted, 1990, The Hague. *Education:* University of Amsterdam. *LANGUAGES:* English. *PRACTICE AREAS:* Labour Law; Competition Law; Intellectual Property Law; Copyright Law.

(This Listing Continued)

MARGOT E. KOKKE, born 1963; admitted, 1990, The Hague. *Education:* Leyden University. *LANGUAGES:* English, French and German. *PRACTICE AREAS:* Labour Law; Intellectual Property Law; (Bio) Chemistry.

BARBARA KLOPPERT, born 1966; admitted, 1990, The Hague. *Education:* Nijmegen University. *LANGUAGES:* English, French and German. *PRACTICE AREAS:* Administrative Law; Environmental Law; Family Law.

MONIQUE T.P.J. VAN OERS, born 1966; admitted, 1990, The Hague. *Education:* Limburg University. (Resident Brussels Office). *LANGUAGES:* English and French. *PRACTICE AREAS:* EC Law.

FRITS J. DE VRIES, born 1959; admitted, 1990, Amsterdam. *Education:* Leyden University. *LANGUAGES:* English. *PRACTICE AREAS:* Administrative Law; Environmental Law.

JAN M. HEIKENS, born 1962; admitted, 1990, The Hague. *Education:* Groningen University. *LANGUAGES:* English, French and German. *PRACTICE AREAS:* General Practice; Landlord Tenant; Construction Law.

MONICA F.M.T. FRANKE, born 1967; admitted, 1990, The Hague. *Education:* Nijmegen University; D.E.A. de droit privé Université de Poitiers. (Also at Eindhoven Office).

JOLANDA KRIJGSMAN, born 1965; admitted, 1990, Amsterdam. *Education:* University of Amsterdam.

JAN-WILLEM DE BOER, born 1964; admitted, 1991, The Hague. *Education:* Rotterdam University.

PETER HABERMEHL, born 1965; admitted, 1991, The Hague. *Education:* Leyden University.

INES A. HOEDEMAEKER, born 1966; admitted, 1991, The Hague. *Education:* Leyden University.

DIRK VAN OOSTVEEN, born 1963; admitted, 1991, Amsterdam. *Education:* University of Amsterdam.

JAAP W. WINTER, born 1963; admitted, 1991, The Hague. *Education:* Groningen University (Ph.D., 1992).

ARMAND KILLAN, born 1966; admitted, 1991, The Hague. *Education:* Groningen University.

JORIS P. VAN DER GOES VAN NATERS, born 1963; admitted, 1992, Amsterdam. *Education:* University of Amsterdam.

MARIE FRANCE ADMIRAAL, born 1967; admitted, 1992, The Hague. *Education:* Leyden University.

GERHARDUS W. VAN DER BEND, born 1967; admitted, 1992, The Hague. *Education:* Leyden University.

MIRJAM DUYSER, born 1965; admitted, 1992, The Hague. *Education:* Free University of Amsterdam.

INGRID BERGWERF, born 1963; admitted, 1992, The Hague. *Education:* Rotterdam University.

JAN EKKES MOLENAAR, born 1959; admitted, 1992, Rotterdam. *Education:* Leyden University.

NICOLIEN H. VAN DEN BIGGELAAR, born 1967; admitted, 1992, The Hague. *Education:* Nijmegen University; European University Institute, Florence (LL.M., 1990).

MARC DE VRIES, born 1962; admitted, 1992, The Hague. *Education:* Utrecht University.

VINCENT-PAUL AARTS, born 1961; admitted, 1992, The Hague. *Education:* Catholic University of Brabant.

BART J. VAN DEN BROEK, born 1966; admitted, 1992, The Hague. *Education:* University of Amsterdam; Columbia Law School (LL.M., 1992).

JOLLING K. DE PREE, born 1967; admitted, 1992, Amsterdam. *Education:* Groningen University.

ROEL J. THEISSEN, born 1968; admitted, 1992, The Hague. *Education:* Nijmegen University.

TOBIAS COHEN JEHORAM, born 1967; admitted, 1992, The Hague. *Education:* Leyden University.

JORIS C.H. VAN MANEN, born 1964; admitted, 1992, Amsterdam. *Education:* University of Amsterdam.

(This Listing Continued)

DE BRAUW BLACKSTONE WESTBROEK, The Hague—Continued

PETRA E.M. BANK, born 1967; admitted, 1992, Amsterdam. *Education:* University of Amsterdam.

RIXT S. DE VRIES, born 1964; admitted, 1993, The Hague. *Education:* Rotterdam University.

MARC G.A.M. CUSTERS, born 1965; admitted, 1993, The Hague. *Education:* Nijmegen University. (Resident, Brussels Office).

LEONTIEN A.A.M. VAN DER HEIJDEN, born 1966; admitted, 1993, The Hague. *Education:* Utrecht University.

JELLE A. KROES, born 1966; admitted, 1993, Amsterdam. *Education:* University of Amsterdam.

RENÉ R. BROUWER, born 1966; admitted, 1993, The Hague. *Education:* University of Amsterdam. (Resident, Amsterdam Office).

ANTOINETTE E. SPRENGER, born 1966; admitted, 1993, The Hague. *Education:* Groningen University.

A. PAULINE SCHOONBROOD-WESSELS, born 1962; admitted, 1993, The Hague. *Education:* Nijmegen University.

OLAF G. TROJAN, born 1965; admitted, 1993, The Hague. *Education:* Leyden University.

FLEUR E. VAN HOEKEN, born 1968; admitted, 1993, The Hague. *Education:* Leyden University.

MARIËLLE DUYN, born 1965; admitted, 1993, The Hague. *Education:* Free University of Amsterdam; Boalt Hall Law School Berkeley U.S.A. (1992).

GEERT H. LANKHORST, born 1962; admitted, 1993, The Hague. *Education:* Leyden University.

MARIE-HÉLÈNE D.B. SCHUTJENS, born 1961; admitted, 1993, The Hague. *Education:* Utrecht University.

JAN HARRO F. SCHULTZ VAN HAEGEN, born 1967; admitted, 1993, The Hague. *Education:* Leyden University.

KARIN SCHADEE, born 1968; admitted, 1993, The Hague. *Education:* University of Amsterdam.

JAN L. STOOP, born 1967; admitted, 1993, The Hague. *Education:* Limburg University.

ADRIENNE L.H. HOEVERS, born 1967; admitted, 1993, The Hague. *Education:* Leyden University.

JAN HEINSIUS, born 1966; admitted, 1994, The Hague. *Education:* Leyden University.

STEVEN GEERLINGS, born 1964; admitted, 1994, The Hague. *Education:* Utrecht University.

ALEXANDER HARMSE, born 1969; admitted, 1994, The Hague. *Education:* Utrecht University.

MARK P. VAN DEN HOEK, born 1965; admitted, 1994, The Hague. *Education:* Utrecht University.

HÉLÈNE M.J.M. TIELEMANS, born 1968; admitted, 1994, The Hague. *Education:* Leyden University.

MIEK J. VAN NIEUWKUYK, born 1967; admitted, 1994, The Hague. *Education:* Leyden University.

LUCIAN F.E. POLLINGTON, born 1961; admitted, 1994, The Hague. *Education:* University of Essex, Colchester, U.K.

JULIA MENDLIK, born 1969; admitted, 1994, The Hague. *Education:* Leyden University.

HANNA G. SEVENSTER, born 1963; admitted, 1994, The Hague. *Education:* Leyden University.

LEGAL ASSISTANTS

LINDA M. CROES, born 1956. *Education:* Rotterdam University.

WILLY T. B. CLAASSEN-DALES, born 1947. *Education:* Leyden University.

MARTŸNTJE K. GRANDE-V.D. BERGE, born 1959. *Education:* Leyden University.

(This Listing Continued)

CIVIL LAW NOTARIES
MEMBERS OF FIRM

WENDA H.G. KROON-WELP, born 1940; appointed Civil Law Notary, 1974, The Hague. *Education:* Groningen University. *LANGUAGES:* English and German. *PRACTICE AREAS:* Construction/Real Estate Law; Notarial Law.

FRANS A.A. DUYNSTEE, born 1941; appointed Civil Law Notary, 1980, The Hague. *Education:* Leyden University. *LANGUAGES:* English, French and German. *PRACTICE AREAS:* Corporate Law; Notarial Law; Private International Law.

H. PIETER A. KLAPWIJK, born 1950; appointed Civil Law Notary, 1988, The Hague. *Education:* Leyden University. *LANGUAGES:* English. *PRACTICE AREAS:* Corporate Law; Notarial Law; Family Law.

HENK J. STEINVOORT, born 1954; appointed Civil Law Notary, 1989, The Hague. *Education:* Leyden University; Columbia Law School (LL.M., 1978). *LANGUAGES:* English, French and German. *PRACTICE AREAS:* Corporate Law; Financial Law; Notarial Law.

ASSOCIATES

KARIN J. TEEUWEN, born 1963. *Education:* Leyden University. *LANGUAGES:* English. *PRACTICE AREAS:* Notarial Law.

JACQUELINE J. BULDER, born 1965. *Education:* Leyden University. *LANGUAGES:* English, French and German. *PRACTICE AREAS:* Corporate Law; Notarial Law.

JAAP H.M. GRYMANS, born 1965. *Education:* Leyden University. *LANGUAGES:* English. *PRACTICE AREAS:* Notarial Law.

GERBRECHT FREHE-OOMS, born 1965. *Education:* Utrecht University. *LANGUAGES.* English. *PRACTICE AREAS:* Notarial Law.

ROBERT COLLENTEUR, born 1965. *Education:* Nijmegen University.

OSKAR N. GIETEMA, born 1968. *Education:* Leyden University.

MADELEINE I.W.E. MUNS, born 1969. *Education:* University of Amsterdam.

CASPAR I.G.J. VON BERGH, born 1969. *Education:* Limburg University.

REVISERS OF THE NETHERLANDS LAW DIGEST FOR THIS DIRECTORY.

(For list of Partners and Counsel of the respective Member Firms see Professional Biographies at: Oppenhoff & Rädler at Munich, Cologne, Frankfurt am Main, Berlin and Leipzig, Germany; De Bandt van Hecke & Lagae at Brussels and Antwerp, Belgium; De Brauw Blackstone Westbroek at The Hague, Rotterdam, Amsterdam and Eindhoven, The Netherlands; Jeantet & Associés, at Paris, France and Warsaw, Poland; Lagerlöf & Leman at Stockholm, Gothenburg and Malmö, Sweden; Uria & Menendez at Madrid and Barcelona, Spain)

DEN HERTOG & KAM

LANGE VOORHOUT 70
2514 EH THE HAGUE, THE NETHERLANDS
Telephone: +31-70-362.41.87
FAX: +31-70-364.84.47

Business and Corporate Law, Intellectual Property, Licensing, Franchising, Employment, Landlord & Tenant, Contract Law.

FIRM PROFILE: *The firm aims to combine the high quality associated with the bigger firms with the flexibility and quick service afforded by its lesser size. The firm has extensive international experience and excellent contacts in most foreign countries without being affiliated to a particular chain of law offices.*

PARTNERS

WILLEM KAM, born 1950; admitted, 1975, Rotterdam Bar; 1989, The Hague Bar. *Education:* Leyden University (Law Degree, 1975).

WILLEM DEN HERTOG, born 1950; admitted, 1978, Rotterdam Bar; 1983, The Hague Bar. *Education:* Leyden University (Law Degree, 1977; Chemistry Degree, 1981).

Languages: English, French, German, Dutch

MAALDRINK BUREN

Advocates Civil-Law-Notaries Tax Advisors

GEBOUW CULTURA
WASSENAARSEWEG 20
2596 CH THE HAGUE, THE NETHERLANDS
Telephone: (31) 70 - 346.96.46
Fax: (31) 70 - 356.04.90

FIRM PROFILE: Maaldrink, civil law notaries and advocates has been established in 1912 as a notarial practice and has joined the Bar in 1955. It has merged with Buren & Co. Tax Advisors in 1991 into Maaldrink Buren to offer a full range of legal services to its clients.

Most of the firm's clients are medium sized Dutch and international companies.

The firm has presently seven partners and a legal support staff of 18 associates and a secretarial and administrative staff of 24.

MEMBERS OF FIRM

GERARD LAURENS MAALDRINK, born February 15, 1943; admitted, 1972, The Netherlands. *Education:* Leyden University (Law Degree and Notarial Degree). Civil Law Notary. *Member:* Bar of the Supreme Court; IBA. *PRACTICE AREAS:* Governmental Administration; Notarial Practice.

ANTON HENDRIK VERMEULEN, born October 11, 1943; admitted, 1977, The Netherlands. *Education:* Leyden University (Law Degree). Member, Rotterdam Bar, 1973-1977. *Member:* Bar of the Supreme Court; IBA. *PRACTICE AREAS:* Corporate Law; Mergers; Contracts; Employment Law; Copyright Law; Industrial Property Law; EC Law; Insurance Law; Transport Law; Civil Litigation.

FRITS-NIELS GROOSS, born June 16, 1946; admitted, 1974, The Netherlands. *Education:* Leyden University (Law Degree). *Member:* Bar of the Supreme Court. *PRACTICE AREAS:* Environmental Law; Ecology Law; Real Estate; Project Development Law.

FRANK NICOLAAS DESSING, born November 7, 1948; admitted, 1974, The Netherlands. *Education:* Leyden University (Law Degree and Notarial Degree). Civil Law Notary. *PRACTICE AREAS:* Notarial Practice.

THIJS VERMEULEN, born March 27, 1949; admitted, 1980, The Netherlands. *Education:* Utrecht University (Law Degree); University of Amsterdam (Notarial Degree); University of Cape Town (MBA). Candidate Notary. *Member:* Bar of the Supreme Court. *PRACTICE AREAS:* Real Estate Law; Lease Law; Oil Explorations Law; Notarial Practice.

JOAN PAULUS REINHARD SCHOLTEN, born May 24, 1950; admitted, 1990, The Netherlands. *Education:* University of Amsterdam (Law Degree). Associate, Debevoise Plimpton, New York, 1980-1981. Member, Amsterdam Bar, 1977-1990. *Member:* Bar of the Supreme Court; IBA. *PRACTICE AREAS:* Corporate Law; Employment Law; Copyright Law; Industrial Property Law; Sports Law; Contracts; Civil Litigation; EC Law.

NICOLAAS LODEVICUS BUREN, born August 9, 1947. *Education:* Amsterdam University (Tax Law Degree, 1978). International Tax Advisor, Loyens and Volkmaars, 1978-1990. Private Practice, 1990. Merged with Maaldrink, 1991. *Member:* IBA.

Languages: Dutch, English, French, German and Spanish

MORET ERNST & YOUNG TAX ADVISERS

CORPORATE LAW ADVISORY GROUP

80 WASSENAARSEWEG
P.O. BOX 90636
2509 LP THE HAGUE, THE NETHERLANDS
Telephone: 31-70-3286542
Fax: 31-70-3244003

Amsterdam Office: 20, Drentestraat, P.O. Box 7925, 1008 AC.
Telephone: 31-20-5497333. Fax: 31-20-6462553.
Rotterdam Office: 51, Marten Meesweg, P.O. Box 2295, 3000 CG.
Telephone: 31-10-4072627. Fax: 31-10-4072612.
Groningen Office: 17, Leonard Springerlaan, P.O. Box 997, 9700 AZ.
Telephone: 31-50-994444. Fax: 31-50-270852.

(This Listing Continued)

Arnhem Office: Kronenburgsingel 12, P.O. Box 30116, 6803 AC.
Telephone: 31-85-209500. Fax: 31-85-235151.

Civil Law (general). Computer Law, Insolvency Law, (International) Contracts, Corporate Law, Environmental Law, EC Law, Intellectual Property, Labour Law and Workers Participation, Mergers and Acquisitions, Taxation.

PARTNERS

HANS VAN GIJZEN, born 1951. *Education:* Leyden University. (Resident).

SENIOR-ADVISORS

DORIEN ALEMAN, born 1958. *Education:* Rotterdam University(1981).

HUUB PLEIJSIER, born 1961. *Education:* Leyden University (1986).

(For Complete data see at Amsterdam, The Netherlands)

PETTEN & DIECKEN

Attorneys at Law and Tax Lawyers

VAN STOLKWEG 10
2585 JP THE HAGUE, THE NETHERLANDS
Telephone: +31 70 350 40 55
Telefax: +31 70 350 61 87

Mailing Address: P.O. Box 80504, 2508 GM The Hague, The Netherlands

Administrative Law, Arbitration, Banking Law, Bankruptcy, Civil Servants Labour Law, Corporate Law, Criminal Law, Distribution/Agency/Franchise Practice, Foreign Investments, General Tax Practice (including International Taxation), Insolvency Practice, Insurance Law, Intellectual Property Practice, International Contracts, International Private Law, Litigation, Mergers and Acquisitions, Real Estate Law, Trade Law.
The attorneys are all qualified to appear before the Dutch High Court and other Courts in The Netherlands.

MEMBERS OF FIRM

HOUWERD PETTEN. *PRACTICE AREAS:* Employment and Labour Law; Civil Servants Labour Law; Arbitration.

JAN-CAREL DIECKEN, *Member:* International Bar Association. *PRACTICE AREAS:* Corporate Law; Intellectual Property Practice; Unfair Competition; Trademarks; Copyrights.

LOUIS PH.J. BARON VAN UTENHOVE. *PRACTICE AREAS:* General Practice; Criminal Law; Litigation.

MARC A.B. SASSEN. *PRACTICE AREAS:* Insurance Law; Real Estate Law; Trade Law.

RUDOLF H.A. WESSEL. *PRACTICE AREAS:* Employment and Labour Law; Civil Servants Labour Law.

MARC C. UDINK. *PRACTICE AREAS:* Banking Law; Insolvency and Bankruptcy Law; International Contracts; Mergers and Acquisitions.

JEROEN J.M. GRIBLING, *Member:* Dutch Tax Bar Association (NOB); International Fiscal Association (IFA). *PRACTICE AREAS:* General Tax Practice; International Tax Law; Foreign Investments.

ASSOCIATES

MARION R.P. DRIELSMA. *PRACTICE AREAS:* Family Law; International Private Law.

MARIE LOU SANDBERG-CROMMELIN. *PRACTICE AREAS:* Social Security Law; Labour and Employment Law.

ADA M.C. MARIUS-VAN EEGHEN. *PRACTICE AREAS:* Administrative Law; Real Estate Law.

ROBERT I. DE JONG, *Member:* Dutch Tax Bar Association (NOB). *PRACTICE AREAS:* Mergers and Acquisitions; International Taxation; Foreign Investments.

INGE E.A.M. SCHUGARD, *Member:* Dutch Tax Bar Association (NOB). *PRACTICE AREAS:* General Tax Practice; Expatriates.

BRUNO J. TIDEMAN. *PRACTICE AREAS:* Intellectual Property Practice; Litigation.

ELLY J.M. OOSTERVEER. *PRACTICE AREAS:* Employment and Labour Law; Civil Servants Labour Law; Family Law.

(This Listing Continued)

PETTEN & DIECKEN, The Hague—Continued

PAUL P. HART. PRACTICE AREAS: Corporate Law; Insolvency and Bankruptcy Law.

OLAV VAN DER KIND. PRACTICE AREAS: Employment and Labour Law; Distributorship; Agency and Franchise Law.

Languages: English, French, German, Dutch, Russian and Bahassa Indonesia

---

PELS RIJCKEN & DROOGLEEVER FORTUIJN

Attorneys and Civil Law Notaries

Established in 1968

KONINGIN JULIANAPLEIN 30-A5

P.O. BOX 11756

2502 AT THE HAGUE, THE NETHERLANDS

Telephone: 011 31-70 3488700

Fax: 011 31-70 3477494; 3476719

Brussels, Belgium Office: Stephanie Square, 65 Avenue Louise, Floor 01, 1050. Telephone: (32-2) 535-7852; 535-7853. Fax: (32.2) 535-7700; 535-7724.

General Practice and Business Law, Corporate Law, EEC Law, Industrial and Intellectual Property, Labour Law, Traffic Law, Administrative Law, Environmental Law and Cassation Matters as well as General Contracts and Tort Law.

FIRM PROFILE: The firm is a merger of two long established law firms in The Hague. It is a member of LOGOS, a group of independent law firms established in all EC member states and has a good working relationship with firms in the United States. The firm offers a full range of legal services and has a large litigation practice, both in civil as in administrative proceedings. In 1991 the firm was joined by 3 civil law notaries. The firm consists of 24 partners and 65 associates.

ATTORNEYS AT LAW
MEMBERS OF FIRM

H.TH. BOUMA, born 1944. **LANGUAGES:** Dutch, English, French and German. **PRACTICE AREAS:** Company and Commercial Law; Insolvency Law; Insurance Law; Traffic Accident Law; Banking and Securities Law; Arbitration.

H.A. GROEN, born 1941. **LANGUAGES:** Dutch, English, French and German. **PRACTICE AREAS:** Cassation; Compulsory Purchase; Law dealing with the Civil Liability of Government; Tax Law; Arbitration.

B.D. WUBS, born 1943. **LANGUAGES:** Dutch, English, French and German. **PRACTICE AREAS:** Company and Commercial Law; Environmental Law; Arbitration.

D. DEN HERTOG, born 1944. **LANGUAGES:** Dutch, English, French and German. **PRACTICE AREAS:** Labour Law; Industrial and Intellectual Property Law; Architect's Law; Planning Law; Information, Telecommunication and Media Law.

A.W. KIST, born 1945. **LANGUAGES:** Dutch, English, French and German. **PRACTICE AREAS:** Company and Commercial Law; Cassation; Banking and Securities Law.

L.A.D. KEUS, born 1952. **LANGUAGES:** Dutch, English, French and German. **PRACTICE AREAS:** EEC Law; Cassation; Law dealing with the Civil Liability of Government; Administrative Law.

JHR J.L. DE WIJKERSLOOTH DE WEERDESTEYN, born 1946. Advocate for the State of the Netherlands. **LANGUAGES:** Dutch, English, French and German. **PRACTICE AREAS:** Cassation; Law dealing with the Civil Liability of Government; Public International Law; Public and Constitutional Law; Administrative Law; Human Rights; Private International Law; Arbitration.

G.R.J. DE GROOT, born 1951. **LANGUAGES:** Dutch, English, French and German. **PRACTICE AREAS:** Labour Law; Public Health Legislation; Administrative Law; Law relating to Civil Servants; Human Rights; Social Security Law.

W. DE VRIES, born 1952. **LANGUAGES:** Dutch, English, French and German. **PRACTICE AREAS:** Agricultural Law; Tenancy and Leasing Law; Environmental Law.

(This Listing Continued)

M.G.J. PARKINS-DE VIN, born 1947. **LANGUAGES:** Dutch, English, French and German. **PRACTICE AREAS:** Immigration Law; Family and Inheritance Law; English (Civil) Law.

R. LUDDING, born 1946. **LANGUAGES:** Dutch, English, French and German. **PRACTICE AREAS:** EEC Law; Labour Law; Industrial and Intellectual Property Law.

G.M.H. HOOGVLIET, born 1955. **LANGUAGES:** Dutch, English, French and German. **PRACTICE AREAS:** Cassation; Immigration Law.

E.J. DAALDER, born 1957. **LANGUAGES:** Dutch, English, French and German. **PRACTICE AREAS:** EEC Law; General Administrative Law; Public Health Legislation; Law relating to Civil Servants; Criminal Law; Extradition Law; Human Rights; American (Civil) Law.

H.AE. UNIKEN VENEMA, born 1957. **LANGUAGES:** Dutch, English, French and German. **PRACTICE AREAS:** Environmental Law; Tenancy and Leasing Law; Planning Law; Agricultural Law.

H.C. GROOTVELD, born 1950. **LANGUAGES:** Dutch, English, French and German. **PRACTICE AREAS:** Transport and Ship Collision Law; Construction Law (Civil Claims); Cassation; Family and Inheritance Law; Private International Law.

E.C.M. SCHIPPERS, born 1958. **LANGUAGES:** Dutch, English, French and German. **PRACTICE AREAS:** Industrial and Intellectual Property Law; Information, Telecommunication and Media Law; Environmental Law.

R. VAN DE KLASHORST, born 1958. **LANGUAGES:** Dutch, English, French and German. **PRACTICE AREAS:** Company and Commercial Law; Banking and Securities Law; Labour Law.

G.J.H. HOUTZAGERS, born 1958. **LANGUAGES:** Dutch, English, French and German. **PRACTICE AREAS:** Company and Commercial Law; Banking and Securities Law.

R.L.H. IJZERMAN, born 1955. **LANGUAGES:** Dutch, English, French and German. **PRACTICE AREAS:** Company and Commercial Law; Tax Law.

M.B. DE WITTE VAN DEN HAAK, born 1959. **LANGUAGES:** Dutch, English, French and German. **PRACTICE AREAS:** Public Health Law; Administrative Law.

H.S. POST, born 1954. **LANGUAGES:** Dutch, English, French and German. **PRACTICE AREAS:** EEC Law; Public International Law; Public and Constitutional Law.

CIVIL LAW NOTARIES
MEMBERS OF FIRM

A. VAN LONKHUŸZEN, born 1931. **LANGUAGES:** Dutch, English, French and German. **PRACTICE AREAS:** Family Law.

P. VAN DULLEMEN, born 1936. **LANGUAGES:** Dutch, English, French and German. **PRACTICE AREAS:** Corporate Law.

R.A. GALLAS, born 1951. **LANGUAGES:** Dutch, English, French and German. **PRACTICE AREAS:** Real Estate Law.

Languages: Dutch, English, French, German, Italian, Russian and Spanish

---

SJÖCRONA VAN STIGT DE ROOS & PEN

Lawyers

Established in 1992

ORANJESTRAAT 7

2514 JB THE HAGUE, THE NETHERLANDS

Telephone: +31 (0) 70/3467472

Telefax: +31 (0) 70/3924378

Amsterdam, The Netherlands Office: Keizersgracht 332, 1016 EZ.
Telephone: +31 (0) 20/6275411. Telefax: +31 (0) 20/6226577.

Rotterdam, The Netherlands Office: Zeemansstraat 11, 3016 CN.
Telephone: +31 (0) 10/4364311. Telefax: +31 (0) 10/4366700.

Commercial Criminal Law and Criminal Procedures.
Firm engaged in Dutch, European and International Criminal Law practise. All lawyers are entitled to plead before the European Commission in Brussels, the European Court of Human Rights in Strassbourg and the Supreme Court of the Netherlands.

(This Listing Continued)

FIRM PROFILE: Established in 1992, Sjöcrona Van Stigt De Roos & Pen is the largest Commercial Criminal Law Firm in the Netherlands. The firm has a broadly based practise with a reputation for offering a full range of quality legal services in the field. The client base is worldwide. The firm has eight partners and four associates practising in three offices. Two members of the firm hold professorships in Criminal Law and Criminal Procedure at Dutch Universities.

MEMBERS OF FIRM

PROF. DR. THEO A. DE ROOS, born 1948; admitted, 1977, Amsterdam. Part-time Professor, Criminal Law and Criminal Procedure, University of Limburg, Maastricht. *Member:* Dutch Lawyers' Society (Advisory Committee on Criminal Law and Criminal Procedure); Dutch Association of Defence Counsel (Chairman). *LANGUAGES:* French, English and German. *PRACTICE AREAS:* Economic and Environmental Criminal law; Supreme Court Litigation.

JURJEN S. PEN, born 1949; admitted, 1977, Amsterdam. *LANGUAGES:* French, English and German. *PRACTICE AREAS:* Criminal Law; Fraud Law; Military Criminal Law.

ARTHUR J.N. VAN STIGT, born 1951; admitted, 1981, Rotterdam. *LANGUAGES:* French, English and German. *PRACTICE AREAS:* Fraud Law; White Collar Crime; Criminal Liability of Companies; Environmental, Economic and Fiscal Criminal Law; Medical Criminal Law; Computer Criminality.

LIAN A.M. MANNHEIMS, born 1953; admitted, 1983, Amsterdam. *LANGUAGES:* French, English and German. *PRACTICE AREAS:* Criminal Law; Extradition and Fraud Law.

PROF. DR. JAN M. SJÖCRONA, born 1956; admitted, 1985, The Hague. Recipient, Dutch Prof. Modderman Award, 1992. Part-time Professor, International Criminal Law, University of Brabant, Tilburg. Former Lecturer, Criminal Law and Criminal Procedure, University of Leyden. *Member:* Dutch Lawyers' Society (Member of Advisory Committee on Criminal Law and Criminal Procedure); Dutch Association of Defence Counsel (Secretary). *LANGUAGES:* French, English, German and Swedish. *PRACTICE AREAS:* International Criminal Law; EC Law; Supreme Court Litigation; White Collar Crime.

BOUDEWIJN C.W. VAN EIJCK, born 1963; admitted, 1987, Rotterdam. *LANGUAGES:* French, English, German and Spanish. *PRACTICE AREAS:* General Criminal Law; Fraud Law.

MARLIES VAN STRIEN, born 1961; admitted, 1988, Rotterdam. *LANGUAGES:* French, English and German. *PRACTICE AREAS:* Environmental Criminal Law; Fraud Law; Traffic Law.

ANNELIES E.M. RÖTTGERING, born 1960; admitted, 1989, Amsterdam. Previously with, European Commission on Human Rights, Strasbourg, France. *LANGUAGES:* French, English and German. *PRACTICE AREAS:* General Criminal Law; Traffic Criminal Law.

ASSOCIATES

CHANTAL P.E. MEEWISSE, born 1964; admitted, 1989, Amsterdam. Former Assistant, Public Defender Service, Washington DC and Miami, Florida. *LANGUAGES:* French, English and German. *PRACTICE AREAS:* General Criminal Law; Fraud Law.

PETER W.J. VAN DER SPEK, born 1962; admitted, 1990, The Hague. Former Assistant, Constitutional Law, University of Leyden. *LANGUAGES:* French, English and German. *PRACTICE AREAS:* Fraud Law; Environmental Criminal Law; Traffic Law.

JETTY A. BULT, born 1966; admitted, 1992, Amsterdam. *LANGUAGES:* French, English and German. *PRACTICE AREAS:* General Law.

DR. STIJN A. FRANKEN, born 1967; admitted, 1993. Former Lecturer, Criminal Law and Criminal Procedure, University of Brabant, Tilburg. *LANGUAGES:* French, English and German. *PRACTICE AREAS:* General Criminal Law; Economic Criminal Law.

TRENITÉ VAN DOORNE

CHURCHILLPLEIN 5
2517 JW THE HAGUE, THE NETHERLANDS
Telephone: 31 (0) 70-338 3131
Telefax: 31 (0) 70-358 4798

Mailing Address: P.O. Box 17207, 2502 CE THE HAGUE

(This Listing Continued)

Amsterdam, Netherlands Office: De Lairessestraat 133. Mailing Address: P.O. Box 75265, 1070 AG AMSTERDAM. Telephone: 31 (0) 20-6789 123. Telex: 16144 tvda nl. Telefax: 31 (0) 20-6789 589.

Rotterdam, Netherlands Office: Weena 666. Mailing Address: P.O. Box 190, 3000 AD ROTTERDAM. Telephone: 31 (0) 10-404 2111. Telefax: 31 (0) 10-404 2333.

Rijswijk, Netherlands Office: Haagweg 175. Mailing Address: P.O. Box 1073, 2280 CB RIJSWIJK. Telephone: 31 (0) 70-390 10 15. Telefax: 31 (0) 70-399 68 44.

Brussels, Belgium Office: Avenue Louise 149, 1050 BRUSSELS. Telephone: 32-2-537 5159. Telefax: 32-2-537 6961.

Willemstad, Curaçao, Netherlands Antilles Office: Promes, Trenité Van Doorne. Julianaplein 22, P.O. Box 504. Telephone: 599-9-613400. Telefax: 599-9-612023.

Tokyo, Japan: Akasaka Wing Building 5 F , 6-6-15 Akasaka, Minato-ku, 107. Telephone: 813-5563-2911. Telefax: 813-5563-2912.

MEMBER OF FIRM
CIVIL LAW NOTARY

AD DE JONG, born 1954; appointed Civil Law Notary by her Majesty the Queen, 1992. *Education:* University of Leiden (1981). *LANGUAGES:* English and German. *PRACTICE AREAS:* Real Estate Law; Family Law; Corporate Law.

RENÉ M. RIETER, born 1961; admitted as Civil Law Notary, 1987, Rijswijk. *Education:* University of Utrecht (1986). *LANGUAGES:* English and German. *PRACTICE AREAS:* Real Estate Law; Corporate Law.

MEMBERS OF FIRM
ATTORNEYS AT LAW

RUTGER J. VAN OOSTEN, born 1949; admitted, 1976, Rotterdam. *Education:* University of Leiden (1975). Substitute Justice, Court of The Hague. *LANGUAGES:* English, French and German. *PRACTICE AREAS:* Corporate Law; Banking Law; Professional Liability; Bankruptcy Law.

BAS T.M. STEINS BISSCHOP, born 1949; admitted, 1975, Amsterdam. *Education:* University of Rotterdam (1974); New York University, Institute of Comparative Law (M.C.J., 1975); Erasmus University Rotterdam (LL.D., 1991). Practised in Brussels, 1980-1981 and Saudi Arabia, 1985-1986. *LANGUAGES:* English, French and German. *PRACTICE AREAS:* International Corporate Finance; Mergers and Acquisitions; Corporate Restructuring; Public Bids and Matters related to the Amsterdam Stock Exchange.

MARIANNE H. VAN COEVERDEN, born 1952; admitted, 1976, Amsterdam. *Education:* University of Amsterdam (1976). *LANGUAGES:* English. *PRACTICE AREAS:* Employment Law; Pension Law.

HANS E. URLUS, born 1955; admitted, 1980, Rotterdam. *Education:* University of Leiden (1978). *LANGUAGES:* English and German. *PRACTICE AREAS:* Corporate Law; Distribution Law; EEC Competition Law; Litigation.

JACK W.C. BERK, born 1957; admitted, 1987, Rotterdam. *Education:* University of Nijmegen (1987). *LANGUAGES:* English and German. *PRACTICE AREAS:* Company Law (Cross-border); Mergers and Acquisitions; Banking and Corporate Finance.

RUDOLPH A.I. SNETHLAGE, born 1961; admitted, 1986, Rotterdam. *Education:* University of Utrecht (1986). *LANGUAGES:* English. *PRACTICE AREAS:* Corporate Law; Mergers and Acquisitions; Corporate Finance; Banking.

ASSOCIATES
ATTORNEY AT LAW

PETER J. FRESACHER, born 1956; admitted, 1985, The Hague. *Education:* University of Leiden (1985). Special Counsel (Vertrauensanwalt) to the Austrian Embassy at The Hague. *LANGUAGES:* German and English. *PRACTICE AREAS:* Litigation; Corporate Law.

BAS WESTERHOUT, born 1964; admitted, 1990, Amsterdam; 1993, The Hague. *Education:* University of Leiden (1989). *LANGUAGES:* English and French. *PRACTICE AREAS:* Corporate Law; Commercial Law; Labor and Employment Law.

DERK RIJPMA, born 1962; admitted, 1991, Rotterdam. *Education:* University of Utrecht (1988). *LANGUAGES:* English. *PRACTICE AREAS:* Litigation; Business Law.

MECHTELD M. VAN DEN BRANDELER, born 1967; admitted, 1992, Rotterdam. *Education:* University of Leiden (1992). *LANGUAGES:*

(This Listing Continued)

TRENITÉ VAN DOORNE, The Hague—Continued

French and English. **PRACTICE AREAS:** Labor Law; Contract Law; Commercial Law.

IEKE E. VAN DOORN, born 1966; admitted, 1992, The Hague. *Education:* University of Amsterdam (1991). **LANGUAGES:** English. **PRACTICE AREAS:** Corporate Law.

ROBERT C.M. VAN MOORSEL, born 1968; admitted, 1993, The Hague. *Education:* University of Leiden (1993). **LANGUAGES:** English. **PRACTICE AREAS:** Corporate Law.

BART L.M. VOORVAART, born 1968; admitted, 1994, The Hague. *Education:* University of Oxford (1993); University of Amsterdam (1994). **LANGUAGES:** English, French and German. **PRACTICE AREAS:** Litigation; Business Law.

MICHEL CHATELIN, born 1965; admitted, 1994, Rotterdam. *Education:* University of Leiden (1993). **LANGUAGES:** French, German and English. **PRACTICE AREAS:** Corporate Law; EEC Law.

ASSOCIATE
CIVIL LAW NOTARY

CHRISTIAAN D. ROSENBERG POLAK, born 1950; admitted as Civil Law Notary, 1979, Rotterdam. *Education:* University of Leiden (J.D., 1978 and Notarial Law, 1979). **LANGUAGES:** English and German. **PRACTICE AREAS:** Corporate Law; Family Law.

SASKIA EELMAN, born 1966; admitted, as Civil Law Notary, 1991, The Hague. *Education:* University of Groningen (1991). **LANGUAGES:** English. **PRACTICE AREAS:** Corporate Law.

Trenité Van Doorne forms together with Wessing Berenberg-Gossler Zimmermann a European Economic interest grouping. Wessing has offices in Berlin, Brussels, Düsseldorf, Hamburg, Leipzig and Munich. Trenité Van Doorne is a member of Lex Mundi.

Languages: English, French and German

DSH DERKS • STAR BUSMANN

Attorneys at Law - Civil Law Notaries - Tax Advisers

2 PYTHAGORASLAAN
3584 BB UTRECHT, THE NETHERLANDS
Telephone: 030-562611
Telefax: 030-562626

Mailing Address: P.O. Box 85250, 3508 AG

Amersfoort, Netherlands Office: Office Building "De Runmolen", 98, Zonnehof, 7th and 8th Floor, 3811 ND, P.O. Box 506, 3800 AM. Telephone: 033-698698. Telefax: 033-698600.

Arnhem, Netherlands Office: Office Building "De Groenveste", 35-I Velperweg, 6824 BE, P.O. Box 3042, 6802 DA. Telephone: 085-511910. Telefax: 085-458169.

Hilversum, Netherlands Office: 37 Borneolaan, 1217 GX, P.O. Box 710, 1200 AS. Telephone: 035-218547. Telefax: 035-215039.

Hilversum, Netherlands Office: 4 Oude Enghweg, 1217 JC, P.O. Box 271, 1200 AG. Telephone: 035-244853. Telefax: 035-284216.

Brussels, Belgium Office: 391 Avenue Louise, B 11, 1050. Telephone: 02-6403525. Telex: 64880 DSHBRU. Telefax: 02-6406904.

Berlin, Germany Office: Bernadottestrasse 66, 14195 Berlin. Telephone: 30-8316300, 8324431, 8325715. Telefax: 30-8316528.

General and International Practice, Commercial, Corporation and EEC Law. Litigation.
Derks • Star Busmann is the Dutch member of DSH, an international consolidation of firms of attorneys at law and civil law notaries of which the members have establishments in the Netherlands, Belgium and France. Members of DSH at present have offices in: The Netherlands: Utrecht, Amersfoort, Arnhem and Hilversum; Belgium: Brussels; France: Paris.

MEMBERS OF FIRM

G.F.Th. Hesselink	P.B. Hamelberg-Scheephorst
L.H.A.J.M. Quant	Carla J.R.A. Schoonderbeek
P.F.J. Rive	C.J. de Tombe
N.Chr.M. Wilke	*******A.R. Bosman
H.C.E. de Vries	F.G. van Hees
E.J.A. Vilé	*R.D. Bos
Th.F.M. Pothof	****F.P. Lomans
H. du Pon	C.H.J. van Leeuwen

(This Listing Continued)

R.P.G.L.M. Verbunt	****I.P.A. van Heijst
F.M. Vermeulen	**T.H.Th. Feringa
*K.H. Pentinga	**J.A. Miedema
M.W. Guensberg	Prof. Dr. E. Lutjens
*****Tj.A. Meijer	******H.M.J. Frijns
A.Th. de Walle	A.M. van Mourik
M. Brink	********Martika M. Jonk
*A.J.A. van Orsouw	H. Struik
***B.ten Doesschate	***Digna M. de Bruin
W.G. Dormaar	****C.M.A. Delissen-Buijnsters
A. van den End	*B. van der Wilt
C.M.B. Diepenhorst	*T.P. van Duuren
***J.W.M. Pothof	******F.L.M. van de Graaff
F.V.B.M. Mutsaerts	*****J.W. Bouman
F.P.J.M. Otten	******A.C.W. graaf van Limburg Stirum

ASSOCIATES

E.P.M. van Veggel	F. Boschma, LL.M.
W.J.M. van Tongeren	H.M. Giezen
Astrid K. Andela	R.L.J. van der Meer
L.M. van der Sluis	******W.P.M. Brantjes
E.M. van Ardenne-Stachiw	******H.C.D. ten Broecke
L.K.M. van Druenen	******Jan Hein Brummelhuis
J.A. Spigt	*Wilma M.C.A. Stouthart
F.M.J.A. Lohuis	*M.N. Bende
*****A.H. van Tets-Asjes	**R. Habermehl
****H.L.J.M. Kersten	*Eveline Müller
R. Imhof	V. van den Brink
W.A.J. Hoorneman	**E.M.E. van der Enden
J.G.J.M. de Zwaan	P. van Steijnen
Drs C. Hellingman	*A.E.H.M. Kerckhaert
M. Bunders	****M.A. Zon
C.J. van Bavel	****H. Bijl
Madeleine J.C.M. Lamers	P. Siegman
A.M. van Riemsdijk	*P.J.G. Erkens
J.L.M. Groenewegen	A.B.A.P.M. Ficq
*****J.A. Dupree	***R.J.L.M. Lambriex
P.B. van den Bos	**D. Lange
***I.E. Nauta	P.M.A. Ober
*****Emma L. Gast	M.R. van Hall
****C.A. Segaar	C.R. Husikes
****J.H. Sassen	C.J.M. Hendriks
***M.G.H. Dukes	Y.R.M. Heijmans
***J.C.J. van Craaikamp	*Marie-Jeanne J.L.A.M. Loos
***C.J.A. Snoukaert van Schauburg-Buchwalt	J.H. Plantenga
***P.A. Hanrath	Drs M. Stempher
*****M.J.M. Bach	M. Scheffer
M.O. Meulenbelt	**Annemiek J.E.M. Vollenbroek
Miranda M.H.B.F. Lambie	C.S. Schoori
M.C.H.I. van der Dussen	Anouk M.M.E. Beijnes
*****J.T.P. Hogendoorn	G.T.M.J. Raaijmakers
P.J. Soede	Dorine H. Bakker
L.J. Böhmer	***I.N. Kwak
A. Haan	***Marike D. Ubbink
Drs. M.S.T. Belt	***Cybèle M. Boon
C.J.G.M. Schippers	W. de Jong
******Christine M. Klein	Ike M.C. Rosier
******J. Hosselet Finkensieper	F.M. Bus
****G.F. van den Berg	**C.H.W. Segers
	J.M. Post

(This Listing Continued)

TAX ADVISORS
MEMBERS

T.H.Th. Feringa   **J.A. Miedema**

ASSOCIATES

R. Habermehl   **D. Lange**
E.M.E. van der Enden   **Annemiek J.E.M. Vollenbroek**

*Civil Law Notary, Utrecht
**Tax Adviser, Utrecht
***Amersfoort
****Arnhem
*****Hilversum
******Civil Law Notary, Hilversum
*******Brussels
********Berlin

Languages: Dutch, English, French, German and Spanish.

HOEGEN DIJKHOF & VAN BRAKEL

Established in 1976

WILHELMINAPARK 24
P.O. BOX 14215, 3508 SH UTRECHT
3581 NE UTRECHT, THE NETHERLANDS
Telephone: (31)-30-520220
FAX: (31)-30-516885

Amsterdam Office: Emmastraat 40, 1075 HW. Telephone: (31) 20-6791801. Fax: (31) 20-6769081.

Mergers Law, International Tax Law, Business Law, Labour Law, Intellectual and Industrial Property, Computer Law, EC Law, Commercial Litigation and Arbitration.

MEMBERS OF FIRM

HANS J. HOEGEN DIJKHOF, born Doetinchem, Netherlands, June 5, 1947; admitted, 1973, Rotterdam; 1976, Utrecht; 1990, Amsterdam. *Education:* Utrecht University Law School (Cand. with Honors, 1970; Doct. with Honors, 1972), specializing in Company Law and Law of International Organizations. Chairman, Integrated Advisory Group IAG International, 1989—, an Association of Independent Professional Firms with 80 offices throughout Europe and the U.S.; Honorary President, 1993—. *Member:* Amsterdam, Dutch and International Bar Associations. (Resident, Amsterdam Office). *LANGUAGES:* Dutch, English, German, French and Italian. *PRACTICE AREAS:* Mergers Law; International Tax Law; Business Law.

HANS C. VAN BRAKEL, born Beesd (Gld), Netherlands, February 28, 1950; admitted, 1974, Maastricht; 1976, Utrecht. *Education:* Utrecht University Law School (Cand. 1970; Doct., 1973); Economic University at Tilburg, Post Doctoral Examination in Analyzing Financial Statements. *Member:* Utrecht, Dutch and International Bar Associations. *LANGUAGES:* Dutch, English, German and French. *PRACTICE AREAS:* Business Law; Intellectual Property Law; Computer Law; Litigation.

ASSOCIATES

LOUISE G. DE GIER, born Bunnik, Netherlands, October 15, 1960; admitted, 1987, Utrecht. *Education:* Utrecht University Law School (Cand., 1982; Doct., 1985); Free University of Brussels (Master, International Comparative Law, LL.M., 1986)). *Member:* Utrecht and Dutch Bar Associations. *LANGUAGES:* Dutch, English, French, German and Italian. *PRACTICE AREAS:* EC Law; International Law; Intellectual Property Law.

RICHARD H.M. RUIJGROK, born Delft, Netherlands, June 27, 1957; admitted, 1990, Amsterdam. *Education:* Leyden University Law School (Doct., 1984). Candidate Notary, Post-doctoral exams in Administrative Law and Criminal Law, 1980-1987. Honorary Consul, 1987— and Honorary Consul-General, 1984—, Thailand in Amsterdam. Business Advisor, specialized in South-East Asia. Member, Order of Notaries. *Member:* Amsterdam and Dutch Bar Associations. (Resident, Amsterdam Office). *LANGUAGES:* Dutch, English, German, French and Thai. *PRACTICE AREAS:* Business Law; International Taxation Law.

RENATE J.E. REIDINGA, born Loenen, Netherlands, April 20, 1966; admitted, 1992, Utrecht. *Education:* Utrecht University of Law School (Doct., 1991). *Member:* Utrecht and Dutch Bar Associations. *LANGUAGES:* Dutch, English, French and German. *PRACTICE AREAS:* Litigation; Administrative Law; Insurance Law.

(This Listing Continued)

J. EDGAR STAM, born Utrecht, Netherlands, February 26, 1965; admitted, 1993, Utrecht. *Education:* Utrecht University of Law School (Cand., 1985; Doct., 1990); Johns Hopkins University School of Advanced International Studies, Bologna, Italy (Bologna Center Diploma, 1990). *Member:* Utrecht and Dutch Bar Associations. *LANGUAGES:* Dutch, English, German, Italian, French and Russian. *PRACTICE AREAS:* Business Law; International Contracts; Labour Law.

AAD DE BRUIJN, born Abidjan, Ivory Coast, April 13, 1967; admitted, 1994, Utrecht. *Education:* University of Amsterdam Law School (Cand., 1990; Doct., 1993); School of Advanced Economic Studies of Amsterdam (International Management, Diploma, 1989); University of Bordeaux (Diplome d'Etudes Francaises, June 1986). *Member:* Utrecht and Dutch Bar Associations. *LANGUAGES:* Dutch, English, German and French. *PRACTICE AREAS:* Insurance Law; Transport Law; Contracts.

VAN BENTHEM & KEULEN

Established in 1940

EUCLIDESLAAN 51
3584 BM UTRECHT, THE NETHERLANDS
Telephone: 31-30-528 528
Telefax: 31-30-528 500

Mailing Address: Postbus 85005 3508 AA, Utrecht, The Netherlands

General Civil Practice, Corporate, Labour, Health Care, Real Estate and Administrative, Insolvency, Intellectual Property, Insurance and Liability, Landlord/Tenant, EEC Antitrust, Family, Criminal.

FIRM PROFILE: H.C.A. van Benthem began as a sole practitioner in 1940, and was later joined by F.B. Keulen in 1946 to form the firm Van Benthem & Keulen. The firm has consciously restricted its growth in order to maintain its tradition of personal service and collegiality.

While the firm originally had a general practice geared toward private individuals, the focus has shifted increasingly toward businesses and governmental entities now served by nine sections, each specialized in a particular area of the law.

The firm has historically strong ties to the region of Utrecht, acting as counsel to both the city and the province of Utrecht. On a national level, the firm also enjoys renown for its insolvency practice, as a result of the appointment of A.L. Leuftink and C. de Jong as receiver or trustee in several highly-publicized bankruptcies and reorganizations. In the international arena, the inclusion of K. Kao (U.S. attorney-at-law) and A. van der Schee (Rechtsanwaltin) further broadens the firm's horizons.

Van Benthem & Keulen has expertise in all principal areas of Dutch law. In addition to the categories of work stated above. Van Benthem & Keulen also has expertise in the fields of venture capital work, commercial litigation, arbitration, EC competition law and landlord/tenant law.

COUNSEL

FERDINAND B. KEULEN, born Amersfoort, the Netherlands, June 4, 1920; admitted, 1946, Utrecht. *Education:* Rijksuniversiteit Utrecht (Law 1946). *LANGUAGES:* Dutch, English, French, German. *PRACTICE AREAS:* Corporate Law; Insolvency Law.

MEMBERS OF FIRM

GERARD H. OLGERS, born Emmen, the Netherlands, March 16, 1944; admitted, 1969, Utrecht. *Education:* Rijksuniversiteit Groningen (Law 1968). Publications: "The Violator Pays," Antidorum: Liber Amicorum mr F.B. Keulen (1990); "Legal and Administrative Issues of Parking within City Limits given art, 258 Zoning Ordinance," Bouwrecht (1982). *LANGUAGES:* Dutch, English, German. *PRACTICE AREAS:* Real Estate Law; Construction Law; Environmental Law; Administrative Law.

ARNOLD L. LEUFTINK, born Amsterdam, the Netherlands, March 4, 1946; admitted, 1972, Utrecht. *Education:* Rijksuniversiteit Groningen (Law 1972). Publications: various publications on insolvency law issues. *Member:* Dutch Association of Insolvency Practitioners (Member, Board of Directors); Bankruptcy Commission of the Dutch Bar Association; Computer Commission of the Dutch Bar Association; Society for Computers and Law; International Bar Association; European Association of Insolvency Practitioners. *LANGUAGES:* Dutch, German, English, French. *PRACTICE AREAS:* Insolvency; Corporate; Computer.

HYLTSJE S. WIARDA, born Wijmbritseradeel, the Netherlands, February 9, 1945; admitted, 1972, Utrecht. *Education:* Universiteit van Amsterdam (Law 1972). Publications: "Some Aspects of the Problems of Maintenance and Improvement of Housing," Antidorum: Liber Amicorum mr F.B.

(This Listing Continued)

VAN BENTHEM & KEULEN, Utrecht—Continued

Keulen (1990); "Leasing Office Space: Risky Consequences," Utrecht Business (1991). *Member:* Appellate Council of the Royal Dutch Medical Society (Chairman); Utrecht Bar Association (Dean); Museum van Speelklok tot Pierement Foundation (Secretary); Mytylschool for Utrecht and surrounding area Foundation (Treasurer); Winter-Heynsius Foundation (Chairman). *LANGUAGES:* Dutch, English, German. *PRACTICE AREAS:* Labour; Landlord/Tenant.

JOHN N. KOPP, born 's-Gravenhage, the Netherlands, August 1, 1946; admitted, 1975, 's-Gravenhage; 1978, Utrecht. *Education:* Rijksuniversiteit Utrecht (Law 1975). Publications: various articles on the legal position of statutory managing directors. Speaker, Dutch Center for Directors. Substitute Judge: Cantonal Court Utrecht; District Court Utrecht. Permanent Arbiter, Dutch Institute for Arbitration (NAI). Member, Special Advisory Committee on Statements of Conduct, Ministries of Interior and Justice (CieVog). *Member:* International Bar Association; Litigation Association; Rotary Club. *LANGUAGES:* Dutch, English, German. *PRACTICE AREAS:* Health Care; Labour (specialty: Legal Position of Managing Directors).

BEREND F. KEULEN, born Utrecht, the Netherlands, April 30, 1947; admitted, 1975, Rotterdam; 1977, Utrecht. *Education:* Rijksuniversiteit Rotterdam (Law 1975). Publications: "Medical Malpractice," Geneeskunst en Recht, 1991. Permanent arbiter: Dutch Institute for Arbitration (NAI); Board of Arbitration Foundation for Metallurgical Industry and Trade. *Member:* Disciplinary Council for the Dutch Bar Association (Clerk); Sportcomplex de Vechtsebanen (Secretary); Association of Personal Injury Attorneys; Health Law Association; Jurisprudence Commission of the Dutch Association for Clinical Chemistry. *LANGUAGES:* Dutch, English. *PRACTICE AREAS:* Health Care; Personal Injury; Insurance.

WILLEM VINK, born Haarlem, the Netherlands, March 31, 1948; admitted, 1975, Utrecht. *Education:* Vrije Universiteit Amsterdam (Law, 1973). Member: Various Boards of Directors. *LANGUAGES:* Dutch, English, German, French and Russian. *PRACTICE AREAS:* Administrative; Construction; Labour; Contracts; Landlord/Tenant.

TOM E. BAX, born De Bilt, the Netherlands, January 25, 1948; admitted, 1975, Rotterdam; 1981, Utrecht. *Education:* Erasmus Universiteit Rotterdam (Law, 1973); Tulane University (LL.M., 1975). *Member:* International Bar Association; Various Supervisory Boards of Directors. *LANGUAGES:* Dutch, English and German. *PRACTICE AREAS:* Corporate; Mergers; Acquisitions; Recapitalization; EEC Antitrust.

CEES DE JONG, born Woerden, the Netherlands, June 10, 1953; admitted, 1978, Rotterdam; 1984, Utrecht. *Education:* Rijksuniversiteit Utrecht (Law, 1978). Secretary, Albert van Koningsbruggen Health Center. *Member:* Labour Law Association; Dutch Association of Insolvency Practitioners; European Association of Insolvency Practitioners. *LANGUAGES:* Dutch, English and German. *PRACTICE AREAS:* Insolvency; Labour.

NICO J. VAN DER GRAAF, born Amsterdam, the Netherlands, August 30, 1947; admitted, 1979, Utrecht. *Education:* Vrije Universiteit Amsterdam (Law, 1979). Publications: various articles covering social security, administrative health care and labour law issues. *LANGUAGES:* Dutch, French, German and English. *PRACTICE AREAS:* Labour; Social Security; Landlord/Tenant; Administrative; Health Care.

ANKE R.J. MULDER, born Borne, the Netherlands, September 30, 1958; admitted, 1982, Utrecht. *Education:* Rijksuniversiteit Utrecht (Law, 1982). Adjunct Clerk. *Member:* Dutch Bar Association (Disciplinary Council); Family Law Association (Founder). *LANGUAGES:* Dutch, English and German. *PRACTICE AREAS:* Family.

HENDRIK DULACK, born Twello, the Netherlands, December 18, 1955; admitted, 1983, Utrecht. *Education:* Rijksuniversiteit Utrecht (Law, 1979). *Member:* German-Dutch Attorneys Conference; European Association of Insolvency Practitioners; Various Boards of Directors. *LANGUAGES:* Dutch, German, English and French. *PRACTICE AREAS:* Labour; Insolvency.

PIM TH. A. SCHERMER, born Apeldoorn, the Netherlands, February 4, 1959; admitted, 1985, Utrecht. *Education:* Rijksuniversiteit Leiden (Law, 1985). *Member:* Dutch Computer Society; Association Internationale des Jeunes Advocats. *LANGUAGES:* Dutch, English and German. *PRACTICE AREAS:* Corporate; Computer; Contracts; EEC Antitrust; EDI (Electronic Data Interchange).

(This Listing Continued)

ASSOCIATES

*KAREN KAO, born Los Angeles, California, U.S.A., September 21, 1959; admitted, 1984, Washington, D.C. *Education:* University of California, Irvine (B.A., 1981); Georgetown University Law Center (J.D., 1984). Publications: "The Netherlands," Attacking Foreign Assets (1992). *Member:* District of Columbia Bar; American Bar Association. *LANGUAGES:* English, Dutch. *PRACTICE AREAS:* Corporate; Contracts; International Commercial Transactions.

MARLIES C. DE GOEDE, born Wormerveer, the Netherlands, February 19, 1962; admitted, 1986, Haarlem; 1989, Utrecht. *Education:* Universiteit van Amsterdam (Law, 1986). Publications: "LPG and Expanding Construction: Conflict between Zoning and Environmental Laws," Bouwrecht (1994). Secretary, Art Commission of the Utrecht Recreational Foundation; Secretary, MKD "De Molenhorst" Institute for the Multi-Disciplinary Treatment of Young Children. *LANGUAGES:* Dutch, English, German, French. *PRACTICE AREAS:* Real Estate; Environmental; Administrative; Construction.

HANS M. VAN NOORT, born Utrecht, the Netherlands, September 25, 1961; admitted, 1987, Utrecht. *Education:* Rijksuniversiteit Utrecht (Law, 1987). Publications: Various articles on electronic banking issues. *LANGUAGES:* Dutch, English and German. *PRACTICE AREAS:* Labour; Landlord/Tenant.

AART H.J.G. VAN VOORTHUIZEN, born Arnhem, the Netherlands, January 21, 1960; admitted, 1988, Utrecht. *Education:* Erasmus Universiteit Rotterdam (Law, 1988). *LANGUAGES:* Dutch, English and German. *PRACTICE AREAS:* Labour; Criminal.

ARNO J.P. VAN BEURDEN, born Papendrecht, the Netherlands, October 12, 1964; admitted, 1989, Utrecht. *Education:* Rijksuniversiteit Leiden (History; Law, 1989). Deputy-Secretary, Appellate Council of the Royal Dutch Medical Society; Board of Directors: Utrecht Historical Costume Museum; Utrecht Centre of History and Culture Foundation. *LANGUAGES:* Dutch, English and French. *PRACTICE AREAS:* Labour; Health Care; Insurance Law.

NICOLETTE M. PARIS-BERENDSEN, born Maastricht, the Netherlands, October 12, 1963; admitted, 1989, Utrecht. *Education:* Rijksuniversiteit Utrecht (Law, 1989). Publications: Divorce and Morrocan Women: Legal Handbook for Service Providers. *Member:* Art Commission of the Utrecht Recreational Foundation (Secretary). *LANGUAGES:* Dutch, French, German, English. *PRACTICE AREAS:* Family.

NATASJA V.M. GEHLEN, born Spaubeek, the Netherlands, October 6, 1964; admitted, 1989, Utrecht. *Education:* Rijksuniversiteit Utrecht (Law, 1989). *LANGUAGES:* Dutch, English. *PRACTICE AREAS:* Real Estate; Environmental; Administrative; Construction.

JAN A. SCHUMAN, born Utrecht, the Netherlands, June 27, 1964; admitted, 1989, Utrecht. *Education:* Rijksuniversiteit Utrecht (Law, 1989). *LANGUAGES:* Dutch, English and German. *PRACTICE AREAS:* Intellectual Property; Media; Entertainment; Contracts; Corporate.

ALICE VAN DER SCHEE, born Rotterdam, the Netherlands, June 4, 1965; admitted, 1990, Utrecht. *Education:* Erasmus Universiteit Rotterdam (Law, 1989). *LANGUAGES:* Dutch, German, English, French. *PRACTICE AREAS:* Labour; Insolvency; German-Dutch Matters.

ANNELIES E. VAN SOLINGE, born Deventer, the Netherlands, August 3, 1964; admitted, 1991, Utrecht. *Education:* Rijksuniversiteit Utrecht (Law, 1990). *Member:* Disciplinary Board, Royal Dutch Medical Society (Deputy-Secretary). *LANGUAGES:* Dutch, English and German. *PRACTICE AREAS:* Family.

CAROLINA TH.I.M. VAN DEN HEUVEL, born Elst, the Netherlands, December 22, 1966; admitted, 1992, Utrecht. *Education:* Rijksuniversiteit Leiden (Law, 1991). *LANGUAGES:* Dutch, English, German, French. *PRACTICE AREAS:* Health Care; Personal Injury.

MAURICE J.J.M. ESSERS, born Kerkrade, the Netherlands, February 20, 1967; admitted, 1992, Utrecht. *Education:* Rijksuniversiteit Utrecht (Law, 1992). *Member:* Dutch Association for EEC Law. *LANGUAGES:* Dutch, English, German, French. *PRACTICE AREAS:* Corporate; Contracts; EEC Law.

ELEONORE A.C. WILDE, born Breda, the Netherlands, August 21, 1966; admitted, 1993, Utrecht. *Education:* Rijksuniversiteit Utrecht (Law, 1992). *LANGUAGES:* Dutch, English, German, French, Italian, Swiss-German. *PRACTICE AREAS:* Labour; Insolvency.

(This Listing Continued)

WOUTER W. VAN DEN ESHOF, born Amsterdam, the Netherlands, March 9, 1963; admitted, 1993, Utrecht. *Education:* Rijksuniversiteit Utrecht (Law, 1993). *LANGUAGES:* Dutch, English, German. *PRACTICE AREAS:* Corporate; Contracts; Computer; EDI (Electronic Data Interchange).

EVELIEN G. TJABBES, born 's-Gravenhage, the Netherlands, December 14, 1965; admitted, 1993, Utrecht. *Education:* Rijksuniversiteit Utrecht (French 1992, Law 1993). *LANGUAGES:* Dutch, French, English, German. *PRACTICE AREAS:* Family.

ISMAEL A.V. EL MECKY, born Beek, the Netherlands, August 5, 1967; admitted, 1994, Utrecht. *Education:* Rijksuniversiteit Utrecht (Law 1993). *LANGUAGES:* Dutch, French, English. *PRACTICE AREAS:* Real Estate; Construction; Environmental; Administrative.

JAN A.H. PADBERG, born Warmond, the Netherlands, August 23, 1966; admitted, 1994, Utrecht. *Education:* Universiteit van Amsterdam (Law 1993). *LANGUAGES:* Dutch, English, German. *PRACTICE AREAS:* Labour; Insolvency; Contracts.

STEPHANIE N. VAN RHEE, born Abidjan, Ivory Coast, September 28, 1968; admitted, 1994, Utrecht. *Education:* Rijksuniversiteit Utrecht (Law1992). *LANGUAGES:* Dutch, English, French, German. *PRACTICE AREAS:* Labour; Social Security.

MECHTELD E. VAN PRAAG SIGAAR, born Amsterdam, the Netherlands, March4, 1968; admitted, 1994, Utrecht. *Education:* Universiteit van Amsterdam (Law 1992). *LANGUAGES:* Dutch, English, French. *PRACTICE AREAS:* Intellectual Property; Corporate; Contracts.

GERRIE TER HUURNE, born Hengelo, the Netherlands, January 15, 1966; admitted, 1993. *Education:* Rijksuniversiteit Groningen (Law 1988). Publications: New Rules for the Transfer of Registered Shares (1994), "Preliminary Advice of the Commercial Law Committee Meeting on Bankruptcy," TVVS (1993); "No Right to Vote Shares after Dissolution Marital Community of Property," TVVS (1992); "Comparative Review of Relativity and Transfer of Registered Shares," TVVS (1991. *LANGUAGES:* Dutch, English, German. *PRACTICE AREAS:* Corporate; Contracts; Mergers; Acquisitions; Recapitalizations.

ADVISORS

WILHELMUS B. VAN DER MIJN, born Rotterdam, the Netherlands, January 12, 1930. *Education:* Rijksuniversiteit Leiden (Law, 1954). Professor, Health Care Law, Erasmus Universiteit Rotterdam, 1982. Publications: Numerous articles and books, including Malpractice Legislation in the Field of Health Care, 3e druk, 1989. Chairman and/or Member, various health care institutions. *LANGUAGES:* Dutch and English. *PRACTICE AREAS:* Health Care Law.

PAUL G.F.A. GEERTS, born Kampala, Uganda, June 25, 1959. *Education:* Katholieke Universiteit Nijmegen (Law 1986). University Lecturer, Intellectual Property Law, Rijksuniversiteit Groningen, 1986. Publications: various articles and books. *LANGUAGES:* Dutch, English, German. *PRACTICE AREAS:* Intellectual Property Law.

*Attorney-at-Law admitted to the District of Columbia Bar (U.S.A.)

VAN MENS & WISSELINK

Attorneys at Law. Tax advisers

WILHELMINAPARK 60-61
P.O. BOX 85450
3508 AL UTRECHT, THE NETHERLANDS
Telephone: + 31 30 544 949
Telefax: + 31 30 522 552

General Practice, Dutch and International Tax Law, Business Law, Corporate and Commercial Law, Mergers and Acquisitions, Employment Law, Intellectual Property, Re-organization, Bankruptcy, Litigation and Arbitration.

FIRM PROFILE: Van Mens & Wisselink offers legal services, including litigation, with emphasis on Dutch and International Tax Law, EEC Law, Commercial and Corporate Law. The firm consists of 8 partners and 12 associates and maintains excellent working relations with other law firms within the EEC. The client base is worldwide. Van Mens & Wisselink combines practical advise with a high academic level.

MEMBERS OF FIRM

J. WISSELINK, (1938 - General Counsel). *PRACTICE AREAS:* Restructuring of Mult-National Corporations.

(This Listing Continued)

PROF. K.L.H. VAN MENS, (1945). *PRACTICE AREAS:* International Family Wealth Planning; Trusts; Company Tax Planning.

G.A. CONYN, (1952). *PRACTICE AREAS:* Corporate Law; Bankruptcy; Banking and Securities Law.

H. KAISER, (1959). *PRACTICE AREAS:* Company Tax Planning; Re-Organization; VAT Issues.

P.TH.M. VAN DEN OORD, (1954). *PRACTICE AREAS:* Fiscal Aspects Affecting Partnerships and Family Business.

F.M.M. DUYNSTEE, (1960). *PRACTICE AREAS:* International Tax Planning; Partnerships; Pensions.

J.G.I. BAAS, (1948). *PRACTICE AREAS:* Company Tax Planning; General Tax Practice.

J. CHR. WEISZ, (1949). *PRACTICE AREAS:* Commercial and Corporate Law; Mergers and Acquisitions; Litigation.

O.J. VAN LEEUWEN, (1960). *PRACTICE AREAS:* Commercial Law; Bankruptcy; Banking and Securities.

ASSOCIATES

Prof. Ph.H. van Huizen	*T.C. van Wagensveld*
I.A. Koele	*H.H. Tan*
R.W.F. Hendriks	*J.P.A.M. van Balen*
J.V. Boonacker	*C.M. Ettema*
P.R. van der Waal	*M.J.M. Verdonk*
	M.J. Wisselink

VAN RIET & ASSOCIEES

Attorneys at Law

EINSTEINDREEF 111
P.O. BOX 9907
3506 GX UTRECHT, THE NETHERLANDS
Telephone: + 31 30 620855
Telefax: + 31 30 615414

Amersfoort, The Netherlands Office: Henri Dunantstraat 32 A. P.O. Box 1236. 3800 BE Amersfoort, The Netherlands. Telephone: + 31 33 553300. Fax: + 31 33 555525.

Amsterdam, The Netherlands Office: Van Nijenrodeweg 475. Telephone: 020-6442140. Telefax: 030-615414.

Minneapolis, Minnesota, USA Office: 4810 Lakeview Drive. Telephone: 1 (0) 612 9277430. Telefax: 1 (0) 612 9259603.

Business Law, Corporate and Commercial Law, Mergers and Acquisitions, Insolvency and Bankruptcy Law, Re-Organization, Employment Law, Intellectual Property, Liability and Insurance Law, Personal Injury and Medical Liability, Real Estate, Leasing Law, Building Law, Personal Family and Estate Law, Litigation and Arbitration.

FIRM PROFILE: Van Riet & Associees attorneys is a multifaceted dynamic alert and quick-witted law firm with a good oriented service which promotes the interests of its clientele expertly and with verve. More than twenty lawyers are associated with the firm.

Van Riet & Associees maintains close relationships with a network of civil notaries, accountants, tax specialists, real estate brokers, appraisers, medical specialists and other experts.

In addition Van Riet & Associees, is member of an organization of more than 30 law firms spread out all over Europe.

ADRIAAN J.M. VAN RIET, admitted, 1966. *LANGUAGES:* English, French and German. *PRACTICE AREAS:* Corporate Law; Insolvency Law.

MARIANNE VAN RIET-HOLST, admitted, 1974. *LANGUAGES:* English, French and German. *PRACTICE AREAS:* Intellectual Property; Labour Law; Family Law.

MARIE JOSÉ COOLS, admitted, 1982. *LANGUAGES:* English, French and German. *PRACTICE AREAS:* Corporate Law; Intellectual Property; Labour Law; Insolvency Law.

JAN JACOB BIJKERK, admitted, 1988. *LANGUAGES:* English and German. *PRACTICE AREAS:* State Administrative Law; Environmental Law; Real Estate; Leasing Law; Building Law.

(This Listing Continued)

VAN RIET & ASSOCIEES, Utrecht—Continued

RONALD VAN DEN BOS, admitted, 1989. *LANGUAGES:* English and German. *PRACTICE AREAS:* Corporate Law; Insolvency Law; Collection of Bills.

BAS BESSELING, admitted, 1989. *LANGUAGES:* English, German and Spanish. *PRACTICE AREAS:* Corporate Law; Insolvency Law.

JAN J. DINGEMANS, admitted, 1989. *LANGUAGES:* English and German. *PRACTICE AREAS:* Corporate Law; Insolvency Law; Collection of Bills.

WILNA J.E. GROEN, admitted, 1990. *LANGUAGES:* English. *PRACTICE AREAS:* Corporate Law; State Administrative Law; Real Estate; Building Law; Leasing Law.

JAAP J. VAN DER HORST, admitted, 1992. *LANGUAGES:* English and German. *PRACTICE AREAS:* Liability/Insurance Law; Personal Injury; Medical Liability.

BARBARA J.E. GEHLEN, admitted, 1994. *LANGUAGES:* English, French and German. *PRACTICE AREAS:* General Practice; Insolvency Law; Family Law.

NELLEKE CRANS, admitted, 1994. *LANGUAGES:* English and German. *PRACTICE AREAS:* General Practice; Insolvency Law; Family Law.

JAAP P.C. OBBINK, admitted, 1985. (Amersfoort Office). *LANGUAGES:* English and German. *PRACTICE AREAS:* Corporate Law; Insolvency Law; Real Estate.

RÚNA P.Y. HONIG, admitted, 1987. (Amersfoort Office). *LANGUAGES:* English and German. *PRACTICE AREAS:* Corporate Law; Labor Law.

ESTHER M. ROGIER, LL.M; admitted 1982. (Amersfoort Office). *LANGUAGES:* English, French and Spanish. *PRACTICE AREAS:* Insolvency Law; Collection of Bills; Family Law.

HERMAN J.F.M. HÜFFER, admitted, 1943. (Minneapolis Office). *LANGUAGES:* English, German, French and Dutch. *PRACTICE AREAS:* Corporate Law; Insolvency Law; Disciplinary Laws; Arbitration.

PAUL F.J.M. VAN VONDEREN, admitted, 1967. (Amersfoort Office). *LANGUAGES:* English and German. *PRACTICE AREAS:* Corporate Law; Insolvency Law; Leasing Law.

ADRIÈNNE G. VAN DOORN, admitted, 1987. (Amersfoort Office). *LANGUAGES:* English. *PRACTICE AREAS:* Liability/Insurance Law; Personal Injury; Medical Liability.

NORTHERN IRELAND

CLEAVER, FULTON & RANKIN

Established in 1893

50 BEDFORD STREET
BELFAST BT2 7FW, NORTHERN IRELAND
Telephone: 243141
Fax: 249096
International Code + 44 1232; UK STD Code 0232 Cable Address:
DOCUMENT BELFAST

Bangor, Northern Ireland Office: 111, Main Street, BT20 4BJ. Telephone: 45611. Fax: 454216; International Code + 44 247; UK STD Code 0247.

Armagh, Northern Ireland Office: 13-15 Market Street, BT61 7QS. Telephone: 525566. Fax: 526651; International Code + 44 861; UK STD Code 0861.

Administration of Estates, Administrative Law, Arbitration, Banking Law, Bankruptcy, Business Law, Commercial Contracts, Company Management and Secretarial Services, Competition Law, Constitutional Law, Construction Law, Consumer Protection Law, Contract and Securities Law, Commercial Conveyancing, Domestic Conveyancing, Corporate Law, Debt Recovery, Defamation Law, EEC Law, Employer's Liability, Environmental Law, Equality Law, Family Law, Food and Drug Regulations, Health Hospital and Malpractice Law, Human Rights Law, Industrial Relations and Labor Law, Insurance Law, Litigation, Media Law, Negligence Law, Personal Injury Law, Private Client Law, Probate, Product Liability Law,

(This Listing Continued)

Property and Real Estate Law, Rent and Lease, Social Security Law, Taxation Law, Transportation Law, Trusts, General Legal Practice.
AGENCY WORK FOR LAWYERS IN OTHER JURISDICTIONS UNDERTAKEN.

FIRM PROFILE: The Practice was founded in 1893 by J.M. Cleaver of a prominent Belfast family. In line with other comparable practices in Belfast, it then expanded gradually but during the past two decades the practice has very considerably increased in size and case load and now has a special emphasis on commercial and company work, work for education and charitable bodies and other public and institutional authorities, and on private client work of all categories. The practice also has branch offices in Armagh and Bangor.

The practice specializes in agency work for lawyers in other jurisdictions and is developing a consultancy and advisory service for its clients on all aspects of Northern Ireland law which includes the impact of the European Community in Northern Ireland.

PARTNERS

PETER JAMES RANKIN, born Northern Ireland. Admitted as Solicitor, 1968. *Education:* Trinity College of Dublin University (B.A., LL.B.). *Member:* The Law Society of Northern Ireland. *PRACTICE AREAS:* Banks and Banking; Commercial Law; Corporate Law; Finance; Mergers; Acquisitions; Charities.

STEPHEN MAITLAND PATRICK CROSS, born Northern Ireland. Admitted as Solicitor, 1965, England; 1968, Northern Ireland. *Member:* The Law Society of Northern Ireland (Member of Council, 1970-1987; President, 1979-1980); International Bar Association (Member, Committee on Labour Law). *PRACTICE AREAS:* Consumer Law; Franchising Law; Labour and Employment; Leases and Leasing; Licensing Law.

WILLIAM PATRICK MARY O'DRISCOLL, born Northern Ireland. Admitted as Solicitor, 1972. *Education:* Queen's University, Belfast (B.Sc.Econ.). *Member:* The Law Society of Northern Ireland. *PRACTICE AREAS:* Debtor and Creditor; Fraud; Libel and Defamation; Litigation; Products Liability.

IAN DAVID DAWSON, born Northern Ireland. Admitted as Solicitor, 1974. *Education:* Emmanuel College, Cambridge (M.A.). *Member:* The Law Society of Northern Ireland. *PRACTICE AREAS:* Banks and Banking; Commercial Law; Corporate Law; Finance; Mortgages.

DAVID EDGAR KANE CARSON, born Northern Ireland. Admitted as Solicitor, 1975. *Education:* Queen's University, Belfast (LL.B.). *Member:* The Law Society of Northern Ireland. *PRACTICE AREAS:* Real Estate; Property; Wills; Trusts; Taxation.

ALASTAIR JOHN RANKIN, born Northern Ireland. Admitted as Solicitor, 1977. *Education:* Trinity College of Dublin University (B.A.). Consultant Institute of Professional Legal Studies, Queen's University, Belfast, 1988-1992. *Member:* The Law Society of Northern Ireland (Member of Council, 1985—; Director, Law Society (NI) Financial Advice, Limited, 1990—); Society for Computers and Law Limited (Director, 1987—); Incorporated Council on Law Reporting for Northern Ireland. *PRACTICE AREAS:* Chancery and Equity; Probate and Family Trust; Taxation; Trusts and Estates; Wills.

NEIL CAMPBELL FARIS, born Northern Ireland. Admitted as Solicitor, 1977. *Education:* Trinity College of Dublin University (M.A.; LL.B.); University of Cambridge (Diploma in International Law). Consultant Institute of Professional Legal Studies, Queen's University, Belfast, 1988-1992. *Member:* The Law Society of Northern Ireland; International Bar Association (Member, Committee on Environment). *PRACTICE AREAS:* Constitutional Law; Consultancy; Construction Law; Environmental Law; Intellectual Property; International Law.

JOY D.E.M.A. SCOTT, born Northern Ireland. Admitted as Solicitor, 1978. *Education:* Queen's University, Belfast (LL.B.). *Member:* The Law Society of Northern Ireland. *PRACTICE AREAS:* Real Estate; Property; Mortgages; General Practice.

M. PAUL SPRING, born Northern Ireland. Admitted as Solicitor, 1983. *Education:* London School of Economics, University of London (LL.B.). *Member:* The Law Society of Northern Ireland; International Bar Association; Young Lawyers International Association (A.I.J.A.); Northern Ireland Young Solicitors Group (Chairman, 1990/91). *PRACTICE*

(This Listing Continued)

AREAS: Contracts; Libel and Defamation; Litigation; Negligence; Personal Injury.

ASSOCIATES

Bryan J. Law
Fionnuala M. Oliver
Geoffrey T.H. Macartney
William D.A. Cross
Rosalie J. Prytherch

C. & H. JEFFERSON

8/9 DONEGALL SQUARE NORTH
BELFAST BT1 5GN, NORTHERN IRELAND
Telephone: (01232) 329-545
Fax: (01232) 244-644

*REVISERS OF THE NORTHERN IRELAND LAW DIGEST FOR
THIS DIRECTORY.*

CONSULTANT

J.B. MCKEE, M.A., LL.B., born Bangor, County Down, Northern Ireland. *Education:* Portora Royal School, Enniskillen; Trinity College of Dublin University, Dublin. Council of Legal Education London. Admitted as Solicitor, 1959. *Member:* Law Society of Northern Ireland; Belfast Solicitors' Association and Northern Ireland Solicitors' European Group. *PRACTICE AREAS:* Company, Commercial, Contract, Commercial Property, Maritime Law.

PARTNERS

H.L.I. JEFFERSON, B.A., born Glasgow, Scotland. *Education:* Campbell College; Queen's University, Belfast. Admitted as Solicitor, 1971. *Member:* Council of the Law Society of Northern Ireland; Belfast Solicitors' Association; Northern Ireland Solicitors' European Group. LANGUAGES: French, Italian. *PRACTICE AREAS:* Accident and Injury Claims; Insurance Litigation.

D.T. TAYLOR, LL.B., born Bangor, County Down, Northern Ireland. *Education:* Bangor Grammar School, Bangor; Queen's University, Belfast. Admitted as Solicitor, 1975. *Member:* Law Society of Northern Ireland: Belfast Solicitors' Association. *PRACTICE AREAS:* Medical Negligence; Accident and Injury Claims; Litigation.

J.M. HENDERSON, LL.B., born Belfast, Northern Ireland. *Education:* Grosvenor High School, Belfast; London University. Admitted as Solicitor, 1979. *Member:* Law Society of Northern Ireland; Belfast Solicitors' Association. *PRACTICE AREAS:* Accident and Injury Claims; Insurance; Litigation; Maritime; Arbitration; Admiralty.

S.D.L. ROCKE, LL.B., born Ballymena, County Antrim, Northern Ireland. *Education:* Armagh Royal School; Queen's University, Belfast. Admitted as Solicitor, 1978. *Member:* Law Society of Northern Ireland; Belfast Solicitors' Association. *PRACTICE AREAS:* Accident and Injury Claims; Insurance; Litigation; Defamation.

M. TINMAN, LL.B., born Lisburn, County Antrim, Northern Ireland. *Education:* Bangor Grammar School, Bangor; Queen's University, Belfast; Institute of Professional Legal Studies. Queen's University of Belfast, 1922. Admitted as Solicitor, 1987. *Member:* Law Society of Northern Ireland; Belfast Solicitors' Association: LANGUAGES: French. *PRACTICE AREAS:* Banking and Finance; Company: Commercial; Contract; Commercial Litigation; Commercial Property; Construction; Mergers and Acquisitions; Intellectual Property; Tax Fiscal; Labour; Employment; Probate.

G.A. JONES, LL.B., born Belfast, Northern Ireland. *Education:* Belfast Royal Academy, Belfast; Queen's University of Belfast, Institute of Professional Legal Studies. Admitted as Solicitor 1986. *Member:* Law Society of Northern Ireland, Belfast Solicitors' Association Committee Member: Young Solicitors' Group. *PRACTICE AREAS:* Insurance; Accident and Injury Claims; Medical Negligence.

D.G. LENNON, LL.B., born Belfast, Northern Ireland. *Education:* Bangor Grammar School, Bangor; University of Nottingham; Institute of Professional Legal Studies. Admitted as Solicitor, 1986. *Member:* Law Society of Northern Ireland; Nottingham University Law Society; Belfast Solicitors' Association. *PRACTICE AREAS:* Accident and Injury Claims; Insurance; Litigation; Media and Entertainment.

(This Listing Continued)

SOLICITORS

G.A. BOWMAN, LL.B., born Bangor, County Down, Northern Ireland. *Education:* Bangor Grammar School, Bangor; Queen's University, Belfast; Queen's University Institute of Professional Legal Studies. Admitted as Solicitor, 1978. *Member:* Law Society of Northern Ireland; Belfast Solicitors' Association. LANGUAGES: German. *PRACTICE AREAS:* Insurance; Litigation.

G.A. CAVANAGH, B.A., born Portrush, County Antrim, Northern Ireland. *Education:* Coleraine Academical Institution, Coleraine; Queen's University, Belfast. Admitted as Solicitor, 1980. *Member:* Law Society of Northern Ireland; Belfast Solicitors' Association. LANGUAGES: French, German. *PRACTICE AREAS:* Insurance; Litigation; Medical Negligence; Accidents and Injury Claims.

KAREN LOUISE FYFFE, B.B.Sc. Hons, born Omagh, County Tyrone, Northern Ireland. *Education:* Portora Royal School, Enniskillen, Queen's University, Belfast, Queen's Institute of Professional Legal Studies. Admitted as Solicitor, 1989. *Member:* Law Society of Northern Ireland; Belfast Solicitors Association. *PRACTICE AREAS:* Insurance; Litigation; Accident and Injury Claims.

R.T. JOHNSTON, LL.B., born Enniskillen, Northern Ireland. *Education:* Regent House Grammar School, Newtownards, County Down; Queen's University, Belfast; Legal Institute in Professional Legal Studies. Admitted as Solicitor, 1984. *Member:* Law Society of Northern Ireland; Belfast Solicitors' Association. *PRACTICE AREAS:* Insurance; Litigation.

ALANA JONES, LL.B., LL.M., born Belfast, Northern Ireland. *Education:* Belfast Royal Academy, Belfast; Queen's University of Belfast; Institute of Professional Legal Studies. Admitted as Solicitor, 1994. *Member:* Law Society of Northern Ireland; Belfast Solicitor's Association. *PRACTICE AREAS:* Employment, Discrimination and Labour Law.

A.C.S. MCCARROLL, LL.B., born Magherafelt, County Londonderry, Northern Ireland. *Education:* Ballymena Academy, Ballymena; Queen's University, Belfast; Institute of Professional Legal Studies. Admitted as Solicitor, 1992. *Member:* Law Society of Northern Ireland; Belfast Solicitors' Association. LANGUAGES: French, German. *PRACTICE AREAS:* Insurance; Litigation; Debt Recovery.

D.B. MCKEE, B.Sc., born Bangor, County Down, Northern Ireland. *Education:* Bangor Grammar School, Bangor; Ulster Polytechnic. Admitted as Solicitor, 1983. *Member:* Law Society of Northern Ireland; Belfast Solicitors' Association. *PRACTICE AREAS:* Litigation; Insurance.

SUSAN MORRISON, LL.B., born Belfast, Northern Ireland. Admitted as Solicitor, 1990. *Education:* Wallace High School, Lisburn, County Antrim, Queen's University, Belfast; Institute of Professional Legal Studies. *Member:* Law Society of Northern Ireland; Belfast Solicitors' Association. *PRACTICE AREAS:* Insurance; Litigation; Matrimonial; Debt Recovery.

KENNETH RUTHERFORD, LL.B., born London, England. *Education:* Belfast Royal Academical Institution, Queen's University, Belfast; Institute of Professional Legal Studies. Admitted as Solicitor, 1989. *Member:* Law Society of Northern Ireland; Belfast Solicitors' Association. *PRACTICE AREAS:* Company; Commercial; Commercial Litigation; Commercial Property; Construction; Insolvency; Conveyancing; E.C. Law; Debt Recovery.

REVISERS OF THE NORTHERN IRELAND LAW DIGEST FOR
THIS DIRECTORY.

L'ESTRANGE & BRETT

Established in 1795

7/9 CHICHESTER STREET
BELFAST BT1 4JG, NORTHERN IRELAND
Telephone: (01232) 230426
Fax: (01232) 246396
*International Code +44 1232; UK STD code 01232 Cable Address:
Landbrett Belfast*

Corporate Law, Commercial Law, Commercial Property, Civil Litigation, Banking, Insolvency, Employment Law and Private Client Business.

VICTOR ALAN HEWITT, born Belfast, Northern Ireland, March, 1941. admitted as a Solicitor, 1967. *Education:* Queen's University, Belfast (LL.B., 1963); University of Michigan (LL.M., 1964). *Member:* Law Society of Northern Ireland (Council Member, 1991—); International Bar Association; Society for Computers and Law (Council Member, 1981-1987). *PRACTICE AREAS:* Commercial Property; Private Client.

(This Listing Continued)

L'ESTRANGE & BRETT, Belfast—Continued

BRIAN LINDSAY HENDERSON, born Belfast, Northern Ireland, December, 1951. admitted as Solicitor, 1976. *Education:* Trinity College, Dublin (Mod), LL.B. Administrative Trainee European Committee. *Member:* Law Society of Northern Ireland; Solicitors European Group (Northern Ireland). *PRACTICE AREAS:* Banking and Finance; Commercial Property.

ADAM THOMAS GARRETT BRETT, born July 9, 1957. admitted as Solicitor, 1981. *Education:* Rugby (M.A. Oxon). *Member:* Law Society of Northern Ireland. *PRACTICE AREAS:* Civil Litigation; Labour Law/Discrimination Law.

SAMUEL ROBERT BECKETT, born Bangor, Northern Ireland, July, 1957. admitted as a Solicitor, 1980. *Education:* Queen's University, Belfast (LL.B., 1979). *Member:* Law Society of Northern Ireland. *PRACTICE AREAS:* Civil Litigation; Insolvency.

JOHN WALTER IRVINE, born Enniskillen, Northern Ireland, September, 1957. admitted as a Solicitor, 1987. *Education:* Queen's University, Belfast (LL.B., 1980); Queen's University, Kingston, Ontario, Canada (LL.M., 1983. Lecturer in Law: Queen's University, Kingston, Ontario, Canada; University of Central Lancashire, 1983-1984. Tutor in Law, University of Exeter, 1984-1985. Consultant, Institute of Professional Legal Studies, Belfast (1992—. *Member:* Law Society of Northern Ireland; Solicitors' European Group (Northern Ireland). *PRACTICE AREAS:* Corporate and Commercial Law.

IRVINE GRAHAM LLEWELLYN PIERCE, born Belfast, Northern Ireland, October 1965. admitted as a Solicitor, 1988. *Education:* Leicester Polytechnic (LL.B., 1986). *Member:* Law Society of Northern Ireland. *PRACTICE AREAS:* Commercial Property.

IAN WILLIAM HUDDLESTON, born Downpatrick, Northern Ireland, September, 1965. admitted as a Solicitor, 1991. *Education:* Queen's University, Belfast (LL.B., 1988); University of Bristol (LL.M., 1989). *Member:* Law Society of Northern Ireland; N.I. Young Solicitors Association. *PRACTICE AREAS:* Commercial Property and Private Client and Environmental Law.

NORWAY

ADVOKATFIRMAET SCHJØDT AS

CHRISTIAN MICHELSENS GATE 1

P.O. BOX 617

N-5001 BERGEN, NORWAY

Telephone: 47 55 90 13 20

Fax: 47 55 90 13 19

Oslo, Norway Office: Dronning Mauds Gate 10, P.O. Box 2444 Solli, N-0201. Telephone: 47 22 83 22 44. Fax: 47 22 83 17 12. Telex: 19789 law n. Data Network Address: 2422 130116.

Trondheim, Norway Office: Ths. Angell Gate 12, P.O. Box 132, N-7001. Telephone: 47 73 52 75 45. Fax: 47 73 51 55 28.

General/Corporate, Commercial, Securities, International Finance, Intellectual Property, Patent, Licensing, Energy/Oil and Gas, Shipping/Admiralty, Environment/Energy, Tax, Government Relations, Products Liability, Personnel/Labour, International General Litigation, Libel Law, Bankruptcy/Insolvency, Construction, Real Estate.

MEMBERS OF FIRM

Per Hagelien	Christopher Brun
Bjarne Hodne	Hans Dale
Lars Dørheim Nilsen	Tor L. Onarheim
Gisle Didriksen	Eilif Utne Riisøen

ASSOCIATES

Marie Vonen

Languages: The Scandinavian Languages and English

(For complete biographical data on all personnel, see Professional Biographies at Oslo, Norway)

THOMMESSEN KREFTING GREVE LUND

VALKENDORFSGATE 1A

P.O. BOX 349

5000 BERGEN, NORWAY

Telephone: 47 55 31 13 50

Fax: 47 55 31 74 75

In Alliance With: Vinge, Sweden and Kromann & Münter, Denmark.

Oslo, Norway Office: Tollbodgaten 27, P.O. Box 413 Sentrum, 0103 Oslo 1. Telephone: 47 22 42 18 10. Telefax: 47 22 42 35 57.

London, England Office: 44/45 Chancery Lane, WC2A 17B. Telephone: 44 171 404 4825. Fax: 44 171 404 1471.

Brussels, Belgium Office: Avenue Louise 475/B 12, 1050. Telephone: 32 2 646 3620. Fax: 32 2 646 4049.

Paris, France Representation Office: 21, Rue Jean Goujon, 75008. Telephone: 331 40.75.37.37. Fax: 331 45.63.05.49.

Hong Kong Representation Office: 2003 Hutchison House, 10 Harcourt Road Central. Telephone: 852 523 6149. Fax: 852 810 5343.

General Business Law. Tax, Corporation, Commercial, Industrial, Shipping, Banking and Government Relations.

RESIDENT MEMBERS

Gunnar Greve	Endre Grande
Jan Einar Greve	Øystein Elgan
Pål W. Lorentzen	Bernt Jacob Pettersen
Dagfinn Heradstveit	Olav Haugland
Hans Olav Lindal	

(For biographical data see Professional Biographies at Oslo, Norway)

WIKBORG, REIN & CO.

Established in 1979

HANDELENS OG SJØFARTENS HUS

OLAV KYRRESGATE 11

5014 BERGEN, NORWAY

Telephone: 47 55318116

Telex: 42516 WRCON

Telefax: 47 55310015

Oslo, Norway Office: Kronprinsesse Märthas plass 1, P.O. Box 1513 Vika, 0117 Oslo. Telephone: 47 22 335510. Telefax: 47 22 418822.

Kobe, Japan Office: Wikborg & Rein, 1-1, 5-Chome Minatojima Nakamachi, Chuo-Ku, 650. Telephone: (78) 303 1772. Telex: 5622404. Telefax: (78) 303 1781.

London, England Office: 1, Knightrider Court, 2nd Floor, EC4V5JP. Telephone: 44 171 236 4598. Telefax: 44 171 236 4599. Telex: 915952.

Company and Commercial Law, Maritime and Shipping, Financing, Securities and Stock Exchange Regulations, Tax, Oil and Gas, Liquidation and Receivership, Aviation. International (hereunder EU/EEA), Environmental, Construction, Information Technology/Telecommunication Law, Law of Torts, Licenses and Cooperation Agreements, General Civil Practice and Litigation.

RESIDENT MEMBERS

Haakon Blaauw	Knud Lorentzen
Øystein Meland	Jon Heimset
Dag Steinfeld	Christian Friis
Stein Pettersen	Peter Frølich
Per Magne Strandborg	

(For complete Biographical data see Professional Biographies at Oslo, Norway).

ARNTZEN, UNDERLAND & CO.

Established in 1923

KARL JOHANSGT. 39

0162 OSLO, NORWAY

Telephone: +47 22 424227

Telefax: +47 22 424851

Telex: JURA 19188

General Business Practice, Mergers and Acquisitions, Tax Law, Insurance Law, International Trade/Middleman Law, Competition Law EC/EEA Law, Financing, Banking/Finance Institutions' Law, Oil and Gas and

(This Listing Continued)

Energy Law, Real Estate Law, Employment Law, Litigation, Arbitration and Mediation.

MEMBERS OF FIRM

MR. ANDREAS ARNTZEN, born June 1, 1928; admitted, 1952; 1960, Supreme Court of Norway. *Education:* University of Oslo (Law Degree, 1952, Candidate in Jurisprudence); Harvard Law School (MCL, 1957). Author: "Insurance of Products," (1971); "Fire Insurance," (1971); "Insurance against water damage," (1972); "Insurance law I," (1974); "Insurance law II," (1975); "Company, Trade and Tax Law in Norway," (1978). Co-Author: "Insurance law," (1993). Assistance Professor, University of Oslo (1953-1955). Chairman of the Public Investigation Committee of Kongsberg Våpenfabrik 1987-1989. *Member:* The Norwegian Bar Association; Norwegian Association of Copy Right. *LANGUAGES:* The Scandinavian languages and English. *PRACTICE AREAS:* Insurance Law; Company Law.

MR. ULF UNDERLAND, born Ski, February 2, 1928; admitted, 1971. *Education:* University of Oslo (Law Degree, 1953, Candidate of Jurisprudence). Co-Author: "Company Trade and Tax Law in Norway," (1978). Practice: Norwegian Ministry of Foreign Affairs (1954-1971). *Member:* The Norwegian Bar Association. *LANGUAGES:* The Scandinavian languages, English, German and French. *PRACTICE AREAS:* General Business Law; International Transactions.

MR. CHRISTIAN FR. MICHELET, born Oslo, December 21, 1953; admitted, 1953, Norway. *Education:* University of Oslo (Law Degree, 1980, Candidate of Jurisprudence); INSEAD, France (Master of Business Administration). Vice President, Total Norge A.S., 1989-1992. Author: Textbook on Tax Law. Co-Author: Textbook on the European Economic Area. *Member:* The Norwegian Petroleum Law Committee, Chairman, Business Policy Council; The Norwegian Oil Industry Association; The Norwegian Bar Association; International Fiscal Association. *LANGUAGES:* The Scandinavian languages, English and French. *PRACTICE AREAS:* Contract Law; Oil, Gas, and Offshore Law; Company Law; Mediation.

MS. VIBECKE GROTH, born Oslo, January 18, 1947; admitted, 1982. *Education:* University of Oslo (Law Degree, 1979, Candidate of Jurisprudence). Education in Mediation Practice; Assistant Judge. Co-Author: Textbook on Maritime Law. *Member:* The Norwegian Bar Association. *LANGUAGES:* The Scandinavian languages and English. *PRACTICE AREAS:* Contract Law; Tort; General Business and Family Law Litigation; Mediation.

MR. FRED A. GADE, born February 19, 1953; admitted, 1987, Norway. *Education:* University of Oslo (Law Degree, 1981, Candidate of Jurisprudence). Attorney, State Attorney's Office. Counsellor in Law Department, Ministry of Justice, Studies at Universitée Aix-en-Provence, France. Assistant Judge. Lecturer, Law Faculty University of Oslo. Co-Author: Textbooks on Maritime Law and Athletics' Law. *Member:* The Norwegian Bar Association. *LANGUAGES:* The Scandinavian languages, English and French. *PRACTICE AREAS:* Company Law; Contract Law.

MR. SVEN IVER STEEN, born February 2, 1959; admitted, 1986. *Education:* University of Oslo (Law Degree, 1984, Candidate of Jurisprudence). Assistant Judge. Co-Author of Commentary to the Act Relating to Financial Activities. Co-Editor of Collection Book on Finance Legislation. Secretary, Public Investigating Committee of Kongsberg Våpenfabrikk, 1987-1989. Principal Secretary, Norwegian Banking Law Commission from 1989. *Member:* The Norwegian Bar Association. *LANGUAGES:* The Scandinavian languages and English. *PRACTICE AREAS:* Banking/Finance Law.

MR. JAN B. JANSEN, born Oslo, December 17, 1958; admitted, 1986. *Education:* University of Oslo (Law Degree, 1984, Candidate of Jurisprudence). Counsellor in the Tax Law Department, Ministry of Finance. Lecturer, Tax Law, University of Oslo. *Member:* The Norwegian Bar Association; International Fiscal Association; Association of International Petroleum Negotiation. *LANGUAGES:* The Scandinavian languages, English and French. *PRACTICE AREAS:* Tax Law.

MR. SIGURD KNUDTZON, born Oslo, December 8, 1956; admitted, 1986. *Education:* University of Oslo (Law Degree, 1982 Candidate of Jurisprudence); American Graduate School of International Management, Arizona, USA (Master Degree). Co-Editor of Collection Book on Finance Legislation. Co-Author; Textbook on the European Economic Area. *Member:* The Norwegian Bar Association; International Bar Association. *LANGUAGES:* The Scandinavian languages and English. *PRACTICE AREAS:* Contract Law; EU/EEA Law.

(This Listing Continued)

MR. RUNE N. JACOBSEN, born March 27, 1957; admitted, 1992. *Education:* University of Oslo (Law Degree, 1983, Candidate of Jurisprudence); Norwegian School of Management (Business Degree). Counsellor, Tax Directorate. Assistant Judge. *Member:* The Norwegian Bar Association. *LANGUAGES:* The Scandinavian languages and English. *PRACTICE AREAS:* Insurance Law.

MR. LARS HOLO, born Baerum, December 5, 1949; admitted, 1979; 1988, Supreme Court of Norway. *Education:* University of Oslo (Candidate in Jurisprudence, 1976). Author: "The Vacation Act with comments," 1988. Assistant Judge, 1978-1980. Legal Advisor, The Parliament's Ombudsman on Public Administrative Affairs, 1976-1978. *Member:* The Norwegian Bar Association. *LANGUAGES:* The Scandinavian languages and English. *PRACTICE AREAS:* Labour Law; Torts.

ASSOCIATES

MS. MIMI K. BERDAL, born Oslo, July 15, 1959; admitted, 1990. *Education:* Universié Catholique d' Angers, Angers, France; Davies' School of English, Cambridge, England; University of Oslo (Law Degree, 1987, Candidate of Jurisprudence). Co-Author: Textbook on Maritime Law. *Member:* The Norwegian Bar Association. *LANGUAGES:* The Scandinavian languages, English and French. *PRACTICE AREAS:* Contract Law.

MR. ERLING HØYTE, born Bergen, May 28, 1957; admitted, 1986. *Education:* University of Oslo (Candidate in Jurisprudence, 1984). Research Assistant: Nordic Institute of Maritime Law. Associate, 1984-1985. Deputy Judge, 1988-1987. Lawyer, 1987-1993. *Member:* The Norwegian Bar Association. *LANGUAGES:* The Scandinavian languages and English. *PRACTICE AREAS:* Bankruptcy; Insolvency; Liquidation.

MR. SVERRE LARHAMMER, born Bodø, July 18, 1962; admitted, 1990. *Education:* University of Oslo (Candidate in Jurisprudence, 1988). Legal Dept. of Christiania Bank, 1990-1991. Legal Advisor, Christiania Bank Lux, 1992-1992. Assistant Judge in Kristiansand. *Member:* The Norwegian Bar Association. *LANGUAGES:* The Scandinavian languages and English. *PRACTICE AREAS:* Negotiations; Contracts; Finance; Banking Law.

MARIE LOUISE ROENNEBERG, born Oslo, June 2, 1961. *Education:* University of Oslo (Law Degree 1989, Candidate of Jurisprudence); Columbus College, USA, Associate of Arts Degree, 1982. Counsellor Tax Directorate. Trainee EC Commission, Brussels. *Member:* The Norwegian Bar Association. *LANGUAGES:* Scandinavian and English. *PRACTICE AREAS:* Petroleum Law.

MR. OLAV A. NYHUS, born Oslo, December 25, 1961; admitted, 1993. *Education:* University of Oslo (Candidate in Jurisprudence, 1988). Tax Law Department, 1989-1992 and Head of Division, 1992-1993, Ministry of Finance. Assistant Judge. Lecturer, Tax Law, Norwegian School of Management, Handelshøyskolen. *Member:* The Norwegian Bar Association. *LANGUAGES:* The Scandinavian languages and English. *PRACTICE AREAS:* Tax Law.

GRETE FUNDERUD, born 1969. *Education:* University of Oslo (Law Degree 1994, Candidate of Jurisprudence). *Member:* The Norwegian Bar Association. *LANGUAGES:* Scandinavian and English. *PRACTICE AREAS:* Contract Law.

MORTEN FOSS, born 1967. *Education:* University of Oslo (Law Degree 1993, Candidate of Jurisprudence). Researcher in EU-law at Institute of Public Law, University of Oslo, 1994. *Member:* The Norwegian Bar Association. *PRACTICE AREAS:* General Business Law; EU/EEA-law.

BRAEKHUS & CO.

Barristers and Solicitors

Established in 1900

TORDENSKIOLDSGT. 6
N-0160 OSLO 1, NORWAY
Telephone: 4722420615
Telefax: 4722336123
Telex: 72768 Merc J N

Sandvikå, Norway Office: 1300 Sandvika, P.B. 216, 1301. Telephone: 4767569660. Telefax: 4767569240. Telex: 19403 cbkab n.

Admitted to all Norwegian Courts. General Civil Practice: Arbitration, Banking, Bankruptcy, Business, Business Crime, Commercial, Company, Composition Proceedings, Computer, Contract, Copyright, Corporation, Creditors Rights, East European Relations, European Community, Financing, Franchising, Industrial Relations, Industrial Law, Inheritance, Insol-

(This Listing Continued)

BRAEKHUS & CO., Oslo—Continued

vency, Litigation, Marketing, Patents, Real Estate, Revenue, Shipping, Tax, Technology, Trade, Trademark, Transport.

FIRM PROFILE: The firm offers a full range of services including litigation, within business law and other areas with emphasis on professional accuracy and client service. The firm employs a total of 30 persons.

MEMBERS OF FIRM

OLE RAADIM, born 1930; admitted, 1958, Norway; 1967, Supreme Court. *Education:* University of Oslo. *LANGUAGES:* English and Scandinavian. *PRACTICE AREAS:* Tax Law; Business Law; Litigation; Arbitration Law.

THOMAS IDSØE, born 1931; admitted, 1960, Norway; 1964, Supreme Court of Norway. *Education:* University of Oslo. Associate Judge. *Member:* Norwegian Aviation Law Association. *LANGUAGES:* English and Scandinavian. *PRACTICE AREAS:* Business Law; Litigation; Banking Law; Criminal Law; International Law; Dealership and Agency Law.

JOHN PETER SANDBORG, born 1936; admitted, 1966, Norway; 1978, Supreme Court. *Education:* University of Oslo. Board Member, Norwegian Taxpayers' Association. *LANGUAGES:* English, German, Spanish and Scandinavian. *PRACTICE AREAS:* Tax Law; Company Law; Inheritance Law; Real Estate Law; Litigation.

CHRISTEN M. GJESDAHL, born 1944; admitted, 1971, Norway; 1988, Supreme Court. *Education:* University of Oslo. Associate Judge in Tynset, 1970-1971. Legal Advisor and Secretary, Board of Directors, Sig, Bergesen d.y. & Co., 1971-1973. Legal Advisor and Secretary, Board of Directors, Norwegian Savings Bank Association, 1973-1977. Assistant Chairman of Directors, Control Committee of Fokus Bank. Legal Advisor and Secretary, Board of Directors, Oslo Shipowners' Association. Managing Partner, Braekhus & Co. *LANGUAGES:* English and Scandinavian. *PRACTICE AREAS:* Banking Law; Bankruptcy Law; Creditors Rights Law; Composition Proceedings; Business Law; Litigation.

JAN KROHN, born 1949; admitted, 1980, Norway. *Education:* University of Oslo. Associate Judge, Ålesund. Ministry of Justice. *LANGUAGES:* English and Scandinavian. *PRACTICE AREAS:* Real Estate Law; Corporate Law; Contract Law; Litigation.

PAL BERG, born 1951; admitted, 1981, Norway; 1993, Supreme Court. *Education:* University of Oslo. Norwegian Tax Directorate. *LANGUAGES:* English and Scandinavian. *PRACTICE AREAS:* International Law; Domestic Tax law.

IVAR A. BARSTAD, born 1945; admitted, 1974, Norway. *Education:* University of Oslo. Police Inspector, Bodø, Associate Judge, Sogndal. Legal Advisor to Fellesbankern A/S. Manager, Sandborg & Co., Eiendom A/S. *LANGUAGES:* English and Scandinavian. *PRACTICE AREAS:* Real Estate Law.

PER BJØRNSEN, born 1956; admitted, 1983, Norway. *Education:* University of Oslo. Associate Judge, Hallingdal. Trainee in New York Firm. *LANGUAGES:* English and Scandinavian. *PRACTICE AREAS:* Corporate Law; Financing Law; Contracts Law.

ESPEN RØNNINGEN, born 1957; admitted, 1986, Norway. *Education:* University of Oslo. Associate Judge, Hønefoss, Norwegian Tax Directorate. *LANGUAGES:* English and Scandinavian. *PRACTICE AREAS:* Business Law; Tax Law; Company Law; Contract Law.

MARIANNE KNOPH KVAMME, born 1944; admitted, 1990, Norway. *Education:* University of Oslo. Legal Advisor: Department of Oil and Industry; Consumers Insurance Office. Associate Judge, District Court, Ringerike. *LANGUAGES:* English and Scandinavian. *PRACTICE AREAS:* Insurance Law; Penal Law; Family Law.

DAG KRISTEN STADHEIM, born 1959; admitted, 1991, Norway. *Education:* University of Oslo; University of North Dakota, Grand Forks, U.S. (Legal studies; Bachelor of economics). Legal Advisor, Tax Directorate. Associate Judge, District Court of Ålesund. *LANGUAGES:* English, German and Scandinavian. *PRACTICE AREAS:* Corporate Law; Tax Law.

EBBE GASTON LARSEN, born 1946; admitted, 1978, Norway. *Education:* University of Oslo. Assistant Police Inspector, Asker and Baerum. Associate, Bull, Løchen & Skirstad. Legal Advisor, Norwegian Tax Directorate. Legal Director, Digital Equipment Corp. A/S. *LANGUAGES:* English and Scandinavian. *PRACTICE AREAS:* Computer Law; Business Law; Contract Law.

(This Listing Continued)

CHRISTIAN SOLEMSLIE, born 1957; admitted, 1987, Norway. *Education:* University of Oslo. Law Firm, Arild Harsson. Union Bank of Norway, Oslo. *LANGUAGES:* English and Scandinavian. *PRACTICE AREAS:* Banking Law; Bankruptcy Law; Business Law; Litigation.

COUNSEL

KIRSTEN ANDENAES, born 1952; admitted, 1990, Norway. *Education:* University of Oslo. Assistant Police Inspector, Asker and Baerum. Assistant Judge, District Court, Eiker, Modum and Sigdal. Member, Kluge ANS. *LANGUAGES:* English and Scandinavian. *PRACTICE AREAS:* Tax Law; Penal Law; Construction Law.

All Partners are members of Norwegian Bar Association and International Bar Association.

BUGGE, ARENTZ-HANSEN & RASMUSSEN

Established in 1966

STRANDEN 1, AKER BRYGGE
P.O. BOX 1524 - VIKA
0117 OSLO 1, NORWAY
Telephone: 22 83 02 70
Telex: 19118 just n
Telecopier: 22 83 07 95/ 22 83 22 75

London, England Office: Bugge, Arentz-Hansen & Rasmussen (UK) ANS, Suite 1A, 99 Gresham Street. Telephone: (0171) 600-0334. Telecopier: (0171) 600-0335.

Corporation, Commercial, Tax, Industrial, Financial, Shipping and International Law, Administrative Law, Government Relations, Inheritance, Litigation.

FIRM PROFILE: Established in 1966, the firm offers a full range of services, including litigation, within Norwegian, EEC and EEA business law. The firm emphasizes professional accuracy, rapid client response and a high degree of client service. The client base is Scandinavian, European and North American. The firm employs a total of 70 persons, of which 40 are lawyers (members and associates).

MEMBERS OF FIRM

FREDERIK M. BUGGE, born Oslo, Norway, October 6, 1923; admitted, 1951, Norway; 1961, Supreme Court of Norway. *Education:* University of Oslo (Candidate in Jurisprudence, 1947); University of Brussels, Belgium. Associate Judge, Ringerike, 1948-1949. *Member:* Norwegian and International Bar Associations. *LANGUAGES:* The Scandinavian Languages, English and French. *PRACTICE AREAS:* Business Law Practice; Directorships.

LARS ARENTZ-HANSEN, born Kristiansund, Norway, November 17, 1927; admitted, 1951, Norway; 1969, Supreme Court of Norway. *Education:* University of Chicago, U.S.A.; Columbia University, U.S.A.; University of Oslo (Candidate in Jurisprudence, 1951); one year studies in France. Associate Judge, Bergen, 1953-1954. Ministry of Foreign Affairs, Legal Section, 1954-1955. *Member:* Norwegian Bar Association. *LANGUAGES:* The Scandinavian Languages, English and French. *PRACTICE AREAS:* Corporation; Contracts; Petroleum Law; Directorships.

KNUT RASMUSSEN, born Drammen, Norway, October 6, 1925; admitted, 1950, Norway; 1965, Supreme Court of Norway. *Education:* University of Oslo (Candidate in Jurisprudence, 1950). Trainee, Haight, Gardner, Poor & Havens, New York, 1951-1952. Associate Judge, Horten, 1953-1954. Legal Advisor, Norwegian Shipowners Association, 1954-1966. *Member:* Norwegian Bar Association; Norwegian Maritime Law Association. *LANGUAGES:* The Scandinavian Languages and English. *PRACTICE AREAS:* Corporate Law; Securities Law; Arbitration.

EVEN WAHR-HANSEN, born Oslo, Norway, March 9, 1942; admitted, 1967, Norway; 1977, Supreme Court of Norway. *Education:* University of Oslo (Candidate in Jurisprudence, 1967). Institute of Comparative Law, New York University, 1972-1973. Associate Judge, Harstad, 1968-1969. Legal teaching, University of Oslo, 1971-1972. Member, Board of Examinators, University of Oslo, 1970-1971. *LANGUAGES:* The Scandinavian Languages and English. *PRACTICE AREAS:* Securities; Corporate; Contract Law.

ANDERS ECKHOFF, born Lier, Norway, November 11, 1943; admitted, 1970, Norway. *Education:* University of Oslo (Candidate in Jurisprudence, 1969); Harvard University (LL.M., 1971). Associate Judge, Strøm-

(This Listing Continued)

men, 1969-1970. *Member:* Norwegian Bar Association. *LANGUAGES:* The Scandinavian Languages and English. *PRACTICE AREAS:* Contracts; Securities; Corporate; Debts Settlement Law.

TIM H. SCHEIE, born Oslo, Norway, April 3, 1944; admitted, 1972, Norway. *Education:* University of Oslo (Candidate in Jurisprudence, 1970). Associate Judge, Salten, 1970-1971. Legal Advisor, Elkem-Spigerverket A/S, 1971-1973. Legal Advisor, 1973-1976 and Managing Director, 1976-1977, Hagb. Waage Shipowners. *Member:* Norwegian Bar Association. *LANGUAGES:* The Scandinavian Languages, English and French. *PRACTICE AREAS:* Financing; Shipping; Corporate Law.

ØYSTEIN ORE, born Oslo, Norway, May 30, 1942; admitted, 1971, Norway. *Education:* University of Oslo (Candidate in Jurisprudence, 1969). Associate Judge, Sunnhordland, 1969-1970. *Member:* Norwegian Bar Association. *LANGUAGES:* The Scandinavian Languages, English and French. *PRACTICE AREAS:* Corporate; Contracts; Financing; Transportation Law.

JAN-FREDRIK RAFEN, born Oslo, Norway, June 30, 1943; admitted, 1972, Norway. *Education:* University of Oslo (Candidate in Jurisprudence, 1969). Author: "Com. on Carriage of Goods by Road Act," Karnov Norway, 1994. *Member:* Norwegian Bar Association. *LANGUAGES:* The Scandinavian Languages and English. *PRACTICE AREAS:* Insurance; Admiralty Law.

EINAR HARBOE, born Oslo, Norway, December, 1950; admitted, 1976, Norway. *Education:* University of Oslo (Candidate in Jurisprudence, 1974). Author: "Inheritance Tax," 1982; "The Property Tax Law," 1984. Co-Author: "The Joint Stock Company, Taxation of Joint Stock Companies and Shareholders," 1990; "The Tax Assessment Act" with comments, 1993. Associate Judge, Eiker, Modum and Sigdal, 1975-1976. Assistant Professor, Civil Law, University of Oslo, 1976-1979. Deputy Director, Tax Law, Ministry of Finance, 1983. *Member:* Norwegian Bar Association. *LANGUAGES:* The Scandinavian Languages and English. *PRACTICE AREAS:* Taxation; Mergers.

ROLF JOHAN RINGDAL, born Oslo, Norway, July 23, 1955; admitted, 1984, Norway. *Education:* University of Oslo (Candidate in Jurisprudence, 1982). Trainee, Haight, Gardner, Poor & Havens, New York, 1979. Associate Judge, Trondenes Sorenskriverembete, 1983-1984. *LANGUAGES:* The Scandinavian Languages and English. *PRACTICE AREAS:* Contracts; Financing; International Joint Ventures Law.

GEIR MIKALSEN, born Bergen, Norway, February 7, 1958; admitted, 1986, Norway. *Education:* University of Oslo (Candidate in Jurisprudence, 1983); British Council Law Course, London, 1986. Associate Judge Hamar Sorenskriverembete, 1985-1986. *LANGUAGES:* The Scandinavian Languages and English. *PRACTICE AREAS:* Corporate; Contract Law; Bankruptcy/Insolvency Law.

RUNE SVOREN, born Drammen, Norway, July 7, 1958; admitted, 1987, Norway. *Education:* University of Oslo (Candidate in Jurisprudence, 1984). Research Assistant, Scandinavian Institute of Maritime Law, Oslo, 1981-1982. Legal Assistant, Office of the Military Judge Advocate, Oslo, 1984-1985. *LANGUAGES:* The Scandinavian Languages and English. *PRACTICE AREAS:* Petroleum; Administrative; Admiralty Law; Financial/Securities Law.

FINN MYHRE, born Oslo, Norway, November 11, 1943; admitted, 1974, Norway. *Education:* University of Oslo (Candidate in Jurisprudence, 1971); International Course in European Integration, Europa Institut, University of Amsterdam, 1971-1972. Assistant Judge, Drammen City Court, 1972-1973. In-house Counsel, Saga Petroleum A. S, 1973-1979. In-house Counsel, Den norske Creditbank, 1979-1982. General Counsel and head of Legal Department, Den norske Creditbank, 1982-1989. *Member:* Norwegian and International (Member, Section on Business Law and Section on Energy and Natural Resources Law). *LANGUAGES:* The Scandinavian Languages and English. *PRACTICE AREAS:* Financing; Petroleum; Banking Law.

TROND SANFELT, born Sarpsborg, Norway, July 5, 1956; admitted, 1983, Norway. *Education:* University of Oslo (Law graduate). Author: 1986 annual revision of Fagernaes: "Referencebook in Tax Law"; "Norwegian Tax Conventions", 1987; "Collection of Norwegian Tax Treaties," 1987; "Maritime Joint Ventures," 1991. Executive Officer, 1980-1981, Senior Executive Officer, 1981-1982, Assistant Judge, 1983-1984, Head of Division, 1984-1985 and Assistant General Director, 1986, Ministry of Finance. *Member:* Norwegian Lawyers Association; International Fiscal Association. *LANGUAGES:* The Scandinavian Languages and English. *PRACTICE AREAS:* Business and Capital Taxation; Domestic and International; Company Law; Acquisitions.

(This Listing Continued)

GUNNAR SORLIE, born Oslo, Norway, September 27, 1952; admitted, 1982, Norway; 1988, Supreme Court of Norway. *Education:* University of Oslo (Candidate in Jurisprudence, 1979). Ministry of Justice, Department of Legislation, 1980-1981. Associate Judge, Ski, 1981-1982. *Member:* Norwegian Bar Association. *LANGUAGES:* The Scandinavian Languages and English. *PRACTICE AREAS:* Litigation; Construction Law; Offshore Contracts; Product Liability.

ERNST RAVNAAS, born Kristiansand, Norway, April 18, 1955; admitted, 1990, Norway. *Education:* Norwegian School of Economics (NHH), Bergen (Bachelor of Commerce, 1980); University of Bergen (Candidate in Jurisprudence, 1988). Author: "Tax Planning for Business," 1987; Tax Economy," 1991; "The Tax Reform - Expectations and Consequences," 1991; "Tax Planning after the 1992 Tax Reform," 1992. Legal Advisor at the Tax Inspectorate, 1980-1982. Associate Professor, Norwegian School of Management, 1983-1990. *Member:* Norwegian Bar Association. *LANGUAGES:* The Scandinavian Languages and English. *PRACTICE AREAS:* Taxation.

GUDMUND KNUDSEN, born Kristiansand, Norway, August 20, 1946; admitted, 1989, Norway. *Education:* University of Oslo (Candidate in Jurisprudence, 1973). Author: "Sports and the Law," 1984; "The Companies Act," 1985; "The Foundation Act" with comments, 1987. Co-Author: "The Joint Stock Companies Act" with comments, 1988. Executive Officer, 1974-1979, Head of Division and Assistant General Director, 1979-1986, and Legal Adviser, 1986-1990, Ministry of Justice, Department of Legislation. Associate Judge, Asker og Baerum Sorenskriverembede, 1976-1978. *Member:* Norwegian Bar Association. *LANGUAGES:* The Scandinavian Languages and English. *PRACTICE AREAS:* Company Law.

KNUT BRUNDTLAND, born Oslo, Norway, July 17, 1961; admitted, 1991. *Education:* University of Oslo (Candidate in Jurisprudence, 1988). *LANGUAGES:* The Scandinavian Languages and English. *PRACTICE AREAS:* Finance; Financial Institutions.

OLA MESTAD, born Oslo, Norway, December 8, 1955; admitted, 1987, Norway. *Education:* University of Oslo (Candidate in Jurisprudence, 1984; Lic. Jur. 1985; Dr. Jur., 1992). Author: "Statoil and Government Regulation and Control," 1984; "On Force Majeure and Contractual Risk," 1991. Research Assistant, Scandinavian Institute of Maritime Law, 1981-1982 and Institute of Public Law, 1982-1984. Assistant and Associate Professor, Scandinavian Institute of Maritime Law, 1984-1989. Research Fellow, University of Munich, Germany, Leopold Wenger Institute, 1984-1985. Associate Professor, University of Bergen, Institute of Private Law, 1988-1990. *Member:* International Bar Association (Member, Section on Energy and Natural Resources Law). *LANGUAGES:* The Scandinavian Languages, English and German. *PRACTICE AREAS:* Energy Law; Offshore Contracts.

BJØRN GABRIEL REED, born Peking, China, September 19, 1958; admitted, 1986, Norway. *Education:* University of Oslo (Candidate in Jurisprudence, 1984). Co-Author: "Shareholders Agreements," 1993. *LANGUAGES:* The Scandinavian Languages and English and French. *PRACTICE AREAS:* Corporate; Contracts Securities.

LONDON REPRESENTATIVES

TERJE SOMMER, Resident Partner, born 1946; admitted, 1974. *Education:* University of Oslo (Candidate in Jurisprudence, 1969). Head of Legal Department Bergen Bank (now Den norske Bank) in Oslo, 1975-1989. General Manager, Bergan Bank/Den norske Bank, London Branch 1989-1991. *LANGUAGES:* The Scandinavian Languages and English. *PRACTICE AREAS:* Banking; Security and Corporate Finance Law.

BEATE MJAALAND, born January 30, 1964. *Education:* University of Oslo (Candidate in Jurisprudence, 1989). Ministry of Consumer Affairs and Government Administration, 1989-1990. Member of the Norwegian Delegation for Competition Law in the EEA Negotiations. EF-Commission, Merger Task Force, 1991-1993. EFTA Surveillance Authority, Competition Directorate, 1993-1995. *LANGUAGES:* The Scandinavian Languages, English, German and French.

ASSOCIATES

ANNE GRO SUNDBY, born Oslo, Norway, April 23, 1953; admitted, 1990, Norway. *Education:* University of Oslo (Candidate in Jurisprudence, 1987). *LANGUAGES:* The Scandinavian Languages and English. *PRACTICE AREAS:* Shipping; Financing.

ØYVIND ERIKSEN, born Tønsberg, Norway, June 1, 1964; admitted, 1992, Norway. *Education:* University of Oslo (Candidate in Jurisprudence, 1990). *LANGUAGES:* The Scandinavian Languages and English. *PRACTICE AREAS:* Corporation Law; Financial Institutions.

(This Listing Continued)

BUGGE, ARENTZ-HANSEN & RASMUSSEN, Oslo—Continued

ARE STENVIK, born June 6, 1966; admitted, 1993, Norway. *Education:* University of Oslo (Candidate in Jurisprudence, 1990). Author: "Com. on Design and Patent Act," Karnov Norway, 1994. Co-Author: "Oil Futures," 1989. Research Assistant, Scandinavian Institute of Maritime Law, 1988-1989. *LANGUAGES:* The Scandinavian Languages and English. *PRACTICE AREAS:* Intellectual Property; Company Law.

LIV MONICA BARGEM, born Kristiansand, Norway, July 24, 1961; admitted, 1990, Norway. *Education:* University of Oslo (Candidate in Jurisprudence, 1987). Censor for the law degree, University of Oslo. Trainee, EEC Commission Brussels, 1991. *LANGUAGES:* The Scandinavian Languages, English and French. *PRACTICE AREAS:* EEC Law; Litigation; Labour Law.

DIDERIK HEIBERG DANBOLT, born Kristiansand, Norway, November 15, 1964; admitted, 1993, Norway. *Education:* University of Oslo (Candidate in Jurisprudence, 1990). Research Assistant, University of Oslo, Institute of Private Law, 1988-1990. *LANGUAGES:* The Scandinavian Languages and English. *PRACTICE AREAS:* Offshore Contracts.

IDA ESPOLIN JOHNSON, born Oslo, Norway, March 1, 1964. *Education:* University of Oslo (Candidate in Jurisprudence, 1990). Research Assistant, University of Oslo, Institute of Private Law, 1988-1989. *LANGUAGES:* The Scandinavian Languages and English.

HANS GEORG WILLE, born Oslo, Norway, August 21, 1958; admitted, 1994, Norway. *Education:* University of Oslo (Candidate in Jurisprudence, 1985); University of California (Economics, 1978-1979). Author: "Corporate Taxation," 1988; "Taxation of Joint Stock Companies - Tax Aspects of De-Mergers," 1988. Member, 1986-1992, Legal Counsellor, 1988 and Director, 1992, Ministry of Finance. On leave to OECD, Division of Fiscal Affairs, 1989-1990. *Member:* International Fiscal Association. *LANGUAGES:* The Scandinavian Languages, English and French. *PRACTICE AREAS:* Business and Capital Taxation; Domestic and International; Company Law.

MARIANNE IVERSEN, born Kristiansand, Norway, December 1, 1956. *Education:* District University of Agder (English Course - part of B.A., 1976); University of Oslo (Candidate in Jurisprudence, 1983). Co-Author: "Manual of Tax Law and Assessment," 1989-1993. Research Assistant, University of Oslo, Institute of Criminal Law, 1981-1982. First Secretary, Ministry of Commerce, 1984. Ministry of Finance, 1984-1992; Head of Division, 1986, Legal Councellor, 1988. *LANGUAGES:* The Scandinavian Languages and English. *PRACTICE AREAS:* Taxation.

AASE GUNDERSEN, born Asker, Norway, August 1, 1962; admitted, 1992, Norway. *Education:* University of Oslo (Candidate in Jurisprudence, 1987). Research Fellow, University of Oslo, Institute of Public Law, 1988-1992. Member, Editorial Board of "Retfaerd" a nordic legal journal. *LANGUAGES:* The Scandinavian Languages and English. *PRACTICE AREAS:* Domestic and International Contract Law; Company Law; Intellectual Property.

STEIN HEGDAL, born Oslo, Norway, August 19, 1953; admitted, 1991, Norway. *Education:* Royal Norwegian Naval Academy, Supply Officer, 1976; University of Bergen (Candidate in Jurisprudence, 1984). Royal Norwegian Navy, 1972-1989. Judge Advocate, 1989-1992. *LANGUAGES:* The Scandinavian Languages, German and English. *PRACTICE AREAS:* Domestic and International Contract Law; Labour Law.

PAAL ESPEN, born Gran, Norway, October 23, 1964. *Education:* University of Oslo (Candidate in Jurisprudence, 1993). *LANGUAGES:* The Scandinavian Languages and English.

JORGEN MONN, born Oslo, Norway, February 14, 1967. *Education:* University of Calgary, 1990; University of Oslo (Candidate of Jurisprudence, 1993). Research Assistant, University of Oslo, 1991-1992. *LANGUAGES:* The Scandinavian Languages and English. *PRACTICE AREAS:* Offshore Contracts.

BJOERN GULESTOEL, born September 23, 1957; admitted, 1986, Norway; 1991, Supreme Court of Norway. *Education:* University of Oslo (Candidate in Jurisprudence, 1984). Various positions in UNI Storebrand AS, Oslo, 1982-1993. Senior Vice President and Head of Legal Department from Feb. 1991. *Member:* Norwegian Bar Association; International Bar Association. *LANGUAGES:* The Scandinavian Languages and English. *PRACTICE AREAS:* Insurance; Tort; Corporate Law; Litigation; Product Liability.

(This Listing Continued)

INGAR OWREN SOLHEIM, born January 16, 1968. *Education:* University of Oslo (Candidate in Jurisprudence, 1993); University of Southampton (Master in Maritime Law, 1994). *LANGUAGES:* The Scandinavian Languages and English.

YNGVILD THUE, born May 5, 1965. *Education:* University of Oslo (Candidate of Jurisprudence, 1993). Author: "The European Court of Justice and Direct Effect of Directives," 1993. *LANGUAGES:* The Scandinavian Languages, English and French.

BJØRN HOGSTAD, born August 7, 1967. *Education:* University of Oslo (Candidate in Jurisprudence, 1993). *LANGUAGES:* The Scandinavian Languages and English.

CARINE SMITH, born October 14, 1962; admitted, 1991, Norway. *Education:* Norwegian School of Economics and Business Administration (M.B.A., 1987); University of Oslo (Candidate in Jurisprudence, 1988); Harvard Law School (LL.M., 1989). Legal Counsel, Kvaerner a.s., 1989-1994. *Member:* Norwegian Bar Association. *LANGUAGES:* The Scandinavian Languages and English. *PRACTICE AREAS:* Corporate Law; Business Law.

IVAR HOBBELHAGEN, born Oslo, Norway, April 7, 1955. *Education:* University of Oslo (Candidate in Jurisprudence, 1983). *LANGUAGES:* The Scandinavian Languages and English. *PRACTICE AREAS:* Taxation Law; Corporate Law.

KNUT ROBERT SVEEN, born Gjøvik, Norway, June 3, 1968. *Education:* University of Oslo (Candidate in Jurisprudence, 1992). Legal Assistant, Office of Judge Advocate General, 1993-1994. *LANGUAGES:* The Scandinavian Languages and English.

HENNING GRØSTAD, born June 26, 1966. *Education:* University of Oslo (Candidate in Jurisprudence, 1994). *LANGUAGES:* The Scandinavian Languages and English.

EINAR BAKKO, born Oslo, Norway, May 1, 1961; admitted, 1994, Norway. *Education:* University of Oslo (Candidate in Jurisprudence, 1988). Ministry of Finance, Tax Law Department, 1989-1993. Associate Judge, Drammen, 1993-1994. *LANGUAGES:* The Scandinavian Languages and English. *PRACTICE AREAS:* Taxation Law.

YNGVE ANDERSEN, born Vadsø, Norway, February 6, 1969. *Education:* University of Oslo (Candidate in Jurisprudence, 1994). *LANGUAGES:* The Scandinavian Languages and English.

STIG EVEN JAKOBSEN, born May 25, 1966. *Education:* Norwegian School of Economics and Business Administration (1991); University of Oslo (Candidate in Jurisprudence, 1995). *LANGUAGES:* The Scandinavian Languages and English.

REFERENCES: US: Haight, Gardner, Poor & Heavens, NY; Seward & Kissel, NY; Sullivan & Cromwell, NY; Healy and Baillie, NY. UK & Hong Kong: Allen & Overy, London; Blake Dawson Waldron, London; Sinclair, Roche & Temperley, London and Hong Kong; Stephenson Harwood, London and Stephenson Harwood & Lo, Hong Kong; Denton Hall, London. France: Clifford Chance, Paris. Bangladesh: Rokanuddin Mahmud, Dhaka.

BULL & CO.

Advokatfirma Ans

Established in 1864

NEDRE VOLLGATE 4
0158 OSLO 1, NORWAY
Telephone: 22-42 70 15
Telefax: (22) 33 64 10

General Business Law, Copyright, Trademark, Patents (Litigation only), Unfair Competition, EDP-Law, Corporation, Commercial and International Law. Creditors Rights, Financial Law, Industrial Law, Shipping, Petroleum Law, Tax Law.

MEMBERS OF FIRM

TORVALD C. LÖCHEN, born Oslo, Norway, May 3, 1928; admitted, 1955, Norway; 1977, Supreme Court of Norway. *Education:* University of Oslo (Candidate in Jurisprudence, 1953). Author: "Praktisk jus. i Markedsforing," (Practical Law in Marketing) 1966, 1970 and 1975. Co-Author, with Hans E. Skirstad and Amund Grimstad, "Juridisk Produktbeskyttelse," (Industrial Property Rights) 1988. Associate Judge, Steinkjer, 1956-1957. *Member:* Norwegian Bar Association (Member of the Council); Norwegian Association for Protection of Industrial Property; Norwegian Association for Copyright Law (Chairman, 1973-1980); Norwegian Association for Marketing Law (Chairman, 1989); Norwegian Association of Jurists.

(This Listing Continued)

LANGUAGES: The Scandinavian languages and English. PRACTICE AREAS: Copyright, Trademark and Patents; Unfair Competition.

HANS E. SKIRSTAD, born Oslo, Norway, May 22, 1939; admitted, 1971, Norway. Education: University of Delaware, U.S.A. (special student, 1961-1962); University of Oslo (Candidate in Jurisprudence, 1967). Associate Judge, Bronnoysund, 1968-1969. Legal Consultant, The Norwegian Guarantee Institute for Export Credit, 1969-1970. Member: Norwegian Bar Association; Norwegian Association for Copyright Law; Norwegian Association of Jurists; International Bar Association. LANGUAGES: The Scandinavian languages, English and German. PRACTICE AREAS: Copyright; Trademark; Unfair Competition; General Business Law.

AMUND GRIMSTAD, born Oslo, Norway, November 13, 1942; admitted, 1976, Norway. Education: University of Oslo (Candidate in Jurisprudence, 1975). Member: Norwegian Bar Association, Norwegian Association of Jurists; Norwegian Copyright Law Association; Norwegian EDP Law Association. LANGUAGES: The Scandinavian languages, English and German. PRACTICE AREAS: Copyright; Trademark; Unfair Competition; Corporation; Commercial and International Law.

HAAKON I. HARALDSEN, born Fredrikstad, Norway, February 18, 1948; admitted, 1977, Norway; 1988, Supreme Court of Norway. Education: University of Oslo (Candidate in Jurisprudence, 1973). Author: "The Board of Conciliation as a means of Solving Conflicts," Oslo, 1978. Co-Author: "Product Liability: An International Manual of Practice," New York, 1987; "Road Traffic Act and Traffic Legislation with Comments," Oslo, 1983; "Family Law Litigation," Tokio, 1984. Assistant Professor, University of Oslo, 1973-1975. Associate Judge, Lillehammer, 1975-1977. Member: Norwegian Bar Association; Norwegian Association for Protection of Industrial Property, AIPPI; Norwegian Association of Jurists; International Bar Association. LANGUAGES: The Scandinavian languages and English. PRACTICE AREAS: General Business Law; Corporation; Commercial and International Law; Petroleum Law.

STEIN INGE SPURKLAND, born Kristiansund, Norway, November 27, 1942; admitted, 1972, Norway. Education: University of Oslo (Candidate in Jurisprudence, 1969; Sociology-Subsidiary subject, 1971). Co-Author: "Bedriftskriser," (Crises in Companies) Oslo, 1988; "Restrukturering av Bedriften," (Reconstruction of Companies) Oslo, 1988. Associate Judge, Tromsø, 1969-1971. Legal Consultant, Ministry of Environment, 1972-1974, Secretary in the Parliament, 1974-1976. Head of Division, Ministry of Eternal Affairs and Labor, 1976-1979. Attorney, Norwegian Industrial Fund, 1979-1984. General Manager, Foenix Industrier A/S, 1984-1985. Member: Norwegian Bar Association; Norwegian Association of Jurists; International Bar Association. LANGUAGES: The Scandinavian languages and English. PRACTICE AREAS: Creditor's Rights; Financial Law; Industrial Law.

KÅRE BJÖRLO, born Oslo, Norway, January 2, 1955; admitted, 1985, Norway. Education: University of Oslo (Candidate in Jurisprudence, 1980). Legal Consultant, State Pollution Control Authority, 1981-1982. Associate Judge, Ski, 1983-1985. Member: Norwegian Bar Association; Norwegian Association of Jurists. LANGUAGES: The Scandinavian languages and English. PRACTICE AREAS: General Business Law; Commercial and International Law; Shipping.

MORTEN WISHMAN, born Oslo, Norway, May 4, 1948; admitted, 1990, Norway. Education: University of Oslo (Candidate in Jurisprudence, 1978). Legal Consultant, Court of Social Affairs, 1978-1980. General Tax Inspector Deputy, Municipal Tax Office of Oslo, 1980-1988. Co-author: "ABC on Assessment 1987 and 1988." Member: Norwegian Bar Association; Norwegian Association of Jurists; International Fiscal Association. LANGUAGES: The Scandinavian languages, French and English. PRACTICE AREAS: Tax Law; General Business Law.

HELGE ALMESTAD, born Oslo, Norway, May 13, 1957; admitted, 1988, Norway. Education: University of Oslo (Candidate of Jurisprudence, 1984). General Tax Inspector Deputy, Municipal Tax Office of Oslo/Akershus, 1985-1986. Associate Attorney, 1986-1988. Attorney with own practice, 1988-1994. Member: Norwegian Bar Association; Norwegian Association of Jurists, International Association. LANGUAGES: The Scandinavian languages and English. PRACTICE AREAS: Tax Law; General Business Law.

ASSOCIATES

ADVOKAT PER LANGSETH. LANGUAGES: The Scandinavian languages and English. PRACTICE AREAS: EDP Law; General Business Law.

(This Listing Continued)

ADVOKAT SISSEL DOMAAS. LANGUAGES: The Scandinavian languages and English. PRACTICE AREAS: General Business Law.

ADVOKAT BENTE HOLMVANG. LANGUAGES: The Scandinavian languages and English. PRACTICE AREAS: General Business Law.

ADVOKAT OLE ANDREAS BAALSRUD. LANGUAGES: The Scandinavian languages and English. PRACTICE AREAS: General Business Law.

ADVOKAT VEGARD LUND. LANGUAGES: The Scandinavian languages and English. PRACTICE AREAS: General Business Law.

Languages: The Scandinavian languages and English.

DALAN SIGMOND HAGEMANN & LOUS

STORTINGSGT 30
N-0161 OSLO, NORWAY
Telephone: 47 22 83 89 09
Fax: 47 22 83 88 38

FIRM PROFILE: Firm includes 10 partners. Firm practices Real Estate related law - zoning and real estate regulations, national and international business law.

Advokatene Dalan, Sigmond, Hagemann & Lous is the result of the merger in 1992 of Advokatene Dalan, Sigmond og Swang and Advokatfirmaet Lous, Hagemann, Arff-Pettersen & Loken.

BJØRN DALAN, born Notodden, Norway, April 4, 1923; admitted, 1949, Norway; 1958, Supreme Court of Norway. Education: University of Oslo (Candidate of Jurisprudence, 1948). LANGUAGES: Scandinavian. PRACTICE AREAS: Business Law; Property Law.

AXEL OTTO CHRISTIAN HAGEMANN, born Andenes, Norway, March 9, 1926; admitted, 1954, Norway; 1963, Supreme Court of Norway. Education: University of Oslo (Candidate of Jurisprudence, 1950). LANGUAGES: Scandinavian and English. PRACTICE AREAS: Real Estate Zoning; Environmental Law; Property Law.

FRITHJOF BARFOD SIGMOND, born Oslo, Norway, June 18, 1930; admitted, 1958, Norway; 1964, Supreme Court of Norway. Education: University of Oslo (Candidate of Jurisprudence, 1955). LANGUAGES: Scandinavian and English. PRACTICE AREAS: Business Law; International Law; Real Estate Zoning; Property Law.

JOHN ARFF-PETERSEN, born Oslo, Norway, January 14, 1941; admitted, 1969, Norway; 1972, Supreme Court of Norway. Education: University of Oslo (Candidate of Jurisprudence, 1966). LANGUAGES: Scandinavian and English. PRACTICE AREAS: Environmental Law; Business Law; Commercial Law; Real Estate; Construction Law.

OLE SWANG, born Oslo, Norway, April 24, 1939; admitted, 1983, Norway;. Education: University of Oslo (Candidate of Jurisprudence, 1967). LANGUAGES: Scandinavian and English. PRACTICE AREAS: Environmental Law; Property Law.

SØREN LORENTZ LOUS, born Oslo, Norway, January 22, 1954; admitted, 1985, Norway. Education: University of Oslo (Candidate of Jurisprudence, 1982). LANGUAGES: Scandinavian and English. PRACTICE AREAS: Business Law; Real Estate Zoning; Property Law.

OLE LØKEN, born June 14, 1944; admitted, 1971, Norway. Education: University of Oslo (Candidate of Jurisprudence, 1969). LANGUAGES: Scandinavian and English. PRACTICE AREAS: International Business Law; Real Estate; Zoning.

HANS P. BJERRING, born Larvik, Norway, November 9, 1953; admitted, 1983, Norway. Education: University of Oslo (Candidate of Jurisprudence, 1979). LANGUAGES: Scandinavian and English. PRACTICE AREAS: Business Law; Contracts; Property Law.

EINER JOYS, born Norway, December 15, 1933; admitted, 1964, Norway; 1993, Supreme Court of Norway. Education: University of Oslo (Candidate of Jurisprudence, 1961). LANGUAGES: Scandinavian and English. PRACTICE AREAS: Business Law.

MATHIESEN HÅKON, born Drammen, Norway, August 9, 1959; admitted, 1990, Norway. Education: University of Oslo (Candidate of Jurisprudence, 1987). LANGUAGES: Scandinavian and English. PRACTICE AREAS: Energy Law; Real Estate.

ADVOKATFIRMAET DE BESCHE & CO.

Established in 1870

TORDENSKIOLDSGATE 4, 0160 OSLO

P.O. BOX 1424 VIKA

0115 OSLO, NORWAY

Telephone: 22 20 60 90

Telex: 71661 beth n

Telefax: 22 33 40 00

General Business Practice, Litigation, Composition Proceedings, Insolvency and Bankruptcy Proceedings, Shipping, Aviation, Banking, Finance, Corporate Law, Tax Law, Mergers and Acquisitions.

MEMBERS OF FIRM

HENNING E. ASHEIM, born Oslo, Norway, January 4, 1948; admitted, 1977, Norway. *Education:* University of Oslo (Candidate in Jurisprudence, 1975); Practical Legal Course arranged by the Norwegian Ministry of Justice, 1975-1976. Worked for Students Legal Aid, University of Oslo. Legal Adviser at the National Insurance Institution, 1976-1977. Scholar, University of Edinburgh, 1981. Worked with Law Office of J & W Burness, Edinburgh, Scotland, 1981. Lecturing at the Law School, University of Oslo. *Member:* Norwegian Bar Association; European Lawyers Association. *LANGUAGES:* Scandinavian Languages and English. *PRACTICE AREAS:* Bankruptcy; Labour and Employment; Litigation.

AKSEL O. HILLESTAD, born Oslo, Norway, June 19, 1948; admitted, 1976, Norway; 1992, Supreme Court of Norway. *Education:* University of Oslo (Candidate in Jurisprudence, 1975); Practical Legal Course arranged by the Norwegian Ministry of Justice (1975-1976); Midwestern State University, Wichita Falls, Texas (Business Law II, 1977); The Southwest Legal Foundation, Dallas, Texas (American and International Law, 1979). Worked with Law Offices of Sherrill & Pace, Wichita Falls, Texas, 1977 and Baker & Botts, Houston Texas, 1978. Worked for the Legal Aid, University of Oslo. Teaching Bankruptcy and Insolvency Law, University of Oslo Law School, 1982-1985. *Member:* Norwegian Bar Association; International Bar Association. *LANGUAGES:* Scandinavian Languages and English. *PRACTICE AREAS:* Business, Corporate and Environmental Laws; Debtor and Creditor.

KARSTEIN J. ESPELID, born Bergen, Norway, July 25, 1949; admitted, 1981, Norway. *Education:* University of Oslo (Candidate in Jurisprudence, 1974). Research Assistant, University of Bergen, Law Faculty, 1971-1972. Public Prosecutor, Bergen, 1974-1977. Lecturer, Private Law, University of Bergen 1974-1977. Public Prosecutor and Head of Office, Investigation Economic and Financial Crimes, Oslo, 1978-1979. Associate Judge, Strømmen, 1980-1981. Attorney at law, Bugge, Arentz-Hansen & Rasmussen, Oslo, 1981-1982. Company Lawyer, Fred Olsen & Co, Oslo, 1982-1985. *Member:* Norwegian Bar Association. *LANGUAGES:* Scandinavian Languages and English. *PRACTICE AREAS:* Commercial and Company Laws; Litigation.

KÅRE I. MOLJORD, born Kristiansand S. Norway, March 28, 1953; admitted, 1984, Norway. *Education:* University of Oslo (Candidate in Jurisprudence, 1978). Counsellor and Head of Office, National Insurance Institution, 1979-1982. Associate Judge, Oslo, 1982-1984. Attorney at Law, KPMG Audit Company, Norway, 1984-1987. Attorney at law, Bugge, Arentz-Hansen & Rasmussen, 1987-1989. Lecturer and Examiner in Tax Law, Norwegian School of Management, 1984—. Lecturer, Tax and Corporate Law, Norwegian Bar Association. Chairman, National Advisory Accounting Board. *Member Norwegian Bar Association; International Fiscal Association. LANGUAGES:* Scandinavian Languages and English. *PRACTICE AREAS:* Mergers and Acquisitions; Taxation; Securities.

HANS HENRIK KVAERNE, born Sandefjord, Norway, May 20, 1959; admitted, 1987. *Education:* University of Oslo (Candidate in Jurisprudence, 1984); University of North Dakota Law School (Courses in Contracts, Torts, Conflicts of Law, Criminal Law and Introduction to the American Legal System, January 1983-May 1983). Worked with Law Offices of Healy & Baillie, New York, N.Y., 1987. *Member:* Norwegian Bar Association. *LANGUAGES:* Scandinavian Languages and English. *PRACTICE AREAS:* Banks and Banking; Contracts; Investments; Aviation; Maritime Law.

TERJE GRANVANG, born Tønsberg, Norway, August 27, 1958; admitted, 1990, Norway. *Education:* University of Oslo (Candidate in Jurisprudence, 1985). Research Assistant, Petroleum Department, Nordic Institute of Maritime Law, University of Oslo, 1983-1984. Legal Counsellor, Royal Ministry of Petroleum and Energy, 1985-1988. Examiner, for the 1st, 2nd and 4th Department Exams, University of Oslo, Faculty of Law,

(This Listing Continued)

1985—. Lecturer, Tort/Compensation Law, Constitution Law and General Legal Methodics, University of Oslo, Law Faculty, 1985—. *Member:* Norwegian Bar Association. *LANGUAGES:* Scandinavian Languages and English. *PRACTICE AREAS:* Constitutional and Administrative Laws; Energy; Natural Resources; Negligence.

ASSOCIATES

OLE KRISTIAN AABØ-EVENSEN, born Oslo, Norway, March 16, 1964; admitted, 1990, Norway. *Education:* University of Oslo (Candidate in Jurisprudence, 1988); Participant at the European Young Lawyer Scholarship Scheme, 1992; King's College, University of London, England (Studies in English Law and International Finance, 1992). Summer Associate, de Besche & Co, 1988. Trainee: Sinclair, Roche & Temperley (Solicitors) London, England, 1992; Four Essex Court, (Barristers), London, England, 1992. *Member:* Norwegian Bar Association; International Bar Association; European Lawyer's Association; International Fiscal Association. *LANGUAGES:* Scandinavian Languages, English and German (Moderate). *PRACTICE AREAS:* Torts; Professional Liability; Debtor and Creditor; Insolvency; Banks and Finance; Mergers and Acquisitions; Fraud.

PER KARSTEN WAHL, born Drammen, Norway, May 22, 1959; admitted, 1988, Norway. *Education:* University of Oslo (Candidate in Jurisprudence, 1985). Legal Consultant, Ministry of Petroleum and Energy, 1986-1988. Associate Judge, Sunnfjord, 1988-1989. Lecturer in Legal Disciplines, Folkeuniversitetet Sør, 1990—. *Member:* Norwegian Bar Association; Norwegian Lawyers Association. *LANGUAGES:* Scandinavian Languages and English. *PRACTICE AREAS:* Property; Real Estate; General Practice; Construction Law; Computers and Software.

STÅLE GJENGSET, born Oslo, Norway, February 16, 1966; admitted, 1993, Norway. *Education:* University of Oslo (Candidate in Jurisprudence, 1991). *Member:* Norwegian Bar Association; Norwegian Lawyers Association. *LANGUAGES:* Scandinavian Languages and English. *PRACTICE AREAS:* Admiralty and Maritime Law; Insurance; Products Liability.

KNUT GLAD, born Tønsberg, Norway, March 4, 1965. *Education:* University of Oslo (Candidate in Jurisprudence, 1993). *Member:* Norwegian Bar Association; Norwegian Lawyers Association. *LANGUAGES:* Scandinavian and English. *PRACTICE AREAS:* Trade Regulation; Consumer Law; Intellectual Property; Leases and Leasing.

PÅL KRISTOFFER SØRVOLL, born Oslo, Norway, January 2, 1967. *Education:* University of Oslo (Candidate in Jurisprudence, 1992). Attorney at Law, Bugge, Arentz-Hansen & Rasmussen, 1992-1994. *Member:* Norwegian Bar Association; Norwegian Lawyers Association. *LANGUAGES:* Scandinavian Languages and English. *PRACTICE AREAS:* Finance; Investments; Trusts and Estates.

JACOB SVERDRUP BJØNNESS-JACOBSEN, born Drammen, Norway, July 16, 1967. *Education:* University of Oslo (Candidate in Jurisprudence, 1993). Legal Consultant, Ministry of Justice, 1993-1994. *Member:* Norwegian Bar Association; Norwegian Lawyers Association. *LANGUAGES:* Scandinavian Languages and English. *PRACTICE AREAS:* Government; Administrative Law; Admiralty; Maritime Law.

STEIN OVE SOLBERG, born Ålesund, Norway, February 23, 1966. *Education:* University of Oslo (Candidate in Jurisprudence, 1994); University of Southampton, UK (courses in European Law and Public International Law, 1991-1992). Research Assistant, University of Oslo, Centre of European Community Law, 1992-1993. Author: Various publications on European Community Law. *Member:* Norwegian Bar Association; Norwegian Lawyers Association. *LANGUAGES:* Scandinavian Languages and English. *PRACTICE AREAS:* European Community Law; Antitrust and Trade Regulation.

ADVOKATFIRMA ENGELSCHIØN & CO.

DA

Established in 1968

AKERSGT. 65 B

P.O. BOX 8333 HAMMERSBORG

0129 OSLO 1, NORWAY

Telephone: +47.22. 36 36 30

Telefax: +47.22. 36 36 80

Mailing Address: P.O. Box 6330 St. Olava Plass, N-0129 Oslo, Norway

London, England Office: 8 Bream's Buildings, EC4A 1HP. Telephone: +44 171 242 3084/1563. Telefax: +44 171 831 8134.

(This Listing Continued)

Paris, France Office: 3 Square Pétrarque, F-75116. Telephone: +33-1-47-55-44-00. Fax: +33-1-47-04-51-31.

Member of Euro-American Lawyers Group with Associated Offices in Europe and America

General Business and Civil Law, Corporate, Commercial, Industrial, Tax and International Law, Computer, Technology, Construction and Real Estate, Trademark, Aviation and Energy Law, Law on Torts and Litigation, Bankruptcies and Liquidation. General Law.

FIRM PROFILE: *The firm was established 25 years ago and offers the full range of all legal services. Through the well reputed EURO-AMERICAN LAWYERS GROUP, at present consisting of more than 700 lawyers connected with associated law offices throughout Europe and America, the complete international legal services exists for our actual and potential clients. We emphasize on General Law with specialization in Commercial, Corporate, Construction and Computer Law, including litigation of any subject of national or international nature.*

MEMBERS OF FIRM

TORE SVERDRUP ENGELSCHIØN, born Oslo, Norway, July 30, 1931; admitted, 1960, Norway; 1965, Supreme Court of Norway. *Education:* Treider Commercial School, Oslo (1953); University of Oslo (Candidate in Jurisprudence, 1957); Columbia University, New York (Master of Law, 1959). Judge, Østre Baerum County Court, 1960-1962. Lecturer in Law, University of Oslo, 1906-1964. Associate, Law Firm Annaeus Schjødt, 1962-1968. Examining Commissioner (Censor), University of Oslo, 1964—. Senior Partner Law Firm Engelschiøn & Co. ANS, 1968—. Judge Advocate, HQ South Norway, 1980—. Government Appointed Board Member, Norwegian Maritime Museum. 1989—. *Member:* Norwegian and International Bar Associations; Deutsche Anwaltverein; The Law Society (UK); Société Internationale de Droit Militaire et de Droit de Guerre; Norwegian Association of Jurists, Deutsch-nordische Juristvereinnung; US, UK, French and Norwegian Chambers of Commerce. [Lt.Col. Norwegian Army (R) 1990—]. *LANGUAGES:* Norwegian, Swedish, Danish, English and German. *PRACTICE AREAS:* Commercial; Corporate; Competition and General Law; Litigation and Arbitration.

FREDRIK BUGGE SIVERTS, born Oslo, Norway, February 17, 1944; admitted, 1973, Norway. *Education:* University of Oslo (Candidate in Jurisprudence, 1969); Oslo Value Added Tax Office (1969-1970). Associate Judge, Bamble, 1970-1972. Legal Consultant, Oslo Tax Office, 1972-1974. Associate Legal Department, Den norske Creditbank, 1974. Partner Law Firm Engelschiøn & Co. ANS, 1976—. *Member:* Norwegian Bar Association. *LANGUAGES:* The Scandinavian languages and English.

HANS CHRISTIAN STEENSTRUP, born Oslo, Norway, June 14, 1950; admitted, 1980, Norway. *Education:* University of Oslo (Candidate in Jurisprudence, 1977). Consultant, Norwegian Employers Confederation, 1977-1979. Associate, Thommessen, Karlsrud, Heyerdahl & Brunsvig, Law Firm, 1980-1984. Partner Law Firm Engelschiøn & Co. ANS, 1984—. *Member:* Norwegian Bar Association; Norwegian Association for Computer Law. *LANGUAGES:* The Scandinavian languages and English.

THOR HENNING PEDERSEN, born Oslo, Norway, May 25, 1955; admitted, 1985, Norway. *Education:* University of Oslo (Candidate in Jurisprudence, 1983). Deputy Chief Constable and Prosecutor, 1983-1984. Associate, Moltke-Hansen, Lorange, Moltke-Hansen, Law Firm, 1984-1985. Associate, 1985-1987 and Partner, 1987—, Law Firm Engelschiøn & Co. ANS. *Member:* Norwegian Bar Association. *LANGUAGES:* The Scandinavian languages and English.

ERIC-JEAN THOMAS, born 1950; admitted, 1980, Paris (Not admitted in Norway). *Education:* University of Paris Pantheon-Sorbonne, IEP Paris (Master in Law, DES). Lecturer, 1975-1985 and Consultant and Study Director, 1979-1982, UNESCO. Partner Law Firm Engelschiøn & Co. 1989—. (Resident, Paris Office). *LANGUAGES:* The Scandinavian languages, English, Spanish and French.

TOR VALE, born Skien, Norway, April 26, 1948; admitted, 1980, Norway. *Education:* University of Oslo (Master, 1977). Author: "Dismissal of leaders," Lov og Rett, 1986. Associate: The Norwegian Society of Chartered Engineers, 1977-1980; Judge Alta, 1978; Law Firm Hr.adv. Per Helweg and Einar Dahl, 1980-1987. Partner, Law Firm Sunde & Co., 1987-1990. Appointed Legal Advisor (Vertrauensanwalt) of the Embassy of Switzerland. *Member:* Norwegian Bar Association. *LANGUAGES:* Scandinavian, English and German.

PER OMRENG, born Stavanger, Norway, March 21, 1953; admitted, 1987, Norway. *Education:* University of Oslo (Candidate in Jurisprudence, 1979). Head of Division, Norwegian Oil Taxation Office, 1984-1985. *Member:*

(This Listing Continued)

ber: Norwegian Bar Association. *LANGUAGES:* The Scandinavian languages and English.

TERJE SØRENSEN, born 1942; admitted, 1974. Deputy Judge Romsdal District Court. Legal Secretary Justice Department. Legal Consultant Chief Administrative Officer of Møre og Romsdal. Legal Department Elkem-Spigerverk AS. Head of office County Administration of Møre og Romsdal. Chief Officer of Molde town. Manager NBBL Utbygging AS. Secretary General of Norwegian Union of Bank Employees. In association with Law Firm Engelschiøn & Co. 1993.

Member of Euro-American Lawyers Group.

EVENSEN & CO.

Advokatfirma ANS

GRENSEN 3

P.O. BOX 334 SENTRUM

0101 OSLO, NORWAY

Telephone: (47) 22 330 331

Telefax: (47) 22 333 208

Telex: 79931 EVEN N

Antwerp, Belgium Office: Lange Lozanastraat 2, 2018 Antwerp. Telephone: (32) 3 248 1818. Telefax: (32) 3 248 5592.

Norwegian, English, Belgian and International Law.
Admirality and Maritime Law, Commercial Law, Bankruptcy and Corporate Insolvency, European Union, Personal Injury, General Norwegian and Belgian Civil Practice, Civil Litigation and Arbitration.

FIRM PROFILE: *Evensen & Co. Advokatfirma ANS provides a wide range of legal services, particularly in the fields of Admiralty and Maritime Law. Although Evensen & Co. is internationally known for its services to the shipping industry, we are devoted to provide quality service over an extensive range of legal services for both individual and corporate clients. The combination of our firm's maritime and legal knowledge as well as the central positions of our offices in Oslo and Antwerp, enable us to provide our clients with an expedite and efficient service.*

MEMBERS OF FIRM

TOM HAUGÅRD EVENSEN, born Oslo, Norway, October 17, 1951; admitted, 1979, Norway. *Education:* University of Oslo (Candidate in Jurisprudence, 1977). Assistant Public Prosecutor, 1977-1978. Practising in Japan, 1981-1984. Member, Law Firm, Wikborg, Rein & Co., 1985-1988. *Member:* Norwegian Bar Association; Norwegian Maritime Law Association. *LANGUAGES:* The Scandinavian Languages and English.

OLA RØTHE, born Oslo, Norway, June 14, 1960; admitted, 1989, Norway. *Education:* Winona State University, USA (Economics, 1980); Norwegian Naval Academy (Navigation Officer/Lieutenant, 1981-1982); University of Oslo (Candidate in Jurisprudence, 1986). Assistant Foreign Exchange Dealer, Den norske Bank, Oslo, 1983. Associate, Law Firm, Wikborg, Rein & Co., 1987-1988; Law Firm, Haugård Evensen, 1990. Associate Judge, Sørumsand, 1989. *Member:* Norwegian Bar Association; Norwegian Maritime Law Association. *LANGUAGES:* The Scandinavian Languages and English.

ANDERS W. FÆRDEN, born Oslo, Norway, February 1, 1962; admitted, 1988, Norway. *Education:* University of Oslo (Candidate in Jurisprudence, 1987); University of Kiel, Germany (Exam in German Contract Law, 1987). Associate, Law Firm, Thommesen, Krefting & Greve AS, Oslo and London, 1988-1991. Associate Judge, Toten, 1989-1990. Trainee, Law Firm, Walker & Corsa, New York, 1991. *Member:* Norwegian Bar Association; Norwegian Maritime Law Association. *LANGUAGES:* Norwegian, Danish, English and German.

DAG RØMMEN, born Tromsø, Norway, August 26, 1955; admitted, 1993, Norway. *Education:* Bergen Naval Academy (Master Mariner, 1982); University of Bergen (Candidate in Jurisprudence, 1987). Seaman, Deck Officer, Operation Manager, Chartering Manager, Leif Hoegh & Co. AS, 1977-1985. Operation Manager, Sale and Purchase Broker, P.F. Bassoe AS & Co., 1985-1990. General Manager, Chartering and Assistant Counsel, Anders Wilhelmsen & Co., 1990-1992. Lecturer, The Norwegian Shipping Academy. Chartering and S and P practice since 1989. Chairman, Intertanko Ad hoc Working Group on Combination Carriers 1991-1992. Assistant Member, BIMCO Documentary Committee, 1991-1992. *Member:* Association of Norwegian Ship Operators; The Norwegian Bar Association; Norwegian Maritime Law Association. *LANGUAGES:* The Scandinavian Languages and English.

(This Listing Continued)

EVENSEN & CO., Oslo—Continued

EINAR ASKVIG, born Oslo, Norway, March 4, 1947; admitted, 1978, Norway. *Education:* Business School of Oslo and Oslo Marketing College (Bachelor in Economics, 1971); University of Oslo (Candidate in Jurisprudence, 1976); Harvard Business School OPM, 1993. Associate Judge, Jaeren, 1976-1977. Associate, Law Firm, Wikborg Rein & Co., 1977-1981 (Resident Lawyer, Rotterdam Office, 1979-1981). Director of European Marketing and Development, Bally Manufacturing Corp., 1981-1985, Law Firm Scanlaw, Antwerp, Belgium, 1985-1993. *Member:* The Norwegian Bar Association. *LANGUAGES:* The Scandinavian Languages, English, German and Dutch.

VÉRONIQUE CARETTE, born Antwerp, Belgium, August 25, 1960; admitted, 1987, Belgium. *Education:* University of Antwerp (Law, 1978-1984), Maritime Law (1984-1986). Practice: Law Firm E. Clijmans, 1984-1987; Law Firm Lange, Naeyaert & Carette, 1987-1993; Law Firm De Roeck, Naeyaert & Carette, 1993-1994. *Member:* Belgian Bar Association. *LANGUAGES:* English, French, Dutch, Spanish and German.

ASSOCIATES

KNUT ERIK WESTAD, born Oslo, Norway, September 6, 1952. *Education:* Oslo Business School (Bachelor of Business Administration, 1976); Arizona State University (Master of Business Administration, 1977); University of Oslo (Candidate in Jurisprudence, 1990). Assistant Controller, Olav Thon, 1977-1980. Director of Finance, Supply-Service AS, 1980-1986. Director, Osco Shipping Services AS, 1986-1989. Director of Finance, Naess, Jahre & Partners AS, 1986-1992. *Member:* Norwegian Bar Association; Norwegian Maritime Law Association; Norwegian Association of Masters in Business Administration. *LANGUAGES:* The Scandinavian Languages and English.

JONE ENGH, born Stavanger, Norway, March 15, 1963; admitted, 1992, Norway. *Education:* University of Bergen (Candidate in Jurisprudence, 1989). Lecturer and Teacher, University of Bergen and Molde College, Commercial Law, 1988-1992. First Legal Advisor, The Register of Business Enterprises, The Brønnøysund Register Centre, 1990. Associate Judge, Romsdal, 1991-1992. *Member:* Norwegian Bar Association; Norwegian Maritime Law Association. *LANGUAGES:* The Scandinavian Languages and English.

SARA GILLINGHAM, born Surrey, March 19, 1964; admitted, 1991, English Solicitor. *Education:* London School of Economics (Economics and International Relations, 1983-1986); The College of Law (1987-1989). Trainee then Solicitor, Ince & Co., London, 1989-1994. *Member:* The Law Society (England); Norwegian Maritime Law Association. *LANGUAGES:* English, French, Spanish and Norwegian.

ADVOKATFIRMAET FØYEN & CO ANS.

OSCARS GATE 52
0258 OSLO, NORWAY
Telephone: +47 22 44 46 40
Telefax: +47 22 44 89 27

Nesbru, Norway Office: P.O. Box 253 Nesbru Senter. Telephone: +47 66 84 52 80. Telefax: +47 66 98 29 30.

London, England Office: 30 Aylesbury Street. EC1R OER. Telephone: +44 171 490 6336. Telefax: +44 171 490 6234.

Maplewood, New Jersey Office: Foyen & Partners, 108 Baker Street, 07040. Telephone: 201-564-6116. Telefax: 201-564-7665.

Stockholm, Sweden Office: Foyen & Partners Advokatbyra, Nybrogatan 15, S-102 46. Telephone: 8-663 02 90. Telefax: 8-662 15 90.

Brussels, Belgium Office: Masons Solicitors. Avenue Louise 391. Telephone: 32 2-646-0260. Telefax: 32 2-646-7323.

Agency Law, Licensing, Distribution Agreements, Copyright Law. Labour Law. Building and Contracting Law, Real Estate, Development Projects, Housing and Rent. Electronic Data Processsing, Information Technology, Telecommunications and Broadcasting Law. Business Development, Strategy and Financing, in Norway and abroad. Division of Estate, Inheritance, Personal Rights Law. Competition Law, Marketing Law and EU/EEC Law. Bankruptcy and Debt Negotiations. Environmental Law. Company Law and Law relating to Shareholders, Stock Exchange and Acquisition of Companies. Taxes, Duties and Indirect Taxes.

(This Listing Continued)

PARTNERS

STEIN A. FØYEN, born Oslo, Norway, February 11, 1935; admitted, 1963, Norway. *Education:* University of Oslo, Faculty of Law (Cand. Jur., 1961). *Member:* Norwegian (MNA) and International Bar Associations; Norwegian Chamber of Commerce; The American Tax Institute in Europe. *LANGUAGES:* English and Scandinavian.

KARL MARTHINUSSEN, born February 15, 1948; admitted, 1977, Norway. *Education:* University of Bergen (Cand. Jur., 1974). Legal Adviser in The State Committee for Revision of the Building Regulation, 1985-1987. *Member:* Norwegian Bar Association (Member of the Board, District of Olson; Member, Law Committee for Building and Planning Legislation, 1983—). *LANGUAGES:* English and Scandinavian.

ARVE FØYEN, born Oslo, Norway, February 28, 1947; admitted, 1984, Norway. *Education:* University of Oslo (Cand. Jur., 1973). Co-author: "EDB-anskaffelser," Computer Purchase, University Press, 1981. Engaged by Ministry of Justice as Consultant suggesting revision to the Personal Registers Act (Privacy in Computer Systems), 1982. Chairman of the Board, Norwegian Society for Computers and Law, 1980-1983. Appointed by the Norwegian Bar Association as Member of its reference Group for Computer Law-Legislation, 1983-1987, 1987—. *Member:* Norwegian Bar Association (MNA). *LANGUAGES:* English and Scandinavian.

HEIKKI GIVERHOLT, born Oslo, Norway, October 24, 1953; admitted, 1982, Norway. *Education:* University of Oslo, Faculty of Law (Cand. Jur., 1978). Consultant, Department of Justice, 1979-1980. Assistant Judge, 1980-1982. Sencor at the University of Oslo. *Member:* Norwegian Bar Association (MNA);. *LANGUAGES:* English and Scandinavian.

GEIR SAND, born June 6, 1955; admitted, 1987, Norway. *Education:* University of Oslo, Faculty of Law (Cand. Jur., 1982). Trainee, Sullivan & Cromwell, New York, 1984-1985. *Member:* Norwegian Bar Association (MNA). *LANGUAGES:* English and Scandinavian.

JOSTEIN RAMSE, born June 5, 1953; admitted, 1984, Norway. *Education:* University of Oslo, Faculty of Law (Cand. Jur., 1979). *Member:* Norwegian Bar Association. *LANGUAGES:* English and Scandinavian.

FRODE MÜLLER, born 1953; admitted, 1988, Norway. *Education:* University of Oslo, Faculty of Law (Cand. Jur., 1979). *Member:* Norwegian Bar Association. *LANGUAGES:* English and Scandinavian.

KARSTEN ØVRETVEIT, born December 19, 1951; admitted, 1979, Norway. *Education:* University of Oslo, Faculty of Law (Cand. Jur., 1975). *Member:* Norwegian Association of Lawyers. *LANGUAGES:* English and Scandinavian.

HANS JØRGEN ARVESEN, born 1959; admitted, 1988, Norway. *Education:* University of Oslo, Faculty of Law (Cand. Jur., 1985). *Member:* Norwegian Bar Association. *LANGUAGES:* English and Scandinavian.

ASSOCIATES

OTTAR F. EGSETH, born 1962; admitted, 1991, Norway. *Education:* University of Bergen, Faculty of Law (Cand Jur., 1988). *Member:* Norwegian Bar Association. *LANGUAGES:* English and Scandinavian.

JOHAN HENRIK VISTER, born 1960; admitted, 1989, Norway. *Education:* University of Oslo, Faculty of Law (Cand Jur., 1986). *Member:* Norwegian Bar Association. *LANGUAGES:* English and Scandinavian.

MARIT NYGAARD, born 1959; admitted, 1988, Norway. *Education:* University of Oslo, Faculty of Law (Cand Jur., 1984). *Member:* Norwegian Bar Association. *LANGUAGES:* English and Scandinavian.

GØSTA W. THOMMESEN, born 1956; admitted, 1992, Norway. *Education:* University of Oslo, Faculty of Law (Cand. Jur., 1987). *Member:* Norwegian Bar Association. *LANGUAGES:* English and Scandinavian.

INGAR HÅLAND, born 1962; admitted, 1993, Norway. *Education:* University of Oslo, Faculty of Law (Cand. Jur., 1990). *Member:* Norwegian Bar Association. *LANGUAGES:* English and Scandinavian.

EINAR NOREIK, born 1958; admitted, 1993, Norway. *Education:* University of Oslo, Faculty of Law (Cand. Jur., 1986). *Member:* Norwegian Bar Association. *LANGUAGES:* English and Scandinavian.

SUNNIVA BERNSTEN, born 1960; admitted, 1994. *Education:* University of Oslo, Faculty of Law (Cand. Jur., 1988). *Member:* Norwegian Bar Association. *LANGUAGES:* English and Scandinavian.

LARS BORCHGREVNIK GRINDAL, born 1963; admitted, 1993. *Education:* University of Oslo, Faculty of Law (Cand. Jur., 1991). *Member:* Norwegian Bar Association. *LANGUAGES:* English and Scandinavian.

(This Listing Continued)

ERIK BØHN, born 1962; admitted, 1994. *Education:* University of Oslo, Faculty of Law (Cand. Jur., 1990). *Member:* Norwegian Bar Association. *LANGUAGES:* English, Scandinavian and Spanish.

MARIANNE RYTTER EVENSEN, born 1968. *Education:* University of Oslo, Faculty of Law (Cand. Jur., 1994). *Member:* Norwegian Bar Association. *LANGUAGES:* English and Scandinavian.

(For complete biographical data on other personnel, see professional biographies in New York, New York, Maplewood, New Jersey, Stockholm and Sweden)

ADVOKATENE HAAVIND & HAGA

DRAMMENSVEIEN 20 A
P.O. BOX 2338-SOLLI
N-0201 OSLO, NORWAY
Telephone: 47-22 447850
Telefax: 47-22 444401

General Business Law, Tax, Company, Commercial and International Law, Public Law, Copyright, Entertainment Law, Trademark, Patents (Litigation only), Unfair Competition, Probate, Real Estate Planning, Bank and Monetary Law, Product Liability, Employment Law, EEA Law.

MEMBERS OF FIRM

JAN DAHL, born Oslo, Norway, February 14, 1931; admitted, 1959, Norway; 1966, Supreme Court of Norway. *Education:* University of Oslo (Candidate in Jurisprudence, 1955). Author: "Incorporation and Registration of Companies." Co-Author: with Einar Hanssen, "Law for domestic use." Co-Editor: Editorial Committee for the Law Review: "Law and Justice." Legal Consultant, Directorate of Prices and Antitrust Control, 1956. Associate Judge, Hadeland and Land, 1957-1958. External Examiner, University of Oslo, 1960-1968. Member, Norwegian Board of the Nordic Jurist Meetings, 1984—(Secretary, 1975-1985). *Member:* Norwegian Bar Association (Chairman and Member, Committee for Corporate Law, 1971-1983). *LANGUAGES:* The Scandinavian Languages, English and French.

HARALD BJELKE, born Oslo, Norway, June 20, 1931; admitted, 1957, Norway; 1966, Supreme Court of Norway. *Education:* University of Oslo (Candidate in Jurisprudence, 1956); Studies Oxford (1959-1960). Associate Judge, Nes, 1957-1959. Chairman the Government's Council of Experts on Copyright Law, 1984—. Chairman Committee for Government Scholarships and Guaranteed Income for Performers of the Fine Arts, 1980-1985. Member, Executive Committee of International Literary and Artistic Association (ALAI), 1980-1992. *Member:* Norwegian Bar Association (Chairman and Member, Permanent Committee for Copyright, 1969-1989); International Bar Association; Norwegian Copyright Society (Vice President, 1972-1980; President, 1980-1992). *LANGUAGES:* The Scandinavian Languages and English.

FINN ARNESEN, born Oslo, Norway, November 7, 1934; admitted, 1963, Norway; 1969, Supreme Court of Norway. *Education:* University of Oslo (Candidate in Jurisprudence, 1960); Studies in England, USA and France. Associate Judge, Hallingdal, 1961-1962. Secretary, Norwegian Board, Nordic Jurist Meetings. *Member:* Norwegian and International Bar Associations; Union International des Avocats; Norwegian Associations for European Law and Competition Law. *LANGUAGES:* The Scandinavian Languages, English and French.

HANS GEORG HAGA, born Oslo, Norway, September 18, 1937; admitted, 1964, Norway. *Education:* University of Oslo (Candidate in Jurisprudence, 1963). Chief Legal Adviser Ministry of Justice, 1963-1964. Author: "Several articles in legal journals and in newspapers. *Member:* Norwegian Bar Association. *LANGUAGES:* The Scandinavian Languages and English.

HARALD ARNKVAERN, born Oslo, Norway, February 5, 1939; admitted, 1966, Norway; 1972, Supreme Court of Norway. *Education:* University of Oslo (Candidate in Jurisprudence, 1964); University of Illinois, Law School (1967-1968). Associate Judge, Ringerike, 1964-1965. With Legal Department Elkem, 1965-1974. Head of Legal Department, 1974-1982 and Deputy Managing Director, 1981-1988, Den norske Creditbank. External Examiner, Bank and Monetary Law, University of Oslo. *Member:* Norwegian Bar Association (Board Member Oslo Branch, 1975-1979); International Bar Association; Norwegian Association of Jurists. *LANGUAGES:* The Scandinavian Languages and English.

ERIK WAHLSTRØM, born Oslo, Norway, March 3, 1946; admitted, 1978, Norway. *Education:* University of Oslo (Candidate in Jurisprudence, 1974). Author: "Shares and Income Tax," 1980; several articles on tax issues

(This Listing Continued)

in legal journals. Legal Consultant, Norwegian Tax Directorate, 1974-1976. *Member:* Norwegian Bar Association (Chairman, permanent committee for Tax Law). *LANGUAGES:* The Scandinavian Languages and English.

BJØRG VEN, born Oslo, Norway, January 28, 1946; admitted, 1974, Norway; 1988, Supreme Court of Norway. *Education:* University of Oslo (Candidate in Jurisprudence, 1972); City of London Polytechnic (English Business Law, 1977). Author: Article, "Distributor's Position when the Contract is Discontinued", Nordic Jurists Meetings, 1984. Associate Judge, Ålesund, 1972-1973. External Examiner, University of Oslo. *Member:* Norwegian Bar Association (Board Member, 1986-1987; Vice President, 1988-1994; President, 1994—; President, Oslo Branch, 1983-1985, Member, Committee for Construction Law). *LANGUAGES:* The Scandinavian Languages, English, French and Spanish.

KJELL T. TORKILDSEN, born Oslo, Norway, April 30, 1945; admitted, 1975, Norway. *Education:* University of Oslo (Candidate in Jurisprudence, 1972). Chief Legal Adviser, Ministry of Justice, 1972-1973 and 1975-1978. Associate Judge, Midhordland, 1973-1975. *Member:* Norwegian Bar Association; Norwegian Association of Jurists; Norwegian Copyrights Society (Member of the Board, 1992—). *LANGUAGES:* The Scandinavian Languages and English.

ARNE HAAVIND, born Oslo, Norway, May 14, 1949; admitted, 1982, Norway; 1988, Supreme Court of Norway. *Education:* University of Oslo (Candidate in Jurisprudence, 1975). Associate Judge, Nedre Romerike, 1978-1979. Chief Legal Adviser and Head of Division Norwegian Tax Directorate, 1976-1981. *Member:* Norwegian Bar Association; Norwegian Association of Jurists; International Fiscal Association. *LANGUAGES:* The Scandinavian Languages and English.

RAGNAR ØSTENSEN, born Oslo, Norway, October 11, 1948; admitted, 1984, Norway. *Education:* University of Oslo (Candidate in Jurisprudence, 1975). Author: of several articles in "Tax Law" and other legal journals. Legal Consultant, Baerum County Council Taxation Authorities, 1975-1978. Legal Consultant and Head of Division Ministry of Finance, 1978-1983. *Member:* Norwegian Bar Association; Norwegian Association of Jurists; International Fiscal Association. *LANGUAGES:* The Scandinavian Languages and English.

ERIK DAVIDSEN, born Oslo, Norway, April 17, 1950; admitted, 1984, Norway. *Education:* University of Oslo (Candidate in Jurisprudence, 1976). Chief Legal Adviser, Ministry of Environment, 1976-1979. Legal Consultant, Nordic Councils of ministers. Secretary, Governmental Committee examining the consequences and preparing remedial actions after the Tsjernobyl-accident. Assistant Professor, Constitutional Law. *Member:* Norwegian Bar Association; Norwegian Association of Jurists. *LANGUAGES:* The Scandinavian Languages and English.

MIKAEL FARSTAD HELLEVIK, born Alesund, Norway, April 13, 1959; admitted, 1988, Norway. *Education:* University of Oslo (Candidate in Jurisprudence, 1978). Editor, "Yngvar Tank: The Inheritance Tax Act, a Commentary," 1984. Legal Consultant Ministry of Finance, 1979-1985. Head of Division, 1983-1985. *Member:* Norwegian Bar Association. *LANGUAGES:* The Scandinavian Languages and English.

DAG ARNE RUUD, born Oslo, Norway, December 29, 1957; admitted, 1987, Norway. *Education:* University of Oslo (Candidate in Jurisprudence, 1982). Legal Adviser, Ministry of Consumers Affairs, 1982-1983. Chief Legal Adviser, Ombudsmann, 1983-1985. Associate Judge, Larvik, 1985-1986. External Examiner, University of Oslo. *Member:* Norwegian Bar Association; Norwegian Association of Jurists. *LANGUAGES:* The Scandinavian Languages and English.

INGER KJERSTI DØRSTAD, born Oslo, Norway, April 5, 1953; admitted, 1984, Norway. *Education:* University of Oslo (Candidate in Jurisprudence, 1980); New York University, School of Law (Master of Comparative Jurisprudence, M.C.J., 1985). Chief Legal Adviser Ministry of Environment, 1980-1983. Associate Judge, Asker og Baerum, 1983-1984. Assistant Professor, Marketing Law, Wang Marketing School and Constitutional Law, University of Oslo, 1983-1984. External Examiner, in Copyright, University of Oslo. *Member:* Norwegian Bar Association; Norwegian Association of Jurists; Norwegian Copyright Society. *LANGUAGES:* The Scandinavian Languages and English.

ANNE MERETE NICOLAYSEN, born Oslo, Norway, August 12, 1946; admitted, 1988, Norway. *Education:* University of Oslo (Candidate in Jurisprudence, 1981). Legal Editor, Grøndahl & Son Publishing House, 1981-1983. Chief Legal Adviser, Ministry of Justice, 1983-1986. Associate Judge, Ringerike, 1986-1988. *Member:* Norwegian Bar Association. *LANGUAGES:* The Scandinavian Languages and English.

(This Listing Continued)

ADVOKATENE HAAVIND & HAGA, Oslo—Continued

SIGMUND SANDALL, born Oslo, Norway, August 4, 1950; admitted, 1979, Norway. *Education:* Naval Academy, Bergen (1969-1970); University of Oslo (Candidate in Jurisprudence, 1976). Chief Executive Officer, Ministry of Justice, 1977-1978. Associate Judge, Hadeland and Land, 1979-1980. Member, Legal Department and Manager, Foreign Department, Union Bank of Norway, 1980-1984. Company Secretary, Norwegian Association of Savings Banks, 1984-1985. Manager, Financial Department, Mutual Insurance, 1985-1987. Senior Consultant and Partner, IKO Management, 1987. Utviklings Partner A/S, 1988-1990. *Member:* Norwegian Bar Association. *LANGUAGES:* Scandinavian Languages, English and Russian.

HANS OTTO MEYER, born Oslo, Norway, October 12, 1954; admitted, 1988, Norway. *Education:* Military Academy (1974-1975); University of Oslo (Candidate in Jurisprudence, 1981). Legal Adviser and Assistant Deputy Director, Ministry of Finance, 1982-1989. Assistant Judge, Sandnes, 1986-1988. *Member:* Norwegian Bar Association. *LANGUAGES:* The Scandinavian Languages and English.

JØRGEN BRUNSVIG, born Baerum, Norway, August 9, 1957; admitted, 1988, Norway. *Education:* Economic College Oslo (1977); University of Oslo (Candidate in Jurisprudence, 1985). Research Assistant, Institute of Civil Law, University of Oslo, 1982-1983. Chief Legal Adviser, Ministry of Justice, 1985-1988. Associate Judge, Toten, 1988-1989. External Lecturer and Examiner, University of Oslo. Author: "Negligence in the medical profession" (Oslo 1983); The patient's right to damages" (Oslo 1985). "Co-author: "Medical responsibility in Norway." *Member:* Norwegian Bar Association; Norwegian Association of Jurists. *LANGUAGES:* The Scandinavian Languages and English.

ASSOCIATES

CECILIE ELISABETH EGELAND, born July 9, 1964. *Education:* University of Oslo (Candidate in Jurisprudence, 1993). *LANGUAGES:* The Scandinavian Languages, English, French and Spanish.

LIV TORILL EVENRUD, born August 20, 1966. *Education:* University of Oslo (Candidate in Jurisprudence, 1992). Research Assistant, University of Oslo, Institute for Civil Law. Legal Consultant, Norwegian Tax Directorate, 1992-1993. Author: "Norwegian Power Prices in Relation to the Rules About State Aid in the EEC Treaty," Art. 92 (1). *LANGUAGES:* The Scandinavian Languages and English.

HELGE OLAV BERGAN, born September 23, 1968. *Education:* University of Oslo (Candidate in Jurisprudence, 1993). *LANGUAGES:* The Scandinavian languages and English.

ELLEN-KATRINE THRAP-MEYER, born Oslo, Norway, March 27, 1962. *Education:* University of Oslo (Candidate in Jurisprudence, 1994). Research Assistant, University of Oslo, Norwegian Center for Computers and Law, 1987 and 1983-1994. Author: "The Consumer Protection Act and Computers," Oslo, 1989. Co-Author: "Computerprogrammes and legal classification," Oslo, 1990. *LANGUAGES:* The Scandinavian Languages and English.

JOHAN K. ENGELSCHIØN, born December 30, 1963; admitted, 1994, Norway. *Education:* University of Oslo (Candidate in Jurisprudence). Legal Consultant, Norwegian Tax Directorate, 1991-1993. Associate, law firm of Aakvaag, Bull Enger & Co. DA, Oslo, 1993-1994. *Member:* Norwegian Association of Jurists. *LANGUAGES:* The Scandinavian languages and English.

ANNE CATHRINE RØED, born August 8, 1968. *Education:* University of Oslo (Candidate in Jurisprudence, 1994). Research Assistant, University of Oslo, Institute for Civil Law, 1992-1993. Author: "Choice of Law and the protection of pieces of Art.". *LANGUAGES:* The Scandinavian languages, English and Italian.

FORENEDE ADVOKATER JOHANSEN OG UNHJEM JOHANSEN A/S

Established in 1975

PILESTREDET 41C
N-0166 OSLO, NORWAY
Telephone: 47-22-208160
Fax: 47-22-208161

Asker, Norway Office: Fekjan 15, P.O. Box 253, N-1362 Nesbru. Telephone: 47-66980730. Fax: 47-66848588.

(This Listing Continued)

Geilo, Norway Office: Torgbygget, P.O. Box 113, N-3580. Telephone: 47-32091911. Fax: 47-32091911.

Associated Offices: "United Lawyers" in several countries including Spain (Alicante, Málaga, Marbella and Madrid).

Barristers and Solicitors, admitted to Norwegian Courts.
General Civil Practice, Corporation, Taxation, Trade, Divorce, Inheritance.

FIRM PROFILE: The firm offers a full range of legal services. It is well known in Real Estate, Family and Inheritance, as well as Commercial and Norway-Spain problems.

MEMBERS OF FIRM

PER EINAR JOHANSEN, born Oslo, January 7, 1942; admitted, 1972, Norway. *Education:* University of Oslo (candidate in Jurisprudence, 1971). Associate, Law Firm Jordan, 1972-1974. Senior Partner, Forenede Advokater Johansen og Unhjem Johansen AS, 1975—. Author, Publication, "Life and Law in Spain," 1991; "International Commercial," 1993; "Spanish-Norwegian Law," 1995. Associate Judge, Court of Oslo, 1971-1972. *Member:* Norwegian Bar Association; International Bar Association. *LANGUAGES:* The Scandinavian Languages, English, German and Spanish. *PRACTICE AREAS:* Real Estate; Trusts and Estates; Trademarks; Commercial; Corporate Business; Company Law; Inheritance; General Practice.

MILDRID UNHJEM JOHANSEN, born Oslo, August 21, 1939. *Education:* candidate in Psychology and Pedagogy, 1972; candidate in Jurisprudence, 1985. Associate, Forenede Advokater Johansen og Unhjem Johansen AS, 1985-1987. *Member:* The Norwegian Bar Association. *LANGUAGES:* The Scandinavian Languages, English and German. *PRACTICE AREAS:* Family Law; Wills; Contracts; Children; Labour and Employment; General Practice.

ADVOKATFIRMA KLUGE ANS

FRIDTJOF NANSENS PL. 7
0160 OSLO, NORWAY
Telephone: 47/22 33 07 60
Fax: 47/22 33 23 80

Stavanger, Norway Office: Gamle Forusvei 17, Box 277, 4033, Forus. Telephone: 47/51 57 14 77. Fax: 47/51 57 65 65.

Firm engaged in Norwegian, European and International Law Practice. Entitled to plead before the Norwegian Supreme Court.
Company Law, Tax Law, Construction Law, Petroleum Law, Contract Law, Labour Law, Public and Administrative Law, Environmental Law, Litigation and International Arbitration.

FIRM PROFILE: Established in 1923, Kluge Ans has become one of Norway's most well recognized and respected law firms. The client base consists mainly of both Norwegian, European and North American companies in trade, industry, and the petroleum and construction industries, financial institutions, as well as branches and agencies of local and central government. The firm has 11 partners and 7 assistants practicing in offices in Oslo and Stavanger, centre of the petroleum industry in Norway. English brochure available upon request.

(For Complete Biographical Data, see Professional Biographies at Stavanger, Norway)

KVALE & CO. ANS

AKERSGATEN 8
P.O. BOX 354 SENTRUM
0101 OSLO, NORWAY
Telephone: +47 22 331616
Fax: +47 22 331615

General Business Law, Commercial, Corporate, and International Law, Bankruptcies and Liquidation, Oil and Energy Law, Competition and Labour Law.

FIRM PROFILE: Kvale & Co provides legal services in the fields of Company and Commercial Law. The firm serves clients ranging from small companies to some of the largest Norwegian Companies, as well as foreign companies doing business in Norway. The clients are involved in a wide range of businesses including banking, oil exploration and production, retailing, real estate and service industries.

ANDERS KVALE, born July 29, 1947; admitted, 1977, Norway. *Education:* Norwegian School of Economics and Business administration (MBA, 1970); University of Oslo (Candidate in Jurisprudence, 1977). *Member:*

(This Listing Continued)

Norwegian Bar Association. *LANGUAGES:* Scandinavian and English. *PRACTICE AREAS:* Civil and International Arbitration; Company Law; Bank Finance; Mergers and Acquisitions.

GUNNAR STAKE-LARSEN, born Oslo, May 31, 1953; admitted, 1982, Norway; 1988, Supreme Court of Norway. *Education:* University of Oslo (Candidate in Jurisprudence, 1980). Research Assistant, University of Oslo, 1978-1979. Associate Judge, Sandnes, 1980-1981. *Member:* Norwegian Bar Association; Norwegian Association for Protection of Industrial Property. *LANGUAGES:* Scandinavian, English and German. *PRACTICE AREAS:* Company Law; Patents; Contract Law; Property Settlements.

ARNE SEEMANN BERG, born 1953; admitted, 1982, Norway. *Education:* University of Oslo (Candidate in Jurisprudence, 1979). Lecturer, Norwegian Law Society. *Member:* Norwegian Bar Association. *LANGUAGES:* Scandinavian and English. *PRACTICE AREAS:* Bankruptcy Law; Insolvency; Reorganizations; Contract Law.

JENS BREDE, born Oslo, February 8, 1958; admitted, 1986, Norway. *Education:* University of Oslo (Candidate in Jurisprudence, 1984). Research Assistant, University of Oslo, 1983-1984. Associate Judge, Lofoten, 1984-1986. *Member:* Norwegian Bar Association. *LANGUAGES:* Scandinavian and English. *PRACTICE AREAS:* Civil and International Arbitration; Aviation (Aircraft); Energy Acquisitions.

JO RODIN, born Oslo, November 20, 1956; admitted, 1985, Norway. *Education:* University of Oslo (Candidate in Jurisprudence, 1983). Legal Adviser, Finance Ministry, 1984. *Member:* Norwegian Bar Association. *LANGUAGES:* Scandinavian, English and French. *PRACTICE AREAS:* Bankruptcy Law; Reorganizations; Bank Collections; Acquisitions and Sales; Restructuring.

PER CHRISTOFFERSEN, born Oslo, September 22, 1955; admitted, 1986, Norway. *Education:* University of Oslo (Candidate in Jurisprudence, 1981). Legal Adviser, Ministry of Justice, 1981-1984. Associate Judge, 1984-1985. *Member:* Norwegian Bar Association. *LANGUAGES:* Scandinavian, English and German. *PRACTICE AREAS:* Company Agency and Distributorships; Restructuring; Acquisitions and Sales; Commercial Contracts.

GEIR LOLLENG, born Oslo, June 9, 1954; admitted, 1986, Norway. *Education:* University of Oslo (Candidate in Jurisprudence, 1981). Legal Adviser, The Norwegian Employers Confederation. Associate Judge, Sandnes, 1984-1985. Director, The Employers Association of Oil Companies. *Member:* Norwegian Bar Association; The Association of Labour Law. *LANGUAGES:* Scandinavian and English. *PRACTICE AREAS:* Labour and Employment; Company Administration; Commercial Contracts; Leveraged and Management Buyouts.

BØRGE KROGSRUD, born Oslo, Norway, November 12, 1954; admitted, 1992, Norway. *Education:* University of Oslo (Candidatus Magistrii, Pedagogics and Psychology, 1981; Candidate in Jurisprudence, 1984). Editor/Author: "Telecommunication laws," Juridisk Forlag, Oslo, 1994. Chief Legal Advisor, Ministry of Health and Social Affairs, Department of Environmental Health, 1984-1986. Head of Law Committee, 1986-1989. *Member:* Norwegian Bar Association; International Bar Association; Norwegian Association for European Law; Norwegian Maritime Law Association. *LANGUAGES:* The Scandinavian Languages and English.

FRODE SAETER, born Oslo, Norway, June 20, 1955; admitted, 1986, Norway. *Education:* University of Oslo (Candidate in Jurisprudence, 1984). Legal Advisor, Hewlett-Packard, 1984-1985; Associate, Føyen & Co., 1985-1987; Research Assistant, Norwegian Research Center of Computers and Law, Norwegian School of Management, 1986-1987; Partner, Law Firm Engelschiøn & Co. ANS, 1988-1994. *Member:* Norwegian Bar Association; International Bar Association; Norwegian Copyright Society; Norwegian Association for Computer Law. *LANGUAGES:* The Scandinavian Languages and English.

PETER L. BRECHAN, born Oslo, Norway, February 5, 1959; admitted, 1989, Norway. *Education:* University of Oslo (Candidate in Jurisprudence, 1985). Trainee, Sinclair Roche & Temperley, London, 1985. Executive Officer: Ministry of Trade, Section of Shipping Affairs, 1985; Den norske Creditbank, International Finance Department, 1986-1988. Legal Counsel, Den norske Creditbank, Legal Department, 1988-1989. Law Firm Schjødt ANS, 1989-1994. Author: "Capital Market in Norway," IFLR, 1995. *Member:* Norwegian Bar Association; International Bar Association; Norwegian Maritime Law Association. *LANGUAGES:* The Scandinavian Languages and English.

DAG THORSTENSEN, born Oslo, Norway, April 9, 1956; admitted, 1986, Norway. *Education:* Engineer Officer Academy (1975-1976); University of Oslo (Candidate in Jurisprudence, 1982). Legal Consultant, County of Oslo, 1982-1983. Deputy Chief Welfare Officer, Council of Oslo, 1983-1984. Associate: Torkildsen & Torkildsen, 1984-1985; Borge & Borge, 1985-1987. Partner, Law Firm Engelschiøn & Co ANS, 1987-1994. *Member:* Norwegian Bar Association; Norwegian Society for Military Law and War Law; International Bar Association. *LANGUAGES:* The Scandinavian Languages and English.

TRYGVE NORUM, born Orkdal, Norway, October 24, 1964; admitted, 1993, Norway. *Education:* University of Oslo (Candidate in Jurisprudence, 1989). *Member:* Norwegian Bar Association; International Bar Association; Norwegian Association for European Law. *LANGUAGES:* The Scandinavian Languages and English.

LOWZOW & CO.

RAADHUSGATEN 27
N-0158 OSLO, NORWAY
Telephone: +47 22 41 68 10
Facsimile: +47 22 41 68 08

Mailing Address: P.O. Box 359 Sentrum, N-0101 Oslo, Norway

Securities Law, Project Finance, Banking, Licenses, Patents, Trademarks, Copyrights, Competition, Computer and Telecommunications Law, Liquidation/Bankruptcy/Receivership, International Transactions/Foreign Investments, Environmental Law, Labour Law, Litigation and General Corporate and Business Law.

MEMBERS OF FIRM

HALFDAN A. LOWZOW, born Oslo, Norway, July 30, 1957; admitted, 1988, Norway. *Education:* University of Bergen, Institute for Psychology (1979); University of Oslo (Candidate in Jurisprudence, 1984). Co-Author: "Shareholders Agreements," Ad Notam Gyldendal, Oslo, 1993. Executive Officer, Ministry of Trade, Section of State Guarantees, 1986-1987. *Member:* Norwegian Bar Association; International Bar Association. *LANGUAGES:* The Scandinavian Languages and English.

GEIR BO STEINBERG, born Oslo, Norway, October 26, 1958; admitted, 1989, Norway. *Education:* University of Oslo (Candidate in Jurisprudence, 1987). Research Assistant, Institute of Private and Commercial Law, University of Oslo, 1985-1986. Co-Author: "Shareholders Agreements," Ad Notam Gyldendal, Oslo, 1993. Editor, Norwegian Business Law Journal, 1994—. *Member:* Norwegian Bar Association; International Bar Association; Norwegian Association for European Law; Norwegian Association for Intellectual Property Law; Norwegian Copyright Society. *LANGUAGES:* The Scandinavian Languages and English.

(This Listing Continued)

ADVOKATFIRMAET MELTVEDT KOMNAES & CO.

Established in 1977

HAAKON VIIS GT. 2
P.O. BOX 1893 VIKA
0124 OSLO, NORWAY
Telephone: Int. 47 22 83 48 00
Telefax: Int. 47 22 83 48 11

General Business Law, Corporation, Commercial, Competition, Tax, Banking, Construction, Labor and Criminal Law, Litigation.

MEMBERS OF FIRM

ARNE MELTVEDT, born Oslo, Norway, June 21, 1935; admitted, 1963, Norway; 1967, Supreme Court of Norway. *Education:* University of Oslo (Candidate in Jurisprudence, 1961). Associate Judge, Porsgrunn, 1961-1963. Member, Board of Examiners, University of Oslo, 1974. Head of Legal Department, Den norske Bank, 1971-1973. Permanent Defense Counsel to the Supreme Court, 1978—. Chairman, Oslo District of the Norwegian Bar Association, 1989-1991. Chairman Board of Directors of the Control Committee of Union Bank of Norway. *Member:* Norwegian Bar Association; International Bar Association (SBL). *LANGUAGES:* English. *PRACTICE AREAS:* General Business Law; Corporation; Banking; Litigation.

ESPEN KOMNAES, born Drammen, Norway, January 19, 1952; admitted, 1976, Norway. *Education:* University of Bergen (Candidate in Jurisprudence, 1979); Santa Barbara City College, California, USA (Political Science). Legal Department, Ministry of Foreign Affairs, 1980-1981. Associate Judge Molde, 1981-1983. *Member:* Norwegian Bar Association; Inter-

(This Listing Continued)

ADVOKATFIRMAET MELTVEDT KOMNAES & CO.,
Oslo—Continued

national Bar Association (SBL). *LANGUAGES:* English. *PRACTICE AREAS:* General Business Law; Corporation; Banking; Insurance.

BJØRN GETZ, born Oslo, Norway, February 10, 1948; admitted, 1978, Norway. *Education:* University of Oslo (Candidate in Jurisprudence, 1974). Ministry of Justice, 1975-1980; Associate Judge, Gjøvik, 1976-1978. Associate, Advokatfirmaet Bull, Løchen og Skirstad, Oslo, 1980-1985. Partner, Advokatfirmaet Meltvedt, Komnaes & Getz, 1987-1991. *Member:* Norwegian Bar Association; International Bar Association (SBL). *LANGUAGES:* English. *PRACTICE AREAS:* Corporation; Commercial; General Business Law; Labour Law; Litigation.

OLAV BRAATEN, born Oslo, Norway, March 25, 1956; admitted, 1989, Norway. *Education:* University of Oslo (Sociology, 1977; Candidate in Jurisprudence, 1985). Legal Adviser, Eksportfinans, 1985-1987. Associate, Law firm of Bugge, Arentz-Hansen & Rasmussen, 1987-1991. *Member:* Norwegian Bar Association; International Bar Association (SBL). *LANGUAGES:* English. *PRACTICE AREAS:* Company Law; Litigation; Contract Law; Financing.

KRISTIN HEGSTAD, born Horten, Norway, September 21, 1959; admitted, 1988, Norway. *Education:* University of Oslo (Candidate in Jurisprudence, 1985). Associate, Bugge, Arentz-Hansen & Rasmussen, Oslo, 1986-1988. Associate Judge, Midhordaland Sorenskriverembede, 1988-1989. Associate, Bugge, Arentz-Hansen & Rasmussen, Oslo, 1990-1992. *Member:* Norwegian Bar Association. *LANGUAGES:* English. *PRACTICE AREAS:* General Business Law; Corporation; Labor Law; Litigation.

NYBORG & BLANCK

HAAKON VII'S GT. 1
0161 OSLO, NORWAY
Telephone: (47) 22 83 40 00
Telefax: (47) 22 83 43 00
Telex: 79078 NBORGn

General Civil and Business Law Practice, Arbitration, Mediation and Litigation, Banking, Commercial, Company and Corporate, Computers and Software, Construction, Contracts, Copyrights and Intellectual Property, Oil and Gas, Real Estate, Shipping and Taxation.

MEMBERS OF FIRM

KJELL NYBORG, born Bø, Vesterålen, Norway, January 19, 1934; admitted, 1964, Norway; 1971, Supreme Court of Norway. *Education:* University of Oslo (Candidate in Jurisprudence, 1962). Research Fellow in law at University of Oslo, 1962-1963. Scholarship for postgraduate law studies at London School of Economics second half, 1963. International Course in Common Market Law, Europa Institutt, University of Amsterdam. Author: "Strict Liability in Criminal Law," Lov og Rett, 1963. Associate Judge, 1964. General Counsel to ABC Bank, 1971-1973. General Counsel and Director to Stolt-Nielsen Group/Stolt Tankers and Terminals (Holdings) S.A., 1973-1984, whereof 7 years in USA. Represented Norwegian Bank Association in Law Committee and Liberian Shipowners Association in Maritime Law Committee of International Chamber of Shipping. *Member:* Norwegian Bar Association. *LANGUAGES:* The Scandinavian Languages and English.

PER G. GULBRANDSEN, born Oslo, April 13, 1939; admitted, 1968, Norway. *Education:* University of Oslo (Candidate in Jurisprudence, 1965). Associate Judge, Kongsvinger, 1966-1967; Legal Counsel, Elkem a.s., 1968-1970;, General Counsel, Norwegian Oil Consortium a.s. & Co. and Saga Petroleum a.s. (Vice President) 1971-1986. *Member:* Norwegian Bar Association. *LANGUAGES:* The Scandinavian Languages, English and German.

TOR NORDLIE, born Oslo, May 12, 1943; admitted, 1972, Norway; 1988, Supreme Court of Norway. *Education:* University of Oslo (Candidate in Jurisprudence, 1969). Associate Judge, Hardanger, 1970-1972. *Member:* Norwegian Bar Association; The Norwegian Society of Construction and Consulting Law. *LANGUAGES:* The Scandinavian Languages and English.

RAGNVALD HOLM LIE, born Oslo, Norway, March 30, 1944; admitted, 1975, Norway. *Education:* Handelsakademie (Vienna), 1964; University of Oslo (Candidate in Jurisprudence, 1971). Research Student, The London School of Economics and Political Science, 1972-1973. Author: Book, "Take-over bid and amalgamation", 1981. Associate Judge, Eidsvoll,

(This Listing Continued)

1973-1975. *Member:* Norwegian Bar Association. *LANGUAGES:* The Scandinavian Languages, English and German.

BERTEL O. STEEN, JR., born Oslo, February 20, 1948; admitted, 1978, Norway. *Education:* University of Oslo (Candidate in Jurisprudence, 1974); University of Aston, England (M.Sc. in Business Administration, 1979). Associate Judge, Orkdal, 1977-1978. Legal Counsel of Stolt-Nielsen Seaway, 1980-1982. *Member:* Norwegian Bar Association. *LANGUAGES:* The Scandinavian Languages and English.

LARS JAKOB BLANCK, born Oslo, February 27, 1948; admitted, 1982, Norway. *Education:* University of Oslo (Candidate in Jurisprudence, 1975). Thesis, "Discretion, Rule application and Computer-assisted Decision making in Public Administration." Editor: "Data Banks and Society," 1972; "Swedish Data Act and Data Inspectorate to protect Personal Integrity," Lov og Rett, 1974; "Court Decisions regarding Computers and Law I," 1980. Scholar, University of Oslo, 1975-1976. University of Oslo: Research Assistant 1972-1974; Research Scholar 1975; Assistant Professor 1976-1980. Consultant, The Data Inspectorate, 1980-1981. Associate Judge, Tromsø, 1981-1982. *Member:* Norwegian Bar Association, Information Technology Law Group/Europe (IT Law Group/Europe). *LANGUAGES:* The Scandinavian Languages and English.

KLAUS DÖSCHER, born Oslo, December 1, 1946; admitted, 1986, Norway. *Education:* University of Oslo (Candidate in Jurisprudence, 1982). Associate Judge, Vardø, 1984-1986. *Member:* Norwegian Bar Association, The Norwegian Society of Construction and Consulting Law. *LANGUAGES:* The Scandinavian Languages and English.

RAEDER, WISLØFF, AASLAND & CO.

Established in 1948

DRAMMENSVEIEN 30
P.O. BOX 2873 SOLLI
0230 OSLO 2, NORWAY
Telephone: +(47) 22 44 68 33
Telecopier: +(47) 22 43 44 28

Corporation, Commercial, Trade, Industrial Construction and Real Estate. Tax, Government Relations, Finance, International Law, Commercial Litigation, Family Law, Inheritance.

MEMBERS OF FIRM

ODD WISLØFF, born November 18, 1936; admitted, 1965, Norway; 1969, Supreme Court of Norway. *Education:* University of Oslo (Candidate in Jurisprudence, 1963). Associate Judge, Harstad, 1964-1965. *Member:* Norwegian Bar Association. *LANGUAGES:* The Scandinavian Languages and English.

CHR. AASLAND, born May 24, 1942; admitted, 1972, Norway. *Education:* University of Oslo (Candidate in Jurisprudence, 1969). Associate Judge, Harstad, 1971-1972. In house Counsel: Andresens Bank, 1975-1978. *Member:* Norwegian Bar Association. *LANGUAGES:* The Scandinavian Languages and English.

KARSTEN H. TORKILDSEN, born November 24, 1947; admitted, 1976, Norway. *Education:* University of Oslo (Candidate in Jurisprudence, 1973). Associate Judge, Sarpsborg, 1975-1976. Legal Advisor, Oslo Tax Authorities, 1976-1979. *Member:* Norwegian Bar Association. *LANGUAGES:* The Scandinavian Languages and English.

LARS OLE EVENSEN, born November 29, 1952; admitted, 1984, Norway. *Education:* University of Oslo (Candidate in Jurisprudence, 1980). Associate Judge, Kristiansand, 1982-1984. *Member:* Norwegian Bar Association. *LANGUAGES:* The Scandinavian Languages and English.

CARL ARTHUR CHRISTIANSEN, born June 27, 1958; admitted, 1987, Norway. *Education:* University of Oslo (Candidate in Jurisprudence, 1984). Associate Judge, Hamar, 1986-1987. *Member:* Norwegian Bar Association. *LANGUAGES:* The Scandinavian Languages and English.

MORTEN OPSTAD, born August 31, 1953; admitted, 1986, Norway. Education Cand, jur 1979. Executive officer and Assistant Secretary Ministry of Finance 1980-1984. Associate Judge, Fredrikstad 1984-1986. Tax lawyer, Deloitte Tax Services and Coopers & Lybrand Tax Services, 1986-1991. *Member:* Norwegian Bar Association. *LANGUAGES:* The Scandinavian Languages and English.

OLE PER SOLUM, born December 12, 1957; admitted, 1987, Norway. *Education:* University of Oslo (Candidate in Jurisprudence, 1984). Skuld P & I Club. *Member:* Norwegian Bar Association. *LANGUAGES:* The Scandinavian Languages and English.

(This Listing Continued)

JENS I. KOBRO, born May 19, 1957; admitted, 1988, Norway. *Education:* University of Oslo (Candidate in Jurisprudence, 1984). Legal Advisor, Central Tax Authorities 1984-1986. Associate Judge Arendal, 1986-1988. Tax Lawyer, Deloitte Tax Services and Cooper & Lybrand, 1988-1991. *LANGUAGES:* The Scandinavian Languages and English.

OF COUNSEL

JACQUES F. RAEDER, born September 26, 1914; admitted, 1945, Norway; 1965, Supreme Court of Norway. *Education:* University of Oslo (Candidate in Jurisprudence, 1939); Harvard Graduate School of Business Administration (1947-1948). Associate Judge, Sand, 1942-1943. *Member:* Norwegian Bar Association. *LANGUAGES:* The Scandinavian Languages and English.

ASSOCIATES

GUNNAR MARTINSEN, born August 24, 1965. *Education:* University of Oslo (Candidate in Jurisprudence, 1993). *LANGUAGES:* Scandinavian and English.

ADVOKATFIRMA SANDER, TRUYEN & CO.

Established in 1979

MUNKEDAMSVEIEN 45 - VIKA ATRIUM
0250 OSLO, NORWAY
Int. Telephone: (47) 22 83 10 40
Int. Telefax: (47) 22 83 10 48

Mailing Address: P.O. Box 1923 Vika, 0125 Oslo, Norway

General Business Practice, Tax and VAT Law, International Contracts, Mergers and Acquisitions, Licensing and Trade Marks, Admiralty Law, Transportation Law, Insurance Law, Labour Law, Dealership Law, Litigation, Valuation, Asset retrieval, Probate Law.
Among clients: Embassies, major insurance companies, international airlines, many international industrial, trading and service companies.

MEMBERS OF FIRM

JENS-JACOB SANDER, born Boraas, Sweden, 1944. *Education:* University of Oslo (1974). Legal Counsel of Tax Assessment Office, 1974-1975. Deputy Judge, 1976. Tax Advisor Peat, Marwich, Mitchell & Co., Oslo, 1977-1979. Author: "International Mergers of Swedish and Norwegian Company and Tax Law," Thesis, 1974; "Recent Developments regarding the Petroleum Tax," European Taxation, 1983; "Fiscal Obstacles to the International Flow of Capital," Cahiers de Droit Fiscal International, 1984. Regular Correspondent Reporting Norwegian Tax Law Developments and Trends to Tax Management International Review. *Member:* Norwegian Bar Association; International Fiscal Association; International Bar Association; Association International des Jeunes Avocats. *LANGUAGES:* English and German. *PRACTICE AREAS:* Commercial and Corporate Law; Tax Law; Property Law.

PIETER TRUYEN, born Roermond, Holland, 1935. *Education:* NIB Nijenrode, Amsterdam (Business Administration, 1957); Oslo University (Candidatus juris, 1976). Legal Counsel: Baerum Tax Assessment Office, 1976-1977; The Ministry of Finance, General Tax Department, 1977-1980. Board Memberships. *Member:* Norwegian Bar Association; International Fiscal Association; UIA; LES. *LANGUAGES:* Dutch, English, French, German and Italian. *PRACTICE AREAS:* Commercial Law; Licensing Law; Tax Law.

JOHAN KJETIL HØGEVOLD, born Oslo, Norway, 1952. *Education:* University of Oslo (Candidatus juris, 1978). Ministry of Finance, 1978-1980. Deputy Judge, Sandefjord, 1980-1982. Trainee Haight, Gardner, Poor & Havens, New York and Houston, 1983-1984. *Member:* Norwegian Bar Association, International Fiscal Association. *LANGUAGES:* English. *PRACTICE AREAS:* Commercial and Corporate Law; Tax Law; Bankruptcy Law.

ØYSTEIN RØD, born Oslo, Norway, 1950. *Education:* University of Oslo (Candidatus juris, 1978); American Graduate School of International Management, Arizona, USA (M.I.M., 1980). Legal Counsel: Ministry of Commerce and Shipping, 1978-1980; Ministry of Finance, 1980; Norwegian Tax Directorate, 1981-1982; Oil Taxation Office, 1982-1983. Attorney at Law, Arthur Andersen & Co., 1984-1985. *Member:* Norwegian Bar Association (Board Member); International Fiscal Association. *LANGUAGES:* English, Norwegian, Swedish and Danish. *PRACTICE AREAS:* Commercial and Corporate Law; Tax Law; Establishment in Norway.

(This Listing Continued)

ERIK BLAKER, born Oslo, Norway, 1951. *Education:* University of Oslo (Candidatus juris, 1977). Head of Legal Department of Association of Marine Underwriters. Chairman of the Bar Association's permanent council for Admiralty Law. *Member:* Norwegian Bar Association. *LANGUAGES:* English. *PRACTICE AREAS:* Transport Law; Insurance Law; Maritime Law.

HANNE ELIZABETH EGE, born Missouri, U.S.A., 1957. *Education:* University of Oslo (Candidatus juris, 1983). Ministry of Justice, 1984-1988. *Member:* Norwegian Bar Association. *LANGUAGES:* English. *PRACTICE AREAS:* Labour Law; Corporate Law; Litigation; Competition; Marketing Law.

RUNAR HANSEN, born Kristiansund, Norway, 1960. *Education:* University of Oslo (Candidatus juris, 1987). Securities Commission, 1987-1988. Deputy Judge, Trondenes, 1989. *Member:* Norwegian Bar Association. *LANGUAGES:* English and German. *PRACTICE AREAS:* Transport Law; Insurance Law; Compensation Law.

ASSOCIATES

TOM OLAV RISA, born Oslo, Norway, 1961. *Education:* University of Oslo (Candidatus juris) 1987. Legal Counsel, Oslo Tax Assessment Office, 1988-1989. *Member:* Norwegian Bar Association. *LANGUAGES:* English and Spanish. *PRACTICE AREAS:* Commercial and Corporate Law; Tax Law.

ANN ELIN SANDHAUG SCHÜSSEL, born Baerum, Norway, 1962. *Education:* University of Oslo (Candidatus juris, 1989). Legal Counsel, Ministry of Finance, 1989-1990. *Member:* Norwegian Bar Association. *LANGUAGES:* Dutch and English. *PRACTICE AREAS:* Commercial Law; Housing Law; Debt Collection.

BJØRN FR. SALVESEN, born Lillehammer, Norway 1958. *Education:* University of Oslo (Candidatus juris, 1985). Legal Counsel: Baerum Tax Assessment Office, 1985-1986; The Ministry of Finance, General Tax Department, 1986-1988. Associate, Norwegian lawfirm, 1988-1992. *Member:* Norwegian Bar Association; International Fiscal Association. *LANGUAGES:* English. *PRACTICE AREAS:* Commercial and Corporate Law; Tax Law.

TRINE STANDAL, born Ålesund, Norway, 1963. *Education:* University of Oslo (Candidatus juris, 1988). Legal Counsel, Ministry of Finance, 1988-1989. Deputy Chief Assistant, Oslo Police Department, 1989-1991. Attorney-at-Law, Realkreditt, 1991-1992. Deputy Judge, Asker and Baerum, 1992-1994. *Member:* Norwegian Bar Association. *LANGUAGES:* English. *PRACTICE AREAS:* Tax and Corporate Law; Detection of Fraud and Retrieval of Assets.

DAG DREVVATNE, born Oslo, Norway, 1955. *Education:* University of Oslo (Candidatus juris, 1983). Legal Counsel, Baerum Tax Assessment Office, 1984-1986. Attorney-at-Law: Arthur Andersen & Co., 1986-1988; Vogt & Co., 1989-1994. *Member:* Norwegian Bar Association. *LANGUAGES:* English. *PRACTICE AREAS:* Tax; Commercial and Corporate Law; Bankruptcy Law; Labour Law; Contracts.

MORTEN O. HURUM, born Oslo, Norway, 1953. *Education:* University of Oslo (Candidatus juris, 1980). Norwegian Patent Office, 1980-1981; Attorney-at-law: 1981-1983, Bratsberg, Ness & Howlid; 1983-1985, Lefac Finance Company; 1985-1986, Havtor Management AS Shipping Company; 1986—Individual Practice. *Member:* Norwegian Bar Association. *LANGUAGES:* English. *PRACTICE AREAS:* Transport Law; Commercial and Corporate Law; Law relating to Fishing Industry; Bankruptcy Law.

Languages: Dutch, English, French, German, Italian and Spanish

ADVOKATFIRMAET SCHJØDT AS

DRONNING MAUDS GATE 10
P.O. BOX 2444 SOLLI
N-0201 OSLO, NORWAY
Telephone: +47 22 83 22 44
Fax: +47 22 83 17 12
Telex: 19789 law n
Data Network Address: 2422 130116

Bergen, Norway Office: Christian Michelsens Gate 1, P.O. Box 617, N-5001. Telephone: 47 55 90 13 20. Fax: 47 55 90 13 19.
Trondheim, Norway Office: Ths. Angell Gate 12, P.O. Box 132, N-7001. Telephone: 47 73 52 75 45. Fax: 47 73 51 55 28.

(This Listing Continued)

ADVOKATFIRMAET SCHJØDT AS, Oslo—Continued

General/Corporate, Commercial, Securities, International Finance, Intellectual Property, Patent, Licensing, Energy/Oil and Gas, Shipping/Admiralty, Environment/Energy, Tax, Government Relations, Products Liability, Personnel/Labour, International General Litigation, Libel Law, Bankruptcy/Insolvency, Construction, Real Estate.

OSLO OFFICE

MEMBERS OF FIRM

A.C. HØEG RASMUSSEN, born Trondheim, Norway, June 29, 1936; admitted, 1962, Norway; 1971, Supreme Court of Norway. *Education:* University of Oslo (Candidate in Jurisprudence, 1960). Associate Judge, Stavanger, 1961-1962. *Member:* Norwegian Bar Association. *LANGUAGES:* The Scandinavian Languages, English and French. *PRACTICE AREAS:* Energy Law; Company Law; Contracts.

OLE CHR. WAERENSKJOLD, born Oslo, Norway, March 30, 1941; admitted, 1967, Norway; 1973, Supreme Court of Norway. *Education:* University of Oslo (Candidate in Jurisprudence, 1964); University of Illinois, 1968-1969. Associate Judge, Sandefjord, 1965-1966. Teaching Assistant in Law, University of Illinois, 1968-1969. *Member:* Norwegian Bar Association. *LANGUAGES:* The Scandinavian Languages and English. *PRACTICE AREAS:* Company Law; Contract; Litigation.

CATO SCHIØTZ, born Oslo, Norway, July 26, 1948; admitted, 1976, Norway; 1985, Supreme Court of Norway. *Education:* University of Oslo (Candidate in Jurisprudence). Assisting Professor, University of Oslo, 1975-1977. Associate Judge, Lillehammer, 1977-1978. *Member:* Norwegian Bar Association. *LANGUAGES:* The Scandinavian Languages and English. *PRACTICE AREAS:* Litigation; Arbitration.

ERLING CHRISTIANSEN, born Oslo, Norway, November 21, 1951; admitted, 1981, Norway. *Education:* University of Oslo (Candidate in Jurisprudence, 1976); Ohlone College, Fremont, California, USA (1970-1971); New York University, New York, N.Y., USA (M.C.J., 1981). Associate Judge, Nord-Hedmark, 1977-1978. Tax Legislation Department of Norwegian Tax Directorate, 1979-1980. *Member:* Norwegian Bar Association. *LANGUAGES:* The Scandinavian Languages and English. *PRACTICE AREAS:* Mergers and Acquisitions; Company Law; Securities Law; Banking/Finance Law.

PETER G. NITTER, born Oslo, Norway, June 24, 1947; admitted, 1976, Norway; 1992, Supreme Court of Norway. *Education:* University of Oslo (Candidate Jurisprudence, 1973). Associate Judge, Sogndal, 1973-1974. Research Assistant, Scandinavian Institute of Maritime Law, 1971-1972. *Member:* Norwegian Bar Association. *LANGUAGES:* The Scandinavian Languages and English. *PRACTICE AREAS:* Intellectual Property; Competition Law.

DAGFINN CLEMETSEN, born Oslo, Norway, February 21, 1944; admitted, 1972, Norway; 1992, Supreme Court of Norway. *Education:* University of Oslo (Candidate in Jurisprudence, 1967). Legal Counsellor/Head of Section, Department of Legislation, Ministry of Justice and Police, 1968-1979. Judge, Kristiansund Town Court, Kristiansund, 1979-1983. Judge, Eidsivating Court of Appeal, Oslo, 1983-1986. *Member:* Norwegian Bar Association. *LANGUAGES:* The Scandinavian Languages and English. *PRACTICE AREAS:* Litigation; Arbitration.

ARNOLD RØRHOLT, born Oslo, Norway, December 21, 1951; admitted, 1983, Norway. *Education:* Economic College, Oslo (1972); University of Oslo (Candidate in Jurisprudence, 1979). Legal Counsellor, Tax Department of Ministry of Finance, 1979-1981. Legal Counsellor, A.S. Norske Shell, 1981-1983. *Member:* Norwegian Bar Association. *LANGUAGES:* The Scandinavian Languages and English. *PRACTICE AREAS:* Energy Law; Company Law; Contracts.

NILS-HENRIK PETTERSSON, born Oslo, Norway, November 19, 1957; admitted, 1984, Norway; 1989, Supreme Court of Norway. *Education:* Economic College, Oslo (1977); University of Oslo (Candidate in Jurisprudence, 1982; Basic Degree in Economics, 1984). Associate Judge, Alstahaug, 1983-1984. *Member:* Norwegian Bar Association; International Fiscal Association. *LANGUAGES:* The Scandinavian Languages and English. *PRACTICE AREAS:* Tax Law; Company Law; Building and Construction Law.

TROND STANG, born Engerdal, Norway, November 9, 1953; admitted, 1988, Norway. *Education:* University of Oslo (Candidate in Jurisprudence, 1980); Canadian Institute of Resources Law; University of Calgary, Canada, 1983-1984. Legal Counsellor, Petroleum Department, Ministry of Petroleum and Energy, 1980-1986. *Member:* Norwegian Bar Association.

(This Listing Continued)

LANGUAGES: The Scandinavian Languages and English. *PRACTICE AREAS:* Energy Law; Labour Law; Computer Contracts.

SVEN RUNE GRENI, born Oslo, Norway, June 21, 1952; admitted, 1990, Norway. *Education:* University of Oslo (Candidate in Jurisprudence, 1971). Legal Counsellor/Deputy Director Norwegian Tax Directorate, 1978-1986. Tax Adviser, Peat, Marwick, Mitchell & Co., 1986-1987. Tax Adviser, Federation of Norwegian Industries, 1987-1989. *Member:* Norwegian Bar Association; International Fiscal Association. *LANGUAGES:* The Scandinavian Languages and English. *PRACTICE AREAS:* Tax Law; Company Law.

WILHELM DAMM, born Oslo, Norway, June 17, 1954; admitted, 1980, Norway. *Education:* University of Oslo (Candidate in Jurisprudence, 1978). Associate Judge, Stjør-og Verdal, 1978-1979. Trainee, Sinclair, Roche & Temperley, London, 1980. Legal Counsellor, Wilh-Wilhelmsen, 1982-1985. *Member:* Norwegian Bar Association. *LANGUAGES:* The Scandinavian Languages and English. *PRACTICE AREAS:* Shipping; International Finance; Contracts.

JAN SYVERSEN, born Oslo, Norway, January 13, 1946; admitted, 1984, Norway. *Education:* University of Oslo (Candidate in Jurisprudence, 1971). Associate Judge, Hadeland & Land, 1972-1973. Legal Counsellor, Oslo Assessment Office, 1974-1975. Head of Section/Assistant Director, Tax Directorate, Oil Taxation Department, later Oil Taxation Office, 1975-1982. Head of Section, Federation of Norwegian Industries, 1983-1984. Research Fellow, Nordic Institute of Maritime Law, 1985-1990, LL.D. *Member:* Norwegian Bar Association. *LANGUAGES:* Scandinavian Languages and English. *PRACTICE AREAS:* Company Law; Tax Law; Petroleum Tax Law.

OLE G. KLEVAN, born Oslo, Norway, September 23, 1959; admitted, 1988, Norway. *Education:* University of Oslo (Candidate in Jurisprudence, 1985). Associate Judge, Oslo, 1986-1988. *Member:* Norwegian Bar Association. *LANGUAGES:* Scandinavian Languages and English. *PRACTICE AREAS:* Company Law; Labour Law; Contracts.

PETTER CHR. SOGN, born Oslo, Norway, January 29, 1952; admitted, 1979, Norway. *Education:* University of Oslo (Candidate of Jurisprudence, 1977). Associate Judge, Sarpsborg, 1978. Legal practice in New York, 1981-1982. Partner of Vogt & Co., 1983-1992. Joined Advokatfirmaet Schjødt, 1993. *Member:* Norwegian Bar Association. *LANGUAGES:* The Scandinavian Languages and English. *PRACTICE AREAS:* Maritime; Insolvency Law.

EINAR IRGENS, born Bergen, Norway, September 26, 1937; admitted, 1966, Norway; 1977, Supreme Court of Norway. *Education:* University of Oslo (Candidate in Jurisprudence, 1962). Associate Judge, Ålesund, 1965. Legal Counsellor, The Central Union of Marine Underwriters, 1966-1968. Partner of Vogt & Co., 1969-1982. General Counsel/Head of Legal Department, Christiania Bank og Kreditkasse, 1982-1994. *Member:* Norwegian Bar Association. *LANGUAGES:* The Scandinavian Languages and English. *PRACTICE AREAS:* Company Law; Banking Law; Maritime Law.

ASSOCIATES

Bertram Vedeler	Aslak Aslaksen
Thorbjørn Gjerde	Vidar Strømme
Jens Otto Moltke-Hansen	Inger-Marie Landfald
Jan Magne Styrmoe	Cathrine Hambro
	Egil Stokka

BERGEN OFFICE

MEMBERS OF FIRM

PER HAGELIEN, born Bergen, Norway, September 16, 1943; admitted, 1970, Norway; 1976, Supreme Court of Norway. *Education:* University of Oslo (Candidate in Jurisprudence, 1968); University d'Aix-en-Provence (1970-1971). Associate Judge, Bergen, 1968-1970. *Member:* Norwegian Bar Association (National Council), 1981-1984); Union Internationale des Avocats (UIA, President, 1983—); Conceil des Barreaux de la Communaute Europeenne (CCBE, Norwegian Representative, 1984—). *LANGUAGES:* The Scandinavian Languages, English, French and German. *PRACTICE AREAS:* Contracts; Company Law; EU and EEA; International Law; Competition Law; Litigation.

BJARNE HODNE, born Bergen, Norway, September 14, 1949; admitted, 1979, Norway. *Education:* University of Bergen (Candidate in Jurisprudence, 1974). Associate Judge, Bergen, 1977-1979. *Member:* Norwegian Bar Association. *LANGUAGES:* The Scandinavian Languages and English. *PRACTICE AREAS:* Employment and Labour Law; Government Relations; Competition Law; Enforcement; Litigation.

(This Listing Continued)

LARS DØRHEIM NILSEN, born Bergen, Norway, April 13, 1943; admitted, 1983, Norway. *Education:* University of Oslo (Candidate in Jurisprudence, 1971). Advisor/Head of Company Tax Department, Ligningstontor, Bergen, 1973-1983. *Member:* Norwegian Bar Association. *LANGUAGES:* The Scandinavian Languages and English. *PRACTICE AREAS:* Tax Law; Company Law; Inheritance.

GISLE DIDRIKSEN, born Bergen, Norway, May 23, 1949; admitted, 1985, Norway. *Education:* University of Bergen (Candidate in Jurisprudence, 1975). Police Intendant I, Hordaland, 1977-1980 and 1982-1985. Associate Judge, Hardanger, 1980-1981. *Member:* Norwegian Bar Association. *LANGUAGES:* The Scandinavian Languages and English. *PRACTICE AREAS:* Criminal Law; Claims/Bankruptcy; Real Property; Compensation.

CHRISTOPHER BRUN, born Bergen, Norway, July 16, 1952; admitted, 1982, Norway. *Education:* University of Bergen (Candidate in Jurisprudence, 1979). Police Intendant II, 1980-1982. *Member:* Norwegian Bar Association (Board Member). *LANGUAGES:* The Scandinavian Languages and English. *PRACTICE AREAS:* Real Property; Company Law; Mortgage/Security; Tax Law; Duty Law.

HANS DALE, born Bergen, Norway, April 29, 1949; admitted, 1978, Norway. *Education:* University of Oslo (Candidate in Jurisprudence, 1975). Associate Judge, Bergen, 1976-1978. Department Manager/Lawyer, Norwegian Employers Association and Confederation of Norwegian Business and Industry, Bergen, 1979-1990. *Member:* Norwegian Bar Association. *LANGUAGES:* The Scandinavian Languages and English. *PRACTICE AREAS:* Employment and Labour Law; Enforcement; Litigation.

TOR L. ONARHEIM, born Bergen, Norway, June 1, 1952; admitted, 1982, Norway. *Education:* University of Bergen (Candidate in Jurisprudence, 1979). Associate Judge, Egersund, 1980-1981. Worked on International matters for Elf Petroleum, 1981-1987 and Norske Shell E&P, 1989-1991; Managing Director, Bergenske Services, 1987-1989. *Member:* Norwegian Bar Association. *LANGUAGES:* The Scandinavian Languages and English. *PRACTICE AREAS:* Energy/Petroleum Law; International Contracts; Government Relations; EU and EEA.

EILIF UTNE RIISØEN, born Bergen, Norway, July 25, 1937; admitted, 1965, Norway. *Education:* University of Oslo (Candidate in Jurisprudence, 1962). Associate Judge, Midthordland, 1963-1965. Legal Counsel, Ministry of Defense. Legal Counsel, shipowners Reksten A/S, 1965-1971. Established Law Firm, 1972. *Member:* Norwegian Bar Association. *LANGUAGES:* The Scandinavian Languages and English. *PRACTICE AREAS:* Company Law; Contracts; Litigation.

ASSOCIATES

Marie Vonen

TRONDHEIM OFFICE

MEMBERS OF FIRM

GUDMUND KUVÅS, born Trondheim, Norway, December 1, 1938; admitted, 1966, Norway; 1970, Supreme Court of Norway. *Education:* University of Oslo (Candidate in Jurisprudence, 1964). Associate Judge, 1965-1966. *Member:* Norwegian Bar Association. *LANGUAGES:* The Scandinavian Languages and English. *PRACTICE AREAS:* Company Law; Tax Law; Contract Law; Real Property.

MAGNE SPILDE, born Oslo, Norway, April 1, 1942; admitted, 1970, Norway; 1980, Supreme Court of Norway. *Education:* University of Oslo (Candidate in Jurisprudence, 1968). Associate Judge, 1969-1970. *Member:* Norwegian Bar Association. *LANGUAGES:* The Scandinavian Languages and English. *PRACTICE AREAS:* Real Property, Building and Construction Law; Expropriation Law; Tort; Public Law; Contract Law.

JOAR GRIMSBU, born Folldal, Norway, April 17, 1952; admitted, 1981, Norway; 1988, Supreme Court of Norway. *Education:* University of Oslo (Candidate in Jurisprudence, 1978). Associate Judge, 1979-1980. *Member:* Norwegian Bar Association. *LANGUAGES:* The Scandinavian Languages and English. *PRACTICE AREAS:* Claim/Bankruptcy; Company Law; Contract Law; Real Property.

ENDRE KOLBJØRNSEN, born Trondheim, Norway, April 9, 1956; admitted, 1984, Norway. *Education:* University of Oslo (Candidate in Jurisprudence, 1982). Associate Judge, 1983-1985. *Member:* Norwegian Bar Association. *LANGUAGES:* The Scandinavian Languages and English. *PRACTICE AREAS:* Company Law; Tax Law; International Law.

ROALD ENGENESS, born Bodø, Norway, October 25, 1942; admitted, 1975, Norway. *Education:* University of Oslo (Candidate in Jurisprudence,

(This Listing Continued)

1971). Associate Judge, 1975-1976. *Member:* Norwegian Bar Association. *LANGUAGES:* The Scandinavian Languages and English. *PRACTICE AREAS:* Maritime Law; Expropriation Law; Tort/Insurance; Labour Law.

ARVE ROSVOLD ALVER, born Stjørdal, Norway, June 8, 1951; admitted, 1979, Norway; 1994, Supreme Court of Norway. *Education:* University of Oslo (Candidate in Jurisprudence, 1976). Associate Judge, 1977-1978. *Member:* Norwegian Bar Association. *LANGUAGES:* The Scandinavian Languages and English. *PRACTICE AREAS:* Expropriation Law; Real Property; Tort and Bankruptcy.

TERJE SKJØNHALS, born Trondheim, Norway, July 10, 1949; admitted, 1982, Norway. *Education:* University of Oslo (Candidate in Jurisprudence, 1977). Associate Judge, 1980-1981. *Member:* Norwegian Bar Association. *LANGUAGES:* The Scandinavian Languages and English. *PRACTICE AREAS:* Banking Law; Company Law; Contract Law; International Law.

ASSOCIATES

Cecilie Amdahl

Languages: The Scandinavian Languages, English, French and German

---

ADVOKATFIRMAET
SELMER & CO. DA
KIRKEGATA 15
N-0153 OSLO 1, NORWAY
Telephone: 47 22 42 64 90
Facsimile: 47 22 33 63 10

Mailing Address: P.O. Box 476 Sentrum, 0105 Oslo, Norway

Business, Contracts, Corporations, Commercial, Tax, Petroleum, Energy, Trade, Shipping, Financial, Computers and Law, Bankruptcy, Litigation, Labour, Legislation, Family and Inheritance Law. Copyrights, Insurance, Real Estate, Environmental Law and Communication Law.

FIRM PROFILE: Advokatfirmaet Selmer & Co. Da is a member of Unilaw which is an international network of well reputed law firms in Europe and Japan. The firm is also a member of Nordic Alliance, a cooperation among the business law firms Nielsen & Nørager, Copenhagen, Advokatfirmaet Selmer & Co. ANS, Oslo and Advokatfirmaen Delphi, Stockholm.

MEMBERS OF FIRM

ASBJØRN BERG, born Oslo, Norway, October 11, 1955; admitted, 1984, Norway. *Education:* University of Oslo (Candidate in Jurisprudence, 1982). *Member:* Norwegian Bar Association. *LANGUAGES:* Scandinavian and English. *PRACTICE AREAS:* Business; Contracts; Insurance Law; Copyright; Computer Law.

ODD-EINAR CHRISTOPHERSEN, born Baerum, Norway, May 23, 1952; admitted, 1982, Norway. *Education:* University of Oslo, Norway (Candidate in Jurisprudence, 1978). Senior Legal Adviser, Department of Rationalization, 1978-1981. *Member:* Norwegian Bar Association. *LANGUAGES:* Scandinavian and English. *PRACTICE AREAS:* Computer and Software Law; Construction Law; Company Law; Real Estate Law.

ANNE-BLANCA DAHL, born Oslo, Norway, December 7, 1946; admitted, 1974, Norway. *Education:* University of Oslo (Candidate in Jurisprudence, 1970). Associate Judge, Sandefjord, Norway, 1973-1974. *LANGUAGES:* Scandinavian and English. *PRACTICE AREAS:* Business; Family; Inheritance; Labour; Employment.

BJØRN KLEIVEN, born Gothenburg, Sweden, April 12, 1950; admitted, 1983, Norway. *Education:* University of Oslo (Candidate in Jurisprudence, 1976). Tax Advisor, Norwegian Tax Authorities, 1976-1978. Peat Marwick, Mitchel & Co., The Hague and Oslo, 1978-1983. Senior Tax Manager and Head of Tax Department, Ernst & Young, 1988-1990. Tax Advisor, Institute of Chartered Accountants, 1983-1985. *Member:* Norwegian Bar Association. *LANGUAGES:* Scandinavian and English. *PRACTICE AREAS:* Business; Contracts; Tax Law; Corporation.

JEPPE NORMANN, born Oslo, Norway, September 15, 1951; admitted, 1983, Norway. *Education:* University of Oslo (Candidate in Jurisprudence, 1979). Deputy Assistant Chief of Police and Associate Judge, 1979-1980. Legal Adviser the Norwegian Revenue Service, 1980-1983. Associate Judge, 1983-1984. Partner, Idsøe, Norman & Sulland ANS, 1986-1994. *Member:* Norwegian Bar Association. *LANGUAGES:* Scandinavian and English. *PRACTICE AREAS:* Liquidation and Bankruptcy; Corporate Law; Contract Law; Business Law.

(This Listing Continued)

ADVOKATFIRMAET SELMER & CO. DA, Oslo— Continued

TRYGVE ØYDNE, born Kvinesdal, Norway, August 17, 1956; admitted, 1985, Norway. *Education:* University of Oslo (Candidate in Jurisprudence, 1980). Legal Adviser, Ministry of Labour and Community Affairs; Legal Adviser, the Ombudsmann of the Norwegian Parliament. Associate Judge, Holmestrand, Norway, 1984-1985. Attorney, Gjensidige Forsikring (insurance), 1986-1987 and Elcon Finans (finance, 1988-1989). *Member:* Norwegian Bar Association. *LANGUAGES:* Scandinavian and English. *PRACTICE AREAS:* Creditors Rights; Computer Law; Business; Contracts; Insurance Law.

CHRISTIAN SELMER, born Trondheim, Norway, April 22, 1946; admitted, 1975, Norway; 1988 Supreme Court of Norway. *Education:* University of Oslo (Candidate in Jurisprudence, 1972). Associate Judge, Orkdal, Norway, 1973-1974. *Member:* Norwegian Bar Association. *LANGUAGES:* Scandinavian and English. *PRACTICE AREAS:* Business; Contracts; Corporation.

JON SKJØRSHAMMER, born Oslo, Norway, November 9, 1956; admitted, 1986, Norway. *Education:* University of Oslo (Candidate in Jurisprudence, 1984). Research Fellow, Norwegian Research Centre for Computers and Law, 1983-1985. *Member:* Norwegian Bar Association. *LANGUAGES:* Scandinavian and English. *PRACTICE AREAS:* Bankruptcy; Intellectual Property; Labour and Employment; Antitrust and Trade Regulations.

ROY M. SLETTVOLD, born Nordreisa, Norway, February 21, 1957; admitted, 1987, Norway. *Education:* University of Oslo (Candidate in Jurisprudence, 1982). Associate Judge, Sarpsborg, Norway, 1986-1987. *Member:* Norwegian Bar Association. *LANGUAGES:* Scandinavian and English. *PRACTICE AREAS:* Business; Contracts; Taxation; Entertainment and the Arts.

SYNNØVE SMEDAL, born Oslo, Norway, June 7, 1957; admitted, 1990, Norway. *Education:* University of Oslo (Candidate in Jurisprudence, 1983). Research Fellow, Norwegian Research Centre for Computers and Law, University of Oslo, 1981. Legal Adviser, Ministry of Environment and Ministry of Justice, 1983-1984. Assistant Secretary, Ministry of Environment, 1987-1988. *Member:* Norwegian Bar Association. *LANGUAGES:* Scandinavian and English. *PRACTICE AREAS:* Business; Company Law; EC Law; Computer Law; Environmental Law.

SVEIN SULLAND, born Oslo, Norway, April 9, 1953; admitted, 1983, Norway. *Education:* University of Oslo (Candidate in Jurisprudence, 1980). Legal Adviser, Norwegian Revenue Service, 1980-1981. Associate Judge, 1981-1983. Partner, Idsøe, Normann & Sulland ANS, 1986-1994. *Member:* Norwegian Bar Association; Norwegian Construction Law Association. *LANGUAGES:* Scandinavian and English. *PRACTICE AREAS:* Construction Law; Liquidation and Bankruptcy; Corporate Law; Business Law.

EILIF TORMA, born Oslo, Norway, September 15, 1943; admitted, 1975, Norway. *Education:* University of Oslo (Candidate in Jurisprudence, 1971); North European Management Institute (1972-1973). Vice-President, Finance and Board Member, Vesta-Hygea Insurance Group, 1984. *Member:* Norwegian Bar Association. *LANGUAGES:* Scandinavian and English. *PRACTICE AREAS:* Business; Contracts; Corporation; Finance.

SVERRE S. TYSLAND, born Trondheim, Norway, April 19, 1952; admitted, 1982, Norway. *Education:* University of Oslo (Candidate in Jurisprudence, 1979); Graduate School of Business Administration, University of California at Berkeley (1980-1981). Research Fellow, Norwegian Research Centre for Computers and Law, University of Oslo, 1976-1979. Head of Natural Gas, LPG, Crude Oil and Products Departments, 1985-1988 and Corporate Counsel, 1981-1984, Norsk Hydro Corporation. *Member:* Norwegian Bar Association. *LANGUAGES:* Scandinavian and English. *PRACTICE AREAS:* Business; Contracts; Shipping; Petroleum; Energy; Corporations; Computer Law.

LARS WEYER-LARSEN, born Baerum, Norway, December 29, 1946; admitted, 1974, Norway. *Education:* University of Oslo (Candidate in Jurisprudence, 1972). Head of Legal Department, Norwegian Savings Bank Association, 1978-1980. Associate Judge, Brønnøysund, 1972-1974. *Member:* Norwegian Bar Association. *LANGUAGES:* Scandinavian and English. *PRACTICE AREAS:* Business; Contracts; Finance; Commercial.

(This Listing Continued)

ASSOCIATES

ARNT ANGELL, born Trondheim, Norway, April 15, 1963; admitted, 1992, Norway. *Education:* Nordland College (Studies of Political Science, 1984); University of Bergen, Norway (Candidate in Jurisprudence, 1990). Associate Judge, Nedre Romerike Herredsrett, 1992-1993. *Member:* Norwegian Bar Association. *LANGUAGES:* Scandinavian and English. *PRACTICE AREAS:* EC Law; Admiralty and Maritime Law; Energy; Corporation; Contracts.

INGE EKKER BARTNES, born Trondheim, Norway, October 31, 1967; admitted, 1995, Norway. *Education:* University of Oslo (Candidate in Jurisprudence, 1993). *Member:* Norwegian Bar Association. *LANGUAGES:* Scandinavian and English. *PRACTICE AREAS:* Corporation; Energy; EC Competition; Taxation.

FREDRIK ASTRUP BORCH, born Oslo, Norway, January 28, 1963; admitted, 1988, Norway. *Education:* University of Oslo (Candidate in Jurisprudence, 1988). Associate, Normann & Sulland ANS, 1988-1994. *LANGUAGES:* Scandinavian and English. *PRACTICE AREAS:* Liquidation and Bankruptcy; Contracts; Corporate Law; Business Law.

MORTEN BØSTERUD, born Drøbak, Norway, June 11, 1965; admitted, 1992, Norway. *Education:* University of Oslo (Candidate in Jurisprudence, 1990). Associate Attorney in Oslo, 1990-1993. *Member:* Norwegian Bar Association. *LANGUAGES:* Scandinavian and English. *PRACTICE AREAS:* Business; Contracts; Creditor Rights; Takeovers.

GUNHILD BUESTAD, born Oslo, Norway, October 10, 1953; admitted, 1987, Norway. *Education:* University of Oslo (Candidate in Jurisprudence, 1980). Tax Advisor, Directorate of Tax and Tax Manager, KPMG Peat Marwick. Executive Advisor, Taxation, Confederation of Norwegian Business and Industry. *LANGUAGES:* Scandinavian and English. *PRACTICE AREAS:* Tax Law; Corporations; Contracts.

SUSAN HALVORSEN, born New Jersey, U.S.A., August 8, 1956; admitted, 1986, Norway. *Education:* University of Oslo (Candidate in Jurisprudence, 1983). First Secretary in the Ministry of Consumer and Administration Affairs, 1983-1984. Assistant Chief of Police Telemark Police Department, 1984-1985. Deputy Chief of Police Oslo Police Department, 1985-1988 and 1990. Associate Judge, Notodden, 1988-1989. *Member:* Norwegian Bar Association. *LANGUAGES:* Scandinavian and English. *PRACTICE AREAS:* Business; Contracts; Family and Inheritance Law.

INGEBJORG HARTO, born Bodø, Norway, January 30, 1961; admitted, 1990, Norway. *Education:* University of Oslo, Norway (Candidate in Jurisprudence, 1988. Associate, Consumers Insurance Office, 1988-1990. Associate Judge, Stjørdal and Verdal, 1990-1991. *Member:* Norwegian Bar Association. *LANGUAGES:* Scandinavian and English. *PRACTICE AREAS:* Insurance; Family and Inheritance Law; Energy; Construction Law.

JAN RAGNAR HERUD, born Kongsvinger, Norway, February 23, 1960; admitted, 1992, Norway. *Education:* University of Oslo (Candidate in Jurisprudence, 1988). Stipendiary Magistrate in the Office of Public Registrar and Notary Public, City of Oslo, 1987-1990. Lawyer, Oslo Tax Assessment Office, 1988-1990. Associate Attorney, Oslo, 1990-1991. Deputy Judge, Sarpsborg City Court, 1991-1993. *LANGUAGES:* Scandinavian and English. *PRACTICE AREAS:* Business Law; Contracts; Property; Taxation.

MARGRETHE HUSEBØ , born Oslo, Norway, April 12, 1966; admitted, 1995, Norway. *Education:* University of California at Santa Barbara (1989-1990); University of Oslo (Candidate in Jurisprudence, 1992). Government Directorate of Taxation, Lawyer, 1992-1993. *Member:* Norwegian Bar Association. *LANGUAGES:* Scandinavian and English. *PRACTICE AREAS:* Contracts; Corporation Law.

GEIR J. KRUGE, born Oslo, Norway, November 11, 1960; admitted, 1988, Norway. *Education:* University of Bergen (Political Science, 1982); University of Oslo (Candidate in Jurisprudence, 1986). Associate Attorney in Oslo, Deputy Chief of Police, Follo Police Department, 1986-1988. Deputy Judge, Horten City Court, 1988-1989. Deputy Chief of Police, Follo Police Department, 1989. Deputy Judge, Oslo City Court, 1989. Circuit Judge, Oslo City Court, 1993. *Member:* Norwegian Bar Association. *LANGUAGES:* Scandinavian and English. *PRACTICE AREAS:* Contracts; Litigation; Companies; Administrative Law.

ANNE HELENE OSBERG, born Oslo, Norway, November 18, 1962; admitted, 1990, Norway. *Education:* University of Oslo, Norway (Candidate in Jurisprudence, 1987); Graduate School of Law, University of North Dakota (1987). Associate Legal Department, Christiania Bank, 1988-1989.

(This Listing Continued)

Associate Judge, Romsdal, 1989-1991. *Member:* Norwegian Bar Association. *LANGUAGES:* Scandinavian and English. *PRACTICE AREAS:* Contracts; Creditors Rights; Family and Inheritance Law.

ADVOKATFIRMAET STABELL DA

Established in 1991

HAAKON VII'S GT. 2

P.O. BOX 1364 VIKA

0114 OSLO 1, NORWAY

Telephone: 22 83 83 60

Telefax: 22 83 73 60

REVISER OF THE NORWAY LAW DIGEST FOR THIS DIRECTORY.

General Civil Practice, Corporation, Commercial, Industrial, Financial, Stock Exchange and Securities, Product Liability, Importer and Dealership, Leasing, Licensing and General Tax Law, Governmental Relations, Damages and Collection of Debt, Real Estate, Insurance, Shipping, Broadcasting and Media Law, Patent and Trademark Law.

FIRM PROFILE: *The firm was established 1991 through a merger of reputable medium sized law firms with long tradition in different areas of practice: STABELL Heiberg & Co., Tellmann Ramm & Co., Strøm Sandaker & Co. and Elde & Co.*

As of 1994 STABELL has grown into an organization of 76 partners and in total 26 fee earners, making STABELL one of the largest Norwegian law firms.

Today STABELL reflects a combination of compatible legal skills and clients, establishment of a flexible organization to service our clients nationally and internationally, adjusted to increased demand for services and diversified skills, at the same time being a better base for development of internal professional skills and specialization.

Areas of Emphasis: STABELL emphasises high accessibility of professional legal assistance, realizing the importance of close partner attention to all clients. The firm has founded a team player concept with clients and are known to give good personal service and new referrals immediate and relevant attention. STABELL is a full service firm with strength in Norwegian and International corporate law, banking and securities, tax, media, building and construction, insurance, property, agricultural law and litigation.

Client Base: STABELL's clients include large corporations in building and construction, insurance, finance, media, property developers, trade, industry and travelling as well as state or community owned companies and institutions.

Firm Activities: All partners and associates participate in internal professional study groups to ensure that the lawyers of the firm are professionally qualified and up to date. All lawyers of the firm are members of the Norwegian Bar Association. Several of the partners are strategically involved with the business community, being Members of Boards of a number of corporations and charitable institutions.

MEMBERS OF FIRM

STEINAR TELLMANN, born Fauske, Norway, December 23, 1936; admitted, 1965, Norway; 1974, Supreme Court of Norway. *Education:* University of Oslo (Candidate in Jurisprudence, 1963). Associate Judge, Sem, 1964-1965. *Member:* Norwegian Bar Association. *LANGUAGES:* The Scandinavian Languages and English. *PRACTICE AREAS:* International Contracts; License; Intermediaries; Competition; Labour Law.

HARALD HESSELBERG, born Larvik, Norway, March 12, 1939; admitted, 1968, Norway. *Education:* University of Oslo (Candidate in Jurisprudence, 1965). Associate Judge, Hardanger, 1966-1968. Consultant, Christiania Bank og Kreditkasse, Oslo, 1968-1969. *Member:* Norwegian Bar Association; Norwegian Association for International Law. *LANGUAGES:* The Scandinavian Languages, English and French. *PRACTICE AREAS:* Administrative Law Related to Real Estate; Corporate Law.

KARL-FREDRIK LINDBLOM, born Oslo, Norway, November 4, 1943; admitted, 1972, Norway. *Education:* University of Oslo (Candidate in Jurisprudence, 1970). Consultant, Norwegian Ministry of Justice, 1970-1971. Associate Judge, Ringerike, 1971-1972. Legal Advisor, The Export Council of Norway, 1972-1974. *Member:* Norwegian Bar Association. *LANGUAGES:* The Scandinavian Languages and English. *PRACTICE AREAS:* General Corporate Law; Banking; Financing; Competition; Contract of Intermediaries; Labour Law.

(This Listing Continued)

EVALD JON STRØM, born Oslo, Norway, February 15, 1942; admitted, 1973, Norway. *Education:* University of Oslo (Candidate in Jurisprudence, 1970). Author: "Maktfordeling og normkontroll" (Constitutional Law), (Jussens Venner 1971, Page 341-368), "Kommentar til odelsloven av 1974" (Odallaw) (Oslo, 1975) "Husnøkkelen" (Real Estate Law) (Oslo, 1985). Research Assistant, 1967-1968, University of Oslo, Institute of Private Law. Associate Judge, Stavanger, 1971-1972. *Member:* Norwegian Bar Association; Norwegian Association for Agricultural Law. *LANGUAGES:* The Scandinavian Languages and English. *PRACTICE AREAS:* Property Law; Inheritance; Estate Management; Corporate Law; The Law of Allodial Rights.

CHRISTIAN MEVATNE, born Bergen, Norway, November 24, 1944; admitted, 1975, Norway. *Education:* University of Oslo (Candidate in Jurisprudence, 1972); International Management Institute, Geneva (M.B.A., 1976). Associate Judge, Karmsund, 1973-1974. Legal Consultant, Oslo Tax Office, 1974-1975. President, Vesta American Insurance Company, Inc., New York, 1984-1987. Legal Counsel, BFP Holding A/S, 1987-1988 and SysScan A/S, 1988-1989. Partner, Law Firm Martens, Bergen, 1978-1983. *Member:* Norwegian Bar Association. *LANGUAGES:* The Scandinavian Languages, English, French and German. *PRACTICE AREAS:* Corporate; Mergers and Acquisitions; Labour Law; International Contracts; Insurance Law.

CHRISTIAN SANDAKER, born Havana, Cuba, January 2, 1948; admitted, 1976, Norway. *Education:* University of Oslo (Candidate in Jurisprudence, 1973). *Member:* Norwegian Bar Association. *LANGUAGES:* The Scandinavian Languages and English. *PRACTICE AREAS:* Building; Construction; Contracts; Leasehold; Corporate Law.

HANS OLAV HELI, born Oslo, Norway, December 11, 1947; admitted, 1977, Norway; 1987, Supreme Court of Norway. *Education:* University of Oslo (Candidate in Jurisprudence, 1973). Associate Judge, Halden, 1976-1977. *Member:* Norwegian Bar Association; Norwegian Insurance Law Association; Norwegian Copyright Law Association. *LANGUAGES:* The Scandinavian Languages and English. *PRACTICE AREAS:* Insurance Litigation; General Litigation; Arbitration; Negotiations.

BREDO STABELL, born Washington, D.C., U.S.A., August 5, 1949; admitted, 1980, Norway. *Education:* University of Oslo (Candidate in Jurisprudence, 1976). Research Assistant in E.D.P. and Law, Faculty of Law, University of Oslo, 1973-1974. Executive Officer, Ministry of Industry, 1977 and Ministry of Petroleum and Energy, 1977-1979. Associate Judge, Holmestrand, 1979-1980. Scholarship Studies, London, 1981. *Member:* Norwegian Bar Association. *LANGUAGES:* The Scandinavian Languages and English. *PRACTICE AREAS:* Loan Agreements; International Contracts; Competition; Marketing Law.

BJØRN HANESTAD, born Oslo, Norway, August 12, 1948; admitted, 1983, Norway. *Education:* University of Bergen (Candidate in Jurisprudence, 1976). *Member:* Norwegian Bar Association; International Fiscal Association. *LANGUAGES:* The Scandinavian Languages and English. *PRACTICE AREAS:* Corporate Law; International Tax; Contracts; Labour Law; Mergers and Acquisitions Duties.

MORTEN POULSSON, born Oslo, Norway, June 12, 1950; admitted, 1983, Norway. *Education:* University of Oslo (Candidate in Jurisprudence, 1975). Associate Judge, Asker og Baerum, 1980-1983. *Member:* Norwegian Bar Association; Norwegian Association for Agricultural Law. *LANGUAGES:* The Scandinavian Languages and English. *PRACTICE AREAS:* Property Law; Labour Law; Inheritance; Joint Estate Law.

HENNING ØGLÆND, born Stavanger, October 12, 1957; admitted, 1985, Norway. *Education:* University of Oslo (Candidate in Jurisprudence, 1983). Member, Oslo Boers committee on Stock Exchange and Securities Law. *Member:* Norwegian Bar Association. *LANGUAGES:* The Scandinavian Languages, German and English. *PRACTICE AREAS:* Media; Securities; Corporate Law; Competition; Private Banking; EU Law.

BJØRN SLAATTA, born Oslo, Norway, May 7, 1954; admitted, 1986, Norway. *Education:* University of Oslo (Candidate of Jurisprudence, 1980). Legal Consultant, Asker Tax Office, 1981; Legal Consultant, Inland Revenue, 1981-1984. Associate, Elde & Co., 1984-1988. *Member:* Norwegian Bar Association. *LANGUAGES:* The Scandinavian Languages and English. *PRACTICE AREAS:* Corporate Law; Norwegian Tax; Tax Treaties; Securities; Contracts; Mergers and Acquisitions.

GEIR FRØHOLM, born Oslo, Norway, January 23, 1954; admitted, 1986, Norway. *Education:* University of Oslo (Candidate in Jurisprudence, 1983). Executive Officer, Directorate of Labour Inspection, 1983; Executive Officer, Ministry of Trade and Shipping, 1984-1985. Associate Judge, Oslo Byfogdembede, 1985-1986. Legal Counsel, Selmer-Sande AS, 1986-1989.

(This Listing Continued)

ADVOKATFIRMAET STABELL DA, Oslo—Continued

Member: Norwegian Bar Association. *LANGUAGES:* The Scandinavian Languages, German and English. *PRACTICE AREAS:* Contracts; Corporate; Building; Construction; Loan Agreements; Mergers and Acquisitions.

BÅRD RACIN MELTVEDT, born Oslo, Norway, October 17, 1958; admitted, 1989, Norway. *Education:* Royal Norwegian Naval Academy (1980); University of Oslo (Candidate in Jurisprudence, 1986). Consultant, Norwegian Shipowners Association 1985. *Member:* Norwegian Bar Association. *LANGUAGES:* The Scandinavian Languages and English. *PRACTICE AREAS:* Building; Construction; Media; Intellectual Property; Litigation.

TORD JOHAN EIDE, born Narvik, Norway, March 19, 1961; admitted, 1990, Norway. *Education:* University of Oslo (Candidate in Jurisprudence, 1987); University of North Dakota, School of Law (Spring Semester, 1985). Scholarships: The Japan-Scandinavian Sasakawa Foundations Scholarship, Japan 1987. Publications: The Defamation Law of the United States of America, an introduction to Civil Defamation Law before and after the New York Times V. Sullivan Case (Det juridiske fakultets skriftserie nr. 13, Bergen 1987; Etableringsretti Japan, Tano (Norway), Norstedts (Sweden) amd Jurist og Økonomiforbundets forlag (Denmark, 1989). *How to Establish Business in Japan*, Kluwer Law and Taxation Publishers, Deventer, The Netherlands and Boston USA. *Member:* Norwegian Bar Association. *LANGUAGES:* The Scandinavian Languages and English. *PRACTICE AREAS:* Corporate Law; Intermediaries; Insurance; International Contracts; Financing; EU Law.

MADS KROHN, born Oslo, Norway, January 13, 1953; admitted, 1983, Norway. *Education:* University of Oslo (Candidate in Jurisprudence, 1977); INSEAD, Fontainebleau, France (MBA, 1980). Associate Attorney Fred Olsen & Co., 1980-1984, Vice President, Jøtunfinans AS, 1984-1987. General Manager, Astor Corporate, 1987-1988. Legal Practice, 1989—. Partner Advokatfirmaet STABELL, 1994—. *Member:* Norwegian Bar Association. *LANGUAGES:* Scandinavian Languages, English and French. *PRACTICE AREAS:* Insolvency; Corporate Law; Financing; Intellectual Property; Litigation.

REVISER OF THE NORWAY LAW DIGEST FOR THIS DIRECTORY.

STABELL, HEIBERG, LINDBLOM, STABELL, HESSELBERG ET MEVATNE

OSLO, NORWAY

(See Advokatfirmaet Stabell DA)

General Civil Practice, Corporation, Commercial, Industrial, Financial, Stock Exchange and Securities, Product Liability, Importer and Dealership, Leasing, Licensing and General Tax Law, Governmental Relations, Damages and Collection of Debt, Real Estate, Insurance, Shipping, Broadcasting and Media Law, Patent and Trademark Law.

ADVOKATFIRMAET STEENSTRUP ANS

FR. NANSENS PLASS 4
0160 OSLO, NORWAY
Telephone: (47) 22-423-336
Fax: (47) 22-423-494

Shipping, Tax Law, Company Law, Banking and Finance, Competition, Marketing and Intellectual Property Rights, Insolvency, EEA and EU Law, Real Estate, Labour Law, Torts, Boards and Management.

FIRM PROFILE: *The law firm Advokatfirmaet Steenstrup ANS provides a full range of services in the field of commercial law, with special emphasis on: tax law, maritime law, banking and finance law, the law of construction and contracting, real estate law, the law of torts and general law of contract.*

Our lawyers act as advisors and negotiate on behalf of Norwegian and foreign clients and also take assignments as counsel in courts and arbitration tribunals. A substantial part of our business consists of assisting foreign companies in Norway, in connection with setting up business here, signing contracts, debt collection, protection of intellectual property rights and negotiations with Norwegian authorities. Our working languages are Scandinavian, English and French.

(This Listing Continued)

MEMBERS OF FIRM

MORTEN STEENSTRUP, born Tønsberg, Norway, April 4, 1953; admitted, 1987, Norway. *Education:* University of Oslo (Bachelor of Arts in Sociology and Political Science, 1976; Law, 1980). The right to plead before the Supreme Court. State Secretary: Ministry of Finance, 1985-1986; to the Prime Minister's Office, 1986. Member, Supervisory Council of Norges Bank. *Member:* Norwegian Parliament Stortinget (1981-1989). *LANGUAGES:* Norwegian and English. *PRACTICE AREAS:* Corporate Law; Arbitration; Litigation; Trademarks; Intellectual Property; Taxation; Banking; Securities; Finance.

TOR KIELLAND, born Oslo, Norway, May 30, 1954; admitted, 1986, Norway. *Education:* University of Oslo (Cand. Jur., 1981). Assistant Judge, Drammen City Court, 1984-1986. *Member:* Norwegian Bar Association. *LANGUAGES:* Scandinavian and English. *PRACTICE AREAS:* Maritime Law; Corporate Law; Banking; Finance.

OLA STRØMSMOEN, born Rendalen, Norway, February 12, 1959; admitted, 1987, Norway. *Education:* University of Bergen (Cand. Jur., 1986). *LANGUAGES:* English, Danish and Swedish. *PRACTICE AREAS:* Construction Law; Consulting Law; Contract Law; Torts; Labour Law.

STEIN GULDBAKKE, born Drøbak, Norway, June 16, 1956; admitted, 1989, Norway. *Education:* University of Oslo (1984). Directorate of taxes, Oslo Tax Office. Assistant Judge, Arendal City Court. Associate, Wiersholm, Melbye & Bech ANS. *LANGUAGES:* Norwegian and English. *PRACTICE AREAS:* Company Law; Taxation; Torts; Bankruptcy; Insolvency; Commercial Law.

OVE-MARTHIN GRANLUND, born Oslo, Norway, January 17, 1959; admitted, 1991, Norway. *Education:* University of Oslo (Cand. Jur., 1986). Author: Several articles in tax law journals. *Member:* Norwegian Bar Association. *LANGUAGES:* Norwegian and English. *PRACTICE AREAS:* Tax Law; Corporate Law.

ASSOCIATES

ODD MOE, born Oslo, Norway, September 18, 1956; admitted, 1988, Norway. *Education:* University of Oslo (Cand. Jur., 1984). Legal Adviser, Tax Law, Ministry of Finance, 1984-1986. Corporate Lawyer with Sparebanken NOR (1989-1993). *Member:* Norwegian Association of Jurists. *LANGUAGES:* Scandinavian and English. *PRACTICE AREAS:* Banking; Finance; Bankruptcy; Insolvency; Corporate Law; Company Law; Real Estate; Litigation.

THOMAS MEINICH, born Oslo, Norway, July 27, 1964; admitted, 1992, Norway. *Education:* University of Oslo (Cand. Jur., 1990). *LANGUAGES:* Scandinavian and English. *PRACTICE AREAS:* Contract Law; Torts.

ELSE LIEN HANSEN, born Bergen, Norway, May 7, 1925; admitted, 1990, Norway. *Education:* University of Bergen (1978). Tax Consultant. *LANGUAGES:* Scandinavian and English.

CATHERINE DE COSTER, born Brussels, Belgium, April 21, 1955; admitted, 1978, Brussels, Belgium; 1993, Norway. *Education:* Belgium (Lic. Jur.); King's College, London, England (1981); University of Louvain, Belgium (Lic. Jur., 1978). Legal Adviser, Belgian and International Law. Authorisation from the Ministry of Justice of Norway. *Member:* E.L.A. (European Lawyers Association). *LANGUAGES:* French, English and Norwegian. *PRACTICE AREAS:* Private International Law; Family Law; European Community Law.

JAN M. DRANGE, born Bergen, Norway, May 10, 1951; admitted, 1994, Norway. *Education:* University of Oslo (Can.jur., 1981); The Norwegian Bank Academy (Economist, 1981-1994). More than 20 years of Experience from domestic and international financial institutions (VP of Den Norske Credit bank; Oslo and Chase Manhattan Bank; Oslo and President of Samuel Montagu, Oslo) concerning legal, financial and investment bank service. *LANGUAGES:* Scandinavian, English and German. *PRACTICE AREAS:* Finance, Banking and Securities; Corporate and Petroleum/Offshore; Mergers and Acquisitions.

FREDRIK SOLLIE, born Oslo, Norway, March 16, 1956; admitted, 1990, Norway. *Education:* University of Oslo (Candidate in Jurisprudence, 1988). Research Assistant, Institute of Public Law, University of Oslo, 1985-1986 (Written thesis on taxation of real estate). Associate Judge, Ytre Follo, 1990-1992. External Examinor, Legal Faculty University of Oslo. *Member:* Norwegian Bar Association. *LANGUAGES:* English and Scandinavian. *PRACTICE AREAS:* Contract Law; Energy Law; Real Estate.

TELLMANN, RAMM & CO.
OSLO, NORWAY

(See Advokatfirmaet Stabell DA)

General Civil Practice, Corporation, Commercial, Industrial, Financial, Stock Exchange and Securities, Product Liability, Importer and Dealership, Leasing, Licensing and General Tax Law, Governmental Relations, Damages and Collection of Debt, Real Estate, Insurance, Shipping, Broadcasting and Media Law, Patent and Trademark Law.

THOMMESSEN KREFTING GREVE LUND

TOLLBODGATEN 27
P.O. BOX 413 SENTRUM
0103 OSLO, NORWAY
Telephone: 47 22 42 18 10
Telexfax: 47 22 42 35 57

In Alliance With: Vinge, Sweden and Kromann & Münter, Denmark.
London, England Office: 44/45 Chancery Lane, WC2A 1JB. Telephone: 44 171 404 4825. Fax: 44 171 404 1471.
Bergen, Norway Office: Valkendorfsgate 1A, P.O. Box 349, 5000. Telephone: 47 55 31 13 50. Fax: 47 55 31 74 75.
Brussels, Belgium Office: Avenue Louise 475/B 12, 1050. Telephone: 32 2 646 3620. Fax: 32 2 646 4049.
Paris, France Representation Office: 21, Rue Jean Goujon, 75008. Telephone: 331 40.75.37.37. Fax: 331 45.63.05.49.
Hong Kong Representation Office: 2003 Hutchison House, 10 Harcourt Road Central. Telephone: 852 523 6149. Fax: 852 810 5343.

General Business Law. Tax, Corporation, Commercial, Industrial, Shipping, Banking and Government Relations.

FIRM PROFILE: With approximately 70 lawyers, Thommessen Krefting Greve Lund is the largest law firm in Norway. The firm's client base includes a considerable number of leading Norwegian corporations as well as several major multinational corporations. The firm is working in an international environment and has experience in the major areas of business life.

MEMBERS OF FIRM

HERM OTTO KREFTING, born Moss, Norway, April 16, 1919; admitted, 1945, Norway; 1952, Supreme Court of Norway. *Education:* University of Oslo (Candidate in Jurisprudence, 1943). Associate Judge, Nes Romerike, 1945-1946. *Member:* Norwegian and International Bar Associations; International Fiscal Association. *LANGUAGES:* Scandinavian Languages and English. *PRACTICE AREAS:* Business; Tax; Mergers; Finance Law.

GUNNAR GREVE, born Norway, 1929; admitted, 1955, Norway. *Education:* University of Bergen (Candidate in Jurisprudence, 1953); Dispasjø. Member, International and Business and tax organisations. (Resident at Bergen, Norway Office). *LANGUAGES:* Scandinavian Languages and English. *PRACTICE AREAS:* Finance; Commercial; Business Law.

HAAKON LØCHEN, born Meråker, Norway, February 17, 1929; admitted, 1962, Norway; 1967, Supreme Court of Norway. *Education:* University of Oslo (1952). Author: "Lease of Real Property and Taxation," Booklet, 1965; "Taxation of Real Property and Capital Gains," Lov og Rett, 1967; "Form and Substance in Taxation," Lov og Rett, 1971; "Taxation of Capital Gains on Shares," 1968 and 1978; "Skattebetalerforeningens Aksjehandbok;" "Determination of the Taxable Profit of Corporations;" "Cahiers de Droit Fiscal International," Vol. LX b, 1977; "Tax Treatment of Abandonment Work and Provision For Such Costs," Vol I Energy Law Seminar, Cambridge, 1979. Co-author: "Tax Avoidance; Tax Evasion," Sweed & Maxwell Ltd., 1982; "Transformation of Partnerships into Limited Corporations," Skatterett 1986. Member: Royal Commission on Taxation of Domestic Houses, 1968; Royal Commission on Company Law, 1975; Royal Commission on Reform of Taxation of Physical Persons, 1981. *Member:* Norwegian, American and International Bar Associations. *LANGUAGES:* Scandinavian Languages and English. *PRACTICE AREAS:* Commercial; Tax; Finance Law.

JAN EINAR GREVE, born Norway, 1933; admitted, 1961, Norway; 1963 Supreme Court. *Education:* University of Oslo (Candidate in Jurisprudence, 1968). *Member:* International Business Association. (Resident at Bergen, Norway Office). *LANGUAGES:* Scandinavian Languages and English. *PRACTICE AREAS:* Inside Trading; Finance; Commercial; Stocks and Bonds Law.

(This Listing Continued)

ANDERS ØSTBYE, born Oslo, Norway, November 10, 1920; admitted, 1955, Norway; 1962, Supreme Court of Norway. *Education:* University of Oslo (Candidate in Jurisprudence, 1947); Harvard Business School (M.B.A., 1950); University of Basel; University of Paris. *Member:* Norwegian Bar Association. *LANGUAGES:* English, German and French. *PRACTICE AREAS:* Commercial; Tax; Inside Trading; Finance Law.

GUNNAR THOMMESSEN, born Oslo, Norway, May 25, 1928; admitted, 1956, Norway; 1962, Supreme Court of Norway. *Education:* University of Oslo (Candidate in Jurisprudence, 1952). Associate Judge, Follo, 1954-1956. *Member:* Norwegian Bar Association; AIPPI; International Fiscal Association. *LANGUAGES:* English. *PRACTICE AREAS:* Commercial; Finance; Contract; Patent; Intellectual Property Law.

ØYSTEIN ESKELAND, born Oslo, Norway, March 12, 1932; admitted, 1961, Norway; 1966, Supreme Court of Norway. *Education:* University of Oslo (Candidate in Jurisprudence, 1957). Legal Secretary, Ministry of Foreign Affairs, 1958-1959. Associate Judge, Lier, Røyken og Hurum, 1959-1960. *Member:* Norwegian Bar Association; Norwegian Maritime Law Association; International Fiscal Association. *LANGUAGES:* English. *PRACTICE AREAS:* Finance; Mergers; Commercial Law.

BENT ØDEGÅRD, born Hamar, Norway, March 14, 1945; admitted, 1972, Norway; 1983, Supreme Court of Norway. *Education:* University of Oslo (Candidate in Jurisprudence, 1970). Associate Judge, Stroemmen District Court, 1970-1971. Legal Consultant: Oslo Tax Office, 1971-1972; Den norske Creditbank, Legal Department, Oslo, 1972-1974. Author: "The Raising of Rent," Lov og Rett, 1972; "Tax Planning in Connection with Insolvency and Bankruptcy," Bedriftsøkonomen, 1978; "Inflation and Taxation," Cahiers de Droit Fiscal International, Vol. LXII a, 1977. *Member:* Norwegian Bar Association; International Fiscal Association. *LANGUAGES:* Scandinavian Languages and English. *PRACTICE AREAS:* Tax; Business; Finance; Mergers and Acquisitions Law.

ERIK SAMUELSEN, born Oslo, Norway, October 21, 1944; admitted, 1972, Norway; 1976, Supreme Court of Norway. *Education:* University of Oslo (Candidate in Jurisprudence, 1968). Author: "Data Banks and Privacy," Universitetsforlaget, 1972. Lecturer of Law, University of Oslo, 1969-1971. Associate Judge, Strømmen, 1971-1972. *Member:* Norwegian Bar Association; AIPPI; Norwegian EDP Law Association; Association for Copyright Law. *LANGUAGES:* English. *PRACTICE AREAS:* Energy; Bankruptcy; Contract; Business; Finance Law.

PÅL W. LORENTZEN, born Norway, 1941; admitted, 1971, Norway; 1976, Supreme Court. *Education:* University of Oslo (Candidate in Jurisprudence, 1968); Period of residence for studying in England, 1970. *Member:* Norwegian Bar Association. (Resident at Bergen, Norway Office). *LANGUAGES:* Scandinavian and English. *PRACTICE AREAS:* Workers Compensation; Construction; Media; Regulatory; Contracts Law.

CARSTEN RIEKELES, born Oslo, Norway, October 25, 1943; admitted, 1974, Norway; 1978, Supreme Court of Norway. *Education:* University of Oslo (Candidate in Jurisprudence, 1970). Lecturer, Tax Law, University of Oslo, 1977-1978. Associate Judge Alta, 1972-1973. Tax Directorate, 1971-1972 and 1973-1974. *Member:* Norwegian Bar Association; IFA; Practicing Tax Lawyers Association (President). *LANGUAGES:* English. *PRACTICE AREAS:* Mediation; Energy; Contracts; Tax; Shipbuilding Law.

FINN E. ENGZELIUS, born Røros, Norway, September 10, 1943; admitted, 1973, Norway; 1981, Supreme Court of Norway. *Education:* University of Oslo (Candidate in Jurisprudence, 1971). External Examiner, Legal Faculty University of Oslo. Associate Judge, Hadeland, 1971-1973. Sulzburg Seminar, American Law & Legal Institutions, 1977. Member, Oslo Tax Assessment Board, 1983-1987. Magistrate, Oslo Superior Tax Assessment Board, 1987—. *Member:* Norwegian Bar Association; International Fiscal Association, International Bar Association. (Resident at Brussels, Belgium Office). *LANGUAGES:* Scandinavian Languages, English and French. *PRACTICE AREAS:* International Arbitration; Bankruptcy; European Union; Petroleum; Tax Law.

CHRISTIAN BRUUSGAARD, born Oslo, Norway, October 11, 1947; admitted, 1978, Norway. *Education:* University of Oslo (Candidate in Jurisprudence, 1974). *Member:* Norwegian Bar Association; International Fiscal Association. *LANGUAGES:* Scandinavian Languages and English. *PRACTICE AREAS:* Finance; Tax; Business Law.

SVERRE E. KOCH, born Oslo, Norway, April 8, 1948; admitted, 1981, Norway. *Education:* Augsburg College, Minneapolis (1968-1969); University of Oslo, (Candidate in Jurisprudence, 1974). Author: "Taxation of Capital Gains on Real Property," Book, Oslo 1981. Directorate of Taxes, 1975-1979. Associate Judge, Lier, Røyken and Hurum District Court, 1979-

(This Listing Continued)

THOMMESSEN KREFTING GREVE LUND, Oslo—
Continued

1981. *Member:* Norwegian Bar Association; International Fiscal Association. *LANGUAGES:* Scandinavian Languages and English. *PRACTICE AREAS:* Mergers and Acquisitions; Tax; Business; Finance Law.

STEPHEN KNUDTZON, born Bergen, Norway, June 6, 1952; admitted, 1979, Norway; 1991, Supreme Court of Norway. *Education:* University of Oslo (Candidate in Jurisprudence, 1976). Scientific Assistant, Scandinavian Institute of Maritime Law, 1974. Attorney, Northern Shipowners Defence Club, 1976-1980, 1981-1984 and 1985-1986. Associate Judge: Indre Follo, 1980-1981; Fred Olsen & Co., 1984-1985. Partner, Lund & Co., 1986-1993. *Member:* Norwegian Bar Association; Norwegian Maritime Law Association; International Bar Association. *LANGUAGES:* Scandinavian Languages, Dutch, French and English.

DAGFINN HERADSTVEIT, born Norway, 1952; admitted, 1980, Norway. *Education:* University of Bergen (Candidate in Jurisprudence, 1977). *Member:* Norwegian Bar Association. (Resident at Bergen, Norway Office). *LANGUAGES:* Scandinavian Languages, English and German. *PRACTICE AREAS:* Real Estate; Maritime; Landlord/Tenant; Finance; Business Law.

ENDRE GRANDE, born Norway, 1950; admitted, 1980, Norway; 1987, Supreme Court. *Education:* University of Bergen (Candidate in Jurisprudence, 1976). *Member:* Norwegian Bar Association. (Resident at Bergen, Norway Office). *LANGUAGES:* Scandinavian Languages, English and German. *PRACTICE AREAS:* Inheritance; Real Estate; Fish Farming; Environmental Law.

ØYSTEIN ELGAN, born April 27, 1955; admitted, 1982, Norway. *Education:* University of Bergen (Candidate in Jurisprudence, 1980). *Member:* Norwegian Bar Association. (Resident at Bergen, Norway Office). *LANGUAGES:* Scandinavian Languages and English. *PRACTICE AREAS:* Workers Compensation; Contract; Finance; Business Law.

TRULS LEIKVANG, born Marseille, France, June 23, 1946; admitted, 1974, Norway. *Education:* University of Oslo (Candidate in Jurisprudence, 1971). Author: Article, "Taxation of Limited Partnerships," Utvalget, 1977; Article, "Tax Questions Concerning Bankruptcy and Administrated Estates," Lov og Rett, 1980; "Deferred Taxation," Bedriftsøkonomen, 1981; Article, "The Tax Authorities use of Accounts," Registered Accountants Yearbook; Article, "Selected Tax questions Concerning Shipbuilding Contracts," Marius nr. 74, 1982; "Selected Tax Questions Concerning Condemnation of Fishing Vessels," Skatterett, nr. 1, 1983; *Tax Procedure Act,* Book published 1984. Lecturer of Law, University of Oslo. Manager, Oslo Tax Office, 1976-1979. Deputy Director General, Ministry of Finance, 1979-1982. *Member:* Norwegian Bar Association; International Fiscal Association; International Bar Association. *LANGUAGES:* Scandinavian Languages, English and French. *PRACTICE AREAS:* Finance; Business; Administrative Tax; Mergers and Acquisitions Law.

JØRGEN LUND, born Oslo, Norway, August 29, 1953; admitted, 1982, Norway. *Education:* University of Oslo (Candidate in Jurisprudence, 1978); American Graduate School of International Management (M.I.M., 1979). Scientific Assistant, Scandinavian Institute of Maritime law, 1976-1977. Attorney for the Attorney General, 1980. Attorney, Northern Ship Owners Defence Club, 1980-1986. Partner, Lund & Co., 1986-1993. *Member:* Norwegian Bar Association; Norwegian Maritime Law Association; International Bar Association. *LANGUAGES:* Scandinavian Languages and English. *PRACTICE AREAS:* Petroleum; Aviation; Transportation; International Arbitration; Maritime Law.

CARL ERIK KREFTING, born Oslo, Norway, October 8, 1953; admitted, 1980, Norway. *Education:* University of Oslo (Candidate in Jurisprudence, 1978). Author: Article, "Taxation of Group of Companies," Bedriftsøkonomen and Utvalget, 1980; Article, "The Taxpayers Right to use the LiFo Principle," Bedriftsøkonomen, 1981; "Taxation of Capital Gains on Real Property," Book, Published in 1981. Directorate of Taxes, 1978-1980. Secretary for the Royal Commission on The Accountants Rights and Duties Towards the State. *Member:* Norwegian Bar Association; International Fiscal Association; International Bar Association. *LANGUAGES:* Scandinavian Languages and English. *PRACTICE AREAS:* Business; Finance Tax Law.

BERNT JACOB PETTERSEN, born Norway, 1954; admitted, 1983, Norway; 1989, Supreme Court. *Education:* University of Bergen (Candidate in Jurisprudence, 1981); Visiting Scholar, University of California at Berkeley. *Member:* Norwegian Bar Association; International Bar Association (Member, Permanent Law Revision Committee). (Resident at Bergen, Norway Office).

(This Listing Continued)

way Office). *LANGUAGES:* Scandinavian Languages and English. *PRACTICE AREAS:* Petroleum; Contract; Business; Finance Law.

OLAV VIKØREN, born Oslo, Norway, December 7, 1955; admitted, 1984, Norway. *Education:* University of Oslo (Candidate in Jurisprudence, 1981). Scientific Assistant, Institute of Private Law, 1978-1979; Haight, Gardner, Poor & Havens, New York, 1981-1982; Northern Ship Owners Defence Club, 1982-1985 and 1986-1987. Associate Judge, Lier Røyken and Hurum, 1985-1986. Partner, Lund & Co., 1987-1993. *Member:* Norwegian Bar Association; Norwegian Maritime Law Association; International Bar Association. *LANGUAGES:* Scandinavian Languages and English. *PRACTICE AREAS:* Transportation; Finance; Maritime; Contracts; Business Law.

KIM DOBROWEN, born Oslo, Norway, July 4, 1957; admitted, 1985, Norway. *Education:* University of Oslo (Candidate in Jurisprudence, 1982). Co-Author: *Shipping and Finance,* Book published by the Scandinavian Institute of Maritime Law, 1981. Scientific Assistant, Scandinavian Institute of Maritime Law, 1980-1981. Lecturer on Bankruptcy Law, University of Oslo, 1984-1985. Legal Consultant, Ministry of Justice, Department of Legislation, 1983-1985. *Member:* Norwegian Bar Association. *LANGUAGES:* Scandinavian Languages and English. *PRACTICE AREAS:* Inside Trading; Business; Finance Law.

KRISTINE SCHEI, born Oslo, Norway, March 14, 1946; admitted, 1988, Norway. *Education:* University of Oslo (Candidate in Jurisprudence, 1970). Counsellor and Head of Section Ministry of Justice, 1970-1984. Associate Judge, Nedre Romerike, 1972-1973. Judge, Oslo City Court, 1984-1988. Scholarship: British Council, London, 1975. *Member:* Norwegian Bar Association. *LANGUAGES:* English. *PRACTICE AREAS:* Patent; Intellectual Property Law.

HENNING NAAS, born Norway, October 7, 1952. *Education:* University of Oslo (Candidate in Jurisprudence); University of Miami (Master of Law, LL.M.). Legal Consultant, Directorate of Taxes, 1979-1980. Baerum Tax Office, Legal Consultant, 1980-1981. *Member:* Norwegian Bar Association; International Fiscal Association. *LANGUAGES:* Scandinavian and English. *PRACTICE AREAS:* Contracts; Tax; Finance; International Law.

ARNE RINGNES, born Oslo, April 28, 1955; admitted, 1987, Norway. *Education:* University of Oslo (Candidate of Jurisprudence, 1982). Counsellor, Ministry of Justice, Department of Legislation, 1983-1985. Associate Judge, Indre Follo, 1985-1986. Scholarship, British Council, Edinburgh, 1986. *Member:* Norwegian Bar Association; AIPPI; Association for Copyright Law. *LANGUAGES:* English. *PRACTICE AREAS:* Petroleum; Patent; European Union; Finance; Business Law.

OLAV HAUGLAND, born Norway, 1952; admitted, 1985, Norway. *Education:* University of Oslo (Candidate in Jurisprudence, 1979). Tax inspector of Oslo, four years. *Member:* Norwegian Bar Association; International Fiscal Association. (Resident at Bergen, Norway Office). *LANGUAGES:* Scandinavian Languages, English and French. *PRACTICE AREAS:* Tax Law.

RUNE SOLBERG, born Norway, June 7, 1954; admitted, 1985, Norway. *Education:* University of Oslo (Candidate in Jurisprudence, 1982). Legal Consultant, Directorate of Taxes, 1983-1985. *Member:* Norwegian Bar Association. *LANGUAGES:* Scandinavian and English. *PRACTICE AREAS:* Tax Law.

GERHARD HOLM, born Tønsberg, Norway, February 11, 1952; admitted, 1983, Norway. *Education:* University of Oslo (Candidate in Jurisprudence, 1979); American Graduate School of International Management (M.I.M., 1982). Legal Consultant, Oslo Tax Office, 1980. Associate Judge, Gjoevik, 1980-1981. With: Krefbing, Løchen, Ødegärd & Sandner; Bø, Lieng, Fakobsen & Holm, Horten, 1985-1989. *Member:* Norwegian Bar Association; International Fiscal Association;. (Resident at Høvik, Norway Office). *LANGUAGES:* Scandinavian Languages and English. *PRACTICE AREAS:* Computer; Tax; Finance; Labor; Bankruptcy Law.

BERIT STOKKE, born Stockholm, Sweden, December 21, 1956; admitted, 1983, Norway. *Education:* Candidate in Jurisprudence (1981); Diplome des Etudes Superieures d'Universite d'Aix-Marseille, France (1983). Co-author: "Ship-Owner and Financial Institutions from a Practical Point of View," Article published by Scandinavian Institute of Maritime Law, 1979; *Ship, Shipyard and Financial Institutions,* Book published by Scandinavian Institute of Maritime Law, 1980. Scientific Assistant, Scandinavian Institute of Maritime Law, 1979-1980. Lecturer in Private Law, Institute for Private Law, Oslo Law Faculty, 1982. Legal Consultant, Civil Servant, Ministry of Justice, 1981. *Member:* Norwegian Bar Association; Association Internationaux des Jeunes Avocats. (Resident at London, England

(This Listing Continued)

Office). *LANGUAGES:* Scandinavian, English and French. *PRACTICE AREAS:* Finance; Maritime; International Tax; Business Law.

KJERSTI RINGDAL, born Oslo, Norway, June 22, 1955. *Education:* University of Oslo (Candidate in Jurisprudence, 1981). Legal Consultant, Directorate of Taxes, 1982-1985. *LANGUAGES:* Scandinavian and English. *PRACTICE AREAS:* Finance; Business; Tax Law.

ERIK NYGAARD, born October 7, 1957; admitted, 1986, Norway. Co-author: "Legal Problems related to Trans-Border Data Flows, OECD-ICCP No. 8, 1983. Scientific Assistant, Institute of Legal Information, University of Oslo. Legal Consultant, Ministry of Justice, Department of Legislation, 1984-1985. Assistant Judge, Indre Follo, 1985-1986. Council Lawyers Office, Oslo, 1986-1989. *LANGUAGES:* Scandinavian Languages and English. *PRACTICE AREAS:* Finance; Administrative; Real Estate; Computer; Business Law.

HANS OLAV LINDAL, born Norway, 1962; admitted, 1989, Norway. *Education:* University of Bergen (Candidate in Jurisprudence, 1987). *Member:* Norwegian Bar Association. (Resident at Bergen, Norway Office). *LANGUAGES:* Scandinavian Languages and English. *PRACTICE AREAS:* Contracts; Maritime Law.

MORTEN FJERMEROS, born Bergen, Norway, September 22, 1958; admitted, 1989, Norway. *Education:* University of Oslo (Candidate in Jurisprudence, 1984). Legal Consultant, Ministry of Finance, 1986-1987. Assistant Judge, Horten District Court, 1987-1988. *LANGUAGES:* Scandinavian Languages and English. *PRACTICE AREAS:* Bankruptcy; Mortgage; Tax; Finance Law.

ASSOCIATES

BØRGE BENUM, born Korea, 1963. *Education:* University of Oslo (Candidate in Jurisprudence, 1990); University of Exeter, England (LL.M. in European Legal Studies, 1991). *Member:* Norwegian Bar Association. *LANGUAGES:* English, Scandinavian and German. *PRACTICE AREAS:* Workers Compensation; European Union; Environmental; Bankruptcy; Landlord/Tenant Law.

ELISABETH HEIEN BERG, born Oslo, Norway, 1956. *Education:* Cleveland State University, 1979, Jurisprudence; University of Oslo (Candidate in Jurisprudence, 1981). *Member:* Norwegian Bar Association. *LANGUAGES:* Scandinavian Languages, English, French and Italian. *PRACTICE AREAS:* Immigration; Finance; Business Law.

KJERSTIN M. BULL-BERG, born Bergen, Norway, January 31, 1958; admitted, 1989, Norway. *Education:* University of Bergen (Candidate of Jurisprudence, 1984). Legal Adviser in the Banking, Insurance and Security Commission, 1984-1990. *Member:* Norwegian Bar Association. (Resident at Brussels, Belgium Office). *LANGUAGES:* Scandinavian Languages and English. *PRACTICE AREAS:* Finance; Business; Inside Trading Law.

TERRANCE W. CONLEY, born Kitchener, Ontario, 1958; admitted, 1986, Ontario; 1991, England and Wales as Solicitor of the Supreme Court. *Education:* University of Western Ontario, London Ontario, Canada (Economics 1979); University of Ottawa (Bachelor of Law, LL.B., 1981); The Centre for International Trade and Investment Contracts, University of Bielefeld, Bielefeld, Germany (Research Fellow, 1985). Attorney with Blake, Cassels and Graydon, Toronto, Ontario, 1987-1991. *LANGUAGES:* English, Norwegian, German, French. *PRACTICE AREAS:* Patent; Mergers; Finance; International; Business Law.

CHRISTIAN GARRICK DITLEV-SIMONSON, born Oslo, Norway, April 6, 1960. *Education:* University of Oslo (Candidate in Jurisprudence, 1988); Georgetown University (LL.M., 1991). Member, The Norwegian Banking, Insurance and Securities Commission. *LANGUAGES:* English and Norwegian.

STEIN FAGERHAUG, born October 7, 1956; admitted, 1986, Norway. *Education:* University of Oslo (Candidate in Jurisprudence, 1982). Legal Consultant, Directorate of Taxes, 1983-1984. Associate, Flod & Flod, 1984-1986. Associate Judge, Vest-Telemark, 1986-1988. *LANGUAGES:* Scandinavian Languages and English. *PRACTICE AREAS:* Tax; Real Estate; Construction; Landlord/Tenant Law.

ØYVIND HANDELAND, born Norway, 1950. *Education:* Batchelor of Commerce, University of Oslo (Candidate in Jurisprudence, 1976). Government Service and Ministry of Industry. Participation in several law-committees on the Corporate Law field. Co-author: Book, *Comments to the Account Act. Member:* Norwegian Bar Association. *LANGUAGES:* Scandinavian Languages, English and German. *PRACTICE AREAS:* Accounting; Tax; Business; Finance; Inside Trading Law.

(This Listing Continued)

KETIL HARDENG, born Bergen, Norway, December 1, 1968; admitted, 1994, Norway. *Education:* University of Bergen (Candidate in Jurisprudence, 1993). *LANGUAGES:* English and Norwegian. *PRACTICE AREAS:* Marine Law; Corporation Law.

HANS HAUGSTAD, born Drammen, Norway, March 19, 1968; admitted, 1994, Norway. *Education:* University of Oslo. *LANGUAGES:* English and Scandinavian. *PRACTICE AREAS:* Corporate Law; Maritime Law.

VIDAR HAVSGARD, born Bergen, Norway, November 20, 1965; admitted, 1994, Norway.

ARE HERREM, born Norway, 1962. *Education:* University of Oslo (Candidate in Jurisprudence, 1990). Research Assistant, University of Oslo, 1989-1990. Written phases on Maritime Joint Venture. *Member:* Norwegian Bar Association. *LANGUAGES:* Scandinavian Languages and English. *PRACTICE AREAS:* Trademark; Business; Contracts; Finance; Maritime Law.

SVERRE HVEDING, born Trondheim, Norway. *Education:* University of Oslo (Candidate of Jurisprudence, 1994). Scientific Assistant, University of Oslo, 1993. *Member:* Norwegian Bar Association. *LANGUAGES:* Scandinavian Languages and English.

JENS A. JACOBSEN, born Norway, 1947; admitted, 1977, Norway. *Education:* University of Oslo (Candidate in Jurisprudence, 1974). Legal Consultant, Ministry of Finance, 1974-1975. Assistant Judge, Tromsø, 1975-1977. Private Law Practice, 1977-1990. *Member:* Norwegian Bar Association. *LANGUAGES:* Scandinavian Languages and English. *PRACTICE AREAS:* Petroleum; Real Estate; Labor Law.

VIDAR KLEPPE, born Askoy, Norway, August 22, 1965; admitted, 1993, Norway. *Education:* University of Bergen (1990). Ministry of Defence, 1990-1991. Associate, Arthur Andersen, 1991-1993; TKGL, 1993—. *Member:* Norwegian Bar Association. *LANGUAGES:* Scandinavian Languages and English. *PRACTICE AREAS:* Finance; Business; Contracts; Tax Law.

KRISTIAN KVAMME, born Oslo, Norway, August 22, 1954; admitted, 1990, Norway. *Education:* University of Oslo (Candidate in Jurisprudence, 1982). Legal Consultant and Office Manager, Directorate of Taxes, 1983-1988. *Member:* Norwegian Bar Association; International Fiscal Association. *LANGUAGES:* English and Scandinavian. *PRACTICE AREAS:* Immigration; Labor; Tax; Business; Finance Law.

ELLEN MULSTAD, born Norway, 1962. *Education:* University of Oslo (Candidate in Jurisprudence, 1987); Hedmark Distrikshøyskole (Regional College), 1981-1983. Oslo Tax Office, 1987-1990. Legal Adviser/Assistant Secretary, Bedriftsøkonomisk Institutt (BI), 1989-1990; EEC (European Economic Community). British Council Scholarship, 1991. *Member:* Norwegian Bar Association. *LANGUAGES:* English and Scandinavian. *PRACTICE AREAS:* Inheritance; Labor; Immigration; Administrative; International Business Law.

CHRISTIAN MÜLLER, born Oslo, Norway, January 8, 1966; admitted, 1994, Norway. *Education:* University of Oslo (Candidate in Jurisprudence, 1991); Law School, University of North Dakota, 1990. *Member:* Norwegian Bar Association. *LANGUAGES:* English and Scandinavian Languages. *PRACTICE AREAS:* Real Estate; Contracts; Procedural Law; Business Law.

TORBJØRN MÆLAND, born Norway, 1966. *Education:* University of Bergen (Candidate in Jurisprudence, 1990). *Member:* Norwegian Bar Association. *LANGUAGES:* English and Scandinavian. *PRACTICE AREAS:* Maritime Law.

PER KAARE NERDRUM, born August 13, 1961; admitted, 1991, Norway. *Education:* University of Oslo (Candidate in Jurisprudence, 1988). Assistant Judge, Indre Follo, 1990. *Member:* Norwegian Bar Association. *LANGUAGES:* Scandinavian Languages and English. *PRACTICE AREAS:* Energy; Contracts; Labor; Real Estate Law.

ANNA ELISABETH NORDBØ, born Norway, 1966. *Education:* University of Bergen (Candidate in Jurisprudence, 1991). *LANGUAGES:* Scandinavian, English and German. *PRACTICE AREAS:* Trademark; Inside Trading; Business Law.

WILLIAM NYBØ, born February 18, 1953; admitted, 1987, Norway. *Education:* University of Oslo (Candidate in Jurisprudence, 1979). Legal Consultant, Ministry of Justice, 1979-1982 and 1984-985. Assistant Judge, Salten, 1982-1984. Office Manager, Oslo City Court, 1985-1987. *LANGUAGES:* Scandinavian Languages and English. *PRACTICE AREAS:* Labor; Real Estate; License Agreement; Contracts; Shipping Law.

(This Listing Continued)

THOMMESSEN KREFTING GREVE LUND, Oslo— Continued

HENRIK NYGAARD, born Norway, 1963. *Education:* University of Bergen (Candidate in Jurisprudence, 1990). *Member:* Norwegian Bar Association. (Resident at Bergen, Norway Office). *LANGUAGES:* English and Scandinavian. *PRACTICE AREAS:* Finance Law.

BRYNJULF NÆSS, born Norway, 1962. *Education:* University of Oslo (Candidate of Jurisprudence, 1989); University of Nort Dakota (1986). Counsellor, Ministry of Justice, Department of Legislation, 1989-1991. Associate Judge, Indre Follo, 1991-1992. *Member:* Norwegian Bar Association. *LANGUAGES:* English. *PRACTICE AREAS:* Tax; Finance; Workers Compensation; Mortgage Law.

ERIK SCHUMANN, born Sarpsborg, Norway, May 16, 1968; admitted, 1995, Norway. *Education:* University of Oslo (Candidate in Jurisprudence, 1992). *LANGUAGES:* English and Norwegian. *PRACTICE AREAS:* Tax Law.

SIV BLANCA SEJERSTED, born Denmark, February 28, 1968. *Education:* University of Oslo (Candidate of Jurisprudence, 1992). *Member:* Norwegian Bar Association. *LANGUAGES:* Scandinavian and English.

MAGNI SKAAR, born Norway, 1964. *Education:* University of Bergen (Candidate in Jurisprudence, 1990). *Member:* Norwegian Bar Association. (Resident at Bergen, Norway Office). *LANGUAGES:* Scandinavian Languages and English. *PRACTICE AREAS:* Personal Injury Law.

JOHN MORTEN SVENDGARD, born Norway, August 14, 1958; admitted, 1990, Norway. *Education:* Norwegian School of Management (Bedriftsøhonom, 1987); University of Oslo (Candidate in Jurisprudence, 1987). Associate Judge, Moss District Court, 1989-1990. Corporate Counsel, 1987-1989; 1990-1994. *Member:* Norwegian Bar Association. *LANGUAGES:* English and Scandinavian Languages. *PRACTICE AREAS:* Real Estate; Energy and Natural Resources; Litigation.

SIRI TEIGUM, born Sunndal, Norway, 1961. *Education:* University of Oslo (Candidate of Jurisprudence, 1987); College of Europe (Postgraduate studies in European Community Law, 1985). Research Assistant, University of Oslo, Faculty of Law, 1986-1987. Ministry of Justice, Department of Legislation, 1988-1989, EFTA Secretariat, Legal Department (European Free Trade Association) 1989-1992 (negotiation of the Agreement on the European Economic Area). Lecturer on i.a. Community Law (main emphasis on competition law) since 1987. *Member:* Norwegian Bar Association; Norwegian Association on European Law. *LANGUAGES:* Scandinavian, English and French. *PRACTICE AREAS:* Administrative; Patent; Trademark; Bankruptcy; Contracts Law.

KAI THØGERSEN, born Oslo, Norway, April 13, 1961; admitted, 1990, Norway. *Education:* University os Oslo (Candidate in Jurisprudence, 1987). Legal Adviser, Oslo Tax Office, 1987-1988. Assistant Judge, Skien & Porsgrunn City Court. *Member:* Norwegian Bar Association; International Fiscal Association. *LANGUAGES:* Scandinavian Languages, English and German. *PRACTICE AREAS:* Finance; Business; Mergers; Maritime Law.

SVEIN AAGE VALEN, born Norway, 1961; admitted, 1990, Norway. *Education:* University of Bergen (Candidate in Jurisprudence, 1987). Prosecutor, 1988-1989. Legal Department, Den norske Bank AS, 1989-1992. *Member:* Norwegian Bar Association. *LANGUAGES:* Scandinavian Languages and English. *PRACTICE AREAS:* Bankruptcy; Criminal; Finance; Business Law.

EIVIND J. VESTERKJÆR, born November 6, 1963. *Education:* University of Oslo (Candidate in Jurisprudence, 1989). *LANGUAGES:* Scandinavian Languages, English and French. *PRACTICE AREAS:* Real Estate; Patent; Bankruptcy; Intellectual Property; International Law.

EIRIK VIKANES, born BÆrum, Norway, March 21, 1968; admitted, 1994, Norway. *Education:* University of Oslo (Candidate in Jurisprudence, 1994). *LANGUAGES:* English and Scandinavian Languages.

THORNES, BERG, MUNDAL & GLOSIMOT

HAAKON VII'S GT 5
0161 OSLO, NORWAY
Telephone: (+47) 22-83-50-00
Fax: (+47) 22-83-07-66

General Civil Practice including Admiralty, Banking, Commercial Competition, Cooperation, Corporate Finance, Creditors Rights, Entertainment, Estate Planning, Family Law, Foreign Investment, Insolvency and Receivership, International Trade, Labour, Litigation, Pension, Probate, Real Estate, Securities, Taxation, Trade Mark and Corporate Law.

MEMBERS OF FIRM

SVERRE A. THORNES, born Aalesund, Norway, 1928; admitted, 1955, Norway; 1978, Supreme Court of Norway. *Education:* University of Oslo (Candidate in Jurisprudence, 1951). Den Norske Creditbank, Legal Department, 1951-1953. Associate Judge, Eiker, Modum og Sigdal Sorenskriverembete, 1953-1955. AS Norske Shell Legal Department, 1955-1957. Attorney-at-Law, 1957. Chairman and Member, Board of Directors of several Norwegian limited companies and foreign owned companies in Norway. *Member:* Norwegian Bar Association. *LANGUAGES:* Scandinavian, English and German.

PAAL OLAV BERG, born Oslo, Norway, 1946; admitted, 1976, Norway. *Education:* University of Oslo (Candidate in Jurisprudence, 1973). Ministry of Local Government and Labour Relations, 1973-1975. Associate Judge, Nedenes Sorenskriverembete, Arendal, 1975-1976. Attorney-at-Law, 1976. Lecturer of Law, University of Oslo, 1977; Member, Board of Examinators, University of Oslo, 1973-74. *Member:* Norwegian Bar Association. *LANGUAGES:* Scandinavian and English, some French, German and Italian.

JENS MUNDAL, born Oslo, Norway, 1952; admitted, 1984, Norway. *Education:* University of Oslo (Candidate in Jurisprudence, 1980). Ministry of Environment, 1980-1984. Associate Judge, Larvik Sorenskriverembete, 1984-1985. Attorney-at-Law, 1985. *Member:* Norwegian Bar Association. *LANGUAGES:* Scandinavian and English.

TOM H. GLOSIMOT, born Tromsø, Norway, 1956; admitted, 1988, Norway. *Education:* University of Oslo (Candidate in Jurisprudence, 1984). Trainee, McMillan, Binch, Toronto, 1984-1985. Directorate of Taxes, Legal Consultant, 1986-1987. Associate Judge, Holt Sorenskriverembete, Tvedestrand, 1987-1988, Bergen Bank, Legal Department, Oslo, 1988-1989. *Member:* Norwegian Bar Association. *LANGUAGES:* Scandinavian and English.

TORKILDSEN, TENNØE & CO.

Established in 1979

BOGSTADVEIEN 36
N-0366 OSLO 3, NORWAY
Telephone: 47 22 46 73 10
Facsimile: 47 22 46 95 17

Corporate and Company Law, Personal and Corporate Taxation, Finance, General Business Law including Contract Negotiations, Litigation, and Real Estate Law including Construction, Purchase, Sale, Rent and Lease of Business Properties.

FIRM PROFILE: The firm was established in 1979 and has since grown evenly till its present size. Further growth can be expected. It offers a full range of legal services, including negotiation as well as litigation regarding corporate and general business law. It is also well known for its wide legal experience regarding business properties.

MEMBERS OF FIRM

TOM A. TORKILDSEN, born Oslo, Norway, June 26, 1947; admitted, 1977, Norway. *Education:* University of Oslo (Cand. Jur., 1974). Trainee, EEC-Commission, Brussels, 1972 and Norton, Rose, Botterell & Roche, London, 1978. Associate Judge, Halden, 1975-1976. *Member:* Norwegian Bar Association. *LANGUAGES:* Scandinavian and English. *PRACTICE AREAS:* Company and Corporate; General Business; Litigation.

JAN TENNØE, born Oslo, Norway, February 12, 1949; admitted, 1977, Norway. *Education:* University of Oslo (Cand. Jur., 1975). Associate Judge, Ringerike, 1976-1977. *Member:* Norwegian Bar Association. *LANGUAGES:* Scandinavian and English. *PRACTICE AREAS:* Construction; Arbitration; Litigation.

(This Listing Continued)

ANDREAS IVERSEN, born Oslo, Norway, August 26, 1952; admitted, 1980, Norway. *Education:* University of Oslo (Cand. Jur., 1977). Deputy Public Prosecutor, 1978-1979. *Member:* Norwegian Bar Association. *LANGUAGES:* Scandinavian, English and German. *PRACTICE AREAS:* Real Estate; General Business.

FABIAN STANG, born Oslo, Norway, August 19, 1955; admitted, 1984, Norway. *Education:* University of Oslo (Cand. Jur., 1984). Deputy Assistant Chief of Police, 1986. Deputy Public Prosecutor, 1986. *Member:* Norwegian Bar Association. *LANGUAGES:* Scandinavian and English. *PRACTICE AREAS:* Real Estate; General Business; Litigation.

HARALD CHRISTENSEN, born Oslo, February 28, 1953; admitted, 1985, Norway. *Education:* University of Oslo (Cand. Jur., 1980). With, Ministry of Justice, 1981-1982 and Oslo Tax Authorities, 1983-1985. Associate Judge, Sandnes, 1982-1983. *Member:* Norwegian Bar Association. *LANGUAGES:* Scandinavian and English. *PRACTICE AREAS:* Tax; Company; General Business.

ASSOCIATES

ELLING Ø. OSE, born 1957; admitted, 1990, Norway. *LANGUAGES:* English and Scandinavian. *PRACTICE AREAS:* Banking Law; Investment Law; General Business.

STIG HVINDEN, born 1951; admitted, 1990, Norway. *LANGUAGES:* English and Scandinavian. *PRACTICE AREAS:* General Business.

VISLIE, ØDEGAARD & KOLRUD ANS

Established in 1935

FR. NANSENS PLASS 6

P.O. BOX 1244 VIKA

0110 OSLO, NORWAY

Telephone: (47) 22 42 02 15

Telefax: (47) 22 42 55 44; (47) 22 42 53 94

Firm engaged in Norwegian, European and International Law Practice. Entitled to plead before Norwegian Courts.

Energy Law, Commercial Law including Offshore Contracts, Construction Law, General International Trade Law, Compulsory Purchase Law, Administrative Law, European Community Law, Litigation and International Arbitration.

FIRM PROFILE: Established in 1935, Vislie, Ødegaard & Kolrud originally was a small specialist firm in compulsory purchase and concession law. Since 1970, it has gradually grown into a larger law firm recognized for several areas of special competence, yet offering a wide range of quality legal services in commercial and administrative law. The areas of special competence are energy and concession law, contract law especially offshore, construction, process plant and industrial delivery contracts, administrative law and compulsory purchase law. It has also developed a comprehensive practice in general international trade law and in international arbitration. The client base is National, European and to some extent North American in scope.

The firm has several big industrial companies in Norway and Europe as clients, besides a couple of Norwegian governmental agencies and a large number of the country's municipalities.

The firm has 11 partners and eight assistants practicing in the office in Oslo. The firm is a member of LEX NORVEGICA, a Norwegian law firm cooperation consisting of four law firms situated in the four largest Norwegian cities, Oslo, Bergen, Stavanger and Trondheim, with more than 45 lawyers. Through LEX NORVEGICA the firm has established a Brussels Office in cooperation with the Norwegian law firm Hjort.

MEMBERS OF FIRM

INGOLF A. VISLIE, born Oslo, Norway, February 22, 1930; admitted, 1957, Norway; 1963, Supreme Court Barrister. *Education:* University of Oslo (Candidate in Jurisprudence, 1954). Partner, 1959—; Deputy Judge, Sandefjord County Court, 1956-1957; Lecturer, Compulsory Purchase Law, Procedural Law and Energy Law. *Member:* Norwegian Bar Association; International Bar Association. *LANGUAGES:* Scandinavian, English and German. *PRACTICE AREAS:* Energy Law; Compulsory Purchase Law; Planning Law; Administrative Law.

KÅRE ØDEGAARD, born Skjåk, Norway, September 15, 1927; admitted, 1962, Norway; 1967, Supreme Court Barrister. *Education:* University of Oslo (Candidate in Jurisprudence, 1956). Partner, 1968—; Deputy Judge, Nord-Hedmark County Court, 1958-1960; Lecturer, Compulsory Purchase Law and the Law of Waterways. *Member:* Norwegian Bar Association.

(This Listing Continued)

LANGUAGES: Scandinavian and English. *PRACTICE AREAS:* Energy Law; Compulsory Purchase Law; Planning Law; Property Law.

HELGE JAKOB KOLRUD, born Bergen, Norway, April 23, 1938; admitted, 1967, Norway; 1970, Supreme Court Barrister. *Education:* University of Oslo (Candidate in Jurisprudence, 1965). Partner, 1972—; Deputy Judge, Lier, Røyken og Hurum County Court, 1965-1967; Co-author, "North Sea Offshore Construction Contracts," 1979, including numerous Articles and Books on Offshore Construction Contracts, Construction Contracts, Product Liability and Compulsory Purchase; Lecturer, Offshore Construction Contracts, Construction Contracts, Product Liability and Compulsory Purchase, National and International Seminars, 1975—. Member, 1976—and Chairman, 1980-1984, Legal Committee of Organisme de Liaison des Fabriques Metalliques Europeenes, ORGALIME. Board Member: Oslo University's Nordic Institute of Maritime and Petroleum Law, 1989—; Arbitration Institute of Oslo Chamber of Commerce, 1985—. *Member:* Norwegian Bar Association (Board Member, 1990—; President, 1991-1994); International Bar Association (Council Member; Head of Norwegian Delegation, CCBE). *LANGUAGES:* Scandinavian, English and German. *PRACTICE AREAS:* Contract Law; Process Plant Contracts; Offshore Contracts; Construction and Delivery Contracts; International Trade Law; Compulsory Purchase Law; International and National Arbitration; Commercial Litigation.

SVEIN ARILD PIHLSTRØM, born Oslo, Norway, March 28, 1945; admitted, 1975, Norway; 1985, Supreme Court Barrister. *Education:* University of Oslo (Candidate in Jurisprudence, 1969). Partner, 1980—; Deputy Judge, Salten County Court, 1972; Storting's Ombudsman (Norwegian Parliament) for Public Administration, 1970-1975; Lecturer, Compulsory Purchase Law. *Member:* Norwegian Bar Association. *LANGUAGES:* Scandinavian and English. *PRACTICE AREAS:* Compulsory Purchase Law; Construction Contracts Law; Administrative Law; Planning Law; Litigation.

HANS OLUF BANG, born Oslo, Norway, February 16, 1944; admitted, 1973, Norway; 1989, Supreme Court Barrister. *Education:* University of Oslo (Candidate in Jurisprudence, 1968). Partner, 1982—; Deputy Judge, Bodø City Court, 1969-1970; Oslo City Tax Office, 1970-1973; Fred, Olsen & Co., 1973-1980. *Member:* Norwegian Bar Association. *LANGUAGES:* Scandinavian and English. *PRACTICE AREAS:* Company and Tax Law; Taxation of Hydro-Electric Power Plants.

OLA BREKKEN, born Lillehammer, Norway, March 21, 1949; admitted, 1981, Norway; 1988, Supreme Court Barrister. *Education:* University of Oslo (Candidate in Jurisprudence, 1975). Partner, 1986—; Archivist and Counsellor, Norwegian National Archives, 1977. Deputy Judge, Nedre Romerike County Court, 1979-1981; Lecturer, Norwegian Property Law. *Member:* Norwegian Bar Association; International Bar Association. *LANGUAGES:* Scandinavian and English. *PRACTICE AREAS:* Compulsory Purchase and Planning Law; Construction Contracts; Property Law.

STEIN ERIK STINESSEN, born Oslo, Norway, July 10, 1951; admitted, 1982, Norway. *Education:* University of Oslo (Candidate in Jurisprudence, 1976). Partner, 1986—; Police Superintendent, Oslo City Police, 1977-1978; Storting's Ombudsmann (Norwegian Parliament) for Public Administration, 1978-1981; Deputy Judge, Nedre Romerike County Court, 1981-1982. Lecturer, Planning Law and Water Administration Law. *Member:* Norwegian Bar Association. *LANGUAGES:* Scandinavian and English. *PRACTICE AREAS:* Energy Law; Planning and Compulsory Purchase Law; Construction Contracts; Administrative Law.

OLAV BERGSAKER, born Arendal, Norway, August 9, 1952; admitted, 1985, Norway. *Education:* University of Oslo (Candidate in Jurisprudence, 1979). Partner, 1990—; Executive Officer, Norwegian Ministry of Local Government, 1979-1984; Deputy Judge, Skien and Porsgrunn City Court, 1984-1985; Lecturer, Taxation of Hydro-Electric Power Plant Companies. *Member:* Norwegian Bar Association. *LANGUAGES:* Scandinavian and English. *PRACTICE AREAS:* Contract Law; Offshore and Construction Contracts; Property Tax; Taxation of Hydro-Electric Power Plant Companies; Commercial Law; International Trade Law; Commercial Litigation.

INGER-JOHANNE LUND, born Oslo, Norway, March 11, 1952; admitted, 1982, Norway. *Education:* University of Oslo (Candidate in Jurisprudence, 1977). Partner, 1991—; Norwegian Bank Inspectorate, 1977-1978; Norwegian Ministry of Trade, 1978-1980; Deputy Judge, Ringerike County Court, 1980-1982. *Member:* Norwegian Bar Association. *LANGUAGES:* Scandinavian and English. *PRACTICE AREAS:* Contract Law; Construction and Delivery Contracts; Property Tax; Taxation of Hydro-Electric Power Plant Companies; Commercial Law; International Private Law; Commercial Litigation.

(This Listing Continued)

VISLIE, ØDEGAARD & KOLRUD ANS, Oslo—
Continued

WILFRED ROHDE GARDER, born Oslo, Norway, March 7, 1958; admitted, 1988, Norway. *Education:* University of Oslo (Candidate of Jurisprudence, 1985). Partner, 1992—; Executive Officer, Norwegian Department of Justice, 1986-1987; Deputy Judge, Heggen and Frøland County Court, 1987-1988. *Member:* Norwegian Bar Association. *LANGUAGES:* Scandinavian and English. *PRACTICE AREAS:* Contract Law; Offshore Contracts; Construction and Delivery Contracts; Commercial Law; International Trade Law; Compulsory Purchase Law; Commercial Litigation.

CAROLINE LUND MELTVEDT, born Oslo, Norway, June 29, 1961; admitted, 1990, Norway. *Education:* University of Oslo (Candidate in Jurisprudence, 1987). Partner, 1993—; Deputy Judge, Horten County Court, 1987-1988. *Member:* Norwegian Bar Association. *LANGUAGES:* Scandinavian, English and French. *PRACTICE AREAS:* Energy Law; Construction Contracts; Administrative Law; Planning and Compulsory Purchase Law.

VOGT & CO.

Member of S.L.G.

(Scandinavian Business Law Group)

Oslo: Vogt & Co.

Copenhagen: Berning Schlüter Hald

Helsinki: Bützow & Co.

Stockholm: Tisell & Co. AB

London: S.L.G.

ROALD AMUNDSENSGATE 6
P.O. BOX 1503 VIKA
0117 OSLO, NORWAY
Telephone: 47-22 41 01 90
Telex: 71 236 lawad
Telefax: 47-22 42 54 85

London, England Office: 2 Suffolk Lane, EC4R 0AT. Telephone: +44 171 623 3121. Fax: +44 171 936 2545.

Maritime, Aviation, Corporate, Banking, Finance, Tax, Insurance, Mergers and Acquisitions, Construction and Oil Offshore Law.

MEMBERS OF FIRM

ARILD DITLEV-SIMONSEN, born Paris, France, March 21, 1931; admitted, 1963, Norway; 1980, Supreme Court. *Education:* Princeton University (B.A., 1952); University of Oslo (Candidate of Jurisprudence, 1958). *Member:* Norwegian Bar Association; Norwegian Maritime Law Association. *LANGUAGES:* English and Scandinavian. *PRACTICE AREAS:* Maritime Law and Marine Insurance; Transportation Law; Contract Law; Tort Law.

BJØRN KJOS, born Norway, July 18, 1946; admitted, 1980, Norway. *Education:* University of Oslo (Candidate of Jurisprudence, 1978). Lecturer, Business Law for Final Examine, University of Oslo, 1981-1985. With, Ministry of Oil and Energy, 1978. Associate Judge, Moss, 1979-1980. *Member:* Norwegian Bar Association; Norwegian Maritime Law Association. *LANGUAGES:* English and Scandinavian. *PRACTICE AREAS:* Maritime Law and Marine Insurance; Aviation Law; Transportation Law; Contract Law including Offshore Construction Contracts.

BJØRN HALVOR KISE, born Holla, Norway, May 16, 1950; admitted, 1979, Norway. *Education:* University of Oslo (Candidate of Jurisprudence, 1978). With, Ministry of Justice, 1978-1980. Associate Judge, Hamar, 1980-1981. *Member:* Norwegian Bar Association; Norwegian Maritime Law Association. *LANGUAGES:* English and Scandinavian. *PRACTICE AREAS:* Corporate Law and Commercial Transactions; Finance; Real Estate Law including Property Development; Contract Law; Tort Law.

MORTEN LUND, born Oslo, Norway, August 3, 1951; admitted, 1984, Norway. *Education:* University of Oslo (Candidate of Jurisprudence, 1978). Author: "Norwegian Petroleum Law," Sjørettsfondet, 1977. Part time Lecturer and Examinor on Law, University of Oslo, 1978-1985. Visiting Lecturer on Law, Energy Law Department, University of Southampton, 1981. Executive Officer, Legislation Department, Ministry of Justice, 1978-1982. *Member:* Norwegian Bar Association; Norwegian Computers and Law Association, Norwegian Maritime Law Association. *LANGUAGES:* English

(This Listing Continued)

and Scandinavian. *PRACTICE AREAS:* Corporate Law; Debt and Equity; Mergers and Acquisitions; Securities Law; Maritime Law and Marine Insurance; Contract Law; Tort Law.

ARVID DAHM, born Oslo, Norway, March 24, 1952; admitted, 1982, Norway. *Education:* University of Oslo (Candidate in Jurisprudence, 1977). With, Ministry of Finance, 1978-1979 and The Taxpayer's Association, 1979-1983. Tax Partner Forum, Touche Toss, 1983-1988. *Member:* Norwegian Bar Association; International Fiscal Association. *LANGUAGES:* English and Scandinavian. *PRACTICE AREAS:* Tax and Accounting Law; Corporate Law; Contract Law.

TROND VERNEGG, born Sandefjord, Norway, April 10, 1958; admitted, 1986, Norway. *Education:* University of Oslo (Candidate of Jurisprudence, 1985). *Member:* Norwegian Bar Association. *LANGUAGES:* English and Scandinavian. *PRACTICE AREAS:* Corporate Law; Debt and Equity; Mergers and Acquisitions; Securities Law; Contract Law.

OLA TOFTEGAARD-HOX, born Oslo, Norway, October 25, 1956; admitted, 1992, Norway. *Education:* University of Oslo (Candidate of Jurisprudence, 1981); Insead Fontaine Bleau, France (M.B.A., 1983); New York Bar Exam (1987). *Member:* Norwegian Bar Association. *LANGUAGES:* English, French and Scandinavian. *PRACTICE AREAS:* Corporate Law; Debt and Equity; Mergers and Acquisitions; Securities Law; Secured and Structured Financing.

PETTER RUSTEN, born Oslo, Norway, September 12, 1962; admitted, 1990, Norway. *Education:* University of Oslo (Candidate of Jurisprudence, 1990). *Member:* Norwegian Bar Association. *LANGUAGES:* English and Scandinavian. *PRACTICE AREAS:* Maritime Law and Marine Insurance; Insolvency Law.

STEIN CHR. HEXEBERG, born Kristiansund, Norway, March 20, 1953; admitted, 1982, Norway. *Education:* University of Oslo (Candidate of Jurisprudence, 1978); University of Pennsylvania Law School (Master of Law-LL.M., 1980). *Member:* Norwegian Bar Association. *LANGUAGES:* English and Scandinavian. *PRACTICE AREAS:* Tort Law; Traffic Law; Contract Law.

WATSON, FARLEY & WILLIAMS

BEDDINGEN 8

AKER BRYGGE

0250 OSLO, NORWAY
Telephone: (47 22) 83 83 08
Telex: 79209 WFW N
Fax: (47 22) 83 83 13

London, England Office: 15 Appold Street, London EC2A 2HB. Telephone: (44 171) 814 8000. Telex: 8955707 WFW LON G. Fax: (44 171) 814 8141.

New York, New York Office: 380 Madison Avenue, 10017. Telephone: 212-922-2200. Telex: 6790626 WFW NY. Fax: 212-922-1512.

Paris, France Office: 19 Rue de Marignan, 75008 Paris. Telephone: (33 1) 45 63 15 15. Telex: WFW PAR 651096 F. Fax: (33 1) 45 61 09 01.

Athens, Greece Office: Alassia Building, Defteras Merarchias 13, 185-35 Piraeus. Telephone: (30 1) 422 3660. Telex: 24 1311 WFW GR. Fax: (30 1) 422 3664.

Moscow, Russia Office: 36 Myaskovskovo Street, Moscow 121019. Telephone: (7 502) 224 1700 (international only); (7 095) 291 8046/5968. Fax: (7 502) 224 1701 (international only); (7 095) 202 9027.

Firm engaged in General International Practice, Corporate, Commercial and Financing, Shipping, Aviation, Banking, Taxation, Commerical Litigation and Arbitration and European Community Law. Not qualified to advise on Norwegian law.

RESIDENT PARTNERS
M.L. Vernell

(For Biographical Data on additional partners, see Professional Biographies at Copenhagen, Denmark, London, England, Paris, France, Pireaus, Greece and Moscow, Russia)

ADVOKATFIRMAET WIERSHOLM, MELLBYE & BECH ANS

Established in 1875

KIRKEGATEN 15
P.O. BOX 400 SENTRUM
N-0103 OSLO 1, NORWAY
Telephone: +47 22 400 600
Fax: Group III +47 22 410 600
Telex: 76761

Administrative, Arbitration, Banking, Bankruptcy, Competition, Corporate, Distributorship, Agency and Franchise, Foreign Investments, International Contracts, Insurance, Employer's Liability, Health, Hospital, Malpractice, Industrial Relations, Labor, Litigation, Maritime, Admiralty, Oil, Mining, Corporate Taxation, Personal Income Taxation, Taxation of Foreign Nationals, Exchange Control, Mergers and Acquisitions Law, General Legal Practice.

FIRM PROFILE: *The firm was established in 1875 and offers a full range of legal services.*

MEMBERS OF FIRM

HARALD SCHJOLDAGER, born Oslo, 1931; admitted, 1958, Norway; 1964, Supreme Court of Norway. *Education:* University of Oslo (Candidate in Jurisprudence, 1956); Yale Law School (LL.M., 1958). *Member:* Norwegian and International Bar Associations. *LANGUAGES:* The Scandinavian Languages, English and German.

NILS J. SEJERSTED, born Oslo, 1934; admitted, 1962, Norway; 1967, Supreme Court of Norway. *Member:* Norwegian and International Bar Associations. *LANGUAGES:* The Scandinavian Languages, English and German.

OLE A. BACHKE, JR., born Oslo, Norway, April 28, 1935; admitted, 1962, Norway and Supreme Court of Norway. *Education:* University of Oslo (Candidate in Jurisprudence, 1960). *Member:* Norwegian and International Bar Associations. *LANGUAGES:* The Scandinavian Languages and English.

ARNLJOT HUSTAD, born Norway, March 22, 1935; admitted, 1968, Norway. *Education:* University of Oslo (Candidate in Jurisprudence, 1966). *Member:* Norwegian and International Bar Associations; International Fiscal Association. *LANGUAGES:* The Scandinavian Languages and English.

JON TENDEN, born Oslo, 1939; admitted, 1968, Norway; 1976, Supreme Court of Norway. *Education:* University of Oslo (Candidate in Jurisprudence, 1965). *Member:* Norwegian and International Bar Associations. *LANGUAGES:* The Scandinavian Languages and English.

ERIK HIRSCH, born Norway, May 20, 1946; admitted, 1975, Norway; 1986, Supreme Court of Norway. *Education:* University of Oslo (Candidate in Jurisprudence, 1971). *Member:* Norwegian Bar Association; International Fiscal Association. *LANGUAGES:* The Scandinavian Languages, French and English.

HANS CHR. BJØNNESS, born Norway, July 30, 1945; admitted, 1975, Norway; 1992, Supreme Court of Norway. *Education:* University of Oslo (Candidate in Jurisprudence, 1969). *Member:* Norwegian and International Bar Association. *LANGUAGES:* The Scandinavian Languages, French and English.

TRYGVE HONNE, born Norway, August 13, 1945; admitted, 1976, Norway. *Education:* University of Oslo (Candidate in Jurisprudence, 1973). *Member:* Norwegian Bar Association. *LANGUAGES:* The Scandinavian Languages and English.

CHRISTIAN B. HERLOFSON, born Arendal, 1952; admitted, 1972, Norway; 1979, Supreme Court of Norway. *Education:* University of Oslo (Candidate in Jurisprudence, 1969). *Member:* Norwegian and International Bar Associations. *LANGUAGES:* The Scandinavian Languages, English and German.

PER F. HETTY, born Norway, April 3, 1948; admitted, 1976, Norway. *Education:* University of Oslo (Candidate in Jurisprudence, 1974). *Member:* Norwegian and International Bar Associations. *LANGUAGES:* The Scandinavian Languages and English.

JAN-FREDRIK WILHELMSEN, born Ardal i Sogn, 1953; admitted, 1982, Norway; 1992, Supreme Court of Norway. *Education:* University of Oslo (Candidate in Jurisprudence, 1979). *Member:* Norwegian and International Bar Associations. *LANGUAGES:* The Scandinavian Languages, English and German.

(This Listing Continued)

BERNHARD MAGNUSSEN, born Norway, February 17, 1951; admitted, 1981, Norway. *Education:* University of Oslo (Candidate in Jurisprudence, 1978). *Member:* Norwegian and International Bar Associations. *LANGUAGES:* The Scandinavian Languages and English.

ERLING LIND, born Norway, June 13, 1955; admitted, 1985, Norway. *Education:* University of Oslo (Candidate in Jurisprudence, 1982). *Member:* Norwegian and International Bar Associations. *LANGUAGES:* The Scandinavian Languages and English.

JENS R. ANDERSEN, born Norway, July 12, 1953; admitted, 1982, Norway. *Education:* University of Oslo (Candidate in Jurisprudence, 1978). *Member:* Norwegian Bar Association. *LANGUAGES:* The Scandinavian Languages and English.

PER RAUSTØL, born Oslo, Norway, May 17, 1953; admitted, 1983, Norway. *Education:* University of Oslo (Candidate in Jurisprudence, 1981). *Member:* Norwegian and International Bar Associations. *LANGUAGES:* The Scandinavian Languages and English.

ANDREAS MELLBYE, born Oslo, 1955; admitted, 1986, Norway. *Education:* University of Oslo (Candidate in Jurisprudence, 1983). *Member:* Norwegian Bar Association. *LANGUAGES:* The Scandinavian Languages and English.

TERJE HOFFMANN, born Oslo, 1956; admitted, 1987, Norway. *Education:* University of Oslo (Candidate in Jurisprudence, 1982). *Member:* Norwegian Bar Association. *LANGUAGES:* The Scandinavian Languages and English.

MAGNUS HELLESYLT, born Norway, October 30, 1959; admitted, 1987, Norway. *Education:* University of Oslo (Candidate in Jurisprudence, 1985). *Member:* Norwegian Bar Association. *LANGUAGES:* The Scandinavian Languages and English.

WILHELM MATHESON, born Oslo, 1955; admitted, 1988, Norway. *Education:* University of Oslo (Candidate in Jurisprudence, 1982). *Member:* Norwegian Bar Association. *LANGUAGES:* The Scandinavian Languages, English and German.

HELGE MORTEN SVARVA, born Levanger, 1954; admitted, 1986, Norway; 1986, Supreme Court of Norway. *Education:* University of Oslo (Candidate in Jurisprudence, 1982). *Member:* Norwegian and International Bar Associations. *LANGUAGES:* The Scandinavian Languages and English.

ANDERS CHR. STRAY RYSSDAL, born Oslo, Norway, October 16, 1955; admitted, 1987, Supreme Court of Norway. *Education:* University of Oslo (Candidate in Jurisprudence, 1983); Harvard Law School (LL.M., 1986). Awarded, H.M. The King's Gold Medal, 1980. Chairman, Norwegian Competition Committee, 1990-1991. *LANGUAGES:* The Scandinavian Languages, English and German.

PER FLEISJE, born Norway, June 2, 1957; admitted, 1987, Norway. *Education:* University of Oslo (Candidate of Jurisprudence, 1985). *Member:* Norwegian Bar Association. *LANGUAGES:* The Scandinavian Languages and English.

NICOLAS BRUN-LIE, born Oslo, Norway, June 24, 1955; admitted, 1985, Norway. *Education:* University of Oslo (Candidate in Jurisprudence, 1983). *Member:* Norwegian Bar Association. *LANGUAGES:* The Scandinavian Languages, English and French.

ERIK RAMM, born Oslo, Norway, May 5, 1950; admitted, 1979, Norway. *Education:* University of Oslo (Candidate in Jurisprudence, 1976). *Member:* Norwegian and International Bar Associations. *LANGUAGES:* The Scandinavian Languages and English.

HARALD WILLUMSEN, born Oslo, Norway, October 17, 1952; admitted, 1982, Norway. *Education:* University of Oslo (Candidate in Jurisprudence, 1978). *Member:* Norwegian Bar Association. *LANGUAGES:* The Scandinavian Languages and English.

KARSTEN STENERSEN, born Norway, April 13, 1952; admitted, 1983, Norway. *Education:* University of Oslo (Candidate in Jurisprudence, 1977). *Member:* Norwegian Bar Association. *LANGUAGES:* The Scandinavian Languages and English.

LEIF JOACHIM MOLTKE-HANSEN, born Oslo, Norway, November 13, 1954; admitted, 1983, Norway. *Education:* University of Oslo (Candidate in Jurisprudence, 1980). *Member:* Norwegian and International Bar Associations. *LANGUAGES:* The Scandinavian Languages and English.

JOHN S. GULBRANSEN, born Oslo, December 14, 1954; admitted, 1990, Norway. *Education:* University of Oslo (Candidate in Jurisprudence,

(This Listing Continued)

**ADVOKATFIRMAET WIERSHOLM, MELLBYE &
BECH ANS, Oslo—Continued**

1985). *Member:* Norwegian Bar Association. *LANGUAGES:* The Scandinavian Languages and English.

JAN FOUGNER, born Fredrikstad, Norway, October 30, 1961; admitted, 1990, Norway; 1992, Supreme Court of Norway. *Education:* University of Oslo (Candidate in Jurisprudence, 1988). *Member:* Norwegian Bar Association. *LANGUAGES:* The Scandinavian Languages, English and German.

HENRIK A. CHRISTENSEN, born Norway, July 10, 1962; admitted, 1992, Norway. *Education:* University of Oslo (Candidate in Jurisprudence, 1989). *Member:* Norwegian Bar Association. *LANGUAGES:* The Scandinavian Languages and English.

WIKBORG, REIN & CO.

Established in 1923

KRONPRINSESSE MÄRTHAS PLASS 1
P.O. BOX 1513 VIKA
0117 OSLO, NORWAY
Telephone: 47 22827500
Telefax: 47 22827501

Bergen, Norway Office: Handelens og Sjøfartens Hus, Olav Kyrresgate 11, 5014. Telephone: 47 55318116. Telex: 42516 WRCON. Telefax: 47 55310015.

Kobe, Japan Office: Wikborg & Rein, 1-1, 5-Chome Minatojima Nakamachi, Chuo-ku, 650. Telephone: (78) 303 1772. Telex: 5622404. Telefax: (78) 303 1781.

London, England Office: 1, Knightrider Court, 2nd Floor, EC4V 5JP. Telephone: 44 171 236 4598. Telefax: 44 171 236 4599. Telex: 915952.

Company and Commercial Law, Maritime and Shipping, Financing, Securities and Stock Exchange Regulations, Tax, Oil and Gas, Liquidation and Receivership, Aviation, International (hereunder EU/EEA). Environmental, Construction, Information Technology/Telecommunication Law, Law of Torts, Licenses and Cooperation Agreements, General Civil Practice and Litigation.

MEMBERS OF FIRM

SIGURD WAELGAARD, born New York, U.S.A., January 30, 1929; admitted, 1957, Norway; 1966, Supreme Court of Norway. *Education:* University of Oslo (Candidate in Jurisprudence). *Member:* Norwegian Bar Association; Norwegian Maritime Law Association. *LANGUAGES:* English, Norwegian, Danish and Swedish.

ERLING C. HJORT, born Hoeyanger, Norway, October 23, 1936; admitted, 1962, Norway; 1970, Supreme Court of Norway. *Education:* University of Oslo (Candidate in Jurisprudence). *Member:* Norwegian Bar Association (Board Member, 1977-1978); Norwegian Maritime Law Association; Norwegian Insurance Law Association (Board Member, 1970-1977). *LANGUAGES:* English, German, Norwegian, Danish and Swedish.

LARS A. CHRISTENSEN, born Oslo, Norway, November 9, 1939; admitted, 1967, Norway; 1977, Supreme Court of Norway. *Education:* University of Oslo (Candidate in Jurisprudence). *Member:* Norwegian Bar Association; Norwegian Maritime Law Association. *LANGUAGES:* English, Norwegian, Danish and Swedish.

HELGE MYHRE, born Oslo, Norway, July 8, 1940; admitted, 1964, Norway; 1975, Supreme Court of Norway. *Education:* University of Oslo (Candidate in Jurisprudence). *Member:* Norwegian Bar Association; Norwegian Maritime Law Association; Norwegian Insurance Law Association (Board Member, 1977-1983). *LANGUAGES:* English, Norwegian, Danish and Swedish.

HAAKON STANG LUND, born Tønsberg, Norway, July 3, 1943; admitted, 1970, Norway; 1981, Supreme Court of Norway. *Education:* University of Oslo (Candidate in Jurisprudence). *Member:* Norwegian Bar Association; Norwegian Maritime Law Association (Board Member, 1985; Chairman of the Board, 1986-1993). *LANGUAGES:* English, Norwegian, Danish and Swedish.

EINAR L. KOEFOED, born Tønsberg, Norway, March 22, 1942; admitted, 1973, Norway. *Education:* University of Oslo (Candidate in Jurisprudence). *Member:* Norwegian Bar Association; Norwegian Maritime Law Association. *LANGUAGES:* English, Norwegian, Danish and Swedish.

(This Listing Continued)

OLAV ERIKSSØN KLINGENBERG, born Oslo, Norway, July 24, 1944; admitted, 1972, Norway. *Education:* University of Oslo (Candidate in Jurisprudence, 1969). Lecturer of Law: Oslo Commercial College, 1972-1976; Norwegian Revenue Service College, 1972-1975. Board Member, 1976 and President, 1987—, Norwegian Tax Association. *Member:* Norwegian Bar Association; Norwegian Law Association; International Fiscal Association. *LANGUAGES:* English, Norwegian, Danish and Swedish.

HAAKON BLAAUW, born Bergen, Norway, September 2, 1949; admitted, 1977, Norway; Supreme Court of Norway. *Education:* University of Bergen (Candidate in Jurisprudence); Columbia Law School, New York (LL.M.). *Member:* Norwegian Bar Association. (Resident, Bergen, Norway Office). *LANGUAGES:* English, Norwegian, Danish and Swedish.

TOM BERNHARD KNUDSEN, born Oslo, Norway, November 21, 1951; admitted, 1981, Norway. *Education:* University of Oslo (Candidate in Jurisprudence). *Member:* Norwegian Bar Association; International Fiscal Association. *LANGUAGES:* English, Norwegian, Danish and Swedish.

ØYSTEIN MELAND, born Bergen, Norway, September 24, 1951; admitted, 1980, Norway. *Education:* University of Bergen (Candidate in Jurisprudence). *Member:* Norwegian Bar Association; Norwegian Maritime Law Association; Bergen Shipowners Association (Secretary). (Resident, Bergen, Norway Office). *LANGUAGES:* English, Norwegian, Danish and Swedish.

JOHN A. REIN, born Oslo, Norway, October 3, 1951; admitted, 1981, Norway. *Education:* University of Oslo (Candidate in Jurisprudence). Research Scholarship Scandinavian Institute of Maritime Law, 1978-1979. *Member:* Norwegian Bar Association; Norwegian Petroleum Association. *LANGUAGES:* English, Norwegian, Danish and Swedish.

ARNE DIDRIK KJØRNAES, born Oslo, Norway, May 23, 1956; admitted, 1982, Norway. *Education:* University of Oslo (Candidate in Jurisprudence, 1980). Associate Professor, 1980-1981, Institute of Private Law, University of Oslo. *Member:* Norwegian Bar Association; Norwegian Maritime Law Association. *LANGUAGES:* English, Norwegian, Danish and Swedish.

DAG STEINFELD, born March 14, 1955; admitted, 1983, Norway; 1988, Supreme Court of Norway. *Education:* University of Bergen (Candidate in Jurisprudence). *Member:* Norwegian Bar Association. (Resident, Bergen, Norway Office). *LANGUAGES:* English, Norwegian, Danish and Swedish.

STEIN PETTERSEN, born Bergen, Norway, April 22, 1953; admitted, 1984, Norway; 1993, Supreme Court of Norway. *Education:* University of Bergen (Candidate in Jurisprudence, 1979). *Member:* Norwegian Bar Association. (Resident, Bergen, Norway Office). *LANGUAGES:* English, Norwegian, Danish and Swedish.

KNUD LORENTZEN, born Bergen, Norway, May 4, 1954; admitted, 1984, Norway. *Education:* University of Bergen (Candidate in Jurisprudence). *Member:* Norwegian Bar Association. (Resident, Bergen, Norway Office). *LANGUAGES:* English, Norwegian, Danish and Swedish.

JON HEIMSET, born Nordfjord, Norway, December 22, 1953; admitted, 1986, Norway. *Education:* University of Bergen (Candidate in Jurisprudence). *Member:* Norwegian Bar Association. (Resident, Bergen, Norway Office). *LANGUAGES:* English, Norwegian, Danish and Swedish.

CHRISTIAN FRIIS, born Bergen, Norway, January 17, 1955; admitted, 1985, Norway. *Education:* University of Bergen (Candidate in Jurisprudence, 1981). *Member:* Norwegian Bar Association. (Resident, Bergen, Norway Office). *LANGUAGES:* English, Norwegian, Danish and Swedish.

MARIUS M. GISVOLD, born Trondheim, Norway, March 24, 1957; admitted, 1986, Norway. *Education:* University of Oslo (Candidate in Jurisprudence). Lecturer, 1982-1983, Nordic Institute of Maritime Law, University of Oslo. *Member:* Norwegian Bar Association; Norwegian Maritime Law Association; Norwegian Petroleum Association. *LANGUAGES:* English, German, Norwegian, Danish and Swedish.

TROND EILERTSEN, born Harstad, Norway, January 8, 1956; admitted, 1985, Norway. *Education:* University of Bergen (Candidate in Jurisprudence). *Member:* Norwegian Bar Association; Norwegian Maritime Law Association. *LANGUAGES:* English, Norwegian, Danish and Swedish.

FINN BJØRNSTAD, born Norway, May 5, 1958; admitted, 1985, Norway. *Education:* University of Bergen (Candidate in Jurisprudence, 1985). *LANGUAGES:* English, Norwegian, Danish and Swedish.

LARS OLAV ASKHEIM, born Eidsvoll, Norway, September 10, 1957; admitted, 1987, Norway. *Education:* University of Oslo (Candidate in Jurisprudence, 1984); University of Calgary (LL.B.). Research Fellow, Scandi-

(This Listing Continued)

navian Institute of Maritime Law, 1984-1987. *Member:* Norwegian Bar Association. (Resident, London, England Office). *LANGUAGES:* English, Norwegian, Danish and Swedish.

JAN L. BACKER, born Kristiansund, Norway, August 15, 1958; admitted, 1988, Norway. *Education:* University of Oslo (Candidate in Jurisprudence). *Member:* Norwegian Bar Association. *LANGUAGES:* English, Norwegian, Danish and Swedish.

LEIF PETTER MADSEN, born Oslo, Norway, June 11, 1957; admitted, 1986, Norway. *Education:* University of Oslo (Candidate in Jurisprudence, 1984). *Member:* Norwegian Bar Association. *LANGUAGES:* English, Norwegian, Danish and Swedish.

BERNHARD HAUKALI, born Stavanger, Norway, January 7, 1958; admitted, 1986, Norway. *Education:* University of Bergen, Faculty of Political Science, Institute of Comparative Politics (1980); University of Bergen (Candidate in Jurisprudence, 1986). *Member:* Norwegian Bar Association. *LANGUAGES:* English, Norwegian, Danish and Swedish.

GEIR OVE RØBERG, born Bergen, Norway, June 4, 1958; admitted, 1986, Norway. *Education:* University of Bergen (Candidate in Jurisprudence); University of Oslo, Institute of Maritime Law (1986). *Member:* Norwegian Bar Association; Norwegian Maritime Law Association. *LANGUAGES:* English, Norwegian, Danish and Swedish.

PETER FRØLICH, born Bergen, Norway, July 20, 1956; admitted, 1985, Norway. *Education:* University of Bergen (Candidate in Jurisprudence, 1984); Mc George School of Law (Diploma in International Legal Practice, 1986). Lecturer of Law and Legal Training, University of Bergen and University of Tromsø. *Member:* Norwegian Bar Association. (Resident, Bergen, Norway Office). *LANGUAGES:* English, Norwegian, Danish and Swedish.

TORLEIF P. DAHL, born Baerum, Norway, July 28, 1959; admitted, 1988, Norway. *Education:* Oslo University (Candidate in Jurisprudence, 1986); Columbia University (LL .M., 1991). *Member:* Norwegian Bar Association. *LANGUAGES:* English, Norwegian, Danish and Swedish.

PER MAGNE STRANDBORG, born Bergen, Norway, July 13, 1959; admitted, 1987, Norway. *Education:* University of Bergen (Candidate in Jurisprudence, 1986). *Member:* Norwegian Bar Association. *LANGUAGES:* English, Norwegian, Danish and Swedish.

SUSANNE MUNCH THORE, born Bergen, Norway, June 24, 1960; admitted, 1990, Norway. *Education:* University of Oslo (Candidate in Jurisprudence, 1987); John Hopkins University, Bologna Center (Diploma in International Affairs, 1985); Georgetown University Law School (LL.M., Masters of Common Law, 1989). *Member:* Norwegian Bar Association; Oslo Bar Association (Board Member). *LANGUAGES:* English, Norwegian, Danish and Swedish.

EINAR J. GREVE, born Bergen, Norway, August 2, 1960; admitted, 1989, Norway. *Education:* University of Oslo (Candidate in Jurisprudence, 1987). *Member:* Norwegian Bar Association; Norwegian Maritime Law Association. *LANGUAGES:* English, German, Norwegian, Danish and Swedish.

BULL, TVEDT, ASSERSON, THINN & HÅLAND

Advokatfirma ANS

Established in 1969

KIRKEGATEN 3

P.O. BOX 8

4001 STAVANGER, NORWAY

Telephone: (47) 51 89 53 20

Telefax: (47) 51 89 53 22

Business Law, Construction Law, Compulsory Purchase Law and Public Law. In Business Law, main interest is Company Law, Tax Law, Banking and Financial Law, including Leasing and Factoring.

FIRM PROFILE: The law firm was established in 1969 and is located in Stavanger, the oil capital of Norway. Today the firm has five partners and one associate. Its main fields are Business Law, Construction Law, Compulsory Purchase Law and Public Law. In Business Law, main interest is Company Law, Tax Law, Banking and Financial Law, including Leasing and Factoring. Bull, Tvedt, Asserson, Thinn & Håland's clients are mostly bigger and smaller companies and organizations in the commercial sector,

(This Listing Continued)

but the firm also represents private clients and municipalities. In addition to general consultancy, the firm engages in extensive litigation.

The firm is a member of LEX NORVEGICA, a Norwegian law firm cooperation consisting of four law firms situated in the four largest Norwegian cities; Oslo, Bergen, Trondheim and Stavanger, with almost 50 lawyers. Through LEX NORVEGICA the firm has established a BRUSSELS office in cooperation with the Norwegian law firm Hjort DA.

MEMBERS OF FIRM

JOHAN CHR. BULL, born 1937. *Education:* University of Oslo, Faculty of Law (1964). Deputy Judge, Ryfylke County Court, 1965-1966; Associate to Supreme Court Barrister Ole Helliesen, 1966-1969; Established law firm in Stavanger, 1969; Supreme Court Barrister, 1970. *Member:* Norwegian Bar Association. *LANGUAGES:* The Scandinavian Languages and English. *PRACTICE AREAS:* Business Law; Tax Law; Building and Construction Law; Law of Torts.

LEIV H. TVEDT, born 1938. *Education:* University of Oslo, Faculty of Law (1965). Deputy Judge, Eiker, Modum and Sigdal County Court, 1965-1966; Associate in law firm, Arnesen, Haavind, Haavind, Dahl & Bjelke, Oslo, 1967-1969; Established law firm in Stavanger, 1969; Supreme Court Barrister, 1973. Former Chairman, Norwegian Law Society's Permanent Committee on Trade, Crafts and Industrial Law; Former Chairman, regional Law Society. *Member:* Norwegian Bar Association. *LANGUAGES:* The Scandinavian Languages and English. *PRACTICE AREAS:* Business Law; Banking and Financial Law; Leasing; Factoring; Company Law; Tax Law.

CHRISTIAN THRANE ASSERSON, born 1954. *Education:* University of Oslo, Faculty of Law (1981). Ministry of Justice, 1981-1982; Deputy Judge, Jaeren County Court, 1982-1983; Associate, Bull, Tvedt, Asserson, Thinn & Håland, 1983-1985; Partner, 1986; Supreme Court Barrister, 1992. *Member:* Norwegian Bar Association. *LANGUAGES:* The Scandinavian Languages and English. *PRACTICE AREAS:* Business Law; Compulsory Purchase Law; Law of Torts; General Practice.

BERNT T. THINN, born 1954. *Education:* University of Bergen, Faculty of Law (1980). Police Superintendent, Stavanger, 1981-1983; Deputy Judge, Public Registrar and Notary Public, Stavanger, 1983-1984; Associate, Bull, Tvedt, Asserson, Thinn & Håland, 1985-1987; Partner, 1987. *Member:* Norwegian Bar Association. *LANGUAGES:* The Scandinavian Languages and English. *PRACTICE AREAS:* Bankruptcy Law; Business Law; Administrative Law; General Practice.

LEIF INGE HÅLAND, born 1958. *Education:* University of Bergen, Faculty of Law (1983). Oslo Tax Inspector's Office, 1983-1984; Police Superintendent, Nord Jarlsberg, 1984-1986; Deputy Judge, Hardanger County Court, 1986-1987; Associate, Bull, Tvedt, Asserson, Thinn & Håland, 1987-1990; Partner, 1991. *Member:* Norwegian Bar Association. *LANGUAGES:* The Scandinavian Languages and English. *PRACTICE AREAS:* Business Law; Banking and Financial Law; Bankruptcy Law; General Practice.

ASSOCIATES

LEIV BJØRNSEN, born 1962. *Education:* University of Bergen, Faculty of Law (1989). Department of Environment, 1989-1990; Police Superintendent, Stavanger, 1990-1991; Deputy Judge at Jaeren County Court, 1991-1992; Associate with firm, 1992. *Member:* Norwegian Bar Association. *LANGUAGES:* The Scandinavian Languages and English. *PRACTICE AREAS:* Criminal Law; Bankruptcy Law; General Practice.

ADVOKATFIRMA KLUGE ANS

GAMLE FORUSVEI 17, BOX 277

4033 FORUS

4033 STAVANGER, NORWAY

Telephone: 47/51 57 14 77

Fax: 47/51 57 65 65

Oslo, Norway Office: Fr. Nansenspl. 7, 0160 Oslo. Telephone: 22 33 07 60. Telefax: 22 33 23 80.

Firm engaged in Norwegian, European and International Law Practice. Entitled to plead before the Norwegian Supreme Court.
Company Law, Tax Law, Construction Law, Petroleum Law, Contract Law, Labour Law, Public and Administrative Law, Environmental Law, Litigation and International Arbitration.

(This Listing Continued)

ADVOKATFIRMA KLUGE ANS, Stavanger—Continued

FIRM PROFILE: Established in 1923, Kluge Ans has become one of Norway's most well recognized and respected law firms. The client base consists mainly of both Norwegian, European and North American companies in trade, industry, and the petroleum and construction industries, financial institutions, as well as branches and agencies of local and central government. The firm has 11 partners and 7 assistants practicing in offices in Oslo and Stavanger, centre of the petroleum industry in Norway. English brochure available upon request.

MEMBERS OF FIRM

CLEMENT ENDRESEN, born 1949. Law degree 1974. Deputy judge 1977-1979. Attorney at the office of the Solicitor General 1979. Supreme Court barrister 1989. *PRACTICE AREAS:* Company Law; Mergers and Acquisitions; Tax Law; Petroleum and Contract Law; International Arbitration.

ODD-SVERRE RAGE, born 1950. Law degree 1976. Admitted to the Bar 1978. *PRACTICE AREAS:* Company Law; Labour Law; Contract Law; Property Law; Expropriation Law.

HARALD S. KOBBE, born 1949. Law degree 1975. Deputy judge 1977-1979. Attorney at the office of the Solicitor General 1979-1987. LL.M. Harvard Law School 1982. Supreme Court Barrister 1983. *PRACTICE AREAS:* Construction Law; Public and Administrative Law; Litigation.

STIG TUFTE-JOHNSEN, born 1951. Law Degree 1978. Counsellor and Chief Counsellor, Tax Directorate, 1979-1981. Attorney at the office of the Solicitor General 1981-1987. Supreme Court Barrister 1987. *PRACTICE AREAS:* Company Law; Contract Law; Tax Law; Litigation; Public and Administrative Law.

ODD R. TVEDT, born 1949. Law degree 1975. Attorney at the office of the City Attorney of Oslo 1981-1986. Chief Legal Counsel AS Veidekke 1986-1987. Supreme Court barrister 1982. *PRACTICE AREAS:* Company and Contract Law; Mergers and Acquisitions; Construction Law.

PER SANDVIK, born 1940. Law degree 1965. Deputy judge 1966-1967. Supreme Court barrister 1973. City Attorney of Oslo 1982-1991. Co-author: "Expropriation," as well as author of numerous articles on tax law, civil procedure, public and administrative law, labour law. *PRACTICE AREAS:* Public and Administrative Law; Tax Law; Expropriation Law; Litigation.

EIRIK JENSEN, born 1950. Admitted to the Bar 1987; Supreme Court Barrister, 1994. Masters degree in philosophy 1976. Law degree 1983. Counsellor at the Treasury 1984-1985. Counsellor at the Oslo Tax Office 1985-1986. Deputy judge 1986-1987. *PRACTICE AREAS:* Company and Contract Law; Tax Law; Construction Law; Litigation; International Arbitration.

SNORRE HAUKALI, born 1959. Admitted to the Bar 1988. Law degree 1986. Deputy judge 1986. *PRACTICE AREAS:* Company and Contract Law; Petroleum Law.

CHRISTIAN WILLE KAISEN, born 1958. Admitted to the Bar 1988. Law degree 1984. Counsellor at the Storting's ombudsmann for public administration 1985-1988. Deputy judge 1988-1989. *PRACTICE AREAS:* Company and Contract Law; Public and Administrative Law.

INGRID SKAANES SØRENSEN, born 1950. Admitted to the Bar 1988. Law degree 1977. Counsellor to the city of Oslo 1980-1985. Deputy judge 1985-1986. Judge Oslo City Court 1987-1988. *PRACTICE AREAS:* Contract Law; Construction Law; Public and Administrative Law.

TROND SELVIKVÅG, born 1959. Admitted to the Bar 1988. Law degree 1986. Deputy judge 1989-1990. *PRACTICE AREAS:* Labour Law; Contract Law.

ADVOKATFIRMAET SCHJØDT, AS

THS. ANGELL GATE 12
P.O. BOX 132
N-7001 TRONDHEIM, NORWAY
Telephone: 47 73 52 75 45
Fax: 47 73 51 55 28

Oslo, Norway Office: Dronning Mauds Gate 10, P.O. Box 2444 Solli, N-0201. Telephone: 47 22 83 22 44. Fax: 47 22 83 17 12. Telex: 19789 law n. Data Network Address: 2422 130116.

(This Listing Continued)

Bergen, Norway Office: Christian Michelsens Gate 1, P.O. Box 617, N-5001. Telephone: 47 55 90 13 20. Fax: 47 55 90 13 19.

General/Corporate, Commercial, Securities, International Finance, Intellectual Property, Patent, Licensing, Energy/Oil and Gas, Shipping/Admiralty, Environment/Energy, Tax, Government Relations, Products Liability, Personnel/Labour, International General Litigation, Libel Law, Bankruptcy/Insolvency, Construction, Real Estate.

MEMBERS OF FIRM

Gudmund Kuvås	Endre Kolbjørnsen
Magne Spilde	Roald Engeness
Joar Grimsbu	Arve Rosvold Alver
	Terje Skjønhals

ASSOCIATES

Cecilie Amdahl

Languages: The Scandinavian Languages and English

(For complete biographical data on all personnel, see Professional Biographies at Oslo, Norway)

POLAND

MILLER, CANFIELD, PADDOCK AND STONE, SP. z o.O.

A Professional Limited Liability Company
Founded in 1852 by Sidney Davy Miller
SUITE 322, DOM TECHNIKA BUILDING
UI. RAJSKA 6
80-850 GDAŃSK, POLAND
Telephone: 011-48-58-312-808
Fax: 011-48-58-314-319

REVISERS OF THE MICHIGAN LAW DIGEST FOR THIS DIRECTORY

Detroit, Michigan Office: 150 West Jefferson, Suite 2500, 48226-4415. Telephone: 313-963-6420. Fax: 313-496-7500. Cable Address: "Stem Detroit."

Ann Arbor, Michigan Office: 101 North Main Street, 7th Floor, 48104-1400. Telephone: 313-663-2445. Fax: 313-747-7147.

Bloomfield Hills, Michigan Office: Suite 100, Pinehurst Office Center, 1400 North Woodward, 48303-2014. Telephone: 313-645-5000. Fax: 313-645-1917.

Grand Rapids, Michigan Office: 1200 Campau Square Plaza, 99 Monroe, N.W., 49503-2639. Telephone: 616-454-8656. Fax: 616-776-6322.

Howell, Michigan Office: 121 South Barnard Street, Suite 4, 48843-2305. Telephone: 517-546-7600. Telecopier: 517-546-6974.

Kalamazoo, Michigan Office: 444 West Michigan Avenue, 49007-3752. Telephone: 616-381-7030. Fax: 616-382-0244.

Lansing, Michigan Office: One Michigan Avenue, Suite 900, 48933-1609. Telephone: 517-487-2070. Fax: 517-374-6304.

Monroe, Michigan Office: The Executive Centre, 214 East Elm Avenue, 48161-2682. Telephone: 313-243-2000. Fax: 313-243-0901.

Washington, D.C. Office: 1225 Nineteenth Street, N.W., Suite 400. 20036. Telephone: 202-429-5575. 785-0600. Fax: 202-331-1118; 785-1234.

Pensacola, Florida Office: 25 West Cedar, 32501. Telephone: 904-469-1088. Fax: 904-432-0677.

St. Petersburg, Florida Office: 100 Second Avenue S., Suite 7045, 33701. Telephone: 813-982-6000. Fax: 813-892-6002.

Warsaw, Poland Office: UI. Marszalkowska 82, Suite 561, 00-517. Telephone: 011-482-623-6457 and 6458. Fax: 011-482-623-6459.

Accounting Litigation, Administrative, Admiralty/Maritime, Antidumping, Antitrust, Licensing & High Technology, Appellate Practice, Banking, Bankruptcy & Reorganization, Commercial Transactions, Computer, Condemnation, Condominiums & Cooperatives, Construction Litigation, Corporate, Domestic Relations, Education, Emerging Business, Environmental, Estate Planning & Administration, Foundations & Nonprofit Organizations, Franchising, Health Care & Hospital, Immigration, Insurance, Intellectual Property, International Law, International Trade & Customs, Labor & Employment, Libel & Slander Litigation, Litigation & Alternative Dispute Resolution, Litigation Management, Mergers & Acquisitions, Mu-

(This Listing Continued)

nicipal & Governmental Law, Nuclear Power Plant Litigation, Oil & Gas, Pension, Profit-sharing & Employee Benefits, Product Liability Consulting & Defense, Professional Malpractice Consulting & Defense, Public Law, Real Estate Development & Investment, Securities (Corporate & Municipal), Securities Litigation, State, Municipal & Public Finance, Taxation, Tax-exempt Financing, Telecommunications, Toxic Torts Litigation, Transportation, Utilities, White Collar Criminal Defense, Zoning.

FIRM PROFILE: Miller, Canfield, Paddock and Stone traces its history to 1852 when Sidney Davy Miller (1830-1904) opened a practice on Detroit's Jefferson Avenue. Today Miller Canfield is one of the largest law firms in Michigan with more than 250 attorneys and over 40 legal assistants. We have a growing national practice and a long-established statewide practice. Our Michigan offices are located in Ann Arbor, Bloomfield Hills, Detroit, Grand Rapids, Howell, Kalamazoo, Lansing and Monroe. We also have offices in Pensacola and St. Petersburg, Florida and in Washington, D.C. Our offices in Gdansk and Warsaw, Poland enable us to serve clients throughout Central and Eastern Europe.

Our practice areas are organized into the following practice groups: Bankruptcy/Workout, Business Services, Employee Benefits, Environmental, Estate Planning, Federal Taxation, Health Care, Intellectual Property, International, Labor and Employment, Product Liability/Tort Litigation, Commercial Litigation, Dispute Resolution, State/Local Taxation, Public Law, Finance and Development.

We represent individuals in their personal law and business concerns, trusts and estates, publicly traded companies, and many start-up, small, and medium sized businesses. Clients also include public bodies such as the state of Michigan and many of its agencies, authorities and universities, cities, counties, townships, school and community college districts, and special authorities throughout the state. We represent many nonprofit, tax-exempt institutions, such as hospitals, charitable corporations, and professional associations.

PARTNER

RICHARD A. WALAWENDER, born Hamtramck, Michigan, December 14, 1960; admitted, 1986, Michigan (Not admitted in Poland). *Education:* University of Michigan (B.A., with high distinction, 1982; J.D., 1986). John B. Angell Scholar. Contributing Editor, University of Michigan Journal of Law Reform, 1985-1986. Member, Supervisory Board Solidarity Chase D.T. Bank S.A. (Poland). Member and General Counsel, Board of Trustees, Cornerstone Schools Association. Member, Advisory Board, University of Michigan Center for Russian and E. European Studies. *Member:* Detroit, Macomb County and American (Member: International Law Section; Business Law Section; Public Law Section) Bar Associations; State Bar of Michigan (Member: International Law Section; Public Law Section); National Association of Bond Lawyers. *LANGUAGES:* Polish. *TRANSACTIONS:* Polish Solidarity Chase D.T. Bank, S.A. Joint Venture, 1990. *PRACTICE AREAS:* Finance (Public and Project Financings); International Corporate Law; Municipal Law; Governmental Law.

SENIOR ATTORNEY

WOJCIECH BABICKI, born Gdańsk, Poland, November 14, 1958; admitted, as barrister, 1988, Poland. *Education:* University of Gdańsk (Masters of Law, 1981). Member: Board of Gdańsk Chamber of Legal Advisors; Lecturer for Committee for Legal Profession Training Committee. *Member:* Polish Bar Association. *LANGUAGES:* Polish, English and Russian. *PRACTICE AREAS:* Business and Commercial Law; International Law.

LEGAL ADVISORS

JACEK KRAJEWSKI, born Warsaw, Poland, January 4, 1965; admitted to Chamber of Legal Advisors, 1992. *Education:* University of Warszawa (Masters of Law, 1990). *LANGUAGES:* Polish, English and Norwegian. *PRACTICE AREAS:* Business and Commercial Law; Real Estate; International Law.

ANDRZEJ CHECHCOWSKI, born Ostróleka, Poland, June 24, 1968; admitted to Chamber of Legal Advisors, 1992. *Education:* University of Warsaw (Masters of Law, 1992). *LANGUAGES:* Polish, English and Russian. *PRACTICE AREAS:* Business and Commercial Law; International Law.

REVISERS OF THE MICHIGAN LAW DIGEST FOR THIS DIRECTORY

(For Complete Biographical Data on all Personnel, see Professional Biographies at Detroit, Michigan)

SCHEELE, SCHWARTZ, ZIELCKE & PARTNER
UL. STOWIANSKI 28A
60-651 POZNAŃ, POLAND
Telephone: 0048-61-485 107
Fax: 0048-61-485 107

Munich, Germany Office: Prinzregentenplatz 15, 81675. Telephone: 089/470 10 02. Fax: 089/470 10 06.

FIRM PROFILE: Scheele, Schwartz, Zielcke & Partner is an international law firm advising business clients and public institutions on all domestic and overseas corporate and commercial matters. The firm specializes in Eastern European and C.I.S. matters. Currently the firm is representing a broad range of clients in Europe, North America, South America, Asia and Africa.

(For biographical data and areas of practice see listing at Munich, Germany)

ALLEN & OVERY
UL. KOPERNIKA 17
IV FLOOR
00-359 WARSAW, POLAND
Telephone: (48 22) 262 226
Facsimile: (48 22) 262 360

London, England Office: One New Change, EC4M 9QQ. Telephone: 0171 330 3000. Facsimile: 0171 330 9999.

Beijing, China Office: Suite 3204, Jing Guang Centre, Hu Jia Lou, Chaoyang District, 100020. Telephone: (86 1) 501 4681. Facsimile: (86 1) 501 4682.

Brussels, Belgium Office: Rue de la Loi 99, Box 8, 1040. Telephone: (32 2) 230 27 91. Facsimile (32 2) 230 66 13.

Budapest, Hungary Office: Mádach Trade Center, Mádach Imre utca 13-14, H-1075. Telephone: (361) 268 1511. Facsimile: (361) 268 1515.

Dubai, United Arab Emirates Office: 501 Al Futtaim Tower,P.O. Box 3251, Deira. Telephone: (971 4) 282296. Facsimile: (971 4) 212860.

Frankfurt, Germany Office: Taunusanlage 11, 11th Floor, 60329. Telephone: (49 69) 242 6120. Facsimile: (49 69) 242 61220.

Hong Kong Office: 9th Floor, Three Exchange Square, 8 Connaught Place. Telephone: (852) 2840 1282. Telex: 68757. Facsimile: (852) 2840 0515.

Madrid, Spain Office: Antonio Maura 7, 6°, 28014. Telephone: (34 1) 521 2654. Facsimile: (34 1) 523 0458.

Moscow, Russia Office: 9 ul Tverskaya, Entrance No 5, 8th Floor, 103009. Telephone: (7 501) 940 4500. Facsimile: (7 501) 940 4501.

New York Office: Swiss Bank Tower, 10 East 50th Street, 10022. Telephone (1-212) 754 3340. Facsimile: (1-212) 754 7903.

Paris, France Office: 1 Avenue Franklin D. Roosevelt, 75008. Telephone (33-1) 49 53 06 37. Telex: 651079. Facsimile: (33-1) 49 53 91 52.

Prague, Czech Republic Office: Jindřišská 34, 110 00 Prague 1. Telephone: (42 2) 2410 3317. Facsimile: (42 2) 2410 3235.

Singapore Office: 20 Raffles Place #08-03, Ocean Towers, 0104. Telephone: (65) 533 0988. Facsimile: (65) 533 1322.

Tokyo, Japan Office: NSE Building, 5th Floor, 1-7-1 Kanda Jinbo-cho, Chiyoda-ku Tokyo 101. Telephone (81 3) 3259 9898. Facsimile (81 3) 3259 9888.

Firm engaged in advising on all legal aspects of doing business in Poland with an international practice and advice on local law provided by qualified local lawyers.

RESIDENT PARTNERS

Stephen Denyer

RESIDENT ASSOCIATES

Chris Moore

RESIDENT SENIOR POLISH LAWYERS

Jacek Michalski
Andrzej Siemiatkowski
Wojoiech Wadolowski

(For Complete Biographical Data on all Personnel, see Professional Biographies at London, England)

ALTHEIMER & GRAY

UL. NOWOGRODZKA 50
WARSAW 00-950, POLAND
Telephone: 48-22-298-357; 48-39-12-1338
Fax: 48-2-628-3640
Telex: 867 817079

REVISERS OF THE POLAND LAW DIGEST FOR THIS DIRECTORY.

Chicago, Illinois Office: 10 South Wacker Drive, 60606. Telephone: 312-715-4000. Fax: 312-715-4800. Telex: RCA 297102 A G UR.

Prague, Czech Republic Office: Platnerska 4, 110 00 Prague 1. Telephone: 42-2-2481-2782. Fax: 42-2-2481-0125 or 232-9595.

Kiev, Ukraine Office: Kontraktova Ploscha 4, Building 3, Room 304, 254145. Telephone: 7-044-230-2534. Fax: 7-044-230-2535.

Bratislava, Slovakia Office: Nam. SNP 15, 810 00. Telephone: 42-7-362-736. Fax: 42-7-367-960.

Istanbul, Turkey Office: Tesvikiye Cad. 107, Tesvikiye Palas 7, Tesvikiye 80200 Istanbul, Turkey. Telephone: 90-212-227-6750. Fax: 90-212-227-6759.

Privatizations and Acquisitions, Joint Ventures and Foreign Investment, Government Affairs, Real Estate Development, Architecture, Engineering and Construction, Banking and Finance, Bankruptcy, Licensing and Distribution, Insurance, Telecommunications, Securities, Taxation and Customs.

DIRECTOR OF THE WARSAW OFFICE &

PARTNER

GABRIEL WUJEK, born Lódź, Poland, March 23, 1952. *Education:* Warsaw University (Master of Law, with distinction, 1973; Doctor of Law, 1978); Europa Institut of the University of Amsterdam (Diploma, with distinction , in Legal Aspects of European Integration, 1976). Author: "Legal Regulation of Multinational Enterprises," (Reglamentacja Prawna Przedsiebiorstw Wielonarodowych - Title in Polish), PWN Warszawa, 1982; "Relations between Foreign Trade and Industrial Enterprises in Poland," Foreign Trade Academy, Budapest, 1978; "Polish Perception of Countertrade," Countertrade and Trading Companies: Trade Trends in the 80's, Law and Business Inc., Harcourt Brace Jovanovich, 1984; "The Bankruptcy Laws of Poland," European Bankruptcy Laws, 2nd Edition, American Bar Association, 1986; "Legal Environment for Doing Business in Poland," How to Joint-Venture in Poland, Polish Foundation, Warsaw, 1990 (Also Edited). Member of Faculty, Foreign Trade, Central School of Planning and Statistics, 1973—. Legal Advisor, Polish Embassy, New York, N.Y., 1980-1985. Deputy Director, 1986-1987 and Director, Legal Department, Ministry of Foreign Economic Relations of the Republic of Poland, 1987-1990. Senior Negotiator, U.S. - Poland Trade Treaty, 1990. *Member:* International Bar Association. *LANGUAGES:* Polish, English, French and Russian.

PARTNER

WLODZIMIERZ RADZIKOWSKI, Sopot, Poland, January 15, 1952; admitted to Advocates Association, 1990, Poland. *Education:* Warsaw University (Master of Law, 1975; post-graduate studies on legal problems of foreign trade, 1981-1982). Post-graduate judge's training, Warsaw Regional Court, 1976-1978. Member of faculty, Institute of Legal Problems of Management, Warsaw University, 1975-1980. Legal Adviser, Ministry of Foreign Trade, Legal Department, 1980-1985. Legal Adviser, Polish Embassy, Moscow, 1985-1989. Deputy Director of Legal Department, Ministry of Foreign Economic Relations of the Republic of Poland, Warsaw, 1989-1990. Member of the Legal Advisors Association since 1984. *LANGUAGES:* Polish, English and Russian.

EUROPEAN COUNSEL

ZBIGNIEW SKORCZYNSKI, born Warsaw, Poland, June 16, 1958; admitted to Advocates Association, 1990, Poland. *Education:* Law Faculty, University of Warsaw (Master of Law Degree, 1982); Central School for Planning and Statistics, Warsaw (Post-Master Study for Foreign Trade Executives, 1987-1988). Legal Advisor, 1986-1988 and Head, 1988-1989 of the Domestic Division of the Legal Department, Ministry of Foreign Economic Relations of the Republic of Poland. Member of the Legal Advisors Association since 1986. *LANGUAGES:* Polish, English and German.

KRZYSZTOF ULEWSKI, born Poland, August 27, 1947. *Education:* Warsaw University (Master of Law, 1974). Director General, Ministry of Industry and Trade, 1991. Director, Legal Department, Ministry of Internal Markets of the Republic of Poland, 1988-1991. Judge, Court of Economic Disputes.

(This Listing Continued)

MAREK WIERZBOWSKI, born Pruszkow, Poland, February 23, 1946. Advocate. *Education:* Warsaw University School of Law (Master of Law, 1968; Doctor of Legal Science, 1972; Doktor Habilitowany, 1977). Visiting Scholar, under auspices of the John Marshall Fellowship program, University of California at Berkeley, School of Law, 1991. Visiting or Adjunct Professor at McGeorge School of Law, University of San Francisco School of Law, Saint Louis University School of Law, Indiana University School of Law (Bloomington), and Capital University School of Law. Extraordinary Professor (granted by the President of Poland), 1988. Professor, Warsaw University School of Law, 1968—. Head of the Department of Public Business Law and Department of Administrative Law and Process. Associate Dean, 1981-1985. Vice-Chancellor, 1985-1990. Member, Advisory Board, Securities and Exchange Commission of the Republic of Poland. Counsel to the Minister of Privatization of the Republic of Poland. Co-Author of Polskie Prawo Administracyjne (The Polish Administrative Law), second edition Panstwowe Wydawnictwo Naukowe, 1992. *LANGUAGES:* Polish, English and Russian.

ASSOCIATES

ANIA M. FRANKOWSKA, born Warsaw, Poland, March 31, 1967; admitted, 1990, Illinois (Not admitted in Poland). *Education:* St. Louis University (B.A., magna cum laude, 1987); University of Illinois (J.D., 1990). Recipient, American Jurisprudence Award. Member, 1988-1989 and Notes and Comments Editor, 1989-1990, University of Illinois Law Review. Author: "Fetal Tissue Transplants: A Proposal to Amend the Uniform Anatomical Gift Act," University of Illinois Law Review, 1989; "Poland: The Law of 1991 on Companies with Foreign Participation," International Legal Materials, 1991; "The Association Treaty Between Poland and the European Community: An Economic and Political Analysis," University of Miami Yearbook of International Law, 1993; "Prohibition of Insider Trading in the United States and the European Community: Providing Guidance to the Legislatures of Eastern Europe," (co-authored) Boston University International Law Journal, 1994. *Member:* Illinois State Bar Association; Advocates Society. (Also at Chicago Office). *LANGUAGES:* English, Polish, French and Russian. *PRACTICE AREAS:* Corporate (Eastern Europe Transactions) Law; Securities Law; Banking Law.

MALGORZATA KACPRZYK, born Gubin, Poland, April 18, 1962. *Education:* Law Faculty, University of Warsaw, Poland (Master of Law, 1986). Participated in the Academy of American and International Law in Dallas, Texas, organized by the Southwestern Legal Foundation. Legal Advisor, Legal Department, Ministry of Foreign Economic Relations of the Republic of Poland, (involved in the preparation of new foreign investment law, foreign exchange law, stock exchange law and custom law), 1986-1991. *LANGUAGES:* Polish, English, Russian and French.

DARIUSZ MICHALSKI, born Lodz, Poland, October 21, 1959. *Education:* Warsaw University (Master of Law with strong civil and commercial law background). Participated in the Academy of American and International Law in Dallas, Texas, organized by the Southwestern Legal Foundation. Legal Department of the Ministry of Foreign Economic Relations of the Republic of Poland (prepared and implemented new customs regulations and participated in concluding the Polish-Hungarian trade and payment agreement), 1988-1990. *LANGUAGES:* Polish, English, German and Russian.

JAROSLAW MYJAK, born Slupsk, Poland, March 13, 1955. *Education:* Faculty of Law and Administration and Faculty of Philology, Adam Mickiewicz University, Poznan (M.A., English Philology, summa cum laude, 1978; Master of Law, summa cum laude, 1981); majored in civil commercial and international law as well as in American Studies at the above university and studied at the University of Toronto (1976-1977). Programs: Columbia, Leyden, Amsterdam Summer program in American Law, 1985; European Comparative Law organized by Association de Droit Compare, 1986; and Japan Productivity Center - JICA Training Program, 1990. Judicial training, District Court in Poznan; passed the Judge exam, 1983; appointed sworn translator in 1981. Member of the Faculty, Law and Administration, Adam Mickiewicz University, 1982—. Published articles on the antidumping regulation of the EEC, principle of nominalism, transfer of property. *LANGUAGES:* Polish, English, French and Russian.

DARIUSZ OKOLSKI, born Warsaw, Poland, July 2, 1967. Advocate Apprentice. *Education:* Faculty of Law and Administration, Warsaw University, (Master of Law, 1991-Thesis: Privatization in Poland with Foreign Investor Participation); Karls Eberhardt Universitat, Tubingen, Germany (Master of Law, LL.M., 1992); DePaul University School of Law, Chicago, 1993 American Constitutional Law and Human Rights Internship for Polish Lawyers. Faculty, Strasbourg, France, 1991, course on Comparative Law. Member, Salzburg Seminar, Austria, 1993, seminar on American Law

(This Listing Continued)

and Legal Institutions. *Member:* Polish Bar Association. *LANGUAGES:* Polish, English and German.

MARIUSZ STAWIARCZYK, born Poland, August 26, 1959. *Education:* Warsaw University (post-university studies in Foreign Trade, 1988); University of Jean, Germany, 1984, Goethe Institute, Schwaebish Hall, Germany, 1983, Preston School of English, U.K., 1976-1977. Deputy Commercial Attache, Commercial Counsellor's Office, Polish Embassy in Norway, 1989-1991; Legal Advisor, Pro-Invest Consulting Company, Warsaw, 1988-1989; Senior Legal Advisor, Legal Department, Ministry of Foreign Economic Relations of the Republic of Poland, 1982-1989. *Member:* Polish Lawyers Organization. *LANGUAGES:* Polish, English, Russian, German, Norwegian.

PIOTR M. TOMASZEWSKI, born Warsaw, Poland, May 11, 1967. *Education:* University of Warsaw, Law Faculty (J.D., 1992); University of Chicago Law School (LL.M., 1994); International Faculty of Comparative Law, Strasbourg, France (Comparative Law Studies); University of Florida School of Law Introduction to the American Law Program, 1990). Attorney with Coudert Brothers, Paris, France, 1991-1993 and Uni-Expert Ltd., University Law and Business Consultants, Warsaw, Poland, 1990-1991 and 1993. Author: "(Poland's) Mass Privatization Legislation Nears Adoption," CCH, Doing Business in Eastern Europe, No. 5, May 18, 1993. Contributing Author: "Foreign Investment in Ukraine: New Laws, Opportunities and Issues," The International Law, Vol. 27, No. 1, Spring 1993.

JOLANTA ZAWALONKA-CECELSKA, born Opole, Poland, October 10, 1958. *Education:* Law Faculty, Warsaw University (Master of Law degree, 1983), Salzburg Seminar on American Commercial and Antitrust Law, EEC Course on company law. Legal Advisor, Ministry of Foreign Economic Relations, 1984-1991 (preparatory work for the Uruguay Round of GATT and the association treaty with the EEC). *LANGUAGES:* Polish and English.

PARTNERS

JAMES E. CARROLL, born Evanston, Illinois, July 31, 1956; admitted, 1982, Illinois (Not admitted in Poland). *Education:* Loras College (B.A., maxima cum laude, 1978); Cambridge University (LL.M. in International Law, 1980); Northwestern University (J.D., 1982). Delta Epsilon Sigma; Phi Alpha Theta. Member, Northwestern Journal of International Law and Business, 1981-1982. Author: "Of Icebergs, Oil Wells and Treaties: Hydrocarbon Exploitation Offshore Antarctica," 19 Stanford Journal of International Law, 1983. Co-author: "Recent Developments in Polish Insurance Law," De Paul Business Law Journal, Spring/Summer 1991. *Member:* Chicago, Illinois State, American and International Bar Associations. (Also at Chicago, Prague, Bratislava, Kiev and Istanbul Offices). *PRACTICE AREAS:* International Law; Finance Law; Mergers and Acquisitions.

HOWARD FRIEDMAN, born Chicago, Illinois, December 19, 1940; admitted, 1964, Illinois (Not admitted in Poland). *Education:* Indiana University (B.S., 1960); Northwestern University (J.D., magna cum laude, 1964). Phi Eta Sigma; Beta Gamma Sigma; Order of the Coif. Managing Editor, Northwestern University Law Review, 1963-1964. Certified Public Accountant, Illinois, 1962. *Member:* Chicago, Illinois State and American Bar Associations. [Capt., JAGC, U.S. Naval Reserve]. (Also at Chicago Office). *PRACTICE AREAS:* Corporate Law; Acquisitions Law; International Transactions; Syndications Law.

LOUIS B. GOLDMAN, born Chicago, Illinois, April 11, 1948; admitted, 1975, California; 1976, New York; 1991, Illinois (Not admitted in Poland). *Education:* University of California at Berkeley (A.B., magna cum laude, 1970); University of Chicago (J.D., cum laude, 1974). Phi Beta Kappa; Order of the Coif. Member, University of Chicago Law Review, 1972-1973. Co-Author: "Repossessing the Spirit of St. Louis: Expanding The Protection of Sections 1110 and 1168 of The Bankruptcy Code," The Business Lawyer, Vol. 41, No. 1, 1985. Co-Author: "Recent Developments in Polish Insurance Law," De Paul Business Law Journal, Spring/Summer 1991. Law Clerk to Judge Charles B. Renfrew, U.S. District Court, Northern District of California, 1974-1975. Member, Chicago-Prague Sister Cities Committee of the City of Chicago. *Member:* State Bar of California; Association of the Bar of the City of New York; Chicago, New York State (Member, Committee on International Banking, Securities and Financial Transactions, Committee on International Investment and Development), American (Member, Sections on: Corporation, Banking and Business Law; Taxation; International Law and Practice) and International Bar Associations; New York County Lawyers Association (Member, Special Committee on the Peoples Republic of China). (Also at Chicago, Prague and Bratislava Offices). *PRACTICE AREAS:* Securities Law; Mergers and Acquisitions Law; International Law.

(This Listing Continued)

JEFFREY NORMAN SMITH, born Milwaukee, Wisconsin, May 5, 1960; admitted, 1985, Illinois (Not admitted in Poland). *Education:* University of Michigan (B.B.A., with high distinction, 1982); Northwestern University (J.D., cum laude, 1985). Phi Beta Kappa; Beta Gamma Sigma. *Member:* Chicago, Illinois State and American Bar Associations. (Also at Chicago, Prague and Bratislava Offices). *PRACTICE AREAS:* Mergers and Acquisitions; Joint Ventures; Privatizations; Finance Law; International Law.

ALEXANDRA R. COLE, born Milwaukee, Wisconsin, September 12, 1955; admitted, 1979, Illinois. *Education:* Schiller College, Heidelberg, West Germany and DePauw University (B.A., cum laude, 1976); University of Chicago (J.D., 1979). *Member:* Chicago, Illinois State (Appointed Member, Real Estate Section Council, 1985-1989) and American (Member, Committee on Design and Construction; Chair of Subcommittee on Architect's Concerns in Design and Construction Contracts, 1989—) Bar Associations. (Also at Chicago Office). *PRACTICE AREAS:* Real Estate; Construction Contracts (Domestic and International); Commercial Transactions.

OF COUNSEL

DAVID J. LESTER, born Kewanee, Illinois, October 23, 1928; admitted, 1955, Illinois (Not admitted in Poland). *Education:* University of Chicago (A.B., 1947; J.D., 1954). *Member:* Illinois State Bar Association. (Also at Chicago Office). *PRACTICE AREAS:* Corporations Law; Contracts Law; Securities Law.

REVISERS OF THE POLAND LAW DIGEST FOR THIS DIRECTORY.

(For complete biographical data on personnel at Chicago, Illinois, Prague, Czech Republic, Kiev, Ukraine, Bratislava, Slovakia and Istanbul, Turkey see Professional Biographies at those locations)

AMHURST BROWN COLOMBOTTI
Established in 1990

UL. KOSZYKOWA 59 M.6
00-660 WARSAW, POLAND
Telephone: 48 (22) 29 16 84; 48 (2) 625 30 51; 48 (2) 625 31 25
Satellite: 48 (39) 12 06 02
Fax: 48 (2) 6213289
Telex: 816370 AMPOL

London, England Office: 2 Duke Street, St. James's, SW1Y 6BJ.
  Telephone: (0171) 930-2366. Telex: 261857 AMBRON. Fax: (0171) 930-2250.

Milan, Italy Office: Via Settembrini 17, 20124. Telephone: (02) 6698 4270. Fax: (02) 6698 4252.

Madrid, Spain Office: Paseo del General Martinez Campos 41 8-B, 28010. Telephone: (91) 410 72 24. Fax: (91) 410 55 92.

General Commercial Practice specializing in Joint Ventures, Tax, Employment, Property and Finance, Privatizations.

MEMBERS OF FIRM

M.S. Duval (Also at London,   **P. Ciecwierz**
  England Office)   **M. Barlowski**
D.J. Eldridge (Also at London,   **T. Zasacki**
  England Office)

(For complete list of Personnel see Professional Biographies at London, England)

BAKER & McKENZIE
JUR GRUSZCZYŃSKI LAW OFFICE

UL. DLUGA 26/28
00-238 WARSAW, POLAND
Telephone: (02) 635 3521; 635 4111; 635 0521; 635 8611; 635 9611;
39121203 (Komertel/satellite)
Intn'l Dialing: (48-2) 635 3521; 635 4111; 635 0521; 635 8611;
635 9611; (48) 39121203 (Komertel/satellite)
Facsimiles: (48-2) 635 9447; (48) 39121213 (Komertel/satellite)

Associated Offices of Baker & McKenzie in: Almaty, Amsterdam, Bangkok, Barcelona, Beijing, Berlin, Bogotá, Brasília, Brussels, Budapest, Buenos Aires, Cairo, Caracas, Chicago, Dallas, Frankfurt, Geneva, Hanoi, Ho Chi Minh City, Hong Kong, Juárez, Kiev, London, Madrid, Manila, Melbourne, México City, Miami, Milan,

(This Listing Continued)

BAKER & McKENZIE JUR GRUSZCZYŃSKI LAW OFFICE, Warsaw—Continued

Monterrey, Moscow, New York, Palo Alto, Paris, Prague, Rio de Janeiro, Riyadh, Rome, St. Petersburg, San Diego, San Francisco, São Paulo, Singapore, Stockholm, Sydney, Taipei, Tijuana, Tokyo, Toronto, Valencia, Washington, D.C. and Zürich.

Correspondent Law Firm: Hadiputranto, Hadinoto & Partners, Jakarta.

Corporate Law, Tax Law, Privatization, Intellectual Property, Commercial.

RESIDENT PARTNERS

JUR GRUSZCZYŃSKI, born Warsaw, Poland, April 10, 1955; admitted, 1987, Poland. *Education:* University of Warsaw (Master of Law, 1981). Member, Bar of Legal Advisers, Warsaw, 1987. *LANGUAGES:* Polish, English and Russian. *PRACTICE AREAS:* Corporate and Partnership Law; Mergers and Acquisitions; Taxation; Communications and Media Law; Banking and Finance.

TOMASZ Z. H. UJEJSKI, born Ontario, Canada, May 29, 1956; admitted, 1984, Alberta, Canada; 1987, Ontario, Canada (Not admitted in Poland). *Education:* University of Toronto (B.A., 1978); Universite de Grenoble (French Diploma, 1979); University of Calgary (LL.B., 1983); Cambridge University (LL.M., 1986). Lecturer on Law, University of Hong Kong, 1987-1991. *Member:* Law Society of Upper Canada; Law Society of Alberta. *LANGUAGES:* English, Polish and French. *PRACTICE AREAS:* Mergers and Acquisitions; Corporate and Partnership Law; Banking and Finance; Securities and Financial Products; Taxation.

RESIDENT ASSOCIATES

WOJCIECH T. BIALIK, born Warsaw, Poland, November 1, 1953; admitted, 1983, Poland. *Education:* University of Vienna; University of Warsaw (LL.M., 1978); New York University (M.L.J., 1981). Commercial Attache (Legal Matters), Embassy of Republic of Poland Commercial Counselor's Office, New York. *Member:* Bar of Legal Advisers. *LANGUAGES:* Polish, English and German. *PRACTICE AREAS:* Communications and Media; Corporate and Partnership Law; Construction and Property Development.

KRZYSZTOF KORZENIEWSKI, born Warsaw, Poland, July 31, 1965; admitted, 1993, Poland. *Education:* Warsaw University (Master of Law). *Member:* Warsaw Bar of Legal Advisers. *LANGUAGES:* Polish and English. *PRACTICE AREAS:* Corporate and Partnership Law; Banking and Finance; Administrative Law; Securities and Financial Products; Labor and Employment Law.

NICHOLAS H. RICHARDSON, born Leeds, England, July 4, 1961; admitted, 1986, England and Wales (Not admitted in Poland). *Education:* Brasenose College (B.A., 1983; M.A., 1987); College of Law (Solicitors' Final Examination, 1984). *Member:* The Law Society; City of London Solicitors' Company; British Polish Legal Association. *PRACTICE AREAS:* Corporate and Partnership Law; Banking and Finance; Mergers and Acquisitions; Securities and Financial Products; English Law.

JERZY SKRZYPOWSKI, born Grodzisk Mazowiecki, Poland, August 14, 1954; admitted, 1983, Poland. *Education:* Warsaw University Faculty of Law (Master, 1978). *Member:* Warsaw District Chamber of Legal Advisers. *LANGUAGES:* Polish, English and Russian. *PRACTICE AREAS:* Corporate and Partnership Law; Arbitration and Dispute Resolution; Bankruptcy, Insolvency and Reorganization; Computers and Technology Law; Intellectual Property Law.

ANDRZEJ TYNEL, born Warsaw, Poland, November 18, 1937; admitted, 1964, Poland. *Education:* Jagiellonian University, Kraków; Central School of Planning, Warsaw (Post Graduate Studies, 1972; 1973). Lecturer on Law, Warsaw University and Silesian University Post Graduate Studies. *Member:* Polish Bar of Legal Advisers; Polish Bar Association; International Law Association. *LANGUAGES:* English, German and Russian. *PRACTICE AREAS:* Trade (International); Commercial Litigation; Arbitration and Dispute Resolution; Intellectual Property Law; Mergers and Acquisitions.

JOSEPH ZUROMSKI, born Kętrzyn, Poland, October 11, 1964; admitted, 1994, Poland. *Education:* University of Warsaw (LL.M., 1989). *Member:* District Chamber of Legal Advisers in Warsaw. *LANGUAGES:* Polish, English and Russian. *PRACTICE AREAS:* Corporate and Partnership Law; Labor and Employment Law; Employee Benefits; Real Estate Law; Intellectual Property Law.

BENDER ZAHN TIGGES

UL. PIEKNA 66A

00-072 WARSAW, POLAND

Telephone: (00482) 628-02-11

Fax: (00482) 628-47-66

Düsseldorf, Germany Office: Thyssen-Haus, August-Thyssen-Straße 1, 40211. Telephone: 0211/86 87-0. Telex: 8 588 246 bend. Telefax: 0211/86 87-100.

Berlin, Germany Office: Kurfürstendamm 170, 10707 Berlin. Telephone: (0 30) 883 23 98/99. Telefax: (0 30) 8 82 45 52.

Chemnitz, Germany Office: Straße der Nationen 37, 09111 Chemnitz. Telephone: (0371/428946/47). Telefax: (0371/428949).

General and International Practice, Corporate and Securities, Banking, Commercial, Bankruptcy, Insolvency and Reorganization, Taxation, Real Estate, Antitrust, Intellectual Property, Environmental and Administrative, Insurance, Litigation, International Trusts, Family and Inheritance Law. Privatization in the former German Democratic Republic. Restitution Claims in the former German Democratic Republic. Commercial and Business Law in Poland.

MEMBER - WARSAW

DR. MICHAEL TIGGES, born Hagen, Germany, 1954; admitted, 1986, Germany. *Education:* Münster University (Law; Doctorate, 1986). Assistant: Institute for International Private Law; University for Administrative Law, Speyer. With Boodle Hatfield, London, 1985. Author: "History and Development of State Supervision of Insurance Companies," Karlsruhe, 1985. Co-Author: "Deutsche Rechtspraxis," München, 1991. *Member:* International Bar Association; Young Lawyers' International Association; West-East German Law Society; German-Japanese Law Society; Society for Banking Law; German-Polish Law Society. (Also at Düsseldorf, Germany Office). *LANGUAGES:* German and English.

Languages: German, English, French, Italian, Polish and Japanese

BOESEBECK, BARZ & PARTNER

Established in 1991

UL. WSPÓLNA 25

00519 WARSAW, POLAND

Telephone: (48) (2) 62 83 029

Telecopier: (48) (22) 29 41 05

Frankfurt am Main, Germany Office: Darmstaedter Landstrasse 125, 60598 Frankfurt am Main. Telephone: (49) (69) 9 62 36-0. Telefax: (49) (69) 9 62 36-100.

Berlin, Germany Office: Schlueterstrasse 37, 10629 Berlin. Telephone: (49) (30) 8857 45-0. Telecopier (49) (30) 88-57 45-99.

Dresden, Germany Office: Heideparkstrasse 4, 01099 Dresden. Telephone: (49) (351) 56 70 550. Telecopier: (49)(351) 50 23 476.

Vienna, Austria Office (Sprechstelle): Graben 29A 1010 Vienna. Telephone (43) (1) 53 55 744. Telecopier (43) (1) 53 50 649.

Zagreb, Croatia Office: Trg bana J. Jelacica 3,41000 Zagreb. Telephone: (385) (41) 42 71 16. Telecopier: (385) (41) 42 87 99.

Commercial, Corporation, Contracts, Mergers and Acquisitions, Banking, Antitrust, Distributorship Agency and Franchising, Computer Law (EDP Law), Patents and Trademarks, Capital Market, Financial Services, Product Liability, Property and Real Estate, Foreign Investment, Administrative, Environmental, Trade Regulations, Food and Drug Regulations.

MEMBER OF FIRM

JOACHIM HILLA, born Benthen/Bytom, Poland, September 11, 1953; admitted, 1991, Germany (Not admitted in Poland). *Education:* University of Silisia; Warsaw University; University of Heidelberg; Academic Tutor, University of Pasau. *LANGUAGES:* German, English, Polish and Russian. *PRACTICE AREAS:* Mergers and Acquisitions; Distributorship; Corporate; Joint Ventures; Finance; Property and Real Estate; Foreign Investments; Polish Commercial Law.

CLIFFORD CHANCE

WARSAW CORPORATE CENTRE
UL. EMILII PLATER 28
00-688 WARSAW, POLAND
Telephone: (48 2) 630 3344
Fax: (48 2) 630 3355

Other Offices: Amsterdam, Bahrain, Barcelona, Brussels, Budapest, Dubai, Frankfurt, Hanoi, Hong Kong, London, Madrid, Milan, Moscow, New York, Paris, Riyadh, Rome, Shanghai, Singapore, Tokyo. (See London for full address details).

RESIDENT MANAGER

NICK FLETCHER, admitted, 1987, Solicitor.

CONSULTOR LTD.

Established in 1985

PIĘKNA 66A I FLOOR
00-672 WARSAW, POLAND
Telephone: (2) 6280211
Fax: (2) 6284766

Administrative Law, Banking Law, Bankruptcy & Reconstruction, Commercial Law, Company Law, Company Acquisitions & Mergers, Company Formation, Competition Law, Contract Law, Intellectual Property, Joint Venture Capital, Commercial Litigation, Privatization, Tax (Avoidance of Double Taxation included).

FIRM PROFILE: Consultor Limited Liability Company has been established in 1985 in Warsaw in order to render the specialized legal assistance to all entities carrying out or undertaking an economic activity in Poland.

The Company provides its clients, both domestic and foreign, with a wide range of legal services including:

— Presentation of options & advising of the most appropriate for intended business,

— Partnerships, companies, foundations formations,

— Drafting of contracts, agreements, statements, notarial deeds and other legal documents,

— Preparing legal opinions and analysis,

— Assisting clients in negotiations and representing them before the courts, government and local authorities and institutions.

Consultor's 11 partners are the members of the Faculty of Law at Warsaw University and Central School of Warsaw, mostly with LL.D.

With a command of English, French, German, Russian and other languages the partners are perfectly able to assist foreign clients and to identify their individual requirements.

JERZY MODRZEJEWSKI, born 1954; admitted, 1976, Poland. *Education:* (LL.M., 1976; LL.D., 1989). Senior Lecturer in Commercial Law, Deputy Dean of Faculty of Law University of Warsaw. Advisor to the Minister of Privatization, 1990. (President, Head of Dept.) (Ptnr.). *LANGUAGES:* Polish, English and French. *PRACTICE AREAS:* Company & Commercial Law; Foreign Investments.

CEZARY WISNIEWSKI, born 1960; admitted, 1984, Poland. *Education:* (LL.M., 1984). Lecturer in Civil Law, University of Warsaw. (Transaction, Privatisation). *LANGUAGES:* Polish and German. *PRACTICE AREAS:* Civil & Company Law; Intellectual Property.

JACEK KRAUSS, born 1949; admitted, 1973, Poland. *Education:* (LL.M., 1973; LL.D., 1985). Senior Lecturer in Commercial Law, University of Warsaw. Member, Legislation Committee on Commercial Law. (Anti-Trust Companies) (Ptnr.). *LANGUAGES:* Polish and French. *PRACTICE AREAS:* Company & Commercial; Anti-Trust & Foreign Investment Law.

WIESLAW OPALSKI, born 1941; admitted, 1963, Poland. *Education:* (LL.M., 1963; LL.D., 1973). Editor-in-Chief, Economic Legislation Review. Senior Lecturer in Commercial Law, University of Warsaw. (Transactions Insolvency) (Ptnr.). *LANGUAGES:* Polish and English. *PRACTICE AREAS:* Civil & Commercial Transactions; Real Estate & Negotiable Instruments.

TADEUSZ KOMOSA, born 1961; admitted, 1985, Poland. *Education:* (Ms.Econ., 1985; LL.M., 1986). Lecturer in Commercial Law, University of Warsaw. (Foreign Investments Securities) (Ptnr.). *LANGUAGES:* Polish,

(This Listing Continued)

English and Russian. *PRACTICE AREAS:* Company Law; Foreign Investments; Negotiable Instruments & Securities.

WITOLD KONIECZNY, born 1948; admitted, 1970, Poland. *Education:* (LL.M., 1970; LL.D., 1981). Editor-in-Chief, Tax Review. Senior Lecturer in Financial Law, University of Warsaw Career, Chief specialist in the Dept. of Taxes Ministry of Finance, 1982-1986. (Head of Dept.) (Ptnr.). *LANGUAGES:* Polish, English and Russian. *PRACTICE AREAS:* Taxation & Budgeting.

MAREK GRZYBOWSKI, born 1953; admitted, 1977, Poland. *Education:* (LL.M., 1977; LL.D., 1986). Senior Lecturer in Financial Law, University of Warsaw. (Taxation) (Ptnr.). *LANGUAGES:* Polish and Russian. *PRACTICE AREAS:* Taxation & Banking.

MARIUSZ ALEKSANDROWICZ, born 1965; admitted, 1990, Poland. *Education:* (LL.M., 1990). Lecturer in Financial Law, University of Warsaw. (Banking Credit, Security) (Ptnr.). *LANGUAGES:* Polish and German. *PRACTICE AREAS:* Banking; Credit & Security; Insolvency.

WOJCIECH BOGUSLAWSKI, born 1955; admitted, 1978, Poland. *Education:* (LL.M., 1978; LL.D., 1988). Senior Lecturer in Civil Law, University of Warsaw. (Head of Dept.) (Ptnr.). *LANGUAGES:* Polish and German. *PRACTICE AREAS:* Company & Commercial Law; Intellectual Property.

MAREK SZUBIAKOWSKI, born 1949; admitted, 1978, Poland. *Education:* (LL.M., 1978; LL.D., 1986). Senior Lecturer in Administrative Law, University of Warsaw. (Head of Dept.) (Ptnr.). *LANGUAGES:* Polish, English, French, Serbocroatian & Arabic. *PRACTICE AREAS:* Administrative Law; Customs & Foreign Exchange Law; Foreign Investments.

SLAWOMIR JEDRZEJEWSKI, born 1961; admitted, 1986, Poland. *Education:* (Ms.Econ., 1986; LL.M., 1987). Lecturer in International & Comparative Law, Department Central School of Commerce. (Dept. Foreign Exchange) (Ptnr.). *LANGUAGES:* Polish, English & Russian. *PRACTICE AREAS:* Foreign Exchange Regulations; Foreign Investment Law; International Taxation; Avoidance of Double Taxation.

STUDIO LEGALE DE CAPOA - GUIDUCCI & ASSOCIATI

UL. BELWEDERSKA 14
WARSAW, POLAND
Telephone: (48-22) 412475
Telefax: (48-22) 412475

Bologna, Italy Office: Via Albertazzi 22,40137. Telephone: (39-51) 343799; 346062; 34835. Telefax: (39-51) 344125.

International and Domestic Commercial Law, General and Civil Practice, Contracts, Litigation, Intellectual Property, EEC and Tax Law.

MEMBERS OF FIRM

Antonio de Capoa   **Elena Baroni**
Michele Draghetti

OF COUNSEL

Robert Smoktunowicz

(For Complete Biographical Data on all Personnel, see Professional Biographies at Bologna, Italy)

DEWEY BALLANTINE THEODORE GODDARD

UL. KLONOWA 8
00-591 WARSAW, POLAND
Telephone: 011-48-22-49-32-88
Fax: 011-48-22-49-80-23

Dewey Ballantine Offices:
New York, New York Office: 1301 Avenue of the Americas, 10019-6092. Telephone: 212-259-8000. Fax: 212-259-6333.
Washington, D.C. Office: 1775 Pennsylvania Avenue, N.W., 20006-4605. Telephone: 202-862-1000. Fax: 202-862-1093.
Los Angeles, California Office: 333 South Hope Street, 90071-1406. Telephone: 213-626-3399. Fax: 213-625-0562.
London, England Office: 150 Aldersgate Street, London EC1A 4EJ, England. Telephone: (44-71) 606-6121. Fax: (44-71) 600-3754.

(This Listing Continued)

DEWEY BALLANTINE THEODORE GODDARD,
Warsaw—Continued

Hong Kong Office: Asia Pacific Finance Tower, Suite 3907, Citibank Plaza, 3 Garden Road, Central, Hong Kong. Telephone: 852-2509-7000. Fax: 852-2509-7088.

Theodore Goddard Offices:

London, England Office: 150 Aldersgate Street, EC1A 4EJ. Telephone: (44-71) 606-8855. Fax: (44-71) 606-4390.

Paris, France Office: Klein Goddard, 44 Avenue des Champs Elysées, 75008. Telephone: (33-1) 4495-2000. Fax: (33-1) 4953-0397.

Brussels, Belgium Office: 79 avenue de Cortenberg/Kortenberglaan 79, B-1040. Telephone: (32-2) 732-2700. Fax: (32-2) 735-2352.

Other Dewey Ballantine Theodore Goddard Offices:

Budapest, Hungary Office: Vadasz utca 31 H-1054. Telephone: (36-1) 111-9620. Fax: (36-1) 112-2272.

Prague, Czech Republic Office: 6th Floor, Revolucni 13, 110 00 Prague 1. Telephone: (42-2) 2481-0283. Fax: (42-2) 231-0983.

Kraków, Poland Office: Pl. Axentowicza 6. 30-034 Kraków Poland. Telephone: 48-12-340-339. Fax: 48-12-333-624.

General Corporate and Commercial Practice.

FIRM PROFILE: *Dewey Ballantine Theodore Goddard is a joint venture between the U.S.-based international law firm of Dewey Ballantine and the British-based international law firm of Theodore Goddard. Dewey Ballantine Theodore Goddard also has offices in Budapest and Prague*

MANAGING LAWYER

BRUCE MCGREGOR, born Cape Town, South Africa, June 2, 1946; admitted, 1973, South Africa; 1981, England (Not admitted in Poland). *Education:* University of Cape Town, South Africa (B.Comm., 1969; LL.B., 1970). *Member:* Law Society of England. [South African Navy, 1965]. *LANGUAGES:* Afrikaans.

RESIDENT ASSOCIATES

PAWEL BAJNO, born Warswa, Poland, July 17, 1970. *Education:* University of Warsaw Law Faculty, Warsaw. *LANGUAGES:* English and Russian.

MARCIN BRUSZEWSKI, born Warsaw, Poland, 1970. *Education:* Warsaw University; British Centre for English Legal Studies 1992. *LANGUAGES:* Polish, English.

RAFAEL EILE, born Cracow, Poland, October 10, 1965; admitted, 1995, England (Not admitted in Poland). *Education:* Courtland Institute of Art, London, England (B.A., 1989); College of Law, London, England (L.S.F., 1993). *LANGUAGES:* English and Polish.

JAROSLAW GRZESIAK, born Cracow, Poland, 1966. *Education:* Jagiellonian University (LL.M., 1990). Research Assistant, Jagiellonian University, 1990-1992. *Member:* Cracow Bar. *LANGUAGES:* Polish, English, Russian.

JENNIFER HANDZ, born Perth, Western Australia, May 14, 1963; admitted, 1987, Western Australia; 1991, England (Not admitted in Poland). *Education:* University of Western Australia, Perth, Western Australia (LL.B., 1985). *LANGUAGES:* Polish.

PIOTR KRÜGER, born Warsaw, Poland, October 30, 1965. *Education:* Reytan High School, Warsaw, Poland (1984); Law Faculty, Warsaw University, War. [aw, Poland (1994)]. *LANGUAGES:* Polish.

ANETA POPLAWSKA, born Olsztyn, Poland, June 1, 1966; admitted, 1992, Poland. *Education:* University of Warsaw, Law Faculty, Warsaw, Poland (1992). *Member:* Warsaw Legal Advisors Chamber; Polish Young Lawyers Association. *LANGUAGES:* English, Polish, Russian, Italian. *PRACTICE AREAS:* Privatisations; Securities; Joint Ventures.

LUKASZ REDZINIAK, born Rzeszow, Poland, 1968. *Education:* Jagiellonian University (LL.M., 1991). Research Assistant, Jagiellonian University, 1990-1991; Trainee at Chamber of Commerce, Graz, Austria. *Member:* Cracow Bar. *LANGUAGES:* Polish, English, German.

COUNSEL

TOMASZ GIZBERT-STUDNICKI, born Cracow, 1948. *Education:* Jagiellonian University (LL.M., 1970; Doctor of Laws, 1974; Habilitation (venia legendi) in Jurisprudence, 1978). Research Fellow, Max Planck Institute for Private Law, Hamburg, Germany, 1978-1979; Research Fellow, University of Gottingen, Germany, 1985-1987; Professor of Law, Jagiel-

(This Listing Continued)

lonian University, 1989—. *Member:* Cracow Bar; Cracow Industrial Society; Supervisory Board of Pioneer First Polish Trust. *LANGUAGES:* Polish, English, German.

DICKINSON, WRIGHT, MOON, VAN DUSEN & FREEMAN, Sp. z o.o.

46 WILCZA STREET, 4TH FLOOR
00-679 WARSAW, POLAND
Telephone: (48-22) 299-241
Facsimile: (48-2) 628-4107
Komertel Satellite Phone: (48-39) 121-510

Detroit, Michigan Office: 500 Woodward Avenue, Suite 4000. Telephone: 313-223-3500. Facsimile: 313-223-3598.

Washington, D.C. Office: Suite 800, 1901 L Street, N.W. Telephone: 202-457-0160. Facsimile: 202-659-1559.

Chicago, Illinois Office: 225 West Washington, Suite 400. Telephone: 312-220-0300. Facsimile: 312-220-0021.

Bloomfield Hills, Michigan Office: 525 North Woodward Avenue. Telephone: 313-433-7200. Facsimile: 313-433-7274.

Lansing, Michigan Office: Suite 200, 215 South Washington Square. Telephone: 517-371-1730. Facsimile: 517-487-4700.

Grand Rapids, Michigan Office: 200 Ottawa Avenue, N.W., Suite 900. Telephone: 616-458-1300. Facsimile: 616-458-6753.

Banking, Commercial and International Law.

RESIDENT PARTNERS

PETER SWIECICKI, born Lancaster, Pennsylvania, June 29, 1954; admitted, 1982, Michigan (Not admitted in Poland). *Education:* Georgetown University (B.S.F.S., cum laude, 1976); Columbia University (M.A., 1977); University of Michigan (J.D., 1982). Administrative Editor, University of Michigan Journal of Law Reform, 1981-1982. *Member:* Detroit, American and International Bar Associations; State Bar of Michigan. *LANGUAGES:* English, Polish. *PRACTICE AREAS:* Banking Law; Commercial Law; International Law.

KRZYSZTOF WIERZBOWSKI, born Zyrardow, Poland, March 8, 1956. admitted, 1986, Poland. Education: University of Warsaw (M.S., 1979). *Member:* Warsaw Bar Association (Member, Committee on Professional Training; Disciplinary Court Judge, 1990-1992). *LANGUAGES:* Polish, English.

RESIDENT OF COUNSEL

PIOTR J. STRAWA, born Warsaw, Poland, May 22, 1955; admitted, 1985, Poland. *Education:* University of Warsaw (M.A., 1981). *Member:* Warsaw Bar Association; Warsaw Council of Legal Advisors. *LANGUAGES:* Polish, English. *PRACTICE AREAS:* Commercial Law; Acquisitions; Tax Law.

RESIDENT ASSOCIATES

MATTHEW V. PIWOWAR, born Marquette, Michigan, March 7, 1965; admitted, 1990, Michigan (Not admitted in Poland). *Education:* St. Mary's College (B.S., magna cum laude, 1986 Salutatorian); Jagiellonian University, Poland; University of Michigan (J.D., 1989). *Member:* Grand Rapids, Detroit and International Bar Associations; State Bar of Michigan. *PRACTICE AREAS:* Corporate and Banking Law; International Law; Securities Law; Tax Law; Privatization.

HENRYK ROMANCZUK, born Markowce, Poland, October 11, 1951. admitted, 1980, Poland. Education: University of Warsaw (Masters, 1974). Author: in "Nowe Prawo" on Adoption; in "Domy Spoldzielcze" on Cooperative Law. Lecturer, Warsaw Bar Association, 1990—. Deputy Secretary, Warsaw Bar Council, 1992—. Judge in Disciplinary Tribunal of Warsaw Bar Council, 1988-1990. Coordinator: Social Committee; Committee of Sport and Tourism; Retired Advocates, 1987-1990. Inspector, Bar Council, 1987-1990. Deputy Prosecutor, The Disciplinary Tribunal, 1985-1988. *Member:* Warsaw Bar Association. *LANGUAGES:* Polish, Russian, English. *PRACTICE AREAS:* Civil Law; Administrative Law.

(This Listing Continued)

Johnson; Kmart Corp.; Kuhlman Corp.; Mallinckrodt Inc.; Mellon Bank, N.A.; Melon-McMahon Real Estate Advisors Inc.; Michigan Bell Telephone Co.; Michigan Consolidated Gas Co.; Michigan Health Care Corp.; Miller Brewing Co.; Ministry of Privatization of the Republic of Poland; NBD Bank, N.A.; Nippondenso America, Inc.; Nissan Research and Development, Inc.; Northwest Airlines; Polish Development Bank; Premark International; Republic Bancorp, Inc.; Ross Roy, Inc.; Suburban Mobility Authority Regional Transportation (SMART); Suzuki Motor Co., Ltd.; The Marmon Group, Inc.; Thiokol Corp.; University of Detroit Mercy; UNO-VEN; W.R. Grace & Co.

(For complete biographical data on all personnel, see Professional Biographies at Detroit, Michigan)

DRZEWIECKI & TOMASZEK

UL. WILCZA 31 M.5
00-544 WARSAW, POLAND
Telephone: (22) 29 36 74; (2) 628 45 19
Fax: (2) 628 45 19

Civil Law, Law of Obligations, Unfair Competition Law, Trademark Law, Intellectual Property Law, Commercial and Corporate Law, Privatisation Law, Real Estate Law, Foreign Exchange Law, Employment Law, Tax and Customs Law, Joint Venture Law, Banking Law, Construction Law.

FIRM PROFILE: Drzewiecki, Tomaszek - Spólka Adwokacka" is a professional Law partnership established in mid-1992.

The firm has the permanent associates among the advocates - members of the Warsaw Bar Association, notaries and legal advisors.

PARTNERS

ZBIGNIEW DRZEWIECKI, born Warsaw, February 20, 1962; admitted, 1987, Warsaw. *Education:* Warsaw University (Degree in Law, 1987). Permanent Associate, Tomasz Wardynski, 1987-1991. Co-author: Article published in the Polish Tax Review on investing in the United Kingdom. *Member:* Polish Bar Association (Elected to Supreme Governing Institutions, 1993). *LANGUAGES:* English. *PRACTICE AREAS:* Commercial Law; Joint Venture Law; Privatisation Law and Foreign Exchange Law; Civil and Criminal Litigation; Intellectual Property Law.

MALGORZATA KACPERSKA, born Warsaw, Poland, March 1, 1966; admitted, 1993, Warsaw. *Education:* Warsaw University (Law Degree, 1989). Permanent Associate of Adwokat Maciej Dubois, Specialising in Company Law, Advertising Law and Civil Law, 1989-1993. Attended York University, Osgoode Law School and the Canadian Law Firm of Gowling, Strathy & Henderson, Familiarised herself with Canadian Corporate Law and Advertising Law, 1991. *LANGUAGES:* English. *PRACTICE AREAS:* Commercial Litigation; Company Law; Civil Law; Advertising Law and Employment Law.

ANDRZEJ TOMASZEK, born Warsaw, Poland, May 26, 1961; admitted, 1989, Warsaw. *Education:* Warsaw University (Degree in Law 1984; History, with distinction, 1986). Permanent Associate, specializing in Employment Law, Tax Law and Industrial Property, Adwokat Tomasz Wardynski, 1989-1991. Specialized in Industrial and Commercial Law and Intellectual Property, Boden Oppenhoff Rasor Raue Law Firm, Cologne, Germany, 1992. Consultant in the preparation of the English language version of the Polish Commercial Code author by Roman Poplawski. Co-author: with Roman Poplawski, Articles "Sources of Polish Business Law" and "The Polish Civil Code," published by International Bar Association. Author: Articles on German Investment Law and Investing in the United Kingdom in the Polish Tax Review. *LANGUAGES:* English, German and Russian. *PRACTICE AREAS:* Industrial and Commercial Law; Intellectual Property Law; Employment Law; Criminal Law; Law on Trademarks; Commercial Litigation; Tax Law.

The Firm is a member of the International Bar Association (IBA).

GIDE LOYRETTE NOUEL

UL. KOPERNIKA 17
00-359 WARSAW, POLAND
Telephone: (48.22) 26.22.21
Fax: (48.22) 26.03.02

Paris, France Office: 26 Cours Albert 1er, 75008. Telephone: (1) 40.75.60.00. Cable Address: "3 Avocagidva Paris 86," Telex: 651261F GILOY. Telecopier: (1) 43.59.37.79.
New York, New York Office: Swiss Bank Tower, 10 East 50th Street, 10022. Telephone: (1-212) 644-1201. Telex: 424353 GIDE. Telecopier: (1-212) 644-1205.

(This Listing Continued)

Brussels, Belgium Office: Rue de la Loi 99.101, B-1040. Telephone: (32.2) 231.11.40. Telecopier: (32.2) 231.11.77.
Riyadh, Saudi Arabia Office: P.O. Box 4615, 11412. Telephone: (966.1) 476.60.39. Telex: 401677 NASHWA. Telecopier: (966.1) 476.18.96.
Tokyo, Japan Office: Homei Building 3F, 3-19 Akasaka 1-Chome, Minato-Ku, 107. Telephone: (81.3) 55.62.03.01. Telecopier: (81.3) 55.62.03.06.
Beijing, People's Republic of China Office: Suite 3309 A, Jing Guang Centre, Hu Jia Lou, Chaoyang District, 100020. Telephone: (86.1) 501 4511. Telecopier: (86.1) 501 4551.
Prague, Czech Republic Office: 34 Jindrisska, 11207. Telephone: (42.2) 24.21.34.65;24.21.36.50. Telecopier: (42.2) 24.21.09.12;24.22.58.53.
St. Petersburg, Russia Office: 34 Souvorovsky Prospect, App 45, P.O. Box 172, 193015. Telephone by satellite: (7.812) 850.16.85. Telecopier by satellite: (7.812) 850.16.86.
Moscow, Russia Office: 9, Ulitsa Tverskaya - App 66, 103009. Telephone by satellite: (7.501) 940.45.00. Telecopier by satellite: (7.501) 940.45.01.
Budapest VII, Hungary Office: EMKE Building, Rákóczi út 42, BP 409, 1072. Telephone: (36.1) 268.1236; 268.1237; 268.1238. Telecopier: (36.1) 268.1239.
Madrid, Spain Office: Antonio Maura 7, 6°, 28014. Telephone: (34.1) 531.25.01. Telecopier: (34.1) 531.35.30.
Hanoi, Vietnam Office: Hanoi Business Centre, 51 Ly Thai To. Telephone: (84.42) 66.122.3. Telecopier: (84.42) 66.030.1.

French and International Law.

RESIDENT ASSOCIATES

Stanislas Dwernicki
Guillaume Rougier-Brierre
Arwid Mednis
Dariusz Tokarczuk
Marzena Matuszyk
Marek Grodek
Piotr Sadownik
Eva Branecka

(For Biographical Data on Personnel, see Professional Biographies at Paris, France).

HOGAN & HARTSON SP.ZO.O

MARSZALKOWSKA 6/6
00-590 WARSAW, POLAND
Telephone: (48 2) 628 0201; Satellite (48) 3912 1413
Fax: (48 2) 628 7787; Satellite (48) 3912 1511

Washington, D.C. Office: Columbia Square, 555 13th Street, N.W. Telephone: 202-637-5600. Telex: 89-2757. Cable Address: "Hogander Washington". Fax: 202-637-5910.
Brussels, Belgium Office: Avenue des Arts 41, 1040. Telephone: (32.2) 505.09.11. Fax: (32.2) 502.28.60.
London, England Office: Veritas House, 125 Finsbury Pavement, EC2A 1NQ. Telephone: (44 171) 638.9595. Fax: (44 171) 638.0884.
Moscow, Russia Office: 33/2 Usacheva Street, Building 3, 119048. Telephone: (7095) 245-5190. Fax: (7095) 245-5192.
Paris, France Office: Cabinet Wolfram, 14, rue Chauveau-Lagarde, 75008. Telephone: (33-1) 44.71.97.00. Fax: (33-1) 47.42.13.56.
Prague, Czech Republic Office: Opletalova 37, 110 00. Telephone: (42-2) 2422-9009. Fax: (42-2) 2421-5105.
Baltimore, Maryland Office: 111 South Calvert Street, 16th Floor. Telephone: 410-659-2700. Fax: 410-539-6981.
Bethesda, Maryland Office: Two Democracy Center, Suite 720, 6903 Rockledge Drive. Telephone: 301-564-5000. Fax: 301-493-5169.
Colorado Springs, Colorado Office: 518 North Nevada Avenue, Suite 200. Telephone: 719-635-5900. Fax: 719-635-2847.
Denver, Colorado Office: One Tabor Center, Suite 1500, 1200 Seventeenth Street. Telephone: 303-899-7300. Fax: 303-899-7333.
McLean, Virginia Office: 8300 Greensboro Drive. Telephone: 703-848-2600. Fax: 703-448-7650.

Foreign Investment, Privatization, Commercial Transactions, Intellectual Property, Taxation, Real Estate, Labor Law, Customs and Litigation, Structured Financings.

(This Listing Continued)

HOGAN & HARTSON SP.ZO.O, Warsaw—Continued

RESIDENT PARTNERS

STEVEN E. BALLEW, born Greenwood, South Carolina, June 17, 1945; admitted, 1978, California; 1981, District of Columbia (Not a Member of the Polish Bar). *Education:* Duke University (A.B., 1967); Indiana University (Ph.D., 1974); University of Southern California (J.D., 1978). Order of the Coif. Author: "Joint Ventures in Poland," Corporate Finance, 1992; "Assignment of Rights, Franchises and Obligations of the Disappearing Corporation in a Merger," The Business Lawyer, 1982. *Member:* District of Columbia Bar; State Bar of California; American Bar Association. *PRACTICE AREAS:* Corporate Law; Securities Law; Financings; International Transactions.

JOSEPH C. BELL, born Louisville, Kentucky, November 11, 1940; admitted, 1968, Massachusetts; 1977, District of Columbia (Not a Member of the Polish Bar). *Education:* University of Colorado (B.A., summa cum laude, 1962); Harvard University (A.M., Economics, 1965); Yale University (LL.B., 1968); University of California at Berkeley. Phi Beta Kappa. Editor, Yale Law Journal, 1967-1968. Attorney: Cabinet Task Force on Oil Import Controls, 1969; Antitrust Division, Department of Justice, 1970-1972. Assistant Professor, Duke Law School and Institute of Policy Studies, 1972-1974. Assistant General Counsel for International and Special Programs, Federal Energy Administration, 1974-1977. Advisor, Polish Ministry of Finance, 1989-1991. Director, Project on Economic Reform in Ukraine, 1990—. *Member:* District of Columbia Bar; Federal Energy and American (Member, Sections on: Administrative Law; International Law; Natural Resource Law) Bar Associations. *PRACTICE AREAS:* Energy and Natural Resources Law; Commercial and Privatization Law; International Law.

RESIDENT EUROPEAN COUNSEL

MACIEJ JAMKA (ADWOKAT), born Cracow, Poland, June 19, 1959; admitted, 1991, Poland. *Education:* Jagiellonian University (Magister of Law, 1985). Co-Author: "Mortgage," 1992. Member, Polish Bar of Advocates with All Rights of Practice, 1992. *LANGUAGES:* Polish, English, German. *PRACTICE AREAS:* Commercial and Corporate Practice; Finance Law.

PIOTR KOCHANSKI (ADWOKAT), born Bielsko-Biala, Poland, June 28, 1961; admitted, 1986, Poland. *Education:* Jagiellonian University (Magister of Law, 1985). Judicial Clerk, Court of Appeals, Cracow, 1985-1986. Founding Partner, Consoft, Ltd. (legal and consulting company), Cracow, 1988. Rimbaud Martell, Paris, 1989. U.S. Chamber of Commerce, Washington, D.C., 1990. Member, Cracow Bar (1987) and Warsaw Bar (1991), with all rights of practice. *LANGUAGES:* Polish, English, French, Russian. *PRACTICE AREAS:* Commercial; Intellectual Property Law; Litigation; Administrative Law; Privatization.

RESIDENT OF COUNSEL

BOGUDAR KORDASIEWICZ, born Olsztryn, Poland, September 10, 1950. *Education:* Warsaw University (Magister, 1972); Institute of Legal Sciences; Polish Academy of Science, Warsaw Poland (Ph.D. in Civil Law, 1975; Doctor Juris Habilitatus (Mass Media Law, 1991). Instructor, Civil Law, Warsaw University, 1988—. Member, President's Council on Mass-Media, 1993—. Auditor, Polish Parliament. *Member:* Association of Polish Lawyer. [Polish Army Training, 1968-1972]. *LANGUAGES:* English, Polish, Russian, German. *PRACTICE AREAS:* Commercial Law; Real Estate; Intellectual Property Law.

RESIDENT ASSOCIATES

ALEKSANDER GALOS, born Krakow, Poland, June 14, 1960; admitted, 1994, Poland. *Education:* Jagiellonian University (M.A., 1984). Zesyty Naukowe UJ; Krakow Casopis Za Pravno Teorijo in Prakso; Ljubljana. Assistant to the Professor, Jagiellonian University, 1984-1992. *LANGUAGES:* Polish, Slovenue, English.

LECH NAJBAUER, born Warsaw, Poland, August 25, 1969 (Not a Member of the Polish Bar). *Education:* Warsaw University (Master of Law, 1993). *LANGUAGES:* Polish, English. *PRACTICE AREAS:* General Commercial and Corporate Law.

KRZYSZTOF STEFANOWICZ, born Warsaw, Polska, October 25, 1955; admitted, 1990, Poland. *Education:* Warsaw University (LL.M., with highest honour, 1978; J.D., 1987). Member, Criminal Law Society, 1989-1993. Author: "Criminal Code Commentary," Poland - Sezam (1991-1992); "White Collar Crimes - Economic Crimes," Poland - MSM, 1993. Assistant Professor, Warsaw University Law School, 1978-1993. Visiting Professor, Capital University, Ohio, U.S.A., 1992. Member: Senate, Warsaw University, 1991-1993; Scientific Board of the Criminal Law Institute, Warsaw

(This Listing Continued)

University, 1988-1993. *Member:* Polish Legal Counsellors Association. *LANGUAGES:* Polish, English, Russian, German. *PRACTICE AREAS:* Commercial Law; Finance Law; Tax Law.

AGNIESIKA SUCHECKA-TARNACKA (ADWOKAT), born Warsaw, Poland, February 6, 1963; admitted, 1991, Poland. *Education:* Warsaw University. Member, Human Rights Committee, National Bar Association. *LANGUAGES:* Polish, English, Russian,. *PRACTICE AREAS:* Civil Law; Commercial Law; Real Estate Law.

ANDRZEJ SUTKOWSKI, born Zambrów, August 22, 1968; (Not a Member of the Polish Bar). *Education:* Warsaw University (Master of Law, 1992). *LANGUAGES:* Polish, English, Russian. *PRACTICE AREAS:* General Commercial and Corporate Law; Tax and Foreign Exchange Regulations.

(For complete biographical data on all personnel, see Professional Biographies at Washington, D.C.)

HUNTON & WILLIAMS
UL. BAGATELA 14, VP.
00-585 WARSAW, POLAND
Telephone: 011 (48-2) 625 21 07
Telecopier: 011 (48-2) 621 83 94

Brussels, Belgium Office: Avenue Louise 106, 1050 Brussels, Belgium. Telephone: 011 (32-2) 646-0010. Fax: 011 (32-2) 646-0246.

Atlanta, Georgia Office: NationsBank Plaza, 600 Peachtree Street, N.E. Telephone: 404-888-4000. Fax: 404-888-4190.

New York, New York Office: 200 Park Avenue. Telephone: 212-309-1000. Cable Addresses: "Huntwand, New York" and "Dialboard." Telex: 424 549 HUNT UI. Fax: 212-309-1100.

Washington, D.C. Office: 2000 Pennsylvania Avenue, N.W., P.O. Box 19230. Telephone: 202-955-1500. Telex: 350 362 H&W WASH UD. Fax: 202-778-2201 (Rapicom); 202-778-2202 (Ricoh230).

Richmond, Virginia Offices: Riverfront Plaza, East Tower, 951 East Byrd Street. Telephone: 804-788-8200. Cable Address "Huntwand." Telex: 804-684-4251. FAX: 804-788-8218. TWX: 710-956-0061 and Church Hill Office: 2300 East Marshall Street. Telephone: 804-775-2248.

Raleigh, North Carolina Office: One Hannover Square, P.O. Box 109. Telephone: 919-899-3000. FAX: 919-899-3096.

Knoxville, Tennessee Office: 2000 Riverview Tower, 900 South Gay Street. Telephone: 615-549-7700. FAX: 615-549-7704.

Fairfax, Virginia Office: 3050 Chain Bridge Road, P.O. Box 1147. Telephone: 703-352-2200. FAX: 703-273-6772.

Norfolk, Virginia Office: Crestar Bank Building, Suite 1000, 500 East Main Street. Telephone: 804-625-5501. Telex: 825 455 H&W NFK. Fax: 804-625-7720.

General and International Practice.
Office engaged in Polish and European Business Law, Regulatory and Administrative practice, including Mergers and Acquisitions, Privatization, Competition, Environmental, Energy, Health and Safety, and related matters.

PARTNERS

CHARLES A. BLANCHARD, born Richmond, Virginia, September 24, 1957; admitted, 1985, Virginia. *Education:* University of Colorado at Boulder (B.A., 1980); Washington & Lee University (J.D., summa cum laude, 1985). Phi Beta Kappa. Order of the Coif. Member, Washington & Lee Law Review, 1983-1985. (Managing Partner) (Also, Brussels, Belgium Office). *LANGUAGES:* English and French.

LEJB FOGELMAN, born Legnica, Poland, June 21, 1949; admitted, 1981, Massachusetts; U. S. District Court, District of Massachusetts. *Education:* State University of New York at Stony Brook (B.A., summa cum laude, 1972); University of Paris-Sorbonne, Paris, France (Cert., 1972); Columbia University (M.A., M.Phil., School of International Aff. Cert.); University of Warsaw, Warsaw, Poland; Harvard University (J.D., 1981). *Member:* American and International Bar Associations. *LANGUAGES:* English, Polish, Russian, French and Italian.

RAY V. HARTWELL, III, born Anniston, Alabama, June 19, 1947; admitted, 1975, Virginia; 1980, District of Columbia. *Education:* Washington & Lee University (B.A., 1969; J.D., summa cum laude, 1975). Omicron Delta Kappa; Order of the Coif; Delta Theta Phi. Winner, John W. Davis Prize, 1975. Editor-in-Chief, Washington & Lee Law Review, 1974-1975. Member, Editorial Advisory Boards, The Antitrust Bulletin and The Journal of Reprints for Antitrust Law and Economics, 1978—; Council Member, 1992—. Chair, Consumer Protection Committee, 1989-1992, Vice-

(This Listing Continued)

Chair, Criminal Practice and Procedure Committee, 1987-1989, American Bar Association Section of Antitrust Law. Chairman, 1979-1980 and Member, Board of Governors, 1977-1981, Antitrust Franchising and Trade Regulation Section, Virginia State Bar. Member, International Bar Association; ABA Sections of Science and Technology, Intellectual Property Law. [Lt.(j.g.), U.S. Navy, 1969-1972]. (Also, Richmond, Virginia, Washington, D.C. and Brussels, Belgium Offices). *LANGUAGES:* English and French.

SPECIAL COUNSEL

ANDRZEJ W. WIŚNIEWSKI, born Warsaw, Poland, January 6, 1950; admitted, (Counsellor at Law) 1982, Poland. *Education:* University of Warsaw (Master of Law, 1971; Doctor of Law, 1978); University of Florida (Introduction to American Law, 1988). Lecturer, International Private and Commercial Law, Warsaw University, 1975—. Member: Court of Arbitration, Polish Chamber of Commerce, 1988—; Working Group for the Reform of Partnership and Company Law, Civil Law Reform Commission, 1989—. *Member:* Polish Arbitration Association; Association of Business Consultants. *LANGUAGES:* Polish, English, Russian, German and French.

ASSOCIATES

ANDREW Z. BLATTER, born New York, N.Y., November 5, 1961; admitted, 1986, Maryland; 1989, District of Columbia; 1992, New York. *Education:* University of Pennsylvania (B.A., summa cum laude, 1983; J.D., 1986). Member, Section of Taxation, American Bar Association. *Member:* The District of Columbia Bar; Maryland State and New York State Bar Associations. (Also in New York, New York Office).

SUSAN S. CUMMINGS, born Washington, D.C., September 29, 1965; admitted, 1992, Illinois; 1994, District of Columbia. *Education:* Princeton University (A.B., 1987); George Washington University (J.D., 1992).

JUDITH Y. GLINIECKI, born Mt. Gilead, Ohio, February 2, 1966; admitted, 1991, Ohio. *Education:* Wellesley College (B.A., magna cum laude, 1988); Harvard Law School (J.D., 1991). Phi Beta Kappa. Author: "Poland's New Copyright Law," Eastern European Reporter (BNA) No. 4 at 321, April 11, 1994; "International Electronic Commerce and Administrative Law: The Need for Harmonized National Reforms," 6 Harv. J.L. & T. 263, 1993; "The Legal Acceptance of Electronic Documents, Writings, Signatures and Notices in International Transportation Conventions: A Challenge in the Age of Global Electronic Commerce," 13 NW. J. Int'l. L & Bus. 117, 1992; "Revenue Procedure 91-59 —Tax Rules for Electronic Commerce," UCC Committee Newsletter (UCC Committee-Section of Business Law of the ABA) November, 1992. *LANGUAGES:* English, Russian and Polish.

RADEK A. GRONET, born Warsaw, Poland, April 27, 1965. *Education:* University of Illinois (M.A., 1990); Warsaw University (LL.M., 1990). Recipient, Dean's Award for Outstanding Results, 1987 and 1988. Co-Author, with Ania Frankowska: "Commentary to the Polish Foreign Investment Law of June, 1991," International Legal Matters, July, 1991. (Teaching Assistant, Criminal Law, University of Illinois). *LANGUAGES:* Polish, English, Russian and German.

ANNA M. HAGOPIAN, born Bialystok, Poland, April 8, 1963. *Education:* Hague Academy of International Law (Cert., 1986); University of Warsaw (Masters of Law, , 1990); Queen Mary and Westfield College, London University (Cert., 1991). Member, E.C. Lawyers Society. *LANGUAGES:* Polish, English and Russian.

DOROTA JAKUBIAK, born Warsaw, Poland, October 13, 1966; admitted, 1994, Poland. *Education:* University of of Warsaw (M.A., 1992). Member, District Chamber of Commerce, Warsaw, 1993. *LANGUAGES:* Polish, Italian, English.

AREK R. KRASNODĘBSKI, born Opole, Poland, December 16, 1965. *Education:* Jagiellonian University (M.A., 1990); University of Stockholm (LL.M., 1992). *LANGUAGES:* Polish, English, Swedish and Russian.

PAULINA MARUSCZYK, born Katowice, Poland, December 18, 1966. *Education:* University of Gdańsk; University of Warsaw (M.A., with honors, 1992); University of Konstanz, Germany (1990-1991). *LANGUAGES:* Polish, German, English and Russian.

P. WATSON SEAMAN, born Durham, North Carolina, September 20, 1960; admitted, 1988, Virginia. *Education:* Williams College (B.A., 1983); University of Virginia (J.D., 1988). (Also Richmond, Virginia Office). *LANGUAGES:* English and French.

JANUSZ TYMCZENKO, born Warsaw, Poland, January 12, 1960; admitted, 1988, Poland. *Education:* Warsaw University School of Law

(This Listing Continued)

(J.D., 1985). Warsaw District Court, 1985-1987. Polish Academy of Science, Civil Law Department, 1986-1989. Lecturer, Civil Law, Warsaw University. *LANGUAGES:* Polish, Russian.

JEANTET POLSKA
UL. WIEJSKA 12A
00-490 WARSAW, POLAND
Telephone: (48) 2/628 24 12; (48) 391 22017
Fax: (48) 2/628 24 11

Paris, France Office: 87, avenue Kléber, 75116. Telephone: (33) 1 45 05 80 08. Fax: (33) 1 47 04 20 41; (33) 1 47 55 95 10.
London, England Office: Royex House, Aldermanbury Square, EC2V 7HR. Telephone: (44) 171 600 36 08. Fax: (44) 171 600 17 18.
Brussels, Belgium Office: Rue Brederode 13 A, B, 1000. Telephone: (32) 2505 02 11. Fax: (32) 2502 26 44.
New York, New York Office: 712 Fifth Avenue, 10019. Telephone: (212) 801 3440. Fax: (212) 801 3445.
Prague, Czech Republic Office: Blanicka 28, 12000. Telephone: (42) 2 256 251. Fax: (42) 2 254 233.
Budapest, Hungary Office: Szemere Utca 17.IV./1, 1054. Telephone: (36) 2 203 40759. Fax: (36) 2 201 63 79.
Bucarest, Romania Office: Strada Docentilor 7, Sector 1. Telephone: (40) 1 312 99 36. Fax: (40) 1 312 97 56.
Moscow, Russia Correspondent Office: Krasnopresnenskaya NAB, 12, International Trade Center, Office 2009, CEI - 123610. Telephone: (7) 502 253 00 41. Fax: (7) 502 253 20 42.

French and International Law.

RESIDENT ASSOCIATES

Christine Fortea
Laurent Xardel
Andrzej Debiec
Justyna Szwech
Ewa Lubowicz
Jacek Lempicki

KALWAS & PARTNERS
LAW OFFICE
Established in 1989

PIEKNA 3 ST.
00-539 WARSAW, POLAND
Tel/fax: (48-2) 621 29 34, (48-2) 628 66 57, (48-22) 29 05 71

Commerical Law, Company Law, Civil Law, Litigation, Land Law, Financial Law, Privatisation issues, Antitrust Law and Custom Duties.

PARTNERS

ANDRZEJ KALWAS, PRESIDENT, born Wtoctawek, Poland, 1936; admitted, 1965, Poland. *Education:* Warsaw University (Master of Law and Administration, 1963). Judge, Parliamentary Judicial Court, 1989-1991. Member, Editorial Boards of Several Legal Publications. *Member:* Warsaw District Chamber of Legal Advisors (President, 1983—). *LANGUAGES:* Polish and Russian. *PRACTICE AREAS:* Trade Law; Civil Law; Administrative Law; Business Law; Antitrust Law.

RYSZARD TYMINSKI, FOUNDER, born Warsaw, Poland, 1948; admitted, 1978, Poland. *Education:* Warsaw University (Master of Law and Administration, 1972). *Member:* Warsaw District Bar Association of Legal Advisors. *LANGUAGES:* Polish. *PRACTICE AREAS:* Trade Law; Ventures with Foreign Capital.

IWONA CHELKOWSKA-KAMIONKA, born Warsaw, Poland, 1942; admitted, 1978, Poland. *Education:* Warsaw University (Master of Law and Administration, 1972); Hamline University (Legal Training). Certification as Judge, Polish Court System, 1977. Attendant of Business Law Seminar, Copenhagen. Legal training at Oppenheimer, Wolff & Donnelly Law Office, St. Paul, Minnesota, 1991. *Member:* Warsaw District Bar of Legal Advisors (Chairperson, Foreign Affairs Committee); Polish-Danish Lawyers' Friendship Association (President). *LANGUAGES:* Polish, English and Russian. *PRACTICE AREAS:* Trade Law; Joint Ventures; Financial Law; Labour Law; Customs Duties.

BOŻENNA ŚWIETLIK, born Warsaw, Poland, 1946; admitted, 1994, Poland. *Education:* Warsaw University (Master of Law and Administra-

(This Listing Continued)

KALWAS & PARTNERS LAW OFFICE, Warsaw—
Continued

tion, 1980). *Member:* Warsaw Bar Association of Legal Advisors. *LAN-
GUAGES:* Polish, Russian. *PRACTICE AREAS:* Civil Law; Land Law.

ASSOCIATES

EDWARD KAMIONKA, born Zgierz, Poland, 1927; admitted, 1962,
Poland. *Education:* University of Lódź (Master in Law, 1959). *LAN-
GUAGES:* Polish, German. *PRACTICE AREAS:* Financial Law; Civil
Law; Trade Law.

ANNA LENGIEWICZ, born Warsaw, Poland, 1965; admitted, 1994,
Poland. *Education:* University of Katowice (Master of Law and Administration, 1989). *Member:* Warsaw District Bar Association of Legal Advisors. *LANGUAGES:* Polish, English. *PRACTICE AREAS:* Commercial
Law; Corporate Law; Business Law.

IWONA KONTOR, born Warsaw, Poland, 1966. *Education:* Warsaw
University (Master of Law, 1993). Legal Training at Watt, Tieder & Hoffar,
McLean, Virginia, USA in 1993, Traineeat Warsaw District Bar Associa-
tion of Legal Advisors. *LANGUAGES:* Polish, English, Russian. *PRAC-
TICE AREAS:* Civil Law; Trade Law.

AGNIESZKA GASIOROWSKA, born Warsaw, Poland, 1970. *Education:* Warsaw University (Master of Law, 1994). British Centre for English
Legal Studies, 1994, Trainee at Warsaw District Bar Association of Legal
Advisors. *LANGUAGES:* Polish, English. *PRACTICE AREAS:* Commercial Law; Corporate Law; Negotiable Instruments Law.

PAWEL KAMELA, born Warsaw, Poland, 1971. *Education:* Warsaw
University (Master of Law, 1994); holder of doctor's scholarship at Warsaw
University. *LANGUAGES:* Polish, English, Russian. *PRACTICE
AREAS:* Commercial Law; Corporate Law; Civil Law.

KUBIAK, LUKOWICZ, ZIELIŃSKI
SOLICITORS

Established in 1990

13 MAZOWIECKA STR.
WARSAW 00-052, POLAND
Telephone: 26-71-39; 27-33-22; 27-36-79
(International) (48) 39 12 05 46
Fax: 26-83-19
(International) (48) 39 12 05 46
Telex: 825486 besar pl

*Administrative Law, Banks and Banking, Business Law, Civil Law, Com-
mercial Law, Company Law, Contracts, Intellectual Property, Copyrights,
Trademarks, Property, Real Estate, Securities, Taxation, Privatization,
Litigation.*

*FIRM PROFILE: Kubiak, Lukowicz, Zieliński Solicitors was founded in
1990. The firm has a substantial experience in the field of privatization
and in providing legal services for major international companies establishing their business in Poland. KLZ is a member of Interlex-an international association of about 40 law firms with over 700 lawyers. KLZ cooperates with major law firms in Gdańsk, Szczecin, Lód ź, Poznań, Katowice.*

PARTNERS

MACIEJ LUKOWICZ, born Ilża, April 22, 1941; admitted, 1966, Po-
land. *Education:* Adam Mickiewicz University in Poznań (Mag.Jur., 1964).
Director: Legal Department, Ministry of Maritime Economy, 1982-1987;
Legal Department, Foreign Investment Agency, 1989-1990. Legal Advisor,
Warimex Polish Trade Companies, 1987-1989. Legal Chief Adviser, Gov-
ernment Foreign Investment Legislation in Poland, 1989-1990. Expert of
the Parliament on the Law of the Sea and Foreign Investment in Poland.
Member: Polish Association (Vice President of the Sea). *LANGUAGES:*
Polish and English. *PRACTICE AREAS:* General Commercial; Privatiza-
tion.

MACIEJ ZIELIŃSKI, born Warszawa, January 22, 1957; admitted,
1988, Poland. *Education:* Warsaw University (Mag.Jur., magna cum laude,
1979; post-graduate studies in international law). Editor, "Solicitor"
monthly of the Solicitors' Bar. Expert, Ministry of Transportation, Maritime and Commercial Law. Speaker at Legal Conferences: ECE, UNC-
TAD, IMO. Legal Expert, Ministry of Economy. Legal Advisor to the
Commercial Companies engaged in International Trade. *Member:* Solici-

(This Listing Continued)

tors' Bar. *LANGUAGES:* Polish, English, French, German and Russian.
PRACTICE AREAS: General Commercial.

JAN CIEĆWIERZ, born Czerwińsk, June 3, 1929; admitted, 1961, Po-
land. *Education:* Warsaw University (Mag.Jur., 1953). *Member:* Polish Bar
Association (Board of Directors, 1980); Supreme Barristers Disciplinary
Court (President, 1989—). *LANGUAGES:* Polish and German. *PRAC-
TICE AREAS:* Litigation.

ASSOCIATES

WALDEMAR WAWRZYNIAK, born 1927. *Education:* Warsaw Uni-
versity (Mag.Jur., 1961; Dr.Jur., 1974). Legal Advisor of the Agency for
Foreign Investment. *LANGUAGES:* Polish, English and German. *PRAC-
TICE AREAS:* General Commercial.

JAROSLAW WIECZORKIEWICZ, born 1965. 1993, Admitted as
Judge. 1994, Admitted as Solicitor. *Education:* Warsaw University (Mag.-
Jur., 1991). *LANGUAGES:* Polish, English and French. *PRACTICE
AREAS:* Litigation.

BOGDAN SĘDLAK, born 1957. *Education:* Maria Sklodowska-Curie
University of Lublin (Mag.Jur., 1981). Expert of the Maritime Economy
Office and of the Ministry of Transportation. *LANGUAGES:* Polish and
Russian. *PRACTICE AREAS:* Labour Law; Real Estate; Property.

DOROTA STRZEPEK, born 1966. *Education:* Warsaw University
(Mag.Jur., 1991). *LANGUAGES:* Polish and English. *PRACTICE
AREAS:* Litigation; Civil Law.

RAFAL CIEĆWIERZ, born 1968. *Education:* Warsaw University
(Mag.Jur., 1993). *LANGUAGES:* Polish and English. *PRACTICE
AREAS:* General Commercial.

CLAIRE DI CRESCENZO, born 1965. *Education:* Universite ASSAS,
Paris II (D.E.A., 1989); Doctorat in progress. *LANGUAGES:* French, English, Polish and German. *PRACTICE AREAS:* General Commercial; European and International Law; Contracts.

DOROTA TEMPICKA, born 1966. *Education:* Warsaw University
(Mag.Jur., 1993). *LANGUAGES:* Polish and English. *PRACTICE
AREAS:* Commercial Law; Taxation.

JOLANTA OKONIECKA, born 1967. *Education:* Warsaw University
(Mag.Jur., 1993). *LANGUAGES:* Polish and English. *PRACTICE
AREAS:* Taxation; Commercial Law.

WERONIKA PELC, born 1969. *Education:* Warsaw University (Mag.-
Jur., magna cum laude, 1994); University of Sussex (1991). *LANGUAGES:*
Polish and English. *PRACTICE AREAS:* General Commercial; Intellec-
tual Property; Trademarks.

JOANNA ROGOWSKA, born 1970. *Education:* Warsaw University
(Mag.Jur., magna cum laude, 1994). *LANGUAGES:* Polish and German.
PRACTICE AREAS: General Commercial; Contracts.

BOZENA SZCZYTOWSKA, born 1963. *Education:* Warsaw University
(Mag.Jur., 1988). *LANGUAGES:* Polish and English. *PRACTICE
AREAS:* Litigation; General Commercial.

HUBERT TUCHOLKA, born 1966. *Education:* Warsaw University
(Mag.Jur., 1990). *LANGUAGES:* Polish, English and Russian. *PRAC-
TICE AREAS:* Commercial and Civil Law.

MAGDALENA TYLIPSKA, born 1967. *Education:* University of tódź
(Mag.Jur., 1990). 1994, qualified as judge. *LANGUAGES:* Polish and English. *PRACTICE AREAS:* Litigation; Civil Law.

LATHAM & WATKINS

ST. SZPITALNA 1
SUITE 49, 9TH FLOOR
Warsaw 00-018 Poland
Telephone: +-48-2-227-9610
Telecopier: +-48-2-227-9610

Los Angeles, California Office: 633 West Fifth Street, Suite 4000, 90071.
  Telephone: 213-485-1234. Telecopier: 213-891-8763.
Costa Mesa, California Office: Suite 2000, 650 Town Center Drive,
  92626-1918. Telephone: 714-540-1235. Telecopier: 714-755-8290.
San Diego, California Office: Suite 2100, 701 B Street, 92101-8197.
  Telephone: 619-236-1234. Telecopier: 619-696-7419.
San Francisco, California Office: 505 Montgomery Street, Suite 1990,
  94111. Telephone: 415-391-0600. Fax: 415-395-8095.

(This Listing Continued)

Washington, D.C. Office: Suite 1300, 1001 Pennsylvania Avenue, N.W., 20004. Telephone: 202-637-2200. Telecopier: 202-637-2201.

Chicago, Illinois Office: Suite 5800 Sears Tower, 60606. Telephone: 312-876-7700. Telecopier: 312-993-9767.

Newark, New Jersey Office: One Newark Center, 07101-3174. Telephone: 201-639-1234. Fax: 201-639-7298.

New York, N.Y. Office: Suite 1000, 885 Third Avenue, 10022-4802. Telephone: 212-906-1200. Telecopier: 212-751-4864.

London, England Office: One Angel Court, EC2R 7HJ. Telephone: +-44-71-374 4444. Telecopier: +-44-71-374 4460.

Moscow, Russia Office: Suite C200, 113/1 Leninsky Prospeckt, 117198. Telephone: +-7 503 956-5555. Fax: +-7 503 956-5556.

Hong Kong Office: 11th Floor Central Building, Number One Pedder Street, Central Hong Kong. Telephone: 011-852-841-7779. Fax: 011-852-7749.

PARTNERS

WILLIAM A. LONG, born Cincinnati, Ohio, May 27, 1937; admitted, 1967, California; 1978, District of Columbia (Not admitted in Poland). *Education:* Xavier University (A.B., magna cum laude, 1959); University of Pennsylvania (M.B.A., 1961); Boston College (J.D., magna cum laude, 1967). Order of the Coif. Member, Board of Editors, Boston College Law Review, 1966-1967. Deputy Under Secretary of Defense (Acquisition Management), 1981-1983. *Member:* Los Angeles County, Federal and American Bar Associations; District of Columbia Bar; State Bar of California. (Also at London, England Office).

JOHN L. SACHS, born Washington, D.C., 1954; admitted, 1980, District of Columbia (Not admitted in Poland). *Education:* Yale University (B.A., magna cum laude, 1976); Harvard University (J.D., 1980). Law Clerk to Charles R. Richey, U.S. District Court, District of Columbia, 1980-1981. Member, Judicial Conference of the District of Columbia Circuit, 1987-1988, 1990-1991. *Member:* District of Columbia Bar; Federal Energy (Member, Committee on International Energy Transactions) and American (Member, Sections on: Natural Resources, Energy and Environmental Law; International Law) Bar Associations. (Also at Washington, D.C. Office).

DENNIS B. NORDSTROM, born Camp Lejeune, North Carolina, February 14, 1961; admitted, 1986, California (Not admitted in Poland). *Education:* College of William & Mary (B.B.A., 1983); Pepperdine University; University of Virginia (J.D., 1986). *Member:* State Bar of California; American Bar Association. (Also at London, England Office).

RESIDENT POLISH COUNSEL

HANNA E. NAPIERALA, born Klukowo, Ciechanow, Poland, February 29, 1960; admitted, 1989, Poland. *Education:* University of Warsaw (M.A. Law, 1983; M.A., Administration, 1983). Member, Legal Advisors Association, Warsaw.

RESIDENT STAFF ATTORNEY

MIROSLAW A. OSTRYNSKI, born Fairford, England, July 25, 1949; admitted 1987, Solicitor of the Supreme Court of England and Wales; (Not admitted in Poland). *Education:* University of London (B.A., Hons. 1st Class, 1973; M.A., 1974); College d'Europe (M.A. Public Administration, 1977); The College of Law (Law Society Finals, 1984). *Member:* Law Society of England and Wales.

(For biographical data on Los Angeles, California, Costa Mesa, California, San Diego, California, San Francisco, California, Washington, D.C., Chicago, Illinois, New York, New York, London, England, Moscow, Russia and Hong Kong personnel, see Professional Biographies at each of those cities)

McKENNA & CO SP. z o.O.

UL.KOPERNIKA 30, SUITE 213

00-950 WARSAW, POLAND

Telephone: (48) 22 26 69 88

Fax: (48) 22 26 41 93

London, England Office: Mitre House, 160 Aldersgate Street, EC1A 4DD. Telephone: 0171 606 9000. Telex: 27251. Fax: 0171-606 9100. CDE Box 724.

London Lloyd's Office: 908 Lloyd's, One Lime Street, London EC3M 7DQ. Telephone: 0171-929 1250. Fax: 0171-626 5749 DX Box 724.

Brussels, Belgium Office: Avenue de Cortenberg 66, Box 10, B-1040. Telephone: (32)(2)735.38.36. Telex: 27122. Fax: (32)(2)735.77.43.

(This Listing Continued)

Budapest, Hungary Office: H-1122. Maros utca 22, 1st Floor. Telephone: (36)(1) 202 6527; (36)(1) 202 6936; (36)(1) 201 9199; (36)(1) 156 5354. Fax: (36)(1) 156 5391.

Moscow, Russia Office: McKenna & Co, International, MosenkáPlaza, 24/27 Sadovaya-Samotyochnaya Street, Russian Federation, Moscow, 103051. Telephone: (7 501) 258 5000. Fax: (7 501)258 5100.

Prague, Czech Republic Office: Betlémský palác, First Floor, Husova 5, 110 00 Prague 1. Telephone: (42)(2) 2424 8518-22. Fax: 42(2) 2424 8524.

Warsaw, Poland Office: McKenna & Co Sp. zo.o., ul. Kopernika 30, Suite 213, 00-950, Warsaw. Telephone: (48) 22 26 69 88. Fax: (48) 22 26 41 93.

Hong Kong Office: 5th Floor, Lippo Tower, 89 Queensway, Hong Kong. Telephone: (852) 846 9100. Fax: (852) 845 3575.

Associated Firms:

Sigle Loose Schmidt-Diemitz and Partners: Stuttgart, Berlin, Leipzig, Frankfurt/Main, Chemnitz and Moscow. .

Minter Ellison: Sydney, Melbourne, Canberra, Brisbane and the Gold Coast.

Firm involved in advising in international tranactions relating to Poland, including privatisations, mergers and acquisitions, joint ventures, banking, property, insurance, information technology, pensions and establishing a business presence in Poland.

RESIDENT PARTNER

ROBERT J. WINDMILL, admitted 1964.

RESIDENT LAWYERS

JANUSZ ADAMKOWASKI

Languages: English and Polish

MILLER, CANFIELD, PADDOCK AND STONE, SP. z o.O.

A Professional Limited Liability Company

Founded in 1852 by Sidney Davy Miller

Ul. MASZALKOWSKA 82

SUITE 561

00-517 WARSAW, POLAND

Telephone: 011-482-623-6457 and 6458

Fax: 011-482-628-5400

REVISERS OF THE MICHIGAN LAW DIGEST FOR THIS DIRECTORY

Detroit, Michigan Office: 150 West Jefferson, Suite 2500, 48226-4415. Telephone: 313-963-6420. Fax: 313-496-7500. Cable Address: "Stem Detroit."

Ann Arbor, Michigan Office: 101 North Main Street, 7th Floor, 48104-1400. Telephone: 313-663-2445. Fax: 313-747-7147.

Bloomfield Hills, Michigan Office: Suite 100, Pinehurst Office Center, 1400 North Woodward, 48303-2014. Telephone: 313-645-5000. Fax: 313-645-1917.

Grand Rapids, Michigan Office: 1200 Campau Square Plaza, 99 Monroe, N.W., 49503-2639. Telephone: 616-454-8656. Fax: 616-776-6322.

Howell, Michigan Office: 121 South Barnard Street, Suite 4, 48843-2305. Telephone: 517-546-7600. Telecopier: 517-546-6974.

Kalamazoo, Michigan Office: 444 West Michigan Avenue, 49007-3752. Telephone: 616-381-7030. Fax: 616-382-0244.

Lansing, Michigan Office: One Michigan Avenue, Suite 900, 48933-1609. Telephone: 517-487-2070. Fax: 517-374-6304.

Monroe, Michigan Office: The Executive Centre, 214 East Elm Avenue, 48161-2682. Telephone: 313-243-2000. Fax: 313-243-0901.

Washington, D.C. Office: 1225 Nineteenth Street, N.W., Suite 400. 20036. Telephone: 202-429-5575; 785-0600. Fax: 202-331-1118; 785-1234.

Pensacola, Florida Office: 25 West Cedar, 32501. Telephone: 904-469-1088. Fax: 904-432-0677.

St. Petersburg, Florida Office: 100 Second Avenue S., Suite 7045, 33701. Telephone:813-982-6000. Fax: 813-892-6002.

Gdańsk, Poland Office: Suite 322, Dom Technika Building, Ul. Rajska 6, 80-850. Telephone: 011-485-831-2808. Fax: 011-485-831-4719.

Accounting Litigation, Administrative, Admiralty/Maritime, Antidumping, Antitrust, Licensing & High Technology, Appellate Practice, Banking, Bankruptcy & Reorganization, Commercial Transactions, Computer, Condemnation, Condominiums & Cooperatives, Construction Litigation, Corpo-

(This Listing Continued)

MILLER, CANFIELD, PADDOCK AND STONE, SP. Z O.O., Warsaw—Continued

rate, Domestic Relations, Education, Emerging Business, Environmental, Estate Planning & Administration, Foundations & Nonprofit Organizations, Franchising, Health Care & Hospital, Immigration, Insurance, Intellectual Property, International Law, International Trade & Customs, Labor & Employment, Libel & Slander Litigation, Litigation & Alternative Dispute Resolution, Litigation Management, Mergers & Acquisitions, Municipal & Governmental Law, Nuclear Power Plant Litigation, Oil & Gas, Pension, Profit-sharing & Employee Benefits, Product Liability Consulting & Defense, Professional Malpractice Consulting & Defense, Public Law, Real Estate Development & Investment, Securities (Corporate & Municipal), Securities Litigation, State, Municipal & Public Finance, Taxation, Tax-exempt Financing, Telecommunications, Toxic Torts Litigation, Transportation, Utilities, White Collar Criminal Defense, Zoning.

FIRM PROFILE: *Miller, Canfield, Paddock and Stone traces its history to 1852 when Sidney Davy Miller (1830-1904) opened a practice on Detroit's Jefferson Avenue. Today Miller Canfield is one of the largest law firms in Michigan with more than 250 attorneys and over 40 legal assistants. We have a growing national practice and a long-established statewide practice. Our Michigan offices are located in Ann Arbor, Bloomfield Hills, Detroit, Grand Rapids, Howell, Kalamazoo, Lansing and Monroe. We also have offices in Pensacola and St. Petersburg, Florida and in Washington, D.C. Our offices in Gdansk and Warsaw, Poland enable us to serve clients throughout Central and Eastern Europe.*

Our practice areas are organized into the following practice groups: Bankruptcy/Workout, Business Services, Employee Benefits, Environmental, Estate Planning, Federal Taxation, Health Care, Intellectual Property, International, Labor and Employment, Product Liability/Tort Litigation, Commercial Litigation, Dispute Resolution, State/Local Taxation, Public Law, Finance and Development.

We represent individuals in their personal and business concerns, trusts and estates, publicly traded companies, and many start-up, small, and medium sized businesses. Clients also include public bodies such as the state of Michigan and many of its agencies, authorities and universities, cities, counties, townships, school and community college districts, and special authorities throughout the state. We represent many nonprofit, tax-exempt institutions, such as hospitals, charitable corporations, and professional associations.

PARTNER

RICHARD A. WALAWENDER, born Hamtramck, Michigan, December 14, 1960; admitted, 1986, Michigan (Not admitted in Poland). *Education:* University of Michigan (B.A., with high distinction, 1982; J.D., 1986). John B. Angell Scholar. Contributing Editor, University of Michigan Journal of Law Reform, 1985-1986. Member, Supervisory Board Solidarity Chase D.T. Bank S.A. (Poland). Member and General Counsel, Board of Trustees, Cornerstone Schools Association. Member, Advisory Board, University of Michigan Center for Russian and E. European Studies. *Member:* Detroit, Macomb County and American (Member: International Law Section; Business Law Section; Public Law Section) Bar Associations; State Bar of Michigan (Member: International Law Section; Public Law Section); National Association of Bond Lawyers. *LANGUAGES:* Polish. *TRANSACTIONS:* Polish Solidarity Chase D.T. Bank, S.A. Joint Venture, 1990. *PRACTICE AREAS:* Finance (Public and Project Financings); International Corporate Law; Municipal Law; Governmental Law.

SENIOR ATTORNEY

WOJCIECH BABICKI, born Gdańsk, Poland, November 14, 1958; admitted, as barrister, 1988, Poland. *Education:* University of Gdańsk (Masters of Law, 1981). Member: Board of Gdańsk Chamber of Legal Advisors; Lecturer for Committee for Legal Profession Training Committee. *Member:* Polish Bar Association. *LANGUAGES:* Polish, English and Russian. *PRACTICE AREAS:* Business and Commercial Law; International Law.

LEGAL ADVISORS

ANDRZEJ W. CZOPSKI, born Pia, Poland, February 1, 1968; admitted to the Chamber of Legal Advisors, 1993, Poland. *Education:* University of Gdańsk (Master of Law, 1992). *LANGUAGES:* Polish, English and Russian. *PRACTICE AREAS:* Business and Commercial Law; International Law; Labor Law.

(This Listing Continued)

EU1130B

NABARRO NATHANSON

UL. SENATORSKA 12
00-082 WARSAW, POLAND
Telephone: 48-2-227 6144/7901/9227
Fax: 48-2-227 4838

London, England Office: 50 Stratton Street, London W1X 5FL, England. Telephone: 0171-493-9933. Telex: 8813144 NABARO G. Fax: 0171-629-7900.

Doncaster, England Office: The Lodge, South Parade, Doncaster DN1 2DQ, England. Telephone: 01302-344455. Fax: 01302-738408.

Hull, England Office: 12Marina Court, Castle Street, Hull HU1 1TJ, England. Telephone: 01482-219111. Fax: 01482-218444.

Budapest, Hungary Office: Istanhegyi ut 9/b, Budapest 1126, Hungary.

Deira, Dubai, United Arab Emirates Office: P.O. Box 13779. Telephone: (9714) 287157. Fax: (0974) 287086.

General Practice.

MEMBERS OF FIRM

MICHAEL DAVIES (Partner). *PRACTICE AREAS:* Company Law; Commercial Law.

BEATA GESSEL. LANGUAGES: Polish and English.

STEVEN SHONE (Partner). *PRACTICE AREAS:* Commercial Real Estate.

PAWEL DEBOWSKI. LANGUAGES: English, Polish and German.

AGNIESZKA DEEG

(For Personnel and Biographical Data, see Professional Biographies at London, England).

NAUMANN - TRELA - ZUCHOWICZ

Attorneys-at-Law
UL. KREDYTOWA 8-53
P.O. BOX 340
WARSAW 00-950, POLAND
Telephone: (+ 48-22) 27.22.00
Fax: (+ 48-22) 27.67.18 E-Mail: NTZ.PL @ applelink.apple.com

Business Law, Corporate, Commercial Law, Mergers and Acquisitions, Contracting Law, Joint Ventures and Foreign Investments Law, Real Property Transactions, Taxation Law, Labour Law, Civil Litigation, Insolvency, Competition Law, Administrative Law, Copyright and Intellectual Property.

FIRM PROFILE: *The firm was founded in 1990 and offers a wide range of business legal advice.*

MEMBERS OF FIRM

JERZY NAUMANN, born Bialystok, Poland, February 14, 1956; admitted, 1984, Poland. *Education:* University of Warsaw (Faculty of Law, 1979). *Member:* Warsaw Bar Association. *LANGUAGES:* Polish and English.

JACEK TRELA, born Warsaw, Poland, August 30, 1956; admitted, 1987, Poland. *Education:* University of Warsaw (Faculty of Law, 1979). Former Judge, Arbitration Court of Warsaw, 1982-1984. *Member:* Warsaw Bar Association; Warsaw Bar Council. *LANGUAGES:* Polish and English.

GRZEGORZ ZUCHOWICZ, born Warsaw, Poland, July 11, 1956; admitted, 1984, Poland. *Education:* University of Warsaw (Faculty of Law, 1979). *Member:* Warsaw Bar Association. *LANGUAGES:* Polish and Russian.

ASSOCIATES

STEFAN JAWORSKI, born Warsaw, Poland, January 20, 1962. *Education:* University of Warsaw (Faculty of Law, 1990). Warsaw Bar Trainee. *LANGUAGES:* Polish and English.

PIOTR WOJNAR, born Warsaw, Poland, January 12, 1967. *Education:* International Institute for Securities Market Development, Washington,

(This Listing Continued)

D.C. (1991); University of Warsaw (Faculty of Law, 1992). Former Member, Polish Securities Commission. Warsaw Bar Trainee. *LANGUAGES:* Polish and English.

OLE NIELSEN & PARTNERS

Law Offices Sp. z o.o.

Established in 1990

UL. LANGIEWICZA 15
PL-02-071 WARSAW, POLAND
Telephone: +48 22 25 53 81-82
Telefax: +48 22 25 03 44

Kolding, Denmark Head Office: Ole Nielsen & Partnere Advokater A/S, Jernbanegade 29, P.O. Box 830. DK-6000 Kolding. Telephone: +45-75 50 40 00. Telefax: +45-75 54 10 50.

Kiel, Germany Office: Ole Nielsen & Partner Dänische Advokaten, Eggerstedtstraße 13, D-24103 Kiel. Telephone: +49 431 97 406 17. Telefax: +49 431 97 406 30.

Vejle, Denmark Office: Ole Nielsen & Partnere Advok ater A/S. Enghavevej 11, Enghavecentret, DK-7000 Vejle. Telephone: +45 75 72 22 22. Telefax: +45 75 72 24 22.

Advice on Business Law including Company, Tax, Distribution, Agency and Licensing Contracts, Franchising, Foreign Investment, Joint Ventures, Privatization.

FIRM PROFILE: *The firm was founded in 1990 as a subsidiary of Ole Nielsen & Partnere Advokater A/S, Denmark, and is offering a full range of business legal advice. During its relatively short period of existence the firm has among other cases participated as legal advisors in one of the first five Polish privatizations. The Company employs four Polish lawyers, one sworn translator, two foreign correspondents, and one administrator.*

Members of the Board: Peter Taerø Nielsen and Susanne Simonsen, Ole Nielsen & Partnere Advokater A/S, Jernbanegade 29, DK-6000 Kolding; Jadwiga Czarnecka, Ole Nielsen & Partners Law Offices sp. z o.o., Warsaw.

MEMBERS OF FIRM

PETER TAERØ NIELSEN, born January 18, 1954; admitted, 1983, Denmark (Not admitted in Poland). *Education:* University of Aarhus (1980); University of Oslo, Norway (Maritime Law, 1979). *Member:* Danish Bar Association; International Bar Association (Member, Council of Eastern European Forum and of Business Law Section, Committee of International Construction Contracts); Danish Society for Construction and Consulting Law. (Resident, Kolding, Denmark Office). *LANGUAGES:* Scandinavian Languages, English and German. *PRACTICE AREAS:* Mergers and Acquisitions; Foreign Investment in Eastern Europe; Privatisation; Joint Ventures; Licensing; Construction Law; Project Financing; Bank Guarantees.

ASSOCIATES

ROBERT KAMIONOWSKI, born September 21, 1964; admitted, 1993, Poland. *Education:* University of Warsaw (Graduate of Law, 1988). *LANGUAGES:* Polish and English. *PRACTICE AREAS:* Company Law; Aviation Law; Commercial Law.

DARIUSZ OBREPALSKI, born May 20, 1964; admitted, 1993, Poland. *Education:* University of Warsaw (Graduate of Law, 1990); judge's exam 1992. *LANGUAGES:* Polish, English and Russian. *PRACTICE AREAS:* Business Law; Commercial Law; Taxation.

BERNARD KORONA, born June 11, 1965. *Education:* University of Warsaw (Graduate of Law, 1993). *LANGUAGES:* Polish, English and Russian.

DOROTA DABROWSKA, born June 23, 1965; admitted, 1993, as Polish Legal Advisor's Trainee. *Education:* University of Warsaw (Graduate of Law, 1990). *LANGUAGES:* Polish, English and Russian.

PHILIP SØREN THORSEN, born March 21, 1966; admitted, 1992, as Danish Advocate's Trainee (Not admitted in Poland). *Education:* International Baccalaureate, Atlantic College (1984); Copenhagen Business College Niels Brock (1985); Aarhus University (Graduate of Law, 1992). (Resident, Kolding, Denmark Office). *LANGUAGES:* Danish, English and French.

NÖRR, STIEFENHOFER & LUTZ

Established in 1993

KANCELARIA ADWOKACKA SP. Z O. O.
UL. NOWOGRODZKA 50
00950 WARSAW, POLAND
Telephone: 48-2-6216232
Telecopier: 48-2-6251976

Munich, Germany Office: Brienner Str. 28, 80333 Munich, Postfach 101121, 80085 Munich. Telephone: 49-89-280111. Telecopier: 49-89-280110.

Frankfurt/Main, Germany Office: Freiherr-vom-Stein-Straße 11, 60323 Frankfurt/Main. Telephone: 49-69-172917. Telecopier: 49-69-172916.

Berlin, Germany Office: Schlüterstraße 36, D-10629 Berlin. Telephone: 49-30-8836700. Telecopier: 49-30-8835052.

Dresden, Germany Office: Böhmertstraße 3, 01099 Dresden. Telephone: 49-351-5671188, 49-351-5671187. Telecopier: 49-351-5671186.

Prague, Czech Republic Office: Masarykovo nábřeži 30, 11000 Prague 1. Telephone: 42-2-24913396, 42-2-24913882. Telecopier: 42-2-24911836.

Budapest, Hungary Office: Becsi utca 5/I. 1-2, 1052 Budapest V. Telephone: 36-1-1174905; 36-1-1378293. Telecopier: 36-1-1184035.

Brussels, Belgium EEC Office: 106 Avenue Louise, 1050 Brussels. Telephone: 32-2-6470650. Telecopier: 32-2-6464729.

Moscow, Russia Office: Ul. Levoberezhnaya, 32. 125475. Telephone: 7-095-4585822; 7-095-4585792. Telecopier: 7-095-4585782.

General and International Practice, Privatization, Mergers and Acquisitions, Joint Ventures, Corporate Law, Commercial Law, Real Estate and Investment Law, Labor Law, Banking and Foreign Exchange Law, Intellectual Property and Trademark Law, Tax and Customs Law, Law relating to Commercial Leases, Competition and Anti-Trust Law.

PARTNERS IN CHARGE

DR. ECKART RABICH, born Berlin, Germany, March 22, 1940; admitted, 1968, Germany (Not admitted in Poland). *Education:* Universities of Berlin, Tübingen and Cologne. *Member:* German Bar Association; German Society for the Protection of Industrial Property and Copyright Law. *LANGUAGES:* German and English. *PRACTICE AREAS:* Corporate Law; Company Law; Joint Ventures.

DR. HANS-PETER ZIER, born Stuttgart, Germany, February 26, 1950; admitted, 1976, Germany (Not admitted in Poland). *Education:* Universities of Geneva, Munich and London (King's College). With Linklaters & Paines, London, 1977-1978. *Member:* International Bar Association; British-German Jurists' Association; German-American Lawyers' Association. *LANGUAGES:* German, English, French and Italian. *PRACTICE AREAS:* Commercial Law; Privatization; Mergers and Acquisitions.

ASSOCIATES

ALINA JOLANTA SZARLAK, born Munich, Germany, May 25, 1958; admitted, 1990, Germany (Not admitted in Poland). *Education:* University of Munich, Hague Academy of International Law. *LANGUAGES:* German, English, French, Polish and Russian. *PRACTICE AREAS:* Polish Law; Commercial Law; Corporate Law; Real Estate; Privatization Law.

PETER WILHELM GORZAWSKI, born Hindenburg, Poland, August 1, 1957; admitted, 1993, Germany (Not admitted in Poland). *Education:* Universities of Katowice and Cologne. Certified translator and interpreter for the Polish language. *LANGUAGES:* German, Polish, Russian, English. *PRACTICE AREAS:* Polish Law; Commercial; Corporate; Labor and Real Estate Law.

OF COUNSEL

BOHDAN OZIEMSKI, born Warsaw, Poland, 1925; admitted, 1958, Poland. *Education:* University of Warsaw. Member of the Warsaw Bar. Judge at the Warsaw Bar Professional Tribunal. *LANGUAGES:* Polish. *PRACTICE AREAS:* Civil and Real Estate Law; Law relating to commercial leases.

JERZY BIEJAT, born Warsaw, Poland, 1921; admitted, 1951, Poland. *Education:* Trade Academy, University Warsaw. Former Vice President of the Warsaw Bar and President of the Warsaw Lawyers Association. *LANGUAGES:* Polish, German, French. *PRACTICE AREAS:* Trade and Administrative Law; Intellectual Property; Competition and Antitrust Law.

German, English, French, Polish and Russian.

PÜNDER, VOLHARD, WEBER & AXSTER

UL. JASNA 1
00-013 WARSAW, POLAND
Telephone: (48) 39 12 21 41
Fax: (48)(22) 27 15 29

Frankfurt/Main, Germany Office: Mainzer Landstrasse 46, 60325 Frankfurt/Main. Telephone: (49)(69) 71 99-01. Fax: (49)(69) 71 99-4000. Telex: 414 827.

Düsseldorf, Germany Office: Cecilienallee 6, 40474 Düsseldorf. Telephone: (49)(211) 43 55-0. Fax: (49)(211) 43 55-600.

Berlin, Germany Office: Katharina-Heinroth-Ufer, 10787 Berlin. Telephone: (49)(30) 2546 5800. Fax: (49)(30) 2546 5900.

Leipzig, Germany Office: Burgplatz 7, 04109 Leipzig. Telephone: (49)(341) 21 49-0. Fax: (49)(341) 21 49-600.

Beijing, People's Republic of China Office: Suite C 603, Beijing Lufthansa Center, 50 Liangmaqiao Road, Beijing 100 016. Telephone: (86)(1) 465 15 68; (86)(1) 465 18 08; (86)(1) 465 13 45. Fax: (86)(1) 467 12 56.

Brussels, Belgium Office: Rue d'Arlon 92, 1040 Bruxelles. Telephone: (32)(2) 230 90 11. Fax: (32)(2) 231 19 55.

Budapest, Hungary Office: Endrödy Sandor utca 48, 1026 Budapest. Telephone: (36) 60 33 26 18 international; (6) 60 33 26 18 national. Fax: (36) 60 33 26 17 international; (6) 60 33 26 17 national.

Moscow, Russia Office: ul. Wolchonka, 18/2, 121 019 Moskwa. Telephone: (7)(095) 202 64 90; (7)(095) 202 65 12; (7)(543) 708 00 900 from Germany; (49)(7545) 893 42 from other countries. Fax: (7)(095) 202 65 14; (7)(543) 708 00 990 from Germany; (49)(7545) 893 43 from other countries.

New York, New York Office: 152 West 57th Street, Carnegie Hall Tower, New York, N.Y. 10019. Telephone: (1)(212) 582 28 28. Fax: (1)(212) 582 24 24.

Administrative Law; Antitrust Law; Arbitration; Auditing and Valuations; Banking, Securities and Finance; Bankruptcy; Building Law; Chinese Law; Commercial Crime; Computer Law; Construction Law; Corporate Law; EU Law; Energy Law; Environmental Law; Franchising; Industrial Property Law; Insolvency; Intellectual Property Law; International and German Business Law; Labor and Employment Law; Litigation; Media Law; Mergers and Acquisitions; Pharmaceutical Law; Privatizations; Product Law; Public Law; Real Estate; Reorganizations; Russian Law; Tax Law; Telecommunications; Unfair Trade Law.

FIRM PROFILE: Member of PÜNDER GROUP

Members:

- *BURUMA MARIS, The Hague, Rotterdam*

- *CERHA, HEMPEL & SPIEGELFELD, Wien*

- *COPPENS, VAN OMMESLAGHE, HORSMANS & FAURES, Bruxelles*

- *DE PARDIEU-LACOURTE G.I.E., Paris*

- *PÜNDER, VOLHARD, WEBER & AXSTER, Frankfurt/Main, Düsseldorf, Berlin, Leipzig*

- *STOFFEL & PARTNER, Zürich, Genève.*

Joint Offices of PÜNDER GROUP:

Beijing - Bruxelles - Budapest - Moskwa - New York - Warszawa

MEMBERS OF FIRM

DR. RAINER MASCHMEIER, born Gniesno, Poland, January 13, 1944; admitted, 1975, Düsseldorf. *Education:* Universities of Berlin, Geneva, Würzburg, Caen (France) and Münster (Dr. jur.). Lecturer, Law School of Warwick University, Coventry, U.K., 1972-1973. Author: "Die Einantwortung der Verlassenschaft nach österreichischem Recht durch deutsche Nachlaßgerichte," 1972. *Member:* Board of Düsseldorf Bar and Düsseldorf Lawyers' Association; German-Italian Association of Commerce. (Also at Düsseldorf, Germany Office). *LANGUAGES:* German, French and English. *PRACTICE AREAS:* International and German Business Law; Corporate Law; Construction Law; Real Estate; Privatizations.

DR. ROLF GIEBELER, born Bonn, Germany, July 5, 1957; admitted, 1988, Frankfurt/Main; 1990, Düsseldorf (Not admitted in Poland). *Education:* University of Bonn (Dr. jur., 1990); University of Pittsburgh; Harvard University (M.P.A., 1987). Author: "Verfahren und Maßstäbe bei der Setzung von Umweltstandards in den USA," 1990. *Member:* German Bar Association; German-American Lawyers' Association; International and Environmental Law Association. *LANGUAGES:* German, English and French. *PRACTICE AREAS:* International Business Law; Corporate Law;

(This Listing Continued)

Mergers and Acquisitions; Environmental Law; Privatizations; Investment Law.

COUNSEL

DR. KRZYSZTOF RASTAWICKI, born Pruszkow, Poland, October 26, 1957; admitted, 1988, Warsaw. *Education:* University of Warsaw (Master of Law, 1980); Polish Academy of Sciences (Dr. jur., 1989). Visiting Scholar of Canadian Bar Association, 1988. *Member:* Polish Bar Association; Polish Society of Criminal Law. *LANGUAGES:* Polish, English and Russian. *PRACTICE AREAS:* Corporate Law; Commercial Crime; Real Estate; Litigation.

ASSOCIATES

JAN F. WREDE, born Düsseldorf, Germany, December 30, 1962; admitted, 1990, New York; 1992, California; 1994, Düsseldorf (Not admitted in Poland). *Education:* Universities of Mannheim and Kiel; Indiana University School of Law, Bloomington; University of California School of Law, Los Angeles (J.D., 1990). Order of the Coif. *Member:* German Bar Association; German-American Lawyers' Association; State Bar of California. *LANGUAGES:* German and English. *PRACTICE AREAS:* International and German Business and Corporate Law; Mergers and Acquisitions; International Financing Transactions; Tax Law.

PETER DASZKOWSKI, born Gdansk, Poland, June 29, 1961; admitted, 1993, Düsseldorf (Not admitted in Poland). *Education:* Universities of Bonn and Speyer. *Member:* German Bar Association. *LANGUAGES:* German, Polish, English and Russian. *PRACTICE AREAS:* Intellectual Property Law; Commercial Law; Real Estate.

DR. WLODZIMIERZ KOZUCHOWSKI, born Sokolow Pudlaski, Poland, April 19, 1963; (Not admitted in Poland). *Education:* Free University of Berlin (1986); University of Warsaw (Master of Law, 1988); University of Trier (Master of Law, 1989; Dr. jur., 1993). Konrad Adenauer Scholar, 1991-1993. Author: "Der internationale Schadenversicherungsvertrag im EG-Binnenmarkt.". *LANGUAGES:* Polish, German, English and Russian. *PRACTICE AREAS:* Banking and Securities Law; Competition Law; Antitrust Law.

PAWEL KUGLARZ, born Krakow, Poland, October 19, 1964; (Not admitted in Poland). *Education:* Jagiellonian University, Krakow (Master of Law, 1989); University of Regensburg (Master of Law, 1988). Assistant to the Law Faculty of Jagiellonian University, 1988-1992. Post-Graduate Doctorate Scholar of German Academic Exchange Service. *LANGUAGES:* Polish, German, English and Russian. *PRACTICE AREAS:* Regulatory Law; Commercial Law.

(For complete biographical data on personnel at Frankfurt/Main, Düsseldorf, Berlin and Leipzig, Germany, Brussels, Belgium, Moscow, Russia, New York, New York, Beijing, People's Republic of China, see Professional Biographies at those locations)

SALANS HERTZFELD & HEILBRONN

UL. PODWALE 7
00-252 WARSAW, POLAND
Telephone: 48.22 31.96.88; 31.25.72; 31.29.20
Fax: 48.22 31.39.32; 31.15.65

Paris, France, Office: 9, Rue Boissy D'Anglas, 75008. Telephone: 42.68.48.00. Telex: 280990 PARILEX. Fax: 42.68.15.45; 42.68.15.46; 42.68.15.47.

New York, N.Y. Office: 750 Lexington Avenue, 10022. Telephone: 212.644.0800. Fax: 212.644.1003.

London, England Office: 103 Mount Street. W1Y-5HE. Telephone: 44.171.491.3735. Fax: 44.171.408 0843.

Moscow, Russia Office: Gazetnyi Pereulok, 17/9, (Ex. UL. Ogareva). 103009. Telephone: 7.501.940.2944. Fax: 7.501.940.2806.

St. Petersburg, Russia Office: Dom Zhurnalistov, 70 Nevskii Prospekt. 191 025. Telephone: 7.812.272.4572; 273.6844. Fax: 7.812.273.6844.

Other St. Petersburg, Russia Office: 6 Inzhenernaya Ulitsa, 191011. Telephone: 7.812.850.1504; 210.4040; 210.4447; 210.4008; 210.4032; 210.4005; 210.4348; 210.4812. Fax: 7.812.850.1505; 210.4114. Office move planned for March 15, 1995.

Kiev, Ukraine Office: Ukrainskii Dim, Vul. Kreshchatik 2 (4th Floor), 252601. Telephone: 7.044.228.5451. Fax: 7.044.228.6398.

Almaty, Kazakhstan Office: 10A Abaya Prospect, Corner "Furmanova," 11th Floor, Suite 5, 480013. Telephone: 7 3272 634 053; 634 049.

Other Almaty, Kazakhstan Office: 86 Gogol Street, 5th Floor, 480091. Office move planned for April 1, 1995.

(This Listing Continued)

MEMBERS OF FIRM

DARIUSZ OLESZCZUK, born Warsaw, Poland, July 8, 1956; qualified as a Judge, 1982; 1983, admitted as legal adviser in Poland. *Education:* Warsaw University (Master of Law, 1979). *LANGUAGES:* Polish, English, Russian. *PRACTICE AREAS:* Acquisitions; Joint Ventures; Privatizations; Corporate Finance; Project Finance; Securities; Telecommunications; Media; Commercial; Corporate.

ASSOCIATES

LUDWIK E. ALLERHAND, born England, May 4, 1949; admitted, 1981, England as Solicitor. *Education:* University of York (B.A., 1977). *LANGUAGES:* Polish and English. *PRACTICE AREAS:* Eastern European Commerce; Telecommunications; Real Estate.

TOMASZ DABROWSKI, born Warsaw, Poland, August 19, 1956. *Education:* Warsaw University (Master of Law, 1992). *LANGUAGES:* Polish and English. *PRACTICE AREAS:* Company; Commercial; Tax; Foreign Exchange; Real Estate.

PIOTR NOWACZYK, born Poznan, Poland, August 25, 1953; admitted, 1984, Poznan; 1993, Paris as Avocat; 1994, Warsaw. *Education:* University of Poznan (Master of Law, 1976). Judge, Poznan Courts, 1978-1981. *LANGUAGES:* Polish, English, German, French, Italian and Russian. *PRACTICE AREAS:* Intellectual Property; Litigation; Competition; Corporate.

AGNIESZKA STEFANOWICZ-BARANSKA, born Warsaw, Poland, August 28, 1968. *Education:* Warsaw University (Master of Law, 1993). *LANGUAGES:* Polish, English and German. *PRACTICE AREAS:* Corporate; Commercial; Intellectual Property.

RAFAL MARCIN SARBINSKI, born Warsaw, Poland, July 2, 1970. *Education:* Utrecht University (EEC Scholarship, 1993); Warsaw University (Master of Law, 1994). *LANGUAGES:* Polish and English. *PRACTICE AREAS:* Intellectual Property; Corporate Law.

ARTHUR PIERRET, born Klodzko, Poland, June 21, 1966; admitted, 1993, Paris as Avocat. *Education:* Université de Paris X (Maîtrise de Droit des Affaires, 1990; D.E.J.A. Droit Anglais et Américain, 1991); Columbia Law School (1991). *LANGUAGES:* French, English, Polish and Spanish. *PRACTICE AREAS:* Commercial Law; Company Law; International Taxation; Media; Mergers and Acquisitions.

AGNIESZKA LEWOCKA-SZCZESNIAK, born Siedlce, Poland, September 17, 1967. *Education:* Warsaw University (Master of Law, 1994); British Centre for English Legal Studies, Warsaw (1994). *LANGUAGES:* Polish and English. *PRACTICE AREAS:* International Contract Law; Franchising; EC Law; Product Liability; Civil Law; Commercial Law.

(For complete biographical data on all personnel, see Paris, France)

SCHEELE, SCHWARTZ, ZIELCKE & PARTNER

UL. ZURAWIA 47
00-680 WARSAW, POLAND
Telephone: 0048-22-6300670
Fax: 0048-22-6300670

Munich, Germany Office: Prinzregentenplatz 15, 81675. Telephone: 089/470 10 02. Fax: 089/470 10 06.

FIRM PROFILE: Scheele, Schwartz, Zielcke & Partner is an international law firm advising business clients and public institutions on all domestic and overseas corporate and commercial matters. The firm specializes in Eastern European and C.I.S. matters. Currently the firm is representing a broad range of clients in Europe, North America, South America, Asia and Africa.

(For biographical data and areas of practice see listing at Munich, Germany)

SIMÉON KARNIOL MALECKI

ALEJE JEROZOLIMSKIE 30
00024 WARSAW, POLAND
Telephone: (48) 22 27 04 64
Fax: (48) 22 27 48 08; 39 12 32 01

Affiliated Siméon & Associes Offices:
Paris, France Office: 5, Avenue Percier, 75008. Telephone: (1) 40 75 08 08. Fax: (1) 40 75 04 50.

(This Listing Continued)

Brussels, Belgium Office: Avenue de Tervuren 13, B-1040. Telephone: (2) 732 69 69. Fax: (2) 732 70 71.
Hanoi, Vietnam Office: 13 Tran Hung Dao. Telephone: (84 4) 251 588; (84 4) 244 345. Fax: (84 4) 251 514.
Ho Chi Minh Ville, Vietnam Office: IBC Centre, 1A Me Linh Square. Telephone: (84) 4 294 890. Fax: (84) 4 294 876.

Polish and International Law Practice.

RESIDENT PARTNERS

JOANNA KARNIOL, born Warsaw, Poland, November 9, 1958; admitted, 1988, Warsaw. *Education:* University of Warsaw (Maîtrise en Droit, 1981). *LANGUAGES:* Polish, French and English.

ROBERT MALECKI, born Warsaw, Poland, December 8, 1960; admitted, 1989, Warsaw. *Education:* University of Warsaw (Maîtrise en Droit, 1985). *LANGUAGES:* Polish, English, Russian and French.

Polish, French, English, German and Russian

(For Complete Biographical Data on all Personnel, see Professional Biographies at Siméon & Associés, Paris, France).

SOLTYSIŃSKI KAWECKI & SZLEZAK

Established in 1991

Legal Advisors, Sp. z o.o.

UL. KONSTRUKTORSKA 1A
02-673 WARSAW, POLAND
Telephone: (048-22) 48 66 08; (International) (48) 39 12 21 93
Fax: (048-22) 48 89 68; (International) (48) 39 12 21 94

Banking and Finance, Corporate & Securities, Commercial Law, Intellectual Property, Commercial Litigation, Customs and Foreign Exchange Regulation, Antitrust Law, Unfair Competition, Civil Law, Tax Law.

MEMBERS OF FIRM

STANISLAW J. SOLTYSIŃSKI, born Poznań, Poland, May 2, 1939; admitted, 1964, Poland. *Education:* University of Poznań Law School (J.D., 1961); Columbia University Law School (LL.M., 1973); London School of Economics (a British Council Research Student, 1966-1967). Visiting Professor, University of Pennsylvania Law School. Professor (part-time), University of Poznań Law School and College of Europe (Brugge). Legal Advisor to the Minister of Finance. *Member:* Poland's Legislative Council; Polish Academy of Art and Sciences; Practicing Law Institute and Commercial Practice; International Chamber of Commerce, Paris; International Association for Protection of Industrial Property, Zurich. *LANGUAGES:* Polish, English and German. *PRACTICE AREAS:* Commercial Law; Company Law; Intellectual Property and Antitrust Law.

ANDRZEJ W. KAWECKI, born Szczecinek, Poland, February 26, 1952; admitted, 1987, New York. *Education:* University of Poznań Law School (J.D., 1975); Institute of State and Law, Polish Academy of Sciences (S.J.D., 1981); University of Pennsylvania Law School (LL.M., 1985). Senior Fulbright Scholar, University of Pennsylvania Law School (1982-1985). Associate, Drinker Biddle & Reath, Philadelphia (1986-1991). Legal Advisor for the Minister of Privatization, Polish Securities Commission and Polish Parliament on Capital and Securities Markets. *Member:* American Bar Association. *LANGUAGES:* Polish, English, Russian and some German. *PRACTICE AREAS:* Corporate and Securities; Investment Companies; Banking and Finance.

ANDRZEJ SZLEZAK, born Poznań, Poland, July 7, 1954; admitted, 1981, Poland. *Education:* University of Poznań Law School (M.A., 1978; J.D., 1979; S.J.D., 1985; Doctor Habilitatus, 1992). Professor, University of Poznań Law School. *LANGUAGES:* Polish, English, French and Russian. *PRACTICE AREAS:* Commercial Law; Company Law; Banking and Finance.

ASSOCIATES

RUDOLF M. OSTRIHANSKY, born Wroclaw, Poland, December 6, 1958; admitted, 1984, Poland. *Education:* University of Warsaw Law School (J.D., 1981; S.J.D., 1988); Institute of Social Studies, The Hague (1985-1986); Asser College Europe International Law of Trade (Research Fellow, 1991). Assistant Professor, University of Warsaw Law School. *Member:* International Law Association (Polish Branch). *LANGUAGES:* Polish, English and Russian. *PRACTICE AREAS:* Commercial Law; Corporate; Customs and Foreign Exchange Regulations.

DARIUSZ JAN SKUZA, born Zabki, Poland, June 26, 1959; admitted, 1983, Poland. *Education:* University of Warsaw Law School (J.D., 1983).

(This Listing Continued)

SOLTYSIŃSKI KAWECKI & SZLEZAK, Warsaw—
Continued

Judge, Warsaw District Court (1983-1993). *Member:* Association of Polish Judges; Warsaw Legal Counsellor Association. *LANGUAGES:* Polish and German. *PRACTICE AREAS:* Civil Law; Commercial Litigation; Intellectual Property Law.

AURELIA NOWICKA, born Komorzewo, Poland, July 26, 1953; admitted, 1979, Poland. *Education:* University of Poznań Law School (J.D., 1976; S.J.D., 1987); The Hague Academy of International Law (1990); Max-Planck Institut für Patent, Urheber und Wettbewersrecht, Munich (1990-1991). Assistant Professor, University of Poznań Law School. *LANGUAGES:* Polish, German and English. *PRACTICE AREAS:* Commercial Law; Banking and Finance; Intellectual Property.

PRZEMYSLAW A. SZMYT, born Poznań, Poland, December 16, 1962; admitted, 1992, Poland. *Education:* University of Poznań Law School (J.D., 1987); Apprenticeship, Poznań Court of Appeals (1987-1989); Fulbright Fellow, University of California, Hastings, College of Law (1991-1992); Georgetown University (Orientation in the U.S. Legal System, 1992); Asser College of Europe (Research Student, 1991). *Member:* Poznań Legal Counsellors' Association. *LANGUAGES:* Polish, English and German. *PRACTICE AREAS:* Civil Law; Commercial Law; Private International Law; International Business Transactions.

JAROSLAW SROCZYŃSKI, born Cracow, Poland, May 15, 1957. *Education:* Academy of Economics, Cracow (M.A., 1981); the Jagiellonian University Law School, Cracow (J.D., 1990). Director, The Antimonopoly Office, Regional Office, Cracow, 1990-1994. The European Commission, Directorate-General IV Competition, Brussels, scagiaire, 1992. Cleary, Cottlieb, Steen & Hamilton, Brussels, scagiaire, 1993-1994. *LANGUAGES:* Polish, English and Russian. *PRACTICE AREAS:* Antitrust Law; Unfair Competition Law; Corporate Law; Civil Law; Commercial Transactions; Intellectual Property Law.

MALGORZATA ANTONIUK, born Warsaw, Poland, February 13, 1958; admitted, 1982, Poland. *Education:* University of Warsaw Law School (J.D., 1981). Judge, Warsaw District Court, 1984-1993. *LANGUAGES:* Polish and English. *PRACTICE AREAS:* Civil Law; Commercial Law; Commercial Litigation; Labor Law.

LECH GILICIŃSKI, born Kolo, Poland, January 3, 1968. *Education:* University of Poznań Law School (J.D., 1980; S.J.D., 1994); University of Oxford visiting scholar (1991-1992). *Member:* Oxford University Law Society. *LANGUAGES:* Polish, English, German and Russian. *PRACTICE AREAS:* Corporate, Commercial Law; Antitrust Law.

JAROSLAW BIEROŃSKI, born Świebodzin, Poland, October 3, 1964. *Education:* University of Poznań Law School (J.D., 1990). Legal and tax advisor, Ernst & Young, Warsaw, 1993. *LANGUAGES:* Polish, English and Russian. *PRACTICE AREAS:* Tax Law; Customs and Foreign Exchange Regulations; Banking Law.

ROBERT GAWALKIEWICZ, born Gniezno, Poland, January 7, 1965; admitted, 1994, Poland. *Education:* University of PoznańLaw School (J.D., 1990); Rheinische Friedrich-Wilhelms Universitat, Bonn (visiting student, 1988-1989; Master of Comparative Law, 1993). *Member:* Poznań Legal Counsellors' Association. *LANGUAGES:* Polish, German, English and Russian. *PRACTICE AREAS:* Company Law; Commercial Law; Civil Law; International Business Transactions.

EWA PODGÓRSKA, born Otwock, Poland, January 6, 1969. *Education:* University of Warsaw Law School (J.D., 1992); Amsterdam-Columbia-Leyden (Summer course in American Law, 1992); Asser College Europe (Research Fellow, 1994). Visiting Attorney, Morrison & Foerster, San Francisco Office, Summer, 1993. *LANGUAGES:* Polish, English and Russian. *PRACTICE AREAS:* Corporate Law; Commercial Law; Civil Law; Polish Constitutional Law.

JANUSZ SIEKANSKI, born Kraków, Poland, April 11, 1968. *Education:* University of Poznań Law School (J.D., 1994). *LANGUAGES:* Polish and English. *PRACTICE AREAS:* Corporate Law; Securities; Commercial Law.

OF COUNSEL

ANDRZEJ MARIA SZAJKOWSKI, born Warsaw, Poland, June 4, 1938; admitted, 1967, Poland. *Education:* University of Warsaw Law School (J.D., 1967); Silesian University Law School (J.S.D., 1974); Ecole des Hautes Etudes en Science Sociales, Paris (1978-1982); Max Planck Institut für Patent, Urheber und Wettbersrecht (1984). Co-Chairman, Foun-

(This Listing Continued)

dation for Promotion of European Law. Professor, Institute of Legal Studies, Polish Academy of Sciences. *Member:* Association International de la Protection de la Propriéte Industrielle. *LANGUAGES:* Polish, French, German and Russian. *PRACTICE AREAS:* Corporate Law; Finance and Banking; Intellectual Property; Unfair Competition.

RYSZARD SKUBISZ, born Biala Podlaska, Poland, January 11, 1950. *Education:* University of Lublin Law School (J.D., 1972; S.J.D., 1978; Doctor Habilitatus, 1988). Professor: Catholic University of Lublin; Maria Sklodowska-Curie University of Lublin. *Member:* European Community Trademark Association; Association Internationale pour la Protection de la Propriété Industrielle. *LANGUAGES:* Polish, French and German and Russian. *PRACTICE AREAS:* Intellectual Property (including Trademarks); Antitrust and Unfair Competition Law.

MACIEJ MISIEWICZ, born Warsaw, Poland, April 20, 1935; admitted, Licensed Patent Attorney. *Education:* Warsaw University of Technology (M.Sc., 1961). Director, Department of Patent Research and Examination of the Polish Patent Office (1970-1989). *Member:* Polish Association of Patent Attorneys. *LANGUAGES:* Polish and English. *PRACTICE AREAS:* Intellectual Property.

WARDYŃSKI & PARTNERS

Established in 1989

ALEJE UJAZDOWSKIE 12
00-478 WARSAW, POLAND
Telephone: (48-2) 622 04 00, (48-22) 29 24 69 Satellite: (48) 39 12 01 48
Telefax: 628 90 40; Satellite: (48) 39 12 01 52
e-mail: wardynsk @ sam. nask. com. pl

Poznań, Poland Office: ul. Ostroroga 8, 60-349. Telephone: (48-61) 688 352. Fax: (48-61) 688 344.

General Commercial Practice, including Banking and Finance, Securities, Privatization, Joint Ventures, Commercial Arbitration and Litigation, Debt Restructuring and Bankruptcy, Real Estate and Property Development, and Copyright, Industrial Property and Competition Law.

PARTNERS

TOMASZ WARDYŃSKI, born Warsaw, Poland, 1947; admitted, 1975, Poland. *Education:* University of Warsaw, Faculty of Law (1970); College of Europe, Bruges, Belgium (1973); University of Strasbourg, France, Institute des Hautes Études Européennes (1974; Faculty of Law, 1975). Visiting Scholar to the American Bar Foundation, 1985. Member, Prime Minister's Advisory Council on Privatization. Honorary Legal Adviser to Her Britannic Majesty's Ambassador in Poland. *Member:* Polish Bar Association (Chairman, Foreign Commission, 1988-1992). *LANGUAGES:* English, French, Polish and Russian. *PRACTICE AREAS:* International Banking; Project Finance; Privatization.

MICHAL LACHERT, born Warsaw, Poland, 1947; admitted, 1979, Poland. *Education:* University of Warsaw, Faculty of Law (1970). Assistant Professor, University of Warsaw, 1973-1976. Arbitrator, State Arbitration Court, Warsaw, 1977-1979. Honorary Legal Advisor to the Belgian Ambassador in Poland. *Member:* Polish Bar Association. *LANGUAGES:* English, Polish and Russian.

DR. JANUSZ ŚLEDZIŃSKI, born Warsaw, Poland, 1922; admitted, 1950, Poland. *Education:* University of Warsaw, Faculty of Law (Ph.D., 1950). Assistant Professor, University of Warsaw, 1951-1953. Legal Advisor, National Bank of Poland, 1951-1964, 1968-1972. Senior Consultant to International Bank of Economic Cooperation, Moscow, 1964-1968. Senior Legal Advisor, Bank Handlowy w Warszawie S.A., 1972-1982. *Member:* Polish Bar Association. *LANGUAGES:* English, German, Polish and Russian. *PRACTICE AREAS:* Civil Law; Commercial Law; Commercial Litigation; Civil Litigation; Debt Restructuring; Bankruptcy; Composition Proceedings.

DR. WIESLAW SZAJ, born Poznań, Poland, 1947. *Education:* University of Poznań, Faculty of Law (Ph.D., 1974). Lecturer, Higher School of Banking and Administration, 1992—. *Member:* Polish Association of Legal Advisors. *LANGUAGES:* Polish and Russian. *PRACTICE AREAS:* Banking; Civil Law; Commercial Law.

WIESLAW SZCZEPIŃSKI, born Poznań, Poland, 1946; admitted, 1976, Poland. *Education:* University of Poznań, Faculty of Law (1969). Legal Advisor, National Bank of Poland, 1972-1976. *Member:* Polish Bar Association (Secretary General, 1980-1983); Warsaw Bar Association (Deputy Dean, 1983-1992). *LANGUAGES:* English, Polish and Russian. *PRACTICE AREAS:* Real Estate; Property Development.

(This Listing Continued)

DR. ANDRZEJ WIERCINSKI, born Poznań, Poland, 1947; admitted, 1982, Poland. *Education:* University of Poznań, Faculty of Law (Ph.D., 1974). Visiting Scholar, Trinity College, Oxford, 1983. Professor, University of Poznań, 1970-1992; Corporate Department, Stephenson Harwood, London, 1990. *Member:* Polish Bar Association. *LANGUAGES:* English, Polish and Russian. *PRACTICE AREAS:* Civil Law; Securities; Privatization and Restructuring of State owned Enterprises.

WEIL, GOTSHAL & MANGES

UL SENATORSKA 12
WARSAW 00-082, POLAND
Telephone: 011-48-22-27-61-44
Telecopier: 011-48-22-27-48-38

New York, N.Y. Office: 767 Fifth Avenue. Telephone: 212-310-8000. Cable Address: "Wegoma". Telex: 424281; 423144. Telecopier: 212-310-8007.

Dallas, Texas Office: 100 Crescent Court, Suite 1300. Telephone: 214-746-7700. Fax: 214-746-7777.

Houston, Texas Office: Suite 1600, 700 Louisiana Street. Telephone: 713-546-5000. Telecopier: 713-224-9511.

Menlo Park, California Office: 2882 Sand Hill Road, Suite 280. Telephone: 415-926-6200. Telecopier: 415-854-3713.

Miami, Florida Office: Suite 2100, 701 Brickell Avenue. Telephone: 305-577-3100. Telecopier: 305-374-7159.

Washington, D.C. Office: Suite 700, 1615 L Street, N.W. Telephone: 202-682-7000. Telecopier: 202-857-0939; 857-0940. Telex: 440045.

Brussels, Belgium Office: 1 Place Madou, Box 34, 1030 Brussels. Telephone: 011-32-2-217-4003. Telecopier: 011-32-2-217-0215.

Budapest, Hungary Office: H-1065 Budapest, Revay Utca 10. Telephone: 011-361-269-1144. Fax: 011-361-269-1233.

London, England Office: 50 Stratton Street, London W1X 5FL. Telephone: 011-44-171-493-9933. Telecopier: 011-44-171-629-7900.

Prague, Czechoslovakia Office: Charles Bridge Center, Krizovnicke nam. 1, 110 00 Prague 1, Czech Republic. Telephone: 011-42-2-24-09-73-00. Telecopier: 011-42-2-24-09-73-10.

General Practice.

RESIDENT PARTNERS

WILLIAM K. SIEVERS, born Fukuoka, Japan, November 23, 1955; admitted, 1981, New York (Not admitted in Poland). *Education:* Hofstra University (B.A., cum laude, 1977); De Paul University (J.D., 1980); New York University School of Law (LL.M., Taxation, 1981). Member, De Paul Law Review, 1979-1980.

RESIDENT ATTORNEYS

AGNIESZKA DEEG-DEBROWSKA, (Not admitted in Poland). *Education:* Law Faculty of Warsaw University. *LANGUAGES:* English, Polish, conversational Italian and Russian.

TOMASZ DOBROWOLSKI, (Not admitted in Poland). *Education:* Law Faculty of the University of Warsaw, post-graduate casework; Law Faculty in Poznan on industrial property, anti-monopoly and anti-dumping laws. *LANGUAGES:* English, Polish.

BARBARA KAMINSKA, (Not admitted in Poland). *Education:* University of Warsaw's Law Faculty. Qualified as advokat and judge. Member, Council of the Warsaw Bar and International Bar Association. *LANGUAGES:* English, Polish, French and Russian.

GRAZYNA KUZMA, (Not admitted in Poland). *Education:* Law Faculty of the Adam Mickiewicz University in Poznan. *LANGUAGES:* English, Polish, German, Russian.

TADEUSZ PIATEK. *Education:* Law Faculty of the Silesian University at Katowice. *LANGUAGES:* English, Polish, Russian.

GRAZYNA POSTEPSKA, (Not admitted in Poland). *Education:* University of Warsaw's Faculty of Law. *LANGUAGES:* English, Polish.

ULRIKE RADTKE-FISCHER, (Not admitted in Poland). *Education:* Johannes-Gutenburg University. *LANGUAGES:* English, German, French.

ROMAN REWALD, born Bydgoszcz, Poland, February 6, 1953; admitted, 1983, Michigan (Not admitted in Poland). *Education:* Copernicus University, Torun, Poland (M.A., 1976; LL.M., 1978); University of Detroit (J.D., 1982).

(This Listing Continued)

PAWEL RYMARZ, Admitted as legal counsel in Poland, 1992. *Education:* University of Warsaw Faculty of Law. *LANGUAGES:* English, Polish, Russian, some French.

THOMAS J.R. STADNIK, born Amityville, New York, March 5, 1952; admitted, 1979, Louisiana, U.S. Court of Appeals, Fifth Circuit and U.S. District Court, Eastern District of Louisiana; 1981, New York and U.S. District Court, Southern and Eastern Districts of New York; 1982, U.S. Court of Appeals, Second Circuit; 1983, U.S. Court of International Trade (Not admitted in Poland). *Education:* University of Pennsylvania (B.A., 1974); The Queens College, Oxford University (B.A. in Jurisprudence, 1976; M.A., 1986); Loyola University of the South (J.D., Civil Law Division, 1979); Tulane University (M.C.L., with distinction, 1980).

MACIEJ TOMASZEWSKI. *Education:* Warsaw University (Doctor of Law). *LANGUAGES:* English, Polish, French.

(For complete biographical data on New York, New York, Dallas, Texas, Houston, Texas, Menlo Park, California, Miami, Florida, Washington, D.C., Brussels, Belgium, Budapest, Hungary, London, England and Prague, Czech Republic, see Professional Biographies at those locations)

WENGER MATHYS PLATTNER LTD.

Established in 1993

UL. NOWOGRODZKA 56/7
PL-00695 WARSAW, POLAND
Telephone: +48-2 621 2750
Telefax: +48-2 621 6753
Komertel: +48-39 12 17 96

Basel, Switzerland Office: Aeschenvorstadt 55, CH-4010. Telephone: +41-61-271 62 62. Telefax: +41-61-272 62 40.

Zürich, Switzerland Office: Mühlebachstrasse 20, CH-8024. Telephone: +41-1-261 07 70. Telefax: +41-1-261 07 88.

General Commercial and Business Practice, Corporate, Contract and Banking Law, Privatization, Mergers and Acquisitions, Tax, Customs and Foreign Exchange Law, Securities Law, Real Estate Law, Bankruptcy Law.

RESIDENT MEMBERS OF FIRM

DR. IUR. EWA BUTKIEWICZ, born 1949; admitted, 1988. *Education:* University of Wroclaw. *LANGUAGES:* Polish, English and Russian. *PRACTICE AREAS:* Corporate and Banking Law; Tax, Customs and Foreign Exchange Law.

MGR. IUR. LESZEK BERGER, born 1953; admitted, 1988. *Education:* University of Lodz. *LANGUAGES:* Polish, German, English and Russian. *PRACTICE AREAS:* Privatisation; Mergers and Acquisitions; Securities Law.

Languages: Polish, English, German and Russian

(For complete Biographical data on all Firm Personnel, see Professional Biographies at Basel and Zurich, Switzerland)

WHITE & CASE (POLAND), LTD.

UL. FOKSAL 1
00-366 WARSAW, POLAND
Telephone/Facsimile: (48-22) 26-80-53. International Telephone/Facsimile: (48-39) 12-19-06

New York, New York: Telephone: 212-819-8200. Facsimile: 212-354-8113.

Washington, D.C.: Telephone: 202-872-0013. Facsimile: 202-872-0210.

Los Angeles, California: Telephone: 213-620-7700. Facsimile: 213-687-0758; 213-617-2205.

Miami, Florida: Telephone: 305-371-2700. Facsimile: 305-358-5744.

Mexico City, Mexico: Telephone: (52-5) 207-9717. Facsimile: (52-5) 208-3628.

Tokyo, Japan: Telephone: (81-3) 3239-4300. Facsimile: (81-3) 3239-4330.

Hong Kong: Telephone: (852) 2822-8700. Facsimile: (852) 2845-9070; Grice & Co., Solicitors, Telephone: (852) 2826-0333. Facsimile: (852) 2526-7166.

Singapore, Republic of Singapore: Telephone: (65) 225-6000. Facsimile: (65) 225-6009.

Bangkok, Thailand: Pacific Legal Group Ltd., In Association With White & Case, Telephone: (662) 236-6154/7. Facsimile: (662) 237-6771.

(This Listing Continued)

WHITE & CASE (POLAND), LTD., Warsaw—Continued

Hanoi, Viet Nam: Representative Office, Telephone: (84-4) 227-575/6/7. Facsimile: (84-4) 227-297.

Bombay, India: Telephone: (91-22) 282-6300. Facsimile: (91-22) 282-6305.

London, England: Telephone: (44-171) 726-6361. Facsimile: (44-171) 726-4314; (44-171) 726-8558.

Paris, France: Telephone: (33-1) 42-60-34-05. Facsimile: (33-1) 42-60-82-46.

Brussels, Belgium: Telephone: (32-2) 647-05-89. Facsimile: (32-2) 647-16-75.

Stockholm, Sweden: Telephone: (46-8) 679-80-30. Facsimile: (46-8) 611-21-22.

Helsinki, Finland: Telephone: (358-0) 631-100. Facsimile: (358-0) 179-477.

Moscow, Russia: Telephone: (7-095) 201-9292/3/4/5. Facsimile: (7-095) 201-9284.

Budapest, Hungary: Telephone: (36-1) 269-0550; (36-1) 131-0933. Facsimile: (36-1) 269-1199.

Prague, Czech Republic: Telephone: (42-2) 2481-1796. Facsimile: (42-2) 232-5522.

Istanbul, Turkey: Telephone: (90-212) 275-68-98; (90-212) 275-75-33. Facsimile: (90-212) 275-75-43.

Ankara, Turkey: Telephone: (90-312) 446-2180. Facsimile: (90-312) 437-9677.

Jeddah, Saudi Arabia: Law Office of Hassan Mahassni, Telephone: (966-2) 651-3535. Facsimile: (966-2) 651-3636.

Riyadh, Saudi Arabia: Law Office of Hassan Mahassni, Telephone: (966-1) 476-7099. Facsimile: (966-1) 479-0110.

Almaty, Kazakhstan: Telephone: (7-3272) 50-7491/2. Facsimile: (7-3272) 61-0842.

General International Practice.

WITOLD DANILOWICZ, born Warsaw, Poland, February 24, 1954; admitted, 1985, Louisiana; 1986, Texas (Not admitted in Poland). *Education:* University of Wroclaw School of Law (M.L., 1977); Institute of Social Studies, The Hague, The Netherlands (Diploma in International Law and Development, 1985); Louisiana State University (J.D., 1985; LL.M., 1985). *Member:* American and International Bar Associations.

RESIDENT OF COUNSEL

ANDRZEJ BURZYNSKI, born Warsaw, Poland, July 17, 1940; admitted, 1990, Poland. *Education:* Foreign Service College, Warsaw (M.A., 1961); Warsaw University (M.L., 1963); Polish Academy of Science (LL.D., 1972).

WITOLD JURCEWICZ, born Wroclaw, Poland, July 16, 1956; admitted, 1987, Poland. *Education:* University of Wroclaw (M.L., 1977); Polish Academy of Sciences (LL.D., 1982).

RESIDENT COUNSEL

GRZEGORZ E. DOMANSKI, born Warsaw, Poland, November 17, 1942; admitted, 1982, Poland. *Education:* Warsaw University (LL.M., 1965; LL.D., 1971; Ph.D., 1980).

JANUSZ FISZER, born Piotrkow Trybunalski, Poland, March 17, 1957; (Not admitted in Poland). *Education:* Warsaw University (M.L., 1980; LL.D., 1986).

ALEXANDER G. FRASER, born 1960; admitted, 1988, New York (Not admitted in Poland). *Education:* Princeton University (B.A.); New York University (J.D.).

JOANNA GOMULA, born Washington, D.C., May 14, 1961; admitted, 1993, New York (Not admitted in Poland). *Education:* University of Warsaw (M.L., 1983); University of Michigan (LL.M., 1992); Polish Academy of Sciences (LL.D., 1992).

STEPHEN HARDER, born Boston, Massachusetts, May 13, 1956; admitted, 1987, New York (Not admitted in Poland). *Education:* Princeton University (B.A., 1979); Columbia University (M.B.A., 1986; J.D., 1986).

BARBARA JASNIEWSKA, born Warsaw, Poland, March 30, 1962; (Not admitted in Poland). *Education:* Warsaw University (M.L., 1986).

ANTONI TOMASZ MINKIEWICZ, born Szczecin, Poland, December 8, 1961; (Not admitted in Poland). *Education:* Warsaw University (M.L., 1987).

(This Listing Continued)

MAREK WISNIEWSKI, born Warsaw, Poland, 1963; (Not admitted in Poland). *Education:* Warsaw University (M.L., 1988).

JULITA ZIMOCH, born Gorzow, Wielkopolski, Poland, August 4, 1966; (Not admitted in Poland). *Education:* Warsaw University (M.L., 1990). *Member:* Warsaw Chamber of Legal Advisors.

(For biographical data as to other locations, see Professional Biographies at New York, New York; Washington, D.C.; Los Angeles, California; Miami, Florida; Mexico City, Mexico; Tokyo, Japan; Hong Kong; Singapore, Republic of Singapore; Bangkok, Thailand; Hanoi, Viet Nam; Bombay, India; London, England; Paris, France; Brussels, Belgium; Stockholm, Sweden; Helsinki, Finland; Moscow, Russia; Budapest, Hungary; Prague, Czech Republic; Istanbul and Ankara, Turkey; Jeddah and Riyadh, Saudi Arabia; Almaty, Kazakhstan).

PORTUGAL

LAW OFFICE OF JOÃO MAXIMIANO

Advocates

RUA CONSELHEIRO BIVAR 10, 1 DTO

8000 FARO, PORTUGAL

Telephone: (89) 803219/803220/803221

Fax: (89) 802293

Lisbon, Portugal Office: Av Antonio Augusto de Aguiar, 17, 2 Esq., 1000. Telephone: (1) 3560152/3/4. Fax: (1) 3527913.

DR. JOÃO MAXIMIANO

DR. JOSÉ CAMPOS DE CARVALHO

DR. LUIS NIZA

DRA. MARGARIDA ANTUNES

Languages: English, French, Portuguese and Spanish.

TEIXEIRA DE FREITAS & JARDIM FERNANDES

Sociedade de Advogados

RUA DO ESMERALDO, 44 - 4° ANDAR

9000 FUNCHAL (MADEIRA), PORTUGAL

Telephone: (351-91) 226950

Fax: (351-91) 230637

Lisbon, Portugal Office: Praça João do Rio, n°8 - 5° Dt°, 1000. Telephone: (351-1) 8461921; (351-1) 8461922. Fax: (351-1) 8461927.

General Corporate, Commercial and Tax Practice, Banking and Finance, International Tax Planning, Real Estate, Foreign Investment, Labor Law, Litigation and Ship Registration.

MEMBERS OF FIRM

LUIZ AUGUSTO TEIXEIRA DE FREITAS, born Rio de Janeiro, Brazil, 1962; admitted, 1986, Brazil; 1991, Portugal. *Education:* Rio de Janeiro State University (LL.B., 1986). With: Skadden, Arps, Slate, Meagher & Flom, New York, 1989; Grant, Herrmann, Schwartz & Klinger, New York, 1989-1990. *Member:* Portuguese Bar Association; Brazilian Bar Association; International Tax Planning Association; Associação Brasileira de Direito Financeiro. Contributor, Madeira Section of the ITO - International Offshore Financial Centres Manual. *LANGUAGES:* Portuguese, English and Spanish.

ROSANA MARIA FREITAS RODRIGUES JARDIM FERNANDES, born Funchal, Madeira, Portugal, 1964; admitted, 1987, Portugal. *Education:* Lisbon University School of Law (LL.B., 1987). Assistant Legal Counsel, to the Vice-President of the Madeira Regional Government, 1989-1991. *Member:* Portuguese Bar Association. *LANGUAGES:* Portuguese, English, French and Spanish.

HENRIQUE ABECASIS, ANDRESEN GUIMARÃES & ASSOCIADOS

Sociedade de Advogados
AV. MIGUEL BOMBARDA, 36-60
1000 LISBON, PORTUGAL
Telephone: (01) 793 41 40
Telefax: (01) 793 40 66/ 795 47 92

Oporto, Portugal Office: Av. da Boavista, 3523, Salas 301 and 302. Tel. (02) 61 01 751/2. Fax: (02) 61 01 755.

Brussels, Belgium Associated Office: Barents & Krans, Advocaten, Av. de la Toison D'Or, 55, Bte. 10-11, B-1050. Tel: (02) 534.97.39. Fax: (02) 534.97.40.

Vigo, Spain Associated Office: Bufete Nunez Arias, Abogados, Manuel Nunez, 2-3 Edificio Derby, 36203. Tel: (86) 22 72 04. Telex: 83716 NUAR E.

Luanda, Angola Office: Av. 4 de Fevereiro, 9 - r/c. Tel: (42) 39.55.31/39.55.80 Fax: 39 02 28.

Milan, Italy Associated Office: Avv. Giorgio Pinotti, Piazza Torre Velasca, 4, 20121. Tel: (02) 8645516. Fax: (02) 8645535.

General Practice, Corporation, Commercial, Business, Banking, Foreign Investment, Taxation, Labour and Industrial Relations, Maritime, Administrative, Civil, Trademark and Copyright and EEC Law, Civil, Commercial and Administrative Litigation before all Courts.

FIRM PROFILE: *The firm has a large experience in the rendering of professional services covering the widest range of legal matters with a special emphasis on business, commercial and company law. Clients can count on personal attention and high level legal service assured by an experienced, committed and well trained Team of Lawyers. Among the Firm's Clients there exist an important number of foreign companies and individuals, from Europe, Africa and the United States of America, the firm being able to assist those clients, prior to the establishment of their local representatives, with professional accommodation and administrative help.*

MEMBERS OF FIRM

HENRIQUE ABECASIS, born Lisbon, 1951; admitted, 1975, Portugal. *Education:* University of Lisbon. Assistant Professor, International Private Law and Labour Law, University of Lisbon (1974, 1975), Consultant to the Minister of Agriculture (1977). *Member:* Portuguese Bar Association. *LANGUAGES:* Portuguese, English, French and Spanish.

ANTÓNIO ANDRESEN GUIMARÃES, born Lisbon, 1953; admitted, 1980, Portugal. *Education:* University of Lisbon. *Member:* Portuguese Bar Association. *LANGUAGES:* Portuguese, English, French and Spanish. *PRACTICE AREAS:* General Practice; Foreign Investment; Commercial; Civil; Maritime; Real Estate; Energy; Litigation.

TIAGO FERREIRA DE LIMA, born Lisbon, 1960; admitted, 1988, Portugal. *Education:* Catholic University of Lisbon (Law Degree; Postgraduation in EEC Law). Stage at the European Community, Brussels. *Member:* Portuguese Bar Association. *LANGUAGES:* Portuguese, English, French and Spanish.

RITA DELGADO VAZ PINTO, born Lisbon, 1963; admitted, 1988, Portugal. *Education:* Catholic University of Lisbon (Law Degree). *Member:* Portuguese Bar Association. *LANGUAGES:* Portuguese, English, French and Spanish. *PRACTICE AREAS:* Corporation; Banking; Civil Law.

GONÇALO ROQUETTE, born Lisbon, 1964; admitted, 1991, Portugal. *Education:* Universidade Autónoma de Lisboa. *Member:* Portuguese Bar Association. *LANGUAGES:* Portuguese, French, English and Spanish.

PEDRO GUERRA, born Luanda, Angola, 1957; admitted, 1991, Portugal. *Education:* University of Lisbon (Law Degree). *Member:* Portuguese Bar Association. *LANGUAGES:* Portuguese, French and English.

MARIA DO ROSARIO GOMES FERREIRA, born Cascais, 1933; admitted, 1992, Portugal. *Education:* Technical University of Lisbon (Politics and Social Studies); University of Lisbon (Law Degree). *Member:* Portuguese Bar Association. *LANGUAGES:* Portuguese, French and English.

ELISABETTA BORTONE, born Milano, Italy, 1960; admitted, 1989, Milano. *Education:* Catholic University of Milano, Italy (Law Degree; Postgraduation in EEC Law). Stage at the European Community, Brussels. *Member:* Milano Bar Association. *LANGUAGES:* Italian, French, Portuguese and English.

(This Listing Continued)

ANTÓNIO CALHEIROS FERRAZ, born Porto, 1961; admitted, 1990, Portugal. *Education:* Universidade Autónoma de Lisboa (Law Degree). *LANGUAGES:* Portuguese, French, English and Spanish.

RUI SACADURA CABRAL, born London, 1967; admitted, 1994, Portugal. *Education:* Catholic University of Lisbon (Law Degree). *Member:* Portuguese Bar Association. *LANGUAGES:* Portuguese, French, English, German and Spanish. *PRACTICE AREAS:* Commercial Law; Contracts.

MAFALDA OLIVEIRA MONTEIRO, born Lisbon, 1969; admitted, 1994, (Not admitted in Portugal). *Education:* Catholic University of Lisbon (Law Degree). *LANGUAGES:* Portuguese, French and English.

LUÍS TEIXEIRA DE MELO, born Porto, 1962; admitted, 1994. *Education:* Universidade Portucalense. *Member:* Portuguese Bar Association. *LANGUAGES:* Portuguese, French and English.

ABREU, CARDIGOS & PARTNERS

RUA MARQUÊS DE SÁ DA BANDEIRA 8, R/C
1000 LISBON, PORTUGAL
Telephone: (351 1) 353 2555
Telefax: (351 1) 353 6347

Banking and Finance, Local and International Taxation and Tax Planning, European Union Law, Mergers and Acquisitions, Real Estate and Environmental Law, General Civil and Commercial Practice, Insurance Law, Competition and Anti-Trust, Foreign Investment and Corporate Law, Local and EEC Litigation.

FIRM PROFILE: *Abreu, Cardigos & Partners is a firm providing legal services particularly addressed to corporate entities which require a wide range of complementary services and specialized assistance in particular fields of law. The firm also offers the services of the Accountancy Firm of Base Cont Lda. which is an officially recognized accountancy firm in good standing with the Portuguese Chartered Accountants Association.*

The firm was incorporated in April 1993 by four Lisbon attorneys with a valuable experience in international law firms. Their professional legal background together with their corresponding expertise was the ground on which the firm was established and allowed it to quickly become known and accepted in four major areas of law: Banking and Finance, Taxation and Tax Planning, European Union Law and Mergers and Acquisitions. The firm's client base includes multinational corporations, international banks and some well known international law firms.

PARTNERS

MIGUEL TEIXEIRA DE ABREU, born Lisbon, Portugal, July 30, 1959; admitted, 1987, Lisbon. *Education:* Universidade Clássica de Lisboa, Faculdade de Direito (Bachelor in Laws); University of London, London School of Economics and Political Science (LL.M., International Business Law). Associate Attorney and Tax Counsel, A.M. Pereira, L. Saragga Leal, Oliveira Martins, Júdice, Torres e Associados, Lisbon, 1989-1991. Associate Attorney, Grupo Legal Português (Simmons & Simmons, J. & A. Garrigues e Pinheiro Neto) Lisbon, 1992. Several works published in the International Tax Planning area. Lecturer, professional training courses and seminars, Tax Law and related areas. Assistant Professor, Tax Law and Public Finances, Faculdade de Direito da Universidade Clássica de Lisboa, 1988—. *Member:* Portuguese Bar Association. *LANGUAGES:* Portuguese, English and Spanish (fluently), French (oral understanding and reading) and German (notions). *PRACTICE AREAS:* International and Local Tax Law; Mergers and Acquisitions; Financing Contracts.

PEDRO CARDIGOS DOS REIS, born Lisbon, Portugal, June 6, 1964; admitted, 1987, Lisbon and São Paulo, Brazil. *Education:* Universidade Católica Portuguesa, Faculdade de Ciências Humanas (Bachelor in Laws); Universidade de São Paulo, Brasil (Pos-Graduate Studies in International Law); ITT - Chicago Kent School of Law (LL.M., American Legal Studies). Associate Attorney: Stroeter, Trench, Veirano e Advogados - today, Trench, Rossi, Watanabe e Advogados - (Baker & McKenzie - São Paulo office) in Brazil, 1987-1989; Baker & McKenzie (Chicago office) 1989-1990; F. Castelo Branco, Nobre Guedes & Associados, Lisbon, 1990-1991. Senior Associate Attorney, Veiga Gomes, Bessa Monteiro, Marques Bom e Associados, 1992. *Member:* Portuguese and Brazilian Bar Associations. *LANGUAGES:* Portuguese, English and French (fluently), Spanish (oral understanding and reading) and German (notions). *PRACTICE AREAS:* Banking Law; Finance Law; International Contracts; Foreign Investment Law.

ANTÓNIO ESTEVES DA FONSECA, born Lisbon, Portugal, May 22, 1959; admitted, 1983, Lisbon. *Education:* Universidade Católica Portuguesa, Faculdade de Ciências Humanas (Bachelor in Laws). Attorney

(This Listing Continued)

ABREU, CARDIGOS & PARTNERS, Lisbon—Continued

with own practice, Lisbon, 1983-1988 and 1991-1993. Tax Counsel, Coopers & Lybrand, 1988-1991. Lecturer, several professional training courses and seminars, Tax Law and related areas. *Member:* Portuguese Bar Association. *LANGUAGES:* Portuguese, English and Spanish (fluently), French (oral understanding and reading) and German (notions). *PRACTICE AREAS:* Real Estate Law; Environmental Law; Company Law; Tax Law; Tax Litigation.

JOÃO PAULO TEIXEIRA DE MATOS, born Lisbon, Portugal, July 14, 1962; admitted, 1985, Lisbon. *Education:* Universidade Católica Portuguesa, Faculdade de Ciências Humanas (Bachelor in Laws); Universidade Católica Portuguesa Pos-Graduate Studies on EEC Law (LL.M., European Community Studies, 1987). Associate Attorney: Assis de Almeida e Associados, Lisbon office, 1985-1988. Founding Partner, F. Castelo Branco, Nobre Guedes e Associados, Lisbon, 1989-1991. Associated to Grupo Legal Português (Simmons & Simmons, J. & A. Garrigues and Pinheiro Neto) in Lisbon, 1991-1992; Simmons & Simmons e J. & A. Garrigues (Brussels) 1992. *Member:* Portuguese Bar Association. *LANGUAGES:* Portuguese, English and French (fluently), Spanish (oral understanding and reading) and German (notions). *PRACTICE AREAS:* European Union Law; Competition Law; Anti-Trust Law; European Union Litigation; Civil Litigation.

OF COUNSEL

ARTUR REIS E SOUSA, born October 7, 1934; admitted, 1963, Portugal. *Education:* Universidade Clássica de Lisboa, Faculdade de Direito (Bachelor in Laws). Fellow: Salzburg Seminar, 1974 and 1981; International Advisory Council of the Salzburg Seminar, 1985—. Deputy District Attorney, 1958-1962. *Member:* Portuguese Bar Association. *LANGUAGES:* Portuguese, English, French, Italian (fluently) and German (understanding). *PRACTICE AREAS:* General Counselling; International and Multinational Representation.

FÁTIMA COELHO, born Lisbon, Portugal, January 19, 1967; admitted, 1989, Lisbon. *Education:* Universidade Católica Portuguesa, Faculdade de Ciências Humanas (Bachelor in Laws); Universidade Católica Portuguesa (Pos-Graduate Studies on EEC Law); King's College of London - LSE (LL.M., International Business Law). Associate Attorney, A.M. Pereira, L. Saragga Leal, Oliveira Martins, Júdice, Torres e Associados, Lisbon, 1989-1991. Attorney-at-Law: Stephenson Harwood (London) 1992. *Member:* Portuguese Bar Association; AIJA. *LANGUAGES:* Portuguese, English and French (fluently), Spanish and Italian (oral understanding and reading) German and Russian (notions). *PRACTICE AREAS:* Banking Law; Finance Law; Capital Markets.

ALEXANDRE BOBONE, Official Patent and Trademark Agent. *PRACTICE AREAS:* Industrial Property.

ASSOCIATES

CARLOS NANDE FILIPE, born Lisbon, Portugal, July 24, 1963; admitted, 1990, Lisbon. *Education:* Universidade Autónoma de Lisboa (Bachelor in Laws). Tax Counsel, Arthur Andersen & Co., 1988-1991. Associate Attorney, Grupo Legal Portuguêse (Simmons & Simmons, J. & A. Garrigues e Pinheiro Neto), Lisbon, 1991-1993. *Member:* Portuguese Bar Association. *LANGUAGES:* Portuguese and Spanish (fluently) English and French (oral understanding and reading). *PRACTICE AREAS:* Litigation.

MARGARIDA RODA SANTOS, born Lisbon, Portugal, July 16, 1968; admitted, 1993, Lisbon. *Education:* Universidade Clássica de Lisboa, Faculdade de Direito (Bachelor in Laws; Post Graduate Studies, European Union Law). *Member:* Portuguese Bar Association. *LANGUAGES:* Portuguese, English (fluently) and German (written and oral understanding).

TRAINEES

Manuel Andrade Neves; Benedita Faria de Carvalho; Vanda do Carmo Rodrigues; Altino Silva Pinto; João Duarte Sousa.

Languages: Portuguese, English, French and German

ABREU & MARQUES E ASSOCIADOS
SOCIEDADE DE ADVOGADOS

Established in 1980

RUA AUGUSTO DOS SANTOS, 2-4°
S. SEBASTIÃO PEDREIRA
1000 LISBON, PORTUGAL
Telephone: (351-1) 3528268
Fax: 527491

London, England Office: Suite C4, City Cloisters, 188-196 Old Street, EC1V 8BP. Telephone: 0171-4904656/9656. Telex: 918573 LEGIS P. Fax: 0171-4904417.

Funchal, Madeira Office: Rua da Carreira, 138, Caixa Postal 57, 9001. Telephone: 091-20697. Fax: 091-22029.

Corporate, Mergers and Acquisitions, Banking and Investment Law, Foreign Investment, Property Inheritance, Maritime, Energy Law, Copyright Arbitration, Administrative Law, Litigation, EC and Competition, Environmental, Tax.

FIRM PROFILE: Abreu & Marques was one of the first three law firms in Portugal. In fact, a law permitting the incorporation and operation of law firms was only introduced in that year. Before that, Dr. Jorge de Abreu and Dr. Paulo Lowndes Marques had already been working together under a private partnership agreement since 1972. The firm deals mainly with Foreign Investment, Commercial and Banking Law as well as Corporate, Real Estate, Mining, Oil, Energy and Maritime Law.

MEMBERS OF FIRM

JORGE DE ABREU, born 1946; admitted, 1970, Portugal. *Education:* Lisbon University (1968); International Faculty of Comparative Law in Strasbourg (Graduated Comparative Law). *Member:* Portuguese (Member, District Council, 1986) and International Bar Associations; Law Society of England (Overseas Member); International and Comparative Law Center, Dallas, USA (Member, Advisory Board); International Association of Petroleum Negotiators, Kitty, Texas, USA. *LANGUAGES:* Portuguese, English, French and Spanish. *PRACTICE AREAS:* Banking Law; Mergers and Acquisitions; Investment Funds; Intellectual Property Law; Maritime Law; Madeira Free Trade Zone; Property Law.

PAULO LOWNDES MARQUES, born 1941; admitted, 1971, Portugal. *Education:* Lisbon University (1965). Author: "The Law of Foreigners," Abreu E Marques, 1986. Legal Advisor to Plessey Telecommunications Limited, 1975-1980. Secretary of State for Foreign Affairs, 1982-1983. *Member:* Portuguese and International Bar Associations; Law Society of England (Overseas Member). *LANGUAGES:* Portuguese, English, French and Spanish. *PRACTICE AREAS:* Corporate Law; Property Law; Competition Law; Banking Law; Mergers and Acquisitions.

MARIA ISABEL DE ANDRADE E SILVA, born 1943; admitted, 1969, Portugal. *Education:* Lisbon University (1967). Legal Advisor to Ministry of Tourism. *Member:* Portuguese Bar Association. *LANGUAGES:* Portuguese, English, French and Spanish. *PRACTICE AREAS:* Property Law; Planning Law.

LUIS BRANCO, born 1958; admitted, 1984, Portugal. *Education:* Catholic University, Lisbon (Graduate in Law; Master in Law). Author: "Current account-structure, nature and statute". Co-author: with Prof. Augusto de Athayde, "Banking Law, Vol. 1. Assistant Professor of Law, Catholic University, Lisbon, 1982. *Member:* Portuguese and International Bar Association. *LANGUAGES:* Portuguese, English, French and Spanish. *PRACTICE AREAS:* Foreign Investment; Taxation; Banking.

DUARTE GARIN, born 1959; admitted, 1985, Portugal. *Education:* Lisbon University (1983). *Member:* Portuguese and International Bar Association. *LANGUAGES:* Portuguese, English, French and Spanish. *PRACTICE AREAS:* Corporate Law; Property Law.

ASSOCIATES

MARIA JOSE DE LENCASTRE, born 1960; admitted, 1988, Portugal. *Education:* Catholic University of Lisbon (1986), EEC Law Course. *Member:* Portuguese Bar Association. *LANGUAGES:* Portuguese, English, French and Spanish. *PRACTICE AREAS:* Foreign Investment Law; Corporate Law; Property Law.

AFONSO BARROSO, born 1963; admitted, 1989, Portugal. *Education:* University of Washington, U.S.A.; Lisbon University (1987). *Member:* Portuguese Bar Association. *LANGUAGES:* Portuguese, English, French and Spanish. *PRACTICE AREAS:* Madeira Free Trade Zone; Corporate Law; Securities.

(This Listing Continued)

TIAGO PITTA E CUNHA, born 1967; admitted, 1992, Portugal. *Education:* Catholic University of Lisbon (Law Degree, 1990). Assistant Professor, Catholic University of Lisbon. *Member:* Portuguese Bar Association. *LANGUAGES:* Portuguese, English, French and Spanish.

AUGUSTO DE ATHAYDE, born 1965; admitted, 1993, Portugal. *Education:* Catholic University of Lisbon (Law Degree, 1990). London Chamber of Commerce and Industry Diplom. *Member:* International Young Lawyers Association (A.I.J.A.). *LANGUAGES:* Portuguese, English, French and Spanish.

ANA MÊGRE PIRES, born 1966; admitted, 1993, Portugal. *Education:* Lusiada University (1991). Legal Advisor of Terrazul, SGPS, SA, 1992. *LANGUAGES:* Portuguese, English, French and Spanish.

FRANSCISCA PERRY VIDAL, born 1965; admitted, 1993, Portugal. *Education:* Catholic University of Lisbon. *LANGUAGES:* Portuguese, English, French and Spanish.

RITA FERREIRA VICENTE, born 1969; Portugal. *Education:* Catholic University of Lisbon (1992). *LANGUAGES:* Portuguese, English, French, Spanish and German.

REPRESENTATIVE CLIENTS: Commission of the European Communities; Bankers Trust; Banque Nationale de Paris (Paris and Lisbon); Barclays Bank Plc (London and Lisbon); Lloyds Bank Plc (London); Finanskandic International S.A.; Banque Canadienne Nationale (Europe); Grindlay's Bank (London); Eksportfinans (Oslo); Den Norske Bank (Oslo); Security Pacific Bank (Madrid); Wells Fargo Bank (Madrid); Cooperative Rabobank (Holland); Societe Generale (Lisbon); ABN-AMRO (Lisbon); Union des Banques Suisses (Zurich); Nordbanken (Luxembourg); Banco Internacional de Credito, S.A. (Lisbon); Midland Montagu (London); J.P. Morgan (London and Geneva); Merrill Lynch (U.K.).
REFERENCES: Julian How, Clifford Chance, London; Audrey Horton, Bootle Hatfield & Co.; Richard Spinogatti, Shea & Gould; Stanley Temko, Covington & Burling; Colin Gravenor, Gravenor Keenan; Guy Sancerres, Banque Nationale de Paris; Peter Harris, Linklaters and Paines; Ernest Podesta, Barclays Bank PLC; David Read; Lloyds Bank PLC.

ALBUQUERQUE & ASSOCIATES

Established in 1961

AVENIDA ANTÓNIO AUGUSTO DE AGUIAR, 126 - 4°

1000 LISBON, PORTUGAL

Telephone: 3525471
Telefax: (351.1) 521156 - 353 55 21

General and International Law Practice, Banking, Corporation, Taxation, EEC, Maritime, Aviation, Insurance, Foreign Investment, Trademark and Copyright, Labor, Commercial, Civil, Administrative, Property, Criminal, Public, Private, European and Administrative Law.

FIRM PROFILE: The firm is one of the oldest and of more tradition in Portugal. The origin of it's practice is situated in 1922 when the predecessor individual lawyers started their legal activity. The two Senior Partners are Senior Professors of Law (Catedráticos). The firm concentrates on business law, in all its main areas, from commercial contracts to finance, banking, insurance, etc. and has a broad range of clients among the largest companies worldwide, as well as some of the most important Portuguese Groups.

MEMBERS OF FIRM

PROF. DR. RUY DE ALBUQUERQUE, born Lisbon, Portugal, October 7, 1933; admitted, 1959, Lisbon; 1968, Portuguese Supreme Court. *Education:* Faculty of Law, Lisbon (Graduate in Law; Post Graduate, Ph.D. in Law). Recipient, Scholarship of the Institute of High Culture, University of Rome, 1962. Lawyer of the Treasury, 1960-1968. Director, Bank Association, 1964-1972. Executive Vice-President, S.T.A.R. Representative, American Express, 1968-1974. Senator, Lisbon University, 1988. Author: "Critical Appreciation of L.L. Fuller and W.R. Pardue the Reliance Interest in Contract Damages," C.T.F., No° 49, Reprisals, Vol. I and II, 1972; "The Brazilian Bank System," 1978; "Habitation of Employees," 1982; "Bank's Credits Set-Off," 1986. Co-Author: "Commercial Law," with Dr. António Braz Teixeira, 1957; "Procedural Law," with Dr. António Braz Teixeira, 1958; "Legal History," with Prof. Dr. Martim de Albuquerque, 8th Edition, 1992; "Responsibility of Managers for Unpaid Tax," with Prof. Menezes Cordeiro, 1986; "Conversion in Bankruptcy of Measures of Execution," with Dr. Prazeres Beleza, 1986; "De Re Philosophica. A Lawyer," 1989; "Critical Appreciation on Santos Justo," - Fictions in Roman Law, 1989; "Law of State, Law of Jurists," 1989. Professor: Law, University of Lisbon, 1961—; Law, International University, 1985. Member: Superior Council of the Social Welfare System, 1959-1960; Governmental Commission for the Creation of the Sidesurgical Industry, 1960; Governmental Commission for the Regula-

(This Listing Continued)

tion of the Aluminium Industry, 1960; Fiscal Board, Banco de Crédito Comercial e Industrial, 1970-1974; Bank Borges & Irmão, Executive Member of the Board, 1970-1974; Fiscal Board of Angol, Associated of Gulf Oil Company, 1970-1974. *Member:* Portuguese Bar Association (O.A.); Brazilian Institute of Solicitors and Barristers (I.A.B.); Association Juridique Henri Capitan; Portuguese Fiscal Association; Portuguese and Brazilian Comparative Jurisprudence Association; International Fiscal Association; Portuguese Association of European Law. *LANGUAGES:* English, French, Spanish, Italian and Portuguese. *PRACTICE AREAS:* Banking Law; Private International Law; Arbitration Law; Maritime Law.

PROF. DR. MARTIM DE ALBUQUERQUE, born S. Domingos de Rana, Portugal, August 18, 1936; admitted, 1968, Portugal and Portuguese Supreme Court. *Education:* Faculty of Law, Lisbon and Complutense de Madrid (Graduate in Law; Post-Graduate, Ph.D.). General Secretary and Legal Advisor, P.L.T., ITT Associated, 1969-1975. Author: "Error Facti and Error Juris in Criminal Law," 1968; "Collection of Treaties and Public International Acts Relating Portugal," 1986; "Enforcement of Judgements in Portuguese Law," 1986; "Equality - Introduction to Jurisprudence," Lisbon, 1993. Co-Author: "Commercial Law," with Prof. Alberto Xavier, 1964; "Legal History," with Prof. Ruy de Albuquerque, 8th Edition, 1992; "Products Liability," Portugal, International Manual of Practice, London - N.Y., I.S.C.S., 1966-1973. Visiting Professor, Lourenço Marques University, 1972. Professor: Law, University of Lisbon, 1977—; Law, International University, 1985—. Member: Commission of Publication of Treaties and Public International Acts Relating Portugal, A.C.P., 1967; Occidental Petroleum Corporation of Portugal, Chairman, 1974-1986. *Member:* Portuguese Bar Association (O.A.); Portuguese Academy of Sciences (Member, Law Section); Association Juridique Henri Capitan; Portuguese and Brazilian Comparative Jurisprudence Association. *LANGUAGES:* English, French, Spanish, Italian and Portuguese. *PRACTICE AREAS:* Fundamental Rights and Freedoms; Commercial Law; Arbitration Law; Criminal Law.

ALEXANDRE DE ALBUQUERQUE, born Lisbon, Portugal, June 8, 1960; admitted, 1985, Portugal. *Education:* Fribourg (Switzerland), Madrid, Cambridge and Lisbon; U.C.P. (Graduate in Law); Post-Graduation in Administration Law. Author: "Silence of the Public Administration," Lisbon, 1990; "Judicial Implication of the Inactivity of Public Administration Tacit Behavour," in *Public Administrative* Dictionary, 1992. Assistant Professor: Law, University of Lisbon, 1985—; Law, Universidade Lusíada, 1986-1987; of UCP; Advisor, Presidency of the Council of Ministers. *Member:* Portuguese Bar Association; The Offshore Institute. *LANGUAGES:* English, French, Spanish, Italian and Portuguese. *PRACTICE AREAS:* Administrative Law; Environmental Law; Urbanism.

PEDRO DE ALBUQUERQUE, born Lisbon, Portugal, December 9, 1962; admitted, 1987, Portugal. *Education:* Fribourg (Switzerland), Madrid, Cambridge and Lisbon; U.C.P. (Graduate in Law; Post-Graduate in Commercial and Corporate Law). Assistant Professor, Law, University of Lisbon, 1988—. Author: "Contracts in Family Law," 1986; "Bankruptcy by Ceasement of Payments", 1989; "Delay of Prescription in Contractual Liability," 1989; "The Portuguese Law of Competition (on the Decree Law 482/83)," 1989; "Essential Effects of Purchase and Sale" (in the collective work "Law of Obligations," Volume III, by Prof. Doctor Menezes Cordeiro), 2ª Ed., 1990. "The Preemptive Right of Shareholders to Subscribe to New Shares," 1993. Co-Author: "Attacking Foreign Assets (Portuguese Chapter)" by Dennis Campbell, Associated Press of London, 1993; "Code of the Special Proceeding of the Recovering of Companies and Bankruptcy," with Professor Teixeira de Sousa, 1993. *Member:* Portuguese Bar Association; The Association of Fellows and Legal Scholars of the Center for International Legal Studies, Salzburg, Austria (Honorary Member). *LANGUAGES:* English, Spanish, French, Italian and Portuguese. *PRACTICE AREAS:* Commercial Law; Corporate Law; Civil Law; Privatizations.

ANTÓNIO DE MENDONÇA RAIMUNDO, born Oporto, Portugal, June 10, 1963; admitted, 1987, Portugal. *Education:* University of Toulouse Le Mirail, France (Diplome Superieur d'Études Françaises); U.C.P. Lisbon (Graduate in Law). Portuguese Correspondent, World Tax Report, Financial Times Business Enterprises Ltd. Author: "Leasing Law in the EEC (Portugal)," Euromoney Books, 1990, 2nd Edition, 1993; "Protecting the Lessor under Portuguese Leasing Law and Practice," Euromoney Conferences, Brussels, 1990; "Contracts of Agency and Distribution," Chamber of Trade and Industry of Valencia, Spain, 1990. Co-Author: "International Execution Against Judgement Debtors," Sweet & Maxwell, London, 1993. *Member:* Portuguese Bar Association; Young Lawyers International Association; Association of Fellows and Legal Scholars of the Center for International Legal Studies, Salzburg, Austria (Honorary Member). *LANGUAGES:* Portuguese, English, French, Spanish and German. *PRACTICE*

(This Listing Continued)

ALBUQUERQUE & ASSOCIATES, Lisbon—Continued

AREAS: Commercial Law; Commercial Contract Law; Taxation Law; Taxation Planning; Corporate Law.

ANTÓNIO DE MACEDO VITORINO, born Lisbon, Portugal, March 18, 1967; admitted, 1991, Portugal. *Education:* Madrid, Lisbon; University of Lisbon (Graduate in Law, Master and Post-Graduate in Contract and Copyright Law). Author: "Pre-Marital Conventions," 1989; "Probability and Evidence - a Procedural Law Study," 1990; "Essay on the Nature of Copyright," 1991; "Copyright Contractual Law," 1994. Assistant Professor, Law, University of Lisbon. *Member:* Portuguese Bar Association. **LANGUAGES:** English, French, Spanish, Italian, German and Portuguese. **PRACTICE AREAS:** Civil Law; Commercial Law; Corporate Law; Copyright Law; Contract Law.

MARGARIDA VINAGRE, born Oliveira de Azemeis, Portugal, January 25, 1964; admitted, 1990, Portugal. *Education:* Universidade Lusíada (1987). **LANGUAGES:** Portuguese, English, Spanish and French. **PRACTICE AREAS:** Commercial Law; Insurance Law; Privatizations.

PAULO CORDEIRO DE SOUSA, born Lisbon, Portugal, June 20, 1966; admitted, 1994, Portugal. *Education:* University of Lisbon (Graduate in Law, 1992); Post-Graduate in Taxation Law. *Member:* Portuguese Bar Association; Portuguese Tax Association. **LANGUAGES:** Portuguese, German, English and French. **PRACTICE AREAS:** Taxation Law; Corporate Law; Finance.

LUÍSA JARDIM GONÇALVES, born Luanda, Angola, October 1963; admitted, 1986, Portugal. *Education:* Montealto (Madrid) and Instituto Español en Lisboa (Graduate in Law, 1986; Post-Graduate, EC Studies by UCP, 1987). Trainee, EC Commission, Tax Division, 1989. Legal Counsel, Studies Department, International Insurance Company, 1987—. Adjunct, Secretary of State for European Affairs, 1990-1993. **LANGUAGES:** Spanish, French and English. **PRACTICE AREAS:** EEC Law.

MÓNICA POMBEIRO, born Lisbon, Portugal, January 3, 1969; admitted, 1992, Portugal. *Education:* F.D.L. (Universidade Clássica, Graduate in Law). **LANGUAGES:** Portuguese, Spanish and English. **PRACTICE AREAS:** Commercial Law; Labour Law.

ANA DA SILVEIRA, born Lisbon, Portugal, January 19, 1969; admitted, 1992, Portugal. *Education:* F.D.L. (Universidade Clássica, Graduate in Law). **LANGUAGES:** Portuguese, English and Spanish. **PRACTICE AREAS:** Commercial Law; Taxation Law.

SUSANA AVELINO, born Lisbon, Portugal, December 25, 1969; admitted, 1993, Portugal. *Education:* F.D.L. (Universidade Clássica, Graduate in Law). **LANGUAGES:** Portuguese, English, German, Spanish and French. **PRACTICE AREAS:** Commercial Law; Environment Law.

MIGUEL ALCOBIA, born Lisbon, Portugal, June 8, 1969; admitted, 1993, Portugal. *Education:* University of Lisbon (Graduate in Law, 1993). **LANGUAGES:** Portuguese, English and Spanish. **PRACTICE AREAS:** Urbanism Law; Taxation Law.

RODRIGO MENDIA DE CASTRO, born Lisbon, Portugal, May 31, 1970; admitted, 1993, Portugal. *Education:* Universidade Lusíada (Graduate in Law, 1987-1992). **LANGUAGES:** Portuguese, English, French and Spanish. **PRACTICE AREAS:** Commercial Law; Taxation Law.

PAULA MILHEIRAO, born Montevideu, Uruguay, June 21, 1970; admitted, 1993, Portugal. *Education:* Lycée du Parc (Lion); University of Lisbon (Graduate in Law). **LANGUAGES:** Portuguese, French, English, Spanish and German. **PRACTICE AREAS:** Commercial Law.

PEDRO FERREIRA MURIAS, born Benavente, Portugal, October 17, 1970; admitted, 1994, Portugal. *Education:* University of Lisbon (Graduate in Law, 1993). **LANGUAGES:** Portuguese, English, German and Spanish. **PRACTICE AREAS:** Banking; Conflicts Law; Tort Law.

AMARAL CABRAL - ADVOGADOS

AV. ANTÓNIO AUGUSTO DE AGUIAR, N.° 25 - 2.° ESQ.
1050 LISBON, PORTUGAL
Telephone: (351-1) 352.72.55; (351-1) 352.72.56
Fax: (351-1) 353.30.76

Corporate and Commercial, Banking and Capital Markets Law, Contracts and Torts, Foreign Investments and International Contracts, Real Estate, Environmental Law, Labour Law, General Litigation, EC Law.

(This Listing Continued)

FIRM PROFILE: *Amaral Cabral - Advogados is a Portuguese law firm registered and licensed by the Portuguese Bar Association to advise and represent clients in all aspects of domestic and international transactions involving Portugal. Amaral Cabral - Advogados is the Portuguese member of GLOBALAW network.*

PARTNERS

RITA AMARAL CABRAL, born 1954, Lisbon, Portugal; admitted, 1978, Portugal. *Education:* Lisbon Law School (Bachelor of Law, 1976). Legal Adviser, Ministry of Housing, 1981-1982. Researcher, Institut für Bügerliches Recht und Zivil Prozessrecht, University of Munich, 1988-1991. Author: "Privity of Contracts," 1984; "Prior Conditions of Bankruptcy," 1987. Assistant Professor, Commercial Law, Contracts and Torts, Lisbon Law School and Portuguese Catholic University, 1977-1989. Member, Commission for Reform of the Commercial Maritime Law, 1986-1987. *Member:* Portuguese Bar Association. **LANGUAGES:** Portuguese, English, French and German. **PRACTICE AREAS:** Contract Law; Tort Law; Commercial Law; Corporate Law; Banking Law; Insurance Law; Finance Law.

PEDRO EIRÓ, born 1956, Lisbon, Portugal; admitted, 1981, Portugal. *Education:* Lisbon Law School (Bachelor of Law, 1979; Master Degree, 1987). Drafting and Negotiation of Contracts and International Contracts. Legal Advice, International Project Finance. Author: "Undue Influence and Unconscionable Bargain in Portuguese Law," 1990. Assistant Professor, Civil Law, Contracts and Torts, Lisbon Law School and Portuguese Catholic University. *Member:* Portuguese Bar Association (Member, District Board). **LANGUAGES:** Portuguese, English, French, Italian, Spanish and German. **PRACTICE AREAS:** Commercial Law; Corporate Law; Contract Law; Tort Law; Banking Law; Insurance Law; Finance Law; Labour Law.

FERNANDO A. FERREIRA PINTO, born Angola, 1959; admitted, 1984, Portugal. *Education:* Portuguese Catholic University (Bachelor of Law, 1983; Master Degree, 1990). Drafting and Negotiation, Cross-Border Unincorporated Joint-Ventures and International Contracts. Legal Advice: International Arbitrations; Conflicts of Laws; Foreign Banks on licenses to operate in Portugal; International Project Finance; International Investment Banks with regard to Bond Issues and Portuguese Capital Markets Law. General Legal Counsel, Portuguese International Businessman Association. Author: "Support obligation in Private International Law," 1992. Co-Author: "Private International Law - Statutes, Projects, International Conventions," 1988. Assistant Professor, Contracts, Torts, and Private International Law, Portuguese Catholic University. *Member:* Portuguese Bar Association. Honorary Member of the Center for International Legal Studies. **LANGUAGES:** Portuguese, English, French, Italian, Spanish and German. **PRACTICE AREAS:** Commercial Law; Corporate Law; Contract Law; Tort Law; International Contract Law; Conflicts of Laws; Banking Law; Insurance Law; Finance Law.

ASSOCIATES

Margarida Cunha	*Helena Franco*
Alexandra Resina da Silva	*Daniel Salgado*
	Susana Simões Correia

AVILLEZ PEREIRA & ASSOCIADOS

Established in 1967
AVENIDA MIGUEL BOMBARDA, N° 36 - 4° F
1000 LISBON, PORTUGAL
Telephone: (01) 793 71 32
Fax: (01) 793 71 39

General Practice.

FIRM PROFILE: *Avillez Pereira & Associados has its roots in the firm founded by Dr. José Manuel de Avillez Pereira in 1960. Following the involvement in mergers with other practices, the firm has undergone a major restructurazation and thereupon is under the name of Avillez Pereira & Associados. The aim of the firm is to provide an efficient quality service for corporate, government and private clients, on a partner-client relationship basis. The Firm enjoys a wide reputation for acting for International Clients. Indeed, through the strong personal commitment of its members and staff the firm is well placed to deal with the affairs of domestic and international clients.*

Albeit being mainly a commercial law firm with particular experience in company, business matters and commercial litigation, the firm provides a comprehensive range of legal services, including foreign investment and international contracts, privatizations and public tenders, mergers and ac-

(This Listing Continued)

quisitions, banking and finance, insurance, telecommunications, agency and distribution, intellectual and industrial property, offshore, EC and competition, maritime, building and construction, arbitration and litigation.

MEMBERS OF FIRM

JOSÉ MANUEL DE AVILLEZ PEREIRA, born Lisbon, Portugal, 1933; admitted, 1960, Portugal. *Education:* University of Lisbon (Licenciatura em Direito). Government Attorney, 1959-1960. General Secretary of Labour Courts, 1960-1963. Executive Vice-President, Occidental Petroleum Corporation of Portugal, 1974-1985. *Member:* Portuguese Bar Association; Law Insurance International Association; Portuguese Fiscal Association; Portuguese Association of European Law; International Bar Association (IBA); American Bar Association (ABA). *LANGUAGES:* Portuguese, English, French and Spanish. *PRACTICE AREAS:* Foreign Investment and International Contracts; Banking Law; Corporate Law; Maritime Law; Privatization; Public Tenders; Mergers and Acquisitions.

MIGUEL DE AVILLEZ PEREIRA, born Lisbon, Portugal, 1965; admitted, 1989, Portugal. *Education:* University of Lisbon (Licenciatura em Direito); University of Edinburgh (LL.M.). Maclay, Murray & Spens, Edinburgh, 1992. Author: "The position of EC banks and non EC banks under the second banking directive," BGDDC, 1994; "Arbitration Issues in EC Law," BGDDC, 1994. *Member:* Portuguese Bar Association; International Bar Association (IBA); Young Lawyers International Association (AIJA). *LANGUAGES:* Portuguese, English, German and Spanish. *PRACTICE AREAS:* Corporate Law; Mergers and Acquisitions; Offshore; EC Law; Competition Law; Agency Law; Distribution; Telecommunications.

NUNO PAIXÃO, born Lisbon, Portugal, 1965; admitted, 1989, Portugal. *Education:* University of Lisbon (Licenciatura em Direito); University of Edinburgh (LL.M.). DG-IV EC Commission, 1993. Author: "Unimplemented Directives and the Interpretative Obligation," BGDDC, 1994; "Eurobond," Revista Da Banca, 1994. *Member:* Portuguese Bar Association. *LANGUAGES:* Portuguese, English, Spanish and French. *PRACTICE AREAS:* Maritime Law; Ec and Competition; Transport; Corporate Law; Insurance.

GUILHERME SANTOS SILVA, born Lisbon, Portugal, 1967; admitted, 1992, Portugal. *Education:* Catholic University of Lisbon (Licenciatura em Direito). Stagnetto & Co., Gibraltar, 1992. Assistant Professor, Modern University of Lisbon. *Member:* Portuguese Bar Association; International Bar Association (IBA); Young Lawyers International Association (AIJA). *LANGUAGES:* Portuguese, English, Spanish and French. *PRACTICE AREAS:* Foreign Investment Law; Corporate Law; Intellectual Property Law; Offshore; Telecommunications.

CATARINA COUTINHO GOUVEIA, born Lisbon, Portugal, 1970; admitted, 1993, Portugal. *Education:* Catholic University of Lisbon (Licenciatura em Direito). Legal Department, BPI-Portuguese Bank of Investment, Lisbon, 1993-1994. *Member:* Portuguese Bar Association. *LANGUAGES:* Portuguese, English, French and Italian. *PRACTICE AREAS:* Banking Law; Taxation; Privatization and Public Tenders; Administrative; Construction Law.

PATRICIA SILVEIRA DA CUNHA, born Lisbon, Portugal, 1971; admitted, 1994, Portugal. *Education:* University of Lisbon (Licenciatura em Direito). *Member:* Portuguese Bar Association. *LANGUAGES:* Portuguese, French, English and German. *PRACTICE AREAS:* Taxation; Competition Law; Corporate Law.

Languages: Portuguese, English, French, German, Spanish and Italian

---

M.P. BARROCAS & ASSOCIADOS

Sociedade de Advogados

AV. FONTES PEREIRA DE MELO, 15-7TH FLOOR
1000 LISBON, PORTUGAL
Telephone: (351.1) 522156
Fax: (351.1) 576202

Correspondent Offices: Oporto; Faro (Algarve); Funchal (Madeira).

FIRM PROFILE: The firm offers a full range of legal services including Corporate and Commercial Law, Banking and Financial Law, Insurance Law, Mergers and Acquisitions, Telecommunications Law, Foreign Investments, Investment Funds and Real Estate, Administrative Law, Agency, Distribution and Franchising, Maritime Law, Labor Law, Tax Law, Intellectual Property, Construction Law, Arbitration and Litigation.

(This Listing Continued)

MANUEL PEREIRA BARROCAS, born Fundão, 1943; admitted, 1968, Portugal. *Education:* University of Lisbon, Law School. Author of the Portuguese chapters of the books: "Business Law in Europe"; "Maritime Law Handbook"; "Pre-Trial and Court Procedures Worldwide"; "Injunction Proceedings in Europe"; "International Tax Planning"; "Security on Movable Property and Receivables in Europe"; "Arbitration and Recognition and Enforcement of Foreign Judgments". Co-Author: "Protections and Remedies for Foreign Sellers of Goods." Professor, Commercial Law, Business School. Consultant to the Ministry of Tourism, 1968-1974. *Member:* International Bar Association (Council Member, SBL). *LANGUAGES:* Portuguese, English, French and Spanish. *PRACTICE AREAS:* Corporate Law; Commercial Law; Banking Law; Finance Law.

ALBANO NUNES DE ALMEIDA SARMENTO, born Oporto, 1954; admitted, 1979, Portugal. *Education:* University of Lisbon, Law School. Consultant to the Ministry of Commerce. Assistant at the University of Lisbon Law School, 1976-1983. Author, Directors and Officers Liability Insurance (Portuguese chapters on International Financial and Banking Law, Tax Law). *LANGUAGES:* Portuguese, English and French. *PRACTICE AREAS:* Construction Law; Insurance Law; Tax Law.

ÁLVARO BRAGA DA CRUZ, born Braga, 1934; admitted, 1959, Portugal. *Education:* University of Coimbra, Law School. Arbitrator, appointed by Government for settling of disputes. *LANGUAGES:* Portuguese, English, French and Spanish. *PRACTICE AREAS:* Taxation Law; Intellectual Property Law.

MÁRIO ALBERTO S. SOARES DE FREITAS, born 1956; admitted, 1980, Portugal; 1985, Montreal, Canada. *Education:* University of Coimbra, Law School; McGill University, Montreal, Canada (Master in Aeronautical and Outerspace Law). *LANGUAGES:* Portuguese, English and French. *PRACTICE AREAS:* Telecommunications Law; Air Law.

HENRIQUE DOS SANTOS PEREIRA, born Lisbon, 1955; admitted, 1979, Portugal. *Education:* Law School of Portuguese Catholic University, Lisbon. Author of the Portuguese chapters of the books: "Foreign Property & Your Client"; "Personal Injuries and Awards in Europe"; "Civil Procedures in Europe"; "Environmental Law"; "Sports Law in Europe". Nationality Law. Rapporteur on Portuguese law and jurisprudence to the European Current Law edited by Sweet & Maxwell. *LANGUAGES:* Portuguese, English and French. *PRACTICE AREAS:* Commercial Law; Maritime Law; Litigation; Real Estate Law.

PEDRO OSÓRIO DE CASTRO, born Lisbon, 1957; admitted, 1982, Portugal. *Education:* University of Lisbon, Law School (Diploma, European Community Law). Co-Author, Portuguese Chapter, "Protections and Remedies for Foreign Sellers of Goods". *LANGUAGES:* Portuguese, English, French and Spanish. *PRACTICE AREAS:* Commercial Law; Mergers and Acquisitions.

JOSÉ SÃO PEDRO CELESTINO, born Castelo Branco, 1946; admitted, 1970, Portugal. *Education:* University of Lisbon, Law School. *LANGUAGES:* Portuguese, English, French and Spanish. *PRACTICE AREAS:* Commercial Law; Maritime Law.

CASSIANO MANUEL SOARES CONSCIÊNCIA, born Oporto, 1949; admitted, 1981, Portugal. *Education:* University of Coimbra, Law School. *LANGUAGES:* Portuguese, English and French. *PRACTICE AREAS:* Administrative Law; Labour Law.

FRANCISCO JOSÉ SARMENTO TOMÁS, born 1964; admitted, 1987, Portugal. *Education:* Portuguese Catholic University, Oporto. (Associate, Oporto Office). *LANGUAGES:* Portuguese, English and French. *PRACTICE AREAS:* Commercial Law; Litigation.

FERNANDO JOSÉ VIEIRA RAMOS, born Funchal, 1959. *Education:* University of Lisbon, Law School. (Associate, Madeira Island Office). *LANGUAGES:* Portuguese, English and French. *PRACTICE AREAS:* Commercial Law; Mergers and Acquisitions.

MARGARIDA CALDEIRA, born Lisbon, 1968. *Education:* Law School of Lisbon University. *LANGUAGES:* Portuguese, English and French. *PRACTICE AREAS:* Corporate Law; Tax Law.

CARMEN RODRIGUES, born 1969. *Education:* Law School of Portuguese Catholic University. *LANGUAGES:* Portuguese, English and French. *PRACTICE AREAS:* Commercial Law; Competition Law; Environmental Law.

BARROS, SOBRAL, XAVIER, G.GOMES & ASSOCIADOS
SOCIEDADE DE ADVOGADOS

AVENIDA INFANTE SANTO, Nº 17 - 8º ESQ.
1300 LISBON, PORTUGAL
Telephone: (01) 396 28 01
Facsimile: (01) 397 31 55
Telex: 65986 INTLAW P

Rio de Janeiro, Brazil Office: Castro, Barros, Sobral e Xavier S.C. Praia de Botafogo, 228, 15º andar, 22250, Rio de Janeiro. Telephone: (021) 551-1149. Fax: (021) 552-1796. Telex: (021) 22887 CABG BR.

São Paulo, Brazil Office: Castro, Barros Sobral E Xavier S.C. Avenida Cidade Jardim, 400, 14º andar, Edificio Dacon, 0145, São Paulo. Telephone: (011) 8166499. Fax: (011) 8144903.

London, England Representative Office for Lisbon and Brazil: Barros, Sobral, Xavier, G. Gomes & Associados, 3rd floor - Globe House, 4 Temple Place, London WC2R 3H. Telephone: 0171-240 17 55. Fax: 0171-240 18 08.

Business Law, Company, Corporate and Commercial Law, Taxation, Contracts, Real Estate, International Financial Transactions, Maritime Law, Aviation, Intellectual Property, Litigation, Labour Law, Banking, Shipping and Administrative Law.

MEMBERS OF FIRM

FÁBIO MONTEIRO DE BARROS, born São José do Rio Preto, S.P., Brazil, 1925; admitted, 1949, São Paulo and Rio de Janeiro; 1989, Portugal. *Education:* University of São Paulo (LL.B., 1948). Post Graduate Research Work on Taxation and Public Finance at Oxford University, U.K., 1953. Assistant Professor of Taxation, School of Economics and Administration, University of São Paulo, 1949-1962. Assistant Professor of Public Finance, University of São Paulo, 1950-1951. Professor of Public Finance, School of Sorocaba, 1958-1961 and Law School of Sorocaba, 1958-1961. Professor of Taxation, School of Economics and Administration of the University of São Paulo, 1963-1980. *Member:* Ordem dos Advogados do Brasil; Associação Advogados de São Paulo; Instituto Brasileiro de Direito Financeiro; Instituto Latino Americano de Direito Tributário; International Fiscal Association; Ordem dos Advogados de Portugal.

SERGIO SOARES SOBRAL FILHO, born São Paulo, S.P., Brazil, 1955; admitted, 1980, Rio de Janeiro and São Paulo; 1988, Portugal. *Education:* University of São Paulo (LL.B., 1977); Bachelor of Business Administration of Fundação Getúlio Vargas, S.P. (1976); Diplôme Supérieur de l'Université de Droit e Sciences Economiques de Paris, Section de Droit Commercial (1979). Resident partner, Bomchil Castro Goodrich Claro, Lavalle & Associés, Paris, France Office, 1978-1980. Author: "Stockholders Agreements under Brazilian Corporate Law," 1981; "The International Contract," Law and Finance Review, 1981; "Aircraft Finance in Brazil," Aircraft Finance, Registration, Security and Enforcement, London, 1990-1991. Member, Editorial Council of Oil and Gas Review. *Member:* Ordem dos Advogados do Brasil; Ordem dos Advogados de Portugal; Associação Brasileira de Direito Financeiro; International Fiscal Association; International Bar Association. (resident, Rio de Janiero Office).

ALBERTO SANTOS PINHEIRO XAVIER, born Lisbon, Portugal, 1942; admitted, 1964, Lisbon; 1975, São Paulo; 1983, Rio de Janeiro. *Education:* University of Lisbon, Faculty of Law (LL.B.; LL.M.; LL.D). Author: Publications in Portugal: "Portugal and the European Economic Integration," Coimbra, 1970; "Budget Policy and Market Economy: The American Experience of the Post War," Lisbon, 1970; "Contributions Towards a Fair Trade Law," Lisbon, 1970; "Fundamentals of Tax Litigation," Lisbon, 1972; "Concept and Nature of Tax (Doctoral Thesis)," Coimbra, 1972; "Market Economy and Social Justice," Lisbon, 1973; "Manual of Fiscal Law I," Lisbon, 1974 (reprint 1981). Publications in Brazil: "Of Administrative Procedures," São Paulo, 1976; "The International Tax Law of Brazil," São Paulo, 1977; "Incorporation of Companies and Income Tax," São Paulo, 1978; The Principle of Legality and the Vagueness Doctrine in Taxation," São Paulo, 1978; "The Situation of the Portuguese in Brazil as Depicted in Brazilian Law," Rio de Janeiro, 1979; "Directors of Companies (Taxation of Income-Publication and Approval of Accounts)," São Paulo, 1979; "Tax Law and Corporate Law-Opinions," Rio de Janeiro, 1982; "Opinions on Tax Law," São Paulo, 1986; "Studies on Income Tax," Belém, 1988; "On Tax Law," Rio de Janeiro, 1991. Other Countries: "The Taxation of Foreign Investment in Brazil," Deventer (Kluwer), 1980; "L'imposition des Investissments Étrangers au Brésil," Paris, 1983. Assistant Professor, Fiscal Law and Corporative Law, 1972, 1975. Professor: Fiscal Law, LL.M Course, 1975,

(This Listing Continued)

EU1142B

Pontifícia Universidade Católica de São Paulo; Escola de Administração Fazendária, 1983. Secretary of State for Planning, Portuguese Government, 1974. Vice-President do Gabinete de Estudos sobre o Amanhã; Director para Assuntos Internacionais do Instituto Internacional de Direito Público e Empresarial. Conselho Deliberativo da Federação das Associações Portuguesas e Luso-Brasileiras. Sócio Grande Benemérito do Real Gabinete Portuguêse de Leitura. *Member:* Ordem dos Advogados de Portugal; Ordem dos Advogados do Brasil; Instituto Brasileiro de Estudos Tributários; Associação Brasileira de Direito Financeiro; Instituto de Advogado de São Paulo; Instituto dos Advogados Brasileiros; Academia Brasileira de Direito Tributário; Academia Internacional de Direito e Economia; International Bar Association; International Fiscal Association. (Resident , Rio de Janiero Office).

JOÃO PEDRO MARQUES GONÇALVES GOMES, born Lisbon, Portugal, 1956; admitted, 1982, Lisbon; 1989, Rio de Janeiro, Brazil. *Education:* Portuguese Catholic University, Lisbon (LL.B., 1983). With Thomson McLitock & Co. Chartered Accountants, 1975-1978. *Member:* Ordem dos Advogados de Portugal; Ordem dos Advogados do Brasil; International Bar Association; A.I.J.A.-Association Internationale des Jeunes Avocats; Euro-American Lawyers Group.

HORACIO BERNARDES NETO, born São Paulo, S.P., Brazil, 1955; admitted, 1978, São Paulo; 1984, Rio de Janeiro; 1990, Portugal. *Education:* University of São Paulo (B.A., 1976; LL.B., 1977; Post-Graduation Studies, 1978-1980); University of Cologne, West Germany (1981-1983). Resident Partner, Bomchil Castro Goodrich Claro Arosemena & Associates, Düsseldorf, West Germany, 1980-1983. Vice-President, Brazilian-German Chamber of Commerce in Rio de Janeiro. Member, German and Brazilian Integrated Commission. *Member:* Ordem dos Advogados do Brasil; Ordem dos Advogados de Portugal; International Bar Association; AIJA-Association Internationale des Jeunes Avocats (Member, Executive Committee); Deutsch-Brasilianische Juristenvereinigung; Gesellschaft für Rechstvergleichung. (Resident, São Paulo Office).

HELENA DE ARAÚJO LOPES XAVIER, born Lisbon, Portugal, 1952; admitted, Munich, 1989 (Rechtskundige fur Portugiesches Recht); 1977, Lisbon, Portugal. *Education:* University of Lisbon, Faculty of Law (LL.B., 1975). Regency of the Chair, Administrative Law, University of Lisbon Faculty of Law (1978-1986). Regency of Administrative Law & Administrative Procedure Law and Auxiliary Professor, University Livre/Universidade Lusía da, Lisbon (1982-1986); Universidade Autónoma Luís de Camões, Lisbon (1991). Lecturer in Seminars of Administrative Law (Secretaria de Estado da Administração Pública, 1984-1986). Guest Researcher, Faculty of Law, University of Munich Institut Fur Politik und Offentliches Recht (1986-1991). Appointed Member of Cabinet Commission for the Preparation of the New Administrative Code, 1981-1983. *Member:* Ordem dos Advogados de Portugal; Ordem dos Advogados do Brasil; Associação Portuguesa dos Jovens Advogados; Deutscher Anwaltverein. (Also member, Castro, Barros, Sobral E. Xavier, Rio de Janeiro, Brazil).

JOÃO RAFAEL LOBO DE CAMPOS, born Lisbon, Portugal, 1958; admitted, 1983, Portugal. *Education:* Colégio Valsassina, Faculdade de Ciências Humanas da Universidade Católica Portuguesa, Lisbon (LL.B., 1983). Auditor of Justice, C.E.J. Ministry of Justice, 1985-1986. *Member:* Ordem dos Advogados de Portugal.

JOÃO MIGUEL SANTOS DE REZENDE ELVAS, born Lisbon, Portugal, April 25, 1960; admitted, 1988, Lisbon, Portugal. *Education:* Faculty of Law of the University of Lisbon (LL.B., 1987). *Member:* Ordem dos Advogados de Portugal.

JOÃO MARQUES PINTO, born Lisbon, Portugal, June 7, 1961; admitted, 1987, Lisbon, Portugal; 1989, KPMG Peat Marwick, Lisbon, Portugal. *Education:* Faculty of Law of the University of Lisbon (LL.B., 1986). Legal Advisor at "Câmara Municipal de Lisboa" (1987-1989); Senior Tax Consultant at KPMG PEAT MARWICK (1989-1991). *Member:* Ordem dos Advogados de Portugal.

BRUNO DE ROSSI CHEVALIER, born Rio de Janeiro, RJ, Brazil, February 3, 1964; admitted, 1987, Rio de Janeiro, Brazil; 1991, Lisbon, Portugal. *Education:* Rio de Janeiro State University (LL.B., 1986); University of London (LL.M., 1989). With Stoneham Langton & Passmore, London 1989-1990. Assistant of Department of Justice, Rio de Janeiro, 1984-1986. *Member:* Ordem dos Advogados do Brasil and Ordem dos Advogados de Portugal; International Bar Association.

ROBERTO LIESEGANG, born Rio de Janeiro, RJ, Brazil, 1963; admitted, 1988, Rio de Janeiro. *Education:* Rio de Janeiro State University (LL.B., 1988); Europa Institut, Faculty of Law, University of Saarland, Germany (LL.M., M. Jur. Eur.). Author: "Die Europaische Atiengesell-

(This Listing Continued)

schaft und das Gesellschaftsrecht Portugals," Saarbrucken, 1991. *Member:* Ordem dos Advogados do Brasil; Ordem dos Advogados de Portugal; Deutsch-Brasilianische Juristenvereinigung.

MARIA RAQUEL MENEZES RIBEIRO BRAVO, born S. Tomé e Príncipe, February 13, 1964; admitted, 1988, Lisbon, Portugal. *Education:* Portuguese Catholic University (LL.B., 1988). *Member:* Ordem dos Advogados de Portugal.

CRISTINA GALHARDO VILÃO, born Lisbon, Portugal, 1964; admitted, 1988, Portugal. *Education:* Faculty of Law, University of Lisbon (LL.B., 1987); McGill University, Institute of Air and Space Law, Montreal, Canada (LL.M., 1991). Legal Adviser: to Secretary for Economic Affairs, Macao Government (1987-1989); to the Cabinet of the Macao Governor (1989-1990). Secretary-General to the Standing Council for Social Concert of Macao (1988-1990). *Member:* Ordem dos Advogados de Portugal; AIJA-Association Internationale des Jeunes Avocats; Institute of Air and Space Law Alumni Association.

MARIA ANTÓNIA CAMEIRA, born Lisbon, Portugal, 1958. *Education:* Faculty of Law, University of Lisbon (LL.B., 1981). Lawyer Assistant: Offices of Assis de Almeida e Associados, Lisbon; Assis de Almeida e Associados, Rio de Janeiro, Brasil, 1981-1984; Lafarge Flecheux et Ghestin, Paris, France, 1984-1985; Doutor Jorge Delaunay Gonçalves Pereira. Tutor: Political Economy, University of Lisbon, 1982-1984; Internacional University of Lisbon, 1985-1986. *Member:* Portuguese Bar Association.

MARIA FILOMENA VIEIRA, born Coimbra, Portugal, 1966. *Education:* Portuguese Catholic University (LL.B., 1989; Administrative, Constitutional and Maritime Law Post-Graduate Studies). Assistant Lecturer of the Chair of Administrative Law at the Faculty of Law, University of Lisbon (1990—). *Member:* Ordem dos Advogados de Portugal.

JOSÉ NÓVOA CORTEZ, born Lourenco Marques, Mocambique, August 26, 1946; admitted, 1980, Portugal. Ordem dos Advogados, 1980. *LANGUAGES:* Portuguese.

Languages: Portuguese, Spanish, French, English, German and Italian.

BORGES NETO E ASSOCIADOS

Sociedade de Advogados

Law Firm

RUA D. JOÃO V, N°11-1° ESQ.
1200 LISBON, PORTUGAL
Telephone: (351) 387 4848
Fax: (351) 387 4950

FIRM PROFILE: *Borges Neto & Associados is a partnership of lawyers with offices in Lisbon, Cascais and the Algarve.*

The firm offers a full range of legal services such as Corporate and Commercial Law, Banking and Financial Law, Insurance Law, Foreign Investments, Investment Funds and Real Estate, Administrative Law, Agency, Distribution and Franchising, Maritime Law, Labour Law, Tax Law, Intellectual Property, Construction Law, Arbitration and Litigation.

It is a member of the British-Portuguese Chamber of Commerce since 1987, a member of the Dutch-Portuguese Chamber of Commerce and the Swedish-Portuguese Chamber of Commerce.

FREDERICO BORGES NETO. *Education:* University of Lisbon Law School (Law Degree, 1984). Awarded, British Council Scholarship, King's College, London, 1987. *Member:* Portuguese Bar Association. *PRACTICE AREAS:* Commercial Law; Real Estate Property; Tax Law; Corporate Law; Maritime Law.

FÁTIMA ABREU E OLIVEIRA. *Education:* Faculty Cândido Mendes, Law School, Rio de Janeiro (Law Degree, 1981).

SÃO MARTINS. *Education:* University of Lisbon, Law School (Law Degree, 1991).

TERESA AMADOR. *Education:* University of Lisbon, Law School (Law Degree, 1993).

LUIS OLIVEIRA ROSA. *Education:* Lusiada University, Law School (Law Degree, 1992).

CARLOS DE SOUSA E BRITO & ASSOCIADOS

Established in 1982

RUA CASTILHO 71 R/C
1200 LISBON, PORTUGAL
Telephone: (351) (1) 3861407
Telex: 42888 Legal P
Telefax: (351) (1) 3861735

FIRM PROFILE: *Carlos de Sousa e Brito & Associados in one of the largest firms in Portugal. It was founded in 1982. It has representative offices in Luanda, Angola and Maputo, Mozambique.*

The firm is in the general practice of law in the areas of corporate, commercial EEC, banking, tax, maritime, mergers and acquisitions, securities, aircraft, real estate, international and antitrust law, patents and trademark law, foreign investment, unfair competition, industrial property rights, arbitration and copyright, pensions, employment and labour law, broadcasting and telecommunications.

CARLOS DE SOUSA E BRITO, born Lisbon, Portugal, April 28, 1942; admitted, 1965, Portugal and Portuguese Supreme Court. *Education:* Lisbon Law School, The Hague, International Law Academy, (Graduate, 1962); Lisbon University (Graduate, 1964). Author: "Wartime Public Finance" Minister for Information and Social Communication, 1980. Arbitrator, Lisbon and O Porto Commercial Association. *Member:* Portuguese Bar Association; EEC. *LANGUAGES:* English, French, German Italian, Portuguese and Spanish. *PRACTICE AREAS:* Banking; Securities; Finance; Commercial Law; EEC.

MARIA MANUEL MAGRO ROMÁO, born Lisbon, Portugal, 1942; admitted, 1968, Portugal. *Education:* Coimbra University (Graduate, 1963) Coimbra University, Lisbon Law Faculty (Ph.D., 1968). *Member:* Portuguese Bar Association. *LANGUAGES:* English, French, German, Portuguese, Italian and Spanish. *PRACTICE AREAS:* EEC; Commercial; Corporate.

ANTÓNIO FRUTUOSO DE MELO, born Viseu, Portugal, November 16, 1948; admitted, 1985, Portugal and Portuguese Supreme Court. *Education:* Coimbra Law School; Lisbon Law School (Graduate, 1979). Author: Several Articles published by International Financial Law Review and other specialized magazines; Co-authorship: "The Portuguese Section of European Mergers and Acquisitions"; "The Portuguese Section of the GT Guide to World Equity Markets" and The Portuguese Section of the Morgan Grenfell Handbook of International Mergers and Acquisitions". Teacher of Administrative Law, Lisbon University , 1977-1980 and Professor by special invitation -Free University of Lisbon, 1985-1987. Administrative Law: Special Proceeding Before the Supreme Administrative Court. *Member:* Portuguese Bar Association. *LANGUAGES:* English, French, Italian, Portuguese and Spanish. *PRACTICE AREAS:* Taxes; Corporate; Mergers and Acquisitions; Banking.

LUIS SOARES DE SOUSA, born Lisbon, Portugal, September 9, 1958; admitted, 1986, Portugal. *Education:* Universidade Livre of Lisbon (Graduate, 1984). *Member:* Portuguese Bar Association. *LANGUAGES:* English, French, Portuguese and Spanish. *PRACTICE AREAS:* Aircraft; Real Estate; MLA.

EDUARDO MENEZES CARDOSO, born Lisbon, Portugal, July 27, 1955. *Education:* University of Lisbon (Graduate, 1977). Legal Counsel, The Foreign Investment Institute (Lisbon, Portugal), 1978-1989 . *LANGUAGES:* French, English and Portuguese. *PRACTICE AREAS:* Commercial.

GUIDA VILA NOVA, born Mozambique, March 29, 1969; admitted, 1990, Portugal. *Education:* Lisbon University (Law, 1988). *Member:* Portuguese Bar Association. *LANGUAGES:* English, French, Italian and Portuguese. *PRACTICE AREAS:* Intellectual Property.

JOSÉ MIRANDA BAPTISTA, born Barcelos, August 31, 1949; admitted, 1980, Portugal. *Education:* Coimbra University (Graduate, 1974). Teacher of Professional Deontology at the Criminal Investigation Police School. Supervising Officer at the Criminal Investigation Police, 1977-1980. State Prosecutor, 1974-1980. *Member:* Portuguese Bar Association. *LANGUAGES:* French, English, Portuguese and Spanish. *PRACTICE AREAS:* Litigation; Court Work.

PEDRO PALMA CARLOS, born Lisbon, Portugal, May 6, 1961; admitted, 1990, Portugal. *Education:* University of Lisbon (Graduate, 1988).

(This Listing Continued)

CARLOS DE SOUSA E BRITO & ASSOCIADOS,
Lisbon—Continued

Member: Portuguese Bar Association. *LANGUAGES:* English, French, Portuguese and Spanish. *PRACTICE AREAS:* Corporate; Commercial.

SOFIA BELARD, born Mocambique, July 5, 1965; admitted, 1989, Portugal. *Education:* University of Lisbon (Graduate, 1989). *Member:* Portuguese Bar Association. *LANGUAGES:* English, French, Portuguese and Spanish. *PRACTICE AREAS:* EEC; Commercial; Labour Law.

DIOGO LEÓNIDAS ROCHA, born Lisbon, Portugal, November 5, 1967; admitted, 1990, Portugal. *Education:* Catholic University of Lisbon (Graduate, 1990). *Member:* Portuguese Bar Association. *LANGUAGES:* English, French and Portuguese. *PRACTICE AREAS:* Banking Law; Securities; Commercial Law.

FERNANDO MAGIOLO MAGARREIRO, born Lisbon, Portugal, December 5, 1964; admitted, 1991. *Education:* Catholic University of Lisbon (Graduate, 1991). *Member:* Portuguese Bar Association. *LANGUAGES:* French, English and Portuguese. *PRACTICE AREAS:* Pensions; Employment; Labour Law.

NUNO BAPTISTA GONÇALVES, born Viseu, Portugal, October 10, 1957. *Education:* Lisbon Law School (Graduate, 1982). Lecturer: Law, Lusíada University, Lisbon; Law, International University, Lisbon. *LANGUAGES:* English, French and Portuguese. *PRACTICE AREAS:* Civil Law; Business Law.

PEDRO PORTO DORDIO, born Coimbra, Portugal, June 20, 1966; admitted, 1992, Portugal. *Education:* Coimbra Law School (Graduate, 1991). *Member:* Portuguese Bar Association. *LANGUAGES:* English, French and Portuguese. *PRACTICE AREAS:* Commercial Law.

ALDA CABEÇAS, born Castelo Branco, Portugal, April 12, 1964; admitted, 1991, Portugal. *Education:* Lisbon Law School (Graduate, 1989). *Member:* Portuguese Bar Association. *LANGUAGES:* English, French and Portuguese. *PRACTICE AREAS:* Litigation; Arbitration.

ANA LÚCIA GUERRA, born Figueira da Foz, Portugal, December 12, 1963. *Education:* Coimbra Law School (Graduate, 1989). Public Notary and Land and Civil Registry. *LANGUAGES:* English, French, German and Portuguese.

Languages: Portuguese, English, French, German, Italian and Spanish

---

CARLOS OLAVO & ASSOCIADOS
LISBON, PORTUGAL

(See Veiga Gomes, Bessa Monteiro, Marques Bom Carlos Olavo & Associados)

F. CASTELO BRANCO, NOBRE GUEDES & P. REBELO DE SOUSA
LISBON, PORTUGAL

(See Grupo Legal Português E.E.I.G.)

COELHO RIBEIRO & ASSOCIADOS
AV. ENG°. DUARTE PACHECO, 19 - 3°
1070 LISBON, PORTUGAL
Telephone: 385 31 82 (8 lines)
Telefax: 385 32 02
Telex: 64066 LEXLUR P

Other Lisbon, Portugal Office: Avenida Sidónio Pais, 8 Cave, 1000 Lisbon, Portugal.

General Business Law Practice, Company and Commercial Law, Banking and Insurance Law, EC Law, Environmental Law, Competition Law, Arbitration, Contracts, Mergers and Acquisitions, Foreign Investment, Taxation, Labour, Administrative and Property Law, Litigation, Patents, Trademarks, Agency, Distribution and Franchising Law.

(This Listing Continued)

JOSÉ MANUEL COELHO RIBEIRO, born Lisbon, December 23, 1930; admitted, 1957, Portugal. *Education:* Law Faculty, Lisbon University. Member, High Council of the Portuguese Public Prosecutor. Invited Professor of Business Law, School of Economics, Universidade Nova de Lisboa (MBA). Founder and First President of APDE (the Portuguese Association for European Law). Honorary Member: Colegio de Abogados de Espana; American Bar Association; Portuguese-Brazilian Institute of Comparative Law. Chairman, RTP (Portuguese State-owned Television), 1985-1992. Nominated "Lawyer of the Year 1993" by the "Lawyers in Europe Association". *Member:* Portuguese Bar Association (Chairman, 1980-1984); CCBE, Council of the Bars and Law Societies of the EC (President, 1992).

MARIA CLARA LOPES, born Aveiro, December 28, 1941; admitted, 1964, Portugal. *Education:* Law Faculty, Lisbon University. *Member:* Portuguese Bar Association (President, Lisbon District Council, 1984-1986.); Union International des Avocats; Association Européene des Avocats.

JAIME MANUEL DE MEDEIROS, born Lisbon, November 13, 1958; admitted, 1981, Portugal. *Education:* Law Faculty, Lisbon University. Former Assistant Professor of Civil Procedural Law and Contracts Law. *Member:* Portuguese Bar Association (Board of the Lisbon District Council); CCBE, Council of the Bars and Law Societies of the EEC (Special Committee on Company Law).

JOSÉ CARLOS GOMES DA SILVA, born Lisbon, June 5, 1957; admitted, 1983, Portugal. *Education:* Law Faculty, Lisbon University. *Member:* Portuguese Bar Association; Portuguese Association of Environmental Law (Director).

JOSÉ PEDRO RIBEIRO, born Angola, September 23, 1966; admitted, 1990, Portugal. *Education:* Law Faculty, Lisbon University. *Member:* Portuguese Bar Association.

RUI BOTICA SANTOS, born Lisbon, March 25, 1968; admitted, 1992, Portugal. *Education:* Law Faculty, Lisbon University. *Member:* Portuguese Bar Association.

ESPERANÇA PEREIRA, born Setubal, October 19, 1970; admitted, 1993, Portugal. *Education:* Law Faculty, Lisbon University. *Member:* Portuguese Bar Association.

Languages: Portuguese, English, Spanish and French

J. HENRIQUES DA SILVA E ASSOCIADOS

Established in 1990

AV. DUQUE DE LOULÉ, 47-6°
1000 LISBON, PORTUGAL
Telephone: 351-1-525302
Telex: 62311 Hensil P
Facsimile: 351-1-3528843

Commercial Law, Company Law, Labour Law, Competition Law, Tax Law.

JOSE HENRIQUES DA SILVA, born Tomar, Portugal, October 30, 1940; admitted, 1969, Portugal. *Education:* University of Lisbon (1969). *LANGUAGES:* Portuguese, English, French and Spanish. *PRACTICE AREAS:* Corporate Law; Corporate Taxation.

RUI PINTO DA SILVA, born Lisbon, Portugal, October 12, 1958; admitted, 1983, Portugal. *Education:* University of Lisbon (1981); Faculty of Law of Lisbon (Graduate, 1981). *Member:* Portuguese Bar Association. *LANGUAGES:* English, French, Spanish and Portuguese. *PRACTICE AREAS:* Commercial Law.

MARIA FERNANDA LOPES, born Lourenço, Marques, April 14, 1958; admitted, 1986, Portugal. *Education:* Universidade Católica Portuguesa (Graduate, 1986). *Member:* Portuguese Bar Association. *LANGUAGES:* English, French, Spanish and Portuguese. *PRACTICE AREAS:* Competition Law; Consumer Law.

ISABEL MARIA FERREIRA SEUANES, born Portimao, Portugal, October 9, 1965; admitted, 1990, Portugal. *Education:* University of Cambridge (Certificate of English Proficiency, 1986); University of Lisbon, College of Law (Master, 1988); European Institute of the Lisbon College of Law (Post-Gradate Degree, 1989). Professor, Labour Law, EEC Sponsored School, 1990. *LANGUAGES:* English, French and Portuguese. *PRACTICE AREAS:* Labour Law.

Member of Network 92.

VIEIRA DE ALMEIDA

Advogados

Established in 1976

AVENIDA FONTES PEREIRA DE MELO, 3-11°
1000 LISBON, PORTUGAL
Telephone: 548154; 548185; 3522203
Cable Address: "Vieiper"
Telex: 42490 VIALP P
Fax: GP 2/3 Cannon 730 Tel. 548939; 548651

General Practice, Corporation and Banking, Commercial, Civil, Tax and Labor Law, Foreign Investment, International Contracts, Patents and Trademarks.

FIRM PROFILE: Established in 1976, Vieira de Almeida Advogados has grown to become one of the leading Portuguese law firms providing a wide range of legal services with a reputation for quality. Its client base is basically European and North American. The firm has been involved in some of the largest foreign investment projects and project finance transactions in Portugal. It now has sixteen lawyers: two partners, twelve associates and two trainees to be co-opted as associates.

MEMBERS OF FIRM

VASCO VIEIRA DE ALMEIDA, born Lisbon, Portugal, 1933; admitted, 1955, Portugal. *Education:* University of Lisbon, Faculty of Law. Author: "Economic Relations between Italy and Portugal," Lisbon, 1968; "Medium and Long Term Financing to Industry," Lisbon, 1969. Lecturer: "The Future of Trade Relations Between the U.K. and Portugal," London, England, 1969; "Evolution and Growth of the Portuguese Economy," New York, New York, 1970; "Perspectives of the Portuguese Economy," Chicago, Illinois, 1970; "Recent Trends in Portuguese Industrialization," Tokyo, Japan, 1971; "Economic Relations Between France and Portugal," Paris, France, 1971; "The Basic Options of the Portuguese Economic Policy," Rio de Janeiro, Brazil, 1972. Member and Director, British Chamber of Commerce, 1967-1969. Vice Chairman, 1969 and Director, 1977, 1978, 1979 and 1980, German Chamber of Commerce. Director, Italian Chamber of Commerce, 1970. Managing Director, Banco Português do Atlântico, 1970-1972. Chairman, Bank Crédito Predial, 1972-1974. Minister of Economic Coordination, Government of Portugal, 1974. Minister of Economic Affairs, Government of Angola (Representing the Portuguese Government), 1975. Roving Ambassador of the Portuguese Government, 1976. Honorary Legal Advisor to the British Ambassador in Portugal, 1980-1990. *Member:* Portuguese and American (Associate) Bar Associations. *LANGUAGES:* Portuguese, English, French, Spanish and German.

JOÃO VIEIRA DE ALMEIDA, born Lisbon, Portugal, 1961; admitted, 1987, Portugal. *Education:* Catholic University of Lisbon, Faculty of Law. *Member:* Portuguese Bar Association; International Bar Association. *LANGUAGES:* Portuguese, English, French and Spanish.

ASSOCIATES

MARIA HELENA SIMÕES, born Oeiras, Portugal, 1960; admitted, 1986, Portugal. *Education:* University of Lisbon, Faculty of Law. *Member:* Portuguese Bar Association. *LANGUAGES:* Portuguese, English and French.

MARGARIDA COUTO, born Vila Real, Portugal, 1964; admitted, 1989, Portugal. *Education:* Catholic University of Lisbon, Faculty of Law; Complementary Graduation, European Legal Studies, 1988. *Member:* Portuguese Bar Association. *LANGUAGES:* Portuguese, English, French and Spanish.

PEDRO CASSIANO SANTOS, born Lisbon, Portugal, 1965; admitted, 1991, Portugal. *Education:* University of Lisbon, Faculty of Law; Complementary Graduation, College of Europe, Bruges, Belgium, 1989-1990. *Member:* Portuguese Bar Association. *LANGUAGES:* Portuguese, English, French and Spanish.

ISABEL FALCÃO DE CAMPOS, born Lisbon, Portugal, 1964; admitted, 1988, Portugal. *Education:* University of Lisbon, Faculty of Law. *Member:* Portuguese Bar Association. *LANGUAGES:* Portuguese, English and Spanish.

TIAGO DE MELO, born Lisbon, Portugal, 1959; admitted, 1987, Portugal. *Education:* Free University of Lisbon, Faculty of Law. *Member:* Portuguese Bar Association. *LANGUAGES:* Portuguese, English and French.

PEDRO CORREIA, born Viseu, Portugal, 1967; admitted, 1991, Portugal. *Education:* University of Coimbra, Faculty of Law. *Member:* Portuguese Bar Association. *LANGUAGES:* Portuguese, English and French.

(This Listing Continued)

MANUEL PROTÁSIO, born Lisbon, Portugal, 1961; admitted, 1992, Portugal. *Education:* Catholic University of Lisbon, Faculty of Law. *Member:* Portuguese Bar Association. *LANGUAGES:* Portuguese, English and French.

PEDRO FERREIRINHA, born Lisbon, Portugal, 1964; admitted, 1989, Portugal. *Education:* University of Lisbon, Faculty of Law. *Member:* Portuguese Bar Association. *LANGUAGES:* Portuguese, English and French.

HELENA VAZ PINTO, born Lisbon, Portugal, 1967; admitted, 1993, Portugal. *Education:* University of Lisbon, Faculty of Law. *Member:* Portuguese Bar Association. *LANGUAGES:* Portuguese, English and French.

DIOGO SALEMA DA COSTA, born Lisbon, Portugal, 1967; admitted, 1993, Portugal. *Education:* University of Lisbon, Faculty of Law. *Member:* Portuguese Bar Association. *LANGUAGES:* Portuguese, English and French.

RUI RAMALHAL, born Lisbon, Portugal, 1967; admitted, 1994, Portugal. *Education:* Catholic University of Lisbon, Faculty of Law. *Member:* Portuguese Bar Association. *LANGUAGES:* Portuguese, English and French.

VANDA CASCÃO, born Beira, Mozambique, 1968; admitted, 1994, Portugal. *Education:* University of Coimbra, Faculty of Law; College of Europe, Bruges, Belgium, 1991-1992. *Member:* Portuguese Bar Association. *LANGUAGES:* Portuguese, English and French.

PINTO DUARTE, MEDEIROS E FERREIRA MALAQUIAS

Sociedade de Advogados

AV. DEFENSORES DE CHAVES, 37 - 1° DT°
1000 LISBON, PORTUGAL
Telephone: (351-1) 315 18 00/1/2/3
Telefax: (351-1) 315 17 99

General Practice, Corporation and Commercial Law, Banking and Financial Law, Insurance Law, Mergers and Acquisitions, Foreign Investments, International Contracts, E.E.C. Law, Family Law, Administrative Law, Real Estate, Labour Law, Debt Recovery and Arbitration.

MEMBERS OF FIRM

ANTÓNIO PINTO DUARTE, born Figueira da Foz, Portugal, 1949; admitted, 1975, Portugal. *Education:* University of Lisbon, Faculty of Law. Ex-Lecturer, Civil Law and Real Estate Law. Ex-Consultant, Ministry of Construction. *LANGUAGES:* Portuguese, English and French.

RUI PINTO DUARTE, born Coimbra, Portugal, 1955; admitted, 1979, Portugal. *Education:* University of Lisbon, Faculty of Law (Master). Author: of several books and articles on Contracts, Companies, Leasing, Factoring and Banking Law. Ex-Lecturer, Commercial Law and Private International Law. *LANGUAGES:* Portuguese, English and French.

MARIA MARGARIDA MEDEIROS, born Chaves, Portugal, 1955; admitted, 1979, Portugal. *Education:* University of Lisbon, Faculty of Law; Catholic University, Faculty of Law (Master in European Law). Ex-Lecturer, Commercial Law, Faculty of Economics. *LANGUAGES:* Portuguese, English and French.

PEDRO FERREIRA MALAQUIAS, born Lisbon, Portugal, 1958; admitted, 1985, Lisbon. *Education:* University of Lisbon, Faculty of Law (1981); College of Europe, Bruges, Belgium (1982). Fonctionnaire, Directorate General of Competition (DG IV) Commission of the EC, 1986-1988. Author: several articles on Banking and Competition. *Member:* Directive Council of the Associacao Portuguesa de Direito Europeu; European Law Portuguese Association. *LANGUAGES:* Portuguese, English and French.

SANTOS FERREIRA, ALMEIDA SAMPAIO, MIGUEL EIRÓ, GOMES DA SILVA & ASSOCIADOS

Established in 1981

AV. ANTÓNIO AUGUSTO AGUIAR, N° 11 - 4° ESQ.
1000 LISBON, PORTUGAL
Telephone: 00351-1-3536924/25/26
Fax: 00351-1-3536927

Company Law, Tax Law, Economic Law, Competition Law, Labour Law, European Law, Banking Law and Maritime Law both at national and international level, as well as in Litigation.

FIRM PROFILE: *The law firm Santos Ferreira, Almeida Sampaio, Miguel Eiró, Gomes da Silva & Associados is a Lisbon based law firm, established in its initial framework in 1981 and with the present composition since 1994. This law firm has expertise in sectors as Banking, Energy, Telecommunications, Transports and relevant Industrial Sectors, as well as, Public Tenders and Privatization. The client base is European, North American and Middle Eastern. The firm has a branch in the off-shore zone of Funchal, Island of Madeira. This firm has four Partners, two Associates and four Junior Associates with a paralegal staff of four. The firm has developed an international network of correspondent law firms with mutual referral agreements in Madrid, London, New York, Toronto, Hong Kong and Sidney.*

MEMBERS OF FIRM

CARLOS SANTOS FERREIRA, born Lisbon, Portugal, 1949. *Education:* Faculty of Law, Lisbon (Graduate, Law). Assistant Professor, Faculty of Law, University of Lisbon and Universidade Católica, 1977/1986. Former Managing Director, ANA-EP. Former President, Board of Fundicao de Oeiras and Airport of Macao Authority. *Member:* Portuguese Bar Association; Tax Reform Commission; Portuguese Fiscal Association. *LANGUAGES:* Portuguese, English and French. *PRACTICE AREAS:* Taxation; Economic Law; Banking; Corporate Law.

CARLOS DE ALMEIDA SAMPAIO, born Porto, Portugal, 1952. *Education:* University of Lisbon (Graduate and Master in Law). Invited Professor, European Studies Centre of the Universidade Católica Portuguesa, 1984—. Assistant Professor, Faculty of Law, University of Lisbon, 1977-1984. Portuguese Prime Minister's Adviser, EEC Affairs, 1987-1991. Member: VAT Governmental Commission, 1981-1984; Governmental Commission for the EEC Affairs, 1985-1991. *Member:* Portuguese Bar Association; International Fiscal Association; Portuguese Fiscal Association. *LANGUAGES:* Portuguese, English, German, French and Spanish. *PRACTICE AREAS:* Taxation; Corporate Law; Public Economic Law; Competition; EEC Law.

MIGUEL EIRÓ, born Lisbon, Portugal, 1949. *Education:* University of Lisbon (Graduate in Law, 1971). Legal Adviser: Portuguese Industrial Association; Major Portuguese Companies. *Member:* Portuguese Bar Association (Board, 1984/1986); Arbitration Center of the Portuguese Bar Association; European Communities Trade Mark Association (Board of Directors). *LANGUAGES:* Portuguese, English and French. *PRACTICE AREAS:* Litigation; Civil Law; Commercial Law; Industrial Property Law; Labour Law.

RUI GOMES DA SILVA, born Porto, Portugal, 1958. *Education:* University of Lisbon (Graduate in Law, 1981). Assistant Professor, University of Lusiada, Lisbon. *Member:* Parliament; Portuguese Bar Association. *LANGUAGES:* Portuguese, English and French. *PRACTICE AREAS:* Commercial Law; Maritime Law; Litigation.

LUIS GALLEGO, CATARINA GALLEGO, FILIPA GALLEGO AND ASSOCIATES

Barristers and Solicitors

Established in 1959

AV. ANTÓNIO AUGUSTO DE AGUIAR, 165 - 4. DTO.
1000 LISBON, PORTUGAL
Telephone: 3873942; 3873283; 3872646
Telefax: 3872349

General Practice, Civil Litigation, Commercial Law, Corporate Law, Commercial, Property, Debt Recovery, Family Law, International Investment and Financial Services, Mergers and Acquisitions, Partnership, Real Estate

(This Listing Continued)

Purchase, Mercantile Law, Banking Law, Arbitration, EEC Law, Agency and Distributorships.

DR. LUIS GALLEGO, born Lisbon, Portugal, February 7, 1936; admitted, 1959, Portugal. *Education:* University of Lisbon, Faculty of Law. Former Member of the Superior Council of the Portuguese Bar Association. Vice President: Portuguese Conciliation and Arbitration Association; European of the Medium and Small Business Union. Former Member of the Portuguese Parliament. *Member:* Portuguese Bar Association; International Bar Association; Union Internationale des Avocats. *LANGUAGES:* Portuguese, English, French and Spanish.

DRA. CATARINA GALLEGO, born Lisbon, Portugal, May 29, 1962; admitted, 1986, Portugal. *Education:* Catholic University of Lisbon, Faculty of Law (Course: European Studies and "Lawyers in Europe"). *Member:* Association Internationale des Jeunes Avocats (AIJA). *LANGUAGES:* Portuguese, English, French and Spanish.

DRA. FILIPA GALLEGO, born Lisbon, Portugal, December 12, 1964; admitted, 1988, Portugal. *Education:* University of Lisbon, Faculty of Law. Annual Course of Fiscal Law in the Commercial Association of Lisbon. *Member:* Association Internationale des Jeunes Avocats (AIJA). *LANGUAGES:* Portuguese, English, French and Spanish.

GRUPO LEGAL PORTUGUÊS E.E.I.G. F. CASTELO BRANCO, NOBRE GUEDES & P. REBELO DE SOUSA

In Association with J & A Garrigues, Simmons & Simmons and

Pinheiro Neto & Co

Established in 1992

RUA CASTILHO, N° 32-9°
1250 LISBON, PORTUGAL
Telephone: 351-1-352 1318
Telecopier: 351-1-352 1418

Business, Corporate Law, Contracts and Torts, Portuguese and International Taxation, International Contracts and Conflict of Laws, Foreign Investment, EEC Law, Intellectual Property, Labour Law, Banking and Capital Markets, Corporate and Project Finance, Privatisation, Telecommunications, Insurance and Finance Law, Real Estate Law, Construction Law, Civil, Criminal and Administrative Litigation.

PRINCIPAL MEMBERS OF FIRM

MIGUEL FERRÃO CASTELO BRANCO, born Lisbon, Portugal, 1955; admitted, 1978, Portugal. *Education:* University of Lisbon Law School (Bachelor of Law); Superior Institute of New Profession. *Member:* Portuguese Bar Association. *LANGUAGES:* Portuguese, French, English and Spanish. *PRACTICE AREAS:* Business Law; Corporate Law; Contracts and Torts; Real Estate Law; Civil Law; Criminal Law; Administrative Litigation.

LUIS NOBRE GUEDES, born Lisbon, Portugal, 1955; admitted, 1978, Portugal. *Education:* University of Lisbon Law School (Bachelor of Law). Associate with Assis de Almeida, Rio de Janeiro Office, 1977-1988. Partner of Assis de Almeida, Lisbon Office, 1981-1988. *Member:* Portuguese Bar Association. *LANGUAGES:* Portuguese, French and English. *PRACTICE AREAS:* Business Law; Corporate Law; Contracts and Torts; Foreign Investments; Insurance Law; Finance Law; Civil Litigation.

PEDRO REBELO DE SOUSA, born Lisbon, Portugal, 1955; admitted, 1977, Brazil; 1993, Portugal. *Education:* University of Lisbon Law School (Bachelor of Law); Getúlio Vargas Business School, São Paulo (MBA). Associate with A.A. Alvim, Lisbon Office, 1976-1977. Senior Lawyer with Citibank N.A., São Paulo, 1977-1982. Assistant General Counsel Citicorp, Brazil, 1982-1985. Vice-President, Citicorp Investment Bank, New York, 1985-1988. Vice-President, Citibank N.A., New York, 1988-1990. President and Chief Executive Officer, Banco Fonsecas & Burnay S.A., Lisbon, 1990-1991. Professor, Lusiada, University of Lisbon, 1990-1994. *Member:* Portuguese Bar Association; Brazilian Bar Association. *LANGUAGES:* Portuguese, English, French and Spanish. *PRACTICE AREAS:* Banking and Capital Markets; Finance Law; Corporate and Commercial Law.

MANUEL PAULINO BRILHANTE SANTOS, born Lisbon, Portugal, 1961; admitted, 1987, Portugal. *Education:* University of Lisbon Law School (Bachelor of Law); Accounting, Audit, International Taxation in Portugal and The Netherlands; Degree on Organizational Development;

(This Listing Continued)

Courses Taught: Real Estate Law, Administrative Law. Experienced Senior Consultant of Arthur Andersen & Co., Tax Department, 1988-1991. *Member:* Portuguese Bar Association; Portuguese Tax Association. *LANGUAGES:* Portuguese, English and French. *PRACTICE AREAS:* Portuguese and International Taxation; Banking; Capital Markets.

WILLIAM PETER HUMPHREY SMITHSON, born London, England, 1963; admitted, 1989, England and Wales (Not admitted in Portugal). *Education:* Universita Italiana, University of Wales (B.A., Hons); College of Law, Guildford. (Simmons & Simmons Contact). *LANGUAGES:* English and Portuguese. *PRACTICE AREAS:* Banking and Capital Markets; Corporate and Commercial.

GONCALO ULRICH DA CUNHA, born Lisbon, Portugal, 1962; admitted, 1985, Portugal. *Education:* Portuguese Catholic University (Bachelor of Law). Associate with D. Antonio D'Orey da Cunha, Lisbon Office, 1985-1992. *Member:* Portuguese Bar Association. *LANGUAGES:* Portuguese, English, French and Spanish. *PRACTICE AREAS:* EEC Law; Business Law; Intellectual Property; Corporate Law; Labour Law; Contracts and Torts; Civil Law and Litigation; Criminal Law; Administrative Litigation.

OCTAVIO CASTELO PAULO, born Luanda, Angola, 1964; admitted, 1987, Portugal. *Education:* University of Lisbon Law School (Bachelor of Law). Assistant Professor, Lusiada, University of Lisbon. *Member:* Portuguese Bar Association. *LANGUAGES:* Portuguese, French, English and Spanish. *PRACTICE AREAS:* Business Law; Corporate Law; Contracts and Torts; Real Estate Law; Civil Law; Criminal Law; Insurance Law; Telecommunications Law; Administrative Law.

ASSISTANTS

VICTOR FÉLIX

MARIA HELENA MACIEIRA PIRES

JOÁO CANIÇO GOMES

GONÇALO MALEITAS CORRÉA

ALEXANDRA BESSONE CARDOSO

CÉSAR SÁ ESTEVES

DUARTE PINHO DE OLIVEIRA

NUNO ASCENSO PIRES

TERESA VASCONCELOS CAEIRO

CRISTINA MARIA PEREZ

MARGARIDA MENEZES CRUZ

TIAGO CORRÈA DE SAMPAIO

PATRÍCIA CASTRO ROSA

RODRIGO JARDIM GONÇALVES

SOFIA BARROS CARVALHOSA

ALEXANDRA C. VALENTE

J.M.'S & ASSOCIADOS
Established in 1990
CÇ MARQUÊS DE ABRANTES N°38 - 3°ESQ.
1200 LISBON, PORTUGAL
Telephone: 351-1-396 96 84
Facsimile: 351-1-397 36 70

Lisbon, Portugal Office: Calçada Marquês de Abrantes - 38 - 3° Esq. Telephone: 395 61 89; 396 96 84. Fax: 397 36 70.

Oporto, Portugal Office: Manuel Marques da Costa - Rua Júlio Diniz, 852 - 4° A. Telephone: 02-69 52 59; 69 52 50. Fax: 600 03 38.

London, England Office: Edmonds Bowen & Co. -4 Old Park Lane, W1Y 3LJ. Telephone: 0171-629 80 00. Fax: 0171-221 93 34; 495 63 82.

Hamburg, Germany Office: Peter Berger & Gerhard Kohnecke, Barmebecker Strasse, 148 - 2000, 60. Telephone: 040-48 14 32; 46 14 78. Fax: 040-480 22 64.

Paris, France Office: 87 Boulevard St. Michel, 75005. nelephone: 46 337 766; 46 346 052.

General Practice, Business, Commercial, Industrial Relations, Civil, EEC, Private International Law.

JORGE MOTA, born Lisbon, Portugal, June 12, 1936; admitted, 1972, Portugal. *Education:* University of Law School (Bachelor of Law). *Member:* Portuguese Bar Association; Center for International Legal Studies. *LAN-*

(This Listing Continued)

GUAGES: Portuguese, English, French, Spanish and Italian. *PRACTICE AREAS:* Commercial Law; Contract Law; Company Law; Banking Law; Finance Law; Arbitration; Private International Law.

JORGE MONTEIRO DOS SANTOS, born Almada, Portugal, February 22, 1941; admitted, 1973, Portugal. *Education:* University of Lisbon Law School (1964). *Member:* Portuguese Bar Association. *LANGUAGES:* Portuguese, English, French and Spanish. *PRACTICE AREAS:* Commercial Law; Contract Law; Company Law; Banking Law; Finance Law; Arbitration; Private International Law.

JORGE MENDIA, born Lisbon, Portugal, March 6, 1959; admitted, 1988, Portugal. *Education:* Lusíada University of Lisbon (Bachelor of Law, 1986). *Member:* Portuguese Bar Association. *PRACTICE AREAS:* General Civil Law; Real Estate Law; Family Law.

ANA CRISTINA VASCONCELOS, born Lisbon, Portugal, March 11, 1963; admitted, 1988, Portugal. *Education:* University of Law School (Bachelor of Law); Portuguese Catholic University (Degree in EEC Law). *Member:* Portuguese Bar Association. *LANGUAGES:* Portuguese, English, French, Spanish and Italian. *PRACTICE AREAS:* Commercial Law; Contract Law; Company Law; Industrial Property Law; EEC Law.

PAULA BAPTISTA COELHO, born Lisbon, Portugal, 1963; admitted, 1989, Portugal. *Education:* University of Law School (Bachelor of Law); Lusíada University of Lisbon. *Member:* Portuguese Bar Association. *LANGUAGES:* Portuguese, English and French. *PRACTICE AREAS:* General Civil Law; Labour Law; Administrative Law; Public International Law; Constitutional Law.

JALLES ADVOGADOS
Established in 1986
AV. ÁLVARES CABRAL, 34 - 6°
P-1250 LISBON, PORTUGAL
Telephone: 351-1-388.40.95
Telefax: 351-1-388.19.55

Brussels, Belgium Office: Rue J-A Demot, 23, B-1040. Telephone: 32-2-230.13.18. Telefax: 32-2-230.79.07.

Foreign Investments, International Trade Law, Private International Law, Recognition and Enforcement of Foreign Judgements, Business Law, Corporate Mergers and Acquisitions and Commercial Law, Debt Collection, Taxation, Contracts, EC Law, Competition Law, Licence and Distributorships, Advertising Law, Immigration, Product Liability, Environmental Law, Energy Law, Investment Funds and Real Estate, Finance and Banking Law, Insurance Law, Aviation, Transportation, Intellectual Property, Entertainment, Property Inheritance, Telecommunication Law, Arbitration and Litigation, Administrative Law.

FIRM PROFILE: The firm is highly specialized in complex negotiations, mainly so far international trade law, business transactions and corporate law, as well as private international law, are concerned, maintaining its original commitment to excellence and to provide cost efficient legal services to their clients through a multi-lingual staff. The firm has its own representative office in Brussels and belongs to the small group of leading Portuguese firms at international level.

Portuguese lawyers may represent clients before all Portuguese courts, before the European Court of Justice and other international courts and are admitted to plead before all courts of the Member States of the European Union.

ISABEL JALLES, born Lisbon, Portugal, July 4, 1949; admitted, 1973, Portugal. *Education:* Universities of Lisbon and Coimbra (Law degree, 1973; Master in Law, 1979); Heidelberg (1978); Hamburg (1978); Max-Planck-Institut Munich (1980); Salzburg Seminar in American Studies (1980). Author: "Portugal" in Handbuch des Werberechts in den EG-Staaten, Oesterreich, Schweiz und USA, Verlag Dr. Otto Schmidt KG, 1995; collaboration with William C. Hoffman, "Cologne Re: Product Liability Book," Kluwer, 1995; "The Liability of the Inland Road Carrier according to Portuguese private law," in Road Carrier's Liability in Europe, The Hague: Stichting Vervoeradres, 1994; "European Economic Interest Groupings (Portugal)," Deventer/Boston: Kluwer Law and Taxation Publishers, 1990; "Das Urteil des EuGH in der Sache 'Rush Portuguesa' - eine Anmerkung," EuZW, 1990; "Public enterprises in Portugal and Spain: An analysis from the point of view of competition law," Luxemburg: Commission of the European Communities, 1988 (coordination of the work); "Extraterritoriality and International Trade. An exercise on American Law," (in Portuguese), Lisbon: Bertrand, 1988; "Consequences of the application of

(This Listing Continued)

JALLES ADVOGADOS, Lisbon—Continued

Directive 85/374/CEE on product liability for the exporters of different Member States," (in Portuguese), RDE, 1988; "Portuguese Competition Law: Analysis and Perspectives on Implementation," (in Portuguese), Concorrência em Portugal nos Anos 80, Lisboa, 1985; "Implications Juridico-constitutionnelles de l'adhésion aux Communautés européennes. Le cas du Portugal," Bruxelles: Bruylant, 1981; "State Monopolies of a Commercial Character (Article 37 of the EEC Treaty) and their Importance in Connection with Portugal's Accession to the European Communities," Georgia J. Int'l & Comp. L. 1980. Visiting Professor, Catholic University of Louvain, 1983-1985. Assistant Professor for European Competition Law and Industrial Property Rights and Litigation in European Court, Catholic University of Lisbon, 1979-1987. Assistant Professor of Private International Law and International Economic Law, University of Lisbon, 1977-1985. Arbitrator, Portuguese Chambers of Commerce and Industry (Lisbon/Oporto). Correspondent for Portugal of EuZW. Portuguese correspondent on the Working Group of Experts of the ILPA - Immigration Law Practitioners' Association, 1990. Correspondent for Portugal of Gaceta Juridica de la CEE (Madrid). *Member:* Portuguese Association for European Law (Vice President); European Advertising Lawyers' Association; Legal Forum of European Direct Mail Association; Union of European Lawyers, AIJA; Cahiers de Droit Européen and of the Newsletter Stratégie Europe (Member, Advisory Board); International Litigation Practitioners' Forum; LAWASIA. *LANGUAGES:* Portuguese, English, French, German, Spanish, Dutch and Italian. *PRACTICE AREAS:* EC and Competition (antitrust) law; Corporate and Company Law; International Law and conflict of laws; Product Liability Law; Advertising and Marketing; Foreign Investments; Administrative Law; Immigration Law; Banking and Finance.

PEDRO CORREIA DE MATOS, born Lisbon, Portugal, January 9, 1963. *Education:* University of Lisbon (Law degree, 1990). Catholic University of Lisbon, Course on Environmental Law, 1990. Newsletter Strategie Europe, collaborator for Portugal. *LANGUAGES:* Portuguese, English, French and Spanish. *PRACTICE AREAS:* Immigration Law; Administrative Law; Environmental Law; Taxation; Consumer Law.

CLARA GUIMARÃES FERNANDES, born Funchal, Portugal, June 11, 1957. *Education:* University of Lisbon (Law degree, 1982). Member, Commission of the European Communities, 1989-1991. *LANGUAGES:* Portuguese, French, English, Spanish and German. *PRACTICE AREAS:* Computers and Software; Entertainment and the Arts; Communications and Media; Intellectual Property; Litigation.

ANA SOTTOMAYOR, born Lisbon, Portugal, January 31, 1962; admitted, 1990, Portugal. *Education:* University of Lisbon (1989). Training, Marketing Studies , Lyons France, 1991. *LANGUAGES:* Portuguese, French and English. *PRACTICE AREAS:* Commercial and Company Law; Successions; Litigation; Labour Law; Family Law.

JOÃO RIBEIRINHO, born Lisbon, Portugal, May 5, 1969. *Education:* Catholic University of Lisbon (Graduated in Law, 1993). *LANGUAGES:* Portuguese, English and French. *PRACTICE AREAS:* General Practice; Civil Law; Consumer Law; Debtor Creditor Law; Family Law.

CRISTINA DEIN, born Schorndorf, Germany, May 8, 1967; admitted, 1993, Portugal. *Education:* University of Coimbra, Portugal (Law Degree, 1993); University of Konstanz, Germany, 1993. Seminars: Europäische Gerichtshöfe, Freiburg, 1992; Umweltschutzrecht, Konstanz, 1993; Consumer Protection, Coimbra, 1993; Community Law, Lisbon, 1993. *LANGUAGES:* German, Portuguese English and French. *PRACTICE AREAS:* Contracts; Corporate and Company Law; Foreign Investments; Real Estate and Property; Transportation Law.

MARTINHO VILLANI, born Lisbon, Portugal, March 11, 1970; admitted, 1994, Portugal. *Education:* University of Lisbon, Portugal (Law Degree, 1994). Member: Hungarian Association in Portugal (Vice-President, 1994). *LANGUAGES:* Portuguese, German, English, French, Spanish, Italian and Hungarian. *PRACTICE AREAS:* Agency and Distributorships; Business Law; Energy; Franchises and Franchising; Sports Law.

OF COUNSEL

PROF. DR. RUI MOURA-RAMOS, born Batalha, Portugal, June 30, 1950; admitted, 1973, Portugal. *Education:* University of Coimbra (Law degree, 1972; Master of Law, 1979; Ph.D., 1991); University of Sorbonne (D.E.A., 1987). Author: *The law governing the international labour agreements* (in Portuguese), Coimbra, 1991; *About the Law of Nationality* (in Portuguese), Coimbra, 1974. Professor of International Law, PIL and European Law, Universities of Coimbra, Porto and Lisbon. Member, Portuguese

(This Listing Continued)

EU1148B

Section of CIEC, 1986—). Director, The Hague Academy of International Law, 1984. Associate Member, UNIDROIT, 1983—. Delegate, The Hague Conference on PIL, 1982—. Governmental representative, UNCITRAL, 1980—. Member, Portuguese Association for European Law. *LANGUAGES:* Portuguese, French, English, German, Spanish and Italian. *PRACTICE AREAS:* Arbitration; Constitutional Law; EEC Law; Private International Law; Industrial Relations and Labour Law; International Contracts.

LEGAL SUPPORT PERSONNEL

DR. PETER G.F. HEILMANN, born Hilversum, The Netherlands, February 7, 1944. *Education:* University of Utrecht, The Netherlands (Ph.D). Expert for the United Nations, 1972. Consultant for the Norwegian Government, 1976. Policy adviser for Dutch authorities, 1980. Director of the Industrial Liaison Office of the University of Utrecht, 1986. Managing Director. *LANGUAGES:* Dutch, English, French and German.

Languages: Portuguese, English, German, French, Dutch, Spanish, Italian and Hungarian.

JARDIM, SAMPAIO, CALDAS E ASSOCIADOS SOCIEDADE PROFISSIONAL DE ADVOGADOS

Established in 1968

AVENIDA DUQUE DE AVILA, 66 - 5TH FLOOR
1000 LISBON, PORTUGAL
Telephone: (351)-1-527925
Cable Address: "Advocat"
Fax: (351)-1 3533363, 3527695

Oporto, Portugal Office: Rua Franca Júnior, 44 - 7° 4450 Matosinhos. Telephone: (351) 2-9372153. Fax: (351) 2-9372154.

General Practice. Business, Commercial, Patent, Industrial Relations, Civil Law and Litigation.

FIRM PROFILE: The firm was established in 1968 with 3 partners and offers a full range of legal services. It is well known for its commercial and civil law, banking and litigation.

Besides Portuguese companies, many clients are multinational ones on several activities. The support staff consists of 20 people.

Usually 5 trainees give their support to the partners and to the associates.

MEMBERS OF FIRM

JOSÉ VERA JARDIM, born Ponte do Sôr, Portugal, January 2, 1939; admitted, 1964, Portugal. *Education:* Faculty of Law, University of Lisbon. Lecturer of Law, University of Lisbon, 1972-1980. *Member:* Portuguese Bar Association. *LANGUAGES:* Portuguese, English, French and German. *PRACTICE AREAS:* Commercial and Civil Law; Mergers and Acquisitions; Foreign Investment.

JÚLIO CASTRO CALDAS, born Lisbon, Portugal, November 19, 1943; admitted, 1970, Portugal. *Education:* Faculty of Law, University of Lisbon. Member of the Parliament, 1980. *Member:* Portuguese Bar Association (President). *LANGUAGES:* Portuguese, French, English, Italian and German. *PRACTICE AREAS:* Commercial and Civil Law; Litigation.

MANUEL MAGALHÃES E SILVA, born Porto, Portugal, December 12, 1944; admitted, 1973, Portugal. *Education:* Faculty of Law, University of Lisbon. *Member:* Portuguese Bar Association. *LANGUAGES:* Portuguese, English, French and German. *PRACTICE AREAS:* Civil and Criminal Law; Labour Law; Litigation.

MARIA DE LOURDES SILVA, born Mozambique, October 6, 1952; admitted, 1977, Portugal. *Education:* University of Lisbon. Lecturer on Law, University of Lisbon, 1976-1979. *Member:* Portuguese Bar Association; AIJA-Association Internationale des Jeunes Avocats. *LANGUAGES:* Portuguese, English and French. *PRACTICE AREAS:* Trademarks; Intellectual Property; Real Estate Law.

PEDRO LEITE ALVES, born Lisbon, Portugal, June 2, 1962; admitted, 1988, Portugal. *Education:* Faculty of Law, University of Lisbon, Catholic University of Lisbon. Lecturer on Law, University of Lisbon, 1980-1982. *Member:* Portuguese Bar Association. *LANGUAGES:* Portuguese, English and French. *PRACTICE AREAS:* Commercial and Civil Law; Banking Law; Foreign Investment.

(This Listing Continued)

ASSOCIATES

HEIKE ENGELKING ALVES, born Zweibrücken, Federal Republic of Germany, April 15, 1962; admitted, 1988, Portugal. *Education:* Faculty of Law, University of Lisbon. *Member:* Portuguese Bar Association. *LANGUAGES:* Portuguese, German, English and French. *PRACTICE AREAS:* Consumer and Commercial Law.

MARIA DO CARMO BARBOSA, born Lisbon, Portugal, July 14, 1964; admitted, 1988, Portugal. *Education:* Faculty of Law, University of Lisbon. *Member:* Portuguese Bar Association. *LANGUAGES:* Portuguese, French and English. *PRACTICE AREAS:* Banking.

HELENA LANCASTRE, born Lisbon, Portugal, July 5, 1965; admitted, 1991, Portugal. *Education:* Faculty of Law, Catholic University of Lisbon. *Member:* Portuguese Bar Association. *LANGUAGES:* Portuguese, English and French. *PRACTICE AREAS:* Commercial and Civil Law; Property Law.

MARGARIDA MACHADO ROSA, born Lisbon, Portugal, April 5, 1967; admitted, 1992, Portugal. *Education:* Faculty of Law, Catholic University of Lisbon. *Member:* Portuguese Bar Association. *LANGUAGES:* Portuguese, English and French. *PRACTICE AREAS:* Patent and Commercial Law; Competition Law.

ANTÓNIO FIGUEIREDO CARVALHO, born Mozambique, August 26, 1968; admitted, 1993, Portugal. *Education:* Faculty of Law, Catholic University of Lisbon. *Member:* Portuguese Bar Association. *LANGUAGES:* Portuguese, English, French and Spanish. *PRACTICE AREAS:* Civil Law; Administrative Law; Commercial Law.

CARLA SANTOS, born Angola, April 2, 1965; admitted, 1991, Portugal. *Education:* Faculty of Law, University of Coimbra. *Member:* Portuguese Bar Association. *LANGUAGES:* Portuguese, English and French. *PRACTICE AREAS:* Banking.

OPORTO PORTUGAL OFFICE

PAULO MAGALHÃES E. SILVA, born Oporto, September 25, 1965; admitted, 1990, Portugal. *Education:* Faculty of Law, Portucalense University of Oporto. *Member:* Portuguese Bar Association. *LANGUAGES:* Portuguese, English and French. *PRACTICE AREAS:* Civil Law; Criminal Law; Labour Law.

AUGUSTO VELLOSO FERREIRA, born Oporto, June 9, 1964; admitted, 1990, Portugal. *Education:* Faculty of Law, Portucalense University of Oporto. *Member:* Portuguese Bar Association. *LANGUAGES:* Portuguese, English and French. *PRACTICE AREAS:* Commercial Law; Civil Law; Labour Law.

MORAIS LEITÃO, J. GALVÃO TELES & ASSOCIADOS

Established in 1978

RUA CASTILHO, 75 - 1ST FLOOR
1200 LISBON, PORTUGAL
Telephone: (351-1) 3863174/3864178/3860730
Fax: (351-1) 3861019/3863177

Oporto, Portugal Office: In Co-operation with Vellozo Ferreira, Cavaleiro Brandão, Pinheiro Torres, Amorim Ferreira & Associados, Alameda Basilio Telles, n°26 - 4100 Porto. Telephone: 351 2 6001245; 351 2 6001246. Fax: 351 2 6001270.

Litigation and Arbitration, Corporate, Business and Commercial Law, Civil Law, Banking, Financial and Securities Law, Foreign Investment, Privatizations, Mergers and Acquisitions, Insurance, Leasing, Domestic and International Taxation, Competition Law, EEC Law, Consumer Law, Agency and Distributorships, Aviation, Franchise, Labour Law, Administrative Law, Real Estate and Urban Planning, Public Procurement, Telecommunications and Media Law.

FIRM PROFILE: *Morais Leitão, Galvão Teles & Associados is the result of the merger of João Morais Leitão & Associados and Galvão Teles, Bleck, Pinto Leite & Associados, two well known Portuguese firms. The resulting firm is of significant dimension in the Portuguese market, and able to offer legal services in most areas of practice.*

(This Listing Continued)

PARTNERS

JOÃO MORAIS LEITÃO, born Covilhã, Portugal, September 4, 1938; admitted, 1961, Portugal. *Education:* University of Lisbon Law School. Minister of Social Affairs, 1980 and Minister of Finance, 1981, of the Portuguese Government. Author: "Satisfaction of a Banking Debt with Treasury Bonds," "Foreign Investment in Portugal," "Capital Markets in Portugal," "The Portuguese Insurance Market." Member of Parliament, 1982-1984. *Member:* Portuguese Bar Association (Vice-President, 1990-1992). *LANGUAGES:* Portuguese, English, French and Spanish. *PRACTICE AREAS:* Litigation; Arbitration; Mergers and Acquisitions; Banking Law; Finance Law; Securities; Competition Law; EEC Law.

JOSÉ MANUEL GALVÃO TELES, born Lisbon, Portugal, April 8, 1938; admitted, 1960, Portugal. *Education:* University of Lisbon Law School. Portuguese Ambassador to the United Nations, 1975-1976. *Member:* Portuguese Bar Association; International Bar Association. *LANGUAGES:* Portuguese, French, English and Spanish. *PRACTICE AREAS:* General Civil Law; Corporate Law; Privatization Law; Insolvency Law; Arbitration; Litigation.

JORGE MARIA BLECK, born Lisbon, Portugal, December 27, 1954; admitted, 1981, Portugal. *Education:* University of Lisbon Law School. Junior Assistant Professor, University of Lisbon Law School. *Member:* Portuguese and International Bar Associations; Portuguese Delegation of International Chamber of Commerce (ICC); Leaseurope - European Federation of Equipment Leasing Companies Association (Member, Legal Committee). *LANGUAGES:* Portuguese, French and English. *PRACTICE AREAS:* Corporate Law; Finance Leasing; Aviation Law; International Contract Law; Foreign Investment Law.

ANTÓNIO MARIA PINTO LEITE, born Lisbon, Portugal, July 24, 1954; admitted, 1981, Portugal. *Education:* University of Lisbon Law School. Junior Assistant Professor: University of Lisbon Law School; Portuguese Catholic University. *Member:* Portuguese Bar Association. *LANGUAGES:* Portuguese, French and English. *PRACTICE AREAS:* Civil Law; Property Law; Expropriation Law; Business Law; Labour Law; Litigation.

FILIPA ARANTES PEDROSO, born Lisbon, Portugal, November 22, 1954; admitted, 1980, Portugal. *Education:* University of Lisbon Law School; University of Louvain, Belgium (Degrees in Law and EEC Law). Stage, Commission of the EEC, Competition Law. Assistant Professor, Political Economics, University of Lisbon Law School, 1977-1979. Author: Several articles on Competition Law, Merger Control, Agency and Distributorship, Insurance and EEC Law. *Member:* Portuguese Bar Association; Portuguese European Law Association. *LANGUAGES:* Portuguese, English, French and Spanish. *PRACTICE AREAS:* Competition Law; Agency and Distributorships; Company Law; Mergers and Acquisitions; Public Procurement; Telecommunications and Media Law.

FERNANDA MATOSO, born Silves, Portugal, July 3, 1961; admitted, 1984, Portugal. *Education:* Universidade Livre, Lisbon (Law Degree). *Member:* Portuguese Bar Association. *LANGUAGES:* Portuguese, English and French. *PRACTICE AREAS:* Litigation; Civil Law.

SEGISMUNDO PINTO BASTO, born Lisbon, Portugal, November 14, 1961; admitted, 1985, Portugal. *Education:* Universidade Livre, Lisbon (Law Degree); Stage at the Commission of the European Communities (1987). *Member:* Portuguese Bar Association. *LANGUAGES:* Portuguese, English and French. *PRACTICE AREAS:* Corporate Law; Business Law; Banking Law; Finance Law; Securities; Mergers and Acquisitions.

FRANCISCO DE SOUSA DA CÂMARA, born Lisbon, Portugal, July 31, 1961; admitted, 1986, Portugal. *Education:* Portuguese Catholic University, Lisbon Law School (Law Degree and Graduate Studies in EEC Law; Master in Tax and Financial Law). Author: several articles published on tax subjects. Contributor: "Commentary on the EC Direct Tax Measures and Member States' Implementation," ed. by I.B.F.D. (original release), and to the "Guides to European Taxation - The Taxation of Companies in Europe," (updated release) ed. by I.B.F.D. Correspondent in Portugal for the European Taxation published by the International Bureau of Fiscal Documentation and for the Tax Letter Europe, published by the European Law Press. *Member:* Portuguese Bar Association (Tax Committee Member, 1990-1992); I.F.A.- International Fiscal Association; ITPA-International Tax Planning Association; Portuguese Fiscal Association (Associate). *LANGUAGES:* Portuguese, English, French and Spanish. *PRACTICE AREAS:* International and Domestic Taxation; Taxation Litigation; Company Law; Administrative Law; Litigation.

NUNO GALVÃO TELES, born Lisbon, Portugal, October 4, 1964; admitted, 1987, Portugal. *Education:* University of Lisbon Law School;

(This Listing Continued)

MORAIS LEITÃO, J. GALVÃO TELES &
ASSOCIADOS, Lisbon—Continued

University of London (LL.M.). *Member:* Portuguese Bar Association. *LANGUAGES:* Portuguese, English and Spanish. *PRACTICE AREAS:* Banking Law; Securities; Corporate Finance Law; Company Law.

ASSOCIATES

PEDRO SIZA VIEIRA, born Lisbon, Portugal, July 14, 1964; admitted, 1988, Portugal. *Education:* University of Lisbon Law School. Assistant Professor, Universidade Autónoma, Lisbon. *Member:* Portuguese Bar Association. *LANGUAGES:* Portuguese, English and French. *PRACTICE AREAS:* Administrative Law; Litigation; Construction Law; Real Estate Law; Urban Planning Law.

MIGUEL PINTO CARDOSO, born Lisbon, Portugal, August 23, 1964; admitted, 1987, Portugal. *Education:* University of Lisbon Law School. *Member:* Portuguese Bar Association. *LANGUAGES:* Portuguese, English and French. *PRACTICE AREAS:* Company Law; Franchise Law; Litigation.

MARIA ANTÓNIA CARDOSO DE MENEZES, born Lisbon, Portugal, April 5, 1966; admitted, 1991, Portugal. *Education:* Portuguese Catholic University, Lisbon Law School (Law Degree). *Member:* Portuguese Bar Association. *LANGUAGES:* Portuguese, French, English and Spanish. *PRACTICE AREAS:* Corporate Law; Mergers and Acquisitions; Bankruptcy Law; Litigation.

JOÃO SERRA, born Lisbon, Portugal, February 28, 1966; admitted, 1991, Portugal. *Education:* University of Lisbon Law School (Law Degree). *Member:* Portuguese Bar Association. *LANGUAGES:* Portuguese, French, English and Spanish. *PRACTICE AREAS:* Litigation; Arbitration; Civil Law; Business Law.

FILIPA MENDES PINTO, born Lisbon, Portugal, February 21, 1968; admitted, 1993, Portugal. *Education:* University of Lisbon Law School. *Member:* Portuguese Bar Association. *LANGUAGES:* Portuguese, English and French. *PRACTICE AREAS:* General Practice; Labour Law; Litigation.

TERESA MORAIS LEITÃO, born Lisbon, Portugal, July 11, 1969; admitted, 1992, Portugal. *Education:* University of Lisbon Law School; European University Institute (LL.M). *Member:* Portugues Bar Association. *LANGUAGES:* Portuguese, English, Spanish and German. *PRACTICE AREAS:* Family Law; Environmental Law.

OF COUNSEL

CARLOS FERREIRA DE ALMEIDA, born Lisbon, Portugal, September 25, 1938. *Education:* University of Lisbon Law School. Professor of Law, University of Lisbon Law School. Legal Banking Advisor. *LANGUAGES:* Portuguese, English, French, Italian and German. *PRACTICE AREAS:* Civil Law; Commercial Law; Banking Law; Consumer Law.

JOÃO DE MENEZES FERREIRA, born Lisbon, Portugal, May 20, 1950; admitted, 1978, Portugal. *Education:* University of Lisbon Law School (Post-Graduate studies on EC Law); College of Europe, Brugges, Belgium. Member, Negotiation Committee, Portuguese Accession to EEC, 1977-1985. Head of Delegation that drafted the Treaty of Accession and European Single Act, 1985. Legal Advisor, Portuguese Permanent Representation to E.C. in Brussels, 1986-1991. Participant, in European Unity Treaty drafting. Visiting Professor: INA (Institute for National Administration); Institute for High Studies on Finance and Taxation. *Member:* Portuguese Bar Association. *LANGUAGES:* Portuguese, English and French. *PRACTICE AREAS:* EC Law; Competition Law.

EU1150B

LOPES DIAS, COSTA BASTO, JORGE VERISSIMO E ASSOCIADOS - SOCIEDADE DE ADVOGADOS

Established in 1986

AV. 24 DE JULHO, NR. 60 2ND FLOOR
1200 LISBON, PORTUGAL
Telephone: 600667; 3954767
Telefax: 3954766

Company and Maritime Law, Competition Law, Foreign Investment, Mergers and Acquisitions, Transfer of Technology, International Contracts, Intellectual Property, Trademarks, Franchising, Patent Law, EC Law, Taxation Law and Procedures, Computer Law, Civil Law Contracts, Family, Real Estate, Conveyancing, Insurance Law, Banking Law, Finance Law, Administrative Law, Wills and Estates, Arbitration, Criminal Law, Litigation in Civil, Administrative and Criminal Courts.

MARIA DE LOURDES LOPES DIAS, born Setúbal, Portugal, 1937; admitted, 1977, Portugal. *Education:* University of Lisbon (Lawyer); The Hague Academy of Private International Law (Seminars on: Arbitration and EC Law; Intensive Courses: EC Law and Company Law). Vice President of Honor, AIJA, 1987. *Member:* International Chamber of Commerce; Association Européene des Avocats; International Bar Association; Computer Law Association; Transnational Taxation Network; International Grouping of Lawyers and Intercounsel. *LANGUAGES:* Portuguese, English, French, German, Spanish and Italian. *PRACTICE AREAS:* Company Law; Maritime Law; Competition Law; Foreign Investment; Mergers and Acquisitions; Transfer of Technology; International Contracts; EC Law; Taxation Law; Computer Law; Arbitration; Administrative Law; Wills and Estates.

ANTONIO DA COSTA BASTO, born 1949; admitted, 1976, Portugal. *Education:* Faculty of Law, Classic University (Graduated, 1973). *Member:* Association Internationale des Droits d'Assurance (Portuguese Section); Association Internationale des Jeunes Avocats; Associação Portuguesa dos Jovens Advogados. *LANGUAGES:* Portuguese, Spanish, French and English. *PRACTICE AREAS:* Civil Law; Insurance Law; Commercial Law; Criminal Law; Company Law; Foreign Investment.

JORGE VERISSIMO, born Lisbon, Portugal, 1949; admitted, 1974, Portugal. *Education:* Faculty of Law, Classic University (Graduated, 1972). *Member:* Association Internationale des Jeunes Avocats; Associazioni Giuristi di Lingua Italiana; Associação Portuguesa de Direito Europeu. *LANGUAGES:* Portuguese, English, French, German, Spanish and Italian. *PRACTICE AREAS:* Civil Law; Contract Law; Company Law; Banking Law; Finance Law; Commercial Law; Foreign Investment.

ANA CARDOSO PERES, born Rio Maior, Portugal, 1960; admitted, 1988, Portugal. *Education:* Lisbon Catholic University (Lawyer). *Member:* International Association of Young Lawyers. *LANGUAGES:* Portuguese and English. *PRACTICE AREAS:* Real Estate; Conveyancing; Lease Law; Property Law; EC Law; Family Law; Wills and Estates; Foreign Investment; Litigation in Civil Courts.

DOMINGOS VAZ DE AZEVEDO, born Lisbon, Portugal, 1938; admitted, 1977, Portugal. *Education:* Faculty of Law, Classic University (Graduated, 1975); Lisbon Catholic University (Master, European Law, 1989). *LANGUAGES:* Portuguese, French, English, Spanish and Italian. *PRACTICE AREAS:* Taxation Law; Company Law; Property Law; EC Law.

M. ROSÁRIO DE ALMEIDA RIBEIRO, born Lisbon, Portugal, 1951; admitted, 1977, Brazil; 1989, Portugal. *Education:* University of the State of Rio de Janeiro Law School (1976). *Member:* Portuguese Bar Association; Brazilian Bar Association. *LANGUAGES:* Portuguese, English and French. *PRACTICE AREAS:* Civil Law; Commercial Law; Criminal Law; Company Law.

DOMINGOS ALVIM, born Lisbon, Portugal, 1966; admitted, 1992, Portugal. *Education:* Portuguese Catholic University. *LANGUAGES:* Portuguese, English, French and Italian. *PRACTICE AREAS:* Civil Law; Commercial Law; Company Law; Foreign Investment; International Contracts; Maritime Law; Insurance Law.

MIGUEL BETTENCOURT DA CAMARA, born Lisbon, Portugal, 1967; admitted, 1992, Portugal. *Education:* Faculty of Law, International University (Graduated, 1990); Classic University (Master, European Law,

(This Listing Continued)

1992). Lecturer: Administrative Law, International and Community Law, Faculty of Law, International University, Lisbon; International Law, Faculty of Law, Lusiada University, Lisbon. *Member:* Association Internationale des Jeunes Avocats. *LANGUAGES:* Portuguese, English and French. *PRACTICE AREAS:* Administrative Law; International Law; EC Law; Litigation; Administrative Courts.

LUSOJURIST

Advogados

Established in 1992

RUA ALMEIDA BRANDÃO, 19
1200 LISBON, PORTUGAL
Telephone: (351 1) 3975180
Fax: (351 1) 3975186; 3975191

Member of EUROJURIST E.E.I.G.

Mergers and Acquisitions, Banks and Banking, Securities, Commodities, Business Law, Corporate Law, Company Law, Foreign Investment, International Arbitration, Contracts, Labor and Employment, Wills, Real Estate, Planning, Land Use, General Practice and Litigation.

MEMBERS OF FIRM

JOÃO PAULO MENEZES FALCÃO, born Oporto, Portugal, 1959; admitted, 1984, Portugal. *Education:* Catholic University, Lisbon. *PRACTICE AREAS:* Commercial Law; Administrative Law; Taxation; Pharmaceutical Regulation.

LUÍS DE GOUVEIA FERNANDES, born Lisbon, Portugal, 1957; admitted, 1985, Portugal. *Education:* Catholic University, Lisbon. Author: "Planning Applications in Portugal," London, 1991; "Reprivatization of Nationalized Companies," London, 1992. *PRACTICE AREAS:* Corporate Contracts; Incorporation; Shareholders Agreements; Privatization; International Arbitration.

LUÍS BARROS DE FIGUEIREDO, born Lisbon, Portugal, 1960; admitted, 1985, Portugal. *Education:* Faculty of Law, Lisbon. Consultant, CEJUR, Cabinet's legal support agency. Author: "The Inheritance of the Right to Inherit," Lisbon, 1989. Assistant Professor, Lusíada University, Lisbon. *PRACTICE AREAS:* Litigation; Civil Law; Contracts; Family Law; Trust and Estates; Wills; Property; Arbitration.

FILIPE FRAÚSTO DA SILVA, born Lisbon, Portugal, 1963; admitted, 1989, Portugal. *Education:* Catholic University, Lisbon. Consultant, CEJUR, Cabinet's legal support agency. Author: "Mergers and Acquisitions in Portugal," London, 1990; "Company Acquisitions in Portugal: Public Offers," London, 1992. *PRACTICE AREAS:* Labor; Employment; Commercial Law; Litigation.

JOÃO DE FREITAS E COSTA, born Lisbon, Portugal, 1962; admitted, 1989, Portugal. *Education:* Faculty of Law, Lisbon. Practice of Law, Macao, 1986-1992. Private Notary, Macao. *PRACTICE AREAS:* Commercial Law; Notarial Services; Contracts; Environmental Law; Agricultural Law; Wills.

JOSÉ GUILHERME FRANQUEIRA DIAS, born Lisbon, Portugal, October 21, 1960; admitted, 1986, Portugal. *Education:* Catholic University, Lisbon. *PRACTICE AREAS:* Civil Law; Corporate Law; Commercial Law; Bankruptcy; Litigation.

OF COUNSEL

PEDRO ROMANO MARTINEZ, born Lisbon, Portugal, 1959; admitted, 1985, Portugal. *Education:* Catholic University, Lisbon. Author: "Subcontract," Coimbra, 1989; "Contractor Agreement," Lisbon, 1991. Professor of Law, Faculty of Law, Lisbon and Catholic University, Lisbon.

PAULO OLAVO DE PITTA E CUNHA, born Lisbon, Portugal, 1961; admitted, 1986, Portugal. *Education:* Catholic University of Lisbon (Master in Law, 1989). Currently preparing PhD Thesis on Commercial and Banking Law. Author: "Sale of Other People's Property", 1987; "Short Note about the Rights of the Members (of the Limited Liability Companies)," 1988; "Special Rights in Public Companies Limited by Shares: the Preference Shares," 1993; "Commercial Law II (Public Companies Limited by Shares/Resume)," 1994. Assistant Professor of Law, Faculty of Law, Lisbon and Catholic University, Lisbon. *PRACTICE AREAS:* Banks and Banking; Company Law; Corporate Law; Capital Markets; Securities; Commodities.

Languages: Portuguese, English, French and Spanish

BELARMINO MARTINS & ASSOCIADOS

Sociedade de Advogados

AV. ENG. DUARTE PACHECO, 19-10 ESQ.
1000 LISBON, PORTUGAL
Telephone: (351-1) 3879540
Fax: (351-1) 3873527

Local and International Business Law, Corporate and Commercial Law, Foreign Investment and International Contracts, EC Law, Mergers and Acquisitions, Real Estate Law.

FIRM PROFILE: The firm is a regulated law firm and is known for offering a full range of legal services to both national and international clients. It is a member of Correspondent Law Firms of Price Waterhouse EEIG and cooperates with member firms and Price Waterhouse firms to render legal services throughout Europe, where appropriate on a multidisciplinary basis. The firm has two members and seven associates.

MEMBERS OF FIRM

BELARMINO GONCALVES MARTINS, born Lisbon, Portugal, February 28, 1938; admitted, 1968, Portugal. *Education:* Faculty of Law, University of Coimbra (1966). *Member:* Portuguese Bar Association; Portuguese Chamber of Statutory Auditors; Technical Standards Committee; European Federation of Accountants (Representative for Corporate Law Matters). *LANGUAGES:* Portuguese, English, French and Spanish. *PRACTICE AREAS:* International Business Taxation; Accounting; Audit; Company Commercial Law.

MARIA ADELAIDE MOURA, born Benguela, Angola, June 6, 1960; admitted, 1987, Portugal. *Education:* Faculty of Law, University of Lisbon (1985). *Member:* Portuguese Bar Association. *LANGUAGES:* Portuguese and English. *PRACTICE AREAS:* Business Reorganizations; International Joint Ventures; Banking; Tax Planning.

ASSOCIATES

MANUEL ANSELMO TORRES, born Lisbon, Portugal, May 17, 1962; admitted, 1990, Portugal. *Education:* Faculty of Law, University of Lisbon (1987); Monterey Institute of International Studies (M.B.A., 1992). *Member:* Portuguese Bar Association; Association Internationale des Jeunes Avocats. *LANGUAGES:* Portuguese, English, German, French and Spanish. *PRACTICE AREAS:* Taxation of Mergers and Acquisitions; International Estate Taxation; Offshore Taxation; Stamp Duties.

CARMO GOMES TEIXEIRA, born Lisbon, Portugal, July 16, 1964; admitted, 1990, Portugal. *Education:* Faculty of Law, Catholic University of Lisbon (1987). *Member:* Portuguese Bar Association. *LANGUAGES:* Portuguese and English. *PRACTICE AREAS:* Labour Taxation; Work Permits; Distribution Agreements.

PAULA ALBERGARIA SILVA, born Azores, Portugal, October 5, 1964; admitted, 1990, Portugal. *Education:* Faculty of Law, University of Lisbon (1987). *Member:* Portuguese Bar Association. *LANGUAGES:* Portuguese, English and Spanish. *PRACTICE AREAS:* Labour Legislation; Industrial Relations; Government Contracts.

Languages: English, French, German, Italian and Spanish.

MATEUS ANDRADE DIAS E ASSOCIADOS

Established in 1962

RUA ANTÓNIO MARIA CARDOSO, N°25-4°
1200 LISBON, PORTUGAL
Telephone: 1-3468134
Telex: 42645 LEXMAR P
Fax: 1-3473746

Admiralty Law, Arbitration and Litigation, Banking Securities and Finance, Commercial Law, Companies and Corporations, Contract, Consumer Law, Business Crime, Tax Law, Accident and Injury Claims.

FIRM PROFILE: The office advocates Maritime cases in court and out of court on behalf of shipowners, P & I Clubs, cargo owners and underwriters and banks. It assists the clients in negotiations of contracts involving shipping interests. The main Activity of the office is on behalf of foreign clients above all Anglo Saxons but it also represents Portuguese companies, other than in the shipping activity, in commercial and business crime disputes, as well as a consultant in tax law. In the recent years because the assistance of the office was requested in matters other than shipping it was decided to have the support of professor Doutor João Calvão da Silva, who is recognized as a leading authority in all fields of private law.

(This Listing Continued)

MATEUS ANDRADE DIAS E ASSOCIADOS, Lisbon—
Continued

PARTNERS

MATEUS ANDRADE DIAS (1934-1994).

ANTÓNIO LABISA, born 1957; admitted, 1980, Portugal. *LAN-GUAGES:* English, French and Spanish.

TERESA ANDRADE DIAS, born 1964; admitted, 1991, Portugal. *LANGUAGES:* English, French and Spanish.

OF COUNSEL

PROFESSOR DOCTOR JOÃO CALVÃO DA SILVA, Professor of Law, University of Coimbra and Lusiada University of Lisbon. *LAN-GUAGES:* English, German, French and Spanish.

Languages: English, French and Spanish.

MOURA, CHAVES & ASSOCIADOS

Sociedade de Advogados

Established in 1988

TRAV. DE SANTO ILDEFONSO, 32-1
1200 LISBON, PORTUGAL
Telephone: (351-1) 3968161
Fax: (351-1) 609105

Member of the Terrelex Network.

Administrative Law, Banking and Financial Assistance, Civil and Commercial Litigation and Arbitration Procedures, Commercial Law, Construction Law, Corporate Law, Foreign Investments, Insurance Law, Labour Law, Real Estate Law and Tax Law.

FIRM PROFILE: The firm Moura, Chaves & Associados, was founded in 1988 with members who came from a previous law firm, founded in 1981, who was the third to be registered in Portugal. Since then, the firm offers its clients a wide scope of assistance in many different fields, making it a full service law firm with emphasis in Business, Corporate and Tax Law.

The firm represents clients ranging from small, medium to large enterprises, from the most diversified ares of business and economy. Insurance companies, agricultural, industrial, and instruction and commercial corporations. The firm also represents individuals and cultural non-profit foundations.

MEMBERS OF FIRM

JOSÉVAZ SERRA DE MOURA, born Lisbon, Portugal, 1947; admitted, 1971, Portugal. *Education:* Lisbon Law University (1969). Member, Board of the Lisbon Bar, 1990-1993. *LANGUAGES:* Portuguese, Spanish, French and English.

HENRIQUE JOSÉ MONTEIRO CHAVES, born Lisbon, Portugal, 1951; admitted, 1979, Portugal. *Education:* Lisbon Law University (1975). Councillor, Lisbon Town Council, 1974-1975. Member: I Extraordinary Congress of the Portuguese Lawyers, 1989; III Ordinary Congress of the Portuguese Lawyers, 1990. *LANGUAGES:* Portuguese, Spanish, French and English.

MARIA PAULA TERRA DA MOTTA DE VASCONCELOS GUIMARAES MOREIRA, born Lisbon, Portugal, 1958; admitted, 1984, Portugal. *Education:* Catholic Law University (1982). Member, III Ordinary Congress of the Portuguese Lawyers, 1990. *LANGUAGES:* Portuguese, French, Spanish and English.

ASSOCIATES

EDUARDO ANTONIO DE MATOS CARDOSO CORREIA DE AZEVEDO, born Peso da Régua, Portugal, 1960; admitted, 1989, Portugal. *Education:* Lisbon Law University (1987). Member, Fiscal Law Studies, Ecla, Lisbon, 1988-1989. *LANGUAGES:* Portuguese, English, French and Spanish.

MIGUEL JOÃO DE MOURA TRINDADE ELIAS, born Lisbon, Portugal, 1968; admitted, 1992, Portugal. *Education:* Catholic Law University (1991). *LANGUAGES:* Portuguese, English, French and Spanish.

SOFIA MIRANDA DA CUNHA, born Lisbon, Portugal, 1968; admitted, 1993, Portugal. *Education:* Catholic Law University (1991); College of Europe (1993). *LANGUAGES:* Portuguese, English, French and Spanish.

(This Listing Continued)

JOANA MERINO, born Lisbon, Portugal, 1970; admitted, 1993, Portugal. *Education:* Universidade Autónoma de Lisboa (1993). *LANGUAGES:* Portuguese, English, Spanish and French.

BUFETE MULLERAT & ROCA

RUA RODRIGO DA FONSECA 149-4
1000 LISBON, PORTUGAL
Telephone: (3511) 387 64 04
Fax; (3511) 385 5310

Barcelona Office: Passeig de Gràcia 81, 08008. Telephone: (343) 487 11 44. Telex: 51575. Fax: (343) 487 96 32; (343) 487 13 32.
Other Barcelona Office: Passeig de Gràcia 122, 08008. Telephone: (343) 237 84 46. Fax: (343) 237 86 30.
Madrid Office: Velàzquez 94, 28006. Telephone: (341) 578 17 62. Telex: 47089. Fax: (341) 575 13 86; (341) 575 27 80.

Banking and financial law, EC law, General Corporate and commercial law, International commercial arbitration, International construction, Litigation, Tax law, Intellectual property, Insolvency and bankruptcy, Administrative and public law, Environmental law, Zoning law.

LLUISA MASUET, born Barcelona, 1961; admitted, 1985, Barcelona. *Education:* Law Faculty of the Barcelona University (1979-1984; Diplomate on EEC Law, 1986; Master in Trade and International Legislation, 1991). *Member:* Barcelona Bar Association. *LANGUAGES:* Spanish, Catalan, French, English and Portuguese.

NORONHA-ADVOGADOS

PRAÇA MARQUÊS DE POMBAL, 16A - 5° PISO
1200 LISBON, PORTUGAL
Telephone: (01) 355-7435/7650
Facsimile: (01) 355-7854

São Paulo, Brazil Office: Av. Brigadeiro Faria Lima, 2100, 3rd Floor, 01452-919. Telephone: (011) 816.6609. Telex: (011) 32677 NMSA BR. Facsimile: (011) 212.2495 (Gps II & III).
Brasília, D.F., Brazil Office: SCS - Q 3, Edifício Planalto - Entrada 40 - s/310, 70300-500. Telephone: (061) 223.8315. Telex: (061) 3888 NMSA BR. Facsimile: (061) 223.8031.
Miami, Florida Office: 1221 Brickell Avenue, Suite 1040, 33131. Telephone: (305) 372.0844. Telex: ITT 441219 NWE. Facsimile: (305) 372.1792 (Gps II & III).
London, England Office: 4th Floor, 193/195 Brompton Road, SW3 1NE. Telephone: (0171) 581.5040. Telex: 849323. Facsimile: (0171) 581.8002.

RESIDENT PARTNER

VERA HELENA DE MORAES DANTAS, born São Paulo, S.P., Brazil, March 3, 1961; admitted, 1985, São Paulo; 1990, Portugal. *Education:* Catholic University Law School, São Paulo, Brazil; University College London - University of London. *Member:* International Bar Association; Club of Brazilian Businessmen of Lisbon (Legal Director). *LANGUAGES:* Portuguese, English and French.

ASSOCIATES

ANA MARIA SANTOS REIS, born Lisbon, Portugal; admitted, 1983, Portugal.

ANA MARGARIDA COSTA ALVES, born Lisbon, Portugal; admitted, 1987, Portugal.

Languages: Portuguese, English, French, Spanish and Italian.

References will be furnished upon request.

PENA, MACHETE & ASSOCIADOS

Established in 1989

AV. MIGUEL BOMBARDA, 61-5°
1000 LISBON, PORTUGAL
Telephone: (01) 3157719
Fax: 52 56 28

Associated with: Carlos Osorio de Castro, Eduardo Verde Pinho e J.J. Vieira Peres-sociedade de advogados -Av. da Boavista n° 1203/1215 6° salas 601/603 4100, Porto, Portugal.

(This Listing Continued)

Administrative, Antitrust and Trade Regulations, Arbitration and Mediation, Banking, Bankruptcy, Business, Civil, Commercial, Company, Constitutional, Construction, Corporate, Criminal, Divestitures, EC and Competition, Energy, Environmental, Family, Finance, Government, Insurance, Investment, Labour, Lease and Leasing, Mergers and Acquisitions, Property Public, Real Estate, Securities, Taxation, Trademark and Patent Law.

FIRM PROFILE: Pena, Machete & Associados was established on the twenty third of September, 1989, by eight partners who had been practicing law together for approximately twenty years.

The firm has the ability to provide every type of legal services required. Our Members includes not only nine partners but also several associates working for the firm.

PARTNERS

RUI PENA, born Torres Novas, 1939; admitted, 1964, Portugal. *Education:* Universidade de Lisboa, Faculty of Law. Author: "Concorrência de Medidas de Seguranca"; "Aval em Letras de Câmbio em Indicacão do Avalizado"; "Obrigacões Convertíveis em Acções." Associate Professor at the Universidade Autónoma de Lisboa. Minister of Portuguese Government, 1978. Member of Parliament, 1976-1982. Member, General Council of Portuguese Bar Association. *LANGUAGES:* Portuguese, English and French. *PRACTICE AREAS:* Administrative Law; Corporate Law; Company Law; Mergers and Acquisitions; Divestitures.

RUI CHANCERELLE MACHETE, born Setúbal, 1940; admitted, 1965, Portugal. *Education:* Universidade de Lisboa, Faculty of Law (LL.B., 1962; LL.M., 1963). Author: "Contribuções para as Relações Entre o Processo Administrativo Gracioso e Contencioso," "Dogmática Juridica Administrativa Contemporanea". Lecturer at Universidade de Lisboa, Faculty of Law; Universidade Católica, Faculty of Law. Minister of Social Affairs, 1976. Minister of Justice, 1983-1985. Deputy Prime Minister, 1985. Minister of Defense, 1985. Member of Parliament, 1985-1990. Chairman of the Budget and Means Committee in Parliament, 1985-1990. President of the Legislation Council, 1987-1989. President of the Luso-American Development Foundation, 1988—. Member, Editorial Commission for the Portuguese Bar Association Magazine. *Member:* Portuguese Bar Association. *LANGUAGES:* Portuguese, German, English and French. *PRACTICE AREAS:* Administrative Law; Business Law; Contract Law; European Community Law; Finance Law; Government Law; Government Contract Law; Securities.

LOPO CANCELLA DE ABREU, born Lisbon, 1943; admitted, 1970, Portugal. *Education:* Universidade de Lisboa, Faculty of Law. *Member:* Portuguese Bar Association. *LANGUAGES:* Portuguese, English and French. *PRACTICE AREAS:* Aviation Law; Aerospace Law; Children's Law; Criminal Law; Drug and Narcotic Law; Environmental Law; Family Law; Insurance Law; Medical Malpractice Law; Insurance Defense Law; Military Law; Personal Injury Law.

HENRIQUE TROCADO, born Lisbon, 1951; admitted, 1978, Portugal. *Education:* Universidade de Lisboa, Faculty of Law. *LANGUAGES:* Portuguese, English and French. *PRACTICE AREAS:* Business Law; Civil Law; Commercial Law; Company Law; Corporate Law; Contract Law; Debtor Creditor Law; General Practice; Labour Law; Employment Law; Lease Law; Litigation; Property Law; Real Estate Law; Resorts and Leisure Law.

PIEDADE DE ALMEIDA GARRETT, born Lisbon, 1953; admitted, 1983, Portugal. *Education:* Universidade de Lisboa, Faculty of Law. *Member:* Portuguese Bar Association. *LANGUAGES:* Portuguese and French. *PRACTICE AREAS:* Business Law; Civil Law; Company Law; General Practice.

LUIS ABREU COUTINHO, born Évora, 1960; admitted, 1988, Portugal. *Education:* Universidade de Lisboa, Faculty of Law. *Member:* Portuguese Bar Association. *LANGUAGES:* Portuguese, English and French. *PRACTICE AREAS:* Business Law; Civil Law; Company Law; Construction Law; Corporate Law; Family Law; Labour Law; Employment Law; Property Law; Taxation Law.

PEDRO MANUEL PENA CHANCERELLE DE MACHETE, born Lisboa, 1965; admitted, 1989, Portugal. *Education:* Universidade Católica Portuguesa, Faculty of Law (Master in Law). Author: "A Suspensão Jurisdicional da Eficácia de Actos Administrativos", O Direito, 1991; "Os Princípios de Articulacão Interna de Ordenamentos Complexos no Direito Comparado", O Direito, 1992; "A ZEE no Direito Internacional", Direito e Justiça , 1991; "Elementos para o Estudo das Relações entre os Actos Legislativos do Estado e das Regiões Autónomas no Quadro da Constituição Vigente", Revista de Direito e Estudos Sociais, 1991; "A Audiência dos Interessados no Procedimento Administrativo," Lisboa, 1994. Assistant Professor, Universidade Católica Portuguesa. *Member:* Portuguese Bar Associ-

(This Listing Continued)

ation. *LANGUAGES:* Portuguese, German, English and French. *PRACTICE AREAS:* Administrative Law; Antitrust Law; Trade Regulation Law; Business Law; Company Law; Constitutional Law; European Community Law; Government Law; Government Contract Law; Lease Law; Public Law.

FRANCISCO CORTEZ, born Évora, 1965; admitted, 1990, Portugal. *Education:* Universidade Católica Portuguese. *Member:* Portuguese Bar Association. *LANGUAGES:* Portuguese, English and French. *PRACTICE AREAS:* Business Law; Commercial Law; Company Law; Corporate Law; Litigation.

DR. JOÃO CALDEIRA, born Lisbon, 1967; admitted, 1992, Portugal. *Education:* Universidade de Lisboa, Faculty of Law. *Member:* Portuguese Bar Association. *LANGUAGES:* Portuguese, English and French. *PRACTICE AREAS:* Business Law; Civil Law; Commercial Law.

MIGUEL NUNO FERREIRA PENA CHANCERELLE DE MACHETE, born Lisbon, 1968; admitted, 1994, Portugal. *Education:* Universidade Católica Portuguesa, Faculty of Law. *Member:* Portuguese Bar Association. *LANGUAGES:* Portuguese, German, English and French. *PRACTICE AREAS:* Administrative Law; European Community Law; Finance Law; Antitrust Law; Business Law; Civil Law; Commercial Law; Company Law; Corporate Law; Contract Law; General Practice; Litigation.

ASSOCIATES

JOÃO PAULO ROSADO CORREIA, born Castelo Branco, 1962; admitted, 1987, Portugal. *Education:* Universidade de Lisboa, Faculty of Law. *Member:* Portuguese Bar Association. *LANGUAGES:* Portuguese, English and French. *PRACTICE AREAS:* Administrative Law; Business Law; Company Law; Corporate Law; Government Law; Government Contract Law.

ANTÓNIO CÔRTE-REAL CRUZ, born Lisbon, 1965; admitted, 1990, Portugal. *Education:* Universidade de Lisboa, Faculty of Law; Universidade Católica European Studies Centre. Author: "Colectânea de Direito da Publicidade Anotada", Rei dos Livros, 1991; "Acordos de Distribuição e Contrato de Agência e Representação Comercial", Gazette, 1991. *Member:* Portuguese Bar Association; European Patent Attorney; European Community Trademark Association (ECTA); Association Internationelle Pour La Protection De La Proprieté Industrielle (AIPPI). *LANGUAGES:* Portuguese, English and French. *PRACTICE AREAS:* Advertising Law; Marketing Law; Computer Software; Consumer Law; Intellectual Property Law; Technology Law; Science Law; Trademark and Patent Law.

JOSE LUIS ARNAUT, born Covilhã, 1963; admitted, 1988, Portugal. *Education:* Universidade Lusiada de Lisboa; UniversitéStrasbourg III, France. Author: "La Marque Tridimensionnelle en Droit Portugais", Ceipi, 1990; "Licensing Agreements in Portuguese Law", Gazette, 1991. *Member:* Portuguese Bar Association; Licensing Executive Society (France); Association Internationelle pour la Protection de la Propreté Industrielle (AIPPI); European Communities Trademark Association (ECTA); Associacão Portuguesa de Consultores em Propriedade Industrial (ACPI); American International Property Law Association; Union des Practiciens Europeens en Propriete Industrielle (UNION); Federation Internationale des Conseils en Pro Priete Industrielle. *LANGUAGES:* Portuguese, English and French. *PRACTICE AREAS:* Antitrust Law; Trade Regulation Law; Intellectual Property Law; Industrial Agreements; Industrial Property Law; Patent and Trademark Law.

LAW OFFICES OF
DR. ARMANDO FELIX PEREIRA

AVENIDA DA REPUBLICA 14-8TH
1000 LISBON, PORTUGAL
Telephone: (351 1) 315 9115, 353 0321
Facsimile: (G. 2/3) (351-1) 52 40 02

General and International Law Practice. Maritime and Aviation Law, Patents, Trademarks and Copyright, Foreign Investment, Transfer of Technology, International Transactions, Insurance and Negligence Law, Corporation, Taxation, Wills and Estates, Matrimonial Law, Real Estate, Mining, Administrative Tribunals and Governmental Agencies, Litigation, Trials and Appeals, EEC Law.

DR. ARMANDO FELIX PEREIRA, born Goa (formerly Portuguese India), December 9, 1922; admitted, 1949, Portugal; 1954, Supreme Court of Justice. *Education:* University of Lisbon, Faculty of Law (LL.B., 1942;

(This Listing Continued)

LAW OFFICES OF DR. ARMANDO FELIX PEREIRA, Lisbon—Continued

LL.M., 1948). Recipient, Diploma in Comparative Law, Luxembourg, 1959. Member, Legal Committee, International Air Transport Association, 1965-1985, Chairman, 1974. *LANGUAGES:* Portuguese, English, French and Spanish. *PRACTICE AREAS:* General Practice; Administrative Law; Admiralty Law; Maritime Law; Aviation Law; Commercial Business; Mining Law; Patent, Trademark and Copyright Law.

DR. ERNESTO DE CARVALHO OLIVEIRA, born 1927; admitted, 1954, Portugal. *Education:* University of Lisbon (LL.B., 1944; LL.M., 1950). Author: "Sumarios Juridicos"; "Informação e Sumario das Leis"; "Reforma de Processo Penal"; "Despedimentos." Attorney for Government, 1951-1954. *LANGUAGES:* Portuguese and French. *PRACTICE AREAS:* Civil Law; Commercial Law; Computer Law.

DR. ANTONIO FARIA BLANC, born 1924; admitted, 1952, Portugal. *Education:* University of Lisbon (LL.B., 1944; LL.M., 1950). *LANGUAGES:* Portuguese, English and French. *PRACTICE AREAS:* Civil Law; Labor Law; Property Law; Family Law.

DR. JOÃO LUIS RODRIGUES, born 1939; admitted, 1969, Portugal. *Education:* University of Coimbra, 1961-1967. *LANGUAGES:* Portuguese, French and English. *PRACTICE AREAS:* Children Law; Civil Law; Commercial Law; Constitutional Law; Contract Law; Copyright Law; Family Law; Insurance Law; Intellectual Property Law; Labor Law; Personal Injury Law; Pharmaceutical Law; Expropriation.

DR. MARIA JOÃO SOLLER, born 1951; admitted, 1975, Portugal. *Education:* University of Lisbon, 1967-1973. *LANGUAGES:* Portuguese, French and English. *PRACTICE AREAS:* Civil Law; Commercial Law; Agency Law; Distribution; Bankruptcy Law; Business Law; Commercial Law; Computers and Software Law; Contract Law; Debtor and Creditor Law; Franchise and Franchising Law; Leases and Leasing Law; Mortgages; Products Liability; Professional Liability; Property Law; Real Estate Law; Wills.

DR. MARIA ALEXANDRA PESTANA, born 1938; admitted, 1979, Portugal. *Education:* University of Lisbon, 1971-1977. *LANGUAGES:* Portuguese, French, English and Spanish. *PRACTICE AREAS:* Civil Law; Commercial Law; Children Law; Criminal Law; Family Law; Foreign Investment Law; Labor Law; Relations; Property Law; Real Estate Law.

Correspond in English, French, Spanish and German.

GONÇALVES PEREIRA, VINHAS, CASTELO BRANCO E ASSOCIADOS

Established in 1928

PRAÇA MARQUÊS DE POMBAL, NR. 1 - 8TH FLOOR
1200 LISBON, PORTUGAL
Telephone: 351-1-3563311
Telex: 12320 ANGPER P
Fax: (1) 3532362; 549784

Porto, Office: Av. da Boavista, nr. 1383, 2nd Floor, 4100, Porto. Telephone: (2) 6001862/3/4. Fax: (2) 6001848.

Civil, Commercial, Company, Banking, Arbitration, Tax, Administrative, Litigation, Property, Aviation and Environmental Law.

FIRM PROFILE: This legal office has been active since 1928 without interruption, first through individual lawyers and thereafter as a legal firm. It has always been primarily concerned with international transactions, or to giving legal advice and representing foreign investors in Portugal. Offices are located in Lisbon and Porto.

PROF. ANDRÉ GONÇALVES PEREIRA, born 1937; admitted, 1959, Lisbon. Professor of International Law, University of Lisbon since 1962. Minister of Foreign Affairs of the Republic of Portugal from January 1981 to June 1982. Holder of Several Decorations and Academic Degrees: Grand Cross Order of Merit, Republic of Italy, 1981; Grand Officer Légion d'Honneur, France, 1982; Grand Cross Cruzeiro do Sul, Brazil, 1982.

LUIS VINHAS, born 1953; admitted, 1979, Lisbon. Former Assistant Professor at Lisbon Law School, M.B.A., Insead 1976.

MANUEL CASTELO BRANCO, born 1953; admitted, 1976, Lisbon. Former Assistant Professor, Lisbon Law School and Lisbon Free University (Law). Former UN Counsellor.

(This Listing Continued)

JOSÉ DE FREITAS, born 1956; admitted, 1982, Porto. (Resident, Porto Office).

MARIA JOÃO RICOU, born 1960; admitted, 1986, Lisbon.

MARIA DA GLORIA LEITÃO, born 1955; admitted, 1987, Lisbon. Assistant Professor ISE.

ISABEL GARCIA, born 1962; admitted, 1987, Lisbon.

JOÃO PEDRO COLLARES PEREIRA, born 1959; admitted, 1987, Lisbon.

ANA MENÉRES, born 1964; admitted, 1989, Lisbon.

FREDERICO PEREIRA COUTINHO, born 1964; admitted, 1990, Lisbon.

MIGUEL DE AZEREDO PERDIGÃO, born 1967; admitted, 1991, Lisbon.

FRANCISCO PINTO LEITE, born 1967; admitted, 1991, Lisbon.

ANA FURTADO VELOSO, born 1966; admitted, 1992, Porto. (Resident, Porto Office).

MANUEL MAGALHÃES, born 1967; admitted, 1993, Porto. (Resident, Porto Office).

DIOGO PERESTRELO, born 1968; admitted, 1992, Lisbon.

ANDREIA LIMA CARNEIRO, born 1969; admitted, 1992, Porto. (Resident, Porto Office).

VERONICA O'SHEA, born 1961. English Solicitor. (Resident, Porto Office).

Languages: Portuguese, English, French, Spanish and Italian.

JOSÉ ALVES PEREIRA E ASSOCIADOS

AVA. DE BERNA, N° 4, 1° DTO.
1000 LISBON, PORTUGAL
Telephone: 7938890/1/2/3/4
Telefax: 7938889

Corporate, Commercial, Civil, Tax, Banking, Aviation, Maritime, Foreign Investment, International Contracts, Licensing and Agency, Mergers and Acquisitions, Property, EEC Law, Patents and Trademark, Copyright, Entertainment and Advertising, Immigration, Insurance, General Practice.

PARTNERS

DR. JOSÉ DE A. ALVES PEREIRA, born Àgueda, Portugal, 1945; admitted, 1968, Portugal. *Education:* University of Lisbon, Faculty of Law. Author: "Basic Aspects of Distribution Agreements under Portuguese Law," 1985; "Brief Summary of the Law and Doctrine on Pre-Contractual Liability," 1986; "Information on Legal Developments in European Countries Concerning the Hague Convention on Taking Evidence Abroad in Civil and Commercial Matters - Note on Portugal", 1987; "Note on Portuguese Employment and Labor Laws", 1988; "Agency and Distribution Agreements in Portugal", 1991; "Insurance Intermediaries - A Survey of the Rules under which Insurance Intermediaries Operate in the European Community (Contribution on Portugal)", 1991; "A Practitioner's Guide to European Corporate Insolvency Law - Contribution on Portugal", 1991. Associate and Area Coordinator for Portugal of the American Bar Association, 1981—. National President of the World Jurist Association. Member, Executive Committee, IAG International-an association of independent professional firms. *Member:* Inter-Pacific Bar Association; International Bar Association; Union of European Lawyers; European Immigration Lawyers Group; Portuguese Bar Association (Member, Executive Committee). *LANGUAGES:* Portuguese, English, French and Spanish. *PRACTICE AREAS:* Corporate; Commercial; Banking; International Contracts; Mergers and Acquisitions; Aviation.

DR. JORGE SILVA MARQUES, born Almada, Portugal, 1961; admitted, 1989, Portugal. *Education:* University of Lisbon, Faculty of Law. *LANGUAGES:* Portuguese, English, French, Spanish. *PRACTICE AREAS:* Corporate; Foreign Investment; Property.

DR. JOÃO NORONHA LOPES, born Lisbon, Portugal, 1966; admitted, 1989, Portugal. *Education:* University of Lisbon, Faculty of Law. *LANGUAGES:* Portuguese, English, French, Spanish. *PRACTICE AREAS:* Corporate; Commercial; Licensing and Agency; Immigration.

DR. CARLOS MIGUEL FERREIRA, born Mozambique, 1967; admitted, 1990, Portugal. *Education:* University of Lisbon, Faculty of Law.

(This Listing Continued)

LANGUAGES: Portuguese, English, French, Spanish. **PRACTICE AREAS:** Civil; Tax; Entertainment; Advertising.

ASSOCIATES

DRA. ANA CAROLINA CARDOSO, born Coimbra, Portugal, 1968; admitted, 1991, Portugal. *Education:* University of Coimbra (Law Degree). LANGUAGES: Portuguese, English, French, Spanish. **PRACTICE AREAS:** Patent and Trademarks; Copyright.

DRA. PATRICIA FARINHA, born Lisbon, Portugal, 1969; admitted, 1992, Portugal. *Education:* Catholic University of Lisbon, Faculty of Law. LANGUAGES: Portuguese, English, French, Spanish. **PRACTICE AREAS:** Civil; Labor; Property.

DR. ANTÓNIO NETO ALVES, born Lisbon, Portugal, 1971; admitted, 1994, Portugal. *Education:* University of Lisbon, Faculty of Law. LANGUAGES: Portuguese, English, French, Spanish. **PRACTICE AREAS:** Corporate; Property.

A.M. PEREIRA, SARAGGA LEAL, OLIVEIRA MARTINS, JUDICE E ASSOCIADOS

Established in 1968

RUA SILVA CARVALHO, NO. 234 - 7°
1296 LISBON CODEX, PORTUGAL
Telephone: 3800700
Cable Address: "Pereiralex"
Telex: 16479 PELEX P; 16678 PELEX P; 64229 EULEX P
Fax: 693841; 693651; 692816; 693771

Foreign Investment, Corporate Law, Construction Law, Mergers and Acquisitions, Constitutional and Administrative Law, Competition and Anti-Trust Law, Tax (Corporate and Personal) Law, Transfer of Technology, International Patents, Trademarks, Software Law, Franchising, Licence and Distributorship Law, Property and Real Estate Law, Banking, Leasing, Insurance and Finance Law, Bankruptcy Law, Capital Markets Law, Immigration, Debt Collection, Product Liability, General Litigation, Labor Law, Environment Law.

MEMBERS OF FIRM

ANTÓNIO MARIA PEREIRA, admitted, 1948, Portugal. *Education:* University of Lisbon Law School, Historical-Juridical Science. *Member:* Portuguese Bar Association; International Bar Association (Chairman, Sales of Goods Committee, 1971-1975); International Lawyers Network; Association Internationale des Avocats; American Bar Association; Portuguese Section of the International Commission of Jurists (President of the Board, 1984—); Honorary Member of the International Committee of the Florida Bar. Delegate in Portugal of the International League for Human Rights, New York (Member of the Board, 1977-1979). Delegate of Portugal in WIPO (World International Property Organization, Geneva) and UNESCO, 1975-1987. Member of the Board, 1977-1979 and President of the Assembly, 1980-1986, Portuguese German Chamber of Commerce. Member of Board, American Club of Lisbon. Member of the Board, AEDBF (European Association of the Financial and Banking Law - Paris). Rewarded by the French Government with "Légion d'Honneur", 1985, "l'Ordre de l'Economie Nationale Française, 1962 and "l'Ordre Nationale du Merite by the Federal Republic of Germany with the "Order of Merit", 1st Class, 1989 and Order of the British Empire awarded by Her Majesty the Queen of Great Britain. LANGUAGES: Portuguese, English, French and Spanish. **PRACTICE AREAS:** Corporate Law; International Law; Intellectual Property Law; Real Estate Law.

LUIS SÁRAGGA LEAL, admitted, 1968, Portugal. *Education:* University of Lisbon. Consultant to the Ministry of Labor, 1969-1973. National Delegate to C.C.B.E. (Commission Consultative des Barreaux de la Communaute Europeenne), 1982-1986. *Member:* Portuguese Bar Association (Vice-President, 1984-1986; Member, International Relations Committee; Ethics Committee, 1978-1980; General Council, 1981-1986); International Bar Association (Member, Tax Committee); Union International des Avocats; International Fiscal Association; International Commission of Jurists (Portuguese Section); Honorary member of the International Law Committee of the Florida Bar. LANGUAGES: Portuguese, English, French and Spanish. **PRACTICE AREAS:** Corporate Law; Tax Law; Finance Law; Securities and Stock Exchange.

FRANCISCO DE OLIVEIRA MARTINS, admitted, 1970, Portugal. *Education:* University of Lisbon. *Member:* Portuguese Bar Association

(This Listing Continued)

(Member, Ethics Committee, 1981-1986; General Council, 1990). LANGUAGES: Portuguese, English, French and Spanish. **PRACTICE AREAS:** Corporate Law; Commercial Law; Mergers and Acquisitions; Real Estate; Tourism Law; Competition Law.

JOSÉ MIGUEL JÚDICE, admitted, 1977, Portugal. *Education:* University of Coimbra. Arbitrator, Center of Commercial Arbitration of the Commercial Association of Lisbon (Portuguese Chamber of Commerce) and Commercial Association of Oporto (Chamber of Commerce and Industry of Oporto). Assistant Professor of Politics and Constitutional Law, Law School of the University of Coimbra, 1972-1977. Assistant Professor, International Law, 1978-1980 and Political Science, 1980-1981, Lisbon University Law School. Member, Portuguese Advisory Board, MAC Group. *Member:* Portuguese Bar Association; International Bar Association; International Commission of Jurists (Director of the Portuguese Section, 1976-1979); Commercial Law Affiliates; GESICA. LANGUAGES: Portuguese, English, French and Spanish. **PRACTICE AREAS:** Construction Law; Real Estate Law; Tourism Law; Administrative Law; Corporate Law; Commercial Law; Litigation.

MARIA HELENA VAZ MAIA, admitted, 1969, Portugal. *Education:* University of Coimbra, Juridical Science, Complementary Graduation. *Member:* Portuguese Bar Association; Young Lawyers International Association. LANGUAGES: Portuguese, English, French and Spanish. **PRACTICE AREAS:** Administrative Law-Municipal Law; Tax Law; Commercial Law; Real Estate; Litigation; Product Liability; Naturalization.

FERNANDO CAMPOS FERREIRA, admitted, 1978, Portugal. *Education:* University of Lisbon. Junior Assistant Professor of Civil Law, University of Lisbon Law School, 1979-1980. *Member:* Portuguese Bar Association. LANGUAGES: Portuguese, English, French and Spanish. **PRACTICE AREAS:** Corporate Law; Finance Law; Commercial Law.

VICTOR REFEGA FERNANDES, admitted, 1980, Portugal. *Education:* University of Coimbra; College of Europe, Bruges, Belgium; Salzburg Seminar in American Studies; Trainee at the Legal Service of the EEC Commission, Brussels. Lecturer, National Institute of Public Administration 1990-1981. *Member:* Portuguese Bar Association. LANGUAGES: Portuguese, English, French and Spanish. **PRACTICE AREAS:** Competition an Anti-trust Law; Product Liability; EEC Law.

PEDRO SÁRAGGA LEAL, admitted, 1978, Portugal. *Education:* University of Lisbon; College of Europe, Bruges, Belgium; Trainee at the EEC Commission, Brussels, Belgium. International Civil Servant in the Council of Europe, Strasbourg, France, 1979-1982. *Member:* Portuguese Bar Association. LANGUAGES: Portuguese, English, French and Spanish. **PRACTICE AREAS:** Commercial Law; Corporate Law; Real Estate.

DULCE FRANCO VILHENA DE CARVALHO, admitted, 1982, Portugal. *Education:* University of Lisbon; Oxford University, International Commercial Contracts. Junior Assistant Professor of Civil Constitutional and Civil Procedure Law, University of Lisbon Law School (1979-1982). *Member:* Portuguese Bar Association (Member, Ethics Committee, 1990-1993). LANGUAGES: Portuguese, English, French and Spanish. **PRACTICE AREAS:** Corporate Law; Real Estate and Construction Law; Foreign Investment; Industrial Licensing.

JOSÉ MANUEL SERRA FORMIGAL, admitted, 1979, Portugal. *Education:* University of Lisbon. Labor Judge , 1956-1978. Arbitrator for several labor collective agreements. Awarded with the "Ordem de S. Tiago da Espada" and the "Medalha de Mérito Cultural" by the Portuguese State; and the "Al Merito della Republica Italiana" by the State of Italy, *Member:* Portuguese Bar Association. LANGUAGES: Portuguese, French, Italian and Spanish. **PRACTICE AREAS:** Labour Law.

J. SILVA HERDEIRO, admitted, 1983, Portugal. *Education:* Portuguese Catholic University. *Member:* Portuguese Bar Association; Young Lawyers International Association, A.I.J.A. **PRACTICE AREAS:** Portuguese Income and Property Tax Laws; Free Zones of Madeira and Azores; Assessment Appeals and Fiscal Litigation; Bankruptcy; Maritime Law; Competition; Factoring; Agency Agreements; Commercial and Civil Litigation.

ISABEL NOLASCO CRESPO, admitted, 1981, Portugal. *Education:* University of Lisbon. *Member:* Portuguese Bar Association. **PRACTICE AREAS:** Litigation; Corporate Law; Family Law; Criminal Law.

NUNO LÍBANO MONTEIRO, admitted, 1987, Portugal. *Education:* University of Lisbon. Member, Commercial Law Affiliates. *Member:* Portuguese Bar Association. LANGUAGES: Portuguese, English and French. **PRACTICE AREAS:** Product Liability Law; Leasing Law; Bankruptcy Law.

(This Listing Continued)

A.M. PEREIRA, SARAGGA LEAL, OLIVEIRA MARTINS, JUDICE E ASSOCIADOS, Lisbon—Continued

GABRIELA RODRIGUES MARTINS, admitted, 1991, Portugal. *Education:* Portuguese Catholic University. *Member:* Portuguese Bar Association, Brasilian Bar Association (Section, S. Paulo). *LANGUAGES:* Portuguese, English, Italian, Spanish and French. *PRACTICE AREAS:* Finance Law; Security and Banking Law; Environmental Law.

ANA TERESA PULIDO, admitted, 1984, Portugal. *Education:* University of Lisbon. *Member:* Portuguese Bar Association. *PRACTICE AREAS:* Copyright; Industrial and Intellectual Property Law.

MARIA DULCE ALEIXO, admitted, 1983, Portugal. *Education:* Portuguese Catholic University; Diplôme de l'Institut Européen des Hautes Etudes Internacionales; Etudes Supérieures des Communautes Européennes. *Member:* Portuguese Bar Association. *PRACTICE AREAS:* Civil and Commercial Law; Product Liability Law; Litigation.

MARIA JOSÉ VERDE, admitted, 1988, Portugal. *Education:* University of Lisbon. *Member:* Portuguese Bar Association. *PRACTICE AREAS:* Corporate Law and Real Estate Investment.

MADALENA FERREIRA, admitted, 1988, Portugal. *Education:* Portuguese Catholic University; Postgraduate Course in European Studies - Portuguese Catholic University (1989-1990). *Member:* Portuguese Bar Association; Association Internacionale des Jeunes Avocats (A.I.J.A.). *PRACTICE AREAS:* Corporate Law; Mergers and Acquisitions.

VASCO MARQUES CORREIA, admitted, 1988, Portugal. *Education:* Portuguese Catholic University; Complementary Course of Environment Law. Trainee period at a leading Portuguese Stock Broker. *Member:* Portuguese Bar Association. *LANGUAGES:* Portuguese, English, Spanish and French. *PRACTICE AREAS:* Corporate Law; Mergers and Acquisitions; Banking; Finance; Privatizations and Marketing; Media Law.

RITA MALTEZ, admitted, 1988, Portugal. *Education:* University of Lisbon. *Member:* Portuguese Bar Association; Association Internacionale des Jeunes Avocats (A.I.J.A.). *PRACTICE AREAS:* Bankruptcy Law.

PEDRO FARIA, admitted, 1989, Portugal. *Education:* University of Lisbon. *Member:* Portuguese Bar Association. *PRACTICE AREAS:* Civil and Criminal Litigation; Bankruptcy; Real Estate; Corporate Law; Automotive Crash.

MANUEL SANTOS VICTOR, admitted, 1989, Portugal. *Education:* University of Lisbon; College of Europe, Bruges, Belgium. *Member:* Portuguese Bar Association. *PRACTICE AREAS:* Financing; Public Tenders; EEC Law; Competition; Corporate and Construction Law.

ANTÓNIO ABRANTES RAIO, admitted, 1987, Portugal. *Education:* Portuguese Catholic University. *Member:* Portuguese Bar Association. *PRACTICE AREAS:* Labour Law.

DORA MAURÍCIO, admitted, 1987, Portugal. *Education:* University of Lisbon. *Member:* Portuguese Bar Association. *PRACTICE AREAS:* Corporate Law; Litigation; Commercial; Environment and Regulatory Law; Investment Funds and Mining.

ANA CRISTINA MARQUES, admitted, 1987, Portugal. *Education:* Portuguese Catholic University. *Member:* Portuguese Bar Association. *PRACTICE AREAS:* Corporate Law; Litigation; Regulatory Law.

ANTÓNIO CAMILO MARTINS, admitted, 1988, Portugal. *Education:* Portuguese Catholic University; Complementary Course of Environment Law. *Member:* Portuguese Bar Association. *PRACTICE AREAS:* Construction Law; Corporate Law; Tourism Law; Competition Law; Advertising Law; Environment Law.

FILIPA SOARES DA CUNHA, admitted, 1989, Portugal. *Education:* Portuguese Catholic University, Faculty of Human Sciences. Trainee period in patent law at the Law Firm Wells and Wells, Washington, D.C. *Member:* Portuguese Bar Association. *PRACTICE AREAS:* Real Estate and Construction Law; Corporate Law; Condominium Law; Shopping Centers; Real Estate Development and Leasing.

BERNARDO ALEGRIA, admitted, 1989, Portugal. *Education:* University of Lisbon. *Member:* Portuguese Bar Association. *PRACTICE AREAS:* Commercial Law; Corporate Finance Law; Real Estate.

JOSÉ FILIPE ABECASIS, admitted, 1989, Portugal. *Education:* Portuguese Catholic University. Legal Advisor, Lisbon City Council, 1988-1991. *Member:* Portuguese Bar Association. *PRACTICE AREAS:* Real Estate; Construction Law.

(This Listing Continued)

EU1156B

JORGE DE BRITO PEREIRA, admitted, 1990, Portugal. *Education:* Portuguese Catholic University. Junior Assistant Professor, Contracts Law, Law School of the University of Lisbon, 1990—. *Member:* Portuguese Bar Association. *PRACTICE AREAS:* International Law; Contracts Law; Mergers and Acquisitions; Stock Exchange Law; Capital Markets Law.

SOFIA AMRAM, admitted, 1990, Portugal. *Education:* Portuguese Catholic University. *Member:* Portuguese Bar Association.

JOSÉ JACOME, admitted, 1990, Portugal. *Education:* University of Lisbon. *Member:* Portuguese Bar Association. *PRACTICE AREAS:* Business and Commercial Law; Civil Practice; Business; Commercial and Civil Litigation.

FERNANDO SILVA FERNANDES, admitted, 1990, Portugal. *Education:* University of Coimbra, Faculty of Law. *Member:* Portuguese Bar Association. *PRACTICE AREAS:* Immigration Law; Labour Law; Social Security and Labor Litigation; Leasing Law.

AIDA FRANCO NOGUEIRA, admitted, 1992, Portugal. *Education:* University of Lisbon, Faculty of Arts, Language and Literature; International University of Lisbon Law School. *Member:* Portuguese Bar Association. *LANGUAGES:* French, English and German. *PRACTICE AREAS:* Landlord and Tenant Law; Commercial Leasing; Environmental Law; Family Law; Advertising and Direct Marketing Law; Data Protection Law.

TERESA DE MELO RIBEIRO, admitted, 1992, Portugal. *Education:* University of Lisbon (Geography Degree); Portuguese Catholic University (Law Degree). Assistant Professor, Law Fundamentals in Economy and Management Studies; Introduction to Public Law. Master in Public Law. *PRACTICE AREAS:* Constitutional and Administrative Law.

LUIS MAGALHÃES GUEDES, admitted, 1991, Portugal. *Education:* Portuguese Catholic University. *Member:* Portuguese Bar Association. *PRACTICE AREAS:* Patents and Trademarks; Copyright; Advertising Law; Immigration.

MONICA PEREIRA PINTO, admitted, 1991, Portugal. *Education:* University of Lisbon. *Member:* Portuguese Bar Association. *PRACTICE AREAS:* Leasing Law.

NUNO DE BRITO LOPES, admitted, 1991, Portugal. *Education:* Lusiada University, Lisbon. Junior Assistant Professor, European Community Law, Lusíada University, Lisbon. *Member:* Portuguese Bar Association. *PRACTICE AREAS:* Contracts and Commercial Law; Takeovers and Securities Law; European Law.

FREDERICO PERRY VIDAL, admitted, 1992, Portugal. *Education:* International University, Lisbon. *Member:* Portuguese Bar Association. *PRACTICE AREAS:* Real Estate; Town Planning; Administrative Law.

MIGUEL NOLASCO CRESPO, admitted, 1981, Portugal. *Education:* University of Lisbon. *Member:* Portuguese Bar Association. *PRACTICE AREAS:* Litigation; Corporate Law; Family Law; Criminal Law.

MARIA CASTELOS, admitted, 1991, Portugal. *Education:* Portuguese Catholic University, Lisbon. *Member:* Portuguese Bar Association. *PRACTICE AREAS:* Corporate and Construction Law; Public Tenders; Banking and Finance.

ANTÓNIO MARQUES VALIDO, admitted, 1991, Portugal. *Education:* University of Lisbon Law School. *Member:* Portuguese Bar Association; AIJA; International Association of Young Lawyers. *LANGUAGES:* Portuguese, English, French and Spanish. *PRACTICE AREAS:* Civil Litigation; Real Estate; Family Law; Bankruptcy.

ANA VERA ARAUJO, admitted, 1991, Portugal. *Education:* University of Lisbon. *Member:* Portuguese Bar Association. *PRACTICE AREAS:* Litigation.

DUARTE DE ATHAYDE, admitted, 1992, Portugal. *Education:* Portuguese Catholic University, College of Europe, Bruges, Belgium. *Member:* Portuguese Bar Association. *PRACTICE AREAS:* EEC Law; Corporate Law; Competition Law.

RITA GAMA ABREU, admitted, 1992, Portugal. *Education:* University of Lisbon Law School. *Member:* Portuguese Bar Association. *PRACTICE AREAS:* Corporate Law; Real Estate; Administrative Law.

M. CARMO TELLES DE FREITAS, admitted, 1991, Portugal. *Education:* Portuguese Catholic University Law School, Lisbon. *Member:* Portuguese Bar Association. *PRACTICE AREAS:* Commercial; Family; Tourism and European Law; Litigation.

RITA OLIVEIRA RAMIRO, admitted, 1991, Portugal. *Education:* University of Lisbon Law School. *Member:* Portuguese Bar Association.

(This Listing Continued)

PRACTICE AREAS: Litigation; Corporate Law; Tourism Law; European Community Law; Product Liability; Criminal Law.

JOÁO MEDEIROS, admitted, 1992, Portugal. *Education:* Portuguese Catholic University Law School, Lisbon. *Member:* Portuguese Bar Association. **PRACTICE AREAS:** Civil; Criminal; Regulatory Law; General Litigation and Automotive Crash.

VASCO PASSANHA, admitted, 1991, Portugal. *Education:* Lusíada University, Lisbon. *Member:* Portuguese Bar Association. **PRACTICE AREAS:** Commercial Law; Company Law; Contracts.

MIGUEL MOURA E. SILVA, admitted, 1991, Portugal. *Education:* Portuguese Catholic University, Law School, Lisbon (Master of EC Law); College of Europe, Bruges, Belgium. Assistant Professor, European Community Law, University of Lisbon, Law School. **LANGUAGES:** Portuguese, English, French and Spanish. **PRACTICE AREAS:** Competition Law; Intellectual Property Law; EC Law.

RODOLFO VASCO LAVRADOR, admitted, 1985, Portugal. *Education:* Portuguese Catholic University, Law School, Lisbon (Master of Tax Law). Assistant Professor: Public Finance, University of Lisbon, Law School; Economic Law, Autonomous University, Lisbon. **LANGUAGES:** Portuguese, English, Spanish and French. **PRACTICE AREAS:** Tax Law; Banking Law; Finance Law.

TERESA BAMOND, admitted, 1987, Portugal. *Education:* Portuguese Catholic University, Lisbon. Officer of Direcção Geral do Turismo, 1988-1994. *Member:* Portuguese Bar Association. **PRACTICE AREAS:** Administrative Law; Town Planning; Tourism Law.

SOFIA FIGUEIREDO LOPES, admitted, 1992, Portugal. *Education:* University of Lisbon Law School. *Member:* Portuguese Bar Association. **PRACTICE AREAS:** Litigation.

TIAGO CORTES, admitted, 1989, Portugal. *Education:* University of Lisbon, Law School. *Member:* Portuguese Bar Association. **PRACTICE AREAS:** Labor Law; Corporate Law; Bankruptcy.

LEILA NYROP, admitted, 1989, Brasil; 1994, Portugal. *Education:* Faculdade Cándido Mendes, Rio de Janeiro. Trainee at the Procuradoria do Estado do Rio de Janeiro, 1989-1990. *Member:* Brazilian Bar Association; Portuguese Bar Association. **LANGUAGES:** Portuguese, English and Spanish. **PRACTICE AREAS:** Family Law; Environmental Law.

JOÁO BRITO E CUNHA, admitted, 1992, Portugal. *Education:* Lusíada University, Lisbon. *Member:* Portuguese Bar Association. **LANGUAGES:** Portuguese, Spanish, English and French. **PRACTICE AREAS:** Contracts and Commercial Law; Banking; Finance and Media Law.

CLÁUDIA VARELA, admitted, 1992, Portugal. *Education:* International University, Lisbon. *Member:* Portuguese Bar Association. **PRACTICE AREAS:** Labor Law; Social Security Law; Commercial Law; Civil Law; Criminal Law.

CRISTINA PORTUGAL, admitted, 1992, Portugal. *Education:* Autonomous University, Lisbon. *Member:* Portuguese Bar Association. **PRACTICE AREAS:** Commercial Law - Contracts; Real Estate; Construction and Transportation Law.

MARIA DA LUZ PASSANHA, admitted, 1993, Portugal. *Education:* Portuguese Catholic University, Lisbon. *Member:* Portuguese Bar Association. **PRACTICE AREAS:** Contracts; Naturalization - Citizenship; Criminal Law.

NUNO MORAIS SARMENTO, admitted, 1984, Portugal. *Education:* Portuguese University, Lisbon. Government Representative in the National Commission for Data Protection. *Member:* Portuguese Bar Association; Atlantic Association of Young Political Leaders. **LANGUAGES:** Portuguese, English, French and Spanish. **PRACTICE AREAS:** Commercial Law; Labor Law; EEC Law; General Litigation.

CARLA BRANCO, admitted, 1993, Portugal. *Education:* University of Lisbon, Law School. *Member:* Portuguese Bar Association. **PRACTICE AREAS:** Contracts; Business Law; Real Estate; Consumer Law; Advertising and Marketing; Computer Copyrights.

NELSON RAPOSO BERNARDO, admitted, 1993, Portugal. *Education:* University of Lisbon, Law School. Assistant Professor of Contracts Law, University of Lisbon Law School and Modern University. *Member:* Portuguese Bar association. **PRACTICE AREAS:** Corporate Law; Banking Law; Bank Holding Companies; Capital Market; Contracts Law; Pharmaceutical Regulation; Tax Planning.

SANDRA SALVAÇÃO BARRETO, admitted, 1993, Portugal. *Education:* University of Lisbon, Law School. Junior Assistant Professor of Inter-

(This Listing Continued)

national Public Law and Administrative Law, Lusíada University Law School, Lisbon. *Member:* Portuguese Bar Association. **PRACTICE AREAS:** Administrative Law; Government Contracts; Municipal Law; European Community Law.

PEDRO GUSTAVO TEIXEIRA, admitted, 1993, Portugal. *Education:* Portuguese Catholic University, Porto. Legal Advisor to the Lisbon Stock Exchange. *Member:* Portuguese Bar Association. **PRACTICE AREAS:** Capital Market; Corporate Law; Contracts Law; Private International Law.

PATRICK DEWERBE, admitted, 1993, Portugal. *Education:* Portuguese Catholic University, Lisbon. *Member:* Portuguese Bar Association. **PRACTICE AREAS:** Fiscal Law; Free Zones of Madeira and Azores; Estate Planning; Commercial Law; Corporate Law; Business Law; Finance.

EMANUEL MACEDO DE MEDEIROS, admitted, 1993, Portugal. *Education:* University of Lisbon, Law School. *Member:* Portuguese Bar Association. **LANGUAGES:** Portuguese, English, French and Spanish. **PRACTICE AREAS:** Civil Law; Commercial Law; Criminal Law; Banking Law; Business Law; Litigation.

SOFIA BARATA, admitted, 1993, Portugal. *Education:* University of Lisbon, Law School. *Member:* Portuguese Bar Association. **PRACTICE AREAS:** Real Estate; Advertising and Marketing; Tax Law; Consumer Law; Contracts.

SUSANA ALBUQUERQUE, admitted, 1993, Portugal. *Education:* University of Lisbon, Law School. *Member:* Portuguese Bar Association. **PRACTICE AREAS:** Commercial Law; Contracts; Telecommunications and Media; Energy.

SUSANA SANTOS AFONSO, admitted, 1993, Portugal. *Education:* Lusíada University, Lisbon. *Member:* Portuguese Bar Association. **PRACTICE AREAS:** Civil Litigation; Litigation; Taxation; Family Law.

Languages: Portuguese, English, French, Spanish, German and Italian

---

ARTUR REIS E SOUSA
ADVOGADO

In Cooperation with law firm Abreu, Cardigos and Partners

Established in 1964

AVENIDA FONTES PEREIRA DE MELO, 25-6TH D
1000 LISBON, PORTUGAL
Telephone: 351-1-529627/525306/529033
Telefax: 351-1-522186 Direct Dial: 351-1-3522484

Civil, Commercial, Labor, Real Estate, Criminal, International and General Matters.

ARTUR REIS E SOUSA, born October 7, 1934; admitted, 1963, Portugal. *Education:* University of Lisbon, Graduate in Law; Lisbon Law School. Fellow, Salzburg Seminar, 1974 and 1981 and Local Representative of same Seminar, 1976—. Member, International Advisory Council of the Salzburg Seminar, 1985—. Deputy District Attorney, 1958-1962. Member, Lawspan International E.E.I. Group. *Member:* Portuguese Bar Association. (Also Counsel, Abreu, Cardigos and Partners, Lisbon, Portugal). **LANGUAGES:** Portuguese, Spanish, French, Italian, English and some German.

CLIENTS: Marriott Corporation, Washington; United Press, London; Canadian Embassy, Lisbon; Australian Embassy, Lisbon; Jaakko Poyry, Helsinki; WH Pipe International, Helsinki; Canadian Saltfish Corp., St John's, Newfoundland; Union des Assurances du Canada, Ottawa; J.I. Case-Tenneco, Madrid; International Press Distributors, London; Case Poclain, SA, France; Columbian Chemicals Europa, GMBH, Hanover.
REFERENCES: Shearman & Sterling, New York, N.Y. (William B. Pennell); Baker & McKenzie, New York, N.Y. (Norman Resnicow); Steptoe & Johnson, Washington, D.C. (Daniel Plaine); Perkins, Coie, Stone, Olsen & Williams, Seattle, Washington (Susan Cole); Victor Mishcon & Co., London (Simon Freeman); Cleary, Gottlieb, Steen & Hamilton, Paris (Laurent Cohen-Tanugy); J. and A. Garrigues, Madrid (Rafael Echegoyen).

MARTIN J.H. REYNOLDS, R.P. RANKINE AND MICHAEL LLOYD

Established in 1927

16 LARGO DA ACADEMIA NACIONAL DE BELAS ARTES

1200 LISBON, PORTUGAL

Telephone: 346 2277; 342 8383

Fax: 346 5079

MARTIN J.H. REYNOLDS IS CO-REVISER OF THE PORTUGAL LAW DIGEST FOR THIS DIRECTORY.

English Lawyers.
Engaged in British, EEC, American and General International Practice Specializing in Foreign Investment, Conveyancing, Local Management and Client Representation, but not being Advogados or Solicitadores, are not authorized to appear before the Portuguese Courts.

MARTIN J.H. REYNOLDS, SOLICITOR, born London, 1929; admitted, 1958, English Solicitor. *Education:* Ampleforth College, York, Oxford University (M.A.). Legal Adviser to the British Ambassador. *LANGUAGES:* English, Portuguese and French. *PRACTICE AREAS:* Commercial Law; Company Law; Conveyancing; Property Law; Estates; International Law.

ROBERT P. RANKINE, SOLICITOR, admitted, 1958, English Solicitor. *Education:* Clifton College, Bristol; Cambridge University (M.A.). European Community Lawyer registered with the Consultative Committee of the Bars and Law Societies of the European Community. *Member:* Law Society of England and Wales. *LANGUAGES:* English and Portuguese. *PRACTICE AREAS:* Commercial Law; Property Law; Wills and Estates; Conflicts of Law; Taxation; Arbitration; International Law.

MICHAEL LLOYD, BARRISTER, born London, 1945; admitted, 1967, Gray's Inn, Barrister. *Education:* Oxford University (M.A.). Lecturer, Law, University of London, King's College, 1968-1974. *LANGUAGES:* English, Portuguese and French. *PRACTICE AREAS:* Company Law; Property Law; Taxation; Conflicts of Laws; EEC Law; Entertainment and the Arts.

Languages: English, Portuguese, Spanish, French and German

MARTIN J.H. REYNOLDS IS CO-REVISER OF THE PORTUGAL LAW DIGEST FOR THIS DIRECTORY.

SERRA LOPES ADVOGADOS

Sociedade de Advogados

CAMPO GRANDE, 28-10° D

1700 LISBON, PORTUGAL

Telephone: (351.1) 7933164

Fax: (351.1) 7974556

General Practice, Company Law, Commercial and Business Law, Maritime Law, Financial and Investment Law, E.E.C. Law, International Contracts, Environment and Mining Law, Civil Law, Arbitration.

MEMBERS OF FIRM

ANTÓNIO SERRA LOPES, born Lisbon, 1934; admitted, 1958, Portugal; 1975, Brazil. *Education:* Lisbon University, 1953-1958; Strasbourg International Comparative Law Faculty, 1965-1967. Former Consultant for Portuguese Government (Foreign Investments in Portugal). *Member:* Portuguese and Brazilian Bar Associations. *LANGUAGES:* Portuguese, Spanish, French, English and Italian.

MARIA DE JESUS SERRA LOPES, born Lisbon, 1933; admitted, 1957, Portugal; 1975, Brazil. *Education:* Lisbon University, 1952-1957; Strasbourg International Comparative Law Faculty, 1965-1967. *Member:* Portuguese Bar Association (Chairman, Ordem dos Advogados, 1989-1992); Brazilian Bar Association. *LANGUAGES:* Portuguese, Spanish, French, English and Italian.

LUÍS MIGUEL CORTES MARTINS, born Santarém, 1962; admitted, 1987, Portugal. *Education:* Catholic University, Lisbon 1985. Assistant Professor of Law: Lisbon University, 1986-1990; Catholic University, 1987. *Member:* Portuguese Bar Association. *LANGUAGES:* Portuguese, French, English and Spanish.

FÁTIMA ANTUNES RODRIGUES, born Torres Vedras, 1957; admitted, 1987, Portugal. *Education:* Lisbon University, Faculty of Law, 1985; Catholic University, EEC Law Course, 1985. Member, European Law Cab-

(This Listing Continued)

inet, Portuguese Ministry of Justice, 1987-1990. *Member:* Portuguese Bar Association. *LANGUAGES:* Portuguese, English, French and Spanish.

MARIA DE FATIMA NUNES, born Estoril, 1957; admitted, 1982, Portugal. *Education:* Lisbon University, 1980. *Member:* Portuguese Bar Association; International Association of Young Lawyers. *LANGUAGES:* Portuguese, English, French, Spanish and German.

CÉLIA MOURA ULLMANN, born Lisbon, 1963; admitted, 1992, Portugal. *Education:* Lisbon University, 1989. *Member:* Portuguese Bar Association. *LANGUAGES:* Portuguese, German, English, French and Spanish.

SERVULO CORREIA, ASDRUBAL CALISTO, JORGE CALISTO & ASSOCIADOS

Sociedade de Advogados

48 B AV. DA REPUBLICA, 4° ANDAR DIREITO

1000 LISBON, PORTUGAL

Telephone: (01) 793.63.43

Fax: (01) 793.69.67

Administrative, Banking and Finance, Bankruptcy/Insolvency, Civil Litigation, Commercial, Commercial Property, Company, Competition, Construction, Debt Recovery, Employment, Entertainment, European Community, Family, Franchising, Investment, Matrimonial, Mergers and Acquisitions, Partnerships, Real Estate, Company Tax and Personal Tax Law.

PARTNERS

PROF. DR. JOSÉMANUEL SERVULO CORREIA, born Angra do Heroísmo, Portugal, December 30, 1937; admitted, 1962, Portugal. *Education:* University of Lisbon (M.B.A., 1968; Doctor Juris, 1987). *Member:* Portuguese Bar Association. *LANGUAGES:* Portuguese, English, French, Spanish and German. *PRACTICE AREAS:* Administrative Law.

DR. ASDRUBAL CALISTO, born Caldas da Rainha, Portugal, March 11, 1937; admitted, 1962, Portugal. *Education:* University of Lisbon. *Member:* Portuguese Bar Association. *LANGUAGES:* Portuguese, English, French and Spanish. *PRACTICE AREAS:* Commercial; Tourism and Gambling; Real Estate; Investment and Financial Services; Corporate Law.

DR. JORGE CALISTO, born Caldas da Rainha, Portugal, April 12, 1941; admitted, 1975, Portugal. *Education:* University of Lisbon. *Member:* Portuguese Bar Association. *LANGUAGES:* Portuguese. *PRACTICE AREAS:* Family; Commercial; Corporate Law.

DR. PEDRO CALISTO, born Caldas da Rainha, Portugal, August 10, 1963; admitted, 1988, Portugal. *Education:* Lusiada University. *Member:* Portuguese Bar Association. *LANGUAGES:* Portuguese, English and French. *PRACTICE AREAS:* Family; Commercial; Civil; Litigation.

DR. HORTENSE MATOS, born Barrancos, Portugal, July 22, 1959; admitted, 1986, Portugal. *Education:* University of Lisbon. *Member:* Portuguese Bar Association. *LANGUAGES:* Portuguese. *PRACTICE AREAS:* Labour; Corporate Law.

DR. JOÃO AMARAL E ALMEIDA, born Mangualde, Portugal, September 3, 1964; admitted, 1991, Portugal. *Education:* Catholic University of Lisbon. *Member:* Portuguese Bar Association. *LANGUAGES:* Portuguese, French, Spanish, German and English. *PRACTICE AREAS:* Administrative Law.

A Member of European Law Firm (ELF) which is a European Economic Interest Group. It has offices in Belgium, France, Germany, Greece, Holland, Italy, Portugal and Spain and Associate offices in Sweden and U.S.A.

Languages: Portuguese, English, French, Spanish and German

SIMMONS & SIMMONS

Grupo Legal Português E.E.I.G. in association with J & A Garrigues, Pinheiro Neto & Co. and F. Castelo Branco, Nobre Guedes & P. Rebelo de Sousa

RUA CASTILHO, N° 32-9°
1250 LISBON
1000 LISBON, PORTUGAL
Telephone: 351-1-352 1318
Fax: 351-1-352 1418

London, England Office: 21 Wilson Street, EC2M 2TQ. Telephone: 44-171-628 2020; 44-171-528 9292. Facsimile: 44-171-628 2070. Telex: 888562SIMMON G.

Paris, France Office: 2, Avenue Bugeaud, 75116. Telephone: 33-1-45016767. Telecopier: 33-1-45012232. Telex: TRANSAV 649381F.

Brussels, Belgium Office: Rue d'Arlon 118, 1040. Telephone: 32-2-280 16 70. Telecopier: 32-2-280 04 84.

Milan, Italy Office in joint practice with Studio Avv. Eugenio Grippo: Via Dei Boschetti 1, 20121. Telephone: 39-2-76003012. Telecopier: 39-2-782770.

Abu Dhabi Office: The Blue Tower, Khalifa Street. P.O. Box 5931. Telephone: 971 2 347882. Telecopier: 971 2 347832.

Hong Kong Office: 24th Floor, Jardine House, One Connaught Place, Central. Telephone: 852-28681131. Telecopier: 852-28105040. Telex: 75888 SANDS HX.

New York, New York Office: 115 East 57th Street, 10022. Telephone: 1-212-688-6620. Telecopier: 1-212-355-3594.

(For complete list of other Partners, see Professional Biographies at London, England and Grupo Legal Português, Lisbon, Portugal)

TEIXEIRA DE FREITAS & JARDIM FERNANDES

Sociedade de Advogados
PRAÇA JOÃO DO RIO, N° 8 - 5° DT°
1000 LISBON, PORTUGAL
Telephone: (351-1) 8461921; (351-1) 8461922
Fax: (351-1) 8461927

Funchal (Madeira), Portugal Office: Rua do Esmeraldo, 44 - 4, 9000. Telephone: (351-91) 226950. Fax: (351-91) 230637.

General Corporate, Commercial and Tax Practice, Banking and Finance, International Tax Planning, Real Estate, Foreign Investment, Labor Law, Litigation and Ship Registration.

MEMBERS OF FIRM

LUIZ AUGUSTO TEIXEIRA DE FREITAS, born Rio de Janeiro, Brazil, 1962; admitted, 1986, Brazil; 1991, Portugal. *Education:* Rio de Janeiro State University (LL.B., 1986). With: Skadden, Arps, Slate, Meagher & Flom, New York, 1989; Grant, Herrmann, Schwartz & Klinger, New York, 1989-1990. *Member:* Portuguese Bar Association; Brazilian Bar Association; International Tax Planning Association; Associação Brasileira de Direito Financeiro. Contributor, Madeira Section of the ITO - International Offshore Financial Centres Manual. *LANGUAGES:* Portuguese, English and Spanish.

ROSANA MARIA FREITAS RODRIGUES JARDIM FERNANDES, born Funchal, Madeira, Portugal, 1964; admitted, 1987, Portugal. *Education:* Lisbon University School of Law (LL.B., 1987). Assistant Legal Counsel, to the Vice-President of the Madeira Regional Government, 1989-1991. *Member:* Portuguese Bar Association. *LANGUAGES:* Portuguese, English, French and Spanish.

ASSOCIATES

ANTONIO SANTA DIOGO, born Lisbon, Portugal, 1964; admitted, 1987, Portugal. *Education:* Lisbon University School of Law (LL.B., 1987). *Member:* Portuguese Bar Association. *LANGUAGES:* Portuguese, Spanish and English.

ANABELA GOMES LOPES, born Lisbon, Portugal, 1962; admitted, 1985, Portugal. *Education:* Lisbon University School of Law (LL.B., 1985). Assistant Professor: International Private, Family Law and Civil Law, Lisbon University; Independent University School of Law. *Member:* Portuguese Bar Association. *LANGUAGES:* Portuguese, French and English.

(This Listing Continued)

ELITA MARIA CORREIA, born London, England, 1970; admitted, 1994, Portugal. *Education:* Lisbon University School of Law (LL.B., 1993; Post Graduation, E.C. Law, 1994). *LANGUAGES:* English, Portuguese and French.

ANA MARGARIDA ALMEIDA DE PINHO NENO, born Lisbon, Portugal, 1969; admitted, 1992, Portugal. *Education:* Catholic University of Lisbon (LL.B., 1992). *LANGUAGES:* Portuguese, French and English.

JOÃO FERNANDES, born Funchal, Madeira, Portugal, 1967; admitted, 1993, Funchal. *Education:* Coimbra University School of Law (LL.B., 1993). *LANGUAGES:* Portuguese, English and Spanish.

OF COUNSEL

MARIA ISABEL ALMEIDA DE PINHO NENO, born Murtosa, Portugal, 1963; admitted, 1986, Portugal. *Education:* Catholic University, Lisbon (LL.B., 1986). Member, Wessing Berenberg Zimmermann, Dusseldorf, 1990. *Member:* Portuguese Bar Association; Young Portuguese Lawyers Association. *LANGUAGES:* Portuguese, French, English, German and Spanish.

LUIS MIGUEL OOM, born Lisbon, Portugal, 1954; admitted, 1986, Portugal. *Education:* Lisbon University School of Law, Lisbon (LL.B., 1986; Post Graduation in E.C. Law, 1987). Assistant Professor, Criminal Law, Lisbon University School of Law, 1987-1990. *Member:* Portuguese Bar Association. *LANGUAGES:* Portuguese, English and Spanish.

NUNO REYNOLDS TELLES PEREIRA

16, LARGO DA ACADEMIA NACIONAL DE BELAS ARTES
1200 LISBON, PORTUGAL
Telephone: (01) 346 22 77
Telex: 13434 REYRAN P
Cable: STONSOLIC LISBON
Fax: (01) 346 50 79

CO-REVISER OF THE PORTUGAL LAW DIGEST FOR THIS DIRECTORY.

NUNO JOSE REYNOLDS TELLES PEREIRA, born Lisbon, Portugal, September 13, 1954; admitted, 1991, Portugal. *Education:* Portuguese Military College; University College Dublin (B.C.L., 1981); Universidade Clássica de Lisboa, Law Faculty (Licenciate at Law, 1988). *Member:* Portuguese Bar Association. *LANGUAGES:* Portuguese, English, French and Spanish. *PRACTICE AREAS:* General Practice; Succession; Company Law; Commercial Law; Land Law; Patent Law; Trademark Law.

CO-REVISER OF THE PORTUGAL LAW DIGEST FOR THIS DIRECTORY.

M. KARIM VAKIL & ASSOCIADOS

Sociedade de Advogados
Established in 1990

AV. ALMIRANTE GAGO COUTINHO, 80
1700 LISBON, PORTUGAL
Telephone: 8472536/37/38/39/40
Fax: 8472542/43

Mergers and Acquisitions, Banking, Company, Competition, Contracts, Real Estate, Foreign Investment, Administrative, Labour, Family and Inheritance Law, General Practice and Litigation.

PARTNERS

M. KARIM VAKIL, born Lourenco Marques, 1945; admitted, 1975, Portugal. *Education:* Universidade de Lisboa. Co-Author: Mergers and Acquisitions in Europe/Chapter on Portugal, London, 1990. *Member:* Portuguese and International Bar Associations; International Fiscal Association; Asia-Pacific Lawyers Association; Young Presidents Association.

TERESA FORJAZ COELHO, born Lisbon, 1962; admitted, 1985, Portugal. *Education:* Universidade Lusiada de Lisboa. *Member:* Portuguese Bar Association.

ASSOCIATES

JOÃO MACEDO VITORINO, born Lisbon, 1965; admitted, 1990, Portugal. *Education:* Universidade de Lisboa. Assistant Professor, Universidade de Lisboa. *Member:* Portuguese Bar Association.

(This Listing Continued)

M. KARIM VAKIL & ASSOCIADOS, Lisbon—Continued

JOSÉ VIEIRA FONSECA, born Cartaxo, 1966; admitted, 1991, Portugal. *Education:* Universidade Católica Portuguesa. Assistant Professor, Universidade Autónoma de Lisboa. *Member:* Portuguese Bar Association.

MAGDA KARIM VAKIL, born Lisbon, 1968; admitted, 1993, Portugal. *Education:* Universidad de Lisboa. Assistant Professor, Instituto Superior de Matematica e Administraçao.

ANA MARCAL GRILLO, born Lisbon, 1967; admitted, 1992, Portugal. *Education:* Universidade de Lisboa. *Member:* Portuguese Bar Association.

ANTONIO GONCALVES, born Tomar, 1966; admitted, 1992, Portugal. *Education:* Universidade Lusiada de Lisboa. *Member:* Portuguese Bar Association.

MIGUEL MACHADO FELDMANN, born Lisbon, 1967; admitted, 1992, Portugal. *Education:* Universidade Catholic Portuguesa. *Member:* Portuguese Bar Association.

Languages: Portuguese, English, French, Spanish, Italian.

VALE E AZEVEDO & ASSOCIADOS

Established in 1983

AVENIDA PRAIA DA VITORIA, N° 5 -1ST FLOOR
1000 LISBON, PORTUGAL
Telephone: 351-1-315 35 56
Facsimile: 351-1-52 58 56

Povoa De Varzim, Portugal Office: Rua da Junqueira, N 19-1st Floor, 4490 Povoa de Varzim. Telephone: 351-52-62 72 84. Facsimile: 351-52-61 17 63.

Luxembourg-G.D. du Luxembourg Office: 5, Rue de La Reine, L-2418 Luxembourg. Telephone: 352-46 35 63. Facsimile: 352-46 29 32.

Geneve, Suisse Office: 16, Place Longemalle, 1204 Geneve - Suisse. Telephone: 41-22-312 03 62/60. Facsimile: 41-22-312 05 20.

Administrative Law, Arbitration, Banking Law, Bankruptcy, Competition Law, Construction Law, Customer Protection Law, Conveyancing, Corporate Law, Customs and Exercise Law, Distribution Agency & Franchise Law, EEC Law, Employer's Liability, Family Law, Finance Law, Food and Drug Regulations, Foreign Investments, Immigration Law, Industrial Relations and Labour Law, International Contracts, International Private Law, Litigation, Property and Real Estate Law, Rent and Lease, Social Security, Trade Regulations, General Legal Practice.
Capital Taxation, Corporate Taxation, Custom Duties, Indirect Taxation, Inheritance, Succession and Donation Taxation, International Taxation, Individual Income Taxation, Sales, Turnover and Value Added Taxes, Taxation of Foreign Nationals, Exchange Control, General Tax Practice.

FIRM PROFILE: The firm is a Member of the Portuguese Bar Association, Portuguese-British Chamber of Commerce, American Chamber of Commerce, Portuguese-Belgium-Luxembourg Chamber of Commerce, Italian Chamber of Commerce, Portuguese-German Chamber of Commerce and Industry, Portuguese-French Chamber of Commerce, Portuguese-Spanish Chamber of Commerce, Portuguese-Venezuelian Chamber of Commerce.

SENIOR PARTNER

DR. JOÃO VALE E AZEVEDO, born Lisbon, Portugal, May 17, 1957. admitted to bar, 1980, Portugal. *Education:* University of Lisbon Law School (Law, 1980). Junior Assistant, Family and Inheritance Law, Lisbon Law University, 1979-1981. Legal Advisor, Portuguese Prime Minister, 1981-1983. Corporate and Tax Law Consultant, Portuguese Industrial Association, (AIP), 1983—. Transport and Tax Law Consultant, International Chamber of Commerce and Industry, Lisbon, 1983-1990. *Member:* Portuguese Bar Association; Young Lawyers International Association (AIJA); European Lawyers' Union. *LANGUAGES:* Portuguese, English, French and Spanish. *PRACTICE AREAS:* International Business Law; Corporate Law; Real Estate Law.

PARTNERS

DR. MANUEL CUNHA GOMES, born Povoa De Varzim, Portugal, May 30, 1959. admitted to bar, 1984, Portugal. *Education:* Catholic University of Oporto (Law, 1984). *Member:* Portuguese Bar Association. *LANGUAGES:* Portuguese, English and Spanish. *PRACTICE AREAS:* Corporate Law; Litigation; Labour Law.

(This Listing Continued)

EU1160B

DR. PEDRO MENDES PINTO, born Lisbon, Portugal, September 8, 1965. admitted to bar, 1990, Portugal. *Education:* University of Lisbon Law School (Law, 1989; Post-graduate course of EEC studies, 1990-1991). *Member:* Portuguese Bar Association. *LANGUAGES:* Portuguese, English, French and Spanish. *PRACTICE AREAS:* EEC Law; Administrative Law; Corporate Taxation Law.

DRA. MARIA DO ROSARIO CARNEIRO PACHECO, born Lisbon, Portugal, October 15, 1964. admitted to bar, 1989, Portugal. *Education:* Catholic University of Lisbon (Law, 1988). *Member:* Portuguese Bar Association. *LANGUAGES:* Portuguese, Spanish and English. *PRACTICE AREAS:* Family Law; Inheritance Law; Succession and Donation Taxation Law; Corporate Law.

DR. VASCO BIVAR AZEVEDO, born Lisbon, Portugal, December 17, 1963. admitted to bar, 1988, Portugal. *Education:* Lusiada University, Lisbon Law School (Law, 1988). Advisor, Jurisdictional Council of the F.P.R. (Portuguese Rugby Federation). *Member:* Portuguese Bar Association. *LANGUAGES:* Portuguese, French and English. *PRACTICE AREAS:* Litigation; Distribution Agency and Franchise Law; Foreign Investment Law.

Languages: English, French, German, Portuguese and Spanish.

REPRESENTATIVE CLIENTS: UOB-United Overseas Bank (Geneva/Luxembourg); J.P. Capital Management (Geneva); Friedrich Naumann Stiftung (Germany); Cereol-Group Ferruzzi (Spain); Cerestar-Group Feruzzi (Italy); Fritz W. Meyer (Germany-Portugal); Cevasa-Group March (Spain); Cenoura (Portugal); Gaz Natural (Spain); COPAM (Portugal); Wrobel (Brasil-Portugal); Bygg Fast Parklane (Sweden-Portugal); Martur Finance (Luxembourg); Gunther Peitz (Germany-Portugal); Advent España (Spain); Portuguese Industrial Association (Portugal); Comercial Solia (Spain); Chiesa de La Madona di Loreto (Italy); Banque Paribas Luxembourg (Luxembourg); Mundial Confiança Insurance Cia. (Portugal); Wacker (Germany); Jet Worldwild (France); Deceuninck (Belgium); G.U. Grestsch-Unitas, Gmbh (Germany).

VASCONCELOS, F. SÁ CARNEIRO, FONTES & ASSOCIADOS

Sociedade de Advogados

RUA ALEXANDRE HERCULANO, 60-7°
1200 LISBON, PORTUGAL
Telephone: (351-1) 387 58 15
Fax: (351-1) 387 58 47

General Corporate and Commercial Law, Banking, Financial and Securities Law, Litigation and Arbitration, Insolvency Law, Mergers and Acquisitions, Tax Law, Property Law, Administrative Law, EC and Competition Law, Labour Law.

PARTNERS

DUARTE PESTANA DE VASCONCELOS, born Lisbon, Portugal, June 7, 1957; admitted, 1983, Portugal. *Education:* Catholic University of Minas Gerais, Brazil; Catholic University, Lisbon Law School. Partner, Coelho Ribeiro & Associados, 1986-1993. Adviser, to the Secretary of State, Fiscal Affairs, 1986-1990. Founding Member, Portuguese Arbitration and Conciliation Committee. *Member:* Special Committee on Competition and Literary Property, CCBE (Council of Bars and Law Societies of the EC, 1989-1992); Legal Committee Leaseurope; Portuguese Bar Association. *LANGUAGES:* Portuguese, English, French and Spanish.

FRANCISCO SÁ CARNEIRO, born Porto, Portugal, March 12, 1958; admitted, 1982, Portugal. *Education:* Portuguese Catholic University, Lisbon Law School; Catholic University of Louvain, Belgium (EC Law). Stagiaire with Oppenheimer, Wolff & Donnelly, Brussels Office, 1983. Partner, João Morais Leitão & Associados, 1982-1993. Correspondent, European Taxation, International Bureau of Fiscal Documentation, 1988. *Member:* Portuguese Bar Association. *LANGUAGES:* Portuguese, English and French.

TITO ARANTES FONTES, born August 9, 1957; admitted, 1982, Portugal. *Education:* Coimbra University, Coimbra Law School. Member, Legal Department, Caixa Geral de Depósitos, 1983-1991; Manager, Legal Department, 1991-1992. Legal Adviser: Secretary of State of Education, 1987- 1991; Secretary of State of the Territory, 1991-1992. General Secretary, Lisbon Association of Trade, 1992-1993. *Member:* Portuguese Bar Association. *LANGUAGES:* Portuguese, English and French.

(This Listing Continued)

ASSOCIATES

JOÃO SANTOS, born Lisbon, Portugal, June 20, 1968; admitted, 1992, Portugal. *Education:* Lisbon University, Lisbon Law School. *Member:* Portuguese Bar Association. *LANGUAGES:* Portuguese, English and Spanish.

VEIGA GOMES, BESSA MONTEIRO, MARQUES BOM

Sociedade de Advogados

Attorneys at Law - Patents and Trademarks

R. MARQUÊS DE FRONTEIRA 8-3° DTO.
P - 1000 LISBON, PORTUGAL
Telephone: 3871940; 3872094; 3871897; 3871931; 3872884; 3871551;
3871982; 3872897; 3872996
Fax: 3873453; 3870335

Banking Law, Competition Law, Corporate Law, Distributorship, Agency and Franchise Law, Mergers and Acquisitions, Foreign Investment, Industrial Relations and Labour, Insurance Law, International Contracts, Litigation, Oil and Mining Law, Property and Real Estate Law, Social Security, General Legal Practice.
Intellectual Property: Copyright Law, Industrial Models, License Negotiation, Patent Litigation, Patent Prosecution, Pharmaceutical Patents, Trademark Litigation, Trademark Prosecution, Transfer of Technology, General Intellectual Property Practice.

PARTNERS

JOAO JOSE VEIGA GOMES, born Lisbon, Portugal, 1940; admitted, 1967, Portugal. *Education:* Lisbon School of Law (Graduated in Law, 1962); Canonical Law Studies Center of the Portuguese Catholic University (Postgraduate course in Matrimonial Canonical Law, 1994). Public Attorney Delegate in Maputo, Mozambique, 1963. Teacher, Economical Law, Lisbon School of Law, 1976-1977. Participant and Moderator, several conferences and seminars. Author: "Sociedades Anónimas-Uma Perspectiva de Direito Económico," Lisboa, 1981. Article on Portugal in "The Lawyers Guide to Transnational Corporate Acquisitions," Kluwer, 1991 and collaboration in "Legal Aspects of Doing Business in Western Europe," West Publishing Co., St. Paul, Minn., USA. Member, Board of Advisors, McGeorge School of Law, University of the Pacific. *Member:* International Association for the Protection of the Industrial Property; EPI and LES; General Council of the Social Security of the Bar Association (1993-1994). *LANGUAGES:* Portuguese, French and English. *PRACTICE AREAS:* International Contracts and Acquisitions; Foreign Investment; Corporate Matters; Licensing, Agency and Distributorship Agreements.

CÉSAR BESSA MONTEIRO, born Vila Real, Portugal, 1944; admitted, 1969, Portugal. *Education:* Lisbon School of Law (Graduated in Law, 1966). Reporter: Portuguese Group, AIPPI Congress of Paris, Committee dealing with the Influence of Laws on Restraint of Trade of Transfer of Technology of Know-how Agreements, 1983; Portuguese Group, AIPPI Congress of London, Committee dealing with the Measures against Counterfeiting of Branded Goods, 1986; Portuguese Group, AIPPI Congress of Amsterdam, Committee dealing with the Protection of the Software, 1989. Vice-President, Board of General Meeting, Portuguese Delegation, International Chamber of Commerce. Author: "Doing Business in Portugal," Common Market Reports, Commerce Clearing House, Inc., Chicago, Illinois, 1986; "Patents throughout the World," Trade Activities Inc., New York; "Trademarks throughout the World," Trade Activities Inc., New York; "Legal Aspects of doing business in Western Europe," West Publishing Co., St. Paul, Minn., USA; "European Franchising Law & Practice in the European Community," Mark Abell, Waterlow Publishers, 1991; "Pre-Emptive Remedies in Europe," Nicholas Rose, Longman Law, Tax and Finance, Longman Group UK Ltd., 1992; "International Franchising Law," General Editor, Dennis Campbell, Matthew Bender, 1983. *Member:* Portuguese Bar Association (Secretary, 1981-1983, Lisbon Delegation; Vice-President, 1984-1986, 1993-1995, Lisbon Delegation); Portuguese Delegation, International Chamber of Commerce (Member, Industrial Property Commission); Portuguese Group, International Association for the Protection of the International Property (Member, Board of Directors); Portuguese Association of the Industrial Property Association Consultants (Member, Ethics Committee); International Federation of the Industrial Property Consultants; European Communities Trademark Association; LES and EPI. *LANGUAGES:* Portuguese, French and English. *PRACTICE AREAS:* Industrial Property Law; Distributorship, Agency and Franchising; Foreign Investment Law.

(This Listing Continued)

FRANCISCO MARQUES BOM, born Coimbra, Portugal, 1950; admitted, 1976, Portugal. *Education:* Coimbra School of Law (Graduated in Law, 1974). *Member:* Portuguese Bar Association (Member, Board of Lisbon Delegation, 1985); Portuguese Association of Young Lawyers (President of the Board, 1987-1988). *LANGUAGES:* Portuguese, English, French and Spanish. *PRACTICE AREAS:* Administrative Law; Real Estate Law; Maritime Law; Litigation; Commercial Law.

MANUEL SALEMA, born Lourenco Marques, Portugal, 1938; admitted, 1969, Portugal. *Education:* Lisbon School of Law (Graduate in Law, 1968). *Member:* Portuguese Bar Association. *LANGUAGES:* Portuguese, French and English. *PRACTICE AREAS:* Corporate Law; Insurance Law; Foodstuff and Labeling; Mergers and Acquisitions.

VITOR MARQUES DA CRUZ, born Leiria, Portugal, 1959; admitted, 1984, Portugal. *Education:* Lisbon School of Law (Graduated in Law, 1982; Graduated in EEC Law, 1983). Participant, several international conferences and seminars. Co-Author: "Legal Aspects of Doing Business in Western Europe," West Publishing Co., St. Paul, Minn, USA. Correspondent, International Company and Commercial Law Review. *Member:* Portuguese Bar Association; Portuguese Association of Young Lawyers. *LANGUAGES:* Portuguese, English and French. *PRACTICE AREAS:* International Contract Law; Real Estate Law; Commercial Law; Oil Law; Mining Law; Foreign Investment Law.

ASSOCIATES

RUI CARLOS COLMONERO, born Lisbon, Portugal, 1959; admitted, 1984, Portugal. *Education:* Lisbon School of Law (Graduated in Law, 1982). *Member:* Portuguese Bar Association; Portuguese Young Lawyers Association. *LANGUAGES:* Portuguese and English. *PRACTICE AREAS:* Insurance Law; Corporate Law; Litigation.

PEDRO ABREU ROCHA, born Lisbon, Portugal, 1964; admitted, 1990, Portugal. *Education:* Lisbon School of Law (Graduated in Law, 1988). *Member:* Portuguese Bar Association. *LANGUAGES:* Portuguese, French and English. *PRACTICE AREAS:* Corporate Law; Litigation.

MARIA DE LURDES SENRA BESSA MONTEIRO, born Lisbon, Portugal, 1953; admitted, 1990, Portugal. *Education:* Lisbon School of Law (Graduate in Law, 1988). *Member:* Portuguese Bar Association; Portuguese Association of Young Lawyers. *LANGUAGES:* Portuguese, English and French. *PRACTICE AREAS:* Immigration Law; Labour Law; Social Security Law; General Legal Practice.

HELENA TAPP BARROSO, born Lisbon, Portugal, 1966; admitted, 1991, Portugal. *Education:* Lisbon Catholic University (Graduate in Law, 1989). Assistant Professor, Contract Law, Lisbon School of Law, 1989—. Publications: Update article on "Portugal," together with J.J. Veiga Gomes and C. Bessa Monteiro, "Legal Aspects of Doing Business in Western Europe," 1991; Chapter on "Portugal," in "Environmental Regulation. Its Impact on Foreign Investment," 1992; Chapter on "Portugal," in "Data Transmission and Privacy," currently being printed. Country Contributor: "European Environmental Law Revision," 1992—; together with V. Marques da Cruz, for the "International Company and Commerical Law Review." *Member:* Portuguese Bar Association. *LANGUAGES:* Portuguese, English and French. *PRACTICE AREAS:* Corporate Law; Contract Law; Environmental Law; Arbitration Law; General Legal Practice.

J.A. MARTINS FERREIRA, born Abrantes, Portugal, 1966; admitted, 1991, Portugal. *Education:* Lisbon University (Graduate in Law, 1989); S.T.Q.E. (EEC Law Course). *Member:* Portuguese Bar Association. *LANGUAGES:* Portuguese, English and French. *PRACTICE AREAS:* Commercial Law; Real Estate Law; Litigation; Financial Law.

MEMBERS OF CARLOS OLAVO & ASSOCIADOS

CARLOS OLAVO, born Lisbon, Portugal, 1947; admitted, 1971. *Education:* State Faculty of Law (Law Degree, 1969); State University of Law, Lisbon, Master of Judicial Science, 1971). Professor of Commercial Law. Official Agent of Industrial Property. *Member:* Portuguese Bar Association; International Union of Lawyers Association (U.I.A.). *LANGUAGES:* Portuguese, French, English and Spanish. *PRACTICE AREAS:* Industrial Property Law; Competition Law; Banking Law; Financial Law; Commercial Law; Taxation Law; Administrative Law.

ISABEL MAGALHÃES OLAVO, born Lisbon, Portugal, 1956; admitted, 1980. *Education:* State University of Law Lisbon (Law Degree, 1978). Vice President of the Portuguese Young Lawyers Association. *Member:* Portuguese Bar Association (General Council); International Lawyers Association (U.I.A.); Portuguese Young Lawyers Association. *LANGUAGES:* Portuguese, French, English and Spanish. *PRACTICE AREAS:* Banking Law; Finance Law; Family Law.

(This Listing Continued)

VEIGA GOMES, BESSA MONTEIRO, MARQUES BOM,
Lisbon—Continued

FERNANDO QUINTAIS LOPES, born Lisbon, Portugal, 1950; admitted, 1977. *Education:* State University of Law, Lisbon (Law Degree, 1975). *Member:* Portuguese Bar Association; Portuguese Young Lawyers Association ; International lawyers Association U.I.A.). *LANGUAGES:* Portuguese, French and English. *PRACTICE AREAS:* Labour Law; Corporate Law; Litigation; General Legal Practice.

Languages: English, French and Spanish.

RONALD CHARLES WOLF

Established in 1970

TRAVESSA DO FERREIRO, 23 - 5D
1200 LISBON, PORTUGAL
Telephone: (351-1) 3964754; (351-61) 6 34 39
Fax: (351-61) 6 34 39

Joint Ventures and Mergers, Establishment of Companies, Competition Law, Foreign Investment, Commercial, Corporation and International Private Law, Common Market Law, Technology Transfer and Distribution Contracts.

FIRM PROFILE: The firm was established in 1970 and offers a full range of legal services with particular experience in acquisitions and mergers as well as the establishment of subsidiaries. The firm participates actively in complex litigation in conjunction with local Portuguese counsel thus ensuring that difficulty in the understanding of complicated legal instruments or American law is not misunderstood because of language or legal subtleties. Dr. Wolf's expertise in American and Portuguese law is often reflected in opinions delivered to the Portuguese courts or other official institutions. Dr. Wolf's recently published "Corporate Acquisitions & Mergers in Portugal" (July 1993, Graham & Trotman Ltd., London) is the first comprehensive treatment in English of Portuguese commercial law. Scheduled for publication in 1994/1995 is Dr. Wolf's "International Joint Ventures," a comprehensive survey of the legal techniques, clauses and documents for forming an international joint venture.

RONALD CHARLES WOLF, born New York, N.Y., March 20, 1932; admitted, 1957, New York; 1965, Vermont. *Education:* University of Wisconsin and New York University (B.A., 1953); Boston University and New York University (LL.B., 1956); University of Manchester, England. Author: "Lessor's Liability for Lessee's Improvements," New York Law Journal, December, 1961; "In Transit—A Definition," Brooklyn Law Review, April, 1963; "Promissory Notes: Their Effect Under the Lien Law," New York State Bar Journal, October, 1963; "Trial by Jury: A Sociological Analysis," Wisconsin Law Review, Summer, 1966; "The Refundable Commitment Fee," The Business Lawyer, July, 1968 ; "Corporate Acquisitions & Mergers in Portugal", Graham & Trotman, London, 1993. Reporter, Competition Law, IBA. Chairman, Board of Tax Appeals, Washington County, Vermont, 1967. *Member:* New York, Vermont and American (Member, Sections on Business Law, Anti-Trust Law, International and Comparative Law) Bar Associations; International Bar Association. *LANGUAGES:* English and Portuguese. *PRACTICE AREAS:* Mergers and Acquisitions; Establishment of Subsidiaries; Competition Law; Complex Litigation.

MRS. MARILYN WOLF, born Newton, Massachusetts (USA), August 20, 1931. *Education:* Boston University and University of Wisconsin (1952). Paralegal and Collaborator on all clients' matters. *LANGUAGES:* English and Portuguese.

PAULO ALEXANDRE DE PINA

advogados

Established in 1980

R.D. PAIO PERES CORREIA, 31/1
8100 LOULÉ, ALGARVE, PORTUGAL
Telephone: +351-89-415 047/8/9, 415 051
Telex: 56982 JURISP P
Telefax: +351-89-415-050

Lisbon, Portugal Office: R. do Alecrim, 75, 2°, 1200. Telephone: (01) 3421778-3426858-3421265. Telefax: 1-342 5956.
(This Listing Continued)

EU1162B

Founding members of LAW—LAWYERS ASSOCIATED WORLDWIDE, an association of lawyers with offices in Amsterdam, Athens, Barcelona, Berne, Boca Raton, Brussels, Cairo, Copenhague, Denver, Derby, Dublin, Dusseldorf, Glasgow, Isle of Man, Jersey, Kingston, Kristianstad, Lagos, Limassol, Lisboa, London, Los Angeles, Malta, Milan, New York, Paris, Quebec City, Saint Tropez, Seattle, Sofia, Toronto, Vancouver, Victoria, Warsaw, Zurich.

PARTNERS

PAULO ALEXANDRE DE PINA, born Lisbon, Portugal, September, 1958; admitted, 1980, Rio de Janeiro; 1981, Portugal. *Education:* Fac. Dir. Cândido Mendes-Ipanema, Rio (1980). Chairman, LAW LAWYERS ASSOCIATED WORLDWIDE. *Member:* Union Internationale des Advocates (UIA); American (International Associate) and International Bar Associations. *LANGUAGES:* Portuguese, English, French and Spanish. *PRACTICE AREAS:* Commercial Law; Foreign Investment; Litigation.

MARIA ISABEL DE PINA, born Coimbra, November, 1959; admitted, 1984, Portugal. *Education:* Catholic University Law School, Lisbon (1982). Training in Banking Law, Banco Português do Atlântico, Lisbon, 1982. *LANGUAGES:* Portuguese, English, French and Spanish. *PRACTICE AREAS:* Real Estate; General Practice.

ASSOCIATES

RUI FALCÃO DE CAMPOS, born Santarém, Portugal; admitted, 1994, Portugal. *Education:* Catholic University Law School, Lisbon, Portugal (1985); Vermont Law School (Environmental Law Studies, 1988). Consultant, Ministry of Environment, 1986-1994. Chief of Cabinet, Minister of Environment. Executive, Portuguese Port Authority. Chief, Portuguese International Delegations related with Environmental and Port Law. *LANGUAGES:* Portuguese, French, English, Spanish and Italian. *PRACTICE AREAS:* Environmental Law; Administrative Law.

SARA CAETANO, born Loulé, Algarve, Portugal; admitted, 1994, Portugal. *Education:* University of Lisbon Law School (1993). *LANGUAGES:* Portuguese and English. *PRACTICE AREAS:* General Practice.

Languages: Portuguese, Spanish, English and French.

FERNANDO BROCHADO COELHO &
MARIA TERESA BROCHADO COELHO

Established in 1962

RUA RODRIGUES SAMPAIO, N°, 117-4° ESQ°
P.O.BOX 4.446-4.007 PORTO CODEX
4000 PORTO, PORTUGAL
Telephone: (2) 200 0011/2
Fax: (2) 200 3314

General Civil and Commercial Law; Property Law; Family; Transport Law; Company Law; Business Law; Banking; Investment; Administrative Law; Criminal Law.
Firm engaged in Portuguese law practice and entitled to plead before the Portuguese courts.

MEMBERS OF FIRM

FERNANDO BROCHADO COELHO, born 1934; admitted, 1962, Portugal. *Education:* University of Lisbon. Magistrate (Public Prosecutor), 1962.

MARIA TERESA BROCHADO COELHO, born 1962; admitted, 1988, Portugal. *Education:* University of Oporto.

MARIO BROCHADO COELHO, born 1939; admitted, 1962, Portugal. *Education:* University of Coimbra.

CARLOS PACHECO MOREIRA, born 1958; admitted, 1982, Portugal. *Education:* University of Coimbra.

Languages: Portuguese, English, French, Italian and Spanish

CLAUDINO PEREIRA

Established in 1967

RUA DOS CLÉRIGOS, 46-1°
4000 PORTO, PORTUGAL
Telephone: (351) 2/2004687; 2/324663; 2/324638
Fax: (351) 2/2087629; 2/319768
Telex: 23102 Perlex P

Commercial, Civil and International Private Law. Patents, Maritime Law.

DR. CLAUDINO PEREIRA, born Oporto, Portugal, April 26, 1943; admitted, 1965, Portugal. *Education:* University of Coimbra. *LANGUAGES:* French, English, German and Portuguese. *PRACTICE AREAS:* Commercial Law; Civil Law; International Private Law; Maritime Law.

DR. FERNANDO OLIVEIRA E SILVA, admitted, 1969. *LANGUAGES:* English, French and Portuguese. *PRACTICE AREAS:* Commercial Law; Civil Law.

LEGAL SUPPORT PERSONNEL

DR. MARIA DO ROSÁRIO VASCONCELOS (Translator).

ANTÓNIO VILAR & ASSOCIATES

Established in 1977

RUA DE CEUTA, 118 - 2°
4000 PORTO, PORTUGAL
Telephone: 351-2-2004281; 351-2-2083496
Fax: 351-2-325914

Paris, France Office: 10, Rue de Richelieu, 75001.
Brussels, Belgium Office: Av. Eugène Demolder, 136, 1030.
Lisbon: Largo do Mastro, 29.

General Practice, Taxation, Commercial, Foreign Investment and International Trade Law, Company and Corporation, Labour, Real Estate, Civil Litigation, Mergers and Acquisitions, Debt Collection, Environmental Law.

MEMBERS OF FIRM

PROF. DR. ANTÓNIO VILAR, born Porto, Portugal, January 19, 1952. *Education:* University of Coimbra (Economic Law). *Member:* International Association of Young Lawyers. (Founding Member). *LANGUAGES:* Portuguese, French, English, German and Spanish. *PRACTICE AREAS:* Company Law; Commercial Law; Labour Law; Foreign Investment.

DRA. MARIA DOS ANJOS GUERRA, born September 19, 1961. *Education:* University of Coimbra; Lusíada University (European Studies). Joined this firm, 1985. *Member:* Euro-Atlantic Institute; Porto Bar Association. *LANGUAGES:* Portuguese, French, English, Spanish and Italian. *PRACTICE AREAS:* Civil Law; Real Estate Law; Corporate Tax.

DR. VÍTOR ROCHA, born November 21, 1965. *Education:* University of Porto. Joined this firm, 1990. *Member:* Porto Bar Association. *LANGUAGES:* Portuguese, English, French and Spanish. *PRACTICE AREAS:* Contracts; Family Law; Commercial Law; Holdings; Offshore.

REPUBLIC OF BELARUS

YURIDICHESKAYA LABORATORIA

Established in 1990

8 CHERNISHEVSKOGO STREET
220012 MINSK, REPUBLIC OF BELARUS
Telephone: 7 (0172) 320554, 691964
Fax: 7 (0172) 320554, 310072

Firm engaged in Belarussian, European and International Law, entitled to plead before Belarussian courts.
International Banking and Business Law, Corporate Law including setting up of Joint Ventures and Companies wholly owned by Foreign Investors in Belarus, Property Law, Mortgages, Commercial Law, Leases and Leasing, Construction, Tax Law, Labour Law, Copyright, Trademarks, Arbitration and Mediation.

(This Listing Continued)

FIRM PROFILE: Established in 1990, Yuridicheskaya Laboratoria has grown to become one of Belarussian leading private law firms specializing in international business law. Although the firm is small in size it has an expanded broadly-based practice, while maintaining a recognizable personal approach to its clients. The firm works in close cooperation with major law firms in Russia, Ukraine and Lithuania. As a member of TerraLex Inc. the firm is included in the international legal network, and has correspondent relations with a number of law firms throughout the world.

The firm has 3 members and 10 assistants.

MEMBERS OF FIRM

LILIA VLASOVA, born 1953; admitted, 1990, Republic of Belarus. *Education:* Belarussian State University (1975; Doctor of Law, International Public Law, 1979). Author: "Succession of States with respect to Treaties," Belarussian State University, 1981. *Member:* Belarussian Association of Lawyers-Businessmen; International Bar Association. *LANGUAGES:* Russian and English. *PRACTICE AREAS:* International Public Law; Corporate Law; Property Law; Tax Law; Litigation; Arbitration.

NATALIA KOZYRENKO, born 1968; admitted, 1990, Republic of Belarus. *Education:* Belarussian State University (1990). *Member:* Belarussian Association of Lawyers-Businessmen; International Bar Association. *LANGUAGES:* Russian and English. *PRACTICE AREAS:* International Banking Law; International Business Law; Commercial Law; Mortgages; Copyright Law; Trademark Law; Labour Law.

EKATERINA MAKARENYA, born 1968; admitted, 1992, Republic of Belarus. *Education:* Belarussian State University (1992). *LANGUAGES:* Russian and English. *PRACTICE AREAS:* International Trade Law; Construction Law; Lease and Leasing Law; Corporate Law; Tax Law.

ROMANIA

G & P CONSULTING AND BUSINESS OFFICE, LTD.

26 ITALIANA STREET
BUCHAREST, ROMANIA
Telephone: +40 1 6145378
Fax: +40 1 3112347

Civil, Corporate and Commercial, Fiscal Law, Banking, Finance, Investment Law, Real Estate, Litigation.

PARTNER

ALEXANDRU GRAMA. *PRACTICE AREAS:* Civil Law; Commercial Law; Litigation; Real Estate.

COUNSEL

MICHAELA GRAMA POPOVICI. *PRACTICE AREAS:* Civil Law; Corporate Law; Commercial Law; Fiscal Law; Banking and Finance; Investment Law.

HALL, DICKLER (ROMANIA), SRL

BOULEVARD EXPOZITIEI, NR. 2
SUITE 225
BUCHAREST 71134, ROMANIA
Telephone: 40-1-611.56.67

REVISERS OF THE ROMANIA LAW DIGEST FOR THIS DIRECTORY

New York, N.Y. Office: Hall, Dickler, Kent, Friedman & Wood. 27th Floor, 909 Third Avenue. Telephone: 212-339-5400.
Los Angeles, California Office: Hall, Dickler, Kent, Friedman & Wood. Suite 3590, 2029 Century Park East. Telephone: 310-203-8410.
White Plains, New York Office: Hall, Dickler, Kent, Friedman & Wood. 11 Martine Avenue. Telephone: 914-428-3232.

General Corporate, Securities, Taxation, International, Real Estate, Estate Planning, Probate, Copyright, Advertising, Marketing, Unfair Competition, Radio, Television (CATV), Entertainment, Trade Regulation, Literary Property, Matrimonial and Federal and State Litigation.

(This Listing Continued)

HALL, DICKLER (ROMANIA), SRL, Bucharest—Continued

MEMBERS OF FIRM

SAMUEL J. FRIEDMAN, (P.C.), born New York, N.Y., August 3, 1932; admitted, 1958, New York (Not admitted in Romania). *Education:* Harvard University (A.B., cum laude, 1954; LL.B., 1957). Co-author: *How To Take Money Out Of a Closely Held Business,* Macmillan, 1966: *Tax Planning To Increase and Keep Executive Take Home Pay,* Macmillan, 1970. Chairman of the Board, 1994—; Director, Executive, Endowment and Personnel Committees and Legal Counsel, American Red Cross of Westchester County, 1981—. Secretary, 1988, Treasurer, 1989, Vice President, 1990 and President, 1991, Estate Planning Council of Westchester County. President, Professional Planners Forum, 1984. *Member:* The Association of the Bar of the City of New York; Westchester County, New York State and American (Member, Section of Taxation) Bar Associations. (Also at White Plains & New York, New York Offices). *PRACTICE AREAS:* Taxation Law; Estate Planning Law; Corporate Law.

DOUGLAS J. WOOD, born Fort Belvoir, Virginia, August 14, 1950; admitted, 1976, New Jersey and U.S. District Court, District of New Jersey; 1977, New York and U.S. District Court, Southern and Eastern Districts of New York; 1982, U.S. Court of Appeals, Fifth Circuit and U.S. Supreme Court (Not admitted in Romania). *Education:* University of Rhode Island (B.A., 1972); Franklin Pierce Law Center (J.D., 1976); New York University (LL.M. in Trade Regulation, 1977). Phi Alpha Delta. Author: "Please be Advised: The Legal Reference Guide for the Advertising Executive," (Cotton States Publishing Co., 1995). Co-author: with Felix H. Kent, *Legal Problems In Advertising,* Matthew Bender & Co., 1984. Columnist on Advertising Law, Retail Advertising Digest, 1988—. Assistant Editor, IDEA, Law Review, Volume 18, No. 1, 1976. Author: "New Hampshire's Evolving Conflict of Laws Doctrine," 17 N.H.B.J. 43, 1975: "Commentary on the Law-Science Relationship in the Admissibility of Scientific Evidence," 18 IDEA 5, 1976. Adjunct Faculty, Legal Business Problems and Solution in Advertising, UCLA, 1990—. President and Member, Board of Directors: Touchdown Club of America, Inc., 1989—; The Natural Guard, 1990—; Romanian American Chamber of Commerce, 1991—; Member, National Panel of Arbitrators, American Arbitration Association. (Also at Los Angeles, California & New York, New York Offices). *PRACTICE AREAS:* Advertising Law; Marketing Law; International Law; Trade Regulation Law.

DR. VICTOR TANASESCU, born Chiajna, Romania, November 21, 1929; admitted, 1954, Bucharest, Romania. *Education:* Faculty of Law and Academy of Economics (1951); University of Bucharest (Doctor of Law, 1954); Europa Institut, University of Amsterdam, The Netherlands (Postgraduate Diploma in European Integration, 1970-1971). Author: "The Contribution of Romanian Legal Doctrine to Substantiating Civil Liability in the Field of the Peaceful Use of Nuclear Energy," Romanian Academy, 1990; "Counter-trade Export, Economic and Legal Problems," Romanian Academy, 1987; "International Sale of Goods," Romanian Academy, 1990; " Establishing Joint Ventures in Romania," Romanian Academy, 1976; "Institutions of International Commercial Law," Romanian Academy, 1992. Member, Special Group of Counsels for Foreign Trade Legal Assistance, 1974-1978. Permanent Member, International Commercial Arbitration Court, Bucharest, Romania, 1981—. Co-arbitrator or Counsel in several cases at International Chamber of Commerce, Court of Arbitration, Paris, France. Romanian observer at UNCITRAL (UN International Trade Law Commission) sessions, 1988-1989; Working Group Experts commissioned by UNCITRAL to draft legal guide on counter-trade transactions, 1989. Chief Counsel, Romanian Ministry of Foreign Trade, 1987-1991. (Resident). *LANGUAGES:* English, French and Romanian. *PRACTICE AREAS:* International Law; Corporate Law; Commercial Transactions.

SERGIU DORU, born Bucharest, Romania, April 13, 1956; admitted, 1982, Bucharest, Romania. *Education:* Faculty of Law, University of Bucharest (1982). Member, National Union of Romanian Lawyers, 1991—. (Resident). *LANGUAGES:* French, Italian and Romanian. *PRACTICE AREAS:* Corporate Law; Commercial Transactions; Inheritance; Real Property.

ALICE R. MACDIARMID, born Teaneck, New Jersey, August 14, 1965; admitted, 1992, Connecticut; 1993, New York (Not admitted in Romania). *Education:* University of Virginia (B.A., 1987); Washington and Lee University School of Law (J.D., 1992). Member, National Moot Court Team, 1992. *Member:* Association of the Bar of the City of New York; American Bar Association. (Resident). *LANGUAGES:* English, Russian.

(This Listing Continued)

PRACTICE AREAS: International Business Law; Commercial Transactions; Joint Ventures.

CORIN TRANDAFIR, born Sibiu, Romania, September 14, 1968; admitted, 1991, Bucharest, Romania. *Education:* Faculty of Law, University of Bucharest (1991); Faculté International e de Droit Compare, Strasbourg, France (Comparative Law, 1991); Fulbright Visiting Scholar, St. John's University, New York, New York (International Transfer Technology, 1991-1992). Member, Congress on Constitutionalism and Democracy in Central and Eastern Europe, Charlottesville, Virginia. Member, National Union of Romanian Lawyers, 1991—. (Resident). *LANGUAGES:* English, French and Romanian. *PRACTICE AREAS:* Corporate Law; Commercial Transactions.

IUSTINA NEGURA, born Piatra Neamt, Romania, September 20, 1971; (Not admitted in Romania). *Education:* Faculty of Law of the Ecology University of Bucharest (1994). (Resident). *LANGUAGES:* Romanian, English, Italian, French, Turkish. *PRACTICE AREAS:* Commercial Law.

ANTHONY V. RAFTOPOL, born Vienna, Australia, February 11, 1969; (admission pending). *Education:* Northwestern University (B.A., 1991); Boston University (J.D., 1994). Book Review and Topics Editor, Boston University International Law Journal, 1993-1994. Author: "Russian Roulette: A Theoretical Analysis of Voucher Privatization in Russia," B.U. Int'L. L.J., Vol. 11, Fall, 1993. (Also at New York, New York Office). *LANGUAGES:* Romanian, French, Italian.

REPRESENTATIVE CLIENTS: President of Romania; Colgate-Palmolive Co.; Coca-Cola; Chevron Corp.; Digital Equipment Corp.; W.R. Grace & Co.; R.J. Reynolds Tobacco Co.; Toraom, SA.

REVISERS OF THE ROMANIA LAW DIGEST FOR THIS DIRECTORY

KINGSTON & PETERSEN

Established in 1992

STR. IULIU TEODORI, NR. 1
BUCHAREST, ROMANIA
Telephone: (+401) 312-5196; (+401) 312-5318
Fax: (+401) 311-0646

Joint Ventures, Foreign Investment, International Trade, Tax and Accounting, Banking and Finance, Securities, Privatization, International Commercial Transactions, Commercial Litigation, Real Estate, Licensing, Distribution, Maritime, Government Regulatory Matters. Dedicated practice group for Intellectual Property Matters.

FIRM PROFILE: Established in 1992, Kingston & Petersen has grown to become the largest law firm in Romania, providing services to companies doing business in Romania and in other Central and Eastern European countries. The client base is European and North American in scope. All members of the firm are skilled international business lawyers who live and work permanently in Bucharest. Their understanding of local conditions enables Kingston & Petersen to provide clients with quick, effective, and reliable assistance in connection with a wide range of international business transactions. The firm also employs highly skilled teams of western-trained paralegals and legal translators fluent in several languages, including Romanian, English, French, Italian and Russian. Client matters involving Romanian litigation or court representation are handled by Romanian lawyers who are members of the Bar Association and who have special expertise representing foreign investors in Romania. The firm's Romanian associates are all experienced in international trade, commercial transactions, and corporate litigation, and include a former prosecutor and judge. All Romanian associates are fluent in Romanian and English, and several associates also are fluent in French and German.

MEMBERS OF FIRM
AMERICAN PRINCIPALS

ANDREW B. KINGSTON, born Rochester, New York, December 17, 1958; admitted, 1987, Washington (Not admitted in Romania). *Education:* University of Virginia (B.A., with high distinction, 1981); Harvard Law School (J.D., cum laude, 1987). Phi Beta Kappa. President, Board of Student Advisors, Harvard Law School, 1986-1987. Law Clerk to Hon. Harold M. Fong, Chief Judge, U.S. District Court, District of Hawaii, 1987-1988. *Member:* Washington State and American Bar Associations.

PATRICIA M. PETERSEN, born Seoul, Korea, March 17, 1960; admitted, 1990, Washington (Not admitted in Romania). *Education:* University of Texas (B.A., summa cum laude, 1987); Harvard Law School (J.D., cum laude, 1990). *Member:* Washington State and American Bar Associations.

(This Listing Continued)

INTELLECTUAL PROPERTY GROUP

MARIANA VASILESCU, born Bucharest, Romania; admitted, Romania, Licensed Patent and Trademark Specialist. *Education:* University of Bucharest (Graduate Degree in Chemical Engineering). *Member:* Romanian Association for Industrial Property; AIPPI; Patent, Trademark, Copyright and Design Associations of Bucharest and Romania. (Director of Intellectual Property Group). *LANGUAGES:* Romanian, English and French.

REPRESENTATIVE CLIENTS: ABB Asea Brown Boveri, Ltd.; Arthur Andersen S.C.; Brau und Brunnen International GmbH; Colgate-Palmolive Romania S.R.L.; DHL International Romania S.R.L.; ICI Seeds/Zeneca International Ltd.; Kraft General Foods International, Inc.; McDermott International Ltd.; Philip Morris Europe S.A.; Quadrant-Amroq Bottling Company Ltd.; Robert Bosch GmbH; Stefanel S.p.A.

VIRGIL POPOVICI LAW OFFICE

STRADA POLONĂ, NO. 36, SECTOR 1
BUCHAREST, ROMANIA
Telephone: 40-1-12.99.36; 12.99.37
Telecopier: 40-1-12.97.56

Other Bucharest, Romania Office: Strada Muzeul Zambaccian, No. 25, Sector 1. Telephone: 40-1-12.99.36; 12.99.37. Telecopier: 40-1-12.97.56.

Civil, Commercial, Criminal, Banking, Finance, Foreign Investment and Privatization.

VIRGIL POPOVICI, born Bîrlad, Romania; admitted, 1946, Romania. *Education:* Law University, Bucharest (Master of Law, 1946). *Member:* Bucharest Bar Association; Romanian National Bar Association (Vice-President); International Bar Association. *LANGUAGES:* Romanian and French. *PRACTICE AREAS:* Civil; Criminal; Commercial Law.

MEMBERS OF FIRM

ERNEST VIRGIL POPOVICI, born Bucharest, Romania; admitted, 1980, Romania; 1991, France, Conseil Juridique. *Education:* Law University of Bucharest (License, 1980); Law University of Clermont, Ferrand (Maîtrise, 1990). *Member:* Bucharest Bar Association; International Bar Association. *LANGUAGES:* Romanian, French, English and Italian. *PRACTICE AREAS:* Commercial; Banking; Finance; Foreign Investment.

ILINCA POPOVICI, born Bucharest, Romania; admitted, 1986, Romania; 1991, France, Conseil Juridique. *Education:* Law University of Bucharest (Law Degree, 1986); Law University of Clermont, Ferrand (Maîtrise, 1990). *Member:* Bucharest Bar Association; International Bar Association. (Also Associate with Jeantet & Associes, Paris, France). *LANGUAGES:* Romanian, French, English and German.

SCHEELE, SCHWARTZ, ZIELCKE & PARTNER

ALEEA NEGRU VODA, NR. 6, BLOC C3
SCARA 2, ETAJ 4, APARTMENT 33
BUCHAREST, ROMANIA
Telephone: 0040 1 7899589
Fax: 0040 1 7899589

Munich, Germany Office: Prinzregentenplatz 15, 81675. Telephone: 089/470 10 02. Fax: 089/470 10 06.

FIRM PROFILE: Scheele, Schwartz, Zielcke & Partner is an international law firm advising business clients and public institutions on all domestic and overseas corporate and commercial matters. The firm specializes in Eastern European and C.I.S. matters. Currently the firm is representing a broad range of clients in Europe, North America, South America, Asia and Africa.

(For biographical data and areas of practice see listing at Munich, Germany)

SINCLAIR ROCHE & TEMPERLEY (ROMANIA) LTD.

SPLAIUL INDEPENDENTEI 7
BLOCK 101, APT. 57, SECTOR 5
BUCHAREST, ROMANIA
Telephone: (401) 312 0411
Fax: (401) 312 0412

Other Offices: London (England), Hong Kong, Singapore, Shanghai (China) and Vietnam.

International Commercial Practice.

(For Complete Biographical Data on all personnel, see Professional Biographies at London, England)

TAYLOR JOYNSON GARRETT

Established in 1993

BD. NICOLAE TITULESCU NR. 1
BLOC A7, SCARA 3, ETAJ 9
APART. 88, SECTOR 1
BUCHAREST, ROMANIA
Telephone: (401) 211 88 98
Facsimile: (401) 211 75 89

London, England Office: Carmelite, 50 Victoria Embankment, Blackfriars, London EC4Y 0DX. Telephone: (44) 171 353 1234. Facsimile: (44) 171 936 2666.
EC Office: 14 Rue Montoyer, 1040 Brussels, Belgium. Telephone: (32) 2 514 0402. Facsimile: (32) 2 514 0088.
Affiliated firms and offices:
Graham & James in San Francisco, Los Angeles, Newport Beach, Sacramento, Palo Alto, Washington DC, New York, Raleigh, Milan. Joint Offices in Bangkok, Guangzhou, Hanoi, Taipei, Beijing. Graham & James affiliated offices in Riyadh, Jeddah, Jakarta, Mexico City, Tokyo, Kuwait, Bahrain, Sydney, Melbourne, Brisbane, Perth, Canberra.
Deacons, Hong Kong.
Haarmann, Hemmelrath & Partner in Düsseldorf, Berlin, Munich, Frankfurt, Leipzig, Prague.

RESIDENT PARTNERS

Richard Pertwee

Languages: Romanian and English

AURELIA TREUILLAUD-PAUN

BD. MAGHERU NR. 7
BIOC D, SC. 3, ET.9, AP.96
P.O. BOX SECTOR 1
BUCHAREST, ROMANIA
Telephone: 40.1.3126021
Telefax: 40.1.3126021

Geneva, Switzerland Office: 3, Avenue Théodore-Weber, 1208. Telephone: 41.22.7364216. Telefax: 41.22.7364266.

General Practice, Commercial, Corporate, Administrative, Real Estate, Banking, International Trade Law, Civil Litigation. Concentration in Industrial and Commercial Operations.

AURELIA TREUILLAUD-PAUN, born Bucharest, Romania, June 15, 1945; admitted, 1972, Romania. *Education:* University of Bucharest, Faculty of Law (Lic.jur., 1969); Academy of High Commercial Studies, Faculty of Trade and International Relations (Graduate, 1979). *Member:* Swiss Society of Lawyers; International Union of Lawyers; Union of Romanian Lawyers; Swiss-Romanian Chamber of Commerce. *LANGUAGES:* French, English and Romanian (Official Translator).

LIGIA DANILA LAW OFFICE

Established in 1989

ZONA MIRCEA CEL BĂTRÎN BLOC 48 SCARA C ETAJ II AP.11
TIMIŞOARA 1900, ROMANIA
Telephone: 056/143.11
Fax: 056/16.25.66; 056/143.11

Commercial Law, Joint Ventures, Intellectual Property, Family Law, Criminal Law, Finance, Civil Law Contracts, Civil and Commercial Litigations, Corporate and Romanian Trade Law.

LIGIA DĂNILĂ, born Timişoara, Romania, February 7, 1965. *Education:* Law University of Bucharest (Law Degree, with high distinction, 1987). Honorary Membership in the Association of Fellows and Legal Scholars of the Center for international legal studies, Salzburg, Austria. Lecturer, University of Timişoara. *Member:* The Romanian Bar Association-Timişoara; International Bar Association. *LANGUAGES:* Romanian, English, French, Italian and German.

POPA CONSTANTIN DRAGOS, born Timişoara, Romania, June 14, 1959. *Education:* Law University Babeş-Bolyai from Cluj Napoca (Law Degree, 1983). Lecturer, University of Timişoara. *Member:* Romanian Bar Association - Timişoara. *LANGUAGES:* Romanian, French and Serbish.

COZAC RODICA MARCELA, born Clopodia, Timiş, Romania, May 13, 1951. *Education:* Law University Babeş-Bolyai from Cluj Napoca (Law Degree, 1975). *Member:* Romanian Bar Association - Timişoara. *LANGUAGES:* Romanian, Italian and English.

RUSSIA

"INTER-LEX" BAR AGENCY

BOLSHAYA SUKHAREVSKAYA STR., 16/18
BLDG. 2., APP. 2
103045 MOSCOW, RUSSIA
Telephone: (7-095) 207 76 54
Fax: (7-095) 207 77 18

Mailing Address: Bolshaya Dmitrovka street, 9 bldg. 6, 103009 Moscow, Russia

Consultations, advise, references and interpretation on legal issues and current legislation; expertise and conclusions on legal issues; representation of physical and juridical persons' interests (including foreign) in the bodies of authority, government, court, other bodies for civil and administrative cases, including abroad; provides legal security of commercial contracts and economic relations between the participants of industrial commercial and other activities; participates in negotiations with clients' partners and counter-agents; on the basis of legal analysis of enterprises' contractual and legal activity works our the measures to obtain cost-effectiveness; researches in certain issues of commercial and activities legal regulation, makes comments to the practice of legal acts application; informs the clients about current law and legal acts of Russian Federation, CIS and other foreign countries, current court and arbitrary practice; prepares documents for publishing of reference books on legal issues; renders other legal assistance in compliance with its goal which does not contradict to legislation in force.

FIRM PROFILE: "INTER-LEX" Bar Agency was founded as a substructure of Moscow City Bar Association, which is the oldest institution of the kind in Moscow and which has a previous history of more than a century.

The main goal of "INTER-LEX" Bar Agency is to assist clients in the most effective, highly qualified and cost-efficient manner. Lawyers provide the clients, which could be either juridical or physical person, Russian or foreign, with all the capabilities to resolve their legal problems.

Lawyers are specialized in various fields of economy, such as business, finance, trade and other practice areas. They also may assist the clients in the following aspects of business: banking, securities, real estate, represent client's interests in dispute resolution.

"INTER-LEX" Bar Agency has an agreement for partnership, professional cooperation and correspondence with law firms and barristers from Germany, France, the USA, Spain, Switzerland, Belgium, Great Britain, Cyprus and other states.

"INTER-LEX" Bar Agency has a great experience in the following fields: international commercial contracts, agreements and foundation documents for juridical persons registration; US, European and multinational law

(This Listing Continued)

relating to international trading and business cooperation, including the UN Convention on the International Sale of Goods and international arbitrary conventions; international tax and property; acquisition, mergers and financing of foreign companies; legal services for banks, other financial institutions, insurance companies, industrial enterprises, media, show business teams, foreign trade associations and firms, other commercial institutions; licensing; financing, debt and equity securities distribution; immigration law; commercial projects and investments into United States and Europe; current European legal issues, including the application of European Community Directives; briefings for senior executives enterprises and other institutions on starting business in foreign market; consultations and information on legal and tax issues; assistance in preparing for negotiations; organization of lectures and seminars on international law and tax matters.

"INTER-LEX" Bar Agency's lawyers in professional activity keep strict confidence according to article 16 of RF Regulations on Bar and legal ethics norms.

Attorneys in the Agency are proficient in main European languages.

"INTER-LEX" Bar Agency as a juridical person in a member of the CIS - USA Trade and Economic Cooperation Board, a member of European Consulting Unit.

Office of the Agency was opened in 1993, it is situated in the centre of Moscow and equipped with the modern communication technologies.

MEMBERS OF THE FIRM

ELENA ORLOVA, admitted, 1979, Moscow. *Education:* Moscow State University (Legal Department Graduate); Ministry of Education and Science of Spain on the grounds of the Royal Decree (Cand.Sc., Doctor of Law Diploma, 1986). Former Member, Foreign Legal Board, representing property interests of CIS residents abroad (in Europe and USA) and foreigners in CIS. Representative, Moscow City Bar Association in Madrid, Spain, 1990-1993. *Member:* International Bar Association; UN Promotion Association (Member, European Consulting Unit); Council for the Trade and Economic Cooperation between CIS and USA; Union of the Capital Bar Association of the Countries (Members of the Black Sea Economic Cooperation). (Senior Partner). *LANGUAGES:* English and Spanish. *PRACTICE AREAS:* International Private Law; Banking and Currency Law; Civil and Commercial Law.

ELENA N. DOUDIY, born Vladivistok, Russia, April 3, 1971; admitted, 1988, Russia. *Education:* Moscow State Law Academy (1994). *LANGUAGES:* English. *PRACTICE AREAS:* Civil Law; Real Estate; Tax Law.

SVETLANA I. RYZHOVA, born Moscow, Russia, July 6, 1967; admitted, 1984, Russia. *Education:* Moscow State Law Academy (1990). *Member:* Union of Moscow Lawyers. *LANGUAGES:* English. *PRACTICE AREAS:* International Arbitration; Corporate Law; Property Law.

ELENA E. DEMENTIEVA, born Moscow, Russia, December 5, 1957; admitted, 1982, Russia. *Education:* Moscow State University (Legal Faculty). *LANGUAGES:* English. *PRACTICE AREAS:* Tax Law; Civil Procedure Law; Arbitration.

ALLA V. JIVINA, born Moscow, Russia, August 3, 1949; admitted, 1967, Russia. *Education:* Moscow State University (Legal Faculty). *LANGUAGES:* English. *PRACTICE AREAS:* Family Law; Civil Law; Criminal Law.

AKIN, GUMP, STRAUSS, HAUER & FELD, L.L.P.

A Registered Limited Liability Partnership including Professional
Corporations

BOLSHOI SUKHAREVSKY PEREULOK 26
BUILDING 1
MOSCOW 103051, RUSSIA
Telephone: 011/7-095-974-2411 or (202) 887-4545
Fax: 011/7-095-974-2412 or (202) 887-4544

Dallas, Texas Office: 1700 Pacific Avenue, Suite 4100. Telephone: 214-969-2800. Telex: 732324. FAX: 214-969-4343.

Austin, Texas Office: 2100 Franklin Plaza, 111 Congress Avenue. Telephone: 512-499-6200.

Houston, Texas Office: Pennzoil Place-South Tower, 711 Louisiana Street, Suite 1900. Telephone: 713-220-5800.

(This Listing Continued)

San Antonio, Texas Office: 300 Convent Street, Suite 1500. Telephone: 210-270-0800.

New York, New York Office: 65 East 55th Street, 33rd Floor. Telephone: 212-872-1000. Fax: 212-872-1002.

Washington, D.C. Office: 1333 New Hampshire Avenue, N.W., Suite 400. Telephone: 202-887-4000.

Brussels, Belgium Office: Akin, Gump, Strauss, Hauer, Feld & Dassesse, 65 Avenue Louise, P.B. #7, B-1050. Telephone: 011-322-535-29-11.

General Civil and Trial Practice. Corporations, Securities, Insurance, Trusts, Probate, Oil and Gas, Taxation, Banking, Bankruptcy, Real Estate, Antitrust, Labor Law, International Law.

RESIDENT PARTNER

JAMES S. FRIEDLANDER, born Chicago, Illinois, March 25, 1942; admitted, 1966, Illinois; 1979, District of Columbia; 1980, U.S. Supreme Court (Not admitted in Russia). *Education:* University of Wisconsin (A.B., 1963); Harvard Law School (J.D., 1966). International Legal Advisor, Ministry of External Affairs, Republic of Malawi, 1968-1971. Attorney, World Bank, 1972-1975. *Member:* The District of Columbia Bar; Illinois State and American Bar Associations.

ASSOCIATES

NATALIA BARATIANTS, born Turkmenia, U.S.S.R., November 5, 1960. *Education:* Moscow State University, Moscow, U.S.S.R. (M.A., 1983); Institute of State and Law of the Academy of Sciences of the U.S.S.R., Moscow (Ph.D., Law, 1987); College of Law, University of Illinois at Champaign-Urbana (LL.M., 1992). *Member:* Russian Association of International Law. *LANGUAGES:* Russian, French.

YURI E. GOLOVANOV, born St. Petersburg, Russia, April 7, 1971; admitted, 1993, Russia. *Education:* MGIMO, Moscow, Russia (LL.M., 1993); Northwestern University School of Law (LL.M., 1994). *LANGUAGES:* Russian, French, Arabic.

All Members and Associates of the firm are members of the State Bar of Texas, except where indicated.

(For Biographical Data of other Firm Personnel, see Professional Biographies at Austin, Dallas, Houston and San Antonio, Texas, New York, New York, Washington, D.C. and Brussels, Belgium)

ALLEN & OVERY

9 UL. TVERSKAYA, ENTRANCE NO. 5
8TH FLOOR
MOSCOW 103009, RUSSIA
Telephone: (7501) 940 4500
Facsimile: (7501) 940 4501

London, England Office: One New Change, EC4M 9QQ. Telephone: 0171 330 3000. Facsimile: 0171 330 9999.

Beijing, China Office: Suite 3204, Jing Guang Centre, Hu Jia Lou, Chaoyang District, 100020. Telephone: (86 1) 501 4681. Facsimile: (86 1) 501 4682.

Brussels, Belgium Office: Rue de la Loi 99, Box 8, 1040. Telephone: (32 2) 230 27 91. Facsimile (32 2) 230 66 13.

Budapest, Hungary Office: Mádach Trade Center, Mádach Imre utca 13-14, H-1075. Telephone: (361) 268 1511. Facsimile: (361) 268 1515.

Dubai, United Arab Emirates Office: 501 Al Futtaim Tower,P.O. Box 3251, Deira. Telephone: (971 4) 282296. Facsimile: (971 4) 212860.

Frankfurt, Germany Office: Taunusanlage 11, 11th Floor, 60329. Telephone: (49 69) 242 6120. Facsimile: (49 69) 242 61220.

Hong Kong Office: 9th Floor, Three Exchange Square, 8 Connaught Place. Telephone: (852) 2840 1282. Telex: 68757. Facsimile: (852) 2840 0515.

Madrid, Spain Office: Antonio Maura 7, 6°, 28014. Telephone: (34 1) 521 2654. Facsimile: (34 1) 523 0458.

New York Office: Swiss Bank Tower, 10 East 50th Street, 10022. Telephone (1-212) 754 3340. Facsimile: (1-212) 754 7903.

Paris, France Office: 1 Avenue Franklin D. Roosevelt, 75008. Telephone (33-1) 49 53 06 37. Telex: 651079. Facsimile: (33-1) 49 53 91 52.

Prague, Czech Republic Office: Jindřišská 34, 110 00 Prague 1. Telephone: (42 2) 2410 3317. Facsimile: (42 2) 2410 3235.

Singapore Office: 20 Raffles Place #08-03, Ocean Towers, 0104. Telephone: (65) 533 0988. Facsimile: (65) 533 1322.

Tokyo, Japan Office: NSE Building, 5th Floor, 1-7-1 Kanda Jinbo-cho, Chiyoda-ku Tokyo 101. Telephone (81 3) 3259 9898. Facsimile (81 3) 3259 9888.

(This Listing Continued)

Warsaw, Poland Office: ul. Kopernika 17, IV Floor, 00-359. Telephone: (48 22) 262 226. Facsimile: (48 22) 262 360.

Firm engaged in English and International Practice.

RESIDENT SENIOR RUSSIAN LAWYERS

Alexander Barmin

RESIDENT ASSOCIATES

Doran Doeh
Peter Lewis

(For Complete List of Firm Personnel, see Professional Biographies at London, England).

ARNOLD & PORTER
REPRESENTATIVE OFFICE

OZERKOVSKAYA NA. 50
113532 MOSCOW, RUSSIA
Telephone: 7095-235-3774
Telefax: 7095-235-5181

Washington, D.C. Office: Thurman Arnold Building, 1200 New Hampshire Avenue, N.W., 20036-6885. Telephone: 202-872-6700. Telecopy: 202-872-6720.

Los Angeles, California Office: 44th Floor, 777 Figueroa Street, 90017-2513. Telephone: 213-243-4000. Telecopy: 213-243-4199.

Denver, Colorado Office: 1700 Lincoln Street, 80203-4540. Telephone: 303-863-1000. Telecopy: 303-832-0428.

New York, New York Office: 399 Park Avenue, 10022-4690. Telephone: 212-715-1000. Telecopy: 212-715-1399.

Budapest, Hungary Representative Office: Retek utca 26, H-1024. Telephone: 36-1-212-1110. Telefax: 36-1-135-7857.

Istanbul, Turkey Representative Office: Büyükdere Caddesi No. 118/10, Esentepe 80280. Telephone: 90-212-275-2160. Fax: 90-212-275-2079.

General and International Practice.

PARTNER IN CHARGE

JEFFREY A. BURT, born Philadelphia, Pennsylvania, April 27, 1944; admitted, 1971, Maryland, District of Columbia; 1983, U.S. Supreme Court. *Education:* Princeton University (A.B., magna cum laude, 1966); Yale University (M.A., in Econ., 1970; LL.B., 1970). Phi Beta Kappa; Omicron Delta Epsilon. Member, Yale Law Journal, 1967-1970. Co-Author: "International Joint Venture," Federal Publications, 1986, revised edition, 1988. Co-editor: "Joint Ventures with International Partners," Butterworth Legal Publishers, 1989, 1991. Adjunct Professor of Law, Georgetown University Law Center, 1988—. Law Clerk to Judge Simon E. Sobeloff, U.S. Court of Appeals, Fourth Circuit, 1970-1971. Chairperson, Committee on Newly Independent States of FSU, Section on International Law, American Bar Association, 1991—. *PRACTICE AREAS:* International.

BAKER & BOTTS, L.L.P.

10 UL. PUSHKINSKAYA
103031 MOSCOW, RUSSIA
Telephone: 7095/921-5300 (Local)
7501/929-7070 (International)
Fax: 7095/921-5390 (Local)
Fax: 7501/929-7073 (International)

REVISERS OF THE TEXAS LAW DIGEST FOR THIS DIRECTORY

Houston, Texas Office: One Shell Plaza, 910 Louisiana. Telephone: 713-229-1234.

Washington, D.C. Office: The Warner, 1299 Pennsylvania Avenue, N.W. Telephone: 202-639-7700.

Austin, Texas Office: 1600 San Jacinto Center, 98 San Jacinto Boulevard. Telephone: 512-322-2500.

Dallas, Texas Office: 2001 Ross Avenue. Telephone: 214-953-6500.

New York, New York Office: 885 Third Avenue, Suite 2000. Telephone: 212-750-5000.

General Practice.
(This Listing Continued)

BAKER & BOTTS, L.L.P., Moscow—Continued

MEMBERS OF FIRM

JAY T. KOLB, born Houston, Texas, March 8, 1953; admitted, 1982, Texas (Not admitted in Russia). *Education:* University of Texas (B.B.A., 1976); University of Houston (J.D., 1982). Certified Public Accountant, Texas, 1978. *Member:* Houston and American Bar Associations; State Bar of Texas.

HOLLY A. NIELSEN, born St. Joseph, Missouri, October 2, 1956; admitted, 1982, Oklahoma; 1986, Texas (Not admitted in Russia). *Education:* Vassar College (A.B., cum laude, 1978); University of Copenhagen, Denmark; University of Kansas (J.D., 1982). Order of the Coif. Editor, Kansas Law Review, 1981-1982. *Member:* Houston and American Bar Associations; State Bar of Texas. *LANGUAGES:* Russian.

REVISERS OF THE TEXAS LAW DIGEST FOR THIS DIRECTORY

(For Complete Personnel and Biographical data on Austin, Texas, Dallas, Texas, Houston, Texas, Washington D.C., New York, New York Offices, see Professional Biographies at Austin, Texas, Houston, Texas, Washington, D.C. and New York, New York)

BAKER & McKENZIE

BOLSHOI STROCHENOVSKY PEREULOK, 22/25
113054 MOSCOW, RUSSIA
Telephone: (095) 230-60-36
Intn'l Dialing: (1-212) 891-3799* (7-095) 230-60-36
Telex: 413671
Answer Back: 413671 BAKER SU
Facsimile: (7-095) 230-60-47

*This number is available as a telephone line from 9:00 a.m. to 9:00 p.m. Moscow time. After 9:00 p.m. Moscow time, the number is switched to serve as a facsimile line.

Associated Offices of Baker & McKenzie in: Almaty, Amsterdam, Bangkok, Barcelona, Beijing, Berlin, Bogotá, Brasília, Brussels, Budapest, Buenos Aires, Cairo, Caracas, Chicago, Dallas, Frankfurt, Geneva, Hanoi, Ho Chi Minh City, Hong Kong, Juárez, Kiev, London, Madrid, Manila, Melbourne, México City, Miami, Milan, Monterrey, New York, Palo Alto, Paris, Prague, Rio de Janeiro, Riyadh, Rome, St. Petersburg, San Diego, San Francisco, São Paulo, Singapore, Stockholm, Sydney, Taipei, Tijuana, Tokyo, Toronto, Valencia, Warsaw, Washington, D.C. and Zürich.
Correspondent Law Firm: Hadiputranto, Hadinoto & Partners, Jakarta.

General Practice. Foreign Trade Country Specialists.

PARTNERS

WILLIAM F. ATKIN, born Cedar City, Utah, March 13, 1949; admitted, 1975, Arizona, U.S.A.; 1976, U.S. Courts of Appeals, Ninth and Tenth Circuits and U. S. Court of International Trade; 1978, U.S. Customs and Patent Appeals Court; 1979, Illinois, U.S.A.; 1983, California, U.S.A. (Not admitted in Russia). *Education:* Brigham Young University (B.A., cum laude, 1972); Arizona State University (J.D., magna cum laude, 1975); Columbia University (LL.M., 1979). Editor-in-Chief, Arizona State Law Journal, 1974-1975. Law Clerk to Hon. David T. Lewis, U.S. Court of Appeals, Tenth Circuit, 1975-1976. Trial Attorney, U.S Department of Justice, Civil Division, 1976-1979. *LANGUAGES:* English and Spanish.

PAUL J. MELLING, born England; admitted, 1982, Solicitor of Supreme Court of England and Wales (Not admitted in Russia). *Education:* Oxford University (M.A., 1982). Faculty Member, Centre for the Study of Socialist Legal Systems, University College, London, 1983—. Visiting Scholar, Institute of State and Law, U.S.S.R. Academy of Sciences, 1984, 1987. *Member:* Law Society of England and Wales; British-Soviet Law Association. *LANGUAGES:* English and Russian.

CAROL A. M. PATTERSON, born Halifax, Nova Scotia, Canada, September 6, 1954; admitted, 1981, Nova Scotia, Canada; 1983, British Columbia, Canada; 1984, Ontario, Canada (Not admitted in Russia). *Education:* Dalhousie University (B.A., with distinction, 1975; LL.B., 1978); Pushkin Language Institute, Moscow (1979); School of Slavonic and East European Studies, University of London (1980). Instructor, Ontario Bar Admission Course, Creditors' and Debtors' Rights, 1978-1989. *Member:* Canadian and International Bar Associations; Law Society of Upper Canada; Nova Scotia Barristers' Society; Law Society of British Columbia. *LANGUAGES:* English, Russian and French.

(This Listing Continued)

OF COUNSEL

ALEXANDER I. FEINSTEIN, born Russia, July 20, 1923; admitted, 1947, Russia. *Education:* Moscow Judicial Society (now the Law Faculty of Moscow State University (LL.M., 1949). Chief Advisor, Legal and Scientific Center at the International Union of Advocates. Consultant, Association of Joint Ventures, International Amalgamations and Organizations. *Member:* Moscow College of Advocates. *LANGUAGES:* Russian.

ASSOCIATES

MARSHA W. BLITZER, born Waukegan, Illinois, July 13, 1956; admitted, 1986, Massachusetts, U.S.A.; 1989, District of Columbia, U.S.A. (Not admitted in Russia). *Education:* Sarah Lawrence College (B.A., 1977); Pushkin Language Institute (1977); School of Languages and Linguistics, Georgetown University (M.S., 1979); University of San Diego School of Law, Moscow and Warsaw (1985); Suffolk University Law School (J.D., 1986). Attorney, U.S. Federal Trade Commission, International Antitrust Division, 1988-1992. *Member:* Massachusetts Bar Association; District of Columbia Bar. *LANGUAGES:* English and Russian.

MARK W. BORGHESANI, born Alexandria, Virginia, May 10, 1962; admitted, 1989, Virginia, U.S.A. and U.S. Court of Appeals, Fourth Circuit; 1990, U.S. Bankruptcy Court and U.S. District Court, Eastern District of Virginia; 1991, District of Columbia, U.S.A. (Not admitted in Russia). *Education:* University of Virginia (B.A., 1984); Leningrad State University; College of William and Mary (J.D., 1989); University of Exeter. *Member:* District of Columbia Bar; Virginia State Bar; American Bar Association. *LANGUAGES:* English and Russian.

JEAN A. BROUGH, born Toronto, Ontario, Canada, June 5, 1962; admitted, 1990, Ontario, Canada (Not admitted in Russia). *Education:* University of Toronto (B.A., 1985); Queens University (LL.B., 1988). *Member:* Canadian Bar Association; Law Society of Upper Canada. *LANGUAGES:* English.

ALEXANDER A. BYCHKOV, born Bryansk, Russia, November 25, 1968; admitted, 1994, Russia. *Education:* Moscow Institute of International Relations (MGIMO), Faculty of International Law (Diploma, 1994). *LANGUAGES:* Russian, English and French.

ALEXANDER CHMELEV, born New York, N.Y., January 23, 1959; admitted, 1986, Massachusetts, U.S.A.; 1987, New York, U.S.A.; 1988, U.S. Court of Appeals for the Federal Circuit (Not admitted in Russia). *Education:* University of Rochester (B.A., 1981); Boston University (J.D., 1986); New York University (LL.M., 1991). *Member:* New York State Bar Association (Member, Committee on Central and Eastern Europe and Central Asian Law, 1992—). *LANGUAGES:* English and Russian.

MARINA DREL, born Moscow, Russia, May 21, 1955; admitted, 1992, Russia. *Education:* Moscow State University (LL.B., 1977; J.D., 1983); Dalhousie Law School (LL.M., 1992). *Member:* Moscow City Bar. *LANGUAGES:* Russian and English.

KAREN M. HANDELSMAN, born New York, N.Y., March 21, 1962; admitted, 1992, New York, U.S.A. (Not admitted in Russia). *Education:* Middlebury College (Vermont) (B.A., 1985); Pushkin Institute (Moscow); Emory University School of Law (J.D., 1991); Leiden University (The Netherlands). Law Clerk, Hon. Thomas J. Aquilino, Jr., United States Court of International Trade, 1991-1993. *Member:* American Bar Association; New York County Lawyers Association. *LANGUAGES:* English, Russian and French.

IGOR S. MARTINOV, born Kashira, Russia, September 18, 1960; admitted, 1988, Russia. *Education:* Moscow State Institute of International Relations (Diploma/Bachelor, 1988); Moscow State Judicial Academy (Postgraduate Student, 1992). *Member:* Russia Association of International Law. *LANGUAGES:* Russian, English and Spanish.

VLADIMIR V. MIRONOV, born Moscow Region, Russia, December 3, 1961; admitted, 1984, Russia. *Education:* Moscow Institute of International Relations, Law Faculty. *LANGUAGES:* Russian, English, French.

GRAHAM J. NICHOLSON, born Lincoln, England; admitted, 1985, England and Wales (Not admitted in Russia). *Education:* London School of Economics & Political Science (LL.B., 1980); Bristol Polytechnic (Final Exam, Law Society (England), 1983); London Business School (M.B.A., 1992). *Member:* Law Society of England and Wales. *LANGUAGES:* English.

MAXIM D. SMYSLOV, born Moscow, Russia, December 26, 1964; admitted, 1987, Russia. *Education:* Moscow Institute of International Relations (MGIMO), Faculty of International Law (Diploma, 1987); European

(This Listing Continued)

University Institute, Department of Law, Florence, Italy (Doctor of Laws, 1993). *LANGUAGES:* Russian, English, French, Hungarian and Italian.

MARK C. SWORDS, born Aurora, Illinois, July 2, 1960; admitted, 1992, Illinois, U.S.A. (Not admitted in Russia). *Education:* University of Illinois (B.A., with high distinction, 1983; M.S., 1988; J.D., 1992). *LANGUAGES:* English.

BENEDIKT M.M. WEIFFENBACH, born Germany, April 7, 1959; admitted, 1988, The Netherlands (Not admitted in Russia). *Education:* Rijksuniversiteit Utrecht (History of Philosophy and Russian Language and Literature, 1985); Rijksuniversiteit Leiden (Civil Law, 1988); Barrister's Professional Training, 1990. *Member:* Amsterdam Bar Association. *LANGUAGES:* Dutch, German, English, French and Russian.

CORINNA M. WISSELS, born Luxemburg, Luxemburg, November 15, 1963; admitted, 1987, The Netherlands (Not admitted in Russia). *Education:* Leyden University (LL.M., 1986); Université Paris II (LL.M., 1987). *Member:* International Young Lawyers Associates; Netherlands Association for European Law. *LANGUAGES:* Dutch, English, French, German and Russian.

BEITEN BURKHARDT MITTL & WEGENER

Rechtsanwälte

UL. ALEKSEJA TOLSTOVO D.30/1
103001 MOSCOW, RUSSIA
Telephone: (095) 202 37 60; 290 05 56
Telefax: (095) 202 37 60; 290 05 56

Munich, Germany Office: Leopoldstrasse 236, D-80807. Telephone: (089) 35065-00. Telefax: (089) 35065-123.

Berlin, Germany Office: Kurfürstenstrasse 72-74, D-10787 Berlin. Telephone: (0 30) 264 71-0. Telefax: (0 30) 264 71-123.

Frankfurt/Main, Germany Office: Arndtstrasse 28, D-60325 Frankfurt/Main. Telephone: (0 69) 75 60 95-0. Telefax: (0 69) 75 60 95-12.

Nürnberg, Germany Office: Obere Turnstrasse 8, D-90429 Nürnberg. Telephone: (09 11) 2 79 71-0. Telefax: (09 11) 2 79 71-99.

Leipzig, Germany Office: Käthe-Kollwitz-Strasse 54, D-04109 Leipzig. Telephone: (03 41) 4 77 25 97. Telefax: (03 41) 4 77 25 99.

Potsdam, Germany Office: Heinrich-Mann-Allee 105 B, D-14473 Potsdam. Telephone: (0331) 33 43 06. Telefax: (0331) 33 43 29.

Hof, Germany Office: Oberer Torplatz 1, D-95028 Hof. Telephone: (09281) 80 23. Telefax: (09281) 1 65 69.

Plauen, Germany Office: Lindenstrasse 5, D-08523 Plauen. Telephone: (03741) 22 35 11; 22 49 62. Telefax: (03741) 22 49 62.

New York, New York Office: 215 East 73rd Street, New York, NY 10021. Telephone: (212) 570-2141. Telefax: (212) 734-7011.

London, England Office: Swedenborg House, 21 Bloomsbury Way, London, WC1A 2TH. Telephone: (0171) 2 42 44 66. Telefax: (0171) 2 42 44 67.

Prague, Czech Republic Office: Na Bojišti 24, 120 00 Prague 2. Telephone: (2) 24 91 5808. Telefax: (2) 24 91 5804.

Budapest, Hungary Office: József Nádor Tér 9, H-1051 Budapest. Telephone: (1) 2 66 18 10. Telefax: (1) 2 66 18 11.

Hong Kong Office: 605 B, Sixth Floor, Peregrine Tower, Lippo Centre, 89 Queensway. Telephone: (852) 2524 6468. Telefax: (852) 2524 7028.

Beijing, People's Republic of China Office: Unit 10, 29th Floor, Jing Guang Centre, Hu Jia Lou, Chao Yang Qu, 100020. Telephone: (86-1) 501 4569; 501 3388 Ext. 2910. Telefax: (86-1) 501 3034.

Commercial Law, Company Law, M & A, Joint Ventures, Finance, Banking, Leasing, Domestic and International Tax, Antitrust, EC Law, Real Property and Private Construction, Electronic Data Processing (Protection and Licensing), Media, Publishing, Unfair Competition, Trademarks, Copyright, Labour, General and Special Administrative Law Particularly Public Construction and Planning Regulations and Public International Law, Environmental Law, Agricultural Law, Privatization and Restitution (former GDR), Probate, Family and Estate Planning, Insolvency and Sports, Insurance, Automobile Accidents and Injuries.

FIRM PROFILE: BEITEN BURKHARDT MITTL & WEGENER is a nation-wide and international law firm with 108 lawyers. The firm's head office is in Munich. All the firm's offices provide a comprehensive range of services in the main areas of civil and commercial law.

(This Listing Continued)

BENNO SCHWARZ, born Osnabrück, 1965; admitted, 1993, Germany (Not admitted in Russia). *Education:* University of Bonn and Munich (law degree, 1989; Dr. jur., 1992). *LANGUAGES:* German, English, French and Russian. *PRACTICE AREAS:* Company Law; Acquisitions and Sales; Restructuring; Expropriation and Restitution; European Community Law.

OLGA N. SOPOVA, born Moscow, 1961; admitted, 1987, Russia. *Education:* University of Moscow (law degree, 1986). *Member:* Moscow Bar and Moscow Lawyers Association. *LANGUAGES:* Russian. *PRACTICE AREAS:* Company Law; Acquisition and Sales; Restructuring; Press Law; Publishing and Radio; Real Estate; Construction Law; Labour and Employment.

BRUCKHAUS WESTRICK STEGEMANN

MALYJ GNEZDNIKOVSKIJ PER. 9 NO. 2
103009 MOSCOW, RUSSIA
Telephone: (7-503) 9562300; (7-501) 9401200
Telefax: (7-503) 9562301; (7-501) 9401211

Düsseldorf, Germany Office: Freiligrathstrasse 1, 40479 Düsseldorf. Telephone: (02 11) 49 79-0. Telefax: (02 11) 49 79-1 03 and 4 98 12 21. Telex: 858 7027 JUS D.

Frankfurt, Germany Office: Taunusanlage 11, 60329 Frankfurt am Main. Telephone: (069) 27308-0. Telefax: (069) 232664. Telex: 41 49 17 WEST CD.

Hamburg, Germany Office: Alsterarkaden 27, 20354 Hamburg. Telephone: (040) 36 90 60. Telefax: (040) 36 906-155. Telex: 212 522 EURO D.

Berlin, Germany Office: Friedrichstrasse 95 (IHZ), 10117 Berlin. Telephone: (030) 26 43-3303. Telefax: (030) 26 43-3366.

Leipzig Office: Grimmaische Strasse 25, 04109 Leipzig. Telephone: (0341) 127230. Telefax: (0341) 1272333.

Brussels, Belgium Office: Rue de la Loi 99/101, B-1040 Brussels. Telephone: (32-2) 2 87 26 11. Telefax: (32-2) 2 30 39 03.

Tokyo, Japan Office: Ark Mori Building, 22F, 12-32, Akasaka 1-chome, Minato-ku, Tokyo 107. Telephone: (81-3) 55610-236. Telefax: (81-3) 55610-238.

New York, New York Office: 767 Fifth Avenue, GM Building, New York 10153. Telephone: (212) 486-1100. Telefax: (212) 759-3151.

Corporate Law, Commercial Law, Mergers, Acquisitions and Divestitures, Joint Ventures, Banks and Banking, Finance, Securities, Capital Markets, Leases and Leasing, Equipment Finance, Aircraft Finance and Leasing, Antitrust and Trade Regulation, German and EC Cartel Law, Competition, Unfair Trade, Intellectual Property (trademarks, patents, copyrights), Taxation, Property, Real Estate, Energy, Natural Resources, Environmental Law, Administrative Law, Computers and Software, Food and Drug, Biotechnology, Labour and Employment, Products Liability, Insurance, Litigation, Arbitration, Broadcasting, Telecommunications, Aviation, Subsidies and State Aids, Construction Law, Zoning, Planning and Land Use, Customs and Foreign Trade Law, European Community Law, German-French Investments, Russian and Post Soviet Commerce.

MEMBERS OF FIRM

Dr. Klaus-Albert Bauer
Yorck Jetter
Irene Engel
Dimitri Kurotschkin

CATLETT & YANCEY
BOLSHOI GNEZDNYKOVSKY PEREULOK 10, SUITE 624
MOSCOW 103009, RUSSIA
Telephone: (7-095) 229-6930
Fax: 229-8332

Little Rock, Arkansas Office: Eighteenth Floor, The Tower Building, 72201. Telephone: 501-372-2121. FAX: 501-372-5566. TELEX: 6503414534.

Business and Estate Planning, Taxation, USSR Business Planning, Real Estate, Litigation.

MEMBERS OF FIRM

H. B. STUBBLEFIELD (1907-1991).

S. GRAHAM CATLETT, born Little Rock, Arkansas, August 12, 1952; admitted, 1977, Arkansas. *Education:* University of Arkansas (B.S.B.A., with high honors, 1974; J.D., with honors, 1977). Blue Key; Beta Alpha Psi.

(This Listing Continued)

CATLETT & YANCEY, Moscow—Continued

Associate Editor, Arkansas Law Review, 1976-1977. Licensed Real Estate Broker, Arkansas, 1972. Certified Public Accountant, Arkansas, 1974. *Member:* Pulaski County, Arkansas (Member, Taxation and Real Estate Committee) and American (Member, Sections on: Taxation; Corporation, Banking and Business Law) Bar Associations; American Institute of Certified Public Accountants. Board Recognized Tax Specialist, Arkansas Board of Legal Specialization. *PRACTICE AREAS:* Taxation Law; Business Planning Law.

GREGORY PADGHAM, born Oklahoma City, Oklahoma, November 29, 1959; admitted, 1991, Arkansas. *Education:* University of Arkansas (B.S., History, 1988; J.D., 1991). *Member:* Arkansas Bar Association. *LANGUAGES:* Russian. *PRACTICE AREAS:* Business Organization; Contracts; Comparative Law.

EVGUINY V. BUREIKO, born Peropavlovsk-Kamchatsky, Russia, December 11, 1957; admitted, 1981, Moscow. *Education:* Moscow State Institute of International Relations of Minister of Foreign Affairs, USSR (Law Degree, 1981). Law Clerk, Minister of Foreign Trade Legal Department, Moscow State Institute of International Relations. Chairman, Scientific Law Society of Law Faculture, Moscow State Institute of International Relations. Author: "Legal Problems of Trade and Economic Relations Between USSR and Western European Countries in the 70th," Moscow State Institute of International Relations. Former Member, State Archive Legal Department, USSR. Committee Member, Youth Organization (CYO) of the USSR, 1985-1991. Member, Moscow Rotary Club. Deputy Director General, Foreign Economic Association "Novocom Inc.," Moscow, Russia, 1991-1993. Recipient: Honorary Citizen of Little Rock Diploma; "Arkansas Traveller" Certificate, signed by Bill Clinton; "Good Will" Certificate, signed by Arkansas Attorney General. *LANGUAGES:* Russian, English and French. *PRACTICE AREAS:* International Law (100%).

REPRESENTATIVE CLIENTS: Catlett & Co.; Citizens Fidelity Insurance Co.; Frost and Company, CPA's; General Properties, Inc.; McKay and Company Residential Realtors; Midwest Lumber Co.; Motel Sleepers, Inc.; National Home Centers, Inc.; The Buffalo Co.; The Hathaway Group, Inc.; The Tower Building; Quality Products International, Inc.; Roller Funeral Homes of Arkansas.

CHADBOURNE & PARKE

38 MAXIM GORKY NABEREZHNAYA
MOSCOW 113035, RUSSIA
Telephone: 7095-974-2424 Telecopier: 7095-974-2425
International satellite lines via U.S.: Telephone: 212-408-1190. Telecopier:
212-408-1199

New York, N.Y. Office: 30 Rockefeller Plaza, 10112. Telephone: 212-408-5100. Telecopier: 212-541-5369.

Los Angeles, California Office: 601 South Figueroa Street, 90017. Telephone: 213-892-1000. Telecopier: 213-622-9865.

Washington, D.C. Office: Suite 900, 1101 Vermont Avenue, N.W., 20005. Telephone: 202-289-3000. Telecopier: 202-289-3002.

London, England Office: 86 Jermyn Street, SW1 6JD. Telephone: 44-171-925-7400. Facsimile: 44-171-839-3393.

Hong Kong Office: Suite 3704, Peregrine Tower, Lippo Centre, 89 Queensway. Telephone: (852) 2842-5400. Telecopier: (852) 2521-7527.

New Delhi, India Office: Chadbourne & Parke Associates, A16-B Anand Niketan, 110 021. Telephone: 91-11-301-7568/7581/7582. Telecopier: 91-11-301-7351.

General Practice.

PARTNER

WILLIAM E. HOLLAND, born Kearney, Nebraska, September 16, 1940; admitted, 1974, Nebraska; 1989, U.S. Supreme Court; 1992, New York (Not admitted in Russia). *Education:* University of Nebraska (B.Sc., with highest distinction, 1963); Oxford University (B.A., 1965), Rhodes Scholar; Stanford University (Ph.D., 1971); Stanford Law School (J.D., 1974). Rhodes Scholar; Phi Beta Kappa; Sigma Tau; Sigma Xi; Order of the Coif. Author: "Techniques for Financing Transactions and Projects in the Soviet Union," ABA National Institute on Change in Eastern Europe and the Soviet Union, American Bar Association, 1990; Nebraska Environmental Law Handbook, C. Hineline and W. Holland, Government Institutes, Inc., Rockville, Maryland, 1991; "New Soviet Law on Investment," Financial Times East European Business Law, March 1991, with Mikhail Rozenberg; "USSR, A Special Report," in Free Market Takeover: A Legal Guide to Investing in Eastern Europe, USSR, China and Vietnam, Euromoney

(This Listing Continued)

Publications, London, 1991, 55-61, with Robert E. Langer and Mikhail Rozenberg; "The Russian Republic Law on Privatization," BNA Eastern Europe Reporter, 88, November 11, 1991; "Rights to Oil and Gas in Russia," Russian Petroleum Investor 52, June, 1992 with Mikhail Rosenberg; "Getting into Business in Russia," American Lawyer, Eye on Russia, November, 1992; "Privatization in Russia," in Columbia University's Parker School Journal of East European Law, June 1994; "Russian Telecommunications: Legal Issues for Foreign Investors," in BNA's Eastern Europe Reporter, March 14, 1994, vol. 4, no. 6, p. 241-244; "The Russian Law on Environmental Protection," in BNA Eastern Europe Reporter, September 13, 1993, vol. 3, no. 19; also in East-West Executive Guide, December 1993, vol. 3, no. 12; "Licensing Mineral Rights," in East/West Executive Guide, May 1993, p. 22-23, with Alexander Buyevitch. *Member:* Nebraska State and New York State Bar Associations.

GENERAL DIRECTOR

GENRIKH P. PADVA, born Moscow, U.S.S.R., 1931; admitted, 1953, Tver, U.S.S.R. *Education:* Moscow Juridical Institute (Law, 1953): Tver Pedagogical Institute (History. 1962). *Member:* Moscow City Bar Association; International Union (Commonwealth) of Advocates (First Vice-President); Union Internationale des Avocats (Vice President); Association of Non-Government Organizations (Member, Executive Committee).

RESIDENT COUNSEL

JOHN T. CONNOR, JR., born New York, N.Y., June 16, 1941; admitted, 1968, New York; 1980, District of Columbia (Not admitted in Russia). *Education:* Williams College (B.A., 1963); Harvard University (J.D., 1967). Phi Beta Kappa. Chairman and Editor, "Legal Aspects of Doing Business with the USSR and Eastern Europe," Practicing Law Institute, 1977. Deputy Director: Office of Economic Policy and Case Analysis, U.S. Pay Board, 1971-1972; Deputy Director: Bureau of East-West Trade, U.S. Department of Commerce, 1972-1973. Consultant, U.S. Department of State, 1976. Member, Legal Committee, 1980— and Senior Vice President and Head, Moscow Office, 1973-1976, U.S.-USSR Trade and Economic Council. *Member:* Association of the Bar of the City of New York (Member, International Law Committee, 1977-1980); New York State (Chairman, Soviet and Eastern European Law Committee, 1990—) and American (Member, Corporate Law Department Committee, 1983-1988 and Chairman, EEC Financial Services Subcommittee, 1991—) Bar Associations. *LANGUAGES:* Russian.

ROBERT E. LANGER, born Chicago, Illinois, September 1, 1960; admitted, 1987, New York (Not admitted in Russia). *Education:* Norwich University Russian School; University of Michigan (B.A., with honors, 1982); Tulane University of Louisiana (J.D., magna cum laude, 1985). Order of the Coif. *Member:* The Association of the Bar of the City of New York. *LANGUAGES:* Russian.

RESIDENT ASSOCIATES

ALEXANDER J. BUYEVITCH, born Smolensk, U.S.S.R., 1961; admitted, 1985, Moscow. *Education:* Moscow State University (Law, Diploma with honors, 1984). *Member:* International Union (Commonwealth) of Advocates; Moscow Regional Bar (Chairman, Council of Young Advocates, 1985-1990); Union of Russian Advocates. *LANGUAGES:* Russian, Belorussian, English.

MIKHAIL A. ROZENBERG, born Moscow, U.S.S.R., 1954; admitted, 1979, Moscow. *Education:* Moscow State University (Economics, Diploma with honors, 1976); All-Union Law Institute, Moscow (Law, Diploma with honors, 1978). *Member:* Internationale Union (Commonwealth) of Advocates; Moscow City Bar (Patron-Tutor, 1988—); Union Internationale des Avocats. *LANGUAGES:* Russian, English, French.

MELISSA J. SCHWARTZ, born New York, N.Y., December 15, 1966; admitted, 1991, New York (Not admitted in Russia). *Education:* Cornell University (B.A., with distinction, 1988); Harvard University (J.D., cum laude, 1991). *LANGUAGES:* Russian.

NATALIE MENSHIKOVA WHITMAN, born Kalinin, Russia, March 4, 1971; admitted, 1994, Russia. *Education:* Trinity College, University of Dublin, Ireland (Law, 1992); Moscow State University Law School, Moscow, Russia (Law, 1994). Vice-President, European Law Students' Association, Moscow, 1989-1991. Legal Scientific Society, MGU, 1988-1989. *LANGUAGES:* Russian and French.

(For Biographical Data of other Personnel, see Professional Biographies at New York, N.Y., Washington, D.C., Los Angeles, California, London, England, Hong Kong and New Delhi, India)

CLIFFORD CHANCE

Established in 1991

UL. SADOVAYA - SAMOTECHNAYA 24/27
2ND FLOOR

103051 MOSCOW, RUSSIA
Telephone: (7 501) 258 50 50
Fax: (7 501) 258 50 51

Amsterdam, The Netherlands Office: Apollolaan 171, 1077 AS, P.O. Box 7301, 1007 JH. Telephone: (31 20) 577 71 11. Fax: (31 20) 676 93 26.

Bahrain, Manama Associated Office: Law Office of Shaikh Isa bin Mohammed Al Khalifa. P.O. Box 20717. Telephone: (973) 531535; 531073. Fax: (973) 536272; 530608.

Barcelona, Spain Office: Pau Claris 102, 08009. Telephone: (34 3) 318 68 64. Fax: (34 3) 317 73 23.

Brussels, Belgium Office: Avenue Louise 65, Box 2, 1050. Telephone: (32 2) 533 59 11. Fax: (32 2) 533 59 59.

Budapest, Hungary Office: Köves & Partners, Clifford Chance. Madách Trade Center, Madách Imre Út 14, 1075. Telephone: (36 1) 268 1600. Fax: (36 1) 268 1610.

Dubai, United Arab Emirates Office: 18th Floor, Dubai World Trade Centre, P.O. Box 9380. Telephone: (971 4) 314333. Fax: (971 4) 313990; 314565.

Frankfurt/Main, Germany Office: Friedrichstraße 2-6, 60323. Telephone: (49 69) 971 4090. Fax: (49 69) 971 40977.

Hanoi, Vietnam Office: 52 Nguyen Binh Khiem. Telephone: (844) 229 182/3/4/5/6. Fax: (844) 229 190.

Hong Kong Office: 30th Floor, Jardine House, One Connaught Place. Telephone: (852) 2810 0229. Fax: (852) 2810 4708; 2810 4858; 2810 4743.

London, England Office: 200 Aldersgate Street, EC1A 4JJ. Telephone: (44 171) 600 1000. Fax: (44 171) 600 5555.

Madrid, Spain Office: Paseo de la Castellana 110, 28046. Telephone: (34 1) 562 7674. Fax: (34 1) 562 49 93.

Milan, Italy Associated Office: Grimaldi e Clifford Chance. Via Gesú, 3, 20121. Telephone: (39 2) 7600 8040. Fax: (39 2) 7600 4950.

New York, New York Office: Swiss Bank Tower, 10 East 50th Street, 10022. Telephone: (1 212) 750 1440. Fax: (1 212) 758 6625.

Paris, France Office: 112 avenue Kléber, BP 163 Trocadéro, 75770 Paris Cedex 16. Telephone: (33 1) 44 05 52 52. Fax: (33 1) 44 05 52 00.

Riyadh, Saudi Arabia Associated Office: The Law Firm of Salah Al-Hejailan. P.O. Box 1454, 11431. Telephone: (966 1) 479 2200. Fax: (966 1) 479 1717.

Rome, Italy Associated Office: Grimaldi e Clifford Chance. Viale G. Rossini 7, 00198. Telephone: (39 6) 807 2251. Fax: (39 6) 807 8201.

Shanghai, People's Republic of China Office: Suite 898, Shanghai Centre, 1376 Nanjing Xi Lu, 200040. Telephone: (86 21) 279 8461. Fax: (86 21) 279 8462.

Singapore Office: 16 Collyer Quay #31-00, 0104. Telephone: (65) 535 1855. Fax: (65) 535 6855.

Tokyo, Japan Office: 6th Floor, South Hill Nagatacho Building, 11-30 Nagatacho 1-chome, Chiyoda-ku, 100. Telephone: (81 3) 3581 4311. Fax: (81 3) 3593 0651.

Warsaw, Poland Office: Warsaw Corporate Centre, ul. Emilii Plater 28, 00-688. Telephone: (48 2) 630 3344. Fax: (48 2) 630 3355.

International Banking and Finance including Project Finance, Joint Ventures, Inward Investment and Privatization.

RESIDENT PARTNER

WILLIAM KNOWLES, admitted, 1976, Solicitor of the Supreme Court of England and Wales. **PRACTICE AREAS:** Commercial Law; Joint Ventures; Russian Law; Finance Law.

(For the Names of Partners Resident in other Offices, see the Professional Biographies for those Offices).

COUDERT BROTHERS

ULITSA STARAYA BASMANNAYA 14
MOSCOW 103064, RUSSIA
Telephone: (7502) 220-4998 International, 262-1611 Local
Telecopier: (7502) 220-4213 International, 262-2351 Local;
Telex: 612158 COUDR SU

REVISERS OF THE FRANCE LAW DIGEST FOR THIS DIRECTORY

New York, New York 10036-7794: 1114 Avenue of the Americas.

Washington, D.C. 20006: 1627 I Street, N.W.

Los Angeles, California 90017: 1055 West Seventh Street, Twentieth Floor.

San Francisco, California 94111: 4 Embarcadero Center, Suite 3300.

San Jose, California 95113: Suite 1250, Ten Almaden Boulevard.

Paris 75008, France: Coudert Frères, 52 Avenue des Champs-Elysees.

London, EC4M 7JP, England: 20 Old Bailey.

Brussels B-1050, Belgium: Tour Louise. 149 Avenue Louise-Box 8.

Beijing, People's Republic of China 100020: Suite 2708-09 Jing Guang Centre Hu Lou, Chao Yang Qu.

Shanghai, People's Republic of China 200002: c/o Suite 1804, Union Building, 100 Yanan Road East.

Hong Kong: 25th Floor, Nine Queen's Road Central.

Sydney N.S.W. 2000, Australia: Suite 2202, State Bank Centre, 52 Martin Place.

Singapore 0104: Tung Centre, 20 Collyer Quay.

Tokyo 107, Japan: 1355 West Tower, Aoyama Twin Towers, 1-1-1 Minami-Aoyama, Minato-ku.

01301 Sao Paulo, SP, Brazil: Machado, Meyer, Sendacz, e Opice, Advogados, Rua da Consolacao, 247, 8 Andar.

Bangkok 10500, Thailand: Bubhajit Building, 20 North Sathorn Road, 10th Floor.

Ho Chi Minh City, Vietnam: c/o Saigon Business Centre, 49-57 Dong Du Street, District 1.

General and International Law Practice.
Firm engaged in American and International Law Practice, not authorized to appear before the Moscow Courts.

RESIDENT PARTNER

JOHN F. SHEEDY, born Boston, Massachusetts, August 11, 1957; admitted, 1983, Texas; 1991, New York (Not admitted in Russia). *Education:* Georgetown University (B.S., magna cum laude, 1979); University of Michigan (J.D., 1983). Phi Beta Kappa. Author: "Indonesia's New Capital Market Regulations," East-Asian Executive Reports (April-May 1988). Co-Author: "Gaining a Foothold in the Soviet Market: How to Establish a Representative Office," 25 The International Lawyer 103 (1991); "Some Legal Considerations for Joint Ventures," Russian Petroleum Investor (August 1992); "Well Repair and Workover Contracts in Russia," Russian Oil and Gas Guide (April 1993); "Overview of Energy Legislation in the Former Soviet Union," Petroleum Economist (May 1993). *Member:* State Bar of Texas; New York State and American Bar Associations. **LANGUAGES:** Russian, French, German, Danish, Norwegian and Indonesian.

RESIDENT ASSOCIATES

Andrew J. Fletcher
(Not admitted in Russia)
Marian M. Hagler
(Not admitted in Russia)

Yevgeny V. Nikiforov
Michael G. Pekowsky
(Not admitted in Russia)
Olga N. Sirodoeva

REVISERS OF THE FRANCE LAW DIGEST FOR THIS DIRECTORY

(For biographical data of the New York personnel, see Professional Biographies at New York, N.Y.).

(For biographical data of the Washington personnel, see Professional Biographies at Washington, D.C.).

(For biographical data of the San Francisco personnel, see Professional Biographies at San Francisco, California).

(For biographical data of the Los Angeles personnel, see Professional Biographies at Los Angeles, California).

(For biographical data of the San Jose Personnel, see Professional Biographies at San Jose, California).

(For biographical data of the Paris personnel, see Professional Biographies at Paris, France).

(For biographical data of the London personnel, see Professional Biographies at London, England).

(For biographical data of the Brussels personnel, see Professional Biographies at Brussels, Belgium).

(This Listing Continued)

COUDERT BROTHERS, Moscow—Continued

(For biographical data of the Beijing personnel, see Professional Biographies at Beijing, People's Republic of China).

(For biographical data of the Hong Kong personnel, see Professional Biographies at Hong Kong).

(For biographical data of the Singapore personnel, see Professional Biographies at Singapore).

(For biographical data of the Tokyo personnel, see Professional Biographies at Tokyo, Japan).

(For biographical data of the Sao Paulo personnel, see Professional Biographies at Sao Paulo, Brazil).

(For biographical data of the Shanghai personnel, see Professional Biographies at Shanghai, People's Republic of China).

(For biographical data of the Sydney personnel, see Professional Biographies at Sydney, Australia).

(For biographical data of the Ho Chi Minh City personnel, see Professional Biographies at Ho Chi Minh City, Vietnam).

DAMEU LEGAL ADVISER

Established in 1991

STRASTNOI BOULEVARD
4, BUILDING 1, SUITE 70
103009 MOSCOW, RUSSIA
Telephone: (095) 209-52-83
Fax: (095) 209-52-33

Moscow Region Office: 15/206 Pobratimov Street, Suite 206, 140013, Lubertsy, Russia. Telephone: (095) 559-08-63

General Civil Practice, Civil Litigation, Contract, Commercial and Corporate Law, Creditor Rights, Tax, Bankruptcy, Joint Ventures, International Transactions and Arbitration.

ALEXANDER M. DOROSHENKO, born Kremenchug, Ukraine, July 25, 1940; admitted, 1968. *Education:* Moscow State University Faculty of Laws, 1968; High Courses of Foreign Languages, 1975. Member: Moscow Regional Bar, 1968-1971; Ministry of Foreign Trade, 1971-1991. Member, Executive Counsel of British-Soviet Chamber of Commerce, 1975-1979, Trade Delegation of the USSR in the United Kingdom, 1975-1979, Trade Representation of the USSR in Norway, 1985-1989. *LANGUAGES:* Russian, English and Ukrainian.

DENTON HALL

A Member of the Denton International Group of Law Firms

AEROSTAR
THIRD FLOOR
LENINGRADSKI PROSPECT
KORPUS 9
MOSCOW, RUSSIA
Telephone: 7-502 224 1494
Fax: 7-502 224 1495

Other Offices: London, England; Milton Keynes, Buckinghamshire, England; Beijing, People's Republic of China; Hong Kong; Los Angeles, California; Singapore; Tokyo, Japan; Brussels, Belgium.

Associated Offices: Amsterdam, Berlin, Chemnitz, Copenhagen, Dusseldorf, Frankfurt, Hamburg, Prague, Rotterdam and Vienna.

PARTNERS

RICHARD METCALF (Also at London, England Office). *LANGUAGES:* French, German. *PRACTICE AREAS:* Energy and Natural Resources.

BLANCHE SAS. PRACTICE AREAS: Energy and Natural Resources.

(For all Firm Personnel, see Professional Biographies at London, England).

DERINGER TESSIN HERRMANN & SEDEMUND

UL. BOLSCHAJA ORDYNKA 21
RF-113035 MOSCOW, RUSSIA
Telephone: 7-095-233 24 50; 231 54 03
Telefax: 7-095-233 43 55

Cologne, Germany Office: Heumarkt 14, D-50667 Cologne. Telephone: 49-221-205070. Telefax: 49-221-2050790. Telex: 8 881 356 ELAW D.

Frankfurt/Main Germany Office: Bockenheimer Landstraße 51-53, D-60325 Frankfurt a.M. Telephone 49-69-971090-0. Telefax: 49-69-971090-90.

Leipzig, Germany Office: Burgplatz 2, D-04109 Leipzig. Telephone: 49-341-711590. Telefax: 49-341-7115999.

Brussels, Belgium Office: Place des Barricades 13, B-1000 Brussels. Telephone: 32-2-219 82 50. Telefax: 32-2-219 88 32.

Mergers and Acquisitions, International Trade Law, Commercial Law, Real Estate, Development Projects, Privatization, Companies, Corporate Law, Employment, Labour.

RESIDENT PARTNERS

KIRSTEN FLOSS, born Münster, Germany, April 11, 1963; admitted, 1993, Cologne. *Education:* University of Münster (Germany), Strasbourg (France), Geneva (Switzerland); Institut Universitaire d'Etudes Européennes, Geneva; Pushkin-Institute, Moscow. Consultant of EC Commission, Brussels, 1990, Stagiaire with Russian Chamber of Commerce, Moscow, 1992; Stagiaire with White & Case, New York, 1992. *Member:* German Bar Association. *LANGUAGES:* German, English, French and Russian.

(For complete biographical data on all personnel, see Professional Biographies at Cologne, Germany)

FRERE CHOLMELEY BISCHOFF

Established in 1993

UL. SADOVAYA-SAMOTYOCHNAYA 24/27
103051 MOSCOW, RUSSIA
Telephone: (7) 095 258 5058
Fax: (7) 095 258 5060
Telex: 412348 ALM SU

London, England Office: 4 John Carpenter Street, London EC4Y ONH. Telephone: 0171-615 8000. Fax: 0171-615 8080. Telex: 27623.

Paris, France Office: 42 Avenue du Président Wilson, 75116. Telephone: (33) (1) 44 34 71 00. Fax: (33) (1) 44 34 71 11.

Rome, Italy Office: and Studio Legale Associato, 47, Viale Bruno Buozzi, 00197. Telephone: (39) (6) 808 0133. Fax: (39) (6) 808 0134.

Milan, Italy Office: and Studio Legale Associato, Piazza Castello 24, 20121 Milan. Telephone: (39) (2) 720 03 457. Fax: (39) (2) 720 03 469. Telephone: (32) (2) 513 8604. Fax: (32) (2) 512 0426.

Monte Carlo, Monaco Office: "Est Ouest", 24 Boulevard Princesse Charlotte, MC 98000. Telephone: (33) (93) 508 570. Fax: (33) (93) 502 210.

Berlin, Germany Office: im Internationalen Handelszentrum, Friedrichstrasse 95, 10117 Berlin. Telephone: (49) (30) 26 43 2000. Fax: (49) (30) 2643 1900. Telex: 305996 KBIHZ D.

Dubai, United Arab Emirates Office (trading as McNeill & Associates): Suite 802, EBIL Building, PO Box 2510, Deira, Dubai. Telephone: (9714) 267085/268336. Fax: (9714) 160206. Telex: 45493 LAWMC EM.

FIRM PROFILE: Frere Cholmeley Bischoff opened an office in Moscow in 1993 to advise the increasing number of companies looking to invest in the CIS. As well as advising national and international clients on specific transactions, this office provides regular updates on the developments of the Russian business environment to the rest of the firm's clients.

MEMBERS OF THE FIRM

DR. JOHANNES POSTH, born Berge, Germany, 1942. *Education:* Humanistisches Gymnasium, (First and Second State Examinations in law). German Ministry of Transport, 1980-1988; German Ministry of Inner-German Relations, 1974-1980; Adviser, German Embassy in Moscow, 1988-1993. Senior Representative of Frere Cholmeley Bischoff's Moscow

(This Listing Continued)

office from September 1993. *LANGUAGES:* German, Russian and English.

(For a full list of the Partners see Professional Biographies, London, England Office)

FRESHFIELDS

Established in 1992

BOLSHAYA POLYANKA UL., 24/2
MOSCOW 109180, RUSSIA
Telephone: (7 502) 222 1098 Domestic: 7 095 237 5852/5951
Fax: (7 502) 222 1099 Domestic: 7 095 237 5478

Other Offices in: Bangkok, Barcelona, Brussels, Frankfurt, Hanoi, Hong Kong, London, Madrid, New York, Paris, Singapore and Tokyo.

RESIDENT PARTNERS

JACKY BAUDON, born Landes Genusson, France, April 26, 1954; admitted, 1975, Avocat (Not admitted in Russia). *Education:* Nantes University Law School (1975); Fondation Nationale de Sciences Politiques, Paris; Moscow State University (Ph.D.). *LANGUAGES:* French, Russian and English. *PRACTICE AREAS:* Real Estate; Construction; Mineral Resources; Oil and Gas; Telecommunications; Privatisation; Distribution.

STEPHEN MCGAIRL, born England, 1951; admitted, 1976, England; 1992, Avocat, Paris (Not admitted in Russia). *Education:* Worcester College, Oxford. *Member:* Law Society; Société Française de Droit Aérien et Spatial. *LANGUAGES:* French, English and Russian. *PRACTICE AREAS:* International Financing; Asset and Project Finance; Investment and Finance in Russia and the CIS.

GIDE LOYRETTE NOUEL

9, ULITSA TVERSKAYA - APP. 66
103009 MOSCOW, RUSSIA
Telephone by satellite: (7.501) 940.45.00
Telecopier by satellite: (7.501) 940.45.01

Paris, France Office: 26 Cours Albert 1er, 75008. Telephone: (1) 40.75.60.00. Cable Address: "3 Avocagidva Paris 86." Telex: 651261F GILOY. Telecopier: (1) 43.59.37.79.

New York, New York Office: Swiss Bank Tower, 10 East 50th Street, 10022. Telephone: (1-212) 644-1201. Telex: 424353 GIDE. Telecopier: (1-212) 644-1205.

Brussels, Belgium Office: Rue de la Loi 99.101, B-1040. Telephone: (32.2) 231.11.40. Telecopier: (32.2) 231.11.77.

Warsaw, Poland Office: Ul. Kopernika 17, 00-359. Telephone: (48.22) 26.22.21. Telecopier: (48.22) 26.03.02.

Riyadh, Saudi Arabia Office: P.O. Box 4615, 11412. Telephone: (966.1) 476.60.39. Telex: 401677 NASHWA. Telecopier: (966.1) 476.18.96.

Tokyo, Japan Office: Homei Building 3F, 3-19 Akasaka 1-Chome, Minato-Ku, 107. Telephone: (81.3) 55.62.03.01. Telecopier: (81.3) 55.62.03.06.

Beijing, People's Republic of China Office: Suite 3309 A, Jing Guang Centre, Hu Jia Lou, Chaoyang District, 100020. Telephone: (86.1) 501 4511. Telecopier: (86.1) 501 4551.

Prague, Czech Republic Office: 34 Jindrisska, 11207. Telephone: (42.2) 24.21.34.65;24.21.36.50. Telecopier: (42.2) 24.21.09.12;24.22.58.53.

St. Petersburg, Russia Office: 34 Souvorovsky Prospect, App 45, P.O. Box 172, 193015. Telephone by satellite: (7.812) 850.16.85. Telecopier by satellite: (7.812) 850.16.86.

Budapest VII, Hungary Office: EMKE Building, Rákóczi út 42, BP 409, 1072. Telephone: (36.1) 268.1236; 268.1237; 268.1238. Telecopier: (36.1) 268.1239.

Madrid, Spain Office: Antonio Maura 7, 6°, 28014. Telephone: (34.1) 531.25.01. Telecopier: (34.1) 531.35.30.

Hanoi, Vietnam Office: Hanoi Business Centre, 51 Ly Thai To. Telephone: (84.42) 66.122.3. Telecopier: (84.42) 66.030.1.

French and International Law.

RESIDENT ASSOCIATES

Mathieu Fabre-Magnan
Katie Guendzekhaze
Helena Kheifets
(This Listing Continued)

Chautal Couteaux
Denis Sukhanov

(For Biographical Data on Personnel, see Professional Biographies at Paris, France).

HOGAN & HARTSON L.L.P.

33/2 USACHEVA STREET
BUILDING 3
119048 MOSCOW, RUSSIA
Telephone: (7095) 245-5190
Fax: (7095) 245-5192

Washington, D.C. Office: Columbia Square, 555 13th Street, N.W., 20004-1109. Telephone: 202-637-5600. Telex: 89-2757. Cable Address: "Hogander Washington". Fax: 202-637-5910.

Brussels, Belgium Office: Avenue des Arts 41, 1040. Telephone: (32.2) 505.09.11. Fax: (32.2) 502.28.60.

London, England Office: Veritas House, 125 Finsbury Pavement, EC2A 1NQ. Telephone: (44 171) 638.9595. Fax: (44 171) 638.0884.

Paris, France Office: Cabinet Wolfram: 14, rue Chauveau-Lagarde, 75008. Telephone: (33-1) 44.71.97.00. Fax: (33-1) 47.42.13.56.

Prague, Czech Republic Office: Opletalova 37, 110 00. Telephone: (42-2) 2422-9009. Fax: (42-2) 2421-5105.

Warsaw, Poland Office: Marszalkowska 6/6, 00-590. Telephone: (48 2) 628 0201; Int'l (48) 3912 1413. Fax: (48 2) 628 7787; Int'l (48) 3912 1511.

Baltimore, Maryland Office: 111 South Calvert Street, 16th Floor. Telephone: 410-659-2700. Fax: 410-539-6981.

Bethesda, Maryland Office: Two Democracy Center, Suite 720, 6903 Rockledge Drive. Telephone: 301-493-0030. Fax: 301-493-5169.

Colorado Springs, Colorado Office: 518 North Nevada Avenue, Suite 200. Telephone: 719-635-5900. Fax: 719-635-2847.

Denver, Colorado Office: One Tabor Center, Suite 1500, 1200 Seventeenth Street. Telephone: 303-899-7300. Fax: 303-899-7333.

McLean, Virginia Office: 8300 Greensboro Drive. Telephone: 703-848-2600. Fax: 703-448-7650.

International Commercial Transactions, Foreign Investment, Telecommunications, Privatization, Project Finance, Public Finance.

RESIDENT PARTNERS

REBECCA B. BRONSON, born Fort Worth, Texas, August 16, 1947; admitted, 1980, Texas (Not admitted in Russia). *Education:* Tulane University of Louisiana (B.A., 1969); University of Texas (M.A., 1977; J.D., 1980). *Member:* State Bar of Texas; American Bar Association; National Association of Bond Lawyers. *PRACTICE AREAS:* Public/Project Finance Law; Securities Law; Financial Institutions Law.

DEAN W. CROWELL, born Ogden, Utah, September 7, 1949; admitted, 1975, Colorado; 1989, District of Columbia (Not admitted in Russia). *Education:* University of Colorado (B.A., 1971); University of California, Hastings College of the Law (J.D., 1974). *Member:* District of Columbia Bar; American Bar Association. *PRACTICE AREAS:* International Commercial Transactions.

RESIDENT ASSOCIATES

ALEXANDER A. DUBITSKY, born Saratov, Russia, April 19, 1965; admitted, 1993, District of Columbia (Not admitted in Russia). *Education:* Kiev State University (J.D., with high honors, 1989); Ukrainian School of International Business (1990); Yale Law School (LL.M., 1992). *Member:* District of Columbia Bar. *LANGUAGES:* Russian, Ukrainian. *PRACTICE AREAS:* Commercial; International.

MICHAEL A. PROETT, born Boulder, Colorado, August 18, 1961; admitted, 1986, Colorado (Not admitted in Russia). *Education:* University of Colorado (B.A., magna cum laude, 1983); Harvard Law School (J.D., cum laude, 1986). Phi Beta Kappa. Author: "Cumulative Impacts of Hydroelectric Development: Beyond the Cluster Impact Assessment Procedure," 11 Harvard Environmental law Review 77, 1987. *Member:* Denver, Colorado and American (Member, Sections on: Business Law; International Law) Bar Associations. *PRACTICE AREAS:* International Transactions; Corporate and Securities.

HOLME ROBERTS & OWEN LLC

Established in 1898

14 KRIVOKOLENNY PR., SUITE 30
101000 MOSCOW, RUSSIA
Telephone: 095-925-7816
Telecopier: 095-923-2726

REVISERS OF THE COLORADO LAW DIGEST FOR THIS DIRECTORY

Denver, Colorado Office: Suite 4100, 1700 Lincoln, 80203. Telephone: 303-861-7000. Telex: 45-4460. Telecopier: 303-866-0200.

Boulder, Colorado Office: Suite 400, 1401 Pearl Street, 80302. Telephone: 303-444-5955. Telecopier: 303-444-1063.

Colorado Springs, Colorado Office: Suite 1300, 90 South Cascade Avenue, 80903. Telephone: 719-473-3800. Telecopier: 719-633-1518.

Salt Lake City, Utah Office: Suite 1100, 111 East Broadway, 84111. Telephone: 801-521-5800. Telecopier: 801-521-9639.

London, England Office: 4th Floor, Mellier House, 26a Albemarle Street, W1X 3FA. Telephone: 44-171-499-8776. Telecopier: 44-171-499-7769.

General and International Practice, including Joint Ventures, Natural Resources, Cable and Telecommunications, Labor, Real Estate, and Environmental Law, International Business and International Tax.

MEMBERS OF FIRM

BRUCE R. KOHLER, born Springfield, Massachusetts, April 15, 1943; admitted, 1970, New York; 1973, Colorado (Not admitted in Russia). *Education:* Harvard University (A.B., magna cum laude, 1965; J.D., cum laude, 1969). Phi Beta Kappa. Chairman, Colorado Italy Council, 1989. U.K. Representative, Colorado International Trade Office. *Member:* International Bar Association. (Co-chair, International Practice). (Co-Director, Moscow Office; Resident, Managing Lawyer, London Office). *LANGUAGES:* English, Italian, Danish. *PRACTICE AREAS:* International Business Law; Corporate Law; Real Estate Lending Law.

JUDITH L. L. ROBERTS, born Seattle, Washington, December 27, 1939; admitted, 1979, Colorado (Not admitted in Russia). *Education:* University of Michigan (A.B., magna cum laude, 1962); University of Tübingen, Germany, Fulbright Scholar; University of Wisconsin (M.A., 1964); University of Denver (J.D., 1979). Phi Beta Kappa. Woodrow Wilson Fellow. Order of St. Ives. Staff, Denver Law Journal, 1977-1979. Member, Colorado Governor's Soviet Advisory Council; Chairman of Board, Denver World Trade Center, 1991-1992; Director, Colorado-Taiwan Trade and Investment Office, 1988-1991; Resident Lawyer, London, 1981-1982. *Member:* Denver, Colorado International Bar Associations. (Co-Chair, International Practice). (Co-Director, London Office; Moscow Office). *PRACTICE AREAS:* International Business Law.

JAMES W. SPENSLEY, born Chicago, Illinois, February 23, 1946; admitted, 1972, Virginia; 1973, District of Columbia; 1983, Colorado (Not admitted in Russia). *Education:* Iowa State University (B.S., 1969); George Washington University (J.D., 1972). Author: "Evolution of U.S. Environmental Law," Buenos Aires, 1993. Adjunct Professor: University of Denver Law School, 1983-1993; Graduate Program on Environmental Policy and Management, 1992-1994. Chairman, Colorado Advanced Technology Institute, 1987-1993. Co-Chairman, 1990-1991 and Board Member, 1994, Colorado Center for Environmental Management. Co-Chairman, Colorado Environmental Business Alliance. Counsel: U.S. House of Representatives Committee on Science and Technology, 1975-1980; National Center for Atmospheric Research, 1982-1984. Manager, New Denver Airport Office, 1984-1988. Board Member, Denver Regional Air Quality Council, 1993-1994. *Member:* Denver, Virginia and Colorado Bar Associations. (Also at Denver, Colorado Office). *PRACTICE AREAS:* Domestic and International Environmental Law; Land Use Planning Law; Administrative Law.

ASSOCIATES

ELENA KURYATNIKOVA. *Education:* Moscow State Institute for Foreign Affairs, Law Department (J.D., equivalent, 1992). *LANGUAGES:* Russian, English and French. *PRACTICE AREAS:* Corporate Law; Licensing; Currency and Central Bank Regulations; Banking.

MARGARET B. MCLEAN, born Kiev, Ukraine, April 10, 1963; admitted, 1992, Colorado (Not admitted in Russia). *Education:* University of Arizona (B.S., magna cum laude, 1983); University of Colorado (M.B.A., 1985); University of Michigan (J.D., cum laude, 1992). Note Editor, Michigan Journal of Law Reform, 1991-1992. Chair, "Doing Business in Eastern Europe and the CIS Roundtable" at World Trade Center, Denver, Colorado, 1992-1993. Author: "Market Transition through Defense Conversion:

(This Listing Continued)

Ukrainian Opportunities," Politichna Dumka, August, 1993; "Russia and the NIS in the World Economy and Business Environment," Prager Publishers (Co-author, Ch. 8). *Member:* Colorado and American Bar Associations. (Resident Managing Lawyer). *LANGUAGES:* English, Russian and Ukrainian. *PRACTICE AREAS:* International Business Law; International Tax Law.

PAUL G. THOMPSON, born Des Moines, Iowa, November 17, 1963; admitted, 1989, Colorado; 1990, District of Columbia (Not admitted in Russia). *Education:* University of Iowa (B.B.A., magna cum laude, 1985); University of Michigan (J.D., 1989). Contributing Author: "Business Ventures in Eastern Europe and the Soviet Union: The Emerging Legal Framework for Foreign Investment," Prentice Hall Law & Business, 1991. Co-Author: "Securities Regulation in Central Europe: Hungary and Czechoslovakia," Denv. J. Int'l L. & Pol'y, 1992; "Roll-Up Transactions," Clark Boardman, 1992; "Securities Regulations in Central Europe: Poland, Hungary and Czech and Slovak Federal Republics," Clark Boardman, 1993. *Member:* Denver, Colorado and American Bar Associations; District of Columbia Bar. (Also at Denver, Colorado and London, England Offices). *PRACTICE AREAS:* International Law; Corporate Law; Securities Law.

RASHID SHARIPOV, born Moscow, 1968; admitted, 1990, Russia. *Education:* Moscow State Institute for International Affairs (J.D. equivalent, Red Diploma, magna cum laude, 1990); California Western School of Law, San Diego (LL.M., 1992). *LANGUAGES:* Russian, English, Persian. *PRACTICE AREAS:* International Law; Russian Business Law; Russian Telecommunications Law.

ALEXANDER UDOVENKO. *Education:* Moscow State Institute for Foreign Affairs, Law Department (J.D., equivalent, 1994). *LANGUAGES:* Russian, English and Spanish. *PRACTICE AREAS:* Administrative Law; Licensing; Company Registration; Currency and Central Bank Regulations; Customs; Intellectual Property.

LEGAL SUPPORT PERSONNEL

KATHERINE FADEEVA, born Moscow, 1965. *Education:* Moscow Pedagogical Institute (English and Geography). (Office Administrator). *LANGUAGES:* Russian, English. *PRACTICE AREAS:* Planning Decisions; Finance; General Administration.

REVISERS OF THE COLORADO LAW DIGEST FOR THIS DIRECTORY

(For Complete Biographical Data on all Personnel, see Professional Biographies at Denver, Colorado)

INIURCOLLEGUIA

Attorneys at Law

5 TVERSKAYA STREET
103009 MOSCOW, RUSSIA
Telephone: 7 (095) 203 6864, 203 0348
Fax: 7 (095) 200 5247
Telex: 411811 Injur Su

St. Petersburg Office: 13, Pushkin Street.

Firm engaged in Russian, European and International Law practice, entitled to plead before Russian courts, General International Trade Law, International Banking and Business Law, Corporate Law including creation of Joint Ventures and Wholly Foreign owned enterprises in Russia, Property Law Commercial Law and Administration Law, Construction Law, Public International Law, Transport Law, Labour Law, Tax Law, Financial Law, Family Law, General Civil Law, Criminal Law, Litigation and International Arbitration, Inheritance Service, Genealogical Research.

FIRM PROFILE: Established in 1937 Iniurcolleguia has grown to one of Russian leading firms with a strong international law practice. The firm has a branch in St. Petersburg and has correspondent agreements with major law firms in the Ukraine, Belarus, Lithuania, Latvia and Estonia. It has strong International contacts, particularly, with Europe and North America. The firm has a world wide network of correspondent lawyers enabling to solve widest range of problems.

The firm has 83 members, all have legal education graduating from law faculty of various Russian universities.

MEMBERS OF FIRM

VALERIY ALPATIKOV, born 1959; admitted, 1989. Chairman of the Presidium of Iniurcolleguia. *LANGUAGES:* Russian and English. *PRACTICE AREAS:* International Public Law; Administrative Law; Construction Law; Corporate Law.

(This Listing Continued)

BORIS Z. SLOBODIN, born 1939; admitted, 1990. *LANGUAGES:* Russian and German. *PRACTICE AREAS:* Administrative Law; Criminal Law; Genealogical Research.

TATYANA V. ALEKSEEVA, born 1953; admitted, 1981. *LANGUAGES:* Russian and English. *PRACTICE AREAS:* Canadian Inheritance Law; General Civil Law; Corporate Law.

NIKOLAY N. POTAPOV, born 1915; admitted, 1951. *LANGUAGES:* Russian. *PRACTICE AREAS:* Inheritance in the USA; General Civil Law.

GALINA M. SAVEIJEVA, born 1953; admitted, 1982. *LANGUAGES:* Russian and English. *PRACTICE AREAS:* General Civil Law; Corporate Law; Family Law; International Arbitration; Shipping Law; Compensation of Damage.

VLADISLAV F. MIRONOV, born 1935; admitted, 1970. *LANGUAGES:* Russian and English. *PRACTICE AREAS:* International Trade Law; Transport Law; Corporate Law; International Arbitration.

TATYANA A. OKSUZIAN, born 1957; admitted, 1981. *LANGUAGES:* Russian, German and Spanish. *PRACTICE AREAS:* Corporate Law; Tax Law; Property Law; International Trade Law.

YURY I. RAKITIN, born 1940; admitted, 1985. *LANGUAGES:* Russian. *PRACTICE AREAS:* General Civil Law; Criminal Law; International Adoption.

DMITRY V. VOROBYOV, born 1966; admitted, 1992. *LANGUAGES:* Russian and English. *PRACTICE AREAS:* International Business Law; International Arbitration; General Civil Law; International Trade Law; Commercial Litigation; Contracts.

ELENA L. RUDNEVA, born 1957; admitted, 1981. *LANGUAGES:* Russian and English. *PRACTICE AREAS:* International Business Law; General Civil Law; International Trade Law; Commercial Litigation; Contracts; Criminal Law.

EKATERINA V. MURADOVA, born 1964; admitted, 1990. *LANGUAGES:* Russian, French and English. *PRACTICE AREAS:* International Business Law; General Civil Law; International Trade Law; Commercial Litigation; Contracts; Criminal Law.

NADEZDA A. LABUTINA, born 1949; admitted, 1979. *LANGUAGES:* Russian and English. *PRACTICE AREAS:* International Business Law; General Civil Law; International Trade Law; Commercial Litigation; Contracts.

OLGA V. BURDONOVA, born 1961; admitted, 1986. *LANGUAGES:* Russian, English and German. *PRACTICE AREAS:* International Business Law; General Civil Law; International Trade Law; Commercial Litigation; Contracts.

ANATOLIY S. EMELIANOV, born 1960; admitted, 1992. *LANGUAGES:* Russian and English. *PRACTICE AREAS:* International Business Law; General Civil Law; International Trade Law; Commercial Litigation; Contracts; Criminal Law; Banking.

JURINFLOT

INTERNATIONAL LAW OFFICE

4TH FLOOR
30 LENINGRADSKY PR.
P.O. BOX 44
MOSCOW 125124, RUSSIA
Telephone: (7-095) 214-6058; 214-7209; 214-0552; 214-2192
International Only: (7-505) 211-301
Telex: 612306 JURIF SU
Fax: 212-8074
International Only: (7-505) 211-306

MEMBERS OF FIRM

NATALIA MIKHAILOVNA BELOVA, born Moscow, Russia, December 7, 1943; admitted, 1969, Russia. *Education:* Moscow Juridical Institute (Master Degree, 1969). *LANGUAGES:* Russian and English. *PRACTICE AREAS:* Commercial Litigation and Arbitration; Maritime Law; Charter Party Disputes; Civil Law.

VADIM GERMANOVICH ERMOLAEV, born Odessa, Ukraine, June 27, 1951; admitted, 1985, Russia. *Education:* Odessa High Engineering Marine School (Graduated, 1973); Odessa State University (Master Degree, 1985); All-Union Academy for Foreign Trade, Faculty of International Economy (Graduated, 1988). Mate and Master-Mariner, sailed ships of

(This Listing Continued)

Black Sea Shipping Co. for 12 years. *LANGUAGES:* Russian, English and Ukrainian. *PRACTICE AREAS:* Transport and Trading; Maritime Matters; Commercial Litigation and Arbitration; Commercial Contracts.

STANISLAV PITIRIMOVICH KONDRASHIN, born Samara, Russia, June 23, 1944; admitted, 1971, Russia. *Education:* Peoples' Friendship University (Master Degree, 1971). *LANGUAGES:* English, French, Spanish, German, Polish and Russian. *PRACTICE AREAS:* Company Law; Commercial Contracts; Asset and Project Financing; Lending and Security; Foreign Investment; Public Sector and Privatisation; Commercial Litigation and Arbitration; Maritime Law.

VALERY VASSILEVICH MANDRIOUC, born Chernovtsi, Ukraine, May 26, 1958; admitted, 1989, Russia. *Education:* Moscow State Institute of International Relations (Master Degree, 1989). Member, Maritime Arbitration Commission, Moscow, 1993—. *LANGUAGES:* Ukrainian, Russian, French, English and Polish. *PRACTICE AREAS:* Company Law; Commercial Contracts; Foreign Investment; Public Sector and Privatisation; Corporate Law; Maritime Law; Commercial Litigation and Arbitration.

VLADIMIR ALEXANDROVICH MEDNIKOV, born Moscow, Russia, November 2, 1953; admitted, 1980, Russia. *Education:* Peoples' Friendship University, Moscow, Russia (Master Degree, 1980); All-Union Marine Research Institute, Moscow, Russia (Postgraduate in Conflict of Laws, Maritime Law by Correspondence, 1982-1986). *LANGUAGES:* Russian and English. *PRACTICE AREAS:* Asset and Project Financing; Lending and Security; Maritime Law; Conflict of Laws; Civil Law; Litigation.

TAISA TROFIMOVNA MISHCHENKO, born Vitebsk, Belarus, September 4, 1948; admitted, 1974, Russia. *Education:* Moscow State Institute of International Relations (Master Degree, 1974). *LANGUAGES:* Bielarussian, Russian, French, English and German. *PRACTICE AREAS:* Transport and Trading; Maritime Law; Commercial Litigation and Arbitration; Civil Law; Charter Party Disputes.

IRINA VICTOROVNA NISTRATOVA, born Evpatoria, Ukraine, June 10, 1956; admitted, 1978, Russia. *Education:* Moscow Juridical Institute (Master Degree, 1978). *LANGUAGES:* Russian and English. *PRACTICE AREAS:* Commercial Litigation and Arbitration; Maritime Law; Charterparties and Contracts of Affreightment; Commercial Contracts.

BORIS VICTOROVICH PAVLOV, born Moscow, Russia, September 29, 1947; admitted, 1976, Russia. *Education:* Moscow State Institute of International Relations (Master Degree, 1976). *LANGUAGES:* Russian and English. *PRACTICE AREAS:* Maritime Law; Insurance Law; Commercial Contracts.

STANISLAV GRIGORIEVICH POKROVSKI, born Saratov, Russia, January 15, 1933; admitted, 1968, Russia. *Education:* Leningrad University (Master Degree, 1968). Arbitrator, Maritime Arbitration Commission, Russian Chamber of Commerce and Industry, Moscow. *LANGUAGES:* Russian and English. *PRACTICE AREAS:* Maritime Law; Insurance Law; Commercial Litigation and Arbitration; Commerical Contracts.

LATHAM & WATKINS

SUITE C200
113/1 LENINSKY PROSPECKT
MOSCOW 117198, RUSSIA
Telephone: +-7 503 956-5555
Fax: +-7 503 956-5556

Los Angeles, California Office: 633 West Fifth Street, Suite 4000, 90071. Telephone: 213-485-1234. Telecopier: 213-891-8763.

Costa Mesa, California Office: Suite 2000, 650 Town Center Drive, 92626-1918. Telephone: 714-540-1235. Telecopier: 714-755-8290.

San Diego, California Office: Suite 2100, 701 B Street, 92101-8197. Telephone: 619-238-1234. Telecopier: 619-238-2895.

San Francisco, California Office: 505 Montgomery Street, Suite 1900, 94111. Telephone: 415-391-0600. Fax: 415-395-8095.

Washington, D.C. Office: Suite 1300, 1001 Pennsylvania Avenue, N.W., 20004. Telephone: 202-637-2200. Telecopier: 202-637-2201.

Chicago, Illinois Office: Suite 5800 Sears Tower, 60606. Telephone: 312-876-7700. Telecopier: 312-993-9767.

Newark, New Jersey Office: One Newark Center, 07101-3174. Telephone: 201-639-1234. Fax: 201-639-7298.

New York, N.Y. Office: Suite 1000, 885 Third Avenue, 10022-4802. Telephone: 212-906-1200. Telecopier: 212-751-4864.

(This Listing Continued)

LATHAM & WATKINS, Moscow—Continued

London, England Office: One Angel Court, EC2R 7HJ. Telephone: +-44-171-374 4444. Telecopier: +-44-171-374 4460.
Warsaw, Poland Office: St. Szpitalna 1, Suite 49, 9th Floor, 00-018. Telephone: +-48-2-227-9610. Telecopier: +-48-2-227-9610.
Hong Kong Office: 11th Floor Central Building, Number One Pedder Street, Central Hong Kong. Telephone: 011-852-841-7779. Fax: 011-852-841-7749.

General Practice.

RESIDENT PARTNERS

RICHARD A. CONN, JR., born Norfolk, Virginia, November 13, 1957; admitted, 1982, California (Not admitted in Russia). *Education:* Dartmouth College (B.A., 1979); Fordham University (J.D., 1982). Member, Fordham University Law Review, 1980-1982. Co-Author: Collier Labor Law and the Bankruptcy Code. Clerk to the Honorable Gordon Thompson, Jr., Chief Judge to the U.S. District Court, Southern District of California, 1982. Managing Partner of Moscow Office. Member: U.S. Committee to Assist Russian Reform; California-USSR Trade Association. President, Russia's International Lawyers Group. Committee Chairman, Moscow American Chamber of Commerce. Columnist: Moscow Tribune; East/West Executive Reports. *Member:* State Bar of California; American Bar Association (Member, Business Bankruptcy Committee and International Bankruptcy Subcommittee). *LANGUAGES:* Russian and Spanish.

RESIDENT OF COUNSEL

THOMAS B. TRIMBLE, born Jacksonville, Florida, July 19, 1959; admitted, 1988, New York and Connecticut; 1989, District of Columbia (Not admitted in Russia). *Education:* Bucknell University (B.A., 1982); Columbia University, School of International Affairs (M.I.A., 1985); The American University, Washington College of Law (J.D., 1987). *Member:* District of Columbia Bar.

KIM ORNELAS CONN, born San Diego, California, August 20, 1955; admitted, 1982, California (Not admitted in Russia). *Education:* Yale College (B.S., 1977); Stanford Business School (M.B.A., 1979); Harvard Law School (J.D., 1982). Member: Russia's International Lawyers Group; Moscow American Chamber of Commerce. Columnist: Moscow Tribune; East/West Executive Reports. *Member:* San Diego County and American Bar Associations; State Bar of California.

LEV S. SIMKIN, born Moscow, Russia, April 6, 1951; (Not admitted in Russia). *Education:* Moscow Law Institute (LL.M., 1973); Moscow State University (LL.D., 1989); High Education Committee (Professor of Law, 1993). Member and President, International Committee of Legal Reform in Russia. Columnist: Izvestiya; Moscow News; Nezavisimaya Gazzetta; Novy Mir; Znamya. *LANGUAGES:* Russian and English.

RESIDENT ASSOCIATES

ANYA GOLDIN, born St. Petersburg, Russia, February 20, 1963; admitted, 1990, California (Not admitted in Russia). *Education:* University of California at Berkeley (B.A., 1987); Boalt Hall School of Law, University of California (J.D., 1990). Phi Beta Kappa; Order of the Coif. Teaching Assistant, Income Tax, Boalt Hall School of Law, 1990. Editor, International Business Lawyer. Member, American Chamber of Commerce, Moscow, Russia. *Member:* American Bar Association; International Lawyers Association. *LANGUAGES:* Russian.

(For biographical data on Los Angeles, California Costa Mesa, California, San Diego, California, San Francisco, California, Washington, D.C., Chicago, Illinois, New York, New York, London, England, Warsaw, Poland and Hong Kong personnel, see Professional Biographies at each of those cities)

EU1176B

LeBOEUF, LAMB, GREENE & MacRAE L.L.P.

A Limited Liability Partnership including Professional Corporations
Formerly LeBoeuf, Lamb, Leiby & MacRae
ULITSA DELEGATSKAYA, 25
103473 MOSCOW, RUSSIAN FEDERATION
Telephone: 011-7-503-956-3935
Facsimile: 011-7-503-956-3936

Eastern United States:
New York, N.Y. Office: 125 West 55th Street, 10019-5389. Telephone: 212-424-8000. Facsimile: 212-424-8500. Telex: 1561363 or 423416.
Washington, D.C. Office: 1875 Connecticut Avenue, N.W., Suite 1200, 20009. Telephone: 202-986-8000. Facsimile: 202-986-8102. Telex: 440274.
Albany, New York Office: One Commerce Plaza, 99 Washington Avenue, Suite 2020. 12210. Telephone: 518-465-1500. Facsimile: 518-465-1585.
Boston, Massachusetts Office: 260 Franklin Street, 02110. Telephone: 617-439-9500. Facsimile: 617-439-0341; 439-0342.
Harrisburg, Pennsylvania Office: 320 Market Street, Suite E400, Strawberry Square, 17108. Telephone: 717-232-8199. Facsimile: 717-232-8720.
Pittsburgh, Pennsylvania Office: 601 Grant Street, 15219. Telephone: 412-594-2300. Facsimile: 412-594-5237.
Hartford, Connecticut Office: Goodwin Square, 225 Asylum Street, 13th Floor. Telephone: 203-293-3500. Facsimile: 203-293-3555.
Newark, New Jersey Office: The Legal Center, One Riverfront Plaza, 07102. Telephone: 201-643-8000. Facsimile: 201-643-6111.
Western United States:
Los Angeles, California Office: 725 South Figueroa Street, Suite 3600, 90017-5422. Telephone: 213-955-7300. Facsimile: 213-955-7399. Telex: 678982.
Salt Lake City, Utah Office: 1000 Kearns Building, 136 South Main Street, 84101. Telephone: 801-320-6700. Facsimile: 801-359-8256.
San Francisco, California Office: One Embarcadero Center, Suite 400, 94111. Telephone: 415-951-1100. Facsimile: 415-951-1180; 951-1181. Telex: 470167.
Denver, Colorado Office: 633 17th Street, Suite 2800, 80202. Telephone: 303-291-2600. Facsimile: 303-297-0422.
Southern United States:
Jacksonville, Florida Office: 50 N. Laura Street, Suite 2800, 32202. Telephone: 904-354-8000. Facsimile: 904-353-1673.
European Community:
Brussels, Belgium Office: 14 rue Montoyer 5th Floor, 1040 Brussels. Telephone: 011-32-2-514-56 50. Facsimile: 011-32-2-514-50 48.
London, England Office: 2 Suffolk Lane, London EC4R OAT. Telephone: 011-44-171-626-3000. Facsimile: 011-44-171-626-2623. Modem: 011-44-171-626-2591.

International Trade and Investment Transactions, Natural Resources Law, Aerospace, Insurance, Tax, Intellectual Property, Commercial Law.

RESIDENT PARTNERS

JOHN I. HUHS, born 1944; admitted, 1971, New York; 1981, District of Columbia (Not admitted in Russia). *Education:* University of Washington (B.A., 1966); Stanford University M.B.A., 1970; J.D., 1970). Order of the Coif. Comment Editor, Stanford Law Review, 1967-1969. Senior Staff Member, White House Office of Management and Budget, National Security and International Affairs Management Division, 1974-1976. Member, Legal Committee, US-USSR Trade and Economic Council, 1976-1992. American Bar Association Representative to the Union International des Avocats. *Member:* The Association of the Bar of the City of New York (Chairman, Subcommittee on Relations with the Legal Profession of the USSR, Special Committee on CIS Affairs, 1989-1991); New York State (Chairman, Committee on International Investment and Development, 1986-1989) and American (Chairman, Committee on International Commercial Transactions, 1986-1990; Chairman, Committee on Soviet and Eastern European Law, 1981-1986; Member, Section of International Law and Practice; Member of Governing Council, 1988-1991; Representative to the Union International des Avocats) Bar Associations. *LANGUAGES:* Russian.

JAMES I. MANDEL, born 1942; admitted, 1983, District of Columbia (Not admitted in Russia). *Education:* Yale University (B.A., cum laude, 1964; LL.B., 1968; M.A., 1969); Columbia University (Ph.D., 1978). International Fellow, Fulbright Scholar. Administrative Officer for New Em-

(This Listing Continued)

bassy Construction, American Embassy, Moscow, 1978-1981. Contracts Administrator and Legal Consultant for Embassy Project, U.S. Department of State, Office of Foreign Buildings, 1982-1985. *LANGUAGES:* Russian.

BRIAN L. ZIMBLER, born 1958; admitted, 1986, California. *Education:* Harvard University (A.B., magna cum laude, 1980; J.D., cum laude, 1986); Fletcher School of Law and Diplomacy (M.A.L.D., 1986); Ecole Normale Superieure, Paris, France, Harvard Fellow, 1980-1981. Pontificia Universidade Catolica, Rio de Janeiro, Brazil, Rotary Fellow, 1985. Editor-in-Chief, Harvard International Law Journal, 1983-1984. Author: "Debtor State Law and Default: Enforcement of Foreign Loan Agreements in Brazilian Courts," 17 Inter-American Law Review 509, 1986; "Peacekeeping Without the UN: The Multinational Force in Lebanon and International Law," 10 Yale Journal of International Law 222, 1985; "Soviet Cooperatives and East West Trade," 17 Whittier Law Review 587, 1989; "Soviet Foreign Investment Laws and Practices, 1987-1990: A Practitioner's Perspective," 4 Transnational Lawyer 85, 1991. *LANGUAGES:* French, Portuguese and Russian.

RESIDENT ASSOCIATES

ROBERT E. D. HAWKINS, born 1963; admitted, 1994, New York. *Education:* Brown University (B.A., magna cum laude, with departmental honors, 1985); Middlebury College (M.A., with honors, 1987); Columbia University (J.D., 1992). Phi Beta Kappa. Recipient, Pushkin Prize. Fulbright-Hays Fellow. Author: (with James Mandel) "Russia Moves to Improve the Safety and Quality of Goods and Services," Survey of East European Law, Vol. 4, pg. 1 (December 1993); (with L. Charles Landgraf) "Russia Establishes a New Legal Framework for the Insurance Industry," Survey of East European Law, Vol. 4, No. 4, pg. 1 (May 1993); "RSFSR Proposes Draft on Foreign Investment," 1 Soviet and East European Law 8 (Oct. 1990); "Greater Economic Autonomy for Soviet Republics," 1 Soviet and East European Law (June/July 1990). (Also at New York, N.Y. Office). *LANGUAGES:* Russian, French, Hungarian.

BEATA I. JOSTMEIER, born 1960; admitted, 1989, New York (Not admitted in Russia). *Education:* Atlantic College, Leantwit Major, United Kingdom (International Baccalaureate, high honors, 1979); Duke University (B.A., magna cum laude, 1983; J.D., 1988). Phi Beta Kappa. (Also at Brussels, Belgium Office). *LANGUAGES:* Polish, English, German, Russian, Spanish.

MARGARITA G. MARTYNOVICH, born 1965; admitted, 1993, Russian Federation. *Education:* Moscow State University School of Law; Dickinson School of Law (LL.M., 1994). Edmund Muskie Fellow. *Member:* Interrepublican Bar Association. *LANGUAGES:* Russian, English, Czech, French.

ILIA E. MINIAEV, born 1963; admitted, 1988, Russian Federation. *Education:* Moscow State University School of Law (L.L.B., 1988; Ph.D., 1991). Consultant to the Russian Federation State Property Management Committee, 1991-1993. Adjunct Professor of Law, Moscow State University Law Faculty, 1991—. *LANGUAGES:* Russian, English.

(Biographical data on all Members of the Firm, Counsel, Of Counsel, in Washington, D.C.; New York, New York; Albany, New York; Boston, Massachusetts; Harrisburg, Pennsylvania; Hartford, Connecticut; Newark, New Jersey; Los Angeles, California; Salt Lake City, Utah; San Francisco, California; Jacksonville, Florida; Pittsburgh, Pennsylvania; Denver, Colorado; London, England and Brussels, Belgium are listed in the respective Biographical Sections)

LeBOEUF, LAMB, LEIBY & MacRAE

MOSCOW, RUSSIA

(See LeBoeuf, Lamb, Greene & MacRae L.L.P.)

MACLEOD DIXON

LARUSHENSKY PERULOK 15
MOSCOW 109017, RUSSIAN FEDERATION
MOSCOW, RUSSIA
Telephone: 231-5833; 231-3464
Fax: 011-7-501-882-4058

Calgary, Alberta, Canada Office: Canterra Tower, 3700, 400 3rd Avenue S.W., Calgary, Alberta, T2P 4H2. Telephone: 403-267-8222. Fax: 403-264-5973.

General Practice, Corporate Law, Commercial Law, International Trade, Banking, Securities, Energy Law, Insolvency, Debt Restructuring, Project Financing, Leveraged Buyouts, Corporate Reorganizations, Aircraft Financing, Litigation, Arbitration and Mediation, Taxation, Estate Planning, Wills, Trusts and Estate Administration, Commercial Property Development, Real Estate Conveyancing, Environmental Law, Insurance Law, Private Business, Regulatory and Administrative Law, Professional Liability Law, Intellectual Property, Pension and Employee Benefits, Personal Legal Services, Product Liability Law, Employment Law.

(For complete Biographical Data on all personnel see Professional Biographies at Calgary, Alberta, Canada)

MANNHEIMER SWARTLING

CHISTOPRUDNY BULVAR 8
101000 MOSCOW, RUSSIA
Telephone: +7 (095) 929 90 05
Telefax: +7 (095) 929 90 06

Stockholm, Sweden Office: Västra Trädgårdsgatan 15, P.O. Box 1650, S-111 86. Telephone: +46-8 613 55 00. Telefax: +46-8 613 55 01. Telex: 13082.
Gothenburg, Sweden Office: Lilla Torget 1, P.O.Box 2235, S-40314. Telephone: +46-31 10 96 00. Telefax: +46-31 10 96 01. Telex: 2591.
Helsingborg, Sweden Office: Södra Storgatan 7 P.O. Box 1384, S-251 13. Telephone: +46-42 18 02 95. Telefax: +46-42 18 42 71.
Malmö, Sweden Office: Stortorget 29, P.O. Box 4291, S-203 14. Telephone: +46-40 25 08 00. Telefax: +46-40 25 08 01. Telex: 32727.
Brussels, Begium Office: Avenue de Tervueren 13A, B-1040. Telephone: +32-2-732 22 22. Telefax: +32-2-732 96 52.
Frankfurt, Germany Office: Bockenheimer Landstrasse 97, D-60325. Telephone: +49-69 974 01 20. Telefax: +49-69 741 01 43.
Berlin, Germany Office: Haus der Schweiz, Friedrichstrasse 155-156, D-10117. Telephone: +49 30 202 20 10. Telefax: +49 30 202 20 110.
New York, New York Office: 101 Park Avenue, 10178. Telephone: +1 212 682-0580. Telefax: +1 212 682-0982.

General Business Law Practice. Joint Venture Law. Admiralty, Maritime and Carriage of Goods Law. Banking. Computer Law. Construction and Engineering Contracts and Disputes. Corporate Taxation. Industrial Property, Copyright and Trademarks. Labor Law. Mergers and Acquisitions. Real Estate Law. Litigation and Arbitration.

RESPONSIBLE PARTNERS

Bengt Sjövall   **Kaj Hobér**

RESIDENT ASSOCIATES

Jonas Bratt   **Alexander Zyuba**
Alexander Kozlovski

(For biographical data on all personnel, see Professional Biographies at Stockholm, Sweden)

McKENNA & CO

MOSENKA PLAZA
24/27 SADOVAYA-SAMOTYOCHNAYA STREET, RUSSIAN FEDERATION
MOSCOW 103051, RUSSIA
Telephone: (7 501) 258 5000
Fax: (7 501) 258 5100

London, England Office: Mitre House, 160 Aldersgate Street, EC1A 4DD. Telephone: 0171 606 9000. Telex: 27251. Fax: 0171-606 9100. CDE Box 724.
London Lloyd's Office: 908 Lloyd's, One Lime Street, London EC3M 7DQ. Telephone: 0171-929 1250. Fax: 0171-626 5749 DX Box 724.

(This Listing Continued)

McKenna & Co, Moscow—Continued

Brussels, Belgium Office: Avenue de Cortenberg 66, Box 10, B-1040. Telephone: (32)(2)735.38.36. Telex: 27122. Fax: (32)(2)735.77.43.

Budapest, Hungary Office: H-1122. Maros utca 22, 1st Floor. Telephone: (36)(1) 202 6527; (36)(1) 202 6936; (36)(1) 201 9199; (36)(1) 156 5354. Fax: (36)(1) 156 5391.

Moscow, Russia Office: McKenna & Co, International, MosenkáPlaza, 24/27 Sadovaya-Samotyochnaya Street, Russian Federation, Moscow, 103051. Telephone: (7 501) 258 5000. Fax: (7 501)258 5100.

Prague, Czech Republic Office: Betlémský palác, First Floor, Husova 5, 110 00 Prague 1. Telephone: (42)(2) 2424 8518-22. Fax: 42(2) 2424 8524.

Warsaw, Poland Office: McKenna & Co Sp. zo.o., ul. Kopernika 30, Suite 213, 00-950, Warsaw. Telephone: (48) 22 26 69 88. Fax: (48) 22 26 41 93.

Hong Kong Office: 5th Floor, Lippo Tower, 89 Queensway, Hong Kong. Telephone: (852) 846 9100. Fax: (852) 845 3575.

Associated Firms:

Sigle Loose Schmidt-Diemitz and Partners: Stuttgart, Berlin, Leipzig, Frankfurt/Main, Chemnitz and Moscow.

Minter Ellison: Sydney, Melbourne, Canberra, Brisbane and the Gold Coast.

Firm advises foreign investors on corporate and corporate finance matters in the Russian Federation, and client companies based in Russia on all aspects of Russian corporate and commercial law (including privatisation, tax, employment, intellectual property, banking, property). Entitled to appear before the Russian Commercial Court.

PARTNER

ELENA KIRILLOVA, LL.B. (N.S.W. Australia), admitted 1991.

RESIDENT LAWYER

TATIANA VINOGRADOVA, admitted, 1974.

Languages: English, French and Russian

MILBANK, TWEED, HADLEY & McCLOY

24/27 SADOVAYA-SAMOTYOCHNAYA
MOSCOW 103051, RUSSIA
Telephone: 7-502-258-5015
Fax: 7-502-258-5014

New York, New York Office: 1 Chase Manhattan Plaza, 10005. Telephone: 212-530-5000. Cable Address: "Miltweed NYK" ITT: 422962; 423893. Fax: 212- 530-5219. ABA/net: Milbank NY.

Midtown Office: 50 Rockefeller Plaza, 10020. Telephone: 212-530-5800. Fax: 212-530-0158.

Los Angeles, California Office: 601 South Figueroa Street, 30th Floor, 90017. Telephone: 213-892-4000. Fax: 213-629-5063. Telex: 678754. ABA/net: Milbank LA.

Washington, D.C. Office: Suite 1100, 1825 Eye Street, N.W., 20006. Telephone: 202-835-7500. Cable Address: "Miltweed Wsh". ITT 440667. Fax: 202-835-7586. ABA/net: Milbank DC.

Tokyo, Japan Office: Nippon Press Center Building, 2-1, Uchisaiwai-cho 2-chome, Chiyoda-ku, Tokyo 100. Telephone: 81-3-3504-1050. Fax: 81-3-3595-2790, 81-3-3502-5192.

London, England Office: Ropemaker Place, 25 Ropemaker Street, EC2Y 9AS. Telephone: 44-171-374-0423. Cable Address: "Miltuk G." Fax: 44-171-374-0912.

Hong Kong Office: 3007 Alexandra House, 16 Chater Road. Telephone: 852-2526-5281. Fax: 852-2840-0792, 852-2845-9046. ABA/net: Milbank HK.

Singapore Office: 14-02 Caltex House, 30 Raffles Place, 0104. Telephone: 65-534-1700. Fax: 65-534-2733. ABA/net: Milbank EDNANG.

Jakarta, Indonesia Correspondent Office: Makarim & Taira S., 17th Floor, Jl, Jend. Sudirman 61, Jakarta. Telephone: 62-211252-1272 or 2460. Fax: 62-21-252-2750 or 2751.

Firm engaged in New York and United States Federal and International Law Practice but not Authorized to appear before Russian Courts or Administrative Agencies or to act as Russian Solicitors.

RESIDENT ASSOCIATE

IRINA MASHLENKO, born Moscow, 1960. *Education:* University of Moscow, Institute of State and Law (1982).

NÖRR, STIEFENHOFER & LUTZ

Established in 1994
UL. LEVOBEREZHNAYA, 32
125475 MOSCOW, RUSSIA
Telephone: 7-095-4585822; 7-095-4585792
Telecopier: 7-095-4585782

Munich, Germany (Head Office): Brienner Str. 28. 80333 Munich, Postfach 1001121, 80085 Munich. Telephone: 49-89-280111. Telecopier: 49-89-280110.

Frankfurt/Main, Germany Office: Freiherr-vom-Stein-Straße 11, 60323 Frankfurt/Main. Telephone: 49-69-172917. Telecopier: 49-69-172916.

Berlin, Germany Office: Schlüterstraße 36, D-10629 Berlin. Telephone: 49-30-8836700. Telecopier: 49-30-8835052.

Dresden, Germany Office: Böhmertstraße 3, 01099 Dresden. Telephone: 49-351-5671188, 49-351-5671187. Telecopier: 49-351-5671186.

Prague, Czech Republic Office: Masarykovo nábřeži 30, 11000 Prague 1. Telephone: 42-2-24913396, 42-2-24913882. Telecopier: 42-2-24911836.

Budapest, Hungary Office: Becsí utca 5/I. 1-2, 1052 Budapest V. Telephone: 36-1-1174905; 36-1-1378293. Telecopier: 36-1-1184035.

Warsaw, Poland Office: Kancelaria Adwokacka Sp. Z o. o. UL. Nowogrodzka 50, 00950 Warsaw. Telephone: 48-2-6216232. Telecopier: 48-2-6251976.

Brussels, Belgium EEC Office: 106 Avenue Louise, 1050 Brussels. Telephone: 32-2-6470650. Telecopier: 32-2-6464729.

General and International Practice, Privatization, Mergers and Acquisitions, Joint Ventures, Corporate Law, Commercial Law, Real Estate and Investment Law, Labour Law, Banking and Foreign Exchange Law, Intellectual Property and Trademark Law, Tax and Customs Law, Law relating to Commercial Leases, Competition and Anti-Trust Law.

PARTNER IN CHARGE

DR. ECKART RABICH, born Berlin, Germany, March 22, 1940; admitted, 1968, Germany. *Education:* Universities of Berlin, Tübingen and Cologne. *Member:* German Bar Association; German Society for the Protection of Industrial Property and Copyright Law. (Also, Partner in charge of Warsaw Office). *LANGUAGES:* German and English. *PRACTICE AREAS:* Corporate Law; Company Law; Joint Ventures.

ASSOCIATES

CHRISTINE HÜPER, born Peine, Germany, June 10, 1961; admitted, 1994, Germany. *Education:* University of Berlin. *LANGUAGES:* German, Russian, English, Spanish. *PRACTICE AREAS:* Civil Law; Public Law; Russian Commercial Law.

OF COUNSEL

GENNADYJ B. LUKIN, born Moscow, Russia, July 27, 1957. *Education:* Moscow State University; Academy of Foreign Trade. *LANGUAGES:* Russian, German. *PRACTICE AREAS:* Commercial Law; Corporate Law; Real Estate; Privatization Law.

Languages: German, English and Russian.

NORTON ROSE

BOLSHOI SUKHAREVSKY PEREULOK 26
103051 MOSCOW, RUSSIA
Telephone: +7 095 244 3639
*Telephone: (Satellite)** +7 502 220 4211*
Fax: +7 095 244 3968
*Fax: (Satellite)** +7 502 220 4212*
***International calls only*

Other Offices: London, Bahrain, Brussels, Hong Kong, Paris, Piraeus, Prague and Singapore.

FIRM PROFILE: Norton Rose is a leading City and International law firm with its principal office in the City of London. The firm provides a wide range of legal services primarily to the business and financial communities as well as to a number of sovereign governments and state organizations. We are known particularly for our corporate and debt finance, banking, company and commercial law, natural resources, insurance, property development, aerospace and maritime practices and wide-ranging expertise on tax matters. Norton Rose has a major litigation department handling all forms of commercial dispute resolution.

In Moscow the firm specialises in assets finance; banking; commercial and residential property; companies, corporations; natural resources; privatisations; project finance; securitisations.

(This Listing Continued)

RESIDENT LAWYERS

MARCIA LEVY, admitted, 1976, England and Wales.

Languages: English, Russian, Ukrainian, French and German

(For Complete Biographical Data on all Personnel, see Professional Biographies at London, England).

PATTERSON, BELKNAP, WEBB & TYLER, LLP

KONUSHKOVSKAYA 26
MOSCOW 123242, RUSSIA
Telephone: 011-7095-253-9607
Telephone/Fax: 011-7502-221-1857; 011-7095-564-8063

New York, New York Office: 1133 Avenue of the Americas. Telephone: 212-336-2000. Fax: 212-336-2222.

General Practice.

MEMBERS OF FIRM

PETER J. PETTIBONE, born Schenectady, New York, December 11, 1939; admitted, 1965, Pennsylvania and District of Columbia; 1968, New York; 1974, U.S. Supreme Court (Not admitted in Russia). *Education:* Woodrow Wilson School, Princeton University (A.B., summa cum laude, 1961, Phi Beta Kappa); Harvard University (J.D., 1964); New York University (LL.M., 1971). U.S. Co-Chairman, Legal Committee of the U.S.-U.S.S.R. Trade and Economic Council, Inc., 1980-1992. Director, U.S.-Russia Business Council, 1992—. Member, Council on Foreign Relations, 1993—. Editor, treatise, *Laws of the USSR,* Parker School, 1989-1991. *Member:* The Association of the Bar of the City of New York (Member: Committee on Housing and Urban Development, 1975-1978; Committee on Foreign and Comparative Law, 1981-1985; Committee on International Law, 1985-1988; Committee on International Trade Law, 1988-1991; Special Committee on the Independent States of the former Soviet Union, 1989—, Chairman, 1991-1994); American Bar Association. *PRACTICE AREAS:* Corporate Law; International Law; Securities Regulation Law.

ASSOCIATES

NATASHA ANTONOVA, *Education:* Moscow Juridical Institute (1988). Assistant Director, Institute of State and Law, 1983-1990. Researcher, All-Union Research Institute of Soviet Legislation, 1981-1983.

ALEXANDER G. DNEPROVSKI, *Education:* Moscow State Institute for International Affairs and International Law (MGIMO); Institute of State and Law (Kandidat). Legal Department, State Committee for Foreign Trade, 1977-1978. With Ministry for International Affairs (IMIMO), Institute of World Economy and Legal Problems, 1978-1979.

MIKHAIL Y. GALYATIN, *Education:* Institute of State and Law (Doctor of Juridical Science, 1984); Columbia University, School of International and Public Affairs (M.P.A., 1990). Assistant to Deputy Prime Minister for Environmental Law and Policy, Assistant to Deputy Prime Minister for Inter-State Economic Relations and Special Advisor to Minister for Foreign Economic Relations, Russian Federation. President and CEO, Rus-Consult.

LUDMILLA JACKOVA, *Education:* Moscow Juridical Institute (1975). Attorney, Tula, 1975-1981. Member, Republican Bar, 1981-1989.

GALINA F. STRIKHANOVA, *Education:* Kharkov Juridical Institute (Ukraine) (1972). Advocate, Dnepeopetrovsk Bar Association, 1972-1975. Attorney, Belgord, 1975-1978.

(For Biographical data on all personnel, see Professional Biographies at New York, New York)

PEPPER, HAMILTON & SCHEETZ

Established in 1890

19-27 GROKHOLSKY PEREULOK
MOSCOW 129010, RUSSIA
Telephone: (7) 095-280-4493
Telecopy: (7) 095-280-5518

Philadelphia, Pennsylvania Office: 3000 Two Logan Square, Eighteenth and Arch Streets, 19103-2799. Telephone: 215-981-4000. Fax: 215-981-4750.

Washington, D.C. Office: 1300 Nineteenth Street, N.W., 20036-1685. Telephone: 202-828-1200. Fax: 202-828-1665.

(This Listing Continued)

Detroit, Michigan Office: 100 Renaissance Center, 36th Floor, 48243-1157. Telephone: 313-259-7110. Fax: 313-259-7926.

Harrisburg, Pennsylvania Office: 200 One Keystone Plaza, North Front and Market Streets, P.O. Box 1181, 17108-1181. Telephone: 717-255-1155. Fax: 717-238-0575.

Berwyn, Pennsylvania Office: 1235 Westlakes Drive, Suite 400, 19312-2401. Telephone: 610-640-7800. Fax: 610-640-7835.

New York, New York Office: 450 Lexington Avenue, Suite 1600, 10017-3904. Telephone: 212-878-3800. Fax: 212-878-3835.

Wilmington, Delaware Office: 1201 Market Street, Suite 1401, P.O. Box 1709, 19899-1709. Telephone: 302-571-6555. Fax: 302-656-8865.

Westmont, New Jersey Office: Sentry Office Plaza, Suite 321, 216 Haddon Avenue, 08108-2811. Telephone: 609-869-9555. Fax: 609-869-9595.

London, England Office: City Tower, 40 Basinghall Street, EC2V 5DE. Telephone: 011-44-171-628-1122. Fax: 011-44-171-628-6010.

PARTNER

EDWARD H. LIEBERMAN, born New York, NY, 1950; admitted, 1975, New York; 1977, District of Columbia; 1978, U.S. Supreme Court; 1982, U.S. Tax Court (Not admitted in Russia). *Education:* City College of the City University of New York (B.A., Valedictorian, 1971); Brooklyn Law School (J.D., 1974); London School of Economics, London, England (LL.M., 1975). Author: "Whether and to What Extent a Foreign Tax Is Creditable under Final Regulations," Journal of Taxation, 1984; "A Foreign Tax Under New Proposed Foreign Tax Credit Regulations," Bulletin for International Fiscal Documentation, 1983; "The Foreign Sales Corporation," Tax Management International Journal, March, 1985; "Analysis of the Foreign Sales Corporation - Temporary Regulations," Tax Management Memorandum, April, 1985; "Foreign Sales Corporation - Recent Developments," Tax Management Memorandum, February, 1986. Co-Author: "The Foreign Sales Corporation," BNA Portfolio, June, 1988; "Comparison of Soviet and Hungarian Legislation on Joint Ventures," Washington University International Law Journal, 1991; "Soviet Income Taxation," CCH Portfolio Series, 1991. Speeches: "The Foreign Tax Credit," World Trade Institute; "The Foreign Sales Corporation," Tax Management Memorandum Board of Advisors; "The Foreign Presence Requirements of the Foreign Sales Corporation," GULC - U.S. Chamber of Commerce FSC Conference; "Proposed Legislation Creating the Foreign Sales Corporation," National Association of Manufacturers Seminar on the Foreign Sales Corporation; "Section 999 - U.S. Boycott Rules," I.R.S. Annual Meeting of Northeast Regional Examination Directors; "Affirmative Use of FSCs to Avoid Independent Factory Pricing," Tax Management Memorandum Board of Advisors; "Soviet Income Taxation," Worldwide Information, Inc.; "U.S. Export Tax Incentives," ALI-ABA; "Hungarian Income Taxation," Toronto Conference on Hungary and the West. Advisor, World Bank and the Hungarian Government on the New Hungarian Income Tax Law, 1989—. Chair, Soviet and Eastern European Tax Subcommittee, National Foreign Trade Council's Soviet and Eastern European Task Force, 1990—. *Member:* International Bar Association. (Also at Washington, D.C. Office). *PRACTICE AREAS:* Taxation Law; Transactional Law; Investment in Russia.

OF COUNSEL

LARISA A. AFANASYEVA, born Samarkand, Former Soviet Union, 1957; admitted, 1980, Russia; 1992, New York. *Education:* Moscow State Institute of International Relations (MGIMO), Russia (Diploma of Lawyer, 1980); Institute of State and Law USSR Academy of Sciences (IGPAN), Moscow, Russia (Ph.D., 1984); Harvard University (LL.M., 1992). Author: *Nuclear Insurance:* Comparative Law Study, (Nauka, 1989); Research Scholar, IGPAN, 1984-1989. Adjunct Professor of International Private Law, MGIMO, 1981-1989. Assistant to Arbitration Court of USSR Chamber of Commerce and Industry, 1984-1989. (Also at Washington, D.C. Office). *LANGUAGES:* Russian, English, Spanish and French. *PRACTICE AREAS:* Russian Law; East-West Trade; Foreign Investments and Privatization.

SALLY J. MARCH, born Algoma, WI, 1955; admitted, 1980, California; 1982, Wisconsin (Not admitted in Russia). *Education:* Lawrence University (B.A., cum laude, 1977); University of California, Hastings (J.D., with honors, 1980); University of London (LL.M., 1987). Author: "Protecting Computer Software: Creative Solutions to Creative Problems," Patent World, July 1987. Co-author: "Joint Ventures in the USSR," World Wide Information, Inc., 1989. *Member:* International Bar Association. (Also at London, England Office). *LANGUAGES:* Russian. *PRACTICE AREAS:* International Law.

WILLIAM B. SIMONS, born Dodgeville, WI, 1949; admitted, 1974, Wisconsin (Not admitted in Russia). *Education:* Carleton College (B.A., cum laude, 1971); University of Wisconsin-Madison (J.D., 1974). Member,

(This Listing Continued)

PEPPER, HAMILTON & SCHEETZ, Moscow—Continued

INTERGU (International Copyright Society). Author: "New Laws Allow Foreign Investment in East Germany," International Financial Law Review, March 1990; *Soviet Foreign Trade and the Economy:* An Overview, Soviet Law and Economy, 1987; *The Soviet Codes of Law,* 2nd ed. 1984; *The Constitutions of the Communist World,* 1980. Co-editor, *The Encyclopedia of Soviet Law,* 2nd rev. ed., 1985. Co-translator, *The Soviet Approach to Private International Law* by M. M. Boguslavskii, 1988. (Also at Washington, D.C. Office). *LANGUAGES:* Russian, German and Dutch. *PRACTICE AREAS:* East/West Practice; Intellectual Property Law.

PÜNDER, VOLHARD, WEBER & AXSTER

UL. WOLCHONKA, 18/2
121019 MOSCOW, RUSSIA
Telephone: (7)(095) 202-64 90; (7)(095) 202 65 12
(7)(543) 708 00 900 from Germany;
(49)(7545) 893 42 from other countries
Fax: (7)(095) 202-65 14;
(7)(543) 708 00 990 from Germany;
(49)(7545) 893 43 from other countries

Frankfurt/Main, Germany Office: Mainzer Landstrasse 46, 60325 Frankfurt/Main. Telephone: (49)(69) 71 99-01. Fax: (49)(69) 71 99-4000. Telex: 414 827.

Düsseldorf, Germany Office: Cecilienallee 6, 40474 Düsseldorf. Telephone: (49)(211) 43 55-0. Fax: (49)(211) 43 55-600.

Berlin, Germany Office: Katharina-Heinroth-Ufer, 10787 Berlin. Telephone: (49)(30) 2546 5800. Fax: (49)(30) 2546 5900.

Leipzig, Germany Office: Burgplatz 7, 04109 Leipzig. Telephone: (49)(341) 21 49-0. Fax: (49)(341) 21 49-600.

Beijing, People's Republic of China Office: Suite C 603, Beijing Lufthansa Center, 50 Liangmaqiao Road, Beijing 100 016. Telephone: (86)(1) 465 15 68; (86)(1) 465 18 08; (86)(1) 465 13 45. Fax: (86)(1) 467 12 56.

Brussels, Belgium Office: Rue d'Arlon 92, 1040 Bruxelles. Telephone: (32)(2) 230 90 11. Fax: (32)(2) 231 19 55.

Budapest, Hungary Office: Endrödy Sandor utca 48, 1026 Budapest. Telephone: (36) 60 33 26 18 international; (6) 60 33 26 18 national. Fax: (36) 60 33 26 17 international; (6) 60 33 26 17 national.

New York, New York Office: 152 West 57th Street, Carnegie Hall Tower, New York, N.Y. 10019. Telephone: (1)(212) 582 28 28. Fax: (1)(212) 582 24 24.

Warsaw, Poland Office: ul. Jasna 1, 00-013 Warszawa. Telephone: (48) 39 12 21 41. Fax: (48)(22) 27 15 29.

Administrative Law; Antitrust Law; Arbitration; Auditing and Valuations; Banking, Securities and Finance; Bankruptcy; Building Law; Chinese Law; Commercial Crime; Computer Law; Construction Law; Corporate Law; EU Law; Energy Law; Environmental Law; Franchising; Industrial Property Law; Insolvency; Intellectual Property Law; International and German Business Law; Labor and Employment Law; Litigation; Media Law; Mergers and Acquisitions; Pharmaceutical Law; Privatizations; Product Law; Public Law; Real Estate; Reorganizations; Russian Law; Tax Law; Telecommunications; Unfair Trade Law.

FIRM PROFILE: *Member of PÜNDER GROUP*

Members:

- *BURUMA MARIS, The Hague, Rotterdam*

- *CERHA, HEMPEL & SPIEGELFELD, Wien*

- *COPPENS, VAN OMMESLAGHE, HORSMANS & FAURES, Bruxelles*

- *DE PARDIEU-LACOURTE G.I.E., Paris*

- *PÜNDER, VOLHARD, WEBER & AXSTER, Frankfurt/Main, Düsseldorf, Berlin, Leipzig*

- *STOFFEL & PARTNER, Zürich, Genève.*

Joint Offices of PÜNDER GROUP:

Beijing - Bruxelles - Budapest - Moskwa - New York - Warszawa

MEMBERS OF FIRM

DR. GERD LENGA, born Stuttgart, Germany, July 8, 1947; admitted, 1988, Stuttgart; 1993, Frankfurt; 1977, sworn Translator for Russian and Polish (Not admitted in Russia). *Education:* Universities of Tübingen, Warsaw and Leningrad. Co-Editor: "WiRO - Wirtschaft und Recht Os-

(This Listing Continued)

teuropas," München 1992 ff. *Member:* German-Russian Forum; Society for Russian-German Economic Law; Society for East European Studies. (Also at Frankfurt/Main, Germany Office). *LANGUAGES:* German, English, Russian, Polish and French. *PRACTICE AREAS:* Law of the Commonwealth of Independent States; Commercial and Corporate Law; Competition and Antitrust Law; Real Estate; Telecommunications; Energy Law.

DR. HERMANN W. SCHMITT, born Kassel, Germany, May 15, 1961; admitted, 1989, Frankfurt/Main. *Education:* Universities of Marburg and Giessen. Judge, Civil Court, 1989-1990. Author: "Die Einrede des Schiedsvertrags im Verfahren des einstweiligen Rechtsschutzes," 1987; "Einstweiliger Rechtsschutz gegen drohende Gesellschafterbeschlüsse in der GmbH?" 1992. Co-Author: "Privatization in Eastern Germany: Legal Concepts and their Possible Value to Others," 1993. *Member:* International Bar Association; Society for Russian-German Economic Law. *LANGUAGES:* German, English and Russian. *PRACTICE AREAS:* Company Law; Arbitration; Privatizations; Mergers and Acquisitions; Project Finance.

ASSOCIATES

LJUDMILA M. LJOSCHINA, born Chmelnizki, Ukraine, May 5, 1954. *Education:* Lomonosow University of Moscow. Activities at the Ministry of Petrochemical Industry of the (former) USSR and at the wholesale association "Rasobuwtorg"; Head of Legal Department of the weekly journal "Stoliza". *LANGUAGES:* Russian, Ukrainian and English. *PRACTICE AREAS:* Company Law; Real Estate; Contract Law; Commercial Leases.

SWETLANA G. BYSTROWA, born Leningrad, USSR, May 9, 1969; admitted, 1992, Russia. *Education:* Lomonosow University of Moscow. *Member:* International Bar Association; Moscow Bar Association. *LANGUAGES:* Russian, German, English and Italian. *PRACTICE AREAS:* Foreign Trade Law; Litigation/Arbitration; Intellectual Property Law; Industrial Property Law.

KONSTANTIN W. SCHACHOW, born Moscow, USSR, March 9, 1969. *Education:* Lomonosow University of Moscow. *LANGUAGES:* Russian, German and English. *PRACTICE AREAS:* Private International Law; Labor Law; Real Estate; Banking; Stock Exchange and Securities Law; Privatizations.

MICHAEL MÜLLER, born Lahnstein, Germany, February 16, 1964; admitted, 1993, Frankfurt/Main. *Education:* Universities of Bonn and Berlin. *Member:* Society for Russian-German Economic Law. *LANGUAGES:* German, English, French and Russian. *PRACTICE AREAS:* Russian Economic Law.

DMITRIJ A. ALPETJAN, born Moscow, USSR, June 23, 1967. *Education:* Lomonosow University of Moscow. *LANGUAGES:* Russian and German. *PRACTICE AREAS:* Constitutional Law; Administrative Law; Banking Law; Real Estate.

TENGIZ G. GUMBARIDZE, born Tbilisi, Republic of Georgia, July 15, 1967. *Education:* Lomonosow University of Moscow. *LANGUAGES:* Georgian, Russian and English. *PRACTICE AREAS:* Civil Law; Labor Law; International Business Law; Foreign Trade Law.

TAX ADVISERS

MAG. MARCO KOSCHIER, born Vienna, Austria, July 31, 1964 (Not admitted to bar). *Education:* University of Graz. Head of the East European Tax and Foreign Exchange group of the Legal department in a major European corporation. *LANGUAGES:* German, English and Russian. *PRACTICE AREAS:* Tax Law; Foreign Exchange and Currency Law; Accounting.

WALENTINA D. LEWKOWITSCH, born Irkutsk, USSR, May 26, 1949. *Education:* Institute for Political Economy in Irkutsk. *LANGUAGES:* Russian and English. *PRACTICE AREAS:* Accounting; Auditing.

(For complete biographical data on personnel at Frankfurt/Main, Düsseldorf, Berlin and Leipzig, Germany, Brussels, Belgium, Warsaw, Poland, New York, New York, Beijing, People's Republic of China, see Professional Biographies at those locations)

PUSCHNER & POIGNER

Established in 1989

STAROKONJUSHENNYI PEREULOK 1
SU-119 034 MOSCOW, RUSSIA
Telephone: +7 095 201 7308
Fax: +7 230 2687
Telex: 413399 ATORG SU

Alternate Number, Vienna, Austria: +43 1 513 80 91.
Vienna, Austria Office: Schubertring 8, A-1010 Wein I. Telephone: +222
513 80 91 series. Telefax: +43 1 513 86 66. Telex: 75 211358 ewla a.
Budapest, Hungary Office: Ferenczy Istvan Ut. 14, H-1053. Telephone &
Fax: Ø137 84 08.

*Banking, Corporate, Commercial, Taxation, Property, Contract and Real
Estate Law, International Transactions and Arbitration.*

DR. JOHANN POIGNER, born Altmünster, Austria, September 26,
1953; admitted, 1990, Austria. *Education:* University of Vienna, Salzburg
(1986). Author: "USSR - The New Stock Corporation Law and New Law
on Limited Liability Companies," Austria Business & Economy, 1990;
"Laws in the First Phase of Economic Reforms," USSR, 1990; "Who Will Be
Able to Cope With The Flood of Laws?" Austria Business & Economy,
1990. *Member:* East-West Lawyers Association; Austria Lawyers Association.

ASSOCIATES

DR. KATALIN LEHNER, born Budapest, Hungary, July 15, 1968. *Education:* University Budapest (Dr. jur., 1992); University Vienna; Professorial Assistant, Institute of Comparative Law. *LANGUAGES:* Hungarian,
German and Russian.

LEGAL SUPPORT PERSONNEL

GRIGORIJ DJOMIN. *Education:* University of Moscow (1992).

Languages: German, English, Russian and Hungarian.

(For biographical data, see Professional Biographies at Vienna, Austria)

RODGERS, MILLER, ELLISON & HOLT P.C.

103798, GSP, MOSCOW K-6 CENTRE
NASTASINSKY 2 R. 303 RUSSIA
MOSCOW, RUSSIA
Telephone: 7095 200 3400
Fax: 7095 209 3757

Bryan, Texas, Office: 4444 Carter Creek Parkway, Suite 208. P.O. Box
4884. Telephone: 409-260-9911. Facsimile: 409-846-7083.

Oil and Gas, Commercial and Taxation Law.

CHARLES A. ELLISON, born Clovis, New Mexico, October 31, 1953;
admitted, 1979, Texas, U.S. District Court, Southern and Western Districts
of Texas and U.S. Court of Military Appeals. *Education:* Texas A & M University (B.B.A., cum laude, 1976); Texas Tech University (J.D., with honors, 1979). Phi Eta Sigma; Phi Alpha Delta. *Member:* Brazos County Bar
Association; State Bar of Texas (Member, Sections on: Real Estate, Probate
and Trust; Corporation, Banking and Business); College of the State Bar of
Texas; Texas Association of Bank Counsel; Independent Banking Association of Texas Attorneys Counsel. [Capt., JAGC, U.S. Army, 1979-1983].
PRACTICE AREAS: Real Estate Law; Banking Law; Business Law; Commercial Litigation.

LEGAL SUPPORT PERSONNEL

EUGENE TITOV (Resident Paralegal).

REPRESENTATIVE CLIENTS: Russian Petroleum Consultants Corporation;
Alexander Khachatryan.

ROTHSTEIN & SHAW, P.C.

BUILDING 1, FIRST FLOOR
26 BOLSHOI SUHAREVSKI PEREULOK
103051 MOSCOW, RUSSIA
*Telephone: 7(095) 208-9839; 7(095) 208-9859; 7(095) 208-9608; 7(501)
207-5593*
Facsimile: 7(095) 208-9822; 7(501) 207-5590; 7(501) 207-5591

Almaty, Kazakhstan Office: 10a Abaia Prospect, 11th Floor, Suite 5,
480018. Telephone: 7(3272) 633-454. Facsimile: 7(3272) 638-637.

Corporate Law, Securities Law, Real Estate Law.
*Firm engaged in the practice of general corporate law in the Russian Fed-
eration and the Republic of Kazakhstan.*

*FIRM PROFILE: Established in 1994 by Mr. Britt Allen Shaw, founder
of the Joint Stock Service Company and Mr. Daniel J. Rothstein, who
formerly practiced as Daniel J. Rothstein & Associates, P.C. The firm consists of two American lawyers and two Russian lawyers and has a broadly-
based practice providing a wide range of legal services to the foreign business community in the Russian Federation and Kazakhstan.*

BRITT ALLEN SHAW, born Springfield, Missouri, August 26, 1960;
admitted, 1989, New York. *Education:* Johns Hopkins University (B.A.,
1986); Columbia University Law School (J.D., 1989). Editor-in-Chief, Columbia Law School News, 1985-1986. Associate, Skadden, Arps, Slate,
Meagher & Flom, New York, N.Y., 1989-1991. President, Joint Stock Service Company, Moscow, Russian Federation, 1992-1994. *LANGUAGES:*
English and Russian.

DANIEL J. ROTHSTEIN, born York, Pennsylvania, July 21, 1956;
admitted, 1986, New York. *Education:* Cornell University (A.B., 1978;
J.D., 1985); Hebrew University of Jerusalem (M.A., cum laude, 1983). Editor-in-Chief, Cornell International Law Journal, 1984-1985. Author: "Adjudication of Freedom of Expression Cases Under Israel's Unwritten Constitution," Cornell International Law Journal, Vol. 18, 1985. Recipient, Justice
Robert H. Jackson Award, Washington Foreign Law Society, 1985. Law
Clerk to: Chief Judge Howard G. Munson, U.S. District Court, Northern
District of New York, 1985-1986; Judge Albert J. Engel, U.S. Court of Ap-
peals, Sixth Circuit, 1986-1987; Judges Aharon Barak and Eliezer Gold-
berg, Israel Supreme Court, 1990-1991. Associate: Stein, Zauderer, Ellen-
hirn, Frischer & Sharp, New York, N.Y., 1987-1990; Coudert Brothers,
Moscow, 1990-1991. Legal Advisor, State Committee for Management of
State Property, Russian Federation, 1992-1993. Member, International
Advisory Board, Russian Federation Bankruptcy Agency. *LANGUAGES:*
English, Russian, Hebrew and German.

ALEXANDER S. GOLUBNICHY, born Moscow, USSR, September
27, 1970; admitted, 1992, Russia. *Education:* Moscow State Institute of
Foreign Relations, International Law Faculty, Department of Private and
Trade Law (1992). Legal Department, H.I. Development Corporation,
1989-1992. Vice-President, Joint Stock Service Company, 1992-1994. *LAN-
GUAGES:* Russian, English and Spanish.

ALEXANDRA SEREDA, born Moscow, USSR, February 10, 1970;
admitted, 1992, Russia. *Education:* Moscow State University, Faculty of
Law (1992). Recipient, Gold Medal, Moscow State University, 1992. Legal
Department, State Foreign-Trade Organization "Sovintersport," 1992-1993.
Sole Practitioner, 1993-1994. *LANGUAGES:* Russian and English.

RUSSIN & VECCHI

International Legal Counselors

DANILOVSKY HOTEL COMPLEX
BOLSHOY STARODANILOVSKY PEREULOK NO. 5
113191 MOSCOW, RUSSIA
Telephone: 7-095-954-0652
Telex: 612506 RVMO SU.
E-Mail: Sprintmail X.400
Fax: 7-095-954-0653

Bangkok, Thailand Office: Russin & Vecchi, International Legal
Counsellors Thailand, Ltd., Sathorn City Tower, 175 South Sathorn
Road, 18th Floor, 10120. Telephone: 662-679-6005, 662-679-6015.
Fax: 662-679-6041, 662-679-6042.
Hanoi, Vietnam Office: Russin & Vecchi, 25 Ly Thuong Kiet Street.
Telephone: (84-4) 251-699/251-700. Fax: (84-4) 251-742.

(This Listing Continued)

EU1181B

RUSSIN & VECCHI, Moscow—Continued

Ho Chi Minh City, Vietnam Office: Russin & Vecchi, OSIC Building, 6/F, 8 Nguyen Hue Street. Telephone: (84-8) 243-026/243-114. Fax: (84-8) 243-113.

New York, New York Office: Russin & Vecchi, 15th Floor, 90 Park Avenue, 10016-1387. Telephone: 212-210-9543. Fax: 212-210-9493.

Puerto Plata, Dominican Republic Office: Russin Vecchi & Heredia Bonetti, Plaza Turisol Local #11A. Telephone: 809-586-5535. Fax: 809-586-5861.

San Francisco, California Office: Russin & Vecchi, 16th Floor, 580 California Street, 94104. Telephone: 415-421-1100. Fax: 415-421-1103.

Santo Domingo, Dominican Republic Office: Russin Vecchi & Heredia Bonetti, Edificio Monte Mirador, Calle El Recodo No 2, Esquina Winston Churchill, Bella Vista, Apartado Postal 425. Telephone: 809-535-9511. Cable Address: "RUSVEC SANTO DOMINGO." Telex: 3264199 RUSVEC. Fax: 809-535-6649.

Taipei, Taiwan Office: Russin & Vecchi, 9th Floor, 205 Tun Hwa N. Road. Telephone: (886-2) 712-8956. Fax: (886-2) 713-4711.

Washington, D.C. Office: Russin & Vecchi, Second Floor, 1140 Connecticut Avenue, N.W., 20036. Telephone: 202-223-4793. Fax: 202-223-4810.

International and Russian Commercial Law. Corporate, Joint Ventures, Foreign Investment, Contracts, Trade, Tax, Labor and Litigation.

JONATHAN RUSSIN, born Kingston, Pennsylvania, 1937; admitted, 1964, District of Columbia (Not admitted in Russia). *Education:* Yale University (B.A., 1959; J.D., 1963). Recipient, Order of Prince St. Vladimir, Russian Orthodox Church. Co-Author: "Forming A Russian Company," sponsored by the Embassy of the Russian Federation in Washington, D.C., 1994; Co-Author: "Forming A Dominican Company," 10th Edition, American Chamber of Commerce of the Dominican Republic, 1987; "Laws Affecting Franchise Operations in Spain," American Bar Association, 1982. With Office of the General Counsel, Agency for International Development, U.S. Department of State, 1964-1969 (Regional Legal Adviser, Caribbean Area, 1967-1969). Chair, Advisory Council, Institute for European, Russian and Eurasian Studies, George Washington University, 1991-1993. General Counsel, Orthodox Church in America. Washington Representative, Russian Orthodox Church. *Member:* The District of Columbia Bar; American Bar Association; Inter-American Bar Association. (Also at Washington, D.C. and Santo Domingo, Dominican Republic Offices). *LANGUAGES:* English, Spanish and Russian.

SERGEI L. LAZAREV, born Kuibyshev (Samara), USSR, 1961; admitted, 1983, Russia. *Education:* Moscow State University Law Faculty (LL.B., 1983; Ph.D., 1990); George Washington University, National Law Center (1992-1993). Author: "International Arbitration," Moscow, International Affairs, 1991; "Ad Hoc Chambers of International Arbitration," Soviet State and Law, No. 11, 1991; Topical Problems of International Arbitration," Soviet State and Law, No. 2, 1991; "Arbitral Settlement of Disputes Arising Out of Bilateral Investment Treaties," Legislation ane Economy, No. 1/2, 1991, and others. *Member:* Russian Association of International Law. *LANGUAGES:* Russian, English.

JOHN A. KNAB, born Buffalo, New York, 1963; admitted, 1993, Maryland (Not admitted in Russia). *Education:* State University of New York at Albany (B.A., 1986); Washington College of Law, The American University (J.D., cum laude, 1992); School of International Service, The American University (M.A., 1993). Co-Author: "Forming A Russian Company," Ventus, Inc., 1994. Associate Executive Editor, American University Journal of International Law & Policy, 1991-1992. (Also at Washington, D.C. Office). *LANGUAGES:* English and Russian.

OF COUNSEL

ALEXANDER A. PODOLSKY, born Moscow, USSR, 1960; admitted, 1986, Moscow. *Education:* Moscow State University Law Faculty, 1982; Institute of State and Law of the Academy of Sciences of the USSR, 1986-1990. Author: "Establishing American Businesses in the Soviet Union: The Role of Soviet Attorneys," The California International Practitioner, Vol. 1, No. 2, 1989-1990; "Forming A Russian Company," Ventus, Inc., 1994. *Member:* American Bar Association (International Member). *LANGUAGES:* Russian, English.

(For Biographical Data on other Personnel, see Professional Biographies at: Washington, D.C., U.S.A.; San Francisco, California, U.S.A.; New York, N.Y., U.S.A.; Bangkok, Thailand; Taipei, Taiwan; Santo Domingo, Dominican Republic; Ho Chi Minh City, Hanoi, S.R. Vietnam).

SALANS HERTZFELD & HEILBRONN

GAZETNYI PEREULOK, 17/9 (EX. UL. OGAREVA)
103009 MOSCOW, RUSSIA
Telephone: 7.501.940.2944
Fax: 7.501.940.2806

Paris, France, Office: 9, Rue Boissy D'Anglas, 75008. Telephone: 42.68.48.00. Telex: 280990 PARILEX. Fax: 42.68.15.45; 42.68.15.46; 42.68.15.47.

New York, N.Y. Office: 750 Lexington Avenue, 10022. Telephone: 212.644.0800. Fax: 212.644.1003.

London, England Office: 103 Mount Street. W1Y-5HE. Telephone: 44.171.491.3735. Fax: 44.171.408 0843.

Warsaw, Poland Office: ul. Podwale 7, 00-252. Telephone: 48.22 31.96.88; 31.25.72; 31.29.20. Fax: 48.22 31.39.32; 31.15.65.

St. Petersburg, Russia Office: Dom Zhurnalistov, 70 Nevskii Prospekt. 191 025. Telephone: 7.812.272.4572; 273.6844. Fax: 7.812.273.6844.

Other St. Petersburg, Russia Office: 6 Inzhenernaya Ulitsa, 191011. Telephone: 7.812.850.1504; 210.4040; 210.4447; 210.4008; 210.4032; 210.4005; 210.4348; 210.4812. Fax: 7.812.850-1505; 210.4114. Office move planned for March 15, 1995.

Kiev, Ukraine Office: Ukrainskii Dim, Vul. Kreshchatik 2 (4th Floor), 252601. Telephone: 7.044.228.5451. Fax: 7.044.228.6398.

Almaty, Kazakhstan Office: 10A Abaya Prospect, Corner "Furmanova," 11th Floor, Suite 5, 480013. Telephone: 7 3272 634 053; 634 049.

Other Almaty, Kazakhstan Office: 86 Gogol Street, 5th Floor, 480091. Office Move planned for April 1, 1995.

International Business, Tax, Finance, Corporate and Securities, Litigation, Arbitration, International Trade Regulation, Customs, Joint Ventures, Labor Law.

MEMBERS OF FIRM

MIRA DAVIDOVSKI, born Baltimore, Maryland, August 13, 1959; admitted, 1986, Maryland; 1988, District of Columbia; 1989, Massachusetts. *Education:* Harvard/Radcliffe College (A.B., 1981); University of Maryland (J.D., 1985). Member, Moot Court Board. Recipient, Joseph Bernstein Prize. Articles Editor, 1984-1985, Maryland Journal of International Law and Trade. Participant, International Research and Exchanges Fellowship, 1985-1986. *LANGUAGES:* English, Russian and French. *PRACTICE AREAS:* Eastern European Commerce.

ROBERT C. SEXTON, born New York, New York, November 12, 1956; admitted, 1985, New York and District of Columbia; 1988, U.S. Supreme Court. *Education:* University of Virginia (B.A., 1978; M.A., 1981); Catholic University of America (J.D., 1984). *LANGUAGES:* English, Russian, Spanish, Italian, French and Polish. *PRACTICE AREAS:* Eastern European Commerce.

JANE V. TARASSOVA, born Moscow, Russia, 1957. *Education:* Moscow State University (Law Degree, 1980). *LANGUAGES:* Russian and English. *PRACTICE AREAS:* Eastern European Commerce.

ASSOCIATES

DEREK A. BLOOM, born Worcester, Massachusetts, April 2, 1959; admitted, 1984, District of Columbia. *Education:* Brown University (B.A., 1981); Boston University (J.D., 1984); Georgetown University (M.L.T., 1989). Staff Editor, Boston University International Law Journal, 1983-1984. *Member:* District of Columbia Bar. *PRACTICE AREAS:* Eastern European Commerce; Banking and Financial Regulatory.

TIMOTHY J.A. ENNEKING, born Minneapolis, Minnesota, September 11, 1958; admitted, 1990, Virginia; Avocat. *Education:* University of Maryland (B.A., 1984); University of Baltimore (M.B.A., 1986); Georgetown University (J.D., 1989; LL.M., 1991). *PRACTICE AREAS:* Eastern European Commerce.

STEVEN HELLMAN, born Detroit, Michigan, October 20, 1964; admitted, 1989, California. *Education:* University of California at Berkeley (B.A.); Leningrad State University, Leningrad (1985); University of California, Boalt Hall School of Law (J.D., 1989). *LANGUAGES:* English and Russian. *PRACTICE AREAS:* Eastern European Commerce.

ERIC K. JOHNSON, born Fort Ord, California, October 22, 1961; admitted, 1992, Pennsylvania. *Education:* University of California at Berkeley (B.A., 1984); Pushkin Institute, Moscow (Certificate, 1984); George Washington University (J.D., 1992). Associate Editor, George Washington University Journal of International Law and Economics, 1991-1992. *LANGUAGES:* English, Russian and German. *PRACTICE AREAS:* Eastern European Commerce.

(This Listing Continued)

BORIS KARABELNIKOV, born Moscow, Russia, April 24, 1968. *Education:* Moscow State University (Law Degree, 1992). *LANGUAGES:* Russian and English. *PRACTICE AREAS:* Eastern European Commerce.

OLEG Y. KONNOV, born Moscow, Russia, September 23, 1970. *Education:* Moscow State Institute for International Relations (Law Degree, 1994). *LANGUAGES:* Russian and English. *PRACTICE AREAS:* Eastern European Commerce.

IRINA V. KRASSIKOVA, born Moscow, April 9, 1949. *Education:* Moscow Governmental Institute of International Relations, School of International Law, Moscow, Russia. *LANGUAGES:* Russian, English and French. *PRACTICE AREAS:* Eastern European Commerce.

SERGEY V. MARINICH, born Krasnodar, Russia, August 10, 1964. *Education:* Law Faculty of the Moscow State University (Law degree, 1986; Candidate of Sciences (Law) degree, 1989). *LANGUAGES:* Russian and English. *PRACTICE AREAS:* Eastern European Commerce.

ANNA L. MISHCHENKOVA, born Kaliningrad, Russia, August 7, 1967. *Education:* Moscow State University (Law Degree, 1989). *LANGUAGES:* Russian and English. *PRACTICE AREAS:* Eastern European Commerce.

(For complete biographical data on all personnel, see Paris, France)

SCHEELE, SCHWARTZ, ZIELCKE & PARTNER

NEM. DANTCHENKO 3
103808 MOSCOW, RUSSIA
Telephone: 007-095-292-8595

Munich, Germany Office: Prinzregentenplatz 15, 81675. Telephone: 089/470 10 02. Fax: 089/470 10 06.

FIRM PROFILE: Scheele, Schwartz, Zielcke & Partner is an international law firm advising business clients and public institutions on all domestic and overseas corporate and commercial matters. The firm specializes in Eastern European and C.I.S. matters. Currently the firm is representing a broad range of clients in Europe, North America, South America, Asia and Africa.

(For biographical data and areas of practice see listing at Munich, Germany)

SECRETAN TROYANOV & PARTNERS

ULITSA USACHEVA 35, SUITE 222
MOSCOW 119048, RUSSIA
Telephone: (+7095) 245.5203
Telefax: (+7095) 244.1663; Satellite Telephone/Telefax from outside Russia: 007.502.220.3137/8

Geneva, Switzerland Office: 2, Rue Charles-Bonnet, P.O. Box 189, 1211 Geneva 12. Telephone: (+4122) 789.7000. Cable Address: "Intercounsel". Telex: 427 475 Setr CH. Telefax: (+4122) 789.7070.
London, England Office: 7/9 Bream's Buildings, Chancery Lane, EC4A 1DY. Telephone: (+44 171) 404-1199. Telefax: (+44 171) 405-0240.

Swiss and General International Practice, including Russian Law, Corporation, Banking and Financial Services, International Estate Planning, Arbitration, Commercial Law.

RESIDENT PARTNER

DR. TIKHON TROYANOV, born Belgrade, Yugoslavia, 1932; admitted, 1963, Switzerland. *Education:* University of Lausanne (Licence en droit, 1956; Doctorat en droit, 1963); Frankfurt am Main (1953-1954); Geneva (1963-1964). Author: "De la Nature Juridique du Contrat Collectif en URSS", Thesis, Lausanne, 1963. Member, Panel of Swiss Arbitrators, International Chamber of Commerce. *Member:* Geneva Bar Association; Geneva Law Society; Swiss Bar Association; Geneva Association of Business Law; Swiss-Russian Chamber of Commerce (Member of the Board); Swiss Arbitration Association; International Bar Association (East European Forum); Geneva Chamber of Commerce; International Lawyers Group, Moscow.

RESIDENT ASSOCIATES

NATHALIA GAIDAIENKO SCHAER, born Moscow, Russia, 1965; Russian lawyer. *Education:* Moscow State Institute for Foreign Relations (Diploma with Honors, Commercial Law, 1987; Doctoral Candidate in Law, 1992). Author: "Limited Liability Companies and Economic Interest Groupings in France," Thesis, Moscow, 1992. Researcher, Parliamentary

(This Listing Continued)

Institute of Legislation and Comparative Law Studies, Moscow, 1987—. *Member:* International Bar Association (East European Forum); International Lawyers Group, Moscow.

MARKUS SCHAER, born Balsthal, Switzerland, 1963; admitted, 1994, Switzerland. *Education:* University of Geneva (Licence es lettres, 1989: Branch A - Russian; Branch B - English; Licence en droit, 1991); GITIS Moscow, Russia, (1987-1988). *Member:* International Bar Association (East European Forum); International Lawyers Group, Moscow.

JULIA MIROSHNIKOVA, born Moscow, Russia, 1968; Russian lawyer. *Education:* Moscow State University (Diploma with Honors, Jurisprudence, 1990).

ALEXANDRE VASSILTCHIKOV, born Geneva, Switzerland, 1966; admitted, 1992, Switzerland (Not admitted in Russia). *Education:* University of Geneva (Licence en droit, 1990); Moscow State University (1991-1992); University of Geneva, Erasmus Program (Banking and Capital Markets Law, 1993).

VERONIKA ODINTSOVA, born Moscow, Russia, 1961; Russian lawyer; (Not admitted in Russia). *Education:* Moscow State University (Diploma with Honors, International Law, 1983; Doctoral Candidate in Law, 1987). Researcher, Parliamentary Institute of Legislation and Comparative Law Studies, Moscow, 1988—. Author: "International Protection of Copyright in the field of Cinematography and Television," Thesis, Moscow, 1987.

Languages: French, English, Russian (Official Translator), German, Italian, Spanish and Hungarian.

(For Complete Biographical Data on all Personnel, see Professional Biographies at Geneva, Switzerland)

SIGLE, LOOSE, SCHMIDT-DIEMITZ & PARTNERS

Established in 1962

SADOVAJA SAMOTJOSCHNAJA
103 051 MOSCOW, RUSSIA
Telephone: 007/095/258 50 55
Fax: 007/095/258 51 55

Stuttgart, Germany Office: Schottlestr 8, P.O. Box 70 02 65. Telephone: 0711-9764-0. Telefax: 0711-9764-900.
Berlin, Germany Office: Friedrichstrasse 130 a, 10117 Berlin. Telephone: 030-308792-0. Telefax: 030-2385849.
Leipzig, Germany Office: August-Bebel-Strasse 38, 04275 Leipzig. Telephone: 0341-3912007. Telefax: 0341-391-2085.
Frankfurt/Main, Germany Office: Schumannstrasse 62, 60325 Frankfurt/Main. Telephone: 069-97 5841-0. Telefax: 069-97 584117.
Chemnitz, Germany Office: Barbarossastraße 46, 09112 Chemnitz. Telephone: 0371-36974-0. Telefax: 0371-3697421.

Commerical Corporation, Mergers and Acquisitions, Banking Investment, Common Market, Antitrust, Unfair Competition, Copyright, Patent and Trademark, License Agreements, Press, Transportation, Insurance, Product Liability, Real Estate, Construction, Probate, Labor, Administrative, Tax, International, Litigation and Arbitration.

RESIDENT ASSOCIATE

DR. THOMAS MUNDRY, born Berlin, Germany, 1962; admitted, 1990, Stuttgart. *Education:* Free University of Berlin (Doctor of Law, 1992). Author: "Darlehen und stille Einlagen im Recht der Kommanditgesellschaft" (Loans and Undisclosed Participations in a Limited Partnership), 1992. Assistant Lecturer in Company, Commercial and Civil Law, Free University of Berlin, 1987-1991, Center of National and International Cartel Law of the Free University of Berlin, 1987-1989. *Member:* German Bar Association. *LANGUAGES:* German, English and French. *PRACTICE AREAS:* Company Law; Commercial Law; Litigation.

SKADDEN, ARPS, SLATE, MEAGHER & FLOM

PLETESHKOVSKY PEREULOK 1
107005 MOSCOW, RUSSIA
Telephone: 011-7-501-940-2304
Fax: 011-7-501-940-2511

New York, New York Office: 919 Third Avenue, 10022. Telephone: 212-735-3000. Fax: 212-735-2000; 212-735-2001. Telex: 645899 Skarslaw.

Boston, Massachusetts Office: One Beacon Street, 02108. Telephone: 617-573-4800. Fax: 617-573-4822.

Washington, D.C. Office: 1440 New York Avenue, N.W., 20005. Telephone: 202-371-7000. Fax: 202-393-5760.

Wilmington, Delaware Office: One Rodney Square, 19899. Telephone: 302-651-3000. Fax: 302-651-3001.

Los Angeles, California Office: 300 South Grand Avenue, 90071. Telephone: 213-687-5000. Fax: 213-687-5600.

Chicago, Illinois Office: 333 West Wacker Drive, 60606. Telephone: 312-407-0700. Fax: 312-407-0411.

San Francisco, California Office: Four Embarcadero Center, 94111. Telephone: 415-984-6400. Fax: 415-984-2698.

Houston, Texas Office: 1600 Smith Street, Suite 4460, 77002. Telephone: 713-655-5100. Fax: 713-766-5181.

Newark, New Jersey Office: One Riverfront Plaza, 07102. Telephone: 201-596-4440. Fax: 201-596-4444.

Tokyo, Japan Office: 12th Floor, The Fukoku Seimei Building, 2-2-2, Uchisaiwaicho, Chiyoda-ku, 100. Telephone: 011-81-3-3595-3850. Fax: 011-81-3-3504-2780.

London, England Office: 25 Bucklersbury EC4N 8DA. Telephone: 011-44-171-248-9929. Fax: 011-44-171-489-8533.

Hong Kong Office: 30/F Peregrine Tower, Lippo Centre, 89 Queensway, Central. Telephone: 011-852-820-0700. Fax: 011-852-820-0727.

Sydney, New South Wales, Australia Office: Level 26-State Bank Centre, 52 Martin Place, 2000. Telephone: 011-61-2-224-6000. Fax: 011-61-2-224-6044.

Toronto, Ontario Office: Suite 1820, North Tower, P.O. Box 189, Royal Bank Plaza, M5J 2J4. Telephone: 416-777-4700. Fax: 416-777-4747.

Paris, France Office: 105 rue du Faubourg Saint-Honoré, 75008. Telephone: 011-33-1-40-75-44-44. Fax: 011-33-1-49-53-09-99.

Brussels, Belgium Office: 523 avenue Louise, Box 30, 1050. Telephone: 011-32-2-648-7666. Fax: 011-32-2-640-3032.

Frankfurt, Germany Office: MesseTurm, 27th Floor, 60308. Telephone: 011-49-69-9757-3000. Fax: 011-49-69-9757-3050.

Beijing, China Office: 1605 Capital Mansion Tower, No. 6 Xin Yuan Nan Road, Chao Yang District, 100004. Telephone: 011-86-1-466-8800. Fax: 011-86-1-466-8822.

Budapest, Hungary Office: Mahart Building, H-1052 Apáczai Csere János u-11, Vl.em. Telephone: 011-36-1-266-2145. Fax: 011-36-1-266-4033.

Prague, Czech Republic Office: Revolucni 16, 110 00. Telephone: 011-42-2-231-75-18. Fax: 011-42-2-231-47-33.

Firm engaged in general practice.

RESIDENT ASSOCIATE

ANDRÉ DE CORT, born Brussels, Belgium, December 12, 1962; admitted, 1986, Brussels (Not admitted in Russia). *Education:* University of Louvain (Lic. Droit, 1986); University of Virginia, U.S.A. (Master of Laws, 1988).

(For Biographical data on other Personnel, see New York, New York Professional Biographies).

STARKEY, LAND & CROWLEY

36 LENINGRADSKY PROSPKT
125190 MOSCOW, RUSSIA
Telephone: 7095/212-8442
Fax: 7095/213-2058

Atlanta, Georgia Office: 1400 Resurgens Plaza, 945 East Paces Ferry Road, 30326. Telephone: 404-237-2500. Fax: 404-365-6560.

General and International Practice Specializing in Joint Ventures, Aviation, Communications, Public Relations and Advertising Law.

G. ROGER LAND, born Goldsboro, North Carolina, May 12, 1943; admitted, 1966, Georgia; 1981, Florida (Not admitted in Russia). *Education:* University of Georgia (B.B.A., 1964); University of Georgia School of

(This Listing Continued)

Law (J.D., 1967). Phi Delta Phi. *Member:* Atlanta Bar Association; State Bar of Georgia; The Florida Bar; Georgia Trial Lawyers Association; Lawyers Club of Atlanta. **PRACTICE AREAS:** International Law.

STEPTOE & JOHNSON

International Affiliate in Moscow
25 TSVETNOY BOULEVARD, BUILDING 3
103051 MOSCOW, RUSSIA
Telephone: 011-7-501-929-9701

Washington, D. C. Office: 1330 Connecticut Avenue, N.W., 20036. Telephone: 202-429-3000. Cable Address "Stepjohn". Telex: 89-2503. Telecopier: 202-429-3902.

Phoenix, Arizona Office: Two Renaissance Square, 40 N. Central, Suite 2400, 85004. Telephone: 602-257-5200.

General Practice. Aviation Law.

MEMBERS

SARAH C. CAREY, born New York, N.Y., August 12, 1938; admitted, 1966, District of Columbia (Not admitted in Russia). *Education:* Radcliffe College (B.A., magna cum laude, 1960); Georgetown University (LL.B., 1965). Member, Georgetown Law Journal, 1964-1965. Member, Board of Directors: Georgetown University Institute for Public Interest Representation, 1971-1984; American Arbitration Association, 1975-1984; Overseas Education Fund, 1982—; New Transcentury Foundation, 1982—; Institute for Soviet American Relations, 1982—; Eurasia Foundation, 1993—; Russian-American Enterprise Fund, 1993—. **PRACTICE AREAS:** International Business Law; International Investment Law; International Practice.

WALTER H. WHITE, JR., born Milwaukee, Wisconsin, August 21, 1954; admitted, 1980, Wisconsin (Not admitted in Russia). *Education:* Amherst College (B.A., 1977); Leningrad Pedagogical Institute, Leningrad, U.S.S.R.; University of California-Berkeley (J.D., 1980). Editor, Black Law Journal, 1979-1980. Wisconsin Commissioner of Securities, 1988-1991. Vice-Chair, 1990-1991, Corporation Finance Section and Chair, 1989-1990, International Corporation Finance Committee, North American Securities Administrators Association. Member, Securities & Exchange Commission Task Force on Canadian Multijurisdictional Disclosure System, 1988-1991. Member, Association Internationale Des Jeunes Avocats, 1985—. *Member:* Milwaukee and American (Member: Commission on Opportunities for Minorities in the Profession, 1986-1988; Chair, Young Lawyers Division, 1989-1990; Forum Committee on Health Law; Business Law Section, Executive Council Liaison, 1989-1991; House of Delegates, 1990-1993; Special Advisory Committee on International Activities, 1990—; Co-Chair, International Law and Practice Section, Soviet Law Committee, 1990—) and International Bar Associations; State Bar of Wisconsin (Member, Board of Governors, 1990-1993); National Bar Association; Milwaukee Young Lawyers Association (President, 1984-1985); National Health Lawyers Association. **LANGUAGES:** Russian. **PRACTICE AREAS:** Business; Securities; International.

ARTHUR RANDOLPH BREGMAN, born Philadelphia, Pennsylvania, December 9, 1946; admitted, 1985, District of Columbia (Not admitted in Russia). *Education:* Columbia University (B.A., 1968); Yale University (M.A., 1969); Georgetown University (J.D., 1985). Adjunct Professor of Soviet Law, Georgetown University, 1986-1989.

ASSOCIATES

DMITRI V. BAKATIN, born Kemerovo, Russia, July 1, 1965; admitted, 1987, Russia. *Education:* Secondary School #1 Kemerovo, Russia (M.A., 1987); Moscow University Law School (J.D., 1987; Ph.D., 1993). Professor, Moscow State University Law School, 1991—. Member of Electoral Commission for State Duma of Russia Elections, 1994. Member, Association of Soviet Lawyers, 1986. Member, Scientific Society Znanie, 1987.

TATIANA KOVALEVA, born Yrozny, Russia, January 12, 1957; admitted, 1988, Russia. *Education:* Secondary, English School #5, Ryazan, Russia (M.A., 1974); Moscow State University Law School (J.D., 1979; Ph.D., 1984). Professor, Moscow State University Law School, 1987—. Consultant Supreme Soviet USSR, 1988-1989. Honorary Member, Young Lawyers Division, American Bar Association, 1990. Member, Scientific Society Znanie, 1985—.

MARINA A. KALDINA, born Chelyabinsk, Russia, October 4, 1964; admitted, 1985, Russia. *Education:* Sverdlovsk Law Institute (1985); Emory University (Certificate with distinction).

(This Listing Continued)

VICTOR KHVESENIA, born Darkmimovtsy, Grodno, Belarls, June 15, 1962; admitted, 1985, Russia; 1993, Belarus. *Education:* Grodno Secondary School #14, Grodno, Belarus (School Certificate, 1979); Buelorassian State University (J.D., 1984).

MARC J. HALSEMA, born Los Angeles, California, August 30, 1959; admitted, 1987, Illinois (Not admitted in Russia). *Education:* University of Notre Dame (B.A., 1981); Northwestern University (J.D., 1985). Member, Northwestern Journal of International Law and Business, 1983-1985. *Member:* Chicago and American Bar Associations.

ALEXANDER V. PANKRATOV, born Moscow, Russia, June 17, 1968; (Not admitted in Russia). *Education:* Moscow State University (LL.B., with highest honors, 1992); University of Pennsylvania (1990-1991); Capital Law School, Ohio (LL.M., 1994).

(For Biographical Data on other Personnel, see Professional Biographies at Washington, D.C. and Phoenix, Arizona)

VINSON & ELKINS L.L.P.

16 ALEXEY TOLSTOY STREET
SECOND FLOOR
MOSCOW 103001, RUSSIA
Telephone: (70-95) 956-1995
Telecopy: (70-95) 956-1996

London, England Office: 47 Charles Street, Berkeley Square, London W1X 7PB, England. Telephone: (44-171) 491-7236. Fax: (44-171) 499-5320.

Mexico City, Mexico Office: Arisóteles 77, 5°Pisco, Colonia Chapultepec Polanco, 11560 Mexico D.F. Telephone: (52-5) 280-7828. Fax: (52-5) 280-9223.

Singapore Office: 50 Raffles Place, #19-05 Shell Tower, Singapore, 0104. U.S. Voice Mailbox: 713-758-3500. Telephone: (65) 536-8300. Fax: (65) 536-8311.

Houston, Texas Office: 1001 Fannin, Suite 2300, 77002-6760. Telephone: 713-758-2222. Fax: 713-758-2346. International Telex: 6868314.

Washington, D.C. Office: The Willard Office Building, 1455 Pennsylvania Avenue, N.W., 20004-1008. Telephone: 202-639-6500. Fax: 202-639-6604.

Dallas, Texas Office: 3700 Trammell Crow Center, 2001 Ross Avenue, 75201-2975. Telephone: 214-220-7700. Fax: 214-220-7716.

Austin, Texas Office: One American Center, 600 Congress Avenue, 78701-3200. Telephone: 512-495-8400. Fax: 512-495-8612.

General Commercial Practice Specializing in Joint Ventures, Banking and Finance (including Project Finance), Asset Acquisitions, Real Estate Developments and Privatization Law.

RESIDENT PARTNERS

JAMES L. CUCLIS, born Berkeley, California, November 9, 1958; admitted, 1981, Texas. *Education:* American University; University of Texas (B.A., 1978; J.D., 1981). *PRACTICE AREAS:* International Law; Natural Resources Law; Corporate Law; Project Finance Law.

J. BRIAN SOKOLIK, born Passaic, New Jersey, June 7, 1944; admitted, 1976, Texas (Not admitted in Russia). *Education:* St. Peter's College (B.S., 1967); St. Mary's University of San Antonio (J.D., 1976); University of Virginia (LL.M., 1977). St. Mary's Law Journal, 1974-1976 (Editor-in-Chief, 1975-1976). Phi Delta Phi. *PRACTICE AREAS:* Commercial Law; Corporate Law; Real Estate Law; International Business Law; Project Finance Law.

RESIDENT ASSOCIATES

PAVEL L. BAKULEV, born Moscow, USSR, November 9, 1964. *Education:* Moscow State University, Lawyer, 1989; Institute of State and Law, 1992. *PRACTICE AREAS:* International Business Law; Corporate Law; Business Litigation.

ALEXEY L. CONDRATCHICK, born Uhta, Republic of Komy, Russian Federation, November 14, 1963. *Education:* Latvian State University School of Law (Degree in Law, with Honors, 1985); Moscow State University School of Law, 1988-1991; New York University (LL.M., 1991). *PRACTICE AREAS:* Russian Taxation Law; Russian Companies Law; International Investments Law.

NATALYA (NATASHA) MOROZOVA, born Moscow, Russia, March 20, 1959. *Education:* Moscow State Pedagogical Institute of Foreign Languages; All-Union Law Institute (J.D., 1988). *LANGUAGES:* Russian,

(This Listing Continued)

English. *PRACTICE AREAS:* International Law; Business Law; Corporate Law; Real Estate Law.

KIRILL YURIEVICH PARINOV, born Moscow, USSR, October 21, 1967. *Education:* Lomonosov Moscow State University (Diploma on Higher Education in Law, 1991); Southern Methodist University (LL.M., Comparative and International Law, 1994). *PRACTICE AREAS:* Foreign Investment; International Petroleum Transactions; Russian Oil and Gas Law.

(Other Offices at Houston, Texas; Austin, Texas; Dallas, Texas; Washington, D.C.; London, England; Mexico City, Mexico and Singapore)

WATSON, FARLEY & WILLIAMS

36 MYASKOVSKOVO STREET
101000 MOSCOW 121019, RUSSIA
Telephone: (7 502) 224 1700 (international only)
(7 095) 291 8046/5968
Fax: (7 502) 224 1701 (international only)
(7 095) 202 9027

London, England Office: 15 Appold Street, London EC2A 2HB. Telephone: (44 171) 814 8000. Telex: 8955707 WFW LON G. Fax: (44 171) 814 8141.

New York, New York Office: 380 Madison Avenue, 10017. Telephone: 212-922-2200. Telex: 6790626 WFW NY. Fax: 212-922-1512.

Paris, France Office: 19 Rue de Marignan, 75008 Paris. Telephone: (33 1) 45 63 15 15. Telex: WFW PAR 651096 F. Fax: (33 1) 45 61 09 01.

Oslo, Norway Office: Beddingen 8, Aker Brygge, 0250 Oslo. Telephone: (47 22) 83 83 08. Telex: 79209 WFW N. Fax: (47 22) 83 83 13.

Athens, Greece Office: Alassia Building, Defteras Merarchias 13, 185-35 Piraeus. Telephone: (30 1) 422 3660. Telex: 24 1311 WFW GR. Fax: (30 1) 422 3664.

Copenhagen, Denmark Office: Lille Kongensgade 20 DK-1074 Copenhagen K. Telephone (45 33) 91 33 03. Fax: (45 33) 91 49 12.

Firm engaged in General International Practice, Corporate, Commercial and Financing, Shipping, Aviation, Banking, Taxation, Commerical Litigation and Arbitration and European Community Law. Not qualified to advise on Russian law.

RESIDENT PARTNERS

M.G.S. GREVILLE, born 1962; admitted, 1990, England. *Education:* LL.B. (Hons.). *PRACTICE AREAS:* Shipping; Oil and Gas; Financing; General Commercial.

(For Biographical Data on additional partners, see Professional Biographies at Copenhagen, Denmark, London, England, Paris, France, Oslo, Norway and Pireaus, Greece)

WHITE & CASE

7, ULITSA TVERSKAYA
103375 MOSCOW, RUSSIA
Telephone: (7-095) 201-929 2/3/4/5
Telex: 612012 WCMOS
Facsimile: (7-095) 201-9284

New York, New York: Telephone: 212-819-8200. Facsimile: 212-354-8113.

Washington, D.C.: Telephone: 202-872-0013. Facsimile: 202-872-0210.

Los Angeles, California: Telephone: 213-620-7700. Facsimile: 213-687-0758; 213-617-2205.

Miami, Florida: Telephone: 305-371-2700. Facsimile: 305-358-5744.

Mexico City, Mexico: Telephone: (52-5) 207-9717. Facsimile: (52-5) 208-3628.

Tokyo, Japan: Telephone: (81-3) 3239-4300. Facsimile: (81-3) 3239-4330.

Hong Kong: Telephone: (852) 2822-8700. Facsimile: (852) 2845-9070; Grice & Co., Solicitors, Telephone: (852) 2826-0333. Facsimile: (852) 2526-7166.

Singapore, Republic of Singapore: Telephone: (65) 225-6000. Facsimile: (65) 225-6009.

Bangkok, Thailand: Pacific Legal Group Ltd., In Association With White & Case, Telephone: (662) 236-6154/7. Facsimile: (662) 237-6771.

Hanoi, Viet Nam: Representative Office, Telephone: (84-4) 227-575/6/7. Facsimile: (84-4) 227-297.

Bombay, India: Telephone: (91-22) 282-6300. Facsimile: (91-22) 282-6305.

(This Listing Continued)

WHITE & CASE, Moscow—Continued

London, England: Telephone: (44-171) 726-6361. Facsimile: (44-171) 726-4314; (44-171) 726-8558.

Paris, France: Telephone: (33-1) 42-60-34-05. Facsimile: (33-1) 42-60-82-46.

Brussels, Belgium: Telephone: (32-2) 647-05-89. Facsimile: (32-2) 647-16-75.

Stockholm, Sweden: Telephone: (46-8) 679-80-30. Facsimile: (46-8) 611-21-22.

Helsinki, Finland: Telephone: (358-0) 631-100. Facsimile: (358-0) 179-477.

Budapest, Hungary: Telephone: (36-1) 269-0550; (36-1) 131-0933. Facsimile: (36-1) 269-1199.

Prague, Czech Republic: Telephone: (42-2) 2481-1796. Facsimile: (42-2) 232-5522.

Warsaw, Poland: Telephone/Facsimile: (48-22) 26-80-53; (48-22) 27-84-86. International Telephone/Facsimile: (48-39) 12-19-06.

Istanbul, Turkey: Telephone: (90-212) 275-68-98; (90-212) 275-75-33. Facsimile: (90-212) 275-75-43.

Ankara, Turkey: Telephone: (90-312) 446-2180. Facsimile: (90-312) 437-9677.

Jeddah, Saudi Arabia: Law Office of Hassan Mahassni, Telephone: (966-2) 651-3535. Facsimile: (966-2) 651-3636.

Riyadh, Saudi Arabia: Law Office of Hassan Mahassni, Telephone: (966-1) 476-7099. Facsimile: (966-1) 479-0110.

Almaty, Kazakhstan: Telephone: (7-3272) 50-7491/2. Facsimile: (7-3272) 61-0842.

General and International Practice.
Firm engaged in American and International Law Practice, but not authorized to appear before the Soviet Courts.

RESIDENT PARTNERS

ALISON M. DREIZEN, born Brooklyn, New York, September 14, 1952; admitted, 1978, New York. *Education:* Cornell University (B.A., 1974); Harvard University (J.D., 1977). *Member:* The Association of the Bar of the City of New York.

MARYANN E. GASHI-BUTLER, born Kingston, Pennsylvania, January 12, 1955; admitted, 1983, District of Columbia; 1984, Massachusetts (Not admitted in Russia). *Education:* Boston College (B.A., 1980); Yale University (M.A., 1980); Harvard University (J.D., 1983).

RESIDENT ASSOCIATES

NATALYA ARTEMYEVA, born Moscow, Russia, July 1, 1961; admitted, 1986, Moscow, Russia. *Education:* Moscow State Institute of International Relations (M.L., 1983; LL.D., 1988). Senior Professor, Moscow State Institute of International Relations, 1984—.

SERGEI M. BARANCHENKOV, born Moscow, Russia, September 7, 1964; admitted, 1986, Russia. *Education:* Moscow State Institute of International Relations (Diploma in International Law, 1986); New York University (LL.M., 1992).

MAYA FISHKIN, born Minsk, Belarus, April 30, 1965; admitted, 1990, California. *Education:* Harvard University (B.A., 1987; J.D., 1990).

ERIC MICHAILOV, born Donetsk, Ukraine, February 2, 1969; admitted, 1991, Australia. *Education:* University of Adelaide (B. EC., 1990; LL.B., 1991).

KALINKA H. MOUDROVA, born Sofia, Bulgaria, March 16, 1960; admitted, 1993, New York. *Education:* Sofia University (LL.M., 1984); Columbia University (LL.M., 1992).

DENIS VINOKUROV, born St. Petersburg, Russia, May 27, 1969; admitted, 1993, Russia. *Education:* Moscow State Institute of International Relations (Doctor of Law, 1993); Central European University, Budapest, Hungary (LL.M., 1995).

(For biographical data as to other locations, see Professional Biographies at New York, New York; Washington, D.C.; Los Angeles, California; Miami, Florida; Mexico City, Mexico; Tokyo, Japan; Hong Kong; Singapore, Republic of Singapore; Bangkok, Thailand; Hanoi, Viet Nam; Bombay, India; London, England; Paris, France; Brussels, Belgium; Stockholm, Sweden; Helsinki, Finland; Budapest, Hungary; Prague, Czech Republic; Warsaw, Poland; Istanbul and Ankara, Turkey; Jeddah and Riyadh, Saudi Arabia; Almaty, Kazakhstan).

OLGA TISSEN

ST. D KOVALCHUK 258-179
630122 NOVOSIBIRSK, RUSSIA
Telephone: (3832) 28-51-94
Fax: (3832) 23-38-74; (3832) 91-21-42

Real Estate and Trade Business, Joint Ventures, Travel Business, Transactions with Securities of Russian Corporations.

OLGA TISSEN, born Novosibirsk, July 28, 1956; admitted, 1979, Russia. *Education:* Sverdlovsk, Russia, 1978.

AGENCY OF PATENT ATTORNEYS "ARS-PATENT"

SHVEDSKY PEREULOK, 2, SUITE 33
P.O. BOX 230
191186 ST. PETERSBURG, RUSSIA
Telephone: (812) 312-35-94
Fax: (812) 312-35-94

Industrial and Intellectual Property Law, Patent, Trademark, Copyright, Design, Licensing and Unfair Competition.

MEMBERS OF FIRM

VLADIMIR MIHAILOVICH SERGEJEV, born St. Petersburg, Russia, May 28, 1937; admitted, 1971, Russia. *Education:* Fine Mechanic and Optic University, St. Petersburg (Diploma, Engineering, 1961); Intellectual Property and Innovation Institute, St. Petersburg (Dr.jur., 1971). *Member:* AIPPI; St. Petersburg Bar of Patent Attorneys. *LANGUAGES:* Russian and German. *PRACTICE AREAS:* Russian and International Industrial Property Law; Trademark Law; Design Law; Copyright Law; Licensing; Franchising; Unfair Competition.

VLADIMIR MOISEJEVICH RYBAKOV, born St. Petersburg, Russia, June 5, 1951; admitted, 1985, Russia. *Education:* State Baltic Technical University, St. Petersburg (Diploma, Engineering, 1974); Intellectual Property and Innovation Institute, St. Petersburg (1985). *Member:* AIPPI; St. Petersburg Bar of Patent Attorneys. *LANGUAGES:* Russian, English and German. *PRACTICE AREAS:* Russian and International Industrial Property Law; Patent Law; Utility Model Law; Trademark Law; Licensing; Copyright Law.

ELENA ALEXANDROVNA ZAITSEVA, born St. Petersburg, Russia, January 31, 1966; admitted, 1992, Russia. *Education:* St. Petersburg Electronical University, St. Petersburg (Diploma, Engineering, 1990); Intellectual Property and Innovation Institute, St. Petersburg (1992). *LANGUAGES:* Russian and English. *PRACTICE AREAS:* Trademark Law; Design Law.

BAKER & McKENZIE

BOLSHAYA MORSKAYA, 57
19000 ST. PETERSBURG, RUSSIA
Telephone: (812) 310-54-46; 310-55-44; 310-01-71;
Int'l Dialing: (7- 812) 310-54-46; 310-55-44; 310-01-71;
(7-812) 850-14-25 (Satellite)
Telex: 612151
Answer Back: 612151 BMSTP
Facsimile: (7-812) 310-59-44 (7-812) 119-60-13 (Satellite)

Associated Offices of Baker & McKenzie in: Almaty, Amsterdam, Bangkok, Barcelona, Beijing, Berlin, Bogotá, Brasília, Brussels, Budapest, Buenos Aires, Cairo, Caracas, Chicago, Dallas, Frankfurt, Geneva, Hanoi, Ho Chi Minh City, Hong Kong, Juárez, Kiev, London, Madrid, Manila, Melbourne, México City, Miami, Milan, Monterrey, Moscow, New York, Palo Alto, Paris, Prague, Rio de Janeiro, Riyadh, Rome, San Diego, San Francisco, São Paulo, Singapore, Stockholm, Sydney, Taipei, Tijuana, Tokyo, Toronto, Valencia, Warsaw, Washington, D.C. and Zürich.
Correspondent Law Firm: Hadiputranto, Hadinoto & Partners, Jakarta.

Foreign Investment, Tax, Real Estate, Privatization, Intellectual Property, Arbitration.

(This Listing Continued)

PARTNERS

ARTHUR L. GEORGE, born Hartford, Connecticut, November 24, 1956; admitted, 1983, District of Columbia, U.S.A. (Not admitted in Russia). *Education:* University of Colorado (B.A., summa cum laude, 1979); George Washington University (J.D., with high honors, 1983). Phi Beta Kappa; Order of the Coif. Editor-in-Chief, The George Washington Journal of International Law and Economics, 1982-1983. *Member:* District of Columbia Bar Association (Member, International Law Section); American Bar Association (Member, International Law Section). *LANGUAGES:* English and Russian.

ASSOCIATES

EVGENY V. ASTAKHOV, born Leningrad, Russia, January 25, 1969; admitted, 1993, Russia. *Education:* Moscow State Institute of International Relations (J.D., 1993). *LANGUAGES:* English, Russian and German.

MAXIM V. KALININ, born Leningrad, Russia, February 15, 1969; admitted, 1993, Russia. *Education:* Moscow State University of International Relations (J.D., 1993). *LANGUAGES:* English, Russian and German.

NICHOLAS M.N. RUMIN, born Montréal, Québec, Canada, May 20, 1962; admitted, 1990, Ontario, Canada (Not admitted in Russia). *Education:* McGill University (B.A., 1984); University of Ottawa (LL.B., 1987). *Member:* Law Society of Upper Canada; Canadian Bar Association (Ontario). *LANGUAGES:* English, Russian and French.

DAVID I. SCOTT, born Bristol, United Kingdom, September 15, 1961; admitted, 1987, England and Wales (Not admitted in Russia). *Education:* King's College London; Université de Paris I (Panthéon-Sorbonne) (LL.B. in English and French Law with First Class Honours, 1984). *LANGUAGES:* English, Russian and French.

CASTRÉN & SNELLMAN A/O

NEVSKY PROSPEKT 22-24/18
191186 ST. PETERSBURG, RUSSIA
Telephone: 7-812-119-8085
Telefax: 7-812-119-8086

Helsinki, Finland Office: Erottajankatu 5A, 00130. Telephone: 358-0-228-581. Telefax: 385-0-655-919, 601 961.

RESIDENT ASSOCIATES

NINA STANISLAVOVNA VASILJEVA, born Leningrad, USSR, October 8, 1966. *Education:* Leningrad State University (Law degree, 1989). *Member:* St. Petersburg Regional Bar Association. *LANGUAGES:* Russian and English.

IGOR LIVSHITS, born Tallinn, Estonia, January 31, 1958. *Education:* University of St. Petersburg (Law degree, 1982). *Member:* Russian Sociological Association; Association of Finnish Lawyers. *LANGUAGES:* Russian, English and Finnish.

J.P. GALMOND

Established in 1983

MILLIONNAYA 27
191186 ST. PETERSBURG, RUSSIA
Telephone: +7 812 315 4860
Fax: +7 812 315 8734

Copenhagen, Denmark Office: H.C. Andersens Boulevard 51, 4.tv., 1553 Copenhagen. Telephone; +45 33 13 45 30. Fax: +45 33 93 55 30.

Hamburg, Germany Office: Bollmann, Kiesselbach & Partner, Neuer Wall 42, 20354 Hamburg. Telephone: +49 40 36 22 41. Fax: +49 40 36 69 30.

Firm engaged in Danish, German, Russian, and International Law Practice. Entitled to plead before the European Commission, Danish and Russian Courts.

European Community Law, Russian Law, International Banking and Business Law, General International Trade Law, Commercial Law and Litigation and International Arbitration.

FIRM PROFILE: Established in 1983. The firm has a broadly-based practice with a reputation of offering a full range of quality legal services. The client base is mainly European and Russian. The firm has one owner and 5 (6) assistants practicing in Denmark and Russia. In addition the

(This Listing Continued)

---

firm has a close association with the Hamburg-based office, Bollmann, Kiesselbach & Partner in Germany.

MEMBERS OF FIRM

JEFFREY PETER GALMOND, born Frederiksberg, Denmark, June 1, 1950; admitted, 1975, Denmark (Not admitted in Russia). *Education:* University of Copenhagen (Master of Law, 1975). *LANGUAGES:* Danish, English and German.

SUNE SKADEGAARD THORSEN, born Hellerup, Denmark, October 14, 1961; admitted, 1990, Denmark (Not admitted in Russia). *Education:* University of Copenhagen (Master of Law, 1986). *LANGUAGES:* Danish, English and German.

LINE HELL HANSEN, born Gentofte, Denmark, December 20, 1966; admitted, 1992, Denmark (Not admitted in Russia). *Education:* University of Copenhagen (Master of Law, 1992). *LANGUAGES:* Danish, English and German.

LARS BRUHN, born Korsør, Denmark, June 12, 1960; admitted, 1994, Denmark (Not admitted in Russia). *Education:* University of Copenhagen (Master of Law, 1986). *LANGUAGES:* Danish, English and German.

VLADISLAV ZABRODIN, born St. Petersburg, Russia, January 13, 1967; admitted, 1991, Russia. *Education:* University of St. Petersburg (Master of Law, 1991). *LANGUAGES:* Russian and English.

IGOR MISHIN, born St. Petersburg, Russia, September 23, 1967; admitted, 1991, Russia. *Education:* University of St. Petersburg (Master of Law, 1991). *LANGUAGES:* Russian and English.

GIDE LOYRETTE NOUEL

34 SOUVOROVSKY PROSPECT
APP 45
P.O. BOX 172
193015 ST. PETERSBURG, RUSSIA
Telephone by satellite: (7.812) 850 16.85
Telecopier by satellite: (7.812) 850 16.86

Paris, France Office: 26 Cours Albert 1er, 75008. Telephone: (1) 40.75.60.00. Cable Address: "3 Avocagidva Paris 86." Telex: 651261F GILOY. Telecopier: (1) 43.59.37.79.

New York, New York Office: Swiss Bank Tower, 10 East 50th Street, 10022. Telephone: (1-212) 644-1201. Telex: 424353 GIDE. Telecopier: (1-212) 644-1205.

Brussels, Belgium Office: Rue de la Loi 99.101, B-1040. Telephone: (32.2) 231.11.40. Telecopier: (32.2) 231.11.77.

Warsaw, Poland Office: Ul. Kopernika 17, 00-359. Telephone: (48.22) 26.22.21. Telecopier: (48.22) 26.03.02.

Riyadh, Saudi Arabia Office: P.O. Box 4615, 11412. Telephone: (966.1) 476.60.39. Telex: 401677 NASHWA. Telecopier: (966.1) 476.18.96.

Tokyo, Japan Office: Homei Building 3F, 3-19 Akasaka 1-Chome, Minato-Ku, 107. Telephone: (81.3) 55.62.03.01. Telecopier: (81.3) 55.62.03.06.

Beijing, People's Republic of China Office: Suite 3309 A, Jing Guang Centre, Hu Jia Lou, Chaoyang District, 100020. Telephone: (86.1) 501 4511. Telecopier: (86.1) 501 4551.

Prague, Czech Republic Office: 34 Jindrisska, 11207. Telephone: (42.2) 24.21.34.65;24.21.36.50. Telecopier: (42.2) 24.21.09.12;24.22.58.53.

Moscow, Russia Office: 9, Ulitsa Tverskaya - App 66, 103009. Telephone by satellite: (7.501) 940.45.00. Telecopier by satellite: (7.501) 940.45.01.

Budapest VII, Hungary Office: EMKE Building, Rákóczi út 42, BP 409, 1072. Telephone: (36.1) 268.1236; 268.1237; 268.1238. Telecopier: (36.1) 268.1239.

Madrid, Spain Office: Antonio Maura 7, 6°, 28014. Telephone: (34.1) 531.25.01. Telecopier: (34.1) 531.35.30.

Hanoi, Vietnam Office: Hanoi Business Centre, 51 Ly Thai To. Telephone: (84.42) 66.122.3. Telecopier: (84.42) 66.030.1.

French and International Law.

RESIDENT ASSOCIATES

Alexandra Nesterenko
Andreï Bushev
Nathalie Andrieux

(For Biographical Data on Personnel, see Professional Biographies at Paris, France).

McDERMOTT, WILL & EMERY

A Partnership including Professional Corporations

Established in 1934

2/2 TCHAIKOVSKY STREET, #517
191187 ST. PETERSBURG, RUSSIA
Telephone: (7) (812) 273-9831
Facsimile: (7) (812) 273-9831

Boston, Massachusetts Office: 75 State Street, Suite 1700, 02109-1807. Telephone: 617-345-5000. Telex: 951324 MILAM BSN. Facsimile: 617-345-5077.

Chicago, Illinois Office: 227 West Monroe Street, 60606-5096. Telephone: 312-372-2000. Telex: 253565 MILAM CGO. Facsimile: 312-984-7700.

Los Angeles, California Office: 2049 Century Park East, 90067-3208. Telephone: 310-277-4110. Facsimile: 310-277-4730.

Miami, Florida Office: 201 South Biscayne Boulevard, 33131-4336. Telephone: 305-358-3500. Telex: 441777 LEYES. Facsimile: 305-347-6500.

Newport Beach, California Office: 1301 Dove Street, Suite 500, 92660-2444. Telephone: 714-851-0633. Facsimile: 714-851-9348.

New York, N.Y. Office: 1211 Avenue of the Americas, 10036-8701. Telephone: 212-768-5400. Facsimile: 212-768-5444.

Washington, D.C. Office: 1850 K Street, N.W., 20006-2296. Telephone: 202-887-8000. Telex: 253565 MILAM CGO. Facsimile: 202-778-8087.

Vilnius, Lithuania Office: Smetonos 6, 2600 Vilnius, Lithuania. Telephone: 370 2 61-43-08. Facsimile: 370 2 22-79-55.

Associated (Independent) Offices:

Brussels, Belgium: Uettwiller Grelon Lippens Dekeyser, 73 avenue Vandendriessche, 1150 Brussels, Belgium. Telephone: (32) (2) 772-87-50. Facsimile: (32) (2) 772-87-52.

London, England: Paisner & Co, Bouverie House, 154 Fleet Street, London EC4A 2DQ, England. Telephone: (44) (71) 353-0299. Facsimile: (44) (71) 583-8621.

Paris, France: Uettwiller Grelon Gout Canat & Associes, 68, boulevard de Courcelles, 75017 Paris, France. Telephone: (33) (1) 48 88 89 00. Facsimile: (33) (1) 48 88 05 50.

General Practice (including Corporate, Employee Benefits, Estate Planning, Health, Litigation and Tax Law).

FIRM PROFILE: Founded in Chicago in 1934, the firm originally focused on federal taxation matters. Over the years it has grown to become a leading international law firm with a diversified business practice. We represent a wide range of industrial, financial, and commercial enterprises, both publicly and privately held. Our clientele includes some of the world's largest corporations as well as individuals and small and medium-sized businesses.

The firm is organized along lines of functional specialization—most attorneys focus on a particular aspect of the law from the outset of their career. The firm's 500 attorneys practice in corporate, employee benefits, estate planning, health, litigation, and tax law. Many attorneys also practice in interdepartmental groups. This structure distinguishes us from many other national law firms of our size and experience and permits maximum flexibility and efficiency in handling client matters.

MEMBERS OF FIRM

VLADIMIR S. AVERYANOV, born St. Petersburg, Russia. *Education:* St. Petersburg University Law School. *LANGUAGES:* Russian and English. *PRACTICE AREAS:* Russian Business Law.

FREDERICK H. DULLES, born New York, N.Y., March 12, 1942; admitted, 1971, District of Columbia; 1972, New York (Not admitted in Russia). *Education:* Harvard College (A.B., 1964); Columbia University Graduate School of Business (M.B.A., 1968); Columbia University School of Law (J.D., 1968). Attorney, Shearman & Sterling, New York & Paris, 1971-1980. Counsel, Assistant General Counsel, Philip Morris Incorporated, New York, 1980-1983. Regional Counsel, EFTA-Eastern Europa-Middle East-Africa Region, Philip Morris Europe S.A., Lausanne, Switzerland, 1983-1992. *Member:* International Bar Association; American Bar Association; The Association of the Bar of the City of New York. *LANGUAGES:* English and French. *PRACTICE AREAS:* Multinational Corporate and Commercial Law; Mergers; Acquisitions; Privatization.

NIKOLAI V. NEMTCHINOV, born Tver (Kolinin), Russia, January 27, 1955. *Education:* St. Petersburg University Law School. *LANGUAGES:* Russian and English. *PRACTICE AREAS:* Commercial Law; Russian Intellectual Property Law; Tax Law.

(This Listing Continued)

DMITRI P. SILTCHENKOV, admitted, 1977, U.S.S.R. *Education:* St Petersburg University Law School. *Member:* St. Petersburg Bar Association. *LANGUAGES:* Russian and English.

(For Biographical data on all firm personnel, see Professional Biographies listings at other office locations)

SALANS HERTZFELD & HEILBRONN

DOM ZHURNALISTOV, 70 NEVSKII PROSPEKT
191 025 ST. PETERSBURG, RUSSIA
Telephone: 7.812.272.4572; 273.6844
Fax: 7.812.273.6844

SALANS HERTZFELD & HEILBRONN. 6 Inzhenernaya Ulitsa, 191011, St. Petersburg, Russia. Telephone: 7.812.850.1504; 210.4040; 210.4447; 210.4008; 210.4032; 210.4005; 210.4348; 210.4812. Fax: 7.-812.850.1505; 210.4114. Office Move Planned for March 15, 1995.

Paris, France, Office: 9, Rue Boissy D'Anglas, 75008. Telephone: 42.68.48.00. Telex: 280990 PARILEX. Fax: 42.68.15.45; 42.68.15.46; 42.68.15.47.

New York, N.Y. Office: 750 Lexington Avenue, 10022. Telephone: 212.644.0800. Fax: 212.644.1003.

London, England Office: 103 Mount Street. W1Y-5HE. Telephone: 44.171.491.3735. Fax: 44.171.408 0843.

Moscow, Russia Office: Gazetnyi Pereulok, 17/9, (Ex. UL. Ogareva). 103009. Telephone: 7.501.940.2944. Fax: 7.501.940.2806.

Warsaw, Poland Office: ul. Podwale 7, 00-252. Telephone: 48.22 31.96.88; 31.25.72; 31.29.20. Fax: 48.22 31.39.32; 31.15.65.

Kiev, Ukraine Office: Ukrainskii Dim, Vul. Kreshchatik 2 (4th Floor), 252601. Telephone: 7.044.228.5451. Fax: 7.044.228.6398.

Almaty, Kazakhstan Office: 10A Abaya Prospect, Corner "Furmanova," 11th Floor, Suite 5, 480013. Telephone: 7 3272 634 053; 634 049.

Other Almaty, Kazakhstan Office: 86 Gogol Street, 5th Floor, 480091. Office move planned for April 1, 1995.

MEMBERS OF FIRM

TIMOTHY STUBBS, born Ann Arbor, Michigan, October 12, 1960; admitted, 1986, Illinois; 1989, New York; 1992, District of Columbia. *Education:* University of Michigan (B.A., 1982; M.A., 1986); University of Michigan (Doctor of Law, 1985). *LANGUAGES:* English, Russian and French. *PRACTICE AREAS:* Eastern European Commerce.

PHILIPP H. WINDEMUTH, born Kassel, Germany February 6, 1959; admitted, 1988, New York; Paris as Avocat. *Education:* Harvard University (B.A., 1982); Leningrad State University, Leningrad, U.S.S.R. (1984); New York University (J.D., 1987). Articles Editor, New York University Annual Survey of American Law, 1986-1987. *LANGUAGES:* English, German, Russian, French and Spanish. *PRACTICE AREAS:* Eastern European Commerce.

ASSOCIATES

ELENA BARIKHNOVSKAYA, born St. Petersburg, Russia, April 7, 1954; admitted, 1976, St. Petersburg. *Education:* Leningrad State University (J.D., 1976). *LANGUAGES:* Russian and English. *PRACTICE AREAS:* Eastern European Commerce.

(For complete biographical data on all personnel, see Paris, France)

SCANDINAVIAN LAW OFFICES A/O

PROLETARSKAYA DIKTATURA SQ. 6, ROOM 309
193124 ST. PETERSBURG, RUSSIA
Telephone: +7-812-8502200 (Int'l.); +7-812-2744347
Telefax: +7-812-8502201 (Int'l.); +7-812-2741146

Helsinki, Finland Office: Eteläranta 8, 00130. Telephone: +358-0-171900. Telefax: +358-0-171950.

Tallinn, Estonia Office: Rüütli 16, EE0001. Telephone: +372-2-666689. Telefax: +372-6-313549.

Corporate, Contract, Business, Financial and Tax Law, International Business Transactions, East-West Trade, Arbitration and Litigation.

MEMBERS OF FIRM

ANSSI JAANTI, born Helsinki, Finland, December 27, 1951; admitted, 1987, Finland (Not admitted in Russia). *Education:* University of Helsinki (LL.M., 1981). *Member:* Finnish Bar Association. *LANGUAGES:* English, Finnish, Swedish and German.

(This Listing Continued)

MARKKU ROPPONEN, born Helsinki, Finland, August 26, 1961; (Not admitted in Russia). *Education:* University of Helsinki (LL.M., 1989). *LANGUAGES:* English, Finnish, Swedish and German.

ASSOCIATES

IGOR HITRUHIN, born Trubtchevsk, Russia, June 4, 1965. *Education:* Moscow State University (LL.M., 1991). *LANGUAGES:* Russian, Finnish and English.

SCHEELE, SCHWARTZ, ZIELCKE & PARTNER

UL. FUHRMANNOWA 6-A III
191187 ST. PETERSBURG, RUSSIA
Telephone: 007-812-2751071

Munich, Germany Office: Prinzregentenplatz 15, 81675. Telephone: 089/470 10 02. Fax: 089/470 10 06.

FIRM PROFILE: Scheele, Schwartz, Zielcke & Partner is an international law firm advising business clients and public institutions on all domestic and overseas corporate and commercial matters. The firm specializes in Eastern European and C.I.S. matters. Currently the firm is representing a broad range of clients in Europe, North America, South America, Asia and Africa.

(For biographical data and areas of practice see listing at Munich, Germany)

CONTRACT LAW FIRM

Established in 1988

142/1 KRASNAYA ARMIYA AVENUE
141300 SERGIEV POSAD, RUSSIA
Telephone: (09654) 4 10 21
Fax: (09654) 2 73 84

Civil Law, Corporate Law, Insurance, International Sales, Real Estate, Russian and International Banking and Business Law, Litigation and International Arbitration.
Firm engaged in Russian and CIS Law practice.

FIRM PROFILE: Established in 1988 Contract Law Firm has a broad-based practice with a reputation for offering a full range of legal services of high quality. The firm has 6 partners and 12 assistants.

ALEXANDER VEDERNIKOV, born 1954; admitted, 1983. *Education:* Moscow Law Institute (1983). *LANGUAGES:* Russian, English, and Spanish. *PRACTICE AREAS:* Civil Law; Business Law; Banking Law; International Trade Law.

GREGORY KOMANDIN, born 1957; admitted, 1984. *Education:* Peoples' Friendship University (1984). *LANGUAGES:* Russian, English, and Hindi. *PRACTICE AREAS:* Business Law; Insurance Law; Banking Law.

VALERIY MAIKOV, born 1947; admitted, 1984. *Education:* Moscow Law Institute (1984). *LANGUAGES:* Russian and German. *PRACTICE AREAS:* Business Law; Estate Law; Construction Law.

LEONID ANUTCHIN, born 1949; admitted, 1981. *Education:* Moscow Law Institute (1981). *LANGUAGES:* Russian. *PRACTICE AREAS:* Civil Law; Business Law; Estate Law; Construction Law.

HELENA SHILINA, born 1966; admitted, 1991. *Education:* Moscow Law Institute (1991). *LANGUAGES:* Russian. *PRACTICE AREAS:* Business Law; Civil Law.

(This Listing Continued)

EUGENIA VESELOVA, born 1973; admitted, 1994. *Education:* Moscow Law Institute (1994). *LANGUAGES:* Russian, English and French. *PRACTICE AREAS:* Estate Law; Civil Law.

SCOTLAND

GRAY AND CONNOCHIE

Solicitors, Notaries and Estate Agents

Established in 1930

106/108 CROWN STREET
ABERDEEN AB9 2BF, SCOTLAND
Telephone: (0224) 586201
Fax: (0224) 575098

Banchory, Scotland Office: 29 High Street. Telephone: (0330) 822188. Fax: (0330) 824691.

Company, Property, Accident Claims, Litigation, Reparation (Tort), Criminal, Wills, Trusts, Estates, Matrimonial, Divorce, Family Affairs, Bankruptcy, International Related Transactions.

FIRM PROFILE: The firm was established in 1930 and offers a full range of legal services including all aspects of purchase, sale and lease of domestic and commercial properties, all company, corporate and business matters and a complete court work service. This five Partner firm has five Legal Support Personnel, including four qualified Legal Assistants.

MEMBERS OF FIRM

HENRY JOHN GRAY CONNOCHIE, born Aberdeen, February 17, 1929; admitted, 1957, Scotland; 1960, Notary Public. *Education:* Edinburgh University; Aberdeen University (B.L., 1957). Life Governor, Imperial Cancer Research Fund, 1979. Tutor on Finance and Investment (Diploma in Legal Practice), Aberdeen University, 1985-1994. *Member:* The Law Society of Scotland; Scottish Law Agents Society; Society of Advocates in Aberdeen, The Stair Society, Scotland; International Bar Association; Institute of Directors (Associate Member). *LANGUAGES:* English. *PRACTICE AREAS:* Employers Liability Law; Insurance Law; Wills and Estates Law.

PETER FORBES EMSLIE, born Aberdeen, December 11, 1941; admitted, 1966, Scotland; Notary Public. *Education:* Aberdeen University (LL.B., 1964). *Member:* The Law Society of Scotland; Scottish Law Agents Society. *LANGUAGES:* English. *PRACTICE AREAS:* Corporate Law; Commercial and Residential Property Law.

KENNETH WILLIAM SHAW, born Aberdeen, March 11, 1953; admitted, 1975, Scotland; Notary Public. *Education:* Aberdeen University (LL.B.). Lecturer on Safety Law and Employers Liability, Aberdeen College of Commerce, 1977-1979. *Member:* Law Society of Scotland; Scottish Law Agents Society. *LANGUAGES:* English. *PRACTICE AREAS:* Reparation (Tort) Law.

NORMAN ROY ADAMS, born Montrose, September 28, 1957; admitted, 1980, Scotland; Notary Public. *Education:* Aberdeen University (LL.B.). *Member:* Law Society of Scotland; Scottish Law Agents Society; Society of Advocates in Aberdeen. *LANGUAGES:* French and English. *PRACTICE AREAS:* Property and Business Law.

JULIE ELIZABETH LONGMUIR, born Culross, March 7, 1961; admitted, 1985, Scotland; Notary Public. *Education:* Aberdeen University (LL.B., 1983; Dip.L.P.). *Member:* Law Society of Scotland; Aberdeen Bar Association. *LANGUAGES:* English. *PRACTICE AREAS:* Matrimonial Law.

KEATY & KEATY

Established in 1978

22 JOHN STREET
ABERDEEN AB1-1BT, SCOTLAND
Telephone: 022463601; Free Call in United Kingdom to the U.S.:
0-800-892276
Telecopier: 0224641544

New Orleans, Louisiana Office: 2140 World Trade Center, No. 2 Canal Street, 70130. Telephone: 504-524-2100; Nationwide Wats: 1-800-899-0039. Telecopier: 0224641544.

(This Listing Continued)

KEATY & KEATY, Aberdeen—Continued

Lafayette, Louisiana Office: One Lafayette Square, 345 Doucet Road, Suite 104, 70503. Telephone: 318-981-7707; Nationwide Wats: 1-800-489-1706. Telecopier: 318-989-0020.

Beaumont, Texas Office: 805 Park Street, Suite 200, 77701. Telephone: 1-800-489-1706.

Firm engaged in American and International Law Practice; not authorized to appear before Scottish Courts.

MEMBERS OF FIRM

ROBERT BURKE KEATY, SR., born Baton Rouge, Louisiana, July 7, 1949; admitted, 1973, Louisiana; 1986, Texas; U.S. District Court, Eastern, Western, and Middle Districts of Louisiana; U.S. Court of Appeals, 5th Circuit; U.S. District Court, Eastern and Southern Districts of Texas (Not admitted in Scotland). *Education:* University of Southwestern Louisiana (B.S., 1971); Tulane University (J.D., 1973). Recipient: Teagle Scholarship, 1972-1973; Sears Roebuck Award, 1971. Most Outstanding Senior, 1971. Most Outstanding Alumni, University Southwestern Louisiana, College of Business Administration, 1991. Listed in: Who's Who in American Colleges and Universities, 1971; Who's Who in New Orleans, Who's Who in America's Southeast, 1991; Who's Who in the World, 1992; Who's Who Among Emerging Leaders, 1991-1993; Who's Who in Finance and Industry, 1991-1993. Author: "Denying Tort Immunity to Offshore Non-Operators," LTLA Winter Convention, 1988; "Recent Developments in Removal and Remand," LTLA Winter Seminar, 1991; "Can a DOHSA Claim be Removed," LTLA Winter Seminar, 1994. Law Clerk to Hon. R. Blake West, Judge, U.S. District Court, Eastern District of Louisiana, 1974-1976. Dean's Committee, Tulane Law School. President's Committee, University of Southwestern Louisiana Offshore Marine Survival Center. Member, University Southwestern Louisiana, College of Business Administration Executive Advisory Council, 1991. Co-Chairman, United Givers Fund, Judicial Section, 1993. Member, Board of Directors, MidSouth National Bank. *Member:* Lafayette, New Orleans, Louisiana State, Federal and American Bar Associations; State Bar of Texas. The Association of Trial Lawyers of America; Louisiana Trial Lawyers Association (Governor, 1990, 1992-1993). Lifetime Fellow, Louisiana Bar Foundation. [Lt., USAR, Hon. Discharge, 1979]. *REPORTED CASES:* Lemelle v. Universl Mfg. Corp., 18 F.3d 1268, 62 USLW 2687, 25 Bankr. Ct. Dec. 792, Bankr. L. Rep. P75,824 (5th Cir. (La.), Apr 15, 1994) (NO. 93-4181); Taylor v. Lloyd's Underwriters of London, 972 F.2d 666, 1994 A.M.C. 607 (5th Cir. (La.), Sep 24, 1992) (NO. 91-3629; Melancon v. Western Auto Supply Co., 628 F.2d 395 (5th Cir.(La.), Oct 15, 1980) (NO. 79-1425); Bazile v. Bisso Marine Co., Inc., 606 F.2d 101 (5th Cir. (La.), Nov 08, 1979) (NO. 77-1015; Roger v. Estate of Moulton, 513 So.2d 1126 (La., May 18, 1987) (NO. 86-C-2266); Miller v. Griffin-Alexander Drilling Co., 715 F.Supp. 164 (W.D.La., Jul 03, 1989) (NO. CIV.A.85-0337-L); Johnson v. Odeco Oil and Gas Co., 864 F.2d 40, 1990 A.M.C. 35 (5th Cir.(La.), Jan 23, 1989) (NO. 87-3872); Davidson v. Enstar Corp., 860 F.2d 167 (5th Cir.(La.), Nov 09, 1988) (NO. 86-3874); Hota v. NHE Hospitals, Inc., 690 F.Supp. 1539 (E.D.La., Aug 02, 1988) (NO. CIV A 86-4385); Parfait v. Bowen, 803 F.2d 810, 15 Soc.-Sec.Rep.Ser. 245, Unempl.Ins.Rep. CCH (P) 17,319 (5th Cir.(La.), Oct. 15, 1986) (NO. 86-3145); Gautreaux v. Tex-Steam Co., 723 F. Supp. 1181, 14 O.S.H. Cos(BNA) 1326 (E.D.La., Oct. 25, 1989) (NO. CIV. A. 87-4396); Duhon. v. Petroleum Helicopters, Inc. 554 So.2d 1270 (La.App. 3 Cir., Dec 13, 1989) (NO. 88-875); Complaint of McDonough Marine Service, a Div. of Marmac Corp., 749 F.Supp. 128, 1991 A.M.C. 319 (E.D.La., Oct 22, 1990) (NO. GIV A 89-2167); Zapata Haynie Corp. v. Arthur, 980 F.2d 287, 1993 A.M.C. 1113 (5th Cir.(La.), Dec 15, 1992) (NO. 91-4432); Byrd v. Bossier Parish School Bd., 604 So.2d 997 (La., Sep 25, 1992) (NO. 92-OC-1612); Ducote v. Cliffs Drilling Co., 624 So.2d 960 (La.App. 3 Cir., Oct 06, 1993) (NO. 93-27). *PRACTICE AREAS:* Admiralty; Aviation; Multiple Death Disaster Litigation; Unsafe Products; Environmental Torts.

THOMAS ST. PAUL KEATY, II, born Baton Rouge, Louisiana, January 3, 1943; admitted, 1972, Louisiana and U.S. District Court, Eastern, Middle and Western Districts of Louisiana; 1974-1982, U.S. Court of Customs and Patent Appeals; 1975, U.S. Court of Appeals, Fifth Circuit; registered to practice before U.S. Patent and Trademark Office; 1980, U.S. District Court, Southern and Western Districts of Texas (Not admitted in Scotland). *Education:* University of Southwestern Louisiana (B.S., in Chem. Eng., 1966); Tulane University (J.D., 1972). Member, Moot Court. Lecturer: on Intellectual Property at Loyola University, New Orleans, Louisiana, 1979-1980; on Project Business, Newman School, New Orleans, Louisiana, 1981, Guest Lecturer at Academy of the Sacred Heart, Economics, New Orleans, Louisiana, 1969-1972. Author: "What the U.S. Businessman should know about Patents, U.S. and Foreign," U.S. Department of Com-

(This Listing Continued)

merce Publication, 1979; "Louisiana Section" of *State Trademark Section of Louisiana, 1982-1984. Member:* Lafayette, New Orleans, Louisiana State, American and Federal (Member, Board of Directors, 1985-1989) Bar Associations; State Bar of Texas; Louisiana Engineering Society; American Society of Chemical Engineers; American Intellectual Property Law Society.

ASSOCIATES

MICHEL P. WILTY, born Baton Rouge, Louisiana, March 20, 1959; admitted, 1985, Louisiana and U.S. District Court, Eastern District of Louisiana; 1987, U.S. Court of Appeals, Fifth Circuit and U.S. District Court, Middle and Western Districts of Louisiana (Not admitted in Scotland). *Education:* Louisiana State University and A. & M. College (B.S., 1981); Tulane University of Louisiana (J.D., cum laude, 1985). Member, Texas Trial Lawyers Association National Moot Court Trial Team, 1985. *Member:* New Orleans, Louisiana State and American Bar Associations.

JEFFREY S. CHOW, born New Orleans, Louisiana, November 14, 1958; admitted, 1985, Louisiana and U.S. District Court, Eastern, Middle and Western Districts of Louisiana (Not admitted in Scotland). *Education:* Tulane University, School of Engineering (B.S., Civil Engineering with Structural Design emphasis, 1980); Tulane University, School of Law (J.D., 1983); Institute of Comparative Law, Grenoble University, Grenoble, France (1981). *Member:* New Orleans, Louisiana State, Federal (Member, National Council, 1986-1988; Director, Young Lawyers Division, 1987) and American (Member, Committee on Arbitration) Bar Associations. Louisiana Society of Engineers, Reservist, Federal Emergency Management Agency.

CHRIS P. PERQUE, born Thibodaux, Louisiana, January 23, 1963; admitted, 1991, Louisiana and U.S. District Court, Western and Middle Districts of Louisiana. *Education:* Louisiana State University and A. and M. College (B.S., 1985) and Tulane University of Louisiana (J.D., 1991). Tulane Environmental Law Society, 1988-1991. *Member:* Louisiana State Bar Association; Society of Petroleum Engineers.

LEGAL SUPPORT PERSONNEL

RORIE CRAIGMYLE, born Aberdeen, Scotland, June 29, 1968. *Education:* Aberdeen College of Commerce (Scottish Higher National Diploma, 1988); University of Aberdeen, Scotland (LL.B., with honours, 1994). (Law Clerk).

REPRESENTATIVE CLIENTS: Guy Scroggins, Inc.; Mr. Cook's; First National Bank of Lafayette; L'eau Claire, Inc.; Citibank; Ramada Inns, Inc.; Quality Inns; Laitram Corp.; Subsea, Inc.; UNIFAB, Inc.; UNEX Corp.; Louisiana World Exposition; Teledyne Industries, Inc.; TBW Industries; Chemfix, Inc.; Friede & Goldman; Frank Craigmyle & Associates; I.C.C. Corporation; Hayden Energy Inc.; Keaty Land Company.
REFERENCES: Whitney National Bank; Bank of Lafayette; Premier Bank.

PROFESSOR S.H. AMIN

Established in 1975

FACULTY OF ADVOCATES
PARLIAMENT HOUSE
EDINBURGH EH1 1RF, SCOTLAND
Telephone: 0131-226 5071
(Clerk) Telephone: 0131-226 2881
Fax: 0131-225 3642

FIRM PROFILE: General Practice: International Commercial Law, Scottish, United Kingdom and European Community Law. Specialist Practice: Expert Opinion and advice on the laws of Islamic countries including Iran, Iraq, Saudi Arabia and the Gulf States.

Admitted to appear before all courts in Scotland, and on appeal in civil and commercial cases before the House of Lords.

PROF. S.H. AMIN, admitted, 1992, Faculty of Advocates, Edinburgh. *Education:* University of Tehran (LL.B., 1969; LL.M., 1972); University of Glasgow (Ph.D., 1978; Pupillage and Bar Exams, 1980-1982). Author: "International and Legal Problems of the Gulf," 1981; "Middle East Legal Systems," 1985; "Islamic Law and Its Implications for the Modern World," 1989; "Legal System of Iraq," 1991; "Commercial Arbitration in Islamic and Iranian Law," 1988; "Marine Insurance in Islamic & Iranian Law," 1989; "Marine Pollution in International and Middle Eastern Law," 1985; "Commercial Law of Iran," 1986; "Islamic Banking and Finance: The Experience of Iran," 1986; "Remedies for Breach of Contract in Islamic and Iranian Law," 1984 and also 30 books on International Islamic and Middle East Laws. Former Iranian Judge. Former Visiting Professor of Law, Tehran University. Former Full-time Professor of Law and Director, Centre for Comparative and International Law, Glasgow Caledonian University.

(This Listing Continued)

LANGUAGES: English, Arabic, Farsi and Kurdish. *PRACTICE AREAS:* Cross-border Litigation and Arbitration; International Law; Conflict of Laws; Islamic and Middle Eastern Laws.

BENNETT & ROBERTSON

Solicitors

16 WALKER STREET
EDINBURGH EH3 7NN, SCOTLAND
Telephone: 0131-225 4001
Telecopier: 0131-225 1107

Glasgow, Scotland Office: Gate House, 201-203 West George Street, G2 2LW. Telephone: 0141-204 0841. Fax: 0141-221 4216.

Agricultural Law, Arbitration, Commercial Law and Contracts. Company Law, Construction Law, Tax Planning, Trusts, Conveyancing, Licensing Law, Litigation, Executry and Investments, Intellectual Property Employment Law, European Law.

PARTNERS OF FIRM

COMMERCIAL DEPARTMENT

David A. Bennett, W.S.	Julie G. Macphail
J.S. Fraser MacGregor	Patricia M. McFarlane
Stuart Duncan, W.S.	Alan C. Bauchop
Roderick G. Alexander, W.S.	

ASSOCIATES

Gillian A. Phillips

LITIGATION DEPARTMENT

John H. Macfie, W.S.	Kenneth M.C. Gray
Gordon Innes, W.S.	A. Wyllie Robertson
Andrew D. Williams, W.S.	

PRIVATE CLIENTS

William C. Stevens	Elspeth M. Paget
John A. Hardy	David B. Milne, W.S.

Founder Members of ACL International, the Association of Commercial Lawyers International with legal contacts across the world.

BRODIES, W.S.

15 ATHOLL CRESCENT
EDINBURGH, SCOTLAND
Telephone: 0131-228-3777
Fax: 0131-228-3878

London, England Office: Telephone: 0171-247-6763. Fax: 0171-377-6293.

FIRM PROFILE: A broadly based practice providing a very wide range of services to commercial and private clients. Brodies offers expertise in the fields of Company Law (including Corporate Taxation), Commercial Property Law, Litigation, Planning and Environmental Law, all aspects of Private Client work, Rural Property Law and Accounting and Taxation. In addition, the firm has an in-house Land & Estate Agency. Brodies is a member of Tenalex and Unilaw.

MEMBERS OF FIRM

ALISTAIR C. CAMPBELL, admitted, 1978, Scotland. *LANGUAGES:* English. *PRACTICE AREAS:* Company Acquisitions; Corporate Mergers and Takeovers; Share Rights; Corporate Tax and VAT; Corporate Finance.

JAMES G. CLARK, admitted, 1970, Scotland. *LANGUAGES:* English. *PRACTICE AREAS:* Residential Property; Trusts; Taxation.

MOIRA E. CLARK, admitted, 1979, Scotland. *LANGUAGES:* English, French and Italian. *PRACTICE AREAS:* Commercial Property; Retail Property.

JOYCE CULLEN, admitted, 1981, Scotland. *LANGUAGES:* English. *PRACTICE AREAS:* Civil Litigation; Labour and Employment Law.

EVAN J. CUTHBERTSON, admitted, 1963, Scotland. Notary Public. *LANGUAGES:* English. *PRACTICE AREAS:* General Practice.

ANDREW M.C. DALGLEISH, admitted, 1975, Scotland. Notary Public. *LANGUAGES:* English. *PRACTICE AREAS:* Trusts; Executries; Taxation Planning; Off-shore Trusts.

(This Listing Continued)

HEW D.K. DALRYMPLE, admitted, 1977, Scotland. Notary Public. *LANGUAGES:* English and French. *PRACTICE AREAS:* Agricultural Law; Agricultural Property; Personal Taxation.

WILLIAM DRUMMOND, admitted, 1982, Scotland. *LANGUAGES:* English. *PRACTICE AREAS:* Commercial Property Law-Investment.

J. RONALD GARDINER, admitted, 1963, Scotland. Senior Partner. *LANGUAGES:* English. *PRACTICE AREAS:* Commercial Property; Liquor Licensing; Banking; Securities.

MICHAEL N.C. GASCOIGNE, admitted, 1973, Scotland. *LANGUAGES:* English and French. *PRACTICE AREAS:* Agricultural Law; Agricultural Property; Trusts.

DAVID W.A. GUILD, admitted, 1981, Scotland. *LANGUAGES:* English, French and German. *PRACTICE AREAS:* Corporate Law; Insolvency; Corporate Re-structuring; Banking Law.

W. JAMES C. HENDERSON, admitted, 1973, Scotland. *LANGUAGES:* English and French. *PRACTICE AREAS:* Residential Property; Trusts.

JOHN E.G. HENDRY, admitted, 1977, Scotland. *LANGUAGES:* English. *PRACTICE AREAS:* Agricultural Law; Agricultural Property.

WILLIAM HOLLIGAN, admitted, 1981, Scotland; 1985, South Australia. Notary Public. *LANGUAGES:* English. *PRACTICE AREAS:* Civil Litigation; Alternative Dispute Resolution; Insurance Law; Maritime.

DAVID H. HOULDSWORTH, admitted, 1974, Scotland. *LANGUAGES:* English and French. *PRACTICE AREAS:* Agricultural Law; Agricultural Property; Personal Taxation.

LINDA M. KINNIBURGH, admitted, 1982, Scotland. Notary Public. *LANGUAGES:* English. *PRACTICE AREAS:* Commercial Property- Securities.

KAREN BRUCE LOCKHART, admitted, 1972, Scotland. Part-time Member, VAT Tribunals, Scotland, 1993. *LANGUAGES:* English and French. *PRACTICE AREAS:* Civil Litigation; Personal Injury Law; Family Law; Reparation Law.

DAVID C. MACARTNEY, admitted, 1977, Scotland. *LANGUAGES:* English. *PRACTICE AREAS:* Commercial Property; Zoning Planning and Land Use; Renewable Energy.

ALAN J. MCANDREW, admitted, 1977, Scotland. *LANGUAGES:* English. *PRACTICE AREAS:* Commercial Property- Retail Property.

SOMERLED M. NOTLEY, admitted, 1979, Scotland. *LANGUAGES:* English and French. *PRACTICE AREAS:* Agricultural Law; Agricultural Property; Personal Taxation.

CHARLES SMITH, admitted, 1987, Scotland. *LANGUAGES:* English and French. *PRACTICE AREAS:* Environmental Law; Company Law.

HUGH J. STEVENS, admitted, 1980, Scotland. Notary Public. *LANGUAGES:* English. *PRACTICE AREAS:* Wills; Trusts; Executries.

K.P. DALE STRACHAN, admitted, 1979, Scotland. *LANGUAGES:* English. *PRACTICE AREAS:* Commercial Property-Development, Shopping Centers.

GEORGE L. TAYLOR, admitted, 1967, Scotland. Managing Partner. *LANGUAGES:* English. *PRACTICE AREAS:* Commercial Property-Investment, Franchising.

JULIAN C.A. VOGE, admitted, 1982, Scotland; 1992, England. Notary Public. *LANGUAGES:* English. *PRACTICE AREAS:* Corporate Law; Franchising Law; Corporate Financial Services Law.

DAVID J. WALKER, admitted, 1968, Scotland. *LANGUAGES:* English and French. *PRACTICE AREAS:* Civil Litigation; Personal Injury Litigation; Debt Recovery.

DAVID S. WILLIAMSON, admitted, 1971, Scotland; as Solicitor Advocate 1993, Scotland. Part-time Industrial Tribunal Chairman, Scotland, 1992. *LANGUAGES:* English. *PRACTICE AREAS:* Civil Litigation; Insolvency Law; Intellectual Property Law.

CONSULTANT

COLIN S. STROYAN, W.S., admitted, 1955, Scotland. *LANGUAGES:* English. *PRACTICE AREAS:* General Practice.

Languages: English, French, German, Italian and Russian

W. & J. BURNESS, WS

Established in 1836

16 HOPE STREET
CHARLOTTE SQUARE
EDINBURGH EH2 4DD, SCOTLAND
Telephone: +44 131-226-2561
Cable Address: "Burness Edinburgh"
Fax: +44 131-225-5075; 3949; 2964

Glasgow, Scotland Office: 242 West George Street. Telephone: 0141-248-4933. Fax: 0141-204-1601.

Guernsey, Channel Islands Office: Suite 9, The Maze, Berthelot Street, St. Peter Port. Telephone: 0481-710867. Fax: 0481-710578.

Corporate Advice, Competition Law, Commercial Property, Commercial Litigation, Intellectual Property, Tax Planning, Trusts, Executry and Investments, Farms and Estates, Residential Property and Construction Law.

MEMBERS OF FIRM

DAVID RONALD REID, born Scotland, June 23, 1937; admitted, 1962, Scotland. *Education:* Edinburgh University (M.A. Hons., 1959; LL.B., 1962). Notary Public. Writer to Her Majesty's Signet. **LANGUAGES:** French. **PRACTICE AREAS:** Commercial Property Law.

WILLIAM BRUCE LOGAN, born Scotland, September 7, 1941; admitted, 1967, Scotland. *Education:* Cambridge University (B.A., Hons., 1962); Edinburgh University (LL.B., 1964). Notary Public. Writer to Her Majesty's Signet. Hon. Consul in Edinburgh for the Republic of Venezuela. **PRACTICE AREAS:** Civil Litigation; Arbitration Law.

ALISTER MACDONALD SUTHERLAND, born England, July 11, 1934; admitted, 1959, Scotland. *Education:* Edinburgh University (M.A., 1954; LL.B., 1956). Notary Public. Writer to Her Majesty's Signet. **PRACTICE AREAS:** Pensions Law; Tax Planning Law; Settlements Law; Trust Law.

GEORGE MACBETH MENZIES, born Scotland, September 18, 1943; admitted, 1973, Scotland. *Education:* Oxford University (B.A. Hons., 1965); Edinburgh University (LL.B., 1967). Notary Public. Writer to Her Majesty's Signet. **LANGUAGES:** French. **PRACTICE AREAS:** Personal Tax Law; Estate Planning Law; Settlement Law; Trust Law.

DAVID ALAN GIFFORD, born Scotland, August 22, 1946; admitted, 1972, Scotland. *Education:* Edinburgh University (M.A. in Modern Languages, 1967; LL.B., 1970). Notary Public. Writer to Her Majesty's Signet. Part Time Conveyancing Tutor, Edinburgh University, 1974-1976. Director of ESPC. **PRACTICE AREAS:** Residential and Commercial Property Law; Conveyancing Law; Licensed Trade Law; Residential Development Law.

MALCOLM GRAHAM STRANG STEEL, born Scotland, November 24, 1946; admitted, 1972, Scotland. *Education:* Trinity College, Cambridge (B.A., 1968); Edinburgh University (LL.B., 1970). Notary Public. Writer to Her Majesty's Signet. External Examiner, Conveyancing Diploma in Legal Practice, Edinburgh University, 1981-1984. Member, Council of Law Society of Scotland, 1984-1990. Convenor, Agricultural Law Committee, 1988. Member, Tax and Law and Parliamentary Committees of Scottish Landowners Federation. Trustee, Scottish Dyslexia Trust, 1988—. **PRACTICE AREAS:** Agricultural Law; Personal Taxation Law; Conveyancing Law.

PAUL DOMINIC PIA, born Scotland, March 29, 1947; admitted, 1970, Scotland. *Education:* University of Edinburgh (LL.B. Hons., Law & Economics, 1968); Perugiz University (Diploma in Italian Language). Notary Public. Writer to Her Majesty's Signet. Co-Author: "Care, Diligence and Skill," a handbook for Company Directors. **LANGUAGES:** French and Italian. **PRACTICE AREAS:** Corporate Law; Commercial Contracts Law; Intellectual Property Law; Overseas Companies and Inward Investments.

JAMES ANGUS MCLEAN, born England, April 25, 1947; admitted, 1972, Scotland. *Education:* Cambridge University (B.A., 1968); Edinburgh University (LL.B., 1970). Writer to Her Majesty's Signet. **LANGUAGES:** French. **PRACTICE AREAS:** Intellectual Property Law; Competition (Antitrust) Law; Commercial Contracts Law.

JOHN CAMPBELL RAFFERTY, born Scotland, June 30, 1951; admitted, 1975, Scotland. *Education:* Edinburgh University (LL.B. Hons, 1973). Notary Public. Writer to Her Majesty's Signet. **LANGUAGES:** French. **PRACTICE AREAS:** Corporate Law.

GORDON LINDSAY KEVAN MURRAY, admitted, 1978, Scotland. *Education:* Edinburgh University (B.A., 1974; LL.B., 1976). Notary Public. Writer to Her Majesty's Signet. President, Scottish Young Lawyers Associ-

(This Listing Continued)

ation, 1977-1978. **LANGUAGES:** Italian. **PRACTICE AREAS:** Property Law.

HUBERT JAMES ROSS, born Scotland, October 26, 1948; admitted, 1974, Scotland. *Education:* Edinburgh University (M.A. Hons., 1970; LL.B., 1972). Notary Public. Writer to Her Majesty's Signet. Parliamentary Draftsman, Lord Advocates Department, 1976-1978. Merchant Banker, Leopold Joseph and Sons Limited, 1977-1983. **LANGUAGES:** French. **PRACTICE AREAS:** Tax Planning Law; Trust Law; Banking Law.

L. ANNETTE PAIRMAN, born England, February 11, 1958; admitted, 1980, Scotland. *Education:* Edinburgh University (LL.B., 1978). Notary Public. Writer to Her Majesty's Signet. **PRACTICE AREAS:** Corporate Law.

SIMON A. MACKINTOSH, born England, February 2, 1957; admitted, 1982, Scotland. *Education:* Cambridge University (B.A. Hons., 1978); Edinburgh University (LL.B., Distinction, 1980). Notary Public. Writer to Her Majesty's Signet. Author: "Revenue Law in Scotland," Butterworths, 1986. Tutor in Law, Edinburgh University, 1980-1983. Scottish Editor, Butterworths Personal Tax Guide. *Member:* Association Internationale Des Jeunes Avocats; Law Society of Scotland (Member, Revenue Law Committee). **LANGUAGES:** French and German. **PRACTICE AREAS:** Private Client Taxation Law; Pension Schemes Law; Trust Law.

MALCOLM J. WOOD, born Scotland, September 12, 1955; admitted, 1980, Scotland. *Education:* Edinburgh University (LL.B. Hons., 1977). Notary Public. Writer to Her Majesty's Signet. Visiting Scholar, University of California, Berkeley, 1977-1978. Tutor, Edinburgh University Legal Practice Unit, 1985-1990. *Member:* The Securities Institute. **PRACTICE AREAS:** Corporate Law; Banking Law; Security Law; Insolvency Law; Commercial Contracts Law.

KENNETH A. ROSS, born Scotland, January 18, 1957; admitted, 1981, Scotland. *Education:* Edinburgh University (LL.B. Hons.). Notary Public. **LANGUAGES:** French. **PRACTICE AREAS:** Commercial Property Law.

DONALD B. CASKIE, born Scotland, March 8, 1941; admitted, 1966, Scotland. *Education:* University of Glasgow (M.A., 1961; LL.B., 1963); Cornell University, USA (Exchange Student, 1963/1964). Notary Public. Writer to Her Majesty's Signet. Author: *Wallace & McNeil's Banking Law,* W. Green & Son Ltd., 10th Edition, 1991. **PRACTICE AREAS:** Trust Law; Banking Law.

CAROLINE STEWART DRUMMOND, born Scotland, May 30, 1959; admitted, 1982, Scotland. *Education:* Aberdeen University (LL.B., 1980); Edinburgh University (DipLP, 1981). Notary Public. Writer to Her Majesty's Signet. **LANGUAGES:** French and German. **PRACTICE AREAS:** Commercial Property Law.

DR. MARTIN SALES, born South Africa, September 26, 1952; admitted, 1984, Scotland. *Education:* Edinburgh University (M.A. Hons., 1975; Ph.D., 1980; LL.B., 1982). Notary Public. Writer to Her Majesty's Signet. Tutor in Law, University of Edinburgh, 1983-1984. **LANGUAGES:** French. **PRACTICE AREAS:** Civil Litigation; Building Law; Construction Law; Arbitration Law.

CHRISTOPHER SCOTT, born Scotland, April 29, 1960; admitted, 1985, Scotland. *Education:* University of Edinburgh (LL.B., Hons., 1982). Notary Public. Writer to Her Majesty's Signet. Tutor in Law, University of Edinburgh, 1982-1987. **LANGUAGES:** German. **PRACTICE AREAS:** Corporate Law.

ANDREW FALCONER SLEIGH, born Scotland, September 11, 1957; admitted, 1981, Scotland. *Education:* University of Glasgow (M.A., 1977; LL.B., 1979); University of Amsterdam (Diploma, European Law, 1982); University of Virginia (LL.M., 1983). **LANGUAGES:** Dutch. **PRACTICE AREAS:** Corporate Law; Commercial Law.

ADAM RICHARD GILLINGHAM, born Scotland, December 31, 1958; admitted, 1983, Scotland. *Education:* Aberdeen University (LL.B., 1981). Notary Public. Writer to Her Majesty's Signet. **LANGUAGES:** French. **PRACTICE AREAS:** Rural Conveyancing Law; Private Client.

DAVID BISSET GIBSON, born Scotland, February 10, 1961; admitted, 1986, Scotland. *Education:* Edinburgh University (LL.B. Hons., 1983). Notary Public. Writer to Her Majesty's Signet. **LANGUAGES:** French. **PRACTICE AREAS:** Commercial Property Law; Company Law.

MARSALI MURRAY, born Scotland, October 14, 1961; admitted, 1986, Scotland. *Education:* Edinburgh University (LL.B. Hons., 1983). **LANGUAGES:** German. **PRACTICE AREAS:** Commercial Litigation; Medical Negligence Law; Employment Law.

(This Listing Continued)

DAVID JOHNSTON, born Scotland, October 20, 1958. *Education:* Edinburgh University (LL.B. Hons., 1981). Notary Public. Writer to Her Majesty's Signet. *Member:* Law Society of Scotland. **LANGUAGES:** French. **PRACTICE AREAS:** Residential, Commercial and Licensed Property Law; Small Business.

ANTHONY JAMES MONTRESOR READ, born Kenya, October 24, 1961; admitted, 1986 Scotland. *Education:* Dundee University (LL.B., 1982); Cambridge University (LL.M., 1984). Notary Public. Writer to Her Majesty's Signet. **LANGUAGES:** French and German. **PRACTICE AREAS:** Intellectual Property Law; Competition (Antitrust) Law; Construction Law; Commercial Contracts Law.

HEATHER THOMPSON, born Northern Ireland, December 7, 1961; admitted, 1986, England and Wales; 1990, Scotland. *Education:* Cambridge University (B.A., Hons., 1983); Chester College of Law (C.P.E., 1984). Notary Public. **LANGUAGES:** French. **PRACTICE AREAS:** Trust Law; Wills and Succession; Tax Planning; Value Added Tax.

J. IAN WATTIE, born Scotland, December 5, 1962; admitted, 1988, Scotland. *Education:* Aberdeen University (LL.B., 1984). Notary Public. **LANGUAGES:** French, German and Italian. **PRACTICE AREAS:** Commercial Property Law.

SHONA MACLEAN, born Scotland, October 18, 1963; admitted, 1985, Scotland. *Education:* Strathclyde University (LL.B., 1983). **PRACTICE AREAS:** Commercial Litigation; Employment Law; Construction Law.

All Partners are members of The Law Society of Scotland.

Languages: English, French, German, Spanish and Italian

DUNDAS & WILSON, C.S.

SALTIRE COURT
20 CASTLE TERRACE
EDINBURGH EH1 2EN, SCOTLAND
Telephone: 0131-228 8000
Fax: 0131-228 8888

Glasgow, Scotland Office: Sutherland House, 149 St. Vincent Street, G2 5NW. Telephone: 0141-221 8586. Fax: 0141-221 8687.

London, England Office: Boston House, 6364 New Broad Street, EC2M 1JR. Telephone: 0171-256 9191. Fax: 0171-256 6464.

Commercial Property, Company and Commercial, Litigation, Private Clients.

J. BRIAN LEGGAT, W.S., CHAIRMAN, admitted, 1971, Scotland. *Education:* Edinburgh (LL.B.). Notary Public.

ROBIN A. EDWARDS, C.B.E., W.S., admitted, 1964, Scotland. *Education:* Edinburgh (M.A., LL.B.). Notary Public.

ROBIN O. BLAIR, W.S., admitted, 1965, Scotland. *Education:* St. Andrews (M.A.); Edinburgh (LL.B.). Notary Public.

JOHN A.D. INNES, W.S., admitted, 1965, Scotland. *Education:* Cambridge (B.A.); Edinburgh (LL.B.).

JAMES S. HODGE, W.S., admitted, 1967, Scotland. *Education:* Edinburgh (LL.B.). Notary Public.

CHRISTOPHER N. ATHANAS, W.S., admitted, 1966, Scotland. *Education:* Aberdeen (M.A., LL.B.). Notary Public.

NEIL A. MACLEOD, W.S., admitted, 1969, Scotland. *Education:* Edinburgh (LL.B.). Notary Public.

EUAN R. MACLEOD, W.S., admitted, 1967, Scotland. *Education:* Edinburgh (LL.B.). Notary Public.

DAVID K. MCLELLAN, W.S., admitted, 1971, Scotland. *Education:* Edinburgh (LL.B.). Notary Public.

ROBERT C. TURCAN, W.S., admitted, 1973, Scotland. *Education:* Oxford (M.A.); Edinburgh (LL.B.).

PHILIP A. DACKER, W.S., MANAGING PARTNER, admitted, 1972, Scotland. *Education:* Edinburgh (LL.B.). Notary Public.

JAMES P. WATT, W.S., admitted, 1976, Scotland. *Education:* Edinburgh (B.Comm.; LL.B., Hons); Harvard (LL.M.). Notary Public.

J. NEIL COCHRAN, W.S., admitted, 1972, Scotland. *Education:* Edinburgh (LL.B.).

IAN W. MOFFETT, W.S., admitted, 1974, Scotland. *Education:* Edinburgh (LL.B., Hons). Notary Public.

(This Listing Continued)

DOUGLAS A. CONNELL, W.S., admitted, 1976, Scotland. *Education:* Edinburgh (LL.B.).

DONALD I. CUMMING, W.S., admitted, 1976, Scotland. *Education:* Edinburgh (LL.B., Hons.). Notary Public.

JOHN S. MURRAY, W.S., admitted, 1979, Scotland. *Education:* Edinburgh (M.A., Hons.; LL.B.).

DAVID HARDIE, W.S., admitted, 1978, Scotland. *Education:* Dundee (LL.B., Hons). Notary Public.

COLIN M. MACLEOD, W.S., admitted, 1979, Scotland. *Education:* Edinburgh (LL.B., Hons.).

MAUREEN S. COUTTS, W.S., admitted, 1983, Scotland. *Education:* St. Andrews (M.A., Hons.).

DONALD G.B. SHAW, W.S., admitted, 1979, Scotland. *Education:* Aberdeen (LL.B.). Notary Public.

KENNETH M. CUMMING, W.S., admitted, 1982, Scotland. *Education:* Edinburgh (LL.B., Hons.).

PHILIP MACKAY, W.S., admitted, 1982, Scotland. *Education:* Edinburgh (LL.B., Hons.).

CHRISTOPHER R.J. CAMPBELL, W.S., admitted, 1982, Scotland. *Education:* Edinburgh (LL.B., Hons.).

MICHAEL P. STONEHAM, W.S., admitted, 1985, Scotland. *Education:* Cambridge (M.A.).

BRIAN W.J. RUTHERFORD, admitted, 1979, Scotland. *Education:* Dundee (LL.B.).

IAN J.C. PATERSON, W.S., admitted, 1985, Scotland. *Education:* Edinburgh (M.A., LL.B.).

IAN R. CLARK, W.S., admitted, 1985, Scotland. *Education:* Edinburgh (LL.B., ATII). Notary Public.

CHRISTIAN R.M. HOOK, admitted, 1988, Scotland. *Education:* Cambridge (B.A. Cantab.).

JONATHAN M. ROBERTSON, W.S., admitted, 1986, Scotland. *Education:* Aberdeen (LL.B.). Notary Public.

LAURENCE C. WARD, W.S., admitted, 1985, Scotland. *Education:* Aberdeen (LL.B.).

HUGH W.D. BRUCE-WATT, admitted, 1984, Scotland. *Education:* Cambridge (M.A.); Edinburgh (LL.B.).

ALAN D. CAMPBELL, admitted, 1986, Scotland. *Education:* Edinburgh (LL.B.).

PAMELA L. LYALL, admitted, 1982, Scotland. *Education:* Aberdeen (LL.B.).

ALAYNE E. SWANSON, admitted, 1983, Scotland. *Education:* Edinburgh (LL.B.).

LINDSAYS WS

Established in 1815
11 ATHOLL CRESCENT
EDINBURGH EH3 8HE, SCOTLAND
Telephone: 031-229 1212
Fax: 031-229 5611
Dx: ED25

Agricultural Property and Estates, Civil Litigation, Commercial (Real Estate) Conveyancing, Corporate Law, Intellectual Property, Residential Conveyancing, Liquor Licensing, Planning Law, Landlord and Tenant, Debt Collection, Employment Law, Building and Construction Law, Road Haulage and Transport, Trusts and Executries, Private Client Work.

PARTNERS

R. J. Elliot, WS	W. B. Robertson, WS
R. G. Shearer, WS	R. J. Arbuthnott
E. O. St.John, WS	N. A. Kellock
W. J. Gay, WS	S. J. Pitches
A. D. MacKay, WS	C. Kennedy
D. S. Reith, WS	C. McClanachan
D. K. Tullis, WS	M. Townsend
J. A. R. Mackie	A.W. Cummings

(This Listing Continued)

LINDSAYS WS, Edinburgh—Continued
A.W. Cummings

ASSOCIATES

A. Gordon	A. Laird
L. Hampton	L. McPhail
G. Hyams	K. Preston

MACLAY MURRAY & SPENS

Established in 1871

3 GLENFINLAS STREET
EDINBURGH EH3 6AQ, SCOTLAND
Telephone: 0131-226 5196
Telex: 727238 Vindex
Fax: 0131-226-3174; 0131-225-9610

Glasgow, Scotland Office: 151 St. Vincent Street, G2 5NJ. Telephone: 0141-248-5011. Cable Address: "Vindex, Glasgow". Telex: 77474 Vindex. Fax: 0141-221-2968; 0141-248-5819.

London, England Office: 10 Foster Lane, EC2V 6HH. Telephone: 0171-606-6130. Fax: 0171-600-0992; 0171-600-0993.

Brussels, Belgium Office: Scotland Europa Centre, 35 Square De Meeus, B-1040. Telephone: 322 927 2001. Fax: 322 927 2401.

RESIDENT PARTNERS

IAN G. INGLIS, admitted, 1959, Scotland. Education: B.A. (Oxon); LL.B. Member: Royal Faculty of Procurators in Glasgow; Law Society of Scotland; Writer to the Signet; Institute of Patent Agents (Associate Member). LANGUAGES: English. PRACTICE AREAS: Admiralty and Maritime; Arbitration; Intellectual Property.

BRUCE R. PATRICK, admitted, 1975, Scotland. Education: B.A. (Oxon); LL.B. Member: Royal Faculty of Procurators in Glasgow; Law Society of Scotland; Writer to the Signet. LANGUAGES: English, French and German. PRACTICE AREAS: Company Law; Corporate Law; Finance.

IAN S. QUIGLEY, admitted, 1972, Scotland. Education: LL.B. Notary Public. Member: Law Society of Scotland; Writer to the Signet. LANGUAGES: English. PRACTICE AREAS: Commercial Property Development and Finance; Leases and Leasing.

IAN G. LUMSDEN, admitted, 1977, Scotland. Education: B.A. (Cantab); LL.B. Notary Public. Member: Royal Faculty of Procurators in Glasgow; International Bar Association; Law Society of Scotland. LANGUAGES: English. PRACTICE AREAS: Corporate Law; Environmental Law; Mergers, Acquisitions and Divestitures.

ROBERT J. LAING, admitted, 1977, England; 1985, Scotland. Education: M.A. (Cantab). Member: Writer to the Signet; International Bar Association; Law Society of Scotland. LANGUAGES: English. PRACTICE AREAS: Corporate Law; Mergers, Acquisitions and Divestitures; Banks and Banking.

EWAN R. EASTON, admitted, 1983, Scotland. Education: LL.B. Member: Law Society of Scotland; Writer to the Signet. LANGUAGES: English. PRACTICE AREAS: Construction; Labour and Employment; Land Development and Planning.

ROBERT PIRRIE, admitted, 1981, Scotland. Education: LL.B. Member: Writer to the Signet; Law Society of Scotland. LANGUAGES: English. PRACTICE AREAS: Company Law; Corporate Law; Finance.

JENNIFER D. JOHNSON, admitted, 1979, Scotland. Education: LL.B. Notary Public. Member: Law Society of Scotland; Writer to the Signet. LANGUAGES: English. PRACTICE AREAS: Commercial Property Development and Finance; Leases and Leasing.

ALASTAIR J.A. MCEWAN, admitted, 1989, Scotland. Education: LL.B.; M.Sc.; LL.M. Member: Law Society of Scotland. LANGUAGES: English and Norwegian. PRACTICE AREAS: Commercial Property Development and Finance; Environmental; Leases and Leasing.

GRAEME E.C. SLOAN, admitted, 1987, Scotland. Education: LL.B. Member: Law Society of Scotland. LANGUAGES: English and French. PRACTICE AREAS: Corporate Law; Mergers, Acquisitions and Divestitures; Securities.

WILLIAM BROWN, admitted, 1983, Scotland; 1989, England and Wales. Education: LL.B. Member: Law Society of Scotland; Law Society of England and Wales; Scottish Lawyers European Group; Solicitors Euro-

(This Listing Continued)

pean Group; AIJA. LANGUAGES: English and French. PRACTICE AREAS: European Community; Competition; Agency and Distributorships.

GILL M. GRASSIE, admitted, 1986, Scotland. Education: LL.B., Hons. Member: Writer to the Signet; Law Society of Scotland. LANGUAGES: English, French, Italian and German. PRACTICE AREAS: Intellectual Property; Admiralty; Professional Liability.

RESIDENT ASSOCIATES

JOHN G. K. HARDING-EDGAR, admitted, 1987, Scotland. Education: LL.B. Associate, Chartered Institute of Bankers. Member: Writer to the Signet; Law Society of Scotland. LANGUAGES: English and French. PRACTICE AREAS: Corporate Law; Banks and Banking; Finance Law.

DOUGLAS J. CRAWFORD, admitted, 1988, Scotland. Education: LL.B. Notary Public. Member: Law Society of Scotland. LANGUAGES: English. PRACTICE AREAS: Corporate Law; Company Law; Finance Law.

TIMOTHY J. EDWARD, admitted, 1989, Scotland. Education: B.A.; LL.B. Writer to the Signet. Member: Scottish Law Agents Society; Scottish European Lawyers Group; Law Society of Scotland. LANGUAGES: English and French. PRACTICE AREAS: Intellectual Property; Insolvency; European Community Law.

OLIVIA R. GILES, admitted, 1989, Scotland. Member: Law Society of Scotland. LANGUAGES: English. PRACTICE AREAS: Commercial Property Development and Finance; Leases and Leasing.

MARK R. HAMILTON, admitted, 1987, Scotland. Education: LL.B. Member: Law Society of Scotland. LANGUAGES: English. PRACTICE AREAS: Labour and Employment; Professional Negligence; Environmental.

(For Complete Personnel and Biographical Data, see Professional Biographies at Glasgow, Scotland)

McCLURE NAISMITH ANDERSON & GARDINER

Established in 1826

49 QUEEN STREET
EDINBURGH EH2 3NH, SCOTLAND
Telephone: 0131-220-1002
Facsimile: 0131-220-1003

Commercial and Company Law, Banking, Commercial Property, Intellectual Property, Civil Litigation, Environmental and Mineral Law, Commercial Contracts.

FIRM PROFILE: Established in 1826, the firm is now one of Scotland's leading commercial law firms.

MEMBERS OF FIRM

WILLIAM D. WALKER, born Keith, Scotland, December 22, 1952; admitted, 1976, Scotland. Education: University of Edinburgh (LL.B., 1974). Member: Law Society of Scotland; Society of the Writers to Her Majesty's Signet. LANGUAGES: English. PRACTICE AREAS: Commercial Litigation; Personal Injuries; Insurance Law.

STEVEN BROWN, born Irvine, Scotland, November 20, 1956; admitted, 1980, Scotland. Education: University of Edinburgh (LL.B., Hons., 1978). Member: Law Society of Scotland; International Bar Association. LANGUAGES: English. PRACTICE AREAS: Banking; Commercial Contracts.

ALAN K. SIMPSON, born Aberdeen, Scotland, November 22, 1951; admitted, 1977, Scotland. Education: University of Dundee (LL.B., 1973; M.A., 1975). Notary Public. Member: Law Society of Scotland; International Bar Association. LANGUAGES: English. PRACTICE AREAS: Mineral Law; Commercial Conveyancing and Leasing; Secured Lending.

PETER C. CAMPBELL, born Huntly, Scotland, January 20, 1953; admitted, 1981, Scotland. Education: University of Aberdeen (LL.B., Hons., 1974). Member: Law Society of Scotland; United Kingdom Environmental Law Association. LANGUAGES: English. PRACTICE AREAS: Commercial Conveyancing; Mineral Law.

JEFFREY A. HUTCHESON, born Irvine, Scotland, July 16, 1957; admitted, 1981, Scotland. Education: University of Aberdeen (LL.B., Hons., 1979). Notary Public. Member: Law Society of Scotland. LANGUAGES:

(This Listing Continued)

EU1194B

English. *PRACTICE AREAS:* Employment; Commercial Litigation; Reparation; Debt Recovery.

CAROLINE DOCHERTY, born Edinburgh, Scotland, February 15, 1960; admitted, 1983, Scotland. *Education:* University of Aberdeen (LL.B., 1981; Dip. L.P., 1982). *Member:* Law Society of Scotland; Society of Writers to Her Majesty's Signet. *LANGUAGES:* English. *PRACTICE AREAS:* Commercial and Residential Property.

ANDREW S.C. MACMILLAN, born Canterbury, England, March 8, 1964; admitted, 1988, Scotland. *Education:* University of Aberdeen (LL.B., Hons, 1986). Notary Public. Seminars: Management Buy Outs, Tourism Law. *Member:* Law Society of Scotland; Association and International Forum of Travel and Tourism Attorneys. *LANGUAGES:* English. *PRACTICE AREAS:* Commercial and Company Law; Banking; Commercial Contracts; Intellectual Property.

McGRIGOR DONALD

ERSKINE HOUSE
68-73 QUEEN STREET
EDINBURGH EH2 4NF, SCOTLAND
Telephone: 44 131 226 7777
Fax: 44 131 226 7700

Glasgow, Scotland Office: Pacific House, 70 Wellington Street, G2 6SB. Telephone: 44 141 248 6677. Facsimile: 44 141 204 1351/221 1390.
London, England Office: 63 Queen Victoria Street, EC4N 4ST. Telephone: 44 171 329 3299. Fax: 44 171 329 4000.
English Affiliated Firm: Morrison Skirrow, Solicitors.

General Practice.

MANAGING PARTNER

JAMES D. YOUNG, born Scotland, February 26, 1950; admitted, 1975, Scotland. *Education:* Glasgow University (LL.B., 1971). *Member:* Industrial Law Group.

(For Complete Biographical Data on all Personnel, see Professional Biographies at Glasgow, Scotland).

MORTON, FRASER MILLIGAN, W.S.

Established in 1800
15 & 19 YORK PLACE
EDINBURGH EH1 3EL, SCOTLAND
Telephone: 0131-556-8444
Telecopier: 0131-557-3778

Other Edinburgh, Scotland Office: Commercial Departments, 18 York Place, EH1 3EP. Telephone: 0131-557-9595. Telecopier: 0131-557-6334.
Brussels, Belgium Office: 119/10 Avenue de la Forêt, B-1050. Telephone: 32-2-673-81-59. Fax: 32-2-673-79-20.

Company, Commercial, Banking, Asset and Project Finance, Commercial and Domestic Real Estate, Environmental. Trust and Executry, Investment, Taxation, Patent, Oil and Gas and Planning Law. Litigation and Arbitration. General Practice.

MEMBERS OF FIRM

JOHN WIGHTMAN, C.B.E., W.S., admitted, 1959, Scotland. *Education:* St. Andrews (M.A., Hons.); Edinburgh (LL.B.). Notary Public. *LANGUAGES:* French. *PRACTICE AREAS:* General Practice; Trusts; Taxation; Estate Planning.

D. JOHN MCNEIL, C.B.E., W.S., admitted, 1962, Scotland. *Education:* Edinburgh (M.A., Hons.; LL.B.). Notary Public. *PRACTICE AREAS:* Commercial Property; Joint Ventures; Oil and Gas Law.

SCOTT A. RAE, W.S., admitted, 1968, Scotland. *Education:* Edinburgh (LL.B., Hons.). Notary Public. *PRACTICE AREAS:* Taxation; Charities; Trusts; Estates; Planning; Pensions Law.

HUGH J.S. HENDERSON, W.S., admitted, 1964, Scotland. *Education:* University of Edinburgh. Notary Public. *PRACTICE AREAS:* Commercial Property; Hotels and Licensing Law; Banking Law.

DAVID L. STEWART, W.S., admitted, 1970, Scotland. *Education:* Cambridge (B.A.); Edinburgh (LL.B.). Notary Public. *LANGUAGES:* French. *PRACTICE AREAS:* Commercial Litigation; Arbitration; European Law; Labor Law.

(This Listing Continued)

DONALD A. REID, W.S., admitted, 1967, Scotland. *Education:* Edinburgh (LL.B.). Notary Public. *PRACTICE AREAS:* Environmental Law; Planning; Agriculture.

G. LEONARD R. MAIR, W.S., admitted, 1975, Scotland. *Education:* Stirling (B.A., Hons.); Edinburgh (LL.B.). Notary Public. *LANGUAGES:* French. *PRACTICE AREAS:* Personal Litigation; Family Law.

R. BRUCE WOOD, W.S., admitted, 1976, Scotland. *Education:* Edinburgh (LL.B., Hons); California, Berkeley (LL.M.). Notary Public. *LANGUAGES:* German. *PRACTICE AREAS:* Corporate Law; Asset and Project Financing; Pensions Law.

GEORGE B. CLARK, W.S., admitted, 1976, Scotland. *Education:* Edinburgh (LL.B., Hons.; LL.M.). Notary Public. *PRACTICE AREAS:* Trusts; Property; General Practice.

H. CRAIG BOWMAN, W.S., admitted, 1978, Scotland. *Education:* Glasgow (M.A.; LL.B., Hons.). Notary Public. *LANGUAGES:* French. *PRACTICE AREAS:* Corporate; Competition Law; Intellectual Property.

GORDON J. KERR, W.S., admitted, 1978, Scotland. *Education:* Edinburgh (LL.B., Hons.). Notary Public. *LANGUAGES:* French. *PRACTICE AREAS:* Employee Relocation; Property; General Practice.

PETER J. BRAID, W.S., admitted, 1982, Scotland. *Education:* Edinburgh (LL.B., Hons.), Notary Public. *PRACTICE AREAS:* Commercial Litigation; Insolvency and Debt.

JAMES H. RUST, W.S., admitted, 1981, Scotland. *Education:* Aberdeen (LL.B.). Notary Public. *PRACTICE AREAS:* Property; General Practice.

LINDA H. URQUHART, W.S., admitted, 1982, Scotland. *Education:* Edinburgh (LL.B.). Notary Public. *LANGUAGES:* French. *PRACTICE AREAS:* Commercial Property; Banking and Securities.

A. SHIRLEY DAVIDSON, W.S., admitted, 1982, Scotland. *Education:* Edinburgh (LL.B. Hons.). Notary Public. *LANGUAGES:* Spanish. *PRACTICE AREAS:* Commercial Property; Banking and Securities.

IAN G.A. HAIGH, W.S., admitted, 1985, Scotland. *Education:* Dundee (LL.B.). Notary Public. *PRACTICE AREAS:* Banking; Planning; Commercial Property.

DOROTHY A. KELLAS, W.S., admitted, 1985, Scotland. *Education:* Edinburgh (LL.B.). Notary Public. *LANGUAGES:* French. *PRACTICE AREAS:* Property; General Practice.

DAVID HOSSACK, admitted, 1987, Scotland. *Education:* Aberdeen (LL.B., Hons.). Notary Public. *PRACTICE AREAS:* Litigation; Reparation; Road Traffic.

ADRIAN E. BELL, admitted, 1990, Scotland. *Education:* Edinburgh (LL.B., Hons.). *PRACTICE AREAS:* Corporate; Corporate Finance.

SENIOR ASSOCIATES

RICHARD S.H. GIRDWOOD. PRACTICE AREAS: Commercial Property.

JOHN TOTHILL. PRACTICE AREAS: Corporate Law.

ANNE STEELE. PRACTICE AREAS: Trusts.

HAZEL LOGAN. PRACTICE AREAS: Property.

PIERGROSSI VILLA MANCA GRAZIADEI

3 WALKER STREET
EDINBURGH EH3 7JY, SCOTLAND
Telephone: +44-131-226.7722
Telefax: +44-131-226.7887

Milan, Italy Office: Via Festa del Perdono 10, 20122 Milan. Telephone: +39-2-58303657 (multiple). Fax: +39-2-58303818.
Rome, Italy Office: Via dei Gracchi 320, 00192 Rome. Telephone: +39-6-3215901 (multiple). Fax: +39-6-3213218.

General Civil and Commercial Practice. Acquisitions, Corporate, Licensing, Patents and Trademarks, International Law. Litigation. Arbitration. Environmental Law, EEC Law.

RESIDENT MEMBER

GIANNI MANCA, born Genoa, Italy, July 21, 1924; admitted, 1952, Italy. *Education:* University of Rome Law School, Italy (J.D., 1948).

(This Listing Continued)

PIERGROSSI VILLA MANCA GRAZIADEI,
Edinburgh—Continued

RESIDENT ASSOCIATES

MASSIMILIANO PINNA, born Sassari, October 14, 1964; admitted, 1992, Italy. *Education:* University of Sassari Law School, Italy (J.D., 1989).

Languages: Italian, English, French, German and Spanish.

SHEPHERD & WEDDERBURN, W.S.

SALTIRE COURT
20 CASTLE TERRACE
EDINBURGH EH1 2ET, SCOTLAND
Telephone: 0131 228 9900
Fax: 031 228 1222

Company, Banking and Commercial Law, Corporate Insolvency, Oil and Gas, Commercial and Residential Real Estate Conveyancing and Leasing, Litigation and Arbitration, Trusts and Tax Planning, Executry Law and General Practice.

MEMBERS OF FIRM

IAN B. INGLIS, W.S., (Senior Partner). admitted, 1967, Scotland. *Education:* Edinburgh (LL.B.). Notary Public.

JAMES W. BRYDIE, W.S., admitted, 1964, Scotland. *Education:* Edinburgh (B.L.). Notary Public.

D. IAN K. MACLEOD, W.S., admitted, 1960, Scotland. *Education:* Edinburgh (M.A.; LL.B.). Notary Public.

THOMAS H. DRYSDALE, W.S., admitted, 1966, Scotland. *Education:* Edinburgh (LL.B.). Notary Public.

IAN S. BOYD, W.S., admitted, 1965, Scotland. *Education:* Cambridge (B.A.); Edinburgh (B.L.). Notary Public.

JOHN DONALD, W.S., admitted, 1970, Scotland. *Education:* Edinburgh (M.A.; LL.B.). Notary Public.

DAVID A. JOHNSTONE, W.S., admitted, 1970, Scotland. *Eduction:* Edinburgh (M.A.; LL.B.). Notary Public.

ROBERT D.D. BERTRAM, W.S., admitted, 1969, Scotland. *Education:* Oxford (M.A.); Edinburgh (LL.B., Hons.).

DAVID A. SMITH, W.S., admitted, 1971, Scotland. *Education:* Edinburgh (LL.B.). Notary Public.

DAVID F. MURBY, W.S., admitted, 1972, Scotland. *Education:* Edinburgh (LL.B.). Notary Public.

THE LORD KINROSS, W.S., admitted, 1975, Scotland. *Education:* Edinburgh (LL.B.). Notary Public.

HUGH R. DONALD, W.S., admitted, 1975, Scotland. *Education:* Edinburgh (LL.B.). Notary Public.

NICHOLAS C. RYDEN, W.S., admitted, 1976, Scotland. *Education:* Aberdeen (LL.B.). Notary Public.

JAMES R. WILL, W.S., admitted, 1978, Scotland. *Education:* Aberdeen (LL.B.). Notary Public.

IAIN M.C. MEIKLEJOHN, W.S., admitted, 1978, Scotland. *Education:* Edinburgh (LL.B., Hons.). Notary Public.

ROBIN D. FULTON, W.S., admitted, 1979, Scotland. *Education:* Edinburgh (LL.B.). Notary Public.

ANDREW D. BIRRELL, W.S., admitted, 1979, Scotland. *Education:* Aberdeen (LL.B.). Notary Public.

LORNA M. SMITH, W.S., admitted, 1975, Scotland. *Education:* Edinburgh (LL.B.). Notary Public.

HUGH D.I. SMITH, admitted, 1978, Scotland. *Education:* Dundee (LL.B.). Notary Public.

PAUL W. HALLY, admitted, 1983, Scotland. *Education:* Edinburgh (LL.B., Hons.).

DOROTHY M. BOYD, W.S., admitted, 1980, Scotland. *Education:* Glasgow (LL.B., Hons.).

KAREEN E. MOFFAT, admitted, 1987, Scotland. *Education:* Edinburgh (LL.B.). Notary Public.

(This Listing Continued)

PATRICK ANDREWS, admitted, 1987, Scotland. *Education:* Aberdeen (LL.B.).

ANDREW N. HOLEHOUSE, admitted, 1981, England; 1990, Scotland. *Education:* Wolverhampton (LL.B., Hons.). Notary Public.

SUSAN P. INGLIS, admitted, 1988, Scotland. *Education:* Aberdeen (LL.B.).

KAY R. MCCORQUODALE, admitted, 1987, Scotland. *Education:* Edinburgh (LL.B.). Notary Public.

JAMES H. SAUNDERS, admitted, 1984, Scotland; 1988, England. *Education:* Glasgow (LL.B., Hons.).

BERMANS

1 CLAREMONT TERRACE
GLASGOW G3 7UQ, SCOTLAND
Telephone: 0141-248 1020
Telex: 779219 LAWMAN G
Fax: 0141-333 0318

Liverpool, England Office: Pioneer Buildings, 65/67 Dale Street, L2 2NS. Telephone: 0151-227 3351. Telex: 627555 LAWMAN G. Fax: 0151-236 2107.

Manchester, England Office: 7 Ralli Courts, West Riverside, New Bailey Street, M3 5FT. Telephone: 0161-834 2442. Telex: 665555 LAWMAN G. Fax: 0161-834 2402.

London, England Office: 1 Angel Court, EC2R 7HJ. Telephone: 011 44 171 600 2448. Fax: 011 44 171 600 2449.

New York, New York Office: Fortieth Floor, 1633 Broadway, 10019-6799. Telephone: (212) 956-7767. Telex: 205562 LAWMAN (RCA). Fax: (212) 956-1099. Superfine Fax: (212) 956-7030.

MEMBERS OF SCOTTISH PARTNERSHIP

J. STUART MORRISON, born Carlisle, England, June 13, 1947; admitted, 1970, Glasgow. *PRACTICE AREAS:* Commercial Property; Property Leasing; Licensing.

STUART CHALMERS, born Edinburgh, Scotland, June 30, 1952; admitted, 1973, Edinburgh. *PRACTICE AREAS:* Commercial Property; Licensing and Insolvency.

ANTHONY F. DEUTSCH, born Glasgow, Scotland, June 9, 1952; admitted, 1978, Edinburgh. *PRACTICE AREAS:* Commercial Litigation; Asset Leasing; Insolvency and Factoring.

ROBERT SWINDELL, born Glasgow, Scotland, September 30, 1958; admitted, 1981, Glasgow. *PRACTICE AREAS:* Commercial Property; Development; Sites Assembly.

JOYCE HELEN WHITE, born Greenock, Scotland, June 29, 1959; admitted, 1983, Glasgow. *PRACTICE AREAS:* Corporate Work and Insolvency.

JOHN D. THOMSON, born Glasgow, Scotland, August 22, 1954; admitted, 1977, Glasgow. (Resident Partner, East Kilbride Office). *PRACTICE AREAS:* Commercial Property and Development.

ROBERT M. BREE, born Sheffield, England, February 2, 1964; admitted, 1986, Glasgow. *PRACTICE AREAS:* Commercial Property and Development.

BRIAN M. CAMERON, born Glasgow, Scotland, September 30, 1964; admitted, 1987, Glasgow. *PRACTICE AREAS:* Commercial Litigation; Factoring.

RESIDENT ASSOCIATES

EDWARD ISAACS, born Lennoxtown, Scotland, February 24, 1953; admitted, 1979, Glasgow.

IAN MCKILLOP, born Glasgow, Scotland, April 16, 1957; admitted, 1981, Edinburgh.

DONALD MACLEOD, born Stirling, Scotland, November 12, 1963; admitted, 1987, Edinburgh.

FIONA MCGOWAN, born London, England, October 24, 1965; admitted, 1990, Edinburgh.

ALEXANDRA BUICK, born Glasgow, Scotland, October 13, 1945; admitted, 1967, Edinburgh.

(For List of other Personnel, see Professional Biographies at Liverpool, England and New York, New York)

BIGGART BAILLIE & GIFFORD, W.S.

Solicitors

Established in 1894

DALMORE HOUSE
310 ST. VINCENT STREET
GLASGOW G2 5QR, SCOTLAND
Telephone: 041-228-8000
Fax: 041-228-8310
Telex: 777997

Edinburgh, Scotland Office: 11 Glenfinlas Street, EH3 6YY. Telephone: 0131 226 5541. Telex: 777997. Fax: 0131 226 2278.

Corporate, Company and Commercial Law, Banking, Investment, Acquisition, Corporate Insolvency, Oil and Gas, Litigation and Arbitration, Commercial Real Estate Conveyancing and Leasing, Planning Law, Trust and Tax Planning, Executry Law and General Practice.

MEMBERS OF FIRM

Alexander Thomson, W.S.	J.M. Brown
T.Norman Biggart, W.S.	Philip J.S. Dry
H.J.L. Allan, W.S.	David H. Kidd, W.S.
R.I.D. Anderson	J.R.B. Corbett
W.W. Campbell Smith	Christine A. Mackenzie
David C.H. Ross	J.Fraser M. Hardie
Gordon M. Wyllie, W.S.	Alexander C. McEwen
Marie E. Brown	Norman R. Oliver
Murray W.A. Shaw	David L. Stevenson
Peter A. Cruickshank	Anthony V. McEwan
James A.R. Roxburgh	David S. Allan
J.H. Mutch, W.S.	Colin B. McKay

BISHOP AND ROBERTSON CHALMERS

Established in 1986

2 BLYTHSWOOD SQUARE
GLASGOW G2 4AD, SCOTLAND
Telephone: (3044) 141-248 4672
Fax: (3044) 141-221 9270

Edinburgh, Scotland Office: 22 Ainslie Place, EH3 6AJ. Tel: (30 44) 131-220 3355 Fax: (30 44) 131-220 3777.

European Community Law; Commercial and Corporate Law; Pensions and Employment Law; Commercial Litigation and Arbitration; Commercial Property Law; Estate and Tax Planning; Corporate Insolvency; Intellectual Property; Trusts; Private Client Services.

FIRM PROFILE: *The firm was formed in 1986 by the merger of Bishop and Company and Robertson Chalmers and Auld. It currently has 19 partners, plus 34 additional fee earners. It is a member of IAG International an International Association of Independent Professional Firms.*

MEMBERS OF THE FIRM

IAN L. DUNSMORE, born December 24, 1936; admitted, 1962, Scotland. *LANGUAGES:* English. *PRACTICE AREAS:* Trusts and Estates; Tax Planning; Private Client Services; Charitable Organizations.

JOHN A. WELSH, born September 9, 1945; admitted, 1968, Scotland. *LANGUAGES:* English and German. *PRACTICE AREAS:* Arbitration Law; Construction Law; Professional Indemnity.

ALASTAIR H. LOCKHART, born September 21, 1946; admitted, 1969, Scotland. *LANGUAGES:* English. *PRACTICE AREAS:* Insurance Defense Law.

HELEN E. STIRLING, born June 2, 1947; admitted, 1972, Scotland. *LANGUAGES:* English. *PRACTICE AREAS:* Commercial Property; Property Development.

DOMINIC L.G. BAYNE, born August 19, 1943; admitted, 1972, Scotland. *LANGUAGES:* English. *PRACTICE AREAS:* Insurance Defense Law.

JAMES A. MILLAR, born February 5, 1949; admitted, 1973, Scotland. *LANGUAGES:* English. *PRACTICE AREAS:* Joint Ventures; Company and Commercial Law.

(This Listing Continued)

IAIN J.S. TALMAN, born July 18, 1952; admitted, 1976, Scotland. *LANGUAGES:* English. *PRACTICE AREAS:* Pensions.

JAMES A.K. WARNOCK, born August 26, 1952; admitted, 1977, Scotland. *LANGUAGES:* English. *PRACTICE AREAS:* Commercial Property.

DAVID D. WHYTE, born July 1, 1954; admitted, 1978, Scotland. *LANGUAGES:* English. *PRACTICE AREAS:* Employment Law.

J. RUSSELL LANG, born April 28, 1952; admitted, 1976, Scotland. *LANGUAGES:* English. *PRACTICE AREAS:* Corporate Insolvency Law.

KENNETH H. FORREST, born October 23, 1953; admitted, 1977, Scotland. *LANGUAGES:* English. *PRACTICE AREAS:* Commercial Litigation; Insurance Defense Law.

KENNETH C. ROSS, born September 30, 1958; admitted, 1982, Scotland. *LANGUAGES:* English. *PRACTICE AREAS:* Environment Law.

IAIN H. TAYLOR, born October 29, 1952; admitted, 1981, Scotland. *Member:* Union des Avocats Européens (Comité Executif); British Law Association for Estonia, Latvia and Lithuania (Committee). *LANGUAGES:* English, French, Russian and Thai. *PRACTICE AREAS:* EEC Law; Intellectual Property.

THOMAS G. MARSHALL, born April 2, 1957; admitted, 1984, Scotland. *LANGUAGES:* English and German. *PRACTICE AREAS:* Commercial Litigation.

MADELEINE S.L. THOMSON, born June 9, 1948; admitted, 1981, Scotland. *LANGUAGES:* English. *PRACTICE AREAS:* Trusts and Estates; Tax Planning Law.

RODGER G. MURRAY, born November 14, 1959; admitted, 1983, Scotland. *LANGUAGES:* English. *PRACTICE AREAS:* Company Law; Finance Law; Resorts and Leisure.

KATHLEEN H. ADAIR, born July 6, 1959; admitted, 1983, Scotland. *LANGUAGES:* English. *PRACTICE AREAS:* Insurance Defense Law.

ALAN D. CALVERT, born March 8, 1961; admitted, 1984, Scotland. *LANGUAGES:* English. *PRACTICE AREAS:* Insurance Defense Law.

JUNE CROMBIE, born May 2, 1962; admitted, 1987, Scotland. *LANGUAGES:* English. *PRACTICE AREAS:* Pension Law.

Languages: French, German, Italian, Spanish, Russian, Thai and English

DIGBY BROWN & CO.

Established in 1906

THE SAVOY TOWER
77 RENFREW STREET
GLASGOW G2 3BZ, SCOTLAND
Telephone: 0141-332-8899
Fax: (Groups 2 & 3) 0141-332 2920

REVISERS OF THE SCOTLAND LAW DIGEST FOR THIS DIRECTORY.

Edinburgh, Scotland Office: 7 Albyn Place. Telephone: 0131-225 8505. Fax: (Groups 2 & 3) 0131-225 8482.
Dundee, Scotland Office: Discovery House, 5 Cowgate. Telephone: (0382) 322197. Fax: (Groups 2 & 3) 0382 200180.

Litigation. Conveyancing, Trusts and Executry and Company Law.

MEMBERS OF FIRM

IAN MAILLIE, admitted, 1955, Scotland. Bachelor of Law (Glasgow); S.S.C.; Notary Public, 1960. *Member:* The Royal Faculty of Procurators in Glasgow; Law Society of Scotland; Scottish Law Agents Society.

ROBERT T. SWANNEY, admitted 1972, Scotland. LL.B. (Glasgow). Notary Public, 1980. *Member:* Law Society of Scotland; The Royal Faculty of Procurators in Glasgow; Glasgow Bar Association.

IAN GRAEME MCKNIGHT, admitted 1973, Scotland. LL.B. (Glasgow). Notary Public, 1980. *Member:* Law Society of Scotland.

ALAN J. DUNIPACE, admitted, 1980, Scotland. LL.B. (Strathclyde). Notary Public, 1982. *Member:* Law Society of Scotland; The Royal Faculty of Procurators in Glasgow; Glasgow Bar Association.

ISHBEL JANE DOW MCLAREN, admitted 1978, Scotland. LL.B. (Edinburgh); S.S.C.; Notary Public, 1980.

(This Listing Continued)

DIGBY BROWN & CO., Glasgow—Continued

JOHN P. MAILLIE, admitted, 1987, Scotland. LL.B. (Strathclyde). Notary Public, 1987. Member: Law Society of Scotland.

REVISERS OF THE SCOTLAND LAW DIGEST FOR THIS DIRECTORY.

HARPER MACLEOD

Solicitors & Notaries

THE CA'D'ORO
45 GORDON STREET
GLASGOW G1 3PE, SCOTLAND
Telephone: 0141-221 8888
Telex: 777967 (ref 444)
Fax: 0141-226 4198

Agency Work, Arbitration, Asset Recovery, Banking Law, Bankruptcy and Reconstruction, Commercial Law, Company Law, Company Acquisitions and Mergers, Company Formation, Competition Law, Construction Law and Disputes, Consumer Protection, Contract Law, Commercial Conveyancing, Domestic Conveyancing, Copyright, Corporate Finance, Corporate Insolvency, Credit Agreements, Creditors Rights, Cross-Border Transactions, Debt Recovery, Discrimination, Sex and Race, Distribution Agency, E.C. Law, Electronic Banking and Data Processing, Employment, Energy Law, Environmental Law, Equal Opportunities, Financial Services, Franchising, Professional Indemnity, Industrial Relations, Inheritance, Insolvency and Reconstruction, Intellectual Property, Intestacy, Joint Ventures, Landlord and Tenant, Libel, Licensing, Betting and Gaming, Litigation, Civil Litigation, Commercial Litigation, Management Buyins and Leverage Buyouts, Manufacturing Licence Agreements, Media and Entertainment Law (Music, Films, Theatre, Publishing), Mergers and Acquisitions, Mining Law, Notary Public, Partnerships, Passing Off, Personnel, Press Law, Private Client, Product Liability, Professional Liability, Commercial Property, Receivership, International Sale of Goods, Secured Lending, Securities, Slander and Defamation, Sport, Succession and Probate, Syndicated Loans, Company Tax, Corporation Tax, Tort, Trade Secrets, Trade Union Law, Trademarks and Anti-Counterfeiting, Transport Law, Industrial and Labour Tribunals, Trusts, Unfair Competition, Wills and Trusts.

FIRM PROFILE: Harper Macleod is the Commercial Division of Ross Harper and Murphy (one of Scotland's largest legal practices). This division handles Company and Commercial work and Conveyancing. The firm has developed particular expertise in Licensing, Management Buyouts and Company Acquisitions and Flotations as well as offering a full range of Company and Commercial work including Insolvency, Commercial Litigation, Employment and Commercial Fraud Work .

All of the partners of Ross Harper & Murphy are Partners of Harper Macleod (and vice versa), but a separate marketing strategy targeting referrals has been established.

Agency work is accepted from other Solicitors; contact Rod McKenzie (Litigation and Employment); Gordon Stoddart (Domestic Conveyancing); Lorne Crerar (Commercial Conveyancing, Leasing, Securities, Banking and Licensing); Leonard Freedman (Corporate and Environmental); Dawn McKenzie (Insolvency).

PARTNERS

PROF. JOHN ROSS HARPER, admitted, 1958, Scotland. Education: C.B.E., M.A., LL.B. Notary Public. International Bar Association (President, 1994—). PRACTICE AREAS: Corporate Law; Political Lobbying; Commercial Fraud; Minerals Law.

LORNE D. CRERAR, admitted, 1978, Scotland. Education: LL.B. Notary Public and Managing Partner. PRACTICE AREAS: Property and Banking Law.

GORDON E. STODDART, admitted, 1972, Scotland. Education: LL.B. Notary Public. PRACTICE AREAS: Conveyancing; Wills and Executries.

RODERICK C. MCKENZIE, admitted, 1980, Scotland. Education: LL.B. Notary Public. ACIA. PRACTICE AREAS: Litigation and Employment Law; Minerals Law.

LEONARD FREEDMAN, admitted, 1979, Scotland. Education: LL.B. Notary Public. PRACTICE AREAS: Corporate and Environmental Law; Minerals Law.

DAWN MCKENZIE, admitted, 1989, Scotland. Education: LL.B.; DIP. L.P. Notary Public. PRACTICE AREAS: Corporate and Insolvency Law.

(This Listing Continued)

STEPHEN MILLER, admitted, 1990, Scotland. Education: LL.B. (Hons.); DIP. L.P. Notary Public. PRACTICE AREAS: Litigation; Sports and Entertainment Law.

SHEILA J. MC CALLUM, admitted, 1977, Scotland. Notary Public. PRACTICE AREAS: Commercial Conveyancing.

ASSOCIATES

PETER M. GILMOUR, admitted, 1980, Scotland. Education: LL.B. (Hons.). PRACTICE AREAS: Litigation Planning; Local Government.

LESLEY STODDART, admitted, 1989, Scotland. Education: LL.B. (Hons.). PRACTICE AREAS: Domestic Conveyancing; Wills and Executries.

W. KIRK TUDHOPE, admitted, 1991, Scotland. Education: LL.B. (Hons.). PRACTICE AREAS: Litigation; Employment Law; Construction Law.

GRAEME B. NISBET, admitted, 1992, Scotland. Education: LL.B. Notary Public. PRACTICE AREAS: Commercial Conveyancing.

MACLAY MURRAY & SPENS

Established in 1871

151 ST. VINCENT STREET
GLASGOW G2 5NJ, SCOTLAND
Telephone: 0141-248-5011
Telex: 77474 Vindex
Fax: 0141-221-2968; 0141-248-5819

Edinburgh, Scotland Office: 3 Glenfinlas Street, EH3 6AQ. Telephone: 0131-226-5196. Telex: 727238 Vindex. Fax: 0131-226-3174; 0131-225-9610.

London, England Office: 10 Foster Lane, EC2V 6HH. Telephone: 0171-606-6130. Fax: 0171-600-0992; 0171-600-0993.

Brussels, Belgium Office: Scotland Europa Centre, 35 Square De Meeus, B-1040. Telephone: 322 927 2001. Fax: 322 927 2401.

General Legal Practice.

PARTNERS

THOMAS M. LAWRIE, admitted, 1961, Scotland. Education: B.A. (Cantab); LL.B. Member: Royal Faculty of Procurators in Glasgow; Law Society of Scotland; International Bar Association. LANGUAGES: English and French. PRACTICE AREAS: Corporate Law; Mergers, Acquisitions and Divestitures; Securities.

IAN G. INGLIS, admitted, 1959, Scotland. Education: B.A. (Oxon); LL.B. Member: Royal Faculty of Procurators in Glasgow; Law Society of Scotland; Writer to the Signet; Institute of Patent Agents (Associate Member). LANGUAGES: English. PRACTICE AREAS: Admiralty and Maritime; Arbitration; Intellectual Property.

ANDREW H. PRIMROSE, admitted, 1964, Scotland; 1993, England and Wales. Education: B.A. (Oxon); LL.B. Notary Public. Member: Royal Faculty of Procurators in Glasgow; International Bar Association; UK Environmental Law Association; Law Society of Scotland. LANGUAGES: English. PRACTICE AREAS: Commercial Property Development and Finance; Environmental; Construction Law; Timeshare.

G. RONALD G. GRAHAM, C.B.E., admitted, 1966, Scotland. Education: M.A. (Oxon); LL.B. Notary Public. Member: Royal Faculty of Procurators in Glasgow; Law Society of Scotland (Council Member; President, 1984-1985). LANGUAGES: English. PRACTICE AREAS: Trusts and Estates; Taxation; Wills.

MALCOLM F. FLEMING, admitted, 1968, Scotland. Education: B.A. (Cantab); LL.B. Member: Royal Faculty of Procurators in Glasgow; Law Society of Scotland. LANGUAGES: English and French. PRACTICE AREAS: Property; Commercial Property Development and Finance; Leases and Leasing.

IAN M. STUBBS, admitted, 1972, Scotland. Education: LL.B.; C.A. Notary Public. Member: Royal Faculty of Procurators in Glasgow; Law Society of Scotland; Institute of Taxation; Institute of Chartered Accountants of Scotland (Council Member). LANGUAGES: English. PRACTICE AREAS: Taxation; Agricultural; Wills.

J. ANTHONY S. MURRAY, admitted, 1973, Scotland; 1992, England and Wales. Education: B.A. (Cantab); LL.B. Member: Royal Faculty of Procurators in Glasgow; British Institute of International and Corporate

(This Listing Continued)

Law; Law Society of Scotland. *LANGUAGES:* English and French. *PRACTICE AREAS:* Securities; Corporate Law; Company Law.

BRUCE R. PATRICK, admitted, 1975, Scotland. *Education:* B.A. (Oxon); LL.B. *Member:* Royal Faculty of Procurators in Glasgow; Law Society of Scotland; Writer to the Signet. *LANGUAGES:* English, French and German. *PRACTICE AREAS:* Company Law; Corporate Law; Finance.

IAN S. QUIGLEY, admitted, 1972, Scotland. *Education:* LL.B. Notary Public. *Member:* Law Society of Scotland; Writer to the Signet. *LANGUAGES:* English. *PRACTICE AREAS:* Commercial Property development and Finance; Leases and Leasing.

RICHARD A.F. CLARK, admitted, 1973, Scotland. *Education:* LL.B. Notary Public. *Member:* Royal Faculty of Procurators in Glasgow; Law Society of Scotland. *LANGUAGES:* English. *PRACTICE AREAS:* Fraud and Deceit; Aviation and Aerospace; Environment.

IAN G. LUMSDEN, admitted, 1977, Scotland. *Education:* B.A. (Cantab); LL.B. Notary Public. *Member:* Royal Faculty of Procurators in Glasgow; International Bar Association; Law Society of Scotland. *LANGUAGES:* English. *PRACTICE AREAS:* Corporate Law; Environmental Law; Mergers, Acquisitions and Divestitures.

MICHAEL J. WALKER, admitted, 1977, Scotland. *Education:* LL.B. Notary Public. *Member:* Royal Faculty of Procurators in Glasgow; Law Society of Scotland; International Bar Association. *LANGUAGES:* English. *PRACTICE AREAS:* Corporate Law; Mergers, Acquisitions and Divestitures; Securities.

IAIN G. MACNIVEN, admitted, 1979, Scotland. *Education:* M.A.; LL.B. Notary Public. *Member:* Royal Faculty of Procurators in Glasgow; Law Society of Scotland. *LANGUAGES:* English. *PRACTICE AREAS:* Commercial Property Development and Finance; Leases and Leasing.

DONALD M. WHITE, admitted, 1982, Scotland. *Education:* B.A. (Oxon). Notary Public. *Member:* Royal Faculty of Procurators in Glasgow; Law Society of Scotland. *LANGUAGES:* English. *PRACTICE AREAS:* Trusts and Estates; Wills; Property.

ROBERT J. LAING, admitted, 1977, England; 1985, Scotland. *Education:* M.A. (Cantab). *Member:* Writer to the Signet; International Bar Association; Law Society of Scotland. *LANGUAGES:* English. *PRACTICE AREAS:* Corporate Law; Mergers, Acquisitions and Divestitures; Banks and Banking.

F. JANE GARVIE, admitted, 1981, Scotland; 1992, England and Wales. *Education:* M.A.; LL.B. *Member:* Law Society of Scotland. *LANGUAGES:* English and French. *PRACTICE AREAS:* Intellectual Property; Labour and Employment; Insolvency and Receiverships.

EWAN R. EASTON, admitted, 1983, Scotland. *Member:* Law Society of Scotland; Writer to the Signet. *LANGUAGES:* English. *PRACTICE AREAS:* Construction; Labour and Employment; Land Development and Planning.

ROBERT PIRRIE, admitted, 1981, Scotland. *Education:* LL.B. *Member:* Writer to the Signet; Law Society of Scotland. *LANGUAGES:* English. *PRACTICE AREAS:* Company Law; Corporate Law; Finance.

MAGNUS P. SWANSON, admitted, 1983, Scotland. *Education:* LL.B. *Member:* Law Society of Scotland; International Bar Association; Insolvency Lawyers Association. *LANGUAGES:* English and French. *PRACTICE AREAS:* Mergers, Acquisitions and Divestitures; Insolvency; Corporate.

JENNIFER D. JOHNSON, admitted, 1979, Scotland. *Education:* LL.B. Notary Public. *Member:* Law Society of Scotland; Writer to the Signet. *LANGUAGES:* English. *PRACTICE AREAS:* Commercial Property Development and Finance; Leases and Leasing.

KENNETH D. SHAND, admitted, 1984, Scotland. *Education:* LL.B. Notary Public. *Member:* Law Society of Scotland; Scottish Lawyers European Group. *LANGUAGES:* English and French. *PRACTICE AREAS:* Corporate Law; Banks and Banking; European Community.

ANDREW S. BIGGART, admitted, 1988, Scotland. *Education:* M.A.; LL.B. Notary Public. *Member:* Royal Faculty of Procurators in Glasgow; Law Society of Scotland; Writer to the Signet. *LANGUAGES:* English. *PRACTICE AREAS:* Agricultural; Trusts and Estates; Wills.

ANDREW S. FLEMING, admitted, 1977, Scotland. *Education:* LL.B. Notary Public. *Member:* Association of Pension Lawyers; Law Society of Scotland. *LANGUAGES:* English. *PRACTICE AREAS:* Pensions and Profit Sharing; Superannuation.

(This Listing Continued)

HILARY A. KANE, admitted, 1986, Scotland. *Education:* LL.B. Notary Public. *Member:* Law Society of Scotland. *LANGUAGES:* English. *PRACTICE AREAS:* Corporate Law; Mergers, Acquisitions and Divestitures; Banks and Banking.

A. GORDON AITKEN, admitted, 1986, Scotland. *Education:* LL.B. *Member:* Law Society of Scotland. *LANGUAGES:* English. *PRACTICE AREAS:* Commercial Property Development and Finance; Leases and Leasing.

ALASTAIR J.A. MCEWAN, admitted, 1989, Scotland. *Education:* LL.B.; M.Sc.; LL.M. *Member:* Law Society of Scotland. *LANGUAGES:* English and Norwegian. *PRACTICE AREAS:* Commercial Property Development and Finance; Environmental; Leases and Leasing.

GRAEME E.C. SLOAN, admitted, 1987, Scotland. *Education:* LL.B. *Member:* Law Society of Scotland. *LANGUAGES:* English and French. *PRACTICE AREAS:* Corporate Law; Mergers, Acquisitions and Divestitures; Securities.

WILLIAM BROWN, admitted, 1983, Scotland; 1989, England and Wales. *Education:* LL.B. *Member:* Law Society of Scotland; Law Society of England and Wales; Scottish Lawyers European Group; Solicitors European Group; AIJA. *LANGUAGES:* English and French. *PRACTICE AREAS:* European Community; Competition; Agency and Distributorships.

MAUREEN A. BURNSIDE, admitted, 1986, Scotland. *Education:* LL.B. *Member:* Law Society of Scotland. *LANGUAGES:* English. *PRACTICE AREAS:* Company Law; Corporate Law; Finance Law.

GILL M. GRASSIE, admitted, 1986, Scotland. *Education:* LL.B., Hons. *Member:* Writer to the Signet; Law Society of Scotland. *LANGUAGES:* English, French, Italian and German. *PRACTICE AREAS:* Intellectual Property; Admiralty; Professional Liability.

FIONA M.M. NICOLSON, admitted, 1986, Scotland. *Education:* M.A.; LL.B. *Member:* Secretary Licensing Executives Society (Scottish Branch); Law Society of Scotland. *LANGUAGES:* English. *PRACTICE AREAS:* Intellectual Property; Company Law; Corporate Law.

ASSOCIATES

CARYN M. AULD, admitted, 1987, Scotland. *Education:* LL.B. *Member:* Law Society of Scotland. *LANGUAGES:* English. *PRACTICE AREAS:* Commercial Property Development and Finance; Leases and Leasing.

JOHN G. K. HARDING-EDGAR, admitted, 1987, Scotland. *Education:* LL.B. Associate, Chartered Institute of Bankers. *Member:* Writer to the Signet; Law Society of Scotland. *LANGUAGES:* English and French. *PRACTICE AREAS:* Corporate Law; Banks and Banking; Finance Law.

KEITH S. BISHOP, admitted, 1987, Scotland. *Education:* M.A. (Edinburgh); LL.B. *Member:* Law Society of Scotland. *LANGUAGES:* English and French. *PRACTICE AREAS:* Insolvency; Construction; General Liability Insurance.

A. GILLIAN S. DUNN, admitted, 1975, Scotland. *Member:* Law Society of Scotland. *LANGUAGES:* English. *PRACTICE AREAS:* Property; Agricultural; Wills.

SUSAN C. GILLON, admitted, 1989, Scotland. *Education:* LL.B., Hons. Notary Public. *Member:* Law Society of Scotland. *LANGUAGES:* English. *PRACTICE AREAS:* Commercial Property Development and Finance; Leases and Leasing.

MARTYN H. JONES, admitted, 1976, Scotland. *Member:* Law Society of Scotland. *LANGUAGES:* English. *PRACTICE AREAS:* Tax Law.

ALISON RICHMOND, admitted, 1988, Scotland. *Education:* LL.B., Hons. Notary Public. *Member:* Law Society of Scotland. *LANGUAGES:* English and French. *PRACTICE AREAS:* Taxation; Agricultural; Wills.

DOUGLAS J. CRAWFORD, admitted, 1988, Scotland. *Education:* LL.B. Notary Public. *Member:* Law Society of Scotland. *LANGUAGES:* English. *PRACTICE AREAS:* Corporate Law; Company Law; Finance Law.

TIMOTHY J. EDWARD, admitted, 1989, Scotland. *Education:* B.A.; LL.B. Writer to the Signet. *Member:* Scottish Law Agents Society; Scottish Lawyers European Group; Law Society of Scotland. *LANGUAGES:* English and French. *PRACTICE AREAS:* Intellectual Property; Insolvency; European Community Law.

(This Listing Continued)

MACLAY MURRAY & SPENS, Glasgow—Continued

OLIVIA R. GILES, admitted, 1989, Scotland. *Member:* Law Society of Scotland. *LANGUAGES:* English. *PRACTICE AREAS:* Commercial Property Development and Finance; Leases and Leasing.

MARK R. HAMILTON, admitted, 1987, Scotland. *Education:* LL.B. *Member:* Law Society of Scotland. *LANGUAGES:* English. *PRACTICE AREAS:* Labour and Employment; Professional Negligence; Environmental.

DAVID F. COOKE, admitted, 1987, England and Wales; 1993, Scotland. *Education:* LL.B.; B.A. (Mod.). *Member:* Law Society of England and Wales; Law Society of Scotland. *LANGUAGES:* English and French. *PRACTICE AREAS:* Corporate Law; Mergers and Acquisitions; Securities.

PETER A.A. TROTTER, admitted, 1987, Scotland. *Education:* LL.B., Hons.; LL.B. Dist. Notary Public. Associate Member, Pensions Management Institute. *Member:* Law Society of Scotland. *LANGUAGES:* English. *PRACTICE AREAS:* Pensions; Profit Sharing; Superannuation; Employee Benefits.

MICHAEL B. LIVINGSTON, admitted, 1981, Scotland. *Education:* LL.B.; LL.M. *Member:* Law Society of Scotland. *LANGUAGES:* English. *PRACTICE AREAS:* Corporate Law; Mergers and Acquisitions; Securities.

McCLURE NAISMITH ANDERSON & GARDINER

Established in 1826

292 ST. VINCENT STREET
GLASGOW G2 5TQ, SCOTLAND
Telephone: 0141-204-2700
Facsimilie: 0141-248-3998

Commercial and Company Law, Banking, Commercial Property, Intellectual Property, Civil Litigation, Environmental Law.

FIRM PROFILE: Established in 1826, the firm is now one of Scotland's leading commercial law firms particularly renowned for its mergers and acquisition work and civil litigation. Practicing from modern offices in Glasgow, Edinburgh and London, the firm has a total staff of over 60 lawyers.

MEMBERS OF FIRM

GORDON W.R. CARLISLE, born Paisley, Scotland, November 22, 1937; admitted, 1963, Scotland. *Education:* University of Glasgow (M.A., 1960; LL.B., 1963). *Member:* Law Society of Scotland; The Royal Faculty of Procurators in Glasgow; Glasgow Bar Association; International Bar Association. *LANGUAGES:* English and French. *PRACTICE AREAS:* Litigation; Matrimonial; Contract; Planning Law.

DR. KENNETH G. CHRYSTIE, born Glasgow, Scotland, November 24, 1946; admitted, 1970, Scotland. *Education:* University of Glasgow (Ph.D., 1971); University of Virginia (Post-Graduate Studies). Contributing Author: "International Handbook on Contracts of Employment"; "Encyclopaedia of the Laws of Scotland," Chapter on Commercial Paper. *Member:* Law Society of Scotland (Scottish Representative, UK Intellectual Property Committee); International Bar Association (Business Section); DTI Committee on Arbitration Law; Insolvency Lawyers Association. *LANGUAGES:* English and French. *PRACTICE AREAS:* Commercial Contracts; Commercial Litigation; Intellectual Property; Banking; Arbitration.

W. MICHAEL B. BROWN, born Glasgow, Scotland, November 4, 1945; admitted, 1970, Scotland. *Education:* University of Edinburgh (LL.B., 1967). Tutor, University of Glasgow, Diploma in Legal Practice, 1982-1987. *Member:* Law Society of Scotland; The Royal Faculty of Procurators in Glasgow.Internati onal Bar Association. *LANGUAGES:* English. *PRACTICE AREAS:* Commercial Property Law.

ALAN S. THOMSON, born Glasgow, Scotland, September 1, 1952; admitted, 1976, Scotland. *Education:* University of Edinburgh (LL.B., Hons., 1974). *Member:* Law Society of Scotland; The Royal Faculty of Procurators in Glasgow. *LANGUAGES:* English. *PRACTICE AREAS:* Civil Litigation; Employment Law.

MORAG CAMPBELL, born Lennoxtown, Scotland, August 3, 1957; admitted, 1981, Scotland. *Education:* University of Glasgow (LL.B., Hons., 1979). *Member:* Law Society of Scotland; The Royal Faculty of Procurators

(This Listing Continued)

---

in Glasgow. *LANGUAGES:* English. *PRACTICE AREAS:* Secured Finance; Leasing; Commercial Property.

T. WILSON AITKEN, born Kilwinning, Scotland, May 23, 1957; admitted, 1980, Scotland. *Education:* University of Glasgow (LL.B., Hons., 1978); McGeorge School of Law (Diploma, International Trade, 1982). *Member:* Law Society of Scotland; The Royal Faculty of Procurators in Glasgow. *LANGUAGES:* English. *PRACTICE AREAS:* Commercial Property; Commercial and Residential Tenancies.

GORDON L. SHEARER, born Glasgow, Scotland, April 2, 1957; admitted, 1980, Scotland. *Education:* University of Glasgow (LL.B., Hons., 1978). *Member:* Law Society of Scotland; The Royal Faculty of Procurators in Glasgow; Scottish Law Agents Society. *LANGUAGES:* English. *PRACTICE AREAS:* Residential Property; Succession; Tax Planning.

FRANK R. JOHNSTONE, born Airdrie, Scotland, October 12, 1957; admitted, 1982, Scotland. *Education:* University of Glasgow (M.A., 1978; LL.B., 1980). Lecturer, Consumer Credit Law and Debt Collection. *Member:* Law Society of Scotland (Convenor of Consumer Law Committee). *LANGUAGES:* English. *PRACTICE AREAS:* Consumer Credit Law; Hire Purchase; Leasing of Moveables; Sale of Goods; Litigation.

ALISTAIR S. BURROW, born Glasgow, Scotland, October 14, 1951; admitted, 1978, Scotland. *Education:* University of Glasgow (M.A., Hons., 1973; LL.B., 1976). Tutor, Diploma in Legal Practice, University of Strathclyde, 1980-1982; University of Glasgow, 1988-1991. *Member:* Law Society of Scotland; The Royal Faculty of Procurators in Glasgow; International Bar Association; Scottish Law Agents Society; Society for Computers and Law. *LANGUAGES:* English. *PRACTICE AREAS:* Corporate Law.

GEORGE W. FRIER, born Crieff, Scotland, November 2, 1962; admitted, 1987, Scotland. *Education:* University of Glasgow (LL.B., Hons, 1984). *Member:* Law Society of Scotland. *LANGUAGES:* English. *PRACTICE AREAS:* Company Law; Mergers and Acquisitions; Commercial Contracts; Banking; Insolvency; Customs and International Trade.

NICHOLAS P. NADDELL, born Glasgow, Scotland, March 15, 1964; admitted, 1986, Scotland. *Education:* University of Strathclyde, Glasgow (LL.B., 1984). *Member:* Law Society of Scotland. *LANGUAGES:* English and French. *PRACTICE AREAS:* Commercial Property Law; Commercial Leasing.

McGRIGOR DONALD

PACIFIC HOUSE
70 WELLINGTON STREET
GLASGOW G2 6SB, SCOTLAND
Telephone: 44 41 248 6677
Facsimile: 44 41 204 1351/221 1390

Edinburgh, Scotland Office: Erskine House, 68-73 Queen Street, EH2 4NF. Telephone: 44 31 226 7777. Facsimile: 44 31 226 7700.
London, England Office: 63 Queen Victoria Street, EC4N 4ST.
Telephone: 44 71 329 3299. Fax: 44 71 329 4000.
English Affiliated Firm: Morrison Skirrow, Solicitors.

General Practice, Acquisitions, Arbitration, Banking, Building, Civil Engineering and Litigation, Commercial, Company, Construction, Contract, Conveyancing, Corporate, Employment, Environmental Law, European Law, Executry Administration, Financial Planning, Insolvency, Intellectual Property, International Tax, Investor Protection, Investment Management, Libel, Licensing, Litigation, Management Buy-outs and Buy-Ins, Media, Partnership, Pensions, Property, Security, Tax, Town and County Planning, Tribunals, Trust and Venture Capital Law.

PARTNERS

ALFRED C. SHEDDEN, born Scotland, June 30, 1944; admitted, 1970, Scotland. *Education:* Aberdeen University (M.A.; LL.B., 1968). *Member:* Royal Faculty of Procurators in Glasgow.

KEVIN SWEENEY, born Scotland, December 16, 1939; admitted, 1963, Scotland. *Education:* Glasgow University (M.A., 1960; LL.B., 1963; C.A., 1966). *Member:* Institute of Chartered Accountants of Scotland.

JOHN NEWALL, born Scotland, August 6, 1942; admitted, 1966, Scotland. *Education:* Edinburgh University (LL.B., 1964). *Member:* Society of Writers to the Signet.

LEONARD W. FOLEY, born Scotland, November 17, 1947; admitted, 1974, Scotland. *Education:* Glasgow University (LL.B. Hons., 1969). External Examiner in Conveyancing, Aberdeen University, 1986—.

(This Listing Continued)

JAMES A. M. SMITH, born Gibraltar, 1945; admitted, 1969, Scotland. *Education:* Glasgow University (LL.B., 1967). *Member:* Royal Faculty of Procurators in Glasgow.

DAVID A. BANKIER, born Scotland, March 24, 1949; admitted, 1977, Scotland. *Education:* Edinburgh University (LL.B., 1970).

ALLAN T. M. NICOLSON, born Scotland, April 25, 1949; admitted, 1972, Scotland. *Education:* Glasgow University (LL.B., 1970).

T. RONALD COLE, born Scotland, October 11, 1950; admitted, 1973, Scotland. *Education:* Glasgow University (LL.B., 1970). *Member:* Royal Faculty of Procurators in Glasgow.

JAMES D. YOUNG, born Scotland, February 26, 1950; admitted, 1975, Scotland. *Education:* Glasgow University (LL.B., 1971). *Member:* Industrial Law Group.

EDWARD M. MACKECHNIE, born England, May 4, 1950; admitted, 1972, Scotland. *Education:* Glasgow University (LL.B., 1970). Tutor, Diploma of Law, Course in Advocacy and Pleading, Glasgow University, 1984-1986. *Member:* Glasgow Bar Association.

J. NIALL SCOTT, born Scotland, May 4, 1952; admitted, 1975, Scotland. *Education:* Aberdeen University (LL.B., 1973). External Examiner, Course of Professional Practice, Glasgow University, 1988—. *Member:* Royal Faculty of Procurators in Glasgow.

ROBERT M. GLENNIE, born Scotland, April 4, 1951; admitted, 1977, Scotland. *Education:* Strathclyde University (LL.B., 1975).

R. CRAIG CONNAL, born England, July 7, 1954; admitted, 1977, Scotland. *Education:* Glasgow University (LL.B., 1975). *Member:* Society of Construction Law.

JAMES A. TAYLOR, born Scotland, February 21, 1951; admitted, 1977, Scotland. *Education:* Aberdeen University (B.Sc., 1972; LL.B., 1975).

KIRKLAND B. MURDOCH, born Scotland, March 7, 1955; admitted, 1978, Scotland. *Education:* Edinburgh University (LL.B., 1976).

TOM D. ANDERSON, born Scotland, March 17, 1954; admitted, 1977, Scotland. *Education:* Edinburgh University (LL.B., 1975).

DEREK PETRIE, born Scotland, March 7, 1956; admitted, 1980, Scotland. *Education:* Aberdeen University (LL.B., 1977).

IAN GORDON, born Scotland, August 15, 1957; admitted, 1981, Scotland. *Education:* Edinburgh University (LL.B. Hons., 1979). *Member:* Association of Pension Lawyers.

KATHLEEN M. STEWART, born Scotland, January 25, 1946; admitted, 1976, Scotland. *Education:* St. Andrews University (M.A., 1968); Sweet Briar College, Virginia, USA; Edinburgh University (LL.B., 1971). Committee Member, Institute of Directors, Edinburgh Branch, 1989—, and Edinburgh Chamber of Commerce, 1988.

I. NEIL D. WALKER, born Scotland, January 3, 1947; admitted, 1969, Scotland. *Education:* Glasgow University (LL.B., 1967). *Member:* Society of Writers to the Signet.

JOHN MACFARLANE, born Scotland, September 18, 1949; admitted, 1973, Scotland. *Education:* Glasgow University (LL.B., 1971). Tutor: Company Law, Strathclyde University, 1983-1987; Edinburgh University, 1988-1990. *Member:* Joint Insolvency Examination Board, 1988—.

NEIL C. MORRISON, born Scotland, December 4, 1948; admitted, 1973, Scotland; 1986, England. *Education:* Edinburgh University (LL.B., 1969).

IAN J. G. LYALL, born Scotland, April 25, 1955; admitted, 1980, Scotland. *Education:* Aberdeen University (LL.B., 1977; M.A., 1978).

BRANDON E. NOLAN, born England, November 4, 1955; admitted, 1980, Scotland. *Education:* Glasgow University (LL.B., 1978). Associate Member, Institute of Arbiters.

MURDO MACLEAN, born Scotland, June 12, 1956; admitted, 1981, Scotland. *Education:* Aberdeen University (LL.B. Hons., 1978); University of British Columbia, Vancouver B.C. (LL.M., 1979).

STEPHEN S. COOK, born Scotland, June 4, 1960; admitted, 1984, Scotland. *Education:* University of Aberdeen (LL.B. Hons., 1981; Dip. L.P., 1982).

RICHARD K. LINTON, born Scotland, May 23, 1958; admitted, 1981, Scotland. *Education:* Strathclyde University (LL.B., 1979).

(This Listing Continued)

ANDREW TAYLOR, born Scotland, March 27, 1954; admitted, 1982, Scotland. *Education:* Glasgow University (B.Sc., 1975); Aberdeen University (LL.B., 1981).

FRANK DORAN, born Scotland, October 12, 1959; admitted, 1984, Scotland. *Education:* Glasgow University (LL.B. Hons., 1982).

MORAG MCNEILL, born Scotland, June 18, 1959; admitted, 1985, Scotland. *Education:* Edinburgh University (LL.B., 1981; Dipl.P, 1982, LL.M., 1983).

COLIN F. GRAY, born Scotland, December 23, 1962; admitted, 1986, Scotland. *Education:* Glasgow University (LL.B., 1983; Dip. L.P., 1984).

SHONAIG MACPHERSON, born Scotland, September 29, 1958; admitted, 1984, England; 1991, Scotland. *Education:* Sheffield University (LL.B. Hons., 1981).

L. DRYSDALE GRAHAM, born Scotland, August 1, 1958; admitted, 1983, Scotland; 1990, England. *Education:* Aberdeen University (LL.B. Hons., 1980).

IAIN A. MACAULAY, born Scotland, April 23, 1960; admitted, 1985, Scotland. *Education:* Aberdeen University (LL.B. Hons, 1982).

THOMAS N. FERRIER, born Scotland, August 13, 1960; admitted, 1985, Scotland. *Education:* Strathclyde University (LL.B. Hons., 1982; Dip. L.P., 1983).

ALISON NEWTON, born Kenya, April 14, 1963; admitted, 1985, Scotland. *Education:* Dundee University (LL.B., 1983; Dip. L.P., 1984).

Languages: English, French, Italian, Spanish and Gaelic

SEMPLE FRASER W.S.

Established in 1990

The Business Law Partnership

130 ST VINCENT STREET
GLASGOW G2 5HF, SCOTLAND
Telephone: 0141-221-3771
Facsimile: 0141-221-3776

Project Development and Investment, Banking, Corporate Work, Contract and Commercial Litigation, Take-overs, Mergers and Acquisitions, Management Buy-outs, Banking and Insolvency, Taxations, Leisure and Recreation Matters, Construction, Property Development and Investment Work including matters relating to Enterprise Zone Trusts, Mortgages and Secured Loans, Taxation Consequences and Implications, Environmental Protection Legislation, Agricultural Tenancies, EC Law.

PARTNERS

DAVID SEMPLE, born Scotland, 1943; admitted, 1967, Scotland. *Education:* Glasgow University (LL.B., 1964). Notary Public. Member, CBI Scottish Council, 1987-1990. Director, Chamber of Commerce. *Member:* International Bar Association; Institute of Directors; Law Society of Scotland. **PRACTICE AREAS:** Corporate; Takeovers; Management Buy-outs; International Contracts; Insolvency/Reconstruction.

ALISTER FRASER, born Scotland, 1955; admitted, 1981, Scotland. *Education:* Edinburgh University (LL.B., Hons., 1977). Notary Public. *Member:* Law Society of Scotland. **PRACTICE AREAS:** Property Investment; Development and Financing; Construction Contracts.

PAUL S. HANIFORD, W.S., born Scotland, 1955; admitted, 1980, Scotland. *Education:* Glasgow University (M.A., 1976; LL.B., 1978). Writer to the Signet. Notary Public. *Member:* Law Society of Scotland. **PRACTICE AREAS:** Property Investment and Development.

ALAN J. STEWART, born Scotland, 1957; admitted, 1979, Scotland. *Education:* Glasgow University (LL.B., 1977). Notary Public. *Member:* Law Society of Scotland; Institute of Directors. **PRACTICE AREAS:** Corporate Finance; Equity Funding; Acquisitions; Listed Company Transactions.

HEATHER M. NISBET, born Scotland, 1962; admitted, 1985, Scotland. *Education:* Edinburgh University (LL.B., 1982). *Member:* Law Society of Scotland. **PRACTICE AREAS:** Property Investment; Property Development; Construction Contracts; Property Taxation.

ANGUS D. MACRAE, W.S., born Scotland, 1963; admitted, 1986, Scotland. *Education:* Aberdeen University (LL.B.). Writer to the Signet. Notary Public. *Member:* Law Society of Scotland. **PRACTICE AREAS:** Commercial Property; Banking; Healthcare.

(This Listing Continued)

SEMPLE FRASER W.S., Glasgow—Continued

SIMON P. ETCHELLS, W.S., born England, 1962; admitted, 1988, Scotland. *Education:* Edinburgh University (LL.B., Hons., 1984). Writer to the Signet. *Member:* Law Society of Scotland. *PRACTICE AREAS:* Commercial Property; Banking; Property Development and Investment; Secured Lending.

ALISON M. GOW, born Scotland, 1959; admitted, 1982, Scotland. *Education:* Edinburgh University (LL.B., Hons.). *Member:* Law Society of Scotland. *PRACTICE AREAS:* Commercial Litigation; Employment Law; Licensing; Insolvency; Property Litigation.

SLOVAKIA

ALTHEIMER & GRAY

NAM. SNP 15
BRATISLAVA, SLOVAKIA
Telephone: 42-7-362-736
Fax: 42-7-367-960

REVISERS OF THE POLAND LAW DIGEST FOR THIS DIRECTORY.

Chicago, Illinois Office: 10 South Wacker Drive, 60606. Telephone: 312-715-4000. Fax: 312-715-4800. Telex: RCA 297102 A G UR.

Prague, Czech Republic Office: Platnerska 4, 110 00 Prague 1. Telephone: 42-2-2481-2782. Fax: 42-2-2481-0125 or 232-9595.

Warsaw, Poland Office: ul Nowogrodzka 50, 00-950. Telephones: 48-22-298-357; 48-39-12-1338. Fax: 48-2-628-3640.

Kiev, Ukraine Office: Kontraktova Ploscha 4, Building 3, Room 304, 254145. Telephone: 7-044-230-2534. Fax: 7-044-230-2535.

Istanbul, Turkey Office: Tesvikiye Cad. 107, Tesvikiye Palas 7, Tesvikiye 80200 Istanbul, Turkey. Telephone: 90-212-227-6750. Fax: 90-212-227-6759.

Privatizations and Acquisitions, Joint Ventures and Foreign Investment, Government Affairs, Real Estate Development, Architecture, Engineering and Construction, Banking and Finance, Bankruptcy, Licensing and Distribution, Insurance, Telecommunications, Securities, Taxation and Customs.

PARTNERS

JAMES E. CARROLL, born Evanston, Illinois, July 31, 1956; admitted, 1982, Illinois (Not admitted in Slovakia). *Education:* Loras College (B.A., maxima cum laude, 1978); Cambridge University (LL.M. in International Law, 1980); Northwestern University (J.D., 1982). Delta Epsilon Sigma; Phi Alpha Theta. Member, Northwestern Journal of International Law and Business, 1981-1982. Author: "Of Icebergs, Oil Wells and Treaties: Hydrocarbon Exploitation Offshore Antarctica," 19 Stanford Journal of International Law, 1983. Co-author: "Recent Developments in Polish Insurance Law," De Paul Business Law Journal, Spring/Summer 1991. *Member:* Chicago, Illinois State, American and International Bar Associations. (Also at Chicago, Warsaw, Prague, Kiev and Istanbul Offices). *PRACTICE AREAS:* International Law; Finance Law; Mergers and Acquisitions.

LOUIS B. GOLDMAN, born Chicago, Illinois, April 11, 1948; admitted, 1975, California; 1976, New York; 1991, Illinois (Not admitted in Slovakia). *Education:* University of California at Berkeley (A.B., magna cum laude, 1970); University of Chicago (J.D., cum laude, 1974). Phi Beta Kappa; Order of the Coif. Member, University of Chicago Law Review, 1972-1973. Co-Author: "Repossessing the Spirit of St. Louis: Expanding The Protection of Sections 1110 and 1168 of The Bankruptcy Code," The Business Lawyer, Vol. 41, No. 1, 1985. Co-Author: "Recent Developments in Polish Insurance Law," De Paul Business Law Journal, Spring/Summer 1991. Law Clerk to Judge Charles B. Renfrew, U.S. District Court, Northern District of California, 1974-1975. Member, Chicago-Prague Sister Cities Committee of the City of Chicago. *Member:* State Bar of California; Association of the Bar of the City of New York; Chicago, New York State (Member, Committee on International Banking, Securities and Financial Transactions, Committee on International Investment and Development), American (Member, Sections on: Corporation, Banking and Business Law; Taxation; International Law and Practice) and International Bar Associations; New York County Lawyers Association (Member, Special Committee on the Peoples Republic of China). (Also at Chicago, Warsaw, Prague and

(This Listing Continued)

Istanbul Offices). *PRACTICE AREAS:* Securities Law; Mergers and Acquisitions Law; International Law.

JEFFREY NORMAN SMITH, born Milwaukee, Wisconsin, May 5, 1960; admitted, 1985, Illinois (Not admitted in Slovakia). *Education:* University of Michigan (B.B.A., with high distinction, 1982); Northwestern University (J.D., cum laude, 1985). Phi Beta Kappa; Beta Gamma Sigma. *Member:* Chicago, Illinois State and American Bar Associations. (Also at Chicago, Warsaw and Prague Offices). *PRACTICE AREAS:* Mergers and Acquisitions; Joint Ventures; Privatizations; Finance Law; International Law.

ASSOCIATES

IVO BARTA, born February 14, 1967. *Education:* Comenius University School of Law, Bratislava (Doctor of Law, summa cum laude); Catholic University of Leuven School of Law (LL.M., magna cum laude, with specialization in the Law of the European Communities, 1992); University of Michigan School of Law (LL.M., in U.S. Business and Financial Law, 1993). Scholar at the Centre for Advanced Legal Studies of the Catholic University of Leuven School of Law. Fulbright Scholar (John Marshall) University of Michigan School of Law. Member, Faculty of Law of Comenius University. (Also at Prague Office). *LANGUAGES:* Slovak, English, Czech, Russian and German.

REVISERS OF THE POLAND LAW DIGEST FOR THIS DIRECTORY.

(For complete biographical data on personnel at Chicago, Illinois, Warsaw, Poland, Prague, Czech Republic, Kiev, Ukraine and Istanbul, Turkey see Professional Biographies at those locations)

BLAHA, ERBEN, NOVÁK & PARTNERS

Established in 1990

BENEDIKTIHO 5
811 05 BRATISLAVA, SLOVAKIA
Telephone: 42/7/498754; 498867; 492942; 492946; 492948
Fax: 42/7/498754; 498867; 492942; 492946; 492948

Business Law, Civil Law, Labour Law, Intellectual Property, Privatization Issues, Competition Law, Litigation, Criminal Law, Real Estate, Corporate Law.

FIRM PROFILE: The firm was established in 1990 right after the private legal practise was enabled by the Law on Legal Profession. It belongs to the largest firms in Slovakia. The client base is European, mainly German, Austrian, British, Greek as well as North American and Canadian.

MEMBERS OF FIRM

JUDR. ANTON BLAHA, born Čadca, Czechoslovakia, 1934; admitted, 1961, Czechoslovakia. *Education:* Law School of Comenius University (Dr.Jur., 1961; PhD., 1982). Co-Author: Textbook of the "Czechoslovak Labour Law." Member, Legislative Commission of the Federal Government of the CSFR and Legislative Council of the Slovak Republic. *Member:* Slovak Bar Association. *LANGUAGES:* German and French. *PRACTICE AREAS:* Business Law; Labour Law.

JUDR. PAVOL ERBEN, born Bratislava, Czechoslovakia, 1952; admitted, 1975, Czechoslovakia. *Education:* Law School of Comenius University (Dr.Jur.). Author: Article, "Immaterial Property and Civil Law." Legal Practise, one of Canada's largest law firms, 3 months. Honorary Counsel for Canada. *Member:* Slovak Bar Association (Commission of Experts). *LANGUAGES:* German, English and Russian. *PRACTICE AREAS:* Business Law; Civil Law; Intellectual Property.

JUDR. ANTON NOVÁK, born Bratislava, Czechoslovakia, 1952; admitted, 1991, Czechoslovakia. *Education:* Law School of Comenius University (Dr.Jur., 1983). Judge, Civil Law, Slovak Antimonopoly Office. *LANGUAGES:* English and Russian. *PRACTICE AREAS:* Business Law; Family Law; Labour Law; Competition Law; Corporate Law.

JUDR. ZUZANA KRÁLOVIČOVÁ, born Bratislava, Slovakia, 1962; admitted, 1985, Slovakia. *Education:* Law School of Comenius University (Dr. Jur., 1985). *Member:* Slovak Bar Association. *LANGUAGES:* German and Russian. *PRACTICE AREAS:* Civil Law; Litigation; Business Law; Corporate Law; Criminal Law.

JUDR. JANA TOMASOVIČOVÁ, born Smolenice, Slovakia, 1962; admitted, 1985, Slovakia. *Education:* Law School of Comenius University

(This Listing Continued)

(Dr. Jur., 1985). *Member:* Slovak Bar Association. *LANGUAGES:* German and Russian. *PRACTICE AREAS:* Civil Litigation; Criminal Law; Real Estate.

ČECHOVÁ, HRBEK

Established in 1990

MARIÁNSKA NO. 3
811 08 BRATISLAVA, SLOVAKIA
Telephone: 011-42-7-323 033; 011-42-7-322 166; 011-42-7-322 168
Fax: 011-42-7-321 254

Civil, Corporate, Commercial and Tax Law, Banking and Finance, Privatisation, Bankruptcy Law, Civil and Commercial Litigation, Competition Law, International Private Law.

FIRM PROFILE: *The firm was established in 1990 and was transferred to the Law Firm Čechová, Hrbek in 1992. It offers a full range of legal services. The client base is in Europe, North America and Australia, especially in Central Europe, France, U.K., Germany, Italy, Austria, U.S.A. and Canada. The firm has three partners, one associate and a legal support staff of four persons consisting of legal trainee, legal assistant and two office administrators.*

MEMBERS OF FIRM

DR. KATARÍNA ČECHOVÁ, born Trnava, Slovakia, November 26, 1960; admitted, 1987, Slovakia. *Education:* Comenius University, Bratislava, Slovakia (Graduated; Dr. Jur., 1984); Ministry of Justice of Slovak Republic (International Private Law Course, 1989). With: Law Offices No. 1, International Department, Bratislava, Czechoslovakia, 1984-1990; Stikeman, Elliott, Montreal, Canada, 1991; Allen & Overy, London, U.K., 1994. *Member:* Slovak Bar Association; International Bar Association; Canadian Bar Association. *LANGUAGES:* English, German, Russian and French. *PRACTICE AREAS:* International Private and Business Law; Commercial and Corporate Law; Bankruptcy Law; Mergers and Acquisitions; Securities Law.

DR. MILAN HRBEK, born Bratislava, Slovakia, January 26, 1961; admitted, 1988, Slovakia. *Education:* Comenius University, Bratislava, Slovakia (Graduated, 1984; Dr.Jur., 1985). With: District Prosecution Office of Bratislava, 1984-1992; Deputy District Prosecutor, 1989-1991; District Prosecutor, 1992; 1993, Allen & Overy, London, U.K. *Member:* Slovak Bar Association; International Bar Association. *LANGUAGES:* English, Russian and German. *PRACTICE AREAS:* Tax Law; Civil and Commercial Litigation; Civil and Corporate Law; Privatization.

DR. IGOR PÁLKA, born Bratislava, Slovakia, November 22, 1966; admitted, 1992, Slovakia. *Education:* Comenian University, Bratislava, Slovakia (Graduated 1988, Dr. Jur., 1989); with Stavoinvesta Bratislava 1988, Law Offices Lučenec 1989-1990. Law Offices No. 1 Bratislava 1990. Individual Private Practice, 1990-1993. *Member:* Slovak Bar Association; International Bar Association. *LANGUAGES:* English, Russian and German. *PRACTICE AREAS:* Commercial, Civil and Corporate Law; Banking and Finance; Property Law and Competition Law.

CSEKES, VILAGI

OBCHODNÁ 21
811 01 BRATISLAVA, SLOVAKIA
Telephone: (42 7) 331 404
Fax: (42 7) 330 568

General Slovak and International Practice.

FIRM PROFILE: *The firm's practice includes establishment of business organizations, privatizations, joint ventures, foreign investments, distribution and franchising, corporate finance, secured transactions, real estate, intellectual property, labor and competition law, commercial litigation and bankruptcy.*

MEMBERS OF FIRM

ERIKA CSEKES, born Hurbanovo, Czechoslovakia, October 1, 1963. *Education:* Comenius University (Doctor of Jurisprudence, 1985). Slovak Counsel: Office of the President of Czechoslovakia, 1991-1992; Squire, Sanders & Dempsey, 1992-1994. Member, Slovak Parliament, 1990. *Member:* Commercial Bar of the Slovak Republic. *LANGUAGES:* Czech, English, Hungarian, Russian and Slovak.

OSZKAR VILAGI, born Dunajska Streda, Czechoslovakia, April 17, 1963. *Education:* Comenius University (Diploma in Law, 1985; Doctor of

(This Listing Continued)

Jurisprudence, 1991). Member: Advocates before the courts of the Slovak Republic; Czechoslovak Federal Assembly, 1990-1992 (Vice Chairman of the Lower Chamber and Vice Chairman of the Constitutional Committee). *LANGUAGES:* Czech, Hungarian, Russian and Slovak.

COUNSEL

ROBERT LYMAN JILLSON, born Detroit, Michigan, May 18, 1936; admitted, 1962, Ohio; 1975, District of Columbia; 1982, New York. *Education:* University of Michigan (B.A., with High Honors in English, 1958; J.D., 1961). Phi Beta Kappa. Articles Editor, Michigan Law Review, 1960-1961. Stagiaire with F.C. Jeantet, Avocat a la Cour d'Appel de Paris, 1961-1962. With, Squire, Sanders & Dempsey, 1962-1994. General Partner, 1971-1994. Managing Partner, Brussels, 1982-1994. Partner in charge of Slovak practice, 1992-1994. *Member:* Bar of the United States Supreme Court; American Bar Association; The Association of the Bar of the City of New York; International Bar Association; Order of the Coif; Chartered Institute of Arbitrators, London (Associate). (Practicing individually in Brussels, Belgium). *LANGUAGES:* English and French.

DETVAI LUDIK MALÝ UDVAROS

CUKROVÁ 14
813 39 BRATISLAVA, SLOVAKIA
Telephone: 0042-7-323-628; 326-015; 326-579
Fax: 0042-7-326-002

Business and Commercial Law, Privatization Issues, Civil Law, Labour Law, Criminal Litigation, Law of Securities.

FIRM PROFILE: *The firm was established in 1991. Since 1993, it exists as Detvai Ludik Malý Udvaros and belongs to the largest law firms in Slovakia with four partners, six associates and five employees.*

The clients are mainly European, American and Asian companies (most of them international) and individuals.

Firm has contractual cooperation with Froriep, Renggli & Associeés, Switzerland and cooperation with several law firms in Austria, Germany, Great Britain and U.S.A.

MEMBERS OF FIRM

DR. ŠTEFAN DETVAI, born Filakovo, Czechoslovakia, 1945; admitted, 1973, Czechoslovakia. *Education:* Law School of Comenius University of Bratislava (1964; Dr.Jur., 1974). Co-Author: "Advocacy Law," draft, 1990. With, Regional Union of Advocates, 1969-1990. *Member:* Slovak Bar Association (President). *LANGUAGES:* German, Hungarian and Russian. *PRACTICE AREAS:* Business and Commercial Law; Patent Law; Criminal Litigation; Labour Law; Law of Securities.

DR. ZOLTÁN LUDIK, born Trnava, Czechoslovakia, 1956; admitted, 1983, Czechoslovakia. *Education:* Law School of Comenius University of Bratislava (1980; Dr.Jur., 1981). Co-Author: "Advocacy Law," draft, 1980. With, Ministry of Justice of Slovak Republic, Regional Union of Advocates, 1981-1990. *Member:* Slovak Bar Association (Supervisory Board); DACH. *LANGUAGES:* German and Hungarian. *PRACTICE AREAS:* Business and Commercial Law; Real Estate; Civil Law.

DR. JOZEF MALÝ, born Bratislava, Czechoslovakia, 1957; admitted, 1991, Czechoslovakia. *Education:* Law School of Comenius University of Bratislava (1980; Dr.Jur., 1982). With: Ministry of Finance, 1980; Central Committee for Sport, 1983-1990. *Member:* Slovak Bar Association; DACH. *LANGUAGES:* English, German and Russian. *PRACTICE AREAS:* Business and Commercial Law; Privatisation Issues; Labour Law.

DR. LADISLAV UDVAROS, born Nové Zámky, Czechoslovakia, 1949; admitted, 1977, Czechoslovakia. *Education:* Law School of Comenius University of Bratislava (1973; Dr.Jur., 1978). Co-Author: "Advocacy Law," draft, 1990. With, Regional Union of Advocates, 1973-1990. *Member:* Slovak Bar Association (Supervisory Board); DACH. *LANGUAGES:* German, Hungarian and French. *PRACTICE AREAS:* Business and Commercial Law; Civil Law; Real Estate.

Languages: German, English, French, Hungarian and Russian

FLASSIK & FLASSIKOVÁ & VALENTOVÁ & VÁSOVÁ

Established in 1994

STETINOVA 5

811 06 BRATISLAVA, SLOVAKIA

Telephone: 42 7 315 860, 314 925, 316 444

Fax: 42 7 335 022

Business Law, Civil Law, Labour Law, Competition Law, Intellectual Property, Privatization, Mergers and Acquisitions, Construction Law.

FIRM PROFILE: The firm was established in 1994 by four lawyers from various law firms dealing basically with business law. The client base is mainly-European. This firm with its four partners has a wide range of collaborators and paralegal staff.

MEMBERS OF FIRM

JUDR. IMRICH FLASSIK, born Bratislava, Slovakia, 1925; admitted, 1994, Solvakia. Education: Law School of Comenius University (Dr.Jur., 1950); University of Economics. Arbitrator, Slovak Arbitration Court. Minister, Antitrust Issues. Judge, Supreme Court. LANGUAGES: English, German and French. PRACTICE AREAS: Business Law; Competition Law; Construction Law; Mergers and Acquisitions.

JUDR. GERTA FLASSIKOVÁ, born Bratislava, Slovakia, 1962; admitted, 1991, Slovakia. Education: Law School of Comenius University (Dr. Jur., 1988). Member: International Bar Association. LANGUAGES: English and German. PRACTICE AREAS: Business Law; Corporate Law; Civil Law; Property Law; Intellectual Property.

JUDR. DAGMAR VALENTOVÁ, born Bratislava, Slovakia, 1959; admitted, 1993, Slovakia. LANGUAGES: German and English. PRACTICE AREAS: Business Law; Privatization Issues; Civil Law; Property Law; Family Law.

JUDR. RUZENA VÁSOVÁ, born Bratislava, Slovakia, 1955; admitted, 1994. Education: Law School of Comenius University (Dr.Jur. 1982). LANGUAGES: German and English. PRACTICE AREAS: Administrative Law; Business Law; Labour Law; Telecommunication Issues.

HAVLÁT, BOREC & PARTNERS

Law Offices

Established in 1990

GORKEHO 6

811 01 BRATISLAVA, SLOVAKIA

Telephone: 00427 361 810; 0042 7 367 392

Telefax: 00427 323 724; 0042 7 367 392

General and International Practice.

JAN HAVLÁT, born Bratislava, Czechoslovakia, May 15, 1953; admitted, 1980, Czechoslovakia. Education: Comenius University at Bratislava, Faculty of Law. Arbitrator of the Court of Arbitration: Czechoslovak Chamber of Commerce in Prague; Austrian Chamber of Commerce in Vienna. Member: Slovak Bar Association. LANGUAGES: Slovak, Czech, English, German and Russian. PRACTICE AREAS: Civil Law; Criminal Law; Commercial Law; Estate Law.

TOMÁŠ BOREC, born Bratislava, Czechoslovakia, January 17, 1967; admitted, 1993, Slovakia. Education: Comenius University at Bratislava, Faculty of Law; Duke University, School of Law; Summer Institute in Transnational Law in Brussels; University of London, Queen Mary & Westfield College; United Kingdom Central European Legal Scholarship Scheme. Member: Slovak Bar Association. LANGUAGES: Slovak, Czech, English and Russian. PRACTICE AREAS: Civil Law; Commercial Law; Corporate Law.

HELLER, LÖBER, BAHN & PARTNERS

Established in 1991

LAURINSKÁ 12

SK-811 01 BRATISLAVA, SLOVAKIA

Telephone: (427) 361439

Fax: (427) 361478

Vienna, Austria Office: Seilergasse 16, A-1010. Telephone: (431) 515 15 0. Fax: (431) 512 63 94.

(This Listing Continued)

Budapest, Hungary Office: János Zsigmond U. 7B, H-1121. Telephone: (361) 2093370. Fax: (361) 1868481.

Prague, Czech Republic Office: Italská 27, CZ-12000. Telephone: (422) 24231006. Fax: (422) 24218375.

Brussels, Belgium Office: Rue de la Loi 99/101, B-1040. Telephone: (322) 237 26 55. Fax: (322) 280 09 83.

Advice and assistance in the preparation, negotiation and conclusion of Foreign Trade Contracts, including advice and assistance in the establishment of Slovak Joint-Venture Companies with foreign participation, including Tax Advice.

PARTNERS

GEORG BAHN, born Vienna, Austria, 1943; admitted, 1973, Austria. Education: University of Vienna Law School (Dr. iur.) and Department of Political Sciences (Dr. rer.pol.); University of California, Santa Barbara, Department for Political Science. Member, Austrian Association on Foreign Policy and International Relations. Member: Vienna Bar Association; Association Internationale des Jeunes Avocats. LANGUAGES: German and English. PRACTICE AREAS: Real Estate.

RESIDENT COUNSELS

EDITA KREJČÍ, born Nitra, Slovak Republic, 1950; admitted, 1991, Slovak Republic. Education: Komenium University of Bratislava Law School (Dr. iur.); Post Graduate Studies at Institute of Foreign Trade (State Bar Examination, Economic Law, Civil Law, Criminal Law and International Private Law). LANGUAGES: Slovak, Czech, Russian, German, English, French. PRACTICE AREAS: Corporate Law; Banking.

JANA MIKULÁŠOVÁ, born Bratislava, Slovak Republic, 1953; admitted, 1991, Slovak Republic. Education: Komenium University of Bratislava Law School (Dr. iur.); Post Graduate Studies at Institute of Foreign Trade (State Bar Examination, Economic Law, Civil Law, Criminal Law and International Private Law). LANGUAGES: Slovak, Czech, Russian, English, German. PRACTICE AREAS: Arbitration; Administrative Law.

JUDR. DUŠAN KUBOVČÁK

Member of IAG International

Established in 1990

ŠTÚROVÁ 1/A

P.O. BOX 36

814 99 BRATISLAVA, SLOVAKIA

Telephone: 00427-36 18 18; 32 15 75

Fax: 00427-32 15 82

Associated Offices in: Prague, České Budějovice, Plzen, Ústí nad Labem, Hradec Králové, Brno, Ostrava, Banská Bystrica, Košice.

Civil and Commercial Law Practice.

Member of IAG International, an integrated advisory group of 42 independent professional firms who provide quick and easy access to advice from other legal, accountancy and taxation firms in 58 cities throughout Europe, including Belgium.

JUDR. DUŠAN KUBOVČÁK, born Trenčín, Czechoslovakia, 1949. Education: University of Comenius, Bratislava (1970); Charles University Law Faculty, Prague (1972; Dr. Jur., 1975). Member: Slovak Bar Association. LANGUAGES: English, German, Russian and Serbo-Croatian. PRACTICE AREAS: Civil Law; Commercial Law.

ASSOCIATES

JUDR. ZDENKA CIMMERMANNOVÁ. PRACTICE AREAS: General Trade; Commercial Law.

ING. POLÁK JOZEF. PRACTICE AREAS: General Tax Law.

SQUIRE, SANDERS & DEMPSEY

MUDRONOVA 37

811 01 BRATISLAVA, SLOVAKIA

Telephone: 011-42-7-315-370

Fax: 011-42-7-313-918

Cleveland, Ohio Office: 4900 Society Center, 127 Public Square, Cleveland, Ohio 44114-1304. Telephone: 216-479-8500. Fax's: 216-479-8780, 216-479-8781, 216-479-8787, 216-479-8795, 216-479-8793, 216-479-8776, 216-479-8788.

Columbus, Ohio Offices: 1300 Huntington Center, 41 South High Street, Columbus, Ohio 43215. Telephone: 614-365-2700. Fax: 614-365-2499.

(This Listing Continued)

Jacksonville, Florida Office: One Enterprise Center, Suite 2100, 225 Water Street, Jacksonville, Florida 32202. Telephone: 904-353-1264. Fax: 904-356-2986.

Miami, Florida Office: 201 South Biscayne Boulevard, Suite 2900 Miami Center, Miami, Florida 33131. Telephone: 305-577-8700. Fax: 305-358-1425.

New York, New York Office: 520 Madison Avenue, 32nd Floor, New York, New York 10022. Telephone: 212-872-9800. Fax: 212-872-9814.

Phoenix, Arizona Office: Two Renaissance Square, 40 North Central Avenue, Suite 2700, Phoenix, Arizona 85004-4441. Telephone: 602-528-4000. Fax: 602-253-8129.

Washington, D.C. Office: 1201 Pennsylvania Avenue, N.W., P.O. Box 407, Washington, D.C. 20044. Telephone: 202-626-6600. Fax: 202-626-6780.

London, England Office: 1 Gunpowder Square, Printer Street, London EC4A 3DE. Telephone: 011-44-71-830-0055. Fax: 011-44-71-830-0056.

Brussels, Belgium Office: Avenue Louise, 165-Box 15, 1050 Brussels, Belgium. Telephone: 011-32-2-648-1717. Fax: 011-32-2-648-1064.

Prague Office: Adria Palace, Jungmannova 31/36, 11000 Prague 1, Czech Republic. Telephone: 011-42-2-231-5661. Fax: 011-42-2-231-5482.

Budapest, Hungary Office: Deak Ferenc Ut. 10, Office 304, H-1052 Budapest V., Hungary. Telephones: 011-36-1-226-2024. Fax: 011-36-1-226-2025.

Kiev, Ukraine Office: vul. Prorizna 9, Suite 20, Kiev 252035, Ukraine. Telephones: 011-7-044-244-3452, 011-7-044-244-3453, 011-7-044-228-8687. Fax: 011-7-044-228-4938.

General and International Practice.

(For Biographical Data on Cleveland and Columbus, Ohio, Miami and Jacksonville, Florida, New York, New York, Phoenix, Arizona, Washington, D.C., London, England, Brussels, Belgium, Prague, Czech Republic, Budapest, Hungary and Kiev, Ukraine Personnel, see Professional Biographies at those Points Respectively).

WEISS-TESSBACH

spol S.R.O.

Established in 1993

PANSKA 31

81102 BRATISLAVA, SLOVAKIA

Telephone: 0042 7 335769
Telecopier: 0042 7 331126

Vienna, Austria Office: Weiss-Tessbach Rechtsanwälte OEG, Rotenturmstrasse 13. A-1010. Telephone: 0043 1 5331651. Telecopier: 0043 1 5335252.

Budapest, Hungary Representative Office: Weiss-Tessbach Kft. Vármegye u.3-5, H-1052. Telephone: 0036 1 2674227; 2674228; 2674229. Telecopier: 0036 1 2674241.

Prague, Czech Republic Representative Office: Weiss-Tessbachspol s.r.o. Celetna 11, 11000. Telephone: 0042 2 2318693; 2317237; 2319963. Telecopier: 0042 2 2317400.

Administrative Law, Advertising Law, Agricultural Law, Antitrust Law, Arbitration, Banking Law, Bankruptcy, Competition Law, Constitutional Law, Construction Law, Conveyancing, Corporate Law, Distributorship Agency and Franchise Law, EEC Law, Employer's Liability, Environmental Law, Foreign Investments, Immigration Law, Industrial Relations and Labor Law, Insurance Law, International Contracts, International Private Law, Litigation, Product Liability Law, Property and Real Estate Law, Rent and Lease, Trade Regulations, General Legal Practice, Copyright Law, Industrial Models, License Negotiation, Patent Litigation, Trademark Litigation, Trademark Prosecution, Transfer of Technology, General Intellectual Property Practice, Capital Taxation, Corporate Taxation, Indirect Taxation, Inheritance, Estate and Gift Taxation, International Taxation, Personal Income Taxation, Sales Turnover, Value Added Taxes, Taxation of Foreign Nationals, Exchange Control, East-West Relations (Countertrade, Joint Ventures), Hungarian Law, Czechoslovakia Law.

FIRM PROFILE: *Founded in 1878, Weiss-Tessbach offers the full range of Eastern European corporate legal services. The firm opened its Bratislava office in 1993 and is currently composed of seven partners, one U.S. attorney and 23 associates and expects to grow in Eastern Europe in particular.*

(This Listing Continued)

PARTNERS IN CHARGE

DR. WIELAND SCHMID-SCHMIDSFELDEN, born St. Pölten, July 1, 1959; admitted, 1989, Austria. *LANGUAGES:* German and English. *PRACTICE AREAS:* Corporate Law; General Commercial Law; The Laws of Eastern European Countries; EEC Law; Banking Finance and Insurance Law; Industrial Installations; Environmental Law; Telecommunication Arbitration.

MAG. DR. STEFAN EDER, born Vienna, April 4, 1962; admitted, 1992, Austria. *LANGUAGES:* German and English. *PRACTICE AREAS:* Corporate Law; General Commercial Law; Computer Law; The Laws of Eastern European Countries; Banking Finance and Insurance Law; Capital Markets; Data Protection; Arbitration.

RESIDENT ASSOCIATES

DR. TINSCHMIDTOVA IVETA, born Zilina, August 16, 1955; admitted, 1991, Slovak Republic as commercial lawyer. *LANGUAGES:* Slovak and German. *PRACTICE AREAS:* Corporate Law; General Commercial Law.

DR. ANNA MAGOVA, born Trnava, July 10, 1961; admitted, 1992, Slovak Republic. *Education:* University of Bratislava (Dr.iur., 1984). *LANGUAGES:* Slovak, German and Russian.

SLOVENIA

SELIH, REMEC & JANEZIC

RESLJEVA 24

61000 LJUBLJANA, SLOVENIA

Telephone: 386-61-313-740
Facsimile: 386-61-133-70-98

Company and Commercial Law, Industrial Property Law, Labour Law. Patent and Trademark.

MEMBERS OF FIRM

RUDI SELIH, born Slovenske Konjice, January 6, 1929; admitted, 1960, Slovenia. *Education:* Celje, Slovenia (1947); Ljubljana, Slovenia (Diploma, 1956). Patent and Trademark Attorney, 1992. *Member:* Slovenian Bar Association; Union Internationale des Avocats. *PRACTICE AREAS:* Company Law; Commercial Law; Industrial Property Law.

NINA REMEC SELIH, born Maribor, February 8, 1960; admitted, 1988, Slovenia. *Education:* Ljubljana, Slovenia (1978., Diploma, 1983). Patent and Trademark Attorney, 1992. *Member:* Slovenian Bar Association; Union Internationale des Avocats; Association Internationale des Jeunes Avocats. *PRACTICE AREAS:* Company Law; Commercial Law; Industrial Property Law; Labour Law.

ALEKSANDRA JANEZIC, born Ljubljana, January 2, 1960; admitted, 1991, Slovenia. *Education:* Ljubljana, Slovenia (1978., Diploma, 1983). Author: Pravna Praksa. Patent and Trademark Attorney, 1992. *Member:* Slovenian Bar Association; Association Internationale des Jeunes Avocats.

(This Listing Continued)

SELIH, REMEC & JANEZIC, Ljubljana—Continued

PRACTICE AREAS: Company Law; Commercial Law; Industrial Property; Labour Law.

ASSOCIATES

SABINA KLUN, born 1970; admitted, 1994, Slovenia.

SPAIN

ARTHUR ANDERSEN
ASESORES LEGALES Y TRIBUTARIOS

Legal and Tax Advisors

MAISONNAVE, 28 BIS
03003 ALICANTE, SPAIN
Telephone: 34-6-5921770
Fax: 34-65-228967

Arthur Andersen Asesores Legales y Tributarios's offices: Alicante, Barcelona, Bilbao, Granada, La Coruña, Madrid, Málaga, Oviedo, Palma de Mallorca, San Sebastian, Sevilla, Valencia, Vigo, Vitoria, Zaragoza.

Associated Law Firms abroad: France, Italy, Germany, Portugal, The Netherlands, Belgium, United Kingdom, South Africa, Colombia and Brazil.

PARTNER

EDUARDO FERNÁNDEZ DE VALDERRAMA, born Madrid, Spain, January 13, 1951; admitted, 1974, Madrid. *Education:* ICADE (Law Degree, 1973; Economics Degree, 1974). *Member:* Madrid Bar Association. **LANGUAGES:** English and Spanish.

RESIDENT ASSOCIATE

RAFAEL JORDA, born Alcoy (Alicante), Spain, November 3, 1966; admitted, 1990, Madrid. *Education:* University of Alicante (Law Degree, 1989). *Member:* Alicante Bar Association. **LANGUAGES:** Spanish and English.

OTHER ASSOCIATES

Susana Bengoa

(For Complete Firm Profile, see data at Madrid, Spain)

CORNO & CARDONA

Abogados

PLAZA CALVO SOTELO 4-2°
03001 ALICANTE, SPAIN
Telephone: (96) 514 02 72 (3 Lines)
Fax: (96) 520 89 33

Corporation, Banking, Foreign Investment, Urbanism, Taxation, EEC, Administrative Law, Accounting, Real Estate, Patents and Trademarks.

PARTNERS

LUIS CORNO CAPARROS, born Alicante, Spain, May 23, 1954; admitted, 1980, Tenerife; 1982, Alicante; 1983, Murcia; 1986, Valencia. *Education:* University of Murcia (1971-1973); Granada University (Law Degree, 1973-1976); Fordham University School of Law, New York (1987). Contributions: Material for Discussion on Spain's Constitution, 1978 (Ed. Aranzadi). Member, Editorial Board "Revista General de Derecho"; Juan March Foundation Law Award, 1984. Assistant Professor of Administrative Law, Alicante University, 1982. Professor of European Community Law at CESA-ICADE, Alicante, 1986. Government Attorney, 1980-1985. Legal Adviser to the Department of Regional Trade with European Economic Community, Autonomous Community of Valencia, 1986. Foreign Associate with Rosenman & Colin, New York, 1987. *Member:* ABA; IBA. **LANGUAGES:** Spanish and English.

PABLO CARDONA MARTIN, born Granada, Spain, September 14, 1952; admitted, 1989, Alicante. *Education:* University of Granada (Law Degree, 1969-1974). Collaborator in the Departments of Financial and Taxation Law of the University of Granada, 1975-1980. State Department of

(This Listing Continued)

Financial and Tax Inspectors, 1980-1989. *Member:* Official Register of Accounting Auditors. **LANGUAGES:** Spanish and French.

ASSOCIATES

ANTONIO GARRIGOS JUAN, born Alicante, Spain, September 12, 1960; admitted, 1990, Alicante and Valencia. *Education:* University of Alicante (Law Degree, 1977-1982; Post-graduate studies in Mercantile Law). Assistant Professor: Mercantile Law; Civil and Mercantile Law, University of Alicante. **LANGUAGES:** Spanish and English.

GONZALO ALCAIDE CRESPO, born Alicante, Spain, November 2, 1961. *Education:* University of Alicante (Economics Degree, 1979-1984); University of Valencia (Master in Business Management, 1988).

JOSE MARIA RUIZ JOVER, born Alicante, Spain, September 22, 1967; admitted, 1992, Alicante. *Education:* University of Alicante (Law Degree, 1985-1990). **LANGUAGES:** Spanish and English.

ANA JUANET ROEL, born La Coruña, October 3, 1969; admitted, 1993, Alicante. *Education:* Universidad Pontificia de Comillas (I.C.-.A.D.E.), Madrid (Law Degree and Diploma in Business Management, (1987-1992). **LANGUAGES:** Spanish and English.

ARTHUR ANDERSEN
ASESORES LEGALES Y TRIBUTARIOS

Legal and Tax Advisors

AVENIDA DIAGONAL, 654
08034 BARCELONA, SPAIN
Telephone: 34-3-280 4040
Fax: 34-3-280 2810; 34-3-280 4563

Arthur Andersen Asesores Legales y Tributarios's offices: Alicante, Barcelona, Bilbao, Granada, La Coruña, Madrid, Málaga, Oviedo, Palma de Mallorca, San Sebastian, Sevilla, Valencia, Vigo, Vitoria, Zaragoza.

Associated Law Firms abroad: France, Italy, Germany, Portugal, The Netherlands, Belgium, United Kingdom, South Africa, Colombia and Brazil.

PARTNERS

PEDRO PABLO RODES, born Palma de Mallorca, Baleares, Spain, July 18, 1955; admitted, 1982, Barcelona. *Education:* University of Barcelona (Economics Degree, 1977; Law Degree, 1979); Barcelona Tax Studies Center (Master, 1979). *Member:* Barcelona Bar Association. **LANGUAGES:** Spanish, French and English.

TOMÁS LÉRIDA, born Madrid, Spain, July 24, 1958; admitted, 1990, Barcelona. *Education:* ICADE (Law Degree, 1982; Economics Degree, 1983); Instituto de Empresa de Madrid (Master, 1984); CESEM (Master, Financial and Tax Management, 1982). Co-Author: "Las nuevas Leyes del Impuesto sobre la Renta y el Patrimonio," Arthur Andersen Asesores Legales y Tributarios, 1992. *Member:* Barcelona Bar Association. **LANGUAGES:** Spanish and English.

ASSOCIATES

JOSE LUIS BLANCO, born Barcelona, Spain, May 17, 1961; admitted, 1987, Barcelona. *Education:* University of Barcelona (Law Degree, 1984); Yale Law School (LL.M., 1986). Professor, Business Law, University of Barcelona. *Member:* Barcelona Bar Association. **LANGUAGES:** Spanish, French, English and Italian.

ENRIQUE ALFREDO CHINCHILLA, born Barcelona, Spain, November 6, 1958; admitted, 1989, Barcelona. *Education:* University of Barcelona (Law Degree, 1981); IESE (Master, Business Administration, 1983). *Member:* Barcelona Bar Association. **LANGUAGES:** Spanish, French and English.

VICTOR ISÁBAL, born Barcelona, Spain, February 28, 1962; admitted, 1985, Barcelona. *Education:* University of Barcelona (Law Degree, 1985). *Member:* Barcelona Bar Association. **LANGUAGES:** Spanish and English.

JOSE LUIS ROS, born Barcelona, Spain, March 8, 1960; admitted, 1990, Baleares. *Education:* INEDE-FERT, UNED (Law Degree, 1982); Barcelona Tax Studies Center (Master, 1985). *Member:* Baleares Bar Association and R.O.A.C. (Official Institute of Auditors). **LANGUAGES:** Spanish and English.

FERNANDO REY, born Barcelona, Spain, December 17, 1961; admitted, 1989, Barcelona. *Education:* University of Barcelona (Law Degree,

(This Listing Continued)

1984). Professor, Tax Law - Personal Income Tax and Wealth Tax, ESADE, Barcelona. *Member:* Barcelona Bar Association. *LANGUAGES:* Spanish and English.

MANUEL MARAGALL, born Barcelona, Spain, June 1, 1964; admitted, 1990, Barcelona. *Education:* University of Madrid (Law Degree, 1987). *Member:* Barcelona Bar Association. *LANGUAGES:* Spanish and English.

RAMÓN GIRBAU, born Sabadell, Barcelona, Spain, January 2, 1961; admitted, 1986, Sabadell; 1988, Barcelona. *Education:* University of Barcelona (Law Degree, 1984); Université Libre de Bruxelles, Institut d'Etudes Européennes (License spéciale en droit européen, 1987); University of Barcelona, Instituto de Economía Pública y Derecho Tributario (1989). Co-Author: "Las cláusulas de no competencia en los contratos de compraventa de empresa y el derecho comunitario de la competencia," Gaceta jurídica de la CEE, 1988; "Commercial Agency and Distribution Agreements: Law and practice in the Member States of the EC Contribution," London, 1989. *Member:* Sabadell and Barcelona Bar Associations. *LANGUAGES:* Spanish, French and English.

LUIS ESQUERRA, born Barcelona, Spain, December 8, 1963; admitted, 1989, Barcelona. *Education:* University of Barcelona (Law Degree, 1986; Doctor, European Community Law, 1987). *Member:* Barcelona Bar Association. *LANGUAGES:* Spanish, French, English and Italian.

ANTONIO VALDIVIA, born Barcelona, Spain, August 25, 1961; admitted, 1990, Barcelona. *Education:* UNED, Madrid (Law Degree, 1987); University of Barcelona (Economics Degree, 1986; Master, Business Administration, 1984). *Member:* Barcelona Bar Association. *LANGUAGES:* Spanish, French and English.

ALBERTO COLLADO, born Barcelona, Spain, September 23, 1964; admitted, 1989, Barcelona. *Education:* University of Barcelona (Law Degree, 1987); Special Course on Corporate Legal Counsel for Tax Expert (1987). *Member:* Barcelona Bar Association. *LANGUAGES:* Spanish, French and English.

JAVIER MIRAVITLLES, born Barcelona, Spain, December 23, 1962; admitted, 1991, Barcelona. *Education:* University of Barcelona (Law Degree, 1985); IESE (Master, Business Administration, 1987). *Member:* Barcelona Bar Association. *LANGUAGES:* Spanish and English.

CLAUDIO DORIA, born Lima, Perú, July 27, 1962; admitted, 1987, Barcelona. *Education:* University of Navarra (Law Degree, 1987). *Member:* Barcelona Bar Association. *LANGUAGES:* Spanish, English, French and Italian.

MARIO SOLER, born Barcelona, Spain, April 2, 1965; admitted, 1989, Barcelona. *Education:* University of Barcelona (Law Degree, 1988). *Member:* Barcelona Bar Association. *LANGUAGES:* Spanish.

PABLO TORRANO, born Tarrasa, Spain, June 13, 1965; admitted, 1989, Barcelona. *Education:* University of Barcelona (Law Degree, 1988). *Member:* Barcelona Bar Association. *LANGUAGES:* Spanish and French.

IGNACIO CALVET, born Barcelona, Spain, August 24, 1965; admitted, 1989, Barcelona. *Education:* University of Barcelona (Law Degree, 1988; Economics Degree, 1991). Actuary of Insurances, 1991. Official Translator of English, 1992. *Member:* Barcelona Bar Association. *LANGUAGES:* Spanish, French and English.

JESÚS DELGADO, born Seville, Spain, March 6, 1964; admitted, 1992, Barcelona. *Education:* University of Barcelona (Law Degree, 1989). *Member:* Barcelona Bar Association. *LANGUAGES:* Spanish and English.

MONTSERRAT TOMÁS, born Barcelona, May 14, 1966; admitted, 1992, Barcelona. *Education:* University of Barcelona (Law Degree, 1989). *Member:* Barcelona Bar Association. *LANGUAGES:* Spanish, French and English.

MISERICORDIA BORRÁS, born Reus, Tarragona, Spain, December 31, 1962; admitted, 1987, Barcelona. *Education:* University of Barcelona (Law Degree, 1987; Master, European Law, 1989). *Member:* Barcelona Bar Association. *LANGUAGES:* Spanish, French and English.

JOSE RAMON MORALES, born Barcelona, Spain, October 26, 1965; admitted, 1992, Barcelona. *Education:* University of Barcelona (Law Degree, 1989). *Member:* Barcelona Bar Association. *LANGUAGES:* Spanish and English.

SILVIA SORRIBAS, born Barcelona, Spain, February 9, 1967; admitted, 1992, Barcelona. *Education:* University of Barcelona (Law Degree, 1990). *Member:* Barcelona Bar Association. *LANGUAGES:* Spanish and English.

(This Listing Continued)

VICTOR XERCAVINS, born Barcelona, Spain, December 27, 1966; admitted, 1990, Barcelona. *Education:* University of Barcelona (Law Degree, 1990); University (C. Abad Oliba, Master in Law, 1991). *Member:* Barcelona Bar Association. *LANGUAGES:* Spanish and English.

BENJAMIN CHASCO, born Barcelona, Spain, February 17, 1967; admitted, 1991, Barcelona. *Education:* University of Barcelona (Law Degree, 1989); ESADE (MBA, 1992). *Member:* Barcelona Bar Association. *LANGUAGES:* Spanish and English.

ELIA LABASTIDA, born Barcelona, Spain, November 1, 1968; admitted, 1992, Barcelona. *Education:* INEDE-FERT, UNED Barcelona (Law Degree, 1991). *Member:* Barcelona Bar Association. *LANGUAGES:* Spanish and English.

LAURA CERVERA, born Barcelona, Spain, February 26, 1962; admitted, 1990, Barcelona. *Education:* University of Barcelona (Law Degree, 1985). *Member:* Barcelona Bar Association and R.O.A.C. (Official Institute of Auditors). *LANGUAGES:* Spanish and English.

MIGUEL ACOSTA, born Málaga, Andalucia, Spain, June 29, 1968; admitted, 1992, Barcelona. *Education:* University of Córdoba (Law Degree, 1991); Université Libre de bruselles (License speciale en droit européen, 1992). *Member:* Barcelona Bar Association. *LANGUAGES:* Spanishy, French and English.

TOMÁS FORNESA, born Barcelona, Spain, January 25, 1968; admitted, 1992, Barcelona. *Education:* University of Barcelona (Law Degree, 1991). *LANGUAGES:* Spanish, English and French.

ANTONI ANGERRI, born Barcelona, Spain, July 3, 1966; admitted, 1994, Barcelona. *Education:* University of Barcelona (Law Degree, 1990); University of Koln, Germany (European Community Lasw Seminar, 1990); Barcelona Tax Studies Center (Master, 1993). *LANGUAGES:* Spanish, Engish and French.

EVA TOSCAS, born Barcelona, Spain, November 27, 1969; admitted, 1991 Barcelona. *Education:* University of Barcelona (Law Degree, 1992). *LANGUAGES:* English.

OTHER ASSOCIATES

Josep Torras	**José Ayllón**
Montserrat Collado	**Patrick de Bonilla**
José Luis Rutz-Flores	**Joaquin Giráldez**
Diego Rodriquez	**Miriam Omedes**
Carlos Heredia	

(For Complete Firm Profile, see data at Madrid, Spain)

B M & A

Abogados y Consultores

Established in 1978

AVDA. DIAGONAL 604, 4° 2ª &
AVDA. PAU CASALS 22, 2°
08021 BARCELONA, SPAIN
Telephone: 414.20.28; 201.59.77
Fax: 200.82.46

General Legal Practice, Company Law, Civil Law, Tax Law, Employment Law, Litigation, International Law, Foreign Investments, CEE Law, Banking and Financing, Bankruptcy, Insurance Law, Commercial, Auditing and General Business Consulting.

FIRM PROFILE: The firm was established in 1978 and offers a full range of legal and consulting services. It is well known for its Commercial and European Community Law.

PARTNER

ENRIQUE MORERA GUAJARDO, born Lisboa, Portugal, February 24, 1955; admitted, 1980, Barcelona; 1980, Madrid; 1982, Gerona; 1982, Lérida. *Education:* University of Barcelona (Law Degree, 1978); Insurance Law Institute (Master, 1979); Law Society Barcelona (Master, Company Law, 1979); Instituto de Estudios Superiores de la Empresa, I.E.S.E., Barcelona (M.B.A., 1980). Author: "La letra de Cambio," IESE, 1986; "La Suspensión de Pagos," IESE, 1987. Lecturer: Commercial Law, Instituto de Estudios Superiores de la Empresa (I.E.S.E.) Secretary, Humanism and Democracy Association, 1990—. *Member:* Colegio de Abogados de Barcelona; Colegio de Abogados de Madrid; Colegio de Abogados de Lérida; Colegio de Abogados de Gerona; Association of Young Employers; Circulo

(This Listing Continued)

B M & A, Barcelona—Continued

de Economía (President and Founder); B.M.&A. (President and Founder). *LANGUAGES:* Spanish, Catalán, English, French and Portuguese.

MEMBERS OF FIRM

TRINIDAD ROIG FARRAN, born Tarragona, Spain, March 25, 1957; admitted, 1982, Barcelona. *Education:* University of Barcelona (Economics Degree, 1980); Instituto de Estudios Superiores de la Empresa, IESE, Barcelona (M.B.A., 1982). *Member:* Registro de Economistas Auditores; Colegio de Economistas de Barcelona (Spain); Registro Oficial de Auditores de Cuentas de Barcelona; Asociación Española de Contabilidad y Administratián de Empresas. *LANGUAGES:* Spanish, Catalán and English.

LORENZO GARCIA ARNAU, born Barcelona, Spain, March 30, 1958. *Education:* University of Barcelona (Law Qualified, 1987); Center of International Economic Studies; Barcelona Tax Law School. Author: Colaborator in "Manual fiscal práctico", Ed. Weka, 1986; "Sobre sociedades anónimas," Instituto de Estudios Superiores de la Empresa, IESE, Barcelona, 1986. *LANGUAGES:* Spanish, Catalán and French.

ANGEL MAZORRA FOLGUERA, born Barcelona, July 16, 1958; admitted, 1983, Barcelona. *Education:* University of Barcelona (Law Degree, 1982); Colegio de Abogados de Barcelona (Legal Practice Course, 1984). *Member:* Colegio de Abogados de Barcelona and Mataró. *LANGUAGES:* Spanish, Catalán and French.

FRANK D. MULLER, born Kreiznach, Germany, October 18, 1960; admitted, 1994. *Education:* University of Maguncia. Junior Barrister Attending The Court in 1987, ESPC in International Civil Law; Assessor International in 1991. Speciality in Criminal Law, Spanish Law Degree Since 1993; German Lawyer Lecturer. *LANGUAGES:* Spanish, German and English.

ASSOCIATES

EMILIO LLORENS MARTINEZ, born Barcelona, Spain, February 22, 1959; admitted, 1991, Barcelona. *Education:* University of Barcelona (History Degree, 1982 and Law Degree, 1991; Catalán Law Civil Course, 1993). *Member:* Colegio de Abogados de Barcelona. *LANGUAGES:* Spanish, Catalán and English.

JAVIER NIÑO BOSCH, born Oviedo, Spain, October 30, 1962; admitted, 1991, Barcelona. *Education:* University of Barcelona (Economics Degree, 1985); Instituto de Estudios Superiores de la Empresa, Barcelona, IESE (M.B.A., 1989). *LANGUAGES:* Spanish, Catalàn and English.

GABRIEL ALBALAT GARRIDO, born Granada, Spain, October 14, 1963; admitted, 1991, Barcelona. *Education:* University of Barcelona (Law Degree, 1990). *Member:* Colegio de Abogados de Barcelona. *LANGUAGES:* Spanish, Catalán and English.

JAVIER RAMOS CHILLON, born Barcelona, Spain, February 17, 1963; admitted, 1991, Barcelona. *Education:* University of Barcelona (Law Degree, 1991). Oficial Administracion de Justicia (en excedencia). *Member:* Colegio de Abogados de Barcelona. *LANGUAGES:* Spanish, Catalán and French.

MARTIN VALLES BOTEY, born Barcelona, Spain, September 18, 1967; admitted, 1992, Barcelona. *Education:* University of Barcelona (Law Degree, 1992; Master en Legislación y Comercio Internacional; Master en Derecho de Sociedades). *Member:* Colegio de Abogados de Barcelona. *LANGUAGES:* Spanish, Catalán, English and French.

JAVIER SEGON ROCA-UMBERT, born Barcelona, Spain, January 31, 1962; admitted, 1992, Barcelona. *Education:* University of Barcelona (Law Degree, 1987); Abad Oliva (Course Finance and Taxes, 1988). *Member:* Colegio de Abogados de Barcelona. *LANGUAGES:* Spanish, Catalán and English.

ELENA PEREIRA PEREZ, born Madrid, Spain, March 7, 1964; admitted, 1993, Barcelona. *Education:* University of Madrid (Law Degree, 1987); Instituto de Estudios Superiores de la Empresa, IESE (M.B.A., 1993). *LANGUAGES:* Spanish and English.

SANTIAGO ESTEVE PARDO, born Barcelona, Spain, February 3, 1970; admitted, 1993, Barcelona. *Education:* University of Barcelona (Law Degree, 1993; Master en Derecho Fiscal; Master Derecho Civil Catalán). *LANGUAGES:* Spanish, Catalán and English.

(This Listing Continued)

LAURA ANGUERA ARMENGOL, born Barcelona, Spain, June 2, 1966; admitted, 1994, Barcelona. *Education:* University of Barcelona (Law Degree, 1992); Instituto de Estudios Superiores de la Empresa, IESE (M.B.A., 1993). *LANGUAGES:* Spanish, Catalán, English and French.

BAKER & McKENZIE
PASSEIG DE GRÀCIA 11, ESC. B, 2°-1°
08007 BARCELONA, SPAIN
Telephone: (93) 302 27 28
Intn'l. Dialing: (34-3) 302 27 28
Facsimile: (34-3) 318 93 88

Associated Offices of Baker & McKenzie in: Almaty, Amsterdam, Bangkok, Beijing, Berlin, Bogotá, Brasília, Brussels, Budapest, Buenos Aires, Cairo, Caracas, Chicago, Dallas, Frankfurt, Geneva, Hanoi, Ho Chi Minh City, Hong Kong, Juárez, Kiev, London, Madrid, Manila, Melbourne, México City, Miami, Milan, Monterrey, Moscow, New York, Palo Alto, Paris, Prague, Rio de Janeiro, Riyadh, Rome, St. Petersburg, San Diego, San Francisco, São Paulo, Singapore, Stockholm, Sydney, Taipei, Tijuana, Tokyo, Toronto, Valencia, Warsaw, Washington, D.C. and Zürich.
Correspondent Law Firm: Hadiputranto, Hadinoto & Partners, Jakarta.

General and International Law Practice.

PARTNERS

PEDRO AGUARÓN, born Sevilla, Spain, September 26, 1955; admitted, 1984, Madrid; 1988, Barcelona. *Education:* Escolapios San Fernando (Bachillerato, 1973); University of Madrid School of Law (Licenciado en Derecho, 1978; Master in Fiscal Advise, 1984). *Member:* Bar Association of Madrid; Bar Association of Barcelona. *LANGUAGES:* Spanish, English and Catalan. *PRACTICE AREAS:* Banking and Finance; Corporate and Partnership Law; Mergers and Acquisitions; Taxation.

JESÚS M. DE ALFONSO, born Barcelona, Spain, February 6, 1946; admitted, 1969, Barcelona; 1983, Madrid. *Education:* Bachillerato Superior I.N.E.M.; Menendez Pelayo (1963); University of Barcelona School of Law (1969). *Member:* Barcelona, Pamplona, Mataro, Terrassa, Soria Bar Associations. *LANGUAGES:* English, Italian, Spanish and Catalan. *PRACTICE AREAS:* Computers and Technology Law; EC Competition and Trade; Intellectual Property Law; Commercial Law; Mergers and Acquisitions.

ALVARO ESPINÓS, born Barcelona, Spain, March 31, 1945; admitted, 1967, Barcelona. *Education:* Jesuitas Barcelona (Bachillerato, 1962); University of Barcelona School of Law (Licenciado en Derecho, 1967). *Member:* Bar Association of Barcelona; Bar Association of Mataro; Bar Association of Sabadell. *LANGUAGES:* English, French, Italian, Spanish and Catalan. *PRACTICE AREAS:* Bankruptcy, Insolvency and Reorganization; Construction and Property Development; Commercial Litigation; Mergers and Acquisitions; Real Estate Law.

ALEJANDRO VALLS, born Barcelona, Spain, September 18, 1960; admitted, 1984, Barcelona. *Education:* Lycée Français (B.A.C. D., 1979); University of Barcelona School of Law (Licenciado en Derecho, 1984). *Member:* Bar Association of Barcelona. *LANGUAGES:* English, French, Spanish and Catalan. *PRACTICE AREAS:* Employee Benefits; Executive Transfers; Immigration Law; Labor and Employment Law.

ASSOCIATES

JOSEP MARIA BALCELLS, born Barcelona, Spain, December 8, 1963; admitted, 1986, Barcelona. *Education:* University of Barcelona (Law, 1986); Universite Libre de Bruxelles (Master EEC Law, 1989); Universitat Autonoma de Bellaterra (Barcelona) (Magister EEC Law, 1991). *LANGUAGES:* Spanish, English and French. *PRACTICE AREAS:* Antitrust Law; Corporate and Partnership Law; EC Competition and Trade; Franchise Law; Mergers and Acquisitions.

FRANCISCO A. BAYGUAL, born Barcelona, Spain, December 30, 1966; admitted, 1993, Barcelona. *Education:* Universidad de Barcelona (Law, 1993). *Member:* Colegio de Abogados de Barcelona. *LANGUAGES:* Spanish, French, Catalan and English.

CRISTINA CALVO, born Barcelona, Spain, May 21, 1969; admitted, 1992, Barcelona. *Education:* Colegio Universitario Abad Oliba (1990); Central Oregon Community College (1988); Copenhaguen Business School (1991); Facultad de Derecho, Barcelona University (1992).

MIGUEL CANALS, born Barcelona, Spain, February 5, 1968; admitted, 1992, Barcelona. *Education:* University of Barcelona Law School (Law, 1992). *LANGUAGES:* Spanish, Catalan and English. *PRACTICE*

(This Listing Continued)

AREAS: Arbitration and Dispute Resolution; Entertainment, the Arts and Sports Law; Commercial Litigation; Civil Litigation.

MARGARITA DOMÉNECH VIÑAS, born Sabadell, Spain, January 1, 1964; admitted, 1987, Sabadell. *Education:* Universidad Autonoma de Barcelona (Law, 1987); Colegio Universitario Abad Oliba, Barcelona (Special Degree on Tax and Corporate Law). *LANGUAGES:* English, French, German, Spanish and Catalan. *PRACTICE AREAS:* Corporate and Partnership Law; Mergers and Acquisitions; Taxation.

JOSÉ RAMÓN FERNÁNDEZ-CASTELLANOS, born Barcelona, Spain, November 22, 1965; admitted, 1993, Barcelona. *Education:* University of Barcelona School of Law (Law, 1989). *LANGUAGES:* Spanish, English and Catalan. *PRACTICE AREAS:* Intellectual Property Law; Commercial Litigation; EC Competition and Trade; Computers and Technology Law; Communications and Media Law.

MA. DEL PILAR T. GARCIA, born Barcelona, Spain, October 3, 1965; admitted, 1989, Barcelona. *Education:* University of Barcelona (Licenciate, 1989). *LANGUAGES:* Spanish, Catalan and English.

RAFAEL JIMÉNEZ-GUSI, born Barcelona, Spain, August 22, 1961; admitted, 1986, Barcelona. *Education:* University of Barcelona School of Law (Licenciado en Derecho, 1984); Spanish Ministry of Foreign Affairs (Diploma in EC Law, 1985); University of California School of Law, Davis (Diploma in U.S. Law, 1990); Various specialization courses in EC and Commercial Law. Practicing lawyer since 1986, including one year with the Chicago office of Baker & McKenzie. *Member:* EC Law Commission of the Barcelona Bar Association. *LANGUAGES:* English, French, Spanish and Catalan. *PRACTICE AREAS:* Mergers and Acquisitions; Corporate and Partnership Law; Arbitration and Dispute Resolution; Real Estate Law; EC Competition and Trade.

XAVIER JUNQUERA, born Barcelona, Spain, April 20, 1962; admitted, 1987, Barcelona. *Education:* Sagrados Corazones (C.O.U., 1980); Universitat Autonoma de Barcelona (Licenciado, 1986). *Member:* Bar Association of Barcelona. *LANGUAGES:* English, Spanish and Catalan. *PRACTICE AREAS:* Administrative Law; Arbitration and Dispute Resolution; Commercial Litigation; Civil Litigation; Real Estate Law.

JOSE MARIA LLULL, born Barcelona, Spain, October 29, 1963; admitted, 1988, Barcelona. *Education:* University of Barcelona (Law, 1988). *LANGUAGES:* Spanish, Catalan, English, French, Italian and German.

FE L. LOPEZ, born Chandeiro-Cervantes (Lugo), Spain, December 28, 1961; admitted, 1993, Barcelona. *Education:* University of Barcelona (Licenciate, 1992); Escola Profesional i de Practica Juridica - Roda Ventura Colegi Advocats de Barcelona (Graduate, 1994). Administrative Clerk: Ministry of Justice, 1990-1994; Social Security Authorities, 1990. *LANGUAGES:* Spanish and English.

ANDRÉS MILLÁN, born Barcelona, Spain, February 28, 1967; admitted, 1992, Barcelona. *Education:* University of Barcelona Law School (Licenciado en Derecho, 1990). *LANGUAGES:* English, Spanish and Catalan. *PRACTICE AREAS:* Employee Benefits; Executive Transfers; Labor and Employment Law.

MA. MERCÈ PUJADAS, born Vic, Barcelona, October 18, 1963; admitted, 1987, Barcelona. *Education:* University of Barcelona School of Law (Licenciado en Derecho, 1986); Colegio Universitario, Abad Oliva (Corporate and Tax Advisor Diploma, 1989). *Member:* Bar Association of Barcelona. *LANGUAGES:* English, French, Spanish and Catalan. *PRACTICE AREAS:* Corporate and Partnership Law; Mergers and Acquisitions; Real Estate Law.

EUSEBIO PUJOL, born Barcelona, Spain, January 30, 1965; admitted, 1990, Barcelona. *Education:* University of Barcelona Law School (Licenciado en Derecho, 1989); University of Pennsylvania Law School, Philadelphia (LL.M., 1991). *LANGUAGES:* English, French, Spanish and Catalan. *PRACTICE AREAS:* Corporate and Partnership Law; Franchise Law; Mergers and Acquisitions.

ESTEBAN RAVENTOS, born Barcelona, Spain, January 27, 1966; admitted, 1994, Barcelona. *Education:* Universidad Central de Barcelona (Law, 1990). Lecturer on Law, Escuela Superior de Direccion y Administracion de Empresas. *Member:* Colegio de Abogados de Barcelona. *LANGUAGES:* Spanish, Catalan and English.

ALEXANDRE SOLSONA, born Barcelona, Spain, November 22, 1964; admitted, 1994, Barcelona. *Education:* University of Barcelona Law School (Licenciado en Derecho, 1993). *Member:* Barcelona Bar Association. *LANGUAGES:* English, Spanish and Catalan. *PRACTICE AREAS:* Criminal

(This Listing Continued)

Law; Civil Litigation; Commercial Litigation; Intellectual Property; Insurance Law.

JOSÉ-LUIS STAMPA, born Barcelona, Spain, August 28, 1965; admitted, 1989, Barcelona. *Education:* University of Barcelona Law School (Licenciado en Derecho, 1989); McGeorge School of Law (LL.M. in Transnational Business Practice, 1991). *Member:* Barcelona Bar Association; Pacific International Law Society; ACTA 25; Spanish-German Jurists' Association. *LANGUAGES:* English, French, German, Italian, Spanish and Catalan. *PRACTICE AREAS:* Corporate and Partnership Law; Mergers and Acquisitions; Intellectual Property Law; Taxation; Commercial Litigation.

ROSANA VELASCO MASÓ, born Barcelona, Spain, December 28, 1967; admitted, 1992, Barcelona. *Education:* Abad Oliba University; University of Barcelona (Law, 1991); University of Sheffield, England (Diploma in European Business Studies, 1993). *Member:* Barcelona Bar Association. *LANGUAGES:* Spanish, Catalan, English and Italian.

MA. TERESA R. VIDAL, born Sabadell (Barcelona), Spain, June 5, 1964; admitted, 1990, Barcelona. *Education:* University of Barcelona (Law, 1987). *Member:* Barcelona Bar Association. *LANGUAGES:* Catalan, Spanish and English.

BALAÑÁ EGUÍA

Loeff Claeys Verbeke

550, 4° 1A AV. DIAGONAL
08021 BARCELONA, SPAIN
Telephone: 34-3-2007177
Telecopier: 34-3-2023098

Madrid, Spain Office: Balana Eguia Antonio Maura 7, 5°, 28014. Telephone: 34-1-5212654. Telecopier: 34-1-5230458.

Amsterdam, The Netherlands Office: 15 Apollolaan, P.O. Box 75088, 1070 AB. Telephone: 31-20-5741200. Telex: 14291 (LEX NL). Telecopier: 31-20-6718775.

Brussels, Belgium Office: 268 A Avenue de Tervueren, A-1150. Telephone: 02-778.22.11. Telecopier: 02-763.21.85.

Paris, France Office: 1, Avenue Franklin D. Roosevelt, 75008. Telephone: 33-1-49539125. Telecopier: 33-1-45610664.

New York, New York Office: Swiss Bank Tower, 23rd Floor, 10 East 50th Street, 10022. Telephone: 212-759-9000. Fax: 212-759-9018.

Rotterdam, The Netherlands Office: 70 Weena, P.O. Box 74, 3000 AB. Telephone: 31-10-4034777. Telex: 23395 (LEX NL). Telecopier: 31-10-4149388.

Singapore Office: 20 Raffles Place, #08-03, Ocean Towers, Singapore 00104. Telephone: 65-5335332. Telecopier: 64-5330313.

Tokyo, Japan Office: NSE Building, 5th Floor, 1-7-1 Kanda Jinbo-cho, Chiyoda-Ku, Tokyo 101, Japan. Telephone: 81-3-32599831. Telecopier: 81-3-32599888.

Antwerp, Belgium Office: "De Hertoghe," 8th floor, 92 Desguinlei, B.8, B-2018. Telephone: 32.3.2385656. Telex: 72748 (EURLAWB). Telecopier: 32.3.2387877.

Jakarta, Indonesia Associated Office: Ali Budiardjo, Nugroho, Reksodiputro, Niaga Tower, 24th floor, Jalan Jenderal Sudirman Kav. 58, 12920. Telephone: 62.21.2505125/2505136. Telecopier: 62.21.2505121/2505001.

Liege, Belgium Office: 13, Rue Simonon, (Place de Bronckart), B-4000. Telephone: 32-41-527722. Telecopier: 32-41-527511.

Luxembourg, Luxembourg Correspondent Office: Zeyen Beghin Feider. 67, Rue Ermesinde, P.O. Box 5017, 1050. Telephone: 352.468946. Telex:60736 (zflaw lu). Telecopier: 352.468947.

PARTNER

JOSÉ MARÍA BALAÑÁ DE EGUÍA, born 1963; admitted, 1987, Barcelona. *Education:* University of Barcelona (Law Degree, 1985) (Degree in Economics, 1985; Catalan Civil Law, 1986). *Member:* International Fiscal Association; Association Internationale des Jeunes Avocats.

ASSOCIATES

GUSTAVO ADOLFO GÓMEZ FERRÉ , born 1964; admitted, 1988, Barcelona. *Education:* University of Barcelona (Law Degree, 1987); University Abad Oliva, Barcelona (Financial and Tax Law, 1990); University of Barcelona (Catalan Civil Law, 1987).

GERARD F. HERNÁNDEZ COLET, born 1965; admitted, 1990, Barcelona. *Education:* University of Barcelona (1988); UAB/Université Catholique de Louvain, Belgium (European Studies, 1990).

(This Listing Continued)

BALAÑÁ EGUÍA, Barcelona—Continued

ANA DE ISABEL Y ESTRADA, born 1966; admitted, 1990, Barcelona. *Education:* University Computense of Madrid (Law Degree 1988).

GEERT PAEMEN, born 1964; admitted, 1988, Brussels, Belgium. *Education:* University of Louvain, Belgium (Law Degree 1987); College of Europe, Bruges, Belgium (European Studies, 1988).

JUAN PABLO PALOMAR LÓPEZ, born 1965; admitted, 1989, Barcelona. *Education:* University of Barcelona (Law Degree. 1989); Centre of Tax and Financial Studies, Barcelona (Degree Tax Law, 1992).

DIAMA GIL PLASENCIA, born 1967; admitted, 1993, Barcelona. *Education:* University of Barcelona (Law Degree 1991); University Abad Oliva, Barcelona (Postgraduate Degree Business Law, 1992).

MANUEL-JULIO VINIEGRA DOMINGUEZ, born 1966; admitted, 1994, Barcelona. *Education:* University of Barcelona (Law Degree, 1989); University of Houston Law Center (LL.M., International Law, 1994).

(Members of the Bar of Barcelona)

Languages: Spanish, Catalan, English, French, Dutch and German

(For Personnel and other data, see Professional Biographics at Amsterdam, Antwerp, Brussels, Liège, New York, Paris, Rotterdam, Singapore and Tokyo)

PEDRO BROSA & ASOCIADOS

Established in 1965

AVDA. DIAGONAL, 598, 1° 2ᵃ , PRAL. 2ᵃ, 5° 2ᵃ
08021 BARCELONA, SPAIN
Telephone: 34-3-200 09 33
Telefax: 34-3-202 29 07

Madrid, Spain Office: Alfonso XII, 18, 3° Izqda., 28014. Telephone: 34-1-522 82 02. Telefax: 34-1-522-39-89.
Bilbao, Spain Office: San Vicente, 8, plta. 9° dpto. 2, 48001. Telephone: 34-4-423 03 06. Telefax: 34-4-423 93 82.
Brussels, Belgium Office: 165, Avenue Louise 9 ème étage, 1050.
Telephone: 32-2-644 16 09. Telefax: 32-2-644 30 25.

General Practice, Civil Litigation, Civil, Commercial, Corporation, Taxation, Foreign Investments, Administrative, Banking and Financing, Bankruptcy Law, Accounting, Auditing and General Business Consulting.

MEMBERS OF FIRM

PEDRO BROSA, born Lérida, Spain, May 30, 1937; admitted, 1964, Barcelona. *Education:* University of Barcelona (Licenciado en Derecho, 1959; Profesor Mercantil, 1960). Lecturer, Taxation Law, University of Barcelona, 1962-1963. *Member:* Barcelona (Member Governing Body) and Madrid Bar Associations; Colegio de Titulares Mercantiles de Barcelona; Fomento del Trabajo Nacional (Member, Advisory Committee); English Chamber of Commerce in Spain. *LANGUAGES:* Spanish, English, French and Catalan. *PRACTICE AREAS:* General Practice; Commercial; Corporation; Banking and Financing; Bankruptcy law; General Business Consulting.

JAUME BROSA, born Barcelona, Spain, August 24, 1967; admitted, 1993, Barcelona. *Education:* University of Barcelona (Licenciado en Derecho, 1992). *Member:* Colegio de Abogados de Barcelona. *LANGUAGES:* Spanish, French, English, Catalan. *PRACTICE AREAS:* Civil; Commercial; Auditing.

JORDI BROSA, born Barcelona, Spain, November 13, 1968; admitted, 1993, Barcelona. *Education:* University of Barcelona (Licenciado en Derecho, 1992). *Member:* Colegio de Abogados de Barcelona. *LANGUAGES:* Spanish, French, English, Catalan. *PRACTICE AREAS:* Civil; Commercial; Auditing.

AGUSTIN BOU, born Barcelona, Spain, September 8, 1956; admitted, 1982, Barcelona. *Education:* University of Barcelona (Licenciado en Derecho, 1981; Master en Ciencias de los Negocios por Management School, 1979). *Member:* Union Internacional de Abogados; Asociacion Internacional de Jovenes Abogados. *LANGUAGES:* Spanish, English, French, Italian and Catalan. *PRACTICE AREAS:* Accounting and Auditing.

RAMON CATALAN, born Barcelona, Spain, December 19, 1952; admitted, 1979, Barcelona. *Education:* University of Barcelona (Licenciado en Ciencias Economica y Empresariales, 1978). Member: Instituto de Censores Jurados de Cuentas de España; Registro Oficial de Auditores de Cuentas; Registro de Economistas Auditores del Ministerio de Economia y Haci-

(This Listing Continued)

enda. *LANGUAGES:* Spanish, French and Catalan. *PRACTICE AREAS:* Taxation and Accounting.

GUILLERMO CARDONA, born Barcelona, Spain, January 23, 1965; admitted, 1991, Barcelona. *Education:* University of Barcelona (Licenciado en Derecho, 1990). *Member:* Barcelona Bar Association. *LANGUAGES:* Spanish, French, English, Italian, German and Catalan. *PRACTICE AREAS:* Commercial.

ISABEL ESCUDERO, born Barcelona, Spain, May 8, 1958; admitted, 1983, Barcelona. *Education:* University of Barcelona (Licenciada en Derecho, 1980, Distinguished); Catedra Durán y Bas (Diploma de Estudios de Derecho Civil Catalán, 1980). Attorney-at-Law, recognized by the Special Canonical Court of the Rota Romana, 1987. *LANGUAGES:* Spanish, English and French. *PRACTICE AREAS:* Litigation and Civil Law.

LOURDES MILLAT, born Barcelona, Spain, July 26, 1967; admitted, 1990, Barcelona. *Education:* University of Barcelona (Diplomada en Ciencias Empresariales, 1991). *LANGUAGES:* Spanish, English and Catalan. *PRACTICE AREAS:* Accounting and Auditing.

HECTOR NICOLAU, born Barcelona, Spain, May 25, 1965; admitted, 1991, Barcelona. *Education:* University of Barcelona (Licenciado en Ciencias Economicas y Empresariales, 1990). *Member:* Colegio de Economistas de Catalunya. *LANGUAGES:* Spanish, French and Catalan. *PRACTICE AREAS:* Accounting and Auditing.

MARIA JOSE POVILL, born Barcelona, Spain, August 7, 1963; admitted, 1988, Barcelona. *Education:* University of Barcelona (Licenciada en Derecho, 1987). *Member:* Barcelona Bar Association. *LANGUAGES:* Spanish, English and French. *PRACTICE AREAS:* Civil and Commercial.

DAVID RAMÍREZ, born Valencia, Spain, December 21, 1964; admitted, 1988, Barcelona. *Education:* University of Valencia (Law Degree, 1988); Business Institute of Madrid (Master in Business Tax). *Member:* Barcelona Bar Association. *LANGUAGES:* English and Spanish. *PRACTICE AREAS:* Taxation; Accounting.

RAMÓN RIBALDA, born Cifuentes, Guadalajara, Spain, August 20, 1952. Master, Instituto Directivos de Empresa, 1989. *LANGUAGES:* Spanish and Catalan. *PRACTICE AREAS:* Taxation and Accounting.

MANUEL ROMANI, born Barcelona, Spain, March 29, 1949; admitted, 1972, Barcelona. *Education:* University of Barcelona (Licenciado en Cicencias Economicas, 1972). *Member:* Colegio de Economistas de Catalunya, Registro Oficial de Auditores de Cuentas. *LANGUAGES:* Spanish, French, English, Catalan. *PRACTICE AREAS:* General Business Practice and Consulting; Accounting and Auditing.

FRANCESC ROS, born Hospitalet de Liobregat, May 27, 1962; admitted, 1991, Barcelona. *Education:* University of Barcelona (Diplomado en Ciencias Empresariales, 1989). *LANGUAGES:* Spanish and Catalan. *PRACTICE AREAS:* Accounting and Auditing.

CARLOS SAHUQUILLO, born Barcelona, Spain, May 10, 1958; admitted, 1982, Barcelona. *Education:* University of Barcelona (Licenciado en Ciencias Económicas y Empresariales, 1981; Licenciado en Derecho, 1982); Cátedra Durán y Bas (Diploma en Estudios de Derecho Civil Catalán, 1982). *Member:* Barcelona and American Bar Associations; International Bar Association; Colegio de Economistas de Catalunya; Instituto de Censores Jurados de Cuentas de España; Asociación Española de Contabilidad y Administración de Empresas; Registro de Economistas Auditores; Registro Oficial de Auditores de Cuentas; International Tax Planning Association. *LANGUAGES:* Spanish, English, French and Catalan. *PRACTICE AREAS:* General Practice; Commercial; Corporation; Foreign Investments; Banking and Financing; General Business Consulting.

ARMANDO TOMAS, born Barcelona, Spain, March 20, 1953; admitted, 1985. *Education:* University of Barcelona (Licenciado en Derecho, 1975; Licenciado en Empresaria;es. 1974; Master in Business Administration (ESADE). Intrenationall Tax Law Professor at ESADE, Commercial Law Professor at INEDE and Legal Environment of Business Professor at Bentley School. Specialist in merers and acquisitions and company strategy at international level. *LANGUAGES:* Spanish and English. *PRACTICE AREAS:* Commercial Law; International Tax Planning.

GINES TORRES, born Tarragona, Spain, February 24, 1947; admitted, 1973, Barcelona. *Education:* University of Barcelona (Licenciado en Derecho, 1975; Profesor Mercantil, 1970; Licenciado en Ciencias Económicas y Empresariales, 1979). *Member:* Colegio de Economistas de Catalunya; Colegio de Titulares Mercantiles de Barcelona; Instituto de Censores Jurados de Cuentas de España; Registro de Economistas de Catalunya; Colegio de Titulares Mercantiles de Barcelona; Instituto de Censors Jurados de

(This Listing Continued)

Cuentas de Espanaña; Registro de Economistas Auditores; Registro de Auditores del Instituto de Contabilidad y Auditores de Cuentas; Asociación de Economistas Asesores Fiscales del Consejo General de Colegios de Economistas de España; Asociación Española de Asesores Fiscales. *LANGUAGES:* Spanish, English, French, Italian and Catalan. *PRACTICE AREAS:* Taxation; Accounting; General Business Consulting.

OF COUNSEL

MANUEL VICENS, born L'Ametlla del Vallés, Barcelona, Spain, October 20, 1937; admitted, 1987, Barcelona. *Education:* University of Barcelona (Licenciado en Derecho, 1959). Author: "EL IVA y el Transporte," 1985; "Régimen del Transporte Multimodal," 1982; "Comentarios sobre el Estatuto de Autonomía de Cataluña," 1987. Lecturer, ESADE, Barcelona, 1982. Letrado Consistorial, 1987. Subsecretario General Adjunto del Gabinete Jurídico Central of the Generalitat de Cataluña, 1987. Counsel of the Spanish Delegation at the Diplomatic Conference at Geneva for the Adoption of an International Treaty Regarding International Multimodal Transportation of Merchandises, 1982. *Member:* Barcelona Bar Association; International Law Association; International Federation of Freight Forwarders Association. *LANGUAGES:* Spanish, English, French and Catalan. *PRACTICE AREAS:* Transportation; EEC and Constitutional Law.

Languages: Spanish, English, French, Italian, German and Catalan

(For Biographical Data of the Madrid and Bilbao, Spain and Brussels, Belgium Personnel, see Professional Biographies at Madrid, Spain and Brussels, Belgium).

BRUGUERAS, GARCIA-BRAGADO, MOLINERO Y ASOCIADOS

PASEO DE GRACIA, 81
08008 BARCELONA, SPAIN
Telephone: (343) 487 21 02; 215 05 62
Telefax: (343) 487 18 53

Brussels Belgium Office: TELFA, Boulevard Brand Whitlock 114/5, B-1200. Telephone: (32) 2 735 4511. Fax: (32) 2 735 3713.

Member of TELFA (Trans European Law Firms Association) in association with Interlega.

TELFA-Interlega is an association of European law firms, whose members have offices in Athens, Arnhem, Barcelona, Brussels, Budapest, Copenhagen, Düsseldorf, Edinburgh, Geneva, Glasgow, Guernsey, Halle, London, Luxembourg, Madrid, Milan, Nijmegen and Paris.

For more details see TELFA-Interlega entry under Brussels, Belgium.

International and Foreign Investments, General Practice, Commercial, Financial, Stock-Exchange, Corporation, Bankruptcy, Taxation, Civil and Real Estate, Administrative, EEC's Law, Litigation, Criminal and Labor Law.

MEMBERS OF FIRM

JUAN-IGNACIO BRUGUERAS, born Barcelona, Spain, October 7, 1941; admitted, 1968, Barcelona. *Education:* University of Barcelona, Faculty of Law (Master in Business Administration for ESADE). Former Member, Council of the Barcelona Bar Association. Chairman, Board of Caixa Advocats (Savings Bank). Board Secretary, Football Club Barcelona; Vice-Secretary, MEFFSA (Future & Options Market). *LANGUAGES:* Spanish, Catalan and French.

JAIME PERIS, born Barcelona, Spain, September 11, 1936; admitted, 1962, Barcelona. *Education:* Faculties of Law of Valladolid and Barcelona; Commercial University of Deusto (Bilbao). *LANGUAGES:* Spanish, Catalan, English and French.

ANTONI ESQUERRA-T., born Barcelona, Spain, June 8, 1947; admitted, 1974, Barcelona. *Education:* Col. legi Ntra. Sra. de les Escoles Pies; University of Barcelona. *LANGUAGES:* Spanish, Catalan, French and English. *PRACTICE AREAS:* Commercial Law; Company Law; Consumer Law.

CÉSAR MOLINERO, born Burgos, Spain; admitted, 1968, Barcelona. *Education:* Barcelona Faculty of Law. Professor of Law, Universidad Autónoma de Barcelona. *Member:* Association International d'Experts Scientifiques du Tourisme; Union Internationale d'Avocats (U.I.A.). *LANGUAGES:* Spanish, Catalan and French. *PRACTICE AREAS:* Zoning, Planning and Land Use; Administrative; Environmental and Public Law; Government; Real Estate; Land and Landowners.

(This Listing Continued)

ALEJANDRO GARCÍA-BRAGADO, born Girona, Spain, 1949; admitted, 1977, Barcelona. *Education:* Barcelona Law Faculty. State Lawyer (on leave). Secretary and Legal Advisor of the Stock Exchange of Barcelona. *LANGUAGES:* Spanish, Catalan, French and English. *PRACTICE AREAS:* Bank and Banking; Corporate Law; Finance; Mergers, Acquisitions and Divestitures; Securities.

CARLOS GINEBREDA, born 1959; admitted, 1984, Barcelona. *Education:* University of Barcelona; City of London Polytechnic (European Business Law). President, Civil Law Commission Barcelona Bar. *LANGUAGES:* Spanish, Catalan, English and French.

CARLOS BAIXERAS, born Málaga, Spain, 1951; admitted, 1974, Barcelona. *Education:* University of Barcelona (Graduate in Law and Modern History). *LANGUAGES:* Spanish and Catalan.

MARIO PASCUAL, born Barcelona, Spain, 1957; admitted, 1981, Barcelona. *Education:* Jesuit Fathers (Col.legi San Ignasi, Barcelona) University of Barcelona (Post graduate course in Corporate Law). Former Legal Advisor, Stock Exchange of Barcelona; Legal Advisor, Real Club de Tenis Barcelona. Lawyer, Catalan Paddle Association. Member of the Board of Real Federación Española de Tenis. *Member:* Barcelona Bar Association (Sports Law Commission). *LANGUAGES:* Spanish, Catalan, English and French. *PRACTICE AREAS:* Bankruptcy; Banks and Banking; Business Law; Civil Law; Commercial Law; Company Law; Construction Law; Corporate Law; Environmental Law; Family Law; Franchises and Franchising; Fraud and Deceit; Leases and Leasing; Litigation; Medical Malpractice; Mergers, Acquisition and Divestitures; Mortgages; Property; Real Estate; Securities; Sports; Trademark; White Collar Crime.

JUAN-CARLOS ROS, born Barcelona, Spain, 1961; admitted, 1984, Barcelona. *Education:* University of Barcelona. Lecturer, Foreign Investments in Spain. Practiced in England, 1988-1989. *LANGUAGES:* Spanish, Catalan and English.

JOSE J. CARBALLEDA, admitted, 1974, Barcelona. *Education:* Colegio La Salle Bonanova, Barcelona; Barcelona University; Rapporteur in several postgraduate courses at San Pablo University Foundation (Abad Oliba). State Finance Inspector, 1990. Professor, INEDE College, 1990. *LANGUAGES:* Spanish, Catalan and French. *PRACTICE AREAS:* Taxation.

CARMEN PASCUAL, born Barcelona, Spain; admitted, 1978, Barcelona. *Education:* University of Barcelona; Abad Oliva College (Diploma in Foreign Investment Law). *Member:* International Bar Association (IBA). *LANGUAGES:* Spanish, Catalan, English and French. *PRACTICE AREAS:* International Franchising; International Investments.

XAVIER PERIS, born Barcelona, Spain; admitted, 1989, Barcelona. *Education:* University of Barcelona, Centro de Estudios Tributarios Abad Oliva. *LANGUAGES:* Spanish, Catalan and English. *PRACTICE AREAS:* Taxation and Business Law.

OF COUNSEL

LUIS CARBALLEDA, admitted, 1974, Barcelona. Inspector of Finance (on leave). *PRACTICE AREAS:* Taxation.

T. BUXEDA - ABOGADOS

Established in 1960

RAMBLA DE CATALUÑA, 53-55 6°A.
08007 BARCELONA, SPAIN
Telephone: (343) 488 02 50; 488 30 10; 488 16 17
Telex: 50439 UNIM-E
Telefax: (3) 488.16.56

General Practice, Commercial, Corporate, Banking and Finance, Foreign Investments, EEC, Real Estate, Mergers and Acquisitions, Technology Transfers, Licensing, Energy, Tax and Administrative Law.

MEMBERS OF FIRM

TOMAS BUXEDA NADAL, born Barcelona, Spain, February 17, 1938; admitted, 1960, Spain. *Education:* University of Barcelona (Licenciate in Law, 1960). Lecturer in Law Procedure, University of Barcelona, 1960-1964. Deputy, Barcelona Bar Association, 1965-1970. *Member:* Barcelona, Madrid and Lérida Bar Associations; U.I.A. *LANGUAGES:* Spanish, Catalan, English and French. *PRACTICE AREAS:* General Practice; Commercial; Corporate; Banking and Finance; Foreign Investments; Real Estate; Mergers and Acquisitions.

(This Listing Continued)

T. BUXEDA - ABOGADOS, *Barcelona—Continued*

JUAN DE TORD FIGUERAS, born Barcelona, Spain, January 6, 1949; admitted, 1972, Spain. *Education:* City of London College (English Law and Comparative Law Course, 1969); University of Barcelona (Licenciate in Law, 1972); Strasbourg University (EEC Law Course, 1972); University of San Francisco (American Business Law Course, 1984). *Member:* Barcelona Bar Association; A.I.J.A. *LANGUAGES:* Spanish, Catalan, English, French, German and Italian. *PRACTICE AREAS:* General Practice; Commercial; Corporate; Foreign Investments; EEC; Technology Transfers; Licensing; Energy; Tax and Administrative Law.

CARMEN LOMEÑA CABALLERO, born Barcelona, Spain, July 16, 1954; admitted, 1977, Spain. *Education:* University of Barcelona (Licenciate in Law, 1977). *Member:* Barcelona Bar Association. *LANGUAGES:* Spanish and Catalan. *PRACTICE AREAS:* General Practice; Commercial; Corporate; Tax and Administrative Law.

ALEJANDRO JAUMANDREU PATXOT, born Barcelona, Spain, September 22, 1949; admitted, 1980, Spain. *Education:* University of Barcelona (Licenciate in Law, 1972); Strasbourg University (EEC Law Course, 1972); Barcelona Institute of Fiscal Studies (Spanish Tax Law Course, 1978-1979). *Member:* Barcelona Bar Association. *LANGUAGES:* Spanish, Catalan and French. *PRACTICE AREAS:* General Practice; Commercial; Corporate; Tax and Administrative Law.

Languages: Spanish, Catalan, English, French, German and Italian.

CERVELLÓ, LÓPEZ-CHICHERI Y ARAGÓN, ABOGADOS

Associated with Ernst & Young International

L'ILLA DIAGONAL, 575-PLANTA 7
08029 BARCELONA, SPAIN
Telephone: (34-3) 410.67.07
Fax: (34-3) 405.37.84

Madrid, Spain Office: Torre Picasso - Planta 3, Plaza Pablo Ruiz Picasso, s/n, 28020. Telephone (34-1) 572-7200. Fax: (34-1) 572-7400/7372.

Bilbao, Spain Office: Colón de Larreátegui, 26, 48009. Telephone: (34-4) 424-3777/423-8746. Fax: (34-4) 424-2745.

General, Commercial and International Practice.

Juan Antonio Roger	Mercedes Sorribas
Carlos Poy Ciuranan	Alvaro Salmarri
Nieves Briz Puertas	Carlos Obeso

CLIFFORD CHANCE

PAU CLARIS 102
08009 BARCELONA, SPAIN
Telephone: (34 3) 318 68 64
Fax: (34 3) 317 73 23

Other Offices: Amsterdam, Bahrain, Brussels, Budapest, Dubai, Frankfurt, Hanoi, Hong Kong, London, Madrid, Milan, Moscow, New York, Paris, Riyadh, Rome, Shanghai, Singapore, Tokyo, Warsaw. (See London for full address details).

RESIDENT MANAGERS

CARLOS VALLS, Abogado.

MARK INSTANCE, admitted, 1988, Solicitor.

BUFETE CLIMENTE & MARINEL-LO

Established in 1990

C/. PAU CLARIS, NO. 154, 2ND FLOOR
08009 BARCELONA, SPAIN
Telephone: 3/4871084
Fax: 3/4871680

General Practice, Foreign Investments, Commercial, Companies, Mergers and Acquisitions, EEC Law, Bankruptcy, Administrative, Tax, Industrial Property, Real Estate, Insurance and International Private Law, Litigation.

(This Listing Continued)

FIRM PROFILE: Bufete Climente and Marinel-Lo was constituted as a consequence of the dissolution of the firm Bufete Bertran y Musitu, one of the oldest and most prestigious Spanish Law Firms.

PARTNERS

ENRIQUE CLIMENTE LUCIO, born Barcelona, Spain, July 18, 1951; admitted, 1974. *Education:* Colegio de San Ignacio, Barcelona; University of Barcelona; Strasbourg University of Comparative Law. Author: "Franchising: Spain," IBA, 1988. *Member:* International Bar Association. *LANGUAGES:* French and English. *PRACTICE AREAS:* Foreign Investments; Corporate; Franchising; Tax Law; Insurance; Administrative and Planning; Commercial Law.

ENRIQUE MARINEL-LO JORDAN, born Barcelona, Spain, March 2, 1959; admitted, 1987. *Education:* German College, Barcelona; University of Barcelona; Strasbourg University of Comparative Law. Author: "Franchising in Spanien," 1991. *Member:* Spanish-German Association of Lawyers; Young Lawyers International Association; German Chamber of Commerce in Barcelona. *LANGUAGES:* German and English. *PRACTICE AREAS:* Foreign Investments; Corporate; Franchising; EEC Law; Insurance; Mergers and Acquisitions; Commercial Law.

JOSÉ LUIS MARTÍN MENDOZA, born Barcelona, Spain, January 17, 1962; admitted, 1985. *Education:* University of Barcelona; Executive Management School (Diploma in Accountancy); Diploma in International Trading Law. Author: Book *Capital-Riesgo*, Venture Capital, 1988. Senior Spanish Counsel, De Pinna, Scorers & John Venn-London, 1988-1990. *Member:* Spanish Chamber of Commerce in Great Britain. *LANGUAGES:* English. *PRACTICE AREAS:* Foreign Investments; Corporate; Venture-Capital; EEC Law; Tax Law; Mergers and Acquisitions; Commercial Law.

JUAN SAULA ADELL, born Barcelona, Spain, November 11, 1968. *Education:* University of Barcelona. *LANGUAGES:* English. *PRACTICE AREAS:* Corporate; Mergers and Acquisitions; Insurance; Private Law; Commercial Law.

Languages: English, French, German and Spanish.

A List of Representative Clients will be furnished upon request.

CORTADA ADVOCATS

AVDA DIAGONAL, 558, 5-2
08021 BARCELONA, SPAIN
Telephone: 34-3 209.65.22
Fax: 34-3 200.41.57

General Practice, Bankruptcy, Business Law, Civil Law, Commercial, Company Law, Foreign Investments, Property, Taxation, Trust and Estates, Franchising.

FIRM PROFILE: Cortada Advocats, founded in 1991 is a young and dynamic law firm offering a full range of legal services to a diverse domestic and international clientele.

MEMBERS OF FIRM

JORDI CORTADA PASOLA, born Barcelona, Spain, October 9, 1961; admitted, 1985, Barcelona. *Education:* University of Barcelona (Law Degree, 1985); Institut d'Etudes Europeennes ULB, Brussels (International and European Law); University of Cambridge (Introduction to English Law; Abad Oliva College (Diploma in Tax and Corporate Legal Adviser). *LANGUAGES:* Spanish, French, English and Catalan. *PRACTICE AREAS:* Bankruptcy; Business Law; Foreign Investments; Franchising; Tax Law; Trusts and Estates.

CLARA PEREZ LAMON, born Zaragoza, November 29, 1967; admitted, 1992, Barcelona. *Education:* University of Barcelona (Law Degree, 1990); London School of Economics (LL.M., Commercial Law, 1991; Postgraduate courses: Property and Company Law). *LANGUAGES:* French and English. *PRACTICE AREAS:* General Practice; Company Law; Commercial Law; Property; Civil Law.

BUFETE CUATRECASAS

BALMES 76
08007 BARCELONA, SPAIN
Telephone: 290.55.00
Fax: 290.55.67

Bilbao, Spain Office: Alameda de Mazarredo 5. Telephone: 424.82.67. Fax: 424.82.34.

(This Listing Continued)

Madrid, Spain Office: Antonio Maura 10. Telephone: 521.94.47. Fax: 522.48.99.

Gerona, Spain Office: Ronda Ferrán Puig, 4-6. Telephone: 22.71.02. Fax: 22.66.61.

Brussels, Belgium Office: 78 Avenue d'Auderghem. Telephone: 735.06.43. Fax: 734.72.34.

All areas of Spanish and EEC business law, including corporate, commercial, taxation, foreign investments, capital markets, finance, regulatory including environmental law, labour law, intellectual property including software licensing and protection, anti-trust law, litigation, criminal law, bankruptcy law and company restructuring.

FIRM PROFILE: Bufete Cuatrecasas founded in 1917, is presently the largest law firm in Spain with a total staff of 236 (20 partners, 150 lawyers and 66 support staff). We offer a full range of legal services from five fully staffed offices (four in Spain and one in Brussels, Belgium).

MEMBERS OF FIRM

PEDRO CUATRECASAS, born Barcelona, Spain, May 28, 1928; admitted, 1952, Barcelona. *Education:* University of Barcelona (Law Degree, 1952). *Member:* Barcelona Bar Association; Spanish Association of Taxation Experts. (Also at Madrid and Bilbao Offices). *LANGUAGES:* French.

EMILIO CUATRECASAS, born Barcelona, Spain, January 12, 1954; admitted, 1977, Barcelona; 1984, Bilbao. *Education:* University of Navarra (Law Degree, 1976); Abad Oliba College (Diploma in International Law). *Member:* Barcelona Bar Association; Bilbao Bar Association; Madrid Bar Association; Association for Development of Industry; IBA. (Also at Madrid and Bilbao Offices). *LANGUAGES:* French and English.

FEDERICO ESPADALER, born Barcelona, Spain, June 12, 1928; admitted, 1952, Barcelona. *Education:* University of Barcelona (Law Degree, 1952). *Member:* Barcelona Bar Association; Financial Club of Barcelona. *LANGUAGES:* French.

JAVIER HERREROS, born Barcelona, Spain, January 17, 1943; admitted, 1964, Barcelona. *Education:* University of Barcelona (Law Degree, 1964); Professional School of the Barcelona Bar Association, Post Graduate Courses in Corporate Law, Foreign Investment Law and International Business Law. *Member:* Barcelona Bar Association; Barcelona Trial Lawyers Association. *LANGUAGES:* French.

RAFAEL FONTANA, born Barcelona, Spain, March 28, 1954; admitted, 1984, Barcelona. *Education:* University of Barcelona (Law Degree, 1977); Post Graduate Course in Taxation; Professional School of the Barcelona Bar Association, Post Graduate Course in Foreign Investment Law. *Member:* Barcelona Bar Association; Spanish Association of Taxation Experts; IFA; IBA. *LANGUAGES:* English and French.

JAVIER CASTRODEZA, born Barcelona, Spain, January 4, 1952; admitted, 1980, Barcelona; 1984, Girona. *Education:* University of Barcelona (Law Degree, 1976); CECO, Madrid (Foreign Commerce Specialist, 1979); School of Diplomacy, Madrid (European Law); International Faculty of Comparative Law, Strasbourg; Centre of Commercial Studies (Rio de Janeiro). *Member:* Barcelona Bar Association; Gerona Bar Association; IBA. *LANGUAGES:* English, French and Portuguese.

ENRIC PICAÑOL, born Barcelona, Spain, October 2, 1952; admitted, 1976, Barcelona. *Education:* University of Barcelona (Law Degree, 1976; Economics and Business Degree, 1977); University of London, LSE (Master of Laws, 1983); International Faculty of Comparative Law, Strasbourg (Diplomé 3ème cycle, 1976). Member, Editorial Board, Revista Juridica de Catalunya. *Member:* Barcelona Bar Association; IBA; ASIL; Law Society of England and Wales (o.m.). (Also at Brussels Office). *LANGUAGES:* English, French and German.

JORGE ARQUÉS, born Barcelona, Spain, July 12, 1958; admitted, 1982, Barcelona. *Education:* University of Barcelona (Economics and Business Degree, 1980). *Member:* Catalonia Economist Association; Institute of Auditors. *LANGUAGES:* French and English.

CARLOS PUIG, born Barcelona, Spain, August 16, 1957; admitted, 1980, Barcelona. *Education:* University of Barcelona (Economics and Business Degree). *Member:* Barcelona Economist Association. *LANGUAGES:* French and English.

EMILIO COCO, born Barcelona, Spain, January 27, 1954; admitted, 1978, Barcelona. *Education:* University of Barcelona (Law Degree, 1978). Professor of Tax Law (ESADE). *Member:* Barcelona Bar Association. (Also at Brussels Office). *LANGUAGES:* English and French.

ALBERTO RAVENTÓS, born Barcelona, Spain, November 15, 1955; admitted, 1981, Barcelona. *Education:* University of Barcelona (Law De-

(This Listing Continued)

gree, 1977). Counsel to the Generalitat de Catalunya (Regional Government of Catalonia). Municipal Government Attorney. Professor, Catalonia School of Public Administration. *Member:* Barcelona Bar Association. *LANGUAGES:* French.

JUAN CARLOS BARTHE, born Barcelona, Spain, July 19, 1958; admitted, 1982, Spain. *Education:* University of Barcelona (Law Degree, 1981). *Member:* Barcelona Bar Association. *LANGUAGES:* French and English.

RAIMON SEGURA, born Barcelona, Spain, January 10, 1961; admitted, 1985, Barcelona. *Education:* University of Barcelona (Law Degree, 1984). *Member:* Barcelona Bar Association. *LANGUAGES:* English.

JOSÉ MIGUEL GÓMEZ-PAPI, born Barcelona, Spain, June 1, 1953; admitted, 1989, Spain. *Education:* University of Barcelona (Law Degree, 1975). *Member:* Barcelona Bar Association. *LANGUAGES:* English.

FRANCISCO VICENT CHULIA, born Valencia, Spain, February 12, 1943; admitted, 1966, Spain. *Education:* University of Valencia (Law Degree, 1966; Doctor in Law, 1970). *Member:* Barcelona and Valencia Bar Associations. *LANGUAGES:* English, French, German and Italian.

TAX CONSULTANTS

LOLITA PAREJA, born Barcelona, Spain, January 25, 1946. *Education:* Specialist in Tax Law. *LANGUAGES:* English.

ASSOCIATES

JUAN ALBALATE, born Barcelona, Spain, August 8, 1958; admitted, 1983, Barcelona. *Education:* University of Barcelona (Economics Degree, 1982). Registered as Official Auditor. *Member:* Catalonia Economist Association. *LANGUAGES:* French and English.

JAVIER ARAZURI, born Zaragoza, Spain, March 1, 1965; admitted, 1991, Barcelona. *Education:* University of Barcelona (Law Degree, 1990). *Member:* Barcelona Bar Association. *LANGUAGES:* English.

ANNA ARIS, born Barcelona, Spain, April 19, 1964; admitted, 1989, Barcelona. *Education:* University of Barcelona (Law Degree, 1989). *Member:* Barcelona Bar Association. *LANGUAGES:* English and French.

MIRO AYATS, born Gerona, Spain, June 21, 1964; admitted, 1989, Barcelona. *Education:* University UNED FERT (Law Degree; Diploma in Economics, 1987). *Member:* Barcelona Bar Association. *LANGUAGES:* English and French.

JORGE BADIA, born Barcelona, Spain, September 13, 1962; admitted, 1988, Barcelona. *Education:* Autonoma University of Barcelona (Law Degree, 1988). *Member:* Barcelona Bar Association. *LANGUAGES:* French and English.

LUIS BASART, born Barcelona, Spain, October 10, 1962; admitted, 1990, Spain. *Education:* University of Barcelona (Law Degree, 1989; Diploma in Hispanic Archeology, 1989). *Member:* Barcelona Bar Association. *LANGUAGES:* English.

LUIS BATLLÓ, born Barcelona, Spain, June 15, 1967; admitted, 1991. *Education:* University of Barcelona (Master, Criminal Law, 1993). *Member:* Barcelona Bar Association; Association of Members of the Master in Criminal Law. *LANGUAGES:* English.

JOAQUIM BOTANCH, born Barcelona, Spain, February 26, 1965; admitted, 1991, Barcelona. *Education:* University of Barcelona (Law Degree, 1990). *Member:* Barcelona Bar Association. *LANGUAGES:* English.

MARIA BRAVO, born Zaragoza, Spain, June 3, 1967; admitted, 1992. *Education:* University of Barcelona (Law Degree, 1990). *Member:* Barcelona Bar Association. *LANGUAGES:* English.

JAVIER CALAF, born Barcelona, Spain, October 8, 1958; admitted, 1981, Barcelona. *Education:* University of Barcelona (Economics Degree, 1980). Registered as Official Auditor. *Member:* Catalonia Economics Association. *LANGUAGES:* English.

MONTSERRAT CAPDEVILA, born Barcelona, Spain, October 7, 1963; admitted, 1986, Barcelona. *Education:* University of Barcelona (Law Degree, 1986). *Member:* Barcelona Bar Association. *LANGUAGES:* English and French.

JORDI CAPELLERAS, born Barcelona, Spain, December 31, 1962; admitted, 1989, Barcelona. *Education:* University of Barcelona (Economics Degree, 1985). Associate Professor of the department of Business Economy of the Autonomous University of Barcelona. Official Register of Auditors. *Member:* Economists Bar Association. *LANGUAGES:* English.

(This Listing Continued)

BUFETE CUATRECASAS, Barcelona—Continued

CARLOS CARBONELL, born Alcoy (Alicante), Spain, September 6, 1963. *Education:* University of Valencia (Science Degree, 1986); Valencia Business School (Master in Tax Advising). Registered as Official Auditor. *LANGUAGES:* English.

VICTOR MANUEL CARRERA, born Madrid, Spain, March 28, 1965; admitted, 1992, Barcelona. *Education:* University of Barcelona (Law Degree, 1991). *Member:* Barcelona Bar Association. *LANGUAGES:* English, French and Portuguese.

EVA CESTER, born Barcelona, Spain, January 12, 1966; admitted, 1989, Barcelona. *Education:* University of Barcelona (Law Degree, 1989). *Member:* Barcelona Bar Association. *LANGUAGES:* English and French.

IÑIGO CISNEROS, born Bilbao, Spain, July 9, 1968; admitted, 1994, Spain. *Education:* University of Deusto, Bilbao (Law Degree, 1992); University Pompeu Fabra (Master in Business Law, 1994). *Member:* Barcelona Bar Association. *LANGUAGES:* English.

ANTONIO CIVERA, born Valencia, Spain, March 5, 1964; admitted, 1989, Barcelona. *Education:* University of Valencia (Law Degree, 1987); University of Johannes Gutenberg, Maguncia (Mainz), Germany (Master of Laws, 1988). *Member:* Barcelona Bar Association. *LANGUAGES:* German, English and Russian.

MARTA COLOMER, born Barcelona, Spain, June 29, 1970; admitted, 1994, Spain. *Education:* ESADE (Economics and Business Degree, 1993); University Pompeu Fabra (Master in Business Law, 1994). *Member:* Barcelona Bar Association. *LANGUAGES:* English, Italian and French.

CARLOS CORBERA, born Barcelona, Spain, July 8, 1966; admitted, 1992, Barcelona. *Education:* University of Barcelona (Law Degree, 1989, Master European Community Law, 1990). *Member:* Barcelona Bar Association. *LANGUAGES:* English.

JOAN DAURA, born Barcelona, Spain, July 24, 1965; admitted, 1993. *Education:* University of Anahuac of México D.F.; University of Barcelona (Law Degree, 1991) University Foundation San Pablo (Master Tax Expert, 1991; University Pompeu Fabra (Master Business Law, 1993). *Member:* Barcelona Bar Association. *LANGUAGES:* English and French.

MANUEL DE CORDOBA, born Granada, Spain, August 17, 1965; admitted, 1989, Barcelona. *Education:* University of Barcelona (Law Degree, 1988). *Member:* Barcelona Bar Association. *LANGUAGES:* French and English.

ALEJANDRO ESCODA, born Barcelona, Spain, March 25, 1963; admitted, 1986, Barcelona. *Education:* University of Barcelona (Law Degree, 1986). *Member:* Barcelona Bar Association. *LANGUAGES:* French, English and Italian.

CONCEPCION FERNANDEZ, born Cartagena, Spain, April 21, 1963; admitted, 1989, Barcelona. *Education:* University of Zaragoza (Law Degree, 1986); Free University of Brussels (European Law Degree, 1987). *Member:* Barcelona Bar Association. *LANGUAGES:* English and French.

JUAN FERRER, born Barcelona, Spain, July 29, 1968; admitted, 1993. *Education:* University of Barcelona (Law Degree, 1991); University Pompeu Fabra (Master, Civil Service and Administrative Law, 1992). *Member:* Barcelona Bar Association. *LANGUAGES:* English and French.

JAVIER GARANTO, born Huesca, Spain, May 18, 1963; admitted, 1988, Barcelona. *Education:* Autonoma University of Barcelona (Law Degree, 1988). *Member:* Barcelona Bar Association. *LANGUAGES:* English and French.

ALBERT GARROFE, born Barcelona, Spain, June 16, 1963; admitted, 1988, Barcelona. *Education:* University of Barcelona (Law Degree, 1986); King College, London (European Law, 1990). *Member:* Barcelona Bar Association. *LANGUAGES:* French, English and Japanese.

ANTONIO GIL, born Barcelona, Spain, August 22, 1960; admitted, 1987, Barcelona. *Education:* University of Barcelona (Law Degree, 1986). *Member:* Barcelona Bar Association. *LANGUAGES:* French and English.

MARTA GISPERT, born Barcelona, Spain, June 21, 1965; admitted, 1989, Barcelona. *Education:* University of Barcelona (Law Degree, 1988). *Member:* Barcelona Bar Association. *LANGUAGES:* English.

MARIA JOSÉ GOMEZ, born Barcelona, Spain, August 12, 1969; admitted, 1994, Spain. *Education:* University of Barcelona (Law Degree, 1992); University Pompeu Fabra (Master in Business Law, 1993). *Member:* Barcelona Bar Association. *LANGUAGES:* English.

(This Listing Continued)

JUAN GRIMA, born Valencia, Spain, June 3, 1966; admitted, 1993. *Education:* University of Valencia (Law Degree, 1989); Business Institute of Madrid (Master, Business Administration, 1992). *Member:* Barcelona Bar Association. *LANGUAGES:* English.

YOLANDA GUERRA, born Zaragoza, Spain, October 23, 1958; admitted, 1985, Barcelona. *Education:* University of Madrid (Law Degree, 1980). City Planning Expert, Local Administration Secretary, Attorney, Generalitat de Catalunya (Regional Government of Catalonia). *Member:* Barcelona Bar Association; Association of Local Administration Secretaries (Supervisor and Treasures, 1982). *LANGUAGES:* French.

GUSTAVO GUTIERREZ, born Barcelona, Spain, April 18, 1961; admitted, 1985, Barcelona. *Education:* University of Barcelona (Law Degree, 1985). *Member:* Barcelona Bar Association. *LANGUAGES:* English and French.

CARLOS HERNANDEZ, born Barcelona, Spain, May 7, 1963; admitted, 1992, Barcelona. *Education:* Commerce and Banking University of Mexico (Economics Degree, 1987). *Member:* Barcelona Economists. *LANGUAGES:* English.

JOSE HERRADOR, born Barcelona, Spain, October 15, 1958; admitted, 1985, Barcelona. *Education:* University of Barcelona (Economics and Business Degree, 1984). *Member:* Catalonia Economist Association. *LANGUAGES:* French and English.

JAVIER HERRERO, born Murcia, Spain, January 6, 1953; admitted, 1979, Barcelona, Sabadell and Matarö. *Education:* University of Barcelona (Law Degree, 1979). *Member:* Barcelona, Sabadell and Matarö Bar Associations.

PERE KIRCHNER, born Barcelona, Spain, March 10, 1965; admitted, 1988, Barcelona. *Education:* Autonoma University of Barcelona (Law Degree, 1988); Master in LLM, (LSE). *Member:* Barcelona Bar Association. *LANGUAGES:* English and French.

FRANCESC LEAL, born Lérida, Spain, October 1, 1965; admitted, 1992, Spain. *Education:* University of Barcelona (Law Degree, 1988). Judge, Social Court, 1989-1992. *Member:* Barcelona Bar Association. *LANGUAGES:* French.

JORGE LE MONNIER, born Barcelona, Spain, January 12, 1957; admitted, 1985, Barcelona. *Education:* University of Barcelona (Law Degree, 1979; Post Graduate Courses in Taxation and Corporate Law). *Member:* Barcelona Bar Association. *LANGUAGES:* English.

ESPERANZA MACARENA LLANSO, born Tarragona, Spain, June 16, 1964; admitted, 1989, Barcelona. *Education:* University of Barcelona (Law Degree, 1987). *Member:* Barcelona Bar Association. *LANGUAGES:* English.

JORDI LLEVAT, born Tarragona, Spain, July 23, 1961; admitted, 1989, Spain. *Education:* University of Barcelona (Law Degree, 1984); University of Chicago Master of Laws (LL.M., 1987-1988). *Member:* New York and Barcelona Bar Associations. *LANGUAGES:* English and French.

JAIME LLOPIS, born Valencia, Spain, January 17, 1964; admitted, 1992. *Education:* University of Valencia (Law Degree, 1987); University of Coimbra, Portugal (Special Degree in European Law); University Pompeu Fabra (Master, Business Law, 1993). *Member:* Valencia Bar Association; Association of European Law and Economy (Portugal). *LANGUAGES:* Portuguese, French and English.

MIGUEL MARTI, born Barcelona, Spain, November 27, 1961; admitted, 1991, Barcelona. *Education:* University of Barcelona (Law Degree, 1991). *Member:* Barcelona Bar Association. *LANGUAGES:* English.

LORENA MASIÁ, born Barcelona, Spain, July 10, 1969; admitted, 1994, Spain. *Education:* University of Barcelona (Law Degree, 1992); London School of Economics (LL.M., 1993); University of Pompeu Fabra (Master in Business Law, 1994). *Member:* Barcelona Bar Association. *LANGUAGES:* French and English.

MIGUEL ANGEL MELERO, born Málaga, Spain, August 13, 1968; admitted, 1994, Spain. *Education:* University of Navarra (Law Degree, 1991); University of London (LL.M., with merit, 1993); University Pompeu Fabra (Master in Business Law, 1994). *Member:* Barcelona Bar Association. *LANGUAGES:* English.

FERNANDO MIER, born Barcelona, Spain, December 22, 1963; admitted, 1989, Barcelona. *Education:* University of Barcelona (Law Degree, 1989). *Member:* Barcelona Bar Association. *LANGUAGES:* English.

ALICIA MOLINERO, born Barcelona, Spain, January 7, 1967; admitted, 1989, Barcelona. *Education:* University of Barcelona (Law Degree,

(This Listing Continued)

1989). *Member:* Barcelona Bar Association. *LANGUAGES:* English and French.

GEMMA OLIVAR, born Barcelona, Spain, December 31, 1965; admitted, 1988, Barcelona. *Education:* University of Barcelona (Law Degree; Courses in Maritime Law, 1988); University of Saarland, Germany (Certificate in European Studies, 1989). *Member:* Barcelona Bar Association; AIJA. *LANGUAGES:* English, French, Italian and German.

ANTONIO PAGES, born Barcelona, Spain, September 29, 1966; admitted, 1989, Barcelona. *Education:* University of Barcelona (Law Degree, 1989). *Member:* Barcelona Bar Association. *LANGUAGES:* English and French.

JOSE M° PARET, born Vic, Spain, May 15, 1963; admitted, 1991. *Education:* University of Barcelona (Law Degree, 1990). *Member:* Barcelona Bar Association. *LANGUAGES:* French.

MONTSERRAT PASTOR, born Barcelona, Spain, March 26, 1965; admitted, 1993, Spain. *Education:* University of Barcelona (Law Degree, 1991); ESADE (Master in Taxation, 1993). *Member:* Barcelona Bar Association. *LANGUAGES:* English.

CRISTINE PAULEAU, born Grenoble, France, April 10, 1969. *Education:* Université de Grenoble, France (Law Degree, 1991); Université de Liège, Belgium (Master in EEC Law, 1992). *LANGUAGES:* English, French and Spanish.

GUILLERMO PÉREZ, born Madrid, Spain, October 5, 1968; admitted, 1993. *Education:* Complutense University of Madrid (Law Degree, 1991); University of Pompeu Fabra (Master, Business Law, 1993). *Member:* Barcelona Bar Association. *LANGUAGES:* English.

CRISTINA PUIG, born Barcelona, Spain, September 16, 1962; admitted, 1986, Barcelona. *Education:* University of Barcelona (Law Degree, 1985). *Member:* Barcelona Bar Association. *LANGUAGES:* English.

VENTURA REBÉS, born La Seu d'Urgell, Spain, June 29, 1965; admitted, 1993. *Education:* University of Barcelona (Law Degree, 1992; University of Barcelona (Master in Tax and Financial Law, 1993). *Member:* Barcelona Bar Association; Lérida Bar Association. *LANGUAGES:* English and French.

SALVADOR REINA, born Barcelona, Spain, September 25, 1962; admitted, 1987, Mataró. *Education:* University of Barcelona (Law Degree, 1986). *Member:* Mataro Bar Association. *LANGUAGES:* French.

RICARDO RIVEROLA, born Barcelona, Spain, June 29, 1961; admitted, 1987, Barcelona. *Education:* University of Barcelona (Law Degree, 1987). *Member:* Barcelona Bar Association. *LANGUAGES:* English.

OLGA ROCA, born Barcelona, Spain, October 30, 1965; admitted, 1994, Spain. *Education:* University of Barcelona (Economics Degree, 1989); ESADE (Master in Taxation, 1992). Associated Professor, University of Barcelona. *Member:* Barcelona Bar Association. *LANGUAGES:* English.

JORGE ALBERTO RODRIGUEZ, born Asturias, Spain, January 9, 1960; admitted, 1989, Barcelona. *Education:* University of Barcelona (Law Degree, 1982). *Member:* Barcelona Bar Association. *LANGUAGES:* French and English.

MARIA DOLORES SABATER, born Barcelona, Spain, November 11, 1940. *Education:* University of Barcelona (Law Degree, 1964). *LANGUAGES:* French and Italian.

RAFAEL SALA, born Barcelona, Spain, March 5, 1962; admitted, 1988, Barcelona. *Education:* University of Barcelona (Law Degree, 1987). *Member:* Barcelona Bar Association.

PEDRO SAN JOSÉ, born Barcelona, Spain, January 20, 1963; admitted, 1986, Spain. *Education:* Autonomous University of Barcelona (Law Degree, 1986). *Member:* Barcelona Bar Association. *LANGUAGES:* English.

JUAN IGNACIO SANZ, born Valladolid, Spain, November 20, 1967; admitted, 1992. *Education:* University of Valladolid (Law Degree, 1990); ESADE (Master, Business Administration, 1992). *Member:* Barcelona Bar Association. *LANGUAGES:* English.

JUAN SOLDEVILA, born Barcelona, Spain, February 20, 1962; admitted, 1986, Barcelona. *Education:* University of Barcelona (Law Degree, 1985). *Member:* Barcelona Bar Association. *LANGUAGES:* English and French.

ANA SOTO, born Barcelona, Spain, March 17, 1966; admitted, 1989, Barcelona. *Education:* University of Barcelona (Law Degree, 1989). *Member:* Barcelona Bar Association. *LANGUAGES:* English and French.

(This Listing Continued)

GEMA TENA, born Barcelona, Spain, February 5, 1967; admitted, 1992. *Education:* UNED (Law Degree, 1990) (Master, Business Law). *Member:* Barcelona Bar Association. *LANGUAGES:* English.

MIGUEL TERRASA, born Barcelona, Spain, April 26, 1962; admitted, 1988, Barcelona. *Education:* University of Barcelona (Law Degree, 1987). *Member:* Barcelona Bar Association. *LANGUAGES:* English.

ANNA VALLS, born Balaguer, Spain, April 21, 1963; admitted, 1986, Barcelona. *Education:* University of Barcelona (Law Degree, 1986). Tax Technical Advisor, Barcelona School of Business Administration. *Member:* Barcelona Bar Association. *LANGUAGES:* English and French.

DAVID VAZQUEZ, born Barcelona, Spain, August 20, 1967; admitted, 1994, Spain. *Education:* Autonomous University of Barcelona (Law Degree, 1991); University Pompeu Fabra (Master in Business Law, 1994). *Member:* Barcelona Bar Association. *LANGUAGES:* English and French.

OLGA VAZQUEZ, born Barcelona, Spain, July 31, 1964; admitted, 1993. *Education:* University of Barcelona (Law Degree, 1987; Diplome in Criminal Law); University Pompeu Fabra (Master Business Law, 1993). *Member:* Barcelona Bar Association. *LANGUAGES:* French.

SONIA VELASCO, born Barcelona, Spain, March 28, 1969; admitted, 1994, Spain. *Education:* University of Barcelona (Law Degree, 1992); University Pompeu Fabra (Master in Business Law, 1994). *Member:* Barcelona Bar Association. *LANGUAGES:* English.

NURIA VILA, born Barcelona, Spain, March 17, 1966; admitted, 1989, Barcelona. *Education:* University of Barcelona (Law Degree, 1989). *Member:* Barcelona Bar Association. *LANGUAGES:* English and French.

JORDI VILALTA, born Reus (Tarragona), Spain, October 22, 1963; admitted, 1989, Barcelona. *Education:* University of Barcelona (Law Degree, 1989). *Member:* Barcelona Bar Association. *LANGUAGES:* English.

ISABEL VILLARO, born Barcelona, Spain, November 19, 1964; admitted, 1988, Barcelona. *Education:* University of Barcelona (Law Degree, 1987). *Member:* Barcelona Bar Association. *LANGUAGES:* English and French.

JAVIER VILLASANTE, born Valencia, Spain, March 29, 1964; admitted, 1990, Barcelona. *Education:* University of Valencia (Law Degree, 1987); Free University of Brussels (Special Degree in European Community Law); Columbia University, School of Law (LL.M.); University of Alcalá de Henares (Diploma in European Community Law). *Member:* Madrid Bar Association. *LANGUAGES:* English and French.

MERITXELL YUS, born Barcelona, Spain, July 12, 1969; admitted, 1994, Spain. *Education:* University of Barcelona (Law Degree, 1992); University Pompeu Fabra (Master in Business Law, 1993). *Member:* Barcelona Bar Association. *LANGUAGES:* English.

REPRESENTATIVE CLIENTS: AbellóOxigeno Linde (Linde GmbH): Acedor, S.A., Aguas de Barcelona; Akzo Coatings, S.A.; Antibioticos (Grupo Montedison); Aristrain, S.A.; Banc Catalàde Crèdit (Gruppo Bancario San Paolo SpA; Bancotrans (Deutsche Bank); Bankers Trust Co.; Cia de Contadores (Schlumberger); Christian Salvensen Plc.; Ciba Geigy, S.A.; CNE Swedbank; Cofir; Cortefiel, S.A.; Den Norsk Bank; Dicalite Española, S.A.; Dresser Industries Inc.; Dunlop Slazenger; Electronic Data Systems; Elf Ibérica Lubricantes, S.A.; Enoxy Quimica S.A. (ENI); Enichem Ibérica, S.A.; Farmitalia Carlo Erba, S.A.; Ferrero Ibérica, S.A.; Ferrovial; Gates Vulca; Grupo Prac, S.A. (Pernod-Ricard); Grupo Prodes; Grupo Puig; Grupo Uralita (Grupo March); ICI Zeltia, S.A.; Ina Rodamientos, S.A. (INA GmbH); Industrias Figueras; La Caixa: Laboratorios Ausonia, S.A.; Laboratorios Labaz (ELF-Aquitana); Laura Ashley, B.V.; Lloyds Bank, Ltd.; Moet Hennessy-Louis Vuitton, S.A.; Mondadori SpA; Nabisco Brands Españ4. S.A.; Nutrexpa, S.A.; Papelera Guarro (Arjomarie); Pinturas Hempel, S.A.; Pirelli SpA; Prenatal, S.A.; Pricoa Vida (Prudential); Quaker Quimica Española, S.A.; Robertson Española, S.A.; Rubbermaid Incorporated; S.A.B.A.; Saica, S.A.; Sanofi; Telemecánica, S.A.

(For complete biographical data on personnel at Bilbao, Madrid and Gerona, Spain and Brussels, Belgium, see Professional Biographies at those locations)

DAGÁ & SAURET

Lawyers

Established in 1986

TORRE BARCELONA
AVENIDA DIAGONAL, NUMBER 477 FLOOR 20
08036 BARCELONA, SPAIN
Telephone: (93) 419-18-18
Fax: (93) 410-25-13

Administrative Law, Banking Law, Commercial Law, Company Law, Company Acquisitions & Mergers, Contract Law, Finance Corporate, Corporate Insolvency, E.C. Law, Foreign Investment, Joint Venture Capital, Licensing, Betting & Gaming, Commercial Litigation, Patents, Private Client, Commercial Property, Revenue Law, Tax, Capital Tax, Company Tax, Corporation Tax, Foreign Nationals Tax, Income Tax, International Tax, Local Tax, National Tax, V.A.T., Venture Capital.

FIRM PROFILE: Dagá & Sauret was constituted in 1986 as a firm of associated lawyers which includes in its team economists, since its object is to provide accurate and profitable professional services to its clients in commercial law as well as in legal, tax and exchange control matters.

The founding partners of the Firm are Tomás Dagá and Carlos Sauret, the third partner Jordi Fábregas, was incorporated to this category six years ago.

Our team is formed by eight lawyers (one of them is also an economist) each of them being a specialist in specific fields. The recruiting and formation of the associated lawyers is very important for our Firm, as well as the permanence of the persons who form it. The Firm is organized into three departments and each department is headed by one of the partners.

PARTNERS

TOMÁS DAGÁ GELABERT, admitted, 1979, Barcelona. **LANGUAGES:** Catalan, Spanish and English. **PRACTICE AREAS:** Business and Company Law.

CARLOS SAURET MANÉN, admitted, 1980, Barcelona. *Education:* B.S. Economics. **LANGUAGES:** Catalan and Spanish. **PRACTICE AREAS:** Business and Company Law.

JORDI FÁBREGAS HUGUET, admitted, 1981, Barcelona. *Education:* B.S., Economics. **LANGUAGES:** Catalan, Spanish and English. **PRACTICE AREAS:** Tax Planning.

ASSOCIATES

NURIA MARTIN BARNÉS, admitted, 1983, Barcelona. **LANGUAGES:** Catalan, Spanish and English. **PRACTICE AREAS:** Business and Company Law.

JORDI MUIXÍ VALLÉS, admitted, 1986, Barcelona. **LANGUAGES:** Catalan, Spanish and English. **PRACTICE AREAS:** Commercial Law.

ANA CLARAMUNT FREIXANET, admitted, 1982, Barcelona. **LANGUAGES:** Catalan, Spanish, French. **PRACTICE AREAS:** Business and Company Law.

XAVIER MIRET CARCELLER, admitted, 1988, Barcelona. **LANGUAGES:** Catalan, Spanish, French and English. **PRACTICE AREAS:** Business and Company Law.

MAITE TERESA GATNAU CASAÑÉ, admitted, 1988, Barcelona. **LANGUAGES:** Catalan, Spanish and English. **PRACTICE AREAS:** Business and Company Law.

RAIMON GRIFOLS ROURA, admitted, 1989, Barcelona. **LANGUAGES:** Catalan, Spanish, English and French. **PRACTICE AREAS:** Commercial Law.

JORGE DANTART MINUÉ, admitted, 1989, Barcelona. *Education:* B.S. Economics. **LANGUAGES:** Spanish and English. **PRACTICE AREAS:** Tax Advisor.

Professional Associations: International Bar Association.

Language: Spanish, Catalan, English, French, German, Italian.

BUFETE DEXEUS, ABOGADOS ASOCIADOS

Established in 1949

8-10 TUSET
08006 BARCELONA, SPAIN
Telephone: 07.93.237.37.01
Fax: 07.93.237.37.20

A law firm specializing in Legal and Financial consulting for Spanish and foreign clients in, inter alia, the following areas: corporate and commercial law, administration (city planning, license applications), drafting and negotiation of contracts, international and EC law, foreign investment, taxation for companies and natural persons, company and shares acquisitions and takeovers, family and inheritance law.

FIRM PROFILE: Founded in 1949 by Juan Dexeus, it expanded in 1955 when Rafael Gomis joined the firm. This law firm has acted in many important property, commercial, Industrial and financial transactions throughout its many years of professional activity, establishing important international relations and acquiring an unparalleled investment expertise both in relation to Spanish clients in the international market and to foreign clients in Spain.

MEMBERS OF FIRM

JUAN DEXEUS, born Barcelona, Spain, February 15, 1926; admitted, 1949, Barcelona. *Education:* University of Barcelona, Extraordinary Graduating Prize; Business Expert, School of Advanced Business Studies (1952). Chartered accountant by competitive exam, Madrid, 1966. Founder of "Praxis Juridico" and Author of the Income Tax section of the same collection; business articles in newspapers and professional journals. General Consul of Luxembourg, Order of Merit (Luxembourg). *Member:* Barcelona Bar Association; Madrid Bar Association; College of Economists of Barcelona; Inst. of Chartered Accountants of Spain; Assn. of Investment Analysts; College of Real Estate Agents; Institut de l'ECU, Brussels and Lyon, France (Member of Directory). **LANGUAGES:** French, Spanish, Catalán and Italian. **PRACTICE AREAS:** Financial Planning Law; Financial Structure and Strategy Law; Tax-Planning Law; Mergers and Acquisitions.

RAFAEL GOMIS, born Barcelona, Spain, August 12, 1930; admitted, 1952, Barcelona. *Education:* University of Deusto (Bilbao) and Valladolid (Diplomas in Specialized courses in Business Law, Fiscal Law and Financial Law). *Member:* Barcelona Bar Association; Financial Law Association. (Real Estate Agent). **LANGUAGES:** French, Spanish and Catalan. **PRACTICE AREAS:** Business Law; Fiscal Law; Financial Law.

JUAN NÚNEZ, born Hamburg, (R.F.A.), December 19, 1956; admitted, 1981, Barcelona. *Education:* Anthonom University of Barcelona; Abad Oliva Private University Barcelona (Graduate in Accounting, Tax Expert and Company Secretarial Services); Europe Institut, University of Amsterdam (Graduate Legal Aspects in European Integration, 1985 and 1987). Lecturer, E.E.C. Law Bar Association; Conferences and seminars A.I.J.A. and Foro Portuguese of Porto. *Member:* Barcelona Bar Association (Secretary of Committee of Community Law); Member A.I.J.A.; Treasurer of the Spanish-German Lawyer Association. **LANGUAGES:** French, English, German, Italian, Spanish and Catalán. **PRACTICE AREAS:** European Community Law; International Trade Law.

CHRISTINA BURGUERA, born Barcelona, Spain, August 13, 1959; admitted, 1984, Barcelona. *Education:* University of Barcelona; Abad Oliva Private University of Barcelona (Graduate Tax Expert and Graduate Accounting in E.A.D.A.). *Member:* Barcelona Bar Association. **LANGUAGES:** French, Spanish and Catalan. **PRACTICE AREAS:** Fiscal Law; Tax Accounting.

ASSOCIATES

SANTIAGO AYESTA, born 1966; admitted, 1994. **LANGUAGES:** English, Spanish and Calalan. **PRACTICE AREAS:** Tax Law.

ANTONIO GILBERT, born 1961; admitted, 1991. **LANGUAGES:** French, English, Spanish and Catalan. **PRACTICE AREAS:** Procedural Law.

GONZALO GOMIS, born 1970; admitted, 1993. *Education:* Master in Business Law. **LANGUAGES:** English, Spanish and Catalan. **PRACTICE AREAS:** Business Law.

LUIS PEREZ-SALA, born 1965; admitted, 1989. Associate Prof., Pompeu Fabra University. **LANGUAGES:** French, English, Spanish and Catalan. **PRACTICE AREAS:** Corporate Law; European Community Law.

(This Listing Continued)

Mª JOSE PORTABELLA, born Barcelona, Spain, December 14, 1934; admitted, 1984, Barcelona. *Education:* University of Barcelona. *LANGUAGES:* French, Spanish and Catalan. *PRACTICE AREAS:* Family Law; Ecclesiastic Court.

ANA RIVERA, born 1966; admitted, 1992. *LANGUAGES:* French, English, Spanish and Catalan. *PRACTICE AREAS:* Trade Law; European Community Law.

ANA MORALES, born 1966; admitted, 1994, Economist. *LANGUAGES:* French, English, Spanish and Catalan.

EVA PASCUAL, (Accounting Department); Born 1965. *LANGUAGES:* English, Spanish and Catalan.

OF COUNSEL

AMPARO FERRANDO, born Guipuzcoa, Spain, June 19, 1945; admitted, 1969, Barcelona. *Education:* University of Madrid; Barcelona law University (Doctor Degree, cum laude). *LANGUAGES:* French, English and Spanish. *PRACTICE AREAS:* Inheritance Law; Commercial Law.

A list of Representative Clients will be furnished upon request.

E.B.A.M.E. & ASOCIADOS

C/ MUNTANER, NO. 292-294
08021 BARCELONA, SPAIN
Telephone: (93) 209-73-44
Fax: (93) 201-83-52

General Corporate Law and International Tax, Administrative Relations, Securities Law, Corporate and Partnership Financing and Organization, Banking Law, Mergers and Acquisitions, Business Litigation, Real Estate Transactions and International Business.

PROF. DR. EDUARD BAJET, born Barcelona, 1949; admitted, 1974, Barcelona. *Education:* Universities of Zaragoza and Barcelona (Doctor of Laws, 1977). University Lecturer, 1981; University Professor, 1983; Dean of the Faculty of Law, 1986-1989. Magistrate of the High Court of Justice in Catalonia, 1989. Director of the Juridical Text Collections and Juridical Formularies. *Member:* Barcelona Bar Association. *LANGUAGES:* Spanish, Catalan, French, English and Italian.

PROF. DR. ANTONI FONT, born Barcelona, 1949; admitted, 1982, Barcelona. *Education:* Universities of Barcelona, Strasbourg, Fribourg and Munich (Doctor of Laws, 1976). Author: "Common Market and Distribution" (Mercado Común y Distribución), Barcelona 1987; "Commerce Code and Complementary Legislation," (Código de Comercio y Legislación Complementaria), Barcelona 1987; "Exchange and Cheque Law," (Llei Canviària i del Xec), Barcelona 1988; "The Public Companies Reform," (La Reforma de las Sociedades Anónimas), Madrid 1987; "Commentaries to the Autonomy Statutes of Catalonia," (Comentaris a l'Estatut d'Autonomia de Catalunya), Barcelona 1989; "New Entities, contractual figures and guaranties in the financial market," (Nuevas Entidades, figuras contractuales y garantias en el mercado financiero), Madrid 1990; "Property Rights and Trademark Rights," Valence 1990. University Lecturer, 1979; University Professor, 1986. Director of the Private Law and Economic Law Department, 1986-1987. Secretary of the Public Council of the University of Barcelona, 1987. *Member:* Barcelona Bar Association; Gesellschaft für Rechtsvergleichung; Deutsch-Spanisch Juristenverein; ALADDA (Spanish ALAI Group); Spanish Association for the Defense of the Free Competition (Spanish LIDC Group). *LANGUAGES:* Spanish, Catalan, German, English, French, Italian and Portuguese.

ADRIA GUAL, born Barcelona, 1912; admitted, 1934, Barcelona. *Education:* University of Barcelona. Professional Experience: Borough Council of Barcelona. President of the Copyright Commission. Advisor-Secretary of the "Foment de les Arts Decoratives," (ADI-FAD). *Member:* Barcelona Bar Association; ALADDA (Spanish ALAI Group). *LANGUAGES:* Spanish, Catalan, French and English.

EDUARDO MEDIAVILLA, born Barcelona, 1957; admitted, 1983, Barcelona. *Education:* University of Barcelona. Professional Experience: Auditor of General Insurances Co. (Mutua General de Seguros), 1983. Associate Lecturer at the University. *Member:* Barcelona Bar Association. *LANGUAGES:* Spanish, Catalan and French.

ALBERT BAJET, born Barcelona, 1957; admitted, 1981, Barcelona. *Education:* University Barcelona; Chamber of Commerce of Barcelona (Diplome Foreign Trading, 1985); Archaeology University of Barcelona (Diplome). Professional Experience: Legal Advisor of Hispamer Financial Corporation for Catalonia Area. *Member:* Barcelona Bar Association; Tenerife *(This Listing Continued)*

(Canary Island) Bar Association. *LANGUAGES:* Spanish, Catalan, English and French.

BENJAMIN NICOLAU, born Capella, 1959; admitted, 1981, Spain. *Education:* Barcelona University (Licenciate of Law); Economists School (Master in Fiscal Law); Salamanca University (Diploma in EEC Law). *Member:* European Community Bar Association Council; Lawyers International Union; Business Law Commission; Young Lawyers International Union; Association Internationale de Droit Penal. *LANGUAGES:* Spanish, Catalan, French, English, Italian and Portuguese.

GEMMA FONTANET, born Barcelona, 1961; admitted, 1985, Barcelona. *Education:* University of Barcelona; Matrimonial Canonical Law Course (1991-1992). *Member:* Barcelona Bar Association. *LANGUAGES:* Spanish, Catalan, French and English.

ADOLF ROUSAUD, born Barcelona, 1968; admitted, 1991 (Not admitted in Spain). *Education:* University of Barcelona. Tax Consultant. Spanish and International Tax Law Course at Centro de Estudios Colegio Universatario Abad Oliva, 1991-1992. Author: "The Stock Company Ltd. Business and their Own Shares," (Los Negocios de la Sociedad Anónima con sus Propias Acciones), Barcelona, 1991. Professor at the Faculty of Economics of the University of Barcelona, 1993. *LANGUAGES:* Spanish, Catalan and English.

MARIA PILAR TORNE, born Barcelona, 1971; (Not admitted in Spain). *Education:* University Ramón Llull (Technical Engineering of Telecommunications, specialized in electronical equipment). Author: "Study Design and Simulation of Commutation Network of Circuits and Packets with Simulation Tools" (1993). Professional Experience: Support Engineer, Epson Ibérica, S.A. Technical Consultant, NexTReT, Technological Transfer Centre of Engineering Technology of the Salle, University Ramón Llull (Barcelona). *LANGUAGES:* Spanish, Catalan, French and English.

MIGUEL ANGEL CAÑIVANO, born Barcelona, 1965. *Education:* University of Barcelona (1991); Attorney Title of Investigation Ability of the University of Barcelona (1994). Author: "The Object of the Cannonical Matrimony Invalidation Process." Notary-Secretary of the Ecclesiastical Tribunal of Barcelona. Cannonical Law Associate of the Autonomic University of Barcelona. *LANGUAGES:* Spanish, Catalan, English and French.

PATRICIA GINER, born Barcelona, 1965; admitted, 1992, Barcelona. *Education:* University of Barcelona; Tulane University, La, U.S.A. *Member:* Barcelona Bar Association. *LANGUAGES:* Spanish, Catalan, French and English.

SANDRA BUISAN, born Barcelona. 1971; (Not admitted in Spain). *Education:* University of Barcelona; Trinity College, Toronto, Ontario (Canada). *LANGUAGES:* Spanish, Catalan, French and English.

ECHECOPAR ABOGADOS

Established in 1976

TRAVESERA DE GRACIA, 17-21, 5° 5A
08021 BARCELONA, SPAIN
Telephone: 209 8922
Telefax: 202.21.14

Madrid, Spain Office: Calle Dr. Fleming, 3, 28036. Telephone: 457-2400. Cable Address: "Lerama". Telefax: 458 7449.

General and International Practice. Administrative, Banking, Civil, Commercial, Corporation, EEC, Foreign Investment, Insurance, Labor, Oil and Gas, Maritime, Real Estate and Tax Law. Litigation.

FIRM PROFILE: This firm provides a broad base of Spanish and transnational clients with a full range of legal services from its locations in Madrid and Barcelona. It has a well established practice in corporate and commercial as well as in tax law and is engaged in extensive international activity. Litigation and labour matters are fields where it has likewise developed strength. Based on the expertise it has acquired this firm feels particularly able to offer valuable assistance in the set-up of new business projects and in M&A work as well as in the wide scope of the attendant areas of the law. These skills and experience are applied to satisfy the day-to-day requirements of its clients.

RESIDENT PARTNER

ANTONIO BUNDÓ MASGORET, born Barcelona, Spain, 1954; admitted, 1978, Spain. *Education:* Universidad Central de Barcelona. *Member:* Ilustre Colegio de Abogados de Barcelona; Ilustre Colegio de Abogados de Madrid; Ilustre Colegio de Abogados de Sabadell; Ilustre Colegio de *(This Listing Continued)*

ECHECOPAR ABOGADOS, Barcelona—Continued

Abogados de Tarragona; Ilustre Colegio de Abogados de Tarrasa; Ilustre Colegio de Abogados de Valencia. *LANGUAGES:* French, Catalan and Spanish.

RESIDENT ASSOCIATE

ANTONIO LLOBET POAL, born Barcelona, Spain, 1960; admitted, 1983, Spain. *Education:* Universidad Autónoma de Barcelona. Member: Ilustre Colegio de Abogados de Barcelona; Ilustre Colegio de Abogados de Madrid. *LANGUAGES:* English, Catalan and Spanish.

(For Complete Biographical Data on all Personnel, see Professional Biographies at Madrid, Spain)

EMO ADVOCATS

BALMES, 163, PRAL 2ª
08008 BARCELONA, SPAIN
Telephone: (343) 217 41 51
Telefax: (343) 217 76 94

General Practice, Foreign Investments, Corporate and Commercial Law, Real Estate, Bankruptcy and Litigation.

MEMBERS OF FIRM

ENRIC EMO, born Barcelona, 1959; admitted, 1984, Barcelona. *Education:* Col.legi Sant Ignasi, Universitat Central de Barcelona. *Member:* Colegio d'Advocats de Barcelona and Colegio de Abogados de Madrid Bar Associations; International Bar Association (IBA); International Association of Young Lawyers (AIJA); American Chamber of Commerce in Spain. *LANGUAGES:* Spanish, Catalan and English. *PRACTICE AREAS:* General Practice; Business; Corporate and Commercial Law; Property; Real Estate; Construction Law and Environment.

ELISABETH EMO, born Barcelona, 1967; admitted, 1992, Barcelona. *Education:* Colegio de la Compañía de Sta Teresa de Jesús, Universitat Central de Barcelona. *LANGUAGES:* Catalan, French and Spanish. *PRACTICE AREAS:* General Practice; Business Law; Company Law; Property.

Languages preferred: Catalan, English and Spanish

FOLCHI & ASOCIADOS, ABOGADOS

Established in 1980
C/CÓRCEGA N° 368
08037 BARCELONA, SPAIN
Telephone: (93) 459.27.00
Intn'l Dialing (343) 459.27-00 Fax: (343) 459-32-80/90

General Practice, Taxation, Civil, Commercial, Company, Banking, Securities, Bankruptcy, Administrative Law, Real Estate and Urban Law, EEC and International Law, Mergers and Acquisitions and Foreign Investments.

FIRM PROFILE: The firm was established in 1980 under the name of "Folchi & De Pascual y Asociados, Abogados" and intends to provide a full comprehensive legal services to companies operating in Spain and its well known for its advice in legal, financial and tax matters.

MEMBERS OF FIRM

JOAN JOSEP FOLCHI, born Zaragoza, Spain, June 21, 1947; admitted, 1980. *Education:* University of Barcelona (Law Degree, 1970). State Lawyer (Abogado del Estado 1974). Co-Author: "Evolución del pensamiento económico," 1992. Minister of Economy and Finance of the Regional Government of Catalonia, 1977-1980. Member of the Catalan Parliament (1984-1987). *Member:* Barcelona Bar Association; Union Internationale des Avocats. *LANGUAGES:* Spanish, French and English. *PRACTICE AREAS:* Domestic and International Taxation; M&A and International Finance.

JOSE CARLOS CALDERON, born Barcelona, Spain, December 6, 1957; admitted, 1991. *Education:* University of Barcelona (Law Degree, 1981). State Lawyer (Abogado del Estado 1985). *Member:* Barcelona Bar Association. *LANGUAGES:* Spanish and English. *PRACTICE AREAS:* Takeovers; M & A; Construction Law.

JOAN FRANCESC PONT, born Barcelona, Spain, January 21, 1957; admitted, 1986. *Education:* University of Barcelona (Law Degree, 1983; MBA, Doctors of Laws, cum laude, 1990). Taxation Professor, Barcelona University (Catedrático de Derecho financiero y tributario). Dean of the Faculty of Business Administration School of Barcelona (Facultad de Em-

(This Listing Continued)

presariales). Author: "El pago fraccionado de los tribulos," 1993. Co-author: "Análisis y aplicación del nuevo IRPF," 1992. *Member:* Barcelona Bar Association. *LANGUAGES:* Spanish, French, English and Italian. *PRACTICE AREAS:* International and Domestic Taxation.

ASSOCIATES

ANTONI VILANOVA, born Reus (Tarragona), Spain, November 11, 1953; admitted, 1989. *Education:* University of Barcelona (Law Degree, 1977). Director-General of Economy and Finance at the Regional Government of Catalonia, 1977-1988. *Member:* Barcelona Bar Association; Union Internationale des Avocats. *LANGUAGES:* Spanish, French and English. *PRACTICE AREAS:* Public Law; Administrative Law and Environment Law.

IGNACIO GONZALEZ-FREIXA, born Barcelona, Spain, January 15, 1957; admitted, 1983. *Education:* University of Barcelona (Law Degree, 1980). *Member:* Barcelona, Madrid and Gerona Bar Associations; Association Internationale des Jeunes Avocats. *LANGUAGES:* Spanish, French and English. *PRACTICE AREAS:* Business and Company Law.

JOAQUIM JUBERT, born Lisbon, March 27, 1961; admitted, 1986. *Education:* University of Barcelona (Law Degree, 1984). Executive PDM at I.E.S.E., 1990. *Member:* Barcelona and Madrid Bar Association; International Bar Association; EC Executive Training Programme in Japan. *LANGUAGES:* Spanish, French, English, Italian and Portuguese. *PRACTICE AREAS:* Business Law; Banking and Securities Law; Aircraft Leasing and Finance.

ROBERT SANAHUJA, born Barcelona, Spain, December 3, 1956; admitted, 1988. *Education:* University of Barcelona (Law Degree, 1980). *Member:* Barcelona Bar Association. *LANGUAGES:* Spanish, French and English. *PRACTICE AREAS:* International and Domestic Taxation.

BLANCA BOIXEDA, born Barcelona, Spain, September 19, 1962; admitted, 1989. *Education:* Autonomous University of Barcelona (Law Degree, 1986). *Member:* Barcelona Bar Association; International Association of Human Rights. *LANGUAGES:* Spanish and English. *PRACTICE AREAS:* Civil Law; Entertainment Law; Company Law.

ANA ROCA, born Barcelona, Spain, February 5, 1964; admitted, 1988. *Education:* University of Barcelona (Law Degree, 1987). *Member:* Barcelona Bar Association. *LANGUAGES:* Spanish and English. *PRACTICE AREAS:* Administrative Law and Real Estate.

HUMBERT BATLLE, born Barcelona, Spain, February 25, 1964; admitted, 1987. *Education:* University of Barcelona (Law Degree, 1987). *Member:* Barcelona Bar Association. *LANGUAGES:* Spanish, French and English. *PRACTICE AREAS:* Civil and Corporate Law.

MARTA DEL COTO, born Barcelona, Spain, August 6, 1968; admitted, 1993. *Education:* University of Barcelona (Law Degree, 1992). *Member:* Barcelona Bar Association. *LANGUAGES:* Spanish, French and English. *PRACTICE AREAS:* Civil and Real Estate Law.

CARLOTA MASDEU, born Barcelona, Spain, February 6, 1966; admitted, 1993. *Education:* University of Barcelona (Law Degree, 1992). *Member:* Barcelona Bar Association. *LANGUAGES:* Spanish and English. *PRACTICE AREAS:* Environmental Law; General Practice.

OF COUNSEL

ANTONIO VERDU, born Palencia, Spain, September 4, 1922. *Education:* University of Barcelona (Degree in Economics, 1965) "Intendente Mercantil"; Doctor in Economics, 1967. Professor of the University of Economics. Member of the Spanish Royal Academy of Economics and Finance Sciences (Académico de la Real Academia de Ciencias Económicas y Financieras). Co-Author: "Evolución del pensamiento económico," 1992. Tax Inspector for the State 1953-1987 (Inspector de Finanzas del Estado).

FRANCISCO VALERO, born Murcia, Spain, March 13, 1922; admitted, 1974. *Education:* University of Barcelona (Law Degree, 1972) Doctor in Laws "Intendente Mercantil". Tax Inspector for the State, 1954-1987 (Inspector de Finanzas del Estado). *Member:* Economists Bar Association.

CARIN LINDA PARKER, born Sussex, England, September 28, 1951. *Education:* University of London; Université de Paris IV, Sorbonne; University of Reading (Master of Arts). Manager of International Operations. *Member:* International Tax Planning Association. *LANGUAGES:* English, French, Spanish, German and Russian.

Languages: Spanish, Catalan, French, English, German, Dutch, Italian, Portuguese and Russian

A list of Representative Clients and References will be furnished upon request.

FRESHFIELDS

DIPUTACIÓ 246 - 2°
08007 BARCELONA, SPAIN
Telephone: (34 3) 301 9758
Fax: (34 3) 301 4234

Other Offices: Bangkok, Brussels, Frankfurt, Hanoi, Hong Kong, London, Madrid, Moscow, New York, Paris, Singapore, Tokyo.

RESIDENT PARTNERS

ANTONI VALVERDE ROY, born Barcelona, Spain, 1961; admitted, 1986, Abogado, Spain. *Education:* Universitat de Barcelona (Licenciat en Dret, 1985); City of London Polytechnic (M.A., Business Law, 1988). (Fortuny Abogados Asociados con Freshfields). *LANGUAGES:* Spanish, Catalan, English and French.

FLAVIA ROSEMBUJ GONZALES-CAPITEL, born Rome, Italy, 1969; admitted, 1991, Abogado, Spain; 1994, Avocat, France. *Education:* Universitat de Barcelona (Licenciat en Dret, 1991); Université de Paris I, Panthéon-Sorbonne (EC Law, Post-graduate Degree, 1992); Université Libre de Bruxelles (EC Law, Post-graduate Degree, 1993). *LANGUAGES:* Spanish, Catalan, English, French and Italian.

DR. FRÜHBECK
ABOGADOS Y ECONOMISTAS

BALMES, 368, PR 2°
08006 BARCELONA, SPAIN
Telephone: (3) 418 63 87
Telex: (3) 418 93 50

Madrid, Spain Office: Marqués del Riscal, 11, 5°, 28010. Telephone: 308-25-22. Telex: 22469; 49214. Telefax: (1) 310 28 82.

Marbella, Spain Office: Ramón Gómez de la Serna, 22, Edif. King Edward, Of. 404, 29600. Telephone: 778589; 778590. Telex: 79827. Telefax: 824-659.

Business Law, Commercial, Administrative, Tax, Exchange Control, Foreign Investment in Spain, Spanish Investment abroad, Labor, Industrial, Patents and Trademarks, Insolvency, Banking, Maritime Law, Civil Law, Inheritances, Real Estate, Criminal Law and Litigation.

CARLOS WIENBERG, born Madrid, Spain, August 26, 1959; admitted, 1988, Berlin; 1992, Madrid; 1993, Barcelona. *Education:* Albert Ludwigs Universität, Freiburg (1984). Author: Die Produkthaftung im deutschen and US-amerikanischen Kollisionsrecht, Centaurus, 1991. *LANGUAGES:* German, Spanish, English, French, Portuguese.

ARNO WILHELM MEUSER, born Hannover, German, July 2, 1959; admitted, 1993, Hamburg (Not admitted in Spain). *Education:* Universität Hannover; Universität, Hamburg; Universidad de Sevilla. *LANGUAGES:* German, English, Spanish and French.

Languages: Spanish, English, German and French.

(For Complete Biographical Data on all Personnel, see Professional Biographies at Madrid, Spain)

VENTURA GARCÉS

FREIXA, 26-28
08021 BARCELONA, SPAIN
Telephone: (34-3) 201.94.44
Telefax: (34-3) 209.83.91
Telex: 54278 VGAR E

Madrid, Spain Office: Alfonso XII, 22, 28014. Telephone: (34-1) 521 7818. Fax: (34-1) 521 7853.

General Practice, Antitrust Law, Arbitration, Banking Law, Bankruptcy, Commercial Law, Company Law, Distribution, Agency and Franchise Law, EEC Law, Fiscal Law, Foreign Investments, International Contracts, Litigation, M&A, Property and Real Estate Law.

FIRM PROFILE: *The firm was founded in 1952 by Ventura Garcés. It has grown steadily during its forty years of existence and now has offices in Madrid as well as Barcelona. The principal activity of the practice is acting as legal advisers to Spanish and foreign firms, and it is well known as specializing in counselling large foreign and multinational companies on*

(This Listing Continued)

---

setting up in Spain. The firm covers practically all fields of law relating to companies, with the exception of criminal law.

VENTURA GARCÉS, admitted, 1952, Barcelona. *Education:* University of Barcelona (Law Degree). Author: *Regimen jurídico de las inversiones extranjeras en España* , 1975 (English edition: Legal Aspects of Foreign Investments in Spain, 1976); *Los contratos de asistencia técnica internactional y su regulación en Espanña* , 1980. Co-Author: "Licensing and Franchising in Spain" and "Tax Treatment of Joint Ventures in Spain," published in International Tax Review (Euromoney Publications, London, 1992). *Member:* Barcelona, Madrid and Balearic Islands Bar Association. *LANGUAGES:* Spanish, Catalan, English, French and Italian.

ANGEL SEGARRA FERRÉ, admitted, 1989, Barcelona. *Education:* Barcelona University (Degree in Economics and Business Studies); Ce ntro de Estudios Tributarios (Postgraduate Course in Taxation). Lecturer, Tax Law, Collegio de Economistas de Cataluña. Author: "Tratamiento de las diferencias entre principios contables y fiscales. Modificaciones de la Ley de Reforma Mercantil y del nuevo Plan Gerneral de Contabilidad" (Gaceta Fiscal) and "Tax Treatment of Joint Ventures in Spain" (International Tax Review). *Member:* Colegio de Economistas de Cataluña; Spanish Institute of Certified Auditors (Instituto de Censores Jurados de Cuentas). Head of the Tax Department. *LANGUAGES:* Spanish, Catalan and English.

RICARD GENÉ, admitted, 1985, Sabadell and Barcelona. *Education:* Barcelona University (Degree in Law). Expert in Property and Administrative Law. Official Translator for English and Catalan. *Member:* Barcelona Bar Association. *LANGUAGES:* Spanish, Catalan, English, French and German.

CLAUDIO GARCÉS, admitted, 1986, Barcelona. *Education:* Barcelona University (Degree in Law); Colegio Abad Oliba (Postgraduate Course in Taxation); University of London (Diploma in International Law). Co-Author: "Licensing and Franchising in Spain" (International Tax Review). *Member:* Barcelona Bar Association. *LANGUAGES:* Spanish, Catalan, French and English.

MARIO BOSCH, admitted, 1990, Barcelona. *Education:* Barcelona University (Degree in Law); Colegio Abad Oliba (Postgraduate Course in Taxation). Lecture, Tax Law, INESE, Barcelona. *Member:* Barcelona Bar Association. *LANGUAGES:* English.

ANA RIBÓ, admitted, 1990, Barcelona. *Education:* Barcelona University (Degree in Law); London University (Master in Commercial Law); Pompeu Fabra University, Barcelona (Diploma in Arbitration Law). *LANGUAGES:* Spanish, Catalan and English.

LUIS VIÑUALES, admitted, 1991, Barcelona. *Education:* Barcelona University (Law Degree, 1990); Colegio de Abogados de Barcelona (Postgraduate course in Company Law); Colegio de Economistas de Barcelona (Diploma in Tax Law. Lecturer, Tax Law, INESE, Barcelona. *Member:* Barcelona Bar Association. *LANGUAGES:* Spanish, Catalan and English.

ANDREA GARCÉS, admitted, 1989, Barcelona. *Education:* Barcelona University (Degree in Law and Spanish Philology); Colegio de Economistas de Barcelona (Diploma in Tax Law). *Member:* Barcelona Bar Association. Specialist in Intellectual Property Law. *LANGUAGES:* Spanish, Catalan, French and English.

IVÁN AZINOVIC, admitted, 1992, Madrid. *Education:* University of Alcalá de Henares (Law Degree, 1989); Washington College of Law, American University, Washington, D.C. (Master in International, specialism: International Commercial Law and Banking Law). *Member:* Madrid Bar Association. *LANGUAGES:* Spanish, Catatlan and English.

TOMAS GARCÉS, admitted, 1992, Barcelona. *Education:* Barcelona University (Degree in Law); Colegio Abad Oliba, Barcelona (Postgraduate course on Corporate Lawyers). *Member:* Barcelona Bar Association. *LANGUAGES:* Spanish, Catalan and English.

JUAN FIGAROLAS, admitted, 1992, Barcelona. *Education:* Barcelona University (Degree in Law); ESADE, Barcelona (Master in Business Administration, specialism: Tax Law). *Member:* Barcelona Bar Association. *LANGUAGES:* Spanish, Catalan and English.

MARTI ADROER. *Education:* Barcelona University (Degree in Economics and Business Studies, 1992); ESADE, Barcelona (Postgraduate course in Tax Law). *Member:* Colegio de Economistas de Cataluña. *LANGUAGES:* Spanish, Catalan and English.

ETIENNE SANZ DE ACEDO, admitted, 1993, Barcelona. *Education:* Alicante University (Degree in Law); Free University of Brussels (LL.M., in European Law). *Member:* Alicante Bar Association. Specialist in Competition Law. *LANGUAGES:* Spanish, Catalan, French, English and Italian.

(This Listing Continued)

VENTURA GARCÉS, Barcelona—Continued

Languages: English, French, German and Italian.

REPRESENTATIVE CLIENTS: Imperial Chemical Industries PLC. (England); Concast Standard AG (Switzerland); BCS S.p.A. (Italy); Perrot Duval Holding (Switzerland); N.W. Ayer International Inc. (U.S.A.); Mattel Inc. (U.S.A.); A/S Thomas Ths. Sabroe & Co. (Denmark); IMI PLC (England); Générale de Transport et d'Industrie (France); The Kendall Co. (U.S.A.); Italstrade, S.p.A. (Italy); Luxottica Group, S.p.A. (Italy); Prima Inmobiliaria, S.A. (Spain); Agrolimen, S.A. (Spain); Lowndes Lambert Group Ltd. (England); Manpower Inc. (U.S.A.); Huurre OY (Finland); International Management Group (Overseas) Inc. (USA); Lexmark International Inc. (USA); Aprilia S.p.A. (Italy); Iso-Roy S.A. (France); NBA Properties Inc. (USA); Carter Wallace Inc. (USA); Metaleurop S.A. (France).
REFERENCES: Debevoise & Plimpton, 21 Avenue George V, Paris.

J. & A. GARRIGUES

MALLORCA, 260-262, 4° 2ª
08008 BARCELONA, SPAIN
Telephone: (34-3) 488-12-11
Telex: 51285 abog
Facsimile: (34-3) 487-53-76; 487-99-26

REVISERS OF THE SPAIN LAW DIGEST FOR THIS DIRECTORY.

Madrid, Spain Office: Antonio Maura, 16, 28014. Telephone: (34-1) 521-21-51. Facsimile: (34-1) 521-40-53; 531-70-16. Telex: 22153 Aboga.
New York, New York Office: 115 East 57th Street, Suite 1230, 10022. Telephone: 1-212-751-9233. Facsimile: 1-212-355-3594. Telex: 14-9543.
Brussels, Belgium Office: Rue D'Arlon, 118, B-1040. Telephone: (32-2) 280-16-60. Facsimile: (32-2) 280-15-60.
Marbella, Spain Office: Avda. Ricardo Soriano, 65 - 5° 1. Telephone: (34-52) 86-22-11. Facsimile: (34-52) 82-68-84.
Oviedo, Spain Office: Marqués de Pidal, 6 - 3°C., 33004. Telephone: (34-8) 527-73-75. Facsimile: (34-8) 527-73-83.
Seville, Spain Office: Zaragoza, 50, 41001. Telephone: (34-5) 456-45-36. Facsimile: (34-5) 456-47-52.
Lisbon, Portugal Office: Grupo Legal Português (EEIG) in association with F. Castelo Branco, Nobre Guedes & P. Rebelo de Sousa, Simmons & Simmons and Pinheiro Neto & Co. Rua Fialhode Almeida, Castilho, n°32 - 9°/ 1200 Lisbon. Telephone: (351-1) 352-13-18. Facsimile: (351-1) 352-14-18.

General Practice, Administrative, Corporation, International, Labor Relations, Oil and Gas, Mines, Foreign Investments, Banking, Estate Law and Taxation, Maritime Law.

RESIDENT LAWYERS

MIGUEL ANGEL PANDO, born Madrid, Spain, 1939; admitted, 1965, Spain. *Education:* University of Madrid. *Member:* Madrid and Barcelona Bar Associations. **LANGUAGES:** English, French. Italian.

JUAN RAMÓN ANDINO VILLASANTE, born Medina de Pomar, Burgos, Spain, 1940; admitted, 1971, Spain. *Education:* University of Barcelona. *Member:* Barcelona and Gerona Bar Associations. **LANGUAGES:** English.

MARIA TERESA HERNANDEZ FALCO, born Barcelona, Spain, 1951; admitted, 1975, Spain. *Education:* University of Barcelona. *Member:* Barcelona Bar Association. **LANGUAGES:** English, French.

SERGIO SANCHEZ SOLE, born Barcelona, Spain, 1964; admitted, 1988, Spain. *Education:* University of Barcelona. Professor, Commercial Law, Colegio Universitario Abad Oliva. *Member:* Barcelona Bar Association. **LANGUAGES:** English, French.

JOSE LUIS MAGRE, born Barcelona, Spain, 1962; admitted, 1987, Spain; 1989, New York. *Education:* University of Barcelona, Barcelona Tax and Financial Studies Center. *Member:* Barcelona Bar Association. **LANGUAGES:** English.

JORDI R. TORRENTS, born Barcelona, Spain, 1955; admitted, 1980, Spain. *Education:* University of Barcelona; Master of International Law, S.M.U. Dallas, Texas, USA. *Member:* Barcelona Bar Association. **LANGUAGES:** English.

IGNACIO CORBERA DALE, born Bilbao, Spain, 1965; admitted, 1990 (Not admitted in Spain). *Education:* Colegio "San Igancio", Barcelona; University of Barcelona Law School; College of Europe (Postgraduate in EEC Law, 1989). *Member:* Barcelona Bar Association. **LANGUAGES:** English, French, Italian.

(This Listing Continued)

SILVIA VALIENTE DOMINGUEZ, born Barcelona, Spain, 1967; admitted, 1992, Spain. *Education:* University of Barcelona; ESADE (Postgraduation in Tax Law, 1992). *Member:* Barcelona Bar Association. **LANGUAGES:** English.

CRISTINA CONTEL BONET, born El Vendrell, Tarragona, Spain, 1965; admitted, 1990, Spain. *Education:* University of Barcelona (Law Degree); Master in Corporate and Business Law. *Member:* Barcelona Bar Association. **LANGUAGES:** English.

JOSEFA MORALES CAÑAS, born Barcelona, Spain, 1958; admitted, 1988, Spain. *Education:* Law School, University of Barcelona; Barcelona University of Arts (History Degree). *Member:* Barcelona Bar Association. **LANGUAGES:** French.

JAVIER VIDAL-QUADRAS TRIAS DE BES, born Barcelona, Spain, 1961; admitted, 1988, Spain. *Education:* Law School, University of Barcelona. Professor of Commercial Law. *Member:* Barcelona Bar Association. **LANGUAGES:** English, Portuguese.

MARIA EUGENIA CARVAJAL, born Madrid, Spain, 1963; admitted, 1987, Spain. *Education:* University of Madrid; Diploma on Advanced European Studies (College of Europe, Bruges). *Member:* Madrid Bar Association.

MONTSE MURO OLLE, born Barcelona, Spain, 1966; admitted, 1993. *Education:* University of Barcelona. **LANGUAGES:** English, French.

REVISERS OF THE SPAIN LAW DIGEST FOR THIS DIRECTORY.

GOMEZ-ACEBO & POMBO

DIAGONAL, 442
08037 BARCELONA, SPAIN
Telephone: (343) 415-74-00
Fax: (343) 415-84-00

Madrid, Spain Office: Castellana, 164, 28046. Telephone: (341) 582 91 00. Fax: (341) 345 36 79; 582 91 14. Cable: Juristas. Telex: 23429 GAPO E.
Bilbao, Spain Office: Gran Vía, 31, 48009. Telephone: (344) 415-62-66/77. Fax: (344) 416-87-49.
Las Palmas (Canary Islands), Spain Office: Viera y Clavijo, 48, 35002. Telephone: (342) 838-38-36. Fax: (342) 838-38-56.
Santiago de Compostela, Spain Office: Casas Reales, 4, 15704. Telephone: (348) 157-33-46. Fax: (348) 157-35-46.
Seville, Spain Office: Av. de la Constitución, 40, 41001. Telephone: (345) 421-66-59; 422-18-93. Fax: (345) 421-08-14.
Valencia, Spain Office: Gran Vía Marqués del Turia, 49, 46005. Telephone: (346) 351-38-35. Fax: (346) 351-60-74.
Brussels, Belgium Office: Rue de la Loi, 99/101, 1040. Telephone: (322) 231-12-20. Fax: (322) 230-80-35.

Manuel Martin
Santiago De Nadal
Eduardo Vila
Iñigo Igartua
Aitana Mendez Vilaplana
Jose Angel Cano
Antonio Jódar
Ignasi Guardans
Clara Pombo

OF COUNSEL

Richard A. Silberstein (Not admitted in Spain)

(For Complete Biographical data on all Personnel, see Professional Biographies at Madrid, Spain).

JAUSAS & TERRICABRAS

Established in 1965

LEÓN XIII NO. 23, ROGER DE LLURIA, 118
08022 BARCELONA, SPAIN
Telephone: (3) 212 61 54; (3) 207.70.60
Telex: 51705 LAWS E
Fax: (3) 418 21 99; (3) 207.14.24

Madrid, Spain Office: Miguel Angel, No. 6-3°, 28010 Madrid. Telephone: (1) 310.01.65. Fax: (1) 308.39.33.

(This Listing Continued)

Pharmaceutical Law, Mergers and Acquisitions, Competition, Trade and Commercial, Corporate, Foreign Investment, EEC Law, Trademarks and Intellectual Property, Labor and Tax Law, Arbitration and Litigation.

FIRM PROFILE: Jausàs & Terricabras is the result of the integration, in 1990 of two law firms based in Barcelona: Estudio Jausàs, in practice since 1965 and Bufete Terricabras, in practice since 1973.

The firm has two main offices in Barcelona and an office in Madrid.

Jausàs & Terricabras intends to provide a fully comprehensive legal service to Spanish and Foreign companies operating in Spain including, inter alia, corporate, trade, labor and tax matters. To achieve this objective, the firm relies on qualified professionals, most of them holding postgraduate degrees and fluent at least in both English and French. Assistants and other personnel of the firm are also fluent in these languages. All documents are directly prepared in English, French or Spanish as each case requires. Official translations (sworn translations) are also provided by the firm.

The clients of the firm consist of important international and domestic companies operating in the main industrial and commercial sectors.

MEMBERS OF FIRM

AGUSTI JAUSAS MARTI, born Bellver de Cerdanya (Lérida), Spain, September 19, 1937; admitted, 1961, Barcelona; 1967, Madrid. *Education:* University of Barcelona (Law, 1960). Editor of "Agency and Distribution Agreements, An International Survey," 1994. Author: "Tratado de Seguridad Social," Bosch, 1971; "Mercado Común," Ode, 1986. *Member:* IBA; Vice-Chairman of Committee M on International Sales and Related Transactions, IBA; Spanish Group of AIPPI; APLA. *LANGUAGES:* Spanish, Catalan, English and French (Sworn Translator in English and French). *PRACTICE AREAS:* Pharmaceutical Law; Mergers and Acquisitions; Commercial Law.

CARLOS TERRICABRAS FELIUS, born Tona (Barcelona), Spain, February 7, 1946; admitted, 1967, Barcelona. *Education:* University of Barcelona (Law, 1967). Master in Tax Law, CEFT, Barcelona, 1968; Former Senior Lecturer in Escuela Superiorde Marketing, Instituto de Estudios Universitarios, UNED Law Faculty. *LANGUAGES:* Spanish, Catalan, English and French. *PRACTICE AREAS:* Tax Law; Finance Law.

CLIMENT BUXADERAS ROQUETA, born Tona (Barcelona), Spain, January 31, 1952; admitted, 1978, Barcelona. *Education:* University of Barcelona (Law, 1978). Senior Lecturer of Tax Law, Business School of Barcelona, 1986-1990. *LANGUAGES:* Spanish and Catalan. *PRACTICE AREAS:* Tax Law; Trade Law.

JAIME CABECERANS CABECERANS, born Barcelona, Spain, October 23, 1958; admitted, 1983, Barcelona. *Education:* Autonomous University of Barcelona (Law, 1983). *LANGUAGES:* Spanish, Catalan, English and French. *PRACTICE AREAS:* Civil Law; Trade Law; Administrative Law.

CRISTINA COLOMA FERNANDEZ, born Badajoz, Spain, March 18, 1948; admitted, 1981, Barcelona. *Education:* University of Barcelona (Law 1980). *LANGUAGES:* Spanish and French. *PRACTICE AREAS:* Tax Law.

JORDI FAUS SANTASUSANA, born Barcelona, Spain, September 7, 1963; admitted, 1987, Barcelona. *Education:* University of Barcelona (Law, 1986). Master in Advanced European Legal Studies, College of Europe, Brugge, 1987. Author: "Legal Aspects of Free Movement of Capitals in the EEC," 1989; "Responsabilite patrimoniale des états par violation de l'article 30 du Traité CEE," 1989; "Pharmaceutical Administrative Regulations Trigger the Attack of Anti-Trust Rules Against Selective Distribution of Cosmetics," 1993; "The Case-Law of Products," 1993; "Consumer Law in Spain," 1994. Former Assistant Lecturer, ESADE, Barcelona, 1989. *LANGUAGES:* Spanish, Catalan, English and French (Sworn Translator in English and French). *PRACTICE AREAS:* EEC Law; Pharmaceutical Law.

JOSE ANTONIO FERNANDEZ BUSTILLO, born Oviedo, Spain, November 20, 1938; admitted, 1964, Barcelona. *Education:* University of Oviedo (Law, 1960). Senior Lecturer, Law Practice School of Barcelona, 1990—. President, Labor Law Section of the Barcelona Bar, 1990—. *LANGUAGES:* Spanish and French. *PRACTICE AREAS:* Labor Law; Social Security Law; Administrative Law.

PEDRO FULGUEIRA PONS, born Ciudadela (Menorca), Spain, July 3, 1946. *Education:* University of Barcelona (Economics, 1974). *LANGUAGES:* Spanish, Catalan and French. *PRACTICE AREAS:* Tax Law.

JOSEP GODALL CASTELL, born Barcelona, Spain, December 23, 1952; admitted, 1978, Barcelona. *Education:* University of Barcelona (Law,

(This Listing Continued)

1974). Master in Tax Law (CETF), 1977. Real Estate Agent, 1987. Senior Lecturer, UNED School of Economics, 1987-1989. *LANGUAGES:* Spanish, Catalan, English, French and Italian. *PRACTICE AREAS:* Tax Law; Trade Law; Civil Law.

JORDI GUARCH RECAJ, born Sabadell, Barcelona, Spain, November 16, 1958. *Education:* University of Barcelona (Economics, 1980). Finance and Tax Inspector, 1984. Senior Lecturer of Accounting, Fundación Bosch Gimpera 1990—. Chief of Inspection Unit in the Barcelona Tax Delegation, 1984-1989. *LANGUAGES:* Spanish, Catalan, English and French. *PRACTICE AREAS:* Tax and Financial Law.

XAVIER MOLINER BERNADES, born Barcelona, Spain, October 30, 1961; admitted, 1987, Barcelona. *Education:* University of Barcelona (Law, 1986). Foreign Trade Courses, Barcelona Bar Association, 1987. *LANGUAGES:* Spanish, Catalan and English. *PRACTICE AREAS:* Procedural Law; Litigation.

FRANCESC ORDEIG FOURNIER, born Barcelona, Spain, July 19, 1956; admitted, 1980, Barcelona. *Education:* University of Deusto-Bilbao (Law, 1978); University of Deusto-Bilbao (Economic Applied Sciences, 1978). Author: "Mercado Común, Tratado Práctico," Ode, 1985. *Member:* IBA. *LANGUAGES:* Spanish, Catalan, English and French. *PRACTICE AREAS:* Trade Law; Corporate Finance Law; Mergers and Acquisitions.

TERESA DEL ROSAL BLASCO, born Granada, Spain, October 26, 1945; admitted, 1979, Madrid. *Education:* University of Madrid (Law, 1977). (Resident, Madrid Office). *LANGUAGES:* Spanish, English and French. *PRACTICE AREAS:* Civil Law; Family Law.

GONZALO SERRACLARA CATALA, born Barcelona, Spain, December 3, 1960; admitted, 1990, Barcelona. *Education:* University of Barcelona (Law, 1984). Program of Instruction for Lawyers, 1989. Author: "Sobre el método del estudio de la Historia del Derecho," IV Jornadas de HD Español, 1984. Senior Lecturer of History of Law, UNED, 1984-1993. Senior Lecturer of History of Law, INEDE, 1984-1990. Senior Lecturer of Political Law, CEURA, 1987-1990. *LANGUAGES:* Spanish, Catalan and English. *PRACTICE AREAS:* Civil Law; Registry Law; Mercantile Law.

AUGUST TORA BARNADAS, born Barcelona, Spain, September 10, 1952; admitted, 1980, Barcelona. *Education:* University of Barcelona (Law, 1977). *Member:* Tourism Law Association of the Barcelona Bar Association. *LANGUAGES:* Spanish, Catalan, English and French. *PRACTICE AREAS:* Labor Law; Administrative Law.

BLANCA USON VEGAS, born Barcelona, Spain, June 18, 1959. *Education:* University of Barcelona (Economics, 1982); Master in Tax Law (CETF, 1984). *LANGUAGES:* Spanish, Catalan, English and French. *PRACTICE AREAS:* Tax Law.

OF COUNSEL

LORENZO RODRIGUEZ ROJO, born León, Spain, March 4, 1948. *Education:* Complutense University of Madrid (Economics, 1977). Finance and Tax Inspector. Head of Financial and Tax Inspection, Catalan Autonomous Government (1985-1992). Senior Lecturer at the School of Economics of the University of Barcelona. Senior Lecturer at E.S.A.D.E. (Barcelona). Author: "Manual del Impuesto Sobre Sucesiones y Donaciones", 1988. *LANGUAGES:* Spanish, Catalan, English and French. *PRACTICE AREAS:* Tax Law.

ANTONIO VENTURA-TRAVESET HERNANDEZ, born Valencia, Spain, April 9, 1931; admitted, 1953, Barcelona and Notary Public. *Education:* University of Valencia (Law, 1953). Author: "Derecho de Propiedad Horizontal," Bosch Barcelona, 1961-1992. *LANGUAGES:* Spanish, English and French. *PRACTICE AREAS:* Real Estate Law.

ASSOCIATES

JOSE LUIS CALVO SORRIBAS, born Barcelona, Spain, September 19, 1966; admitted, 1991, Barcelona. *Education:* University of Barcelona (Law, 1991). *LANGUAGES:* Spanish and French. *PRACTICE AREAS:* Labor Law.

ALBERTO CANALS ALVAREZ, born Barcelona, Spain, October 27, 1969. *Education:* University of Zaragoza (Law, 1992). *LANGUAGES:* Spanish, Catalan and English. *PRACTICE AREAS:* Tax Law.

MARIA BELEN CASTRO BAÑERES, born Barbastro (Huesca), Spain, March 5, 1968; admitted, 1991, Barcelona. *Education:* U.N.E.D. (Law, 1991). *LANGUAGES:* Spanish, English and French. *PRACTICE AREAS:* Administrative Law; Corporate Law.

NURIA CLEMENTE FARRE, born Barcelona, Spain, January 8, 1962; admitted, 1993, Barcelona. *Education:* University of Barcelona (Law 1992).

(This Listing Continued)

JAUSAS & TERRICABRAS, Barcelona—Continued

LANGUAGES: Spanish, Catalan, English and French. **PRACTICE AREAS:** Corporate Law.

MARIA DEL CARMEN CHIVITE OTERO, born Barcelona, Spain, February 14, 1956. Education: University of Barcelona (Economics, 1987). **LANGUAGES:** Spanish and English. **PRACTICE AREAS:** Tax Law.

MARGARITA FERRER SANTAMARIA, born Barcelona, Spain, March 27, 1962. Education: Labor School, University of Barcelona (Diploma in Labor Law, 1992). **LANGUAGES:** Spanish, Catalan, English and French. **PRACTICE AREAS:** Labor Law.

MARIA JOSE MARCO MOGALLON, born Tarragona, Spain, September 23, 1965. Education: University of Barcelona (Law, 1988). **LANGUAGES:** Spanish, English and French. **PRACTICE AREAS:** Administrative Law; Corporate Law.

TERESA OTERO GINER, born Valencia, Spain, September 23, 1943. Education: Labor School, University of Barcelona (Diploma in Labor Law, 1982). **LANGUAGES:** Spanish, Catalan, English. **PRACTICE AREAS:** Labor Law.

CRISTINA PELLON ROMEU, born Barcelona, Spain, July 13, 1967. Education: University of Barcelona (Law, 1992). **LANGUAGES:** Spanish, Catalan, English. **PRACTICE AREAS:** Labor Law.

MARIA TERESA SIVATTE FONT, born Barcelona, Spain, November 5, 1968; admitted, 1992, Barcelona. Education: University of Barcelona (Law, 1991); Instituto de Empresa, Madrid (Master in Legal Counseling, 1992). **LANGUAGES:** Spanish, Catalan and English. **PRACTICE AREAS:** Procedural Law; Litigation.

ASSUMPCIO SOLER CARNE, born Rubi (Barcelona), Spain, December 12, 1966. Education: Labor School, University of Barcelona (Diploma in Labor Law, 1990). **LANGUAGES:** Spanish, Catalan, English and French. **PRACTICE AREAS:** Labor Law.

CHRISTOPHER LEE

DIAGONAL 506, 8°2ª

08006 BARCELONA, SPAIN

Telephone: (010 343) 217 64 33

Fax: (010 343) 217 64 33

FIRM PROFILE: An English solicitor, Christopher Lee works together with Spanish lawyers for English-speaking clients who have interests throughout Spain. Not being linked to any single Spanish law firm ensures that the most appropriate firms are selected for each case. Matters dealt with include: company and business law, commercial and residential property, civil litigation, regulatory issues, residency, matrimonial, wills and succession. Christopher Lee is also available for consultations in London each month.

CHRISTOPHER LEE, born 1959; admitted as an English Solicitor, 1984. Education: B.A. (Hons). **LANGUAGES:** English and Spanish.

ESTUDIO LEGAL ABOGADOS

AVDA. DIAGONAL, 442

08037 BARCELONA, SPAIN

Telephone: 3. 415.95.82

Telecopier: 416.18.03

Madrid, Spain Office: c/Velázquez, 51-28001. Telephone: 1. 578.06.43. Telecopier: 1. 431.21.52.

Paris, France Office: c/o Bureau Francis Lefebvre 3, Villa Emile Bergerat. Telephone: (1) 47385500. Fax: 47385555.

Brussels, Belgium Office: 45, Rue du Luxembourg. Telephone: 2. 502.20.30. Telecopier: 2. 502.32.78.

General Practice. Corporation, Mergers and Acquisitions Insolvency, Taxation, Foreign Investments, Banking, Securities, Administrative, Planning, Labour, Oil, Mining and Gas, Civil, International/EEC Law, Litigation, Antitrust, Distributorship, Agency and Franchise Law, Arbitration, Intellectual Property, Environmental, Entertainment, Pharmaceutical, Transport, Telecommunications.

(This Listing Continued)

RESIDENT PARTNER

ANTONIO CAÑADAS ALONSO, born Madrid, 1950; admitted, 1979, Spain. Education: Lycée Français, Madrid; University of Madrid, Faculty of Law; College d'Europe, Brugge, Belgium; International Law Academy, The Hague, The Netherland (Diploma, EEC Law). Assistant Professor of International Law, Universidad Autónoma de Madrid. Member: Colegio de Abogados de Madrid. (Resident Partner).

ASSOCIATES

INMACULADA UMBERT MILLET, born Barcelona, 1952; admitted, 1984, Spain. Education: Marymount School, Sagrado Corazón; University of Barcelona, Faculties of Law and Philosophy (Degree in Tax Studies). Member: Colegio de Abogados de Barcelona.

NOEL E. LERYCKE PAQUET, born Thysville, Zaire, 1949; admitted, 1976, Barcelona; 1983, Balearic Islands. Education: Lycée Français, Kinshasa; Ecole Saint Pierre, Brussels; Colegio Teatinos, Mallorca; University of Barcelona, Faculty of Law, Center for Taxes and Economic Studies (Master in EEC Law). Member: Colegio de Abogados de Barcelona and Balearic Islands.

FRANCESCA RUIZ GURBALA, born La Ricamarie, Saint Etienne, France, 1958; admitted, 1986, Barcelona. Education: Lycée Français, P. Andorra; Instituto de Enseñanza Media, P. Andorra; University of Barcelona, Faculty of Law; School of Juridical Practice. Member: Colegio de Abogados de Barcelona.

MANUEL FELIPE SESMA GARCIA, born Ciudad Real, 1961; admitted, 1986, Barcelona. Education: La Salle Horta-Menendez Pelayo and La Salle Condal (Barcelona); University of Barcelona, Faculty of Law; School of Juridical Practice. Member: Colegio de Abogados de Barcelona.

MA. MARIA TERESA ROIG VIDAL, born Barcelona, Spain, 1964. Education: Colegio Sant Nicolau (Sabadell); University School Abad Oliba (Barcelona); University of Barcelona, Faculty of Law. Member: Colegio de Abogados de Barcelona, 1991—.

ANTONIA LOBO FEMENIA, born Palma, Spain, 1966. Education: Colegio Jesús María (Jerez de la Frontera, Cádiz) and Sagrad a Familia (Madrid); Universities of Madrid and Barcelona, Faculties of Law. Master in Practice of Corporate Social Security Management at Adams Academy of Barcelona. Member: Colegio de Abogados de Barcelona, 1990—.

Languages: Spanish, English, French, Italian and German

MEMBRILLERA & RODRIGUEZ MOLNAR

Bufetes Asociados

Established in 1993

AVENIDA DIAGONAL, 419 - 2°, 1ª

08008 BARCELONA, SPAIN

Telephone: (34-3) 416 17 20 / 11 91

Fax: (34-3) 416 10 38

Madrid, Spain Office: Velázquez, 78 - 5° Izq., 28001 Madrid. Telephone: (34-1) 431 67 95. Fax: (34-1) 575 81 90.

General International Practice, EEC, Foreign Investments, Real Estate, Corporate, Commercial, Acquisitions, Industrial and Intellectual Property, Commercial Litigation, Environmental and Telecommunications.

FIRM PROFILE: Membrillera & Rodriquez Molnar was established in 1993 as an association between the Madrid based firm of Rodriquez Molnar & Asociados (established in 1984) and the Barcelona Law Office of Mr. Rafael G. de Membrillera (established in (1976). The client base is substantially European and North American in nature.

MEMBERS OF FIRM

RAFAEL G. DE MEMBRILLERA DOLSET, born July 22, 1943. Education: Universidad de Barcelona (1965); Universidad de Paris (1966). Member: Barcelona and Madrid Bar Associations; International Bar Association. **LANGUAGES:** Spanish, English and French. **PRACTICE AREAS:** Corporate Law; International Law.

LUIS GIBERT VIDAURRE, born April 12, 1937. Education: University of Barcelona (1960). Member: Barcelona, Madrid and Bilbao Bar Association; International Association of Trademark Agents. **LANGUAGES:** Spanish, English and Catalán. **PRACTICE AREAS:** Industrial and Intellectual Property.

GERMAN MINGUELL ZANUY, born February 29, 1952. Education: University of Barcelona. Member: Barcelona Bar Association. **LAN-**

(This Listing Continued)

GUAGES: Spanish, French and Catalán. **PRACTICE AREAS:** Commercial Litigation.

ALEJANDRO SANVICENTE IBIRICU, born September 22, 1950. *Education:* University of Palma de Mallorca (1977). *Member:* Barcelona Bar Association. **LANGUAGES:** Spanish. **PRACTICE AREAS:** Litigation; Criminal Law.

OF COUNSEL

ALEJANDRO SANVICENTE SAMA, born May 3, 1918. *Education:* University of Zaragoza. Former General Prosecutor of Tarragona, Palma de Mallorca, Valencia y Barcelona. *Member:* Barcelona Bar Association. **LANGUAGES:** Spanish. **PRACTICE AREAS:** Criminal Law.

BUFETE MULLERAT & ROCA

PASEIG DE GRÀCIA, 81
08008 BARCELONA, SPAIN
Telephone: (343) 487 11 44
Telex: 51575
Fax: (343) 487 96 32; (343) 487 13 32

Other Barcelona Office: Paseig de Gràcia 122, 08008. Telephone: (343) 237 84 46. Fax: (343) 237 86 30.
Madrid Office: Velázquez, 94, 28006. Telephone: (341) 578 17 62. Telex: 47089. Fax: (341) 575 1386; (341) 575 27 80.
Lisbon Office (Correspondent firm): Rua Rodrigo da Fonseca 149-4, 1000 Lisbon. Telephone: (3511) 387 64 04. Fax: (3511) 385 5310.

Banking and financial law, EC law, General Corporate and commercial law, International commercial arbitration, International construction, Litigation, Tax law, Intellectual property, Insolvency and bankruptcy, Administrative and public law, Environmental law, Zoning law.

PARTNERS

RAMÓN M. MULLERAT, born Barcelona, Spain, 1939; admitted, 1962, Barcelona; 1979, Madrid. *Education:* Law Faculty of Barcelona University (1957-1961). Co-Author: "Legislación sobre inversiones extranjeras," 1993; "EEC Legal Systems (Spanish Chapter)," Butterworths, 1992; "European Product Liability (Spanish Chapter)," Butterworths, 1992. Author: "Spain's Capital Gain," 1992; "La etiqueta ecológica," 1992; "Overhauling Spanish Unfair Competition," 1992; "La responsabilidad del prestador de servicios (Propuesta de Directiva del Consejo, CEE)," 1992; "Directors' Civil Liability Under Spanish Company Law," 1991; "Management and Leveraged Buy-outs," 1991; Integrating Spanish Company Law into the Community," 1990; "La responsabilidad civil del fabricante," 1988; "La Directiva CEE de 25 de Julio de 1985 y el Derecho Español," 1988; "Setting up a Company in Spain," 1987; "Liberalization of Foreign Investments in Spain," 1987; "La adquisición de bienes inmuebles por Extranjeros en España," 1986; "Transfer of Foreign Technology and Technical Assistance Contracts in Spain," 1985; "Legislación sobre Inversiones Extranjeras Directas," 1985; "El acceso al crédito interior por parte de sociedades españolas con participación extranjera," 1985; "Foreign Investments in Spain Real Estate," 1985; "Direct Foreign Investments in Spain," 1984; "La responsabilidad civil del fabricante derivada de los productos defectuosos," 1984; " La liberación de las garantías extranjeras O.M. 23 de enero 1982"; "Unas palabras acerca de la U.I.A.," 1978; "La responsabilidad de los productos," 1977. Assistant Professor, Barcelona University, 1970-1980. Professor, Legal Practice School, Barcelona Bar Association, 1975-1992. Honorary Legal Adviser the British Chamber of Commerce since 1970. President, British Chamber of Commerce of Barcelona, 1988-1989. Deputy Director for Research of the International Union of Lawyers (UIA), 1987-1989. Spanish Representative in the Council of the Bars and Law Societies of the European Community (CCBE)-Company Law Committee, 1987. Vice-President of the CCBE. *Member:* Barcelona (Member of Council, 1987-1990); Madrid and Tarragona Bar Associations; The Florida Bar (Honorary Member, International Law Committee); Union Internationale des Avocats, President of the Barcelona Conference of the U.I.A., 1989. **LANGUAGES:** Spanish, Catalan, French and English.

SEBASTIA ROCA, born Artés (Barcelona), 1936; admitted, 1963, Barcelona. *Education:* Law Faculty of the Barcelona University (1960). General Counsel: Banco Condal, 1968-1980; Banco Garriga Nogués, 1980-1984. Seminars: on banking matters: Moscow, St. Petersburg and Kiev (1990); Trias de Bes i Giró summer University: report on bankruptcy in Spain (1990); UIA, Mexico Congress: report on modern concept of ownership (1991). *Member:* Council of Barcelona Bar Association (1985-1988), Zaragoza, Tarragona, Reus, Manresa, Malaga, Sabadell and Tortosa Bar Associations; Union Internationale des Advocats; Patronat Fundació:

(This Listing Continued)

study and justice Lluís de Peguera. **LANGUAGES:** Spanish, Catalan and English.

ROSER RAFOLS, born Barcelona, 1950; admitted, 1974, Barcelona. *Education:* Law Faculty of the Barcelona University (1973). Professor of International Law, Autonomous University of Barcelona, 1992. Reporter in Master on International Trade Law in the Law Practice School of the Barcelona Bar. *Member:* Barcelona, Madrid and Girona Bar Associations; Union Internationale des Advocats. **LANGUAGES:** Spanish, Catalan, French and English.

CARLES PRAT, born Barcelona, Spain, 1959; admitted, 1981, Barcelona. *Education:* Law Faculty of the Barcelona University (1981; Diplomate of Law of the European Economic Communities, 1982). Author: "La responsabilidad del fabricante en derecho español"; "La Situació Actual de l'Exequatur a Espanya," 1988; "Spain: A New Approach to Competition Issues?" 1992; "El Control de las Fusiones y Concentraciones de Empresas en Derecho Español"; "El Ordenamiento Juríd ico Español ante la Venta Directa," 1993. Visiting Lecturer, Department of Law, Bristol Polytechnic, 1991-1992. *Member:* Barcelona Bar Association; Association Internationale des Jeunes Avocats (AIJA), 1989-1991. **LANGUAGES:** Spanish, Catalan, English and French.

CARLES TORTRAS, born Barcelona, Spain, 1942; admitted, 1970, Barcelona; 1973, Madrid. *Education:* Law Faculty of the Barcelona University (1965; Diplomate of Law of the European Economic Communities). Author: "La Protección Jurídica de los Programas de Ordenador," 1987; "El Delito Informático," 1988; "El Contrato de Leasing sobre Bienes Informáticos," 1990; "Computers in Spain," 1991; "Software and Intellectual Property in Spain," 1993; "La Protección Legal de las Obras de Diseño," 1993. Collaborator: Comillas Pontifical University - ICADE (Madrid); Summer University, "Universidad Nacional de Educación a Distancia (UNED). Professor, Legal Practice School, Barcelona Bar Association. Lecturer, University Nebrisensis. *Member:* Madrid, Barcelona (Chairman, Commission on Unfair Competition; Vice President, Copyright Section), Granollers, Mataró and Sabadell Bar Associations; Spanish Association for the Protection of the Trademark and the Intellectual Property (APMPI) (Foundation Member and Member, Board of Directors); Association of European Trademark Proprietors; Spanish Association of Users of Information Technology (AESUTI); Literary and Artistic Association for the Defence of the Author's Royalties (ALAI). **LANGUAGES:** Spanish, Catalan and French.

DOLORS ROCA, born Barcelona, 1955; admitted, 1981, Barcelona. *Education:* Law Faculty of the Barcelona University (1973-1979); Institute of Administrative Law, Madrid (Diplomas in Zoning Law). Seminars: Civil Catalan Law; Hypothecary Law; New Legislation of Joint Stock Companies, 1990. *Member:* Barcelona, Girona, Terrassa and Granollers Bar Associations. **LANGUAGES:** Spanish, French and Catalan.

MIGUEL TORRES, born Barcelona, 1962; admitted, 1987, Barcelona. *Education:* Law Faculty of the Barcelona University (1981-1986). Author: "Las Agrupaciones Europeas de Interés Económico," 1990; "EEIG in Spain," 1991; "Banking Law in Spain," 1992; "La Comercialización de Valores Emitidos en el Extranjero y las Emisiones de No Residentes en España," 1992. Co-Author: "Legislación sobre inversiones extranjeras"; "Securities Lending in Spain," 1993. Professor, Private International, Faculty of Law, Barcelona University. *Member:* Barcelona Bar Association; Union Internationale des Avocats. **LANGUAGES:** Spanish, Catalan, French and English.

OF COUNSEL

ENRIQUE BADÍA, born Barcelona, 1917; admitted, 1951, Barcelona. *Education:* Escuela Superior de Altos Estudios Mercantiles of Barcelona (1935); University of Zaragoza (1945). Former Professor of Legal Architecture, Escuela Práctica Superior de Arquitectura, Barcelona, 1955-1958. *Member:* Barcelona Bar Association. **LANGUAGES:** Spanish, Catalan, French, English and Italian.

JOSEP Mª CALPE, born Tarragona, 1929; admitted, 1954, Tarragona. *Education:* Law Faculty of the Barcelona University (Doctor in Law, 1946-1952); University of Perugia (Course on Compared Commercial Law, 1955 and Pisa, Italy, 1956). Professor of Commercial Law, Faculty of Law, 1951-1960 and Insurance Law, Economic Science Faculty, 1957-1993, Barcelona University. Diplomate in European Economic Communities. Course on Commercial Advice, Commercial and Consumption Department, Generalitat of Catalonia. General Secretary and current Honorary General Secretary and Member, Arbitration Body, Industry and Navigation of Barcelona, Chamber of Commerce, "Consul de Mar." Member: Barcelona Arbitration Court; Chartered Insurance Institute and Chartered Institute of

(This Listing Continued)

BUFETE MULLERAT & ROCA, Barcelona—Continued

Arbitrations. *Member:* Tarragona Bar Association. *LANGUAGES:* Spanish, Catalan, French, English and Italian.

HUGH MCCAIRLEY, born London, England, 1961; admitted, 1987, England and Wales. *Education:* University of St. Andrews, Scotland (1980-1984); Polytechnic of Central London (1986); Course in European Community Law, University of Exeter. Inns of Court School of Law, 1987. Co-author: "Securities Lending in Spain," 1993; "Labor Law Reform in Spain," 1994. *LANGUAGES:* English and Spanish.

ASSOCIATES

MERCEDES CARAL, born Barcelona, 1958; admitted, 1983, Barcelona. *Education:* Law Faculty of the Barcelona University (1975-1980). Professor of Civil Law, School of Law, Autonomous University of Barcelona. *Member:* Barcelona (Secretary, Civil Law Section), Tarragona and Reus Bar Associations. *LANGUAGES:* Spanish, Catalan, French and English.

ROSA Mª MUÑOZ, born Barcelona, 1959; admitted, 1983. *Education:* Law Faculty of the Barcelona University (1983); School of Europe of Bruges (1988); Advanced Studies on Local Administration (1985). Former Member, Council, Barcelona Bar Association. *LANGUAGES:* Spanish, Catalan and Italian.

SONIA CORTES, born Barcelona, 1964; admitted, 1988, Barcelona. *Education:* Law Faculty of the Barcelona University (1983-1988); London City Polytechnic (English Law Certificate, 1987); School of Europe of Bruges (European Community Law Certificate, 1988). Co-Author: "Product Liability in Spain," in "Product Liability in Europe," Butterworths, 1991; "Sports Marketing in Spain," in "Sports Marketing Europe," Kluwer, 1993; "Competition Law in Spain," Financial Law Review, 1993. *Member:* Barcelona Bar Association; Union Internationale des Avocats. *LANGUAGES:* Spanish, Catalan, French and English.

JOAN ALBOS, born Barcelona, 1963; admitted, 1987. *Education:* Law Faculty of the Barcelona University (1981-1986); Instituto de Empresas (Madrid) (Master de Asesoría Juridica de Empresa, 1987-1988). Course of European Community Law, Exeter University. Author: "La fiscalidad en la transmisión de inmuebles: Disposición Adicional 4°. Ley de tasas," 1989. *Member:* Barcelona Bar Association. *LANGUAGES:* Spanish, Catalan, French and English.

JORGE ADELL, born Barcelona, 1964; admitted, 1987, Barcelona. *Education:* Law Faculty of the Barcelona University (1982-1987); University of Chicago (Master in Laws, 1992-1993). Author: "Financial Instruments of the International Capital Markets," Revista de Derecho Bancario y Bursatil, 1994. *Member:* Barcelona Bar Association. *LANGUAGES:* Spanish, Catalan, English and French.

SOPHIE-ANNE CARTON, born Brussels, 1959; admitted, 1986, Barcelona. *Education:* Law Faculty of Barcelona University (1977-1982). *Member:* Barcelona Bar Association. *LANGUAGES:* Spanish, Catalan, French and English.

JUAN C. FABREGAT, born Barcelona, 1962; admitted, 1985. *Education:* Law Faculty of the Universidad Autonoma de Barcelona (1980-1985). *Member:* Barcelona Bar Association. *LANGUAGES:* Spanish, Catalan and French.

SERGIO GIMENEZ, born Barcelona, 1966; admitted, 1989, Barcelona. *Education:* Law Faculty of the Barcelona University (1984-1989); Law Faculty of the Freiburg University, Germany (1984-1985); Patronat Catala pro Europa (EEC Law Certificate, 1985-1986; Master in Private International Law, LL.M., Münster, 1990). Author: "EWIV in Spanien: Bestimmung dos subsidiär anwendbaren Rechts," 1990. Co-Author: "Il Diritto di Agenzia in Europa," 1991; "Guarantees and Securities under Spanish Law," 1992. *Member:* Barcelona Bar Association; Barcelona Young Lawyers Association (Member, Executive Committee). *LANGUAGES:* Spanish, Catalan, German and English.

ORIOL RAFOLS, born Barcelona, 1967; admitted, 1991. *Education:* Law Faculty of the Barcelona University (1985-1990); University of Exeter (LL.M., European Legal Studies, 1992). *Member:* Barcelona Bar Association. *LANGUAGES:* Spanish, Catalan, French and English.

ANDREU PARERA, born Barcelona, 1963; admitted, 1991. *Education:* Law Faculty of the Barcelona University (1985-1990); Abad Olivia (Commercial Law, 1990); Summer University Trias de Bes i Giró(1992, 1993). *Member:* Barcelona Bar Association. *LANGUAGES:* Spanish, Catalan and French.

(This Listing Continued)

MONTSERRAT JANE, born Calafeil (Tarragona), 1966; admitted, 1992. *Education:* Law Faculty of the Barcelona University (1990). Visiting lawyer: Glaisyers Solicitors, Manchester, England, 1990-1991; Rogers, Towers, Bailey, John & Gay, Jacksonville, Florida, 1991. *Member:* Barcelona Bar Association. *LANGUAGES:* Spanish, Catalan, French and English.

ANGELES SUBIRA, born Barcelona, 1965; admitted, 1991. *Education:* Law Faculty of the Barcelona University (1991). *Member:* Barcelona Bar Association. *LANGUAGES:* Spanish, Catalan, English and French.

MARIONA BALDO, born Barcelona, 1968; admitted, 1992. *Education:* Law Faculty of the Barcelona University (1986-1991); Law Faculty of Liege University, Belgium (Erasmus Scholarship, 1990); Law Faculty of Toulouse 1 University, France (1991-1992). *Member:* Barcelona Bar Association. *LANGUAGES:* Spanish, Catalan, English and French.

RICARD BOSCH, born Vilafranca de Penedès (Barcelona), 1965; admitted, 1993. *Education:* Law Faculty of Barcelona University (1991); Abad Oliva (Business Law, 1991). *Member:* Barcelona Bar Association. *LANGUAGES:* Spanish, Catalan and French.

JOSE MARIA BRUGUERA CHAVARRIA, born Barcelona, 1969; admitted, 1993. *Education:* Law Faculty of Madrid University (1992). *Member:* Madrid Bar Association. *LANGUAGES:* Spanish, Catalan and English.

JOSEP ENCESA, born Girona, 1964. *Education:* Law Faculty of Barcelona, 1989; Instituto de Empresa (Madrid) Masters in Legal Advice to Companies, 1991; Summer University Trias de Bes i Girń, 1992. *Member:* Barcelona Bar Association. *LANGUAGES:* Catalan, Spanish, French and English.

OSCAR DE SANTIAGO, born Barcelona, 1968. *Education:* Law Faculty of Barcelona University (1986-1991; EEC Law, 1990-1991). Erasmus Scholarship, Law Faculty of Essex University, England, 1991-1992. *Member:* Barcelona Bar Association. *LANGUAGES:* Spanish, Catalan and English.

Mª TERESA CUBIERTA LLOBET, born Barcelona, 1965. *Education:* Central University of Barcelona (Degree in Law, 1991) College of Property and Commercial Registrars of Spain (Specialist Course in Company Law, 1992-1993). *LANGUAGES:* Spanish, Catalan and French.

BUFETE PINTÓ RUIZ

Abogados & Economistas

BEETHOVEN, 13, 7°

08021 BARCELONA, SPAIN

Telephone: 34 (3) 414 58 85

Fax: 34 (3) 414 38 85

All areas of Spanish and EEC Law, including General Practice, Corporate and Commercial, Licensing and Banking, M & A, Environmental Law, Media and Sport Law, Litigation and Arbitration, Tax Law, Real Estate and Construction Law, as well as Civil Law.

FIRM PROFILE: BUFETE PINTO RUIZ develops its practice in Barcelona, since 1889, and several correspondent offices in the main cities of Spain.

MEMBERS OF FIRM

JOSÉ JUAN PINTÓ RUIZ, born Barcelona, April 16, 1927; admitted, 1949, Barcelona. *Education:* Central University of Barcelona (Licensed in Law, 1949; Doctor of Law, cum laude, 1959). Councillor, Consejo Nacional de la Abogacía Española. Former President, Academia de Jurisprudencia y Legislación de Cataluña. Member, Academia de Doctores y Licenciados del Distrito Universitario de Barcelona. Former Member, Consejo de Estudios de la Cátedra "Durán i Bas" de Derecho Civil de Cataluña. Magistrate, High Court of La Mitra de Andorra. Vice-President, Consejo General de la Abogacía. Former Director, Consejo de Redacción de la Revista Jurídica de Cataluña. President, Caixa de Barcelona, July 9, 1982-July 27, 1990. President, Fundació "La Caixa"; Vice-President, Caixa d'Estalvis i Pensions de Barcelona; President, Caixabank. Former President, Spanish Confederation of Savings Bank. Member of the Board of Directors, Saving Banks Association of the EEC. President, Consejo de Administración de Autopistas de Cataluña, S.A. Ex Vice-President, Consejo de Administracñn de Autopistas, Cocesionaria Española, S.A. Member, Real Acadamia de Ciencias Económicas y Financieras de Cataluña. Author: "Naturaleza Jurídica del pago," RJC 1949; "En torno a la llamada condición resolutoria Tácita," RJC 1954; "El usufructo general de viudedad en el ante-

(This Listing Continued)

proyecto a la Compilación especial de Derecho Civil de Cataluña," ADC 1953; "Incumplimiento de Obligaciones Civiles," RJC 1964; "Identificación y determinación de dincas y su publicación," RJC 1959; "La resolución del derecho del arrendador y subsistencia del derecho del arrendatario," RJC 1965. *Member:* Barcelona Bar Association (4th Member of the Governing Board); Madrid Bar Association. *PRACTICE AREAS:* Civil Bank and Business Law.

FRANCISCO BELLAVISTA ARIMANY, born Granollers, Barcelona, 1954. *Education:* Escurela Universitaria de Estudios Empresariales, Autonomous University of Barcelona (Ciencias Empresariales Degree, 1976); Ciencias Empresariales, Faculty of Economics and Business Science, Autonomous University of Barcelona (Licensed in Ciencias Económicas y Empresariales, 1978). Member, Instituto de Censores Jurados de Cuentas de España, 1978. Assistant of the Manager of the Coordination and Studies Department, Torras Hostench, S.A., 1975-1977. Collaboration in Research and Teaching, Professorship of Undertaking's Economy, Escuela Universitaria de Estudio Empresariales of the Autonomous University of Barcelona, 1977-1978 and 1978-1979. Assistant Teacher, Organization and Administration of Undertakings, 1979-1980. Professor of Economy of Undertakings, 1983, Escuela Universitaria de Estudios Empresariales, Autonomous of Barcelona, 1980-1981 and 1981-1982. Professor, University School, Department of Economy of Undertakings, Autonomous University of Barcelona, 1983-1987. *Member:* Economist Professional Association of Barcelona. (Economist and Auditor). *LANGUAGES:* Spanish, Catalan and English. *PRACTICE AREAS:* Tax Law, Mergers and Acquisitions.

JOSÉ JUAN PINTÓ SALA, born Barcelona, 1951; admitted, 1973, Barcelona. *Education:* Elementary and High School San Ignacio de los Reverendos Padres Jesuitas; Central University of Barcelona (Licensed in Law, 1973). Vice-President, Economic Committee of Identirama. Member, Board of Directors, European G.E.I.E. Pannone de Backer. *Member:* Barcelona Bar Association (Course for Secretaries of Board of Directors; Member, Judges and Lawyers Commission); Madrid Bar Association. *LANGUAGES:* Spanish, Catalán, English, French and Italian. *PRACTICE AREAS:* Company and Business Law; Mergers and Acquisitions.

ALEJANDRO PINTÓSALA, born Barcelona, 1957; admitted, 1983, Barcelona. *Education:* Nelly and Abad Oliba, Barcelona; Central University of Barcelona (Licensed in Law, 1983); Studies in the School of Juridical Practice "Roda Ventura of the Gereralitat de Catalunya; Abad Oliba (Course on informatics applied to Law; Course on Practical Application of the European Communities Law in Spain). Court Solicitor Office Ranera Cahís. Member, Legal Counsel, Department of the Banco Guipuzcoano. Former Board of Directors Member, Joven Cámara de Cataluña. *Member:* Barcelona Bar Association (Member and Delegate Board of Directors; President, Infiltration Commission); Legal Adviser of the Employer's Organization for the National Work Promotion; Director of the legal magazine "Economist & Jurist.". *LANGUAGES:* Catalan, Spanish and French. *PRACTICE AREAS:* Real State Law, Company Law and Litigation.

JUAN SANTAMARIA TRILLO, born Barcelona, January 31, 1963; admitted, 1987, Barcelona. *Education:* Viaró de Sant Cugat del Vallés, Barcelona; Autonomous University of Barcelona (Licensed in Law, 1987). *Member:* Barcelona Bar Association; Inter-American Lawyer's Federation; Urban Land Institute. *LANGUAGES:* Spanish, Catalán and English. *PRACTICE AREAS:* Company and Business Law; Acquisitions.

JUAN VIDAL DE LLOBATERA GELI, born Barcelona, 1958; admitted, 1981, Barcelona. *Education:* School Decroly, Barcelona; Central University of Barcelona (Licensed in Law, 1981); Financial and Tributary Studies Center (Financial and Tax Studies, 1981); Ministry of Foreign Affairs, Barcelona (European Communities Law, 1982); Course on European Business Law and International Law, London, 1982; Illustrious Lawyers College, Barcelona (European Communities Law); Leiden & Columbia & Amsterdam Universities, Leiden (Commercial Law U.S.A., 1984);. Colegio de Abogados de Barcelona, 1984. *Member:* Barcelona Bar Association (Member, EEC Law Commission). *LANGUAGES:* Spanish, English, French and Catalán. *PRACTICE AREAS:* Company and Business Law; Commercial Litigation; Real Estate.

JORGE PINTÓ SALA, admitted, 1991, Barcelona. *Member:* Barcelona Bar Association. *LANGUAGES:* Spanish, Catalán, English and French. *PRACTICE AREAS:* Company and Business Law.

FRANCESC TORRELLA CABELLO, admitted, 1985, Barcelona. *Member:* Barcelona Bar Association. *LANGUAGES:* Spanish, Catalán, Italian and French. *PRACTICE AREAS:* Business and Sport Law.

(This Listing Continued)

MARGARITA GINESTA DE PUIG, admitted, 1984, Barcelona. *Member:* Barcelona Bar Association. *LANGUAGES:* Spanish, Catalán and English. *PRACTICE AREAS:* Civil Law and Litigation.

FRANCISCO JAVIER OBISPO CASTILLO. Education: Ciencias Empresariales, Faculty of Economics and Business Science, Autonomous University of Barcelona (Licensed in Ciencias Económicas y Empresariales, 1978; Ciencias Empresariales Degree, 1982). Former Lecturer, School of Industrial Mastership. *PRACTICE AREAS:* Tax Law; Accountancy and Financial.

MARIA LUISA DE ALARCON ELORRIETA, admitted, 1985, Barcelona. *Member:* Barcelona and Madrid Bar Associations. (Economist and Lawyer). *LANGUAGES:* Spanish, English and French. *PRACTICE AREAS:* Company and Tax Law.

JOAQUÍN MALVESI MARTINEZ, Member: Professional Association of Business Holders of Barcelona. (Economist). *PRACTICE AREAS:* Specialist in Tax, and Financial Law.

CAMIL RAICH PUYOL, admitted, 1986, Barcelona. *Member:* Granollers Bar Association. *PRACTICE AREAS:* Company and Business Law.

RAMÓN MARIA PARCERISAS BUNDO, admitted, 1990, Barcelona. *Member:* Barcelona Bar Association. *LANGUAGES:* Spanish, Catalán and English. *PRACTICE AREAS:* Tax Law.

ALBERT FAUS ROSANAS, admitted, 1991, Barcelona. *Member:* Barcelona Bar Association. *LANGUAGES:* Spanish, Catalán, English and French. *PRACTICE AREAS:* Business Law and Litigation.

JORGE SÁNCHEZ RODRÍGUEZ, admitted, 1991, Barcelona. *Member:* Barcelona Bar Association. *LANGUAGES:* Spanish, Catalán and English. *PRACTICE AREAS:* Company and Business Law.

FRANCISCO DE PUIG EGIDO, admitted, 1992, Barcelona. *Member:* Barcelona Bar Association. *LANGUAGES:* Spanish, Catalán, English, French and German. *PRACTICE AREAS:* Company and Business Law.

MONSTERRAT PRIETO RUIZ, admitted, 1986, Barcelona. (Accountant and Economic Adviser).

ANDREU PUJADAS CASAS. LANGUAGES: Spanish, Catalán, English and French. *PRACTICE AREAS:* Real Estate and Litigation.

SILVIA HERNÁNDEZ ALEGRE, admitted, 1992, Granollers. *LANGUAGES:* Spanish, Catalán and English. *PRACTICE AREAS:* Company and Business Law.

MANUEL CANTUESO, admitted, 1992, Granollers. *LANGUAGES:* Spanish, Catalán and French. *PRACTICE AREAS:* Labor Law.

PERE MIRALBELL GUERIN, admitted, 1994, Barcelona. *Member:* Barcelona Bar Association. *LANGUAGES:* Spanish, Catalán and English. *PRACTICE AREAS:* Civil Law and Litigation.

MARIA JOSE RODRIGUEZ CAMINO. LANGUAGES: Spanish, Catalán and French. *PRACTICE AREAS:* Company and Business Law.

BUFETE PLASENCIA ABOGADOS ASOCIADOS

Established in 1954

AVENIDA DIAGONAL, 550 PRAL. 2A.
08021 BARCELONA, SPAIN
Telephone: (34-3) 200.61.22; 65.21; 67.21
Facsimile: (34-3) 209.41.57

Madrid, Spain Office: C/. Velazquez, 26 3° A, 28001. Telephone: (34-1) 576.69.42; 578.20.35. Fax: (34-1) 578.22.83

Commercial, Foreign Investments, CEE, International, Civil and Company Law, Litigation.

FIRM PROFILE: *The Firm was established in 1969. It is well known for its clients and also correspondents which are all over Europe and North America.*

MEMBERS

ANTONIO PLASENCIA MONLEON, born Barcelona, Spain, July 28, 1930; admitted, 1954, Barcelona and Madrid. *Education:* Facultad de Derecho, Universidad de Barcelona (licenciatura, 1952); Faculte de Droit, Paris (Diplome Doctorat Universite, 1953). President, Decano Colegio de Abogados de Barcelona (Barcelona's Bar), 1983-1986. *Member:* A.I.J.A. (President, 1969-1970; U.I.A. (General Secretary, 1977-1982); C.C.B.E. (Mem-

(This Listing Continued)

BUFETE PLASENCIA ABOGADOS ASOCIADOS,
Barcelona—Continued

ber, Spanish Delegation, 1983-1986). *LANGUAGES:* Spanish, English, French and Italian. *PRACTICE AREAS:* Foreign Investments; Commercial and Company Land; Banking Law; C.E.E.; Civil Law; International Law.

CLAUDIO GRAU HOYOS, born Barcelona, Spain, November 17, 1932; admitted, 1956, Barcelona, Gerona, Lérida and Tarragona. *Education:* Barcelona Law School. *LANGUAGES:* Spanish, English and French. *PRACTICE AREAS:* Civil Law; International Law; Company and Commercial Law; Litigation.

MA. FATIMA PINEDA PEREZ, born Mataro (Barcelona), Spain, November 25, 1953; admitted, 1979, Barcelona; 1985, Valencia. *Education:* Facultad de Derecho, Universidad de Barcelona (Licenciatura, 1976). *LANGUAGES:* Spanish, English and French. *PRACTICE AREAS:* Civil Law; International Law; Industrial Law; Intellectual Property; Commercial Law; Litigation.

MIQUEL LLIMONA BALCELLS, born Barcelona, Spain, September 19, 1955; admitted, 1979, Barcelona. *Education:* Barcelona Law School (Lawyer, 1979). *Member:* Barcelona Law Association; Young Lawyers International Association (Member, Executive Committee). *LANGUAGES:* Spanish, English, French and Portuguese. *PRACTICE AREAS:* Foreign Investments; Civil Law; International Law; Commercial and Company Law.

ASSOCIATES

ALBERT MARRUGAT DE LA IGLESIA, born Barcèlona, Spain, January 16, 1958; admitted, 1985, Barcelona. *Education:* Universidad Central de Barcelona (Licenciate, 1985). *Member:* Colegio de Abogados de Barcelona. *LANGUAGES:* Spanish, English and French. *PRACTICE AREAS:* Litigation; Civil Law; Commercial Law.

FRANCISCO VAZQUEZ DE SOLA Y GALINDO, born Granada, Spain, August 1, 1956; admitted, 1985, Madrid; 1989, Barcelona. *Education:* University College Cardenal Cisneros; Universidad Complutense de Madrid (Lawyer, 1982). *LANGUAGES:* Spanish, English and French. *PRACTICE AREAS:* Commercial and Company Law; Litigation.

ESTEVE ECHE COSTA, born Barcelona, Spain, Mars 27, 1968; admitted, 1992, Barcelona. *Education:* Universidad Central de Barcelona (Licenciate, 1991); Universidas Pompeu Fabra (Master Company Law, 1992-1993). *LANGUAGES:* Spanish, English, French. *PRACTICE AREAS:* Civil Law; Commercial; Company Law; Litigation; Advertising; Unfair Competition.

JORGE ANGLADA PERLETTI, born Barcelona, Spain, May 10, 1968; admitted, 1994, Madrid. *Education:* Centro de Estudios Universitarios San Pablo, CEU (Licenciate, 1991); Université Catholique de Louvain-La-Neuve, UCL (EEC Law, 1992). *Member:* Colegio de Abogados de Mardid. *LANGUAGES:* Spanish, English, French and Italian. *PRACTICE AREAS:* EC Law; Commercial Law.

RAMOS & ARROYO

PASEO DE GRACIA, 92 (LA PEDRERA)
08008 BARCELONA, SPAIN
Telephone: (3) 487 11 12; (3) 215 77 11
Fax: (3) 487 35 62

Cadiz, Spain Office: Avenida Ramón de Carranza, 20, 11006. Telephone: (56) 25 22 00. Fax: (56) 26 16 55. Telex: 76192 Hull E.

Fuengirola, Málaga, Spain Office: Córdoba, Edificio Centro Comercial Reyes, 6°B, 29640. Telephone: (5) 258 45 72; (5) 258 45 90. Fax: (5) 258 45 72.

Madrid, Spain Office: Serrano 89-7°, 28006. Telephone: (1) 5629200. Fax: (1) 561 49 03.

Oviedo, Spain Office: Cimadevilla 19-2°B, 33003. Telephone: (8) 520 42 80. Fax: (8) 520 42 80.

Admiralty, Arbitration, Bankruptcy, Commercial, Competition, Construction, Copyright, Corporation, EEC, General Practice, Insurance, Labour, Litigation, Taxation, Trademarks & Patents and Real Estate Law.

(This Listing Continued)

EU1226B

MEMBERS OF FIRM

FRANCISCO RAMOS MENDEZ, born Orense, Spain, April 18, 1947; admitted, 1977, Barcelona and Madrid. *Education:* University of Santiago de Compostela, School of Law, Spain (LL.B., 1969); University of Oviedo, Spain (Doctor of Laws, 1972). Author: "Derecho Procesal Civil," 1980, 5th ed., 1992; "La Jurisdiccion Voluntaria en los Negocios de Comercio," 1978; "Las Medidas Cautelares en el Proceso Civil," 1974; "La Anotación Preventiva de Demanda," 1980; "Código Procesal Civil International," Barcelona, 1985, 2nd ed., 1991; "Arbitraje y Proceso Internacional," 1987; "El Proceso Penal," 1988, 3nd ed., 1993. Professor of Civil Procedure, University of Barcelona. Member, Commercial Panel of Arbitrators, American Arbitration Association. Member, Spanish Court of Arbitration. General Editor of Procedural Library. Editor, Justicia. *Member:* Barcelona (Former Member of the Board) and Madrid Bar Associations; UIA; IBA; ILA; Wissenschaftliche Vereinigung für Schiedsgerichtswesen e. V. (Also at Madrid, Spain Office). *LANGUAGES:* Spanish, German, French, English, Italian and Portuguese.

IGNACIO ARROYO MARTINEZ, born Bilbao, Spain, July 28, 1948; admitted, 1971, Barcelona. *Education:* University of Deusto, School of Law (LL.B., 1970); University of Bologna, Italy (Doctor of Laws, 1972); Harvard Law School (LL.M., 1975). General Editor, Yearbook Maritime Law, 1991. Author: "Spanish Code of Commerce," 6th, 1990; "Código de Legislación Bancaria," 3rd ed., 1990; "Legislación de Sociedades Mercantiles," 3rd, 1990; "Promissory Notes," 1986. Professor of Commercial Law, University of Barcelona. Member of the Board of JBLL, ETL, RDM, ADM, IFL Rev. and LMCLQ. *Member:* IBA; UIA; ILA; CMI. (Also at Madrid, Spain Office). *LANGUAGES:* English, French, Italian, Portuguese and Spanish.

JORGE ARROYO MARTINEZ, born Bilbao, Spain, March 15, 1956; admitted, 1988, Spain. *Education:* University of Barcelona (LL.B., 1987). *Member:* Barcelona Bar Association. *LANGUAGES:* Spanish, English, French and Italian.

PILAR ROMEU FERRE, born Barcelona, Spain, September 19 1951; admitted, 1975, Spain. *Education:* Barcelona University, School of Law (Licenciada); Doctor of Phil., 1990. *Member:* Barcelona Bar Association. *LANGUAGES:* Spanish, French, English, German, Italian and Hebrew.

ASSOCIATES

NURIA NOLLA ZAYAS, born Barcelona, Spain, June 26, 1956; admitted, 1980, Spain. *Education:* Barcelona University, School of Law (Licenciada, LL.B.). *Member:* Barcelona Bar Association (Governing Committee); YLIA; Spanish Association of Tax Experts. *LANGUAGES:* French, Italian, English and Spanish.

URSULA VESTWEBER HAAS, born Duisburg, West Germany, October 6, 1935; admitted, 1983, Barcelona. *Education:* Interpreters and Translators Institute, Mainz, West Germany; Central University, Barcelona, Spain (Licenciada). *Member:* Barcelona Bar Association. *LANGUAGES:* Spanish, German and English.

JOSEP QUEROL BENET, born Barcelona, Spain, March 25, 1961; admitted, 1985, Spain. *Education:* University Autonoma of Barcelona School of Law (LL.B., Licenciado); London School of Economics. *Member:* Barcelona Bar Association. *LANGUAGES:* English, French, German and Spanish.

MANUEL CACHON CADENAS, born Leon, Spain, 1956; admitted, 1981, Barcelona. *Education:* University Autonoma of Barcelona, School of Law (LL.B., 1981). Author: "El Embargo," 1989. Professor of Procedure, UAB. *Member:* Barcelona Bar Association. *LANGUAGES:* French, Italian and Spanish.

JUST FRANCO ARIAS, born Barcelona, Spain, 1951; admitted, 1981, Barcelona. *Education:* University of Barcelona, Faculty of Law (LL.B., 1981; Doctor of Laws, 1986). Author: "El Procedimiento de Apremio," 1987. Professor of Procedure, UAB. *Member:* Barcelona Bar Association. *LANGUAGES:* French, English, Italian and Spanish.

MIGUEL VIVES SUÑÉ, born Barcelona, Spain, May 9, 1962; admitted, 1989, Spain. *Education:* University of Barcelona (LL.B., 1989). *LANGUAGES:* Spanish, German and English.

OF COUNSEL

EDUARDO ALEMANY ZARAGOZA, born 1944, Barcelona; admitted, 1979, Barcelona. LL.B., Labor Law.

Languages: Spanish, German, French, English, Italian and Portuguese.

RIBALTA & MARTI DE VESES

AVDA. DIAGONAL, 442 BIS, 4°
08037 BARCELONA, SPAIN
Telephone: 415.46.00
Fax: 416.01.92

Madrid, Spain Office: Plaza Manolete, 3, 6°A, 28020. Telephone: 556.15.57. Telecopier: 556.73.03.

Corporate, Banking, Taxation, Foreign Investment, Contracts, Litigation, Patent and City Planning Law.

MEMBERS OF FIRM

JUAN RIBALTA AGUILERA, born Barcelona, Spain, January 2, 1934; admitted, 1957, Barcelona; 1977, Madrid. *Education:* Instituto de Estudios Superiores de Empresa; University of Barcelona (Iuris Doctor, 1957). Professor, Tax Law, University of Barcelona, 1957-1960. *Member:* Barcelona and Madrid Bar Associations. *LANGUAGES:* Spanish, French and Italian.

JOSÉ JAVIER MARTI DE VESES PUIG, born Barcelona, Spain, June 16, 1927; admitted, 1951, Barcelona; 1960, Madrid and Gerona. *Education:* University of Valencia (Iuris Doctor, 1951). Author: "Studies and Reports on Intellectual Property," AIPPI, 1977. Manager, Law Department, Fuerzas Electricas de Cataluña, S.A. 1956-1988. *Member:* Barcelona, Madrid, Gerona, Sabadell, San Feliu and Granollers Bar Associations; International Law Association; AIPPI. *LANGUAGES:* Spanish, French and Italian.

MANUEL BUENO PARALS, born Barcelona, Spain, October 16, 1948; admitted, 1980, Barcelona. *Education:* University of Barcelona (Iuris Doctor, 1972). Professor, Tax Law, University of Barcelona, 1979-1984. Tax Inspector, 1973-1980. *Member:* Barcelona Bar Association. *LANGUAGES:* Spanish, English and French.

MARIA CONCEPCION HORS CASANOVAS, born Barcelona, Spain, November 4, 1941; admitted, 1975, Barcelona. *Education:* University of Barcelona (Iuris Doctor, 1975). Author: "Inversiones Extranjeras," French Chamber of Commerce, 1986. *Member:* Barcelona Bar Association. *LANGUAGES:* Spanish, English, French and Italian.

PABLO USANDIZAGA USANDIZAGA, born Barcelona, Spain, January 9, 1964; admitted, 1987, Barcelona; 1989, New York. *Education:* University of Barcelona (Iuris Doctor, 1987); Harvard University (Master of Laws). *Member:* Barcelona Bar Association; New York State Bar Association. *LANGUAGES:* Spanish, English and French.

ASSOCIATES

JUAN CASALS FRADERA, born Barcelona, Spain, April 19, 1951; admitted, 1976, Barcelona; 1983, Sevilla; 1984, Valencia. *Education:* University of Barcelona (Iuris Doctor, 1975). *Member:* Barcelona, Sevilla and Valencia Bar Associations. *LANGUAGES:* Spanish, English and French.

AUGUSTO ESCARPIZO LORENZANA, born Barcelona, Spain, August 30, 1945; admitted, 1969, Barcelona; 1982, Gerona. *Education:* University of Barcelona (Iuris Doctor, 1969). *Member:* Barcelona and Gerona Bar Associations. *LANGUAGES:* Spanish, English, German and French.

CHRISTINA RIBALTA NOGUERA, born Barcelona, Spain, March 16, 1964; admitted, 1987, Barcelona. *Education:* University of Barcelona (Iuris Doctor, 1987). *Member:* Barcelona Bar Association. *LANGUAGES:* English, French and Italian.

JAVIER MARTI DE VESES ESTADES, born Barcelona, Spain, June 19, 1961; admitted, 1985, Barcelona; 1986, Tarragona and Gerona. *Education:* Instituto de Empresa Madrid (Masters, 1987); University of Barcelona (Iuris Doctor, 1985). Attorney, Fuerzas Electricas de Cataluña, S.A., 1985-1989. *Member:* Barcelona, Tarragona, Gerona, Tortosa and Sabadell Bar Associations. *LANGUAGES:* Spanish and French.

MARIA DEL CARMEN REÑAGA RUBIN, born Barcelona, Spain, November 14, 1964; admitted, 1987, Barcelona. *Education:* University of Barcelona (Iuris Doctor, 1987). *Member:* Barcelona Bar Association. *LANGUAGES:* Spanish, English and French.

DAVID BARA FERNÁNDEZ, born Barcelona, Spain, February, 28, 1964; admitted, 1989, Barcelona. *Education:* University of Barcelona (Iuris, Doctor, 1987); University of London (LL.M., Commercial and Corporate Law, 1988). *Member:* Barcelona and Madrid Bar Associations. *LANGUAGES:* English, Spanish and German.

BLANCA OCHOA GOMEZ, born Barcelona, Spain, August 10, 1964; admitted, 1990, Barcelona. *Education:* University of Barcelona (Juris Doc-

(This Listing Continued)

tor, 1987). *Member:* Barcelona Bar Association. *LANGUAGES:* Spanish, English and French.

PILAR COLOMA BELLVER, born Valencia, Spain, March 1, 1964; admitted, 1990, Barcelona. *Education:* University of Barcelona (Juris Doctor, 1988); Universite de Sciences Sociales de Toulouse (Master in International and European Law). Lecturer, Constitutional Law, Universite de Sciences Souoles de Tourouse, France, 1988-1989. *Member:* Barcelona Bar Association. *LANGUAGES:* Spanish, English, French and Italian.

ANTONIO MUÑOZ DE GISPERT, born Barcelona, Spain, February 11, 1968; admitted, 1991, Barcelona. *Education:* University of Barcelona (Iuris Doctor, 1991). *Member:* Barcelona Bar Association. *LANGUAGES:* Spanish, English and French.

MARIA LUISA DE URQUIA DE SOLA, born Barcelona, Spain, January 29, 1967; admitted, 1991, Barcelona. *Education:* University of Barcelona (Iuris Doctor, 1991). *Member:* Barcelona Bar Association. *LANGUAGES:* Spanish and English.

JEAN FRANÇOIS GIBIER, born Nancy, France, August 31, 1963; admitted, 1991, Barcelona. *Education:* University of Bordeaux, France (Maître en droit, 1989); University of Zaragoza, Spain (Curso quinto de derecho, 1990); University of Toulouse, France (Master in International Commercial Law option Financial Contracts, 1991). Author: "Change and Interest Rate Risk: Management and Tax Consequences," University of Toulouse, 130 pp. *LANGUAGES:* French, English and Spanish.

XAVIER FORASTER BASAGAÑA, born Barcelona, Spain, June 16, 1963; admitted, 1992, Barcelona. *Education:* University of Barcelona (Juris Doctor, 1986). Curso de Abogados de Empresa, Abad Oliba (1990-1991); Arthur Andersen (1991-1992). *Member:* Barcelona Bar Association. *LANGUAGES:* Spanish, English and French.

CARMEN MORENO CARMONA, born Almeria, Spain, March 29, 1967; admitted, 1992, Madrid. *Education:* Universidad Complutense de Madrid; Master Instituto de Empresa. *Member:* Madrid Bar Association. *LANGUAGES:* English and French.

MARTA SANZ-DIEZ DE ULZURRUN LLUCH, born Madrid, Spain, August 25, 1963; admitted, 1992, Madrid. *Education:* Universidad Complutense de Madrid, Oposiciones Abogado del Estado, Curso de Contabilidad, Curso Derecho Paramentario. *Member:* Madrid Bar Association. *LANGUAGES:* English and French.

CARMEN CAMPS PAPIOL, born Barcelona, Spain, November 17, 1966; admitted, 1989, Barcelona. *Education:* Law Degree (1989). *Member:* Barcelona Bar Association. *LANGUAGES:* French and English.

Languages: Spanish, English, French and Italian.

REPRESENTATIVE CLIENTS: Nestle; Michelin; Penn-Central Corp.; General Biscuits; Groupe Societe Generale; Groupe Merlin-Gerin; Henkel Iberica S.A.; Akzo Group; Groupe L'Oreal; Banco de Sabadell; Groupe Carrefour; Philips; Crouzet S.A.; Martini & Rossi; French Chamber of Commerce; Dym-Panel; Barnices Valentine; Swissair; Cointreau; Groupe Eugene; Clinica Platon, S.A.

BUFETE ROCA PUIG

Established in 1962

AVENIDA DIAGONAL 506, 5°, 2ª
08006 BARCELONA, SPAIN
Telephone: (343) 415 81 16
Fax: (343) 415 17 62

General and International Practice, Civil, Commercial, Corporation, Foreign Investments, Litigation and German Law.

FIRM PROFILE: Bufete Roca Puig was founded in 1962 by Antonio Roca Puig. Taking advantage of its considerable commercial experience, the firm places a strong emphasis on corporate and international work. With associates in Frankfurt/Main, Baden (Zürich-Switzerland), Lisboa, Parma, Madrid, Palma de Mallorca and Tarragona, the firm's overseas links ensure that its clients receive legal services in the most significant jurisdictions.

MEMBERS OF FIRM

ANTONIO ROCA PUIG, born Mataró, Barcelona, Spain, September 12, 1937; admitted, 1959, Spain. *Education:* Colegio de Hermanos Maristas, Escuela de Altos Estudios Mercantiles of Barcelona; University of Barcelona; Academy for International Trade, University of Frankfurt/Main (Titles: Accountant, Lawyer). Recipient, Big Cross of Civil Merit of the First Class Awarded by the President of the German Federal Republic. *Member:* Colegios de Abogados, Barcelona, Madrid, Valencia, Bilbao, Las Palmas de

(This Listing Continued)

BUFETE ROCA PUIG, Barcelona—Continued

Gran Canaria, Palma de Mallorca, Tarragona, Gerona, Alicante, Badajoz, Cantabria, Manresa, Vich, Sabadell, San Feliu de Llobregat and Malaga. *LANGUAGES:* Spanish, German, English and French. *PRACTICE AREAS:* General and International Practice; Civil; Commercial; Corporate; Foreign Investment; Litigation; German Law.

GERARDO S. ROCA IDELBERGER, born Mataró, Barcelona, Spain, May 15, 1963; admitted, 1986, Spain. *Education:* University of Barcelona. *Member:* Colegios de Abogados Barcelona and Madrid. *LANGUAGES:* Spanish, German and English. *PRACTICE AREAS:* General and International Practice; Civil; Commercial; Corporate; Foreign Investment; Litigation; German Law.

Languages: Spanish, German, English and French.

BUFETE ROFES & ASOCIADOS

Abogados

PASEO DE GARCIA, 21, 1ST FLOOR
08007 BARCELONA, SPAIN
Telephone: 34-3-487-0637
Fax: 34-3-487-0504

New York, New York Corresponding Office: Kevin MacCarthy Associates. 444 Madison Avenue. Telephone: 212-752-67-00. Fax: 212-319-75-84.

General Practice. Administrative Law, Arbitration and Mediation, Bankruptcy, Banks and Banking, Business Law, Charitable organizations, Company Law, Competition Law and Trade Regulation, Corporate Law Contracts, Management Contracts, Criminal Law, Debtor and Creditors, European Community Law, Family Law, Finance, International Law, Sales and Transactions, Investments, Litigation, Trademarks, Tourism Law.

MEMBERS OF FIRM

JOSE ROFES MENDIOLAGARAY, born Barcelona, 1956; admitted, 1979, Spain. *Education:* Barcelona University, Licenciate of Law. Author: EADA "Impago de Cuotas Obreras - Apropiacion indebida." Barcelona University: "El delito de prevaricacion judicial," in course Revision of Bankruptcy Treaty of J.A. Ramirez Lopez. Teacher of Criminal Law in Universidad Nacional de Education a Distancia. *Member:* Lawyers International Union; Lawyers European Union; Tourism Law Commission; Barcelona Bar Association. *LANGUAGES:* Spanish, French and English. *PRACTICE AREAS:* Criminal Law; Administrative and Civil Law; Bankruptcy; Torts; EEC and Tourism Law.

MARIA ISABEL GALOBARDES MENDOZA, born Barcelona, 1959; admitted, 1981, Spain. *Education:* Licenciate of Law, Diploma EEC Law, Diploma Corporate Law. *Member:* Fiscal Law and Administrative Law Commission; Barcelona Bar Association. *LANGUAGES:* Spanish, French and English. *PRACTICE AREAS:* Business and Corporate Law.

ASSOCIATES

CARLOS BARONET ALDABO, born Barcelona, 1961; admitted, 1988, Spain. *Education:* Barcelona University Licenciate of Law. *Member:* EEC Law, Mercantile Law, Civil Law and Sports Law, Barcelona Bar Association. *LANGUAGES:* Spanish, French and English. *PRACTICE AREAS:* EEC Law; Administrative and Civil Law.

MAITE MASCARO MIRALLES, born May 24, 1961; admitted, 1993, Barcelona. *Education:* University of Barcelona, Licenciate of Law; University of Brussels (U.L.B.), Licenciate of EEC Law; Master in Tax Law; Diploma Corporate Law. *Member:* International Young Lawyers Association; International Business Law and Tax Commission (Executive Committee); Barcelona Bar Association; EEC Law and Tax Commission. *LANGUAGES:* Spanish, Catalan, French and English. *PRACTICE AREAS:* Commercial and Corporation Law; Tax Law.

LUCIA CANO CANO, born Barcelona, 1963; admitted, 1987, Spain. *Education:* Barcelona University, Licenciate of Law, Civil Law Diploma. *Member:* Penal Law, Proceedings Law, Civil Law Barcelona Bar Association. *LANGUAGES:* Spanish and English. *PRACTICE AREAS:* Civil and Family Law; Real Estate and Property Law.

ANA MARIA MENDOZA ZARAGOZA, born Barcelona, 1963; admitted, 1993, Spain. *Education:* Barcelona University (Licentiate of Law; General Course of EEC; Course of Management; Inspection and Revision of Taxes in Foreign Trade; Diploma of Catalan Civil Law). *LANGUAGES:* Spanish, English and French. *PRACTICE AREAS:* Civil; Business and Administrative.

(This Listing Continued)

Mª ROSA RIBO HERRERO, born August 8, 1966; admitted, 1989, Barcelona. *Education:* University of Barcelona, Licenciate of Law; Course in Accounting, Diploma in Personal Income Tax Law. *Member:* Barcelona Bar Association; Corporate Law Commission. *LANGUAGES:* Spanish and English. *PRACTICE AREAS:* Commercial and Corporate Law.

CARLES BOQUERA MIRALLES, born October 5, 1967; admitted, 1991, Barcelona. *Education:* University of Barcelona, Licenciate of Law; Diploma in Administrative Local Law. *Member:* Barcelona Bar Association; Litigation and Business Law Commission. *LANGUAGES:* Spanish, Catalan and English. *PRACTICE AREAS:* Litigation and Torts.

JOSEP RIBA CIURANA, born December 25, 1967; admitted, 1993, Barcelona. *Education:* University of Barcelona, Licenciate of Law; Diploma in Maritime Law; Diploma in Criminal Law. *Member:* Barcelona Bar Association; Criminal Law Commission. *LANGUAGES:* Spanish, Catalan and English. *PRACTICE AREAS:* Criminal Law Torts.

Correspondents Offices in all Important Cities in Spain and Europe.

Languages: Spanish, French, Catalan, English, Italian and Russian.

BUFETE ROIG ARAN

AVDA DIAGONAL 399, 4° 2ª
08008 BARCELONA, SPAIN
Telephone: (34-3) 416 14 61
Telefax: (34-3) 416 05 87
Telex: 53920 LGAL-E

Advertising and Marketing, Agency and Distributorships, Alternative Dispute Resolution, Antitrust and Trade Regulations, Banks and Banking, Business, Contracts, Finance, Franchising, Intellectual Property, Leases and Leasing, Litigation, Mergers, Acquisitions and Divestitures, Property and Real Estate, Securities, Taxation, Business, Civil, Commercial, Company, Construction, Corporate, EEC, Foreign Investments, Labour, Environmental and Bankruptcy Law.

MEMBERS OF FIRM

JAVIER SANS ROIG, born Barcelona, Spain, 1944; admitted, 1968, Barcelona. *Education:* University of Barcelona; Strasbourg University; Salzburg Seminar in American Studies. *Member:* Colegio de Abogados de Barcelona for Terrassa and Elche; International Bar Association (Chairman, Ethics Committee); Europäische Präsidentenkonferenz Wiener Advokatengespräche (Member, Permanent Senate). *LANGUAGES:* English, French and Italian.

FÉLIX VILASECA, born Barcelona, Spain, 1950; admitted, 1974, Barcelona. *Education:* University of Barcelona; University of Strasbourg. *LANGUAGES:* French and English.

JOSÉ LUIS RODRÍGUEZ HERRERA, born Barcelona, Spain, 1955; admitted, 1982, Barcelona. *Education:* University of Barcelona. ESADE. Head Counsel, Banco Atlántico, Barcelona. *LANGUAGES:* English.

IGNACIO LÓPEZ-BALCELLS, born Barcelona, Spain, 1961; admitted, 1985, Barcelona. *Education:* University of Barcelona; City of London Polytechnic (London); Centre of Finance and Tax Studies, Barcelona; School of Commerce, Barcelona. *LANGUAGES:* English and French.

ELVIRA CUXART FONOLLEDA, born Barcelona, Spain, 1963; admitted, 1986, Barcelona. *Education:* University of Barcelona; City of London Polytechnic (London); Master in Real Estate and Planning Law, Barcelona. *LANGUAGES:* English and French.

CRISTINA PONT VILADOMIU, born Barcelona, Spain, 1965; admitted, 1989, Barcelona. *Education:* University of Barcelona (Master in Register Law). *LANGUAGES:* English.

SERGIO ROMERO PLA, born Barcelona, Spain, 1966; admitted, 1989, Barcelona. *Education:* Instituto Europeo de Derecho y Econónicas, Barcelona; Colegio Abad Oliba, Barcelona; Instituto de Empresas, Madrid (Diploma in Environmental Law); Post-graduate course in Taxation. *LANGUAGES:* English.

MIREIA BLANCH OLIVE, born Barcelona, Spain, 1968; admitted, 1992, Barcelona. *Education:* Instituto Europeo de Derecho y Económicas, Barcelona; City of London Polytechnic (London). *LANGUAGES:* English and French.

CARLOS DE YZAGUIRRE, born Barcelona, Spain, 1968; admitted, 1992, Barcelona. *Education:* University of Navarra; Master in Corporate Legal Counseling, Madrid; Post-graduate courses on Corporate Law,

(This Listing Continued)

American Legal System and International Economic Policy, Harvard Extension University, Cambridge, MA. *LANGUAGES:* English.

MARTA SANROMÁ LEON, born Barcelona, Spain, 1966. *Education:* University of Barcelona; Specialized in Taxation; Post-graduate course on Autonomous Government Taxation, Catalan Autonomous Government Headquarters, Barcelona. Teacher at the CEEM (Centre of Economics and Business Studies), Barcelona. *LANGUAGES:* English.

ROBERT GIRALT LEINWEBER, born Barcelona, Spain, 1968. *Education:* University of Barcelona; Post-graduate course on Comparative and German Civil Law, University of Kiel, Germany. *LANGUAGES:* English, German and French.

Languages: English, French, Italian, German, Dutch, Romanian

REPRESENTATIVE CLIENTS: AEG Telefunken, Aldus Europe Ltd. (Scotland); Alpha Therapeutic Corporation (USA); Aprilia SpA. (Italy); Benetton Group Spa (Italy); BBA Group Plc (England); B. Braun Melsungen AG (Germany); Bostik, S.A.; Compañía General de Tabacos de Filipinas S.A.; COOB'92, S.A. (organiser of the Olympic games in Barcelona 1992); Echlin International Group Plc (England); Fabra & Coats, Gestetner, S.A.; ECA (Entidad Colaboradora de la Administración S.A.); General de Transporte y de Industria (GTI), S.A. (VIA); Green Cross Corporation (USA); Higgs & Hill Plc (England); Ibérica de Inversiones Industriales S.A.(3i); Interchem Europa S.A.; International Management Group (Overseas) Inc. (USA); KGK Knutsson AB (Sweden), Laboratorios Virbac, S.A.; Ladbroke Group Plc (England); Lovable Spa (Italy); NBA Properties Inc. (USA); Pechiney España S.A.; Quinton Hazell Plc (England), Roche Bobois España; Sligos S.A. (France); Sealed Air Corporation (USA); Telephone International Media Ltd. (England); Trefilunión G.m.b.H (Germany); Union Kaffee Rösterei GmbH & Co. (Germany).

SARDA, CALOMARDE, CASTELO & ASOCIADOS

MUNTANER, 407 1ST FLOOR
08021 BARCELONA, SPAIN
Telephone: 3/201.64.66; 201 74 56
Fax: 3/202.00.96

Valencia, Spain Office: Cronista Carreres, 13 4° 8°. Telephone: 6/352.96.03. Fax: 6/394.26.86.
Madrid, Spain Office: P° de la Castellana, 228, 3°, 28046. Telephone: 1/314.19.34. Fax: 1/314.19.52.

European Community Law, International Banking and Business Law, Foreign Investment Law, General International Trade Law, Corporate, Civil and Criminal Litigation, Competition and Copyright Law, Insurance Law, Family Law, Procedural Law, Bankruptcy Law and Tax Law.

FIRM PROFILE: *The firm, established in 1993 is the result of the association of three Lawyer's offices: Sardá y Asociados in Barcelona, established in 1964, Mas Millet y Calomarde, established in Valencia in 1978 and Castelo y Larraz, established in Madrid in 1975. It is a member of LEGALLIANCE (EEIG) a large union of European lawyers with offices in Brussels, Paris, London, Berlin, Frankfurt, Cologne, Leipzig, Milan, Bologna, Padua, The Hague and Stockholm.*

RESIDENT MEMBERS OF FIRM

JUAN IGNACIO SARDA ANTON, born San Sebastian, Guipuzcoa, June 27, 1937; admitted, 1961, Barcelona; 1971, Madrid. *Education:* University of Barcelona (1961). *Member:* Barcelona, Madrid, Girona, Baleares and Alicante Bar Associations. *LANGUAGES:* Catalan, Spanish, French and English. *PRACTICE AREAS:* International Banking and Business Law; General International Trade Law; Foreign Investment Law; Bankruptcy Law.

MARIA JOSE MORENO HUMET, born Barcelona, January 22, 1956; admitted, 1981, Barcelona. *Education:* University of Barcelona (Lic. Jur., 1979); Course of European Community Law Collège d'Europe of Bruges (Diploma, 1988). *Member:* Barcelona and Pamplona Bar Associations. *LANGUAGES:* English, Italian, French, Catalan and Spanish. *PRACTICE AREAS:* Company Law; European Community Law; Family Law.

LLUIS LLADO I FONT, born Igualada, July 7, 1940; admitted, 1967. *Education:* University of Barcelona (Lic. Jur., 1964). *Member:* Barcelona Bar Association. *LANGUAGES:* Catalan, Spanish and English. *PRACTICE AREAS:* Procedural Law; Insurance Law; Consumers Law.

ALEJANDRO MIRO VALVERDE, born Madrid, June 18, 1929; admitted, 1964, Barcelona. *Education:* University of Barcelona (Lic. Jur., 1953). *Member:* Barcelona Bar Association. *LANGUAGES:* Spanish, English, Catalan and French. *PRACTICE AREAS:* International Financial Law; Administrative Law.

SILVA & RIBA, ABOGADOS

ARAGÓN, 284 BIS, 6° 2A
08007 BARCELONA, SPAIN
Telephone: (34-3) 487.59.83
Telefax: (34-3) 487.44.89

General Practice on national and international level, Corporate Law, Government, Business Law, Civil Law, Labour Law, Administrative Law, Tax Law, Tax Crimes, Suspension of Payments, Bankruptcies and Litigation.

MEMBERS OF FIRM

MANUEL J. SILVA SÁNCHEZ, born Piedrahita (Avila), Spain, December 30, 1960; admitted, 1991, Barcelona. *Education:* Autonomous University of Barcelona, School of Law (summa cum laude, 1982). State Attorney on leave ("Abogado del Estado excedente"). Chief of Legal Department, Spanish State in Barcelona, 1985-1992. Member, Executive Board, SEFES. Author: "El Proceso Contencioso Tributario", published by Marcial Pons, Madrid 1992; also various articles in newspapers and magazines as "La Ley"; "Gaceta Fiscal"; "Impuestos"; "Cinco Dias"; "El País". *Member:* Barcelona Bar Association. *LANGUAGES:* English, Spanish and Catalan. *PRACTICE AREAS:* Administrative Law; Government; Taxation; Economic Crimes; Tax Crimes.

JOSÉ RIBA VIDAL, born Sabadell, Spain, December 21, 1958; admitted, 1984, Barcelona. *Education:* Autonomous University of Barcelona, School of Law (summa cum laude, 1982). Attorney, Spanish Navy, 1983-1988. Assistant Professor, Corporate Law, Autonomous University of Barcelona, School of Law, 1984-1985. Assistant Professor, Process Law, University of Pompeu Fabra, School of Law, Barcelona, 1992. *Member:* Barcelona Bar Association. *LANGUAGES:* English, Spanish and Catalan. *PRACTICE AREAS:* Bankruptcy; Insolvency; Business Law; Corporate Law; Banking and Finance; Mergers, Acquisitions and Divestitures; Litigation.

ASSOCIATES

JAN WILLEM DE HAAN, born Haarlem, The Netherlands, June 5, 1960; admitted, 1988, Utrecht; 1989, Amsterdam; 1991, Madrid; 1992, Barcelona. *Education:* University of Amsterdam School of Law (J.D., 1986). *Member:* Amsterdam, Madrid and Barcelona Bar Associations. *LANGUAGES:* English, Dutch, German, French and Spanish. *PRACTICE AREAS:* International Business; International Commercial Law; Corporate Law; Bankruptcy; Insolvency; Agency and Distributorships; Mergers, Acquisitions and Divestitures; Debt Recovery.

CARLOS MENÉNDEZ MARTÍNEZ, born Barcelona, Spain, January 3, 1966; admitted, 1989, Barcelona. *Education:* Central University of Barcelona, School of Law (1989). *Member:* Barcelona Bar Association. *LANGUAGES:* English, Spanish and Catalan. *PRACTICE AREAS:* Administrative Law; Municipal Law; Governmental; Subsidies and State Aids; Environmental.

JUAN JOSÉ BURGOS-BOSCH ORTEGA, born Barcelona. Spain, June 22, 1966; admitted, 1991, Barcelona. *Education:* Abad Oliba College; Central University of Barcelona, School of Law (1990) Central University of Barcelona (Master Program for Corporate Lawyers, with merit, 1991). *Member:* Barcelona Bar Association. *LANGUAGES:* English, Spanish and Catalan. *PRACTICE AREAS:* Administrative Law; Tax Law; Tax Crimes; Tax Litigation.

ANNA LLOBET MONCLÚS, born Barcelona, Spain, March 19, 1967; admitted, 1991, Barcelona. *Education:* Autonomous University of Barcelona, School of Law (1991); School of Legal Practice of Barcelona Bar (1993); Central University of Barcelona (preparing Ph.D. on Civil Law). *Member:* Barcelona Bar Association. *LANGUAGES:* English, Spanish and Catalan. *PRACTICE AREAS:* Civil Law; Civil Litigation; Commercial Litigation.

RAMÓN MOLÍAS SENTÍS, born Reus, Spain, October 5, 1967; admitted, 1993, Barcelona. *Education:* Autonomous University of Barcelona, School of Law (1990). *Member:* Barcelona Bar Association. *LANGUAGES:* English, Spanish and Catalan. *PRACTICE AREAS:* Commercial Contracts; Corporate Law; Debt Recovery; Agency and Distributorships.

FRANCISCO HERNANDEZ DE URQUIA, born Barcelona, Spain, February 26, 1967; admitted, 1991, Barcelona. *Education:* Abad Oliba College; Central University of Barcelona School of Law (1991); School of Legal Practice of Barcelona Bar (1992); Master in International Commerce and Law (1994). *Member:* Barcelona Bar Association. *LANGUAGES:* English,

(This Listing Continued)

SILVA & RIBA, ABOGADOS, Barcelona—Continued

Spanish, French and Catalan. **PRACTICE AREAS:** International Business; Commercial Litigation; European Community Law; Labour Law.

SUSANA ROMÁN ABRIL, born Granada, Spain, November 20, 1969; admitted, 1993, Barcelona. *Education:* Central University of Barcelona, School of Law (1992). *Member:* Barcelona Bar Association. **LANGUAGES:** French, Spanish and Catalan. **PRACTICE AREAS:** Products Liability; Company Commercial Law; Debtor and Creditor Collections..

URÍA & MENÉNDEZ

Established in 1941

DIAGONAL, 514
08036 BARCELONA, SPAIN
Telephone: 415.50.05.
Fax: 415.90.61; 415.94.49

Madrid, Spain Office: Hermosilla, 30, 28001. Telephone: 586.04.00. Telex: 48141 URME E. Fax: 586.04.04/03.
Brussels, Belgium Office: Rue Bréderode 13A, 1000. Telephone: 505.02.11. Fax: 502.26.44.
New York, New York Office: 712 Fifth Avenue, 30th Floor, 10019. Telephone: 801-3460. Fax: 801-3465.
London, England Office: Royex House, Aldermanbury Square, EC2V 7HR. Telephone: (44) 171 600.36.10. Fax: (44) 171 600.17.18.
Prague, Czech Republic Office: Branická, 28, CZ 120 00 Prague 2. Telephone: 20.70.50. Fax: 25.42.23.

Commercial, Corporate, Banking and Financing, Foreign Investment, Transfer of Technology, Admiralty, Insurance, European Communities, Litigation, General Practice, Environmental Law.
Member of Alliance of European Lawyers (EEIG) which regroups six law firms from Continental Europe. The Alliance consists of De Bandt, van Hecke & Lagae at Brussels and Antwerp; De Brauw Blackstone Westbroek at The Hague, Amsterdam, Rotterdam and Eindhoven; Jeantet & Associés at Paris and Warsaw; Lagerlöf & Leman at Stockholm, Gothenburg and Malmö; Oppenhoff & Rädler at Berlin, Cologne, Frankfurt am Main, Leipzig and Münich; Uria & Menendez at Madrid and Barcelona.

RESIDENT MEMBERS OF FIRM

LUIS DE CARLOS BERTRAN, born 1960; admitted, 1983. Professor of Banking and Securities Law, Universidad Comillas-ICADE. **LANGUAGES:** English and French.

CARLOS VILADÁS JENE, born 1952; admitted, 1976. *Education:* University of Barcelona (Doctor of Law, 1980); Stanford Law School (Vis. Sch., 1982). Lecturer, 1984—, University of Barcelona. Associate Dean for Studies Programs, Instituto de Criminología, University of Barcelona, 1983—. **LANGUAGES:** English and French.

IGNACIO ALBIÑANA CILVETI, born 1961; admitted, 1984, Madrid; 1987, Barcelona. **LANGUAGES:** English.

ASSOCIATES

ALBERTO NUÑEZ-LAGOS BURGUERA, born 1964; admitted, 1987. **LANGUAGES:** English, German and French.

EDUARDO GELI FERNANDEZ-PEÑAFLOR, born 1964; admitted, 1988. **LANGUAGES:** English.

MIGUEL ANGEL MARTÍNEZ CONDE, born 1964; admitted, 1989. **LANGUAGES:** English and French.

MARIONA XICOY CRUELLS, born 1965; admitted, 1989. **LANGUAGES:** French.

JAVIER VALLE ZAYAS, born 1965; admitted, 1990. Lecturer of Commercial Law, University of Barcelona. **LANGUAGES:** English and French.

ELENA UBEDA HERNANDEZ, born 1966; admitted, 1990. *Education:* LL.M. (London School of Economics and Political Science). **LANGUAGES:** English and French.

ARIADNA CAMBRONERO GINES, born 1967; admitted, 1990. **LANGUAGES:** English.

CARMEN BIGATA VISCASILLAS, born 1967; admitted, 1991. *Education:* London School of Economics (LL.M.). **LANGUAGES:** English and French.

(This Listing Continued)

JUAN ANTONIO FERNANDEZ-VELILLA HERNANDEZ, born 1962; admitted, 1988. **LANGUAGES:** English and French.

JAVIER AMANTEGUI LORENZO, born 1965; admitted, 1992. *Education:* Master in Legal Business (Instituto de Empresa, Madrid). **LANGUAGES:** English and French.

JORDI CASAS THIO, born 1969; admitted, 1993. *Education:* Master in EEC Law (ULB). **LANGUAGES:** English and French.

CORAL CASTAÑE MAGNO, born 1968; admitted, 1994. *Education:* Master of European Law (Institute des Etudes Europées, ULB). **LANGUAGES:** English and French.

JOAN ROCA SAGARRA, born 1969; admitted, 1992. *Education:* LL.M. (Yale University). **LANGUAGES:** English and French.

MARIO IBAÑEZ LOPEZ, born 1969; admitted, 1992. *Education:* Master in Company Law, University Pompeu-Fabra (Barcelona). **LANGUAGES:** English, French and Italian.

OF COUNSEL

RAMÓN VILADÁS MONSONÍS, born 1921; admitted, 1946. Conseiller Juridique, Paris, 1958-1964.

(For list of Partners and Counsel of the respective Member Firms of The Alliance of European Lawyers see Professional Biographies of: Oppenhoff & Rädler at Munich, Cologne, Frankfurt a/Main and Berlin, Germany; De Bandt van Hecke & Lagae at Brussels, Belgium; De Brauw Blackstone Westbroek at The Hague, Rotterdam and Amsterdam, The Netherlands; Jeantet & Associés at Paris and Strasbourg, France and Abidjan, Ivory Coast; Lagerlöf & Leman at Stockholm, Malmö and Göthenburg, Sweden, London, England, Paris, France, Berlin, Germany and New York, New York; Uria & Menendez at Madrid and Barcelona, Spain).

ARTHUR ANDERSEN
ASESORES LEGALES Y TRIBUTARIOS

Legal and Tax Advisors

RODRÍGUEZ ARIAS, 15
48008 BILBAO, SPAIN
Telephone: 34-4-447 7000
Fax: 34-4-444 7998

Arthur Andersen Asesores Legales y Tributarios's offices: Alicante, Barcelona, Bilbao, Granada, La Coruña, Madrid, Málaga, Oviedo, Palma de Mallorca, San Sebastian, Sevilla, Valencia, Vigo, Vitoria, Zaragoza.
Associated Law Firms abroad: France, Italy, Germany, Portugal, The Netherlands, Belgium, United Kingdom, South Africa, Colombia and Brazil.

PARTNER

ANA MARÍA ARMESTO, born Bilbao, Spain, February 7, 1956; admitted, 1987, Bilbao; 1991, Madrid. *Education:* University of Deusto (Law Degree, 1978). *Member:* Bilbao and Madrid Bar Associations. **LANGUAGES:** Spanish, English and French.

ASSOCIATES

VÍCTOR ECHEVARRÍA, born Bilbao, Spain, March 17, 1961; admitted, 1991, Madrid. *Education:* University of Deusto (Law Degree, 1984); Escuela de Administración Marítima (Course, Maritime Law, 1985). *Member:* Madrid Bar Association. **LANGUAGES:** Spanish and English.

ANTONIO REGO, born Baracaldo, Vizcaya, Spain, March 26, 1962; admitted, 1990, Bilbao. *Education:* University of Deusto (Law Degree, 1985). Lecturer, Master in Taxation (University of Deusto). *Member:* Bilbao Bar Association. **LANGUAGES:** Spanish and English.

SABINA HERNÁNDEZ, born Madrid, Spain, January 10, 1962; admitted, 1988, Bilbao. *Education:* University of Navarra (Law Degree, 1989). *Member:* Bilbao Bar Association. **LANGUAGES:** Spanish and English.

BEGOÑA DE FRUTOS, born Bilbao, Spain, April 25, 1966; admitted, 1992, Bilboa. *Education:* University of Deusto - Bilbao (Law Degree, 1989).

(This Listing Continued)

Master Spanish System, 1990. *Member:* Vizcaya Bar Association. *LANGUAGES:* Spanish and English.

OTHER ASSOCIATES

Iñaki Núñez	Alfonso Peña
Daniel Armesto	Verónica Lópezde Aragón
José Antonio Olivera	José Maria Ruiz Ilundáin
Alex García	

(For Complete Firm Profile, see data at Madrid, Spain)

BUFETE BARRILERO & ASOCIADOS

ALAMEDA DE URQUIJO, N°12, ENTREPLANTA IZDA
48008 BILBAO, SPAIN
Telephone: 34-4-416.55.00
Fax: 34-4-416.84.37

Madrid, Spain Office: Ortega y Gasset, n° 30 - Bajo, 28006. Telephone: 576.34.24. Fax: 575.75.17.

Taxation, Commercial, Corporation, Civil, Banking, Bankruptcy, Administrative, EEC and International Law, General Practice.

MEMBERS OF FIRM

EDUARDO BARRILERO, born Madrid, Spain, October 6, 1957. *Education:* University of Deusto, Bilbao (Law Degree, 1979). *Member:* Basque Country Bar Association. *LANGUAGES:* English.

JULIO LECANDA, born Guecho, Spain, February 29, 1960. *Education:* University of Deusto, Bilbao (Law Degree, 1982). *Member:* Basque Country Bar Association. *LANGUAGES:* English.

ANTONIO TENA, born Bilbao, Spain, December 17, 1959. *Education:* University of Deusto, Bilbao (Law Degree; Diploma in Economics, 1982). *Member:* Basque Country Bar Association. *LANGUAGES:* English.

MARGARITA BIDEGORRI, born Guecho, Spain, February 27, 1962. *Education:* University of Deusto, Bilbao (Law Degree, 1985). *Member:* Basque Country Bar Association. *LANGUAGES:* English.

ALBERTO FERREIRO, born Bilbao, Spain, September 1, 1961. *Education:* University of Deusto, Bilbao (Law Degree; Diploma in Economics, 1984). *Member:* Basque Country Bar Association. *LANGUAGES:* English.

RESIDENT ASSOCIATES

INES IDIGORAS, born Bilbao, Spain, May 13, 1963. *Education:* University of Deusto, Bilbao (Law Degree, Diploma in Economics, 1986); College of Europe-Bruges (Diploma on Advanced European Studies, 1987). *Member:* Basque Country Bar Association. *LANGUAGES:* English and French.

JAVIER GONZALEZ YABAR, born Bilbao, Spain, September 22, 1965. *Education:* University of Deusto, Bilbao (Law Degree, 1988). *Member:* Basque Country Bar Association. *LANGUAGES:* English and Bisque.

GONZALO GRIJELMO, born Bilbao, Spain, September 8, 1964. *Education:* University of Deusto, Bilbao (Law Degree, 1988). *Member:* Basque Country Bar Association. *LANGUAGES:* English and French.

FERNANDO LAFITA, born Bilbao, Spain, August 10, 1965. *Education:* University of Deusto, Bilbao (Law Degree, 1990). *Member:* Basque Country Bar Association. *LANGUAGES:* English.

BEATRIZ CASTELAR, born Bilbao, Spain, March 16, 1967. *Education:* University of Deusto, Bilbao (Law Degree, 1989). *Member:* Basque Country Bar Association. *LANGUAGES:* English.

MARIO MONSMA, born Valencia, Spain, July 24, 1965. *Education:* University of Deusto, Bilbao (Law Degree, Diploma in Economics, 1989; Master in Business Legal Advising, 1990). *Member:* Basque Country Bar Association. *LANGUAGES:* English.

FRANCISCO MONTERO, born Bilbao, Spain, June 27, 1967. *Education:* University of Deusto, Bilbao (Law Degree, 1991; Diploma in Tax Advising, 1992). *Member:* Basque Country Bar Association. *LANGUAGES:* English.

JAVIER SAENZ-CORTABARRIA, born Bilbao, Spain, April 19, 1966. *Education:* University of Deusto, Bilbao (Law Degree, 1989). *Member:* Basque Country Bar Association. *LANGUAGES:* English.

CARLOS ARANGUREN, born Madrid, Spain, February 21, 1968. *Education:* Complutense University, Madrid (Law Degree, 1991); University of

(This Listing Continued)

Navarra (Master in Business Law, 1992). *Member:* Basque Country Bar Association. *LANGUAGES:* English.

OLATZ IMAZ, born Olaberría, (Guipuzcoa), Spain, August 23, 1966. *Education:* University of Valencia (Law Degree, 1989). *Member:* Basque Country Bar Association. *LANGUAGES:* English, French and Basque.

MIGUEL ETCHART, born Bilbao, Spain, November 11, 1968. *Education:* University of Deusto, Bilbao (Law Degree, 1991). *Member:* Basque Country Bar Association. *LANGUAGES:* English.

IDOIA INGRID BENGOA, born Bilbao, Spain, March 23, 1970. *Education:* University of Deusto, Bilbao (Law Degree; Diploma in Economics, 1993). *Member:* Basque Country Bar Association. *LANGUAGES:* English, German and French.

ALEX LINACISORO, born Bilbao, Spain, April 12, 1967. *Education:* University of Deusto, Bilbao (Law Degree, 1991). *Member:* Basque Country Bar Association. *LANGUAGES:* English.

Mª JOSE PAREDES, born Bilbao, Spain, February 9, 1970. *Education:* University of Deusto, Bilbao (Law Degree, diploma in Economics, 1993); Business Institute, Madrid (Master in Business Legal Advising, 1994). *Member:* Basque Country Bar Association. *LANGUAGES:* English, French.

RODRIGO HERVAS, born Bilbao, Spain, August 26, 1968. *Education:* University of Deusto, Bilbao (Law Degree, Diploma in Economics, 1991; Master in Tax Advising, 1994). *Member:* Basque Country Bar Association. *LANGUAGES:* English, French.

PEDRO BROSA & ASOCIADOS

SAN VICENTE, 8, PLTA 9°, DPTO. 2 EDIFICIO ALBIA I
48001 BILBAO, SPAIN
Telephone: 34-4-423 03 36
Telefax: 34-4-423 93 82

Barcelona, Spain Office: Avda. Diagonal, 598. 1° 2°, Pral, 2° y 5° 2°, 08021. Telephone: 34-3-200 09 33. Telefax: 34-3-202 29 07.
Madrid, Spain Office: Alfonso XII, 18, 3° Izqda., 28014. Telephone: 34-1-522 82 02. Telefax: 34-1-522-39-89.
Brussels, Belgium Office: 165, Avenue Louise, 9 ème. étage, 1050. Telephone: 32-2-644 16 09. Telefax: 32-2-344 30 25.

General Practice, Civil Litigation, Civil, Commercial, Corporation, Intellectual Property, Taxation, Foreign Investments, Administrative, Banking and Financing, Bankruptcy Law, Accounting, Auditing and General Business Consulting.

MEMBERS OF FIRM

PEDRO BROSA, born Lérida, Spain, May 30, 1937; admitted, 1964, Barcelona. *Education:* University of Barcelona (Licenciado en Derecho, 1959; Profesor Mercantil, 1960). Lecturer, Taxation Law, University of Barcelona, 1962-1963. *Member:* Barcelona (Member Governing Body) and Madrid Bar Associations; Colegio de Titulares Mercantiles de Barcelona; Fomento del Trabajo Nacional (Member, Advisory Committee); English Chamber of Commerce in Spain. *LANGUAGES:* Spanish, English, French and Catalan. *PRACTICE AREAS:* General Practice; Commercial; Corporation; Banking and Financing; Bankruptcy law; General Business Consulting.

CARLOS SAHUQUILLO, born Barcelona, Spain, May 10, 1958; admitted, 1982, Barcelona. *Education:* University of Barcelona (Licenciado en Ciencias Económicas y Empresariales, 1981; Licenciado en Derecho, 1982); Cátedra Durán y Bas (Diploma en Estudios de Derecho Civil Catalán, 1982). *Member:* Barcelona and American Bar Associations; International Bar Association; Colegio de Economistas de Catalunya; Instituto de Censores Jurados de Cuentas de España; Asociación Española de Contabilidad y Administración de Empresas; Registro de Economistas Auditores; Registro Oficial de Auditores de Cuentas; International Tax Planning Association. *LANGUAGES:* Spanish, English, French and Catalan. *PRACTICE AREAS:* General Practice; Commercial; Corporation; Foreign Investments; Banking and Financing; General Business Consulting.

ALMUDENA ORTIZ, born Madrid, Spain, May 31, 1960; admitted, 1983, Madrid. *Education:* University of Madrid (Licenciada en Derecho, 1983); University of Brussels, Institute of European Studies (LL.M. in Eu-

(This Listing Continued)

PEDRO BROSA & ASOCIADOS, Bilbao—Continued

ropean Law, 1985). *LANGUAGES:* English and Spanish. *PRACTICE AREAS:* Commercial Law; Civil Law.

(For Biographical Data of the Madrid and Barcelona, Spain and Brussels, Belgium Personnel, see Professional Biographies at Madrid, Barcelona, Spain and Brussels, Belgium).

CERVELLÓ, LÓPEZ-CHICHERI Y ARAGÓN, ABOGADOS

Associated with Ernst & Young International

COLÓN DE LARREÁTEGUI, 26
48009 BILBAO, SPAIN
Telephone: (34-4) 424-3777/423-8746
Fax: (34-4) 424-2745

Madrid, Spain Office: Torre Picasso - Planta 3, Plaza Pablo Ruiz Picasso, s/n, 28020. Telephone: (34-1) 572-7200. Fax: (34-1) 572-7400/7372.
Barcelona, Spain Office: L'Illa Diagonal, 575; 08029. Telephone: (34-3) 410.67.07. Fax: (34-3) 405.37.84.

General, Commercial and International Practice.

Sabiniano Medrano Irazola

BUFETE CUATRECASAS

ALAMEDA DE MAZARREDO, 5
48001 BILBAO, SPAIN
Telephone: 424.82.67
Fax: 424.82.34

Barcelona, Spain Office: Balmes 76. Telephone: 290.55.00. Fax: 290.55.67.
Madrid, Spain Office: Antonio Maura 10. Telephone: 521.94.47. Fax: 522.48.99.
Gerona, Spain Office: Ronda Ferrán Puig, 406. Telephone: 22.71.02. Fax: 22.66.61.
Brussels, Belgium Office: 78 Avenue d'Auderghem. Telephone: 735.06.43. Fax: 734.72.34.

All areas of Spanish and EEC business law, including corporate, commercial, taxation, foreign investments, capital markets, finance, regulatory including environmental law, labour law, intellectual property including software licensing and protection, anti-trust law, litigation, criminal law, bankruptcy law and company restructuring.

MEMBERS OF FIRM

PEDRO CUATRECASAS, born Barcelona, Spain, May 28, 1928; admitted, 1952, Barcelona. *Education:* University of Barcelona (Law Degree, 1952). *Member:* Barcelona Bar Association; Spanish Association of Tax Advisors. (Also at Barcelona and Madrid Offices). *LANGUAGES:* French.

EMILIO CUATRECASAS, born Barcelona, Spain, January 12, 1954; admitted, 1977, Barcelona; 1984, Bilbao. *Education:* University of Navarra (Law Degree, 1976); Abad Oliba College (Diplom in International Law). *Member:* Barcelona Bar Association; Bilbao Bar Association; Madrid Bar Association; Association for Development of Industry; IBA. (Also at Barcelona and Madrid Offices). *LANGUAGES:* French and English.

ANTÓN PÉREZ DE IRIONDO, born Bilbao, Spain, July 26, 1956; admitted, 1991. *Education:* University of Deusto (Law Degree, 1977). *Member:* State Financial and Tax Inspectors. *LANGUAGES:* French.

RESIDENT ASSOCIATES

LUIS ALBA, born Bilbao, Spain, September 30, 1962; admitted, 1991, Bilbao. *Education:* University of Deusto (Law Degree, 1989); Diplomed in Marlleg London. *Member:* Bilbao Bar Association. *LANGUAGES:* English.

IGNACIO ALLENDE, born Bilbao, Spain, September 30, 1962; admitted, 1991, Bilbao. *Education:* University of Deusto (Law Degree, 1986); Master in Business Legal Advice. *Member:* Bilbao Bar Association. *LANGUAGES:* English.

FRANCISCO AZPIRI, born Bilbao, Spain, June 1, 1965; admitted, 1992. *Education:* University of Deusto (Law Degree, 1989), (Business Science Diploma, 1989); Business Institute of Madrid (Master, Tax Advising,

(This Listing Continued)

1990). *Member:* Bilbao Bar Association. *LANGUAGES:* English and French.

DIEGO BILBAO, born Bilbao, Spain, June 20, 1964. *Education:* University of Deusto, Bilbao, (Law Degree, 1987); Business Institute (Master of Business Law, 1988). *Member:* Bilbao Bar Association. *LANGUAGES:* English.

JAVIER CHALBAUD, born Caracas, Venezuela, May 29, 1948; admitted, 1978, Spain. *Education:* University of Deusto, Bilbao (Law Degree, 1977). *Member:* Bilbao Bar Association. *LANGUAGES:* English.

IGNACIO GARCÍA, born Las Arena, Spain, July 31, 1959; admitted, 1989, Bilbao. *Education:* University of Deusto, Bilbao (Law Degree, 1985); Master of Taxation of the Center of Financial Studies of Madrid, Degree in Corporate Tax. *Member:* Bilbao Bar Association. *LANGUAGES:* English and French.

RAFAEL HERRERA, born Bilbao, Spain, December 29, 1964; admitted, 1992. *Education:* University of Deusto (Law Degree, 1989); Business Institute of Madrid (Master, Tax Advising). *Member:* Bilbao Bar Association. *LANGUAGES:* English.

JUAN IZAGUIRRE, born Bilbao, Spain, February 28, 1959; admitted, 1984, Spain. *Education:* University of Deusto, Bilbao (Law Degree, 1984). *Member:* Bilbao Bar Association. *LANGUAGES:* French and English.

AMAYA LATORRE, born Bilbao, Spain, April 5, 1965; admitted, 1990, Spain. *Education:* University of Deusto, Bilbao (Law Degree; Diploma in Economics, 1988). *Member:* Bilbao Bar Association. *LANGUAGES:* English.

JOSE CARLOS LOUREDA, born Barakaldo (Vizcaya), Spain, August 9, 1967; admitted, 1992. *Education:* University of Deusto (Bilbao) (Law Degree, 1990). *Member:* Bilbao Bar Association. *LANGUAGES:* English.

JOSE MARIA MENDIETA, born Bilbao, Spain, October 14, 1960; admitted, 1985, Bilbao. *Education:* University of Deusto, Bilbao (Law Degree; Diploma in Economics, 1982). Assistant Professor in Tax Law, University of Deusto. *Member:* Bilbao Bar Association. *LANGUAGES:* English.

IÑIGO QUINTANA, born Bilbao, Spain, March 25, 1962; admitted, 1987, Bilbao. *Education:* University of Deusto (Law Degree; Economics and Business, 1987). *Member:* Vizcaya Bar Association. *LANGUAGES:* French and English.

AITOR SOLOETA, born Bilbao, Spain, March 25, 1964; admitted, 1990, Spain. *Education:* University of Deusto, Bilbao (Law Degree; Diploma in Economics, 1987). *Member:* Bilbao Bar Association. *LANGUAGES:* English.

(For complete biographical data on personnel at Barcelona, Madrid and Gerona, Spain and Brussels, Belgium, see Professional Biographies at those locations)

GOMEZ-ACEBO & POMBO

GRAN VÍA, 31
48009 BILBAO, SPAIN
Telephone: (344) 415-62-66; 415-62-77
Fax: (344) 416-87-49

Madrid, Spain Office: Castellana, 164, 28046. Telephone: (341) 582 91 00. Fax: (341) 345 36 79; 582 91 14. Cable: Juristas. Telex: 23429 GAPO E.
Barcelona, Spain Office: Diagonal 442, 08037. Telephone: (343) 415-74-00. Fax: (343) 415-84-00.
Las Palmas (Canary Islands), Spain Office: Viera y Clavijo, 48, 35002. Telephone: (342) 838-38-36. Fax: (342) 838-38-56.
Santiago de Compostela, Spain Office: Casas Reales, 4, 15704. Telephone: (348) 157-33-46. Fax: (348) 157-35-46.
Seville, Spain Office: Av. de la Constitución, 40, 41001. Telephone: (345) 421-66-59; 422-18-93. Fax: (345) 421-08-14.
Valencia, Spain Office: Gran Vía Marqués del Turia, 49, 46005. Telephone: (346) 351-38-35. Fax: (346) 351-60-74.
Brussels, Belgium Office: Rue de la Loi, 99/101, 1040. Telephone: (322) 231-12-20. Fax: (322) 230-80-35.

Joaquin Lopez Ante
Josu Larrauri
(This Listing Continued)

Miren Arbulu
Jesus Gonzalez

(For Complete Biographical Data on all Personnel, see Professional
Biographies at Madrid, Spain).

RAMOS & ARROYO

AVENIDA RAMÓN DE CARRANZA, 20

11006 CADIZ, SPAIN

Telephone: (56) 25 22 00

Fax: (56) 26 16 55

Telex: 76192 Hull E

Barcelona, Spain Office: Paseo de Gracia 92 (La Pedrera), 08008.
Telephone: (3) 487 11 12; (3) 215 77 11. Fax: (3) 487 35 62.

Fuengirola, Málaga, Spain Office: Córdoba, Edificio Centro Comercial
Reyes, 6°B, 29640. Telephone: (5) 258 45 72; (5) 258 45 90. Fax: (5)
258 45 72.

Madrid, Spain Office: Serrano 89-7°, 28006. Telephone: (1) 5629200. Fax:
(1) 561 49 03.

Oviedo, Spain Office: Cimadevilla 19-2°B, 33003. Telephone: (8) 520 42
80. Fax: (8) 520 42 80.

*Admiralty, Arbitration, Bankruptcy, Commercial, Competition, Construc-
tion, Copyright, Corporation, EEC, General Practice, Insurance, Labour,
Litigation, Taxation, Trademarks & Patents and Real Estate Law.*

MEMBERS OF FIRM

JOSE LUIS RODRIGUEZ CARRION, born Almeria, Spain, 1936;
admitted, 1960, Cadiz. *Education:* University of Seville (Master Marine,
LL.B.); University of Barcelona (Doctor of Laws, cum laude). Professor of
Commercial Law, University of Cadiz. Spanish Delegate UNCTAD &
IMO. *Member:* Cadiz, Jerez, Huelva and Jaen Bar Associations.

MARIA VICTORIA ORDOÑEZ ANDREY, born Cadiz, Spain, 1963;
admitted, 1987, Cadiz. *Education:* University of Cadiz. *Member:* Cadiz Bar
Association.

(For complete biographical data on all personnel, see Professional
Biographies at Barcelona, Spain).

ADECO ABOGADOS

Established in 1988

BOULEVARD 3 - 1° - D

20003 DONOSTIA-SAN SEBASTIAN, SPAIN

Telephone: 34-(43)-42.67.44

Fax: 34-(43)-43.06.37

*Private International Law, European Community Law, Business Law,
General International Trade Law, Tax Law, Civil and Commercial Litigation.*

FIRM PROFILE: *The firm was established in 1988 and offers a full
range of legal services. Our law office is known in the region to be dedicated exclusively to International, European and Comparative Law.*

MEMBERS OF FIRM

JON ETXABE JAUREGI, born Zumaia, Gipuzkoa, Spain, January 3,
1959; admitted, 1986, Spain. *Education:* University of the Basque Country,
1984; University of Louvain, Belgium (Licence in European Law, 1986);
Free University of Brussels, Belgium (Post Graduate Master in International and Comparative Law, 1987). Lecturer in Law in the Business Administration Faculty, University of Deusto in Donostia-San Sebastian.
LANGUAGES: Spanish, Basque, French and English. *PRACTICE
AREAS:* European Community Law; International Law; Litigation.

ELISABETH LAGARDE NOULENS, born Mirande, Gers, France,
August 5, 1957; admitted, 1987, Spain. *Education:* University of Bordeaux,
France, 1981; (Post Graduate Studies in Business and Tax Law, 1983).
LANGUAGES: Spanish, French and English. *PRACTICE AREAS:* Tax
Law; International Litigation; Trade Law.

RAMOS & ARROYO

CÓRDOBA, EDIFICIO CENTRO COMERCIAL REYES, 6°B

29640 FUENGIROLA, MALAGA, SPAIN

Telephone: (5) 258 45 72; (5) 258 45 90

Fax: (5) 258 45 72

Barcelona, Spain Office: Paseo de Gracia 92 (La Pedrera), 08008.
Telephone: (3) 487 11 12; (3) 215 77 11. Fax: (3) 487 35 62.

Cadiz, Spain Office: Avenida Ramón de Carranza, 20, 11006. Telephone:
(56) 25 22 00. Fax: (56) 26 16 55. Telex: 76192 Hull E.

Madrid, Spain Office: Serrano 89-7°, 28006. Telephone: (1) 5629200. Fax:
(1) 561 49 03.

Oviedo, Spain Office: Cimadevilla 19-2°B, 33003. Telephone: (8) 520 42
80. Fax: (8) 520 42 80.

*Admiralty, Arbitration, Bankruptcy, Commercial, Competition, Construc-
tion, Copyright, Corporation, EEC, General Practice, Insurance, Labour,
Litigation, Taxation, Trademarks & Patents and Real Estate Law.*

MEMBERS OF FIRM

JOSE-MARIA SAEZ SAEZ, born Avila, Spain, November 14, 1957;
admitted, 1986, Malaga. *Education:* University of Salamanca (1985). *LAN-
GUAGES:* Spanish and English.

MARIA-ANGELES VALLE ALARCON, born Málaga, Spain, August
30, 1965; admitted, 1989, Malaga. *Education:* University of Málaga (1988).
LANGUAGES: Spanish, English and French.

(For complete biographical data on all personnel, see Professional
Biographies at Barcelona, Spain).

BUFETE CUATRECASAS

RONDA FERRAN PUIG, 4-6

17001 GERONA, SPAIN

Telephone: 22.71.02

Fax: 22.66.61

Barcelona, Spain Office: Balmes 76. Telephone: 290.55.00. Fax:
290.55.67.

Madrid, Spain Office: Antonio Maura 10. Telephone: 521.94.47. Fax:
522.48.99.

Bilbao, Spain Office: Alameda de Mazarredo 5. Telephone 424.82.67.
Fax: 424.82.34.

Brussels, Belgium Office: 78 Avenue d'Auderghem. Telephone: 735.06.43.
Fax: 734.72.34.

*All areas of Spanish and EEC business law, including corporate, commer-
cial, taxation, foreign investments, capital markets, finance, regulatory
including environmental law, labour law, intellectual property including
software licensing and protection, anti-trust law, litigation, criminal law,
bankruptcy law and company restructuring.*

MEMBERS OF FIRM

PEDRO CUATRECASAS, born Barcelona, Spain, May 28, 1928; admitted, 1952, Barcelona. *Education:* University of Barcelona (Law Degree,
1952). *Member:* Barcelona Bar Association; Spanish Association of Taxation Experts. (Also at Barcelona, Madrid and Bilbao Offices). *LAN-
GUAGES:* French.

EMILIO CUATRECASAS, born Barcelona, Spain, January 12, 1954;
admitted, 1977, Barcelona; 1984, Bilbao. *Education:* University of Navarra
(Law Degree, 1976); Abad Oliba College (Diploma in International Law).
Member: Barcelona Bar Association; Bilbao Bar Association; Madrid Bar
Association; Association for Development of Industry; IBA. (Also at Bar-
celona, Madrid and Bilbao Offices). *LANGUAGES:* French and English.

RAFAEL FONTANA, born Barcelona, Spain, March 28, 1954; admitted, 1984, Barcelona. *Education:* University of Barcelona (Law Degree,
1977); Post Graduate Course in Taxation; Professional School of the Barcelona Bar Association, Post Graduate Course in Foreign Investment Law.
Member: Barcelona Bar Association; Spanish Association of Taxation Experts; IFA; IBA. *LANGUAGES:* English and French.

RESIDENT ASSOCIATE

SILVIA ALBERTI, born Barcelona, Spain, March 25, 1963; admitted,
1986, Spain. *Education:* University of Barcelona (Law Degree, 1986). *Member:* Barcelona Bar Association. *LANGUAGES:* English.

(For complete biographical data on personnel at Barcelona, Madrid and
Bilbao, Spain and Brussels, Belgium, see Professional Biographies at
those locations)

EU1233B

ARTHUR ANDERSEN
ASESORES LEGALES Y TRIBUTARIOS

Legal and Tax Advisors

AVENIDA DE LA CONSTITUCIÓN, 22
18012 GRANADA, SPAIN
Telephone: 34-58-288967
Fax: 34-58-289704

Arthur Andersen Asesores Legales y Tributarios's offices: Alicante, Barcelona, Bilbao, Granada, La Coruña, Madrid, Málaga, Oviedo, Palma de Mallorca, San Sebastian, Sevilla, Valencia, Vigo, Vitoria, Zaragoza.

Associated Law Firms abroad: France, Italy, Germany, Portugal, The Netherlands, Belgium, United Kingdom, South Africa, Colombia and Brazil.

PARTNER

DAVID MORENO, born Madrid, Spain, December 4, 1956; admitted, 1989, Seville. *Education:* University of Deusto (Law Degree, 1979); ICADE (Master, Business Administration); Instituto de Empresa (Master, Corporation Taxes Counsel, 1983); Instituto Internacional San Telmo (Graduate, Corporation Management, 1990). Professor, Business Law, University of Seville. Co-Author: "El IVA verde," 1986; "Adaptación de su Empresa a la Reforma Mercantil," 1989. *Member:* Seville Bar Association. *LANGUAGES:* Spanish and English.

RESIDENT ASSOCIATES

FRANCISCO JAVIER MERINO, born Malaga, May 29, 1961. *Education:* University of Granada (Law Degree, 1984). *LANGUAGES:* Spanish and English.

ELENA CAZORLA, born Granada, October 16, 1966. *Education:* University of Granada (Law Degree, 1989). *LANGUAGES:* Spanish and English.

OTHER ASSOCIATES

JUAN BAQUERO

(For Complete Firm Profile, see data at Madrid, Spain)

FERNANDO SCORNIK GERSTEIN

Abogados, Lawyers, Rechtsanwalte, Counsellors at Law

Established in 1978

FRANCHY Y ROCA 5
PLANTA 4, OFICINA 10
035007 LAS PALMAS
GRAN CANARIA, (CANARY ISLANDS), SPAIN
Telephone: (28) 273724; 273728
Fax: (28) 223877

Gran Canaria (Canary Islands-Maspalomas), Playa del Ingles Office: Edificio Mercurio, Torre II, Planta 4B, 35100 Playa del Ingles. Telephone: (928) 762306, 767867. Fax: (928) 766667.

Lanzarote (Canary Islands), Spain Office: Calle Ginés de Castro 12, 3rd Floor, 35500 Arrecife de Lanzarote. Telephone: (928) 815262; 815258. Fax: (928) 814892.

Tenerife (Canary Islands), Spain Office: Edificio Valdes Center, Torre A., Piso 2, Oficina 1, 38650 Los Cristianos, Arona. Telephone: (922) 794412; 750060. Fax: (922) 794208.

Fuerteventura (Canary Islands) Spain Office: Prof. Juan Tadeo Cabrera 10 Piso 1B, 356000 Puerto de Rosario. Telephone: (928) 532 266. Fax: (928) 532 241.

Madrid, Spain Office: Calle Alberto Alcocer, No. 7, 3-Izda. Telephone: (34) 1-3507262. Fax: (34) 1-3507306.

London, England Office: 32 St. James's Street, 3rd Floor, SW1A 1HD. Telephone: (071) 930-3593; 930-0769. Fax: (071) 930-3385.

Buenos Aires, Argentina Office: Avda Corrientes 330, Piso 4, 1378 Buenos Aires, Argentina. Telephone: (541) 311 1273. Fax: (541) 313 5268.

(This Listing Continued)

General Practice, Civil and Commercial, Taxes, Foreign Investments, Banking, Finance, Real Estate, Litigation and Criminal Law, Immigration, Family Law, Probate, Maritime and Intellectual Property.

(For complete Biographical Data on all personnel, see Biographies at Madrid, Spain).

GOMEZ-ACEBO & POMBO

VIERA Y CLAVIJO, 48
LAS PALMAS
35002 GRAN CANARIA, (CANARY ISLANDS), SPAIN
Telephone: (342) 838-38-36
Fax: (342) 838-38-56

Madrid, Spain Office: Castellana, 164, 28046. Telephone: (341) 582 91 00. Fax: (341) 345 36 79; 582 91 14. Cable: Juristas. Telex: 23429 GAPO E.

Barcelona, Spain Office: Diagonal 442, 08037. Telephone: (343) 415-74-00. Fax: (343) 415-84-00.

Bilbao, Spain Office: Gran Vía, 31, 48009. Telephone: (344) 415-62-66/77. Fax: (344) 416-87-49.

Santiago de Compostela, Spain Office: Casas Reales, 4, 15704. Telephone: (348) 157-33-46. Fax: (348) 157-35-46.

Seville, Spain Office: Av. de la Constitución, 40, 41001. Telephone: (345) 421-66-59; 422-18-93. Fax: (345) 421-08-14.

Valencia, Spain Office: Gran Vía Marqués del Turia, 49, 46005. Telephone: (346) 351-38-35. Fax: (346) 351-60-74.

Brussels, Belgium Office: Rue de la Loi, 99/101, 1040. Telephone: (322) 231-12-20. Fax: (322) 230-80-35.

José Miguel Bravo de Laguna
Jose Manuel Melian

(For Complete Biographical Data on all Personnel, see Professional Biographies at Madrid, Spain).

ANDRES TUELLS JUAN
AGUSTIN GOERLICH LOPEZ

Established in 1963

AV. IGNACIO WALLIS, 21, 2°
07800 IBIZA (BALEARIC ISLANDS) SPAIN
Telephone: 34-71-391909
Fax: 34-71-391817

General Practice, Civil, Mercantil and Penal Law, Litigation, Debt Recovery, Family, Wills and Probates, Real Estate Purchase. Administrative, Commercial and Insurance Company Law.

ANDRÉS TUELLS JUAN. *Education:* University of Barcelona (License of Law). *Member:* Balearic Islands and Madrid Bar Associations. *LANGUAGES:* Spanish, Catalán English and French.

AGUSTIN GOERLICH LÓPEZ. *Education:* University of Castilla-La Mancha (License of Laws). *Member:* Balearic Islands Bar Association. *LANGUAGES:* Spanish, Catalán, German and English.

ALBORS, GALIANO & CO.
ABOGADOS

Established in 1990

46 NÚÑEZ DE BALBOA 1ST FLOOR
28001 MADRID, SPAIN
Telephone: 34 1 435 66 17
Fax: 34 1 576 74 23
Telex: 41521 ALBEN

Shipping and Admiralty Law, Aviation, Carriage by road, International and Domestic Commercial Law, Insurance, Arbitration, EC Law, Civil Professional Liability, Labour and General Practice.

FIRM PROFILE: The partners are litigators in the above areas and are admitted in the majority of Spanish Bar Associations. The firm has correspondents throughout Spain.

(This Listing Continued)

PARTNERS

EDUARDO ALBORS, born Valencia, Spain, 1954. *Education:* Faculty of Law, University of Valencia (Specialty in Private Law), 1977; Doctorate Courses, University of Madrid; Master in Maritime Law, University of Madrid, 1980; Master in EC Law, Centre for Constitutional Studies, 1985. Titular Member, International Maritime Committee. *Member:* Spanish Maritime Law Association; Iberoamerican Maritime Law Institute; International Bar Association. *LANGUAGES:* Spanish and English.

JAVIER GALIANO, born Orgaz (Toledo), Spain, 1951. *Education:* Faculty of Law, University of Madrid, 1974; Master in Bankruptcy Law, University of Madrid, 1978; Master in Maritime Law and Master in Tax Law, University of Madrid, 1980; Master in EC Law, University of Madrid, 1988. *Member:* Spanish Maritime Law Association; Iberoamerican Maritime Law Institute. *LANGUAGES:* Spanish and English.

ASSOCIATES

JAVIER PORTALES, born Santander, Spain, 1965. *Education:* Faculty of Law, University of Santander, 1989; European Institute of Maritime Studies, Gijón (Master in Maritime Law, 1990). *LANGUAGES:* Spanish and English.

CARLOS PEREZ, born Algeciras, Spain, 1964. *Education:* Faculty of Law, University of Seville, 1988; Spanish Maritime Institute-ICADE, Madrid (Master in Maritime Law and Maritime Business, 1989). *LANGUAGES:* Spanish and English.

LUIS SOUTO, born La Coruña, Spain, 1967. *Education:* Faculty of Law, University of La Coruña , 1991; European Institute of Maritime Studies, Gijón (Master in Maritime Law, 1992). *LANGUAGES:* Spanish and English.

ALLEN & OVERY

ANTONIO MAURA 7, 6°
28014 MADRID, SPAIN
Telephone: (34 1) 521 2654
Facsimile: (34 1) 523 0458

London, England Office: One New Change, EC4M 9QQ. Telephone: 0171 330 3000. Facsimile: 0171 330 9999.

Beijing, China Office: Suite 3204, Jing Guang Centre, Hu Jia Lou, Chaoyang District, 100020. Telephone: (86 1) 501 4681. Facsimile: (86 1) 501 4682.

Brussels, Belgium Office: Rue de la Loi 99, Box 8, 1040. Telephone: (32 2) 230 27 91. Facsimile (32 2) 230 66 13.

Budapest, Hungary Office: Mádach Trade Center, Mádach Imre utca 13-14, H-1075. Telephone: (361) 268 1511. Facsimile: (361) 268 1515.

Dubai, United Arab Emirates Office: 501 Al Futtaim Tower,P.O. Box 3251, Deira. Telephone: (971 4) 282296. Facsimile: (971 4) 212860.

Frankfurt, Germany Office: Taunusanlage 11, 11th Floor, 60329. Telephone: (49 69) 242 6120. Facsimile: (49 69) 242 61220.

Hong Kong Office: 9th Floor, Three Exchange Square, 8 Connaught Place. Telephone: (852) 2840 1282. Telex: 68757. Facsimile: (852) 2840 0515.

Moscow, Russia Office: 9 ul Tverskaya, Entrance No 5, 8th Floor, 103009. Telephone: (7 501) 940 4500. Facsimile: (7 501) 940 4501.

New York Office: Swiss Bank Tower, 10 East 50th Street, 10022. Telephone (1-212) 754 3340. Facsimile: (1-212) 754 7903.

Paris, France Office: 1 Avenue Franklin D. Roosevelt, 75008. Telephone (33-1) 49 53 06 37. Telex: 651079. Facsimile: (33-1) 49 53 91 52.

Prague, Czech Republic Office: Jindřišská 34, 110 00 Prague 1. Telephone: (42 2) 2410 3317. Facsimile: (42 2) 2410 3235.

Singapore Office: 20 Raffles Place #08-03, Ocean Towers, 0104. Telephone: (65) 533 0988. Facsimile: (65) 533 1322.

Tokyo, Japan Office: NSE Building, 5th Floor, 1-7-1 Kanda Jinbo-cho, Chiyoda-ku Tokyo 101. Telephone (81 3) 3259 9898. Facsimile (81 3) 3259 9888.

Warsaw, Poland Office: ul. Kopernika 17, IV Floor, 00-359. Telephone: (48 22) 262 226. Facsimile: (48 22) 262 360.

Firm engaged in advising on all forms of financing activities and transactions and providing Spanish and English legal assistance on all aspects of cross-border transactions involving Spain.

(This Listing Continued)

CONTACT PARTNERS

Peter F. Schulz (Also at London, England)

RESIDENT ASSOCIATES

Alfonso Lopez-Ibor

(For Complete Biographical Data on all Personnel, see Professional Biographies at London, England)

ESTUDIO JURIDICO ALMAGRO

C/CONSUEGRA N°3
28036 MADRID, SPAIN
Telephone: 383.01.92
Fax: 767.25.61

General Practice. Administrative, Commercial, Company, Contract, EEC, Foreign Investments in Spain, Industrial and Intellectual Property, Labor, Litigation, Local and State Taxes, Mining and Hydrocarbons, Real Estate, Trademarks and Zoning Law.

FIRM PROFILE: Established in 1970, E.J.A. with 11 partners and 14 assistants is now one of the Spain's medium size leading commercial law firms, with high reputation in tax, business and real estate and intellectual property law. E.J.A. is member of the European Law Group, a group of European law firms specializing in transactions involving several European countries.

MEMBERS OF FIRM

JOSE A. DE FRANCISCO BLANCO, born Gijón, Asturias, Spain, August 9, 1940; admitted, 1967, Madrid. *Education:* Auseva College, Marists, Oviedo; Universities of Oviedo and Valencia (Master in Law; Licenciado). *Member:* Madrid Bar Association; Candas Association of Tax Lawyers (Founding Member). *LANGUAGES:* English and French. *PRACTICE AREAS:* Contract-Company and Tax Law.

JOSE ANTONIO BOCCHERINI SANCHEZ, born Madrid, Spain, March 31, 1930; admitted, 1963, Spain. *Education:* El Pilar College; University of Madrid (Master in Law; Licenciado). *Member:* Madrid Bar Association. *LANGUAGES:* English and French. *PRACTICE AREAS:* Real Estate and Contract Law.

JOSE MARIA MARGOLLES LOPEZ, born S. Esteban Pravia, Asturias, March 8, 1939; admitted, 1975, Bilbao; 1979, Madrid. *Education:* Auseva College Marists, Oviedo; University of Rome (Master in Philosophy); University of Frankfurt (Ph.D.); University of Oviedo (Master in Law; Licenciado). Head of Hamburg Immigration Office of Spain at the Spanish Embassy in Germany, 1972-1975. *Member:* Madrid Bar Association; Hispano-German Lawyers Association. *LANGUAGES:* German and Italian. *PRACTICE AREAS:* Zoning and Labor Law.

FERNANDO HERCE MELENDREZ, born La Coruña, Spain, January 26, 1953; admitted, 1975, Spain. *Education:* Chamartin College, Jesuits, Madrid; San Pablo Law School, CEU, Madrid; University of Madrid (Master in Law; Licenciado). *Member:* Madrid Bar Association; Candas Association of Tax Lawyers. *LANGUAGES:* French and English. *PRACTICE AREAS:* Commercial Law; Mergers and Acquisitions.

MARIA PAZ ROMERO MELERO, born Madrid, Spain, December 1, 1953; admitted, 1980, Madrid. *Education:* University of Deusto (Bachelor in Business Administration; Master in Law; Licenciada). *Member:* Madrid Bar Association. *LANGUAGES:* English. *PRACTICE AREAS:* Tax Law.

SANTOS SESEÑA DIEZ, born Madrid, Spain, November 4, 1935; admitted, 1966, Madrid. *Education:* El Pilar College, Madrid; University of Madrid (English and Philosophy Majors); Cornell College, USA (English and Mathematics); University of Madrid (Master in Law; Licenciado). *Member:* Madrid Bar Association; Candas Association of Tax Lawyers. *LANGUAGES:* English, French and Portuguese. *PRACTICE AREAS:* Intellectual Property; Trademark and Tax Law.

CARLOS CASANOVA CABALLERO, born Madrid, Spain, August 26, 1951; admitted, 1976, Madrid. *Education:* St. Estanislao de Kostka College; Deusto University, ICADE (Master in Business Administration; Licenciado; Master in Law; Licenciado). *Member:* Madrid Bar Association; Candas association of Tax Lawyers (Founding Member). *LANGUAGES:* English. *PRACTICE AREAS:* Tax Law.

JOSE IGNACIO OLLEROS IZARD, born Madrid, Spain, March 31, 1961; admitted, 1984, Madrid. *Education:* Chamartin College, Jesuits, Madrid; Universite de Caen (Summer Courses); University of Madrid (Master

(This Listing Continued)

ESTUDIO JURIDICO ALMAGRO, Madrid—Continued

in Law; Licenciado). *Member:* Madrid Bar Association. *LANGUAGES:* English and French. *PRACTICE AREAS:* Company Law; Tax Law.

RAMIRO PEREZ ALVAREZ, born Cortiguera Leon, Spain, May 17, 1964; admitted, 1989, Madrid. *Education:* Instituto Mendana de Ponferrada; University of Leon (Master in Law, 1987). *LANGUAGES:* French. *PRACTICE AREAS:* Litigation and Administrative Law.

ANGEL IGNACIO RIVAS PINO, born Madrid, Spain, November 25, 1963; admitted, 1987, Spain. *Education:* Madrid University (Master in Law, 1987); Instituto de Empresa, Madrid (Master in Business Law, 1989). *LANGUAGES:* English. *PRACTICE AREAS:* Contract and Company Law.

MARTA GOMEZ PEREZ-MANZUCO, born Almería, Spain, July 1968; admitted, 1992, Spain. *Education:* Universidad Pontificia de Comillas, ICADE (Jesuits School of Law). *LANGUAGES:* English and French. *PRACTICE AREAS:* Company and Administrative Law.

Languages: Spanish, English, French, German, Italian and Portuguese.

REPRESENTATIVE CLIENTS: Blue Bell Inc.; Ceselsa; Praxair; Groupe Promodes General Electric Technical Services Co.; Wiggins Teape; International Paper Co.; Terrain IB; Aresbank; Loctite; Alfa Laval; Courage; Peat Marwick; Mitchell Co.; British Council; British Steel; Eagle Star; Florimex; Tupperware; Tberfomento; British American Tobacco; Vanity Fair; Groupo Prisa (El Pais); Groupo Timon; ARKOPHARMA.
REFERENCES: Jeffrey Weinberger, Munger, Tolles and Olson, Los Angeles, California; John P. Williams, Duncan, Allen & Mitchell, Washington, D.C.; Manuel Rodriguez Aragon, Arthur Young, Madrid, Spain; Enrique Jimenez Batalla, Gomez-Acebo & Pombo, Madrid, Spain; Antonio Selas, Baker & McKenzie; Joaquin de Rojas, M. Vega Penichet.

ALONSO UREBA & ASOCIADOS

Established in 1986

C/ VELAZQUEZ, 86 DUPLICADO, (3°DCHA.)
28006 MADRID, SPAIN
Telephone: 5775875
Fax: 5775881

General Practice, Commercial, Corporation, Banking, Finance, Foreign Investments, Taxation, Administrative, EEC Law, International, Accounting.

PARTNERS

ALBERTO ALONSO UREBA, born Sevilla, Spain, July 3, 1953; admitted, 1986, Madrid. *Education:* Complutense University of Madrid (Law, 1975; Doctorate (Law, 1984); Bonn University, West Germany. Professor Head of Merchantile Law Department, University of Albacete, 1989. Professor, Merchantile Law Department, ICADE Madrid University and San Pablo Institute. Spanish Government Representative on Company Law EEC Directives Commission. Author: "State Enterprises," 1985; "Stock Companies as the vehicle of local state-owned enterprises," 1988; "Legal Reforms in stock company regulations," 1987. Co-author: "New entities, contracts and guarantees in financial markets," 1990. *LANGUAGES:* Spanish, German and English. *PRACTICE AREAS:* Corporate Law; Competition Law; Public Enterprises.

FRANCISCO JOSE BAUZÁ MORÉ, born Barcelona, Spain, November 25, 1956; admitted, 1984, Madrid. *Education:* Navarra University (Law, 1978), Doctorate (Law, 1982); Bonn University, West Germany. Professor at ICADE Madrid University and Instituto de Empresa. Co-author: "Legal Reforms in stock Company regulations," 1987; "New Entities contracts and guarantees in financial Markets," 1990. *Member:* Spanish-German Association of Lawyers. [With Spanish Air Force Legal Corps]. *LANGUAGES:* Spanish, German and English. *PRACTICE AREAS:* Corporate Law; Financial Law; Mergers and Acquisitions; Venture Capital Structures; Litigation.

ASSOCIATES

JULIO MORENO MORENO, born Valladolid, Spain, October 29, 1944; admitted, 1977, Madrid. *Education:* Complutense University of Madrid (Law, 1976). *LANGUAGES:* Spanish and French. *PRACTICE AREAS:* Litigation; Civil Law.

FERNANDO MARROQUÍN MOCHALES, born Madrid, Spain, July 9, 1961; admitted, 1994, Madrid. *Education:* Complutense University of Madrid (Law, 1984). *LANGUAGES:* Spanish and English. *PRACTICE AREAS:* Corporate Law; Civil Law.

(This Listing Continued)

EU1236B

REPRESENTATIVE CLIENTS: Alcatel, S.A.; Dragados y Construcciones, S.A.; Midland Bank plc, Sucursal en España; Midland Montagu Ventures, S.A.; J. Henry Schröder Wagg and Co. Limited; Banco Gallego, S.A.; Deutsche Krankenversicherung AG, Madrid; Agencia EFE, S.A.; Ayuntamiento de Madrid; Compañía General de Inversiones, S.A.; SAFEI-SAMEDI, Sociedad de Valores, S.A.; Schroders y Asociados, S.A.; Caja De Ahorros De Valencia; Castellon y Alicante (Bancaja); Honesta Manzaneque, S.A.; Banco Central Hispanoamericano, S.A.; Valenciana de Cementos, S.A.; Laboratorios Leti, S.A.; Inespal, S.A.

IBERFORO-MADRID
ALZAGA, CARO, MARAÑÓN,
SÁNCHEZ-TERÁN & ASOCIADOS,
ABOGADOS

Established in 1967

MARQUES DE CUBAS, 6
28014 MADRID, SPAIN
Telephone: 521-82-19
Fax: 521-54-26; 521-87-82

IberForo's offices: Alicante, Almería, Barcelona, Bilbao, Burgos, Cāceres, Cantabria, Ceuta, Ciudad Real, Córdoba, Gerona, Guadalajara, Huesca, Ibiza, Jaén, La CoruÑa, Las Palmas de Gran Canaria, León, Logroño, Madrid, Málaga, Marbella, Menorca, Murcia, Navarra, Oviedo, Palma de Mallorca, Pamplona, Salamanca, San Sebastián, Santa Cruz de Tenerife, Teruel, Toledo, Valencia, Valladolid, Vigo, Vitoria, Zaragoza.

Corporate, Mercantile, Civil, Taxation, Administrative, Foreign Investment, Spanish Litigation, Banking and Labour Law.

FIRM PROFILE: *The firm was established in 1967 covering all areas of business law. In 1990 the firm Iberforo was founded which intigrates 38 Offices established through the Spanish Territory.*

MEMBERS OF FIRM

OSCAR ALZAGA VILLAAMIL, born Madrid, Spain, May 29, 1942; admitted, 1965, Spain. *Education:* Universidad Complutense de Madrid. Author: "Comentario sistemático a la Constitución Española de 1978." Public Law Professor at the University in Madrid. Member of Parliament, 1977-1987. President, Justice Committee in the Congress, 1979. Member, Codification General Committee, Department of Justice, 1979-1982. Member, General Council for Education, 1978. Advisor to the Prime Minister, 1982. *Member:* Madrid Bar Association. *LANGUAGES:* Spanish, English and French. *PRACTICE AREAS:* Constitutional Law; Civil Law; Litigation.

ANIBAL CARO CEBRIAN, born Zaragoza, Spain, November 13, 1941; admitted, 1977, Spain. *Education:* Universidad de Zaragoza. Governmental Finance Inspector, 1967. Associate Director of "Control Presupuestario, S.A.," (Business Consulting, 1974). Member of the Editorial Staff of the magazines "Partida Doble" (Accounting) and "Carta Tributaria" (Tax). Lecturer of numerous training courses at public and private centres. Associate President of "Club Tributario". *LANGUAGES:* Spanish and French. *PRACTICE AREAS:* Tax Law; Financial Law; Litigation.

GREGORIO MARAÑON Y BERTRAN DE LIS, born Madrid, Spain, October 25, 1942; admitted, 1965, Madrid. *Education:* Law School at the Universidad Complutense de Madrid; Master in Business Administration at the I.E.S.E. Chairman and Board Member of prestigious Spanish and multinational companies. *LANGUAGES:* Spanish, English and French. *PRACTICE AREAS:* Financial Law; Commercial Law.

MIGUEL ANGEL SANCHEZ-TERAN, born Logroño, Spain, March 8, 1942; admitted, 1976, Madrid. *Education:* Universidad Complutense de Madrid. Author: "Impuesto Sobre Transmisiones Patrimoniales Intervivos," Madrid, 1976; "Las Sociedades Inmobiliarias," Madrid, 1977. Lecturer: Instituto de Formación y Estudio, 1972-1974; Centro de Estudios Tributarios y Económicos, 1973-1976; Escuela Superior de Dirección de Empresas, (I.C.A.D.E.) 1973-1976. Abogado del Estado, Secretario General Técnico y Sub Secretario del Ministerio de Educación y Ciencia, 1977-1979. Member, Arbitration Spanish Court. *Member:* Madrid, Barcelona and SeTua Bar Associations. *LANGUAGES:* Spanish and French. *PRACTICE AREAS:* Administrative Law; Litigation.

FERNANDO JAVIER GOMEZ REY, born Madrid, Spain, March 18, 1955; admitted, 1979, Madrid. *Education:* Universidad Autónoma de Madrid and Training on syndicated loans, Norton, Rose, Botterell & Roche, London, England. Author: "La Base Imponible del I.V.A." U.A.M., 1979;

(This Listing Continued)

"El Control de Cambios en Espana," Madrid, 1980; "Creditos y Prestamos Internacionales," 1982; "Banks Abroad", collective book, 1985; "Actual Spanish Commercial Law", Collective book, 1991. Lecturer on Private International Law, Faculty of Law, 1979-1986, Madrid. *Member:* Madrid Bar Association. *LANGUAGES:* Spanish and English. *PRACTICE AREAS:* Banking Law; Financial Law; International Law.

ASSOCIATES

JOSE MIGUEL LOPEZ LOPEZ-OLEAGA, born Madrid, March 3, 1963; admitted, 1988, Madrid. *Education:* Universidad Autónoma de Madrid (Law Degree). *Member:* Madrid Bar Association. *LANGUAGES:* Spanish, English and French. *PRACTICE AREAS:* Civil Law; Administrative Law; Commercial Law.

JUAN MANUEL BALLESTEROS Y ALLUE, born Madrid, Spain, June 3, 1961; admitted, 1986, Madrid. *Education:* Universidad Complutense de Madrid (Law Degree, 1985; Diploma in Enterprise Legal Advising, 1989). Lecturer, Universidad Pontificia Comillas, ICADE. *Member:* Madrid, Alcalá de Henares and Sevilla Bar Associations; Real Academia de Jurisprudencia. *LANGUAGES:* Spanish, French and English. *PRACTICE AREAS:* Litigation; Commercial Law.

CRISTINA MARCO CANO, born Madrid, Spain, December 11, 1959; admitted, 1984, Madrid. *Education:* Universidad Complutense de Madrid. *Member:* Madrid Bar Association. *LANGUAGES:* Spanish and French. *PRACTICE AREAS:* Labour Law.

PABLO RON CRUCELEGUI, born Eibar, Guipuzcoa, Spain, September 19, 1966; admitted, 1991, Madrid. *Education:* Universidad de Salamanca. *Member:* Madrid Bar Association. *LANGUAGES:* Spanish and English. *PRACTICE AREAS:* Labour Law; Commercial Law.

MARIA LUISA DE MEER MADRID, born Alcalá de Henares, Madrid, Spain, October 31, 1967; admitted, 1992, Madrid. *Education:* Universidad de Alcalá, Madrid (Law Degree, 1990); Instituto de Empresa, Madrid (Master in Enterprise Legal Counsel, 1991). *Member:* Madrid Bar Association. *LANGUAGES:* Spanish and English. *PRACTICE AREAS:* Public Administrative Law; Litigation.

MARIA FUENTES BUESO, born Madrid, Spain, February 28, 1967; admitted, 1993, Madrid. *Education:* Universidad Complutense de Madrid, Colegio C.E.U. San Pablo (Law Degree, 1990); Instituto de Empresa, Madrid (Master in Enterprise Legal Counsel, 1991). *Member:* Madrid Bar Association. *LANGUAGES:* Spanish, English and French. *PRACTICE AREAS:* Commercial Law; Corporate Law.

MARIA VICTORIA FERNANDEZ LOPEZ, born Madrid, Spain, September 30, 1965; admitted, 1993, Madrid. *Education:* Universidad Complutense de Madrid (Law Degree, 1988). *Member:* Madrid Bar Association. *LANGUAGES:* Spanish and English. *PRACTICE AREAS:* European Community Law; Commercial Law.

PABLO ALBERT ALBERT, born Madrid, Spain, May 4, 1970; admitted, 1994, Madrid. *Education:* Universidad Complutense de Madrid. *Member:* Madrid Bar Association; Segovia Bar Association. *LANGUAGES:* Spanish, English and French. *PRACTICE AREAS:* Litigation; Civil Law.

TAX DEPARTMENT

JOSE IGNACIO ALARCON ELORRIETA, born Madrid, Spain, January 14, 1964; admitted, 1990, Madrid. *Education:* Universidad Pontificia de Comillas ICADI-ICADE, Madrid (Law Degree, 1987; Business Administration Degree, 1988). Member of "Club Tributario". *LANGUAGES:* Spanish and English. *PRACTICE AREAS:* Tax law; Financial Law; Litigation.

VICENTE CLEMENTE CLEMENTE, born Guadalajara, Spain, November 2, 1961; admitted, 1985, Madrid. *Education:* Universidad Pontificia de Comillas, Madrid (Degree in Law and Diploma in Business Administration 1984); Legal Practice School, Universidad Complutense (1985); Centre for Tax Studies. Lecturer at the Instituto de Empresa. Member of "Club Tributario", Academia de Jurisprudencia. *LANGUAGES:* Spanish and English. *PRACTICE AREAS:* Tax; Financial Law; Litigation.

JAVIER ZAPATA FERRER, born Madrid, Spain, January 15, 1966; admitted, 1990, Madrid. *Education:* Universidad Pontificia de Comillas ICADE-ICADE, Madrid (Law Degree, 1989; Business Administration Degree, 1990). Member of "Club Tributario". *LANGUAGES:* Spanish and English. *PRACTICE AREAS:* Tax; Financial Law; Litigation.

(This Listing Continued)

GARCIA AÑOVEROS & PÉREZ-LLORCA

Established in 1983

LAGASCA, 28-2° IZQD.
28001 MADRID, SPAIN
Telephone: 435-20-10/69
Telefax: 4354736

Seville, Spain Office: Avenida República Argentina, 13 - 6, Seville 41011. Telephone: (954) 27.08.02.

International Commercial Law. EEC, Corporate, Taxation, Foreign Investments, Administrative, Financing, Banking and Insurance Law. Commercial Arbitration, Property.

SENIOR PARTNERS

JAIME GARCIA AÑOVEROS, born Teruel, Spain; admitted, 1960, Spain. *Education:* University of Valencia (Law Degree, Honors); University of Bologna, Italy (Doctor in Law, Honors). Professor, Tax Law, University of Sevilla, 1961—. Founder of the Business School of the University of Sevilla, 1966—. Member of Parliament, 1977 and 1979. Chairman, Public Finance Committee, 1977. Minister of Finance, April, 1979/December, 1982. *LANGUAGES:* Spanish, English, French and Italian.

JOSE PEDRO PÉREZ-LLORCA, born Cádiz, Spain; admitted, 1965, Spain. *Education:* Freiburg and Munich; University of Madrid (Law Degree, Honors). Career Diplomat, 1964. Letrado de las Cortes Generales, 1967. Professor of Law, Diplomatic School, 1967. Legal Advisor to the Ministry of Foreign Affairs, 1967. Minister in Charge of the Prime Minister Office (Ministro de la Presidencia del Gobierno), April 1979. Minister of Relations with Parliament, subsequently, Minister of Foreign Affairs, September, 1980/December, 1982. *LANGUAGES:* Spanish, English, German and French.

ASSOCIATES

LUIS FERNANDO ZURERA DELGADO, born Puente Genil (Cordoba), Spain, June 3, 1962; admitted, 1988, Madrid. *Education:* Facultad de Derecho de Cordoba (Law Degree); Instituto de Empresa (Master's degree in Corporate Legal Counsel). *LANGUAGES:* Spanish, English and French.

JUAN LUIS RODRIGUEZ AMBLES, born Madrid, Spain, May 29, 1958; admitted, 1988, Madrid. *Education:* Universidad Complutense, Madrid (Law Degree, 1980; Political Science Degree, 1982). Professor, Constitutional Law, Universidad Complutense, Madrid, 1988-1990. *LANGUAGES:* Spanish, English and German.

MONTSERRAT SOTO RODRIGUEZ, born Santiago de Compostela (La Coruña), Spain, April 7, 1965; admitted, 1990, Madrid. *Education:* Universidad de Santiago (Law Degree); Escuela Libre de Derecho, Economia (Master's Degree in Corporate Law and Economy). *LANGUAGES:* Spanish and English.

MARTIN VALLE DURAN, born Madrid, Spain, December 28, 1965; admitted, 1992, Madrid. *Education:* Universidad Complutense, Madrid (Law Degree); Instituto de Empresa (Masters degree in Corporate Legal Counsel). *LANGUAGES:* Spanish, French and English.

OF COUNSEL

ANTONIO JIMÉNEZ BLANCO, born Granada, Spain; admitted, 1955, Spain. *Education:* University of Sevilla (Law Degree, Honors). Senator for Granada, 1977 and 1979. President, Council of State, October, 1980/December, 1982. *LANGUAGES:* Spanish and French.

Languages: Spanish, English, French, Italian and German.

A List of Representative Clients and References furnished upon request.

BUFETE ARBOLEYA

GENERAL ORAA, 68
28006 MADRID, SPAIN
Telephone: 562.24.15
Cable Address: "Arbolaw Madrid"
Telecopier: 564.50.44

General Practice. Admiralty, Corporation, Tax, Administrative, Foreign Investment and Labor Law. Patents and Trademarks. Oil and Gas.

MEMBERS OF FIRM

ANTONIO ARBOLEYA GÓMEZ, born Ceuta, Spain, February 12, 1938; admitted, 1961, Madrid. *Education:* Maristas College (B.A., 1956); Faculty of Law, University of Madrid (LL.B., 1960); Columbia University Law School, New York, N.Y. (Master of Comparative Law, 1962). Author: "Spanish Corporate Taxation." *Member:* Madrid Bar Association. *LANGUAGES:* Spanish, English and French. *PRACTICE AREAS:* Oil and Gas; Admiralty; Corporate; Foreign Investment.

EMILIO CASSINELLO, born Ciudad Real, Spain, July 7, 1936; admitted, 1958, Mexico; 1961, Madrid. *Education:* University Center of Mexico (B.A., 1953); National Autonomous University of Mexico (LL.B., 1957); Faculty of Law, University of Madrid (LL.B., 1958); Harvard University Law School, Cambridge, Mass. (LL.M., 1960). Spanish Attorney, Office of Staff Judge Advocate, 1961-1962. *LANGUAGES:* Spanish, English and French. *PRACTICE AREAS:* Contract Law.

PILAR CEBALLOS PEREZ, born Torrelavega, February 1, 1951; admitted, 1981, Spain. *Education:* El Pilar College, Irún (B.A., 1969); Faculty of Law, University of Madrid (LL.B., 1980); University of Miami Law School (Master of Comparative Law, 1981). *LANGUAGES:* Spanish and English. *PRACTICE AREAS:* Contract Law; Labor; Corporate.

RAFAEL MUNOZ-ROJAS, born Malaga, November 24, 1935; admitted, 1975, Spain. *Education:* Pilar (B.A., 1952); Institute of Political Studies (Sociology Diploma, 1953-1954); Faculty of Law, University of Madrid (LL.B., 1957). *LANGUAGES:* Spanish, English and French. *PRACTICE AREAS:* Corporate; Tax Law.

Languages: Spanish, English, French and German.

REPRESENTATIVE CLIENTS: Continental Can Co.; Conoco Inc.; Continental Carbon Co.; Hydrauliska Industri, A.B. (Sweden); Mobil Oil Corp.; Svenska Handelsbanken (Sweden); Timex Corp. (Switzerland); Data General Corp. (USA); Procordia AB (Sweden); Partek AB (Finland).
REFERENCES: The Chase Manhattan Bank, 1 Chase Manhattan Plaza, New York, N.Y., 10015; Dewey, Ballantine, Bushby, Palmer & Wood, 140 Broadway, New York, N.Y., 10005; Morgan Guarantee Trust Co.; Davis Polk, New York.

BUFETE JOSE M. ARMERO

Established in 1952

CALLE VELÁZQUEZ, 21
28001 MADRID, SPAIN
Telephone: 431-31-00; 431-33-58
Cable Address: "Unilaw"
Telex: 23543-Ulaw-E
Fax: 431-85-76

General Practice. Administrative, Civil, Mercantile, Banking, Mining, Foreign Investment, Corporation, Tax, Labor and International Law.

MEMBERS OF FIRM

JOSE MARIO ARMERO, born Valladolid, Spain, 1927; admitted, 1952, Spain. *Education:* Colegio del Pilar, Madrid (Bachelor, 1944); University of Madrid (Licencite in Law, 1950); Degree in Journalism, University of Navarra, Spain. *Member:* Madrid Bar Association. *LANGUAGES:* Spanish and English. *PRACTICE AREAS:* General Practice.

FERNANDO ESCARDÓ, born Madrid, Spain, 1932; admitted, 1956, Spain. *Education:* British Institute, 1939-1941 and Colegio del Pilar, Madrid (Bachelor, 1950); University of Madrid (Licencite in Law, 1955). *Member:* Barcelona and Madrid Bar Associations. *LANGUAGES:* Spanish, English and French. *PRACTICE AREAS:* Bank and Banking.

JUAN JOSÉ CAYUELA, born Totana (Murcia), Spain, 1933; admitted, 1977, Spain. *Education:* Institutos de San Isidro y Ramiro de Maeztu, Madrid (Bachelor, 1967); University of Madrid (Licentiate in Law, 1977). *Member:* Madrid Bar Association. *LANGUAGES:* Spanish and English. *PRACTICE AREAS:* Commercial Law.

(This Listing Continued)

COLOMA ARMERO, born Madrid, Spain, 1954; admitted, 1979, Spain. *Education:* University of Madrid (Licentiate in Law, 1977). *Member:* Madrid Bar Association. *LANGUAGES:* Spanish, English and French. *PRACTICE AREAS:* Commercial Law.

JUAN DEL CARRE, born Madrid, Spain, 1933; admitted, 1962, Spain. *Education:* Colegio del Pilar, Madrid (Bachelor, 1950); University of Madrid (Licentiate in Law, 1955). *Member:* Madrid Bar Association. *LANGUAGES:* Spanish, English and French. *PRACTICE AREAS:* Real State.

JOSÉ F. CARBALLO, born Havana, Cuba, 1920; admitted, 1971, Spain. *Education:* Escuelas Pias, Havana (Bachelor, 1938); University of Havana (Doctor in Law, 1942); University of Salamanca (Licentiate in Law, 1970). *Member:* Alcala, Barcelona and Madrid Bar Associations. *LANGUAGES:* Spanish and English. *PRACTICE AREAS:* General Practice.

JOSÉ MERINO, born Málaga, Spain, 1935; admitted, 1962, Spain. *Education:* University of Madrid (Licentiate in Law, 1962); Graduate in Business Administration ICADE, University of Comillas, Spain (1966). Sworn interpreter for the English and French languages. *Member:* Madrid Bar Association. *LANGUAGES:* Spanish, English and French. *PRACTICE AREAS:* Commercial Law.

LUIS VIDAL, born New York, New York, 1945; admitted, 1979, Madrid, Spain. *Education:* American School of Madrid (Graduated, 1963); University of Madrid (Licentiate in Law, 1968 and Licenciate in Political Science). *Member:* Madrid Bar Association. *LANGUAGES:* English and Spanish. *PRACTICE AREAS:* Company Law.

EMILIO LUCAS, born Madrid, Spain, 1940; admitted, 1974, Spain. *Education:* Colegio San Antón, Madrid (Bachelor, 1956); University of Madrid (Licentiate in Law, 1961). *Member:* Madrid Bar Association. *LANGUAGES:* Spanish. *PRACTICE AREAS:* Commercial Law.

FELIPE MARTINEZ DE ARAGON, born Vitoria, Spain, 1926; admitted, 1964, Spain. *Education:* Colegio del Pilar, Vitoria; Liceo Frances, Madrid (Bachelor, 1944); University of Madrid (Licentiate in Law, 1950); Centro de Estudios Tributarios y Económicos (Titulado de Empresas). Sworn translator for the French language. *Member:* Madrid Bar Association. *LANGUAGES:* Spanish and French. *PRACTICE AREAS:* Litigation.

JOSÉ MANUEL SORIANO, born Zaragoza, Spain, 1952; admitted, 1975, Spain. *Education:* Colegio San Agustin, Madrid (Bachelor, 1969); University of Deusto (Licentiate in Law, 1974); Graduated in Ciencias Empresariales (ICADE, 1976), Madrid, Spain. *Member:* Madrid Bar Association. *LANGUAGES:* Spanish and English. *PRACTICE AREAS:* Commercial Law.

FRANCISCO JAVIER RUIZ, born Madrid, 1953; admitted, 1975, Spain. *Education:* Institute Ramiro de Maeztu and San Damaso College; Higher Education at San Isidro Institute; Complutense University, Madrid (Licentiate in Law, 1978); post graduate courses, Pontificia University of Comillas, Master in Company Law, Instituto de Empresa, Madrid. *Member:* Madrid, Barcelona, Valencia, Málaga, Pamplona and Vigo Bar Associations. *LANGUAGES:* Spanish. *PRACTICE AREAS:* Litigation.

FRANK J. WIRGA, born England, 1950; (Not admitted in Spain). *Education:* King's College; University of London (Licentiate in Law, 1972). *LANGUAGES:* English and Spanish. *PRACTICE AREAS:* Commercial Law.

MERCEDES COSTA, born Lerida, Spain, 1964; admitted, 1989, Spain. *Education:* Colegios Mater Salvtoris, Lerida; Jesus Maria, Barcelona; University of Barcelona (Licentiate in law, 1987); Master in Company Law, Instituto de Empresa, Madrid. *Member:* Madrid Bar Association. *LANGUAGES:* Spanish and English. *PRACTICE AREAS:* Commercial Law.

BORJA SANZ, born Córdoba, Spain, 1964; admitted, 1991, Spain. *Education:* Colegio Cervantes (Maristas); University of Córdoba (Licentiate in Law, 1988); Instituto de Empresa, Madrid (Master in Company Law; Graduate of the Legal Practice School). *Member:* Madrid Bar Association. *LANGUAGES:* Spanish. *PRACTICE AREAS:* Labor and Employment.

GREGORY J. MARSDEN, born United States, 1964; admitted, 1991, California (Not admitted in Spain). *Education:* University of California, Hastings College of the Law (J.D., 1990); University of the Pacific, McGeorge School of Law (Postdoctoral Diploma, 1990). *LANGUAGES:* English and Spanish. *PRACTICE AREAS:* Commercial Law.

CAROLINA CUEVAS, born Madrid, Spain, 1968; admitted, 1994. Spain. *Education:* Colegio Ntra. Sra. Santa María, Madrid, Autonoma University of Madrid (Licenciate in Law, 1991); University of Convain la

(This Listing Continued)

EU1238B

Neuve (Master in International and European Law, 1992). *Member:* Madrid Bar Association. *LANGUAGES:* Spanish, English and French. *PRACTICE AREAS:* EC and Competition Law.

NICOLAS CHAPA, born Madrid, Spain, 1968; admitted, 1994, Spain. *Education:* Colegio Rosales, Madrid, University of Madrid (Licenciate in Law, 1991); Instituto de Empresa, Madrid (Master in Company Law, 1993). *Member:* Madrid Bar Association. *LANGUAGES:* Spanish and English. *PRACTICE AREAS:* Bank and Banking.

SUSANA BUCETA, born Pontevedra, Spain, 1968; admitted, 1994, Spain. *Education:* Sánchez Cantón Institute, Pontevedra (Bachelor, 1986); Complutense University Madrid (Licenciate in Law, 1992); I.E.S. Fundación Universitaria San Pablo-C.E.U., Madrid (Master in Private Law, 1993). *LANGUAGES:* Spanish and English. *PRACTICE AREAS:* Litigation.

BEATRIZ DE PAZ, born Léoon, Spain, 1969; admitted, 1994, Spain. *Education:* Colegio Santa Teresa, León (Bachelor, 1987); Complutense University, Madrid - C.E.U. San Pablo (Licenciate in Law, 1992); I.E.S. Fundación Universitaria San Pablo - C.E.U. (Master in Private Law, 1993). *Member:* Madrid Bar Association. *LANGUAGES:* Spanish and English. *PRACTICE AREAS:* Litigation.

FEDERICO ROIG, born San Sebastián, Spain, 1966; admitted, 1992, Spain. *Education:* Colegio Santa María (Marianistas); University of Salamanca (Licenciate in Law, 1989); Instituto de Empresa, Madrid (Master in Company Law, 1991). *Member:* Madrid Bar Association. *LANGUAGES:* Spanish, English and French. *PRACTICE AREAS:* Commercial Law.

ALVARO SÁNCHEZ, born Madrid, Spain, 1967; admitted, 1991, Spain. *Education:* Colegio Fundación Caldeiro (Terciarios Capuchinos) Madrid (Bachelor, 1985); University of Madrid (Licenciate in Law, 1990); Notarial College of Madrid (Master in Documentary Law); Member, Litigation Department, (Investigation), University of Madrid. *Member:* Madrid Bar Association. *LANGUAGES:* Spanish and English. *PRACTICE AREAS:* Litigation.

BORJA ESCRIVA DE ROMANI, born Madrid, Spain, 1968; admitted, 1992, Spain. *Education:* Jesuit School, Madrid; C.E.U. San Pablo Complutense University (Licenciate in Law, 1991). *Member:* Madrid Bar Association. *LANGUAGES:* Spanish and English. *PRACTICE AREAS:* Taxation.

Languages: Spanish, French, English, Italian and Portuguese.

ARTHUR ANDERSEN
ASESORES LEGALES Y TRIBUTARIOS

Legal and Tax Advisors
RAIMUNDO FERNÁNDEZ VILLAVERDE, 65
28003 MADRID, SPAIN
Telephone: 34-1-597 0000
Fax: 34-1-556 6469

Arthur Andersen Asesores Legales y Tributarios's offices: Alicante, Barcelona, Bilbao, Granada, La Coruña, Madrid, Málaga, Oviedo, Palma de Mallorca, San Sebastian, Sevilla, Valencia, Vigo, Vitoria, Zaragoza.

Associated Law Firms abroad: France, Italy, Germany, Portugal, The Netherlands, Belgium, United Kingdom, South Africa, Colombia and Brazil.

Business, Corporate and Commercial Law, Tax Law, International Business Law, International and Foreign Investments, Mergers and Acquisitions, Business Litigation, International Contracts and Real Estate Law, Joint Ventures, Corporate Restructuring, EC Law, Employment Law, Banking and Financing, Environment, Transfer Pricing, Stock Exchange Authority, Bankruptcy, Competition Law, Arbitration Assistance and General Practice.

FIRM PROFILE: Arthur Andersen Asesores Legales y Tributarios is a law firm with a total staff of 239 (168 of them are lawyers listed in this guide as members of the firm in the city of their residence) which offers a full range of business legal services on both a national and international basis.

PARTNERS

SANTIAGO ILUNDÁIN, born Madrid, Spain, July, 1945; admitted, 1973, Madrid. *Education:* University of Madrid (Law Degree, 1967); ICADE (Economics Degree, 1968); Madrid Tax Studies Center, (Master). Co-Author: "La reforma de la Legislación Mercantil," Editorial CDN, 1990.

(This Listing Continued)

Member: Madrid and International Bar Associations. *LANGUAGES:* Spanish and English.

JESÚS YUSTE, born Cáceres, Spain, March 23, 1944; admitted, 1984, Madrid. *Education:* University of Madrid (Law Degree, 1968); ICADE (Economics Degree, 1969) Madrid Tax Studies Center, (Master). Professor, Tax Systems and Tax Law, Madrid Chamber of Commerce. *Member:* Madrid Bar Association. *LANGUAGES:* Spanish and English.

JOSÉ MANUEL BURGOS, born Madrid, Spain, September 2, 1945; admitted, 1967, Madrid. *Education:* University of Madrid (Law Degree, 1967). Professor, Civil Law, Madrid University. Co-Author: "La reforma de la Legislación Mercantil," Editorial CDN, 1990. *Member:* Madrid and International Bar Associations. *LANGUAGES:* Spanish and English.

MIGUEL GORDILLO, born Madrid, Spain, July 4, 1952; admitted, 1989, Madrid. *Education:* University of Deusto (Law Degree, 1973); ICADE (Master, Business Administration, 1974; Master, Tax Counsel, 1975). Professor, Instituto de Empresa. Co-Author: "Las nuevas Leyes del Impuesto sobre la Renta y el Patrimonio," Arthur Andersen Asesores Legales y Tributarios. *Member:* Madrid Bar Association. *LANGUAGES:* Spanish and English.

ERNESTO JIMÉNEZ, born Madrid, Spain, July 8, 1956; admitted, 1989, Madrid. *Education:* University of Madrid (Law Degree, 1979); Instituto de Empresa (Master, Corporation Tax Counsel, 1982). Professor, Master in Financial and Insurance Entities, Instituto de Estudios Superiores de Seguros. Co-Author: "Las nuevas Leyes del Impuesto sobre la Renta y el Patrimonio," 1991. *Member:* Madrid Bar Association. *LANGUAGES:* Spanish, English and French.

RAFAEL NEBREDA, born Bilbao, Spain, May, 1954; admitted, 1993, Madrid. *Education:* University of Deusto, Bilbao (Law Degree, 1979). *Member:* Madrid Bar Association. *LANGUAGES:* Spanish and English.

PABLO OLÁBARRI, born Bilbao, Spain, July 16, 1960; admitted, 1989, Madrid. *Education:* University of Navarra (Law Degree, 1983). Co-Author: "La reforma de la Legislación Mercantil," Editorial CDN, 1990. *Member:* Madrid Bar Association. *LANGUAGES:* Spanish and English.

JAVIER ESCUDERO, born Madrid, Spain, January, 1957; admitted, 1993, Madrid. *Education:* Universidad Complutense (Law Degree, 1979). *Member:* Madrid Bar Association. *LANGUAGES:* Spanish and English.

JOSÉ RAMÓN MARTÍNEZ, born Valencia, Spain, September 11, 1956; admitted, 1989, Madrid. *Education:* University of Madrid (Law Degree, 1979); ICADE (Course, Tax Counsel, 1983); Instituto de Empresa (Course, Legal Counsel, 1984). *Member:* Madrid Bar Association. *LANGUAGES:* Spanish and English.

JOSÉ PALACIOS, born Jaén, Spain, January, 1954; admitted, 1993, Madrid. *Education:* Universidad Complutense (Law Degree, 1976); Instituto de Empresa (Tax Counsel Master, 1982/1984). *Member:* Madrid Bar Association. *LANGUAGES:* Spanish, English and French.

ASSOCIATES

ANTONIO MOLINS, born Alicante, Spain, November 2, 1960; admitted, 1984, Madrid. *Education:* ICADE (Law Degree, 1983; Economics Degree, 1984). *Member:* Madrid Bar Association. *LANGUAGES:* Spanish and English.

GEORGE HUNTER, born Buffalo, New York, January 27, 1957; admitted, 1982, Massachusetts; 1987, Madrid. *Education:* Atlantic College in Wales, U.K. (International Baccalaureate, 1974); New York University (B.A., cum laude, 1978); Boston University (J.D., 1981). Professor, Business Law, Instituto de Empresa, 1990-1992. *Member:* Madrid Bar Association; International Bar Association; Massachusetts Bar Association. *LANGUAGES:* English, Spanish and French.

DANIEL MÉNDEZ, born Madrid, Spain, September 21, 1961; admitted, 1985, Madrid. *Education:* ICADE (Law Degree, 1984; Economics Degree, 1985). *Member:* Madrid Bar Association. *LANGUAGES:* Spanish and English.

ANGEL CALLEJA, born Madrid, Spain, July 11, 1961; admitted, 1991, Madrid. *Education:* ICADE (Economics Degree, 1985; Law Degree, 1986). *Member:* Madrid Bar Association. *LANGUAGES:* Spanish, English and German.

MARTA HERNÁNDEZ, born Madrid, Spain, April 6, 1960; admitted, 1991, Madrid. *Education:* University of Madrid (Law Degree, 1982). *Member:* Madrid Bar Association. *LANGUAGES:* Spanish and English.

FERNANDO VIVES, born Madrid, Spain, October 8, 1962; admitted, 1986, Madrid. *Education:* ICADE (Law Degree, 1985; Economics Degree,

(This Listing Continued)

ARTHUR ANDERSEN, ASESORES LEGALES Y TRIBUTARIOS, Madrid—Continued

1986); Instituto de Empresa (Master, Tax Counsel, 1988). Professor, ICADE, Accounting, 1988-1989; Business Management, 1989-1992. *Member:* Madrid Bar Association. *LANGUAGES:* Spanish and English.

MÓNICA MARTÍN DE VIDALES, born Madrid, Spain, December 1, 1963; admitted, 1991, Madrid. *Education:* ICADE (Law Degree, 1986; Graduate, Business Administration, 1986). Assistant Professor, Civil Law, ICADE, 1985-1986. *Member:* Madrid Bar Association. *LANGUAGES:* Spanish and English.

GONZALO GALLARDO, born Baena, Córdoba, Spain, April 15, 1962; admitted, 1986, Madrid. *Education:* ICADE (Law Degree, 1985; Economics Degree, 1986). *Member:* Madrid Bar Association. *LANGUAGES:* Spanish and English.

EDUARDO GARDETA, born Zaragoza, Spain, December, 1963; admitted, 1986, Madrid. *Education:* Universidad Complutense (Law Degree, 1986); Instituto de Empresa (Master Tax Counsel, 1987/1989). Program of Instruction for Lawyers, Harvard University. *Member:* Madrid Bar Association. *LANGUAGES:* Spanish and English.

DAVIER POVEDANO, born Madrid, Spain, May 1963; admitted, 1986, Madrid. *Education:* ICADE (Law Degree, 1986, Economics Degree, 1987). *Member:* Madrid Bar Association. *LANGUAGES:* Spanish and English.

ALEJANDRO ORTIZ, born Jaén, Spain, November 18, 1964; admitted, 1990, Madrid. *Education:* ICADE (Law Degree, 1987; Economics Degree, 1988); Centro de Estudios Tributarios y Económicos, Madrid Chamber of Commerce (Master, Tax Counsel, 1990); ICADE (Graduate, European Community Law, 1987). *Member:* Madrid Bar Association. *LANGUAGES:* Spanish, English and French.

LOURDES RAMOS, born Madrid, Spain, August 29, 1963; admitted, 1989, Madrid. *Education:* ICADE (Law Degree, 1986; Economics Degree, 1987; Graduate, European Community Law, 1987; Master, Tax Counsel, 1989). *Member:* Madrid Bar Association. *LANGUAGES:* Spanish and English.

ROSA ZARZA, born Madrid, Spain, May 14, 1966; admitted, 1991, Madrid. *Education:* University of Madrid (Law Degree, 1989; Master, Tax and Labour Law Counsel, 1989). *Member:* Madrid Bar Association. *LANGUAGES:* Spanish and English.

CARLOS GARDEAZÁBAL, born Madrid, Spain, January 10, 1963; admitted, 1987, Madrid. *Education:* University of Navarra (Law Degree, 1986). *Member:* Madrid Bar Association. *LANGUAGES:* Spanish and English.

RAMÓN CARBALLÁS, born Vigo, Pontevedra, Spain, July 8, 1965; admitted, 1992, Madrid. *Education:* ICADE (Law Degree, 1988; Economics Degree, 1989). *Member:* Madrid Bar Association. *LANGUAGES:* Spanish and English.

MARÍA PEÑA, born Madrid, Spain, September 12, 1966; admitted, 1990, Madrid. *Education:* ICADE (Law Degree, 1989; Graduate, Business Administration, 1989). *Member:* Madrid Bar Association. *LANGUAGES:* Spanish and English.

CARMEN ALONSO, born Zamora, Spain, December, 1967; admitted, 1991, Madrid. *Education:* ICADE (Law Degree, 1990, Business Degree, 1991). *Member:* Madrid Bar Association. *LANGUAGES:* Spanish, English and German.

EDUARDO GRACIA, born Madrid, Spain, January, 1967; admitted, 1991, Madrid. *Education:* ICADE (Law Degree, 1990). *Member:* Madrid Bar Association. *LANGUAGES:* Spanish, English and French.

ALBERTO DE MIGUEL, born Madrid, Spain, February, 1966; admitted, 1991, Madrid. *Education:* Universidad Complutense, Madrid, (Law Degree, 1989). *Member:* Madrid Bar Association. *LANGUAGES:* Spanish and English.

PILAR MARCHÁN, born Madrid, Spain, April, 1966; admitted, 1991, Madrid. *Education:* Universidad Complutense of Madrid, (Law Degree, 1990). *Member:* Madrid Bar Association. *LANGUAGES:* Spanish and English.

JOAQUÍN VALCÁRCEL, born Madrid, Spain, October, 1965; admitted, 1991, Madrid. *Education:* Universidad of Madrid, CEU (Law Degree, 1988). *Member:* Madrid Bar Association. *LANGUAGES:* Spanish, English and French.

(This Listing Continued)

EU1240B

JORGE SANZ, born Madrid, Spain, May, 1966; admitted, 1993, Madrid. *Education:* Universidad Autónoma Madrid (Economics Degree, 1989); UNED (Law Degree, 1991). *Member:* Madrid Bar Association. *LANGUAGES:* Spanish and French.

OTHER ASSOCIATES

JoséMaría Gil-Robles	Sara Rojas
José Ignacio García	Alfredo Fernández
Andrés Sánchez	Juan Rejg
Santiago Díez	Jaime Muguiro
Renata Mendaña	Barbara López-Chicheri
Margarita Madrigal	Dolores Herrera
Carlos Arenas	Amaya Llovet
Carlos Gómez	José Manuel Martín
Juan Luis Zayas	Juan José Barragán
Remigio Abad	Ramon Tejada
Antonio Viñuela	Carmen Gutiérrez
Carmen Aquerreta	Lorenzo Clemente
Félix Plaza	Pedro de Rojas
Luis María Viñuales	Vicente Bootello
Eduardo Cosmen	Antonio Entrena
Juan Jiménez	Alvaro Luna
Rafael Giménez-Arnau	Cristina Rica
Alfredo Manero	Juan Rincón
Eva Holgado	Patricia Gutiérrez
Nieves García	Pedro Rodríguez
Javier Navarro	Ismael Clemente
Fernando Ortiz	Carlos Olmedo

ASESORES LEGALES Y DE INVERSIONES ABOGADOS

Established in 1991

MARIA DE MOLINA, 5
28006 MADRID, SPAIN
Telephone: 564-3383
Telefax: 564-0020

General Practice, Foreign Investments, Banking and Financial Law, Corporate Finance, Taxation, Commercial, Real Estate and Patent Law, International Arbitration, Litigation, Restructuring, Labour Law and Aeronautical.

FIRM PROFILE: *The firm was established in 1991 and offers a full range of legal services. Although a young firm, some of the partners and associates have a large experience in International and Domestic Law for more than 20 years.*

PARTNERS

JAVIER ALVAREZ-CIENFUEGOS COIDURAS, born Granada, Spain, 1952. *Education:* University of Granada (LL.B., 1976); Bolonia Law School (Ph.D., 1979). Professor, University Autonoma of Madrid. *Member:* Madrid Bar Association. *LANGUAGES:* Spanish and Italian. *PRACTICE AREAS:* General Practice; Corporate Finance; Commercial and Real Estate.

GREGORIO FRAILE BARTOLOMÉ, born Madrid, Spain, 1954. *Education:* University Autónoma, Madrid (LL.B., 1978); Harvard University/Instituto de Empresa (P.I.L., 1989). *Member:* Madrid Bar Association; Instituto de Finanzas. *LANGUAGES:* Spanish and English. *PRACTICE AREAS:* General Practice; Corporate Finance; Commercial and Real Estate.

SANTIAGO GASTÓN DE IRIARTE MEDRANO, born Madrid, Spain, 1947. *Education:* University of Barcelona (LL.B., 1969); ICADE (M.B.A., 1970). Professor, Private Law, Universidad Complutense, Madrid. *Member:* Madrid and International Bar Associations. *LANGUAGES:* Spanish, French and English. *PRACTICE AREAS:* General Practice; Corporate Finance; Commercial; Real Estate; Litigation; Banking and Patent Law.

(This Listing Continued)

TOMÁS PELAYO MUÑOZ, born Zaragoza, Spain, 1955. *Education:* University of Navarra (LL.B., 1978); Instituto de Empresa, Madrid (LL.M., 1986); Financial Assessment, Banco de España (1987); Harvard University/Instituto de Empresa (P.I.L., 1989). Professor, Instituto de Empresa. *Member:* Madrid and Burgos Bar Associations. *LANGUAGES:* Spanish and French. *PRACTICE AREAS:* General Practice; Corporate Finance; International Arbitration; Commercial; Real Estate; Labour Law; Litigation and Aeronautical.

TOMÁS PELAYO ROS, born Zaragoza, Spain, 1928. *Education:* University of Zaragoza (LL.B., 1951). General Prosecutor, Tarragona, Zaragoza, Madrid. Member, Spanish Olympic Committee. *Member:* Madrid, La Coruña, Zamora, Tarragona, León and Tenerife Bar Associations. *LANGUAGES:* Spanish and English. *PRACTICE AREAS:* General Practice; Corporate Finance; Commercial; Real Estate; White Collar Criminal Law and Litigation.

ASSOCIATES

ITZIAR BALLESTEROS AGUIRRE, born Madrid, Spain, 1970. *Education:* Universidad Complutense, Madrid (LL.B., 1993). *Member:* Madrid Bar Association. *LANGUAGES:* Spanish and English. *PRACTICE AREAS:* General Practice; Corporate and Civil Law; Commercial; Foreign Investments; Real Estate; Litigation.

MARIA DEL PILAR GARCIA ZARANDIETA Y GIMENEZ, born Madrid, Spain, 1969. *Education:* Universidad Complutense, Madrid (LL.B., 1992). *Member:* Madrid Bar Association. *LANGUAGES:* Spanish, English and French. *PRACTICE AREAS:* General Practice; Corporate and Civil Law; Commercial; Foreign Investments; Real Estate; Litigation.

F. JAVIER ECHAVARRI LÓPEZ, born Pamplona, Spain, April 10, 1969; admitted, 1995, Spain. *Education:* University of Navarra (LL.B., 1993); Instituto De Empresa (LL.M., 1995). *Member:* Madrid Bar Association. *PRACTICE AREAS:* General Practice; Corporate Finance; Commercial; Real Estate; Litigation.

SPECIAL COUNSEL

JUAN BUTRAGUEÑORODRÍGUEZ-BORLADO, born Madrid, Spain, April 11, 1963; admitted, 1988, Madrid. *Education:* Complutense University of Madrid (LL.B., 1986). *Member:* Madrid Bar Association. *LANGUAGES:* Spanish, English and French. *PRACTICE AREAS:* General Practice; Corporate and Civil Law; Commercial; Foreign Investments; Real Estate; Litigation.

BAKER & McKENZIE

PINAR 18
MADRID 28006, SPAIN
Telephone: (91) 411-3062
Intn'l. Dialing: (34-1) 411-3062
Facsimiles: (34-1) 562-2425; 564-6035

Associated Offices of Baker & McKenzie in: Almaty, Amsterdam, Bangkok, Barcelona, Beijing, Berlin, Bogotá, Brasília, Brussels, Budapest, Buenos Aires, Cairo, Caracas, Chicago, Dallas, Frankfurt, Geneva, Hanoi, Ho Chi Minh City, Hong Kong, Juárez, Kiev, London, Manila, Melbourne, México City, Miami, Milan, Monterrey, Moscow, New York, Palo Alto, Paris, Prague, Rio de Janeiro, Riyadh, Rome, St. Petersburg, San Diego, San Francisco, São Paulo, Singapore, Stockholm, Sydney, Taipei, Tijuana, Tokyo, Toronto, Valencia, Warsaw, Washington, D.C. and Zürich.
Correspondent Law Firm: Hadiputranto, Hadinoto & Partners, Jakarta.

General and International Law Practice.

JOSÉ A. ARCILA, born Madrid, Spain, July 31, 1951; admitted, 1973, Madrid; 1987, Barcelona. *Education:* University of Madrid School of Law (Licenciado en Derecho, 1973). *Member:* Bar Association of Madrid; Bar Association of Barcelona. *LANGUAGES:* English and Spanish.

JAMES A. BAKER, born Chicago, Illinois, January 16, 1931; admitted, 1956, Illinois, U.S.A.; 1970, Madrid. *Education:* Harvard College (B.A., 1952); Harvard Law School, Chicago-Kent College of Law (J.D., 1956); Université Libre de Brussels (Docteur en Droit, 1966); University of Valladolid (Law Degree, 1970). *LANGUAGES:* Spanish and English.

CRISTINA BUSTILLO MUÑOZ, born Avila, Spain, March 20, 1952; admitted, 1979, Madrid. *Education:* University of Madrid (Law Degree, 1977). *LANGUAGES:* Spanish and English.

(This Listing Continued)

EDUARDO GARCÍA CALLEJA, born Madrid, Spain, February 18, 1951; admitted, 1976, Madrid; 1982, Barcelona. *Education:* University of Madrid (Law Degree). *LANGUAGES:* Spanish and English.

ANTONIO LÓPEZ BARRIO, born Madrid, Spain, August 2, 1944; admitted, 1965, Madrid. *Education:* University of Madrid (Law Degree, 1965). *LANGUAGES:* Spanish, English and French.

ALBERTO PÉREZ-FONTÁN ESTEFANIA, born Madrid, Spain, October 17, 1945; admitted, 1971, Madrid. *Education:* Colegio Fray Luis de Leon (Bachiller, 1963); University of Madrid (Law Degree, 1969). *LANGUAGES:* Spanish and English.

FERNANDO PÉREZ-FONTÁN ESTEFANIA, born Madrid, Spain, January 3, 1950; admitted, 1973, Madrid. *Education:* Colegio Fray Luis de Leon (Bachiller 1966); Consejo Superior de Investigaciones Científicas de España, Instituto de Tecnicas Sociales, University of Madrid (Law Degree, 1973). *LANGUAGES:* Spanish and English.

CARLOS E. RUBIO, born Orihuela (Alicante), Spain, October 31, 1941; admitted, 1963, Madrid. *Education:* Colegio Fray Luis de Leon (Bachiller, 1958); University of Madrid (Law Degree, 1963). *LANGUAGES:* Spanish, English and French.

ANTONIO SELAS LOPEZ, born Madrid, Spain, June 11, 1940; admitted, 1964, Madrid. *Education:* Colegio Fray Luis de Leon (Bachiller, 1958); University of Madrid (Law Degree, 1963). *LANGUAGES:* Spanish and English.

OF COUNSEL

JOSÉ MARIA DELGADO COBOS, born Tetuan (Marruecos), Spain, July 24, 1953; admitted, 1979, Madrid. *Education:* University of Madrid (B.A.; Law Degree, 1975); Universite Libre de Bruxelles (EEC Studies, 1981-1982). *LANGUAGES:* Spanish, English and French.

ASSOCIATES

CARMEN ARAUJO, born Madrid, Spain, January 14, 1963; admitted, 1989, Madrid. *Education:* Madrid University (Law, 1987); University of Miami, Coral Gables, Florida (LL.M., 1989). *Member:* Madrid Bar Association. *LANGUAGES:* Spanish, English and French.

MARÍA BARRAGÁN, born Madrid, Spain, March 26, 1971; admitted, 1994, Madrid. *Education:* Madrid University (Complutense) (Law Degree, 1994). *LANGUAGES:* Spanish, English and French.

JOSÉ ANTONIO CAINZOS, born La Coruña, Spain, June 12, 1960; admitted, 1982, Madrid. *Education:* University of Santiago de Compostela (Licenciado en Derecho, 1982); Abogado del Estado (State Attorney, 1985). Professor of Civil and Procedural Law at Instituto de Empresa, Madrid. *LANGUAGES:* Spanish and English.

JUAN MANUEL DE CASTRO, born Madrid, Spain; admitted, 1990, Madrid. *Education:* University of Madrid (Law Degree, 1987); Escuela Libre de Derecho y Economía (Masters, 1991). *LANGUAGES:* Spanish and English.

LETICIA DÍEZ DE LA LASTRA, born Madrid, Spain; admitted, 1990, Madrid. *Education:* Icade (Law Degree, 1990). *LANGUAGES:* Spanish and English.

MAITE DÍEZ VERGARA, born Bilbao, Spain, January 13, 1963; admitted, 1988, Madrid. *Education:* University of Deusto (Law Degree, 1986); University of Exeter, United Kingdom (LL.M. in International Business Legal Studies). *LANGUAGES:* Spanish and English.

ISABEL FERNÁNDEZ, born Madrid, Spain, December 21, 1967; admitted, 1993, Madrid. *Education:* University of Alcalá de Henares, Madrid (Law Degree, 1993; General Practice Law Degree, 1993); School of Law Practice (Labor Law Degree, 1994). *LANGUAGES:* Spanish, English and French.

BEATRIZ GARCIA CIENFUEGOS, born Washington, D.C., June 16, 1966; admitted, 1990, Madrid. *Education:* University of Madrid (Law, 1987); ICADE (M.B.A., 1988). *Member:* Madrid Bar Association. *LANGUAGES:* Spanish, English and French.

CARLOS IRIBARREN, born Pamplona, Spain, January 31, 1966; admitted, 1989, Pamplona (Navarra). *Education:* University of Navarra (Law, 1989); City of London Polytechnic (M.A., Business Law, 1990). *LANGUAGES:* Spanish, English and French.

ADELA LARIO, born Madrid, Spain, December 6, 1963; admitted, 1986, Madrid; 1988, Barcelona. *Education:* Institut Saint Dominique, F.C.E. (Bachillerato, 1981); University of Madrid School of Law (Licenciada en Derecho, 1986); Universite Libre de Bruxelles (License Speciale en

(This Listing Continued)

BAKER & McKENZIE, Madrid—Continued

Droit Europeen, 1987). *Member:* Bar Association of Madrid; Bar Association of Barcelona. *LANGUAGES:* Spanish, French, English and Portuguese.

CONCEPCIÓN MARTÍN, born Madrid, Spain; admitted, 1991, Madrid. *Education:* Madrid Business School (Business Administration, 1989); University of Madrid (Law Degree, 1987); School of Law Practice (Labor Law Degree, 1992; Tax Law Degree, 1992). *LANGUAGES:* Spanish and English.

JAVIER MORERA, born Madrid, Spain. April 8, 1963; admitted, 1986, Madrid. *Education:* University of Madrid (Law, 1986); Madrid Economics School (Tax Law, 1988). *Member:* Madrid Bar Association. *LANGUAGES:* Spanish and English.

CECILIA PASTOR CABALLERO, born Madrid, Spain, October 31, 1962; admitted, 1989, Madrid. *Education:* Liverpool Law Faculty (Bachelor in Law, 1983); University of Madrid (Law Degree, 1988). *LANGUAGES:* Spanish and English.

LUIS PEINADO MATAIX, born Madrid, Spain, July 23, 1962; admitted, 1990, Madrid. *Education:* Murcia University (Law Degree, 1989). *LANGUAGES:* Spanish and English.

ELIZABETH A. POWERS, born New York, N.Y., March 3, 1948; admitted, 1978, Madrid. *Education:* Trinity College, Washington, D.C. (B.A., 1969); University of Madrid (Law Degree, 1977). *LANGUAGES:* Spanish and English.

IÑIGO RODRIGUEZ SASTRE, born Madrid, Spain, November 6, 1965; admitted, 1991, Madrid. *Education:* University of Madrid (Law, 1988); Instituto de Empresa (Master in Corporate Legal Consulting, 1990). *Member:* Madrid Bar Association. *LANGUAGES:* Spanish, English, French.

ENRIQUE VALERA, born San Sebastian, Spain, August 11, 1967; admitted, 1991, Madrid. *Education:* Madrid University (Law, 1990). *Member:* Madrid Bar Association. *LANGUAGES:* Spanish, English and French.

BALAÑÁ EGUÍA

Loeff Claeys Verbeke

ANTONIO MAURA 7, 5°
28014 MADRID, SPAIN
Telephone: 34-1-5312501
Telecopier: 34-1-5313530

Barcelona Office: Avenida Diagonal 550, 4° 1A, 08021. Telephone: 34-3-2007177. Telecopier: 34-3-203098.

Amsterdam, The Netherlands Office: 15 Apollolaan, P.O. Box 75088, 1070 AB. Telephone: 31-20-5741200. Telex: 14292. Telecopier: 31-20-6718775.

Brussels, Belgium Office: 268, A Avenue de Tervueren, A-1150. Telephone: 02-778.22.11. Telecopier: 02-763.21.85.

New York, New York, U.S.A. Office: Swiss Bank Tower, 23rd Floor, 10 East 50th Street, 10022. Telephone: 212-759-9000. Fax: 212-759-9018.

Paris, France Office: 1 Avenue Franklin D. Roosevelt, 75008. Telephone: 1-49539125. Telecopier: 1-45610664.

Rotterdam, The Netherlands Office: 70 Weena, P.O. Box 74, 3000 AB. Telephone: 31-10-4034777. Telex: 23395 (LEX NL). Telecopier: 31-10-4149388.

Singapore Office: 20 Raffles Place, #08 03, Ocean Towers, Singapore 0104. Telephone: 65-5335332. Telecopier: 65-5330313.

Tokyo, Japan Office: NSE Building, 5th Floor, 1-7-1 Kanda Jinbo-cho, Chiyoda-Ku, Tokyo 101. Telephone: 81-3-32599831. Telecopier: 81-3-32599888.

Jakarta, Associated Office: Ali Budiardjo, Nugroho, Reksodiputro, Niaga Tower, 24th floor, Jalan Jenderal Sudirman Kav. 58, 12920. Telephone: 62.21.2505125/2505136. Telecopier: 62.21.2505121/2505001.

Antwerp, Belgium Office: "De Hertoghe," 8th floor, 92 Desguinlei, B.8, B-2018. Telephone: 32.2.2385656. Telex: 72748 (EURLAWB). Telecopier: 32.2.2387877.

Liège, Belgium Office: 13, Rue Simonon, (Place de Bronckart), B-4000. Telephone: 32-41-527722. Telecopier: 32-41-527511.

Luxembourg, Luxembourg Correspondent Office: Zeyen Beghin Feider. 67, Rue Ermesinde, P.O. Box 5017, 1050. Telephone: 352.468946. Telex: 60736 (AFLAW LU). Telecopier: 352.468947.

(This Listing Continued)

EU1242B

PARTNER

JOSÉ MARÍA BALAÑÁ DE EGUÍA, born 1963; admitted, 1987, Barcelona. *Education:* University of Barcelona (Law Degree, 1985) (Degree in Economics, 1985; Catalan Civil Law, 1986). *Member:* International Fiscal Association; Association Internationale des Jeunes Avocats. (Barcelona Office).

ASSOCIATES

PABLO ALCAZAR SIRVENT, born 1968; admitted, 1993, Madrid. *Education:* University of Pontificia de Comillas, Madrid (Law Degree, 1993).

WERNER VON TABOUILLOT, born 1959; admitted, 1987, Madrid. *Education:* University of Heidelberg, Germany (German law Degree, 1984); University of Alcaláde Henares, Madrid (Spanish Law Degree, 1987); University of Innsbruck, Austria (Doctorate in Law, 1989). Associate Professor, University of Alcaláde Henares, Madrid and the National Institute for Administrative Studies.

Languages: Dutch, English, French, German, Italian, Japanese, Russian and Spanish.

(For personnel and other data, see Professional Biographics at Amsterdam, Antwerp, Brussels, Liège, New York, Paris, Rotterdam, Singapore and Tokyo).

BUFETE BARRILERO & ASOCIADOS

ORTEGA Y GASSET, N° 30 - BAJO
28006 MADRID, SPAIN
Telephone: 576.34.24
Fax: 575.75.17

Bilbao, Spain Office: Alameda Urquijo, n° 12, Entreplanta Izda., 48008. Telephone 34-4-416.55.00. Fax: 34-4-416.84.37.

Taxation, Commercial, Corporation, Civil, Banking, Bankruptcy, Administrative, EEC and International Law, General Practice.

MEMBERS OF FIRM

EDUARDO BARRILERO, born Madrid, Spain, October 6, 1957. *Education:* University of Deusto, Bilbao (Law Degree, 1979). *Member:* Basque Country Bar Association. *LANGUAGES:* English.

JULIO LECANDA, born Guecho, Spain, February 29, 1960. *Education:* University of Deusto, Bilbao (Law Degree, 1982). *Member:* Basque Country Bar Association. *LANGUAGES:* English.

ANTONIO TENA, born Bilbao, Spain, December 17, 1959. *Education:* University of Deusto, Bilbao (Law Degree, Diploma in Economics, 1982). *Member:* Basque Country Bar Association. *LANGUAGES:* English.

MARGARITA BIDEGORRI, born Guecho, Spain, February 27, 1962. *Education:* University of Deusto, Bilbao (Law Degree, 1985). *Member:* Basque Country Bar Association. *LANGUAGES:* English.

ALBERTO FERREIRO, born Bilbao, Spain, September 1, 1961. *Education:* University of Deusto, Bilbao (Law Degree; Diploma in Economics, 1984). *Member:* Basque Country Bar Association. *LANGUAGES:* English.

RESIDENT ASSOCIATES

BEATRIZ LADERO, born Bilbao, Spain, May 4, 1966. *Education:* University of Deusto, Bilbao (Law Degree, 1989); Business Institute, Madrid (Master in Business Legal Advising, 1990). *Member:* Madrid Bar Association. *LANGUAGES:* English.

Mª ASUNCION MUGICA, born Bilbao, Spain, September 12, 1966. *Education:* University of Deusto, Bilbao (Law Degree, 1991). *Member:* Basque Country Bar Association. *LANGUAGES:* English.

BEATRIZ ECHANIZ, born Azkonitia, Guipuzcoa, Spain, October 14, 1969. *Education:* ICADE, Madrid (Law Degree, 1993). *Member:* Madrid Bar Association. *LANGUAGES:* English and French.

ANGELICA FERNANDEZ-IRIONDO, born San Sebastian, Guipuzcoa, Spain, June 28, 1967. *Education:* Complutense University, Madrid (Law Degree, 1991). *Member:* Madrid Bar Association. *LANGUAGES:* English and French.

(For Complete Biographical Data on all Personnel, see Professional Biographies at Bilbao, Spain)

BIGNON & LEBRAY

CASTELLO 35
MADRID 28001, SPAIN
Telephone: (34.1) 577.26.66
Telecopier: (34.1) 577.61.89

Paris, France Office: 4, Rue Bayard, 75008. Telephone: (1) 42.56.64.00. Telex: BIGLEX 649 526 F. Telecopier: (1) 45.61.09.50.

Aix-en-Provence, France Office: 3, cours Mirabeau, 13100. Telephone: 42.38.58.38. Telecopier: 42.26.92.37.

Lille, France Office: 19, boulevard de la Liberté, 59800. Telephone: 20.57.90.90. Telecopier: 20.57.90.95.

Lyon, France Office: 29, rue Gasparin, 69002. Telephone: 78.37.03.17. Telecopier: 78.92.82.94.

General French, European Community and International Practice. Corporate, Reorganization, Real Estate, Construction, Commercial Leases, Banking, Financial, Securities, Stock Exchange Regulations, International Contracts, Antitrust, Unfair Competition, Distributorship, Agency, Franchise, Product Liability, Patent and Trademark, Environment, Labor, Taxation, Litigation, Arbitration. Admitted to appear before all French Courts and The European Community Court of Justice. Some Lawyers of the firm are admitted to appear before certain foreign courts.

FIRM PROFILE: Originally founded in 1982, Bignon & Lebray is dedicated to providing corporate law assistance. Composed of a multidisciplinary team, it renders legal advice and counselling or litigation in all branches of business law, from a domestic, European and international perspective.

The firm counsels and assists French and foreign corporations, comprising major groups as well as smaller competitive companies, with varied activities including industry, banking, finance, portfolio management, distribution, real estate, transportation, computer and tourism.

While the firm maintains an extensive network of correspondents in the rest of France and in most major foreign cities, it has began an expansion program to open branch offices in several major cities in France and in other countries of Europe. At present, it has three branch offices in France, in Lille, in Lyon and in Aix-en-Provence and one in Spain, in Madrid.

RESIDENT LAWYERS

CHRISTINE SABAS-BIDEGAIN, born Boulogne-Billancourt, France, March 9, 1959; admitted, 1986, Paris. *Education:* Université de Paris XI (Maîtrise en droit privé, 1980); Université de Paris I (D.E.A. de Droit International Privé et Droit du Commerce International, 1981; D.E.A. de droits anglais et nord-américain des affaires, 1982); University of Illinois (M.C.L., 1983). *Member:* Paris Bar Association. *LANGUAGES:* French, Spanish and English. *PRACTICE AREAS:* Foreign Investments; Corporate law; Industrial Property Law; International Contracts.

FRANCISCO JAVIER CARBONELL RODRIGUEZ, born Cartagena, Spain, December 14, 1958; admitted, 1982, Madrid. *Education:* University Autonome of Madrid (Licence in Law, 1982). *Member:* Madrid Bar Association. *LANGUAGES:* Spanish, French and English. *PRACTICE AREAS:* Commercial Law; Civil Law; Intellectual Property; Maritime Law; Bankruptcy Law.

(For List of Partners and Associates, see Professional Biographies at Paris, France)

BRIONES, ALONSO & MARTIN

PASEO DE LA CASTELLANA 126 8ÓDCHA
28046 MADRID, SPAIN
Telephone: 34 (1) 563 77 53
Telefax: 34 (1) 563 66 67

Barcelona, Affiliated Office: Rodes & Sala, C/Pau Casals, 15-08021, BARCELONA - TEL: 34 (3) 200 15 55. FAX: 34 (3) 209 89 96.

International and Domestic Tax Planning and Advise, Tax Litigation.

SENIOR PARTNERS

LUIS BRIONES FERNANDEZ, born Madrid, Spain, 1954. *Education:* Deusto University, Bilbao, Spain, (J.D., 1976) University of Madrid - Complutense - 1991 (Licenciate in Psychology); I.C.A.D.E., Madrid, 1978 (Licenciate in Business Administration; Harvard University, U.S.A., 1986 (LL.M. and International Tax Program). Inspector of Finances at the Ministry of Finance on Leave. Professor from 1981 at the School of Financial and Tax Inspection, Business Institute and School of Public Finance,

(This Listing Continued)

among other institutions. *Member:* Madrid Bar Association. *LANGUAGES:* Spanish and English.

FELIPE ALONSO FERNANDEZ, born Madrid, Spain, 1953. *Education:* University of Madrid- Autónoma - 1978 (Law Degree). Inspector of Finances at the Ministry of Finance, on leave. Professor at the University of Madrid - Autónoma - School of Financial and Tax Inspection, Business Institute and Economic School Editor of the "Value Added Tax Monographies". *Member:* Madrid Bar Association. *LANGUAGES:* Spanish and English.

ALFONSO MARTIN MUNCHARAZ, born Toledo, Spain, 1953. *Education:* Deusto University, Bilbao-Spain, 1975 (Law Degree). Inspector of Finances at the Ministry of Finance, on leave. Professor at the School of Public Finance, Business Institute, and Centre for Tax and Business Studies - CETE. Director of Master on Tax Advise of ICADE and of the Master on Tax Planning of SEK. *Member:* Madrid Bar Association. *LANGUAGES:* Spanish and French.

OF COUNSEL AND ASSOCIATES

ANGEL SERRANO GUTIERREZ, born Madrid, Spain, 1954. *Education:* University of Madrid - Complutense -1976 (Licenciate in Economics). Inspector of Finance at the Ministry of Finance, on leave. Professor at the School of Financial and Tax Inspection and the Business Institute. *Member:* Madrid Economist Association. *LANGUAGES:* Spanish and English.

ROMAN CARNICERO PERALES, born Santa Cruz de Tenerife, Spain, 1948. *Education:* University of Madrid - Politécnica - , 1975 (Industrial Engineering Degree). Associated Tax Inspector at the Ministry of Finance, on leave. *LANGUAGES:* Spanish and German.

ENRIQUE LEON SANCHEZ, born Romanshorn, Switzerland, 1964. *Education:* University of Zaragoza, 1987 (Law Degree); Business Institute Madrid (Master in Taxation, 1990). *Member:* Madrid Bar Association. *LANGUAGES:* Spanish, French and English.

ENRIQUE FERNANDEZ OTERO, born Madrid, Spain, 1962. *Education:* Madrid, 1986 (Law Degree); Business Institute, Madrid (Master in Taxation, 1989). *Member:* Of the Madrid Bar Association. *LANGUAGES:* Spanish.

JUAN PUJOL JAEN, born Madrid, Spain, 1954. *Education:* University of Madrid - Complutense - 1976 (Law Degree). Associated Tax Inspector at the Ministry of Finance, on leave. Technical Director, of EDERSA-FRANCIS LEFEBVRE (Legal Publications). *LANGUAGES:* Spanish and French.

PEDRO BROSA & ASOCIADOS

Established in 1965

ALFONSO XII, 18, 3° IZQDA.
28014 MADRID, SPAIN
Telephone: 34-1-522 82 02
Telefax: 34-1-522 39 89

Barcelona, Spain Office: Avda. Diagonal, 598, 1° 2ª, pral. 2ª y 5° 2ª, 08021. Telephone: 34-3-200 09 33. Telefax: 34-3-202 29 07.

Bilbao, Spain Office: San Vicente, 8, Plta 9° dpto. 2, 48007. Telephone: 34-4-423 03 36 Telefax: 34-4-423 93 82.

Brussels, Belgium Office: 165, Avenue Louise, 9 ème. étage, 1050. Telephone: 32-2-644 16 09. Telefax: 32-2-644 30 25.

General Practice, Civil Litigation, Civil, Commercial, Corporation, Intellectual Property Taxation, Foreign Investments, Administrative, Banking and Financing, Bankruptcy Law, Accounting, Auditing and General Business Consulting.

MEMBERS OF FIRM

PEDRO BROSA, born Lérida, Spain, May 30, 1937; admitted, 1964, Barcelona. *Education:* University of Barcelona (Licenciado en Derecho, 1959; Profesor Mercantil, 1960). Lecturer, Taxation Law, University of Barcelona, 1962-1963. *Member:* Barcelona (Member Governing Body) and Madrid Bar Associations; Colegio de Titulares Mercantiles de Barcelona; Fomento del Trabajo Nacional (Member, Advisory Committee); English Chamber of Commerce in Spain. *LANGUAGES:* Spanish, English, French and Catalan. *PRACTICE AREAS:* General Practice; Commercial; Corporation; Banking and Financing; Bankruptcy Law; General Business Consulting.

DOLORES ALEMANY, born Madrid, Spain, 1961; admitted, 1987, Madrid. *Education:* University of Madrid (Licenciada en Derecho, 1985);

(This Listing Continued)

PEDRO BROSA & ASOCIADOS, Madrid—Continued

Instituto de Empresa of Madrid (Master en Asesoría Jurídica de Empresa, 1987). *Member:* Madrid Bar Association. *LANGUAGES:* Spanish and French. *PRACTICE AREAS:* Civil and Commercial.

AGUSTIN BOU, born Barcelona, Spain, September 8, 1956; admitted, 1982, Barcelona. *Education:* University of Barcelona (Licenciado en Derecho, 1981; Master en Ciencias de los Negocios por Management School, 1979). *Member:* Union Internacional de Abogados; Asociacion Internacional de Jovenes Abogados. *LANGUAGES:* Spanish, English, French, Italian and Catalan. *PRACTICE AREAS:* Accounting and Auditing.

FERNANDO GONZALEZ, born Madrid, Spain, September 3, 1964; admitted, 1989, Madrid; 1933, Soria. *Education:* University of Madrid (Licenciado en Derecho); Master in Business ConsultancyInstituto de Empresa (Busisness and Civil Law). *PRACTICE AREAS:* Commercial and Litigation.

RICARDO REBATE, born Madrid, Spain, 1960; admitted, 1989, Madrid. *Education:* University of Madrid (Licenciado en Derecho, 1982); Instituto de Empresa of Madrid (Master en Asesoría Juridica de Empresa, 1986); Centro de Estudios Tributarios y Económicos (Diplomado en Estudios Tributarios, 1988). *Member:* Madrid Bar Association. *LANGUAGES:* Spanish and English. *PRACTICE AREAS:* Commercial; Intellectual Property; Show Business.

CARLOS SAHUQUILLO, born Barcelona, Spain, May 10, 1958; admitted, 1982, Barcelona. *Education:* University of Barcelona (Licenciado en Ciencias Económicas y Empresariales, 1981; Licenciado en Derecho, 1982); Cátedra Durán y Bas (Diploma en Estudios de Derecho Civil Catalán, 1982). *Member:* Barcelona, American Bar Association; International Bar Association; Colegio de Economistas de Catalunya; Instituto de Censores Jurados de Cuentas de España; Asociación Española de Contabilidad y Administración de Empresas; Registro de Economistas Auditores; Registro Oficial de Auditores de Cuentas; International Tax Planning Association. *LANGUAGES:* Spanish, English, French and Catalan. *PRACTICE AREAS:* General Practice; Commercial; Corporation; Foreign Investment; Banking and Financing; General Business Consulting.

JUAN SÁNCHEZ, born Madrid, Spain, February 21, 1970. *Education:* University of Madrid (Licenciado en Derecho, 1994). *LANGUAGES:* English and Spanish. *PRACTICE AREAS:* Civil Law; Commercial Law; Auditing.

Languages: Spanish, English, French, Italian, German and Catalan.

(For Biographical Data on Barcelona, Spain, Bilbao, Spain and Brussels, Belgium Personnel, see Professional Biographies at Barcelona, Spain, Bilbao, Spain and Brussels, Belgium).

BUFETE INTERNACIONAL

Abogados y Economistas

GURTUBAY 6
28001 MADRID, SPAIN
Telephone: 34 3 414 56 86
Fax: 34 3 414 56 97

Barcelona Spain Office: Diagonal, 600, 08021. Telephone: +34 3 416 5697. Fax: +34 3 414 5686.

FIRM PROFILE: Multidisciplinary firm integrating Lawyers and Business Consultants experienced in international corporate matters. It provides a complete range of legal services, being specially well prepared, due to its multidisciplinarity, to deal with matters involving complex business situations. Its main areas of practice are: Corporate and Commercial Law, Banking and Finance, Property and Real Estate, Mergers and Acquisitions, Civil Law, Public Administration, Litigation, Spanish and International Taxation.

Associated to ICC INTERCONTINENTAL CONSULTANTS.

PARTNERS

Pedro Pascual   **Juan Calderon**

Languages: Spanish, English, French, German, Italian and Catalan.

CASTRO, SUEIRO & VARELA

Established in 1987

CLAUDIO COELLO, 46, 4°
28001 MADRID, SPAIN
Telephone: 577.50.20
Fax: 431.59.31

Commercial, Corporate, Banking and Financing, Insurance, Aviation, Foreign Investment, Labor, Litigation, Administrative and General Practice.

MEMBERS OF FIRM

JUAN CARLOS CASTRO RICO, born 1958; admitted, 1982, Madrid. *Education:* University of Madrid (Degree in General Practice and Tax Studies). Author: Chapter on Spain for the 'International Handbook on Contracts of Employment," Kluwer Publishers, 1990-1994. *LANGUAGES:* Spanish and English. *PRACTICE AREAS:* Commercial; Corporate; Banking and Financing; Aviation; Foreign Investment; Labor; Litigation; General Practice.

MIGUEL SUEIRO SEOANE, born 1958; admitted, 1982, Madrid. *Education:* University of Madrid. *LANGUAGES:* Spanish and English. *PRACTICE AREAS:* Commercial; Corporate; Banking and Financing; Insurance; Aviation; Foreign Investment; General Practice.

JOSE RAMON VARELA DIAZ, born 1958; admitted, 1986, Madrid; 1988, Santander. *Education:* University of Madrid. *LANGUAGES:* Spanish, English and French. *PRACTICE AREAS:* Commercial; Corporate; Banking and Finance; Foreign Investment; Labor; Litigation; Administrative; General Practice.

ASSOCIATES

VALERIA MENDEZ DE VIGO MONTOJO, born 1965; admitted, 1990, Madrid. *Education:* University of Madrid. *LANGUAGES:* Spanish, English and German. *PRACTICE AREAS:* Commercial; Corporate; Banking and Financing; Insurance; Foreign Investment; General Practice.

SUSANA NAVARRO NICOLAS, born 1964; admitted, 1989, Madrid. *Education:* University of Madrid. *LANGUAGES:* Spanish and English. *PRACTICE AREAS:* Commercial; Corporate; Foreign Investment; Labor; General Practice.

SANTIAGO CRUCES TITO, born 1967; admitted, 1992, Madrid. *Education:* University of Madrid. *LANGUAGES:* Spanish and English. *PRACTICE AREAS:* Commercial; Corporate; Foreign Investment; Labor; Litigation; General Practice.

DAVID DIAZ ZAFORAS, born 1970; admitted, 1994, Madrid. *Education:* University of Madrid. *LANGUAGES:* Spanish, English and French. *PRACTICE AREAS:* Commercial; Corporate; Insurance; Foreign Investments; Labor; General Practice.

JOSE ANTONIO RODRIGUEZ GARCIA, born 1964; admitted, 1994. *Education:* University of Seville (Company Law Speciality); Doctor in Hispanic Philology (Literary theory); Business Institute ("Instituto de Empresa") (Master in Corporate Legal Advice). *LANGUAGES:* Spanish, English and Arabic. *PRACTICE AREAS:* Commercial; Corporate; Litigation; General Practice.

CERVELLÓ, LÓPEZ-CHICHERI Y ARAGÓN, ABOGADOS

Associated with Ernst & Young International

TORRE PICASSO - PLANTA 3
PLAZA PABLO RUIZ PICASSO, S/N
28020 MADRID, SPAIN
Telephone: (34-1) 572-7200
Fax: (34-1) 572-7400/7372

Barcelona, Spain Office: L'Illa Diagonal, 575; 08029. Telephone: (34-3) 410.67.07. Fax: (34-3) 405.37.84.
Bilbao, Spain Office: Colón de Larreátegui, 26, 48009. Telephone: (34-4) 424-3777/423-8746. Fax: (34-4) 424-2745.
Associated Offices in Spain: Las Palmas de Gran Canaria, Málaga, Palma de Mallorca, Pamploma, Santa Cruz de Tenerife, Sevilla, Valencia and Vigo.
Associated Law Practices Abroad: Belgium, France, Germany, Hungary, Italy, The Netherlands and Portugal.

(This Listing Continued)

General Practice, Corporate, Commercial, Administrative, Litigation, Foreign Trade and Investment, Banking, Finance, Real Estate, EV Law, Intellectual Property, Tax, and Labor Law.

PARTNERS / DIRECTORS

JOSÉ MARÍA CERVELLÓ GRANDE, born Cádiz, Spain, December 11, 1947; admitted, 1975, Madrid. *Education:* University of Seville (Law Degree, 1969); University of Madrid (Art History Degree, 1980). Former Senior Govt. Attorney. Founding Member, Civil and Mercantile Court of Arbitration (CIMA). Professor of Law: UNED 1975-1978; School of Public Treasury, 1982-1989; Instituto de Empresa, 1979—. Instituto de Empresa: Secretary, Advisory Committee, 1984—; Director, Masters Program in Business Law, 1986—. *Member:* Madrid Bar Association. *LANGUAGES:* Spanish, English and French.

JAIME LÓPEZ-CHICHERI DABAN, born Madrid, Spain, June 13, 1948; admitted, 1975, Madrid. *Education:* University of Madrid (Law Degree, 1975). Advisory Committee of the Masters Program of the Instituto de Empresa. *Member:* Madrid Bar Association; National Union of Tax Attorneys; National Association of Tax Advisers; and Tax Club. *LANGUAGES:* Spanish, English and French.

MANUEL ARAGÓN ARAGÓN, born Madrid, Spain, January 17, 1948; admitted, 1973, Madrid. *Education:* University of Madrid (Law Degree, 1973). Censor Jurado de Cuentas (CPA). *Member:* Madrid Bar Association. *LANGUAGES:* Spanish and English.

JAVIER DÍAZ-GÁLVEZ, born Madrid, Spain, December 3, 1952; admitted, 1979, Madrid, Alcalá de Henares. *Education:* University of Madrid (Law Degree, 1976). Real Estate Agent. *Member:* Madrid and Alcalá de Henares Bar Associations. *LANGUAGES:* Spanish, English and French.

ADOLFO MENÉNDEZ MENÉNDEZ, born Gijón, Spain, February 1, 1958; admitted, 1986, Madrid; 1988, Toledo. *Education:* University of Madrid (Law Degree, 1980). Former Senior Govt. Attorney. Founding member, Civil and Mercantile Court of Arbitration (CIMA). Professor of Law: University of Madrid and Instituto de Empresa. *Member:* Madrid and Toledo Bar Associations. *LANGUAGES:* Spanish, English and French.

ALVARO REQUEIJO PASCUA, born Madrid, Spain, April 3, 1958; admitted, 1989, Madrid. *Education:* ICADE (Law Degree, 1980; Business Degree, 1981). Former Senior Government Attorney. *Member:* Madrid Bar Association.

MEMBERS OF FIRM

Javier Arroyo Ramos	Manuela Dumas Kremer
Miguel Angel	Ana Luisa Collazo Lugo
Rodríguez-Sahagún	Ramón Del Avellanal Calzadilla
Borja Otero De Navascués	Sofía Del Pozo Jiménez
Carmen Pérez Fontes	José Domínguez Leandro
Herbert F. Riband (U.S. Lawyer,	Alfonso Javier Lara Garay
not admitted in Spain)	Pilar Foncillas
Elena Fraile Chiarri	Jaime Beltrán
María Victoria Apaolaza	Alejandro Rebollo Rico
	Paz Mendoza

Languages: Spanish, English, French, German and Italian.

CLIFFORD CHANCE

Established in 1980

PASEO DE LA CASTELLANA 110
28046 MADRID, SPAIN
Telephone: (34 1) 562 76 74
Fax: (34 1) 562 49 93

Amsterdam, The Netherlands Office: Apollolaan 171, 1077 AS, P.O. Box 7301, 1007 JH. Telephone: (31 20) 577 71 11. Fax: (31 20) 676 93 26.
Bahrain, Manama Associated Office: Law Office of Shaikh Isa bin Mohammed Al Khalifa. P.O. Box 20717. Telephone: (973) 531535; 531073. Fax: (973) 536272; 530608.
Barcelona, Spain Office: Pau Claris 102, 08009. Telephone: (34 3) 318 68 64. Fax: (34 3) 317 73 23.
Brussels, Belgium Office: Avenue Louise 65, Box 2, 1050. Telephone: (32 2) 533 59 11. Fax: (32 2) 533 59 59.
Budapest, Hungary Office: Köves & Partners, Clifford Chance. Madách Trade Center, Madách Imre Út 14, 1075. Telephone: (36 1) 268 1600. Fax: (36 1) 268 1610.

(This Listing Continued)

Dubai, United Arab Emirates Office: 18th Floor, Dubai World Trade Centre, P.O. Box 9380. Telephone: (971 4) 314333. Fax: (971 4) 313990; 314565.
Frankfurt/Main, Germany Office: Friedrichstraße 2-6, 60323. Telephone: (49 69) 971 4090. Fax: (49 69) 971 40977.
Hanoi, Vietnam Office: 52 Nguyen Binh Khiem. Telephone: (844) 229 182/3/4/5/6. Fax: (844) 229 190.
Hong Kong Office: 30th Floor, Jardine House, One Connaught Place. Telephone: (852) 2810 0229. Fax: (852) 2810 4708; 2810 4858; 2810 4743.
London, England Office: 200 Aldersgate Street, EC1A 4JJ. Telephone: (44 171) 600 1000. Fax: (44 171) 600 5555.
Milan, Italy Associated Office: Grimaldi e Clifford Chance. Via Gesú, 3, 20121. Telephone: (39 2) 7600 8040. Fax: (39 2) 7600 4950.
Moscow, Russia Office: Ul. Sadovaya - Samotechnaya 24/27, 2nd Floor, 103051. Telephone: (7 501) 258 50 50. Fax: (7 501) 258 50 51.
New York, New York Office: Swiss Bank Tower, 10 East 50th Street, 10022. Telephone: (1 212) 750 1440. Fax: (1 212) 758 6625.
Paris, France Office: 112 avenue Kléber, BP 163 Trocadéro, 75770 Paris Cedex 16. Telephone: (33 1) 44 05 52 52. Fax: (33 1) 44 05 52 00.
Riyadh, Saudi Arabia Associated Office: The Law Firm of Salah Al-Hejailan. P.O. Box 1454, 11431. Telephone: (966 1) 479 2200. Fax: (966 1) 479 1717.
Rome, Italy Associated Office: Grimaldi e Clifford Chance. Viale G. Rossini 7, 00198. Telephone: (39 6) 807 2251. Fax: (39 6) 807 8201.
Shanghai, People's Republic of China Office: Suite 898, Shanghai Centre, 1376 Nanjing Xi Lu, 200040. Telephone: (86 21) 279 8461. Fax: (86 21) 279 8462.
Singapore Office: 16 Collyer Quay #31-00, 0104. Telephone: (65) 535 1855. Fax: (65) 535 6855.
Tokyo, Japan Office: 6th Floor, South Hill Nagatacho Building, 11-30 Nagatacho 1-chome, Chiyoda-ku, 100. Telephone: (81 3) 3581 4311. Fax: (81 3) 3593 0651.
Warsaw, Poland Office: Warsaw Corporate Centre, ul. Emilii Plater 28, 00-688. Telephone: (48 2) 630 3344. Fax: (48 2) 630 3355.

International and Domestic Banking, Capital Markets, Corporate Law, Management Buy-outs, Commercial Law, Aircraft Finance, Takeovers and Mergers, Corporate Restructurings, Joint Ventures, Commercial Property, EC Law and Litigation.
Firm engaged in English, Spanish and General International Practice.

RESIDENT PARTNERS

PETER C.E. CORNELL, (Not admitted in Spain). Solicitor of the Supreme Court of England and Wales, 1978. *LANGUAGES:* English, French and Spanish. *PRACTICE AREAS:* Project Finance; Asset Based Lending; Leveraged Buyouts; Mergers and Acquisitions.

JAIME DE SAN ROMAN DIEGO, admitted, 1978, Madrid. *Education:* Universidad Complutense de Madrid (1975). Lecturer, Commercial Law, Universidad de Comillas ICADE, 1985. *LANGUAGES:* Spanish, English and French. *PRACTICE AREAS:* Banking Law; Corporate Law; Commercial Law.

IGNACIO OJANGUREN, Abogado. *PRACTICE AREAS:* Mergers, Acquisitions and Divestitures; Joint Ventures; Securities; Cross Border Mergers and Acquisitions; Corporate Finance.

CLIVE VERO, Solicitor of the Supreme Court, 1969; Conseil Juridique inscrit sur la Liste du Tribunal de Grande Instance de Paris, 1973; Universidad Complutense de Madrid; Licencaido en Derecho, 1980; Abogado admitted, 1985. *LANGUAGES:* English and Spanish. *PRACTICE AREAS:* Property Law; Construction Law; Corporate Law.

(For names of Partners resident in other offices, see Professional Biographies for those offices)

CORONEL DE PALMA & ASOCIADOS

Abogados

Established in 1986

ANTONIO MAURA, 18
MADRID 28014, SPAIN
Telephone: 532.38.52 532.62.15 532.09.22
Telefax: 532.39.47

General Practice, Business, Banking, Tax and European Law. Commercial, Civil and Administrative Law. Litigations.

(This Listing Continued)

CORONEL DE PALMA & ASOCIADOS, Madrid—
Continued

MEMBERS OF FIRM

LUIS CORONEL DE PALMA, born Madrid, Spain, May 3, 1925; admitted, 1957, Madrid and Barcelona. *Education:* University of Madrid (Dr. Jur. with distinction, 1946). Public State Notary, 1951. State Lawyer, 1953. Magistrate in the Administrative Court of the Interamerican Development Bank, 1955. Professor, University of Madrid. Lecturer at the Spanish Chamber of Commerce in New York, Zurich and Milan and University of Santander, Barcelona and Lima, Peru. *Member:* Royal Academy of Jurisprudence and Legislation (Academician); Spanish Institute; Royal Academy of Economic and Financial Sciences (Academician). *LANGUAGES:* English and French. *PRACTICE AREAS:* Banking; Financial.

FEDERICO CACHO-ZABALZA SCHNEIDER, born Madrid, Spain, May 19, 1941; admitted, 1971, Madrid. *Education:* University of Madrid (Jur. Lic., 1968); Centro de Estudios Universitarios of Madrid (Master Foreign Trade, 1971); Institute Cooperativo (Diploma in Coo perative Societies). *LANGUAGES:* English and French. *PRACTICE AREAS:* Commercial; Civil; Administrative; Litigation.

CARLOS DE LA MATA GOROSTIZAGA, born Madrid, Spain, July 16, 1947. *Education:* University of Madrid (C.E.U.)(Jur.Lic. 1973). State Lawyer, 1973. Chief State Lawyer in the Delegations of the Ministry of Finance in Alava, Navarra and Guadalajara. Director of Law Dept. of Tres Cantos, Auxini. Vice-Secretary of Instituto Nacional de Industria. Assistant General Manager of Iberia Air Lines. Chairman of Iber-Swiss Catering. General Secretary of Dorna S.A. *LANGUAGES:* English. *PRACTICE AREAS:* Civil; Commercial; Corporate Law; Investments; Air Lines.

ALFONSO CORONEL DE PALMA, born Madrid, Spain, December 29, 1963; admitted, 1989, Madrid. *Education:* University of Madrid (C.E.U.) (Jur.Lic.1986). Doctorate studies in Philosofical, Moral & Political Rights. Studies in Politi cal Sciences and Corporate Rights. Co-Author: "Centessimus Annus," (C.E.U.). Professor, Corporate Rights, I.T.E. Member, Governing Body of the Law School of the University of Madrid, 1985. Member, Royal Academy of the Jurisprudence and Legislation. *LANGUAGES:* English. *PRACTICE AREAS:* Civil, Penal and Corporate Law; Litigation.

MIGUEL ANGEL MEDIERO HERNANDEZ, born Madrid, Spain, April 6, 1957; admitted, 1989, Madrid. *Education:* University of Madrid (Jur.Lic.1987); Technical Engineering; Masters in Taxes and Financial Advisement (C.E.F.); Diploma, General Accounting, Economic and Financial Analysis; Diploma, Corporate Taxes; Diploma, Labor Rights). *Member:* Spanish Fiscal Advisor Association. *LANGUAGES:* Italian. *PRACTICE AREAS:* Fiscal, Taxes and Finance Law; Civil and Business Law.

REPRESENTATIVE CLIENTS: Banco Hispano-Americano, B.N.P.; Finazauto-Caterpillar; Cristaleria, ESP; St. Gobain; Consejo Superior de Camaras Prop. Urbano; I.N.G. Group.

J. Y B. CREMADES Y ASOCIADOS

GOYA 18, 2ND FLOOR
28001 MADRID, SPAIN
Telephone: 431.8354
Fax: 576.9794

Paris, France Office: J. et B. Cremades et Associes, 51, Avenue Georges Mandel, 75116. Telephone: 45.53.55.50. Fax: 45.53.55.49.
Brussels, Belgium Office: Av. Louise, 391, 1050. Telephone: 648.9840. Fax: 647.8351.

General Practice. Commercial, Corporate, Foreign Investment, Licensing, Insurance, Banking and Finance, Oil and Gas, Real Estate and Patent Law, Aeronautical/Transportation, Commercial Arbitration, EEC, Competition Law, Customs Regulations, Environmental Law, Public Procurement.

PARTNERS

JUAN ANTONIO CREMADES, born Zaragoza, Spain, January 1, 1940; admitted, 1961, Zaragoza; 1966, Madrid; 1986, Paris. *Education:* University of Zaragoza (Law Degree, 1960); University of Paris (Law Degree, 1960; Ph.D., 1968); International Faculty of Comparative Law (1961). President, Union Internationale des Avocats, 1990-1991; Representative of the Paris Bar, 1992; Chairman, Committee of Regulation of Contracts of the International Chamber of Commerce, 1979-1980; International Maritime Arbitration Organization (CMI-ICC), 1979-1980. President, Spanish

(This Listing Continued)

Chamber of Commerce in France since 1987. *Member:* Madrid Bar Association; Ordre des Avocats à la Cour de Paris; ICC International Court of Arbitration since 1969; Honorary member, Zaragoza, Mexico and Dominican Republic Bar Associations. (Also at Paris, France and Brussels, Belgium Offices). *LANGUAGES:* Spanish, French and English.

BERNARDO M. CREMADES, born Zaragoza, Spain, July 20, 1943; admitted, 1969, Madrid; 1986, Paris, France. *Education:* University of Cologne (Ph.D., German Law, 1967); University of Seville (Ph.D., Spanish Law, 1968). Professor, Law Faculty, University of Madrid, 1975—. Author, Litigating in Spain (Kluwer, 1989). Arbitration in Spain (Butterworths, 1991) and Business Law in Spain (Butterworths, 1992). *Member:* Madrid Bar Association; International Council of Commercial Arbitration; International Bar Association; American Bar Association; Avocat à la Cour de Paris. (Also at Paris, France and Brussels, Belgium Offices). *LANGUAGES:* Spanish, French, German and English.

JOSÉ I. GARCÍA GOIZUETA, born San Sebastián, Spain, July 18, 1947; admitted, 1975, Madrid. *Education:* University of Zaragoza (Law Degree, 1969); The Hague Academy of International Law (Private International Law). Member, Unión Internacional de Abogados (UIA). *Member:* Madrid, Zaragoza, Barcelona, Guipúzcoa and Oviedo Bar Associations. *LANGUAGES:* Spanish, French and English.

ANGEL M. TEJADA, born Madrid, Spain, February 27, 1953; admitted, 1980, Madrid. *Education:* University of Madrid (Law Degree, 1976). Visiting Lecturer at the Augustine of Bethencourt Foundation: College of Civil Engineering of the Complutense University of Madrid. *Member:* Madrid, Barcelona, Málaga and Jerez de la Frontera Bar Associations; European Lawyers' Union. *LANGUAGES:* Spanish, French and English.

FERNANDO VON CARSTENN-LICHTERFELDE MENÉNDEZ, born Madrid, Spain, May 28, 1956; admitted, 1980, Madrid. *Education:* University of Madrid (Law Degree, 1979). *Member:* Madrid, Las Palmas de Gran Canaria and International Bar Associations. *LANGUAGES:* Spanish, German and English.

JORGE RICHTER ECHEVARRÍA, born Bilbao, Spain, June 27, 1956; admitted, 1982, Madrid. *Education:* University of Madrid (Law Degree, 1982). Professor, Center for Iberoamerican Studies, University of Paris, Sorbonne, 1982-1987. Chargé d'enseignement de la Faculté de Droit de l'université Paris V René Descartes, 1983-1987. *Member:* Madrid Bar Association. *LANGUAGES:* Spanish, French and English.

CARLOS PAZOS, born Orense, Spain, January 8, 1962; admitted, 1988, Orense. *Education:* University of Madrid (Law Degree, 1987); College of Europe, Bruges (Diploma in High European Studies, 1988); London School of Economics, University of London (LL.M., Master of Laws, 1989). *Member:* Madrid Bar Associations. *LANGUAGES:* Spanish, English, French and Portuguese.

ASSOCIATES

CALVIN A. HAMILTON, born Guyana, South America, December 21, 1952; admitted, 1987, New York; 1991, Madrid. *Education:* C.W. Post College of Long Island University (B.Sc., 1977); Brooklyn Law School (J.D., 1983); Fletcher School of Law and Diplomacy (M.A.L.D., 1985). *Member:* New York Bar Association; Madrid Bar Association; American Society of International Law; International Bar Association. *LANGUAGES:* English, Spanish and French.

CARMEN NÚÑEZ-LAGOS, born Madrid, Spain, May 24, 1966; admitted, 1989, Madrid. *Education:* University of Zaragoza (Law Degree, 1989); University of Bologne (1988-1989); University of Exeter (LL.M., International Business Legal Studies, 1990). *Member:* Madrid Bar Association. *LANGUAGES:* Spanish, French, English and Italian.

ROSARIO LUNA GARCIA-MINA, born Pamplona, Spain, February 11, 1966; admitted, 1991, Madrid. *Education:* Universidad Pontificia de Comillas, Madrid, ICADE (Law Degree, 1989; Economics Degree, 1990). *Member:* Madrid Bar Association. *LANGUAGES:* Spanish and English.

JAVIER SANTOS RAMIREZ, born Madrid, Spain, July 2, 1964; admitted, 1991, Madrid. *Education:* Universidad Pontificia de Comillas, ICADE, Madrid (Law Degree, 1987); London School of Economics (LL.M., Commercial and Corporate Law, 1991). *Member:* Madrid Bar Association. *LANGUAGES:* Spanish and English.

GONZALO STAMPA CASAS, born Granada, July 20, 1968; admitted, 1991, Madrid. *Education:* University of Madrid (Law Degree, 1991); University of London (LL.M., Commercial and Corporate Law, 1993). *Member:* Madrid Bar Association; International Bar Association; London Court

(This Listing Continued)

of International Arbitration. *LANGUAGES:* Spanish, English and German.

PABLO GONZALEZ SCHWITTERS, born Madrid, November 13, 1966; admitted, 1991, Madrid. *Education:* Universidad Complutense de Madrid (Law Degree, 1990); Instituto de Empresa, Madrid, Masters in Corporate Counselling, 1991. *Member:* Madrid Bar Association. *LANGUAGES:* Spanish, German and English.

ALICIA ARROYO APARICIO, born Colmenar Viejo, Madrid, Spain, October 31, 1968; admitted, 1991, Madrid. *Education:* Universidad Pontificia de Comillas ICADE (Law Degree, 1991); Graduado Superior en Ciencias Jurídicas, 1991); City Polytechnic of London (European Business Law Seminar, 1991); School of Legal Practice (Diploma, 1992). Member "Real Academia de Jurisprudencia y Legislación" (Royal Academy of Jurisprudence and Legislation). Member, "Real Sociedad Económica Matritense" (Royal Economics Society of Madrid). *Member:* Madrid Bar Association. *LANGUAGES:* Spanish, French and English.

JUAN-JESUS BLANCO MORENO, born Alburquerque, Badajóz, Spain, August 21, 1959; admitted, 1992, Madrid. *Education:* University of Extremadura (Law Degree, 1983). *Member:* Madrid Bar Association. *LANGUAGES:* Spanish and English.

ANA M. CAMACHO Y MENDOZA, born Madrid, Spain, October 6, 1963; admitted, 1986, Madrid. *Education:* Fundación Univeritaria San Pablo CEU (Law Degree, 1986); Instituto de Empresa, Madrid (Masters Degree in Corporate Counselling, 1992); Ilustre Colegio Notarial, Madrid (Masters in Documentary Law, 1992). *Member:* Madrid Bar Association. *LANGUAGES:* Spanish, French, English and German.

GONZALO ARANZABAL, born San Sebastian, Spain, January 13, 1963; admitted, 1987, Madrid. *Education:* Universidad Pontificia de Comillas, ICADE, Madrid (Law Degree, 1986; Degree in Corporate, Business and Legal Advising, 1986). *Member:* Madrid Bar Association. *LANGUAGES:* Spanish and English.

ANA HIDALGO ALBERCA, born Hamburg, Germany, October 3, 1967; admitted, 1993, Madrid and Murcia. *Education:* University of Murcia (Law Degree, 1991); Carlos III University, Madrid (Masters in European Law, 1992). *Member:* Madrid and Murcia Bar Associations. *LANGUAGES:* Spanish, German, English and French.

JOSE MIGUEL BENITO NOTARIO, born Barcelona, Spain, November 21, 1966; admitted, 1991, Madrid. *Education:* Universidad de Alcalá de Henares, 1989 (Masters in Corporate and Business Law, 1991); Instituto de Empresa de Madrid; Escuela de Prática Jurídica de Madrid (Diploma, Labor Law, 1993). *Member:* Madrid Bar Association. *LANGUAGES:* English, French and Spanish.

FRANCISCO JAVIER ORTS CASTRO, born Madrid, Spain, March 17, 1966; admitted, 1993, Madrid. *Education:* Universidad Complutense de Madrid (Law Degree, 1989). *Member:* Madrid Bar Association. *LANGUAGES:* Spanish and English.

JAVIER CATALAN MEZQUIRIZ, born Pamplona, Spain, October 29, 1967; admitted, 1993, Pamplona; 1994, Madrid. *Education:* Universidad de Navarra (Law Degree, 1990); American University of Paris (Diploma, International Trade Law, 1992); University of London, King's College (LL.M., International Business Law, 1993). *Member:* Madrid Bar Association. *LANGUAGES:* Spanish, English and French.

JOSEP MARIA JULIÁ INSENSER, born Barcelona, Spain, January 1, 1966; admitted, 1993, Barcelona; 1994, Madrid. *Education:* Universitat Autónoma de Barcelona (Law Degree, 1989); College of Europe of Bruges (Diploma and Masters in European Studies, 1991); Université Libre de Bruxelles (Masters in Comparative Law, 1992); University of London, London School of Economics (LL.M., International Business Law, 1993). *Member:* Madrid and Barcelona Bar Associations. *LANGUAGES:* Catalan, Spanish, English and French.

TAX CONSULTANT

F. JAVIER RODRIGUEZ SANTOS, born Leon, Spain, November 5, 1951; admitted, 1978, Madrid. *Education:* Universidad Autónoma de Madrid (Law Degree, 1978); Centro de Estudios Constitucionales, Madrid (Degree in Constitutional Law and Politica Science, 1979). Tax Inspector, Spanish Ministry of Finance, 1983-1992. *Member:* Madrid Bar Association. *LANGUAGES:* Spanish, English and French.

Languages: Spanish, French, English, German, Italian and Portuguese.

BUFETE CUATRECASAS
ANTONIO MAURA, 10
28014 MADRID, SPAIN
Telephone: 521.94.47
Fax: 522.48.99

Barcelona, Spain Office: Balmes 76. Telephone: 290.55.00. Fax: 290.55.67.
Bilbao, Spain Office: Alameda de Mazarredo 5. Telephone: 424.82.67. Fax: 424.82.34.
Gerona, Spain Office: Ronda Ferrán Puig, 4-6. Telephone: 22.71.02. Fax: 22.66.61.
Brussels, Belgium Office: 78 Avenue d'Auderghem. Telephone: 735.06.43. Fax: 734.72.34.

All areas of Spanish and EEC business law, including corporate, commercial, taxation, foreign investments, capital markets, finance, regulatory including environmental law, labour law, intellectual property including software licensing and protection, anti-trust law, litigation, criminal law, bankruptcy law and company restructuring.

MEMBERS OF FIRM

PEDRO CUATRECASAS, born Barcelona, Spain, May 28, 1928; admitted, 1952, Barcelona. *Education:* University of Barcelona (Law Degree, 1952). *Member:* Barcelona Bar Association; Spanish Association of Taxation Experts. (Also at Barcelona and Bilbao Offices). *LANGUAGES:* French.

EMILIO CUATRECASAS, born Barcelona, Spain, January 12, 1954; admitted, 1977, Barcelona; 1984, Bilbao. *Education:* University of Navarra (Law Degree, 1976); Abad Oliba College (Diploma in International Law). *Member:* Barcelona Bar Association; Bilbao Bar Association; Madrid Bar Association; Association for Development of Industry; IBA. (Also at Barcelona and Bilbao Offices). *LANGUAGES:* French and English.

JULIAN GARCIA RUBI, born Madrid, Spain, December 4, 1952; admitted, 1983, Madrid. *Education:* Complutense University of Madrid (Law and Business Management Degrees). *Member:* Madrid Bar Association; Institute of Auditors; IBA. *LANGUAGES:* English and French.

JAVIER LAORDEN, born Madrid, Spain, February 17, 1955; admitted, 1981, Madrid. *Education:* University of Deusto, ICADE (Law Degree, 1975); ICADE (Economics and Business Degrees). Professor of Legal Practices, ICADE. *Member:* Madrid Bar Association; Spanish Financial Law Association; Registered as Official Auditor; Insurance Agents Association. *LANGUAGES:* English and French.

PILAR CAVERO, born Madrid, Spain, October 12, 1959; admitted, 1990, Spain. *Education:* Complutense University Madrid (Law Degree; Master of Labor and Social Security Law); ESADE (Labor Law Diploma); School of Legal Practices (Labor Law Diploma). *Member:* Madrid Bar Association; Spanish Association of Labor Law. *LANGUAGES:* English and French.

ANTONIO SÁNCHEZ-PEDREÑO, born United Kingdom, July 25, 1959; admitted, 1982, Madrid; 1986, New York. *Education:* Complutense University of Madrid (Law Degree, 1981); University of London, U.K. (Master in Common Law, 1983); New York University (Master in Comparative Jurisprudence, 1984). *Member:* Madrid Bar Association; New York State Bar Association. *LANGUAGES:* English and French.

ASSOCIATES

CRISTINA ALUM, born Madrid, Spain, March 12, 1963; admitted, 1988, Madrid. *Education:* Complutense University of Madrid (Law Degree, 1987). *Member:* Barcelona Bar Association; Madrid Bar Association; Registered as Official Auditor. *LANGUAGES:* English.

ALVARO ANTON, born Madrid, Spain, October 31, 1964; admitted, 1991. *Education:* Complutense University of Madrid (Law Degree, 1988). *Member:* Madrid Bar Association. *LANGUAGES:* English.

LUIS MIGUEL BRAVO, born Madrid, Spain, September 13, 1966; admitted, 1990. *Education:* Complutense University of Madrid (Law Degree, 1989) Center for Financial Studies, Madrid (Master, Tax Advising). *Member:* Madrid Bar Association. *LANGUAGES:* English.

JORGE CAPELL, born Madrid, Spain, March 28, 1969; admitted, 1989. *Education:* University of Madrid (Law Degree, 1991); School of Diplomacy (Diplome in EC Law, 1991); University of the Pacific (Sacramento)-London (Diplome in International Law, 1992); University Pompeu Fabra (Master Business Law, 1993). *Member:* Madrid Bar Association. *LANGUAGES:* English and French.

(This Listing Continued)

BUFETE CUATRECASAS, Madrid—Continued

FLORENTINO CARREÑO, born Madrid, Spain, January 11, 1964; admitted, 1991, Madrid. *Education:* University of Navarra, Pamplona, Spain (Law Degree, 1987); College of Europe, Brugge, Belgium (Diploma of Advanced European Studies, 1989). *Member:* Madrid Bar Association. *LANGUAGES:* English and French.

ALICIA DE CARLOS, born Madrid, Spain, December 14, 1969; admitted, 1994, Spain. *Education:* University Pontificia Comillas, Madrid (Law Degree, 1993); University Pompeu Fabra (Master in Business Law, 1994). *Member:* Madrid Bar Association. *LANGUAGES:* English.

CAROLINA FERNANDEZ, born Santander, Spain, April 26, 1966; admitted, 1992. *Education:* University of Navarra, Pamplona (Law Degree, 1989); Europa College, Bruges, Belgium (Diplome in European Studies, 1990); Washington University, St. Louis, MO (Certificate in International Affairs, M.A. Program, 1991); University Pompeu Fabra (Master Business Law, 1993). *Member:* Pamplona Bar Association. *LANGUAGES:* English and French.

JOSE RAFAEL GARCIA DE LA CALLE, born Madrid, Spain, January 10, 1966; admitted, 1990, Spain. *Education:* University of Madrid (Law Degree, 1989). *Member:* Madrid Bar Association. *LANGUAGES:* English and French.

MARTA GOMEZ-LUENGO, born Orense, Spain, June 24, 1965; admitted, 1989, Madrid. *Education:* University of Madrid (Law Degree, 1988); Business Institute (Master of Business Law). *Member:* Madrid Bar Association. *LANGUAGES:* English and French.

CESAR GONZALEZ, born Córdoba, Spain, June 5, 1967; admitted, 1992. *Education:* ICADE (Law Degree, 1991) (Economics Degree, 1991). *Member:* Madrid Bar Association. *LANGUAGES:* English and French.

JAVIER HERVAS, born Madrid, Spain, November 1, 1965; admitted, 1990, Madrid. *Education:* University of Madrid (Law Degree, 1988). Expert in Industrial Relations. *Member:* Madrid Bar Association. *LANGUAGES:* English and Italian.

JUAN JOSE LAZARO, born Cuenca, Spain, October 1, 1959; admitted, 1989. *Education:* University of Madrid (Law Degree, 1982); Business Institute (Master in Tax Advice, 1986). *Member:* Madrid Bar Association. *LANGUAGES:* English.

ALEJO LOPEZ-MELLADO, born Madrid, Spain, February 15, 1964; admitted, 1987, Madrid. *Education:* University of Madrid (Law Degree, 1987); San Pablo College (CEU). *Member:* Madrid Bar Association. *LANGUAGES:* English.

LUCIA LORENTE, born Bilbao, Spain, November 23, 1964; admitted, 1990, Spain. *Education:* ICADE (Law Degree, 1988); Free University of Brussels (Special Degree in European Law, 1989). *Member:* Madrid Bar Association. *LANGUAGES:* English and French.

LUIS LORENZO, born Madrid, Spain, May 5, 1963; admitted, 1988, Madrid. *Education:* Complutense University of Madrid (Law Degree, 1987). *Member:* Madrid Bar Association. *LANGUAGES:* English.

JAVIER LUCAS, born Madrid, Spain, February 9, 1966; admitted, 1991. *Education:* Complutense University of Madrid (Law Degree, 1990); Know-How Business College of Madrid (Master, Law Practice). *Member:* Madrid Bar Association. *LANGUAGES:* English.

CRISTINA MARQUEZ, born Paris, France, June 12, 1970; admitted, 1994, Spain. *Education:* University of Paris, France (Law Degree, 1992); Institut Supérieur d'Interprétariat et Traduction, Paris (1988-1992); Complutense University of Madrid (Master in EEC Law, 1993); University Pompeu Fabra (Master in Business Law, 1994). *Member:* Madrid Bar Association. *LANGUAGES:* English and French.

ALVARO MENDIOLA, born Pamplona, Spain, June 8, 1966; admitted, 1994, Spain. *Education:* University of Navarra, Pamplona, Spain (Law Degree, 1989); College of Europe, Brugge, Belgium (Diploma of Advanced European Studies, 1990). *Member:* Madrid Bar Association. *LANGUAGES:* English, French and Italian.

ALBERTO MOYA, born Madrid, Spain, June 11, 1965; admitted, 1990, Spain. *Education:* University of Madrid (Law Degree, 1988); Business Institute (Master of Business Law, 1989). *Member:* Madrid Bar Association. *LANGUAGES:* English.

ANTONIO PLAZA, born Madrid, Spain, July 19, 1962; admitted, 1985, Madrid. *Education:* ICADE (Law Degree, 1985; Economics Degree, 1986). *Member:* Madrid Bar Association. *LANGUAGES:* French and English.

(This Listing Continued)

MARIA PALOMA VIA, born Madrid, Spain, June 28, 1963; admitted, 1987, Madrid. *Education:* Complutense University of Madrid (Law Degree, 1986). *Member:* Madrid Bar Association; Registered as Official Auditor. *LANGUAGES:* English and French.

MARIA LUISA RUIZ, born Murcia, Spain, September 19, 1959; admitted, 1990, Madrid. *Education:* Complutense University of Madrid (Law Degree, 1987); EEC Law. *Member:* Madrid Bar Association. *LANGUAGES:* English.

OF COUNSEL

ANTONIO HIERRO, born Madrid, Spain, March 7, 1959; admitted, 1983. *Education:* University of Madrid (Law Degree, 1981). Spanish Representative in the Maastricht Treaty. Spanish Agent, Court of Justice of EC, 1989-1993. *Member:* Madrid Bar Association. *LANGUAGES:* English and French.

RAMIRO SÁNCHEZ DE LERÍN, born Madrid, Spain, September 14, 1954; admitted, 1976, Spain. *Education:* University of Deusto, Bilbao (Law Degree, 1976); I.C.A.D.E. (Master in Business Law, 1976). State Attorney. *Member:* Madrid Bar Association. *LANGUAGES:* German, English and French.

Languages: Spanish, English, French, Portuguese, Italian and German.

(For complete biographical data on personnel at Barcelona, Bilbao and Gerona, Spain and Brussels, Belgium, see Professional Biographies at those locations)

DAVIES ARNOLD COOPER

SERRANO ANGUITA
10-5 DCHA
28004 MADRID, SPAIN
Telephone: 1-446 3566
Facsimile: 1-445 1600

London, England Offices: 6-8 Bouverie Street, EC4Y 8DD. Telephone: 71-936 2222. Telex: 262894. Facsimile: 71-936 2020 and Room 991 Lloyd's Building, 1 Lime Street. Telephone: 71-283 8658. Facsimile: 71-283 8063.

Manchester, England Office: 60 Fountain Street, M2 2FE. Telephone: 61-839 8396. Facsimile: 61-839 8309.

Commercial/Mercantile Law (general), Mergers and Acquisitions, Real Property (Commercial, Residential and Development); Construction, Admiralty and Maritime, Arbitration and Litigation, Banking, Company, Employment, Insurance and Reinsurance, Planning, Intellectual Property.

MEMBERS OF FIRM

Pablo Wesolowski   **Paulino Fajardo**

(For complete list of personnel, see Professional Biographies at London, England)

DE LORENZO ABOGADOS

Established in 1955

VELAZQUEZ, 124
28006 MADRID, SPAIN
Telephone: (34-1) 561.17.12 (7 Lines); (34-1) 411.66.98
Telex: 49286 DLOR E
Fax: (34-1) 411.41.07; (34-1) 564.07.91

General Practice, Medical and Pharmaceutical Law, Labor, Civil, Commercial, Corporation, Health, Food and Drug.

FIRM PROFILE: *De Lorenzo was founded in 1955 and is a nationally leading firm engaged primarily in the practice of Medical and Pharmaceutical Law. Handling all aspects of health care, including medical malpractice, negligence, liability, civil, labor, and financing, the firm represents both individuals and corporations providing a wide range of legal services. De Lorenzo's commercial practice is also active, serving privately-owned businesses, partnerships, professional bodies, institutions and corporations.*

MEMBERS OF FIRM

DON. ANTONIO DE LORENZO SANCHEZ (Founder, 1922-1989).

DON. RICARDO DE LORENZO Y MONTERO, born 1950; admitted, 1973, Spain. *Education:* Attorney at Law, University of Madrid (Universidad Complutense). Professor at the School of Medical Law, Medicine Faculty, Universidad Complutense of Madrid. President of the Spanish

(This Listing Continued)

Medical Law Association. *Member:* Madrid Bar Association; International Bar Association; World Medical Association; Food and Drug Law Institute. *LANGUAGES:* English and French.

DON. MANUEL AULLO CHAVES, born 1951; admitted, 1973, Spain. *Education:* Attorney at Law, University of Madrid; Instituto de Empresa, Madrid (Master in Legal Practice, 1982). Professor, Civil Law, University of Madrid (Universidad Autónoma). *Member:* Madrid Bar Association. *LANGUAGES:* English and French.

ASSOCIATES

DON. ALFONSO CAVALLE SESE, born 1944; admitted, 1967, Spain. *Education:* Attorney at Law, University of Madrid; Centro Superior de Estudios Empresariales (M.B.A., 1986; Master in Finance and Tax Advisor, 1991); Cámara de Comercio de Madrid (Diploma in Insurance Broking, 1993). President of the Spanish Commercial Broadcasting Association. Vice-Chairman of the International Broadcasting Association. Vice-Chairman of the European Broadcasting Association. *Member:* Madrid Bar Association. *LANGUAGES:* English.

DOÑA. MARIA DOLORES DE HARO MARTINEZ, born 1966; admitted, 1990, Spain. *Education:* Attorney at Law, University of Madrid; Centro de Estudios Financieros, Madrid (Master in Tax Law, 1992). *Member:* Madrid Bar Association. *LANGUAGES:* English.

DON. JOSE WOLTERS Y DIEZ, born 1956; admitted, 1983, Spain. *Education:* Attorney at Law, University of Madrid. *Member:* Madrid Bar Association. *LANGUAGES:* German and English.

DOÑA. ELENA FERNANDEZ FERNANDEZ, born 1968; admitted, 1991, Spain. *Education:* Attorney at Law, University of Madrid. Diplomate in Labor Law, Escuela de Práctica Jurídica, 1994. *Member:* Madrid Bar Association. *LANGUAGES:* English and French.

DON. IÑIGO DE ZUNZUNEGUI VALLERO DE BERNABE, born 1956; admitted, 1981, Spain. *Education:* I.C.A.D.E. E-3 (Attorney at Law, 1978; Degree in Economics, 1978). *Member:* Madrid Bar Association; Madrid Association of Counsellors of Tax and Finance. *LANGUAGES:* English.

DON. CARLOS SAINZ RUBIO, born 1957. *Education:* University of Madrid; Universidad Complutense (Degree in Economics, 1982). Economic Advisor of the Madrid City Council in "excedencia" (special leave for civil servants). *Member:* Madrid Economists Association; Economists and Fiscal Advisors Register. *LANGUAGES:* English.

DON. ANGEL FERNANDEZ SAÑUDO, born 1959. *Education:* University of Madrid, Universidad Complutense (Degree in Economics, 1982). *Member:* Madrid Economists Association; Economists and Fiscal Advisors Register. *LANGUAGES:* French.

DOÑA. PILAR JIMENEZ PRIETO, born 1969; admitted, 1993, Spain. *Education:* University of Madrid (Attorney at Law); ICADE (Practice Legal Course, 1994). Madrid Bar Association. *LANGUAGES:* English.

REPRESENTATIVE CLIENTS: Iltre. Colegio Oficial de Odontólogos y Estomatólogos de la I Región (Madrid Dental Association); Consejo General de Colegios de Médicos Gallegos; Iltres. Colegios Oficiales de Médicos de Madrid, La Coruña, Lugo, Orense, Pontevedra, Tarragona Lérida (Medical Associations); The Medical Defence Union (U.K.); Kalon Plc (U.K.); Krieg Zivy (F). REFERENCES: Consejo General de Colegios de Médicos de España (Spanish Medical Associations); Consejo General de Colegios de Odontólogos y Estomatólogos de España (Spanish Dental Associations); Sindicatos Médicos (Spanish Medical Unions); Danish Wind Technology A/S (D); Laboratorios Sintex; Smyth Morris S/A (Kalon Plc).

BUFETE DIAZ-ARIAS

PLAZA DE LAS CORTES, 4
28014 MADRID, SPAIN
Telephone: (341) 4294517
Fax: (341) 4294505

Barcelona, Spain Office: Avenida Diagonal 506, 08006. Telephone: (343) 415.0404. Fax: (343) 415.7514. Additional Barcelona address: C/Gran Via de las Corts Catalanas, 295-301, 08014. Telephone: (343) 4234047. Fax: (343) 4263188.

Miami, Florida (USA) Office: 1925 Brickell Avenue, Suite 206, Fl. 33129. Telephone: (305) 8588853. Fax: (305) 8588857.

Los Angeles, California (USA) Office: 711 Ocean Avenue, Suite 123, Huntington Beach, Ca. 92648. Telephone: (714) 9692509. Fax: (714) 9695349.

(This Listing Continued)

Taxation: (Corporate, Taxation, International Taxation, Value Added Taxes, Personal Income Taxation, Taxation of Oil and Mining Companies). Corporate, Foreign Investments, Commercial, Bankruptcy, International Private Law, EEC, Exchange Control.
Litigation Services: Fraud Investigation, Post Acquisition Disputes, Taxation Proceedings.
Associated with a European network of professional offices and a Mexican Tax Law firm.

JOSE MANUEL DIAZ-ARIAS, born Madrid, Spain, 1950; admitted, 1972, Madrid; 1973, Barcelona. *Education:* University of Madrid (Law Degree); LL.M. in Taxation; Diploma in Corporate Law; Diploma in International Tax Law. Head of law firm Bufete Diaz-Arias of Madrid, Barcelona, California and Miami (Florida). President and Director of GACETA FISCAL. President of Gabinete juridico fiscal de gestores administrativos-asesores fiscales. Lecturer and Coordinator for seminars on tax law organized by the Madrid Bar Association. Reporter for the Unión Iberoamericana de Colegios y Agrupaciones de Abogados (South American Lawyers Association). Member of the Examining Tribunal of candidates to be appointed judges. Author of numerous publications on tax law. Frequent contributor of articles on tax and legal questions to "El Pais" and other newspapers and specialist publications. Holder of the judicial award, the "Cruz de Honor de San Raimundo de Peñafort.".

JAMIE TREBOLLE FERNANDEZ, born Orense, Spain, 1946; admitted, 1968, Madrid. *Education:* University of Madrid (Law Degree). Professor of Tax Law at the I.C.A.D.E. University. Former Tax Inspector with the National Revenue Authority in Zaragoza, Orense and Oviedo (1970-1977). Member, Central Economic-Administrative Tribunal (1986-1989). Vice President, representing Spain, of CEDRE, based in Strasbourg (1984-1985). President, International Committee of the Association for the Construction of the Transeuropa based in Bordeaux, 1985. *Member:* Spanish Tax Law Association; Regional Science Association of Spain.

MANUEL SORIA CABRERA, born Madrid, 1958; admitted, 1980, Madrid; 1989, Barcelona. *Education:* University of Madrid (Law Degree); LL.M. in Taxation for Corporations; Diploma in Corporate; Diploma in International Tax Law. Reporter, Seminars on Tax Law organized by the Madrid Bar Association. Co-Director, Monthly Tax Review GACETA FISCAL. Co-Author: "Basic Tax Law" and several books on Tax Matters.

FRANCISCO PLACER SANCHEZ, born Madrid, 1957; admitted, 1979, Madrid; 1989, Barcelona. *Education:* University of Madrid (Law Degree); LL.M. in Taxation; Diploma in Corporate Law; Diploma in Labour Law. Adviser, Tax Magazine, GACETA FISCAL. Co-Director, Budiar Gage Corporations. Lecturer in Seminars on Tax Law, organized by the Madrid Bar Association and I.C.A.D.E. University.

ALFONSO MONGE MOLINA, born Madrid, 1959; admitted, 1981, Madrid; 1989, Barcelona. *Education:* University of Madrid (Law Degree); LL.M. in Taxation; I.C.A.D.E. University (Bachelor of Science in Economics); Diploma in Corporate Law. Co-Author; "Basic Tax Law". Adviser, Tax Magazine GACETA FISCAL. Reporter in Seminars on Tax Law, organized by Madrid Bar Association.

CARLOS PALAO TABOADA, born Orense, Spain, 1941; admitted, 1983, Madrid; Licensed as Foreign Legal Consultant to the Supreme Court of New York State. *Education:* University of Madrid (Law Degree with high Honors and Bachelor of Science in Economics); University of Bologna, Italy (Ph.D. in Law); New York University Law School (LL.M.). Tenured Professor of Tax Law, Universidad Autónoma de Madrid.

LUIS ROMAN CARERO, born Buenos Aires, Argentina, 1914; admitted, 1980, Madrid. Former Inspector of Taxes. Subdirector General at the Ministry of Revenue and Finance. Senior Advisor to the Central Economic-Administrative Tribunal.

TAX ADVISOR

ANDRES VALLES CAMPS, born Barcelona, Spain, 1949. *Education:* Diploma in Taxation; Diploma in Corporate Law. Qualified Real Estate Manager. Co-Author: "Basic Tax Law". Contributor, Articles, on Tax to specialized press, General Manager of the Firm in Catalonia (Spain).

OTHER LAWYERS & ECONOMISTS

Fernando Justel Eusebio	*Jose Vazquez Rojas*
Juan Antonio Gonzalez Perez	*Alejandra Ortega de la Pena*
Jose Maria Lastra Bermudez	*Daniel Garcia del Cura*
Miguel Sanchez Iniesta	*Nuria Diaz-Varela Arrese*
Elena Sobrino Arias	*Sara Muniz*
Maria Luisa Maestre Gomez	*Antonio Monge Molina*

(This Listing Continued)

BUFETE DIAZ-ARIAS, Madrid—Continued

Nicolas Sierra Muñoz	Constantino Montero Luna
Marta de Penaranda	Pilar Diaz-Arias Perez
Gonzalez-Robatto	Ursula Zabalza De Frutos
Maria Dolores Coba Alameda	Mariano Salinas Marti
Marta Rico Donovan	Melinda Huyette
Jose Carlos de Nicolas Ortells	Javier Catalina Lapuente
Maria Ruiz Jarabo Pelayo	Gracia Soria Cabrera
M. Isabel de las Heras Castellvi	Jose Maria Diaz Crespo
Arturo Javier Jimenez Contento	Juan Carlos Bernal Morales
Juan Plaza Echevarria	Araceli Sanchez Lopez
Mireia Valles Camps	Antonio Herrero Castillo
Jose Aranda Vides	Manuel Gonzalez Cayuela
Maria Nicolas Jimenez	Antonio Gonzalez Helguera
Christina Calleja Cazorla	Federico Escorial Bonet
Maria Teresa Cavero Rincon	Javier Gil Pecharroman
Gonzalo Delagado Lusson	Jose Luis Cuesta Sanfiz
	Antonio Diaz De Neira

DIAZ-BASTIEN & TRUAN ABOGADOS

Established in 1978

HERMOSILLA, 21, 2° IZDA
MADRID 28001, SPAIN
Telephone: (91) 577.36.60; 577.36.61; 577.36.62
Facsimile: (91) 575.54.68

Marbella, Málaga Office: Sierra Blanca, 2, 3° A, 29600 Marbella.
   Telephone: (5) 277.63.62; 277.63.03. Facsimile: (5) 282.54.52.
London, England Office: 111 Park Street, Mayfair, W1Y 3FB.
   Telephone: (171) 409.20.18; 491.33.08. Facsimile: (171) 629.29.02.

Administrative, Anti-Trust, Arbitration. Aviation, Banking and Finance, Bankruptcy/Insolvency, Civil Litigation, Commercial, Commercial Property, Company, Competition, Constitutional, Construction, Debt Recovery, Distribution, Employment, Entertainment, European Community, Franchising, House Purchase/Conveyancing, Import/Export, Insolvency, Insurance, Intellectual Property, International, Investment and Financial Services, Media, Mergers and Acquisitions, Mortgages/Hypothecates, Partnerships, Pharmaceutical, Planning, Real Estate Purchase, Shipping/Admiralty, Tax-Company, Tax-International, Tax-Offshore, Transport, Wills and Probate.

MEMBERS OF FIRM

CONRADO TRUAN, admitted, 1976, Spain. *Education:* Universidad Complutense de Madrid.

ERNESTO DIAZ-BASTIEN, admitted, 1977, Spain. *Education:* Universidad Complutense de Madrid.

PALOMA PEMAN DOMECQ, admitted, 1984, Spain. *Education:* Universidad Pontificia de Comillas (ICADE).

JUAN JOSE NUÑEZ, admitted, 1985, Spain. *Education:* Universidad Complutense de Madrid.

EDUARDO MOLINA, admitted, 1979, Spain. *Education:* Universidad Complutense de Madrid (CEU).

VERÓNICA GONZÁLEZ, admitted, 1986, Spain. *Education:* Universidad Complutense de Madrid (CEU).

Languages: Spanish, English and French

ECHARRI & BRINDLE

PASEO DE LA CASTELLANA 28
28046 MADRID, SPAIN
Telephone: (34.1) 578.0875
Fax: (34.1) 576.0028

Associated Offices in Barcelona, Bilbao, Halaga.

General Practice, Corporate, Commercial and Civil, Mergers and Acquisitions, Banking and Finance, Securities, Foreign Trade and Investment, International Contracts, Joint Ventures, Franchising, Licensing, Insolvency, Real Estate, EEC Law, Tax, Labor and Litigation.

ALBERTO ECHARRI, born Montreal, Canada, 1959; admitted, 1982, Madrid. *Education:* University of Madrid, Faculty of Law (Master in Business Law). Professor of Law, Institute de Empresa. Chairman, Spanish Ca-

(This Listing Continued)

nadian Business Association. *Member:* International Bar Association; Association Internationale de Jeunes Avocats; Rotary International. *LANGUAGES:* Spanish, French and English. *PRACTICE AREAS:* Business Law; Banking; Corporate Law; Mergers and Acquisitions; Securities; Franchise.

SANTIAGO MAIZ, born Santiago de Compostela, Spain, August 31, 1960; admitted, 1983, Madrid. *Education:* University of Madrid, Faculty of Law (Master in Business Law and Taxation). *Member:* International Bar Association; Association Internationale Jeunes Avocats; Rotary International. *LANGUAGES:* Spanish and English. *PRACTICE AREAS:* Business Law; Corporate Law; Property and Real Estate; Franchising.

PILAR BRINDLE, born Madrid, Spain, February 28, 1960; admitted, 1983, Madrid. *Education:* University of Madrid, Faculty of Law (Master in Business Law). *Member:* International Bar Association. *LANGUAGES:* Spanish and English. *PRACTICE AREAS:* Business Law; Corporate Law; Litigation; White Collar Crime.

ALFONSO RIVEIRO, born Vigo, Spain, June 16, 1964; admitted, 1988, Madrid. *Education:* University of Santiago de Compostela, Faculty of Law (Master in Business Law). *Member:* International Bar Association. *LANGUAGES:* Spanish, English, German and Portuguese. *PRACTICE AREAS:* Business Law; Banking; Corporate Law; Mergers and Acquisitions; Securities.

E. G. MADARIAGA, born Madrid, Spain, October 26, 1966; admitted, 1991, Madrid. *Education:* University of Madrid, Faculty of Law (Master in Business Law). Professor of Law, Masters Program in Business Law, Institute de Empresa. *LANGUAGES:* Spanish and English. *PRACTICE AREAS:* Business Law; Banking; Corporate Law; Mergers and Acquisitions; Securities.

M.L. MAIZ, born Santiago de Compostela, Spain. *Education:* University of Madrid, Faculty of Law, State Lawyer. *LANGUAGES:* Spanish, English and French. *PRACTICE AREAS:* Administrative Law; Contracts and Environmental Law.

M.E. SEBASTIAN DE ERICE, born Madrid, Spain; admitted, 1991, Madrid. *Education:* University of Madrid, Faculty of Law (Master in Business Law). *LANGUAGES:* Spanish, English and French. *PRACTICE AREAS:* Business Law; Banking; Corporate Law; Mergers and Acquisitions.

JUAN LUIS DELGADO, born Salamanca, February 24, 1969; admitted, 1994, Madrid. *Education:* University of Salamanca, Faculty of Law (Master in Business Law). *LANGUAGES:* Spanish and English. *PRACTICE AREAS:* Business Law; Corporate Law; Franchise.

FELI ECHARRI, born Montreal, Canada, March 19, 1962; (Not admitted in Spain). *Education:* University of Madrid, Faculty of Economics (Master in Foreign Trade). *Member:* Madrid Chamber of Commerce. *LANGUAGES:* Spanish, French and English. *PRACTICE AREAS:* Investments; Taxation.

ECHECOPAR ABOGADOS

Established in 1976

CALLE DR. FLEMING 3
28036 MADRID, SPAIN
Telephone: 457-2400
Cable Address: "Lerama"
Telefax: 458 7449

Barcelona, Spain Office: Travesera de Gracia, 17 - 21, 5° 5a, 08021.
   Telephone: 209 8922. Telefax: 202.21.14.

General and International Practice. Administrative, Banking, Civil, Commercial, Corporation, EEC, Foreign Investment, Insurance, Labor, Oil and Gas, Maritime, Real Estate and Tax Law. Litigation.

FIRM PROFILE: This firm provides a broad base of Spanish and transnational clients with a full range of legal services from its locations in Madrid and Barcelona. It has a well established practice in corporate and commercial as well as in tax law and is engaged in extensive international activity. Litigation and labour matters are fields where it has likewise developed strength. Based on the expertise it has acquired this firm feels particularly able to offer valuable assistance in the set-up of new business projects and in M&A work as well as in the wide scope of the attendant areas of the law. These skills and experience are applied to satisfy the day-to-day requirements of its clients.

(This Listing Continued)

MEMBERS OF FIRM

LUIS ECHECOPAR REY, born Lima, Perú, 1936; admitted, 1961, Perú; 1971, Spain. *Education:* Pontificia Universidad Católica del Perú. *Member:* Ilustre Colegio de Abogados de Madrid; Ilustre Colegio de Abogados de Alava; Ilustre Colegio de Abogados de Barcelona; Ilustre Colegio de Abogados de Las Palmas; Ilustre Colegio de Abogados de San Sebastián; Ilustre Colegio de Abogados de Vizcaya; Ilustre Colegio de Abogados de Lima; Ilustre Colegio de Abogados del Callao. (Also Counsel to Estudio Luis Echecopar García, Lima, Perú). *LANGUAGES:* English, French and Spanish.

ANTONIO BUNDÓ MASGORET, born Barcelona, Spain, 1954; admitted, 1978, Spain. *Education:* Universidad Central de Barcelona. *Member:* Ilustre Colegio de Abogados de Barcelona; Ilustre Colegio de Abogados de Madrid; Ilustre Colegio de Abogados de Sabadell; Ilustre Colegio de Abogados de Tarragona; Ilustre Colegio de Abogados de Tarrasa; Ilustre Colegio de Abogados de Valencia. (Resident, Barcelona, Spain Office). *LANGUAGES:* French, Catalan and Spanish.

LUIS ERNESTO ECHECOPAR FLÓREZ, born Lima, Perú, 1962; admitted, 1985, Spain. *Education:* Universidad Autónoma de Madrid. *Member:* Ilustre Colegio de Abogados de Madrid; Ilustre Colegio de Abogados de Barcelona. *LANGUAGES:* English and Spanish.

J. MARIANO RIOJA NIETO, born Madrid, Spain, 1954; admitted, 1978, Spain. *Education:* Universidad Complutense de Madrid. *Member:* Ilustre Colegio de Abogados de Madrid; Ilustre Colegio de Abogados de Barcelona. *LANGUAGES:* English and Spanish.

ELICIA RIVAS MANGA, born Madrid, Spain, 1952; admitted, 1978, Spain. *Education:* Universidad Complutense de Madrid. *Member:* Ilustre Colegio de Abogados de Madrid; Ilustre Colegio de Abogados de Alcalá de Henares; Ilustre Colegio de Abogados de Barcelona; Ilustre Colegio de Abogados de Cádiz; Ilustre Colegio de Abogados de Las Palmas; Ilustre Colegio de Abogados de Málaga; Ilustre Colegio de Abogados de Sevilla. *LANGUAGES:* French and Spanish.

ANTONIO GARICANO CIRUJEDA, born Madrid, Spain, 1946; admitted, 1970, Spain. *Education:* Universidad Complutense de Madrid. *Member:* Ilustre Colegio de Abogados de Madrid; Ilustre Colegio de Abogados de Barcelona; Ilustre Colegio de Abogados de Las Palmas. *LANGUAGES:* Spanish.

ASSOCIATES

MIGUEL OLAIZOLA ARES, born Bilbao, Spain, 1962; admitted, 1989, Spain. *Education:* Universidad de Deusto; University of Exeter. *Member:* Ilustre Colegio de Abogados de Madrid; Ilustre Colegio de Abogados de Barcelona. *LANGUAGES:* English and Spanish.

JAIME MOREY JAUME, born Palma de Mallorca, Spain, 1962; admitted, 1989, Spain. *Education:* Universidad de Navarra; Université Libre de Bruxelles (Institut d'Etudes Européennes); College d'Europe; London School of Economics. *Member:* Ilustre Colegio de Abogados de Madrid; Ilustre Colegio de Abogados de Barcelona. *LANGUAGES:* English, French, Catalan and Spanish.

FERNANDO GOLMAYO ALONSO, born Madrid, Spain, 1961; admitted, 1986, Spain. *Education:* Universidad Complutense de Madrid. *Member:* Ilustre Colegio de Abogados de Madrid; Ilustre Colegio de Abogados de Barcelona. *LANGUAGES:* English, French and Spanish.

FERNANDO BOBO GUMPERT, born Madrid, Spain, 1962; admitted, 1987, Spain. *Education:* Universidad Autónoma de Madrid. *Member:* Ilustre Colegio de Abogados de Madrid; Ilustre Colegio de Abogados de Barcelona. *LANGUAGES:* Spanish.

DIEGO ECHECOPAR ROSSELLÓ, born Lima, Perú, 1965; admitted, 1990, Spain. *Education:* Universidad Complutense de Madrid. *Member:* Ilustre Colegio de Abogados de Madrid; Ilustre Colegio de Abogados de Barcelona. *LANGUAGES:* English and Spanish.

ANTONIO BARRAGAN GARCIA, born Madrid, Spain, 1965; admitted, 1990, Spain. *Education:* Universidad Complutense de Madrid. *Member:* Ilustre Colegio de Abogados de Madrid. *LANGUAGES:* English and Spanish.

AGUSTIN FERNANDEZ Y FERNANDEZ-ARROYO, born Madrid, Spain, 1967; admitted, 1990, Spain. *Education:* Universidad Pontificia de Comillas-ICADE (Law Degree, 1990; Economics Degree, 1991). *Member:* Ilustre Colegio de Abogados de Madrid. *LANGUAGES:* English and Spanish.

(This Listing Continued)

ELADIO SANCHEZ MARTINEZ, born Logroño, Spain, 1967; admitted, 1992, Spain. *Education:* Universidad de Deusto. *Member:* Ilustre Colegio de Abogados de Madrid. *LANGUAGES:* English and Spanish.

ANTONIO LLOBET POAL, born Barcelona, Spain, 1960; admitted, 1983, Spain. *Education:* Universidad Autónoma de Barcelona. *Member:* Ilustre Colegio de Abogados de Barcelona; Ilustre Colegio de Abogados de Madrid. (Resident Barcelona, Spain Office). *LANGUAGES:* English, Catalán and Spanish.

MARIANO PEREZ DE CACERES, born Badajoz, Spain, 1970; admitted, 1994, Spain. *Education:* Universidad Complutense de Madrid. *Member:* Ilustre Colegio de Abogados de Madrid. *LANGUAGES:* English and Spanish.

PABLO HENRIQUEZ DE LUNA LOSADA, born Ciudad Real, Spain, 1969; admitted, 1994, Spain. *Education:* Universidad Complutense de Madrid. *Member:* Ilustre Colegio de Abogados de Madrid. *LANGUAGES:* English and Spanish.

Languages: Spanish, Catalan, English and French.

ESTUDIO JURIDICO CASTELLANA

CARACAS, 23 1°
28010 MADRID, SPAIN
Telephone: (34-1) 310 43 91
Fax: (34-1) 310 42 68

Spanish and International Commercial Law (including Mergers and Acquisitions, Banking Transactions), EEC Law, Administrative Law, Exchange Control and Foreign Investment, Civil Law, Litigation, Tax Advice and Labor Law.

MEMBERS OF FIRM

ALBERTO URETA BUCKLEY, born Lima, Perú, 1935; admitted, 1961, Perú; 1975, Spain. *Education:* Pontificia Universidad Católica del Perú (Law Degree, 1961). *Member:* Ilustre Colegio de Abogados de Madrid; Ilustre Colegio de Abogados de Barcelona. *LANGUAGES:* Spanish and English.

ERNESTO CORREA REY, born Lima, Perú, 1943; admitted, 1968, Perú; 1975, Spain. *Education:* Pontificia Universidad Católica del Perú and Universidad Nacional de Trujillo, Perú (Law Degree, 1968). *Member:* Ilustre Colegio de Abogados de Madrid; Ilustre Colegio de Abogados de Barcelona. *LANGUAGES:* Spanish, English and French.

JAIME LIGUÉS CREUS, born San Sebastián, Spain, 1952; admitted, 1981, Spain. *Education:* Universidad Complutense de Madrid (Law Degree, 1978). *Member:* Ilustre Colegio de Abogados de Madrid; Ilustre Colegio de Abogados de Barcelona. *LANGUAGES:* Spanish and English.

ALMUDENA ORTIZ SÁNCHEZ, born Madrid, Spain, 1960; admitted, 1985, Spain. *Education:* Universidad Complutense de Madrid (Law Degree, 1982); Institute of European Studies, University of Brussels (Special Degree in EEC Law). *Member:* Ilustre Colegio de Abogados de Madrid; Ilustre Colegio de Abogados de Barcelona. *LANGUAGES:* Spanish, English and French.

JULIAN URBISTONDO ROMERO, born Madrid, Spain, June 4, 1959; admitted, 1988, Madrid. *Education:* Universidad Complutense de Madrid (Law Degree, 1981). *Member:* Ilustre Colegio de Abogados de Madrid. *LANGUAGES:* Spanish and English.

ALFONSO DE MEDINA CLARET, born Madrid, Spain, 1945; admitted, 1970, Spain. *Education:* Universidad Complutense de Madrid (Law Degree, 1970). *Member:* Ilustre Colegio de Abogados de Madrid. *LANGUAGES:* Spanish.

CRISTINA MARQUEZ DORSCH, born Madrid, Spain, 1967; admitted, 1992, Spain. *Education:* Universidad Complutense de Madrid (Law Degree, 1991). *Member:* Ilustre Colegio de Abogados de Madrid. *LANGUAGES:* Spanish and English.

SANTIAGO ALVAREZ-SALA SANJUAN, born Madrid, Spain, 1965; admitted, 1992, Spain. *Education:* Universidad Complutense de Madrid (Law Degree, 1991). *Member:* Ilustre Colegio de Abogados de Madrid. *LANGUAGES:* Spanish and English.

FIGAREDO & ASOCIADOS

PASEO DE LA HABANA, 182
28036 MADRID, SPAIN
Telephone: (34-1) 359 64 05
Fax: (34-1) 359 64 17

Offices in Vigo, Algerciras, Barcelona and Bilbao.
ALL CONNECTIONS SHALL BE MADE THROUGH THE
MADRID OFFICE CONTACTING WITH TOMAS
FERNANDEZ-QUIROS.

General Practice, Corporate, Commercial, Mergers and Acquisitions, Foreign Investments, Maritime Law, Insurance, Transport Law, International Arbitration, EEC Law, International Contracts, Environmental, Telecommunicati ons

LUIS FIGAREDO, *Member:* Madrid, Gijon, and Bilbao Bar Associations. *LANGUAGES:* Spanish, English, French and German. *PRACTICE AREAS:* Mergers and Acquisitions; Corporate Law; International Arbitration; Admiralty.

TOMAS FERNANDEZ-QUIROS, *Member:* Madrid, Tenerife, Las Palmas and Sabadell Bar Associations. *LANGUAGES:* Spanish, English and French. *PRACTICE AREAS:* International and Domestic Litigation and Arbitration; Commercial; Admiralty.

AMPARO GONZALEZ, *Member:* Madrid Bar Association. *LANGUAGES:* Spanish and English. *PRACTICE AREAS:* Banking and Tax Law.

JUAN CARLOS LOPEZ-QUIROGA, *Member:* Madrid and Lugo Bar Associations. *LANGUAGES:* Spanish, English and Portuguese. *PRACTICE AREAS:* International Sales Contract; Ship Finance and Registration; EEC Law.

AURORA DELGADO, *Member:* Madrid Bar Association. *LANGUAGES:* Spanish, English and French. *PRACTICE AREAS:* Commercial and Tax Law; Company Law.

JULIO LOPEZ-QUIROGA, *Member:* Madrid Bar Association. *LANGUAGES:* Spanish and English. *PRACTICE AREAS:* Environmental Law; Administration Law.

ROBERTO SANZ, *Member:* Madrid Bar Association. (Bilbao Office). *LANGUAGES:* Spanish, English and French. *PRACTICE AREAS:* Admiralty; Shipping; Transport Law; International Sales.

ALBERTO PENELAS, *Member:* Vigo and La Coruña Bar Associations. (Vigo Office). *LANGUAGES:* Spanish, English and Portuguese. *PRACTICE AREAS:* Admiralty; Commercial and Administration Law.

BEATRIZ GOICOECHEA, *Member:* Vigo and La Coruña Bar Associations. (Vigo Office). *LANGUAGES:* Spanish, French and Portuguese. *PRACTICE AREAS:* General Practice; Litigation.

INES ALVEAR, *Member:* Madrid Bar Association. *LANGUAGES:* Spanish, English and French. *PRACTICE AREAS:* International Commercial Law; Telecomunications.

ALMUDENA JIMENEZ, *Member:* Madrid Bar Association. *LANGUAGES:* Spanish and English. *PRACTICE AREAS:* Insurance and Tax Law.

GONZALO VALLEJO, *Member:* Madrid Bar Association. *LANGUAGES:* Spanish and English. *PRACTICE AREAS:* Maritime and Transport Law.

RAFAEL PÉREZ DE VARGAS LÓPEZ, *Member:* Cádiz and Seville Bar Association. *LANGUAGES:* Spanish and English. *PRACTICE AREAS:* Mercantile and Civil Law.

PAZ VIOZCAINO. *LANGUAGES:* Spanish, English, French and Catalan. *PRACTICE AREAS:* Environmental.

ELENA GARCÍA-SAÑUDO, *Member:* Madrid Bar Association. *LANGUAGES:* Spanish, English and Italian. *PRACTICE AREAS:* Insurance and Transport.

Languages: Spanish, English, French, German, Catalan, Italian, and Portuguese.

FRANCIS, RYAN AND FARRELL
ASESORIA INTERNACIONAL

PRINCIPE DE VERGARA, 17 - PISO 8°
MADRID 28001, SPAIN
Telephone: (91) 575-2219
Intn'l Dialing: (34-1) 575-0370
Fax: (34-1) 431-1153

International, Commercial and Civil, Corporations, Taxations, Foreign Investment, Oil and Gas, Mining, Real Estate, Transfer of Technology, Patents, Copy Right, Licensing Agreement, Common Market Law, Banking, Franchising and Telecommunications.

EDWARD F. FARRELL, admitted, 1958, District of Columbia; 1959, New Jersey (Not admitted in Spain). *Education:* Georgetown Law School (LL.D.); Notre Dame University (LL.B.); International Law Academy, The International Court, The Hague, Holland. Co-Author: "Doing Business in Spain," First Edition, Commerce Clearing House, 1976-1985. Professor of Business Law, St. Louis University, Madrid, 1987-1988. Professor of Business Law, University of ALCALA de Henares, Madrid, 1988-1989. Executive Secretary, American Business Council, Madrid. Past Co-Chairman, European Law Committee, 1974-1978. *Member:* American Bar Association (Member, International Law Section).

JUAN CASTELLÓ REQUEMA, admitted, Madrid and Barcelona. *Education:* University of Madrid (LL.D., 1951). Former Business Law Professor, University of Navarra, 1963. *Member:* Association of Prestigious Spanish Attorneys (Founder, 1956 and 1960; President, 1984).

JUAN ANTONIO BERJANO LEIRA, admitted, Malaga.

JOSE MANUEL GARCIA MARTINEZ, admitted, Madrid.

Languages: English, Spanish, French and German.

REPRESENTATIVE CLIENTS: Carte Blanche; Compaq Computer; European Software Company; Insurance Company of North America; Commission for Atlantic Tuna; Netherland Sea Drilling; Southwire Incorporated; Tideland Inc.; Western Crude Oil Inc.; Associated Natural Gas Company.

FRESHFIELDS

Established in 1991

FORTUNY, 6-3°
28010 MADRID, SPAIN
Telephone: (34 1) 319 1024
Fax: (34 1) 308 4636/2353

Other Offices in: Bangkok, Barcelona, Brussels, Frankfurt, Hanoi, Hong Kong, London, Moscow, New York, Paris, Singapore and Tokyo.

FIRM PROFILE: Freshfields provides a wide range of commercial legal advice internationally including mergers and acquisitions, joint ventures, capital markets, banking, project and specialist finance, tax, commercial property, intellectual property, agency, energy, environmental, pensions and competition law. Freshfields Madrid offers English, French, EC and (through its associated Spanish team) Spanish law advice.

RESIDENT PARTNERS

JOHN N. BYRNE, born Ayr, Scotland, 1953; admitted, 1978 in England and Wales as Solicitor; (Not admitted in Spain). *Education:* Gonville & Caius College, Cambridge (B.A., Hons, 1975; M.A.). *LANGUAGES:* English, Spanish and French.

TIMOTHY W. JONES, born England, 1957; admitted, 1984, England (Not admitted in Spain). *Education:* Wadham College, Oxford. *Member:* Law Society. *LANGUAGES:* Spanish, French and English. *PRACTICE AREAS:* Corporate Law; Corporate Finance Law; Mergers and Acquisitions; Privatisations.

JAVIER GOMEZ-ACEBO, born Madrid, Spain, 1953; admitted, 1980, Abogado and Letrado del Consejo de Estado, Spain. *Education:* Universidad Complutense-Madrid, Spain (1975) "Letrado Asesor del Consejo de Estado". (Fortuny Abogados Asociados con Freshfields). *LANGUAGES:* Spanish, English and French.

JUAN GOMEZ-ACEBO, born San Sebastian, Spain, 1954; admitted, 1983, Abogado, Spain. *Education:* Universidad Autónoma de Madrid (1977) Ministry of Defence Legal Advisory Body (1978). (Fortuny Abogados Asociados con Freshfields). *LANGUAGES:* Spanish, English and French.

(This Listing Continued)

FRANCISCO CANTOS BAQUEDANO, born Madrid, Spain, 1962; admitted, 1986, Abogado, Spain. *Education:* Universidad Autónoma de Madrid (Licenciado en Derecho, 1985); College d'Europe, Bruges, Belgium (EC Law, Post-graduate Degree, 1988). (Fortuny Abogados Asociados con Freshfields). *LANGUAGES:* Spanish, English and French.

JOSÉ IGNACIO YSASI-YSASMENDI, born Madrid, Spain, 1966; admitted, 1992, Abogado, Spain. *Education:* Universidad Complutense Madrid, Spain (1989); University of London (LL.M., Master in Laws, 1990). (Fortuny Abogados Asociados con Freshfields). *LANGUAGES:* Spanish, English and French.

PAUL ROEBUCK, born Bath, England, 1963; admitted, 1990, Solicitor, England and Wales (Not admitted in Spain). *Education:* Emmanuel College, Cambridge (B.A., Hons., 1985; M.A.). *LANGUAGES:* English and Spanish.

ANTONIA SERRA CLAPES, born Ibiza, Spain, February 17, 1967; admitted, 1989, Baleares, Abogado; 1991, Madrid, Abogado. *Education:* Universidad Complutense de Madrid (Licenciado en Derecho, 1989). *LANGUAGES:* Spanish, Catalan, English, German and Rumanian.

DR. FRÜHBECK
ABOGADOS Y ECONOMISTAS

Established in 1952

MARQUÉS DEL RISCAL, 11, 5°
28010 MADRID, SPAIN
Telephone: 308 25 22
Telex: 22469; 49214
Telefax: (1) 310 28 82

Barcelona, Spain Office: Balmes, 368 pr 2°, 08006. Telephone: (3) 418 63 87. Telex: (3) 418 93 50.

Marbella, Spain Office: Ramón Gómez de la Serna, 22, Edif. King Edward, Of. 404, 29600. Telephone: 778589; 778590. Telex: 79827. Telefax: 824-659.

Business Law, Commercial, Administrative, Tax, Exchange Control, Foreign Investment in Spain, Spanish Investment abroad, Labor, Industrial, Patents and Trademarks, Insolvency, Banking, Maritime Law, Civil Law, Inheritances, Real Estate, Criminal Law and Litigation.

PARTNERS

DR. GUILLERMO FRÜHBECK FRÜHBECK, born Burgos, Spain, September 30, 1926; admitted, 1952, Madrid; 1958, Burgos; 1978 Tenerife; 1981, Santander; 1982, Málaga; 1985, Oviedo; 1986, Las Palmas. *Education:* Universities of Valladolid and Madrid (Dr. in Law, 1963). Seminar for Doctorandi in the Spanish Institute of Comparative Law, 1987. *Member:* German-Spanish Law Association (Vice-President, 1984—). *LANGUAGES:* Spanish, English, German and French.

GUILLERMO FRÜHBECK OLMEDO, born Madrid, Spain, December 30, 1953; admitted, 1976, Madrid. *Education:* University Complutense of Madrid. *LANGUAGES:* Spanish, English and German.

FEDERICO FRÜHBECK OLMEDO, born Madrid, Spain, January 27, 1955; admitted, 1978, Madrid; 1982, Bilbao; 1985, Málaga, Oviedo and Baleares. *Education:* University Complutense of Madrid. *LANGUAGES:* Spanish, English, German and French.

ASSOCIATES

FERNANDO FRÜHBECK OLMEDO, born Madrid, Spain, May 30, 1967; admitted, 1990, Madrid. *Education:* Colegio Universitario San Pablo C.E.U. (University Complutense of Madrid), 1990. *LANGUAGES:* Spanish, German, French, English.

DR. FRANCISCA HERNANZ SANCHEZ, born Madrid, Spain, September 29, 1954; admitted, 1987, Madrid. *Education:* Universidad Complutense de Madrid (Lic. en Derecho); Rheinische Friedrich-Wilhelm Universität, Boon (Dr. Jur.); Boalt Hall, University of California, Berkeley (LL.M.); University of California, Hastings College of Law (J.D.). Author: "La reforma del Derecho Internacional Privado en la República Federal de Alemania," vol. LXXII, Revista de Derecho Privado 1988; "Recognition-Exequator-of Foreign Judgements, Especially of U.S. Divorce Judgements in Spain," vol. 38, The American Journal of Comparative Law 1990; "Das Kollisions-, Zuständigkeits- und Anerkenungsrecht der internationalen Ehescheidung in Spanien," Duncker & Humblot 1987. *LANGUAGES:* Spanish, English and German.

(This Listing Continued)

DR. JÖRG OLIVER HELRICH, born Frankfurt, Germany, September 14, 1961; admitted, 1993, Düsseldorf. *Education:* Rheinische Friedrich-Wilhelm Universität, Bonn and Albert Ludwigs Universität, Freiburg. Author: "Rechtsschutz der Mode," Nomos 1993. *LANGUAGES:* German, Spanish and English.

INMACULADA ESTEVE SERNA, born Alicante, Spain, April 7, 1967; admitted, 1993, Alicante, Madrid. *Education:* Universidad de Alicante; Universidad de Castilla La Mancha, Albacete. *LANGUAGES:* Spanish and English.

JORGE AGUINACO MORENO, born Vitoria, Spain, November 1, 1968; admitted, 1993, Madrid. *Education:* Universidad de Deusto, Bilbao; M.A.J. Instituto de Empresa, Madrid. *LANGUAGES:* Spanish, English and German.

Languages: Spanish, English, German and French.

VENTURA GARCÉS

ALFONSO XII, 22
28014 MADRID, SPAIN
Telephone: (34-1) 521 7818
Telefax: (34-1) 521 7853

Barcelona, Spain Office: Freixa, 26-28, 08021. Telephone: (34-3) 201 94 44. Telefax: (34-3) 209 83 91.

General Practice, Antitrust Law, Arbitration, Banking Law, Bankruptcy, Commercial Law, Company Law, Distribution, Agency and Franchise Law, EEC Law, Fiscal Law, Foreign Investments, International Contracts, Litigation, M&A, Property and Real Estate Law.

MEMBERS OF FIRM

VENTURA GARCÉS, admitted, 1952, Barcelona. *Education:* University of Barcelona (Law Degree). Author: *Regimen jurídico de las inversiones extranjeras en España* , 1975 (English edition: Legal Aspects of Foreign Investments in Spain, 1976); *Los contratos de asistencia técnica internactional y su regulación en Espanña* , 1980. Co-Author: "Licensing and Franchising in Spain" and "Tax Treatment of Joint Ventures in Spain," published in International Tax Review (Euromoney Publications, London, 1992). *Member:* Barcelona, Madrid and Balearic Islands Bar Association. *LANGUAGES:* Spanish, Catalan, English, French and Italian.

RICARD GENÉ, admitted, 1985, Sabadell and Barcelona. *Education:* Barcelona University (Degree in Law). Expert in Property and Administrative Law. Official Translator for English and Catalan. *Member:* Barcelona Bar Association. *LANGUAGES:* Spanish, Catalan, English, French and German.

CLAUDIO GARCÉS, admitted, 1986, Barcelona. *Education:* Barcelona University (Degree in Law); Colegio Abad Oliba (Postgraduate Course in Taxation); University of London (Diploma in International Law). Co-Author: "Licensing and Franchising in Spain" (International Tax Review). *Member:* Barcelona Bar Association. *LANGUAGES:* Spanish, Catalan, French and English.

IVÁN AZINOVIC, admitted, 1992, Madrid. *Education:* University of Alcalá de Henares (Law Degree, 1989); Washington College of Law, American University, Washington, D.C. (Master in International, specialism: International Commercial Law and Banking Law). *Member:* Madrid Bar Association. *LANGUAGES:* Spanish, Catatlan and English.

Languages: Spanish, Catalan, English, French, German and Italian.

(For Complete Biographical Data on all Personnel and for Representative Clients, see Professional Biographies at Barcelona, Spain)

LUIS GARRIDO

Abogados

SEGRE, 20
28002 MADRID, SPAIN
Telephone: 564.77.47; 564.77.37
Telefax: 564.77.60

General Practice, Corporate, Commercial, Tax, Insurance and Reinsurance, Foreign Investments, License Technical Assistance and Distribution Agreements, Arbitration, Labor Relations, Insolvency, EEC and International Law.

LUIS GARRIDO, born Madrid, Spain, 1930; admitted, 1953, Spain. *Education:* Colegio de Nuestra Señora del Pilar (Bachelor, 1947); University

(This Listing Continued)

LUIS GARRIDO, Madrid—Continued

of Madrid (Licentiate in Law, 1952); New York University (Master of Comparative Jurisprudence, 1958); Graduate in Foreign Trade, Centro de Estudios Universitarios, Madrid. Diploma in License and Transfer of Technology Agreements, CEU, Madrid. *Member:* Colegio de Abogados de Madrid; Real Academia de Legislacion y Jurisprudencia; American Bar Association. *LANGUAGES:* Spanish, French and English.

ASSOCIATES

PATRICIA GARRIDO, born Madrid, Spain, 1963; admitted, 1986, Spain. *Education:* I.C.A.D.E., University of Madrid (Licenciate in Law, 1986; Diplomas in Inco me Tax, 1988; Corporation Law, 1988; Added Value Tax, 1989). Member, Madrid Chamber of Commerce and Industry. *Member:* Colegio de Abogados de Madrid. *LANGUAGES:* Spanish, French and English.

SOLEDAD MURUBE, born Madrid, Spain, 1966; admitted, 1992, Spain. *Education:* University of Madrid (Licenciate in Law, 1990); Instituto de Empresa, Madrid (Master of Corporate and Business Law, 1991). *Member:* Colegio de Abogados de Madrid. *LANGUAGES:* Spanish and English.

LETICIA R. ETCHEVERRIA, born Madrid, Spain, 1969; admitted, 1993, Spain. *Education:* University of Madrid (Licenciate in Law, 1992); Diploma in Juridical Practice, CEU, Madrid, 1991; Instituto de Empresa, Madrid (Master of Corporate and Business Law, 1993). *Member:* Colegio de Abogados de Madrid. *LANGUAGES:* Spanish, English and French.

Languages: Spanish, English and French.

REPRESENTATIVE CLIENTS: *USA:* Allegiance Capital Partners; American Mutual Liability Insurance Co.; Atlantic Southern Insurance Co.; Employers Reinsurance Corp.; General Reinsurance Corp.; Hay Associates; International Reinsurance Corp.; Johnson & Johnson; Loews Hotels, Inc.; Pan-American Life Insurance Co.; Peninsular Life Insurance Co.; Petroéleos de Venezuela; Westport Insurance Corp. *EUROPE:* Baltica Expat, S.A.; British Caledonian Airways; Danica-Baltica I, Life Insurance Co.; Eurodollar Ren-A-Car Ltd.; Forsikringsaktieselskabet Kompas; Jardine Insurance Brokers; Kompan International A/S; Luis Caballero, S.A.; Lloyd's Register of Shipping; New Chappel Inc.; Rank Hotels Ltd.; Reemtsma Cigarettenfabriken GmbH; Sterling Airways; Waldorf-Astoria International GmbH.

J. & A. GARRIGUES

ANTONIO MAURA, 16
28014 MADRID, SPAIN
Telephone: (34-1) 521.21.51
Facsimile: TLM (34-1) 521.40.53, 531.70.16, 521.39.73, 532.96.38
Telex: 22153 - 44189

REVISERS OF THE SPAIN LAW DIGEST FOR THIS DIRECTORY.

Barcelona, Spain Office: Mallorca, 260-262, 4°, 2ª, 08008. Telephone: (34-3) 488-12-11. Facsimile: (34-3) 487-53-76; 487-99-26. Telex: 51285.

New York, New York Office: 115 East 57th Street, Suite 1230, 10022. Telephone: 1-212-751-9233. Facsimile: 1-212-355-3594. Telex: 14-9543.

Brussels, Belgium Office: Rue D'Arlon, 118. B - 1040. Telephone: (32-2) 280-16-60. Facsimile: (32-2) 280-15-60.

Marbella, Spain Office: Avda. Ricardo Soriano, 65 - 5° 1. Telephone: (34-52) 86-22-11. Facsimile: (34-52) 82-68-84.

Oviedo, Spain Office: Marqués de Pidal, 6 - 3°C., 33004. Telephone: (34-8) 527-73-75. Facsimile: (34-8) 527-73-83.

Seville, Spain Office: Zaragoza, 50, 41001. Telephone: (34-5) 456-45-36. Facsimile: (34-5) 456-47-52.

Lisbon, Portugal Office: Grupo Legal Português (EEIG) in association with F. Castelo Branco, Nobre Guedes & P. Rebelo de Sousa, Simmons & Simmons and Pinheiro Neto & Co. Rua, Castilho, n°- 9°/ 1200 Lisbon. Telephone: (351-1) 352-13-18. Facsimile: (351-1) 352-14-18.

General Practice, Administrative, Corporation, International Labor Relations, Oil and Gas, Mines, Foreign Investments, Banking, Estate Law and Taxation, Maritime Law.

MEMBERS OF FIRM

ANTONIO GARRIGUES WALKER, born Madrid, Spain, 1934; admitted, 1959, Spain. *Education:* University of Madrid. *Member:* Madrid and American (Honorary Member) Bar Associations.

RAMON LLADO FERNANDEZ-URRUTIA, born Barcelona, Spain, 1939; admitted, 1966, Spain. *Education:* University of Madrid. Assistant Professor of Commercial Law, University of Madrid, 1963-1970. *Member:* Madrid and Barcelona Bar Associations.

(This Listing Continued)

DANIEL GARCIA-PITA-PEMAN, born Cadiz, Spain, 1947; admitted, 1969, Spain. *Education:* University of Madrid. Faculty of Economic Science, 1964-1968. Assistant Professor of Commercial Law, University of Madrid, 1969. *Member:* Madrid Bar Association.

CARLOS LORING MARTINEZ DE IRUJO, born Mieres, Asturias, Spain, 1947; admitted, 1969, Spain. *Education:* University of Madrid; University College of Dublin. *Member:* Madrid and Malaga Bar Associations.

ALFREDO ZABALJAUREGUI CHICOTE, born Manila, Philippine Is., 1933; admitted, 1962, Spain. *Education:* Universities of Deusto and Valladolid, School of Legal Practice and Center of Tax Studies. *Member:* Madrid Bar Association.

ANTONIO ALONSO-LASHERAS, born Valladolid, Spain, 1942; admitted, 1967, Spain. *Education:* University of Valladolid. Assistant Professor, Administrative Law. *Member:* Madrid and Valladolid Bar Associations.

ARTURO DELGADO DE ALMEIDA, born Lisbon, Portugal, 1939; admitted, 1965, Spain. *Education:* Universities of Madrid and Salamanca. Professional relations with Portugal. *Member:* Madrid Bar Association.

MIGUEL ANGEL PANDO, born Madrid, Spain, 1939; admitted, 1965, Spain. *Education:* University of Madrid. *Member:* Madrid and Barcelona Bar Associations. *LANGUAGES:* English, French and Italian.

RAMON BUSTILLO AGUIRRE, born Seville, Spain, 1946; admitted, 1971, Spain. *Education:* University of Seville, Spain. *Member:* Madrid Bar Association.

EDUARDO SEBASTIAN DE ERICE, born Madrid, Spain, 1940; admitted, 1975, Spain. *Education:* Universities of Deusto and Valladolid. Former Head of Spanish Trade Office in Chicago, (Commercial Attache) and Head of Department of Spanish Investments. *Member:* Madrid Bar Association.

EMILIO DEL SOL RODRIGUEZ, born Madrid, Spain, 1951; admitted, 1974, Spain. *Education:* University of Madrid. *Member:* Madrid Bar Association.

JOSE MARIA ALONSO PUIG, born Madrid, Spain, 1953; admitted, 1978, Spain. *Education:* University of Madrid; Escuela of Practica Juridica (Diploma in Communitary Law). Professor of Procedural Law, Madrid Bar Association, 1988-1989. *Member:* Madrid, Burgos and Leon Bar Associations.

IGNACIO URBISTONDO Y GAYTAN DE AYALA, born San Sebastián, Spain, 1952; admitted, 1976, Spain. *Education:* University of Salamanca, Spain, School of Filosofía y Letras, Salamanca, Spain (Licenciate in Philosophy, 1975); Master of Laws, Columbia Law School (LL.M., 1978). *Member:* Madrid and Vizcaya Bar Associations.

JUAN RAMON ANDINO VILLASANTE, born Medina de Pomar, Burgos, Spain, 1940; admitted, 1971, Spain. *Education:* University of Barcelona. *Member:* Barcelona and Gerona Bar Associations. *LANGUAGES:* English, French.

RAFAEL ECHEGOYEN ENRIQUEZ, born Madrid, Spain, 1952; admitted, 1974, Spain. *Education:* University of Madrid; Dale Carnegie Course, Public Relations; Fordham University, N.Y., International Foreign Transactions Course. *Member:* Madrid Bar Association.

IGNACIO DE LAS CUEVAS, born Madrid, Spain, 1946; admitted, 1986, Spain. *Education:* University of Madrid. State Fiscal Inspector. Lecturer, Instituto de Empresa. *Member:* Madrid Bar Association.

FERNANDO BAUTISTA SAGÜÉS, born Madrid, Spain, 1957; admitted, 1982, Spain. *Education:* University of Deusto (Bilbao) Graduated in Economic Sciences (I.C.A.D.E. Madrid). *Member:* Madrid Bar Association.

ENRIQUE FONSECA CAPDEVILA, born Madrid, Spain, 1956; admitted, 1979, Spain. *Education:* University of Madrid. *Member:* Madrid Bar Association.

MANUEL ZUMALACARREGUI, born Madrid, Spain, 1952; admitted, 1978, Spain. *Education:* University of Madrid; Centro de Estudios Universitarios (CEU), Madrid. *Member:* Madrid Bar Association.

MARIA JOSE MORA, born Madrid, Spain, 1949; admitted, 1979, Spain. *Education:* University of Madrid. *Member:* Madrid Bar Association.

MIGUEL MOSCARDO MORALES-VARA DE REY, born Madrid, Spain, 1953; admitted, 1978, Spain. *Education:* University of Madrid; Es-

(This Listing Continued)

cuela Diplomática of Madrid, Spain (Diploma in European Communities Course). Assistant Professor of Procedure Law, University of Madrid, 1977-1979. Professor Procedure Law, Madrid Bar Associations. Teacher of Master's degree course at the College of Architecture of Madrid University, 1987-1989. *Member:* Madrid, Almería, Murcia, Cartagena (Murcia) and Lorca (Murcia) Bar Associations.

ALVARO SAINZ MARTIN, born Madrid, Spain, 1958; admitted, 1985, Spain. *Education:* University of Madrid. *Member:* Madrid Bar Association.

JAVIER PEREZ-ARDA CRIADO, born La Coruña, Spain, 1954; admitted, 1986, Spain. *Education:* University of Santiago de Compostela. Abogado del Estado, 1980-1986 (retired). Chief Legal Adviser, Public Treasury, 1982-1986. Professor of Administrative Law (UNED), 1984-1986. *Member:* Madrid and La Coruña Bar Associations.

JOSE ANTONIO SANFULGENCIO, born Cartagena (Murcia), Spain, 1953; admitted, 1978, Spain. *Education:* University Autónoma of Madrid (Degree in Corporate, Economic and Labor Studies). Lecturer in Labor Law, Escuela Social of Madrid. *Member:* Madrid Bar Association.

OF COUNSEL

ANDRES TRUJILLO ROSEÑADA, born Colón, Cuba, 1919; admitted, 1970, Spain. *Education:* University of Havana (Doctor of Law, 1945) and Madrid. Full Professor of Roman and Civil Law, Villanova University, Havana, 1946-1960. *Member:* Madrid Bar Association.

ALEJO LOPEZ MELLADO, born Laujar, Spain, 1923; admitted, 1966, Spain. *Education:* Universities of Granada and Madrid. Former Assistant Professor, University of Madrid and Center of University Studies. Former Superior Court Judge. *Member:* Madrid Bar Association.

GUILLERMO SENÉN DE LA FUENTE, born Madrid, Spain, 1929; admitted, 1953, Spain. *Education:* University of Madrid (Doctor of Law). Assistant Professor, 1953-1959 and Associate Professor, 1964-1970, Commercial Law, University of Madrid. *Member:* Madrid Bar Association.

ASSOCIATES

MANUEL FILLOL CIORRAGA, born Torrenueva, Ciudad Real, Spain, 1931; admitted, 1965, Spain. *Education:* University of Madrid; Diploma of Social Science, School of Legal Practice. *Member:* Madrid Bar Association.

JOSE LUIS SAN PIO, born Saragossa, Spain, 1939; admitted, 1961, Spain. *Education:* Universities of Madrid and Saragossa. *Member:* Madrid Bar Association; International Law Association; Union Internationale D'Avocats.

GONZALO SOSA ALGUACIL, born Madrid, Spain, 1958; admitted, 1982, Spain. *Education:* University of Madrid. *Member:* Madrid Bar Association.

FELIPE YANNONE, born Madrid, Spain, 1960; admitted, 1983, Spain. *Education:* University of Madrid; Instituto de Empresa (Master's Degree in Corporate Legal Consultancy, 1983). *Member:* Madrid Bar Association.

MARIO PEÑA FERNANDEZ-PEÑA, born Madrid, Spain, 1956; admitted, 1985, Spain. *Education:* University of Madrid. *Member:* Madrid Bar Association.

ANTONIO FERNANDEZ RODRIGUEZ, born Madrid, Spain, 1960; admitted, 1985, Spain. *Education:* University of Madrid. Assistant, Commercial Law and Conflict Law Departments, University of Madrid, 1983-1986. International Commercial Law doctorate studies. Assistant Professor, Procedure Law at the Madrid Bar Association, 1988-1989. *Member:* Madrid Bar Association.

JUAN JOSE TOME, born Madrid, Spain, 1959; admitted, 1986, Spain. *Education:* University Pontificia de Comillas (I.C.A.D.E.). *Member:* Madrid Bar Association.

CARMEN MARTIN-PEÑA GARCIA, born Madrid, Spain, 1959; admitted, 1984, Spain. *Education:* University of Madrid, Instituto de Empresa: Master's Degree in Corporate Legal Consultancy, 1986. *Member:* Madrid Bar Association.

MIGUEL JORDANA DE POZAS, born Madrid, Spain, 1955; admitted, 1981, Spain. *Education:* University of Madrid. *Member:* Madrid Bar Association.

MARIA TERESA HERNANDEZ FALCO, born Barcelona, Spain, 1951; admitted, 1975, Spain. *Education:* University of Barcelona. *Member:* Barcelona Bar Association. *LANGUAGES:* English and French.

(This Listing Continued)

IÑIGO BASTARRECHE SAGÜES, born Madrid, Spain, 1963; admitted, 1988, Spain. *Education:* University of Madrid. *Member:* Madrid Bar Association.

STEPHEN PICKARD, born Canberra, Australia, 1954; admitted, 1979, Solicitor England and Wales; 1985, New York (Not admitted in Spain). *Education:* Oxford Polytechnic (B.A., 1976, Law, Politics and Economics); Johns Hopkings University, Bologna (Graduate Diploma, 1980); Columbia University School of Law, New York (LL.M., 1983). (Resident Lawyer, Brussels Office).

IÑIGO RAMILO RODRIGUEZ DE ROBLES, born Vigo, Pontevedra, Spain, 1960; admitted, 1983, Spain. *Education:* University of Madrid; Universidad de Comillas (Diplomado en Comunidades Europeas). *Member:* Madrid Bar Association.

CAROLINA CAPARROS ALVAREZ, born Madrid, Spain, 1964; admitted, 1987, Spain. *Education:* University of Madrid. *Member:* Madrid Bar Association.

ISABEL FERRER LOPEZ, born Alicante, Spain, 1962; admitted, 1985, Spain. *Education:* University of Alicante; University of Amsterdam (Diploma on European Integration, 1986). *Member:* Elche and Málaga Bar Associations.

SERGIO SANCHEZ SOLE, born Barcelona, Spain, 1964; admitted, 1988, Spain. *Education:* University of Barcelona. Professor, Commercial Law, Colegio Universitario Abad Oliva. *Member:* Barcelona Bar Association. *LANGUAGES:* English, French.

JAVIER YBAÑEZ RUBIO, born Porto Alegre, Brazil, 1963; admitted, 1988, Spain. *Education:* University of Madrid. *Member:* Madrid Bar Association.

RAFAEL GONZALEZ GALLARZA, born Madrid, Spain, 1964; admitted, 1989, Spain. *Education:* University of Madrid. *Member:* Madrid Bar Association.

MARIA EUGENIA CARVAJAL, born Madrid, Spain, 1963; admitted, 1987, Spain. *Education:* University of Madrid; Diploma on Advanced European Studies (College of Europe, Bruges). *Member:* Madrid Bar Association.

MARIA TERESA FERNANDEZ MATEOS, born Madrid, Spain, 1965; admitted, 1988, Spain. *Education:* University of Madrid; Master's Degree in Corporate Legal Consultancy. *Member:* Madrid Bar Association.

ERNESTO TRIGUEROS GOMEZ-DEGANO, born Madrid, Spain, 1956; admitted, 1980, Spain. *Education:* University of Madrid. *Member:* Madrid Bar Association.

CARLOS BUSTILLO MUÑOZ, born Avila, Spain, 1956; admitted, 1985, Spain. *Education:* University of Madrid. *Member:* Malaga Bar Association.

JUAN JOSE YAGO LUJAN, born Albacete, Spain, 1957; admitted, 1980, Spain. *Education:* University of Madrid; Diploma en delitos economicos (University Pontificia of Comillas ICAI). *Member:* Madrid Bar Association.

MARCOS ARAUJO, born Madrid, Spain, 1963; admitted, 1990, Spain. *Education:* University of Alicante (Law Degree, 1986; Doctorate Courses, 1989). *Member:* Madrid Bar Association.

CONCEPCION CURIEL MANRESA, born Murcia, Spain, 1963; admitted, 1986, Spain. *Education:* University of Madrid; College of Europe, Bruges (Diploma of Advanced Studies). *Member:* Madrid Bar Association.

GONZALO FERNANDEZ-ATELA, born Mexico, D.F, Mexico, 1959; admitted, 1986, Spain. *Education:* University of Madrid, Colombia Law School (Master of Laws, 1987). *Member:* Madrid Bar Association.

JOSE RAMON F. VILLAR, born Vitoria, Spain, 1961; admitted, 1984, Spain. *Education:* Basque University Law School (J.D., 1984); Basque University (Licentiate in Philosophy, 1986); Santa Clara Law School, California, U.S.A. (Visiting Scholar, 1987); University of Iowa Law School, U.S.A. (LL.M., 1988). Phi Alpha Delta Law Fraternity International. Member, Board of Directors, Spain-USA Chamber of Commerce. *Member:* Basque Country, Madrid, American and International Bar Associations; American Foreign Law Association.

PALOMA RODRIGUEZ DE RAVENA, born Madrid, Spain, 1965; admitted, 1990, Spain. *Education:* University Pontificia of Comillas (ICADE); Licenciada en Derecho y Diplomada en Ciencias Empresariales (Letrado Asesor de Empresas). *Member:* Madrid Bar Association.

(This Listing Continued)

J. & A. GARRIGUES, Madrid—Continued

JOSE LUIS MAGRE, born Barcelona, Spain, 1962; admitted, 1987, Spain; 1989, New York. *Education:* University of Barcelona, Barcelona Tax and Financial Studies Center. *Member:* Barcelona Bar Association. *LANGUAGES:* English.

JORDI R. TORRENTS, born Barcelona, Spain, 1955; admitted, 1980, Spain. *Education:* University of Barcelona; Master International Law, S.M.U. Dallas, Texas, USA. *Member:* Barcelona Bar Association. *LANGUAGES:* English.

ROCIO BELDA DE MERGELINA, born Madrid, Spain, 1963; admitted, 1986, Spain. *Education:* University of Valencia (Licenciatura en Derecho, 1988); Vrije Universiteit Brussel (LL.M., Master on International and Comparative Law, 1988). Trainee, EEC Commission, Legal Service, 1989. *Member:* APILCA; Association of Former Trainees of the EEC Commission. *LANGUAGES:* English and French.

GUILLERMO RUIZ ZAPATERO, born Soria, Spain, 1958; admitted, 1990, Spain. *Education:* University of Madrid. *Member:* Madrid Bar Association; Institute of Chartered Accountants.

IGNACIO CORBERA DALE, born Bilbao, Spain, 1965; admitted, 1990 (Not admitted in Spain). *Education:* Colegio "San Igancio", Barcelona; University of Barcelona Law School; College of Europe (Postgraduate Course in EEC Law, 1989). *Member:* Barcelona Bar Association. *LANGUAGES:* English, French and Italian.

ALFONSO BARON BASTARRECHE, born Madrid, Spain, 1953; admitted, 1979, Spain. *Education:* University of Madrid; Master degree on Tax Law of "Instituto de Empress," Madrid, Spain. *Member:* Madrid Bar Association.

CESAR ALBIÑANA GARCIA-QUINTANA, born Alar del Rey, Palencia, 1920; admitted, 1948, Spain. *Education:* University of Madrid (Doctorate in Law). Professor of Taxation, Complutense University. *Member:* Madrid Bar Association; International Bar Association.

DOLORES MOLINA FERNANDEZ, born Priego, Cordoba, Spain, 1967; admitted, 1990, Spain. *Education:* University of I.C.A.D.E. - Comillas - Madrid. *Member:* Malaga Bar Association.

TERESA ARRANZ CACERES, born Segovia, Spain, 1966. *Education:* University of Madrid. *Member:* Madrid Bar Association.

ANGELES MANZANO, born Madrid, Spain, 1957; admitted, 1980, Spain. *Education:* University of Madrid. *Member:* Madrid Bar Association.

MIGUEL ANGEL SERRANO, born Madrid, Spain, 1964; admitted, 1991, Spain. *Education:* Pontifical University of Comillas (I.C.A.D.E.)-Madrid. Assistant Professor, Dept. of Criminal and Procedural Law, Pontifical University of Comillas (I.C.A.D.E.). *Member:* Madrid Bar Association.

MIGUEL FUERTES SUAREZ, born Oviedo, Spain, 1951; admitted, 1983. *Education:* University of Oviedo; Europa College, Brugge, Belgium; Diplomatic School, Madrid. *Member:* Oviedo Bar Association. (Resident Lawyer, Oviedo Office).

CARLOS GONZALEZ, born Madrid, Spain, 1966; admitted, 1991, Spain. *Education:* University of Madrid (Doctorate in Law). *Member:* Madrid Bar Association.

SUSANA PIZARROSO GONZALEZ, born Madrid, Spain, 1963; admitted, 1988. *Education:* Lycée français de Madrid - University of Madrid - Diplomatic School. *Member:* Madrid Bar Association (Labor Specialization). *LANGUAGES:* French, English.

SILVIA VALIENTE DOMINGUEZ, born Barcelona, Spain, 1967; admitted, 1992, Spain. *Education:* University of Barcelona; ESADE (postgraduation in tax law, 1992). *Member:* Barcelona Bar Association. *LANGUAGES:* English.

FERNANDO GONZALEZ DE LA PEÑA YSERN, born Jerez de la Frontera, Spain, 1956; admitted, 1981, Spain. *Education:* University of Sevilla (licenciatura en Derecho, 1979). *Member:* Sevilla, Huelva and Jerez de la Frontera, Cádiz and Jaen Bar Associations. *LANGUAGES:* English.

RAFAEL DORREGO GONZALEZ, born Madrid, Spain, 1951; admitted, 1992, Spain. *Education:* Nuestra Señora de El Pilar School in Madrid-University Complutense of Madrid, 1976. *Member:* Madrid-Alcalá de Henares Bar Association (Labor Law Specialization, 1976—). *LANGUAGES:* French and English.

(This Listing Continued)

JAVIER URBANO, born Burgos, Spain, 1967; admitted, 1992, Spain. *Education:* ICADE (Law Degree, 1990); Harvard University (LL.M., 1992). *Member:* Madrid Bar Association.

CARLOS DE LOS SANTOS, born Madrid, Spain, 1966; admitted, 1991. *Education:* University Pontificia de Comillas (ICADE), Law Degree, 1989. *Member:* Madrid Bar Association. *LANGUAGES:* English.

MARISA LOPEZ VILLALBA, born Madrid, Spain, 1968; admitted, 1992, Spain. *Education:* University of Madrid (Law Degree); Master in Labour Law, Labor Specialization. *Member:* Madrid Bar Association. *LANGUAGES:* English, Italian and French.

DULCE MIRANDA, born Madrid, Spain, 1968; admitted, 1993, Madrid. *Education:* University of Madrid (Law Degree). *Member:* Madrid Bar Association. *LANGUAGES:* English and French.

CRISTINA CONTEL BONET, born El Vendrell, Tarragona, Spain, 1965; admitted, 1990, Spain. *Education:* University of Barcelona (Law Degree); Master in Corporate and Business Law. *Member:* Barcelona Bar Association. *LANGUAGES:* English.

MIGUEL RIAÑO POMBO, born Madrid, Spain, 1967; admitted, 1993, Madrid. *Education:* University of Madrid (Master in European Community Law). *Member:* Madrid Bar Association. *LANGUAGES:* English.

PEDRO YSASY-YSASMENDI, born Cadiz, Spain, 1967; admitted, 1993, Madrid. *Education:* University of Madrid; New York University (M.C.J., Master in Comparative Jurisprudence, 1992). *Member:* Madrid Bar Association. *LANGUAGES:* English and French.

JOSE MARIA REQUENA LAVIÑA, born Madrid, Spain, 1962; admitted, 1993, Madrid. *Education:* University of Madrid. *Member:* Madrid Bar Association. *LANGUAGES:* English.

SANTIAGO GARRIDO DE LAS HERAS, born Madrid, Spain, 1967; admitted, 1992, Madrid. *Education:* University of Madrid (Law Degree). *Member:* Madrid Bar Association. *LANGUAGES:* English.

PILAR DE HOYOS MAROTO, born Zaragoza, Spain, 1964; admitted, 1993, Madrid. *Education:* University of Madrid. *Member:* Madrid Bar Association. *LANGUAGES:* English.

LUIS FERNANDEZ DE LA GANDARA, born Valladolid, Spain, 1941; admitted, 1994, Madrid. *Education:* University of Alicante (Professor in Commercial Law). *LANGUAGES:* English, German, Italian and French.

JOSEFA MORALES CAÑAS, born Barcelona, Spain, 1958; admitted, 1988, Spain. *Education:* Law School, University of Barcelona; Barcelona University of Arts (History Degree). *Member:* Barcelona Bar Association. *LANGUAGES:* French.

JAVIER VIDAL-QUADRAS TRIAS DE BES, born Barcelona, Spain, 1961; admitted, 1988, Spain. *Education:* Law School, University of Barcelona. Professor of Commercial Law. *Member:* Barcelona Bar Association. *LANGUAGES:* English and Portuguese.

ALVARO PEREZ ARBIZU, born Sevilla, Spain, 1968. *Education:* University of Sevilla (Licenciatura de Derecho, 1991); Postgraduate Studies in Financial and Taxation Law. *Member:* Sevilla Bar Association.

AURELIO ORRILLO LARA, born La Linea, Spain, 1967; admitted, 1993, Spain. *Education:* University of Navarra (Law Degree and Master in Business Law). *Member:* Sevilla Bar Association. *LANGUAGES:* English.

JOSE GUARDO GALDON, born Valencia, Spain, 1969; admitted, 1994, Spain. *Education:* University of Valencia School of Law (Master in European Law); University Carlos III of Madrid. *Member:* Madrid Bar Association. *LANGUAGES:* English, French and Italian.

LORETO SALVADOR OLEA, born Bilbao, Spain, 1969; admitted, 1994, Spain. *Education:* University of Madrid. *Member:* Madrid Bar Association. *LANGUAGES:* English.

MONTSE MURO OLLE, born Barcelona, Spain, 1966; admitted, 1993. *Education:* University of Barcelona. *LANGUAGES:* English, French.

BARCELONA OFFICE
RESIDENT LAWYERS

MIGUEL ANGEL PANDO LOPEZ, born Madrid, Spain, 1939; admitted, 1965, Spain. *Education:* University of Madrid. *Member:* Madrid and Barcelona Bar Associations. *LANGUAGES:* English, French and Italian.

JUAN RAMON ANDINO VILLASANTE, born Medina de Pomar, Burgos, Spain, 1940; admitted, 1971, Spain. *Education:* University of Barce-

(This Listing Continued)

lona. *Member:* Barcelona and Gerona Bar Associations; International Law Association. *LANGUAGES:* English.

MARIA TERESA HERNANDEZ FALCO, born Barcelona, Spain, 1951; admitted, 1986, Spain. *Education:* University of Barcelona. *Member:* Barcelona Bar Association. *LANGUAGES:* English and French.

SERGIO SANCHEZ SOLE, born Barcelona, Spain, 1962; admitted, 1985, Spain. *Education:* University of Barcelona. *Member:* Barcelona Bar Association. *LANGUAGES:* English and French.

JOSE LUIS MAGRE, born Barcelona, Spain, 1962; admitted, 1987, Spain; 1989, New York. *Education:* University of Barcelona, Barcelona Tax and Financial Studies Center. *Member:* Barcelona Bar Association. *LANGUAGES:* English.

JORDI R. TORRENTS, born Barcelona, Spain, 1955; admitted, 1980, Spain. *Education:* University of Barcelona; Master, International Law, S.M.U. Dallas, Texas USA. *Member:* Barcelona Bar Association. *LANGUAGES:* English.

IGNACIO CORBERA DALE, born Bilbao, Spain, 1965; admitted, 1990 (Not admitted in Spain). *Education:* Colegio "San Igancio", Barcelona; University of Barcelona Law School; College of Europe (Postgraduate Course in EEC Law, 1989). *Member:* Barcelona Bar Association. *LANGUAGES:* English, French and Italian.

SILVIA VALIENTE DOMINGUEZ, born Barcelona, Spain, 1967; admitted, 1992, Spain. *Education:* University of Barcelona; ESADE (Postgraduation in Tax Law, 1992). *Member:* Barcelona Bar Association. *LANGUAGES:* English.

CRISTINA CONTEL BONET, born El Vendrell, Tarragona, Spain, 1965; admitted, 1990, Spain. *Education:* University of Barcelona (Law Degree); Master in Corporate and Business Law. *Member:* Barcelona Bar Association. *LANGUAGES:* English.

JOSEFA MORALES CAÑAS, born Barcelona, Spain, 1958; admitted, 1988, Spain. *Education:* Law School, University of Barcelona; Barcelona University of Arts (History Degree). *Member:* Barcelona Bar Association. *LANGUAGES:* French.

JAVIER VIDAL-QUADRAS TRIAS DE BES, born Barcelona, Spain, 1961; admitted, 1988, Spain. *Education:* Law School, University of Barcelona. Professor of Commercial Law. *Member:* Barcelona Bar Association. *LANGUAGES:* English and Portuguese.

MARIA EUGENIA CARVAJAL, born Madrid, Spain, 1963; admitted, 1987, Spain. *Education:* University of Madrid; Diploma on Advanced European Studies (College of Europe, Bruges). *Member:* Madrid Bar Association.

MONTSE MURO OLLE, born Barcelona, Spain, 1966; admitted, 1993. *Education:* University of Barcelona. *LANGUAGES:* English, French.

NEW YORK OFFICE
RESIDENT LAWYER

JOSE RAMON F. VILLAR, born Vitoria, Spain, 1961; admitted, 1984, Spain. *Education:* Basque University Law School (J.D., 1984); Basque University (Licentiate in Philosophy, 1986); Santa Clara Law School, California, U.S.A. (Visiting Scholar, 1987); University of Iowa Law School, U.S.A. (LL.M., 1988). Phi Alpha Delta Law Fraternity International. Member, Board of Directors, Spain-USA Chamber of Commerce. *Member:* Basque Country, Madrid, American and International Bar Associations; American Foreign Law Association.

BRUSSELS OFFICE
RESIDENT LAWYERS

STEPHEN PICKARD, born Canberra, Australia, 1954; admitted, 1979, Solicitor England and Wales; 1985, New York (Not admitted in Spain). *Education:* Oxford Polytechnic (B.A., 1976, Law, Politics and Economics); Johns Hopkins University, Bologna (Graduate Diploma, 1980); Columbia University School of Law, New York (LL.M., 1983). *LANGUAGES:* English, Spanish and French.

DIEGO MELLADO PASCUA, born Almeria, Spain, 1967; admitted, 1993, Spain (Not admitted in Belgium). *Education:* University of Granad (Law Degree, 1990); Institut d'études européenes, Brussels, Belgium (Master in European Community Law). *Member:* Madrid Bar Association. *LANGUAGES:* French, English and German.

(This Listing Continued)

MARBELLA OFFICE
RESIDENT LAWYERS

CARLOS BUSTILLO MUÑOZ, born Avila, Spain, 1956; admitted, 1985, Spain. *Education:* University of Madrid. *Member:* Malaga Bar Association.

ISABEL FERRER LOPEZ, born Alicante, Spain, 1962; admitted, 1985, Spain. *Education:* University of Alicante; University of Amsterdam (Diploma on European Integration, 1986). *Member:* Elche and Málaga Bar Association.

DOLORES MOLINA FERNANDEZ, born Priego, Cordoba, Spain, 1967; admitted, 1990, Spain. *Education:* University of I.C.A.D.E. - Comillas - Madrid. *Member:* Malaga Bar Association.

OVIEDO OFFICE
RESIDENT LAWYER

MIGUEL FUERTES SUAREZ, born Oviedo, Spain, 1951; admitted, 1983. *Education:* University of Oviedo; Europa College, Brugge, Belgium; Diplomatic School, Madrid. *Member:* Oviedo Bar Association.

SEVILLA OFFICE
RESIDENT LAWYERS

FERNANDO GONZALEZ DE LA PEÑA YSERN, born Jerez de la Frontera, Spain, 1956; admitted, 1981, Spain. *Education:* University of Sevilla (Licenciatura en Derecho, 1979). *Member:* Sevilla, Huelva, Jerez de la Frontera, Cádiz and Jaen Bar Associations. *LANGUAGES:* English.

ALVARO PEREZ ARBIZU, born Sevilla, Spain, 1968. *Education:* University of Sevilla (Licenciatura de Derecho, 1991); Postgraduate Studies in Financial and Taxation Law. *Member:* Sevilla Bar Association.

AURELIO ORRILLO LARA, born La Linea, Spain, 1967; admitted, 1993, Spain. *Education:* University of Navarra (Law Degree and Master in Business Law). *Member:* Sevilla Bar Association. *LANGUAGES:* English.

REPRESENTATIVE CLIENTS: Avon Products, Inc.; Bank of Tokyo; Beecham Group, Ltd.; The Bendix Corp.; BMW, AG; The Borden Co.; Bristol Myers Co.; Cabot Corp.; Caisse des Depots; The Chase Manhattan Bank; Colgate Palmolive International Inc.; Credit Suisse; E.I. du Pont de Nemours & Co.; The First National Bank of Chicago; Ford Motor Co.; The Goodyear Tire & Rubber Co.; Gillette Co.; Hewlett Packard; Hitachi Data Systems; Honeywell; The Hong Kong & Shanghai Banking Corp.; I.B.M. World Trade Corp.; The Industrial Bank of Japan; International Finance Corp. (World Bank); International General Electric; John Deere Co.; Minnesota Mining and Manufacturing Co.; McDonnell Douglas; Morgan Guaranty Trust Co.; Nissho Iwai Co. Ltd.; Oscar Mayer Co.; Pepsi-Cola Co.; Phillip Morris Inc.; Revlon International Corp.; Rolex Holding; Sea Land Service; Stanley Home Products; Steel Corp.; Sterling Drug Inc.; Toshiba España, S.A.; Westinghouse Electric Corp.; Westinghouse Nuclear Services, S.A.; Ermenegildo Zegna.

REVISERS OF THE SPAIN LAW DIGEST FOR THIS DIRECTORY.

FERNANDO SCORNIK GERSTEIN

Established in 1978

CALLE ALBERTO ALCOCER, NO. 7. 3-IZDA
28036 MADRID, SPAIN
Telephone: (34) 1-3507262
Fax: (34) 1-3507306

Gran Canaria (Canary Islands), Las Palmas Office: Franchy y Roca 5, Planta 4, oficina 10, 035007 Las Palmas. Telephone: (928) 273724, 273728. Fax: (928) 223877.

Gran Canaria (Canary Islands-Maspalomas), Playa del Ingles Office: Edificio Mercurio, Torre II, Planta 4B, 35100 Playa del Ingles. Telephone: (928) 762306; 767867. Fax: (928) 766667.

Lanzarote (Canary Islands), Spain Office: Calle Ginés de Castro 12, 3rd Floor, 35500 Arrecife de Lanzarote. Telephone: (928) 815262; 815258. Fax: (928) 814892.

Tenerife (Canary Islands), Spain Office: Edificio Valdes Center, Torre A., Piso 2, Oficina 1, 38650 Los Cristianos, Arona. Telephone: (922) 794412; 750060. Fax: (922) 794208.

Fuerteventura (Canary Islands), Spain Office: Prof. Juan Tadeo Cabrera 10, Piso 1B, 35600 Puerto del Rosario. Telephone: (928) 532 266. Fax: ((28) 532 241.

London, England Office: 32 St. James's Street, 3rd Floor, SW1A1HD. Telephone: (071) 930-3593; 930-0769. Fax: (071) 930-3385.

Buenos Aires, Argentina Office: Avda Corrientes 330, Piso 4, 1378 Buenos Aires, Argentina. Telephone: (541) 311 1273. Fax: (541) 313 5628.

(This Listing Continued)

FERNANDO SCORNIK GERSTEIN, Madrid—Continued

General Practice, Civil and Commercial, Taxation, Foreign Investments, Banking, Finance, Real Estate, Litigation and Criminal Law, Immigration, Family Law, Probate, Maritime Law and Intellectual Property.

FIRM PROFILE: The firm was founded by Mr. Fernando Scornik Gerstein on the Island of Gran Canaria in 1978. It grew rapidly to become one of the largest law firms in the Canary Islands with offices also in Tenerife, Lanzarote and Fuerteventura. In 1986 a branch was opened in London at 32 St James's Street, where it is still functioning. Many important UK Solicitors and Accountancy firms are their clients.

The firm now has its central offices in Madrid, dealing with its traditional British, German, American, Japanese and South American clients.

The expertise of this firm is mainly in foreign investments, civil, commercial and criminal law, taxation, personal injury, family law and immigration. The firm also has expertise in Argentinean law and working agreements with Chilean and Mexican Law Firms.

SENIOR PARTNER

FERNANDO SCORNIK GERSTEIN, born Buenos Aires, Argentina, March 4, 1937; admitted, 1965, Buenos Aires, Argentina; 1978, Las Palmas and Madrid. *Education:* University of Buenos Aires, Argentina (Graduated, 1962); University of La Laguna, Spain (1977); Seminars and Special Studies: University of Santiago de Chile, Cambridge University; Institute of Development Studies, University of Sussex, England. Author: "France, Agrarian Law," Argentina, 1967; "The Land Tax," Argentina, 1971; "The Policy of the United States towards Latin American Agrarian Sector," Argentina, 1974; "Basis for a Taxation System," Argentina, 1973; "Market Versus Administrative Methods in a Process of Change," presented at IDS, University of Sussex, 1973; "Migration, Immigration and Asylum in Canary Islands, Spain," presented at IBA, Section on General Practice Conference, Madrid, 1985; "Law of Corporations"; "Further Developments towards 1992 in the European Community for Business Migration," The Spanish Case, presented in Committee 14, IBA, 1991. "The True Importance of Local Taxation Reform," London, 1991. Offices held: Director of Practical Studies for Agrarian and Mining Law, University of Buenos Aires; Advisor to the Argentinean Minister of Economy, 1973 and Agriculture, 1974-1975; Legal Advisor to the Argentinean Cooperatives, 1966-1975; Director of the Land Taxation Group, Argentina, 1975. *Member:* International Bar Association (Chairman, Committee 14, Migration and Nationality Law); Union International des Avocats; Spanish-German Chamber of Commerce for Spain; British-Spanish Chamber of Commerce in London; Argentinian Club in Spain (President, 1993-1995); Camara Hispano Argentina de Comercio (Madrid). IAG (International Advisory Group). (Also at London, England, Gran Canaria, Lanzarote and Tenerife, Canary Islands, Spain Offices). *LANGUAGES:* Spanish, English, French and German. *PRACTICE AREAS:* Civil Law; Taxation; Immigration; Company Law.

PARTNERS

EILEEN IZQUIERDO LAWLOR, born Las Palmas, Spain; admitted, 1986, Las Palmas. *Education:* University Autonoma of Madrid, Spain (Graduated, 1985). *Member:* International Bar Association. (Resident, Lanzarote, Canary Islands, Spain Office). *LANGUAGES:* English and Spanish. *PRACTICE AREAS:* Civil Law; Commercial Law; General Practice; Time-Share Regulations.

JORGE DE LA CUEVA TERRER, born Madrid, Spain; admitted, 1987, Las Palmas. *Education:* University Complutense of Madrid, Spain (Graduated, 1986). (Resident, Lanzarote, Canary Islands, Spain Office). *LANGUAGES:* English and Spanish. *PRACTICE AREAS:* Litigation; Personal Injury; Civil Law; Commercial Law.

ISABEL LINDEMANN RUIZ, born Santa Cruz de Tenerife, Spain, May 18, 1962; admitted, 1988. *Education:* University of La Laguna, Tenerife, Spain (Graduated, 1988). *Member:* International Bar Association. (Resident, Tenerife, Canary Islands, Spain Office). *LANGUAGES:* German, English and Spanish. *PRACTICE AREAS:* Litigation; Civil Law; Personal Injury; Torts; Commercial Law; Criminal Law; Company Law; Insurance Law.

SANTIAGO LLEO FERNANDEZ, born Madrid, Spain, 1962; admitted, 1990, Las Palmas. *Education:* Universidad Complutense de Madrid (Degree in Law, 1986); City of London, Polytechnic (Degree in International Law, 1986). Trainee, Legal Services, Commission of the European Communities, Brussels, 1987. (Resident, Lanzarote, Canary Islands, Spain Office). *LANGUAGES:* English, French, Italian and Spanish. *PRACTICE AREAS:* Civil Law; Commercial Law; Company Law; Litigation.

(This Listing Continued)

ISABEL GONZALEZ DAVIDEIT, born Den Haage, Holland, 1962; admitted, 1987, Madrid; 1988, Las Palmas. *Education:* University Autonoma of Madrid (Graduated, 1987). (Resident, Madrid, Director of the Madrid office, Spain). *LANGUAGES:* Spanish, English and German. *PRACTICE AREAS:* Civil Law; Commercial Law; Company Law; Litigation; Intellectual Property.

ALBERTO PEREZ CEDILLO, born Madrid, Spain, 1963; admitted, 1992, Madrid. *Education:* ICADE, Madrid (Graduated, 1987); City of London Polytechnic (Master in Business Law). (Resident, London, England Office, Director, London Office). *LANGUAGES:* Spanish and English. *PRACTICE AREAS:* Civil Law; Commercial Law; Conveyancing; Intellectual Property.

MARIANO EZEQUIEL ZUNINO SIRI, born Buenos Aires, Argentina, 1964; admitted, 1991, Las Palmas. *Education:* University of Buenos Aires, Argentina (Graduated, 1988). (Resident, Tenerife, Canary Islands, Spain Office). *LANGUAGES:* German, English and Spanish. *PRACTICE AREAS:* Currency; Foreign Investment; Litigation; Immigration; Administrative Law; Inheritance Law; Company Law; Insurance Law.

ASSOCIATES

NATALIA RODRIGUEZ JIMENEZ, born Sevilla, Spain, 1965; admitted, 1989, Las Palmas. *Education:* University de Sevilla (Graduated, 1989). (Resident, Fuenteventura, Canary Islands, Spain Office). *LANGUAGES:* Spanish. *PRACTICE AREAS:* Civil and Criminal Law; Personal Injury; Litigation.

OLGA MARIA VILORIA HERNANDO, born Valladolid, Spain, 1964; admitted, 1989, Valladolid. *Education:* University of Valladolid (Graduated, 1988). *Member:* International Bar Association. (Resident, London, England Office). *LANGUAGES:* English and Spanish. *PRACTICE AREAS:* Civil Law; Personal Injury; Commercial Law and Insurance Law.

JAIME VALERA MARTOS, born Geneve, Switzerland, 1971. *Education:* University Complutense of Madrid (Degree, 1993); University Paris XI (Diplome de droit francaise, 1993). (Resident, Madrid Office). *LANGUAGES:* English, Spanish and French. *PRACTICE AREAS:* Civil and Commercial; Intellectual Property.

CINTA LOPEZ GALVEZ, born Las Palmas, 1970; admitted, 1993, Las Palmas. *Education:* University of Las Palmas, Spain (1993). (Resident, Las Palmas, Gran Canaria, Canary Islands). *LANGUAGES:* German, English and Spanish. *PRACTICE AREAS:* Civil Law; Commercial Law; Criminal Law.

IGNACIO CASTELEIRO CULLEN, born Sevilla, Spain, 1964. *Education:* University of Las Palmas (1992). (Resident, Gran Canaria, Canary Island, Spain). *LANGUAGES:* Spanish and English. *PRACTICE AREAS:* Personal Injury; Civil and Commercial Law; Litigation.

MONICA DE BENITO INGLADA, born 1964; admitted, 1993, Tenerife. *Education:* University of Cantabria (1989). (Resident, Tenerife, Canary Islands, Spain Office). *LANGUAGES:* English and Spanish. *PRACTICE AREAS:* Litigation.

CARLOS LOPEZ PEREZ-CEJUELA, born Madrid, 1967; admitted, 1993, Madrid. *Education:* University Complutense of Madrid (Degree, 1993). (Resident, Lanzarote, Office). *LANGUAGES:* English, German and Spanish. *PRACTICE AREAS:* Civil, Commercial and Criminal Law.

CESAR GONZALEZ ZARZA, born Madrid, Spain, 1968; admitted, 1994. *Education:* University of Deusto (Graduated 1991); University of Pau (EC Law). (Resident, Fuerteventura Office). *LANGUAGES:* English, French and Spanish. *PRACTICE AREAS:* Civil and Commercial Law.

MERCEDES ANTON ESCALONA, born Madrid, 1967; admitted, 1994. *Education:* ICADE, Madrid (Graduated 1990; Master in European Community Law, 1991). (Resident, London office, England). *LANGUAGES:* English, French, German and Spanish. *PRACTICE AREAS:* EC Law; Taxation; Civil and Commercial Law.

ANTONIO COLLAR CABRERA, born Las Palmas, Spain, 1967; admitted, 1992. *Education:* Universidad Complutense of Madrid (Graduated 1991); Master in Taxation Law (Madrid 1993). (Resident, Las Palmas Office, Gran Canaria, Canary Islands). *LANGUAGES:* German, English and Spanish. *PRACTICE AREAS:* Taxation and Commercial Law.

FEDERICO TOLEDO GUADALUPE, born Lanzarote, Spain, 1968. *Education:* University Complutense de Madrid (Degree in Law, 1994). (Resident, Lanzarote Office). *LANGUAGES:* English, Spanish. *PRACTICE AREAS:* Labour Law; Litigation; Civil Law; General Practice.

(This Listing Continued)

PEDRO MEDINA JIMENEZ, born Tenerife, Spain, 1968. *Education:* Europe Institute of Law and Economics, Barcelona, INEDE (1992); National University of Distance Education (Law) UNED (1992). Master in Legibus, LL.M legal aspects of Sea Affairs by the University of Cardiff (1994); Institute of Finance and Insurance (average adjuster) INESE 1995. *LANGUAGES:* Spanish, English, German. *PRACTICE AREAS:* Commercial Law; Maritime Law; Insurance Law; Civil Law.

LEGAL SUPPORT PERSONNEL

ESTER BOTZ JETTER, born Argentina, 1961. (Interpreter of German, English and Spanish; Resident, Playa del Ingles, Gran Canaria, Canary Islands, Spain). *LANGUAGES:* English, German and Spanish. *PRACTICE AREAS:* Accounting; Tax Law.

OLGA CENTURION ROBUSTELLI, born Buenos Aires, Argentina, 1939. *Education:* Alliance Francaise. (French Interpreter; Resident, Las Palmas, Gan Canaria, Canary Island). *LANGUAGES:* French and Spanish. *PRACTICE AREAS:* Administration.

BEGONA RUIZ TOBALINA, born Burgos, Spain, 1966. *Education:* University of Valladolid (1990). Economist. (Resident, London, England Office). *LANGUAGES:* Spanish, English. *PRACTICE AREAS:* Accounting; Finance; Administration.

REPRESENTATIVE CLIENTS: Masons-Solicitors; MacFarlanes-Solicitors; Cameron Markby Hewitt-Solicitors; Rakison-Solicitors; Shakespeares-Solicitors; Tokyo Marine Research Institute; Kirin Brewery; Thomson Electronics AG, Nrv-Rechtsschutzversicherung; ARAG-Rechtsschutzversicherung AG; Juan A Calzado-Comisario de Averias-SA; SeaSide Hotels-SA; Allen Edmonds Shoe Corporation; Austin Powder of Chile; INASA-(Industrias Navarras del Aluminio); Grupo General del Cable; Agrippina Rechtsschutzversicherung A; Allianz-Lebensversicherung AG; DAS Defensa Juridica; Bayerische Vereinsbank, Munich; ITM International Transportmittlung GmbH; Lincos Finance, SA; Senatsverwaltungs fuer Justiz, Berlin; Auxiliair, SA; Grupo Barcelo, Elsafe SA; Club La Santa S.A.; Sun Alliance S.A.; H.O.H. Canarias S.A.; Morrocan Consulate in Madrid; Konica Corporation; Kenippi Ox; Rank Xerox Limited; J. Garcia Carrion S.A.

GIDE LOYRETTE NOUEL

ANTONIO MAURA 7, 6°
28014 MADRID, SPAIN
Telephone: (34.1) 531.25.01
Telecopier: (34.1) 531.35.30

Paris, France Office: 26 Cours Albert 1er, 75008. Telephone: (1) 40.75.60.00. Cable Address: "3 Avocagidva Paris 86." Telex: 651261F GILOY. Telecopier: (1) 43.59.37.79.

New York, New York Office: Swiss Bank Tower, 10 East 50th Street, 10022. Telephone: (1-212) 644-1201. Telex: 424353 GIDE. Telecopier: (1-212) 644-1205.

Brussels, Belgium Office: Rue de la Loi 99.101, B-1040. Telephone: (32.2) 231.11.40. Telecopier: (32.2) 231.11.77.

Warsaw, Poland Office: Ul. Kopernika 17, 00-359. Telephone: (48.22) 26.22.21. Telecopier: (48.22) 26.03.02.

Riyadh, Saudi Arabia Office: P.O. Box 4615, 11412. Telephone: (966.1) 476.60.39. Telex: 401677 NASHWA. Telecopier: (966.1) 476.18.96.

Tokyo, Japan Office: Homei Building 3F, 3-19 Akasaka 1-Chome, Minato-Ku, 107. Telephone: (81.3) 55.62.03.01. Telecopier: (81.3) 55.62.03.06.

Beijing, People's Republic of China Office: Suite 3309 A, Jing Guang Centre, Hu Jia Lou, Chaoyang District, 100020. Telephone: (86.1) 501 4511. Telecopier: (86.1) 501 4551.

Prague, Czech Republic Office: 34 Jindrisska, 11207. Telephone: (42.2) 24.21.34.65;24.21.36.50. Telecopier: (42.2) 24.21.09.12;24.22.58.53.

St. Petersburg, Russia Office: 34 Souvorovsky Prospect, App 45, P.O. Box 172, 193015. Telephone by satellite: (7.812) 850.16.85. Telecopier by satellite: (7.812) 850.16.86.

Moscow, Russia Office: 9, Ulitsa Tverskaya - App 66, 103009. Telephone by satellite: (7.501) 940.45.00. Telecopier by satellite: (7.501) 940.45.01.

Budapest VII, Hungary Office: EMKE Building, Rákóczi út 42, BP 409, 1072. Telephone: (36.1) 268.1236; 268.1237; 268.1238. Telecopier: (36.1) 268.1239.

Hanoi, Vietnam Office: Hanoi Business Centre, 51 Ly Thai To. Telephone: (84.42) 66.122.3. Telecopier: (84.42) 66.030.1.

(This Listing Continued)

French and International Law.

RESIDENT ASSOCIATES

Philippe Esposito

(For Biographical Data on Personnel, see Professional Biographies at Paris, France).

GABINETE JURIDICO JULIAN GIL

PLAZA DE LA INDEPENDENCIA 5, 4° IZDA.
28001 MADRID, SPAIN
Telephone: 575 25 03
Fax: 576 48 88

General Practice. Foreign Investments, Civil, Mercantile, International and Fiscal Law.

MEMBERS OF FIRM

JULIAN GIL NAVARRO, born Madrid, Spain, December 29, 1942; admitted, 1969, Spain. *Education:* Colegio del Pilar, Madrid; Colegio La Salle, Valencia; University of Madrid (Licenciate in Law, 1969). Graduate in Business Administration at ICADE, 1964-1969. *Member:* Madrid Bar Association. *LANGUAGES:* Spanish and English. *PRACTICE AREAS:* Foreign Investments Law; Exchange Control Law.

MIGUEL SAGÜÉS NAVARRO, born Madrid, Spain, April 24, 1954; admitted, 1977, Spain. *Education:* Madrid University (Licenciate in Law, 1976). *Member:* Madrid and Barcelona Bar Association. *LANGUAGES:* Spanish and English. *PRACTICE AREAS:* Labor Law; Civil Law; Criminal Litigation.

MIGUEL GARCIA-HERRANZ MARTINEZ, born Madrid, Spain, December 18, 1957; admitted, 1990, Spain. *Education:* Instituto Ramiro de Maeztu; Universidad Complutense de Madrid (1990). *Member:* Madrid Bar Association. *LANGUAGES:* Spanish, English and French. *PRACTICE AREAS:* Mercantile Law; International Law; Fiscal Law.

Languages: Spanish, English and French.

REPRESENTATIVE CLIENTS: Budget Rent a Car International, Inc.; Carrefour; Cuétara, S.A.; Hispano Foxfilm, S.A.E.; Slavenburg's Bank (Holland); 20th Century Fox; Arthur Bell & Sons, Ltd.; Arista Films, Chesterfield Ronson; Computer Machinery Corporation (C.M.C.); Institut Pasteur Production; Sanofi; Laboratorios Labaz, S.A.; Institut Pasteur Foundation; Avalmadrid, S.G.R.

GOMEZ-ACEBO & POMBO

CASTELLANA, 164
28046 MADRID, SPAIN
Telephone: (341) 582 91 00
Fax: (341) 345 36 79 / 582 91 14
Cable: Juristas
Telex: 23429 GAPO E

Barcelona, Spain Office: Diagonal 442, 08037. Telephone: (343) 415 74 00. Fax: (343) 415 84 00.

Bilbao, Spain Office: Gran Vía, 31, 48009. Telephone: (344) 415 62 66/77. Fax: (344) 416 87 49.

Santiago de Compostela, Spain Office: Casas Reales, 4, 15704. Telephone: (348) 157 33 46. Fax: (348) 157 35 46.

Valencia, Spain Office: Gran Vía Marqués del Turia, 49, 46005. Telephone: (346) 351 38 35. Fax: (346) 351 60 74.

Las Palmas, Canarias, Spain Office: Viera y Clavijo, 48, 35002. Telephone: (342) 838 38 36. Fax: (342) 838 38 56.

Sevilla, Spain Office: Av. de la Constitución, 40, 41001. Telephone: (345) 421 66 59/422 18 93. Fax: (345) 421 08 14.

European Law Office: Rue de la Loi, 99/101, 1040 Brussels, Belgium. Telephone: (322) 231 12 20. Fax: (322) 230 80 35.

Banking, Mergers and Acquisitions, Commercial and Corporate, Securities, Insolvency, Foreign Investment, Licensing, Franchising and Computers, Intellectual Property (Contentious and Non-Contentious), Taxation, Real Estate and Development, Mining and Energy, Government Contracts, EC Law, Telecommunications, Entertainment/Media, Administrative, Employment/Labour Law, Maritime, Aircraft, Litigation and Arbitration (Domestic and International), Insurance, Product Liability, Inheritance, Environmental Law.

(This Listing Continued)

GOMEZ-ACEBO & POMBO, Madrid—Continued

SENIOR PARTNERS

IGNACIO GOMEZ-ACEBO, born Madrid, 1932; admitted, 1962, Madrid. *Education:* Universities of Madrid and Salamanca. Chartered Patent Agent and Insurance Agent. Chairman of the Boards: Cofic; Peugeot Leasing; PSA Credit. President of Intermediaciones y Finanzas, S.A. (INFIN). *Member:* New York Stock Exchange for Europe; Axa-Insurance-; Centro de Estudios Universitarios (CEU), Madrid (Trustee); AIPPI; LES. *LANGUAGES:* Spanish, English and French.

FERNANDO POMBO, born Santander, 1943; admitted, 1971, Madrid; 1975, Burgos; 1982, Bilbao; 1983, Valencia; 1986, Seville; 1987, Barcelona. *Education:* Universities of Madrid, Geneva, Munich (LL.D. Studies, Max Planck); Dundee (Oil and Gas Law); Amsterdam (Europa Institut). Author: "Doing Business in Spain," (loose leaf format), Publishers Matthew Bender; Co-Author: Spanish Section of "Merger Control in the EEC," Publishers Kluwer, 1993 and "Environmental Liabilities and Regulation in Europe," International Business Publishing, 1993; Contributor to "Digest of Commercial Laws of the World," Oceana Publications. Correspondent of "International Financial Law Review," and other. Professor of Law, CPE, 1965-1968. Professor of Licensing Law, CEU, Madrid, 1974-1979. Visiting Professor, Institute on International Legal Studies, Salzburg, 1985—. IBA Secretary (SGP). President of LES International, 1984. *Member:* Spanish Arbitration Court; ABA; AIPPI; AEPPC. *LANGUAGES:* Spanish, English, French and German.

PARTNERS

EMILIO SALAS, born Murcia, 1939; admitted, 1976, Madrid. *Education:* Granada University (Diploma on EEC Law). Member, Agricultura, 1968-1973. Lawyer, Instituto Español de Reforma y Desarrollo Agrario (IRYDA), 1973-1975. Contributing author for articles on brand names, patents and technology, 1987—. *Member:* LES. *LANGUAGES:* Spanish and English.

ENRIQUE J. BATALLA, born Málaga, 1944; admitted, 1973, Madrid. *Education:* Granada University; Georgetown University, Washington, D.C.; U.S. Patent Office. International Legal Practice in Washington, 1972. *Member:* LES. *LANGUAGES:* Spanish and English.

GONZALO DE ULLOA, born Madrid, 1952; admitted, 1975, Madrid. *Education:* Universities of Madrid and Strasbourg. President of LES España, 1990. *Member:* LES; AIPPI; LICD. *LANGUAGES:* Spanish, French and English.

JOAQUIN GARCIA-ROMANILLOS, born Granada, 1944; admitted, 1969, Granada; 1973, Madrid. *Education:* Granada University. Professor of Civil Law, Granada University, 1966-1969. Member of Parliament, 1977-1982. Secretary of the Parliamentary Commission on Justice, 1977-1982. Legal Adviser to the Ministry of Justice, 1979-1980. Director General of Justice, 1981-1982. Permanent Member of the General Commission on the Codification of the Law. *LANGUAGES:* Spanish, French and English.

FERNANDO HUIDOBRO, born Madrid, 1947; admitted, 1972, Madrid. *Education:* Universities of Granada (LL.B.), Bologna (LL.D.), Madrid (LL.D.); European Community Law, Europa Institut, University of Amsterdam, 1985-1986. Professor of Civil Procedure, Madrid University, since 1971. Secretary of the Spanish Insurance Arbitration Tribunal, 1979-1985. Summer Associate, Rosenman, Colin, Freund, Lewis & Cohen, New York, N.Y., 1982-1983. *LANGUAGES:* Spanish, Italian, French and English.

FRANCISCO A. PEÑA, born Ribadesella, 1952; admitted, 1982, Madrid; 1984, Oviedo. *Education:* Madrid University (Master in Tax Law, 1975). Foreign Associate with City Law firm, London. Secretary and Legal Counsel to Venture Capital Co. and its industrial group (S.R.P. Principality of Asturias). *LANGUAGES:* Spanish and English.

LUIS BAZAN, born Tetuán, Morocco, 1937; admitted, 1974, Burgos; 1976, Madrid. *Education:* Complutense University of Madrid, Law, 1959; Political Science, 1960. Government Attorney, 1963, assigned to the Ministry of Finance in Gerona, Burgos and Madrid, to the Presidential Offices, Development and Planning Commission and General Directorate of the Litigation Section of the Government. Deputy and Assistant Judge of Monetary Crimes, 1968-1970. Chief Counsel of Legal Services of the Banco de Crédito Industrial, 1971-1978. *LANGUAGES:* Spanish and French.

FERNANDO DE LAS CUEVAS, born Bilbao, 1959; admitted, 1983, Madrid. *Education:* Deusto University, Bilbao (Law and Business Administration, 1981); Instituto de Estudios Europeos, Bilbao, 1981; College of Europe, Bruges, 1982. Official EFTA Research Fellowship, 1982-1983. Foreign Associate with Shearman & Sterling, New York, N.Y., 1985-1986;

(This Listing Continued)

Harvard Law School (P.I.L.), 1990. *Member:* IBA; AIJA. *LANGUAGES:* Spanish, English and French.

VICTORIA LLAVERO, born Madrid, 1955; admitted, 1985, Madrid. *Education:* University of Madrid, 1978; Kings College (University of London) EEC Law, 1982. Commission of the European Communities (external relations and legal service), 1983. Author: Papers of Community Law "Legal Issues of European Integration," (Europa Institut), 1984. *LANGUAGES:* Spanish, English and French.

FERNANDO IGARTUA, born Eibar, 1959; admitted, 1984, Madrid. *Education:* Deusto University, Bilbao (Law and Business Administration, 1981). Professor of Civil Law: University of the Basque Country, 1981-1983 and Madrid University, 1983-1990. Visiting Scholar, University of California, Berkeley, 1987-1988; U.S.A.-Spain, Joint Committee Fellowship, 1987. Foreign Associate, Linklaters & Paines, London, 1991-1992. *LANGUAGES:* Spanish, English and French.

JESUS MUÑOZ-DELGADO, born Madrid, 1959; admitted, 1986, Madrid. *Education:* Complutense Madrid University, 1981; I.E. (Master in Business Law, 1987); Harvard Law School (P.I.L., 1989). *Member:* LICD. *LANGUAGES:* Spanish and English.

ALMUDENA ARPON DE MENDIVIL, born Madrid, 1961; admitted, 1985, Madrid. *Education:* ICADE, 1985; College of Europe, Bruges, 1986-1987 (Scholarship of the Ministry of Foreign Affairs); European Business Law, City of London Polytechnic, 1986; Catholic University of Louvain, 1986; Harvard Law School (P.I.L.), 1990. The Academy of American and International Law, SWLF, Dallas, 1993. *LANGUAGES:* Spanish, English and French.

ASSOCIATES

SALVADOR J. MARISCAL, born Madrid, 1957. *Education:* Madrid University (1978; Real Estate Law Course, 1982; Financing Real-Estate Acquisition, 1985; Zoning and Planning Regulations Law, 1991); Complutense University (Master in Mortgage Law, 1992). Administrative Law Agent, 1981. *LANGUAGES:* Spanish and English.

JOSE MARIA ALVAREZ, born Madrid, 1962; admitted, 1988, Madrid. *Education:* Complutense University of Madrid (1987; Master in Business Law, 1988); Harvard Law School (P.I.L.), 1992. *LANGUAGES:* Spanish and English.

JUAN MANUEL S. PADROS, born Madrid, 1962; admitted, 1988, Madrid. *Education:* Madrid University, 1987; Notarial Law, Madrid, 1984; Inheritance Law in ICAI-ICADE, 1988; Complutense University of Madrid (Master in Mortgage Law, 1992). *LANGUAGES:* Spanish and English.

MANUEL J. MARTIN, born Madrid, 1965; admitted, 1989, Madrid. *Education:* Complutense University of Madrid, 1988; Master in Business Law, Madrid, 1989. *LANGUAGES:* Spanish and English.

FRANCISCO ALDAVERO, born Moral de Calatrava, 1964; admitted, 1987, Madrid. *Education:* Autonomous University of Madrid, 1987; Master in Business Law, Madrid, 1989. *LANGUAGES:* Spanish and English.

SILVIA DE LA FUENTE, born Orense, 1964; admitted, 1989, Madrid. *Education:* Complutense University of Madrid, 1988. *LANGUAGES:* Spanish and English.

MARIA ARPON DE MENDIVIL, born Madrid, 1966; admitted, 1992, Madrid. *Education:* Complutense University of Madrid, 1989; London School of E & P Sciences (LL.M., 1991). *LANGUAGES:* Spanish, English and French.

JOSE Mª BENEYTO, born Valencia, 1956; admitted, 1980, Pamplona; 1991, Madrid, New York and Berlin. *Education:* University of Navarra (J.D., 1979); Harvard University (LL.M.); University of Münster, Germany (Ph.D. in law, 1982; Ph.D. in History, 1986). EEC officer at the European Parliament, 1986-1989. Visiting Professor: Harvard University, 1989-1991; Universities of Bonn, Trier and Maryland. Professor, International Business Law, Instituto de Empresa, Madrid and University of Miami, Florida. Author: "The World's Largest Market, A Business Guide to Europe 1991," Amacom, New York, 1990; "Europe 1992, Internal Market and European Political Cooperation," Civitas, Madrid, 1989. *LANGUAGES:* Spanish, German, English, French and Russian.

MIGUEL BERMUDEZ DE CASTRO, born Salamanca, 1965; admitted, 1992, Madrid. *Education:* Salamanca University, 1988; I.E. (Master in Business Law, 1990). Legal Adviser, Banco del Comercio, S.A., Madrid, 1991. *LANGUAGES:* Spanish and English.

(This Listing Continued)

VICTOR CASARRUBIOS, born Madrid, 1967; admitted, 1992, Madrid. *Education:* ICADE (Law and Business Administration, 1991). Author: "Company Mergers and Splits, Taxation," ICADE, 1990. The Academy of International Law, SWLF, Dallas, 1994. *LANGUAGES:* English and Spanish.

INES FONTES, born Madrid, 1967; admitted, 1992, Madrid. *Education:* University of Madrid, 1991; Master in Business Law, 1992. *LANGUAGES:* Spanish and English.

CARLOS RUEDA, born Madrid, 1965; admitted, 1992, Madrid. *Education:* ICADE, 1988. *LANGUAGES:* Spanish and English.

JULIA TELLEZ, born Madrid, 1969; admitted, 1993, Madrid. *Education:* Club Europeo (Business Management Course, 1990); ICADE (International Tax Course, 1991). Legal Adviser of Companies, ICADE, 1992. Collaborator of Administrative Law and Political Economics, ICADE. Titleholder of Insurance Agent Broker, 1992. *LANGUAGES:* Spanish and English.

IGNACIO GABILONDO, born San Sebastian, 1968; admitted, 1993, Madrid. *Education:* Autonomous University of Madrid, 1991; I.E. (Master in Business Law, 1993). *LANGUAGES:* Spanish, English and French.

PABLO DIAZ DE RABAGO, born Madrid, 1965. *Education:* ICADE (1988; B.A. in Economics, 1989); Harvard Law School (LL.M.; Ph.D. in Financial Regulation, 1994). *LANGUAGES:* Spanish, English, German and French.

ANGEL VARELA, born Avila, 1962; admitted, 1993, Madrid. *Education:* University of Salamanca (1985; School of Legal Practice, 1986); Institute of Stock Market Studies, Madrid (Masters in Stock Market and Securities, 1989). Lecturer of Financial Statements Analysis in the Complutense University of Madrid. Author of articles regarding the Stock Market, 1989-1993. *LANGUAGES:* Spanish and English.

RAMON NOVO, born Jerez de la Frontera, 1963; admitted, 1994, Madrid. *Education:* University of Madrid (CEU), 1986; Harvard Business School (M.B.A., 1992-1994). Government Attorney, Department of Justice, 1989. Law Clerk to the Spanish Judge at the European Court of First Instance, Luxembourg, 1991. Legal Advisor to the Madrid Tax Court, Department of Finance, 1991-1992. *LANGUAGES:* Spanish, English and French.

LUIS FERNANDEZ NOVOA, born La Estrada, December 2, 1963; admitted, 1993, Madrid. *Education:* University of Santiago de Compostela, 1989; Antitrust Law and Intellectual Property Law, University of Pennsylvania, 1990-1991. *LANGUAGES:* Spanish and English.

EMILIANO GARAYAR, born Torrelavega, 1966; admitted, 1991, Madrid. *Education:* University of Deusto, 1989; University of La Sorbonne, Paris (Language and French Civilization, 1990); College of Europe, Bruges (High European Legal Studies, 1991). Scholarship, Spanish Ministry of Foreign Affairs, 1990-1991. Visiting Professor, Institute of European Studies, University of Deusto; Laureate of EC legal concourse COM/A/715, 1991. *LANGUAGES:* Spanish, French and English.

ANTONIO CAMUÑAS, born Madrid, 1959; admitted, 1988, Madrid. *Education:* University of Madrid and Granada, 1983; New York University, 1985; Harvard University, 1989. Deputy Executive Director, Spain-USA Chamber of Commerce, 1985-1988. Member, International Committee and Representative in Spain, Global Economic Action Institute. Fellow of the Carnegie Council for Ethics and International Relations. *LANGUAGES:* Spanish and English.

LABOUR DEPARTMENT

ENRIQUE RAYON, born Oviedo, 1944; admitted, 1980, Madrid. *Education:* Legal Spanish Institute of Rome (scholarship, 1968); University of Oviedo (with high honors, 1972). Associate Professor of Labor Law of the University of Oviedo, Spain, 1967. Current Professor of Labour Law at the University of Madrid since 1975. Author: Studies on Law Labour, Trade Uniones and National Health Issues. Contributor to scientific magazines. *LANGUAGES:* Spanish, Italian and French.

JOSE RAMON GARCIA, born Mexico, D.F., 1960; admitted, 1989, Madrid. *Education:* Complutense University of Madrid, 1986; I.E. (Master in Business Law, 1988). Foreign Associate, Norton Rose M5 Group, London. *LANGUAGES:* Spanish and English.

TAX DEPARTMENT

CARLOS BENITEZ, born Madrid, 1942; admitted, 1967, Madrid. *Education:* University of Madrid, 1965; School of Commerce, Madrid (Master in Business Law, 1970). *LANGUAGES:* Spanish, English and French.

(This Listing Continued)

LUIS RICO, born Aspe, 1927; admitted, 1978, Madrid. *Education:* University of Barcelona. Professor of Economics. Tax Inspector for the Ministry of Finance, 1958-1992. *LANGUAGES:* Spanish and English.

OF COUNSEL

ROBIN M. SMEATON, born Surrey, England, 1930; admitted as Solicitor of the Supreme Court of England and Wales, 1954; (Not admitted in Spain). *Education:* St. John's School, Leatherhead and London University. Practiced with Herbert Smith & Co., London, 1964-1985 (Associate Partner, 1965-1968; Partner, 1968-1985). *Member:* Law Society; Chartered Institute of Arbitrators. *LANGUAGES:* English, Spanish and French.

ROGER A. LANDHOLM, born St. Paul, U.S.A., 1948; admitted, 1973, Colorado; 1982, California (Not admitted in Spain). *Education:* Dartmouth College; Tulane University School of Law, with honors. Member, Tulane Law Review, 1971-1973. Law Clerk to Hon. James K. Groves, Associate Justice of the Colorado Supreme Court, 1973-1974. Associate with: Calkins, Kramer, Grimshaw and Harring, Denver, Colorado, 1975-1981; Hill, Gould, Pearson and Mendelson, Los Angeles, California, 1982-1983; Kim and Chang, Seoul, Korea, 1983-1985. *Member:* IBA; ABA. *LANGUAGES:* English and Spanish.

BARCELONA

MANUEL MARTIN, born Madrid, 1958; admitted, 1984, Madrid; 1987, Las Palmas; 1990, Barcelona. *Education:* Madrid University, 1981; LSE University of London (1982-1984); Harvard Law School (P.I.L., 1990). Administrative Law under fellowship of Spanish Government. Assistant to Professor of Administrative Law, Complutense University, 1981-1985. Member of the Governing Council of the British Chamber of Commerce in Spain, 1985-1990. *LANGUAGES:* Spanish and English.

SANTIAGO DE NADAL, born Barcelona, 1955; admitted, 1986, Barcelona. *Education:* Universities of Barcelona, Louvain, Amsterdam and Dundee; University of Strasbourg (Comparative Law); Barcelona Law Society (Master in EEC Law). *LANGUAGES:* Spanish, Catalan, English and French.

EDUARDO VILA, born Vic, 1966; admitted, 1991, Barcelona. *Education:* University of Barcelona; University Trías de Bes (Course on private International Law, 1987); Notarial and Registry Law (1988); Master in Urban Law (Fundacion San Pablo, Barcelona), 1990; Queen Mary & Westfield College (University of London) LL.M., 1991; Harvard Law School (P.I.L.), 1992. Foreign Associate with Nagashima and Ohno, Tokyo, Japan, 1994. *LANGUAGES:* Spanish, Catalan, English and Japanese.

IÑIGO IGARTUA, born Oñate, 1965; admitted, 1990, Madrid; 1992, Barcelona. *Education:* University of the Basque Country, 1988; Institut d'Etudes Européennes (Free University of Brussels), 1990 (Master in European Law); Scholarship Basque Government, 1990. *LANGUAGES:* Spanish, French and English.

AITANA MENDEZ VILAPLANA, born Barcelona, 1966; admitted, 1991, Barcelona. *Education:* Fundación Universitaria San Pablo, 1987; Barcelona University, 1989; University of Toronto, School of Continuing Studies, 1990. Fellowship: Instituto Italiano di Cultura for the Faculta di Lingue Straniere dell Universita di Perugia, 1991. Master in Business Law, Barcelona. *LANGUAGES:* Spanish, Italian, English and Catalan.

JOSE ANGEL CANO, born Barcelona, 1964; admitted, 1991, Barcelona. *Education:* Barcelona University, 1987; Postgraduate in Tax and Finance Law, 1991; Scholarship from the Fundación Bosch i Gimpera. *LANGUAGES:* Spanish, French, Catalan and English.

ANTONIO JÓDAR, born Manresa, 1964; admitted, 1991, Barcelona; 1993, Tarrasa. *Education:* University of Barcelona, 1988; Abad Oliba University (Master in Corporate Law), 1990; University of Edinburgh (Summer Programs, 1992); Columbia University, New York, 1993-1994. *LANGUAGES:* Spanish, Catalan, English and French.

IGNASI GUARDANS, born Barcelona, 1964; admitted, 1993, Barcelona. *Education:* University of Navarra, 1987; Ph.D., 1992. Scholarships from Ministry of Education, 1991, German DAAD, 1991. Lecturer of Private International Law, University of Navarra, 1987-1992. Professor, University of Barcelona, 1992 and Colegio Universitario "Abad Oliba," 1993. *LANGUAGES:* Spanish, Catalan, English, French, German and Italian.

CLARA POMBO, born Geneva, Switzerland, 1970; admitted, 1993, Madrid and Barcelona. *Education:* Complutense University of Madrid, 1992; Harvard Law School (P.I.L.), 1992; Göttingen University, Germany, 1993. *LANGUAGES:* Spanish, English, German and French.

(This Listing Continued)

GOMEZ-ACEBO & POMBO, Madrid—Continued

OF COUNSEL

RICHARD A. SILBERSTEIN, born St. Louis, U.S.A., December 18, 1958; admitted, 1986, California (Not admitted in Spain). *Education:* Bates College; University of Maryland; McGeorge School of Law, Sacramento and Salzburg (Post Graduate Studies), 1986. *Member:* ABA. *LANGUAGES:* English, Spanish and French.

BILBAO

JOAQUIN LOPEZ ANTE, born Bayona, 1946; admitted, 1974, Bilbao. *Education:* ICADE (Law and Business Administration). Professor of Civil Law, Bilbao University, 1974-1977. Legal Counsel, Firestone Hispania, S.A., 1973-1982. President of the British Chamber of Commerce in Bilbao, 1986. *LANGUAGES:* Spanish, English and French.

JOSU LARRAURI, born Mungia, 1958; admitted, 1982, Bilbao. *Education:* Deusto University, Bilbao (Law and Business Administration), 1980. *LANGUAGES:* Spanish, Basque and French.

MIREN ARBULU, born Bilbao, 1962. *Education:* University of Deusto. Professor, Labor Law at the University of Deusto and School of Commerce. Deputy Director, School of Commerce, Bilbao. *LANGUAGES:* Spanish and French.

JESUS GONZALEZ, born Barakaldo, May 4, 1962; admitted, 1992, Bilbao. *Education:* University of Deusto, Bilbao, 1990; Master in Business Law, 1991. *LANGUAGES:* Spanish and French.

LAS PALMAS (CANARY ISLANDS)

JOSÉ MIGUEL BRAVO DE LAGUNA, born Las Palmas, 1944; admitted, 1974, Las Palmas. *Education:* Complutense University, Madrid, 1967. Government Attorney, 1973; Member, Parliament, 1977-1989; Director General of Parliamentary Relations, 1977-1981; Deputy Minister of State of the National Budget and Public Expenditure, 1981-1982; Vice-President of House of Parliament, 1982-1986; Councillor, Cabildo Insular of Gran Canaria, 1987-1991. *Member:* Academy of Legislation and Jurisprudence. *LANGUAGES:* Spanish and English.

JOSE MANUEL MELIAN, born Las Palmas, 1967; admitted, 1992, Las Palmas. *Education:* Deusto University, Bilbao (Law and Business Administration), 1990; Master in Business Law (IE), Madrid, 1991. *LANGUAGES:* Spanish, English and German.

SANTIAGO DE COMPOSTELA

CARLOS FERNANDEZ NOVOA, born La Estrada, 1933; admitted, 1987, La Corvña; 1989, Madrid. *Education:* Universities of Santiago de Compostela, Madrid and Munich (LL.D., Max Planck). Professor of Commercial Law, Santiago de Compostela University, 1964—. Director of the periodical, "Actas de Derecho Industrial." Author of works on commercial and industrial property and other contributions published in Spanish, English and German. Author: "The International Protection of Geographic Names of Products;" "Fundamentals of Trademark Law;" "Studies in Advertising Law;" "Trademark Law." Co-Author: "Towards a New Patent System;" The Modernization of Spanish Patent Law.". *LANGUAGES:* Spanish, English and French.

SEVILLA

LUIS JAVIER FERNANDEZ-PALACIOS, born Sevilla, 1947; admitted, 1973, Seville; 1989, Malaga and Granada; 1994, Cadiz. *Education:* Seville University, 1972. Professor of Legal Rules of Marketing, Business Administration School, Seville University, 1978-1980. *Member:* LES; AIPPI. *LANGUAGES:* Spanish, Italian and English.

MANUEL BELLIDO, born Melilla, 1961; admitted, 1987, Seville; 1994, Jérez de la Frontera. *Education:* Seville University and ICADE (Master in European Communities), 1990; Special Courses EEC Law, EEC Economy and Competition Law, 1988; The Reform of Spanish Company Law, 1989; The New Income Tax Law, 1990. *LANGUAGES:* Spanish, English and French.

ISABEL CARMONA, born Cordoba, 1966; admitted, 1992, Madrid. *Education:* University of Granada, 1989; Special Course in Foreign Trade; Master in European Community Law, 1991 (ICADE, Madrid). *LANGUAGES:* Spanish, English and French.

JOSE JOAQUIN SILVA, born Sevilla, 1961; admitted, 1993, Madrid. *Education:* University of Seville, Private Law, 1984. Current Assistant Professor, Financial Department, Seville University of Law. *LANGUAGES:* Spanish and English.

(This Listing Continued)

MANUEL DORADO, born Paris, France, 1965; admitted, 1995, Sevilla. *Education:* University of Alcaláde Henares, 1991; Foreign Trade, Chamber of Commerceand Shipping, Sevilla, 1990;Legal Advice for Business (LL.M.), Institute of L egal and Business, Sevilla, 1992; Mercantile Law (Ph.D.), Sevilla, 1994; Associate Professor of Mercantile Law, University of Sevilla, Since 1994. *LANGUAGES:* Spanish, English, French and Italian.

MACARENA CALVILLO, born Sevilla, 1967; admitted, 1995, Sevilla. *Education:* University of Sevilla, 1990; Legal Practice Course. *Member:* Bar Association of Sevilla. *LANGUAGES:* Spanish and English.

VALENCIA

IGNACIO ALAMAR, born Valencia, 1956; admitted, 1984, Valencia. *Education:* Valencia University (Specializing in Private Law), 1979; Course on Economics, International Menéndez Pelayo University, Santander, 1984; Courses on Community Law, Valencia, 1984-1986. Real Estate Property Agent, 1982. *Member:* Assembly of the Court of Arbitration of Valencia, 1989-1990; IBA; Chairman of the British Chamber of Commerce in Levante, 1989-1991. Professor of Foreign Investments of the Chamber of Commerce of Valencia and Castellón, 1990. *LANGUAGES:* Spanish, English and Italian.

FRANCISCO FITA, born Valencia, 1962; admitted, 1992, Valencia. *Education:* University of Valencia (1985); CEU (Master in Business Law, 1986). *LANGUAGES:* Spanish and English.

JUANA MARIA FORES, born Valencia, May 21, 1962; admitted, 1992, Valencia. *Education:* University of Valencia, 1986;. District Attorney Substitute of the Superior Court of the Valencian Community, 1989-1991. Professor, of Administrative Law, 1991. *LANGUAGES:* Spanish, English and French.

ANA FITA, born Valencia, 1959; admitted, 1985, Valencia. *Education:* University of Valencia (1982). *LANGUAGES:* Spanish and English.

EUROPEAN LAW OFFICE

RICARDO GARCIA VICENTE, born Zaragoza, 1957; admitted, 1985, Madrid. *Education:* University of Zaragoza (with honours); Centre Européen University of Nancy. Director of Department of EEC Law of University of Deusto (Bilbao), 1982-1985. Professor of the Centre of Technical/-Business Studies of Santander, 1983-1985. *LANGUAGES:* Spanish, French and English.

MARIA LUISA TIERNO, born Madrid, June 21, 1968; admitted, 1992, Madrid. *Education:* Complutense University of Madrid, 1991; Licence Spéciale en Droit Européen, University Libre of Brussels, 1992. *LANGUAGES:* Spanish, French and English.

ROSA CHOVER, born Valencia, May 26, 1969; admitted, 1994, Valencia. *Education:* University of Valencia, 1992; Droit Euroéen des Affaires, University RenéDescartes, Paris V, 1993. *LANGUAGES:* Spanish, French and English.

GOÑI & CO.

ABOGADOS

Established in 1964

SERRANO, 91 - 4°

28006 MADRID, SPAIN
Telephone: (34+1) 563.47.40
Fax: (34+1) 563.11.43
Telex: 42344 MARL E

Shipping and Admiralty, Aviation and Aerospace, Insurance, Civil and Commercial Law, Corporate Law, International Law, Foreign Investments and Financing, Products Liability, Environmental Law, EEC and Competition Law. Licensed to act both in Litigation and Arbitration all over Spain.

PARTNERS

JOSÉ LUIS GOÑI, born Vitoria, Spain, July 19, 1935. *Education:* Santiago University School of Law, Complutense University of Madrid School of Law (LL.B., 1957). Past President, Spanish Maritime Law Association. Former Professor of Maritime Law, Universidad Autónoma de Madrid. Arbitrator. *Member:* Titular Member of the Comité Maritime International; Spanish Maritime Law Association; Spanish Court of Arbitration; Counsel of Spanish Chambers of Commerce and Navigation; International Bar Association; Association Internationale des Despacheurs Européens; Spanish Association of Average Adjusters; Iberoamerican Institute of Maritime Law. *LANGUAGES:* Spanish, English, French, Italian and Portu-

(This Listing Continued)

guese. *PRACTICE AREAS:* Shipping and Admiralty; Transportation Law; Civil Law; Marine Insurance; Arbitration.

RODOLFO A. GONZALEZ-LEBRERO, born Buenos Aires, Argentina, October 18, 1929. *Education:* University of Buenos Aires School of Law (LL.B., 1948; S.J.D., 1952). *Member:* Titular Member of the Comité Maritime International; Argentine, French and Spanish Maritime Law Associations; Spanish Association of Maritime Arbitrators; Iberoamerican Institute of Air and Space Law; ICC's Committee for Air Transport; Iberoamerican Institute of Maritime Law; International Bar Association; Spanish Association of Average Adjusters; Interamerican Committee of Legal Experts on Air and Space Law; International Court of Aviation and Space Arbitration; Mediterranean Maritime Arbitration Association. *LANGUAGES:* Spanish, English, French and Italian. *PRACTICE AREAS:* Shipping and Admiralty; Transportation Law; Civil Law; Marine Insurance; Arbitration.

FRANCISCO GOÑI, born Madrid, Spain, February 14, 1962. *Education:* Autonomous University of Madrid School of Law (LL.B., 1985); Institute of Science and Technology (UWIST), Cardiff, UK (LL.M., 1986). Trainee with Phelps, Dunbar, Marks, Cleverie & Sims, New Orleans, 1986 and with Haight, Gardner, Poor & Havens, New York, 1987. *Member:* Titular Member of the Comité Maritime International; Spanish Maritime Law Association. *LANGUAGES:* Spanish and English. *PRACTICE AREAS:* Shipping and Admiralty; Insurance; International Trade; Transportation Law; Commercial Law; Arbitration.

MANUEL GOMEZ-ACEBO, born Malaga, Spain, April 5, 1956. On leave. Currently a member of the Spanish Diplomatic Corps.

OF COUNSEL

VICENTE SERRA Y PONCE DE LEON, born Vigo, Spain, September 18, 1927. *Education:* Santiago University School of Law (LL.B., 1951). *Member:* International Association of Financial Law; Government Attorney (Rtd.); Former Head of the Cabinet of the Minister of Finance; Former Secretary to the Board of Directors and Head of the Legal Department of the Banco de Crédito Agrícola; Former Member of the Central Economic Administrative Court. *LANGUAGES:* Spanish, French and English. *PRACTICE AREAS:* Corporate; Commercial and Finance Law.

ASSOCIATES

BORJA CAMILLERI, born Madrid, Spain, October 11, 1968. *Education:* Complutense University of Madrid School of Law (LL.B., 1992); Instituto de Empresa, Madrid (Master on Corporate Law, LL.M., 1993). *LANGUAGES:* Spanish and English. *PRACTICE AREAS:* Corporate and Commercial Law.

MARIA DEL AMOR DE MIRANDA, born San Sebastián, Spain, March 26, 1968. *Education:* Alcalá de Henares University School of Law, Luis Vives Institute (LL.B., 1993); Alcalá se Henares University (Master on EEC Law (LL.M., 1993). *LANGUAGES:* Spanish, French and English. *PRACTICE AREAS:* EEC and Competition Law; Products Liability; Transportation Law; Environmental Law.

CARMEN CODES, born Jaén, Spain, November 23, 1970. *Education:* Complutense University of Madrid School of Law (LL.B., 1994); IMEFE, Madrid (Master on International Trade, LL.M., 1994). *LANGUAGES:* Spanish and English. *PRACTICE AREAS:* Commercial and Corporate Law; Mergers and Acquisitions; International Contracts.

MARIA DEL PILAR BLANCO, born St. Andrews, Scotland, U.K., November 15, 1967. *Education:* University of Granada School of Law (LL.B., 1992); IME-ICADE (Master on Maritime Law and Shipping Business, LL.M., 1993). Trainee with Richards Butler, London, U.K. *LANGUAGES:* Spanish and English. *PRACTICE AREAS:* Shipping and Aviation; Corporate Law; Finance Law.

GERMAN MILLAN, born Barcelona. Spain, July 1, 1965. *Education:* University of Barcelona School of Law (LL.B., 1988); San Francisco State University, San Francisco, U.S.A. (Master on Business Administration, M.B.A., 1991); Barcelona Chamber of Commerce, Industry and Navigation, Barcelona (Diploma on International Trade, 1987). *LANGUAGES:* Spanish, English and French. *PRACTICE AREAS:* Commercial and Corporate Law; Shipping; International Trade.

LAURA ESTEBAN, born Madrid, Spain, January 31, 1969. *Education:* University College San Pablo, C.E.U. School of Law (LL.B., 1992); University Lille II, Lille, France (DESS on the Law of the Seas and of Shipping

(This Listing Continued)

Activities, 1993). *LANGUAGES:* Spanish, French and English. *PRACTICE AREAS:* Shipping Law; EU and Administrative Law; Deep Sea Fishing.

BUFETE J.Y. HERNANDEZ-CANUT

PASEO DE LA CASTELLANA 144-7°E
28046 MADRID, SPAIN
Telephone: 457 60 00
Telefax: 344 03 27

General Practice, Commercial and Corporate Law, Securities and Banking Law; International Transactions including Foreign Investments in Spain and Spanish Investments Abroad; Litigation; Administrative Law; Labor Law; Real Estate Law; Civil Law; Immigration and Naturalization.

LAWYERS

JUAN-YAGO HERNANDEZ-CANUT, born Madrid, 1954; admitted, 1977. *Education:* Universidad de Deusto-ICADE, Madrid (Law Degree, (1976); Business Administration Degree (1977). *Member:* Madrid Bar Association. *LANGUAGES:* Spanish, English and French. *PRACTICE AREAS:* Commercial Law; Corporate Law; Securities; Litigation.

FELIX PARADELA, born Madrid, 1936; admitted, 1964. *Education:* Universidad Complutense de Madrid (Law Degree, 1963). *Member:* Madrid and Alcala de Henares Bar Associations. *PRACTICE AREAS:* Litigation.

JAVIER MALDONADO, born Madrid, 1962; admitted, 1985, Madrid, Spain; 1988, Illinois. *Education:* Northwestern University School of Law, Chicago, Il. (Juris Doctor Degree, 1988); U.N.E.D., Spain (Law Degree, 1984). *Member:* American, Illinois, Chicago and Madrid Bar Associations. *LANGUAGES:* Spanish and English. *PRACTICE AREAS:* Corporate Law; International Business Law; Taxation Law.

MARIA A. CENTENERA, born Madrid, 1961; admitted, 1985, Madrid. *Education:* Universidad Complutense Madrid (Law Degree, 1984). *Member:* Madrid Bar Association. *LANGUAGES:* Spanish and English. *PRACTICE AREAS:* Litigation; Immigration Law.

LUIS FELIPE UTRERA, born Sevilla, 1968; admitted, 1992. *Education:* Universidad Pontificia de Comillas-ICADE, Madrid (Law Degree, 1991). Corporate Legal Advisor, ICADE, Madrid, 1991. *Member:* Madrid Bar Association. *LANGUAGES:* Spanish and English. *PRACTICE AREAS:* Labor Law; Administrative Law; Real Estate Law.

MIGUEL TOLEDANO, born Toledo, 1969; admitted, 1993, Spain. *Education:* Universidad de Comillas-ICADE, Madrid (Law Degree, 1992); ICADE, Madrid (Business Administration Degree). *Member:* Madrid Bar Association. *LANGUAGES:* Spanish, English, French and German. *PRACTICE AREAS:* Commercial Law.

Languages: Spanish, English, French and German

REPRESENTATIVE CLIENTS: AB VOLVO (Sweden); MO och Domsjö, AB MoDo (Sweden); Holmens Bruk AB (Sweden); Borregaard Industries Ltd. (Norway); Pfisterer GMBH (Germany); SocietéGenerale de Surveillance (SGS) S.A. (Switzerland); Arthur Flury AG (Switzerland); Redland Plc. (United Kingdom); FMC Corporation Europe (Belgium); ABN-AMRO Bank (Holland), and Spain: Uralita S.A.; SGS Española de Control S.A.; CM Capital Markets Holding S.A.; CM Capital Markets Brokerage Agencia de Valores S.A.; ABN-AMRO Sociedad de Valores y Bolsa S.A.; MoDo Iberia S.A.; VOLVO PENTA España S.A.; VOLVO Truck España S.A.; ITAL Rent a Car SL.; Redland Ibérica S.A.; Fibrotubo-Bonna S.A.

HERRERO & ASOCIADOS

Established in 1982
C/ALCALÁ, 21
28014 MADRID, SPAIN
Telephone: (1)-522-74-20
Telefax: (1)-522-62-49
Telex: 47014 Hyal e

Patent & Trademark Law, Copyright, Advertising and Unfair Competition.

MEMBERS OF FIRM

JOSÉ ANTONIO HERNÁNDEZ RODRIQUEZ, born Segovia, Spain, 1942,; admitted, 1972. *Education:* University Complutense of Madrid (Licenciate in law, 1971). *Member:* Colegio de Abogados de Madrid and Barcelona.

FRANCISCO CARPINTERO LÓPEZ, born Guadalajara, Spain, 1948; admitted, 1977, Spain. *Education:* University Complutense of Madrid (Licenciate in Law, 1971). *Member:* Colegio de Abogados de Madrid.

(This Listing Continued)

HERRERO & ASOCIADOS, Madrid—Continued

COUNSEL

JOSÉ MARIA CASTELLÓ COLCHERO, born Madrid, Spain, 1922; admitted, 1946, Spain. *Education:* University Complutense of Madrid (Licenciate in Law, 1945). *Member:* Colegio de Abogados de Madrid.

ASSOCIATES

JUAN CASULÁ OLIVER, born Barcelona, Spain, 1964; admitted, 1987. *Education:* Autonoma University of Madrid (Licenciate in Law, 1987). *Member:* Colegio de Abogados de Madrid, Barcelona, Bilbao, Seville and Valencia.

MIGUEL AZNAR ALONSO, born Segovia, Spain, 1961; admitted, 1992. *Education:* University of Complutense of Madrid (Licenciate in Law, 1984). *Member:* Colegio de Abogados de Madrid.

PATRICIA KOCH MORENO, born Madrid, Spain, 1967; admitted, 1993. *Education:* Icade University of Madrid (Licenciate in Law, 1990; Business Degree, 1991; Patent Attorney, 1991). *Member:* Colegio de Abogados de Madrid, Barcelona and Valencia.

Languages: Spanish, English, French and German.

REPRESENTATIVE CLIENTS: Unilever; Merck & Co., Inc.; Bayer AG; Beecham Group; Grupo Z; Fagor; Hasbro; Samsonite.

HUANG & ASSOCIATES

P° DE SAN FRANCISCO DE SALES, 4
28003 MADRID, SPAIN
Telephone: 34-1-544 52 03/04
Fax: 34-1-544 52 02

General Practice, International Commercial and Corporate Law, Trade and Joint Ventures, Mergers and Acquisitions, Security and Banking Law, International Transactions and Contracts, Foreign Investments in Spain and Spanish Investment Abroad, Administrative Law, Labor Law, Real Estate Law, Immigration and Naturalization, International Tax Counselling, EEC Legal and Business Consultancy, Advertising Law, Intellectual Property, Copyright, Trademarks, Patents, Licensing Agreements, Transfer of Technology, Opening of New Branches and Subsidiaries, Inheritance, Legal Separation and Divorce, Residence and Work Permits in Spain, Automobile Accidents and Injuries, Bankruptcy, and Counsel for International Affairs.

FIRM PROFILE: The firm was established in 1980 at Madrid and offers a full range of business legal services on both a national and international basis. It is a multidisciplinary law office with international projections, devoted to, as its fundamental mission, besides the legal consultancy in general, litigation of all kinds of cases before Spanish courts. It is particularly active in the international tax and commercial areas.

Correspondent & Associated Lawyers throughout Spain and in major countries: The United States, Japan, Taiwan, Hong-Kong, People's Republic of China, Great Britain, France, Germany, Belgium, Portugal, Italy, Russia and Sweden.

GEORGE M.C. HUANG, born Taiwan, Republic of China, May 28, 1933 (Spanish National and Chinese National). *Education:* Taiwan Normal University (B.A., Liberal Arts); Madrid University (M.A., Political Science and Economics; Doctorate, Political Science); Madrid University Law School (LL.M.); Madrid School of Business Administration of the Spanish Association of Arbitration (Diplomas of Business Administration); Madrid School of Legal Practice, University of Madrid (Corporate Legal Consulting); Faculty of Philosophy and Letters University of Madrid (Hispanic Studies). EEC Law, Association for the European Integration, and Madrid Bar Association. Attorney-at-Law; Political Scientist; Certified sworn Interpreter and Official Translator of Chinese and Japanese Languages; Spanish Ministry of Foreign Affairs, Professional Corporate Manager. Appointed by the Spanish Ministry of Foreign Affairs, official interpreter of Chinese language to: His Majesty the King of Spain; Prime Minister; Minister of Foreign Affaires; the Secretary of State for Foreign Affairs; the Minister of Culture; the Minister of Labor; the Minister of Industry and Energy; the Minister of Public Administrations and the Mayor of Madrid. Appointed, by the Ministry of Education and Science. Member, Examination Committee for the State Examination of Professor of the Chinese and Japanese languages of the Official School of Languages of Madrid. Appointed by the Ministry of Culture, the Adviser of the Chinese and Japanese language to the Committee for the International Award of "Promotion to the

(This Listing Continued)

Translation of Spanish Authors to other Languages." Legal interpreter of Spanish courts in Chinese and Japanese languages. Legal advisor to the Delegation Office in Spain, Ministry of Foreign Affairs, Republic of China. Foreign Trade and International Investment Consultant. Legal and Technical Translator. Professional Corporate Manager. *Member:* Madrid Bar Association; Inter-American Bar Association (Washington, D.C.); Valladolid Bar Association; American Society of International Law (Washington, D.C.); World Association of Lawyers (Washington, D.C.); International Law Association (London); Spanish Society of Constitutional Law; Royal Academy of Jurisprudence and Legislation; Iberoamerican Aviation Law; Association of the Spanish Environmental Law; Latino American Association of Air and Space Law; Spanish Society of Political Science; Spanish Association of Political Scientists; Spanish Association of Professional Translators and Interpreters' Spanish Association of Industrial Organizations and Business Administration' Spanish Association of Japanese Culture; Spanish-Japanese Association; Inter-Pacific Bar Association (Tokyo); The Chinese Society of International Law (Taipei).

Languages: Spanish, English, Chinese, Japanese, German, Portuguese, French, Italian and Russian

IUSFINDER

Established in 1985

C/ GOYA 48 BAJO DCHA.
28001 MADRID, SPAIN
Telephone: (34) 91.431.37.75; 91.431.37.02
Fax: (34) 91.575.61.64

Bilbao, Spain Office: C/ Diputación 10 - 4° dcha. dcha. - 48008-BILBAO. Teléfono: 94.415.13.91. Fax: 94.415.64.69.
Barcelona, Spain Office: C/Cardenal Reig, 19-1° 3 - 08028-BARCELONA. Teléfono: 93.440.23.49.
Zaragoza, Spain Office: C/ Fco. de Vitoria, 16- Pricipal C. 50008-ZARAGOZA. Teléfono: 976.21.21.64. Fax: 976.23.12.83.
Pamplona, Spain Office: C/San Fermín, 43-1° 31004 PAMPLONA. Teléfono: 948.23.69.50. Fax: 948.15.26.36.
Palma de Mallorca, Spain Office: C/San Miguel n° 30-Edificio Antoniet 6° H. 07002-PALMA DE MALLORCA. Teléfono: 971.71.35.85. Fax: 971.71.35.85.
Valencia, Spain Office: C/Serrano Morales n° 3 -4° 10ª 46004-VALENCIA. Teléfono: 96.373.75.61. Fax: 96.374.15.99.
Valladolid, Spain Office: C/ Santiago, 24.1 Dcha. 47001 VALLADOLID Telephone: (34) 983.35.96.99. Fax: 983.35.97.99.
Cairo, Egypt Office: Nile Tower 21, Giza Street 17th Floor, Giza EGYPT. Telephone: (202).571.63.40/41. Fax: (202).571.63.42.

General Practice, Civil, Commercial, Company, Insolvency, Banking, Finance, Securities, Taxation, International, EEC, Administrative, Real Estate, Mergers and Acquisitions, Foreign Investment, Licensing, Patent, Trademark and Copyright Law, Maritime.

MEMBERS OF FIRM
MADRID OFFICE

FRANCISCO JAVIER BARRILERO YARNOZ, born Bilbao, Spain, October 18, 1952; admitted, 1977, Madrid. *Education:* University of Navarra and University Complutense of Madrid (Licenciado en Derecho); Graduated at School of Judicial Practices, University Complutense of Madrid. Member of the Spanish Association of Finance Law. President of the Young Lawyers Madrid Bar Association. *Member:* Madrid, Malaga and Cartagena Bar Associations; Asociación Española de Derecho Tributario; International Bar Association. *LANGUAGES:* English and French.

ALFREDO ARISTONDO MARURI, born Bilbao, Spain, June 3, 1961; admitted, 1986, Vizcaya; 1990, Madrid. *Education:* University of Deusto, Bilbao (Law Degree); Masters in Company Law and Fiscal Law at Instituto de Empresa, Madrid; Shipping Management Diploma, Bilbao. *LANGUAGES:* English.

ELENA VALLEJO CAYRE, born Madrid, Spain, June 13, 1968; admitted, 1993, Madrid. *Education:* University Complutense of Madrid (Licenciado en Derecho); Master in Company Law at the Instituto de Empresa, Madrid. *Member:* Madrid Bar Association. *LANGUAGES:* English and French.

EMILIO RAMOS CALZON, born Orense, Spain, June 28, 1965; admitted, 1994, Madrid. *Education:* University Complutense of Madrid (Licenciado en Derecho); Private and Public Law Programme; Manchester (LL.M., International Business Law, Insolvency); Universities of Rotterdam, Hamburg (also at the Max Planck Institute); Aix-Marseille (European

(This Listing Continued)

Master in Law and Economics). European Union Fellowship. *Member:* Madrid Bar Association. Author: "The Futures Market of Companies under Rescue Mechanisms (FMCRM).". *LANGUAGES:* English, French and Portuguese.

OF COUNSEL

TOMAS MAESTRE AZNAR, born Madrid, Spain, December 24, 1925. *Education:* University of Madrid (Law Degree). Founding Father of the Young Lawyers of Madrid Bar Association. Corresponding Academician of the Royal Academy of Jurisprudence and Legislation of Spain. Member of de L'Académie International de Tourisme. Formerly President of Aviaco and several companies concerning the development of the tourism of La Manga del Mar Menor (Spain) as well as President of the Spanish Tourism Commission; Also member of the Board of Directors of Entursa and Frenos y Señales.

FRANCISCO JAVIER MONEDERO SANMARTIN, born Madrid, Spain, August 25, 1957. *Education:* University of Complutense (Law Degree). Notary Public of Madrid since 1994. Former Professor of the School of Judicial Practices (San Sebastian).

BILBAO OFFICE

JAVIER BICARREGUI GARAY, born London, United Kingdom, October 19, 1962; admitted, 1990, Vizcaya. *Education:* University of Deusto, Bilbao (Licenciado en Derecho); Graduated in Business Administration at C.E.O.E., Madrid; Graduated in Maritime Law (Esuela de Administración Marítima del Gobierno Vasco). *Member:* Vizcaya Bar Association; International Bar Association. *LANGUAGES:* English.

LUIS GOMEZA ALCIBAR, born Bilbao, Spain, February 24, 1963; admitted, 1987, Vizcaya. *Education:* University of Deusto, Bilbao (Licenciado en Derecho); Masters in Tax Assessment at Instituto de Empresas, Madrid. *Member:* Vizcaya Bar Association. *LANGUAGES:* English and French.

JOSE RAMÓN SAN ROMAN CARNEROS, born Bilbao, Spain, July 13, 1961; admitted, 1986, Vizcaya. *Education:* University of Deusto, Bilbao (Licenciado en Derecho) M.B.A. Graduated at Escuela de Organización Industrial, Madrid; Graduated at Judicial Practice, Bilbao. *Member:* Vizcaya Bar Association. *LANGUAGES:* English.

IÑIGO ZAVALA ORTIZ DE LA TORRE, born Bilbao, Spain, April 24, 1963; admitted, 1987, Vizcaya. *Education:* University of Deusto, Bilbao (Licenciado en Derecho) Graduated in Common Market Law at Instituto de Estudios Europeos (University of Deusto, Bilbao); Graduated in Accounting at Chamber of Industry and Commerce, Bilbao. *Member:* Vizcaya Bar Association; Asociacióde Jóvenes Empresarios de Vizcaya. *LANGUAGES:* English and French.

GUILLERMO ALONSO OLARRA, born Bilbao, Spain, November 8, 1963; admitted, 1987, Vizcaya. *Education:* University of Deusto, Bilbao (Licenciado en Derecho); Graduate in Spanish Register Law; Graduated at Judicial Practice, Bilbao.

BARCELONA OFFICE

AGUSTIN DE PASCUAL MASPONS, born Barcelona, Spain, September 15, 1952; admitted, 1975, Barcelona (Cataluña). *Education:* University of Navarra. Lawyer of Caja de Ahorros y Pensiones de Barcelona. *LANGUAGES:* French, English and Catalán.

PAMPLONA OFFICE

JOSE-MIGUEL GOMARA URDIAIN, born Pamplona (Navarra), Spain, November 21, 1963; admitted, 1987, Pamplona (Navarra). *Education:* University of Deusto, Bilbao and University of Pais Vasque, San Sebastián (Licenciado en Derecho); University of Navarra (Private Law Doctorate Program). *Member:* Pamplona (Navarra) Bar Association. *LANGUAGES:* English.

ZARAGOZA OFFICE

JOSE MIGUEL REVILLO PINILLA, born Zaragoza, Spain, December 10, 1957; admitted, 1981, Zaragoza; 1992, Huesca. *Education:* University of Zaragoza (Licenciado en Derecho); Graduated at Judicial Practice, Zaragoza. *Member:* Zaragoza and Huesca Bar Associations. *LANGUAGES:* French.

FRANCISCO JAVIER MONFORTE FRANCIA, born Zaragoza, Spain, April 17, 1955; admitted, 1981, Zaragoza. *Education:* University of Madrid; University of Zaragoza (Licenciado en Derecho); Graduated at Judicial Practice, Zaragoza. *Member:* Zaragoza Bar Association. *LANGUAGES:* French.

(This Listing Continued)

PALMA DE MALLORCA OFFICE

LUIS CLAR BARCELO, born Madrid, Spain, June 21, 1967; admitted, 1993, Palma de Mallorca. *Education:* University of Islas Baleares (Licenciado en Derecho). *LANGUAGES:* English.

RAMON PITA DA VEIGA MONTIS, born Palma de Mallorca, Spain, December 13, 1967; admitted, 1993, Palma de Mallorca. *Education:* University of Pontificia de Comillas (ICADE), Graduated in Business and Law; Masters in urbanistic laws and planning at Fundación Universitaria San Pablo (CEU), Madrid. *LANGUAGES:* English.

VALENCIA OFFICE

ENRIQUE LOPEZ SALVA, born Valencia, Spain, January 19, 1934; admitted, 1965, Valencia. *Education:* University of Valencia. *Member:* Valencia Bar Association. Specialized in Judicial Practice and in Civil and Commercial Law. *LANGUAGES:* English and French.

ALVARO LOPEZ-JAMAR CABALLERO, born Valencia, Spain, March 19, 1966; admitted, 1992, Valencia. *Education:* City of London Polytechnic University; Academie du Droit Internacional de La Haye. Specialized in Fiscal and Financial Law. *LANGUAGES:* English.

VALLADOLID OFFICE

CARLOS GONZALEZ CASCOS Y JIMENEZ, born Madrid, Spain, March 15, 1961; admitted, 1994, Valladolid. *Education:* University of Navarra and University of Valladolid (Licenciado en Derecho); University of Valladolid (Doctor in Civil Law). *Member:* Valladolid, Palencia and Burges Bar Associations. *LANGUAGES:* English and French.

CAIRO OFFICE

LISSET DUMIT DE SARKIS, born Santo Domingo, Dominican Republic, September 13, 1969; admitted, 1994. *Education:* University Nacional Pedro Enriques Ureña (Law Degree); University of Manchester (LL.M.). Formerly Associated with Messina & Messina. Honorary Consul of the Dominican Republic. *LANGUAGES:* Arab, Spanish, English and French.

Languages: English, French, Italian, Portuguese, German, Spanish and Catalan.

REPRESENTATIVE CLIENTS: N.H. Hoteles; Chupa-Chups; Globewide Española; Air Truck; Grupo PAS, IBERIA de Seguros; M.A. MARTIN; Casino del Mar Menor; Casino del Principado; Hotel Doble Casino; Eurosegur Correduría de Seguros; Villa Dolores SA; ENISA; Credit Agricole (Spain); Egon Zehnder International; Porcelano S.A.; Abvale Properties Ltd.; Landale Properties Ltd.; Bardon Limited; Mr. Stanley Ho; Fercam; Aeroleasing S.A.; Aglomerados Numancia II S.A.; Aleph, Producciones Cinematogràficas; Asycore Company Ltd.; Cooper Ltd.; Colbyco Ltd.; Avenida Company Ltd.; China Fullion International Development Company; Embajada de la Replíca Popular China en España; China State Construction Engineering Company; De Benedetti S.A.; Dialsur S.L.; Earlwood Development Company; East Holdings Ltd.; Green Hoteles S.A.; Jagomen S.A.; Linguasec S.A.; LTC Productions S.A.; Maglificio Espagnol S.A.; *Bankers:* United Bank of Kuwait, Ltd.; Barclays Bank, Banco Hispano Americano; National Westminster Bank PLC; Firestone Bilbao.

JAUSAS & TERRICABRAS

Established in 1965

MIGUEL ANGEL, NO. 6-3°
28010 MADRID, SPAIN
Telephone: (1) 310 01 65
Fax: (1) 308 39 33

Barcelona, Spain Office: León XIII, No. 23, Roger de Lluria, 118, 08022 Barcelona. Telephone: (3) 212.61.54; (3) 207.70.60. Telex: 51707 LAWS E. Fax: (3) 418.21.99; (3) 207.14.24.

Pharmaceutical Law, Mergers and Acquisitions, Competition, Trade and Commercial, Corporate, Foreign Investment, EEC Law, Trademarks and Intellectual Property, Labor and Tax Law, Arbitration and Litigation.

RESIDENT PARTNER

TERESA DEL ROSAL BLASCO, born Granada, Spain, October 26, 1945; admitted, 1979, Madrid. *Education:* University of Madrid (Law, 1977). *LANGUAGES:* Spanish, English and French. *PRACTICE AREAS:* Civil Law; Family Law.

(This Listing Continued)

JAUSAS & TERRICABRAS, Madrid—Continued

ASSOCIATE

MARIA TERESA CABEZA, born Madrid, Spain. April 1, 1963; admitted, 1993, Madrid. *Education:* Complutense University of Madrid (Law, 1992). *LANGUAGES:* Spanish and English. *PRACTICE AREAS:* Commercial Law.

(For complete biographical data on all personnel, see Professional Biographies at Barcelona, Spain)

KPMG ESTUDIO JURIDICO Y TRIBUTARIO

Established in 1987

EDIFICIO TORRE EUROPA
PASEO DE LA CASTELLANA, 95
28046 MADRID, SPAIN
Telephone: 34 (1) 555 53 63
Fax: 34 (1) 555 01 32

Barcelona Office: Edificio Masters, Pedro í Pons, 9-11, 08034. Telephone: 34 (3) 280 03 04. Fax: 34 (3) 280 49 16.
Bilbao Office: Edificio Aurora Polar, Iparraguirre, 29-2a olanta, 48011. Telephone: 34 (4) 416 21 00. Fax: 34 (4) 415 29 67.
Seville, Office Edificio Forum: Avda. Luis de Morales, 32 41018, Seville. Telephone: 34 (54) 453 28 01. Fax: 34 (54) 453 93 43.
Valencia, Office Edificio: Condes de Buñol, Isabel la Catolica, 8 46004, Valencia. Telephone: 34 (6) 352 68 19. Fax: 34 (6) 351 27 29.

A law Firm for Spanish and Foreign Clients in Inter alia, the following areas: Fiscal, Commercial Law. European Community, Civil, International and Administration. Among the service provided are Tax Planning for Companies and Individuals, Assistance with Tax Inspections, Evaluation of Tax Contingencies, Information on Current Policies. Legislation, Acting as Tax Representative for Non-Residents, Formation and Registration of Companies and Branches, Advice on Import and Export Operations, Mergers and Transformation of Entities, Purchase, Sale and Leasing Agreements.

FIRM PROFILE: *Formed in June, 1987 and with offices in Madrid, Barcelona, Bilbao, Valencia and Seville, KPMG ESTUDIO JURIDICO Y TRIBUTARIO employs a large number of lawyers with broad knowledge and the experience required to meet each client's specific needs. Our lawyers have broad knowledge of not only Spanish legislation, but also of EC Law and that of the other countries where KPMG operates, thus providing Spanish companies seeking to expand their business outside of Spain with information about the most important fiscal and legal matters which affect their overseas activities.*

MEMBERS OF FIRM

MERCEDES DE ROJAS, born La Habana, Cuba, January 14, 1944; admitted, 1983 as partner, Madrid. *Education:* Complutense University of Madrid (Law Degree, 1969). *Member:* Madrid and Barcelona Bar Association; Spanish Institute of Chartered Accountants. *LANGUAGES:* Spanish and English. *PRACTICE AREAS:* Tax and Legal Advice; Leasing; Foreign Investment; Company Law; Non-Resident and International Taxation and International Contracts.

VICENTE MUÑOZ SEÑORANS, born Orense, Spain, October 22, 1947; admitted, 1985 as partner, Madrid. *Education:* Complutense University of Madrid (Law Degree, 1969). *Member:* Madrid and Barcelona Bar Association; Spanish Institute of Chartered Accountants. *LANGUAGES:* Spanish, English and French. *PRACTICE AREAS:* Tax and Legal Advice; Pharmaceutical Industry; Real Estate and Construction.

ANTONIO GONZALEZ LOBON, born Madrid, January 20, 1954; admitted, 1987 as partner, Madrid. *Education:* Complutense University of Madrid (Law Degree, 1977); University of Deusto (Master Degree, Tax Law, 1978). Tax Bank and Finance Coordinator for Spain, 1991. *Member:* Madrid and Barcelona Bar Associations; Spanish Institute of Chartered Accountants. *LANGUAGES:* Spanish, English and French. *PRACTICE AREAS:* Fiscal; Mercantile; Civil Law and European Economic Community Legislation.

JOSE MARIA REVUELTA, born Madrid, Spain, January 16, 1955; admitted, 1987 as partner, Madrid. *Education:* Deusto University (Law Degree, 1978); The Catholic Institute of Business Administration (ICADE) (1978); The Fiscal and Economics Study Center (CETE) (Economics,

(This Listing Continued)

1982). *Member:* Madrid, Barcelona and Valencia Bar Associations; Spanish Tax Attorney's Association; Spanish Institute of Chartered Accountants. *LANGUAGES:* Spanish, English and French. *PRACTICE AREAS:* Fiscal and Legal Advice; Insurance; Manufacturing; Foreign Investments and Company Law.

XAVIER MIRAVALLS, born Barcelona, Spain, December 7, 1950; admitted, 1989 as partner, Barcelona. *Education:* Central University of Barcelona (Law Degree, 1973); University of Strasbourg (Master in European Comparative Law, 1973). Auditor, Legal Services EC Community, Brussels, 1982. *Member:* Barcelona Bar Association. *LANGUAGES:* Spanish, Catalonian, English, German and French. *PRACTICE AREAS:* Foreign Investments; Corporate Law; EC Law; Litigation (Commercial and Bankruptcy Cases).

JAVIER MUÑOZ ZAPATERO, born Madrid, Spain, January 20, 1958; admitted, 1989 as partner, Madrid. *Education:* Catholic University of Commillas (Law Degree, 1980; Economics Degree, 1981); Catholic Institute of Business Administration (Master's Degree in Taxation, 1983). *Member:* Madrid and Barcelona Bar Associations. *LANGUAGES:* Spanish and English. *PRACTICE AREAS:* Manufacturing and Pharmaceutical Industry; Expatriate and International Taxation.

MARIA JOSE AGUILO, born Madrid, December 15, 1960; admitted, 1992 as partner, Madrid. *Education:* Complutense University of Madrid (Law Degree, 1982); Financial Studies Center (Master Degree in Taxation, 1983); International Menéndez Pelayo University (Master in EC Legislation, 1985). *Member:* Madrid Bar Association. *LANGUAGES:* Spanish, English and French. *PRACTICE AREAS:* Drafting of Commercial Contracts; Supervising Tax Inspections; Incorporating Companies.

JOAQUÍN HERRERA, born Barcelona, Spain, December 16, 1958; admitted, 1994, as Partner, Barcelona. *Education:* Central University of Barcelona (Law Degree, 1983; Economics Degree, 1982); Diploma in Tributary Law from the Abad Olia College in 1985. *Member:* Spanish Institute of Chartered Accountants. *LANGUAGES:* Spanish, Caralonian, English and French. *PRACTICE AREAS:* Mercantile Law and Taxation; Specializing in VAT.

MADRID ASSOCIATES

Isabel de Otaola	Javier Sabau
Celso Garcia	Borja Montesino-Espartero
Ramón Pallares	José Antonio de San Roman
Juan Rivero	Victor Mendoza
Joaquín Latorre	Nicolas Martin
Fernando Gómez	Natalia Pastor

SPANISH PROVINCES ASSOCIATES

Joaquín Torruella	Pilar Sarrias
Fco. Javier Pelegay	Juan Garcia-Mochales
María Angeles Campo	María Teresa Urruticoechea
Alain Casanovas	Francisco Farinós

LAGO & LOPEZ ACOSTA ABOGADOS

Established in 1992

VELAZQUEZ, 109, 5TH FLOOR
28006 MADRID, SPAIN
Telephone: (34-1) 561 5101
Fax: (34-1) 561 5066

General Civil Practice, International Business Law, Corporate, Tax, Foreign Investment, Litigation, Environmental and Labor Law.

PARTNERS

SANTIAGO LAGO BORNSTEIN, born Madrid, Spain, September 12, 1952. *Education:* University of Madrid (Law Degree, 1973); Instituto de Estudios Superiores de la Empresa, Madrid (I.E.S.E.) (M.B.A., 1986). *Member:* Madrid Bar Association. *LANGUAGES:* Spanish. *PRACTICE AREAS:* Corporate and Business Law; Civil Law; Administrative Law.

IGNACIO LÓPEZ ACOSTA, born La Habana, Cuba, October 10, 1956. *Education:* University of Navarra, Spain (Law Degree, 1977); Escuela Diplomática, Ministry of Foreign Affairs, Madrid (Diploma, EEC Law, 1986). *Member:* Madrid Bar Association; Barcelona Bar Association. *LANGUAGES:* Spanish, English and French. *PRACTICE AREAS:* International Business Law; Corporate Law; Environmental Law.

(This Listing Continued)

ASSOCIATES

MERCERES BARDERAS MARTIN, born Arenas de San Pedro, Avila, Spain, September 23, 1964. *Education:* University of Salamanca (Law Degree, 1989); I.C.A.D.E., Madrid (Master in Tax Law, 1991). *Member:* Madrid Bar Association. *LANGUAGES:* Spanish, French and Portuguese. *PRACTICE AREAS:* Corporate Law; Civil Law.

JOHN R. GUSTAFSON, born Torreión de Ardoz, Madrid, November 10, 1965. *Education:* C.E.U. San Pablo, Madrid University (Law Degree, 1988). Assistant, Public Defender's Office of Albany, New York. *Member:* Madrid Bar Association; León Bar Association. *LANGUAGES:* Spanish and English. *PRACTICE AREAS:* Civil and Commercial Litigation; Arbitration and Insolvency Proceedings.

MIGUEL LOPEZ ACOSTA, born Madrid, Spain, December 9, 1968. *Education:* C.E.U. San Pablo, University of Madrid (Law Degree, 1992). *Member:* Madrid Bar Association. *LANGUAGES:* Spanish and English. *PRACTICE AREAS:* Corporate Law; Civil Law.

AMAYA PEREZ-NIEVAS VIZCAINO, born Newark, New Jersey, U.S.A., June 22, 1966. *Education:* C.E.U. San Pablo, University of Madrid (Law Degree, 199). *Member:* Madrid Bar Association. *LANGUAGES:* Spanish and English. *PRACTICE AREAS:* Tax Law; Commercial Law.

SEBASTIAN RIVERO GALAN, born Cádiz, Spain, July 9, 1966. *Education:* University of Seville (Law Degree, 1989); Instituto de Empresa, Madrid (Master in Corporate Law, 1990). Assistant, Department of Labor Law, University of Seville, 1988-1989. *Member:* Madrid Bar Association. *LANGUAGES:* Spanish, English and French. *PRACTICE AREAS:* Corporate Law; Real Estate Law; Civil Litigation.

JOSE CARLOS RUIZ SANCHEZ-MURILLO, born Ciudad Real, Spain, January 12, 1960. *Education:* University of Extremadura (Law Degree, 1982). *Member:* Madrid Bar Association; Cáceres Bar Association. *LANGUAGES:* Spanish and English. *PRACTICE AREAS:* Corporate Law; Civil Law; Civil Litigation.

DESPACHO LUIS LAMANA, ABOGADOS

CALLE DE MONTALBAN NO. 5
28014 MADRID, SPAIN
Telephone: (34 1) 531 22 39; 531 14 34; 531 41 83; 5315268
Cable Address: "Lamanabogs"
Fax: 5328732/5319821

Canary Islands Office: Villalba Hervás, Santa Cruz de Tenerife. Telephone: (34 22) 24 61 77. Fax: (34 22) 24 48 70.

Administrative Law, Advertising Law, Aeronautical Law, Agricultural Law, Antitrust Law, Arbitration, Banking Law, Bankruptcy, Business Law, Competition Law, Constitutional Law, Consumer Protection Law. Conveyancing, Corporate Law, Criminal Law, Customs and Excise Law, Distributorship, Agency and Franchise Law, EEC Law, Employer's Liability, Entertainment Law, Environmental Law, Family Law, Food and Drug Regulations, Foreign Investments, Health, Hospital and Malpractice Law, Immigration Law, Industrial Relations and Labour Law, Insurance Law, International Contracts, International Private Law, Litigation, Negligence Law, Oil and Mining Law, Pension Law, Personal Injury Law, Product Liability Law, Property and Real Estate Law, Rent and Lease, Social Security, Trade Regulations, Transportation Law, General Legal Practice.

LUIS LAMANA DE HOYOS, born Madrid, Spain, December 12, 1930; admitted, 1954, Spain. *Education:* University of Madrid (Licenciado and Doctor Degrees); The Hague (International Law). Author: *Spain in Planning Subsidiary Operations in Selected European Countries,* Prentice Hall, 1963, 1964, 1965 Editions, and *Informacion Comercial Espanola,* Madrid, January, 1965; "Iron Ore Mining in Spain," *Revista Industrial,* Madrid; "Foreign Investments in Spain Milano." Professor of Economics, University of Madrid, 1955-1964. *Member:* Ilustre Colegio de Abogados de Madrid; A.A. de la Academia de Derecho Internacional de la Haya; Chevalier de la Légion d'Honneur. *LANGUAGES:* Spanish, French.

ASSOCIATES

Fermin Santiago Velasco	*Cristina Lamana Chico*
Emilio Perez Sendino	*Ana Ferrando*
Ignacio Lamana de Hoyos	*Eduardo Arguelles*
Luis Lamana Chico	*Ernesto Juarez*
	Alberto Pinazo Osuna

Languages: English, French, German and Spanish

(This Listing Continued)

REPRESENTATIVE CLIENTS: Ingersoll-Rand Co.; Banque Nationale de Paris; Telemecanica Electrica S.A.; Telemecanique; Construcciones y Auxiliar de Ferrocarriles S.A.; Van Leer (The Netherlands); Bonduelle; Knoll Lab.; Greenland; Skania; CAF; Legrand; GAN; Groupe de la Mutuell d Mans a Madrid; Maus Freres S.A.; French Embassy; Belgium Embassy; Ericsson; Financial Insurance Group (G.E. Group).

ESTUDIO LEGAL ABOGADOS

VELÁZQUEZ, 51
28001 MADRID, SPAIN
Telephone: 578.06.43 (30 lines)
Telex: 44159 ESLE
Telecopier: 431 21 52
Cable Address: "Estleg"

Barcelona, Spain Office: Avda. Diagonal, 442, 08037. Telephone: 3. 415.95.82. Telecopier: 3. 416.18.03.
Paris, France Office: c/o Bureau Francis Lefebvre 3, Villa Emile Bergerat. Telephone: (1) 47385500. Fax: 47385555.
Brussels, Belgium Office: 45, Rue du Luxembourg. Telephone: 2. 502.20.30. Telecopier: 2. 502.32.78.

General Practice. Corporation, Mergers and Acquisitions Insolvency, Taxation, Foreign Investments, Banking, Securities, Administrative, Planning, Labour, Oil, Mining and Gas, Civil, International/EEC Law, Litigation, Antitrust, Distributorship, Agency and Franchise Law, Arbitration, Intellectual Property, Environmental, Entertainment, Pharmaceutical, Transport, Telecommunications.

SENIOR PARTNERS

ANTONIO BARRAGAN LOZANO, born Mieres (Asturias), 1932; admitted, 1962, Spain. *Education:* Instituto Jovellanos, Gijón; University of Madrid, Faculty of Law, School of Juridical Practice (Ph.D. Studies). *Member:* Colegio de Abogados de Madrid.

LUIS FERNANDO LOPEZ-CHICHERI Y DABAN, born Gijón (Asturias), 1942; admitted, 1969, Spain. *Education:* Sagrados Corazones; University of Madrid, Faculty of Law, Center of Tax and Economic Studies. Former Professor of Tax Law, School of Juridical Practice, University of Madrid. *Member:* Colegio de Abogados de Madrid.

LUIS FERNANDO MARTIN PEREZ, born Madrid, 1942; admitted, 1969, Spain. *Education:* Instituto Ramiro de Maeztu; University of Madrid, Faculty of Law. Former Assistant Professor of Commercial Law, University of Madrid. Senior Board of Civil Administrators of the State (on leave). *Member:* Colegio de Abogados de Madrid.

PARTNERS

ANTONIO CAÑADAS ALONSO, born Madrid, 1950; admitted, 1979, Spain. *Education:* Lycée Français, Madrid; University of Madrid, Faculty of Law; College d'Europe, Brugge, Belgium; International Law Academy, The Hague, The Netherland (Diploma, EEC Law). Assistant Professor of International Law, Universidad Autónoma de Madrid. *Member:* Colegio de Abogados de Madrid. (Resident, Barcelona Office).

MARTA ORTIZ PEÑALVER, born Madrid, 1957; admitted, 1981, Spain. *Education:* Liceo Italiano, Madrid; University of Madrid, Faculty of Law, Center of Tax and Economic Studies, School of Juridical Practice (Master in EEC Law). *Member:* Colegio de Abogados de Madrid.

MIGUEL PINTOS DEL VALLE, born Valencia, 1952; admitted, 1976, Spain. *Education:* Instituto Ramiro de Maeztu, Madrid and San José, Valencia; Universidad Navarra, Faculty of Law, School of Juridical Practice. *Member:* Colegio de Abogados de Madrid.

MARTA DE LARREA Y GARCIA-MORATO, born Madrid, 1959; admitted, 1984, Spain. *Education:* Instituto Veritas; Universidad Pontificia de Comillas, ICADE (Licenciate in Law and Graduate in Business Administration); Centre for Tax and Economic Studies (Master in EEC Law). *Member:* Colegio de Abogados de Madrid.

COUNSEL

FERNANDO BORRACHERO RIVAS, born Madrid, Spain, 1936; admitted, 1965, Spain. *Education:* British Institute; Colegio Nuestra Señora de las Maravillas (Lasalle); University of Madrid, Faculty of Law, School of Juridical Practice, Center for Tax and Economic Studies. *Member:* Colegio de Abogados de Madrid.

(This Listing Continued)

ESTUDIO LEGAL ABOGADOS, Madrid—Continued

ASSOCIATES

INMACULADA UMBERT MILLET, born Barcelona, 1952; admitted, 1984, Spain. *Education:* Marymount School, Sagrado Corazón; University of Barcelona, Faculties of Law and Philosophy (Degree in Tax Studies). *Member:* Colegio de Abogados de Barcelona. (Resident, Barcelona Office).

JAIME ESPEJO Y VALDELOMAR, born Madrid, 1961; admitted, 1986, Spain. *Education:* Colegio Alamán and Colegio Fray Luis de León, Universidad Pontificia de Comillas, ICADE (Licenciate in Law; Diploma in Company Tax Advise); Instituto de Empresa (Master's Degree in Foreign Trade). *Member:* Colegio de Abogados de Madrid.

FRANCISCO JAVIER DE DIOS MORALES, born Madrid, 1962; admitted, 1985, Madrid. *Education:* Nuestra Señora del Recuerdo (PP.JJ.); Universidad Pontificia de Comillas, ICADE (Licenciate in Law and Graduate in Business Administration); School of Juridical Practice (Diploma in Tax Advise). Assistant Professor of Mercantile Law, Nuestra Señora del Recuerdo (PP.JJ.) Madrid and I.C.A.D.E. University of Madrid, 1985, 1986 and 1987. *Member:* Colegio de Abogados de Madrid.

ISIDRO DEL SAZ CORDERO, born Madrid, Spain, 1961; admitted, 1984, Spain. *Education:* University of Madrid, Faculty of Law and Economics; Master on Spanish Tax System and European Tax Senior School, The Netherlands; Degree on Public Economy of the Economic Science, University of Madrid. *Member:* Colegio de Abogados de Madrid.

JAVIER MARTIN MARTIN, born Madrid, 1959; admitted, 1982, Madrid. *Education:* Nuestra Señora del Loreto; Universidad Pontificia de Comillas, ICADE (Licenciate in Law and Graduate in Business Administration); Center of Tax and Economic Studies. *Member:* Colegio de Abogados de Madrid.

ALFONSO VEGA IMAÑA, born Madrid, 1960; admitted, 1983, Spain. *Education:* Colegio Foundatión Calderio; University of Madrid, Faculty of Law (Masters in Economics and Corporations); Colegio de Abogados of Madrid (Masters). *Member:* Colegio de Abogados de Madrid.

JOSE RAMON CADAHIA CASLA, born Madrid, 1960; admitted, 1987, Spain. *Education:* Instituto Ramiro de Maeztu; University of Madrid, Faculty of Law; Master in Business School of Madrid. *Member:* Colegio de Abogados de Madrid.

MIGUEL ANGEL ALCARAZ GARCIA, born Madrid, 1955; admitted, 1980, Spain. *Education:* Colegio Sagrados Corazones; University of Madrid, Faculty of Law (Specialist in Labor and Employment Law; Degree in Description Appraisal System HAY). *Member:* Colegio de Abogados de Madrid.

JAVIER CAVESTANY MANZANEDO, born Cartagena, Murcia, 1961; admitted, 1988, Madrid. *Education:* Hermanos Maristas, Cartagena; Colegio Huérfanos de la Armada, Madrid; University of Madrid, Faculty of Law, Centro San Pablo, C.E.U.; Center for Taxes and Economic Studies, Specialized in Civil Law. *Member:* Colegio de Abogados de Madrid.

NOEL E. LERYCKE PAQUET, born Thysville, Zaire, 1949; admitted, 1976, Barcelona; 1983, Balearic Islands. *Education:* Lycée Français, Kinshasa; Ecole Saint Pierre, Brussels; Colegio Teatinos, Mallorca; University of Barcelona, Faculty of Law, Center for Taxes and Economic Studies (Master in EEC Law). *Member:* Colegio de Abogados de Barcelona and Balearic Islands. (Resident, Barcelona Office).

FRANCESCA RUIZ GURBALA, born La Ricamarie, Saint Etienne, France, 1958; admitted, 1986, Barcelona. *Education:* Lycée Français, P. Andorra; Instituto de Enseñanza Media, P. Andorra; University of Barcelona, Faculty of Law; School of Juridical Practice. *Member:* Colegio de Abogados de Barcelona. (Resident, Barcelona Office).

CONSUELO DIEZ MARTIN, born Madrid, 1950; admitted, 1990, Madrid. *Education:* Colegio Sagrados Carazones; University of Madrid, Faculty of Law (Master's Degree in Corporate Law). *Member:* Colegio de Abogados de Madrid.

LUIS RUFILANCHAS SOLARES, born Madrid, 1961; admitted, 1990, Madrid. *Education:* Colegio Base and Centro San Pablo (CEU); University of Madrid, Faculty of Law; Legal Defense Corps (Course in Maritime Law). Specialized in Administrative Law. Legal Adviser to the Ministry of Defense. Ex-Naval Judge number 9 (Palma de Mallorca). *Member:* Colegio de Abogados de Madrid.

ISABEL GARRIDO ARSUAGA, born Madrid, 1965; admitted, 1990, Madrid. *Education:* Colegio Mater Salvatoris; University of Madrid, Fac-

(This Listing Continued)

ulty of Law (Master's Salvatoris); University of Madrid, Faculty of Law (Master's Degree in Corporate Law). *Member:* Colegio de Abogados de Madrid.

LUCIA FIERROS PEREZ, born Madrid, 1964; admitted, 1989, Madrid. *Education:* Colegio Santa Maria del Camino; University of Madrid, Centro San Pablo (CEU). *Member:* Colegio de Abogados de Madrid.

CARMEN ROZPIDE ORBEGOZO, born San Sebastian, 1964; admitted, 1989, Madrid. *Education:* Santa Maria de los Rosales; University of Madrid, Faculty of Law, Centro San Pablo (CEU); Business Consulting Master at the School of Juridical Practice; Master of Law (LL.M.) at the Washington College of Law, The American University. *Member:* Colegio de Abogados de Madrid.

MANUEL FELIPE SESMA GARCIA, born Ciudad Real, 1961; admitted, 1986, Barcelona. *Education:* La Salle Horta-Menendez Pelayo and La Salle Condal (Barcelona); University of Barcelona, Faculty of Law; School of Juridical Practice. *Member:* Colegio de Abogados de Barcelona. (Resident, Barcelona Office).

JOSE MARTOS MATINEZ, born Valladolid, 1965; admitted, 1989, Madrid. *Education:* Colegio Estudio; University of Madrid, Faculty of Law. Master of Legal Counselling to Companies at the Madrid Business Institute and Centre of Taxation Studies. *Member:* Colegio de Abogados de Madrid.

ALVARO KLECKER ALONSO DE CELADA, born Madrid, 1964. *Education:* Colegio Cuesta de las Perdices, I.N.B Ortega y Gasset; University of Madrid, Faculty of Law (Master of Law); Business Institute of Madrid. *Member:* Colegio de Abogados de Madrid, 1987—.

MARIA TERESA ROIG VIDAL, born Barcelona, Spain, 1964. *Education:* Colegio Sant Nicolau (Sabadell); University School Abad Oliba (Barcelona); University of Barcelona, Faculty of Law. *Member:* Colegio de Abogados de Barcelona, 1991—. (Resident, Barcelona Office).

ANTONIA LOBO FEMENIA, born Palma, Spain, 1966. *Education:* Colegio Jesús María (Jerez de la Frontera, Cádiz) and Sagrad a Familia (Madrid); Universities of Madrid and Barcelona, Faculties of Law. Master in Practice of Corporate Social Security Management at Adams Academy of Barcelona. *Member:* Colegio de Abogados de Barcelona, 1990—. (Resident, Barcelona Office).

ELENA LOPEZ-HENARES SANCHO, born Madrid, Spain, 1965. *Education:* St. Anne's School (Madrid); New Hall School (Essex, England); University of Madrid, Faculty of Law, Centro San Pablo (C.E.U.); Master of Law, Business Institute of Madrid. *Member:* Colegio de Abogados de Madrid, 1989—.

JOSE LUIS HUERTA GONZALEZ, born Bauenberg, Germany, 1962. *Education:* Colegio Nuestra Señora del Pilar (Pola de Lena, Asturias); University of Oviedo, Faculty of Law (Master of Law); Business Institute of Madrid; Master of Law (LL.M.) at QMW, University of London. *Member:* Colegio de Abogados de Madrid, 1992—.

ALEJANDRA PUIG RUANO, born Madrid, 1963. *Education:* Colegio Madalaine Michelis (Paris); Universidad Pontifica de Comillas (ICADE); Master in European Community Law (ICADE). *Member:* Colegio de Abogados de Madrid, 1986—.

JUAN CARLOS CALVO, born Reus (Tarragona). *Education:* Ntra Sra del Recuerdo; University of Alcalá de Henares, Madrid, Faculty of Law (graduate in Political Science and Arts). Lecturer, Financial Law and Government Finance at the UNED; Government Attorney, 1985—. *Member:* Madrid Bar Association.

Languages: Spanish, English, French, Italian and German

REPRESENTATIVE CLIENTS: Agfa Gevaert; Alcan; American Home Products; ARA; Atlas Copco; Bache; Baker Industries; Bechtel Corp.; Bridgestone/Firestone Inc.; Cadbury Schweppes; Campbell Tagart; Carlsberg; Compagnie Generale d'Electricite; Coparex; Dart & Kraft Inc.; Electrolux; ELF Aquitaine; Fiat, S.p.A.; Iveco; J. Walter Thompson Co.; Kodak; Lubrizol; Makro; Memorex; Prudential Bache; Roche; Scannia; Schering; Sotheby's; Stanhome; Tetra Pak; Texas Instruments; Upjohn Co.; Volvo Group; Warner Lambert; W.R. Grace and Co.

LOPEZ LOZANO, CREMADES & SANCHEZ PINTADO

GUZMAN EL BUENO 21
28015 MADRID, SPAIN
Telephone: 341 549 8080
Fax: 341 549 8280

General Practice, Telecommunications, Intellectual, Property, Trademarks, Banking, European Union Law, Financing, International Contracts, Litigation, Merger & Acquisitions, Taxation, Arbitration.

PARTNERS

MIGUEL ANGEL LOPEZ LOZANO, born Càdiz, Spain, 1955; admitted, 1979. *Education:* University of Seville; University of Granada (J.D., 1978); University of Navarra, IESE (M.B.A., Major in Finance, 1989); New York School of Law (Master of Comparative Jurisprudence, 1994). *LANGUAGES:* Spanish and English. *PRACTICE AREAS:* Company and Commercial Law; Banking; Finance and Securities; Taxation.

DR. JAVIER CREMADES, born Ceuta, 1965; admitted, 1992. *Education:* University of Malaga, Universidad Nacional de Educación a Distancia (J.D., 1989); University of Regensburg, Germany (Dr. jur. German Law, 1992); UNED (Ph. D. Spanish Law, 1992); University Carios III of Madrid (Assistant Professor, 1992); Univesidad Nacional de Educación a Distancia (Associate Professor, 1993). Author: Gesellschaftsrecht in Spanien (Jehle-Rehm, 1992); Gesellschaftsrecht in Portugal (Jehle-Rehm, 1993), Das Grundrecht der Meinungsfreiheit in der spanischen Verfassung (Duncker & Humblot, 1994), Los límites de la libertad de expresion en el ordenamiento jurídíco español (La Ley, 1995). Legal Advisor: Latvian Government in the Framework of the PHARE-PROJECT, 1994-1996). *LANGUAGES:* Spanish, German and English. *PRACTICE AREAS:* Copyright and Intellectual Property; Telecommunications; Media and Entertainment Law; Public and Administrative Law; Patent and Trademarks.

EMILIO SANCHEZ PINTADO, born Toledo, Spain, 1933; admitted, 1965. *Education:* Complutense University of Madrid (J.D, 1955); study of Government Institutions in U.K. (arranged by U.S.A. International Cooperation Administration, 1959); Complutense University of Madrid (Professor, 1960); Commissariat, Economic Development, Minister's Secretary Technical 1969; European Management Institute (Professor, EC Law, 1988). Foreign Office Director, General Minister's Cabinet, 1973. *LANGUAGES:* Spanish, English and French. *PRACTICE AREAS:* Public and Administrative Law; Arbitration and Litigation; EC Law; Competition.

ASSOCIATES

RAFAEL DEL POZO GONZALEZ, born Madrid, Spain, 1957; admitted, 1982. *Education:* Complutense University of Madrid (J.D., 1981); Instituto de Empresa, Madrid (M.B.A., 1984); ICADE, Madrid (Master in Finance, 1987); University of Navarra, IESE (M.B.A., 1989); European Management Institute (Professor, 1990). *LANGUAGES:* Spanish and English. *PRACTICE AREAS:* Banking; Finance and Securities.

ALBERTO VALDES ALONSO, born Madrid, Spain, 1966; admitted, 1993. *Education:* Complutense University of Madrid (J.D., 1990). National Institute of Safety and Hygiene at Work (Work and Health Conditions, Security at Work, Certified, 1994). *LANGUAGES:* Spanish and English. *PRACTICE AREAS:* Labour Law; Litigation and Arbitration.

LIONEL DIEGO FERNANDEZ GARCIA, born Córdoba, Spain, 1965; admitted, 1988. *Education:* University of Extremadura (J.D., 1987); Instituto de Empresa, Madrid (Master in Business Law, 1994; Associate Professor of Administrative Law and Intellectual Property, 1994). *LANGUAGES:* Spanish, English and Portuguese. *PRACTICE AREAS:* Telecommunications; Company and Commercial Law; Public and Administrative Law.

JACOBO SOUVIRON GAYTAN DE AYALA, born San Sebastian, Spain, 1967; admitted, 1995. *Education:* Complutense University of Madrid (J.D., 1990). *Member:* Madrid Bar Association. *LANGUAGES:* Spanish and English. *PRACTICE AREAS:* Copyright; Intellectual Property; Corporate and Commercial Law.

JESUS MENOR CANTADOR, born Madrid, Spain, 1965; admitted, 1993. *Education:* Autónoma University of Madrid (J.D., 1991); ICADE-Spanish Maritime Institute (Master in Business Shipping, 1991); Faculty of Law of the City of London Polytechnic (Maritime Law and Export Trade, 1989); Commercial Studies Center-Commercial State Secretary and Madrid

(This Listing Continued)

Chamber of Commerce and Industry (Politics and Institutions of European Community. *LANGUAGES:* Spanish and English. *PRACTICE AREAS:* Patents and Trademark; Civil and Commercial Law.

MARISCAL, MONEREO & MEYER

Established in 1989

11, BÁRBARA DE BRAGANZA, 2ND FLOOR
28004 MADRID, SPAIN
Telephone: (34-1) 319 96 86
Fax: (34-1) 308 53 68

General Practice, Maritime Law, Distribution Agreements, International Distribution, Insolvency, International Bankruptcy, Liquidations, Banking Litigation, Finance Law, Loans, Joint Ventures, Civil Law, Civil Litigation, International Civil Law, Conflict of Laws, International Civil Litigation, Commercial Law, Sale of Goods, Company Law, Fiscal Law, Company Acquisitions and Sales, Company Commercial Law, Company Contracts, Cross Border Contracts, Corporate Law, Creditors Rights, International Franchising, International Law, Company Investment, Labor and Employment. Leasing, Cross Border Leasing, Mortgages, Personal Injury, Accidents, Real Estate, Taxation, Cargo Claims, Carriage of Goods, International Transportation, Shipping, Successions.

PARTNERS

MIGUEL MARISCAL FLORES, born Salamanca, 1960; admitted, 1984, Madrid. *Education:* Centro Estudio Universitarios San Pablo, Madrid. *LANGUAGES:* Spanish and English.

ANDRES MONEREO VELASCO, born Madrid, 1961; admitted, 1986, Madrid. *Education:* Universidad Pontificia Commillas ICADE, Madrid. *LANGUAGES:* Spanish and English.

STEFAN MEYER, born West-Berlin, Germany, 1960; admitted, 1989, Madrid and Berlin. *Education:* University Berlin, Genever and Freiburg i. Br. *LANGUAGES:* German, Spanish and English.

ASSOCIATES

SONIA GUMPERT MELGOSA, born Madrid, 1966; admitted, 1993, Madrid. *Education:* University Autónoma Madrid. *LANGUAGES:* Spanish, German and English.

Languages: Spanish, German and English

ABOGADOS MARITIMOS Y ASOCIADOS

Established in 1982

C/ MIGUEL ANGEL, 16, 5° DCHA.
28010 MADRID, SPAIN
Telephone: (34+1) 308 30 95
Telefax: (34+1) 310 35 16
Telex: 49438 LEXM E

Marbella, Spain Office: Jacinto Benavente, 4, 4°. Telephone: (34+5) 286 39 95. Telefax: (34+5) 286 39 92.

General Practice. Shipping and Admiralty. Commercial Law. Aviation. Insurance. Litigation and Arbitration. Foreign Investments and Financing. Corporation. EEC Law. Environmental Law. International Contracts. Mergers and Acquisitions.

PARTNERS

JOSE MARIA ALCANTARA, born Malaga, Spain, January 22, 1944; admitted, 1972, Madrid. *Education:* University of Madrid School of Law (LL.B., 1968). Titular Member, Comité Maritime Internacional and of AIDE. Member, ICC's Arbitration Committee and Committee for Maritime Transport. Arbitrator of the Monaco's Chambre Arbitrale Maritime. *Member:* Spanish Association of Maritime Arbitration; Spanish and Argentine Maritime Law Associations; International Bar Association; Spanish Association of Average Adjusters; Ibero-American Institute of Maritime Law; Mediterranean Maritime Arbitration Association. *LANGUAGES:* Spanish, English and French.

LUIS DE SAN SIMON, born Madrid, Spain, September 24, 1956. *Education:* University of Madrid School of Law (LL.B., 1978). Titular Member, Comité Maritime Internacional. *Member:* Spanish Maritime Law Association; International Bar Association; Ibero-American Institute of Maritime Law; Mediterranean Maritime Arbitration Association; Center For International Legal Studies, Salzburg (Honourary Membership). *LANGUAGES:* Spanish and English.

(This Listing Continued)

ABOGADOS MARITIMOS Y ASOCIADOS, Madrid— *Continued*

ASSOCIATES

JOSE LUIS ORTIZ, born Bilbao, Spain, October 4, 1952. *Education:* University of San Sebastian School of Law (LL.B., 1983). *Member:* Spanish Maritime Law Association. *LANGUAGES:* Spanish and English.

JESUS ORTEGA, born Malaga, Spain, November 9, 1963. *Education:* University of Madrid School of Law (LL.B., 1986); Spanish Maritime Institute (Master in Maritime Law). *Member:* Spanish Maritime Law Association; Ibero-American Institute of Maritime Law. *LANGUAGES:* Spanish and English.

F. DE ASIS DE MORA, born Lucena, Spain, January 6, 1931. *Education:* University of Seville School of Law (LL.B., 1954). *LANGUAGES:* Spanish.

P. G. DE CASTRO ANDREWS, born Las Palmas de Gran Canaria, Spain, December 4, 1966. *Education:* University of Madrid School of Law (LL.B., 1991); University of Kent (BA, English Law). *LANGUAGES:* Spanish and English.

MERCEDES DUCH, born Madrid, Spain, May 28, 1965. *Education:* University of San Pablo School of Law (LL.B., 1990). *LANGUAGES:* Spanish, English and French.

JOSE LUIS BENITEZ, born Malaga, Spain, January 16, 1943. *Education:* University of Madrid School of Law (LL.B., 1969). *Member:* Spanish Maritime Law Association. *LANGUAGES:* Spanish.

ESTHER ZARZA, born Madrid, Spain, August 16, 1967. *Education:* University of Madrid School of Law (LL.B., 1990); University of Wales, College of Cardiff (LL.M., 1991). *LANGUAGES:* Spanish and English.

MARIA DOLORES PERTEJO, born Lugo, Spain, August 2, 1967. *Education:* University of San Pablo (CEU); University of Wales, College of Cardiff (LL.M., 1991). *LANGUAGES:* Spanish, English and Greek.

MARTIN & MAYNADIER

C. RAIMUNDO FERNANDEZ VILLAVERDE, 30
28003 MADRID, SPAIN
Telephone: 34-1-535-37-64; 34-1-535-38-07
Telefax: 34-1-554-73-91

Paris, France Office: 198, Avenue Victor Hugo, 75116. Telephone: (33) (1) 45.04.84.84. Telefax: (33) (1) 45.04.87.22.
New York, New York Office: 324 East 51st Street, 10022. Telephone: (212) 754-3390. Telefax: (212) 754-3397.

General Spanish, European Community and International Corporate, Commercial, Financial and Tax Practice. Mergers, Acquisitions, Joint Ventures, Corporate Restructurings and Reorganizations, Intellectual Property Rights, Trademark and Technology Transfers, Real Estate, Banking and Trusts and Estates. Litigation and Arbitration.

MEMBERS OF FIRM

FRANÇOIS MARTIN, born Paris, France, March 28, 1935; admitted, 1958, Paris; Licensed Legal Consultant, New York (Not admitted in Spain). *Education:* University of Paris (Licence en Droit, 1958; D.E.S. Economie Politique; D.E.S. Sciences Politiques; D.E.S. Droit Public); Institut des Sciences Politiques de Paris; Centre de Perfectionnement dans l'Administration des Affaires (C.P.A.; Diplôme, 1971). Member, Board of Trustees, University of Paris-Sorbonne, 1989—. *Member:* Confédération Nationale des Avocats; Union Internationale des Avocats (President, 1985-1987); Association of the Bar of the City of New York; American Bar Association (Member, Section on International Law and Practice). *LANGUAGES:* French and English. *PRACTICE AREAS:* Mergers and Acquisitions; Joint Ventures; Corporate Restructuring and Reorganization; Takeovers.

ALAIN MAYNADIER, born Limoges, France, April 8, 1946; admitted, 1968, Paris; 1989, Madrid. *Education:* University of Poitiers (Licence en Droit, 1968); University of Paris (Doctorat d'Etat en Droit, 1977); Institut des Hautes Etudes d'Amérique Latine. Recipient: Laureat du Concours Général des Facultés de Droit de France, 1966; Premier Prix de Droit International Privé de la Faculté de Droit de Poitiers, 1968. Professor of Contract Law, Faculté Autonome de Paris, 1972-1978. Lecturer in Private International Law, Faculté de Droit de Nanterre, France, 1969. Lecturer, Universidad Trias de Bes de Barcelona, 1985. *Member:* Confédération Na-

(This Listing Continued)

tionale des Avocats; Union Internationale des Avocats. *LANGUAGES:* French, English and Spanish. *PRACTICE AREAS:* Intellectual Property Rights; Trademarks and Technology Transfers; Banking; Contracts; Licensing and Distribution.

FRANÇOISE NAMIN-MARTIN, born Paris, France, May 14, 1933; admitted, 1958, Paris (Not admitted in Spain). *Education:* Institut des Sciences Politiques de Paris (1952-1953); University of Paris (Licence en Droit, 1958). *Member:* Confédération Nationale des Avocats. *LANGUAGES:* French and English. *PRACTICE AREAS:* Litigation; Contracts; Family Law; Trusts and Estates; Franchising.

ASSOCIATE

MARIO CELAYA, born Madrid, Spain, December 7, 1958; admitted, 1989, Madrid. *Education:* Paris University (Licence en Droit, Maîtrise en Droit Communautaire, D.E.A. en Droit Communautaire, 1983); Institut d'Etudes Politiques de Paris (1983). *LANGUAGES:* Spanish, French, English. *PRACTICE AREAS:* European Community and International Corporate Contracts; Trademarks and Technology Transfers.

Languages: Spanish, English and French

MARTINEZ LAGE & ASOCIADOS

Established in 1985

SERRANO, 25
28001 MADRID, SPAIN
Telephone: 34-1-435 84 83
Fax: 34-1-577 37 74

Administrative Law, Antitrust and Trade Regulation, Arbitration and Mediation, Banks and Banking, Broadcasting, Business Law, Commercial Law, Communications and Media, Company Law, Contracts, Copyrights, Corporate Law, Entertainment and the Arts, Environmental Law, European Community Law, Intellectual Property, Mergers, Acquisitions and Divestitures, Real Estate, Sports, Taxation, Telecommunications.

MEMBERS OF FIRM

SANTIAGO MARTINEZ LAGE, born 1946. *Education:* Madrid University (Certificates for Advanced International Studies and Studies of the European Community, Lawyer). Supernumerary Member, Spanish Diplomatic Corps.; Former Chief Legal Counsel at the Office of the Secretary of State for Relations with the European Community. Editor, Gaceta Jurídica de la CE y de la Competencia (EC and Competition Law Gazette). Secretary General, Spanish Society for the Study of European Law. FIDE (Former Secretary General, International Federation for European Law).

RAFAEL ALLENDESALAZAR CORCHO, born 1960. *Education:* Madrid University (Certificated in Advanced European Studies from the European College, Lawyer); London Polytechnic, (European Business Law and International Law). Subeditor, EC Law Gazette.

ERNESTO VALLEJO LOBETE, born 1962. *Education:* Navarra University (Certificate in Advanced European Studies, Lawyer); ULB, Brussels ICADE (Master's Degree, Business Tax Advisor). Supernumerary Member, Legal of the EC Court of Justice. Chief Subeditor, EC Law Gazette.

JAVIER VIAS ALONSO, born 1959. *Education:* Universidad Autóde Madrid, Paris University (Certificate on EC Law, Lawyer). Senior Subeditor, EC Law Gazette. Member, Steering Committee of the Spanish Society for the Study of European Law.

JAIME PÉREZ-BUSTAMANTE KÖSTER, born 1964. *Education:* Universidad Autónoma de Madrid; Brussels Free University (Master's Degree in European Law, Lawyer). Subeditor, EC Law Gazette. Member, Competition Defence Committee of the Spanish Business Confederation C.E.O.E.

ANTONIO MARTINEZ SANCHEZ, born 1966. *Education:* Universidad Autónoma de Madrid; ULB, Brussels (Special Master's Degree, European Law, Lawyer). Chief Subeditor, EC Law Gazette.

Languages: Spanish, English, French and German.

DESPACHO MELCHOR DE LAS HERAS ABOGADOS

Established in 1960

JOSÉ ABASCAL, 58

28003 MADRID, SPAIN

Telephone: 4421077

Cable Address: "LEGISPANIA"

Telex: 42297 LEGE E

Telefax: 4426045

General Practice, Foreign Investments, Banking and Financial Law, Corporate, International Transactions, EEC Law, Administrative, Taxation, License and Technical Assistance Agreements, Labor, Litigations.

FOUNDER OF FIRM

D. ANTONIO MELCHOR DE LAS HERAS died August 1986.

MEMBERS OF FIRM

DR. JOSÉ LUIS LÓPEZ SÁNCHEZ, born Córdoba, Spain, March 26, 1935; admitted, 1961, Spain. *Education:* University of Madrid. *LANGUAGES:* English, French and Spanish.

DR. VÍCTOR M. CARRASCAL FELGUEROSO, born Madrid, Spain, October 24, 1930; admitted, 1957, Spain. *Education:* University of Madrid. *LANGUAGES:* English, French and Spanish.

DR. FERNANDO SATRÚSTEGUI AZNAR, born Madrid, Spain, March 1, 1942; admitted, 1967, Spain. *Education:* University of Madrid; University of Southern California, Los Angeles. *LANGUAGES:* English and Spanish.

DR. JESÚS M. MELCHOR SANTAOLALLA, born Madrid, Spain, December 26, 1950; admitted, 1972, Spain. *Education:* University of Madrid. *LANGUAGES:* English, French and Spanish.

DR. RAFAEL SUÁREZ DE LEZO CRUZ-CONDE, born Córdoba, Spain, April 14, 1954; admitted, 1978, Spain. *Education:* University of Deusto, Bilbao. *LANGUAGES:* English and Spanish.

DR. JOSÉ LUIS ANTÓN SUANZES, born Madrid, Spain, February 11, 1955; admitted, 1980, Spain. *Education:* University of Madrid. *LANGUAGES:* English and Spanish.

ASSOCIATES

DR. LUIS RUIZ-JIMÉNEZ CABALLO, born Madrid, Spain, January 7, 1937; admitted, 1972, Spain. *Education:* University of Madrid. *LANGUAGES:* English, French and Spanish.

DR. RAFAEL ORTIZ DE SOLÓRZANO CUBILLO, born Madrid, Spain, September 9, 1957; admitted, 1983, Spain. *Education:* University of Madrid. *LANGUAGES:* English and Spanish.

DR. ALFREDO SANFELIZ MEZQUITA, born La Coruña, Spain, March 28, 1962; admitted, 1986, Spain. *Education:* University of Madrid. *LANGUAGES:* English and Spanish.

DR. MARIANO BAUTISTA SAGÜES, born Madrid, Spain, June 5, 1963; admitted, 1986, Spain. *Education:* University of Comillas. *LANGUAGES:* English, French and Spanish.

DR. PEDRO JIMENEZ-POYATO PEREZ, born Córdoba, Spain, July 3, 1957; admitted, 1986, Spain. *Education:* University of Madrid. *LANGUAGES:* English and Spanish.

DR. GRACIA SAINZ MUÑOZ, born Madrid, Spain, May 27, 1956; admitted, 1980, Spain. *Education:* University of Madrid. *LANGUAGES:* English and Spanish.

DR. CARLOS PEÑA BOADA, born Madrid, Spain, June 17, 1959; admitted, 1987, Spain. *Education:* University of Madrid; Provence University (Master Maritime Law Aix). *LANGUAGES:* English, French and Spanish.

DR. PILAR MELCHOR SANTAOLALLA, born Madrid, Spain, November 6, 1953; admitted, 1987, Spain. *Education:* University of Madrid. *LANGUAGES:* French, English and Spanish.

DR. MARTA GIL DE BIEDMA SALMONES, born Madrid, Spain, March 17, 1965; admitted, 1987, Spain. *Education:* University of Madrid. *LANGUAGES:* English, French and Spanish.

DR. JAVIER CARRASCAL SATRÚSTEGUI, born Madrid, Spain, October 24, 1962; admitted, 1987, Spain. *Education:* University of Madrid. *LANGUAGES:* English and Spanish.

(This Listing Continued)

PAZ PUIG DE LA BELLACASA AZNAR, born Madrid, Spain, February 20, 1964; admitted, 1989, Spain. *Education:* University of Madrid. *LANGUAGES:* English, French, Italian and Spanish.

INMACULADA LOPEZ PERICAS, born Madrid, Spain, October 25, 1966; admitted, 1989, Spain. *Education:* University of Madrid. *LANGUAGES:* English and Spanish.

JESUS ALMOGUERA GARCIA, born Madrid, Spain, January 21, 1964; admitted, 1990, Spain. *Education:* ICADE - Universidad Pontificia Comillas", Madrid (LL.M., 1987 and M.B.A., 1988); College of Europe, Bruges (Diploma in Advanced European Legal Studies, 1989). "Laureat" - Lawyer of the Commission of the European Communities (Open Competition of 1989). *LANGUAGES:* Spanish, English and French.

ALFREDO LAFITA TORRES, born Madrid, Spain, January 6, 1967; admitted, 1993, Spain. *Education:* University of Madrid (I.C.A.D.E.). *LANGUAGES:* English and Spanish.

ELENA ARROYO BOTANA, born Madrid, January 15, 1963; admitted, 1992. *Education:* University of Madrid. *LANGUAGES:* English and Spanish.

JUAN JOSÉ GONZÁLEZ RAMIREZ, born Tarazona (Zaragoza), Spain, April 26, 1963. *Education:* University of Navarra. *LANGUAGES:* English and Spanish.

JUAN GUERRERO-BURGOS Y PEREIRO, born Madrid, Spain, October 30, 1955. *Education:* University of Madrid (CEU). *LANGUAGES:* English, French and Spanish.

OF COUNSEL

DR. ANTONIO MARÍA MELCHOR SANTAOLALLA, born Madrid, Spain; admitted, 1974, Spain. *Education:* University of Madrid. Former Counsel to the Spanish State, 1973-1983. *LANGUAGES:* English, French and Spanish.

REPRESENTATIVE CLIENTS: National Westminster Bank; CITIBANK; Bank of Montreal; Banco Central; Banco de Santander; Samsonite; Spencer & Stuart; Gates Rubber Co,; BASS; Armstrong Equipment; American Express; Mitsubishi Leasing; Merrill Lynch, Pierce, Fenner & Smith; Phillips Petroleum Co.; Buhler Miag, S.A.; Holderbank; Honeywell Bull; Renault; British Leyland; Eaton Limited; Polaroid; Pfizer; Schering Plough; L'Air Liquide; John Laing Construction LTD.; Sulzer España, S.A.; Bahlsen International, A.G.

MEMBRILLERA & RODRIGUEZ MOLNAR

Bufetes Asociados

Established in 1993

VELAZQUEZ, 78-5° IZQ

28001 MADRID, SPAIN

Telephone: (34-1) 431 67 95

Telefax: (34-1) 575 81 90

Barcelona, Spain Office: Avenida Diagonal, 419 - 2°, 1ª, 08008 Barcelona. Telephone: (34-3) 416 17 20/11 91. Fax: (34-3) 416 10 38.

General International Practice, EEC, Foreign Investments, Real Estate, Corporate, Commercial, Acquisitions, Industrial and Intellectual Property, Commercial Litigation, Environmental and Telecommunications.

FIRM PROFILE: Membrillera & Rodriquez Molnar was established in 1993 as an association between the Madrid based firm of Rodriquez Molnar & Asociados (established in 1984) and the Barcelona Law Office of Mr. Rafael G. de Membrillera (established in (1976). The client base is substantially European and North American in nature.

SENIOR PARTNER

HÉCTOR RODRIGUEZ MOLNAR, born Buenos Aires, Argentina, November 25, 1950; admitted, 1974, Argentina; 1978, Spain. *Education:* Catholic University of Argentina (LL.B., 1973); Universidad Complutense de Madrid (LL.B., 1977); International School of Comparative Law, Strasbourg (EEC Law, 1979); University of Pennsylvania (LL.M., 1981). *Member:* Madrid, Zaragoza and Bilbao Bar Association; International Bar Association; American Foreign Law Association; International Council of Environmental Law (ICEL); Spanish Environmental Law Association. *LANGUAGES:* Spanish, English and French. *PRACTICE AREAS:* International; Corporate; Foreign Investment; Environmental.

(This Listing Continued)

MEMBRILLERA & RODRIGUEZ MOLNAR *Bufetes Asociados, Madrid—Continued*

ASSOCIATE

BEGOÑA GONZALEZ DEL TANAGO RODRIGUEZ, born Madrid, Spain, January 10, 1966; admitted, 1991, Spain. *Education:* Universidad Complutense de Madrid (Licenciado, 1989); Université de Droit, d'Economie et de Sciences Sociales de Paris, Paris 2 (Diplôme d'Etudes Approfondies de Droit Communautaire, 1990). *Member:* Madrid Bar Association. *LANGUAGES:* Spanish, English and French. *PRACTICE AREAS:* Corporate.

OF COUNSEL

FRANCISCO GRACIA CEBOLLA, born Zaragoza, Spain, July 29, 1940; admitted, 1967, Spain. *Education:* University of Zaragoza (LL.B., 1963). *Member:* Madrid and Zaragoza Bar Associations. *LANGUAGES:* Spanish. *PRACTICE AREAS:* Taxation.

BUFETE MULLERAT & ROCA

VELÁZQUEZ, 94
28006 MADRID, SPAIN
Telephone: (341) 578 17 62
Telex: 47089
Fax: (341) 575 13 86; (341) 575 27 80

Barcelona Office: Passeig de Gràcia, 81, 08008. Telephone: (343) 487 11 44. Telex: 51575. Fax: (343) 487 96 32; (343) 487 13 32.

Other Barcelona Office: Passeig de Gràcia, 122, 08008. Telephone: (343) 237 84 46. Fax: (343) 237 86 30.

Lisbon Office (Correspondent firm): Rua Rodrigo da Fonseca 149-4, 1000 Lisbon. Telephone: (3511) 387 64 04. Fax: (3511) 385 5310.

Banking and financial law, EC law, General corporate and commercial law, International commercial arbitration, International construction, Litigation, Tax law, Intellectual property, Insolvency and bankruptcy, Administrative and public law, Environmental law, Zoning law.

PARTNERS

JAVIER DIAZ DE BUSTAMANTE, born Madrid, 1957; admitted, 1981, Madrid. *Education:* Law Faculty of the Madrid University; University of Wales (Maritime Law Master, 1982). *Member:* Madrid Bar Association; Maritime Law Spanish Association. *LANGUAGES:* Spanish and English.

FERNANDO LOPEZ-OROZCO, born Madrid, 1959; admitted, 1983, Madrid. *Education:* Law Faculty of the Madrid University (1982). *Author:* Spanish Chapter of "A Practitioner's Guide to European Corporate Insolvency Law," 1992. Collaborator to the Business Law Commission of the AIJA. *Member:* Madrid Bar Association. *LANGUAGES:* Spanish and English.

ENRIQUE SANZ, born Madrid, 1957; admitted, 1983, Madrid. *Education:* Law Faculty of the Madrid University (1980); Companies Administration and Management Institute, ICADE (Diploma, 1983; Diploma on Financing of Ships, 1984; Master in Maritime Business, 1987; Average Adjuster, 1987). Postgraduate Courses, Bank of Spain, Joint Stock Companies and crisis of companies and suspension of payments, bankruptcy, 1984-1986. Author: "Banking Law in Spain," 1992. *Member:* Madrid Bar Association; Maritime Law Spanish Association; UNCTAO-IMO Mixed Intergovernment Group of Experts im Maritime Privileges and Mortgages. *LANGUAGES:* Spanish, French and English.

ASSOCIATES

ROMAN MARTINEZ DE ARAGON, born Madrid, 1958; admitted, 1984, Madrid. *Education:* Law Faculty of the Madrid University (1983). *LANGUAGES:* Spanish, French and English.

F. JAVIER GARCIA-CAMACHO, born Madrid, 1959; admitted, 1990, Madrid. *Education:* Law Faculty of the Madrid University (1981); Universidad Politécnica de Comillas, (Master, Fiscal Audit, 1990). *Member:* Madrid Bar Association. *LANGUAGES:* Spanish and English.

EMILIO ALONSO, born Madrid, 1959; admitted, 1985, Madrid. *Education:* Law Faculty of Madrid University (1982). European Patent Attorney. Lecturer, Intellectual Property, Instituto de Empresa, Madrid. *Member:* Madrid Bar Association; Institute of Professional Representatives before the European Patent Office; Spanish Group of the International Association for the Protection of Industrial Property (AIPPI). *LANGUAGES:* Spanish, English and Italian.

JOSÉ PEÑA, born Madrid, 1962; admitted, 1985, Madrid. *Education:* Law Faculty of University of Madrid (1980-1985). *Member:* Madrid Bar Association. *LANGUAGES:* Spanish and English.

PATRICIA MANCA, born Madrid, 1966; admitted, 1991, Madrid. *Education:* Law Faculty of the Madrid University (1990). *Member:* Madrid Bar Association. *LANGUAGES:* Spanish, French and English.

Mª DOLORES GARAYALDE, born Madrid, 1965; admitted, 1992, Madrid. *Education:* Law Faculty of the Madrid University (1988). *Member:* Madrid Bar Association. *LANGUAGES:* Spanish, French and English.

MARIA DOLORES BUENO, born Madrid, 1967; admitted, 1993. *Education:* Law Faculty of Madrid University (1991); Madrid University (Doctorate in Civil Law, 1992-1994). *Member:* Madrid Bar Association. *LANGUAGES:* Spanish and English.

(For Complete Biographical Data on all Personnel, see professional biographies at Barcelona, Spain).

NAUTA DUTILH

Attorneys, Civil Law Notaries, Tax Advisers

HERMOSILLA 29-1°
E-28001 MADRID, SPAIN
Telephone: (34-1) 4359764
Telecopier: (34-1) 4359815

MEMBERS OF FIRM ATTORNEYS AT LAW

ERLEND MENSING, born 1947; admitted, 1975, The Netherlands (Not admitted in Spain). *Education:* Amsterdam University.

RAFA ALONSO, born 1961; admitted, 1984, Spain. *Education:* Barcelona University.

MEMBER OF FIRM TAX ADVISER

EDGAR A. BROOD, born 1956. *Education:* Rotterdam and Tilburg Universities.

ASSOCIATES ATTORNEYS AT LAW

FERNANDO GONZÁLEZ, born 1960; admitted, 1985, Spain. *Education:* Madrid University.

ANGEL L. SÁNCHEZ, born 1959; admitted, 1988, Spain. *Education:* Madrid University.

(For Complete Biographical Data on all Personnel, see Professional Biographies at Rotterdam, The Netherlands)

RAMON C. PELAYO ABOGADOS

Established in 1981

P° PINTOR ROSALES, 20-1°
28008 MADRID, SPAIN
Telephone: 34-1-5477184
Fax: 34-1-5416318

Marbella, Spain Office: C/Maria Auxiliadora, 2. Telephone: 34-52-773154. Telefax: 34-52-776208.

General Practice, Commercial and Company Law, Administrative Law, EEC and International Law, Foreign Investment, Competition Law, Industrial Property Law, Arbitration, Litigation, Taxation and Constitutional Law.

FIRM PROFILE: One partner firm, headed by a former State Lawyer and specialized mainly in Administrative and Commercial matters. Our clients are both national and international medium size companies and we have corresponding law firms in all EEC countries.

RAMON C. PELAYO, born 1954; admitted, 1979, Madrid and Málaga. *Education:* Universidad Complutense de Madrid, Centro de Estudios Universitarios (Law Degree, 1976). State Lawyer, 1978. Professor: Business Law, Málaga University, 1984-1985; Instituto de Empresa, Madrid, 1986-1987; Competition Law, CEU, 1992. *Member:* Sociedad Española de Arbitraje; Corte Civil y Mercantil de Arbitraje. *LANGUAGES:* Spanish and English. *PRACTICE AREAS:* Business; Administrative; Constitutional; Arbitration; Litigation.

(This Listing Continued)

ASSOCIATES

ALEXIS MORALES BULJAN, born 1958; admitted, 1983, Málaga. *Education:* University of Granada (Law Degree, 1983). *LANGUAGES:* Spanish, English and Italian. *PRACTICE AREAS:* Business; Real Estate; Family Law.

ANTONIO MARIA ALCALA DE LIMA, born 1955; admitted, 1982, Málaga. *Education:* Universidad Complutense de Madrid (Law Degree, 1979). *LANGUAGES:* Spanish and English. *PRACTICE AREAS:* Business Law; Real Estate Law; Taxation.

CONCEPCION PELAYO, born 1949; admitted, 1983, Madrid. *Education:* Universidad Complutense de Madrid (Law Degree, 1983). *LANGUAGES:* Spanish. *PRACTICE AREAS:* Procedural Law; Civil Law.

Mª DEL PILAR BLANCO MARTIN, born 1961; admitted, 1989, Madrid. *Education:* Universidad Autónoma de Madrid (Law Degree, 1984). Building and Estate Manager Licence, 1984. Real Estate Agent Licence, 1989. *Member:* Vice-Secretary of the Real Estate Agents, Madrid. *LANGUAGES:* Spanish and English. *PRACTICE AREAS:* Business Law; Civil Law; Real Estate Law.

JOSE Mª BUXEDA, born 1965; admitted, 1988, Barcelona; 1991, Madrid. *Education:* Instituto Europeo de Derecho y Economía, Barcelona (Law Degree, 1988); Institut d'Etudes Européennes, Brussels (Special Degree, EEC Law, 1990). Professor, Competition Law, CEU, 1992. *Member:* International Young Lawyers Association (A.I.J.A.). *LANGUAGES:* Spanish, English, French and Catalan. *PRACTICE AREAS:* Business International; EEC Law.

TERESA NIETO HERNANDEZ, born 1967; admitted, 1990, Madrid. *Education:* Universidad Autónoma de Madrid (Law Degree, 1990); CEU (Master in Competition Law, 1993). *LANGUAGES:* Spanish and English. *PRACTICE AREAS:* Business Law; Civil Law.

Languages: Spanish, English, French, Italian and Catalan

BUFETE M. VEGA PENICHET

ALCALÁ, 115
28009 MADRID, SPAIN
Telephone: (341) 431-55-00 (10 Lines)
Cable Address: "Lawyer"
Telex: 22714 (Mavep E); 46125 (Mavep E)
Telefax: (Groups 2 and 3) (341) 431-5938/276-0434

General Practice. Civil, Mercantile, Banking, Mining, Foreign Investment, Taxes, Labor, Corporation, Real Estate, International, E.E.C. and Entertainment Law.

FIRM PROFILE: The firm was founded in 1962 and provides full legal services, other than criminal or family cases, with great experience and complete dedication, with a professional staff of 18 lawyers and three paralegals assisted by a clerical staff of about 20 persons.

MEMBERS OF FIRM

MANUEL VEGA PENICHET (1918-1983).

JOAQUÍN DE ROJAS, born 1916; admitted, 1966, Spain. Doctor in Law, University of Havana, Cuba, 1940; Attorney at Law, University of Salamanca, Spain. *LANGUAGES:* English and Spanish. *PRACTICE AREAS:* Commercial Law; Banking Law.

JOAQUIN MUÑOZ, born 1929; admitted, 1958, Spain. Attorney at Law, University of Madrid. *LANGUAGES:* English and Spanish. *PRACTICE AREAS:* Foreign Investment; Regulatory; Administrative Law.

MANUEL GUASCH, born 1942; admitted, 1976, Spain. Attorney at Law, University of Deusto, Spain. *LANGUAGES:* English, French and Spanish. *PRACTICE AREAS:* Commercial Law.

FRANCISCO M. MONTESINOS, born 1928; admitted, 1954, Spain. Attorney at Law, University of Granada. *LANGUAGES:* Spanish. *PRACTICE AREAS:* Civil; Labor Law.

PILAR MOLINA GOMEZ-ARNAU, born 1953; admitted, 1979, Spain. Attorney at Law, University of Madrid. *LANGUAGES:* English and Spanish. *PRACTICE AREAS:* Tax Law.

JORGE VEGA-PENICHET, born 1956; admitted, 1980, Spain. Attorney at Law, University of Madrid. *LANGUAGES:* English and Spanish. *PRACTICE AREAS:* Corporate Law.

(This Listing Continued)

IGNACIO VEGA-PENICHET, born 1955; admitted, 1981, Spain. Attorney at Law, University of Madrid. *LANGUAGES:* English and Spanish. *PRACTICE AREAS:* Commercial; Mining Law.

LUIS VEGA-PENICHET, born 1958; admitted, 1983, Spain. Attorney at Law, University of Madrid. *LANGUAGES:* English and Spanish. *PRACTICE AREAS:* Civil; European Community Law.

ENRIQUE VEGA-PENICHET, born 1953; admitted, 1984, Spain. Attorney at Law, University of Madrid. *LANGUAGES:* English and Spanish. *PRACTICE AREAS:* Litigation; Administrative Law.

ASSOCIATES

FRANCISCO PANIZO, born 1944; admitted, 1972, Spain. Attorney at Law, University of Oviedo. *LANGUAGES:* English and Spanish. *PRACTICE AREAS:* Corporate Law.

CLEMENTE VARCARCEL, born 1963; admitted, 1987, Spain. Attorney at Law, University of Madrid. *LANGUAGES:* English and Spanish. *PRACTICE AREAS:* Civil Law.

MARISA VARGAS-MACHUCA, born 1964; admitted, 1987, Spain. Attorney at Law, University of Madrid. *LANGUAGES:* English, French and Spanish. *PRACTICE AREAS:* Administrative Law.

JUAN VEGA-PENICHET, born 1960; admitted, 1989, Spain. Attorney at Law, University of Madrid. *LANGUAGES:* Spanish and English. *PRACTICE AREAS:* Corporate Law.

MARIA DEL VALLE GARCIA DE NOVALES, born 1966; admitted, 1990, Spain. Attorney at Law, University of Seville. *LANGUAGES:* Spanish, English and French. *PRACTICE AREAS:* Commercial Law.

CRISTINA ECED, born 1964; admitted, 1991, Spain. Attorney at Law, University of Madrid. *LANGUAGES:* Spanish, English and French. *PRACTICE AREAS:* Labor Law.

OF COUNSEL

VICENTE CUELLO CALON, born 1926; admitted, 1954, Spain. Attorney at Law, University of Madrid. *LANGUAGES:* Spanish. *PRACTICE AREAS:* Litigation.

JOSE CARDONA GARCIA, born 1938; admitted, 1975, Spain. Attorney at Law, University of Murcia. *LANGUAGES:* Spanish. *PRACTICE AREAS:* Labor Law.

REPRESENTATIVE CLIENTS: AMF (U.S.); Asea Brown Boveri A.B. (Sw); Ares Serono N.V. (HL); Bank of America (U.S.); Banque NMB Interunion (Gr.); Bethlehem Steel (U.S.); Black & Decker (Belgium); Bovis Ltd. (U.K.); CBS Inc. (U.S.); Central Soya Co., Inc. (U.S.); Computervision (U.S.); Eagle-Picher Industries (U.S.); Enso Gutzait OY (Fin.); Export Credit Guarantee Department (U.K.); Export Development Corp. (Canada); Exxon Corp. (U.S.); F.M.C. (U.S.); Forte PLC (U.S.); General Motors Corp. (U.S.); Lorimar-Telepictures (U.S.); Marsh & McLennan (U.S.); Mohawk Data Sciences-MDS (U.S.); Nissho Iwai Corp. (Japan); Nokia (Finland); Playtex Apparel (U.S.); Recognition Equipment Inc. (U.S.); R.J. Reynolds Tobacco (U.S.); Sony Music Entertainment (U.S.); Sumitomo Corp. (Japan); The Boeing Co (U.S.); Times Mirror (U.S.); Unisys Corp. (U.S.); U.S. Playing Card Corp. (U.S.); Western Union International Inc. (U.S.); Westinghouse Electric Co. (U.S.).

PRICE WATERHOUSE JURIDICO Y FISCAL S.L.

PASEO DE LA CASTELLANA, 43
28046 MADRID, SPAIN
Telephone: (34-1) 3083500
Telefax: (34-1) 3083566; 3083571
Telex: 42164 (PWCO E)

Barcelona Office: Torre Catalunya, Avda. de Roma 2 y 4 - 08014.
 Telephone: (34-3) 4231581. Telecopier: (34-3) 4243801.
Bilbao Office: Avda. de Zugazarte, 8 - 48930 Las Arenas (Vizcaya).
 Telephone: (34-4) 4640032. Telecopier: (34-4) 4640693.
Sevilla Office: Avda. de la Republica Argentina 13 AAC - 41011.
 Telephone: (34-5) 4275400. Telecopier: (34-5) 4280507.
Valencia Office: Edificio Gran Via. Gran Via Marqués del Turia, 49 - 46005. Telephone: (34-6) 3527017. Telecopier: (34-6) 3518657.

Local and International Business Law and Taxation. Corporate and Commercial Law, Labour and Employment Law, Banking and Financing Law, M&A, EEC Law, Litigation, Property Law, Civil Law. Corporate and Individual Taxation, International Taxation, VAT, US Taxes, Customs, Indirect Taxes.

(This Listing Continued)

PRICE WATERHOUSE JURIDICO Y FISCAL S.L., Madrid—Continued

FIRM PROFILE: The firm is a multiprofessional law firm and offers a full range of legal and tax services to both national and international clients. It is a member of Correspondent Law Firms of Price Waterhouse EEIG and cooperate with member firms and Price Waterhouse firms to render legal services throughout Europe, where appropriate, on a multidisciplinary basis. The firm has approximately 100 associates.

MEMBERS OF FIRM

JOSE LUIS BEOTAS, born Avila, Spain, June 22, 1953; admitted, 1983. *Education:* Universidad Compultense, Madrid (Law Degree, 1976). Government Attorney, 1980-1985. Legal Adviser for the Public Works Ministry. *Member:* Madrid Bar Association. *LANGUAGES:* Spanish and French. *PRACTICE AREAS:* Civil Law; Commercial Law; Litigation.

RAFAEL COLLANTES, born Cadiz, Spain, July 9, 1950. *Education:* University of Sevilla (Law Degree, 1974). *LANGUAGES:* Spanish and English. *PRACTICE AREAS:* Tax and Commercial Law.

TOMÁS FERNÁNDEZ DE PINEDO, born Madrid, Spain, October 1, 1945; admitted, 1971. *Education:* University of Barcelona and Madrid (Law Degree, 1970); IESE, Madrid (M.B.A., 1978). *Member:* Madrid Bar Association. *LANGUAGES:* Spanish and English. *PRACTICE AREAS:* Commercial Law and M&A.

CESAR RODRIGUEZ, born Madrid, Spain, December 10, 1950. *Education:* ICADE (Law Degree, 1974). *LANGUAGES:* Spanish and English. *PRACTICE AREAS:* Tax and Commercial Law.

JOSE MARIA TAJADURA, born Burgos, Spain, August 28, 1948. *Education:* ICADE (Law Degree, 1971). *LANGUAGES:* Spanish and English. *PRACTICE AREAS:* Tax and Commercial Law.

AGUSTIN ANTUNEZ, born Montevideo, Paraguay, December 19, 1945. *Education:* University of Paris IV, Sorbonne ("Expert comptable," France, Latin American Studies, 1976). *LANGUAGES:* Spanish, English and French. *PRACTICE AREAS:* M&A; International Taxation; Transfer Pricing.

SIRO ARIAS, born Barcelona, Spain, January 29, 1951. *Education:* Universidad de Barcelona (Economics Degree, 1973). Lecturer in International Tax Planning. Professor, colaborador en la Cátedra Hacienda Pública de la Facultad de Económicas. *LANGUAGES:* Spanish, Catalan, English and French. *PRACTICE AREAS:* Tax Law.

JOSE MARIA ORTEGA, born July 9, 1948. *Education:* Economics Degree. Tax Inspector. *LANGUAGES:* Spanish and English. *PRACTICE AREAS:* Corporate and Individual Taxation; VAT.

ASSOCIATES

PAULINO BORRALLO, born Madrid, January 11, 1961. *Education:* CEU, San Pablo, Madrid (Law Degree, 1985). *Member:* Madrid Bar Association. *LANGUAGES:* Spanish and English. *PRACTICE AREAS:* Labour Law; Litigation and Commercial Law.

ABELARDO BRACHO, born Huelva, Spain, June 29, 1958. *Education:* Universidad de Sevilla (Law Degree, 1982); Université Libre de Bruxelles (Licence en Droit Européen). *Member:* Sevilla Bar Association. *LANGUAGES:* Spanish, French and English. *PRACTICE AREAS:* Commercial and Labour Law.

MARTA CASAS, born Terrassa, Barcelona, Spain; June 27, 1959; admitted, 1983. *Education:* Universidad Autónoma de Barcelona (Law Degree, 1982). *Member:* Barcelona Bar Association. *LANGUAGES:* Spanish, Catalan, English and French. *PRACTICE AREAS:* Corporate Law; Real Estate Law; Civil Law.

LUIS COMAS, born Barcelona, Spain, October 28, 1960. *Education:* University of Barcelona; Harvard Law University (PIL); Université Libre de Bruxelles (Licence Speciale en Droit Europeen). *Member:* Barcelona Bar Association. *LANGUAGES:* Spanish, Catalan, English and French. *PRACTICE AREAS:* International Business Law; Corporate Law; European Community Law.

PEDRO HUERTA, born Madrid, Spain, September 27, 1959. *Education:* Universidad Complutense, Madrid (Law Degree). *Member:* Madrid Bar Association. *LANGUAGES:* Spanish and English. *PRACTICE AREAS:* Corporate and Commercial Law; M&A.

JAVIER MACEIRA, born El Ferrol, Spain, August 21, 1962. *Education:* Universidad Pontificia de Comillas ICADE, Madrid (Law Degree,

(This Listing Continued)

1986). *Member:* Madrid Bar Association. *LANGUAGES:* Spanish, English and French. *PRACTICE AREAS:* Banking and Financial Law.

JOSE LUIS MARTIN BALLESTERO, born Bilbao, Spain, March 24, 1961. *Education:* University of Deusto (Law Degree, 1984). *Member:* Madrid Bar Association. *LANGUAGES:* Spanish and English. *PRACTICE AREAS:* Commercial and Corporate Law.

LUIS REALES, born Barcelona, Spain, September 11, 1933. *Education:* Universidad Central de Barcelona (Law Degree). *Member:* Barcelona Bar Association; Málaga Bar Association. *LANGUAGES:* Spanish, Catalan and English. *PRACTICE AREAS:* Litigation and Insolvency.

VICTOR SAVAL, born January 20, 1959. *Education:* University of Valencia (Law Degree, 1983). *Member:* Valencia Bar Association. *LANGUAGES:* Spanish and English. *PRACTICE AREAS:* Commercial Law and Litigation.

MIGUEL TRIAS, born Barcelona, Spain, October 23, 1957; admitted, 1981. *Education:* University of Barcelona (Law Degree, 1980); ESADE (M.B.A.). Lecturer, Commercial Law and International Tax, ESADE, *Member:* Barcelona Bar Association. *LANGUAGES:* Spanish, Catalan, English and French. *PRACTICE AREAS:* Corporate Law; M&A.

SERGIO UNSAIN, born Barcelona, Spain, November, 1961; admitted, 1988. *Education:* University of Barcelona (Law Degree, 1988). *Member:* Barcelona Bar Association. *LANGUAGES:* Spanish, Catalan and English. *PRACTICE AREAS:* Litigation; Corporate Law.

MARIA VIDAL, born Madrid, Spain, June 15, 1960; admitted, 1987. *Education:* University Complutense, Madrid (Law Degree, 1983). *Member:* Barcelona Bar Association. *LANGUAGES:* Spanish and French. *PRACTICE AREAS:* Social Security; Labour Law.

PROL Y ASOCIADOS

Abogados

EDUARDO DEL PALACIO 4
28002 MADRID, SPAIN
Telephone: (34-1) 563 06 01
Fax: (34-1) 563 00 20

Barcelona, Spain Office: Enrique Granados 137-3° 1ª, 08008. Telephone: (34-3) 415.07.28. Fax: (34-3) 217.03.91.

General Practice, Banking and Financial Law, Foreign Investments, Corporate, Mergers and Acquisitions, International Transactions, Technology Law, Oil and Gas, Labour Law, Commercial Litigation and Arbitration.

MEMBERS OF FIRM

FRANCISCO G. PROL, born Madrid, Spain, September 28, 1953. *Education:* University of Madrid (Centro de Estudios Universitarios-CEU) (Law Degree, 1975). *Member:* Colegio de Abogados de Madrid; European Society for Banking and Financial Law (E.S.B.F.L.) (Founder); International Bar Association; Union Internationale Des Avocats; International Network for Technology Law. *LANGUAGES:* Spanish, French and English.

MANUEL MORENO, born Madrid, Spain, September 15, 1955. *Education:* University of Valladolid, Spain (Law Degree, 1977). *Member:* Colegio de Abogados de Madrid, Vizcaya and Vigo. *LANGUAGES:* Spanish and English.

JOSEFINA GARCIA, born Léon, Spain, July 24, 1950. *Education:* University of Madrid (Law Degree, 1985). *Member:* Colegio de Abogados de Madrid. *LANGUAGES:* Spanish and French.

JUAN MANUEL LOPEZ MOMPEAN, born Madrid, Spain, December 22, 1951. *Education:* University of Madrid (Centro de Estudios Universitarios-CEU) (Law Degree, 1973). *Member:* Colegio de Abogados de Madrid. *LANGUAGES:* Spanish and French.

ASSOCIATES

AVELINA DE LEON, born Madrid, Spain, November 4, 1962. *Education:* University of Madrid (Law Degree, 1988). *Member:* Colegio de Abogados de Barcelona. (Resident, Barcelona Office). *LANGUAGES:* Spanish, Catalan, English and French.

ANTONIO PRIETO, born Madrid, Spain, December 1, 1961. *Education:* University of Madrid (Centro de Estudios Universitarios-CEU) (Law Degree, 1984); Instituto De Empresa (Master Company Legal Advice, 1989). *Member:* Colegio de Abogados de Madrid. *LANGUAGES:* Spanish, English and French.

(This Listing Continued)

TERESA DE LA TORRE, born Santiago de Compostela, Spain, August 6, 1961. *Education:* University of Santiago de Compostela (Law Degree, 1984); Instituto de Empresa (Master Company Legal Advise, 1990). *Member:* Colegio de Abogados de Madrid. *LANGUAGES:* Spanish, English and French.

ROLDAN MARTINEZ, born Barcelona, Spain, August 6, 1965. *Education:* Central University of Barcelona (Law Degree, 1990); Instituto de Empresa (Master Company Legal Advice, 1991). *Member:* Colegio de Abogados de Barcelona and Baleares. (Resident, Barcelona Office). *LANGUAGES:* Spanish, Catalan, English and French.

L. IGNACIO ALONSO, born Madrid, Spain, February 16, 1965. *Education:* University of Comillas (ICADE), Madrid (Law Degree, 1988); Institut d'Etudes Européennes ULB, Brussels (Master European Community Law, 1991). *Member:* Colegio de Abogados de Madrid. *LANGUAGES:* Spanish, French, English and Italian.

SUSANA PERIS SOS, born Castellón, Spain, May 16, 1967. *Education:* University of Valencia (Law Degree, 1990); Master on Labour Law. Scholarship, Institute Tax Studies. *Member:* Colegio de Abogados de Madrid and Sevilla. *LANGUAGES:* Spanish, English and Catalán.

MIGUEL PELAYO MUÑOZ, born Zaragoza, Spain, January 15, 1965. *Education:* University of Madrid (Law Degree, 1988). *Member:* Colegio de Abogados de Barcelona. (Resident, Barcelona Office). *LANGUAGES:* Spanish, Catalan and English.

A list of Representative Clients and References furnished upon request.

PURROY, CANUT & DE LA VEGA

VELAZQUEZ, 11
28001 MADRID, SPAIN
Telephone: 435.50.10
Fax: 576.90.88

General Corporate Practice and Related Litigation, and Foreign Investments in Spain, including Tax, Corporate, Environmental, Labor, Banking, Real Estate and European Union Law.

PARTNERS

ANTONIO RODRIGUEZ PURROY, born Pamplona, Spain, 1964; admitted, 1990, Madrid. *Education:* University of Navarra (law degree); Business Institute (Instituto de Empresa), Madrid (LL.M.); Harvard University (C.S.S. Program). *LANGUAGES:* English and Spanish.

JUAN CANUT GUILLEN, born Madrid, Spain, 1961; admitted, 1991, Madrid. *Education:* Universidad Complutense, Madrid (law degree); University of San Diego, California (Master in Comparative Law); Universidad Pontificia de Comillas (ICADE), Madrid (diploma for graduate studies in European Community law). *LANGUAGES:* English and Spanish.

F. JAVIER DE LA VEGA JIMENEZ, born Madrid, Spain, 1967; admitted, 1990, Madrid. *Education:* Universidad Pontificia de Comillas (ICADE), Madrid (law degree and Masters in European Community Law). *LANGUAGES:* Italian, English and Spanish.

OF COUNSEL

DAVID A. VAUGHAN, born Toledo, Ohio, U.S.A., 1965; admitted, 1991, New York (Not admitted in Spain). *Education:* Bowling Green State University, Bowling Green, Ohio (B.A., cum laude); Georgetown University Law Center (J.D., cum laude). *LANGUAGES:* Spanish and English.

RAMOS & ARROYO

SERRANO 89-7°
28006 MADRID, SPAIN
Telephone: (1) 5629200
Fax: (1) 5614903

Barcelona, Spain Office: Paseo de Gracia 92 (La Pedrera), 08008. Telephone: (3) 487 11 12; (3) 215 77 11. Fax: (3) 487 35 62.

Cadiz, Spain Office: Avenida Ramón de Carranza, 20, 11006. Telephone: (56) 25 22 00. Fax: (56) 26 16 55. Telex: 76192 Hull E.

Fuengirola, Málaga, Spain Office: Córdoba, Edificio Centro Comercial Reyes, 6°B, 29640. Telephone: (5) 258 45 72; (5) 258 45 90. Fax: (5) 258 45 72.

Oviedo, Spain Office: Cimadevilla 19-2°B, 33003. Telephone: (8) 520 42 80. Fax: (8) 520 42 80.

(This Listing Continued)

Admiralty, Arbitration, Bankruptcy, Commercial, Competition, Construction, Copyright, Corporation, EEC, General Practice, Insurance, Labour, Litigation, Taxation, Trademarks & Patents and Real Estate Law.

MEMBERS OF FIRM

IGNACIO ARROYO MARTINEZ, born Bilbao, Spain, July 28, 1948; admitted, 1971, Barcelona. *Education:* University of Deusto, School of Law (LL.B., 1970); University of Bologna, Italy (Doctor of Laws, 1972); Harvard Law School (LL.M., 1975). General Editor, Yearbook Maritime Law, 1991. Author: "Spanish Code of Commerce," 6th, 1990; "Código de Legislación Bancaria," 3rd ed., 1990; "Legislación de Sociedades Mercantiles," 3rd, 1990; "Promissory Notes," 1986. Professor of Commercial Law, University of Barcelona. Member of the Board of JBLL, ETL, RDM, ADM, IFL Rev. and LMCLQ. *Member:* IBA; UIA; ILA; CMI. (Also at Barcelona, Spain Office). *LANGUAGES:* English, French, Italian, Portuguese and Spanish.

FRANCISCO RAMOS MENDEZ, born Orense, Spain, April 18, 1947; admitted, 1977, Barcelona and Madrid. *Education:* University of Santiago de Compostela, School of Law, Spain (LL.B., 1969); University of Oviedo, Spain (Doctor of Laws, 1972). Author: "Derecho Procesal Civil," 1980, 5th ed., 1992; "La Jurisdiccion Voluntaria en los Negocios de Comercio," 1978; "Las Medidas Cautelares en el Proceso Civil," 1974; "La Anotación Preventiva de Demanda," 1980; "Código Procesal Civil International," Barcelona, 1985, 2nd ed., 1991; "Arbitraje y Proceso Internacional," 1987; "El Proceso Penal," 1988, 3nd ed., 1993. Professor of Civil Procedure, University of Barcelona. Member, Commercial Panel of Arbitrators, American Arbitration Association. Member, Spanish Court of Arbitration. General Editor of Procedural Library. Editor, Justicia. *Member:* Barcelona (Member of the Board) and Madrid Bar Associations; UIA; IBA; ILA; Wissenschaftliche Vereinigung für Schiedsgerichtswesen e. V. (Also at Barcelona, Spain Office). *LANGUAGES:* Spanish, German, French, English, Italian and Portuguese.

OF COUNSEL

JOSE LUIS GARCIA GABALDON, born Madrid, Spain, April 26, 1948. *Education:* University of Madrid (Master Marine, LL.B.); University of Carlos III, Madrid (Doctor of Laws, cum laude). Professor, Commercial Law. Ex-Deputy General Director, Spanish Merchant Marine. Ex-President, Spanish EEC Commission Sea Transport. Member, Spanish Delegate UNCTAD and IMO. *LANGUAGES:* Spanish, English, French and Italian.

(For complete biographical data on all personnel, see Professional Biographies at Barcelona, Spain).

L.C. RODRIGO ABOGADOS

VELÁZQUEZ, 75 - 1ST FLOOR
28006 MADRID, SPAIN
Telephone: 435 12 44/ 435 54 12
Telex: 42360 REMM E
Telefax: 576 67 16/ 578 07 41

Lima, Peru Office: Rodrigo, Elias & Medrano. Avda. San Felipe, 758, 11. Telephone: 633232. Telex: 25622 PE LUCARO. Telefax: 637300.

Associated Offices:

London, England Office: Bomchil, Castro, Goodrich, Claro, Arosemena and Associates, New Loom House - 101 Back Church Lane - London E1 1LU. Telephone: 488 09 33. Telefax: 488 09 47.

Düsseldorf, Germany Office: Bomchil, Königsallee 92 A - P.O. Box 8508, D - 4000 Düsseldorf. Telephone: 37 0864. Telex: 8581914 WESSD. Telefax: 32 36 16.

Paris, France Office: Goodrich, Riquelme and Associates. 15 Rue Greuze, F - 75116 Paris. Telephone: 47 27 03 10. Telex: 610469 LATALOI. Telefax: 47 27 37 81.

Lisboa, Portugal Office: Barros, Sobral, Xavier e Gomes. Av. Infante Santo, 17 -8° Esq. - 1300 Lisboa. Telephone: 60 10 37. Telex 65986 INTLAW P. Telefax: 397 31 55.

Corporate Law, Banking, Company Law, Foreign Investment, Administrative Law, Taxation, Labor, Civil Law, Litigation, International Law, Insurance, Arbitration and European Community Law.

MEMBERS OF FIRM

LUIS CARLOS RODRIGO, born January 20, 1929; admitted, 1953, Lima; 1973, Madrid. *Education:* Catholic University of Peru (Lawyer, 1953; Economist, 1966); Harvard Law School International Tax Program and Graduate in Tax Studies in the Tax and Economical Studies Centre of Spain. Professor of Tax Law, Catholic University of Peru, 1963. *Member:*

(This Listing Continued)

L.C. RODRIGO ABOGADOS, Madrid—Continued

International Bar Association; Inter-American Bar Association (Vice President, X Committee of Tax Law); International Academy of Trial Lawyers; Tax Institute of America; International Commission of Jurists (Peruvian Section); Tax Advisors Association of Spain; Tax Law Association of Spain; Lima and Madrid Bar Associations. *LANGUAGES:* Spanish and English. *PRACTICE AREAS:* Taxation; Corporate Law.

CARLOS DULANTO, born March 8, 1942; admitted, 1968, Lima; 1974, Madrid. *Education:* Catholic University of Peru (Bachelor of Laws, 1967; Lawyer, 1968); University of Madrid. *Member:* International Bar Association; Lima and Madrid Bar Associations. *LANGUAGES:* Spanish and English. *PRACTICE AREAS:* Business Law; Corporate Law; Mergers and Acquisitions.

JORGE ANGELL, born August 15, 1946; admitted, 1971, Lima; 1974, Madrid. *Education:* Catholic University of Peru (Bachelor of Laws, 1971; Lawyer, 1971); University of Madrid. *Member:* International Bar Association; Lima and Madrid Bar Associations. *LANGUAGES:* Spanish and English. *PRACTICE AREAS:* Civil Law; Litigation; Insurance; Foreign Investments; International Law; Corporate Law; Arbitration.

MATEO AMICO, born December 13, 1948; admitted, 1975, Lima; 1992, Madrid. *Education:* Catholic University of Peru (Bachelor of Laws, 1974); Lawyer, 1975); Tax and Economical Studies Centre of Spain. *Member:* Lima and Madrid Bar Associations. *LANGUAGES:* Spanish and English. *PRACTICE AREAS:* Corporate Law; International Law; Trade Law.

MARTÍN ECHÁNIZ, born June 13, 1952; admitted, 1977, Madrid. *Education:* Deusto University and Graduate in Tax and Economical Studies Centre of Spain. *Member:* International Bar Association; Madrid and Valladolid Bar Associations. *LANGUAGES:* Spanish, English and French. *PRACTICE AREAS:* Taxation; Company Law; Commercial Law; Corporate Law.

ALEX ROY MORRIS, born April 8, 1955; admitted, 1979, Lima; 1990, Madrid. *Education:* Catholic University of Peru (Bachelor of Laws, 1979; Lawyer, 1979); Tax and Economical Studies Centre of Spain. *Member:* Lima and Madrid Bar Associations. *LANGUAGES:* Spanish and English. *PRACTICE AREAS:* Taxation; International Tax Planning; Corporate Law.

ASSOCIATES

MAURICIO ZAROBE, born February 27, 1958; admitted, 1983, Madrid. *Education:* University of Madrid. *Member:* Madrid Bar Association. *LANGUAGES:* Spanish, English and French. *PRACTICE AREAS:* Administrative Law; European Community Law; Foreign Investment.

MANUEL RODRÍGUEZ-PIÑERO, born May 26, 1963; admitted, 1987, Madrid. *Education:* University of Seville (Law Degree, 1986); College of Eur ope, Bruges, Belgium (Diploma of Advanced European Studies, 1987). Professor, EEC Law, I.C.A.D.E., Madrid. *Member:* Madrid Bar Association. *LANGUAGES:* Spanish, English and French. *PRACTICE AREAS:* Civil Law; Litigation; Labor; Corporate Law; European Community Law.

ANGEL BRIOSO, born November 27, 1957; admitted, 1986, Madrid. *Education:* University Complutense of Madrid. *Member:* Madrid and Ciudad Real Bar Associations. *LANGUAGES:* Spanish. *PRACTICE AREAS:* Litigation; Labor; Civil Law; Consumer Law; Products Liability.

JESUS MARIA REDONDO, born June 8, 1962; admitted, 1986, Madrid. *Education:* University Autónoma of Madrid; I.C.A.D.E. (Master of Taxation, 1986). *Member:* Madrid Bar Association. *LANGUAGES:* Spanish and English. *PRACTICE AREAS:* Taxation.

JUAN ALBERTO URRENGOECHEA, born June 15, 1962; admitted, 1989, Madrid. *Education:* University of Duesto (Bilbao); Instituto de Empresa, Madrid (Master's Degree in Corporate Legal Consultancy, 1988); Instituto de Empresa, Madrid (Master's Degree in Tax Law, 1989). Lecturer, University of Dijon, France, Faculty of Law. Professor of Commercial and Tax Law, Instituto de Empresa, Madrid. *Member:* Madrid Bar Association. *LANGUAGES:* Spanish, French and English. *PRACTICE AREAS:* Taxation.

REPRESENTATIVE CLIENTS: A.T. Cross Co.; A.T. Cross España, S.A.; ABC Group (Canada); American International Group (AIG Europe); Asefa, S.A. (Insurance); Asociación Fonográfica y Videográfica Española (Discos CBS, S.A.; EMI Odeón, S.A.; HISPAVOX, S.A.; POLYGRAM IBERICA, S.A.: RCA, S.A.); Cámara de Comercio Hispano-Finlandesa; Cooper Gay Holdings Ltd.; Castellanos y Compañía, S.A.; Citibank España, S.A.; Codetel Computer Graphics, S.A. (Gte International Telephone Inc.); Continental Europe Ltd.;

(This Listing Continued)

Embajada de Finlandia; Ganaderia Samuel Flores; Genencor International Europe Ltd.; Grupo Fosforera, S.A.; Industrias y Almacenes Pablos, S.A.; Kone Corporation; Laminados Oviedo Córdoba, S.A. (LOCSA); O.Y.E. Sarlin, AB; Pearson Overseas Holdings Ltd. (Finantial Times); S & C Correduria de Seguros,S.A.; Sol Nutritivo Inc. (Slim Fast); Skandia Industrial Insurance Company Ltd.; Tapón Corona Ibérica, S.A.; Textron Atlantic Inc.; Unat Direct, S.A.; Van Ommeren International B.V.; Warner Music Spain, S.A.; Westinghouse Electric, S.A.; Wilis Corron;
REFERENCES: Swiss Bank Corp., New York (Mrs. Weidlich); Harvard Law School (Professor Oliver Oldman); Banco Luso Español (Mr. F. Garcia de la Noceda); Sindicato de Banqueros de Barcelona, S.A. (Mr. Juan González de Mendoza).

LUPICINIO RODRIGUEZ-ABOGADOS

Established in 1979

VILLANUEVA 29
MADRID 28001, SPAIN
Telephone: (91) 5775502 International: (34-1) 5775502
Fax: (91) 4310413 / (91) 578 24 99
Telex: 48564 LUPRE

Barcelona, Spain Office: Paseo de Gracia 85, 7° B, 08008 , Barcelona 08006. Telephone: (34-3) 488 28 02. Fax: (34-3) 488 27 33.
London, England Associated Office: 43 Brook Street, W1Y 2BL London. Telephone 071 629 7411. Fax: (071) 629 2621.
Bonn, Germany Associated Office: Oxfordstrasse 24, 5300 Bonn 1. Telephone: 0228/726250. Fax: 0228/650479.
Paris, France Associated Office: 250 bis, Boulevard Saint Germain, Paris 75007. Telephone: 1 49 54 90 00. Fax: 1 49 54 90 04.
Houston, Texas, United States Associated Office: 2900 South Tower, Pennzoil Place, 77002-2781 Houston. Telephone: (713) 223-2900. Fax: (713) 221-1212.

Corporate and Partnership Formation, Joint Ventures, Mergers, Acquisitions and Sale of Public and Private Companies, Securities Issues, Commercial Agreements, Employment Law and Arbitration. Spanish Inward and Outward Investment, Energy Law, EC Industrial Assistance, Central and Regional Turnkey Contracts. Patents, Trademarks, Copyright and Know-How Protection, Licensing and Litigation. Purchase, Sale, Leasing and Management of Commercial Premises. Agricultural Law, Resort and Leisure Complexes and Residential Property. Mining Concessions, Licenses, Royalties, Environmental Reconstruction. National and International Tourism Investment, Hotels. Timesharing. Sports Clubs, Charter, Commercial and Leisure Aviation. Income, Corporation, Value Added and Local Taxation, Double Taxation. Tax and Fiscal Planning. International Corporate Structures. Commercial and Civil Litigation throughout Spain. Administrative Procedures, National and International Arbitration. Reconversion of Companies in Crisis. Bankruptcy Proceedings. International Commerce and Finance. Banking Operations and Leasing. Syndicate Loans. SWAPS. Issue of Securities on National and International Markets. Assessment of Stockbroking Operations in Spain and Abroad. Options and Future Contracts. Environmental Law. Zoning, Planning and Land Use. Telecommunications.

FIRM PROFILE: *The firm was founded in 1979. Bufete Lupicinio Rodríguez is a multidisciplinary Law Firm with an international scope. The Firm currently has a team of 25 lawyers (including 8 partners) and five consultants, which along with the number of cases handled, places it among the top Law Firms in Spain.*

The Bufete Lupicinio Rodríquez is particularly active in the fields of financial and commercial Law, the complexity of which have grown as a consequence of the increasing internationalization of the world's markets, the creation of increasingly sophisticated financial instruments and aggressive domestic and international competition.

It is a primary object of the Firm to ensure the management presence of a senior partner in every case undertaken by the Firm.

Our well coordinated links with prestigious Law Firms abroad ensure that all cases submitted to our attention will be handled in a practical and integrated fashion, which have proven extremely useful for both Spanish and foreign business executives and entrepreneurs who wish to internationalize their markets in a safe and rational manner.

FOUNDING PARTNERS

LUPICINIO RODRIGUEZ JIMÉNEZ, born Avila, Spain. *Education:* University of Deusto, Bilbao (Law School, School of Economics); City of London Polytechnic (Diploma in Shipping Law); Postgraduate Studies in European Business and Maritime Law. *Member:* Madrid, Jerez and International Bar Associations. *LANGUAGES:* Spanish, English and French. *PRACTICE AREAS:* Commercial and Corporate Law; International Cor-

(This Listing Continued)

porate Taxation; Mergers and Acquisitions; Capital Markets; Industrial and Energy Law.

LEÓN BARRIOLA URRUTIOECHEA, born San Sebastian, Spain. *Education:* University of Navarra's Civil Engineering School (Civil Engineer Degree); University of Madrid (Law Degree). *Member:* Madrid and International Bar Associations. *LANGUAGES:* Spanish, English and French. *PRACTICE AREAS:* Fiscal Law; Tax Planning; International Corporate Finance.

SENIOR PARTNERS

GASPAR ARIÑO, born Valencia, Spain. *Education:* University of Valencia (Masters in Law); University of Madrid (Ph.D. in Law). Scholarships from: United Nations Organization; The Ford Foundation; Joint Commission Spain-USA; Fulbright Commission. *Member:* Madrid, Valencia and Toledo Bar Association. *LANGUAGES:* French, English and Spanish. *PRACTICE AREAS:* Administrative Law; Public Works; Utilities, Electricity, Oil and Gas, Water Companies; Transportation and Telecommunications.

ANTONIO IRASTORZA RUIGOMEZ, Spanish Lawyer and English Solicitor resident in London. *Education:* University of Navarra (Law School). Solicitor to the Supreme Court of England. (Also Partner, Boodle Hatfield, London). *LANGUAGES:* Spanish, English and French. *PRACTICE AREAS:* Finance and Banking.

LUIS MANUEL GARCÍA LÓPEZ, born Madrid, Spain. *Education:* University of Madrid (Law Degree). *Member:* Madrid and International Bar Associations. *LANGUAGES:* Spanish, English and French. *PRACTICE AREAS:* Corporate Law; Mergers and Acquisitions; Foreign Investments; Telecommunications Law.

IGNACIO LACORZANA BARINAGARREMENTERIA, born Bilbao, Spain. *Education:* University of Deusto (Law Degree); London University (Degree in Maritime Law). Formerly Lawyer of the Diputación Foral de Vizcaya. *LANGUAGES:* Spanish, English and French. *PRACTICE AREAS:* Real Estate; Property; Government and Administrative Law.

FRANCISCO CARRION NAVARRO, born Cuenca, Spain. *Education:* Complutense University of Madrid (Law Degree). Judge and Dean of the Province of Valencia. Former Judge of the Third Hall of the Central Employment Court. Associate Professor, Department of Labour Law of the Compultense University of Madrid. Professor of Labour Law at the University Pontifica de Comillas. Distinguished Cross, First Class, San Raimundo de Peñafort (1981). Work Cross. Work Medal. *PRACTICE AREAS:* Labour Law.

HERMENEGILDO ALTOZANO GARCÍA-FIGUERAS, born Madrid, Spain. *Education:* Colegio Retamar (Bachiller, 1980); University of Madrid (Law Degree, 1986). Resident in Houston, Texas. *Member:* Madrid and international Bar Associations. *LANGUAGES:* Spanish and English. *PRACTICE AREAS:* Timeshares; Tourism; Corporate Law; Privatizations.

SALVADOR ESCRIBANO GUZMÁN, born Madrid, Spain. *Education:* University of Madrid (Law Degree; Diploma in European Community Law; Diploma in Business Law). Member, Royal Academy of Jurisprudence and Legislation. *Member:* Madrid Bar Association. *LANGUAGES:* Spanish and English. *PRACTICE AREAS:* Environmental Law; Company Investments and Government Subsidies; Mergers and Acquisitions; Foreign Investments.

PEDRO MEJÍAS VILLATORO, born Alicante, Spain. *Education:* University of Alicante (Law Degree); Instituto de Empresa, Madrid (Master in Business Law); INESFI, Madrid (Diploma in Specialization of Intermediary and Financial Operations). *Member:* Madrid and International Bar Associations. *LANGUAGES:* Spanish and English. *PRACTICE AREAS:* Mergers and Acquisitions; Finance Law; Tax Planning.

JOSE MANUEL SALA ARQUER, born Barcelona, Spain. *Education:* University of Navarra (Doctor of Law Degree). *LANGUAGES:* French, English and Spanish. *PRACTICE AREAS:* Public Contracting; Criminal Administrative Law; Public Economic Law; Regulation of the Energy Sector; Legal Structure of Major Public Services; Public Banking; Stock Exchange Law.

FRANCISCO JAVIER CARRIÓN GARCIA DE PARADA, born Madrid, Spain. *Education:* University of Madrid (Law Degree). ember: Madrid and International Bar Associations. *LANGUAGES:* Spanish and English. *PRACTICE AREAS:* Collections; Litigation; Bankruptcy Proceedings.

(This Listing Continued)

SENIOR ASSOCIATES

CARLOS DIAZ MARQUINA, born Madrid, Spain. *Education:* University of Madrid (Law Degree). *Member:* Madrid Bar Association. *LANGUAGES:* Spanish , English and French. *PRACTICE AREAS:* Collections and Commercial Litigation; Insurance Law.

ANGEL VALDÉS BURGUI, born Madrid, Spain. *Education:* University of Madrid (Law Degree); College of Brugges, Belgium (Graduate in European Legal Studies, 1989). *Member:* Madrid Bar Association. *LANGUAGES:* Spanish, English and French. *PRACTICE AREAS:* European Community Law; Government Subsidies.

ANA FERNÁNDEZ LUNA, born Madrid, Spain. *Education:* Colegio Jesús María (Bachiller); University of Madrid (Law Degree); Instituto de Empresa, Madrid (Master in Business Law). *Member:* Madrid Bar Association. *LANGUAGES:* Spanish and English. *PRACTICE AREAS:* Corporation Law.

JAVIER LASA. *Education:* University of Valladolid (Law School); Master in European Community Law, Brussels. Senior Associate, Resident in London. Professional experience in Brussels, Madrid and London. *LANGUAGES:* Spanish, English and French. *PRACTICE AREAS:* European Community Law.

ASSOCIATES

VALENTÍN GANUZA FÉRREO, born Madrid, Spain. *Education:* University of Madrid (Law Degree); Madrid Law Practice School (Graduate). *Member:* Madrid Bar Association. *LANGUAGES:* Spanish. *PRACTICE AREAS:* Collections and Litigation; Leases; Housing.

ANGEL LAVÍN MARTÍNEZ, born Bilbao, Spain. *Education:* German School (Bachiller); University of Madrid (Law Degree). *Member:* Madrid Bar Association. *LANGUAGES:* Spanish, German and English. *PRACTICE AREAS:* Real Estate and Commercial Property Development; Foreign Investments in Spain.

GEMMA VEGA CALVO, born Madrid, Spain. *Education:* University of Madrid (Law Degree). *Member:* Madrid Bar Association. *LANGUAGES:* Spanish, French and English. *PRACTICE AREAS:* Corporate Law.

JOSE IGNACIO MARTINEZ PEREZ, born Madrid, Spain. *Education:* University of Madrid (Law Degree). *Member:* Madrid Bar Association. *LANGUAGES:* Spanish and English. *PRACTICE AREAS:* Intellectual Property Law; Patents; Corporate Development.

JOSE MARIA AGUILERA ANEGON, born Madrid, Spain. *Education:* Complutense University of Madrid (Law Degree); Complutense University of Madrid Law Practice School (Graduate). *Member:* Madrid Bar Association. *LANGUAGES:* Spanish and English. *PRACTICE AREAS:* Collections and Litigation.

ELENA AGÚNDEZ AGÚNDEZ, born Madrid, Spain. *Education:* University of Madrid (Law Degree). *Member:* Madrid Bar Association. *LANGUAGES:* Spanish and English. *PRACTICE AREAS:* Real Estate and Property; Government and Administrative Law.

MARÍA VICTORIA LACORZANNA BARINAGARREMENTERIA, born Bilbao, Spain. *Education:* University of Deusto (Law Degree); Institute of General Studies (Masters Degree in Finance and Stock Market Studies). *LANGUAGES:* Spanish and English. *PRACTICE AREAS:* Fiscal Law.

ANA ANTUÑA PELEGRÍ, born Oviedo, Spain. *Education:* University of the Basque Country (Law Degree); University of Sapienza, Rome (Matrimony Law). *Member:* Madrid Bar Association. *LANGUAGES:* Spanish and French. *PRACTICE AREAS:* Fiscal Law.

ROSA MARIA FATSINI PIQUE, born Bogotá , Colombia. *Education:* University of Madrid (Law Degree). *LANGUAGES:* Spanish and Catalán. *PRACTICE AREAS:* Documentation.

CONSULTANTS

ALFREDO GALLEGO ANABITARTE, Senior Consultant. Lawyer and Professor of Administrative Law. *Education:* University of Madrid (Law Degree) Law School; University of Paris X "Nanterre"; University of Paris V "René Descartes". *PRACTICE AREAS:* Constitutional and Administrative Law.

THOMAS SHORTT, Senior Consultant. Certified Chartered Accountant of England and Wales.

(This Listing Continued)

LUPICINIO RODRIGUEZ-ABOGADOS, Madrid—
Continued

DANIEL TOBAR, Senior Consultant in Company Hardware and Software.

MARIA GONZÁLEZ CHAVES, Senior Consultant. Director of Arenaria-Personnel Selection Agency.

Languages: Spanish, English, French, German, Italian and Catalán.

ESTUDIO JURIDICO
SANCHEZ CALERO & CO.

CALLE QUINTANA N° 2, 2°
(EDIFICIO BUEN SUCESO)
28008 MADRID, SPAIN
Telephone: 548-2805
Fax: 548-0986

General Practice. Administrative, Banking, Securities, Civil, Commercial, Corporate, Criminal, Foreign Investments, International, Labor, Litigation and Taxation Law.

MEMBERS OF FIRM

FERNANDO SÁNCHEZ CALERO, born Valladolid, Spain, September 25, 1928; admitted, 1963, Bilbao; 1976, Madrid. Author: "Curso de Derecho de Seguro privado," 1961; "Instituciones de Derecho Mercantil," 17th Edition, 1994; "Comentario de la Ley de Contrato de Seguro," Madrid, Vol. I, 1984, Vol. 2, 1986, Vol. 3, 1989. General Editor of the Revista de Derecho Bancario y Bursátil, 1981. Professor of Commercial Law, University Complutense of Madrid, 1977. Dean, University of Bilbao, 1961-1965. Director, Instituto de Estudios Bancarios Bursátiles, 1967-1977. Legal Adviser, Bolsa of Bilbao, 1970-1977. President, Asociación Española de Derecho Marítimo, 1977-1980. President, Spanish Section of the International Association of Insurance Law, 1986. Standing Committee Member, Comisión General de Codificación, 1970. Vice-Chairman, Securities Law Reform Commission, 1977-1978. *Member:* International Association of Insurance Law (Member, Executive Committee); International Maritime Committee. *LANGUAGES:* Spanish, French and Italian.

FERNANDO GISBERT CALABUIG, born Villena, Alicante, Spain, April 22, 1929; admitted, 1957, Madrid. Contributor, "Revista Derecho Procesal" and "PRETOR", Madrid, 1964. Author: "Doctrina de Suplicación", Madrid, 1964. Professor, Facultad de Derecho, 1961-1967, Universidad Pontificia de Comillas, 1967-1985. Diplomate at the Escuela de Práctica Jurídica de Madrid in Labor Law, 1981. *LANGUAGES:* Spanish.

JUAN SANCHEZ-CALERO GUILARTE, born Roma, Italy, June 24, 1956; admitted, 1983, Madrid. Doctor (University of Madrid). Assistant Editor of the Revista de Derecho Bancario y Bursátil, 1984. Adviser of Spain's Cooperative Banks Association, 1986. Professor of Commercial Law, University of Madrid, 1982. *LANGUAGES:* Spanish, English, German and French.

JOSE LUIS REDONDO DIAZ DE CORCUERA, born Sepulveda (Segovia), Spain, June 16, 1934; admitted, 1960, Bilbao. *Education:* University of Valladolid (Licenciado en Derecho, 1956). Professor, Commercial Law, Universidad del País Vasco, 1959. Legal Adviser, Bilbao Stock Exchange. *Member:* International Association of Insurance Law (Spanish Section). *LANGUAGES:* Spanish.

MIGUEL SANCHEZ-CALERO GUILARTE, born Bilbao, Spain, July 9, 1960; admitted, 1983, Bilbao; 1987, Madrid. *Education:* Deutsche Schule (Abitur); Universidad Complutense of Madrid (Licenciado en Derecho, 1983); Harvard Law School, Program of Instruction for Lawyers (June 1987). Legal Adviser, Bilbao Stock Exchange, 1983-1986. *LANGUAGES:* Spanish, English and German.

ALBERTO TAPIA HERMIDA, born Vigo, Spain, April 11, 1960; admitted, 1990, Madrid. *Education:* Licenciate of Law, University of Madrid; Doctor (University of Madrid). Professor of Commercial Law, University of Madrid, 1983. Legal Adviser, National Securities Commission, 1988-1990. *LANGUAGES:* Spanish, English and Portuguese.

ALFONSO GUILARTE GUTIERREZ, born Valladolid, Spain, July 23, 1963; admitted, 1988, Valladolid; 1992, Madrid. *Education:* University of Valladolid (Licenciado en Derecho, 1987). Professor of Taxation U.N.E.D., 1992. Legal Adviser Unión Nacional de Cooperativas. *LANGUAGES:* Spanish and English.

(This Listing Continued)

PABLO MARIN LARRINAGA, born Bilbao, Spain, September 6, 1955; admitted, 1986, Madrid. *Education:* Deutsche Schule (Bilbao), University of Deusto (Bilbao) Law Degree and Graduate in Economics, M.B.A. Chamber of Commerce Madrid; Scholarship of the Spanish Ministry of Trade and Commerce. Commercial Office in Tokyo, Japan, 1982. Legal Adviser of Dresdner Bank AG Sucursal en España, 1983-1990. Secretary General and Legal Adviser of Banco Cooperativo Español S.A. and Gescooperativo S.A. S.G.I.I.C.. 1990-1993. *LANGUAGES:* Spanish, German, English and French.

OF COUNSEL

PEDRO ARAGONESES ALONSO, born Mansilla de las Mulas, Leon, Spain, January 8, 1922; admitted, 1945, Madrid. Professor, Facultad de Derecho, Universidad Complutense de Madrid, 1965. Professor and Director, Escuela de Práctica Jurídica, Facultad de Derecho, University of Madrid, 1955. Standing Committee Member, Comisión General de Codificación, 1960. Head of the Gabinete de Estudios, 1968-1971. Technical Secretary, Gabinete de Estudios, 1968-1971. Technical Secretary, Ministries of Education, 1971-1974 and Justice, 1976-1977. General Secretary, Consejo Nacional de Educación, 1972-1977. Member, Executive Staff, Consejo Superior de Investigación Científica, 1971-1974. Foundation Member and General Secretary, Instituto Español of Procedural Law, 1949. (Judge on leave).

Languages: Spanish, French, English, German, Italian and Portuguese.

SARDA, CALOMARDE, CASTELO & ASOCIADOS

PASEO DE LA CASTELLANA, 228, 3°
28046 MADRID, SPAIN
Telephone: 1/314.19.34
Fax: 1/314.19.52

Barcelona, Spain Office: Muntaner, 407, 1° 2°, 08021. Telephone: 3/201.64.66. Fax: 3/202.00.96.

Valencia, Spain, Office: Cronista Carreres, 13, 3° 8°, 46003. Telephone: 6/352.96.03. Fax: 6/394.26.83.

European Community Law, International Banking and Business Law, Foreign Investment Law, General International Trade Law, Corporate, Civil and Criminal Litigation, Competition and Copyright Law, Insurance Law, Family Law, Procedural Law, Bankruptcy Law and Tax Law.

FIRM PROFILE: The firm, established in 1993 is the result of the association of three Lawyer's offices: Sardá y Asociados in Barcelona, established in 1964, Mas Millet y Calomarde, established in Valencia in 1978 and Castelo y Larraz, established in Madrid in 1975. It is a member of LEGALLIANCE (EEIG) a large union of European lawyers with offices in Brussels, Paris, London, Berlin, Frankfurt, Cologne, Leipzig, Milan, Bologna, Padua, The Hague and Stockholm.

RESIDENT MEMBERS OF FIRM

D. EMILIO CASTELO BEREGUIAIN, born 1948; admitted, 1975, Madrid. *Education:* University Complutense of Madrid (lic.jur.); Post Graduate course of companies' legal advisement; Specialised courses in Real Estate Law. *Member:* Madrid, Alcalá de Henares and Guadalajara Bar Associations. *LANGUAGES:* Spanish and English. *PRACTICE AREAS:* Business Law; Company Law; Bankruptcy Law; Real Estate Law; Civil and Criminal Law and Litigation.

D. ALFONSO LARRAZ ISTURIZ, born 1952; admitted, 1975, Madrid. *Education:* Complutense University of Madrid (Lic.jur.); Post graduate courses of Tax Law and European community Law. *Member:* Madrid Bar Association. *LANGUAGES:* Spanish, French and English. *PRACTICE AREAS:* Tax Law; Commercial Law; International Law; European Community Law; Company Law; Corporate Law.

D. FERNANDO DOMINGUEZ DE POSADA Y DE MIGUEL, born 1950; admitted, 1975, Madrid. *Education:* University Complutense of Madrid (Doctor E.T.). Post Graduate course of Financial Interdrises E.O.I. Official in Public Administration by Opposition (Excedent). *LANGUAGES:* Spanish and English. *PRACTICE AREAS:* Tax Law; Commercial Law; Company Law; Corporate Law; Public and Administration Law.

STEPHENSON HARWOOD

Established in 1991

FERNANDO EL SANTO 15-3°
28010 MADRID, SPAIN
Telephone: (341) 319 1212
Fax: (341) 319 1940

London, England Office: One St. Paul's Churchyard, EC4M 8SH. Telephone: (44) 0171 329 4422. Telex: 886789 SHSPC G. Fax: (44) 0171 606 0822.

Brussels, Belgium Office: Avenue du Diamant 139, 1040. Telephone: (322) 735 9190. Fax: (322) 732 2237.

Guangzhou, People's Republic of China Associated Office: Stephenson Harwood & Lo, Room 516, China Hotel, Liu Hua Lu, 510015. Telephone: (8620) 669 3490. Telex: 44888 CHLGZ CN. Fax: (8620) 669 3479.

Hong Kong Associated Office: Stephenson Harwood & Lo, 18th Floor, Edinburgh Tower, The Landmark, 15 Queen's Road Central. Telephone: 852-2868 0789. Telex: 66278 SHL HX. Fax: 852-2868 1504.

Kuwait Associated Office: Al Sarraf, Al Ruwayeh & Stephenson Harwood, Salhiya Complex, Gate 1, 3rd Floor, P.O. Box 1448, Safat 13015. Telephone: 965 240 0061/2/3. Fax: 965 240 0064.

RESIDENT PARTNERS

KENNETH L. BONAVIA, born January 10, 1957; admitted, 1982. *Education:* Prior Park College, Bath and King's College, University of London, England. *LANGUAGES:* English, French, Spanish and Italian. *PRACTICE AREAS:* Corporate; Commercial; Property.

NICOLAS MARTIN DE VIDALES, Abogado, born June 4, 1962; admitted, 1985. *Education:* ICADE Law School, Madrid. Former Senior Legal Advisor to the Madrid Stock Exchange. *LANGUAGES:* Spanish, English and French. *PRACTICE AREAS:* Stock Exchange; Banking; Corporate; Commercial.

ENRIQUE ARMIJO, Abogado, born November 29, 1961; admitted, 1986. *Education:* ICADE Law School, Madrid (LL.M.); American University, Washington, D.C. *LANGUAGES:* Spanish, English and French. *PRACTICE AREAS:* Litigation; Corporate; Commercial; Banking.

MONICA CORNET, Abogado, born April 7, 1965; admitted, 1989. *Education:* C.E.U. San Pablo Law School (Master Degree in EC Law). *LANGUAGES:* Spanish, English and French. *PRACTICE AREAS:* Banking; Corporate; Commercial; Finance; EC Law.

(For Complete List of Stephenson Harwood's Overseas Offices, Please see London, England Office)

TENA, MUÑOZ Y ASOCIADOS

JOSÉ ORTEGA Y GASSET 34
28006 MADRID, SPAIN
Telephone: 576.0450
Fax: 435.7076

Corporate Law, Securities, Banking and Finance, Tax, Civil, Real Estate and Competition Law, Bankruptcy and Insolvency, Litigation and Arbitration.

PARTNERS

JUAN I. TENA, born Madrid, Spain, January 4, 1952; admitted, 1977, Madrid. *Education:* Complutense University of Madrid (Law , 1973; Political Science, 1973). Advisor to the Minister's Cabinet, Ministry of Education and Science (1973-1974). Head of the President's Cabinet of the Spanish Federation of Business Organizations-CEOE (1978-1979). *Member:* Madrid and Barcelona Bar Associations; International Bar Association. *LANGUAGES:* Spanish, English and French.

LUIS M. MUÑOZ, born Salamanca, Spain, April 26, 1952; admitted, 1985, Madrid. *Education:* University of Salamanca (Law, 1976); Instituto de Empresa, Madrid (Master in Legal Counseling for Companies, 1981-1982). *Member:* Madrid Bar Association. *LANGUAGES:* Spanish, English and French.

MERCEDES FERNANDEZ, born Oviedo, Spain, March 22, 1960; admitted, 1985, Madrid. *Education:* University of Oviedo (Law, 1982). Professor of Private International Law, University of Oviedo (1982-1985). *Member:* Madrid Bar Association. *LANGUAGES:* Spanish, English and French.

(This Listing Continued)

FEDERICO MERINO, born Segovia, Spain, June 24, 1960; admitted, 1986, Madrid. *Education:* Complutense University of Madrid (Law, 1982); Georgetown University and American University, Washington, D.C. (Master in Law, 1985). *Member:* Madrid Bar Association. *LANGUAGES:* Spanish and English.

LUIS RIESGO, born Madrid, Spain, October 8, 1965; admitted, 1989, Madrid. *Education:* University of Comillas ICADE (Law, 1988; Economics, 1989; Diploma in Community Law, 1988); Madrid Bar Association (Diploma in Taxation, 1990). *Member:* Madrid Bar Association. *LANGUAGES:* Spanish and English.

TAX LAWYER

PABLO BASCHWITZ, born Madrid, Spain, June 9, 1965; admitted, 1990, Madrid. *Education:* CEU, San Pablo Complutense University of Madrid (Law, 1988); Instituto de Empresa, Madrid (Master in Taxation, 1993). *Member:* Madrid Bar Association. *LANGUAGES:* Spanish, English and German.

URÍA & MENÉNDEZ

Established in 1941

HERMOSILLA, 30
28001 MADRID, SPAIN
Telephone: 586.04.00
Telex: 48141 URME E
Fax: 586.04.04/03

Barcelona, Spain Office: Diagonal, 514, 08036. Telephone: 415.50.05. Fax: 415.90.61; 415.94.49.

Brussels, Belgium Office: Rue Bréderode 13A, 1000. Telephone: 505.02.11. Fax: 502.26.44.

New York, New York Office: 712 Fifth Avenue, 30th Floor, 10019. Telephone: 801-3460. Fax: 801-3465.

London, England Office: Royex House, Aldermanbury Square, EC2V 7HR. Telephone: (44) 171 600.36.10. Fax: (44) 171 600.17.18.

Prague, Czech Republic Office: Blanická, 28 CZ 120 00 Prague 2. Telephone: 20.70.50. Fax: 25.42.23.

Commercial, Corporate, Banking and Financing, Foreign Investment, Transfer of Technology, Admiralty, Insurance, European Communities, Litigation, General Practice, Environmental Law.

Member of Alliance of European Lawyers (EEIG) which regroups six law firms from Continental Europe. The Alliance consists of De Bandt, van Hecke & Lagae at Brussels and Antwerp; De Brauw Blackstone Westbroek at The Hague, Amsterdam, Rotterdam and Eindhoven; Jeantet & Associés at Paris and Warsaw; Lagerlöf & Leman at Stockholm, Gothenburg and Malmö; Oppenhoff & Rädler at Berlin, Cologne, Frankfurt am Main, Leipzig and Münich; Uria & Menendez at Madrid and Barcelona.

MEMBERS OF FIRM

RODRIGO URÍA GONZÁLEZ, born 1906; admitted, 1940. *Education:* University of Oviedo (Licenciate of Law; Doctor Honoris Causa); University of Madrid (Doctor of Law). *Author:* "Commercial Law", 21st Edition, 1994; "Commentary on the Spanish limited liability Company Law", 3rd Edition, 1976. Chaired Professor of Commercial Law, University of Madrid, 1953-1976. *Member:* Royal Academy of Legislation and Jurisprudence; National Commission on Codification. *LANGUAGES:* French and Italian.

AURELIO MENÉNDEZ MENÉNDEZ, born 1927; admitted, 1972. *Education:* University of Oviedo (Licenciate of Law); University of Madrid (Doctor of Law). Chaired Professor of Commercial Law, University of Madrid, 1970-1993. Dean of the Law School, University of Madrid, 1970-1973. Minister of Education and Science, 1976-1977. Justice of the Spanish Constitutional Court, 1980. *Member:* State Council; General Commission on Codification (President, Commercial Law Section). *LANGUAGES:* French.

RODRIGO URÍA, JR., born 1941; admitted, 1972. Consultant, Curtis, Mallet-Prevost, Colt & Mosle, New York 1974-1975. Member: Royal Board of Trustees, The Prado Museum, 1988—; Board of Trustees, Foundation Collection Thyssen-Bornemisza; Spanish Court of Arbitration; Asociación de Amistad Hispano Francesa (Vice-Chairman). *LANGUAGES:* English, French and Italian.

JUAN LUIS IGLESIAS PRADA, born 1941; admitted, 1982. *Education:* University of Oviedo (Doctor of Law). Chaired Professor of Commercial Law, University of Madrid, 1975—. Vice-Dean of the Law School and

(This Listing Continued)

URÍA & MENÉNDEZ, Madrid—Continued

University of Madrid, 1975-1976. *Member:* General Commission on Codification. *LANGUAGES:* French and Italian.

CHARLES CORWIN COWARD, born 1946; admitted, 1975, New York; 1981, Madrid; 1987, Barcelona. *Education:* Columbia University (A.B., 1968; M.B.A., 1975; J.D., 1974); University of Madrid (Licenciate of Law, 1980). *LANGUAGES:* English and Spanish.

JOSÉ PÉREZ SANTOS, born 1950; admitted, 1976. *LANGUAGES:* English and French.

FERNANDO REVILLA MACHO, born 1944; admitted, 1975. Former Judicial Officer. *LANGUAGES:* English, French and Italian.

JUAN FERNÁNDEZ-ARMESTO, born 1953; admitted, 1978. *Education:* University Autónoma of Madrid (Doctor of Law). Chaired Professor of Commercial Law, University of Comillas-ICADE. *LANGUAGES:* German, English and French.

JUAN CADARSO PALAU, born 1947; admitted, 1979. *Education:* University of Valladolid (Doctor of Law). Chaired Professor of Civil Law, University of Alcalá. *LANGUAGES:* French.

JOSÉ MARÍA SEGOVIA CAÑADAS, born 1951; admitted, 1980. *Education:* New York University (Master of Comparative Jurisprudence, Institute of Comparative Law). *LANGUAGES:* English and French.

LUIS PASTOR RIDRUEJO, born 1935; admitted, 1963. *Education:* University of Madrid (Doctor of Law). Law Officer of The State, 1969-1974. General Secretary of ENPETROL and CAMPSA, 1975-1988. *LANGUAGES:* English and French.

EMILIO DÍAZ RUIZ, born 1957; admitted, 1980. *Education:* University Complutense of Madrid (Doctor of Law). Lecturer of Commercial Law, University Complutense of Madrid, 1986—. *LANGUAGES:* English and French.

CARLOS VILADÁS JENE (Resident in Barcelona. For Complete Biographical Data, see Professional Biographies at Barcelona, Spain).

JUAN MIGUEL GOENECHEA DOMINGUEZ, born 1959; admitted, 1982. Lecturer of Commercial Law, University of Comillas-ICADE, 1984—. *LANGUAGES:* English and French.

RAFAEL SEBASTIAN, born 1955; admitted, 1980, Spain; Licensed in New York as Legal Consultant. Lecturer of Commercial Law, University of Comillas-ICADE. (Resident, New York Office). *LANGUAGES:* English and French.

LUIS DE CARLOS BERTRAN (Resident, Barcelona Office. For Complete Biographical Data, see Professional Biographies at Barcelona, Spain).

IGNACIO ALBIÑANA CILVETI (Resident in Barcelona. For Complete Biographical Data, see Professional Biographies at Barcelona, Spain).

JAIME FOLGUERA CRESPO, born 1954; admitted, 1978. Senior Civil Servant. Deputy Director, Finance and Budget Department, Ministry of Economy and Budget Department for the European Community. Senior Counsel, EEC Law, (INI). (Resident, Brussels Office). *LANGUAGES:* English and French.

ASSOCIATES

FERNANDO PEREZ DE LA SOTA, born 1962; admitted, 1986. *LANGUAGES:* French, English and German.

JOSE ANTONIO ESCALONA DE MOLINA, born 1962; admitted, 1986. *LANGUAGES:* English.

JUAN FRANCISCO FALCÓN RAVELO, born 1963; admitted, 1987. *LANGUAGES:* English and German.

ALBERTO NUÑEZ-LAGOS BURGUERA (Resident, Barcelona Office. For Complete Biographical Data, see Professional Biographies at Barcelona, Spain).

CHRISTIAN HOEDL EIGEL, born 1964; admitted, 1987. Master in Tax Law. Master in Real Estate Law. *LANGUAGES:* English, German and French.

EDUARDO GELI FERNANDEZ-PEÑAFLOR (Resident in Barcelona; For Complete Biographical Data, see Professional Biographies at Barcelona, Spain).

JUAN IGNACIO GONZALEZ RUIZ, born 1965; admitted, 1987. *LANGUAGES:* English, German and Italian.

(This Listing Continued)

SALVADOR SANCHEZ-TERAN SANCHEZ-ARJONA, born 1964; admitted, 1988. Lecturer of Commercial Law, Universidad Comillas (ICADE), Madrid. *LANGUAGES:* English.

EDUARDO TRIGO SIERRA, born 1960; admitted, 1988. *LANGUAGES:* English.

CARLOS DE MIGUEL PERALES, born 1964; admitted, 1988. *Education:* University of Comillas-ICADE (Doctor of Law). Lecturer of Civil Law, University of Comillas-ICADE, 1988—. *LANGUAGES:* English.

RODRIGO MENÉNDEZ GARCÍA, born 1964; admitted, 1989. Lecturer of Commercial Law, University Autónoma of Madrid. *LANGUAGES:* English.

MARINA ALVAREZ ROYO-VILLANOVA, born 1965; admitted, 1988. *Education:* Harvard Law School (LL.M.). (Resident, New York Office). *LANGUAGES:* English and French.

RAMIRO RIVERA ROMERO, born 1966; admitted, 1989. Lecturer of Commercial Law, Universidad Comillas (ICADE), Madrid. *LANGUAGES:* English.

ESTEBAN ASTARLOA HUARTE-MENDICOA, born 1966; admitted, 1989. *LANGUAGES:* English.

MARIONA XICOY CRUELLS (Resident in Barcelona. For Complete Biographical Data, see Professional Biographies at Barcelona, Spain).

CARLOS DE CARDENAS SMITH, born 1966; admitted, 1990. *LANGUAGES:* English.

JAVIER VALLE ZAYAS (Resident in Barcelona. For Complete Biographical Data, see Professional Biographies at Barcelona, Spain).

RAFAEL GARCIA LLANEZA, born 1964; admitted, 1990, Spain. *LANGUAGES:* English and French.

ELENA UBEDA HERNANDEZ (Resident in Barcelona. For Complete Biographical Data, see Professional Biographies at Barcelona, Spain).

PABLO GONZALEZ-BUENO CATALAN DE OCON, born 1964; admitted, 1987. *Education:* Degree in EEC Law (College of Europe Bruges); University of Michigan (LL.M.). *LANGUAGES:* English, French and German.

EDUARDO RODRIGUEZ ROVIRA, born 1965; admitted, 1990. *Education:* Licenciate of European Law (Institute Etudes Européens, U.L.B., Brussels). *LANGUAGES:* English and French.

JORGE MARTI MORENO (Resident, London Office, For Complete Biographical Data, see Professional Biographies at London, England).

ARIADNA CAMBRONERO GINES (Resident in Barcelona. For Complete Biographical Data, see Professional Biographies at Barcelona, Spain).

PEDRO ALEMAN LAIN, born 1964; admitted, 1990. *Education:* New York University (Master of Comparative Jurisprudence). *LANGUAGES:* English and French.

DAVID GARCIA-OCHOA MAYOR, born 1968; admitted, 1991. *LANGUAGES:* English, French and German.

CARMEN BIGATA VISCASILLAS (Resident, Barcelona Office, For Complete Biographical Data, see Professional Biographies at Barcelona, Spain).

RAFAEL FUSTER TOZER, born 1967; admitted, 1991. *LANGUAGES:* English.

EDURNE NAVARRO-VARONA, born 1965; admitted, 1988. *Education:* University of Barcelona (Doctor of Law); University of Brussels (Lic. Eur. Law); University of Michigan (LL.M.). (Resident, Brussels Office). *LANGUAGES:* English, French, German and Italian.

ALVARO LOPEZ DE ARGUMEDO, born 1968; admitted, 1992. *LANGUAGES:* English.

JUAN ANTONIO FERNANDEZ-VELILLA HERNANDEZ (Resident, Barcelona Office. For Complete Biographical Data, see Professional Biographies at Barcelona, Spain).

IÑIGO DIAZ DE BERRICANO, born 1965; admitted, 1989. *LANGUAGES:* English.

TERESA PAZ-ARES (Resident, London Office. For Complete Biographical Data, see Professional Biographies at London, England).

JULIO GARRIDO AMADO, born 1942; admitted, 1964. *Education:* Graduate in Taxation, Centro de Estudios Tributarios; English Law De-

(This Listing Continued)

gree, City of London College. Lecturer of Civil Law, University of Madrid, 1964-1975. *LANGUAGES:* English and French.

JAVIER AMANTEGUI LORENZO (Resident, Barcelona Office. For Complete Biographical Data, see Professional Biographies at Barcelona, Spain).

LOURDES MARTIN FLOREZ, born 1964; admitted, 1987. *LANGUAGES:* English and French.

ANA BUITRAGO MONTORO, born 1969; admitted, 1992. *Education:* London Institute on International Business and Commercial Law (Diploma of International Business Law). *LANGUAGES:* English and French.

RAFAEL VARGAS MORENO, born 1963; admitted, 1987. Professor of Internacional Tax Planning, Instituto de Empresa and Chamber of Commerce, Madrid. *LANGUAGES:* English.

RAMON VIDAL PUIG, born 1964; admitted, 1989. *Education:* Diploma of Alliance European Legal Studies, College of Europe, Bruges; University of Michigan (LL.M.). (Resident, Brussels Office). *LANGUAGES:* English and French.

JOSE LUIS GONZALO PECES, born 1965; admitted, 1989. *Education:* Master of Law in Transnational Business Practice, McGeorge School of Law, University of the Pacific. *LANGUAGES:* English and French.

PEDRO PEREZ LLORCA, born 1968; admitted, 1993. *LANGUAGES:* English, French, German and Italian.

FERNANDO AZOFRA VEGAS, born 1969; admitted, 1993. *LANGUAGES:* English.

RAFAEL MOLINA NAVARRO, born 1966; admitted, 1989, Madrid; 1991, England and Wales; 1993, New York. *Education:* New York University, Institute of Comparative Law (Master of Comparative Jurisprudence). *LANGUAGES:* English.

PATRICIA MACIAS SERFATY, born 1970; admitted, 1993. *Education:* Diploma of European Law (University San Pablo-CEU). *LANGUAGES:* English.

MONICA GONZALEZ MUÑOZ, born 1969; admitted, 1994. *LANGUAGES:* English.

GABRIEL NUÑEZ FERNANDEZ, born 1970; admitted, 1994. *LANGUAGES:* English and French.

PABLO GONZALEZ-ESPEJO, born 1971; admitted, 1994. *LANGUAGES:* English and French.

EMILIO SAMUEL HERNANDEZ MUÑOZ, born 1971; admitted, 1994. *LANGUAGES:* English.

VICENTE CONDE VIÑUELAS, born 1968; admitted, 1994. *Education:* Licenciate of European Law (U.L.B.). *LANGUAGES:* English and French.

IDOYA AGUIRRE OLORIZ, born 1968; admitted, 1992. *Education:* Degree in EEC Law (College of Europe, Bruges); University of Columbia (LL.M.). *LANGUAGES:* English, French and German.

OF COUNSEL

RAMÓN VILADÁS MONSONÍS (Resident in Barcelona. For Complete Biographical Data, see Biographical Card at Barcelona, Spain).

JAIME ALFONSIN ALFONSO, born 1956; admitted, 1983. Law Officer of the State; General Secretary of Barclays Bank, S.A.E., 1984-1992. *LANGUAGES:* English.

ROMANA SADURSKA, born 1951; (Not admitted in Spain). *Education:* University of Warsaw (LL.B.; LL.M.); Yale University (LL.M.); Polish Academy of Sciences (Ph.D.). Senior Lecturer, Faculty of Law, University of Sydney. *LANGUAGES:* English, French, Polish, Russian and Spanish.

(For list of Partners and Counsel of the respective Member Firms of the Alliance of European Lawyers see Professional Biographies of: Oppenhoff & Rädler at Munich, Cologne, Frankfurt a/Main and Berlin, Germany; De Bandt van Hecke & Lagae at Brussels, Belgium; De Brauw Blackstone Westbroek at The Hague, Rotterdam and Amsterdam, The Netherlands; Jeantet & Associés at Paris and Strasbourg, France and Abidjan, Ivory Coast; Lagerlöf & Leman at Stockholm, Malmö and Göthenburg, Sweden, London, England, Paris, France, Berlin, Germany and New York, New York; Uria & Menendez at Madrid and Barcelona, Spain).

ANTONIO VINAL & CO.

Established in 1986

MORETO 15
28014 MADRID, SPAIN
Telephone: 420 24 27
Fax: 420 12 33

Associates in Other Countries: Hamburg, Germany; Brussels, Belgium; Prague, Czech Republic; Copenhagen, Denmark; New York, United States; Helsinki, Finland; Paris, France; London, England; Edinburgh, Scotland; Athens, Greece; Rotterdam, The Netherlands; Budapest, Hungary; Dublin, Ireland; Milan, Italy; Luxembourg; Warsaw, Poland; Lisbon, Portugal; Malmo, Sweden.

Corporate Law, Industrial and Intellectual Property Law, Transportation Law, Insurance Law. European Community Law, and Criminal Law.

FIRM PROFILE: *Antonio Vinal & Co. is a law firm established in 1986. From that time it has been concentrating in Commercial Law, and, in that sense, has been offering its services as a whole, which includes all necessary legal advice to its clients. In this respect it is important to indicate, among other things, the firm's involvement with the following: Establishing, merging, acquisition and sale of companies; international commerce including exporting and importing, which also involves the elements of transporting and insurance, customs and tariffs; special handling of fiscal aspects of mercantile transactions, and representation and defense before the ordinary and arbitration tribunals, both national and international.*

MEMBERS OF FIRM

ANTONIO VINAL. *Education:* Universidad de Santiago de Compostela (Lawyer); Columbia University, New York (Master of Law); School of Foreign and Comparative Law, New York (Graduate in Comparative Law). Minister, Plenipotentiary. *LANGUAGES:* Spanish, English, French and Italian. *PRACTICE AREAS:* International Contracts; Industrial and Intellectual Property Law; Arbitration.

EDUARDO VILARINO. *Education:* Universidad de Santiago de Compostela (Lawyer); Diplomacy and Consular Law, Universidad Complutense de Madrid (Escuela Diplomatica). Professor. *LANGUAGES:* Spanish, French and English. *PRACTICE AREAS:* European Community Law; Transportation Law; Insurance Law.

JESUS CASAS. *Education:* Universidad Complutense de Madrid (Lawyer); Centro de Estudios Comerciales, Madrid (Graduate in European Community Law); Seatrade Academy, Cambridge, England (Maritime Law). *LANGUAGES:* Spanish, English and Italian. *PRACTICE AREAS:* Transportation Law.

ASSOCIATE

MARIA GONZALEZ. *Education:* Universidad Complutense de Madrid (Lawyer); Universidad Americana "McGeorge School of Law-Salzburg" (International and Mercantile Law). *LANGUAGES:* Spanish and English. *PRACTICE AREAS:* Criminal Law.

CRISTINA HEVIA. *Education:* Universidad de Oviedo (Lawyer); Instituto de Empresa de Madrid-P.I.L. through Harvard University (Commercial). *LANGUAGES:* Spanish, English and French. *PRACTICE AREAS:* Corporate Law.

CONSULTANTS

ALEXANDER GRANT, Solicitor (Supreme Court of England and Wales). *LANGUAGES:* English, Spanish and French.

ARTHUR ANDERSEN ASESORES LEGALES Y TRIBUTARIOS

Legal and Tax Advisors

CALLE HILERA Nº 8
29007 MÁLAGA, SPAIN
Telephone: 34-52-276454
Fax: 34-52-277740

Arthur Andersen Asesores Legales y Tributarios's offices: Alicante, Barcelona, Bilbao, Granada, La Coruña, Madrid, Málaga, Oviedo, Palma de Mallorca, San Sebastian, Sevilla, Valencia, Vigo, Vitoria, Zaragoza.

Associated Law Firms abroad: France, Italy, Germany, Portugal, The Netherlands, Belgium, United Kingdom, South Africa, Colombia and Brazil.

(This Listing Continued)

ARTHUR ANDERSEN, ASESORES LEGALES Y TRIBUTARIOS, Málaga—Continued

PARTNER

DAVID MORENO, born Madrid, Spain, December 4, 1956; admitted, 1989, Seville. *Education:* University of Deusto (Law Degree, 1979); ICADE (Master, Business Administration); Instituto de Empresa (Master, Corporation Taxes Counsel, 1983); Instituto Internacional San Telmo (Graduate, Corporation Management, 1990). Professor, Business Law, University of Seville. Co-Author: "El IVA verde," 1986; "Adaptación de su Empresa a la Reforma Mercantil," 1989. *Member:* Seville Bar Association. *LANGUAGES:* Spanish and English.

ASSOCIATES

AURELIO LÓPEZ, born Algeciras, Cádiz, Spain, December 31, 1959; admitted, 1992, Málaga. *Education:* University of Seville (Law Degree, 1981); Escuela Superior de Administración y Dirección de Empresas (Master, Business Administration, 1984); Colegio de Abogados of Seville (Course, Legal Practice, 1981). *Member:* Málaga Bar Association. *LANGUAGES:* English and Spanish.

JESÚS NUÑO, born Málaga, Spain, July 3, 1961; admitted, 1992, Málaga. *Education:* University of Málaga (Law Degree, 1987; Doctorate Course, Economics, 1991). *Member:* Málaga Bar Association. *LANGUAGES:* English and Spanish.

LOURDES DEL MONTE, born Malaga, May 5, 1965; admitted, 1988, Malaga. *Education:* University of Comillas, ICADE (Law Degree, 1988). *Member:* Malaga Bar Association. *LANGUAGES:* Spanish and English.

EMIGDIO DEL TORO, born Villalba del Alcor (Huelva), February 14, 1963; admitted, 1989, Malaga. *Education:* University of Seville (Law Degree, 1986). *Member:* Malaga Bar Association. *LANGUAGES:* Spanish and English.

JOSE ANTONIO FERNANDEZ, born Malaga, Spain, May 14, 1966; admitted, 1990, Malaga. *Education:* University of Comillas, ICADE (Law Degree, 1989; Economic Degree, 1990). *Member:* Malaga Bar Association. *LANGUAGES:* Spanish and English.

ALEJANDRO BEIGVEDER, born Malaga, Spain, May 1967; admitted, 1991, Malaga. *Education:* University of Malaga (Law Degree, 1990). *Member:* Malaga Bar Association. *LANGUAGES:* Spanish and English.

OTHER ASSOCIATES

Antonio Cabello   Manuel Pino
Jose Luis Mapelli

(For Complete Firm Profile, see data at Madrid, Spain)

RAFAEL BERDAGUER

Abogados
RAMIRO CAMPOS TURMO 10 A
29600 MARBELLA, SPAIN
Telephone: (5) 282 23 21; (5) 282 30 85
Telefax: (5) 282 42 46

General Practice, Administrative Law, Civil and Commercial Law, Company Law and Foreign Investment in Spain, Fiscal Law, Family Law, International Law, Domicile, Litigation in all Courts.

PARTNERS

RAFAEL BERDAGUER BARBADILLO, born Málaga, Spain, January 26, 1961; admitted, 1986, Málaga. *Education:* University of Granada (Law); Postgraduate Course General Taxation. *LANGUAGES:* Spanish, English and French.

LOURDES HIJANO UTRERA, born Málaga, Spain, October 15, 1960; admitted, 1986, Málaga. *Education:* University of Málaga (Law). *LANGUAGES:* Spanish, English, French and Italian.

ASSOCIATED MEMBERS

CHARLOTTE TROMEL, born Frankfurt, Germany, July 1, 1964; admitted, 1992, Málaga. *Education:* University Málaga (Economics). *LANGUAGES:* Spanish, English and German.

(This Listing Continued)

MARGARITA OTAOLAURRUCHI, born Sanlúcar de Barrameda, Spain, October 2, 1968. *Education:* University of Navarra (Law); Postgraduate Course Corporate Law. *LANGUAGES:* Spanish and English.

REFERENCES: Barclays Bank; NatWest March; Lloyds Bank; Price Waterhouse (insolvency department; London Bridge 1, London); Y.J. Lovell (España) S.A.

DE LA RIVA Y CRUZ CONDE

C/SANTA ANA 1
EDIF. CITY CENTER
29600 MARBELLA, SPAIN
Telephone: 277-10-94; 277-10-45; 277-30-31
Telefax: 277-10-12

Madrid, Spain Office: San Quintin, 10, 1° Dcha (Plaza de Oriente), 28013. Telephone: 542-31-51; 542-13-39; 542-16-23. Telefax: 247-83-15.

Córdoba, Spain Office: Duque de Hornachuelos, 3-3°, 14002. Telephone: 47-45-70; 47-89-60. Telefax: 47-69-71.

General Practice, Foreign Investments, Civil and Tax Litigation, Corporation, Administrative and Maritime Law.

MEMBERS OF FIRM

ANTONIO DE LA RIVA BOSCH, born Jerez de los Caballeros, Badajoz, May 19, 1931; admitted, 1963, Cordoba; 1982, Málaga. *Education:* University of Sevilla. State Attorney, 1959-1963. *LANGUAGES:* Spanish, Portuguese, English and French.

RAFAEL CRUZ CONDE Y SUAREZ DE TANGIL, born La Granja, Segovia, August 12, 1944; admitted, 1980, Cordoba; 1981, Málaga; 1983, Granada, Almeria and Madrid. *Education:* University of Madrid, ICADE (Law and Master in Business Administration). *LANGUAGES:* Spanish and English.

GUZMAN DE LACALLE Y DE NORIEGA, born Madrid, January 1, 1959; admitted, 1984, Málaga. *Education:* University of Madrid (Law). *LANGUAGES:* Spanish and English.

ASSOCIATES

MANUEL RENEDO OMAECHEVARRIA, born Guernica, Vizcaya, December 31, 1945; admitted, 1978, Cordoba; 1981, Madrid. *Education:* University of Navarra (Law); University of Madrid (Political Science). State Attorney, 1975-1982. Lecturer, Tax Law, University of Cordoba, 1978-1982. *LANGUAGES:* Spanish and French.

MANUEL LACLAUSTRA ARROYO, born Madrid, September 17, 1963; admitted, 1986, Madrid; 1990, Málaga. *Education:* University of Madrid (Law). *LANGUAGES:* Spanish and English.

CARMEN MOLINA SERRANO, born Priego, Córdoba, February 11, 1963; admitted, 1991, Málaga. *Education:* University of Granada (Law). *LANGUAGES:* Spanish and English.

VALLE DE LA RIVA LARA, born Castellón, February 4, 1962; admitted, 1986, Córdoba; 1988, Madrid; 1990, Guadalajara. *Education:* University of Córdoba (Law). *LANGUAGES:* Spanish and English.

LUIS GERMAN BURGOS RUIZ, born Granada, December 25, 1959; admitted, 1993, Málaga. *Education:* University of Granada (Law). *LANGUAGES:* Spanish.

MATTHIAS REINHOLD SCHIEMANN, born Kassel, Germany, April 23, 1956; admitted, 1991. *Education:* Georg August Universität Göttingen (Law). *LANGUAGES:* Spanish, German and English.

REPRESENTATIVE CLIENTS: Bacardi y Cia; Pedro Domecq S.A.; Gonzalez Byass and Co.; Hiram Walker; Destilerias y Crianza del Whisky S.A.
REFERENCES: Banco Español de Crédito S.A.; Banco de Andalucía S.A.; Barclays Bank S.A.E.; Banco de Bilbao-Vizcaya S.A.; Banco de Jerez S.A.

DE LA ROSA & ASOCIADOS

AVDA. RICARDO SORIANO, 22
(EDIFICIO SABADELL)
29600 MARBELLA, SPAIN
Telephone: 34-5-286-3387
Fax: 34-5-286-3559

Seville Office: Santillana 10, 41004, Seville. Telephone: 34-5-456-1162; 34-5-456-3689. Fax: 34-5-421-2954.

General Practice, Foreign Investments, Residential and Commercial Real Estate Developments, Sales, Purchases and Timeshares, Litigation.

DIAZ-BASTIEN & TRUAN ABOGADOS

Established in 1978

SIERRA BLANCA 2, 3° A
29600 MARBELLA, MÁLAGA, SPAIN
Telephone: (5) 277.63.62; 277.63.03; 277.75.04
Facsimile: (5) 282.54.52

Madrid, Spain Office: Hermosilla 21, 2° Izda, 28001. Telephone: (91) 577.36.60; 577.36.61; 577.36.62. Facsimile: (91) 575.54.68.
London, England Office: 111 Park Street, Mayfair, W1Y 3FB. Telephone: (71) 409.20.18, 491.33.08. Facsimile: (71) 629.29.02.

Administrative, Anti-Trust, Arbitration. Aviation, Banking and Finance, Bankruptcy/Insolvency, Civil Litigation, Commercial, Commercial Property, Company, Competition, Constitutional, Construction, Debt Recovery, Distribution, Employment, Entertainment, European Community, Franchising, House Purchase/Conveyancing, Import/Export, Insolvency, Insurance, Intellectual Property, International, Investment and Financial Services, Media, Mergers and Acquisitions, Mortgages/Hypothecates Partnerships, Pharmaceutical, Planning, Real Estate Purchase, Shipping/Admiralty, Tax-Company, Tax-International, Tax-Offshore, Transport, Wills and Probate.

RESIDENT MEMBERS

Hector Diaz-Bastien   Javier Guerrero
Luis Manrique Juega   Maria Jose Rodriguez
Pedro Villalba   Belen Fernandez

Languages: Spanish, English and French

DR. FRÜHBECK
ABOGADOS Y ECONOMISTAS

RAMÓN GÓMEZ DE LA SERNA, 22
EDIF. KING EDWARD, OF. 404
29600 MARBELLA, SPAIN
Telephone: 778589; 778590
Telex: 79827
Telefax: 824-659

Madrid, Spain Office: Marqués del Riscal, 11, 5°, 28010. Telephone: 308-25-22. Telex: 22469; 49214. Telefax: (1)310 28 82.
Barcelona, Spain Office: Balmes, 368, pr 2°, 08006. Telephone: (3) 418 63 87. Telex: (3) 418 93 50.

Business Law, Commercial, Administrative, Tax, Exchange Control, Foreign Investment in Spain, Spanish Investment abroad, Labor, Industrial, Patents and Trademarks, Insolvency, Banking, Maritime Law, Civil Law, Inheritances, Real Estate, Criminal Law and Litigations.

PARTNERS

DR. GUILLERMO FRÜHBECK FRÜHBECK, born Burgos, Spain, September 30, 1926; admitted, 1952, Madrid; 1958, Burgos; 1978 Tenerife; 1981, Santander; 1982, Málaga; 1985, Oviedo; 1986, Las Palmas. *Education:* Universities of Valladolid and Madrid (Dr. in Law, 1963). Seminar for Doctorandi in the Spanish Institute of Comparative Law, 1987. *Member:* German-Spanish Law Association (Vice-President, 1984—). *LANGUAGES:* Spanish, English, German and French.

GUILLERMO FRÜHBECK OLMEDO, born Madrid, Spain, December 30, 1953; admitted, 1976, Madrid. *Education:* University Complutense of Madrid. *LANGUAGES:* Spanish, English and German.

FEDERICO FRÜHBECK OLMEDO, born Madrid, Spain, January 27, 1955; admitted, 1978, Madrid. *Education:* University Complutense of Madrid. *LANGUAGES:* Spanish, English, German and French.

(This Listing Continued)

ASSOCIATE

JOSÉ LUIS PALANCO BÜHRLEN, born Granada, Spain, May 21, 1965; admitted, 1992, Málaga. *Education:* C.E.U. (University Complutense of Madrid). *LANGUAGES:* Spanish, German, English and French.

(For Complete Biographical Data on all Personnel, see Professional Biographies at Madrid, Spain).

J. Y A. GARRIGUES

AVDA. RICARDO SORIANO, 65 - 5° 1
29600 MARBELLA, SPAIN
Telephone: (952) 86-22-11
Facsimile: (952) 82-68-84

REVISERS OF THE SPAIN LAW DIGEST FOR THIS DIRECTORY.

Madrid, Spain Office: Antonio Maura, 16, 28014. Telephone: (34-1) 521-21-51. Facsimile: (34-1) 521-40-53; 531-70-16. Telex: 22153 Aboga.
Barcelona, Spain Office: Mallorca, 260-262, 4°, 2ª, 08008. Telephone: (34-3) 488-12-11. Facsimile: (34-3) 487-53-76; 487-99-26. Telex: 51285.
New York, New York, Office: 115 East 57th Street, Suite 1230, 10022. Telephone: 1-212-751-9233. Facsimile: 1-212-355-3594. Telex: 14-9543.
Brussels, Belgium Office: Rue D'Arlon, 118, B-1040. Telephone: (32-2) 280-16-60. Facsimile: (32-2) 280-15-60.
Oviedo, Spain Office: Marqués de Pidal, 6 - 3°C., 33004. Telephone: (34-8) 527-73-75. Facsimile: (34-8) 527-73-83.
Seville, Spain Office: Zaragoza, 50, 41001. Telephone: (34-5) 456-45-36. Facsimile: (34-5) 456-47-52.
Lisbon, Portugal Office: Grupo Legal Português (EEIG) in association with F. Castelo Branco, Nobre Guedes & P. Rebelo de Sousa, Simmons & Simmons and Pinheiro Neto & Co. Rua Castilho, n°- 9°/ 1200 Lisbon. Telephone: (351-1) 352-13-18. Facsimile: (351-1) 352-14-18.

General Practice, Administrative, Corporation, International Labor Relations, Oil and Gas, Mines, Foreign Investments, Banking, Estate Law and Taxation, Maritime Law.

RESIDENT LAWYERS

CARLOS BUSTILLO MUÑOZ, born Avila, Spain, 1956; admitted, 1985, Spain. *Education:* University of Madrid. *Member:* Malaga Bar Association.

ISABEL FERRER LOPEZ, born Alicante, Spain, 1962; admitted, 1985, Spain. *Education:* University of Alicante; University of Amsterdam (Diploma on European Integration, 1986). *Member:* Elche and Malaga Bar Associations.

DOLORES MOLINA FERNANDEZ, born Priego, Cordoba, Spain, 1967; admitted, 1990, Spain. *Education:* University of I.C.A.D.E. - Comillas - Madrid. *Member:* Malaga Bar Association.

REVISERS OF THE SPAIN LAW DIGEST FOR THIS DIRECTORY.

PEREZ DE VARGAS ABOGADOS

C/Mª AUXILIADORA N° 2
EDIFICIO PATA-PATA 5° IZDA.
29600 MARBELLA, SPAIN
Telephone: (95) 778848; 824160
Telefax: (95) 825159

Estepona, Spain Office: C/Buenavista 2, Edificio Peñas Blancas 1° 9, 28680. Telephone: (52) 801431; 800006. Telefax: (52) 803994.

General Practice, Commercial and Civil Law, Litigations, Banking, Company Law, Foreign Investment and Tax Advice, Administrative Law, Urbanism and Planning, Real Estate Promotions, Inheritances.

MEMBERS OF FIRM

IGNACIO PEREZ DE VARGAS LOPEZ, born Estepona, Málaga, September 25, 1948; admitted, 1973, Málaga; 1978, Granada; 1981, Sevilla and Cádiz. *Education:* University of Granada (Law Degree, 1973). *LANGUAGES:* Spanish and English. *PRACTICE AREAS:* General Practice; Administrative Law; Municipal Law and Local Government; Expropriation; Land Development.

MARIA ISABEL FUENTES VILLAR, born Málaga, October 19, 1952; admitted, 1977, Málaga. *Education:* University of Granada (Law Degree,

(This Listing Continued)

PEREZ DE VARGAS ABOGADOS, Marbella—Continued

1976). *LANGUAGES:* Spanish and English. *PRACTICE AREAS:* General Practice; Banks and Banking; Banking Litigation; Banking Regulation; Finance Law.

AURORA HERRERA LLAMAS, born Málaga, September 20, 1962; admitted, 1986, Madrid; 1987, Málaga. *Education:* University of Madrid ICADE (Law and Company Advisor Degree, 1985). *LANGUAGES:* Spanish and English. *PRACTICE AREAS:* General Practice; Banks and Banking; Banking Litigation; Banking Regulation; Finance Law.

ASSOCIATES

INMACULADA SANCHEZ FALQUINA, born Segovia, October 27, 1965; admitted, 1991, Málaga. *Education:* University of Segovia (Law Degree, 1989). *LANGUAGES:* Spanish and English. *PRACTICE AREAS:* General Practice; Banks and Banking; Banking Litigation; Banking Regulation; Mortgages and Enforcement of Mortgages.

ENRIQUE BALMASEDA FERNANDEZ, born Málaga, June 12, 1967; admitted, 1991, Málaga. *Education:* University of Granada (Law Degree, 1991). *LANGUAGES:* Spanish and English. *PRACTICE AREAS:* General Practice; Banks and Banking; Banking Litigation; Banking Regulation; Mortgages and Enforcement of Mortgages.

ARTHUR ANDERSEN
ASESORES LEGALES Y TRIBUTARIOS

Legal and Tax Advisors

PLAZA DE LA ESCANDALERA, 3-3°Y 4°A
33003 OVIEDO, SPAIN
Telephone: 34-85-219849
Fax: 34-85-218857

Arthur Andersen Asesores Legales y Tributarios's offices: Alicante, Barcelona, Bilbao, Granada, La Coruña, Madrid, Málaga, Oviedo, Palma de Mallorca, San Sebastian, Sevilla, Valencia, Vigo, Vitoria, Zaragoza.

Associated Law Firms abroad: France, Italy, Germany, Portugal, The Netherlands, Belgium, United Kingdom, South Africa, Colombia and Brazil.

PARTNER

JOSÉ MANUEL BURGOS, born Madrid, Spain, September 2, 1945; admitted, 1967, Madrid. *Education:* University of Madrid (Law Degree, 1967). Professor, Civil Law, Madrid University. Co-Author: "La reforma de la Legislación Mercantil," Editorial CDN, 1990. *Member:* Madrid and International Bar Associations. *LANGUAGES:* Spanish and English.

ASSOCIATES

Manuel Alvarez	*Fernando Herrero*
Pablo Alvarez De Linera	*Alma Menéndez*
	Enrique Señaris

(For Complete Firm Profile, see data at Madrid, Spain)

J. Y A. GARRIGUES

MARQUES DE PIDAL, 6-3° C
33004 OVIEDO, ASTURIAS, SPAIN
Telephone: (98) 527-73-75
Facsimile: (98) 527-73-83

REVISERS OF THE SPAIN LAW DIGEST FOR THIS DIRECTORY.

Madrid, Spain Office: Antonio Maura, 16, 28014. Telephone: (34-1) 521-21-51. Facsimile: (34-1) 521-40-53; 531-70-16. Telex: 22189 Aboga.

Barcelona, Spain Office: Mallorca, 260-262, 4°, 2ª, 08008. Telephone: (34-3) 488-12-11. Facsimile: (34-3) 487-53-76; 487-99-26. Telex: 51285.

New York, New York Office: 115 East 57th Street, Suite 1230, 10022. Telephone: 1-212-751-9233. Facsimile: 1-212-355-3594. Telex: 14-9543.

Brussels, Belgium Office: Rue D'Arlon, 118, B-1040. Telephone: (32-2) 280-16-60. Facsimile: (32-2) 280-15-60.

Marbella, Spain Office: Avda. Ricardo Soriano, 65 - 5° 1. Telephone: (34-52) 86-22-11. Facsimile: (34-52) 82-68-84.

Seville, Spain Office: Zaragoza, 50, 41001. Telephone: (34-5) 456-45-36. Facsimile: (34-5) 456-47-52.

(This Listing Continued)

Lisbon, Portugal Office: Grupo Legal Portuguêse (EEIG) in association with F. Castelo Branco, Nobre Guedes & P. Rebelo de Sousa, Simmons & Simmons and Pinheiro Neto & Co. Rua Castilho, n°32 - 9°/ 1200 Lisbon. Telephone: (351-1) 352-13-18. Facsimile: (351-1) 352-14-18.

RESIDENT LAWYER

MIGUEL FUERTES SUAREZ, born Oviedo, Spain, 1951; admitted, 1983. *Education:* University of Oviedo; Europa College, Brugge, Belgium; Diplomatic School, Madrid. *Member:* Oviedo and Gijon Bar Associations.

REVISERS OF THE SPAIN LAW DIGEST FOR THIS DIRECTORY.

RAMOS & ARROYO

CIMADEVILLA 19-2°B
33003 OVIEDO, SPAIN
Telephone: (8) 520 42 80
Fax: (8) 520 42 80

Barcelona, Spain Office: Paseo de Gracia 92 (La Pedrera), 08008. Telephone: (3) 487 11 12; (3) 215 77 11. Fax: (3) 487 35 62.

Cadiz, Spain Office: Avenida Ramón de Carranza, 20, 11006. Telephone: (56) 25 22 00. Fax: (56) 26 16 55. Telex: 76192 Hull E.

Fuengirola, Málaga, Spain Office: Córdoba, Edificio Centro Comercial Reyes, 6°B, 29640. Telephone: (5) 258 45 72; (5) 258 45 90. Fax: (5) 258 45 72.

Madrid, Spain Office: Serrano 89-7°, 28006. Telephone: (1) 5629200. Fax: (1) 561 49 03.

Admiralty, Arbitration, Bankruptcy, Commercial, Competition, Construction, Copyright, Corporation, EEC, General Practice, Insurance, Labour, Litigation, Taxation, Trademarks & Patents and Real Estate Law.

MEMBERS OF FIRM

JOSE-ALEJO RUEDA MARTINEZ, born Escobar de Campos, Spain, August 18, 1954; admitted, 1988, Oviedo. *Education:* University of Oviedo (LL.B.); University Autonoma of Barcelona (Doctor of Laws, cum laude, 1988). Author: "Código de Legislación Empresarial"; "Compraventa de buques." Professor, Commercial Law. *LANGUAGES:* Spanish, English, French and Italian.

AMPARO LESMES GONZALEZ, born Oviedo, Spain, June 6, 1961; admitted, 1988, Gijón and Oviedo. *Education:* University of Oviedo (LL.B.). *LANGUAGES:* Spanish and English.

(For complete biographical data on all personnel, see Professional Biographies at Barcelona, Spain).

ARTHUR ANDERSEN
ASESORES LEGALES Y TRIBUTARIOS

Legal and Tax Advisors

BARÓN DE PINOPAR, 22
07012 PALMA DE MALLORCA, SPAIN
Telephone: 34-71-719272
Fax: 34-71-710098

Arthur Andersen Asesores Legales y Tributarios's offices: Alicante, Barcelona, Bilbao, Granada, La Coruña, Madrid, Málaga, Oviedo, Palma de Mallorca, San Sebastian, Sevilla, Valencia, Vigo, Vitoria, Zaragoza.

Associated Law Firms abroad: France, Italy, Germany, Portugal, The Netherlands, Belgium, United Kingdom, South Africa, Colombia and Brazil.

PARTNER

PEDRO PABLO RODES, born Palma de Mallorca, Baleares, Spain, July 18, 1955; admitted, 1982, Barcelona. *Education:* University of Barcelona (Economics Degree, 1977; Law Degree, 1979); Barcelona Tax Studies Center (Master, 1979). *Member:* Barcelona Bar Association. *LANGUAGES:* Spanish, French and English.

(This Listing Continued)

RESIDENT ASSOCIATES

JOSE LUIS ROS, born Barcelona, Spain, March 8, 1960; admitted, 1990, Baleares. *Education:* INEDE-FERT, UNED (Law Degree, 1982); Barcelona Tax Studies Center (Master, 1985). *Member:* Baleares Bar Association and R.O.A.C. (Official Institute of Auditors). *LANGUAGES:* Spanish and English.

JOSE MANUEL CARDONA, born Ibiza, Spain, June 14, 1964; admitted, 1987, Baleares. *Education:* University of Baleares (Law Degree, 1987); Instituto de Empresa, Madrid (Master Company Taxation, 1990). *Author:* "Los expolits en el derecho foral balear," Ed University of Islas Baleares. *Member:* Baleares Bar Association. *LANGUAGES:* Spanish and English.

FRANCISCO ROSSELLÓ, born Palma de Mallorca, Baleares, Spain, May 29, 1965; admitted, 1991, Palma de Mallorca. *Education:* University of Baleares (Law Degree, 1990); Instituto de Empresa, Madrid (Master Company Taxation, 1991). *Member:* Baleares Bar Association. *LANGUAGES:* English.

(For Complete Firm Profile, see data at Madrid, Spain)

BUFETE FELIU

Established in 1927

PASEO MALLORCA 2
07012 PALMA DE MALLORCA (BALEARIC ISLANDS), SPAIN
Telephone: (34 71) 714849 / 713287
Fax: (34 71) 721546

Firm engaged in Spanish Law Practice, especially Mercantile Law, Civil Law, Tax Law, Labour Code, Foreign Investment, Law of Real Estate, Patents, Community Law.

FIRM PROFILE: In 1927 José Feliu Rosselló founded the Legal Office which has been developed into BUFETE FELIU with the incorporation of his sons, first José Feliu Vidal in 1962, then Alejandro Feliu Vidal in 1971 and Gabriel Feliu Vidal in 1973. More recently, in 1988, his grandson Miguel Feliu Bordoy joined the family firm, and in 1990 Francisca Ochogavia Bennassar. Apart from the above mentioned Lawyers, Bufete Feliu has a Tax advisory Department, run by the founder's grandson José Luis Feliu Bordoy since 1991, and a Department dealing with Labour matters.

In principle the firm covers all aspects of Legal Practice however, due to the touristic influx since the Fifties, mainly engaged in assessment and administration of foreign, and later national, investments in Spain and also abroad, specifically in United Europe, N. Africa and S. America.

In the last decade, with the incorporation of new members, the firm has specialized not only in Mercantile Law, but in Civil, Penal, Tax and Labour Laws.

Association:

Member of CONSULEGIS (European Joint Consulting) EEIG Management Office: Auguststraße 14, D-22085 Hamburg, Germany.

Member of DEUTSCH-SPANISH JURISTENVEREINIGUNG e.V. (Assn. of German & Spanish Lawyers) General Sekretariat: C/Enrique Granados, 114, 08006 Barcelona, Spain.

MEMBERS OF FIRM

JOSE FELIU VIDAL, born Palma, March 6, 1936; admitted, 1962, Spain. Experience in Legal Office in Bournemouth G.B. Real Estate Agent since 1970. Qualified by E.S.I.T.E. Accountancy and Financial Analysis (1985). *Member:* College of Lawyers of Balearic Islands. *LANGUAGES:* Spanish, English, French and Catalonian. *PRACTICE AREAS:* Civil; Corporate; Mercantile Law; Foreign Investment; Real Estate.

ALEJANDRO FELIU VIDAL, born Palma, June 17, 1946; admitted, 1971, Spain. *Education:* University of Barcelona. Experience in Legal Office in London, Paris and Geneva (1970). Estate Administrator. Representative of Financing Group Abbey National in the Balearic Islands. *Member:* College of Lawyers of Balearic Islands. *LANGUAGES:* Spanish, English, French, Italian and Catalonian. *PRACTICE AREAS:* Civil Law; Conveyancing; Foreign Investment; Property Development; Golf Courses; Mortgages.

GABRIEL FELIU VIDAL, born Palma, January 4, 1949; admitted, 1973, Spain. *Education:* University of Barcelona (2 years study of Economics; 1976, History and Geography). Professor, Private Law, Balearic Island School of Tourism (1978-1979). *Member:* College of Lawyers of the Balearic

(This Listing Continued)

Islands. *LANGUAGES:* Spanish, French, English, German, Italian and Catalonian. *PRACTICE AREAS:* Civil Law; Conveyancing; Foreign Investment; Nautical Matters.

MIGUEL FELIU BORDOY, born Palma, July 15, 1965; admitted, 1988, Spain. *Education:* University of Balearic Islands; University of Alcalá de Henares. *Member:* College of Lawyers of Balearic Islands. *LANGUAGES:* Spanish, English and Catalonian. *PRACTICE AREAS:* Litigation; Civil Law; Mercantile Law.

FRANCISCA OCHOGAVIA BENNASSAR, born Palma, July 14, 1966; admitted, 1990, Spain. *Education:* University of Balearic Islands. *Member:* College of Lawyers of Balearic Islands. *LANGUAGES:* Spanish, English and Catalonian. *PRACTICE AREAS:* Civil Law; Matrimonial; Family Matters; Penal Law; Mercantile Law.

JOSE LUIS FELIU BORDOY, born Palma, July 21, 1964. *Education:* University of Balearic Islands (Economics and Business Management, 1988); Management Study Center in Madrid (Master in Tax and Fiscal Assessment, 1989). *Member:* Spanish Association of Tax Assessors; Balearic Islands Association of Tax Assessors (Board Member, 1990). *LANGUAGES:* Spanish, English, German and Catalonian. *PRACTICE AREAS:* Corporate Fiscal Policy; Accounting; Taxation Counselling and Service.

ARTHUR ANDERSEN
ASESORES LEGALES Y TRIBUTARIOS

Legal and Tax Advisors

AVENIDA INFANTA CRISTINA, 11
2008 SAN SEBASTIAN, SPAIN
Telephone: 34-943-217033
Fax: 34-943-218479

Arthur Andersen Asesores Legales y Tributarios's offices: Alicante, Barcelona, Bilbao, Granada, La Coruña, Madrid, Málaga, Oviedo, Palma de Mallorca, San Sebastian, Sevilla, Valencia, Vigo, Vitoria, Zaragoza.

Associated Law Firms abroad: France, Italy, Germany, Portugal, The Netherlands, Belgium, United Kingdom, South Africa, Colombia and Brazil.

PARTNER

ANA MARÍA ARMESTO, born Bilbao, Spain, February 7, 1956; admitted, 1987, Bilbao; 1991, Madrid. *Education:* University of Deusto (Law Degree, 1978). *Member:* Bilbao and Madrid Bar Associations. *LANGUAGES:* Spanish, English and French.

RESIDENT ASSOCIATES

JORGE IBÁÑEZ, born Bilbao, Spain, September 17, 1960; admitted, 1990, Guipuzcoa. *Education:* University of Deusto (Bilbao) (Law Degree, 1984). Economist Specialty. *Member:* Guipuzcoa Bar Association. *LANGUAGES:* Spanish and French.

IGNACIO IRIGOYEN, born Vigo, Spain, December 3, 1965; admitted, 1991, Madrid. *Education:* University of Deusto (Bilbao) (Law Degree, 1988); Instituto de Empresa (Master, Corporation Counsel, 1990). *Member:* Madrid Bar Association. *LANGUAGES:* Spanish and English.

OTHER ASSOCIATES

Francisco Javier de Miguel   Juan Abrisqueta
Jesús Alvarez   Roberto Delgado

(For Complete Firm Profile, see data at Madrid, Spain)

GOMEZ-ACEBO & POMBO

CASAS REALES, 4
15704 SANTIAGO de COMPOSTELA, SPAIN
Telephone: (348) 157-33-46
Fax: (348) 157-35-46

Madrid, Spain Office: Castellana, 164, 28046. Telephone: (341) 582 91 00. Fax: (341) 345 36 79; 582 91 14. Cable: Juristas. Telex: 23429 GAPO E.

Barcelona, Spain Office: Diagonal 442, 08037. Telephone: (343) 415-74-00. Fax: (343) 415-84-00.

Bilbao, Spain Office: Gran Vía, 31, 48009. Telephone: (344) 415-62-66/77. Fax: (344) 416-87-49.

(This Listing Continued)

GOMEZ-ACEBO & POMBO, Santiago de Compostela— Continued

Las Palmas (Canary Islands), Spain Office: Viera y Clavijo, 48, 35002. Telephone: (342) 838-38-36. Fax: (342) 838-38-56.

Seville, Spain Office: Av. de la Constitución, 40, 41001. Telephone: (345) 421-66-59; 422-18-93. Fax: (345) 421-08-14.

Valencia, Spain Office: Gran Vía Marqués del Turia, 49, 46005. Telephone: (346) 351-38-35. Fax: (346) 351-60-74.

Brussels, Belgium Office: Rue de la Loi, 99/101, 1040. Telephone: (322) 231-12-20. Fax: (322) 230-80-35.

Carlos Fernandez Novoa

(For Complete Biographical Data on all Personnel, see Professional Biographies at Madrid, Spain).

ARTHUR ANDERSEN
ASESORES LEGALES Y TRIBUTARIOS

Legal and Tax Advisors

AVENIDA DE BLAS INFANTE, 8
41011 SEVILLE, SPAIN
Telephone: 34-54-456811
Fax: 34-54-459975

Arthur Andersen Asesores Legales y Tributarios's offices: Alicante, Barcelona, Bilbao, Granada, La Coruña, Madrid, Málaga, Oviedo, Palma de Mallorca, San Sebastian, Sevilla, Valencia, Vigo, Vitoria, Zaragoza.

Associated Law Firms abroad: France, Italy, Germany, Portugal, The Netherlands, Belgium, United Kingdom, South Africa, Colombia and Brazil.

PARTNER

DAVID MORENO, born Madrid, Spain, December 4, 1956; admitted, 1989, Seville. *Education:* University of Deusto (Law Degree, 1979); ICADE (Master, Business Administration); Instituto de Empresa (Master, Corporation Taxes Counsel, 1983); Instituto Internacional San Telmo (Graduate, Corporation Management, 1990). Professor, Business Law, University of Seville. Co-Author: "El IVA verde," 1986; "Adaptación de su Empresa a la Reforma Mercantil," 1989. *Member:* Seville Bar Association. *LANGUAGES:* Spanish and English.

ASSOCIATES

ÁLVARO SILVA, born San Fernando, Cádiz, Spain, April 29, 1961; admitted, 1985, Seville. *Education:* ICADE (Law Degree, 1984; Economics Degree, 1987). Professor, Collaboration at Business Law, University of Seville. *Member:* Seville Bar Association. *LANGUAGES:* Spanish and English.

ANTONIO JESÚS UCEDA, born Palma del Río, Córdoba, Spain, October 26, 1964; admitted, 1987, Seville. *Education:* University of Seville (Law Degree, 1987). *Member:* Seville Bar Association. *LANGUAGES:* Spanish and English.

RAFAEL BENÍTEZ, born Seville, July, 1963; admitted, 1990, Seville. *Education:* University of Madrid, Complutense (Law Degree, 1986), Diploma School of Legal Practice, University of Madrid, Complutense. *LANGUAGES:* Spanish and English.

OTHER ASSOCIATES

Ignacio Montaño	Lázaro Cepas
Salvador Carrero	Maria Romero
Ignacio Cantillana	Juan Alarcón
	Miguel Oñate

(For Complete Firm Profile, see data at Madrid, Spain)

DE LA ROSA & ASOCIADOS

SANTILLANA, 10
41004 SEVILLE, SPAIN
Telephone: 34-5-456-1162; 34-5-456-3689
Fax: 34-5-421-2954

Marbella, Spain Office: Avda. Ricardo Soriano 22. Telephone: 34-5-286-3387. Fax: 34-5-286-3559.

(This Listing Continued)

Corporate and Commercial Law, Foreign Investments, Joint Ventures, Intellectual Property, Transfer of Technology and Licensing, Real Estate, Insurance, Arbitration, "ARD", Litigation.

FIRM PROFILE: The Firm specialises in Foreign Private and Business Investments in Spain, in general, and in Andalucía, in particular, and offers its international corporate and individual clients a high quality, efficient, experienced and personalised service at competitive rates.

JOSÉ DE LA ROSA, born Seville, Spain, December 10, 1948; admitted, 1975, Seville; 1980, Madrid and Zaragoza; 1988, Málaga. *Education:* University of Seville (1972); Georgetown University (1979); New York University (M.C.J., 1980); Course on American Legal Institutions, Salzburg Seminar, 1981; Course on International Transactions, Salzburg Seminar, 1984; Course on European Law, Salzburg Seminars, 1993. *Member:* IBA; ABA; INTA; Fulbright Association.

ASSOCIATES

Gregorio Peralta	Francisco Bono
Luis Carlos Leal	Jorge Moreno
Magdalena Cerero	Jesus Suárez
Javier Tirado	(Industrial Property Agent)

Languages: Spanish, English and French

J. Y A. GARRIGUES

ZARAGOZA, 50
41001 SEVILLE, SPAIN
Telephone: (95) 456 45 36
Facsimile: (95) 456 47 52

REVISERS OF THE SPAIN LAW DIGEST FOR THIS DIRECTORY.

Madrid, Spain Office: Antonio Maura, 16, 28014. Telephone: (34-1) 521-21-51. Facsimile: (34-1) 521-40-53; 531-70-16. Telex: 22153 Aboga.

Barcelona, Spain Office: Mallorca, 260-262, 4°, 2ª, 08008. Telephone: (34-3) 488-12-11. Facsimile: (34-3) 487-53-76; 487-99-26. Telex: 51285.

New York, New York Office: 115 East 57th Street, Suite 1230, 10022. Telephone: 1-212-751-9233. Facsimile: 1-212-355-3594. Telex: 14-9543.

Brussels, Belgium Office: Rue D'Arlon, 118. B - 1040. Telephone: (32-2) 280-16-60. Facsimile: (32-2) 280-15-60.

Marbella, Spain Office: Avda. Ricardo Soriano, 65 - 5° 1. Telephone: (34-52) 86-22-11. Facsimile: (34-52) 82-68-84.

Oviedo, Spain Office: Marqués de Pidal, 6 - 3°C., 33004. Telephone: (34-8) 527-73-75. Facsimile: (34-8) 527-73-83.

Lisbon, Portugal Office: Grupo Legal Portuguêse (EEIG) in association with F. Castelo Branco, Nobre Guedes & P. Rebelo de Sousa, Simmons & Simmons and Pinheiro Neto & Co. Rua Castilho, n°32 9°/ 1200 Lisbon. Telephone: (351-1) 352-13-18. Facsimile: (351-1) 352-14-18.

General Practice, Administrative, Corporation, International Labor Relations, Oil and Gas, Mines, Foreign Investments, Banking, Estate Law and Taxation, Maritime Law.

FERNANDO GONZALEZ DE LA PEÑA YSERN, born Jerez de la Frontera, Spain, 1956; admitted, 1981, Spain. *Education:* University of Sevilla (licenciatura en Derecho, 1979). *Member:* Sevilla, Huelva and Jerez de la Frontera, Cádiz and Jaen Bar Associations. *LANGUAGES:* English.

ALVARO PEREZ ARBIZU, born Sevilla, Spain, 1968. *Education:* University of Sevilla (Licenciatura de Derecho, 1991); Postgraduate Studies in Financial and Taxation Law). *Member:* Sevilla Bar Association. *LANGUAGES:* English.

AURELIO ORRILLO LARA, born La Linea, Spain, 1967; admitted, 1993, Spain. *Education:* University of Navarra (Law Degree and Master in Business Law). *Member:* Sevilla Bar Association. *LANGUAGES:* English.

REVISERS OF THE SPAIN LAW DIGEST FOR THIS DIRECTORY.

GOMEZ-ACEBO & POMBO

AV. DE LA CONSTITUCIÓN, 40
41001 SEVILLE, SPAIN
Telephone: (345) 421-66-59; 422-18-93
Fax: (345) 421-08-14

Madrid, Spain Office: Castellana, 164, 28046. Telephone: (341) 582 91
00. Fax: (341) 345 36 79; 582 91 14. Cable: Juristas. Telex: 23429
GAPO E.

Barcelona, Spain Office: Diagonal 442, 08037. Telephone: (343)
415-74-00. Fax: (343) 415-84-00.

Bilbao, Spain Office: Gran Vía, 31, 48009. Telephone: (344)
415-62-66/77. Fax: (344) 416-87-49.

Las Palmas (Canary Islands), Spain Office: Viera y Clavijo, 48, 35002.
Telephone: (342) 838-38-36. Fax: (342) 838-38-56.

Santiago de Compostela, Spain Office: Casas Reales, 4, 15704. Telephone:
(348) 157-33-46. Fax: (348) 157-35-46.

Valencia, Spain Office: Gran Vía Marqués del Turia, 49, 46005.
Telephone: (346) 351-38-35. Fax: (346) 351-60-74.

Brussels, Belgium Office: Rue de la Loi, 99/101, 1040. Telephone: (322)
231-12-20. Fax: (322) 230-80-35.

Luis Javier Fernandez-Palacios
Manuel Bellido
Isabel Carmona
Jose Joaquin Silva
Manuel Dorado
Macarena Calvillo

(For Complete Biographical Data on all Personnel, see Professional
Biographies at Madrid, Spain).

ARTHUR ANDERSEN
ASESORES LEGALES Y TRIBUTARIOS

Legal and Tax Advisors

PASCUAL Y GENÍS, 1
46002 VALENCIA, SPAIN
Telephone: 34-6-352 9125
Fax: 34-6-394-42-34

Arthur Andersen Asesores Legales y Tributarios's offices: Alicante,
Barcelona, Bilbao, Granada, La Coruña, Madrid, Málaga, Oviedo,
Palma de Mallorca, San Sebastian, Sevilla, Valencia, Vigo, Vitoria,
Zaragoza.

Associated Law Firms abroad: France, Italy, Germany, Portugal, The
Netherlands, Belgium, United Kingdom, South Africa, Colombia and
Brazil.

PARTNER

EDUARDO FERNÁNDEZ DE VALDERRAMA, born Madrid, Spain,
January 13, 1951; admitted, 1974, Madrid. *Education:* ICADE (Law De-
gree, 1973; Economics Degree, 1974). *Member:* Madrid Bar Association.
LANGUAGES: English and Spanish.

ASSOCIATES

JOSE LUIS DE TOMÁS, born Valencia, Spain, May 23, 1961; admit-
ted, 1986, Valencia. *Education:* University of Valencia (Law Degree, 1984;
Economics Degree, 1985). *Member:* Valencia and Murcia Bar Associations.
LANGUAGES: English and Spanish.

RAMÓN TRENOR, born Valencia, Spain, April, 1962; admitted, 1991,
Valencia. *Education:* ICADE (Law Degree, 1985; Economics Degree,
1986). *Member:* Valencia and Albacete Bar Associations. *LANGUAGES:*
English and Spanish.

CARLOS PEIRÓ, born Gandía, Valencia, Spain, July 27, 1963; admit-
ted, 1991, Valencia. *Education:* University of Valencia (Law Degree, 1988);
Instituto de Empresa (Master, Legal Counsel, 1989); Escuela de Economía
(Master, Tax Counsel, 1990). *Member:* Valencia Bar Association. *LAN-
GUAGES:* Spanish and English.

(This Listing Continued)

LUIS SEBASTIA, born Valencia, June 3, 1964; admitted, 1992, Valencia. *Education:* University of Valencia (Law Degree, 1988). *Member:* Valencia Bar Association. *LANGUAGES:* Spanish and English.

OTHER ASSOCIATES

Antonio Lon   **Isabel Pellicer**
                    Maria José Calvet

(For Complete Firm Profile, see data at Madrid, Spain)

DURAN Y LALAGUNA

Abogados

AV. ARAGON, 12
46021 VALENCIA, SPAIN
Telephone: 34-6- 337 2383
Fax: 34-6-3371519

General Practice, Banking and Business Law, Civil Law, Corporate and
Competition Law, Property Law, Patents.

FIRM PROFILE: The Firm was established in 1984 and offers a full
range services. There are three partners and a legal support staff of paralegals. This firm has an associate program with other firms in Spain and the
rest of Europe. The legal firm has associate lawyers and economists and
an adequate staff of office administrators.

MEMBERS OF FIRM

MARIANO DURAN LALAGUNA, (Founding Member) born Valen-
cia, Spain. *Education:* Valencia University Law: School Bachelor and Master Private Law (1981); Jurisprudence Academy Valencia: Judicial Practice
Program (1984); Chamber of Commerce, Valencia: European Community
Law Postgraduate studies (1985); Law School Jaime I University: Doctoral
thesis (Commercial and Business Law, 1991). *Member:* Valencia Bar Association; Alicante Bar Association; International Lawyers Union; Lawyers
of Europe; Banking Commission of International Union Lawyers. *PRAC-
TICE AREAS:* Banking and Business Law.

ENRIQUE DURAN LALAGUNA, born Melilla, Spain. *Education:* Valencia University Law School: Bachelor and Master Private Law (1976);
Jurisprudence Academy, Valencia: Juridical Practice Program (1978); Valencia University Law School: Doctoral Program, Civil Law (1982). Lecturer in Law (Civil Branch). *Member:* Valencia Bar Association. *PRAC-
TICE AREAS:* Civil Law; Patents; International Law.

PALOMA DURAN LALAGUNA, born Valencia, Spain. *Education:*
Navarre University Law School (1982); Navarre University Canon Law,
Ph.D, (1983); Navarre University Law School, Ph.D. (1987). Lecturer in
Law (Legal theory). Visiting Scholar: Columbia University, USA, 1990;
Visiting Scholar, McGill University, Canada (1991). Visiting Professor,
Oxford University, (1992). Author: "Economic analysis of law"; "The juris-
prudence of the European Court of Human Rights"; "On Human Right."
Member: Valencia Bar Association; International Association of Consul-
tants on Human Rights. *PRACTICE AREAS:* Human Rights; Canon
Law; Family Law.

ASSOCIATES

Jesus De Obeso Corbalan   **Vicente Carbonell Pastor**

Languages: Spanish, English, French and Italian.

GOMEZ-ACEBO & POMBO

GRAN VÍA MARQUÉS DEL TURIA, 49
46005 VALENCIA, SPAIN
Telephone: (346) 351-38-35
Fax: (346) 351-60-74

Madrid, Spain Office: Castellana, 164, 28046. Telephone: (341) 582 91
00. Fax: (341) 345 36 79; 582 91 14. Cable: Juristas. Telex: 23429
GAPO E.

Barcelona, Spain Office: Diagonal 442, 08037. Telephone: (343)
415-74-00. Fax: (343) 415-84-00.

Bilbao, Spain Office: Gran Vía, 31, 48009. Telephone: (344)
415-62-66/77. Fax: (344) 416-87-49.

Las Palmas (Canary Islands), Spain Office: Viera y Clavijo, 48, 35002.
Telephone: (342) 838-38-36. Fax: (342) 838-38-56.

Santiago de Compostela, Spain Office: Casas Reales, 4, 15704. Telephone:
(348) 157-33-46. Fax: (348) 157-35-46.

(This Listing Continued)

GOMEZ-ACEBO & POMBO, Valencia—Continued

Seville, Spain Office: Av. de la Constitución, 40, 41001. Telephone: (345) 421-66-59; 422-18-93. Fax: (345) 421-08-14.
Brussels, Belgium Office: Rue de la Loi, 99/101, 1040. Telephone: (322) 231-12-20. Fax: (322) 230-80-35.

Ignacio Alamar
Francisco Fita
Juana Maria Fores
Ana Fita

(For Complete Biographical Data on all Personnel, see Professional Biographies at Madrid, Spain).

SARDA, CALOMARDE, CASTELO & ASOCIADOS

CRONISTA CARRERES, 13, 4° 8°
46003 VALENCIA, SPAIN
Telephone: 6/352.96.03
Fax: 6/394.26.86

Barcelona, Spain Office: Muntaner, 407, 1° 2°, 08021. Telephone: 3/201.64.66. Fax: 3/202.00.96.
Madrid, Spain Office: P° de la Castellana, 228, 3°, 28046. Telephone: 1/314.19.34. Fax: 1/314.19.52.

European Community Law, International Banking and Business Law, Foreign Investment Law, General International Trade, Corporate, Civil and Criminal Litigation, Competition and Copyright Law, Insurance Law, Family Law, Procedural Law, Bankruptcy Law and Tax Law.

FIRM PROFILE: *The firm, established in 1993 is the result of the association of three Lawyer's offices: Sardá y Asociados in Barcelona, established in 1964, Mas Millet y Calomarde, established in Valencia in 1978 and Castelo y Larraz, established in Madrid in 1975. It is a member of LE-GALLIANCE (EEIG) a large union of European lawyers with offices in Brussels, Paris, London, Berlin, Frankfurt, Cologne, Leipzig, Milan, Bologna, Padua, The Hague and Stockholm.*

RESIDENT MEMBERS OF FIRM

JOSE MARIA MAS MILLET, born Gandía (Valencia), October 14, 1953; admitted, 1978, Valencia. *Education:* University of Valencia (1976). *Member:* Valencia and Madrid Bar Associations. **LANGUAGES:** Valencian, Spanish and English. **PRACTICE AREAS:** International Banking and Business Law; Foreign Investment Law; Bankruptcy Law; Company Law.

ENRIQUE CALOMARDE RODRIGO, born Valencia, July 3, 1957; admitted, 1982, Valencia. *Education:* University of Valencia (1979). *Member:* Valencia, Castellon, Alicante Bar Associations. **LANGUAGES:** Spanish and English. **PRACTICE AREAS:** International Banking and Business Law; Foreign Investment Law; Bankruptcy Law; Company Law.

JAVIER PLA MAS, born OLIVA (Valencia, May 15, 1956; admitted, 1991, Valencia. *Education:* University of Navarra (1978). *Member:* Valencia Bar Association. **LANGUAGES:** Valencian, Spanish and French. **PRACTICE AREAS:** Company Law; Civil and Criminal Litigation.

ASSOCIATE MEMBERS

Rafael Mas Millet   **Javier Alvarez Alonso**
Amparo Pont Perez

ARTHUR ANDERSEN
ASESORES LEGALES Y TRIBUTARIOS

Legal and Tax Advisors
POLICARPO SANZ, 3
36202 VIGO, SPAIN
Telephone: 34-86-433766
Fax: 34-86-430316

(Costa Rica, 5 - 15004 LA CORUÑNA - SPAIN; Telephone: 34-81-264695, Fax: 34-81-276248).
Arthur Andersen Asesores Legales y Barcelona, Bilbao, Granada, La Coruña, Madrid, Málaga, Oviedo, Palma de Mallorca, San Sebastian, Sevilla, Valencia, Vigo, Vitoria, Zaragoza.

(This Listing Continued)

Associated Law Firms abroad: France, Italy, Germany, Portugal, The Netherlands, Belgium, United Kingdom, South Africa, Colombia and Brazil.

RESIDENT ASSOCIATES

JAVIER BÚA, born Vigo, Spain, May 21, 1963; admitted, 1987, Madrid; 1991, Vigo. *Education:* University of Madrid (Law Degree, 1986; Master, Tax Law, 1987). *Member:* Vigo and Madrid Bar Associations. **LANGUAGES:** Spanish and English.

OTHER ASSOCIATES

Víctor Jaúregui   Pedro Regojo
Silvia de Francisco   Alfredo Fernández
Eduardo Sánchez   Antonio Losada

OTHER ASSOCIATES RESIDENT IN LA CORUÑA

Antonio Ulloa

(For Complete Firm Profile, see data at Madrid, Spain)

ARTHUR ANDERSEN
ASESORES LEGALES Y TRIBUTARIOS

Legal and Tax Advisors
ARCA 2
01005 VITORIA, SPAIN
Telephone: 34-45-145118
Fax: 34-45-145191

Arthur Andersen Asesores Legales y Tributarios's offices: Alicante, Barcelona, Bilbao, Granada, La Coruña, Madrid, Málaga, Oviedo, Palma de Mallorca, San Sebastian, Sevilla, Valencia, Vigo, Vitoria, Zaragoza.
Associated Law Firms abroad: France, Italy, Germany, Portugal, The Netherlands, Belgium, United Kingdom, South Africa, Colombia and Brazil.

PARTNER

ANA MARÍA ARMESTO, born Bilbao, Spain, February 7, 1956; admitted, 1987, Bilbao; 1991, Madrid. *Education:* University of Deusto (Law Degree, 1978). *Member:* Bilbao and Madrid Bar Associations. **LANGUAGES:** Spanish, English and French.

RESIDENT ASSOCIATES

JOSE MANUEL PEÑA, born Bilbao, Spain, October 18, 1961; admitted, 1985, Bilboa. *Education:* University of Deusto - Bilbao (Law Degree, 1984); ESADE (Master Business Administration). *Member:* Vizcaya Bar Association. **LANGUAGES:** Spanish and English.

OTHER ASSOCIATES

Antonio Matute

(For Complete Firm Profile, see data at Madrid, Spain)

ARTHUR ANDERSEN
ASESORES LEGALES Y TRIBUTARIOS

Legal and Tax Advisors
PLAZA DE ARAGÓN, 10
5004 ZARAGOZA, SPAIN
Telephone: 34-76-214675
Fax: 34-76-216495

Arthur Andersen Asesores Legales y Tributarios's offices: Alicante, Barcelona, Bilbao, Granada, La Coruña, Madrid, Málaga, Oviedo, Palma de Mallorca, San Sebastian, Sevilla, Valencia, Vigo, Vitoria, Zaragoza.
Associated Law Firms abroad: France, Italy, Germany, Portugal, The Netherlands, Belgium, United Kingdom, South Africa, Colombia and Brazil.

(This Listing Continued)

PARTNER

PEDRO PABLO RODES, born Palma de Mallorca, Baleares, Spain, July 18, 1955; admitted, 1982, Barcelona. *Education:* University of Barcelona (Economics Degree, 1977; Law Degree, 1979); Barcelona Tax Studies Center (Master, 1979). *Member:* Barcelona Bar Association. *LANGUAGES:* Spanish, French and English.

RESIDENT ASSOCIATES

JUAN CARLOS TENA, born Zaragoza, July 27, 1968. *Education:* University of Zaragoza (Law Degree, 1991). *LANGUAGES:* Spanish, English and German.

OTHER ASSOCIATES

VICTOR ANGUREL

(For Complete Firm Profile, see data at Madrid, Spain)

SWEDEN

STYRBJÖRN GÄRDE ADVOKATBYRÅ

STORA KYRKOGATAN 4
P.O. BOX 305
S-501 05 BORÅS, SWEDEN
Telephone: +46 (33) 11 59 00
Telefax: +46 (33) 13 79 00

Stockholm, Sweden Office: Nybrogatan 34, P.O. Box 5208. Telephone: +46 (8)-665 00 40. Telefax: +46 (8)-665 00 41.

Gothenburg, Sweden Office: Kastellgatan 1, S-413 07. Telephone: +46 (31)-11 36 30 . Telefax: +46 (31)-13 73 68.

Malmö, Sweden Office: Norra Vallgatan 64, S-211. Telephone: +46 (40)-10 48 10. Telefax: +46 (40)-23 52 31.

Helsingborg, Sweden Office: Garnisonsgatan 10, S-254 66. Telephone: +46-(42) 20 10 80. Telefax: +46 (42)-20 18 38.

Borås, Sweden Office: Stora Kyrkogatan 4, P.O. Box 305, S-501 05. Telephone: +46 (33) 11 59 00. Telefax: +46 (33) 13 79 00.

Paris, France Office: 41, Rue de Passy, F-75016. Telephone: +33 (1) 45 27 95 22. Telefax: +33 (1) 40 50 90 31.

Representative Offices:
Schweiz: Stadelgarden, Stadelhofer Strasse 40, CH-8024 Zürich. Telephone: +41 (1)-261 52 60. Telefax: +41 (1)-261 55 29.

Sweden: HAGA Företagscenter, Brogatan 25, S-334 33 Anderstorp. Telephone: +46 (371)-174 80. Telefax: +46 (371)-169 67.

Admitted to Practice in Sweden. General Swedish and International Business Law Practice. Company Law, Contracts and Disputes, Real Estate Law, Building and Construction Law, Mergers and Acquisitions, Intellectual Property, Copyright and Trademarks, Marketing and Unfair Competition, Computer and Telecommunication Law, Transportations and Maritime Law, EC and EEA Law, Labour Law, Banking and Insolvency Law, Corporate Financing and Securities Law, Trusts, Corporate Taxation, Insurance Law and Claims, Litigation and Arbitration. All Swedish Courts.

MEMBERS OF FIRM

CHRISTER ERIKSON, born Borås, Sweden, 1944. *Education:* University of Lund (LL.B., 1971). Served in County Administration and County Administrative Court of Älvsborg, 1971-1974. Member, Enforcement Office of Borås, 1974-1978. Member: Arne Gullacks Law Firm, 1978-1984; Law Firm of Erikson & Öjerklint, 1984-1994. *Member:* Swedish Bar Association. *LANGUAGES:* English and Swedish.

ULF ÖJERKLINT, born Lidhult, Sweden, 1951. *Education:* University of Lund (LL.B., 1977). Served in District Court of Malmö, 1977-1979. Corporate Lawyer, Dahlén International AB, 1979-1980. *Member:* Swedish Bar Association and Rotary. *LANGUAGES:* English and Swedish.

LARS SVENSSON, born Borås, Sweden, 1946. *Education:* University of Lund (LL.B., 1971). Served in District Court of Borås, 1971-1974 and Court of Appeal in Gothenburg. Assistant Judge, Court of Appeal, 1984 and Magistrate, 1980-1985. *Member:* Swedish Bar Association. *LANGUAGES:* English and Swedish.

SVEN-INGE SANDBERG, born Borås, Sweden, 1957. *Education:* University of Uppsala (LL.B., 1981). Served in District Court of Gothenburg, 1981-1984 and Court of Appeal in Gothenburg, 1984-1986. Assistant Judge, Court of Appeal, 1985 and Assistant Judge in District Court of

(This Listing Continued)

Borås, 1986-1988. *Member:* Swedish Bar Association and Round Table. *LANGUAGES:* English and Swedish.

ASSOCIATES

STEFAN RISÖ, born Gothenburg, Sweden, 1957. *Education:* University of Umeå and Lund (LL.B., 1986). Served in: District Court of Borås, 1986-1989; Public Law Office, 1989-1993; Law Firm Erikson & Öjerklint, 1994. *Member:* Swedish Bar Association. *LANGUAGES:* English and Swedish.

ANDERS SEGERBLOM, born Borås, Sweden, 1966. *Education:* University of Lund (LL.B., 1991). Served in: District Court of Ljungby, 1992-1993; Office of the Public Prosecutor of Borås, 1994. *LANGUAGES:* English and Swedish.

Languages: Swedish, English, German, French, Finnish, Hungarian, Portuguese and Russian.

(For Biographical data on other Personnel, see Professional Biographies at Stockholm, Gothenburg, Helsingborg and Malmö Sweden).

BERGLUND & COMPANY ADVOKATBYRÅ

Established in 1986

BERZELIIGATAN 14
P.O. BOX 53166
S-400 15 GOTHENBURG, SWEDEN
Telephone: +46 31 81 98 00
Telefax: +46 31 16 99 81

General Business and Corporation Law, European Community Law, Competition Law, Mergers and Acquisitions, Real Estate Law, Labour Law, Swedish and International Taxation, Arbitration and Litigation in Civil Matters.

FIRM PROFILE: The firm was established in 1986 by four partners with experience from large sized firms. The firm, which provides a full range of legal services in the business area benefits from the advantages of being small. The clients are mainly medium sized companies, both in Sweden and within the Common Market.

CHRISTER BERGLUND, born 1939. *Education:* University of Lund (LL.B., jur.kand., 1967). *Member:* Swedish Bar Association (Member of Board, 1974-1980; Chairman, Board of Western District, 1985-1990. Chairman, Professional Board, 1987-1989.; International Bar Association. *LANGUAGES:* Swedish and English. *PRACTICE AREAS:* Business Law; Corporate Law; Mergers and Acquisitions.

LEIF JOHANSSON, born 1944. *Education:* Gothenburg School of Economics and Business Administration (M.B.A., Civilekonom, 1970). With County Tax Administration and National Tax Board, 1970-1980. Tax Partner of Arthur Young & Co. AB, Sweden, 1980-1986. *Member:* International Fiscal Association. *LANGUAGES:* Swedish and English. *PRACTICE AREAS:* Swedish and International Taxation.

STEFAN RUBEN, born 1950. *Education:* University of Gothenburg (Faculty of Economics); University of Lund (LL.B., jur.kand., 1976). *Member:* Swedish Bar Association (Member of Board, Western District, 1990—); International Bar Association; Swedish Maritime Law Association. *LANGUAGES:* Swedish and English. *PRACTICE AREAS:* Labor Law; Arbitration; Litigation in Civil Matters.

CLAES SJÖLIN, born 1947. *Education:* University of Lund (LL.B., jur.kand., 1973). Studies at: The Scandinavian Institute of Maritime Law at Oslo, Norway (1975-1976); The London School of Economics (European Community Law and English Law, 1977). Assistant Average Adjuster of Gothenburg, 1980-1987. *Member:* Swedish Bar Association (Member of Board of Due Process, 1990—); Association for European Law; International Bar Association; American Bar Association (Associate Member); Swedish Maritime Law Association. *LANGUAGES:* Swedish and English. *PRACTICE AREAS:* Business Law; Corporate Law; EC Law; Competition Law; Real Estate Law.

LARS SÖDERLUND, born 1957. *Education:* University of Gothenburg (Master of Science in Business and Public Law, 1981); University of Lund (LL.B., jur.kand. 1986). *Member:* Swedish Bar Association; International Fiscal Association. *LANGUAGES:* Swedish and English. *PRACTICE AREAS:* Business Law; Corporate Law; Swedish and International Law.

FOLKE BRANDT ADVOKATBYRÅ

Established in 1970

P.O. BOX 7086
S-402 32 GOTHENBURG 7, SWEDEN
Telephone: +46-31-113478
Telefax: +46-31-135373

Swedish and International Commercial Law, Corporate Law, Agency Law, Private Law, Estates, Wills and Successions, Intellectual Law, Transportation and Accident Law, Arbitration, Litigation in all Swedish Courts.

FOLKE BRANDT, born 1932; admitted, 1966, Sweden. *Education:* University of Lund (LL.B., 1961); Business Institute of Göteborg; City of London College. Counsel to the British and German General Counsulates in Gothenburg. *Member:* Swedish and International Bar Associations; European Consultants Unit; Verein Europäischen Rechtsanwäite; Euro-Link for Lawyers; Gothenburg Maritime Law Association.

Languages: English, German, French and Italian.

FRIMAN & CARLANDER ADVOKATBYRÅ

Established in 1874

ÖSTRA HAMNGATAN 29
411 10 GOTHENBURG, SWEDEN
Telephone: 031-178810
Telefax: Sweden (46)-31-139469

General Practice. Corporation, Business, Taxation, International, Bankruptcy, Environment and Labor Law.

BO BJÖRCK, born 1919. *Education:* University of Uppsala (LL.B., Jur. kand., 1942). *Member:* Swedish Bar Association (Secretary of Board, Western District, 1959-1965; Member of Board, 1966-1974; Vice President, 1967-1969; 1971-1974); International Bar Association (IBA). *LANGUAGES:* English, German and Swedish. *PRACTICE AREAS:* Arbitration; Water Law.

HANS JOHNSON, born 1919. *Education:* University of Uppsala (LL.B., Jur. kand., 1946). *Member:* Swedish Bar Association (Member of Board, Gothenburg District, Legal Aid Committee, 1975; Member of Disciplinary Committee, 1978-1982). *LANGUAGES:* English, German and Swedish. *PRACTICE AREAS:* Insolvency; Family Law.

JAN MELIN, born 1925. *Education:* University of Uppsala (LL.B., Jur. kand., 1949). *Member:* Swedish Bar Association; International Bar Association (IBA). *LANGUAGES:* English, German and Swedish. *PRACTICE AREAS:* Insolvency; Company Commercial Law.

BENGT BOGREN, born 1938. *Education:* University of Lund (LL.B., Jur.kand., 1963). *Member:* Swedish Bar Association. *LANGUAGES:* English, German and Swedish. *PRACTICE AREAS:* Insolvency; Company Law; Real Estate.

HÅKAN ROTH, born 1941. *Education:* University of Uppsala (LL.B., Jur. kand., 1969). *Member:* Swedish Bar Association (Member of Board, Western District, 1983-); International Bar Association (IBA). *LANGUAGES:* English and Swedish. *PRACTICE AREAS:* Successions; Separation; Agreements; Real Estate; Compensation Claims.

CLAES KARLZÉN, born 1951. *Education:* University of Lund (LL.B., Jur. kand., 1975). *Member:* Swedish Bar Association; International Bar Association (IBA); Young Lawyers' International Association (AIJA). *LANGUAGES:* Spanish, English, German and Swedish. *PRACTICE AREAS:* Business Law; International Law; Insolvency.

HANS L. BERGQVIST, born 1953. *Education:* University of Lund (LL.B., Jur. kand., 1979). *Member:* Swedish Bar Association; International Bar Association (IBA). *LANGUAGES:* English and Swedish. *PRACTICE AREAS:* Business Law; Insolvency; Environmental Law.

ROLF KARLSSON, born 1956. *Education:* University of Lund (LL.B., Jur. kand., 1981). *Member:* Swedish Bar Association. *LANGUAGES:* English, German and Swedish. *PRACTICE AREAS:* Business Law.

JAN STENEBY, born 1943. *Education:* University of Lund (LL.B., Jur.-kand., 1972); University of Stockholm (Doctor of Contract Law, Jur.Dr., 1981). *Member:* Swedish Bar Association. *LANGUAGES:* English, German and Swedish. *PRACTICE AREAS:* Contracts; Company Law.

HÅKAN HEDSTRÖM, born 1947. *Education:* University of Uppsala (LL.B., Jur.kand., 1973). *Member:* Swedish Bar Association. *LAN-*

(This Listing Continued)

GUAGES: English and Swedish. *PRACTICE AREAS:* Business Law; Banks and Banking.

LARS JAKTLING, born 1933. *Education:* University of Stockholm (LL.B., Jur.kand., 1963). *Member:* Swedish Bar Association. *LANGUAGES:* English, German and Swedish. *PRACTICE AREAS:* Commercial Law; Company Law; Transportation.

TORGNY ANDERSSON, born 1964. *Education:* University of Lund (LL.B., Jur.kand., 1992). *LANGUAGES:* English and Swedish. *PRACTICE AREAS:* Insolvency; Business Law.

ANDERS STRID, born 1964. *Education:* University of Lund (LL.B., Jur.kand., 1990). *LANGUAGES:* English, German and Swedish. *PRACTICE AREAS:* Business Law; Insolvency; Commercial Real Estate.

Languages: English, German, French and Spanish.

ADVOKATHUSET GAMLESTADEN

Established in 1982

SÄVEÅNS STRANDGATA 4
S-415 05 GOTHENBURG, SWEDEN
Telephone: +46-31-84 00 50
+46-31-21 00 99

FIRM PROFILE: *Established as a general practice 1982, and admitted to the Swedish Bar Association 1985, we have developed a wide skill in litigation in most areas of business law in and outside court in Sweden, having a wide range of clients, from smaller companies to cities, even other law firms from U.S.A., Germany, England, Ireland, Denmark, Norway and Sweden.*

MEMBERS OF FIRM

ULF LUNDMAN, born Helsingborg, Sweden, 1953. *Education:* University of Lund (Juris kandidat, LL.B., 1978; cum gradis in jurisprudence, 1979). Alingsås tingsrätt, Kammarrätten i Göteborg, längrätten i Göreborgs och Bohus län, Sjuhäradsbygdens tingsrätt, 1978-1982. District Attorney, Gothenburg, 1979. Attorney, and founder of this firm 1982—. Author: Valutabrott "Currencyfraud," Lunds Universiter, 1978. *Member:* Swedish Bar Association. *LANGUAGES:* Swedish, English and German. *PRACTICE AREAS:* Business Litigation; Contracts; Entertainment Law; Transport Law; Trade Law; Computer Law.

KENT CAJVERT, born Gothenburg, Sweden, 1952. *Education:* University of Lund (Jur kand, LL.B., 1982). Company-Lawyer, Göteborg Energi AB, 1982-1991, (distributors of energy). Lecturer, Law, University of Gothenburg. Seminar-Leader, Business in Law and Litigation. Attorney, Advokathuser Gamlestaden, 1991—. Author: "Lille Inkasso-Jätten," a hand book on practical execution. *LANGUAGES:* Swedish and English. *PRACTICE AREAS:* Business Litigation; Contract Law; Trade Law; Energy Law; Construction Law; Planning Law.

ANNA-KARIN REÜTER, born Kungälv, Sweden, 1962. *Education:* University of Uppsala (Jur kand, LL.B., 1987). Lawyer, employment law, City of Stockholm, 1987-1989. Court of Årnål, 1989-1991. Attorney, Advokahusct Gamlestaden, 1991—. *LANGUAGES:* Swedish, English and German. *PRACTICE AREAS:* Civil Litigation; Employment Law; Real Estate Law.

STYRBJÖRN GÄRDE ADVOKATBYRÅ

KASTELLGATAN 1
S-413 07 GOTHENBURG, SWEDEN
Telephone: +46 (31)-11 36 30
Telefax: +46 (31)-13 73 68

Stockholm, Sweden Office: Nybrogatan 34, P.O. Box 5208, S-102 45. Telephone: +46 (8)-665 00 40. Telefax: +46 (8)-665 00 41.
Malmö, Sweden Office: Norra Vallgatan 64, S-211. Telephone: +46 (40)-10 48 10. Telefax: +46 (40)-23 52 31.
Helsingborg, Sweden Office: Garnisonsgatan 10, S-254 66. Telephone: +46 (42)-20 10 80. Telefax: +46 (42)-20 18 38.
Borås, Sweden Office: Stora Kyrkogatan 4, P.O. Box 305, S-501 05. Telephone: +46 (33) 11 59 00. Telefax: +46 (33) 13 79 00.

(This Listing Continued)

Paris, France Office: 41, Rue de Passy, F-75016. Telephone: +33 (1) 45 27 95 22. Telefax: +33 (1) 40 50 90 31.

Representative Offices:

Schweiz: Stadelgarden, Stadelhofer Strasse 40, CH-8024 Zürich. Telephone +41 (1)-261 52 60. Telefax: +41 (1)-261 55 29.

Sweden: HAGA Företagscenter, Brogatan 25, S-334 33 Anderstorp. Telephone: +46 (371)-174 80. Telefax: +46 (371)-169 67.

Admitted to Practice in Sweden, The Law Firm's Primary Activities are Concentrated on Swedish and International Business, Tax Law and Insolvency Law.

MEMBERS OF FIRM

ROBERT SVAN, born Gothenburg, Sweden, 1947. *Education:* University of Lund (LL.B., 1972). Served in District Court of Alingsås, 1973-1975. Legal practice at an American law firm 1989. *Member:* Swedish Bar Association. *LANGUAGES:* English and Swedish. *PRACTICE AREAS:* Joint Ventures; Mergers and Acquisitions; Commercial Litigation; Arbitration; Company Law; Corporate Law; Contracts.

HANS JOSEFSON, born Gothenburg, Sweden, 1940. *Education:* University of Lund (LL.B., 1969). Served in District Court of Stockholm, 1969-1972. Associate, Jörgensen & Samzelius, 1972-1973. Legal Counsel to Investment AB Beijer, 1973-1974, Sjöförsäkrings AB Hansa, 1974-1975, Investment AB Asken, 1975-1978. Chief Counsel, Kema Nobel AB, 1978-1981. Partner, law firm Carler, 1981-1990; law firm Cicero, 1990-1993. *Member:* Swedish Bar Association. *LANGUAGES:* English, German, French, Spanish and Swedish. *PRACTICE AREAS:* Mergers and Acquisitions; Intellectual Property Law; Corporate Law; Commercial Matters.

STIG-ERIK SÖDERHOLM, born Helsinki, Finland, 1947. *Education:* University of Uppsala (LL.B., 1973). *Member:* Swedish Bar Association. *LANGUAGES:* Finnish, English, German and Swedish. *PRACTICE AREAS:* Insurance Law; Criminal Law.

ERIK BERGENHEM, born Gothenburg, Sweden, 1948. *Education:* University of Lund (LL.B., 1975). Served in District Court of Gothenburg, 1976-1978, Administrative Court of Appeals in Gothenburg, 1978-1980, Court of Appeals of Västra Sverige, 1981. Assistant Judge, Court of Appeals, 1979. *Member:* Swedish Bar Association. *LANGUAGES:* English, German and Swedish. *PRACTICE AREAS:* Banking; Financing; Joint Ventures; Mergers and Acquisitions.

CLAES ÅBERG, born Vänersborg, Sweden, 1957. *Education:* University of Lund (LL.B., 1982). Served in District Court of Borås, 1982-1984 and Court of Appeals of Västra Sverige, 1984-1986. Assistant Judge, Court of Appeals, 1985. *Member:* Swedish Bar Association. *LANGUAGES:* English and Swedish. *PRACTICE AREAS:* Real Estate Law; Construction Law; Commercial Litigation; Arbitration.

ARNE WOXLIN, born Edsbyn, Sweden, 1957. *Education:* University of Uppsala (LL.B., 1982). Served in District Court of Gothenburg, 1983-1985 and Court of Appeals of Västra Sverige, 1985-1987. Assistant Judge, Court of Appeals, 1986. *Member:* Swedish Bar Association. *LANGUAGES:* English and Swedish. *PRACTICE AREAS:* Company Law; Corporate Law; Contracts.

ASSOCIATES

GÖRAN INSULÁN, born Gothenburg, Sweden, 1949. *Education:* University of Lund (LL.B., 1976). Served in District Court of Norrköping, 1976-1979. Crown Bailiff, 1979-1989. *Member:* Swedish Bar Association. *LANGUAGES:* English and Swedish.

ULF TOLLHAGE, born Mölndal, Sweden, 1960. *Education:* University of Lund (LL.B., 1988). Served in District Court of Helsingborg, 1988-1990 and Court of Appeals of Västra Sverige, 1990-1991. Assistant Judge, Court of Appeals, 1991. *LANGUAGES:* English and Swedish.

Languages: Swedish, English, German, French and Spanish

(For Biographical data on other Personnel, see Professional Biographies at Malmo, Stockholm, Helsingborg and Borås Sweden).

LAGERLÖF & LEMAN
VÄSTRA HAMNGATAN 24
P.O. BOX 2252
S-403 14 GOTHENBURG, SWEDEN
Telephone: Int. 46-31-17 10 00
Telefax: Int. 46-31-13 56 62
Telefax: Maritime department: Int. 46-31-11 65 37

Stockholm, Sweden Office: Strandvägen 7A, P.O. Box 5402, S-114 84, Stockholm. Telephone: Int. 46-8-665 66 00. Telefax: Int. 46-8-667 68 83. Telex: 17715 Laglaw S.

Malmö, Sweden Office: Stortorget 8, S-211 34, Malmö. Telephone: Int. 46-40-704 50. Telefax: Int. 46-40-97 19 17.

London, England Office: Royex House, Aldermanbury Square, London EC2V 7HR. Telephone: Int. 44-171-606 17 15. Telefax: Int. 44-171-600 17 18.

Berlin, Germany Office: Meinekestrasse 13, D-10719 Berlin. Telephone: Int. 49-30-884 710. Telefax: Int. 49-30-882 4852.

Paris, France Office: 87 Avenue Kléber, F-75116 Paris. Telephone: 33-1-45 05 1208. Telefax: 33-1-47 55 0975.

New York, N.Y. Office: 712 Fifth Avenue, 30th Floor, New York, N.Y. 10019-4102 U.S.A. Telephone: Int. 1-212-801-3450. Telefax: Int. 1-212-801-3455.

Corporate and Commercial law, including Tax, Banking, Financing, Insurance, Real Estate, Computer, Patent, Trademark, Copyright, Labor, Trade Regulation and Antitrust Law. International Legal Transactions. Arbitration and Litigation in Civil Matters. EC Law. International Private Law. Maritime and Admiralty Law.
Member of Alliance of European Lawyers (EEIG).

PARTNERS

TORSTEN LEMAN, born Gothenburg, Sweden, 1940. *Education:* University of Uppsala (juris kandidat, LL.M., 1965). Service with Swedish Courts. Uppsala County Administrative Board, Extra Tax Inspector, 1965-1966. *Member:* Swedish and International Bar Associations; Gothenburg Maritime Law Association. *LANGUAGES:* Swedish and English. *PRACTICE AREAS:* General Commercial Law; Corporate Law; Real Estate Law; Tax Law.

TRYGGVE WAHLIN, born Stockholm, Sweden, 1942. *Education:* University of Lund (juris kandidat, LL.M., 1967). Service with Swedish Courts. *Member:* Swedish and International Bar Associations. *LANGUAGES:* Swedish, English and German. *PRACTICE AREAS:* General Commercial Law; Corporate Law; Computer Law.

PETER EGNELL, born Jonkoping, Sweden, 1942. *Education:* University of Uppsala (juris kandidat LL.M., 1968). Service with Swedish Courts. *Member:* Swedish and International Bar Associations. *LANGUAGES:* Swedish and English. *PRACTICE AREAS:* General Commercial Law; Corporate Law; Real Estate Law.

TOMAS SETTERBERG, born Gothenburg, Sweden, 1945. *Education:* University of Lund (juris kandidat, LL.M., 1971). Service with Swedish Courts. *Member:* Swedish and International Bar Associations. *LANGUAGES:* Swedish, English and German. *PRACTICE AREAS:* General Commercial Law; Corporate Law; Real Estate Law.

LARS MELIN, born Malmo, Sweden, 1949. *Education:* University of Lund (juris kandidat, LL.M., 1975). Service with Swedish Courts; Judgeship, Administrative Court of Appeal and Court of Appeal, 1978-1979. *Member:* Swedish Bar Association (1982; Appointed Chairman, Professional Board, 1993—); International Bar Association; International Fiscal Association. *LANGUAGES:* Swedish and English. *PRACTICE AREAS:* General Commercial Law; Corporate Law; Real Estate Law; Financing Law.

MAX SLOTTE, born Kronoby, Finland, 1935. *Education:* University of Stockholm (juris kandidat, LL.M., 1967); Nautical College of Aland Islands (Master Mariner, 1963). Service with Swedish Courts. General Counsel Tor Line AB 1969-1981. *Member:* Swedish and International Bar Associations; Swedish Maritime Law Society. *LANGUAGES:* Swedish, English, German, Finnish and Spanish. *PRACTICE AREAS:* Shipping General Transport Law.

JÖRGEN ESTVING, born Gothenburg, Sweden, 1952. *Education:* University of Lund (juris kandidat, LL.M., 1976). Service with Swedish Courts. Judgeship, Court of Appeal, 1979-1981. *Member:* Swedish Bar Association. *LANGUAGES:* Swedish and English. *PRACTICE AREAS:* General Commercial Corporate Law; Real Estate Law.

(This Listing Continued)

LAGERLÖF & LEMAN, Gothenburg—Continued

BJÖRN OHDE, born Umea, Sweden, 1946. *Education:* University of Lund (juris kandidat, LL.M., 1973). Service with Swedish Courts. *Member:* Swedish and International Bar Associations; International Fiscal Association. *LANGUAGES:* Swedish and English. *PRACTICE AREAS:* Corporate Law; Swedish and International Tax Law; International Financial Law.

JUNE LASSESSON, born Karlskrona, Sweden, 1954. *Education:* University of Lund (juris kandidat, LL.M., 1979); University of California, Los Angeles (Master of Arts, 1979). Service with Swedish Courts. Judgeship, Administrative Court of Appeal, 1982-1983. *Member:* Swedish and International Bar Associations. *LANGUAGES:* Swedish and English. *PRACTICE AREAS:* General Commercial Law; Company Law; Bankruptcy Law.

MATS BERTER, born Trelleborg, Sweden, 1953. *Education:* University of Lund (juris kandidat, LL.M., 1978). Service with Swedish Courts. Judgeship, Administrative Court of Appeal, 1981-1982. *Member:* Swedish Bar Association; Young Lawyers International Association. *LANGUAGES:* Swedish, English and German. *PRACTICE AREAS:* General Commercial Law; Corporate Law; Bankruptcy Law.

JOHAN WILKENS, born Gothenburg, Sweden, 1949. *Education:* University of Lund (juris kandidat, LL.M., 1978). Service with Swedish Courts. *Member:* Swedish and International Bar Associations. *LANGUAGES:* Swedish and English. *PRACTICE AREAS:* General Commercial Law.

ANDERS I. BENGTSSON, born Kalmar, Sweden, 1946. *Education:* University of Lund (juris kandidat, LL.M., 1972). Service with Swedish Courts. Judgeship, Court of Appeal, 1974-1980; Judge, Court of Appeal, 1980-1985. *Member:* Swedish and International Bar Associations. *LANGUAGES:* Swedish, English and German. *PRACTICE AREAS:* General Commercial Law; Corporate Law; Real Estate Law; Litigation.

EVA JONASSON-MELIN, born Huskvarna, Sweden, 1951. *Education:* University of Lund (juris kandidat, LL.M., 1975). Service with Swedish Courts. Judgeship: Administrative Court of Appeal, 1978-1980, National Tax Board, 1980-1983. Judge, Administrative Court of Appeal 1983-1985. Tax Lawyer, KPMG Bohlins, 1985-1990. *Member:* Swedish Bar Association; International Fiscal Association. *LANGUAGES:* Swedish and English. *PRACTICE AREAS:* Tax Law.

LENA BRYNTESSON, born Torup, Sweden, 1948. *Education:* University of Lund (juris kandidat, LL.M., 1982). Service with Swedish Courts. Judgeship, Administrative Court of Appeal, 1985-1986. Tax Lawyer, KPMG Bohlins, 1986-1990. *Member:* Swedish Bar Association; International Fiscal Association. *LANGUAGES:* Swedish and English. *PRACTICE AREAS:* Tax Law; Corporate Law.

MAGNUS DAHLÉN, born Eskilstuna, Sweden, 1958. *Education:* University of Uppsala (juris kandidat, LL.M., 1984). Service with Swedish Courts. *Member:* Swedish Bar Association. *LANGUAGES:* Swedish and English. *PRACTICE AREAS:* General Commercial Law; Computer Law.

ASSOCIATES

ELISABET OLSSON, born Uddevalla, Sweden, 1960. *Education:* University of Lund (juris kandidat, LL.M., 1985). Service with Swedish Courts. Judgeship, Administrative Court of Appeal, 1988-1989. *LANGUAGES:* Swedish, English and French.

PETER ANDEBY, born Karlstad, Sweden, 1958. *Education:* University of Uppsala (juris kandidat, LL.M., 1985). Service with Swedish Courts. *Member:* Swedish Bar Association. *LANGUAGES:* Swedish and English. *PRACTICE AREAS:* Commercial Law; Corporate Law; Bankruptcy Law; Reconstruction; Labour Law.

HÅKAN SCHILLER, born Uppsala, Sweden, 1960. *Education:* University of Uppsala (juris kandidat, LL.M., 1987); Scandinavian Institute of Maritime Law, University of Oslo 1985. Service with Swedish Courts. *Member:* Swedish Bar Association. *LANGUAGES:* Swedish and English.

MATS ROMELL, born Gothenburg, Sweden, 1961. *Education:* University of Lund (juris kandidat, LL.M., 1987). Service with Swedish Courts. Judgeship, Administrative Court of Appeal, 1989-1990. *Member:* Swedish Bar Association. *LANGUAGES:* Swedish and English. *PRACTICE AREAS:* Bankruptcy Law; Industrial Property Law.

JOHAN SÖDERLUND, born Karlshamn, Sweden, 1960. *Education:* University of Lund (juris kandidat, LL.M., 1986); University of California at Los Angeles (LL.M., 1988); Eberhard-Karls-Universität, Tübingen (LL.M., 1990). Service with Swedish Courts. *Member:* Swedish Bar Association. *LANGUAGES:* Swedish and English.

(This Listing Continued)

MAGDALENA PERSSON, born Hoting, Sweden, 1963. *Education:* University of Uppsala (juris kandidat, LL.M., 1988). Service with Swedish Courts. *LANGUAGES:* Swedish and English.

HELEN BECKMAN, born Gothenburg, Sweden, 1966. *Education:* University of Lund (juris kandidat, LL.M., 1990). Service with Swedish Courts. *LANGUAGES:* Swedish and English. *PRACTICE AREAS:* Corporate Law.

DAN BULLARBO, born Strömstad, Sweden, 1959. *Education:* University of Uppsala (juris kandidat, LL.M., 1989). Service with Swedish Courts. Judgeship, Court of Appeal, 1992-1993. *LANGUAGES:* Swedish and English. *PRACTICE AREAS:* Commercial Law.

OLOF STENSTRÖM, born Lerum, Sweden, 1964. *Education:* University of Lund (juris kandidat, LL.M., 1989); University of London (LL.M., 1993). Service for Swedish Courts. *LANGUAGES:* Swedish, English and German.

OF COUNSEL

TOR SETTERBERG, born Gothenburg, Sweden, 1910. *Education:* Uppsala University (juris kandidat LL.M., 1934). Service with Swedish Courts. *Member:* Swedish Bar Association. *LANGUAGES:* Swedish and English. *PRACTICE AREAS:* General Commercial Law; Corporate Law.

ROLF LEMAN, born Gothenburg, Sweden, 1910. *Education:* Uppsala University (juris kandidat, LL.M., 1936). Service with Swedish Courts. *Member:* Swedish Bar Association. *LANGUAGES:* Swedish and English.

ESKIL WEIBULL, born Lund, Sweden, 1922. *Education:* Lund University (juris kandidat, LL.M., 1947). Service with Swedish Courts. *Member:* Swedish Bar Association. *LANGUAGES:* Swedish, English, German and French.

ADVOKATFIRMAN LINDAHL

ÖSTRA HAMNGATAN 36

P.O. BOX 11911

S-404 39 GOTHENBURG, SWEDEN

Telephone: +46-31 80 34 30

Telefax: +46-31 15 82 85

Helsingborg, Sweden Office: Mariagatan 10. Mailing Address: P.O. Box 1214, S-251 12 Helsingborg. Telephone: 46-42 18 31 80. Telefax: 46-42 11 96 78 and 46-42 24 12 86. Telex: 72715 Counsel S.

Kristianstad, Sweden Office: Västra Vallgatan 26. Mailing Address: P.O. Box 167, S-291 22 Kristianstad. Telephone: 46-44 10 07 80. Telex: 32584 LUNDLAW S. Telefax: 46-44 11 85 14.

Malmö, Sweden Office: Hjälmaregatan 3, Scandinavian Center, S-211 18 Malmö. Telephone: 46-40 17 44 40. Telex: 32584 LUNDLAW S. Telefax: 46-40 11 13 54.

Stockholm, Sweden Office: Strandvägen 5 A. Mailing Address: P.O. Box 14240, S-104 40 Stockholm. Telephone: 46-8 670 5800. Telex: 19609 LINDAHL S. Telefax: 46-8 667 73 80.

Örebro, Sweden Office: Vasastrand 11-13. Mailing Address: P.O. Box 143, S-701 42 Örebro. Telephone: 46-19 10 48 00. Telefax: 46-19 10 44 45.

Brussels, Belgium Office: 33 Blvd de la Cambre, Bte 13, B-1050 Brussels. Telephone: 32-2 646 46 90. Telefax: 32-2 646 45 80.

General Swedish and International Business Law Practice, Admiralty and Maritime Law, Insolvency, Antitrust, Marketing and Unfair Competition, Banking, Computer Law, Construction and Engineering Contracts and Disputes, Corporate Financing and Securities Law, International Taxation, EC Law, Environmental Energy and Natural Resources Law, Industrial Property, Copyright and Trademarks, Labor Law, Mergers and Acquisitions, Real Estate Law, Reorganizations, Space Law, Litigation and Arbitration, Family Law and Successions.

MEMBERS OF FIRM IN GOTHENBURG

BENGT ELFVIN, born Gothenburg, Sweden, April 20, 1926. *Education:* University of Uppsala (LL.M., 1951). Junior Judgeship, District Court of Trollhättan, 1952-1953. *Member:* Swedish Bar Association, 1956; International Bar Association. *LANGUAGES:* English. *PRACTICE AREAS:* General Commercial Law; Corporate Law; Estate Administration.

ALLAN LINDEN, born Helsingborg, Sweden, December 15, 1929. *Education:* University of Lund (LL.M., 1956). Junior Judgeship, District Court of Sölvesborg, 1956-1958. *Member:* Swedish Bar Association, 1962 (Member, General Council, 1978-1984; Chairman of Western Section, 1983-1986); International Bar Association; Union Internationale des Avocats.

(This Listing Continued)

LANGUAGES: English, French, German. *PRACTICE AREAS:* Arbitration Law; Commercial Dispute Resolution; Corporate Law; General Commercial Law; Professional Liability.

BJÖRN MAGNUSSON, born Gothenburg, Sweden, April 4, 1939. *Education:* University of Lund (LL.M., 1964). Junior Judgeship, City Court of Gothenburg, 1964-1967. *Member:* Swedish Bar Association, 1970 (Member, Professional Committee, 1984-1991, Vice Chairman, 1989-1990); International Bar Association; Association Internationale des Jeunes Avocats (Member, Executive Committee, 1982-1984). *LANGUAGES:* English, French, German and Spanish. *PRACTICE AREAS:* Arbitration Law; Litigation; Contract Law; General Commercial Law; Corporate Law; Real Estate Law.

RICKARD STRÖM, born Örebro, Sweden, April 28, 1946. *Education:* University of Uppsala (LL.M., 1973); University of Lund (Company and Tax Law, 1987). Junior Judgeship, District Court of Strömstad, 1973-1976. Associate Judge, Fiscal Court of Appeal and Court of Appeal, Gothenburg, 1976-1978. *Member:* Swedish Bar Association, 1981 (Secretary, Western Section, 1989—). *LANGUAGES:* English. *PRACTICE AREAS:* General Commercial Law; Corporate Law; Taxation; Insolvency; Litigation.

JAN BJÖRKLUND, born Gothenburg, Sweden, June 8, 1952. *Education:* University of Lund (LL.M., 1978). Junior Judgeship, District Court of Gothenburg, 1979-1981. *Member:* Swedish Bar Association, 1984. *LANGUAGES:* English. *PRACTICE AREAS:* General Commercial Law; Insolvency; Reconstruction.

PER BÄCKLUND, born Gothenburg, Sweden, August 3, 1952. *Education:* University of Lund (LL.M., 1978). Junior Judgeship, District Court of Gothenburg, 1978-1980. Associate Judge, Court of Appeal, Gothenburg, 1980-1983. *Member:* Swedish Bar Association, 1986. *LANGUAGES:* English. *PRACTICE AREAS:* General Commercial Law; Corporate Law; Real Estate Law; Insolvency.

LENNART MOLANDER, born Stockholm, Sweden, May 18, 1949. *Education:* University of Lund (LL.M., 1976). Junior Judgeship, District Court of Stenungsund, 1976-1978. Associate Judge, 1978-1987, and Deputy Judge, 1988, Court of Appeal, Gothenburg. Reading Clerk to Committee of the Swedish Parliament, 1988-1989. *Member:* Swedish Bar Association (1993). *LANGUAGES:* English. *PRACTICE AREAS:* General Commercial Law; Corporate Law; Litigation.

ASSOCIATES IN GOTHENBURG

GÖRAN THALEN, born Sollefteå, Sweden, April 23, 1951. *Education:* University of Stockholm (LL.M., 1978). Junior Judgeship, District Court of Karistad, 1978-1981. Associate Judge, Court of Appeal, Gothenburg, 1981-1983. *Member:* Swedish Bar Association, 1986. *LANGUAGES:* English. *PRACTICE AREAS:* General Commercial Law; Labour Law; Personal Injury.

ANNA REHNBERG, born Stockholm, Sweden, October 5, 1962. *Education:* University of Lund (LL.M., 1987). Junior Judgeship, District Court of Uddevalla, 1987-1989. *Member:* Swedish Bar Association (1993). *LANGUAGES:* English and German. *PRACTICE AREAS:* General Commercial Law; Bankruptcy Litigation.

ANDERS NILSSON, born Härnösand, Sweden, June 12, 1959. *Education:* University of Lund (LL.M., 1987). Junior Judgeship, District Court of Boras, 1987-1989. Associate Judge, Court of Appeal, Gothenburg, 1989-1991. *Member:* Swedish Bar Association. *LANGUAGES:* English. *PRACTICE AREAS:* General Commercial Law; Bankruptcy Law.

AXEL WEIBULL, born Lund, Sweden, June 6, 1960. *Education:* University of Lund (LL.M., 1987). Junior Judgeship, District Court of Gothenburg, 1987-1990. Associate Judge, Court of Appeal, Gothenburg, 1990-1991. *LANGUAGES:* English. *PRACTICE AREAS:* General Commercial Law; Bankruptcy Law.

(For Biographical data on all Personnel, see Professional Biographies at Helsingborg, Kristianstad, Lund, Malmö, Stockholm, Örebro and Brussels)

MANNHEIMER SWARTLING

LILLA TORGET 1
P.O. BOX 2235
S-403 14 GOTHENBURG, SWEDEN
Telephone: +46-31 10 96 00
Telefax: +46-31 10 96 01
Telex: 2591

Stockholm, Sweden Office: Västra Trädgårdsgatan 15, P.O. Box 1650, S-111 86. Telephone: +46-8 613 55 00 Telefax: +46-8 613 55 01 Telex: 13082.

Malmö, Sweden Office: Stortorget 29, P.O. Box 4291, S-203 14. Telephone: +46-40 25 08 00. Telefax: +46-40 25 08 01. Telex: 32727.

Helsingborg, Sweden Office: Södra Storgatan 7, P.O. Box 1384, S-251 13. Telephone: +46-42 18 02 95. Telefax: +46-42 18 42 71.

New York, New York Office: 101 Park Avenue, 10178. Telephone: +1 212 682-0580. Telefax: +1 212 682-0982.

Brussels, Belgium Office: Avenue de Tervueren 13A, B-1040. Telephone: +32-2-732 22 22. Telefax: +32-2-736 96 52.

Frankfurt, Germany Office: Bockenheimer Landstrasse 97, D-60325. Telephone: +49-69 974 01 20. Telefax: +49-69 741 01 43.

Berlin, Germany Office: Haus der Schweiz, Friedrichstrasse 155-156, D-10117. Telephone: +49 30 202 20 10. Telefax: +49 30 202 20 110.

Moscow, Russia Office: Chistoprudny Bulvar 8, 101000 Moscow. Telephone: +7 (095) 929 90 05. Telefax: +7 (095) 929 90 06.

General Swedish and International Business Law Practice. Admiralty and Maritime Law. Antitrust, Marketing and Unfair Competition. Banking. Computer Law. Construction and Engineering Contracts and Disputes. Corporate Financing and Securities Law. Corporate Taxation. EC Law. Environmental Energy and Natural Resources Law. Industrial Property, Copyright and Trademarks. Labor Law. Mergers and Acquisitions. Real Estate Law. Reorganizations. Space Law. Litigation and Arbitration.

RESIDENT PARTNERS

Lars Rahmn	**Claes Lundblad**
Claes Beyer	**Jerker Sellén**
Hans-Elof Olsson	**Peter Nordquist**
Torbjörn Molander	**Anders Wikström**
Hans Strempel (Also at	**Göran Kraft**
Frankfurt and Berlin Offices)	**Kerstin Engström**
	Kristina Leffler

RESIDENT ASSOCIATES

Maria Hemberg	**Stefan Brocker**
Christer Hagberg	**Fredrik Ahlberg**
Anders Hedbrandh	**Lennart Johansson**
Fredrika Hörlin	**Helena Hallgarn**
Richard Hammarvid	

RESIDENT CONSULTANTS

Lennart Hagberg

(For biographical data on all personnel, see Professional Biographies at Stockholm, Sweden)

ADVOKATAKTIEBOLAGET
NORDIC LAW

Established in 1987

MÄSSANS GATA 14
P.O. BOX 5043
GOTHENBURG S-402 21, SWEDEN
Telephone: 46 31 81 51 00
Telefax: 46 31 20 82 52

Lund, Sweden Office: Kungsgatan 2 C, S-223 50 Lund. Telephone: +46 46 15 10 00. Telefax: +46 46 18 94 40.

Stockholm, Sweden Office: Sky City, P.O. Box 182, S-190 45 Stockholm-Arlanda. Telephone: 46 8 593 600 04. Telefax: 46 8 593 600 05.

Brussels, Belgium Office: Avenue Louise 177, BTE. 1, B-1050. Telephone: 32 26 40 04 29. Telefax: 32 26 48 34 39.

Helsinki, Finland Office: Mikonkatu 2 D, SF-00100 Helsinki. Telephone: 358 0 64 87 11. Telefax: 358 0 60 50 43.

(This Listing Continued)

ADVOKATAKTIEBOLAGET NORDIC LAW,
Gothenburg—Continued

General Corporation Business Law, Commercial Tax, Financing, Real Estate, Transport, Trade Regulations and Antitrust Law, Copyright, International Legal Transactions, Arbitration and Litigation, European Community Law.

MEMBERS OF FIRM

B.G. NILSON, born Gothenburg, Sweden, 1932; admitted, 1963, Sweden. *Education:* University of Uppsala, Law Faculty (LL.M., 1955); University College, London. Assistant Judge to the District Court of Skövde, 1957-1960. With Vinge Law Office; Broström Shipping Legal Department. Chairman: Atlantic Container Line Gothenburg; Hoverspeed, Dover. President, Intercontinental Transport BV, Rotterdam. Councillor and Member, Arbitration Council of Western Sweden Chamber of Commerce. *Member:* Swedish Bar Association. *LANGUAGES:* Swedish, English, German, Dutch and French.

ANDERS J. BERGVIST, born Gothenburg, Sweden, 1961; admitted, 1993, Sweden. *Education:* University of Lund, Law Faculty (LL.M., 1988). *Member:* Swedish Bar Association. *LANGUAGES:* Swedish and English.

ASSOCIATES

PER NICLAS AURELL, born Alingsås, Sweden, 1966. *Education:* University of Lund, Law Faculty (LL.M., 1989); University of Amsterdam, Amsterdam School of International Relations (LL.M., 1993). Assistant Judge to the District Court of Varberg, 1990-1992. *LANGUAGES:* Swedish and English.

REPRESENTATIVE CLIENTS AND REFERENCES: Western Sweden Chamber of Commerce.

ADVOKATFIRMAN VINGE KB

NILS ERICSONSGATAN 17
P.O. BOX 11025
S-404 21 GOTHENBURG, SWEDEN
Telephone: +46 31-80 51 00
Telex: 21119 VINGE S
Telefax: +46-31-15 88 11

For offices in Stockholm, Malmö and Helsingborg, Sweden see those cities.

London, England Office: 44/45 Chancery Lane, WC2A 1JB. Telephone: +44 171 404 4825. Telex: 25585 VINGE G. Telefax: +44 171 831 6860.

Paris, France Office: 21 Rue Jean Gougjor, F-75008. Telephone: +33 4075 3737. Telefax: +33-1-45630579.

Hong Kong Office: 2003 Hutchison House, 10 Harcourt Road, Central. Telephone: +852 2523 6149. Telefax: +852 2810 5343.

Brussels, Belgium Office: Avenue Louise 475/B 12, 1050. Telephone: +32 (2) 646 36 20; (2) 646 36 80. Telefax: +32 (2) 646 41 46.

Admiralty, Transport, Corporate, Labor, Environmental, Tax, Contracting, Antitrust, Patent, Trademark and Bankruptcy Law.

MEMBERS OF FIRM

ROBERT ROMLÖV, born 1936. *Education:* University of Lund (LL.M., Jur. kand., 1961; Diplôme Superieur de droit comparé, 1960). Trainee with Haight, Gardner, Poor and Havens, New York, 1961-1962. *Member:* Swedish Bar Association (1966, Member of the Board, 1989-1994); International Bar Association (1972); Swedish Maritime Law Association (Member of the Board, 1978-1992); International Law Association; Comité Maritime International (Titular Member). *LANGUAGES:* English and French. *PRACTICE AREAS:* Maritime Law; Business Law; Arbitration.

HANS-ERIK ÅHMAN, born 1940. *Education:* University of Lund (LL.M., Jur. kand., 1965). *Member:* Swedish Bar Association (1971); International Bar Association (1972); Association Internationale des Jeunes Avocats (1975); Swedish Association for European Community Law; Inter-Pacific Bar Association (1991). *LANGUAGES:* Swedish, English, French, German. *PRACTICE AREAS:* Corporate Law.

JOHAN WETTER, born 1941. *Education:* University of Uppsala (LL.M., Jur. kand., 1967). *Member:* Swedish Bar Association (1973); International Bar Association; Swedish Maritime Law Association; Association Internationale des Jeunes Avocats. *LANGUAGES:* Swedish, English, German, French and Spanish. *PRACTICE AREAS:* Maritime and Transport Law; Business Law; Arbitration.

BJÖRN ASCHAN, born 1942. *Education:* University of Uppsala (juris kandidat, LL.M., 1968). Service with Swedish Courts, 1968-1970. Associated with the firm since 1970. *Member:* Swedish Bar Association. *LANGUAGES:* Swedish, English, French, Spanish, German. *PRACTICE AREAS:* Mergers and Acquisitions; Corporate Law; Insolvency Law.

TORSTEN JACOBSSON, born 1940. *Education:* University of Lund (LL.M., Jur. kand., 1965). *Member:* Swedish Bar Association (1974); International Bar Association; Swedish Association for European Community Law; Swedish Maritime Law Association; Swedish Association for Market Law. *LANGUAGES:* Swedish, English, German and Norwegian. *PRACTICE AREAS:* Maritime Law; Business Law; Market and Industrial Property Law.

GÖRAN PETERSSON, born 1942. *Education:* University of Lund (LL.M., Jur. kand., 1967). *Member:* Swedish Bar Association (1977); International Bar Association. *LANGUAGES:* Swedish, English and German. *PRACTICE AREAS:* Mergers and Acquisitions; Real Estate; Corporate Law.

THOMAS MACDOWALL, born 1945. *Education:* University of Stockholm (LL.M., Jur.kand., 1972). Chairman, Swedish Chamber of Commerce in Hong Kong, 1990-1991. Resident, Hong Kong, Office, 1985-1987, 1989-1992. *Member:* Hong Kong Law Society; Swedish and International Bar Associations. *LANGUAGES:* Swedish and English. *PRACTICE AREAS:* Swedish and International Commercial Law; Corporate Law; Mergers and Acquisitions; Insolvency; Labour Law.

TORBJÖRN SKÖLD, born 1945. *Education:* University of Stockholm (LL.M., Jur.Kand., 1970). Vice President and General Counsel of AB Volvo, 1982-1988. Senior Vice President, Secretary to the Board and General Counsel of Scandinavian Airlines System (SAS), 1988-1990. Chairman, Swedish Corporate Counsels Association (Bolagsjuristernas förening, 1988-1990). *Member:* Swedish Bar Association (1975-1982, 1990—); International Bar Association; American Bar Association; Licensing Executives Society. *LANGUAGES:* Scandinavian, English and German. *PRACTICE AREAS:* Corporate Law; Competition Law; Joint Ventures; Mergers and Acquisitions; Domestic and International Trade.

MICHAEL STERNER, born 1946. *Education:* University of Lund (juris kandidat LL.M., 1973). Instructor in Law, University of Lund, 1973-1974. Practised with: Wiberg, Jonsson, Wikander Advokatbyrå, Gothenburg, 1974-1976; Shearman & Sterling, New York, 1982-1983. Member of this firm since, 1976. *Member:* Swedish (1979) and International Bar Associations; Swedish Maritime Law Association. *LANGUAGES:* Swedish, English, German and Portuguese. *PRACTICE AREAS:* Corporate Law; Bank Finance; Insolvency Law.

FREDRIK VINGE, born 1951. *Education:* University of Lund (LL.M., Jur. kand., 1973). *Member:* Swedish Bar Association (1982); Swedish Maritime Law Association. *LANGUAGES:* Swedish, English and German. *PRACTICE AREAS:* Admiralty Law; Corporate Law.

PER SETTERGREN, born 1948. *Education:* University of Lund (LL.M., Jur. kand. 1976). *Member:* Swedish Bar Association (1981). *LANGUAGES:* Swedish, English and French. *PRACTICE AREAS:* Corporate Law; Mergers and Acquisitions; Insolvency Law; Reorganisations.

PER-OLOV SKÖLD, born 1949. *Education:* University of Stockholm (LL.M., Jur.kand., 1976). *Member:* Swedish Bar Association (1984); International Bar Association; Association Internationale des Jeunes Avocats; Swedish Maritime Law Association. *LANGUAGES:* Swedish and English. *PRACTICE AREAS:* Company and Commercial Law; Maritime Law; Transportation Law.

ANDERS AHLM, born 1956. *Education:* University of Uppsala (LL.M., Jur.kand., 1982). Junior Judge at District Court, 1982-1984. Law Clerk in Court of Appeal, 1985-1986. *Member:* Swedish Bar Association (1989). *LANGUAGES:* Swedish and English. *PRACTICE AREAS:* Company Law; Intellectual Property Law.

ULF OHRLING, born 1957. *Education:* University of Linköping, (Economics, 1976-1977); University of Uppsala (LL.M., Jur.kand., 1984). Assistant at the Faculty of Law, University of Uppsala, 1982-1984. Service and Junior Judgeships at the District Court of Stockholm, 1984-1986. *Member:* Swedish Bar Association (1989); International Bar Association; Licensing Executives Society. *LANGUAGES:* Swedish and English. *PRACTICE AREAS:* Corporate Law; Mergers and Acquisitions.

(This Listing Continued)

(This Listing Continued)

ASSOCIATES

JAN-ERIC ASKENSTRÖM, born 1948. *Education:* Gothenburg School of Economics and Business Administration (Master of Business Administration, civilekonom, 1970). With Swedish Tax Authorities, 1971-1983. Head, Department of Education, Swedish National Tax Board, 1975-1979. Instructor, Tax Law, University of Gothenburg, University of Lund and Gothenburg School of Economics and Business Administration, 1979-1988. Tax Consultant, KPMG, 1983-1989. *Member:* Gothenburg Tax Law Society (President); Tax Law Council of the Western Sweden Chamber of Commerce; International Fiscal Association. *LANGUAGES:* Swedish and English. *PRACTICE AREAS:* International Tax Law.

RAOUL SVENSSON, born 1958. *Education:* University of Gothenburg (LL.M., Jur.kand., 1992). *Member:* International Fiscal Association; Association Internationale des Jeunes Avocats. *LANGUAGES:* Swedish and English. *PRACTICE AREAS:* Tax Law.

OLOF JISLAND, born 1963. *Education:* University of Uppsala (LL.M., Jur.Kand., 1988); University of Minnesota Law School (degrees in contracts, torts and products liability, 1986); University of Oslo (Sjörättsexamen, Maritime Law Degree, 1988). *Member:* Swedish Bar Association (1993); Swedish Maritime Law Association; International Bar Association; Associationale des Jeunes Avocats. *LANGUAGES:* Swedish and English.

PAULO FOHLIN, born 1961. *Education:* University of Minnesota Law School (1985); University of Uppsala (LL.M., Jur.kand., 1988). Assistant Faculty of Law, University of Uppsala, 1986-1988. Teacher in Contracts and Sales Law at the Faculty of Law, University of Uppsala, 1987-1988. *LANGUAGES:* Swedish and English.

TOMMY NILSSON, born 1940. *Education:* University of Lund (LL.M., Jur. kand., 1966). *Member:* Swedish Bar Association (1992). *LANGUAGES:* Swedish and English. *PRACTICE AREAS:* Environmental Law; Building and Planning Law; Public Law.

OLLE LINDÉN, born 1960. *Education:* University of Uppsala (LL.M., Jur.kand., 1986). Service with Swedish Courts, 1986-1988. *Member:* Swedish Bar Association. *LANGUAGES:* Swedish and English.

JAN SVENSSON, born 1963. *Education:* University of Gothenburg (Master in Law, 1987); College of Europe (Diploma in Advanced European Studies, 1988); University of Lund (LL.M., 1989). *LANGUAGES:* Swedish, English and French.

MORGAN HALLEN, born 1962. *Education:* University of Gothenburg (LL.M., Jur.Kand, 1988). Master in Law, 1987. Service with Swedish Courts, 1988-1991. *LANGUAGES:* Swedish and English.

FREDRIK TENGSTRÖM, born New York, USA, November 12, 1950. *Education:* University of Lund (Jur. kand., LL.M., 1975). Assistant Judge, 1975-1977. Execution Officer, 1977-1980. Government Supervisor, 1980-1990. Government Counsel of Bankruptcy Trustees, 1990. *Member:* Swedish Bar Association (1993). *LANGUAGES:* Swedish and English. *PRACTICE AREAS:* Insolvency Law.

AGNETA E. DANIELSSON, born 1963. *Education:* University of Gothenburg (Master in Law, 1989); University of Lund (LL.M., 1990). *LANGUAGES:* English, French and Swedish.

INGMARIE PERSSON, born 1966; admitted, 1990, Sweden. *Education:* University of Lund (LL.M., Jur.kand., 1990); Maîtrise de Droit International (1991). Service with Swedish Courts, 1992-1993. *LANGUAGES:* Swedish, French and English.

BARNEY FYMAN, born 1958; admitted, 1986, New York and U.S. District Court Southern District of New York; 1994, Gothenburg. *Education:* Queens College (B.A., 1980); Benjamin N. Cardozo School of Law (J.D., 1985); University of Gothenburg (LL.M., Jur.kand., 1994). Lecturer: Johnson & Wales University, Gothenburg Campus, Spring 1994; University of Gothenburg, School of Economics, Spring 1993; University of Gothenburg, School of Law, Spring 1993. *Author:* "Impaired Capital and Director Liability," article, Sweden; "European Business Law Review," Publication, January, 1995. Member, County Board Sandhult Township, October 1993 - December 1994. *Member:* New York Bar Association (Sections: International Law and Practice); American Bar Association (Sectionss: International Law and Practice, Committees: International Litigation, International Commercial Transactions, Immigration, Business Law Section). *LANGUAGES:* English and Swedish.

(This Listing Continued)

OF COUNSEL

KURT MARK, born 1929. *Education:* University of Uppsala (LL.M., Jur. kand., 1954). *Member:* Swedish Bar Association (1960). (Resident, Paris Office). *LANGUAGES:* Swedish, English, French, German.

Languages: English, French, German, Russian, Spanish and Scandinavian

---

ADVOKATFIRMAN WÅHLIN

VÄSTRA HAMNGATAN 5
P.O. BOX 2240
S-403 14 GOTHENBURG, SWEDEN
Telephone: (0) 31 101710
Telefax: (0) 31 111123

Corporation and Business Law, Labour Law, Taxation, International Legal Transactions, Insolvency, Mergers and Acquisitions, General Practice.

MEMBERS OF FIRM

PETER WÅHLIN, born Lund, Sweden, June 25, 1927; admitted, 1954, Sweden. *Education:* University of Lund (Jur. kand., LL.B., 1951). Chairman of Arbitration Institute of Swiss Chamber of Commerce in Sweden. *Member:* Swedish Bar Association (1954); International Bar Association; Interlaw; International Fiscal Association. *LANGUAGES:* Swedish, English, German, Danish and Norwegian. *PRACTICE AREAS:* Business Law; Mergers and Acquisitions; Litigation; Arbitration; Corporate Tax.

LARS P. WÅHLIN, born Gothenburg, Sweden, August 10, 1954; admitted, 1985, Sweden. *Education:* University of Lund (Jur. kand., LL.B., 1980). *Member:* Swedish Bar Association (1985); Young Lawyers International Association. *LANGUAGES:* Swedish, English, German, Danish and Norwegian. *PRACTICE AREAS:* Business Law; Insolvency.

PER WÅHLIN, born Gothenburg, Sweden, December 31, 1956; admitted, 1987, Sweden. *Education:* University of Lund (Jur. kand., LL.B., 1982). *Member:* Swedish Bar Association (1987); Young Lawyers International Association. *LANGUAGES:* Swedish, English, German, Danish and Norwegian. *PRACTICE AREAS:* Corporation; Business Law; International Legal Transactions; Banking Law.

LEIF RAMBERG, born Gothenburg, Sweden, May 5, 1956; admitted, 1989, Sweden. *Education:* University of Lund (Jur. kand., LL.B., 1982). Assistant Judge, 1982-1985. Student Lecturer on Law, University of Lund, 1979-1982. *Member:* Swedish Bar Association (1989). *LANGUAGES:* Swedish, English, Danish and Norwegian. *PRACTICE AREAS:* Corporation; Business Law; Labour Law; Insolvency.

ASSOCIATE

TOM SCHLOSSMAN, born Gothenburg, Sweden, October 27, 1964; (Not admitted in Sweden). *Education:* University of Lund (Jur. kand., LL.B., 1989). Editor of the Law Review University of Lund, 1988. Assistant Judge, 1990-1992. *LANGUAGES:* Swedish, English, Danish and Norwegian. *PRACTICE AREAS:* Corporation; Business Law; Litigation; Labour Law; Insolvency.

Members of INTERLAW, an International Association of Law firms in Major World Centers.

REFERENCES: Skandinaviska Enskilda Banken; Gotabanken; Swiss Chamber of Commerce in Stockholm, Sweden.

ADVOKATFIRMAN WISTRAND

LILLA BOMMEN 1
S-411 04 GOTHENBURG, SWEDEN
Telephone: +46-31 771 21 00
Telex: 21322 GOTLEX S
Telefax: +46-31 7712150

Stockholm, Sweden Office: Kungsgatan 4A, P.O. Box 7414, S-103 91. Telephone: +46-8211325. Telefax: +46-8 212305.

Company and commercial, banking and finance, maritime and transport, competition, insolvency, intellectual property, construction, environmental, litigation and arbitration, EU and EEA law.

MEMBERS OF FIRM

FOLKE WISTRAND, born 1926. *Education:* University of Uppsala (LL.M., 1947). *Member:* Swedish Bar Association (1956). *LANGUAGES:* Swedish, English and German.

(This Listing Continued)

ADVOKATFIRMAN WISTRAND, Gothenburg—Continued

BO HANSSON, born 1940. *Education:* University of Lund (LL.M., 1966). *Member:* Swedish Bar Association (1971). *LANGUAGES:* Swedish and English.

JONAS LAURITZEN, born 1942. *Education:* University of Lund (LL.M., 1967). *Member:* Swedish Bar Association (1973, Member of the Board, 1983-1990, Chairman for Western Sweden, 1990—). *LANGUAGES:* Swedish and English.

PETER HEDBORG, born 1943. *Education:* University of Uppsala (LL.M., 1967). Practice with the law firm Haight, Gardner, Poor & Havens, New York, 1970-1971. *Member:* Swedish Bar Association (1974, Member of the Board, 1990—). *LANGUAGES:* Swedish and English.

TORSTEN ROSELL, born 1939. *Education:* University of Lund (LL.M., 1965). *Member:* Swedish Bar Association (1976). *LANGUAGES:* Swedish and English.

BJÖRN AGRELL, born 1946. *Education:* University of Lund (LL.M., 1971). *Member:* Swedish Bar Association (1976). *LANGUAGES:* Swedish and English.

CHRISTER ELANDER, born 1947. *Education:* University of Lund (LL.M., 1973). *Member:* Swedish Bar Association (1978). *LANGUAGES:* Swedish and English.

STEFAN LINDSKOG, born 1951. *Education:* University of Lund (LL.M., 1974); University of Stockholm (LL.D., 1985). Professor, Institute of Commercial Law, University of Gothenburg. *Member:* Swedish Bar Association (1980). *LANGUAGES:* Swedish and English.

MATTHIAS VON LEMPRUCH, born 1947. *Education:* University of Lund (LL.M., 1973). *Member:* Swedish Bar Association (1981); German Bar Association (1986). *LANGUAGES:* Swedish, English and German.

KAI DITTMER, born 1947. *Education:* University of Lund (LL.M., 1971). *Member:* Swedish Bar Association (1981). *LANGUAGES:* Swedish and English.

THOMAS DREIJER, born 1949. *Education:* University of Lund (LL.M., 1976). *Member:* Swedish Bar Association (1982). *LANGUAGES:* Swedish, English and French.

MARGARETA ANDERSSON, born 1950. *Education:* University of Lund (LL.M., 1974). *Member:* Swedish Bar Association (1983). *LANGUAGES:* Swedish and English.

ANNE-MARIE POUTEAUX, born 1951. *Education:* University of Lund (LL.M., 1975). *Member:* Swedish Bar Association (1984). *LANGUAGES:* Swedish, English and French.

BO STEFAN ARLEIJ, born 1952. *Education:* University of Lund (LL.M., 1977). *Member:* Swedish Bar Association (1985). *LANGUAGES:* Swedish and English.

ULF JAKOBSSON, born 1954. *Education:* University of Uppsala (LL.M., 1979). *Member:* Swedish Bar Association (1987). *LANGUAGES:* Swedish and English.

JOACIM ÖBERG, born 1959. *Education:* University of Lund (LL.M., 1984). *Member:* Swedish Bar Association (1990). *LANGUAGES:* Swedish and English.

MÅRTEN HULTERSTRÖM, born 1960. *Education:* University of Lund (LL.M., 1986). *Member:* Swedish Bar Association (1991). *LANGUAGES:* Swedish and English.

LAVE BECK-FRIIS, born 1947. *Education:* University of Stockholm (LL.M., 1972). *Member:* Swedish Bar Association (1991). *LANGUAGES:* Swedish and English.

ASSOCIATES

MICHAEL PLOGELL, born 1961. *Education:* University of Stockholm (LL.M., 1987). *Member:* Swedish Bar Association (1993). *LANGUAGES:* Swedish and English.

HANS POTILA STRÖMSNES, born 1960. *Education:* University of Lund (LL.M., 1988). *Member:* Swedish Bar Association. *LANGUAGES:* Swedish and English.

GÖRAN HÄRSTEDT, born 1965. *Education:* University of Lund (LL.M., 1989). *Member:* Swedish Bar Association. *LANGUAGES:* Swedish and English.

(This Listing Continued)

RUDOLF LAURIN, born 1966. *Education:* University of Lund(LL.M., 1991). *LANGUAGES:* Swedish, English, French and Czech.

JÖRGEN AXELSSON, born 1964. *Education:* University of Uppsala (LL.M., 1991). *LANGUAGES:* Swedish and English. *PRACTICE AREAS:* General Commercial Law.

JESPER GRÜNBAUM, born 1964. *Education:* University of Stockholm (LL.M., 1990). *LANGUAGES:* Swedish and English.

BOB LEE, born 1967. *Education:* University of Lund (LL.M., 1991). *LANGUAGES:* Swedish, English and Chinese.

Member of Legal Network International (LNI).

STYRBJÖRN GÄRDE ADVOKATBYRÅ

GARNISONSGATAN 10
S-254 66 HELSINGBORG, SWEDEN
Telephone: +46 (42)-20 10 80
Telefax: +46 (42)-20 18 38

Stockholm, Sweden Office: Nybrogatan 34, P.O. Box 5208, S-102 45. Telephone: +46 (8)-665 00 40. Telefax: +46 (8)-665 00 41.

Gothenburg, Sweden Office: Kastellgatan 1, S-413 07. Telephone: +46 (31)-11 36 30. Telefax: +46 (31)-13 73 68.

Malmö, Sweden Office: Norra Vallgatan 64, S-211. Telephone: +46 (40)-10 48 10. Telefax: +46 (40)-23 52 31.

Borås, Sweden Office: Stora Kyrkogatan 4, P.O. Box 305, S-501 05. Telephone: +46 (33) 11 59 00. Telefax: +46 (33) 13 79 00.

Paris, France Office: 41, Rue de Passy, F-75016. Telephone: +33 (1)-45 27 95 22. Telefax: +33 (1) 40 50 90 31.

Representative Offices:

Schweiz: Stadelgarden, Stadelhofer Strasse 40, CH-8024 Zürich. Telephone: +41 (1)-261 52 60. Telefax: +41 (1)-261 55 29.

Sweden: HAGA Företagscenter, Brogatan 25, S-334 33 Anderstorp. Telephone: +46 (371)-174 80. Telefax: +46 (371)-169 67.

Admitted to Practice in Sweden, The Law Firm's Primary Activities are Concentrated on Swedish and International Business, Tax Law and Insolvency Law.

MEMBERS OF FIRM

PETER BERGGREN, born Säffle, Sweden, 1943. *Education:* University of Lund (LL.B., 1970). Served in the District Court of Sunne, 1970-1973. *Member:* Swedish Bar Association; Swedish Chamber of Commerce. *LANGUAGES:* Swedish, English and German. *PRACTICE AREAS:* Company Law; Corporate Law; Contracts; Licensed Trade.

BENGT GESSLE, born Halmstad, Sweden, 1951. *Education:* University of Lund (LL.B., 1985). Served in County Administrative Court, 1985-1987. Administrative Court of Appeals in Jönköping, 1988. Deputy Judge, Court of Appeals, 1988. *Member:* Swedish Bar Association. *LANGUAGES:* Swedish and English. *PRACTICE AREAS:* Company Law; Corporate Law; Contracts; Insolvency Law.

ASSOCIATES

MATS KROON, born Ödeshög, Sweden, 1955. *Education:* University of Uppsala (LL.B., 1982). Served in District Court of Klippan, 1982-1984; Municipality of Värnamo, 1985-1988; Society of Landlords of Norra Skåne, 1988-1990. *Member:* Swedish Bar Association. *LANGUAGES:* Swedish and English. *PRACTICE AREAS:* Corporate Law; Real Estate; Contracts.

RIKARD BONDESSON, born Eslöv, Sweden, 1964. *Education:* University of Lund (LL.B., 1988). Served in District Court of Malmö, 1989-1992; Court of Appeal, 1992. District Court of Kalmar, 1992-1993. *LANGUAGES:* Swedish and English. *PRACTICE AREAS:* Company Law; Corporate Law; Contracts; Commercial Litigation.

RIKARD MAURITZON, born Örkelljunga, Sweden, 1961. *Education:* University of Lund (LL.B., 1986). Served in District Court of Lidköping, 1987-1989; The Central Office for Composition, 1990-1993. *LANGUAGES:* Swedish and English. *PRACTICE AREAS:* Corporate Law; Contracts; Insolvency Law; Bankruptcy Law.

Languages: Swedish, English, German and French

(For Biographical data on other Personnel, see Professional Biographies at Gothenburg, Stockholm, Malmö and Borås Sweden).

ADVOKATFIRMAN LINDAHL

MARIAGATAN 10
P.O. BOX 1214
251 12 HELSINGBORG, SWEDEN
Telephone: 46-42 18 31 80
Telefax: 46-42 11 96 78 and 46-42 24 12 86
Telex: 72715 Counsel S

Gothenburg, Sweden Office: Östra Hamngatan 36. Mailing Address: P.O. Box 11911, S-404 39 Göteborg. Telephone: 46-31 80 34 30. Telex: 21915 MAGLAW S. Telefax: 46-31 15 82 85.

Kristianstad, Sweden Office: Västra Vallgatan 26. Mailing Address: P.O. Box 167, S-291 22 Kristianstad. Telephone: 46-44 10 07 80. Telex: 32584 LUNDLAW S. Telefax: 46-44 11 85 14.

Malmö, Sweden Office: Hjälmaregatan 3, Scandinavian Center, S-211 18 Malmö. Telephone: 46-40 17 44 40. Telex: 32584 LUNDLAW S. Telefax: 46-40 11 13 54.

Stockholm, Sweden Office: Strandvägen 5 A. Mailing Address: P.O. Box 14240, S-104 40 Stockholm. Telephone: 46-8 670 5800. Telex: 19609 LINDAHL S. Telefax: 46-8 667 73 80.

Örebro, Sweden Office: Vasastrand 11-13. Mailing Address: P.O. Box 143, S-701 42 Örebro. Telephone: 46-19 10 48 00. Telefax: 46-19 10 44 45.

Brussels, Belgium Office: 33 Blvd de la Cambre, Bte 13, B-1050 Brussels. Telephone: 32-2 646 46 90. Telefax: 32-2 646 45 80.

MEMBERS OF FIRM IN HELSINGBORG

GÖRAN RAMBERG, born Väla, Sweden, January 28, 1930. *Education:* University of Stockholm (LL.M., 1953). Legal Research 1954-1955. Junior Judgeship, District Court of Södertörn, 1956-1957. *Member:* Swedish Bar Association, 1961 (Member of the Board, 1969-1975; Chairman, Professional Committee, 1978-1982; Chairman, Southern Section, 1980-1984). *LANGUAGES:* English. *PRACTICE AREAS:* General Commercial Law; Contracts; Corporate Law; litigation; Arbitration.

KJELL STENSTRÖM, born Lund, Sweden, June 12, 1940. *Education:* University of Lund (LL.M., 1970). *Member:* Swedish Bar Association, 1977 (Chairman, Professional Committee, 1989-1993; Vice Chairman, Southern Section, 1992—). *LANGUAGES:* English. *PRACTICE AREAS:* General Commercial Law; Contracts; Corporate Law; Real Estate Law; Litigation; Arbitration.

MAGNUS RAMBERG, born Östersund, Sweden, January 20, 1960. *Education:* University of Lund (LL.M., 1986). Chairman of Lund's University Students Association, 1985. During period as associate trainee in Travers Smith Braithwaite, London, 1991-1992. *Member:* Swedish Bar Association (1992—). *LANGUAGES:* English, Scandinavian Languages. *PRACTICE AREAS:* General Commercial Law; Corporate Law; Contracts; Litigation; Arbitration.

ASSOCIATE IN HELSINGBORG

JOHAN KARLEFORS, born Lund, Sweden, 1960. *Education:* University of Oslo, Norway (1983); University of Lund (LL.B., 1986). Served in County Administrative Court of Kalmar, 1986-1988. *Member:* Swedish Bar Association. *LANGUAGES:* English and Swedish. *PRACTICE AREAS:* General Commercial Law; Corporate Law; Labour Legislation.

(For Biographical data on all Personnel, see Professional Biographies at Gothenburg, Kristianstad, Lund, Malmö, Stockholm, Örebro and Brussels)

MANNHEIMER SWARTLING

SÖDRA STORGATAN 7
P.O. BOX 1384
S-251 13 HELSINGBORG, SWEDEN
Telephone: +46-42 18 02 95
Telefax: +46-42 18 42 71

Stockholm, Sweden Office: Västra Trädgårdsgatan 15, P.O. Box 1650, S-111 86. Telephone: +46-8 613 55 00. Telefax: +46-8 613 55 01. Telex: 13082.

Gothenburg, Sweden Office: Lilla Torget 1, P.O. Box 2235, S-403 14. Telephone: +46-31 10 96 00. Telefax: +46-31 10 96 01. Telex: 2591.

Malmö, Sweden Office: Stortorget 29, P.O. Box 4291, S-203 14. Telephone: +46-40 25 08 00. Telefax: +46-40 25 08 01. Telex: 32727.

New York, New York Office: 101 Park Avenue, 10178. Telephone: +1 212 682-0580. Telefax: +1 212 682-0982.

(This Listing Continued)

Brussels, Belgium Office: Avenue de Tervueren 13A, B-1040. Telephone: +32-2-732 22 22. Telefax: +32-2-736 96 52.

Frankfurt, Germany Office: Bockenheimer Landstrasse 97, D-60325. Telephone: +49-69 974 01 20. Telefax: +49-69 741 01 43.

Berlin, Germany Office: Haus der Schweiz, Friedrichstrasse 155-156, D-10117. Telephone: +49 30 202 20 10. Telefax: +49 30 202 20 110.

Moscow, Russia Office: Chistoprudny Bulvar 8, 101000 Moscow. Telephone: +7 (095) 929 90 05. Telefax: +7 (095) 929 90 06.

General Swedish and International Business Law Practice. Admiralty and Maritime Law. Antitrust, Marketing and Unfair Competition. Banking. Computer Law. Construction and Engineering Contracts and Disputes. Corporate Financing and Securities Law. Corporate Taxation. EC Law. Environmental Energy and Natural Resources Law. Industrial Property, Copyright and Trademarks. Labor Law. Mergers and Acquisitions. Real Estate Law. Reorganizations. Space Law. Litigation and Arbitration.

RESIDENT PARTNER

Ragnar Lindqvist

RESIDENT ASSOCIATE

Björn Mullaart
Lars Palmqvist

(For biographical data on all personnel, see Professional Biographies at Stockholm, Sweden)

ADVOKATBOLAGET WIKLUND, GUSTAVII, OHLIN

Established in 1983
DROTTNINGGATAN 30-36
S-252-21 HELSINGBORG, SWEDEN
Telephone: +46 42 12 79 45
+46 42 13 60 47

Corporate Law, Mergers and Acquisitions, Tax Law, Civil and Trade Litigation, International Family Law.

FIRM PROFILE: *The firm has two divisions, one for Business Law and one for Family Law. The firm is well known for its competence in especially Mergers and Acquisition cases as well as cases concerning international Family Law. The four partner firm has a legal support staff of seven consisting of lawyers and office administrators. The firm has a subsidiary in London and a reception office in Malmö.*

MEMBERS OF FIRM

JOHAN WIKLUND, born Helsingborg, Sweden, July 19, 1951; admitted, 1983, Sweden. *Education:* University of Lund (jur kand and fil kand, 1976). Junior Judgeship, District Court of Kristianstad, 1978-1979. Author: "Protection of Minority Interest in Companies", Balans, 1991. *Member:* Swedish Bar Association, Association International Jeunes Avocats (AIJA). *LANGUAGES:* English and Scandinavian. *PRACTICE AREAS:* Mergers and Acquisitions; International Trade Law; Corporate Trade Litigation.

LARS GUSTAVII, born Göteborg, Sweden, July 22, 1942; admitted, 1977, Sweden. *Education:* University of Lund (jur kand, 1971). *Member:* Swedish Bar Association. *LANGUAGES:* English, German and Scandinavian. *PRACTICE AREAS:* Mergers and Acquisitions; International Trade Law; Corporate Trade Litigation.

INGRID WIKLUND, born Lund, Sweden, February 9, 1952; admitted, 1987, Sweden. *Education:* University of Lund (jur kand 1977). *Member:* Swedish Bar Association and Association International Jeunes Avocats (AIJA). *LANGUAGES:* English, German and Scandinavian. *PRACTICE AREAS:* International Family Law; Personal Injury; Civil Litigation.

HANS OHLIN, born Lund, Sweden, August 9, 1946; admitted, 1987, Sweden. *Education:* University of Lund (jur kand 1973 and civ.ek 1970). Junior Judgeship, District Court of Halmstad, 1973-1975. *Member:* Swedish Bar Association. *LANGUAGES:* English and Scandinavian. *PRACTICE AREAS:* Mergers and Acquisitions; International Trade Law; Corporate Trade Litigation; Tax Law.

HELENE EK, born Lund, Sweden, March 19, 1955. *Education:* University of Lund (Filkand 1979 and Jur Kand 1987). Junior Judgeship, District Court of Helsingborg, 1987-1990. Public Prosecutor, Authority of Helsingborg, 1990-1991. *LANGUAGES:* English, German and Scandinavian. *PRACTICE AREAS:* Family Law; Personal Injury; Civil Litigation.

(This Listing Continued)

ADVOKATBOLAGET WIKLUND, GUSTAVII, OHLIN,
Helsingborg—Continued

LARS ANDERSSON, born Lund, Sweden, December 10, 1960; admitted, 1994, Sweden. *Education:* University of Lund (Jur Kand 1988). Junior Judgeship, District Court of Helsingborg, 1988-1991. *Member:* Swedish Bar Association. *LANGUAGES:* English and Scandinavian. *PRACTICE AREAS:* Mergers and Acquisitions; International Trade Law; Corporate Trade Litigation; Civil Litigation.

ADVOKATFIRMAN, SYLL & CO.

HAMNGATAN 2
P.O. BOX 684
S-55119 JÖNKÖPING, SWEDEN
Telephone: 36-100-250
FAX: 36-165-579

PARTNERS

ERIK KARL INGVAR SYLL, born Kisa, January 13, 1930; admitted, 1962, Sweden. *Education:* University of Uppsala (LL.B., 1955). AGM, INSEAD, Fontainebleau, France, 1970. *LANGUAGES:* English, French and German. *PRACTICE AREAS:* General Business Law; International Contracts; Construction Contracts; Timber Trade.

STAFFAN G. LINDBLAD, born Skärstad, June 5, 1948; admitted, 1978, Sweden. *Education:* University of Lund (LL.B., 1973). *LANGUAGES:* Swedish, English and German. *PRACTICE AREAS:* Corporate Law; General Contract Law; Banking and Securities.

GUNNAR HJERTQUIST, born Stockholm, February 12, 1949; admitted, 1979, Sweden. *Education:* University of Stockholm (LL.B., 1973). Claims Adjuster at AB Indemnitas Insurance Company. Associate at Erik Berglund Law Firm, 1976-1983. Managing Director, Swedish Association of Marine Underwriters, 1984-1988. Chairman, Freedom of Insurance Committee in the International Union of Marine Insurance, 1986-1988. *Member:* Swedish Bar Association. *LANGUAGES:* English, German and French. *PRACTICE AREAS:* General Commercial Law; Maritime and Transportation Law; Insurance Law; Insolvency Law; Law of Tort.

HANS-GÖRAN E. FRICK, born Jönköping, April 16, 1957; admitted, 1989, Sweden. *Education:* University of Lund (LL.B., 1982). *LANGUAGES:* English and German. *PRACTICE AREAS:* General Business Law; International Contracts; Intellectual Property Law.

KRISTER JAN OLOF HAVERT, born Gislaved, May 23, 1960; admitted, 1993, Sweden. *Education:* University of Lund (LL.B., 1986). *LANGUAGES:* English. *PRACTICE AREAS:* General Business Law; Bankruptcy Law.

ASSOCIATES

PETER BO FLODIN, born Jönköping, February 21, 1967. *Education:* University of Stockholm (LL.B., 1991). *LANGUAGES:* English. *PRACTICE AREAS:* General Business Law; Property and Real Estate Law; International Contracts.

ADVOKATFIRMAN LINDAHL

VÄSTRA VALLGATAN 26
P.O. BOX 167
S-291 22 KRISTIANSTAD, SWEDEN
Telephone: 46-44 10 07 80
Telex: 325 84 LUNDLAW S
Telefax: 46-44 11 85 14

Gothenburg, Sweden Office: Östra Hamngatan 36. Mailing Address: P.O. Box 11911, S-404 39 Göteborg. Telephone: 46-31 80 34 30. Telefax: 46-31 15 82 85.

Helsingborg, Sweden Office: Mariagatan 10. Mailing Address: P.O. Box 1214, S-251 12 Helsingborg. Telephone: 46-42 18 31 80. Telefax: 46-42 11 96 78 and 46-42 24 12 86. Telex: 72715 Counsel S.

Malmö, Sweden Office: Hjälmaregatan 3, Scandinavian Center, S-211 18 Malmö. Telephone: 46-40 17 44 40. Telex: 32584 LUNDLAW S. Telefax: 46-40 11 13 54.

Stockholm, Sweden Office: Strandvägen 5 A. Mailing Address: P.O. Box 14240, S-104 40 Stockholm. Telephone: 46-8 670 5800. Telex: 19609 LINDAHL S. Telefax: 46-8 667 73 80.

(This Listing Continued)

Örebro, Sweden Office: Vasastrand 11-13. Mailing Address: P.O. Box 143, S-701 42 Örebro. Telephone: 46-19 10 48 00. Telefax: 46-19 10 44 45.

Brussels, Belgium Office: 33 Blvd de la Cambre, Bte 13, B-1050 Brussels. Telephone: 32-2 646 46 90. Telefax: 32-2 646 45 80.

General Swedish and International Business Law Practice, Admiralty and Maritime Law, Insolvency, Antitrust, Marketing and Unfair Competition, Banking, Computer Law, Construction and Engineering Contracts and Disputes, Corporate Financing and Securities Law, International Taxation, EC Law, Environmental Energy and Natural Resources Law, Industrial Property, Copyright and Trademarks, Labor Law, Mergers and Acquisitions, Real Estate Law, Reorganizations, Space Law, Litigation and Arbitration, Family Law and Successions.

MEMBER OF FIRM IN KRISTIANSTAD

GÖRAN RISE, born Mariestad, Sweden, December 29, 1940. *Education:* University of Lund (LL.M., 1966). Junior Judgeship, District Court of Sölvesborg, 1966-1968. Bank Manager, Svenska Handelsbanken, Lund, 1983-1986. *Member:* Swedish Bar Association, 1971. *LANGUAGES:* English and German.

ASSOCIATES IN KRISTIANSTAD

SVEN HOLMGREN, born Trollhatttan, Sweden, January 5, 1961. *Education:* University of Lund (LL.M., 1987). Junior Judgeship, District Court of Ystad, 1987-1990. *LANGUAGES:* English and German.

THORVALD PERSSON, born Malmö, Sweden, September 16, 1951. *Education:* University of Lund (LL.M., 1975). Junior Judgeship, District Court of Karlshamn, 1978-1980. Bank Manager, Gota Bank, Malmö, 1983-1991. *LANGUAGES:* English and German.

(For Biographical data on all Personnel, see Professional Biographies at Gothenburg, Helsingborg, Malmö, Stockholm, Örebro and Brussels)

ADVOKATFIRMAN L.J.B AB

STORA TORGET 4
P.O. BOX 465
S-581 05 LINKÖPING, SWEDEN
Telephone: +46-13 12 30 40
Fax: +46-13 14 12 20

Commercial and Corporate Transactions; Banking, Finance and Investment; Property Development and Construction; Insolvency, Receivership and Corporate Reorganization; Commercial Litigation; EU and Competition Law; Intellectual Property; Employment and Labour Relations; Equestrian Transactions and Disputes.

MEMBERS OF FIRM

ERIK FOCK, born 1938; admitted, 1966, Sweden. *Education:* University of Uppsala (Law Graduate, 1964). Service in Swedish Courts, 1964-1966. *Member:* Swedish Bar Association. *LANGUAGES:* Swedish and English. *PRACTICE AREAS:* Receivership; Insolvency; Employment Law; General Commercial Law; Equestrian Transactions and Disputes.

BENGT EHRENBORG, born 1945; admitted, 1976, Sweden. *Education:* University of Lund (Law Graduate, 1970; B.A. Econ., 1971). Service in Swedish Courts, 1971-1973. *Member:* Swedish Bar Association. *LANGUAGES:* Swedish and English. *PRACTICE AREAS:* General Business Law; Company Law; Property Law; Reconstructions and Insolvency; Receivership and International Law.

GÖRAN M. KARLSSON, born 1955; admitted, 1988, Sweden. *Education:* University of Uppsala (Law Graduate, 1983). Service in Swedish Courts, 1983-1985. *Member:* Swedish Bar Association; International Bar Association. *LANGUAGES:* Swedish, English, French and German. *PRACTICE AREAS:* International Business Law; Company Law; Contract Law; General Commercial Law.

MAGNUS NEDSTRAND, born 1960; admitted, 1991, Sweden. *Education:* University of Uppsala (Law Graduate, 1985). Service in Swedish Courts, 1986-1988. *Member:* Swedish Bar Association. *LANGUAGES:* Swedish and English. *PRACTICE AREAS:* Receivership; Insolvency; Intellectual Property Law; General Business Law.

CARL-GÖSTA LJUNGMARK, born 1924; admitted, 1956, Sweden. *Education:* University of Uppsala (Law Graduate, 1949). Service in Swedish Courts, 1950-1952. *Member:* Swedish Bar Association. (Former Partner). *LANGUAGES:* Swedish and English. *PRACTICE AREAS:* Bankruptcy

(This Listing Continued)

Law; Insolvency; Leasehold; Landlord and Tenant Law; General Business Law; Probate Law.

ASSOCIATES

CHRISTOPHER BONA, born 1965. *Education:* University of Heidelberg 1991 (EC Law); University of Lund (Law Graduate, 1992). Service in Swedish Courts, 1992-1994. *LANGUAGES:* Swedish, German and English.

CLAES HÁKANSON, born 1965. *Education:* University of Lund (Law Graduate, 1991); King's College, University of London 1991-1992 (EC Law). Service in Swedish Courts, 1992-1993. *LANGUAGES:* Swedish and English.

ADVOKATAKTIEBOLAGET
NORDIC LAW

Established in 1987

KUNGSGATAN 2 C
S-223 50 LUND, SWEDEN
Telephone: +46 46 15 10 00
Telefax: +46 46 18 94 40

Gothenburg, Sweden Office: Mässans gata 14, P.O. Box 5043, S-402 21 Gothenburg. Telephone: 46 31 81 51 00. Telefax: 46 31 20 82 52.

Stockholm, Sweden Office: Sky City, P.O. Box 182, S-190 45 Stockholm-Arlanda. Telephone: 46 8 593 600 04. Telefax: 46 8 593 600 05.

Brussels, Belgium Office: Avenue Louise 177, BTE. 1, B-1050. Telephone: 32 26 40 04 29. Telefax: 32 26 48 34 39.

Helsinki, Finland Office: Mikonkatu 2 D, SF-00100 Helsinki. Telephone: 358 0 64 87 11. Telefax: 358 0 60 50 43.

General Corporation Business Law, Commercial Tax, Financing, Real Estate, Transport, Trade Regulations and Antitrust Law, Copyright, International Legal Transactions, Arbitration and Litigation, European Community Law.

MEMBERS OF FIRM

BJÖRN WELINDER, born Stockholm, Sweden, 1954; admitted, 1988, Sweden. *Education:* University of Lund, Law Faculty (LL.B., 1982). Assistant Judge to the District Court of Ystad, 1982-1985. Legal Adviser to the Association of Real Estate Owners, 1979-1982. *Member:* Swedish Bar Association. *LANGUAGES:* Swedish, English and French.

DAN LINDMARK, born Örebro, Sweden, 1958; admitted, 1994, Sweden. *Education:* University of Lund, Law Faculty (LL.B., 1981; LL.M., 1987). Author: Books, *Industrial Product Liability; Swedish Insurance Law, An Introduction* (together with C-M Roos); *European Community and Political Union,* published Nordstedts, 1987. Law Consultant, 1982. Assistant Professor in Torts, Insurance and Products Liability Law, University of Lund, Law Faculty, 1983—. *LANGUAGES:* Swedish, English and German.

ASSOCIATES

ULLA ANDRÉASSON NEPPELBERG, born Falkenberg, Sweden, 1958; admitted, 1992, Sweden. *Education:* University of Lund, Law Faculty (LL.B., 1985; LL.M., 1991). Assistant Judge to the District Court of Trelleborg, 1985-1988. *LANGUAGES:* Swedish, English and French.

PER SAMUELSSON, born Halmstad, Sweden, 1955. *Education:* University of Lund, Law Faculty (LL.B., 1985; LL.D., 1991). Dissertation: Information and Remedies. Listed Companies and Their Responsibility for False and Misleading Information in the Stock Market. Lecturer in Company Law and Securities Law, University of Lund, 1984—. Research Fellow, University of Lund, 1991—. *LANGUAGES:* Swedish and English.

JONAS OLSSON, born Växjö, Sweden, 1967. *Education:* University of Lund, Law Faculty (LL.B., 1993). *LANGUAGES:* Swedish and English.

REPRESENTATIVE CLIENTS AND REFERENCES: Kungsörnen AB; Sapa Skandinaviska Aluminium Profiler AB; Industriforsikring A/S (owned by Norsk Hydro A/S); Papyrus-Kopparfors AB; Fiskeby AB; Nolato AB; Hackman OY/AB; Cerealia AB.

STYRBJÖRN GÄRDE ADVOKATBYRÅ

NORRA VALLGATAN 64, S-211
S-211 25 MALMÖ, SWEDEN
Telephone: +46 (40)-10 48 10
Telefax: +46 (40)-23 52 31

Stockholm, Sweden Office: Nybrogatan 34, P.O. Box 5208, S-102 45. Telephone: +46 (8)-665 00 40. Telefax: +46 (8)-665 00 41.

Gothenburg, Sweden Office: Kastellgatan 1, S-413 07. Telephone: +46 (31)-11 36 30. Telefax: +46 (31)-13 73 68.

Helsingborg, Sweden Office: Garnisonsgatan 10, S-254 66. Telephone: +46 (42)-20 10 80. Telefax: +46 (42)-20 18 38.

Borås, Sweden Office: Stora Kyrkogatan 4, P.O. Box 305, S-501 05. Telephone: +46 (33) 11 59 00. Telefax: +46 (33) 13 79 00.

Paris, France Office: 41, Rue de Passy, F-75016. Telephone: +33-(1) 452 795 22. Telefax: +33 (1) 40 50 90 31.

Representative Offices:

Swhweiz: Stadelgarden, Stadelhofer Strasse 40, CH-8024 Zürich. Telephone: +41 (1)-261 52 60. Telefax: +41 (1)-261 55 29.

Sweden: HAGA Företagscenter, Brogatan 25, S-334 33 Anderstorp. Telephone: +46 (371)-174 80. Telefax: +46 (371)-169 67.

Admitted to Practice in Sweden, The Law Firm's Primary Activities are Concentrated on Swedish and International Business, Tax Law and Insolvency Law.

MEMBERS OF FIRM

KRISTER BRUZELIUS, born Malmö, Sweden, 1947. *Education:* University of Lund (LL.B., 1970). Served in the District Court of Malmö, 1971-1973. Associate, Mannheimer & Zetterlöf, Malmö, 1973-1976. Company Lawyer and Chief Legal Officer, Kockums AB, Malmö, 1976-1979. Company Lawyer, Swedyards Corp., Gothenburg, 1979-1980. Advisor to the Swedish Governmental Official Investigation on Mortgages, 1979-1982. *Member:* Swedish and International Bar Associations; Swedish Society for Computers and Law (ADBJ); Licensing Executive Society (Board Member, Scandinavian Chapter). *LANGUAGES:* English and Swedish. *PRACTICE AREAS:* Intellectual Law; Property Law; Contractual Law; Computer Law.

CLAES SANDBERG, born Östersund, Sweden, 1949. *Education:* University of Lund (LL.B., 1974). Served in District Court of Landskrona, 1974-1977. Juristfirman Sandberg & Winklerfelt, 1977-1981. Lecturer, University of Lund, 1978-1984. Advokatgruppen Claes Sandberg, 1981-1992. *Member:* Swedish Bar Association. *LANGUAGES:* English and Swedish.

HANS ANTONSON, born Jönköping, Sweden, 1955. *Education:* University of Lund (LL.B., 1980). District Court of Lund, 1980-1983. Administrative Court of Appeals, Jönköping, 1983-1984. County Administrative Court of Kalmar, 1984-1985. Assistant Judge, Administrative Court of Appeals, 1984. *Member:* Swedish Bar Association. *LANGUAGES:* English and Swedish. *PRACTICE AREAS:* Tax Law.

ANNA RADING-PLOMAN, born Östra Ljungby, Sweden, 1956. *Education:* University of Lund (LL.B., 1979). Served in the District Court of Kristianstad, 1979-1984; Administrative Court of Appeals in Göteborg, 1982-1983; Court of Appeals, 1988. Allmänna Advokatbyrån (Public Defenders Office) in Kristianstad, 1984-1985; Peters & Co. Consultants in Malmö, 1986-1987; Advokatfirman Nordic Law in Lund, 1987-1992. *Member:* Swedish Bar Association. *LANGUAGES:* English and Swedish.

ANDERS BRYNJE, born Linköping Sweden, 1958. *Education:* University of Lund (LL.B., 1984). Served in the District Court of Ronneby, 1984-1986, Administrative Court of Appeals, Stockholm, 1987 and Court of Appeals of Skåne and Blekinge, 1988. *Member:* Swedish Bar Association. *LANGUAGES:* English and Swedish. *PRACTICE AREAS:* Contractual Law; Tax Law.

ASSOCIATES

PER ERICSSON, born Norrköping, Sweden, 1965. *Education:* University of Lund (LL.B., 1990). Served in the District Court of Örnsköldsvik, 1990. *LANGUAGES:* English and German.

Languages: Swedish, English, German and French

(For Biographical data on other Personnel, see Professional Biographies at Gothenburg, Stockholm, Helsingborg and Borås Sweden).

LAGERLÖF & LEMAN

STORTORGET 8
S-211 34 MALMÖ, SWEDEN
Telephone: Int. 46-40-704 50
Telefax: Int. 46-40-97 19 17

Stockholm, Sweden Office: Strandvägen 7A, P.O. Box 5402, S-114 84. Stockholm. Telephone: Int. 46-8-665 66 00. Telefax: Int. 46-8-667 68 83. Telex: 17715 Laglaw S.

Gothenburg, Sweden Office: Västra Hamngatan 24, P.O. Box 2252, S-403 14, Gothenburg. Telephone: Int. 46-31-17 10 00. Telefax: Int. 46-31-13 56 62. Telefax Maritime department: Int. 46-31-11 65 37.

London, England Office: Royex House, Aldermanbury Square, London EC2V 7HR. Telephone: Int. 44-171-606 17 15. Telefax: Int. 44-171-600 17 18.

Berlin, Germany Office: Meinekestrasse 13, D-10719 Berlin. Telephone: Int. 49-30-884 710. Telefax: Int. 49-30-882 4852.

Paris, France Office: 87 Avenue Kléber, F 75116 Paris. Telephone: 33-1-45 05 1208. Telefax: 33-1-47 55 0975.

New York, N.Y. Office: 712 Fifth Avenue, 30th Floor, New York, N.Y. 10019-4102 U.S.A. Telephone: Int. 1-212-801-3450. Telefax: Int. 1-212-801-3455.

Corporate and Commercial law, including Tax, Banking, Financing, Insurance, Real Estate, Computer, Patent, Trademark, Copyright, Labor, Trade Regulation and Antitrust Law. International Legal Transactions. Arbitration and Litigation in Civil Matters. EC Law. International Private Law. Maritime and Admiralty Law.
Member of Alliance of European Lawyers (EEIG).

PARTNERS

LARS ANDERSSON, born Lund, Sweden, 1942. *Education:* University of Lund (juris kandidat, LL.M., 1969). Service with Swedish Courts. *Member:* Swedish Bar Association. *LANGUAGES:* Swedish and English. *PRACTICE AREAS:* General Commercial Law; Corporate Law; Insolvency Law; Real Estate Law.

CARL GUSTAF TRÄGÅRDH, born Malmo, Sweden, 1946. *Education:* University of Lund (juris kandidat, LL.M., 1971). Service with Swedish Courts. Judgeship, Gothenburg Administrative Court of Appeal, 1974-1975. *Member:* Swedish Bar Association. *LANGUAGES:* Swedish and English. *PRACTICE AREAS:* General Commercial Law; Corporate Law; Insolvency Law; Real Estate Law.

ULLA TRÄGÅRDH, born Gavle, Sweden, 1947. *Education:* University of Lund (juris kandidat, LL.M., 1973). Service with Swedish Courts. *Member:* Swedish Bar Association. *LANGUAGES:* Swedish and English. *PRACTICE AREAS:* General Commercial Law; Corporate Law; Insolvency Law; Real Estate Law.

CARL EKBERG, born Hassleholm, Sweden, 1948. *Education:* University of Lund (juris kandidat, LL.M., 1973). Service with Swedish Courts. Judgeship, Administrative Court of Appeal, 1975-1978. *Member:* Swedish Bar Association; International Fiscal Association. *LANGUAGES:* Swedish and English. *PRACTICE AREAS:* Tax Law.

THOMAS MOLL, born Simrishamn, Sweden, 1955. *Education:* Lund University (juris kandidat, LL.M., 1981). Service with Swedish Courts. Judgeship, Scania and Blekinge Court of Appeal, 1983-1984. *Member:* Swedish Bar Association. *LANGUAGES:* Swedish and English. *PRACTICE AREAS:* General Commercial Law; Corporate Law; Real Estate Law.

ASSOCIATES

MADELEINE JACOBSSON, born Falkenberg, Sweden, 1958. *Education:* University of Lund (juris kandidat, LL.M., 1981). Service with Swedish Courts. *Member:* Swedish Bar Association. *LANGUAGES:* Swedish and English. *PRACTICE AREAS:* General Commercial Law; Corporate Law; Real Estate Law; Environmental Law.

STEFAN WENDÉN, born Hassleholm, Sweden, 1959. *Education:* University of Lund (juris kandidat, LL.M., 1984). Service with Swedish Courts. *Member:* Swedish Bar Association. *LANGUAGES:* Swedish and English. *PRACTICE AREAS:* Commercial Law; Corporate Law; European Community Law; Real Estate Law.

ANDERS PERBORN, born Karlskrona, Sweden, 1958. *Education:* University of Lund (juris kandidat, LL.M., 1986). Service with Swedish Courts. *Member:* Swedish Bar Association. *LANGUAGES:* Swedish and English. *PRACTICE AREAS:* Commercial Law; Corporate Law; Finance Law.

(This Listing Continued)

BO SVENSSON, born Kalmar, Sweden, 1954. *Education:* University of Lund (juris kandidat, LL.M., 1983). Service with Swedish Courts. Judgeship, Administrative Court of Appeal, 1985-1986. *Member:* Swedish Bar Association. *LANGUAGES:* Swedish and English. *PRACTICE AREAS:* Insolvency Law; Tax Law.

MATS ANDERSSON, born Karlskrona, Sweden, 1961. *Education:* University of Lund (juris kandidat, LL.M., 1986). Service with Swedish Courts. Judgeship, Administrative Court of Appeal, 1988-1989; Gothenburg Administrative Court of Appeal, 1989-1990. *Member:* Swedish Bar Association. *LANGUAGES:* Swedish and English.

MIKAEL KARLSSON, born Lund, Sweden, 1964. *Education:* University of Lund (juris kandidat, (LL.M., 1991). Service with Swedish Courts. *LANGUAGES:* Swedish and English. *PRACTICE AREAS:* International Commercial Law; Corporate Law; Insolvency Law; Real Estate Law.

MARC TULLGREN, born Vevey, Switzerland, 1965. *Education:* University of Lund (juris kandidat, LL.M., 1990). Service with Swedish Courts. *LANGUAGES:* Swedish and English. *PRACTICE AREAS:* General Commercial Law.

ADVOKATFIRMAN LINDAHL

HJÄLMAREGATAN 3
SCANDINAVIAN CENTER
S-211 18 MALMÖ, SWEDEN
Telephone: 46-40 17 44 40
Telefax: 46-40 11 13 54

Gothenburg, Sweden Office: Östra Hamngatan 36. Mailing Address: P.O. Box 11911, S-404 39 Göteborg. Telephone: 46-31 80 34 30. Telefax: 46-31 15 82 85.

Helsingborg, Sweden Office: Mariagatan 10. Mailing Address: P.O. Box 1214, S-251 12 Helsingborg. Telephone: 46-42 18 31 80. Telefax: 46-42 11 96 78 and 46-42 24 12 86. Telex: 72715 Counsel S.

Kristianstad, Sweden Office: Västra Vallgatan 26. Mailing Address: P.O. Box 167, S-291 22 Kristianstad. Telephone: 46-44 10 07 80. Telex: 32584 LUNDLAW S. Telefax: 46-44 11 85 14.

Stockholm, Sweden Office: Strandvägen 5 A. Mailing Address: P.O. Box 14240, S-104 40 Stockholm. Telephone: 46-8 670 5800. Telex: 19609 LINDAHL S. Telefax: 46-8 667 73 80.

Örebro, Sweden Office: Vasastrand 11-13. Mailing Address: P.O. Box 143, S-701 42 Örebro. Telephone: 46-19 10 48 00. Telefax: 46-19 10 44 45.

Brussels, Belgium Office: 33 Blvd de la Cambre, Bte 13, B-1050 Brussels. Telephone: 32-2 646 46 90. Telefax: 32-2 646 45 80.

General Swedish and International Business Law Practice, Admiralty and Maritime Law, Insolvency, Antitrust, Marketing and Unfair Competition, Banking, Computer Law, Construction and Engineering Contracts and Disputes, Corporate Financing and Securities Law, International Taxation, EC Law, Environmental Energy and Natural Resources Law, Industrial Property, Copyright and Trademarks, Labor Law, Mergers and Acquisitions, Real Estate Law, Reorganizations, Space Law, Litigation and Arbitration, Family Law and Successions.

MEMBERS OF FIRM IN MALMÖ

LARS LAURIN, born Landskrona, Sweden, July 8, 1935. *Education:* University of Lund (LL.M., 1960). Junior Judgeship, District Court of Landskrona, 1960-1962. *Member:* Swedish Bar Association, 1965 (Member, General Council, 1971-1976; Member, Professional Committee, 1978-1981; Chairman, Southern Section, 1984-1988); International Bar Association. *LANGUAGES:* English.

LARS DOMINIQUE, born Jönköping, Sweden, November 12, 1942. *Education:* Universities of Lund and Stockholm (LL.M., 1969). Junior Judgeship, District Court of Mjölby, 1969-1971. *Member:* Swedish Bar Association, 1975. *Member:* International Bar Association. *LANGUAGES:* English and German. *PRACTICE AREAS:* Insolvency; Labour Law.

LEIF LJUNGHOLM, born Falkenberg, Sweden, September 12, 1945. *Education:* University of Lund (LL.M., 1972). Junior Judgeship, District Court of Malmö, 1972-1974. *Member:* Swedish Bar Association, 1977 (Member, General Council, 1988—; Member, Professional Committee, 1981-1987, Vice Chairman, 1986-1987). *Member:* International Bar Association. *LANGUAGES:* English. *PRACTICE AREAS:* Insolvency; Creditor's Rights; Litigation.

SVEN-OLOF ABDON, born October 7, 1943. *Education:* University of Lund (B.A., 1971; LL.M., 1972). Service and Junior Judgeships in Swedish

(This Listing Continued)

Courts, 1972-1976. *Member:* Swedish Bar Association, 1979 (Member, Legislation Committee, 1981—); International Bar Association.

GLENN BRORSTRÖM, born Malmö, Sweden, July 20, 1950. *Education:* University of Lund (LL.M., 1975). Junior Judgeship, District Court of Jönköping, 1975-1977. *Member:* Swedish Bar Association, 1980. *LANGUAGES:* English and German.

KRISTIAN LUNDIUS, born Malmö, Sweden, May 18, 1956. *Education:* University of Lund (LL.M., 1982). Junior Judgeship, District Court of Västervik, 1983-1984. *Member:* Swedish Bar Association, 1987. *LANGUAGES:* English. *PRACTICE AREAS:* Real Estate Law including Right of Use.

LENNART ARVIDSON, born Örnsköldsvik, Sweden, May 9, 1955. *Education:* University of Lund (LL.M., 1981); Institute of Maritime Law, University of Oslo, Oslo, Norway. Junior Judgeship, District Court of Lund, 1983-1984. *Member:* Swedish Bar Association, 1988. *LANGUAGES:* English.

LENNART IWAR, born Gothenburg, Sweden, July 22, 1955. *Education:* University of Lund (LL.M., 1981). Junior Judgeship, District Court of Västervik, 1981-1983. Associate Judge, Court of Appeal, Gothenburg, 1983-1985. Corporate Lawyer, Sydkraft AB, 1985-1988. *Member:* Swedish Bar Association, 1990. *LANGUAGES:* English.

ANNIKA BOSTRÖM, born Borås, Sweden, July 7, 1957. *Education:* University of Lund (LL.M., 1982). Junior Judgeship, District Court of Landskrona, 1982-1984. Associate Judgeship, Court of Appeal, Stockholm, 1984-1986. Legal Counsel, Swedish Export Credits Guarantee Board (EKN), 1986-1988. *Member:* Swedish Bar Association, 1991. *LANGUAGES:* English. *PRACTICE AREAS:* Insolvency.

ASSOCIATES IN MALMÖ

GÖRAN OHLSON, born Gothenburg, Sweden, August 8, 1951. *Education:* University of Uppsala (LL.M., 1977). Graduate, Nordic Institute of Maritime Law, University of Oslo, 1977. Junior Judgeship, District Court of Gothenburg, 1977-1978. Associate, Maritime Department, Mannheimer & Zetterlöf, Gothenburg, 1978-1983. Corporate Counsel, Alfa-Laval AB, Stockholm, 1983-1987. General Counsel, Secretary and Vice President, Alfa-Laval, Inc., 1987-1991. Vice President Alfa-Laval Food Engineering AB and Chairman of Alfa-Laval Middle East Co. Ltd., 1991. *Member:* Swedish Bar Association, 1982. *LANGUAGES:* English.

CHRISTIAN ZÄTTERSTRÖM, born Lund, Sweden, August 29, 1958. *Education:* University of Lund (LL.M., 1988). Junior Judgeship, District Court of Kristianstad, 1989-1991. *LANGUAGES:* English and French.

CHRISTIAN RASMUSSON, born Lund, Sweden, April 14, 1963. *Education:* University of Lund (LL.M., 1988). Junior Judgeship, District Court of Vaxjo, 1989-1991. *Member:* Swedish Bar Association, 1994. *LANGUAGES:* English and German.

MARIE LAGERLÖF, born Malmo, Sweden, March 31, 1959. *Education:* University of Lund (LL.M., 1984). Junior Judgeship, District Court of Eslov, 1985-1987. Reporting Clerk, Court of Appeal, Malmö, 1987-1988. Assistant Judge, District Court of Malmö, 1989-1992. *LANGUAGES:* English.

MAGNUS BERLIN, born Lund, Sweden, February 7, 1961. *Education:* University of Lund (LL.M., 1987). Junior Judgeship, District Court of Eslov, 1987-1989. Reporting Clerk, Court of Appeal, Malmö, 1989-1990. Assistant Judge, District Court of Helsingborg, 1991. Associate Judge, Court of Appeal, Malmö, 1992. *LANGUAGES:* English.

THORVALD PERSSON, born Malmö, Sweden, September 16, 1951. *Education:* University of Lund (LL.M., 1975). Junior Judgeship, District Court of Karlshamn, 1978-1980. Bank Manager, Gota Bank, Malmö, 1983-1991. *Member:* Swedish Bar Association, 1993. *LANGUAGES:* English and German. *PRACTICE AREAS:* Banks and Banking; Insolvency; General Commercial Law.

(For Biographical data on all Personnel, see Professional Biographies at Gothenburg, Helsingborg, Malmo, Stockholm, Orebro and Brussels)

MANNHEIMER SWARTLING

STORTORGET 29
P.O. BOX 4291
S-203 14 MALMÖ, SWEDEN
Telephone: +46-40 25 08 00
Telefax: +46-40 25 08 01
Telex: 32727

Stockholm, Sweden Office: Västra Trädgårdsgatan 15, P.O. Box 1650, S-111 86. Telephone: +46-8 613 55 00. Telefax: +46-8 613 55 01. Telex: 13082.
Gothenburg, Sweden Office: Lilla Torget 1, P.O. Box 2235, S-403 14. Telephone +46-31 10 96 00. Telefax: +46-31 10 96 01. Telex: 2591.
Helsingborg, Sweden Office: Södra Storgatan 7 P.O. Box 1384, S-251 13. Telephone: +46-42 18 02 95. Telefax: +46-42 18 42 71.
New York, New York Office: 101 Park Avenue, 10178. Telephone: +1 212 682-0580. Telefax: +1 212 682-0982.
Brussels, Belgium Office: Avenue de Tervueren 13A, B-1040. Telephone: +32-2-732 22 22. Telefax: +32-2-736 96 52.
Frankfurt, Germany Office: Bockenheimer Landstrasse 97, D-60325. Telephone: +49-69 974 01 20. Telefax: +49-69 741 01 43.
Berlin, Germany Office: Haus der Schweiz, Friedrichstrasse 155-156, D-10117. Telephone: +49 30 202 20 10. Telefax: +49 30 202 20 110.
Moscow, Russia Office: Chistoprudny Bulvar 8, 101000 Moscow. Telephone: +7 (095) 929 90 05. Telefax: +7 (095) 929 90 06.

General Swedish and International Business Law Practice. Admiralty and Maritime Law. Antitrust, Marketing and Unfair Competition. Banking. Computer Law. Construction and Engineering Contracts and Disputes. Corporate Financing and Securities Law. Corporate Taxation. EC Law. Environmental Energy and Natural Resources Law. Industrial Property, Copyright and Trademarks. Labor Law. Mergers and Acquisitions. Real Estate Law. Reorganizations. Space Law. Litigation and Arbitration.

RESIDENT PARTNERS

Göran Linders	Pär Andersson
Tore Wiwen-Nilsson	Louise Widén
Jan Wetterberg	Jan Kansmark
Göran Miörner	Michael Karlsson
Mikael Ekdahl	Claes Albinsson

RESIDENT ASSOCIATES

Peter Idsäter	Johan Hegethorn
Maria Hallengren	Hans Peterson
Lars Kongstad	Johan Granehult
Anna Bjerkelund	Fredrik Forssman
	Henrik Olshov

(For biographical data on all personnel, see Professional Biographies at Stockholm, Sweden)

ADVOKATBYRÅN SIGEMAN WERNBRO & CO.

Established in 1991

KANSLIGATAN 1 A
S-211 22 MALMÖ, SWEDEN
Telephone: +46-40-11 46 00
Telecopier: +46-40-11 00 10

Commercial Law, Corporate Law, Employment Law, Intellectual Property, Litigation.

MEMBERS OF FIRM

JOHAN SIGEMAN, born 1957. *Education:* Universities of Uppsala and Lund (LL.M., 1982). Teaching Assistant in Law, University of Lund, 1980-1982. Service and Junior Judgeships in Swedish Courts, including Court of Appeal, 1983-1987. Associate with Carl Swartling Advokatbyrå/Mannheimer Swartling Advokatbyrå, 1987-1991. *Member:* Swedish Bar Association; Association Internationale des Jeunes Avocats. *LANGUAGES:* Swedish and English. *PRACTICE AREAS:* Commercial Law; Litigation; Employment Law.

PER ISINGER, born 1956. *Education:* University of Lund (LL.M., 1985). Service at District Court, 1985-1987. Associate with Mannheimer and Zetterlöf/Mannheimer Swartling Advokatbyrå, 1987-1991. *Member:* Swedish Bar Association. *LANGUAGES:* Swedish and English. *PRAC-*

(This Listing Continued)

ADVOKATBYRÅN SIGEMAN WERNBRO & CO.,
Malmö—Continued

TICE AREAS: Mergers and Acquisitions; Foreign Establishments; Corporate Law.

HUGO WERNBRO, born 1957. *Education:* University of Lund (LL.M., 1985). Associate with Lars Holmqvist Patentbyrå, 1984-1986. Associate with Carl Swartling Advokatbyrå/Mannheimer Swartling Advokatbyrå, 1986-1991. Corporate Counsel for Trelleborg Group, 1988-1990. *Member:* Swedish Bar Association. *LANGUAGES:* Swedish and English. *PRACTICE AREAS:* Intellectual Property.

MAGNUS NEDSTRÖM, born 1959. *Education:* University of Lund (LL.M., 1985). Service at District Court, 1985-1987. Associate with Mannheimer and Zetterlöf/Mannheimer Swartling Advokatbyrå, 1988-1991. *Member:* Swedish Bar Association. *LANGUAGES:* Swedish and English. *PRACTICE AREAS:* Commercial Law; Insolvency Law; Corporate Law.

MIKAEL HENRIKSSON, born 1959. *Education:* University of Lund (LL.M., 1986). Service in Swedish Courts, 1986-1988. Associate with Mannheimer and Zetterlöf/Mannheimer Swartling Advokatbyrå, 1989-1991. *Member:* Swedish Bar Association; Rotary. *LANGUAGES:* Swedish, English and German. *PRACTICE AREAS:* Commercial Law; Property Law.

ASSOCIATE

EVA MUNCK AF ROSENSCHÖLD, born 1949. *Education:* University of Lund (LL.M., 1975), International Private Law at Tokyo University, 1976. Associate with Lena Ström Advokatbyrå, 1982. Service at District Court, 1983-1984. Legal counsel of AB Leo, 1986-1987. Head of legal department of Pharmacia LEO Therapeutics AB, 1988-1990. Legal counsel of Procordia AB, 1991-1992. *Member:* Swedish Bar Association. *LANGUAGES:* Swedish, English, German and French. *PRACTICE AREAS:* Commercial Law; Competition Law.

ADVOKATFIRMAN VINGE KB

ÖSTERGATAN 30
P.O. BOX 4255
S-203 13 MALMÖ, SWEDEN
Telephone: 040-748 40
Telefax: 040-97 27 72

For offices in Gothenburg, Helsingborg and Stockholm, Sweden, see those cities.

London, England Office: 44/45 Chancery Lane, WC2A 1JB. Telephone: +44-71-404 4825. Telex: 25585 VINGE G. Telefax: +44-71-8316860.

Paris, France Office: 21, rue Jean Goujon, F-75008. Telephone: +33-1-40 75 373. Telefax: +33-1 45 63 0549.

Hong Kong Office: 2003 Hutchison House, 10 Harcourt Road, Central. Telephone: 852-5-236149. Telefax: 852-8105343.

Brussels, Belgium Office: Avenue Louise 475/B12, B-1050. Telephone: +32 2 646 36 20; +32 2 646 36 80. Telefax: +32 2 646 41 46.

General Corporation and Business Law, International Legal Transactions, Taxation, Antitrust, All Swedish Courts.

MEMBERS OF FIRM

BENGT ALMGREN, born Malmo, Sweden, November 5, 1922. *Education:* University of Lund, Sweden, Law Examination (juris kandidatexamen, LL.B., 1948). *Member:* Swedish Bar Association (Member of Council, 1976-1982); International Bar Association (Corresponding Member); Union Internationale des Avocats (Delegué au Conseil).

PETER BENGTSSON, born Bjärnum, Sweden, February 22, 1944. *Education:* University of Lund, Sweden, Law Examination (juris kandidatexamen, LL.B., 1969). Assistant Prosecutor, 1969-1970. Service with Swedish Courts, 1970-1972, Legal Counsel for the Swedish Forest Services, 1972-1976. Associated with this firm since 1976. *Member:* Swedish Bar Association (1979); International Bar Association.

LARS GILDÉUS, born Malmo, Sweden, June 16, 1950. *Education:* University of Lund, Sweden, Law examination (juris kandidatexamen, LL.B., 1974). Services in Swedish District Court and Court of Appeal, 1975-1979. *Member:* Swedish Bar Association (1982); International Bar Association; Licensing Executives Society.

JAN ÖRTENHOLM, born Helsingborg, Sweden, March 6, 1947. *Education:* University of Lund, Sweden, Law Examination (juris kandidatexamen, LL.B., 1972). Services in Swedish District Court and Court of Appeal,

(This Listing Continued)

1972-1976. Legal Counsel for Farming Association, 1977-1982. *Member:* Swedish Bar Association (1984); International Bar Association.

TOMMY HED, born Hallstahammar, Sweden, June 26, 1947. *Education:* University of Uppsala, Sweden, Law Examination (juris kandidatexamen, LL.B., 1971). Service in Swedish District Court and Court of Appeal, 1971-1982. *Member:* Swedish Bar Association (1984); International Bar Association.

PETER OSCARSSON, born S. Hestra, Sweden, November 1, 1952. *Education:* University of Lund, Sweden, Law Examination (juris kandidatexamen, LL.B., 1979). Services in Swedish District Court, 1979-1981. *Member:* Swedish Bar Association (1984); International Bar Association.

LENNART ATTERYD, born Landskrona, Sweden, May 30, 1953. *Education:* University of Lund, Sweden, Law Examination (juris kandidatexamen, LL.B., 1982). Service in Swedish District Court, 1982-1984. *Member:* Swedish Bar Association (1987, 1991).

ARNE KÄLLÉN, born Copenhagen, Denmark, May 20, 1958. *Education:* University of Lund, Sweden, Law Examination (juris kandidatexamen, LL.B., 1983). Service in Swedish District Court, 1983-1985. *Member:* Swedish Bar Association (1988).

ASSOCIATES

PETER LINDEROTH, born Malmo, Sweden, July 12, 1962. *Education:* University of Lund, Sweden, Law Examination (juris kandidatexamen, LL.M., 1987). Service in Swedish District Court, 1988-1989. *Member:* Swedish Bar Association (1993); Association Internationale des Jeunes Avocats (AIJA).

ERIK GABRIELSON, born Karlshamn, Sweden, May 10, 1962. *Education:* University of Lund, Sweden, Law Examination (juris kandidatexamen, LL.B., 1 989). Service in Swedish District Court, 1989-1991. *Member:* Swedish Bar Association (1994); Association Internationale des Jeunes Avocats (AIJA).

INGELA MALMBORG, born Brösarp, Sweden, January 8, 1959. *Education:* University of Lund, Sweden, Law Examination (juris kandidatexamen, LL.B., 1984). Service in Swedish Court and Administration Court of Appeal, 1985-1990. *Member:* Swedish Bar Association (1993); Association Internationale des Jeunes Avocats (AIJA).

FINN MADSEN, born Kalix, Sweden, January 14, 1953. *Education:* University of Lund, Sweden, Law Examination (juris kandidatexamen, LL.B., 1980). Service in Swedish District Courts and Court of Appeal, 1980-1986. Associated with Hägglund & Ramm Eriksson, Stockholm, 1986-1988 and Johnsson & Johnson, Stockholm, 1988-1991. Head of Legal Department, Gota Bank, Malmö, 1991-1993. *Member:* Swedish Bar Association (1989-1991, 1993—).

ANDERS FORKMAN, born Malmö, Sweden, December 29, 1964. *Education:* University of Lund, Sweden, Law Examination (juris kandidatexamen, LL.B., 1991). Service in Swedish District Court, 1991-1993.

Languages: English, French, German and Scandinavian.

ADVOKATFIRMAN LINDAHL

VASASTRAND 11 13
P.O. BOX 143
S-701 42 ÖREBRO, SWEDEN
Telephone: 46-19 10 48 00
Telefax: 46-19 10 44 45

Gothenburg, Sweden Office: Östra Hamngatan 36. Mailing Address: P.O. Box 11911, S-404 39 Göteborg. Telephone: 46-31 80 34 30. Telex: 21915 MAGLAW S. Telefax: 46-31 15 82 85.

Helsingborg, Sweden Office: Mariagatan 10. Mailing Address: P.O. Box 1214, S-251 12 Helsingborg. Telephone: 46-42 18 31 80. Telefax: 46-42 11 96 78 and 46-42 24 12 86. Telex: 72715 Counsel S.

Kristianstad, Sweden Office: Västra Vallgatan 26. Mailing Address: P.O. Box 167, S-291 22 Kristianstad. Telephone: 46-44 10 07 80. Telex: 32584 LUNDLAW S. Telefax: 46-44 11 85 14.

Malmö, Sweden Office: Hjälmaregatan 3, Scandinavian Center, S-211 18 Malmö. Telephone: 46-40 17 44 40. Telex: 32584 LUNDLAW S. Telefax: 46-40 11 13 54.

Stockholm, Sweden Office: Strandvägen 5 A. Mailing Address: P.O. Box 14240, S-104 40 Stockholm. Telephone: 46-8 670 5800. Telex: 19609 LINDAHL S. Telefax: 46-8 667 73 80.

Brussels, Belgium Office: 33 Blvd de la Cambre, Bte 13, B-1050 Brussels. Telephone: 32-2 646 46 90. Telefax: 32-2 646 45 80.

(This Listing Continued)

General Swedish and International Business Law Practice, Admiralty and Maritime Law, Insolvency, Antitrust, Marketing and Unfair Competition, Banking, Computer Law, Construction and Engineering Contracts and Disputes, Corporate Financing and Securities Law, International Taxation, EC Law, Environmental Energy and Natural Resources Law, Industrial Property, Copyright and Trademarks, Labor Law, Mergers and Acquisitions, Real Estate Law, Reorganizations, Space Law, Litigation and Arbitration, Family Law and Successions.

MEMBERS OF FIRM IN ÖREBRO

STAFFAN CARLBÄCK, born Hedemora, Sweden, September 29, 1931. *Education:* University of Uppsala (LL.M., 1958). Junior Judgeship, District Court of Kristinehamn, 1958-1960. *Member:* Swedish Bar Association, 1964 (Member, General Council, 1977-1984). *LANGUAGES:* English.

JAN LINDSTRÖM, born Trelleborg, Sweden, October 25, 1942. *Education:* University of Lund (LL.M., 1968). Junior Judgeship, District Court of Motala, 1968-1970. *Member:* Swedish Bar Association, 1974. *LANGUAGES:* English.

BENGT STRIDH, born Sandviken, Sweden, April 10, 1944. *Education:* University of Uppsala (LL.M., 1971). Junior Judgeship, District Court of Sjuhäradsbygden, Borås, 1971-1974. *Member:* Swedish Bar Association, 1977; International Bar Association. *LANGUAGES:* English.

ANDERS SANDBERG, born Örebro, Sweden, October 1, 1950. *Education:* University of Uppsala (LL.M., 1977). *Member:* Swedish Bar Association, 1986. *LANGUAGES:* English.

OLA PETTERSSON, born Örebro, February 10, 1952. *Education:* University of Uppsala (LL.M., 1980). Junior Judgeship, District Court of Uppsala, 1980-1982. *Member:* Swedish Bar Association, 1986. *LANGUAGES:* English.

ASSOCIATES IN ÖREBRO

PETER BREDELIUS, born Gothenburg, Sweden, December 5, 1959. *Education:* Universities of Lund and Stockholm (LL.M., 1988). Junior Judgeship, District Court of Nyköping, 1988-1990. *Member:* Swedish Bar Association, 1994. *LANGUAGES:* English.

ULRIKA BENGTSSON, born Sundsvall, Sweden, April 19, 1963. *Education:* University of Uppsala (LL.M., 1990). Junior Judgeship, District Court of Linköping, 1990-1993. *LANGUAGES:* English.

(For Biographical data on all Personnel, see Professional Biographies at Gothenburg, Kristianstad, Malmö , Stockholm, Helsingborg and Brussels)

ADVOKATKOLLEGIET KB

Established in 1986

BIRGER JARLSGATAN 55, 5TR
111 45 STOCKHOLM, SWEDEN
Telephone: +46-8-14 45 90
Fax: +46-8-24 20 80

Business Law, Banking Law, Contract and Land Law, Civil Litigation, all courts and Criminal Law.

MEMBERS OF FIRM

ANN LIVERUD, born Stockholm, Sweden, February 14, 1948; admitted, 1983, Sweden. *Education:* University of Stockholm (Master of Law, 1977; Master of Arts, 1972). *Member:* Swedish Bar Association. *LANGUAGES:* English and German. *PRACTICE AREAS:* Company Law; Financial Law; Contract Law; Real Estate Law; Criminal Law.

ANDERS PETHRUS, born Stockholm, Sweden, February 2, 1950; admitted, 1984, Sweden. *Education:* University of Stockholm (Master of Law, 1976). *Member:* Swedish Bar Association. *LANGUAGES:* English. *PRACTICE AREAS:* Company Law; Financial Law; Contract Law; Real Estate Law; Criminal Law.

BERTIL NAESLUND, born Karlstad, Sweden, June 20, 1952; admitted, 1985, Sweden. *Education:* University of Uppsala (Master of Law, 1979). *Member:* Swedish Bar Association. *LANGUAGES:* English. *PRACTICE AREAS:* Company Law; Financial Law; Contract Law; Real Estate Law; Criminal Law.

LENA GUSTAFSSON, born Stockholm, Sweden, July 9, 1954; admitted, 1991, Sweden. *Education:* University of Stockholm (Master of Law, 1984). *Member:* Swedish Bar Association. *LANGUAGES:* English. *PRAC-*

(This Listing Continued)

TICE AREAS: Company Law; Financial Law; Contract Law; Real Estate Law; Criminal Law.

KJELL LARSSON, born Högsby, Sweden, April 7, 1953; admitted, 1989, Sweden. *Education:* University of Lund (juris kandidat LL.M., 1979); University of Illinois, College of Law (Master of Comparative Law, 1980). Instructor in Law, University of Lund, 1978-1979. Advokatfirman Vinge, Gothenburg, 1981-1983; London, 1984-1994. *Member:* Swedish and International Bar Associations. *LANGUAGES:* English. *PRACTICE AREAS:* Commercial; Corporate Law.

ASSOCIATES

LARS DAHLSTRÖM, born Stockholm, Sweden, December 14, 1960; admitted, 1994, Sweden. *Education:* University of Lund (Master of Law, 1987). *LANGUAGES:* English and Danish. *PRACTICE AREAS:* Company Law; Financial Law; Contract Law; Real Estate Law; Criminal Law.

PETER BROMS, born New York, USA, November 1, 1963. *Education:* University of Stockholm (Master of Law, 1991). *LANGUAGES:* English. *PRACTICE AREAS:* Company Law; Contract Law; Real Estate Law; European Community Law.

ADVOKATFIRMAN BILL ANDRÉASSON

SMÅLANDSGATAN 14
S-111 46 STOCKHOLM, SWEDEN
Telephone: 46 8 678 05 60
Fax: 46 8 611 46 05

Taxation Law Practice: Corporate and Individual Income Taxation, Value Added Tax, Excise Duties, Gift and Inheritance Taxation, Payroll Taxes.

MEMBERS OF FIRM

BILL ANDRÉASSON, born Smålandsstenar, Sweden, December 7, 1941. *Education:* University of Lund (LL.M., 1966). Service and Junior Judgeship in Swedish Courts, 1966-1971. Service in the Supreme Administrative Court, 1971-1972. Head of the Office of the Committee for Advance Rulings, Swedish National Tax Board, 1972-1975. Head of Tax Department, Axel Johnson and Nordstjernan Groups, 1975-1985. *Member:* Swedish Bar Association; International Fiscal Association. *LANGUAGES:* English and German.

ASSOCIATES

VIESTURS BERZINS, born Riga, Latvia, April 12, 1944. *Education:* University of Stockholm (LL.M., 1974). Tax Lawyer, Office of the Committee for Advance Rulings, Swedish National Tax Board, 1974-1990. *Member:* International Fiscal Association. *LANGUAGES:* English.

JONAS DANIELSON, born Lidköping, Sweden, November 10, 1962. *Education:* University of Uppsala (LL.M., 1989). Tax Lawyer, County Tax Authority, Stockholm County, 1987-1991. Associate, Mannheimer Swartling, 1991-1994. *Member:* International Fiscal Association. *LANGUAGES:* English.

MICHAEL ASPLUND, born Gothenburg, Sweden, July 19, 1966. *Education:* University of Stockholm (LL.M., 1993). *LANGUAGES:* English.

BAKER & McKENZIE ADVOKATBYRÅ

ERIKSBERGSGATAN 46
P.O. BOX 26163
100 41 STOCKHOLM, SWEDEN
Telephone: (08) 676 77 00
Intn'l Dialing: (46-8) 676 77 00
Facsimile: (46-8) 24 89 20

REVISERS OF THE SWEDEN LAW DIGEST FOR THIS DIRECTORY

Associated Offices of Baker & McKenzie in: Almaty, Amsterdam, Bangkok, Barcelona, Beijing, Berlin, Bogotá, Brasília, Brussels, Budapest, Buenos Aires, Cairo, Caracas, Chicago, Dallas, Frankfurt, Geneva, Hanoi, Ho Chi Minh City, Hong Kong, Juárez, Kiev, London, Madrid, Manila, Melbourne, México City, Miami, Milan, Monterrey, Moscow, New York, Palo Alto, Paris, Prague, Rio de Janeiro, Riyadh, Rome, St. Petersburg, San Diego, San Francisco, São Paulo, Singapore, Sydney, Taipei, Tijuana, Tokyo, Toronto, Valencia, Warsaw, Washington, D.C. and Zürich.
Correspondent Law Firm: Hadiputranto, Hadinoto & Partners, Jakarta.

Business and Corporate Law.

(This Listing Continued)

BAKER & McKENZIE ADVOKATBYRÅ, Stockholm—Continued

MEMBERS OF FIRM

JONAS BENEDICTSSON, born Sweden, 1955. *Education:* University of Stockholm (LL.M., juris kandidat, 1983). Served in the District Court, 1984-1986 and in the Court of Appeal, 1986-1987. *Member:* Swedish Bar Association, 1990. *LANGUAGES:* English and German. *PRACTICE AREAS:* Arbitration; Commercial Litigation; Insolvency.

CLAES CRONSTEDT, born Sweden, 1943. *Education:* University of Stockholm (LL.M., juris kandidat, 1969). *Member:* Swedish Bar Association, 1975; International Bar Association; Swedish Association of International Maritime Law; AIJA; International Law Association. *LANGUAGES:* English. *PRACTICE AREAS:* Aviation; Banking and Finance; Corporate Law; Mergers and Acquisitions.

ROBERT FRÖMAN, born Sweden, 1948. *Education:* Duke University, N.C. (1967-1968); University of Stockholm (B.A., filosofie kandidat, 1973; LL.M., juris kandidat, 1978). Served in the District Court, 1978-1980. *Member:* Swedish Bar Association, 1983; International Bar Association. *LANGUAGES:* English. *PRACTICE AREAS:* Corporate Law; Commercial Law; Intellectual Property Law.

LEIF G. GUSTAFSSON, born Sweden, 1950. *Education:* University of Stockholm (LL.M., juris kandidat, 1975); University of Amsterdam (Postgraduate Diploma eq., LL.M., 1976). Assistant Royal Commission on Foreign Take Overs of Swedish Enterprises, 1974. Served in the District Court, 1975-1978; EEC Commission, Brussels, 1977. Resident Lawyer, Brussels, 1978-1982. *Member:* Swedish Bar Association, 1981; International Bar Association; AIJA. *LANGUAGES:* English and French. *PRACTICE AREAS:* EC Competition and Trade; Corporate Law; Commercial Law; Mergers and Acquisitions.

BO LINDQVIST, born Sweden, 1950. *Education:* University of Uppsala (LL.M., juris kandidat, 1976). Served in the Administrative District Court, 1977-1979. Served as Taxation Superintendent in the County Fiscal Authority, 1979-1980. Served in the Administrative Court of Appeal, 1981-1982. *Member:* Swedish Bar Association, 1985. *LANGUAGES:* English. *PRACTICE AREAS:* Corporate Law; Taxation; Litigation.

MAURITZ SILFVERSTOLPE, born Sweden, 1945. *Education:* University of Stockholm (LL.M., juris kandidat, 1973). *Member:* Swedish Bar Association, 1978. *LANGUAGES:* English. *PRACTICE AREAS:* Real Estate Law.

LOCAL PARTNER

STEN BAUER, born Sweden, 1959. *Education:* University of Stockholm (LL.M., juris kandidat, 1985); University of Geneva and the Graduate Institute of International Studies, Geneva (1985-1986). Served in the District Court, 1986-1987. *Member:* Swedish Bar Association, 1991. *LANGUAGES:* English and French. *PRACTICE AREAS:* Labor and Employment Law; Corporate Law; Mergers and Acquisitions.

COUNSEL

SVEN HARALD BAUER, born Sweden, 1924. *Education:* University of Stockholm (LL.M., juris kandidat, 1947). Served in the District Court, 1947-1950. *Member:* Swedish Bar Association, 1953 (Board Member, 1969-1975; President, 1981-1985; Chairman, Disciplinary Committee, 1989-1992). *LANGUAGES:* English. *PRACTICE AREAS:* Corporate Law; Arbitration.

BENGT BERGENDAL, born Sweden, 1926. *Education:* University of Stockholm (LL.M., juris kandidat, 1951). Served in the District Court, 1951-1954. *Member:* Swedish Bar Association, 1957 (Board Member, 1968-1974; Secretary General, 1979-1987). *LANGUAGES:* English and German. *PRACTICE AREAS:* Administrative Law; Real Estate Law; Environmental Law.

CARL GÖRAN RISBERG, born Sweden, 1929. *Education:* The Stockholm School of Economics (1952-1953); University of Lund (LL.M., juris kandidat, 1952). Served in the District Court, 1953-1955. Swedish Chamber of Commerce, London, 1955-1956. *Member:* Swedish Bar Association, 1959; International Bar Association; International Fiscal Association. *LANGUAGES:* English and German.

(This Listing Continued)

EU1304B

ASSOCIATES

JEANETTE ALMSÄTTER, born Sweden, 1960. *Education:* University of Stockholm (LL.M., juris kandidat, 1989); Duke University, N.C. (LL.M., 1990). Served in the County Administrative Court, 1990-1991. *LANGUAGES:* English.

RIKARD BENTELIUS, born Sweden, 1964. *Education:* University of Lund (LL.M., juris kandidat, 1990). Served in Local Enforcement Agency, 1990; District Court, 1990-1992; Court of Appeal, 1992-1993. *LANGUAGES:* English.

AGNETA GUSTAFSSON, born Sweden, 1964. *Education:* University of Uppsala (LL.M., juris kandidat, 1991). Served in the County Administrative Court, 1991-1992; District Court, 1992-1993; Court of Appeal, 1993. *LANGUAGES:* English.

FREDRIK NIKLASSON, born Sweden, 1967. *Education:* University of Stockholm (LL.M., juris kandidat, 1993); University of Toulouse (LL.M., EC Law, 1994). *LANGUAGES:* English and French.

MICHAEL NYMAN, born Sweden, 1965. *Education:* University of Uppsala (LL.M., juris kandidat, 1990). Served in District Court, 1992-1994. *LANGUAGES:* English.

ANNA-KARIN OLSSON, born Sweden, 1965. *Education:* University of Lund (LL.M., juris kandidat, 1988); University of Amsterdam (LL.M., EC Law, 1991). Served in the District Court, 1988-1991; Court of Appeal, 1991. *LANGUAGES:* English, French and German.

TOMAS RUDENSTAM, born Colombia, 1962. *Education:* University of Lund (LL.M., juris kandidat, 1990). Served in the District Court, 1990-1992. *LANGUAGES:* English, Spanish.

CARL M. SVERNLÖV, born Sweden, 1964; admitted, 1991, New York, U.S.A. and U.S. District Court, Southern District of New York. *Education:* Uppsala University, Sweden (B.A., 1989; LL.M., 1989); Harvard University (LL.M., juris kandidat, 1990). *Member:* American and International Bar Associations. [1st Lt. Swedish RAF, 1983-1985]. *LANGUAGES:* English.

REVISERS OF THE SWEDEN LAW DIGEST FOR THIS DIRECTORY

ADVOKATFIRMAN CARLER

Established in 1960

ENGELBREKTSPLAN 2
S-114 34 STOCKHOLM, SWEDEN
Telephone: 46-8 6796360
Telex: 11900 Carler S
Telefax: 46-8 6112605

Gothenburg, Sweden Office: Engelbrektsgatan 28, S-411 37. Telephone: 46 31 18 02 50. Fax: 46 31 18 02 51.

Gävle, Sweden Office: P.O. Box 1346, S-801 38. Telephone: 46 26 12 51 30. Fax: 46 26 12 89 20.

Helsingborg, Sweden Office: Hamntorget 5, S-252 21. Telephone: 46-42.187060. Telex: 721 40 Carler S. Telefax: 46-42-184753.

Linköping, Sweden Office: Slattefors Herrgård, S-585 93. Telephone: 46-13 160350. Fax: 46-13 160355.

Paris, France Office: 36, rue Tronchet, F-75009. Telephone: 33-1-42661449. Telefax: 33-1-42665945.

Nice, France Office: 22, rue Maréchal Joffre, F-06000. Telephone: 33 93 88 88 96. Fax: 33 93 88 94 98.

Milan, Italy Office: Via Silvio Pellico 12, I-20121. Telephone: 39-2-860968; 39-2-8059439. Telefax: 39-2-86465445.

International Business Law, Intellectual Property Law, European Community Law, Corporate, Competition and Administrative Law, Labor Law, Civil Litigation, Mergers and Acquisitions.

FIRM PROFILE: The firm was established in 1960 and offers services relating to International Business Law. The firm has 26 lawyers. Its offices are located in Stockholm, Gothenburg, Gävle, Helsingborg, Linkoping, Milan, Nice and Paris. Its objective is to improve the quality of business transactions thereby increasing the profitability of the client.

MEMBERS OF FIRM

GUNNAR CARLER, born 1928; admitted, 1971, Conseil Juridique; 1992, Avocat at Barreau de Paris. *Education:* LL.M. (Jur.kand.) 1954. District Court, 1954-1956. Private Legal Practice, 1956-1960. Founder of Advokatfirman Carler, 1960. Appointed Chairman of Arbitral Tribunal by the

(This Listing Continued)

International Chamber of Commerce, Paris. Chairman or Member, Board of Directors of Swedish Subsidiaries of foreign Companies such as Reynolds, Sharp Corporation, Marubeni Corporation, Rhône Poulenc, L'Oréal, Legrand, Essilor, Thomson and Legal Counsel for the French, Belgian and Italian Embassy in Stockholm. *Member:* Swedish Bar Association; Barreau de Paris. *LANGUAGES:* Swedish, French, English and German.

ANDERS ANGELSTIG, born 1957. *Education:* LL.M. (Jur. Kand.) University of Uppsala, 1981; M.B.A. (Civilekonom) Stockholm School of Economics, 1983, Uppsala District Court, 1983-1985. Private legal practice since 1986. *Member:* Swedish Bar Association. (Resident, Linköping Office). *LANGUAGES:* Swedish and English.

STAFFAN BERGLING, born 1942. *Education:* LL.M. (Jur. kand.) University of Stockholm, 1968. Stockholm District Court, 1968-1970. Assistant Secretary of the Swedish Bar Association, 1970-1971. Board Member, Stockholm Bar Association, 1980-1985. Private legal practice since 1971. Board Member of Swedish subsidiaries to foreign companies. Representative Clients: Suomen Aldata Oy; Fuji Hunt; 3M (Minnesota Mining and Manufacturing Co.) Warner Bros.; Warner/Chappell Music; Yoshida Kogyo K.K. *Member:* Swedish Bar Association. (Resident, Linköping Office). *LANGUAGES:* Swedish and English.

BERNDT FÜRST, born 1947. *Education:* LL.M. (Jur. Kand) 1971. Law Clerkship: District Court 1971-1973 and Court of Appeal 1973-1974. Associate Judge 1974-1976. Private legal practice since 1976. Foreign Associate Shearman & Sterling, New York 1980. Legal Consultant New York 1982-1983. *Member:* Swedish Bar Association; International Bar Association; American Bar Association (Associate). (Resident, Gothenburg Office). *LANGUAGES:* Swedish, Danish, English and German.

STEN HOLDO, born 1954. *Education:* LL.M. (Jur.kand.) University of Uppsala, 1981. Falun District Court, 1982-1984. Private legal practice since 1984. Authorized representative for Ackordscentralen (creditors organization), Stockholm. *Member:* Swedish Bar Association. (Resident, Gävle Office). *LANGUAGES:* Swedish and English.

CHRISTER F. NORDÉN, born 1946. *Education:* LL.M. (Jur. Kand.); University of Stockholm 1973. Corporate Counsel, ICA, 1972-1975. Corporate Counsel, 1975-1979 and Head of Legal Department, 1979-1982, Astra AB. Vice President and General Counsel, Ahlsell AB, 1982-1986. *Member:* Swedish Bar Association. (Resident, Stockholm Office). *LANGUAGES:* Swedish and English.

ANDERS NORLANDER, born 1947. *Education:* LL.M. (Jur. Kand.) University of Lund, 1970. District Court, 1971-1974. Court Appeal, 1974-1975. Assistant Judge: District Court, 1975-1979; Court of Appeal, 1980-1981. Corporate Counsel, Axel Johnson Group, 1981-1984. General Counsel, Axel Johnson Group, 1984-1992. (Resident, Stockholm Office). *LANGUAGES:* Swedish, English and German.

MATS OLOFSON, born 1932. *Education:* University of Toronto, 1952, LL.M., (Jur. Kand.); University of Uppsala (1958). Secretary, Swedish Board of Commerce, 1958-1961. Appointed expert to Swedish bilateral foreign trade delegations and mixed commissions for foreign trade, District Court of Lund, 1961-1963. Academie de Droit International de la Haye, 1962. Associate of Swedbergs Advokatbyrå, Gothenburg, 1963-1970. Corporate Counsel for Facit AB, 1970-1973. Corporate Counsel and Head of Legal Department of AB Electrolux, 1973-1981. Secretary to the Board of AB Electrolux, 1978-1981. *Member:* Swedish Bar Association. (Resident, Stockholm Office). *LANGUAGES:* Swedish, English and French.

HÅKAN PIHL, born 1944. *Education:* LL.M. (Jur.kand) University of Lund, 1970, District Court of Mora, 1970-1973, University of Gothenburg and Oslo, 1974. Associate: Lillick McHose and Charles, San Francisco, 1975-1977; Thommessen Karlsrud, Heyerdahl and Brunsvig, Oslo and New York, 1977-1980. General Counsel, Vice President, ESAB Aktiebolag, Gothenburg, 1980-1993. (Resident, Gothenburg Office). *LANGUAGES:* Swedish, English and German.

JOHAN ROSENLUND, born 1936. *Education:* LL.M. (Jur. Kand.) 1962. District Court, 1963-1965. Private Legal Practice since 1965. *Member:* Swedish Bar Association; Barreau de Nice. (Resident, Nice Office). *LANGUAGES:* Swedish, French and English.

JERKER SWANSTEIN, born 1952. *Education:* LL.M. (Jur. Kand.), 1978; B.A. (Fil. Kand.), 1980. Studies for Doctor's degree in Topics of Antitrust. Author: "Comparative Agency Law," 1979. Assistant Professor, University of Lund, School of Law, 1978-1986. Private legal practice since 1980. *Member:* Swedish Bar Association; International Bar Association. (Resident, Helsingborg Office). *LANGUAGES:* Swedish and English.

(This Listing Continued)

K.J. WESTMAN, born 1939. *Education:* LL.M. (Jur.kand), 1968. Assistant at the Department of Law, Uppsala University, 1966-1968, District Court of Uppsala, 1968-1970. Legal Counsel Svenska Handelsbaken, Stockholm, 1970-1994. Secretary to the Board of Svenska Handelsbaken. (Resident, Stockholm Office). *LANGUAGES:* Swedish and English.

INGEMAR WIKSTRÖM, born 1938. *Education:* LL.M. (Jur. Kand.), 1964. Taxation Authority, 1964-1965. District Court, 1965-1968. In-house Counsel, 1968-1974 and Director, 1974-1978, S-E Bank. Private legal practice since 1978. *Member:* Swedish Bar Association. (Resident, Helsingborg Office). *LANGUAGES:* Swedish, English, German and French.

ASSOCIATES

CARINA ABRAHAMSSON, born 1961. *Education:* LL.M. (Jur.kand.) University of Surrey, London, 1985; University of Uppsala, 1986. District Court of Mora 1986-1989. Administrative Court of Appeal, Sundsvall, 1989-1990. Private legal practice since 1990. *Member:* Swedish Bar Association. (Resident, Gävle Office). *LANGUAGES:* Swedish and English.

PETER ABRAHAMSSON, born 1963. *Education:* LL.M. (Jur. Kand., 1989) University of Lund; Motala District Court, 1989-1990. (Resident, Helsingborg Office). *LANGUAGES:* Swedish and English.

ANNIKA ARVIDSSON, born 1946. *Education:* LL.M. (Jur. Kand.) 1971; Paris II Maîtrise de droit. The District Court of Sala 1973-1974, Paris II 1974-1975, The District Court of Sala 1975-1977. *Member:* Swedish Bar Association. (Resident, Paris Office). *LANGUAGES:* Swedish, French and English.

MASSIMO CAIAZZA, born 1961. *Education:* University of Trieste, Italy (J.D., 1985). Private legal practice since 1988. Advokatfirman Carler since 1986. (Resident, Italy Office). *LANGUAGES:* Italian, Swedish and English.

BO CALLGREN, born 1935. *Education:* LL.M. (Jur.kand.) University of Uppsala, 1961. District Court, 1961-1963. Associate, Advokaterna Kaiding & Ljungdahl, Skellefteå, 1963-1969. Partner, Lindbergs Advokatbyrå, Gävle, 1970-1980. Managing Director, Gävle Galvan AB, Gävle, 1981-1993. Private legal practice since 1993. *Member:* Swedish Bar Association, 1966. (Resident, Gävle Office). *LANGUAGES:* Swedish, English and German.

NATHALIE COSSA, born 1964. *Education:* Maîtrise de droit; DEA. (Resident, Nice Office). *LANGUAGES:* French and English.

PETER DEXFALK, born 1962. *Education:* LL.M. (Jur. Kand.) University of Minnesota Law School, 1989. University of Uppsala, 1990. Norrköping District Court, 1990-1992. (Resident, Linköping Office). *LANGUAGES:* Swedish and English.

LARS-ERIK ERIKSSON, born 1961. *Education:* LL.M. (Jur.kand.), University of Uppsala, 1986. Taxation Authority, 1987-1993. (Resident, Gävle Office). *LANGUAGES:* Swedish and English.

PETER JONSSON, born 1953. *Education:* LL.M. (Jur. Kand.) University of Lund 1983. District Court, 1984-1985. Legal Counsel Swedish Employers' Confederation, 1986-1987. Company legal Counsel, 1988-1990. (Resident, Helsingborg Office). *LANGUAGES:* Swedish, English and German.

JACQUES MERRET, born 1963. admitted, 1991, Conseil Juridique; 1992, Avocat at Barreau de Paris. *Education:* Université de Paris II (Maîtrise de droit affaires et fiscalité). (Resident, Paris Office). *LANGUAGES:* French, Swedish, English and German.

MIKAEL NIKLASSON, born 1957. *Education:* LL.M. (Jur. Kand.) University of Lund 1984. District Court, 1984-1987. Appeal Court, 1987-1989. *Member:* Swedish Bar Association. (Resident, Helsingborg Office). *LANGUAGES:* Swedish, English and German.

HELENA NORD, born 1961. *Education:* LL.M. (Jur. Kand.) University of Lund 1986. District Court, 1987-1989, Court of Appeals, 1989-1991. (Resident, Gothenburg Office). *LANGUAGES:* Swedish, English and German.

BARBARA SEGESVARY, *Education:* LL.M. (Jur. Kand.) 1975, University of Uppsala. Former positions: Rotary International, Zürich; Lutheran World Federation, Geneva; Carborundum International, Geneva; European Organization for Nuclear Research, Geneva; International Life Insurance Co., Geneva; Office of District Attorney, Uppsala; District Court of Uppsala. Chairman or Member of Board of Directors of a number of swedish subsidiaries to foreign companies. *Member:* Swedish Bar Association; International Bar Association. (Resident, Stockholm Office). *LANGUAGES:* Swedish, English, German, French and Italian.

(This Listing Continued)

ADVOKATFIRMAN CARLER, Stockholm—Continued

GILLIS ÅKESSON, born 1966. *Education:* LL.M. (Jur. kand) University of Stockholm, 1991. Solna District Court, 1991-1993. (Resident, Stockholm Office). *LANGUAGES:* Swedish and English.

ADVOKATFIRMAN CEDERQUIST KB

Established in 1953

NYBROKAJEN 15

P.O. BOX 1670

111 96 STOCKHOLM, SWEDEN

Telephone: +46 8 463 65 00

Telecopier: +46 8 678 01 70

London, England Office: 16, Black Friars Lane, EC4V 6EB. Telephone: +44 71 489 14 31. Telecopier: +44 71 236 21 06.

Domestic and International Corporate and Commercial Law, Labour, Tax and Real Estate Law, Marketing and Antitrust Law, Copyright, Patent and Trademark Law, Domestic and International Licensing, Litigations and Arbitrations in Civil Matters.

MEMBERS OF FIRM

AXEL LIDBECK, born 1931. *Education:* University of Stockholm (juris kandidat [LL.B.], 1957). Service in Swedish Courts, 1957-1960. Associated with this Firm, 1960. Entered this Firm, 1964. *Member:* Swedish Bar Association. *LANGUAGES:* Swedish, English and German. *PRACTICE AREAS:* General Commercial and Corporate Law; Intellectual Property Law.

GÖSTA WESTRING, born 1931. *Education:* University of Stockholm (juris kandidat [LL.B.], 1956). Service in Swedish Courts, 1956-1960. Associated with Advokaterna Pehrsson & Bjerke, Stockholm, 1960-1964. Various position Swedish Government, 1965-1979. Entered this firm 1979. The World Bank, Washington, D.C., 1985-1991, The United Nations, Geneva, Switzerland, 1991-1993. Reentered this firm 1994. *Member:* Swedish Bar Association; International Bar Association. *LANGUAGES:* Swedish, English and French. *PRACTICE AREAS:* International Contracts; Public Procurement.

ERIC AGER, born 1940. *Education:* University of Stockholm (juris kandidat [LL.B.], 1966). Service in Swedish Courts, 1966-1968. Advokatfirman Lagerlöf, 1968-1982. Entered this Firm, 1982. *Member:* Swedish and American (Associated Member) Bar Associations. *LANGUAGES:* Swedish and English. *PRACTICE AREAS:* General Commercial and Corporate Law.

MATS BENDRIK, born 1944. *Education:* University of Stockholm (juris kandidat [LL.B.], 1969). Service in Swedish Courts, 1970-1972. Associated with this Firm, 1972. Entered this Firm, 1977. *Member:* Swedish Bar Association. *LANGUAGES:* Swedish and English. *PRACTICE AREAS:* General Commercial and Corporate Law; Real Estate Law; Litigation.

JOHAN HAGGREN, born 1945. *Education:* University of Stockholm (juris kandidat [LL.B.], 1969). Service in Swedish Courts, 1970-1972. National Tax Board, 1973-1976. Advokatfirman Lagerlöf, 1976-1982. Entered this Firm, 1982. *Member:* Swedish and International (Member, Section on Business Law) Bar Associations; International Fiscal Association. *LANGUAGES:* Swedish and English. *PRACTICE AREAS:* General Commercial and Corporate Law; Tax Law; Litigation; Real Estate Law.

ROLF ANDERSSON, born 1949. *Education:* University of Stockholm (juris kandidat [LL.B.], 1974). Service in Swedish Courts, 1974-1977. Associated with this Firm, 1977. Entered this Firm, 1981. *Member:* Swedish Bar Association. *LANGUAGES:* Swedish and English. *PRACTICE AREAS:* General Commercial and Corporate Law; Intellectual Property Law.

OLOF NILSSON, born 1949. *Education:* University of Stockholm (juris kandidat [LL.B.] 1974). Service in Swedish Courts, 1974-1976. Advokatfirman Lagerlöf, 1976-1980. Associated with this Firm, 1980. Entered this Firm, 1982. *Member:* Swedish Bar Association; International Bar Association (Member, Section on Business Law). *LANGUAGES:* Swedish and English. *PRACTICE AREAS:* General Commercial and Corporate Law; Real Estate Law; Litigation.

OLLE JANSSON, born 1949. *Education:* University of Stockholm (juris kandidat [LL.B.], 1977). Legal Executive, Office of the Anti Trust Ombudsman, 1977-1978. Service in Swedish Courts, 1978-1979 and Labour Court of Sweden, 1979-1980. Associated with Carl Swartling Advokatbyrå, Stockholm, 1980-1984 and with this Firm since 1984. Entered this Firm, 1985. *Member:* Swedish Bar Association; International Bar Association.

(This Listing Continued)

LANGUAGES: Swedish and English. *PRACTICE AREAS:* General Commercial and Corporate Law; Antitrust Law; Labour Law.

LENNART KANTER, born 1956. *Education:* University of Uppsala (juris kandidat [LL.B.], 1980). Service in Swedish Courts, 1980-1982. Associated with this Firm, 1982. Entered this Firm, 1990. *Member:* Swedish and International Bar Associations. *LANGUAGES:* Swedish and English. *PRACTICE AREAS:* General Commercial and Corporate Law; Intellectual Property Law; Litigation.

KERSTIN CALISSENDORFF, born 1955. *Education:* Stephens College (A.A., 1975); University of Stockholm (juris kandidat [LL.B.], 1981). Service in Swedish Courts, 1982-1984. Associated with this Firm, 1984. Entered this Firm, 1991. *Member:* Swedish Bar Association; International Bar Association. *LANGUAGES:* Swedish and English. *PRACTICE AREAS:* General Commercial and Corporate Law; Intellectual Property Law.

LENA FRÅNSTEDT LOFALK, born 1958. *Education:* University of Stockholm (juris kandidat [LL.B.], 1983). Service in Swedish Courts, 1983-1985. Associated with this Firm, 1985. Entered this Firm, 1992. *Member:* Swedish Bar Association. *LANGUAGES:* Swedish and English. *PRACTICE AREAS:* General Commercial and Corporate Law; Litigation; Real Estate Law.

WILHELM LÜNING, born 1959. *Education:* University of Stockholm (juris kandidat, [LL.B.], 1987). Associated with Företagsjuridik Nord & Co AB, 1985-1990, Advokatfirman Vinge KB, 1990-1993. Entered this firm 1993. *Member:* Swedish Bar Association. *LANGUAGES:* Swedish and English. *PRACTICE AREAS:* General Commercial and Corporate Law; Securities Law.

ANDERS FÄLLMAN, born 1962. *Education:* University of Stockholm (juris kandidat [LL.B.], 1986); University of Michigan Law School (Master of Laws [LL.M.], 1987). Associated with this Firm, 1987. Entered this firm, 1995. *Member:* Swedish Bar Association; International Bar Association. *LANGUAGES:* Swedish, English and German. *PRACTICE AREAS:* General Commercial and Corporate Law; Securities Law; Finance Law.

ASSOCIATES

PETTER WIRELL, born 1963. *Education:* University of Lund (juris kandidat [LL.B.], 1988). Service in Swedish Courts, 1988. Associated with this Firm, 1988. *Member:* Swedish Bar Association. *LANGUAGES:* Swedish and English. *PRACTICE AREAS:* General Commercial and Corporate Law; Patent Law.

LARS JOHANSSON, born 1957. *Education:* University of Stockholm (juris kandidat [LL.B.], 1985). Research Assistant and Instructor, Faculty of Law, University of Stockholm, 1985-1987. Service in Swedish Courts, 1988-1989. Associated with this Firm, 1989. *Member:* Swedish Bar Association. *LANGUAGES:* Swedish and English. *PRACTICE AREAS:* General Commercial and Corporate Law; Intellectual Property Law; Competition Law; Computer Law.

PER NORDENSON, born 1959. *Education:* University of Stockholm (juris kandidat [LL.B.], 1987). Service in Swedish Courts, 1987-1989. Associated with Advokatbyrån Frie AB, Stockholm, 1989-1991. Associated with this Firm, 1991. *Member:* Swedish Bar Association. *LANGUAGES:* Swedish and English. *PRACTICE AREAS:* General Commercial and Corporate Law; Litigation; Competition Law.

JENS TILLQVIST, born 1962. *Education:* University of Stockholm (juris kandidat [LL.B.], 1988). Service in Swedish Courts, 1988-1990. Lecturer, Faculty of Law, University of Stockholm since 1988. Associated with this Firm, 1991. *Member:* Swedish Bar Association. (Resident, London Office). *LANGUAGES:* Swedish and English. *PRACTICE AREAS:* General Commercial and Corporate Law; Insolvency Law; Labour Law.

KARL OLE MÖLLER, born 1963. *Education:* University of Uppsala (juris kandidat [LL.B.], 1990); Scandinavian Institute of Maritime Law (1990). Service in Swedish Courts, 1990-1991. Associated with this Firm, 1991. *LANGUAGES:* Swedish and English. *PRACTICE AREAS:* General Commercial and Corporate Law.

ERIKA ÅSLUND, born 1964. *Education:* University of Stockholm (juris kandidat [LL.B.], 1990). Service in Swedish Courts, 1990-1991. Associated with this Firm, 1991. *LANGUAGES:* Swedish, English and Spanish. *PRACTICE AREAS:* General Commercial and Corporate Law.

HANS RAMBERG, born 1963. *Education:* University of Uppsala (juris kandidat [LL.B.], 1989); Scandinavian Institute of Maritime Law (1990). Service in Swedish Courts, 1990. Associated with Advokatfirman Mattson & Ramberg, 1990-1991. Trainee with Haight, Gardner, Poor & Havens,

(This Listing Continued)

New York, 1991-1992. Associated with this Firm, 1992. *LANGUAGES:* Swedish and English. *PRACTICE AREAS:* General Commercial and Corporate Law.

OLA HANSSON, born 1967. *Education:* University of Lund (juris kandidat [LL.B.], 1992). Service in Swedish Courts, 1992-1994. Associated with this firm 1994. *LANGUAGES:* Swedish and English. *PRACTICE AREAS:* General Commercial and Corporate Law.

MARIA-PIA MIDENBÄCK, born 1969. *Education:* University of Lund (juris kandidat, [LL.B.], 1993); Harvard Law School (Master of Laws, LL.M., 1994). Tutor, EC Law, University of Edinburgh, 1994—. Associated with this firm, 1994. (Resident, London Office). *LANGUAGES:* Swedish, English and French. *PRACTICE AREAS:* General Commercial and Corporate Law; EC Law.

FREDRIK LINDER, born 1969. *Education:* University of Stockholm (juris kandidat [LL.B.], 1994). Associated with this firm 1994. *LANGUAGES:* Swedish and English. *PRACTICE AREAS:* General Commercial and Corporate Law.

DAVID BONNIER, born 1968. *Education:* University of Stockholm, (Juris kandidat [LL.B.], 1994). Trainee with Feddersen, Laule, Scherzberg & Ohle Hansen Ewerwahn, Hamburg, Germany 1994. Associated with this firm 1995. *LANGUAGES:* Swedish, English and German. *PRACTICE AREAS:* General Commercial and Corporate Law.

ADVOKATFIRMAN CHRYSANDER

Established in 1933

KUNGSGATAN 26, 4 TR

P.O. BOX 7494

S-103 92 STOCKHOLM, SWEDEN

Telephone: +46 8 453 48 00
Telefax: +46 8 796 80 40

Uppsala, Sweden Office: Kungsängsgatan 17-19, P.O. Box 1203, S-751 42 Uppsala. Telephone: +46 18 16 18 50. Telefax: +46 18 14 46 79.

Swedish and International Business Law including Corporate and Commercial Law, Litigation, Arbitration, Banking and Financing, Mergers and Acquisitions, Cross Border Transactions, Joint Ventures, Intellectual Property, Franchising, Insolvency and Bankruptcy Law, Taxation, Liquidation, Composition and Debtors' Reconstruction, Creditors' Rights, Local Government and Administrative Law, Government Contracts, European Community Law, Property.

FIRM PROFILE: *Advokatfirman Chrysander is a major Swedish law firm, founded in 1933, with offices in Uppsala and Stockholm with eighteen partners, one associate and one legal research consultant. The firm offers a full range of legal services with concentration on Swedish and International Business law. The firm is a member of Integrated Advisory Group, IAG International, an association of independent professional legal, tax and accountancy firms in Europe, with its head office in Brussels.*

MEMBERS OF FIRM

KURT WINBERG, born 1916. *Education:* University of Uppsala (LL.M., 1939). District Court of Uppsala, 1939-1940. Associate, 1940; Partner, 1944. *Member:* Swedish Bar Association. *LANGUAGES:* Swedish and English. *PRACTICE AREAS:* Commercial and Corporate Law; Real Estate; Inheritance Law.

STIG RINDBORG, born 1929. *Education:* University of Stockholm (LL.M., 1956). Private Legal Practice, 1956-1958 and 1961-1964. Court Work, 1958-1960. Advokatfirman Rindborg, 1964-1993. Chairman of the Board of small and medium sized enterprises. Counseillor of the Town Council of Stockholm, 1966-1982. Chairman of the Board of the Conservative Party of the County Council, 1979-1988. Chairman of the Executive Committee of the County Council, 1978-1981 and 1986-1988. Vice Chairman of the Executive Committee of the County Council, 1982-1985. County Council Planning Commissioner, 1978-1979. Public Health Commissioner, 1980-1981. Finance and Personnel Commissioner, 1986-1988. Vice Chairman of the Swedish Association of Free Enterprise, 1979-1985, Chairman, 1988-1991. Chairman of the Swedish Federation of Free Enterprise, 1990-1992, Partner, 1993. *Member:* Swedish Bar Association (Board Member, 1982-1988); Swedish Parliament (1985 and 1992—). *LANGUAGES:* Swedish and English. *PRACTICE AREAS:* Commercial and Corporate Law; European Community Law; Property and Tenancy Law; Local Government Law; Arbitration; Banking and Financing; Insolvency and Bankruptcy Law; Liquidation; Composition and Debtors' Reconstruction; Creditors' Rights; Litigation.

GUNNAR LJUNGMAN, born 1938. *Education:* University of Uppsala (LL.M., 1963). District Court of Uppsala, 1963-1965. Associate, 1965; Partner, 1970. *Member:* Swedish Bar Association (Board Member, 1989—). *LANGUAGES:* Swedish and English. *PRACTICE AREAS:* Insolvency and Bankruptcy Law; Composition and Debtors' Reconstruction; Real Estate Law.

TOMAS MATSSON, born 1940. *Education:* University of Uppsala (LL.M., 1963). District Court of Uppsala, 1964-1966. Associate, 1966; Partner, 1970. Chairman of Olle Olsson Bolagen AB, 1980—. Chairman of publishing company Atlantis, 1988—. Chairman of the Chamber of Commerce for Uppsala County, 1989—. Chairman of the Swedberg Laboratory, 1990—. Treasurer of the Royal Academy of Arts and Sciences of Uppsala, 1988—. *Member:* Swedish Bar Association. *LANGUAGES:* Swedish and English. *PRACTICE AREAS:* Commercial and Corporate Law.

SARA RINDBORG, born 1926. *Education:* University of Stockholm (LL.M., 1960). Court Work, 1960-1962. Chief Tax Inspector, 1962-1963. Advokatfirman Rindborg, 1964-1993. Vice President of the National Swedish Defence Society, 1980-1991. Partner, 1993. *Member:* Swedish Bar Association (Accountant of the Stockholm Branch, 1978-1990). *LANGUAGES:* Swedish, English and German. *PRACTICE AREAS:* Insolvency and Bankruptcy Law; Liquidation; Local Government Law.

ANDERS FRIGELL, born 1943. *Education:* University of Uppsala (LL.M., 1970). District Court of Stockholm, 1970-1971. Senior University Lecturer, University of Uppsala, 1971-1974. Associate, 1974; Partner, 1979. *Member:* Swedish Bar Association. *LANGUAGES:* Swedish and English. *PRACTICE AREAS:* Commercial and Corporate Law; Franchising; Real Estate; Litigation.

ANNE-CATHERINE MATSSON, born 1943. *Education:* University of Uppsala (LL.M., 1978; M.A. Fil lic, 1969). Associate, 1978; Partner, 1983. *Member:* Swedish Bar Association. *LANGUAGES:* Swedish, English and French. *PRACTICE AREAS:* Insolvency and Bankruptcy Law; Composition and Debtors' Reconstruction.

TORBJÖRN GELFGREN, born 1946. *Education:* University of Uppsala (LL.M., 1970). Taxation Court of Uppsala, 1971-1976. Private Legal Practice, 1976-1982. Associate, 1982; Partner, 1984. *Member:* Swedish Bar Association; International Fiscal Association; International Tax Planning Association. *LANGUAGES:* Swedish and English. *PRACTICE AREAS:* Commercial and Corporate Law; Mergers and Acquisitions; Banking and Financing; Tax Law; Real Estate Law.

JÖRGEN SANDSTRÖM, born 1955. *Education:* University of Uppsala (LL.M., 1986); University of Minnesota, Law School (1985). District Court of Uppsala, 1986-1987. Associate, 1987; Partner, 1991. *Member:* Swedish Bar Association. *LANGUAGES:* Swedish and English. *PRACTICE AREAS:* Commercial and Corporate Law; Contracts; Tax Law.

BENGT BOLIN, born 1959. *Education:* University of Uppsala (LL.M., 1986). District Court of Uppsala, 1986-1987. Associate, 1987; Partner, 1991. *Member:* Swedish Bar Association. *LANGUAGES:* Swedish, English and Russian. *PRACTICE AREAS:* Commercial and Corporate Law; Contracts; Litigation; Arbitration.

LARS HASP, born 1957. *Education:* University of Uppsala (LL.M., 1984); University of California, Berkeley (LL.M., 1985). National Tax Board, 1985. Arthur Andersen & Co. (tax division) 1986-1988. Associate, 1988; Partner, 1991. *Member:* Swedish Bar Association; International Association of Boalt Alumni. *LANGUAGES:* Swedish and English. *PRACTICE AREAS:* Commercial Law; Corporate Law; Tax Law; Mergers and Acquisitions; Cross Border Transactions and Reorganizations.

HENRIK EDSTAM, born 1958. *Education:* University of Uppsala (LL.M., 1986). Private Legal Practice, 1986-1989. Associate, 1989; Partner, 1992. *Member:* Swedish Bar Association. *LANGUAGES:* Swedish and English. *PRACTICE AREAS:* Commercial and Corporate Law; Banking and Financing; Contracts; Real Estate Law; Labour and Employment Law.

LARS LA FLEUR, born 1950. *Education:* University of Uppsala (LL.M., 1983). District Court of Katrineholm, 1983-1985; Administrative Court of Appeal, Sundsvall, 1985-1986. Private Legal Practice, 1986-1991. Partner, 1991. *Member:* Swedish Bar Association. *LANGUAGES:* Swedish and English. *PRACTICE AREAS:* Insolvency and Bankruptcy Law; Composition and Debtors' Reconstruction; Real Estate Law; Criminal Law.

GÖRAN SOHLBERG, born 1956. *Education:* University of Stockholm (LL.M., 1981). The County Administration Board of Stockholm, 1981-1986. Arthur Andersen & Co., 1986-1989, (tax division). Associate, 1989; Partner, 1991. *Member:* Swedish Bar Association. *LANGUAGES:* Swedish

(This Listing Continued)

(This Listing Continued)

ADVOKATFIRMAN CHRYSANDER, Stockholm—
Continued

and English. **PRACTICE AREAS:** General Commercial Law; Tax Law; Corporate Law.

TOMMY GRÖNBERG, born 1955. *Education:* University of Stockholm (LL.M., 1985); University of Umea (B.A., 1978). National Tax Board, 1986. District Court of Nacka, 1986-1987. Private Legal Practice, 1988-1990. Associate, 1990; Partner, 1991. *Member:* Swedish Bar Association. **LANGUAGES:** Swedish and English. **PRACTICE AREAS:** Commercial Law; Corporate Law; Mergers and Acquisitions; Cross Border Transactions; Joint Ventures; Intellectual Property and Litigation.

TOMMY LUNDQVIST, born 1954. *Education:* University of Stockholm (LL.M., 1983). Private Legal Practice, 1983-1984. The County Administration Board of Stockholm, 1984-1987. Arthur Andersen & Co. (tax division), 1987-1989. Private legal practice, 1989-1992. Partner, 1992. *Member:* Swedish Bar Association; International Fiscal Association. **LANGUAGES:** Swedish and English. **PRACTICE AREAS:** General Commercial Law; Corporate Law; Tax Law; Insolvency and Bankruptcy Law.

GUNNAR MATTSSON, born 1964. *Education:* University of Uppsala (LL.M., 1989); University of Minnesota Law School (1987). Swedish Foreign Office, 1989. Associate, 1990. Partner, 1994. **LANGUAGES:** Swedish and English. **PRACTICE AREAS:** General Commercial law; Insolvency and Bankruptcy Law; Competition Law; European Community Law.

HAKAN RUDSTRÖM, born 1957. *Education:* University of Minnesota Law School (1983); University of Uppsala (LL.M., 1985). District Court of Uppsala, 1985-1988. Corporate Lawyer at Scandinavian Airline System (SAS), 1988-1991. Associate, 1991. Partner, 1994. **LANGUAGES:** Swedish and English. **PRACTICE AREAS:** General Commercial Law; Corporate Law; Computers and Software; Insolvency and Bankruptcy Law.

PER LUTHANDER, born 1964. *Education:* University of Stockholm (LL.M., 1992). District Court of Arvika, 1992-1994. Associate, 1994. **LANGUAGES:** Swedish and English. **PRACTICE AREAS:** General Commercial Law; Corporate Law.

CONSULTANT

GÖRAN LJUNGBERG, born 1930. *Education:* University of Stockholm (LL.M., 1954). Service and Judgeships in Swedish Courts, 1955-1970. Secretary of the Government Committee regarding Laws on Privacy, 1966-1970. Expert of the same Committee, 1971-1978. Head of the Legal Department of the Stockholm County Council, 1971-1979. Executive Director of the Executive Committee of the County Council, 1980-1989. Representative of the County Council's Union on the Labor Litigation's Court, 1986-1989. **LANGUAGES:** Swedish and English. **PRACTICE AREAS:** Corporate Law; Insolvency and Bankruptcy Law; Local Government Law; Arbitration.

DAHLMAN MAGNUSSON ADVOKATBYRÅ AB

BIRGER JARLSGATAN 15
P.O. BOX 7009
S-103 86 STOCKHOLM, SWEDEN
Telephone: +46 (8) 679 82 00
Telefax: +46 (8) 679 75 65

General Corporate and Business Law including Banking, Financing, Taxation, Contract, Industrial Property, Copyright and Trademarks, Licensing, Labour Law, Mergers and Acquisitions, Aviation, Arbitration and Litigation, Environmental Law, Competition Law, EC Law and Entertainment Law.

MEMBERS OF FIRM

ROLAND DAHLMAN, born Stockholm, Sweden, November 2, 1945. *Education:* University of Stockholm (juris kandidat, LL.B., 1970); Harvard Law School (LL.M., 1974); Columbia Law School (Dipl., 1974); New York University Graduate School of Business Administration (Dipl., 1976). Co-author: of a Manual on International Aspects of Swedish Taxation. Author: "Business Operations in Sweden," 985 Tax Management. Associated with Messrs. Cleary, Gottlieb, Steen & Hamilton, New York and Brussels, 1976-1980. Associate (1981-1982) and Partner (1983-1991), Advokatfirman Södermark. Vice President, Harvard Law School Association of Europe, 1983—. *Member:* Swedish Bar Association (1982); International Bar Association; International Fiscal Association; American Society of International Law.

BO HJALMARSSON, born Landskrona, Sweden, February 21, 1957. *Education:* University of Stockholm (LL.M., 1983). Assistant Judge, 1983-1985. Lecturer in Law, Stockholm School of Economics, 1983-1985. Associate: Advokatfirman Tisell & Co, 1985-1989; Mannheimer Swartling Advokatbyra, 1989-1991. *Member:* Swedish Bar Association (1988).

PER MAGNUSSON, born Stockholm, Sweden, September 27, 1959. *Education:* University of Stockholm (LL.M., 1984). Assistant Judge, 1984-1986. Associate, Advokatfirman Tisell & Co, 1986-1990. Partner, Advokatfirman Chrysander, 1990-1991. *Member:* Swedish Bar Association (1989).

LARS ISACSSON, born Nacka, Sweden, February 18, 1961. *Education:* University of Uppsala (LL.M., 1987); University of Oxford (Diploma in Legal Studies, 1988). Associate: Carl Swartling Advokatbyrå, 1988-1990; Resident, New York Office, Mannheimer Swartling Advokatbyra, 1990-1992. *Member:* Swedish Bar Association (1993); International Bar Association; Association Internationale des Jeunes Avocats; American Bar Association (International Associate); Aircraft Financing and Contracts Division of ABA Forum on Air and Space Law.

WILHELM DAHLBORN, born Stockholm, Sweden, September 20, 1959. *Education:* University of Stockholm (LL.M., 1986). Assistant Judge, 1987-1989. Lawyer at the Swedish Finance Inspectorate 1989-1990. Lawyer at the Swedish Securities Register Centre, 1990-1991.

ASSOCIATES

MARGARETHA HÖGBERG, born Falun, Sweden, November 13, 1935. *Education:* University of Stockholm (LL.M., 1985). Associate, Advokatfirman Chrysander, 1988-1991. *Member:* Swedish Bar Association (1993).

ERIK BERGENSTRÅHLE, born Stockholm, August 18, 1960. *Education:* University of Stockholm (LL.M., 1985). Assistant Judge, 1986. Assistant Attorney, Scandinavian Airlines System (SAS), 1986-1987. Associate: Carl Swartling Advokatbyrå, 1987-1990; Mannheimer Swartling Advokatbyrå, 1990-1993. *Member:* Swedish Bar Association (1991); Association Internationale des Jeunes Avocats.

TORBJÖRN CLAESON, born Sweden, 1958; (Not admitted in Sweden). *Education:* University of Stockholm (LL.M., 1984). Assistant Judge, 1984-1987. Associate, Advokatfirman Vinge, 1987-1988. General Counsel, Swedegas AB, 1988-1991. Partner, Advokatfirman Nordia, 1991-1994. *Member:* Swedish Bar Association (1991); International Bar Association.

ROBERT HANSSON, born 1955. *Education:* University of Stockholm (LL.M., 1991). Service in Swedish Courts, 1981-1983. Associate: Hedberg & Johnsson, 1983-1985. Legal Counsel: AB Electrolux, 1985-1991. Associate: Advokatfirman Vinge, 1991-1994. *Member:* Swedish Bar Association (1991).

PETER SJÖGREN, born Strangnas, Sweden, January 24, 1962. *Education:* University of Uppsala (LL.M., 1989). Taxation Consultant, Trygg-Hansa SPP, 1989-1993.

ANNA BOVALLER, born Trollhättan, Sweden, February 12, 1963. *Education:* University of Lund (LL.M., 1988). Associate, Michelsons Advokatbyra, 1988-1989. Assistant Judge, 1990-1993.

JOHAN SUNDIN, born Gävle, Sweden, September 23, 1965. *Education:* University of Uppsala (LL.M., 1990). Assistant Judge, 1990-1993. Judge Referee to the Court of Appeal, 1993.

MARIA WALL, born Solna, Sweden, September 28, 1963. *Education:* University of Stockholm (LL.M., 1990). Assistant Judge, 1990-1993. Judge Referee to the Court of Appeal, 1993. Associate Judge of the Court of Appeal, 1994.

HELEN OLINDER, born Falkenberg, Sweden, July 15, 1964. *Education:* University of Lund (LL.M., 1989). Assistant Judge, 1989-1992. Counsel at Scandinavian Multi Access Systems AB, 1992-1994.

MARIA ROSÉN, born Stockholm, Sweden, January 28, 1967. *Education:* University of Stockholm (LL.M., 1994).

JOHAN RAMBERG, born 1965. *Education:* University of Stockholm. Service in Swedish Courts, 1993. Associate: Haight, Gardner, Poor & Havens, 1994.

Languages: Swedish, English, French and German

DANOWSKY & PARTNERS ADVOKATBYRÅ

Established in 1993

HOVSLAGARGATAN 5

P.O. BOX 16097

S-103 22 STOCKHOLM, SWEDEN

Telephone: +46-8-614 64 00

Telefax: +46-8-678 09 25

PETER DANOWSKY, born Solna, Sweden, 1949. *Education:* University of Uppsala (LL.M., 1972); Collège d' Europe (1974); Columbia University (LL.M., 1975). Partner, Lagerlöf & Leman, 1988-1993. *Member:* Swedish Bar Association. *LANGUAGES:* English, French and German. *PRACTICE AREAS:* Intellectual Property Law; Media and Communication; Professional Liability; International Arbitration and Litigation; Domestic Arbitration and Litigation.

ULF SALLNÄS, born Linköping, Sweden, 1956. *Education:* University of Linköping (MBA, 1979); University of Uppsala (LL.M., 1981). Junior Judgeship, Svea Court of Appeal, 1984. Legal Counsel, Boliden AB, 1984-1988. Associated with Lagerlöf & Leman, 1988-1993. *Member:* Swedish Bar Association. *LANGUAGES:* English. *PRACTICE AREAS:* Corporate; Commercial; Real Estate; Debtor/Creditor; Secured Transactions.

PETER BÄÄRNHIELM, born Stockholm, Sweden, 1958. *Education:* University of Uppsala (LL.M., 1985; Doctoral Studies, 1985-1987); University of Minnesota Law School (1983). Associated with Lagerlöf & Leman, 1990-1992. Legal Counsel, Enskilda Law, Skandinaviska Enskilda Banken, 1992-1993. *Member:* Swedish Bar Association. *LANGUAGES:* English. *PRACTICE AREAS:* Corporate; Commercial; Securities; Mergers and Acquisitions; Banking and Lending; Intellectual Property.

JOHAN CERVIN, born Lund, Sweden, 1960. *Education:* University of Lund (LL.M., 1984); Scandinavian Institute of Maritime Law (1983). Trelleborg and Uppsala District Courts, 1984-1987. Associated with Wesslau & Lindskog, 1987-1989. Legal Counsel, Enskilda Law, Skandinaviska Enskilda Banken, 1989-1993. *Member:* Swedish Bar Association. *LANGUAGES:* English. *PRACTICE AREAS:* Corporate Law; Commercial; Securities; Banking and Lending; Mergers and Acquisitions.

STEFAN PETTERSSON, born Lund, Sweden, 1963. *Education:* University of Lund (LL.M., 1989). Gothenburg District Court, 1989-1992. Associated with Mannheimer Swartling Advokatbyrå, 1992-1994. *LANGUAGES:* English.

ULF ISAKSSON, born Fredrika, Sweden, 1964. *Education:* University of Uppsala (LL.M., 1990); University of Amsterdam, ASIR (LL.M., 1992-1993). Stockholm District Court, 1990-1993. *LANGUAGES:* English.

MÅRTEN LUNDMARK, born Urneå, Sweden, 1963. *Education:* University of Lund (LL.M., 1989). Alingsås District Court, 1990-1992. Court of Appeal, 1992-1993. Appointed Judge, Härnösand District Court, 1993. *LANGUAGES:* English and French.

JOHAN LIDBECK, born Stockholm, Sweden, 1964. *Education:* University of Stockholm (LL.M., 1990); University of Illinois College of Law (LL.M., 1994). Stockholm City Court, 1991-1993. *LANGUAGES:* English.

ASSOCIATE

MARGARETA BONTHRON MALIN, born Uppsala, Sweden March 22, 1967. *Education:* Uppsala, Sweden (LL.M., 1991). Clerk of Court, Sollentuna, Sweden, 1992-1994. Applicant for Reporting Clerk, 1994—. *LANGUAGES:* English.

ADVOKATFIRMAN DELPHI

Established in 1984

SERGELS TORG 12, 6TR

P.O. BOX 1432

S-111 84 STOCKHOLM, SWEDEN

Telephone: +46 8 677 54 00

Telex: 12511 DELPHI S

FAX: +46 8 20 18 84

General Commercial, Corporate and Securities Law, Antitrust, Industrial Property and Copyright Law, Labor Law and Industrial Relations, Taxation, International and Comparative Law, Maritime and Transportation Law, Admiralty, Communications Law, Insolvency Law, Arbitration and Litigation, all Swedish Courts.

(This Listing Continued)

FIRM PROFILE: *Advokatfirman Delphi was established in 1984. Its practice encompasses both Swedish and international business law. A major focus of its practice is rendering services to foreign enterprises doing business in Sweden, the Nordic Regim and Northern Europe as well as Nordic enterprises operating abroad. Advokatfirman Delphi is a member of UNILAW, which is an international network of well reputed law firms in Europe and Japan. Advokatfirman Delphi is also a member of Nordic Alliance, which is a co-operation among Advokatfirmaet Selmer & Co., Oslo, Nielsen & Nørager Advokatkontor, Copenhagen and Advokatfirman Delphi, Stockholm.*

PARTNERS

SVEN-GÖRAN ALM, born 1947. LL.B., Uppsala, 1973. Asst. Judge, 1973-1976. Erik Berglunds Advokatbyrå, 1976-1983. Advokatfirman Delphi, 1984—. *Member:* Swedish Bar Association; Swedish Insurance Law Association; Asian Pacific Lawyers Association. *LANGUAGES:* Swedish and English. *PRACTICE AREAS:* Swedish and International Business Law; Mergers and Acquisitions.

PER-ERIK ANDERSSON, born 1948. LL.B., Uppsala, 1976. Negotiator for the Swedish Association of Graduate Engineers, 1976-1978. Asst. Judge, 1978-1981. Legal Adviser to Swedish Television and Radio, 1981-1984. Advokatfirman Delphi, 1984—. *Member:* Swedish Bar Association; International Bar Association; Inter Pacific Bar Association. *LANGUAGES:* Swedish and English. *PRACTICE AREAS:* Media Law; Copyright and Trademark Law; Entertainment Law; Telecommunication Law; Mergers and Acquisitions.

PER BERGLÖF, born 1952. LL.B., Uppsala, 1978. Asst. Judge, 1978-1980. Erik Berglunds Advokatbyrå, 1980-1983. Advokatfirman Delphi, 1984—. *Member:* Swedish Bar Association; Swedish Market Law Association; International Bar Association; AIJA. *LANGUAGES:* Swedish and English. *PRACTICE AREAS:* Swedish and International Business Law; Mergers and Acquisitions; Banking and Finance.

KARL-JOHAN DHUNÉR, born 1947. LL.B., Lund, 1971. University of Amsterdam, Europa Institut, International Course on European Integration, Business Law Section (LL.M., 1973). Asst. Judge, 1975-1977. Counsel, National Swedish Board of Consumer Policies, 1977-1979. Morssing & Nycander, Stockholm, 1979-1989. Advokatfirman Delphi, 1989—. *Member:* Swedish Bar Association; International Bar Association; AIJA; Swedish Maritime Law Association; Swedish Association for European Law (Secretary); Swedish Market Law Association; Swedish Insurance Law Association; AIDA (Board Member); ICC Competition Commission. *LANGUAGES:* Swedish, English, German and French. *PRACTICE AREAS:* International Trade; Transport; Insurance; Swedish and EC Antitrust.

CHRISTER A. HOLM, born 1954. LL.B. Stockholm, 1979. The Office of the Public Prosecutor of Stockholm, 1979-1980. Asst. Judge, 1980-1981. Mannheimer & Zetterlöf KB, 1981-1985. Advokatfirman Delphi, 1985—. *Member:* Swedish Bar Association; Asia Pacific Lawyers Association; International Bar Association. *LANGUAGES:* Swedish and English. *PRACTICE AREAS:* Insurance Law; Competition Law; Mergers and Acquisitions; Distribution Law; Computer Law; Product Liability.

AGNE LINDBERG, born 1962. LL.B., Uppsala, 1987. Asst. Judge, 1987-1989. Advokatfirman Delphi, 1989-1990; Advokatfirman Smitt, 1990-1992; Advokatfirman Delphi, 1992—. *Member:* Swedish Bar Association; Swedish Society for Computers & Law (Member of the Board, 1992—). *LANGUAGES:* Swedish and English. *PRACTICE AREAS:* Computer Law; Intellectual Property.

LENNART OLSSON, born 1952. LL.B., Uppsala, 1980. Asst. Judge, 1980-1983. In-house lawyer at Svenska Handelsbanken, 1983-1987; Hökerberg & Söderqvist Advokatbyrå AB, 1987-1992; Advokatfirman Delphi, 1992—. *Member:* Swedish Bar Association. *LANGUAGES:* Swedish and English. *PRACTICE AREAS:* General Business Law; Litigation and Insolvency Law.

LARS ERIK REJE, born 1951. LL.B., Stockholm, 1980. Asst. Judge, 1980-1982. Lindstedts Advokatbyrå, 1982-1983; In-house Lawyer, Svenska Handelsbanken, 1983-1988; Erik Berglunds Advokatbyrå, 1988-1990; Hökerberg & Söderqvist Advokatbyrå, 1990-1992; Advokatfirman Delphi, 1992—. *Member:* Swedish Bar Association; International Bar Association. *LANGUAGES:* Swedish and English. *PRACTICE AREAS:* General Business Law; Insolvency Law; Litigation.

PETER SKOGLUND, born 1956. LL.B., Uppsala, 1981. Asst. Judge, 1982-1984. Advokatfirman Delphi, 1984—. *Member:* Swedish Bar Association; Swedish Market Law Association. *LANGUAGES:* Swedish and En-

(This Listing Continued)

ADVOKATFIRMAN DELPHI, Stockholm—Continued

glish. *PRACTICE AREAS:* Intellectual Property; Antitrust; Litigation; Mergers and Acquisitions.

PETER UTTERSTRÖM, born 1947. LL.B., Stockholm, 1973. Associate of Law Firm, 1973-1974. Asst. Judge, Tax Court, 1974-1977. National Tax Board (Advance Private Rulings), 1977. With Tax Department of Arthur Anderson & Co., Stockholm, 1978-1982. Associate of Law Firm, 1982-1983. With Erik Berglunds Advokatbyrå, 1984-1990. Advokatfirman Landahl, 1991-1993. Advokatfirman Delphi, 1993—. *Member:* Swedish Bar Association; International Bar Association; International Fiscal Association. *LANGUAGES:* Swedish and English. *PRACTICE AREAS:* Swedish and International Business Law; Swedish and International Tax Law; Real Estate Law; Mergers and Acquisitions.

ASSOCIATES

TALBOT S. LINDSTRÖM, born 1934. B.A., Stanford University, 1956; J.D., 1958. LL.M., University of California, Berkeley, 1965. M.C.L., University of Stockholm, 1966. Associate of McCutchen, Doyle, Enersen & Brown; Peart, Baraty & Hassard; Kaiser Industries Legal Division; Safeway Stores Contract Division, 1960-1963. U.S. Department of Justice, Antitrust Division, Trial Attorney, 1963-1969. Department of Defense, International Security Affairs, Executive Officer to Deputy Assistant Secretary of Defense, 1969-1970. Counsel, Export-Import Bank of U.S., Office of General Counsel, 1971-1973. Washington Partner, Whitman & Ransom, 1973-1980. Chief, Unfair Import Investigation Division, U.S. International Trade Commission, 1981. Deputy Director, Office of Export Administration, Department of Commerce, 1981-1982. Special Assistant to Under Secretary for Policy, Department of Defense, 1982. Deputy Under Secretary of Defense for International Programs and Technology, Department of Defense, 1983-1986. Deputy Director, Defense Technology Security Administration, Department of Defense, 1986-1990. Assistant Director, Bureau of Competition, Federal Trade Commission (responsible for International Antitrust Division), 1990-1994. Advokatfirman Delphi, 1994—. *Member:* District of Columbia Bar Association; California State Bar Association; American Bar Association; International Bar Association; American Arbitration Association; Advisory Group, ABA Committee on Law and National Security; Global Strategy Council. *LANGUAGES:* English and Swedish. *PRACTICE AREAS:* Antitrust; Trade Law; Export Control; General Business Law; International Law.

MAGNUS BRORSSON, born 1961. LL.B., Stockholm, 1987. Asst. Judge, 1987-1990. Advokatfirman Delphi, 1990—. *Member:* Swedish Bar Association. *LANGUAGES:* Swedish and English. *PRACTICE AREAS:* Litigation; Corporate Law; General Business Law.

PETER BENGTSSON, born 1961. LL.B., Lund, 1987. Asst. Judge, 1988-1990. Advokatfirman Delphi 1990—. *Member:* Swedish Bar Association. *LANGUAGES:* Swedish and English. *PRACTICE AREAS:* Mergers and Acquisitions; Intellectual Property and Commercial Contracts.

ULF HANSON, born 1952. LL.B., Stockholm, 1979. Asst. Judge, 1980-1982. The Swedish Law & Informatics Research Institute, 1982-1986. Advokatfirman Foyen & Pedersen, 1987-1990. Legal Counsel of the Swedish Agency for Administrative Development, 1990-1991. General Counsel of the Swedish Agency for Administrative Development, 1991-1994. Advokatfirman Delphi, 1994—. *Member:* Swedish Bar Association. *LANGUAGES:* Swedish and English. *PRACTICE AREAS:* Computer Law.

JAN HOLMQVIST, born 1949. LL.M., Stockholm, 1975. Legal Counsel, Head of Insurance and Credit Department of Swedish Philips Organization (subsidiary of Philips Electronics N.V.), 1976-1991; Advokatfirman Delphi, 1992—. *Member:* Swedish Bar Association. *LANGUAGES:* Swedish, English and German. *PRACTICE AREAS:* Bankruptcy and Reorganization; Swedish and International Business Law.

ULF HÅRDEMAN, born 1958. LL.M., Stockholm, 1988. Asst. Judge, 1988-1990. Advokatfirman Landahl, 1990-1994; Advokatfirman Delphi, 1994—. *Member:* Swedish Bar Association. *LANGUAGES:* Swedish and English. *PRACTICE AREAS:* Litigation; Real Estate Law; General Law.

AGNETA BERN, born 1964. LL.B., Stockholm, 1990. Asst. Judge, 1990-1992. Advokatfirman Delphi, 1992—. *LANGUAGES:* Swedish and English. *PRACTICE AREAS:* General Business Law; Insolvency Law.

MARITA CEDERHOLM, born 1959. LL.B., Stockholm, 1992. Advokatfirman Delphi, 1992—. *LANGUAGES:* Swedish and English. *PRACTICE AREAS:* General Business Law; Insolvency Law.

(This Listing Continued)

OF COUNSEL

JÖRGEN BENGTSSON, born 1924. LL.B., Uppsala, 1945. Asst. Judge, 1946. Employed in Sweden, Belgium and Western Germany, 1946-1950. Practiced Law in Stockholm, 1950-1955. House Counsel, L.M. Ericsson Telephone Company, 1955-1965. With Erik Berglunds Advokatbyrå, 1966-1990. Advokatfirman Landahl, 1990-1993. Advokatfirman Delphi, 1993—. *LANGUAGES:* Swedish, English and German.

Languages: Swedish, English, German and French.

FALKS ADVOKATBYRÅ

Established in 1938

ARTILLERIGATAN 24

P.O. BOX 5436

S-114 84 STOCKHOLM, SWEDEN

Telephone: 46 8-667 05 20

Telefax: 46 8-662 59 44

General Business, Commercial and Corporate Law, Bankruptcy, Antitrust and Trade Regulation, Copyright and Trademark, Civil Litigation, Entertainment, European Union Law, Labour Law, Landlord and Tenant Law, Taxation.

PARTNERS OF THE FIRM

ULF FALK, born Söderhamn, Sweden, 1934; admitted, 1965, Sweden. *Education:* University of Stockholm (LL.B., 1959). District court, 1959-1961. *Member:* Swedish Bar Association. *LANGUAGES:* Swedish and English. *PRACTICE AREAS:* General Business Law; Entertainment.

HANS DAHLBECK, born Stockholm, Sweden, 1941; admitted, 1973, Sweden. *Education:* University of Stockholm (LL.B., 1966). District court, 1966-1969. *Member:* Swedish Bar Association. *LANGUAGES:* Swedish, English and French. *PRACTICE AREAS:* General Business Law; Antitrust and Trade Regulation; Copyright and Trademark; European Union Law.

JOHAN OBEL, born Stockholm, Sweden, 1944; admitted, 1977, Sweden. *Education:* University of Stockholm (LL.B., 1970). District court, 1970-1972. *Member:* Swedish Bar Association. *LANGUAGES:* Swedish and English. *PRACTICE AREAS:* General Business Law; Landlord and Tenant Law.

ÅSA THORELL, born Stockholm, Sweden, 1958; admitted, 1989, Sweden. *Education:* University of Uppsala (LL.B., 1983). Administrative Court, 1983-1985. *Member:* Swedish Bar Association. *LANGUAGES:* Swedish and English. *PRACTICE AREAS:* General Business Law.

ASSOCIATES

ULF FREDHOLM, born Stockholm, Sweden, 1929. *Education:* University of Uppsala (LL.B., 1955). District court, 1955-1957. Administrative Court of Appeal, 1956-1968 (Kammarrätten i Stockholm). Taxation consultant, SE-Banken, 1969-1992. *LANGUAGES:* Swedish and English. *PRACTICE AREAS:* Taxation.

ULF HÖKEBERG, born Uppsala, Sweden, 1958; admitted, 1994, Sweden. *Education:* University of Uppsala (LL.B., 1987). District court, 1987-1989. Administrative Court of Appeal, 1989-1990 (Kammarrätten i Stockholm). *LANGUAGES:* Swedish and English. *PRACTICE AREAS:* General Business Law; Litigation.

BO SÖDERBERG, born Stockholm, Sweden, 1928. *Education:* University of Stockholm (LL.B., 1948). District court, 1949-1951. *LANGUAGES:* Swedish and English. *PRACTICE AREAS:* Labour Law.

GUY LOFALK, born Stockholm, Sweden, 1955. *Education:* University of Stockholm (LL.M., 1985). District Court, 1985-1987. *Member:* Swedish Bar Association. *LANGUAGES:* Scandinavian and English. *PRACTICE AREAS:* Business Law; Bankruptcy; Litigation.

SUSANNE BRITZ, born Stockholm, Sweden, 1964. *Education:* University of Stockholm (LL.B., 1991). *LANGUAGES:* Swedish and English. *PRACTICE AREAS:* General Business Law.

FOYEN & PARTNERS

NYBROGATAN 15
P.O. BOX 5294
S-102 46 STOCKHOLM, SWEDEN
Telephone: 8-663 02 90
Telefax: 8-662 15 90

New York, N.Y. Office: 80 Third Avenue, 23rd Floor - NTC, 10022-7604. Telephone: 212-265-2555. Telefax: 212-838-0374.

Maplewood, New Jersey Office: 108 Baker Street, 07040. Telephone: 201-762-5800. Telefax: 201-762-5801.

Oslo, Norway Office: Advokatfirmaet Foyen & Co Ans, Oscarsgate 52, N-0258 Oslo 2. Telephone: 02-44 46 40. Telefax: 02-44 89 27.

Falun, Sweden Office: Magasinsgatan 7, P.O. Box 81, S-791 22. Telephone: 23-190 70. Telefax: 23-190 77.

Malmo, Sweden Office: Davidhallsgatan 27A, S-211 45. Telephone: 40-2377 55. Telefax: 40-97 12 44.

International, Finance, Banking, Admiralty, Commercial Litigation and Arbitration, Real Estate, Construction Law, Trusts and Estates, Fiscal, General Commercial and Corporate Law.

MEMBERS OF FIRM

JAN SALLNÄS, born 1945; admitted, 1979, Sweden. *Education:* University of Uppsala (LL.B., 1971). District Court, 1973-1979. The Court of Appeal for Western Sweden, 1975-1976. *Member:* Swedish Bar Association; Swedish Insurance Law Association. *LANGUAGES:* English, Spanish and Scandinavian.

JENS PEDERSEN, born 1948; admitted, 1980, Sweden. *Education:* University of Stockholm (B.A., Econ.); University of Uppsala (LL.B.). *Member:* Swedish Bar Association. *LANGUAGES:* English and Scandinavian.

JOHAN ÖSTERLING, born 1946; admitted, 1982, Sweden. *Education:* University of Stockholm (LL.B., 1973; M.Sc Economics, 1977); Language Studies University of Grenoble, 1973-1974; Institute of Air and Space Law, McGill University, Montreal, Canada, 1975-1976, Diploma Air and Space Law. Council of Europe, Legal Department, Strasbourg, 1974. Rechtsanwâlte Dr. Ostertag Grub, Dr. Frank Ludwigsburg/Stuttgart, Germany, 1975. District Court, 1977-1979. *Member:* Swedish Bar Association; International Association of Young Lawyers. (Also at Falun Office). *LANGUAGES:* Scandinavian, English and German..

PATRIK ADERSTEG, born 1956; admitted, 1988, Sweden. *Education:* University of Uppsala (LL.B., 1981). District Court, 1982-1984. *Member:* Swedish Bar Association. *LANGUAGES:* English and Scandinavian.

INGEMAR ALFROST, born 1947; admitted, 1990, Sweden. *Education:* University of Lund (LL.B., 1973). District Court, 1973-1975. The Court of Appeal for Western Sweden, 1976. *Member:* Swedish Bar Association. *LANGUAGES:* English and Scandinavian.

PETER FALK, born 1952; admitted, 1990, Sweden. *Education:* University of Lund (LL.B., 1979). District Court, 1980-1982. *Member:* Swedish Bar Association. (Resident, Malmo Office). *LANGUAGES:* English and Scandinavian.

ANDERS JANSON, born 1954; admitted, 1992, Sweden. *Education:* University of Stockholm (LL.B., 1980). District Court, 1980-1982. *Member:* International Fiscal Association. *LANGUAGES:* English and Scandinavian.

ASSOCIATES

PER HÅRD, born 1949; admitted, 1987, Sweden. *Education:* University of Stockholm (LL.B., 1977). District Court, 1979-1981. The Court of Appeal for Northern Sweden, 1981-1984. *Member:* Swedish Bar Association. *LANGUAGES:* English and Scandinavian.

PER GRAPP, born 1957; admitted, 1991, Sweden. *Education:* University of Uppsala (LL.B., 1984). District Court, 1984-1987. *Member:* Swedish Bar Association. *LANGUAGES:* English, German and Scandinavian.

LARS BRAUN, born 1964; admitted, 1994, Sweden. *Education:* University of Lund (LL.B., 1989). District Court, 1988-1991. The Court of Appeal, Göta hovrätt, 1991. *LANGUAGES:* English and Scandinavian.

MIKAEL ROSÉN, born 1955; (Not admitted in Sweden). *Education:* University of Lund (LL.B., 1983). (Resident Falun Office). *LANGUAGES:* English and Scandinavian.

(This Listing Continued)

MARIA GUSTAFSSON, born 1962; (Not admitted in Sweden). *Education:* University of Uppsala (LL.B., 1986). District Court, 1986-1988. Fiscal Court of Appeal, 1989-1992. *LANGUAGES:* English and Scandinavian.

LARS HAG, born 1961; (Not admitted in Sweden). *Education:* University of Uppsala (LL.B., 1989). District Court, 1990-1992. (Resident, Falun Office). *LANGUAGES:* English and Scandinavian.

(For complete biographical data on other personnel in New York, Maplewood, Oslo, see those listings)

ADVOKATBYRAN FRIE

Established in 1985
NYBROGATAN 34
P.O. BOX 55547
S-102 04 STOCKHOLM, SWEDEN
Telephone: +46 8 660 0460
Fax: +46 8 665 7888

Member of Commercial Law Affiliates, CLA.
Company and Commercial Law, Mergers and Acquisitions, Intellectual Property.

FIRM PROFILE: Advokatbyrån Frie is a well-established firm based in Stockholm practising Swedish and international commercial law. The firm was founded in 1985 by Michael Frie and Rickard Poppelman and has - over the years - sustained steady growth and expansion without recourse to merger. The clients are mainly small and medium sized companies, but the firm also acts as legal adviser to larger companies on specific matters or individual projects.

Advokatbyrån Frie's organisation is compact and structured as a single legal entity which provides clients with access to the expertise and resources of all of the lawyers of the firm. A designated partner will at all times be the key contact person with responsibility for any necessary co-ordination of work. The firm is thus able to provide first-rate, speedy and cost-efficient legal assistance.

The firm is a member of Commercial Law Affiliates (CLA), an international association of independent highly qualified medium sized business and litigation law firms. CLA currently has members in over 160 cities worldwide and is the only international network where member firms must meet strict quality control criteria. Only one firm with a general commercial practice is accepted from each area. With 225 offices in cities, worldwide, CLA is the largest legal affiliation of its kind.

Advokatbyrån Frie provides a broad range of legal services in corporate affairs and business transactions. Principal areas of expertise include company and commercial law with particular emphasis on mergers and acquisitions. The firm's intellectual property expertise includes trademark, design and copyright law as well as marketing law. Other notable areas of expertise are commercial litigation and property, competition, computer and information law, media and entertainment law.

MEMBERS OF FIRM

MICHAEL FRIE, PARTNER, born Kalmar, Sweden, January 29, 1953; admitted, 1984, Sweden; 1988, Belgium. *Education:* University of Lund and Stockholm (Juris kandidat, LL.B., 1978). Advokatfirman Tisell & Co., 1979-1985. *Member:* Swedish Bar Association; Brussels Bar Association; International Bar Association; Union International des Avocats. *LANGUAGES:* Scandinavian and English. *PRACTICE AREAS:* Company and Commercial Law; Mergers and Acquisitions; Commercial Litigation.

RICKARD D. POPPELMAN, PARTNER, born Stockholm, Sweden, October 10, 1952. *Education:* University of Stockholm (Juris kandidat, LL.B., 1979). Service in Swedish Courts, 1980-1982. Advokatfirman Tisell & Co. AB, 1982-1985. *Member:* Swedish Bar Association. *LANGUAGES:* Swedish and English. *PRACTICE AREAS:* Commercial and Company Law; Mergers and Acquisitions; Estate Planning; Tax.

PETER VON HEIDENSTAM, PARTNER, born Walton on Thames, Surrey, January 24, 1959; admitted, 1990, Sweden. *Education:* Oslo University (Maritime Law, 1982); Uppsala University; Stockholm University (Juris kandidat, LL.B., 1985). Service in Swedish Courts, 1985-1987. *Member:* Swedish Bar Association; International Bar Association; Association Internationale Pour la Protection de la Propriété Industrielle. *LANGUAGES:* Swedish and English. *PRACTICE AREAS:* Intellectual Property Law; Competition Law; Computer Law; General Commercial Law.

(This Listing Continued)

ADVOKATBYRAN FRIE, Stockholm—Continued

HANS NICANDER, PARTNER, born Gothenburg, Sweden, October 19, 1960; admitted, 1991, Sweden. *Education:* University of Stockholm (Juris kandidat, LL.B., 1985). Service in Swedish Courts, 1986-1988. *Member:* Swedish Bar Association. *LANGUAGES:* Swedish and English. *PRACTICE AREAS:* Commercial and Company Law; Competition Law; Media and Entertainment Law; Litigation.

ASSOCIATES

ÅKE THEBLIN, born Stockholm, Sweden, June 9, 1961; admitted, 1993, Sweden. *Education:* University of Stockholm (juris kandidat, LL.B., 1987). Service in Swedish Courts, 1987-1989. Advokatfirman Vinge, London, 1990. *Member:* Swedish Bar Association. *LANGUAGES:* Swedish and English. *PRACTICE AREAS:* Real Estate Law; Tenancy Law; General Commercial Law.

HELENA ÖSTBLOM, born Stockholm, Sweden, May 16, 1963. *Education:* University of Stockholm (juris kandidat, LL.B., 1989). Service in Swedish Courts, 1989-1991. *LANGUAGES:* Swedish and English. *PRACTICE AREAS:* General Commercial Law.

ANDERS BOVALLER, born Stockholm, Sweden, September 4, 1965. *Education:* University of Stockholm (juris kandidat, LL.B., 1991). Service in Swedish Courts, 1991-1993. *LANGUAGES:* Swedish, English and German. *PRACTICE AREAS:* General Commercial Law; Litigation.

ADVOKATFIRMAN FRITZ ENGSTRÖM AB

STOCKHOLM, SWEDEN

(See Rydin & Carlsten Advokatbyrå AB)

ADVOKATFIRMAN FYLGIA

Established in 1986

HAMNGATAN 2

P.O. BOX 7814

S-103 96 STOCKHOLM, SWEDEN

Telephone: +46 8 679 50 60

Telefax: +46 8 611 39 54

General International Business Law, European Community Law, Computer Law, Intellectual Property, Insolvency, Real Estate and Construction, Maritime, Litigation and Arbitration.

PARTNERS

STIG FRIBERG, born Stockholm, Sweden, September 24, 1945; admitted, 1971, Sweden. *Education:* University of Stockholm (LL.M., 1971). Mariestad District Court, 1971-1973. *Member:* Swedish Bar Association. *LANGUAGES:* English. *PRACTICE AREAS:* Corporate Law; Real Estate; Construction Law; Insurance Law.

JAN FELLENIUS, born Stockholm, Sweden, July 19, 1945; admitted, 1974, Sweden. *Education:* University of Stockholm (LL.M., 1974). Regional Tax Court, 1974-1975. Hudiksvalls District Court, 1976-1978. Lecturer, Stockholm University, 1979-1982. *Member:* Swedish Bar Association. *LANGUAGES:* English. *PRACTICE AREAS:* Corporate Law; Insolvency Law.

BO H REUTERDAHL, born Västerås, Sweden, February 19, 1949; admitted, 1974, Sweden. *Education:* University of Uppsala (LL.M., 1974). Stockholm District Court, 1975-1977. Göta Court of Appeal, 1977-1978. *Member:* Swedish Bar Association. *LANGUAGES:* English. *PRACTICE AREAS:* Corporate Law.

JONAS REINER, born Stockholm, Sweden, December 12, 1950; admitted, 1978, Sweden. *Education:* University of Stockholm (LL.M., B.M.A., 1978). Jakobsberg District Court, 1979-1981. *Member:* Swedish Bar Association. *LANGUAGES:* English. *PRACTICE AREAS:* Corporate Law; Insolvency Law.

STAFFAN CASSMER, born Stockholm, Sweden, July 22, 1951; admitted, 1980, Sweden. *Education:* University of Stockholm (LL.M., 1980). *Member:* Swedish Bar Association. *LANGUAGES:* English. *PRACTICE AREAS:* Corporate Law; Insolvency Law.

(This Listing Continued)

MÅRTEN ANDERSSON, born Norberg, Sweden, May 6, 1945; admitted, 1978, Sweden. *Education:* University of Stockholm (LL.M., 1978). Construction Engineer, 1966. Contracting Company, 1967-1974. Handen District Court, 1978-1980. *Member:* Swedish Bar Association. *LANGUAGES:* English. *PRACTICE AREAS:* Corporate Law; Contract Law; Real Estate Law.

INGVAR ZÖÖGLING, born Stockholm, Sweden, April 5, 1949; admitted, 1975, Sweden. *Education:* University of Stockholm (LL.M., 1975). Stockholm District Court, 1975-1977. *Member:* Swedish Bar Association. *LANGUAGES:* English and German. *PRACTICE AREAS:* Corporate Law.

CHRISTER PEHRSON, born Borås, Sweden, October 23, 1945; admitted, 1974, Sweden. *Education:* University of Uppsala (LL.M., 1974). Lecturer, Institute for Legal Research, Gothenburg, 1974-1976. With, Haight Gardner Poor and Havens, New York, 1977. *Member:* Swedish Bar Association. *LANGUAGES:* English. *PRACTICE AREAS:* Corporate Law; Maritime Law; Transport Law.

JAN RAMKVIST, born August 15, 1945; admitted, 1972, Sweden. *Education:* University of Uppsala (LL.M., 1972). Västerås District Court, 1972-1975. Stockholm City, 1975-1980. Kooperativa Förbundet, 1980-1982. Hewlett-Packard, 1982-1987. Lecturer, Stockholm University, 1979-1983. Member, Licensing Executives Society. *Member:* Swedish Bar Association. *LANGUAGES:* English. *PRACTICE AREAS:* Corporate Law; Computer Law; Industrial and Intellectual Property Law.

ANDERS ASPEGREN, born Stockholm, Sweden, January 15, 1960; admitted, 1985, Sweden. *Education:* University of Stockholm (LL.M., 1985). Stockholm District Court, 1985-1988. *Member:* Swedish Bar Association. *LANGUAGES:* English. *PRACTICE AREAS:* Corporate Law; Insolvency Law; Real Estate Law.

ASSOCIATES

ROGER SÖDERSTRÖM, born Stockholm, July 10, 1961; admitted, 1987, Sweden. *Education:* University of Uppsala (LL.M., 1987). Västerås District Court, 1987-1989. *Member:* Swedish Bar Association. *LANGUAGES:* English. *PRACTICE AREAS:* Corporate Law; Insolvency Law.

LARS NYLUND, born Ludvika, Sweden, January 1, 1962; admitted, 1987, Sweden. *Education:* University of Uppsala (LL.M., 1987). Stockholm District Court, 1987-1989. Svea Court of Appeal, 1990-1991. *Member:* Swedish Bar Association. *LANGUAGES:* English. *PRACTICE AREAS:* Corporate Law; Insolvency Law.

DIMITRIJ TITOV, born Stockholm, Sweden, November 5, 1962; admitted, 1988, Sweden. *Education:* University of Stockholm (LL.M., 1988). Gävle District Court, 1990-1991. *Member:* Swedish Bar Association. *LANGUAGES:* English, French and Italian. *PRACTICE AREAS:* Corporate Law; Insolvency Law.

PER MATSON, born October 13, 1961; admitted, 1987, Sweden. *Education:* University of Uppsala (LL.M., 1987). Falu District Court, 1987-1989. Swedish Telecom, 1989-1991. *Member:* Swedish Bar Association. *LANGUAGES:* English. *PRACTICE AREAS:* Corporate Law; Insolvency Law; Competition Law.

EVA BLONDE, born Stockholm, Sweden, April 29, 1963; admitted, 1988, Sweden. *Education:* University of Uppsala (LL.M., 1988). Sandviken District Court, 1989-1991. The Criminal Injuries Compensation Board, 1991-1992. *LANGUAGES:* English and French. *PRACTICE AREAS:* Corporate Law; Intellectual Property Law; Insolvency Law.

MIKAEL MORITZ, born 1963; admitted, 1989, Sweden. *Education:* LL.M., 1989. Västerås District Court, 1989-1992. *LANGUAGES:* English. *PRACTICE AREAS:* Corporate Law; Insolvency Law.

BJÖRN NORDIN, born Stockholm, Sweden, February 11, 1959; admitted, 1987, Sweden. *Education:* University of Uppsala (LL.M., 1987). Falu District Court, 1987-1990. Reporting Clerk, Court of Appeal, 1990-1992. *LANGUAGES:* English. *PRACTICE AREAS:* Corporate Law.

BJÖRN DJUPMARK, born Eskilstuna, Sweden, March 7, 1959; admitted, 1987, Sweden. *Education:* University of Stockholm (LL.M., 1987). County Administrative Court Nyköping, 1987-1990. *Member:* Swedish Restaurateurs Employers' Association. *LANGUAGES:* English. *PRACTICE AREAS:* Corporate Law; Labour Law.

MAINA SANCHO, born 1940; admitted, 1963, Sweden. *Education:* LL.M., 1963. Södertörns Judicial District, 1963-1965. Malmöhus County Council, 1966-1967. Insurance Lawyer, Folksam, 1967-1971. Company

(This Listing Continued)

Lawyer, Folksam, 1971-1975, KF, 1975-1984. General Counsel, Nordico AB, 1984-1993. *LANGUAGES:* English and German. *PRACTICE AREAS:* Corporate Law; EC Law; Competition Law.

STYRBJÖRN GÄRDE ADVOKATBYRÅ

Established in 1957

NYBROGATAN 34

P.O. BOX 5208

S-102 45 STOCKHOLM, SWEDEN

Telephone: +46 (8)-665 00 40

Telefax: +46 (8)-665 00 41

Gothenburg, Sweden Office: Kastellgatan 1, S-413 07. Telephone: +46 (31)-11 36 30 . Telefax: +46 (31)-13 73 68.

Malmö, Sweden Office: Norra Vallgatan 64, S-211. Telephone: +46 (40)-10 48 10. Telefax: +46 (40)-23 52 31.

Helsingborg, Sweden Office: Garnisonsgatan 10, S-254 66. Telephone: +46-(42) 20 10 80. Telefax: +46 (42)-20 18 38.

Borås, Sweden Office: Stora Kyrkogatan 4, P.O. Box 305, S-501 05. Telephone: +46 (33) 11 69 00. Telefax: +46 (33) 13 79 00.

Paris, France Office: 41, Rue de Passy, F-75016. Telephone: +33 (1) 45 27 95 22. Telefax: +33 (1) 40 50 90 31.

Representative Offices:

Schweiz: Stadelgarden, Stadelhofer Strasse 40, CH-8024 Zürich. Telephone: +41 (1)-261 52 60. Telefax: +41 (1)-261 55 29.

Sweden: HAGA Företagscenter, Brogatan 25, S-334 33 Anderstorp. Telephone: +46 (371)-174 80. Telefax: +46 (371)-169 67.

Admitted to Practice in Sweden. General Swedish and International Business Law Practice. Company Law, Contracts and Disputes, Real Estate Law, Building and Construction Law, Mergers and Acquisitions, Intellectual Property, Copyright and Trademarks, Marketing and Unfair Competition, Computer and Telecommunication Law, Transportations and Maritime Law, EC and EEA Law, Labour Law, Banking and Insolvency Law, Corporate Financing and Securities Law, Trusts, Corporate Taxation, Insurance Law and Claims, Litigation and Arbitration. All Swedish Courts.

FIRM PROFILE: *The law firm of Gärde was founded almost forty years ago by Styrbjörn Gärde and is today one of the major law firms in Sweden with offices in Stockholm, Gothenburg, Malmö, Helsingborg and Borås as well as a branch office in Paris, France. Styrbjörn Gärde Advokatbyrå has well established relations with other law firms in Scandinavia and in other countries and is a member of worldwide legal networks.*

MEMBERS OF FIRM

HANS STYRBJÖRN GÄRDE, born Stockholm, Sweden, 1920. *Education:* University of Upsala (LL.B., 1943). Legal practice at the law firm of Covington & Burling, Washington, D.C., 1956. Author: articles, "Tidskrift för Sveriges Advokatsamfund," Swedish Bar Journal; "Svensk Skattetidning," Swedish Tax Journal; "Svensk Juristtidning," Swedish Law Journal; "Tax Avoidance, Tax Evasion," International Bar Association, London, 1982; "Corporate Migration," International Bar Association, Vienna, 1984. *Member:* Swedish and International Bar Associations; American Arbitration Association; Swedish-German Chamber of Commerce; German-Swedish Chamber of Commerce; German-Nordic Lawyers Association. Fellow, The American College of Probate Counsel. *LANGUAGES:* English, French, German, Finnish and Swedish. *PRACTICE AREAS:* Company Law; Insurance Law; Licensed Trade; Financing; Mergers and Acquisitions.

OLOF NYSTRÖM, born Stockholm, Sweden, 1932. *Education:* University of Stockholm (LL.B., 1958). Served in District Court of Södra Roslag, 1960, Svea Court of Appeal, 1961-1963, and Assistant Judge, District Court of Västernärke, 1962. *Member:* Swedish Bar Association; German-Nordic Lawyers Association; Swedish Association for Industrial Property Rights; Swedish Association for Design; Swedish Association for Legal Practitioners within the Insurance Field; Swedish Copyright Association; Licensing Executives Society, Scandinavian Chapter. *LANGUAGES:* English, German, French and Swedish. *PRACTICE AREAS:* Commercial Litigation; Arbitration; Intellectual Property; Licensed Trade; Construction Law.

ULF GÄRDE, born Stockholm, Sweden, 1949. *Education:* University of Stockholm (LL.B., 1975). Served in District Court of Linköping, 1975-1978 and Svea Court of Appeal, 1978-1979. Assistant Judge, Court of Appeal, 1979. *Member:* Swedish and International Bar Associations; British-Swedish Chamber of Commerce; Swedish Association for Industrial Property Rights; Swedish American Chamber of Commerce; American Club of

(This Listing Continued)

Sweden (Treasurer). *LANGUAGES:* English, German and Swedish. *PRACTICE AREAS:* Mergers and Acquisitions; Corporate Law; Contracts on Agents and Distribution; Unfair Competition and Marketing Law; Copyright and Trademarks.

TORBJÖRN WIDEMAR, born Stockholm, Sweden, 1949. *Education:* University of Stockholm (LL.B., 1976). Served in District Court of Ängelholm, 1977-1979, Court of Appeal of Skäne and Blekinge, 1960 and District Court of Helsingborg, 1981-1984. *Member:* Swedish and International Bar Associations. *LANGUAGES:* English and Swedish. *PRACTICE AREAS:* Commercial Litigation; Arbitration; Insolvency Law; Labour Law.

BENGT GÄRDE, born Stockholm, Sweden, 1952. *Education:* University of Stockholm (LL.B., 1980); University of Pau, France (1981). Served in the District Court of Trelleborg, 1982-1984. Author of article in Finnish-Swedish Chamber of Commerce's Year Book "Insurance Issues." *Member:* Swedish Bar Association; Finnish-Swedish Chamber of Commerce. *LANGUAGES:* English and Swedish. *PRACTICE AREAS:* Corporate Law; Telecommunication; Real Estate Law; Commercial Litigation; Banking; Construction Law.

KRISTER LEVIN, born Lund, Sweden, 1955. *Education:* University of Lund (LL.B., 1982); Scandinavian Institute of Maritime Law, University of Oslo (Scholarship). Served in District Court of Oskarshamn, 1983-1984 and District Court of Varberg, 1987-1988. *Member:* Swedish and International Bar Associations. *LANGUAGES:* English, German and Swedish. *PRACTICE AREAS:* Insolvency Law; Company Law; Contract Law; Trade Law.

NIKLAS HAAK, born Malmö, Sweden, 1957. *Education:* University of Stockholm (LL.B., 1984). Served in District Court of Oskarshamn, 1985-1987. *Member:* Swedish Bar Association; Swedish Association for Industrial Property Rights; Swedish Association for Legal Practitioners within the Insurance Field. *LANGUAGES:* English, German and Swedish. *PRACTICE AREAS:* Company Law; Contracts; Unfair Competition; Licensed Trade; Trade Law.

MIKAEL NORDLIN, born Stockholm, Sweden, 1957. *Education:* University of Stockholm (LL.B., 1983). Served in District Court of Huddinge, 1984-1986, Svea Court of Appeals, 1986-1987, District Court of Köping, 1987-1988 and District Court of Stockholm, 1988-1989. Authorised as Expert on Swedish Law by Amtsgericht Hamburg, Germany. *Member:* Swedish Bar Association; Swedish Association for Industrial Property Rights; Swedish Association for Legal Practitioners within the Insurance Field; German-Nordic Lawyers Association; Swedish-German Chamber of Commerce. *LANGUAGES:* German, English, French and Swedish. *PRACTICE AREAS:* International Law; Commercial Law; Litigation and Arbitration.

BJÖRN ULVGÅRDEN, born Stockholm, Sweden, 1961. *Education:* University of Stockholm (LL.B., 1987). Served in District Court of Uppsala, 1988-1989. *Member:* Swedish Bar Association. *LANGUAGES:* English, Hungarian and Swedish. *PRACTICE AREAS:* Commercial Litigation; Contract Law; Insolvency Law.

ASSOCIATES

THOMAS NYMAN, born Jukkasjäärvi, Sweden, 1961. *Education:* University of Lund (LL.B., 1988. Served in the County Administrative Court, 1988-1990 and District Court, 1989-1990. Legal Practice at Advokatfirmam Landahl, 1991-1992. *Member:* Swedish Bar Association. *LANGUAGES:* English and Swedish.

STEN GISSELBERG, born Stockholm, Sweden, 1951. *Education:* University of Stockholm (LL.B., 1982); Axel Axison Johnson's Institute for Maritime and Transport Law (1982-1983). Served in District Court of Nyköping, 1983-1985. Legal Counsel: Swedish Association for Road Carriers, 1985-1989; Sirius Industrial & Marine Insurance Co. Ltd., Stockholm, 1989-1992. *Member:* International and Swedish Bar Associations. *LANGUAGES:* English and Swedish. *PRACTICE AREAS:* Transport Law; Maritime Law.

AGNETA MUNTHER, born Sundsvall, Sweden, 1961. *Education:* University of Uppsala (LL.B., 1988). Served in District Court of Solna, 1989-1991. *Member:* Swedish Bar Association. *LANGUAGES:* English and Swedish.

ANN-MARIE WIDEMAR, born Stockholm, Sweden, 1964. *Education:* University of Stockholm (LL.B., 1988); University of Kiel, Germany (LL.M., 1989). Served in District Court of Solna, 1989-1991. *Member:* Nordic-German Lawyers Association. *LANGUAGES:* German, English and Swedish.

(This Listing Continued)

STYRBJÖRN GÄRDE ADVOKATBYRÅ, Stockholm— Continued

URBAN WALL, born Sollentuna, Sweden, 1962. *Education:* University of Stockholm (LL.B., 1989). Legal Practice at the Law Firm of Advokatforum, 1989-1992. *LANGUAGES:* Swedish and English.

JÜRGEN CONZEN, born Stockholm, Sweden, 1964. *Education:* University of Lund (LL.B., 1989); University of Trier, Germany (LL.M., 1990). Served at Karlshamns District Court, 1990-1993. *Member:* German-Nordic Lawyers Association. *LANGUAGES:* German, English and Swedish.

STAFFAN OLSSON, born Gothenburg, Sweden, 1958. *Education:* University of Stockholm (LL.B., 1984); Stockholm School of Economics (B.S., Economics, 1984). Legal Counsel: Swedish Metal Trades Employers' Association, 1984-1986; SIAR-Bossard, 1986-1987; Gyllenhammar & Partners and Mercurius-Group, 1987-1991. Legal Chief Counsel, Probo-Group, 1991-1993. *LANGUAGES:* English, Russian and Swedish.

PEHR JACOBSON, born Stockholm, Sweden, 1952. *Education:* University of Stockholm (LL.B., 1978). Served in District Court of Västervik, 1979-1981. Legal Chief Counsel: District Board of Housing Finance; Swedish Association of Building Proprietors. *Member:* Swedish Society for Construction and Consulting Law. *LANGUAGES:* English and Swedish. *PRACTICE AREAS:* Constructing and Consulting Law; Real Estate Law; Arbitration; Environmental Law.

PER HENDAR, born Eksjö, Sweden, 1956. *Education:* University of Lund (LL.B., 1981). Served in: Public Prosecution Authority of Gothenburg and District Court of Mölndal, 1982-1984; Court of Appeal of Västra Sverige, 1984-1987. Assistant Judge, Court of Appeal, 1985. Associate, Advokatfirman Lindahl, 1987-1989 and Advoaktfirman Vinge, 1989-1994. *Member:* Swedish Bar Association; Association Internationale des Jeunes Avocats (AIJA). *LANGUAGES:* English and Swedish. *PRACTICE AREAS:* Commercial Law; Corporate Law; Insolvency Law.

Languages: Swedish, English, German, French, Finnish, Hungarian, Portuguese and Russian.

(For Biographical data on other Personnel, see Professional Biographies at Gothenburg, Helsingborg, Malmö and Borås Sweden).

BJÖRN GÄRDES, ADVOKATBYRÅ AB

Established in 1987

ENGELBREKTSGATAN 5, 4 TR

P.O. BOX 26035

S-100 41 STOCKHOLM, SWEDEN

Telephone: 468-679 70 95

Telefax: 46 8-611 71 95

Swedish and International Business Law, General Business and Corporate Law, Swedish and International Tax Law, Real Estate Business in Sweden and in Western Europe, Arbitration and Civil Court Cases, Patents, Trade Marks and Designs.

FIRM PROFILE: *The firm is an associated member of Euro American Lawyers Group EALG which includes law firms in Belgium, Cyprus, Denmark, England, France, Germany, Greece, Ireland, Italy, Luxembourg, Norway, Panama, Portugal, Scotland, Spain, Switzerland, USA (Chicago, Denver and New York).*

MEMBER OF FIRM

BJÖRN GÄRDE, born 1947. *Education:* University of Stockholm (LL.M.); University of Zürich (LL.M.). Previous employers: Pestalozzi & Gmür, Zürich; Styrbjörn Gärdes Advokatbyrå AB. *Member:* Swedish Bar Association; International Bar Association; International Fiscal Association. *LANGUAGES:* Swedish, English and German. *PRACTICE AREAS:* Tax Law; International and Swedish Corporate Law; International Law; M & A.

ASSOCIATES

TOMMY BERGQUIST, born 1958. *Education:* University of Lund (LL.M.). District Court, 1983-1985. Previous employer, Styrbjörn Gärdes Advokatbyrå AB. *LANGUAGES:* Swedish and English. *PRACTICE AREAS:* Company Acquisitions; Tax Law.

LEIF RYDSTRÖM, born 1946. *Education:* University of Stockholm (LL.M.). *LANGUAGES:* Swedish and English. *PRACTICE AREAS:* Swedish Corporate Law; Debt Collections; Trademarks.

(This Listing Continued)

GUY R. ASTERIUS, born 1946. *Education:* University of Uppsala (LL.M.). District Court, 1972-1974. Previous employers, Bank Director, PK-banken. General Counsel, Uddeholms AB. *Member:* International Bar Association; Swedish Bar Association. *LANGUAGES:* Swedish, English and German. *PRACTICE AREAS:* International and Swedish Commercial and Corporate Law; Arbitration.

ADVOKATFIRMAN LEVANDER GAWELL

Established in 1976

HOVSLAGARGATAN 5

S-111 48 STOCKHOLM, SWEDEN

Telephone: Int. 46-8-463 88 00

Telefax: Int. 46-8-678 37 35

Falun, Sweden Office: Åsgatan 12, S-791 71. Telephone: 46-23-481 00. Telefax: 46-23-481 80.

Sandviken, Sweden Office: Storgatan 29, S-811 31. Telephone: 46-26-27 54 90. Telefax: 46-26-25 45 22.

Valbonne, France Office: Route des Dolines, Sophia Antipolis, 06560. Telephone: Int. 33-93-65 41 60. Telefax: Int. 33-93-65 40 90.

General Business Law Practice including Tax, Mergers and Acquisitions, Property, Banking, Securities and Financing, Liquidation and Reorganizations, Franchising, Arbitration and Pharmaceuticals.

MEMBERS OF FIRM

KJELL BERGMAN, born Stockholm, Sweden, August 17, 1948. *Education:* University of Stockholm (LL.M., 1974). Associated with the firm, 1977—. Member of this firm, 1980—. *Member:* Swedish Bar Association.

PETER W. BOMAN, born Stockholm, Sweden, November 12, 1947. *Education:* University of Stockholm (LL.M., 1975). Member of this firm, 1985—. *Member:* Swedish Bar Association.

JAN LITBORN, born Alingsås, Sweden, August 8, 1951. *Education:* Stockholm School of Economics, University of Stockholm (LL.M., 1982). Associate, Advokatfirman Sohlberg AB, 1982-1990. Member of this firm, 1990—. *Member:* Swedish Bar Association.

CARL AXEL WREDE, born Lund, Sweden, September 22, 1942. *Education:* University of Lund (LL.M., 1967). *Member:* District Court of Middle Halland, Falkenberg, 1967-1969; District Court of Mölndal, Gothenburg, 1970. Associate: Frykman & Herslow Advokatfirma, 1970; Birger Johanssons Advokatfirma, 1974-1980. General Counsel and Head of Legal Department, KabiVitrum AB, 1981-1987. Member of this firm, 1987—. *Member:* Swedish Bar Association.

Languages: Swedish, English, French and German

GEDDA & EKDAHL ADVOKATBYRÅ

STUREPLAN 2

P.O. BOX 5348

S-102 47 STOCKHOLM, SWEDEN

Telephone: 46 8 6118090

Cable Address: "Affärsjurist"

Telex: 17059 Esox-S

Telefax: 46 8 6113551

Aerospace and Aviation Finance, Banking, Commercial Real Estate, Company and Commercial, Competition, Computers and Software, Construction, Engineering Contracts, Entertainment, Equipment Finance and Leasing, Insolvency, Insurance, Intellectual Property, Litigation, Mergers, Acquisitions and Divestitures, Products Liability, Securities and Stock Exchange Regulation, Taxation.

FIRM PROFILE: *Established in 1917, the services provided by Gedda & Ekdahl cover virtually all the needs of a Swedish company or business client as well as non-Swedish investors in a Swedish enterprise. Clients range from large industries to banking and financial institutions and small and medium size businesses. Legal advice is provided in all areas of commercial, corporate, financial and tax law, including litigation and arbitration in these and related areas.*

Member of ABLE, Associated Business Lawyers in Europe, comprising of law firms with a total of 350 attorneys with offices in Antwerp, Brussels, Hamburg, London, Paris and Stockholm.

(This Listing Continued)

MEMBERS OF FIRM

PER H. GEDDA, born Gothenburg, Sweden, August 28, 1914; admitted, 1946, Sweden. *Education:* University of Uppsala (juris kandidat LL.B.).

HANS HERRLIN, born Ljungarum/Jönköping, June 26, 1919. *Education:* University of Stockholm (juris kandidat LL.B., 1943).

GÖRAN EKDAHL, born Stockholm, Sweden, March 7, 1940; admitted, 1970, Sweden. *Education:* University of Stockholm (juris kandidat LL.B., 1965).

MATS MÜLLERN, born 1944; admitted, 1977, Sweden. *Education:* University of Stockholm (LL.M., 1971).

SÖREN HÄRNBLAD, born Stockholm, Sweden, June 22, 1945; admitted, 1979, Sweden. *Education:* University of Stockholm (juris kandidat LL.B.).

STAFFAN BOSTRÖM, born Lund, Sweden, May 27, 1950; admitted, 1980, Sweden. *Education:* University of Stockholm (juris kandidat LL.B.).

JÖRGEN EKSTRÖM, born Västerås, Sweden, September 19, 1955; admitted, 1986, Sweden. *Education:* University of Uppsala (juris kandidat, LL.B.).

BÖRJE RYHN, born Stockholm, Sweden, April 19, 1956; admitted, 1988, Sweden. *Education:* University of Stockholm (juris kandidat, LL.B., 1981).

ASSOCIATES

MARIE EKSTRÖM, born 1958; admitted, 1989, Sweden. *Education:* University of Stockholm (LL.M., 1983).

MÄRIT E. ELIASSON, born Uppsala, Sweden, September 7, 1955; admitted, 1990, Sweden. *Education:* University of Uppsala (Master of Business Administration, 1980; juris kandidat, LL.M., 1985).

LENNART STEN, born Gothenburg/Partille, March 18, 1959; admitted, 1992, Sweden. *Education:* University of Stockholm (juris kandidat, LL.M., 1987).

GUNNAR ERLAND THURESSON, born Stockholm, Sweden, June 28, 1953. *Education:* University of Uppsala (juris kandidat, LL.M., 1980). *PRACTICE AREAS:* Tax Law.

PIA JANSON, born Linköping, Sweden, March 15, 1961. *Education:* University of Uppsala (juris kandidat, LL.M., 1987).

PETTER HETTA, born Umea, Sweden, April 8, 1963. *Education:* University of Uppsala (juris kandidat, LL.M., 1988); University of Amsterdam (Certificate of Executive in International Relations, 1990).

PETTER NILSSON, born Jönköping, Sweden, July 20, 1962. *Education:* University of Stockholm (juris kandidat, LL.M., 1988).

NIKLAS BJÖRKQVIST, born Södertälje, Sweden, May 21, 1962. *Education:* University of Stockholm (juris kandidat, LL.M., 1987).

Languages: Swedish, English and German.

GERNANDT & DANIELSSON
ADVOKATBYRÅ

NYBROGATAN 11
P.O. BOX 5747
S-114 87 STOCKHOLM, SWEDEN
Telephone: Int. 46-8 670 6600
Telefax: Int. 46-8 662 6101
Telex: 10175 gerlaw

General Swedish and International Law Practice, Litigation and Arbitration.

FIRM PROFILE: *The firm was established in 1992. All of the firm's partners were previously partners of or associated with one of the major Swedish firms. The firm represents Swedish authorities, banks, insurance companies and other enterprises, both foreign and Swedish, of various sizes.*

PARTNERS

JOHAN GERNANDT, born Stockholm, Sweden, 1943. *Education:* University of Stockholm (juris kandidat, LL.B., 1969). Junior Judgeship Fiscal Court of Appeal, 1972-1973. *Member:* Swedish and International Bar Associations; International Fiscal Association. *LANGUAGES:* Swedish, En-

(This Listing Continued)

glish, German and French. *PRACTICE AREAS:* General Commercial Law; Litigation; Arbitration.

KARL-ERIK DANIELSSON, born Stockholm, Sweden, 1946. *Education:* University of Stockholm (juris kandidat, LL.B., 1972). Junior Judgeship Court of Appeal, 1974-1975 and Fiscal Court of Appeal, 1975-1976. *Member:* Swedish Bar Association; International Bar Association. *LANGUAGES:* Swedish and English. *PRACTICE AREAS:* Corporate Law; Banking Law; Litigation; Arbitration.

ANDERS LUNDIN, born Stockholm, Sweden, 1952. *Education:* University of Stockholm (juris kandidat, LL.B., 1977); New York University (Master of Comparative Jurisprudence, M.C.J., 1978). Studies of Maritime Law in New York in the Offices of Haight, Gardner, Poor & Havens, 1978-1979. *Member:* Swedish and International Bar Associations. *LANGUAGES:* Swedish and English. *PRACTICE AREAS:* General Commercial Law; Corporate Law; Licensing Law.

ANDERS WALLÉN, born Stockholm, Sweden, 1956. *Education:* University of Stockholm (juris kandidat, LL.B, 1981). *Member:* Swedish Bar Association. *LANGUAGES:* Swedish and English. *PRACTICE AREAS:* General Commercial Law; Corporate Law; Financing Law.

MATHS HEUMAN, born Ljungby, Sweden, 1954. *Education:* University of Lund (juris kandidat, LL.B., 1980); Scandinavian Institute of Maritime Law, Oslo, 1980. Junior Judgeship, Court of Appeal, 1985-1986. *Member:* Swedish Bar Association. *LANGUAGES:* Swedish and English. *PRACTICE AREAS:* General Commercial Law; Corporate Law.

STEFAN DE GEER, born Kristianstad, Sweden, 1956; admitted, 1983, New York. *Education:* University of Stockholm (juris kandidat, LL.B., 1981); New York University (Master of Comparative Jurisprudence, M.C.J., 1982). Associated with Hale Russell & Gray, New York, 1982-1984, and Reid & Priest, New York, 1984-1985. *Member:* Swedish, American and International Bar Associations. *LANGUAGES:* Swedish and English. *PRACTICE AREAS:* General Commercial Law; Financing Law; Telecommunications Law.

BJÖRN TUDE, born Visby, Sweden, 1956. *Education:* University of Stockholm (juris kandidat, LL.B., 1982). Junior Judgeship Court of Appeal, 1985-1987. *Member:* Swedish Bar Association. *LANGUAGES:* Swedish and English. *PRACTICE AREAS:* General Commercial Law; Corporate Law; Litigation; Arbitration.

ASSOCIATES

LOTTA BOHMAN, born Stockholm, Sweden, 1955. *Education:* University of Stockholm (juris kandidat, LL.B., 1982); Scandinavian Institute of Maritime Law, Oslo (1983). Studies of Maritime Law in New York in the Offices of Haight, Gardner, Poor & Havens, 1982-1983. *Member:* Swedish Bar Association. *LANGUAGES:* Swedish and English. *PRACTICE AREAS:* General Commercial Law; Corporate Law.

JONAS EKLUND, born Stockholm, Sweden, 1958. *Education:* University of Stockholm (juris kandidat, LL.B., 1985). *Member:* Swedish Bar Association. *LANGUAGES:* Swedish and English. *PRACTICE AREAS:* General Commercial Law; Corporate Law.

MARIA SNÖBOHM, born Stockholm, Sweden, 1961. *Education:* University of Stockholm (juris kandidat, LL.B., 1985). *Member:* Swedish Bar Association. *LANGUAGES:* Swedish and English. *PRACTICE AREAS:* General Commercial Law; Corporate Law.

ANNIKA KYRÖLÄINEN, born Kalmar, Sweden, 1961. *Education:* University of Lund (juris kandidat, LL.B., 1985). *LANGUAGES:* Swedish and English. *PRACTICE AREAS:* General Commercial Law; Corporate Law.

LARS NYBERG, born Östersund, Sweden, 1961. *Education:* University of Stockholm (juris kandidat, LL.B., 1987). *LANGUAGES:* Swedish and English. *PRACTICE AREAS:* General Commercial Law; Corporate Law.

CHRISTER DANIELSSON, born Ludvika, Sweden, 1961. *Education:* University of Uppsala (juris kandidat, LL.B., 1990). *LANGUAGES:* Swedish and English. *PRACTICE AREAS:* General Commercial Law; Corporate Law.

DICK LUNDQVIST, born Malmö, Sweden, 1962. *Education:* University of Lund (juris kandidat, LL.B., 1987). *LANGUAGES:* Swedish, English and German. *PRACTICE AREAS:* General Commercial Law; Corporate Law; Financing Law.

PETER WESSMAN, born Malmö, Sweden, 1964. *Education:* University of Stockholm (juris kandidat, LL.B., 1990); College of Europe, Bruges (Master of Advanced European Legal Studies, 1991). Commission of the

(This Listing Continued)

GERNANDT & DANIELSSON ADVOKATBYRÅ, Stockholm—Continued

European Communities, Directorate General for Competition, Brussels, 1991-1992. Author: "Competition Law in Hungary," 15, 1992 World Comp. 4; "Competition sharpens in Sweden," 17, 1993 World Comp. 1. Co-Author: "Handbok om konkurrensreglerna," 1994. *LANGUAGES:* Swedish, English and French. *PRACTICE AREAS:* General Commercial Law; Competition Law; European Community Law.

ÅSA SUNDBERG, born Örebro, Sweden, 1965. *Education:* University of Uppsala (juris kandidat, LL.B., 1990). *LANGUAGES:* Swedish and English.

MANFRED LÖFVENHAFT, born Örebro, Sweden, 1967. *Education:* University of Uppsala (juris kandidat, LL.B., 1993). *LANGUAGES:* Swedish and English.

MATS HUGOSON, born Helsingborg, Sweden, 1967. *Education:* University of Stockholm (juris kandidat, LL.B., 1991). *LANGUAGES:* Swedish and English.

MATS BERGLING, born Hudiksvall, Sweden, 1965. *Education:* University of Stockholm (juris kandidat, LL.B., 1989); Christian Albrechts University, Kiel (LL.M., 1992). Junior Judgeship, Court of Appeal, 1993-1994. *LANGUAGES:* Swedish, English and German.

BOB JOHANSON, born Forserum, Sweden, 1967. *Education:* University of Stockholm (juris kandidat, LL.B., 1992). *LANGUAGES:* Swedish and English.

JAN JENSEN, born Järfälla, Sweden, 1965. *Education:* University of Stockholm (juris kandidat, LL.B., 1993); Harvard Law School (LL.M., 1994). *LANGUAGES:* Swedish, English, German and Finnish.

ORMONDE GOLDIE ADVOKATBYRÅ AB

BIRGER JARLSGATAN 15
P.O. BOX 7730
S-103 95 STOCKHOLM, SWEDEN
Telephone: +46 8 679 52 70
Telecopier: +46 8 611 43 61

London, England Office: 16, Berkeley Street, W1X 5AE. Telephone: +44 71 493 0362; +44 71 491 1010. Telecopier: +44 71 629 0796.

Domestic and International General Corporate and Business Law, Marketing and Antitrust Law, Agency & Distributorships, Civil and Commercial Litigation, Air and Space Law, Arbitration.

ORMONDE GOLDIE, born Grantown-on-Spey, Scotland, September 15, 1926; admitted, 1963, Sweden. *Education:* University of Lund (juris kandidat LL.B., 1953). Served as Prosecutor, 1953. Served in: District Court, 1954-1956; Court of Appeals, 1956-1958. Assistant Judge, Court of Appeals, 1957. Appointed Commander of the British Empire for legal work in connection with Anglo-Swedish matters. *Member:* Swedish Bar Association; International Bar Association. *LANGUAGES:* Swedish, English, German and French. *PRACTICE AREAS:* Domestic and International Corporate Law; Business Law; Marketing Law; Arbitration.

ASSOCIATES

I. H. CATHARINA W. MARKBORN-SÖRÅS, born Lund, Sweden, July 28, 1944. *Education:* University of Lund (juris kandidat, LL.B., 1969). Served in: District Court, 1969-1971; Court of Appeals, 1971-1972. Solicitor in Malmö, 1973-1975 and in Stockholm, 1975-1977. Ministry of Justice, 1978-1983; Swedish Parliament, 1983-1985, Working as Solicitor in Stockholm, 1986—. *Member:* Swedish Bar Association. *LANGUAGES:* Swedish, English, German and French. *PRACTICE AREAS:* Marketing Law; Commercial Law.

G. FREDRIK BRANDEL, born Jönköping, Sweden, January 12, 1957. *Education:* University of Uppsala (juris kandidat, LL.B., 1982); McGill University, Montreal, Canada (Diploma, Air and Space Law, 1983; Master of Laws, LL.M., 1984). Served in: Government Entity of Company Registration, 1984-1985, District Court, 1986-1987. Solicitor, Torsby and Avesta, 1988. Working as Solicitor in Stockholm, 1989—. *Member:* Swedish Bar Association; McGill International Air and Space Law Society. *LANGUAGES:* Swedish and English. *PRACTICE AREAS:* Air and Space Law.

W. JOHN F. GOLDIE, born Stockholm, Sweden, March 18, 1964; admitted, 1990, Sweden. *Education:* University of Lund (juris kandidat,

(This Listing Continued)

LL.B., 1990). Served in: District Court, 1993. *Member:* International Bar Association. *LANGUAGES:* English and Swedish. *PRACTICE AREAS:* Agency and Distributorships.

N. JOHN P. HANE, born Stockholm, Sweden, May 31, 1961. *Education:* University of Stockholm (juris kandidat, LL.B., 1988). Served in: Administrative and District Court, 1988-1990; Court of Appeals, 1991. Assistant Judge, District Court, 1992. Lecturer, International Law, University of Stockholm, 1988-1992. *LANGUAGES:* Swedish and English. *PRACTICE AREAS:* Antitrust Law.

Legal Adviser to British Embassy in Stockholm.

G. GRÖNBERGS ADVOKATBYRÅ AB

Established in 1928

BIRGER JARLSGATAN 16
P.O. BOX 7418
S-103 91 STOCKHOLM, SWEDEN
Telephone: 8 614 49 00
Cable Address: "Jura"
Telex: 11772 Jura S
Telefax: 8 611 04 04

International, Commercial, Corporate, Entertainment, Labour, Tax, Estate and Probate Law, Copyright, Trademark, Litigations in Civil Matters.

MEMBERS OF FIRM

STIG ASSARSON, born Worcester, Mass., U.S.A., April 17, 1918. *Education:* University of Stockholm (jur. kand., LL.B., 1944). *Member:* Swedish Bar Association, 1959.

CLAES FELLÄNDER, born Stockholm, Sweden, March 20, 1939. *Education:* University of Stockholm (jur. kand., LL.B., 1963). *Member:* Swedish Bar Association, 1969.

BENGT-ÅKE FRITJOFSSON, born Uppsala, Sweden, October 22, 1947. *Education:* University of Uppsala (jur. and fil. kand, 1974). *Member:* Swedish Bar Association, 1980.

BERNDT WESTERLUND, born Trosa, Sweden, November 17, 1950. *Education:* University of Stockholm (jur. kand., LL.B., 1976). Chairman of the Board: Pronegus AB; Tricum AB; Swedish subsidiaries of Grapha Holding AG; Sciaky Industries SA. Member of the Board, EssNet AB of Henkel KGaA subsidiaries in Sweden. *Member:* Swedish Bar Association, 1982.

EINAR WANHAINEN, born Luleå, Sweden, October 8, 1953. *Education:* University of Uppsala (jur. kand. LL.B., 1977). Served in District Court and Svea Hovrätt, Court of Appeal, 1978-1981. *Member:* Swedish Bar Association, 1984.

PER ÅGREN, born Gävle, Sweden, May 5, 1956. *Education:* University of Uppsala (jur. kand., LL.B., 1981). *Member:* Swedish Bar Association, 1988.

ROLAND SUNDQVIST, born Arjeplog, Sweden, February 5, 1944. *Education:* University of Uppsala (jur. kand., LL.B., 1970). *Member:* Swedish Bar Association, 1979.

LARS WIKING, born Västanfors, Sweden, January 30, 1961. *Education:* University of Uppsala (jur.kand., LL.M., 1986); University of Oslo (Maritime Law Degree, 1986); University of Minnesota Law School (1986). Service in Swedish Courts 1987-1988. With: Carl Swartling Advokatbyrå, 1988-1990; Mannheimer Swartling Advokatbyrå, 1990. Associated with this firm since 1991. *Member:* Swedish Bar Association, 1992.

ASSOCIATES

BRITT-MARIE FORSBERG, born Göteborg, Sweden, July 8, 1959. *Education:* University of Uppsala (jur. kand., LL.B., 1983). *Member:* Swedish Bar Association, 1990.

ANDERS FLINCK, born Karlstad, Sweden, December 28, 1956. *Education:* University of Uppsala (jur. kand. LL.B., 1984). Corporate Lawyer, Nordbanken, 1988-1992. *Member:* Swedish Bar Association, 1993.

HENRIK BÖRJESSON, born Gällivare, Sweden, July 31, 1959. *Education:* University of Uppsala (jur.kand., LL.B., 1986). *Member:* Swedish Bar Association, 1993.

LENA MELINDER, born Falun, Sweden, July 11, 1957. *Education:* University of Uppsala (jur. kand., LL.B., 1983).

(This Listing Continued)

MATS JANSSON, born Vansbro, Sweden, November 23, 1961. *Education:* University of Stockholm (jur. kand., LL.B., 1990).

LARS LUNDBERG, born Hudiksvall, Sweden, June 29, 1965. *Education:* University of Uppsala (jur. kand., LL.M., 1991); University of Minnesota Law School (1990). Service in District Court, Uppsala, 1991-1993.

Languages: Swedish, English and German.

ADVOKATFIRMAN HÄGGLUND & RAMM-ERICSON KB

Established in 1983

KUNGSGATAN 6

P.O. BOX 1729

S-111 87 STOCKHOLM, SWEDEN

Telephone: 248110; Int + 46 8 248110

Telefax: 214911; Int + 46 8 214911

General Business Law Practice, Trademark and Patent Law, Domestic and International Licensing, International Legal Transactions, Banking, Arbitration, Real Estate, Construction Law, Insolvency, Liquidation and Reorganizations.

MEMBERS OF FIRM

KENT HÄGGLUND, born Stockholm Sweden, January 18, 1947. *Education:* University of Stockholm (LL.B., 1975). Work at the National Patent and Registration Office, Company department, 1974-1976. Court work, Stockholm District Court, 1976-1978. Associated with Advokatfirman Rindborg, 1978-1982. Member of this firm since 1983. *Member:* Swedish Bar Association; Swedish Association for Intellectual Property Law; International Bar Association; Inter-Pacific Bar Association. *PRACTICE AREAS:* General Corporate Law; Mergers and Acquisitions; Intellectual Property.

MICHAEL RAMM-ERICSON, born Stockholm, Sweden, April 13, 1946. *Education:* University of Stockholm and Lund (LL.B., 1974). Court work, Sollentuna District Court, 1974-1975. Associated with Hedberg & Runeland Advokatbyrå, 1975-1976. Legal counsel at the Stockholm Chamber of Commerce, 1977-1981. Associated with Advokatfirman Rindborg, 1981-1982. Member of this firm since 1983. *Member:* Swedish Bar Association; International Bar Association; International Law Association; ICC Commission on Taxation. *PRACTICE AREAS:* Business Law; Commercial Law; Company Law; Intellectual Property; Litigation.

LARS EHRSTEDT, born Sundsvall, Sweden, January 19, 1953. *Education:* University of Lund (LL.B., 1979). Court work, Nyköping District Court and Svea Appeal Court, 1980-1983. Associated with this firm since 1983 and member of the firm since 1986. *Member:* Swedish Bar Association; International Bar Association; Swedish Association for Intellectual Property Law. *PRACTICE AREAS:* Bankruptcy; Business Law; Company Law; Computers and Software; Litigation.

ULF MÅRTENSSON, born Malmö, Sweden, August 11, 1955. *Education:* University of Lund (B.Sc., 1978; LL.B., 1980). Court work, Stockholm District Court and Svea Appeal Court, 1980-1984. Associated with this firm since 1984 and member of the firm since 1988. *Member:* Swedish Bar Association. *PRACTICE AREAS:* Bankruptcy; Business Law; Company Law; Corporate Law; Securities.

CLAES-GÖRAN WESTERBERG, born Stockholm, Sweden, June 22, 1956. *Education:* University of Stockholm (LL.B., 1981). Court work, Katrineholm District Court, 1982-1984. Associated with Friberg & Wallander Advokatbyrå, 1984-1988. Associated with this firm since 1989 and member of the firm since 1990. *Member:* Swedish Bar Association. *PRACTICE AREAS:* Bankruptcy; Business Law; Company Law; Labor and Employment; Securities.

PETER NÄSLUND, born Helsingborg, Sweden, October 19, 1962. *Education:* University of Lund (LL.B., 1987). Court work, Stenungsund District Court, 1987-1990. Associated with this firm since 1990 and member of the firm since 1993. *Member:* Swedish Bar Association. *PRACTICE AREAS:* Bankruptcy; Business Law; Commercial Law; Company Law; Corporate Law.

BO LINANDER, born Lund, Sweden, May 24, 1955. *Education:* University of Lund (LL.B., 1980). Court work, Hässleholm District Court, 1981-1983; Fiscal Court of Appeal in Gothenburg, 1984; Gota Appeal Court, 1985. Associated with Friberg & Wallander Advokatbyrå, 1986-1989. Legal counsel at the Swedish Construction Federation, 1989-1993.

(This Listing Continued)

Member of this firm from September 1993. *Member:* Swedish Bar Association. *PRACTICE AREAS:* Antitrust and Trade Regulation; Bankruptcy; Construction Law; Property; Zoning, Planning and Land Use.

ASSOCIATES

PETER SJÖLUND, born Örnsköldsvik, Sweden, October 12, 1961. *Education:* University of Uppsala (LL.B., 1987); University of Minnesota Law School (J.D., 1989). Associated with this firm since 1989. *Member:* New York State Bar. *PRACTICE AREAS:* General Corporate Law; Mergers and Acquisitions; Agency and Distributorships; European Community and Competition Law.

PER MILDNER, born Lund, Sweden, September 10, 1965. *Education:* University of Lund (LL.B., 1989). Court work, Sölvesborg District Court, 1990. Associated with this firm since 1991. *PRACTICE AREAS:* Company Law; Contracts; European Community Law; Labor and Employment; Litigation.

ULF MULLO, born Gävle, Sweden, April 18, 1964. *Education:* University of Uppsala (LL.M., 1989). Court work, Umeå District Court, 1990-1992. Associated with this firm since 1992. *PRACTICE AREAS:* Bankruptcy; Business Law; Commercial law; Company Law; Property.

PETER LÖHR, born Sigtuna, Sweden, September 2, 1964. *Education:* University of Stockholm (LL.M., 1992). Associated with this firm since 1992. *PRACTICE AREAS:* Bankruptcy; General Business Law; General Corporate Law; Debtor and Creditor; General Taxation.

FREDRIK JÄRUND, born Umeå, Sweden, October 31, 1962. *Education:* University of Lund (LL.M., 1990). Court work, Huddinge District Court, 1990-1993. Associated with this firm since 1993. *PRACTICE AREAS:* General Corporate Law; Property Law; Insolvency and Bankruptcy Law.

HAMILTON & CO. ADVOKATBYRÅ

JAKOBS TORG 3

P.O. BOX 715

S-101 33 STOCKHOLM, SWEDEN

Telephone: +468-231075 (Day); +468-231079 (Night)

Telefax: +468-202946

Växjö, Sweden Office: Kungsgatan 4, Box 124, S-351 04. Telephone: +46470-45190. Telefax: +46470-47990.

London, England Office: 29, Abingdon Road, W8 6 AH. Telephone: +4471-938 5408. Telex: 291802 MDAC G. Telefax: +4471-938 1649.

General Commercial and Corporate Law, Insolvency and Bankruptcy Law, Liquidation, Banking and Financing, Corporate Matters, Composition and Debtors Reconstruction, European Community Law, International Law, International Law of Properties, Laws on Real Property and Tenancy Right, Local Government Law, Family Law, Arbitration, Incorporeal Property Law, General Legal Practice, Taxation, Insurance and Reinsurance Law, Creditors Right, Litigation.

MEMBERS OF FIRM

LARS WENNE, born Stockholm, Sweden, 1951; admitted, 1983, Sweden. *Education:* University of Uppsala (B.Sc., Econ, 1974; LL.B., 1978). Vice Chief Tax Inspector, 1975-1978. Court Work, 1978-1980. Chairman of the Board, Edske Bruk AB, 1988—. *Member:* Swedish Bar Association (Secretary, 1980-1983); International Bar Association. *LANGUAGES:* Swedish and English. *PRACTICE AREAS:* Commercial and Corporate Law; Real Property and Tenancy Right; Arbitration; General Practice; Taxation; Insurance and Reinsurance Law; Banking and Financing; Insolvency and Bankruptcy Law; Composition and Debtors Reconstruction.

DAG DI MEO, born Stockholm, Sweden, 1949; admitted, 1984, Sweden. *Education:* University of Stockholm (LL.B., 1978). Court Work, City Court and Court of Appeal, 1979-1981. County Division Police Commissioner, 1981-1982. *Member:* Swedish Bar Association; International Bar Association. *LANGUAGES:* Swedish, English and Italian. *PRACTICE AREAS:* Banking and Financing; Insolvency and Bankruptcy Law; Credit Law; Commercial and Corporate Law; Arbitration; Litigation.

CHRISTOFFER HAMILTON, born Stockholm, Sweden, 1952; admitted, 1987, Sweden. *Education:* University of Uppsala (LL.B. and B.A., 1980). *Member:* Swedish Bar Association. *LANGUAGES:* Swedish, English and French. *PRACTICE AREAS:* Company Law; Insolvency and Bankruptcy Law; Liquidation.

LARS-ERIC GUSTAFSSON, born Fagerhult, Sweden, 1956; admitted, 1988, Sweden. *Education:* University of Uppsala (B.Sc. Business Adminis-

(This Listing Continued)

HAMILTON & CO. ADVOKATBYRÅ, Stockholm— Continued

tration, 1980); University of Stockholm (LL.B., 1983). With, J M Byggnads & Fastighets AB, 1979-1981. Ackordscentralen Composition Center of Creditors Organization in Stockholm, 1983-1985. *Member:* Swedish Bar Association. *LANGUAGES:* Swedish, English and French. *PRACTICE AREAS:* Credit Law; Insolvency and Bankruptcy Law; Business Reorganization with Creditors.

PETER NORDFELDT, born Stockholm, Sweden, 1945; admitted, 1979, Sweden. *Education:* University of Lund (LL.B., 1972). Court Work, City Court Work, Court of Appeal, 1972-1977. With: Gunnar Reinholtz Advokatbyrå, Växjö, 1977-1985; Advokatbyrån Nordfeldt & Pyrell HB, 1985-1989. *Member:* Swedish Bar Association. *LANGUAGES:* Swedish and English. *PRACTICE AREAS:* Commercial and Corporate Law; Construction Law; Litigation and Arbitration.

JAN PYRELL, born St. Jät, Sweden, 1949; admitted, 1984, Sweden. *Education:* University of Lund (LL.B., 1976). Court Work, City Court, Court of Appeal, 1976-1982. With, Allmänna Advokatbyrån i Växjö, 1982-1984. Advokatbyrån Nordfeldt & Pyrell HB, 1985-1989. Chairman of the Board, Trensums Musteri AB, 1989—. Member of the Board: Olle Svenssons Partiaffär, 1989—; Blekinge Invest AB, 1988—. *Member:* Swedish Bar Association. *LANGUAGES:* Swedish and English. *PRACTICE AREAS:* Insolvency Law; Contract Law; Business Law.

MICHAEL LEVIN, born Stockholm, Sweden, 1953; admitted, 1989, Sweden. *Education:* University of Stockholm (LL.B., 1984). With, The Building Committee of Private Commerce and Industry in Sweden, 1982-1985. *Member:* Swedish Bar Association. *LANGUAGES:* Swedish and English. *PRACTICE AREAS:* Real Estate Law; Commercial and Corporate Law; Insolvency and Bankruptcy Law.

ASSOCIATES

HANS RENMAN, born Gäddede, Sweden, 1961; admitted, 1992, Sweden. *Education:* University of Stockholm (LL.M., 1986). Court Work, 1987-1989. *Member:* Swedish Bar Association; Association Internationale des Jeunes Avocats (AIJA). *LANGUAGES:* Swedish and English. *PRACTICE AREAS:* Commercial and Corporate Law; Arbitration; Banking and Financing; Insolvency and Bankruptcy Law; Litigation.

THOMAS NYGREN, born Norrköping, Sweden, 1962; admitted, 1993, Sweden. *Education:* University of Uppsala (LL.M., 1986). Court Work, City Court and Court of Appeals, 1987-1990. Junior Judge, 1990. *Member:* Swedish Bar Association; Association Internationale des Jeunes Avocats (AIJA). *LANGUAGES:* Swedish, English and German. *PRACTICE AREAS:* Commercial and Corporate Law; Insurance and Reinsurance Law; Banking and Financing; Insolvency and Bankruptcy Law; Composition and Debtors Reconstruction; Creditors Rights; Litigation.

JOHAN LINDER, born Södertälje, 1962; admitted, 1994, Sweden. *Education:* University of Stockholm (LL.M., 1988). Court Work, 1988-1990. *Member:* Swedish Bar Association. *LANGUAGES:* Swedish and English. *PRACTICE AREAS:* Insolvency and Bankruptcy Law.

PER NILSSON, born Ängelholm, Sweden, 1962. *Education:* University of Stockholm (LL.M., 1988). Court Work: Administrative Court and City Court, 1988-1991. *LANGUAGES:* Swedish and English. *PRACTICE AREAS:* Commercial and Corporate Law; Insolvency and Bankruptcy Law; Liquidation.

JENS MJÖBERG, born Växjö, Sweden, 1959. *Education:* University of Lund (LL.B., 1987). Court Work, City Court Work, Court of Appeal, 1987-1991. *LANGUAGES:* English. *PRACTICE AREAS:* Commercial Law; Insolvency Law; Family Law.

LARS BÄCKMAN, born Undersåker, Sweden, 1961. *Education:* University of Stockholm (LL.M., 1992). *LANGUAGES:* Swedish, English and French. *PRACTICE AREAS:* Commercial and Corporate Law; Insolvency and Bankruptcy Law; Creditors Rights.

PETER HALONEN, born Ängelholm, Sweden, 1963. *Education:* University of Lund (LL.M., 1989). *LANGUAGES:* Swedish and English. *PRACTICE AREAS:* Commercial and Corporate Law; Insolvency and Bankruptcy Law; Creditors Rights.

ULRICA CEDERBRATT, born Uddevalla, Sweden, 1965. *Education:* University of Lund (LL.M., 1991). Court Work, City Court, 1991-1993. *LANGUAGES:* Swedish and English. *PRACTICE AREAS:* Commercial and Corporate Law; Insolvency and Bankruptcy Law; Creditors Rights.

(This Listing Continued)

Languages: English, German, French and Italian.

REFERENCES: Götabanken; Skandinaviska Enskilda Banken; Svenska Handelsbanken; Östgötabanken; Sparbankernas Bank; Skanska Banken; PK-Banken; Swedish Savings Banks Association-Stockholm; Stockholm Chamber of Commerce; The Swedish American Chamber of Commerce-New York; The British-Swedish Chamber of Commerce in Sweden.

HEDBERG & CO. ADVOKATBYRÅ AB

Established in 1972

STRANDVÄGEN 5 A
114 51 STOCKHOLM, SWEDEN
Telephone: 660 95 70
Telex: 19741 Hedberg S
Telefax: 667 31 35

General Business Law Practice, Corporation, Mergers and Acquisitions, Antitrust, Marketing Practices Law, Intellectual Property, Environmental Law, Securities and Financing, Insurance and Reinsurance, Insurance Law, Litigation and Arbitration.

MEMBERS OF FIRM

JAN O. HEDBERG, born Stockholm, Sweden, January 6, 1939. *Education:* University of Stockholm (juris kandidat, LL.M., 1965); Södra Roslags District Court (1965-1967). Associated with Wetter & Swartling Advokatbyrå, 1968-1972. Member, Advisory Board, International and Comparative Law Center, The Southwestern Legal Foundation, Dallas, Texas, 1989—. Chairman, Board of Directors, Local Subsidiaries of Otis Elevator Company, 1976—, Colgate Palmolive Company, 1986—, The Reader's Digest Association Inc., 1980—, American Home Products Corporation, 1989—, Microsoft Corporation, 1986-1992, National Semiconductor Corporation, 1972—, Hitachi Data Systems, 1981— and Asahi Optical Co. Ltd., 1982—. *Member:* Swedish Bar Association. *LANGUAGES:* Swedish and English. *PRACTICE AREAS:* Corporate Law; Mergers and Acquisitions; Advertising and Marketing; Consumer Law; Reinsurance Law; Arbitration.

STEFAN BRANDT, born Stockholm, Sweden, July 8, 1955. *Education:* University of Stockholm (juris kandidat, LL.M., 1982); Stockholm District Court (1982-1985). Associated with Advokatfirman Vinge, London, 1985-1987. *Member:* Swedish Bar Association; International League of Competition. *LANGUAGES:* Swedish and English. *PRACTICE AREAS:* Advertising and Marketing; Antitrust and Competition; Intellectual Property; Environmental Law; Litigation and Arbitration.

ASSOCIATES

JIM K. BLOMQVIST, born Stockholm, Sweden, September 24, 1959. *Education:* University of Uppsala (juris kandidat, LL.M., 1986); University of Minnesota Law School (J.D., 1988). Associate, Oppenheimer Wolff and Donnely, Minneapolis, Minnesota, 1988-1990. *Member:* Minnesota State and American Bar Associations; Swedish Bar Association. *LANGUAGES:* Swedish and English. *PRACTICE AREAS:* General Business Law; Labour Law; Litigation and Arbitration.

OLA WÄLIMAA, born Boden, Sweden, November 7, 1966. *Education:* University of Minnesota Law School, 1989, University of Uppsala (juris kandidat, LLM., 1992). Enköping District Court, 1992. *LANGUAGES:* Swedish and English. *PRACTICE AREAS:* General Business Law; Antitrust; Intellectual Property.

STEFAN BESSMAN, born Danderyd, Sweden, December 23, 1962. *Education:* University of Stockholm (juris kandidat, LL.M., 1989). Sollentuna District Court, 1989-1992, Svea Court of Appeal, 1992. *LANGUAGES:* Swedish and English. *PRACTICE AREAS:* General Business Law; Insurance and Reinsurance Law; Bankruptcy; Litigation and Arbitration.

MATS UEBEL, born Uppsala, Sweden, July 16, 1961. *Education:* University of Stockholm (juris kandidat, LL.M., 1990). Gävle District Court, 1990-1992, National Board of Consumer Policies/the Consumer Ombudsman's Office, 1988-1990, Secretary, the Competition Commission, 1990, Svea Court of Appeal, 1992-1993. *LANGUAGES:* Swedish, English and German. *PRACTICE AREAS:* General Business Law; Advertising and Marketing; Environmental Law; Antitrust.

OF COUNSEL

ERIK NEREP, born Stockholm, Sweden, December 12, 1951. *Education:* University of Stockholm (juris kandidat, LL.M., 1976); New York University School of Law (MCJ, 1977); University of Stockholm (Juris Doktor, J.S.D., 1982). Assistant Professor, International Market Law, University of Stockholm, 1979-1982. Professor, International Trade Law,

(This Listing Continued)

Stockholm School of Economics, 1985—. Author: "Extraterritorial Control of Competition under International Law," Stockholm, 1982. Contributor to World Competition Law, Matthew Bender, 1982 (Swedish Competition Laws). *LANGUAGES:* Swedish, English and German.

Languages: Swedish, English and German.

REPRESENTATIVE CLIENTS: Colgate-Palmolive Co.; Microsoft Corp.; Asahi Optical Co. Ltd. (Pentax); United Technologies Group (Otis Elevator, Pratt & Whitney, Sikorsky, Hamilton Standard, UTC Automotive); National Semiconductor Corp.; Hitachi Data Systems; National Advanced Systems Inc.; American Home Products Corporation; The Reader's Digest Association Inc.; Brunswick Corp.; Advanced Technology Laboratories; Swiss Reinsurance Co.; Munich Reinsurance Co.; Cigna Reinsurance Co.; Trade Indemnity Pic.

HELLSTRÖM & PARTNERS
ADVOKATBYRÅ HB

KUNGSGATAN 33
P.O. BOX 7305
S-103 90 STOCKHOLM, SWEDEN
Telephone: +46 8 220900
Telefax: +46 8 204090

Corporate Finance, Banking and Capital Markets, Company Law, Commercial Law, Admiralty Law and Law related to Carriage by Sea, Air, Road and Rail, Intellectual Property Law, Litigation.

MEMBERS OF FIRM

PETER SEDEROWSKY, born March 28, 1957. *Education:* University of Lund (LL.B., 1982); University of California at Berkeley-Boalt Hall (LL.M., 1984). Served in District Court 1984-1986. Fulbright Fellow. Author: "The U.S. Tax Reform"; The Swedish Tax Review, 1987; "Insider Trading in Sweden"; International Business Lawyer, 1991; "Ending Share Restrictions", International Financial Law Review, 1991. Previously legal counsel with Swedish Match AB and Stora Kopparbergs Bergslags AB, and with Advokatfirman Vinge. *Member:* Swedish Bar Association.

HANS LILJEBLAD, born February 26, 1957. *Education:* University of Oslo Scandinavian Institute of Maritime Law (1983); University of Stockholm (LL.B., 1985); New York University (Studies in Maritime Law, 1986). Served in Taxation Court, 1986-1987 and in District Court, 1987-1988. Author: "Legal Liabilities of Swedish Ports," Swedish Shipping Gazette, 1994. Previously with, Messrs Healy & Baillie, New York. *Member:* Swedish Bar Association.

MATS HELLSTRÖM, born March 7, 1959. *Education:* University of Stockholm (LL.B., 1984); University of Sorbonne, Paris (1984). Served in District Court, 1986-1988. Previously with EFTA, Geneva; the International Chamber of Commerce (ICC), Paris and Advokatfirman Carler, Paris. *Member:* Swedish Bar Association.

ASSOCIATES

THOMAS EVERS, born November 22, 1957. *Education:* University of Lund (LL.B., 1984). Served in District Court, 1984-1987 and Administrative Court of Appeal, 1987-1988. Previously legal counsel with Kooperativa förbundet (KF), ekonomisk förening, and with Advokatfirman Delphi.

HANS RUDBERG, born August 30, 1960. *Education:* Stockholm University (LL.B., 1989). Served in District Court (1989-1992).

JONAS ARMTOFT, born August 13, 1962. *Education:* University of Lund (LL.B., 1989); University of London, QMW College (LL.M., 1993). Served in District Court, 1989-1992.

ANDERS LUNDBERG, born February 14, 1962. *Education:* University of Minnesota Law School (1989); Uppsala University (LL.B., 1991); University of Aberdeen (LL.M., 1994). Served in County Administrative Court, 1991-1993. Author: "Compliance with the Obligations of the Berne Convention - Some Questions Raised by the United States Implementation of Article 6bis," Nordic Intellectual Property Law Review, 1993.

BENGT OLOVSSON, born April 18, 1951. *Education:* University of Lund (LL.B., 1991); University of California at Davis, School of Law (1988-1990); London School of Economics and Political Science (1993-1994). Served in District Court, 1991-1993. *Member:* State Bar of California; American Bar Association.

(This Listing Continued)

JOAKIM BERGSTRÖM, born November 21, 1960. *Education:* University of Stockholm (LL.B., 1985); Georgetown University Law School (LL.M., 1986). Fulbright Fellow. Served in District Court, 1986-1988, 1993-1994.

Languages: Swedish, French and English.

HÖKERBERG & SÖDERQVIST
ADVOKATBYRÅ AB

Established in 1985
KUNGSGATAN 54
P.O. BOX 3206
S-103 64 STOCKHOLM, SWEDEN
Telephone: +46 8 790 50 90
Telefax: +46 8 790 30 90

Securities, Banking and Financial Law, Insolvency Law, General Commercial and Corporate Law, Arbitration and Litigation, Mergers and Acquisitions, Insurance Law, Labour Law.

FIRM PROFILE: Hökerberg & Söderqvist Advokatbyrå AB is one of the leading commercial law firms in Sweden, specializing in Securities, Banking and Financial Law as well as Insolvency Law. Within the practice areas of Securities, Banking and Financial Law, the firm represents several of the financial sector's leading banks, brokerage firms, insurance companies and investors. With many years of experience in Insolvency Law, the firm's attorneys are regularly appointed as trustees in bankruptcy by the district courts in Stockholm and throughout Sweden.

PARTNERS

KLAS HÖKERBERG, born 1944. *Education:* University of Stockholm (LL.M., 1969). District Court, 1970-1972. *Member:* Swedish Bar Association. *LANGUAGES:* Swedish, English and French. *PRACTICE AREAS:* Insolvency Law; Mergers and Acquisitions; General Commercial and Corporate Law.

LARS SÖDERQVIST, born 1953. *Education:* University of Stockholm (LL.M., 1978). District Court, 1979-1981. *Member:* Swedish Bar Association. *LANGUAGES:* Swedish and English. *PRACTICE AREAS:* Securities; Banking and Financial Law; Insolvency Law; General Commercial and Corporate Law; Mergers and Acquisitions; Insurance Law.

ERIK STRÖMQVIST, born 1952. *Education:* University of Stockholm (LL.M., 1980). District Court, 1980-1982. *Member:* Swedish Bar Association. *LANGUAGES:* Swedish, English and German. *PRACTICE AREAS:* Insolvency Law; Mergers and Acquisitions; General Commercial and Corporate Law.

CHARLOTTE SANDART, born 1955. *Education:* University of Stockholm (LL.M., 1980). District Court, 1980-1984. *Member:* Swedish Bar Association. *LANGUAGES:* Swedish and English. *PRACTICE AREAS:* Securities; Banking and Financial Law.

MIKAEL CELVIN, born 1957. *Education:* University of Stockholm (LL.M., 1986). District Court, 1986-1988. *Member:* Swedish Bar Association. *LANGUAGES:* Swedish and English. *PRACTICE AREAS:* Securities; Banking and Financial Law; Insolvency Law; General Commercial and Corporate Law; Mergers and Acquisitions.

ULF BLOMMÉ, born 1958. *Education:* University of Uppsala (LL.M., 1983). County Administrative Court, 1983-1986. Administrative Court of Appeal, 1986-1987. *Member:* Swedish Bar Association. *LANGUAGES:* Swedish and English. *PRACTICE AREAS:* Insolvency Law; Mergers and Acquisitions; General Commercial and Corporate Law; Tax Law.

PER ASPENDAL, born 1958. *Education:* University of Stockholm (LL.M., 1986). District Court, 1987-1989. *Member:* Swedish Bar Association. *LANGUAGES:* Swedish and English. *PRACTICE AREAS:* Insolvency Law; General Commercial and Corporate Law.

DAN ENGSTRÖM, born 1960. *Education:* University of Uppsala (LL.M., 1986). District Court, 1987-1988. *Member:* Swedish Bar Association. *LANGUAGES:* Swedish and English. *PRACTICE AREAS:* Arbitration and Litigation; General Commercial and Corporate Law; Banking and Financial Law; Insurance Law; Labour Law.

(This Listing Continued)

HÖKERBERG & SÖDERQVIST ADVOKATBYRÅ AB,
Stockholm—Continued

ASSOCIATES

RICHARD BERLIN, born 1958. *Education:* University of Stockholm (LL.M., 1987). District Court, 1987-1989. Court of Appeal, 1989-1991 and 1992-1993. *LANGUAGES:* Swedish and English. *PRACTICE AREAS:* Arbitration and Litigation; Securities and Financial Law.

TORSTEN LAVETT, born 1949. *Education:* University of Stockholm (LL.M., 1990). District Court, 1990-1992. *LANGUAGES:* Swedish and English. *PRACTICE AREAS:* Insolvency Law; General Commercial and Corporate Law.

MAX BJÖRKBOM, born 1966. *Education:* University of Stockholm (LL.M., 1990). District Court, 1990-1992. *LANGUAGES:* Swedish and English. *PRACTICE AREAS:* Litigation; Securities Law; General Commercial and Corporate Law.

BILL KRONQVIST, born 1963. *Education:* University of Stockholm (LL.M., 1990). District Court, 1991-1992. *LANGUAGES:* Swedish and English. *PRACTICE AREAS:* Insolvency Law; General Commercial and Corporate Law; Litigation.

ELISABETH IVARSSON, born 1966. *Education:* University of Uppsala (LL.M., 1990). District Court, 1990-1992. *LANGUAGES:* Swedish and English. *PRACTICE AREAS:* Securities; Banking and Financial Law.

SVANTE OLOFSSON, born 1961. *Education:* University of Uppsala (LL.M., 1989). District Court, 1989-1991. *LANGUAGES:* Swedish and English. *PRACTICE AREAS:* Insolvency Law; General Commercial and Corporate Law.

MAGNUS GRÖNDAL, born 1963. *Education:* University of Uppsala (LL.M., 1989); Universiteit van Amsterdam, 1991-1992. District Court, 1989-1991 and 1992-1993. *LANGUAGES:* Swedish and English. *PRACTICE AREAS:* Securities; Banking and Financial Law; General Commercial and Corporate Law.

EVA SJÖBERG, born 1964. *Education:* University of Stockholm (LL.M., 1991). District Court, 1991-1993. *LANGUAGES:* Swedish and English. *PRACTICE AREAS:* Securities; Banking and Financial Law.

NICLAS NELSON, born 1964. *Education:* University of Lund (LL.M., 1989). District Court, 1990-1992. *LANGUAGES:* Swedish, English and German. *PRACTICE AREAS:* Securities; Banking and Financial Law.

ÅSA KJELLANDER, born 1965. *Education:* University of Uppsala (LL.M., 1991). District Court, 1991-1993. *LANGUAGES:* Swedish, English and French. *PRACTICE AREAS:* Securities; Banking and Financial Law.

JÖRGEN BERGLUND, born 1962. *Education:* University of Uppsala (LL.M., 1989). District Court, 1990-1992. Court of Appeal, 1992-1994. *LANGUAGES:* Swedish and English. *PRACTICE AREAS:* Securities; Banking and Financial Law; Litigation.

ÅSA ENGSTRÖM, born 1963. *Education:* University of Stockholm (LL.M., 1990); University of London (LL.M., 1993). District Court, 1991-1992 and 1993-1994. *LANGUAGES:* Swedish, English and French. *PRACTICE AREAS:* Securities; Banking and Financial Law; Labour Law.

JOHNSSON & JOHNSON ADVOKATBYRÅ AB

Established in 1989

STRANDVÄGEN 5 A
114 51 STOCKHOLM, SWEDEN
Telephone: +46 8 665 90 70
Telex: 19735 JLAW S
Telefax: +46 8 665 08 55

General Business Law Practice, Corporation, International Trade, Securities, Financing, EEC Law, Arbitration, Admiralty Law related to Carriage by Sea, Air, Road and Rail, Marine and Transport Insurance, all Swedish courts.

FIRM PROFILE: Johnsson & Johnson Advokatbyrå was established in 1989. It offers a comprehensive legal service to commercial clients, while concentrating its expertise in the areas of corporation, financing and banking, transportation, commercial property, international trade and arbitration. From its inception the firm has always had strong international con-

(This Listing Continued)

---

nections with an emphasis on Europe/North America. Although the firm works closely with a network of law firms in commercial centers of the world, it is not tied to any formal association of law firms.

MEMBERS OF FIRM

BENGT Å. JOHNSSON, born Kristianstad, Sweden, February 11, 1945. *Education:* University of Lund (juris kandidat, LL.B., 1972); Studies of Maritime Law and Marine Insurance at Scandinavian Institute of Maritime Law, Oslo (1971), and in the Offices of Sinclair, Roche & Temperley; Ernest Robert Lindley & Sons, London (1974). Associated with Mannheimer & Zetterlöf, 1975. Co-author "Aircraft Finance, Registration, Security & Enforcement," 1989. *Member:* Swedish Bar Association; Interpacific Bar Association; Union Internationale des Avocats; Association Suisse de l'Arbitrage. *LANGUAGES:* Swedish, English and French.

CLAES JOHNSON, born Linköping, Sweden, May 20, 1951. *Education:* University of Uppsala (juris kandidat, LL.B., 1976); Malmö District Court, (1977-1979); Southwestern Legal Foundation, Dallas (1982). *Member:* Swedish Bar Association. *LANGUAGES:* Swedish and English.

JOHAN HESSIUS, born Örnsköldsvik, Sweden, February 10, 1958. *Education:* University of Stockholm (juris kandidat, LL.B., 1985); Södra Roslags District Court (1983-1985); Southwestern Legal Foundation, Dallas (1987). *Member:* Swedish Bar Association. *LANGUAGES:* Swedish and English.

ASSOCIATES

OLOF RAGMARK, born Norrköping, Sweden, February 22, 1958. *Education:* University of Uppsala (juris kandidat LL.B., 1985); Studies of Maritime Law and Marine Insurance at Scandinavian Institute of Maritime Laws, Oslo (1983); District Court of Linköping (1985-1987); Svea Court of Appeal (1987-1988). *Member:* Swedish Bar Association. *LANGUAGES:* Swedish and English.

TOM NYGREN, born Gävle, June 8, 1959. *Education:* University of Stockholm (juris kandidat, LL.B., 1985); Studies of Maritime Law and Marine Insurance at Scandinavian Institute of Maritime Law, Oslo (1984); Sollentuna District Court (1986-1987); Svea Court of Appeal (1988-1989). *Member:* Swedish Bar Association. *LANGUAGES:* Swedish and English.

SUZANNE HENRIKSSON, born Aaland, Finland, January 12, 1948. *Education:* University of Stockholm (juris kandidat, LL.B., 1988); Stockholm District Court (1988-1990). *Member:* Swedish Bar Association. *LANGUAGES:* Swedish, English and German.

MARTIN AXELSSON, born Danderyd, Sweden, September 30, 1966. *Education:* University of Stockholm (juris kandidat, LL.B., 1991); District Court of Nyköping (1992-1994). *LANGUAGES:* Swedish, English and French.

Languages: Swedish, English, French and German.

ADVOKATFIRMAN LAGERLÖF

STOCKHOLM, SWEDEN

(See Lagerlöf & Leman)

LAGERLÖF & LEMAN

STRANDVÄGEN 7A
P.O. BOX 5402
S-114 84 STOCKHOLM, SWEDEN
Telephone: Int. 46-8-665 66 00
Telefax: Int. 46-8-667 68 83
Telex: 17715 Laglaw S

Gothenburg, Sweden Office: Västra Hamngatan 24, P.O. Box 2252, S-403 14, Gothenburg. Telephone: Int. 46-31-17 10 00. Telefax: Int. 46-31-13 56 62. Telefax Maritime department: Int. 46-31-11 65 37.

Malmö, Sweden Office: Stortorget 8, S-211 34, Malmö. Telephone: Int. 46-40-704 50. Telefax: Int. 46-40-97 19 17.

London, England Office: Royex House, Aldermanbury Square, London EC2V 7HR. Telephone: Int. 44-171-606 1715. Telefax: Int. 44-171-600 1718.

Berlin, Germany Office: Meinekestrasse 13, D-10719 Berlin. Telephone: Int. 49-30-884 710. Telefax: Int. 49-30-882 4852.

(This Listing Continued)

Paris, France Office: 87 Avenue Kléber, F-75116 Paris. Telephone: 33-1-45 05 1208. Telefax: 33-1-47 55 0975.

New York, N.Y. Office: 712 Fifth Avenue, 30th Floor, New York, N.Y. 10019-4102 U.S.A. Telephone: Int. 1-212-801-3450. Telefax: Int. 1-212-801-3455.

Corporate and Commercial law, including Tax, Banking, Financing, Insurance, Real Estate, Computer, Patent, Trademark, Copyright, Labor, Trade Regulation and Antitrust Law. International Legal Transactions. Arbitration and Litigation in Civil Matters. EC Law. International Private Law. Maritime and Admiralty Law.

Member of Alliance of European Lawyers (EEIG) which regroups six law firms from Continental Europe. The Alliance consists of De Bandt, van Hecke & Lagae at Brussels and Antwerp; De Brauw Blackstone Westbroek at The Hague, Amsterdam, Rotterdam and Eindhoven; Jeantet & Associés at Paris and Warsaw; Lagerlöf & Leman at Stockholm, Gothenburg and Malmö; Oppenhoff & Rädler at Berlin, Cologne, Frankfurt am Main, Leipzig and Munich; Uria & Menendez at Madrid and Barcelona. The Alliance member firms have joint offices at Brussels, London, New York and Prague.

PARTNERS

DAG WERSÉN, born Stockholm, Sweden, August 28, 1939. *Education:* Stockholm University (juris kandidat, LL.M., 1961). Service with Swedish Courts. Secretary in the Commission on the Execution of Foreign Judgments in Civil Actions, 1961-1967. *Member:* Swedish and International Bar Associations. *LANGUAGES:* Swedish, English, German and French. *PRACTICE AREAS:* General Commercial Law; Corporate Law; Procedural Law.

JAN LUNDBERG, born Stockholm, Sweden, September 23, 1940. *Education:* Stockholm University (juris kandidat, LL.M., 1965). Service with Swedish Courts. *Member:* Swedish and International Bar Associations; Swedish Group of AIPPI. *LANGUAGES:* Swedish, English and German. *PRACTICE AREAS:* General Commercial Law; Computer Law; Trademark Law; Copyright Law; Drug Law.

ALLAN STENSHAMN, born Karlskrona, Sweden, September 3, 1933. *Education:* Stockholm University (juris kandidat, LL.M., 1965). Service with Swedish Courts; Judgeship, Stockholm Administrative Court of Appeal, 1968-1969. Author: "The Taxation of Unincorporated Associations, Foundations and Funds," Forum AB Publishing Company, 1967. *Member:* Swedish and International Bar Associations; International Fiscal Association. *LANGUAGES:* Swedish, English, French and German. *PRACTICE AREAS:* General Commercial Law; Corporate Law; Tax Law.

PER-ERIK HASSELBERG, born Gävle, Sweden, May 18, 1944. *Education:* Stockholm University (juris kandidat, LL.M., 1969). Service with Swedish Courts. *Member:* Swedish and International Bar Associations. *LANGUAGES:* Swedish, English and German. *PRACTICE AREAS:* General Commercial Law; Corporate Law; Financing Law.

STEFAN BERNHARD, born Mora, Sweden, August 29, 1944. *Education:* Stockholm University (juris kandidat, LL.M., 1969). Service with Swedish Courts; Judgeship, Court of Appeal, 1973-1974. Expert of the Government Committee of 1983 on Copyright and Computer Technology. *Member:* Swedish Bar Association; International Chamber of Commerce, Paris (Chair WP: on Computer Software, Integrated Circuits and Data Bases; on Computing and information Technology). *LANGUAGES:* Swedish, English, German and French. *PRACTICE AREAS:* Corporate Law; Computer Law; Trademark Law; Copyright Law.

CHRISTER HÅKANSSON, born Härnösand, Sweden, July 12, 1949; admitted, Service with Swedish Courts. *Education:* Uppsala University (juris kandidat, LL.M., 1972). *Member:* Swedish and International Bar Associations; International Fiscal Association. *LANGUAGES:* Swedish, English, French and German. *PRACTICE AREAS:* General Commercial Law; Corporate Law; Financing Law; Commercial Litigation.

INGVAR ZANDER, born Stockholm, Sweden, November 17, 1949. *Education:* Stockholm University (juris kandidat, LL.M., 1974). Service with Swedish Courts. *Member:* Swedish Bar Association. *LANGUAGES:* Swedish, English and German. *PRACTICE AREAS:* General Commercial Law; Corporate Law; Financing Law.

LARS PERHARD, born Stockholm, Sweden, 1950. *Education:* Stockholm University (Juris Kandidat, LL.M., 1973). Service with Swedish Courts. *Member:* Swedish Bar Association; International Bar Association; International Association of Young Lawyers, AIJA (National Vice President, 1990—). *LANGUAGES:* Swedish, English, German and French.

(This Listing Continued)

PRACTICE AREAS: Arbitration Law; Litigation; Computer Law; Contract Law; General Commercial Law; Corporate Law; Real Estate Law.

SIGBJÖRN OLSSON, born Lidingö, Sweden, 1949. *Education:* Stockholm University (juris kandidat, LL.M., 1974). Service with Swedish Courts; Judgeship, Svea Court of Appeal, 1977-1978. *Member:* Swedish Bar Association. *LANGUAGES:* Swedish, English, French and German. *PRACTICE AREAS:* General Commercial Law; Corporate Law; Corporate Finance; Company Law.

MARIANNE LUNDIUS, born Malmö, Sweden, April 28, 1949; admitted, Service with Swedish Courts. *Education:* Lund University (juris kandidat, LL.M., 1976). *Member:* Swedish and International Bar Associations. *LANGUAGES:* Swedish, English and German. *PRACTICE AREAS:* General Commercial Law; Corporate Law.

CLAES SÖDERSTRÖM, born Stockholm, Sweden, May 28, 1942. *Education:* Uppsala University (juris kandidat, LL.M., 1968). Service with Swedish Courts; Judgeship, Administrative Court of Appeal. Legal Advisor to the Minister of Finance, 1972-1978. Lecturer in Tax Law at the University of Uppsala, 1977-1984. Author: "Taxation of International Transactions," Liber Publications, 1982. *Member:* Swedish and International Bar Associations. *LANGUAGES:* Swedish, English, French and German. *PRACTICE AREAS:* General Commercial Law; Corporate Law; Tax Law.

STEN ÅKE ZETHRAEUS, born Umeå, Sweden, July 23, 1942. *Education:* Stockholm University (juris kandidat, LL.M., 1967). Service with Swedish Courts; Judgeship, Svea Court of Appeal, 1971-1975. Secretary: of the Government Committee Regarding Laws on Security of Employment, 1972-1973; of the Labour Court, 1973-1975; of the Government Committee on New Laws Regarding Partnerships and Unlimited Companies, 1974-1978. Expert of the Government Committee of 1980 Regarding a New Law on Security of Employment. *Member:* Swedish Bar Association. *LANGUAGES:* Swedish and English. *PRACTICE AREAS:* Labor Law; Litigation.

PONTUS KÅGERMAN, born Kristianstad, Sweden, 1948. *Education:* Stockholm University (juris kandidat, LL.M., 1976; M.A., 1971). Service with Swedish Courts. *Member:* Swedish Bar Association. *LANGUAGES:* Swedish and English. *PRACTICE AREAS:* Corporate Law; Financing Law.

THOMAS RAJALA, born Piteå, Sweden, 1947. *Education:* Stockholm University (juris kandidat, LL.M., 1978). Service with Swedish Courts. Lecturer, Company Law, University of Stockholm. *Member:* Swedish Bar Association. *LANGUAGES:* Swedish and English. *PRACTICE AREAS:* General Commercial Law; Corporate Law; Real Estate Law.

MARTIN BÖRRESEN, born Solna, Sweden, 1950. *Education:* Stockholm University (juris kandidat, LL.M ., 1974); McGill University, Montreal (Diploma in Air and Space Law, 1980). Service with Swedish Courts; Judgeship, Court of Appeal, 1977-1979. *Member:* Swedish Bar Association. *LANGUAGES:* Swedish, English and German. *PRACTICE AREAS:* General Commercial Law; Corporate Law; Competition Law; Transportation Law.

TOM JOHANSSON, born Karlskoga, Sweden, 1948. *Education:* Uppsala University (juris kandidat, LL.M., 1974). Service with Swedish Courts. Judgeship, Court of Appeal and Administrative Court of Appeal, 1978-1979. Secretary Labour Court, 1979-1981. Member, Government Committee, 1979-1983. *Member:* Swedish Bar Association. *LANGUAGES:* Swedish and English. *PRACTICE AREAS:* General Commercial Law; Litigation; Arbitration; Labor Law; Insolvency Law.

HENRIK BIELENSTEIN, born Stockholm, Sweden, 1949. *Education:* Stockholm University (juris kandidat, LL.M.; jur pol mag, 1979; fil kand, M.A., 1975). Service with Swedish Courts. Lecturer, Torts, Civil Law, University of Stockholm. *Member:* Swedish Bar Association. *LANGUAGES:* Swedish and English. *PRACTICE AREAS:* General Commercial Law; Corporate Law; Insurance Law; Contract and Tort Law; Professional Indemnity; Product Liability; Litigation.

CHRISTIAN LUTHMAN, born Stockholm, Sweden, 1952. *Education:* Stockholm University (juris kandidat, LL.M., 1979). Service with Swedish Courts. *Member:* Swedish Bar Association. *LANGUAGES:* Swedish and English. *PRACTICE AREAS:* General Commercial Law; Financing Law; Tax Law.

THOMAS LINDQVIST, born Stockholm, Sweden, 1950. *Education:* Stockholm University (juris kandidat, LL.M., 1977). Service with Swedish Courts. *Member:* Swedish Bar Association. *LANGUAGES:* Swedish and English. *PRACTICE AREAS:* General Commercial Law; Corporate Law; Industrial Property Rights Law; Labor Law.

(This Listing Continued)

LAGERLÖF & LEMAN, Stockholm—Continued

PEDER HAMMARSKIÖLD, born Stockholm, Sweden, 1955. *Education:* University of Hamburg, Germany (Diploma in Civil Law, 1974); Uppsala University (juris kandidat, LL.M., 1979). Assistant to the Professor of International Law and Lecturer in Company Law, Uppsala University, 1977-1981. Service with Swedish Courts. Lecturer in Law, Stockholm School of Economics, 1982—. Author: Swedish Sections of "Banks Abroad-Establishment, Operation, Supervision," Kluwer Law Publisher, 1986; "A World Guide to Exchange Control Regulations," Euromoney Publications, 1986. Lecturer in Law, Stockholm University, 1985—. *Member:* Swedish and International Bar Associations. *LANGUAGES:* Swedish, English, German, French and Russian. *PRACTICE AREAS:* General Commercial Law; Corporate Law; Banking, Insurance and Financing Law.

MATHIAS ANDRÉ, born Malmberget, Sweden, 1950. *Education:* Lund University (juris kandidat, LL.M., 1975; fil. kand. M.A., 1976); Harvard Law School, Boston, Massachusetts (LL.M., 1981); Stockholm University (juris doktor, LL.D., 1984). Service with Swedish Courts. Chairman of the Student Organization, University of Lund, 1974; Docent, 1984. Lecturer, University of Stockholm, 1979-1989. *Member:* Swedish Bar Association. *LANGUAGES:* Swedish and English. *PRACTICE AREAS:* Competition Law; General Commercial Law; Industrial Property Rights Law.

BENGT KÄRDE, born Stockholm, Sweden, 1948. *Education:* Stockholm University (juris kandidat, LL.M., 1973; fil. kand., M.A., 1974). Service with Swedish Courts. Assistant Director, Legal Department of the Swedish National Debt Office, 1978-1984. *Member:* Swedish and International Bar Associations. *LANGUAGES:* Swedish, English and French. *PRACTICE AREAS:* General Commercial Law; Corporate Law; Financing; Litigation.

JÖRGEN DURBAN, born Stockholm, Sweden, 1956. *Education:* Stockholm University (juris kandidat, LL.M., 1983). Service with Swedish Courts. *Member:* Swedish Bar Association. *LANGUAGES:* Swedish, English and German. *PRACTICE AREAS:* General Commercial Law; Corporate Law; Financing Law.

ROLF JOHANSSON, born Linköping, Sweden, 1952. *Education:* Uppsala University (juris kandidat, LL.M., 1978). Service with Swedish Courts; Judgeship, Court of Appeal, 1981-1982. Assistant Professor, University of Uppsala, 1982-1985. *Member:* Swedish Bar Association. *LANGUAGES:* Swedish and English. *PRACTICE AREAS:* General Commercial Law; Corporate Law; Real Estate Law.

SUZANNE KNÖÖS, born Landskrona, Sweden, 1949. *Education:* Lund University (juris kandidat, LL.M., 1971). Service with Swedish Courts; Judgeship, Administrative Court of Appeal, 1974-1976. Legal Advisor to the Minister of Finance, 1976-1977. Judge Administrative Court of Appeal, 1977-1981. Secretary Supreme Administrative Court, 1981-1983. Head of the Secretariat for the Inter-Municipal Fiscal Court of Appeal, 1983-1985. *Member:* Swedish and International Bar Associations; International Fiscal Association. *LANGUAGES:* Swedish, English and French. *PRACTICE AREAS:* General Commercial Law; Corporate Law; Tax Law.

JÖRGEN AXELSSON, born Kristianstad, Sweden, 1957. *Education:* Lund University (juris kandidat, LL.M., 1982). Service with Swedish Courts. *Member:* Swedish Bar Association. *LANGUAGES:* Swedish and English. *PRACTICE AREAS:* General Commercial Law; Corporate Law; Real Estate Law.

LENA HASSELGREN, born Stockholm, Sweden, 1957. *Education:* Uppsala University (juris kandidat, LL.M., 1982). Service with Swedish Courts; Judgeship, Court of Appeal, 1984-1985. *Member:* Swedish and International Bar Associations. *LANGUAGES:* Swedish and English. *PRACTICE AREAS:* General Commercial Law; Corporate Law; Banking and Financing Law.

ANDERS HEDMAN, born Ljusdal, Sweden, 1958. *Education:* Stockholm University (juris kandidat, LL.M., 1983). Service with Swedish Courts. Author: "Medical Liability and Compensation," in Swedish, Juristförlaget, Stockholm, 1984; "The Determination of the Tax Base for Real Property," Cahier, Kluwer, 1991; Chapter on Sweden in "Product Liability - European Laws and Practise," edited by Chris Hodger, Sweet & Maxwell, 1993. *Member:* Swedish and International Bar Associations; International Fiscal Association; Swedish Insurance Law Association. *LANGUAGES:* Swedish and English. *PRACTICE AREAS:* Corporate Law; Taxation; Product Liability.

KLAS FALKENBORN, born Sävsjö, Sweden, 1957. *Education:* Lund University (juris kandidat, LL.M., 1982). Service with Swedish Courts.

(This Listing Continued)

Judgeship, Administrative Court of Appeal, 1984-1985, 1986. *Member:* Swedish Bar Association. *LANGUAGES:* Swedish and English. *PRACTICE AREAS:* General Commercial Law; Corporate Law; Real Estate Law.

ASSOCIATES

HANS FORSSELL, born Solna, Sweden, 1940. *Education:* Uppsala University (juris doctor, LL.D., 1976). Service with Swedish Courts. Docent, Assistant Professor, University of Uppsala, 1976. *Member:* Swedish Bar Association. *LANGUAGES:* Swedish, German, English and French. *PRACTICE AREAS:* Corporate Law; Industrial Property Law; Litigation; Insurance Law.

PER SUNDIN, born Nacka, Sweden, 1957. *Education:* Uppsala University (juris kandidat, LL.M., 1982). Service with Swedish Courts; Judgeship, Court of Appeal, 1985-1987. *Member:* Swedish Bar Association. *LANGUAGES:* Swedish and English. *PRACTICE AREAS:* General Commercial Law; Corporate Law; Financial Law.

PETER TRAUNG, born Södertälje, Sweden, 1961. *Education:* Uppsala University (juris kandidat, LL.M., 1985). Service with Swedish Courts. *Member:* Swedish Bar Association. *LANGUAGES:* Swedish and English. *PRACTICE AREAS:* General Commercial and Corporate Law; Litigation; Arbitration.

SÖREN DRUVE, born Svenljunga, Sweden, 1958. *Education:* Uppsala University (juris kandidat, LL.M., 1985). Service with Swedish Courts. *Member:* Swedish Bar Association. *LANGUAGES:* Swedish and English. *PRACTICE AREAS:* General Commercial Law; Corporate Law; Competition Law.

LARS PETTERSSON, born Gislaved, Sweden, 1961. *Education:* Lund University (juris kandidat, LL.M., 1985). Service with Swedish Courts. Author: Chapter on Sweden in "The Taxation of Private Investment" edited by EIAM. *Member:* Swedish Bar Association. *LANGUAGES:* Swedish, English and French. *PRACTICE AREAS:* General Commercial Law; Corporate Law; Tax Law.

PER GUSTAF EKBOM, born Sundsvall, Sweden, 1960. *Education:* Stockholm University (juris kandidat, LL.M., 1985). Service with Swedish Courts. *Member:* Swedish Bar Association. *LANGUAGES:* Swedish and English. *PRACTICE AREAS:* General Commercial Law; Corporate Law; Financial Law.

YLVA LINDQUIST, born Stockholm, Sweden, 1961. *Education:* Stockholm University (juris kandidat, LL.M., 1985). Service with Swedish Courts. *Member:* Swedish Bar Association. *LANGUAGES:* Swedish and English. *PRACTICE AREAS:* General Commercial Law; Corporate Law; Financing Law.

PETER HÖGSTRÖM, born Stockholm, Sweden, 1961. *Education:* Lund University (juris kandidat, LL.M., 1986). Diploma from the University of Amsterdam (Europe Institute). Service with Swedish Courts. *Member:* Swedish Bar Association. *LANGUAGES:* Swedish, English and German. *PRACTICE AREAS:* General Commercial Law; Corporate Law; Antitrust; Banking; Financial and Insurance related Law.

MAGNUS LIDMAN, born Uppsala, Sweden, 1960. *Education:* Uppsala University (juris kandidat, LL.M., 1986). Service with Swedish Courts. *Member:* Swedish Bar Association. *LANGUAGES:* Swedish and English. *PRACTICE AREAS:* General Commercial Law; Real Estate Law; Litigation.

BIRGITTA JACOBSSON, born Hammerdal, Sweden, 1959. *Education:* Uppsala University (juris kandidat, LL.M., 1986). Service with Swedish Courts. *LANGUAGES:* Swedish and English. *PRACTICE AREAS:* General Commercial Law.

PIA SODEMANN, born Copenhagen, Denmark, 1959. *Education:* Lund University (juris kandidat, LL.M., 1985); Scandinavian Institute of Maritime Law, Olso, 1984. Service with Swedish Courts. *LANGUAGES:* Swedish, Danish, English and French. *PRACTICE AREAS:* General Commercial Law; Corporate Law.

JOAKIM LAVÉR, born Stockholm, Sweden, 1962. *Education:* Stockholm University (juris kandidat, LL.M., 1988). Service with Swedish Courts. *Member:* Swedish Bar Association. *LANGUAGES:* Swedish and English. *PRACTICE AREAS:* General Commercial Law; Competition Law.

SOPHIE DEGENNE, born Stockholm, Sweden, 1963. *Education:* Stockholm University (juris kandidat, LL.M., 1988). Service with Swedish

(This Listing Continued)

Courts. *LANGUAGES:* Swedish and English. *PRACTICE AREAS:* General Commercial Law.

MATS ANDERSON, born Stockholm, Sweden, 1956. *Education:* Stockholm University (juris kandidat, LL.M., 1982). Service with Swedish Courts. Judgeship, Administrative Court of Appeal, 1985-1987. Secretary of the Inter-Municipal Fiscal Court of Appeal, 1987-1988. Judge, Administrative Court of Appeal, 1989-1991. *LANGUAGES:* Swedish, English and German. *PRACTICE AREAS:* General Commercial Law; Tax Law; Corporate Law.

ANDREAS SELIN, born Örebro, Sweden, 1962. *Education:* Uppsala University (juris kandidat, LL.M., 1989). Service with Swedish Courts. *LANGUAGES:* Swedish and English. *PRACTICE AREAS:* General Commercial Law; Corporate Law.

CLAES LANGENIUS, born Stockholm, Sweden, 1962. *Education:* Stockholm University (juris kandidat, LL.M., 1988); University of London, Queen Mary & Westfield College (LL.M., 1991). Service with Swedish Courts. *Member:* Swedish Bar Association. *LANGUAGES:* Swedish and English. *PRACTICE AREAS:* General Commercial Law; European Community Law; Competition Law.

PER NYBERG, born Stockholm, Sweden, 1964. *Education:* Uppsala University (juris kandidat, LL.M., 1990). Service with Swedish Courts. *LANGUAGES:* Swedish, English and French. *PRACTICE AREAS:* Company Law; Securities.

ERIK SWARTLING, born Stockholm, Sweden, 1963. *Education:* Stockholm University (juris kandidat, LL.M., 1990). Service with Swedish Courts. *LANGUAGES:* Swedish and English. *PRACTICE AREAS:* General Commercial Law; EEC Law; Competition Law.

ERIK NERPIN, born Stockholm, Sweden, 1961. *Education:* Uppsala University (juris kandidat, LL.M., 1990); Boston University School of Law (LL.M., 1992). Service with Swedish Courts. *LANGUAGES:* Swedish and English. *PRACTICE AREAS:* General Commercial Law.

JACK WANGENHEIM, born Stockholm, Sweden, 1963. *Education:* Stockholm University (juris kandidat, LL.M., 1990). Service with Swedish Courts. *LANGUAGES:* Swedish and English. *PRACTICE AREAS:* General Commercial Law.

KARIN DUNÉR, born Stockholm, Sweden, 1963. *Education:* Stockholm University (juris kandidat, LL.M., 1988). Service with Swedish Courts. *LANGUAGES:* Swedish, English and French. *PRACTICE AREAS:* General Commercial Law.

PETER NORDBECK, born Gothenburg, Sweden, 1963. *Education:* Lund University (juris kandidat, LL.M., 1988). Service with Swedish Courts; Judgeship, Administrative Court of Appeal, 1991-1992; Court of Appeal, 1992-1993. *LANGUAGES:* Swedish and English. *PRACTICE AREAS:* General Commercial Law.

JEANETTE PIETZSCH, born Danderyd, Sweden, 1965. *Education:* Stockholm University (juris kandidat, LL.M., 1990); Scandinavian Institute of Maritime Law, Oslo (Maritime Law Studies, 1990). Trainee: Haight, Gardner, Poor & Havens, New York, 1990-1991. Sinclair, Roche & Temperley, 1991-1992. *LANGUAGES:* Swedish, English and German. *PRACTICE AREAS:* General Commercial Law; Maritime Law.

LARS ULRICHS, born Stockholm, Sweden, 1962. *Education:* Stockholm University (juris kandidat, LL.M., 1990). Service with Swedish Courts. Judgeship, Svea Court of Appeal, 1993. *LANGUAGES:* Swedish and English. *PRACTICE AREAS:* General Commercial Law; Litigation.

CECILIA VERNERSON, born Stockholm, Sweden, 1964. *Education:* Stockholm University (juris kandidat, LL.M., 1992). Service with Swedish Courts. *LANGUAGES:* Swedish, English and French. *PRACTICE AREAS:* General Commercial Law.

HELENA BORGLUND, born Gothenburg, Sweden, 1967. *Education:* Lund University (juris kandidat, LL.M., 1991). Service with Swedish Courts. *LANGUAGES:* Swedish, English and French. *PRACTICE AREAS:* General Commercial Law.

ANDERS NORDSTRÖM, born Karlskrona, Sweden, 1961. *Education:* Lund University (juris kandidat, LL.M., 1986). Service with Swedish Courts. Judgeship, Svea Court of Appeal, 1989-1992; Labour Court, Secretary, 1991; Judge, Svea Court of Appeal, 1992-1994. Expert, Government Committee on Labour Legislation, 1992. *LANGUAGES:* Swedish and English. *PRACTICE AREAS:* Labour Law; Litigation; Arbitration; General Commercial Law.

(This Listing Continued)

KRISTER HANSEN, born Täby, Sweden, 1966. *Education:* Stockholm University (juris kandidat, LL.M., 1992). Service with Swedish Courts. *LANGUAGES:* Swedish and English. *PRACTICE AREAS:* General Commercial Law.

LARS HÅBÄCK, born Lima, Sweden, 1945. *Education:* Uppsala University (juris kandidat, LL.M., 1981; fil. kand., M.A., 1981). Service with Swedish Courts. Legal Counsel with Kema Nobel AB and Nobel Industries AB. *LANGUAGES:* Swedish and English. *PRACTICE AREAS:* General Commercial Law; Corporate Law.

MARIA WESTERLUND, born Vasteras, Sweden, 1965. *Education:* Stockholm University (juris kandidat, LL.M., 1989); EC Law at the University of Amsterdam (LL.M., 1993). Service with Swedish Courts. Associated Lawyer with the London firm Osmond, Gaunt & Rose, 1990. Judgeship Svea Court of Appeal, 1993-1994. *LANGUAGES:* Swedish and English. *PRACTICE AREAS:* General Commercial Law; Company Law.

SOFIE KROOK, born Växjö, Sweden, 1967. *Education:* Uppsala University (juris kandidat, LL.M., 1992). Service with Swedish Courts. *LANGUAGES:* Swedish, English and French. *PRACTICE AREAS:* General Commercial Law; Environmental Law.

RICHARD ÅKERMAN, born Stockholm, Sweden, 1966. *Education:* Stockholm University (juris kandidat, LL.M., 1991; Diploma in political economy, 1990); Assistant to the professor of General Jurisprudence; Columbia University, New York, NY (LL.M., 1994). Service with Swedish Courts. *LANGUAGES:* Swedish and English. *PRACTICE AREAS:* General Commercial Law.

PETER SARKIA, born Helsinki, Finland, 1967. *Education:* Uppsala University (juris kandidat, LL.M., 1994). *LANGUAGES:* Swedish, Finnish, English and French. *PRACTICE AREAS:* General Commercial Law; Finance Law.

(For list of Partners and Counsel of the respective Member Firms see Professional Biographies at: Oppenhoff & Rädler at Munich, Berlin, Cologne, Frankfurt am Main and Leipzig, Germany; De Bandt van Hecke & Lagae at Brussels and Antwerp, Belgium; De Brauw Blackstone Westbroek at The Hague, Rotterdam and Amsterdam, The Netherlands; Jeantet & Associés, at Paris, France and Warsaw, Poland; Lagerlöf & Leman at Stockholm, Gothenburg and Malmö, Sweden; Uria & Menendez at Madrid and Barcelona, Spain. For joint offices in Brussels, see under Boden De Bandt De Brauw Jeantet Lagerlöf & Uria. For joint offices in London and New York, see under the name of the respective member firms. For joint offices in Prague, see under the name Alliance Prague).

ADVOKATFIRMAN LANDAHL

Established in 1942

CARDELLGATAN 1
P.O. BOX 5209
S-102 45 STOCKHOLM, SWEDEN
Telephone: +46 8 66 66 700
Telex: 11061 LANDLAW S
Cable Address: Landlaw
Telefax: +46 8 661 49 20; +46 8 663 77 58

Corporate Law, Mergers and Acquisitions, Taxation, Commercial, Litigation, Property, Insolvency, Aviation, Intellectual Property, EC Law and Competition.

MEMBERS OF FIRM

HANS ULRIK VON DER ESCH, born Germany, 1928; admitted, 1966, Sweden. *Education:* Gothenburg School of Economics (civilekonom, M.B.A., 1951); University of Stockholm (LL.B., juris kandidat, 1954). Served in the District Court, 1954-1956. Deputy Judge, Stockholm City Court, 1957. *Member:* Swedish Bar Association; American Bar Association (Associate); Lawyer-Pilots Bar Association; International Law Association; International Fiscal Association. *LANGUAGES:* Swedish, English, German, French and Spanish. *PRACTICE AREAS:* Corporate Law; Aviation Law; Litigation; Product Liability; Arbitration; Mergers and Acquisitions.

LARS ROSENGREN, born Sweden, 1928; admitted, 1959, Sweden. *Education:* University of Lund (LL.B., juris kandidat, 1954). Served in the District Court, 1954-1955 and 1956-1957. *Member:* Swedish Bar Association (Member of Board, Stockholm Section, 1970 and 1972-1975). *LANGUAGES:* Swedish, English and German. *PRACTICE AREAS:* Business Law; Commercial Law; Swedish Tax Law; Civil Litigation/Arbitration; Mergers and Acquisitions; Money and Capital Markets.

(This Listing Continued)

ADVOKATFIRMAN LANDAHL, Stockholm—Continued

RICHARD W. HJELT, born England, 1931; admitted, 1966, Sweden. *Education:* University of Stockholm (LL.B., juris kandidat, 1956). Served in the District Court, 1957-1959. *Member:* Swedish Bar Association; International Bar Association. *LANGUAGES:* Swedish, English, Finnish and French. *PRACTICE AREAS:* Business Law; Commercial Law; Civil Litigation/Arbitration.

STEN-ÅKE STENSHAMN, born Sweden, 1944; admitted, 1974, Sweden. *Education:* University of Stockholm (LL.B., juris kandidat, 1968). Served in the District Court, 1969-1971. *Member:* Swedish Bar Association. *LANGUAGES:* Swedish and English. *PRACTICE AREAS:* Business Law; Commercial Law; Real Estate Law.

FELIX KÖRLING, born Sweden, 1944; admitted, 1979, Sweden. *Education:* University of Stockholm (LL.B., juris kandidat, 1972). Served in the District Court, 1973-1975 and the Administrative Court of Appeal, 1975-1976. *LANGUAGES:* Swedish and English. *PRACTICE AREAS:* Business Law; Commercial Law; Swedish Tax Law; Real Estate Law; Civil Litigation/Arbitration; Mergers and Acquisitions; Industrial Property; Insolvency Law.

LENNART F. LINDSTRÖM, born Malmö, Sweden, May 20, 1945; admitted, 1979, Sweden. *Education:* University of Lund (LL.B., juris kandidat, 1971); Europa Institute, University of Amsterdam (Diploma in European Integration, 1973). Served in the District Court, 1973-1976. *Member:* Swedish Bar Association; International Bar Association (Area Reporter, Banking, 1986); Asia-Pacific Lawyers Association. *LANGUAGES:* Swedish and English. *PRACTICE AREAS:* Corporate Law; Commercial Law; Real Estate Law; Civil Litigation/Arbitration; European Community Law; Mergers and Acquisitions; Energy Law; Antitrust Law.

STEFAN HOLMBERG, born Sweden, 1946; admitted, 1980, Sweden. *Education:* University of Uppsala (LL.B., juris kandidat, 1972). Served in the District Court, 1973-1975, the Court of Appeal, 1976 and as judge in the District Court, 1977. *Member:* Swedish Bar Association; AIJA; International Bar Association. *LANGUAGES:* Swedish and English. *PRACTICE AREAS:* Business Law; Commercial Law; Insolvency Law.

ÖRJAN JARVIN, born Sweden, 1947; admitted, 1981, Sweden. *Education:* University of Stockholm (LL.B., juris kandidat 1973). Served in the District Court, 1973-1976. *Member:* Swedish Bar Association; AIJA; IBA. *LANGUAGES:* Swedish, English, German and French. *PRACTICE AREAS:* Business Law; Commercial Law; Insolvency Law.

TOMAS K. NORDBERG, born 1948; admitted, 1981, Sweden. *Education:* University of Uppsala (juris kandidat LL.B., 1975). Fiscal Court Work, 1975-1978. Associate, Law Firm Gedda & Ekdal Advokatbyrå, 1978-1984. Own Law Firm, 1984-1986. Partner of Advokatfirman Sandart, 1986-1990. With the firm since 1991. *Member:* Swedish Bar Association, 1981. *LANGUAGES:* Swedish, English and German. *PRACTICE AREAS:* Business Law; Commercial Law; Civil Litigation/Arbitration; Intellectual Property Law; Mergers and Acquisitions; Contract Law.

STEN HAMBERG, born 1946. *Education:* (LL.B. juris kandidat, 1968). County Tax Inspector, 1968-1970. Court Work, 1970-1972. Associate of Law Firm, 1972-1973. Court Work in Tax Court, 1973-1976. Employee of National Tax Board, 1976. With Tax Department of Arthur Anderson & Co., Stockholm, 1977-1982 (tax partner, 1978-1982). Own Law Firm, 1982-1983. With Erik Berglunds Advokatbyrå, 1984-1990. With the firm since 1991. *Member:* Swedish Bar Association. *LANGUAGES:* Swedish, English and French. *PRACTICE AREAS:* Mergers and Acquisitions; Money and Capital Markets.

MIKAEL NILSSON, born Sweden, 1949; admitted, 1986, Sweden. *Education:* Florida State University (Economics, 1972); University of Lund (LL.B., juris kandidat, 1977). *Member:* Swedish Bar Association; AIJA. *LANGUAGES:* Swedish, English and French. *PRACTICE AREAS:* Business Law; Commercial Law; Real Estate Law; Insolvency Law.

SVEN BLANKE, born Sweden, 1951; admitted, 1984, Sweden. *Education:* University of Stockholm (LL.B., juris kandidat, 1977). Served in Swedish Tax Courts, 1978-1980. Bank Lawyer, 1980-1982. *Member:* Swedish Bar Association; International Fiscal Association. *LANGUAGES:* Swedish and English. *PRACTICE AREAS:* Business Law; Commercial Law; Swedish Tax Law; Mergers and Acquisitions.

DAG SANDART, born 1955. *Education:* University of Stockholm (juris kandidat [LL.B.], 1980). Associate of Law Firm Advokatfirman Sandart, 1980-1985. Partner of Advokatfirman Sandart, 1986-1990. *Member:* Swedish Bar Association (1985); Association Internationale des Jeunes Avocats;

(This Listing Continued)

Swedish Copyright Society. *LANGUAGES:* Swedish, English and German. *PRACTICE AREAS:* Industrial Property; Copyright; Marketing Law.

KARL-ARNE OLSSON, born Sweden, 1952; admitted, 1986, Sweden. *Education:* University of Stockholm (LL.B., juris kandidat, 1980). Served in the District Courts, 1980-1983. *Member:* Swedish Bar Association. *LANGUAGES:* Swedish, English and German. *PRACTICE AREAS:* Business Law; Commercial Law; Agency/Distributor Agreements; Mergers and Acquisitions; Civil Litigation/Arbitration.

MAGNUS ODIN, born Sweden, 1956; admitted, 1991, Sweden. *Education:* University of Stockholm (LL.B., juris kandidat, 1986). *Member:* Swedish Bar Association; AIJA. *LANGUAGES:* Swedish and English. *PRACTICE AREAS:* Business Law; Commercial Law; Real Estate Law; Insolvency Law.

LENNART DE VERDIER, born 1941; admitted, 1992, Sweden. *Education:* University of Stockholm (LL.B., juris kandidat, 1968). Served in the District Courts, 1968-1970, the fiscal Court of Appeal, 1971-1974 and the Supreme Administrative Court, 1975-1981, including time at the Ministry of Finance, 1976-1977, the National Tax Board, 1981-1989, with Vinge Grosskopf Tax Advisers, 1989-1991. *LANGUAGES:* Swedish and English. *PRACTICE AREAS:* Business Law; Commercial Law; Swedish Tax Law; International Tax Law.

BJÖRN ROHDIN, born Sweden, 1949; admitted, 1993. *Education:* University of Stockholm (LL.B., juris kandidat, 1977). Served in the District Court, 1977-1980, Administrative Court of Appeal, 1980-1986. Expert in International Tax Matters at the National Tax Board, 1986-1987. Head of the International Legal Section at the National Tax Board, 1988-1991. *LANGUAGES:* Swedish and English. *PRACTICE AREAS:* Business Law; Commercial Law; Swedish Tax Law; International Tax Law.

ERIC M. RUNESSON, born 1960; admitted, 1993. *Education:* Stockholm University (LL.B., juris kandidat, 1986); Harvard Law School (LL.M., 1989). *LANGUAGES:* Swedish, English and German. *PRACTICE AREAS:* Commercial Contracts; Civil Litigation/Arbitration; Mergers and Acquisitions.

ASSOCIATES

KERSTIN WISS HOLMDAHL, born Sweden, 1954; admitted, 1993. *Education:* University of Uppsala (LL.B., juris kandidat, 1982). Served in the Administrative District Court, 1982-1984, the District Court, 1984-1985 and the Administrative Court of Appeal, 1985-1986. *LANGUAGES:* Swedish and English. *PRACTICE AREAS:* Business Law; Commercial Law; Swedish Tax Law; Real Estate Law.

GUNNAR BLOMBERG, born 1961; admitted, 1993. *Education:* Stockholm University (LL.B., juris kandidat, 1986). Court Work, 1987-1989. *LANGUAGES:* Swedish and English. *PRACTICE AREAS:* Business Law; Commercial Law; Civil Litigation/Arbitration; Industrial Property.

KATARINA HELLSÉN, born Sweden, 1962; admitted, 1993. *Education:* University of Stockholm (LL.B., juris kandidat, 1987). Served in the District Court, 1987-1990. *LANGUAGES:* Swedish and English. *PRACTICE AREAS:* Business Law; Commercial Law; Insolvency Law.

MARIE GERREVALL, born Sweden, 1962; admitted, 1994. *Education:* University of Lund (LL.B., juris kandidat, 1988). Served in the District Court. *LANGUAGES:* Swedish and English. *PRACTICE AREAS:* Business Law; Commercial Law; Insolvency Law.

MÅRTEN STENSTRÖM, born Sweden, 1966. *Education:* University of Stockholm (1990). Served in the District Court, 1990-1991. *LANGUAGES:* Swedish, English and German. *PRACTICE AREAS:* Business Law; Commercial Law; Real Estate Law; Civil Litigation/Arbitration.

ANNA CARBELL, born Sweden, 1962. *Education:* University of Stockholm (LL.B., juris kandidat, 1989). Served in the District Court, 1989-1991 and the Court of Appeal, 1991-1992. *LANGUAGES:* Swedish and English. *PRACTICE AREAS:* Business Law; Commercial Law; Insolvency Law.

OF COUNSEL

SIXTEN WEGNELIUS, born Sweden, 1919; admitted, 1956, Sweden. *Education:* University of Lund (LL.B., juris kandidat, 1948). Served in the District Court, 1948-1951 and the Court of Appeal, 1951-1953. *Member:* Swedish Bar Association. *LANGUAGES:* Swedish, English and German. *PRACTICE AREAS:* Family Law; Succession Law.

STEN HELLNER, born Sweden, 1923; admitted, 1955, Sweden. *Education:* University of Stockholm (LL.B., juris kandidat, 1948). Served in the District Court, 1948-1950. *Member:* Swedish Bar Association; International Bar Association. *LANGUAGES:* Swedish, English, German and French.

(This Listing Continued)

PRACTICE AREAS: International Private Law; Business Law; Commercial Law; Family Law; Succession Law.

STEN G. CARLSTON, born Sweden, 1926; admitted, 1956, Sweden. *Education:* University of Stockholm (LL.B., juris kandidat, 1950). Served in the District Court, 1950-1953. *Member:* Swedish and American (Associated Member) Bar Associations. *LANGUAGES:* Swedish, English, German and French. **PRACTICE AREAS:** Business Law; Commercial Law; Swedish Tax Law; Real Estate Law; Civil Litigation/Arbitration; Mergers and Acquisitions; Money and Capital Markets; Industrial Property.

CARL MICHAEL VON QUITZOW, born 1962. *Education:* University of Lund (Master of Laws, LL.M., 1986). Tax Advisor, Peters & Co., 1986. Assistant Professor, EC Law, Institute of European Market Law, Copenhagen, 1987-1989 and University of Lund. Adviser to the Swedish Ministry of Foreign Affairs, Trade Department and the National Board of Trade, Stockholm, 1989-1991. With the firm since 1991. Lecturer, EC Law, Faculties of Law, Lund and Stockholm. *Member:* Danish Association of European Law (Member of the Board, 1987-1989); F.I.D.E.; Swedish Association of European Law; International Wine Law Association. *LANGUAGES:* Swedish, German, Danish, English and French. **PRACTICE AREAS:** Business Law; International Commercial Law; EC Law; Agricultural Law; Intellectual Property Law; Competition law; Anti-dumping Law; Insurance and Financing.

TORGNY LEBENBERG ADVOKATBYRÅ AB

KARLAVÄGEN 76, IV
S-114 59 STOCKHOLM, SWEDEN
Telephone: + 46 8 661 14 14
Telefax: + 46 8 661 11 55

FIRM PROFILE: *Established in 1982, Torgny Lebenberg Advokatbyrå AB has concentrated on civil law matters. The firm assists with litigation, legal research and contracts concerning commercial and private matters. The firm is also engaged in administration of estates, preferably with commercial and international complications.*

TORGNY LEBENBERG, born Stockholm, Sweden, 1943. *Education:* University of Stockholm (LL.B.) jur kand 1968. Served in District Court, 1968-1970. Kronofogdemyndighet, 1970-1972. Kammarkollegiet, 1972-1977. Ministry of Budget and Economic Affairs, 1977-1980. Private Legal Practice, 1980—. *Member:* Swedish Bar Association; International Bar Association; A.I.J.A.; British-Nordic Lawyers Association. *LANGUAGES:* English and Swedish.

ASSOCIATES

HELENA HYTTING, born Stockholm, Sweden, 1964. *Education:* University of Stockholm (LL.B.) jur kand 1989. Served in S-E-Banken, Kronofogdemyndighet, District Court, 1989-1991. *LANGUAGES:* English and Swedish.

TORBJÖRN LINDMARK, born Stockholm, Sweden, 1965. *Education:* University of Stockholm (LL.B.) jur kand 1990. Served in District Court, 1990-1993. *LANGUAGES:* English and Swedish.

ADVOKATFIRMAN LINDAHL

STRANDVÄGEN 5 A
P.O. BOX 14240
S-104 40 STOCKHOLM, SWEDEN
Telephone: 46-8 670 5800
Telex: 19609 LINDAHL S
Telefax: 46-8 667 73 80

Gothenburg, Sweden Office: Östra Hamngatan 36. Mailing Address: P.O. Box 11911, S-40439 Göteborg. Telephone: 46-31 80 34 30. Telefax: 46-31 15 82 85.
Helsingborg, Sweden Office: Mariagatan 10. Mailing Address: P.O. Box 1214, S-251 12 Helsingborg. Telephone: 46-42 18 31 80. Telefax: 46-42 11 96 78 and 46-42 24 12 86.
Kristianstad, Sweden Office: Västra Vallgatan 26. Mailing Address: P.O. Box 167, S-291 22 Kristianstad. Telephone: 46-44 10 07 80. Telefax: 46-44 11 85 14.
Malmö, Sweden Office: Hjälmaregatan 3, Scandinavian Center, S-211 18 Malmö. Telephone: 46-40 17 44 40. Telefax: 46-40 11 13 54.

(This Listing Continued)

Örebro, Sweden Office: Vasastrand 11-13. Mailing Address: P.O. Box 143, S-701 42 Örebro. Telephone: 46-19 10 48 00. Telefax: 46-19 10 44 45.
Brussels, Belgium Office: 33 Blvd de la Cambre, Bte 13, B-1050 Brussels. Telephone: 32-2 646 46 90. Telefax: 32-2 646 45 80.

General Swedish and International Business Law Practice, Admiralty and Maritime Law, Insolvency, Antitrust, Marketing and Unfair Competition, Banking, Computer Law, Construction and Engineering Contracts and Disputes, Corporate Financing and Securities Law, International Taxation, EC Law, Environmental Energy and Natural Resurces Law, Industrial Property, Copyright and Trademarks, Labor Law, Mergers and Acquisitions, Real Estate Law, Reorganizations, Space Law, Litigation and Arbitration, Family Law and Successions.

MEMBERS OF FIRM IN STOCKHOLM

GÖRAN RISE, born Mariestad, Sweden, December 29, 1940. *Education:* University of Lund (LL.M., 1966). Junior Judgeship, District Court of Sölvesborg, 1966-1968. Bank Manager, Svenska Handelsbanken, Lund, 1983-1986. *Member:* Swedish Bar Association, 1971. *LANGUAGES:* English and German. **PRACTICE AREAS:** Insolvency; General Commercial Law; Business Law; Banks and Banking.

ROLF B. ÅBJÖRNSSON, born Stockholm, Sweden, August 25, 1941. *Education:* University of Stockholm (LL.M., 1967). Junior Judgeship, District Court of Stockholm, 1967-1969. Bank Manager, Svenska Handelsbanken, Lund, 1983-1986. *Member:* Swedish Bar Association, 1972 (Member, Professional Committee, 1989-1991). *LANGUAGES:* English. **PRACTICE AREAS:** Insolvency Law and Litigation.

TONY SANDELL, born Stockholm, Sweden, August 24, 1943. *Education:* University of Stockholm (LL.M., 1969). *Member:* Swedish Bar Association, 1974 (Member, General Council, 1986-1987); Licensing Executive Society (Board Member, 1974-1979); International Bar Association. *LANGUAGES:* English. **PRACTICE AREAS:** Joint Venture; Intellectual Property; Project Financing; Company Acquisitions.

LARS FREDBORG, born Uppsala, Sweden, December 30, 1945. *Education:* University of Stockholm (LL.M., 1969). Co-Author: A Manual on Swedish International Taxation (Loose-Leaf). Junior Judgeship, District Court of Västervik, 1970-1972. Associate Judge, Fiscal Court of Appeal, Gothenburg, 1972-1973. *Member:* Swedish Bar Association, 1976; International Bar Association. *LANGUAGES:* English, French and German. **PRACTICE AREAS:** Financial Law; Corporate Law; International Taxation; Mergers and Acquisitions.

ANDERS CHRISTNER, born Stockholm, Sweden, July 11, 1950. *Education:* University of Stockholm (LL.M., 1976). Junior Judgeship, District Court of Stockholm, 1976-1978. *Member:* Swedish Bar Association, 1981. *LANGUAGES:* English and German. **PRACTICE AREAS:** Mergers and Acquisitions; Information Technology; Telecommunications; Computers and Software.

LARS STENBERG, born Borås, Sweden, October 15, 1944. *Education:* University of Lund (LL.M., 1972; B.A.). Junior Judgeship, District Court of West Stockholm, 1974-1975. *Member:* Swedish Bar Association, 1981. *LANGUAGES:* English. **PRACTICE AREAS:** Corporate Law; Commercial Law.

ROLF G. SON SJÖBERG, born Stockholm, Sweden, October 21, 1949. *Education:* University of Stockholm (LL.M., 1977). *Member:* Swedish Bar Association, 1983; International Bar Association. *LANGUAGES:* English. **PRACTICE AREAS:** Commercial and Corporate Law; Insolvency Law; Litigation; Real Estate and Property; Wills; Successions; International Successions.

ODD SWARTING, born Stockholm, Sweden, May 26, 1957. *Education:* University of Stockholm (LL.M., 1982). Junior Judgeship, District Court of Handen, 1983-1985. *Member:* Swedish Bar Association, 1988. *LANGUAGES:* English. **PRACTICE AREAS:** Corporate Law; Mergers and Acquisitions; Insolvency; Securities; Financing.

ERIK SELANDER, born Östersund, Sweden, April 4, 1959. *Education:* University of Uppsala (LL.M., 1986). Junior Judgeship, District Court of Södra Roslag, 1987-1988. *Member:* Swedish Bar Association. *LANGUAGES:* English.

(This Listing Continued)

ADVOKATFIRMAN LINDAHL, Stockholm—Continued

SVANTE HULTQVIST, born Kalmar, Sweden, April 11, 1959. *Education:* University of Stockholm (LL.M., 1987). Junior Judgeship, District Court of Södra Roslag, 1987-1989. *Member:* Swedish Bar Association, 1992. *LANGUAGES:* English. *PRACTICE AREAS:* Financing; Corporate Law; Mergers and Acquisitions.

ERIK LINNARSSON, born Linköping, Sweden, April 25, 1957. *Education:* University of Stockholm (LL.M., 1983). Corporate Lawyer, AB Indemnitas, 1983-1987. Cool Carriers AB, 1987-1990. *Member:* International Bar Association. *LANGUAGES:* English. *PRACTICE AREAS:* Admiralty; Maritime; Financing.

MICHAEL MOHAMMAR, born Stockholm, Sweden, November 29, 1941. *Education:* University of Stockholm (LL.M., 1964). Junior Judgeship, District Court of Södertörn, 1964-1967. Reporting Clerk to the Court of Appeal in Stockholm, 1967-1973. Associate Judge of Appeal, 1973-1978. Reporting Clerk to the Supreme Court, 1978-1984. Judge, District Court of Södra Roslag, 1984-1990. *Member:* Swedish Bar Association (1991). *LANGUAGES:* English. *PRACTICE AREAS:* Litigation.

ASSOCIATES IN STOCKHOLM

MARIE FREDBORG, born Ljusdal, Sweden, August 3, 1955. *Education:* University of Uppsala (LL.M., 1980); University of Georgia School of Law, Athens, Georgia, USA (1980-1981). Junior Judgeship, District Court of Södertälje, 1982-1984. *Member:* Swedish Bar Association, 1988. *LANGUAGES:* English. *PRACTICE AREAS:* Insolvency; Commercial Law.

EVA SCHYBERG, born Örnsköldsvik, Sweden, May 3, 1958. *Education:* University of Lund (LL.M., 1984); University of The Pacific, McGeorge School of Law, Sacramento, U.S.A. (LL.M., Business and Taxation, 1985). Junior Judgeship, District Court of Helsingborg, 1987-1990. Law Clerk, Flehr, Hohbach, Test, Albritton & Herbert, San Francisco, U.S.A., 1985-1986. *Member:* Swedish Bar Association, 1993. *LANGUAGES:* English and German. *PRACTICE AREAS:* Intellectual Property; Commercial Law.

SVEN HOLMGREN, born Trollhatttan, Sweden, January 5, 1961. *Education:* University of Lund (LL.M., 1987). Junior Judgeship, District Court of Ystad, 1987-1990. *LANGUAGES:* English and German.

LENA BLIXT, born Skara, Sweden, March 30, 1960. *Education:* University of Stockholm (LL.M., 1988). Junior Judgeship, District Court of Stockholm, 1988-1990. *Member:* Swedish Bar Association, 1993. *LANGUAGES:* English. *PRACTICE AREAS:* Insolvency; Commercial.

MARIE HOLMBERG LÜNING, born Jönköping, Sweden, October 17, 1963. *Education:* University of Stockholm (LL.M., 1988). Junior Judgeship, District Court of Stockholm, 1988-1990. *Member:* Swedish B ar Association, 1993. *LANGUAGES:* English. *PRACTICE AREAS:* Insolvency; Commercial.

MARIA FORSGREN, born Sollentuna, Sweden, June 1, 1963. *Education:* University of Stockholm (LL.M., 1988). Junior Judgeship, District Court of Sollentuna, 1988-1990. Associate Judge, Court of Appeal, Umeå, 1990-1991; *Member:* Swedish Bar Association, 1994. *LANGUAGES:* English. *PRACTICE AREAS:* Insolvency; Commercial.

HANS STENBERG, born Stockholm, Sweden, November 20, 1932. *Education:* University of Stockholm (LL.M., 1956; LL.D., 1974). Junior Judgeship, District Court of Köping, 1959-1961. President, Swedish Institute of Foreign Law Ltd., 1979-1992. Chairman, Swedish Association for European Law. *LANGUAGES:* English, French, Spanish and German.

HANS RAMBERG, born Helsingborg, Sweden, April 2, 1963. *Education:* University of Lund (LL.M., 1989). *LANGUAGES:* English. *PRACTICE AREAS:* Commercial; Corporate; Mergers and Acquisitions.

MATS HILMERSSON, born Norrtälje, Sweden, November 10, 1956. *Education:* University of Stockholm (LL.M., 1989). Junior Judgeship, District Court of Sodra Roslagen, 1989-1991. *LANGUAGES:* English. *PRACTICE AREAS:* Insolvency; Commercial; Inheritance Law.

LARS WIDHAGEN, born Stockholm, Sweden, February 4, 1966. *Education:* University of Stockholm (LL.M., 1991). *LANGUAGES:* English. *PRACTICE AREAS:* Insolvency.

PETER HELLE, born Stockholm, Sweden, May 6, 1962. *Education:* University of Stockholm (LL.M., 1990). Junior Judgeship, District Court of Stockholm, 1990-1992. *LANGUAGES:* English. *PRACTICE AREAS:* Insolvency; Computer Law.

(This Listing Continued)

EU1326B

PETER BÄVERLID, born Stockholm, Sweden, May 28, 1965. *Education:* University of Stockholm (LL.M., 1991). Junior Judgeship, District Court of Jakobsberg, 1991-1993. *LANGUAGES:* English. *PRACTICE AREAS:* Admiralty; Maritime Law; Insolvency.

LARS-HENRIK ANDERSSON, born Gnarp, Sweden, 1962. *Education:* University of Uppsala (LL.M., 1991). Served in the Prime Ministers Office 1991-1994. *PRACTICE AREAS:* Insolvency; Company Law; Environmental Law.

(For Biographical data on all Personnel, see Professional Biographies at Gothenburg, Kristianstad, Lund, Malmö, Helsingborg, Örebro and Brussels)

ADVOKATFIRMAN LINDBERG & SAXON

Established in 1974

REGERINGSGATAN 66

P.O. BOX 7712

103 95 STOCKHOLM, SWEDEN

Telephone: (+46 8) 791 45 90

Telefax: (+46 8) 791 45 01

Telex: 12442 FOTEX S, ATT. SAXONLAW

General Business and Corporate Law, Contracts, Copyright, Licensing and Trademarks, Bankruptcy, Financing, Acquisitions, Labor Law, Litigation and Arbitration.

MEMBERS OF FIRM

BENGT GUSTAWSSON, born Stockholm, Sweden, September 17, 1929; admitted, 1963, Sweden. *Education:* University of Stockholm (Juris Kandidat, LL.M., 1957). Assistant judge, 1957-1960. *Member:* Swedish Bar Association. *LANGUAGES:* Scandinavian. *PRACTICE AREAS:* Insolvency; Receiverships; Computer Law; Contract; Litigation; Estate Administration.

JAN LINDBERG, born Stockholm, Sweden, July 27, 1942; admitted, 1973, Sweden. *Education:* University of Stockholm (Juris Kandidat, LL.M., 1967). Service in Swedish Courts, 1967-1969. *Member:* Swedish Bar Association. *LANGUAGES:* Scandinavian, English and German. *PRACTICE AREAS:* Intellectual Property; Copyright; Patents; Contracts; Company Law; Corporate Law; Labor and Employment.

ANDERS SAXON, born Stockholm, Sweden, March 7, 1938; admitted, 1969, Sweden. *Education:* University of Stockholm (Juris Kandidat, LL.M., 1962); Yale Law School (LL.M., 1963). Assistant Public Prosecutor, 1963. Assistant Judge, 1963-1965. *Member:* Swedish Bar Association (Board Member, Stockholm Department, 1972-1976). *LANGUAGES:* Scandinavian, English and French. *PRACTICE AREAS:* Company Law; Contract; Intellectual Property; Licensing; Arbitration; Travel Industry.

JAN FLOOD, born Stockholm, Sweden, June 20, 1945; admitted, 1979, Sweden. *Education:* University of Stockholm (Juris Kandidat, LL.M., 1970). Assistant judge, 1970-1973. Service in Swedish Courts, 1973-1974. Legal adviser to the Swedish Union of Clerical and Technical Employees in Industry and the Swedish Association of Supervisers, 1975-1977. *Member:* Swedish Bar Association. *LANGUAGES:* Scandinavian and English. *PRACTICE AREAS:* Insolvency; Receiverships; Labor and Employment; Company Law; Contract.

LARS ZACHAROFF, born Gothenburg, Sweden, February 12, 1956; admitted, 1988, Sweden. *Education:* Universities of Stockholm and Uppsala (Juris Kandidat, LL.M., 1983). Assistant Judge, 1983-1985. *Member:* Swedish Bar Association; International Bar Association. *LANGUAGES:* Scandinavian and English. *PRACTICE AREAS:* Finance; Leasing; Company Law; Contracts; Labor and Employment; Litigation; Arbitration.

PETER THORELL, born Linköping, Sweden, June 14, 1952; admitted, 1990, Sweden. *Education:* University of Linköping (B.Sc. Econ., 1976); University of Stockholm (Juris Kandidat, LL.M. 1984). Assistant Judge in Swedish Courts, 1985-1986. *Member:* Swedish Bar Association. *LANGUAGES:* Scandinavian and English. *PRACTICE AREAS:* Company Law; Finance; Creditors Rights; Leasing; Contracts; Litigation; Arbitration.

ASSOCIATES

JACOB LANDEN, born Dalby, Sweden, April 25, 1965. *Education:* University of Uppsala (Juris Kandidat, LL.M., 1989). Assistant Judge, 1989-1990. *LANGUAGES:* Scandinavian and English. *PRACTICE AREAS:* Litigation; Contracts; Creditors Rights.

HENRIK SUNDELL, born Stockholm, Sweden, March 30, 1964. *Education:* University of Stockholm (Juris Kandidat, LL.M., 1988). Swedish

(This Listing Continued)

Competition Office, 1989. Corporate Lawyer, 1990-1991. *LANGUAGES:* Scandinavian, English and French. *PRACTICE AREAS:* European Community Law; Competition; Intellectual Property; Trademarks; Contracts; Corporate Law.

STEFAN WIDENHOLM, born Stockholm, Sweden, November 16, 1964. *Education:* University of Stockholm (Juris Kandidat, LL.M., 1990). Service in Swedish District Court, 1991-1992. *LANGUAGES:* Scandinavian and English. *PRACTICE AREAS:* Insolvency; Company Law; Contract; Real Estate; Litigation.

FREDRIK SUNDIN, born Boras, Sweden, August 25, 1962. *Education:* University of Lund (Juris Kandidat, LL.M., 1987). Assistant judge, 1988-1990, City of Stockholm's Department, 1990-1993. *LANGUAGES:* Scandinavian and English. *PRACTICE AREAS:* Company Law; Insolvency; Contract; Real Estate; Litigation.

GUNNAR LINDHS ADVOKATBYRÅ HB

Established in 1940

REGERINGSGATAN 42

P.O. BOX 7315

S-103 90 STOCKHOLM, SWEDEN

Telephone: 08-701 78 00

Facsimile: 08-796 82 23. 20 90 04

Corporate, Commercial, Tax, Real Estate, Intellectual Property, Labor, Banking, Securities, International Legal Transactions, Arbitration and Litigation in Civil Matters.

FIRM PROFILE: Established in 1940, Gunnar Lindhs Advokatbyrå has grown to become one of Sweden's leading commercial law firms. The firm has a broadly based practice with a reputation for offering a range of high quality legal services within its area of services. The firm is a member of Pannone Law Group EEIG, which includes law firms with offices in London, Manchester, Guernsey, Paris, Lyon, Bourg-en-Bresse, Annecy, Hamburg, Frankfurt am Main, Rome, Milan, Madrid, Barcelona, Brussels, Geneva, Lisbon and Andorra.

MEMBERS OF FIRM

NILS ERIK SEGERFORS, born Stockholm, Sweden, July 28, 1919. *Education:* University of Stockholm (juris kandidat, LL.B., 1945). *Member:* Swedish Bar Association. (Senior Partner). *LANGUAGES:* Swedish, English, French and German. *PRACTICE AREAS:* Corporate; Commercial; Arbitration.

OLA WETTERGREN, born Gothenburg, Sweden, February 11, 1920. *Education:* University of Uppsala (juris kandidat, LL.B., 1945). *Member:* Swedish Bar Association. (Senior Partner). *LANGUAGES:* Swedish, English and German. *PRACTICE AREAS:* Corporate; Family.

PARTNERS

TORE STENHOLM, born Jönköping, Sweden, February 17, 1936. *Education:* University of Stockholm (juris kandidat, LL.B., 1962). *Member:* Swedish and International Bar Associations; Licensing Executives Society. *LANGUAGES:* Swedish and English. *PRACTICE AREAS:* Corporate; Commercial; Civil Litigation.

TOMMY EKHOLM, born Helsinki, Finland, November 13, 1938. *Education:* University of Stockholm (juris kandidat, LL.B., 1964). *Member:* Swedish Bar Association. *LANGUAGES:* Swedish, English, German and French (limited Spanish and Finnish). *PRACTICE AREAS:* Corporate, Commercial and International Legal Transactions.

TOM RUNE, born Stockholm, Sweden, July 30, 1937. *Education:* University of Stockholm (juris kandidat, LL.B., 1963). Former Associate Judge, Fiscal Court of Appeal, 1966-1969. *Member:* Swedish Bar Association. *LANGUAGES:* Swedish, English, French and German. *PRACTICE AREAS:* Corporate; Commercial; Real Estate; Litigation; Arbitration.

RONALD ADOLFSSON, born Stockholm, Sweden, January 4, 1936. *Education:* University of Stockholm (juris kandidat, LL.B., 1963). Former Associate Judge, Fiscal Court of Appeal, 1966-1969. *Member:* Swedish Bar Association; International Fiscal Association. *LANGUAGES:* Swedish, French, English and German. *PRACTICE AREAS:* Corporate; Commercial; Tax; International Tax.

JAN BERGMAN, born Överkalix, Sweden, October 4, 1946. *Education:* University of Stockholm (juris kandidat, LL.B., 1972). Former Associate Judge, Fiscal Court of Appeal, 1974-1976. *Member:* Swedish Bar Associa-

(This Listing Continued)

tion. *LANGUAGES:* Swedish and English. *PRACTICE AREAS:* Real Estate.

PER BJÖRKMAN, born Stockholm, Sweden, January 8, 1951. *Education:* London School of Foreign Trade (1972-1973); University of Lund (Juris kandidat, LL.B., 1974). *Member:* Swedish and International Bar Associations; International Law Association; Swedish Copyright Association; Arbitration Panel of American Film Market Association. *LANGUAGES:* Swedish, English and French. *PRACTICE AREAS:* Intellectual Property; Telecommunications; International Legal Transactions.

PETER KINDBLOM, born Västerås, Sweden, October 20, 1950. *Education:* University of Stockholm (juris kandidat, LL.B., 1975). *Member:* Swedish Bar Association. *LANGUAGES:* Swedish and English. *PRACTICE AREAS:* Corporate; Commercial; Real Estate; Labour.

STEFAN SANDÉN, born Jönköping, Sweden, December 25, 1950. *Education:* University of Uppsala (juris kandidat, LL.B., 1975). *Member:* Swedish Bar Association. *LANGUAGES:* Swedish, English, German and French. *PRACTICE AREAS:* Corporate; Commercial; Civil Litigation; Arbitration.

SVEN RASMUSSON, born Jönköping, Sweden, March 12, 1953. *Education:* University of Stockholm (juris kandidat, LL.B., 1980). *Member:* Swedish Bar Association. *LANGUAGES:* Swedish and English. *PRACTICE AREAS:* Corporate; Commercial; Real Estate; Banking; Securities.

MILLERT CARLSSON, born Östhammar, Sweden, July 15, 1945. *Education:* Stockholm School of Economics (M.B.A., 1972); University of Stockholm (juris kandidat, LL.B., 1973). *Member:* Swedish Bar Association. *LANGUAGES:* Swedish and English. *PRACTICE AREAS:* Corporate; Commercial; Tax; Civil Litigation.

GUNNAR JOHANSSON, born Karlstad, Sweden, April 22, 1955. *Education:* University of Stockholm (juris kandidat, LL.B., 1981). Junior Judgeship Court of Appeal, 1984. *Member:* Swedish Bar Association. *LANGUAGES:* Swedish and English. *PRACTICE AREAS:* Corporate; Commercial; Real Estate; Banking; Securities.

SVEN ERFORS, born Nyköping, Sweden, February 22, 1956. *Education:* University of Stockholm (juris kandidat, LL.B., 1982). *Member:* Swedish Bar Association. *LANGUAGES:* Swedish and English. *PRACTICE AREAS:* Labour.

PETER ORANDER, born Stockholm, Sweden, 1953. *Education:* University of Stockholm (juris kandidat, LL.B., 1979). Junior Judgeships Court of Appeal and Fiscal Court of Appeal, 1982-1984. *Member:* Swedish Bar Association. *LANGUAGES:* Swedish and English. *PRACTICE AREAS:* Corporate; Commercial; Civil Litigation.

PER RÖNSTRÖM, born Stockholm, Sweden, April 24, 1959. *Education:* University of Stockholm (juris kandidat, LL.B., 1984). *Member:* Swedish Bar Association. *LANGUAGES:* Swedish and English. *PRACTICE AREAS:* Corporate, Commercial and International Legal Transactions.

JAN RÅSSJÖ, born Lindesberg, Sweden, December 9, 1958. *Education:* University of Stockholm (juris kandidat, LL.B., 1984). Service in Administrative Court of Appeal, 1987-1988. *Member:* Swedish Bar Association. *LANGUAGES:* Swedish and English. *PRACTICE AREAS:* Corporate; Commercial; Banking and Securities.

ASSOCIATES

HENRIK WOLLSÉN, born Sundsvall, Sweden, April 17, 1959. *Education:* University of Stockholm (juris kandidat, LL.B., 1986). Associated, Hans Göran Francks Advokatbyrå, 1986. *Member:* Swedish Bar Association. *LANGUAGES:* Swedish, English and Spanish. *PRACTICE AREAS:* Corporate; Commercial; Civil Litigation.

INGRID ELIASSON, born Skellefteå, Sweden, October 10, 1953. *Education:* University of Uppsala (juris kandidat, LL.B., 1986). *Member:* Swedish Bar Association. *LANGUAGES:* Swedish and English. *PRACTICE AREAS:* Corporate; Commercial.

MATS BORGSTRÖM, born Örebro, Sweden, February 18, 1956. *Education:* University of Stockholm (juris kandidat, LL.B., 1984). Service in Administrative Court of Appeals, 1987. *Member:* Swedish Bar Association. *LANGUAGES:* Swedish and English. *PRACTICE AREAS:* Corporate; Commercial; Labour.

JAN BRYME, born Stockholm, Sweden, July 30, 1960. *Education:* University of Stockholm (juris kandidat, LL.B., 1987). *Member:* Swedish Bar Association. *LANGUAGES:* Swedish and English. *PRACTICE AREAS:* Corporate; Commercial; Market; Competition.

(This Listing Continued)

GUNNAR LINDHS ADVOKATBYRÅ HB, Stockholm—Continued

HÅKAN GIRELL, born Stockholm, Sweden, November 1, 1950. *Education:* University of Uppsala (juris kandidat, LL.B., 1977). Counsel to: HSB's Riksförbund, 1979-1981; The Swedish Federation for Rental Property Owners, 1981-1984. General Counsel, AB Arsenalen (Subsidiary of SE-Banken), 1984-1992. *LANGUAGES:* Swedish and English. *PRACTICE AREAS:* Real Estate.

GUSTAF BODIN, born Stockholm, Sweden, March 5, 1961. *Education:* University of Stockholm (juris kandidat, LL.B., 1989); New York University, School of Law (LL.M., 1991). *LANGUAGES:* Swedish and English. *PRACTICE AREAS:* Corporate; Commercial.

GABRIELLA FORSSELL, born Gothenburg, Sweden, April 7, 1965. *Education:* University of Lund (juris kandidat, LL.B., 1990). *LANGUAGES:* Swedish and English. *PRACTICE AREAS:* Corporate; Commercial.

ERIKA BRÄNNSTRÖM, born Stockholm, Sweden, August 17, 1965. *Education:* University of Stockholm (juris kandidat, LL.B., 1989). Junior Judgeship Court of Appeal, 1991-1993. *LANGUAGES:* Swedish and English.

THOMAS POUSETTE, born Stockholm, Sweden, August 11, 1964. *Education:* University of Stockholm (juris kandidat, LL.B., 1989); King's College, University of London (LL.M., 1990). Service in Administrative Court of Appeal, 1993-1994. *LANGUAGES:* Swedish, English, Spanish and French.

Languages: English, French, German and Spanish.

MALMSTRÖM & MALMENFELT ADVOKATBYRÅ AB

Solicitors and Barristers

4TH AND 5TH FLOOR
HOVSLAGARGATAN 5 B
P.O. BOX 1665
S-111 96 STOCKHOLM, SWEDEN
Telephone: (+46 8) 679 69 50
Fax: (+46 8) 611 57 55

Administrative Law, Agriculture, Arbitration, Civil Litigation, Commercial, Commercial Property, Company, Construction, Debt Recovery, Environment, Franchising, House Purchase, Conveyancing, Insolvency, Insurance, International, Investment and Financial Services, Mergers and Acquisitions, Mortgages, Hypothecs, Oil and Gas, Energy, Partnerships, Planning, Real Estate Purchase, Trusts, Wills and Probate.

PARTNERS

KARL-GUSTAV GRIPENVIK, born Klippan, Sweden, April 9, 1948; admitted, 1984, Sweden. *Education:* University of Stockholm (Law Degree, 1977). *Member:* Swedish Bar Association. *LANGUAGES:* Swedish and English. *PRACTICE AREAS:* Business Law; Real Estate Law; Construction Law; Litigation; Arbitration.

BENGT LJUNGQVIST, born Stockholm, Sweden, August 13, 1937; admitted, 1970, Sweden. *Education:* University of Stockholm (Law Degree, 1965). *Member:* International Bar Association; Swedish Bar Association. *LANGUAGES:* Swedish and English. *PRACTICE AREAS:* Business Law; Real Estate Law; Construction Law; Litigation; Arbitration.

LENNART MELCHIOR, born Stockholm, Sweden, March 20, 1943; admitted, 1978, Sweden. *Education:* University of Stockholm (Law Degree, 1975). *Member:* International Bar Association; Swedish Bar Association. *LANGUAGES:* Swedish and English. *PRACTICE AREAS:* Business Law; Real Estate Law; Construction Law; Litigation.

HANS KINDSTRAND, born Norrköping, Sweden, September 22, 1949; admitted, 1984, Sweden. *Education:* University of Stockholm (Law Degree, 1975). *Member:* Swedish Bar Association. *LANGUAGES:* Swedish, English and German. *PRACTICE AREAS:* Business Law; Real Estate Law; Construction Law; Litigation.

LARS STRÖMBERG, born Stockholm, Sweden, November 5, 1950; admitted, 1987, Sweden. *Education:* University of Stockholm (Law Degree, 1977). *Member:* Swedish Bar Association. *LANGUAGES:* Swedish, En-

(This Listing Continued)

glish and Spanish. *PRACTICE AREAS:* Business Law; Real Estate Law; Construction Law; Litigation.

A Member of European Law Firm (ELF) which is an European Economic Interest Group. It has offices in Belgium, France, Germany, Greece, The Netherlands, Italy, Portugal and Spain. Associate office in USA.

Languages: Danish, English, French, German, Norwegian, Spanish and Swedish.

MANNHEIMER SWARTLING

VÄSTRA TRÄDGÅRDSGATAN 15
P.O. BOX 1650
S-111 86 STOCKHOLM, SWEDEN
Telephone: +46-8 613 55 00
Telefax: +46-8 613 55 01
Telex: 13082

Gothenburg, Sweden Office: Lilla Torget 1, P.O. Box 2235, S-403 14. Telephone: +46-31 10 96 00. Telefax: +46-31 10 96 01. Telex: 2591.
Malmö, Sweden Office: Stortorget 29, P.O. Box 4291, S-203 14. Telephone: +46-40 25 08 00. Telefax: +46-40 25 08 01. Telex: 32727.
Helsingborg, Sweden Office: Södra Storgatan 7, P.O. Box 1384, S-251 13. Telephone: +46-42 18 02 95. Telefax: +46-42 18 42 71.
New York, New York Office: 101 Park Avenue, 10178. Telephone: +1 212 682-0580. Telefax: +1 212 682-0982.
Brussels, Belgium Office: Avenue de Tervueren 13A, B-1040. Telephone: +32-2-732 22 22. Telefax: +32-2-736 96 52.
Frankfurt, Germany Office: Bockenheimer Landstrasse 97, D-60325. Telephone: +49-69 974 01 20. Telefax: +49-69 741 01 43.
Berlin, Germany Office: Haus der Schweiz, Friedrichstrasse 155-156, D-10117. Telephone: +49 30 202 20 10. Telefax: +49 30 202 20 110.
Moscow, Russia Office: Chistoprudny Bulvar 8, 101000 Moscow. Telephone: +7 (095) 929 90 05. Telefax: +7 (095) 929 90 06.

General Swedish and International Business Law Practice. Admiralty and Maritime Law. Antitrust, Marketing and Unfair Competition. Banking. Computer Law. Construction and Engineering Contracts and Disputes. Corporate Financing and Securities Law. Corporate Taxation. EC Law. Environmental Energy and Natural Resources Law. Industrial Property, Copyright and Trademarks. Labor Law. Mergers and Acquisitions. Real Estate Law. Reorganizations. Space Law. Litigation and Arbitration.

MEMBERS OF FIRM

PER HÅKAN OSVALD, born August 28, 1928. *Education:* University of Uppsala (LL.M., 1952). Service in Swedish Courts, 1953-1955. Associate, 1955-1963, and Member, 1963-1978, Advokatfirman Lagerlöf. Member, Carl Swartling Advokatbyrå, 1978-1990, and Mannheimer Swartling Advokatbyrå, 1990—. Member, The Stock Market Panel, 1986-1991. *Member:* Swedish Bar Association, 1959 (Deputy Member of Board, 1975-1978; Member of Board, 1978-1982; Chairman, Stockholm Section, 1977-1979); International Bar Association; Union Internationale des Avocats. *PRACTICE AREAS:* Commercial Arbitration; Company Law.

LARS RAHMN, born August 16, 1933. *Education:* University of Lund (LL.M., 1959). Studies of Marine Insurance and Maritime Law in London in the offices of W.K. Webster & Co., Ince & Co., Thos. R. Miller & Son and English Courts, 1961 and 1963. Associate, 1959-1966 and Member, 1966-1990, Mannheimer & Zetterlöf. Member, 1990—, Mannheimer Swartling Advokatbyrå. *Member:* Swedish Bar Association, 1964 (Member of the Board, 1974-1978; Delegate to the CCBE, 1972-1992 and Head of delegation, 1986-1992; Chairman, Committee on European Community Law, 1989-1992); Swedish Maritime Law Association; International Bar Association. (Resident, Gothenburg Office). *PRACTICE AREAS:* Admiralty and Maritime Law; Alternative Dispute Resolution; Commercial and International Commercial Arbitration; European Community Law; Transportation.

KJELL M. WALLMAN, born January 21, 1933. *Education:* Amherst College, Massachusetts, U.S.A.; University of Stockholm (LL.M., 1958). Service in Swedish Courts, 1959-1961. Associate, 1961-1967 and Member, 1968-1974, Wetter & Swartling Advokatbyrå. Member, Carl Swartling Advokatbyrå, 1974-1990, and Mannheimer Swartling Advokatbyrå, 1990—. *Member:* Swedish Bar Association, 1964; International Bar Association.

GÖRAN LINDERS, born September 28, 1933. *Education:* University of Lund (LL.M., 1958); Studies in England and France. Assistant Professor in Business Economics and Company Taxation at the University of Lund, 1962-1967. Company lawyer at AB SKF, Gothenburg 1971-1973. Member, Mannheimer & Zetterlöf, 1973-1990, and Mannheimer Swartling Advokat-

(This Listing Continued)

byrå, 1990—. *Member:* Swedish Bar Association, 1973; International Bar Association; International Fiscal Association. (Resident, Malmö Office). *PRACTICE AREAS:* Corporate Law; Mergers, Acquisitions and Divestitures; Securities.

BENGT ELFGREN, born January 19, 1936. *Education:* University of Stockholm (LL.M., 1963). Assistant to Dean of Law Faculty, University of Stockholm, 1963-1964. Service in Swedish Courts, 1964-1967. Associate, 1967-1971 and Member, 1972-1974, Wetter & Swartling Advokatbyrå. Member, Carl Swartling Advokatbyrå, 1974-1990, and Mannheimer Swartling Advokatbyrå, 1990—. Member of Board of Studies of Law Faculty, University of Stockholm, 1977-1986. *Member:* Swedish Bar Association, 1970 (Member of Board, Stockholm Section, 1977-1983); International Bar Association. *PRACTICE AREAS:* Aircraft Finance and Leasing; Joint Ventures; Company Acquisitions and Sales.

CLAES BEYER, born November 24, 1936. *Education:* University of Lund (LL.M., 1961); Institut de Droit Comparé de l'Université de Paris, (Diplomé de Droit Comparé, 1963); College of Law, University of Illinois (LL.M., 1962). Avocat-conseil de l'Ambassade de France en Suède. Associate, 1963-1970 and Member, 1970-1990, Mannheimer & Zetterlöf. Member, 1990—, Mannheimer Swartling Advokatbyrå. *Member:* Swedish Bar Association, 1967 (President, 1985-1989); Union Internationale des Avocats; International Bar Association; Swedish Association for European Law (Board Member, 1976—); The Institute of Company and Securities Law (Board Member, 1986—); The Swedish Industry and Commerce Stock Exchange Committee, 1989—; Export of the Government Committee on Due Process in Tax Matters, 1992—; UNICE (Vice President, Company Affairs Committee); New York Bar Association. (Resident, Gothenburg Office). *PRACTICE AREAS:* Company Law; Stock Exchange Regulations; International Mergers and Acquisitions; Arbitration; Mediation and Alternative Dispute Resolution.

HANS-ELOF OLSSON, born March 16, 1942. *Education:* University of Lund (LL.M., 1967). Member, Advisory Board, South-Western Legal Foundation, Dallas, Texas. Member, Mannheimer & Zetterlöf, 1974-1990, and Mannheimer Swartling Advokatbyrå, 1990—. *Member:* Swedish Bar Association, 1972; International Bar Association; American Bar Association (International Associate). (Resident, Gothenburg Office). *PRACTICE AREAS:* Mergers and Acquisitions; Business Organizations; Company Commercial Law; Joint Ventures; Private Placements.

TORE WIWEN-NILSSON, born March 4, 1944. *Education:* University of Lund (LL.M., 1967). General Counsel of AB Asea-Atom, Västerås, 1972-1974. Member, Mannheimer & Zetterlöf, 1974-1990, and Mannheimer Swartling Advokatbyrå, 1990—. *Member:* Swedish Bar Association, 1976; International Nuclear Law Association; International Bar Association (Vice Chairman, Committee M, 1992—, and Chairman Subcommittee, "Turn Key Heavy Plant Contracts" of Committee T, 1989-1993 and Chairman Subcommittee, "International Contract Forms" of Committee T); International Law Association; Licensing Executives Society; Swedish Association for European Law; Swedish Association of Construction and Consultancy Law (Deputy Member of the Board). (Resident, Malmö Office). *PRACTICE AREAS:* Cross Border Investments; International Commercial Arbitration; International Construction; Contracts; International Joint Ventures; Nuclear Energy.

TORBJÖRN MOLANDER, born February 27, 1941. *Education:* University of Uppsala (LL.M., 1969). Studies of Commercial Law in the Offices of Coward Chance, London, 1973-1974. Associate, 1971-1974 and Member, 1975-1990, Mannheimer & Zetterlöf. Member, Mannheimer Swartling Advokatbyrå, 1990—. *Member:* Swedish Bar Association, 1974; Union Internationale des Avocats; International Bar Association. (Resident, Gothenburg Office). *PRACTICE AREAS:* Commercial Real Estate; Company Commercial Law; Construction Contracts; Construction Arbitration; Landlord and Tenant Law.

HANS STREMPEL, born January 16, 1939. *Education:* Albert-Ludwigs-Universität, Freiburg i. Br., Germany (LL.M., 1964); University of Lund (LL.M., 1967). Judge Referee of the Court of Appeal for Western Sweden. Secondment to Coward Chance, London, 1975. Associate, 1972-1977 and Member, 1977-1990, Mannheimer & Zetterlöf. Member, Mannheimer Swartling Advokatbyrå, 1990—. *Member:* Swedish, German and International Bar Associations. (Gothenburg, Frankfurt and Berlin Offices). *PRACTICE AREAS:* International Corporate and Commercial Law; Commercial Arbitration.

MAGNUS KINDSTRAND, born September 6, 1943. *Education:* University of Uppsala (B.A., 1965; LL.M., 1969); Centre Européen Universitaire de Nancy (D.E.S. Europ., 1971). Assistant to Dean of Law Faculty, University of Uppsala, 1968-1969. Associate, Wetter & Swartling Advokat-

(This Listing Continued)

byrå, Stockholm, 1970-1974. Associate, 1974-1976 and Member, 1976-1990, Carl Swartling Advokatbyrå. Member, Mannheimer Swartling Advokatbyrå, 1990—. *Member:* Swedish Bar Association, 1975; International Bar Association. *PRACTICE AREAS:* Agricultural Property; Company Law; Employee Stock Ownership Plans; Family Trusts; Successions.

CLAES LUNDBLAD, born March 5, 1946. *Education:* University of Lund (LL.M., 1969). Associate, 1972-1977 and Member, 1977-1990, Mannheimer & Zetterlöf. Resident, Rotterdam Office, 1974-1977. Member, Mannheimer Swartling Advokatbyrå, 1990—. *Member:* Swedish Bar Association, 1975; International Bar Association; Swedish Maritime Law Association; American Bar Association (International Associate). (Resident, Gothenburg Office). *PRACTICE AREAS:* Admiralty and Maritime Law; Banking Litigation; Commercial Dispute Resolution; Litigation.

PER-OLOF HEMMAR, born September 1, 1936. *Education:* University of Stockholm (LL.M., 1962). Assistant to Dean of Law Faculty, University of Stockholm, 1961-1962. Service in Swedish Courts, 1962-1965. General Counsel, AB Statens Skogsindustrier (ASSI) 1965-1977. Associate, 1977-1978 and Member, 1979-1990, Carl Swartling Advokatbyrå. Member, Mannheimer Swartling Advokatbyrå, 1990—. *Member:* Swedish Bar Association, 1979 (Member of Board, Stockholm Section, 1982-1987; Member, Legislation Committee, 1981—). *PRACTICE AREAS:* Joint Ventures; Commercial Arbitration; Company Acquisitions and Sales.

CHRISTIAN VINGE, born November 4, 1935. *Education:* University of Lund (LL.M., 1963). Service in Swedish Courts, 1963-1965. Associate, Karl Axel Vinges Advokatbyrå, Gothenburg, 1965-1968. General Counsel, Mölnlycke AB, 1968-1977. General Counsel and Vice President, Svenska Cellulosa Aktiebolaget SCA, 1977-1986. Member, Carl Swartling Advokatbyrå, 1986-1990, and Mannheimer Swartling Advokatbyrå, 1990—. *Member:* Swedish Bar Association, 1986. *PRACTICE AREAS:* Agency and Distributorships; Commercial Law; Company Law; Contracts.

JAN WETTERBERG, born September 21, 1939. *Education:* University of Lund (LL.M., 1965). Assistant Justice of the Court of Appeal for Western Sweden. Law Studies in the Offices of Andrews & Kurth, Houston, Texas, 1979. Associate, 1976-1979 and Member, 1979-1990, Mannheimer & Zetterlöf. Member, Mannheimer Swartling Advokatbyrå, 1990—. *Member:* Swedish Bar Association, 1978; International Bar Association; International Association of Lawyers. (Resident, Malmö Office). *PRACTICE AREAS:* Banks and Banking; Business Law; Finance; Intellectual Property; Securities.

JOHAN COYET, born November 4, 1947. *Education:* University of Stockholm (LL.M., 1973). Junior Legal Advisor, Swedish Board of Commerce, 1973-1974. Associate, Wetter & Swartling Advokatbyrå, 1974. Associate, 1974-1981 and Member, 1982-1990, Carl Swartling Advokatbyrå. Member, Mannheimer Swartling Advokatbyrå, 1990—. *Member:* Swedish Bar Association, 1978. *PRACTICE AREAS:* Advertising and Marketing; Antitrust.

SVEN UNGER, born October 8, 1947. *Education:* Universities of Uppsala and Lund (LL.M., 1972). Service in Swedish Courts, 1973-1974. Assistant secretary of the Swedish Bar Association 1975-1976. Associate, 1976-1982 and Member, 1983-1990, Carl Swartling Advokatbyrå. Member, Mannheimer Swartling Advokatbyrå, 1990—. *Member:* Swedish Bar Association, 1978 (Deputy Member of Board, 1986; Member of Board, 1987-1992; President, 1992—; Vice Chairman, 1987 and Chairman, Stockholm Section, 1988-1992; Member, Editorial Committee, Journal of the Swedish Bar Association, 1982-1992). *PRACTICE AREAS:* Aviation; Commercial Law; Company Law; Contracts; Litigation.

GÖRAN MIÖRNER, born December 15, 1947. *Education:* University of Lund (LL.M., 1975; M.B.A., 1976). Associate, 1977-1982 and Member, 1983-1990, Mannheimer & Zetterlöf. Member, Mannheimer Swartling Advokatbyrå, 1990—. *Member:* Swedish Bar Association, 1980; International Fiscal Association; International Bar Association. (Resident, Malmö Office). *PRACTICE AREAS:* Aircraft Finance and Leasing; Commercial Mergers and Acquisitions; Joint Ventures; International Taxation.

MIKAEL EKDAHL, born July 1, 1951. *Education:* University of Lund (LL.M., 1975). Associate, 1974-1984 and Member, 1984-1990, Mannheimer & Zetterlöf. Member, Mannheimer Swartling Advokatbyrå, 1990—. *Member:* Swedish Bar Association, 1982; International Bar Association. (Resident, Malmö Office). *PRACTICE AREAS:* Business Law; Company Law; Construction Law; Corporate Law; Mergers, Acquisitions and Divestitures.

JERKER SELLÉN, born March 18, 1951. *Education:* University of Lund (LL.M., 1976). Associate, 1976-1984 and Member, 1984-1990, Mannheimer & Zetterlöf. Member, Mannheimer Swartling Advokatbyrå,

(This Listing Continued)

MANNHEIMER SWARTLING, Stockholm—Continued

1990—. *Member:* Swedish Bar Association, 1983; International Bar Association. (Resident, Gothenburg Office). *PRACTICE AREAS:* Admiralty and Maritime Law; Transportation; Insurance; General Commercial Law.

THORSTEN LEIJONHIELM, born May 26, 1947. *Education:* University of Stockholm (LL.M., 1973). Junior Legal Advisor, Swedish Central Bureau of Statistics, 1973-1975. Service and Junior Judgeships in Swedish Courts, 1975-1978. Associate, 1979-1984 and Member, 1985-1990, Carl Swartling Advokatbyrå. Member, Mannheimer Swartling Advokatbyrå, 1990—. *Member:* Swedish Bar Association, 1981; International Bar Association, 1993. *PRACTICE AREAS:* Commercial Litigation and Arbitration; Company Law; Professional Liability; (especially Directors and Officers Liability).

MAGNUS WALLANDER, born March 3, 1952. *Education:* University of Lund (LL.M., 1976). Associate, 1979-1985 and Member, 1985-1990, Mannheimer & Zetterlöf. Member, Mannheimer Swartling Advokatbyrå, 1990—. *Member:* Swedish Bar Association, 1982; International Bar Association; Licensing Executives Society. *PRACTICE AREAS:* Company Commercial Law; Energy Acquisitions; Energy Regulation; International Mergers and Acquisitions; Leveraged and Management Buyouts.

AXEL CALISSENDORFF, born May 25, 1953. *Education:* University of Stockholm (LL.M., 1978). Service and Junior Judgeships in Swedish Courts, 1978-1981. Associate, 1981-1986 and Member, 1986-1990, Mannheimer & Zetterlöf. Member, Mannheimer Swartling Advokatbyrå, 1990—. *Member:* Swedish Bar Association, 1984. *PRACTICE AREAS:* Company Acquisitions and Sales; Commercial Contracts; Copyright Infringement; Litigation.

PETER NORDQUIST, born October 13, 1946. *Education:* University of Lund (LL.M., 1972; B.A., 1973). Service in Swedish Courts, 1973-1983. Assistant Judge and Head of the Secretariat, Fiscal Court of Appeal, 1979-1983. General Counsel and Member of the Executive Group of the National Swedish Tax Board, 1983-1986. Associate, 1986-1987 and Member, 1987-1990, Carl Swartling Advokatbyrå. Member, Mannheimer Swartling Advokatbyrå, 1990—. Member, Fiscal Expert Group, Stockholm Chamber of Commerce, 1987—. *Member:* Swedish Bar Association and International Fiscal Association. (Resident, Gothenburg Office). *PRACTICE AREAS:* Corporate Taxation; Cross Border Leasing; International Taxation.

PÄR ANDERSSON, born January 8, 1954. *Education:* University of Lund (LL.M., 1979). Associate, 1982-1987 and Member, 1987-1990, Mannheimer & Zetterlöf. Member, 1990—, Mannheimer Swartling Advokatbyrå. Studies in the offices of Reboul, MacMurray, Hewitt, Maynard & Kristol, New York, 1985-1986. *Member:* Swedish Bar Association, 1985; International Bar Association. (Resident, Malmö Office). *PRACTICE AREAS:* Partnerships; Commercial Arbitration; Company Acquisitions and Sales; International Commercial Contracts; Automation Engineering.

ULF AF KLINTBERG, born July 9, 1935. *Education:* University of Stockholm (LL.M., 1960). Service in Swedish Courts, 1960-1981; Judge of Appeal, 1981; Deputy Chairman of the National Swedish Franchise Board for Environmental Protection, 1981-1988. Associate, Carl Swartling Advokatbyrå, 1988-1990. Member, Mannheimer Swartling Advokatbyrå, 1990—. *Member:* Swedish Bar Association, 1990. *PRACTICE AREAS:* Environmental Law.

CARL OLOF BLOMQVIST, born March 15, 1951. *Education:* University of Uppsala (LL.M., 1978). Teaching Assistant in Law, University of Uppsala, 1974-1976. Service and Junior Judgeships in Swedish Courts, 1978-1982. Associate, 1982-1986 and Member, 1987-1990, Carl Swartling Advokatbyrå. Member, Mannheimer Swartling Advokatbyrå, 1990—. Licensed under New York State Law as a Legal Consultant. *Member:* Swedish Bar Association, 1985. (Resident, New York Office). *PRACTICE AREAS:* International Business; International Finance; International Contracts; International Commercial Law; International Mergers and Acquisitions.

ANDERS WIKSTRÖM, born June 12, 1949. *Education:* University of Lund (LL.M., 1973). Judge of the Court of Appeal for Western Sweden. Associate, 1983-1988 and Member, 1988-1990, Mannheimer & Zetterlöf. Member, 1990—, Mannheimer Swartling Advokatbyrå. *Member:* Swedish Bar Association, 1986. (Resident, Gothenburg Office). *PRACTICE AREAS:* Company Law; Finance; Property; Mergers and Acquisitions; Leases and Leasing.

LOUISE WIDÉN, born March 23, 1950. *Education:* University of Stockholm (LL.M., 1975). Research and Teaching Assistant in Law, University of Stockholm, 1973-1975. Service and Junior Judgeships in Swedish Courts, 1975-1980. Associate, 1980-1987 and Member, 1987-1990, Carl Swartling Advokatbyrå. Member, Mannheimer Swartling Advokatbyrå, 1990—. *Member:* Swedish Bar Association, 1983; International Bar Association; Association Internationale des Jeunes Avocats. (Resident, Malmö Office). *PRACTICE AREAS:* Advertising and Marketing; Antitrust and Trade Regulation; Commercial Law; European Community Law; Litigation.

TOM HÅRD, born December 11, 1945. *Education:* University of Stockholm (LL.M., 1974) Service in Swedish Courts, 1974-1976. Legal Department, Federation of Swedish Industries, 1976-1985 (Head, 1981-1985). Secretary General, Swedish National Committee of ICC, 1985-1986. Director General, Stock Market Panel, 1986-1989. Associate, Mannheimer & Zetterlöf, 1990. Associate, 1990-1992, and Member, 1993—, Mannheimer Swartling Advokatbyrå. *Member:* Swedish Bar Association, 1992.

KAJ HOBÉR, born Ramnäs, Sweden, August 2, 1952. *Education:* University of Uppsala (fil. kand. B.A., 1974; juris kandidat LL.B., 1977); University of Illinois, College of Law (M.C.L., 1978). Junior Judgeships in Swedish Courts, 1978-1982; Associate, Wetter & Wetter, Stockholm, 1982-1983; Associate, White & Case, Stockholm, 1983-1989, Member, White & Case, Stockholm, 1989-1994. Member, Mannheimer Swartling Advokatbyrå, 1994—. *Member:* Swedish Bar Association, 1985; American Bar Association; International Bar Association. (Resident, Moscow, Russia Office). *PRACTICE AREAS:* Antitrust and Trade Regulation; Business Law; Commercial Law; International Law; Securities.

CARL G. DE GEER, born September 5, 1955. *Education:* University of Stockholm (LL.M., 1979); University of Pennsylvania (1981). Foreign Associate, Donovan Leisure Newton & Irvine, New York, 1981-1982. Associate, 1983-1988 and Member, 1988-1990, Carl Swartling Advokatbyrå. Member, Mannheimer Swartling Advokatbyrå, 1990—. *Member:* New York Bar, 1982; Swedish Bar Association, 1986; International Bar Association. *PRACTICE AREAS:* Banks and Banking; Company Law; Corporate Law; Finance.

BIÖRN RIESE, born December 26, 1953. *Education:* University of Stockholm (LL.M., 1978; M.B.A., 1980). Service in Swedish Courts, 1980-1982. Associate, Åbjörnsson & Rausing Advokatbyrå, 1982-1983. Associate, 1984-1988 and Member, 1989-1990, Carl Swartling Advokatbyrå. Member, Mannheimer Swartling Advokatbyrå, 1990—. *Member:* Swedish Bar Association, 1985; International Bar Association; Association Internationale des Jeunes Avocats. *PRACTICE AREAS:* Bankruptcy; Business Law; Telecommunications; Computers and Software; Professional Liability.

BRITA MUNCK-PERSSON, born October 10, 1950. *Education:* University of Lund (LL.M., 1974); University of Linköping (M.B.A., 1977). Service and Junior Judgeships in Swedish Courts, 1975-1981. Principal Administrative Officer, National Swedish Tax Board, 1981-1986. Tax Adviser, Hagström & Olsson AB (Arthur Young), 1986-1989. Associate, Carl Swartling Advokatbyrå, 1989-1990. Associate, Mannheimer Swartling Advokatbyrå, 1990-1991, and Member, 1991—. *Member:* Swedish Bar Association, 1991; ICC, Commission on taxation, Swedish Committee; International Fiscal Association; International Bar Association. *PRACTICE AREAS:* Corporate Taxation; International Taxation; Cross Border Leasing; Tax Planning; Taxation of Mergers and Acquisitions.

JAMES F. FARRINGTON, JR., born September 22, 1952; admitted, 1984, Connecticut; 1985, New York (Not admitted in Sweden). *Education:* University of Notre Dame (B.Ch.E., 1974); University of Bridgeport (J.D., magna cum laude, 1984). Associate Editor, Bridgeport Law Review, 1981-1984. Member, Mannheimer Swartling Advokatbyrå, 1991—. (Resident, New York Office). *PRACTICE AREAS:* Acquisitions and Mergers; Licensing; Pharmaceutical Strategic Alliances; Commercial Contracts.

ÅKE KJELLSON, born September 1, 1955. *Education:* University of Uppsala (LL.M., 1980); Assistant to the Professor of Jurisprudence, University of Uppsala (1978-1980); Harvard Law School (LL.M., 1982). Service in Swedish Courts, 1982-1984. Associate, Carl Swartling Advokatbyrå, 1984-1990. Member, Mannheimer Swartling Advokatbyrå, 1990—. *Member:* Swedish Bar Association, 1987. *PRACTICE AREAS:* International Mergers and Acquisitions; Litigation.

RAGNAR LINDQVIST, born September 10, 1955. *Education:* University of Lund (LL.M., 1981). Assistant Judge, District Court of Helsingborg, 1981-1983. Associate, Mannheimer & Zetterlöf, 1983-1990. Member, Mannheimer Swartling Advokatbyrå, 1990—. *Member:* Swedish Bar Association, 1987; Asia Pacific Lawyers Association. (Resident, Helsingborg Office). *PRACTICE AREAS:* Business Law; Company Law; Corporate Law; Investments; Mergers, Acquisitions and Divestitures.

(This Listing Continued)

(This Listing Continued)

JAN KANSMARK, born August 14, 1955. *Education:* University of Lund (LL.M., 1981). Associate, Mannheimer & Zetterlöf, 1985-1990. Associate, Mannheimer Swartling Advokatbyrå, 1990-1991, and Member, 1991—. *Member:* Swedish Bar Association, 1987; Licensing Executives Society. (Resident, Malmö Office). *PRACTICE AREAS:* Corporate Law; Commercial Law; Company Law; Construction Law; Intellectual Property Law.

GÖRAN KRAFT, born April 4, 1953. *Education:* University of Lund (LL.M., 1981). Associate, Mannheimer & Zetterlöf, 1985-1990. Associate, Mannheimer Swartling Advokatbyrå, 1990-1991, and Member, 1991—. *Member:* Swedish Bar Association, 1988. (Resident, Gothenburg Office). *PRACTICE AREAS:* Civil Litigation and Arbitration; Intellectual Property and Trademark Law; Media Law.

MICHAEL KARLSSON, born May 27, 1955. *Education:* University of Lund (LL.M., 1980). Associate, Mannheimer & Zetterlöf, 1985-1990. Associate, Mannheimer Swartling Advokatbyrå, 1990-1991, and Member, 1991—. *Member:* Swedish Bar Association, 1986. (Resident, Malmö Office). *PRACTICE AREAS:* Construction Law; Mergers and Acquisitions; General Business Law.

BENGT SJÖVALL, born October 24, 1947. *Education:* University of Lund (B.A., 1973; LL.M., 1973). Teaching Assistant in Law, University of Lund, 1970-1973. Service and Junior Judgeships in Swedish Courts, 1973-1982. Associate Judge, Court of Appeal, 1983. Secretary to Legislation Committees, Ministry of Justice and Ministry of Energy and Environment, 1983-1987. Associate, Carl Swartling Advokatbyrå, 1987-1990. Associate, Mannheimer Swartling Advokatbyrå, 1990-1993, and Member, 1993—. *Member:* Swedish Bar Association, 1989; International Bar Association; ICC East-West Committee. *PRACTICE AREAS:* International Arbitration; Litigation; East West Trade.

TOMMY PETTERSSON, born September 5, 1958. *Education:* University of Uppsala (LL.M., 1985). Service in Swedish Courts, 1985-1987. Associate, Mannheimer & Zetterlöf, 1987-1990. Associate, Mannheimer Swartling Advokatbyrå, 1990-1993, and Member, 1993—. Secondment to Clifford Chance, Brussels, 1990-1991. *Member:* Swedish Bar Association, 1990. (Resident, Brussels Office). *PRACTICE AREAS:* European Community Law; Antitrust and Trade Regulation; Business Law; Commercial Law; Company Law.

KERSTIN ENGSTRÖM, born April 13, 1958. *Education:* University of Lund (LL.M., 1983). Service and Junior Judgeships in Swedish Courts, 1983-1987. Associate, Mannheimer & Zetterlöf, 1987-1990. Associate, Manheimer Swartling Advokatbyrå, 1990-1993, and Member, 1993—. *Member:* Swedish Bar Association, 1990. (Resident, Gothenburg Office). *PRACTICE AREAS:* Insolvency; Real Estate; Litigation.

EVA HÄGG, born August 10, 1959. *Education:* University of Stockholm (LL.M., 1983). Service in Swedish Courts, 1983-1985. Associate, Carl Swartling Advokatbyrå, 1986-1990. Associate, Mannheimer Swartling Advokatbyrå, 1990-1994, and Member, 1994—. *Member:* Swedish Bar Association, 1989. *PRACTICE AREAS:* Banks and Banking; Company Law; Finance; Leases and Leasing; Securities.

KRISTINA LEFFLER, born June 12, 1955. *Education:* University of Lund (LL.M., 1982). Service and Junior Judgeships in Swedish Courts, 1982-1985. Associate, Mannheimer & Zetterlöf, 1986-1990. Associtae, Mannheimer Swartling Advokatbyrå, 1990-1994, and Member, 1994—. *Member:* Swedish Bar Association, 1988. (Resident, Gothenburg Office). *PRACTICE AREAS:* Commercial Mergers and Acquisitions; Management Buyouts; Insolvency; Reconstructions.

ANDRÉ ANDERSSON, born August 10, 1959. *Education:* University of Lund (LL.M., 1986; M.B.A., 1986); University of Oxford (Diploma Legal Studies, 1987). Associate, Carl Swartling Advokatbyrå, 1987-1990. Visiting Lawyer, Slaughter and May, London, 1991-1992. Associate, Mannheimer Swartling Advokatbyrå, 1990-1994, and Member, 1994—. *Member:* Swedish Bar Association, 1993; Association Internationale des Jeunes Avocats; Association Internationale Protéction de la Propriété Intellectuelle; International Trademark Association. *PRACTICE AREAS:* Aviation and Aerospace; Banks and Banking; Finance; Leases and Leasing; Securities.

CLAES ALBINSSON, born May 7, 1959. *Education:* University of Lund (LL.M., 1985). Service in Swedish Courts, 1985-1987. Associate, Mannheimer & Zetterlöf, 1988-1990. Associate, 1990-1993, and Member, 1994—, Mannheimer Swartling Advokatbyrå. *Member:* Swedish Bar Association, 1991. (Resident, Malmö Office). *PRACTICE AREAS:* Business Law; Company Law; Mergers, Acquisitions and Divestitures; Corporate Law; Securities.

MARIA TUFVESSON SHUCK, born June 2, 1959. *Education:* University of Lund (LL.M., 1985); Harvard Law School (LL.M., 1987). Assistant in International Law, University of Lund, 1984-1985. Service in Swedish Courts, 1985-1986. Foreign Associate, White & Case, New York, 1987-1988. Associate, Carl Swartling Advokatbyrå, 1988-1990, and Mannheimer Swartling Advokatbyrå, 1990-1994, and Member, 1995—. *Member:* Swedish Bar Association, 1992; Association of the Bar of the City of New York, New York State, American and International Bar Associations. (Resident, New York Office). *PRACTICE AREAS:* International Business; International Finance; International Contracts; International Leasing; International Mergers and Acquisitions.

THOMAS KAISER, born May 1, 1960. *Education:* University of Mainz (1. juristische Staatsexamen, 1985; Dr.rer.pol., 1989); University of Nice (European Studies, 1982); London School of Economics (LL.M., 1986). Private Practice, Frankfurt am Main, 1989-1990. Treuhandanstalt, Legal Department, 1990-1991. Author: "Klauseln in Unternehmenskaufverträgen mit der Treuhandanstalt," 1992. Associate, Mannheimer Swartling Advokatbyrå, 1991-1994, and Member, 1995—. (Resident, Berlin Office). *PRACTICE AREAS:* Mergers and Acquisitions; Real Estate Law; Company and Commercial Law; Construction Law.

ASSOCIATES

CLAS NYBERG, born July 18, 1958. *Education:* University of Lund (LL.M., 1984). Service and Junior Judgeships in Swedish Courts, 1984-1987. Associate, Mannheimer & Zetterlöf, 1987-1990. Resident, New York Office, 1989-1990. Associate, Mannheimer Swartling Advokatbyrå, 1990-1991. Corporate Legal Counsel, AB Volvo, 1991-1994. Associate, Mannheimer Swartling Advokatbyrå, 1994—. *Member:* Swedish Bar Association, 1990-1991 and 1994—; Legal and Taxation Committee of Association des Constructeurs Européennes des Automobiles, 1992-1994. (Resident, Gothenburg Office). *PRACTICE AREAS:* Agency and Distributorships; Antitrust and Trade Regulation; European Community Law; Mergers, Acquisitions and Divestitures.

HELÉN WAXBERG, born December 17, 1956. *Education:* University of Lund (LL.M., 1982). Service and Junior Judgeships in Swedish Courts, 1983-1987. Associate, Carl Swartling Advokatbyrå, 1987-1990, and Mannheimer Swartling Advokatbyrå, 1990—. *Member:* Swedish Bar Association, 1990. *PRACTICE AREAS:* Advertising and Marketing; Antitrust and Trade Regulation; European Community Law.

ALEXANDER FOERSTER, born May 22, 1961. *Education:* Universities of Cologne, Bonn and Lausanne (Juristische Staatsexamen, Düsseldorf, 1986)); University of Stockholm (M.C.L., 1988; LL.M., 1989). Associate, Mannheimer & Zetterlöf, 1988-1990, and Mannheimer Swartling Advokatbyrå, 1990—. *Member:* Swedish Bar Association, 1993; Frankfurt a.m. Bar Association. (Resident, Frankfurt Office). *PRACTICE AREAS:* Alternative Dispute Resolution; Litigation; Commercial Law; Company Law; European Community Law.

MARTIN ERICSSON, born April 11, 1962. *Education:* University of Stockholm (LL.M., 1986). Associate, Mannheimer & Zetterlöf, 1988-1990, and Mannheimer Swartling Advokatbyrå, 1990—. Mannheimer Swartling, New York, 1993. *Member:* Swedish Bar Association, 1991. *PRACTICE AREAS:* Agency and Distributorships; Company Law; Contracts; Litigation; Mergers, Acquisitions and Divestitures.

KARIN FAXÉN ÅGRUP, born July 30, 1960. *Education:* University of Stockholm (LL.M., 1985). Assistant in Jurisprudence, University of Stockholm 1981-1982. Service in Swedish Courts, 1986-1989. Associate, Carl Swartling Advokatbyrå, 1989-1990, and Mannheimer Swartling Advokatbyrå, 1990—. *Member:* Swedish Bar Association, 1991.

PETER IDSÄTER, born July 17, 1960. *Education:* University of Lund (LL.M., 1986). Service in Swedish Courts, 1986-1988. Associate, Mannheimer & Zetterlöf, 1989-1990, and Mannheimer Swartling Advokatbyrå, 1990—. *Member:* Swedish Bar Association, 1992. (Resident, Malmö Office). *PRACTICE AREAS:* Commercial Mergers and Acquisitions; Securities; International Joint Ventures; Asia-Pacific Investment; Construction Law.

MARIA HALLENGREN, born October 6, 1961. *Education:* University of Lund (LL.M., 1987). Service in Swedish Courts, 1988-1989. Associate, Mannheimer & Zetterlöf. 1989-1990, and Mannheimer Swartling Advokatbyrå, 1990—. *Member:* Swedish Bar Association, 1992. (Resident, Malmö Office). *PRACTICE AREAS:* Business Law; Contracts; Company Law; Finance; Computers and Software.

HELENA REMPLER, born October 31, 1958. *Education:* University of Lund (LL.M., 1985). Service and Junior Judgeships in Swedish Courts,

(This Listing Continued)   *(This Listing Continued)*

MANNHEIMER SWARTLING, Stockholm—Continued

1985-1989. Associate, Carl Swartling Advokatbyrå, 1988-1990, and Mannheimer Swartling Advokatbyrå, 1990—. *Member:* Swedish Bar Association, 1992; International Fiscal Association. *PRACTICE AREAS:* Corporate Taxation; International Corporate Taxation; International Taxation; Tax Planning.

CECILIA BJELLE, born October 17, 1960. *Education:* University of Stockholm (LL.M., 1985). Service and Junior Judgeships in Swedish Courts, 1985-1990. Associate, Mannheimer Swartling Advokatbyrå, 1990—. *Member:* Swedish Bar Association, 1992. *PRACTICE AREAS:* Corporate Law; Company Law; Securities.

JAN E. FRYDMAN, born September 9, 1958. *Education:* University of Oregon (B.B.A., 1980); University of Stockholm (LL.M., 1989). Corporate Banking Officer and Scandinavian Representative, The First National Bank of Chicago, 1984-1987. Vice President, American Professionals Insurance Company, 1987-1988. Associate, Carl Swartling Advokatbyrå, 1989-1990, and Mannheimer Swartling Advokatbyrå, 1990—. *Member:* Swedish Bar Association, 1994; New York State Bar Association; American Bar Association (International Associate); International Bar Association; Association Internationale des Jeunes Avocats. *PRACTICE AREAS:* Banks and Banking; Company Law; Corporate Law; Mergers, Acquisitions and Divestitures; Securities.

JONAS BRATT, born April 10, 1963. *Education:* University of Uppsala (LL.M., 1988); University of Minnesota Law School; Scandinavian Institute of Maritime Law. Service in Swedish Courts, 1988-1989. Associate, Mannheimer & Zetterlöf, 1990, and Mannheimer Swartling Advokatbyrå, 1990—. *Member:* Swedish Bar Association, 1993. (Resident, Moscow, Russia Office). *PRACTICE AREAS:* Business Law; Commercial Law; Securities; Arbitration.

MARIA HEMBERG, born December 25, 1964. *Education:* University of Lund (LL.M., 1988). Service in Swedish Courts, 1988-1989. Associate, Mannheimer Swartling Advokatbyrå, 1990—. *Member:* Swedish Bar Association, 1993. (Resident, Gothenburg Office). *PRACTICE AREAS:* Business Law; Company Law; Labour and Employment Law; Real Estate.

LARS KONGSTAD, born May 31, 1963. *Education:* University of Lund (LL.M., 1988). Service in Swedish Courts, 1988-1990. Associate, Mannheimer Swartling Advokatbyrå, 1990—. *Member:* Swedish Bar Association, 1993. (Resident, Malmö Office). *PRACTICE AREAS:* General Business Law; Construction Law; Real Estate.

MONIQUE WADSTED, born September 19, 1957. *Education:* University of Stockholm (LL.M., 1988). Service in Swedish Courts, 1988-1990. Associate, Mannheimer Swartling Advokatbyrå, 1991—. *Member:* Swedish Bar Association, 1994. *PRACTICE AREAS:* Litigation; Advertising and Marketing; Intellectual Property; Air Law; Human and Civil Rights; Personal Injury.

SVEN-ÅKE BERGKVIST, born May 7, 1955. *Education:* University of Uppsala (LL.M., 1980). Assistant to the Professors of Company law, Real Estate law and Labour law, 1978-1981. Associate, Nydahl Advokatbyrå, 1980. Lecturer on Tax law, 1981-1984. Tax Adviser, Industriens Skattebyrå, 1984-1987; Skattejuristerna HB, 1987-1989; Trygg Hansa, 1989-1993. Associate, Mannheimer Swartling Advokatbyrå, 1993—. *Member:* Swedish Bar Association, 1994. *PRACTICE AREAS:* Corporate Taxation; Taxation of Mergers and Acquisitions; Tax Planning; International Taxation.

HANS HAMMARBÄCK, born May 19, 1960. *Education:* University of Uppsala (LL.M., 1987). Service in Swedish Courts, 1987-1990. Associate, Mannheimer Swartling Advokatbyrå, 1990—. Visting Lawyer, Slaughter & May, London, 1994. *Member:* Swedish Bar Association, 1994. *PRACTICE AREAS:* Securities; Commercial Law; Company Law.

CARL-OLOF BOUVENG, born July 6, 1963. *Education:* University of Stockholm (LL.M., 1988); Duke University (LL.M., 1989). Lawyer from abroad, Covington & Burling, Washington, D.C., 1989-1990. Associate, Mannheimer Swartling Advokatbyrå, 1990—. *Member:* New York State Bar, 1991. *PRACTICE AREAS:* Corporate Law; Insurance; International Law; Mergers, Acquisitions and Divestitures.

DR. CHRISTIAN BLOTH, born July 31, 1961. *Education:* Freie Universität Berlin; Universität Munster (1. juristische Staatsexamen, 1986; 2. juristische Staatsexamen 1990; Dr. of Laws, 1993); Stockholm (Diploma in Graduate Legal Studies, 1987); Traineeship 1988-1990. Associate, Mannheimer Swartling Advokatbyrå, 1991—. *Member:* Deutscher Anwaltsverein; Deutscher Juristentag; Deutsch-Nordische Juristengesellschaft.

(This Listing Continued)

(Resident, Frankfurt Office). *PRACTICE AREAS:* Litigation; Commercial Law; Company Law; Labour and Employment; Product Liability.

PER MOLANDER, born March 24, 1960. *Education:* University of Lund (LL.M., 1984). Service and Junior Judgeships in Swedish Courts, 1984-1989. Legal secretary at the National Franchise Board for Environment Protection, 1988. Corporate Counsel, Ovako AB, 1990-1991. Associate, Mannheimer Swartling Advokatbyrå, 1991—. *PRACTICE AREAS:* Chemicals and Chemistry; Energy; Environmental Law; Natural Resources; Zoning, Planning and Land Use.

HELENA HEDMAN, born September 7, 1962. *Education:* University of Uppsala (LL.M., 1987); University of Minnesota Law School. Assistant, Criminal Law, University of Uppsala, 1985-1987. Service and Junior Judgeships in Swedish Courts, 1988-1991. Associate, Mannheimer Swartling Advokatbyrå, 1991—. *PRACTICE AREAS:* Corporate Law; Mergers, Acquisitions and Divestitures; Commercial Litigation.

THOMAS WALLINDER, born December 8, 1964; admitted, 1992, New York. *Education:* University of Stockholm (LL.M., 1990); Duke University (LL.M., 1991). Service in Swedish Courts, 1990. Editor, Duke Journal of International and Comparative Law. Associate, Mannheimer Swartling Advokatbyrå, 1991—. *Member:* New York State Bar Association; Association Internationale des Jeunes Avocats.

ANNA BJERKELUND, born July 5, 1960. *Education:* University of Uppsala (LL.M., 1987). Service in Swedish Courts, 1988-1990. Associate, Mannheimer Swartling Advokatbyrå, 1991—. (Resident, Malmö Office). *PRACTICE AREAS:* Bankruptcy; Business Law; Commercial Law; Company Law; Trademarks.

PATRICK LINDBERG, born April 16, 1964. *Education:* University of Gothenburg (M.Sc., Business and Public Law, 1990); University of Lund (LL.M., 1990); University of Amsterdam (EC Law, 1991). Associate, Mannheimer Swartling Advokatbyrå, 1991—. (Resident, Brussels Office). *PRACTICE AREAS:* European Community Law; Antitrust and Trade Regulation; Contracts.

NINA LINDSTRÖM, born February 7, 1968. *Education:* University of Uppsala (LL.M., 1993); University of Maastricht (Magister Juris Communis LL.M., 1994). Associate, Mannheimer Swartling Advokatbyri, 1994—. (Resident, Brussels Office). *PRACTICE AREAS:* European Community Law; Antitrust and Trade Regulation; Intellectual Property.

CONRAD WALLENRODHE, born November 14, 1957. *Education:* University of Stockholm (LL.M., 1989). Service in Swedish Courts, 1987-1991. Associate, Mannheimer Swartling Advokatbyrå, 1991—. *PRACTICE AREAS:* Agency and Distributorship; Company Law; Contracts; Labour and Employment; Real Estate.

PATRICIA KAVEE MELICK, born New York, New York, October 19, 1962; admitted, 1988, New York. *Education:* Lehigh University (B.A., 1984); University of Chicago (J.D., 1987). Associate, Mannheimer Swartling Advokatbyrå, 1991—. (Resident, New York Office). *PRACTICE AREAS:* Mergers and Acquisitions; Joint Ventures; Licensing; General Corporate and Commercial Contracts.

MALCOLM LIDBECK, born March 26, 1963. *Education:* University of Stockholm (LL.M., 1989). Service in Swedish Courts 1990-1991. Associate, Mannheimer Swartling Advokatbyrå, 1991—. *PRACTICE AREAS:* Business Law; Mergers, Acquisitions and Divestitures; Finance.

MAGNUS ARVE, born May 20, 1964. *Education:* University of Stockholm (LL.M., 1990). Service in Swedish Courts, 1990-1991. Associate, Mannheimer Swartling Advokatbyrå, 1991—. *PRACTICE AREAS:* Commercial Litigation; International Commercial Arbitration; Insolvency Real Property.

JOHAN WINNERBLAD, born February 22, 1967. *Education:* University of Stockholm (LL.M., 1990). Assistant Corporate Lawyer, IBM Svenska AB, 1990-1991. Associate, Mannheimer Swartling Advokatbyrå, 1992—. *Member:* The Swedish Society for Computers and Law; Association Internationale des Jeunes Avocats. *PRACTICE AREAS:* Business Law; Communications and Media; Computers and Software; Intellectual Property; Mergers, Acquisitions and Divestitures.

TOMAS JOHANSSON, born September 11, 1963. *Education:* University of Uppsala (LL.M., 1990). Senior Administrative Officer, National Tax Board, 1990-1992. Associate, Mannheimer Swartling Advokatbyrå, 1992—. *PRACTICE AREAS:* Corporate Taxation Law.

BO SÖDERBERG, born September 23, 1964. *Education:* University of Uppsala (LL.M., 1989); Christian-Albrechts-Universität Kiel (LL.M., 1992). Service in Swedish Courts, 1989-1991. Associate, Mannheimer Swar-

(This Listing Continued)

tling Advokatbyrå, 1992—. *PRACTICE AREAS:* Business Law; Company Law; Mergers and Acquisitions; Labour and Employment; Contracts.

ANDERS MÅNSSON, born February 18, 1961. *Education:* University of Uppsala (LL.M., 1990). Lecturer in Law, 1989-1990. Service in Swedish Courts, 1990-1991. Associate, Mannheimer Swartling Advokatbyrå, 1992—. *PRACTICE AREAS:* Commercial Arbitration; Computer Contracts; Commercial Contracts; Creditors Rights.

BJÖRN MULLAART, born November 6, 1962. *Education:* University of Lund (LL.M., 1989). Assistant, 1988-1989. Service in Swedish Courts, 1990-1992. Associate, Mannheimer Swartling Advokatbyrå, 1992—. (Resident, Helsingborg Office). *PRACTICE AREAS:* Business Law; Copyrights; Company Law; Computers and Software.

JOHAN CARLE, born June 18, 1966. *Education:* University of Uppsala (LL.M., 1991); University of Amsterdam (LL.M., 1992). Service in Swedish Courts, 1991-1993. Associate, Mannheimer Swartling Advokatbyrå, 1993—. *PRACTICE AREAS:* Antitrust and Trade Regulation; Energy; European Community Law.

CHRISTER HAGBERG, born May 29, 1963. *Education:* University of Stockholm (LL.M., 1989). Service in Swedish Courts, 1989-1992. Associate, Mannheimer Swartling Advokatbyrå, 1992—. (Resident, Gothenburg Office). *PRACTICE AREAS:* Construction Law; Labour and Employment Law; Real Estate Law.

ANDERS HEDBRANDH, born December 1, 1964. *Education:* University of Lund (LL.M., 1990). Service in Swedish Courts, 1990-1993. Associate, 1993—, Mannheimer Swartling Advokatbyrå. (Resident, Gothenburg Office). *PRACTICE AREAS:* Civil Law; Communications and Media; Computers and Software; Franchises and Franchising; Charitable Organizations.

ALEXANDER ZYUBA, born March 16, 1965. *Education:* Moscow Institute of International Relations (MM.L., 1991). Associate, Mannheimer Swartling Advokatbyrå, 1992—. (Resident, Moscow Office). *PRACTICE AREAS:* Business Law; Commercial Law; Securities; Privatization.

JOSEF HERMES, born May 21, 1963. *Education:* Bonn Law School (l.juristische Staatsexamen, 1987); Georgetown University Law Center, Washington D.C. (LL.M., 1988). Bertelsmann Foundation, Guetersloh, 1991-1993. Associate, Mannheimer Swartling Advokatbyrå, 1993—. *Member:* Berlin Bar Association. (Resident, Berlin Office). *PRACTICE AREAS:* Corporate Law; Construction Law; Unfair Trade Law; Government Procurement Law.

JÜRGEN BUSCH, born September 15, 1961. *Education:* Albert Ludwigs Universität Freiburg (1989); Kammergericht Berlin (1992). *Member:* Deutsch-Nordische Juristenvereinigung; Deutscher Anwaltsverien; Berliner Anwaltsverein. Associate, Mannheimer Swartling Advokatbyrå, 1992—. (Resident, Berlin Office). *PRACTICE AREAS:* Antitrust and Trade Regulation; Business Law; Environmental Law; European Community Law.

FREDRIKA HÖRLIN, born October 12, 1965. *Education:* University of Lund (LL.M., 1990). Service in Swedish Courts, 1990-1993. Associate, Mannheimer Swartling Advokatbyrå, 1993—. (Resident, Gothenburg Office). *PRACTICE AREAS:* Litigation; Insolvency.

STEFAN BROCKER, born April 2, 1966. *Education:* University of Gothenburg (LL.M., 1993); M.Sc. Business and Public Law, 1993. *Member:* Swedish Maritime Law Association; Association Internationale des Jeunes Avocats. Associate, Mannheimer Swartling Advokatbyrå, 1994—. *PRACTICE AREAS:* Admiralty and Maritime Law; Corporate Law; Transportation.

FREDRIK AHLBERG, born March 13, 1965. *Education:* University of Uppsala (LL.M., 1993). Associate, Mannheimer Swartling Advokatbyrå, 1993—. (Resident, Gothenburg Office). *PRACTICE AREAS:* Environmental Law; Natural Resources; Contracts and Company Law.

ANDREAS GAST, born June 28, 1963. *Education:* University of Uppsala (LL.M., 1992). Service in Swedish Courts, 1992-1993. Associate, Mannheimer Swartling Advokatbyrå, 1993—. *PRACTICE AREAS:* Mergers and Acquisitions; Energy.

JOHAN HEGETHORN, born January 26, 1964. *Education:* University of Lund (LL.M., 1990). Service and Junior Judgeships in Swedish Courts, 1990-1993. Associate, Mannheimer Swartling Advokatbyrå, 1994—. (Resident, Malmö Office). *PRACTICE AREAS:* General Practice.

LENNART JOHANSSON, born July 29, 1965. *Education:* University of Lund (LL.M., 1990). Service in Swedish Courts, 1990-1994. Associate,

(This Listing Continued)

Mannheimer Swartling Advokatbyrå, 1994—. (Resident, Gothenburg Office). *PRACTICE AREAS:* Commercial Law; Company Law.

HELENA HALLGARN, born August 19, 1967. *Education:* University of Uppsala (LL.M., 1993; B.Sc., 1993). Associate, Mannheimer Swartling Advokatbyrå, 1994—. (Resident, Gothenburg Office). *PRACTICE AREAS:* Corporate Taxation.

ALEXANDER KOZLOVSKI, born September 16, 1965. *Education:* 1986-1991, Moscow State Institute for International Relations, International Law Faculty, Customs Legislation Department; 1991-1992, Post graduate course at the Moscow State Institute for International Relations at the Chair of Administrative Law. Associate, Mannheimer Swartling Advokatbyrå, 1994—. (Resident, Moscow Office). *PRACTICE AREAS:* Business Law; Commercial Law; Customs Legislation.

ANNA HASSELBERG, born December 19, 1967. *Education:* University of Uppsala (LL.M., 1992); Collège d'Europe, Bruges, EC law (LL.M., 1993). Associate, Mannheimer Swartling Advokatbyrå, 1994—. *PRACTICE AREAS:* European Community Law; Antitrust and Trade Regulation.

JOACIM SJÖBERG, born October 3, 1964. *Education:* University of Stockholm (LL.M., 1990). Service and Junior Judgeships in Swedish Courts (District Court and Court of Appeal) 1991-1994. Associate, Mannheimer Swartling Advokatbyrå, 1994—. *PRACTICE AREAS:* Litigation.

HANS PETERSON, born July 15, 1966. *Education:* University of Lund (LL.M., 1992). Service in Swedish Courts, 1992-1994. Associate, Mannheimer Swartling Advokatbyrå, 1994—. (Resident, Malmö Office). *PRACTICE AREAS:* General Practice.

SVEN G. LEXNER, born October 24, 1956. *Education:* Denison University, Granville (B.A., 1978); University of Uppsala (LL.M., 1988); Université de Paris II (Dipl. de Dr. Compare, 1990). Service and Junior Judgeships in Swedish Courts, 1988-1991. Associate, White & Case, Stockholm, 1992-1993, and Moscow, 1993-1994. Associate, Mannheimer Swartling Advokatbyrå, 1994—. *PRACTICE AREAS:* East European Law (particularly Russian and Polish); Commercial Contracts.

RICHARD HAMMARVID, born December 14, 1965. *Education:* University of Stockholm (LL.M., 1992). Service in Swedish Courts, 1992-1994. Associate, Mannheimer Swartling Advokatbyrå, 1994—. (Resident, Gothenburg Office). *PRACTICE AREAS:* Maritime Law; Business Law; Company Law.

KATHARINA BARTOVICS, born September 25, 1946. *Education:* Universität Frankfurt a.M. (1. juristische Staatsexamen, 1971); OLG-Bezirk Frankfurt a.M. (2. juristische Staatsexamen, 1975). Notarius Publicus, Berlin, 1987. Associate, Mannheimer Swartling Advokatbyrå, 1994—. (Resident, Berlin Office). *PRACTICE AREAS:* Real Estate Law; Company and Business Law; Notarization.

HANS RAGNHÄLL, born July 30, 1965. *Education:* University of Stockholm (LL.M., 1990). Service in Swedish Courts, 1990-1993. IBM Svenska AB, Corporate Legal Counsel, 1993-1994. Associate, Mannheimer Swartling Advokatbyrå, 1994—. *PRACTICE AREAS:* General Practice.

CHRISTIAN PFEIFF, born April 10, 1965. *Education:* University of Lund (LL.M., 1990); University of Illinois, Urbana-Champaign (LL.M., 1991); University of Amsterdam, The Netherlands (LL.M., 1994). Service in Swedish Courts, 1991-1993. Associate, Mannheimer Swartling Advokatbyrå, 1994—. *PRACTICE AREAS:* General Practice.

KARIN SYNNERSTAD, born November 22, 1965. *Education:* University of Stockholm (LL.M., 1992); Stockholm School of Economics (M.B.A., 1992). Service in Swedish Courts, 1992-1993. Assistant to the professors and lecturer at the Faculty of Law, Stockholm School of Economics, 1993-1994. Guest Lecturer at the Faculty of Law, University of Stockholm, 1994. Associate, Mannheimer Swartling Advokatbyrå, 1994—. *PRACTICE AREAS:* Intellectual Property; Advertising and Marketing.

HANS ANDRÉASSON, born October 30, 1965. *Education:* University of Stockholm (LL.M., 1992). Assistant Teacher, Computer Law, at the University of Stockholm. Service in Swedish Courts, 1992-1994. Associate, Mannheimer Swartling Advokatbyri, 1994—. *PRACTICE AREAS:* General Practice.

DIRK R. RISSEL, born March 24, 1965. *Education:* University of San Diego. Associate, Mannheimer Swartling Advokatbyri, 1994—. (Resident, Frankfurt Office). *PRACTICE AREAS:* European Community Law; International Law; Commercial Law; Litigation.

(This Listing Continued)

MANNHEIMER SWARTLING, Stockholm—Continued

GABRIELLA LEBENBERG, born November 26, 1968. *Education:* University of Stockholm (LL.M., 1992). Service in Swedish Courts, 1992-1994. Associate, Mannheimer Swartling Advokatbyrå, 1994—. *PRACTICE AREAS:* General Practice.

FREDRIK FORSSMAN, born February 14, 1964. (Resident, Malmo Office). *PRACTICE AREAS:* General Practice.

LARS PALMQVIST, born April 17, 1965. *Education:* University of Lund (LL.M., 1990). Service and Junior Judgeships in Swedish Courts, 1990-1994. Associate, Mannheimer Swartling Advokatbyri, 1994—. (Resident, Helsingborg Office). *PRACTICE AREAS:* Alternative Dispute Resolution; Contracts; Corporate Law; Company Law; Litigation.

JOHAN GRANEHULT, born June 3, 1968. *Education:* University of Lund (LL.M., 1992). Service in Swedish Courts, 1992-1994. Associate Mannheimer Swartling Advokabyri, 1994—. (Resident, Malmo Office). *PRACTICE AREAS:* General Practice.

DIMITRI PASHOV. *Education:* Budapest University, 1989; Havana University, Cuba, 1990-1991; Moscow State University Law School (J.D., with honors, 1991); State University of New York (business administration and management-international business, M.B.A., 1994). LeBoeuf, Lamb, Greene & MacRae, New York, 1993; Russin & Vecchi, Moscow, 1994. Associate, Mannheimer Swartling Advokatbyri, 1994—. *PRACTICE AREAS:* Commercial Law; Securities; Taxation.

HENRIK OLSHOV, born January 19, 1966. *Education:* University of Lund (LL.M., 1992). Service in Swedish Courts, 1993-1994. Associate Mannheimer Swartling Advokatbyri, 1995—. (Resident, Malmo Office). *PRACTICE AREAS:* General Practice.

CONSULTANTS

LENNART HAGBERG, born April 7, 1919. *Education:* University of Lund (LL.M., 1942). Law Studies with Mr. J.V. Naisby, Q.C., London, and English Courts, 1946-47 and in office of M. Leopold Dor Avocat à la Cour d'Appel de Paris and French Courts, 1947. Associate, 1948-1950, and Member, 1950-1990, Mannheimer & Zetterlöf. Member, Mannheimer Swartling, 1990-1991. Expert on Maritime Law to Governmental Committee revising the Maritime Code of Sweden, 1958-1972. Member of Governmental Committee revising the Maritime Code of Sweden, 1978-1989. Deputy Director of Scandinavian Institute of Maritime Law at Oslo, 1961-1969. Assistant Average Adjuster of Gothenburg, 1968-1972. *Member:* Swedish (1948, Member of the Board, 1968-1972) and American (International Associate) Bar Associations; Swedish Maritime Law and International Law Associations; International Bar Association (Council Member, Section on Business Law, 1978-1984); Union Internationale des Avocats. (Resident, Gothenburg Office). *PRACTICE AREAS:* International Maritime and Transport Law; International Commercial Law; International Arbitration.

SIGVARD ORANDER, born August 3, 1919. *Education:* University of Stockholm (LL.M., 1945). Service and Judgeships in Swedish Courts 1945-1953. Associate, 1954-1957 and Member, 1958-1974, Wetter & Swartling Advokatbyrå, Stockholm. Member, 1974-1984 and Consultant, 1985-1990, Carl Swartling Advokatbyrå, Stockholm. Consultant, 1991—, Mannheimer Swartling Advokatbyrå, Stockholm. *Member:* Swedish Bar Association, 1956 (Member, Disciplinary Board, 1976-1980; Vice Chairman and Chairman, 1980-1985). *PRACTICE AREAS:* Business Law.

GOTTHARD CALISSENDORFF, born September 24, 1921. *Education:* University of Uppsala (LL.M., 1947). Service in Swedish Courts, 1947-1948. Associate, 1949-1957 and Member, 1958-1974, Wetter & Swartling Advokatbyrå. Member, Carl Swartling Advokatbyrå, 1974-1990. Member, Mannheimer Swartling, 1990-1991. *Member:* Swedish Bar Association, 1952 (Deputy Member of Board, 1972-1974; Member of Board, 1975-1981; Vice Chairman, 1979-1981); International Bar Association; ICC (Member, Executive Board, Swedish National Committee, 1983-1993). *PRACTICE AREAS:* Business Law; Arbitration.

STIG OLOF SVÄRD, born October 15, 1924. *Education:* University of Stockholm (LL.M., 1949). Service and Judgeships in Swedish Courts, 1949-1971. Deputy Chairman, 1971-1981 and Chairman, 1981-1989, National Swedish Franchise Board of Environmental Protection. *PRACTICE AREAS:* Environmental Law.

GUNNAR HERMANSON, born September 21, 1929. *Education:* University of Uppsala (LL.M., 1956). Service and Junior Judgeships in Swedish Courts, 1957-1969; Service in Swedish Ministry of Commerce, 1969-1973; Deputy Antitrust Ombudsman, 1973-1985; Antitrust Ombudsman, 1985-1992; Director General, Swedish Ministry of Industry and Commerce,

(This Listing Continued)

1992-1993. *PRACTICE AREAS:* Antidumping; Competition; EC Competition.

BERTIL SJÖLANDER, born May 8, 1927. *Education:* Royal Institute of Technology, Stockholm, 1952. Service in Wales Power Companies, 1952-1965. Engineer at Water Rights Court, 1965-1971. Technical Memberof Swedish Licensing Board for Environmentment Protection, 1972-1993. *PRACTICE AREAS:* Technical Application of Environmental Law.

ULF K. NORDENSON, born May 20, 1924. *Education:* University of Uppsala (LL.M., 1949); University of Stockholm (Jur. dr h.c., 1980). Service and Judgeships in Swedish Courts, 1949-1960. Service in Swedish Ministry of Justice, 1960-1974 (Chief Legal Officer, 1969; Under-Secretary of State, 1973). Justice of the Swedish Supreme Court, 1974-1983. Independent legal consultant and arbitrator, 1983—. *PRACTICE AREAS:* Civil Law; Procedural Law; International Law.

Languages: English, French, German, Russian, Polish and Swedish

---

MICHELSONS ADVOKATBYRÅ

ENGELBREKTSPLAN 2
P.O. BOX 5156
S-102 44 STOCKHOLM, SWEDEN
Telephone: 678 11 00; International 46 8 678 11 00
Telefax: 678 11 70; International 46 8 678 11 70

General Business Law Practice, Corporation, Banking, Mergers and Acquisitions, Land and Building Law, Environmental Law, Intellectual and Industrial Property, Copyright, Trademark, Litigations in Civil Matters, Insolvency and Reorganizations.

MEMBERS OF FIRM

GUNNAR MICHELSON, born Arbrå, Sweden, May 25, 1908; admitted, 1946, Sweden. *Education:* University of Stockholm (juris kandidat LL.B., 1932); University of Gothenburg (filosofie kandidat, Bachelor of Arts, 1974). *Member:* SBA.

STAFFAN MICHELSON, born Alingsås, Sweden, April 1, 1948; admitted, 1976, Sweden. *Education:* University of Uppsala (juris kandidat, LL.B.). *Member:* SBA; AIJA; IBA.

THOMAS EKENBERG, born Västerås, Sweden, November 19, 1959; admitted, 1990, Sweden. *Education:* University of Uppsala (juris kandidat, LL.M.). *Member:* SBA; AIJA.

MAGNUS CEDERLÖV, born Karlstad, Sweden, November 29, 1956; admitted, 1986, Sweden. *Education:* University of Uppsala (Juris kandidat, LL.M.). *Member:* SBA.

MATS ÅBERG, born Själevad, Sweden, December 16, 1951; admitted, 1992, Sweden. *Education:* University of Stockholm (juris kandidat, LL.M.). *Member:* SBA; AIJA.

INGEMAR GROSS, born Falkenberg, Sweden, April 9, 1951; admitted, 1988, Sweden. *Education:* University of Lund (juris kandidat, LL.M.). *Member:* SBA.

MAGNUS RÄMSELL, born Håbol, Sweden, May 7, 1959; admitted, 1992, Sweden. *Education:* University of Lund (juris kandidat, LL.M.). *Member:* SBA.

ASSOCIATES

GUNNAR IVARSSON, born Örebro, Sweden, June 1, 1956; admitted, 1990, Sweden. *Education:* University of Uppsala (juris kandidat, LL.M.); Université de Paris II. *Member:* SBA.

BEATRICE RÄMSELL, born Kristdala, Sweden, March 26, 1963; admitted, 1993, Sweden. *Education:* University of Uppsala (juris kandidat, LL.M.). *Member:* SBA.

HANS ÖJEMARK, born Hamburg, Germany, November 16, 1960. *Education:* University of Lund (juris kandidat, LL.M.).

ANDERS LORENTZON, born Malmö, Sweden, May 27, 1964. *Education:* University of Lund (juris kandidat, LL.M.).

INGELA GERDÉN KYLEVIK, born Uddevalla, Sweden, October 11, 1965. *Education:* University of Gothenburg, University of Lund (juris kandidat, LL.M.) *Member:* AIJA.

(This Listing Continued)

MONIQUE CARDEN AMUNDSON, born Poona, India, June 24, 1967. *Education:* University of Lund (juris kandidat, LL.M.) *Member:* AIJA.

ISMO SALMI, born Miehikkälä, Finland, July 8, 1964. *Education:* University of Uppsala (juris kandidat, LL.M.).

Languages: English, German and French.

ADVOKATFIRMA MÖLLER, AB
ODENGATAN 62
P.O. BOX 6240
S-102 34 STOCKHOLM, SWEDEN
Telephone: +468-31 00 60
Fax: +468-34 48 48

International Trade Law, Arbitration and EEC Law, Intellectual Property Rights and General Legal Practice.

LENNART H.A. MÖLLER, born Helsinki, Finland, March 24, 1928; admitted, 1963, Sweden. *Education:* University of Stockholm (Jur. kand., 1953). Honorary Consul in Sweden of Benin. *Member:* International Bar Association; Swedish Bar; The Swedish Lawyers' Association; Club Oasis (practitioners of the legal profession in 17 countries). *LANGUAGES:* Swedish, English, German, French and Finnish. *PRACTICE AREAS:* International Trade Law; Arbitration; EC Law.

CAROLINE E.V. SWARTLING, born Stockholm, Sweden, May 1, 1962. *Education:* University of Stockholm (Jur. kand., 1992). *LANGUAGES:* Swedish and English. *PRACTICE AREAS:* Intellectual Property Rights; General Legal Practice.

ADVOKATFIRMAN
MORSSING & NYCANDER
Established in 1880
SVEAVÄGEN 31
P.O. BOX 3299
S-103 66 STOCKHOLM, SWEDEN
Telephone: +46-8-23 79 50
Telex: 17348 ANWALT S
Telefax: +46-8-21 80 21

Admiralty related to Carriage by Sea, Air, Road and Rail, Marine and Transport Insurance, General Corporation and Business Law, International Legal Transactions, Intellectual Property, Law related to Products Liability and Environmental Protection, all Swedish Courts.

FIRM PROFILE: Morssing & Nycander is above all well known in the maritime and admiralty law and marine insurance field. The firm also provides a comprehensive range of legal services in most other insurance fields related to transport including road, rail, aviation and forwarding and to property, product liability and other kinds of liability in tort. An increasing sector of the firms activities is reinsurance, Morssing & Nycander also has a strong practice in traditional commercial matters and covers all aspects of court litigation and arbitration. All lawyers are admitted to all courts in Sweden.

MEMBERS OF FIRM

JAN MELANDER, born Stockholm, Sweden, May 21, 1934; admitted, 1966, Sweden. *Education:* University of Lund (jur. kand., LL.B., 1961). Assistant Judge, City Court of Sodra Roslag, Stockholm, 1961-1963. Lecturer on Law, School of Navigation, Stockholm, 1961-1981. *Member:* Swedish Bar Association; Swedish Maritime Law Association; Association Internationale de Droit des Assurances; Swedish Insurance Law Association; International Bar Association. *LANGUAGES:* Swedish, English and German. *PRACTICE AREAS:* Maritime and Transportation Law; Admiralty and Maritime Law; Insurance Law; Arbitration and Litigation; Products Liability.

LARS BOMAN, born Stockholm, Sweden, July 31, 1944; admitted, 1974, Sweden. *Education:* University of Stockholm (jur. kand., LL.B., 1967). Lecturer on Maritime Law, School of Navigation Stockholm, 1974-1981. Assistant Judge, City Court of Stockholm, 1967-1969. Judge Referee, Svea Court of Appeal, 1969-1970. Deputy Judge, District Court of Stockholm, 1970. *Member:* Swedish Bar Association; Swedish Maritime Law Association (Member of Board, 1982); Swedish Insurance Law Association; International Bar Association. *LANGUAGES:* Swedish, English and German—

(This Listing Continued)

man. *PRACTICE AREAS:* Maritime and Transportation Law; Insurance and Reinsurance Law; Arbitration and Litigation; Finance and Leasing; International Law.

HANS JENDER, born Stockholm, Sweden, February 22, 1941; admitted, 1973, Sweden. *Education:* University of Stockholm (jur. kand., LL.B., 1965). Assistant Judge, City Court of Solna, 1965-1968. Reading Clerk, National Swedish Insurance Court, 1968-1969. Judge Referee, Svea Court of Appeal, 1969-1970. *Member:* Swedish Bar Association; Swedish Maritime Law Association; Swedish Insurance Law Association; International Bar Association. *LANGUAGES:* Swedish, English and German. *PRACTICE AREAS:* Maritime and Transportation Law; Insurance Law; General Commercial Law; Arbitration and Litigation.

ANDERS HÖGLUND, born Uppsala, Sweden, April 28, 1951; admitted, 1984, Sweden. *Education:* University of Stockholm (jur. kand., LL.B., 1978). Assistant Judge, City Court of Jakobsberg, 1979-1981. *Member:* Swedish Bar Association; Swedish Maritime Law Association; Swedish Insurance Law Association; International Bar Association. *LANGUAGES:* Swedish and English. *PRACTICE AREAS:* Business Law; Arbitration and Litigation; Products Liability; Maritime and Transportation Law.

PETER HOLBORN, born Stockholm, Sweden, June 29, 1948; admitted, 1986, Sweden. *Education:* University of Stockholm (jur. kand., LL.B., 1974). Assistant Average Manager, Vegete Insurance Company, 1976-1980. Notary, County Fiscal Court of Appeal, 1974-1976. *Member:* Swedish Insurance Law Association; Swedish Bar Association. *LANGUAGES:* Swedish, English and German. *PRACTICE AREAS:* Maritime and Transportation Law; Insurance Law; Business Law.

PER-OLOV HÅKANSON, born Eksjö, Sweden, July 15, 1952; admitted, 1986, Sweden. *Education:* University of Uppsala (jur Kand., LL.B., 1978); University of Oslo (Diploma in Shipping Law, 1978); University of London, University College (Postgraduate Diploma in Shipping Law, 1981). Assistant Judge, City Courts of Gothenburg and Sollentuna, 1978-1982. *Member:* Swedish and International Bar Associations; Swedish Insurance Law Association. *LANGUAGES:* Swedish and English. *PRACTICE AREAS:* Maritime and Transportation Law; General Commercial Law; Insurance Law; Contracts; Corporate Law.

MIKAEL KÖVAMEES, born Linköping, Sweden, July 9, 1958; admitted, 1991, Sweden. *Education:* University of Stockholm (jur. kand., LL.B., 1984); University of Pennsylvania Law School (Master of Law, LL.M., 1985). Assistant Judge, City Court of Stockholm, 1985-1987. Service at the Commission of the European Communities, Brussels, 1987. *Member:* Swedish and International Bar Associations; Swedish Maritime Law Association. *LANGUAGES:* Swedish and English. *PRACTICE AREAS:* Commercial and Corporate Law; Contracts; Finance and Leasing; Ships Financing; Project Financing.

Languages: English, German and French.

ADVOKATAKTIEBOLAGET
NORDIC LAW
Established in 1987
SKY CITY
P.O. BOX 182
S-190 45 STOCKHOLM (ARLANDA), SWEDEN
Telephone: 46 8 593 600 04
Telefax: 46 8 593 600 05

Gothenburg, Sweden Office: Mässans gata 14, P.O. Box 5043, S-402 21 Gothenburg. Telephone: 46 31 81 51 00. Telefax: 46 31 20 82 52.

Lund, Sweden Office: Kungsgatan 2 C, S-233 50 Lund. Telephone: +46 46 15 10 00. Telefax: +46 46 18 94 40.

Brussels, Belgium Office: Avenue Louise 177, BTE. 1, B-1050. Telephone: 32 26 40 04 29. Telefax: 32 26 48 34 39.

Helsinki, Finland Office: Mikonkatu 2 D, SF-00100 Helsinki. Telephone: 358 0 64 87 11. Telefax: 358 0 60 50 43.

General Corporation Business Law, Commercial Tax, Financing, Real Estate, Transport, Trade Regulations and Antitrust Law, Copyright, International Legal Transactions, Arbitration and Litigation, European Community Law.

(For Biographical Data, See Professional Biographies at Lund and Gothenburg, Sweden.)

ADVOKATFIRMAN NOVA

Established in 1992

GREV TUREGATAN 13 A
114 46 STOCKHOLM, SWEDEN
Telephone: +46 8 783-0780
Fax: +46 8 661-3917

FIRM PROFILE: *The partners of the firm were all partners of a larger City firm until the establishing of NOVA. The firm offers a full range of legal services to the business community. Each attorney of the firm is a general commercial law practitioner, serving as counsel to small and mid-size corporations. Our definition of general commercial law is: Corporate Law, Contract Law, Employment Law, European Community Law, Finance and Banking Law, Intellectual Property, Licensing, Litigation and Arbitration, Mergers and Acquisitions, Rescue and Insolvency, Trade Law.*

Each and every attorney also has at least one special field in which he can serve as general counsel to all sizes of corporations, national and international.

PARTNERS

STEPHANE PLEIJEL, born 1949; admitted, 1985. *Education:* LL.M. (Stockholm, 1977). Law clerk at County Court, 1979-1980. *Member:* International Bar Association; Swedish Bar Association; Swedish-French Chamber of Commerce; International Chamber of Commerce. *LANGUAGES:* French, English and German. *PRACTICE AREAS:* Business Taxation; Financial Planning.

ANDERS FERNLUND, born 1956; admitted, 1988. *Education:* AFS Foreign Exchange Student (Calif., USA, 1973); LL.M. (Stockholm, 1982); M.B.A. (Stockholm, 1985). Lecturer in Law, Stockholm School of Economics, 1981—. Law clerk at District Court, 1983-1985. Author: "Franchising and Vicarious Liability," 1985. Co-Author: "Franchising - A Way of Exporting," 1990; "Scandinavian Franchising," 1992; "Franchising - A Manual," 1994. *Member:* International Bar Association; Swedish Bar Association; Stockholm Chapter of Swedish Bar Association (Secretary, 1989-1993; Board Member, 1991—); Associate of the American Bar Association; International Chamber of Commerce; Swedish-American Chamber of Commerce; International Franchise Association; Swedish Franchise Association; General Counsel to Effectum Franchise Management; Swedish representative in EuroFranchise Lawyers. *LANGUAGES:* English. *PRACTICE AREAS:* Franchising and Distribution Law; Intellectual Property; Competition Law.

JACK SJÖGREN, born 1953; admitted, 1989. *Education:* LL.M. (Stockholm, 1980). Law clerk at District Court, 1982-1984. Judge in Court of Appeal, 1984-1986. *Member:* International Bar Association; Swedish Bar Association. *LANGUAGES:* English. *PRACTICE AREAS:* Construction Law.

CARL-GUSTAV LÖNNBORG, born 1951; admitted, 1991. *Education:* LL.M. (Stockholm, 1979). General Counsel and President of the Swedish Real Estate Agents Association. *Member:* International Bar Association; Swedish Bar Association. *LANGUAGES:* English. *PRACTICE AREAS:* Real Estate; Rental Law; Corporate Rescue and Insolvency.

URBAN HJELM, born 1956; admitted, 1991. *Education:* LL.M. (Stockholm, 1986). *Member:* International Bar Association; Swedish Bar Association; Swedish Bankruptcy Lawyers Association (1982-1985); Swedish Champion in Troup Gymnastics. *LANGUAGES:* English. *PRACTICE AREAS:* Bankruptcy; Insolvency and Corporate Rescue.

ASSOCIATES

JOHAN ENGBORG, born 1962; admitted, 1992. *Education:* LL.M. (Lund, 1987). Law clerk at District Court, 1987-1989. *Member:* Swedish Bar Association. *LANGUAGES:* English. *PRACTICE AREAS:* Leasing; Franchising; Intellectual Property.

MATS WILLMAN, born 1961; admitted, 1993. *Education:* LL.M. (Lund, 1987). Law clerk at District Court, 1987-1989. *Member:* Swedish Bar Association. *LANGUAGES:* English. *PRACTICE AREAS:* Construction Law.

JAN LUNDSTRÖM, born 1965. *Education:* LL.M. (Stockholm, 1989). Law clerk at County Court, 1990-1993. *LANGUAGES:* English. *PRACTICE AREAS:* Business Taxation.

RIKARD LJUNGBERG, born 1965. *Education:* LL.M. (Stockholm, 1989); LL.M. (German Law, magna cum laude, Cologne, Germany, 1991). Co-Author: "Telders International Law Moot Court Competition," 1989.

(This Listing Continued)

Member: German-Swedish Chamber of Commerce. *LANGUAGES:* German, English and French. *PRACTICE AREAS:* Bankruptcy; Insolvency; German Law.

CLAËS PALME & CO.

STUREGATAN 36 B
S-114 36 STOCKHOLM, SWEDEN
Telephone: (0) 8-679 95 40; 667 65 00
Telefax: 8-611 20 37

Admiralty, Air, Road and Rail, Marine and Transport Insurance, General Corporation and Business Law, Labor Law and Disputes, International Legal Transactions, Arbitration, all Swedish Courts.

J. CLAËS W. PALME, born Stockholm, May 31, 1917. *Education:* University of Uppsala, Sweden (LL.B., 1943). Representative for the Swedish Government at Diplomatic Conferences: in Brussels, 1957-1959-1967 and 1969; in London, 1967, 1968 and 1969. Chairman of the Board Engelbrekt Church, Stockholm, 1963-1989. Member of Board Stockholm Administrative and Economic Church Org., 1963-1989. Assisted Stockholm Chamber of Commerce in Revision of the Rules of its own Arb. Institute. Chairman of Board i.a: Johns Manville Scandinavian Corp., 1958-1980; Bekaert Scandinavia, 1974-1993; Dumex, 1959-1979; Nordiska Unipol AB, Matreco AB, 1983-1989 ; Finncarriers AB. Member of Board i.a: Skandia Insurance Comp., Sweden, 1970-1988; Skuld Maritime Insurance Company, Sweden, 1968-1992; Arvid Nordquist HAB, Sweden, 1981-1990; Bonnierdata AB, Sweden; Royal Jordanian Airlines, Amman; Member, Expert Stockholm Law Court, 1969. Member of the Board of Scandinavian Institute of Maritime Law, 1970-1989. Titular Member, International Maritime Committee, 1957. Member, Panel of Arbitrators, American Arbitration Association. *Member:* Swedish Bar Association; Swedish Maritime Law Association (Board Member and Secretary, 1951-1987; Honorary Member, 1987—); International Law Association (Vice President, Swedish Branch, 1965—). *LANGUAGES:* Swedish, English, German and French.

ASSOCIATE

GUNNAR SÖDERHIELM, born Valbo, August 14, 1928. *Education:* University of Stockholm (Master Mariner, 1953; LL.B., 1958). Author: Book, "Maritime Law for Students at Navigational School". Lecturer on Law, Navigational School at Stockholm. Seminars on Maritime Law, Stockholm University. Member, Board of Directors, Messrs. Inter Ocean Ltd. and Messrs. John E. Sandström & Co. Ltd., Stockholm. *Member:* Swedish Association of International Maritime Law; Comité Maritime International (National Branch). *LANGUAGES:* Swedish, English, German and French.

REPRESENTATIVE CLIENTS: EFFOA, Helsinki, Finland; The Export-Import Bank of Japan, Tokyo; Hamburgerische Versicherungs Verein, Hamburg; Badische Anilin- und Soda-Fabrik AG, Ludwigshafen; Shell Tankers, Rotterdam; Nordisk Skibsrederforening, Oslo; Ministry for Foreign Affairs; Skandia Insurance Comp., Stockholm, Sweden; N.V. Bekaert S.A., Belgium; Danish East Asiatic Comp., Copenhagen; A.P Möller Shipowners (Maersk Line), Denmark; Leading P&I-clubs in London and Scandinavia; Danish Ship Owners Defense Organization; Dres Schön & Pflüger, Hamburg; Hasche, Albrecht, Hamburg; Dres Lebuhn & Puchta, Hamburg; Dabelstein & Passehl, Hamburg; Morflot, Moscow, Latvian Shipping Co.; Riga, Baltic Shipping Company, Leningrad; Black Sea Shipping Co., Odessa; Ciech, Poland; Insurance Company, New Hampshire/AIU; China Shipowners' Mutual Assurance Association; Beijing Sudoimport, Moscow.
REFERENCES: Swedish Shipowners' Assn.; Messrs. Haight, Gardner, Poor & Havens, New York; Healy & Baillie, New York; Messrs. Lillick, McHose & Charles, San Francisco, Calif.; Palmer Biezup & Henderson, Philadelphia, Pennsylvania; Terriberry, Carroll & Yancey, New Orleans, Louisiana; Richards, Butler & Co., London; Ince & Co., London; Norton, Rose, Botterell & Roche, London; Freshfields, London; Messrs. Ebsworth & Ebsworth, Sydney; Swedish Chamber of Commerce, Stockholm; Hill, Dickinson & Co., London; Professor Francesco Berlingieri, Genoa, Italy; Holman, Fenwick & Willan, London; Jean Warot, Paris.

ADVOKATFIRMAN CLAËS RENSTRÖM A.B.

Established in 1964

BIRGER JARLSGATAN 13
S-111 45 STOCKHOLM, SWEDEN
Telephone: 8-611 88 40
Telefax: 8-611 83 20

International Private Law, Matrimonial and Probate Law and International Taxation. Litigation. Trust Law, Criminal Law, Custody including Child Abduction.

(This Listing Continued)

MEMBER OF FIRM

CLAËS RENSTRÖM, born Filipstad, Sweden, September 19, 1929; admitted, 1959, Sweden. *Education:* University of Uppsala, Sweden, LL.B. (jur Kand) 1954. District Court, 1954-1956. Private Legal Practice, 1956-1964. Founder of own Firm, 1964. Appointed Chairman of Family Law Committee, International Bar Association, 1976-1981. Legal Counsel for the Austrian Embassy in Stockholm. *Member:* Swedish Bar Association; International Academy of Matrimonial Lawyers; International Bar Association; American Bar Association (associated member). *LANGUAGES:* English and German (Limited). *PRACTICE AREAS:* International Private Law; Matrimonial and Probate Law; International Taxation; Litigation; Criminal Law; Custody Law.

ASSOCIATE

FREDRIC RENSTRÖM, born Stockholm, Sweden, September 21, 1962; admitted, 1993, Sweden. *Education:* University of Uppsala (juris kandidat, LL.B., 1988). *Member:* Swedish Bar Association. *LANGUAGES:* English. *PRACTICE AREAS:* International Private Law; Matrimonial and Probate Law; International Taxation; Litigation; Trust Law; Custody Law.

RYDIN & CARLSTEN ADVOKATBYRÅ AB

Established in 1983

NORRMALMSTORG 1
P.O. BOX 1766
S-111 87 STOCKHOLM, SWEDEN
Telephone: +46 8 679 51 70
Telefax: +46 8 611 48 50

General Corporation and Business Law, International Commercial Transactions, Finance and Banking Law, Industrial Property Law, Litigation, Arbitration and Taxation.

FIRM PROFILE: Rydin & Carlsten Advokatbyrå AB is a medium-sized general business law practice, with an emphasis on international transactions, mergers and acquisitions, intellectual property law, in particular patent litigation, banking and finance law, commercial litigation and arbitration. The firm also has a tradition of advising U.S., Japanese and European corporate clients on issues pertaining to their Swedish subsidiaries and other investment law matters.

MEMBERS OF FIRM

HÅKAN O. BORGENHÄLL, born Växjö, Sweden, May 5, 1959. *Education:* University of Lund (juris kandidat LL.M., 1984); Teknikum College (B.Sc., 1979). Law Clerk, National Enforcement Authority, 1985. Junior Judge, District Court, 1985-1987. Associate, 1987-1990, Advokatfirman Fritz Engström. Member of the Board, subsidiary of FABEGE. *Member:* Swedish Bar Association (1990); Association Internationale pour la Protection de la Propriété Industrielle. *LANGUAGES:* Swedish and English. *PRACTICE AREAS:* Advertising and Marketing; Commercial Law; Computer Regulation; Copyright; Intellectual Property; Patents; Technology and Science; Trade Marks.

HANS M. CARLSTEN, born Linköping, Sweden, January 10, 1944. *Education:* University of Stockholm (juris kandidat, LL.M., 1969). Junior Judge, District Court, 1970-1972. Judge in the Stockholm Tax Court of Appeal, 1973. Associated with Wetter & Swartling Advokatbyrå, Stockholm, 1974 and Wetter & Wetter Advokatbyrå, Stockholm, 1974-1982. Board Member, Swedish subsidiaries of: Seiko Corporation; Baxter International Inc.; SmithKline Beecham Corporation; NEC Corporation; Lotus Development Corporation. *Member:* Swedish (1977) and International Bar Associations. *LANGUAGES:* Swedish and English. *PRACTICE AREAS:* Computer Contracts; International Commercial Contracts; International Joint Ventures; International Mergers and Acquisitions; Pharmaceutical Regulations; Company Taxation; Nuclear Law.

ULF DAHLGREN, born Sollefteå, Sweden, October 2, 1943; admitted, 1975, Sweden. *Education:* University of Lund (juris kandidat, LL.M., 1969). Junior Judge, District Court, 1969-1972. Assistant Secretary of Swedish Bar Association, 1972-1975. Associate 1975-1980, Partner 1980-1990, Advokatfirman Fritz Engström AB, Stockholm. Member of the Board of the Swedish Association for the Protection of Industrial Property; Member of the Board of the Swedish National Group of AIPPI. *Member:* Swedish Bar Association; AIPPI and LES. *LANGUAGES:* Swedish, English and German. *PRACTICE AREAS:* Antitrust and Trade Regulations; (Unfair Competition, Licensing); Business Law; Corporate Law; Contracts; Copyright; Intellectual Property; Patent (Patent Litigations, Licensing); Technology and Science; Trade Marks.

(This Listing Continued)

FRITZ ENGSTRÖM, born Malmberget, January 16, 1926; admitted, 1956, Sweden. *Education:* University of Stockholm (juris kandidat, LL.M., 1950). Junior Judge, 1951-1953. With the Legal Aid Office in Stockholm, 1953-1956. With Advokat Kjell Sjöstedt and Advokat Gösta Åkerlund, 1957-1962. Partner Advokatfirman Fritz Engström AB, 1962-1990. Member of the Governmental Legislative Committee on Patent Litigation, 1979-1983. Chairman of the Board of IWS Sweden AB. Author: Chapter on Sweden in Book International Patent Litigation, 1983. *Member:* Swedish (Member of Board, Stockholm Section, 1966-1971; 1973-1975; Member of Board, 1970-1977) and International Bar Associations. *LANGUAGES:* Swedish, English, German and French. *PRACTICE AREAS:* Antitrust and Trade Regulations (Unfair Competition); Licensing; Business Law; Corporate Law; Contracts; Copyright; Intellectual Property; Patent (Patent Litigations, Licensing); Technology and Science; Trade Marks.

ERIK T.A. LIND, born Stockholm, Sweden, March 11, 1949. *Education:* University of Uppsala (juris kandidat, LL.M., 1975). Junior Judge in a Swedish Court, 1975-1976. Associated with Wetter & Wetter Advokatbyrå, Stockholm, 1976-1982. Board Member, Swedish subsidiaries of Fanuc Ltd., Federal Express Corp., Commercial Shearing Inc., Analog Devices Inc., Emerson Electric Co., Lafarge Coppee, and NEC Scandinavia AB. *Member:* Swedish (1981) and International Bar Associations; International Law Association. *LANGUAGES:* Swedish and English. *PRACTICE AREAS:* Environmental Law; Business and Company Law; Computers and Software; International Contracts; Labour Law; Mergers and Acquisitions; Securities.

RAGNAR LUNDGREN, born 1945. *Education:* LL.M. (Jur.Kand.) University of Stockholm, 1969. District Court 1969-1972. Private legal practice 1972-1980. General Counsel SKF Steel, 1980-1985. Montagu & Co., 1985-1987. Karo Bio AB (Executive Vice President 1989-1991) 1987-1991. *Member:* Swedish Bar Association (1975). *LANGUAGES:* Swedish and English. *PRACTICE AREAS:* Antitrust and Trade Regulations (Unfair Competition); Licensing; Business Law; Corporate Law; Contracts; Copyright; Intellectual Property; Patent (Patent Litigations, Licensing); Pharmaceutical Regulations, Technology and Science; Trade Marks.

BO G.H. NILSSON, born Härnösand, Sweden, April 13, 1950. *Education:* University of Uppsala (Fil. kand. B.A., 1973; juris kandidat, LL.M., 1975). Lecturer, University of Uppsala, 1973-1975. Junior Judge, District Court, 1975-1977 and Junior Judge in a Court of Appeal, 1978-1979. Associated with Wetter & Wetter Advokatbyrå, Stockholm, 1979-1982. *Member:* Swedish (1982) and International Bar Associations. *LANGUAGES:* Swedish, English and Russian. *PRACTICE AREAS:* Arbitration and Litigation.

SVANTE P.A. NYMAN, born 1945. *Education:* University of Stockholm (Juris Kandidat, LL.M., 1970); University of Minnesota Law School, Graduate School (LL.M., 1974). City Attorney's Office of Stockholm, 1970-1972. Associated with: Dorsey & Whitney, Minneapolis, Minnesota, 1972-1974; Advokatfirman Carlers, 1974-1979. Partner, Advokatfirman Carlers, 1979-1984. Chairman of the Board of the Swedish subsidiaries of: Elf Sanofi S.A., (Sanofi Winthrop AB), ITT Corporation (ITT Flygt AB). Member of the Board of Gradic Wire AB. Appointed Special Attorney to the Attorney General of the State of Minnesota, 1984. Honorary Trade Representative of Minnesota Trade Office, 1988—. *Member:* Swedish (1977) and International Bar Associations. *LANGUAGES:* Swedish and English. *PRACTICE AREAS:* Agency and Distributorships; Anti-trust and Trade Regulations; Finance Law; Business and Company Law; Arbitration and Litigation; Mergers and Acquisitions.

P. ANDERS RYDIN, born Gävle, Sweden, May 24, 1945. *Education:* University of Uppsala (juris kandidat, LL.M., 1970); Harvard University Law School (LL.M., 1971). Lecturer, University of Uppsala, 1969-1970. Assistant Secretary to the Committee on the Constitution of the Swedish Parliament, 1970. Junior Judge, District Court, 1971. Associated with Wetter & Swartling Advokatbyrå, Stockholm, 1972-1974 and Wetter & Wetter Advokatbyrå, Stockholm, 1974-1982. Chairman of the Board, Swedish subsidiaries of Paloheimo OY, Ford Motor Company and Ryder System, Inc. Member of the Board, Swedish subsidiaries of Redland PLC and Metsä-Serla Oy. *Member:* Swedish (1976) and International Bar Associations. *LANGUAGES:* Swedish and English. *PRACTICE AREAS:* Antitrust and Trade Regulations; Business and Company law; Contracts; Mergers and Acquisitions; Divestitures; Entertainment and Sports Law.

(This Listing Continued)

RYDIN & CARLSTEN ADVOKATBYRÅ AB,
Stockholm—Continued

ASSOCIATES

CARSTEN W. ANGSMARK, born Falun, Sweden, April 9, 1958. *Education:* University of Uppsala (juris kandidat, LL.M., 1983); University of Minnesota Law School (1983). Law Clerk, National Tax Board, 1984. Junior Judge, District Court, 1984-1986. Associate Counsel, Farmer's Association, 1986-1988. *Member:* Swedish Bar Association (1991); Young Lawyers' International Association. *LANGUAGES:* Swedish and English. *PRACTICE AREAS:* Business and Company Law; Labour Law; Litigation; Real Estate.

NINA M. MACPHERSON, born Gothenburg, Sweden, March 1, 1958. *Education:* University of Stockholm (juris kandidat, LL.M., 1984). Associate Counsel, Saléninvest AB 1982-1985 and Rederi AB Reut, 1985-1988. Member of the Board, subsidiary of Trek Bicycle Corp. *Member:* Swedish Bar Association (1993); Young Lawyers' International Association; International Law Association; Lawyers Committee for Human Rights. *LANGUAGES:* Swedish and English. *PRACTICE AREAS:* Antitrust and Trade Regulation; Company Law; Mergers and Acquisitions; Divestitures; Product Liability.

C. JESPER TIBERG, born Vallentuna, Sweden, August 4, 1963. *Education:* University of Uppsala (juris kandidat, LL.M., 1992); Europa-Institut, University of Saarland, Germany (1990-1991). *LANGUAGES:* Swedish, English and German. *PRACTICE AREAS:* Antitrust and Trade Regulation; Contracts; Litigation.

JONAS H. WESTERBERG, born Stockholm, Sweden, August 24, 1961. *Education:* University of Uppsala (juris kandidat, LL.M., 1989); University of Minnesota Law School (1988). *Member:* Young Lawyers International Association. *LANGUAGES:* Swedish and English. *PRACTICE AREAS:* Antitrust and Trade Regulation; Arbitration and Litigation; Mergers and Acquisitions; Intellectual Property Law; Patents; Business and Company Law.

G. SANDSTRÖMS ADVOKATBYRÅ

STOCKHOLM, SWEDEN

(See Advokatfirman Vinge KB)

Admiralty, Corporate, Contracts, Tax, Labor, Transport, Antitrust, Copyright, Trademark and Patent, Bankruptcy Law, Litigation, Banking and International Finance Law.

SETTERWALLS

Nils Setterwalls Advokatbyrå AB

ARSENALSGATAN 6
S-111 47 STOCKHOLM, SWEDEN
Telephone: +46 (8) 678 78 78
Telex: 176 73 SETLAW S
Fax: +46 (8) 611 46 30 *Cables: Nilsetterwall*

London, England Office: 10, Hill Street, W1X 7FU. Telephone: 0171-409 1843. Fax: 0171-493 1106.
Singapore Office: Straits Trading Building, 9, Battery Road, 17-08, 0104. Telephone: 535 31 12 Telex: 25430 COOMA RS.

Admiralty and Maritime, Aircraft and Ship Finance, Arbitration and Litigation, Banking and Securities, General Business and Corporate, Insurance, Intellectual Property Rights, Taxation.

FIRM PROFILE: Setterwalls was established already in 1878. The firm ranks as a medium size law firm in Sweden with representative offices in London and Singapore and it has over the past century assisted business clients in such areas as commercial and corporate law, maritime and aviation law, banking and finance, intellectual property, taxation and insurance and litigation and arbitration national as well as international.

MEMBERS OF FIRM

KLAS G. KLEBERG, born Stockholm, Sweden, 1936. *Education:* University of Stockholm (LL.B., 1960). *Member:* Swedish Bar Association (1966). *LANGUAGES:* Swedish, English and French. *PRACTICE AREAS:* Commercial and Corporate Law; Maritime Law.

J.G. RUDBECK, born Stockholm, Sweden, 1937. *Education:* University of Stockholm (LL.B., 1962). *Member:* Swedish Bar Association (1969).

LANGUAGES: Swedish and English. *PRACTICE AREAS:* Commercial Law; Maritime and Transportation Law; Insurance Law; Litigation and Arbitration.

CLAES BROMAN, born Stockholm, Sweden, 1942. *Education:* University of Stockholm (LL.B., 1967). *Member:* Swedish Bar Association (1974). *LANGUAGES:* Swedish and English. *PRACTICE AREAS:* Commercial and Corporate Law; Maritime and Transportation Law; Litigation and Arbitration.

FRED WENNERHOLM, born Stockholm, Sweden, 1945. *Education:* University of Stockholm (LL.B., 1969). *Member:* Swedish Bar Association (1974). *LANGUAGES:* Swedish, English and German. *PRACTICE AREAS:* Commercial and Corporate Law; Banking and Finance; Litigation and Arbitration.

OTTO RYDBECK, born Malmö, Sweden, 1945. *Education:* University of Lund (LL.B., 1971). *Member:* Swedish Bar Association (1977). *LANGUAGES:* Swedish and English. *PRACTICE AREAS:* Banking and Finance; Securities; Commercial and Corporate Law.

ERIK AF PETERSENS, born Stockholm, Sweden, 1942. *Education:* University of Stockholm (LL.B., 1969). *Member:* Swedish Bar Association (1975). *LANGUAGES:* Swedish and English. *PRACTICE AREAS:* Commercial and Corporate Law; Intellectual Property Law; Litigation and Arbitration.

MATS WAERING, born Stockholm, Sweden, 1946. *Education:* University of Stockholm (LL.B., 1972). *Member:* Swedish Bar Association (1990). *LANGUAGES:* Swedish and English. *PRACTICE AREAS:* Aircraft Finance; Aviation Law; Commercial and Corporate Law.

HARALD NORDENSON, born Stockholm, Sweden, 1946. *Education:* University of Stockholm (LL.B., 1973). *Member:* Swedish Bar Association (1991). *LANGUAGES:* Swedish, English and French. *PRACTICE AREAS:* Foreign Investments; Joint Ventures and Technology Transfer.

ÅKE J. FORS, born Kalmar, Sweden, 1958. *Education:* University of Lund (LL.B., 1982). *Member:* Swedish Bar Association (1990). *LANGUAGES:* Swedish, English and German. *PRACTICE AREAS:* Banking and Finance; Aircraft Finance.

HÅKAN FOHLIN, born Södertälje, Sweden, 1957. *Education:* University of Stockholm (LL.B., 1981). *Member:* Swedish Bar Association (1990). *LANGUAGES:* Swedish, English and Spanish. *PRACTICE AREAS:* Banking and Finance; Ship Finance; Commercial and Corporate Law.

ASSOCIATES

ANNA SURTEVALL, born Västervik, Sweden, 1955. *Education:* University of Uppsala (LL.B., 1980). *Member:* Swedish Bar Association (1992). *LANGUAGES:* Swedish and English. *PRACTICE AREAS:* Maritime and Transportation Law; Commercial and Corporate Law.

OWE HJELMQVIST, born Stockholm, Sweden, 1958. *Education:* University of Stockholm (LL.B., 1987). *Member:* Swedish Bar Association (1992). *LANGUAGES:* Swedish and English. *PRACTICE AREAS:* Commercial and Corporate Law; Intellectual Property Law.

MARIA CHAMBERS, born Nykoping, Sweden, 1958. *Education:* University of Stockholm (LL.M., 1984); Fordham University (Certificate Program in Corporate Finance, 1989). *Member:* Swedish Bar Association, 1991. *LANGUAGES:* Swedish and English. *PRACTICE AREAS:* Commercial and Corporate Law.

THOMAS MYRDAL, born Uppsala, Sweden, 1965. *Education:* University of Uppsala (LL.B., 1991). *LANGUAGES:* Swedish and English. *PRACTICE AREAS:* Banking and Finance; Commercial and Corporate Law.

ULF DJURBERG, born Borås, Sweden, 1963. *Education:* University of Uppsala (LL.B., 1989); University of Amsterdam (LL.M. in European Integration, 1990). *LANGUAGES:* Swedish and English. *PRACTICE AREAS:* EC and EEA Law; Commercial Law.

CHRISTINA ÅKERHED, born Karlskrona, Sweden, 1967. *Education:* University of Lund (LL.B., 1990). *LANGUAGES:* Swedish and English. *PRACTICE AREAS:* Commercial and Corporate Law.

THOMAS MYHR, born Stockholm, Sweden, 1964. *Education:* University of Stockholm (LL.B., 1991). *LANGUAGES:* Swedish, English and French. *PRACTICE AREAS:* Commercial and Corporate Law.

MAGNUS SJÖDIN, born Vasteras, Sweden, 1963. *Education:* University of Uppsala (LL.B., 1990). *LANGUAGES:* Swedish, English and German. *PRACTICE AREAS:* Maritime Law; Commercial Law.

(This Listing Continued)

(This Listing Continued)

CONSULTANT

MATS HILDING, born Gothenburg, Sweden, 1917. *Education:* University of Stockholm. Former Chief Justice *inter alia,* Maritime and Admiralty Court of Stockholm. Former Chairman at the Swedish Association of International Maritime Law. Former Teacher at the University of Stockholm. Arbitrator for the Arbitration Institute, Stockholm Chamber of Commerce.

Languages: English, French and German

SÖDERLUND & PARTNERS

BIRGER JARLSGATAN 16
S-114 34 STOCKHOLM, SWEDEN
Telephone: +46-8-614 48 00
Fax: +46-8-611 24 85

Geneva, Switzerland Office: 15, Boulevard Helvétique. CH-1207.
Telephone: +41-22-735 40 87. Fax: +41-22-735 40 07.

General Corporation and Business Law. International Legal Transactions, Finance and Banking Law, Aviation and Transportation Law, Intellectual Property Law, Litigation and International Arbitration.

MEMBERS OF FIRM

CHRISTER SÖDERLUND, born Piteå, Sweden, December 9, 1953. *Education:* University of Uppsala (jur. kand., LL.M., 1981). Junior Judge at Hudiksvall District Court, 1981-1983. Associated with Erik Berglunds Advokatbyrå, 1983-1987. Own practice since 1987. *Member:* Swedish Bar Association. *LANGUAGES:* Swedish and English.

CHEDDI LILJESTRÖM, born Kungälv, Sweden, September 15, 1954. *Education:* University of Uppsala (jur. kand., LL.M., 1979); New York University School of Law (M.C.J., 1981; LL.M., 1982). Assistant in Penal Law, University of Uppsala, 1977-1980. Legal Research Instructor, New York University, School of Law, 1981-1982. Intern at UNITAR, 1981-1982. Associated with Wetter & Wetter Advokatbyrå, Stockholm, 1982-1983. Junior Judge at Stockholm District Court, 1983-1985. Associated with Rydin & Carlsten Advokatbyrå, 1985-1988. In house counsel Scandinavian Airlines System (SAS), 1988-1993. *Member:* Swedish Bar Association; New York State and American Bar Associations. *LANGUAGES:* Swedish and English.

MARTIN LUNDQUIST, born Stockholm, Sweden, February 26, 1959. *Education:* University of Stockholm (jur. kand., LL.M., 1985). Junior Judge at Stockholm District Court, 1985-1988. Associated with Advokatfirman Ekelund, Ekholm, Lindberg & Saxon, 1988-1989; Advokatfirman Ekholm & Hesselman, 1989-1992. Partner Advokatfirman Ekholm & Söderlund, 1992-1993. *Member:* Swedish Bar Association. *LANGUAGES:* Swedish and English.

ASSOCIATES

KATARINA DIEDEN, born Umeå, Sweden, April 1, 1945. *Education:* University of Stockholm (jur. kand., LL.M., 1987). Junior Judge at Gävle District Court, 1987-1990. Associated with Advokatfirman Raoul Smitt, 1990-1993; Advokatfirman Ekholm & Söderlund, 1993. *Member:* Swedish Bar Association. *LANGUAGES:* Swedish and English.

ÅSA BITTEL PETTERSSON, born Stockholm, Sweden, November 19, 1962. *Education:* University of Stockholm (jur. kand., LL.M., 1987). ICC International Court of Arbitration, Paris, 1986-1987. European Free Trade Association (EFTA), Geneva, 1987-1988. Associated with Cabinet Juridique Merlotti, Geneva, 1990-1992; Advokatfirman Ekholm & Söderlund, 1992-1993. (Resident in Geneva). *LANGUAGES:* Swedish, French and English.

PER FRANKOW, born Stockholm, Sweden, April 29, 1954. *Education:* University of Stockholm (jur. kand., LL.M., 1982); Stockholm School of Economics (Diploma, 1989). With Skandinaviska Enskilda Banken, 1982. In house counsel FinansSkandic AB, 1983-1985. General Counsel, Finansor AB, 1985-1991; Optimum Kredit AB, 1991-1993. *LANGUAGES:* Swedish and English.

MARITA GRÖNDAHL, born Stockholm, Sweden, December 11, 1966. *Education:* University of Stockholm (jur. kand., LL.M., 1990); University of Exeter (LL.M. in European Legal Studies, 1994). Junior Judge at Stockholm District Court, 1990-1994. *LANGUAGES:* Swedish, English and French.

ADVOKATFIRMAN SÖDERMARK

Established in 1925

STRANDVÄGEN 1
P.O. BOX 14055
S-104 40 STOCKHOLM, SWEDEN
Telephone: +46 (8) 670 57 50
Telex: 117 65 Soder-S
Telefax: +46 (8) 663 67 20

General Corporate and Commercial Practice, including Banking, Finance, Mergers and Acquisitions, Insurance, Maritime, Transportation, Litigation and Arbitration (Domestic and International).

MEMBERS OF FIRM

BERTIL HENRIQUES, born 1919. *Education:* University of Stockholm (juris kandidat, LL.B., 1944). Served in District Court, 1944-1947. *Member:* Swedish Bar Association (1950) (Member of Board, Stockholm Section, 1958-1962). *LANGUAGES:* Swedish and English.

BERTIL SÖDERMARK, born 1935. *Education:* University of Stockholm (juris kandidat, LL.B., 1959). Served in District Court, 1960-1962. *Member:* Swedish Bar Association (1965). *LANGUAGES:* Swedish and English.

ANDERS BECK-FRIIS, born 1942. *Education:* University of Stockholm (juris kandidat, LL.B., 1968). Served in District Court, 1968-1970. *Member:* Swedish Bar Association (1973). *LANGUAGES:* Swedish and English.

PETER J. LINDSKOG, born 1947. *Education:* University of Stockholm (juris kandidat, LL.B., 1971). Advanced Studies of Maritime Law. Served in District Court, 1972-1974. Judge Referee to the Svea Court of Appeal, 1974-1975. Associated with Advokatfirman Morssing & Nycander, 1975-1981. Partner of Advokatfirman Wesslau & Lindskog, 1981-1989. *Member:* Swedish Bar Association (1978); Swedish Maritime Law Association; Swedish Insurance Law Association. *LANGUAGES:* Swedish, English and German.

HÅKAN ROCKSTRÖM, born 1947. *Education:* University of Stockholm (juris kandidat, LL.B., 1972). Served in District Court, 1972-1974. *Member:* Swedish Bar Association (1977). *LANGUAGES:* Swedish and English.

PETER BOLMSTEDT, born 1954. *Education:* University of Uppsala (juris kandidat, LL.B., 1980). Served in District Court, 1981-1984 and Administrative Court of Appeals, 1984-1985. *Member:* Swedish Bar Association (1988). *LANGUAGES:* Swedish and English.

THOMAS TENDORF, born 1959. *Education:* University of Uppsala (juris kandidat, LL.B., 1982); University of London, London School of Economics (LL.M., 1985). Served in District Court, 1983-1984 and 1985-1986. Corporate Counsel, AB Hägglund & Söner, 1988-1989. *Member:* Swedish and International Bar Associations (1990). *LANGUAGES:* Swedish and English.

TORGNY WETTERBERG, born 1961. *Education:* University of Lund (juris kandidat, LL.B., 1985). Served in District Court, 1985-1988. *Member:* Swedish Bar Association (1991). *LANGUAGES:* Swedish and English.

ASSOCIATES

PETER HAGLUND, born 1959. *Education:* University of Stockholm (juris kandidat, LL.B., 1985). Served in District Court, 1986-1988. *Member:* Swedish Bar Association (1992). *LANGUAGES:* Swedish and English.

LARS GÖTHLIN, born 1943. *Education:* University of Uppsala (juris kandidat, LL.B., 1968). Served in District Court, 1968-1971. Assistant Director, Stockholm Chamber of Commerce. Secretary, Arbitration Institute, Stockholm Chamber of Commerce, 1971-1975. Legal Counsel: Rederiaktiebolaget Nordstjernan, 1975-1979; ASSI, 1979-1981. General Counsel and Company Secretary, AB Bofors, 1981-1985. General Counsel and Member, Group Executive Committee, Company Secretary, Nobel Industries AB, 1985-1992. *LANGUAGES:* Swedish and English.

LARS SANDBERG, born 1964. *Education:* University of Uppsala (juris kandidat, LL.B., 1989); University of Minnesota Law School (1987). Served in District Court, 1990-1992. *LANGUAGES:* Swedish and English.

PONTUS SELDERMAN, born 1966. *Education:* University of Uppsala (juris kandidat, LL.B., 1991); University of Minnesota Law School (1989); University of Oslo (juridisk embetseksamen, Maritime Law, 1992). Served in District Court, 1991-1993. *LANGUAGES:* Swedish and English.

(This Listing Continued)

ADVOKATFIRMAN SÖDERMARK, Stockholm—
Continued

HÅKAN LINDGREN, born 1967. *Education:* University of Stockholm (juris kandidat, LL.B., 1992). Served in District Court, 1992-1994. *LANGUAGES:* Swedish and English.

STEN LINDSKOG ADVOKATBYRÅ

Established in 1942

NARVAVÄGEN 32

P.O. BOX 27707

S-115 91 STOCKHOLM, SWEDEN

Telephone: +46 8 670 85 20

Telefax: +46 8 670 85 50

Swedish and International Business Law, Litigation and Arbitration, Bankruptcy and Insolvency Law.

FIRM PROFILE: The firm represents Swedish authorities, banks, insurance companies and other enterprises, both foreign and Swedish of various sizes and provides a full range of legal services in the business area.

PARTNERS

PETER WADSTED, born 1927. *Education:* University of Stockholm (LL.M., juris kandidat, 1952). *Member:* Swedish Bar Association. *LANGUAGES:* English, Danish and German. *PRACTICE AREAS:* General Commercial Law; Family Law; Estates; Real Estate and Land Use.

LARS NYCANDER, born 1931. *Education:* University of Stockholm (LL.M., juris kandidat, 1957). Junior Judgeship, Court of Appeal, 1960-1962. *Member:* Swedish Bar Association. *LANGUAGES:* English. *PRACTICE AREAS:* General Commercial Law; Corporate Law; Bankruptcy and Insolvency Law; Litigation and Arbitration.

GÖRAN MÖRNER, born 1927. *Education:* University of Stockholm (LL.M., juris kandidat, 1957). *Member:* Swedish Bar Association. *LANGUAGES:* English. *PRACTICE AREAS:* General Commercial Law; Corporate Law; Trusts and Estates.

MAGNUS ULLMAN, born 1946. *Education:* University of Stockholm (LL.M., juris kandidat, 1970). Junior Judgeship, Court of Appeal, 1970-1972. *Member:* Swedish Bar Association. *LANGUAGES:* English and German. *PRACTICE AREAS:* General Commercial Law; Corporate Law; Patent Law; Litigation and Arbitration.

GUNNAR LINDSKOG, born 1948. *Education:* University of Stockholm (LL.M., juris kandidat, 1975). *Member:* Swedish Bar Association. *LANGUAGES:* English. *PRACTICE AREAS:* General Commercial Law; Corporate Law.

THOMAS OLROG, born 1946. *Education:* University of Stockholm (LL.M., juris kandidat, 1975). *Member:* Swedish Bar Association. *LANGUAGES:* English. *PRACTICE AREAS:* General Commercial Law; Corporate Law; Bankruptcy and Insolvency Law.

ASSOCIATES

GÖRAN GRUNDÉN, born 1958. *Education:* University of Stockholm (LL.M., juris kandidat, 1984). Junior Judgeship, Court of Appeal, 1986-1989. *Member:* Swedish Bar Association. *LANGUAGES:* English. *PRACTICE AREAS:* General Commercial Law; Corporate Law; Bankruptcy and Insolvency Law.

MIKAEL KLERBRO, born 1957. *Education:* University of Uppsala (LL.M., juris kandidat, 1984). Junior Judgeship, Court of Appeal, 1987-1988. The Housing Court, 1988-1989. *Member:* Swedish Bar Association. *LANGUAGES:* English. *PRACTICE AREAS:* General Commercial Law; Corporate Law; Bankruptcy and Insolvency Law; Tenancy Right.

JENNY GRUNDÉN, born 1961. *Education:* University of Stockholm (LL.M., juris kandidat, 1990). *LANGUAGES:* English and German. *PRACTICE AREAS:* General Commercial Law; Bankruptcy and Insolvency Law.

OLA SELLERT, born 1959. *Education:* University of Lund (LL.M., juris kandidat, 1985). Fiscal Court of Appeal, 1988-1990. Junior Judgeship, Court of Appeal, 1989. Ackordscentralen Stockholm, 1990-1992. *LANGUAGES:* English. *PRACTICE AREAS:* General Commercial Law; Corporate Law; Bankruptcy and Insolvency Law.

(This Listing Continued)

ANDERS BURÉN, born 1966. *Education:* University of Stockholm (LL.M., juris kandidat, 1992). *LANGUAGES:* English and German. *PRACTICE AREAS:* General Commercial Law; Bankruptcy and Insolvency Law.

JG TENGSTRÖM ADVOKATBYRÅ AB

Established in 1982

KUNGSGATAN 33, V.

P.O. BOX 14054

S-104 40 STOCKHOLM, SWEDEN

Telephone: 46 8 660 38 55

Fax: 46 8 667 56 86

Criminal Law, Business and General Crimes. Computer Law and Computer-related Crimes. Human Rights. Labour Law. Family Law. Indemnity Law.

JOHAN G. TENGSTRÖM, born November 21, 1941; admitted, 1981, Sweden. *Education:* University of Uppsala, University of Stockholm (LL.M., 1975). International Law Studies in Bern, Switzerland and Hamburg, Germany, 1963-1966. Trainee at Haight, Gardner, Poor and Havens, New York, 1976-1977. Assistant Judge, District Court of Haparanda, 1977-1978. Notary Public, 1977-1978. Vice President, Kriminalpolitiska Sällskapet (Criminal Political Society), 1988-1990. President: ECU (European Consultants Unit), Sweden, 1989-1994. Representative of International Legal Defense Counsel (ILDC). Secretary, Criminal Law Committee, International Bar Association, 1994—. *Member:* Swedish Bar Association; International Bar Association. *LANGUAGES:* Swedish, Finnish, German and English. *PRACTICE AREAS:* Business and General Crimes; Indemnity Law; Labour Law; Family Law.

ADVOKATFIRMAN TISELL & CO. AB

Member of SLG

(Scandinavian Business Law Group)

Copenhagen: Berning Schlüter, Hald

Helsinki: Bützow & Co.

Oslo: Vogt & Co.

Stockholm: Tisell & Co.

BIRGER JARLSGATAN 32 A

P.O. BOX 7324

103 90 STOCKHOLM, SWEDEN

Telephone: +46 86142200

Telefax: +46 86112255

General Corporate and Business Law, Banking, Financing, Taxation, Contract, Licensing, Trademark, Copyright, Labor Law and Mergers and Acquisition. Arbitration and Litigation in Civil Matters.

MEMBERS OF FIRM

LARS-HENRIK TISELL, born Stockholm, Sweden, 1938. *Education:* University of Stockholm (juris kandidat, LL.B). Assistant Judge, 1964-1966. *Member:* Swedish Bar Association (1969).

PETER LÖNNQUIST, born Stockholm, Sweden, 1943. *Education:* University of Stockholm (juris kandidat, LL.B.). *Member:* Swedish Bar Association (1980).

PER WINNBERG, born Stockholm, Sweden, 1944. *Education:* University of Stockholm (juris kandidat, LL.B.). Assistant Judge, 1969-1971. Fiscal Court of Appeal, 1971-1972. *Member:* Swedish Bar Association (1977).

CHRISTER THINGVALL, born Stockholm, Sweden, 1946. *Education:* University of Stockholm (juris kandidat, LL.B.). Assistant Judge, 1972-1974. *Member:* Swedish Bar Association (1977).

OLLE WIDELL, born Stockholm, Sweden, 1950. *Education:* University of Stockholm (juris kandidat, LL.B.). Assistant judge, 1976-1978. Svea Court of Appeal, 1978-1979. *Member:* Swedish Bar Association (1983).

LARS-OLOF SVENSSON, born Kalmar, Sweden, 1955. *Education:* University of Lund (juris kandidat, LL.B.). Assistant Judge, 1980-1982. *Member:* Swedish Bar Association (1985).

CLAS DALEN, born Stockholm, Sweden, 1945. *Education:* University of Stockholm (juris kandidat, LL.B.). Assistant Judge, 1973-1975. *Member:* Swedish Bar Association (1980).

(This Listing Continued)

EVA-MAJ I. MÜHLENBOCK, born Motala, Sweden, 1959. *Education:* University of Stockholm (juris kandidat, LL.B.). Assistant and Teacher at the Faculty of Law, University of Stockholm, 1979-1982. Law practice in Seattle, USA, 1982-1983. Assistant Judge, 1983-1985. *Member:* Swedish Bar Association (1989).

MATS LARSSON, born Stockholm, Sweden, 1957. *Education:* University of Stockholm (juris kandidat, LL.B.). Assistant Judge 1982-1985. Fiscal Court of Appeal, 1985-1986. *Member:* Swedish Bar Association.

MAGNUS BJÖRCK, born Gävle, Sweden, 1958. *Education:* University of Uppsala (juris kandidat, LL.B.). Assistant at the Faculty of Law, University of Uppsala, 1982-1983. Assistant Judge, 1984-1986. *Member:* Swedish Bar Association.

CHRISTER BRANTHEIM, born Östersund, Sweden, 1959. *Education:* University of Uppsala (juris kandidat, LL.B.). Assistant at the Faculty of Law, University of Uppsala, 1984. Assistant Judge, 1984-1986. *Member:* Swedish Bar Association.

OLOF ALFFRAM, born Stockholm, Sweden, 1953. *Education:* University of Stockholm (juris kandidat, LL.B.). Assistant Judge, 1985-1987. Fiscal Court of Appeal, 1987-1988. *Member:* Swedish Bar Association.

ASSOCIATES

STIG TORSTENIUS, born Stockholm, 1924. *Education:* University of Uppsala (juris kandidat, LL.B.). Assistant Judge, 1951-1952. Law Practice, 1952-1957. Member, Swedish Bar Association, 1956-1957. Manager of Regional Trust Department, Sundsvallsbanken, 1957-1969. Dito Uplandsbanken, 1969-1982. Manager of Regional Legal Department, Uplandsbanken/Nordbanken, 1982-1987. Assistant to Chief Legal Advisor, Nordbanken, 1987-1988.

STEN V.D. OSTEN-SACKEN, born Greifswald, Germany, 1922. *Education:* University of Stockholm (juris kandidat, LL..B.). Service at Swedish Courts 1947-1990. Magistrate 1965-1976. Chief Judge in District Courts 1976-1989.

KRISTINA FORSBACKA, born Vasa, Finland, 1958. *Education:* University of Stockholm (juris kandidat, LL.B.). Assistant Judge, 1985-1987. Fiscal Court of Appeal, 1988. *Member:* Swedish Bar Association.

PETER LEXENBERG, born Stockholm, Sweden, 1962. *Education:* University of Stockholm (juris kandidat, LL.B.). Assistant Judge, 1988-1991. *Member:* Swedish Bar Association.

CHRISTIAN BERGQUIST, born Stockholm, Sweden, 1962. *Education:* University of Stockholm (juris kandidat, LL.B.). Assistant Judge, 1988-1991. *Member:* Swedish Bar Association.

HARRY BERGMAN, born Stockholm, Sweden, 1961. *Education:* University of Stockholm (juris kandidat, LL.B.). Teacher, Faculty of Law, University of Stockholm, 1988-1990. Assistant Judge, 1988-1991. *Member:* Swedish Bar Association.

TORBJÖRN HULTSBERG, born Västervik, Sweden, 1955. *Education:* University of Lund (juris kandidat, LL.B.). Assistant Judge, 1980-1983, Sveq Court of Appeal 1983-1987. Junior Judge at District Court of Stockholm 1987. *Member:* Swedish Bar Association.

ROBERT KULLGREN, born Solna, Sweden, 1964. *Education:* University of Stockholm (juris kandidat, LL.B.); Christian Albrecht's University, Kiel, Germany (LL.M., 1989). Assistant Judge, 1990-1992.

CHRISTER KARLERÖ, born Jönköping, Sweden, 1961. *Education:* University of Stockholm (juris kandidat, LL.B.). Assistant Judge, 1987-1989. Göta Court of Appeal, 1989-1993.

SUSANNE THEMPTANDER, born Lidingö, Sweden, 1959. *Education:* University of Stockholm (juris kandidat, LL.B.). Assistant Judge, 1991-1993.

KATARINA HEDBERG-JANSSON, born Göteborg, Sweden, 1966. *Education:* University of Stockholm (juris kandidat, LL.B.). Assistant Judge, 1992-1994.

LENNART ERNSTSON, born Stockholm, Sweden, 1965. *Education:* University of Stockholm (juris kandidat, LL.B.). Assistant Judge, 1991-1993. Assistant City Lawyer, 1993-1995.

(This Listing Continued)

CLAES JOHANSSON, born Ange, Sweden, 1959. *Education:* University of Uppsala (juris kandidat, LL.B.). Assistant Judge, 1985-1987. Fiscal Court of Appeal, 1987-1988. Tax Consultant, 1989 and 1991-1992.

Languages: English, German, French and Scandinavian.

REFERENCES: Öhrlings Revisionsbyra AB/Coopers & Lybrand, Stockholm; Price Waterhouse, Stockholm, Sweden.

ADVOKATFIRMAN VERUM

BIBLIOTEKSGATAN 11
P.O. BOX 7149
S-103 87 STOCKHOLM, SWEDEN
Telephone: +46-8 6117705
Telex: 12442 FOTEX S, Attn. Verumlex
Facsimile: +46-8 6117190

Singapore Office: 8 Shenton Way, 44-02 Treasury Building, 0106. Telephone: 224 97 44. Telex: RS 65661. Telefax: 224 04 71.

General Corporate and Business Law, Finance and Banking Law, Securities Regulations, Maritime Law, Litigation and Arbitration.

MEMBERS OF FIRM

HUGO WENNBERG, born Orebro, Sweden, 1931; admitted, 1962, Sweden. *Education:* University of Stockholm (juris kandidät, LL.B., 1957). Held Junior Judgeship, 1957-1959. Lecturer on Law, University of Stockholm, 1963-1974 and Stockholm School of Economics, 1965-1974. Partner, Advokatfirman Södermark, 1975-1985 and Advokatfirman Hugo Wennberg AB, 1985-1989. *Member:* Swedish Bar Association (1962) (Board Member, Stockholm Section, 1969-1973); International Bar Association. **LANGUAGES:** Swedish, English and German.

CHRISTER HOLM, born Stockholm, Sweden, 1940; admitted, 1973, Sweden. *Education:* University of Stockholm (juris kandidat, LL.B., 1966). Served in Swedish Courts, 1967-1970. Associated with Carl Swartling Advokatbyrå, 1971-1976. Associate Counsel Gränges AB, 1976-1977. General Counsel Swedish Steel Corporation (SSAB), 1977-1981. Partner Wesslau, Holm & Co., 1981-1985. *Member:* Swedish Bar Association; International Bar Association. **LANGUAGES:** Swedish and English.

CLAES ESSÉN, born Stockholm, Sweden, 1941; admitted, 1973, Sweden. *Education:* University of Stockholm (juris kandidat, LL.B., 1966); Stockholm School of Economics (M.B.A., 1968). Assistant to the Dean of Law Faculty, University of Stockholm, 1965-1966. Held Junior Judgeship, 1968-1970. Partner, Advokatfirman Södermark, Stockholm, 1975-1985. *Member:* Swedish Bar Association (Board Member, Stockholm Section, 1979-1984); International Bar Association. **LANGUAGES:** Swedish and English.

HANS G. WESSLAU, born Sundsvall, Sweden, 1942; admitted, 1976, Sweden. *Education:* Universities of Stockholm and Uppsala (juris kandidat, LL.B., 1970). Legal Studies London, 1966 and 1967. Guest Lecturer on International Trade and Business Law, 1972-1974. Held Junior Judgeship, 1971-1972. Associated with Advokatfirman Morssing & Nycander, 1972-1974. Counsel to the Swedish Investment Bank, 1974-1976. Advokatfirman Morssing & Nycander, 1976-1981 (Resident Lawyer in Brussels, 1978-1980). Partner, Wesslau, Holm & Co., 1981-1989. *Member:* Swedish and International Bar Associations; Swedish Maritime Law Association; Swedish Insurance Law Association; International Law Association; Asia-Pacific Lawyers Association. **LANGUAGES:** Swedish and English.

CLAS ROMANDER, born Stockholm, Sweden, 1955; admitted, 1987, Sweden. *Education:* University of Stockholm (juris kandidat, LL.B., 1981). Lecturer on Law, University of Stockholm, 1987—. Legal Affairs, European Free Trade Association, Geneva, 1981-1982. Held Junior Judgeship, 1982-1983. Associated with Wesslau, Holm & Co., 1983-1986 and with White & Case, 1986-1988. *Member:* Swedish Bar Association; International Bar Association; Swedish Association for Foreign and Comparative Law; American Bar Association (International Associate); American Chamber of Commerce, Sweden (Founding Father). **LANGUAGES:** Swedish, English and French.

HÅKAN PETRELIUS, born Stockholm, Sweden, 1951; admitted, 1988, Sweden. *Education:* University of Stockholm (juris kandidat, LL.B., 1978). Held Junior Judgeship, 1978-1980. Counsel Wermlandsbanken, 1981-1986. *Member:* Swedish Bar Association.

MATS HULTMAN, born August 21, 1951; admitted, 1991, Sweden. *Education:* University of Uppsala (Juris Kandidat, LL.B., 1978). Served in District Court and Court of Appeals, 1979-1982. Corporate Legal Counsel: AGA AB, 1982-1985; Haight, Gardner, Poor & Havens, New York, 1985;

(This Listing Continued)

ADVOKATFIRMAN VERUM, Stockholm—Continued

AB Volvo, 1985-1989. Counsel, White & Case, Stockholm, 1989-1992. *Member:* Swedish Bar Association; International Bar Association; Swedish Insurance Law Association. *LANGUAGES:* Swedish and English.

ASSOCIATES

JAN LJUNGAR, born Stockholm, Sweden, 1957; admitted, 1992, Sweden. *Education:* University of Stockholm (M.B.A., 1979, juris kandidat, LL.B., 1985). Junior Judgeship, City Court of Norrtälje, 1985-1988. *Member:* Swedish Bar Association; International Bar Association. *LANGUAGES:* Swedish, English and German.

JOHN KADELBURGER, born Stockholm, Sweden, 1958; admitted, 1992, Sweden. *Education:* Universities of Stockholm and Uppsala (juris kandidat LL.B., 1987); The Bologna Center of the Paul H. Nitze School of Advanced International Studies; John Hopkins University (Studies in Law, Economy and International Relations, Graduate Diploma in International Affairs, 1986). Associated with White & Case, 1987-1988; Advokatfirman J. Gillis Wetter AB, 1988-1993. *Member:* Swedish Bar Association; International Bar Association; Associazione Giuristi di Lingua Italiana. *LANGUAGES:* Swedish, English, Italian and German.

MAGNUS ANDERSSON, born Visby, Sweden, 1959; admitted, 1993, Sweden. *Education:* University of Uppsala (Juris kandit LL.B., 1986); Studies at University of Minnesota Law School, 1986. Junior Judge, City Court of Varberg, 1987-1988. Judge Referee, Court of Appeal of Vastra Sverige, 1989-1990. *Member:* Swedish Bar Association. *LANGUAGES:* Swedish and English.

SUSANNE RICHTER, born Stockholm, Sweden, 1964. *Education:* University of Surrey, studies in English Law, 1988; University of Stockholm (LL.B., 1988); London School of Economics (LL.M., 1989). Lecturer of Law, University of Stockholm, 1989—. Junior Judge, City Court of Stockholm, 1990. *Member:* Swedish Bar Association; International Bar Association. *LANGUAGES:* Swedish, English and French.

TAX CONSULTANT

LEIF ANDERSON, born Åmål, Sweden, 1949; admitted, 1990, Sweden. *Education:* University of Uppsala (Juris Kandidat, LL.B., 1975). Deputy Judge, Fiscal Court of Appeal, 1975-1976. *Member:* Swedish Bar Association; International Franchise Association; International Bar Association; Association International des Jeunes Avocats. *LANGUAGES:* Swedish and English.

Languages: Swedish, English, German, French and Italian

ADVOKATFIRMAN VINGE KB

SMÅLANDSGATAN 20

P.O. BOX 1703

S-111 87 STOCKHOLM, SWEDEN

Telephone: 08-6143000

Telex: 11150 VINGE S

Telefax: 08-6119037

Gothenburg, Sweden Office: Nils Ericsonsgatan 17, P.O. Box 11025, S-404 21. Telephone: 031-80 51 00. Telex: 21119 VINGE S. Telefax: 031-15 88 11.

Malmö, Sweden Office: Östergatan 30, P.O. Box 4255, S-203 13. Telephone: 040-748 40. Telex: 8305122 VINGE S. Telefax: 040-97 27 72.

Helsingborg, Sweden Office: Kullagatan 60, P.O. Box 1064, S-251 10. Telephone: 042-18 33 70. Telex: 8335079 VINGE S. Telefax: 042-18 23 04.

London, England Office: 44/45 Chancery Lane, WC2A 1JB. Telephone: +44-1-404 4825. Telex: 25585 VINGE G. Telefax: +44-1-831 6860.

Paris, France Office: 8, Avenue Bertie Albrecht, F-75008. Telephone: +33-1-45 63 97 97. Telex: 280918 INTAVOC F. Telefax: +33-1-42 56 24 39.

Hong Kong Office: 2003 Hutchison House, 10 Harcourt Road, Central. Telephone: +852-5 23 61 49. Telefax: 852-8105343.

Brussels, Belgium Office: Avenue Louise 475/B12, B-1050. Telephone: (2) 646 36 20; (2) 646 36 80. Telefax: +32 (2) 646 41 46.

Admiralty, Corporate, Contracts, Tax, Labor, Transport, Antitrust, Copyright, Trademark and Patent, Bankruptcy Law, Litigation, Banking and International Finance Law.

(This Listing Continued)

MEMBERS OF FIRM

ANDERS R. ÖHMAN, born September 10, 1925. *Education:* University of Stockholm (juris kandidat LL.B., 1950). Notary Public, 1958-1971. Expert to the Drafts Legislation Committee, 1963-1971. Member of the Swedish Bankruptcy Committee, 1971-1980. President of Union Internationale des Avocats (UIA). Associated with this firm since 1950. *Member:* Swedish Bar Association (1954; Member of the Board, 1964-1970). *LANGUAGES:* French, German and English. *PRACTICE AREAS:* Commercial Law.

CARL MALCOLM (MAC) FALLENIUS, born May 17, 1935. *Education:* University of Stockholm (juris kandidat, LL.B., 1960). Service with Swedish Courts, 1960-1963. *Member:* Swedish Bar Association (1967). *LANGUAGES:* German and English. *PRACTICE AREAS:* Commercial Law.

JOHAN AF PETERSENS, born September 17, 1934. *Education:* University of Stockholm (juris kandidat, LL.B., 1963). Service in Swedish Courts, 1963-1965. Associated with this firm since 1966. *Member:* Swedish Bar Association (1969). *LANGUAGES:* French, German and English. *PRACTICE AREAS:* Commercial Law.

JAN WIDLUND, born October 21, 1941. *Education:* University of Stockholm (juris kandidat LL.B., 1966); Stockholm School of Economics (B.Sc. Econ., 1970). With Department of Justice, 1966-1968. Associated with this firm since 1968. *Member:* Swedish Bar Association (1973). *LANGUAGES:* French, German and English. *PRACTICE AREAS:* Commercial Law.

LEIF BAECKLUND, born February 8, 1940. *Education:* (juris kandidat LL.B., 1967). Service with Swedish Courts, 1967-1970. Associated with this firm since 1970. *Member:* Swedish Bar Association (1973). *LANGUAGES:* English. *PRACTICE AREAS:* Commercial Law.

OLOF WAERN, born March 23, 1944. *Education:* University of Stockholm (juris kandidat, LL.B., 1969). Service with Swedish Courts, 1969-1971. *Member:* Swedish Bar Association (1975); International Bar Association. *LANGUAGES:* French, German and English. *PRACTICE AREAS:* Commercial Law.

CHRISTER SÖDERLUND, born August 5, 1941. *Education:* University of Minnesota, Minnesota, U.S.A.; University of Stockholm (juris kandidat LL.B., 1969). Service in Swedish Courts, 1969-1972. Associated with this firm since 1972. *Member:* Swedish Bar Association (1976). *LANGUAGES:* French, German, Spanish, Russian and English. *PRACTICE AREAS:* Commercial Law.

BJÖRN LINDAHL, born August 18, 1944. *Education:* University of Stockholm (juris kandidat LL.B., 1972). Bank lawyer, 1972-1974. Practised with: Hovden & Bongenhielm Advokatbyra, 1974-1976; Advokatfirman S. Hovden, 1976-1980. Associated with this firm since 1980. *Member:* Swedish Bar Association (1977). *LANGUAGES:* English. *PRACTICE AREAS:* Commercial Law.

PETER MORAWETZ, born May 22, 1946. *Education:* University of Stockholm (juris kandidat, LL.B., 1972). Service with Swedish Courts, 1972-1974. Practised with: Otto Nordstrand Advokatbyrå, Stockholm, 1974-1978; Ormonde Goldie Advokatbyrå, Stockholm, 1978-1982 (Resident at London Branch Office, 1980-1982). Associated with this firm since June, 1982. *Member:* Swedish Bar Association. (1977). *LANGUAGES:* German and English. *PRACTICE AREAS:* Commercial Law.

HANS WIBOM, born March 26, 1949. *Education:* University of Uppsala (juris kandidat, LL.B., 1974). Service with Swedish Courts, 1974-1977. Treasurer, Swedish Export Credit Corporation (SEK), 1983-1985. *Member:* Swedish Bar Association (1980); International Bar Association. *LANGUAGES:* English. *PRACTICE AREAS:* Commercial Law.

LENNART TENGROTH, born March 11, 1949. *Education:* University of Uppsala (juris kandidat LL.B., 1975). Service with Swedish Courts, 1975-1977. Associated with this firm since 1978. *Member:* Swedish Bar Association (1981). *LANGUAGES:* French and English. *PRACTICE AREAS:* Commercial Law.

MIKAEL BROOMÉ, born September 9, 1952. *Education:* University of Stockholm and Lund (juris kandidat LL.B., 1976). Service with Swedish Courts, 1977-1979. Associated with this firm since 1979. *Member:* Swedish Bar Association (1982). *LANGUAGES:* English. *PRACTICE AREAS:* Commercial Law.

THOMAS EHRNER, born November 11, 1949. *Education:* University of Stockholm (juris kandidat LL.B., 1975). Service with Swedish Courts, 1976-1978. Associated with this firm since 1979. *Member:* Swedish Bar As-

(This Listing Continued)

sociation (1982). *LANGUAGES:* English. *PRACTICE AREAS:* Commercial Law.

KARIN GRAUERS, born September 14, 1953. *Education:* University of Lund (juris kandidat, LL.B., 1977). Associated with this firm since 1981. *Member:* Gothenburg Maritime Law Association; Swedish Bar Association (1984). *LANGUAGES:* English. *PRACTICE AREAS:* Commercial Law.

ELISABET FURA-SANDSTRÖM, born March 28, 1954. *Education:* University of Stockholm (juris kandidat LL.B., 1979). Service with Swedish Courts, 1979-1982. Associated with this firm since 1982. *Member:* Swedish Bar Association (Member of Board, 1988—); Association Internationale des Jeunes Avocats - AIJA (First Vice President, 1990—). (Also Member, Advokatfirman Vinge, Paris, France). *LANGUAGES:* French and English. *PRACTICE AREAS:* Commercial Law.

LARS EDLUND, born July 20, 1952. *Education:* University of Uppsala (juris kandidat, LL.B., 1976). Service and Junior Judgeships in Swedish Courts, 1976-1982. Associated with Advokatfirman Palm-Jensen & Roos, Stockholm, 1982-1983, Carl Swartling Advokatbyrå, Stockholm, 1983-1986 and with this firm since 1986. *Member:* Swedish Bar Association, 1985. *LANGUAGES:* English. *PRACTICE AREAS:* Litigation; Corporate Law; Commercial Law.

BJÖRN GUSTAVSSON, born December 27, 1951. *Education:* University of Lund (B.Sc., Econ., 1974; juris kandidat, LL.B., 1979); University of Colorado at Boulder, U.S.A. (1975-1976); Collège d'Europe, Brügge, Belgium (1979-1980). Trainee at the European Communities and the Law Office of Dechert, Price & Rhoads, Brussels, 1980-1981. With the National Swedish Board for Technical Development, 1981-1983. Associated with this firm since 1983. *Member:* Swedish Bar Association (1986). *LANGUAGES:* French, German and English. *PRACTICE AREAS:* Commercial Law.

STEFAN DE HEVESY, born June 8, 1955. *Education:* University of Stockholm (juris kandidat, LL.B., 1980). Service with Swedish Courts, 1980-1983. *Member:* Swedish Bar Association (1986). *LANGUAGES:* English. *PRACTICE AREAS:* Commercial Law.

JOHAN GÖTHBERG, born June 30, 1954. *Education:* University of Uppsala (juris kandidat LL.B., 1980). Research Assistant Stockholm School of Economics, 1980-1981. Service with Swedish Courts, 1981-1982. Associated with this firm since 1982. *Member:* Swedish Bar Association (1986). *LANGUAGES:* French and English. *PRACTICE AREAS:* Commercial Law.

THOMAS SJÖBERG, born November 8, 1956. *Education:* University of Uppsala (juris kandidat LL.B., 1981). Service with Swedish Courts, 1981-1983. Associated with this firm since 1983. *Member:* Swedish Bar Association (1986). *LANGUAGES:* English. *PRACTICE AREAS:* Commercial Law.

ANDERS FRITZELL, born April 10, 1954. *Education:* University of Stockholm (juris kandidat, LL.B., 1981). Junior Judge at District Court, 1981-1983. Law Clerk in Court of Appeal, 1983-1985. Associated with this firm since 1985. *Member:* Swedish Bar Association (1988). *LANGUAGES:* English. *PRACTICE AREAS:* Commercial Law.

BERTIL RICKARD EFFE VILLARD, born April 7, 1952. Junior Judge at District Court, 1977-1978. Employers Confederation, 1978-1980. Associate, Erik Berglunds Advokatbyrå, 1980-1982. Counsel, Legal Department, Swedish Match AB, 1982-1988. Counsel, Stora Kopparbergs Bergslags AB, 1988-1989. General Counsel Essalte AB, 1990-1992. Associated with this firm since 1990. *LANGUAGES:* English. *PRACTICE AREAS:* Mergers and Acquisitions; General Corporate; Commercial Law.

CHRISTOFFER SAIDAC, born 1959. *Education:* University of Uppsala (juris kandidat, LL.B., 1984); Stockholm School of Economics (M.B.A., 1984). Practiced with the Stockholm office of this firm, 1984-1986. *LANGUAGES:* French and English. *PRACTICE AREAS:* Commercial Law.

PER JOHAN ECKERBERG, born August 23, 1957. *Education:* University of Uppsala (juris kandidat, LL.B., 1982). Service with Swedish Courts, 1982-1985. Associated with this firm since 1985. *Member:* Swedish Bar Association (1988). *LANGUAGES:* French and English. *PRACTICE AREAS:* Commercial Law.

ROBERT WIKHOLM, born 1953. *Education:* Uppsala Universitet (juris kandidat, 1980); Kings College London, University of London (LL.M., 1981). Service in Swedish Courts, 1981-1983. Associated with this firm since 1983. Partner since 1990. *Member:* Swedish Bar Association (1988—). *LANGUAGES:* English. *PRACTICE AREAS:* Commercial Law.

(This Listing Continued)

BO ADRIANZON, born 1958. *Education:* University of Stockholm (juris kandidat, LL.B., 1983). Junior Judge at District Court of Stockholm, 1983-1985. Associated with this firm 1985-1989. Corporate counsel, Stora Kopparbergs Bergslags AB, 1989-1992. Partner of this firm since 1993. *LANGUAGES:* English. *PRACTICE AREAS:* Banking and Finance; Mergers and Acquisitions; Commercial Law.

PER ERIC ALVSING, born October 12, 1955. *Education:* University of Lund (juris kandidat, LL.B., 1982). Service with Swedish District Courts and Court of Appeal, 1982-1986. Secretary to the Swedish Bar Association, 1986-1987. Associated with this firm since 1987. *LANGUAGES:* English and Swedish. *PRACTICE AREAS:* Intellectual Property; Marketing; Media; Commercial Law.

MICHAEL WIGGE, born 1957; admitted, 1983, Stockholm; 1989, Gothenburg. *Education:* University of Stockholm Faculty of Law (LL.M., 1983). Junior Judge at District Court, 1983-1986. Associated with this firm since 1986. *Member:* Swedish Bar Association (1989). *LANGUAGES:* English. *PRACTICE AREAS:* Bank and Financing; General Corporate Law; Commercial Law.

ASSOCIATES

PETER TÖRNGREN, born November 10, 1958. *Education:* University of Stockholm (juris kandidat, LL.B., 1984). Service in Swedish District Courts and Court of Appeal, 1984-1988. Associated with this firm since 1988. *LANGUAGES:* Finnish and English. *PRACTICE AREAS:* Commercial Law.

CARL JOHAN AF PETERSENS, born July 6, 1962. *Education:* University of Stockholm (juris kandidat, LL.B., 1988). Associated with this firm since 1988. *LANGUAGES:* French and English. *PRACTICE AREAS:* Telecommunications Law; Computer Law; Competition Law; Commercial Law.

PETER ALHANKO, born November 11, 1958. *Education:* Stockholm School of Economics (Civilekonom, M.B.A., 1982); University of Stockholm (juris kandidat, LL.B., 1984); Columbia Law School, New York (Master of Laws, LL.M., 1987). Service in Swedish Courts, 1987-1989. Associated with this firm since 1989. *Member:* Swedish Bar Association (1992). *LANGUAGES:* Swedish, Finnish and English. *PRACTICE AREAS:* Commercial Law.

FREDRIK VON BAUMGARTEN, born July 17, 1959. *Education:* University of Stockholm (juris kandidat, LL.B., 1985); The Johns Hopkins University (Bologna, It.), Washington, D.C. (Master of Arts in International Relations, M.A., 1987). Service in Swedish Administrative Court, 1987-1989. Associated with this firm since 1989. *LANGUAGES:* English. *PRACTICE AREAS:* Commercial Law.

MONICA PETERSSON, born June 19, 1963. *Education:* University of Lund (juris kandidat, LL.B., 1985; B.Sc. in Business Administration and Economics, 1987); University of Illinois at Urbana-Champaign (LL.M., 1988). Fulbright grantee. Legal Intern with Winthrop Stimson Putnam & Roberts, Washington, D.C., USA, 1988-1989. Service with Swedish Courts, 1989-1990. Associated with G. Sandströms Advokatbyrå HB (1990) until the merger with Advokatfirman Vinge KB in 1991. *Member:* New York Bar Association. *LANGUAGES:* English. *PRACTICE AREAS:* Commercial Law.

SIGTRYGG SIGUNGER, born March 8, 1956. *Education:* University of Stockholm (juris kandidat, LL.B., 1982). Service in Swedish Courts, 1983-1986. Associated with this firm since 1990. *Member:* Swedish Bar Association (1990). *LANGUAGES:* English. *PRACTICE AREAS:* Commercial Law.

KARIN ULBERSTAD, born August 1, 1960. *Education:* University of Stockholm (juris kandidat, LL.B., 1986). Service in Swedish Courts, 1986-1989. Associated with this firm since 1990. *Member:* Swedish Bar Association (1992). *LANGUAGES:* Swedish and English. *PRACTICE AREAS:* Commercial Law.

ANNA KATARINA NORDBLOM, born Stockholm, Sweden, April 10, 1963; admitted, 1988, Sweden. *Education:* University of Stockholm (Master of Law, 1988). Stockholm Tingsrätt (+District Court of Stockholm), 1988-1991. *LANGUAGES:* English and German. *PRACTICE AREAS:* Commercial Law.

CHRISTINE LAGER, born 1962. *Education:* University of Uppsala (juris kandidat, LL.B., 1987). Service and Junior Judgeships in the District Court of Uppsala and the Svea Court of Appeal in Stockholm, 1987-1991. Associated with this firm since 1992. *LANGUAGES:* English. *PRACTICE AREAS:* Litigation; Commercial Law.

(This Listing Continued)

ADVOKATFIRMAN VINGE KB, Stockholm—Continued

EVA BÖRJESSON, born 1959. *Education:* University of Lund (juris kandidat, LL.B., 1986). Legal Counsel, Nordic Investment Bank (N10), Heldinki, 1986-1989. Service with the Swedish Courts, 1989-1991. Associated with this firm since 1991. *LANGUAGES:* English. *PRACTICE AREAS:* Commercial Law.

MONICA STEDING KARLSSON, born 1958; admitted, 1990, Sweden. *Education:* University of Stockholm (juris kandidat, LL.B., 1987). Lecturer, Labour Law, University of Stockholm, 1985-1990. Service with Swedish Courts, 1990-1991. Associated with this firm since 1991. *LANGUAGES:* English. *PRACTICE AREAS:* Commercial Law.

ERIC ERICSSON, born 1965. *Education:* University of Lund, Faculty of Law (LL.B., 1989). Associated with this firm since 1992. Author: "EG: s Fusionsförordning," Juridisk Tidskrift, No. 4, 1990-1991; "Immaterialrätts-slig Konsumtion," Svensk Juristtidning, No. 2, 1992. Head of Section, National Board of Trade, 1989-1992. *Member:* Association Internationale des Jeunes Avocats - A.I.J.A. *LANGUAGES:* English. *PRACTICE AREAS:* Commercial Law.

ROBERT HANSSON, born 1955. *Education:* University of Stockholm (juris kandidat, 1981). Former Legal Counsel, AB Electrolux, Sweden. Service with Swedish Courts, 1981-1983. *Member:* Swedish Bar Association. *LANGUAGES:* English. *PRACTICE AREAS:* Commercial Law.

OLLE FLYGT, born 1965. *Education:* (juris kandidat, LL.M., 1991). Service with Swedish Courts, 1991-1992. Associated with this firm since 1992. *LANGUAGES:* English. *PRACTICE AREAS:* Commercial Law.

MARTIN BACKMAN, born 1962. *Education:* University of Lund (juris kandidat, LL.B., 1986). Service and Junior Judgeship in Swedish Courts, 1986-1990. *LANGUAGES:* English. *PRACTICE AREAS:* Commercial Law.

JAN BYSTROM, born 1964. *Education:* University of Uppsala (juris kandidat, LL.M., 1990); University of London (LL.M., 1992). Service in Swedish Courts, 1991-1993. *LANGUAGES:* English. *PRACTICE AREAS:* Commercial Law.

FREDRIK WILKENS, born 1962. *Education:* University of Stockholm (juris kandidat LL.B., 1989). Junior Judge at District Court, 1989-1992. Associated with this firm since 1992. *LANGUAGES:* Swedish and English. *PRACTICE AREAS:* Commercial Law.

URBAN E. FUNERED, born 1966. *Education:* University of Lund (Civilekonom, 1991; juris kandidat, 1988); University of London (LL.M., 1992). *LANGUAGES:* English. *PRACTICE AREAS:* Financial Law; Corporate Law; Commercial Law.

KARL JOHAN KARLSSON, born 1967. *Education:* University of Leuven, Belgium (1992); University of Uppsala (juris kandidat, LL.M., 1993). *LANGUAGES:* Swedish and English. *PRACTICE AREAS:* EC-/EEA Law; Competition Law; Commercial Law.

ULRIKA ÅSA MALMBERG, born July 3, 1968. *Education:* University of Lund (juris kandidat, 1993). *PRACTICE AREAS:* Commercial Law.

ERIK ULFSSON ÅSTRÖM, born June 10, 1963. *Education:* University of Uppsala (juris kandidat, LL.M., 1991). Service in Swedish Courts, 1991-1993. *LANGUAGES:* English. *PRACTICE AREAS:* Commercial Law.

MAX MENNFORT, born August 5, 1969. *Education:* University of Stockholm (juris kandidat, LL.M., 1994); University of Stockholm School of Economics (civilekonom, M.B.A., 1994). *LANGUAGES:* English and German. *PRACTICE AREAS:* Commercial Law.

MATS PATRIK MIKAEL ROOTH, born June 7, 1967. *Education:* University of Stockholm (LL.M., 1990); University of Oslo (1991); University of Cambridge (LL.M., 1994); Trinity College. Service in Swedish Courts, 1991-1993. *LANGUAGES:* English. *PRACTICE AREAS:* Commercial Law.

Languages: Swedish, English, French, German and Italian.

WETTER & PRIEM ADVOKATBYRÅ AB

ERIK DAHLBERGS ALLÉ 15, 4TH FLOOR
115 20 STOCKHOLM, SWEDEN
Telephone: +46 (8) 663 61 70
Telecopier: +46 (8) 660 56 32

General International and Domestic Swedish Practice, International and Domestic Arbitration.

(This Listing Continued)

PARTNERS

J. GILLIS WETTER, born Stockholm, Sweden, June 4, 1931. *Education:* University of Stockholm (juris kandidat LL.B., 1954); King's College, University of London; University of Chicago Law School (LL.M., 1958; J.S.D., 1959); Harvard University Law School; University of Stockholm (Jur.dr.(h.c.), 1984). Solicitor-Royal of Sweden, 1974—. Service as chairman, arbitrator, secretary and counsel, respectively, in numerous ICSID, ICC, SCC and ad hoc international arbitrations in Sweden and abroad, 1955—. *Member:* Swedish Bar Association (1964). *LANGUAGES:* Swedish, English and French.

CHARL PRIEM, born Kalmar, Sweden, November 4, 1956. *Education:* University of Uppsala (juris kandidat, LL.M., 1981). Studies in Business Economics, University of Uppsala. Service in Swedish Courts, 1981-1983. Research Fellow, T.M.C. Asser Instituut, The Hague, 1984. Service as secretary and counsel, respectively, in a number of ICC, SCC and ad hoc international arbitrations in Sweden and abroad, 1985—. *Member:* Swedish Bar Association (1993). *LANGUAGES:* Swedish, English and French.

WHITE & CASE ADVOKAT AB

BIRGER JARLSGATAN 14
BOX 5573
S-114 85 STOCKHOLM, SWEDEN
Telephone: (46-8) 679-80-30
Facsimile: (46-8) 611-21-22

New York, New York: Telephone: 212-819-8200. Facsimile: 212-354-8113.
Washington, D.C.: Telephone: 202-872-0013. Facsimile: 202-872-0210.
Los Angeles, California: Telephone: 213-620-7700. Facsimile: 213-687-0758; 213-617-2205.
Miami, Florida: Telephone: 305-371-2700. Facsimile: 305-358-5744.
Mexico City, Mexico: Telephone: (52-5) 207-9717. Facsimile: (52-5) 208-3628.
Tokyo, Japan: Telephone: (81-3) 3239-4300. Facsimile: (81-3) 3239-4330.
Hong Kong: Telephone: (852) 2822-8700. Facsimile: (852) 2845-9070; Grice & Co., Solicitors, Telephone: (852) 2826-0333. Facsimile: (852) 2526-7166.
Singapore, Republic of Singapore: Telephone: (65) 225-6000. Facsimile: (65) 225-6009.
Bangkok, Thailand: Pacific Legal Group Ltd., In Association With White & Case, Telephone: (662) 236-6154/7. Facsimile: (662) 237-6771.
Hanoi, Viet Nam: Representative Office, Telephone: (84-4) 227-575/6/7. Facsimile: (84-4) 227-297.
Bombay, India: Telephone: (91-22) 282-6300. Facsimile: (91-22) 282-6305.
London, England: Telephone: (44-171) 726-6361. Facsimile: (44-171) 726-4314; (44-171) 726-8558.
Paris, France: Telephone: (33-1) 42-60-34-05. Facsimile: (33-1) 42-60-82-46.
Brussels, Belgium: Telephone: (32-2) 647-05-89. Facsimile: (32-2) 647-16-75.
Helsinki, Finland: Telephone: (358-0) 631-100. Facsimile: (358-0) 179-477.
Moscow, Russia: Telephone: (7-095) 201-9292/3/4/5. Facsimile: (7-095) 201-9284.
Budapest, Hungary: Telephone: (36-1) 269-0550; (36-1) 131-0933. Facsimile: (36-1) 269-1199.
Prague, Czech Republic: Telephone: (42-2) 2481-1796. Facsimile: (42-2) 232-5522.
Warsaw, Poland: Telephone/Facsimile: (48-22) 26-80-53; (48-22) 27-84-86. International Telephone/Facsimile: (48-39) 12-19-06.
Istanbul, Turkey: Telephone: (90-212) 275-68-98; (90-212) 275-75-33. Facsimile: (90-212) 275-75-43.
Ankara, Turkey: Telephone: (90-312) 446-2180. Facsimile: (90-312) 437-9677.
Jeddah, Saudi Arabia: Law Office of Hassan Mahassni, Telephone: (966-2) 651-3535. Facsimile: (966-2) 651-3636.
Riyadh, Saudi Arabia: Law Office of Hassan Mahassni, Telephone: (966-1) 476-7099. Facsimile: (966-1) 479-0110.
Almaty, Kazakhstan: Telephone: (7-3272) 50-7491/2. Facsimile: (7-3272) 61-0842.

General International Practice.
Firm engaged in Swedish, American and International Law Practice.

(This Listing Continued)

RESIDENT PARTNERS

GÖRAN ÅSEBORN, born Karlstad, Sweden, November 4, 1945. *Education:* University of Uppsala (juris kandidat LL.B., 1972). *Member:* Swedish Bar Association.

ROLF OLOFSSON, born Stenkyrka, Sweden, May 4, 1947. *Education:* University of Uppsala (LL.M., 1974). *Member:* Swedish Bar Association.

CLAES ZETTERMARCK, born Örebro, Sweden, August 24, 1947. *Education:* University of Stockholm (juris kandidat LL.B., 1972). *Member:* Swedish Bar Association.

COUNSEL

JAN GREGORSSON, born Gothenburg, Sweden, February 17, 1949. *Education:* University of Uppsala (juris kandidat LL.B., 1975).

LARS G. KJELLMAN, born Stockholm, Sweden, December 20, 1948. *Education:* University of Uppsala (LL.B., 1977).

RESIDENT ASSOCIATES

CECILIA AHRBOM, born Danderyd, Sweden, April 3, 1994. *Education:* University of Uppsala (jur. kan., 1991).

PENELOPE E. CODRINGTON, born August 17, 1967; admitted, 1993, New York (Not admitted in Sweden). *Education:* Harvard University (B.A., 1989; J.D., 1992).

THOMAS ENGWALL, born Malmo, Sweden, October 12, 1958. *Education:* University of Lund (juris kandidat LL.B., 1985); University of Chicago Law School (LL.M., 1990).

JAN GUSTAVSSON, born Orebro, Sweden, May 29, 1966; admitted, 1993, New York (Not admitted in Sweden). *Education:* University of Uppsala (LL.M., 1991); Harvard University (LL.M., 1992).

ULF JOHANSSON, born Lund, Sweden, December 7, 1961. *Education:* University of Lund (juris kandidat (LL.B., 1987).

ANDRÉ LINDEKRANTZ, born Polanica, Poland, February 4, 1963. *Education:* University of Lund (jur. kand., 1991).

FREDRIK SCHULTZ, born Falun, Sweden, March 24, 1955. *Education:* University of Stockholm (juris kandidat LL.B., 1983). *Member:* Swedish Bar Association.

(For biographical data as to other locations, see Professional Biographies at New York, New York; Washington, D.C.; Los Angeles, California; Miami, Florida; Mexico City, Mexico; Tokyo, Japan; Hong Kong; Singapore, Republic of Singapore; Bangkok, Thailand; Hanoi, Viet Nam; Bombay, India; London, England; Paris, France; Brussels, Belgium; Helsinki, Finland; Moscow, Russia; Budapest, Hungary; Prague, Czech Republic; Warsaw, Poland; Istanbul and Ankara, Turkey; Jeddah and Riyadh, Saudi Arabia; Almaty, Kazakhstan).

ADVOKAT KJELL WIDMARK, J.D.

BJÖRNGÅRDSGATAN 3
P.O. BOX 171 98
S-104 62 STOCKHOLM, SWEDEN
Telephone: +46 8 702 09 60
Fax: +46 8 640 15 34

Swedish and American Corporate Law, Arbitration Law, Civil Litigation, Products Liability and Tort Law.

KJELL WIDMARK, born Stockholm, Sweden, March 29, 1945. *Education:* Valparaiso University (J.D., 1982); Stockholm University (LL.B., 1985). Associate of Advokatfirman Carler, Stockholm, 1985-1989. *Member:* Swedish Bar Association; International Bar Association; Inter-Pacific Bar Association.

ADVOKATFIRMAN CHRYSANDER

UPPSALA, SWEDEN

(See Stockholm, Sweden)

Swedish and International Business Law including Corporate and Commercial Law, Litigation, Arbitration, Banking and Financing, Mergers and Acquisitions, Cross Border Transactions, Joint Ventures, Intellectual Property, Franchising, Insolvency and Bankruptcy Law, Taxation, Liquidation, Composition and Debtors' Reconstruction, Creditors' Rights, Local Government and Administrative Law, Government Contracts, European Community Law, Property.

SWITZERLAND

HUNZIKER SCHOLL & PARTNER

Advokatur und Notariat

Established in 1977

P.O. BOX LAURENZENVORSTADT 19
CH-5001 AARAU, SWITZERLAND
Telephone: 064 22 23 02
Fax: 064 22 25 00

Zurich, Switzerland Office: Kupper & Lehner, Löwenstrasse 11, CH-8039 Zurich. Telephone: 01 225 47 47. Fax: 01 225 47 77.
Lugano, Switzerland Office: Kupper & Lehner, Viale S. Franscini 1, CH-6901 Lugano. Telephone: 091 21 30 33. Fax: 091 21 30 35.

Contracts, Corporate, Banking, Tax, EC, Property and Inheritance Law, Notary Public, Litigation and Arbitration.

MEMBERS OF FIRM

DR. BRUNO HUNZIKER, born 1930; admitted, 1957, Aarau. *Education:* University of Basel (Dr.iur.). Former Member, Swiss Parliament (1977-1991). Former Member, Government of Canton of Argovie (1968-1976). *Member:* Bar Association of the Canton of Argovie; Swiss Bar Association. *LANGUAGES:* German, English, French and Italian. *PRACTICE AREAS:* Commercial Law; Corporate Law; Energy Industry Law; Banking Law; Insurance Law; Company Law.

HERBERT H. SCHOLL, born 1948; admitted, 1978, Aarau. *Education:* University of Zurich (lic.iur.). Member, Parliament of the Canton of Argovie, 1981—. *Member:* Bar Association of the Canton of Argovie; Swiss Bar Association. *LANGUAGES:* German, English and French. *PRACTICE AREAS:* Administrative Law; Civil Servants Law; Environmental Law; Planning Law; Construction Law; Commercial Law; Corporate Law; Contract Law.

GUSTAV LIENHARD, born 1955; admitted, 1985, Aarau. *Education:* University of Zurich (lic.iur.). Notary Public. *Member:* Bar Association of the Canton of Argovie; Notary Association of the Canton of Argovie; Swiss Bar Association; Swiss Notary Association. *LANGUAGES:* German and French. *PRACTICE AREAS:* Family Law; Real Estate Law; Commercial Law; Company Law; Equity Law; Securities Law; Inheritance Law; Estate Law; Competition Law; Tort Law.

DR. CONRAD M. WALTHER, born 1957; admitted, 1985, Aarau. *Education:* Universities of Basel and Berne (Dr.iur.). *Member:* Bar Association of the Canton of Argovie; Swiss Bar Association; International Fiscal Association; Swiss Association of International Law. *LANGUAGES:* German, English, French and Italian. *PRACTICE AREAS:* Tax Law; Commercial Law; Corporate Law; Competition Law; Insurance Law; Contract Law; Inheritance Law; Estate Law; Debt Collection Law.

DR. ARMIN SCHAETTI, born 1960; admitted, 1988, Aarau. *Education:* University of Zurich (Dr.iur.). *Member:* Bar Association of the Canton of Argovie; Swiss Bar Association. *LANGUAGES:* German, English and French. *PRACTICE AREAS:* Employment Law; Contract Law; Commercial Law; Corporate Law; Criminal Law; Family Law.

(For Complete Biographical Data on all Personnel, see Professional Biographies at Zurich, Switzerland)

BÖCKLI & THOMANN

Established in 1982

ST. JAKOBS-STRASSE 41
CH-4002 BASEL, SWITZERLAND
Telephone: 061-313 50 25
Telefax: 061-313 87 11

Contracts, Corporation, Banking and Securities, Fiscal, Intellectual Property, Computer, Software, Competition, Private International, EC, Property and Inheritance Law, Litigation and Arbitration Law.

FIRM PROFILE: The firm is active in all fields of Business Law (including, in particular, Tax, Corporate, Banking, Securities, Intellectual Property, Competition, Computer and Software Law), in Property, Inheritance, Contracts, Private International and EC Law. It handles Litigation and Arbitration and provides full Notarial Service where under Swiss Law a

(This Listing Continued)

BÖCKLI & THOMANN, Basel—Continued

notary has to act (in particular in connection with the incorporation and restructuring of corporations, real estate transactions, matrimonial property agreements, wills etc).

MEMBERS OF FIRM

PROF. DR. PETER BÖCKLI, born Basel, Switzerland, 1936; admitted, 1962, Switzerland. *Education:* University of Basel (Dr.iur., 1960). Professor of Tax and Business Law, University of Basel. *Member:* Basel and Swiss Bar Associations; Swiss Arbitration Association; American Bar Association (International Associate); International Fiscal Association; Association of the Bar of the City of New York (Non-Resident). *LANGUAGES:* English, German and French. *PRACTICE AREAS:* Tax; Corporate; Banking; Securities; Inheritance and Contract Law; Business Law Arbitration.

DR. FELIX H. THOMANN, born Basel, Switzerland, 1936; admitted, 1962, Switzerland. *Education:* Universities of Zurich and Basel (Dr.iur., 1960). *Member:* Basel and Swiss Bar Associations; Swiss Arbitration Association; Swiss Association for the Protection of Intellectual Property; Swiss Association for Copyright and Media Law; Association Swiss Legal Data Bank; American Bar Association (International Associate); International Bar Association; International Association for the Protection of Industrial Property (AIPPI); German Association for the Protection of Industrial Property and Copyright (GRUR); American Intellectual Property Law Association (AIPLA); Computer Law Association. *LANGUAGES:* English, German and French. *PRACTICE AREAS:* Patents; Computers and Software; Trademarks; Copyrights; Litigation; Competition; Corporate; Banking; Contracts; Arbitration.

DR. PATRICK H. WAMISTER, born Basel, Switzerland, 1954; admitted, 1981, Switzerland; Notary Public. *Education:* University of Basel (Lic.iur., 1979; Dr.iur., 1982). *Member:* Basel and Swiss Bar Associations; Basel and Swiss Notaries Association; Association of the Bar of the City of New York (Non-Resident). *LANGUAGES:* English, German and French. *PRACTICE AREAS:* Corporate; Contracts; Real Estate and Inheritance Law; Banking; Litigation; Computers and Software.

DR. BERNHARD BODMER, born Bern, Switzerland, 1952; admitted, 1982, Switzerland; Notary Public. *Education:* University of Basel (Lic.iur., 1976; Dr.iur., 1982). *Member:* Basel and Swiss Bar Associations; Association of the Bar of the City of New York (Non-Resident); International Fiscal Association. *LANGUAGES:* English, German and French. *PRACTICE AREAS:* Corporate; Contracts; Real Estate and Inheritance Law; Arbitration; Litigation; Tax; Intellectual Property; Competition.

Languages: German, English and French

CHRIST, LÖW, BRÜCKNER & STAEHELIN

BÄUMLEINGASSE 22
POSTFACH 1564
4001 BASEL, SWITZERLAND
Telephone: 061/272 30 60
Telex: 963 939 dres
Telecopier: 061/272 04 14

MEMBERS OF FIRM

DR. BERNHARD CHRIST, born Basel, Switzerland, December 9, 1942; admitted, 1970, Switzerland. *LANGUAGES:* German, French and English.

DR. CHRISTOPH LÖW, born Basel, Switzerland, October 11, 1940; admitted, 1968, Switzerland. *LANGUAGES:* German, English and French.

DR. CHRISTIAN BRÜCKNER, LL.M., born Basel, Switzerland, December 31, 1942; admitted, 1970, Switzerland. *LANGUAGES:* German, English, French and Italian.

DR. ERNST STAEHELIN, LL.M., born Basel, Switzerland, June 4, 1951; admitted, 1978, Switzerland. *LANGUAGES:* German, English and French.

ASSOCIATES

LIC. IUR. URSULA HUBSCHMID-FLURY, born Wil, Switzerland, May 12, 1947; admitted, 1980, Switzerland. *LANGUAGES:* German, French and English.

DR. THOMAS GELZER, LL.M., born Basel, Switzerland, July 1, 1955; admitted, 1984, Switzerland. *LANGUAGES:* German, English and French.

(This Listing Continued)

EU1346B

DR. LEONZ MEYER, born Basel, Switzerland, February 5, 1964; admitted, 1990, Switzerland. *LANGUAGES:* German, English, French and Italian.

DR. ROLAND M. MÜLLER, LL.M., born Zurich, Switzerland, May 3, 1963; admitted, 1991, Switzerland. *LANGUAGES:* German, English and French.

COUNSEL

PROF. DR. FRANK VISCHER, born Basel, Switzerland, September 11, 1923; admitted, 1948, Switzerland. Member," Institut de Droit International." Former Rector, University of Basel. Former Dean, Law Faculty, University of Basel. Dr. h.c., University of Freiburg i. Brg. (Germany). Corresponding Fellow of the British Academy. *LANGUAGES:* German, English and French.

Languages: German, English, French and Italian

ELBERT, MAYER, HUBER, ZELLWEGER

FALKNERSTRASSE 4
P.O. BOX 660
CH-4001 BASEL, SWITZERLAND
Telephone: 061/ 251 17 52
Fax: 061/ 261 18 65

BODO F.O. ELBERT, born Frankfurt-Main/FRG, 1951; admitted, 1979, Switzerland. *Education:* Goethe School, (Arbitur, 1970); Universities of Frankfurt/FRG, Freiburg/FRG, Cambridge/UK, and Basel (Lic. iur., 1975). *LANGUAGES:* German and English. *PRACTICE AREAS:* General Practice.

FELIX MAYER, born Reinfelden, 1952; admitted, 1980, Switzerland. *Education:* University of Basel (Lic. iur., 1976; Dr. jur., 1986). *LANGUAGES:* German and French. *PRACTICE AREAS:* Traffic Law; Transportation Law (Road Transports).

HEIDI MAYER JÜLICH, born Rheinfelden, 1955; admitted, 1983, Switzerland. *Education:* University of Basel (Lic. iur., 1979). *LANGUAGES:* German, French and English. *PRACTICE AREAS:* Family Law; Landlord and Tenant Law; Wills / Successions.

DR. LUCIUS A. HUBER, born Donaueschingen, 1957; admitted, 1986, Switzerland. *Education:* University of Basel (Lic. iur., 1983; Dr. iur., 1989). *LANGUAGES:* German, English and French. *PRACTICE AREAS:* International Commercial Law; International Commercial Arbitration; Joint-Ventures; EC-Competition Law; Corporate Law.

DR. CASPAR ZELLWEGER, born Basel, 1960; admitted, 1986, Switzerland. *Education:* University of Basel (Lic. iur., 1983; Dr. iur., 1988); University of Michigan (LL.M., 1990). *LANGUAGES:* German, English and French. *PRACTICE AREAS:* International Business Law; International Civil Litigation; Conflicts of Law.

EULAU KAUFMANN GIAVARINI & RECHER

Advokatur and Notariat
Established in 1943
MARKTPLATZ 18
4001 BASEL, SWITZERLAND
Telephone: 061-261 18 11
Telecopier: 061-261 01 22

General Practice; Business Law; Commercial, Corporate and Banking Law; Securities, Leasing, Taxation, International Law; Administrative Law; Litigation and Arbitration.

MEMBERS OF FIRM

WERNER EULAU, born Basel, Switzerland, 1914; admitted, 1941, Switzerland. *Education:* University of Basel (Dr.iur., 1938). *PRACTICE AREAS:* General Practice; Corporation Law.

PETER H. EULAU, born Basel, Switzerland, 1946; admitted, 1972, Switzerland. *Education:* University of Basel (lic.iur., 1970; Dr.iur., 1976); Harvard Law School (1976-1977). With Csaplar & Bok, Boston, Massachusetts, 1977-1978. *Member:* Basel and Swiss Bar Associations; International Bar Association; Swiss Arbitration Association. *PRACTICE*

(This Listing Continued)

AREAS: International Law; Corporate Finance; Leasing; Banking; Arbitration; Taxation; Company Law.

MARCO GIAVARINI, born Basel, Switzerland, 1961; admitted, 1990, Switzerland. *Education:* University of Basel (lic.iur., 1986). *Member:* Basel and Swiss Bar Associations. *PRACTICE AREAS:* Unfair Competition; Bankruptcy; Trust's and Estates; Products Liability; Taxation; Buying and Selling; Separation and Divorce.

PETER RECHER, born Lucerne, Switzerland, 1947; admitted, 1974, Switzerland. *Education:* University of Basel (lic.iur., 1971). With Midland Bank, London, England, 1980. *Member:* Basel and Swiss Bar Associations. *PRACTICE AREAS:* Finance and Securities; Retail Banking; Bank Collections; Mortgages, Real Estate, Zoning Planning and Land Use; Debtor and Creditor; Taxation.

Languages: German, English and French

FROMER, SCHULTHEISS AND STAEHELIN

Established in 1943

ST. JAKOBS-STRASSE 7

P.O. BOX 2879

CH-4002 BASEL, SWITZERLAND

Telephone: 061/271 52 00

Telefax: 061/272 71 35

General Practice.

MEMBERS OF FIRM

DR. LEO FROMER, born 1911; admitted, 1938, Switzerland. *Education:* Universities of Basel and Paris (Dr. iur.). *Member:* International Fiscal Association. *LANGUAGES:* French, Italian, English and German. *PRACTICE AREAS:* Tax Law; Corporate Law.

DR. HERMANN SCHULTHEISS, born 1912; admitted, 1939, Switzerland; 1943, Notary Public. *Education:* University of Basel (Dr. iur.). *LANGUAGES:* French, English and German. *PRACTICE AREAS:* Family Law; Property Law; Succession Law; Contract Law; Company Law; Fiscal Law.

DR. THOMAS STAEHELIN, born 1947; admitted, 1975, Switzerland. *Education:* University of Basel (Dr. iur.). *Member:* International Fiscal Association; International Bar Association. *LANGUAGES:* French, Italian, English and German. *PRACTICE AREAS:* Corporation Law; Tax Law; Succession Law; Mergers and Acquisitions Law; Contract Law; International Private Law; Civil and Commercial Law.

CORINA EICHENBERGER-WALTHER, born 1954; admitted, 1981, Switzerland. *Education:* University of Basel (lic. iur.). *LANGUAGES:* French, Italian, English and German. *PRACTICE AREAS:* Commercial Law; Corporate Law; Arbitration Law; Labor Law; Civil Law.

DR. BEAT SCHULTHEISS, born 1954; admitted, 1981, Switzerland; 1982, Notary Public. *Education:* University of Basel (Dr. iur.). *LANGUAGES:* French, English and German. *PRACTICE AREAS:* Family Law; Property Law; Succession Law; Contract Law; Company Law; Administrative Law.

PETER A. ZAHN, born 1951; admitted, 1983, Switzerland. *Education:* Universities of Basel and Zürich (lic. iur.). *Member:* Young Lawyer's International Association (AIJA); International Fiscal Association; Swiss Arbitration Association. *LANGUAGES:* French, English and German. *PRACTICE AREAS:* Commercial Law; Contract Law; Corporation Law; Mergers and Acquisitions Law.

FLAVIO ROMERIO, born 1964; admitted, 1992, Switzerland. *Education:* University of Basel (lic.iur., 1989); University of California at Berkeley (LL.M., 1993). *LANGUAGES:* English, French and German. *PRACTICE AREAS:* Commercial Law; Contract Law; Conflict of Laws; Tort Law; Environmental Law.

All Members of the Firm are Members of the Basel and Swiss Bar Associations.

GELZER, ALDER, BAUMGARTNER, CRON, GEBHARDT

ST. ALBAN-VORSTADT 21

CH-4052 BASEL, SWITZERLAND

Telephone: 061-272 45 11

Fax: 061-272 45 35

General Practice, offering all legal services including civil litigation and administrative procedures, contracts, EC law.

MEMBERS OF FIRM

DR. BERNHARD GELZER, born 1928; admitted, 1956, Switzerland. *Education:* University of Basel (Dr. iur). Notary Public. *LANGUAGES:* German, English and French.

DR. CLAUDIUS ALDER, born 1938; admitted, 1964, Switzerland. *Education:* University of Basel (Dr. iur); College of Europe, Bruges (Belgium). *LANGUAGES:* German, English, French and Italian.

DR. HANNES BAUMGARTNER, born 1946; admitted, 1974, Switzerland. *Education:* Universities Basel and Geneva (Dr. iur). Notary Public. *LANGUAGES:* German, English and French.

LIC.IUR. CAROLINE CRON, born 1960; admitted, 1987, Switzerland. *Education:* University of Basel (lic. iur). *LANGUAGES:* German, English and French.

LIC.IUR. DANIEL GEBHARDT, born 1960; admitted, 1990, Switzerland. *Education:* University of Basel (lic. iur). *LANGUAGES:* German, English, French and Italian.

All Members of the Firm are Members of the Basel and Swiss Bar Associations.

Languages: German, English, French and Italian.

GFELLER CHRISTEN HENTZ

KIRSCHGARTENSTRASSE 7 / STERNENGASSE 20

P.O. BOX 257

CH 4010 BASEL, SWITZERLAND

Telephone: 061 272 30 44

Telecopier: 061 272 30 07.

Telex: 061 963 651

MEMBERS OF FIRM

RUDOLF GFELLER, born Basel, Switzerland, November 7, 1925; admitted, 1953, Basel. *Education:* University of Basel (Dr. iur.). *LANGUAGES:* English, French and German.

BERNHARD CHRISTEN, born Basel, Switzerland, September 3, 1956; admitted, 1986, Basel. *Education:* University of Basel (Dr. iur.). *LANGUAGES:* English, French and German.

THOMAS HENTZ, born Basel, Switzerland, January 24, 1956; admitted, 1986, Basel. *Education:* University of Basel (lic. iur.). *LANGUAGES:* English, French and German.

ASSOCIATE

DANIEL STAEHELIN, born Basel, Switzerland, June 5, 1960; admitted, 1991, Basel. *Education:* University of Basel and Neuchâtel (Dr. iur.). *LANGUAGES:* English, French, Italian and German.

DOMINIQUE ERHART, born Basel, Switzerland, November 27, 1963; admitted, 1990, Basel. *Education:* University of Basel (lic.iur.). *LANGUAGES:* English, French, German and Italian.

Languages: English, French, German and Italian

GLOOR SCHIESS & PARTNERS

AESCHENVORSTADT 4

POSTFACH 526

CH-4010 BASEL, SWITZERLAND

Telephone: 061-279 33 00

Telecopier: 061-279 33 10

Cable Address: "Schiesslaw"

Telex: 963 547

(This Listing Continued)

GLOOR SCHIESS & PARTNERS, Basel—Continued

MEMBERS OF FIRM

PETER GLOOR, born Basel, Switzerland, April 24, 1926; admitted, 1952, Basel. *Education:* University of Basel (Dr. iur.). *LANGUAGES:* English, French and German. *PRACTICE AREAS:* Mergers and Acquisitions; Arbitration; Litigation.

NIKLAUS E. SCHIESS, born Basel, Switzerland, June 26, 1940; admitted, 1967, Basel. *Education:* University of Basel (Dr. iur.). *LANGUAGES:* English, French, Italian and German. *PRACTICE AREAS:* National and International Business Law.

MICHAEL PFEIFER, born Innsbruck, Austria, September 30, 1947; admitted, 1976, Basel. *Education:* University of Basel (Dr. iur.). *LANGUAGES:* English, French and German. *PRACTICE AREAS:* Tax Law; International Business Law.

SEBASTIAN BURCKHARDT, born Basel, Switzerland, September 26, 1954; admitted, 1980, Basel; 1987, New York. *Education:* University of Basel (Dr. iur.); New York University (M.C.J.). *LANGUAGES:* English, French, German and Italian. *PRACTICE AREAS:* Euro-American Contracts; Competition Law; Licensing.

DAVID JENNY, born Basel, Switzerland, June 3, 1960; admitted, 1990, Basel. *Education:* University of Basel (Dr.iur.); University of Michigan (LL.M.). *LANGUAGES:* English, French and German. *PRACTICE AREAS:* Litigation; Mergers and Acquisitions.

ASSOCIATES

BEATRICE WAGNER PFEIFER, born Basel, Switzerland, March 8, 1955; admitted, 1984, Basel. *Education:* University of Basel (Dr. iur.). *LANGUAGES:* English, French and German. *PRACTICE AREAS:* Environmental Law; European Law.

FELIX HEUSLER, born Basel, Switzerland, November 11, 1962; admitted, 1990, Basel. *Education:* University of Basel (Lic.iur); University of London (LL.M.). *LANGUAGES:* English, French, German and Italian. *PRACTICE AREAS:* International Business Law; International Litigation.

AGNES DORMANN BESSENICH, born Lucerne, Switzerland, October 12, 1962; admitted, 1990, Lucerne. *Education:* University of Basel (Dr.iur.). *LANGUAGES:* English, French and German. *PRACTICE AREAS:* Litigation.

MATTHIAS STAEHELIN, born Liestal, Switzerland, October 13, 1965; admitted, 1992, Basel. *Education:* University of Basel (Dr. iur.); College of Europe, Bruges (Master of Advanced European Studies). *LANGUAGES:* German, English, French and Italian. *PRACTICE AREAS:* Banking Law; European Law.

Languages: English, French, Italian and German.

HOLLIGER PFROMMER & PARTNER

ST. ALBAN-GRABEN 8
P.O. BOX 421
CH-4010 BASEL, SWITZERLAND
Telephone: 061-271 14 77
Telefax: 061-271 14 66

General Practice.

DR. PAUL HOLLIGER, born 1925; admitted, 1952. Notary Public. *PRACTICE AREAS:* Business Law; Transportation; Unfair Competition Law; Corporate Law; Criminal Law.

DR. URS BEAT PFROMMER, born 1941; admitted, 1970. *PRACTICE AREAS:* Insurance; Social Insurance; Family Law; Traffic Law; Labour Law.

DR. PAUL RUEST, born 1946; admitted, 1973. Notary Public. *PRACTICE AREAS:* Construction Law; Company Law; Administrative Law; Intellectual Property.

DR. THOMAS BURCKHARDT, born 1950; admitted, 1975. *Education:* Harvard Law School (LL.M.). *PRACTICE AREAS:* National Business Law; International Business Law; International Law; Arbitration; Maritime Law.

LIC.IUR. SUSANNA MARTI, born 1959; admitted, 1988. *PRACTICE AREAS:* Family Law; Litigation; Criminal Law; Unfair Competition Law; Computers and Software.

(This Listing Continued)

DR. HEINER SCHAERRER, born 1949; admitted, 1976. *PRACTICE AREAS:* Insurance; Banking Law; Tax Law; Product and Professional Liability.

LIC.IUR. BERNHARD SIMONETTI, born 1962; admitted, 1990. *PRACTICE AREAS:* Banking Law; Tax Law; Agency and Distributorships; Intellectual Property.

Languages: German, English, French, Spanish, Italian and Portuguese.

NAGY UND TRÓCSÁNYI RECHTSBERATUNG GMBH

BIRSIGSTRASSE 2
CH-4054 BASEL, SWITZERLAND
Telephone: (41) 61-281-2170
Telefax: (41) 61-281-2001

REVISERS OF THE HUNGARIAN LAW DIGEST FOR THIS
DIRECTORY.

Budapest, Hungary Office: Pálya 9, H-1012. Telephone: (36) 1-212-0444. Telefax: (36) 1-212-0443.

New York, New York Office: 1114 Avenue of the Americas, 10036-7794. Telephone: (1) 212-626-4206. Telefax: (1) 212-626-4208.

International Tax Planning, Taxation, Business Law, Finance.

RESIDENT PARTNER

PÉTER P. NAGY, admitted, 1983, Hungary; Legal Consultant, 1994, New York. *Education:* Eötvös Loránd University, Faculty of Law, Budapest (Doctor of Administration and Law, 1980); Université de Strasbourg, Faculté Internationale de Droit Comparé (Diplôme Superieure, 1985). Lawyers Exchange Program, American Bar Association, 1990-1991. *Member:* Budapest Bar Association; International Association of Students and Former Students in Comparative Law; Association of Attenders and Alumni of The Hague Academy of International Law. *LANGUAGES:* Hungarian, English, French and German. *PRACTICE AREAS:* Arbitration; Banks and Banking; Business Law; Commercial Law; Construction Law; Environmental Law; Finance; International Law; Litigation; Securities; Taxation; Media.

ILDIKÓ VARGA, admitted, 1991, New York; 1993, Hungary. *Education:* Eötvös Loránd University, Faculty of Arts, Faculty of Law, Budapest (Ph.D., 1984; Doctor of Administration and Law, 1988); New York University, Faculty of Arts and Law School (M.A., 1990); Universite de Strasbourg, Faculte Internationale de Droit Compare (1987). *Member:* Budapest Bar Association. *LANGUAGES:* Hungarian and English. *PRACTICE AREAS:* Agency and Distributorship; Business Law; Company Law; Construction Law; Energy; Corporate Law; Government; International Law.

RESIDENT ASSOCIATES

ISTVÁN TÓTH, (admission pending). *Education:* University of Trier (1992); University of Miskolc, Faculty of Law (Doctor of Administration and Law, 1993). *LANGUAGES:* Hungarian, English and German. *PRACTICE AREAS:* Contracts; Business Law; Real Estate.

REVISERS OF THE HUNGARIAN LAW DIGEST FOR THIS
DIRECTORY.

SIMONIUS & PARTNERS

Established in 1960
FREIE STRASSE 39
CH-4001 BASEL, SWITZERLAND
Telephone: 061 261 30 11
Telefax: 061 261 38 90

PARTNERS

PROF. DR. PASCAL SIMONIUS, born Basel, Switzerland; admitted, 1959, Switzerland. *PRACTICE AREAS:* International Banking; International Civil Law; Company Law; Real Estate; Arbitration and Mediation; Antitrust Law.

LIC.IUR. EMANUEL WIEMKEN, born Basel, Switzerland; admitted, 1975, Switzerland. *PRACTICE AREAS:* General Practice; Business Law; Commercial Law; Debt Collection; Insurance.

DR. ALESSANDRA CERESOLI, LL.M., born Basel, Switzerland; admitted, 1991, Switzerland. *PRACTICE AREAS:* Family Law; Children's Law; Criminal Law; Bankruptcy; Taxation.

(This Listing Continued)

LIC.IUR. KLAUS FEGER, born Basel, Switzerland; admitted, 1989, Switzerland. **PRACTICE AREAS:** Contracts; Conflict of Laws; Copyrights; Intellectual Property; Litigation.

OSCAR BATTEGAY, born Basel, Switzerland; admitted, 1989, Switzerland. **PRACTICE AREAS:** Company Law; Banks and Banking; Mergers and Acquisitions; Wills; Litigation.

Languages: German, French, English and Italian

STIEGER DÜRR & PARTNERS

Established in 1972

AESCHENVORSTADT 37

P.O. BOX 558

CH-4010 BASEL, SWITZERLAND

Telephone: 41 61 271 27 70

Telefax: 41 61 272 04 17

Commercial and Business Law, Company and Corporate Law, Mortgages and Real Estate, Litigation, Intellectual Property, Administration Law, Taxation, EC Law.

FIRM PROFILE: The firm offers a full range of legal services: consultancy and appraisals; representation in negotiations and disputes before courts of law and public authorities; preparation and conduct of business transactions; co-operation and joint casework with other consultants in one or more disciplines; comprehensive assistance, management and permanent support; preferably in the domestic and international areas mentioned above.

MEMBERS OF FIRM

DR. ARMIN STIEGER, born 1939; admitted, 1967. Notary Public, 1969. Education: Universities of Basel and Paris, studies at University of California at Berkeley. LANGUAGES: German, English, French and Italian. PRACTICE AREAS: Joint Ventures; Family Business; Restructuring; Takeovers; Hotels and Resorts; Trusts and Estates.

PD. DR. DAVID DÜRR, LL.M., born 1952; admitted, 1977. Notary Public, 1979. Education: Universities of Basel and Geneva; Harvard Law School. Lecturer on Law, University of Zurich. Member: International Young Lawyers' Association; International Law Association. LANGUAGES: German, English and French. PRACTICE AREAS: Arbitration and Mediation; Business Law; Company Law; European Community Law; Real Estate.

DR. GEORG ANDRÉ SCHLAGER, born 1947; admitted, 1975. Notary Public, 1983. Education: University of Basel. LANGUAGES: German, English, French and Swedish. PRACTICE AREAS: Construction Law; Family Law; Notarial Real Estate; Debt Collection; Wills.

DR. THOMAS HERZOG, born 1953; admitted, 1984. Education: University of Basel. LANGUAGES: German, English and French. PRACTICE AREAS: Banks and Banking; Contracts; Company Law; Mergers, Acquisitions and Divestitures; Taxation.

DR. STEPHAN FREY, born 1958; admitted, 1987. Education: University of Basel. LANGUAGES: German, English and French. PRACTICE AREAS: Company Law; Intellectual Property; Industrial Property Rights; Trademarks, Licensing and Distribution.

DR. CHRISTOPH NERTZ, born 1960; admitted, 1989. Notary Public, 1995. Education: University of Basel. LANGUAGES: German, English and French. PRACTICE AREAS: Administration Law; Business Law; Commercial Law; Copyrights; Litigation.

All Members of the Firm are Members of the Basel and Swiss Bar Associations.

WENGER MATHYS PLATTNER

Established in 1980

AESCHENVORSTADT 55

CH-4010 BASEL, SWITZERLAND

Telephone: +41-61-271 62 62

Telefax: +41-61-272 62 40

Zurich, Switzerland Office: Mühlebachstrasse 20, CH-8024. Telephone: +41-1-261 07 70. Telefax: +41-1-261 07 88.

Warsaw, Poland Office: ul. Nowogrodzka 56/7, PL-00695. Telephone: +48-39-121796 (satellite) and +48-2 621 2750. Telefax: +48-2-621 6753. Komertel: +48-39 12 17 96.

(This Listing Continued)

General Civil and Commercial Practice, Corporate, Contract and Banking Law, Swiss and International Taxation, Real Estate Law, Leases and Construction Law, Transportation and Shipping Law, Intellectual Property and Competition Law, Labor Law and Pension Plans, Family and Inheritance Law, Bankruptcy Law, Swiss and International Arbitration, Commercial Litigation, Entertainment Law, Telecommunication Law, Swiss and International Estate Planning and Asset Management, Public Notary Services.

RESIDENT MEMBERS OF FIRM

DR. WERNER WENGER, born 1940; admitted, 1967. Education: University of Basel. Notary Public, 1970. LANGUAGES: German, French, English and Italian. PRACTICE AREAS: Contract and Corporate Law; Real Estate Law; Inheritance Law and Estate Planning; International Commercial Arbitration.

DR. PETER MATHYS, born 1941; admitted, 1967. Education: Universities of Basel and St. Gallen. Notary Public, 1970. LANGUAGES: German, French, English and Italian. PRACTICE AREAS: Corporate and Tax Law; Real Estate Law; Mergers and Acquisitions; Financial Reorganizations; Inheritance Law and Estate Planning; Portfolio Management.

DR. PETER MOSIMANN, born 1947; admitted, 1973. Education: Universities of Basel and Geneva. LANGUAGES: German, French and English. PRACTICE AREAS: Corporate and Contract Law; Mergers and Acquisitions; Labor Law; Copyright and Media Law.

LIC. IUR. STEPHAN CUENI, born 1950; admitted, 1978. Education: University of Basel. Notary Public, 1981. Member: Titular Member of International Maritime Committee (CMI). LANGUAGES: German and English. PRACTICE AREAS: Corporate and Commercial Law; Transportation Law; Real Estate and Construction Law; Inheritance Law; Public Notary Services.

DR. MARKUS METZ, born 1948; admitted, 1974. Education: University of Basel. LANGUAGES: German, English, Italian and French. PRACTICE AREAS: Corporate and Contract Law; Litigation; Industrial Property Law and Competition Law; Family and Inheritance Law; Environmental Law.

DR. DIETER GRÄNICHER, born 1950; admitted, 1980. Education: Universities of Basel, Zürich and Neuchâtel. Notary Public, 1985. LANGUAGES: German, English and French. PRACTICE AREAS: Civil, Commercial and Corporate Law; Bankruptcy Law; Trademark and Copyright Law; Competition Law; E.C. Law; Estate Planning and Administration; Public Notary Services.

DR. JOLANTA SAMOCHOWIEC, born 1950; admitted, 1987. Education: Universities of Katowice and Basel. Certified Legal Adviser, Poland, 1993. LANGUAGES: German, English, Polish, Russian, French and Italian. PRACTICE AREAS: Swiss and Polish Commercial and Corporate Law; Joint-Ventures; Mergers and Acquisitions; International Arbitration; Administration Law; Labor Law; Family and Inheritance Law.

DR. THOMAS W. RIHM, born 1961; admitted, 1988. Education: University of Basel. LANGUAGES: German, English and French. PRACTICE AREAS: Swiss and International Taxation; E.C. Law; General Business Law; Litigation.

Languages: German, English, French, Italian, Polish and Russian

---

BADER, BASLER & PARTNER

MÜNSTERGASSE 34

CH-3011 BERN, SWITZERLAND

Telephone: ++41 31 312 25 25

Telefax: ++41 31 312 26 30

Zofingen, Switzerland Office: Luzernerstrasse 1, 4800. Telephone: ++41 62 521 606. Telefax: ++41 62 521 367.

Prague, Czech Republic Office: Narodni 32, 110 00 P. 1. Telephone: ++422 266 146. Telefax: ++422 226 995.

General Practice, National and International Commercial and Corporate Law including Arbitration and Litigation, Specialized in Counseling International Companies for Business and Legal Matters in Eastern Europe (Czech Republic, Hungary, Russia, Poland, Bulgaria, Albania, Slovakia, Romania).

MEMBERS OF FIRM

MICHAEL BADER, born 1957; admitted, 1985, Switzerland. Education: University of Bern (1985). Member: Bernese and Swiss Bar Association; International Union of Lawyers (UIA). LANGUAGES: German, English and French.

(This Listing Continued)

BADER, BASLER & PARTNER, Bern—Continued

MARTIN BASLER, born 1963; admitted, 1992, Switzerland. *Education:* University of Bern (1992). *Member:* Argovian and Swiss Bar Association. *LANGUAGES:* German and English.

BRAND, MAESCHI & PARTNERS

MARIENSTRASSE 18
CH-3000 BERN 6, SWITZERLAND
Telephone: 031 / 351 49 43
Fax: 031 / 351 28 83

General Practice, Administrative Law, Corporate and Banking Law, International Private Law, Contracts, Competition and Intellectual Property Law, Liability, Family Law, Construction Law.

MEMBERS OF FIRM

ANDREAS MAESCHI, born 1940; admitted, 1967, Switzerland.

DANIEL BRAND, born 1945; admitted, 1973, Switzerland.

DR. JÜRG RIEBEN, born 1946; admitted, 1971, Switzerland.

CHRISTINE BIGLER-GEISER, born 1949; admitted, 1979, Switzerland.

FRITZ ROTHENBÜHLER, born 1958; admitted, 1986, Switzerland.

ASSOCIATE

ANDREAS DAMKE, born 1963; admitted, 1990, Switzerland.

All Members and Associates of the Firm are Members of the Bernese and Swiss Bar Associations

Languages: German, English, French and Italian

BRATSCHI EMCH & PARTNERS

Established in 1979

BOLLWERK 15
P.O. BOX 5576
3001 BERN, SWITZERLAND
Telephone: 031 312 01 33
Telefax: 031 311 95 38

Zürich, Switzerland Office: Bahnhofstrasse 106, P.O. Box 7689, 8023. Telephone: 01/211 16 64. Telefax: 01/211 16 69.

FIRM PROFILE: The firm was established in Bern in 1976. In 1979 the office in Zurich was opened. The firm in Bern and Zurich offers a full range of legal services to international and domestic business, corporate and private clients in all areas of civil, criminal and public law. It specializes in contract law, commercial law and banking law.

MEMBERS OF FIRM

DR. PETER BRATSCHI, born 1941; admitted, 1967, Switzerland. *Education:* University of Bern; Georgetown University, Washington, D.C. Federal Government (Taxes, Foreign Economic Relations). *LANGUAGES:* German (native language), English, French.

DR. URS EMCH, born 1941; admitted, 1968, Switzerland. *Education:* University of Bern. Federal Department of Finance, 1970-1972. Legal Counsel, Bank Hofmann AG Zürich, 1973-1976.

DR. CHRISTIAN SCHMID, born 1949; admitted, 1978, Switzerland. *Education:* University of Zürich; University of Michigan Law School (M.C.L.). Superior Court of Zürich, 1978.

DR. MARKUS HÜNIG, born 1946; admitted, 1973, Switzerland. *Education:* University of Zürich.

FRANZ SZOLANSKY, born 1950; admitted, 1981, Switzerland. *Education:* University of Zürich; University of Lausanne; University of Georgia, USA. *LANGUAGES:* Hungarian.

URS GASCHE, born 1955; admitted, 1982, Switzerland. *Education:* University of Bern. Bernese Department of Construction, 1982-1988.

DR. CHRISTOPH BORN, born 1952; admitted, 1980, Switzerland. *Education:* University of Bern. Legal Department, Swiss Volksbank Zürich, Legal Counsel, Jean Frey/Curti Medien AG, Zürich.

DR. JÜRGEN BRÖNNIMANN, born 1955; admitted, 1981, Switzerland. *Education:* University of Bern; Free University of Berlin. Lecturer,

(This Listing Continued)

Swiss School for Chartered Accountants and Tax Experts. Assistant Lecturer, Commercial Law and Civil Procedure Law, University of Bern.

MARK INEICHEN, LL.M., born 1958; admitted, 1985, Switzerland. *Education:* University of Bern; Georgetown University, Washington, D.C.

ASSOCIATES

MARC STUCKI, born 1963; admitted, 1990, Switzerland. *Education:* University of Bern. Legal Services Group of Union Bank of Switzerland (UBS), Zürich, 1990-1991. *LANGUAGES:* Italian and Spanish.

DIETER HAAS, born 1962; admitted, 1988, Switzerland. *Education:* University of Bern. Bernese Department of Construction, 1989-1992.

HERMANN BECHTOLD, born 1963; admitted, 1991, Switzerland. *Education:* University of Bern.

PETER KELLER, born 1965; admitted, 1993. *Education:* University of Bern.

RENÉ ZAHUD, born 1966; admitted, 1994, Switzerland. *Education:* University of Bern. *LANGUAGES:* German (native language), English, French, Italian.

Languages: German, French, English, Italian and Spanish

FRIEDLI & SCHNIDRIG

BAHNHOFPLATZ 5
P.O. BOX 6233
CH-3001 BERN, SWITZERLAND
Telephone: 031/311.57.33/34/35
Fax: 031/311.69.07

MEMBERS

GEORG FRIEDLI, born Solothurn, Switzerland, January 1, 1952; admitted, 1977, Bernese. *Education:* University of Bern (Fuersprecher); George Washington University (M.C.L.). With Justice Department of Bern, 1978-1980; with Swiss Bank Corporation, General Management, 1981-1983. *Member:* Bernese and Swiss Bar Associations. *LANGUAGES:* German, English, French and Spanish.

GERHARD PETER SCHNIDRIG, born Bern, Switzerland, August 3, 1960; admitted, 1986, Bern. *Education:* University of Bern (Fuerspecher). Member, Department of Construction, 1986-1988. *Member:* Bernese and Swiss Bar Association. *LANGUAGES:* German, English and French.

ASSOCIATE

GREGOR MARCOLLI, born Burgdorf, Switzerland, May 2, 1966; admitted, 1992, Bern. *Education:* University of Berne (Fuersprecher). *Member:* Bernese and Swiss Bar Associations. *LANGUAGES:* German, English and French.

Languages: German, English, French and Spanish

KELLERHALS & PARTNER

Established in 1917

MARKTGASSE 55
CH-3011 BERN, SWITZERLAND
Telephone: + +41 31 312 50 55
Facsimile: + +41 31 312 50 86

Commercial Law, Tax and Finance Law, Industrial Property Rights, Administrative Law, Arbitration.

MEMBERS OF FIRM

PROF. DR. FRANZ KELLERHALS, born Bern, Switzerland, October 15, 1939; admitted, 1964, Switzerland. *Education:* Universities of Geneva (1958-1959), Bern (1959-1964), Chicago (1965-1966) and Stanford (1966) (Dr. iur., 1970). Professor, Law School at the University of Bern, 1986—. *Member:* Bernese Bar Association (President, 1984-1987); Swiss Bar Association (Vice-President, 1986-1991); International Union of Lawyers (UIA, Member, of the Board, 1980-1989). *LANGUAGES:* German, French and English. *PRACTICE AREAS:* Commercial Law; Arbitration.

URS HOFER, born Bern, Switzerland, March 31, 1939; admitted, 1965, Switzerland. *Education:* University of Berne, Switzerland (1965). *Member:* Bernese and Swiss Bar Associations. *LANGUAGES:* German, French and English. *PRACTICE AREAS:* Administrative Law; Trade Law; Industrial Property Rights; Social Insurance Law.

(This Listing Continued)

DR. CLAUDE E. THOMANN, LL.M., born Bern, Switzerland, December 22, 1951; admitted, 1978, Switzerland. *Education:* University of Bern (Attorney at Law, 1978; Dr. iur., 1980); University of Chicago Law School (LL.M., 1979); University of Strasbourg, France (1979). *Member:* Bernese and Swiss Bar Associations; Swiss Federation of Lawyers; International Union of Lawyers (UIA). *LANGUAGES:* German, English, French and Italian. *PRACTICE AREAS:* Commercial Law; Arbitration.

ERNST HAUSER, born Bern, Switzerland, April 6, 1955; admitted, 1982, Switzerland. *Education:* University of Bern (Attorney at Law, 1982). Clerk, Supreme Court of Switzerland, 1983-1988. *Member:* Bernese and Swiss Bar Associations; Swiss Federation of Lawyers; International Bar Association. *LANGUAGES:* German, French, English and Italian. *PRACTICE AREAS:* Commercial Law; Administrative Law; Arbitration.

ASSOCIATES

JEAN-LOUIS SCHEURER, born Neuchâtel, Switzerland, June 21, 1942; admitted, 1970, Switzerland. *Education:* University of Neuchâtel (Lic. iur., 1968). *Member:* Bernese and Swiss Bar Associations; Swiss Federation of Lawyers; International Union of Lawyers (UIA). *LANGUAGES:* French, German and English. *PRACTICE AREAS:* Commercial Law; Administration Law.

THOMAS EICHENBERGER, born Bern, Switzerland, August 5, 1963; admitted, 1989, Switzerland. *Education:* University of Bern (1982-1989). *Member:* Bernese and Swiss Bar Associations. *LANGUAGES:* German, French and English. *PRACTICE AREAS:* Commercial Law; Administrative Law.

DR. NICOLAS VON WERDT, LL.M., born Bern, Switzerland, September 15, 1959; admitted, 1985, Switzerland. *Education:* University of Bern (Dr. iur., 1991); Cornell University (LL.M., 1987). *Member:* Bernese and Swiss Bar Associations; Swiss Federation of Lawyers; International Union of Lawyers (UIA). *LANGUAGES:* German, English and French. *PRACTICE AREAS:* Commercial Law; Administrative Law; Intellectual Property Law.

NOTTER BLATTER DAVIDOFF & PARTNER

SCHWANENGASSE 9
3001 BERN, SWITZERLAND
Telephone: (41-31) 312 53 12
Facsimile: (41-31) 311 07 49

Zurich, Switzerland Office: Zimmergasse 16, 8008 Zurich. Telephone: (41-1) 261 15 55. Facsimile: (41-1) 262 35 42.
Gevena, Switzerland Office: 16, Avenue Jules Crosnier, 1206 Geneva. Telephone: (41-22) 346 24 74. Facsimile: (41-22) 347 09 21. Brussels, Belgium Office: Avenue de Tevueren 12, 1040 Brussels.

General Corporate and Commercial Practice, Finance and Banking, International Contracts, International Arbitration, Taxation, Real Estate, Intellectual and Industrial Property and Copyright, Administrative Matters, Inheritance and Estate Planning, Civil Litigation.

FIRM PROFILE: The firm is the result of a merger of three firms in Bern, Geneva and Zurich based on a new service-oriented concept offering an integrated full legal service for the whole of Switzerland. Notary public services are provided by the Bern office. The Zurich office includes professional auditing and controlling services. The firm maintains a well developed network of correspondence law firms.

MEMBERS OF FIRM

HANS LEONZ NOTTER, born 1948; admitted, 1976, Canton of Bern. *Education:* University of Bern Law School. State Examination as Public Notary, Canton of Bern, 1978. *Member:* Bern and Swiss Bar Association. *PRACTICE AREAS:* Business Law; Liquidations; Joint Ventures; Public Administration; Commercial Real Estate.

ASSOCIATES

ANTOINETTE WERNLI-SCHMIDT, born 1963; State Examination as Public Notary, Canton of Bern, 1989. *Education:* University of Bern Law School. *PRACTICE AREAS:* Mortgages; Successions, Notarial Real Estate.

ROLAND GEIGER, born 1959; admitted, 1987, Canton of Bern. *Education:* University of Bern Law School. Court Clerk, State Court for Administrative Law, Bern, 1987-1990. *Member:* Bern and Swiss Bar Associa-

(This Listing Continued)

tion. *PRACTICE AREAS:* Administrative Law; Construction Law, Zoning, Planning and Land Use; Employment Relations.

MICHAEL F. BOLT, born 1960; admitted, 1993, Canton of Vaud. *Education:* University of Lausanne Law School (B.A. in Law, 1982; J.D., in Law, 1988). Banking activity in Lausanne, New York and Zurich, 1988-1991. *PRACTICE AREAS:* Contracts; Banking; Sports.

Languages: German, English, French and Italian.

NOTTER & PARTNERS

Established in 1984
THUNSTRASSE 73
3000 BERN 16, SWITZERLAND
Telephone: 031-356 58 58
Fax: 031-356 58 50
E-Mail: 100101, 1052

Zurich, Switzerland Office: St. Annagasse 16, 8027. Telephone: 01-212 72 74. Fax: 01-212 72 79.
Fribourg, Switzerland Associated Office: Boivin & Nussbaumer, rue de Lausanne 91, 1700. Telephone: 037-22 25 68. Fax: 037-22 19 36.

International Commercial Practice, Taxation, Corporate, Contract, Unfair Competition, Banking and Finance, Corporate Restructuring, Mergers & Acquisitions, Industrial and Intellectual Property Law, Licensing, Arbitration, European Community Law, Commercial Litigation, Insurance Law, Third Party Liability, Administrative and Regulatory Matters, Immigration Law (Residence and Working Permits), Notarial Practice, Deeds, Wills, Testamentary Pacts, Estate Planning, Trusts, Real Estate.
Member of LAW-Lawyers Associated Worldwide, a network of independent law firms with offices throughout Europe, the Middle East, Australasia and the Americas.

MEMBERS OF THE FIRM

MARC GRÜNINGER, born 1959; admitted, 1986, Switzerland. *Education:* University of Bern (Fürsprecher, 1986); New York University School of Law (M.C.J., 1987). Co-Author: "New Commentary on the Swiss Code of Obligations.".

BRUNO HUNZIKER, born 1960; admitted, 1987, Switzerland. *Education:* University of Bern (Fürsprecher, 1987); Tulane Law School (LL.M., 1989). Co-Author: "New Commentary on the Swiss Code of Obligations.".

BERNHARD KOROLNIK, born 1960; admitted, 1990, Switzerland. *Education:* University of Zurich (lic.iur., 1986).

ANDREAS B. NOTTER, born 1953; admitted, 1981, Switzerland; 1983, Notary. *Education:* University of Fribourg (lic.iur., 1978); University of Bern (Fürsprecher, 1981; Notary, 1983). Co-Author: "New Commentary on the Swiss Code of Obligations." *Member:* Secretary General, Association of Swiss Notaries.

JÜRG HUNZIKER, born 1949; admitted, 1976, Switzerland. *Education:* University of Bern (Fürsprecher, 1976). Head of Claims Service Department, La Vaudoise Assurance, Lausanne, Switzerland, 1979-1987.

GERHARD ROTH, born 1965; admitted, 1992, Switzerland. *Education:* University of Bern (Fürsprecher, 1992). Member of Tax Department, Arthur Andersen A.G., Bern, Switzerland, 1992-1994.

PIERRE BOIVIN, born 1942; admitted, 1975, Switzerland; 1978, Notary. *Education:* University of Lausanne (lic. rer. pol., 1966; lic.iur., 1967); Institute of International Studies, Geneva (1969). Assistant Professor, University of Geneva, European Law Studies Center, 1967-1969. *Member:* Executive Council, City of Fribourg, 1979-1991; State Legislature of Fribourg, 1986 and Chairman, 1993. (Also at Boivin & Nussbaumer, Fribourg, Switzerland Associated Office).

ALBERT NUSSBAUMER, born 1957; admitted, 1983, Switzerland; 1986, Notary. *Education:* University of Fribourg (lic.iur., 1980). Assistant Professor, University of Fribourg, 1983-1986. Member and Chairman, Expropriation Committee of the State of Fribourg, 1986. (Also at Boivin & Nussbaumer, Fribourg, Switzerland Associated Office).

Languages: German, English, French and Italian

PIRENNE PYTHON SCHIFFERLI PETER & PARTNERS

SULGENRAIN 14
3007 BERN, SWITZERLAND
Telephone: (41 31) 372 40 46
Telefax: (41 31) 372 45 11

Geneva, Switzerland Office: 3, Rue Bellot, 1206. Telephone: (41 22) 347 46 45. Telex: 427 994 PPSP CH. Telefax: (41 22) 346 85 76; 347 80 54.

Nyon, Switzerland Office: 6, Avenue Reverdil, 1260. Telephone: (41 22) 361 18 04. Telefax: (41 22) 362 37 75.

Commercial and Contract Law, Banking, Corporate Finance, Swiss and International Taxation, Litigation, International Arbitration, Construction Law, Residence and Work Permits.

RESIDENT PARTNERS

FRANCESCO BERTOSSA, born Bern, Switzerland, December 23, 1952; admitted, 1981, Bern. *Education:* University of Bern Law School, Assistant of Public Law Department (Doctorate, 1984); Harvard Law school (LL.M., 1985). *Member:* Swiss and Bernese Association of Lawyers; Swiss Arbitration Association. **LANGUAGES:** German, French, English and Italian.

KURT MOLL, born Kreuzlingen, Switzerland, June 1, 1965; admitted, 1993, Bern. *Education:* University of Bern Law School (Bar exam, 1993). **LANGUAGES:** German, French, English and Italian.

COUNSEL

BERNHARD MÜLLER, born Bern, Switzerland, January 12, 1921; admitted, 1946, Bern. *Education:* University of Lausanne and Bern Law Schools (Graduated as Attorney). Author: "The Practice of the Swiss Federal Banking Commission," in German, 1985, in French, 1987 and in English, 1988. Head of the Legal Department, Federal Department of Finances, 1954-1976. Chief Executive of the Federal Banking Commission, 1976-1986. Member, Standing Committee for Banking Legislation and Supervisory Practices (Cooke Committee), Bank for International Settlements. *Member:* Swiss and Bernese Association of Lawyers; Swiss Arbitration Association; Geneva Association of Business Law. **LANGUAGES:** German, French, English and Italian.

Languages: French, English, German and Italian

(For Complete Biographical data on all Firm Personnel, see Professional Biographies at Geneva, Switzerland).

WEBER & SOMMERHALDER

MUENZGRABEN 2
P.O. BOX 1041
3000 BERN 7, SWITZERLAND
Telephone: (41 31) 311 57 58
Telefax: (41 31) 311 74 70

MEMBERS OF FIRM

ALEXANDER K. WEBER, LL.M., born 1946; admitted, 1976, Switzerland.

RUDOLF H. SOMMERHALDER, born 1931; admitted, 1958, Switzerland.

ASSOCIATE

PIERRE DE RAEMY, born 1958; admitted, 1984, Switzerland.

Languages: German, French and English

MICHAEL BRANDON

P.O. BOX 1
1291 COMMUGNY, SWITZERLAND
Telephone: Geneva 776 14 00; 776 15 00
Cable Address: "Movements Geneva"
Telex: 419328 mb ch
Telecopier: GENEVA 776 55 18

Arbitration, Contract, Corporate, Commercial, Family Law, International Litigation, Tax, Trusts, Wills and Estates.
Engaged in International Law Practice but not authorized to appear before the Swiss Courts.

(This Listing Continued)

MICHAEL BRANDON, born Bromley, England; admitted, 1952, England (Not admitted in Switzerland). *Education:* Cambridge University (B.A., 1947; LL.B., 1948; LL.M., 1955); Yale University (M.A., 1949). Author: "Recent Developments in English Law Affecting International Transactions", The International Lawyer, Vol. 15, No., 4, Fall, 1981; "Recent Developments in English Law Affecting International Transactions - II", The International Lawyer, Vol. 18, No., 4, Fall, 1984; "Immunity from Attachment and Execution", International Financial Law Review, July, 1982; "English Wills & Trust in Switzerland", International Legal Practitioner, November 1977; "Claims Against Wills and Trusts of UK Citizens Domiciled in Switzerland", International Legal Practitioner, November, 1979; "The Convention on the Registration of Wills 1972 and the Convention on International Wills 1973", The International and Comparative Law Quarterly, Vol. 32, 1983; "Matters Arising from an Election of a Foreign Law to Govern a Will in Switzerland," International Legal Practitioner, June 1986; "Swiss Banking Wills and post mortem Powers of Attorney," Tolley's Trust Law International, Vol. 7, No. 2, 1993. Representative of the International Bar Association to the United Nations at Geneva, 1960—. Member, Commercial Panel of Arbitrators of the American Arbitration Association; Swiss Arbitration Association; Member, European Council of the London Court of International Arbitration. Fellow, Chartered Institute of Arbitrators, London. *Member:* American (Member, Sections of International Law and Practice and of Real Property, Probate and Trust Law) and International (Member, Sections on: Business Law; General Practice) Bar Associations; American Foreign Law Association; Society of Trust and Estate Practitioners; The International Academy of Estate and Trust Law. **LANGUAGES:** English, French and German.

OBERSON THIÉBAUD & ASSOCIÉS

Established in 1981

RUE DE LAUSANNE 82
P.O. BOX 933
1701 FRIBOURG, SWITZERLAND
Telephone: (037) 22 32 15
Fax: (037) 23 13 41

Geneva, Switzerland Office: 20, Rue de Candolle, 1205. Telephone: (022) 320.18.88. Fax: (022) 320.16.70.

Swiss and International Tax Laws, Corporate and Finance Laws, Administration Law.

FIRM PROFILE: Oberson, Thiébaud and Partners represent the merger of the practice Oberson and Partners, Geneva, which was founded in 1961 with the law office Thiébaud and Von der Weid, Fribourg, organized in 1981. The joint law firms main activities are tax and business laws. The practice scope covers Swiss and International tax planning, tax litigation, corporate and finance law. In addition, the firm has a close affiliation with the United States firm Jones Day Reavis and Pogue.

MEMBERS OF FIRM

PIERRE-ALAIN THIÉBAUD, born July 22, 1945; admitted, 1972, Fribourg. *Education:* University of Fribourg (Licence en droit, 1967). ATAG Ernst & Young, Bern, 1972-1977. Head of the Tax Department of Canton of Fribourg, 1977-1980. *Member:* Fribourg Bar Association; Swiss Bar Association; Swiss Fiscal Experts Association; International Fiscal Association; International Bar Association; International Association of Lawyers. **LANGUAGES:** French, English and German. **PRACTICE AREAS:** Swiss and International Fiscal Laws; Business; Corporate and Finance Laws; Estate Planning.

FRANÇOIS VON DER WEID, born May 16, 1950; admitted, 1977, Geneva; 1985, Fribourg. *Education:* University of Fribourg Law School (Licence en droit, 1975). *Member:* Fribourg Bar Association; Swiss Bar Association; International Bar Association. **LANGUAGES:** French, English and German. **PRACTICE AREAS:** Swiss and International Taxation; Commercial and Contract Law.

ASSOCIATES

LUKE H. GILLON, born January 14, 1959; admitted, 1987, Fribourg. *Education:* University of Fribourg (Licence en droit, 1983); Tulane Law School (LL.M., 1988). *Member:* Fribourg Bar Association; Swiss Bar Association. **LANGUAGES:** French, English, German and Dutch. **PRACTICE AREAS:** Civil and Commercial Law; Arbitration; Civil and State Litigation.

DENIS ESSELVA, born May 5, 1964; admitted, 1992, Fribourg. *Education:* University of Fribourg (Lic. en droit, 1989); Universitat Augsburg

(This Listing Continued)

(LL.M., 1993). *Member:* Fribourg Bar Association; Swiss Bar Association. *LANGUAGES:* French, English and German. *PRACTICE AREAS:* Civil and Commercial Law; Civil and State Litigation.

(For complete Biographical Data on all Personnel, see Professional Biographies at Geneva, Switzerland)

APPLEBY, SPURLING & KEMPE
ICC, COINTRIN

20 ROUTE DE PRE-BOIS
P.O. BOX 1908
CH 1215 GENEVA 15 SWITZERLAND
Telephone: (41) 22 788 2453
Facsimile: (41) 22 788 2476

Isle of Man Office: Finch Chambers, Finch Road, Douglas, Isle of Man, IM1 2PS. Telephone: (44) 1624 629401. Facsimile: (44) 1624 673566.

Hamilton, Bermuda Office: Cedar House, 41 Cedar Avenue, P.O. Box HM1179, Hamilton HM EX. Telephone: (809) 295-2244. Facsimile: (809) 292-8666.

Hong Kong Office: 2217 Jardine House, 1 Connaught Place, Central, Hong Kong. Telephone: (852) 523 8123. Facsimile: (852) 524 5548.

Banking, Insurance, Re-insurance, Unit Trust, Mutual Fund, Syndicated Loans, Aviation, Insurance Treaties, Trusts, Offshore Companies, Foreign Investment, Overseas Property, Immigration and Nationality, Shipping, Common Law, Taxation, Pensions, Investment, Personal Business.

JOHN D. CAMPBELL, Q.C.. PRACTICE AREAS: Insurance.

DIANNA P. KEMPE, Q.C.. PRACTICE AREAS: Litigation; Liquidations.

GERARD F.B. MACQUILLAN. PRACTICE AREAS: Company, Finance, Trusts, Settlements.

DAVID J. DOYLE

RICHARD D. SPURLING, M.P.

KENNETH E.T. ROBINSON

F. CHESLEY WHITE

JAY W. KEMPE

MICHAEL J. SPURLING (Resident, Hong Kong Office).

ALAN W. DUNCH. PRACTICE AREAS: Litigation.

PETER BUBENZER. PRACTICE AREAS: Company Finance.

MONICA J. JONES. PRACTICE AREAS: Trusts; Settlements.

JOHN BARRITT, M.P.

JUDITH COLLIS

THE HON. C. JEROME DILL, J.P., M.P.

WARREN CABRAL. PRACTICE AREAS: Captive Insurance.

SENIOR COUNSEL

Geoffrey R. Bell, Q.C.

ASSISTANT SOLICITOR

JAMES CUNNINGHAM-DAVIS. PRACTICE AREAS: Intellectual Property.

Languages: English, French and German

BERGER, RECORDON, DE SAUGY

Established in 1985

9, BOULEVARD DES PHILOSOPHES
CH-1205 GENEVA, SWITZERLAND
Telephone: (41 22) 320 12 12
Telefax: (41 22) 320 13 31

General and International Law Practice, Business, Corporate, Banking, Tax, Contracts, Attachment and Bankruptcy, International Arbitration, Estate, Family (National and International), Torts, Insurance and Criminal Law. Litigation.

(This Listing Continued)

MEMBERS OF FIRM

ALAIN BERGER, born Geneva, Switzerland, 1950; admitted, 1974, Geneva. *Education:* University of Geneva (Licence en droit, 1974). *Member:* Geneva and Swiss Bar Associations; Swiss Society of Criminal Law. *LANGUAGES:* French, German and English. *PRACTICE AREAS:* Private Counselling; Estate; Family; Torts; Insurance and Criminal Law; Litigation.

PIERRE-ALAIN RECORDON, born Geneva, Switzerland, 1944; admitted, 1973, Geneva. *Education:* University of Lyon (Licence en droit, 1965); University of Geneva (Doctorat en droit, 1973); Yale University (Visiting Scholar and Fellow, Swiss National Fund for Scientific Research, 1971-1973). Professor of Contracts, Corporation and Commercial Laws, University of Geneva, 1982—. *Member:* Geneva and Swiss Bar Associations; Geneva Law Society; Geneva Association of Business Law; Swiss Society of Jurists; Swiss Arbitration Association; International Union of Lawyers; Swiss Association of University Professors. *LANGUAGES:* French, English and Spanish. *PRACTICE AREAS:* International Arbitration; Business Law; Company; Corporate Law; Construction Law; Mergers and Acquisitions; Tax Law.

JEAN DE SAUGY, born Geneva, Switzerland, 1951; admitted, 1974, Geneva. *Education:* University of Geneva (Licence en droit, 1973; Diplôme d'études juridiques supérieures, 1974). Author: Swiss Reports IUL, (New York, 1981, Luxembourg, 1983, The Hague, 1985), YLIA (Munich, 1988, New Dehli, 1989, various National and General Reports on International Commercial Arbitration, 1987-1992), APLA (Beijing, 1990). *Member:* Geneva and Swiss Bar Associations; Geneva Law Society; Geneva Association of Business Law; Swiss Society of Jurists; Swiss Arbitration Association; International Union of Lawyers; Young Lawyers International Association (President, International Arbitration Commission); International Bar Association; Asia-Pacific Lawyers Association; Inter-Pacific Bar Association; ICC Institute of International Business Law and Practice. *LANGUAGES:* French and English. *PRACTICE AREAS:* Commercial Law; International Arbitration; Contracts; International; Banks and Banking; Arbitration and Mediation; Bankruptcy.

JEAN-PAUL VULLIETY, born Geneva, Switzerland, 1959; admitted, 1987, Geneva. *Education:* University of Geneva (Licence en droit, 1982; Diplôme d'études supérieures en droit, 1988). Research Assistant, Contracts, Corporation and Commercial Laws, 1982-1987 and Lecturer, Civil Law, 1989—, University of Geneva. *Member:* Geneva and Swiss Bar Associations. *LANGUAGES:* French, German, English and Norwegian. *PRACTICE AREAS:* General Practice; Business Law; Contracts and Torts; Litigation.

ASSOCIATES

PATRICK CHENAUX, born Lausanne, Switzerland, 1963; admitted, 1989, Geneva. *Education:* University of Lausanne (Licence en droit, 1988). *LANGUAGES:* French, German and English. *PRACTICE AREAS:* General Practice; Contracts and Torts; Litigation.

MICHÈLE EL ZAYADI, born Geneva, Switzerland, 1971; admitted, 1994, Geneva. *Education:* University of Geneva (Licence en droit, 1994). *LANGUAGES:* French, English, German and Spanish.

FLORENCE PRINI, born Geneva, Switzerland, 1971; admitted, 1994, Geneva. *Education:* University of Lausanne (Licence en sciences économiques, 1993); University of Geneva (Licence en droit, 1994). *LANGUAGES:* French, English, German and Italian.

COUNSEL

WILLIAM K. DABAGHI, born Huntsville, Texas, July 20, 1945; admitted, 1972, Texas; 1979, District of Columbia; Partner, Arter & Hadden, Washington, D.C. *Education:* Harvard College and Corpus Christi University (B.S., 1969); University of Texas (J.D., 1972). Delta Theta Phi. Director, Office of Congressional Affairs, Office of the Secretary U.S. Department of Transportation, 1982-1983. Federal Legislative Counsel, American Bankers Association, 1976-1982. Attorney, Office of General Counsel, Small Business Administration, 1974-1976. *Member:* The District of Columbia Bar; State Bar of Texas; Federal, International, Inter-Pacific and American (Member, Section on Corporation, Banking and Business Law; Banking Law and Consumer Financial Services Committee) Bar Associations; Union Internationals des Avocats (Member, Financial Services Working Group); Institute of International Bankers (Member, Professional Liaison Committee). *PRACTICE AREAS:* Banking and International Trade Policy.

(This Listing Continued)

BERGER, RECORDON, DE SAUGY, Geneva—Continued

The Firm is a member of the Swiss Committee of the International Chamber of Commerce (ICC); of the London Court of International Arbitration (LCIA/European Council); of the Geneva Chamber of Commerce and Industry; of the Swiss Chamber of Commerce in France.

Languages: French, English, German, Spanish, Italian and Norwegian

BERNHEIM, MING, HALPERIN ET DUCRET-BURGER

Established in 1965

5, AVENUE LÉON-GAUD
1206 GENEVA, SWITZERLAND
Telephone: 41 22 347 71 51
Telex: 429 036 HELP CH
Cable Address: Bermiura
Telefax: 41 22 347 68 31

General and International Law Practice, Business, Corporate, Banking, Contracts and Commercial Law, Civil, Administrative and Criminal Litigations, Attachment and Bankruptcy Procedures, International Arbitration, Estate and Inheritance Law, Real Estate and Family Law, Torts and Insurance, International Legal Assistance, European Law, Mergers and Acquisitions, Purchases of Swiss Real Estate, Constructions and Immigration Law (Residence and Work Permits).

MEMBERS OF FIRM

ARIEL R. BERNHEIM (1931-1989).

HANS-ULRICH MING, born 1943; admitted, 1969, Obwalden; 1970, Geneva. *Education:* Licence en droit. *LANGUAGES:* German, French, English and Italian.

MICHEL A. HALPERIN, born 1948; admitted, 1974, Geneva. *Education:* University of Geneva (French Baccalauréat; Licence en droit; Diplôme d'études juridiques supérieures). *Member:* Geneva Bar Association (Bar Council Member, 1986—; Bâtonnier, Chairman, 1990-1992). *LANGUAGES:* French, English, Italian and Hebrew.

DOMINIQUE DUCRET-BURGER, born 1955; admitted, 1979, Geneva. *Education:* Law Degree. *LANGUAGES:* French, English and German.

ASSOCIATES

PIERRE FAUCONNET, born 1949; admitted, 1974, Geneva. *Education:* Law Degree. *LANGUAGES:* French, English and German.

MATTEO INAUDI, born 1956; admitted, 1984, Geneva. *Education:* University of Zürich (Law Degree). *LANGUAGES:* French, English, Italian and German.

GEORGES REYMOND, born 1957; admitted, 1991, Geneva. *Education:* Law degree; Licence spéciale de droit Européen Bruxelles (1993). Legal Counsel at the Federal Department of Justice and Police, Bern, 1980-1981. Law Clerk of the Supreme Court of the Canton de Vaud, 1982-1989. *LANGUAGES:* French, English, Italian and German.

YOUSSEF S. TAKLA, born 1937; admitted, 1964, Beirut; 1993, Paris. *Education:* Licence de droit de la Faculté de Lyon et Ecole de droit de Beirut (1961). *LANGUAGES:* French, English and Arabic.

CATHERINE MING, born 1958; admitted, 1982, Geneva. *Education:* Law Degree. Co-Author of Commentary: "Vienna Convention on Contracts for the International Sales of Goods," Lausanne, 1993. *LANGUAGES:* French, English, German and Italian.

Languages: German, French, English, Italian, Hebrew and Arabic

BONNANT, PEYROT & PARTNERS

3, RUE DE BEAUMONT
1206 GENEVA, SWITZERLAND
Telephone: (+41-22) 347 60 20
Telefax: (+41-22) 346 06 13

Commercial, Corporate, Civil, Criminal Practice, Commercial Litigation, Banking, Private and Public International Law, International Arbitration, Motion Picture Industry, Real Estate and Estate Law, Bankruptcy.

(This Listing Continued)

MEMBERS OF FIRM

NICOLAS PEYROT, born 1942; admitted, 1969, Geneva. *Education:* Schenectady College, N.Y.; University of Geneva Law School (Law Degree, 1967); University of Geneva Economics School (Economics Degree, 1969). Auxiliary Judge, Geneva Administrative Court. *Member:* Geneva Bar Association; Swiss Federation of Lawyers; Swiss Air Law Association; Geneva Business Law Association; Swiss Association for Foreign Policy; Society for Promoting Swiss Centers of European Law Studies; Swiss Arbitration Association.

MARC BONNANT, born 1944; admitted, 1971, Geneva. *Education:* University of Geneva Law School (Law Degree, 1968). *Member:* Geneva Bar Association (President, 1986-1987).

GEORGES BONNANT, born 1915; admitted, 1940, Geneva. *Education:* University of Geneva Law School (Law Degree, 1937; Doctorat en droit, 1949).

FREDERIC MARTI, born 1955; admitted, 1982, Geneva. *Education:* University of Geneva Law School (Law Degree, 1979). *Member:* Geneva Bar Association; Swiss Federation of Lawyers.

JEAN-FRANCOIS DUCREST, born 1958; admitted, 1985, Fribourg; 1986, Geneva. *Education:* University of Fribourg (Licence en droit, 1981); Institut fur Internationales Recht, Munich, 1981-1982; Duke University School of Law (LL.M., 1990). Research Assistant to Professor of Contracts and Commercial, University of Fribourg, 1985. *Member:* Geneva Bar; Swiss Federation of Lawyers; Swiss Law Society; Geneva Association of Business Law; Swiss Sports Law Association; Swiss Arbitration Association.

FRANCOISE MARKARIAN, born 1965; admitted, 1992, Geneva. *Education:* University of Geneva Law School (Law Degree, 1987). Research Assistant to Professor of Contracts, University of Geneva, 1987-1990. *Member:* Geneva Bar Association; Swiss Federation of Lawyers.

BRIGITTE OEDERLIN, born 1962; admitted, 1993, Geneva. *Education:* University of Geneva Law School (Law Degree, 1989). *Member:* Geneva Bar Association; Swiss Federation of Lawyers.

Languages: French, English, German, Italian and Spanish

BOREL & BARBEY

Established in 1907

2, RUE DE JARGONNANT
1207 GENEVA, SWITZERLAND
Telephone: (4122) 736.11.36
Telefax: (4122) 736.45.88
Telex: 41.31.61

Mailing Address: P.O. Box 6045, 1211 Geneva 6

General Civil and Commercial Practice, Banking and Finance Law, Corporate Law, Commercial and Contract Law, Mergers and Acquisitions, Competition Law, Residence and Work Permits, Real Estate Law, Inheritance and Estate Planning, Trusts, Civil and Administrative Litigation, Arbitration, Debt and Bankruptcy Law, Swiss and International Taxation, Private International Law.

OF COUNSEL

ALFRED BOREL, born Neuchâtel, Switzerland, 1902; admitted, 1924, Switzerland. *Education:* University of Geneva (Lic. of Law, 1924). Member of Counsel: Swiss Federation of Lawyers; Geneva Law Society; International Society for Labor Law and Social Security (Honorary President).

GUSTAVE BARBEY, born Geneva, Switzerland, 1911; admitted, 1936, Switzerland. *Education:* University of Geneva (Lic. of Law, 1936). *Member:* Swiss Federation of Lawyers; Swiss Society of Jurists; Swiss Air Law Association; International Law Association; International Tax Association. *LANGUAGES:* French, English and German.

MEMBERS OF FIRM

PIERRE DE CHARMANT, born Budapest, Hungary, 1926; admitted, 1959, Switzerland. *Education:* University of Geneva (Lic. of Law, 1948); Hague Academy of International Law; McGill University, Montreal, Canada (B.C.L., 1954); University of Comparative Studies, Luxembourg (Dipl. Comp. L., 1958); Graduate Institute of International Studies, Geneva. *Member:* Geneva Bar Association; Swiss Federation of Lawyers; Geneva Law Society; ILA (Swiss Branch). *LANGUAGES:* French, English, German, Italian, Spanish and Hungarian.

LUCIEN PERRET (1936-1985).

(This Listing Continued)

OLIVIER DUNANT, born Sevenoaks, England, 1946; admitted, 1969, Switzerland. *Education:* University of Geneva (Lic. of Law, 1969); Southern Methodist University Law School, Dallas, Texas, USA (Master of Comparative Law, 1973). *Member:* Geneva Bar Association; Swiss Federation of Lawyers; Geneva Business Law Association. *LANGUAGES:* French and English.

LUC HAFNER, born Geneva, Switzerland, 1945; admitted, 1970, Switzerland. *Education:* University of Geneva (Lic. of Law, 1970). *Member:* Geneva Bar Association; Geneva Law Society; Swiss Federation of Lawyers; Swiss Arbitration Association; Swiss Fiscal Association. *LANGUAGES:* French, English and German.

MICHÈLE WASSMER, born Geneva, Switzerland, 1956; admitted, 1979, Switzerland. *Education:* University of Geneva (Lic. of Law, 1978). *Member:* Geneva Bar Association; Swiss Federation of Lawyers. *LANGUAGES:* French and English.

NICOLAS PIÉRARD, born Geneva, Switzerland, 1957; admitted, 1980, Switzerland. *Education:* University of Geneva (Lic. of Law, 1979). *Member:* Geneva Bar Association; Swiss Society of Jurists; International Bar Association; Swiss Arbitration Association. *LANGUAGES:* French, English and Italian.

MARC FISCHER, born Leopoldville, Congo-Belge, 1955; admitted, 1981, Switzerland. *Education:* University of Geneva (Lic. of Law, 1981). *Member:* Geneva Bar Association; Swiss Federation of Lawyers. *LANGUAGES:* French, English, German and Italian.

PATRICK BLASER, born Geneva, Switzerland, 1954; admitted, 1976, Switzerland. *Education:* University of Geneva (Lic. of Law, 1976); Advanced Legal Studies Diploma (DES en droit, 1979); University of Geneva (Assistant Intellectual Property Law, 1979-1980). Former Deputy Public Prosecutor. Investigating Magistrate and Judge of the District Court of Geneva, 1981-1993. *Member:* Geneva Bar; Swiss Federation of Lawyers. *LANGUAGES:* French, German and English.

ASSOCIATES

CARL HEGGLI, born Fribourg, Switzerland 1963; admitted, 1985, Switzerland. *Education:* University of Geneva (Lic. of Law, 1984); Advanced Legal Studies Diploma (DES en droit, 1992); Certified Tax Consultant (1992). *Member:* Geneva Bar Association; Swiss Federation of Lawyers; Swiss Institute of Certified Accountants and Tax Consultants; International Fiscal Association. *LANGUAGES:* French and English.

NICOLAS A. KILLEN, born Geneva, Switzerland, 1964; admitted, 1986, Switzerland; 1991, New York. *Education:* University of Geneva (Lic. of Law, 1986); Duke University School of Law (LL.M., 1990). *Member:* Geneva Bar Association, Swiss Federation of Lawyers; New York Bar Association. *LANGUAGES:* French and English.

PHILIPPE HOUMAN, born Geneva, Switzerland, 1964; admitted, 1988, Switzerland. *Education:* University of Geneva (Lic. of Economy, 1986; Lic. of Law, 1988). *Member:* Geneva Bar Association; Swiss Federation of Lawyers. *LANGUAGES:* French, English and Italian.

LOUIS BOISSIER, born Geneva, Switzerland, 1963; admitted, 1988, Switzerland. *Education:* University of Geneva (Lic. of Law, 1988). *Member:* Geneva Bar Association; Swiss Federation of Lawyers. *LANGUAGES:* French and English.

EDOUARD CUENDET, born Geneva, Switzerland, 1967; admitted, 1992, Switzerland. *Education:* University of Bern (Lic. of Law, 1991). *Member:* Geneva Bar Association. *LANGUAGES:* French, English and German.

BOURQUIN & BINER BRADLEY

6 AVENUE DE FRONTENEX
PLACE DES EAUX-VIVES
1207 GENEVA, SWITZERLAND
Telephone: (41-22) 786-8640
Facsimile: (41-22) 786-8311

Mailing Address: P.O. Box 3023, 1211 Geneva 3, Switzerland

St. Peter, Jersey, Channel Islands Associated Office: Biner Bradley Nigel Harris & Partners. Oak Walk, JE3 7EF. Telephone: (0534) 44291. Telex: 4192303 Global G Lex. Facsimile: (0534) 42703.

Corporate, Tax, Real Estate, International, Arbitration, Estate Planning, Accounting, Construction and Environmental Law.

(This Listing Continued)

MEMBERS OF FIRM

GERALD BOURQUIN, born Geneva, Switzerland, April 29, 1923; admitted, 1948, Geneva. *Education:* University of Geneva (Licence en Droit, 1946; Licence en Sciences Commerciales et Industrielles, 1947; Expert Comptable Diplômé, 1960; Docteur en Droit, 1976). Author: "Le Principe de Sincérité du Bilan," Librairie de l'Université Georg and Cie, Genève, 1976. Professor of Law, 1973-1988 and Honorary Professor, 1988, University of Geneva. *Member:* Geneva Bar Association; Swiss Federation of Lawyers; Swiss Chamber of Accountants (Chambre Fiduciaire Suisse). *LANGUAGES:* French, German and Italian.

CATHERINE BINER BRADLEY, born Lausanne, Switzerland, January 19, 1954; admitted, 1981, Valais; 1987, Geneva. *Education:* University of Geneva (1976); University of Neuchâtel, Switzerland (Licence en Droit, 1978). *Member:* Geneva Bar Association; Swiss Federation of Lawyers; Swiss Society of Jurists; International Association of Young Lawyers (AIJA). *LANGUAGES:* French and English.

OF COUNSEL

RUSS V. V. BRADLEY, JR., born Washington, D.C., November 27, 1941; admitted, 1978, Massachusetts (Not admitted in Switzerland). *Education:* Williams College (B.A., 1963); Massachusetts Institute of Technology (M.Arch., 1971); Harvard Law School (J.D., 1978). *Member:* Boston, Massachusetts and American Bar Associations. *LANGUAGES:* English and French.

BRUNSCHWIG WITTMER

13, QUAI DE L'ILE
P.O. BOX 5245
1211 GENEVA 11, SWITZERLAND
Telephone: (41.22) 781.33.22
Telefax: (41.22) 781.31.00
Telex: 429.207

Banking and Finance Law, Securities Regulations, Commercial and Contract Law, Company Law, Mergers and Acquisitions, Corporate Law and Finance, Swiss and International Taxation, Real Estate, Construction, Environment Law, Product Liability, Unfair Competition, Intellectual Property, Civil and Administrative Litigation, Arbitration, Debt Collection and Bankruptcy Law, International Legal Assistance, Estate Planning, Trusts, Maritime Law, Private International Law, European Community Law, Residence and Work Permits.

MEMBERS OF FIRM

FRANCOIS BRUNSCHWIG, born Geneva, Switzerland, 1923; admitted, 1947, Geneva. *Education:* University of Geneva (Licence en droit, 1945). President, Geneva Bar Association, 1989-1990. *LANGUAGES:* French, English, German. *PRACTICE AREAS:* Commercial and Contract Law; Corporate Law; Estate Planning; Arbitration.

JACQUES WITTMER, born Payerne, Switzerland, 1935; admitted, 1977, Geneva. *Education:* University of Fribourg (Licence en droit, 1958; Doctorat en droit, 1959); Max-Plank-Institute for International Private Law, Hamburg and New York University (1960-1962). *LANGUAGES:* French, English, German. *PRACTICE AREAS:* Bank and Finance; Securities Regulations; International Estate and Tax Planning; Trusts; Mergers and Acquisitions.

RAPHAËL BIAGGI, born Martigny, Switzerland, 1942; admitted, 1969, Geneva. *Education:* University of Geneva Law School (Licence en droit, 1967). *LANGUAGES:* French, Italian, German, English. *PRACTICE AREAS:* Civil and Administrative Litigation; International Legal Assistance; Construction Law; Commercial and Contract Law; Residence and Work Permits.

LAURENT LEVY, born Sao Paulo, Brazil, 1948; admitted, 1974, Geneva. *Education:* University of Paris Law School (Licence en droit, 1969; Doctorat en droit, 1983); University of Geneva (Licence en droit, 1972). Assistant with the Universities of Paris, 1969-1970, Wurzburg (Germany), 1973-1974 and Geneva, 1974-1977. *LANGUAGES:* French, English, German. *PRACTICE AREAS:* Commercial and Contract Law; Civil and Commercial Litigation; Arbitration; International Legal Assistance; Debt Collection and Insolvency.

BERNARD S. VISCHER, born Schaffhouse, Switzerland, 1956; admitted, 1980, Geneva. *Education:* University of Geneva (Licence en droit, 1978); University of Pennsylvania (LL.M., 1983). Assistant at University of Geneva, 1981-1984. *LANGUAGES:* French, German, English. *PRAC-*

(This Listing Continued)

BRUNSCHWIG WITTMER, Geneva—Continued

TICE AREAS: Bank and Finance; Securities Regulations; Corporate Law; Commercial and Contract Law; Mergers and Acquisitions; Maritime Law.

YVES JEANRENAUD, born Geneva, Switzerland, January 3, 1960; admitted, 1987, Geneva. *Education:* University of Zürich Law School (Lic.iur., 1983); Northwestern University School of Law, Chicago (LL.M., 1985). *LANGUAGES:* French, German, English. *PRACTICE AREAS:* Real Estate and Construction Law; Environment Law; Administrative Law; Unfair Competition; Antitrust and Trade Law; Intellectual Property; European Community Law; Civil and Administrative Litigation.

UTE RUEDE-BUGNION, born Hamburg, Germany, 1936; admitted, 1973, Zürich; 1974, Geneva. *Education:* University of Hamburg Law School (Referendar, 1958); University of Geneva Law School (Diplôme d'études supérieures en droit, 1972; Doctorat en droit, 1975). Patent and Trade Mark agent with Bugnion SA Geneva, 1959-1969. *LANGUAGES:* German, French, English. *PRACTICE AREAS:* Intellectual Property and Competition; Commercial and Contract Law; Arbitration.

ASSOCIATES

JOËLLE DE SÉPIBUS, born Geneva, Switzerland, 1967; admitted, 1992, Obwald and Geneva. *Education:* University of Bern Law School (Lic.iur., 1991). *LANGUAGES:* German, French, English.

PHILIPPE METZGER, born Bern, Switzerland, 1964; admitted, 1992, Bern and Geneva. *Education:* University of Bern (Lic.iur., 1992); College of Europe (LL.M. in EC Law, 1994). *LANGUAGES:* German, French, English.

KELLY MASSEY-CARLIER, born Durham, North Carolina, 1962; admitted, 1992, Virginia (Not admitted in Switzerland). *Education:* Georgetown University, School of Foreign Service (B.S., 1984); Institut d'etudes politiques de Paris (Certificat, 1983); Institut des Hautes Etudes Internationales de Genève (Certificat, 1990); University of Virginia (J.D., 1992; M.A., Foreign Affairs, 1992). *LANGUAGES:* English, French.

ALEXANDRE CARATSCH, born Bern, Switzerland, 1966; admitted, 1989, Geneva. *Education:* University of Neuchâtel (Licence en droit, 1987). *LANGUAGES:* French, German, English.

ELISABETH ALFONSO VON LAUN, born 1958; admitted, 1984, Geneva. *Education:* University of Geneva (Licence en droit, 1981); University of London (LL.M., 1985). *LANGUAGES:* French, German, English, Spanish.

DIDIER ZUMBRUNN, born Geneva, Switzerland, 1968; admitted, 1993, Geneva. *Education:* University of Geneva (Licence en droit, 1990). *LANGUAGES:* French, English.

MARIA CLARA POLIDURA PICO, born Bogota, Colombia, 1965; admitted, 1989, Colombia. *Education:* University of El Rosario (Doctorate, 1988); University of London (LL.M., 1990). *LANGUAGES:* Spanish, English, French.

LIONEL AESCHLIMANN, born Bienne, Switzerland, 1966; admitted, 1992, Bern and Geneva. *Education:* University of Bern Law School (Lic. iur., 1992); Universidad de Sevilla (Diploma de Derecho Communitario, 1993); College of Europe (LL.M., in EC Law, 1994). *LANGUAGES:* French, German, Spanish and English.

BUDIN AND PARTNERS

20, RUE SÉNEBIER

P.O. BOX 166

1211 GENEVA 12, SWITZERLAND

Telephone: (41) 22 818 08 08

Cable Address: "Legalive, Geneva"

Telex: 427 464 LEGA CH

Telecopier: (41) 22 818 08 18

Business Law and Contracts, International Arbitration, Banking and Financial Law, Litigation, Tax Law, Acquisitions, Mergers and Divestitures, Immigration, Real Estate Law, Intellectual Property, Estate Law and Franchising.

(This Listing Continued)

MEMBERS OF FIRM

ROGER-PHILIPPE BUDIN, admitted, 1952, Geneva. *Education:* University of Geneva (Lic. jur.). Former Partner, Lalive, Budin & Partners. *Member:* Geneva Bar Association; International Bar Association; Geneva Law Society; Swiss Arbitration Association; Swiss Society of Jurists. *LANGUAGES:* French, English, German, Spanish and Italian.

PIERRE-ANDRÉ BÉGUIN, admitted, 1971, Geneva. *Education:* University of Geneva (Lic. jur.). Deputy Secretary, Supervisory Board according to the Swiss Banks' Agreement of Conduct with regard to the Exercise of Due Diligence. Former Partner, Lalive, Budin & Partner. *Member:* Geneva Bar Association; Geneva Law Society; Geneva Association of Business Law; Swiss Arbitration Association; International Lawyers Club. *LANGUAGES:* French, English and German.

PATRICK SCHELLENBERG, admitted, 1977, Geneva. *Education:* University of Geneva (Lic. jur.). Deputy Judge, Geneva Court of Appeal. Former Partner, Lalive, Budin & Partners. *Member:* Geneva Bar Association; Geneva Law Society; Geneva Association of Business Law; Swiss Arbitration Association. *LANGUAGES:* French, English and German.

FRANZ J. ZIMMERMANN, admitted, 1974, Solothurn; 1977, Geneva. *Education:* Universities of Geneva and Paris (Lic. jur.). Former Partner, Lalive, Budin & Partners. Honorary General Counsel of Austria. *Member:* Geneva Bar Association; Geneva Association of Business Law. *LANGUAGES:* German, French and English.

ANDRE H. KAPLUN, admitted, 1970, Geneva. *Education:* University of Geneva, Law School (LL.M.); Graduate Institute of International Studies, IHEI. Rapporteur to International Colloquium on "Institutional and ad hoc Arbitration in Oil Conflicts," 1969. Research Assistant, University of Geneva and Graduate Institute of International Studies, 1970. Salzburg Seminar in American Studies, 1977. Corporate Counsel, Trans World Capital, Geneva, 1972-1974. Associate Area Attorney, Union Carbide Europe, Geneva, 1974-1984. Substitute Area Attorney, Union Carbide Eastern, Hong-Kong, 1981. Chairman Geneva Committee of the Swiss American Chamber of Commerce, 1986-1988. Member, Parliament City of Geneva. Former Partner, Lalive, Budin & Partners. *Member:* Geneva Business Law Association; American International Club (Chairman, Corporate Relations Committee); Switzerland-Russia Association (Chairman). *LANGUAGES:* French, English, Italian and German.

CAMILLE FROIDEVAUX, admitted, 1974, Lugano. *Education:* University of Fribourg, Law School (Lic.jur.). Counsel, Paribas Bank, Geneva, 1975-1984. General Counsel, Trade Development Bank, American Express Bank, Geneva, 1985-1990. *Member:* Geneva and Lugano Bar Associations. *LANGUAGES:* French, English, Italian and German.

PATRICK T. BITTEL, admitted, 1983, Geneva. *Education:* University of Geneva (Lic. jur.). Attorney, Shearman & Sterling, New York, 1984-1985. *Member:* Geneva and Zurich Bar Associations. *LANGUAGES:* French, English and German.

ASSOCIATES

DR. SILVIA TEVINI DU PASQUIER, admitted, 1987, Geneva. *Education:* University of Geneva School of Law (LL.M.; LL.D.). Graduate Assistant, Contract and Banking Law, University of Geneva School of Law, 1979-1984. *Member:* Geneva Bar Association. *LANGUAGES:* Italian, French, English, German and Spanish.

ISABEL VON FLIEDNER, born Lisbon, Portugal; admitted, 1988, Geneva. *Education:* Hochschule St. Gall (lic. oec. HSG, 1976); University of Geneva Law School (Lic. jur.). Chief Economic Analyst for Europe, Business Environment Risk Index 1976-1981. Graduate Assistant, Swiss Tax Law, University of Geneva School of Law, 1984-1985. *Member:* Geneva Bar Association; Geneva Association of Business Law; Swiss Society of Jurists; Swiss-Portuguese Association, Geneva. *LANGUAGES:* Spanish, German, English, French and Portuguese.

SYLVIE CHALLANDE, admitted, 1993, Geneva. *Education:* University of Geneva, School of Law (Lic.jur.). *Member:* Geneva Bar Association. *LANGUAGES:* French, English, Italian, Spanish and German.

JEAN-CHRISTOPHE LIEBESKIND, admitted, 1990, Geneva. *Education:* University of Geneva, Faculty of Law (Licence en Droit, 1987); The London School of Economics & Political Science (LL.M., European Law, 1993). Delegate, International Committee of the Red Cross, 1991-1992. Estudio Legal and Bureau Francis Lefebvre, Madrid, 1992. *Member:* Geneva Bar Association. *LANGUAGES:* French, English, Spanish and German.

(This Listing Continued)

ERIC BECHENIT, admitted, 1992, Geneva. *Education:* University of Geneva, Law School (Lic. jur.); Victoria University of Manchester (LL.M. in International Business Law, 1994). *Member:* Geneva Bar Association; Swiss Society of Jurists. *LANGUAGES:* French, English and German.

GABRIEL A. BENEZRA, admitted, 1994, Geneva. *Education:* University of Geneva, Law School (Lic. jur.). With: Trade Development Bank, Geneva, 1989-1990; International Capital Bank, Geneva, 1992. *Member:* Geneva Bar Association. *LANGUAGES:* French, English, Italian and German.

COUNSEL

STEVEN J. STEIN, born New York, New York, December 9, 1939; admitted, 1964, New York; 1978, Florida. *Education:* Cornell University (B.S., 1961); New York University School of Law (LL.B., 1964). Author: "The Drafting of Effective Choice of Law Clauses," Journal of International Arbitration, September, 1991; "Increasingly Effective Use of Summary Judgment," Wiley Law Publications, 1990. Co-Author: "International Arbitration in the 80's: A Comparative Study of the Major Arbitral Systems and Rules," Business Lawyer, Summer 1983 Ed.; "International Commercial Arbitration in New York," Transnational Publishers, Inc., 1986. General Counsel, United Nations Watch, 1993—. Member, Arbitration Study Group of the Secretary of State's Committee on Private International Law, 1982-1986. U.S. Delegate to International Conference "L'Entreprise Algerienne et Arbitrage Commercial," (Algerian Business and Commercial Arbitration), Algiers, November, 1989. Member, Advisory Committee, World Arbitration Institute, 1984—. Member, Departmental Disciplinary Committee of the First Judicial Department, 1979-1980. Member, Corporate Counsel Committee, 1985— and International Law Committee, 1980—, American Arbitration Association. *Member:* The Association of the Bar of the City of New York (Chair, Committee on International Law, 1986-1989; Member, Council on Foreign Affairs, 1986-1990; Committee on Arbitration and Alternate Dispute Resolution, 1989-1992; Advisory Committee on Arbitration and Alternate Dispute Resolution, 1993-1994; Committee on the Civil Court, 1970-1973; Committee on Special Requirements of the Courts, 1974-1977; Committee on Grievances, 1977-1979; Chair, Committee on the Civil Court, 1974-1977; Committee on International Law, 1981-1985; Committee on Foreign and Comparative Law, 1985-1986); New York State (Member, International Law Committee, 1984-1987) and American (Vice-Chair, International Arbitration Committee, 1992—; Member, International Law and Practice Section and Section Liaison to ABA Standing Committee on World Order Under Law); Bar Associations. (Also with, Boulanger, Hicks, Stein & Churchill, New York, New York). *LANGUAGES:* English and French. *PRACTICE AREAS:* International; Commercial Law.

ELIZABETH CAROLINE DOUGHERTY, admitted, 1977, New York; 1991, Geneva. *Education:* Georgetown University (B.S., cum laude, Fulbright Scholar, 1968); Georgetown University Law Center (J.D., cum laude, 1977); University of Geneva (LL.M., 1987). Editor-in-Chief, Black Law Journal. *Member:* Geneva Bar Association; American Bar Association; National Bar Association; International Bar Association; Geneva Law Society; Swiss Arbitration Association; Association of International Business Lawyers. *LANGUAGES:* English, French, Spanish and German.

CANONICA, CLOSTRE & ASSOCIES

Established in 1953

2, RUE BELLOT

1206 GENEVA, SWITZERLAND

Telephone: (022) 347 47 47

Fax: (022) 346 40 27

FIRM PROFILE: Established in 1953, the firm is divided into a number of specialised departments offering clients, both Swiss and international, services predominantly in the areas of banking law, commercial law, business law, tax law, intellectual property, litigation and international arbitration. The firm is pleased to advise as well as to litigate in these areas of law throughout Switzerland.

The firm also advises private clients in all areas of civil law and, in particular, in relation to tax planning, probate and succession. One particular department in the firm specialises in financial penal law and international cooperation in penal matters.

In addition, the firm is member of the Pannone Law Group with offices in Paris (France), Milano (Italy), Manchester and London (England), Andorra, Stockholm (Sweden), Madrid (Spain), Lisboa (Portugal) and Bruxelles (Belgium). Therefore, Canonica, Clostre & Associés offers to advise

(This Listing Continued)

as well as litigate all over Europe through its Pannone Law Group associated offices.

MEMBERS OF FIRM

JEAN CLOSTRE, born in Geneva, Switzerland, 1936. *LANGUAGES:* French and German. *PRACTICE AREAS:* Civil and Commercial Litigation; International Law; Construction Law; Administrative Law; Labor Law.

DANTE CANONICA, born in Geneva, Switzerland, 1953. *LANGUAGES:* French, English and Italian. *PRACTICE AREAS:* Commercial Law; International Law; Tax Law; National and International Arbitration; Commercial Litigation.

FRANCOIS CANONICA, born in Geneva, Switzerland, 1958. *LANGUAGES:* French, English and Italian. *PRACTICE AREAS:* Business Law; Criminal Law; Civil and Commercial Litigation; International Mutual Aid; Bankruptcy.

JESSICA BACH, born in Geneva, Switzerland, 1956. *LANGUAGES:* French. *PRACTICE AREAS:* Civil Law; Family Law; Inheritances; Civil Litigation.

LAURENCE BOUTELLIER, born in Geneva, Switzerland, 1964. *LANGUAGES:* French. *PRACTICE AREAS:* Intellectual Property; Industrial Property; Trademarks; Licenses; Contract Law.

CATHERINE BROIDO, born in Geneva, Switzerland, 1969. *LANGUAGES:* French, English and Italian. *PRACTICE AREAS:* Commercial Law; International Law; Contract Law; Civil and Commercial Litigation.

COMBE, DE BAVIER & DE SENARCLENS

37, QUAI WILSON

1211 GENEVA 21, SWITZERLAND

Telephone: (22) 741 01 01

Telefax: (22) 741 01 27

Commercial, Corporate, Business, Swiss and International Taxation, Banking and Finance Law, Mergers and Acquisitions, Estate and Trust Law, Intellectual Property and Trademarks, Unfair Competition, Insurance, Distribution Law, Agency, Franchising, European Law, Commercial Litigation, International Arbitration, Debt Collection and Bankruptcy Law.

PARTNERS

CHRISTIANE M. DE SENARCLENS, born Geneva, Switzerland, February 22, 1950; admitted, 1973, Geneva; 1978, New York; 1980, Zurich; 1982, Basle. *Education:* University of Geneva (Licence en droit, 1972); University of Munich (1972-1973). *Member:* Geneva, Swiss and International Bar Associations; Geneva Association of Business Law; Swiss Arbitration Association; Young Lawyers' International Association; International Fiscal Association. *LANGUAGES:* French, English, German and Spanish.

CHARLES DE BAVIER, born Rome, Italy, May 10, 1948; admitted, 1972, Geneva; 1982, New York; 1990, Zurich. *Education:* University of Geneva (Licence en droit, 1972). *Member:* Geneva, Swiss and International Bar Associations; Geneva Association of Business Law; Society of Trust and Estate Practitioners; Associazione Giuristi di Lingua Italiana. *LANGUAGES:* French, English, Italian and Spanish.

JEAN-ERIC COMBE, born Geneva, Switzerland, September 23, 1948; admitted, 1975, Berne; 1980, Geneva; 1982, Basle; 1990, Zurich. *Education:* University of Basle (lic.jur.utr., 1974); University of Berne (Fürsprecher, 1978). Co-Author: "La Législation Suisse protège par des mesures conservatoires les entreprises en cas de conflits internationaux," Fiscalité Européenne, Revue, 1982; "Vorsorgliche Massnahmen zum Schutz Schweizerischer Unternehmen im Falle von Internationalen Konflikten," F.J.S., Geneva, 1982. *Member:* Geneva, Swiss and International Bar Associations; Geneva Association of Business Law; Union Internationale des Avocats; Swiss Association of Arbitration; International Fiscal Association; Associazione Giuristi di Lingua Italiana. *LANGUAGES:* French, English, German, Italian and Spanish.

ASSOCIATES

PIERRE-OLIVIER ALLAZ, born Geneva, Switzerland, November 11, 1956; admitted, 1987, Geneva; 1990, Zurich. *Education:* University of Geneva (degree in political sciences, 1981; Licence en droit, 1986). *LANGUAGES:* French, English and German.

DOMINIQUE CHRISTIN, born Lausanne, Switzerland, June 28, 1964; admitted, 1987, Geneva; 1991, Zurich. *Education:* University of Lausanne

(This Listing Continued)

COMBE, DE BAVIER & DE SENARCLENS, Geneva—
Continued

(Licence en droit, 1986); University of London (LL.M., 1992). *LAN-GUAGES:* French and English.

KRISTOF KALAPOS, born Zurich, Switzerland, September 17, 1969. *Education:* University of Lausanne (Licence en Droit, 1992). *LAN-GUAGES:* French, German, English and Italian.

CROISIER & GILLIOZ

Established in 1971

61, RUE DU RHÔNE

P.O. BOX 3127

CH 1211 GENEVA 3, SWITZERLAND
Telephone: 022.310.12.33
Telecopier: 022.310.81.92

Zürich, Switzerland Associated Office: Meyer Lustenberger & Partners. Forchstrasse 452, 8029 Zürich. Telephone: 01/391.41.61. Telecopier: 01/391.27.81. Telex: 817.804 kmlw.

International, Financial, Commercial, Civil and Tax Practice, Arbitration, Conflict of Laws, Banking, Joint Ventures.

FIRM PROFILE: The firm has its office in the commercial district of Geneva. It provides comprehensive legal services to Swiss and foreign individuals and corporate clients: general contract and commercial law, corporation law (including mergers and acquisitions), art law, federal and cantonal taxation (including international double taxation), labor law (including work permits for foreigners), banking law, international legal assistance, inheritance law and estate planning (including trusts and foundations), product liability, reorganizations and bankruptcy, international arbitrations.

MEMBERS OF FIRM

JEAN-PAUL CROISIER, born Geneva, Switzerland, 1938; admitted, 1964, Geneva; 1967, Fribourg. *Education:* Universities of Bern and Geneva (Licence en droit, 1961; Licence in business administration, 1963). *Member:* Geneva Bar Association; Geneva Law Society; Swiss Federation of Lawyers; Geneva Association of Business Law; International Fiscal Association. *LANGUAGES:* French, English, German and Italian. *PRACTICE AREAS:* Joint Ventures; Mergers and Acquisitions; Trusts and Foundations; Taxation; Art Law.

ANDRÉ GILLIOZ, born St-Maurice, Switzerland, 1937; admitted, 1967, Geneva. *Education:* University of Geneva (Licence en droit, 1959; Licence in business administration, 1960); New York University (M.C.J., 1965). *Member:* Geneva Bar Association; Geneva Law Society; Swiss Federation of Lawyers; Geneva Association of Business Law; International Fiscal Association. *LANGUAGES:* French, English and German. *PRACTICE AREAS:* Mergers and Acquisitions; Reorganizations and Insolvency Law; Taxation; International Arbitration; Estate Planning.

ASSOCIATES

PHILIPPE PROST, born Geneva, Switzerland, 1960; admitted, 1986, Geneva. *Education:* University of Geneva (Licence en droit, 1983). *Member:* Geneva Bar Association; Swiss Federation of Lawyers; Young Lawyers International Association. *LANGUAGES:* French and English. *PRACTICE AREAS:* Commercial Litigation; Arbitration; General Contract Law.

PAULINE GILLIOZ, born Geneva, Switzerland, 1965; admitted, 1990, Geneva; 1991, Zurich. *Education:* Calvin College, Geneva (Maturity, 1984); University of Geneva (LL.B., 1988); Bar exam, Geneva (1990). Author: "Le nouveau droit des sociétés anonymes Weka," Zurich, 1993. Member, Ordre des avocats, 1988—. *Member:* Geneva Bar Association; Swiss Federation of Lawyers. *LANGUAGES:* French and German. *PRACTICE AREAS:* Corporate Law; Insolvency; Litigation; Contract Law.

EU1358B

DONALD CRONSON

4, RUE BONIVARD

1201 GENEVA, SWITZERLAND
Telephone: (022) 738 71 81
Fax: (022) 738 76 75

International Financial, Commercial and Tax Practice, Arbitration, Trusts. Engaged in General International Law Practice, but not authorized to appear before the Swiss Courts as Avocat.

DONALD CRONSON, born Chicago, Illinois, 1922; admitted, 1948, Illinois; 1949, New York; 1954, U.S. Supreme Court (Not admitted in Switzerland). *Education:* University of Chicago Law School (J.D., 1948). Law Clerk to Justice Jackson, U.S. Supreme Court, 1952-1953. Associate, Cravath, Swaine & Moore, 1953-1961. Counsel to European Headquarters, Mobil Oil Corporation, 1964-1977. Legal Adviser to Credit Suisse-First Boston Group, 1977-1981. *LANGUAGES:* English, French and German.

ROGER DAGON

Established in 1970

12-14 RUE DU MARCHÉ

1204 GENEVA, SWITZERLAND
Telephone: 022/311 19 77
Telefax: 022/311 20 32

Zurich, Switzerland Associated Office: Frick & Partner, Dufourstrasse 60, 8702 Zollikon/Zürich.

Zug, Switzerland Associated Office: Lic. Peter B. Arnold, 14, Chamerstrasse, 6301.

Lugano, Switzerland Associated Office: Lic. Joseph Wicki, 9 Via F. Soave, 6900.

Corporate, Commercial, Tax, Banking, Real Estate, Trust, License and Trademarks, Unfair Competition and Aviation Law, Litigation, Notarial Acts.

ROGER DAGON, born Zürich, Switzerland, October 11, 1931; admitted, 1961, Zürich; 1962, Geneva. *Education:* University of Zürich (Dr.jur., 1960). Research Fellow, University of Michigan, USA, 1968-1970. Salzburg Seminar in American Studies. Author: "Regulation of Capital Influx," The American Journal of Comp. L., 1965. *Member:* Geneva Bar Association; Swiss Arbitration Association. *LANGUAGES:* French, German and English. *PRACTICE AREAS:* International Arbitration ICC; Civil Arbitration; Mediation; Corporate Law; Insolvency; White Collar Crime; Computer Contracts.

ASSOCIATES

MARILYN NAHMANI, born Tunis, Tunisia, February 27, 1961; admitted, 1987, Geneva. *Education:* University of Geneva (lic.iur., 1986). Training at Administrative Court of Geneva, Attorney at Law, 1989. *LANGUAGES:* French and German. *PRACTICE AREAS:* Litigation; Divorce; Civil Law; Estate Law; Immigration Law; Lease Contracts; Commercial Litigation; Criminal Law; Insolvency.

DES GOUTTES, FIECHTER, GANZONI, BARTH & PIERREHUMBERT

Established in 1834

4, AVENUE DE CHAMPEL

1206 GENEVA, SWITZERLAND
Telephone: (022) 347 36 00
Telecopier: (022) 346 79 93

FIRM PROFILE: The firm was founded in 1834 by Adolphe Des Gouttes. While it is clearly weighted toward corporate and commercial law, both local and international, the firm's legal practice also includes a significant volume of administrative regulations, banking, taxation, labour and insurance law, immigration matters as well as arbitration and litigation. The firm provides a broad range of legal services to a diversified clientele encompassing banks, financial and trading companies as well as other businesses and many individuals. The firm has been fully involved in the foundation of Euravocat, a European group of economic interests aimed at providing prompt and efficient services throughout Europe.

(This Listing Continued)

MEMBERS OF FIRM

RENÉ DES GOUTTES, born Geneva, 1906; admitted, 1930, Switzerland. *Education:* University of Geneva (Licence en droit, 1927; Docteur en droit, 1938). *Member:* Geneva Law and Legislation Society; Swiss Society of Jurists. *LANGUAGES:* French, English and German.

ARNOLD SCHLAEPFER, born Geneva, 1916; admitted, 1939, Switzerland. *Education:* University of Geneva (Licence en droit, 1939; Docteur en droit, 1948). Former Secretary at the Federal Tribunal of Insurances, 1944-1949. Member, Swiss Arbiter List of the International Chamber of Commerce of Paris, 1975. *Member:* Geneva Law and Legislation Society; Swiss Society of Jurists. *LANGUAGES:* French, German, English and Spanish.

ROBERT FIECHTER, born Geneva, 1952; admitted, 1979, Switzerland. *Education:* University of Geneva (Licence en droit, 1976); Tulane University (LL.M., 1980). *Member:* Geneva, Zurich and Swiss Bar Associations; Swiss Arbitration Association; Swiss Society of International Law; American Society of International Law; Swiss Society of Jurists. *LANGUAGES:* French, English and German.

PHILIPP GANZONI, born Basel, 1952; admitted, 1980, Switzerland. *Education:* University of Geneva (Licence en droit, 1976; Licence ès sciences commerciales, 1978). *Member:* Geneva, Zurich, Neuchatel and Swiss Bar Associations; Geneva Association of Business Law; AIJA International Association of Young Lawyers; Swiss Society of Jurists. *LANGUAGES:* French, English, German, Spanish, Italian and Portuguese.

DOMINIQUE BARTH, born Geneva, 1956; admitted, 1984, Switzerland. *Education:* University of Geneva (Licence en droit, 1981). *Member:* Geneva and Swiss Bar Associations; Geneva Association of Business Law. *LANGUAGES:* French, English and German.

MURIEL PIERREHUMBERT, born Geneva, 1954; admitted, 1979, Switzerland. *Education:* University of Geneva (Licence en droit, 1979). *Member:* Geneva and Swiss Bar; Swiss Arbitration Association; Swiss Society of Jurists. *LANGUAGES:* French, English and German.

COUNSEL

STUART ROBINSON, born Springfield, Illinois, 1930; admitted, 1961, New York (Not admitted in Switzerland). *Education:* Hamilton College, Northwestern University (Sc. B., 1952); Harvard University (Juris.Doc., 1960); University of Geneva (Doc. Sc. Pol., 1972). Adjunct Professor, International Financial and Monetary Law, Graduate Institute of International Studies, Geneva. Former Senior Director and Secretary of Governing Council, GATT, Geneva. *Member:* American Bar Association; International Law Association; American Foreign Law Association; Geneva Association of Business Law. *LANGUAGES:* English, French and Spanish.

OLIVIER CHERPILLOD, born Lausanne, 1969; admitted, 1994, Switzerland. *Education:* University of Lausanne (Licence en droit, 1991). *Member:* Geneva and Swiss Bar Associations; Swiss Society of Jurists. *LANGUAGES:* French, English and German.

Languages: French, English, German, Italian, Spanish and Portuguese.

DINICHERT, DE LAVALLAZ, VULLIEMIN

3. RUE DE LA VALLÉE
1204 GENEVA, SWITZERLAND
Telephone: (41-22) 311 01 01
Telefax: (41-22) 311 01 09

Mailing Address: P.O. Box 3267, 1211 Geneva 3, Switzerland

Commercial, Corporate and Civil Practice. International Contracts, Aviation Transactions, Medical Law and Ethics, Debt Collection and Insolvency, Commercial and Civil Litigation, Commercial Arbitration, Mediation.

MEMBERS OF FIRM

NICOLAS DINICHERT, born Neuchâtel, Switzerland, 1951; admitted, 1987, Geneva; 1988, New York. *Education:* University of Geneva (Licence en droit, 1984); University of Chicago Law School (LL.M., 1988). *Member:* Geneva, American and International Bar Associations; Geneva Business Law Association; Swiss Air and Space Law Association; Swiss Federation of Lawyers. *LANGUAGES:* French, English and German. *PRACTICE AREAS:* Commercial; Corporate and Contract Law; Private International Law (commercial and civil matters); Aviation Transactions; Commercial Litigation; Debt Collection; Insolvency.

(This Listing Continued)

CONSTANCE GILLIOZ DE LAVALLAZ, born Lausanne, Switzerland, 1950; admitted, 1982, Geneva. *Education:* University of Geneva (Licence en droit, 1974). Research Assistant to Professor of Contract and Commercial Law and Lecturer in Civil Law, University of Geneva, 1984-1987. *Member:* Geneva Bar Association; Swiss Federation of Lawyers; Swiss Medical Law Association; Swiss Medical Ethics Society. *LANGUAGES:* French and English. *PRACTICE AREAS:* Commercial Law; Corporate Law; Contract Law; Consumer Law; Medical Law; Commercial Litigation; Civil Litigation; Mediation.

JEAN-MARIE VULLIEMIN, born Lausanne, Switzerland, 1958; admitted, 1989, Geneva. *Education:* University of Lausanne Law School (Licence en droit, 1980; Doctorat en droit, 1988); Doctor en Derecho, Spain, 1990; Hague Academy of International Law, 1987 (Certificate of Center of International Studies: Arbitration and State Contracts); Graduated Assistant at Institut d'Etudes de Droit International. Guest Lawyer, Russell and Dutloulin, Vancouver, 1990. *Member:* Geneva Bar Association; Swiss Federation of Lawyers; Swiss Arbitration Association; Spanish-Swiss Economic Association. *LANGUAGES:* French, Spanish, English. *PRACTICE AREAS:* Private International Law (commercial and civil matters; more specifically with Spanish speaking countries); Commercial, Corporate and Contract Law; Civil and Commercial Litigation; International Commercial Arbitration.

DIXON & DIXON, LTD., L.L.P.

A Registered Limited Liability Partnership including Professional
Corporations
AVENUE GIUSEPPE-MOTTA 52
CH-1211 GENEVA 16, SWITZERLAND
Telephone: 022-734-2343
FAX: 022-734-0322

Omaha, Nebraska Office: Suite 1800, One First National Center, Sixteenth & Dodge Streets, 68102. Telephone: 402-345-3900. Fax: 402-345-0965 or 402-345-3341.
Washington, D.C. Office: 1850 M Street, N.W., Suite 450, 20036. Telephone: 202-452-1034. Fax: 202-452-1822.
Dallas, Texas Office: Suite 2500, Fountain Place, 1445 Ross Avenue, 75202. Telephone: 214-754-0155. Fax: 214-754-0704.
Los Angeles, California Office: Suite 2000, Wells Fargo Center, 333 South Grand Avenue, 90071. Telephone: 213-346-8310. Fax: 213-620-1811.
Kuwait City Office: Al-Hilali Street, Murgab, Al-Burrak Building 2, P.O. Box 22833 SAFAT, Kuwait 13089. Telephone: 011-965-241-5617. Fax: 011-965-240-7030.

International Claims, Banking, Securities, Corporate, Bankruptcy, Real Estate, Insurance, Legislation, Regulation, Environmental, Insurance and Litigation.

INGRID HABERSATTER, admitted, Switzerland. (Resident).

(For Biographical Data on Personnel at Los Angeles, California, Washington, D.C., Omaha, Nebraska, Dallas Texas and Kuwait, Kuwait, see Professional Biographies at those locations)

DUCRET DUCREST VAN LOON & ASSOCIES

8 RUE ST-LÉGER
1205 GENEVA, SWITZERLAND
Telephone: (CH: 41) 022-311 09 44
Telefax: (CH: 41) 022-310 08 39

General and International Business Law, Corporate, Civil Law, Banking, Administrative Law, Intellectual Property, Antitrust and Unfair Competition, Trusts, Domestic and International Taxation, Labour, Bankruptcy, European Community Law.

MEMBERS OF THE FIRM

DOMINIQUE DUCRET, born Geneva, Switzerland, 1943; admitted, 1971, Switzerland. *Education:* University of Geneva (Licence en Droit, 1965-1968). *Member:* Swiss National Council; Geneva Bar Association; Swiss Federation of Lawyers; Swiss Society of Jurists; Geneva Business Law Association.

EMMANUEL DUCREST, born Fribourg, Switzerland, 1942; admitted, 1971, Switzerland. *Education:* University of Fribourg (Licence en Droit,

(This Listing Continued)

DUCRET DUCREST VAN LOON & ASSOCIES,
Geneva—Continued

1963-1967). *Member:* Geneva Bar Association; Geneva Law Society; Geneva Business Law Association; Swiss Arbitration Association.

JOHANNES-POTTER VAN LOON, born Rotterdam, Netherland, 1956; admitted, 1980, Switzerland. *Education:* University of Geneva (Licence en Droit 1976-1979). *Member:* Geneva Bar Association; Swiss Federation of Lawyers; International Bar Association; European Lawyers Association; International Union of Lawyers.

OLIVIER CARRARD, born Fribourg, Switzerland, 1956; admitted, 1981, Switzerland. *Education:* University of Fribourg (Licence en Droit 1977-1981). *Member:* Geneva Bar Association; Swiss Society of Jurists; Swiss Federation of Lawyers; Swiss Association of Law for the Sport; Geneva Business Law Association.

YVES SIEGRIST, born Geneva, Switzerland, 1957; admitted, 1981, Geneva. *Education:* University of Geneva (Licence en Droit 1977-1980). *Member:* Geneva Bar Association; Swiss Federation of Lawyers; International Association of Young Lawyers; Swiss Association for the Study of the Competition Law.

ASSOCIATES

CAROLINE FERRERO, born Geneva, Switzerland, 1966; admitted, 1989, Switzerland. *Education:* University of Geneva (Licence en Droit 1985-1988). *Member:* Geneva Bar Association; International Association of Young Lawyers.

FREDERIC DESPONT, born Geneva, Switzerland, 1967; admitted, 1993, Switzerland. *Education:* University of Geneva (Licence en Droit, 1987-1991); University Robert Schuman, Strasbourg (D.E.S.S. Industrial Property, 1991-1992).

OLIVIER RAPIN, born Montreux, Switzerland, 1969; admitted, 1993, Geneva. *Education:* University of Lausanne (Licence en Droit, 1987-1991; Postgraduated in European Community Law, 1991-1992).

DAVID GARRIDO, born Geneva, Switzerland, 1969; admitted, 1994, Geneva. *Education:* University of Geneva (Licence en Droit, 1989-1993).

LEGAL SUPPORT PERSONNEL

POTTER VAN LOON, born Jakarta, Indonesia, 1913; admitted, 1938, Indonesia; 1950, The Netherlands. *Education:* University of Leyden, Netherlands (Doctoraal Recht 1937). *Member:* Rotterdam Bar and International Fiscal Association. (Paralegal).

Languages: French, English, German, Dutch, Italian and Spanish

---

ALBERT LOUIS DUPONT-WILLEMIN

10 BIS, RUE DU VIEUX-COLLÈGE
P.O. BOX 3194
1211 GENEVA 3, SWITZERLAND
Telephone: (022) 311 40 22
Cable Address: DUPONWIL GENEVE
Telex: 428462 DWAV
Facsimile: (022) 311 74 59

Corporate Law, Business Law, Banking and Commercial Law, Civil and Commercial Litigation, Labour Law, Insurance Law, Bankruptcy Law.

ALBERT LOUIS DUPONT-WILLEMIN, born Geneva, Switzerland, October 8, 1934; admitted, 1961, Switzerland. *Education:* Geneva University Faculty of Law and Commercial Sciences (Licences en droit et sciences commerciales, 1958); Brevet d'avocat, 1961. Author: Le secret professionnel et l'Indépendance de l'avocat, Bulletin de la Fédération Suisse des Avocats, N° 101, 1986 and Juriste International, 1986; Salariat et Indépendance de l'Avocat, Bulletins de la Fédération Suisse des Avocats, N° 115, 116, 118, 1988. Secretary, Young Lawyers International Association, 1975-1980. President, Société Genevoise de Droit et de Législation, 1977-1978. *Member:* Geneva Bar Association (President, 1984-1986); Swiss Federation of Lawyers; International Union of Lawyers (First Vice President, 1993). *LANGUAGES:* French, Spanish, English, German and Italian.

(This Listing Continued)

EU1360B

ASSOCIATES

MADELEINE PASQUIER, born Romont, Switzerland, October 15, 1945; admitted, 1982, Switzerland. *Education:* Geneva University Faculty of Law (Licence en droit, 1978); Brevet d'avocat, 1982. *Member:* Geneva Bar Association; Swiss Federation of Lawyers. *LANGUAGES:* French and English.

MARTINE TABAN, born Geneva, Switzerland, March 5, 1957; admitted, 1985, Switzerland. *Education:* Geneva University Faculty of Law (Licence en droit, 1982); Brevet d'avocat, 1985. *Member:* Geneva Bar Association; Swiss Federation of Lawyers. *LANGUAGES:* French and English.

KATIA FABBRI RATCLIFF, born Geneva, Switzerland, May 19, 1967; admitted, 1992, Switzerland. *Education:* Geneva University Faculty of Law (Licence en droit, 1989); Brevet d'avocat, 1992. *Member:* Geneva Bar Association; Swiss Federation of Lawyers. *LANGUAGES:* French, Spanish, Italian and English.

ETUDE
ETIENNE, BLUM, STEHLÉ, MANFRINI ET ASSOCIÉS

(Associated Office of Baker & McKenzie)

RUE BELLOT 6
1206 GENEVA, SWITZERLAND
Telephone: (022) 346 76 08; 346 70 70
Intn'l. Dialing: (41-22) 346 76 08; 346 70 70
Facsimile: (41-22) 347 02 84

MEMBERS OF FIRM

DENIS BERDOZ, born Geneva, Switzerland, 1953; admitted, 1975, Switzerland. *Education:* University of Geneva (Licence en droit, 1975). *Member:* Geneva and Swiss Lawyers' Associations. *LANGUAGES:* French, English and German. *PRACTICE AREAS:* Taxation; Mergers and Acquisitions; Corporate and Partnership Law; Banking and Finance; Securities and Financial Products.

FRANÇOIS BLUM, born La Chaux-de-Fonds, Switzerland, 1941; admitted, 1964, Switzerland. *Education:* Universities of Geneva and Neuchâtel, Switzerland (Licence en droit, 1964); New York University School of Law (M.C.J., 1970). *Member:* Geneva and Swiss Lawyers' Associations; Association of the Bar of the City of New York. *LANGUAGES:* French, English and German. *PRACTICE AREAS:* Intellectual Property Law; Mergers and Acquisitions; Franchise Law; Computers and Technology Law; EC Competition and Trade.

DONALD ETIENNE, born Bern, Switzerland, 1932; admitted, 1956, Switzerland. *Education:* University of Geneva (Licence en droit, 1954); Harvard Law School (LL.M., 1960). *Member:* Geneva and Swiss Bar Associations. *LANGUAGES:* French, English, German, Italian and Spanish. *PRACTICE AREAS:* Taxation; Corporate and Partnership Law; Arbitration and Dispute Resolution.

LOUIS GAILLARD, born Fribourg, Switzerland, 1947; admitted, 1974, Switzerland. *Education:* University of Geneva (Licence en droit, 1972; Licence en science politique, 1973; Diplôme d'Etudes Supérieures, 1984). *LANGUAGES:* French, English. *PRACTICE AREAS:* Commercial Litigation; Civil Litigation; Arbitration and Dispute Resolution; Bankruptcy, Insolvency and Reorganization; Criminal Law.

GABRIELLE KAUFMANN, born Mulhouse, France, 1952; admitted, 1974, Switzerland; 1982, New York, U.S.A. *Education:* University of Geneva (Licence en droit, 1974); University of Basel (Doctorat en droit, 1979). *Member:* Geneva and Swiss Lawyers' Associations. *LANGUAGES:* French, English and German. *PRACTICE AREAS:* Arbitration and Dispute Resolution.

PIERRE LOUIS MANFRINI, born Monteggio, Switzerland, 1949; admitted, 1977, Switzerland. *Education:* University of Geneva (Licence en droit, 1972; Diplome d'etudes superieures, 1975; Doctorat en droit, 1977). *Member:* Geneva and Swiss Lawyers' Associations. *LANGUAGES:* French, Italian and English. *PRACTICE AREAS:* Commercial Litigation; Administrative Law; Banking and Finance; Environmental Law.

DANIEL ANTONIO PEREGRINA, born Bienne, Switzerland, 1955; admitted, 1983, Switzerland. *Education:* Geneva University (Lic. Jur. and D.E.S.). Teaching Assistant at Geneva University, 1978-1983. *Member:* Swiss Lawyers Association. *LANGUAGES:* French, Spanish, German and

(This Listing Continued)

English. *PRACTICE AREAS:* Commercial Litigation; Environmental Law; Administrative Law; Communications and Media Law; Real Estate Law.

ALAIN STEHLÉ, born Geneva, Switzerland, 1939; admitted, 1964, Switzerland. *Education:* University of Geneva (Licence en droit, 1964); University of Texas at Austin (M.C.J., 1972). *Member:* Geneva and Swiss Bar Associations. *LANGUAGES:* French, English and German. *PRACTICE AREAS:* Labor and Employment Law; Immigration Law; Executive Transfers; Commercial Litigation; Employee Benefits.

LOCAL PARTNERS

QUENTIN BYRNE-SUTTON, born Manchester, England, 1959; admitted, 1990, Switzerland. *Education:* University of Geneva, Faculty of Law (Bachelor's, 1981; Master's, 1984; Ph.D., Law, 1987). Tutor, Private International Law, Geneva University Law Faculty, 1981-1986. *LANGUAGES:* English, French, German and Spanish. *PRACTICE AREAS:* Arbitration and Dispute Resolution; Entertainment, the Arts and Sports Law; Commercial Litigation; Intellectual Property Law; Trust, Probate and Estate Planning.

SYLVIE M. A. GURRY-VEIT, born Belfort, France, February 14, 1960. *Education:* University of Strasbourg (Law Degree, 1981); University of Melbourne (Master of Laws, 1984). Research Assistant in International Monetary Law at the Institute of International Studies, Geneva. *Member:* Association Suisse d'Etude de la Concurrence. *LANGUAGES:* French and English. *PRACTICE AREAS:* Intellectual Property Law; Computers and Technology Law; Franchise Law; EC Competition and Trade; Entertainment, the Arts and Sports Law.

JOËLLE ZUMOFFEN, born Sierre, Switzerland, 1953; admitted, 1989, Switzerland. *Education:* University of Lausanne (Licence HEC, 1976); University of Geneva (Examen d'Etat/Licence en Droit, 1989). Certified Tax Expert, 1984. *Member:* International Fiscal Association; Ordre Romand des Experts Fiscaux Diplômés; Chambre Fiduciaire Suisse, Association Suisse des Experts Fiscaux Diplômés. *LANGUAGES:* French and English. *PRACTICE AREAS:* Taxation; Corporate and Partnership Law; Mergers and Acquisitions; Trust, Probate and Estate Planning; Employee Benefits.

RESIDENT ASSOCIATES

MARTIN S. ANDERSON, born Geneva, Switzerland, July 31, 1965; admitted, 1992, Switzerland. *Education:* University of Geneva (Business Administration, 1987; Law, 1990). Assistant in Finance, 1987-1990. *Member:* Geneva Bar Association; Geneva Business Law Association. *LANGUAGES:* French, English and German. *PRACTICE AREAS:* Banking and Finance; Securities and Financial Products; Mergers and Acquisitions; Corporate and Partnership Law; Bankruptcy, Insolvency and Reorganization.

FRANÇOIS BELLANGER, born Boulogne Billancourt, France, August 24, 1963; admitted, 1992, Switzerland. *Education:* University of Geneva (Law, 1986; Diploma of Superior Study in Law, 1988; Doctor in Law, 1990). Lecturer of Law, Geneva University, 1991-1993. Master of European Community Law (Bruges, 1994). Assistant in Public Law, Geneva University, 1986-1990. *Member:* Geneva Bar Association; Geneva Business Law Association. *LANGUAGES:* French, English and German. *PRACTICE AREAS:* Administrative Law; EC Law; Banking and Finance; Commercial Litigation; Bankruptcy, Insolvency and Reorganization.

YVES BONNARD, born Lausanne, December 27, 1964; admitted, 1992, Switzerland. *Education:* Lausanne University School of Law (Lic., 1988). *LANGUAGES:* French, English and German. *PRACTICE AREAS:* Corporate Law; Taxation.

CHRISTOPHE C. ZELLWEGER, born Geneva, Switzerland, 1962; admitted, 1991, Switzerland. *Education:* Geneva University, Faculté des sciences economiques et sociales (Licence, 1985; Licence, 1988). *LANGUAGES:* French, English and German. *PRACTICE AREAS:* Commercial Litigation; Banking and Finance; Bankruptcy, Insolvency and Reorganization; Real Estate Law; Criminal Law.

FONTANET & JEANDIN

84, RUE DU RHONE
CH-1204 GENEVA, SWITZERLAND
Telephone: (022) 310.90.07
Telex: 422.550 GFT CH
Telecopier: 310.90.42 (Group 2 & 3)

General and International Law Practice.

(This Listing Continued)

MEMBERS OF FIRM

GUY L. FONTANET, born July 27, 1927; admitted, 1949, Geneva. *Education:* University of Geneva Law School (Licence en droit, 1949). Research Assistant, 1951-1952. Member, Legislature, State of Geneva, 1957-1973. Member, Federal Legislature, 1971-1978. Minister of Justice and Police, State of Geneva, 1973-1985. President of the Government, State of Geneva, 1979-1980. Chairman of the Caisse D'Epargne (Bank of the State of Geneva), 1985—. *Member:* Geneva and Swiss Bar Associations; Swiss Society of Jurists; Geneva Association of Business Law.

BENEDICT D. FONTANET, born November 26, 1960; admitted, 1984, Geneva. *Education:* University of Geneva Law School (Licence en droit, 1982). Research Assistant, 1982-1983. *Member:* Geneva and Swiss Bar Associations; Swiss Society of Jurists; Geneva Association of Business Law.

NICOLAS JEANDIN, born Geneva, January 2, 1959; admitted, 1984, Geneva. *Education:* University of Geneva Economics School (Licence en sciences économiques, 1984); University of Geneva Law School (Licence en droit, 1981; Diplôme d'études supérieures en droit, 1986; Docteur en droit, 1993). Research Assistant, 1987—. *Member:* Geneva and Swiss Bar Associations.

ASSOCIATES

PAULINE WENGER STUDER, born Neuchâtel, November 21, 1954; admitted, 1985, Geneva. *Education:* University of Geneva Law School (Licence en droit, 1984). *Member:* Geneva and Swiss Bar Associations; Geneva Association of Business Law.

MOURAD SEKKIOU, born Argenteuil, France, October 10, 1957; admitted, 1985, Geneva. *Education:* University of Lausanne (Licence en droit français, 1982; Licence en droit suisse, 1984). *Member:* Geneva and Swiss Bar Associations.

PAOLA CAMPOMAGNANI, born Geneva, March 5, 1963; admitted, 1990, Geneva. *Education:* University of Geneva Law School (Licence en droit, 1985). *Member:* Geneva and Swiss Bar Associations.

ALAIN TRIPOD, born Beirut, Lebanon, May 8, 1968; admitted, 1991, Geneva. *Education:* University of Geneva Law School (Licence en droit, 1991). *Member:* Geneva and Swiss Bar Associations.

ALEXANDRE S. SABETI, born Geneva, June 6, 1969; admitted, 1993, Geneva. *Education:* University of Geneva (Licence en droit, 1990; Licence en sciences économiques, 1992). *Member:* Geneva and Swiss Bar Associations.

CHRISTINE DUNAND, born Geneva, August 12, 1969; admitted, 1993, Geneva. *Education:* University of Geneva (Licence en droit, 1992). *Member:* Geneva and Swiss Bar Associations.

FRORIEP RENGGLI

4, RUE CHARLES-BONNET
1206 GENEVA, SWITZERLAND
Telephone: (+41)-22 347 18 18
Telex: 423651 frob ch
Telecopier: (+41)-22 347 71 59

Zurich, Switzerland Office: Bellerivestrasse 201, 8034. Telephone: (+41)1 386 60 00. Telecopier: (+41)1 383 60 50 (Address until April 30, 1995: General-Strasse 10, 8027. Telephone: (+41) 12017420. Telex: 815596 frp ch. Telecopier: (+41) 12023666).
Zug, Switzerland Office: Baarerstrasse 75, 6300. Telephone: (+41)-42 21 33 71. Telecopier: (+41)-42 23 07 15.
London, England Office: 1 Knightrider Court, EC4V 5JP. Telephone: (+44)171 236 60 00. Fax: (+44)171 248 02 09.
Fuerth (Nürnberg), Germany Office: Friedrichstrasse 6, 90762. Telephone: (+49)-911 77 39 82. Telecopier: (+49)-911 749 84 51.

Commercial, Corporate and Civil Practice, International Business Transactions, Commercial Litigation and International Commercial Arbitration, Private and Public International Law, Banking, Taxation, Immigration, Bankruptcy, International Judicial Assistance, Trade Marks and Copyrights, EEC Law, Estate, Real Property and Aviation Law.

FIRM PROFILE: *Established in 1966, Froriep Renggli has grown to be one of the leading and largest Swiss law firms with principal offices in Zurich, Geneva and Zug. The firm is engaged in a broad range of Swiss and International practice. Froriep Renggli currently has a total of thirty-two lawyers, twelve of whom are partners. Two of the associates are qualified German lawyers, four lawyers are also admitted in New York and one is an English solicitor. Most of the lawyers have had, in addition to their*

(This Listing Continued)

FRORIEP RENGGLI, Geneva—Continued

Swiss training, legal education in England or the United States and/or have practice as foreign consultants with law firms there or elsewhere abroad. The firm has a three lawyers strong London office, an office in Fürth/Nürnberg, Germany, and an associated office in Bratislava, Slovakia. These, combined with an extensive network of correspondent lawyers, enhance the firm's international advisory, transactional and litigation capabilities.

RESIDENT PARTNERS

NICOLAS JUNOD, born Geneva, Switzerland, May 3, 1947; admitted, 1974, Switzerland. *Education:* University of Geneva (Lic. iur., 1971); New York University Institute of Comparative Law (M.C.J., 1978). *LANGUAGES:* French, English, Italian and German. *PRACTICE AREAS:* Commercial Law; Banking; Contract Law; Corporate Law.

ROLAND KAUFMANN, born Geneva, Switzerland, August 18, 1947; admitted, 1974, Switzerland. *Education:* University of Geneva (Lic. iur., 1973); New York University, Institute of Comparative Law (M.C.J., 1980). *LANGUAGES:* French, English, Italian and German. *PRACTICE AREAS:* Commercial Law; Company Law; Contract Law; Sponsoring; Sports.

DOMINIQUE BROWN-BERSET, born Villarsiviriaux, Switzerland, February 23, 1953; admitted, 1980, Switzerland. *Education:* University of Lausanne (Lic.iur., 1976); Paris I Panthéon-Sorbonne (DEA, 1978); Harvard Law School (Master of Laws, 1980). Former Editor, Journal of International Arbitration. Associate Member, Chartered Institute of Arbitrators. *LANGUAGES:* French, English and German. *PRACTICE AREAS:* Commercial and Contract Law; International Arbitration and ADR; International Litigation and Procedure; Company Law; Finance and Securities.

RESIDENT ASSOCIATES

GILLIAN ROTH, born London, England, February 25, 1960; admitted, 1986, England and Wales as Solicitor (Not admitted in Switzerland). *Education:* Oxford University (B.A., 1982; M.A., 1986); City of London Polytechnic School of Law (C.P.E., 1983); Guildford (Solicitors' Final Exam, 1984). *LANGUAGES:* English, French and German. *PRACTICE AREAS:* Company Law; Banking Law; Contract Law; International Trusts and Estates.

THOMAS P. BISCHOF, born Lichtensteig, Switzerland, September 22, 1959; admitted, 1986, Switzerland. *Education:* University of St. Gall (Lic. iur. 1985); Harvard Law School, Cambridge (LL.M., 1989). *LANGUAGES:* German, French and English. *PRACTICE AREAS:* Commercial Law; Corporate Law; Banking; International Arbitration.

PHILIPPE BERTA, born Geneva, Switzerland, August 8, 1959; admitted, 1985, Switzerland. *Education:* University of Geneva (Lic. iur., 1983). *LANGUAGES:* French and English. *PRACTICE AREAS:* Litigation; Arbitration; Banking Law; Commercial Law.

NICOLAS GENOUD, born Fribourg, Switzerland, May 20, 1964; admitted, 1990, Switzerland; 1994, New York. *Education:* University of Fribourg (Lic. iur., 1988); University of Pennsylvania Law School (LL.M., 1993). *LANGUAGES:* French and English. *PRACTICE AREAS:* Corporate Law; Torts; Contract Law.

(For Biographical Data on all Members, see Zurich Professional Biographies)

HEGETSCHWEILER

Established in 1949

13, RUE CHANTEPOULET

1201 GENEVA, SWITZERLAND

Telephone: (022) 738 17 00

Telefax: (022) 738 17 70

General Practice, Commercial Law, Criminal Law, Public and Administrative Law.

DR. JEAN HEGETSCHWEILER, born Basel, Switzerland, 1924; admitted, 1949, Geneva. *Education:* University of Geneva (Docteur en Droit, 1950). Author: "La Vente à Distance," International Trade, Charles Rohr & Cie Bienne, 1960. Chairman of the Board, Jaeger Le Coutre, 1970-1974. *Member:* Geneva and Swiss Bar Associations; International Bar Association; Union Internationale des Avocats; Associazione Giuristi Di Lingua

(This Listing Continued)

Italiana. *LANGUAGES:* French, German, English, Italian and Spanish. *PRACTICE AREAS:* Insurance; Injury; Civil; Commercial; Intellectual Property.

HENRY & GRAZ

11 BIS. RUE TOEPFFER

1206 GENEVA, SWITZERLAND

Telephone: (41 22) 346 52 60

Telex: 422 328 HEGR CH

Telecopier: (41 22) 346 59 39

International Business Law. Commercial Corporate and Administrative Law. Litigation, Arbitration, Banking and Finance. Tax Planning and Immigration (work and residence permits).

MEMBERS OF FIRM

Dr. Gerald Henry   Me. Jean-Pierre Graz

Languages: English, French, Spanish and Italian

HORNUNG & LÉVY

Established in 1982

16 BOULEVARD DES TRANCHÉES

P.O. BOX 345

1211 GENEVA 12, SWITZERLAND

Telephone: (4122) 789 0011

Telecopier: (4122) 789 0076

Telex: 422500 txc ch

Commercial, Corporate and Banking Law, International Arbitration, Torts, Private and Administrative Law.

FIRM PROFILE: The law firm Hornung & Levy was founded for the purpose of offering a full range of specialized legal services to business firms and individuals engaged in domestic and international business, particularly advice and assistance in drafting and negotiating commercial contracts, establishing corporations and joint ventures. The firm also devotes special attention to the relations between clients and banks, and banking regulations. Furthermore, the law firm has experienced litigation, particularly in business, commercial, torts, corporate and criminal law. Special attention is also devoted to European Community Law (EC antitrust and EC competition).

MEMBERS OF FIRM

DOUGLAS HORNUNG, born Geneva, Switzerland, April 5, 1952; admitted, 1980, Geneva. *Education:* College Voltaire Geneva (Bachelor, 1972); Geneva University (Licence en Droit, 1977; Bar Exam., Lawyer Degree, Brevet, 1980). Trainee, Audeoud & Gautier, Lawyers, 1978-1980. *Member:* Geneva Bar Association (Member, Young Lawyer's Committee, 1989-1991); Swiss Federation of Lawyers; AIJA International Association of Young Lawyers (Member, Executive Committee, 1983-1992; First Vice-President, 1992-1993; President, 1993-1994); Association of International Business Lawyers (President, 1986-1988); Union Internationale des Avocats; Swiss Arbitration Association; Association of Business Law. *LANGUAGES:* French and English. *PRACTICE AREAS:* Banking Law; Contract Law; Torts; Litigation; Arbitration.

ALAIN LÉVY, born Tangier, Morocco, 1956; admitted, 1986, Geneva. *Education:* Collège Claparède, Geneva (Bachelor, 1975); Geneva University School of Law (Law Degree, 1986; Bar Exam, 1988; Assistant, 1989); Columbia University (Master of Laws, LL.M., 1990). Trainee, Law Firm of Poncet Warluzel & Partners, Geneva, 1990-1993. Summer Associate, Law Firm of Donovan Leisure, Rogovin, Huge & Schiller, Washington, D.C., 1991. *Member:* Geneva Bar Association; Swiss Federation of Lawyers; Geneva Society of Law and Legislation; Swiss Arbitration Association; International Chamber of Commerce; American Bar Association. *LANGUAGES:* French, English and Spanish. *PRACTICE AREAS:* Banking Law; Contract Law; Commercial Law; European Community Law; Litigation; International Commercial Arbitration.

Languages: French, English, Spanish and German.

LAW OFFICES OF JEAN-PIERRE AND CHRISTOPHE IMHOOS & PARTNERS

Established in 1959

1, PLACE DU PORT
1204 GENEVA, SWITZERLAND
Telephone: (41-22) 311 97 33
Telefax: (41-22) 311 45 21
Telex: 429 483 Imos ch
Cable:"Imosavoc"

General and International Practice, including Tax Planning, Banking, Commercial, Contract, Inheritance and Civil Practice, International Commercial Arbitration and Litigation.

MEMBERS OF FIRM

JEAN-PIERRE IMHOOS, born Rabat, Morocco, September 25, 1929; admitted, 1958, Geneva. *Education:* University of Geneva Law School (Law Degree, 1956). *Member:* Geneva and Swiss Bar Associations. **LANGUAGES:** French and English. **PRACTICE AREAS:** International Practice; Tax Planning; Banking; Commercial; Contract; Inheritance.

CHRISTOPHE IMHOOS, born Geneva, Switzerland, June 17, 1959; admitted, 1985, Geneva. *Education:* University of Geneva Law School (Law Degree, 1983); New York University, School of Law, Institute of Comparative Law (M.C.J., 1987). Former Counsel, ICC International Court of Arbitration, 1987-1991. *Member:* Geneva and Swiss Bar Associations; International Bar Association; International Union of Young Lawyers; American Bar Association (International Associate); American Arbitration Association (Member, Panel of Arbitrators); Chartered Institute of Arbitrators (Associate); French Committee on Arbitration; Swiss Arbitration Association. **LANGUAGES:** French, English and German. **PRACTICE AREAS:** General Practice; International Practice; International Commercial Arbitration; Litigation.

LILIANE ZWAHLEN-STAMM, born Geneva, Switzerland, July 15, 1950; admitted, 1976, Geneva. *Education:* University of Geneva Law School (Law Degree, 1974). Deputy Judge, Geneva Tribunal of First Instance, 1992—. *Member:* Geneva and Swiss Bar Associations. **LANGUAGES:** French, English and German. **PRACTICE AREAS:** General Practice; Civil Practice.

NATHALIE BERTOCCHI-IMHOOS, born Geneva, Switzerland, November 7, 1964; (Not admitted in Switzerland). *Education:* University of Geneva Law School (Law Degree, 1989). **LANGUAGES:** French, English and Italian. **PRACTICE AREAS:** General Practice; Civil Practice.

Languages: French, English, Italian and German

JONES, DAY, REAVIS & POGUE

20, RUE DE CANDOLLE
CH-1205 GENEVA, SWITZERLAND
Telephone: 011-41-22-320-2339
Telecopier: 011-41-22-320-1232

In Atlanta, Georgia: 3500 One Peachtree Center, 303 Peachtree Street, N.E. Telephone: 404-521-3939. Cable Address: "Attorneys Atlanta". Telex: 54-2711. Telecopier: 404-581-8330.

In Brussels, Belgium: Avenue Louise 480, 7th Floor. B-1050 Brussels. Telephone: 32-2-645-14-11. Telecopier: 32-2-645-14-45.

In Chicago, Illinois: 77 West Wacker. Telephone: 312-782-3939. Telecopier: 312-782-8585.

In Cleveland, Ohio: North Point, 901 Lakeside Avenue. Telephone: 216-586-3939. Cable Address: "Attorneys Cleveland." Telex: 980389. Telecopier: 216-579-0212.

In Columbus, Ohio: 1900 Huntington Center. Telephone: 614-469-3939. Cable Address: "Attorneys Columbus." Telecopier: 614-461-4198.

In Dallas, Texas: 2300 Trammell Crow Center, 2001 Ross Avenue. Telephone: 214-220-3939. Cable Address: "Attorneys Dallas." Telex: 730852. Telecopier: 214-969-5100.

In Frankfurt, Germany: Triton Haus, Bockenheimer Landstrasse 42, 60323 Frankfurt am Main. Telephone: 49-69-9726-3939. Telecopier: 49-69-9726-3993.

In Hong Kong: 1501 One Exchange Square, 8 Connaught Place. Telephone: 852-2526-6895. Telecopier: 852-2810-5787.

In Irvine, California: 2603 Main Street, Suite 900. Telephone: 714-851-3939. Telex: 194911 Lawyers LSA. Telecopier: 714-553-7539.

In London, England: One Mount Street. Telephone: 44-71-493-9361. Cable Address: "Surgoe London WI." Telecopier: 44-71-493-9666.

In Los Angeles, California: 555 West Fifth Street, Suite 4600. Telephone: 213-489-3939. Telex: 181439 UD. Telecopier: 213-243-2539.

In New York, New York: 599 Lexington Avenue. Telephone: 212-326-3939. Cable Address: "JONESDAY NEWYORK." Telex: 237013 JDRP UR. Telecopier: 212-755-7306.

In Paris, France: 62, rue du Faubourg Saint-Honore. Telephone: 33-1-44-71-3939. Cable Address: "Surgoe Paris." Telex: 290156 Surgoe. Telecopier: 33-1-49-24-0471.

In Pittsburgh, Pennsylvania: 500 Grant Street, 31st Floor. Telephone: 412-391-3939. Cable Address: "Attorneys Pittsburgh". Telecopier: 412-394-7959.

In Riyadh, Saudi Arabia: Law Offices of Saud M.A. Shawwaf, P.O. Box 2700. Telephones: (966-1) 465-6543, (966-1) 464-8534 or (966-1) 464-8540. Telex: 401831 SAUCON SJ. Telecopier: (966-1) 464-8480.

In Taipei, Taiwan: 8th Floor, 2 Tun Hwa South Road, Section 2. Telephone: (886-2) 704-6808. Telecopier: (886-2) 704-6791.

In Tokyo, Japan: Toranomon MT Building, 4th Floor, 10-3, Toranomon 3-Chome, Minato-Ku, Tokyo 105, Japan. Telephone: 81-3-3433-3939. Telecopier: 81-3-5401-2725.

In Washington, D.C.: Metropolitan Square, 1450 G Street, N.W. Telephone: 202-879-3939. Cable Address: "Attorneys Washington." Telex: 89-2410 ATTORNEYS WASH. Telecopier: 202-737-2832.

General and International Practice.

MEMBER OF FIRM IN GENEVA

ROY F. RYAN, III, born New London, Connecticut, November 22, 1946; admitted to bar, 1974, Ohio; 1980, Maryland; (Not admitted in Switzerland). *Education:* Yale University (B.A., 1968); University of Virginia (J.D., 1974). Order of the Coif.

OF COUNSEL

MOHAMED AMERSI, born Mombasa, Kenya, April 20, 1960; admitted, 1986, England and qualified as a Solicitor (Not admitted in Switzerland). *Education:* University of Sheffield (B.A., 1984); Cambridge University (LL.B., 1985).

Languages: English, French.

KEPPELER, MAURER, KROO & SPIRGI

Established in 1964

32, ROUTE DE MALAGNOU
1208 GENEVA, SWITZERLAND
Telephone: (022) 735.26.28
Telecopier: (022) 786.55.09

International and General Practice, Commercial and Corporate Law, Banking Law, Aviation Law, International Legal Assistance, Business Crime, Arbitration and Litigation.

MEMBERS OF FIRM

BRUNO KEPPELER, born Rheineck, Switzerland, February 2, 1932; admitted, 1956, Geneva. *Education:* University of Geneva (Licence en Droit, 1953); University of Madrid (Doctor juris, 1956); Academy of International Law, The Hague (Diploma, 1957). Assistant to Professor of Law, University of Geneva, 1956-1958. *Member:* Swiss Arbitration Association; Lawyer-Pilots Bar Association. **LANGUAGES:** French, English, German, Spanish and Italian.

PASCAL MAURER, born Paris, France, February 12, 1951; admitted, 1975, Geneva. *Education:* University of Geneva (Licence en Droit). *Member:* Geneva and Swiss Bar Associations; Geneva Association of Business Law; Swiss Federation of Lawyers; Swiss Association of Criminal Law. **LANGUAGES:** French, English and Italian.

MICHAEL KROO, born Prague, Czech Republic; admitted, 1981, Geneva; 1994, Czech Republic. *Education:* University of Geneva (Licence en Droit, 1979). *Member:* Geneva and Swiss Bar Associations. **LANGUAGES:** French, Czech, English and Hungarian.

FABIO SPIRGI, born Geneva, Switzerland, January 24, 1961; admitted, 1986, Geneva; 1989, New York. *Education:* University of Geneva (Licence en Droit, 1984); New York University, Institute of Comparative Law (M.C.J., 1988). *Member:* Geneva, Swiss, New York State, American and International Bar Associations; Swiss Arbitration Association; International Commercial and Industrial Arbitration Association; Geneva Association of Business Law. **LANGUAGES:** French and English.

(This Listing Continued)

(This Listing Continued)

KEPPELER, MAURER, KROO & SPIRGI, Geneva—Continued

ASSOCIATES

CHRISTIAN VALENTINI, born San Francisco, California, USA, December 30, 1961; admitted, 1993, Geneva; 1994, Valais. *Education:* University of Fribourg (Licence en Droit, 1988). Assistant to Professor of Law, University of Fribourg, 1989-1990. *Member:* Geneva, Valais and Swiss Bar Associations. *LANGUAGES:* French, English and Italian.

PIERRE-ALAIN KILLIAS, born Beijing, People's Republic of China, October 26, 1962; admitted, 1989, Geneva; 1993, Zurich. *Education:* University of Fribourg (Licence en Droit, 1986); University of Exeter (LL.M., 1994). *Member:* Geneva and Swiss Bar Associations; Licensing Executive's Society, Swiss Arbitration Association. *LANGUAGES:* French, English and German.

LACHENAL BRECHBÜHL COTTIER & ROGUET

3, PLACE DU MOLARD
P.O. BOX 3199
1211 GENEVA 3, SWITZERLAND
Telephone: (022) 310 65 11
Telefax: (022) 310 38 66

Other Geneva, Switzerland Office: 19, Place Longenalle, 1211 Geneva 3.

General Practice with special emphasis on Civil, Commercial and Contract Law, Banking, Mergers and Acquisitions, Taxation, Trusts and Estate Planning, Residence and Work Permits, Swiss Real Estate, Civil and Administrative Litigation, Private International Law, Arbitration.

FIRM PROFILE: *The firm has been established in 1881 and provides a large range of legal services mainly in the areas of corporate, contract and civil law. The firm consists of five partners and has a total staff of 26.*

MEMBERS OF FIRM

JEAN-ADRIEN LACHENAL, born Geneva, Switzerland, 1917; admitted, 1943, Switzerland. *Education:* University of Geneva (Licence en Droit, 1938; Doctorat en Droit, 1941). Retired Professor of the University of Geneva. *Member:* Swiss Federation of Lawyers; Geneva Bar Association; Geneva Business Law Association. *LANGUAGES:* French, English and German.

JACQUES COTTIER, born Geneva, Switzerland, 1929; admitted, 1952, Switzerland. *Education:* University of Geneva (Licence en Droit, 1952; Licence es Sciences Economiques, 1952). *Member:* Swiss Federation of Lawyers; Geneva Bar Association (President 1981-1982); Geneva Business Law Association; Geneva Law Society. *LANGUAGES:* French and English.

CLAUDE BRECHBUHL, born Geneva, Switzerland, 1944; admitted, 1975, Switzerland. *Education:* University of Geneva (Licence en Droit, 1971). *Member:* Swiss Federation of Lawyers; Geneva Bar Association; Geneva Business Law Association. *LANGUAGES:* French, English and German.

BERNARD LACHENAL, born Geneva, Switzerland, 1949; admitted, 1977, Switzerland. *Education:* University of Geneva (Licence en Droit, 1972); University of California at Berkeley (Master of Laws, 1978). *Member:* Swiss Federation of Lawyers; Geneva Bar Association; Geneva Business Law Association; American Tax Institute; Society of Trust and Estate Practitioners S.T.E.P. *LANGUAGES:* French and English.

JEAN-CHARLES ROGUET, born Geneva, Switzerland, 1942; admitted, 1967, Switzerland. *Education:* University of Geneva (Licence en Droit, 1965). *Member:* Swiss Federation of Lawyers; Geneva Bar Association (Member of the Executive Committee); Geneva Business Law Association. *LANGUAGES:* French and English.

ASSOCIATES

MARIE-CLAUDE CHEVALLIER, born Mies, Switzerland, 1927; admitted, 1952, Switzerland. *Education:* University of Geneva (Licence en Droit, 1949). *Member:* Swiss Federation of Lawyers; Geneva Bar Association; Geneva Business Law Association. *LANGUAGES:* French and English.

DONATELLA AMADUCCI, born Torre Pellice, Italy, 1945; admitted, 1978, Switzerland. *Education:* University of Geneva (Licence en Droit, 1969). *Member:* Swiss Federation of Lawyers; Geneva Bar Association;

(This Listing Continued)

Geneva Business Law Association. *LANGUAGES:* French, Italian and English.

GREGORY J. CONNOR, born Vevey, Switzerland, 1965; admitted, 1992, Switzerland. *Education:* University of Lausanne (Licence en Droit, 1989). *Member:* Swiss Federation of Lawyers; Geneva Bar Association. *LANGUAGES:* English and French.

GILLES CRETTOL, born Sierre, Switzerland, 1963; admitted, 1990, Switzerland. *Education:* University of Berne and Geneva (Licence en Droit, 1988). *Member:* Swiss Federation of Lawyers; Geneva Bar Association. *LANGUAGES:* French, German and English.

PHILIPPE COTTIER, born Geneva, Switzerland, 1963; admitted, 1989, Switzerland. *Education:* University of Geneva (Licence en droit, 1987). *Member:* Swiss Federation of Lawyers; Geneva Bar Association. *LANGUAGES:* French, English, Spanish and Portuguese.

LALIVE & PARTNERS

6, RUE DE L'ATHÉNÉE
1205 GENEVA, SWITZERLAND
Telephone: (022) 319 87 00
Telecopier: (022) 319 87 60

General Practice with special emphasis on Business Law, International Contracts, International Arbitration, Commercial Litigation, Banking and Finance, Tax Law, Conflict of Laws, International and Transnational Law, EC Law, Aeronautical Law, Medical Law.

MEMBERS OF FIRM

DR. JEAN-FLAVIEN LALIVE, admitted, 1940, Geneva. *Education:* University of Geneva (LL.M., LL.D.); Graduate Institute of International Studies; Fletcher School of Law and Diplomacy (A.M.); Harvard Law School and Columbia University School of Law (1936-1938). Secretary General, Joint Relief Commission of the International Red Cross, 1941-1945. First Secretary of the International Court of Justice, The Hague, 1947-1953. General Counsel of United Nations Relief and Works Agency, Beirut, Lebanon, 1953-1958. Secretary General of the International Commission of Jurists, Geneva, 1958-1961. Honorary Consul General of Thailand. Board of Geneva Opera, Chairman, 1965-1990; Honorary President, 1990—. Elected Member, Institute of International Law, 1977. *Member:* Geneva Bar; Geneva Law Society; Swiss Arbitration Association; Swiss Society of Jurists; Swiss Society of International Law; Geneva Association of Business Law; ILA (Swiss Branch); International Bar Association; Union Internationale des Avocats; British Institute of International and Comparative Law; American Society of International Law; Southwestern Legal Foundation (Member, Advisory Board). *LANGUAGES:* French, English and German.

PIERRE LALIVE, admitted, 1951, Geneva. *Education:* University of Geneva (Lic. lit., Lic. jur.); Graduate Institute of International Studies; Cambridge University (Ph.D.). Professor of Law, Geneva Law School, 1955-1993 and Graduate, Institute of International Studies, Geneva, 1961-1986. Presently, Professor Emeritus and Formerly Dean of Geneva Law School; Visiting Professor: Columbia University, Parker School; Cambridge University; Brussels University, U.L.B.; Hague Academy of International Law. President, 1989-1991 and Elected Member, Institute of International Law; President, INTELSAT, Group of Legal Experts; President, 1981-1991 and Honorary President, Swiss Arbitration Association; President, ICC Institute of International Business Law and Practice, 1979—. Awarded Balzan Prize, PhD and LLD (honoris causa), Universities of Paris, Lyon and Brussels. *Member:* International Council for Commercial Arbitration, ICCA; AAA (Panel of Arbitrators); London Court of International Arbitration; Geneva Law Society; Swiss Society of Jurists; Swiss Society of International Law; ILA (Swiss Branch); British Institute of International and Comparative Law; International Academy of Comparative Law. *LANGUAGES:* French, English, German and Italian.

MICHAEL E. SCHNEIDER, admitted, 1971, Munich, Germany (Not admitted in Switzerland). *Education:* Universities of Munich, Bonn and Geneva; AIESEC Traineeship Shell Co., Sierra Leone, West Africa (1962); Graduate Institute of International Studies, Geneva (1965-1968). Teaching Assistant, Geneva University Law School, 1965-1967. Service as Referendar in Germany, 1967-1970. Associate and Counsel, Lalive Budin and Partners, 1970-1994. Collaborateur scientifique at the Graduate Institute of International Studies, International Contracts and Related Matters, Geneva (1972-1983). Counsel, UNEFICO, Swiss Bank Corporation Consultants Group, 1978-1987; Director of Studies, Center for Studies and Research in International Law and International Relations at the Hague

(This Listing Continued)

Academy of International Law, 1987 (Transnational Law and State Contracts). General Counsel, European Community-Japan Initiative, 1992—. Member of Editorial Advisory Board and Correspondent for Switzerland, International Construction Law Review, 1983—. *Member:* Swiss Arbitration Association (Executive Board); UNCITRAL Expert Groups (Guide for Industrial Works Contracts, 1983-1985 and Arbitral Practice, 1993—); ICC Commission on International Arbitration (Working Parties on Arbitration and Construction, 1980-1983 and Arbitral Referee Procedure, 1980-1989); WIPO Arbitration and Consultative Commission (1994—); American Bar Association. *LANGUAGES:* German, English and French.

TERESA GIOVANNINI, admitted, 1983, Geneva. *Education:* University of Fribourg Law School (Lic.jur.). Lecturer, International Development Institute; ICC Institute of International Business Law and Practice, Paris; China International Economy, Science-Technology, Law and Expertise Society. Legal Counsel, Department of Public Health, Cantonal Government of Fribourg, 1974-1977; Legal Counsel, Cantonal, University Hospital, Geneva, 1977-1981; Internship with Law Firm Turrettini and L'Huilier, Geneva, 1981-1983; Foreign Counsel with Chiomenti & Partners, Rome, 1983-1985; Associate and Partner, Lalive Budin and Partners, Geneva, 1985-1994. *Member:* Geneva Bar; Swiss Society of Jurists; Swiss Society for International Law; Swiss Arbitration Association; International Chamber of Commerce; Swiss National Committee (Panel of Arbitrators); Institute of International Business Law and Practice (Corresponding Member). *LANGUAGES:* French, Italian, English and German.

NICOLAS PONCET, admitted, 1982, Geneva. *Education:* University of Geneva Law School. Assistant to Vice-Chairman and Managing Director of Banque Privée Edmond de Rothschild S.A., Geneva, 1983-1989; Private Practice, 1989-1994. *Member:* Geneva Bar; Geneva Business Law Association; Association of Aeronautical Law; Swiss Association of Sports Law; Licence as Professional Pilot, 1982. *LANGUAGES:* French, English, Spanish, German and Italian.

PATRICE LE HOUELLEUR, admitted, 1986, Geneva. *Education:* University of Geneva (Lic. jur.). Associate, Lalive Budin & Partners, 1989-1994. *Member:* Geneva Bar; Geneva Law Society; Geneva Association of Business Law. *LANGUAGES:* French, English, German and Italian.

PIERRE-YVES GUNTER, admitted, 1989, Neuchâtel. *Education:* University of Neuchâtel Law School (Lic.jur.); Harvard Law School (LL.M., 1990-1991). Teaching Assistant, Neuchâtel Law School, 1989-1990. Associate, LaliveBudin & Partners, 1991-1993. Foreign Associate, Clifford Chance, London and Paris, 1993-1995. Foreign Correspondent, The Arbitration and Dispute Resolution Journal. *Member:* Geneva and Neuchâtel Bar Associations; Swiss Arbitration Association; Swiss Federation of Lawyers; Swiss Society of Jurists; Swiss Society of International Law; Geneva Law Society; Geneva Association of Business Law; Harvard Law School Association of Europe. *LANGUAGES:* French, English and German.

IAN L. MEAKIN, admitted, 1991, England and Wales (Not admitted in Switzerland). *Education:* King's College, London (B.D., A.K.C.); Gray's Inn (Dipl. Law); Inns of Court School of Law. Counsel, Lalive Budin & Partners, 1992-1994. Editorial Secretary, Bulletin Swiss Arbitration Association. *Member:* Honourable Society of Gray's Inn; Bar of England and Wales; Swiss Arbitration Association. *LANGUAGES:* English and French.

MATTHIAS C. SCHERER, admitted, 1992, Bern. *Education:* University of Bern Law School; University of Lausanne Law School (Master of European Law, 1993). Associate, Lalive Budin & Partners, 1993-1994. Editorial Secretary, Bulletin Swiss Arbitration Association. *Member:* Swiss Arbitration Association; Bernese Jurists' Association. *LANGUAGES:* German, English and French.

LENZ & STAEHELIN

Established in 1991

25, GRAND' RUE

CH-1211 GENEVA 11, SWITZERLAND

Telephone: 022 319 06 19

Telex: 422 476 LSB

Telecopier: 022 319 06 00

Lausanne, Switzerland Office: 2, place St-François, CH-1003. Telephone: 021-320.79.72. Telex: 422.476 LSB. Telecopier: 021-312.97.45.
Zürich, Switzerland Office: 58 Bleicherweg, CH-8027. Telephone: 01-204.12.12. Cable Address: "Staehelinjur" Telex: 815656 LAW CH. Telecopier: 01/204.12.00.

(This Listing Continued)

Swiss and International Taxation, Banking and Finance Law, Capital Market Transactions, Share Issues and Listing, International Commercial Arbitration, Commercial and Contract Law, Company Law, Mergers and Acquisitions, Corporate Finance, Competition Law, Residence and Work Permits, Purchase of Swiss Real Estate, Product Liability, Civil, Criminal and Administrative Litigation, Debt and Bankruptcy Law, International Legal Assistance, Estate Planning, Trusts, Charitable Foundations, Private International Law, Unfair Competition, Copyright, Patent and Trademark Law, Environmental Law, European Law.

FIRM PROFILE: Lenz & Staehelin is the result of the merger on January 1, 1991 of the Geneva law firm Lenz, Schluep, Briner & De Coulon established in 1951 by Raoul Lenz and of the Zurich law firm Staehelin, Hafter, Jagmetti, Lutz & Partners which was founded in 1917 by Conrad Staehelin.

The firm consists of 61 lawyers with 29 partners. It has offices in Zurich, Geneva and Lausanne. Two of the Geneva partners are British solicitors.

MEMBERS OF FIRM

RAOUL LENZ, born Geneva, Switzerland, April 30, 1918; admitted, 1943, Geneva; 1970, Fribourg. *Education:* University of Geneva (Licence en droit, 1941; Licence ès sciences commerciales, 1942; Doctorat en droit, 1951). *LANGUAGES:* French, English, German, Italian and Spanish. *PRACTICE AREAS:* Swiss and International Taxation; Estate Planning; Charitable Foundations; Private International Law.

MARTIN SCHLUEP, born Drugehnen, Germany, June 20, 1929; admitted, 1955, Bern; 1959, Geneva; 1970, Fribourg. *Education:* University of Fribourg (Licence en droit, 1953); University of Michigan at Ann Arbor (Master of Comparative Law, 1957). *LANGUAGES:* German, English, French and Italian. *PRACTICE AREAS:* Mergers and Acquisitions; Corporate Finance; Commercial and Contract Law.

PHILIPPE DE COULON, born Neuchâtel, Switzerland, June 26, 1930; admitted, 1954, Geneva; 1971, Fribourg. *Education:* University of Geneva (Licence en droit, 1952). *LANGUAGES:* French, German and English. *PRACTICE AREAS:* International Commercial Arbitration; Commercial and Contract Law; Unfair Competition; Copyright, Patent and Trademark Law.

ROBERT BRINER, born Zurich, Switzerland, April 18, 1930; admitted, 1959, Zurich; 1961, Geneva; 1971, Fribourg. *Education:* University of Zurich (Doctorat en droit, 1957). *LANGUAGES:* French, German and English. *PRACTICE AREAS:* International Commercial Arbitration; Commercial and Contract Law; Swiss and International Taxation.

JEAN-PAUL AESCHIMANN, born Neuchâtel, Switzerland, August 28, 1933; admitted, 1960, Neuchâtel; 1964, Geneva; 1974, Fribourg. *Education:* University of Neuchâtel (Licence en droit, 1958); Harvard University (Certificate of Graduate Studies, 1963). *LANGUAGES:* French, German and English. *PRACTICE AREAS:* Banking and Finance Law; Share Issues and Listing; Capital Market Transactions; Swiss Taxation.

PIERRE OEDERLIN, born Geneva, Switzerland, September 4, 1927; admitted, 1953, Geneva. *Education:* University of Geneva (Licence en droit, 1951). *LANGUAGES:* French and English. *PRACTICE AREAS:* Civil, Criminal and Administrative Litigation; Debt and Bankruptcy Law; International Legal Assistance.

OLIVIER MACH, born Geneva, Switzerland, December 21, 1939; admitted, 1968, Geneva. *Education:* University of Geneva (Licence en droit, 1963); Graduate Institute of International Studies, Geneva (Doctorat ès sciences politiques, 1973). *LANGUAGES:* French, German and English. *PRACTICE AREAS:* Residence and Work Permits; Purchase of Swiss Real Estate; European Law.

RICHARD PEASE, born Exeter, England, October 18, 1940; admitted, as Solicitor, 1967, England and Wales (Not admitted in Switzerland). *Education:* Cambridge University, England (M.A., 1962; LL.M., 1965). *LANGUAGES:* English and French. *PRACTICE AREAS:* Estate Planning; Trusts.

CAROLINE DELETRA, born Birmingham, England, March 7, 1945; admitted, as Solicitor, 1974, England and Wales (Not admitted in Switzerland). *Education:* University College London, England (LL.B. Hons., 1969). *LANGUAGES:* English and French. *PRACTICE AREAS:* Estate Planning; Trusts.

DOMINIQUE ROCHAT, born Geneva, Switzerland, December 20, 1949; admitted, 1975, Geneva. *Education:* University of Geneva (Licence en droit, 1972); Cambridge University, England (D.C.L.S., 1973). *LAN-*

(This Listing Continued)

LENZ & STAEHELIN, Geneva—Continued

GUAGES: French, German and English. **PRACTICE AREAS:** Banking and Finance Law; Share Issues and Listing; Mergers and Acquisitions.

ANDREAS VON PLANTA, born Basel, Switzerland, July 11, 1955; admitted, 1982, Basel; 1983, Geneva. *Education:* University of Basel (Licence en droit, 1978; Doctorat en droit, 1981); Columbia University, School of Law (LL.M., 1983). **LANGUAGES:** French, German and English. **PRACTICE AREAS:** Mergers and Acquisitions; Capital Market Transactions; Share Issues and Listing; Product Liability.

BENOÎT CHAPPUIS, born Geneva, Switzerland, December 3, 1956; admitted, 1984, Geneva. *Education:* University of Geneva (Licence en droit, 1979; Diplôme d'études supérieures en droit, 1982). **LANGUAGES:** French and English. **PRACTICE AREAS:** Civil, Criminal and Administrative Litigation; Debt and Bankruptcy Law; International Legal Assistance.

HENRI TORRIONE, born Martigny, Switzerland, July 27, 1952; admitted, 1983, Valais; 1985, Geneva. *Education:* University of Fribourg (Licence en philosophie, 1976; Licence en droit, 1980; Doctorat en droit, 1989); Georgetown University Law School (LL.M., 1983); Expert fiscal diplômé, 1988. **LANGUAGES:** French, German and English. **PRACTICE AREAS:** Swiss and International Taxation; Commercial and Contract Law; Mergers and Acquisitions.

GILLES FAVRE, born Neuchâtel, Switzerland, November 30, 1948; admitted, 1975, Neuchâtel; 1976, Geneva; 1981, Lausanne, Vaud. *Education:* University of Neuchâtel (Licence en droit, 1973). (Resident Partner of Lausanne Office). **LANGUAGES:** French and English. **PRACTICE AREAS:** Civil Litigation; Contract Law; Debt and Bankruptcy Law; Private International Law.

SHELBY DU PASQUIER, born Le Havre, France, December 9, 1960; admitted, 1986, Geneva; 1989, New York (USA). *Education:* University of Geneva (Licence ès sciences commerciales et industrielles, 1981; Licence en droit, 1983); Columbia University School of Law, New York City (LL.M., 1988). **LANGUAGES:** French, English and German. **PRACTICE AREAS:** Banking and Finance Law; Share Issues and Listing; Capital Market Transactions; Environmental Law.

ASSOCIATES

JEAN-CLAUDE HALDIMANN, born Neuchâtel, Switzerland, May 26, 1933; admitted, 1958, Neuchâtel; 1962, Bern; 1972, Geneva. *Education:* University of Neuchâtel (Licence en droit, 1956; Licence ès sciences commerciales, 1957). **LANGUAGES:** French and English.

EUGÈNE IBIG, born Zurich, Switzerland, May 29, 1945; admitted, 1981, Geneva. *Education:* University of Geneva (Licence en droit, 1979). **LANGUAGES:** French, German and English.

BERNARD BALLANSAT, born Geneva, Switzerland, September 22, 1948; admitted, 1974, Geneva. *Education:* University of Geneva (Licence en droit, 1971; Diplôme d'études supérieures en droit, 1981). **LANGUAGES:** French, English and German.

JACQUES BUSSET, born Geneva, Switzerland, January 18, 1946; admitted, 1978, Geneva. *Education:* University of Geneva (Licence en droit, 1973). **LANGUAGES:** French, German and English.

ANNE CHRISTINE DÖLLING, born Hamburg, Germany, September 28, 1958; admitted, 1983, Geneva. *Education:* University of Geneva (Licence en droit, 1981). **LANGUAGES:** French, German, English and Finnish.

MARIE-FRANCE BERSET, born Fribourg, Switzerland, October 25, 1952; admitted, 1976, Neuchâtel; 1980, Geneva. *Education:* University of Neuchâtel (Licence en droit, 1974; Doctorat en droit, 1988); University of Pennsylvania (LL.M., 1978). **LANGUAGES:** French, English and German.

MARK BARMES, born Port Moresby, Papua and New Guinea, June 22, 1961; admitted, as Solicitor, 1987, Queensland, Australia; 1992, England and Wales (Not admitted in Switzerland). *Education:* University of Queensland, Australia (LL.B. Hons., 1984; BECON, 1984). **LANGUAGES:** English and French.

CHRISTIAN LENZ, born Baden, Switzerland, September 22, 1958; admitted, 1983, Geneva. *Education:* University of Geneva (Licence en droit, 1982); Boalt Hall School of Law, University of California, Berkeley (LL.M., 1986); University of Zürich (Doctorat en droit, 1992). **LANGUAGES:** French, German and English.

URSULA CASSANI, born Zurich, Switzerland, May 29, 1956; admitted, 1989, Geneva. *Education:* University of Geneva (Licence en droit, 1979;

(This Listing Continued)

Diplôme d'études supérieures en droit, 1983; Doctorat en droit, 1986). **LANGUAGES:** French, English and German.

MANUEL ISLER, born Neuchâtel, Switzerland, August 30, 1963; admitted, 1987, Neuchâtel; 1989, Geneva. *Education:* University of Neuchâtel (Licence en droit, 1986); Vanderbilt Law School, Nashville, TN. **LANGUAGES:** French, English and German.

RABAB YASSEEN, born Baghdad, Iraq, October 10, 1962; admitted, 1989, Geneva. *Education:* University of Geneva (Licence en droit, 1986). **LANGUAGES:** French, English, Arabic and German.

GIORDANO REZZONICO, born Milano, Italy, September 10, 1967; admitted, 1991, Geneva; 1995, New York (U.S.A.). *Education:* University of Geneva (Licence en droit, 1988); Duke University School of Law, Durham, North Carolina (LL.M., 1994). **LANGUAGES:** Italian, French, English and German.

GUY VERMEIL, born Zurich, Switzerland, June 2, 1961; admitted, 1988, Geneva; 1990, New York (USA). *Education:* University of Geneva (Licence en droit, 1984); Duke University School of Law, Durham, North Carolina (LL.M., 1989). **LANGUAGES:** French, English and German.

JEAN-BLAISE ECKERT, born Délémont, Switzerland, September 28, 1963; admitted, 1989, Neuchâtel; 1991, Geneva. *Education:* University of Neuchâtel (Licence en droit, 1987); University of California, Berkeley (M.B.A., 1991). **LANGUAGES:** French, English and German.

FRANÇOIS RAYROUX, born Boston, Massachusetts, U.S.A., April 7, 1961; admitted, 1989, Geneva; 1991, Zurich. *Education:* University of Zurich (Licence en droit, 1986; Doctorat en droit, 1993); University of Chicago Law School (LL.M., 1990). **LANGUAGES:** French, German, English and Italian.

ALEXANDER DE DARANYI, born London, England, March 10, 1966; admitted, 1990, Geneva. *Education:* University of Geneva (Licence en droit, 1987). **LANGUAGES:** French, English, German and Hungarian.

JEAN-CHRISTOPHE PERRIG, born Sion, Switzerland, January 12, 1966; admitted, 1991, New York (U.S.A.); 1994, Geneva. *Education:* University of Lausanne (Licence en droit, 1987; Doctorat en droit, 1990); New York University Law School (M.C.J., 1991). **LANGUAGES:** French, English and German.

PAOLO MICHELE PATOCCHI, born Bern, Switzerland, July 23, 1955; admitted, 1985, Geneva; 1992, Zurich. *Education:* University of Geneva (Licence en droit, 1977; Diplôme d'etudes supérieures en droit, 1980; Doctorat en droit, 1983); Hague Academy of International Law (Diploma, 1982); University of London, King's College (LL.M., 1987). Lecturer in Law, University of Geneva, 1989. **LANGUAGES:** Italian, French, English and German.

GILDA MODOIANU, born Bucharest, Romania, June 19, 1964; admitted, 1989, Geneva; 1994 New York (U.S.A). *Education:* University of Geneva (Licence en droit, 1987; Diplôme d'études supérieures en droit, 1993); New York University Law School (M.C.J., 1994). **LANGUAGES:** French, English and Romanian.

DANIEL EDUARDO TUNIK, born Santiago, Chile, May 7, 1967; admitted, 1993, New York (USA); 1994, Geneva. *Education:* University of Geneve (Licence en droit, 1989);; Graduate Institute of International Studies, Geneva (Diplôma d' études supérieures en droit, 1991); Georgetown University Law Center, Washington, D.C. (LL.M, 1992). **LANGUAGES:** French, Spanish, English and German.

MAGNIN AND DUNAND

Established in 1972

2, RUE CHARLES BONNET
CH-1206 GENEVA, SWITZERLAND
Telephone: (022) 347 62 62
Telex: 427754 MAGAV
Cable Address: "Avvocati Geneve"
Telecopier: (022) 347 67 96

Business Law, Corporation Law, Swiss and International Taxation, Banking, Commerical and Contract, Bankruptcy, Administrative, International Legal Assistance, Litigation and International Arbitration.

(This Listing Continued)

MEMBERS OF FIRM

JEAN-JACQUES MAGNIN, born Geneva, Switzerland, February 24, 1940; admitted, 1963, Geneva. *Education:* Calvin College, Geneva (Maturité, 1959); University of Geneva (Licencié ès sciences politiques and Licencié ès sciences commerciales, 1963); University of Geneva Law School (Licence en droit, 1962; Doctorat en droit, 1971); Boston University School of Law (Special Student in International Taxation, 1967-1968). Author: "The Taxation of Undistributed Income, a New Weapon Against International Tax Evasion?" Georg et Cie, Geneva, 1971. *Member:* Geneva and Swiss Bar Associations; International Bar Association; International Fiscal Association; Swiss Arbitration Association; Swiss Society of Jurists; Geneva Association of Business Law; American Chamber of Commerce in Switzerland. *LANGUAGES:* French, English and German. *PRACTICE AREAS:* General Practice; Corporation Law; Banking; Swiss and International Taxation; Trust and Estate Planning; Litigation; International Arbitration; Commercial Law; Bankruptcy.

BAUDOUIN DUNAND, born St-Germain en Laye, France, December 5, 1954; admitted, 1976, Geneva. *Education:* Calvin College, Geneva (1965-1971); Lycée Jean-Jacques Rousseau, Thonon, France (Baccalauréat, 1972); University of Geneva Law School (Licence en droit, 1975). *Member:* Geneva and Swiss Bar Associations; International Bar Association; International Fiscal Association; Swiss Arbitration Association; Geneva Association of Business Law; Arabo-Swiss Chamber of Commerce. *LANGUAGES:* French, English, Italian and German. *PRACTICE AREAS:* General Practice; Corporation Law; Banking; Swiss and International Taxation; Trust and Estate Planning; Litigation; International Arbitration; Commercial Law; Bankruptcy.

ASSOCIATES

OTTO ROBERT GUTH, born Budapest, Hungary, November 22, 1950; admitted, 1981, Geneva. *Education:* University of Geneva (Licence ès letters); University of Geneva Law School (Licence en droit, 1980). *Member:* Geneva Bar Association; Young Lawyers International Association. *LANGUAGES:* German, French, English, Italian and Hungarian.

MOHAMED MARDAM BEY, born Damascus, Syria, October 19, 1962; admitted, 1985, Geneva; 1990, New York. *Education:* University of Geneva Law School (Licence en droit, 1985); New York University School of Law (M.C.J., 1989). *Member:* New York State and American Bar Associations. *LANGUAGES:* French, English and German.

CHRISTIAN FISCHELE, born Geneva, Switzerland, May 1, 1965; admitted, 1987, Geneva. *Education:* University of Geneva Law School (Licence en droit, 1987). *Member:* Geneva and Swiss Bar Associations. *LANGUAGES:* French, English, German, Spanish and Italian.

URS SEIDEL, born Dearborn, Michigan, March 20, 1969; admitted, 1993, Geneva. *Education:* University of Lausanne School of Law (Licence en droit, 1991). *Member:* Geneva and Swiss Bar Associations. *LANGUAGES:* French, English and German.

DOMINIQUE KAEGI, born Geneva, Switzerland, July 19, 1972; admitted, 1994, Geneva. *Education:* University of Geneva Law School (Master in European Law, 1994; Licence en Droit, 1993). *LANGUAGES:* French, English and German.

ALEXANDRE SENBOGLOU, born Lausaane, Switzerland, April 15, 1970. *Education:* University of Geneva Law School (License en Droit, 1993). *LANGUAGES:* French, English and German.

Languages: French, English, German, Spanish, Italian and Hungarian

MICHAEL C. MALZACHER

70, ROUTE DE FLORISSANT
CH-1211 GENEVA 3, SWITZERLAND
Telephone: (41-22) 789.55.55
FAX: (41-22) 789.55.44

International Banking and Commerce Law, Estate and Trust Law, Cross Border Merger and Acquisition, Travel and Tourism Law, International Real Estate, General Contract Law.

MICHAEL C. MALZACHER, born Geneva, Switzerland; admitted, 1974, Geneva. *Education:* University of Geneva (Licence en droit, 1974). Law Associate Teacher, Geneva Business School, 1970-1972. Delegate for the International Committee of the Red Cross (I.C.R.C.) in Bangladesh, 1972. Financial Analyst at Chase Manhattan Bank, Paris and Geneva, 1972-1973. Associate Lawyer at Moser Law Firm - Specialized in Corporate Law, 1974-1976. Arbitrator and Member, Geneva Industrial Court,

(This Listing Continued)

1975-1987; President of the Court, 1977-1988 for Liberal Professions. *Member:* Geneva Bar Association (ODA); International Association of Young Lawyers (AIJA); International Bar Association (IBA) and Geneva Chamber of Commerce (CGCI). *LANGUAGES:* French, English and Italian.

MAYOR, BALSER, HEYER

Established in the 19th Century
25, BOULEVARD HELVÉTIQUE
1207 GENEVA, SWITZERLAND
Telephone: (022) 786 86 86
Telefax: (022) 786 87 88

General Civil Practice. Commercial, Contract and Corporate Law. Financial, Banking, Fiscal, Family and Estate. International Private Law and Judicial Assistance. Legal advisors to Corporate and Private clients. Litigation and Arbitration.

MEMBERS OF FIRM

MATHIAS MAYOR, born 1932; admitted, 1955, Switzerland. *Education:* University of Geneva (Lic.jur.).

EDOUARD C. BALSER, born 1946; admitted, 1972, Switzerland. *Education:* University of Geneva (Lic.jur.); Columbia University (LL.M., 1976).

ELISABETH HEYER, born 1947; admitted, 1980, Switzerland. *Education:* University of Geneva (Lic.jur.).

BEATRIX LEROY JEANDIN, born 1958; admitted, 1986, Switzerland. *Education:* University of Geneva (Lic.jur.; Lic.sc.pol.).

CEDRIC-LAURENT MICHEL, born 1966; admitted, 1991, Switzerland. *Education:* University of Geneva (Lic.jur.).

All Members of the Firm are Members of the Geneva and Swiss Bar Associations; Swiss Society of Jurists; Swiss Federation of Lawyers; Geneva Association of Business Law; American Chamber of Commerce in Switzerland.

Languages: French, English, German and Italian

MÉGEVAND, GROSJEAN & REVAZ

1, RUE ETIENNE-DUMONT
1211 GENEVA 3, SWITZERLAND
Telephone: (41 22) 312 1122; 312 1161
Telefax: (41 22) 312 1155

Mailing Address: P.O. Box 585, CH-1211 Geneva 3, Switzerland

General Swiss and International Law with emphasis on: Swiss and International Litigation in Banking, Real Property/Construction, Commercial Contract, Commodity and Trading and Corporate Matters, including International Judicial Assistance; International Commercial and Maritime Arbitration; Maritime Law, Ship Finance and Mortgages, Charter Parties, Claims; Swiss and International Taxation, including Commercial Structuring for International Business Development; Trusts, Personal Structuring and International Estate Planning, including Asset Protection; Corporate Acquisitions, Mergers and Management Buyouts; Insurance and Construction Law.

MEMBERS OF FIRM

CHRISTIAN GROSJEAN, born Geneva, Switzerland, 1952; admitted, 1978, Geneva. *Education:* University of Geneva (Licence en droit, 1980); University of California at Berkeley (1982). Author: "Private Insurance in the European Community and the Agreement between the Community and Switzerland," Association Internationale pour l'Etude de l'Economie de l'Assurance, Etudes et Dossiers no. 149-152, Genève, 1990-1991. *Member:* Geneva and Swiss Bar Associations. *PRACTICE AREAS:* Construction Law; Insurance Law; Business Law; International Business Law; Corporate Law.

BRUNO MÉGEVAND, born Geneva, Switzerland, 1957; admitted, 1982, Geneva. *Education:* University of Geneva (Licence en droit, 1980). *Member:* Geneva and Swiss Bar Associations. *PRACTICE AREAS:* Banks and Banking Law; Litigation; Agriculture Law; Real Estate Law.

DAVID A. LAWSON, III, born Annapolis, Maryland, USA, 1943; admitted, 1972, California; 1978, U.S. Supreme Court (Not admitted in Switzerland). *Education:* Rensselaer Polytechnic Institute, Troy, N.Y. (B.S., Nuclear Physics, 1965); Golden Gate University School of Law, San Francisco, Ca. (J.D., 1971); Hague Academy of International Law (Diploma, 1972); Oxford University, England (D. Phil., Law, 1974). Author: "Govern-

(This Listing Continued)

MÉGEVAND, GROSJEAN & REVAZ, Geneva— Continued

mental Interest Analysis and Other Policy-Oriented Choice-of-Law Theories," Oxford, 1974. Physics Instructor, U.S. Navy Nuclear Power Program, Vallejo, California, 1965-1970; Adjunct Lecturer in Conflict of Laws, Golden Gate University Law School, 1974-1976; Founding Editor-in-Chief, Golden Gate Law Review, 1969-1970. *Member:* California Bar Association; American Bar Association; Registered with Geneva Bar Association. *PRACTICE AREAS:* Admiralty and Maritime Law; Arbitration and Mediation; Computers and Software; Commodities; International Law.

JEAN-MARIE REVAZ, born Geneva, Switzerland, 1938; admitted, 1968, Geneva. *Education:* University of Geneva (Licence en droit, 1967). *Member:* Geneva and Swiss Bar Associations. *PRACTICE AREAS:* Insurance Law; Business Law; Arbitration.

COUNSEL

ROGER MERKELBACH, born Geneva, Switzerland, 1925; admitted, 1952, Geneva; 1960, Basel. *Education:* University of Geneva (Licence en droit, 1950). Author: "Private Insurance in the European Community and the Agreement between the Community and Switzerland," Association Internationale pour l'Etude de l'Economie de l'Assurance, Etudes et Dossiers no. 149-152, Genève, 1990-1991. *Member:* Geneva and Swiss Bar Associations. *PRACTICE AREAS:* Insurance Law; European Community Law; Commercial Law; Torts; Negligence Law.

ASSOCIATES

MICHEL ARNOUX, born Geneva, Switzerland, 1957; admitted, 1982, Geneva. *Education:* University of Geneva (Licence en droit, 1979). *PRACTICE AREAS:* Landlord and Tenant Law; Administrative Law; Litigation.

MICHEL HOTTELIER, born Geneva, Switzerland, 1958; admitted, 1990, Geneva. *Education:* University of Geneva (Licence en droit, 1980; Docteur en Droit, 1985). Adjunct Lecturer: University of Geneva, 1990-1992; University of California at Berkeley, 1993-1994. *PRACTICE AREAS:* Administrative Law; Public Law; Human and Civil Rights.

SAMUEL M. LOHMAN, born Portland, Oregon, USA, 1960; admitted, 1985, Oregon (Not admitted in Switzerland). *Education:* Portland State University (B.S., 1982); Oklahoma City University School of Law (J.D., 1984); Salzburg University, University of the Pacific, McGeorge School of Law, Salzburg, Austria (Diploma, 1988). Author: "Switzerland's new Money Laundering Legislation," the International Lawyer, Fall, 1991; "Special Considerations in Transferring Assets," the Asset Protection Forum, 1993 "What Every Practitioner Should Know about Going Offshore," European Study Conference, 1993; "The Trading Trust and Massachusetts Trust," European Study Conference, 1993; "Due Diligence and Administrative Considerations in Reviewing New Business From the U.S. and Elsewhere," European Study Conference, 1993; "Asset Protection Planning; The Use of Trusts, Companies and other Vehicles," ATI in Europe, 1991. *Member:* Oregon Bar Association; American Bar Association; Registered with the Geneva Bar Association; International Bar Association; Society of Trust and Estate Practitioners; The Offshore Institute. *PRACTICE AREAS:* Offshore Trusts and Corporations; International Business Law; International Corporate Law; Protection of Wealth-Trusts and Estates; Tax Planning.

JEAN DONNET, born Sion, Switzerland, 1959; admitted, 1988, Geneva. *Education:* University of Geneva (Licence en droit, 1985). *Member:* Geneva and Swiss Bar Associations. *PRACTICE AREAS:* Corporate Law; Business Law; Contracts; Taxation; Bankruptcy Law.

CLAUDE BRETTON-CHEVALLIER, born Geneva, Switzerland, 1963; admitted, 1989, Geneva. *Education:* University of Geneva (Licence en droit, 1986). *Member:* Geneva and Swiss Bar Associations. *PRACTICE AREAS:* Bank and Banking Law; Contracts; Insurance Law; Construction Law; Torts.

MALIKA SALEM, born Geneva, Switzerland, 1968; admitted, 1993, Geneva. *Education:* University of Geneva (Licence en droit, 1991). *Member:* Geneva and Swiss Bar Associations. *PRACTICE AREAS:* Construction Law; Litigation; Commercial Law; Contracts.

MARC OEDERLIN, born Geneva, Switzerland, 1963; admitted, 1993, Geneva. *Education:* University of Fribourg (Licence en droit, 1991). *Member:* Geneva and Swiss Bar Associations. *PRACTICE AREAS:* Criminal Law; Litigation.

Languages: French, English and German

MENTHA MAYSTRE MORAND & AMSLER

4, RUE DE L'ATHÉNÉE
CH-1211 GENEVA 12, SWITZERLAND
Telephone: 022/ 311 22 23
Telecopier: 022 / 781 12 12

General Practice, Banking and Finance Law, Commercial, Corporate, Domestic and International Taxation, Bankruptcy Law, Intellectual Property and Unfair Competition, International and Domestic Arbitration, Labour and Social Security Regulations.

MEMBERS OF FIRM

JACQUES MENTHA, born Geneva, Switzerland, December 19, 1921; admitted, 1948, Geneva. *Education:* University of Geneva Law School (Licence en droit, 1945). Former President, Geneva Bar Association. *Member:* Geneva and Swiss Bar Association. *LANGUAGES:* French and German. *PRACTICE AREAS:* Civil Law; Commercial Law.

MICHEL MAYSTRE, born Geneva, Switzerland, April 1, 1944; admitted, 1970, Geneva. *Education:* University of Geneva Law School (Licence en droit, 1967). *Member:* Geneva and Swiss Bar Association. *LANGUAGES:* French and English. *PRACTICE AREAS:* Civil Law; Insurance Law; Lease Law; Administrative Law.

PIERRE ANDRE MORAND, born Bulle, Switzerland, August 21, 1943; admitted, 1971, Geneva. *Education:* University of Fribourg Law and Economics School (Licence es sciences économiques, 1964; Licence en droit, 1969). Author: "La Clause Arbitrale dans les Contrats Internationaux," Marchés Étrangers No.1, 1984; "Les lois cantonales relatives aux brevets" in "Kernprobleme des Patentrechts," 1988; "Protection of Trade and Technical Secrets in Switzerland," Euromoney Publication, Dec. 1991; "Le taux de l'intérêt moratoire applicable aux créances libellées en monnaie étrangère payables en Suisse," RSDA 4/92. Deputy Judge at the Court of Appeal of Geneva. *Member:* Geneva and Swiss Bar Association; International Bar Association; Geneva Association of Business Law; Swiss Arbitration Association; Swiss National Committee of the ICC; Swiss Arbitrator of the ICC; International Association for the Intellectual Property. *LANGUAGES:* French, English and German. *PRACTICE AREAS:* Commercial Banking Law; Arbitration Law; Intellectual Property; Unfair Competition Law.

PHILIPPE AMSLER, born Lausanne, Switzerland, November 28, 1949; admitted, 1980, Geneva. *Education:* University of Lausanne Law School (Licence en droit, 1973; Doctorat, 1979). Author: "Donation à cause de mort et désignation du bénéficiaire d'une assurance de personnes," Stæmpfli 1979. *Member:* Geneva and Swiss Bar Association; International Bar Association; Geneva Association of Business Law; Swiss Association of Environmental Law. *LANGUAGES:* French, English and German. *PRACTICE AREAS:* Banking and Finance Law; Mutual Funds Law; Corporate Law; Inheritance Law; Environment Law.

ASSOCIATES

MICHEL BERTSCHY, born London, England, July 7, 1960; admitted, 1987, Geneva. *Education:* University of Geneva Law School (Licence en droit, 1986). Part-time Secretary of the Labour Court of Geneva, 1982-1990. *Member:* Geneva and Swiss Bar Association. *LANGUAGES:* French, English, German and Spanish. *PRACTICE AREAS:* Labour Law; Social Security Law.

NATHALIE HUBERT, born Neuchâtel, Switzerland, August 19, 1964; admitted, 1994, Geneva. *Education:* University of Lausanne Law School (Licence en droit, 1986), Certificate in Management (HEC Lausanne, 1987). Audit Assistant with Arthur Anderson, Zurich, 1987-1989. *Member:* Geneva and Swiss Bar Association. *LANGUAGES:* French, English and German. *PRACTICE AREAS:* Civil Law; Commercial and Corporate Law; Litigation.

MONROE PARTNERS INTERNATIONAL, P.C.

72 BLVD. SAINT-GEORGES
GENEVA 1205, SWITZERLAND
Telephone: 41 (22) 329-9420
Fax: 41 (22) 329-9404

New York, New York Office: The Bertelsmann Building, 1540 Broadway. Telephone: 212-782-1040. Fax: 212-782-1043.

(This Listing Continued)

General International and Domestic Corporate, Securities, Litigation, Trademark, Trusts and Estates, Software, Real Estate and Health Care Law Practices.

SANDRA FELGOISE-SINGER, born Philadelphia, Pennsylvania, August 22, 1950; admitted, 1976, New York; 1978, Pennsylvania and U.S. District Court, District of Pennsylvania. *Education:* University of Pennsylvania (B.A., cum laude, 1972); New York University (J.D., 1975). Author: "U.S. Issues for Nonresident Aliens," International Bar Association, 1992. Speaker: ABA-IBA Seminar, "International Wealth Transfers," Use of Offshore Trusts by Residents or Nationals of Common Law Jurisdictions, February 1995. Lecturer, (in Corporate Law), The American Woman's Economic Development Corporation. Member, National Association for the Advancement of Psychoanalysis. Director, American-Israel Chamber of Commerce. *Member:* The Association of the Bar of the City of New York; New York State (International Law Section), American and International Bar Associations; The Financial Woman's Association (Board of Trustees, 1988—).

PAUL J. GIACOMO, JR., born Greenwich, Connecticut, October 1, 1953; admitted, 1979, New York and U.S. District Court, Southern and Eastern Districts of New York; 1984, U.S. Court of Appeals, Second Circuit; 1989, U.S. Court of Appeals, Sixth Circuit. *Education:* College of William and Mary (B.A., 1975); University of Notre Dame (J.D., 1978). Phi Alpha Delta (Justice, 1977-1978). Law Clerk to Hon. Charles L. Brieant, U.S. District Court, Southern District of New York, 1978-1979. *Member:* The Association of the Bar of the City of New York (Member, Committee on Ethical Issues in Complex Corporate and Commercial Litigation); New York State (Member, Commercial and Federal Litigation Section) and American Bar Associations; Federal Bar Council.

KAREN A. MONROE, born Mineola, New York, November 22, 1955; admitted, 1984, New York. *Education:* Institute des Etudes Americaines, Paris, France; State University of New York at Binghamton (B.A., 1979); Washington College of Law of The American University (J.D., 1983). *Author:* "An Overview of the U.S. Federal Securities Laws as they Relate to Securities Offerings, Continuous Reporting Obligations, and American Depositary Receipt Programs," International Business Transactions - Standard Forms and Documents, Kluwer Law and Taxation Publishers, 1995. Lecturer, Negotiation and Business Law, American Women's Economic Development Corp. *Member:* Swiss-American Chamber of Commerce; Austrian-U.S. Chamber of Commerce; Association of the Bar of the City of New York; American (Member, Section on International and Business Law) and International Bar Associations; International Trademark Association. *LANGUAGES:* French and German.

ALFRED F. ROHLS, born Staten Island, New York, September 17, 1936; admitted, 1965, New York; 1976, U.S. District Court, Southern and Eastern Districts of New York. *Education:* Wagner College (B.A., 1957); Fordham University (J.D., 1965). Contributing Author: International Intellectual Property Law Yearbook; International Legal Studies, Salzburg, Austria (1995); American Corporate Counsel Association. Chairman, Greater New York Chapter, Intellectual Property Committee, 1991-1993. *Member:* International Trademark Association. [US Army, 1958-1960]

MINDY B. MERDINGER, born Mount Vernon, N.Y., January 16, 1966; admitted, 1993, New York. *Education:* Mount Holyoke College (A.B., 1988); University of Detroit London Law Programme (1991); Benjamin N. Cardozo School of Law (J.D., 1992). Phi Alpha Delta. Member: Mount Holyoke Club of Bergen County, Alumnae Admissions Representative, 1993-1995; Mount Holyoke College Development Office Class Agent, 1988—. *Member:* Association of the Bar of the City of New York; New York State and American (Member, Sections on Real Estate and International Law) Bar Associations; New York County Bar Association; American Society of International Law. *LANGUAGES:* Spanish.

ETUDE DE MAITRES MUDRY & IGLEHART

Established in 1968

4, RUE CHARLES BONNET, CASE 269
1211 GENEVA 12, SWITZERLAND
Telephone: 41+22+ 347 40.66
Telex: 429 356 LMM CH
Facsimile: 41+22+ 346.04.11

London, England Office: 20 Old Bailey, 5th Floor, EC4M 7JP. Telephone: (0171) 248-8006. Telefax: (0171) 248-3001.

(This Listing Continued)

Contracts, Corporate Law (Swiss and International), Swiss Taxation (Individuals and Companies), U.S. Taxation (Individuals), Treaty Taxation, Banking Law, Administrative Law and Procedure, Labor Law, International Commercial Arbitration, International Business Transactions, Estate Law, Real Property Law, Trusts.

MEMBERS OF FIRM

LOUIS MARC MUDRY, born 1933; admitted, 1962, Geneva. *Education:* Columbia University (Master of Comparative Law, 1960). *LANGUAGES:* French and English.

JOHN HAWES IGLEHART, born Lancaster, Pennsylvania, U.S.A., 1947; admitted, 1981, Geneva. *Education:* University of Geneva (Licence en droit, 1976). Research Assistant, 1976-1977. *Member:* Geneva Bar; American Bar Association; Federal Bar Association; Swiss Society of Jurists; Geneva Association of Business Law. *LANGUAGES:* French, English and German.

ASSISTANT

JOHN D. HILTON, born 1971. *Education:* University of Geneva (Licence en Droit, 1993). *LANGUAGES:* French and English.

Languages: French, English and German

NIKLAUS & BRUTTIN

8, RUE DU MONT-DE-SION
1206 GENEVA, SWITZERLAND
Telephone: (41 22) 347 16 52
Facsimile: (41 22) 346 68 38

General Commercial, Civil and Criminal Practice, Corporate, Real Estate, Banking, Private International Law, Arbitration, Insurance Liability, Work Permits, Bankruptcy, Litigation.

MEMBERS OF FIRM

ROLAND NIKLAUS, born Geneva, Switzerland, January 5, 1928; admitted, 1959, Geneva. *Education:* University of Geneva Law School (Law Degree, 1954). Honorary Consul General of Iceland. *Member:* Geneva Bar Association; Swiss Federation of Lawyers.

REYNALD P. BRUTTIN, born Geneva, Switzerland, December 4, 1957; admitted, 1983, Geneva. *Education:* University of Geneva Law School (Law Degree, 1981). Attorney, Sutherland Asbill & Brennan, Washington D.C., 1984-1985. *Member:* Geneva Bar Association; Swiss Federation of Lawyers; Geneva Business Law Association.

ASSOCIATES

DANIELE FALTER, born Geneva, Switzerland, July 31, 1966; admitted, 1991, Geneva. *Education:* University of Geneva Law School (Law Degree, 1988). *Member:* Geneva Bar Association; Swiss Federation of Lawyers.

Languages: French, German and English

NOTTER BLATTER DAVIDOFF & PARTNER

16, AVENUE JULES CROSNIER
1205 GENEVA, SWITZERLAND
Telephone: (41-22) 346 24 74
Facsimile: (41-22) 347 09 21

Zurich, Switzerland Office: Zimmergasse 16, 8008 Zurich. Telephone: (41-1) 261 15 55. Facsimile: (41-1) 262 35 42.

Bern, Switzerland Office: Schwanengasse 9, 3001 Bern. Telephone: (41-31) 312 53 12. Facsimile: (41-31) 311 07 49.

Brussels, Belgium Office: Avenue de Tevueren 12, 1040 Brussels.

General Corporate and Commercial Practice, Finance and Banking, International Contracts, International Arbitration, Taxation, Real Estate, Intellectual and Industrial Property and Copyright, Administrative Matters, Inheritance and Estate Planning, Civil Litigation.

FIRM PROFILE: The firm is the result of a merger of three firms in Bern, Geneva and Zurich based on a new service-oriented concept offering an integrated full legal service for the whole of Switzerland. Notary public services are provided by the Bern office. The Zurich office includes professional auditing and controlling services. The firm maintains a well developed network of correspondence law firms.

(This Listing Continued)

NOTTER BLATTER DAVIDOFF & PARTNER,
Geneva—Continued

MEMBERS OF FIRM

JEAN-JACQUES MARTIN, born 1950; admitted, 1981, Canton of Geneva. *Education:* University of Geneva Law School. *Member:* Geneva and Swiss Bar Association.

ALEXANDRE DAVIDOFF, born 1950; admitted, 1976, Canton of Geneva. *Education:* University of Geneva Law School. *Member:* Geneva and Swiss Bar Association. *PRACTICE AREAS:* Banking Law; Business Law; Corporate Law; Offshore Trusts and Corporations; Leverage Buy Outs; Distribution Agreements.

VERONIQUE ENGEL, born 1950; admitted, 1976, Canton of Geneva. *Education:* University of Geneva Law School. Deputy Judge in the Geneva Court of Appeal. *Member:* Geneva and Swiss Bar Association; Swiss Arbitration Association; Alumna of the Salzburg Seminar in American Studies. *PRACTICE AREAS:* International Arbitration; Negotiable Instruments; Environmental Law; Art Law.

COSTIN VAN BERCHEM, born 1961; admitted, 1990, Canton of Geneva. *Education:* University of Basel Law School. *Member:* Geneva and Swiss Bar Association. *PRACTICE AREAS:* Business Law; Contracts; Family Business; Historic Houses; Bankruptcy.

ASSOCIATES

PASCAL DUCLOS, born 1967; admitted, 1991, Canton of Geneva. *Education:* University of Geneva Law School. *Member:* Geneva and Swiss Bar Association. *PRACTICE AREAS:* Civil Law; Taxation.

OF COUNSEL

JEAN-FRANÇOIS MARTIN, born 1911; admitted, 1936, Canton of Geneva. *Education:* University of Geneva Law School. *Member:* Geneva and Swiss Bar Association.

Languages: French, English, German, Italian and Spanish

OBERSON THIÉBAUD & ASSOCIÉS

Established in 1961

20, RUE DE CANDOLLE
1205 GENEVA, SWITZERLAND
Telephone: (022) 320.18.88
Fax: (022) 320.16.70

Fribourg, Switzerland Office: 82, Rue de Lausanne, 1701. Telephone:
(037) 22 32 15. Fax: (037) 23 13 41.

Swiss and International Tax Laws, Corporate and Finance Laws, Administrative Law.

FIRM PROFILE: Oberson, Thiébaud and Partners represent the merger of the practice Oberson and Partners, Geneva, which was founded in 1961 with the law office Thiébaud and Von der Weid, Fribourg, organized in 1981. The joint law firms main activities are tax and business laws. The practice scope covers Swiss and International tax planning, tax litigation, corporate and finance law. In addition, the firm has a close affiliation with the United States firm Jones Day Reavis and Pogue.

MEMBERS OF FIRM

RAOUL OBERSON, born Fribourg, May 10, 1930; admitted, 1957, Geneva. *Education:* University of Fribourg (lic.jur., 1953; Dr.jur., 1955). Professor in Tax Law at the University of Geneva since 1967. *Member:* Geneva Bar Association; Swiss Bar Association; Swiss Fiscal Experts Association; International Fiscal Association; International Law Association. *LANGUAGES:* French, English, German and Italian. *PRACTICE AREAS:* Swiss and International Fiscal Laws; Tax Litigation; Planning; Mergers and Restructuring.

XAVIER OBERSON, born Geneva, July 23, 1961; admitted, 1987, Geneva. *Education:* University of Geneva (Lic.jur., 1984; Dr.jur., 1991); Harvard Law School (ITP/LLM, 1992). Lecturer in Administrative and Tax Laws at the University of Geneva. *Member:* Geneva Bar Association; Swiss Bar Association; International Bar Association; International Fiscal Association. *LANGUAGES:* French, English, German and Spanish. *PRACTICE AREAS:* Swiss and International Fiscal Laws; Administrative; Banking and Finance Laws.

(This Listing Continued)

ASSOCIATES

DOMINIQUE GAY, born Geneva, January 6, 1960; admitted, 1985, Geneva. *Education:* University of Geneva (Lic.jur., 1983). Civil Servant, Geneva Tax Administration, 1985-1990. *LANGUAGES:* French and English. *PRACTICE AREAS:* Swiss and International Fiscal Laws; Tax Litigation.

ALFRED GIROD, born July 16, 1956. Swiss Certified Tax Expert, 1990. *Education:* Geneva University (Commercial and Industrial Sciences License, 1990); ATAG Ernst & Young, Geneva (1986-1993); Moore Stephens, Geneva/Tax Department (1991-1993). *Member:* Swiss Tax Expert Association. *LANGUAGES:* French, English and Italian. *PRACTICE AREAS:* Taxation of Individuals and Companies; Mergers and Restructuration.

PIERRE DAYER, born Geneva, June 26, 1965; admitted, 1992, Geneva. *Education:* University of Geneva (Lic. jur., 1990); Exeter University, England (IBLS/LLM, 1994). *Member:* Geneva Bar Association; Swiss Bar Association. *LANGUAGES:* French and English. *PRACTICE AREAS:* International Business; European Law.

COUNSEL

CHRISTINE DOLLFUS, born France, June 10, 1949; admitted, 1974, Paris (Not admitted in Switzerland). *Education:* University of Paris (Master in Law, 1975); INSEAD (M.B.A., 1976). *Member:* International Fiscal Association; International Business Lawyers Association. *LANGUAGES:* French, English, German and Italian.

SYLVIE BUHAGIAR, born France, July 20, 1960; admitted, 1990, Geneva. *Education:* University of Geneva Law School (Lic.iur., 1986); Columbia University School of Law, New York (LL.M., 1988). *LANGUAGES:* French, English, Russian and Italian. *PRACTICE AREAS:* Finance; Corporate Law.

OLTRAMARE HOCHSTAETTER EARDLEY REISER & ASSOCIES

Established in 1981

16 RUE DE CANDOLLE
1205 GENEVA, SWITZERLAND
Telephone: 22/320 42 42; 22/320 47 20
Cable Address: Candolex
Facsimile: 22/320 41 09

Commercial, Corporate, Banking and Tax Law. Civil and Commercial Litigation, Public and Administrative Law, Arbitration, Private International Law and Commercial Criminal Law.

MEMBERS OF FIRM

GABRIEL C. OLTRAMARE, born Geneva, Switzerland, September 1, 1925; admitted, 1959, Geneva. *Education:* College of Glarisegg, Thurgau; University of Geneva (Law Degree, 1949); Harvard Business School (1951); George Washington University (Master of Comparative Law, 1954). *Member:* Geneva and International Bar Association; Societe Suisse des Juristes; Societe Genevoise de Droit et de Legislation. *LANGUAGES:* French, English and German.

JACQUES A. HOCHSTAETTER, born Geneva, Switzerland, July 19, 1928; admitted, 1952, Geneva. *Education:* College Calvin (1947); University of Geneva (Law Degree, 1950). Author: *Elementary Commercial Law Guide,* 1966. Auxiliary Judge, 1971-1991. Member, Court of Arbitration for Sport, 1985—. *Member:* Geneva Bar Association; Young Lawyers's International Association (Former President); International Association of Lawyers. *LANGUAGES:* French.

JOHN F. EARDLEY, born Brentwood, England, August 4, 1949; admitted, 1976, Geneva. *Education:* College Calvin; University of Geneva (Law Degree, 1974). Former Auxiliary Judge at Geneva High Court, 1984-1992. *Member:* Geneva and International Bar Associations. *LANGUAGES:* French, English, and Spanish.

CHRISTIAN M. REISER, born Geneva, Switzerland, July 2, 1950; admitted, 1976, Geneva. *Education:* Institut Florimont; Swiss Federal Baccalaureat (1970); University of Geneva (Law Degree, 1974); Harvard Law School (Program of Instruction for Lawyers, 1981). *Member:* Geneva Bar Association; Competition Law Swiss Association. *LANGUAGES:* French and English.

MARCO J. BRÜSCHWEILER, born Geneva, Switzerland, November 26, 1953; admitted, 1981, Geneva. *Education:* College Calvin; University of

(This Listing Continued)

Geneva (Law Degree, 1979). *Member:* Geneva Bar Association. *LANGUAGES:* French and English.

ANNE REISER, born Strasbourg, France, November 13, 1958; admitted, 1984, Geneva. *Education:* University of Geneva (Law Degree, 1982). *Member:* Geneva and International Bar Associations. *LANGUAGES:* French, English and German.

ASSOCIATES

EMMANUÈLE M. ARGAND-REY, born Montana, Switzerland, September 14, 1959; admitted, 1986, Geneva. *Education:* University of Fribourg (Law Degree, 1982). *Member:* Geneva Bar Association. *LANGUAGES:* French, English, German and Italian.

PHILIPPE MEIER, born Bienne, Switzerland, September 2, 1966; admitted, 1990, Neuchâtel; 1993, Geneva. *Education:* College of Bienne, Bern; University of Neuchâtel (Law Degree, 1988); University of Fribourg (Doctorate in Law, 1994). Lecturer, Family Law, University of Neuchatel. *Member:* Geneva Bar Association; Neuchâtel Bar Association; Sociét é de Droit et de Législation. *LANGUAGES:* French, English and German.

MICHEL A. BOSSHARD, born Zurich, April 4, 1961; admitted, 1993, Geneva and Zurich. *Education:* Ecole Francaise Zurich (French Baccalaureat); University of Geneva (Law Degree, 1991). *Member:* Geneva Bar Association.

Languages: French, English, German, Italian, Spanish and Portugese.

PATRY, JUNET, SIMON ET LE FORT

GENEVA, SWITZERLAND

(See Pestalozzi Gmuer & Patry)

PERRÉARD, DE BOCCARD, KOHLER, ADOR & PARTNERS

Established in 1912

44, AVENUE KRIEG
1208 GENEVA, SWITZERLAND
Telephone: (4122) 839 11 11
Telecopier: (4122) 839 11 00

Mailing Address: P.O. Box 45, 1211 Geneva 17, Switzerland

International Legal Practice, Banking, Insurance, Finance & Securities, Mergers & Acquisitions, Contract Law, Intellectual Property Right, Entertainment & Performers, Labor law, Financial Services, Tax Law, Tax Planning, Family Law, Wills Trust & Estate, Administrative Law, Aviation Law, Construction and Leases. Immigration Law, Arbitration, Litigation, Attachment, Bankruptcy Law, Insolvency, White Collar Litigation.

MEMBERS OF FIRM

FRANCOIS PERRÉARD (Deceased).

GEORGES-F. PERRÉARD, born 1923; admitted, 1946, Geneva and Switzerland. *Education:* University of Geneva, Law School (Licence en droit, 1946). Alternate Judge to the Court of Justice of the State of Geneva, 1980-1989. *Member:* Geneva, Swiss and International Bar Associations.

ANDRÉ TOMBET, born Geneva, Switzerland, March 2, 1927; admitted, 1952, Geneva and Switzerland. *Education:* University of Geneva (Licence en droit, 1950); School of Laws of London University College and Yale University Law School (LL.M., 1954). Associate with White & Case, New York, 1954-1956. *Member:* Interlex Group; Geneva Bar Association (Member of Council); Swiss Federation of Attorneys at Law.

F. PHILIPPE DE BOCCARD, born 1949; admitted, 1972, Geneva and Switzerland. *Education:* University of Zurich; University of Geneva, Law School (Licence en droit, 1972). Alternate Judge to the Administrative Court of the State of Geneva, 1983—. Vice-Consul of Panama, 1979-1982. *Member:* Geneva and Swiss Bar Associations.

THIERRY F. ADOR, born 1954; admitted, 1981, Geneva and Switzerland; 1986, New York USA. *Education:* University of Zurich and Geneva, Business School (Licence ès sciences economiques et Industrielles mention gestion d'entreprise, finance, 1977); Law School (Licence en droit, 1980); University of Columbia, Law School (LL.M., 1985). *Member:* American

(This Listing Continued)

Swiss Chamber of Commerce; Geneva, Swiss, New York and American Bar Associations; Geneva Association of Business Law; International Association of Lawyers; Young Lawyer's International Association; IBA; President of International Commercial and Industrial Arbitration Association (ARICI).

ANTOINE P. KOHLER, born 1956; admitted, 1980, Geneva and Switzerland. *Education:* University of Geneva, Law School (Licence en droit, 1978); Graduate Institute of International Studies. *Member:* Geneva and Swiss Bar Associations; Swiss Federation of Lawyers; Swiss Association for Arbitration.

ANNE SONNEX, born 1962; admitted, 1984, Geneva and Switzerland. *Education:* University of Geneva, Law School (Licence en droit, 1984). *Member:* Geneva and Swiss Bar Associations; Swiss Society of Jurists; Swiss Federation of Lawyers.

ASSOCIATES

Tal Schibler   *Philippe Pulfer*
Yasmine Dubois-Ferriere   *Patrick Richard*
Guido Caratsch   *Sarah Currat*
Steven Street   *Philippe Goetz*
              Philippe Ehrenstrom

Languages: French, English, German, Spanish and Italian.

PESTALOZZI GMUER & PATRY

Established in 1911

15, BD DES PHILOSOPHES
CH-1205 GENEVA, SWITZERLAND
Telephone: 0041 22/320 78 33
Telex: 427079 PJS CH
Telefax: 0041 22/320 43 41

REVISERS OF THE SWITZERLAND LAW DIGEST FOR THIS DIRECTORY.

Zürich, Switzerland Office: Loewenstrasse 1, 8001. Telephone: 411/217 91 11. Telefax: 0041 1/217 92 17. Telex: 812754. Cable Address: "Henggelerjur"

Brussels, Belgium Office: 221, Avenue Louise, 1050. Telephone: 322/646 60 10. Telecopier: 322/646 75 34.

International Commercial, Corporate, Tax and Arbitration Practice, European Law, Industrial Property and Copyright, Immigration and Administrative Matters, Banking and Financial Law, Estate Planning, Civil Litigation.

MEMBERS OF FIRM

JEAN PATRY, born Geneva, 1939; admitted, 1968, Geneva. *Education:* University of Geneva (Licence en droit, 1964). *LANGUAGES:* French, English, German and Spanish. *PRACTICE AREAS:* Contracts; Corporations; Banking; Finance; International Arbitration.

BERNARD JUNET, born Geneva, 1941; admitted, 1968, Geneva. *Education:* University of Geneva (Licence en droit, 1965). *LANGUAGES:* French, English and German. *PRACTICE AREAS:* Contracts; Corporations; Industrial Property and Copyright; Estate Planning; Litigation.

ROBERT SIMON, born Lausanne, 1945; admitted, 1974, Geneva. *Education:* University of Fribourg (Licence en droit, 1971). *LANGUAGES:* French, English and Italian. *PRACTICE AREAS:* Contracts; Corporations; Banking; Finance; Bankruptcy.

ALAIN LE FORT, born Bern, 1953; admitted, 1977, Geneva. *Education:* University of Geneva (Licence en droit, 1975). *LANGUAGES:* French and English. *PRACTICE AREAS:* Contracts; Corporations; Banking; Immigration; Merger and Acquisition.

GUY-PHILIPPE RUBELI, born Geneva, 1956; admitted, 1982, Geneva. *Education:* University of Geneva (Licence en droit, 1978). *LANGUAGES:* French and English. *PRACTICE AREAS:* Contracts; Corporations; Banking; Taxes; Litigation; Bankruptcy.

ASSOCIATES

FRANCOIS DUGAST, born Geneva, 1962; admitted, 1988, Geneva. *Education:* University of Lausanne (Licence en droit, 1986). *LANGUAGES:* French, German and English.

DENIS GOBET, born Lausanne, 1965; admitted, 1990, Geneva. *Education:* University of Lausanne (Licence en droit, 1988). *LANGUAGES:* French and English.

(This Listing Continued)

PESTALOZZI GMUER & PATRY, Geneva—Continued

CHRISTIAN SCHILLY, born Geneva, 1965; admitted, 1990, Geneva. *Education:* University of Geneva (Licence en droit, 1988). *LANGUAGES:* French, German and English.

CORNEL FUERER, born Basilea, 1966; admitted, 1990, Geneva; 1993, New York. *Education:* University of Geneva (Licence en droit, 1988); New York University, Institute of Comparative Law (M.C.J., 1993). *LANGUAGES:* French, English, German and Spanish.

Languages: French, English, German, Spanish and Italian

REVISERS OF THE SWITZERLAND LAW DIGEST FOR THIS DIRECTORY.

DE PFYFFER, ARGAND, TROLLER & PARTNERS

Established in 1968

6, RUE BELLOT

1206 GENEVA, SWITZERLAND

Telephone: 022 346 33 30

Telex: 429 782 hapf ch

Telefax: 022 346 40 53

Swiss Correspondent Firms:

Troller, Hitz & Troller, Schweizerhofquai 2, CH-6004 Lucerne, Switzerland. Telephone: 041 51 40 17. Fax: 041 51 65 71.

Carrard, Paschoud, Heim & Associes, 6 rue de la Grotte, CH-1003 Lausanne, Switzerland. Telephone: 021 20 41 01. Fax: 021 20 44 90.

FIRM PROFILE: The firm was established in 1968 and is since well known in the swiss and international banking and financial community. The client base is both national and international, and the firm offers a wide general practice as well as its partners various areas of specialization, which are as diverse as Banking Law, regular litigation, commercial, arbitration or industrial property. Business and Banking Law, Corporate and Mergers and Acquisitions are a particular tradition of the firm, as has now become Sports Law.

PARTNERS

ANDRÉ DE PFYFFER, born Lucerne, November 3, 1928; admitted, 1952, Geneva. *Education:* Fribourg (baccalauréat 1946), Berne, Geneva (licence en droit 1950). *LANGUAGES:* French, English, German and Italian. *PRACTICE AREAS:* Commercial Law; Company Law; Banking Law; Trusts and Estates.

KAMEN TROLLER, born Lucerne, March 1, 1935; admitted, 1961, Lucerne; 1973, Geneva; 1977, Berne. *Education:* Université de Fribourg (licence en droit, 1958; doctor jurisutriusque , 1962). *LANGUAGES:* French, English and German. *PRACTICE AREAS:* Industrial Property; Franchising; International Arbitration; Arab Commercial Law; Swiss and International Taxation; Konzern Law.

JEAN-JACQUES FIVAZ, born Geneva, September 23, 1942; admitted, 1966, Geneva. *Education:* Collège de Genèva (maturité, 1962); Université de Genèva (licence en droit, 1966). *LANGUAGES:* French, English and German. *PRACTICE AREAS:* Civil and Commercial Law; Company Law; Real Estate Law; Construction Law; Real Estate Taxation; Contract Law; Bankruptcy Law.

LUC ARGAND, born Geneva, January 7, 1948; admitted, 1974, Geneva. *Education:* High School Geneva (maturité in 1969); University of Geneva (lic. jur. 1972), Masters Degree of Business Administration (INSEAD) Paris 1976. *LANGUAGES:* French, English, German and Italian. *PRACTICE AREAS:* Commercial Law; Banking Law; Trust and Estates; International Taxation; Immigration Law; Sports Law.

CHRISTA BALSER, born Joaobello, Mozambique, September 2, 1948; admitted, 1972, Geneva. *Education:* University Geneva Law School (lic. jur. 1972); Interpreter's School of the University of Geneva (dipl. parliamentary interpreter 1971). *LANGUAGES:* French, English and German. *PRACTICE AREAS:* Commercial Law; Estates; Immigration Law; Civil Litigation; Divorce and Family Matters.

BLAISE GROSJEAN, born Neuchâtel, March 9, 1950; admitted, 1977 Neuchâtel; 1979, Geneva. *Education:* Neuchâtel and Sion High Schools (marutiré 1970), University of Newchâtel Law School (lic. jur. 1974). *LANGUAGES:* French and English. *PRACTICE AREAS:* Commercial Law;

(This Listing Continued)

Industrial Property; Immigration Law; Civil Litigation; Contract Law; Bankruptcy Law.

JEAN-CÉDRIC MICHEL, born Geneva, April 19, 1963; admitted, 1987, Geneva; 1989, Vaud. *Education:* Collège Vaudois, High School Geneva (maturité, 1980); University of Geneva Law School (lic. jur., 1985). *LANGUAGES:* French and English. *PRACTICE AREAS:* Litigation; Sports Law; Arbitration; Bankruptcy Law; Criminal Law; International Judicial Assistance; Civil and Commercial Law; Corporate.

ALEXANDRE MONTAVON, born Geneva, May 2, 1959. *Education:* High School Geneva (Maturité1979); University of Geneva Law School (lic. jur. 1983). *LANGUAGES:* French, English and Italian. *PRACTICE AREAS:* Litigation; Arbitration; Civil and Commercial Law; Bankruptcy Law; Contract Law; Immigration Law; Labour Law.

ASSOCIATES

NOVIN TABATABAY, born Stockholm, October 20, 1959; admitted, 1985, Geneva. *Education:* High School Geneva (Maturité1979); University of Geneva (lic. jur. 19 82). *LANGUAGES:* French, English and Swedish. *PRACTICE AREAS:* Industrial Property; Litigation; Civil and Commercial Law; Contract Law.

FREDERIOUE FLOURNOY, born Geneva, October 19, 1967; admitted, 1991, Geneva. *Education:* International School of Geneva, High School Geneva (Maturité1985); University of Geneva Law School (Lic.iur. 1988); London School of Economics (LL.M. 1989). *LANGUAGES:* French and English. *PRACTICE AREAS:* Civil and Commercial Law; Contract Law; International Law; Intellectual Property.

Languages: French, German, English, Spanish, Italian

PIRENNE PYTHON SCHIFFERLI PETER & PARTNERS

3, RUE BELLOT

1206 GENEVA, SWITZERLAND

Telephone: (41 22) 347 46 45

Telex: 427 994 PPSP CH

Telecopier: (41 22) 346 85 76;347 80 54; 789 53 31

Bern, Switzerland Office: Sulgenrain 14, 3007. Telephone: (41 31) 372 40 46. Telefax: (41 31) 372 45 11.

Nyon, Switzerland Office: 6, Avenue Reverdil, 1260. Telephone: (41 22) 361 18 04. Telefax: (41 22) 362 37 75.

Commercial and Contract Law, Banking, Corporate Finance, Swiss and International Taxation, Litigation, International Arbitration, Construction Law, Residence and Work Permits.

MEMBERS OF FIRM

YVES PIRENNE, born Brussels, Belgium, May 10, 1947. Admitted, 1978, Geneva. *Education:* University of Geneva (Licence en droit); Graduate School of International Studies, Geneva. *Member:* Geneva and Swiss Bar Associations; Geneva Association of Business Law; International Bar Association; Swiss Arbitration Association. *LANGUAGES:* French, English and Italian.

JACQUES PYTHON, born Fribourg, Switzerland, June 12, 1943. Admitted, 1973, Zurich; 1978, Geneva and New York. *Education:* Max-Planck-Institute for International Private Law, Hamburg (Auditor, 1983); Columbia University Business School (B.B.A., 1976); University of Fribourg (Licence en droit). *Member:* Geneva and Swiss Bar Associations; Geneva Association of Business Law; International Bar Association; Swiss Arbitration Association. *LANGUAGES:* French, German and English.

PETER SCHIFFERLI, born Geneva, Switzerland, November 2, 1947. Admitted, 1975, Geneva. *Education:* University of Geneva (Licence en droit). Assistant, Faculty of Law, Intellectual Property, University of Geneva, 1971-1974. *Member:* Geneva and Swiss Bar Associations; International Bar Association; Swiss Arbitration Association. *LANGUAGES:* French, German, English and Italian.

WOLFGANG PETER, born Münster, Germany, March 25, 1949. Admitted, 1979, Geneva. *Education:* Graduate Institute of International Studies, Geneva (Degree in Political Science, 1974); University of Lausanne (Doctorate in Economics, 1975); University of Frankfurt (Doctorate in Law, 1986); Harvard Law School (1982-1983). Author: "Arbitration and Renegotiation of International Investment Agreements", Kluwer Academic Publishers Group, Dordrecht, 1986. Secretary of the Federal Expert Commission on Swiss Company Law, 1979-1980. Advisor to the Federal Minis-

(This Listing Continued)

ter of Justice and Police, 1980-1982. *Member:* Geneva and Swiss Bar Associations; Geneva Association of Business Law; International Bar Association; Swiss Arbitration Association. *LANGUAGES:* German, French and English.

BERNHARD CRON, born Basel, Switzerland, April 9, 1946. Admitted, 1978, St. Gall and Zurich; 1981, Geneva; 1986, Vaud. *Education:* University of St. Gall (M.B.A., joined program of economics and law); University of Michigan Law School (LL.M., 1981). Assistant, Institute of Finance Economy and Tax Law, University of St. Gall, 1974-1975. *Member:* Geneva and Swiss Bar Associations; International Bar Association; Swiss Arbitration Association. (Resident, Nyon Office). *LANGUAGES:* French, German and English.

JACQUES JONES, born Raleigh, North Carolina, August 29, 1946. Admitted, 1976, New York; 1979, District of Columbia; (Not admitted in Switzerland). *Education:* Columbia University Law School (J.D., 1975); Graduate Faculties in Political Science (1968-1969); University of Virginia (B.A., 1968). *Member:* American Bar Association; International Bar Association; Geneva Association of Business Law; Maritime Law Association of the United States (Associate Member). *LANGUAGES:* English and French.

DANIEL RICHARD, born Yverdon, Switzerland, August 4, 1950; admitted, 1977, Geneva; 1979, Zurich. *Education:* University of Geneva (Licence en droit, 1974). Attorney with Lachenal, Dutoit, Brechbuhl et Cottier, Geneva, 1974-1977. Attorney with Haight, Gardner, Poor and Havens, New York, 1978-1979. Attorney with Bär and Karrer, Zurich, 1979-1981. Legal Counsel with Tradax Gestion S.A., Geneva, 1982-1985. *Member:* Geneva, Zurich and Swiss Bar Associations; International Bar Association; Swiss Arbitration Association. *LANGUAGES:* French, English and German.

FRANCESCO BERTOSSA, born Bern, Switzerland, December 23, 1952; admitted, 1981, Bern. *Education:* University of Bern Law School, Assistant of Public Law Department (Doctorate, 1984); Harvard Law school (LL.M., 1985). *Member:* Swiss and Bernese Association of Lawyers; Swiss Arbitration Association. (Resident, Bern Office). *LANGUAGES:* German, French, English and Italian.

CHARLES OCHSNER, born Neuchâtel, Switzerland, May 4, 1951; admitted, 1977, Geneva. *Education:* University of Geneva (Licence en Droit). General Counsel, CH Projects Management Ltd., Tokyo, Japan; Vice-President, Chamber of Commerce and Industry in Japan, Tokyo. *Member:* Geneva and Swiss Bar Associations. *LANGUAGES:* French, English, Japanese and German.

PHILIPPE BONVIN, born Lucerne, Switzerland, August 30, 1947; admitted, 1976, Geneva. *Education:* University of Lausanne (Licence en Droit, 1973). Attorney with Lalive & Budin, Geneva, 1974-1976. Attorney with Dr. Jean-Jacques Magnin, Geneva, 1976-1979. Legal Advisor of WW Finance S.A. (a Credit Suisse First Boston subsidiary), Geneva, 1980-1983. Legal Advisor of Gulf Credit S.A., Geneva, 1983-1985. *Member:* Geneva and Swiss Bar Associations. *LANGUAGES:* French, English and German.

DOMINIQUE HENCHOZ, born Geneva, Switzerland, March 9, 1957; admitted, 1981, Geneva. *Education:* University of Geneva Law School (Lic. iur.); New York University, School of Law (Master of Comparative Jurisprudence, 1982). Auxiliary Judge. *Member:* Geneva Bar; Swiss Society of International Law; Swiss Arbitration Association; Geneva Association of Business Law. *LANGUAGES:* French, English and German. *PRACTICE AREAS:* Commercial Law; Corporate Law; Litigation; Arbitration.

CLARENCE PETER, born Plainfield, New Jersey, March 9, 1960; admitted, 1985, Geneva. *Education:* University of Geneva (Licence en Droit, 1982). Author: "Insider Trading in Switzerland," Kluwer, Law and Taxation Publishers Deventer, Boston. *Member:* Geneva and Swiss Bar Associations. *LANGUAGES:* French, English and German.

WILLIAM BALZLI, born Geneva, Switzerland, March 28, 1953; admitted, 1979, Geneva. *Education:* (Licence en Droit, 1977). Manager of the Civil Liability Department of Winterthur Assurance, Geneva, 1980-1981. Legal Adviser of Ferrier, Lullin & Cie, SA, Geneva, 1981-1985. Legal Adviser and Manager of Fidinam Fiduciaire SA, Geneva, 1985-1989. *Member:* Geneva Bar Association; Geneva Association of Business Law. *LANGUAGES:* French, English, German and Italian.

THOMAS STEINMANN, born Bern, Switzerland, November 2, 1961; admitted, 1990, Geneva. *Education:* University of Lausanne (Licence en Droit, 1984; Licence en Sciences Politiques, 1984; Doctorat en Droit, 1991). Author: "Les transferts de technologies et de marques en droit fiscal international," Schulthess, Zürich, 1991. Visiting Attorney, Gibson, Dunn and

(This Listing Continued)

Crutcher, New York, 1990-1991. *Member:* Geneva and Swiss Bar Associations; American Foreign Law Association; International Fiscal Association. *LANGUAGES:* French, English and German.

ASSOCIATES

CAROLINE FREYMOND, born Geneva, Switzerland, June 25, 1961; admitted, 1987, Geneva. *Education:* University of Geneva Law School. *LANGUAGES:* French, English, German, Spanish and Italian.

BERNADETTE SCHINDLER VELASCO, born Neuchâtel, Switzerland, January 6, 1957; admitted, 1982, Neuchâtel; 1990, Geneva and Vaud. *Education:* University of Neuchâtel (Licence en droit, 1979); Graduate Institute of International Studies, Geneva (1985). (Also at Nyon Office). *LANGUAGES:* French, English, German and Spanish.

NICOLAS HOFFMANN, born Geneva, February 3, 1962; admitted, 1987, Geneva. *Education:* University of Geneva (Licence en droit, 1987). Portfolio Manager, Credit Suisse, Geneva, 1988-1990. *Member:* Geneva Bar Association. *LANGUAGES:* French, English and Italian.

THOMAS LEGLER, born Bern, February 19, 1961; admitted, 1988, Bern; 1991, Geneva. *Education:* University of Bern (Bar Exam, 1988); University of Geneva (registered for a doctorate degree). Legal Counsel, Swiss Union of Private Railways, 1988-1991. Member, Swiss Expert Commission Treating Legal Questions on Skiing, 1988-1991. *Member:* Geneva and Swiss Bar Associations. *LANGUAGES:* German, French, English, Italian and Spanish.

ALEXANDRA VON WUSSOW, born Munich, Germany, April 22, 1963; admitted, 1990, Geneva. *Education:* University of Geneva (Licence en droit, 1985). Trainee Lloyd's Bank, Geneva, 1986-1987. *LANGUAGES:* French, English, German.

MARC JOORY, born Geneva, Switzerland, September 15, 1965; admitted, 1990, Geneva; 1992, New York. *Education:* University of Geneva (Licence en Droit, 1986); New York University (LL.M., Corporate Law, 1991). Attorney with Paul, Weiss, Rifking, Wharton & Garnison, New York, 1991-1992. *Member:* Geneva and Swiss Bar Associations; New York State Bar Association. *LANGUAGES:* French, English, Portuguese, Spanish and Hebrew.

NICOLAS DE GOTTRAU, born Fribourg, Switzerland, December 12, 1961; admitted, 1987, Geneva; 1992, New York. *Education:* University of Geneva (Licence en droit, 1984); Duke University School of Law (LL.M., 1991). *Member:* Geneva and Swiss Bar Associations; Geneva Association of Business Law. *LANGUAGES:* French, English and German.

LISA HAUERT, born Santa Monica, California, January 31, 1967; admitted, 1993, Geneva. *Education:* University of Geneva (Licence en droit, 1989). *Member:* Geneva Bar Association. *LANGUAGES:* French, English and Italian.

BEAT MUMENTHALER, born Milano, Italy, October 19, 1962; admitted, 1990, Bern; 1991, Geneva. *Education:* University of Bern (Fürsprecher, 1990). *Member:* Geneva and Swiss Bar Associations. *LANGUAGES:* German, Italian, French and English.

STELLA FAZIO, born Geneva, Switzerland, May 7, 1957; admitted, 1993, Geneva. *Education:* University of Geneva (Licence en droit, 1984). *Member:* Geneva and Swiss Bar Associations. *LANGUAGES:* French, Italian and English.

GIOVANNI M. ROSSI, born Rome, Italy, May 13, 1969; admitted, 1993, Geneva and Vaud. *Education:* University of Geneva (Licence en Droit, 1991). *Member:* Geneva and Swiss Bar Associations; Swiss Arbitration Association. (Also at Nyon Office). *LANGUAGES:* French, Italian, English and German.

HENRIC IMMINK, born Vevey, Switzerland, May 27, 1965; admitted, 1994, Geneva. *Education:* University of Geneva (Licence en droit, 1988). Senior Tax Advisor, PRICE WATERHOUSE, Zurich. *Member:* Geneva and Swiss Bar Associations. *LANGUAGES:* French, German, English and Dutch.

KURT MOLL, born Kreuzlingen, Switzerland, June 1, 1965; admitted, 1993, Bern. *Education:* University of Bern Law School (Bar exam, 1993). (Resident, Bern Office). *LANGUAGES:* German, French, English and Italian.

COUNSEL

PROFESSOR PHILIPPE CAHIER, born Paris, France, March 31, 1932; (Not admitted in Switzerland). *Education:* University of Paris (Licence en droit, 1953); Lyon (DES in Economy, 1956); Graduate Institute of International Studies, Geneva (Doctorat, 1959); Columbia University, New

(This Listing Continued)

PIRENNE PYTHON SCHIFFERLI PETER & PARTNERS, Geneva—Continued

York (Research Fellow, 1961-1962). Counsel: of Spain in the Barcelona Traction case, I.C.J., 1969; for Guinea in the Arbitration Dubai-Sharjah, 1978-1981; of the Boundary Court of Arbitration Dubai-Sharjah, 1978-1981; of the Administrative Tribunal of the UNIDROIT, Rome, 1978—(President, 1984—); of the CARICI, Geneva, 1984—. Professor of International Law, Geneva, 1967—. *Member:* International Law Association; Société Française de Droit International; Société Suisse de Droit International. *LANGUAGES:* French, Italian and English.

BERNHARD MÜLLER, born Bern, Switzerland, January 12, 1921; admitted, 1946, Bern. *Education:* University of Lausanne and Bern Law Schools (Graduated as Attorney). Author: "The Practice of the Swiss Federal Banking Commission," in German, 1985, in French, 1987 and in English, 1988. Head of the Legal Department, Federal Department of Finances, 1954-1976. Chief Executive of the Federal Banking Commission, 1976-1986. Member, Standing Committee for Banking Legislation and Supervisory Practices (Cooke Committee), Bank for International Settlements. *Member:* Swiss and Bernese Association of Lawyers; Swiss Arbitration Association; Geneva Association of Business Law. (Also at Bern Office). *LANGUAGES:* German, French, English and Italian.

Languages: French, English, German, Italian, Japanese, Spanish, Hungarian, Portuguese

---

PONCET TURRETTINI AMAUDRUZ & NEYROUD

Established in 1921

8-10, RUE DE HESSE
P.O. BOX 5715
CH-1211 GENEVA 11, SWITZERLAND
Telephone: (+41 22) 319 11 11
Telecopier: (022) 312 14 31

MEMBERS OF FIRM

ROBERT TURRETTINI, born Geneva, Switzerland, June 3, 1922; admitted, 1948, Geneva. *Education:* University of Geneva (Licence en droit, 1946); Harvard Law School and Geneva Law School (Doctorat en droit, 1948). *LANGUAGES:* French, English and German.

DOMINIQUE PONCET, born Geneva, Switzerland, August 31, 1929; admitted, 1951, Geneva. *Education:* University of Geneva (Licence en droit, 1951; Doctorat en droit, 1967). Professor of Law, Geneva Law School, 1976—. *LANGUAGES:* French, English, German and Italian.

MICHEL AMAUDRUZ, born Lausanne, Switzerland, December 26, 1939; admitted, 1966, Geneva. *Education:* University of Lausanne (Licence en droit, 1964); University of Lausanne (Doctorat en droit, 1968). *LANGUAGES:* French, English and German.

PHILIPPE NEYROUD, born Geneva, Switzerland, January 15, 1950; admitted, 1972, Geneva. *Education:* University of Geneva (Licence en droit, 1972); University of California, Berkeley (Master of Laws, 1976). *LANGUAGES:* French, English, Italian and German.

DOMINIQUE AMAUDRUZ, born Geneva, Switzerland, May 14, 1954; admitted, 1975, Geneva. *Education:* University of Geneva (Licence en droit, 1975). *LANGUAGES:* French, English and German.

PAUL GULLY-HART, born London, England, March 22, 1956; admitted, 1978, Geneva. *Education:* University of Geneva (Licence en droit, 1977). *LANGUAGES:* French, English, Italian, German and Spanish.

GÉRALD PAGE, born Fribourg, Switzerland, January 13, 1953; admitted, 1981, Geneva; 1985, Zurich. *Education:* University of St. Gallen (Lizenziat in Wirtschaftswissenschaften, 1976; Doktorat der Rechtswissenschaften, 1982); University of Geneva (Licence en droit, 1980); Harvard Law School (Visiting Scholar, 1980-1981). *LANGUAGES:* French, English and German.

CARLO LOMBARDINI, born Milano, Italy, May 7, 1964; admitted, 1984, Geneva. *Education:* University of Geneva (Licence en droit, 1984). *LANGUAGES:* French, English, German and Italian.

MAURICE TURRETTINI, born Geneva, Switzerland, March 2, 1961; admitted, 1986, Geneva. *Education:* University of Geneva (Licence en droit, 1984); Boston University (LL.M. in Banking Law, 1986). *LANGUAGES:* French, English and German.

(This Listing Continued)

MICHEL BERGMANN, born Montevideo, Uruguay, October 21, 1951; admitted, 1987, Geneva. *Education:* University of Lausanne (Licence en droit, 1978). *LANGUAGES:* French, English, German and Spanish.

ROBERT ASSAEL, born Geneva, Switzerland, December 14, 1953; admitted, 1981, Geneva. *Education:* University of Geneva (Licence ès sciences commerciales et industrielles, 1975; Licence en droit, 1980). *LANGUAGES:* French, English and German.

OLIVIER WEHRLI, born Geneva, Switzerland, July 30, 1963; admitted, 1986, Geneva. *Education:* University of Geneva (Licence en droit, 1985); Boston University (LL.M. in Banking Law, 1990). *LANGUAGES:* French, English and German.

ALESSANDRA CAMBI, born Zurich, Switzerland, July 19, 1965; admitted, 1988, Geneva. *Education:* University of Geneva (Licence en droit, 1988). *LANGUAGES:* French, Italian, English and German.

VINCENT SOLARI, born Geneva, Switzerland, October 12, 1964; admitted, 1990, Geneva. *Education:* University of Geneva (Licence en droit, 1986). *LANGUAGES:* French, Italian, German and English.

ISABELLE PONCET, born Geneva, Switzerland, June 1, 1970; admitted, 1992, Geneva. *Education:* University of Geneva (Licence en droit, 1992). *LANGUAGES:* French, English and German.

EMMA LOMBARDINI, born Zurich, Switzerland, February 16, 1971; admitted, 1992, Geneva. *Education:* University of Geneva (Licence en droit, 1992). *LANGUAGES:* French, Italian, English and German.

MONICA BERTHOLET, born Zurich, Switzerland, October 29, 1959; admitted, 1993, Geneva. *Education:* University of Geneva (Licence en droit, 1987). *LANGUAGES:* French, German and English.

FLORENCE KRAUSKOPF, born Bern, Switzerland, May 4, 1969; admitted, 1993, Geneva. *Education:* University of Fribourg (Licence en droit, 1993). *LANGUAGES:* French, German and English.

RORY F.B. COOPER, born Cork, Ireland, September 17, 1970; admitted, 1994, Geneva. *Education:* University of Lausanne (Licence en droit, 1993). *LANGUAGES:* French, English and German.

ALAIN MACALUSO, born Montreux, Switzerland, April 9, 1969; admitted, 1994, Geneva. *Education:* University of Lausanne (Licence en droit, 1993). *LANGUAGES:* French, Italian, English and German.

JEAN-LUC EPARS, born Geneva, Switzerland, May 16, 1966; admitted, 1994, Geneva. *Education:* University of Geneva (Licence en droit, 1989). *LANGUAGES:* French, German and English.

EMMANUELLE FELLEY, born Martigny, Switzerland, April 14, 1966; admitted, 1994, Geneva. *Education:* University of Geneva (Licence en droit, 1994). *LANGUAGES:* French, English, German and Spanish.

LUCA PIAZZA, born Locarno, Switzerland, September 11, 1961; admitted, 1994, Geneva. *Education:* University of Fribourg (Licence en droit, 1989). *LANGUAGES:* French, English, German, Italian and Arabic.

Languages: French, English, German, Italian, Spanish and Arabic

---

PONCET WARLUZEL & PARTNERS

14, COURS DES BASTIONS
P.O. BOX 18
1211 GENEVA 12, SWITZERLAND
Telephone: (4122) 311 00 10
Telcopier: (4122) 311 00 20

Contract, Corporate, Civil and Criminal Litigation, Banking and Business Law, Arbitration, Corporate and Commercial Law, International Estate Planning, Media Law, Competition and Administrative Law and Bankruptcy.

MEMBERS OF FIRM

DR. CHARLES PONCET, born Geneva, Switzerland, 1946; admitted, 1969, Switzerland. *Education:* University of Geneva Law School (Law Degree, 1969); Georgetown University (Master of Comparative Law, 1973); University of Geneva Law School (Doctorate in Law, 1982). Corresponding Editor, International Legal Materials (ASIL) and World Arbitration and Mediation Report. Author: "Challenges to the jurisdiction of international arbitrators, an important decision of the Swiss Supreme Court," 50 Arbitration, 1984; "Excerpt on international arbitration from the Swiss draft statute on private international law," XXIII International Legal Materials, 1984; "Swiss Supreme Court opinions in the first and second SANTA Fe

(This Listing Continued)

cases, XXII International Legal Materials," 1983 and XXIV International Legal Materials, 1985; "Swiss Supreme Court opinion in the matter of EL NASR EXPORT IMPORT & Co. v. ANGLO FRENCH STEEL CORPORATION S.A.," X Yearbook Commercial Arbitration, 1985; "The new Swiss statute on international arbitration," XXVII International Legal Materials, 1988; *"La censure cinématographique en droit administratif suisse et en droit genevois,"* Semaine judiciaire, 1979; "Censure cinématographique et délégation législative," Schweizerisches Zentralblatt für Staats- und Gemeindeverwaltung, 1980; "La liberté d'information du journaliste: un droit fondamental? Etude de droit Suisse et comparé," Revue internationale de droit comparé, 1980; "La surveillance de l'état sur l'information radio-télévisée en régime de monopole public," Bâle, 1985 Ed. Helbing & Lichtenhahn. *Member:* Geneva Bar Association; Swiss Federation of Lawyers; Swiss Arbitration Association; American Bar Association; British Chartered Institute of Arbitrators; American Arbitration Association; American Society of International Law. *LANGUAGES:* French, Italian, English and German.

DOMINIQUE WARLUZEL, born Geneva, Switzerland, 1957; admitted, 1980, Switzerland. *Education:* University of Geneva Law School (Law Degree, 1980). *Member:* Geneva Bar Association; Swiss Federation of Lawyers; Swiss Criminal Law Association. *LANGUAGES:* French, English and German.

ERIC ALVES DE SOUZA, born Paris, France, 1961; admitted, 1984, Switzerland. *Education:* University of Geneva Law School (Law Degree, 1983). Deputy Judge, Court of Appeals of Geneva. *Member:* Geneva Bar Association; Swiss Federation of Lawyers; Geneva Association of Business Law. *LANGUAGES:* French, English, German and Italian.

OLIVIER PECLARD, born Geneva, Switzerland, 1958; admitted, 1980, Switzerland; 1987, New York. *Education:* University of Geneva Law School (Law Degree, 1980); Duke University (Master of Laws, LL.M., 1986). *Member:* Geneva Bar Association; Swiss Federation of Lawyers; American Bar Association; International Association of Young Lawyers. *LANGUAGES:* French and English.

ASSOCIATES

DIDIER BOTTGE, born Geneva, Switzerland, 1962; admitted, 1986, Switzerland. *Education:* University of Geneva Law School (Law Degree, 1986). *Member:* Geneva Bar Association; Swiss Society of Criminal Law; Swiss Federation of Lawyers. *LANGUAGES:* French and English.

ISABELLE HAGMANN, born Geneva, Switzerland, 1966; admitted, 1990, Switzerland. *Education:* University of Geneva Law School (Law Degree, 1989). *Member:* Geneva Bar Association. *LANGUAGES:* French, English and German.

JOHANNA GRAZIANO-VON BURG, born Geneva, Switzerland, 1950; admitted, 1973, Switzerland. Co-author: *"Le Secret bancaire suisse,"* Berne, 1994 Ed. Stäampfli & Cie S.A.m. *LANGUAGES:* French, English and German.

DOMINIQUE RITTER, born Geneva, Switzerland, 1966; admitted, 1988, Switzerland. *Education:* University of Geneva Law School (Law Degree, 1988). *Member:* Geneva Bar Association. *LANGUAGES:* French, English and German.

SANDOZ, MOREILLON & REYMOND

13, COURS DE RIVE
P.O. BOX 3477
CH-1211 GENEVA 3, SWITZERLAND
Telephone: 41-22-735 35 31
Telefax: 41-22-735 78 51
Cable Address: SANDAVOCAT GENEVE

Arbitration, Bankruptcy, Commercial, Corporate, Family, International Contracts and Tax Law, General Legal Practice.

MEMBERS OF FIRM

MICHEL W. SANDOZ, born 1930; admitted, 1952, Geneva. *Education:* University of Geneva (Lic. jur.).

CLAUDE MOREILLON, born 1938; admitted, 1962, Geneva. *Education:* University of Geneva (Lic. jur.). Deputy Judge, Court of Appeals of Geneva.

(This Listing Continued)

JACQUES-ANDRÉ REYMOND, born 1937; admitted, 1964, Geneva. *Education:* University of Geneva (Lic. ec., Lic. jur; Dr. jur.). Professor of Tax and Corporation Law, University of Geneva. Former Dean, Geneva Law School.

Languages: French, English and German

SCHELLENBERG & HAISSLY

4, PLACE NEUVE
1211 GENEVA 11, SWITZERLAND
Telephone: 022 / 328 67 22
Telecopier: 022 / 328 79 61

Zürich, Switzerland Office: P.O. Box 6333, Löwenstrasse 19, 8023, Zurich. Telephone: 01 / 211 60 40. Telecopier: 01 / 221 11 65.

Commercial, Corporate, Contracts, Mergers and Acquisitions, Banking and Finance, Securities, Capital Markets, Litigation, Arbitration, Insolvency and Bankruptcy, International Judicial Assistance, Enforcement of Foreign Judgements, Taxation, Trusts and Estates, EC Law, Intellectual Property, Competition, Insurance and Liability, Trade and Transportation, Admiralty and Aviation.

MEMBERS OF FIRM

JEANNE TERRACINA, born 1946; admitted, 1970, Switzerland. *Education:* University of Geneva (lic.iur., 1969); New York University (M.C.J., 1976). *Member:* Swiss and Geneva Bar Associations. *LANGUAGES:* French, English and German. *PRACTICE AREAS:* Banking; Commercial; Bankruptcy; Judicial Assistance in Civil and Criminal Matters.

BERNARD HAISSLY, born 1947; admitted, 1971, Switzerland. *Education:* University of Geneva (lic.iur., 1969). *Member:* Swiss and Geneva Bar Associations. *LANGUAGES:* French, English, Italian and German. *PRACTICE AREAS:* Banking and Finance; Mergers and Acquisitions; Trusts and Estates; Litigation and Arbitration.

MAURICE AUBERT, born 1924; admitted, 1953, Switzerland. *Education:* University of Geneva (Dr.iur., 1951). *Member:* Swiss and Geneva Bar Associations. *LANGUAGES:* French and English. *PRACTICE AREAS:* Banking and Finance; Contract and Labour; Immigration Law; Trusts and Estates.

ROBERT P. BRINER, born 1955; admitted, 1981, Switzerland. *Education:* University of Geneva (lic.iur., 1978). *Member:* Swiss and Geneva Bar Associations. *LANGUAGES:* French, English, German, Italian and Spanish. *PRACTICE AREAS:* Corporate; Mergers and Acquisitions; Information Technology; Art Law.

CHRISTIAN G. GIROD, born 1960; admitted, 1985, Switzerland. *Education:* University of Geneva (lic.iur., 1982); Harvard Law School, Cambridge, Mass. (LL.M., 1986). *Member:* Swiss and Geneva Bar Associations. *LANGUAGES:* French, English and German. *PRACTICE AREAS:* Banking; Commercial; Bankruptcy; Litigation; Private International Law.

OF COUNSEL

JAQUES VERNET, born 1926; admitted, 1951, Switzerland. *Education:* University of Geneva (lic.iur., 1948). Member of Government, Canton of Geneva, 1973-1989. *Member:* Swiss and Geneva Bar Associations. *LANGUAGES:* French, English and German. *PRACTICE AREAS:* Insurance and Liability; Corporate; Trusts and Estates; Public and Administrative Law.

PROF. ANNE PETITPIERRE, born 1943; admitted, 1970, Switzerland. *Education:* Translators School Geneva (Translator Diploma, 1967); University of Geneva (Dr.iur., 1975). Lecturer at Law Faculty, University of Geneva, 1987-1993; Professor at Law Faculty, University of Geneva, 1993. *Member:* Swiss and Geneva Bar Associations. *LANGUAGES:* French, Italian, English and German. *PRACTICE AREAS:* Corporate; Finance; Environmental.

ASSOCIATES

CATHERINE DE PREUX, born 1959; admitted, 1988, Switzerland. *Education:* University of Geneva (lic.iur., 1985). *Member:* Swiss and Geneva Bar Associations. *LANGUAGES:* French and English. *PRACTICE AREAS:* Insurance; Domestic and International Commercial Litigation; Rental Law; Work and Service Contracts.

RAPHAËL TREUILLAUD, born 1960; admitted, 1987, Switzerland. *Education:* University of Geneva (lic.iur., 1985). *Member:* Swiss and Geneva Bar Associations. *LANGUAGES:* French, English and Italian. *PRAC-*

(This Listing Continued)

SCHELLENBERG & HAISSLY, Geneva—Continued

TICE AREAS: Litigation and Arbitration; Judicial Assistance in Criminal Matters; Bankruptcy; Banking.

SYLVIE NAUDY, born 1965; admitted, 1991, Switzerland. *Education:* University of Neuchâtel (lic.iur., 1988). *Member:* Swiss and Geneva Bar Associations. *LANGUAGES:* French, English and German. *PRACTICE AREAS:* Domestic and International Commercial Litigation; Insolvency and Bankruptcy; Contracts.

PIERRE O. KOBEL, born 1961; admitted, 1988, Switzerland. *Education:* University of Geneva (lic.iur., 1983); New York University (D.E.S., LL.M., 1991). *Member:* Swiss and Geneva Bar Associations. *LANGUAGES:* French, English, German and Italian. *PRACTICE AREAS:* Antitrust; International Trade; Litigation.

JACQUES R. BONVIN, born 1968; admitted, 1990, Switzerland. *Education:* University of Geneva (lic.iur., 1989). *Member:* Swiss and Geneva Bar Associations. *LANGUAGES:* French, English and German. *PRACTICE AREAS:* Commercial Litigation; Arbitration; International Private Law; Contract; Company; Commercial Law.

SECRETAN TROYANOV & PARTNERS

Established in 1967

2, RUE CHARLES-BONNET
P.O. BOX 189
1211 GENEVA 12, SWITZERLAND
Telephone: (+4122) 789.7000
Cable Address: "Intercounsel"
Telex: 427 475 Setr CH
Telefax: (+4122) 789.7070

London, England Office: 7/9 Bream's Buildings, Chancery Lane, EC4A 1DY. Telephone: (+44 171) 404-1199. Telefax: (+44 171) 405-0240.
Moscow, Russia Office: Ulitsa Usacheva 35, Suite 222, Moscow 119048. Telephone: (+7095) 245.5203. Telefax: (+7095) 244.1663.
Telephone/Telefax by satellite from outside Russia: 007.502.220.3137/8.

Swiss and General International Practice, Corporation, Banking and Financial Services, International Estate Planning, Arbitration, Commercial Law, Russian Law.

MEMBERS OF FIRM

DR. HUBERT SECRETAN, born Lausanne, Switzerland, 1933; admitted, 1964, Switzerland. *Education:* University of Lausanne (Licence en droit, 1956; Doctorat en droit, 1964); New York University, Institute of Comparative Law (M.C.J., 1960). Author: "La Protection des Dessins et Modèles Industriels et des Oeuvres d'Art Appliqué aux Etats-Unis et en Suisse, Etude de droit comparé", Thesis, Lausanne, 1964. Member, Panel of Swiss Arbitrators, International Chamber of Commerce. *Member:* Geneva Bar Association; Geneva Law Society; Swiss Bar Association; Geneva Association of Business Law; Cercle des Juristes Internationaux; Swiss Arbitration Association; Geneva Chamber of Commerce; Swiss-American Chamber of Commerce.

DR. TIKHON TROYANOV, born Belgrade, Yugoslavia, 1932; admitted, 1963, Switzerland. *Education:* University of Lausanne (Licence en droit, 1956; Doctorat en droit, 1963); Frankfurt am Main (1953-1954); Geneva (1963-1964). Author: "De la Nature Juridique du Contrat Collectif en URSS", Thesis, Lausanne, 1963. Member, Panel of Swiss Arbitrators, International Chamber of Commerce. *Member:* Geneva Bar Association; Geneva Law Society; Swiss Bar Association; Geneva Association of Business Law; Swiss-Russian Chamber of Commerce (Member of the Board); Swiss Arbitration Association; International Bar Association (East European Forum); Geneva Chamber of Commerce; International Lawyers Group, Moscow. (Resident Partner, Moscow, Russia Office).

ERIC W. FIECHTER, born Geneva, Switzerland, 1949; admitted, 1975, Switzerland. *Education:* University of Geneva (Licence en droit, 1973); University of Basle; New York University, Institute of Comparative Law (M.C.J., 1976). *Member:* Geneva Bar Association; Geneva Law Society; Swiss Bar Association; Geneva Association of Business Law; Swiss Jurists Society; Swiss Arbitration Association; Geneva Chamber of Commerce; Swiss Law Database Association (ABSD).

HORACE GAUTIER, born Geneva, Switzerland, 1956; admitted, 1980, Switzerland. *Education:* University of Geneva (Licence en droit, 1979).

(This Listing Continued)

Member: Geneva Bar Association; Geneva Law Society; Swiss Bar Association; Geneva Association of Business Law; Holborn Law Society; International Bar Association; International Litigation Practitioners Forum; British-Swiss Chamber of Commerce; British Institute of International and Comparative Law. (Partner in Charge of London, England Office).

DIDIER DE MONTMOLLIN, born Neuchâtel, Switzerland, 1957; admitted, 1981, Switzerland. *Education:* University of Neuchâtel (Licence en droit, 1981). Member, Secretariat, Swiss Bankers Association, Basle, 1983-1986. Deputy Secretary to Commission of Inquiry of Swiss Bankers Association for Agreement XVI ("U.S.-related Insider Trading"), 1985-1986. Secretary to Swiss Arbitration Commission, ICC Swiss National Committee and to the Board of Swiss Arbitration Association, 1985-1986. Member, Panel of Swiss Arbitrators, International Chamber of Commerce, 1988—. Investigative Counsel appointed by Swiss Bankers Association ("Due Diligence Agreement"), 1989—. *Member:* Geneva Bar Association; Geneva Law Society; Swiss Bar Association; Geneva Association of Business Law; Swiss Arbitration Association; International Bar Association.

CYRIL TROYANOV, born Lausanne, Switzerland, 1957; admitted, 1980, Switzerland; 1987, New York. *Education:* University of Geneva (Licence en droit, 1980); University of Vienna; New York University, Institute of Comparative Law (M.C.J., 1985); University College, London/Centre for the Study of Socialist Legal Systems, Moscow (1990). *Member:* Geneva Bar Association; Geneva Law Society; Swiss Bar Association; Geneva Association of Business Law; International Bar Association (Eastern European Forum; Business Law Section); Swiss Jurists Society. (Partner in Charge of Russian Department, Geneva, and Hiring Partner).

ASSOCIATES

DAVID G. FORBES-JAEGER, born Greensburg, Indiana, USA, 1956; admitted, 1984, Florida (Not admitted in Switzerland). *Education:* Rheinische Friedrich-Wilhelms Universität, Bonn, Federal Republic of Germany (1976-1977); University of Florida (B.A., 1978; M.A., 1979; J.D., 1982); The Hague Academy of International Law (1985). *Member:* The Florida Bar Association (International Law Section; Central and Eastern European Law Committee; Corporate and Business Law Section; Real Property, Probate and Trust Law Section; Tax Law Section); Geneva Association of Business Law.

EVA P. STORMANN, born Geneva, Switzerland, 1962; admitted, 1986, Switzerland. *Education:* University of Geneva (Licence en droit, 1985); University of Lausanne (Post-graduate Degree in European Law, 1993). *Member:* Geneva Bar Association; Geneva Law Society; Swiss Bar Association; Geneva Association of Business Law; Holborn Law Society; Observer, Association of Overseas Young European Community Lawyers in the United Kingdom.

BEATRIZ VIERTL, born Geneva, Switzerland, 1965; admitted, 1988, Switzerland. *Education:* University of Geneva (Licence en droit, 1987). *Member:* Geneva Bar Association; Geneva Law Society; Swiss Bar Association; Swiss Jurists Society; Geneva Association of Business Law.

MARKUS SCHAER, born Balsthal, Switzerland, 1963; admitted, 1994, Switzerland. *Education:* University of Geneva (Licence es lettres, 1989: Branch A - Russian; Branch B - English; Licence en droit, 1991); GITIS Moscow, Russia, (1987-1988). *Member:* International Bar Association (East European Forum); International Lawyers Group, Moscow. (Resident Associate, Moscow, Russia Office).

MICHEL NUSSBAUMER, born Fribourg, Switzerland, 1963; admitted, 1988, Switzerland. *Education:* University of Fribourg (Licence en droit, 1986); University of California at Berkeley (LL.M., 1990); Moscow State University (1991). *Member:* Geneva Bar Association; Swiss Bar Association. (Resident Associate, London, England Office).

NATHALIA GAIDAIENKO SCHAER, born Moscow, Russia, 1965; Russian lawyer (Not admitted in Switzerland). *Education:* Moscow State Institute for Foreign Relations (Diploma with Honors, Commercial Law, 1987; Doctoral Candidate in Law, 1992). Author: "Limited Liability Companies and Economic Interest Groupings in France," Thesis, Moscow, 1992. Researcher, Parliamentary Institute of Legislation and Comparative Law Studies, Moscow, 1987—. *Member:* International Bar Association (East European Forum); International Lawyers Group, Moscow. (Resident Associate, Moscow, Russia Office).

ALEXANDRE VASSILTCHIKOV, born Geneva, Switzerland, 1966; admitted, 1992, Switzerland. *Education:* University of Geneva (Licence en droit, 1990); Moscow State University (1991-1992); University of Geneva, Erasmus Program (Banking and Capital Markets Law, 1993). (Resident Associate, Moscow, Russia Office).

(This Listing Continued)

JULIA MIROSHNIKOVA, born Moscow, Russia, 1968; Russian lawyer (Not admitted in Switzerland). *Education:* Moscow State University (Diploma with Honors, Jurisprudence, 1990). (Resident Associate, Moscow, Russia Office).

ALISON ROCHAT-SPECHTER, born Geneva, Switzerland, 1964; admitted, 1993, United Kingdom (Not admitted in Switzerland). *Education:* University of Buckingham (LL.B., 1991); Inns of Court School of Law (1992). *Member:* Honorable Society of Gray's Inn.

PATRICE AUBRY, born Geneva, Switzerland, 1967; admitted, 1991, Switzerland. *Education:* University of Geneva (Licence en droit, 1991). *Member:* Geneva Bar Association.

DR. PHILIPP GREMPER, born Basle, Switzerland, 1964; admitted, 1994, Switzerland. *Education:* University of Basle (Licence en droit, 1988; Doctorat en droit, 1992). Author: "Arbeitsrechtliche Aspekte der Ausuebung verfossungsmaessiger Rechte," Thesis, Basle, 1992. *Member:* Geneva Bar Association; Swiss Jurists Society.

VERONIKA ODINTSOVA, born Moscow, Russia, 1961; Russian lawyer; (Not admitted in Switzerland). *Education:* Moscow State University (Diploma with Honors, International Law, 1983; Doctoral Candidate in Law, 1987). Researcher, Parliamentary Institute of Legislation and Comparative Law Studies, Moscow, 1988—. Author: "International Protection of Copyright in the field of Cinematography and Television," Thesis, Moscow, 1987.

ANNE-VALÉRIE JACQUIER, born Geneva, Switzerland, 1966; admitted, 1992, Switzerland; 1994, New York. *Education:* University of Geneva (Licence en droit, 1989); New York University (LL.M., 1994). *Member:* Geneva Bar Association.

Languages: French, English, Russian (Official Translator), German, Italian, Spanish and Hungarian

---

SPIESS BRUNONI SAMBUC & PARTNERS

14, COURS DE RIVE
CH-1211 GENEVA 3, SWITZERLAND
Telephone: (022) 786 20 20
Telecopier: (022) 786 40 40

Lugano, Switzerland Office: Spiess Brunoni & Partners, Via Pioda 14, CH-6901. Telephone: (091) 28 64 11. Telecopier: (091) 23 94 68. Telex: 844100.

Locarno, Switzerland Office: Cotti Spiess Brunoni & Partners, Largo F. Zorzi 12, 6601 Locarno. Telephone: (093) 31 37 96. Telecopier: (093) 31 66 41.

General and International Practice, Administrative Law, Family Law, Wills, Criminal Law, Contracts, Personal Injury, Business Law, Commercial Law, Corporate Law, Company Law, Banking and Financial Services, Notary Public, Real Estate Transactions, National and International Taxation, Arbitration and Litigation, Mergers Acquisitions and Divestitures, Property.

FIRM PROFILE: Established in 1959 as Tettamanti-Spiess and Partners, changed to Spiess Brunoni & Partners since 1992, it has grown to become one of the largest firms of Switzerland with 15 lawyers, practicing in four different offices in the country. The client base is European, principally Swiss and Italian.

PARTNERS

GIANGIORGIO SPIESS, born 1933; admitted, 1959. *Education:* University of Bern (Lic. iur., 1957). Notary Public. *Member:* International Bar Association. *LANGUAGES:* Italian, French, German and English. *PRACTICE AREAS:* Commercial Law; Banking and Financial Services; Corporate Law; Business Law; Notary.

BRENNO BRUNONI, born 1948; admitted, 1976. *Education:* University of Bern (Lic. iur., 1973). Notary Public. *LANGUAGES:* Italian, French, German and English. *PRACTICE AREAS:* Litigation and Arbitration; Contracts; Civil Law; International Private Law; Administrative Law; Notary.

MASSIMO PEDRAZZINI, born 1963; admitted, 1989. *Education:* University of Geneva (Lic. iur., 1985). *LANGUAGES:* Italian, French, German and English. *PRACTICE AREAS:* Corporate Law; Business Law; International Law; Contracts.

ANDREA MOLINO, born 1963; admitted, 1991. *Education:* University of Zurich (Lic. iur., 1988). *LANGUAGES:* Italian, French, German and

(This Listing Continued)

English. *PRACTICE AREAS:* Commercial Law; Banking and Financial Services; Corporate Law.

HENRI-PHILIPPE SAMBUC, born 1950; admitted, 1978, Geneva Bar. *Education:* University of Lausanne (Lic. iur., 1974). *LANGUAGES:* French and English. *PRACTICE AREAS:* Business Law; Commercial Law; National and International Taxation; International and Private Law; Arbitration and Litigation; Chinese Law.

DR. ARMANDO PEDRAZZINI, born 1923; admitted, 1950. *Education:* University of Bern (Dr. iur., 1947). Notary Public. *LANGUAGES:* Italian, French and German. *PRACTICE AREAS:* Civil Law; Contracts; Litigation; Notary.

ASSOCIATES

JOHN ROSSI, born 1938; admitted, 1968. *Education:* University of Bern (Lic. iur., 1965). Notary Public. *LANGUAGES:* Italian, French, German and English. *PRACTICE AREAS:* Criminal Law; Civil Law; Administrative Law; Litigation; Notary.

MARIA CRISTINA BONFIO, born 1960; admitted, 1987. *Education:* University of Lausanne (Lic. iur., 1984). Notary Public. *LANGUAGES:* Italian, French and German. *PRACTICE AREAS:* Real Estate Transactions; Corporate Law; Contracts; Notary.

DONATELLA MONTI LANG, born 1960; admitted, 1990. *Education:* University of Fribourg (Lic. iur., 1987). *LANGUAGES:* Italian, French and German. *PRACTICE AREAS:* Civil Law; Family Law; Litigation.

DR. DOMENICO PIOVESANA, born 1958; admitted, 1987, Court of Venice (Not admitted in Switzerland). *Education:* University of Bologna (Dr. iur., 1983); University of Turin (M.B.A., 1985). *LANGUAGES:* Italian and English. *PRACTICE AREAS:* Corporate Law; International and National Taxation.

MICHEL DE LUIGI, born 1963; admitted, 1989. *Education:* University of Fribourg (Lic. iur., 1987). Notary Public. *LANGUAGES:* Italian, French, German and English. *PRACTICE AREAS:* International and National Taxation; Real Estate Transactions; Corporate Law; Notary.

MICHELA HOHL, born 1965; admitted, 1992. *Education:* University of Fribourg (Lic.iur., 1989). Notary Public. *LANGUAGES:* Italian, French, German and English. *PRACTICE AREAS:* Commercial Law; Civil Law; Inheritance; Notary.

STEFANO PIZZOLA, born 1963; admitted, 1990. *Education:* University of Geneva (Lic.iur., 1987). *LANGUAGES:* Italian, French and German. *PRACTICE AREAS:* Civil Law; Criminal Law; Litigation; Insolvency.

STOFFEL & PARTNER

WORLD TRADE CENTER
RTE AÉROPORT 10, CP 515
1215 GENEVA 15, SWITZERLAND
Telephone: 022/798 27 28
Telecopier: 022/798 27 37

Zurich, Switzerland Head Office: Dufourstrasse 40, 8008 Zurich. Telephone: 01/252 16 16. Telecopier: 01/252 27 00.

Brussels Office: 81, Avenue Louis, B-1050. Telephone: 32 2 542 88 88. Telecopier: 32 2 542 89 89.

New York Office: 152 West 57th Street, 10019. Telephone: 212-582-2828. Telecopier: 212-582-2424.

FIRM PROFILE: Joint Offices with PÜNDER GROUP:

- New York, Brussels, Beijing

- Moscow, Budapest, Warsaw

Commercial Law (general), Companies, Corporations, Mergers and Acquisitions, Banking, Securities and Finance, Tax, Arbitration and Litigation, International Legal Assistance, Intellectual Property, Competition, Anti-Trust, Bankruptcy, Insolvency, EC Law.

RESIDENT PARTNER

DR.IUR. LAURENT MOREILLON, born 1956. *Education:* University of Lausanne (Dr.iur., 1988). Author: "The Repressive Control of the Cinematographic Expression," 1983. Lecturer, Property Law, University of Lausanne. *Member:* Swiss Federation of Lawyers; International Association for the Protection of Industrial Property.

(This Listing Continued)

STOFFEL & PARTNER, Geneva—Continued

DR.IUR. AMEDEE KASSER, born 1962. *Education:* University of Lausanne (Dr.iur., 1991). Author: "The Right of Pardon under Federal Law and the Laws of the Canton of Vaud", 1991.

RESIDENT ASSOCIATES

LIC.IUR. JACQUELINE RONCONI, born 1964. *Education:* University of Fribourg (Lic.iur., 1987); Collège d'Europe, Bruges, Belgium (LL.M., 1993). Notary Exam, Canton of Ticino, 1992.

DR.IUR. CHRISTOPHE GEORGES WILHELM, born 1965. *Education:* University of Lausanne (Dr.iur., 1991). Author: "Introduction and mandatory force of international treaties in the Swiss juridical system", 1991.

Member of PÜNDER GROUP: Buruma Maris, The Hague, Rotterdam; Cerha, Hempel & Spiegelfeld, Vienna; Coppens, van Ommeslaghe, Horsmans & Faures, Brussels; De Pardieu-Lacourte G.I.E., Paris; Pünder, Volhard, Weber & Axster, Frankfurt, Düsseldorf, Berlin, Leipzig; Stoffel & Partner, Zurich, Genève.

Languages: German, English, French, Italian and Spanish

TAVERNIER, GILLIOZ, DE PREUX, DORSAZ

Established in 1981

11, RUE TOEPFFER
1206 GENEVA, SWITZERLAND
Telephone: (+41-22) 347-77-07
Telex: 423665 TAGI CH
Cable Address: Tavergill
Telefax: (+41-22) 347-97-89

General Commercial Practice, Banking, Corporate and Finance, Securities Regulations, Commercial and Contract Law, Mergers and Acquisitions, Commercial Litigation and Arbitration, Criminal Litigation and International Legal Assistance Procedure, Estate Planning, Bankruptcy, Administrative and Environmental Law Intellectual and Industrial Property, Antitrust and Unfair Competition, Product Liability.

MEMBERS OF FIRM

EDMOND TAVERNIER, born Martigny, Switzerland, October 28, 1946; admitted, 1975, Geneva. *Education:* University of Geneva (Licence en droit, 1971); Académie de Droit International The Hague (Summer, 1972); Cambridge University, U.K. (Diploma in Comparative Law, 1973); Max-Planck Institute, Munich (1973-1974); Graduate Institute of International Studies, Geneva (Diploma, 1977); Harvard Law School (LL.M. and Certificate International Tax program, 1978). Author: "Trademarks and Parallel Imports," Cambridge, 1973; "Le phénomène des transferts indirects de bénéfices entre sociétés apparentées et les conditions d'application de différentes réglementations nationales en la matière (CH, FR, RFA, UK, USA)," Geneva, 1977. Member of the Cantonal Tax Administration of the Canton of Geneva, January 1976-March 1977. *Member:* Geneva Bar Association; Swiss Federation of Lawyers; International Bar Association; International Fiscal Association; Swiss Arbitration Association; Geneva Association of Business Law. *LANGUAGES:* French, English and German. *PRACTICE AREAS:* Banking Law; Corporate and Finance; Commercial Matters and Contracts; Mergers and Acquisitions; Estates Planning and Trusts.

PIERRE GILLIOZ, born Martigny, Switzerland, July 14, 1947; admitted, 1973, Geneva. *Education:* University of Geneva (Licence en droit, 1970). Research Assistant to Professor of Tax Law, University of Geneva, 1970-1972. Member, Swiss Federal Tax Administration in Bern (Division of International Affairs, Double Taxation Agreements), 1976-1978. *Member:* Geneva Bar Association; Swiss Federation of Lawyers; International Bar Association; International Fiscal Association (Member, Executive Board, Swiss Branch). *LANGUAGES:* French, English and German. *PRACTICE AREAS:* Tax Law; Mergers and Acquisitions; Corporate Law; Administrative Law.

BRUNO DE PREUX, born Sion, Switzerland, September 14, 1946; admitted, 1974, Geneva. *Education:* University of Geneva (Licence en droit, 1970); Universities of Strasbourg and Paris (Diploma of Advanced Studies in European Law). Deputy Public Prosecutor and Former Judge, Republic and Canton of Geneva, 1974-1978. Assistant: European Law Institute of Geneva, 1971-1972; to Professor of EEC Law, University of Geneva, 1972-1973. *Member:* Geneva Bar Association (President, 1992-1994); Swiss Federation of Lawyers; Swiss Association of Criminal Law; Swiss Arbitration

(This Listing Continued)

Association. *LANGUAGES:* French, English and German. *PRACTICE AREAS:* Commercial and Criminal Litigation; International Legal Assistance; White Collar Crime.

BERNARD DORSAZ, born La Chaux-de-Fonds, Switzerland, March 17, 1948; admitted, 1973, Geneva. *Education:* Institute Florimont Geneva (Maturité Fédérale Classique, 1966); University of Geneva (Licence en droit, 1969; Advanced Legal Studies, Diploma, 1973). Member, Legal Department of the European Organization for Nuclear Research (CERN), 1975-1976. Member, Legal Department of the Bank Paribas (Switzerland) SA, 1973-1974. Author: "Enforcement of Money Judgments in Switzerland," in "Enforcement of Money Judgments Abroad" (Matthew Bender). *Member:* Geneva Bar Association; Swiss Federation of Lawyers; International Bar Association; Swiss Arbitration Association. *LANGUAGES:* French, English and German. *PRACTICE AREAS:* Arbitration; Commercial Litigation; Corporate Law; Intellectual Property.

PIERRE-YVES TSCHANZ, born Geneva, Switzerland, October 8, 1952; admitted, 1978, Switzerland; 1981, New York; 1988, Paris. *Education:* University of Geneva, Switzerland (Licence en droit, 1975). Author: International Commercial Arbitration, New York, 1983 (collective course book); International Arbitration in Switzerland, Basle, 1989 (with A. Bucher); "Contributions of the Aminoil Award to the Law of State Contracts," 18 Int'l Law 245 (1984); "Contrats d'Etat et mesures unilatérales de l'Etat devant l'arbitre international," 74 Rev. crit. dr. int'l privé 47 (1985); "International Arbitration in the United States: the Need for a New Act," 3 Arb. Int'l 309 (1967). Member, Panel of Arbitrators, American Arbitration Association. *Member:* Geneva, New York State and International Bar Associations; Swiss Arbitration Association. *LANGUAGES:* French, English and German. *PRACTICE AREAS:* Arbitration; Commercial Litigation; International Transactions.

CHRISTIAN BOVET, born Fribourg, Switzerland, April 24, 1959; admitted, 1985, Geneva. *Education:* University of Fribourg, Switzerland (Licence en droit, 1983; Doctorat en droit, 1990); Columbia University School of Law (LL.M., 1988). Research Assistant to Professor of Contracts and Commercial Law, University of Fribourg, 1985-1986. Author: "La nature juridique des syndicats de prêt et les obligations des banques dirigeantes et gérantes," Fribourg, 1991; "Concurrence et liberté économique," in La protection de la personnalité, Bilan et perspectives d'un nouveau droit, Contributions en l'honneur de Pierre Tercier pour ses cinquante ans, Fribourg, 1993. *Member:* Geneva Bar Association; Swiss Federation of Lawyers; International Association of Young Lawyers; International League of Competition Law. *LANGUAGES:* French, English and German. *PRACTICE AREAS:* Banking Law; Antitrust and Trade Regulation; Corporate Law.

VINCENT JEANNERET, born Geneva, Switzerland, July 9, 1960; admitted, 1989, Geneva. *Education:* University of Geneva (Licence en droit, 1982; Advanced Legal Studies Diploma in International Bankruptcy, 1986; Licence en sciences commerciales et industrielles, mention gestion d'entreprise, 1986); University of Dubrovnik, Postgraduate Diploma (The International Sale of Goods, The Vienna Convention, 1985). Research Assistant to Professor of Commercial Law, University of Geneva, 1982-1986. *Member:* Geneva Bar Association; Swiss Law Society; Swiss Federation of Lawyers; International Association of Young Lawyers. *LANGUAGES:* French, English and German. *PRACTICE AREAS:* Bankruptcy Law; Commercial and Criminal Litigation; International Legal Assistance.

SENIOR ASSOCIATES

STEPHANE VAN CAUTER, born Brussels, Belgium, March 26, 1963; admitted, 1990, Geneva. *Education:* University of Geneva, Switzerland (Licence en droit, 1988). *Member:* Geneva Bar Association; Swiss Federation of Lawyers. *LANGUAGES:* French and German.

XAVIER MO COSTABELLA, born Geneva, Switzerland, December 8, 1964; admitted, 1990, Geneva. *Education:* University of Geneva (Licence en droit, 1988). *Member:* Geneva Bar Association; Swiss Federation of Lawyers. *LANGUAGES:* French, German and English.

RAPHAEL SPAHR, born Sion, Switzerland, July 2, 1963; admitted, 1991, Geneva. *Education:* University of Geneva (Licence en sciences commerciales et industrielles, mention économie politique, 1986; Licence en droit, 1989). *Member:* Geneva Bar Association; Swiss Federation of Lawyers. *LANGUAGES:* French, German and English.

SILVIO VENTURI, born Fully, Switzerland, September 20, 1962; admitted, 1993, Geneva. *Education:* University of Fribourg, Switzerland (Licence en droit, 1987; Doctorat en droit, 1993). Research Assistant to Professors: Contracts, Commercial Law and Conflict of Laws, University of Fribourg, 1987-1990; Max-Planck Institute, Hamburg, 1990-1991. Author: "La réduction du prix de vente en cas de défaut ou de non-conformité de la

(This Listing Continued)

chose. Le Code suisse des obligations et la Convention de Vienne sur les contrats de vente internationale de marchandises," Fribourg, 1993. *Member:* Geneva Bar Association; Swiss Federation of Lawyers. **LANGUAGES:** French, Italian and German.

MANUEL BIANCHI, born Lausanne, Switzerland, December 16, 1962; admitted, 1993, Geneva. *Education:* University of Lausanne, Switzerland (Licence en droit, 1986; Doctorat en droit, 1990); Columbia University School of Law (LL.M., 1991). Research Assistant to Professor of Administrative Law, University of Lausanne, 1986-1989; Research Assistant to Professor of Constitutional Law, University of Geneva, 1991-1992. Author: "La révision du plan d'affectation communal," Lausanne, 1990. *Member:* Geneva Bar Association; Swiss Federation of Lawyers. **LANGUAGES:** French, English, German and Italian.

Languages: French, English, German and Italian

VALTICOS, VEUILLET, REYMOND & MOSIMANN

15, RUE FERDINAND-HODLER
1207 GENEVA, SWITZERLAND
Telephone: (41.22) 700.28.28
Facsimile: (41.22) 700.28.38

General, Commercial, Civil and Criminal Practice, Corporate, Banking, Copyright, Private International Law, Arbitration, Art Transactions, Sponsoring, Insurance Liability, International Legal Assistance.

MEMBERS OF FIRM

MICHEL VALTICOS, born Geneva, Switzerland, June 3, 1955; admitted, 1979, Geneva. *Education:* University of Geneva Law School (Law Degree, 1976). *Member:* Geneva Bar Association (Member of Council); Swiss Federation of Lawyers; Swiss Society of Jurists; Geneva Law Society; Swiss Arbitration Association; Geneva Business Law Association.

ALAIN-LUC VEUILLET, born Geneva, Switzerland, October 19, 1953; admitted, 1981, Geneva. *Education:* University of Geneva Economics School (Economic Degree, 1976); University of Geneva Law School (Law Degree, 1978). *Member:* Geneva Bar Association; Swiss Federation of Lawyers.

ALEC REYMOND, born Bern, Switzerland, June 29, 1956; admitted, 1981, Geneva. *Education:* Geneva College; University of Geneva Law School (Law Degree, 1978). *Member:* Geneva Bar Association; Swiss Federation of Lawyers; Geneva Business Association; Swiss Criminal Law Association.

YVES-ALAIN MOSIMANN, born Geneva, Switzerland, March 18, 1951; admitted, 1981, Geneva. *Education:* University of Geneva Law School (Law Degree, 1979); University of Geneva Economics School. *Member:* Geneva Bar Association; Swiss Federation of Lawyers; Swiss Arbitration Association.

ASSOCIATE

ERIC HESS, born Zurich, Switzerland, October 1, 1963; admitted, 1988, Geneva. *Education:* University of Geneva Law School (Law Degree, 1986). *Member:* Geneva Bar Association.

FABIENNE MARIETHOZ, born Switzerland, January 29, 1968; admitted, 1992, Geneva. *Education:* University of Geneva Law School (Law Degree, 1989). *Member:* Geneva Bar Association.

Languages: French, German, English, Italian and Portuguese

WINSTON & STRAWN

Established in 1853
43 RUE DU RHONE
1204 GENEVA, SWITZERLAND
Telephone: (4122) 7810506
Fax: (4122) 7810361

Chicago, Illinois Office: 35 West Wacker Drive, 60601. Telephone: 315-558-5600. Cable Address: "Winston Chicago." Facsimile: 312-558-5700.

Washington, D.C. Office: 1400 L Street, N.W., 20005-3502. Telephone: 202-371-5700. Telecopier: 202-371-5950. Telex: 440574 INTLAW UI.

New York, N.Y. Office: 175 Water Street, 10038. Telephone: 212-269-2500. Telecopier: 212-952-1474/5. Cable Address: "Coledeitz, NYK." Telex: (RCA) 232459.

(This Listing Continued)

Corporate and Securities, Financial Transactions, Litigation, Antitrust, Insolvency, Bankruptcy and Business Reorganization, Real Estate, Tax, Energy, Employment Relations, Employee Benefits, Intellectual Property, Environmental Law, Health Law, Government and Legislative Matters, Bank and Federal Regulatory Law, Telecommunications, Maritime Law and Trusts and Estates.

FIRM PROFILE: Winston & Strawn, founded in 1853, is one of the nation's oldest and largest law firms. With nearly 500 attorneys in offices in Chicago, New York and Washington, DC, the firm provides a full range of legal services to clients throughout the United States and abroad, including Fortune 500 companies, major commercial and financial institutions, individuals and entrepreneurs from virtually every industry.

MEMBERS OF FIRM

CHARLES C. ADAMS, JR., born Belfast, Northern Ireland, August 25, 1947; admitted, 1973, Virginia; 1975, District of Columbia; 1993, Avocat, Paris France (Not admitted in Switzerland). *Education:* Dartmouth College (B.A., 1968); University of Virginia (J.D., 1973). **LANGUAGES:** French, German, Italian and English.

NICOLAS C. ULMER, born Washington, D.C., August 5, 1952; admitted, 1979, District of Columbia; 1980, California (Not admitted in Switzerland). *Education:* Brown University (A.B., 1974); University of California at Hastings (J.D., 1979). Author: "Drafting the International Arbitration Clause," 20 International Lawyer 1335, 1986; "Discovery Abroad for Domestic Suits," California Lawyer, November 1987; "Le Droit de l'Arbitrage Interne et International en Suisse," (book review) 18 International Business Lawyer 186, 1990; "Winning the Opening Stages of an ICC Arbitration," Journal of International Arbitration 33, 1991. Co-Author: "Recognition and Enforcement of Foreign Civil Judgements in Switzerland," 27 International Lawyer 317, 1993. *Member:* The District of Columbia Bar; State Bar of California; American Bar Association (Member, Section on International Law); Association Suisse de l'Arbitrage. **LANGUAGES:** English, French, Spanish, German and Italian.

MARC S. PALAY, born Chicago, Illinois, January 16, 1952; admitted, 1977, Virginia; 1978, District of Columbia; 1979, U.S. District Court, District of Columbia; 1988, U.S. Court of Appeals, Ninth Circuit; 1990, U.S. Supreme Court and U.S. Court of Appeals, Federal Circuit (Not admitted in Switzerland). *Education:* Washington University (A.B., cum laude, 1973); George Washington University (J.D., with high honors, 1977). Order of the Coif. Member, The George Washington Law Review, 1976-1977. *Member:* District of Columbia Bar. **PRACTICE AREAS:** Complex Litigation; International Commercial Arbitration; International Trade Law.

ASSOCIATE

James A. Tidmarsh

LAW OFFICES
SUZANNE WOLFE MARTIN

15, RUE DU CENDRIER
1201 GENEVA, SWITZERLAND
Telephone: (41-22) 732.31.33
Telefax: (41-22) 738.60.73
Telex: 412838 LWYR CH

General International Business Practice.

SUZANNE WOLFE MARTIN, born New York, New York, August 29, 1934; admitted, 1966, District of Columbia; (not admitted in Switzerland but registered with Geneva Bar). *Education:* New York University (B.A., 1955); Catholic University of America Law School (J.D., 1964); University of Paris (Doctoral studies in Law, 1965). *Member:* American Bar Association; International Chamber of Commerce Paris; Commission on International Commercial Arbitration; Swiss Arbitration Association; Chartered Institute of Arbitrators London; Geneva Association of Business Law. **LANGUAGES:** English and French. **PRACTICE AREAS:** Arbitration; Litigation; Fraud; Eastern European Commerce.

KONSTANTIN RAZUMOV, born Dniepropetrovsk, USSR, November 7, 1952; admitted, 1989, Moscow (Not admitted in Switzerland). *Education:* Law Faculty, Institute of International Relations, USSR Ministry of Foreign Affairs (1975; Post Graduate Studies, 1978); Moscow, Doctor Juris (1979). Professor, Department of International Private Law, Institute of International Relations, 1975-1978. *Member:* Russian Federation Arbitration Court at the Chamber of Commerce and Industry; Arbitration Center,

(This Listing Continued)

LAW OFFICES SUZANNE WOLFE MARTIN, *Geneva—Continued*

Federal Economic Chamber of Austria; Working Group on Arbitration, International Chamber of Commerce, Paris. *LANGUAGES:* Russian, French, English, Spanish and Romanian. *PRACTICE AREAS:* Commercial Arbitration; International Business Transactions; Eastern European Commerce.

MEISSER & MEISSER

Established in 1979

BAHNHOFSTRASSE 8
CH-7250 KLOSTERS, SWITZERLAND
Telephone: (0) 81 69 61 61
Telefax: (0) 81 69 41 81
Telex: 853323 medu ch

Trademarks, Commercial and General Practice.

DR. IUR. J. DAVID MEISSER, born 1947; admitted, 1976, Zurich.

DR. IUR. URS MEISSER, born 1957; admitted, 1988, Switzerland.

LIC.IUR. DANIEL BOHREN, born 1963; admitted, 1994, Switzerland.

Languages: German and English

BAUMGARTNER, WELLAUER, DISERENS, LEI RAVELLO

BEL-AIR-MÉTROPOLE 1
1002 LAUSANNE, SWITZERLAND
Telephone: (4121) 320.77.51
Cable Address: BAUMAVOCAT
Facsimile: (4121) 320.20.64

General Practice and Arbitration.

MEMBERS OF FIRM

Jacques Baumgartner   Pierre-Olivier Wellauer
Jean-Christophe Diserens   Robert Lei Ravello

Languages: French, English, German and Italian

BOURGEOIS, MULLER, PIDOUX, CAMPICHE, CHENAUX, CHERPILLOD, & MASMEJAN

Established in 1954

MONTBENON 2
P.O. BOX 2293
1002 LAUSANNE, SWITZERLAND
Telephone: (021) 320 74 51
Fax: (021) 320 74 54

MEMBERS OF FIRM

OLIVIER BOURGEOIS, born Ballaigues, Switzerland, October 5, 1938; admitted, 1967, Vaud, Switzerland. *Education:* University of Lausanne, Business School (HEC, 1959); University of Lausanne, Law School (licence en droit, 1960; Dr.Jur., 1964). *Member:* Vaud and Swiss Bar Associations; International Fiscal Association; Swiss Society of International Law. *LANGUAGES:* French, English and German.

GEORGES MULLER, born Lausanne, Switzerland, January 23, 1940; admitted, 1974, Vaud, Switzerland. *Education:* University of Lausanne, Business School (HEC, 1963); University of Lausanne, Law School (licence en droit, 1963; Dr.Jur., 1973); Harvard University (LL.M., 1969). Professor, Corporate Law, University of Lausanne. *Member:* Vaud and Swiss Bar Associations; Swiss Arbitration Association; International Fiscal Association. *LANGUAGES:* French, English and German.

PHILIPPE PIDOUX, born Lausanne, Switzerland, June 17, 1943; admitted, 1973, Vaud, Switzerland. *Education:* University of Lausanne (Licence en droit, 1966; Dr.Jur., 1969); University of Texas, Austin (M.C.J., 1970). Member: Government of canton de Vaud, (1986-1994); Swiss Parlia-

(This Listing Continued)

ment, (1983-1995). *Member:* Vaud and Swiss Bar Associations; Swiss Arbitration Association. *LANGUAGES:* French, English and German.

ANTOINE CAMPICHE, born Lausanne, Switzerland, November 26, 1959; admitted, 1988, Vaud, Switzerland. *Education:* University of Lausanne (Licence en droit, 1981; Dr.Jur., 1986); University of Chicago (M.B.A., 1991). *Member:* Vaud and Swiss Bar Associations. *LANGUAGES:* French, English and German.

IVAN CHERPILLOD, born Lausanne, Switzerland, January 24, 1959; admitted, 1989, Vaud, Switzerland. *Education:* University of Lausanne (Licence en droit, 1981; Dr.Jur., 1985). Professor, Intellectual Property, University of Lausanne. *Member:* Vaud and Swiss Bar Association; Licensing Executives Society. *LANGUAGES:* French, English and German.

JEAN-LUC CHENAUX, born Neuchâtel, Switzerland, September 24, 1960; admitted, 1991, Vaud, Switzerland. *Education:* University of Lausanne (Licence en droit, 1982; Dr.Jur., 1990). *Member:* Vaud and Swiss Bar Associations; Swiss Lawyers Association; Swiss Arbitration Association; Swiss Society of International Law. *LANGUAGES:* French, English and German.

LUCIEN MASMEJAN, born Lausanne, Switzerland, December 14, 1961; admitted, 1992, Vaud, Switzerland. *Education:* University of Lausanne (Licence en droit, 1983; Dr.Jur., 1989). *Member:* Vaud and Swiss Bar Associations; International Fiscal Association. *LANGUAGES:* French, English and German.

DUDAN & RICHARD

ATTORNEYS

18, RUE DU PETIT-CHÊNE
P.O. BOX 2593
CH-1002 LAUSANNE, SWITZERLAND
Telephone: (41-21) 320 50 61
Telefax: (41-21) 320 53 30

General and International Practice, Real Estate and Corporate Law, Business and Finance Law, Administrative Law, International Arbitration, Litigation.

MEMBERS OF FIRM

PHILIPPE DUDAN, born 1920; admitted, 1948, Lausanne. President (Bâtonnier) of the State Bar Association, 1978-1980. (Senior Partner).

PHILIPPE RICHARD, born Lausanne, Switzerland, July 29, 1943; admitted, 1973, Lausanne. *Education:* University of Lausanne (Licence en droit, 1968; Doctorat en droit, 1971). President (Bâtonnier) of the State Bar Association, 1994-1996. Author: "La convention de Tokyo," Pont Frères, Lausanne, 1971; "Les arrêtés fédéraux urgents contre la spéculation foncière," Cédidac 19, Lausanne, 1991; "Articles 269 CO et 269 a CO, méthodes absolue et relative, rapport entre les articles, état de la question," Cahiers du bail 3/92, Lausanne, 1992; "Die allgemeinen Bestimmungen des neuen Mietrechts," Mietrechtpraxis MP, Basel, 1991, p. 39-68. *Member:* Vaud (Vice President, 1992-1993 and President, 1994) and Swiss Bar Associations; Swiss Lawyers Association; Swiss Arbitration Association; Geneva Association of Business Law; International Association of Lawyers. *LANGUAGES:* French, English and German.

ASSOCIATES

CORNELIA SEEGER TAPPY, born Aarau, Switzerland, June 5, 1959; admitted, 1991, Lausanne. *Education:* University of Lausanne (J.D., 1981; Licenciée avec thèse, 1989). Clerk, County Court of Vaud, 1985-1989. Vice-President, Riviera District Court, 1993—. Author: "Nullité de mariage, divorce et séparation de corps à Genève, au temps de Calvin," Méta-Editions, Lausanne, 1989; "Etapes de l'unification du droit matrimonial suisse: de la République Helvétique à la loi de 1874," in L'Unification du droit privé suisse au XIXe siècle, Méthodes et problèmes Fribourg, 1986, p. 57-74. *Member:* Vaud and Swiss Bar Associations. *LANGUAGES:* French, German, Swiss, German and English.

GLORIA NANCY CAPT, born Switzerland, October 10, 1959; admitted, 1991, Lausanne. *Education:* University of Lausanne (J.D., 1985; Ph.D., 1989); Case Western Reserve School of Law, Cleveland, Ohio, USA. Scientific Co-Worker, Swiss Department of Justice, Office of Justice, 1991-1992. Assistant Professor, Administrative Law, University of Lausanne, School of Law, 1992—. Author: "Les procédures administrative en droit américain," ("Administrative Procedures in American Law"), Chabloz, SA, Tolochenaz, 1989. *Member:* Vaud and Swiss Bar Associations; International Association of Lawyers. *LANGUAGES:* English, French and German.

(This Listing Continued)

MICHEL ROSSINELLI, born Lausanne, Switzerland, March 6, 1952; admitted, 1979, Geneva, Switzerland; 1993, Lausanne. *Education:* University of Geneva (Licence en droit, 1974; Diplôme d'études jur. sup., 1985; Doctorat en droit, 1986). Office fédéral de la Justice, Berne, Chef de division suppléant, 1991-1993. Lecturer, Université de Genève, Chef de travaux, 1986-1991. Author: "Les libertés non écrites," Payot, Lausanne, 1987; "La liberté de la radio-télévision en droit comparé," Published, Paris, 1991. *Member:* Vaud and Swiss Bar Associations. *LANGUAGES:* French, German and English.

Languages: French, English, German and Swiss-German

LENZ & STAEHELIN

2, PLACE ST-FRANÇOIS
CH-1003 LAUSANNE, SWITZERLAND
Telephone: 021-320.79.72
Telex: 422.476 LSB
Telecopier: 021-312.97.45

Geneva, Switzerland Office: 25, Grand' Rue, CH-1211 Geneva 11.
Telephone: 022 319 06 19. Telex: 422.476 LSB. Fax: 022 319 06 00.
Zürich, Switzerland Office: 58 Bleicherweg, CH-8027. Telephone: 01-204.12.12. Cable Address: "Staehelinjur" Telex: 815656 LAW CH. Telecopier: 01/204.12.00.

Swiss and International Taxation, Banking and Finance Law, Capital Market Transactions, Share Issues and Listing, International Commercial Arbitration, Commercial and Contract Law, Company Law, Mergers and Acquisitions, Corporate Finance, Competition Law, Residence and Work Permits, Purchase of Swiss Real Estate, Product Liability, Civil, Criminal and Administrative Litigation, Debt and Bankruptcy Law, International Legal Assistance, Estate Planning, Trusts, Charitable Foundations, Private International Law, Unfair Competition, Copyright, Patent and Trademark Law, Environmental Law, European Law.

RESIDENT PARTNER

GILLES FAVRE, born Neuchâtel, Switzerland, November 30, 1948; admitted, 1975, Neuchâtel; 1976, Geneva; 1981, Lausanne, Vaud. *Education:* University of Neuchâtel (Licence en droit, 1973). *LANGUAGES:* French and English. *PRACTICE AREAS:* Civil Litigation; Contact Law; Debt and Bankruptcy Law; Private International Law.

ASSOCIATE

SILVIA TOMBESI, born Ancona, Italy, September 16, 1964; admitted, 1991, Geneva; 1992, Lausanne, Vaud. *Education:* University of Bern (Licence en droit, 1989). *LANGUAGES:* Italian, French, German and English.

MATILE, GROSS, BRON, MATHYER, BRANDT & LOGOZ

Established in 1972
20, AVENUE DES MOUSQUINES
P.O. BOX 31
CH-1000 LAUSANNE 5, SWITZERLAND
Telephone: (41 21) 320 22 65
Telefax: (41 21) 320 22 78

MEMBERS OF FIRM

JACQUES MATILE, born 1928; admitted, 1954, Vaud. *Education:* University of Lausanne (Licence en droit, 1950; Doctorat en droit, 1952). Author: "Problèmes du droit suisse des cartels", 89 Revue de Droit Suisse II 159-164, 1970. Co-Author: "Droit vaudois de la construction", 1987. Deputy Justice, Supreme Court of Switzerland, 1975—. President, Federal Appellate Commission for Scientific Research Matters, 1984—. *Member:* Vaud (Chairman, 1982-1984), Swiss and International Bar Associations; Swiss Law Society (Chairman, 1979-1982). *PRACTICE AREAS:* General Practice except Litigation.

JEAN-PIERRE GROSS, born 1942; admitted, 1969, Vaud. *Education:* University of Lausanne (Licence en droit, 1964; Doctorat en droit, 1967); University of California at Berkeley (LL.M., 1970). *Member:* Vaud, Swiss and International Bar Associations; Swiss Law Society; International Fiscal Association. *PRACTICE AREAS:* General Practice.

JACQUES-HENRI BRON, born 1941; admitted, 1976, Vaud. *Education:* University of Lausanne (Licence en droit, 1971). *Member:* Vaud and

(This Listing Continued)

Swiss Bar Associations; Swiss Law Society. *PRACTICE AREAS:* General Practice.

PIERRE MATHYER, born 1950; admitted, 1981, Vaud. *Education:* University of Lausanne (Licence en droit, 1974). *Member:* Vaud and Swiss Bar Associations; Swiss Law Society; Swiss Criminal Law Society. *PRACTICE AREAS:* General Practice.

DOMINIQUE BRANDT, born 1952; admitted, 1987, Vaud. *Education:* University of Lausanne (Licence en droit, 1977; Doctorat en droit, 1986). *Member:* Vaud and Swiss Bar Associations; Swiss Law Society. *PRACTICE AREAS:* General Practice.

FRANCOIS LOGOZ, born 1963; admitted, 1993, Vaud. *Education:* University of Lausanne (License en droit, 1984; Doctorat en droit, 1991). *Member:* Vaud and Swiss Bar Associations; Swiss Law Society. *PRACTICE AREAS:* General Practice.

Languages: French, English, German, Italian and Spanish

PIGUET, SUBILIA, GELLER & DUPUIS

2, CHEMIN DE PRIMEROSE
P.O. BOX 1224
1001 LAUSANNE, SWITZERLAND
Telephone: (International 4121) 617 75 91
Telecopier: (International 4121) 616 52 64

OF COUNSEL

JEAN-FRANÇOIS PIGUET, born Lausanne, Switzerland, 1922; admitted, 1952, Vaud and Federal Courts. *Education:* University of Lausanne (Licence en droit, 1947; Docteur en droit, 1950). *Member:* State Bar Association (Vice-President, 1978-1980; President, 1980-1982); Swiss Federation of Lawyers.

PARTNERS

JEAN-LUC SUBILIA, born Lausanne, Switzerland, 1945; admitted, 1973, Vaud and Federal Courts. *Education:* University of Lausanne (Licence en droit, 1967; Docteur en droit, 1972). Deputy Justice, State Court of Appeals, 1982-1986. *Member:* State Bar Association; Swiss Federation of Lawyers.

BERNARD GELLER, born Pully, Switzerland, 1948; admitted, 1982, Vaud and Federal Courts. *Education:* University of Lausanne (Licence en droit, 1970; Docteur en droit, 1980). Member and General Secretary, 1972-1979, Swiss Musicians Association. *Member:* State Bar Association; Swiss Federation of Lawyers.

CHRISTOPHE PIGUET, born Lausanne, Switzerland, 1955; admitted, 1984, Vaud and Federal Courts; 1986, New York. *Education:* University of Lausanne (Licence en droit, 1978; Docteur en droit, 1983); New York University (M.C.J., 1985). Legal Advisor, State Department of Justice, 1984. Foreign Associate, Brown and Wood, New York, 1986. *Member:* State Bar Association; Swiss Arbitration Association; Swiss Federation of Lawyers.

MICHEL DUPUIS, born Yvorne, Switzerland, 1949; admitted, 1986, Vaud and Federal Courts. *Education:* University of Lausanne (Licence en droit, 1977; Docteur en droit, 1982). Investigating Magistrate, District of Lausanne, 1981-1984. *Member:* State Bar Association; Swiss Federation of Lawyers.

SYLVAINE PERRET-GENTIL, born Yverolon, Switzerland, 1965; admitted, 1994, Vaud. and Federal Courts. *Education:* University of Lausanne (License en droit, 1988; thèse, 1992). *Member:* State Bar Association; Swiss Federation of Lawyers.

Languages: German, English, French and Italian

REYMOND, BONNARD, MAIRE, FREYMOND, TSCHUMY

Established in 1912
5, RUE DU GRAND-CHÊNE
P.O. BOX 3633
1002 LAUSANNE, SWITZERLAND
Telephone: (41) (21) 320 68 51
Telecopier: (41) (21) 320 82 49

General and International Practice, Corporate Law, Business and Finance Law, International Arbitration, Litigation.

(This Listing Continued)

REYMOND, BONNARD, MAIRE, FREYMOND, TSCHUMY, Lausanne—Continued

MEMBERS OF FIRM

CLAUDE REYMOND, born 1923; admitted, 1951, Vaud. *Education:* Lausanne University (Licence en droit, 1946; Doctorat en droit, 1948). Co-Author: "The Law of Municipal and International Arbitration in Switzerland," 1989. Professor of Laws, Lausanne University School of Economics, 1965-1981. Associate Professor of Laws, Geneva University School of Laws, 1972-1989. Professor Emeritus, Lausanne University, 1981. Paul Foriers Professor, Brussels University, 1984-1985. *Member:* Vaud and Swiss Bar Associations; Swiss Lawyers Association; Swiss Arbitration Association (Vice-President d'honneur); Swiss Society of International Law; French Arbitration Committee. Fellow, Chartered Institute of Arbitrators (London).

ALEXANDRE BONNARD, born 1928; admitted, 1958, Vaud. *Education:* Lausanne University (Licence en droit, 1953; Doctorat en droit, 1955). *Member:* Vaud and Swiss Bar Associations; Swiss Lawyers Association.

JEAN-PAUL MAIRE, born 1942; admitted, 1975, Vaud. *Education:* Lausanne University (Licence en droit, 1967; Doctorat en droit, 1972); University of Texas at Austin (M.C.J., 1969). President, Young Bar Association of the Canton de Vaud, 1977-1978. *Member:* Vaud and Swiss Bar Associations; Swiss Lawyers Association; Swiss Society of International Law; Swiss Arbitration Association; Geneva Association of Business Law; French Arbitration Committee.

OLIVIER FREYMOND, born 1952; admitted, 1980, Vaud. *Education:* Lausanne University (Licence en droit, 1975; Doctorat en droit, 1978). Deputy Justice, Supreme Court of the Canton de Vaud, 1986. President, Young Bar Association of the Canton de Vaud, 1986-1988. *Member:* Vaud and Swiss Bar Associations; Swiss Lawyers Association; Swiss Society of International Law; Swiss Arbitration Association; International Association of Young Lawyers.

JEAN-LUC TSCHUMY, born 1959; admitted, 1988, Vaud. *Education:* Lausanne University (Licence en droit, 1983; Doctorat en droit, 1987). *Member:* Vaud and Swiss Bar Associations; Swiss Lawyers Association.

OF COUNSEL

PIERRE RAMELET, born 1918; admitted, 1944, Vaud. *Education:* Lausanne University (Licence en droit, 1942; Doctorat en droit, 1944). Senior Partner, 1960-1979. President (Bâtonnier), State Bar Association (1974-1976). *Member:* Vaud and Swiss Bar Associations; Swiss Lawyers Association.

Languages: French, German and English

COTTI SPIESS BRUNONI & PARTNERS

LARGO F. ZORZI 12
CH-6601 LOCARNO, SWITZERLAND
Telephone: (093) 31 37 96
Telecopier: (093) 31 66 41

Lugano, Switzerland Office: Spiess Brunoni & Partners, Via Pioda 14, CH-6901. Telephone: (091) 28 64 11. Telecopier: (091) 23 94 68. Telex: 844100.

Geneva, Switzerland Office: Spiess Brunoni Sambuc & Partners, 14, Cours de Rive, P.O. Box 373, CH-1211 Geneva 3. Telephone: (022) 786 20 20. Telecopier: (022) 786 40 40.

General and International Practice, Administrative Law, Family Law, Wills, Criminal Law, Contracts, Personal Injury, Business Law, Commercial Law, Corporate Law, Company Law, Banking and Financial Services, Notary Public, Real Estate Transactions, National and International Taxation, Arbitration and Litigation, Mergers Acquisitions and Divestitures, Property.

FIRM PROFILE: Established in 1959 as Tettamanti-Spiess and Partners, changed to Spiess Brunoni & Partners since 1992, it has grown to become one of the largest firms of Switzerland with 15 lawyers, practicing in four different offices in the country. The client base is European, principally Swiss and Italian.

PARTNERS

GIANFRANCO COTTI, born 1929; admitted, 1956. *Education:* University of Bern and Fribourg (Lic. iur. 1954). Notary Public. *LANGUAGES:* Italian, French, German and English. *PRACTICE AREAS:* Commercial Law; Corporate Law; Banking and Finance; Business Law.

(This Listing Continued)

GIANGIORGIO SPIESS, born 1933; admitted, 1959. *Education:* University of Bern (Lic. iur., 1957). Notary Public. *Member:* International Bar Association. *LANGUAGES:* Italian, French, German and English. *PRACTICE AREAS:* Commercial Law; Banking and Financial Services; Corporate Law; Business Law; Notary.

BRENNO BRUNONI, born 1948; admitted, 1976. *Education:* University of Bern (Lic. iur., 1973). Notary Public. *LANGUAGES:* Italian, French, German and English. *PRACTICE AREAS:* Litigation and Arbitration; Contracts; Civil Law; International Private Law; Administrative Law; Notary.

MASSIMO PEDRAZZINI, born 1963; admitted, 1989. *Education:* University of Geneva (Lic. iur., 1985). *LANGUAGES:* Italian, French, German and English. *PRACTICE AREAS:* Corporate Law; Business Law; International Law; Contracts.

ANDREA MOLINO, born 1963; admitted, 1991. *Education:* University of Zurich (Lic. iur., 1988). *LANGUAGES:* Italian, French, German and English. *PRACTICE AREAS:* Commercial Law; Banking and Financial Services; Corporate Law.

DR. ARMANDO PEDRAZZINI, born 1923; admitted, 1950. *Education:* University of Bern (Dr. iur., 1947). Notary Public. *LANGUAGES:* Italian, French and German. *PRACTICE AREAS:* Civil Law; Contracts; Litigation; Notary.

ASSOCIATES

JOHN ROSSI, born 1938; admitted, 1968. *Education:* University of Bern (Lic. iur., 1965). Notary Public. *LANGUAGES:* Italian, French, German and English. *PRACTICE AREAS:* Criminal Law; Civil Law; Administrative Law; Litigation; Notary.

HENRI-PHILIPPE SAMBUC, born 1950; admitted, 1978, Geneva Bar. *Education:* University of Lausanne (Lic. iur., 1974). *LANGUAGES:* French and English. *PRACTICE AREAS:* Business Law; Commercial Law; National and International Taxation; International and Private Law; Arbitration and Litigation; Chinese Law.

MARIA CRISTINA BONFIO, born 1960; admitted, 1987. *Education:* University of Lausanne (Lic. iur., 1984). Notary Public. *LANGUAGES:* Italian, French and German. *PRACTICE AREAS:* Real Estate Transactions; Corporate Law; Contracts; Notary.

DONATELLA MONTI LANG, born 1960; admitted, 1990. *Education:* University of Fribourg (Lic. iur., 1987). *LANGUAGES:* Italian, French and German. *PRACTICE AREAS:* Civil Law; Family Law; Litigation.

DR. DOMENICO PIOVESANA, born 1958; admitted, 1987, Court of Venice (Not admitted in Switzerland). *Education:* University of Bologna (Dr. iur., 1983); University of Turin (M.B.A., 1985). *LANGUAGES:* Italian and English. *PRACTICE AREAS:* Corporate Law; International and National Taxation.

MICHEL DE LUIGI, born 1963; admitted, 1989. *Education:* University of Fribourg (Lic. iur., 1987). Notary Public. *LANGUAGES:* Italian, French, German and English. *PRACTICE AREAS:* International and National Taxation; Real Estate Transactions; Corporate Law; Notary.

MICHELA HOHL, born 1965; admitted, 1992. *Education:* University of Fribourg (Lic.iur., 1989). Notary Public. *LANGUAGES:* Italian, French, German and English. *PRACTICE AREAS:* Commercial Law; Civil Law; Inheritance; Notary.

STEFANO PIZZOLA, born 1963; admitted, 1990. *Education:* University of Geneva (Lic.iur., 1987). *LANGUAGES:* Italian, French and German. *PRACTICE AREAS:* Civil Law; Criminal Law; Litigation; Insolvency.

BÄR & KARRER

RIVA CACCIA 1A (CENTRAL PARK)
6901 LUGANO, SWITZERLAND
Telephone: (+ +91) 55 00 64
Telefax: (+ +91) 55 02 36

Zürich, Switzerland Office: Seefeldstrasse 19, 8024 Zürich 8. Telephone: (+ +1) 261 51 50. Telefax: (+ +1) 251 30 25. Telex: 815 463 bkz.

General Commercial Practice, Corporate, Banking and Underwriting, Finance, International Arbitration, International Contracts, European Law, Taxation, Real Estate, Intellectual and Industrial Property and Copyright,

(This Listing Continued)

Construction, Administrative Matters, Inheritance and Estate Planning, Civil Litigation in all Swiss Courts.

FIRM PROFILE: see the profile of the main office in Zurich.

MEMBERS OF FIRM

DR. THOMAS A. BÄR, born 1937; admitted, 1964, Switzerland. *Education:* University of Zürich (Dr.iur.); Harvard Law School (LL.M.). Author: "Take-overs, their Financing and Financial Defenses.".

DR. ROBERT KARRER, born 1937; admitted, 1965, Switzerland. *Education:* University of Zürich (Dr.iur.); University of Chicago Law School (M.C.L.). Judge (part-time), Zurich Court of Cassation, since 1982.

DR. FELIX R. EHRAT, born 1957; admitted, 1985, Switzerland. *Education:* University of Lausanne; University of Zürich (Dr.iur.); University of the Pacific, McGeorge School of Law, Sacramento (LL.M.). Swiss Correspondent, World Tax Report. Author: "Commentary on Articles 151-163 of the Swiss Code of Obligations"; various other Reports in the field of contract and corporate law.

ASSOCIATES

LIC. IUR. GIANPAOLO ARRIGONI, born 1960; admitted, 1988, Switzerland; 1992, New York. *Education:* University of St. Gallen for Business Administration, Economics, Law and Social Sciences; New York University School of Law (M.C.J.). Author: "Swiss Report on Business Organizations.".

LIC. IUR. RENATO L. BLOCH, born 1958; admitted, 1987, Switzerland. *Education:* University of Geneva (Faculty of Economics and Faculty of Law). Also admitted and practising as notary public.

LIC. IUR. THEOBALD BRUN, born 1962; admitted, 1988, Switzerland. *Education:* University of Zürich; University of San Diego School of Law. Author: "Share Companies-Mergers, A Review of Relevant Swiss Laws and Regulations.".

Languages: Italian, English, German and French

BOLLA BONZANIGO & ASSOCIATI

VIA CANONICA 8
6901 LUGANO, SWITZERLAND
Telephone: 091 923 2581
Telefax: 091 922 6375

General and International Practice, Business, Corporate, Banking and Financial Services, Intellectual Property, Tax Law, Litigation, Estate Law, International Arbitration.

ROCCO C.G. BONZANIGO, born 1945; admitted, 1971, Switzerland. *Education:* University of Geneva (Licence en droit, 1969); University of British Columbia, Vancouver (LL.M., Taxation Law, 1972).

STEFANO BOLLA, born 1946; admitted, 1974, Switzerland. *Education:* University of Berne (Lic. iur., 1972).

FRANCO L. BRUSA, born 1957; admitted, 1984, Switzerland. *Education:* University of Berne (Lic.iur, 1981).

MICHAEL K. BECKER, born 1957; admitted, 1987, Switzerland and New York; 1988, U.S. District Court, Southern and Eastern Districts of New York. *Education:* University of Geneva (Licence en droit, 1982); New York University (M.C.J., 1986; LL.M., Corporate Law, 1989).

LORENZO MOOR, born 1966; (Not admitted in Switzerland). *Education:* University of Zürich (Lic.iur., 1991).

Editors of Repertorio di Giurisprudenza Patria.

Languages: Italian, German, French, English and Spanish

FELDER, RIVA & SOLDATI

Established in 1898

VIA PRETORIO 7
6901 LUGANO, SWITZERLAND
Telephone: 091 23 54 71
Fax: 091 23 38 73

General and International Practice, Business, Corporate, Banking and Financial Services, Intellectual Property, Litigation and Arbitration.

(This Listing Continued)

MEMBERS OF FIRM

FRANCO FELDER, born 1929; admitted, 1955, Switzerland. *Education:* University of Fribourg and Heidelberg. Notary Public. **LANGUAGES:** Italian, German and French. **PRACTICE AREAS:** Family Law; Successions; Corporate Law.

PIERFRANCO RIVA, born 1940; admitted, 1970, Switzerland. *Education:* University of Fribourg, Munich and Berlin. Notary Public, Doctor in law. **LANGUAGES:** Italian, German and French. **PRACTICE AREAS:** Banking, Trusts and Estates; Immigration Law.

FABIO SOLDATI, born 1957; admitted, 1986, Switzerland. *Education:* University of Zürich; University of California (LL.M.). Notary Public. **LANGUAGES:** Italian, German, French and English. **PRACTICE AREAS:** International Civil Law; Copyright Law.

FRANCESCA BARZAGHINI, born 1964; admitted, 1993, Switzerland. *Education:* University of Zurich. **LANGUAGES:** Italian, German and French. **PRACTICE AREAS:** Family Law.

GAMBAZZI & BERRA

VIA DOGANA VECCHIA 2/VIA NASSA
6900 LUGANO, SWITZERLAND
Telephone: 091 22.70.91
Fax: 091 23.68.62
Telex: 844 021 trd ch

General and International Practice, Business, Corporate, Banking and Financial Law and Services, Real Estate Transactions, Litigation and Arbitration.

PARTNERS

GIAMPIERO BERRA, born 1950; admitted, 1978, Switzerland. *Education:* University of Geneva and University of Munich (Licence en droit, 1974). Notary Public, 1983. *Member:* Swiss and International Bar Associations. **LANGUAGES:** Italian, English, German and French.

MARCO GAMBAZZI, born 1937; admitted, 1965, Switzerland. *Education:* University of Lausanne (Licence en droit, 1962). Notary Public, 1965. *Member:* Swiss and International Bar Associations. **LANGUAGES:** Italian, English, German, French and Spanish.

ASSOCIATES

PATRIZIA CASONI DELCÕ, born 1965; admitted, 1992, Switzerland. *Education:* University of Zurich (Lic.iur., 1990). *Member:* Swiss and International Bar Associations. **LANGUAGES:** Italian, German and French.

KUPPER & LEHNER

Established in 1977

VIALE S. FRANSCINI 1
Ch-6901 LUGANO, SWITZERLAND
Telephone: 091 21 30 33
Fax: 091 21 30 35

Zurich, Switzerland Office: Kupper & Lehner, Löwenstrasse 11, CH-8039 Zurich. Telephone: 01 225 47 47. Fax: 01 225 47 77.
Aarau, Switzerland Office: Hunziker Scholl & Partner, Laurenzenvorstadt 19, CH-5001 Aarau. Telephone: 064 22 23 02. Fax: 01 202 64 33.

Contracts, Corporate, Banking, Tax, EC, Property and Inheritance Law, Notary Public, Litigation and Arbitration.

MEMBERS OF FIRM

DR. WERNER KUPPER, born 1941; admitted, 1968, Zurich. *Education:* University of Zurich (Dr.iur.). Author: "Stille Reserven und Aktionärsinteressen," Bern, 1967. *Member:* Swiss, Zurich and International Bar Association; Bar Association of the Canton of Ticino. **LANGUAGES:** German, English, Italian and French.

DR. GEORGE LEHNER, LL.M., born 1951; admitted, 1978, Zurich. *Education:* University of Zurich (lic.iur., 1975); University of California at Berkeley (LL.M., 1976); Faculté Internationale de Droit Comparé Strasbourg (1979); University of Basel (Dr.iur., 1981). Author: "Die Verantwortlichkeit der Leitungsorgane von Aktiengesellschaften," Zurich, 1981. *Member:* Swiss and Zurich Bar Associations; Bar Association of the Canton of Ticino; Association of University of California at Berkeley Alumni. **LANGUAGES:** German, English and French.

(This Listing Continued)

KUPPER & LEHNER, Lugano—Continued

GIANLUCA BOSCARO, born 1958; admitted, 1985, Ticino. *Education:* University of Zurich (lic.iur., 1982). Notary public, Ticino, 1986. *Member:* Bar Association of the Canton of Ticino; Swiss Bar Association. (Resident Partner). *LANGUAGES:* Italian, German, English and French. *PRACTICE AREAS:* Family Law; Estate Law; Inheritance Law; Commercial Law; Corporate Law; Real Estate Registry Law; Constitutional Law.

(For Complete Biographical Data on all Personnel, see Professional Biographies at Zurich, Switzerland)

PIZZOTTI - GUGGIARI - JÖRG

CORSO ELVEZIA 14
CASELLE POSTALE 3249
6901 LUGANO, SWITZERLAND
Telephone: 091-922-04-04
Telefax: 091-923-72-01
Telephone & Telefax Number: Effective October 15, 1995

General and International Practice, Business, Corporate, Banking and Financial Services, Property, Family and Inheritance Law, Litigation and Arbitration.

MEMBERS OF FIRM

CLAUDE C. PIZZOTTI, born 1949; admitted, 1977, Switzerland. *Education:* University of Lausanne (Licence en droit, 1974). Notary Public.

ROSSANO GUGGIARI, born 1957; admitted, 1985, Switzerland. *Education:* University of Fribourg (Licence en droit, 1982). Notary Public.

DANIELE JÖRG, born 1955; admitted, 1988, Switzerland. *Education:* University of Fribourg (Licence en droit, 1982). Notary Public.

STEFANO GUGGIARI, born 1963; admitted, 1993, Switzerland. *Education:* University of Zurich (Licence en droit, 1990).

Languages: Italian, French, German, English.

SPIESS BRUNONI & PARTNERS

Established in 1959

(Formerly Tettamanti-Spiess & Partners)

VIA PIODA 14
6901 LUGANO, SWITZERLAND
Telephone: (091) 28 64 11
Telex: 844100
Telecopier: (091) 23 94 68

Geneva, Switzerland Office: Spiess Brunoni Sambuc & Partners, 14, Cours de Rive, P.O. Box 873, CH- 1211 Geneva 3. Telephone: (022) 786 20 20. Telecopier: (022) 786 40 40.

Locarno, Switzerland Office: Cotti Spiess Brunoni & Partners, Largo F. Zorzi 12, 6601 Locarno. Telephone: (093) 31 37 96. Telecopier: (093) 31 66 41.

General and International Practice, Administrative Law, Family Law, Wills, Criminal Law, Contracts, Personal Injury, Business Law, Commercial Law, Corporate Law, Company Law, Banking and Financial Services, Notary Public, Real Estate Transactions, National and International Taxation, Arbitration and Litigation, Mergers Acquisitions and Divestitures, Property.

FIRM PROFILE: Established in 1959 as Tettamanti-Spiess and Partners, changed to Spiess Brunoni & Partners since 1992, it has grown to become one of the largest firms of Switzerland with 15 lawyers, practicing in four different offices in the country. The client base is European, principally Swiss and Italian.

PARTNERS

GIANGIORGIO SPIESS, born 1933; admitted, 1959. *Education:* University of Bern (Lic. iur., 1957). Notary Public. *Member:* International Bar Association. *LANGUAGES:* Italian, French, German and English. *PRACTICE AREAS:* Commercial Law; Banking and Financial Services; Corporate Law; Business Law; Notary.

BRENNO BRUNONI, born 1948; admitted, 1976. *Education:* University of Bern (Lic. iur., 1973). Notary Public. *LANGUAGES:* Italian, French, German and English. *PRACTICE AREAS:* Litigation and Arbi-

(This Listing Continued)

---

tration; Contracts; Civil Law; International Private Law; Administrative Law; Notary.

MASSIMO PEDRAZZINI, born 1963; admitted, 1989. *Education:* University of Geneva (Lic. iur., 1985). *LANGUAGES:* Italian, French, German and English. *PRACTICE AREAS:* Corporate Law; Business Law; International Law; Contracts.

ANDREA MOLINO, born 1963; admitted, 1991. *Education:* University of Zurich (Lic. iur., 1988). *LANGUAGES:* Italian, French, German and English. *PRACTICE AREAS:* Commercial Law; Banking and Financial Services; Corporate Law.

DR. ARMANDO PEDRAZZINI, born 1923; admitted, 1950. *Education:* University of Bern (Dr. iur., 1947). Notary Public. *LANGUAGES:* Italian, French and German. *PRACTICE AREAS:* Civil Law; Contracts; Litigation; Notary.

ASSOCIATES

JOHN ROSSI, born 1938; admitted, 1968. *Education:* University of Bern (Lic. iur., 1965). Notary Public. *LANGUAGES:* Italian, French, German and English. *PRACTICE AREAS:* Criminal Law; Civil Law; Administrative Law; Litigation; Notary.

HENRI-PHILIPPE SAMBUC, born 1950; admitted, 1978, Geneva Bar. *Education:* University of Lausanne (Lic. iur., 1974). *LANGUAGES:* French and English. *PRACTICE AREAS:* Business Law; Commercial Law; National and International Taxation; International and Private Law; Arbitration and Litigation; Chinese Law.

MARIA CRISTINA BONFIO, born 1960; admitted, 1987. *Education:* University of Lausanne (Lic. iur., 1984). Notary Public. *LANGUAGES:* Italian, French and German. *PRACTICE AREAS:* Real Estate Transactions; Corporate Law; Contracts; Notary.

DONATELLA MONTI LANG, born 1960; admitted, 1990. *Education:* University of Fribourg (Lic. iur., 1987). *LANGUAGES:* Italian, French and German. *PRACTICE AREAS:* Civil Law; Family Law; Litigation.

DR. DOMENICO PIOVESANA, born 1958; admitted, 1987, Court of Venice (Not admitted in Switzerland). *Education:* University of Bologna (Dr. iur., 1983); University of Turin (M.B.A., 1985). *LANGUAGES:* Italian and English. *PRACTICE AREAS:* Corporate Law; International and National Taxation.

BRENNO MARTIGNONI, born 1962; admitted, 1989. *Education:* University of Zurich (Lic. jur. 1987). Notary Public. *LANGUAGES:* Italian, French and German. *PRACTICE AREAS:* Civil Law; Criminal Law; Administrative Law; Litigation; Insolvency; Notary.

MICHEL DE LUIGI, born 1963; admitted, 1989. *Education:* University of Fribourg (Lic. iur., 1987). Notary Public. *LANGUAGES:* Italian, French, German and English. *PRACTICE AREAS:* International and National Taxation; Real Estate Transactions; Corporate Law; Notary.

MICHELA HOHL, born 1965; admitted, 1992. *Education:* University of Fribourg (Lic.iur., 1989). Notary Public. *LANGUAGES:* Italian, French, German and English. *PRACTICE AREAS:* Commercial Law; Civil Law; Inheritance; Notary.

STEFANO PIZZOLA, born 1963; admitted, 1990. *Education:* University of Geneva (Lic.iur., 1987). *LANGUAGES:* Italian, French and German. *PRACTICE AREAS:* Civil Law; Criminal Law; Litigation; Insolvency.

VELO & ASSOCIATI

5, VIA SOAVE
6901 LUGANO, SWITZERLAND
Telephone: (091) 22.05.92
Telefax: (091) 23.58.73

Geneva, Switzerland Office: Velo, Villa & Associés. 3, Rue de la Vallée, 1204. Telephone: (022) 312.04.44. Telefax: (022) 312.05.55.

International and General Practice. Corporation, Taxation, Banking Law. Litigation, Contracts.

MEMBERS OF FIRM

LUCIO VELO, born 1951; admitted, 1981, Lugano and Geneva. *Education:* University of Lausanne, Switzerland (degree in Political Science); University of Geneva, Switzerland (degree in Law). *Member:* International Bar Association; Bar Association of Lugano; Bar Association of Geneva. *LANGUAGES:* Italian, English, French, Spanish, German.

(This Listing Continued)

FRANCO VILLA, born 1956; admitted, 1982, Geneva; 1987, Lugano. *Education:* University of Geneva, Switzerland (degree in Law). *Member:* Bar Association of Lugano; Bar Association of Geneva. (In charge of Geneva Office). *LANGUAGES:* Italian, French, English, German.

PATRIZIA GALIMBERTI, born 1959; admitted, 1984, Lugano. *Education:* University of Zürich, Switzerland (degree in Law). *LANGUAGES:* Italian, German, French, English.

GIANNI MASERA, born 1961; admitted, 1988, Lugano. *Education:* University of Geneva, Switzerland (degree in Law). *LANGUAGES:* Italian, French, German, English.

EMANUELE ALEMAGNA, born 1964; admitted, 1992, Lugano. *Education:* University of Lausanne, Switzerland (degree in Law); University of Pennsylvania (LL.M.). *LANGUAGES:* Italian, French, English.

CARLO VITALINI, born 1961; admitted, 1993, Lugano. *Education:* University of Pavia, Italy (degree in Law). *LANGUAGES:* Italian, French, English, German.

MARCO SOLDATI, born 1963; admitted, 1994, Lugano. *Education:* University of Fribourg, Switzerland (degree in Law). *LANGUAGES:* Italian, French, English, German.

TANJA CAVALLI ZÜRCHER, born Locarno, Switzerland, October 9, 1966; admitted, 1994, Switzerland. *Education:* Locarno, Switzerland (1987); Zurich, Switzerland (1991). *LANGUAGES:* Italian, French, German, English, Spanish.

DR. JUR. GIANMARIA BIANCHETTI, born 1959. *Education:* University of Milan, Italy (degree in Law). *LANGUAGES:* Italian, French, German.

SHAISTA RUGGIA-SATTAR, born 1964; admitted, 1992, London (Barrister). *Education:* University of Draka, Bangladesh (degree in Law); University of Buckingham, U.K. (degree in Law). Member, Honourable Society of the Inner Temple, London, U.K. *LANGUAGES:* English, Italian, Urdu, Hindi, Bengali.

DR. JUR. ILARIA RUGGERI D'URSO, born 1966. *Education:* University of Milan, Italy (degree in Law). *LANGUAGES:* Italian, French, English, Spanish.

DR. JUR. NICOLA GIANOLI, born 1964. *Education:* University of Milan, Italy (degree in Law). *LANGUAGES:* Italian, French, English, German.

LIC. JUR. ENEA PETRINI, born 1967. *Education:* University of Fribourg, Switzerland (degree in Law). *LANGUAGES:* Italian, French, English, Spanish, German.

DARDEL ET MEYLAN

RUE DE LA TREILLE 3
2001 NEUCHÂTEL, SWITZERLAND
Telephone: 038/24.77.47
Telecopier: 038/25.00.18

Business Organizations, Insurance, International Sales and Related Commercial Transactions, Family Law, Individual Tax and Estate Planning, Wills, Trusts and Their Administration, Business Migration, Immigration and Nationality Law, Intellectual Property.

FIRM PROFILE: The firm has a broadly-based practice with a reputation for offering a full range of quality legal services such as real estate, commercial law, corporate law, banking and business law. The firm is also active in property, inheritance, contracts, debt collection and bankruptcy law.

It handles litigation and provides full notarial service where under Swiss law a notary has to act, in particular in connection with the incorporation or restructuring of corporations, real estate, matrimonial property, agreements, etc.

MEMBERS OF FIRM

AMIOD DE DARDEL, born Neuchâtel, Switzerland, October 29, 1933; admitted, 1958, Neuchâtel; 1963, Notary. *Education:* Gymnase of Neuchâtel (Bachelor of Arts, 1951); University of Neuchâtel (Licence en Droit, 1956). *LANGUAGES:* French and German. *PRACTICE AREAS:* Corporate; Contracts; Inheritance Law; Administrative; Insurance; Tax; Real Estate; Estate Planning.

LUC A. MEYLAN, born Vevey, Switzerland, July 21, 1947; admitted, 1973, Notary in Neuchâtel; admitted attorney, 1986, Neuchâtel; 1987,

(This Listing Continued)

Bern; 1988, Zürich; 1989 Genèva. *Education:* College of Bern (Bachelor of Arts, 1967); University of Neuchâtel (Licence en Droit, 1971). *LANGUAGES:* French, English and German. *PRACTICE AREAS:* Corporate; Contracts; Inheritance Law; Administrative; Real Estate.

MARTINE FAVARGER, born Neuchâtel, Switzerland, February 13, 1955; admitted, 1982, Neuchâtel and Geneva. *Education:* University of Neuchâtel (Licence en droit, 1980); Northwestern University (LL.M., 1983). *LANGUAGES:* French, English and German. *PRACTICE AREAS:* Corporate; Contracts; Commercial Law; Banking; Civil Litigation.

PIRENNE PYTHON SCHIFFERLI PETER & PARTNERS

6, AVENUE REVERDIL
1260 NYON, SWITZERLAND
Telephone: (41 22) 361 18 04
Telefax: (41 22) 362 37 75

Geneva, Switzerland Office: 3, Rue Bellot, 1206. Telephone: (41 22) 347 46 45. Telex: 427 994 PPSP CH. Telecopier: (41 22) 346 85 76;347 80 54.

Bern, Switzerland Office: Sulgenrain 14, 3007. Telephone: (41 31) 372 40 46. Telefax:(41 31) 372 45 11.

Commercial and Contract Law, Banking, Corporate Finance, Swiss and International Taxation, Litigation, International Arbitration, Construction Law, Residence and Work Permits.

RESIDENT PARTNER

BERNHARD CRON, born Basel, Switzerland, April 9, 1946. Admitted, 1978, St. Gall and Zurich; 1981, Geneva; 1986, Vaud. *Education:* University of St. Gall (M.B.A. joined program of economics and law); University of Michigan Law School (LL.M., 1981). Assistant, Institute of Finance Economy and Tax Law, University of St. Gall, 1974-1975. *Member:* Geneva and Swiss Bar Associations; International Bar Association; Swiss Arbitration Association. *LANGUAGES:* French, German and English.

ASSOCIATES

BERNADETTE SCHINDLER VELASCO, born Neuchâtel, Switzerland, January 6, 1957; admitted, 1982, Neuchâtel; 1990, Geneva and Vaud. *Education:* University of Neuchâtel (Licence en droit, 1979); Graduate Institute of International Studies, Geneva (1985). (Also at Geneva Office). *LANGUAGES:* French, English, German and Spanish.

GIOVANNI M. ROSSI, born Rome, Italy, May 13, 1969; admitted, 1993, Geneva and Vaud. *Education:* University of Geneva (Licence en Droit, 1991). *Member:* Geneva and Swiss Bar Associations; Swiss Arbitration Association. *LANGUAGES:* French, Italian, English and German.

Languages: French, English, German, Italian and Spanish

(For complete Biographical data on all Firm Personnel, see Professional Biographies at Geneva, Switzerland).

DRES. KUNDERT, SCHILLER, DENZLER & DUBS

CASINOSTRASSE 2
CH-8401 WINTERTHUR, SWITZERLAND
Telephone: 011 41/52 212 72 31
Telex: 76 596 KURE
Telefax: 011 41/52 212 39 81

MEMBERS OF FIRM

Dr. Heinz Kundert	Dr. Beat Denzler,
Dr. Kaspar Schiller, Diploma in	LL.M. (Harvard Law School)
Financial Studies (Heriot-Watt	Dr. Jürg Dubs
University, Edinburgh)	

ASSOCIATES

lic.iur. Daniel Maritz, LL.M.	Dr. Heinrich Hempel
(Free University of Brussels)	

Languages: German, English, French and Italian

FRICK & FRICK

UNTER ALTSTADT 28
P.O. BOX 234
CH-6301 ZUG, SWITZERLAND
Telephone: +41-42/22.66.30
Fax: +41-42/22.66.36

Zurich, Switzerland Office: Uraniastrasse 12, P.O. Box 996, CH-8021.
Telephone: +41-1/211.29.11. Fax: +41-1/211.29.30.
Prague, Czech Republic Office: Office 422a, 4th Floor, Národni trida 10,
CZ-11319 Prague 1. Telephone: +42-2/24.91.30.44. Fax:
+42-2/24.91.34.35.
Sofia, Bulgaria Office: Boulevard Witoscha 25, P.O. Box 475, BG-1000.
Telephone: +359-2/81.33.88. Telefax: +359-2/81.33.85.
In Association with Law Office s in China: Beijing - Qingdao - Shanghai.

General Commercial Practice, Corporate Law, International Contracts,
Law on Unfair Competition, Matters of Product Liability, Mergers and
Acquisitions, Joint Venture Contracts, Privatization Projects, National and
International Arbitration, Litigation, Intellectual Property and Advertising
Law, Real Estate and Construction Law, Tax Law, Inheritance and Estate
Planning, Administrative Matters, Landlords Law.

MEMBERS OF FIRM

Hans Frick	Peter Hofer
Georges Frick	Dr. Titus J. Pachmann
	George Hunziker

The Firm is a Member of CONSULEGIS EEIG Attorneys at Law, a European-Wide grouping of Law Firms.

Languages: German, English, French, Italian, Spanish and Bulgarian

(For Complete Biographical Data on all Personnel see, Zurich,
Switzerland)

FRICK WIDMER VUILLE NEUPERT & PARTNERS

Established in 1851

CHAMERSTRASSE 14
6301 ZUG, SWITZERLAND
Telephone: 042 21 65 91
Telefax: 042 21 83 73

Zollikon/Zürich, Switzerland Office: Dufourstrasse 60, 8702. Telephone:
01/391 33 11. Cable Address: "Feye CH." Telex: 817 600. Telefax:
01/391 38 40.

Corporate, Commercial Tax, Banking, Real Estate, Trust, License and
Trademarks, Unfair Competition and Aviation Law, Litigation, Notarial
Acts.

RESIDENT PARTNER

LIC. PETER B. ARNOLD, born New York, U.S.A., December 2, 1958;
admitted, 1987, Zurich. Education: University of Zurich (Lic.iur., 1984).
Notary Public to the Canton of Zug/Switzerland since 1987. Member: Zurich and Swiss Bar Associations. LANGUAGES: German, English and
French.

FRORIEP RENGGLI

BAARERSTRASSE 75
6300 ZUG, SWITZERLAND
Telephone: (+41)-42 21 33 71
Telecopier: (+41)-42 23 07 15

Zürich, Switzerland Office: Bellerivestrasse 201, 8034. Telephone: (+41)1
386 60 00. Telecopier: (+41)1 383 60 50 (Address until April 30,
1995: General Wille-Strasse 10, 8027. Telephone: (+41) 12017420.
Telex: 815596 frp ch. Telecopier: (+41) 12023666).
Geneva, Switzerland Office: 4, Rue Charles-Bonnet, 1206. Telephone:
(+41)-22 347 18 18. Telex: 423651 frob ch. Telecopier: (+41)-22 347
71 59.
London, England Office: 1 Knightrider Court, EC4V 5JP. Telephone:
(+44)171 236 60 00. Fax: (+44)171 248 02 09.
Fuerth (Nürnberg), Germany Office: Friedrichstrasse 6, 90762. Telephone:
(+49)-911 77 39 82. Telecopier: (+49)-911 749 84 51.

(This Listing Continued)

Commercial, Corporate and Civil Practice, International Business Transactions, Commercial Litigation and International Commercial Arbitration,
Private and Public International Law, Banking, Taxation, Immigration,
Bankruptcy, International Judicial Assistance, Trade Marks and Copyrights, Estate, Real Property, Aviation and EEC Law.

FIRM PROFILE: Established in 1966, Froriep Renggli has grown to be
one of the leading and largest Swiss law firms with principal offices in
Zurich, Geneva and Zug. The firm is engaged in a broad range of Swiss
and International practice. Froriep Renggli currently has a total of thirty-two lawyers, twelve of whom are partners. Two of the associates are qualified German lawyers, four lawyers are also admitted in New York and one
is an English solicitor. Most of the lawyers have had, in addition to their
Swiss training, legal education in England or the United States and/or
have practice as foreign consultants with law firms there or elsewhere
abroad. The firm has a three lawyers strong London office, an office in
Fürth/Nürnberg, Germany, and an associated office in Bratislava, Slovakia. These, combined with an extensive network of correspondent lawyers,
enhance the firm's international advisory, transactional and litigation capabilities.

PARTNERS

HANS STUBER, born Risch, Switzerland, May 1, 1943; admitted, 1979,
Switzerland. Education: University of Zurich (Lic.iur., 1975). LANGUAGES: German, English and French. PRACTICE AREAS: Commercial Law; Corporate Law; International Trusts and Estates; Leases; Taxation; Real Estate; Wills; Inheritance; Insurance; Eastern European Commerce; Notarial Services.

RESIDENT ASSOCIATES

HERBERT C. SCHLAUBITZ, born Meikirch, Switzerland, April 19,
1959; admitted, 1986, Bern and Zurich. Education: University of Berne
(Fuersprecher, 1986). LANGUAGES: German, French and English.
PRACTICE AREAS: Commercial Law; Corporate Law; Arbitration; Intellectual Property.

GABRIELA GRIMM, born Zug, Switzerland, September 15, 1965; admitted, 1992, Switzerland. Education: University of Zurich (Lic. iur. 1990).
LANGUAGES: German, English and French. PRACTICE AREAS: Corporate Law; Contract Law; Product Liability; Immigration; Family Law
and Estates; Leases; Notarial Services.

OF COUNSEL

DR. GUIDO M. RENGGLI, born Zug, Switzerland, April 27, 1931;
admitted, 1959, Switzerland. Education: Universities of Fribourg and Berne
(Dr.iur., 1955). LANGUAGES: German, Swedish, English, French and
Italian. PRACTICE AREAS: Commercial Law; Corporate Law; International Contract Law; Arbitration.

(For Biographical Data on all Members, see Professional Biographies at
Zurich, Switzerland).

HARTMANN & MEYER AND PARTNERS

GRAFENAUWEG 8
6300 ZUG, SWITZERLAND
Telephone: (+41) 42-22 30 40
Telecopier: (+41) 42 22 23 53

Zürich, Switzerland Office: Zürichbergstrasse 66 CH-8044 Zürich.
Telephone: (+41) 1-251 77 12. Telecopier: (+41) 1-251 78 11.

Business and Corporate Law, International Trade, Commercial Contracts,
Banking and Tax Law, Unfair Competition, Transportation Law, Industrial Property Rights (Patent, Trademark, Know-how) Law, Licensing,
Agency and Distribution Law, Debt Collection and Bankruptcy Law, Employment Law, International Judicial Assistance Law, Arbitration and Litigation.

FIRM PROFILE: Full range of legal services with emphasis on business
and corporate law. Work conducted in German, English and French. Advanced office automation systems. Access to national and international
data bases in the legal and economic fields. Extensive network of correspondent national and international law firms.

(This Listing Continued)

MEMBERS OF FIRM

DR. JÜRG E. HARTMANN, born 1949; admitted, 1975. *Education:* University of Zürich (Dr.iur., 1974); University of California at Berkeley. Author: "Der Akkreditiveröffnungsauftrag," Zurich, 1974, "Der Kaufvertrag in der Handelspraxis," Zurich, 1979. Co-Author: "Der Alleinvertriebsvertrag," Zurich, 1984; "Neues schweizerisches Aktienrecht," Zurich 1992. *Member:* Swiss and Zurich Bar Associations; International Bar Association. *LANGUAGES:* German, English and French. *PRACTICE AREAS:* Business Law and Corporate Law; Banking Law; Antitrust Law; Tax Law; International Litigation and Arbitration.

DR. BERNHARD F. MEYER-HAUSER, LL.M., born 1946; admitted, 1975. *Education:* University of Zurich (Dr.Iur., 1979); Northwestern University School of Law, Chicago (LL.M., 1977). Author: "Swiss Banking Secrecy and Its Legal Implications in the United States," Article, New England Law Review 14, No. 1, 1979. Co-Author: "Swiss Work Permit Regulations," Overview and Translation of Limitation Ordinance, Swiss-American Chamber of Commerce, 1989; "Enforcement of a Money Claim in Switzerland, Zurich 1994"; "Agency and Distribution Agreements in Switzerland," 1991; "Swiss Contract Law" and "Swiss Company Law," English translations of official text of Swiss Code of Obligations, 1992. *Member:* Swiss and Zurich Bar Associations; International Bar Association; American Bar Association; Swiss Arbitration Association. *LANGUAGES:* German, English and French. *PRACTICE AREAS:* Business and Corporate Law; Company Foundations; Employment Law and Work Permits; Licensing, Agency and Distribution Law; Unfair Competition Law; International Litigation and Arbitration.

DR. NIKLAUS B. MÜLLER, LL.M., born 1951; admitted, 1977. *Education:* University of Berne (Dr.Iur., 1979); University of California at Berkeley (LL.M., 1980). Author: "Die Rechtsprechung des Bundesgerichts zum Grundsatz der verfassungskonformen Auslegung," Bern, 1980. *Member:* Swiss and Zurich Bar Associations; International Bar Association; Swiss Arbitration Association. *LANGUAGES:* German, English and French. *PRACTICE AREAS:* International Litigation and Arbitration; Banking Law; Contracts Law; Patents Law; Taxes and Bankruptcy Law.

DR. CHRISTOPH P.A. MARTIG, born 1956; admitted, 1987. *Education:* University of Zürich (Dr.jur., 1983); University of California at Berkeley. born 1956; admitted, 1987. *Education:* University of Zurich (Dr. iur., 1983); University of California at Berkeley. Author: "Reederhaftung im Rheinfrachtgeschäft," Basel, 1984; "Ermittlung und Anwendung materiellen Rechts im schweizerischen See- und Rheinfrachtrecht," Zurich 1992. *Member:* Swiss and Zurich Bar Associations. *LANGUAGES:* German, English and French. *PRACTICE AREAS:* Business and Corporate Law; Shipping and Transportation Law; Industrial Property Law; Residential Property and Inheritance Law.

DR. FELIX W. EGLI, LL.M., born 1960; admitted, 1987. *Education:* University of St. Gallen (Dr.Iur., 1989); Southern Methodist University Dallas (LL.M., 1988). Author: "Der Nichtdiskriminierungsbegriff im Versicherungsabkommen Schweiz - EWG," Hartung-Gorre Verlag, Konstanz, 1989; "Die Anerkennung und Vollstreckung deutscher, österreichischer und liechtensteinischer Gerichtsentscheidungen in Zivil- und Handelssachen in der Schweiz," RIW 12/1991. Co-Author: "Agency and Distribution Agreements in Switzerland," 1991. *Member:* Swiss and Zurich Bar Associations; Swiss Arbitration Association. *LANGUAGES:* German, English, French and Italian. *PRACTICE AREAS:* Business and Corporate Law; Company Law; Intellectual Property; International Trade Law; Conflicts of Law; Litigation and Arbitration.

ASSOCIATES

DR. JÜRG BORER, born 1958; admitted 1990. *Education:* University of St. Gall (Dr. Iur., 1988). Author: "Massnahmen gleicher Wirkung wie mengenmässige Einfuhrbeschränkungen im Freihandelsabkommen Schweiz-EWG," Bern 1988; "Grundlagen des Warenverkehrs im Freihandelsabkommen Schweiz-EWG," 1988; "Spruchpraxis zum EG-Wettbewerbsrecht," 1990; *Member:* Swiss and Zurich Bar Associations. *LANGUAGES:* German, English and French. *PRACTICE AREAS:* Business and Corporate Law; Antitrust Law; European Community Law; International Law; Conflicts of Law.

HANS-ULRICH SCHOCH. *Education:* University of Zürich (lic.iur., 1988). born 1962; admitted 1991. *Education:* University of Zurich (lic.iur., 1988). Co-Author: "Neues schweizerisches Aktienrecht," Zurich 1992. *Member:* Swiss and Zurich Bar Associations. *LANGUAGES:* German, English and French. *PRACTICE AREAS:* Business and Corporate Law; Debt Enforcement and Bankruptcy Law; Agency and Distribution Law; Unfair Competition Law.

(This Listing Continued)

DR. GION-ANDRI DECURTINS, born, 1964; admitted 1994. *Education:* University of Fribourg (Dr.jur., 1992); University of San Diego School of Law (M.C.L., 1991). Author: "Die rechtliche Stellung der Behörde im Abstimmungskamf", Fribourg 1992. *Member:* Swiss and Zurich Bar Associations. *LANGUAGES:* German, English, Italian and French. *PRACTICE AREAS:* Business and Corporate Law; Agency and Distribution Law; Intellectual Property Law; Inheritance Law; Debt Enforcement and Bankruptcy Law; Employment Law; Administrative Law.

LUKA MÜLLER, born 1964, admitted 1992. *Education:* University of Zurich (lic.jur., 1990); London School of Economics (LL.M. 1994). *Member:* Swiss and Zurich Bar Associations. *LANGUAGES:* German, English, French. *PRACTICE AREAS:* Business and Corporate Law; Unfair Competition; Insurance Law; Torts and Product Liability.

(For complete Biographical Data on all Members and Associates of the Firm, see Professional Biographies at Zürich/Switzerland).

HANS A. VOGEL

Established in 1983

GUBELSTRASSE 17
ZUG CH-6300, SWITZERLAND
Telephone: 042-21 31 20
Telefax: 042. 21 31 21

General Commercial, Corporate and Notarial Practice, International Company, Licensing, Contract, Estate and Tax Law, Arbitration, Litigation.

DR. HANS A. VOGEL, born Zurich, Switzerland, November 17, 1946; admitted, 1977, Switzerland. *Education:* Universities of Cologne and Zurich (lic. iur., 1971; Dr. iur., 1973). Department Manager, International Licensing and Legal Matters, F. Hoffmann-La Roche & Co. AG, Basel, 1978-1982. *Member:* Swiss and International Bar Associations. *LANGUAGES:* German, English, French, Italian and Spanish.

WINTER & PARTNER

BAHNHOFSTRASSE 16
CH-6300 ZUG, SWITZERLAND
Telephone: (042) 22 18 20
Facsimile: (042) 23 44 23

Zürich, Switzerland Office: Kirchgasse 40, CH-8024. Telephone: (01) 251 81 00. Facsimile: (01) 251 81 28. Telex: 816981 wint ch.

Budapest, Hungary Office: Benczur U, 13, H-1068 Budapest. Telephone: (1) 122 98 40. Facsimile: (1) 122 62 67. Telex: 22 65 70.

Commercial, Corporate and Civil Practice, International Trade and Commodities, Banking and Finance, Mergers and Acquisitions, Commercial Litigation and Arbitration, Estate Planning.

MEMBERS OF FIRM

Dr. Herbert Winter

(For complete biographical data on all personnel, see Professional Biographies at Zürich, Switzerland)

ALTENBURGER & PARTNERS

ALTE LANDSTRASSE 128
8702 ZOLLIKON/ZÜRICH, SWITZERLAND
Telephone: (1) 392.00.07
Telecopier: (1) 392.00.86

Contracts, Corporate, Business, Swiss and International Taxation, Banking and Finance Law, Mergers and Acquisitions, Intellectual Property and Trademarks, Unfair Competition, Insurance, Distribution and Franchising, European Law, Commercial Litigation and International Arbitration, Residence and Work Permits, Debt Collection and Bankruptcy Law, Securitization.

PARTNERS

DR. PETER ROBERT ALTENBURGER, born Zürich, Switzerland, February 3, 1945; admitted, 1973, Zürich; 1990, Geneva. *Education:* European Institute of Business Administration, Fontainebleau, France (M.B.A., 1971); Universities of Zürich and Basle (lic.iur, 1969; Dr.jur., 1977); University of Michigan Law School (Master of Comparative Law, 1970). Member: Tax Management International Forum, 1980—. Co-Author: "Survey of Foreign Laws and Regulations Affecting International Franchising," American Bar Association, 1982; "Tax Management Foreign Income Portfolios -

(This Listing Continued)

ALTENBURGER & PARTNERS, Zürich—Continued

Business Operations in Switzerland." *Member:* Swiss and International Bar Associations; American Bar Association (International Associate). *LANGUAGES:* German, English, French and Italian. *PRACTICE AREAS:* International Taxation Law; Merger and Acquisitions Law; Corporate Law.

LEONHARD J. TOENZ, born Vals, Switzerland, September 20, 1956; admitted, 1981, Graubünden; 1986, Genf; 1990, Zürich. *Education:* University of Fribourg, Switzerland (lic.iur., 1980). *Member:* Swiss and International Bar Associations. *LANGUAGES:* German, French and English. *PRACTICE AREAS:* Insurance Law; Swiss and International Taxation; Banking Law; General Commercial law.

DR. ARMIN A. STRUB, born Zürich, Switzerland, July 20, 1937; admitted, 1966, Zürich; 1993, Aargau and Basle. *Education:* University of Zürich (Dr.iur., 1962); University of Chicago Law School (M.C.L., 1964). Editor and Co-author: Aktuelles Handbuch zum Unternehmenskauf und -verkauf 1991 (handbook on acquisition and divestitures). *Member:* Swiss Bar Association; Swiss Private Equity and Corporate Finance Association. *LANGUAGES:* German, English, French and Italian. *PRACTICE AREAS:* Distribution; Licensing; EEC Antitrust; Reorganizations; Joint Ventures; Acquisitions and Divestitures; MBO; Labor Law; Decedents' Estates; Pension Laws; Executive Pension Plans; Litigation.

GITTI HUG KETTMEIR, born Zürich, Switzerland, March 12, 1951; admitted, 1982, Zürich. *Education:* Kantonsschule, Neuchâtel, Switzerland (Matura H, 1972); University of St. Gallen, Switzerland (lic.oec., HSG, 1976); University of Zürich (cand.iur., 1980). Author: "Schutz der Photographie aus schweizerischer Sicht, ZKM, Zeitschrift für Urheber - und Medienrecht," 12/1989, Baden-Baden, 1989. *Member:* Swiss Bar Association; Zürich Bar Association; Licensing Executives Society; INGRES. *LANGUAGES:* German, French, English and Italian. *PRACTICE AREAS:* Copyright; Neighboring Right.

ASSOCIATES

BJÖRN BAJAN, born Biel, Switzerland, July 22, 1960; admitted, 1989, Zurich. *Education:* University of Zurich (lic.iur., 1986); University of London, Queen Mary and Westfield College (LL.M., 1994). *Member:* Swiss Bar Association; Swiss Association of Arbitrators; Chartered Institute of Arbitrators, London. *LANGUAGES:* German, French and English. *PRACTICE AREAS:* Litigation and Arbitration; Bankruptcy Law; Commercial and Corporate Law; Trade Law and Trade Finance.

JÜRG A. KOEFERLI, born Zürich, Switzerland, June 29, 1963; admitted, 1991, Zürich. *Education:* Kantonsschule, Zürich, Switzerland (Matura E, 1982); University of Zürich (l ic.iur., 1988; Dr.iur., 1994). *Member:* Swiss Bar Association; Zurich Bar Association. *LANGUAGES:* German, English and French. *PRACTICE AREAS:* Litigation; Commercial and Corporate Law; Contract Law; Bankruptcy Law.

COUNSELS

MARKUS J. KROLL, born Zürich, Switzerland, July 26, 1960. *Education:* University of Zürich (lic.oec.publ., 1987; Dr.oec.publ., 1991; lic.iur., 1991); London School of Economics and Political Science (LL.M., 1992). *Member:* International Bar Association; Swiss Association of Arbitrators; Chartered Institute of Arbitrators, London. *LANGUAGES:* German, English, Italian and French. *PRACTICE AREAS:* Banking Law; Financial Services; Asset Finance; Securitization; Project Finance; Capital Markets; Trade Finance; Restructurings.

FRANCIS A. ZOLLER, born Zürich, Switzerland, June 22, 1950. *Education:* Swiss based; completed CPA exams in 1976. *Member:* Swiss Auditors' Association. *LANGUAGES:* German, English, French and Italian.

BAKER & McKENZIE

(Achermann, Müller, Heini & Wehrli)

ZOLLIKERSTRASSE 225
8034 ZÜRICH, SWITZERLAND
Telephone: (01) 384 14 14
Intn'l. Dialing: (41-1) 384 14 14
Facsimile: (41-1) 384 12 84
Postal Address: P.O. Box 57

General Corporate, Mergers and Acquisitions, Tax, Banking and Finance, Intellectual Property, Antitrust and Unfair Competition, Commercial Litigation, Arbitration, Administrative and Regulatory Matters.

(This Listing Continued)

EU1388B

PARTNERS

LIC. IUR. PETER ACHERMANN, born Lucerne, Switzerland, 1932; admitted, 1957, Switzerland. *Education:* Universities of Berne, Paris and Geneva (Lic. iur., 1955); University of Chicago Law School (M.C.L., 1958). *Member:* Zurich and Swiss Bar Associations.

PROF. DR. ANTON C. HEINI, born Lucerne, Switzerland, 1930; admitted, 1962, Switzerland. *Education:* Universities of Zurich and Fribourg (Dr.iur., 1957); City of London College and New York University School of Law. Professor of Law, University of Zurich. *Member:* Zurich and Swiss Bar Associations.

PHILIP MARCOVICI, born Montreal, Canada, 1956; admitted, 1982, New York, U.S.A.; 1986, British Columbia, Canada; 1991, England and Wales and Hong Kong (Not admitted in Switzerland). *Education:* Vanier College, Canada (D.C.S.); McGill University; University of Ottawa (LL.B., 1980); Harvard Law School (LL.M., 1983). *Member:* New York County Lawyers Association; Canadian and American Bar Associations (Tax Sections); Canadian Tax Foundation; International Fiscal Association.

DR. JOHANNES J. MÜLLER, born Buch/Frauenfeld, Switzerland, 1930; admitted, 1961, Switzerland; 1966, Illinois, USA. *Education:* University of Fribourg (lic.iur., 1956; Dr.iur., 1961); Yale Law School (LL.M., 1958); Stanford University and Chicago-Kent College of Law (J.D., 1966). *Member:* Zurich and Swiss Bar Associations.

DR. FRANZ W. SCHENKER, born Solothurn, Switzerland, 1955; admitted, 1986, Switzerland. *Education:* University of Fribourg (lic.iur., 1981; Dr.iur., 1988); University of California, Berkeley, Boalt Hall School of Law (LL.M., 1988). *Member:* Zurich and Swiss Bar Associations.

DR. URS SCHENKER, born Zurich, Switzerland, 1957; admitted, 1986, Switzerland. *Education:* University of Zurich (lic.iur., 1981; Dr.iur., 1984); Harvard Law School (LL.M., 1985). *Member:* Zurich and Swiss Bar Associations.

DR. MAX WEHRLI, born Zurich, Switzerland, 1942; admitted, 1971, Switzerland. *Education:* University of Zurich (lic.iur., 1966; Dr.iur., 1969); University of Michigan (M.C.L., 1972). *Member:* Zurich and Swiss Bar Associations.

OF COUNSEL

PROF. DR. OSCAR VOGEL, born Zürich, Switzerland, 1926; admitted, 1956, Switzerland. *Education:* Gymnasium (Matur, 1946); University of Zurich (Dr., 1952). Judge, Zurich Appeal Court and Commercial Court, 1973-1993. President, Appeal Court, 1988-1992. President, Commercial Court, 1987-1993. *Member:* Zurich and Swiss Bar Associations; Swiss Lawyers Association; Swiss Arbitration Association.

ASSOCIATES

DR. MARKUS AFFENTRANGER, born Zurich, Switzerland, 1956; admitted, 1989, Switzerland. *Education:* University of Zurich (lic.iur., 1982; Dr.iur., 1987). *Member:* Zurich and Swiss Bar Associations.

DR. MARKUS H. BERNI, born St. Gallen, Switzerland, 1958; admitted, 1988, Switzerland. *Education:* University of St. Gallen (lic.iur., 1984; Dr.iur., 1992); University of Virginia (LL.M., 1991). *Member:* Zurich and Swiss Bar Associations.

FÜRSPRECHER MARTIN FREY, born Berne, Switzerland, 1956; admitted, 1984, Switzerland. *Education:* University of Berne (Fürsprecher, 1984); Georgetown University Law Center (LL.M., 1987). Practice in Washington, D.C., with Arnold & Porter. *Member:* Zurich and Swiss Bar Associations.

DR. JOACHIM G. FRICK, born Zurich, Switzerland, 1965; admitted, 1994, Switzerland. *Education:* Universities of Zurich and Paris (lic.iur., 1989; Dr.iur., 1992). *Member:* Zurich and Swiss Bar Associations.

DR. MARCEL GIGER, born St. Gallen, Switzerland, 1962; admitted, 1991, Switzerland. *Education:* University of St. Gallen (lic.iur., 1987; Dr.iur., 1992). *Member:* Zurich and Swiss Bar Associations.

LIC. IUR. KILIAN PERROULAZ, born Fribourg, Switzerland, 1964; admitted, 1993, Switzerland. *Education:* University of Fribourg (lic.iur., 1990). *Member:* Zurich and Swiss Bar Associations.

DR. PETER URS PAUL REINERT, born Zurich, Switzerland, 1962; admitted, 1993, Switzerland. *Education:* University of Zurich (Faculty of Law) (lic.iur., 1989; Dr.iur., 1992). *Member:* Zurich and Swiss Bar Associations.

DR. ROLF C. SCHMID, born Rapperswil, Switzerland, 1962; admitted, 1992, Switzerland. *Education:* University of St. Gallen (lic.iur., 1990;

(This Listing Continued)

Dr.iur., 1994); University of New York (M.C.J., 1994). *Member:* Zurich and Swiss Bar Associations.

DR. THOMAS STÄHELI, born Zurich, Switzerland, 1961; admitted, 1992, Switzerland. *Education:* Universities of Zurich and Basel (lic.iur., 1986; Dr.iur., 1989); College d'Europe Bruges, Belgium (D.H.E.E., 1991). *Member:* Zurich and Swiss Bar Associations.

DR. MICHAEL TREIS, born Alingsås, Sweden, 1957; admitted, 1988, Germany (Not admitted in Switzerland). *Education:* Universities of Munich and Lausanne (Referendar, 1985; Dr. jur., 1990). Max Planck Institute for Intellectual Property Law, Munich, 1985-1988. *Member:* Frankfurt and German Bar Associations.

DR. URS ZENHÄUSERN, born Zurich, Switzerland, 1960; admitted, 1993, Switzerland. *Education:* University of Fribourg (lic.iur., 1986; Dr.iur., 1991). *Member:* Zurich and Swiss Bar Associations.

Languages: German, English, French, Italian, Spanish and Swedish.

BÄR & KARRER

Established in 1938

SEEFELDSTRASSE 19
8024 ZÜRICH 8, SWITZERLAND
Telephone: (++41) 261 51 50
Telefax: (++41) 251 30 25
Telex: 815 463 bkz

Lugano, Switzerland Office: Riva Caccia 1A (Central Park), 6901 Lugano. Telephone: (++91) 55 00 64. Telex: (++91) 55 02 36.

General Commercial Practice, Corporate, Banking and Underwriting, Finance, International Arbitration, International Contracts, European Law, Taxation, Real Estate, Intellectual and Industrial Property and Copyright, Construction, Administrative Matters, Inheritance and Estate Planning, Civil Litigation in all Swiss Courts.

FIRM PROFILE: The law firm dates back to 1938. It is organized as a partnership of at present 11 partners employing 19 associates, all of them admitted to practice in the Canton of Zürich as well as in most other Cantons, including Basel, Bern, Geneva, Ticino and Zug. The main office is located in Zurich; a branch office is established in Lugano and notary public services are carried out in Lugano as well as in Zug. The firm represents Swiss and foreign corporate and individual clients. An extensive network of correspondent law firms around the globe is maintained.

MEMBERS OF FIRM

DR. THOMAS A. BÄR, born 1937; admitted, 1964, Switzerland. *Education:* University of Zürich (Dr.iur.); Harvard Law School (LL.M.). Author, "Take-overs, their Financing and Financial Defenses.".

DR. ROBERT KARRER, born 1937; admitted, 1965, Switzerland. *Education:* University of Zürich (Dr.iur.); University of Chicago Law School (M.C.L.). Judge (part-time), Zurich Court of Cassation, since 1982.

DR. MARTIN KARRER, born 1939; admitted, 1966, Switzerland. *Education:* University of Zürich (Dr.iur.); Osgoode Hall Law School, Toronto. Author, "The Swiss Company Limited by Shares." *Member:* The International Academy of Estate and Trust Law.

DR. HANS-ULRICH FREIMÜLLER, born 1940; admitted, 1965, Switzerland. *Education:* University of Berne (Dr.iur.); University of Paris Law School. Author: "Hybrid Corporate Securities: International Legal Aspects;" "Interim Court Remedies in Support of Arbitration.".

DR. MARC BLESSING, born 1944; admitted, 1972, Switzerland. *Education:* University of Geneva; University of Zürich (Dr.iur.); City of London Polytechnic. President, Swiss Arbitration Association (since 1991); Co-Chairman: Court of Arbitration of the Zürich Chamber of Commerce (since 1989); Member, London Court of International Arbitration (since 1993); Member, Arbitration Council of the World Intellectual Property Organization (since 1994); President, General Section, International Federation of Commercial Arbitration Institutions (IFCAI); listed on the panels of arbitrators of ICC, WIPO, AAA, LCIA, Chartered Institute of Arbitrators (ACIArb), Arbitration Courts of Stockholm, Vienna, Poland, Hungary, Bulgaria, PR of China, AAA/Russian Federation Agreement, CPR International Panel of Mediators. Author: "The New International Arbitration Law in Switzerland;" "The Major Western and Soviet Arbitration Rules;" "Proper Law and Dispute Resolution arising out of East-West Joint Ventures;" "The ICC Arbitral Process;" "Becoming a Centre for International Arbitration: The Major Requirements and Expectations of the Parties, their Counsel and Arbitrators;" "Drafting Arbitration Clauses;" "Extension of the

(This Listing Continued)

Arbitration Clause to Non-Signatories Group of Companies Doctrine;" numerous other publications in the field of international arbitration.

DR. PETER J. KIENAST, born 1945; admitted, 1975, Switzerland. *Education:* University of Zürich (Dr.iur.); Columbia University School of Law (LL.M.).

DR. CHRISTIAN E. STEINMANN, born 1950; admitted, 1978, Switzerland. *Education:* University of Zürich (Dr.iur.); University of California at Berkeley (LL.M.). Past Chairman, U.I.A. Permanent Commission for Tax Law, 1985-1991. Author: "Commentary on Articles 1157-1186 of the Swiss Code of Obligations.".

DR. NEDIM PETER VOGT, born 1952; admitted, 1984, Switzerland. *Education:* University of Zürich (Dr.iur.); Harvard Law School (LL.M.). Lecturer, University of Zürich, 1985 and University of St. Gallen for Business Administration, Economics, Law and Social Sciences, 1986-1989. Author: "Share Transfer Restrictions under Swiss Law and Hostile Take-Overs"; "Transfer of Corporate Domicile"; Co-Author: "International Corporate Governance" (Swiss Report); "Mergers and Acquisitions in Switzerland"; "Joint Ventures in Europe"; "Trial and Court Procedures Worldwide" (Swiss Report); "International Execution against Foreign Judgment Debtors" (Swiss Report). Co-Editor of a new Commentary on the Swiss Code of Obligations, the Swiss Civil Code and the new Swiss Private International Law.

DR. NICO H. BURKI, born 1950; admitted, 1979, Switzerland. *Education:* University of Basel (Dr.iur.); University of St. Gallen for Business Administration, Economics, Law and Social Sciences (Lic.oec.). Certified Swiss Tax Accountant. Board Member of Tax Chapter of the Swiss-American Chamber of Commerce; Country Correspondent for Tax Letter Europe; Member of the Tax Appeal Court.

DR. FELIX R. EHRAT, born 1957; admitted, 1985, Switzerland. *Education:* University of Lausanne; University of Zürich (Dr.iur.); University of the Pacific, McGeorge School of Law, Sacramento (LL.M.). Swiss Correspondent, World Tax Report. Author: "Commentary on Articles 151-163 of the Swiss Code of Obligations"; various other Reports in the field of contract and corporate law.

PD DR. ROLF WATTER, born 1958; admitted, 1986, Switzerland. *Education:* University of Zürich (Dr.iur.); Georgetown University, Washington, D.C. (LL.M.). Associate Professor (Privatdozent), University of Zürich, since 1990. Author: "Unternehmensübernahmen" (take-overs, changes of control by share purchase, tender offer and merger); "Market Manipulation and Price Stabilization"; "Prospectus Liability." Co-Author: "International Corporate Governance"; "Mergers and Acquisitions in Switzerland"; "Joint Ventures in Europe"; Commentaries on numerous Articles of the Swiss Company Law; various further publications in the field of banking law, corporate securities law. Co-Editor of the Swiss law journal "Aktuelle Juristische Praxis.".

ASSOCIATES

LIC. IUR. RENATA JUNGO, born 1961; admitted, 1989, Switzerland. *Education:* University of Fribourg.

LIC. IUR MARKUS SCHNURRENBERGER, born 1958; admitted, 1985, Switzerland. *Education:* University of Zürich. Also admitted and practising as notary public in the Canton of Zug.

LIC. IUR. DAVID F. KÄNZIG, born 1959; admitted, 1987, Switzerland; 1991, New York. *Education:* University of Zürich; New York University School of Law (M.C.J.).

LIC. IUR. GIANPAOLO ARRIGONI, born 1960; admitted, 1988, Switzerland; 1992, New York. *Education:* University of St. Gallen for Business Administration, Economics, Law and Social Sciences; New York University School of Law (M.C.J.). Author: "Swiss Report on Business Organizations.".

LIC. IUR. RENATO L. BLOCH, born 1958; admitted, 1987, Switzerland. *Education:* University of Geneva (Faculty of Economics and Faculty of Law). Also admitted and practising as notary public.

DR. ROLF AUF DER MAUR, born 1962; admitted, 1991, Switzerland. *Education:* University of Zürich (Dr.iur.); University of California, Los Angeles.

LIC. IUR. STEFAN D. NAEGELI, born 1962; admitted, 1988, Switzerland. *Education:* University of Zürich; New York University School of Law (M.C.J.).

LIC. IUR. DANIEL HOCHSTRASSER, born 1960; admitted, 1986, Switzerland. *Education:* University of Zürich; Cornell University, Ithaca

(This Listing Continued)

BÄR & KARRER, Zürich—Continued

(LL.M.). Author: "The Recognition and Enforcement of International Arbitral Awards in the United States: Tolerance of Lack of Control?"; "Choice of Law and 'Foreign' Mandatory Rules in International Arbitration.".

LIC. IUR. MICHAEL TRIPPEL, born 1961; admitted, 1992, Switzerland. *Education:* University of Zürich. Author: "Legal Summary" (Co-Author, Euromoney Publications).

LIC. IUR. PETER REINARZ, born 1958; admitted, 1987, Switzerland. *Education:* University of Zürich. Certified Swiss Tax Accountant. Author: "Foreign Tax and Treaty Issues Relevant to U.S. Business Operations"; "The New Swiss Federal Security Stamp Tax Law"; "Dutch Finance Companies with Branches in Switzerland - A Tool for Tax Efficient Intra-Group Financing"; other publications in the field of tax law.

DR. MARC AMSTUTZ, born 1962; admitted, 1993, Switzerland. *Education:* University of Bern; University of Zürich (Dr.iur.). Author: "Commentary on Article 793-804 and 818 Swiss Code of Obligations"; further publications on corporate law.

LIC. IUR. MARIE-THERESE MÜLLER, born 1961; admitted, 1994, Switzerland. *Education:* University of Bern; New York University School of Law (M.C.J.). Author: Publications on the Vienna Sales Convention and in the field of corporate law.

LIC. IUR. ERIC STUPP, born 1965; admitted, 1994, Switzerland. *Education:* University of St. Gallen for Business Administration, Economics, Law and Social Sciences.

DR. PETER HÄNSELER, born 1964; admitted, 1993, Switzerland. *Education:* University of Zürich (Dr.iur.); Georgetown University, Washington, D.C. (LL.M.).

FUERSPRECHER PETER SCHMID, born 1961; admitted, 1992, Switzerland. *Education:* University of Bern; Tulane University, New Orleans (LL.M.).

LIC. IUR. ALESSANDRA VON PLANTA, born 1965; admitted, 1991, Switzerland. *Education:* University of Geneva; New York University (LL.M.).

LIC.IUR. MICHELE BERNASCONI, born 1963; admitted, 1992, Switzerland. *Education:* University of Zürich.

DR. MARTINA WITTIBSCHLAGER, born 1964; admitted, 1993, Switzerland. *Education:* University of Basel; Yale Law School (LL.M.).

DR. RALPH MALACRIDA, born 1964; admitted, 1993,. *Education:* University of Zürich.

COUNSEL

DR. KLAUS HUG, born 1940; admitted, 1971, Switzerland. *Education:* University of Zürich (Dr.iur.). Former Assistant to the Federal Minister of Justice; former Director General of the Swiss Federal Office for Industry, Trade and Labour in Berne, 1984-1991. Author: various publications on the Swiss economy, the labour market and labour legislation.

All Attorneys of the Firm are Members of the Zürich and Swiss Bar Associations.

Languages: German, English, French and Italian

BAUR, SCHUMACHER & PARTNERS

Established in 1954

BAHNHOFPLATZ 9

8001 ZÜRICH, SWITZERLAND

Telephone: +41 (1) 212 80 90

Fax: +41 (1) 212 80 91

Other Offices: Baur, Schumacher & Partners, Attorneys-at-Law and Notary's offices, Oberstadtstrasse 7, CH - 5400 Baden. Telephone: +41 (56) 22 84 55. Fax: +41 (56) 22 65 23.

General Commercial Practice, Civil Litigation and Arbitration, International Business Transactions, Construction and Engineering Law, Commercial Contracts, Industrial Consortiums, Real Estate, Taxation and Tax Planning, Corporations, Trust and Wills, Bankruptcy Law, Torts, Administrative Law and Environmental Law.

(This Listing Continued)

OF COUNSEL

DR. HANS BAUR, born 1923; admitted, 1953, Switzerland. *Education:* University of Bern (lic.iur., 1949; Dr.iur., 1950). Notary Public, Canton of Aargau. Author: "Die wohlerworbenen Rechte des Aktionärs und ihre Ausgestaltung," Diss Bern, 1950; "Bemerkungen zum Anwaltsrecht," Festschrift: Aarg. Rechtspflege im Gang der Zeit, 1969. *Member:* Swiss Bar Association; Zurich Bar Association; Aargovian Bar Association; Notary's Association of Switzerland and Canton of Aargau.

PARTNERS

DR. RAINER SCHUMACHER, born 1932; admitted, 1961, Switzerland. *Education:* University of Fribourg (lic.iur., 1954; Dr.iur., 1960). Author: "Die Presseäusserung als Verletzung der persönlichen Verhältnisse, insbesondere ihre Widerrechtlichkeit," Diss. Fribourg, 1960; "Das Bauhandwerkerpfandrecht," Systematische Darstellung der Praxis, 2. Auflage, Zürich, 1982; "Gutachten zur Neuregelung der Bauhandwerkersicherungs hypothek (§ 648 Abs. 1 BGB)," Zweiter Bericht der Kommission für Insolvenzrecht, hsg. vom Bundesministerium der Justiz, Köln, 1986, S. 263 ff.; "Die Haftung des Architekten aus Vertrag," in GAUCH P./TERCIER P. (Herausgeber), Das Architektenrecht/ Le droit de l'architecte, 2. Auflage, Fribourg, 1989, S. 105 ff.; "Die Haftung des Grundstückverkäufers," in A. Koller (Herausgeber), Der Grundstückkauf, St. Gallen, 1989, S. 197 ff.; "Beweisprobleme im Bauprozess," in FS Eichenberger, Aarau, 1990, S. 157 ff.; "Kommentar zur SIA-Norm 118, Art. 38-156," in GAUCH/-SCHUMACHER, Zürich, 1992. *Member:* Swiss Bar Association; Zurich Bar Association; Aargovian Bar Association; Swiss Society of Construction Law.

DR. JÜRG BAUR, born 1950; admitted, 1978, Switzerland. *Education:* University of Zurich (lic.iur., 1974; Dr.iur., 1979). Notary Public, Canton of Aargau. Author: "Auskünfte und Zusagen der Steuerbehörden an Private im schweiz Steuerrecht," Diss. Zürich, 1979; "Kommentar zum aargauischen Steuergesetz," Co-Author: BAUR/KLÖTI-WEBER/KOCH/MEIER-/URSPRUNG, 1991. *Member:* Swiss Bar Association; Zurich Bar Association; Aargovian Bar Association; Notary's Association of Switzerland and Canton of Aargau.

DR. ROLAND HÜRLIMANN, LL.M. born 1957; admitted Switzerland. *Education:* University of Fribourg (Lic.iur., 1981; Dr.Jur., 1984); University of California, Berkeley, Boalt Hall School of Law (LL.M., 1987). Author: "Teilnichtigkeit von Schuldverträgen nach Art. 20 Abs. 2 OR," Diss. Fribourg, 1984; "Die Verantwortlichkeit des Architekten im amerikanischen Haftpflichtrecht Zeitschrift Baurecht 4/88, S. 75 ff; "Der Experte - Schlüsselfigur des Bauprozesses," in: In Sachen Baurecht, FS GAUCH, hsg. von TERCIER/HÜRLIMANN, Freiburg, 1990; S. 129 ff; "Reform of medical malpractice law: Liability or insurance? - National report of Switzerland," Co-Author Prof. P. GAUCH: Zürich 1990, vol 12: p. 71 ff; "Gerichtsstandsvereinbarungen unter Berücksichtigung der neuen IPRG," in: FS EICHENBERGER, Aarau 1990, S. 85 ff; "Subcontracting in Switzerland," in: The International Construction Law Review, London, Volume 8, 1991, p. 151; "International Arbitration in Switzerland," Arbitration and Dispute Resolution-Journal, 2, 1993. *Member:* Swiss Bar Association; Zurich Bar Association; Aargovian Bar Association; International Bar Association; Swiss Society of Construction Law; Swiss Arbitration Association.

LIC.IUR. ALFRED L. SCHWARTZ, born 1952; admitted, 1979, Switzerland. *Education:* University Zurich (lic.iur., 1976). Author: "Kommentar zum Schweizerischen OR, Art. 839-851 (zum Genossenschaftsrecht)." *Member:* Swiss Bar Association; Zurich Bar Association; Aargovian Bar Association; Chamber of Commerce Switzerland-Germany and Switzerland-Hungary.

LIC.IUR. WALTER HUG, born 1950; admitted, 1981, Switzerland. *Education:* University of Zurich (lic.iur., 1975). Notary Public, Canton of Aargau. Former Vice-Secretary Legal Department, Canton of Aargau. *Member:* Swiss Bar Association; Zurich Bar Association; Aargovian Bar Association; Notary's Association of Switzerland and Canton of Aargau.

ASSOCIATES

DR. ERICH RÜEGG, LL.M., born 1962; admitted, 1987, Switzerland; 1992, New York. *Education:* University of Fribourg (Lic.Jur., 1986; Dr.Jur., 1990); University of Chicago Law School (LL.M., 1991). Notary Public, Canton of Lucerne and Aargau. Author: "Leistung des Schuldners an einen Nicht-Gläubiger," Diss. Fribourg, 1990. *Member:* Swiss Bar Association; Zurich Bar Association; Aargovian Bar Association; New York Bar Association.

LIC.IUR. MARTIN IMTHURN, born 1951; admitted, 1979, Switzerland. *Education:* University of Zurich (lic.iur., 1976). Former Vice Secre-

(This Listing Continued)

tary, Building and Urban Planning Authority, Canton of Thurgau; Former General Counsel and Vice President of an International Industrial Holding. *Member:* Swiss Bar Association; Zurich Bar Association; Aargovian Bar Association; American Corporate Counsel Association.

Languages: English, German, French, Italian and Hungarian

BECCHIO WEHINGER JURI

KANTSTRASSE 14
P.O. BOX 472
CH-8044 ZÜRICH, SWITZERLAND
Telephone: 01/262 42 77
Fax: 01/252 05 51

Banking and Finance Law, Company and Commercial Law, Estate Law, Industrial Property Law, International Law, Leasing Law and Taxation Law.

MEMBERS OF FIRM

DR.IUR. BRUNO G. BECCHIO, born Canton of Ticino, Switzerland, September 5, 1941. *Education:* Universities of Zürich, Cologne and Oxford (lic.iur., 1964; Dr.iur., 1971). Advisor to the Government of Liechtenstein on Industrial Property Rights; Represented the Principality, European Conferences on Harmonisation of Patent Law in Luxembourg. *Member:* Zürich and Swiss Bar Associations. *LANGUAGES:* German, Italian, English and French. *PRACTICE AREAS:* Industrial Property Law; Company Law; Commercial Law.

DR.IUR. URS WEHINGER, born January 23, 1945. *Education:* University of Zürich (lic.iur., 1970; Dr.iur., 1975). Legal Counsel to Union Bank of Switzerland and Swiss Volksbank Zürich, 1970-1980. *Member:* Zürich and Swiss Bar Associations. *LANGUAGES:* German, English and French. *PRACTICE AREAS:* Banking and Financing Law; Company Law; International Private Law; Leasing Law; Estate Law.

DR.IUR. RENE JURI, born Lucerne, Switzerland, April 24, 1950. *Education:* University of Zürich (lic.iur., 1976; Dr.iur., 1982); University of Basel. Lawyer at Swiss Banking Commission, Bern, 1978-1980. *Member:* Zürich, Swiss and Ticino Bar Associations. *LANGUAGES:* German, Italian, English and French. *PRACTICE AREAS:* Banking Law; Commercial Law; Company Law.

LIC.IUR. PETER-JUERG REUTIMANN, born Zürich, Switzerland, December 25, 1953. *Education:* University of Zürich (lic.iur., 1983). *LANGUAGES:* German, English and French. *PRACTICE AREAS:* Commercial Law; Taxation; International Private Law.

FÜRSPRECHER AURELIO F. FERRARI, born Bern, Switzerland, May 6, 1956. *Education:* University of Bern (Fürsprecher, 1983). Legal Practice with Law Firms in Germany and the US, 1983-1985. *Member:* Zürich and Swiss Bar Associations. *LANGUAGES:* German, English, French and Italian. *PRACTICE AREAS:* Banking and Financing Law; Company Law; Commercial Law; International Private and Civil Law; Taxation Law.

BEGLINGER HOLENSTEIN & PARTNER

UTOQUAI 29
8008 ZÜRICH, SWITZERLAND
Telephone: 41-1-251 84 00
Fax: 41-1-251 8409

International Banking and Business Law, General International Trade Law, Tax Law, Corporate Commercial Law, Mergers and Acquisitions, Telecommunication, Intellectual Property Rights, Civil Litigation, International Judicial Assistance, Arbitration and Real Estate.

DR. PETER BEGLINGER, born Zurich, Switzerland, September 20, 1945; admitted, 1974, Zurich. *Education:* University of Zurich (Dr.iur.). *LANGUAGES:* German, English and French. *PRACTICE AREAS:* Company and Contract Law; Mergers and Acquisitions.

DR. PATRIZIA HOLENSTEIN, admitted, 1985, Zurich. *Education:* London School of Economics (Dr.iur., LL.M.); University of Zurich (Dr.Iur.). *LANGUAGES:* German, English, French and Italian. *PRACTICE AREAS:* Telecommunication; Banking and Commercial Law; Litigation; International Judicial Assistance.

DR. REINMAR FÜLLEMANN, admitted, 1980, Zurich. *Education:* University of Zurich (Dr.iur.). *LANGUAGES:* German, English and French. *PRACTICE AREAS:* Tax Law; Commercial Law; Real Estate Law.

(This Listing Continued)

DR. FRANCO LORANDI, admitted, 1991, Zurich. *Education:* University of St. Gallen (Dr.iur.). *LANGUAGES:* German, English and French. *PRACTICE AREAS:* Bankruptcy Law; Litigation.

DR. PETER KUNZ, admitted, 1991, Berne. *Education:* University of Berne (Dr.iur.). *LANGUAGES:* German, English and French. *PRACTICE AREAS:* Company Law; International Business Transactions; Intellectual Property Rights.

DR. FRANZ SATMER, admitted, 1989, Zurich. *Education:* University of Chicago Law School (LL.M.); University of Zurich (Dr. iur.). *LANGUAGES:* German, English, French and Hungarian. *PRACTICE AREAS:* Commercial Law; Corporate Law; Litigation; Arbitration.

LIC.IUR. RUDOLF MÜLLER, admitted, 1994, Zurich. *Education:* University of St. Gallen. *LANGUAGES:* German, English and French.

DR. MONIKA ROELL, admitted, Hamburg, Germany. German Lawyer. *LANGUAGES:* German and English. *PRACTICE AREAS:* Media Law; Press Law.

All Members and Associates are Members of the Swiss and International Bar Associations.

BENZ & PARTNERS

DUFOURSTRASSE 24
8008 ZÜRICH, SWITZERLAND
Telephone: 01/251 17 77
Telex: 817 700 BENZ CH
Telecopier: 01/251 18 38

Commercial and Corporate Law; Contracts; Banking; Insurance; Transportation Law (Maritime, Air and Land); Agency/Distributorship; Licenses; Franchising; Bankruptcy; Real Estate; Products Liability; Arbitration and Commercial Litigation.

MEMBERS OF FIRM

DR. CHRISTIAN E. BENZ, born Zürich, Switzerland, March 31, 1944; admitted, 1975, Switzerland. *Education:* Universities of Lausanne and Zurich (lic.iur., 1969; Dr.iur., 1973). *LANGUAGES:* German, English, French and Italian.

DR. THOMAS SAUBER, born Zurich, Switzerland, November 9, 1956; admitted, 1986, Switzerland. *Education:* University of Zurich (lic.iur., 1983; Dr.iur., 1986). *LANGUAGES:* German, English and French.

DR. STEFAN SCHALCH, born Zürich, Switzerland, May 16, 1960; admitted, 1991, Switzerland. *Education:* University of Zurich (lic.jur., 1984; Dr.iur., 1990). *LANGUAGES:* German, English and French.

JVO GRUNDLER, born Uzwil, Switzerland, March, 1966; admitted, 1993, Switzerland. *Education:* University of St. Gallen Law School (lic.iur., 1991). GHF Award, Thesis for Diploma, "Remedies under Swiss Intellectual Property Law," 1991. *LANGUAGES:* German, English and French.

BERGER HAUSER & HEPP

Established in 1989
KIRCHGASSE 22
CH-8024 ZÜRICH, SWITZERLAND
Telephone: 01/261 11 66
Telefax: 01/261 59 24

Commercial and Corporate Law, Estate Planning, Labor Law, Product Liability, Communications and Mass Media Law, Litigation, Judicial Assistance.

MEMBERS OF FIRM

DR. HANS BERGER, born Geneva, Switzerland, September 6, 1944; admitted, 1970, Geneva and Federal Courts; 1971, Zurich. *Education:* College of Geneva (Matura, 1964); University of Geneva (lic., 1968); University of Zurich (Dr. iur., 1974); University of Michigan, Ann Arbor, Michigan (Research Scholar, 1974). *Member:* Zurich, Swiss and International Bar Associations. *LANGUAGES:* German, French and English. *PRACTICE AREAS:* Business Law; Commercial Law; Company Law; International Law; Litigation.

DR. MARC T. HAUSER, born Zurich, Switzerland, September 15, 1951; admitted, 1981, Zurich and Federal Courts; 1984, Basel, Bern and Graubünden; 1985, Thurgau. *Education:* Gymnasium (Matura, 1970); University of Zurich (lic.iur, 1975 and Dr.iur., 1978). Practical Training in Lake

(This Listing Continued)

BERGER HAUSER & HEPP, Zürich—Continued

Success, New York, 1982-1983. *Member:* Zurich, Swiss and International Bar Associations. *LANGUAGES:* German, English, French and Italian. *PRACTICE AREAS:* Business Law; Company Law; Labor Law; Product Liability; Litigation; Wills; Judicial Assistance.

LIC.IUR. MARIANNE HEPP, born Uetikon am See, Switzerland, November 25, 1958; admitted, 1988, Zurich and Federal Courts. *Education:* Gymnasium (Matura, 1977); University of Zurich (lic.iur., 1982). *Member:* Zurich and Swiss Bar Associations. *LANGUAGES:* German, English, French and Italian. *PRACTICE AREAS:* Business Law; Commercial Law; Family Law; Wills; Zoning; Planning.

Languages: German, French, English and Italian

BERNASCONI & BERNASCONI
KUTTELGASSE 1/RENNWEG 25
CH-8023 ZÜRICH, SWITZERLAND
Telephone: 01 212 53 53
Telecopier: 01 212 53 54

Killwangen, Aargau Office: Bernasconi & Bernasconi, Rütihalde 12, CH-8956 Killwangen. Telephone: 056 71 58 25. Telecopier: 056 71 58 35.

Commercial Practice, Liability and Insurance Law, Corporations, Taxation, Banking, Securities, Foreign Investment, International Trade Law, Law of Eastern European Countries, Commercial litigation, Real Estate Law.

MEMBERS OF FIRM

EVELYNE C. BERNASCONI-MAMIE, born Zurich, Switzerland, June 2, 1960; admitted, 1989, Basle. *Education:* University of Geneva and St. Gallen (lic. iur. HSG 1985, Dr. iur. HSG 1994); New York University School of Law (LL.M. 1987). *Member:* Swiss Bar Association. *LANGUAGES:* German, French, English, Russian, Spanish. *PRACTICE AREAS:* Commercial Practice; Liability and Insurance Law; Foreign Investment; International Trade Law; Law of Eastern European Countries.

BRUNO M. BERNASCONI, born Zurich, Switzerland, March 14, 1959; admitted, 1990, Basle. *Education:* University of St. Gallen (lic. iur. HSG 1985); New York University School of Law (LL.M. 1987). *Member:* Swiss Bar Association. *LANGUAGES:* German, French, English, Italian, Spanish. *PRACTICE AREAS:* Commercial Practice; Corporations; Taxation; Banking; Securities; Foreign Investment; Commercial Litigation; Real Estate Law.

Languages: German, French, English, Russian, Italian, Spanish.

BLOCH & PARTNER
ZIMMERGASSE 16
8008 ZÜRICH, SWITZERLAND
Telephone: (01) 261 15 61 Telecopier: (01) 261 15 11

General Corporate and Commercial Practice, International Contracts, Finance and Banking, Taxation, Real Estate, Inheritance and Estate Planning, Civil Litigation.

FIRM PROFILE: *The founder of the firm, Dr. Heinz Bloch, has practiced in the United States from 1966 through 1974, in Brussels from 1974 through 1979 and in Zurich since 1979. The firm specializes in advising U.S. clients in Europe and European clients on doing business in the U.S.A. The firm also is extensively engaged in all legal aspects of hotel development, management and financing. The firm is associated with PARKER CHAPIN FLATTAU & KLIMPL, New York, NY 10036, and with NOTTER BLATTER DAVIDOFF & PARTNER with offices in Zurich, Berne, Geneva and Brussels.*

DR. HEINZ BLOCH, born Berne, Switzerland, September 17, 1932; admitted, 1958, Canton of Berne, Switzerland; 1966, New York. *Education:* University of Berne, Switzerland (B.A. in Law and in Economics, 1958; Ph.D. in Economics, 1961); New York University (J.D., 1966). *Member:* American Bar Association; Swiss Bar Association; International Bar Association; Swiss-American Chamber of Commerce. (Of Counsel to Parker Chapin Flattau & Klimpl, New York, NY and Notter Blatter Davidoff & Partner, Zurich, Berne and Geneva, Switzerland and Brussels, Belgium).

(This Listing Continued)

LANGUAGES: English, French and German. *PRACTICE AREAS:* Resorts and Leisure; International Law; Corporate Law; Real Estate; Business Law.

BRATSCHI EMCH & PARTNERS

Established in 1979

BAHNHOFSTRASSE 106
P.O. BOX 7689
8023 ZÜRICH, SWITZERLAND
Telephone: 01/211 16 64
Telefax: 01/211 16 69

Bern, Switzerland Office: Bollwerk 15, P.O. Box 5576, 3001. Telephone: 031 312 01 33. Telefax: 031 311 95 38.

FIRM PROFILE: *The firm was established in Bern in 1976. In 1979 the office in Zurich was opened. The firm in Bern and Zurich offers a full range of legal services to international and domestic business, corporate and private clients in all areas of civil, criminal and public law. It specializes in contract law, commercial law and banking law.*

MEMBERS OF FIRM

DR. PETER BRATSCHI, born 1941; admitted, 1967, Switzerland. *Education:* University of Bern; Georgetown University, Washington, D.C. Federal Government (Taxes, Foreign Economic Relations). *LANGUAGES:* German (native language), English, French.

DR. URS EMCH, born 1941; admitted, 1968, Switzerland. *Education:* University of Bern. Federal Department of Finance, 1970-1972. Legal Counsel, Bank Hofmann AG Zürich, 1973-1976.

DR. CHRISTIAN SCHMID, born 1949; admitted, 1978, Switzerland. *Education:* University of Zürich; University of Michigan Law School (M.C.L.). Superior Court of Zürich, 1978.

DR. MARKUS HÜNIG, born 1946; admitted, 1973, Switzerland. *Education:* University of Zürich.

FRANZ SZOLANSKY, born 1950; admitted, 1981, Switzerland. *Education:* University of Zürich; University of Lausanne; University of Georgia, USA. *LANGUAGES:* Hungarian.

URS GASCHE, born 1955; admitted, 1982, Switzerland. *Education:* University of Bern. Bernese Department of Construction, 1982-1988.

DR. CHRISTOPH BORN, born 1952; admitted, 1980, Switzerland. *Education:* University of Bern. Legal Department, Swiss Volksbank, Züruich, Legal Counsel, Jean Frey/Curti Medien AG, Zürich.

DR. JÜRGEN BRÖNNIMANN, born 1955; admitted, 1981, Switzerland. *Education:* University of Bern, Free University of Berlin. Lecturer, Swiss School for Chartered Accountants and Tax Experts. Assistant Lecturer, Commercial Law and Civil Procedure Law, University of Bern.

MARK INEICHEN, LL.M., born 1958; admitted, 1985, Switzerland. *Education:* University of Bern; Georgetown University, Washington, D.C.

ASSOCIATES

MARC STUCKI, born 1963; admitted, 1990, Switzerland. *Education:* University of Bern. Legal Services Group of Union Bank of Switzerland (UBS), Zürich, 1990-1991. *LANGUAGES:* Italian and Spanish.

DIETER HAAS, born 1962; admitted, 1988, Switzerland. *Education:* University of Bern. Bernese Department of Construction, 1989-1992.

HERMANN BECHTOLD, born 1963; admitted, 1991, Switzerland. *Education:* University of Bern.

PETER KELLER, born 1965; admitted, 1993. *Education:* University of Bern.

RENÉ ZAHUD, born 1966; admitted, 1994, Switzerland. *Education:* University of Bern. *LANGUAGES:* German (native language), English, French, Italian.

Languages: German, French, English, Italian and Spanish

BRINER HESS STREULI WIGET

82 KREUZSTRASSE
8032 ZÜRICH, SWITZERLAND
Telephone: (1) 261 18 81
Telecopier: (1) 261 18 11

General Commercial, Corporate and Civil Practice, Industrial Property, Unfair Competition. International and ECC Law. Probate, Trusts, Wills. Labour Law. Leasing Law. Computer and Software Law. Licensing. Litigation and Arbitration.

DR. NIKLAUS WIGET, born 1944; admitted, 1972, Zürich. *Education:* University of Zürich (Doctor of Law); Postgraduate Studies at the Universities of Cambridge (GB) and Tours (F).

DR. MAGDA STREULI-YOUSSEF, born 1953; admitted, 1980, Zürich. *Education:* University of Zurich (Doctor of Law).

DR. MARKUS HESS, born 1953; admitted, 1980, Zurich. *Education:* University of Zürich (Doctor of Law).

DR. ROBERT G. BRINER, born 1949; admitted, 1981, Zürich. *Education:* University of Zürich (Doctor of Law).

All Attorneys of the Firm are Members of the Swiss and Zürich Bar Associations.

Languages: German, English and French

BRUPPACHER, HUG & PARTNER

ZOLLIKERSTRASSE 58, ZOLLIKON-ZÜRICH
P.O. BOX 186
CH-8702 ZOLLIKON/ZÜRICH, SWITZERLAND
Telephone: 01 396 31 31
Telecopier: 01 396 31 32

General Practice. Commercial, Corporate and Private Law. Distribution, Franchising, Time-Sharing, Tax, Estate and Labor Law. Domestic and International Licensing, International Business Law, International Legal Transactions, Bankruptcy Law and Civil Litigation, Arbitration.

FIRM PROFILE: The firm offers a full range of legal services.

MEMBERS OF FIRM

DR. C. MARK BRUPPACHER, born Washington, D.C., October 23, 1946; admitted, 1975, Switzerland. *Education:* University of Zürich (Dr.iur., 1973); University of Amsterdam (Columbia University Summer Program in American Law). Author: "Die aktienrechtlichen Bewertungsvorschriften (im Hinblick auf eine Teilrevision des Aktienrechtes; mit Berücksichtigung des deutschen Aktiengesetzes)". *Member:* Zürich and Swiss Bar Associations; International Bar Association; The Law Society; American Arbitration Association; EFL European Franchising Lawyers; Swiss Chapter of Licensing Executives Society; International Forum of Travel and Tourism Advocates. *LANGUAGES:* English, French and German. *PRACTICE AREAS:* Commercial; Corporate; Trade Law; Tax Law; International Transactions; Franchising; Timesharing; Leasing.

DR. DIETER HUG, born Zürich, Switzerland, August 6, 1952; admitted, 1981, Switzerland. *Education:* University of Zürich (Dr.iur., 1984); United Nations (18th Graduate Study Program, 1980). Author: "Die Rechtsstellung der in der Schweiz niedergelassenen internationalen Organisationen". *Member:* Zürich and Swiss Bar Associations; International Bar Association. *LANGUAGES:* English, French and German. *PRACTICE AREAS:* Civil Litigation; Arbitration; Insurance and Liability Law; Bankruptcy Law; Commercial Law; Estate and Labour Law.

ASSOCIATE

URS O. KRAFT, born Olten, Switzerland, January 2, 1960; admitted, 1992, Switzerland. *Education:* University of Zurich (lic.iur., 1989). *Member:* Zurich and Swiss Bar Associations. *LANGUAGES:* English, French and German. *PRACTICE AREAS:* Civil Litigation; Labour Law; Commercial Law; Residence and Work Permits; Intellectual and Industrial Property and Copyright.

Languages: German, English and French

GUIDO VON CASTELBERG

BAHNHOSSTRASSE 106
8001 ZÜRICH, SWITZERLAND
Telephone: 01/212 00 05
Cable Address: "Casteliur", Zurich
Fax: 01/211'16'69

DR. GUIDO VON CASTELBERG, born Zurich, Switzerland, September 6, 1927; admitted, 1955, Switzerland. *Education:* University of Zurich (Doctor of Economics; Doctor of Law). *LANGUAGES:* German, English, French and Italian.

DE BEER ATTORNEYS AT LAW

SCHLOSSBERGSTRASSE 22
P.O. BOX 22
CH-8702 ZOLLIKON/ZÜRICH, SWITZERLAND
Telephone: (01) 392 18 92
Fax: (01) 392 17 92

Banking and Finance, International Trade, Estate Planning, Mergers and Acquisitions, Arbitration, General Corporate and Commercial Practice.

PROF. DR. ALEXANDER I. DE BEER, born Pully, Switzerland, May 9, 1948; admitted, 1985, Zug and Zurich. *Education:* University of Zurich (lic.oec.publ., 1972; Dr.iur., 1978); University of Chicago (LL.M., 1979). Visiting Scholar, Harvard Law School, 1979-1980. Professor of Corporate Law, University of Fribourg, 1980—. Board Member, Institute of Swiss Labor Law, 1982—. *Member:* Zurich and Swiss Bar Associations; Swiss Arbitration Association. *LANGUAGES:* German, English and French.

DE CAPITANI, KRONAUER & WENGLE

LIMMATQUAI 3
8001 ZÜRICH, SWITZERLAND
Telephone: 01/261 04 51; 01/262 46 85; 01/262 46 74
Telecopier: 01/252 98 04

International Commercial Practice, Banking, Mergers and Acquisitions, Joint Ventures, Corporate, Taxation, Commercial Litigation, Arbitration, Administrative Matters.

MEMBERS OF FIRM

DR. SILVIO DE CAPITANI, born Zurich, Switzerland, July 30, 1925; admitted, 1954, Canton of Zurich. *Education:* University of Zurich (Dr.iur., 1952). *LANGUAGES:* German, English, French and Italian.

DR. MARIO KRONAUER, born Zurich, Switzerland, September 19, 1943; admitted, 1969, Canton of Zurich. *Education:* University of Berlin, University of Zurich (Dr.iur., 1972); Harvard Law School (LL.M., 1973); Diploma of The Hague Academy of International Law (1970). *LANGUAGES:* German, English, French and Italian.

DR. RICHARD H. WENGLE, born Kreuzlingen, Switzerland, March 3, 1943; admitted, 1969, Canton of Zurich. *Education:* University of Zurich (Dr.iur., 1967); Columbia School of Law (LL.M., 1971). Harlan Fiske Stone Fellowship. *LANGUAGES:* German, English, French and Italian.

DIETRICH, BAUMGARTNER & PARTNERS

SIHLPORTE 3/TALSTRASSE
P.O. BOX 200
8021 ZÜRICH, SWITZERLAND
Telephone: 01-211 10 55
Fax: 01-211 10 54

Commercial and Corporate Law, Banking, Insurance, Taxation, Bankruptcy, Securities Law, Computers and Software, Construction Law, International Finance, Intellectual Property, Real Estate, Probate, Trusts and Estates, Civil and Commercial Litigation, Environmental Law, International Judicial Assistance, Arbitration.

MEMBERS OF FIRM

DR. URS DIETRICH, born Zurich, Switzerland, 1940; admitted, 1970, Switzerland. *Education:* University of Zurich (Dr.iur., 1967). *LANGUAGES:* German, English and French.

(This Listing Continued)

DIETRICH, BAUMGARTNER & PARTNERS, Zürich—
Continued

DR. ANDRES BAUMGARTNER, born Zurich, Switzerland, 1961; admitted, 1988, Switzerland. *Education:* University of Zurich (lic.iur., 1984); University of Freiburg (Dr.iur., 1987); University of California, Berkeley, Boalt Hall School of Law (LL.M., 1989). Law Clerk: Sedgwick, Detert, Moran & Arnold, San Francisco, 1989; Morrison & Foerster, San Francisco, 1989. *LANGUAGES:* German, English, French and Italian.

LIC.IUR. ROLF HERTER, born Zurich, Switzerland, 1963; admitted, 1993, Switzerland. *Education:* University of Zurich (lic.iur., 1989). *LANGUAGES:* German, English and French.

EGLI PATENT ATTORNEYS

HORNEGGSTRASSE 4
P.O. BOX 473
CH-8034 ZÜRICH, SWITZERLAND
Telephone: +41 1 422 02 55
Cable Address: Pategli Zürich
Telex: 817 435 EPAT-CH
Telefax: +41 1 422 04 77

Munich, Germany Office: Egli European Patent Attorneys, Widenmayerstrasse 5, 80538. Telephone: +49 89 229462. Telefax: +49 89 299465.

New York, New York Office: Egli International, 150 E. 52nd Street, 10022. Telephone: (212) 421 2400. Telefax: (212) 421 2255.

Tokyo, Japan Office: Egli International, Kudan Flower Home, Room 707, 4-3-20, Kudan Kita, Chiyoda-ku, Tokyo 102. Telephone: +81 3 3239-4828. Telefax: +81 3 3239-4799.

Intellectual Property Consultants including Patent, Trademark, Design, Copyright, Know How, Licensing and Contract Law and Litigation.

Richard A. Egli
Dr. François Köver
Dr. Wolfgang Wagner
Werner Gloor
Maurice Corten
Dr. Adrian Zimmerli
Josefine Weitzenbeck
Dr. Raoul Bussmann

VON ERLACH KLAINGUTI STETTLER WILLE & PARTNERS

Rechtsanwälte - Attorneys at Law

Established in 1966

DREIKOENIGSTRASSE 7
P.O. BOX CH 8022 ZURICH
8002 ZÜRICH, SWITZERLAND
Telephone: 01 283 21 11
Telecopier: 01 202 07 07
Cable Address: "Erlawcable"
Telex: 815 888 lex ch

International Practice, Commercial and Contract Law, Company Law, Banking and Securities Law, Mergers & Acquisitions, Swiss and International Taxation, International and Domestic Arbitration, European Union Law, Antitrust and Competition Law, Aviation Law, Real Estate, Labor and Immigration Law, Debt Enforcement and Bankruptcy Law, Administrative and Regulatory Law, Intellectual Property, International Law, Estate Planning and Probate Law, Trusts, International Judicial Assistance, Civil Litigation in Swiss courts.

FIRM PROFILE: *The firm was established in 1966. It offers a full range of legal services to international and domestic business, corporate and private clients. The international client base includes important European, American and Japanese groups.*

FÜRSPRECHER WOLFGANG VON ERLACH, born 1918; admitted, 1955, Bern. *LANGUAGES:* German, English, French and Italian. *PRACTICE AREAS:* Swiss and International Taxation; Banks and Banking; Finance and Securities; Corporate and Commercial Law; Wills and Estates.

(This Listing Continued)

DR. ERNEST KLAINGUTI, LL.M., born 1941; admitted, 1972, Zürich. *LANGUAGES:* German, English, French, Italian and Spanish. *PRACTICE AREAS:* Banks and Banking; Contracts; International Trusts and Estates; Art Law; Real Estate Law.

FÜRSPRECHER DIETRICH K. STETTLER, born 1942; admitted, 1969, Bern. *LANGUAGES:* German, English and French. *PRACTICE AREAS:* Commercial and Corporate Law; Immigration and Work Permits; Wills and Estates and Probate Law; Trusts; Intellectual Property Law; Commercial Real Estate.

FÜRSPRECHER JOHANN H. WILLE, M.C.L., born 1947; admitted, 1973, Bern. *LANGUAGES:* German, English and French. *PRACTICE AREAS:* Banking; Finance and Securities Law; Taxation; Commercial Litigation and Arbitration; Competition and Licensing.

DR. RUDOLF VON ERLACH, M.C.L., born 1945; admitted, 1977, Zürich. *LANGUAGES:* German, English and French. *PRACTICE AREAS:* Mergers and Acquisitions Law; Commercial Contracts; Taxation; Immigration and Work Permits; Intellectual Property Laws.

DR. BEAT VON RECHENBERG, M.C.J., born 1950; admitted, 1977, Zürich. *LANGUAGES:* German, English and French. *PRACTICE AREAS:* International Trade Law; Stock Exchange and Securities Law; Commercial Litigation and Arbitration; International Legal Assistance; Mergers and Acquisitions.

DR. MAX ALBERS-SCHÖNBERG, LL.M., born 1953; admitted, 1981, Zürich. *LANGUAGES:* German, English and French. *PRACTICE AREAS:* Corporate and Commercial Law; International Arbitration and Litigation; Swiss and International Taxation; Trusts and Estate Planning; European Union Law; Aircraft Financing.

DR. EDGAR H. PALTZER, LL.M., born 1956; admitted, 1984, Zürich; 1988, New York. *LANGUAGES:* German, English and French. *PRACTICE AREAS:* Commercial Contracts; Swiss and International Taxation; Litigation and Arbitration; White Collar Crime; Trusts and Foundations.

DR. NICOLÀ BARANDUN FURSPRECHER, born 1957; admitted, 1985, Bern. *LANGUAGES:* German, English and French. *PRACTICE AREAS:* Export and Commercial Finance; Intellectual Property Law; Mergers and Acquisitions; European Union Law; Computers and Software.

FLORIAN BAUMANN, H.E.E., born 1961; admitted, 1989, Zürich. *LANGUAGES:* German, English and French. *PRACTICE AREAS:* Litigation and Arbitration; European Union Law; Debtor and Creditor Law; Agency and Distributorship Law; Cross-Border Transactions.

MICHAEL HESS, LL.M., born 1962; admitted, 1990, Zürich. *LANGUAGES:* German, English, French, Italian and Spanish. *PRACTICE AREAS:* Corporate and Commercial Law; Debt and Bankruptcy Law; Litigation; Real Estate Law; Administrative Law.

DR. STEFAN GERSTER, born 1963; admitted, 1993, Zurich. *LANGUAGES:* German, English and French. *PRACTICE AREAS:* Commercial and Business Law; Secured Transactions and Finance; Debtor and Creditor Law; Employment Law; Landlord and Tenant Law.

DAMIANO BRUSA, born 1964; admitted, 1993, Zurich. *LANGUAGES:* Italian, German, French and English. *PRACTICE AREAS:* Corporate and Commercial Law; Litigation; Torts; Property and Construction Law; Seizure and Attachments.

PHILIPP HAAS, born 1965; admitted, 1994, Zürich. *LANGUAGES:* German, English and French. *PRACTICE AREAS:* Corporate and Commercial Law; Securities; Unfair Competition; Litigation.

DR. KASPAR E. LANDOLT, LL.M., born 1964; admitted 1991, Zürich. *LANGUAGES:* German, English and French. *PRACTICE AREAS:* Corporate Law; Contract Law; Intellectual Property Law; Debt and Bankruptcy Law; Commercial Litigation.

DR. ALFRED S. FARHA

Counselor at Law

BAHNHOFSTRASSE 71
8001 ZÜRICH, SWITZERLAND
Telephone: 41 1/212 71 21
Fax: 41 1/212 71 29

International Trade and Commerce involving Mergers and Acquisitions, Reorganizations, Venture Capital Investments, Banking and Finance, Sales and Marketing, Distribution and Representation Agreements, Insurance, Real Estate, European Community and Environmental Law.

(This Listing Continued)

ALFRED S. FARHA, born Kansas City, Missouri, October 13, 1933; admitted, 1961, Kansas; 1962, Missouri; 1965, Michigan (Not admitted in Switzerland). *Education:* University of Kansas (A.B., International Relations, 1955; J.D., 1961). Associate with, Shughart, Thomson & Kilroy, Kansas City, Missouri, 1961-1965. Corporate Attorney, The Dow Chemical Company, Midland, Michigan, 1965-1973; Transferred to, Dow Europe, Horgen, Switzerland, 1973; General Manager, Dow Chemical Middle East; Retired as, Director, Dow Europe for Regulatory Affairs, September, 1993 to enter private practice in Zürich. Citizenship: U.S and Swiss. Board of Advisors, Northwestern University Journal of International Law & Business; Advisory Board, New York State Bar Association International Law Review; MBA Instructor, City University, Zürich. *Member:* American Bar Association; Swiss-American Chamber of Commerce; American Club of Zürich (President, 1991-1992).

LAW FIRM
DR. KONRAD FISCHER

TÖDISTRASSE 17

P.O. BOX 5002

8022 ZÜRICH, SWITZERLAND
Telephone: 01/202 44 11
Telefax: 01/202 44 40

General Practice, Commercial, Corporate and Contract Law, Banking Law, Capital Market Transactions, Trusts and Estates, Litigation.

DR. KONRAD FISCHER, born Aarau, Switzerland, August 16, 1944; admitted, 1973, Zurich. *Education:* Universities of Basle, Rome and Zurich (Dr.iur., 1971). Foreign associate with bank legal department and with law firm in San Francisco. *Member:* Zurich and Swiss Bar Associations. *LANGUAGES:* German, English, French and Italian. *PRACTICE AREAS:* Commercial, Corporate and Contract Law; Banking Law; Capital Market Transactions; Trusts and Estates; Litigation.

ASSOCIATES

LIC. GIOVANNI IADEMARCO, born Zurich, Switzerland, April 2, 1958; admitted, 1993, Switzerland. *Education:* University of Zurich (lic.iur., 1989). *Member:* Zurich and Swiss Bar Associations. *LANGUAGES:* German, English, French and Italian. *PRACTICE AREAS:* General Practice.

LIC. ANDREA DAENIKER-MAYERHÖFER, born Darmstadt, Germany, July 26, 1965; admitted, 1993, Switzerland. *Education:* University of Zurich (lic.iur., 1990). *Member:* Zurich and Swiss Bar Associations. *LANGUAGES:* German, English and French. *PRACTICE AREAS:* General Practice.

DR. MARTIN HESS, born Langnau, Switzerland, April 26, 1954; admitted, 1987, Zurich. *Education:* University of Zurich (Dr.iur., 1984). Author, "Legal Aspects of Payment Systems and Electronic Fund Transfers in Switzerland." Assistant Director and Legal Adviser, Swiss National Bank (Central Bank), 1987-1994. Substitute Member, Zurich Tax Appeal Court. *Member:* Zurich and Swiss Bar Associations. *LANGUAGES:* German, English and French. *PRACTICE AREAS:* Banking Law; Payment and Netting Systems; General Practice.

FISCHER & PARTNER

Advocates

Established in 1978

OBERDORFSTRASSE 8
CH-8024 ZÜRICH, SWITZERLAND
Telephone: 41 1 262 28 00
Telefax: 41 1 262 29 33

General Civil, Commercial and Corporate Practice, International, Finance and Tax Law, Intellectual Property and International Arbitration.

MEMBERS OF FIRM

DR.IUR. ROLF FISCHER, born 1942; admitted, 1975, Switzerland. *Education:* Zurich (Dr. iur.); London (LL.M.). *LANGUAGES:* English, French and German.

LIC.IUR. DANIEL PAGNAMENTA, born 1961. *Education:* Zurich (Lic.iur.). *LANGUAGES:* English, French and German.

Languages: German, English and French

FRICK & FRICK

URANIASTRASSE 12

P.O. BOX 996

CH-8021 ZÜRICH, SWITZERLAND
Telephone: +41-1/211.29.11
Cable Address: Fricklaw, Zurich
Telex: 813 863 fric ch
Fax: +41-1/211.29.30

Zug, Switzerland Office: Unter Altstadt 28, P.O. Box 234, CH-6301. Telephone: +41-42/22.66.30. Telefax: +41-42/22.66.36.

Prague, Czech Republic Office: Office 422a, 4th Floor, Národni trida 10, CZ-11319 Prague 1. Telephone: +42-2/24.91.30.44. Fax: +42-2/24.91.34.35.

Sofia, Bulgaria Office: Boulevard Witoscha 25, P.O. Box 475, BG-1000. Telephone: +359-2/81.33.88. Telefax: +359-2/81.33.85.

In Association with Law Offices in China: Beijing - Qingdao - Shanghai.

General Commercial Practice, Corporate Law, International Contracts, Joint Venture Contracts, Privatization Projects, International Arbitration, Mergers and Acquisitions, Intellectual Property, Construction, Tax Law, Immigration, Inheritance Law, Advertising Law, Litigation and Real Estate Law.

MEMBERS OF FIRM

HANS FRICK, born Sofia, Bulgaria, September 6, 1940; admitted, 1979, Zurich, Switzerland. *Education:* University of Zurich (lic.iur., 1966). Lecturer on Law, Swiss Institute for Business Management (SIB - Schweizerisches Institut ür Betriebsökonomie, Zurich (up to 1982), Higher Marketing and Administration School; (HWV - Höhere Wirtschafts- und Verwaltungsschule, Zurich (up to 1987). Honorary Consul, Republic of Senegal. Examiner on Construction Law for Federal Masters Builders Degree, up to 1987. *Member:* Zurich and Swiss Bar Association; International Bar Association (IBA); Swiss Arbitration Association; UIA Union Internationale des Avocats (International Association of Lawyers); Chamber of Commerce, Switzerland and Bulgaria (Secretary). *LANGUAGES:* German, English, French, and Bulgarian.

GEORGES FRICK, born Sofia, Bulgaria, August 8, 1946; admitted, 1978, Zurich, Switzerland. *Education:* University of Zurich (lic.iur., 1974). Lecturer on Law at Swiss Institute for Business Management (SIB - Schweizerisches Institut für Betriebsökonomie), Higher Marketing and Administration School, Zurich (HWV - Höhere Wirtschafts- und Verwaltungsschule). Examiner, Commercial Law for Federal Sales-Promoters Masters Degree, until 1985. *Member:* Zurich and Swiss Bar Associations; Swiss Lawyers Association; Swiss Arbitration Association; International Chamber of Commerce; International Bar Association; Chambers of Commerce (Board Member) Switzerland-Czech Republic and Switzerland-Slovak Republic; Membership in Chamber of Commerce: CH/USA and 3rd CH. *LANGUAGES:* German, English, French and Bulgarian.

PETER HOFER, born Zurich, Switzerland, September 25, 1957; admitted, 1987, Zurich, Switzerland. *Education:* University of Zurich (lic.iur., 1984). Co-Author: "Advertising Law in Europe and North America," Kluwer, Deveuter, Boston, 1992. Lecturer on Law for HWV Höhere Wirtschafts- und Verwaltungsschule (Higher Marketing and Administration School), Zurich (since 1986) and Handelsschule des kaufmännischen Verbandes (Business School), Zurich (since 1985). Examiner, Construction Law for Federal Master Builders Degree, 1987—and on Advertising Law for Federal Advertising Managers and PR Consultants, 1991—. *Member:* Swiss and Zurich Bar Associations; AIJA (Young Lawyers' Degree International Association); European Advertising Lawyers' Association EWIV. *LANGUAGES:* German, English, French, Italian and Spanish.

DR. TITUS J. PACHMANN, born Munich, Germany, August 12, 1949; admitted, 1983, Obwalden, Switzerland. *Education:* Universities of Munich and Zurich (Dr.iur., 1979); City University of Bellevue (M.B.A., 1992). Author: publications in criminal proceedings and competition law of the EEC/EEA. Examiner, Construction Law, Federal Master Builders Degree. Notary Public, 1985—. *Member:* Zurich and Swiss Bar Associations; International Society of Technology, Law and Insurance. *LANGUAGES:* German and English.

GEORGE HUNZIKER, born Paris, France, June 16, 1954; admitted, 1981, Zürich. *Education:* University of Geneva Law School (1973-1974); University of Zürich Law School (lic.iur., 1978); Georgetown University Law Center, Washington D.C. (LL.M., 1982). *Member:* Swiss, Zurich and American (International Associate) Bar Associations. *LANGUAGES:* German, English and French.

(This Listing Continued)

FRICK & FRICK, Zürich—Continued

ASSOCIATES

SANDRO SOSIO, born Chur, Switzerland, January 25, 1961; admitted, 1992, Zurich. *Education:* University of Zurich (lic.iur., 1988). *Member:* Zurich and Swiss Bar Associations. *LANGUAGES:* German, English, French, Brazilian and Portuguese.

ROLAND MEIER, born Zug, Switzerland, March 14, 1962; admitted, 1990, Zug. *Education:* University of Zürich (Dr. iur., 1993). *Member:* Zürich and Swiss Bar Associations. *LANGUAGES:* German, English and French.

BEAT BARTHOLD, born Switzerland, June 26, 1963; admitted, 1988, Zürich. *Education:* University of Basl. *Member:* Zürich and Swiss Bar Associations. *LANGUAGES:* German and English.

COUNSEL

YUAN JIE, born P.R., China, July 21, 1962; admitted, 1985. *Education:* East China Institute of Politics and Law, 1983. Security Lawyer of Shanghai Economic Relations & Trade Law Firm. *LANGUAGES:* Chinese, English.

The Firm is a Member of CONSULEGIS EEIG Attorneys at Law, a European-Wide grouping of Law Firms.

FRICK WIDMER VUILLE NEUPERT & PARTNERS

Established in 1851

DUFOURSTRASSE 60
8702 ZOLLIKON/ZÜRICH, SWITZERLAND
Telephone: 01/391 33 11
Cable Address: "Feye CH"
Telex: 817 600
Telefax: 01/391 38 40

Zug, Switzerland Office: Chamerstrasse 14, 6301. Telephone: 042 21 65 91. Telefax: 042 21 83 73.

Corporate, Commercial, Tax, Banking, Real Estate, Trust, License and Trademarks, Unfair Competition and Aviation Law, Litigation, Notarial Acts.

MEMBERS OF FIRM

DR. WILLY N. FRICK (1926-1993).

DR. RAOUL E. WIDMER, born Gränichen, Switzerland, 1934; admitted, 1965, Zurich. *Education:* University of Bern (Dr.iur., 1960). *LANGUAGES:* German, English, French, Italian and Spanish.

DR. JEAN-MARC VUILLE, born Zurich, Switzerland, November 17, 1939; admitted, 1968, Zurich. *Education:* University of Witwatersrand, Johannesburg, South Africa (1958); University of Zurich (Dr.iur., 1966). Author: "Die Umwandlung einer Personengesellschaft in eine Aktiengesellschaft," P.G. Keller, 1966. *Member:* Zurich and Swiss Bar Association. *LANGUAGES:* German, English, French and Italian.

DR. DIETER W. NEUPERT, born Zurich, Switzerland, 1942; admitted, 1977, Zurich. *Education:* University of Zurich (Lic.iur., 1969; Dr.iur., 1976). *LANGUAGES:* German, English, French, Italian and Spanish.

DR. URS TREPP, born Zurich, Switzerland, March 22, 1944; admitted, 1978, Zurich. *Education:* Dartmouth College (B.A., 1966); Stanford University (M.A., 1971); University of Zurich (Ph.D., 1984). Author: "Der Begriff des Kleinkreditvertrages," Schulthess, 1985. Lecturer on Law, University of Zurich, 1982-1983. *Member:* Zurich and Swiss Bar Associations. *LANGUAGES:* German, English, French and Italian.

URS A. KAELIN, born Zurich, Switzerland, February 12, 1948; admitted, 1976, Zurich. *Education:* Universities of Geneva and Zurich (Lic.iur., 1972). *Member:* Zurich and Swiss Bar Association. *LANGUAGES:* German, English, French and Italian.

LIC. PETER B. ARNOLD, born New York, U.S.A., December 2, 1958; admitted, 1987, Zurich. *Education:* University of Zurich (Lic.iur., 1984). Notary Public to the Canton of Zug/Switzerland since 1987. *Member:* Zurich and Swiss Bar Associations. (Resident Partner, Zug Switzerland Office). *LANGUAGES:* German, English and French.

LIC. THOMAS H. ROHRER, born Zurich, Switzerland, July 1, 1959; admitted, 1988, Zurich. *Education:* University of Zurich (Lic.iur., 1985).

(This Listing Continued)

Member: Zurich and Swiss Bar Associations. *LANGUAGES:* German, English and French.

DR. CHRISTOPH P. JEZLER (Of Counsel).

ASSOCIATES

Dr. Roger Dagon
Lic. Joseph Wicki
Dr. Bruno Stierli, LL.M.
Patrick M. O'Neill
Lic. Maria Heer
Dr. Denis G. Humbert

Languages: German, English, French, Italian and Spanish

FRORIEP RENGGLI

BELLERIVESTRASSE 201
P.O. BOX 130
8034 ZÜRICH, SWITZERLAND
Telephone: (+41)1 386 60 00
Telex: 815596 frp ch
Telecopier: (+41)1 383 60 50

Address until April 30, 1995: General Wille-Strasse 10, 8027. Telephone: (+41)12017420. Telex: 815596 frp ch. Telecopier: (+41) 12023666.

Geneva, Switzerland Office: 4, Rue Charles-Bonnet, 1206. Telephone: (+41)-22 347 18 18. Telex: 423651 frob ch. Telecopier: (+41)-22 347 71 59.

Zug, Switzerland Office: Baarerstrasse 75, 6300. Telephone: (+41)-42 21 33 71. Telecopier: (+41)-42 23 07 15.

London, England Office: 1 Knightrider Court, EC4V 5JP. Telephone: (+44)171 236 60 00. Fax: (+44)171 248 02 09.

Fuerth (Nürnberg), Germany Office: Friedrichstrasse 6, 90762. Telephone: (+49)-911 77 39 82. Telecopier: (+49)-911 749 84 51.

Commercial, Corporate and Civil Practice, International Business, Commercial Litigation and International Commercial Arbitration, Private and Public International Law, Banking, Taxation, Immigration, Bankruptcy, International Judicial Assistance, Trade Marks and Copyrights, EEC Law, Estate, Real Property and Aviation Law.

FIRM PROFILE: Established in 1966, Froriep Renggli has grown to be one of the leading and largest Swiss law firms with principal offices in Zurich, Geneva and Zug. The firm is engaged in a broad range of Swiss and International practice. Froriep Renggli currently has a total of thirty-two lawyers, twelve of whom are partners. Two of the associates are qualified German lawyers, four lawyers are also admitted in New York and one is an English solicitor. Most of the lawyers have had, in addition to their Swiss training, legal education in England or the United States and/or have practice as foreign consultants with law firms there or elsewhere abroad. The firm has a three lawyers strong London office, an office in Fürth/Nürnberg, Germany, and an associated office in Bratislava, Slovakia. These, combined with an extensive network of correspondent lawyers, enhance the firm's international advisory, transactional and litigation capabilities.

MEMBERS OF FIRM

DR. ANDREAS L. FRORIEP, born Halberstadt, Germany, June 23, 1931; admitted, 1958, Switzerland. *Education:* Universities of Zurich and Berne (Dr.iur., 1956). *LANGUAGES:* German, English and French. *PRACTICE AREAS:* Commercial Law; Corporate Law; Mergers and Acquisitions; Taxation; Banking; International Trust and Estates.

DR. ERIC A. HAYMANN, born Zurich, Switzerland, October 21, 1945; admitted, 1975, Switzerland. *Education:* University of Zurich (Dr.iur., 1973). *LANGUAGES:* German, French, English and Italian. *PRACTICE AREAS:* Contract Law; Corporate Law; Mergers and Acquisitions; Arbitration; International Trusts and Estates.

BRUNO W. BOESCH, born Stockholm, Sweden, April 5, 1949; admitted, 1976, Switzerland. *Education:* University of Geneva (Lic.iur., 1972); New York University Institute of Comparative Law (M.C.J., 1975). (Resident, London Office). *LANGUAGES:* French, German, English and Swedish. *PRACTICE AREAS:* International Contract Law; Finance; Banks and Banking; Cross-Border Transactions; Joint-Ventures; International Arbitration; Litigation; Acquisitions and Financing; International Mergers and Acquisitions; Hotels and Resorts; International Trade and Estates; White Collar Crime.

(This Listing Continued)

NICOLAS JUNOD, born Geneva, Switzerland, May 3, 1947; admitted, 1974, Switzerland. *Education:* University of Geneva (Lic.iur., 1971); New York University Institute of Comparative Law (M.C.J., 1978). (Resident, Geneva Office). *LANGUAGES:* French, English, Italian and German. *PRACTICE AREAS:* Commercial Law; Banking; Contract Law; Corporate Law.

CLAUDIA KÄLIN-NAUER, born Zurich, Switzerland, March 4, 1947; admitted, 1975, Switzerland. *Education:* University of Zurich (Lic.iur., 1972). *LANGUAGES:* German, English, French and Italian. *PRACTICE AREAS:* Arbitration; Litigation.

WALTER J. WEBER, born Littleborough, England, November 16, 1953; admitted, 1981, Switzerland; 1985, New York. *Education:* University of Zurich (Lic.iur., 1978). *LANGUAGES:* German, English and French. *PRACTICE AREAS:* International Commercial Law; Corporate Law; Mergers and Acquisitions; Litigation; Arbitration; Immigration.

ROLAND KAUFMANN, born Geneva, Switzerland, August 18, 1947; admitted, 1974, Switzerland. *Education:* University of Geneva (Lic. iur., 1973); New York University, Institute of Comparative Law (M.C.J., 1980). (Resident, Geneva Office). *LANGUAGES:* French, English, Italian and German. *PRACTICE AREAS:* Commercial Law; Company Law; Contract Law; Sponsoring; Sports.

JEAN-LUC HERBEZ, born Geneva, Switzerland, March 27, 1945; admitted, 1976, Switzerland. *Education:* University of Geneva (Lic. oec., 1970; Lic. iur., 1976); University of Pennsylvania Law School, Center for Study of Financial Institutions, Philadelphia (LL.M., 1981). (Resident, London Office). *LANGUAGES:* French, German, English and Italian. *PRACTICE AREAS:* Commercial Law; Corporate Law; Contract Law; Taxation; Finance; Banking; Finance and Securities.

DOMINIQUE BROWN-BERSET, born Villarsiviriaux, Switzerland, February 23, 1953; admitted, 1980, Switzerland. *Education:* University of Lausanne (Lic.iur., 1976); Paris I Panthéon-Sorbonne (DEA, 1978); Harvard Law School (Master of Laws, 1980). Former Editor, Journal of International Arbitration. Associate Member, Chartered Institute of Arbitrators. (Resident, Geneva Office). *LANGUAGES:* French, English and German. *PRACTICE AREAS:* Commercial and Contract Law; International Arbitration and ADR; International Litigation and Procedure; Company Law; Finance and Securities.

HANS STUBER, born Risch, Switzerland, May 1, 1943; admitted, 1979, Switzerland. *Education:* University of Zurich (Lic.iur., 1975). (Resident, Zug Office). *LANGUAGES:* German, English and French. *PRACTICE AREAS:* Commercial Law; Corporate Law; International Trusts and Estates; Leases; Taxation; Real Estate; Wills; Inheritance; Insurance; Eastern European Commerce; Notarial Services.

PETER J. MERZ, born Kreuzlingen, Switzerland, August 6, 1951; admitted, 1983, Switzerland. *Education:* University of Zurich (Lic.iur., 1978). *LANGUAGES:* German, English and French. *PRACTICE AREAS:* Commercial Law; Corporate Law; Contract Law; Antitrust and Trade Regulation; International Legal Assistance; Litigation; Computer Contracts.

FELIX M. MATHIS, born Zurich, Switzerland, March 31, 1953; admitted, 1985, Switzerland; 1989, New York. *Education:* University of Zurich (Lic.iur., 1980); New York University (M.C.J., 1988). *LANGUAGES:* German and English. *PRACTICE AREAS:* Corporate Law; Securitization; Commercial and Contract Law; Litigation; Aviation.

RESIDENT ASSOCIATES

DR. ALESSANDRO L. CELLI, born Milano, Italy, July 29, 1962; admitted, 1990, Switzerland (Not admitted in Switzerland). *Education:* University of Zurich (Dr. iur., 1993). *LANGUAGES:* German, English and French. *PRACTICE AREAS:* Intellectual Property; Trademarks; Copyrights; Antitrust and Trade Regulation; Art Law; International Law; Commercial Law; Corporate Law; Company Law; Securities.

DR. MICHAEL W. KNELLER, born Zurich, Switzerland, October 25, 1959; admitted, 1988, Switzerland. *Education:* University of Zurich (Dr. iur., 1993); New York University (M.C.J., 1991). *LANGUAGES:* German, French and English. *PRACTICE AREAS:* Contract Law; Corporate Law; Trusts and Estates; International Private Law.

TINA WUESTEMANN, born Zurich, Switzerland, December 30, 1964; admitted, 1994, Switzerland. *Education:* University of Zurich (Lic. iur., 1990). *LANGUAGES:* German, English and French. *PRACTICE AREAS:* Corporate Law; Contract Law; Product Liability.

MARCEL CARL STEINEGGER, born Zurich, Switzerland, September 1, 1961; admitted, 1992, Switzerland. *Education:* University of Zurich (Lic.

(This Listing Continued)

iur., 1988). *LANGUAGES:* German, English, French. *PRACTICE AREAS:* Commercial Law; Public Law; Criminal Law.

PATRICK MARTIN O'NEILL, born England, October 1, 1962; admitted, 1994, Switzerland. *Education:* University of Berne (Lic. iur., 1988); University of St. Gallen (Certificate of EU-Commercial Law, 1993). *LANGUAGES:* English and German. *PRACTICE AREAS:* Swiss and European Commercial Law; Litigation.

OF COUNSEL

DR. GUIDO M. RENGGLI, born Zug, Switzerland, April 27, 1931; admitted, 1959, Switzerland. *Education:* Universities of Fribourg and Berne (Dr.iur., 1955). (Zug and Nürnberg Offices). *LANGUAGES:* German, Swedish, Norwegian, English, French and Italian. *PRACTICE AREAS:* Commercial Law; Corporate Law; International Contract Law; Arbitration.

GAYLER, HEGETSCHWEILER & PARTNER

ZÜRICH, SWITZERLAND

(See Staiger, Schwald & Sauter)

GIPSON HOFFMAN & PANCIONE

A PROFESSIONAL CORPORATION

ZEPPELINSTRASSE 28
CH-8057 ZÜRICH, SWITZERLAND
Telephone: 011-411-261-7555
Telefax: 011-411-364-2713

Los Angeles, California Office: Suite 1100, 1901 Avenue of the Stars, 90067-6002. Telephone: 310-556-4660. Telex: 910-490-2531 GHST LAW: Fax: 310-556-8945, 310-556-4301.

MARKUS W. BARMETTLER, born Lucerne, Switzerland, April 28, 1960; admitted, 1986, Switzerland. *Education:* Bern University (Dr.iur, summa cum laude, 1986). *LANGUAGES:* German, French, Spanish, Italian and English. *PRACTICE AREAS:* International Tax; Corporate Restructuring; International Co-productions.

VINCENT H. CHIEFFO (Resident, Los Angeles, California Office).

ROBERT H. STEINBERG (Resident, Los Angeles, California Office).

(For Complete Biographical Data on all Personnel, see Professional Biographies at Los Angeles, California)

GIROUD & ANDERES

ALTE LANDSTRASSE 55
8802 KILCHBERG-ZÜRICH, SWITZERLAND
Telephone: 01/715 07 15
Telefax: 01/715 06 15

General Corporate and Commercial Practice, Contract Law, International Private Law, Insolvency and Bankruptcy Law, Competition Law, Antitrust Law, Intellectual Property, Law of Inheritance, Litigation and Arbitration.

MEMBERS OF FIRM

DR. ROGER GIROUD, born 1952; admitted, 1982, Switzerland. *Education:* University of Zurich (lic.iur., 1975; Dr.iur., 1980); University of London (LL.M., 1987). *LANGUAGES:* German and English. *PRACTICE AREAS:* International Arbitration; Corporate and Commercial Law; Contract Law; Insolvency and Bankruptcy Law; Conflict of Laws; Competition Law.

LIC.IUR. LUCAS ANDERES, born 1954; admitted, 1984, Switzerland. *Education:* University of Zurich (lic.iur., 1978). *LANGUAGES:* German and English. *PRACTICE AREAS:* Corporate and Commercial Law; Contract Law; Insolvency and Bankruptcy Law; Litigation; Inheritance.

DR. MARIANNE BIERI-GUT, born 1954; admitted, 1984, Switzerland. *Education:* University of Zurich (lic.iur., 1981; Dr.iur., 1993); New York University (M.C.J., 1991). *LANGUAGES:* German and English.

(This Listing Continued)

GIROUD & ANDERES, Zürich—Continued

PRACTICE AREAS: Intellectual Property; Competition Law; Antitrust Law; Agency and Distributorships; Corporate and Commercial Law; Litigation.

Languages: German and English

LAW FIRM
DR. MAX GLAUSER

Established in 1969

SEEFELDSTRASSE 7

P.O. BOX 903

CH-8034 ZÜRICH, SWITZERLAND

Telephone: 01-261 33 81

Telefax: 01-261 08 49

DR. MAX GLAUSER, born Hergiswil, Switzerland, July 27, 1943; admitted, 1968, Zürich. *Education:* Kantonales Gymnasium Zurich; University of Zurich (Dr.iur., 1969). *LANGUAGES:* German, English and French. *PRACTICE AREAS:* International Commercial Practice; Corporate; Contracts; Estates; Real Estate; Taxes; Trusts.

GLOOR & SIEGER

UTOQUAI 37

P.O. BOX 581

CH-8024 ZÜRICH, SWITZERLAND

Telephone: 01/261 36 37

Telefax: 01/261 42 74

San José, Costa Rica Office: P.O. Box 6610, San José 1000, Costa Rica.

Business, Commercial and Corporate Law, International Trade, Contracts, Banking and Tax Law, Intellectual Property, Insurance, Trust and Estates, Debt Collection and Bankruptcy Law, International Judicial Assistance, International Arbitration in Commercial and Construction Law Disputes, Commercial Litigation.

DR. ALAIN GLOOR, born 1950; admitted, 1979, Switzerland. *Education:* University of Zurich (Dr.iur., 1982); University of Michigan School of Law, Ann Arbor (LL.M., 1980). *Member:* Swiss and Zurich Bar Associations. *LANGUAGES:* German, English and French.

DR. KURT SIEGER, born 1948; admitted, 1983, Switzerland. *Education:* University of Zurich (Dr.iur., 1979); Columbia University School of Law (LL.M., 1980). Legal Practitioner, Shutts & Bowen, Miami, 1980-1982. *Member:* Swiss, Zurich, International and American Bar Associations. *LANGUAGES:* German, English and French.

DR. DANIEL WEHRLI, born 1950; admitted, 1978, Switzerland. *Education:* University of Zurich (Dr.iur., 1976). Associate with: Rosenman & Colin, New York, 1989-1990; Studio Legale Ardito, Rome, 1990-1991. *Member:* Swiss, Zurich and International Bar Associations; Swiss Arbitration Association. *LANGUAGES:* German, English, Italian and French.

STEPHAN W. FEIERABEND, born 1962; admitted, 1989, Switzerland. *Education:* University of Zurich (lic.iur., 1986). *Member:* Swiss and Zurich Bar Associations. *LANGUAGES:* German, English and French.

DR. B. GINO KOENIG, born 1956; admitted, 1985, Switzerland; 1988, Virginia. *Education:* University of Zurich (Dr.iur., 1989); University of Virginia School of Law (LL.M., 1988). Associate with: Shaw, Pittman, Potts & Trowbridge, Washington, D.C., 1989-1990. *Member:* Swiss, Zurich and International Bar Associations; Virginia State Bar; American Bar Association; Swiss Arbitration Association. *LANGUAGES:* German, English.

GNAEGI, BELSER & ALTORFER
LAW OFFICES

DUFOURSTRASSE 56

CH-8008 ZÜRICH, SWITZERLAND

Telephone: 01 / 252 91 00

Telex: 816077 IUS CH

Telecopier: G-3 01/252 97 93

General Commercial and Corporate Practice, Banking and Finance, Securities, Contracts, Commercial Litigation, Arbitration, Inheritance and Estate Planning, Taxation, Real Estate, Employment, Work and Residence Permits.

MEMBERS OF FIRM

DR.IUR. ALBERT GNAEGI, born 1944; admitted, 1973, Switzerland. *Education:* University of Zurich (Dr. iur., 1969); University of Rome (1966-1967; 1970-1971).

DR.IUR. PETER M. BELSER, born 1945; admitted, 1976, Switzerland. *Education:* University of Zurich (Dr. iur., 1975); University of Michigan Law School (M.C.L., 1977).

DR.IUR. PETER ALTORFER, born 1953; admitted, 1982, Switzerland. *Education:* University of Zurich (Dr. iur., 1980); IMD Lausanne (1987).

COUNSEL

DR.IUR. MAX P. FISCHER, born 1925. *Education:* University of Zurich (Dr. iur., 1952); University of Paris (1949).

ASSOCIATES OF FIRM

DR.IUR. MICHAEL HUBER, born 1959; admitted, 1990, Switzerland. *Education:* University of Zurich (Dr.iur., 1988); University of Edinburgh, Europa Institute (LL.M., 1993).

DR.IUR. HANS REINHARD, born 1960; admitted, 1988, Switzerland. *Education:* University of Berne (Dr.iur., 1993).

GEORG ZONDLER, born 1961; admitted, 1993, Switzerland. *Education:* University of Zurich (Lic. iur., 1988).

ROLAND VETTERLI, born 1960; admitted, 1989, Switzerland. *Education:* University of St. Gall (Dr. iur., 1989).

Languages: German, French, English and Italian.

HAFNER & HOCHSTRASSER

Established in 1992

GENFERSTRASSE 21

CH-8002 ZÜRICH, SWITZERLAND

Telephone: +41-1 201 95 01

Telefax: +41-1 201 95 41

Corporate, Commercial and Banking Law-Intellectual Property- Transnational Transactions-Estate Planning-General Litigation.

FIRM PROFILE: Established in 1992, Hafner & Hochstrasser is a young Law Firm combining the broad experience of its partners in particular in the corporate, commercial and financial areas to offer a full range of quality legal services.

MEMBERS OF FIRM

BENNO P. HAFNER, born Lucerne, Switzerland, November 4, 1950; admitted, 1979, Lucerne. *Education:* College of Sarnen (Business Degree); University of Bern (Law Degree); Zurich University. Author: "Die Willensbildung bei der Aktiengesellschaft," Zurich, 1985; "Die Kleinaktiengesellschaft," Zurich, 1981. Clerk to the Court, 1978; Legal Adviser with Swiss Trust and Fiduciary Company (Schweizerische Treuhandgesellschaft Coopers & Lybrand AG), Zurich, 1980-1985; Head of Legal Department of Kontron Holding AG, former Sub-Group of F. Hoffmann-La Roche AG, Zurich, 1986-1990; Partner in Law Firm, Werder & Schaub, Zurich, 1990-1992. *LANGUAGES:* German, English, French and Italian. *PRACTICE AREAS:* Business Law; Commercial Law; Banks and Banking; Agency and Distributorships; Company Law; Corporate Law; Unfair Competition; Art Law; Asset Protection; Estate Planning.

EMANUEL C. HOCHSTRASSER, born Lucerne, Switzerland, April 27, 1952; admitted, 1980, Zurich; 1983, New York. *Education:* University of Bern, Switzerland (lic. iur., 1978); New York University. Author: "Das arbeitsrechtliche Risiko des schlechten Geschäftsganges," Bern, 1977. Clerk

(This Listing Continued)

to the Court, 1978-1979; Associated with: Law Firm in Zurich and New York, 1979-1984; Law Firm in Zurich, 1984-1986; General Counsel/Secretary, Board of Inspectorate International Ltd., Neuchâtel, 1986-1989; Partner in Law Firm, Hochstrasser, Attorneys-at-Law, Lucerne, 1990-1992. *Member:* Swiss, Lucerne and New York Bar Associations. *LANGUAGES:* German, English, French and Spanish. *PRACTICE AREAS:* Arbitration and Mediation; International Arbitration; Banks and Banking; Asset Recovery; Business Law; Contracts; General Practice; Litigation.

GUDRUN STEIGER, born Wunstorf/Hanover, Germany, November 9, 1942. *Education:* University of Zurich, Switzerland (Dr.iur., 1981). Author: "Der Leistungsschutz des Schauspielers," Zurich, 1980; "Zum Urheberrecht an Bühnenwerken," Bern, 1983. Head of Legal Department, SUISA, Swiss Copyright Society for Composers, Songwriters and Music Publishers, Zurich, 1982-1994; Vice President, SAFE, Swiss Anti-Piracy Federation, Bern, 1987-1994. *LANGUAGES:* German, English and French. *PRACTICE AREAS:* National and International Copyright and Neighboring Rights; Intellectual Property; Artist Agency and Consultation; Contracts; General Practice; Arbitration; Litigation.

HARTMANN & MEYER
AND PARTNERS

Established in 1983

ZÜRICHBERGSTRASSE 66
CH-8044 ZÜRICH, SWITZERLAND
Telephone: (+41) 01-251 77 12
Telex: 815198 HMZH
Telecopier: (+41) 01-251 78 11

Zug, Switzerland Office: Grafenauweg 8, 6300 Zug. Telephone: (+41) 42-22 30. 40. Telecopier: (+41) 42-22 23 53.

Business and Corporate Law, International Trade, Commercial Contracts, Banking and Tax Law, Unfair Competition, Transportation Law, Industrial Property Rights (Patent, Trademark, Know-how) Law, Licensing, Agency and Distribution Law, Debt Collection and Bankruptcy Law, Employment Law, International Judicial Assistance Law, Arbitration and Litigation.

FIRM PROFILE: Full range of legal services with emphasis on business and corporate law. Work conducted in German, English and French. Advanced office automation systems. Access to national and international data bases in the legal and economic fields.

MEMBERS OF FIRM

DR. JÜRG E. HARTMANN, born 1949; admitted, 1975. *Education:* University of Zürich (Dr.iur., 1974). Author: "Der Akkreditiveröffnungsauftrag," Zurich, 1974, "Der Kaufvertrag in der Handelspraxis," Zurich, 1979. Co-Author: "Der Alleinvertriebsvertrag," Zurich, 1984; "Neues schweizerisches Aktienrecht," Zurich 1992. *Member:* Swiss and Zurich Bar Associations; International Bar Association. *LANGUAGES:* German, English and French. *PRACTICE AREAS:* Business Law and Corporate Law; Banking Law; Antitrust Law; Tax Law; International Litigation and Arbitration.

DR. BERNHARD F. MEYER-HAUSER, LL.M., born 1946; admitted, 1975. *Education:* University of Zurich (Dr.Iur., 1979); Northwestern University School of Law, Chicago (LL.M., 1977). Author: "Swiss Banking Secrecy and Its Legal Implications in the United States," Article, New England Law Review 14, No. 1, 1979. Co-Author: "Swiss Work Permit Regulations," Overview and Translation of Limitation Ordinance, Swiss-American Chamber of Commerce, 1989; "Enforcement of a Money Claim in Switzerland, Zurich 1994"; "Agency and Distribution Agreements in Switzerland," 1991; "Swiss Contract Law" and "Swiss Company Law," English translations of official text of Swiss Code of Obligations, 1992. *Member:* Swiss and Zurich Bar Associations; International Bar Association; American Bar Association; Swiss Arbitration Association. *LANGUAGES:* German, English and French. *PRACTICE AREAS:* Business and Corporate Law; Company Foundations; Employment Law and Work Permits; Licensing, Agency and Distribution Law; Unfair Competition Law; International Litigation and Arbitration.

DR. NIKLAUS B. MÜLLER, LL.M., born 1951; admitted, 1977. *Education:* University of Berne (Dr.Iur., 1979); University of California at Berkeley (LL.M., 1980). Author: "Die Rechtsprechung des Bundesgerichts zum Grundsatz der verfassungskonformen Auslegung," Bern, 1980. *Member:* Swiss and Zurich Bar Associations; International Bar Association; Swiss Arbitration Association. *LANGUAGES:* German, English and

French. *PRACTICE AREAS:* International Litigation and Arbitration; Banking Law; Contracts Law; Patents Law; Taxes and Bankruptcy Law.

DR. CHRISTOPH P.A. MARTIG, born 1956; admitted, 1987. *Education:* University of Zurich (Dr. Iur., 1983); University of California at Berkeley. Author: "Reederhaftung im Rheinfrachtgeschäft," Basel, 1984; "Ermittlung und Anwendung materiellen Rechts im schweizerischen See- und Rheinfrachtrecht," Zurich 1992. *Member:* Swiss and Zurich Bar Associations; Swiss Arbitration Association. *LANGUAGES:* German, English and French. *PRACTICE AREAS:* Business and Corporate Law; Shipping and Transportation Law; Industrial Property Law; Residential Property and Inheritance Law.

DR. FELIX W. EGLI, LL.M., born 1960; admitted, 1987. *Education:* University of St. Gallen (Dr.Iur., 1989); Southern Methodist University Dallas (LL.M., 1988). Author: "Der Nichtdiskriminierungsbegriff im Versicherungsabkommen Schweiz - EWG," Hartung-Gorre Verlag, Konstanz, 1989; "Die Anerkennung und Vollstreckung deutscher, österreichischer und liechtensteinischer Gerichtsentscheidungen in Zivil- und Handelssachen in der Schweiz," RIW 12/1991. Co-Author: "Agency and Distribution Agreements in Switzerland," 1991. *Member:* Swiss and Zurich Bar Associations; Swiss Arbitration Association. *LANGUAGES:* German, English, French and Italian. *PRACTICE AREAS:* Business and Corporate Law; Company Law; Intellectual Property; International Trade Law; Conflicts of Law; Litigation and Arbitration.

ASSOCIATES

DR. JÜRG BORER, born 1958; admitted 1990. *Education:* University of St. Gall (Dr. Iur., 1988). Author: "Massnahmen gleicher Wirkung wie mengenmässige Einfuhrbeschränkungen im Freihandelsabkommen Schweiz-EWG," Bern 1988; "Grundlagen des Warenverkehrs im Freihandelsabkommen Schweiz-EWG," 1988; "Spruchpraxis zum EG-Wettbewerbsrecht," 1990; *Member:* Swiss and Zurich Bar Associations. *LANGUAGES:* German, English and French. *PRACTICE AREAS:* Business and Corporate Law; Antitrust Law; European Community Law; International Law; Conflicts of Law.

DR. HANS-ULRICH SCHOCH, born 1962; admitted 1991. *Education:* University of Zurich (Dr.Iur. 1994). Author: "Die verwandten Schutzrechte der ausübenden Künstler, der Ton-und Tonbildtrager-hersteller und der Sendeunternehmen in schweizerischen Recht". Co-Author: "Neues schweizerisches Aktienrecht," Zurich 1992. *Member:* Swiss and Zurich Bar Associations. *LANGUAGES:* German, English and French. *PRACTICE AREAS:* Business and Corporate Law; Debt Enforcement and Bankruptcy Law; Agency and Distribution Law; Unfair Competition Law.

DR. GION-ANDRI DECURTINS, born, 1964; admitted 1994. *Education:* University of Fribourg (Dr.jur., 1992); University of San Diego School of Law (M.C.L., 1991). Author: "Die rechtliche Stellung der Behörde im Abstimmungskamf", Fribourg 1992. *Member:* Swiss and Zurich Bar Associations. *LANGUAGES:* German, English, Italian and French. *PRACTICE AREAS:* Business and Corporate Law; Agency and Distribution Law; Intellectual Property Law; Inheritance Law; Debt Enforcement and Bankruptcy Law; Employment Law; Administrative Law.

LUKA MÜLLER, born 1964, admitted 1992. *Education:* University of Zurich (lic.jur., 1990); London School of Economics (LL.M. 1994). *Member:* Swiss and Zurich Bar Associations. *LANGUAGES:* German, English, French. *PRACTICE AREAS:* Business and Corporate Law; Unfair Competition; Insurance Law; Torts and Product Liability.

HAYMANN & BALDI

Established in 1977

HOTTINGERSTRASSE 17
CH-8032 ZÜRICH, SWITZERLAND
Telephone: 01/262 10 10
Cable Address: "Counsel"
Telecopier: (01) 2 62 18 22

MEMBERS OF FIRM

MICHEL H.L. HAYMANN, born Zurich, Switzerland, November 20, 1942; admitted, 1975, Zurich. *Education:* University of Zurich (Dr.iur.). *LANGUAGES:* German, English, French and Italian. *PRACTICE AREAS:* International Business Law; EC Law; Corporate Law; Banking Law; Commercial Litigation; Arbitration.

PETER J. BALDI, born Brunnen, Switzerland, March 3, 1946; admitted, 1977, Zurich. *Education:* University of Zurich (Dr.iur., 1974). *LANGUAGES:* German, English, French and Italian. *PRACTICE AREAS:*

(This Listing Continued)

(This Listing Continued)

HAYMANN & BALDI, Zürich—Continued

International Business Law; Corporate Law; Banking Law; Intellectual Property Law; Property Law; Commercial Litigation.

ASSOCIATES

MICHELE A. CARATSCH, born St. Gall, Switzerland, July 3, 1963; admitted, 1991, Zurich. *Education:* University of Zurich (lic. iur., 1988). *LANGUAGES:* German, English, Italian and Spanish. *PRACTICE AREAS:* International Business Law; EC Law; Corporate Law; Commercial Litigation; Banking Law.

BEAT MÜLLER, born Zurich, Switzerland, July 15, 1968; admitted, 1994, St. Gall. *Education:* University of St. Gall (Dr.iur., 1994). *LANGUAGES:* German, English and French. *PRACTICE AREAS:* Private International Law; International Business Law; Corporate Law; Commercial Litigation.

LAURENT OLIVIER KYD, born 1967; admitted, 1993, Geneva. *Education:* University of Geneva, Law School (lic. iur., 1991). *LANGUAGES:* French, English, German and Italian. *PRACTICE AREAS:* International Business Law; Banking Law; Intellectual Property Law; Commercial Litigation.

CLAUDIA KASPER, born Zurich, Switzerland, March 28, 1965; admitted, 1994, Zurich. *Education:* University of Zurich (lic.iur., 1990). *LANGUAGES:* German, English and French. *PRACTICE AREAS:* International Business Law; Corporate Law; Commercial Litigation; Banking Law.

LUKAS HEMMELER, born Brugg, Switzerland, February 17, 1968; admitted, 1994, Berne. *Education:* University of Berne (lic.iur, 1994). *LANGUAGES:* German, English and French. *PRACTICE AREAS:* Corporate Law; Commercial Litigation; Intellectual Property Law; Trusts and Wills.

HENRICI, WICKI & GUGGISBERG

Established in 1937

HOTTINGERSTRASSE 21
CH-8032 ZÜRICH, SWITZERLAND
Telephone: 41-1-251 66 55
Telecopier: 41-1-252 59 84
X-400: C=CH/ADMD=ARCOM/PRMD=HWG/S=HDSK

Mailing Address: Postfach 526 CH-8024 Zürich, Switzerland

Arbitration Law, Banking Law, Bankruptcy Law, Business Law, Buying and Selling of Businesses, Civil (General Civil) Practice, Commercial Law, Commodities Law, Contract Law, Corporate Law, Estate Planning, Extradition, Finance Law, Immigration and Nationality or Naturalization Law, Insolvency Law, International Business Law, EEC Law, Litigation, Mergers and Acquisitions, Tort Law.

MEMBERS OF FIRM

DR. ANDREAS K. HENRICI, born Zurich, Switzerland, 1934; admitted, 1962, Switzerland. *Education:* Universities of Zurich (Dr.iur., 1960) and Berlin. Author of a Thesis on Philosophy of Law, 1960. Deputy Justice, Swiss Federal Supreme Court, 1985-1990. Lecturer, Civil and Commercial Law, Universities of Fribourg and Zurich, 1978-1990. *Member:* Zurich, Swiss and International Bar Associations; Swiss Lawyers' Association. *LANGUAGES:* German, French and English. *PRACTICE AREAS:* Commercial and Corporate Law; Mergers and Acquisitions; Estate Planning.

DR. ANDRÉ ALOYS WICKI, born Lucerne, Switzerland, 1940; admitted, 1975, Switzerland. *Education:* University of Zurich (Dr.iur., 1965). Author: "Zur Dogmengeschichte der Parteiautonomie im Internationalen Privatrecht," Zurich, 1965; "Aktuelle Fragen des Dokumentarakkreditivs," Zurich, 1978; "Obtaining Discovery Abroad," Chapter on Switzerland, American Bar Association, Chicago, 1990. Legal Counsel of a major Swiss Bank, 1966-1975. *Member:* Zurich, Swiss and International Bar Associations; Swiss Lawyers' Association; Swiss Panel of Arbitrators, International Chamber of Commerce, Zurich. *LANGUAGES:* German, English and French. *PRACTICE AREAS:* Banking; Commercial; Corporate; International Legal Assistance in Civil and Criminal Matters; Arbitration.

JÜRG GUGGISBERG, born Zurich, Switzerland, 1949; admitted, 1978, Switzerland. *Education:* University of Zurich (lic.iur., 1975). Legal Counsel of a Swiss Bank, 1977-1981. *Member:* Zurich, Swiss and International Bar Associations. *LANGUAGES:* German, English and French. *PRACTICE AREAS:* Banking; Corporate; Commercial; Contracts.

(This Listing Continued)

DR. HANS-PETER SCHAAD, born Laupersdorf, Switzerland, 1944; admitted, 1972, Switzerland. *Education:* University of Zurich (lic.iur., 1968; Dr.iur., 1972). Author: "Das Depotstimmrecht der Banken nach schweizerischem und deutschem Recht," Zurich, 1972. Legal Counsel of a major Swiss Bank, 1971-1990. *Member:* Zurich, Swiss and International Bar Associations; Swiss Lawyers' Association. *LANGUAGES:* German, English and French. *PRACTICE AREAS:* Banking; Finance; Securities; Corporate; Commercial; Insolvency; Trust and Estate Planning; Arbitration.

DR. ANDREAS D. LÄNZLINGER, born Zurich, Switzerland, 1959; admitted, 1986, Switzerland. *Education:* University of Zurich (lic.iur., 1983; Dr.iur., 1992). Author: "Die Haftung des Kreditgebers - Beurteilung möglicher Haftungstatbestände nach schweizerischem und amerikanischem Recht," Zurich, 1992, (Thesis on Lender Liability). *Member:* Zurich, Swiss and International Bar Associations. *LANGUAGES:* German, English and French. *PRACTICE AREAS:* Banking; Commercial; Corporate; Litigation of Commercial Matters; Legal Assistance in Civil and Criminal Matters.

ASSOCIATES

DANIELA GULLO EHM, born Bern, Switzerland, 1958; admitted, 1989, Switzerland. *Education:* University of Bern (lic.iur., 1984). *Member:* Zurich, Swiss and International Bar Associations. *LANGUAGES:* German, English and French. *PRACTICE AREAS:* Banking; Commercial and Corporate Law; Arbitration.

CLAUDIO MÖHR, born Zurich, Switzerland, 1960; admitted, 1989, Switzerland. *Education:* University of Zurich (lic.iur., 1985). Officer in legal department of a major Swiss Banking Group in Zurich and London, 1988-1991. *Member:* Zurich, Swiss and International Bar Associations; Swiss Lawyers' Association. *LANGUAGES:* German, English, French and Italian. *PRACTICE AREAS:* Banking and Securities Law; Company Law; Arbitration.

BALTHASAR WICKI, born Lucerne, Switzerland, 1963; admitted, 1993, Switzerland. *Education:* University of Zurich (lic.iur., 1989). *Member:* Zurich, Swiss and International Bar Associations; AIJA (Association Internationale de Jeunes Avocats). *LANGUAGES:* German, English and French. *PRACTICE AREAS:* Banking and Securities Law; Commercial and Corporate Law.

THOMAS ZEMP, born Sursee, Switzerland, 1965; admitted, 1993, Switzerland. *Education:* University of St. Gallen (lic.iur. HSG, 1990). *Member:* Zurich, Swiss and International Bar Associations. *LANGUAGES:* German, English and French. *PRACTICE AREAS:* Banking; Commercial; Corporate; Bankruptcy and Insolvency; Contracts.

HOMBERGER, KORACH & PARTNER

LIMMATQUAI 1
CH 8001 ZÜRICH, SWITZERLAND
Telephone: 01/251 68 10
Cable Address: "Kohegro"
Telecopier: 01/252 59 58

MEMBERS OF FIRM

DR. HANS ULRICH HOMBERGER, born Zurich, Switzerland, May 14, 1945; admitted, 1971, Zurich. *Education:* University of Zurich (Lic.iur., 1969; Dr.iur., 1973). *LANGUAGES:* German, English and French. *PRACTICE AREAS:* Corporate Law; Commercial Law; Contractual Law.

DR. ALEXANDER KORACH, born Debrecen, Hungary, July 8, 1946; admitted, 1977, Zurich. *Education:* University of Zurich (Lic.iur., 1970; Dr.iur., 1973). *LANGUAGES:* German, English, French and Hungarian. *PRACTICE AREAS:* Corporate Law; Commercial Law; Contractual Law.

PROF. DR. PASCAL SIMONIUS, born Basel, Switzerland, April 26, 1929; admitted, 1960, Basel. *Education:* University of Basel (Dr.iur., 1955). *LANGUAGES:* German, French, Italian and English. *PRACTICE AREAS:* Commercial Law; Corporate Law; Contractual Law.

DR. BARBARA STREHLE, born Zurich, November 20, 1949; admitted, 1981, Zurich. *Education:* Universities of Lausanne and Zurich (lic.iur. 1973; Dr.iur., 1980). Deputy Judge, District Court of Zurich. Substitute Member, Tax Appeal Commission of the Canton of Zurich. *LANGUAGES:* German, English and French. *PRACTICE AREAS:* Commercial Law; Corporate Law; Contractual Law; Litigation.

DR. STEFAN KNECHT, born Zurich, Switzerland, October 27, 1949; admitted, 1977, Switzerland. *Education:* University of Zurich (Lic.iur., 1974; Dr.iur., 1980); University of Miami School of Law (LL.M., 1983).

(This Listing Continued)

Thesis in Procedural Law, 1980. Lecturer, University of Zurich, 1983—. *LANGUAGES:* German, English and French. *PRACTICE AREAS:* Corporate Law; Commercial Law; Insurance Law; Wills and Estates; International Business Transactions; Litigation.

Languages: German, English, French, Italian and Hungarian

HOMBURGER RECHTSANWÄLTE

Established in 1958

WEINBERGSTRASSE 56/58
8006 ZÜRICH, SWITZERLAND
Telephone: (01) 265 3535
Intn'l Dialing: (41-1) 265 3535
Cable Address: ABOGADO
Telex: 816824
Answer Back: 816824 ABOG CH
Facsimile: (01) 265 3511

Mailing Address: P.O. Box 326, 8035 Zürich

General Corporate, Mergers and Acquisitions, Tax, Banking and Finance, Antitrust and Unfair Competition, Commercial Litigation, Arbitration, Administrative and Regulatory Matters, Intellectual Property, Labor, Law and Immigration.

MEMBERS OF FIRM

DR. DIETER V. SCHULTHESS, born Zurich, Switzerland, 1937; admitted, 1964, Zurich, Switzerland. *Education:* University of Zurich (Dr.iur., 1962); Harvard Law School (LL.M., 1965).

DR. PETER WIDMER, born Zurich, Switzerland, 1940; admitted, 1967, Zurich, Switzerland. *Education:* University of Zurich (Dr.iur., 1965); University of Chicago Law School (M.C.L., 1968).

DR. JENS DROLSHAMMER, born Zurich, Switzerland, 1944; admitted, 1976, Zurich, Switzerland. *Education:* University of Zurich (Dr.iur., 1975); Graduate Institute of International Studies, Geneva; University of Michigan Law School (M.C.L., 1971); Harvard University, Department of Government, Law School, Visiting Scholar.

DR. MARKUS H. WIRTH, born Bern, Switzerland, 1945; admitted, 1977, Zurich, Switzerland. *Education:* University of Zurich (Dr.iur., 1976); University of Toronto Faculty of Law (LL.M., 1972).

DR. PETER A. KURER, born Zurich, Switzerland, 1949; admitted, 1980, Zurich, Switzerland. *Education:* University of Zurich (Dr.iur., 1978); University of Chicago Law School (LL.M., 1976).

DR. FELIX KLAUS, born St. Gallen, Switzerland, 1952; admitted, 1979, St. Gallen, Switzerland. *Education:* University of Fribourg (Dr.iur., 1978); Cornell Law School, Ithaca, N.Y. (LL.M., 1981).

DR. HEINZ SCHÄRER, born Zurich, Switzerland, 1953; admitted, 1982, Zurich, Switzerland. *Education:* University of Fribourg (Dr.iur., 1981); Southern Methodist University School of Law, Dallas (M.C.L., 1981).

DR. THOMAS MÜLLER, born Winterthur, Switzerland, 1949; admitted, 1976, Zurich, Switzerland. *Education:* University of Zurich (Dr.iur., 1982); University of California Law School, Los Angeles (LL.M., 1983).

DR. HAROLD GRÜNINGER, born Basel, Switzerland, 1954; admitted, 1981, Basel, Switzerland. *Education:* University of Basel (Dr.iur., 1983); University of Pennsylvania Law School (LL.M., 1983).

LIC. IUR. UELI HUBER, born Affoltern am Albis, Switzerland, 1955; admitted, 1984, Zurich, Switzerland. *Education:* University of Zurich (lic.iur., 1981); University of California, Los Angeles (LL.M., 1986).

LIC. IUR. WERNER STIEGER, born St. Gallen, Switzerland, 1946; admitted, 1985, Zurich, Switzerland. *Education:* University of Zurich (lic.iur., 1970).

DR. EVELINE M. OECHSLIN-SAUPPER, born Savognin, Switzerland, 1958; admitted, 1987, Zurich, Switzerland. *Education:* University of St. Gallen (lic.iur., 1983; Dr.iur., 1994). Certified Swiss Federal Tax Consultant, 1988.

DR. FRANZ HOFFET, born Bern, Switzerland, 1956; admitted, 1986, Zurich and Geneva, Switzerland. *Education:* Universities of Bern and Zurich; University of Chicago Law School (LL.M., 1988).

(This Listing Continued)

ASSOCIATES

FÜRSPRECHER FRANZ PROBST, born Bern, Switzerland, 1955; admitted, 1983, Bern and Zurich, Switzerland. *Education:* Universities of Zurich and Bern (Fürsprecher, 1983); University of Michigan Law School, Ann Arbor, Michigan (LL.M., 1989).

PD DR. HANS CASPAR VON DER CRONE, born Zurich, Switzerland, 1957; admitted, 1988, Zurich, Switzerland. *Education:* University of Zurich (Dr.iur., 1988); Yale Law School (LL.M., 1990).

DR. GEORG RAUBER, born Zurich, Switzerland, 1958; admitted, 1988, Zurich, Switzerland. *Education:* University of Zurich (Dr.iur., 1987).

DR. RENÉ BÖSCH, born Zurich, Switzerland, 1959; admitted, 1990, Switzerland. *Education:* University of Zurich, Switzerland (Dr.iur., 1987); University of Chicago (LL.M., 1991).

LIC. IUR. STEPHAN NEIDHARDT, born Zurich, Switzerland, 1959; admitted, 1989, Switzerland. *Education:* University of St. Gallen, Switzerland (Lic.iur., HSH, 1986).

DR. SABINE KILGUS, born Zurich, Switzerland, 1958; admitted, 1990, Switzerland. *Education:* University of Zurich (lic.iur., 1982; Dr.iur., 1987); University of Pennsylvania, Philadelphia (LL.M., 1993).

DR. ROBERTO DALLAFIOR, born Zurich, Switzerland, 1961; admitted, 1990, Zurich, Switzerland. *Education:* University of Zurich (Dr.iur., 1990); College of Europe, Brugge, Belgium (H.E.E., 1992).

DR. PATRICK HOLTZ, born Munsterlingen, Switzerland, 1959; admitted, 1990, Switzerland. *Education:* University of St. Gallen (Dr.iur., 1989).

LIC. IUR. REGULA E. WALTER, born Schaffhausen, Switzerland, 1963; admitted, 1990, Zurich, Switzerland. *Education:* University of Zurich (lic.iur., 1988); College of Europe, Brugge, Belgium (H.E.E., 1991).

DR. FELIX DASSER, born Zurich, Switzerland, 1958; admitted, 1991, Zurich, Switzerland. *Education:* University of Zurich (Dr.iur., 1989); Harvard Law School (LL.M., 1990).

DR. DANIEL DAENIKER, born Basel, Switzerland, 1963; admitted, 1990, Zurich, Switzerland. *Education:* Universities of Neuchâtel and Zurich (Dr.iur., 1992).

LIC. IUR. ANDREA GRIMM, born Zurich, Switzerland, 1964; admitted, 1992, Zurich, Switzerland. *Education:* University of Zurich (lic.iur., 1989).

DR. IVO BAUMGARTNER, born St. Gallen, Switzerland, 1962; (Not admitted in Switzerland). *Education:* University of Zurich (Dr.oec.publ.). Certified in Business Administration.

LIC. IUR. EDITH BLUNSCHI, born Einsiedeln, Switzerland, 1951; admitted, 1993, Zurich, Switzerland. *Education:* University of St. Gallen (lic.iur., 1990), Certified accountant.

LIC. IUR. HANS FRICKER, born Weymouth, United Kingdom, 1961; admitted, 1993, Zurich, Switzerland. *Education:* University of Zurich (lic.iur., 1990).

LIC. OEC. RICHARD ALLEMANN, born Zurich, Switzerland, 1954; admitted, 1993, Zurich, Switzerland. *Education:* University of St. Gallen (lic.oec., 1982).

DANIELLE GAUTHEY, born Hinsdale, United States, 1969; admitted, 1993, Geneva, Switzerland. *Education:* University of Lausanne (lic.iur., 1991).

DR. PATRIK DUCREY, born Fribourg, Switzerland, 1963; admitted, 1994, Zurich, Switzerland. *Education:* University of Fribourg (Dr.iur., 1991).

DR. CLAUDE LAMBERT, born Zurich, Switzerland, 1964; admitted, 1994, Zurich, Switzerland. *Education:* University of Zurich (Dr.iur., 1992).

LIC. IUR. BENEDIKT MAURENBRECHER, born St. Gallen, Switzerland, 1964; admitted, 1992, Zurich, Switzerland. *Education:* University of Bern (lic.iur., 1989).

OF COUNSEL

PROF. DR. ERIC E. HOMBURGER, born St. Gallen, Switzerland, 1920; admitted, 1949, Zurich, Switzerland. *Education:* Universities of Geneva and Zurich (Dr.iur., 1947); Harvard Law School (LL.M., 1956). Member of the firm until 1992.

PROF. DR. ERNST HOEHN, born Olten, Switzerland, 1930; admitted, 1957, Zurich, Switzerland. *Education:* University of Zurich (Dr.iur., 1955).

(This Listing Continued)

HOMBURGER RECHTSANWÄLTE, Zürich—Continued

DR. BRUNO SCHMIDHAUSER, born Wintherthur, Switzerland, 1931; (Not admitted in Switzerland). *Education:* University of Zurich (Dr.iur., 1959).

Languages: German, English, French and Italian

HÜRLIMANN URECH & UHLMANN

BAHNHOFSTRASSE 3
P.O. BOX 4930
8022 ZÜRICH, SWITZERLAND
Telephone: 411/211'39'57
Cable Address: JURDOC
Telecopier: 411/221'12'08

Washington, D.C. Office: The Army and Navy Building, 1627 Eye Street, N.W., 20006-4007 USA. Telephone: (202) 857-1700. Telecopier: (202) 857-1737 (in association with McGuire, Woods, Battle & Boothe, L.L.P.).

Commercial, Corporate, Banking and Finance and Industrial Property Law, Estate and Trust Matters, Civil Litigation (including International Arbitration), International Judicial Assistance and International Corporate Taxation.

MEMBERS OF FIRM

DR. CASPAR HÜRLIMANN, born Zürich, Switzerland, 1935; admitted, 1964, Zürich; 1974, Aargau; 1976, Zug and St. Gallen; 1985, Bern. *Education:* University of Zürich and University of Geneva, Law School and Interpreter School (1956-1957); University of Zürich Law School (lic. iur. 1960; Dr. iur. 1963); University of Virginia Law School (LL.M., 1968). *Member:* The Parlex Group of European Lawyers. *PRACTICE AREAS:* Commercial Law; Estate and Trust Law; International Judicial Assistance.

DANIEL URECH, born Schaffhausen, Switzerland, 1938; admitted, 1964, Bern; 1982, Zurich and Geneva. *Education:* University of Geneva Interpreter School (1957-1958); University of Princeton, Woodrow Wilson School (1958-1959); University of Geneva Law School (1957-1958); University of Bern Law School (Law Degree Combined with Admission to Bar, Spring, 1964). Swiss Correspondent, Journal of International Banking Law. Member, Board of Zurich Bar Association, 1991—; Chairman, 1995—. Member: Regulatory Committee of European Managed Futures Association, 1991—; Swiss Council, Euro-Arab Arbitration System, 1987—. *PRACTICE AREAS:* Company Law; Securities Law; Banking and Insurance.

DR. PETER UHLMANN, born Schaffhausen, Switzerland, 1935; admitted, 1967, Zürich; 1970, Schaffhausen; 1971, Bern; 1975, Zug. *Education:* University of Zürich Law School (lic. iur., 1961; Dr. iur., 1964). *Member:* The Interlex Group. *PRACTICE AREAS:* Commercial Law; Banking Law; International Private Law; Arbitration.

DR. SANDRO VISINI, born Zürich, Switzerland, 1957; admitted, 1985, Zurich and Geneva; 1991, New York. *Education:* University of Zurich Law School (Dr.iur., 1983); University of Virginia, Charlottesville (LL.M., 1989). *PRACTICE AREAS:* Corporate Law; Contracts; International Judicial Assistance; Arbitration.

CHRISTOPH FREY, born Zürich, Switzerland, 1962; admitted, 1992, Zürich; 1993, Lucerne. *Education:* University of Zürich Law School (lic.iur., 1988). *PRACTICE AREAS:* Commercial Law; Product Liability; Insurance.

TAX COUNSEL

FRANK L. WEIDEMA, born São Paolo, Brazil, 1960; admitted, 1994, Brussels. *Education:* University of Amsterdam (Tax Law, 1986). *LANGUAGES:* Dutch, English and German. *PRACTICE AREAS:* International Taxation.

All Swiss Attorneys of the Firm are Members of the Swiss and Zurich Bar Associations.

Languages: English, German and French

HÜSSY FORSTER von GRAFFENRIED

BELLERIVESTRASSE 10, POSTFACH
8034 ZÜRICH, SWITZERLAND
Telephone: 01/383 87 34
Telecopier: 01/383 15 14

Commercial, Corporate, Banking, Inheritance, International Law, Litigation and Arbitration, Intellectual Property and Competition Law, Bankruptcy, Taxation, General Practice.

MEMBERS OF FIRM

DR. HANS HÜSSY, born 1930; admitted, 1956. *Education:* Universities Zürich, Geneva (lic.iur., 1954) and Neuchâtel (Dr.iur., 1958). *LANGUAGES:* German, English, French and Italian.

DR. GERTRUD FORSTER, born 1926; admitted, 1954. *Education:* University of Zürich (Dr.iur., 1952). *LANGUAGES:* German, English, French and Italian.

DR. CHRISTOPH VON GRAFFENRIED, born 1954; admitted, 1982. *Education:* University of Zürich (lic.iur., 1979); University of Basel (Dr. iur); Max Planck Institute for Foreign and International Patent, Copyright and Competition Law, Munich, Germany (1983). *LANGUAGES:* German, English and French. *PRACTICE AREAS:* Commercial; Corporate; Banking; Trusts and Estates; Copyrights; Trademarks; Art Law; Communications and Media; Litigation.

Languages: German, English, French and Italian

ISLER & KLAUS

LÖWENSTRASSE 40
CH-8001 ZÜRICH, SWITZERLAND
Telephone: (01) 211 43 97
Telecopier: (01) 211 55 25

Civil Law Practice, Commercial Law, Company Law, Law of Contracts, Law of Succession, Bankruptcy Law, Arbitration, Litigation.

MEMBERS OF FIRM

DR. EUGEN ISLER, born 1925; admitted, 1952, Zürich. *Education:* University of Zürich (Dr.iur., 1950). *Member:* Zürich and Swiss Bar Associations. *LANGUAGES:* German, English and French.

DR. ROMAN KLAUS, born 1942; admitted, 1975, Zürich. *Education:* University of Zürich (Dr.iur., 1971). *Member:* Zürich and Swiss Bar Associations. *LANGUAGES:* German, English, French and Italian.

LIC.IUR. PETER G. ISLER, born 1956; admitted, 1988, Zurich. *Education:* Universities of Zurich and Fribourg (lic.iur., 1984). *Member:* Zurich and Swiss Bar Associations. *LANGUAGES:* German, English and French.

ISLER & PEDRAZZINI AG

European Patent Attorneys
Established in 1910

STAMPFENBACHSTRASSE 48
CH-8023 ZÜRICH, SWITZERLAND
Telephone: (01) 362 95 82
Telex: 817020 ISL CH
Telecopier: (01) 361 33 40

Mailing Address: P.O. Box 6940, CH-8023 Zurich, Switzerland

Intellectual Property Law including Patent, Trademark and Design Prosecution; Corporate Law in particular Start-up Companies, Intellectual Property Litigation, Unfair Competition, Copyright and EEC Intellectual Property and Antitrust Law.

FIRM PROFILE: *Established in 1910, Isler & Pedrazzini AG (formerly Patentanwalts-Bureau Isler AG) has grown to become one of Switzerland's largest Patent Attorneys Firms. The firm is offering a full range of services in respect of Intellectual Property Law as well as to related legal fields. The firm has 5 Patent Attorneys with technical background and 3 lawyers. The professional staff is 30.*

MEMBERS OF FIRM

LIC.IUR. VINCENZO M. PEDRAZZINI, born 1960. *Education:* University of Freiburg (i.Ue., lic.iur., 1988); Georgetown University, Washington D.C. (U.S. Legal System, summer program, 1985). *LANGUAGES:* German, Italian, English and French. *PRACTICE AREAS:* Intellectual

(This Listing Continued)

Property Law; Corporate Law; Unfair Competition; Copyright Law.

DR.SC.NAT. MANFRED GRONER, born 1945; admitted, 1987, European Patent Office. *Education:* Swiss Federal Institute of Technology (Dipl. Natw., 1974; Dr.sc.nat., 1979). *LANGUAGES:* German, English and French. *PRACTICE AREAS:* European and International Patent; Industrial Design Prosecution.

DIPL.ING. OTTO MUENCH, born 1938. *Education:* Swiss Federal Institute of Technology (Mechanical Engineering). Professional Experience in R&D in Switzerland and USA, seven years as examiner in the Swiss and European Patent Office. *LANGUAGES:* German, French and English. *PRACTICE AREAS:* European and International Patent; Industrial Design Prosecution.

DR. CARL SCHICK, born 1932; admitted, 1981, European Patent Office. *Education:* Swiss Federal Institute of Technology (Dipl. El. Ing., 1959; Dr. Ing., 1971; Postgraduate Studies). Professional Experience as Patent Attorney with Siemens, in field of communications and electronics. *LANGUAGES:* German, French, English, Italian and Spanish. *PRACTICE AREAS:* European and International Patent; Industrial Design Prosecution.

DIPL.ING.CHEM. DAISY JUSTITZ, born 1919; admitted, 1978, European Patent Office. *Education:* Swiss Federal Institute of Technology. *LANGUAGES:* German, French, English and Italian. *PRACTICE AREAS:* European and International Patent Prosecution (esp. Chemical and Pharmaceutical Patents).

MICHAEL DEGKWITZ, RECHTSASSESSOR, born 1957. *Education:* University of Grenoble, France, Freiburg and Heidelberg, Germany and Geneva, Switzerland (German Bar Exam, 1987). *LANGUAGES:* German, English and French. *PRACTICE AREAS:* Trademark and Industrial Design Prosecution and Counselling.

DR.RER.NAT.DIPL.BIOL ELLEN KUETTEL, born 1960. *Education:* Justus-Liebig University Giessen, Germany (Dipl.Biol., 1985; Dr.rer.nat., 1989); Philipps University Marburg. Postdoctoral Education at Sloan-Kettering Cancer Center, New York and Cornell University Medical College, 1989-1992. *LANGUAGES:* German and English. *PRACTICE AREAS:* European and International Patent Prosecution (esp. Biotech).

DR.IUR. CHRISTIAN HILTI, born 1957; admitted, 1988, Switzerland as Attorney-at-Law. *Education:* University of Freiburg (i.Ue.); University of Zurich (Dr.iur., 1986); University of California at Berkeley, Boalt Hall (LL.M., 1990). *LANGUAGES:* German, English and French. *PRACTICE AREAS:* Intellectual Property Litigation; Counselling in EEC Intellectual Property and Competition Law; Licensing and Spin-Off Companies.

KOHLI & PARTNERS

Established in 1979

GENERAL WILLE-STRASSE 10
8027 ZÜRICH, SWITZERLAND
Telephone: (01) 202-8700
Telecopier: (01) 201-4832
Internet: urs.kohli@roche.com

General, Corporate, Company Formations Worldwide, Inheritance, Tax, Banking and Finance, Informatic Strategies, Business Innovation, Administrative and Regulatory Matters, Real Estate, Commercial Litigation, Arbitration.

FIRM PROFILE: Internationally oriented law firm, mainly active in the fields of corporate, commercial, banking and inheritance law areas including civil litigation, asset protection, arbitration and European community law. Also active in innovative areas such as information technology and informatic strategies for business innovation.

MEMBERS OF FIRM

DR. IUR. ULRICH A. KOHLI, Fürsprecher, born 1942; admitted to bar, 1969, Bern; 1970, Zürich. *Education:* University and Law School of Bern. Judge, Administrative and Tax Court of Zurich until 1993. Former Inhouse Counsel, large Swiss bank. *Member:* Zürich and Swiss Bar Association. *LANGUAGES:* German, English, French, Italian and Spanish. *PRACTICE AREAS:* Corporate; Banking Law; Estate Planning; Trusts; Offshore Investment; Asset Protection; Film Production; Taxation; Work and Residence Permits.

LIC. IUR. MATTHIAS MEISTER, Rechtsanwalt, born 1954; admitted to bar, 1982, Zürich. *Education:* University and Law School of Zürich (Lic. Iur., 1979). *Member:* Zürich and Swiss Bar Association. *LAN-*

(This Listing Continued)

GUAGES: German, English, French and Italian. *PRACTICE AREAS:* Corporate; Commercial and Contract Law; Construction Law; Litigation; Judicial Assistance; Biological Patents; Wills and Successions; Labor and Employment.

COUNSEL

DR. IUR. URS W. KOHLI, Rechtsanwalt, born 1940; admitted to bar, 1967, Bern; 1994, Zürich. *Education:* University and Law School of Bern. Executive Director, information management of large multinational pharmaceutical company, 1986-1994. *Member:* Advisory Board of Center of Research and Technology in Information, New Delhi. *PRACTICE AREAS:* Business Innovation; Information Technology; Computers and Software.

ASSOCIATES

DR. IUR. GEROLD R. ZOLLIKOFER, Rechtsanwalt, born, 1947; admitted to bar, 1975, Zurich. *Education:* University of Zurich. *Member:* Appellate Court of the Canton of Thurgau, Zurich and Swiss Bar Association. *LANGUAGES:* German, English and French. *PRACTICE AREAS:* Arbitration; Civil Litigation; Business Successions; Family Law.

LIC. IUR. ALFRED GERBER, RECHTSANWALT, born 1959; admitted, 1991, Zurich. *Education:* University and Law School of Zürich; University of London (LL.M., 1994). *Member:* Zurich and Swiss Bar Associations. *LANGUAGES:* German, English and French. *PRACTICE AREAS:* European Community Law; International Joint Ventures; Partnerships; Real Estate Finance; Securities; Offshore Trusts; Company Formation.

PETER STEIN, FUERSPRECHER, born 1965; admitted, 1992, Bern; 1993, Zürich. *Education:* University and Law School of Bern. *Member:* Zurich and Swiss Bar Associations. *LANGUAGES:* German, English and French. *PRACTICE AREAS:* Administrative Law; Aviation; Bankruptcy; Civil Litigation; Commercial Contracts; Criminal Law; Personal Injury; Transportation.

KOPP & PARTNERS

Established in 1972

28, KURHAUSSTRASSE
CH-8032 ZÜRICH, SWITZERLAND
Telephone: 01/261 70 07
Telefax: 01 /262 59 52

Mailing Address: P.O. Box CH-8030, Zürich, Switzerland

Budapest, Hungary Office: Madach I. út. 8.I/5, H-1075.
Telephone: +36-1/269.66.77. Telefax: +36-1/267.88.79.

Commercial and Corporate Law including Arbitration, Litigation, Tax Law and Tax Planning, Trusts and Estates, Communications and Mass Media Law.

FIRM PROFILE: The firm was established at its present location in 1972 and offers a full range of legal services. It specializes in counseling national and international companies and individual clients in legal matters. The four members of the firm have a support staff of 15 to 17 consisting of paralegal personnel, accountant and office administrators. Correspondence in Hungarian is feasible.

MEMBERS OF FIRM

DR. HANS W. KOPP, born Lucerne, Switzerland, June 12, 1931; admitted, 1960, Zurich and Federal Courts. *Education:* Gymnasium/Lyzeum (Matura, 1951); University of Zurich (Dr.iur., 1957); University of Dijon, France; University of Michigan, Ann Arbor, Michigan (LL.M., 1958). Author, main publications: Parlamente, Information in der Demokratie". *Member:* American and International Bar Associations. *LANGUAGES:* German, English, French and Italian. *PRACTICE AREAS:* Commercial and Corporate Law; Taxes; Communication; Mass Media Law.

DR. MARTIN DÜNNER, born St. Gall, Switzerland, July 18, 1944; admitted, 1975, Basle and Federal Courts. *Education:* Gymnasium (Matura, 1965); University of Basle (Dr.iur., 1974). *LANGUAGES:* German and English. *PRACTICE AREAS:* Commercial and Corporate Law; Arbitration; Trusts; Litigation; Estates.

LIC.IUR. JEAN-CHRISTOPHE SCHAI, born Zurich, Switzerland, December 24, 1962; admitted, 1991, Zurich and Federal Courts. *Education:* Gymnasium (Matura, 1982); University of Zurich (Lic.iur., 1988). *LANGUAGES:* German, English and French. *PRACTICE AREAS:* Commercial and Corporate Law; Arbitration; Trusts; Litigation; Estates.

(This Listing Continued)

KOPP & PARTNERS, Zürich—Continued

LIC.IUR. BRIGITT SCHAI-KOPP, born Zurich, Switzerland, December 10, 1963; admitted, 1992, Zurich and Federal Courts. *Education:* Gymnasium (Matura, 1982); University of Zurich (Lic.iur., 1988). *LANGUAGES:* German, English, French and Italian. *PRACTICE AREAS:* Commercial and Corporate Law; Penal Law.

LIC.IUR. ERIC VULTIER, born Zurich, Switzerland, October 1, 1962; admitted, 1991, Aargau and Federal Courts. *Education:* Gymnasium (Matura, 1982); University of Zurich (Lic.iur., 1988). *LANGUAGES:* German, English and French. *PRACTICE AREAS:* Commercial and Corporate Law; Real Estate Law; Penal Law; Litigation.

CARMEN KLECKNER, born Mettlach, Germany, March 28, 1954; admitted, 1992, Constance, Germany and Bordeaux, France. *Education:* Universities of Heidelberg and Paris (Sorbonne). *Member:* German Bar Association; DACH. *LANGUAGES:* German, English and French. *PRACTICE AREAS:* German Business Law; Mass Media Law; European Law.

KORTH NEFF ESSLINGER

KREUZPLATZ 20
CH-8032 ZÜRICH, SWITZERLAND
Telephone: 41 1 251 5040
Fax: 41 1 251 5087

Telecommunications, Computer Contracts, Unfair Competition, Aviation Accidents, Personal Injury, Professional and Products Liability, Patent Licensing, Copyrights, Trademarks, Intellectual Property, Bankruptcy and Corporate Law.

MEMBERS OF FIRM

JÜRGEN O. KORTH, born Hannover, Germany, August 12, 1942; admitted, 1979, Switzerland. *Education:* Universities of Göttingen/D. (German Junior Lawyer, 1970; Dr. jur., 1976); Munich/D. Zurich (Swiss Lawyer, 1979). *LANGUAGES:* German and English. *PRACTICE AREAS:* Aviation Accidents; Personal Injury; International Legal Assistance; Professional Liability; Product Liability.

EMIL F. NEFF, born Zurich, Switzerland, February 10, 1947; admitted, 1976, Switzerland. *Education:* University of Zurich (Dr. jur., 1973). *LANGUAGES:* German, English, French. *PRACTICE AREAS:* Computers and Software; Information Technology; Telecommunications; Computer Contracts; Unfair Competition.

THOMAS F. ESSLINGER, born Zurich, Switzerland, November 12, 1958; admitted, 1987, Switzerland. *Education:* University of Zurich (Lic. jur., 1985); Georgetown University, Washington, D.C. (LL.M., 1991). *LANGUAGES:* German, English and French. *PRACTICE AREAS:* Communications; Media; Copyrights; Litigation; Trade Marks.

JAMES T. PETER, born Palo Alto, California, USA, July 17, 1963; admitted, 1992, Switzerland. *Education:* University of Zurich (Dr. jur., 1994). *LANGUAGES:* German, English and French. *PRACTICE AREAS:* Privacy and Publicity; Intellectual Property; Commercial Contracts; Bankruptcy Law; Corporate Law.

KUPPER & LEHNER

Established in 1977

LÖWENSTRASSE 11
CH-8039 ZÜRICH, SWITZERLAND
Telephone: (01) 225 47 47
Telecopier: (01) 225 47 77

Aarau, Switzerland Office: Hunziker Scholl & Partner, Laurenzenvorstadt 19, CH-5001 Aarau. Telephone: 064 22 23 02. Fax: 064 22 25 00.
Lugano, Switzerland Office: Kupper & Lehner, Viale S. Franscini 1, CH-6901 Lugano. Telephone: 091 21 30 33. Fax: 091 21 30 35.

Contracts, Corporate, Banking, Tax, EU, Estate and Antitrust Law, Litigation and Arbitration.

MEMBERS OF FIRM

DR. WERNER KUPPER, born 1941; admitted, 1968, Zurich. *Education:* University of Zurich (Dr.iur.). Author: "Stille Reserven und Aktionärsinteressen," Bern, 1967. *Member:* Swiss, Zurich and International Bar Association; Bar Association of the Canton of Ticino. *LANGUAGES:* German, English, Italian and French. *PRACTICE AREAS:* International Commercial Law; International Taxation Law; Building Law; Planning Law; Inheritance Law; Arbitration.

DR. GEORGE LEHNER, LL.M., born 1951; admitted, 1978, Zurich. *Education:* University of Zurich (lic.iur., 1975); University of California at Berkeley (LL.M., 1976); Faculté Internationale de Droit Comparé Strasbourg (1979); University of Basel (Dr.iur., 1981). Author: "Die Verantwortlichkeit der Leitungsorgane von Aktiengesellschaften," Zurich, 1981. *Member:* Swiss and Zurich Bar Associations; Bar Association of the Canton of Ticino; Association of University of California at Berkeley Alumni. *LANGUAGES:* German, English and French. *PRACTICE AREAS:* International Commercial Law; Tax Law; Corporate Law; Contract Law; International Inheritance Law.

DR. THOMAS W. SCHREPFER, born 1958; admitted, 1987, Zurich. *Education:* University of Berne (Dr.iur., 1984); Harvard Law School (LL.M., 1988). Phi Alpha Delta. Author: "Datenschutz und Verfassung," Berne, 1985; "Constitutional Aspects of the Regulation of Access to State-held Information," Cambridge, 1988. *Member:* Swiss, Zurich and International Bar Association; Swiss Association for International Law; Harvard Law School Association. *LANGUAGES:* German, English and French. *PRACTICE AREAS:* Corporate Law; Banking Law; Tax Law; Competition Law; Constitutional Law; International Commercial Law; EU Law; Procedural Law.

GIANLUCA BOSCARO, born 1958; admitted, 1985, Ticino. *Education:* University of Zurich (lic.iur., 1982). Notary public, Ticino, 1986. *Member:* Bar Association of the Canton of Ticino; Swiss Bar Association. (Resident Partner at Lugano Office). *LANGUAGES:* Italian, German, English and French.

DR. CHRISTOPH WILDHABER, born 1964; admitted, 1992, Aarau. *Education:* University of St. Gallen (Dr.iur., 1991). Author: "Franchising," 1991. *Member:* Swiss, Zurich and International Bar Association. *LANGUAGES:* German, English and French. *PRACTICE AREAS:* Commercial Law; Corporate Law; National Distribution Law; International Distribution Law; Franchising Law; License Agreements; Tax Law.

LEHNER GUTZWILLER EGGER

BEUSTWEG 12
8032 ZÜRICH, SWITZERLAND
Telephone: 01/252 77 11
Telecopier: 01/252 77 27

Banking, Corporate, International Contracts, Commercial Litigation, Arbitration, Insurance, Inheritance.

DR. THOMAS LEHNER, born 1944; admitted, 1975, Zurich. *Education:* University of Zurich (Dr.iur., 1975). Author: "Impact of Mergers on Long Term Contracts under Special Consideration of License Contracts." Legal Counsel, major Swiss Bank, 1977-1984. *LANGUAGES:* German, English and French.

DR. P. CHRISTOPH GUTZWILLER, born 1939; admitted, 1968, Basel; 1980 Zurich. *Education:* Universities of Basel, Geneva and Cologne; New York University (Dr. iur., 1969; Master of Comparative Jurisprudence, 1971). Legal Advisor, Swiss National Bank, 1972-1977. Counsellor for Financial Affairs, Swiss Embassy, Washington, D.C., 1977-1980. *LANGUAGES:* German, English and French.

DR. WALTER H. EGGER, born 1942; admitted, 1969, Zurich. *Education:* University of Zurich (Dr.iur., 1967). Legal Counsel, major Swiss Bank, 1971-1988. Lecturer on Commercial Law, University of Zurich, 1981-1988. *LANGUAGES:* German and English.

LENHERR & MÜLLER

SEEFELDSTRASSE 62
CH-8008 ZÜRICH, SWITZERLAND
Telephone: 01/383 07 77
Fax: 01/383 07 09

Commercial and General Practice, Contracts, Corporations, Competition, Taxation, Banking and Securities, Wills, Trusts and Estates, Liability, Insurance, Family Law, Criminal Law, Litigation, Arbitration.

FIRM PROFILE: Dr. Lenherr and Dr. Müller having split off from larger organizations, the firm offers personalized legal services to its international and domestic business, corporate and private clientele. The members of the firm are members of the Zurich and the Swiss Bar Associations. Dr.

(This Listing Continued)

(This Listing Continued)

MAYR & GILGEN, Zürich—Continued

MEMBERS OF FIRM

ALFRED GILGEN, born 1955; admitted, 1984, Switzerland; 1988, New York. *Education:* University of St. Gallen (lic. oec. 1978); University of Bern (lic. iur. 1980); New York University School of Law (LL.M., 1987). *Member:* Zurich, Swiss, New York State and American Bar Associations. *LANGUAGES:* German, English and French. *PRACTICE AREAS:* Corporate Law; Mergers, Acquisitions and Divestitures; Taxation; Bankruptcy; Unfair Competition.

MARC D. MAYR, born 1952; admitted, 1982, Switzerland. *Education:* University of Zurich (lic. iur. 1979);. *Member:* Zurich and Swiss Bar Associations; International Association of Young Lawyers. *LANGUAGES:* German, French and English. *PRACTICE AREAS:* Contracts; Business Law; Litigation; Divorce; Criminal Law.

McGUIRE, WOODS, BATTLE & BOOTHE

BAHNHOFSTRASSE 3
P.O. BOX 4930
8022 ZÜRICH, SWITZERLAND
Telephone: (41 1) 225 20 00
Fax: (41 1) 225 20 20

REVISERS OF THE VIRGINIA LAW DIGEST FOR THIS DIRECTORY

Alexandria, Virginia Office: Transpotomac Plaza, Suite 1000, 1199 North Fairfax Street, 22314-1437. Telephone: 703-739-6200. Fax: 703-739-6270.

Baltimore, Maryland Office: The Blaustein Building, One North Charles Street, 21201-3793. Telephone: 410-659-4400. Fax: 410-659-4599.

Charlottesville, Virginia Office: Court Square Building, P.O. Box 1288, 22902-1288. Telephone: 804-977-2500. Fax: 804-980-2222.

Jacksonville, Florida Office: Barnett Center, Suite 2750, 50 North Laura Street, 32202-3635. Telephone: 904-798-3200. Fax: 904-798-3207.

McLean, (Tysons Corner) Virginia Office: 8280 Greensboro Drive, Suite 900, Tysons Corner, 22102-3892. Telephone: 703-712-5000. Fax: 703-712-5050.

Norfolk, Virginia Office: World Trade Center, Suite 9000, 101 West Main Street, 23510-1655. Telephone: 804-640-3700. Fax: 804-640-3701.

Richmond, Virginia Office: One James Center, 901 East Cary Street, 23219-4030. Telephone: 804-775-1000. Fax: 804-775-1061.

Washington, D.C. Office: The Army and Navy Club Building, 1627 Eye Street, N.W., 20006-4007. Telephone: 202-857-1700. Fax: 202-857-1737.

Brussels, Belgium Office: 250 Avenue Louise, Bte. 64, 1050. Telephone: (32 2) 629 42 11. Fax: (32 2) 629 42 22.

General Practice.

FIRM PROFILE: *McGuire, Woods, Battle & Boothe is among the largest law firms in the United States, with over 400 attorneys practicing in ten cities. From modest local beginnings in the nineteenth century to a thriving national practice in the twentieth, McGuire, Woods balances the character of its history with the vitality of its growth. From its locations in Alexandria, Baltimore, Charlottesville, Jacksonville, Norfolk, Richmond, Tysons Corner, Washington, D.C., Brussels, Belgium, and Zurich, Switzerland, the firm serves the Mid-Atlantic region and other U.S. and foreign corporate centers. This concentration of lawyers in one of the fastest growing, most populous areas of the nation, coupled with a long tradition of excellence and individual attention, distinguishes the firm from most others.*

The firm is organized into business, litigation, real estate, and tax departments. Its strengths have long been recognized in public finance, securities, mergers and acquisitions, tax, product liability, litigation, retailing, real estate and land use, banking and financial services, and intellectual property. Specialization within the firm's nearly 50 areas of expertise often develops along with the particular needs of its clients and their industries. Among the industries represented by the firm are banking, computer equipment and software, real estate development, health care, insurance, telecommunications, manufacturing, distribution, and retailing. Its clients range from individuals to multinational corporations. Many client relationships have lasted for decades as fledgling businesses have evolved into Fortune 500 companies.

(This Listing Continued)

EU1406B

RESIDENT MEMBER

DANIEL URECH, born Schaffhausen, Switzerland, 1938; admitted, 1964, Bern; 1982, Zurich and Geneva. *Education:* University of Geneva Interpreter School (1957-1958); University of Princeton, Woodrow Wilson School (1958-1959); University of Geneva Law School (1957-1958); University of Bern Law School (Law Degree Combined with Admission to Bar, Spring, 1964). Swiss Correspondent, Journal of International Banking Law. Member, Board of Zurich Bar Association, 1991—; Chairman, 1995—. Member: Regulatory Committee of European Managed Futures Association, 1991—; Swiss Council, Euro-Arab Arbitration System, 1987—. *PRACTICE AREAS:* Company Law; Securities Law; Banking and Insurance.

REVISERS OF THE VIRGINIA LAW DIGEST FOR THIS DIRECTORY

(For Complete Biographical data on all Personnel, see Professional Biographies at Richmond, Virginia).

DR. O.C. MEIER-BOESCHENSTEIN

Established in 1972

GENERAL GUISON QUAI 22
CH-8002 ZÜRICH, SWITZERLAND
Telephone: 01-285 79 79
Cable Address: OCM LAW
Telex: 815818
Fax: 01 202 67 38

General and International Law Practice. International Business, Corporation, Contracts, Unfair Competition, Intellectual Property, Taxation, Banking, Labor, Wills, Estates and Trusts, Administration Law, Civil Aviation and Travel Law, Litigation and Arbitration.

DR. O.C. MEIER-BOESCHENSTEIN, born Zurich, Switzerland, September 9, 1943; admitted, 1970, Zurich. *Education:* University of Zurich (lic.iur., 1967; Dr. of Laws); University of Toronto, Canada (Post graduate studies). Author: "Die Liechtensteinische Privatrechtliche Anstalt," (Thesis), 1969; "Le nuove restrizioni concernenti l'investimento di fondi stranieri in Svizzera," Rivista degli Scambi Italo-Svizzeri No. 4, 1978; "Rechtsprobleme bei internationalen Warenverkäufen zwischen Italien und der Schweiz," Handelszeitung Nr. 45, November, 1984; "Leitfaden zur Unternehmensgründung. Die rechtlichen und steuerlichen Ueberlegungen," Band 2, Verlag Organisator Zürich, 1988; "Die Internationalisierung des Rechtes am Beispiel der schweizerisch-italienischen Beziehungen," Rivista degli Scambi Italo-Svizzeri, No. 2, February, 1990; "Aspetti della garanzia bancaria nel diritto svizzero," Rivista degli Scambi Italo-Svizzeri, No 4, April, 1990; "Das EWR-Abkommen," Rivista degli Scambi Italo-Svizzeri, No. 7/8, Luglio/Agosto, 1992; The new law regarding joint stock companies to be published in the Apla Journal and the Journal of Planning. Honorary Consul, Republic of Seychelles in Zurich, 1978—; Member, Town Council in Greifensee, responsible for finances; Member, Executive Committee and Arbitration Committee, Italian Chamber of Commerce in Switzerland. *Member:* Swiss and International Bar Associations; Zurich Law Society; Asia-Pacific Lawyers Association; Associazione Giuristi di Lingua Italiana.

ASSOCIATES

LIC.IUR. HSG DIETER LÜTHI, born Berne, Switzerland, August 23, 1959; admitted, 1993, Zurich. *Education:* University of St. Gallen (lic.iur., 1985). With: Audit Department, Price Waterhouse, 1986-1988; Law Firm of Dr. O.C. Meier-Boeschenstein, 1993—.

LIC. IUR. MARINA PETER, born Zurich, Switzerland, October 26, 1963; admitted, 1992, Switzerland. *Education:* University of Zurich (lic.iur., 1988). With: District Court in Meilen, 1989; Law Firm of Dr. O.C. Meier-Boeschenstein, 1989—.

LIC.IUR. CHRISTIANE BREM, born March 30, 1962. *Education:* University of Lausanne (lic.iur., 1985). With Legal Department, Association of Swiss Engineers and Architects, 1986-1990; Law Firm of Dr. O.C. Meier-Boeschenstein, 1991-1992 and 1993—.

Languages: German, English, Italian and French

Müller is also a member of the Swiss Institute of Certified Accountants and Tax Consultants and a member of the International Fiscal Association.

MEMBERS OF FIRM

PAUL LENHERR, born Bern, Switzerland, February 10, 1940; admitted, 1973, Switzerland. *Education:* University of Zurich (Dr.iur., 1969). *LANGUAGES:* German, English and French. *PRACTICE AREAS:* Litigation and Arbitration; Contracts; Law of Succession; Family Law; Liability and Insurance Law; Criminal Law.

DR. PAUL R. MÜLLER, born Herisau, Switzerland, May 30, 1937; admitted, 1968, Switzerland. *Education:* University of St. Gallen (Dr.rer.-publ., 1970). Certified Tax Expert, 1986. *LANGUAGES:* German, English, Italian and French. *PRACTICE AREAS:* Commercial, Corporate and Competition Law; Banking and Securities; Trusts, Wills and Estates; Taxation; Arbitration.

LENZ & STAEHELIN

58 BLEICHERWEG
CH-8027 ZÜRICH, SWITZERLAND
Telephone: 01-204 12 12
Cable Address: "Staehelinjur"
Telex: 815656 Law CH
Telecopier: 01-204 12 00

Geneva, Switzerland Office: 25 Grand'Rue, CH-1211 Geneva 11. Telephone: 022 319 06 19. Telex: 422.476 LSB. Telecopier: 022 319 06 00.

Lausanne, Switzerland Office: 2, place St. François, CH-1003. Telephone: 021-320 79 72. Telex: 422.476 LSB. Telecopier: 021-312 97 45.

Swiss and International Taxation, Banking and Finance Law, Capital Market Transactions, Share Issues and Listing, International Commercial Arbitration, Commercial and Contract Law, Company Law, Mergers and Acquisitions, Corporate Finance, Competition Law, Residence and Work Permits, Purchase of Swiss Real Estate, Product Liability, Civil, Criminal and Administrative Litigation, Debt and Bankruptcy Law, International Legal Assistance, Estate Planning, Trusts, Charitable Foundations, Private International Law, Unfair Competition, Copyright, Patent and Trademark Law, Environmental Law, European Law.

MEMBERS OF FIRM

DR. PETER HAFTER, born 1931; admitted, 1958, Switzerland. *Education:* University of Zurich (Dr.iur., 1957); Harvard Law School (LL.M., 1962). *LANGUAGES:* German, English, French and Russian.

DR. MARCO A. JAGMETTI, born 1935; admitted, 1963, Switzerland. *Education:* Universities of Zurich, Geneva and Paris (Lic.iur., 1958; Dr.iur., 1961); Academy of International Law, The Hague (Diploma, 1961); University of Michigan Law School (M.C.L., 1965). *LANGUAGES:* German, English, French and Italian.

DR. MARTIN J. LUTZ, born 1939; admitted, 1964, Switzerland. *Education:* Universities of Zurich, Berlin, Munich (Lic.iur., 1963; Dr.iur., 1964); University of Michigan Law School (M.C.L., 1967). *LANGUAGES:* German, English, French and Italian.

DR. PETER MAX GUTZWILLER, born 1941; admitted, 1970, Switzerland. *Education:* Universities of Basel and Geneva (lic.iur., 1964; Dr.iur., 1967); Harvard Law School (LL.M., 1968). *LANGUAGES:* German, English and French.

DR. ROBERT HEBERLEIN, born 1941; admitted, 1969, Switzerland. *Education:* University of Zurich (Lic.iur., 1966; Dr.iur., 1969); University of Michigan Law School (M.C.L., 1970). *LANGUAGES:* German, English and French.

DR. MARTIN H. ESCHER, born 1944; admitted, 1971, Switzerland. *Education:* Universities of Geneva (Licence en droit, 1967); Zurich (Dr.iur., 1971); European Institute of Business Administration (Diploma 1972). *LANGUAGES:* German, English, French and Italian.

DR. CHRISTOPH F. REINHARDT, born 1945; admitted, 1973, Switzerland. *Education:* University of Zurich (Lic.iur., 1969; Dr.iur., 1971). *LANGUAGES:* German, English, French and Italian.

DR. RUDOLF TSCHÄNI, born 1950; admitted, 1979, Switzerland; 1982, New York. *Education:* University of Zurich (Lic. iur., 1973; Dr. iur., 1978); College of Europe, Belgium (Diploma, 1976); Harvard Law School (LL.M., 1980). *LANGUAGES:* German, English and French.

(This Listing Continued)

DR. URS L. BAUMGARTNER, born 1948; admitted, 1974, Switzerland. *Education:* University of Zurich (Lic. iur., 1973; Dr. iur., 1978); University of Chicago Law School (LL.M., 1979); American University, Eastern European Summer Law Program (1979). *LANGUAGES:* German, English and French.

LIC. URS ROHNER, born 1959; admitted, 1986, Switzerland; 1990, New York. *Education:* University of Zurich (Lic. iur., 1983). *LANGUAGES:* German, English and French.

DR. PATRICK HÜNERWADEL, born 1959; admitted, 1987, Switzerland. *Education:* University of St. Gallen (Lic. iur., 1984; Dr. iur, 1989); Boston University, Law School, Morin Center of Banking Law (1989). *LANGUAGES:* German, French and English.

DR. STEFAN P. BREITENSTEIN, born 1957; admitted, 1986, Switzerland. *Education:* University of Zurich (Lic.iur., 1983; Dr.iur., 1989); College of Europe, Belgium (Diploma, 1984); Harvard Law School (LL.M., 1989). *LANGUAGES:* German, English and French.

COUNSEL

DR. WILLIAM R. STAEHELIN, born 1917; admitted, 1944, Switzerland. *Education:* University of Zurich; University of Geneva; Harvard University, Cambridge, Mass.; University of California at Los Angeles. *LANGUAGES:* German, English, French and Italian.

PROF. DR. MARIO M. PEDRAZZINI, born 1925; admitted, 1954, Switzerland. *Education:* Universities of Zurich, Rome and Marburg (Germany). *LANGUAGES:* German, Italian, French and English.

SENIOR ATTORNEYS

DR. PETER HEINRICH, born 1943; admitted, 1974, Switzerland. *Education:* University of Zurich (Lic. iur., 1966; Dr. iur., 1972). *LANGUAGES:* German, English, French and Italian.

LIC. CORINNE C. JAGMETTI, born 1945; admitted, 1972, Switzerland. *Education:* Universities of Zurich, Heidelberg and Lausanne (Lic. iur., 1969); Stanford University Law School (Summer, 1975). *LANGUAGES:* German, English, French and Italian.

LIC. BARBARA C. FREI, born 1960; admitted, 1985, Switzerland. *Education:* University of Basel (Lic. iur., 1983); Harvard University (Summer, 1982); International Law Institute, Georgetown University Law Center (Summer, 1985). *LANGUAGES:* German, English and French.

ASSOCIATES

DR. MATTHIAS OERTLE, born 1961; admitted, 1988, Switzerland. *Education:* University of Zurich (Lic. iur., 1986; Dr.iur., 1990). *LANGUAGES:* German, English, French and Italian.

DR. LUKAS C. HANDSCHIN, born 1959; admitted, 1988, Switzerland. *Education:* University of Basel (Lic. iur., 1986; Dr. iur., 1987). *LANGUAGES:* German, English and French.

LIC. WILFRIED HEINZELMANN, born 1963; admitted, 1991, Switzerland. *Education:* University of Zurich (Lic. iur., 1988). *LANGUAGES:* German, English and French.

LIC. YVONNE GRAF, born 1963; admitted, 1991, Switzerland. *Education:* Universities of Zurich and Lausanne (Lic. iur., 1988). *LANGUAGES:* German, English and French.

DR. PATRICK K. OESCH, born 1957; admitted, 1992, Switzerland. *Education:* University of Zurich (Lic. iur., 1981; Dr.iur., 1990). *LANGUAGES:* German, English and French.

LIC. LEYLA KUTSAN, born 1964; admitted, 1992, Switzerland. *Education:* University of Zurich (Lic. iur., 1989). *LANGUAGES:* German, English, French and Turkish.

MAYR & GILGEN

APOLLOSTRASSE 2
CH-8032 ZÜRICH, SWITZERLAND
Telephone: ++41-1-383 55 20
FAX: ++41-1-383 57 76

Swiss and International Practice, Formation, Governance and Reorganisation of Companies and Joint Ventures, Mergers and Acquisitions, Taxation, Work Permits, Trademarks, Trade Practices, Product Liability, Litigation in Corporate, Commercial, Divorce and Criminal Matters, Sale of Goods, Distributorship, Licensing, Service and Employment Contracts, Sequestration, Collection and Bankruptcy, International Legal Assistance, Wills, Trusts and Estate, Immigration.

(This Listing Continued)

MEYER LUSTENBERGER & PARTNER

FORCHSTRASSE 452
8029 ZÜRICH, SWITZERLAND
Telephone: 01/391.41.61
Telecopier: 01/391.27.81
Telex: 817.804 kmlw

Geneva, Switzerland Associated Office: Croisier & Gillioz. 61, Rue du Rhône, P.O. Box 3127, 1211 Geneva 3. Telephone: 022-310 12 33. Telex: 422 349 cogi. Telecopier: 022-310 81 92.

Commercial Practice, Corporations, Taxation, Banking, Securities, Foreign Investment, Commercial Litigation, Arbitration, Trusts and Foundations, Inheritance, Matrimonial Property and Intellectual Property Law.

MEMBERS OF FIRM

DR. FERDINAND MEYER, born 1937; admitted, 1968, Zurich. *Education:* University of Berne (Dr.iur.); Lausanne and Kansas University. **LANGUAGES:** German, English and French. **PRACTICE AREAS:** Corporate and Business Law; Estate Taxation; Business Planning.

DR. THOMAS LUSTENBERGER, born 1951; admitted, 1979, Lucerne; 1980, Zurich. *Education:* University of Berne (Dr.iur.); University of Exeter (LL.M.); Harvard Law School (LL.M.). **LANGUAGES:** German, English, French and Italian. **PRACTICE AREAS:** Taxation; Mergers and Acquisitions; Corporate and Business Law.

CORINNE SIEGER-RONNER, born 1951; admitted, 1977, Zurich. *Education:* University of Zurich (lic.iur.); Columbia University School of Law (LL.M.). **LANGUAGES:** German, English, French and Italian. **PRACTICE AREAS:** Estate Planning and Matrimonial Property Law; Inheritance Law; Trusts and Foundations.

DR. MARCEL LUSTENBERGER, born 1958; admitted, 1987, Zurich. *Education:* University of Zurich (Dr.iur.). **LANGUAGES:** German, English, French. **PRACTICE AREAS:** Commercial Litigation; Arbitration; Tort and Liability Law.

DR. MARTIN AMMANN, born 1952; admitted, 1988, Zurich. *Education:* University of St. Gallen (Dr.iur.; lic.oec.); University of Geneva (lic.iur.); Harvard Law School (LL.M.). **LANGUAGES:** German, English and French. **PRACTICE AREAS:** EC Law; Competition Law; Agency and Distribution Agreements; Product Liability; Computer Law; Work and Residence Permits.

DR. CHRISTOPH HEIZ, born 1956; admitted, 1984, Zurich; 1991, Geneva. *Education:* University of Zurich (Dr.iur.); University of Pennsylvania, School of Law (LL.M.). **LANGUAGES:** German, English, French and Italian. **PRACTICE AREAS:** Corporate and Business Law; Finance and Securities; Bankruptcy, Insolvency and Reorganization Law.

DR. ARMIN ZUCKER, born 1955; admitted, 1986, Zurich. *Education:* Universities of Geneva and Zurich (Dr.iur.). **LANGUAGES:** German, English and French. **PRACTICE AREAS:** Corporate and Business Law; Taxation; Labour and Employment Law; Rent Law.

DR. MICHAEL RITSCHER, born 1959; admitted, 1988, Zurich. *Education:* University of Zurich (Dr.iur.); Georgetown University (LL.M.); Max Planck Institute (Foreign and International Patent, Copyright and Competition Law), Munich. **LANGUAGES:** German, English and French. **PRACTICE AREAS:** Intellectual Property Law; Design and Advertising Law.

ASSOCIATES

PATRICIA CAMENZIND-GUERRA, born 1959; admitted, 1989, Zurich; 1991, New York. *Education:* University of Geneva (lic.iur.); University of Michigan Law School (LL.M.). **LANGUAGES:** Spanish, French, English, German, Portuguese and Italian. **PRACTICE AREAS:** Corporate and Business Law; General Contract Law; Matrimonial Property Law; Inheritance Law.

ALEXANDER VOGEL, born 1964; admitted, 1992, Zurich. *Education:* University of St. Gallen (lic.iur. HSG); Northwestern University (LL.M.). **LANGUAGES:** German, English, French. **PRACTICE AREAS:** Corporate and Business Law; Mergers and Acquisitions; Finance.

ADRIAN J. HALTER, born 1964; admitted, 1991, Berne; 1993, New York. *Education:* University of Berne (Fürsprecher, 1991); Cornell University (LL.M., 1992). **LANGUAGES:** German, English, French. **PRACTICE AREAS:** Corporate and Business Law.

SALLY MEYER PETERSEN, born 1953; admitted, 1978, Michigan (Not admitted in Switzerland). *Education:* University of Detroit School of

(This Listing Continued)

Law (J.D.). **LANGUAGES:** English. **PRACTICE AREAS:** U.S. Law; Corporate and Business Law; International Commercial Transactions.

DR. URS BEHNISCH, born 1959; admitted, 1986, Berne. *Education:* University of Berne (Dr.iur.). **LANGUAGES:** German. **PRACTICE AREAS:** Tax Counsel.

DR. CHRISTOPH M. MUELLER

HAUS ZUM SCHWERT
WEINPLATZ 10
CH-8001 ZÜRICH, SWITZERLAND
Telephone: 0041 1-221 08 00
Telefax: 0041 1-221 08 02

General and International Business, Corporate, Contract, Banking and Finance, Securities, Insurance and Liability, Inheritance and Tax Law, Litigation, Arbitration.

DR. CHRISTOPH M. MUELLER, born 1948; admitted, 1978, Switzerland. *Education:* University of Zurich (Dr. iur., 1977). Author: "Die Bewilligung zum Geschäftsbetrieb einer nach schweizerischem Recht organisierten Bank", Paul Haupt Verlag, Bern/Stuttgart, 1978. *Member:* Zurich, Swiss and International Bar Associations; Swiss Arbitration Association; Swiss Lawyers' Association. **LANGUAGES:** German, English, French and Italian.

MUELLER, MERONI & LANTER

Established in 1906
UTOQUAI 43
P.O. BOX
CH-8032 ZÜRICH, SWITZERLAND
Telephone: 01/251 69 90
Telecopier: 01/251 69 44

International Commercial Practice, Corporate, Banking, Finance, International Arbitration and Litigation, Taxation, Intellectual Property Rights, Mergers and Acquisitions, Estate Planning.

FIRM PROFILE: *Since the first decade of this century, the firm serves international corporate and private clients in all areas of national and international legal work with particular emphasis on all business related matters mainly in the above mentioned areas. The firm maintains an intensive network of contacts with national and international law firms in all major business centers of the world.*

MEMBERS OF FIRM

DR. KURT MUELLER, born Lucerne, Switzerland, 1937; admitted, 1966, Switzerland. *Education:* Groton School, Groton, Mass, USA (1954-1955); University of Zurich Law School (Doctor of Law, 1964); University of Paris Law School (1960). District Court of Lucerne, 1965. Superior Court of the Canton of Lucerne, 1966-1968. Associate, law firm in Geneva. **LANGUAGES:** German, English, French and Italian. **PRACTICE AREAS:** Corporate; Contract; Intellectual Property Law; Mergers and Acquisitions; International Taxation; Estate Planning.

DR. RUDOLF MERONI, born Bellinzona, Switzerland, 1953; admitted, 1980, Switzerland. *Education:* University of Zurich Law School (lic.iur., 1978); New York University, New York City, USA (Master of Comparative Jurisprudence, 1982); University of Zurich Law School (Doctor of Law, 1984). District Court of Horgen, Zurich, 1978-1979. Associate, law firm in Zurich, 1979-1980 and 1983-1986. **LANGUAGES:** German, English and French. **PRACTICE AREAS:** International Commercial Transactions and Finance; Banking Law; International Arbitration and Litigation.

DR. MARCO LANTER, born Lucerne, Switzerland, 1954; admitted, 1981, Switzerland. *Education:* University of Zurich Law School (lic.iur., 1978); New York University, New York City, USA (Master of Comparative Jurisprudence, 1982); University of Zurich Law School (Doctor of Law, 1984). District Court of Horgen, Zurich, 1978-1979. Associate, law firm in Zurich, 1983-1986. Head, legal department, trust and auditing company, Zurich, 1986-1988. **LANGUAGES:** German, English and French. **PRACTICE AREAS:** Corporate; Contract Law; Banking Law; Business Law; Civil Litigation and Arbitration; Estate Planning; Charitable Organizations.

DR. HERBERT TRACHSLER, born Wetzikon, Switzerland, 1957; admitted, 1987, Switzerland. *Education:* University of St. Gallen Law

(This Listing Continued)

MUELLER, MERONI & LANTER, Zürich—Continued

School (lic.iur. HSG, 1984); University of St. Gallen (Doctor of Law, 1991). Assistant, University of St. Gallen, Institute for Financial Economics and Law, 1984-1985. Associate, law firms in Zurich and Toronto, 1986-1992. *LANGUAGES:* German, English, French and Spanish. *PRACTICE AREAS:* Corporate and Commercial Law; Civil Litigation; International Legal Assistance in Criminal and Civil Matters; Trusts and Estates.

DR. RAOUL BUSSMANN, born Egolzwil, Switzerland, 1949; admitted, 1981, Switzerland. *Education:* University of Zurich Law School (lic.iur, 1975); University of Zurich Law School (Doctor of Law, 1977). Associate, law firm in Zug, 1980. Legal Counsel, Corporate legal department, Swiss multinational Group, Winterthur, 1981-1986. General Counsel, Swiss multinational Group, Zug, 1986-1991. Practising Attorney at Law, 1991-1994. *LANGUAGES:* German, English, French, Italian and Spanish. *PRACTICE AREAS:* International Commercial Transactions; Mergers and Acquisitions; Intellectual Property Law; International Arbitration and Litigation.

DR. STEFAN J. SCHMID, born Zurich, Switzerland, 1962; admitted, 1989, Switzerland. *Education:* University of Zurich Law School (lic.iur., 1987); University of Berne Law School (Doctor of Law, 1993). Trainee, major Swiss bank, Zurich, 1981-1982. *LANGUAGES:* German, English and French. *PRACTICE AREAS:* Corporate; Contract Law; Banking Law; Litigation and Arbitration; Commercial Transactions; Business Law; Charitable Organizations.

ADRIAN KUENZLER, born Zürich, Switzerland, 1963; admitted, 1991, Switzerland. *Education:* University of Zürich Law School (lic.iur., 1988). District Court of Zurich, 1989-1990. *LANGUAGES:* German, English and French. *PRACTICE AREAS:* Bankruptcy and Debt Collection Law; Civil Litigation; Inheritance Law; Corporate Law; Labor Law; Social Security Law.

MARKUS FELDMANN, born Langenthal, Switzerland, 1966; admitted, 1994, Switzerland. *Education:* Trainee, Swiss bank, Langenthal, 1986-1987; University of Berne Law School (Fürsprecher, 1994). District Court of Aarwangen, 1990-1991. *LANGUAGES:* German, English and French. *PRACTICE AREAS:* International Contracts; Corporate and Commercial Law; International Family Law; Labor Law; Alien Law; Civil Litigation.

Languages: German, English, French, Italian and Spanish

MUELLER, WEHRLI & PARTNERS

ZÜRICH, SWITZERLAND

(See Mueller, Meroni & Lanter)

International Commercial Practice, Corporate, Banking, Finance, International Arbitration and Litigation, Taxation, Intellectual Property Rights, Mergers and Acquisitions, Estate Planning.

MÜLLHAUPT & CHOQUARD

Established in 1986

WALDMANNSTRASSE 10
P.O. BOX 316
8024 ZÜRICH, SWITZERLAND
Telephone: (0) 252 46 16
Telefax-Telecopier: (01) 252 47 32

General Commercial Practice. International Business, Contracts, Corporation, Torts, USA/EEC/Swiss Products Liability, Industrial Consortiums, Taxation, Banking, Unfair Competition, Arbitration, Transportation, Labor and Working Permits, Wills, Estate and Trusts, Intellectual Property, Computer Law, Franchising.

MEMBERS OF FIRM

WALTER MÜLLHAUPT, born Baden, Switzerland, 1946; admitted, 1974, St. Gallen; 1975, Zurich; 1978, Zug; 1979, Lucerne; 1985, Thurgau. *Education:* St. Gallen School of Economics (Ph.D., in Economics, 1974); Boalt Hall School of Law, University of California, Berkeley (LL.M., 1975). Author: Publications in Commercial and Tax Laws. Associate, Zurich Law Firm, 1975-1979. Chief Executive Officer, Zurich based business conglomerate, 1979-1982. Attorney-at-law, Zurich 1982—. *Member:* Swiss and Zurich Bar Associations. *LANGUAGES:* German, English, French and Italian. *PRACTICE AREAS:* Tax; Corporation; Banking; Labor and Working Permits.

(This Listing Continued)

MAURICE P. CHOQUARD, born Quebec, Canada, 1951; admitted, 1977, Geneva; 1980, California, U.S.A.; 1986, Zurich and Schwyz. *Education:* Geneva Law School (J.D., 1974); Golden Gate University Law School (1978); Boalt Hall School of Law, University of California, Berkeley (LL.M., 1979). Legal Practice: Junior-attorney, international law firm in Geneva, 1974-1977. Foreign lawyer, c/o Bernard Petrie, Esq., San Francisco, 1978-1979; c/o Lillick McHose & Charles, San Francisco, 1979-1980. Legal Counsel to the General Consulate of Switzerland, San Francisco, 1977-1980. In House Counsel, BBC Brown Boveri & Cie, Switzerland, 1980-1984. General Counsel, Kuehne & Nagel International, Ltd., Switzerland, 1984-1986. Attorney-at-law, Zurich, 1986—. Administrator, Zurich Chapter of the French-Swiss Chamber of Commerce and Industries. *Member:* State Bar of California; American, International, Zurich and Swiss Bar Associations; Swiss Arbitration Association; Canadian-Swiss Association (Secretary-Treasurer); Swiss-American Chamber of Commerce; French-Swiss Chamber of Commerce and Industries (President, Zurich Chapter and Business Club). *LANGUAGES:* French, English and German. *PRACTICE AREAS:* Contracts; Corporation; Torts; Computer Law.

ASSOCIATES

BARBARA PFENNINGER, born Zurich, Switzerland, 1967; admitted, 1994, Zurich. *Education:* Zurich Law School (J.D., 1991). Junior Attorney, Müllhaupt & Choquard, 1991-1994. *LANGUAGES:* German, French and English.

CHRISTOPH M. BERTISCH, born Schaffhausen, Switzerland, 1960; admitted, 1991, Zurich, Basle-City, Basle-Country, Lucerne, Aargau, St. Gallen, Schaffhausen. *Education:* Basle Law School (J.D., 1987; Ph.D., 1989); New York University School of Law (LL.M., 1994). Librarian's Assistant, Basle Law School, 1982-1986. Clerk, Hochdorf District Court, Switzerland, 1987. Research Assistant to Prof. Karl Spiro, 1987-1989. Junior Attorney with R. Keuchler, esq. Lucerne, Switzerland, 1989-1990.

Languages: English, German, French and Italian

NAEGELI SCHAUB & STREICHENBERG

Established in 1969

STOCKERSTRASSE 38
8002 ZÜRICH, SWITZERLAND
Telephone: (01) 202 25 33
Fax: (01) 201 44 11

General Practice. Domestic and International Contracts, Commercial, Corporate Law, Banking Law, Bankruptcy, Industrial Property Rights, Unfair Competition, Tax Law, Real Estate and Property, Planning and Property Development, Construction Law, Wills and Estates, Administrative Law, Immigration, Litigation, Arbitration.

MEMBERS OF FIRM

DR. BERNHARD SCHAUB, born Zurich, Switzerland, October 12, 1929; admitted, 1959, Switzerland. *Education:* Universities of Zurich (Dr.iur., 1956) and Geneva; Harvard Law School (LL.M., 1957). *LANGUAGES:* German, English and French. *PRACTICE AREAS:* Contracts; Commercial Law; Wills and Estates; Arbitration.

DR. KURT NAEGELI, born Winterthur, Switzerland, October 19, 1935; admitted, 1963, Switzerland. *Education:* Universities of St. Gallen, Hamburg, Paris and Zurich (Dr.iur., summa cum laude, 1961). *LANGUAGES:* German, English and French. *PRACTICE AREAS:* Contracts; Corporations; Real Estate and Property; Construction; Wills and Estates; Arbitration.

DR. MARTIN STREICHENBERG, born St. Gall, Switzerland, September 3, 1942; admitted, 1970, Switzerland. *Education:* University of Zurich (Dr.iur., 1970). *Member:* International Bar Association. *LANGUAGES:* German, English, French and Italian. *PRACTICE AREAS:* Commercial and Corporate; Inheritance; Banking and Finance.

LIC.IUR. ANDREAS LAKI, born Budapest, Hungary, January 12, 1957; admitted, 1984, Switzerland. *Education:* University of Zurich (lic.iur., 1982). *LANGUAGES:* German, English French, Italian and Hungarian. *PRACTICE AREAS:* Contracts; Corporate Law; Industrial Property Rights; Wills and Estates; Litigation.

(This Listing Continued)

ASSOCIATES

LIC.IUR. HANSPETER WÜSTINER, born Basel, Switzerland, September 19, 1954; admitted, 1985, Switzerland; 1988, New York. *Education:* Universities of Basel and Neuchâtel (lic.iur., 1982). *LANGUAGES:* German, English and French. *PRACTICE AREAS:* Corporate Law; Contracts; Banking and Finance; Civil Litigation.

DR.IUR. MARC STROLZ, born Caracas, Venezuela, January 12, 1964; admitted, 1992, Switzerland. *Education:* University of Zurich (Dr.iur., 1991). *LANGUAGES:* German, French and English. *PRACTICE AREAS:* Contracts; Commercial and Corporate; European Law.

LIC.IUR. FRANZISKA BUOB, born Brugg, Switzerland, February 7, 1961; admitted, 1992, Switzerland. *Education:* University of Zurich (lic.iur., 1988). *LANGUAGES:* German, English and French. *PRACTICE AREAS:* Contracts; Commercial and Corporate; International Law; Litigation.

LIC.IUR. ALEXANDER RABIAN, born Zurich, Switzerland, June 13, 1961; admitted, 1992, Switzerland. *Education:* University of Zurich (lic.iur., 1988). *LANGUAGES:* German, English, French and Spanish. *PRACTICE AREAS:* Banking and Finance; Commercial and Corporate; Litigation.

All members and associates of the firm are members of the Zurich and the Swiss Bar Associations.

NIEDERER KRAFT & FREY

Established in 1937

BAHNHOFSTRASSE 13
8001 ZÜRICH, SWITZERLAND
Telephone: (01) 217-1000
International Dialing: (41-1) 217-1000
Telecopier/Telefax: Groups II & III (41-1) 217-1400
Telex: 813910
Answer Back: 813910 NKF CH
Cable Address: NIKRA ZURICH

Commercial, Corporate, Mergers and Acquisitions, Banking, Securities, Competition Law, EC Law, Environmental Law, Real Estate, Estate Planning, Inheritance Law, Administrative Law, International and National Taxation, Litigation, Arbitration, Judicial Assistance and General Practice.

MEMBERS OF FIRM

DR. HUGO A. FREY, born 1910; admitted, 1936, Zurich, Switzerland. *Education:* Universities of Geneva and Zurich (Dr.iur., 1935). *Member:* Swiss and Zurich Bar Associations. *LANGUAGES:* German, English and French.

DR. STEFAN KRAFT, born 1934; admitted, 1961, Zurich, Switzerland. *Education:* University of Zurich (Dr.iur., 1959); Harvard Law School, U.S.A. (LL.M., 1963). *Member:* Swiss and Zurich Bar Associations. *LANGUAGES:* German, English and French. *PRACTICE AREAS:* Commercial and Contract Law; Corporate; Banking Law; Estate Planning; Administration; Arbitration.

DR. ADOLF E. KAMMERER, born 1936; admitted, 1966, Zurich, Switzerland. *Education:* University of Zurich (Dr.iur., 1963); Harvard Law School, U.S.A. (LL.M., 1965). *Member:* Swiss and Zurich Bar Associations. *LANGUAGES:* German, English and French. *PRACTICE AREAS:* Corporate; Commercial and Contract Law; Banking Law; International Private Law; Arbitration; Mergers and Acquisitions.

DR. HANS NIEDERER, born 1941; admitted, 1971, Zurich, Switzerland. *Education:* University of Zurich (Dr.iur., 1968); University of California, Berkeley, U.S.A. (LL.M., 1970). *Member:* Swiss and Zurich Bar Associations. *LANGUAGES:* German, English, French and Dutch. *PRACTICE AREAS:* Capital Market Law; Securities Law; Banking Law; Corporate; Contract Law.

PROF. DR. PETER B. FORSTMOSER, born 1943; admitted, 1971, Zurich, Switzerland. *Education:* University of Zurich (Dr.iur., 1970); Harvard Law School, U.S.A. (LL.M., 1972). Professor, University of Zurich, Law School, 1974. *Member:* Swiss and Zurich Bar Associations. *LANGUAGES:* German, English and French. *PRACTICE AREAS:* Corporate Law; Banking Law; Securities Law; Contract Law.

DR. WALTER MEIER, born 1931; admitted, 1966, Zurich, Switzerland. *Education:* University of Zurich (Dr.iur., 1963); Harvard Law School, U.S.A. (LL.M., 1972). *Member:* Swiss and Zurich Bar Associations. *LANGUAGES:* German, English and French. *PRACTICE AREAS:* Swiss Tax Law; International Tax Law; Corporate; Banking Law; Estate Planning; Administration; Litigation in Tax Matters.

DR. PETER R. ISLER, born 1946; admitted, 1977, Zurich, Switzerland. *Education:* University of Zurich (Dr.iur., 1973); Harvard Law School, U.S.A. (LL.M., 1974). *Member:* Swiss and Zurich Bar Associations. *LANGUAGES:* German, English and French. *PRACTICE AREAS:* Commercial and Contract Law; Corporate; Banking Law; Capital Market Law; Property Law; General Practice.

DR. CHRISTIAN P. MEISTER, born 1945; admitted, 1971, Zurich, Switzerland. *Education:* University of Zurich (Dr.iur., 1977). *Member:* Swiss and Zurich Bar Associations. *LANGUAGES:* German, English, French and Italian. *PRACTICE AREAS:* Corporate; Commercial and Contract Law; Banking Law; Estate Planning; Litigation; Arbitration; General Practice.

DR. ULRICH BENZ, born 1951; admitted, 1978, Aargau, Switzerland. *Education:* University of Zurich (Dr.iur., 1981). *Member:* Swiss and Zurich Bar Associations. *LANGUAGES:* German and English. *PRACTICE AREAS:* Corporate and Contract Law; Matrimonial and Inheritance Law; Banking Law; General Practice.

DR. ROLF P. JETZER, born 1950; admitted, 1981, Zurich, Switzerland. *Education:* University of Zurich (Dr.iur., 1979); College of Europe, Bruges, Belgium (H.E.E., 1981). *Member:* Swiss and Zurich Bar Associations. *LANGUAGES:* German, English and French. *PRACTICE AREAS:* Corporate; Commercial and Contract Law; Antitrust and Unfair Competition; European Community Law; EDP Law; Work and Residence Permits; Environmental.

DR. ERNST F. SCHMID, born 1952; admitted, 1981, Zurich, Switzerland. *Education:* University of Zurich (Dr.iur., 1979); University of Cambridge, England (LL.M., 1984). *Member:* Swiss and Zurich Bar Associations. *LANGUAGES:* German, English, French and Italian. *PRACTICE AREAS:* Corporate; Commercial and Contract Law; Litigation; Arbitration; EDP Law; Banking Law; General Practice.

DR. PETER C. HONEGGER, born 1955; admitted, 1987, Zurich, Switzerland. *Education:* University of Zurich (Dr.iur., 1986); University of Virginia Law School, U.S.A. (LL.M., 1983). *Member:* Swiss and Zurich Bar Associations. *LANGUAGES:* German, English and French. *PRACTICE AREAS:* Corporate; Commercial and Contract Law; Banking Law; Judicial Assistance; Tax Law; Environmental; International Law.

DR. GAUDENZ G. ZINDEL, born 1954; admitted, 1987, Zurich, Switzerland. *Education:* University of Zurich (Dr.iur., 1984); University of California, Los Angeles, U.S.A. (LL.M., 1988). *Member:* Swiss and Zurich Bar Associations. *LANGUAGES:* German and English. *PRACTICE AREAS:* Securities Law; Corporate; Commercial and Contract Law; European Community Law; Banking Law.

ASSOCIATES

DR. FRANÇOIS M. BIANCHI, born 1955; admitted, 1984, Zurich, Switzerland. *Education:* University of Zurich (Dr.iur., 1981); University of Miami, School of Law, U.S.A. (LL.M., 1986). *Member:* Swiss and Zurich Bar Associations. *LANGUAGES:* German, English, French and Spanish. *PRACTICE AREAS:* Corporate; Commercial and Contract Law; Banking Law; Securities Law; General Practice.

DR. MARKUS A. FREY, born 1956; admitted, 1987, Zurich, Switzerland. *Education:* Universities of Geneva and Zurich (Dr.iur., 1985); University of Miami, School of Law, U.S.A. (LL.M., 1988). *Member:* Swiss and Zurich Bar Associations. *LANGUAGES:* German, English, French and Spanish. *PRACTICE AREAS:* Corporate; Commercial and Contract Law; International Tax Law; International Private Law; Estate Planning and Administration; General Practice.

DR. URS PULVER, born 1957; admitted, 1989, Zurich, Switzerland. *Education:* University of Zurich (Dr.iur., 1986). *Member:* Swiss and Zurich Bar Associations. *LANGUAGES:* German, English, French and Italian. *PRACTICE AREAS:* Corporate; Commercial and Contract Law; Securities Law; Banking Law; Contract Law; Competition Law.

LIC. STEPHANIE COMTESSE, born 1965; admitted, 1990, Geneva, Switzerland. *Education:* University of Geneva (Lic.iur., 1987). *Member:* Swiss and Zurich Bar Associations. *LANGUAGES:* English, French and German. *PRACTICE AREAS:* Corporate; Commercial and Contracts Law; International Private Law; Property Law; General Practice.

DR. ADRIAN PLÜSS, born 1961; admitted, 1991, Zurich, Switzerland. *Education:* University of Zurich (Dr.iur., 1990). *Member:* Swiss and Zurich Bar Associations. *LANGUAGES:* German, French and English. *PRAC-*

(This Listing Continued)

(This Listing Continued)

NIEDERER KRAFT & FREY, Zürich—Continued

TICE AREAS: Corporate; Commercial and Contract Law; Tax Law; Development, Land Use and Zoning Law; Environmental.

DR. THOMAS SPRECHER, born 1957; admitted, 1992, Zurich, Switzerland. *Education:* University of Zurich (Dr.phil. 1985; Lic.iur., 1989). *Member:* Swiss and Zurich Bar Associations. *LANGUAGES:* German, English and French. *PRACTICE AREAS:* Corporate; Commercial and Contract Law; General Practice.

DR. THOMAS A. FRICK, born 1961; admitted, 1992, Zurich, Switzerland. *Education:* University of Zurich (Dr.iur., 1993). *Member:* Swiss and Zurich Bar Associations. *LANGUAGES:* German, English and French. *PRACTICE AREAS:* Company Law; Protection of Personality Law; Competition Law; Intellectual Property Law.

DR. ANDREAS C. LIMBURG, born 1964; admitted, 1991, Zurich, Switzerland. *Education:* University of Zurich (Dr.iur., 1993); London School of Economics and Political Science, LSE (LL.M., 1993). *Member:* Swiss and Zurich Bar Associations. *LANGUAGES:* German, English, French and Spanish. *PRACTICE AREAS:* Commercial Law; Competition Law; Capital Market Law; International Private Law; International Litigation.

DR. ANDREAS I. CASUTT, born 1963; admitted, 1993, Zurich, Switzerland. *Education:* University of Zurich (Dr.iur., 1991). *Member:* Swiss and Zurich Bar Associations. *LANGUAGES:* German, English and French. *PRACTICE AREAS:* Corporate; Commercial and Contract Law; Employment Law.

DR. ANDRÁS A. GUROVITS, born 1960; admitted, 1991, Zurich, Switzerland. *Education:* University of Zurich (Dr.iur., 1993). *Member:* Swiss and Zurich Bar Associations. *LANGUAGES:* German, English, French and Hungarian. *PRACTICE AREAS:* Corporate; Commercial and Contract Law; International Private Law; Intellectual Property Law; EDP Law; Product Liability Law.

Languages: German, English, French, Italian, Spanish, Dutch and Hungarian

---

NIEDERMANN RECHTSANWÄLTE

UTOQUAI 37
CH-8008 ZÜRICH, SWITZERLAND
Telephone: (01) 252 34 00
Telecopier: (01) 252 35 36

General Civil and Commercial Practice, Corporate, Banking, Antitrust and Unfair Competition, Industrial Property, Inheritance, Labor, Commercial Litigation and Arbitration, International Judicial Assistance, Extradition.

MEMBERS OF FIRM

DR. MARCO N. NIEDERMANN, born Zurich, Switzerland, 1949; admitted, 1981, Switzerland. *Education:* University of Zurich (Dr.iur., 1976); University of Virginia (LL.M., 1983). Lecturer, University of Zurich, 1977-1982. Clerk, Commercial Court of Zurich, 1978-1982, Judge ad hoc Commercial Court of Zurich, 1981. *Member:* Zurich, Swiss and International Bar Associations. *LANGUAGES:* German, English and French.

ASSOCIATES

ROBIN P. GRAND, born St. Gallen, Switzerland, 1963; admitted, 1991, Switzerland. *Education:* University of Zurich (lic.iur., 1988). Clerk, Zurich District Court, 1989-1990. *Member:* Zurich and Swiss Bar Associations. *LANGUAGES:* German, English and French.

MAX BAUMGARTNER, born Zurich, Switzerland, 1962; admitted, 1993, Switzerland. *Education:* University of Zurich (lic.iur., 1990). Clerk, Zurich District Court, 1991-1992. *Member:* Zurich and Swiss Bar Associations. *LANGUAGES:* German, English, French, Italian and Spanish.

ISABELLE VOGT, born Basel, Switzerland, 1966; admitted, 1993, Switzerland. *Education:* University of Zurich (lic.iur., 1990). Clerk, Milen District Court, 1991-1992. *Member:* Zurich and Swiss Bar Associations. *LANGUAGES:* German, French and English.

Languages: German, English, French and Italian

NOBEL & HUG

Established in 1983
DUFOURSTRASSE 29
P.O. BOX 6A
8032 ZÜRICH, SWITZERLAND
Telephone: 01/262 22 12
Telecopier: 01/262 00 92

Commercial, Corporate, Banking and Media Law, Litigation, Arbitration and General Practice.

MEMBERS OF FIRM

PROF. DR. PETER NOBEL, born 1945; admitted, 1980, Canton of Zurich. *Education:* University of St. Gallen (Dr.rer.publ., 1973); University of Goettingen, Germany; Columbia Law School (Visiting Scholar, 1976-1978). *LANGUAGES:* German, English, French and Italian.

DR. HANS-JUERG HUG, born 1942; admitted, 1972, Canton of Zurich. *Education:* University of Zurich (Dr.iur., 1971). *LANGUAGES:* German, English and French.

DR. MATTHIAS SCHWAIBOLD, born 1956; admitted, 1985, Canton of Zurich. *Education:* Zurich University (Dr. iur., 1984); Faculté Internationale, Strasbourg (Diplôme de droit comparé). *LANGUAGES:* German, English, French and Italian.

DR. BENNO BERNET, born 1957; admitted, 1985, Canton of Zurich. *Education:* University of Zurich (Dr.iur., 1989). *LANGUAGES:* German, English and French.

ASSOCIATES

DR. CHRISTOPH PETER, born 1960; admitted, 1988, Canton of Zurich. *Education:* University of Zurich (Dr. iur., 1991); University of Exeter (LL.M., 1995). *LANGUAGES:* German, English, French and Portuguese.

DR. ANDREAS MEILI, born 1963; admitted, 1991, Canton of Zurich. *Education:* University of Zurich (Dr.iur., 1990). *LANGUAGES:* German, English and French.

IRENE SPAENI, born 1956; admitted, 1987, Canton of Zurich. *Education:* University of Zurich (lic. iur., 1982). *LANGUAGES:* German, English and French.

NOTTER BLATTER DAVIDOFF & PARTNER

ZIMMERGASSE 16
8008 ZÜRICH, SWITZERLAND
Telephone: (41-1) 261 15 55
Facsimile: (41-1) 262 35 42

Mailing Address: P.O. Box 32, 8032 Zurich, Switzerland

Geneva, Switzerland Office: 16, avenue Jules Crosnier, 1206 Geneva. Telephone: (41-22) 346 24 74. Facsimile: (41-22) 347 09 21.
Bern, Switzerland Office: Schwanengasse 9, 3001 Bern. Telephone: (41-31) 312 53 12. Facsimile: (41-31) 311 07 49.
Brussels, Belgium Office: Avenue de Tervueren 12, 1040 Brussels.

General Corporate and Commercial Practice, Finance and Banking, International Contracts, International Arbitration, Taxation, Real Estate, Intellectual and Industrial Property and Copyright, Administrative Matters, Inheritance and Estate Planning, Civil Litigation.

FIRM PROFILE: The firm is the result of a merger of three firms in Bern, Geneva and Zurich based on a new service-oriented concept offering an integrated full legal service for the whole of Switzerland. Notary public services are provided by the Bern office. The Zurich office includes professional auditing and controlling services. The firm maintains a well developed network of correspondent law firms.

MEMBERS OF FIRM

DR. ANTON W. BLATTER, born 1952; admitted, 1978, Canton of Bern. *Education:* University of Bern Law School (B.A., Law, 1978); J.D., Law, 1981); University of Geneva (Diplôme d'Etudes Superieures en Droit, 1980); Academy of American and International Law, Dallas, Texas. *Member:* Zurich and Swiss Bar Association; AIJA. *PRACTICE AREAS:* Corporate Law; Banks and Banking; Taxation; Liquidation; Receiverships; Sports.

(This Listing Continued)

LIC.IUR. THOMAS REIMANN, born 1960; admitted, 1989, Canton of Zurich. *Education:* University of Zurich Law School (B.A. in Law, 1986); University of Madison, Wisconsin (International and US Law, 1992). *Member:* Zurich and Swiss Bar Association; DACH International Association. *PRACTICE AREAS:* Business Law, Contracts; Agency and Distributorships; Computers and Software; Trademarks; Mergers, Acquisitions and Divestitures.

ASSOCIATES

LIC. IUR. THOMAS H. BLATTMANN, born 1958; admitted, 1990, Canton of Zurich. *Education:* University of Zurich Law School (B.S. in Law, 1985); California Western School of Law, San Diego (Master of Comparative Law, 1992). Recipient, American Jurisprudence Award in Legal Skills, 1991. *Member:* Zurich and Swiss Bar Association. *PRACTICE AREAS:* Civil Law, Litigation; International Law; Trusts and Estates; Real Estates; Immigration and Naturalization.

LEGAL SUPPORT STAFF

HANS-PETER LANZ, born 1949. Certified Accountant/Controller, 1979. *Member Swiss Institute of Certified Accountants and Tax Consultants.*

OF COUNSEL

DR. HEINZ BLOCH, born 1932; admitted, 1958, Canton of Bern; 1966, New York. *Education:* University of Bern Law School (B.A. in Law and in Economics, 1958; Ph.D. in Economics, 1961); New York University (J.D., 1966). *Member:* Zurich and Swiss Bar Association; American Bar Association; International Bar Association; Swiss-American Chamber of Commerce. (Also Member of Bloch & Partner, Zurich and Counsel to Parker Chapin Flattau & Klimpl, New York, N.Y.). *PRACTICE AREAS:* Resorts and Leisure; International Law; Corporate Law; Real Estate; Business Law.

Languages: German, English and French

NOTTER & PARTNERS

Established in 1984

ST. ANNAGASSE 16
8027 ZÜRICH, SWITZERLAND
Telephone: 01-212 72 74
Fax: 01-212 72 79
E-Mail: 100101, 1052

Bern, Switzerland Office: Thunstrasse 73, 3000 16. Telephone: 031-356 58 58. Fax: 031-356 58 50.
Fribourg, Switzerland Associated Office: Boivin & Nussbaumer, rue de Lausanne 91, 1700. Telephone: 037-22 25 68. Fax: 037-22 19 36.

International Commercial Practice, Taxation, Corporate, Contract, Unfair Competition, Banking and Finance, Corporate Restructuring, Mergers & Acquisitions, Industrial and Intellectual Property Law, Licensing, Insurance Law, Third Party Liability, Arbitration, Estate Planning, Trusts, European Community Law, Commercial Litigation, Administrative and Regulatory Matters, Immigration Law (Residence and Working Permits).
Member of LAW-Lawyers Associated Worldwide, a network of independent law firms with offices throughout Europe, the Middle East, Australasia and the Americas.

MEMBERS OF THE FIRM

MARC GRÜNINGER, born 1959; admitted, 1986, Switzerland. *Education:* University of Bern (Fürsprecher, 1986); New York University School of Law (M.C.J., 1987). Co-Author: "New Commentary on the Swiss Code of Obligations.".

BRUNO HUNZIKER, born 1960; admitted, 1987, Switzerland. *Education:* University of Bern (Fürsprecher, 1987); Tulane Law School (LL.M., 1989). Co-Author: "New Commentary on the Swiss Code of Obligations.".

BERNHARD KOROLNIK, born 1960; admitted, 1990, Switzerland. *Education:* University of Zurich (lic.iur., 1986).

ANDREAS B. NOTTER, born 1953; admitted, 1981, Switzerland; 1983, Notary. *Education:* University of Fribourg (lic.iur., 1978); University of Bern (Fürsprecher, 1981; Notary, 1983). Co-Author: "New Commentary on the Swiss Code of Obligations." *Member:* Secretary General, Association of Swiss Notaries.

JÜRG HUNZIKER, born 1949; admitted, 1976, Switzerland. *Education:* University of Bern (Fürsprecher, 1976). Head of Claims Service Department, La Vaudoise Assurance, Lausanne, Switzerland, 1979-1987.

(This Listing Continued)

GERHARD ROTH, born 1965; admitted, 1992, Switzerland. *Education:* University of Bern (Fürsprecher, 1992). Member of Tax Department, Arthur Andersen A.G., Bern, Switzerland, 1992-1994.

PIERRE BOIVIN, born 1942; admitted, 1975, Switzerland; 1978, Notary. *Education:* University of Lausanne (lic. rer. pol., 1966; lic.iur., 1967); Institute of International Studies, Geneva (1969). Assistant Professor, University of Geneva, European Law Studies Center, 1967-1969. Member: Executive Council, City of Fribourg, 1979-1991; State Legislature of Fribourg, 1986 and Chairman, 1993. (Also at Boivin & Nussbaumer, Fribourg, Switzerland Associated Office).

ALBERT NUSSBAUMER, born 1957; admitted, 1983, Switzerland; 1986, Notary. *Education:* University of Fribourg (lic.iur., 1980). Assistant Professor, University of Fribourg, 1983-1986. Member and Chairman, Expropriation Committee of the State of Fribourg, 1986. (Also at Boivin & Nussbaumer, Fribourg, Switzerland Associated Office).

Languages: German, English, French and Italian

PESTALOZZI GMUER & PATRY

Established in 1911

LOEWENSTRASSE 1
8001 ZÜRICH, SWITZERLAND
Telephone: 411/217 91 11
Telefax: 0041 1/217 92 17
Telex: 812754
Cable Address: "Henggelerjur"

REVISERS OF THE SWITZERLAND LAW DIGEST FOR THIS DIRECTORY.

Geneva, Switzerland Office: 15, Bd des Philosophes, CH-1205. Telephone: 0041 22/320 78 33. Telex: 427079 PJS CH. Telefax: 0041 22/320 43 41.
Brussels, Belgium Office: 221, Avenue Louise, 1050. Telephone: 322/646 60 10. Telecopier: 322/646 75 34.

International Commercial, Corporate, Tax and Arbitration Practice. European Law, Industrial Property and Copyright. Fiscal, Construction and Administrative Matters. Banking and Financial Law. Estate Planning. Civil Litigation, all Swiss Courts.

MEMBERS OF FIRM

DR. IUR. DR. OEC. ANTON PESTALOZZI, born Zurich, 1915; admitted, 1947, Switzerland. *Education:* Economics and legal studies, University of Zurich (Dr.oec.publ., 1942; Dr.iur., 1947). Author: Articles on taxation and arbitration. *LANGUAGES:* German, English and French. *PRACTICE AREAS:* Contracts; Corporations; Tax Law; International Arbitration.

DR. PAUL GMUER, born Zurich, 1915; admitted, 1942, Switzerland. *Education:* Legal Studies, University of Zurich (Dr.iur., 1939). *LANGUAGES:* English, French and German. *PRACTICE AREAS:* Company Law; Corporate Law; Taxation; Trusts and Estates; Charitable Organizations.

DR. RUDOLF HEIZ, born St. Gallen, 1930; admitted, 1961, Switzerland. *Education:* Legal studies, University of Zurich (Dr.iur., 1958); Paris, University of Michigan, Ann Arbor. Author: Foreign Public Law in International Conflict of Laws. *LANGUAGES:* English, French and German. *PRACTICE AREAS:* Contracts; Corporations; Banking Law; Tax Law; Conflict of Laws.

DR. KARL ARNOLD, born Luzern, 1940; admitted, 1968, Switzerland. *Education:* Legal studies, Fribourg, Cambridge and Luxembourg; Diplôme de droit comparé, Luxembourg 1967; University of Fribourg (Dr.iur, 1969). Author or Contributor: Switzerland's Private International Law Statute, 2d ed., 1994; The Guide to Foreign Exchange Regulations, 4th edition, 1990; Handbook of Comparative Business Law, 1979; Legal Aspects of Doing Business in Western Europe, 1983. *LANGUAGES:* English, French and German. *PRACTICE AREAS:* Contracts; Corporations; International Arbitration; Litigation; Banking Law; Bankruptcy.

DR. HANS BOLLMANN, born Zurich, 1943; admitted, 1972, Switzerland. *Education:* Legal Studies, University of Zurich (Dr.iur., 1970). Author: "Swiss Bank Secrecy," 1992; "International Handbook on Employment Contracts," 1993. *LANGUAGES:* English, French, German and Italian. *PRACTICE AREAS:* General Practice; Business Law; Litigation.

DR. PIERRE A. KARRER, born Zurich, 1941; admitted, 1969, Switzerland. *Education:* Legal studies, University of Zurich (Dr.iur., 1967); Göttin-

(This Listing Continued)

PESTALOZZI GMUER & PATRY, Zürich—Continued

gen, Padova, The Hague and Yale (LL.M., 1970). Author: Switzerland's Private International Law Statute, 2d ed. 1994; articles on international arbitration. *LANGUAGES:* English, French, German, Italian and Dutch. *PRACTICE AREAS:* Arbitration and Mediation; International Arbitration; Construction Law Arbitration; Alternative Dispute Resolution; Conflict of Laws; Art Law.

DR. MAX WALTER, born Bern, 1945; admitted, 1972, Switzerland. *Education:* Legal studies, University of Zurich (Dr.iur., 1971). *LANGUAGES:* German and English. *PRACTICE AREAS:* Administrative Law; Insolvency; Liquidations; Waste Disposal; Condominiums; Zoning.

DR. PETER PESTALOZZI, born Zurich, 1945; admitted, 1976, Switzerland. *Education:* Legal studies, University of Zurich (Dr.iur., 1974). *LANGUAGES:* German, English, French and Italian. *PRACTICE AREAS:* Contracts; Corporations; Industrial Property; Copyright; Unfair Competition; Licensing Agreements.

DR. URS JORDI, born Wildegg, 1946; admitted, 1972, Switzerland. *Education:* Legal studies, Bern and Zurich; University of Bern (Dr.iur., 1974). *LANGUAGES:* German, French and English. *PRACTICE AREAS:* Contracts; Corporations; Litigation, Trusts and Estates.

LIC. IUR. LIC. OEC. CHRISTOPH R. RAMSTEIN, born Basel, 1951; admitted, 1980, Switzerland. *Education:* Studies in business administration and law, St. Gallen and Zurich; lic.oec. HSG/M.B.A. Graduate School for Economics, St. Gallen 1976; University of Zurich (lic.iur, 1978). *LANGUAGES:* German, English and French. *PRACTICE AREAS:* Banks and Banking; Business Law; Company and Corporate Law; Litigation/Arbitration.

DR. MARCUS DESAX, born Chur, 1948; admitted, 1975, Switzerland. *Education:* Legal Studies, Fribourg and Alabama; University of Fribourg (Dr.iur., 1977); University of Alabama, (M.C.L., 1977). Author: "Swiss Stamp Tax Legislation,", Swiss-American Chamber of Commerce, 2nd ed., 1993; "EC Law: How to Look For? Where to Find?" 1992; "Business Law Guide to Switzerland," ed. 1991; "Swiss Supreme Court Practice in Tax Matters," 1991; Swiss Reporter IFA Congress, 1989; "The Disregard of Legal Entity." Member, Executive Committee, The International Fiscal Association (IFA); Treasurer of the Swiss National Branch of IFA. *LANGUAGES:* English, French and German. *PRACTICE AREAS:* Taxation; International Arbitration; International Civil Law; Mergers, Acquisitions and Divestitures; Agency and Distributorships.

DR. ROBERT FURTER, born Zurich, 1953; admitted, 1979, Switzerland. *Education:* Legal studies, University of Zurich (Dr.iur., 1979). Author: publications on Banking, Securities and Labor Law. *LANGUAGES:* German, English, French and Dutch. *PRACTICE AREAS:* Bank and Banking; Business Law; Company Law; Litigation; Securities.

DR. SILVIA ZIMMERMANN, born Zurich, 1952; admitted, 1978, Switzerland. *Education:* Legal studies, Zurich and Georgetown; University of Zurich (Dr.iur., 1980); Georgetown University (LL.M., 1982). Author: Articles on taxation, Swiss reporter IFA Congress, 1987: "The fiscal residence of companies.". *LANGUAGES:* English, French and German. *PRACTICE AREAS:* Taxation; International Tax; Income Tax; Estate and Gift Tax; Expatriate Tax.

PROF. DR. CHRISTIAN J. MEIER-SCHATZ, born Grenchen, 1950; admitted, 1980, Switzerland. *Education:* Legal studies in Bern and Berkeley; University of Bern (Dr.iur., 1979); University of California, Berkeley (LL.M.. 1985). Author: "Selective Distribution and EEC Competition Law," 1979; "Economic Law and Disclosure," 1989; "Labour Law," 1991; Handbook: "International Capital Market Law and Securities Regulation, Switzerland,", 1991; "The New Swiss Company Law" (ed), 1992; "Cooperation and Joint Venture Agreements", 1994. Professor of Law and Director of the Institute for European Law, University of St. Gallen. *LANGUAGES:* English, French and German. *PRACTICE AREAS:* Corporate Law; Mergers, Acquisitions and Divestitures; Antitrust and Trade Regulations; Community Law; Business Law.

WALTER H. BOSS, born Bern, 1952; admitted, 1980, Switzerland. *Education:* Legal studies, University of Bern (Fürsprecher 1980); New York University (LL.M. Taxation, 1988). Author: Publications on International Taxation. Swiss Reporter IFA Congress 1993 "Non-discrimination Rules in International Taxation"; Senior Correspondent, Tax Notes International. *LANGUAGES:* English, German, Italian, French. *PRACTICE AREAS:* Taxation; International Tax Planning; Corporate Law; Mergers, Acquisitions and Divestitures.

(This Listing Continued)

DR. SILVAN HUTTER, born St. Gallen, 1961; admitted, 1989, Switzerland. *Education:* Legal studies, Yale University (LL.M., 1987); University of Fribourg (Dr.iur., 1989). Author: "International Commercial Arbitration in Thailand"; general publications on dispute resolution in Thailand and Japan and comparative constitutional law. *LANGUAGES:* English, French, German and Thai. *PRACTICE AREAS:* Corporations; Contracts; Conflict of Laws; International Arbitration; Administrative Law.

OF COUNSEL

DR. REGULA PESTALOZZI, born Zurich, 1921; admitted, 1959, Switzerland. *Education:* Legal Studies, Zurich and Geneva; University of Zurich (Dr.iur., 1948). *LANGUAGES:* English, French and German. *PRACTICE AREAS:* Corporations; Tax Law; Trusts and Estates.

PROF. DR. MARKUS REICH, born Baden, 1949; (Not admitted in Switzerland). *Education:* Legal Studies University of Zurich (Dr.iur., 1976). Author: Publications on Corporate National and International Taxation; VAT, Constitutional Law. Professor of Tax Law, University of Zurich. *LANGUAGES:* German, English and French. *PRACTICE AREAS:* Taxation; International Tax; Income Tax; Value Added Tax (VAT); Estate and Gift Tax.

ASSOCIATES

DR. PETER A. STRAUB, born Basel, 1959; admitted, 1987, Switzerland. *Education:* University of Zurich (Dr.iur., 1988); London School of Economics and Political Science (LL.M., 1991). *LANGUAGES:* English, German, French. *PRACTICE AREAS:* Banking; Finance; Corporate Law; Bankruptcy; Mergers, Acquisitions and Divestitures.

PETER R. ACKERMANN, born Basel, 1958; admitted, 1987, Switzerland. *Education:* Legal Studies, University of Bern (lic.iur., 1986; Fürsprecher and Notary, 1987); New York University (M.C.J., 1989). *LANGUAGES:* English, German, French. *PRACTICE AREAS:* Contracts; Corporations; Banking Law; Intellectual Property; Data Processing Law.

DR. JAKOB HOEHN, born Horgen, 1960; admitted, 1988, Switzerland. *Education:* University of Zurich (Dr.iur., 1990); Georgetown University (LL.M., 1991). *LANGUAGES:* English, German, French, Italian. *PRACTICE AREAS:* Contracts; Corporations; Administrative Law.

DR. LAURENT KILLIAS, born Zurich, 1961; admitted, 1990, Switzerland. *Education:* University of Zurich (Dr.iur., 1993). Author: "The Prorogation of Jurisdiction Under The Lugano Convention 1988," 1989. *LANGUAGES:* English, German and French. *PRACTICE AREAS:* Litigation; Contracts; Conflict of Laws.

DR. CHRISTIAN A. MEYER, born Schaffhausen, 1961; admitted, 1987, Switzerland. *Education:* University of Saint-Gall (Dr. iur., 1991); University of Brussels (Post Graduate in European Community Law, U.L.B., 1993). Author: "Sole Distribution, Typology, Contractual Obligations and Questions of Private International Law (Conflict of Laws)", 1990; "Sole Distribution", 1992. *LANGUAGES:* English, French and German. *PRACTICE AREAS:* European Community Law; Competition Law; Commercial Law; Contracts; Conflict of Laws.

DR. THOMAS MEISTER, born Schaffhausen, 1963; admitted, 1991, Switzerland. *Education:* University of St. Gallen (Dr. iur., 1995). *LANGUAGES:* German, French and English. *PRACTICE AREAS:* Corporate Law; Taxation; Administrative Law.

OF COUNSEL

DR. SIBYLLE PESTALOZZI-FRÜH, born Altstätten, 1953; admitted, 1983, Switzerland. *Education:* Legal studies, University of Zurich (Dr.iur., 1982). *LANGUAGES:* German, English, French and Italian. *PRACTICE AREAS:* Contracts; Corporate Law; Litigation; International Arbitration.

DR. ANNE-CATHERINE IMHOFF-SCHEIER, born St. Gallen, 1952; (Not admitted in Switzerland). *Education:* Legal studies, University of Geneva (Dr.iur., 1980). Author: "Torts and Unjust Enrichment in the New Swiss Conflict of Laws," 1990; articles on advertising, unfair competition and consumer protection. *LANGUAGES:* French, German, English and Italian. *PRACTICE AREAS:* International Contracts; Torts; International Arbitration; Unfair Competition; Consumer Protection.

REVISERS OF THE SWITZERLAND LAW DIGEST FOR THIS DIRECTORY.

PESTALOZZI HAEGI & WETTENSCHWILER

MÜHLEBACHSTR. 54
CH-8032 ZÜRICH, SWITZERLAND
Telephone: 01-262 11 12
Fax: 01-262 11 13

General Commercial Practice, Corporate, Contracts, Banking, Underwriting, Mergers and Acquisitions, Arbitration, Wills and Estates, Tax Law and Tax Planning, Administrative Matters, Residence and Work Permits, Civil Litigation in all Swiss Courts, International Judicial Assistance, Intellectual Property, Unfair Competition Law.

MEMBERS OF FIRM

DR. CHRISTOPH M. PESTALOZZI, M.C.J., born Zurich, Switzerland, 1950; admitted, 1979, Switzerland. Education: University of Zurich (Dr. iur., 1977); New York University, School of Law (M.C.J., 1982).

URS W. HAEGI, born Zurich, Switzerland, 1957; admitted, 1989, Switzerland. Education: University of St. Gallen for Business Administration, Economics; University of Zurich (Lic.iur., 1987).

DR. SUZANNE M. WETTENSCHWILER, born Zurich, Switzerland, 1955; admitted, 1984, Switzerland; Education: University of Geneva (Licenciée en droit, 1977); University of Zurich (Dr.iur., 1982).

ERWIN R. GRIESSHAMMER, born Biel, Switzerland, 1948; admitted, 1978, Switzerland. Education: University of St. Gallen for Business Administration (lic.oec. HSG, 1973); University of Berne (lic.iur., 1976).

DR. MARC A. RUSSENBERGER, born Zurich, Switzerland, May 13, 1957; admitted, 1988, Switzerland. Education: University of Zurich (Dr. iur., 1988).

ASSOCIATES

HANSJÜRG RHYNER, born Glarus, Switzerland, 1961; admitted, 1991, Switzerland. Education: University of St. Gallen for Business Administration, School of Law; University of Fribourg (lic.iur., 1989); University of Exeter, UK, (LL.M., 1993).

MARIO C. BAUDACCI, born 1958; admitted, 1986, Zurich. Education: University of Zurich (lic.iur., 1983).

(All Attorneys of the Firm are Members of the Zurich and Swiss Bar Associations.)

Languages: German, English, French and Italian

PEYER, VOGEL, BUSSIEN, BURCKHARDT, STUTZER

LÖWENSTRASSE 17
P.O. BOX 7678
CH-8023 ZÜRICH, SWITZERLAND
Telephone: 01/221 13 71
Telefax: 01/221 28 63

General Practice, Civil and Commercial Law, Banking Law, Company Law, Construction Law, Law of Succession, Litigation, Insolvency Law.

PARTNERS

DR. JÜRG PEYER, born 1943; admitted, 1973, Zürich. Education: Universities of Geneva and Zürich (Dr.iur., 1974). Author: "Der Widerruf im Auftragsrecht." Member: Zürich and Swiss Bar Associations. **PRACTICE AREAS:** Commercial Law.

DR. UELI VOGEL-ETIENNE, born 1952; admitted, 1979, Zürich. Education: University of Zürich (Dr.iur., 1980). Author: "Strafrechtlicher Tierschutz." Member: Zürich and Swiss Bar Associations; International Commission of Jurists. **PRACTICE AREAS:** Civil Law; Criminal Law; Litigation.

DR. RENÉ BUSSIEN, born 1951; admitted, 1978, Zürich. Education: Universities of Fribourg and Zürich (Dr.iur., 1981). Author: "Hinterlegung im Zürcher Zivilprozessrecht." Member: Zürich, Swiss and International Bar Associations. **PRACTICE AREAS:** Criminal Law; Litigation; Construction Law.

DR. CHRISTOPH BURCKHARDT, born 1956; admitted, 1988, Zürich. Education: Universities of Bern and Zürich (Dr.iur., 1986). Author: "Die Vermächtnisforderung." Member: Zürich and Swiss Bar Associations;

(This Listing Continued)

Association International des Jeunes Avocats. **PRACTICE AREAS:** Successions; Litigation; Civil Law.

LIC. IUR. MAYA STUTZER-MÜLLER, born 1950; admitted, 1978, Zürich. Education: University of Zürich (Lic.iur., 1976). Member: Zürich and Swiss Bar Associations. **PRACTICE AREAS:** Family Law; Private International Law; Civil Litigation.

ASSOCIATES

LIC. IUR. FELIX RUTSCHMANN, born 1954; admitted, 1992, Zürich. Education: University of Zürich (Lic.iur., 1989). Accountant. Member: Zürich and Swiss Bar Associations. **PRACTICE AREAS:** Commercial Law; Insolvency Law.

LIC. IUR. THOMAS GATTLEN, born 1959. Education: University of Bern and Zürich (Lic.iur., 1988). **PRACTICE AREAS:** Commercial Law; Insolvency Law.

Languages: German, English, French and Italian.

PRAGER DREIFUSS & PARTNER

ZOLLIKERSTRASSE 183
8008 ZÜRICH, SWITZERLAND
Telephone: 41-1 422 77 11
Telefax: 41-1 422 77 14

Litigation, Arbitration, International Commercial Practice, Mergers and Acquisitions, International Contracts, Banking, Taxation, Real Estate, International Construction, Industrial Property, EC Law, Competition Law, Labor Law, Immigration.

MEMBERS OF FIRM

DR. ERIC L. DREIFUSS, born Zurich, Switzerland, 1943; admitted, 1974, Zurich. Education: Universities of Zurich and Bern (Ph.D., 1970; lic.iur., 1972). Lecturer, University of Zurich.

DR. TIS PRAGER, born Zurich, Switzerland, 1948; admitted, 1978, Zurich. Education: University of Zurich (lic.iur., 1972; Dr.iur., 1975); Max-Planck-Institute, Hamburg, (1976).

PIERRE L. WOOG, born Bern, Switzerland, 1938; admitted, 1964, Bern. Education: Universities of Bern and Paris (Fürsprecher, 1964).

GAUDENZ F. DOMENIG, born Zurich, Switzerland, 1956; admitted, 1984, New York; 1989, Zurich. Education: Universities of Helsinki and Zurich (lic.iur., 1981); New York University (LL.M., 1983).

DR. URS BRUNNER, born Zurich, Switzerland, 1951; admitted, 1989, Zurich. Education: University of Zurich (lic.iur., 1975; Dr.iur., 1985).

DR. STEPHEN V. BERTI, born Carshalton, England, 1956; admitted, 1989, Zurich. Education: University of Zurich (lic.iur., 1983; Dr.iur., 1989). (Also with Schraner & Berti).

ASSOCIATES

DR. ANDRÉ E. LEBRECHT, born Casablanca, Morocco, 1959; admitted, 1989, Zurich; 1992, New York. Education: University of St. Gall (lic.iur., 1983; Dr. iur., 1987); University of Miami (LL.M., 1991).

JANNES SCHOCH, born Tunis, Tunesia, 1958; admitted, 1988, Zurich. Education: University of Basel (lic.iur., 1985).

DR. ANDREAS C. MOLL, born Basel, Switzerland, 1960; admitted, 1987, Basel; 1991, Zurich; 1992, New York. Education: University of Basel (lic.iur., 1985; Dr.iur., 1989); New York University (M.C.J., 1991).

RALPH BUTZ, born Zurich, Switzerland, 1958; admitted, 1987, Zurich. Education: University of Zurich (lic.iur., 1982); University of Edinburgh (LL.M., 1992).

MARKUS GOTTSTEIN, born Zurich, Switzerland, 1962; admitted, 1993, Zurich. Education: University of Zurich (lic.iur., 1989).

VERENA GUGGENBÜHL, born Zurich, Switzerland, 1965; admitted, 1993, Zurich. Education: University of Zurich (lic.iur., 1989).

STEFAN WAESPI, born Winterthur, Switzerland, 1959; admitted, 1988, St. Gallen; 1991, New York; 1992, Zurich. Education: University of St. Gallen (lic.iur., 1984); University of Chicago (LL.M., 1989).

(This Listing Continued)

PRAGER DREIFUSS & PARTNER, Zürich—Continued

DR. CHRISTOPH K. GRABER, born Langenthal, Switzerland, 1961; admitted, 1987, Berne; 1990, Zurich. *Education:* University of Berne (Fürsprecher, 1987; Dr.iur., 1990).

Languages: German, English and French

REBER DIETSCHI HAGMANN WYSS UHL

DUFOURSTRASSE 43
8008 ZÜRICH, SWITZERLAND
Telephone: (01) 251 80 88
Telecopier: (01) 262 53 16

General, Corporate, Tax, Banking, Antitrust and Unfair Competition, Industrial Property, Estate Planning, Commercial Litigation and Arbitration.

PARTNERS

DR. ALFRED REBER, born Zurich, Switzerland, 1935; admitted, 1965, Switzerland. *Education:* University of Zurich (Dr.iur., 1962). Deputy Judge, Zurich District Court. Member, Swiss Panel of Arbitrators, International Chamber of Commerce (ICC). *Member:* Association of the Bar of the City of New York (Non-Resident); Zurich, Swiss and International Bar Associations; American Foreign Law Association. *LANGUAGES:* German, English and French. *PRACTICE AREAS:* Banking Law; Company Law; International Business Law; Inheritance Law; International Arbitration; Litigation.

DR. WILLI DIETSCHI, born Lenzburg, Switzerland, 1944; admitted, 1973, Switzerland. *Education:* University of Paris (1969-1970); University of Bern (Dr.iur., 1971); New York University School of Law (1971-1972). Clerk, 1972-1973, Associate Lawyer, 1974-1978, Vice President and Partner, 1978-1992, ATAG Ernst & Young AG. *Member:* Zurich and Swiss Bar Associations. *LANGUAGES:* German, English, French and Italian. *PRACTICE AREAS:* Company Law; Contract Law; Bankruptcy Law; Taxation Law; Estate Planning.

MARKUS C. HAGMANN, born Zurich, Switzerland, 1946; admitted, 1975, Switzerland. *Education:* University of Zurich (lic.iur., 1971). Legal and Tax Counsel and Deputy Vice President, Swiss Auditing Company (Revisuisse Price-Waterhouse), Zurich, 1976-1986. *Member:* Zurich and Swiss Bar Associations; International Fiscal Association. *LANGUAGES:* German, English, French and Italian. *PRACTICE AREAS:* Taxation Law; Tax Litigation; Tax Planning; Company Law; Commercial Law.

DR. THOMAS E. WYSS, born Zurich, Switzerland, 1952; admitted, 1982, Switzerland. *Education:* University of Zurich (Dr.iur., 1983). Associate Lawyer, 1984-1987. *Member:* Zurich and Swiss Bar Associations. *LANGUAGES:* German, English, French and Italian. *PRACTICE AREAS:* Contract Law; Commercial Law; Corporate Law; Torts; Insurance Law; Construction Law; Litigation.

DR. MARKUS UHL, born Zurich, Switzerland, 1954; admitted, 1984, Switzerland. *Education:* University of Zurich (Dr.iur., 1987). Associate Lawyer, 1982-1987. Vice President, Fides Trust Company, Zurich, 1988-1991. *Member:* Zurich and Swiss Bar Associations; Industrial Property Law Associations. *LANGUAGES:* German, English and French. *PRACTICE AREAS:* Company Law; Contract Law; Industrial Property Law; Software Law; Bankruptcy Law; Litigation.

THOMAS KLOOZ, born Zurich, Switzerland, 1954; admitted, 1984, Switzerland. *Education:* University of Zurich (lic.iur., 1980); University of Miami (LL.M., 1985). Vice President and Legal Counsel, ISL Marketing AG, Lucerne, 1985-1992. *Member:* Zurich and Swiss Bar Associations; Sport-Link Worldwide (Alliance of Sports Lawyers). *LANGUAGES:* German, English and French. *PRACTICE AREAS:* Contract Law; Commercial Law; Corporate Law; Sports Law.

ASSOCIATES

MATHIS A. BERGER, born Zurich, Switzerland, 1964; admitted, 1994, Switzerland. *Education:* University of Zurich (lic.iur., 1991). *Member:* Zurich and Swiss Bar Associations. *LANGUAGES:* German, English and French. *PRACTICE AREAS:* Contract Law; Company Law; Competition Law; International Business Law; Bankruptcy Law; Litigation.

Languages: German, English, French and Italian

DR. IUR. WERNER A. RECHSTEINER

Established in 1987
SUSENBERGSTRASSE 101
8044 ZÜRICH, SWITZERLAND
Telephone: (41) (1) 251 86 15
Fax: (41) (1) 251 49 31

International, Corporate, Commercial and Tax Practice, Arbitrations, Trust and Estate Matters.

DR. IUR. WERNER A. RECHSTEINER, born Zürich, Switzerland, 1943; admitted, 1978, Zürich. *Education:* University of Zürich (lic.iur., 1967; Dr.iur., 1978); Columbia University (LL.M., 1973). Author: "Die Volksschule im Bundesstaat" ("Primary Schools in Federal States"), Schulthess (Zürich), 1978. Lecturer, Civil Law, University of Zürich, 1984—. *Member:* Zürich and Swiss Bar Associations; Association of Civil Procedure; Association Suisse de l'arbitrage. *LANGUAGES:* German, English and French.

REICHENBACH & PARTNER

Established in 1938
TALACKER 50
8001 ZÜRICH, SWITZERLAND
Telephone: National: 01-221 26 53 /211 70 07
International: + 411 212 44 77
Telecopier: 01 221 26 56

Corporate, Insurance, Banking, Aviation, Commercial, Estate and International Law, Media and Copyright Law.

MEMBERS OF FIRM

DR. IUR. FRANZ REICHENBACH, C.B.E., born Switzerland, 1909; admitted, 1937, Zurich. *Education:* Universities of Zurich and Berlin (Doctor of Law). Professional training in Solicitors Firm in London from 1937-1938. *Member:* Zurich and Swiss Bar Associations; International Bar Association (past President, 1982-1984). *LANGUAGES:* German, English and French.

DR. IUR. CURT TUCHSCHMID, born St. Gall, Switzerland, November 25, 1918; admitted, 1951, Zurich. *Education:* Universities of Zurich and Bern (Doctor of Law). *Member:* Zurich and Swiss Bar Associations. *LANGUAGES:* German, English and French.

DR. IUR. DONALD REICHENBACH, born Zurich, Switzerland, July 27, 1945; admitted, 1975, Zurich. *Education:* University of Zurich (Doctor of Law). Professional training in New York, N.Y., Mendes & Mount from 1971-1972. Author: "The Aircraft Owner's and Operator's Liability for Noise Damage and its Insurance Aspects". *Member:* Zurich and Swiss Bar Associations; International Bar Association (Chairman, Insurance Committee, Section of Business Law). *LANGUAGES:* German, English and French.

DR. IUR., LIC. OEC. ALFRED MEILI, born Lucerne, Switzerland, September 28, 1947; admitted, 1977, Zurich, Switzerland. *Education:* Universities of Berne and St. Gall (Licentiate of Economy); University of Zurich (Doctor of Law). Author: "The History and Development of the Swiss Purchase Law," published by Schulthess Polygraphischer Verlag AG, Zurich, 1976. *Member:* Zurich and Swiss Bar Associations; International Bar Association; International Association of Young Lawyers. *LANGUAGES:* German, English, French and Italian.

DR. IUR. AUGUST SCHUBIGER, born Uznach, Switzerland, May 10, 1937; admitted, 1971, Zurich. *Education:* Universities of Fribourg (Doctor of Law) and Zurich. Professional training in Liechtenstein, 1974-1975, Präsidial-Anstalt, Auditing Company. Author: "Legal aspects of the Leasing Contract", publisher: Jos. Zehnder & Co., St. Gall, 1970. *Member:* Zurich, Basel and Swiss Bar Associations; International Bar Association; International Association of Young Lawyers. *LANGUAGES:* German, English and French.

DR. IUR. RETO THOMAS RUOSS, born Zurich, Switzerland, June 7, 1955; admitted, 1987, Zurich. *Education:* University of Zurich (Doctor of Law). Author: "Legal Aspects of Art Auctions", published by Schulthess Polygraphischer Verlag AG, Zurich, 1984. *Member:* Zurich and Swiss Bar Associations; International Association of Young Lawyers. *LANGUAGES:* German, English and French.

DR. FELIX ZULLIGER, born Zurich, Switzerland, April 2, 1954; admitted, 1988, Zurich. *Education:* University of Zurich (Doctor of Law,
(This Listing Continued)

1988). Author: "Interference of third parties with contractual rights", published by Schulthess Polygraphischer Verlag AG, Zurich, 1988. *Member:* Zurich and Swiss Bar Associations; Swiss Association of International Law. *LANGUAGES:* German, English, French and Italian.

DR. IUR. ANDREAS HAFFTER, born Zurich, Switzerland, November 3, 1957; admitted, 1988, Zurich. *Education:* University of Zurich (Doctor of Law). Author: "The child support in private and public law", published by Schulthess Polygraphischer Verlag AG, Zurich, 1985. *Member:* Zurich and Swiss Bar Associations. *LANGUAGES:* German, English and French.

LIC. IUR. HSG THOMAS HÄLG, born St. Gall, Switzerland, March 11, 1962; admitted, 1991, Zurich. *Education:* University of St. Gall HSG (Licentiate of law). *Member:* Zurich and Swiss Bar Associations. *LANGUAGES:* German, English and French.

LIC. IUR. HANSPETER KASPAR, born Fribourg, Switzerland, April 30, 1962; admitted, 1992, Zurich. *Education:* University of Zurich (Licentiate of Law). *Member:* Zurich and Swiss Bar Associations. *LANGUAGES:* German, English and French.

LIC. IUR. PIO RUOSS, born Zurich, Switzerland, October 19, 1962; admitted, 1994, Zurich. *Education:* University of Zurich (Licentiate of Law). *Member:* Zurich and Swiss Bar Associations. *LANGUAGES:* German, English and French.

Languages: German, English, French and Italian

BÜRO DR. RICKENBACH

SCHLOSSBERGSTRASSE 22, ZOLLIKON-ZÜRICH

P.O. BOX 104

CH-8702 ZOLLIKON/ZÜRICH, SWITZERLAND

Telephone: 01 391 44 77

Telecopier: 01 391 77 35

General Practice, Commercial, Corporate and Private Law, Franchising, Tax, Estate and Labor Law, Domestic and International Licensing, International Business Law, International Legal Transactions, Bankruptcy Law and Civil Litigation, Arbitration, Intellectual Property, Trust and Estate Settlement, Joint Ventures, Offshore Investment, Trust Formation, Mergers and Acquisitions, Offshore Trusts, Work Permits.

MEMBERS OF FIRM

DR. ANDREAS M. RICKENBACH, born Samedan, Switzerland, April 28, 1927; admitted, 1953, Switzerland. *Education:* University of Paris; University of Zürich (Dr.iur., 1951). *Member:* Zürich and Swiss Bar Associations.

RINDERKNECHT GLAUS & STADELHOFER

Rechtsanwalte / Attorneys at Law

BEETHOVENSTRASSE 7

P.O. BOX 4451

CH-8022 ZÜRICH, SWITZERLAND

Telephone: +41-(0) 1-287 24 24

Telecopier: +41-(0) 1-287 24 00

Telex: 815 338

Swiss and International Practice in Business, Banking, Tax and Estate Law, Commercial Litigation and Arbitration.

PARTNERS

THOMAS M. RINDERKNECHT, DR.IUR., born 1954; admitted, 1982, Switzerland. *Education:* Law Schools of Zurich and Munich University (lic.iur. 1979; Dr.iur. 1982). *PRACTICE AREAS:* General Corporate; International Tax and Investments; Leasing Law.

HANNES GLAUS, DR.IUR., born 1953; admitted, 1983, Switzerland; 1985, New York. *Education:* Law School of Zurich University (lic.iur. 1979; Dr.iur. 1982); Harvard Law School, Massachusetts (LL.M. 1985). *PRACTICE AREAS:* General Corporate; Banking, Tax and Estate Planning.

CARL STADELHOFER, LIC.IUR., born 1953; admitted, 1982, Switzerland. *Education:* Law Schools of Zurich and Berne University (lic.iur. 1979). *PRACTICE AREAS:* General Corporate; Banking; International Legal Assistance.

(This Listing Continued)

LIC. IUR. THOMAS KLEIN, LIC.IUR., born 1957; admitted, 1985, Switzerland. *Education:* Universities of Basel and Geneva, Law Schools. *PRACTICE AREAS:* General Corporate; Commercial Litigation and Arbitration; International Legal Assistance.

ASSOCIATES

GERRIT STRAUB, LIC.IUR., born 1966; admitted, 1991, Switzerland. *Education:* Law School of Berne.

MARKUS JORDI, LIC.IUR., born 1963; admitted, 1993, Switzerland. *Education:* Law School of Zurich; Interamerican Law Institute of the New York University (Master of Comparative Jurisprudence, 1991).

RALF ROSENOW, LIC.IUR., born 1962; admitted, 1989, Switzerland. *Education:* Law Schools of Zurich and University College London.

HORST WEBER, DR.IUR., born 1960; admitted, 1994, Switzerland. *Education:* Law School of Zurich.

NATHALIE DOMENICONI, LIC.IUR., born 1969. *Education:* Law School of Zurich.

Languages: German, English, French, Italian and Spanish

ROHNER & PARTNER

SEESTRASSE 131

8027 ZÜRICH, SWITZERLAND

Telephone: 411 281 1000

Telefax: 411 281 0000

Commercial Law (General), International Civil Litigation, Contract, Mergers and Acquisitions, Tax, Banking and Finance, Competition and Business Law.

DR. LOUIS ROHNER, born Switzerland, September 11, 1949; admitted, 1977, Switzerland. *Education:* Universities of Zurich and Montpellier (Lic. iur., 1974; Dr.iur., 1976); Harvard University (LL.M., 1978). Author: "Computerkriminalität, Strafrechtliche Probleme bei Zeitdiebstahl und Manipulationen," Schulthess, Zürich, 1976. *Member:* Zurich and Swiss Bar Associations; American Bar Association; International Bar Association. *LANGUAGES:* German, English, French and Spanish. *PRACTICE AREAS:* Arbitration; Banking; Computer Law; Entertainment Law; Trusts and Estates Law; International Successions.

DR. MEN RAUCH, born Switzerland, December 4, 1954; admitted, 1983, Switzerland. *Education:* University of Zurich (Lic. iur., 1980; Dr. iur., 1985). Author: "Die Besteuerung des Eigenmietwertes" (Doctor Thesis); "Kompaktkommentar zum Doppelbesteuerungsabkommen (DBA) Deutschland - Schweiz," German-Swiss Chamber of Commerce, Zurich, 1992. Schweizer Aktiengesell schaft nach neuem Recht, German - Swiss Chamber of Commerce, Zurich, 1992. Legal Department at Tax Administration of the Canton of Zurich, 1985-1991. Head of Legal and Tax Department Switzerland at German - Swiss Chamber of Commerce, 1989-1994. *Member:* Zurich and Swiss Bar Associations. *LANGUAGES:* German, English, French and Italian. *PRACTICE AREAS:* International Taxation; Tax Planning; Fiscal Law; Offshore Taxation; Federal Taxation; Trust Taxation.

FÜRSPRECHER JÜRG M. AMMANN, born Switzerland, April 24, 1965; admitted, 1993, Switzerland. *Education:* University of Bern. *Member:* Zurich and Swiss Bar Associations. *LANGUAGES:* German, English and French. *PRACTICE AREAS:* Antitrust; Trade Regulations; Bankruptcy; Receivership; Debtor and Creditor; Securities Law.

COUNSEL

DR. OTTO N. ROHNER, born Switzerland, September 6, 1917; admitted, 1944, Switzerland. *Education:* University of Fribourg (Dr.iur.). Author: "Der strafrechtliche Schutz der Schweizerischen Neutralität," Heerbrugg, 1944. Member, Appellate Court of the Canton of St. Gallen, 1968. *Member:* Zurich and Swiss Bar Associations. *LANGUAGES:* German, English, Italian and French.

Languages: German, English, French, Spanish and Italian.

SCHELLENBERG & HAISSLY

LÖWENSTRASSE 19
P.O. BOX 6333
8023 ZÜRICH, SWITZERLAND
Telephone: 01 / 211 60 40
Telecopier: 01 / 221 11 65

Geneva, Switzerland Office: 4 Place Neuve, 1211 Geneva 11. Telephone: 022 / 328 67 22. Telecopier: 022 / 328 79 61.

Commercial, Corporate, Contracts, Mergers and Acquisitions, Banking and Finance, Securities, Capital Markets, Litigation, Arbitration, Insolvency and Bankruptcy, International Judicial Assistance, Enforcement of Foreign Judgements, Taxation, Trusts and Estates, EC Law, Intellectual Property, Competition, Insurance and Liability, Trade and Transportation, Admiralty and Aviation.

MEMBERS OF FIRM

DR. GEORG VON SEGESSER, born 1944; admitted, 1972, Switzerland. *Education:* University of Zurich (Dr.iur., 1973). *Member:* Swiss and Zurich Bar Associations. **LANGUAGES:** German, English and French. **PRACTICE AREAS:** Corporate; Banking and Finance.

DR. MARC RONCA, born 1941; admitted, 1967, Switzerland. *Education:* University of Geneva (Dr.iur., 1971); University of Michigan (M.C.L., 1969). *Member:* Swiss and Zurich Bar Associations. **LANGUAGES:** German, English, French and Italian. **PRACTICE AREAS:** International Business Transactions; Technology Transfer; Arbitration.

DR. CLAUS SCHELLENBERG, born 1938; admitted, 1965, Switzerland. *Education:* University of Zurich (Dr.iur., 1968). *Member:* Swiss and Zurich Bar Associations. **LANGUAGES:** German and English. **PRACTICE AREAS:** Banking and Finance; Trusts and Estates.

DR. MARTIN BERNET, born 1954; admitted, 1982, Switzerland. *Education:* University of Zurich (lic.iur., 1979; Dr.iur., 1986). *Member:* Swiss and Zurich Bar Associations. **LANGUAGES:** German, English and French. **PRACTICE AREAS:** Litigation and Arbitration; International Business Transactions; Insurance and Liability.

DR. THOMAS BOLLIGER, born 1955; admitted, 1987, Switzerland. *Education:* University of Zurich (Dr.iur., 1983); Harvard Law School, Cambridge, Mass. (LL.M., 1985). *Member:* Swiss and Zurich Bar Associations. **LANGUAGES:** German and English. **PRACTICE AREAS:** Litigation; Corporate; Contract and Labor.

DR. CHRISTINE BEUSCH-LIGGENSTORFER, born 1955; admitted, 1983, Switzerland. *Education:* University of Bern (lic.iur., 1979; Dr.iur., 1982). *Member:* Swiss and Zurich Bar Associations. **LANGUAGES:** German, English and French. **PRACTICE AREAS:** Banking and Finance; Contract and Labor; Immigration Law; Inheritance.

DR. BRIGITTE VON DER CRONE, born 1957; admitted, 1986, Switzerland. *Education:* University of Zurich (Dr.iur., 1986). *Member:* Swiss and Zurich Bar Associations. **LANGUAGES:** German, English and French. **PRACTICE AREAS:** Banking and Finance; Corporate.

DR. MARTIN WEBER, born 1958; admitted, 1986, Switzerland. *Education:* University of Zurich (lic.iur., 1982; Dr.iur., 1993); University of Chicago Law School (LL.M., 1988). *Member:* Swiss and Zurich Bar Associations. **LANGUAGES:** German, English and French. **PRACTICE AREAS:** Mergers and Acquisitions; Corporate; Contracts; Intellectual Property.

DR. ALEXANDER VON ZIEGLER, born 1957; admitted, 1988, Switzerland. *Education:* University of Zurich (Dr.iur., 1989); Tulane University, New Orleans, LA. (LL.M., 1984). *Member:* Swiss and Zurich Bar Associations. **LANGUAGES:** German, English and French. **PRACTICE AREAS:** International Trade; Transportation and Maritime Law.

DR. MARTIN LANZ, born 1958; admitted, 1983, Switzerland. *Education:* Universities of Basel and Neuchâtel (Dr.iur., 1985). *Member:* Swiss and Zurich Bar Associations. **LANGUAGES:** German, English and French. **PRACTICE AREAS:** Banking and Finance; Securities; Corporate; International Business Transactions.

ASSOCIATES

DR. SALOME ZIMMERMANN OERTLI, born 1955; admitted, 1984, Switzerland. *Education:* University of Zurich (lic.iur., 1979; Dr.iur., 1981). *Member:* Swiss and Zurich Bar Associations. **LANGUAGES:** German, English and French. **PRACTICE AREAS:** Contract; Corporate; Inheritance; Banking.

(This Listing Continued)

ALEXANDER JOLLES, born 1957; admitted, 1988, Switzerland. *Education:* University of Bern (lic.iur., 1985). *Member:* Swiss and Zurich Bar Associations. **LANGUAGES:** German, English and French. **PRACTICE AREAS:** Arbitration; Litigation; Intellectual Property; Art Trade Law.

ANDREA MONDINI, born 1962; admitted, 1991, Switzerland. *Education:* University of Zurich (lic.iur., 1987). *Member:* Swiss and Zurich Bar Associations. **LANGUAGES:** German, Italian, English and French. **PRACTICE AREAS:** Contract; Corporate.

DR. NATHALIE VOSER, born 1963; admitted, 1990, Switzerland. *Education:* University of Basel (lic.iur., 1988; Dr. iur., 1993); Columbia University School of Law, New York (LL.M., 1994). *Member:* Swiss and Zurich Bar Associations. **LANGUAGES:** German, French, English and Italian. **PRACTICE AREAS:** Contract; Arbitration.

SCHÜRMANN, RAUSCH UND ROHRER

Established in 1979
LIMMATQUAI 3
8001 ZÜRICH, SWITZERLAND
Telephone: 01/262 46 00
Telecopier: 01/262 50 05

Commercial Practice including related Litigation and Arbitration.

MEMBERS OF FIRM

PROF. DR. IUR. HERIBERT RAUSCH, born 1942; admitted, 1969, Switzerland.

DR. IUR. HANS J. ROHRER, born 1945; admitted, 1973, Switzerland.

DR. IUR. HANS-JÜRG SCHÜRMANN, born 1944; admitted, 1972, Switzerland.

DR. IUR. TEDDY S. STOJAN, born 1957; admitted, 1987, Switzerland.

DR. IUR. THOMAS HEINIGER, born 1957; admitted, 1986, Switzerland.

ASSOCIATES

LIC.IUR. ANDREA MATHIS, born 1962; admitted, 1993.

DR. IUR. HANS RUDOLF TRUEEB, LL.M., born 1961; admitted, 1993.

FÜRSPRECHER MARCO A. RIZZI, born 1968; admitted, 1994.

Languages: German, English, French, Italian and Russian.

SCHWEIZER DUBLER DAY

AM GUGGENBERG 20
CH-8053 ZÜRICH, SWITZERLAND
Telephone: 41-1-422 6640
Fax: 41-1-422 6676

General Commercial and Corporate Law, Industrial Property Rights including Trademarks and Patents, Unfair Competition, Mergers, Acquisitions and Joint Ventures, Commercial Contracts, Agency, Distributorships, Licensing and Franchising, Trusts and Estates, Litigation and Arbitration.

MEMBERS OF FIRM

DR. HEINZ SCHWEIZER, born Zürich, Switzerland, April 29, 1938; admitted, 1969, Switzerland. *Education:* University of Zürich (Dr.iur., 1979).

LIC.IUR. ANDREAS M. DUBLER, born Zürich, Switzerland, May 9, 1957; admitted, 1985, Switzerland. *Education:* University of Zürich (lic.iur., 1982).

LIC.IUR. STEFAN H. DAY, born Zürich, Switzerland, January 8, 1957; admitted, 1985, Switzerland. *Education:* University of Zürich (lic.iur., 1982).

All Attorneys of the Firm are Members of the Swiss and Zürich Bar Association.
The Firm is a Member of the "ILG International Lawyers' Group," an independent network of correspondent business law firms around the globe.

Languages: German, English and French

SEDGWICK, DETERT, MORAN & ARNOLD

SPLUEGENSTRASSE 3
ZÜRICH CH-8002, SWITZERLAND
Telephone: 011-41-1-201-1730
Fax: 011-41-1-201-4404

San Francisco, California Office: 16th Floor, One Embarcadero Center. Telephone: 415-781-7900. Cable Address: "Sedma". Fax: 415-781-2635.

Los Angeles, California Office: 9th Floor, Wilshire Colonnade, 3701 Wilshire Boulevard. Telephone: 213-386-2833. Fax: 213-487-5456.

Irvine, California Office: 3 Park Plaza, 17th Floor. Telephone: 714-852-8200. Fax: 714-852-8282.

Chicago, Illinois Office: The Rookery Building, Seventh Floor, 209 South LaSalle Street. Telephone: 312-641-9050. Fax: 312-641-9530.

New York, New York Office: 41st Floor, 59 Maiden Lane. Telephone: 212-422-0202. Fax: 212-422-0925.

London, England Office: Lloyds Avenue House, 6 Lloyds Avenue, EC3N 3AX. Telephone: 071-929-1829. Fax: 071-929-1808.

American and International Law.

ERIK J. STENBERG, born Montreal, Canada, July 10, 1957; admitted, 1983, California and U.S. District Court, Northern District of California; 1984, U.S. District Court, Eastern District of California (Not admitted in Switzerland). *Education:* University of Cincinnati (B.M., 1979); Hastings College of the Law, University of California (J.D., 1983). Articles Editor, Hastings International and Comparative Law Review, 1982-1983. *Member:* State Bar of California; American Bar Association (Member: Section on Tort and Insurance Practice); Defense Research Institute; International Bar Association. (Also at London, England Office). *LANGUAGES:* German.

(For complete biographical data on all personnel at Los Angeles, San Francisco and Irvine, California, Chicago, Illinois, New York, New York and London, England, see Professional Biographies at those locations).

SHOOK, HARDY & BACON

BAHNHOFSTRASSE 20, THALWIL
CH-8800 ZÜRICH, SWITZERLAND
Telephone: 011-41-1-721-00385
Facsimile: 011-41-1-721-2384

Kansas City, Missouri, Shook, Hardy & Bacon, P.C. Office: 1200 Main, One Kansas City Place.

Overland Park, Kansas, Shook, Hardy & Bacon, P.C. Office: 40 Corporate Woods.

London, England Office: Manning House, 22 Carlisle Place, SW1P 1JA. Telephone: 011-44-171-821-5595. Facsimile: 011-44-171-834-5918.

Milan, Italy, Shook, Hardy & Bacon Italia S.R.I. Office: Via Meravigli 3, 3rd Floor, 20123. Telephone: 011-392-723-371. Fax: 011-392-7200-3637.

Practice in all major areas of U.S. and International Commercial Practice. Product Liability, Litigation and Arbitration.

OF COUNSEL

VINCENZO CARATTI, born Genova, Italy, 1927; admitted, 1960, Italy (Not admitted in Switzerland). *Education:* State University, Genova, Italy (Degree, cum laude, 1952). Co-Author: Study on International Arbitration, Dalloz & Sirley, Paris, France, 1956. *LANGUAGES:* Italian, French, German. *PRACTICE AREAS:* Corporate Finance; Banking.

(For complete biographical data on all personnel and list of Representative Clients, see Professional Biographies at Kansas City, Missouri)

DR. HARALD SIEGERT

IM LOORAIN 2
CH-8803 RUESCHLIKON/ZÜRICH, SWITZERLAND
Telephone: 41-1-7242650
Telefax: 41-1-7240703

Transportation (Sea, River, Air, Road, Railroad, Multimodal), Insurance, Reinsurance, Insurance-Intermediaries, Banking, Travel, Trademarks, Commercial Law, Debt Collection, Est. of Companies, Arbitration, Mediation, Litigation at Courts of Solothurn and Swiss Federal Courts.

DR.IUR. HARALD SIEGERT, FCIARB., born Cleves, Germany, December 1, 1936; admitted, 1970, Dusseldorf. *Education:* Universities of Munich, Freiburg, Bonn, Cologne, Geneva (Docteur en Droit, 1966). Legal

(This Listing Continued)

Trainee, courts, authorities and private commercial institutions, Germany and England. Qualified for Judge (Assessor), Department of Justice, Dusseldorf, 1967. Bank-Trainee, Head-Office Deutsche Bank AG. Fellow Chartered Institute of Arbitrators, London. Counsel and Financial Manager, W. Decher Wholesales and ABC Verbrauchermarkt GmbH, Duisburg and Braunschweig. Counsel, August-Thyssen-Hütte AG, Duisburg. Counsel, Swiss Watch Factories, Solothurn and La Chaux-de-Fonds. Senior Counsel, Kühne & Nagel International Ltd., Pfaffikon (Forwarders). *LANGUAGES:* German, English and French.

STAIGER, SCHWALD & SAUTER

Established in 1961

(Formerly Gayler, Hegetschweiler & Partner)

GENFERSTRASSE 24
P.O. BOX 677
8002 ZÜRICH, SWITZERLAND
Telephone: 01/283 86 86
Cable Address: "GANELAWYER"
Telex: 813 273 GNP CH
Telecopier: 01/283 87 87

Associated Office: Hancock, Rothert & Bunshoft, Four Embarcadero Center, San Francisco, California. 94111-4168. Telephone: 415-981-5550. Telex: 470369. Telecopy: 415-955-2599.

Member of Integrated Advisory Group IAG International (Association of Independent Legal, Tax and Accountancy Firms).
Commercial Law, Company Law, Banking Law, Litigation and Arbitration, Insolvency Law, Trusts, Estates and Inheritance Law, Taxation, Environmental Law, EC Law, Contract Law.

MEMBERS OF FIRM

DR. HANS-RUDOLF STAIGER, born Frauenfeld, Switzerland, February 12, 1945; admitted, 1975, Switzerland. *Education:* University of Zurich (lic.iur., 1970; Dr.iur., 1975). *LANGUAGES:* German, English and French. *PRACTICE AREAS:* Company Law; Contract Law; Inheritance Law; Banking Law; Litigation and Arbitration.

DR. DANIEL R. SAUTER, born Zürich, Switzerland, May 7, 1952; admitted, 1983, Switzerland. *Education:* University of Zürich (Dr.iur., 1982). *LANGUAGES:* German, English and French. *PRACTICE AREAS:* Contract Law; Inheritance Law; Arbitration; Commercial Law; Competition Law.

HANS-PETER SCHWALD, born Zürich, Switzerland, September 12, 1959; admitted, 1988, Switzerland. *Education:* University of St. Gallen (lic.iur., HSG., 1985). *LANGUAGES:* German, French, English and Italian. *PRACTICE AREAS:* Commercial Law; Company Law; Contract Law; Litigation; Insolvency Law; Environmental Law.

PHILIPP KAENZIG, born Zürich, Switzerland, April 28, 1959; admitted, 1989, Switzerland. *Education:* University of Zürich (lic.iur., 1986). *LANGUAGES:* German, English and French. *PRACTICE AREAS:* Contract Law; Company Law; Labour Law; Landlord and Tenant Law; Unfair Competition; Bankruptcy Law.

DR. MARC BERNHEIM, born Zürich, Switzerland, May 18, 1962; admitted, 1989, Zürich. *Education:* University of Zürich (lic.iur., 1986; Dr.iur., 1993); College of Europe, Bruges (LL.M., 1993). *LANGUAGES:* German, English, French and Italian. *PRACTICE AREAS:* Contract Law; Company Law; Banking Law; Insolvency Law; Litigation; EC Competition Law.

ASSOCIATES

THOMAS TREICHLER, born Zürich, Switzerland, February 14, 1963; admitted, 1991, Zürich. *Education:* University of Zürich (lic.iur., 1988). *LANGUAGES:* German and English. *PRACTICE AREAS:* Contract Law; Company Law; Property Law; Inheritance Law; Litigation; Landlord and Tenant Law; Labor Law.

DR. MICHAEL HAMM, born Luzern, Switzerland, January 25, 1962; admitted, 1990, Zürich. *Education:* Universities of Zürich and Lausanne (lic.iur., 1987; Dr.iur., 1993). *LANGUAGES:* German, English and French. *PRACTICE AREAS:* Commercial Law; Contract Law; Intellectual Property Law; Corporate Law; Planning and Construction Law.

MARC METZGER, born Lausanne, Switzerland, August 29, 1967; admitted, 1993, Berne. *Education:* University of Berne (Fuersprecher), 1993). *LANGUAGES:* German, English, French and Italian. *PRACTICE*

(This Listing Continued)

STAIGER, SCHWALD & SAUTER, Zürich—Continued

AREAS: Contractual Law; Banking Law; Corporate Law; Exploration Law.

COUNSEL

DR. RUDOLF HEGETSCHWEILER, born Zürich, Switzerland, February 21, 1923; admitted, 1948, Switzerland. *Education:* Universities of Zürich and Lausanne (Dr.iur., 1946). **LANGUAGES:** German, French, English and Italian. **PRACTICE AREAS:** Company Law; Banking Law; Contract Law; Inheritance Law; Insolvency Law.

STEINBRÜCHEL & FURGER

Established in 1951

GROSSMÜNSTERPLATZ 8
CH-8001 ZÜRICH, SWITZERLAND
Telephone: (01) 252 40 36
International: (41-1) 252 40 36
Facsimile: (01) 252 04 20

General Practice, Litigation and Arbitration, Commercial, Corporate, Contract, Insurance and Liability, Real Property, Construction, Zoning, Estate Planning, Probate, Administrative Matters.

MEMBERS OF FIRM

DR. RICO A. STEINBRÜCHEL, born Zuoz/GR, 1921; admitted, 1947, Zurich. *Education:* University of Zurich (Doctor of Law, 1946); Lincolns Inn, London (1948-1949). **PRACTICE AREAS:** Business Law; Contract and Corporate Law; Trust and Estate Planning.

DR. JÜRG U. FURGER, born Vals/GR, 1930; admitted, 1959, Zurich. *Education:* University of Zurich (Doctor of Law, 1956). **PRACTICE AREAS:** Litigation and Arbitration; Trusts and Estates; Real Estate; Corporate Liability.

DIETER R. BRUNNER, born Zurich, 1956; admitted, 1984, Zurich; 1989, New York. *Education:* University of Zurich (Lic. iur., 1981). **PRACTICE AREAS:** Business Planning and Organizations; Agency and Distributorship; International Contracts.

GERHARD HOFMANN, born Kreuzlingen/TG, 1958; admitted, 1987, Thurgau. *Education:* University of Zurich (Lic. iur., 1984). **PRACTICE AREAS:** Construction Law; Leases and Leasing; Litigation and Arbitration.

MATHIS ZIMMERMANN, born Zurich, Switzerland, 1954; admitted, 1988, Zurich. *Education:* University of Zurich (Lic. iur., 1979; Lic. phil., 1984). **PRACTICE AREAS:** Landlord and Tenant; Litigation and Arbitration.

ASSOCIATES

NIKLAUS A. LÜCHINGER, born Zürich, 1959; admitted, 1989, Zürich. *Education:* University of Freiburg (Lic. phil., 1983; Lic. iur., 1987). **PRACTICE AREAS:** Contracts; Insurance and Liability; Conflicts of Law.

MARK S. FURGER, born Vals, Switzerland, 1960; admitted, 1989, Zürich. *Education:* University of Zürich (Lic. iur., 1985). **PRACTICE AREAS:** Labor and Employment.

CHRISTIAN H. JUCHLER, born Kirchberg/SG, Switzerland, 1965; admitted, 1993, Zurich. *Education:* University of Zurich (Lic.iur., 1990). **PRACTICE AREAS:** Administrative Law; Personal Injury.

Languages: German, English, French, Swedish and Italian

STIFFLER & NATER

Established in 1973

DUFOURSTRASSE 101
CH-8034 ZÜRICH, SWITZERLAND
Telephone: 01/383 04 72
Telefax: 01/383 07 36

General Practice, Corporate, Insurance, Civil Liability, Banking, Bankruptcy and Commercial Litigation, Sports Law, Real Estate, Wills, Arbitration, International Judicial Assistance and Criminal Law.

(This Listing Continued)

MEMBERS OF FIRM

DR. HANS KASPAR STIFFLER, born 1932; admitted, 1960, Switzerland. *Education:* University of Zurich (Dr.iur.). **PRACTICE AREAS:** Torts; Negligence; Insurance; Wills.

DR. HANS NATER, born 1943; admitted, 1972, Switzerland. *Education:* University of Zurich (Dr.iur.); University of Edinburgh; Harvard Law School (LL.M.). **PRACTICE AREAS:** Civil Arbitration; International Arbitration; Commercial Law; Corporate Law; Products Liability.

DR. HEINZ KLARER, born 1953; admitted, 1982, Switzerland. *Education:* University of Zurich (Dr.iur.). **PRACTICE AREAS:** Commercial Law; Banking; Bankruptcy; Real Estate; Business Law; Wills.

DR. MIRKO ROŠ, born 1951; admitted, 1985, Switzerland. *Education:* University of Zurich (Dr.iur.); Harvard Law School (LL.M.). **PRACTICE AREAS:** Business Law; International Joint Ventures; Computers and Software; Litigation; White Collar Crime.

DR. STEPHAN NETZLE, born 1957; admitted, 1987, Switzerland. *Education:* University of Zurich (Dr.iur.); University of Virginia (LL.M.). **PRACTICE AREAS:** Agency and Distributorships; Communications and Media; Sports Law.

OF COUNSEL

ANDREAS DONATSCH, born 1952; admitted, 1979, Switzerland. *Education:* University of Zurich (Dr.iur., 1981). Professor, University of Zurich, 1987. **PRACTICE AREAS:** Business Crimes; Business Fraud; White Collar Crime.

ASSOCIATES

LIC. PASCALE WALDVOGEL-BAERTSCHI, born 1966; admitted, 1992, Switzerland. *Education:* University of Lausanne (lic.iur.).

LIC. MARC NATER, born 1965. *Education:* University of Zurich (lic.iur.).

DR. REGULA BERGSMA, born 1959; admitted, 1988, Switzerland. *Education:* University of Lausanne (lic.iur.); University of Zurich (Dr.iur.).

NATHAN LANDSHUT, born 1965; admitted, 1994, Switzerland. *Education:* University of Zurich (lic., iur.).

Languages: German, English, French, Spanish, Italian and Norwegian

STOFFEL & PARTNER

DUFOURSTRASSE 40
8008 ZÜRICH, SWITZERLAND
Telephone: 01/252 16 16
Telecopier: 01/252 27 00

Geneva, Switzerland Office: World Trade Center, rte Aéroport 10, CP 515, 1215 Geneva 15. Telephone: 022/798 27 28. Telecopier: 022/798 27 37.

Brussels Office: 81, Avenue Louise, B-1050. Telephone: 32 2 542 88 88. Telecopier: 32 2 542 89 89.

New York Office: 152 West 57th Street, 10019. Telephone: 212-582-2828. Telecopier: 212-582-2424.

FIRM PROFILE: *Joint Offices with PÜNDER GROUP:*

- *New York, Brussels, Beijing*

- *Moscow, Budapest, Warsaw*

Commercial Law (general), Companies, Corporations, Mergers and Acquisitions, Banking, Securities and Finance, Tax, Arbitration and Litigation, International Legal Assistance, Intellectual Property, Competition, Anti-Trust, Bankruptcy, Insolvency, EC Law.

PARTNERS

DR.IUR. MARCO STOFFEL, born 1951. *Education:* University of Fribourg (Dr.iur., 1981); University of Leyden, The Netherlands (1978); Max-Planck-Institute, Heidelberg, Germany (1980); Harvard Law School, Cambridge, Massachusetts (LL.M., 1980). Author: "Bidding Procedure in Contracts", 1981.*Member:* Swiss Federation of Lawyers; International Bar Association; Swiss Arbitration Association.

PROF.DR.IUR. VIKTOR AEPLI, born 1954. *Education:* University of Fribourg (Dr.iur., 1980; Ph.D., 1988). Professor of Law at the University of Fribourg. Author: "Fundamental Rights and Private Law, 1980"; Gauch-/Aepli/Casanova, "Practice of the Supreme Court with respect to the Swiss Code of Obligations," general and special part, 1992-1993; "The Termination of an Obligation, 1991." Co-editor, "The Zurich Commentary to the

(This Listing Continued)

Swiss Civil Code." *Member:* Swiss Federation of Lawyers; Swiss Arbitration Association; German Banking Law Association.

DR.IUR. URS ISENEGGER, born 1955. *Education:* University of Basel (Dr.iur., 1983). Notary Exam, Canton of Solothurn, 1985. Author: "Copyright Issues Concerning Retransmittance of Media Programming", 1983. *Member:* Swiss Federation of Lawyers; International Bar Association; International Association for the Protection of Industrial Property; Associazione Internazionale Giuristi di Lingua Italiana.

DR.IUR. LOUIS BOCHUD, born 1952. *Education:* University of Berne (Lic.rer.pol., 1984; Dr.iur., 1989). Author: "Loans to Shareholders from the Economic, Contractual and Taxation Viewpoint, 1991". Lecturer for Tax Law at the University of Berne. *Member:* Swiss Federation of Lawyers.

DR.IUR. LAURENT MOREILLON, born 1956. *Education:* University of Lausanne (Dr.iur., 1988). Author: "The Repressive Control of the Cinematographic Expression," 1983. Lecturer for Property Law, University of Lausanne. *Member:* Swiss Federation of Lawyers; International Association for the Protection of Industrial Property.

DR.IUR. MARKUS BILL, born 1958. *Education:* University of St. Gallen (Dr.iur., 1991). Author: "The obligation of the third parties to give information in tax assessment and the tax appeal preceedings", 1990. *Member:* Swiss Federation of Lawyers.

ASSOCIATES

LIC.IUR. DANIELA GMÜNDER PERRIG, born 1956. *Education:* University of Fribourg (Lic.iur., 1983); Harvard Law School, Cambridge, Massachusetts (LL.M., 1986). Assistant Editor, Swiss Civil Code and Swiss Code of Obligations by Schoenenberger/Gauch.

LIC.IUR. JACQUELINE RONCONI, born 1964. *Education:* University of Fribourg (Lic.iur., 1987); Collège d'Europe, Bruges, Belgium (LL.M., 1993). Notary Exam, Canton of Ticino, 1992.

Member of PÜNDER GROUP: Buruma Maris, The Hague, Rotterdam; Cerha, Hempel & Spiegelfeld, Vienna; Coppens, van Ommeslaghe, Hormans & Faures, Brussels; De Parieu-Lacourte G.I.E., Paris; Pünder, Volhard, Weber & Axster, Frankfurt, Düsseldorf, Berlin, Leipzig; Stoffel & Partner, Zurich, Genève.

Languages: German, English, French, Italian and Spanish

STUCKI & ALTENBURGER
ZÜRICH, SWITZERLAND
(See Altenburger & Partners)

THOUVENIN STUTZER EGGIMANN & PARTNERS
Established in 1983
LIMMATQUAI 4
P.O. BOX 125
CH-8024 ZÜRICH, SWITZERLAND
Telephone: 01/262 22 21
Telecopier: 01/262 45 72

General Corporate and Commercial Practice, Estate Planning, Immigration, Litigation and Arbitration, Merger and Acquisitions, Bankruptcy, Intellectual Property Rights, Banking, International Judicial Assistance.

MEMBERS OF FIRM

DR. ANDRÉ THOUVENIN, born Olten, Switzerland, 1946; admitted, 1974, Zürich. *Education:* University of Zurich (lic.iur., Dr.iur.). *Member:* Zurich and Swiss Bar Associations; Swiss Arbitration Association. **LANGUAGES:** German, English and French. **PRACTICE AREAS:** Corporate and Commercial Law; Arbitration; General Liability; Trade; Competition; Litigation.

DR. HANSJÖRG STUTZER, born Zürich, Switzerland, 1947; admitted, 1977, Zürich. *Education:* University of Zurich (lic.iur., Dr.iur.). *Member:* Zurich and Swiss Bar Associations; International Bar Association; Swiss Arbitration Association. **LANGUAGES:** German, English, French and Italian. **PRACTICE AREAS:** Joint Ventures; Reorganization; Licensing; International Arbitration; Litigation.

(This Listing Continued)

DR. BRUNO EGGIMANN, born Zürich, Switzerland, 1946; admitted, 1979, Zürich. *Education:* University of Zurich (lic.iur., Dr.iur.). *Member:* Zurich and Swiss Bar Associations. **LANGUAGES:** German, English and French. **PRACTICE AREAS:** Corporate and Commercial Law; Trusts and Estates; Successions; Immigration; Litigation; Arbitration.

DR. DANIEL STOLL, born Zürich, Switzerland, 1957; admitted, 1986, Zürich. *Education:* University of Zurich (lic.iur.; Dr.iur.). *Member:* Zurich and Swiss Bar Associations. **LANGUAGES:** German, English and French. **PRACTICE AREAS:** Banks and Banking; Finance and Securities; Fraud Investigations; Insolvency; Corporate and Commercial Litigation.

Languages: German, English, French and Italian

UMBRICHT, BADERTSCHER & ROESLE
Established in 1970
BAHNHOFSTRASSE, 22
P.O. BOX 4174
8022 ZÜRICH, SWITZERLAND
Telephone: 01/211 25 50
Telecopier: 01/221 25 52
Cable Address: "Lex"
Telex: 813639 Lex ch

General Practice. Commercial, Insolvency, Tax, Banking, Capital Markets, Mergers and Acquisitions, Competition, Real Estate, Estate Planning, Constitutional and Administrative Law, International Judicial Assistance, Conflicts, International Commercial Arbitration.

MEMBERS OF FIRM

DR. ROBERT P. UMBRICHT, born 1935; admitted, 1966, Switzerland. *Education:* Universities of Zurich and Paris (lic.iur., 1960; Dr.iur., 1963); Boalt Hall School of Law, University of California, Berkeley, USA (LL.M., 1966). Co-Author: "Switzerland's Federal Code on Private International Law," Edition Payot, Lausanne, 1989; "The Direct Federal Tax Law," Zurich, 1993.

DR. BEAT BADERTSCHER, born 1951; admitted, 1979, Switzerland. *Education:* University of Zurich (lic.iur., 1976; Dr.iur., 1980); University of Michigan, Ann Arbor, USA (LL.M., 1983).

DR. MAX C. ROESLE, born 1949; admitted, 1977, Switzerland. *Education:* Universities of Zurich and Geneva (Lic.iur., 1975; Dr.iur., 1982); Swiss Banking School. With Shearman & Sterling in New York and Paris, 1979-1980; Former First Vice President of Credit Suisse, 1986-1989, and Senior Executive of CS Holding, 1989-1991. Co-Author: "The Swiss Capital Market," 1985.

DR. MARKUS DÖRIG, born 1960; admitted, 1987, Switzerland. *Education:* Universities of Zurich and Geneva (Lic.iur., 1984; Dr.iur., 1987). With Gardner Carton & Douglas, Chicago, 1988. Author: "Zurich Procedural Law," Zurich, 1987; "Guide to Family Law in Europe," ed. Solicitors Family Law Association, London, 1992.

DR. TOMAS POLEDNA, born 1959; admitted, 1990, Switzerland. *Education:* University of Zurich (lic.iur., 1984; Dr.iur., 1988). Lecturer (Privatdozent), University of Zurich, 1990—. Author: "Wahlrechtsgrundsätze und kantonale Parlamentswahlen," Zurich, 1988; "Praxis zur Europäischen Menschenrechtskonvention aus schweizerischer Sicht," Zurich, 1993; "The Ownership and Economic Structure in former Czechoslovakia," 2 East-West Report 33, 1993.

GEORG STEIGER, born 1959; admitted, 1988, Switzerland. *Education:* University of Zurich (lic.iur., 1985). With Fulbright & Jaworski in Houston and New York, 1992-1993.

OF COUNSEL

PROF. DR. TOBIAS JAAG, born 1947; admitted, 1979, Switzerland. *Education:* University of Zurich (lic.iur., 1972; Dr.iur., 1976); University of Michigan, Ann Arbor, USA (LL.M., 1975). Lecturer (Privatdozent), University of Zurich, 1985-1990. Professor of Constitutional and Administrative Law, University of Zurich, 1990.

ASSOCIATES

FELIX GRETHER, born 1959; admitted, 1992, Switzerland. *Education:* Swiss Federal Institute of Technology (Dipl. Ing. ETH, 1983); University of Zurich (lic.iur., 1990).

(This Listing Continued)

UMBRICHT, BADERTSCHER & ROESLE, Zürich—Continued

THOMAS C. HIPPELE, born 1964; admitted, 1992, Switzerland. *Education:* University of Zurich (lic.iur., 1990). Co-Author: "New Commentary on the Swiss Code of Obligations," 1994.

FÜRSPRECHER JÜRG BRAND, born 1962; admitted, 1990, Switzerland. *Education:* University of Bern (Fürsprecher, 1990).

DR. ERIK JOHNER, born 1963; admitted, 1991, Switzerland. *Education:* University of Basel (lic.iur., 1988; Dr.iur., 1994); University of Exeter, Great Britain (LL.M., 1994).

DIETER HOFMANN, born 1965; admitted, 1994, Switzerland. *Education:* University of Zurich (lic.iur., 1991).

TIZIANA MARENCO, born 1967; admitted, 1994, Switzerland. *Education:* University of Zurich (lic.iur., 1992).

U.S. RESIDENT COUNSEL

REBECCA PETERS, born Wichita, Kansas, U.S.A., 1958; admitted, 1985, Pennsylvania; 1986, District of Columbia (Not admitted in Switzerland). *Education:* Colby College (B.A., cum laude, 1980); University of Rochester (M.A., 1981); University of Pennsylvania (J.D., 1985); University of Zurich (1987-1989). Author: "Protection against Hostile Takeover and the Exercise of Shareholder Rights in Switzerland," 11 U.Pa. J Int'l Bus Law 519 (1990); Co-Author: "The Direct Federal Tax Law," Zurich, 1993.

All Swiss Attorneys of the Firm are Members of the Swiss and Zurich Bar Associations.

Languages: German, English, French, Italian and Czech

DR. BERNHARD H. L. VISCHER

Established in 1988

TALACKER 50
8001 ZÜRICH, SWITZERLAND
Telephone: (01) 212 50 80
Fax: (01) 212 50 88

Commercial Law, Banking Law and Litigation.

DR. BERNHARD H. L. VISCHER, born 1948; admitted, 1978, Switzerland. *Education:* University of Zürich (Dr.iur.); Visiting Scholar Yale Law School (1975). *LANGUAGES:* English, German and French.

VON MEISS BLUM & PARTNERS

USTERISTRASSE 14
P.O. BOX 548
CH-8021 ZÜRICH, SWITZERLAND
Telephone: 01/211 98 88
Cable Address: Thumeiur
Telex: 813114 TMP CH
Telecopier: 01/211 29 88

General Practice, Commercial, Corporation, EC-Law, Taxation, Estate Planning, Insurance, Intellectual Property, Real Estate, Banking, Securities, Arbitration, Sport and Entertainment, Civil Litigation, Merger and Acquisitions.

PARTNERS

DR. FLORIAN H. VON MEISS, born Berne, Switzerland, March 19, 1945; admitted, 1976, Zurich. *Education:* Law School of Zurich University (lic.iur., 1971; Dr. iur., 1973) Law School of Columbia University (LL.M., 1977). *Member:* Swiss and Zurich Bar Associations; International Bar Association. *LANGUAGES:* German, English, French and Dutch.

DR. CLAUDE P. BLUM, born Berne, Switzerland, June 12, 1949; admitted, 1984, Zurich. *Education:* Law School of Southern Methodist University (Master of Comparative Law, 1977); Law School of Zurich University (lic.iur., 1975; Dr.iur., 1979). *Member:* Swiss and Zurich Bar Associations. *LANGUAGES:* German, English and French.

DR. PHILIPPE MEYER, born Zurich, Switzerland, February 8, 1954; admitted, 1980, Zurich. *Education:* Law School of Lausanne and Zurich Universities (lic.iur., 1976; Dr.iur., 1984); New York University, Law School (Master of Comparative Jurisprudence, 1984). *Member:* Swiss, Zurich and International Bar Associations; American Bar Association (International Associate). *LANGUAGES:* German, French and English.

(This Listing Continued)

DR. HANS BODMER, born Weinfelden, Switzerland, June 24, 1955; admitted, 1986, Thurgau. *Education:* Law School of St. Gallen University (lic.iur., 1984; Dr.iur., 1989); University of San Diego, Law School (Master of Comparative Law, 1988). *Member:* Swiss and Zurich Bar Associations. *LANGUAGES:* German, English and French.

COUNSEL

JEANNETTE B. THURNHERR, born Zurich, Switzerland, July 19, 1925; admitted, 1965, Zurich. *Education:* Law School of Zurich University. *Member:* Swiss and Zurich Bar Associations. *LANGUAGES:* German, English, French and Italian.

ASSOCIATES

DR. ALBRECHT LANGHART, born Winterthur, Switzerland, August 7, 1961; admitted, 1988, Zurich. *Education:* Law School of Zurich University (lic.iur., 1986; Dr.iur., 1993). *Member:* Swiss and Zurich Bar Associations. *LANGUAGES:* German, English, French and Spanish.

DR. DANIEL GLASL, born Zurich, Switzerland, April 27, 1961; admitted, 1989, Zurich. *Education:* Law School of Zurich University (lic.iur., 1986; Dr.iur., 1993). *Member:* Swiss and Zurich Bar Associations. *LANGUAGES:* German, English and French.

JUDITH HAMBURGER, born Zurich, Switzerland, January 21, 1951; admitted, 1981, Zurich. *Education:* Law School of Zurich University (lic.iur., 1977). *Member:* Swiss and Zurich Bar Associations. *LANGUAGES:* German, English, Italian and French.

DR. JÜRG BURGER, born Davos, Switzerland, February 6, 1959; admitted, 1991, Zurich. *Education:* Law School of St. Gallen University (lic.iur., 1985); Law School of Chicago University (Master of Laws, 1987). *Member:* Swiss and Zurich Bar Associations. *LANGUAGES:* German, English and French.

DR. ANDRE WAHRENBERGER, born Baden, Switzerland, May 13, 1961; admitted, 1989, Aargau. *Education:* Law School of Zurich University (lic.iur., 1986; Dr. iur., 1991). *Member:* Swiss and Zurich Bar Associations. *LANGUAGES:* German, English and French.

ALEXANDRA VON WILLISEN, born Kilchberg, Switzerland, August 7, 1964; admitted, 1992, Zurich. *Education:* Law School of Zurich University (lic.iur., 1989).

DR. RONALD U. RUEPP, born Solothurn, Switzerland, May 28, 1962; admitted, 1990, Zurich; 1994, California. *Education:* Law School of Zurich University (Lic.iur., 1987; Dr.iur., 1994); University of San Diego, Law School (Master of Comparative Law, 1993). *Member:* Swiss and Zurich Bar Associations; State Bar of California. *LANGUAGES:* German, English and French.

Languages: German, English, French, Italian, Spanish and Dutch.

WALDER WYSS & PARTNERS

MÜNSTERGASSE 2
P.O. BOX 4081
CH-8022 ZÜRICH, SWITZERLAND
Telephone: 01/265 75 11
Fax: 01/265 75 50

General Civil Practice, Arbitration, Banking, Bankruptcy, Commercial, Corporate, Estate, Insurance, Intellectual Property, European Community, Competition, Real Estate and Securities.

MEMBERS OF FIRM

DR. HANS B. WYSS, born Zürich, Switzerland, January 31, 1935; admitted, 1965, Switzerland. *Education:* Kantonales Literar Gymnasium Zürich, University of Paris (Sorbonne) and University of Zürich (Dr. iur., 1963); Harvard Law School (LL.M., 1967). Secretary to District Court, 1963-1966. *Member:* Zürich and Swiss Bar Associations; Swiss Lawyers' Association. *LANGUAGES:* German, English and French. *PRACTICE AREAS:* Corporate; Banking; Law of Succession; International Contracts.

DR. PETER A. BOSSHARD, born Zürich, Switzerland, May 15, 1942; admitted, 1969, Switzerland. *Education:* Gymnasium Schaffhausen and University of Zürich (Dr. iur., 1968). Secretary to District Court, 1965-1967. Assistant District Attorney, 1968. Associate, New York Law Firm, 1969-1970. *Member:* Zürich and Swiss Bar Associations. *LANGUAGES:* German, English and French. *PRACTICE AREAS:* Corporate; Commercial; Banking; Insolvency.

(This Listing Continued)

DR. HANS RUDOLF E. STEINER, born Zürich, Switzerland, November 3, 1942; admitted, 1970, Switzerland. *Education:* Kantonales Literar Gymnasium Zürich and University of Zürich (Dr. iur., 1968); Harvard Law School (LL.M., 1971). Secretary to District Court, 1969. *Member:* Zurich, Swiss and International Bar Associations; Swiss Arbitration Association. *LANGUAGES:* German, French, English, Italian and Spanish. *PRACTICE AREAS:* Banking; Finance; Securities; International Contracts and Arbitration.

DR. LUCAS DAVID, born Zürich, Switzerland, September 6, 1936; admitted, 1963, Switzerland. *Education:* Universities of Geneva and Zürich (Dr.iur., 1961). *Member:* Zürich and Swiss Bar Associations; Swiss Institute for Industrial Property Law (INGRES); International Association for the Protection of Industrial Property (AIPPI); The International League for Competition Law (LIEC); The International Literary and Artistic Association (ALAI). *LANGUAGES:* German, English and French. *PRACTICE AREAS:* Trademarks, Patents and other Intellectual Property Rights; Copyrights; Unfair Competition; Licensing and Distribution; Publishing Contracts.

DR. DANIEL R. WYSS, born Zürich, Switzerland, October 17, 1944; admitted, 1973, Switzerland. *Education:* Kantonales Literargymnasium Zürich and University of Zürich (Dr.iur , 1970); Harvard Law School (LL.M., 1974). *Member:* Zürich, Swiss and International Bar Associations; Swiss Arbitration Association. *LANGUAGES:* German, English and French. *PRACTICE AREAS:* Civil Liability; Commercial; Banking; International Contracts; Arbitration; Litigation.

CHRISTOPH STÄUBLI, born Muri/BE, Switzerland, July 24, 1949; admitted, 1978, Switzerland. *Education:* Freies Gymnasium Bern, St. Gall (Switzerland); Graduate School of Economics and Business Administration (lic. oec. HSG, 1973); University of Zürich (lic. iur., 1976); Georgetown University Law Center (MCL., 1980). Secretary/Referee for Debtors' Compositions to District Court, 1974-1979. *Member:* Zürich, Swiss and International Bar Associations. *LANGUAGES:* German, English and French. *PRACTICE AREAS:* Corporate; Insolvency; Banking; Commercial Litigation.

DR. MARTIN KURER, born Zürich, Switzerland, March 9, 1954; admitted, 1985, Switzerland. *Education:* Collegium Stella Matutina (Feldkirch, Austria); University of Zürich (Dr. iur., 1987); Queen Mary College, London University (LL.M., 1987). Secretary to District Court, 1984-1986. Member, Editorial Board, "Trademark World" and "Copyright World". Vice-Chairman, Committees of the International Bar Association. Chairman, Committee Q 123 of AIPPI. *Member:* Zürich, Swiss and International Bar Associations; International Association for the Protection of Intellectual Property (AIPPI); Swiss Institute for Industrial Property Law (INGRES); International Trademark Association (INTA). *LANGUAGES:* German, English and French. *PRACTICE AREAS:* Intellectual Property; Competition; EC Competition; Commercial.

DR. MARKUS D. VISCHER, born Wädenswil, Switzerland, August 26, 1960; admitted, 1988, Switzerland. *Education:* Kantonales Gymnasium (Zürich-Oerlikon); University of Zürich (Dr. iur., 1986); Queen Mary and Westfield College, London University (LL.M., 1991). Secretary to District Court, 1986-1987. *Member:* Zürich, Swiss and International Bar Associations; International Association for Young Lawyers (AIJA). *LANGUAGES:* German, English and French. *PRACTICE AREAS:* Civil and Commercial Law with emphasis on Arbitration; Mergers and Acquisitions; European Law; Tax Law.

ASSOCIATES

VÉRONIQUE GUBSER, born Zürich, Switzerland, May 9, 1962; admitted, 1990, Switzerland. *Education:* Kantonales Literargymnasium, Züurich; University of Zürich Law School (Lic.iur., 1987); University of California of Berkley, School of Law (LL.M., 1994). Secretary to District Court, 1987-1988. *Member:* Zürich and Swiss Bar Associations. *LANGUAGES:* German, English and French. *PRACTICE AREAS:* Corporate; Commercial; Employment; Bankruptcy and Litigation.

ERICH VON ARX, born Zürich, Switzerland, May 22, 1963; admitted, 1991, Switzerland. *Education:* Kantonsschule Winterthur; University of Zürich Law School (Lic.iur., 1989). Secretary to District Court, 1990. *Member:* Zürich and Swiss Bar Associations. *LANGUAGES:* German, English and French. *PRACTICE AREAS:* Corporate; Commercial; Insolvency; Litigation; Arbitration.

DIDIER SANGIORGIO, born Winterthur, Switzerland, May 9, 1959; admitted, 1989, Switzerland. *Education:* Kantonsschule Winterthur; University of Zürich (Lic.iur, 1984); Georgetown University Law Center, Washington D.C. (LL.M., 1992). Secretary to District Court, 1985. *Mem-*

(This Listing Continued)

ber: Zürich, Swiss and International Bar Associations; Swiss Arbitration Association; AIPPI; INGRES. *LANGUAGES:* German, French and English. *PRACTICE AREAS:* Corporate; Commercial; Joint Venture; Intellectual Property; Arbitration.

DR. JASMIN GHANDCHI, born Karlsruhe, Germany, March 26, 1965; admitted, 1993, Switzerland. *Education:* Schloss Salem and Wirtschaftsgymnasium Kantonsschule Luzern; University of Zurich (lic.iur., 1989; Dr.iur., 1991). Research Assistant, University of Zürich, 1989-1991. Notary Public Examination (1993). *Member:* Zürich, Lucern and Swiss Bar Associations; DACH. *LANGUAGES:* German, English, Spanish and French. *PRACTICE AREAS:* International Law; Business Law; Corporate Law; Contracts; Civil Law.

STEFANO CODONI, born Mendrisio, Switzerland, September 16, 1967; admitted, 1994, Switzerland. *Education:* Liceo Cantonale Mendrisio; University of Zürich (Lic.iur.,1991). Secretary to District Court, 1992. *LANGUAGES:* German, Italian, French and English. *PRACTICE AREAS:* Corporate; Commercial.

MASSIMO CALDERAN, born Zürich, Switzerland, March 23, 1962; admitted, 1991, Switzerland. *Education:* Kantonales Gymnasium (Zürich-Oerlikon); University of Zürich (lic.iur., 1986). Secretary to District Court, 1987-1989. Secretary to Commercial Register, 1991-1994. *LANGUAGES:* German, Italian, English, French and Spanish. *PRACTICE AREAS:* Corporate; Contracts; Immigration; Social Insurance.

MONIKA MÜLLER, born Zürich, Switzerland, May 30, 1964; admitted, 1994, Switzerland. *Education:* Kantonales Literargymnasium (Zürich); University of Zürich Law School (lic.iur., 1990). Associate with Pro Litteris, Zürich (Swiss Copyright Royalty Collecting Company for Works of Literature and Art), 1990. Secretary to District Court, 1991-1992. *Member:* Zürich and Swiss Bar Associations; The International Association of Young Lawyers (AIJA); International Association for the Protection of Intellectual Property (AIPPI); Swiss Institute for Industrial Property Law (INGRES); International League of Competition Law (LIDC); Swiss Association for Copyright and Law of the Media (SVUM); Licensing Executives Society (LES). *LANGUAGES:* German, English and French. *PRACTICE AREAS:* Intellectual Property; Unfair Competition; Publicity; Contracting and Litigation.

DR. MARK A. REUTTER, born St. Gallen, Switzerland, December 11, 1964. *Education:* Kantonsschule St. Gallen, Switzerland; Universities of Lausanne and Zürich (lic.iur., 1989; Dr.iur., 1992). Research Assistant, Swiss Federal Institute of Technology, Zürich, Department of Law and Economics, 1991-1992. Secretary to District Court, 1992-1994. *LANGUAGES:* German, English and French. *PRACTICE AREAS:* Corporate; Contracts; Insolvency; Art Law; Intellectual Property.

DR. MARKUS PFENNINGER, born Zürich, Switzerland, July 3, 1963; admitted, 1991, Switzerland. *Education:* Freies Gymnasium, Zürich and University of Zuürich (lic.iur., 1989; Dr.iur., 1995); Morin Center of Banking Law Studies, Boston University (LL.M. , 1994). Assistant Controller, Stock Exchange of Zürich, 1985-1989. Associate, Reichenbach & Partner, Zürich, 1989-1993. Counsel, Batterymarch Financial Management, Boston, 1994. *LANGUAGES:* German, English and French. *PRACTICE AREAS:* Banking; Finance; Securities; Contracts and Litigation.

OF COUNSEL

DR. ERNST WALDER, born Gossau, Switzerland, December 9, 1929; admitted, 1956, Switzerland. *Education:* Kantonales Literar Gymnasium Winterthur and University of Zürich (Dr. iur., 1955). *Member:* Zürich and Swiss Bar Associations; Swiss Lawyers' Association; International Fiscal Association; Swiss Association for Insurance Law. *LANGUAGES:* German, French, English, Italian and Spanish. *PRACTICE AREAS:* Banking; Insurance; Civil Liability; Arbitration; Law of Succession; Taxes.

DR. GERD F. KUNZE, born Mannheim, Germany, October 10, 1934; admitted, 1963, Germany. *Education:* University of Heidelberg (Dr.iur., 1963). Legal career with Nestlé: attorney responsible for market oriented law of the German group until 1974; after transfer to Nestlé's headquarters in Switzerland during 15 years Chief Trademark Counsel and since 1992 Intellectual Property Consultant; since 1981 member of the senior management. Member, Standing Working Group on Trademarks of Union des Confédérations de l'Industrie et des Employeurs d'Europe (UNICE). *Member:* International Association for the Protection of Intellectual Property (Chairman, Committee Q 92D (Harmonization of Trademark Formalities) and Committee Q 115 (Effective Protection against Unfair Competition under art 10 bis of the Paris Convention)(AIPPI); Swiss Institute for Industrial Property Law (INGRES); European Communities Trademark Association (ECTA); European Association of Industries of Branded Products

(This Listing Continued)

WALDER WYSS & PARTNERS, Zürich—Continued

(Chairman, Trademark Committee) (AIM); International Trademark Association (Member, International Committee; Past Secretary and International Officer)(INTA). *LANGUAGES:* German, English, French and Spanish. *PRACTICE AREAS:* Problems of Trademark Structure and International Trademark Conflicts; International License and similar Agreements related to Intellectual Property Rights.

Languages: German, English, French, Italian and Spanish

WARTMANN & MERKER

FRAUMÜNSTERSTRASSE 29
CH-8022 ZÜRICH, SWITZERLAND
Telephone: (01) 212-1011
International Dialing: (41-1) 212-1011
Telecopier: (41-1) 212-1511

General Corporate and Commercial Practice, Banking and Finance, Reorganization and Insolvency, Inheritance and Estate Planning, Commercial Litigation, Arbitration, Aviation Law.

MEMBERS OF FIRM

DR. THOMAS WARTMANN, born 1945; admitted, 1975, Switzerland. *Education:* University of Zürich (Dr.iur., 1974). *Member:* Zürich and Swiss Bar Associations. *LANGUAGES:* German, English and French.

DR. RUDOLF MERKER, born 1947; admitted, 1975, Switzerland. *Education:* University of Zürich (Dr.iur., 1975); Yale Law School (LL.M., 1977). *Member:* Zürich and Swiss Bar Associations; Swiss Arbitration Association. *LANGUAGES:* German, English, French and Italian.

WEHRLI LUTZ ZIMMERMANN & PARTNER

Established in 1942

FORCHSTRASSE 2/KREUZPLATZ
POSTFACH 24
CH-8032 ZÜRICH, SWITZERLAND
Telephone: 01 382 30 11; 383 61 78
Telefax: 01 382 30 02; 383 06 25

General Corporate and Commercial Practice, Banking and Tax Law, Intellectual Property Law, Inheritance and Estate Planning, European Community Law, Finance and Banking, Immigration and Labour Law, Administrative and Environmental Law, Civil Litigation and Arbitration.

MEMBERS OF FIRM

DR. EDMUND WEHRLI-BLEULER, born 1904; admitted, 1929, Zürich. *Education:* University of Zürich (Doctor of Law). *Member:* Zürich and Swiss Bar Associations. *LANGUAGES:* German, English and French.

DR. REINHARD LUTZ, born 1926; admitted, 1954, Zürich. *Education:* Universities of St. Gall and Zürich (Doctor of Law). *Member:* Zürich and Swiss Bar Associations. *LANGUAGES:* German, English and French.

DR. BERNHARD WEHRLI, born 1932; admitted, 1957, Zürich. *Education:* University of Zürich (Doctor of Law). *Member:* Zürich and Swiss Bar Associations. *LANGUAGES:* German, English and French.

DR. STEPHAN ZIMMERMANN, born 1946; admitted, 1976, Zürich. *Education:* University of Zürich (Doctor of Law). *Member:* Zürich, Swiss and International Bar Associations. *LANGUAGES:* German, English and French. *PRACTICE AREAS:* Arbitration; Commercial Law; Banking; Securities and Finance; Contract Law.

DR. ANTON FLACHSMANN, born 1946; admitted, 1973, Zürich. *Education:* University of Zürich (Doctor of Law). *Member:* Zürich and Swiss Bar Associations. *LANGUAGES:* German, Italian, English and French. *PRACTICE AREAS:* Liability Law.

DR. PETER LUTZ, born 1959; admitted, 1988, Zürich. *Education:* Universities of Geneva, Zürich (Doctor of Law) and London (LL.M., European Law). *Member:* Zürich and Swiss Bar Associations. *LANGUAGES:* German, English and French. *PRACTICE AREAS:* Corporation Law; Commercial Law; Product Liability Law; European Community Law; Competition Law; Litigation.

DR. MARTINA ALTENPOHL, born 1957; admitted, 1988, Zurich. *Education:* University of Zürich (Doctor of Law). *Member:* Zurich and

(This Listing Continued)

Swiss Bar Associations. *LANGUAGES:* German, English and French. *PRACTICE AREAS:* Commercial, Corporation and Contract Law; Intellectual Property Law; Competition Law; Communications and Media Law; European Community Law; Litigation and Arbitration.

ASSOCIATES

LIC. IUR. ROMEO DA RUGNA, born 1962; admitted, 1990, Zürich. *Education:* University of Zürich (lic.iur., 1988). *Member:* Zürich and Swiss Bar Associations. *LANGUAGES:* German, English and French.

WENGER MATHYS PLATTNER

Established in 1980

MÜHLEBACHSTRASSE 20
CH-8024 ZÜRICH, SWITZERLAND
Telephone: +41-1-261 07 70
Telefax: +41-1-261 07 88

Basel, Switzerland Office: Aeschenvorstadt 55, CH-4010. Telephone: +41-61-271 62 62. Telefax: +41-61-272 62 40.
Warsaw, Poland Office: ul. Nowogrodzka 56/7, PL-00695. Telephone: +48-2 621 2750. Telefax: +48-2-621 6753. Komertel: +49-39 12 17 96.

General Civil and Commercial Practice, Corporate, Contract and Banking Law, Swiss and International Taxation, Real Estate Law, Leases and Construction Law, Transportation and Shipping Law, Intellectual Property and Competition Law, Labor Law and Pension Plans, Family and Inheritance Law, Bankruptcy Law, Swiss and International Arbitration, Commercial Litigation, Entertainment Law, Telecommunication Law, Swiss and International Estate Planning and Asset Management.

RESIDENT MEMBERS OF FIRM

DR. JÜRG PLATTNER, born 1942; admitted, 1979. *Education:* Universities of Geneva and Zürich. *LANGUAGES:* German, English and French. *PRACTICE AREAS:* Contract and Corporate Law; National and International Tax Planning; Banking Law; Litigation in Commercial and Corporate Matters.

LIC. IUR. KARL WÜTHRICH, born 1953; admitted, 1983. *Education:* University of Zürich. *LANGUAGES:* German, English and French. *PRACTICE AREAS:* Bankruptcy Law; Debt Restructuring and Reorganizations; Corporate and Commercial Law; Real Estate and Property Right Law; Litigation.

LIC. IUR. FILIPPO TH. BECK, born 1956; admitted, 1985, Switzerland; 1987, Connecticut; 1988, New York. *Education:* Universities of Basel and Geneva; New York University School of Law (M.C.J.). *LANGUAGES:* German, English, French and Italian. *PRACTICE AREAS:* Banking Law; Corporate and Commercial Law; Social Security Law; Labor Law; International Legal Assistance in Criminal Procedures.

Languages: German, English, French, Italian, Polish and Russian

(For complete Biographical data on all Firm Personnel, see Professional Biographies at Basel, Switzerland)

WENGER VIELI GUT & PARTNER

Established in 1971

SEEGARTENSTRASSE 2
8034 ZÜRICH, SWITZERLAND
Telephone: (01) 383 65 60
Cable Address: "Jwengerlaw"
Telex: 816 542 WEVI CH
Telecopier: (01) 383 81 33

Civil and Commercial Law, Corporate Law, Banking Law, Capital Market Transactions, Unfair Competition, Media Law, Estates, Arbitration and Litigation. General Practice.

FIRM PROFILE: The firm was established in 1971 and offers a full range of legal services.

MEMBERS OF FIRM

DR. JEAN-CLAUDE WENGER, born 1926; admitted, 1955, Zurich. *Education:* University of Zurich (Dr. iur.), Consul of Luxembourg in Zurich. *Member:* Zurich and Swiss Bar Associations. *LANGUAGES:* German, English and French. *PRACTICE AREAS:* Commercial, Corporate and Contract Law; Trusts and Estates; Banking Law; Arbitration; General Practice.

(This Listing Continued)

DR. LELIO VIELI, born 1928; admitted, 1956, Zurich. *Education:* University of Paris (Sorbonne, licence ès lettres), University of Zurich (Dr. iur.). Foreign Associate with New York law firm. *Member:* Zurich and Swiss Bar Associations. *LANGUAGES:* German, French, English and Italian. *PRACTICE AREAS:* Commercial, Corporate and Contract Law; Trusts and Estate Banking Law; Arbitration; General Practice.

DR. URS GUT, born 1942; admitted, 1971, Zurich. *Education:* University of Zurich (Dr. iur.). *Member:* Zurich and Swiss Bar Associations. *LANGUAGES:* German, English, French and Italian. *PRACTICE AREAS:* Commercial, Corporate and Contract Law; Trusts and Estates; Banking Law; Administrative Law; Arbitration; General Practice.

DR. PETER VON SALIS, born 1952; admitted, 1982, Zurich. *Education:* University of Zurich (Dr. iur.); Cornell University Law School (LL.M.). *Member:* Zurich and Swiss Bar Associations. *LANGUAGES:* German, English and French. *PRACTICE AREAS:* Commercial, Corporate and Contract Law; Trusts and Estates; Banking Law; Arbitration; General Practice.

DR. CHRISTOPH SCHMID, born 1954; admitted, 1985, Zurich. *Education:* University of Zurich (Dr. iur.). Foreign Associate with Washington DC law firm. *Member:* Zurich and Swiss Bar Associations. *LANGUAGES:* German, English and French. *PRACTICE AREAS:* Commercial, Corporate and Contract Law; Trusts and Estates; Communications and Media Law; Banking Law; Arbitration; General Practice.

DR. MARCO CEREGHETTI, born 1962; admitted, 1989, Zurich. *Education:* University of Zurich (lic. iur.). Foreign Associate with London, Washington and Milan law firms. *Member:* Zurich and Swiss Bar Associations. *LANGUAGES:* German, English, French and Italian. *PRACTICE AREAS:* Commercial, Corporate and Contract Law; Trusts and Estates; Family Law; Arbitration; General Practice.

LIC. BIGNIA VIELI, born 1960; admitted, 1988, Zurich. *Education:* University of Zurich (lic.iur.); New York University, School of Law (LL.M.). Foreign Associate with New York law firm. *Member:* Zurich and Swiss Bar Associations. *LANGUAGES:* German, English and French. *PRACTICE AREAS:* Commercial, Corporate and Contract Law; Banking Law; International Litigation; International Private Law; Commercial Arbitration; Trusts and Estates; Intellectual Property; General Practice.

ASSOCIATES

DR. RUDOLF OTTOMANN, born 1949; admitted, 1978, Zurich. *Education:* University of Zurich (Dr. iur.). Lecturer on Law, University of Zurich. *Member:* Zurich and Swiss Bar Associations. *LANGUAGES:* German, English and French. *PRACTICE AREAS:* Commercial, Corporate and Contract Law; Trusts and Estates; Family Law; Civil Procedures; General Practice.

LIC. BARBARA KOHL, born 1961; admitted, 1989, Zurich. *Education:* University of Zurich (lic. iur.). *Member:* Zurich and Swiss Bar Associations. *LANGUAGES:* German, English and French. *PRACTICE AREAS:* Commercial, Corporate and Contract Law; Trusts and Estates; Arbitration; General Practice.

DR. DANIEL L. GIRSBERGER, born 1960; admitted, 1987, Zurich. *Education:* University of Zurich (Dr.iur.); Georgetown University Law Center (LL.M.). Foreign Associate with Washington DC law firm. *Member:* Zurich and Swiss Bar Associations. *LANGUAGES:* German, English, French and Spanish. *PRACTICE AREAS:* Commercial, Corporate and Contract Law; International Civil Litigation; International Private Law; Commercial Arbitration; Trusts and Estates; General Practice.

LIC. REBECCA ZOPPETTI, born 1964; admitted, 1989, Geneva. *Education:* University of Geneva (lic.iur.). *Member:* Zurich and Swiss Bar Association. *LANGUAGES:* French, English, German and Italian. *PRACTICE AREAS:* Commercial, Corporate and Contract Law; Banking Law; Intellectual Property; Trusts and Estates; Family Law; General Practice.

LIC. FELIX FISCHER, born 1963; admitted, 1991, Aargan. *Education:* University of Fribourg and University of Zürich (lic.iur.); Tulane University School of Law (M.C.L.). *Member:* Zürich and Swiss Bar Associations. *LANGUAGES:* German, English and French. *PRACTICE AREAS:* Commercial, Corporate and Contract Law; International Civil Litigation; Civil Procedures; International Private Law; Intellectual Property; European Union Law; Trusts and Estates; Family Law; General Practice.

(This Listing Continued)

HUGGER MARKUS, born 1955. *Education:* Akademikergesellschaft für Erwachsenenfortbildung AG, Zurich (1985). Certified Accountant-/Controller. *LANGUAGES:* German, English and French.

WENNER ESCHMANN & PARTNER

Established in 1985

BAHNHOFSTRASSE 37
P.O. BOX 6128
8023 ZÜRICH 1, SWITZERLAND
Telephone: 01/221 29 20
Telefax: 01/221 29 40

Zug, Switzerland Office: Bundesplatz 16, P.O. Box 4747, CH-6304. Telephone: 042-22 27 60. Fax: 042/22 37 30.
Winterthur, Switzerland Office: Metzgasse 14, P.O. Box 276, CH-8401. Telephone: 052/213 80 40. Fax: 052/213 73 78.

General Practice, Civil and Commercial Law, Corporate Law, Estate Planning, Banking Law, Insurance Law, Construction Law, Bankruptcy Law, Criminal Law, International Judicial Assistance, Arbitration and Litigation.

FIRM PROFILE: Wenner Eschmann & Partner is a partnership, established in 1985. The firm is offering a full range of quality legal services. The client's base is worldwide. The firm has five partners and three assistants practicing in three offices in Switzerland.

MEMBERS OF FIRM

DR. MARTIN A. WENNER, born Zurich, 1949; admitted, 1984, Zurich. *Education:* School of Law University of Zurich (Lic.iur., 1975; Dr.iur., 1977); Graduate School of Economics and Business School, University of Washington, Seattle; Graduate School, University of California, Berkeley (LL.M., 1979). *Member:* Swiss and International Bar Associations. *LANGUAGES:* German, English, Italian and French. *PRACTICE AREAS:* Litigation and Arbitration; Banking Law.

DR. STEPHAN ESCHMANN, born Zurich, 1952; admitted, 1979, Zurich. *Education:* School of Law University of Zurich (Lic.iur., 1977; Dr.iur., 1984). *Member:* Swiss and International Bar Associations. *LANGUAGES:* German, English and French. *PRACTICE AREAS:* Corporate Law; Estate Planning; Investment Banking; International Judicial Assistance.

RAFFAEL J. WEIDMANN, born Zurich, 1948; admitted, 1987, Zurich. *Education:* Commerce-School, School of Law University of Zurich (Lic.iur., 1983); Swiss Federal University of Technology (Environment Planning, 1985). *Member:* Swiss Bar Association. (Resident Zug, Switzerland Office). *LANGUAGES:* German, English, French and Italian. *PRACTICE AREAS:* Construction Law; Litigation.

WALTER H. SCHÄPPI, born Winterthur, 1955; admitted, 1988, Zurich. *Education:* School of Law University of Zurich (Lic. iur., 1983). *Member:* Swiss Bar Association. (Resident Winterthur, Switzerland Office). *LANGUAGES:* German, English and French. *PRACTICE AREAS:* Criminal Law.

MARCO O. DEL FABRO, born Zurich, 1956; admitted, 1990, Zurich. *Education:* University of St. Gallen for Business, Administration, Economics, Law and Social Sciences (Lic.iur., 1984; Dr.iur., 1992). *Member:* Swiss Bar Association. *LANGUAGES:* German and English. *PRACTICE AREAS:* Commercial Law; Estates; Sports Law.

WERDER & SCHAUB

GENERAL GUISAN-QUAI 36
CH-8002 ZÜRICH, SWITZERLAND
Telephone: 01-201 77 33
Telex: 817 585 224 COM CH,
Facsimile: 01-201 23 69

General Commercial and Corporate Law, Banking and Finance, Patent Litigation, Contract, Transnational Transactions (Mergers and Acquisitions), Estates and Trusts.

MEMBERS OF FIRM

DR. MICHAEL WERDER, born Engen, Germany, March 2, 1947; admitted, 1978, Zurich. *Education:* University of Berlin and Berne (Dr.iur., 1978). Author: "Eigentum und Verfassungswandel," Ruegger, 1978. Assistant, Commercial Law (Professor Schluep) and Constitutional Law (Profes-

(This Listing Continued)

WERDER & SCHAUB, Zürich—Continued

sor Müller), University of Berne, 1972-1977. *Member:* Swiss, Zurich and International Bar Associations; Swiss Association of International Law. *LANGUAGES:* German, English and French. *PRACTICE AREAS:* General Practice; Business Law; Corporate Law; Estate Planning Law; Intellectual Property Law; Industrial Property Law.

DR. RUDOLF P. SCHAUB, born Zurich, Switzerland, January 12, 1948; admitted, 1983, Zurich. *Education:* University of Basel and Berne (Dr.iur., 1979). Author: "Der Engineeringvertrag," Schulthess, 1979; "Zur Problematik des Internationalen Konkursrechts der Schweiz," ZSR, 1982; "Die Nachfolgeklausel im Personengesellschaftsvertrag," SAG, 1984. Assistant and Lecturer: Professor Bucher, Civil Law, University of Berne, 1977-1978; Professor Schluep, University of Zurich, 1979-1980. Substitute Clerk of the Court, 1980-1981. *Member:* Swiss, Zurich and International Bar Associations. *LANGUAGES:* German and English. *PRACTICE AREAS:* General Practice; Business Law; Corporate Law; Patent Law; Intellectual Property Law; Industrial Property Law.

STEFAN FANKHAUSER, born Langnau i/E, Switzerland, March 31, 1963; admitted, 1992, Berne, Switzerland. *Education:* University of Berne (Fürsprecher, 1992). *Member:* Swiss and Zurich Bar Association. *LANGUAGES:* German, English and French. *PRACTICE AREAS:* General Practice; Business Law; Corporate Law; European Community Law.

WHYTE HIRSCHBOECK DUDEK S.C.

FORCHSTRASSE 452
CH-8034 ZÜRICH, SWITZERLAND
Telephone: (011) 411-391-23-43
Facsimile: (011) 411-391-27-81
Telex: 817804 KMLAW

Milwaukee, Wisconsin Office: 111 E. Wisconsin Avenue. Telephone: 414-273-2100. Facsimile: 414-223-5000. Telex: 262012 WHLAW.

Madison, Wisconsin Office: One East Main Street. Telephone: 608-255-4440. Facsimile: 608-258-7138.

Menomonee Falls, Wisconsin Office: N89 W16800 Appleton Avenue, P.O. Box 1028. Telephone: 414-251-0660. Fax: 414-258-7138.

Manitowoc, Wisconsin Office: 21 Maritime Drive. Telephone: 414-683-3600. Fax: 414-683-9844.

General Practice including Antitrust and Trade Regulation, Banking, Bankruptcy, Civil Litigation, Commercial, Corporate, Employee Benefits, Environmental, Government Contracts, Hospital and Health, Intellectual Property, International, Labor, Mergers and Acquisitions, Real Estate, Securities, Taxation, Trusts and Estates.
Firm Engaged in International Law Practice, but not authorized to appear before the Swiss Courts.

G. HANS MOEDE, III, born Madison, Wisconsin, February 28, 1938; admitted, 1963, Wisconsin (Not admitted in Switzerland). *Education:* Harvard University (A.B., magna cum laude, 1960; LL.B., 1963). *Member:* Milwaukee and American (Member, International Law and Practice Section) Bar Associations; State Bar of Wisconsin (Director, International Transaction Section, 1986-1989). (Also at Milwaukee, Wisconsin). *LANGUAGES:* English and German.

MARTIN WIEBECKE

KIRCHSTRASSE 3
P.O. BOX 1612
CH 8700 KUSNACHT/ZÜRICH, SWITZERLAND
Telephone: 01 / 912 01 02
Telecopier: 01 / 912 01 14

Commercial, Corporate and Contract Law, Arbitration, International Arbitration and Litigation, White Collar Crime, Immigration, Labour Law, Trusts and Estates, International Judicial Assistance, General Practice.

MARTIN WIEBECKE, born Hamburg, Germany, 1957; admitted, 1985, New York; 1987, Germany; 1991, Switzerland. *Education:* Universities of Freiburg/Brsg., Geneva, Göttingen (J.D., 1983); Columbia Law School (LL.M., 1984); University of Basel (Lic.iur., 1986). *LANGUAGES:* German, English and French.

WIEDERKEHR FORSTER & WEBER

Established in 1939
BAHNHOFSTRASSE 44
8023 ZÜRICH, SWITZERLAND
Telephone: 211 13 32
Telecopier: 211 80 68
Cable Address: 81 33 53 AWI CH

General, Contracts, Corporate, Banking, Tax, Antitrust and Unfair Competition, Estate Planning, Commercial Litigation, Arbitration.

MEMBERS OF FIRM

DR. ARTHUR WIEDERKEHR, born Zurich, Switzerland, July 29, 1910; admitted, 1933, Zurich. *Education:* University of Zurich (Dr.iur.); Universities of Paris and Rome. Consul General of the Republic of Panama in Zurich, 1952-1980. *Member:* Zurich and Swiss Bar Associations. *LANGUAGES:* German, English, French, Spanish and Italian. *PRACTICE AREAS:* Retail Banking; International Corporate.

DR. ALFRED J. WIEDERKEHR, born Zurich, Switzerland, February 24, 1936; admitted, 1967, Zurich; 1969, Geneva. *Education:* University of Zurich (Dr.iur.); University of Michigan Law School (MCL). Consul of the Republic of Peru in Zurich, 1984—. *Member:* Zurich and Swiss Bar Associations. *LANGUAGES:* German, English, French, Spanish and Italian. *PRACTICE AREAS:* Contracts; International; International Finance; Tax Planning.

DR. MARTIN FORSTER, born Frauenfeld, Switzerland, November 11, 1942; admitted, 1968, Zurich. *Education:* University of Zurich (Dr.iur.); Southern Methodist University, Dallas (MCL). *Member:* Zurich and Swiss Bar Associations. *LANGUAGES:* German, English and French. *PRACTICE AREAS:* Retail Banking; Company Law; Commercial; Commercial Litigation; International Trust and Estates.

DR. GEORG R. WIEDERKEHR, born Zurich, Switzerland, May 27, 1938; admitted, 1978, Zurich. *Education:* University of Zurich (Dr.iur.); University of Lausanne. Consul of Island in Zurich, 1979—. *Member:* Zurich and Swiss Bar Associations. *LANGUAGES:* German, English, French, Spanish and Italian. *PRACTICE AREAS:* Retain Banking; Business Law; Contracts; Succession.

PROF. DR. ROLF H. WEBER, born Zurich, Switzerland, June 9, 1951; admitted, 1978, Zurich. *Education:* University of Zurich (Dr.iur.); Harvard Law School (Visiting Scholar, 1980-1981). Professor at the University of Zurich. *Member:* Zurich and Swiss Bar Associations. *LANGUAGES:* German, English and French. *PRACTICE AREAS:* International Banking; Company Law; Acquisitions and Sales; Telecommunications; Computer Contracts.

MARKUS A. HUGELSHOFER, born Winterthur, Switzerland, July 11, 1956; admitted, 1984, Zürich; 1987, Aargau; 1990, Zug. *Education:* University of Zurich (lic.iur., 1980); Columbia University School of Law, New York (LL.M., 1986). *Member:* Zurich and Swiss Bar Associations. *LANGUAGES:* German, English, French and Italian. *PRACTICE AREAS:* Bankruptcy; Reorganization; Company Law; Contracts.

STEFAN KOLLER, born Zug, Switzerland, September 23, 1958; admitted, 1986, Zug. *Education:* University of Zurich (lic.iur., 1983); New York University School of Law (M.C.J.). *Member:* Zurich and Swiss Bar Associations. *LANGUAGES:* German, English and French.

MONIKA D. WEISSHAUPT, born Zurich, Switzerland, May 1, 1960; admitted, 1992, Zurich. *Education:* University of Zurich (lic.iur., 1988). *Member:* Zurich and Swiss Bar Associations. *LANGUAGES:* German, English and French.

DR. IUR. EGBERT WILMS

Established in 1985
SEMPACHERSTRASSE 12
P.O. BOX 16
CH-8030 ZÜRICH, SWITZERLAND
Telephone: (0041) 1 422 23 23
Telecopier: (0041) 1 251 54 90

Firm engaged in Switzerland, Benelux and Scandinavia, dealing with International Business Law, International Tax Law and Intellectual Property Law.

(This Listing Continued)

DR. EGBERT WILMS, born Amsterdam, The Netherlands, March 2, 1949; admitted, 1973, Switzerland and The Netherlands. *Education:* University of Utrecht (Dr., 1984); University of Tübingen; University of Zurich. Thesis on Product Liability and Trademarks, 1984. Member: Nederlandse Orde van Advocaten, Zürcher Juristenverein. *LANGUAGES:* Dutch, English, German and Norwegian. *PRACTICE AREAS:* International Business Law; European Community Law; Intellectual Property; Antitrust/State Aid.

WINTER & PARTNER

Established in 1986

KIRCHGASSE 40
CH-8024 ZÜRICH, SWITZERLAND
Telephone: (01) 251 81 00
Facsimile: (01) 251 81 28
Telex: 816981 wint ch

Zug, Switzerland Office: Bahnhofstrasse 16, 6300. Telephone: (042) 22 18 20. Facsimile: (042) 23 44 23.
Budapest, Hungary Office: Benczur U, 13, H-1068 Budapest. Telephone: (1) 122 98 40. Facsimile: (1) 122 62 67. Telex: 22 65 70.

Commercial, Corporate and Civil Practice, International Trade and Commodities, Banking and Finance, Mergers and Acquisitions, Commercial Litigation and Arbitration, Estate Planning.

MEMBERS OF FIRM

DR. HERBERT WINTER, born Zurich, Switzerland, December 6, 1946; admitted, 1972, Zurich and Zug. *Education:* University of Zurich (Dr.iur., 1974). Tutorage, University of Zurich, 1972-1973. *Member:* Zurich and Swiss Bar Associations; International Bar Association; Swiss Arbitration Association. *LANGUAGES:* German, English and French.

DR. JANOS BURAI-KOVACS, born Budapest, Hungary, November 14, 1950; admitted, 1976, Budapest, Hungary (Not admitted in Switzerland). *Education:* University of Law in Budapest, postgraduate degree in International Corporate and Trade Law, 1977 (Dr. iur., 1974). *Member:* Hungarian Bar Association. (Resident at Budapest Office). *LANGUAGES:* Hungarian, English and German.

ASSOCIATE

RETO HAUSER, born Wettingen, Switzerland, October 12, 1961; admitted, 1992, Zurich and Zug. *Education:* University of Zurich (lic. iur., 1989). *Member:* Zurich and Swiss Bar Associations. *LANGUAGES:* German, English and French.

ZÜRCHER, BLICKENSTORFER & WIDMER

LÖWENSTRASSE 61, P.O. BOX
8023 ZÜRICH, SWITZERLAND
Telephone: (00411) 224 66 00
Telecopier: (00411) 224 66 24

General Commercial Practice, Corporate, Contracts, Banking, Computer and Software Law, Intellectual and Industrial Property and Copyright, Taxation, Real Estate, Administrative Matters, Residence and Work Permits, Inheritance and Estate Planning, Arbitration and Litigation.

FIRM PROFILE: The firm offers a full range of legal services. It counsels and represents Swiss and foreign corporate and individual clients. An extensive network of correspondent law firms around the globe is maintained.

MEMBERS OF FIRM

LIC. IUR. ANDREAS CH. ZÜRCHER, born 1956; admitted, 1986, Switzerland. *Education:* University of Zurich (Lic.iur.). Co-Author: "Auswirkungen des neuen Aktienrechts für die private Aktiengesellschaft," Corporate Law. *Member:* Zurich and Swiss Bar Associations. *PRACTICE AREAS:* Corporate Law; Commercial Law; Computers and Software; Administrative Law; Government; Environmental Law.

DR. KURT U. BLICKENSTORFER, born 1956; admitted, 1984, Switzerland. *Education:* University of Zurich (Dr.iur.); University of Miami (LL.M.). Author: "Joint Ventures in Switzerland"; "Die genossenschaftsrechtliche Verantwortlichkeit," Company Law. Co-Author: "Auswirkungen des neuen Aktienrechtes für die private Aktiengesellschaft," Company Law. *Member:* Zurich, Swiss and International Bar Associations. *PRAC-*

(This Listing Continued)

TICE AREAS: Company Law; Business Law; Mergers and Acquisitions; Trusts and Estates; International Arbitration; Litigation.

LIC. IUR. ERNST A. WIDMER, born 1956; admitted, 1986, Switzerland; 1989, New York. *Education:* University of Berne (Lic.iur., 1982). Co-Author: Commentary on the Swiss Code of Obligations, Section of Securities Law. *Member:* Zurich and Swiss Bar Associations. *PRACTICE AREAS:* Business Organisation; International Business; Litigation; Intellectual Property; Bankruptcy; Trusts and Estates.

ASSOCIATES

LIC. IUR. ANDREAS HÜNERWADEL, born 1964; admitted, 1993, Switzerland. *Education:* University of Zurich (Lic.iur.). *Member:* Zurich and Swiss Bar Associations.

Languages: German, English and French

TURKEY

ARIHAN & ARIHAN

ILKIZ SOKAK 5/10, SIHHIYE
06430 ANKARA, TURKEY
Telephone: (90-4) 231 83 93; (90-4) 231 83 94
Telefax: (90-4) 231 41 21

Privatization, Foreign Investments, Acquisitions and Mergers, Environmental Law, Patent, Trade Mark and Copyright, Unfair Competition, Contracts, Corporations, Companies, Real Estate.

OKTAY ARIHAN. *Education:* Atatürk Lycee, Law Faculty of Ankara University. Sole practice 1964-1990. *Member:* Ankara Bar Association; Ankara Middle-East Lions Club.

TAYLAN ARIHAN. *Education:* Ankara College, Law Faculty of Ankara University; Commercial Law and Banking Institute, Institute d'Etudes Français. Author: Wetlands of Turkey (IBA publication). *Member:* Ankara Bar Association; Eastern European Forum; International Bar Association; American Bar Association.

Languages: Turkish, English and French

GÜROL EMIN

MESRUTIYET CAD. 12/29
06640 ANKARA, TURKEY
Telephone: (312) 417 64 25; 417 64 26; Evenings: (312) 426 76 23
Telex: 46804 KTX-TR
Telefax: (312) 418 08 92

General Practice in Civil and Commercial Law. Establishment of Foreign and Local Companies.

FIRM PROFILE: The firm had been established in 1954 and during the period offered legal services for several local and foreign companies from the U.S., U.K., Germany, Hungary, Switzerland, Holland, Italy and Turkey etc., as permanent legal advisor for some of them starting from the foundation of companies.

GÜROL EMIN, born Konya, Turkey, November 5, 1925; admitted, 1954, Turkey. *Education:* University of Ankara. *Member:* Ankara Bar Association; Ankara Rotary Club (Chairman, 1975-1976); Turkish American Association (Board Member and Chairman, 1986-1989); American Arbitration Association. *LANGUAGES:* Turkish and English. *PRACTICE AREAS:* Commercial Firms Disputes and Cases; Founding Firms in Turkey.

MERAL MÜREN, admitted, 1972, Turkey. *Education:* University of Ankara. *Member:* Ankara Bar Association; Çayyolu Lions Club.

ERSOY LEGAL OFFICE

Established in 1972

UĞUR MUMCU CADDESI 82/2

06700 ANKARA, TURKEY

Telephone: (90-312) 446 87 58 (3 lines)

Fax: (90-312) 446 87 61

FIRM PROFILE: *Ersoy Legal Office was established in 1972 by Yüksel Ersoy. Its principal areas of occupation are Civil Law, Company and Commercial Law, Commercial Transactions, Computer Law, Joint Ventures and Consortium, General International Trade Law, Licensing and Management Agreements, Proprietary Information Agreements, Rights on Literary and Artistic Works, Construction Law, Indemnity Law, International Arbitration, Administrative Law and Criminal Law. This firm is composed of four lawyers, a secretary and office personnel.*

MEMBERS OF FIRM

YÜKSEL ERSOY, born Artvin, Turkey, 1936; admitted, 1968, Turkey. *Education:* Ankara University Law School (Law Degree, 1959); Rome University Law School (Ph.D. in Law). Author: Thesis on, "Ignoranza ed Errore nel Diritto Penale " (Ignorance and Error in Criminal Law), Rome University Law School. Assistant Professor and Professor, Criminal Law and Criminology, Ankara University, 1966—. Researched, International Criminal Law, Boalt Hall School of Law at the University of California at Berkeley, 1975. Visiting Scholar and Researcher, International Law Department, University of Virginia in Charlottesville, 1978. *Member:* Ankara Bar Association; International Bar Association; Association of European Lawyers; Associazione Internazionale Giuristi di Lingua Italiana; Jurist Europe; Lawyers Associated Worldwide. *LANGUAGES:* Turkish, Italian, English and French. *PRACTICE AREAS:* Company Law; Commercial Law; Commercial Transactions; Joint Ventures; International Trade Law; Licensing; Civil Law; Computer Law; Construction Law; International Arbitration; Criminal Law.

AHMET NAMIK KÖSEBALABAN, born Van, Turkey, 1963; admitted, 1989, Turkey. *Education:* Istanbul University Law School (Law Degree, 1988). *Member:* Ankara Bar Association. *LANGUAGES:* Turkish. *PRACTICE AREAS:* Indemnity Law; Administrative Law; Civil Law.

A. BERNA KAYAALP, born Merzifon, Turkey, 1961; admitted, 1987, Turkey. *Education:* Ankara University Law School (Law Degree, 1985). *Member:* Ankara Bar Association. *LANGUAGES:* Turkish and English. *PRACTICE AREAS:* Contract Law; Commercial Law; Civil Law; Literary; Artistic Works Law.

M. FIRAT POLAT, born Ankara, Turkey, 1969; admitted, 1994, Turkey. *Education:* Ankara University Law School (Law Degree, 1990). *Member:* Ankara Bar Association. *LANGUAGES:* Turkish and English. *PRACTICE AREAS:* Contract Law; Commercial Law; International Arbitration; Civil Law.

YILMAZ OZ

TURAN EMEKSIZ SOKAK 3, PARK AP. B-7

GAZI OSMAN PASA

06700 ANKARA, TURKEY

Telephone: (90-312) 426 1224

Telecopier: (90-312) 427 4855

REVISER OF THE TURKEY LAW DIGEST FOR THIS DIRECTORY.

Contract Law, Investment, Licensing, Tax Matters and Energy Law. Advice on Host Government Relations, Private and Public International Law.

FIRM PROFILE: *Established in 1956, the firm advocates the idea of "Preventive Counselling" as it stresses the need for and encourages its clients (mostly North American, European and Japanese Corporations) to seek professional assistance at pre-contract and contract-administration stages with a view to eschew or minimize prospects of future litigation. The firm regards this as of particular importance in a legal environment such as that exists in Turkey where legislative arrangements are fast-changing and ever-expanding with increased chances of careless lawmaking often resulting in ambiguities which lead to varying or contradictory interpretations.*

YILMAZ OZ, born Ankara, Turkey, April 10, 1930; admitted, 1956, Ankara, Turkey. *Education:* University of Ankara (LL.B., 1951); Yale University (LL.M., 1952). Author: (Articles in Turkish) "Preventive Counselling", The Ankara Bar Journal, Vol. 5, 1965; "Space Law," The Ankara Bar Journal, Vol. 6, 1966; "The Jury System," The Ankara Bar Journal, Vol. 2,

(This Listing Continued)

1968; "The Continental Shelf," The Ankara Bar Journal, Vol. 3, 1968; "Law and Automation," The Ankara Bar Journal, Vol. 1, 1969; "Turkish American Treaties: Yesterday and Today," The Turkish Daily *Milliyet*, June 23, 1976; (Articles in English) "The Rule of Law," The Turkish Daily News, June 1965; "Summary of Turkish Petroleum Legislation," written and periodically revised for "Petroleum Legislation," New York, last revised, January, 1, 1990; "Some Old Turkish American Treaties Revisited," The Turkish Daily News, June 30, 1976; "Quotations from ATATURK," 1981; Chapter on "Turkey" in M. Kurkela's "Comparative Report on Force Majeure in Western Europe," 1982. President: Turkish-American Association, 1965-1974; Ankara Rotary Club, 1966-1967. *Member:* Ankara Bar; World Jurist Association. *LANGUAGES:* Turkish, English and French.

ASSOCIATE

(MRS.) NIHAL OZ. *Education:* Yale Law School (LL.M., 1952).

Languages: Turkish, English and French

REPRESENTATIVE CLIENTS: *Energy:* AGIP; Allied Chemical; Amoco; Ashland; Arco; Chevron; Conoco; Huffco; Marathon; Pennzoil; RWE-DEA; Unocal; Union; Wintershall. *Manufacturing, Service and Miscellaneous:* Beechcraft; Bombardier; British Gas; Cabot; C.Itoh; BNP; Chiyoda; Cooper; Diebold; Dun & Bradstreet; FMC; Hughes; General Electric; General Motors; IBM; Isuzu; Kleinwanzlebener Saatzucht; Loral; Magnavox; Martin Marietta; Mallinckrodt; 3M Co.; McDonnell-Douglas; Mitsui; National Can; Northern Electric; SAIC; SNC-Lavalin; Singer; TRW; Texas Instruments; United Technologies. *Non-Profit Governmental:* Ford Foundation; Population Council; Rockefeller Foundation; UNDP (Turkey); U.S. Department of Justice.

REVISER OF THE TURKEY LAW DIGEST FOR THIS DIRECTORY.

SEZA REISOĞLU - ERDEN KUNTALP - BÜLENT ENSARI

Established in 1985

GÜNEŞ SOKAK, 17/5

KAVAKLIDERE

06690 ANKARA, TURKEY

Telephone: (312) 467 91 03; (312) 467 48 96

Telefax: (312) 467 46 92

General Practice. Administrative, Arbitration, Banking, Business, Capital Market, Civil, Commercial, Foreign Currency, Foreign Investment Legislations, Corporate Law, International Trade, Labor, Law of Bankruptcy and Execution, Law of Obligation, Leasing, Factoring, Defense Industry, Joint Venture, Private International Law and Privatization.

MEMBERS OF FIRM

AV. PROF. DR. SEZA REISOĞLU, born Istanbul, Turkey, February 3, 1931; admitted, 1956, Turkey. *Education:* Ankara University (Doctor, 1958; Associate Professor, 1961; Professor, 1968). Author: "General Rules of an Unjust Richment Action," 1961; "Contract of Guarantee," 1963; "Turkish Suretyship Law," 1964; "Pledge without Delivery," 1965; "Collective Labor Agreements in Turkish and Comparative Laws," 1967; "Contract of Service," 1968; "Rules of Law of Obligations Concerning Banking," 1970; "Commentary of Law on Collective Labor Agreement and Strike and Lockout," 1971; "German Labor and Social Security Law about Foreign Labors," 1973; "Common Market Law," 1973; "Credit Transactions and Participations in Accordance with the Decree No. 70 on Banks," 1985; "Cheque in Turkish Jurisprudence and Banking Practice," 1985; "Commentary of Collective Labor Agreement-Strike and Lock-out Law," 1986; "Commentary of Banks Act," 1988; "Letters of Guarantee and Counter-Guarantee," 1990, "Surety," 1992, All in Ankara. Instructor, Law Faculty of Ankara University, 1956-1982. Research in Max-Planck-Institute in Hamburg, 1958-1959, Lozanne University, 1959-1960 and Visiting Professor Freie Universität, Berlin, 1971-1972. Chief Legal Advisor: Capital Market Board, 1982-1985; Türkiye Iş Bank, 1987—; Bank Association of Turkey. *Member:* Turkish Law Society; Bar of Ankara. *LANGUAGES:* Turkish, German, French and English.

AV. PROF. DR. ERDEN KUNTALP, born Aydin, Turkey, November 8, 1934; admitted, 1960, Turkey. *Education:* Law Faculty of Istanbul University; Ankara University (Doctor, 1964; Associate Professor, 1970; Professor, 1980). Author: "Sales Contract with Delivery One from the Other," 1968; "Contract with Mixed Content," 1971; "Legal Regulation of Off-Shores," 1981; "Contract of Financial Leasing," September, 1986; "Mortgage Created For Certain Amount and Mortgage Created for Maximum Amount," 1989, All in Ankara; Instructor, Law Faculty of Ankara University, 1960-1985. Chief Legal Counsel, Turkish Tourism Bank, 1972-1978 and DESIYAB (State Labor and Investment Bank), 1978-1982. Legal Ad-

(This Listing Continued)

visor, Türkiye Iş Bank, 1983—. *Member:* Turkish Law Society; Bar of Ankara. *LANGUAGES:* Turkish, French and German.

AV. BÜLENT ENSARI, born Mardin, Turkey, January 23, 1950; admitted, 1980, Turkey. *Education:* Law Faculty of Ankara University (Masters degree in Law). Legal Advisor, Türkiye Iş Bank, 1980—. *Member:* Bar of Ankara; International Bar Association. *LANGUAGES:* Turkish, English and Arabic.

ASSOCIATES

AV. ASLI BUDAK, born Ankara, Turkey, April 20, 1966; admitted, 1987, Turkey. *Education:* Law Faculty of Ankara University; Research Institute, Programme of Banking and Commercial Law (Commercial Law Certificate, 1988). *Member:* Bar of Ankara. *LANGUAGES:* Turkish and English.

AV. GOKSEN ACAR, born Ankara, Turkey, November 1, 1967; admitted, 1992, Turkey. *Education:* Law Faculty of Ankara University. *Member:* Bar of Ankara. *LANGUAGES:* Turkish and English.

Languages: English, German, French and Arabic

REPRESENTATIVE CLIENTS: Türk Ekonomi Bankasi A.S., Istanbul, Turkey; Türk Eximbank A.S., Ankara, Turkey; Türk Dis Ticaret Bankasi A.S. (Disbank), Istanbul, Turkey; Baser Kimya Sanayi ve Ticaret A.S., Istanbul, Turkey; Güney Sanayi ve Ticaret Isletmeleri A.S., Adana, Turkey; Prime Ministry Public Participation Administration of Republic of Turkey, Ankara, Turkey; Türkiye Elektrik Kurumu, Ankara, Turkey; Perma Sharp Celik Sanayi A.S., Istanbul, Turkey; Permatik Celik ve Plastik Sanayi A.S., Istanbul, Turkey; Karbon Celik Sanayi A.S., Istanbul, Turkey; Krom Celik Ticaret ve Sanayi A.S., Istanbul, Turkey; Man Kamyon ve Otobüs Sanayi A.S., Istanbul, Turkey; Man Motor Sanayi A.S., Ankara, Turkey; Bastas Baskent Cimento Sanayi ve Ticaret A.S., Ankara, Turkey; Elektrik Tesisleri Mühendislik Hizmetleri ve Ticaret A.S. (Eltem Tek), Ankara, Turkey; Metas Izmir Metalurji Fabrikasi T.A., Izmir, Turkey; Euroturk Bank, Istanbul, Turkey; Nasco Nasreddin Holding A.S., Istanbul, Turkey; International Finance Corporation, Washington, D.C., U.S.A.; Polly Peck International Plc. (In Administration), London, England; Deutsche Bank Aktiengesellschaft, Frankfurt, Germany; Eurolease S.A., Brussels, Belgium; GPA Group Limited, Co. Clare, Ireland; BHF Bank, Frankfurt, Germany; Klöckner & Co, Germany; Deutsche Genossenschoftsbank, Frankfurt, Germany; Itochu Corporation, Tokyo, Japan; Computer Associates International, Inc., Islandia, U.S.A.; On-Line Software International, Inc., Islandia, U.S.A.; Coopers & Lybrand, London, England; Export Development Corporation, Ontario, Canada; Beghin-Say, Paris, France; Milbank, Tweed, Hadley & McCloy, London, England.
REFERENCE: Türkiye Is Bankasi A.S., Ankara, Turkey; The Banks Association of Turkey, Ankara, Turkey; The World Bank.

TURUNÇ & SAVAŞÇIN

Established in 1990

GÜNES SOKAK, 25/7
KAVAKLIDERE
06690 ANKARA, TURKEY
Telephone: (312) 428 52 80
Fax: (312) 468 19 93

Istanbul, Turkey Office: Hüsrev Gerede Caddesi, 126/6, 80200, Tesvikiye. Telephone: (212) 259 45 36; (212) 259 45 37. Facsimile: (212) 259 45 38.
Izmir, Turkey Office: Cumhuriyet Bulvari, 140/2, K. 5, 35210, Alsancak. Telephone: (232) 463 49 07; (232) 463 49 08. Fax: (232) 463 49 09.

Government contracts, foreign investment, joint ventures, registrations, commercial and corporate law, banking and financial law, labour law, mining law, litigation and arbitration.

MEMBERS OF FIRM

MUSTAFA BOZCAADALI, born Ankara, Turkey, February 2, 1945; admitted, 1973, Turkey. *Education:* Law School of Ankara (LL.B., 1971; LL.M., 1980). *Member:* Ankara Bar Association. *LANGUAGES:* Turkish and English.

MEHTAP BENINGTAN, born Istanbul, Turkey, January 6, 1948; admitted, 1973, Turkey. *Education:* Law School of Ankara (LL.B., 1971). *Member:* Ankara Bar Association. *LANGUAGES:* Turkish.

YÜCEL EZBERCI, born Ankara, Turkey, April 25, 1948; admitted, 1973, Turkey. *Education:* Law School of Ankara (LL.B., 1971). *Member:* Ankara Bar Association. *LANGUAGES:* Turkish.

EROL SUNER, born Nazilli, Turkey, January 1, 1940; admitted, 1970, Turkey. *Education:* Law School of Istanbul (LL.B., 1966). *Member:* Izmir Bar Association. *LANGUAGES:* Turkish and English.

(For biographical data on other personnel, see Professional Biographies at Izmir, Turkey and Istanbul, Turkey).

WHITE & CASE

ZIYA UR RAHMAN CADDESI 17/5
06700 GAZIOSMANPAŞA
ANKARA, TURKEY
Telephone: (90-312) 446-2180
Facsimile: (90-312) 437-9677

New York, New York: Telephone: 212-819-8200. Facsimile: 212-354-8113.
Washington, D.C.: Telephone: 202-872-0013. Facsimile: 202-872-0210.
Los Angeles, California: Telephone: 213-620-7700. Facsimile: 213-687-0758; 213-617-2205.
Miami, Florida: Telephone: 305-371-2700. Facsimile: 305-358-5744.
Mexico City, Mexico: Telephone: (52-5) 207-9717. Facsimile: (52-5) 208-3628.
Tokyo, Japan: Telephone: (81-3) 3239-4300. Facsimile: (81-3) 3239-4330.
Hong Kong: Telephone: (852) 2822-8700. Facsimile: (852) 2845-9070; Grice & Co., Solicitors, Telephone: (852) 2826-0333. Facsimile: (852) 2526-7166.
Singapore, Republic of Singapore: Telephone: (65) 225-6000. Facsimile: (65) 225-6009.
Bangkok, Thailand: Pacific Legal Group Ltd., In Association With White & Case, Telephone: (662) 236-6154/7. Facsimile: (662) 237-6771.
Hanoi, Viet Nam: Representative Office, Telephone: (84-4) 227-575/6/7. Facsimile: (84-4) 227-297.
Bombay, India: Telephone: (91-22) 282-6300. Facsimile: (91-22) 282-6305.
London, England: Telephone: (44-171) 726-6361. Facsimile: (44-171) 726-4314; (44-171) 726-8558.
Paris, France: Telephone: (33-1) 42-60-34-05. Facsimile: (33-1) 42-60-82-46.
Brussels, Belgium: Telephone: (32-2) 647-05-89. Facsimile: (32-2) 647-16-75.
Stockholm, Sweden: Telephone: (46-8) 679-80-30. Facsimile: (46-8) 611-21-22.
Helsinki, Finland: Telephone: (358-0) 631-100. Facsimile: (358-0) 179-477.
Moscow, Russia: Telephone: (7-095) 201-9292/3/4/5. Facsimile: (7-095) 201-9284.
Budapest, Hungary: Telephone: (36-1) 269-0550; (36-1) 131-0933. Facsimile: (36-1) 269-1199.
Prague, Czech Republic: Telephone: (42-2) 2481-1796. Facsimile: (42-2) 232-5522.
Warsaw, Poland: Telephone/Facsimile: (48-22) 26-80-53; (48-22) 27-84-86. International Telephone/Facsimile: (48-39) 12-19-06.
Istanbul, Turkey: Telephone: (90-212) 275-68-98; (90-212) 275-75-33. Facsimile: (90-212) 275-75-43.
Jeddah, Saudi Arabia: Law Office of Hassan Mahassni, Telephone: (966-2) 651-3535. Facsimile: (966-2) 651-3636.
Riyadh, Saudi Arabia: Law Office of Hassan Mahassni, Telephone: (966-1) 476-7099. Facsimile: (966-1) 479-0110.
Almaty, Kazakhstan: Telephone: (7-3272) 50-7491/2. Facsimile: (7-3272) 61-0842.

General International Practice.

RESIDENT PARTNER

HUGH VERRIER, born Portsmouth, United Kingdom, June 8, 1956; admitted, 1988, Massachusetts; 1989, New York (Not admitted in Turkey). *Education:* University of Montreal (B.A., 1980); University of Ottawa (LL.B., 1981); Harvard University (LL.M., 1982). *Member:* Massachusetts, New York State, American, Canadian and International Bar Associations; New York County Lawyers' Association.

RESIDENT ASSOCIATES

MESUT CAKMAK, born Izmit, Turkey, January 8, 1967; admitted, 1991, Ankara. *Education:* Ankara University Law Faculty (LL.B., 1990).

ANNE E. LEDERER, born Milwaukee, Wisconsin, December 11, 1964; admitted, 1991, California (Not admitted in Turkey). *Education:* University of Wisconsin (B.S., 1985); University of California at Los Angeles (J.D., 1991).

(This Listing Continued)

WHITE & CASE, Ankara—Continued

ZEYNEP ONALAN, born Ankara, Turkey, June 18, 1967; admitted, 1990, Ankara. *Education:* Ankara University Faculty of Law (LL.B., 1989).

(For biographical data as to other locations, see Professional Biographies at New York, New York; Washington, D.C.; Los Angeles, California; Miami, Florida; Mexico City, Mexico; Tokyo, Japan; Hong Kong; Singapore, Republic of Singapore; Bangkok, Thailand; Hanoi, Viet Nam; Bombay, India; London, England; Paris, France; Brussels, Belgium; Stockholm, Sweden; Helsinki, Finland; Moscow, Russia; Budapest, Hungary; Prague, Czech Republic; Warsaw, Poland; Istanbul, Turkey; Jeddah and Riyadh, Saudi Arabia; Almaty, Kazakhstan).

ALTHEIMER & GRAY

TESVIKIYE CAD. 107
TESVIKIYE PALAS 7
ISTANBUL (TESVIKIYE) 80200, TURKEY
Telephone: 011-90-212-227-6750
Fax: 011-90-212-227-6759

REVISERS OF THE POLAND LAW DIGEST FOR THIS DIRECTORY.

Chicago, Illinois Office: 10 South Wacker Drive, 60606. Telephone: 312-715-4000. Fax: 312-715-4800. Telex: RCA 297102 A G UR.
Warsaw, Poland Office: ul. Nowogrodzka 50, 00-950, Warsaw. Telephone: 011-48-22-298-357; 011-48-39-12-1338. Fax: 48-2-628-3640.
Prague, Czech Republic Office: Platnerska 4, 110 00 Prague 1. Telephone: 011-42-2-2481-2782. Fax: 011-42-2-2481-0125 or 232-9595.
Kiev, Ukraine Office: Kontraktova Ploscha 4, Building 3, Room 304, 254145. Telephone: 011-7-044-230-2534. Fax: 011-7-044-230-2535.
Bratislava, Slovakia Office: Nam. SNP 15, 811 06. Telephone: 011-42-7-362-736. Fax: 011-42-7-367-960.

Privatizations and Acquisitions, Joint Ventures and Foreign Investment, Government Affairs, Real Estate Development, Architecture, Engineering and Construction, Banking and Finance, Bankruptcy, Licensing and Distribution, Insurance, Telecommunications, Securities, Taxation and Customs.

PARTNERS

JAMES E. CARROLL, born Evanston, Illinois, July 31, 1956; admitted, 1982, Illinois (Not admitted in Turkey). *Education:* Loras College (B.A., maxima cum laude, 1978); Cambridge University (LL.M. in International Law, 1980); Northwestern University (J.D., 1982). Delta Epsilon Sigma; Phi Alpha Theta. Member, Northwestern Journal of International Law and Business, 1981-1982. Author: "Of Icebergs, Oil Wells and Treaties: Hydrocarbon Exploitation Offshore Antarctica," 19 Stanford Journal of International Law, 1983. Co-author: "Recent Developments in Polish Insurance Law," De Paul Business Law Journal, Spring/Summer 1991. *Member:* Chicago, Illinois State, American and International Bar Associations. (Also at Chicago, Prague, Warsaw, Bratislava and Kiev Offices). *PRACTICE AREAS:* International Law; Finance Law; Mergers and Acquisitions.

GEORGE I. COWELL, born Grand Rapids, Michigan, July 11, 1926; admitted, 1958, Illinois (Not admitted in Turkey). *Education:* St. John's College and Mexico City College (B.A., cum laude, 1951); University of Chicago (J.D., 1957). Member, Board of Editors, University of Chicago Law Review, 1956-1957. *Member:* Chicago, Illinois State and American Bar Associations. (Also at Chicago Office). *PRACTICE AREAS:* Real Estate; National and International Transactions.

LOUIS B. GOLDMAN, born Chicago, Illinois, April 11, 1948; admitted, 1975, California; 1976, New York; 1991, Illinois (Not admitted in Turkey). *Education:* University of California at Berkeley (A.B., magna cum laude, 1970); University of Chicago (J.D., cum laude, 1974). Phi Beta Kappa; Order of the Coif. Member, University of Chicago Law Review, 1972-1973. Co-Author: "Repossessing the Spirit of St. Louis: Expanding The Protection of Sections 1110 and 1168 of The Bankruptcy Code," The Business Lawyer, Vol. 41, No. 1, 1985. Co-Author: "Recent Developments in Polish Insurance Law," De Paul Business Law Journal, Spring/Summer 1991. Law Clerk to Judge Charles B. Renfrew, U.S. District Court, Northern District of California, 1974-1975. Member, Chicago-Prague Sister Cities Committee of the City of Chicago. *Member:* State Bar of California; Association of the Bar of the City of New York; Chicago, New York State (Member, Committee on International Banking, Securities and Financial Transactions, Committee on International Investment and Development), American (Member, Sections on: Corporation, Banking and Business Law; Taxation; International Law and Practice) and International Bar Associations;

(This Listing Continued)

New York County Lawyers Association (Member, Special Committee on the Peoples Republic of China). (Also at Chicago, Prague, Warsaw and Bratislava Offices). *PRACTICE AREAS:* Securities Law; Mergers and Acquisitions Law; International Law.

EUROPEAN COUNSEL

HALUK CAN OZEL, born Osmaniye, Turkey, April 5, 1952; admitted, 1976, Istanbul. *Education:* Istanbul University Law Faculty (1974). Legal Apprenticeship at Istanbul Courts, 1975-1976. English Language Courses, Exeter, England. Legal Counsel, Deva Holdings, 1977-1978. Partner, Ozel & Ozel, 1979-1993. Author: "Copyright Protection in Turkey," (1985), provider for the part of Turkey in the "International Execution Against Judgement Debtors," by Sweet & Maxwell. *Member:* Istanbul, International and American (International Associate) Bar Associations; American Turkish Businessman Association (Legal Counsel); British Chamber of Commerce in Turkey (Board Member). *LANGUAGES:* Turkish and English.

ASSOCIATE

ALI MURAT DIZDAR, born Zonguldak, Turkey, October 6, 1960; admitted, 1990, Istanbul. *Education:* Law Faculty of Istanbul University (1982); Social Sciences Institute of Istanbul University (LL.M., 1985). Assistant Professor of Commercial Law; Law Faculty of Istanbul University, 1982-1989.

ONUR KORDEL, born Gölcük, Turkey, March 16, 1968; admitted, 1991, Istanbul. *Education:* Marmara University Law Faculty (1988). Apprenticeship at Kadiköy Courts and Cumhur Onur former Chief Legal Advisor to Turkish Maritime Bank Law Office. English Language courses in San Jose and San Francisco, California. In House Counsel to BNP AK Dresdner Bank A.Ş(1991-1993). *LANGUAGES:* Turkish and English.

REVISERS OF THE POLAND LAW DIGEST FOR THIS DIRECTORY.

(For complete biographical data on personnel at Chicago, Illinois, Warsaw, Poland, Prague, Czech Republic, Kiev, Ukraine and Bratislava, Slovakia see Professional Biographies at those locations)

ARNOLD & PORTER
REPRESENTATIVE OFFICE

BÜYÜKDERE CADDESI NO. 118/10
ESENTEPE
80280 ISTANBUL, TURKEY
Telephone: 90-212-275-2160
Telefax: 90-212-275-2079

Washington, D.C. Office: Thurman Arnold Building, 1200 New Hampshire Avenue, N.W., 20036-6885. Telephone: 202-872-6700. Telecopy: 202-872-6720.
Los Angeles, California Office: 44th Floor, 777 Figueroa Street, 90017-2513. Telephone: 213-243-4000. Telecopy: 213-243-4199.
Denver, Colorado Office: 1700 Lincoln Street, 80203-4540. Telephone: 303-863-1000. Telecopy: 303-832-0428.
New York, New York Office: 399 Park Avenue, 10022-4690. Telephone: 212-715-1000. Telecopy: 212-715-1399.
Budapest, Hungary Representative Office: Retek utca 26, H-1024. Telephone: 36-1-212-1110. Telefax: 36-1-135-7857.
Moscow, Russia Representative Office: Ozerkovskaya NA. 50, 113532. Telephone: 7095-235-3774. Telefax: 7095-235-5181.

General and International Practice.

PARTNER IN CHARGE

PAUL S. BERGER, born Blakely, Pennsylvania, August 25, 1932; admitted, 1958, New York; 1961, District of Columbia (Not admitted in Turkey). *Education:* University of Scranton (B.S., 1954); New York University (LL.B., 1957). Alpha Sigma Nu. Comment Editor, New York University Law Review, 1956-1957. Trustee, New York University Law Center Foundation, 1981—. (Also at Washington, D.C. Office).

OF COUNSEL

J. BRADWAY BUTLER, born Orange, New Jersey, February 10, 1941; admitted, 1969, District of Columbia; 1974, U.S. Court of Appeals for the District of Columbia Circuit. *Education:* Harvard University (B.A., 1963); University of Minnesota (LL.B., 1966); George Washington University (LL.M., 1968). (Also at Washington, D.C. Office).

(This Listing Continued)

AFFILIATED COUNSEL

METIN SOMAY, born Istanbul, Turkey, 1958. *Education:* Istanbul University Law School (Law Degree, with Honors, 1981); Catholic University (Master in Tax and Accounting, 1985); Georgetown University Law Center (LL.M., 1987). Foreign Associate, Arnold & Porter, Washington D.C., 1987-1989. (Also Member, Somay Hukuk Bürosu).

AHMET ATALAY LAW FIRM

Established in 1981

YÜZBAŞI KAYA ALDOĞAN SOKAK
SERHAN APT. 3/3 80300, ZINCIRLIKUYU
ISTANBUL, TURKEY
Telephone: 90-1-273 13 67; 288 16 36; 267 20 59; 267 22 11
Telecopier: 90-1-288 16 37

Patent and Trademark Litigation and Prosecution, Litigation in Civil Matters, Corporate and Maritime Law, Contracting, Franchising, Licensing, International Legal Transactions, Foreign Investment Problems and Real Estate.

FIRM PROFILE: *The firm was founded in 1981 on the premise that efficient and effective representation for domestic and foreign corporations require high level of expertise in addition to legal experience. The firm strives to provide its clients with responsive and insightful representation and to obtain them the best possible protection with the most efficient use of the client's time. The firm has three partners with two office administrators.*

MEMBERS OF FIRM

AHMET ATALAY, born Kirklareli, Turkey, January 6, 1950; admitted, 1978, Istanbul. *Education:* Robert College, Faculty of Law, University of Istanbul. *Member:* Istanbul Bar Association. *LANGUAGES:* Turkish and English. *PRACTICE AREAS:* Trademark and Patent Litigation and Prosecution; Maritime Law; International Legal Transactions; Foreign Investment Law.

FAHRI ÖNER, born Konya, Turkey, May 27, 1964; admitted, 1989, Istanbul. *Education:* Faculty of Law, University of Istanbul. *Member:* Istanbul Bar Association. *LANGUAGES:* Turkish and English. *PRACTICE AREAS:* Litigation; Civil Law; Corporate Law.

BIRGÜL ÖNER, born Van, Turkey, 1966; admitted, 1989, Istanbul. *Education:* Faculty of Law, Diyarbakir University. *Member:* Istanbul Bar Association. *LANGUAGES:* Turkish. *PRACTICE AREAS:* Real Estate Law; Execution Law.

REPRESENTATIVE CLIENTS: *Bahrain:* Bahrain Arab International Bank. *Italy:* Lloyd Triestino; Maritalia s.r.l.; Tarros s.p.a. *Germany:* Triumph-Adler; Fresenius AG; Emden g.m.b.h. *United Kingdom:* James Marine Services Ltd.; Hoover p.l.c.; IGI Insurance Co. *Finland:* Oy Partek AB; Oy Wilh Schauman AB. *U.S.A.:* Proctor & Gamble Co.; Sterling Drug Inc.; Allergan Inc.; RCI Inc.; Fuddruckers Inc.; Sutton & Sutton; Mead Corporation; Acme Resin Corporation; Borden, Inc.; Life Industries Inc. *Israel:* Mepro Kibbutz Hagoshrim Ltd. *Hong Kong:* Polycity Industrial Ltd. *Taiwan:* Formosa Coral Trade Co. *S. Korea:* Daewoo Corporation. *Turkey:* Arkas Shipping & Trading Inc.; Ege Container Inc.; Netyapi; Türkpetrol; Palmet.
REFERENCES: Prof. Desmond Cahil, Royal Melbourne Institute of Technology, Australia; Mr. Barry Carter, Denco Ltd., United Kingdom; Mr. Spyros Metaxa, Greece; Dr. Reinhard E. Ingerl, Rechtsanwalt, Lorenz Seidler Gossel, Münich, Germany; Capt. Della Valle, Tarros S.p.a., Istanbul; Mr. Can Abravay, RCI Istanbul Liaison Office; Baser Kimya A.S.; Duran Ofset; Dogu Ilaç.

AYBAY & AYBAY

SIRASELVILER CAD. 87
YENI HAYAT APT. KAT. 1 DA. 3, TAKSIM
80060 ISTANBUL, TURKEY
Telephone: (212) 245 57 35; (212) 243 44 76
Telex: 25511 GAYB TR
Facsimile: (212) 245 39 49

Admiralty and Maritime Law, Transportation Law, Aviation, Insurance, International Trade, Arbitration, Private International Law, Foreign Investments, Administrative, Citizenship and General Practice.

MEMBERS OF FIRM

GÜNDÜZ AYBAY, born Istanbul, Turkey, January 16, 1931; admitted, 1965, Istanbul. *Education:* Merchant Marine Academy (Licence, 1953); University of Istanbul Faculty of Law (Licence, 1964). Fellow, Salzburg Seminar in American Studies, American Law, 1974. Author: "An Analysis of the Decisions on Admiralty Rendered by the Supreme Court," Aybay

(This Listing Continued)

Publications, 1987. Co-Author: *Maritime Law Handbook (Turkey),* International Bar Association - Kluwer, 1989; "Cargo Operations and Stowage in Tankers and Dry Cargo Ships," Aybay Publications, 1988; "The Perpackage Limitation of Carrier's Liability," Sixth Symposium on Commercial Law and Supreme Court's Decisions, 1989. Professor, State Merchant Marine Academy, 1970-1980. Vice President, Maritime Law Association, Turkey. Former President, Maritime Academy Alumni Association, 1975-. Former President, Ocean Going Shipmasters Association. *Member:* Mediterranean Maritime Arbitration Association. *LANGUAGES:* Turkish and English.

AYDIN AYBAY, born Istanbul, Turkey, June 4, 1929; admitted, 1958, Istanbul. *Education:* University of Istanbul Faculty of Law (Licence, 1953; Dr.iur, 1958); Venia Legendi (Habilitation, 1963). Fellow, Salzburg Seminar in American Studies, American Law, 1973. Author: "Provisional Inscription in Land Register," 1962; "Partition of Co-ownership," 1966; *Law of Obligations,* Text book, 10th edition, 1991. Co-Author: "Commercial Agencies and Distributorships," Turkey, Prentice Hall, 1992. Professor of Civil Law, University of Istanbul Faculty of Law, 1974-1983. Professor of Civil Law and former Vice Dean, Istanbul University, Faculty of Political Science, 1979—. *LANGUAGES:* Turkish, English and German.

RONA AYBAY, born Istanbul, Turkey, May 10, 1935; admitted, 1973, Istanbul. *Education:* University of Istanbul Faculty of Law (Licence, 1959; Dr.iur., 1966); Columbia University Law School (M.C.L., 1964); Venia Legendi (Habilitation, 1973). Senior Fulbright-Hays Fellow, Iowa University, College of Law, 1971-1972. Fellow, Salzburg Seminar in American Studies, American Law, 1972. Author: "Legal Aspects of Doing Business in the Middle East (Turkey)," Kluwer Law and Taxation Publishers, The Netherlands, 1986. Co-Author: *Maritime Law Handbook (Turkey),* International Bar Association - Kluwer, 1989; "Commercial Agencies and Distributorships" (Turkey), Prentice Hall, 1992. Dean, Faculty of Administrative Sciences, Middle East Technical University, 1975-1976. Professor of Private International Law and former Vice-Dean, Faculty of Political Science, Ankara University, 1978-1994. Professor of Private International Law, Faculty of Political Science, University of Istanbul, 1994—. President, Aybay Foundation for Legal Studies. *Member:* International Bar Association; Asia Pacific Lawyers' Association; American Foreign Law Association. *LANGUAGES:* Turkish, English and French.

SEVIN ÖZAYDIN KARTAL, born Maras, Turkey, December 15, 1960; admitted, 1984, Istanbul. *Education:* University of Istanbul Faculty of Law (Licence, 1983). Author: "Master's Order," published in Master's Voice Journal of Turkish Ocean Going Master's Association, 1987; "A Brief Summary on Bulk Carriers," Published in Seahorse, Journal of State Maritime Academy Alumni Association, 1988. *LANGUAGES:* Turkish and English.

ERGUN ERSOY, born Antalya, Turkey, November 1, 1954; admitted, 1986, Istanbul. *Education:* Naval Academy (Licence, 1974); University of Istanbul Faculty of Law (Licence, 1983). Co-Author: "Cargo Operations and Stowage in Tankers and Dry Cargo Ships", Aybay Publications House, 1988. Captain of Navy Ships, Retired, Lieutenant (1985). Legal Advisor of D.B. Turkish Cargo Lines, 1987-1991. *Member:* Turkish Maritime Law Association (Founder); Turkish Ocean-Going Shipmasters Association. *LANGUAGES:* Turkish and English.

KERIM ATAMER, born Istanbul, Turkey, April 26, 1965; admitted, 1989, Istanbul. *Education:* University of Istanbul Faculty of Law (Licence, 1987). Author: "Shipowner's Limited Liability - A Comparison between Turkish Commercial Code and Code of Obligations," (published in memory of Late Professor M. Sarica), Aybay Publications, 1988; "Clean Bill of Lading and Letter of Indemnity," Journal of Istanbul Bar Association, 62/7-9 (1988) pp. 495-507; Interpretation and Procedural Assertion of the "whether in berth or not" clause, Journal of Istanbul Bar Association, 65/1-3 (1991). Co-Author: "The Perpackage Limitation of Carrier's Liability," Sixth Symposium on Commercial Law and Supreme Court's Decisions, 1989. *Member:* Turkish Maritime Law Association; German-Turkish Lawyers Association, Hamburg; International Bar Association (SBL(A)) ; American Trial Lawyers Association; Mediterranean Maritime Arbitration Association; German High School Alumni Association. *LANGUAGES:* Turkish, German and English.

ASSOCIATES

MAHMUT KARAMAN, born Sinop, Turkey, September 17, 1962; admitted, 1990, Istanbul. *Education:* Merchant Marine Academy (Licence, 1983); University of Istanbul Faculty of Law (Licence, 1989). Author: "Legal Regime of Territorial Waters and International Sea," Seahorse, Journal of State Maritime Academy Alumni Association, Volumes 2-3, 4-5, 1992. Marine Chief Engineer: D.B. Turkish Cargo Lines, 1983-1984; Turkish Maritime Lines, 1986-1992. *Member:* Turkish Maritime Law Association;

(This Listing Continued)

AYBAY & AYBAY, Istanbul—Continued

State Maritime Academy Alumni Association; Chamber of Marine Engineers. *LANGUAGES:* Turkish and English.

BARIS AYBAY, born Istanbul, Turkey, July 13, 1966; admitted, 1991, Istanbul. *Education:* University of Ankara Faculty of Law (Licence, 1990). *LANGUAGES:* Turkish and English.

CONSULTANTS

ATILLA AYBAY, born Istanbul, Turkey, March 4, 1927. *Education:* University of Istanbul School of Economics; University of Kansas, 1959-1960; Fulbright Scholar, 1959-1960. Eisenhower Fellow, 1970. Vice-President, TKI, 1966-1972. Director, Turkish Bureau of Mines, 1972-1975. Chairman and President, ETIBANK, 1975 and 1978-1979. Consultant, Economics and Foreign Business Relations, Aybay & Aybay, 1981—. Director, Aybay Foundation for Legal Studies. *Member:* Association of Administrators; Alumni Association School of Economics; Touring and Automobile Club; Propeller Club; Association of Salzburg Seminar Fellows in Turkey; Economic and Social Studies Conference Board. *LANGUAGES:* Turkish and English.

BULENT EROL, born Bursa, Turkey, March 16, 1931. *Education:* Maritime Academy of Istanbul (Licence, 1953); University of Wales of Cardiff (British Council Scholar, 1968-1969). Assistant Traffic Manager, Turkish Cargo Lines, 1965-1978. Assistant European Representative, Turkish Cargo Lines, 1969-1974. Assistant General Manager, DITAS, 1979-1983. Consultant, Shipping Group of ASLAN, 1987-1990. *Member:* Maritime Academy Alumni Association; Circle d'Orient; Fenerbahce Club. *LANGUAGES:* Turkish and English.

ASSISTANTS

FEYZI ERCIN. *Education:* University of Istanbul, Faculty of Law (Graduated, 1993).

GULISTAN BALTACI. *Education:* University of Izmir, Faculty of Law (Graduated, 1993).

GOKSEL GEZER. *Education:* University of Istanbul, Faculty of Law (Graduated, 1993).

Languages: Turkish, English, German and French

CEBE & BEKEM
LAW FIRM

Established in 1952

ENIS AKAYGEN SOK. BIRLIK APT.
3/4 VISNEZADA - MACKA
80680 ISTANBUL, TURKEY
Telephone: (212) 227 73 33; (212) 258 64 42
Fax: (212) 258 64 42

Civil Law, Civil Litigation, Economic Law, Corporate Law, Insurance Law and Commercial Papers to Contracts, Leasing, Law concerning Investment and Establishment of Foreign Companies and Banks, Joint Ventures, Real Estate Purchase, Mortgages, Hypothecs, Successions, Creditors Rights of Debt, Recovery, Intellectual Property, Copyright, Unfair Trade, Unfair Competition, International Transportation, Inheritance, Shipping Law, Damage Claims, Bill of Leading and Charterparty Disputes.

FIRM PROFILE: The firm was established in 1952 and offers legal counselling as well as full litigation services and has clients from USA, UK, Europe as well as local clients. The Firm's field of expertise ranges from civil law, economic law, foreign investments and incentives, establishment of foreign companies and banks, commercial, corporate, intellectual property, copyright, trademarks, international commercial arbitration, debt recovery and maritime law.

MEMBERS OF THE FIRM

ORHAN CEBE, born Istanbul, Turkey, March 21, 1918; admitted, 1951, Turkey. *Education:* Ankara Lycee. Law Faculty, University of Ankara. *Member:* Istanbul Bar Association. *LANGUAGES:* Turkish, English, French. *PRACTICE AREAS:* Intellectual Property; International Commercial practice; Arbitration.

CIGDEM CEBE BEKEM, born Ankara, Turkey, March 4; admitted, 1985, Turkey. *Education:* Ankara College. Law Faculty, University of Istanbul. *Member:* Istanbul Bar Association. *LANGUAGES:* Turkish, English

(This Listing Continued)

---

glish. *PRACTICE AREAS:* Joint Venture; Foreign Investments; Commercial and Corporate Law; Unfair Competition; Trademarks Copyright; General Trade Litigation.

CERRAHOĞLU ETÜD VE *MÜŞAVIRLIK*
A.Ş.

(Consulting Services Inc.)

Established in 1981

ŞEHIT MUHTAR CADDESI 26/6
80090 TAKSIM
ISTANBUL, TURKEY
Telephone: (212) 250 52 85; (212) 250 04 17
Telex: 25521 FCR TR
Fax: (212) 250 32 84

Business, Commercial, Execution, Bankruptcy, Labor, Taxation, Banking, Criminal Law and Foreign Investment.

MEMBERS OF FIRM

PROF. DR. M. FADLULLAH CERRAHOĞLU, born Hendek, Turkey, April 30, 1941; admitted, 1973, Istanbul. *Education:* University of Istanbul Law School (License, 1965); Marmara University (Doctor, 1971). Dean: School of Journalism, 1975-1976; Faculty of Technical Education, 1985-1987. Professor of Commercial Law: Bosphorus University, 1978-1983; Marmara University, 1980—. Trustee of the Robert College of Istanbul, 1982-1985. *Member:* Istanbul Bar Association. (Also of Counsel to White & Case, New York, New York). *LANGUAGES:* Turkish and English.

DR. BEKIR AROMA, born 1942. *Education:* Marmara University, (Business, 1966). *LANGUAGES:* English, Turkish and French.

SIBEL M. YURTTUTAN, born 1964. *Education:* University of London (LL.B., hons.). *LANGUAGES:* Turkish, English and French.

COUNSEL

DR. KÖKSAL BAYRAKTAR, Admitted Istanbul Bar, 1980. Professor of Criminal Law. *LANGUAGES:* Turkish and French. *PRACTICE AREAS:* Criminal Law.

DR. ADNAN TEZEL, Admitted Istanbul Bar, 1967. Professor of Taxation Law. *LANGUAGES:* Turkish and English. *PRACTICE AREAS:* Tax Law.

DR. NURI ÇELIK, Admitted Istanbul Bar. Professor of Labor Law. *LANGUAGES:* German and Turkish. *PRACTICE AREAS:* Labor Law.

ASSOCIATES

SELALE KARTAL, born 1954; admitted, 1977, Istanbul. *Education:* University of Istanbul Law School. *LANGUAGES:* Turkish and English.

FATIH VOLKAN, born 1958; admitted, 1985, Istanbul. *Education:* University of Istanbul Law School (1983). *LANGUAGES:* Turkish.

ALEV G. TOPSAKAL, born 1966; admitted, 1992, Istanbul. *Education:* University of Istanbul Law School. *LANGUAGES:* Turkish and English.

GÜLPERI S. YÖÜKER, born 1969; admitted, 1993, Istanbul. *Education:* University of Istanbul Law School (1990); American University (LL.M., 1992). *LANGUAGES:* Turkish and English.

GÜLPERI SAHBAL, born 1969. *Education:* University of Istanbul Law School (LL.M.); The American University. *LANGUAGES:* Turkish and English.

EMINE ERENSOY, born 1967; admitted, 1993, Istanbul. *Education:* University of Istanbul Law School. *Member:* Istanbul Bar Association. *LANGUAGES:* Turkish and English.

Languages: Turkish and English.

(This Listing Continued)

Switzerland; CMB, France; Harlequin Enterprises, Canada; SEB International, France; SCB Leisure, Spain-Holland; Euro Market; Grecian Magnesite, Greece; SAS Service Partner, Denmark; Chiquita Brands International, USA; NRG International, British Isles; Ottoman Bank (Turkey); Autoliv (Sweden); Electrolux (Sweden); Allgon (Sweden); Swiss Bank International (Switzerland); Baxter (USA); Hughes Network Systems (USA); Carnaudmetalbox (France); SEB Development (France); Louis Leitz Ivo GmbH & Co. (Germany); PPG Industries International, Inc. (France); Laboratoire Guerbet (France).

DINAR LAW OFFICES

SET USTU DERYA HAN, KABATAŞ

ISTANBUL, TURKEY

Telephone: (90-212) 245 01 83; (90-212) 245 01 84

Telecopier: (90-212) 249 48 10

Telex: 25514 JUR TR Cable Addresses: Mordodinar Istanbul; Congechile Istanbul

Commercial and Civil Law, Corporate Law, European Common Market Laws and Jurisprudence, Investments, Joint Ventures, Transfer of Technology, Franchise and Licensing, Private and Public International Law, Arbitrations, Fiscality relating to the above.

MORDO DINAR, born Istanbul, Turkey; admitted, 1947, Istanbul. *Education:* College of Galatasaray and Faculty of Law, University of Istanbul. Honorary Consul General of Chile in Turkey, 1955—. *Member:* Istanbul Bar Association; American Bar Association; American Arbitration Association.

Languages: Turkish, French, English, Spanish, Italian and Portuguese

REPRESENTATIVE CLIENTS: Bristol-Myers Squibb; Continental Grain Co.; Pepsico, Inc.; Digital Equipment Corp.; CBS, Inc.; Warner-Lambert, Inc.; Fremantle/Talbot, NBA; Pechiney; Club Mediterranée; Yves Saint-Laurent; Peugeot Citroen Group; GEC Alsthom; Synthelabo; Sony; Mitsui; Alenia S.p.A.; Meridien Group; Svenska Handelsbanken.

GAYRET CONSULTANT SERVICES

Established in 1985

ABDÜLHAKHAMIT CADDESI 34

TAKSIM

ISTANBUL 80090, TURKEY

Telephone: (90-212) 235-4151; 235-4152

Telecopier: (90-212) 253-5262

Matters of Industrial and Intellectual Property, Joint Ventures and Technology Transfers. Representations before Governmental Agencies, Administrative Appeals and Litigations. Pharmaceutical, Corporate, Financing and Labor Laws. Debt Collection.

FIRM PROFILE: Our firm has profound experience in pharmaceutical companies: Creation, development, management of articles of associations, partnership directors; Registration, cancelling and transferring permits, unfair competition. Our firm also can investigate the financial statute of the commercial firms.

OSMAN MACIT SÖYLEMEZ, born Istanbul, Turkey, March 22, 1948; admitted, 1978, Ankara; 1979, Istanbul. *Education:* Ankara University Law School (LL.B., 1976). Assistant Commercial Counsellor, Dutch Embassy of Turkey, Ankara, Turkey, 1975-1977. Consultant, Kiska Holding Company, Ankara, Turkey, 1975-1979. Corporate Counsel, Ottoman Bank (Affiliate with Banque de Paribas), Istanbul, Turkey, 1979-1985. *Member:* Istanbul Bar Association; Association Commerciale Turquie-France; Galatasaraylilar Derneği; Grand Lodge of Free and Accepted Masons of Turkey; Propeller Club; Union Internationale des Avocats.

Languages: Turkish, English and French

REPRESENTATIVE CLIENTS: Servier; Pasteur Merieux; UCB; Farmitalia Carlo Erba affiliate with Kabi Pharmacia ; Guerbet; Runlite; ABN-AMRO, Hollandsche Bank Unie N.V.; Banca di Roma; T.C. Ziraat Bankasi; Pyramid Stock Exchange; Swarovski; Hotelplan, Horizonte; DHL; Technology Marketing Group; Aksan; Tenex.

MEHMET GÜN & CO.

Established in 1988

ZINCIRLIKUYU KOREŞEHITLERI CAD.

NO: 30, KAT 4, DAIRE: 13

ISTANBUL, TURKEY

Telephone: (212) 288 52 32/ 288 52 33/ 275 90 03/ 274 49 21

Fax: (212) 274 20 95

Intellectual Property, Patent, Trademark and Copyright, Unfair Competition and Litigation, Distributorship, Mergers and Acquisitions, Joint Ventures, Consortiums, International Leasing, Agency and Franchise Law, Foreign Investments, International Commercial Arbitration, International Contracts, Shipping Law, International Trade, Corporation Law, Trade Regulations, Arbitration, Maritime Law, Administrative Law, Customs, and Excise Law, Property and Real Estate Law, General Practice.

FIRM PROFILE: The firm was established in 1988, offers a full range of legal services and has clients from USA, UK, Europe and Russia including Balkan states as well as local clients. Firm concentrates mostly on Foreign Investments, Commercial, Corporate, Intellectual Property, Copyright, International Banking and Finance, Joint Ventures, Consortiums, International Leasing, International Trade, International Commercial Arbitration, Shipping Law (Damage Claims, Bill of Lading and Charterparty Disputes), Maritime Law (Ship Mortgages, Salvage, Towage, Admiralty Jurisdiction), Bankruptcy and Insolvency.

MEMBERS OF THE FIRM

MEHMET GÜN, born Konya, Turkey, April 28, 1959; admitted, 1976, Istanbul. *Education:* Teaching College Çanakkale; Faculty of Law, University of Istanbul. Author: Essay on, "Responsibilities of Owners in Time-Charters"; Essay on, "Recognition, Enforcement and Execution of Foreign Arbitral Awards in Turkey"; Study on, "Necessary Amendments to Turkish Trade Marks Act", in View of the Paris Convention. *Member:* Istanbul Bar Association. *LANGUAGES:* Turkish and English. *PRACTICE AREAS:* Intellectual Property; Unfair Competition; Franchising; Copyright; International Commercial Practice; Arbitration; Maritime Law.

SELMA TOPLU, born Eskişehir, Turkey, July 31, 1968; admitted, 1991, Istanbul. *Education:* Izmit Lycee, Law Faculty, Marmara University. *Member:* Istanbul Bar Association. *LANGUAGES:* Turkish and English. *PRACTICE AREAS:* Patents, Trademarks, Copyright; General Trade Litigation; Real Estate Law; Unfair Competition.

NEYYIR KITAPCI, born Ankara, Turkey, January 1, 1962; admitted, 1987, Turkey. *Education:* University of Istanbul, Faculty of Law; University of Kent at Canterbury (Diploma, International Commercial Law). *Member:* Istanbul Bar Association. *LANGUAGES:* Turkish and English. *PRACTICE AREAS:* Banking Law; Bankruptcy and Insolvency; Joint Venture; Consortiums; Leasing; Corporate Law.

METIN ÇALIŞ, born Muğla, Turkey, January 1, 1968; admitted, 1990, Turkey. *Education:* University of Istanbul, Faculty of Law. *Member:* Istanbul Bar Association. *LANGUAGES:* Turkish and English. *PRACTICE AREAS:* Commercial and Corporate; Contract Law; Business Law; Foreign Investments; Intellectual Property; Unfair Competition.

VOLKAN HIDAYETOĞLU, born Zonguldak, Turkey, August 23, 1969; admitted, 1994, Turkey. *Education:* Kadiköy Anatolian High School; Istanbul University Faculty of Law; Marmara University E.C. Institute (M.A.); University of London (LL.M., International Business Law). Author: Essay, "The Jurisdiction of the Arbitrators in International Arbitration." *Member:* Maarifliler Cemiyeti. *LANGUAGES:* Turkish, English and German. *PRACTICE AREAS:* International Commercial Arbitration; Complete International Trade Law; Shipping Law; Maritime Law; E.C. Law.

ASSOCIATES

HALIL CEVAT YAYLALI, born September 8, 1944, Istanbul, Turkey; admitted, 1977, Istanbul. *Education:* Galatasaray College, Istanbul Law Faculty, Law Faculty of Paris University. *Member:* Istanbul Bar Association. *LANGUAGES:* Turkish and French. *PRACTICE AREAS:* General Commercial Practice.

Languages: Turkish, English, French and German

REPRESENTATIVE CLIENTS: Polly Peck Int. Plc. Administration; Bulfracht Shipbrokers; Procter and Gamble AG; Kmart Co.; Sagra Group of Companies; Enak Brokering Co.; C.A. Blockers Inc.; Karginlar Co.; Kendir Keten T.A.s.-;Deka Maritime Co.; Reklamlar; Denge Film Making; Abbott Laboratories, Turkey; Dyteks Turkey; Baush & Lomb, Inc.; Von Hogen Car Rental; Sagra Special Franchising; Marsch Import Export Germany; The Henley Group Inc.; Pall Italia Srl.; All Union Sovexportfilm; Wynn's International Inc.; The Publish-

(This Listing Continued)

MEHMET GÜN & CO., Istanbul—Continued

ers Association, UK; Simon & Schuster, UK; Zinser Gmbh, Reuters, Tesmo-Don, Cambridge University Press; Oxford University Press, UK; Logman Group, UK; McMillan Press Ltd., UK; MacMillan Inc., USA; Mc Graw-Hill USA; Harcourt Brace, John Wiley & Sons, Heinemann, Mosby Year Book, Addison Wesley.

REFERENCES: Cameron Markby Hewitt, UK; Coopers & Lybrand, UK; Lawrence & Graham, UK; Sagra Gida A.S. Ordu/Turkey; Nordelbe GmbH., Germany; Nupra Nut Products Wien and Hamburg; Belgo Factors, Belgium; Alexander, Unikel, Zalewa & Tenenbaum U.S.A.; Gükçe Industry, Turkey; Samuel & Partner, Germany, Turkey; Vinge, Sweden.

HERGÜNER, BILGEN, PAKSOY & GÜRCAN

Established in 1988

INÖNÜ CAD. MITHATPASA APT. 92-94 KAT 2 D.4
ISTANBUL, TURKEY
Telephone: 2453939, 2435225
Telex: 27624 biln tr
Fax: 2452121

Contracts, Corporate Law, International Business Transactions, International Franchising and Licensing, Banking Law, Maritime Law, Foreign Investment Law, Collection Law and Litigation, International Dispute Settlement, Law of Securities and Financings, Energy Law, Privatiation Law.

FIRM PROFILE: *The firm offers a full range of legal services. It is well known for its expertise in any matter involving an international business transaction. The client base is European, North American and Japanese in scope.*

MEMBERS OF FIRM

MS. AYSE BILGEN, born 1959; admitted, 1981, Turkey. *Education:* Istanbul University School of Law (Law Diploma, 1980; Graduate Legal Studies, 1980-1982). Sole practice, 1981-1988. *Member:* Istanbul Bar Association; Young Businessmen Association of Turkey; State Planing Organization Permanent Special Commission on Turkish-EC Legislation Harmonization; Istanbul Catalceşme Lions Club. *LANGUAGES:* French (reading).

MR. ÜMIT HERGÜNER, born 1957; admitted, 1980, Turkey. *Education:* Istanbul University School of Law (Law Diploma, 1979; Graduate Legal Studies, 1980-1982); Georgetown University International Law Institute (Certificate Study on the US Legal System, 1983); Washington College of Law, The American University (LL.M., International Legal Studies, 1984); Internship at International Finance Corporation (World Bank), Legal Department, Spring, 1984; University of Virginia School of Law (LL.M., 1985). Recipient: Dupont Fellowship, 1984-1985; Fulbright Scholarship, 1983-1985; Stipendium, granted by Goethe Institut, Göttingen, Germany, 1980. Assistant Professor of Public International Law, Istanbul University School of Law, 1981-1984. Lecturer on International Business Law, Koc University, Faculty of Economies and Administrative Sciences, MBA Program, 1955. Lecturer on International Business and Organization, Marmara University, School of Business Administration (English Section), 1989-1990. Special Counsel on Foreign Law, Reid & Priest, Attorneys at Law, New York, USA, 1985-1988. *Member:* Istanbul Bar Association; American Bar Association (International Associate); International Bar Association; American Turkish Friendship Council; American Society of International Law; The Propeller Club of the U.S. Port of Istanbul, Turkey; Istanbul Suadiye Rotary Club; Turkish- American Businessmen Association; Blackseatrade Inc. (Member, Board of Directors). *LANGUAGES:* English, German (reading) and French (reading).

MR. SERDAR PAKSOY, born 1962; admitted, 1985, Turkey. *Education:* Istanbul University School of Law (Law Diploma, 1984); Istanbul University School of Business (Graduate Program in International Management, English Section, 1987); Southampton University, Institute of Maritime Law (18th Maritime Law Course). Author: "Franchising in Turkey," International Franchising Law, Matthew Bender Company, 1993. Sole practice, 1985-1988. Foreign Law Associate, Reid & Priest, Attorneys at Law, New York, USA, 1988-1989. *Member:* Istanbul Bar Association; International Bar Association; Inter-Pacific Bar Association; Turkish Franchise Association (Member of the Board of Directors); The British Chamber of Commerce of Turkey; JCI, Jaycees Young Entrepreneurs Organization of Turkey; Association of Fellows and Legal Scholars of the Center for International Legal Studies, Salzburg, Austria (Honorary Member). *LANGUAGES:* English.

(This Listing Continued)

MR. CÜNEYD GÜRCAN, born 1954; admitted, 1982, Turkey. *Education:* Istanbul University School of Law (Law Diploma, 1979; Graduate Legal Studies, 1981-1983; Master of Laws Degree). Sole Practice, 1990-1992. General Counsel, Holantse Bank-Uni N.V. - Istanbul, 1983-1990. Lecturer, Ministry of Tourism, 1990. Assistant Professor, Commercial Law, Marmara University School of Business Administration, 1979-1983. *Member:* Istanbul Bar Association; French Chamber of Commerce of Turkey; Saint Benoit Association; Association of Professional Guides; Moda Maritime Club. *LANGUAGES:* French, English (reading) and Italian (reading).

ASSOCIATES

MR. ERHAN BAKI SELEK, born 1963; admitted, 1992, Turkey. *Education:* Istanbul German High School (1984); Istanbul University School of Law (Law Diploma, 1990). Assistant Professor of Public International Law, Marmara University School of Law, 1991-1992. *Member:* Istanbul Bar Association. *LANGUAGES:* German and English.

MR. TOLGA DANIŞMAN, born 1964; admitted, 1994, Turkey. *Education:* Istanbul Saint Benoit French High School for Boys (1985); Istanbul University School of Law (Law Diploma, 1992). Insurance Agent for Turkish subsidiary of La Preservatrice Fonciere Assurances (PFA), 1985-1990. *Member:* Saint Benoit Association; ELSA-European Law Students Association-Turkey. *LANGUAGES:* French and English (reading).

MS. AYSE DAI, born 1967; admitted, 1990. *Education:* Carleton University, Ottawa, Canada (Certificate of ESL, 1991; Istanbul University School of Law (Law Diploma, 1989). Sole Practice (1992-1994). *Member:* Istanbul Bar Association; Cobro International de Morosos, Barcelona, Spain (Organization of International Lawyers). *LANGUAGES:* English, French (reading).

MS. ESIN TABOĞLU, born 1965; admitted, 1987, Turkey. *Education:* Harvard University School of Law (LL.M., 1990); Istanbul University School of Law (Law Diploma, 1986). Legal Advisor, Set Group Holding A.S., Turkey (1990-1994). Member, of the Board of Directors, Harvard Club-Istanbul. *Member:* Istanbul Bar Association. *LANGUAGES:* English.

KARAKO LAW OFFICE

RUMELI CAD. ZAFER SOK. 55/9
NISANTASI
80220 ISTANBUL, TURKEY
Telephone: (90-212) 230 40 28; (90-212) 231 72 39
Telefax: (90-212) 231 91 09

Commercial and Civil Law, International Business and Investments, Corporations, Tax Matters, Labour Law, Litigations, Real Estate, Public and Private International Matters.

MEMBERS OF FIRM

NEDIM KARAKO, born Istanbul, Turkey, 1945. *Education:* Istanbul University (1967). Advocate and Attorney-at-Law. *Member:* Istanbul Bar Association and International Union of Lawyers. *LANGUAGES:* English and French.

ERSOY YÜCE, born Diyadin-Ağri, Turkey, November 8, 1969. *Education:* Istanbul Marmara Law School (1992).

Languages: English and French.

REPRESENTATIVE CLIENTS: Pakistan Airlines, Int. Mars Corporation, The Belgium Societe General de Bank, Dikarpa Leather Company, Step Ltd., Office National de Ducroire Prayon de Pauw, Telemecanique, Clement Magasins Generaux, Leroy-Somer Intermetro, Valtur.

McDERMOTT, WILL & EMERY

BÜYÜKDERE CADDESI
YAPI KREDI PLAZA
"C" BLOK, KAT. 8, NO. 23/A
ISTANBUL 80620, TURKEY
Telephone: 90-212-2702077
Fax: 90-212-2703457

International Practice.

MARY BELLE FELTENSTEIN, born Chicago, Illinois, July 3, 1947; admitted, 1976, New York; 1978, Florida; 1983, Massachusetts (Not admitted in Turkey). *Education:* Harvard University (B.A., 1969); University of Chicago, Graduate School of Business; Columbia University (J.D.,

(This Listing Continued)

MEMBERS OF FIRM

NOYAN TURUNÇ, born Izmir, Turkey, July 16, 1948; admitted, 1975, Turkey. *Education:* Law School of Ankara (LL.B., 1971; LL.M., 1980). *Member:* Izmir Bar Association; International Bar Association. (Also at Izmir, Turkey Office). *LANGUAGES:* Turkish and English.

MUSTAFA BOZCAADALI, born Ankara, Turkey, February 2, 1945; admitted, 1973, Turkey. *Education:* Law School of Ankara (LL.B., 1971; LL.M., 1980). *Member:* Ankara Bar Association. *LANGUAGES:* Turkish and English.

SIMHAN SAVAŞÇIN, born Ankara, Turkey, April 23, 1962; admitted, 1985, Turkey. *Education:* Law School of Izmir (LL.B., 1984). *Member:* Izmir Bar Association. *LANGUAGES:* Turkish and English.

ADNAN TÖRE, born Ankara, Turkey, April 15, 1943. *Education:* Law School of Ankara (LL.B., 1967). *LANGUAGES:* Turkish and English.

FÜSUN BOLDAG, born Adiyaman, Turkey, March 23, 1966; admitted, 1987, Turkey. *Education:* Law School of Istanbul (LL.B., 1986). *Member:* Istanbul Bar Association. *LANGUAGES:* Turkish and English.

(For biographical data on other personnel, see Professional Biographies at Izmir, Turkey and Ankara, Turkey).

WHITE & CASE

MAYA AKAR CENTER
BUYUKDERE CADDESI 101-102
B BLOK, KAT 17
80280 ESENTEPE
ISTANBUL, TURKEY
Telephone: (90-212) 275-75-33; (90-212) 275-68-98
Facsimile: (90-212) 275-75-43

New York, New York: Telephone: 212-819-8200. Facsimile: 212-354-8113.
Washington, D.C.: Telephone: 202-872-0013. Facsimile: 202-872-0210.
Los Angeles, California: Telephone: 213-620-7700. Facsimile: 213-687-0758; 213-617-2205.
Miami, Florida: Telephone: 305-371-2700. Facsimile: 305-358-5744.
Mexico City, Mexico: Telephone: (52-5) 207-9717. Facsimile: (52-5) 208-3628.
Tokyo, Japan: Telephone: (81-3) 3239-4300. Facsimile: (81-3) 3239-4330.
Hong Kong: Telephone: (852) 2822-8700. Facsimile: (852) 2845-9070; Grice & Co., Solicitors, Telephone: (852) 2826-0333. Facsimile: (852) 2526-7166.
Singapore, Republic of Singapore: Telephone: (65) 225-6000. Facsimile: (65) 225-6009.
Bangkok, Thailand: Pacific Legal Group Ltd., In Association With White & Case, Telephone: (662) 236-6154/7. Facsimile: (662) 237-6771.
Hanoi, Viet Nam: Representative Office, Telephone: (84-4) 227-575/6/7. Facsimile: (84-4) 227-297.
Bombay, India: Telephone: (91-22) 282-6300. Facsimile: (91-22) 282-6305.
London, England: Telephone: (44-171) 726-6361. Facsimile: (44-171) 726-4314; (44-171) 726-8558.
Paris, France: Telephone: (33-1) 42-60-34-05. Facsimile: (33-1) 42-60-82-46.
Brussels, Belgium: Telephone: (32-2) 647-05-89. Facsimile: (32-2) 647-16-75.
Stockholm, Sweden: Telephone: (46-8) 679-80-30. Facsimile: (46-8) 611-21-22.
Helsinki, Finland: Telephone: (358-0) 631-100. Facsimile: (358-0) 179-477.
Moscow, Russia: Telephone: (7-095) 201-9292/3/4/5. Facsimile: (7-095) 201-9284.
Budapest, Hungary: Telephone: (36-1) 269-0550; (36-1) 131-0933. Facsimile: (36-1) 269-1199.
Prague, Czech Republic: Telephone: (42-2) 2481-1796. Facsimile: (42-2) 232-5522.
Warsaw, Poland: Telephone/Facsimile: (48-22) 26-80-53; (48-22) 27-84-86. International Telephone/Facsimile: (48-39) 12-19-06.
Ankara, Turkey: Telephone: (90-312) 446-2180. Facsimile: (90-312) 437-9677.
Jeddah, Saudi Arabia: Law Office of Hassan Mahassni, Telephone: (966-2) 651-3535. Facsimile: (966-2) 651-3636.
Riyadh, Saudi Arabia: Law Office of Hassan Mahassni, Telephone: (966-1) 476-7099. Facsimile: (966-1) 479-0110.

(This Listing Continued)

Almaty, Kazakhstan: Telephone: (7-3272) 50-7491/2. Facsimile: (7-3272) 61-0842.

General International Practice.

RESIDENT PARTNER

ASLI F. BASGOZ, born Ankara, Turkey, August 24, 1957; admitted, 1984, New York (Not admitted in Turkey). *Education:* Indiana University (B.A., 1979); University of Dijon (1980); University of Michigan (J.D., 1983). *Member:* American Bar Association.

RESIDENT COUNSEL

PROF. DR. M. FADLULLAH CERRAHOĞLU, born Hendek, Turkey, April 30, 1941; admitted, 1973, Istanbul. *Education:* University of Istanbul Law School (License, 1965); Marmara University (Doctor, 1971). Professor of Commercial Law, Marmara University, 1980—. *Member:* Istanbul Bar Association. (Also Member, Cebe & Bekem Law Firm).

RESIDENT ASSOCIATES

SEBNEM ISIK KAPLANOGLU, born Mersin, Turkey, February 2, 1969; admitted, 1993, Istanbul. *Education:* Istanbul University Faculty of Law (J.D., 1992).

REFIKA TULAY TUZUN, born Antalya, Turkey, July 26, 1967; admitted, 1993, Istanbul. *Education:* Ankara University Faculty of Law (LL.B., 1988).

ALDORU ULUATAM, born Berkeley, California, June 25, 1965; admitted, 1992, New York (Not admitted in Turkey). *Education:* University of Maryland (B.A., 1988); Cornell University (J.D., 1991).

DENIZ ULUSOY, born Siirt, April 30, 1964; admitted, 1986, Istanbul. *Education:* Istanbul University Faculty of Law (1981-1986).

MELTEM USLUAKOL, born Istanbul, Turkey, February 18, 1970; admitted, 1991, Turkey. *Education:* Istanbul University (1987-1991).

CAN VERDI, born Mersin, Turkey, September 9, 1961; admitted, 1986, Mersin. *Education:* Ege University Law Faculty (LL.B., 1985); Boston University School of Law (LL.M., 1989).

CHRISTOPHER G. WILKINSON, born Amsterdam, New York, March 6, 1962; admitted, 1991, New York (Not admitted in Turkey). *Education:* Yale University (B.A., 1985); Columbia University (J.D., 1990).

SERAP ZUVIN, born Nevsehir, Turkey, October 13, 1960; admitted, 1988, Istanbul. *Education:* University of Istanbul, Law Faculty (1986). *Member:* Istanbul Bar Association.

(For biographical data as to other locations, see Professional Biographies at New York, New York; Washington, D.C.; Los Angeles, California; Miami, Florida; Mexico City, Mexico; Tokyo, Japan; Hong Kong; Singapore, Republic of Singapore; Bangkok, Thailand; Hanoi, Viet Nam; Bombay, India; London, England; Paris, France; Brussels, Belgium; Stockholm, Sweden; Helsinki, Finland; Moscow, Russia; Budapest, Hungary; Prague, Czech Republic; Warsaw, Poland; Ankara, Turkey; Jeddah and Riyadh, Saudi Arabia; Almaty, Kazakhstan).

DUYGUN YARSUVAT & ÖMÜR YARSUVAT LAW OFFICES

HACI ADIL SOK 44
2. LEVENT
ISTANBUL 80620, TURKEY
Telephone: 90 212 282 45 03; 212 282 7898
Telecopier: 90 212 282 7910

New York, New York-Affiliated Office: Walter, Conston, Alexander & Green P.C. 90 Park Avenue, 10016-1387.

Corporate and Commercial Law including media law, finance, mergers & acquisitions, intellectual property and litigation.

DR. DUYGUN YARSUVAT, born Istanbul, 1937; admitted, 1966, Istanbul. *Education:* University of Istanbul School of Law (J.D., Equiv., 1961; Dr.Iur., 1966); Columbia University School of Law (M.C.L., 1967). Professor of Penal Law, Press Law, 1972—. Professor of Intellectual Property Law (University of Istanbul: School of Law, Marmara University, School of Journalism, School of Law); Director, Chair of Legal Studies, University of Istanbul, School of Political Sciences, 1983—. *Member:* Istanbul Bar Association; Galatasaraylilar Dernegi (President). *LANGUAGES:* French and English.

(This Listing Continued)

DUYGUN YARSUVAT & ÖMÜR YARSUVAT LAW OFFICES, Istanbul—Continued

ÖMÜR YARSUVAT, born Istanbul, 1962; admitted, 1990, New York; 1992, Istanbul. *Education:* University of Istanbul School of Law (J.D. equiv. 1985); Columbia University School of Law (LL.M., 1987). *Member:* The Bar Association of the City of New York; American Bar Association; Alman Liseliler Dernegi. *LANGUAGES:* English and German.

AYSE N. YARSUVAT, born Istanbul, 1940; admitted, 1968, Istanbul. *Education:* University of Istanbul School of Law (J.D., equiv., 1963). Southwestern Legal Foundation, Academy of International Comparative Law Seminar, 1980. *Member:* Istanbul Bar Association. *LANGUAGES:* English.

MÜMTAZ EZDIL, born 1937; admitted, 1970, Istanbul. *Education:* University of Istanbul, School of Law (J.D., equiv., 1961). *Member:* Istanbul Bar Association.

KAYHAN AYDEMIR, born 1968; admitted, 1991, Istanbul. *Education:* University of Istanbul School of Law (J.D/ equiv., 1980); Marmara University School of Law (European Community Law, 1991—). *Member:* Istanbul Bar Association. *LANGUAGES:* English.

OF COUNSEL

DR. PERTEV BILGEN, admitted, 1983, Istanbul. *Education:* University of Istanbul School of Law (J.D., equiv. 1958; Ph.D., 1968). Professor, Administrative Law, 1974—. Dean, University of Istanbul School of Political Sciences, 1993—. Consultant to the Turkish State Television Network, 1993. Chairman, Chair of Administrative Legal Studies, University of Istanbul School of Law, 1992. *Member:* Istanbul Bar Association. *LANGUAGES:* English.

HALÛK ÜNDES, born 1959; admitted, 1984, Istanbul. *Education:* University of Istanbul School of Law (J.D. equiv., 1981). *Member:* Istanbul Bar Association. *LANGUAGES:* English.

Commercial Law Affiliates: (A Woldwide Affiliation of Independent Business and Litigation Firms) 420 North Fifth Street, Suite 970.

References and a list of representative clients are available upon request.

YARSUVAT LAW FIRM

Established in 1947

**BÜYÜKDERE CADDESI, YAPI KREDI PLAZA
B BLOK, KAT:9, 4 LEVENT 80620
ISTANBUL, TURKEY**
*Telephone: (90-1) 268-4124/268-4139/268-4151/268-4153
Telefax: 268 41 88*

New York, New York-Affiliated Office: Walter, Conston, Alexander & Green, P.C., 90 Park Avenue, 10016-1387. Telephone: (212) 210-9400. Telefax: (212) 210-9444.

Lausanne, Switzerland-Affiliated Office: Dr. Louis Bagi, Avenue J-J. Cart 8, 1006. Telephone: (021) 275535. Telefax: (021) 264331.

Ankara-Afiliated Office: Fulya Duru. Kaptanpasa Sok. 27/2 Gaziosmanpasa-Ankara. Telephone (0312) 446-7116.

General Practice, including Corporate, Commercial, Penal, Intellectual Property, Bankruptcy, Domestic Relations, Real Estate, International Property, Banking Law, International Commercial Contracts and International Law.

MEMBERS OF THE FIRM

HÜSEYIN YARSUVAT, born 1943; admitted, 1968, Istanbul. *Education:* University of Istanbul School of Law (J.D., equiv. 1967). The Lawyer who made the discussions of the Turkey Textile Industry Employers Trade Union 1963-1967, Ministry of the Interior Gendarmery Commandership Labour and Worker Relations Partial Director 1967-1969, Istanbul Police Education Academy Penalty Procedure Teacher 1983-1990, Law Teacher of the Galatasaray High School. Member, Istanbul Stock Market, Discipline Committee (1990-1993). *Member:* Istanbul Bar Association; Galatasaraylilar Dernegi. *LANGUAGES:* French.

ASSOCIATES

KEMALEDDIN NOMER, born 1931; admitted, 1953, Istanbul. *Education:* University of Istanbul, School of Law (J.D., equiv., 1949). *Member:* Istanbul Bar Association.

(This Listing Continued)

TURGUT SENGIR, born 1926; admitted, 1951, Ankara. *Education:* University of Ankara, School Of Law (J.D., equiv., 1951); University of Paris, School of Law, Panthéon-Sorbonnc (Dr.iur., 1953). Chief Justice of 4. Commercial Court, Istanbul, 1955-1980. Arbitrator (Commercial Law). *Member:* Istanbul Bar Association; Galatasaraylilar Dernegi. *LANGUAGES:* English and French.

DR. ERDENER YURTCAN, born 1942; admitted, 1981, Istanbul. *Education:* University of Istanbul School of Law (J.D. equiv. 1966, Jur. Dr. 1972. Professor of Penal Law 1982 University of Istanbul School of Law. *Member:* Istanbul Bar Association. *LANGUAGES:* German and English.

TANER SERIM, born 1937. *Education:* University of Istanbul, School of Law (J.D., Equiv, 1961). Retired Public Prosecutor. *Member:* IFSAK.

ALI ÖZKIRIS, born 1950; admitted, 1976, Istanbul. *Education:* University of Istanbul, School of Law (J.D., eqiv., 1973). *Member:* Istanbul Bar Association. *LANGUAGES:* German.

NURTEKIN DENIZ, born 1943; admitted, 1972, Istanbul. *Education:* University of Istanbul School of Law (J.D., equiv, 1969). *Member:* Istanbul Bar Association; Foundation of the Bakirkoy Sport Club.

SAIME DALYAN, born 1955; admitted, 1980, Ankara. *Education:* University of Istanbul, School of Business Administration, Institute of Management Economics (1980). *Member:* Istanbul Bar Association; Economic and Legal Research Foundation. *LANGUAGES:* English.

SEHNAZ CELEP, born 1966; admitted, 1990, Istanbul. *Education:* University of Istanbul, School of Law (J.D., equiv., 1988). *Member:* Istanbul Bar Association.

Z. HÜLYA ÖNDER, born 1965; admitted, 1990, Istanbul. *Education:* University of Istanbul, School of Law (J.D., equiv., 1988). *Member:* Istanbul Bar Association.

TURAN YUCEL, born 1966; admitted, 1994. *Education:* University of Istanbul, School of Law (J.D., equiv. 1992). *Member:* Istanbul Bar Association, Galatasarlilar Dernegi, Sports Club of Galatasaray, ESLA, Association of Protection of Natural Life. *LANGUAGES:* French and English.

BIGE KIRAZ, born 1966; admitted, 1988, Istanbul. *Education:* University of Ankara, School of Law (J.D., equiv. 1987, master degree in private law 1990). *Member:* Istanbul Bar Association; European Association of Turkish Academics. *LANGUAGES:* English and French.

OF COUNSEL

SAIT GÜRAN, born 1936; admitted, Istanbul. *Education:* University of Istanbul, School of Law (J.D,, equiv., 1958; Dr., 1967); Columbia University of Law (M.C.L., 1963). Professor of Administrative Law, (1981—), University of Istanbul: School of Law: *Member:* Istanbul Bar Association. *LANGUAGES:* German and English.

METIN ARIYEL, admitted, 1968, Istanbul. *Education:* University of Istanbul, School of Law (J.D., equiv., 1964). *Member:* Istanbal Bar Association.

References and a List of Representative Clients is Available Upon Request.

TURUNÇ & SAVAŞÇIN

Established in 1990

**CUMHURIYET BULVARI, 140/2, K. 5
ALSANCAK
35210 IZMIR, TURKEY**
*Telephone: (232) 463 49 07; (232) 463 49 08
Fax: (232) 463 49 09*

Ankara, Turkey Office: Günes Sokak, 25/7 Kavaklidere, 06690. Telephone: (312) 428 52 80. Fax: (312) 468 19 93.

Istanbul, Turkey Office: Husrev Gerede Caddesi, 126/6, Tesvikiye, 80200. Telephone: (212) 259 45 36; (212) 259 45 37. Facsimile: (212) 259 45 38.

Foreign investment, joint ventures, commercial and corporate law, banking and financial law, securities and stock market, tax law, insurance, leasing, distribution, franchising and licensing, intellectual property including computers, food laws, labour law, property law, litigation and arbitration as well as foreign investment and joint ventures in the Russian, Federation, Azerbaijan, Kazakhstan, Kyrgyzstan, Turkmenistan, Romania and Bulgaria.

(This Listing Continued)

MEMBERS OF FIRM

NOYAN TURUNÇ, born Izmir, Turkey, July 16, 1948; admitted, 1975, Turkey. *Education:* Law School of Ankara (LL.B., 1971; LL.M., 1980). *Member:* Izmir Bar Association; International Bar Association. (Also at Istanbul, Turkey Office). *LANGUAGES:* Turkish and English.

DEMIR SAVAŞÇIN, born Nigde, Turkey, April 28, 1927; admitted, 1952, Turkey. *Education:* Law School of Ankara (LL.B., 1950); School of Administration (1958). *Member:* Izmir Bar Association. *LANGUAGES:* Turkish.

ILKER ERDEM, born Istanbul, Turkey, July 20, 1942; admitted, 1971, Turkey. *Education:* Law School of Istanbul (LL.B., 1967). *Member:* Izmir Bar Association. *LANGUAGES:* Turkish.

FUNDA BALTALI, born Fethiye, Turkey, August 22, 1962; admitted, 1986, Turkey. *Education:* Law School of Izmir (LL.B., 1985); Harvard Summer Law School (1993). *Member:* Izmir Bar Association. *LANGUAGES:* Turkish and English.

(For biographical data on other personnel, see Professional Biographies at Ankara, Turkey and Istanbul, Turkey).

SÖNMEZ LAW FIRM

Established in 1954

URAY CAD. 4/18
SEZER ISHANI
33100 MERSIN, TURKEY
Telephone: (324) 231 20 60; (324) 232 01 89; (324) 232 39 82
Fax: (324) 233 65 11

FIRM PROFILE: Established in 1954 by Kemalettin Sönmez and offers a full range of legal services. Well known in South Part of Turkey for its services in Maritime and Transport Law, Banking Law, Insurance Law, Enforcement Law, Corporate Law, General Practice and in forming Turkish companies with foreign capital including Joint Ventures, Export and Import disputes, arbitration. Firm has a legal support staff of five paralegal personnel, four legal consultants and four associate lawyers.

M. CENGIZ SÖNMEZ, admitted, 1981, Turkey. *Education:* Tarsus American College (1975); Law Faculty, Istanbul University (1979). Honorary Consul of Brazil. *LANGUAGES:* Turkish, English and Spanish.

FETHI DEMIRÖZ, admitted, 1980, Turkey. *Education:* Law Faculty, Istanbul University. *LANGUAGES:* Turkish and English.

UKRAINE

ALTHEIMER & GRAY

KONTRAKTOVA PLOSCHA 4
BUILDING 3, ROOM 304
254145 KIEV, UKRAINE
Telephone: 011-7-044-230-2534
Fax: 011-7-044-230-2535

REVISERS OF THE POLAND AND UKRAINE LAW DIGEST FOR THIS DIRECTORY.

Chicago, Illinois Office: 10 South Wacker Drive, 60606. Telephone: 312-715-4000. Fax: 312-715-4800. Telex: RCA 297102 A G UR.

Warsaw, Poland Office: ul Nowogrodzka 50, 00-950. Telephones: 011-48-22-298-357; 011-48-39-12-1338. Fax: 011-48-2-628-3640.

Prague, Czech Republic Office: Platnerska 4, 110 00 Prague 1. Telephone: 011-42-2-2481-2782. Fax: 011-42-2-2481-0125 or 232-9595.

Bratislava, Slovakia Office: Nam. SNP 15, 810 00. Telephone: 011-42-7-362-736. Fax: 011-42-7-367-960.

Istanbul, Turkey Office: Tesvikiye Cad. 107, Tesvikiye Palas 7, Tesvikiye 80200 Istanbul, Turkey. Telephone: 011-90-212-227-6750. Fax: 011-90-212-227-67598.

Privatizations and Acquisitions, Joint Ventures and Foreign Investment, Government Affairs, Real Estate Development, Architecture, Engineering and Construction, Banking and Finance, Bankruptcy, Licensing and Distribution, Insurance, Telecommunications, Securities, Taxation and Customs.

(This Listing Continued)

DIRECTOR OF KIEV OFFICE & PARTNER

JAROSLAWA ZELINSKY JOHNSON, born Brody, Ukraine; admitted, 1977, Wisconsin; 1978, Illinois and U.S. Court of Appeals, Seventh Circuit. *Education:* Goucher College (B.A., 1965); University of Wisconsin-Madison (J.D., 1977). Member, 1976 and Editor-in-Chief, 1977, Wisconsin Law Review. Author: Comment, "Equitable Remedies: An Analysis of Judicial Utilization of Neoreceivers to Implement Large Scale Institutional Change," 1976 Wisconsin Law Review 1161. Co-Author: "Bid-Rigging in the Construction Industry," Construction Bidding Law, Wiley, 1989. Law Clerk to Chief Judge Thomas E. Fairchild, U.S. Court of Appeals, Seventh Circuit, 1977-1979. Member, Panel of Arbitrators, American Arbitration Association. Co-Founder and Chair of American Ukraine Business Council, 1991—. *Member:* Chicago, Illinois State and American Bar Associations; State Bar of Wisconsin; National Association of Women in Construction. *LANGUAGES:* Ukrainian, Russian, Polish, French and English. *PRACTICE AREAS:* International Corporate.

PARTNERS

JAMES E. CARROLL, born Evanston, Illinois, July 31, 1956; admitted, 1982, Illinois (Not admitted in Ukraine). *Education:* Loras College (B.A., maxima cum laude, 1978); Cambridge University (LL.M. in International Law, 1980); Northwestern University (J.D., 1982). Delta Epsilon Sigma; Phi Alpha Theta. Member, Northwestern Journal of International Law and Business, 1981-1982. Author: "Of Icebergs, Oil Wells and Treaties: Hydrocarbon Exploitation Offshore Antarctica," 19 Stanford Journal of International Law, 1983. Co-author: "Recent Developments in Polish Insurance Law," De Paul Business Law Journal, Spring/Summer 1991. *Member:* Chicago, Illinois State, American and International Bar Associations. (Also at Chicago, Warsaw, Prague, Bratislova and Istanbul Offices). *PRACTICE AREAS:* International Law; Finance Law; Mergers and Acquisitions.

GEORGE KOVAC, born Chicago, Illinois, November 30, 1951; admitted, 1976, Illinois; 1978, Florida. *Education:* Yale University (B.A., cum laude, 1973); University of Chicago (J.D., 1976). *Member:* Chicago and American Bar Associations; The Florida Bar. *PRACTICE AREAS:* Real Estate; Real Estate Financing; Domestic and International Hotel Transactions; Gaming Regulation.

ASSOCIATES

BRADLEY J. HASKINS, born Battle Creek, Michigan, July 7, 1959; admitted, 1985, Texas; 1987, New York (Not admitted in Ukraine). *Education:* University of Michigan, Honors College (A.B., cum laude, 1982); University of Michigan (J.D., cum laude, 1985). Phi Delta Phi. Member: International Law Society, Appellate Law Program; Christian Law Students. Project Chairman, Jaycees project expanding Michigan's international trading opportunities with East Europe, Michigan to East Europe, 1991-1992. (Also at Prague Office). *PRACTICE AREAS:* Corporate; Banking; International.

YEVGENIYA V. KLYMENKO, born Kiev, Ukraine, November 10, 1972. *Education:* Kiev National University (J.D., 1994). *LANGUAGES:* Russian and English.

IHOR V. MYKHAILENKO, born Kiev, Ukraine, October 31, 1967. *Education:* Kiev State University (J.D., with honors in International Law, 1991). Lawyer, "Proxen" Law Firm, 1991-1992. Legal Department Officer, International Law and Affairs, Ukrainian Foreign Ministry, 1992-1993. Assistant to the First Deputy Foreign Minister of Ukraine, 1993-1994. *LANGUAGES:* Russian and English.

SERGEI V. ONISHCHENKO, born February 18, 1964, Kharkov, Ukraine. *Education:* Cornell Law School (LL.M., 1994); Kharkov Law Institute (diploma in jurisprudence with honors, 1988). Attorney, District Procurator's Office, 1988-1989. Law Instructor, Kharkiv Law Academy, 1990-1992. *LANGUAGES:* Ukrainian, Russian and English. *PRACTICE AREAS:* Corporate Law; Foreign Investments in Ukraine; Administrative Law.

REVISERS OF THE POLAND AND UKRAINE LAW DIGEST FOR THIS DIRECTORY.

(For complete biographical data on personnel at Chicago, Illinois, Warsaw, Poland, Prague, Czech Republic, Bratislava, Slovakia and Istanbul, Turkey see Professional Biographies at those locations)

BAKER & McKENZIE

PANKIVSKA 5
FIFTH FLOOR
KIEV, UKRAINE
Telephone: (044) 244-2964; 223-5531
Int'l Dialing: (7-044) 244-2964; 223-5531
Facsimile: (7-044) 223-6184

Associated Offices of Baker & McKenzie in: Almaty, Amsterdam, Bangkok, Barcelona, Beijing, Berlin, Bogotá, Brasília, Brussels, Budapest, Buenos Aires, Cairo, Caracas, Chicago, Dallas, Frankfurt, Geneva, Hanoi, Ho Chi Minh City, Hong Kong, Juárez, London, Madrid, Manila, Melbourne, México City, Miami, Milan, Monterrey, Moscow, New York, Palo Alto, Paris, Prague, Rio de Janeiro, Riyadh, Rome, St. Petersburg, San Diego, San Francisco, São Paulo, Singapore, Stockholm, Sydney, Taipei, Tijuana, Tokyo, Toronto, Valencia, Warsaw, Washington, D.C. and Zürich.
Correspondent Law Firm: Hadiputranto, Hadinoto & Partners, Jakarta.

Corporate, Foreign Investment, Tax, Real Estate.

PARTNER

JOHN P. HEWKO, born Detroit, Michigan, November 18, 1957; admitted, 1987, Pennsylvania, U.S.A.; 1988, District of Columbia, U.S.A. (Not admitted in Ukraine). *Education:* Hamilton College (A.B., 1979); Oxford University (M.Litt., 1981) Marshall Scholar; Harvard University (J.D., 1985). *Member:* Ukrainian-American and American Bar Associations. *LANGUAGES:* Ukrainian, Russian, Spanish, Portuguese and English.

LOCAL PARTNER

BORYS Y. DACKIW, born Hempstead, New York, August 17, 1961; admitted, 1987, New York, U.S.A. (Not admitted in Ukraine). *Education:* Georgetown University, School of Foreign Service (B.S.F.S., 1983); Columbia University Law School (J.D., 1986). *Member:* American and International Bar Associations. *LANGUAGES:* Ukrainian, French and English.

ASSOCIATES

SERHIY V. CHORNY, born Kiev, Ukraine, January 19, 1965; admitted, 1987, Ukraine. *Education:* Kiev State University (LL.B., 1987); Kiev Institute of State and Law (LL.M., 1992); University of Essex (LL.M., 1994). Secretary, Ukrainian Peace Committee, 1987. *LANGUAGES:* Ukrainian, English and Russian.

OLEKSI V. LEVENETS, born Kiev, Ukraine, March 3, 1961; admitted, 1983, Ukraine. *Education:* Kiev State University (Diploma in International Law; LL.M., 1983). Ministry of Finance, Foreign Investment Department, Deputy Head, 1990-1991. *LANGUAGES:* Ukrainian, Russian and English.

ALEXANDER MARTINENKO, born City of Saratov, Russia, December 16, 1961; admitted, 1983, Ukraine. *Education:* Kiev State University (Diploma in International Law; LL.M., 1983; Ph.D., Law, 1991); Harvard University (LL.M., 1994). Visiting Professor: Kiev Polytechnic Institute, 1990-1991; Golden Gate Law School, San Francisco, 1991-1992. *LANGUAGES:* Ukrainian, English, Russian and French.

PETER Z. TELUK, born Baltimore, Maryland, October 25, 1966; admitted, 1993, Maryland, U.S.A. (Not admitted in Ukraine). *Education:* LaSalle University (B.A., 1988); University of Pennsylvania (M.G.A., 1990); Pepperdine School of Law; University of Maryland School of Law (J.D., 1993). Order of the Coif. *LANGUAGES:* English and Ukrainian.

FRAU & PARTNERS
STUDIO LEGALE ASSOCIATO

KIBALCHICHA 12
253125 KIEV, UKRAINE
Telephone: (044) 5127292 - 5128109
Telefax: (044) 5143305

Milan Office: Via Carlo Poerio, 15, 20129. Telephone: (02) 76003199 (r.a.). Telefax: (02) 7600331.
Rome Office: Via Barberini, 29, 00187. Telephone: (06) 4871151. Telefax: (06) 4827513.
Verona Office: Pizza San Nicolõ, 3, 37121. Telephone (045) 8001533. Telefax: (045) 8003115.

International Business Law, Corporate, Banking, Financing, Syndicated Loans, Eurobonds, Commodities, Asset Finance, Bond Issues, Aircraft Finance, Leasing, Merger and Acquisitions, Project Finance. Letters of

(This Listing Continued)

Credit, Commercial Property, Securitization, Foreign Investments, Contracts, EEC, Antitrust and Competition, Real Estate, Building and Construction, International and Domestic Arbitration, International and Domestic Arbitration Litigation, International and Domestic Taxation, Aviation, Transportation, Tort and Intellectual Property, Licensing, Patent and Trademark, Distributorship, Agency and Franchising, Environmental and Media, Sport, Mining and Mineral.

AVENTINO FRAU, born Piovene, Italy, March 3, 1939; admitted, 1965 Italy; Supreme Court of Cassation. *Education:* State University of Parma (J.D., 1963). Assistant Lecturer of International Law, 1966-1968. Law and Economics Lecturer , Secretary and President, ICEPS (International Economics Corporation Institute), 1967-1978. Former President of Italian Trade Missions to Tunisia, Kenya, Somalia, Jordan, Rumania. Member of the Board, Companies involved in International Trade. Reporter at Law Conventions. Former Rapporteur for the Italian Financial Law. Member, Italian Parliament, 1972-1976. Parliament Deputy: Member, of Parliamentary Committee of Finance and Treasury; Member of Parliamentary Committee of Defence; Member of Parliamentary Committee of Finance Reform. Former Mayor of the City of Gardone Riviera, Italy. Former President of the "Comunità del Garda" (Association of the Regional areas around the Lake of Garda). Former President of ANIT (Italian Association of Tourist Cities). Vice President of "Fondazione del Vittoriale degli Italiani" (Vittoriale National Foundation). *LANGUAGES:* Italian, English and French.

(For Complete Biographical Data on all Personnel, see Professional Biographies at Milan, Italy).

FRISHBERG & PARTNERS

Established in 1991

16-22 LENIN STREET, SUITE 405
252030 KIEV, UKRAINE
Telephone: (044) 224-8314
Fax: (044) 225-6342
Internet: gfpkiev@sovamsu.sovusa.com

Real Property Transactions, Privatization, Registration of Joint Ventures, Wholly-Owned Foreign Subsidiaries and Representative Offices, Taxation and Currency Regulation Advice, Labor Relations, Intellectual Property, and Import-Export.

FIRM PROFILE: Firm offers a full range of corporate legal services. We are the largest Ukrainian law firm with foreign participation in Kiev, specializing in the areas of real real property, company formation and intellectual property.

PARTNERS

ALEXANDER FRISHBERG, born Kiev, Ukraine; admitted, 1988, Pennsylvania; 1990, District of Columbia; 1992, Ukraine; 1992, Licensed to advise on privatization matters by the Ukrainian State Property Fund. *Education:* University of Missouri, St. Louis (B.A., 1985); Washington University School of Law (J.D., 1988). Chairman, Legal, Government Relations and Economic Committee, American Chamber of Commerce in Ukraine, 1992—. Author: "Large Scale Privatization," Financial Times East European Business Law, 93-IV; "Changes for Foreign Investors," Financial Times East European Business Law, 93-5; "Ukrainian Real Property Laws," BNA's Eastern Europe Reporter, 3-11. *Member:* The District of Columbia Bar; American Bar Association (Member, International Law and Practice Section). *LANGUAGES:* English, Russian and Ukrainian. *PRACTICE AREAS:* Formation of Joint Ventures, Subsidiaries and Representative Offices; Real Estate Transfer; Privatization.

MARKIAN B. SILECKY, born September 14, 1962; admitted, 1988, Ohio, District of Columbia and U.S. District Court, Northern Districts of Ohio and New Jersey ; 1989, New Jersey; 1994, Ukraine. *Education:* University of Toledo (B.A., International Relations, 1984); Case Western Reserve University (J.D., 1987). Phi Alpha Theta, International History Honorary; Journal of International Law, Executive Board; Dunmore Moot Court Competition; Phi Delta Phi, Legal Fraternity. *Member:* American Bar Association; Ukrainian American Bar Association. *LANGUAGES:* Ukrainian, English, Russian, Spanish and German. *PRACTICE AREAS:* Real Estate; Foreign Investment; Privatization; Mergers and Acquisitions; International Corporate.

(This Listing Continued)

ASSOCIATES

BENJAMIN A. GUDIM, born Russia, 1942; admitted, 1970, Moscow. *Education:* Moscow State University, International Law Faculty (1970). *LANGUAGES:* English, Russian and Ukrainian. *PRACTICE AREAS:* Formation of Joint Ventures, Subsidiaries, and Representative Offices; Import/Export Activities.

SERGEI IVANIUK, born February 23, 1968; admitted, 1994, Ukraine. *Education:* Kiev State University, International Relations and International Law Faculty (1994); Lomonosov State University, Moscow (1988). *LANGUAGES:* English, Russian, Ukrainian and Spanish (limited knowledge, French and German). *PRACTICE AREAS:* Drafting of International Commercial Agreements, Engaging in Import/Export activities; Drafting and setting up legal and representative entities in Ukraine.

VLADIMIR LUKOVICH, born June 2, 1966; admitted, 1994, Ukraine. *Education:* Kiev State University, International Relations and International Law Faculty and the Faculty of Foreign Languages (1994). *LANGUAGES:* Russian, French and Rumanian (working knowledge of English). *PRACTICE AREAS:* Organization of Legal and Representative entities in Ukraine.

ASHLEIGH LOUFER, born London, England; admitted, 1992, Pennsylvania and Ukraine. *Education:* George Washington School of Law (J.D., with high honors, Order of the Coif); King's College, University of London (B.Sc., Mathematics and Business). Member, George Washington University Law Review. Graduated in top 1% of class, Kings College University of London. Author: "US-Ukraine Tax Treaty Signed," Financial Times East European Business Law," 94-V; "Final Version of Ukraine's Law on Patents for Inventions and Utility Models," BNA's Eastern Europe Reporter, 4-15; "The Trade and Service Mark Law," East/West Executive Guide, May 1994, vol. 4 no. 5; "Investors Should Consider Tax Treaties When Determining Where to Base Joint Venture Partner," East/West Executive Guide, March 1994, vol. 4, no. 3. *LANGUAGES:* English and Russian. *PRACTICE AREAS:* Formation of Joint Ventures and Wholly-Owned Subsidiaries; Real Estate Transactions and Intellectual Property.

ADAM M. MYCYK, born Trenton, New Jersey, June 26, 1966; admitted, 1991, Maryland; 1993, District of Colombia. *Education:* George Washington University (B.A., 1988); Catholic University of America, Columbus School of Law (J.D., 1991). Author: Comment, United States Fair Employment Law in the Transnational Employment Arena: The Case for the Extraterritorial Application of Title VII of the Civil Rights Act of 1964, 39 Catholic University Review. 1109, 1990. *Member:* American Bar Associations; the Ukrainian-American Bar Association; Maryland State Bar Association, D.C. Bar Association. *LANGUAGES:* English, Ukrainian and Russian. *PRACTICE AREAS:* International Corporate Law; Transportation Law.

MYRON B. RABIJ, born Utica, New York, May 31, 1966; admitted, 1988, Pennsylvania and New Jersey; 1993, Ukraine and Certified Privatization Consultant Ukrainian State Property Fund. *Education:* Colgate University (B.A. magna cum laude, 1988); University of Pennsylvania (J.D., 1991). Phi Beta Kappa; Pi Sigma Alpha; Phi Alpha Theta; Phi Eta Sigma. Managing Editor, Ukrainian Legal and Economic Bulletin, American Chamber of Commerce in Ukraine. Author: "Import-Export Regulation" (co-author) and "Non Profit Organizations," Financial Time East European Business Law; "Changes in Foreign Investment," East/West Executive Guide. Legal Consultant, Council of Advisors to the Parliament of Ukraine, 1991-1992. *Member:* Ukrainian-American, Pennsylvania and New Jersey Bar Associations. *LANGUAGES:* Ukrainian and English (working knowledge of Russian). *PRACTICE AREAS:* Privatization; Formation of Joint Ventures and Wholly-Owned Subsidiaries, and Import-Export.

VLADIMIR ZAKHVATAEV, born Ukraine, October 26, 1952; admitted, 1979, Ukraine. *Education:* Odessa State University, Faculty of Law (Honors, 1978); Law Center of Georgetown University (LL.M., 1994). Author: "The Preparation and Pleading of Cases on Private Accusation in Courts," Soviet Law. *LANGUAGES:* English, Russian and Ukrainian. *PRACTICE AREAS:* Intellectual Property; Formation of Joint-Ventures and Subsidiaries; Foreign Trade and Real Estate.

RESIDENT OF COUNSEL ON INTELLECTUAL PROPERTY

SEMEN PETROVICH TARTAKOVSKY, born Kiev, Ukraine, October 10, 1919. *Education:* Kiev Polytechnic Institute (1941); Military Academy (1942). *LANGUAGES:* Russian and Ukrainian. *PRACTICE AREAS:* Intellectual Property Law; Patents, Trademarks and Licensing.

REPRESENTATIVE CLIENTS: Westinghouse; Rothmans of Pall Mall (International) Limited; Digital Equipment; Intel; Honeywell; Kelloggs; Alcatel CIT; Rhone Poulenc Animal Nutrition; Hotpoint, Ltd.; Philips International; KLM

(This Listing Continued)

Royal Dutch Airlines; The Royal Dutch Embassy; The United States Embassy; The Canadian Embassy; The Royal Norwegian Embassy; Seagrams Ukraine; American Chamber of Commerce in Ukraine; Austrian Chamber of Commerce and Industry; Ernst & Young; The British Know-How Fund, among others.

JURVNESHSERVICE

Established in 1988

57/3 CHERVONOARMEYSKAYA STREET, SUITE 224
KIEV 252005, UKRAINE
Telephone: 007 44 227 23 70
Fax: 007 44 227 20 54

Firm engaged in Ukrainian and International Law Practice, Business Law, General International Trade Law, Corporate Law, Commercial Law, Administrative Law, Litigation and International Arbitration.

FIRM PROFILE: *Established in 1988 Jurneshservice has known now all over the Ukraine. The Firm has a broadly-based practice with a reputation for offering a full range of quality legal service. The firm has 6 partners. Firm is a member of European Council of LCIA and a member of world wide network Kreditschutzverbsnd von 1870.*

MEMBERS OF FIRM

GENNADY A. TSYRAT, born Taganrog, Russia, November 26, 1962; admitted, 1989, Ukraine. *Education:* Kiev Institute of International Law and International Relations. Firm's Nominative Representative in the LCIA European Council. *Member:* Kiev Region Bar Association. *LANGUAGES:* English, German and Spanish. *PRACTICE AREAS:* Business Law; General International Trade Law; Corporate Law; Commercial Law; Litigation; International Arbitration; Privatization.

JURY A. HKRAPLY, born Berdyansk, Ukraine, November 22, 1962; admitted, 1989, Ukraine. *Education:* Kiev Institute of International Law and International Relations. Chief Consultant of the Department dealing with Issuance of Bulletin. *Member:* Kiev Regional Bar Association. *LANGUAGES:* German. *PRACTICE AREAS:* Tax Legislation; Trade Law; Corporate Law; Industrial Property; Customs and Exchange Control; Law Regulations of Foreign Investments in the Ukraine.

OLEG JU. ALJOSHIN, born Gorlovka, Ukraine, September 13, 1967; admitted, 1993, Ukraine. *Education:* Kiev Institute of International Law and International Relations. *LANGUAGES:* English. *PRACTICE AREAS:* Litigation; Tax Legislation; Trade Law; Corporate Law; Privatization.

VALERY N. KLOCHE, born Sakhalin, Russia, August 27, 1965; admitted, 1989, Ukraine. *Education:* Kiev Institute of International Law and International Relations. *LANGUAGES:* English. *PRACTICE AREAS:* Tax Legislation; Trade Law; Corporate Law; Industrial Property; Customs and Exchange Control Law.

ANNA V. TSYRAT, born Kiev, Ukraine, December 5, 1966; admitted, 1990, Ukraine. *Education:* Kiev State Shevchenko University. Firm's Nominative Representative in Kreditschutzerband von 1870. *LANGUAGES:* English and Italian. *PRACTICE AREAS:* Business Law; Corporate Law; Commercial Law; Litigation; International Arbitration; Privatization.

VLADLMIR V. RATUSHNYAK, born Vinnitsa, Ukraine, December 26, 1966; admitted, 1993, Ukraine. *Education:* Kiev Institute of International Law and International Relations. *LANGUAGES:* English. *PRACTICE AREAS:* Tax Legislation; Trade Law; Corporate :aw; Industrial Property; Patent Law.

VASIL KISIL & PARTNERS

Established in 1987

Attorney at Law & Counselors

57/3, CHERVONOARMIYSKA STREET, SUITE 222
KIEV 252005, UKRAINE
Telephone: 7 (044) 227-1262
Fax: 7 (044) 227-3643

Firm engaged in Ukrainian and International Law Practice.
General Corporate Mergers, Acquisitions, Amalgamation, Registration of Foreign Clients' Representative Offices, Joint Ventures and 100 percent Foreign Owned Ventures; Privatization of State Owned Enterprises in Industry and Agriculture, Contracting, Government Contracting, Countertrade, Leasing, Customs Law, Civil Law Claims (Torts), Local and Inter-

(This Listing Continued)

VASIL KISIL & PARTNERS, Kiev—Continued

national Litigation (Arbitration), Bank Law, Financial Law, Taxation, Copyright, Mineral Rights and Concessions.

FIRM PROFILE: Founded in 1987, as a matter of fact, at the very beginning of a real democratic change in the Soviet society, well known around the world as "Perestroyka," VASIL KISIL & PARTNERS under the name of JURVNESHSERVICE has become one of the first centers of the advanced legal thinking and practice in the Ukraine. Founded by legal scientist and practitioners of similar thinking VASIL KISIL & PARTNERS was one of the very first to practice methods and techniques of working with clients generally accepted in the western world. This made it a real center of legal support for increasing investment activity of the Ukrainian and foreign companies in the territory of the Ukraine and abroad. The firm is also a founding member of TERRALEX, a network of independent law firms specializing in international legal matters.

MEMBERS OF FIRM

VASILIY I. KISIL, born Kiev, Ukraine, October 28, 1948; admitted, 1976, Ukraine. *Education:* Law School of Kiev State University (1976; Ph.D. in International Private Law, 1980). Professor, International Private Law; Chair, International Law School of Kiev University. Reads Courses on Comparative Civil Law, Legal Regulation of Foreign Economic Relations of the Ukraine, Legal Regime of Foreign Investment at the Ukraine, Law School of Keiv University. Author: "Dissolutions of Marriage in the International Private Law," 1980; "Foreigners and Soviet Law," 1982; "Rights and Duties of Parents and Children," 1985; International Private Law" (textbook), 1986; "Civil Law in Questions and Answers," 1987," 1987; "Legal Status of Foreigners in the USSR," 1987; "Family Law for Young People," 1990; "Realization of International Law Standards in the Domestic Legislation," 1982; "International Family Law" (students' manual) 1993. Senior Scientific Consultant, Economic Reform Committee, Supreme Soviet of the Ukraine (Ukrainian Parliament). Member, Government Committee on development of the Ukrainian Civil Code. Participant in development of Laws of the Ukraine: Family Law; Law on Foreign Economic Activityl Law on Business Partnerships; Customs Code; Law on Foreign Investments; Law on Bankruptcy; Law on Mortgage. *Member:* Kiev City Bar; Ukrainian Bar Association (Vice-President) Ukrainian Chamber of Commerce and Industry (Vice-Chairman, Law Section). *LANGUAGES:* Russian, Ukrainian and French. *PRACTICE AREAS:* Civil Law; International Family Law.

SERGEY I. FINOGIN, born Lipetsk, Russian, July 5, 1963; admitted, 1989, Ukraine. *Education:* University of Tampere, Finland (Ph.D., International Joint Venture Economics , 1993). International Economics Chair, Kiev State University (Ukrainian Institute of International Relations), 1989. *LANGUAGES:* Russian, Ukrainian and English. *PRACTICE AREAS:* Foreign Investment Feasibility Studies (TEO); International Crediting and Account Settlement; Contracts Payment Terms; Banking and Taxation.

ALEXEY N. VOLKOV, born Simferopol, Ukraine, January 27, 1962; admitted, 1987, Ukraine. *Education:* International Law School of Kiev State University (1987); International Law Institute, Washington, D.C. (U.S. Law training course); Welborn Dufford Brown & Tooley, P.C., Denver, Colorado (Internship Program). Senior Legal Advisor, Electron Production and Director of Foreign Trade Firm, Amalgamation, Sumy, 1991. Winner, International Contest held by ABA. *LANGUAGES:* Russian, Ukrainian and English. *PRACTICE AREAS:* Contract Law; Corporations and Partnerships; Securities; Mineral Rights and Concessions; Joint Ventures.

OLEG A. MAKAROV, born Kiev, Ukraine, June 24, 1965; admitted, 1989, Ukraine. *Education:* International Law School of Kiev State University (1989); Ukrainian Institute of International Relations and International Law; Finntory Oy, Polyglot Oy, Finland (Legal Training). *LANGUAGES:* Russian, Ukrainian, German and English. *PRACTICE AREAS:* Property Law; Joint Ventures; Investments; Securities; Tax Law.

PAVEL B. RIABIKIN, born Sevastopol, Ukraine, June 6, 1965; admitted, 1989, Ukraine. *Education:* International Law School of Kiev State University (1989); Ukrainian Institute of International Relations and International Law; Law School of Leipzig University, Germany and Law School of Kiev University, Germany (Legal Training). *LANGUAGES:* Russian, Ukrainian, German and English. *PRACTICE AREAS:* Real Estate; Foreign Investments; Securities.

LOGUSH, BORSUK, BRONFMAN & KALISHEVYCH

VUL. MALA ZHYTOMYRSKA ST., 5, SUITE 12
252001 KIEV, UKRAINE
Telephone: 7-044-228-59-19
Fax: 7-044-293-64-34; 7-044-228-59-19

Lviv Office: vul. Sichovykh Stritsiv St., 10, Suite 1, 290000 Ukraine. Telephone: 7-0322-72-16-60; 7-0322-72-09-00. Fax: 7-0322-52-18-50.
Affiliate Office in Major Cities of Ukraine
Philadelphia, Pennsylvania, USA Associated Office: Law Firm of Andre Michniak and Associates, 1700 Walnut Street, Suite 803, 19103. Telephone: 215-790-1700. Fax: 215-790-0811.

Commercial and Trade Law and Contracts; Foreign Investment and Joint Ventures; Privatization; Taxation and Finance; Project Finance and Investment; Real Estate Transactions and Development, including Industrial Property; Intellectual and Industrial Property Protection; Commercial, Civil, and Criminal Dispute Resolution and Indemnity; Labor, Employment, Pension, Benefits Law; Agricultural and Agribusiness Law and Regulations; Legislative Environment, Administrative and Regulatory Law; Licensing, Registration, Government Contracts; Legal Counsel on Ukrainian Law, Decrees and Regulations and On-going Comprehensive Legal Serving.

FIRM PROFILE: Our law firm was one of the first private law firms in Ukraine to be formed under the new Law Concerning the Advocature and the first to open a second office. Its Lviv office draws upon a long pre-Soviet tradition of legal practice in western Ukraine and serves the region. The Kyiv office serves clients in the capital and represents their interests before all government ministries and agencies as well as all courts, including the Supreme Court of Ukraine and arbitration courts. The firm has close relations with law firms in other major cities of Ukraine, the US and Canada, Europe and Israel. Our firm and our attorneys are advocates, licensed by the Ministry of Justice. Unlike other categories of attorneys, as advocates we have enhanced access to government agencies and we are legally licensed to represent our client interests directly before all civil, arbitration and criminal courts of Ukraine. Our firm was among the very first few firms to be listed in the authoritative Martindale-Hubbell International Directory.

Our multilingual staff consists of experienced attorneys with the finest legal education, advisors and consultants in all specialties from law school and university management faculities throughout Ukraine and abroad as well as from parliament and government agencies, legal assistants, paraprofessionals, translators, and a support staff in offices in two cities in Ukraine.

MEMBERS OF FIRM

LYUBOV LOGUSH, born Lviv, Ukraine, June 24, 1951; admitted, 1975, Lviv and all courts of the Ukraine. *Education:* Lviv University Law Faculty (1974; Ph.D. Law, candidate, 1992); Kharkov Law Institute (Post Graduate Program, 1978, 1989); Fordham University School of Law, New York (attended LL.M. Program, 1992-1993). Lecturer in Law: Lviv University; Graduate School of Business Administration, Fordham University. Co-Translator: "US Uniform Commercial Code," in Ukrainian, Lviv University Press, 1994; "German Commercial Code," in Ukrainian, Lviv University Press, 1993. Author: "Defense of Legal Rights of US Agricultural Workers and Implications for Ukraine," Ukrayinske Pravo, 1993. Co-Author: "Overview of US Uniform Commercial Code," Lviv University Press, 1992; "The US Uniform Commercial Code - Implications for Ukraine's Future Commercial Code," Ukrayinske Pravo (the journal of the Ministry of Justice and the Ukrainian Bar Association published monthly in Kiev); "Farming in Ukraine - Legal Foundations," Ukrayinske Pravo, 1993. Co-Editor and Co-Author: "Prefaces" of the multivolume series "Major Legislation of Ukraine," Lviv University Press, Issue I: Laws Governing Foreign Economic Activity, 1992. *Member:* Lviv Collegium of Advocates; Union of Advocates of Ukraine (Ukrainian Bar Association); American Bar Association; International Bar Association; Ukrainian-American Bar Association (Representative, Ukrainian Bar Association to US). (Chairperson, Board of Partners, Head of Kiev Office). *LANGUAGES:* English, Ukrainian, Russian and Polish.

PETRO BORSUK, born Lviv, Ukraine, March 8, 1953; admitted, 1979, Lviv and all courts of Ukraine. *Education:* Lviv University Law Faculty (1978); Kharkov Law Institute (Post Graduate Program, 1981). Lecturer in Law: Lviv University. Co-Editor and Co-Author: "Prefaces" of the multivolume series "Major Legislation of Ukraine," Lviv University Press, Issue I:

(This Listing Continued)

Laws Governing Foreign Economic Activity, 1992. *Member:* Lviv Collegium of Advocates (Presidium Deputy Chairman); Union of Advocates of Ukraine. (President, Head of Lviv Office). *LANGUAGES:* English, Ukrainian, Russian and Polish.

PETRO BRONFMAN, born Lviv, Ukraine, September 30, 1952; admitted, 1978, Lviv and all courts of Ukraine. *Education:* Lviv University Law Faculty (1977); Kharkov Law Institute (Post Graduate Program, 1982). *Member:* Lviv Collegium of Advocates; Union of Advocates of Ukraine. *LANGUAGES:* English, Ukrainian, Russian and Polish.

OLEKSANDER KALISHEVYCH, born Lviv, Ukraine, June 15, 1955; admitted, 1982, Lviv and all courts of Ukraine. *Education:* Lviv University Law Faculty (1980). Lecturer in Law: Lviv University. *Member:* Lviv Collegium of Advocates; Union of Advocates of Ukraine. *LANGUAGES:* Ukrainian, Russian and Polish.

OF COUNSEL

ANDRE MICHNIAK, born Pittsburgh, Pennsylvania, January 24, 1951; admitted, 1983, Pennsylvania; 1985, U.S. District Court, Eastern District of Pennsylvania; U.S. Court of Appeals, Third Circuit (Not admitted in Ukraine). *Education:* John Carroll University (B.S., Biology, cum laude, 1979); Temple University School of Law (J.D., 1982). *Member:* Philadelphia Bar Association; American Bar Association; Ukrainian-American Bar Association; American Immigration Lawyers Association. (United States Counsel; Also Practices Individually at Andre Michniak and Associates, Philadelphia, Pa.). *LANGUAGES:* English and Ukrainian.

MANAGEMENT & BUSINESS CONSULTING CENTER OF OUR LAW FIRM

DR. GEORGE LOGUSH. *Education:* CCNY (B.S., Engineering and Economics, 1968); NYU (M.A., 1971; Ph.D., Econometrics, 1973). CEO, CFO: firms in U.S. General Manager, major multinational firm in Ukraine. Professor, Graduate School of Business Administration, Fordham University, New York City. Co-Translator, "US Uniform Commercial Code," in Ukrainian, Lviv University Press, 1994. Author: articles and books on business, management, finance. President, International Business Services, Ltd., New York City, Kyiv, Lviv. (Director of Center). *LANGUAGES:* English, Ukrainian, Polish, Russian, German and Spanish.

REPRESENTATIVE CLIENTS: in Ukraine: RJR-Nabisco, Ukraine; Foreign Trade Association "UKRIMPEX" (the State import-export agency); PromInvest-Bank (the largest bank in Ukraine); Svitoch Confectionery Co.; Lviv Medical Institute; Ukrainian Institute for Reproductive Medicine; Ukrainian State Railways Health Care Delivery System; Academy of Cybernetics and Technology; Ukrainian Academy of Sciences (National Progress); Dilo (the largest circulation business newspaper in Ukraine; Kremenchuh Tobacco Factory and RJ Reynolds Tobacco-Kremenchuk Joint Venture; Lviv Tobacco Factory and RJ Reynolds Tobacco-Lviv Joint Venture; Dnipropetrovsk Tobacco Factory; Kamyanets-Podilsky Tobacco Factory and Fermentation Plant; Berehove Tobacco Fermentation Plant; Symferopol Tobacco Fermentation Plant; Zabolotiv Tobacco Fermentation Plant; West Ukrainian Philantropic Fund; Lviv Electronic Engineering Research Institute; Lviv Polytechnical Institute firms Formula (patent development) and Technopolis (construction technologies); Lviv University Press; Lviv Fashion Design Center and Textile Co.; in Europe: R. J. Reynolds Tobacco International, S.A., Geneva, Switzerland; Odette Nicos Petrides Co., Kavala, Greece; in the US: General Accounting Office of the US Congress; Monk-Austen Inernational; Republic National Bank of New York; Pharmavite Corporation; ICMA Corporation of Washington, D.C.; in Asia: ACOTEX Far East, Ltd. (Hong Kong and other Asian affiliates).

SALANS HERTZFELD & HEILBRONN
UKRAINSKII DIM, VUL. KRESHCHATIK 2 (4TH FLOOR)
252601 KIEV, UKRAINE
Telephone: 7.044.228.5451
Fax: 7.044.228.6398.

Paris, France, Office: 9, Rue Boissy D'Anglas, 75008. Telephone: 42.68.48.00. Telex: 280990 PARILEX. Fax: 42.68.15.45; 42.68.15.46; 42.68.15.47.

New York, N.Y. Office: 750 Lexington Avenue, 10022. Telephone: 212.644.0800. Fax: 212.644.1003.

London, England Office: 103 Mount Street. W1Y-5HE. Telephone: 44.171.491.3735. Fax: 44.171.408 0843.

Moscow, Russia Office: Gazetnyi Pereulok, 17/9, (Ex. UL. Ogareva). 103009. Telephone: 7.501.940.2944. Fax: 7.501.940.2806.

Warsaw, Poland Office: ul. Podwale 7, 00-252. Telephone: 48.22 31.96.88; 31.25.72; 31.29.20. Fax: 48.22 31.39.32; 31.15.65.

St. Petersburg, Russia Office: Dom Zhurnalistov, 70 Nevskii Prospekt. 191 025. Telephone: 7.812.272.4572; 273.6844. Fax: 7.812.273.6844.

(This Listing Continued)

Other St. Petersburg, Russia Office: 6 Inzhenernaya Ulitsa, 191011. Telephone: 7.812.850.1504; 210.4040; 210.4447; 210.4008; 210.4032; 210.4005; 210.4348; 210.4812. Fax: 7.812.850.1505; 210.4114. Office move planned for March 15, 1995.

Almaty, Kazakhstan Office: 10A Abaya Prospect, Corner "Furmanova," 11th Floor, Suite 5, 480013. Telephone: 7 3272 634 053; 634 049.

Other Almaty, Kazakhstan Office: 86 Gogol Street, 5th Floor, 480091. Office move planned for April 1, 1995.

OLEG BATYUK, born Chernigov, Ukraine, July 18, 1963; admitted before Ukrainian Courts. *Education:* University of Kiev (Law Degree, 1985); Candidate of Science (Law Degree, 1988). Recipient, UK's Foreign & Commonwealth Office Fellowship for Postgraduate Studies, Queen Mary & Westfield College University of London, 1991-1992. Lecturer of Laws, University of Kiev, 1988—. *LANGUAGES:* Ukrainian, Russian and English. *PRACTICE AREAS:* Eastern European Commerce.

ALEXANDER FEFELOV, born Kiev, Ukraine, February 15, 1967. *Education:* Kiev State University; Ukrainian Institute of International Relations (International Law Department; Law Degree, 1991). *LANGUAGES:* Ukrainian, Russian and English. *PRACTICE AREAS:* Eastern European Commerce.

(For complete biographical data on all personnel, see Paris France)

SCHEELE, SCHWARTZ, ZIELCKE & PARTNER
UL. ZOLOTI VOROTA 2-A
252034 KIEV, UKRAINE
Telephone: 007-044-2245208
Fax: 007-044-2292835

Munich, Germany Office: Prinzregentenplatz 15, 81675. Telephone: 089/470 10 02. Fax: 089/470 10 06.

FIRM PROFILE: Scheele, Schwartz, Zielcke & Partner is an international law firm advising business clients and public institutions on all domestic and overseas corporate and commercial matters. The firm specializes in Eastern European and C.I.S. matters. Currently the firm is representing a broad range of clients in Europe, North America, South America, Asia and Africa.

(For biographical data and areas of practice see listing at Munich, Germany)

SMITH, LYONS, TORRANCE, STEVENSON & MAYER
SUITE 175, 5TH FLOOR
PREDSLAVYNSKA STREET, 38
KIEV 252006, UKRAINE
Telephone: 7-044-268-4181
Facsimile: 7-044-268-3171

Toronto, Ontario Office: Suite 6200 Scotia Plaza, 40 King Street West. Telephone: 416-369-7200. Facsimile: 416-369-7250.

Ottawa, Ontario Office: Suite 1700, 45 O'Connor Street. Telephone: 613-230-3988. Facsimile: 613-230-7085.

Vancouver, British Columbia Office: World Trade Centre, 550-999 Canada Place. Telephone: 604-662-8082. Facsimile: 604-685-8542.

Hong Kong: In Association with Fred Kan & Co., 31st Floor, Central Plaza, 18 Harbour Road, Wanchai, Hong Kong. Telephone: 011 852 598 1318. Facsimile: 011 852 588 1318.

Taipei, Taiwan: In Association with Formosa Transnational, 15th Floor, Lotus Building, 136 Jen Ai Road, Section 3. Telephone: 011 886 755-7366. Facsimile: 011 886 755-6486.

Member of Smith Lyons, Langlois Robert, Bryan, González Vargas: Toronto, Ottawa, Vancouver, Hong Kong, Taipei, Kiev, Montréal, Québec, New York, México City, Ciudad Juárez, Chihuahua, Matamoros, Tijuana, Mexicali.

General Practice.
(This Listing Continued)

**SMITH, LYONS, TORRANCE, STEVENSON &
MAYER, Kiev—Continued**

MEMBER OF FIRM

MARK Y. KOWALSKY, born Saskatoon, Saskatchewan, October 9, 1959; admitted, 1989, Ontario (Not admitted in Ukraine). *Education:* Gemological Institute of America; University of Toronto (B.A., Hons., 1984); Osgoode Hall (LL.B., 1987). *Member:* Canadian Bar Association.

(For biographical data on Toronto, Ontario, Ottawa, Ontario and Vancouver, British Columbia personnel, see Professional Biographies at those locations)

SQUIRE, SANDERS & DEMPSEY

VUL. PRORIZNA 9, SUITE 20
KIEV 252035, UKRAINE
Telephone: 011-7-044-244-3452, 244-3453, 228-8687
Fax: 011-7-044-228-4938

Cleveland, Ohio Office: 4900 Society Center, 127 Public Square, Cleveland, Ohio 44114-1304. Telephone: 216-479-8500. Fax's: 216-479-8780, 216-479-8781, 216-479-8787, 216-479-8795, 216-479-8777, 216-479-8793, 216-479-8776, 216-479-8788.

Columbus, Ohio Offices: 1300 Huntington Center, 41 South High Street, Columbus, Ohio 43215. Telephone: 614-365-2700. Fax: 614-365-2499.

Jacksonville, Florida Office: One Enterprise Center, Suite 2100, 225 Water Street, Jacksonville, Florida 32202. Telephone: 904-353-1264. Fax: 904-356-2986.

Miami, Florida Office: 201 South Biscayne Boulevard, Suite 2900 Miami Center, Miami, Florida 33131. Telephone: 305-577-8700. Fax: 305-358-1425.

New York, New York Office: 520 Madison Avenue, 32nd Floor, New York, New York 10022. Telephone: 212-872-9800. Fax: 212-872-9814.

Phoenix, Arizona Office: Two Renaissance Square, 40 North Central Avenue, Suite 2700, Phoenix, Arizona 85004-4441. Telephone: 602-528-4000. Fax: 602-253-8129.

Washington, D.C. Office: 1201 Pennsylvania Avenue, N.W., P.O. Box 407, Washington, D.C. 20044. Telephone: 202-626-6600. Fax: 202-626-6780.

London, England Office: 1 Gunpowder Square, Printer Street, London EC4A 3DE. Telephone: 011-44-071-830-0055. Fax: 011-44-071-830-0056.

Brussels, Belgium Office: Avenue Louise, 165-Box 15, 1050 Brussels, Belgium. Telephone: 011-32-2-648-1717. Fax: 011-32-2-648-1064.

Prague Office: Adria Palace, Jungmannova 31/36, 11000 Prague 1, Czech Republic. Telephone: 011-42-2-231-5661. Fax: 011-42-2-231-5482.

Bratislava Office: Mudronova 37, 811 01 Bratislava, Slovak Republic. Telephone: 011-42-7-313-362; 011-42-7-315-370. Fax: 011-42-7-313-918.

Budapest, Hungary Office: Deak Ferenc Ut. 10, Office 304, H-1052 Budapest V., Hungary. Telephone: 011-36-1-226-2024; 011-36-1-226-5038. Fax: 011-361-226-2025.

General and International Practice.

RESIDENT PARTNER

HELEN Z. KRYSHTALOWYCH, born Bad Werishofen, Germany, 1945; admitted, 1980, Ohio; U.S. District Court, Northern District of Ohio; U.S. Court of Appeals, Sixth Circuit. *Education:* Ohio State University (B.A., B.S., 1967); Kent State University (M.Ed., magna cum laude, 1971); Cleveland-Marshall College of Law (J.D., magna cum laude, 1980). *Member:* American Bar Association, International, Employment Law, and Rail and Airline Committees; Ohio State Bar Association; Cleveland Bar Association, International Law Committee; Ukrainian-American Bar Association; Ohio-Ukraine Judiciary Committee; Secretary, American Chamber of Commerce in Ukraine. *LANGUAGES:* Ukrainian and Russian. *PRACTICE AREAS:* International Commercial and Corporate Law; Labor and Employment Law.

PARTNER

MICHAEL R. SILVERMAN, born Liberty, New York, 1947; admitted, 1973, District of Columbia. *Education:* Syracuse University (B.A., magna cum laude, Phi Beta Kappa, 1969), International Law Institute in Washington, D.C. and Frankfurt, Germany (Schulte Zur Hausen Fellow, 1972-1975); Georgetown University Law Center (J.D., 1972; LL.M., International Law, 1975). *Member:* American Bar Association. (Also at Washing-
(This Listing Continued)

ton, D.C. Office). *PRACTICE AREAS:* International Commercial and Corporate Law; Financing Law.

COUNSEL

EVGEMY V. GOUSSEV, born Donetsk City, Ukraine, 1950. *Education:* Kiev University Faculty of Law (Law Degree, 1972; LL.M., 1979). *Member:* Ukrainian Bar Association for International Affairs; Union of Ukrainian Lawyers. *LANGUAGES:* Ukrainian (native), Russian, English. *PRACTICE AREAS:* International Commercial and Corporate Law.

ASSOCIATE

TARAS G. SZMAGALA, JR., born Parma, Ohio, 1966; admitted, 1991, Ohio. *Education:* University of Virginia (B.A., Economics, 1988); University of Virginia School of Law (J.D., 1991). Member, Ukrainian National Association By-Laws Revision Committee, Ukrainian-American Bar Association, D.C. Bar Association, Cleveland Bar Association. (Also at Cleveland, Ohio Office). *LANGUAGES:* English (native), Ukraine. *PRACTICE AREAS:* International Commercial and Corporate Law.

(For Biographical Data on Cleveland, Ohio, Columbus, Ohio, Miami and Jacksonville, Florida, New York, New York, Phoenix, Arizona, Washington, D.C., London, England, Brussels, Belgium, Prague and Czech Republic, Bratislava, Slovak Republic and Budapest, Hungary Personnel, see Professional Biographies at those Points Respectively).

B.C. TOMS & CO

18 PROREZNAYA STREET, APTS 1/2
KIEV 252001, UKRAINE
Telephone: (7044) 228-1000, 225-2032
Telecopier: (7044) 228-6508

Odessa, Ukraine Office: Ulitsa Kirova 47, Flat 5, 270014. Telephone (7) 0482-218-704. Fax: 7 0482 259 265.

London, England Office: 64 London Wall, EC2M 5TP. Telephone: (44) (171) 638-7711. Fax: (44) (171) 382-9360.

Paris, France Office: 46, Avenue d'Iena, 75116. Telephone: (33) (1) 47234724. Telecopier: (33) (1) 47238053. Telex: 613237F.

Other Associated Offices: Minsk, Belarus; Milan, Italy; Moscow, Russia.

Admitted as locally qualified lawyers since Ukraine's independence in 1991. Practice areas include Establishing and Registering Ukrainian Joint Ventures, Subsidiaries and Branches, Negotiating and Preparing Contractual Documentation in Ukrainian and Russian as well as English, French and other Languages; Real Estate, Investment, Privatisation, Corporate, Construction, Project Finance, Oil and Gas, Banking, Arbitration, Agency, Distribution, Licensing, Insolvency and Intellectual Property Law.

BATE C. TOMS, III, born Virginia, 1949; admitted, 1975, Virginia; 1977, District of Columbia; 1982, France (as avocat) (Not admitted in Ukraine). *Education:* Institut d'Etudes Politiques de Paris-Soviet Studies (1969-1970); Washington and Lee University (B.A., magna cum laude, 1971); Cambridge University, Magdalene College (Law, 1972-1973); Yale Law School (J.D., 1975). Phi Beta Kappa. Editor: Yale Law Journal, 1975-1976; Journal of International Banking Law, 1986—; Oil and Gas Law and Taxation Review, 1984—; 6; "Ukrainian Real Estate Law," Buterworths' Central and East European Business Law J., March 1994; BOT and Non-Recourse Projects-Proceedings of the Second Intl. Construction Projects Conference, 1989; "Privatisation in Ukraine," Euromoney IFLR, September 1992; "Ukrainian Oil and Gas Licensing," 13 (2) Oil and Gas Law and Tax Rev., 1995; "Ukrainian Law," Interforum Books-1995 in Press, with Dr. F. Burchak, Legal Advisor to Ukrainian Pres.; "Ukrainian Law on Banking," J. of Intl. Banking Law, June 1992; "Ukrainian Special Economic Zones; CCH Doing Business in Europe 1992; Ukrainian Tax Law," November 1992—Interforum Conference on Doing Business in Ukraine; "Offshore Share Offerings," 1 J. Intl. Banking L. 36, 1986; "Belarussian Intellectual Property," Intel Prop News, November 1994, with N. Kandrusora. *Member:* District of Columbia Bar; Virginia State Bar; American and International Bar Associations.

COUNSEL

PETER FULLERTON, born UK, 1943; admitted, 1978, California (Not admitted in Ukraine). *Education:* Gonville & Caius College, Cambridge University (Tapp Major Scholar; 1st class honours; B.A., 1964; M.A., 1968) Yale University (Henry Fellow; M.A., 1968); Stanford Law School (J.D., 1978). Member, Board of Editors, Stanford Law Review. President Cambridge Union Society, 1965; Member, Gray's Inn.

VLADIMIR N. PETRINA, born Ukraine, 1956; admitted, 1990, Ukraine. *Education:* Kiev State University Law School (LL.B., 1982). Di-
(This Listing Continued)

rector of Kiev Centre for Legal Studies (Soros Foundation); Assoc. Professor of Law, Kiev State University. Member Advisory Council, Ukraine Institute of Bankers; Legal Counsel GradoBank, 1993-1994.

YLADIMIR V. YANCHUK, born Ukraine, 1956; admitted, 1983, Ukraine. *Education:* Kiev State University Law School (LL.B., 1983); Moscow University (LL.D., 1983). Professor of Law. Member, Union of Agrarian Lawyers of Ukraine.

PAVEL F. KULINICH, born Ukraine, 1956; admitted, 1993, Ukraine. *Education:* Kiev State University Law School (LL.B., 1980). Associate Professor of Law, Kiev State University Law School, 1989-1994. Member, Institute of Government of Cabinet of Ministers. Legal advisor to Land Reform Commission of Cabinet of Ministers.

ASSOCIATES

RONALD D.A. SALLOWS, born England, 1966; admitted, 1994, Solicitor, England (Not admitted in Ukraine). *Education:* University of London (B.Sc, Hons., 1988); London Guildhall University Law School (C.P.E., 1991).

DMITRIY A. SERDYUK, born Ukraine, 1973; admitted, 1995, Ukraine. *Education:* Kiev State University Law School (LL.B., 1995).

OF COUNSEL

VLADISLAV IVONOVICH KALNYI, born Ukraine, 1940; admitted, 1977, Ukraine. *Education:* Kiev State University Law School (LL.B., LL.M., 1964). Publications: The System of Advocates in Ukraine. *Member:* Kiev Bar Association (President); International Union of Lawyers (Vice-President).

Languages: Ukrainian, Russian, English, French, German and Bulgarian.

(For Additional Biographical Entries, see London, England)

YUGOSLAVIA

MILOŠ B. MARKOVIĆ,
SLOBODAN B. MARKOVIĆ

TAKOVSKA 11

11000 BELGRADE, YUGOSLAVIA

Telephone: (38-111) 3224-682

Fax: (38-111) 3227-449

Telex: 72876 advomayu

Business Law, Commercial Law, Foreign Agencies, Foreign Investments, Commercial Disputes, Arbitration, Collections, Litigations and Copyright.

MEMBERS OF FIRM

SLOBODAN B. MARKOVIĆ, born Belgrade, Yugoslavia, April 11, 1952; admitted, 1974, Belgrade. *Education:* Faculty of Law, University of Belgrade (LL.B., 1974). *LANGUAGES:* English and German.

MILOŠ B. MARKOVIĆ, born Belgrade, Yugoslavia, January 27, 1947; admitted, 1981, Belgrade. *Education:* Faculty of Law, University of Belgrade (LL.B., 1970). *LANGUAGES:* English.

REPRESENTATIVE CLIENTS: Lawyers to the German Embassy in Belgrade; Listed Lawyer for the Embassy of the United States of America in Belgrade; Air India; Alitalia; Austrian Airlines; Lufthansa AG; Qantas Airways; The Association of Serbian Writers; Motion Picture Association of America in Rome; Deutsche Bank AG Mannheim; Avis GmbH Frankfurt; Sumitomo Corp.; C. Itoh & Co., Ltd.; Aviation Sales Co., Inc.; Warner Bros.; Converse, Inc.; Kodak Limited; Sandvik International; Procter & Gamble; Deutsche Shell AG; Inter-Continental Hotels Corp.; Delta Airlines; F. Hoffmann-La Roche, Ltd.; Kanematsu Corp.; Dairy Queen; Nichimen Corp.; Fiat; Coca-Cola; Boots PLC.; Marubeni Corp.

MIKIJELJ & JANKOVIĆ

Patent and Trademark Agents

Established in 1973

VLAJKOVIĆEVA 28

11101 BELGRADE, YUGOSLAVIA

Telephone: 381 11 331 970; 381 11 346 185

Cable Address: MIKIJELJ Beograd

Telex: 12910 MIKIELJ YU

Telefax: 381 11 346 065

Patent and Trademark Law, Commercial, Foreign Agencies, Long Term Cooperation, Transfer of Technology, Joint Venture Agreements, Civil Procedures, Trials and Appeals.

MEMBERS OF FIRM

RADE DJ. MIKIJELJ, born Skoplje, Yugoslavia, August 21, 1938; admitted, 1961, Belgrade. *Education:* Faculty of Law, University of Belgrade (LL.B., 1961). *Member:* Belgrade Bar Association; International Association of Lawyers; American Bar Association; International Association of Young Lawyers (Member, Executive Council, 1967-1979); International Association for the Protection of Industrial Property; The Chartered Institute of Patent Agents in London (Overseas Member); The Institute of Trade Mark Agents in London (Overseas Member); The Institute of Patent Attorneys of Australia (Overseas Member); The United States Trademark Association; Licensing Executive Society; Patent and Trademark Institute of Canada. *LANGUAGES:* Serbian, English, German and French. *PRACTICE AREAS:* Patent and Trademark Law; Corporate Law; International Business Law.

DR. IVAN D. JANKOVIĆ, born Belgrade, Yugoslavia, June 8, 1946; admitted, 1986, Belgrade. *Education:* Faculty of Law, University of Belgrade (LL.B., 1968; LL.M., 1972); Institute of Criminology, Cambridge University, England (Diploma in Criminology, 1971); University of California, Santa Barbara, USA (Ph.D. in Sociology, 1977). Patent and Trademark Agent, 1985. *Member:* Belgrade Bar Association. *LANGUAGES:* Serbian, English, French and Russian. *PRACTICE AREAS:* Copyright Law; Commercial Law.

REPRESENTATIVE CLIENTS: American Home Products Corporation, USA; Beecham Group plc., UK; British Petroleum Co. Ltd., UK; Ciba-Geigy AG, Switzerland; Diamond Shamrock Chemicals Co., USA; Fisons Ltd., UK; FMC Corporation, USA; Glaxo Group Ltd., UK; Grünenthal GmbH, FDR; Institute Francais du Petrole des Carburants et Lubrifiants, France; Regie Nationale de Usiness RENAULT; Shell International Research Maatschappij B.V., Holland; Shin-Etsu Chemical Co., Japan; USS Engineers and Consultants, Inc., USA; The Wellcome Foundation Ltd., UK; Astra AB, Sweden; The Goodyear Tire & Rubber Co., USA; Knorr Nährmittel AG, Switzerland; Yardley & Co. Ltd., UK.

NINKOVIC

Established in 1938

MILOVANA MILOVANOVICA 1

11000 BELGRADE, YUGOSLAVIA

Telephone: 381-11 644-084; 381-11 644-545

Cable Address: "Ninlex"

Telex: 12560 NINLEXYU

Telefax: 381-11 684-374

London, England Office: 21 Penton Court, Staines, Middx., TW18 2JU. Telephone and Fax: (01784) 454 242.

Commercial, Company, International Private, Aviation, Insurance, Banking, Intellectual Property, Civil and Criminal Law.

MEMBERS OF FIRM

DJURDJE M. NINKOVIC, born Belgrade, Yugoslavia, April 26, 1942; admitted, 1964, Yugoslavia. *Education:* Belgrade University, Faculty of Law (Dipl. Iur., 1964); Institute of World Affairs, University College London, Postgraduate Course in International Aviation Law (Diploma, 1968). *LANGUAGES:* English and French. *PRACTICE AREAS:* Aviation; Insurance; Banking; International Private Law.

BRANISLAV M. NINKOVIC, born Belgrade, Yugoslavia, February 1944; admitted, 1970, Yugoslavia. *Education:* Belgrade University, Pristina Faculty of Law (Dipl. Iur., 1969). *LANGUAGES:* Serbo-Croatian. *PRACTICE AREAS:* Civil Law; Criminal Law; Company Law; Commercial Law.

(This Listing Continued)

NINKOVIC, Belgrade—Continued

PATENT AGENT

MIRJANA T. NINKOVIC, born Belgrade, Yugoslavia, August 19, 1941. *Education:* Faculty of Electrical Engineering, University of Belgrade (Dipl. ing., 1965). *Member:* The Institution of Electrical Engineering (C. Eng., M.I.E.E.). *LANGUAGES:* English, French and Serbo-Croatian. *PRACTICE AREAS:* Patents and Trade Marks.

BORJANA SUBOTIC, born B.Gradiska, Yugoslavia, August 9, 1959. *Education:* Faculty of Law, Banjaluka University (Dipl.Iur., 1981). Court Interpreter for the English Language.

Languages: English and French.

REPRESENTATIVE CLIENTS: Lawyers to the Swedish Embassy in Belgrade; Lawyers to the Danish Embassy in Belgrade; Lawyers on the list of U.S.A. Embassy in Belgrade; Lawyers on the list of U.K. Embassy in Belgrade; Lawyers to SAS in Belgrade; Lawyers to British Airways in Belgrade; Automobile Association of England; Carrier Corporation of USA; Nichimen Co. Ltd. of Japan; Toyo Menka Kaisha Ltd. of Japan; Honeywell Information Systems Inc. of U.S.A.; Air France; Qantas; Le Foyer Insurance Co.; Svenska Handelsbanken; VTG GmbH of Hamburg; Embassy of Japan; Mitsubishi Corp; Air France; Dresdner Bank AG; Toyota Tsusho Corporation; Lauda Air; Univank Plc; Intermerkur AG; Transakta, Chemapol, Petrimex, Technoexport of Prague; Vitkovice of Ostrava; Rempo, Drevounia of Bratislava; Polimex-Cekop of Warsaw Agrimpex, Magyar Alamvasutak of Budapest; Costain Ltd.; Adria Airways.

POPOVIC, POPOVIC, SAMARDZIJA & POPOVIC

TAKOVSKA 19

11000 BELGRADE, YUGOSLAVIA

Telephone: (381) 339-442
Cable Address: "Lex Beograd"
Telex: 12252 YU Popovic
Telecopier: 342-646

REVISER OF THE YUGOSLAVIA LAW DIGEST FOR THIS DIRECTORY

Corporation Banking and Business Law, Joint Venture, Loan Agreements, Commercial, Foreign Agencies, Civil Procedures, Maritime Law, Trials and Appeals, Industrial Property, Technology Transfer.

MEMBERS OF FIRM

MIODRAG P. POPOVIC (1907-1987).

SRDJA M. POPOVIĆ, born Belgrade, Yugoslavia, February 24, 1937; admitted, 1961, Yugoslavia. *Education:* Faculty of Law, University of Belgrade (LL.B., 1961). Recipient, American Bar Association Rule of Law Award, 1993. *Member:* Belgrade Bar Association; International Union of Lawyers; World Association of Lawyers (Founding Member). *LANGUAGES:* English and French. *PRACTICE AREAS:* Industrial Property; Transfer of Technology; Criminal Law.

GORDANA M. POPOVIĆ, born Belgrade, Yugoslavia, December 20, 1933; admitted, 1966, Yugoslavia. *Education:* Faculty of Philology (M.A., 1956); Faculty of Law, University of Belgrade (LL.B., 1964). Assistant, Institute of Social Sciences, 1961-1966. *Member:* Belgrade Bar Association; International Association of Young Lawyers (Honorary Vice President, 1989); European Association of Lawyers (Founder Member); Federation International des Conseillers en Propriete Industrielles (FICPI). *LANGUAGES:* English and French. *PRACTICE AREAS:* Industrial Property; Transfer of Technology; Trials and Appeals.

PETAR A. SAMARDŽIJA, born Belgrade, Yugoslavia, April 24, 1950; admitted, 1979, Yugoslavia. *Education:* Faculty of Law, University of Belgrade (LL.B., 1976). *Member:* Belgrade Bar Association. *LANGUAGES:* English. *PRACTICE AREAS:* Corporations; Joint Ventures; Foreign Agencies; Maritime Law.

BORIS S. POPOVIĆ, born Yugoslavia, December 2, 1962. *Education:* Faculty of Law, University of Belgrade (LL.B., 1990). *Member:* Belgrade Bar Association; International Association of Young Lawyers. *LANGUAGES:* English and French. *PRACTICE AREAS:* Civil Procedures; Trials and Appeals; Industrial Property; Loan Agreements.

(This Listing Continued)

ASSOCIATE

KATARINA B. KOSTIĆ, born Belgrade, Yugoslavia, May 3, 1965; admitted, 1990, Belgrade, Yugoslavia. *Education:* Faculty of Law, University of Belgrade (LL.B., 1990). *Member:* International Association of Young Lawyers. *LANGUAGES:* French and English. *PRACTICE AREAS:* Commercial Law; Trials and Appeals; Industrial Property.

Languages: English, German and French

REPRESENTATIVE CLIENTS: American Express International Banking Corp., New York, N.Y. 10020; The Chase Manhattan Bank, N.A., 1 Chase Manhattan Plaza, New York, N.Y., 10015; Manufacturers Hanover Trust Co., 7 Princes St., London EC2; Irving Trust Co., One Wall St., New York, N.Y. 10015; IBM, Zurich Patent Dept,. Saumerstrasse 4, 8803 1 Ruschlikon, Switzerland; United California Bank, 707 Wilshire Blvd., Los Angeles, California; Texas Instruments, Inc., Dallas, Texas; Standard Oil Company, 200 East Randolph Drive, Chicago, Illinois; Bank of Tokyo and Detroit (International) Limited, 18, Finsbury Circus, London EC2; Citibank N.A., 339 Park Avenue, New York, N.Y. 10022; Unilever N.V., Museumpark 1, Rotterdam; Borg-Warner Corp., 200 South Michigan Ave., Chicago, Illinois; Export Development Corp.; Ottawa, Ontario, Canada; General Electric Technical Services Co., Inc.; Overseas Nuclear Power Operation, 175 Curtner Avenue, San Jose, California 95125; Black & Decker Manufacturing Co., Towson, Maryland; P. Lorillard Co., New York, N.Y. 10017; Fried, Krupp GmbH. Krupp Industrieund Stahlbau, Helenstrasse 149, 43 Essen, BRD; Bristol-Myers Co., New York, N.Y. 10020; Bank of America National Trust and Savings Assn., World Headquarters (42nd floor), San Francisco, California; Bank of Montreal, International Banking, P.O. Box 6002, Montreal, Que., Canada; Barclays Bank International Ltd., 54 Lombard St., London EC3; East-West United Bank S.A., 22 Boulevard Royal, Luxembourg; The Trade Development Bank, 2 Place du Lac, Geneva, Switzerland; Westdeutsche Landesbank Girozentrale, Friedrichstrasse 56, 4000 Dusseldorf 1, W. Germany; Dunlop Limited, Dunlop House, Ryder Street, St. James', London S WIY 6PX, England; Norddeutsche Landesbank Girozentrale, Postfach 290, Georgsplatz 1, 3 Hanover 1, West Germany; The Coca-Cola Export Corporation Atlanta, Georgia; Rank Xerox Limited, 338 Euston Road, London, NW1 3BH, England; The Long Term Credit Bank of Japan Ltd., 2-4, Otemachi 1-Chrome, Chiyoda-ku Tokyo 100, Japan; Boeing Co., P.O. Box 3707, Seattle, Wa. 98124.

REVISER OF THE YUGOSLAVIA LAW DIGEST FOR THIS DIRECTORY

IGOR PRLJA

Established in 1978

CARA LAZARA 15

11000 BELGRADE, YUGOSLAVIA

Telephone: (11) 630 214
Fax: (11) 624 195
Telex: 72 887
Cable Address: LAW Belgrade

All kind of Civil and Trade Litigations, International Arbitrations, International Insurance for various transports and forwarding, Property Settlements, Trusts, Wills, Estates, Real Estate, Genealogical Research.

FIRM PROFILE: Gradual growth, careful selection of graduate students and thorough training, computerised data of theoretical legal articles of main legal fields.

IGOR PRLJA, born Belgrade, December 4, 1946; admitted, 1978, Belgrade. *Education:* College of Law University of Belgrade (1970).

ASSOCIATES

Branko Božanskć	*Sanja Marinković*
Dejan Slavić	*Dragan Tomić*
	Mirjana Perović

Languages: English, French, Italian and Romanian.

REPRESENTATIVES CLIENTS: Swiss Embassy in Belgrade, Italian Auto Club, Swiss Auto Club, S.A.I. Torino, AHV Geneva, AA Lloyds Policy England, Mapfre Madrid, Plansikring Danemark, Abeille Paris, AXA Belgium, Nieuwe Hollandse Lloyd Holland, Pearl Greece, ITC Beiruth, US Consulate listed.

RISTIC & RISTIC

Established in 1955

SUITE 4

CARA LAZARA STREET 7

11000 BELGRADE, YUGOSLAVIA

Telephone: (381) 620-662

Cable Address: "Rispat Beograd"

Telex: 12185 YU Ristic

Telefax: (381) 620-823

Commercial Law, Local Patents, Trademarks, Copyrights and related matters, including International Patents and Trademarks and related matters in Croatia, Slovenia, Macedonia, in Eastern Europe, The Commonwealth of Independent States and PR of China, Foreign Investment and Agreements, Trials, Appeals and Licensing.

FIRM PROFILE: The firm was established in 1955 and offers the full range of legal and professional services in industrial property locally and internationally in more than twenty (20) countries. It is well known locally and internationally in Croatia, Slovenia and Macedonia, Eastern Europe, Commonwealth of Independent States and PR of China in filing, prosecution and maintenance of industrial and intellectual property rights. The firm is also involved in foreign investment and joint-venture agreements, trials and appeals. The three partners firm has the support staff of seven assisting experts in various industrial property fields. The client base is East and West Europe, The Commonwealth of Independent States, North America, Japan and Far East.

MEMBERS OF FIRM

MIHAILO J. RISTIC (1909-1972).

DRAGOSLAV M. RISTIC, born Skopje, Yugoslavia, May 14, 1939; admitted, 1965, Yugoslavia. *Education:* Second Belgrade Gymnasium (B.A., 1958); University of Belgrade (LL.B., 1965); New York University. Author: Manual for Industrial Property for Eastern European Countries, New York, 1974; "Ristic's Manual of Industrial Property Rights in Eastern Europe and PR China," Edition 1991. Law Department, Johnson & Johnson, New Brunswick, New Jersey, 1971-1972 (Awarded Certificate of Appreciation). Recipient, Awarded Medal and Certificate of the USSR Chamber of Commerce & Industry, Moscow, USSR, 1982. *Member:* Belgrade and Yugoslavia Bar Associations; International Association for the Protection of Industrial Property; The New York Patent Law Association (Associate Foreign Member); International Trademark (INTA). Association (Foreign Member); The Chartered Institute of Patent Agents in London (Overseas Member); The Institute of Trademark Agents in London (Overseas Member); The Patent and Trademark Institute of Canada (Non-Resident Associate); APLA (Asia-Pacific Lawyers Association). *LANGUAGES:* Serbian, English, French, Italian, German and Russian. *PRACTICE AREAS:* Commercial Law; Local and International Patents and Trademarks; Copyrights Law; Foreign Investment and Agreements; Trials; Appeals and Licensing Law.

DUŠANKA M. RISTIC, born Loznica, Yugoslavia, December 15, 1943. *Education:* Gymnasium of Vuk Karadzic (B.A., 1963); University of Technology and Metallurgy of Belgrade (B.Ch.Eng., 1967). *LANGUAGES:* Serbian, English and French. *PRACTICE AREAS:* Industrial Property Law; Patent and Trademark Law.

VLADAN MALEŠEVIĆ, born Belgrade, Yugoslavia, November 4, 1960. *Education:* Tenth Belgrade Gymnasium (B.A., 1979; University of Belgrade (LL.B., 1988). *Member:* International Trademark Association (Foreign Member). *LANGUAGES:* Serbian and English. *PRACTICE AREAS:* Local and International Patents and Trademarks.

LEGAL SUPPORT PERSONNEL

PARALEGAL

LJILJANA MILETIC, born Zemun, Yugoslavia, November 24, 1963. *Education:* High School of Economy, Belgrade; Expert Diploma of Educational Centre, Belgrade. Training in industrial property activities, client correspondence, trademark prosecution and filing, file investigations and research. *LANGUAGES:* Serbian and English.

BOJANA RISTIC, born Belgrade, Yugoslavia, May 10, 1969. *Education:* High School of Economy, Belgrade. Training in industrial property activities, client correspondence, trademark prosecution and filing, file investigations and research. *LANGUAGES:* Serbian and English.

(This Listing Continued)

LEGAL ASSISTANT

MILA VULETIĆ, born Zemun, Yugoslavia, January 13, 1973. *Education:* High School of Technical, Zemun. Training in industrial property activities, client correspondence, trademark prosecution and filing, file investigations and research. *LANGUAGES:* Serbian and English.

Languages: English, French, Italian, German and Russian.

REPRESENTATIVE CLIENTS: *United States and Canada:* International Tel. & Tel., New York; Chesebrough-Pond's Inc., Greenwich, Connecticut; Combustion Engineering, Inc., Windsor, Connecticut; Canadian Industries Ltd., Montreal, Quebec; Noranda Mines Ltd., Pointe Claire, Quebec; B.F. Goodrich Co., Akron, Ohio; Gould Inc., Rolling Meadows, Illinois; Babcock & Wilcox Company, New York, N.Y.; *European Clients:* Patent Department of SOJUZPATENT, Moscow, C.I.S. (Russia); Patentbureau Danubia, H-1368 Budapest 5, Hungary; PATENTSERVIS, Praha 1, Kampa, Czechoslovakia; Bulgarian Chamber of Commerce & Industry, Sofia, Bulgaria; POLSERVICE, Warszawa, Poland; Standard Elktrik Lorenz AG, Stuttgart, West Germany; BBC Brown Boveri, Zurich, Switzerland.

JASNA ALEKSIC SPASIC

CARICE MILICE 8

YU-11000 BELGRADE, YUGOSLAVIA

Telephone: (381-11) 625-204

Telefax: (381-11) 626-594

Intellectual Property Law and Related Litigation, Food and Drug Law, Commercial Law, Inheritance, Family Law, Real Estate, General Practice.

JASNA ALEKSIC SPASIC, born Novi Sad, Yugoslavia, August 27, 1956; admitted, 1980, Yugoslavia. *Education:* Faculty of Law, University of Novi Sad (LL.B., 1979); Faculty of Philology, University of Novi Sad (1979-1981); Faculty of Law, University of Belgrade (1987-1989). Patent and Trademark Attorney recognized by Yugoslav Patent Office. Official Court Interpreter Appointed by the Ministry of Justice. *Member:* Belgrade Bar Association; Association Internationale des Jeunes Avocats (ALJA); Association Internationale pour la Protection de la Propriete Industrielle (AIPPI). *LANGUAGES:* English; German; French..

LAW OFFICE
LJUBIŠA D. VUČETIĆ

Established in 1989

KNEZA OD SEMBERLJE 14

11000 BELGRADE, YUGOSLAVIA

Telephone: 381 11 459-786; 381 11 458-172

Fax: 381 11 459-786

Administrative Law, Arbitration, Conveyancing, Corporate Law, Distributorship Agency & Franchise Law, Intellectual Property Law, Family Law, Insurance Law, International Contacts, International Private Law, Litigation, Property and Real Estate Law, Rent and Lease, Trade Regulations, Transportation Law, Joint Ventures, General Legal Practice.

PARTNERS

LJUBIŠA VUČETIĆ, born Vršac, Yugoslavia, November 19, 1955; admitted, 1989. *Education:* University of Beograde, School of Law (B.A. Degree, Law, 1981; Master Degree, International Trade Contracts, 1984); (Bar Exam, 1985). Authorized Agent for Industrial Property. Federal Department of Industrial Property, 1990. *Member:* Beograd's Bar Association. (President). *LANGUAGES:* Serbo-Croatian, English and Russian.

BERISLAV TOMAC, born Beograde, Yugoslavia, August 6, 1937; admitted, 1966. *Education:* University of Beograde, School of Law (B.A. Degree, Law, 1962; Master Degree, International Law, 1973); (Bar Exam, 1965). *LANGUAGES:* Serbo-Croatian, English and German.

CONSULTANT

MIROSLAV RADIC, born Beograde, Yugoslavia, May 26, 1956. *Education:* University of Beograde, School of Economics (B.A., International Trade, 1983); University of Beograde, School of Law (Master Degree, International Trade Contracts, 1985); Harvard University, Cambridge, Massachusetts (Certified Special Studies, Administration and Management, 1988). *LANGUAGES:* Serbo-Croatian and English.

BANGLADESH

DR. KAMAL HOSSAIN & ASSOCIATES

Established in 1980

CHAMBER BUILDING, 2ND FLOOR
122-124 MOTIJHEEL C.A.
DHAKA 1000, BANGLADESH
Telephone: (8802) 864966; 232946
Cable Address: Equity (DHAKA)
Telex: 632352 Anie BJ
Fax: (8802) 863409; 863378; 864966

Admiralty, Banking, Commercial Arbitration, Constitutional and Administrative Law, Criminal Law, Human Rights, Oil and Gas, Insurance, Shipping, Trademark and Patents, Corporate and General Practice.

DR. KAMAL HOSSAIN, born Calcutta, April 20, 1937; admitted, 1959, England, Pakistan and High Court, Dhaka; 1971, Bangladesh. *Education:* University of Notre Dame (A.B., 1955); University of Oxford (B.A., Hons, 1957; B.C.L., 1958; Doctor of Philosophy, International Law, 1964). Author: "Law and Policy in Petroleum Development," Frances Pinter, London, 1979. Member of Parliament, 1972-1975. Chairman, Constitution Drafting Committee, Constituent Assembly of Bangladesh, 1972. Minister of Law, 1972, Petroleum and Minerals, 1974 and Foreign Affairs, 1973-1975, Government of Bangladesh. Visiting Fellow, All Souls College, Oxford, 1975. International Consultant, Clifford Chance, London. Member, United Nations Compensation Commission; Advisory Board, ICSID Review, Foreign Investment Law Journal. *Member:* International Law Association (Chairman, Committee on Legal Aspects of Sustainable Development); International Bar Association (Member, Gas Law Committee, Energy Section); LAWASIA (Member, Executive Council); Supreme Court Bar Association, Bangladesh (President, 1990-1991); Bangladesh Bar Council (Vice-Chairman, 1989—). *LANGUAGES:* English and Bengali. *PRACTICE AREAS:* Admiralty; Banking; International and Commercial Arbitration; Constitutional Law; Administrative Law; Oil and Gas.

ASSOCIATES

KAZI SHAHABUDDIN AHMED, born Dhaka, January, 1932; admitted, 1963, High Court, Dhaka. *Education:* Dhaka University (B.A., 1952; LL.B., 1958). Former Member of Parliament. *LANGUAGES:* English and Bengali. *PRACTICE AREAS:* Corporate and General; Litigation.

ZAHIRUL ISLAM, born Cox's Bazar, 1939; admitted, 1968, Cox's Bazar; 1991, High Court Division, Supreme Court. *Education:* Dhaka University (B.A., 1960; LL.B., 1967). Former Professor, Law College, Cox's Bazaar. Former Member of Parliament, 1970-1973. Former President of Cox's Bazar District Bar Association. Member of Bangladesh Bar Council (1991—). *LANGUAGES:* Bengali and English. *PRACTICE AREAS:* Criminal; General; Litigation.

SHAMIM HASNAIN, born Dhaka, April 24, 1952; admitted, 1980, Bangladesh, High Court Division, Supreme Court; 198 7, Pennsylvania. *Education:* University of the Punjab (B.A., Hons; M.A.); University of Dhaka (LL.B.); Dickinson School of Law, Pennsylvania (M.C.L.). *LANGUAGES:* English and Bengali. *PRACTICE AREAS:* Admiralty; Banking; Corporate Matters; Litigation.

SARA HOSSAIN, born March 2, 1967; admitted, 1989, England; 1990, Dhaka; 1992, High Court Division, Supreme Court. *Education:* University of Oxford (B.A. Hons., 1988). *LANGUAGES:* English and Bengali. *PRACTICE AREAS:* Corporate and General Matters; Human Rights; Litigation.

RAMZAN ALI SIKDER, born Dhaka, January 11, 1967; admitted, 1993, Dhaka. *Education:* Dhaka University (B.Com., 1989; LL.B., 1992). *LANGUAGES:* Bengali and English. *PRACTICE AREAS:* Trade Mark and Patents; General Practice; Litigation.

SYED QAMRUZZAMAN, born Madaripur, October 25, 1963; admitted, 1994, High Court Division, Supreme Court. *Education:* Rajshaln University (LL.B., Hons., 1987; LL.M., 1988). *LANGUAGES:* Bengali and English. *PRACTICE AREAS:* Criminal; General Practice.

HUQ AND COMPANY

47/1, PURANA PALTAN
DHAKA 1000, BANGLADESH
Telephone: (880-2) 232196; 235953
Telex: 642520 ABBL BJ; 642944 ABBL BJ
Fax: 880-2-860229

Banking, Commercial, Company Matters, Tax Matters, Arbitration, Shipping, Constitutional, Joint-Venture Companies.

FIRM PROFILE: *The firm is one of the largest legal firms in Bangladesh. It is legal adviser and consultant to most of the banks and prominent business houses in Bangladesh, with experience in National and International Commercial matters, including International Arbitrations and negotiation for Joint-Venture Companies.*

SENIOR PARTNER

RAFIQUE-UL HUQ, M.A.; LL.B. Barrister-at-Law. Senior Advocate, Supreme Court of Bangladesh; Former Attorney General of Bangladesh.

ASSOCIATES

*Enayet Hussain Khan, B.Com.; LL.B.	**M.C. Debnath,* B.Com.; LL.B.
*Shorful Islam Khan, B.A.; LL.B.	**Mustafa Adil,* B.Com.; LL.B.
	*Dilruba Dawood, M.A.; LL.B.
*M. Moniruzzaman Khan, B.A. (Hons.) Law, U.K.;	**Shahrina Salam Bari,* LL.B. (Hons)
Barrister-at-Law, Attorney-at-Law (State of New York, U.S.A.)	*Faheem-ul Huq,* LL.B. (Hons.) (U.K.)
	Rokeya Sultana, B.SS. (Hons.); LL.B. (Hons.) (U.K.)

*Advocate of the Supreme Court of Bangladesh

Languages: English and Bengali

KABIR & ASSOCIATES

Established in 1983

BAR ASSOCIATION BUILDING
ROOM NO. 2/11, SUPREME COURT
DHAKA, BANGLADESH
Telephone: (880-2) 237-154
Fax: (880-2) 863-357

Chittagong, Bangladesh: 40 Panchlish Residential Area. Telephone: 031-211- 423. Fax: 880-31-610-089.

Khulna, Bangledesh: Room No. 8, 1st Floor, District Bar Association Building. Telephone: 031-211-423. Fax: 880-31-610-089.

Maritime Law, Commercial, Trademark and Patents, Civil Litigation, Oil and Gas, Banking and Finance, Commercial Collection, Company Law and Arbitration.

FIRM PROFILE: *The firm originally started as a sole practice, but has now extended to three offices; Dhaka, Chittagong and Khulu. With 7 Partners and 6 Associates who are well experienced in all the Fields stated in the areas of practice.*

MEMBERS OF FIRM

AHSANUL KABIR, born June 1, 1952; admitted, 1980, Bangladesh. *Education:* University of Chittagong (M.Com., 1975); Chittagong Law College (LL.B., 1978).

GOLAM QUDDUS

OSMAN GHANI

KHURSHED ALAM KHAN

SK AMJAD HOSSAIN

JAVED AHMAD

KAZI SALEH AHMAD

ASSOCIATES

Azizu Hoque   **Habibure Rahman**
Abul Kalam Azad

THE LAW ASSOCIATES

Established in 1968

GLOBE CHAMBER (2ND FLOOR)
104 MOTIJHEEL COMMERCIAL AREA
DHAKA 1000, BANGLADESH
Telephone: 234098; 252694; 863927
Fax: 880-2-863927
Telex: 671132 BJ

International Trade, Joint Venture, Banking, Investment, Capital, Security Regulations, Construction, Admiralty, Shipping, Trademark, Corporate and General Practice.

FIRM PROFILE: *M. Amir-Ul Islam founded the firm in the name "The Law Consultants" in 1968. In 1968 Mr. Moudud Ahmed joined the firm as junior partner. The Law Consultants dissolved in 1982 and transformed as The Law Associates. Many noted lawyers joined the firm and offered a full range of legal services meeting virtually every client need. The firm represents clients on both national and international level. The firm is assisted by a full staff of legal support personnel and many are fluent in foreign languages.*

SENIOR COUNSEL

M. AMIR-UL ISLAM, born Bangladesh, February 2, 1936; admitted, 1961, England; 1963, Dhaka High Court and Senior Advocate, Bangladesh Supreme Court; 1966, Pakistan Supreme Court. *Education:* Dhaka University (B.A., 1956); Council of Legal Education, Holborn Law College (1956-1961); Lincoln's Inn (Barrister-at-Law, 1961); Fletcher School of Law and Diplomacy (Law and Development); Harvard Law School (P.I.L.). Chambers of Mr. John Platts-Mills Q.C., 1961-1963. Teaching Constitutional Law; Lawyer's Skills; CLE Course Bar Council. Lecturer: Commercial Law, Central Law College (1963-1964); Law and Development, Tufts University, 1977. Special Envoy, 1972-1973, Minister of Food, 1973-1974 and Law Officer, 1977-1979, United Nations, Head Quarter, New York. Founder Honorary Secretary General, Bangladesh Institute of Law and International Affairs since 1972. President, Asia Pacific Organization on Mediation, 1987-1990. President, South Asian Association for Right to Development since 1984. Chairman: Bangladesh Bar Council Legal Education Committee. SAARC Law, Bangladesh Chapter; Vice Chairman: ILA Bangladesh; IFA Bangladesh. Country Correspondent and Contributor to: Lloyd's International Ship Arrest, Euromoney's Laws on International Banking and Security. *LANGUAGES:* English, Bengali, Urdu and Hindi. *PRACTICE AREAS:* General; Corporate; Constitutional; Banking; Shipping; Investment and Business Practice.

ASSOCIATES

MOHIUDDIN AHMED, born Bangladesh, April 10, 1939; admitted, 1973, Dhaka; 1982, Bangladesh Supreme Court. *Education:* Dhaka University (B.A., 1963; LL.B., 1972). *LANGUAGES:* Bengali and English. *PRACTICE AREAS:* Insurance Law; Construction; Claim Recovery.

A.H.M. JAHANGIR CHOWDHURY (RATAN), born Bangladesh, December 12, 1964; admitted, 1987, Dhaka; 1989, Supreme Court of Bangladesh. *Education:* University of Dhaka (LL.B. Hons., 1986); University of Dhaka (LL.M., 1988); University of Brussels (LL.M., 1991). *LANGUAGES:* English, Bengali and French. *PRACTICE AREAS:* International Trade; Banking; Shipping; Admiralty.

MS. TANYA AMIR, born Bangladesh, September 27, 1964; admitted, 1990, Dhaka and Advocate, Bangladesh Supreme Court. *Education:* Buckingham, U.K. (LL.B., 1989); Grays Inn (Barrister-at-Law, 1991). Practiced, Bar of England and Wales, April, 1993. *LANGUAGES:* English, Bengali, French and Hindi. *PRACTICE AREAS:* Foreign Investment; Joint Collaboration; International Trade; Banking; Security Regulations.

MISS SHIRIN AHMED CHOWDHURY, born Bangladesh, March 31, 1964; admitted, 1986, Bangladesh Supreme Court. *Education:* Dhaka University (B.A., 1984; LL.B., 1986). *LANGUAGES:* Bengali and English. *PRACTICE AREAS:* Litigation; Matrimony; General Practice; Admiralty.

MS. SHIRIN SHARMEEN CHOWDHURY, born Bangladesh, October 6, 1966; admitted, 1992. *Education:* University of Dhaka (LL.B. Hons., 1989; LL.M., 1990). *LANGUAGES:* English, Bengali and Hindi. *PRACTICE AREAS:* Legal Research; Arbitration; Corporate Law; Real Estate.

SAYEED MIZANUR RAHMAN, born Bangladesh, January 1, 1970; admitted, 1994, Bangladesh. *Education:* Chittagong Government College (Higher Secondary, 1987); Dhaka University (LL.B. Hons., 1991; LL.M., 1992). Author: "The Rule of Law and Democracy: Bangladesh Perspective," Onmookta, First Issue 1990, Cox's Bazar. Member, Bangladesh Research

(This Listing Continued)

Academy for the Information of New Society (Brains), 1989—; Human Rights Education and Development Project, Cox's Bazar, 1990—. Vice President, Human Rights Education and Development Project, Cox's Bazar, Bangladesh. Former Director, Bangladesh Research Academy for the Information of New Society, Dhaka. *LANGUAGES:* Bengali, English and Hindhi. *PRACTICE AREAS:* Legal Research; Drafting; Legal Pleadings; Deposition Summary.

TAX ADVISERS

FEROZUDDIN BHUIYAN, C.A.. LANGUAGES: Bengali and English. *PRACTICE AREAS:* Tax.

A.T.M. ABDUL BARI, C.A.. LANGUAGES: English and Bengali. *PRACTICE AREAS:* Tax.

OF COUNSEL

Justice (Ret.) K.M. Subhan

REPRESENTATIVE CLIENTS: Bank of New York; British Telecommunication; U.S. Department of Justice; HSBC Holdings plc.; General Motors; AMP (U.S.A.); American Cynamide; Honda Motor Co., Ltd. (Japan); Berjaya (Malaysia); American Cyanamid Co.; C. Itoh & Co., Ltd., Allibe, France; Itoman Corp.; HBO Asia; Daiwoo Textile; Hyundai Corp.; Samsung Corp.; Kukje-ICC Corp.; Motorola Asia Ltd. (Hong Kong); Motorola Singapore Ltd.; Bengal Shipping Lines Ltd.; National Bank Ltd.; Uttara Bank Ltd.; ANZ Grindlays Bank; Wishbone Trading Corp; American Express Ibc.

THE LAW CONSULTANTS

V.I.P. ROAD
35/A PURANA PALTAN LINE
DHAKA 1000, BANGLADESH
Telephone: (880-2) 841405; 839427; 812637
Facsimile: (880-2) 839427; 886629

Administrative Law, Admiralty & Maritime Law, International Banking & Business Law, Bankruptcy, Constitutional Law, Conveyancing, Copyright Law, Corporate Law, Criminal Law, Customs & Excise Law, Environmental Law, Family Law, Foreign Investments, General Legal Practice, General Intellectual Practice, General Tax Practice, Industrial Relations & Labour Law, Insolvency, Insurance Law, Litigation, Patent, Design & Trademark.

FIRM PROFILE: *The firm offers a full range of legal services. It is well known for its Commercial, Shipping Law Practice and General intellectual practice. The firm represents clients on both national and international level. The firm is assisted by a full staff of legal support personnel and office administrators.*

SENIOR COUNSELS

JUSTICE A.K.M. NURUL ISLAM, born Bangladesh, January 1, 1925; admitted, 1951, Advocate, Dhaka High Court; 1956, Pakistan Supreme Court. *Education:* University of Calcutta (B.A., 1945; M.A., 1947); University Law College, Calcutta (LL.B., 1950). Articled, Calcutta High Court, 1950-1951. Justice, Pakistan Supreme Court and Bangladesh Supreme Court, 1968-1977. Chief Election Commissioner of Bangladesh, 1977 and 1982. Senior Minister, Ministry of Law and Justice, 1985-1986. Member of Parliament, 1986-1988. Vice-President, People's Republic of Bangladesh, 1986-1989. Professor, City Law College, Dhaka. Founder President, Governing Body of Bangladesh Red Cross Society. Member, Former East Pakistan Red Cross Society, 15 years; Chairman, Red Cross Society, 1969 and 1971. Leader, Bangladesh delegation, Commonwealth Observer Group for the famous election held in 1980, Rhodesia. Leader, Bangladesh delegation United Nations Sessions, 1987. *LANGUAGES:* English, Bengali, Urdu and Hindi. *PRACTICE AREAS:* Administrative; Arbitration; Civil; Commercial; Constitutional; Shipping; Legal Consultancy.

KHONDKER MAHBUBUDDIN AHMED, born Bangladesh, December 7, 1925; admitted, 1959, Pakistan Supreme Court, Senior Advocate, Supreme Court of Bangladesh. *Education:* University of Calcutta (B.A., Hons., in English, 1945; M.A., in English, 1946); Presidency College, Calcutta (LL.B., 1948). President, Dhaka Rotary Club. Permanent Member: Holly Family Red Crescent Hospital. *Member:* Supreme Court Bar Association (President, 1979-1980; 1992-1993); National Bar Association (President); Bangladesh Bar Council (Member, 1986-1989; Vice-Chairman, 1979-1982, 1989-1992, 1992-1995). *LANGUAGES:* English, Bengali and Hindi. *PRACTICE AREAS:* Admiralty; Arbitration; Civil Matters; Company Law; Constitutional Law; International Banking; Shipping.

DR. MOHIUDDIN FAROOQUE, born Bangladesh, December 31, 1954; admitted, 1977, Advocate, Supreme Court of Bangladesh. *Education:* University of Dhaka (LL.B., Hons., 1977; LL.M., 1979); Institute of Con-

(This Listing Continued)

stitutional & Parliamentary Studies, India (Diploma, Constitutional Law, 1981); Manchester University (Diploma, International Law, 1985; Ph.D., International Law, 1988). Parliamentary Fellowship, Parliamentary Institutions and Procedure, 1981. Special Courses: The United Nations (Diploma, 1990); International Law (UNILC); The Netherlands, International Water Law and Management (Diploma, 1990); Upsala University Conflict Resolution "(Diploma, 1990); East-West Centre, Hawaii, Social Forestry (1991). Lecturer: Law of the Sea and International Law, Bangladesh Navy, 1989; Law of the Sea, Defence Services Command and Staff College, 1989—; International Law, Bangladesh Civil Services Institute. *Member:* Supreme Court Bar Association; Bangladesh Red Crescent Society; Society for Rule of Law; Bangladesh Society of International Studies; Bangladesh Research Bureau; International Association for Water Law, Italy; Asia Forum of Environmental Lawyers, Nepal; International Environmental Law Commission, Bonn; Environmental Law Alliance Worldwide; Bangladesh Environmental Lawyers Association (Secretary General); Country Correspondent and Contributor to: International Environmental Law, U.S.A. *LANGUAGES:* English, Bengali, Urdu and Hindi. *PRACTICE AREAS:* Admiralty; Shipping; Intellectual Property; Corporate; Constitutional; International Banking; Environmental Law.

COUNSELS

KHONDKER SHAMSUDDIN MAHMOOD, born Bangladesh, November 24, 1953; admitted, 1981, Advocate, Supreme Court of Bangladesh. *Education:* University of Dhaka (LL.B., Hons., 1978); University of London (LL.M., 1980). Senior Lecturer, Central Law College, Dhaka. Honourary Lecturer, Institute of Bankers. Member, Rotary Club of Dhaka South, Rotary International. *Member:* Dhaka Bar Association; Supreme Court Bar Association; Bangladesh Environmental Lawyers Association, BELA (Founder Member); Bangladesh Law Association (Vice-President); Lawyers Group (BD) Amnesty International (Executive Member); Bangladesh Red Crescent Society (Life Member). *LANGUAGES:* English, Bengali and Hindi. *PRACTICE AREAS:* Corporate Law; Company; Constitutional; Foreign Investment; Insolvency.

MIRZA QUAMRUL HASAN, born Bangladesh, January 12, 1954; admitted, 1979, Advocate, Supreme Court of Bangladesh. *Education:* University of Dhaka (LL.B., Hons., 1977; LL.M., 1979). Legal Training, Environmental Law, San Francisco, CA, U.S.A. Joint Secretary, Rotary Club of Dhaka, Rotary International. *Member:* Dhaka Bar Association; Supreme Court Bar Association; Bangladesh Environmental Lawyers Association, BELA (Treasurer). *LANGUAGES:* English, Bengali and Hindi. *PRACTICE AREAS:* Commercial Law; Civil; Company; Trademark; Patent and Design; Contract Law; Environmental Law.

RAQUIBUL HAQUE MIAH, born Bangladesh, January 25, 1964; admitted, 1990, Advocate, Supreme Court of Bangladesh. *Education:* University of Rajshahi (LL.B., Hons., 1987; LL.M., 1988). *Member:* Dhaka Bar Association; National Bar Association. *LANGUAGES:* English, Bengali and Hindi. *PRACTICE AREAS:* Administrative; Bankruptcy; Criminal; International Property; General Intellectual Practice; Family Law.

DELWAR HOSSAIN, born Bangladesh, March 3, 1959; admitted, 1992, Advocate, Supreme Court of Bangladesh. *Education:* University of Dhaka (B.A., 1984; LL.B., 1989). *Member:* Dhaka Bar Association; National Bar Association. *LANGUAGES:* English and Bengali. *PRACTICE AREAS:* Foreign Investment; Drafting Legal Pleadings; Company; Legal Research; Deposition Summaries.

JESMIN SULTANA SHAMSAD, born Bangladesh, July 2, 1965; admitted, 1990, Advocate, Supreme Court of Bangladesh. *Education:* University of Rejshahi (LL.B., Hons., 1987; LL.M., 1988). *Member:* Chittagong Bar Association; National Bar Association. *LANGUAGES:* English and Bengali. *PRACTICE AREAS:* Legal Pleadings; Family Law; General Legal Practice; Conveyancing; Trademark; Patent and Design.

AKRAM HOSSAIN, born Bangladesh, December 31, 1965; admitted, 1991, Advocate, Supreme Court of Bangladesh. *Education:* University of Rajshahi (LL.B., Hons., 1987); University of Dhaka (LL.M., 1988). *LANGUAGES:* English and Bengali. *PRACTICE AREAS:* Civil; Legal Pleadings; Drafting.

MD. ABDUL HAKIM, born Bangladesh, August 14, 1964; admitted, 1991, Advocate, Supreme Court of Bangladesh. *Education:* University of Rajshahi (LL.B., Hons., 1987); University of Dhaka (LL.M., 1988); HEAB-IHEU Netherlands (Diploma, Human Rights and Legal Aid). Assistant Coordinator, CLEP, Bangladesh Bar Council. *Member:* Dhaka Bar Association. *LANGUAGES:* English and Bengali. *PRACTICE AREAS:* General Practice; Tax.

(This Listing Continued)

INTELLECTUAL PROPERTY EXPERT

H.A. AKON, born Bangladesh, March 2, 1921; admitted, 1980, Advocate, Supreme Court of Bangladesh. *Education:* University of Calcutta (B.Sc., 1941); University of Dhaka (M.Sc., 1943; LL.B., 1972); National University of Australia (Legal Course on Intellectual Property, 1952). With, Commonwealth Patent Office, Canberra, Australia, 1952-1953. Controller, Patents & Designs and Registrar of Trade Marks (People's Republic of Bangladesh), 1974-1980. Chairman, 1982—. *Member:* Inventors' Association of Bangladesh (affiliated member of IFIA-Geneva); Asian Patent Attorneys Association, Tokyo. *LANGUAGES:* English, Bengali, Urdu & Arabic. *PRACTICE AREAS:* General Intellectual Property.

TAX ADVISER

DEWAN ASHRAFUL ISLAM, born Bangladesh, 1962; admitted, 1986, Advocate, Supreme Court of Bangladesh. *Education:* University of Rajshahi (LL.B., Hons., 1984; LL.M., 1986). *Member:* Dhaka Tax's Bar. *LANGUAGES:* English and Bengali.

NOTARY PUBLIC

M. ABDUR RAZZAQUE, M.A., LL.B., Advocate, Supreme Court of Bangladesh.

OF COUNSELS

DR. M. SHAH ALAM, born Bangladesh, December 31, 1951. *Education:* Patrice Lumumba University, Moscow (LL.M., Honours, 1978; Ph.D., Legal Aspects of the Exclusive Economic Zone, Law of Sea and Interpretation of International Treaties, 1982 and 1992). Assistant Professor, Rajshahi University; Associate Professor and Dean, Faculty of Law, Chittagong University 1992—. *LANGUAGES:* English, Bengali and Russian.

DR. M. MIZANUR RAHMAN, born Bangladesh, January 1, 1956. *Education:* Friendship University, Moscow (LL.M., 1981; Ph.D., 1984); Stockholm University, Sweden (P.G.D., 1985; M.C.L., 1991; Research Fellow, 1990-1992). Associate Professor of Law, University of Dhaka, 1985—. Lecturer, Bangladesh Civil Service Academy, President, Law Review. Founding Member, SAARCLAW. Chief Coordinator, CLEP. *Member:* Bangladesh Bar Council. *LANGUAGES:* Bengali, English, Spanish, Swedish and Russian.

LEGAL SUPPORT PERSONNEL

MD. MOHASIN, B.A., LL.B.

MS. SHAILA HOSSAIN, M.Sc.

REPRESENTATIVE CLIENTS: Sony Corporation, Japan; Mobile Television Engineering, Australia; American Air Lines; Bajaj Automobiles; Rangs Electronics Ltd.; Investment Corporation of Bangladesh; Uttara Bank Ltd.; Transorient Shipping Lines Ltd.; Frontline Clothings Ltd., Hong Kong; Sunset Apparels Ltd.; Security Consultants; Sarwar Jute Mills Ltd.; Quasem Group of Companies.

THE LAW COUNSEL

Established in 1990

MALEK MANSION (1ST FLOOR)
128, MOTIJHEEL COMMERCIAL AREA
DHAKA 1000, BANGLADESH
Telephone: (8802)246492; 817780
Telex: 642525 IBANK BJ
Fax: 880-2-863675; 880-2-867604

London, England Associated Office: A.T.M. Abdullah & Co., Solicitors, 217 High Street North, East Ham, London, E6 2JA. Telephone: 081-471-9693; 081-470-1015. Fax: 081-471-0630.

Admiralty, Banking, Insurance, Shipping, Trademark and Patents, Joint Collaboration, Arbitration, Corporate and General Practice.

FIRM PROFILE: Although formally established in 1990, the Law Counsel traces its origin back to the eighties when it started its journey in the form of a sole partnership by Mr. Abdur Razzaq. The Law Counsel is now one of the leading law firms in Bangladesh with an associated office in London. The firm provides a wide range of legal services and acts as legal advisor to many commercial banks and business houses, and assisted by efficient legal support personnel it represents clients from both home and abroad.

Our primary objective is the success of our clients. In pursuing this objective we have built on our traditions of excellence and integrity and gathered together, in one firm, an outstanding group of lawyers each with di-

(This Listing Continued)

THE LAW COUNSEL, Dhaka—Continued

verse talents to serve a broad client base. The firm's senior counsel is qualified to practice in more than one jurisdiction.

SENIOR COUNSEL

ABDUR RAZZAQ, born Bangladesh, December 31, 1949; admitted, 1980, England; 1986, Dhaka; 1988, Bangladesh Supreme Court. *Education:* Chittagong University (B.A., Hons., M.A., 1970); Holborn Law College (1975-1980); Lincoln's Inn (Barrister-at-Law, 1980). Chambers of Sir Michael Havers, Q.C., 1981-1982; Chambers of Lord Peter Rawlinson, Q.C., 1982-1983. Practiced in England from professional Chambers at 9 Stone Buildings, Lincoln's Inn, London, 1983-1985; Member of the Bar of England and Wales. Author: "The New International Economic Order"; "The International Economic Structures," World Jurist Association, Washington, D.C., 1991 and 1993; "The Supreme Court and the Constitutional Crisis" (The New Nation Dhaka, 1987). Co-Author: "Street Children in Bangladesh and the UN Convention on the Rights of the Child," (Radda Barnen, Bangladesh, 1991). Lecturer: Dhanmondi Law College (1986-1987). Secretary General, Centre for Human Rights and Third World Affairs. *Member:* Bangladesh Supreme Court Bar Association. *LANGUAGES:* Bengali, English, Urdu and Arabic. *PRACTICE AREAS:* General Corporate; Banking.

ASSOCIATES

SHAMIN KHALLED AHMED, born Bangladesh, 1951; admitted, 1986, Bangladesh Supreme Court. *Education:* Dhaka University (B.A. Hons., 1972; M.A., 1974); Lincoln's Inn (Barrister-at-Law, 1978); London University (LL.B., 1981); University of South Hampton (LL.M., 1983). *LANGUAGES:* Bengali and English. *PRACTICE AREAS:* Shipping and Insurance.

MAHBUBUDDIN AHMAD, born Bangladesh, 1953; admitted, 1987, Bangladesh Supreme Court. *Education:* Dhaka University (B.A. Hons, 1973; M.A., 1976); University of Sheffield, England (LL.B., 1981); Lincoln's Inn (Barrister-at-Law, 1985). *LANGUAGES:* English and Bengali. *PRACTICE AREAS:* Admiralty.

LEGAL SUPPORT PERSONNEL

NAZMUL HUQ, born Bangladesh, 1954. *Education:* Dhaka University (B.A. Hons., 1978; M.A., 1980; LL.B., 1982). *LANGUAGES:* English and Bengali. *PRACTICE AREAS:* Legal Research and Drafting.

MUHAMMAD RAFIQULLAH, born Bangladesh, 1967. *Education:* University of Dhaka (B.A., 1987; LL.B., 1990). *LANGUAGES:* English and Bengali. *PRACTICE AREAS:* Legal Pleading; Correspondence; Chambers Administration.

FOREIGN LEGAL CONSULTANT

HON. MICHAEL J. BELOFF, Q.C., admitted, 1967, England; 1981, Queens Counsel. Deputy High Court Judge, Queen's Bench Division. Master of the Bench, Gray's Inn. *PRACTICE AREAS:* Commercial Law; Administrative Law.

OF COUNSEL

DR. F.K.M.A. MUNIM, born 1924; admitted, 1959, England. *Education:* University of London (Doctor of Philosophy in Constitutional Law, 1964). Advocate General of East Pakistan, 1970. Judge of the High Court of East Pakistan, 1970-1971. Judge of Supreme Court of Bangladesh, 1972-1982. Chief Justice of Bangladesh, 1982-1989. Member, Expert Committee for drafting the Statute for the International Islamic Court of Justice sponsored by the Organization of Islamic Conference (OIC), 1981. *LANGUAGES:* Bengali and English. *PRACTICE AREAS:* Administrative Law; Judicial Review.

REPRESENTATIVE CLIENTS: Bank of America NT & SA, San Francisco, U.S.A.; Korean Exchange Bank, Seoul, Korea; Al-Rajhi Banking and Investment Corporation, Saudi Arabia; H.R. Johnson (Malaysia) Berhard, Kualalampur, Malaysia; Islami Bank Bangladesh Ltd.; Pubali Bank Limited; Technological Services Ltd.; Milan Apparels Limited; Century Fashion Wear Limited; Agragami Engineers Limited.

BRUNEI DARUSSALAM

HILBORNE, HAWKIN & CO.

Legal Consultants, Advocates and Solicitors

Trademark, Copyright & Patent Agents

Established in 1965

BRUNEI SERVICE ADDRESS FOR TRADEMARK REGISTRATION:
SUITE 31, 3RD FLOOR, BRITANNIA HOUSE
38 JALAN CATOR

BANDAR SERI BEGAWAN 2085, BRUNEI DARUSSALAM
Telephone: 6732-228382
Facsimile: 6732-228389

Orange, California Administrative Office: 2534 N. Santiago Blvd., 92667. Telephone: (714) 283-1155. Facsimile: (714) 283-1555; 532-2713.

Hong Kong Office: M2-3, New Henry House, 10, Ice House Street, Central. Telephone: 852-869-0828. Facsimile: 852-810-1703.

Singapore Service Address for Trademark Registration: c/o Loke & Seah, 3 Shenton Way, #21-10, Shenton House, Singapore, 0106. Telephone: 65-223-7088. Facsimile: 65-223-7028.

Malaysian Service Address for Trademark Registration: Lots 1708/9, 17th Floor Wisma Hla, Jalan Rajah Chulan, 50200, Kuala Lumpur, West Malaysia. Telephone: 03-2414823. Facsimile: 03-241-4641.

FIRM PROFILE: The firm's clientele consists of multi-national corporations and select "private and entrenched" individuals. Founded in 1965, the firm offers a full range of legal services and is well known internationally in areas of intellectual property, licensing, franchising, joint ventures and international business transactions. Subject to local bar rules, the firm accepts instructions for representation in Singapore, Malaysia, Brunei, Hong Kong, England and Wales.

MEMBERS OF FIRM

VINI KUMAR, born 1935; admitted, 1965, Malaysia; 1966, Brunei; 1969, Singapore; 1961, England and Wales. Certified as a Legal Consultant by the State Bars of New York and California for these jurisdictions.

ALAN H. DAY, born 1943; admitted, 1971, England and Wales; 1972, Hong Kong.

OF COUNSEL

KEITH E. KLINE, born 1955; admitted, 1986, California. Registered Patent Attorney (USPTO).

Please direct all inquiries to our Administrative Office in California, USA.

Y.C. LEE & COMPANY

SUITES 507-508, 5TH FLOOR
KOMPLEKS JALAN SULTAN
51-55 JALAN SULTAN

BANDAR SERI BEGAWAN 2085, BRUNEI DARUSSALAM
Telephone: 02-228725; 02-221917; 02-244646
Fax: 02-240786

Kuala Belait, Brunei Darussalam Office: No. 82, 2nd Floor, Jalan Bunga Tanjong, Kuala Belait 6083. Telephone: 03-331116. Fax: 03-331116.

Arbitration, Civil Litigation, Banking, Commercial, Company, Construction, Intellectual Property, Shipping, Admiralty.

(This Listing Continued)

MEMBERS OF FIRM

YEW CHOH LEE, born Brunei Darussalam, 1961. *Education:* University of Bristol (Barrister of Lincolns Inn, 1986). Advocate and Solicitor of the Supreme Court of Brunei. Brunei Correspondent, Asian Section, The Singapore Journal of Legal Studies. Legal Advisor, The Embassies of France and Germany in Brunei.

Languages: English, Malay and Chinese

CAMBODIA

DELANEY & CO. INDOCHINA LIMITED

THE ALLSON STAR, 138, MONIVONG BOULEVARD
PHNOM PENH, CAMBODIA

Thailand Office: 28/11 Soi Ruamrudee, Wireless Road, Bangkok 10330. Telephone (662) 253-8528. Telecopy: (662) 253-4256. Mobile GSM: (661) 811-1787. Phonelink: (151, 152) 441069. Mailing Address: MBE Asoke Suite #347, 44/1-3 Asoke Road, Bangkok 10110.

Myanmar Office: The Liberty Hotel, 343, Pyay (Prome) Road, San Chaung Township, Yangon, Union of Myanmar. Telecopy: (951) 34144.

New York Office: 167 East 67th Street, Suite 5A, New York, New York 10021, United States of America.

Washington, D.C. Office: 2916 Fessenden Street, N.W., Washington, D.C. 20008 Unites States of America. Telephone: (202) 364-6742. Fax: (202) 364-6749.

Direct Co-Investment, General Corporate, Mergers and Acquisitions, Securities, Corporate Finance, Structured Finance, Public Finance, Leasing, Banking, Restructuring, Private Investment Funds, Futures and Options, Interest Rate and Currency Swaps, Labor, Immigration, Joint Ventures, Venture Capital, Legislative, Lobbying, Government Bidding, Privatizations, Public Concessions, Energy, Environmental, Media and Telecommunications, Oil and Gas, Utilities, Real Estate, Construction, Tax, Trust and Estates, Intellectual Property, General Litigation, Criminal Litigation, Arbitration and Mediation.

(For complete biographical data on all personnel, see Professional Biographies at Bangkok, Thailand)

MBANDO CONSULTING GROUP LAW OFFICES

60 NORODOM BOULEVARD
P.O. BOX 2354
PHNOM PENH H3, CAMBODIA
Telephone: 855-15-913713
Fax: 855-23-26462

Oil and Gas, Energy (Natural Resources), Privatization, International Trade/Investment, Environmental Law, Corporations, Banking, Commercial and International Arbitration.

MBELLA JKOMI NGONGI, born Victoria, Cameroon, March 18, 1954; admitted, 1979, Nigeria; 1992, Cameroon. *Education:* University of Lagos Law School (LL.B., 1978); Nigerian Law School (B.L., 1979); University of Brussels Law School (LL.M., 1982); Harvard University, U.S.A. (LL.M., 1991). Author: "Legal Aspects of Doing Business in Cameroon," Kluwer, IBS vol. 4; "Country Handbook on Cameroon," ILM Country Handbooks Suppl. May 4, 1992, Kluwer; "Country Handbook on Cambodia," 1995; International Contract Manual Country Handbooks To Be Published, 1995. Visiting Professor, International Economic Law, 1991, University of Puerto Law School, P.R.; United Nations Environmental Law and Institutions; Instructor To Officials of the Ministry of Environmental Kingdom of Cambodia, 1993-1994. Member, Chief Counsel, National Hydrocarbons Corporation, Cameroon's State-Owned Oil and Gas Corporation, 1984-1990; Legal Officer United Nations Transitional Authority in Cambodia, 1992-1993. Environmental Lawyer/Contracts Specialist/Acting Chief Technical Adviser, Cambodia Environmental Advisory Team/Secretary-General 1993-1994 UNDP; "MBanDo YA MOKPE" A Grassroots Development Association of Cameroon-More than 20,000 Members, 1988-1990. *Member:* Nigerian, Cameroon (Chairman, Cambodia Lawyers Roundtable) and International Bar Associations. *LANGUAGES:* English, French, Mokpe, Duala, Pidgin, Spanish, German and Khmer

(This Listing Continued)

(Cambodian). *SPECIAL AGENCIES:* United Nations Transitional Authority in Cambodia; United Nations Development Programme. *PRACTICE AREAS:* Oil and Gas, Energy (Natural Resources); Privatization; International Trade/Investment; Environmental Law; Corporations, Banking, Commercial; International Arbitration.

REPRESENTATIVE CLIENTS: Government of Cambodia.

POBLADOR, AZADA & BUCOY

HOUSE NO. 223, RUE NO. 1
KHAND DONPENH, SANGKAT THSAR KANDAL 1, ALANG
MAKANG
PHNOM PENH, CAMBODIA
Telefax: + 855 (23) 27434

Metro Manila, Republic of the Philippines Office: 7th Floor, State Condominium I, 186 Salcedo Street, Legaspi Village, Makati, 1229. Telephone: (632) 892-07-86. Cable Address: "POBLAW" Manila. Telex: (632) 63207. Telefax: (632) 818 3858; (632) 761 0311. Mailing Address: P.O. Box 7340 & 7384, Airmail Distribution Center, Manila International Airport, Philippines.

Patents, Trademarks and Copyrights.

MEMBERS OF FIRM

Honorio U. Poblador, Jr.	*Antonio Audie Z. Bucoy*
(1917-1985)	*Cipriano Azada*
	Manuel A. Poblador, Sr.

ASSOCIATES

Susanna Cruz-Pingol	*Loreto Alano Madarang*
Luis M. Duka, Jr.	*Luz B. Buensuceso*
Augusto Yparraguirre Arreza, Jr.	*Erwin B. Fernandez*
Amelita H. Purugganan	*Gilbert Mario Abril de la Cruz*
Enrique Sahagun Madarang	

OF COUNSEL

Horacio Umali Poblador	*Jesus I. Santos*

PEOPLE'S REPUBLIC OF CHINA

ALLEN & OVERY

SUITE 3204, JING GUANG CENTRE
HU JIA LOU, CHAOYANG DISTRICT
BEIJING (PEKING) 100020, PEOPLE'S REPUBLIC OF CHINA
Telephone: (86 1) 501 4681
Facsimile: (86 1) 501 4682

London, England Office: One New Change, EC4M 9QQ. Telephone: 0171 330 3000. Facsimile: 0171 330 9999.

Brussels, Belgium Office: Rue de la Loi 99, Box 8, 1040. Telephone: (32 2) 230 27 91. Facsimile (32 2) 230 66 13.

Budapest, Hungary Office: Mádach Trade Center, Mádach Imre utca 13-14, H-1075. Telephone: (361) 268 1511. Facsimile: (361) 268 1515.

Dubai, United Arab Emirates Office: 501 Al Futtaim Tower,P.O. Box 3251, Deira. Telephone: (971 4) 282296. Facsimile: (971 4) 212860.

Frankfurt, Germany Office: Taunusanlage 11, 11th Floor, 60329. Telephone: (49 69) 242 6120. Facsimile: (49 69) 242 61220.

Hong Kong Office: 9th Floor, Three Exchange Square, 8 Connaught Place. Telephone: (852) 2840 1282. Telex: 68757. Facsimile: (852) 2840 0515.

Madrid, Spain Office: Antonio Maura 7, 6°, 28014. Telephone: (34 1) 521 2654. Facsimile: (34 1) 523 0458.

Moscow, Russia Office: 9 ul Tverskaya, Entrance No 5, 8th Floor, 103009. Telephone: (7 501) 940 4500. Facsimile: (7 501) 940 4501.

New York Office: Swiss Bank Tower, 10 East 50th Street, 10022. Telephone (1-212) 754 3340. Facsimile: (1-212) 754 7903.

Paris, France Office: 1 Avenue Franklin D. Roosevelt, 75008. Telephone (33-1) 49 53 06 37. Telex: 651079. Facsimile: (33-1) 49 53 91 52.

Prague, Czech Republic Office: Jindřišská 34, 110 00 Prague 1. Telephone: (42 2) 2410 3317. Facsimile: (42 2) 2410 3235.

Singapore Office: 20 Raffles Place #08-03, Ocean Towers, 0104. Telephone: (65) 533 0988. Facsimile: (65) 533 1322.

(This Listing Continued)

ALLEN & OVERY, Beijing (Peking)—Continued

Tokyo, Japan Office: NSE Building, 5th Floor, 1-7-1 Kanda Jinbo-cho, Chiyoda-ku Tokyo 101. Telephone (81 3) 3259 9898. Facsimile (81 3) 3259 9888.

Warsaw, Poland Office: ul. Kopernika 17, IV Floor, 00-359. Telephone: (48 22) 262 226. Facsimile: (48 22) 262 360.

Firm engaged in English and International Practice.

CONTACT PARTNERS

Kenneth Chan (Resident Partner in Hong Kong)

RESIDENT ASSOCIATES

Xiaoyang Li

(For Complete List of Firm Personnel, see Professional Biographies at London, England).

ARNBERGER, KIM, BUXBAUM & CHOY

SUITE 2523, CHINA WORLD TRADE CENTRE
NO. 1 JIAN GUO MEN WAI AVENUE
BEIJING (PEKING), PEOPLE'S REPUBLIC OF CHINA
Telephone: (86)(1) 505-2288 (Ext. 2523)
Fax: (86)(1) 505-2638

REVISER OF THE PEOPLE'S REPUBLIC OF CHINA LAW AND MONGOLIA LAW DIGESTS FOR THIS DIRECTORY.

Hong Kong Office: 3201 Citibank Tower, 3 Garden Road, Central. Telephone: (852) 2523-7001. Fax: (852) 2845-0947.

Guangzhou (Canton), People's Republic of China Office: China Hotel Office Tower, Suite 512. Telephone: (86)(20) 666-3388. Ext. 2512. Fax: (86)(20) 669-1217.

Xiamen, People's Republic of China Office: Foreign Trade Centre, Suite 519, No. 15 Hu Bing North Road, Xiamen City. Telephone: (86)(592) 506-3059. Facsimile: (86)(592) 511-1044 Ext. 519.

Shenzhen, People's Republic of China Office: Shenzhen Development Center, Suite 2103, Renmin Nan Lu, Shenzhen. Telephone: (86)(755) 229-8009. Facsimile: (86)(755) 229-8011.

Shanghai, People's Republic of China Office: 7th Floor, Block 2, Jing Ming Building, No. 8 Zun Yi Road, Shanghai. Telephone: (86)(21) 219-4180. Facsimile: (86)(21) 219-7421.

Ulaanbaatar, Mongolia Office: Ulaanbaatar Supreme Court Building, Room 429, 432. Telephone: (976)(1) 31-0711. Fax: (976)(1) 32-5102.

New York Office: 100 Maiden Lane, 16th Floor, Suite 1600B, New York, New York 10038. Telephone: (212) 504-6109. Fax: (212) 412-7016.

Los Angeles Office: 3731 Wilshire Boulevard, Suite 910, West Tower, Los Angeles, California, 90010. Telephone (213) 380-5798. Facsimile: (310) 358-0226; (213) 380-5798.

San Francisco Office: 44 Montgomery Street, Suite 500, San Francisco, California, 94104. Telephone: (415) 955-0553. Fax: (415) 753-1235.

Alhambra Office: 320 South Garfield, Suite 206, Alhambra, California 91801. Telephone: (818) 281-9088. Fax: (818) 281-7189.

Corporate, Employment Law, Commodities, Securities, Complex Commercial Litigation, International Transactions, Intellectual Property, Aircraft and Equipment Leasing Financing and Taxation.

MEMBERS OF FIRM

DAVID C. BUXBAUM, born New York, N.Y., July 16, 1933; admitted, 1970, New York and U.S. District Court, Southern, Eastern, Northern and Western Districts of New York; 1971, U.S. Court of Appeals, Second Circuit; 1974, U.S. Supreme Court; 1975, U.S. Court of Appeals, Seventh and Fourth Circuits; 1978, U.S. Court of Appeals, Eighth Circuit; 1979, U.S. Court of Appeals, First Circuit; 1981, California; 1989, U.S. District Court, Central District of California; 1991, U.S. District Court, Northern District of California; U.S. Court of Appeals, Ninth Circuit. *Education:* New York University (B.A., 1954); University of Michigan (J.D., 1959); concurrent graduate studies, University of Michigan Graduate School; graduate study, Harvard University and University of Washington (M.A., 1963; Ph.D., 1968). Member, Far East Honor Society, University of Michigan. Author: *Articles:* "Preliminary Trends in the Development of the Legal Institutions of Communist China and the Nature of the Criminal Law," International and Comparative Law Quarterly, January, 1962, reprinted in *Government of Communist China,* Chandler, San Francisco, 1966; "Horizontal and Vertical Influences Upon the Substantive Criminal Law of Mainland Chinese, Some Preliminary Observations," Osteuropa Recht, No. 1, 1964; "Chinese

(This Listing Continued)

Family Law in Common Law Setting: A Note on the Institutional Environment and the Substantive Family Law of the Chinese in Malaysia and Singapore," Journal of Asian Studies, August, 1966; "Some Aspects of Civil Procedure and Practice at the Trial Level in Tanshui and Hsinchu...," XXX Journal of Asian Studies, 1971; *Lawyer's Challenge in China Trade: New and Developing Legal System,* New York Law Journal, International Law Finance and Trade, February, 1979; *Commodities Trade with China,* New York Law Journal, December, 1978; *Regulation of Commodity Futures Exchanges in Japan,* New York Law Journal, October, 1978; *Commodities Transactions in China and Hong Kong,* New York Law Journal, June, 1978; *Jurisdiction Over Foreign Transactions and Foreign Nationals,* New York Law Journal, April, 1978; *Two Cases of Dispute Settlement,* U.S.-China Business Review, Vol. 1, No. 2, March/April, 1974; *Two Cases of Dispute Settlement,* Arbitration and Dispute Settlement in Trade with China, Special Report No. 4 for Members of the National Council for United States-China Trade, February, 1974; *Negotiation with the Chinese,* Trade with China, 1973; *American Trade with the People's Republic of China: Some Preliminary Perspectives,* Columbia Journal of Transnational Law, Vol. 12, No. 1, 1973; *Liability of Federal Officials in Damage for Acts Unconstitutional or in Excess of their Authority; Expanding the Concept of the Rule of Law,* Capital University Law Review, Vol. 8, Issue 4, 1979; *Taking on the Government Alone; Sole Practitioner Battles Way to Supreme Court and Wins,* Legal Times of Washington, December, 1978; *Disclosure of Management Remuneration, Transaction, Litigation and Employment History,* Los Angeles Daily Journal, March, 1979; *Contracts in China,* China Trade, Praeger, 1982. Monthly Columnist, New York Law Journal on Commodities Law, 1976-1982; *Contract Law in China, The Dynamics of Statutory Development and Practice,* Doing Business in China, 1990, Streng et al, ed. Contracts in China during the Qing Dynasty: Key to the Civil Law, Journal of Oriental Studies, University of Hong Kong, 1993. *The Commercial Laws of China,* and *Patents Law and Practice, Trademark Law and Practice, The People's Republic of China,* Digest of the Commercial Laws of the World, 1982-1993. *M.A. Dissertation:* "Legal Institutions of Contemporary Mainland China," University of Washington, 1962. *Ph.D. Dissertation:* Some Aspects of Substantive Family Law and Social Change in Rural China, 1896-1967," University of Washington, 1968. *Case Note:* "Freedom of Marriage in a Pluralistic Society," Malaya Law Review, 1963. Editor: *Traditional and Modern Legal Institutions in Asia and Africa, Journal of Asian and African Studies,* Supplement Edition, 1967; *Family Law and Customary Law in Asia: A Contemporary Legal Perspective,* 1968; *Law and Social Change: A Case Study of Family Law and Social Change in China and Other Developing Areas,* University of Washington Press, 1978; *Transition and Permanence: Chinese History and Culture, A Festschrift in Honor of Dr. Kung-Chan Hsiao,* 1971; *Chinese Family Law and Social Change in Historic and Comparative Perspective,* University of Washington Press, 1978; *China Trade: Prospects and Perspectives,* Prager, 1982; Sole Counsel for Successful Respondents, *Butz v. Economou,* 438 US 478, 1978. Associate Professor, Chinese Law, Comparative Law and Domestic Relations, University of Washington, 1968-1969. Assistant Lecturer, Chinese Law, Domestic Relations, Labor Law, Jurisprudence, Comparative Law, University of Singapore, 1963-1964. Adjunct Professor of Law: Touro Law School, 1980; Southwestern University School of Law, 1983-1988. Member, Commission on Labor Law, Singapore, 1963-1964. Member, Panel of Arbitrators, American Arbitration Association. *Member:* American Bar Association (Member, Committee on Far Eastern Law, Section of International and Comparative Law, 1965-1971); New York Trial Lawyers Association (Member, Liaison Committee with Judicial Conference, 1971-1978). *LANGUAGES:* Chinese, French, German and Japanese (specialized reading). *PRACTICE AREAS:* International Law; Complex International Litigation; Complex International Contract; Joint Venture Contract; Investment Law; Trademark, Copyright and Patent Protection and Enforcement; Commodities and Securities.

KENNETH Y. CHOY, born Hong Kong, May 24, 1956; admitted, 1987, New York; U.S. District Court, Southern and Eastern Districts of New York; 1990, California; 1991, Central and Northern Districts of California and U.S. Court of Appeals, 9th Circuit (Not admitted in China). *Education:* San Francisco State University (B.A., 1977); Northeastern University (J.D., 1986). Judicial Intern to Hon. Dolores K. Sloviter, U.S. Court of Appeals for the Third Circuit, 1985-1986. *Member:* American Bar Association (Member, Section on Labor and Employment Law); American Immigration Lawyers Association. (New York Office). *LANGUAGES:* Chinese (Cantonese and Mandarin). *PRACTICE AREAS:* Litigation and Transactions in U.S. and People's Republic of China.

H. BENNETT ARNBERGER, born Globe, Arizona, July 8, 1953; admitted, 1983, California and U.S. District Court, Northern and Central Districts of California. *Education:* University of California at Berkeley

(This Listing Continued)

(A.B., with honors and distinction, 1977); University of San Francisco (J.D., 1983). Phi Delta Phi. Author: "Ensuring Compliance Through Intellectual Property Audits," 5 International Legal Strategy 54 (1994); "Avoiding The Hidden Liabilities of Independent Contractors," I Foreign Assignments (Kaigai Chuzai) 99 (1994); "Proactive Prevention of Cross-Cultural Disputes," 6 International Legal Strategy 60 (1994); "Protecting Against Misappropriation of Trade Secrets," 10 International Legal Strategy 63 (1993); "Taxation and Legal Requirements of California Corporations," 16 International Business Law Journal (Kokusai Shoji Homu) 202 (1988). Associate, Yuasa & Hara, Tokyo, Japan, 1987-1989. Contract Administrator, Chemsult AG, Saudi Arabia, 1977-1980. *Member:* San Francisco and American (Member, Section on International Law) Bar Associations; State Bar of California; International Bar Association (Member, Section on Business Law); Japan Society of Northern California; California-Southeast Asia Business Association; American Chamber of Commerce in Japan (Member, Committee on Licensing, Patents & Trademarks, 1987-1989). (San Francisco Office).

DAVID S. KIM, born Seoul, South Korea, February 17, 1961; admitted, 1990, California and U.S. District Court, Northern and Central Districts of California. *Education:* Western Illinois University (B.B.A., 1983; M.B.A., 1985); Southwestern University School of Law, Los Angeles (J.D., 1989). Recipient, Bradley and Pollack Scholarship, 1990. *Member:* State Bar of California; California Trial Lawyers Association; Los Angeles Trial Lawyers Association; California Korean Bar Association. (Los Angeles Office). *LANGUAGES:* English and Korean. *PRACTICE AREAS:* Litigation; Real Estate.

DOUGLAS L. BRYAN, born Whittier, California, September 7, 1960; admitted, 1991, California and U.S. District Court, Central District of California; 1992, U.S. Court of Appeals, Ninth Circuit. *Education:* California Polytechnic State University (B.S., 1983); Southwestern University School of Law (J.D., 1991). *Member:* State Bar of California; American Bar Association. (Los Angeles Office). *PRACTICE AREAS:* Tax Law; Corporate Law; Corporate Reorganizations; Constitutional Law; Insurance.

ROBERT W. MULCAHY, born Boston, Massachusetts, May 8, 1940; admitted, 1970, New York; 1971, District of Columbia; 1976, California; 1991, State Bar of Texas. *Education:* Boston College (B.S., Chemistry, 1963); George Washington University (J.D., 1968). *Member:* District of Columbia; State Bar of California; American Bar Association; The Licensing Executive Society. The Houston Volunteer Lawyers Association; Houston Intellectual Property Law Association. (Alhambra Office). *PRACTICE AREAS:* Intellectual Property; Patent Agent; Copyright Law; Trademark Law; Trade Secrets and Licensing.

OF COUNSEL

DEBORAH S. CHEW, born Singapore, May 27, 1964; admitted, 1988, Singapore; 1991, California. *Education:* National University of Singapore (LL.B., with honors, 1987). Associate, Arthur Loke & Partners, Singapore, 1988-1991. *Member:* State Bar of California; American Immigration Lawyers Association; Singapore American Business Association (Founding Member and Director); Hong Kong Association of California (Director); Asian Business Association; Law Society of Singapore and Academy of Law of Singapore. (San Francisco Office). *LANGUAGES:* English and Chinese (Mandarin, Cantonese, Taiwanese and Chiu-chow dialect).

CHRISTINA Y. CHEN, born Canton, China, May 2, 1943; admitted, 1983, California. *Education:* San Francisco State University (B.A., 1969); Hastings College of the Law, University of California (J.D., 1979). (Of Counsel, San Francisco, California Office). *LANGUAGES:* English and Chinese (Mandarin, Cantonese and Toisan dialect).

ROGER S. SAXTON, born Martins Ferry, Ohio, April 30, 1952; admitted, 1979, Sweden (as Jurist); 1980, Pennsylvania and U.S. District Court, Western District of Pennsylvania; 1992, New South Wales, Australia. *Education:* Case Western Reserve University (J.D., 1979); Studies in Japanese Law, Sophia University and University of Tokyo, Tokyo, Japan (1977-1980); Studies in Australian Law, University of Sydney (1989-1991). *Member:* Pennsylvania Bar Association; Law Society of New South Wales; Inter Pacific Bar Association. (Of Counsel, Sydney, Australia). *LANGUAGES:* English, Swedish and Japanese.

KAZUKO ITOH, born Tokyo, Japan, January 17, 1923; admitted, 1959, Japan (Not admitted in the U.S.). *Education:* Tsuda College; Tokyo Bunrika University. Legal Advisor to Her Britanic Majesty's Ambassador, Tokyo, 1976—. Legal Consultant to the American Embassy, Tokyo, 1976—. *Member:* Tokyo Bar Association; International Bar Association. (Of Counsel, Tokyo, Japan). *LANGUAGES:* Japanese, English, French and Spanish.

(This Listing Continued)

PRACTICE AREAS: General Civil and Trial Practice; International Arbitration; Patent Litigation.

DUCK-SOON CHANG, born Korea, July 23, 1960; admitted, 1985, Korea and Korea Patent Bar; 1991, New York; 1992, California. *Education:* Judicial Training and Research Institute of the Supreme Court of Korea (198 3-1984); College of Law, Seoul National University (B.Jur,. 1983); Harvard Law School (LL.M., 1990). Author: "Technology Transfer, Cooperation and Joint Venture Agreements with Korea", Chapter 4 of Legal Aspects of Business Transactions and Investment in the Far East (Kluwer, 1988); "Arbitration Procedures in Korea," Vol. 1, Asia Law and Practice 7 (1989); "Arbitration in South Korea," Vol. 14 East Asian Executive Reports 1 (1992). Lecturer, International Patent Training and Research Institute of the Korean Industrial Property Office. Arbitrator, Korean Commercial Arbitration Board. *Member:* New York State and American Bar Associations; State Bar of California; Korean Bar Association; Korean Patent Bar Association; International Trademark Association. (Of Counsel, Seoul, Korea). *LANGUAGES:* Korean, English, Japanese (reads only). *PRACTICE AREAS:* Joint Venture; Licensing; Commercial Arbitration; Intellectual Property.

ASSOCIATES

JIA LIN, born China; admitted, 1989, China; 1991, California. *Education:* Zhongshan University, Guangzhou, China (LL.B.); People's University Beijing, China (LL.M.). Lecturer, People's University, 1989—.

PEIZHONG GAN, born China, May 8, 1956; admitted, 1988, China (not admitted in the United States). *Education:* The Department of Law, Beijing University (LL.B., 1983; LL.M., 1989). Chief Editor, Encyclopedia of Commercial Law of China and the Encyclopedia of Corporate Law. Author: 21 articles and 3 books, e.g. "Legal Issues on Contracting Management in the Enterprises Owned by the Whole People," "Several Legal Issues on Corporate Reorganization in China". Lecturer, 1988. Associate Professor, 1994, Lectures on Corporate and Companies Law, 1984-1985. Assessor in the Beijing Intermediate Court. *LANGUAGES:* Chinese, English. *PRACTICE AREAS:* Corporate Law; Commercial Law; Litigation; Intellectual Property.

YUAN JIANG, born Fujian Province, China, April 15, 1956; admitted, 1983, China (Not admitted in the United States). *Education:* China University of Political Science and Law, 1979-1983; Part-time graduate student at China University of Political Science and Law, international private law, 1986-1989. Cadre at Research Department, China Lawyer Association, 1989-1990. Reporter, China Lawyer Magazine, 1990-1993. *LANGUAGES:* Chinese. *PRACTICE AREAS:* Labor Law; Leasing; Litigation.

XIAODONG HAO, born Inner Mongolia, China, March 9, 1965; admitted, 1990, China. *Education:* Inner Mongolia University (B.S.); China University (LL.B., Political Science and Law, 1991). *LANGUAGES:* Chinese, English, Japanese. *PRACTICE AREAS:* Litigation; Business Law; Intellectual Property.

SIYANG LIAO, born Shanghai Province, China, April 15, 1970. *Education:* China Political/Legal University (LLB, 1992). *LANGUAGES:* Chinese, English. *PRACTICE AREAS:* Contract Law; Joint Venture Law; Intellectual Property Law.

YAOWU RONG, born Wei Chen County, Ji Bei, March 19, 1979; admitted, 1993, China; (Not admitted in the United States). *Education:* Xiamen University (B.A., 1992); (Now Mid. Graduated College of Xiamen University). (Xiamen Office). *LANGUAGES:* Chinese, English. *PRACTICE AREAS:* Civil Law; Commercial Law.

VINCENT I.S. HSIEH, born Taipei, Taiwan, January 15, 1964; admitted, 1993, New York. *Education:* National Taiwan University (LL.B., 1987) Boston University (LL.M., in International Banking, 1992). *Member:* American Bar Association; New York County Lawyers Association. (New York Office). *LANGUAGES:* Mandarin Chinese.

ZHOUGEN LI, born Shunde, Guangdong Province, PRC, October 1, 1935; (Not admitted in the United States). *Education:* Yue Xue Teachers Training College. 1985-1991, Judge (ret.) Guangzhou Middle People's Court, Civil Division and Director of Administration. Recipient, 1984, 1985 Guangzhou City Court Systems Advance Specialist of the Year; 1988, Guangdong Province Outstanding Judge of the year; 1989 Third Degree Honor awarded by the Guangdong Province High Court. *LANGUAGES:* Chinese (Mandarin and Cantonese). *PRACTICE AREAS:* Litigation; Contract; Intellectual Property.

JIANXIN LI, born Jiangmen, China, October, 1966; admitted, 1988, China (Not admitted in the United States). *Education:* Guangzhou University (Law Department, 1984-1986); Zhongshan University (Economic Man-

(This Listing Continued)

ARNBERGER, KIM, BUXBAUM & CHOY, Beijing (Peking)—Continued

agement Department, 1987-1990). Attorney, Guangzhou Second Foreign Economic Law Office, 1986-1990. (Guangzhou Office). **LANGUAGES:** English, Chinese (Mandarin and Cantonese). **PRACTICE AREAS:** Intellectual Property Litigation; Contracts; Real Estate; Trade; Insurance Law; Adoption Law.

YIKUN ZHU, born Sichuan Province, China, August 1967; admitted, 1993, China (Not admitted in the United States). *Education:* Southwest College of Politics & Law (L.L.M., 1991). [Chinese, Russian, French, and English]. (Guangzhou Office). **PRACTICE AREAS:** Foreign Investment; Securities Law; Company Law; Intellectual Property; Tax Law; International Trade Dispute; Contracts.

DACHTCEREN ENKHBOLD, born Ulaanbaatar, Mongolia, March 11, 1946; admitted, 1973, Mongolia; (Not admitted in the United States). *Education:* International Relations Institute of Moscow (expert of Western Countries - U.S.A., Canada); Mongolian State University (Teacher of English Language). (Mongolia Office). **LANGUAGES:** Russian, English. **PRACTICE AREAS:** Economic Entities and Foreign Investment, Civil Law.

BYAMBAA BAYARMAA, born Moscow, Russia, November 6, 1960; admitted, 1982, Mongolia; (Not Admitted in the United States). *Education:* Moldova State University, Law Faculty, 1982; Passed State Examination on Bar Practice, March, 1994. (Mongolia Office). **LANGUAGES:** Russian, German, Romania, English. **PRACTICE AREAS:** Commercial and Contract Law.

JIANXIONG HUANG, born Rongyan City, Fujian, January 15, 1964; admitted, 1987 (Not admitted in the United States). *Education:* South-West Politics & Law College (B.A., 1984); College of Xiamen University (Master of Law, 1990). (Xiamen Office). **LANGUAGES:** Chinese, Taiwanese, English. **PRACTICE AREAS:** Civil Law; Commercial Law; Investment Law; Real Estate Law.

MINGLIANG LAN, born Hainan Province, China, August 12, 1927; admitted, 1989 (Not admitted in the United States). *Education:* Beijing Zhengfa University of Politics and Law (1956). Publications: Outline of Administrative Law; General Situation of International Organization; International Constitution (Teaching Material); Outline and Guidance on International Law. *Member:* Asian-Africa Development Committee, China International Legal Study Committee; National Lawyer Committee; China-Hong Kong Law Study Committee; China Investment Consultancy Experts Committee; China Political and Legal Management Leaders Institution; China Trade Committee; Foreign Economic and Trade Arbitration Committee (Arbitrator); National Overseas Federation Legal Consultant Committee. (Shenzhen Office). **LANGUAGES:** Chinese, English. **PRACTICE AREAS:** Public International Law; Intellectual Property.

ALFRED YONG LIN, born Fuzhou, China, October 10, 1969; admitted, 1993, China (not admitted in the United States). *Education:* Xiamen University Law Department (B.A., 1992). (Shanghai Office). **LANGUAGES:** Chinese, English and Fuzhou. **PRACTICE AREAS:** General Civil Law; International Investment; Corporation Law.

HONGLIANG WU, born Shanghai, China, 1935; admitted, 1985, China; registered patent agent (not admitted in the United States). *Education:* Beijing Iron and Steel Institute (B.S., 1960). (Shanghai Office). **LANGUAGES:** Chinese (Shanghai dialect) and English. **PRACTICE AREAS:** Patent and Trademark Law; Intellectual Property.

JIANG-XIONG HUANG, born Rongyan City, Fujian Province, China, January 15, 1946; admitted, 1987, China (Not admitted in the United States). *Education:* Institute of Political Science and Law in South-west China (B.A. in Law, 1984); Post-graduate Institute of Xiamen University (LL.M. in civil law, 1990). Author: An Introduction to Civil Law, published by house of Xiamen University; Examples of Lawsuits, published by house of Xiamen University; A Guide for Taiwan People to Invest in Mainland China, published by Beijing Huayi Publishing House. Lecturer: Civil Law; Law of Estate and Practice, Law Department, Xiamen University. *Member:* China Jurisprudence Society; Fujian Jurisprudence Society; Xiamen Jurisprudence Society; Fujian Society of Administrative; Association for Industry and Commerce; Xiamen Society of Administration for Industry and Commerce; Xiamen Bar Association. (Xiamen Office). **LANGUAGES:** Chinese, Taiwanese, English. **PRACTICE AREAS:** Economic; Commercial; Civil; Criminal; Investment Law, and Real Estate Law in China.

(This Listing Continued)

ZHOUGEN LI, born Shunde, Guangdong Province, China, October 1, 1935; (Not admitted in the United States). *Education:* Yue Xue Teachers Training College. 1985-1991, Judge (ret.) Guangzhou Middle People's Court, Civil Division and Director of Administration. Recipient, 1984, 1985 Guangzhou City Court Systems Advance Specialist of the Year; 1988, Guangdong Province Outstanding Judge of the year; 1989 Third Degree Honor awarded by the Guangdong Province High Court. (Hong Kong Office). **LANGUAGES:** Chinese (Mandarin and Cantonese). **PRACTICE AREAS:** Litigation; Contract; Intellectual Property.

LEGAL SUPPORT PERSONNEL

ZHANGQUING WU, born Shantou Guangdong Province, PRC October 15, 1967. *Education:* Shenzhen University (LL.B., 1991). (Shenzhen Office).

SHIJIE CHEN, born Xiamen, Fujian Province, China, November 18, 1970. *Education:* Xiamen University (LL.B., 1992). (Xiamen Office). **LANGUAGES:** English, Chinese. **PRACTICE AREAS:** Adoption Law; Contracts; Insurance; Trade.

SONG GAO, born Fujian Province, China, April 2, 1969. *Education:* Hau Qiao University (LL.B.). (Shenzhen Office).

REVISER OF THE PEOPLE'S REPUBLIC OF CHINA LAW AND MONGOLIA LAW DIGESTS FOR THIS DIRECTORY.

BAKER & McKENZIE

SUITE 2526 CHINA WORLD TOWER
CHINA WORLD TRADE CENTER
1 JIANGUOMENWAI DAJIE
100004 BEIJING (PEKING), PEOPLE'S REPUBLIC OF CHINA

Telephone: 505-0591; 505-0592; 505-4867; 505-4967; 505-4969; 505-2288, Ext. 2596

Intn'l. Dialing: (86-1) 505-0591; 505-0592; 505-4867; 505-4967; 505-4969; 505-2288, Ext. 2526

Cable: ABOGADO BEIJING
Telex: 22907
Answer Back: 22907 ABOGA CN
Facsimiles: (86-1) 505-2309; 505-0378

Associated Offices of Baker & McKenzie in: Almaty, Amsterdam, Bangkok, Barcelona, Berlin, Bogotá, Brasília, Brussels, Budapest, Buenos Aires, Cairo, Caracas, Chicago, Dallas, Frankfurt, Geneva, Hanoi, Ho Chi Minh City, Hong Kong, Juárez, Kiev, London, Madrid, Manila, Melbourne, México City, Miami, Milan, Monterrey, Moscow, New York, Palo Alto, Paris, Prague, Rio de Janeiro, Riyadh, Rome, St. Petersburg, San Diego, San Francisco, São Paulo, Singapore, Stockholm, Sydney, Taipei, Tijuana, Tokyo, Toronto, Valencia, Warsaw, Washington, D.C. and Zürich.

Correspondent Law Firm: Hadiputranto, Hadinoto & Partners, Jakarta.

International Trade and Investment Matters, including Joint Ventures, Wholly Foreign-Owned Ventures, Contracted Projects, Securities, Taxation, Arbitration, Regulatory Compliance, Finance and Real Estate Development.

PARTNER

MICHAEL J. MOSER, born New York, N.Y., U.S.A.; admitted, 1981, New York, U.S.A.; 1989, District of Columbia, U.S.A. (Not admitted in China). *Education:* School of Foreign Service, Georgetown University (B.S.F.S., magna cum laude,); Columbia University (Ph.D. with distinction); Harvard Law School (J.D.). Phi Beta Kappa. Appointments: Panel of Arbitrators: China International Economic and Trade Arbitration Commission, Beijing (one of five foreign nationals appointed); Singapore International Arbitration Centre; Hong Kong International Arbitration Centre; American Arbitration Association. Member, Governing Council and Management Committee, Hong Kong International Arbitration Centre. Associate, Chartered Institute of Arbitrators, London (Member, Governing Committee, Hong Kong Branch). Member, United Nations Working Group on official translations of Chinese foreign investment legislation. *Member:* New York State and International Bar Associations; District of Columbia Bar; Harvard Alumni Association of China (Chairman). (Also at Hong Kong). **LANGUAGES:** English and Chinese (Mandarin).

LOCAL PARTNER

YUEHUA LIU, born Hebei, China, May 14, 1944. *Education:* The University of Hong Kong (LL.M., 1992). **LANGUAGES:** Chinese and English.

(This Listing Continued)

ASSOCIATES

MICHAEL A. ALDRICH, born New York, U.S.A., 1960; admitted, 1992, California, U.S.A.; 1993, District of Columbia, U.S.A. (Not admitted in China). *Education:* Georgetown University School of Foreign Service (B.S.F.S., 1982); State University of New York at Stony Brook (M.A., 1984); Columbia University School of Law (J.D., 1990). *Member:* State Bar of California; District of Columbia Bar; American Bar Association. *LANGUAGES:* Mandarin Chinese.

JON S. EICHELBERGER, born Mineola, New York, U.S.A., July 20, 1956; admitted, 1991, New York, U.S.A. (Not admitted in China). *Education:* Stanford University (A.B., with distinction, 1981); Harvard Law School (J.D., cum laude, 1990). *Member:* American Bar Association. *LANGUAGES:* Mandarin Chinese.

ALLAN K. A. MARSON, born Leavenworth, Washington, U.S.A., August 29, 1952; admitted, 1983, Washington, U.S.A.; 1993, Connecticut, U.S.A. and New York, U.S.A. (Not admitted in China). *Education:* Wenatchee Valley College; Evergreen State College (B.A., 1974); University of Washington; Inter-University Program for Chinese Language; Lewis & Clark Law School (J.D., 1982); Columbia University Law School (LL.M., 1992). *Member:* Washington State (Inactive), Connecticut and New York State Bar Associations. *LANGUAGES:* Mandarin Chinese.

PAUL D. MCKENZIE, born Vancouver, Canada, 1963; admitted, 1990, British Columbia, Canada (Not admitted in China). *Education:* University of Toronto (B.A., 1985; LL.B., 1989). *Member:* Canadian Bar Association. *LANGUAGES:* English and Chinese (Mandarin).

JOHN W. SULLIVAN, III, born Bronx, New York, U.S.A., July 31, 1962; admitted, 1991, New York, U.S.A. (Not admitted in China). *Education:* Lehigh University (B.A., 1984); Suffolk University (J.D., 1990). Member, The American Chamber of Commerce (Beijing) (Member, Board of Governors, 1994). *Member:* The Bar Association of the City of New York; New York State Bar Associations. *LANGUAGES:* English and Mandarin Chinese.

CONSULTANT

XIANGYANG GE, born Beijing, China, February 20, 1969. *Education:* Peking University Law School (LL.B., 1991). *LANGUAGES:* English and Chinese.

BEITEN BURKHARDT MITTL & WEGENER

Rechtsanwälte

UNIT 10, 29TH FLOOR, JING GUANG CENTRE

HU JIA LOU, CHAO YANG QU

100020 BEIJING (PEKING), PEOPLE'S REPUBLIC OF CHINA

Telephone: (86-1) 501 4569; 501 3388 Ext. 2910

Telefax: (86-1) 501 3034

Munich, Germany Office: Leopoldstrasse 236, D-80807. Telephone: (089) 35065-00. Telefax: (089) 35065-123.

Berlin, Germany Office: Kurfürstenstrasse 72-74, D-10787 Berlin. Telephone: (0 30) 264 71-0. Telefax: (0 30) 264 71-123.

Frankfurt/Main, Germany Office: Arndtstrasse 28, D-60325 Frankfurt/Main. Telephone: (0 69) 75 60 95-0. Telefax: (0 69) 75 60 95-12.

Nürnberg, Germany Office: Obere Turnstrasse 8, D-90429 Nürnberg. Telephone: (09 11) 2 79 71-0. Telefax: (09 11) 2 79 71-99.

Leipzig, Germany Office: Käthe-Kollwitz-Strasse 54, D-04109 Leipzig. Telephone: (03 41) 4 77 25 97. Telefax: (03 41) 4 77 25 99.

Potsdam, Germany Office: Heinrich-Mann-Allee 105 B, D-14473 Potsdam. Telephone: (0331) 33 43 06. Telefax: (0331) 33 43 29.

Hof, Germany Office: Oberer Torplatz 1, D-95028 Hof. Telephone: (09281) 80 23. Telefax: (09281) 1 65 69.

Plauen, Germany Office: Lindenstrasse 5, D-08523 Plauen. Telephone: (03741) 22 35 11; 22 49 62. Telefax: (03741) 22 49 62.

New York, New York Office: 215 East 73rd Street, New York, NY 10021. Telephone: (212) 570-2141. Telefax: (212) 734-7011.

London, England Office: Swedenborg House, 21 Bloomsbury Way, London, WC1A 2TH. Telephone: (0171) 2 42 44 66. Telefax: (0171) 2 42 44 67.

Moscow, Russia Office: Ul. Alekseja Tolstovo D.30/1, 103001 Moscow. Telephone and Telefax: (095) 202 37 60; 290 05 56.

(This Listing Continued)

Prague, Czech Republic Office: Na Bojišti 24, 120 00 Prague 2. Telephone: (2) 24 91 5808. Telefax: (2) 24 91 5804.

Budapest, Hungary Office: József Nádor Tér 9, H-1051 Budapest. Telephone: (1) 2 66 18 10. Telefax: (1) 2 66 18 11.

Hong Kong Office: 605 B, Sixth Floor, Peregrine Tower, Lippo Centre, 89 Queensway. Telephone: (852) 2524 6468. Telefax: (852) 2524 7028.

Commercial Law, Company Law, M & A, Joint Ventures, Finance, Banking, Leasing, Domestic and International Tax, Antitrust, EC Law, Real Property and Private Construction, Electronic Data Processing (Protection and Licensing), Media, Publishing, Unfair Competition, Trademarks, Copyright, Labour, General and Special Administrative Law Particularly Public Construction and Planning Regulations and Public International Law, Environmental Law, Agricultural Law, Privatization and Restitution (former GDR), Probate, Family and Estate Planning, Insolvency and Sports, Insurance, Automobile Accidents and Injuries.

FIRM PROFILE: BEITEN BURKHARDT MITTL & WEGENER is a nation-wide and international law firm with 108 lawyers. The firm's head office is in Munich. All the firm's offices provide a comprehensive range of services in the main areas of civil and commercial law.

JÜRGEN BURKHARDT, born Konstanz, 1940; admitted, 1967, Germany. *Education:* Universities of Munich (law degree, 1963) and Zurich (Swiss law degree, 1966; Dr. jur., 1966). With Axel Springer Verlag, 1965-1968. In-house counsel with Gruner+Jahr, Munich, 1969-1971. Member: Advisory Board, Vogel Medien GmbH & Co. KG, Würzburg; Supervisory Board, rotring international, Hamburg; Legal Committee, German Association of Publishers (VDZ); German-American Chamber of Commerce. Lecturer, Cartel, Competition and Media Law, University of Erlangen-Nürnberg, 1990—. *LANGUAGES:* German, English and Italian. *PRACTICE AREAS:* Company Law; Acquisitions and Sales; Restructuring; Press Law; Publishing and Radio; Cartels; Probate and Family Law.

ZHANG XI, born Shenyang, China, 1963. *Education:* University of Beijing (LL.B., Commercial Law, 1985; Joint Ventures, 1987); University of Tübingen (LL.M., 1988; DAAD Scholarship, Dr.jur., 1994). With, Heidian, Beijing, 1984; Dr. A. Wolff, Vienna, 1989; Blake, Cassels & Graydon, Toronto, 1994 and United Nations Commission on International Trade Law (UNCITRAL) - Office of Legal Affairs, Vienna, 1993. *Member:* German-Chinese Legal Fellow Association. *LANGUAGES:* Chinese (Mandarin), English and German. *PRACTICE AREAS:* Financial Services; Expropriation and Restitution.

C & M LAW OFFICE

25TH FLOOR, CHINA TRAVEL SERVICE TOWER

2 BEI SAN HUAN EAST ROAD

BEIJING (PEKING) 100027, PEOPLE'S REPUBLIC OF CHINA

Telephone: 86-01-4612505; 4612506

86-01-4622288 Ext. 2501, 2502

Fax: 86-01-4612507

Firm engaged in Chinese and International Law practice, entitled to practice before all courts in China including the Supreme People's Court of China.

Foreign (International) Economic and Trade, Maritime and Admiralty, including Investment, Joint-Ventures, Compensatory Trade, Banking, Intellectual Property, Technology Transfer, Taxation, Securities, Bonds, Marine Insurance, Shipping, Civil and Criminal, Arbitration and Litigation both International and Domestic.

FIRM PROFILE: Established in May, 1992, following legal reform in China. C & M is one of the leading private partnership law firms in Beijing, China, similar to private firms in western countries. C & M provides superior legal services to clients from around the world.

XIAO FENG GAO, born Beijing, China. *Education:* People's University of China. Co-Author: "Questions and Answers to Economic Contract Law." *Member:* China Law Society; China Economic Law Society; Asia-Pacific Law Society. Partner. *LANGUAGES:* Chinese and English. *PRACTICE AREAS:* Litigation and Arbitration; Trade-Mark; Contracts; Corporation; Joint-Ventures; Securities and Bonds; Criminal.

LU YE, born Sichuan Province, China. *Education:* Beijing University, Chinese Academy of Social Sciences (Master of Law); Harvard Law School (LL.M., 1994). Author: "Introduction to International Practice" and "Damages Under International Sales Contract." *Member:* Asia-Pacific Law Society; China International Law Society. Partner. *LANGUAGES:* Chinese and

(This Listing Continued)

C & M LAW OFFICE, Beijing (Peking)—Continued

English. **PRACTICE AREAS:** International Investment and Trade; Joint-Ventures; Commercial and Corporation; Real-Estate; International Finance and Banking; Securities and Bonds; Intellectual Property; Contracts; Arbitration and Litigation.

PETER WU SI JIANG, born Anhui Province, China. *Education:* Shanghai Maritime Institute. Co-translator: "Arrest of Vessel" and "The Oxford Companion to Law." *Member:* China Maritime Law Association; Asia-Pacific Law Society; Union International Des Avocats. Partner. **LANGUAGES:** Chinese and English. **PRACTICE AREAS:** Maritime Law and International Trade; Carriage of Goods by Sea; Collision; Shipping; Personal Injury; Marine Insurance; Marine Arbitration and Litigation.

CHUN MING TAO, born Hubei Province, China. *Education:* Huazhong Normal University, Jilin University (Master of Law). Former Section Chief of China International Economic and Trade Arbitration Commission. Author: "Copy-right Hand-Book"; "Theory and Practice of Arbitration Procedure for China International Economic and Trade." *Member:* Arbitrator of CIETAC, Mediator of Beijing Conciliation Center; China International Law Society; China Maritime Law Association; Commission for Procedure Disputes under China Maritime Law Association. Partner. **LANGUAGES:** Chinese and English. **PRACTICE AREAS:** International Business and Trade; Corporation; Contracts; Investment; Joint-Ventures; Arbitration and Litigation.

WILLIAM JUN DING, born Beijing, China. *Education:* Dalian Maritime University. *Member:* China Maritime Law Association. Associate. **LANGUAGES:** Chinese and English. **PRACTICE AREAS:** Maritime and Shipping Law; International Trade; Arbitration and Litigation.

AMY XIAO JUN SONG, born Xinjiang, China. *Education:* China University of Political Science and Law. Associate. **LANGUAGES:** Chinese and English. **PRACTICE AREAS:** International Trade and Maritime Law; Joint-Ventures; Contracts; Corporation; Arbitration and Litigation.

COUDERT BROTHERS

JING GUANG CENTRE, SUITE 2708-09

HU JIA LOU, CHAO YANG QU

BEIJING (PEKING) 100020, PEOPLE'S REPUBLIC OF CHINA

Telephone: 501-2851, 501-2852

Telecopier: 501-2856

REVISERS OF THE FRANCE LAW DIGEST FOR THIS DIRECTORY

New York, New York 10036-7794: 1114 Avenue of the Americas.

Washington, D.C. 20006: 1627 I Street, N.W.

Los Angeles, California 90017: 1055 West Seventh Street, Twentieth Floor.

San Francisco, California 94111: 4 Embarcadero Center, Suite 3330.

San Jose, California 95113: Suite 1250, Ten Almaden Boulevard.

Paris 75008, France: Coudert Frères, 52, Avenue des Champs-Elysées,

London, EC4M 7JP England: 20 Old Bailey.

Brussels B-1050, Belgium: Tour Louise. 149 Avenue Louise-Box 8.

Shanghai, People's Republic of China 200002: c/o Suite 1804, Union Building, 100 Yanan Road East.

Hong Kong: 25th Floor, Nine Queen's Road Central.

Singapore, 0104: Tung Centre, 20 Collyer Quay.

Sydney N.S.W. 2000, Australia: Suite 2202, State Bank Centre, 52 Martin Place.

Tokyo 107, Japan: 1355 West Tower, Aoyama Twin Towers, 1-1-1 Minami-Aoyama, Minato-ku.

Moscow, Russia: Ulitsa Staraya Basmannaya 14.

01301 Sao Paulo, SP, Brazil: Machado, Meyer, Sendacz, e Opice, Advogados, Rua Da Consolacao, 247, 8 Andar.

Bangkok 10500, Thailand: Bubhajit Building, 20 North Sathorn Road, 10th Floor.

Ho Chi Minh City, Vietnam: c/o Saigon Business Centre, 49-57 Dong Du Street, District 1.

General and International Law Practice.

Firm engaged in American and International Law Practice. Not authorized to practice Chinese Law. Attorneys not admitted in China.

(This Listing Continued)

PARTNER

DOUGLAS R. ADEN, born Evanston, Illinois, October 2, 1946; admitted, 1975, California; 1977, New York. *Education:* Stanford University (A.B., 1968); Boalt Hall School of Law, University of California, Berkeley (J.D., 1975). *Member:* Association of the Bar of the City of New York; American Bar Association. **LANGUAGES:** Indonesian.

ASSOCIATES

Phillip William Chritton	*Jingzhou Tao*
Bruce R. Schulberg	*Ning Zhu*

REVISERS OF THE FRANCE LAW DIGEST FOR THIS DIRECTORY

(For biographical data of the Washington personnel, see Professional Biographies at Washington, D.C.).

(For biographical data of the New York personnel, see Professional Biographies at New York, N.Y.).

(For biographical data of the San Francisco personnel, see Professional Biographies at San Francisco, California).

(For biographical data of the Los Angeles personnel, see Professional Biographies at Los Angeles, California).

(For biographical data of the San Jose personnel, see Professional Biographies at San Jose, California).

(For biographical data of the London personnel, see Professional Biographies at London, England).

(For biographical data of the Paris personnel, see Professional Biographies at Paris, France).

(For biographical data of the Hong Kong personnel, see Professional Biographies at Hong Kong).

(For biographical data of the Singapore personnel, see Professional Biographies at Singapore).

(For biographical data of the Tokyo personnel, see Professional Biographies at Tokyo, Japan).

(For biographical data of the Sao Paulo personnel, see Professional Biographies at Sao Paulo, Brazil).

(For biographical data of the Shanghai personnel, see Professional Biographies at Shanghai, People's Republic of China).

(For biographical data of the Sydney personnel, see Professional Biographies at Sydney, Australia).

(For biographical data of the Brussels personnel, see Professional Biographies at Brussels, Belgium).

(For biographical data of the Moscow personnel, see Professional Biographies at Moscow, U.S.S.R.).

(For biographical data of the Ho Chi Minh City personnel, see Professional Biographies at Ho Chi Minh City, Vietnam).

DENTON HALL

A Member of the Denton International Group of Law Firms

3325 CHINA WORLD TOWER

CHINA WORLD TRADE CENTRE

1 JIANGUOMENWAI AVENUE

BEIJING (PEKING) 100004, PEOPLE'S REPUBLIC OF CHINA

Telephone: 86-1 505 4891/2

Fax: 86-1 505 4893

Other Offices: London, England; Milton Keynes, Buckinghamshire, England; Brussels, Belgium; Hong Kong; Los Angeles, California; Singapore; Tokyo, Japan; Moscow, Russia.

Associated Offices: Amsterdam, Berlin, Chemnitz, Copenhagen, Dusseldorf, Frankfurt, Hamburg, Prague, Rotterdam and Vienna.

OF COUNSEL

DAVID BEN KAY. LANGUAGES: Mandarin. **PRACTICE AREAS:** Commercial; Corporate.

JOHN KUZMIK (Also at Hong Kong Office). **LANGUAGES:** Mandarin. **PRACTICE AREAS:** Commercial; Corporate.

(For all Firm Personnel, see Professional Biographies at London, England).

GIDE LOYRETTE NOUEL

SUITE 3309 A, JING GUANG CENTRE
HU JIA LOU, CHAOYANG DISTRICT
BEIJING (PEKING) 100020, PEOPLE'S REPUBLIC OF
CHINA
Telephone: (86.1) 501 4511
Telecopier: (86.1) 501 4551

Paris, France Office: 26 Cours Albert 1er, 75008. Telephone: (1) 40.75.60.00. Cable Address: "3 Avocagidva Paris 86." Telex: 651261F GILOY. Telecopier: (1) 43.59.37.79.

New York, New York Office: Swiss Bank Tower, 10 East 50th Street, 10022. Telephone: (1-212) 644-1201. Telex: 424353 GIDE. Telecopier: (1-212) 644-1205.

Brussels, Belgium Office: Rue de la Loi 99.101, B-1040. Telephone: (32.2) 231.11.40. Telecopier: (32.2) 231.11.77.

Warsaw, Poland Office: Ul. Kopernika 17, 00-359. Telephone: (48.22) 26.22.21. Telecopier: (48.22) 26.03.02.

Riyadh, Saudi Arabia Office: P.O. Box 4615, 11412. Telephone: (966.1) 476.60.39. Telex: 401677 NASHWA. Telecopier: (966.1) 476.18.96.

Tokyo, Japan Office: Homei Building 3F, 3-19 Akasaka 1-Chome, Minato-Ku, 107. Telephone: (81.3) 55.62.03.01. Telecopier: (81.3) 55.62.03.06.

Prague, Czech Republic Office: 34 Jindrisska, 11207. Telephone: (42.2) 24.21.34.65;24.21.36.50. Telecopier: (42.2) 24.21.09.12;24.22.58.53.

St. Petersburg, Russia Office: 34 Souvorovsky Prospect, App 45, P.O. Box 172, 193015. Telephone by satellite: (7.812) 850.16.85. Telecopier by satellite: (7.812) 850.16.86.

Moscow, Russia Office: 9, Ulitsa Tverskaya - App 66, 103009. Telephone by satellite: (7.501) 940.45.00. Telecopier by satellite: (7.501) 940.45.01.

Budapest VII, Hungary Office: EMKE Building, Rákóczi út 42, BP 409, 1072. Telephone: (36.1) 268.1236; 268.1237; 268.1238. Telecopier: (36.1) 268.1239.

Madrid, Spain Office: Antonio Maura 7, 6°, 28014. Telephone: (34.1) 531.25.01. Telecopier: (34.1) 531.35.30.

Hanoi, Vietnam Office: Hanoi Business Centre, 51 Ly Thai To. Telephone: (84.42) 66.122.3. Telecopier: (84.42) 66.030.1.

French and International Law.

RESIDENT ASSOCIATES

Olivier Dauchez
Stéphane Luo
Dan Huang
Stéphane Grand

(For Biographical Data on Personnel, see Professional Biographies at Paris, France).

GRAHAM & JAMES

SUITE 1903, CITIC BUILDING
19, JIANGUOMENWAI DAJIE
BEIJING, 100004, PEOPLE'S REPUBLIC OF CHINA
Telephone: (861) 507-8557
Fax: (861) 500-2557
Telex: 22969 GJPEK CN

Associated Offices of Deacons, Graham & James and Sly & Weigall: Bangkok, Hanoi, Hong Kong, Jakarta, Taipei, Tokyo, Brisbane, Canberra, Melbourne, Perth, Sydney, Los Angeles, Newport Beach, New York, Palo Alto, Sacramento, San Francisco, Washington, D.C., Mexico City.

Other Associated Offices: Berlin, Brussels, Bucharest, Düsseldorf, Frankfurt, Leipzig, London, Milan, Munich, Prague.

RESIDENT PARTNER

KEVIN HOBGOOD-BROWN, (Not admitted in China). admitted, 1980, Texas; 1987, California. *Education B.A. (Southern Methodist University); J.D. (Southern Methodist University). Member:* American, Texas, California and San Francisco Bar Associations. **PRACTICE AREAS:** Business Law; Corporate Law; Inter-Trade and Investment Law; Chinese Law.

(This Listing Continued)

RESIDENT ASSOCIATES

FENGMING LIU, admitted, 1988, Washington (Not admitted in China). *Education:* LL.B. (Beijing U.); J.D. (Hamline U.); LL.M. (U. Washington). Author: "China's Resumption of Gatt Membership: A Step Toward Entry into the World Economy.". *LANGUAGES:* Mandarin and English. *PRACTICE AREAS:* International Trade; Foreign Investment; Maritime; Immigration.

MANAGING PARTNER

SALLY HARPOLE, admitted, 1978, California (Not admitted in China). *Education:* J.D. (U. Washington); A.B. (U. Calif., Berkeley). Arbitrator, China International Economic and Trade Arbitration Commission, Chartered Institute of Arbitrators. President, American Chamber of Commerce in PRC, 1985-1986. General Editor, CCH, China Business Law Guide. (Also U.S. Law Consultant at Deacons, Hong Kong Office). *LANGUAGES:* Mandarin, Cantonese, French and German. *PRACTICE AREAS:* China Trade and Investment; Arbitration; U.S. Corporate and Trade Law.

JINGTIAN ASSOCIATES

SUITE 815, BLOCK B, XINGFU BUILDING
3 DONG SANHUAN BEI ROAD
BEIJING (PEKING) 100027, PEOPLE'S REPUBLIC OF
CHINA
Telephone: 86-1-4615753; 86-1-4615723
Fax: 86-1-4615750

Banking and Finance, Investment, Corporate, Intellectual Property, International Trade and Commerce, Securities, Real Estate, Taxation, Bankruptcy and Liquidation, Maritime Commerce, Aviation, Product Liability, Energy and Environment, Labor Management and the Settlement of Labor Disputes, Litigation, Arbitration and Settlement of Disputes.

FIRM PROFILE: One of the first and leading private partnership law firms within P. R. China engaged in Chinese and international law practice, entitled to practice before all courts and arbitration tribunals in China. Provides first class legal services to clients all over the world.

MEMBERS OF FIRM

WEI BAI, born Nanjing, China. *Education:* Peking University (Bachelor of Law); Foreign Affairs College (Master of Law). *Member:* All China Lawyers Association; The China Society of International Law. *LANGUAGES:* Chinese and English. *PRACTICE AREAS:* Banking and Finance; Corporate; Securities; Intellectual Property Protection; International Commercial Arbitration.

CHARLES F. LIANG, born Beijing, China. *Education:* Peking University (Bachelor of Law, Master of Law); Columbia University, School of Law (Certificate). *Member:* All China Lawyers Association; Licensing Executives Society (LES). *LANGUAGES:* Chinese and English. *PRACTICE AREAS:* Foreign Investment; International Procurement and Technology Transfer; Corporate; Contracts; International Commercial Arbitration.

XUEJUN PENG, born Zhengzhou, China. *Education:* Peking University (Bachelor of Law, Master of Law). *Member:* All China Lawyers Association; The China Society of International Law. *LANGUAGES:* Chinese and English. *PRACTICE AREAS:* International Procurement and Technology Transfer; Corporate; International Intellectual Property Protection; International Aviation Law; International Commercial Arbitration.

XUSHENG ZHANG, born Hefei, China. *Education:* Anhui University (Bachelor of Law); Peking University (Master of Law). *Member:* All China Lawyers Association; The China Society of International Law. *LANGUAGES:* Chinese and English. *PRACTICE AREAS:* Aircraft Financing and Leasing; Maritime Law; Securities.

ERIC F. FU, born Handan, China. *Education:* Peking University (Bachelor of Law); University of International Business and Trade (Certificate). *Member:* All China Lawyers Association; The China Society of Maritime Law. *LANGUAGES:* Chinese and English. *PRACTICE AREAS:* International Engineering and Contracting; International Tendering and Bidding; Real Estate; Litigation.

FRANK YAO WU XU, born Anhui Province, China. *Education:* Anhui University (Bachelor of Law); Wuhan University (Master of Law); Hawaii University Law School. *Member:* All China Lawyers Association; The China Society of Private International Law. *LANGUAGES:* Chinese and English. *PRACTICE AREAS:* Corporate Law; Contracts; Securities; Real Estate; Tax; Technology Transfer; International Investment.

(This Listing Continued)

JINGTIAN ASSOCIATES, Beijing (Peking)—Continued

XIANGZHI BAO, born Beijing, China. *Education:* Wuhan University (Bachelor of Law); Peking University (Master of Law). *Member:* All China Lawyers Association. *LANGUAGES:* Chinese and English. *PRACTICE AREAS:* Foreign Investment; Corporate; Contracts; Real Estate; Technology Transfer; International Commercial Arbitration; International Intellectual Property Protection.

YUGUO LI, born Shenyang, China. *Education:* Hei.ongjiang University (Bachelor of Arts); Foreign Affairs College (Master of Law); The University of British Columbia (LL.M.). *Member:* Council of China Society of the Law of the Sea; All China Lawyers Association; The China Society of International Law. *LANGUAGES:* Chinese and English. *PRACTICE AREAS:* Corporate; Securities; Technology Transfer and International Investment.

HELEN H. ZHANG, born Changchun, China. *Education:* Jilin University (Bachelor of Law). *Member:* All China Lawyers Association. *LANGUAGES:* Chinese and English. *PRACTICE AREAS:* Arbitration, Banking and Finance.

JULIA H. YE, born Zhejiang Province, China. *Education:* Peking University (Bachelor of Law; Master of Law). *Member:* All China Lawyers Association. *LANGUAGES:* Chinese and English. *PRACTICE AREAS:* Litigation and Arbitration; Corporate Law; Contracts; Real Estate; Technology Transfer; International Investment; International Intellectual Property Protection.

JUN HE LAW OFFICE

19TH FL PEACE HOTEL
BEIJING (PEKING) 100004, PEOPLE'S REPUBLIC OF CHINA
Telephone: (86-1) 512-8833 (Ext. 1909-1914)
Fax: (86-1) 513-4570

New York, New York Office: 36 W. 44th St., Suite 704, 10036. Telephone: (212) 354-5823. Fax: (212) 354-5831.

Shanghai, China Office: BLDG 2#160 Taiyuan Road. Telephone: (86-21) 437-5450 (Ext. 61-62). Fax: (86-21) 431-4986.

Haikou, China Office: Nan Yang BLDG, Binhai Road, 57005. Telephone: (86-898) 8 512544, 512065. Fax: (86-898) 8 513514.

General practice including: International Trade and Investment, Joint Ventures, Wholly Foreign-owned Ventures, Regulatory Compliance, Real Estate Development, Taxation, Contracted Projects, Finance, Intellectual Property, Securities Law Matters, Arbitration and Litigation, Labor and Employment.

PARTNERS

Olivia Hu	Zhi Long Wang
Gong Jun	Jim (Xiaoji) Wu
Jason Han	Xiaolin Zhou
Lu Jianeng	Yan Shi Zhao
Pan Yue Xin	Ya Dong Wang
Shiao Wei	Linfei Liu

KAYE, SCHOLER, FIERMAN, HAYS & HANDLER

SCITE TOWER, SUITE 708
22 JIANGUOMENWAI DAJIE
100004 BEIJING (PEKING), PEOPLE'S REPUBLIC OF CHINA
Telephone: 861-5124755
Telex: 222540 KAY CN
Facsimile: 861-5124760

New York, N.Y.: 425 Park Avenue, 10022. Telephone: 212-836-8000. Telex: 234860 KAY UR. Facsimile: 212-836-8689.

Washington, D.C.: McPherson Building, 901 Fifteenth Street, N.W., Suite 1100, 20005. Telephone: 202-682-3500. Telex: 897458 KAYSCHOL WSH. Facsimile: 202-682-3580.

Los Angeles, California: 1999 Avenue of the Stars, Suite 1600, 90067. Telephone: 213-788-1000. Facsimile: 213-788-1200.

Hong Kong: 9 Queen Road Centre, 18th Floor. Telephone: 852-8458989. Telex: 62816 KAY HX. Facsimile: 852-8453682; 852-8452389.

(This Listing Continued)

International Trade and Investment Matters, including Joint Ventures and other Foreign Investment Entities, Dispute Resolution, Contracted Projects, Natural Resources Projects, Intellectual Property and Technology Transfers.

PARTNERS

FRANKLIN D. CHU, admitted, 1976, District of Columbia (Not admitted in China). *Education:* Harvard College (A.B., magna cum laude, 1971); L'Institut de'Etudes Politiques, Paris, France, 1968-1969; Yale University (J.D., 1976). Member, Board of Editors, Yale Law Journal, 1975-1976. Panel Arbitrators of American Arbitration Association. *Member:* The District of Columbia Bar; American, International and Inter-Pacific Bar Associations. (Also at Hong Kong Office). *LANGUAGES:* English, Chinese (Mandarin) and French. *PRACTICE AREAS:* International Investment and Finance.

(For complete biographical data on all personnel, see Professional Biographies at New York, New York)

LOVELL WHITE DURRANT

OFFICE 5D, CITIC BUILDING
19 JIANGUOMENWAI DAJIE
BEIJING (PEKING) 100004, PEOPLE'S REPUBLIC OF CHINA
Telephone: (861) 506 3588
Fax: (861) 500 1972

London, England Office: 65 Holborn Viaduct, EC1A 2DY. Telephone: 0171 236 0066. Fax: 0171 248 4212; 236 0084; 248 7273. Telex: 887122 LWD G.

New York, New York Office: 527 Madison Avenue, 10th Floor, 10022. Telephone: (212) 758 3773. Fax: (212) 486 0367.

Paris, France Office: 37 Avenue Pierre 1er de Serbie, 75008. Telephone: (1) 49 52 04 26. Fax: (1) 47 23 96 12.

Brussels, Belgium Office: Avenue Louise 523, Bte 24, 1050. Telephone: (2) 647 0660. Fax: (2) 647 1124.

Prague, Czech Republic Office: U Prasne brany 3, State Mesto, 1. Telephone: (2) 2481 1672. Fax: (2) 2481 1608.

Ho Chi Minh City, Vietnam Office: 141 Vo Van Tan Street, District 3. Telephone: (848) 298 787. Fax: (848) 392 868.

Hong Kong Office: 11th Floor, Peregrine Tower, Lippo Centre, Queensway. Telephone: 2810 4770. Fax: 2868 4051.

Tokyo, Japan Office: Shin-Kasumigaseki Building, 20th Floor, 3-3-2 Kasumigaseki, Chiyoda-ku, 100. Telephone: (3) 3503 2571. Fax: (3) 3503 0699.

Shanghai, People's Republic of China Associated Office: Room 1703, Shanghai International Trade Centre, 2200 Yan An Road (W). Telephone: (21) 219 4419. Fax: (21) 219 5462.

Arbitration, Aviation, Banking, Building and Engineering, China, Collective Investment Schemes, Commercial, Commodities, Competition and Trade Regulation, Computers, Construction, Corporate Finance, Corporate Law, East-West Trade, EEC, Employment, Energy, Environmental Law, Financial Services, Fraud and Asset Recovery, Insolvency, Insurance, Intellectual Property, Litigation, Management Buy-Outs and Venture Capital, Media Law, Mergers and Acquisitions, Pensions, Planning, Product Liability, Property, Rating, Shipping, Taxation, Trusts and Estate Planning.

Ambrose Chua

(For List of Partners see Professional Biographies at London, England)

PAUL, WEISS, RIFKIND, WHARTON & GARRISON

BEIJING OFFICE
SUITE 1910, SCITE TOWER
22 JIANGUOMENWAI DAJIE
BEIJING, 100004, PEOPLE'S REPUBLIC OF CHINA
Telephone: (86-1) 5123628-30; (86-1) 5122288X1910
Telex: 210169 PWRWG CN
Telecopier: (86-1) 5123631

New York, N.Y. Office: 1285 Avenue of the Americas, 10019-6064. Telephones: 212-373-3000, TDD 212-373-2000. Cable Address: "Longsight, New York". Telex: WUI 666-843. Facsimile: 212-757-3990.

(This Listing Continued)

Washington, D.C. Office: 1615 L Street, N.W, Suite 1300, 20036-5694. Telephones: 202-223-7300, TDD 202-223-7490. Telex: 248237 PWA UR. Facsimile: 202-223-7420. Cable Address: "Longsight, Washington".

Paris, France Office: 199, Boulevard Saint Germain, 75007. Telephone: (33-1) 45.49.33.85. Telex: 269940F. Facsimile: (33-1) 42-22-64-38.

Tokyo, Japan Office: 11th Floor, Main Tower, Akasaka Twin Tower, 17-22 Akasaka 2-chome, Minato-Ku. 107. Telephone: (81-3) 3505-0291. Facsimile: (81-3) 3505-4540. Telex: 02428120 PWRWGT.

Hong Kong Office: 13th Floor, Hong Kong Club Building, 3A Chater Road, Central Hong Kong. Telephone: (011-852) 2536-9933. Facsimile: 011 (852) 2536-9622.

Approved by the Ministry of Justice of the PRC to establish a foreign law office in China. Firm engaged in American and International Law Practice but not authorized to appear before the Chinese Courts.

RESIDENT ASSOCIATES

NICHOLAS C. HOWSON, born Montreal, Quebec, October 6, 1961; admitted, 1989, New York (Not admitted in China). *Education:* Williams College (B.A., with highest honors, 1983, magna cum laude, Phi Beta Kappa); Middlebury College Chinese School (Summer, 1983); Fudan University, Shanghai (Graduate Exchange Fellow, 1983-1985); Columbia Law School (J.D., 1988);. Harlan Fiske Stone Scholar, Samuel I. Rosenman Prize, Parker School Achievement with Honors in International Law, David M. Berger Memorial Prize (Public International Law), Head Notes Editor, Columbia Journal of Transnational Law; Beijing University, Law Department (Visiting Research Scholar in Qing law, Fall 1988). Author: Note, "Breaking The Ice: The Canadian-American Dispute Over The Arctic's Northwest Passage," Columbia Journal of Transnational Law, Volume 26, 1988, Number 2; Article, "Cao Siyuan: A 'Responsible Reformer' Silenced," UCLA Pacific Basin Law Journal, Volume 8, Spring 1990, Number 2; Article, with Dr. Lutz-Christian Wolff, "Die Vollstreckung von Schiedsspruchen in der VR China" (The Enforcement of Arbitration Awards in the PRC"), Recht der Internationalen Wirtschaft, Heidelberg, February 1993; Reviews, The China Quarterly, London. Consultant: The Ford Foundation, 1991, co-author with Professor Jerome A. Cohen of report "Assisting Legal Education and Research in China," October, 1991. *Member:* American Bar Association, Lawyers Committee for Human Rights, Charter 88 (U.K.), Article 19, British Association of Chinese Studies. *LANGUAGES:* Chinese (Mandarin), French and English.

HELENA K. KOLENDA, born Houston, Texas, December 24, 1954; admitted, 1990, New York (Not admitted in China). *Education:* Rice University; University of California at Santa Cruz; Inter-University Program for Chinese Language Studies, Taipei, Taiwan; University of California, Berkeley (A.B., with highest honors, 1980); Harvard Law School; University of Texas School of Law (J.D., 1989). Phi Beta Kappa. Departmental Citation for Great Distinction in General Scholarship. American Association of University Women Selected Professions Fellowship, 1988-1989. Author: Note, "A Happy Ending: Buy-Out in Chinese-Foreign Joint Ventures," Texas International Law Journal, Volume 24, 1989; Article, "One Party, Two Systems: Corruption in the People's Republic of China and Attempts to Control It," Journal of Chinese Law, Columbia University, Volume 4, 1991. Co-Author with J.A. Cohen: "People's Republic of China," Encyclopedia of International Commercial Litigation, A. Colman, ed., Graham & Trotman (1991). *Member:* Association of the Bar of the City of New York; Lawyer's Committee for Human Rights. *LANGUAGES:* Chinese (Mandarin). *PRACTICE AREAS:* Law of the People's Republic of China.

(For Biographical Data of other Personnel, see Professional Biographies at New York, Washington, D.C., Paris, France, Tokyo, Japan, and Hong Kong)

PÜNDER, VOLHARD, WEBER & AXSTER

SUITE C 603, BEIJING LUFTHANSA CENTER
50 LIANGMAQIAO ROAD
BEIJING (PEKING) 100 016, PEOPLE'S REPUBLIC OF CHINA

Telephone: (86)(1) 465 15 68; (86)(1) 465 18 08; (86)(1) 465 13 45 Fax: (86)(1) 467 12 56

Frankfurt/Main, Germany Office: Mainzer Landstrasse 46, 60325 Frankfurt/Main. Telephone: (49)(69) 71 99-01. Fax: (49)(69) 71 99-4000. Telex: 414 827.

Düsseldorf, Germany Office: Cecilienallee 6, 40474 Düsseldorf. Telephone: (49)(211) 43 55-0. Fax: (49)(211) 43 55-600.

(This Listing Continued)

Berlin, Germany Office: Katharina-Heinroth-Ufer, 10787 Berlin. Telephone: (49)(30) 2546 5800. Fax: (49)(30) 2546 5900.

Leipzig, Germany Office: Burgplatz 7, 04109 Leipzig. Telephone: (49)(341) 21 49-0. Fax: (49)(341) 21 49-600.

Brussels, Belgium Office: Rue d'Arlon 92, 1040 Bruxelles. Telephone: (32)(2) 230 90 11. Fax: (32)(2) 231 19 55.

Budapest, Hungary Office: Endrödy Sandor utca 48, 1026 Budapest. Telephone: (36) 60 33 26 18 international; (6) 60 33 26 18 national. Fax: (36) 60 33 26 17 international; (6) 60 33 26 17 national.

Moscow, Russia Office: ul. Wolchonka, 18/2, 121 019 Moskwa. Telephone: (7)(095) 202 64 90; (7)(095) 202 65 12; (7)(543) 708 00 900 from Germany; (49)(7545) 893 42 from other countries. Fax: (7)(095) 202 65 14; (7)(543) 708 00 990 from Germany; (49)(7545) 893 43 from other countries.

New York, New York Office: 152 West 57th Street, Carnegie Hall Tower, New York, N.Y. 10019. Telephone: (1)(212) 582 28 28. Fax: (1)(212) 582 24 24.

Warsaw, Poland Office: ul. Jasna 1, 00-013 Warszawa. Telephone: (48) 39 12 21 41. Fax: (48)(22) 27 15 29.

Administrative Law; Antitrust Law; Arbitration; Auditing and Valuations; Banking, Securities and Finance; Bankruptcy; Building Law; Chinese Law; Commercial Crime; Computer Law; Construction Law; Corporate Law; EU Law; Energy Law; Environmental Law; Franchising; Industrial Property Law; Insolvency; Intellectual Property Law; International and German Business Law; Labor and Employment Law; Litigation; Media Law; Mergers and Acquisitions; Pharmaceutical Law; Privatizations; Product Law; Public Law; Real Estate; Reorganizations; Russian Law; Tax Law; Telecommunications; Unfair Trade Law.

FIRM PROFILE: Member of PÜNDER GROUP

Members:

- *BURUMA MARIS, The Hague, Rotterdam*

- *CERHA, HEMPEL & SPIEGELFELD, Wien*

- *COPPENS, VAN OMMESLAGHE HORSMANS & FAURES, Bruxelles.*

- *DE PARDIEU-LACOURTE G.I.E., Paris*

- *PÜNDER, VOLHARD, WEBER & AXSTER, Frankfurt/Main, Düsseldorf, Berlin, Leipzig*

- *STOFFEL & PARTNER, Zürich, Genève.*

Joint Offices of PÜNDER GROUP:

Beijing - Bruxelles - Budapest - Moskwa - New York - Warszawa

MEMBER OF FIRM

DR. JOACHIM GLATTER, born Wuppertal, Germany, August 14, 1958; admitted, 1990, Frankfurt/Main (Not admitted in China). *Education:* Universities of Münster, Lausanne, Göttingen (Dr. jur.) and Nanjing (People's Republic of China). Author: "Rechtsgrundlagen für Handel und wirtschaftliche Kooperation in der Volksrepublik China (ausserhalb des Equity-Joint-Venture-Bereiches)." *Member:* China International Economic and Trade Arbitration Commission (Arbitrator); German-Chinese Lawyers' Association. *LANGUAGES:* German, English, French and Chinese. *PRACTICE AREAS:* German Business Law; Chinese Business Law.

ASSOCIATES

DR. STEFANIE TETZ, born Göttingen, Germany, April 16, 1960; admitted, 1991, Frankfurt/Main (Not admitted in China). *Education:* Universities of Bonn (Dr. jur.), Geneva, Beijing (Beida) and Shanghai (Fudan). Author: "Abschluß und Wirksamkeit von Verträgen in der Volksrepublik China," 1994. *Member:* German Bar Association; European Association for Chinese Law; German Association for Chinese Law. *LANGUAGES:* German, English and Mandarin. *PRACTICE AREAS:* Chinese Business Law; Commercial Law; Corporate and Business Law.

(For complete biographical data on personnel at Frankfurt/Main, Düsseldorf, Berlin and Leipzig, Germany, Brussels, Belgium, Moscow, Russia, Warsaw, Poland and New York, New York, see Professional Biographies at those locations)

RICE FOWLER

BEIJING INTERNATIONAL CONVENTION CENTRE
SUITE 7024
NO. 8 BEICHENDONG ROAD
CHAOYANG DISTRICT
BEIJING (PEKING) 100101, PEOPLE'S REPUBLIC OF
CHINA
Telephone: (861) 493-4250
Telecopier: (861) 493-4251

New Orleans, Louisiana Office: 36th Floor, Place St. Charles, 201 St. Charles Avenue, 70130. Telephone: 504-523-2600. Telecopier: 504-523-2705. Telex: 9102507910. ELN: 62548910.

San Francisco, California Office: Embarcadero Center West, 275 Battery Street, 27th Floor, 94111. Telephone: 415-399-9191. Telecopier: 415-399-9192. Telex: 451981.

San Diego, California Office: Emerald-Shapery Center, 402 W. Broadway, Suite 850, 92101. Telephone: 619-230-0030. Telecopier: 619-230-1350.

London, England Office: Suite 692, Level 6 Lloyd's, 1 Lime Street, London EC3M 7DQ England. Telephone: 071-327-4222. Telecopier: 071-929-0043.

Bogota, Colombia Office: Avenida Jimenez #4-03 Officina 10-05. Telephone: (571) 342-1062. Telecopier: (571) 342-1062.

General Civil Litigation Practice in State and Federal Courts. Maritime, Insurance, International Business, Oil and Gas Law and Environmental Law.

ZHANG LIXING, born Beijing, Peoples Republic of China, November 20, 1953; admitted, 1983, Peoples Republic of China. *Education:* Peking University (LL.B., 1977); Tulane University (LL.M. in Admiralty, with distinction, 1982; S.J.D., 1983). Recipient: Young Scholar Research Award for ChinaLaw Computer-Assisted Legal Research System from Peking University, October, 1985; Young Scholar Research Award for research paper on China Law Computer-Assisted Legal Research from Peking Municipality, 1987; Second Place Award for a Chinese Economic Law Retrieval System, November, 1987; Excellent Teacher Award, granted by Peking University, 1988. Co-Author: Books: *Dictionary of Economic Law,* China Law Publishing House, July, 1987; with Professors Wu Huanning and Zhu Cengjie, *Admiralty and Maritime Law,* (in Chinese), China Law Publishing House, 1988. Articles: "Multimode Transport and the UN Convention on Multimode Transport," Science of Law Abroad, Volume 67, 1984; "The Impact of the Computer Revolution of the World of Law," 3 Journal of Peking University (Philosophy and Social Sciences) 81 (1986); "Legal Aspects of Foreign Investment in China," (in Chinese), *Chinese Economic Law,* Chinese University of Hong Kong, 1987. Lecturer of Law, 1983-1987, Assistant Professor of Law, 1987-1988 and Associate Professor of Law, 1988—, Peking University. Deputy Director, International Economic Law Division, 1985—. Director, China Law Computer-Assisted Legal Research Center, 1985—. *Member:* China Law Association; China International Law Association; China Economic Law Association. *LANGUAGES:* English and Chinese. *PRACTICE AREAS:* International Investment Law; Maritime Law; Aviation Law.

(For Biographical Data on Other Personnel, see Professional Biographies at New Orleans, Louisiana and San Francisco, California)

SHEARMAN & STERLING

SUITE #2205, CAPITAL MANSION
NO. 6, XIN YUAN NAN ROAD
CHAO YANG DISTRICT
BEIJING (PEKING) 100004, PEOPLE'S REPUBLIC OF
CHINA
Telephone: (861) 465-4574
Fax: (861) 465-4578

New York, N.Y. Office: 599 Lexington Avenue, New York, New York 10022-6069 and Citicorp Center, 153 East 53rd Street, New York, New York 10022-4676. Telephone: (212) 848-4000. Telex: 667290 Num Lau. Fax: 599 Lexington Avenue: (212) 848-7179. Citicorp Center: (212) 848-5252.

Abu Dhabi, United Arab Emirates Office: P.O. Box 2948. Telephone: (971-2) 324477. Fax: (971-2) 774533.

Budapest, Hungary Office: Szerb utca 17-19, 1056 Budapest. Telephone: (36-1) 266-3522. Fax: (36-1) 266-3523.

(This Listing Continued)

Düsseldorf, Federal Republic of Germany Office: Königsallee 46, D-40212 Düsseldorf. Telephone: (49-211) 13 62 80. Telex: 8 588 294 NYLO. Fax: (49-211) 13 33 09.

Frankfurt, Federal Republic of Germany Office: Bockenheimer Landstrasse 55, D-60325 Frankfurt am Main. Telephone: (49-69) 97-10-70. Fax: (49-69) 97-10-71-00.

Hong Kong, Hong Kong Office: Standard Chartered Bank Building, 4 Des Voeux Road Central, Hong Kong. Telephone: (852) 2978-8000. Fax: (852) 2978-8099.

London, England Office: 199 Bishopsgate, London EC2M 3TY. Telephone: (44-71) 920-9000. Fax: (44-71) 920-9020.

Los Angeles, California Office: 725 South Figueroa Street, 21st Floor, 90017-5421. Telephone: (213) 239-0300. Fax: (213) 239-0381, 614-0936.

Paris, France Office: 12 rue d'Astorg, 75008. Telephone: (33-1) 44-71-17-17. Telex: 282964 Royale. Fax: (33-1) 44-71-01-01.

San Francisco, California Office: 555 California Street, 94104-1522. Telephone: (415) 616-1100. Fax: (415) 616-1199.

Taipei, Taiwan Office: 7th Floor, Hung Kuo Building, 167 Tun Hwa North Road. Telephone: (886-2) 545-3300. Fax: (866-2) 545-3322.

Tokyo, Japan Office: Shearman & Sterling (Thomas Wilner Gaikokuho-Jimu-Bengoshi Jimusho), Fukoku Seimei Building, 5th Fl. 2-2-2, Uchisaiwaicho, Chiyoda-ku, Tokyo 100, Japan. Telephone: (81 3) 5251-1601. Fax: (81 3) 5251-1602.

Toronto, Ontario, Canada Office: Commerce Court West, Suite 4405, P.O. Box 247, M5L 1E8. Telephone: (416) 360-8484. Fax: (416) 360-2958.

Washington, D.C. Office: 801 Pennsylvania Avenue, N.W., Suite 900, 20004-2604. Telephone: (202) 508-8000. Fax: (202) 508-8100.

Firm engages in General American and International Financial and Commercial Practice. Not authorized to appear before P.R.C. courts or to act as P.R.C. lawyers.

FIRM PROFILE: Shearman & Sterling, founded in 1873, has more than 500 lawyers in 15 offices throughout the world. The firm's practice encompasses most major areas of business law, including: Antitrust and Trade Regulation; Banking; Bankruptcy and Corporate Reorganization; Compensation and Benefits; Environmental; Finance (including Corporate Finance, Domestic Private Finance, Financial Institutions, International Private Finance and Project Finance); Individual Clients, Trusts and Estates; Insurance; International Trade and Government Relations; Litigation and Arbitration; Mergers and Acquisitions; Oil and Gas; Privatizations; Real Estate; and Tax. The Firm is also engaged in the practice of French, German and Hungarian law through its offices in France, Germany and Hungary.

RESIDENT ASSOCIATES

HONG LIU, born 1955; admitted, 1990, New York (Not admitted in China). *Education:* Columbia University (J.D., 1990).

(For Biographical data of all Partners, see Professional Biographies at New York, New York).

SKADDEN, ARPS, SLATE, MEAGHER & FLOM

1605 CAPITAL MANSION TOWER
NO. 6 XIN YUAN NAN ROAD
CHAO YANG DISTRICT
100004 BEIJING, PEOPLE'S REPUBLIC OF CHINA
Telephone: 011-86-1-466-8800
Fax: 011-86-1-466-8822

New York, New York Office: 919 Third Avenue, 10022. Telephone: 212-735-3000. Fax: 212-735-2000; 212-735-2001. Telex: 645899 Skarslaw.

Boston, Massachusetts Office: One Beacon Street, 02108. Telephone: 617-573-4800. Fax: 617-573-4822.

Washington, D.C. Office: 1440 New York Avenue, N.W., 20005. Telephone: 202-371-7000. Fax: 202-393-5760.

Wilmington, Delaware Office: One Rodney Square, 19899. Telephone: 302-651-3000. Fax: 302-651-3001.

Los Angeles, California Office: 300 South Grand Avenue, 90071. Telephone: 213-687-5000. Fax: 213-687-5600.

Chicago, Illinois Office: 333 West Wacker Drive, 60606. Telephone: 312-407-0700. Fax: 312-407-0411.

(This Listing Continued)

San Francisco, California Office: Four Embarcadero Center, 94111. Telephone: 415-984-6400. Fax: 415-984-2698.

Houston, Texas Office: 1600 Smith Street, Suite 4460, 77002. Telephone: 713-655-5100. Fax: 713-655-5181.

Newark, New Jersey Office: One Riverfront Plaza, 07102. Telephone: 201-596-4440. Fax: 201-596-4444.

Tokyo, Japan Office: 12th Floor, The Fukoku Seimei Building, 2-2-2, Uchisaiwaicho, Chiyoda-ku, 100. Telephone: 011-81-3-3595-3850. Fax: 011-81-3-3504-2780.

London, England Office: 25 Bucklersbury EC4N 8DA. Telephone: 011-44-71-248-9929. Fax: 011-44-71-489-8533.

Hong Kong Office: 30/F Peregrine Tower, Lippo Centre, 89 Queensway, Central. Telephone: 011-852-820-0700. Fax: 011-852-820-0727.

Sydney, New South Wales, Australia Office: Level 26-State Bank Centre, 52 Martin Place, 2000. Telephone: 011-61-2-224-6000. Fax: 011-61-2-224-6044.

Toronto, Ontario Office: Suite 1820, North Tower, P.O. Box 189, Royal Bank Plaza, M5J 2J4. Telephone: 416-777-4700. Fax: 416-777-4747.

Paris, France Office: 105 rue du Faubourg Saint-Honoré, 75008. Telephone: 011-33-1-40-75-44-44. Fax: 011-33-1-49-53-09-99.

Brussels, Belgium Office: 523 avenue Louise, Box 30, 1050. Telephone: 011-32-2-648-7666. Fax: 011-32-2-640-3032.

Frankfurt, Germany Office: MesseTurm, 27th Floor, 60308. Telephone: 011-49-69-9757-3000. Fax: 011-49-69-9757-3050.

Budapest, Hungary Office: Mahart Building, H-1052 Apáczai Csere János u.11, Vl.em. Telephone: 011-36-1-266-2145. Fax: 011-36-1-266-4033.

Prague, Czech Republic Office: Revolucni 16, 110 00. Telephone: 011-42-2-231-75-18. Fax: 011-42-2-231-47-33.

Moscow, Russia Office: Pleteshkovsky Pereulok 1, 107005. Telephone: 011-7-501-940-2304. Fax: 011-7-501-940-2511.

Firm engaged in general American and International law practice, but not authorized to appear before the Chinese Courts.

GREGORY G.H. MIAO, born Guangzhou, China, 1954; admitted, 1988, New York (Not admitted in China). *Education:* East China Normal University (LL.B., 1982); New York University (LL.M., 1985). (Also at Hong Kong Office).

(For Biographical data on other Personnel, see Professional Biographies at New York, New York).

ARNBERGER, KIM, BUXBAUM & CHOY

CHINA HOTEL OFFICE TOWER, SUITE 512
GUANGZHOU (CANTON), GUANGZHOU, PEOPLE'S REPUBLIC OF CHINA

Telephone: (20) 666-3388 (Ext. 2512)
Facsimile: 86)(20) 669-1217

REVISER OF THE PEOPLE'S REPUBLIC OF CHINA AND MONGOLIA LAW DIGESTS FOR THIS DIRECTORY.

Hong Kong Office: 3201 Citibank Tower, 3 Garden Road, Central. Telephone: (852) 2523-7001. Fax: (852) 2845-0947.

Beijing (Peking), People's Republic of China Office: China World Trade Centre, Suite 2523, No. 1 Jian Guo Men Wai Avenue. Telephone: (86)(1) 505-2288 Ext: 2523. Fax: (86)(1) 505-2638.

Xiamen, People's Republic of China Office: Foreign Trade Centre, Suite 519, No. 15 Hu Bing North Road, Xiamen City. Telephone: (86)(592) 506-3059. Facsimile: (86)(592) 511-1044 Ext. 519.

Shenzhen, People's Republic of China Office: Shenzhen Development Center, Suite 2103, Renmin Nan Lu, Shenzhen. Telephone: (86)(755) 229-8009. Facsimile: (86)(755) 229-8011.

Shanghai, People's Republic of China Office: 7th Floor, Block 2, Jing Ming Building, No. 8 Zun Yi Road, Shanghai. Telephone: (86)(21) 219-4180. Facsimile: (86)(21) 219-7421.

Ulaanbaatar, Mongolia Office: Ulaanbaatar Supreme Court Building, Room 429, 432. Telephone: (976)(1) 31-0711. Fax: (976)(1) 32-5102.

New York Office: 100 Maiden Lane, 16th Floor, Suite 1600B, New York, New York 10038. Telephone: (212) 504-6109. Fax: (212) 412-7016.

San Francisco Office: 44 Montgomery Street, Suite 500, San Francisco 94104. Telephone: (415) 955-0553. Fax: (415) 753-1235.

Los Angeles Office: 3731 Wilshire Boulevard, Suite 910, West Tower, Los Angeles, California, 90010. Telephone: (213) 380-7780. Facsimile: (310) 358-0226; (213) 380-5798.

Alhambra Office: 320 South Garfield, Suite 206, Alhambra, California 91801. Telephone: (818) 281-9088. Fax: (818) 281-7189.

(This Listing Continued)

Corporate, Employment Law, Commodities, Securities, Complex Commercial Litigation, International Transactions, Intellectual Property, Aircraft and Equipment Leasing Financing and Taxation.

MEMBERS OF FIRM

DAVID C. BUXBAUM, born New York, N.Y., July 16, 1933; admitted, 1970, New York and U.S. District Court, Southern, Eastern, Northern and Western Districts of New York; 1971, U.S. Court of Appeals, Second Circuit; 1974, U.S. Supreme Court; 1975, U.S. Court of Appeals, Seventh and Fourth Circuits; 1978, U.S. Court of Appeals, Eighth Circuit; 1979, U.S. Court of Appeals, First Circuit; 1981, California; 1989, U.S. District Court, Central District of California; 1991, U.S. District Court, Northern District of California; U.S. Court of Appeals, Ninth Circuit (Not admitted in China). *Education:* New York University (B.A., 1954); University of Michigan (J.D., 1959); concurrent graduate studies, University of Michigan Graduate School; graduate study, Harvard University and University of Washington (M.A., 1963; Ph.D., 1968). Member, Far East Honor Society, University of Michigan. Author: *Articles:* "Preliminary Trends in the Development of the Legal Institutions of Communist China and the Nature of the Criminal Law," International and Comparative Law Quarterly, January, 1962, reprinted in *Government of Communist China,* Chandler, San Francisco, 1966; "Horizontal and Vertical Influences Upon the Substantive Criminal Law of Mainland Chinese, Some Preliminary Observations," Osteuropa Recht, No. 1, 1964; "Chinese Family Law in Common Law Setting: A Note on the Institutional Environment and the Substantive Family Law of the Chinese in Malaysia and Singapore," Journal of Asian Studies, August, 1966; "Some Aspects of Civil Procedure and Practice at the Trial Level in Tanshui and Hsinchu...," XXX Journal of Asian Studies, 1971; *Lawyer's Challenge in China Trade: New and Developing Legal System,* New York Law Journal, International Law Finance and Trade, February, 1979; *Commodities Trade with China,* New York Law Journal, December, 1978; *Regulation of Commodity Futures Exchanges in Japan,* New York Law Journal, October, 1978; *Commodities Transactions in China and Hong Kong,* New York Law Journal, June, 1978; *Jurisdiction Over Foreign Transactions and Foreign Nationals,* New York Law Journal, April, 1978; *Two Cases of Dispute Settlement,* U.S.-China Business Review, Vol. 1, No. 2, March/April, 1974; *Two Cases of Dispute Settlement,* Arbitration and Dispute Settlement in Trade with China, Special Report No. 4 for Members of the National Council for United States-China Trade, February, 1974; *Negotiation with the Chinese,* Trade with China, 1973; *American Trade with the People's Republic of China: Some Preliminary Perspectives,* Columbia Journal of Transnational Law, Vol. 12, No. 1, 1973; *Liability of Federal Officials in Damage for Acts Unconstitutional or in Excess of their Authority; Expanding the Concept of the Rule of Law,* Capital University Law Review, Vol. 8, Issue 4, 1979; *Taking on the Government Alone; Sole Practitioner Battles Way to Supreme Court and Wins,* Legal Times of Washington, December, 1978; *Disclosure of Management Remuneration, Transaction, Litigation and Employment History,* Los Angeles Daily Journal, March, 1979; *Contracts in China,* China Trade, Praeger, 1982. Monthly Columnist, New York Law Journal on Commodities Law, 1976-1982; *Contract Law in China, The Dynamics of Statutory Development and Practice,* Doing Business in China, 1990, Streng et al, ed. Contracts in China during the Qing Dynasty: Key to the Civil Law, Journal of Oriental Studies, University of Hong Kong, 1993. *The Commercial Laws of China,* and *Patents Law and Practice, Trademark Law and Practice, The People's Republic of China,* Digest of the Commercial Laws of the World, 1982-1993. *M.A. Dissertation:* "Legal Institutions of Contemporary Mainland China," University of Washington, 1962. *Ph.D. Dissertation:* Some Aspects of Substantive Family Law and Social Change in Rural China, 1896-1967," University of Washington, 1968. *Case Note:* "Freedom of Marriage in a Pluralistic Society," Malaya Law Review, 1963. Editor: *Traditional and Modern Legal Institutions in Asia and Africa, Journal of Asian and African Studies,* Supplement Edition, 1967; *Family Law and Customary Law in Asia: A Contemporary Legal Perspective,* 1968; *Law and Social Change: A Case Study of Family Law and Social Change in China and Other Developing Areas,* University of Washington Press, 1978; *Transition and Permanence: Chinese History and Culture, A Festschrift in Honor of Dr. Kung-Chan Hsiao,* 1971; *Chinese Family Law and Social Change in Historic and Comparative Perspective,* University of Washington Press, 1978; *China Trade: Prospects and Perspectives,* Prager, 1982; Sole Counsel for Successful Respondents, *Butz v. Economou,* 438 US 478, 1978. Associate Professor, Chinese Law, Comparative Law and Domestic Relations, University of Washington, 1968-1969. Assistant Lecturer, Chinese Law, Domestic Relations, Labor Law, Jurisprudence, Comparative Law, University of Singapore, 1963-1964. Adjunct Professor of Law: Touro Law School, 1980; Southwestern University School of Law, 1983-1988. Member, Commission on Labor Law, Singapore, 1963-1964. Member, Panel of Arbitrators, American Arbitration Association. *Member:* American Bar Association

(This Listing Continued)

ARNBERGER, KIM, BUXBAUM & CHOY, Guangzhou (Canton), Guangzhou—Continued

(Member, Committee on Far Eastern Law, Section of International and Comparative Law, 1965-1971); New York Trial Lawyers Association (Member, Liaison Committee with Judicial Conference, 1971-1978). *LANGUAGES:* Chinese, French, German and Japanese (specialized reading). *PRACTICE AREAS:* International Law; Complex International Litigation; Complex International Contract; Joint Venture Contract; Investment Law; Trademark, Copyright and Patent Protection and Enforcement; Commodities and Securities.

KENNETH Y. CHOY, born Hong Kong, May 24, 1956; admitted, 1987, New York; U.S. District Court, Southern and Eastern Districts of New York; 1990, California; 1991, Central and Northern Districts of California and U.S. Court of Appeals, 9th Circuit (Not admitted in China). *Education:* San Francisco State University (B.A., 1977); Northeastern University (J.D., 1986). Judicial Intern to Hon. Dolores K. Sloviter, U.S. Court of Appeals for the Third Circuit, 1985-1986. *Member:* American Bar Association (Member, Section on Labor and Employment Law); American Immigration Lawyers Association. (New York Office). *LANGUAGES:* Chinese (Cantonese and Mandarin). *PRACTICE AREAS:* Litigation and Transactions in U.S. and People's Republic of China.

H. BENNETT ARNBERGER, born Globe, Arizona, July 8, 1953; admitted, 1983, California and U.S. District Court, Northern and Central Districts of California. *Education:* University of California at Berkeley (A.B., with honors and distinction, 1977); University of San Francisco (J.D., 1983). Phi Delta Phi. Author: "Ensuring Compliance Through Intellectual Property Audits," 5 International Legal Strategy 54 (1994); "Avoiding The Hidden Liabilities of Independent Contractors," I Foreign Assignments (Kaigai Chuzai) 99 (1994); "Proactive Prevention of Cross-Cultural Disputes," 6 International Legal Strategy 60 (1994); "Protecting Against Misappropriation of Trade Secrets," 10 International Legal Strategy 63 (1993); "Taxation and Legal Requirements of California Corporations," 16 International Business Law Journal (Kokusai Shoji Homu) 202 (1988). Associate, Yuasa & Hara, Tokyo, Japan, 1987-1989. Contract Administrator, Chemsult AG, Saudi Arabia, 1977-1980. *Member:* San Francisco and American (Member, Section on International Law) Bar Associations; State Bar of California; International Bar Association (Member, Section on Business Law); Japan Society of Northern California; California-Southeast Asia Business Association; American Chamber of Commerce in Japan (Member, Committee on Licensing, Patents & Trademarks, 1987-1989). (San Francisco Office).

DAVID S. KIM, born Seoul, South Korea, February 17, 1961; admitted, 1990, California and U.S. District Court, Northern and Central Districts of California. *Education:* Western Illinois University (B.B.A., 1983; M.B.A., 1985); Southwestern University School of Law, Los Angeles (J.D., 1989). Recipient, Bradley and Pollack Scholarship, 1990. *Member:* State Bar of California; California Trial Lawyers Association; Los Angeles Trial Lawyers Association; California Korean Bar Association. (Los Angeles Office). *LANGUAGES:* English and Korean. *PRACTICE AREAS:* Litigation; Real Estate.

DOUGLAS L. BRYAN, born Whittier, California, September 7, 1960; admitted, 1991, California and U.S. District Court, Central District of California; 1992, U.S. Court of Appeals, Ninth Circuit. *Education:* California Polytechnic State University (B.S., 1983); Southwestern University School of Law (J.D., 1991). *Member:* State Bar of California; American Bar Association. (Los Angeles Office). *PRACTICE AREAS:* Tax Law; Corporate Law; Corporate Reorganizations; Constitutional Law; Insurance.

ROBERT W. MULCAHY, born Boston, Massachusetts, May 8, 1940; admitted, 1970, New York; 1971, District of Columbia; 1976, California; 1991, State Bar of Texas. *Education:* Boston College (B.S., Chemistry, 1963); George Washington University (J.D., 1968). *Member:* District of Columbia; State Bar of California; American Bar Association; The Licensing Executive Society. The Houston Volunteer Lawyers Association; Houston Intellectual Property Law Association. (Alhambra Office). *PRACTICE AREAS:* Intellectual Property; Patent Agent; Copyright Law; Trademark Law; Trade Secrets and Licensing.

OF COUNSEL

DEBORAH S. CHEW, born Singapore, May 27, 1964; admitted, 1988, Singapore; 1991, California. *Education:* National University of Singapore (LL.B., with honors, 1987). Associate, Arthur Loke & Partners, Singapore, 1988-1991. *Member:* State Bar of California; American Immigration Lawyers Association; Singapore American Business Association (Founding

(This Listing Continued)

Member and Director); Hong Kong Association of California (Director); Asian Business Association; Law Society of Singapore and Academy of Law of Singapore. (San Francisco Office). *LANGUAGES:* English and Chinese (Mandarin, Cantonese, Taiwanese and Chiu-chow dialect).

CHRISTINA Y. CHEN, born Canton, China, May 2, 1943; admitted, 1983, California. *Education:* San Francisco State University (B.A., 1969); Hastings College of the Law, University of California (J.D., 1979). (Of Counsel, San Francisco, California Office). *LANGUAGES:* English and Chinese (Mandarin, Cantonese and Toisan dialect).

ROGER S. SAXTON, born Martins Ferry, Ohio, April 30, 1952; admitted, 1979, Sweden (as Jurist); 1980, Pennsylvania and U.S. District Court, Western District of Pennsylvania; 1992, New South Wales, Australia. *Education:* Case Western Reserve University (J.D., 1979); Studies in Japanese Law, Sophia University and University of Tokyo, Tokyo, Japan (1977-1980); Studies in Australian Law, University of Sydney (1989-1991). *Member:* Pennsylvania Bar Association; Law Society of New South Wales; Inter Pacific Bar Association. (Of Counsel, Sydney, Australia). *LANGUAGES:* English, Swedish and Japanese.

KAZUKO ITOH, born Tokyo, Japan, January 17, 1923; admitted, 1959, Japan (Not admitted in the U.S.). *Education:* Tsuda College; Tokyo Bunrika University. Legal Advisor to Her Britanic Majesty's Ambassador, Tokyo, 1976—. Legal Consultant to the American Embassy, Tokyo, 1976—. *Member:* Tokyo Bar Association; International Bar Association. (Of Counsel, Tokyo, Japan). *LANGUAGES:* Japanese, English, French and Spanish. *PRACTICE AREAS:* General Civil and Trial Practice; International Arbitration; Patent Litigation.

DUCK-SOON CHANG, born Korea, July 23, 1960; admitted, 1985, Korea and Korea Patent Bar; 1991, New York; 1992, California. *Education:* Judicial Training and Research Institute of the Supreme Court of Korea (198 3-1984); College of Law, Seoul National University (B.Jur,. 1983); Harvard Law School (LL.M., 1990). Author: "Technology Transfer, Cooperation and Joint Venture Agreements with Korea", Chapter 4 of Legal Aspects of Business Transactions and Investment in the Far East (Kluwer, 1988); "Arbitration Procedures in Korea," Vol. 1, Asia Law and Practice 7 (1989); "Arbitration in South Korea," Vol. 14 East Asian Executive Reports 1 (1992). Lecturer, International Patent Training and Research Institute of the Korean Industrial Property Office. Arbitrator, Korean Commercial Arbitration Board. *Member:* New York State and American Bar Associations; State Bar of California; Korean Bar Association; Korean Patent Bar Association; International Trademark Association. (Of Counsel, Seoul, Korea). *LANGUAGES:* Korean, English, Japanese (reads only). *PRACTICE AREAS:* Joint Venture; Licensing; Commercial Arbitration; Intellectual Property.

ASSOCIATES

JIANXIN LI, born Jiangmen, China, October, 1966; admitted, 1988, China. *Education:* Guangzhou University (Law Department, 1984-1986); Zhongshan University (Economic Management Department, 1987-1990). Attorney, Guangzhou Second Foreign Economic Law Office, 1986-1990. *LANGUAGES:* English, Chinese (Mandarin and Cantonese). *PRACTICE AREAS:* Intellectual Property Litigation; Contracts; Real Estate; Trade; Insurance Adoption Law.

YIKUN ZHU, born Sichuan Province, China, August 1967; admitted, 1993, China. *Education:* Southwest College of Politics & Law (LL.M., 1991). [Chinese, English, Russian and French]. *PRACTICE AREAS:* Foreign Investment; Securities Law; Company Law; Intellectual Property; Tax Law; International Trade Dispute; Contracts.

VINCENT I.S. HSIEH, born Taipei, Taiwan, January 15, 1964; admitted, 1993, New York. *Education:* National Taiwan University (LL.B., 1987) Boston University (LL.M., in International Banking, 1992). *Member:* American Bar Association; New York County Lawyers Association. (New York Office). *LANGUAGES:* Mandarin Chinese.

ZHOUGEN LI, born Shunde, Guangdong Province, PRC, October 1, 1935; (Not admitted in the United States). *Education:* Yue Xue Teachers Training College. 1985-1991, Judge (ret.) Guangzhou Middle People's Court, Civil Division and Director of Administration. Recipient, 1984, 1985 Guangzhou City Court Systems Advance Specialist of the Year; 1988, Guangdong Province Outstanding Judge of the year; 1989 Third Degree Honor awarded by the Guangdong Province High Court. *LANGUAGES:* Chinese (Mandarin and Cantonese). *PRACTICE AREAS:* Litigation; Contract; Intellectual Property.

YAOWU RONG, born Wei Chen County, Ji Bei, March 19, 1979; admitted, 1993, China; (Not admitted in the United States). *Education:* Xia-

(This Listing Continued)

men University (B.A., 1992); (Now Mid. Graduated College of Xiamen University). (Xiamen Office). *LANGUAGES:* Chinese, English. *PRACTICE AREAS:* Civil Law; Commercial Law.

YUAN JIANG, born Fujian Province, China, April 15, 1956; admitted, 1983, China (Not admitted in the United States). *Education:* China University of Political Science and Law, 1979-1983; Part-time graduate student at China University of Political Science and Law, international private law, 1986-1989. Cadre at Research Department, China Lawyer Association, 1989-1990. Reporter, China Lawyer Magazine, 1990-1993. (Beijing Office). *LANGUAGES:* Chinese. *PRACTICE AREAS:* Labor Law; Leasing; Litigation.

XIAODONG HAO, born Inner Mongolia, China, March 9, 1965; admitted, 1990, China (Not admitted in the United States). *Education:* Inner Mongolia University (B.S.); China University of Political Science and Law (LL.B., 1991). (Beijing Office). *LANGUAGES:* Chinese, English, Japanese. *PRACTICE AREAS:* Litigation; Business Law; Intellectual Property.

SIYANG LIAO, born Shanghai Province, China, April 15, 1970. *Education:* China Political/Legal University (L.L.B., 1992). (Beijing Office). *LANGUAGES:* English, Chinese. *PRACTICE AREAS:* Contract Law; Joint Venture Law; Intellectual Property Law.

PEIZHONG GAN, born China, May 8, 1956; admitted, 1988, China (not admitted in the United States). *Education:* The Department of Law, Beijing University (LL.B., 1983; LL.M., 1989). Chief Editor, Encyclopedia of Commercial Law of China and the Encyclopedia of Corporate Law. Author: 21 articles and 3 books, e.g. "Legal Issues on Contracting Management in the Enterprises Owned by the Whole People," "Several Legal Issues on Corporate Reorganization in China". Lecturer, 1988. Associate Professor, 1994, Lectures on Corporate and Companies Law, 1984-1985. Assessor in the Beijing Intermediate Court. (Beijing Office). *LANGUAGES:* Chinese, English. *PRACTICE AREAS:* Corporate Law; Commercial Law; Litigation; Intellectual Property.

DACHTCEREN ENKHBOLD, born Ulaanbaatar, Mongolia, March 11, 1946; admitted, 1973, Mongolia; (Not admitted in the United States). *Education:* International Relations Institute of Moscow (expert of Western Countries - U.S.A., Canada); Mongolian State University (Teacher of English Language). (Mongolia Office). *LANGUAGES:* Russian, English. *PRACTICE AREAS:* Economic Entities and Foreign Investment, Civil Law.

BYAMBAA BAYARMAA, born Moscow, Russia, November 6, 1960; admitted, 1982, Mongolia; (Not Admitted in the United States). *Education:* Moldova State University, Law Faculty, 1982; Passed State Examination on Bar Practice, March, 1994. (Mongolia Office). *LANGUAGES:* Russian, German, Romania, English. *PRACTICE AREAS:* Commercial and Contract Law.

JIANXIONG HUANG, born Rongyan City, Fujian, January 15, 1964; admitted, 1987 (Not admitted in the United States). *Education:* South-West Politics & Law College (B.A., 1984); College of Xiamen University (Master of Law, 1990). (Xiamen Office). *LANGUAGES:* Chinese, Taiwanese, English. *PRACTICE AREAS:* Civil Law; Commercial Law; Investment Law; Real Estate Law.

MINGLIANG LAN, born Hainan Province, China, August 12, 1927; admitted, 1989 (Not admitted in the United States). *Education:* Beijing Zhengfa University of Politics and Law (1956). Publications: Outline of Administrative Law; General Situation of International Organization; International Constitution (Teaching Material); Outline and Guidance on International Law. *Member:* Asian-Africa Development Committee, China International Legal Study Committee; National Lawyer Committee; China-Hong Kong Law Study Committee; China Investment Consultancy Experts Committee; China Political and Legal Management Leaders Institution; China Trade Committee; Foreign Economic and Trade Arbitration Committee (Arbitrator); National Overseas Federation Legal Consultant Committee. (Shenzhen Office). *LANGUAGES:* Chinese, English. *PRACTICE AREAS:* Public International Law; Intellectual Property.

ALFRED YONG LIN, born Fuzhou, China, October 10, 1969; admitted, 1993, China (not admitted in the United States). *Education:* Xiamen University Law Department (B.A., 1992). (Shanghai Office). *LANGUAGES:* Chinese, English and Fuzhou. *PRACTICE AREAS:* General Civil Law; International Investment; Corporation Law.

HONGLIANG WU, born Shanghai, China, 1935; admitted, 1985, China; registered patent agent (not admitted in the United States). *Education:* Beijing Iron and Steel Institute (B.S., 1960). (Shanghai Office). *LAN-*

(This Listing Continued)

GUAGES: Chinese (Shanghai dialect) and English. *PRACTICE AREAS:* Patent and Trademark Law; Intellectual Property.

JIANG-XIONG HUANG, born Rongyan City, Fujian Province, China, January 15, 1946; admitted, 1987, China (Not admitted in the United States). *Education:* Institute of Political Science and Law in South-west China (B.A. in Law, 1984); Post-graduate Institute of Xiamen University (LL.M. in civil law, 1990). Author: An Introduction to Civil Law, published by house of Xiamen University; Examples of Lawsuits, published by house of Xiamen University; A Guide for Taiwan People to Invest in Mainland China, published by Beijing Huayi Publishing House. Lecturer: Civil Law; Law of Estate and Practice, Law Department, Xiamen University. *Member:* China Jurisprudence Society; Fujian Jurisprudence Society; Xiamen Jurisprudence Society; Fujian Society of Administrative; Association for Industry and Commerce; Xiamen Society of Administration for Industry and Commerce; Xiamen Bar Association. (Xiamen Office). *LANGUAGES:* Chinese, Taiwanese, English. *PRACTICE AREAS:* Economic; Commercial; Civil; Criminal; Investment Law, and Real Estate Law in China.

ZHOUGEN LI, born Shunde, Guangdong Province, China, October 1, 1935; (Not admitted in the United States). *Education:* Yue Xue Teachers Training College. 1985-1991, Judge (ret.) Guangzhou Middle People's Court, Civil Division and Director of Administration. Recipient, 1984, 1985 Guangzhou City Court Systems Advance Specialist of the Year; 1988, Guangdong Province Outstanding Judge of the year; 1989 Third Degree Honor awarded by the Guangdong Province High Court. (Hong Kong Office). *LANGUAGES:* Chinese (Mandarin and Cantonese). *PRACTICE AREAS:* Litigation; Contract; Intellectual Property.

JIA LIN, born China; admitted, 1989, China; 1991, California. *Education:* Zhongshan University, Guangzhou, China (LL.B.); People's University Beijing, China (LL.M.). Lecturer, People's University, 1989—. (Beijing Office).

LEGAL SUPPORT PERSONNEL

ZHANGQUING WU, born Shantou Guangdong Province, PRC October 15, 1967. *Education:* Shenzhen University (LL.B., 1991). (Shenzhen Office).

SHIJIE CHEN, born Xiamen, Fujian Province, China, November 18, 1970. *Education:* Xiamen University (LL.B., 1992). (Xiamen Office). *LANGUAGES:* English, Chinese. *PRACTICE AREAS:* Adoption Law; Contracts; Insurance; Trade.

SONG GAO, born Fujian Province, China, April 2, 1969. *Education:* Hau Qiao University (LL.B.). (Shenzhen Office).

REVISER OF THE PEOPLE'S REPUBLIC OF CHINA AND MONGOLIA LAW DIGESTS FOR THIS DIRECTORY.

BECKER & POLIAKOFF, P.A.

Established in 1972

A-1 UNIT, ROOM 1506
371-375 HUAN SHI DONG ROAD
GUANGZHOU (CANTON), GUANGZHOU, PEOPLE'S REPUBLIC OF CHINA
Telephone: 86-20-778-1663
Fax: 86-20-777-9738

Miami, Florida Office: 6161 Blue Lagoon Drive, Suite 250. Telephone: 305-262-4433.

West Palm Beach, Florida Office: 500 Australian Avenue, 9th Floor. Telephone: 407-655-5444.

Sarasota, Florida Office: 630 South Orange Avenue. Telephone: 813-366-8826.

Clearwater, Florida Office: The Clearwater Tower, 33 North Garden Avenue, Suite 960. Telephone: 813-443-3781.

Fort Myers, Florida Office: 13515 Bell Tower Dr., Suite 101. Telephone: 813-433-7707.

Tampa, Florida Office: One North Dale Mabry, Suite 820. Telephone: 813-874-7550.

Orlando, Florida Office: Maitland Center, 901 North Lake Destiny Drive, Suite 145, Maitland, Florida. Telephone: 407-875-0955.

St. Petersburg, Florida Office: 5999 Central Ave., Suite 104. Telephone: 813-345-3420.

Prague, Czech Republic Office: Zastoupeni V CR, Apolinarska 06, 128 00, Praha 2. Telephone: 011 42 2 29 8005. Fax: 011 42 2 296807.

(This Listing Continued)

BECKER & POLIAKOFF, P.A., Guangzhou (Canton), Guangzhou—Continued

Advice and Assistance with foreign investments in People's Republic of China.

Michael X. Zhang
(Not admitted in China)

Gary A. Poliakoff
(Not admitted in China)

Alan S. Becker
(Not admitted in China)

Lana Chiu (admission pending)

OF COUNSEL

Caroly Pedersen (Not admitted in China)

(For complete Biographical data on all Personnel see Professional Biographies at Fort Lauderdale, Florida)

DEACONS

ROOM 1405 14/F NORTH TOWER
WORLD TRADE CENTRE
371-375 EAST HUANSHI ROAD

GUANGZHOU, GUANGZHOU, PEOPLE'S REPUBLIC OF CHINA

Telephone: (86 20) 778 1178/778 1278
Fax: (86 20) 778 9618

Associated Offices of Deacons, Graham & James/Sly Weigall: Bangkok, Beijing, Hanoi, Hong Kong, Jakarta, Taipei, Tokyo, Brisbane, Canberra, Melbourne, Perth, Sydney, Milan, Los Angeles, Newport Beach, New York, Palo Alto, Sacramento, San Francisco, Washington, D.C., Berlin, Brussels, Bucharest, Dusseldorf, Frankfurt, Leipzig, London, Milan, Munich, Prague, Jeddah, Kuwait, Riyadh, Mexico City.

RESIDENT PARTNER

ALEX LAI, LL.B., P.C.LL. (Univ. of Hong Kong), Diploma in Chinese Law (Univ. of East Asia), admitted, 1987, Hong Kong. *LANGUAGES:* Chinese (Mandarin and Cantonese). *PRACTICE AREAS:* Construction; Litigation; Arbitration.

STEPHENSON HARWOOD & LO

Established in 1994

ROOM 516, CHINA HOTEL
LIU HUA LU

GUANGZHOU (CANTON), GUANGZHOU 510015, PEOPLE'S REPUBLIC OF CHINA

Telephone: (8620) 669 3490
Telex: 44888 CHLGZ CN
Fax: (8620) 669 3479

Hong Kong Office: Stephenson Harwood & Lo, 18th Floor Edinburgh Tower, The Landmark, 15 Queen's Road Central. Telephone: 852 2868 0789. Telex: 66278 SHL HX. Fax: 852 2868 1504.

Hong Kong Associated Office: Lo and Lo, Swire House, 11th Floor, Chater Road Central. Telephone: 852 2523 8181. Telex: 73145 HX. Fax: 852 2810 5351.

Other Associated Offices in: London, England; Brussels, Belgium; Kuwait and Madrid, Spain.

International and Local Corporate, Commercial, Banking, Litigation, Property and Shipping Law.

CONTACT PARTNERS

Michael Hoddinott

(For Complete List of Stephenson Harwood's Overseas Offices, Please see London, England Office)

ARNBERGER, KIM, BUXBAUM & CHOY

7TH FLOOR, BLOCK 2, JING MING BUILDING
NO. 8, ZUN YI ROAD
SHANGHAI 90010, PEOPLE'S REPUBLIC OF CHINA
Telephone: (86)(21) 219-4180
Facsimile: (86)(21)219-7421

REVISER OF THE PEOPLE'S REPUBLIC OF CHINA AND MONGOLIA LAW DIGESTS FOR THIS DIRECTORY.

Hong Kong Office: 3201 Citibank Tower, 3 Garden Road, Central. Telephone: (852) 2523-7001. Fax: (852) 2845-0947.

Beijing (Peking), People's Republic of China Office: China World Trade Centre, Suite 2523, No. 1 Jian Guo Men Wai Avenue. Telephone: (86)(1) 505-2288 Ext: 2523. Fax: (86)(1) 505-2638.

Guangzhou (Canton), People's Republic of China Office: China Hotel Office Tower, Suite 512. Telephone: (86)(20) 666-3388. Ext. 2512. Fax: (86)(20) 669-1217.

Xiamen, People's Republic of China Office: Foreign Trade Centre, Suite 519, No. 15 Hu Bing North Road, Xiamen City. Telephone: (86)(592) 506-3059. Facsimile: (86)(592) 511-1044 Ext. 519.

Shenzhen, People's Republic of China Office: Shenzhen Development Center, Suite 2103, Renmin Nan Lu, Shenzhen. Telephone: (86)(755) 229-8009. Facsimile: (86)(755) 229-8011.

Shanghai, People's Republic of China Office: 7th Floor, Block 2, Jing Ming Building, No. 8 Zun Yi Road, Shanghai. Telephone: (86)(21) 219-4180. Facsimile: (86)(21) 219-7421.

Ulaanbaatar, Mongolia Office: Ulaanbaatar Supreme Court Building, Room 429, 432. Telephone: (976)(1) 31-0711. Fax: (976)(1) 32-5102.

New York Office: 100 Maiden Lane, 16th Floor, Suite 1600B, New York, New York 10038. Telephone: (212) 504-6109. Fax: (212) 412-7016.

Los Angeles Office: 3731 Wilshire Boulevard, Suite 910, West Tower, Los Angeles, California, 90010. Telephone: (213) 380-7780. Facsimile: (510) 358-0226; (213) 380-5798.

San Francisco Office: 44 Montgomery Street, Suite 500, San Francisco 94104. Telephone: (415) 955-0553. Fax: (415) 753-1235.

Alhambra Office: 320 South Garfield, Suite 206, Alhambra, California 91801. Telephone: (818) 281-9088. Fax: (818) 281-7189.

Corporate, Employment Law, Commodities, Securities, Complex Commercial Litigation, International Transactions, Intellectual Property, Aircraft and Equipment Leasing Financing and Taxation.

MEMBERS OF FIRM

DAVID C. BUXBAUM, born New York, N.Y., July 16, 1933; admitted, 1970, New York and U.S. District Court, Southern, Eastern, Northern and Western Districts of New York; 1971, U.S. Court of Appeals, Second Circuit; 1974, U.S. Supreme Court; 1975, U.S. Court of Appeals, Seventh Circuit and Fourth Circuits; 1978, U.S. Court of Appeals, Eighth Circuit; 1979, U.S. Court of Appeals, First Circuit; 1981, California; 1989, U.S. District Court, Central District of California; 1991, U.S. District Court, Northern District of California; U.S. Court of Appeals, Ninth Circuit (Not admitted in China). *Education:* New York University (B.A., 1954); University of Michigan (J.D., 1959) concurrent graduate studies, University of Michigan Graduate School; graduate study, Harvard University and University of Washington (M.A., 1963; Ph.D., 1968). Member, Far East Honor Society, University of Michigan. Author: *Articles:* "Preliminary Trends in the Development of the Legal Institutions of Communist China and the Nature of the Criminal Law," International and Comparative Law Quarterly, January, 1962, reprinted in *Government of Communist China,* Chandler, San Francisco, 1966; "Horizontal and Vertical Influences Upon the Substantive Criminal Law of Mainland Chinese, Some Preliminary Observations," Osteuropa Recht, No. 1, 1964; "Chinese Family Law in Common Law Setting: A Note on the Institutional Environment and the Substantive Family Law of the Chinese in Malaysia and Singapore," Journal of Asian Studies, August, 1966; "Some Aspects of Civil Procedure and Practice at the Trial Level in Tanshui and Hsinchu...," XXX Journal of Asian Studies, 1971; *Lawyer's Challenge in China Trade: New and Developing Legal System,* New York Law Journal, International Law Finance and Trade, February, 1979; *Commodities Trade with China,* New York Law Journal, December, 1978; *Regulation of Commodity Futures Exchanges in Japan,* New York Law Journal, October, 1978; *Commodities Transactions in China and Hong Kong,* New York Law Journal, June, 1978; *Jurisdiction Over Foreign Transactions and Foreign Nationals,* New York Law Journal, April, 1978; *Two Cases of Dispute Settlement,* U.S.-China Business Review, Vol. 1, No. 2, March/April, 1974; *Two Cases of Dispute Settlement,* Arbitration and Dispute Settlement in Trade with China, Special Report No. 4 for Members of the National Council for United States-China Trade, February, 1974; *Nego-*

(This Listing Continued)

tiation with the Chinese, Trade with China, 1973; *American Trade with the People's Republic of China: Some Preliminary Perspectives*, Columbia Journal of Transnational Law, Vol. 12, No. 1, 1973; *Liability of Federal Officials in Damage for Acts Unconstitutional or in Excess of their Authority; Expanding the Concept of the Rule of Law*, Capital University Law Review, Vol. 8, Issue 4, 1979; *Taking on the Government Alone; Sole Practitioner Battles Way to Supreme Court and Wins*, Legal Times of Washington, December, 1978; *Disclosure of Management Remuneration, Transaction, Litigation and Employment History*, Los Angeles Daily Journal, March, 1979; *Contracts in China*, China Trade, Praeger, 1982. Monthly Columnist, New York Law Journal on Commodities Law, 1976-1982; *Contract Law in China, The Dynamics of Statutory Development and Practice*, Doing Business in China, 1990, Streng et al, ed. Contracts in China during the Qing Dynasty: Key to the Civil Law, Journal of Oriental Studies, University of Hong Kong, 1993. *The Commercial Laws of China*, and *Patents Law and Practice, Trademark Law and Practice, The People's Republic of China*, Digest of the Commercial Laws of the World, 1982-1993. *M.A. Dissertation:* "Legal Institutions of Contemporary Mainland China," University of Washington, 1962. *Ph.D. Dissertation:* Some Aspects of Substantive Family Law and Social Change in Rural China, 1896-1967," University of Washington, 1968. *Case Note:* "Freedom of Marriage in a Pluralistic Society," Malaya Law Review, 1963. Editor: *Traditional and Modern Legal Institutions in Asia and Africa, Journal of Asian and African Studies*, Supplement Edition, 1967; *Family Law and Customary Law in Asia: A Contemporary Legal Perspective*, 1968; *Law and Social Change: A Case Study of Family Law and Social Change in China and Other Developing Areas*, University of Washington Press, 1978; *Transition and Permanence: Chinese History and Culture, A Festschrift in Honor of Dr. Kung-Chan Hsiao*, 1971; *Chinese Family Law and Social Change in Historic and Comparative Perspective*, University of Washington Press, 1978; *China Trade: Prospects and Perspectives*, Prager, 1982; Sole Counsel for Successful Respondents, *Butz v. Economou*, 438 US 478, 1978. Associate Professor, Chinese Law, Comparative Law and Domestic Relations, University of Washington, 1968-1969. Assistant Lecturer, Chinese Law, Domestic Relations, Labor Law, Jurisprudence, Comparative Law, University of Singapore, 1963-1964. Adjunct Professor of Law: Touro Law School, 1980; Southwestern University School of Law, 1983-1988. Member, Commission on Labor Law, Singapore, 1963-1964. Member, Panel of Arbitrators, American Arbitration Association. *Member:* American Bar Association (Member, Committee on Far Eastern Law, Section of International and Comparative Law, 1965-1971); New York Trial Lawyers Association (Member, Liaison Committee with Judicial Conference, 1971-1978). *LANGUAGES:* Chinese, French, German and Japanese (specialized reading). *PRACTICE AREAS:* International Law; Complex International Litigation; Complex International Contract; Joint Venture Contract; Investment Law; Trademark, Copyright and Patent Protection and Enforcement; Commodities and Securities.

KENNETH Y. CHOY, born Hong Kong, May 24, 1956; admitted, 1987, New York; U.S. District Court, Southern and Eastern Districts of New York; 1990, California; 1991, Central and Northern Districts of California and U.S. Court of Appeals, 9th Circuit (Not admitted in China). *Education:* San Francisco State University (B.A., 1977); Northeastern University (J.D., 1986). Judicial Intern to Hon. Dolores K. Sloviter, U.S. Court of Appeals for the Third Circuit, 1985-1986. *Member:* American Bar Association (Member, Section on Labor and Employment Law); American Immigration Lawyers Association. (New York Office). *LANGUAGES:* Chinese (Cantonese and Mandarin). *PRACTICE AREAS:* Litigation and Transactions in U.S. and People's Republic of China.

H. BENNETT ARNBERGER, born Globe, Arizona, July 8, 1953; admitted, 1983, California and U.S. District Court, Northern and Central Districts of California. *Education:* University of California at Berkeley (A.B., with honors and distinction, 1977); University of San Francisco (J.D., 1983). Phi Delta Phi. Author: "Ensuring Compliance Through Intellectual Property Audits," 5 International Legal Strategy 54 (1994); "Avoiding The Hidden Liabilities of Independent Contractors," I Foreign Assignments (Kaigai Chuzai) 99 (1994); "Proactive Prevention of Cross-Cultural Disputes," 6 International Legal Strategy 60 (1994); "Protecting Against Misappropriation of Trade Secrets," 10 International Legal Strategy 63 (1993); "Taxation and Legal Requirements of California Corporations," 16 International Business Law Journal (Kokusai Shoji Homu) 202 (1988). Associate, Yuasa & Hara, Tokyo, Japan, 1987-1989. Contract Administrator, Chemsult AG, Saudi Arabia, 1977-1980. *Member:* San Francisco and American (Member, Section on International Law) Bar Associations; State Bar of California; International Bar Association (Member, Section on Business Law); Japan Society of Northern California; California-Southeast Asia Business Association; American Chamber of Commerce in Japan (Member,

(This Listing Continued)

Committee on Licensing, Patents & Trademarks, 1987-1989). (San Francisco Office).

DAVID S. KIM, born Seoul, South Korea, February 17, 1961; admitted, 1990, California and U.S. District Court, Northern and Central Districts of California. *Education:* Western Illinois University (B.B.A., 1983; M.B.A., 1985); Southwestern University School of Law, Los Angeles (J.D., 1989). Recipient, Bradley and Pollack Scholarship, 1990. *Member:* State Bar of California; California Trial Lawyers Association; Los Angeles Trial Lawyers Association; California Korean Bar Association. (Los Angeles Office). *LANGUAGES:* English and Korean. *PRACTICE AREAS:* Litigation; Real Estate.

DOUGLAS L. BRYAN, born Whittier, California, September 7, 1960; admitted, 1991, California and U.S. District Court, Central District of California; 1992, U.S. Court of Appeals, Ninth Circuit. *Education:* California Polytechnic State University (B.S., 1983); Southwestern University School of Law (J.D., 1991). *Member:* State Bar of California; American Bar Association. (Los Angeles Office). *PRACTICE AREAS:* Tax Law; Corporate Law; Corporate Reorganizations; Constitutional Law; Insurance.

ROBERT W. MULCAHY, born Boston, Massachusetts, May 8, 1940; admitted, 1970, New York; 1971, District of Columbia; 1976, California; 1991, State Bar of Texas. *Education:* Boston College (B.S., Chemistry, 1963); George Washington University (J.D., 1968). *Member:* District of Columbia; State Bar of California; American Bar Association; The Licensing Executive Society. The Houston Volunteer Lawyers Association; Houston Intellectual Property Law Association. (Alhambra Office). *PRACTICE AREAS:* Intellectual Property; Patent Agent; Copyright Law; Trademark Law; Trade Secrets and Licensing.

OF COUNSEL

DEBORAH S. CHEW, born Singapore, May 27, 1964; admitted, 1988, Singapore; 1991, California. *Education:* National University of Singapore (LL.B., with honors, 1987). Associate, Arthur Loke & Partners, Singapore, 1988-1991. *Member:* State Bar of California; American Immigration Lawyers Association; Singapore American Business Association (Founding Member and Director); Hong Kong Association of California (Director); Asian Business Association; Law Society of Singapore and Academy of Law of Singapore. (San Francisco Office). *LANGUAGES:* English and Chinese (Mandarin, Cantonese, Taiwanese and Chiu-chow dialect).

CHRISTINA Y. CHEN, born Canton, China, May 2, 1943; admitted, 1983, California. *Education:* San Francisco State University (B.A., 1969); Hastings College of the Law, University of California (J.D., 1979). (Of Counsel, San Francisco, California Office). *LANGUAGES:* English and Chinese (Mandarin, Cantonese and Toisan dialect).

ROGER S. SAXTON, born Martins Ferry, Ohio, April 30, 1952; admitted, 1979, Sweden (as Jurist); 1980, Pennsylvania and U.S. District Court, Western District of Pennsylvania; 1992, New South Wales, Australia. *Education:* Case Western Reserve University (J.D., 1979); Studies in Japanese Law, Sophia University and University of Tokyo, Tokyo, Japan (1977-1980); Studies in Australian Law, University of Sydney (1989-1991). *Member:* Pennsylvania Bar Association; Law Society of New South Wales; Inter Pacific Bar Association. (Of Counsel, Sydney, Australia). *LANGUAGES:* English, Swedish and Japanese.

KAZUKO ITOH, born Tokyo, Japan, January 17, 1923; admitted, 1959, Japan (Not admitted in the U.S.). *Education:* Tsuda College; Tokyo Bunrika University. Legal Advisor to Her Britanic Majesty's Ambassador, Tokyo, 1976—. Legal Consultant to the American Embassy, Tokyo, 1976—. *Member:* Tokyo Bar Association; International Bar Association. (Of Counsel, Tokyo, Japan). *LANGUAGES:* Japanese, English, French and Spanish. *PRACTICE AREAS:* General Civil and Trial Practice; International Arbitration; Patent Litigation.

DUCK-SOON CHANG, born Korea, July 23, 1960; admitted, 1985, Korea and Korea Patent Bar; 1991, New York; 1992, California. *Education:* Judicial Training and Research Institute of the Supreme Court of Korea (198 3-1984); College of Law, Seoul National University (B.Jur,. 1983); Harvard Law School (LL.M., 1990). Author: "Technology Transfer, Cooperation and Joint Venture Agreements with Korea", Chapter 4 of Legal Aspects of Business Transactions and Investment in the Far East (Kluwer, 1988); "Arbitration Procedures in Korea," Vol. 1, Asia Law and Practice 7 (1989); "Arbitration in South Korea," Vol. 14 East Asian Executive Reports 1 (1992). Lecturer, International Patent Training and Research Institute of the Korean Industrial Property Office. Arbitrator, Korean Commercial Arbitration Board. *Member:* New York State and American Bar Associations; State Bar of California; Korean Bar Association; Korean Patent Bar Association; International Trademark Association. (Of Counsel, Seoul,

(This Listing Continued)

ARNBERGER, KIM, BUXBAUM & CHOY, Shanghai—
Continued

Korea). *LANGUAGES:* Korean, English, Japanese (reads only). *PRACTICE AREAS:* Joint Venture; Licensing; Commercial Arbitration; Intellectual Property.

ASSOCIATES

ALFRED YONG LIN, born Fuzhou, China, October 10, 1969; admitted, 1993, China (not admitted in the United States). *Education:* Xiamen University Law Department (B.A., 1992). (Shanghai Office). *LANGUAGES:* Chinese, English and Fuzhou. *PRACTICE AREAS:* General Civil Law; International Investment; Corporation Law.

HONGLIANG WU, born Shanghai, China, 1935; admitted, 1985, China; registered patent agent (not admitted in the United States). *Education:* Beijing Iron and Steel Institute (B.S., 1960). (Shanghai Office). *LANGUAGES:* Chinese (Shanghai dialect) and English. *PRACTICE AREAS:* Patent and Trademark Law; Intellectual Property.

VINCENT I.S. HSIEH, born Taipei, Taiwan, January 15, 1964; admitted, 1993, New York. *Education:* National Taiwan University (LL.B., 1987) Boston University (LL.M., in International Banking, 1992). *Member:* American Bar Association; New York County Lawyers Association. (New York Office). *LANGUAGES:* Mandarin Chinese.

ZHOUGEN LI, born Shunde, Guangdong Province, PRC, October 1, 1935; (Not admitted in the United States). *Education:* Yue Xue Teachers Training College. 1985-1991, Judge (ret.) Guangzhou Middle People's Court, Civil Division and Director of Administration. Recipient, 1984, 1985 Guangzhou City Court Systems Advance Specialist of the Year; 1988, Guangdong Province Outstanding Judge of the year; 1989 Third Degree Honor awarded by the Guangdong Province High Court. *LANGUAGES:* Chinese (Mandarin and Cantonese). *PRACTICE AREAS:* Litigation; Contract; Intellectual Property.

YAOWU RONG, born Wei Chen County, Ji Bei, March 19, 1979; admitted, 1993, China; (Not admitted in the United States). *Education:* Xiamen University (B.A., 1992); (Now Mid. Graduated College of Xiamen University). (Xiamen Office). *LANGUAGES:* Chinese, English. *PRACTICE AREAS:* Civil Law; Commercial Law.

YUAN JIANG, born Fujian Province, China, April 15, 1956; admitted, 1983, China (Not admitted in the United States). *Education:* China University of Political Science and Law, 1979-1983; Part-time graduate student at China University of Political Science and Law, international private law, 1986-1989. Cadre at Research Department, China Lawyer Association, 1989-1990. Reporter, China Lawyer Magazine, 1990-1993. (Beijing Office). *LANGUAGES:* Chinese. *PRACTICE AREAS:* Labor Law; Leasing; Litigation.

XIAODONG HAO, born Inner Mongolia, China, March 9, 1965; admitted, 1990, China (Not admitted in the United States). *Education:* Inner Mongolia University (B.S.); China University of Political Science and Law (LL.B., 1991). (Beijing Office). *LANGUAGES:* Chinese, English, Japanese. *PRACTICE AREAS:* Litigation; Business Law; Intellectual Property.

SIYANG LIAO, born Shanghai Province, China, April 15, 1970. *Education:* China Political/Legal University (L.L.B., 1992). (Beijing Office). *LANGUAGES:* English, Chinese. *PRACTICE AREAS:* Contract Law; Joint Venture Law; Intellectual Property Law.

PEIZHONG GAN, born China, May 8, 1956; admitted, 1988, China (not admitted in the United States). *Education:* The Department of Law, Beijing University (LL.B., 1983; LL.M., 1989). Chief Editor, Encyclopedia of Commercial Law of China and the Encyclopedia of Corporate Law. Author: 21 articles and 3 books, e.g. "Legal Issues on Contracting Management in the Enterprises Owned by the Whole People," "Several Legal Issues on Corporate Reorganization in China". Lecturer, 1988. Associate Professor, 1994, Lectures on Corporate and Companies Law, 1984-1985. Assessor in the Beijing Intermediate Court. (Beijing Office). *LANGUAGES:* Chinese, English. *PRACTICE AREAS:* Corporate Law; Commercial Law; Litigation; Intellectual Property.

JIANXIN LI, born Jiangmen, China, October, 1966; admitted, 1988, China (Not admitted in the United States). *Education:* Guangzhou University (Law Department, 1984-1986); Zhongshan University (Economic Management Department, 1987-1990). Attorney, Guangzhou Second Foreign Economic Law Office, 1986-1990. (Guangzhou Office). *LANGUAGES:* English, Chinese (Mandarin and Cantonese). *PRACTICE AREAS:* Intel-

(This Listing Continued)

lectual Property Litigation; Contracts; Real Estate; Trade; Insurance Law; Adoption Law.

YIKUN ZHU, born Sichuan Province, China, August 1967; admitted, 1993, China (Not admitted in the United States). *Education:* Southwest College of Politics & Law (L.L.M., 1991). [Chinese, Russian, French, and English]. (Guangzhou Office). *PRACTICE AREAS:* Foreign Investment; Securities Law; Company Law; Intellectual Property; Tax Law; International Trade Dispute; Contracts.

DACHTCEREN ENKHBOLD, born Ulaanbaatar, Mongolia, March 11, 1946; admitted, 1973, Mongolia; (Not admitted in the United States). *Education:* International Relations Institute of Moscow (expert of Western Countries - U.S.A., Canada); Mongolian State University (Teacher of English Language). (Mongolia Office). *LANGUAGES:* Russian, English. *PRACTICE AREAS:* Economic Entities and Foreign Investment, Civil Law.

BYAMBAA BAYARMAA, born Moscow, Russia, November 6, 1960; admitted, 1982, Mongolia; (Not Admitted in the United States). *Education:* Moldova State University, Law Faculty, 1982; Passed State Examination on Bar Practice, March, 1994. (Mongolia Office). *LANGUAGES:* Russian, German, Romania, English. *PRACTICE AREAS:* Commercial and Contract Law.

JIANXIONG HUANG, born Rongyan City, Fujian, January 15, 1964; admitted, 1987 (Not admitted in the United States). *Education:* South-West Politics & Law College (B.A., 1984); College of Xiamen University (Master of Law, 1990). (Xiamen Office). *LANGUAGES:* Chinese, Taiwanese, English. *PRACTICE AREAS:* Civil Law; Commercial Law; Investment Law; Real Estate Law.

MINGLIANG LAN, born Hainan Province, China, August 12, 1927; admitted, 1989 (Not admitted in the United States). *Education:* Beijing Zhengfa University of Politics and Law (1956). Publications: Outline of Administrative Law; General Situation of International Organization; International Constitution (Teaching Material); Outline and Guidance on International Law. *Member:* Asian-Africa Development Committee, China International Legal Study Committee; National Lawyer Committee; China-Hong Kong Law Study Committee; China Investment Consultancy Experts Committee; China Political and Legal Management Leaders Institution; China Trade Committee; Foreign Economic and Trade Arbitration Committee (Arbitrator); National Overseas Federation Legal Consultant Committee. (Shenzhen Office). *LANGUAGES:* Chinese, English. *PRACTICE AREAS:* Public International Law; Intellectual Property.

JIANG-XIONG HUANG, born Rongyan City, Fujian Province, China, January 15, 1946; admitted, 1987, China (Not admitted in the United States). *Education:* Institute of Political Science and Law in South-west China (B.A. in Law, 1984); Post-graduate Institute of Xiamen University (LL.M. in civil law, 1990). Author: An Introduction to Civil Law, published by house of Xiamen University; Examples of Lawsuits, published by house of Xiamen University; A Guide for Taiwan People to Invest in Mainland China, published by Beijing Huayi Publishing House. Lecturer: Civil Law; Law of Estate and Practice, Law Department, Xiamen University. *Member:* China Jurisprudence Society; Fujian Jurisprudence Society; Xiamen Jurisprudence Society; Fujian Society of Administrative; Association for Industry and Commerce; Xiamen Society of Administration for Industry and Commerce; Xiamen Bar Association. (Xiamen Office). *LANGUAGES:* Chinese, Taiwanese, English. *PRACTICE AREAS:* Economic; Commercial; Civil; Criminal; Investment Law, and Real Estate Law in China.

ZHOUGEN LI, born Shunde, Guangdong Province, China, October 1, 1935; (Not admitted in the United States). *Education:* Yue Xue Teachers Training College. 1985-1991, Judge (ret.) Guangzhou Middle People's Court, Civil Division and Director of Administration. Recipient, 1984, 1985 Guangzhou City Court Systems Advance Specialist of the Year; 1988, Guangdong Province Outstanding Judge of the year; 1989 Third Degree Honor awarded by the Guangdong Province High Court. (Hong Kong Office). *LANGUAGES:* Chinese (Mandarin and Cantonese). *PRACTICE AREAS:* Litigation; Contract; Intellectual Property.

JIA LIN, born China; admitted, 1989, China; 1991, California. *Education:* Zhongshan University, Guangzhou, China (LL.B.); People's University Beijing, China (LL.M.). Lecturer, People's University, 1989—. (Beijing Office).

(This Listing Continued)

LEGAL SUPPORT PERSONNEL

ZHANGQUING WU, born Shantou Guangdong Province, PRC October 15, 1967. *Education:* Shenzhen University (LL.B., 1991). (Shenzhen Office).

SHIJIE CHEN, born Xiamen, Fujian Province, China, November 18, 1970. *Education:* Xiamen University (LL.B., 1992). (Xiamen Office). *LANGUAGES:* English, Chinese. *PRACTICE AREAS:* Adoption Law; Contracts; Insurance; Trade.

SONG GAO, born Fujian Province, China, April 2, 1969. *Education:* Hau Qiao University (LL.B.). (Shenzhen Office).

REVISER OF THE PEOPLE'S REPUBLIC OF CHINA AND MONGOLIA LAW DIGESTS FOR THIS DIRECTORY.

CLIFFORD CHANCE

SUITE 898, SHANGHAI CENTRE
1376 NANJING XI LU
SHANGHAI 200040, PEOPLE'S REPUBLIC OF CHINA
Telephone: (86 21) 279 8461
Fax: (86 21) 279 8462

Other Offices: Amsterdam, Bahrain, Barcelona, Brussels, Budapest, Dubai, Frankfurt, Hanoi, Hong Kong, London, Madrid, Milan, Moscow, New York, Paris, Riyadh, Rome, Singapore, Tokyo, Warsaw. (See London for full address details).

RESIDENT MANAGER

ELIZABETH OWEN, admitted, 1990, Solicitor.

COUDERT BROTHERS

C/O SUITE 1804, UNION BUILDING
100 YANAN ROAD EAST
SHANGHAI 200002, PEOPLE'S REPUBLIC OF CHINA
Telephone: 3265800
Telecopier: 3200203

REVISERS OF THE FRANCE LAW DIGEST FOR THIS DIRECTORY

New York, New York 10036-7794: 1114 Avenue of the Americas.
Washington, D.C. 20006: 1627 I Street, N.W.
Los Angeles, California 900171: 1055 West Seventh Street, Twentieth Floor.
San Francisco, California 94111: 4 Embarcadero Center, Suite 3300.
San Jose, California 95113: Suite 1250, Ten Almaden Boulevard.
Paris 75008, France: Coudert Frères, 52, Avenue des Champs-Elysées,
London, EC4M 7JP England: 20 Old Bailey.
Brussels B-1050, Belgium: Tour Louise. 149 Avenue Louise-Box 8.
Beijing, People's Republic of China 100020: 2708-09, Jing Guang Centre Hu Jia Lou, Chao Yang Qu.
Hong Kong: 25th Floor, Nine Queen's Road Central.
Singapore, 0104: Tung Centre, 20 Collyer Quay.
Sydney N.S.W. 2000, Australia: Suite 2202, State Bank Centre, 52 Martin Place.
Tokyo 107, Japan: 1355 West Tower, Aoyama Twin Towers, 1-1-1 Minami-Aoyama, Minato-ku.
Moscow, Russia: Ulitsa Staraya Basmannaya 14.
01301 Sao Paulo, SP, Brazil: Machado, Meyer, Sendacz, e Opice, Advogados, Rua da Consolacao, 247, 8 Andar.
Bangkok 10500, Thailand: Bubhajit Building, 20 North Sathorn Road, 10th Floor.
Ho Chi Minh City, Vietnam: c/o Saigon Business Centre, 49-57 Dong Du Street, District 1.

General and International Law Practice.
Firm engaged in American and International Law Practice. Not authorized to practice Chinese Law. Attorneys not admitted in China.

PARTNERS

ADAM FREMANTLE, born London, England, March 18, 1934; admitted, 1958, England; 1967, New York. *Education:* Oxford University (B.A., Jurisprudence, 1954; M.A., 1962); Fordham University (J.D., 1966). Author: "The Regulation of Banking in Saudi Arabia," International Financial Review, October 1985; Note, "The Foreign Concept Practices Act Amend-

(This Listing Continued)

---

ments of 1988," 23 The International Lawyer 755, 1989. Editor, Commercial Agencies and Distributorships, An International Guide.

RESIDENT ASSOCIATES

Kenneth Tung

REVISERS OF THE FRANCE LAW DIGEST FOR THIS DIRECTORY

(For biographical data of the Washington personnel, see Professional Biographies at Washington, D.C.).
(For biographical data of the New York personnel, see Professional Biographies at New York, N.Y.).
(For biographical data of the San Francisco personnel, see Professional Biographies at San Francisco, California).
(For biographical data of the Los Angeles personnel, see Professional Biographies at Los Angeles, California).
(For biographical data of the San Jose personnel, see Professional Biographies at San Jose, California).
(For biographical data of the London personnel, see Professional Biographies at London, England).
(For biographical data of the Paris personnel, see Professional Biographies at Paris, France).
(For biographical data of the Hong Kong personnel, see Professional Biographies at Hong Kong).
(For biographical data of the Singapore personnel, see Professional Biographies at Singapore).
(For biographical data of the Tokyo personnel, see Professional Biographies at Tokyo, Japan).
(For biographical data of Sao Paulo personnel, see Professional Biographies at Sao Paulo, Brazil).
(For biographical data of the Sydney personnel, see Professional Biographies at Sydney, Australia).
(For biographical data of the Beijing personnel, see Professional Biographies at Beijing, People's Republic of China).
(For biographical data of the Brussels personnel, see Professional Biographies at Brussels, Belgium).
(For biographical data of the Moscow personnel, see Professional Biographies at Moscow, U.S.S.R.).
(For biographical data of the Ho Chi Minh personnel, see Professional Biographies at Ho Chi Minh City, Vietnam).

DAVIS WRIGHT TREMAINE

SUITE 1008/1009, JIN JIANG HOTEL
59 MAO MING ROAD SOUTH
SHANGHAI 200020, PEOPLE'S REPUBLIC OF CHINA
Telephone: 011-8621-472-3344; 011-8621-415-3002; 011-8621-258-2582
Ext. 1008/1009
Facsimile: 011-8621-415-3003

Anchorage, Alaska Office: Suite 1450, 550 W. Seventh Avenue. 99501. Telephone: 907-257-5300. FAX: 907-257-5399.
Bellevue, Washington Office: 1800 Bellevue Place, 10500 NE 8th Street. 98004. Telephone: 206-646-6100. FAX: 206-646-6199.
Boise, Idaho Office: Suite 911, 999 Main Street, 83702-9010. Telephone: 208-338-8200. FAX: 208-338-8299.
Honolulu, Hawaii Office: 1360 Pauahi Tower, 1001 Bishop Street, 96813. Telephone: 808-538-3360. FAX: 808-526-0101.
Los Angeles, California Office: Suite 600, 1000 Wilshire Boulevard. 90017. Telephone: 213-229-9600. FAX: 213-627-4874.
Portland, Oregon Office: 2300 First Interstate Tower, 1300 SW Fifth Avenue. 97201. Telephone: 503-241-2300. FAX: 503-778-5299.
Richland, Washington Office: Suite 260, 1100 Jadwin Avenue. 99352. Telephone: 509-946-5369. FAX: 509-946-4211.
San Francisco, California Office: Suite 1500, 235 Pine Street, 94104. Telephone: 415-765-5333. FAX: 415-421-6619.
Seattle, Washington Office: 2600 Century Square, 1501 Fourth Avenue. 98101. Telephone: 206-622-3150. FAX: 206-628-7040.
Washington D.C. Office: Suite 700, 1155 Connecticut Avenue N.W. 20036. Telephone: 202-508-6600. FAX: 202-508-6699.

Davis Wright Tremain has been officially authorized to maintain a law office in Shanghai by the Ministry of Justice of the People's Republic of China. Areas of practice include advising foreign companies doing business in China.
Under current Chinese regulations, foreign law firms, including Davis Wright Tremaine, are not authorized to practice Chinese law.

(This Listing Continued)

DAVIS WRIGHT TREMAINE, Shanghai—Continued

RESIDENT PARTNER

J. H. JERRY ZHU, born Shanghai, China, February 26, 1941; admitted, 1987, Washington (Not admitted in China). *Education:* The Law Research Institute of Shanghai Academy of Social Sciences; University of Washington School of Law (LL.M., 1982). Lecturer, Chinese Law, University of Washington School of Law, 1983-1987, 1992. *LANGUAGES:* Mandarin Chinese and Shanghai Dialect.

OF COUNSEL

ZHI-YING JAMES FANG, born Shanghai, China, February 19, 1950; admitted, 1991, New York (Not admitted in China). *Education:* Shanghai Academy of Social Sciences Law Institute (Master in Law, 1982); University of Washington School of Law (LL.M., 1986; Ph.D., 1991). Law Professor and Deputy Director, East China Institute of Political Science and Law, 1982-1985. Visiting Guest Lecturer, University of Washington School of Law and Willamette University College of Law, 1986-1988. *Member:* State Bar of California; New York State Bar Association; People's Republic of China Bar. *LANGUAGES:* Mandarin Chinese and Shanghai Dialect.

ASSOCIATES

R.Z. MARGARET LU, born Shanghai, People's Republic of China, June 26, 1949; admitted, 1992, Washington. *Education:* University of Washington (B.A., magna cum laude, 1989; J.D., 1992). *LANGUAGES:* Mandarin Chinese and Shanghai Dialect.

JAMES M. MEI, born Shanghai, P.R. China, June 21, 1956; admitted, 1989, Oregon; 1990, Washington (Not admitted in China). *Education:* Shanghai University (B.A., 1983); Beijing University; Willamette University (J.D., 1988). Faculty Member, East China Institute of Politics and Law, 1983-1985. *Member:* Washington State Bar Association; Oregon State Bar. *LANGUAGES:* Mandarin Chinese and Shanghai Dialect.

(For Complete Biographical Data on Personnel at Anchorage, Alaska, Los Angeles and San Francisco, California, Honolulu, Hawaii, Boise, Idaho, Portland, Oregon, Bellevue, Richland and Seattle Washington and Washington, D.C., see Professional Biographies at those locations)

SCHULZ NOACK BÄRWINKEL

Established in 1959

APARTMENT 1106, GALAXY HOTEL
888 ZHONGSHAN XI LU
200051 SHANGHAI, PEOPLE'S REPUBLIC OF CHINA
Telephone: (8621) 2196829
Fax: (8621) 2196829

Hamburg, Germany Office: Mönckebergstrasse 7. Telephone: 040/32 55 72-0. Fax: 040/326302.

Rostock, Germany Office: Alter Markt 15. Telephone: 0381/454860. Fax: 0381/4548614.

Commercial, Corporations, Competition, Banking, Insurance, Labour, Media Law, Wills, International Law.

DR. BERND-UWE STUCKEN, born Hamburg, December 21, 1956; admitted, 1990, Hamburg. *Education:* Universities of Cologne, Geneva, Bonn and Göttingen (Dr. jur. 1989). Deputy Director of the German-Chinese Institute for Economic Law at Nanjing/China (1989-1993). Author: "The Legal Framework of China's Economic Reforms," "Bürokratie in China - Ein Leitfaden für das Geschäftsleben". *LANGUAGES:* German, English, French and Chinese. *PRACTICE AREAS:* Chinese Corporate and Investment Law; China-Trade Arbitration.

PROF. DR. XU GUOJIAN, born Jiangsu, China, October 19, 1962; (Not admitted in China). *Education:* University of Hamburg, Germany (Dr. jur., 1994). Research Fellow, Research Institute of International Law, Wuhan University, China. Visiting Scholar. Author: "Internationales Privat- und zivilverfahrensrecht," Zürich 1994; Anwendungsprobleme des chinesischen internationalen Kaufrechts," Frankfurt a.M. 1994". *LANGUAGES:* Chinese, German, English. *PRACTICE AREAS:* Chinese Relations.

SHANGHAI FUDAN V & L BUSINESS CONSULTATION CO., LTD.

Established in 1994

158 YU PING SOUTH ROAD, HONGQIAO DISTRICT
SHANGHAI 200051, PEOPLE'S REPUBLIC OF CHINA
Telephone: 86 21 233-1281
Fax: 86 21 241-4095

Taipei, Taiwan, ROC Office: Concordia Consulting, Ltd., Section 1, Suite 704, 432 Keelung Road. Telephone: 886 2 729-0268; 886 2 729-8976. Fax: 886 2 729-9837.

Hong Kong Liaison Office: Concordia Consulting, Ltd., 6F, Bank of America Tower, 12 Harcourt Road, Central, Hong Kong. Fax: 852 810-0502.

U.S. Immigration and Naturalization Law, Commercial Trade Law, Consultation and Franchising, Business Agreements, Joint-Venture Business and Commercial Law.

FIRM PROFILE: Shanghai Fudan V & L Business Consultation Co., Ltd. was licensed in Mainland China in 1994 and is a joint venture between Concordia Consulting and Shanghai Fudan University Law School, a well respected and recognized institution of higher learning in Shanghai. Concordia Consulting is a Hong Kong based company, established in 1987 with its branch office in Taipei, Taiwan established in 1994. The President of Concordia Consulting and Partner in Shanghai Fudan V & L, Fredrick N. Voigtmann, has practiced U.S. Immigration Law, Business and Commercial Law and Family Law in Taipei, Taiwan for fifteen years. Concordia Consulting is a well respected member of the Taipei community, known for providing pro bono and legal aid to the expatriate community. Concordia is an active, motivating force behind the first formal legal assistance program offered by foreign legal counsel in Taiwan which will begin in early 1995. The firm is also a member of the American Chamber of Commerce in Taiwan and in Shanghai, China.

MEMBERS OF FIRM

FREDRICK N. VOIGTMANN, born Iowa, July 14, 1940; admitted, 1965, Iowa Supreme Court (Not admitted in China). *Education:* Valparaiso University (B.A., 1962); Valparaiso University Law School (J.D., 1965). U.S. Air Force intensive Mandarin language training, Monterey, California, 1970. With: United States Air Force Office of Special Investigations, Special Agent, Active Duty, 1967-1981; United States Air Force Reserves, Manila, Republic of the Philippines, 1981-1992. Lt. Col. U.S.A.F. Retired. Graduated Squadron Officer's School, Air Command and Staff College. *Member:* Iowa Bar Association; American Bar Association, International Law Division; American Immigration Lawyers Association. (Also Member, Concordia Consulting, Ltd.). *LANGUAGES:* English and Chinese (Mandarin). *PRACTICE AREAS:* U.S. Immigration Law; Business Law; Commercial Law; Family Law; General Practice.

FREDRICK W. VOIGTMANN, born Texas, April 27, 1967; admitted, 1993, Ohio Supreme Court (Not admitted in China). *Education:* Ohio State University (B.A., 1990); Capital Law School (J.D., Order of the Curia, 1993). Internship, Ohio State Bar Association, Ethics and Professional Responsibility Section, 1991. *Member:* Ohio State Bar Association; Columbus Bar Association; American Bar Association, International Law Division; American Immigration Lawyers Association. (Also Member, Concordia Consulting, Ltd.). *LANGUAGES:* English and Chinese (Mandarin). *PRACTICE AREAS:* U.S. Immigration Law; Business Law; Commercial Law; Family Law.

BRIAN J. GROSSMAN, born Canton, Ohio, November 20, 1965; admitted, 1993, Oregon Supreme Court (Not admitted in China). *Education:* Colorado College (B.A., 1988); Willamette University (J.D., 1993; Certification in Dispute Resolution, 1993). *Member:* Oregon State Bar Association; American Bar Association, International Law Division; American Immigration Lawyers Association; American Chamber of Commerce, Shanghai, China. (Also Member, Concordia Consulting, Ltd.). *LANGUAGES:* English and Chinese (Mandarin). *PRACTICE AREAS:* U.S. Immigration Law; International Business Law; International Commercial Law; Joint Venture Law.

SINCLAIR ROCHE & TEMPERLEY

25TH FLOOR, JF NEWS TOWER
300 HAN KOU ROAD
SHANGHAI 200001, PEOPLE'S REPUBLIC OF CHINA
Telephone: (8621) 3512312
Fax: (8621) 3512056

Other Offices: London (England), Hong Kong, Singapore, Vietnam and Bucharest (Romania).

International Commercial Practice.

(For Complete Biographical Data on all personnel, see Professional Biographies at London, England Office)

THIEFFRY ET ASSOCIÉS

Established in 1977

ROOM 1406, RUIJIN BUILDING
205 MAOMING NAN LU
20020 SHANGHAI, PEOPLE'S REPUBLIC OF CHINA
Telephone: (86-21) 472 79 93; 472 70 96
Fax: (86-21) 472 43 92

Paris, France Office: 23 avenue Hoche, 75008. Telephone: (1) 45.62.45.54. Telex: "THIEFRY 640 689 F". Telefax: (1) 42.25.80.07.

New York, N.Y. Office: 780 Third Avenue, 10017. Telephone: 212-750-0080. Telefax: 212-750-0054.

Brussels, Belgium Office: 100, Avenue de Tervueren, 1040. Telephone: (2) 733.97.15. Telefax: (2) 733.97.16.

Hong Kong Office: Bank of China Tower, 21st Floor, 1 Garden Road. Telephone: (852) 25 23 4833. Telefax: (852) 25 24 6438.

Associated Offices: Shenzhen, People's Republic of China; Beirut, Lebanon; Cairo, Egypt; Jeddah, Saudi Arabia Office.

Transnational Arbitration, Litigation and Transactions (Acquisitions, Transfers of Technology, Joint Ventures, General Corporate, Tax and Contractual Practice, Environmental and Intellectual Property Law).

VINCENT MERCIER, born Nice, France, May 24, 1960; admitted, 1988, Paris. *Education:* Paris II University (D.E.A. de Droit Privé Général, 1985); Paris I University (D.E.S.S. de Droit du Commerce Exterieur, 1987). *Member:* American Bar Association (Vice Chair, TIPS-International Torts and Insurance Practice Committee, 1991-1992). (Also at Hong Kong Office). *LANGUAGES:* French and English.

MING JIE ZHANG, born Henan, People's Republic of China, April 12, 1964. *Education:* Wuhan University (Legal Diploma, 1984; Graduate Studies in Law, 1984-1986; Doctorate in Law, 1989); Fribourg University (Doctorate in Law, 1995). Visiting Scholar, Swiss Institute of Comparative Law, 1989-1990. Of Counsel to the Guangdong Nuclear Project, 1987-1988. *LANGUAGES:* Mandarin, French, English and German.

JIAN MING XU, born Anqin, People's Republic of China, June 9, 1954. *Education:* Shanghai Institute of Humanities (Diploma in Humanities, 1982); University of Wuhan (Chinese Law Diploma, 1986); Paris I University (DESS de Droit Bancaire et Financier, 1994). Professor of Law, East China Institute of Political Sciences and Law, Shanghai. *LANGUAGES:* Mandarin, Shanghainese, French, English and Japanese.

ARNBERGER, KIM, BUXBAUM & CHOY

SHENZHEN DEVELOPMENT CENTER, SUITE 2103
RENMIN NAN LU
SHENZHEN, PEOPLE'S REPUBLIC OF CHINA
Telephone: (755) 229-8009
Facsimile: (755) 229-8011

REVISER OF THE PEOPLE'S REPUBLIC OF CHINA AND MONGOLIA LAW DIGESTS FOR THIS DIRECTORY.

Hong Kong Office: 3201 Citibank Tower, 3 Garden Road, Central. Telephone: (852) 2523-7001. Fax: (852) 2845-0947.

Beijing (Peking), People's Republic of China Office: China World Trade Centre, Suite 2523, No. 1 Jian Guo Men Wai Avenue. Telephone: (86)(1) 505-2288 Ext: 2523. Fax: (86)(1) 505-2638.

Guangzhou (Canton), People's Republic of China Office: China Hotel Office Tower, Suite 512. Telephone: (86)(20) 666-3388. Ext. 2512. Fax: (86)(20) 669-1217.

(This Listing Continued)

Xiamen, People's Republic of China Office: Foreign Trade Centre, Suite 519, No. 15 Hu Bing North Road, Xiamen City. Telephone: (86)(592) 506-3059. Facsimile: (86)(592) 511-1044 Ext. 519.

Shanghai, People's Republic of China Office: 7th Floor, Block 2, Jing Ming Building, No. 8 Zun Yi Road, Shanghai. Telephone: (86)(21) 219-4180. Facsimile: (86)(21) 219-7421.

Ulaanbaatar, Mongolia Office: Ulaanbaatar Supreme Court Building, Room 429, 432. Telephone: (976)(1) 31-0711. Fax: (976)(1) 32-5102.

New York Office: 100 Maiden Lane, 16th Floor, Suite 1600B, New York, New York 10038. Telephone: (212) 504-6109. Fax: (212) 412-7016.

San Francisco Office: 44 Montgomery Street, Suite 500, San Francisco 94104. Telephone: (415) 955-0553. Fax: (415) 753-1235.

Los Angeles Office: 3731 Wilshire Boulevard, Suite 910, West Tower, Los Angeles, California, 90010. Telephone: (213) 380-5798. Facsimile: (310) 358-0226; (213) 380-5798.

Alhambra Office: 320 South Garfield, Suite 206, Alhambra, California 91801. Telephone: (818) 281-9088. Fax: (818) 281-7189.

Corporate, Employment Law, Commodities, Securities, Complex Commercial Litigation, International Transactions, Intellectual Property, Aircraft and Equipment Leasing Financing and Taxation.

MEMBERS OF FIRM

DAVID C. BUXBAUM, born New York, N.Y., July 16, 1933; admitted, 1970, New York and U.S. District Court, Southern, Eastern, Northern and Western Districts of New York; 1971, U.S. Court of Appeals, Second Circuit; 1974, U.S. Supreme Court; 1975, U.S. Court of Appeals, Seventh Circuit and Fourth Circuits; 1978, U.S. Court of Appeals, Eighth Circuit; 1979, U.S. Court of Appeals, First Circuit; 1981, California; 1989, U.S. District Court, Central District of California; 1991, U.S. District Court, Northern District of California; U.S. Court of Appeals, Ninth Circuit (Not admitted in China). *Education:* New York University (B.A., 1954); University of Michigan (J.D., 1959) concurrent graduate studies, University of Michigan Graduate School; graduate study, Harvard University and University of Washington (M.A., 1963; Ph.D., 1968). Member, Far East Honor Society, University of Michigan. Author: *Articles:* "Preliminary Trends in the Development of the Legal Institutions of Communist China and the Nature of the Criminal Law," International and Comparative Law Quarterly, January, 1962, reprinted in *Government of Communist China,* Chandler, San Francisco, 1966; "Horizontal and Vertical Influences Upon the Substantive Criminal Law of Mainland Chinese, Some Preliminary Observations," Osteuropa Recht, No. 1, 1964; "Chinese Family Law in Common Law Setting: A Note on the Institutional Environment and the Substantive Family Law of the Chinese in Malaysia and Singapore," Journal of Asian Studies, August, 1966; "Some Aspects of Civil Procedure and Practice at the Trial Level in Tanshui and Hsinchu...," XXX Journal of Asian Studies, 1971; *Lawyer's Challenge in China Trade: New and Developing Legal System,* New York Law Journal, International Law Finance and Trade, February, 1979; *Commodities Trade with China,* New York Law Journal, December, 1978; *Regulation of Commodity Futures Exchanges in Japan,* New York Law Journal, October, 1978; *Commodities Transactions in China and Hong Kong,* New York Law Journal, June, 1978; *Jurisdiction Over Foreign Transactions and Foreign Nationals,* New York Law Journal, April, 1978; *Two Cases of Dispute Settlement,* U.S.-China Business Review, Vol. 1, No. 2, March/April, 1974; *Two Cases of Dispute Settlement,* Arbitration and Dispute Settlement in Trade with China, Special Report No. 4 for Members of the National Council for United States-China Trade, February, 1974; *Negotiation with the Chinese,* Trade with China, 1973; *American Trade with the People's Republic of China: Some Preliminary Perspectives,* Columbia Journal of Transnational Law, Vol. 12, No. 1, 1973; *Liability of Federal Officials in Damage for Acts Unconstitutional or in Excess of their Authority; Expanding the Concept of the Rule of Law,* Capital University Law Review, Vol. 8, Issue 4, 1979; *Taking on the Government Alone; Sole Practitioner Battles Way to Supreme Court and Wins,* Legal Times of Washington, December, 1978; *Disclosure of Management Remuneration, Transaction, Litigation and Employment History,* Los Angeles Daily Journal, March, 1979; *Contracts in China,* China Trade, Praeger, 1982. Monthly Columnist, New York Law Journal on Commodities Law, 1976-1982; *Contract Law in China, The Dynamics of Statutory Development and Practice,* Doing Business in China, 1990, Streng et al, ed. Contracts in China during the Qing Dynasty: Key to the Civil Law, Journal of Oriental Studies, University of Hong Kong, 1993. *The Commercial Laws of China,* and *Patents Law and Practice, Trademark Law and Practice, The People's Republic of China,* Digest of the Commercial Laws of the World, 1982-1993. *M.A. Dissertation:* "Legal Institutions of Contemporary Mainland China," University of Washington, 1962. *Ph.D. Dissertation:* Some Aspects of Substantive Family Law and Social Change in Rural China, 1896-1967," University of Washington, 1968. *Case Note:*

(This Listing Continued)

ARNBERGER, KIM, BUXBAUM & CHOY, Shenzhen— Continued

"Freedom of Marriage in a Pluralistic Society," Malaya Law Review, 1963. Editor: *Traditional and Modern Legal Institutions in Asia and Africa, Journal of Asian and African Studies,* Supplement Edition, 1967; *Family Law and Customary Law in Asia: A Contemporary Legal Perspective,* 1968; *Law and Social Change: A Case Study of Family Law and Social Change in China and Other Developing Areas,* University of Washington Press, 1978; *Transition and Permanence: Chinese History and Culture, A Festschrift in Honor of Dr. Kung-Chan Hsiao,* 1971; *Chinese Family Law and Social Change in Historic and Comparative Perspective,* University of Washington Press, 1978; *China Trade: Prospects and Perspectives,* Prager, 1982; Sole Counsel for Successful Respondents, *Butz v. Economou,* 438 US 478, 1978. Associate Professor, Chinese Law, Comparative Law and Domestic Relations, University of Washington, 1968-1969. Assistant Lecturer, Chinese Law, Domestic Relations, Labor Law, Jurisprudence, Comparative Law, University of Singapore, 1963-1964. Adjunct Professor of Law: Touro Law School, 1980; Southwestern University School of Law, 1983-1988. Member, Commission on Labor Law, Singapore, 1963-1964. Member, Panel of Arbitrators, American Arbitration Association. *Member:* American Bar Association (Member, Committee on Far Eastern Law, Section of International and Comparative Law, 1965-1971); New York Trial Lawyers Association (Member, Liaison Committee with Judicial Conference, 1971-1978). *LANGUAGES:* Chinese, French, German and Japanese (specialized reading). *PRACTICE AREAS:* International Law; Complex International Litigation; Complex International Contract; Joint Venture Contract; Investment Law; Trademark, Copyright and Patent Protection and Enforcement; Commodities and Securities.

KENNETH Y. CHOY, born Hong Kong, May 24, 1956; admitted, 1987, New York; U.S. District Court, Southern and Eastern Districts of New York; 1990, California; 1991, Central and Northern Districts of California and U.S. Court of Appeals, 9th Circuit (Not admitted in China). *Education:* San Francisco State University (B.A., 1977); Northeastern University (J.D., 1986). Judicial Intern to Hon. Dolores K. Sloviter, U.S. Court of Appeals for the Third Circuit, 1985-1986. *Member:* American Bar Association (Member, Section on Labor and Employment Law); American Immigration Lawyers Association. (New York Office). *LANGUAGES:* Chinese (Cantonese and Mandarin). *PRACTICE AREAS:* Litigation and Transactions in U.S. and People's Republic of China.

H. BENNETT ARNBERGER, born Globe, Arizona, July 8, 1953; admitted, 1983, California and U.S. District Court, Northern and Central Districts of California. *Education:* University of California at Berkeley (A.B., with honors and distinction, 1977); University of San Francisco (J.D., 1983). Phi Delta Phi. Author: "Ensuring Compliance Through Intellectual Property Audits," 5 International Legal Strategy 54 (1994); "Avoiding The Hidden Liabilities of Independent Contractors," I Foreign Assignments (Kaigai Chuzai) 99 (1994); "Proactive Prevention of Cross-Cultural Disputes," 6 International Legal Strategy 60 (1994); "Protecting Against Misappropriation of Trade Secrets," 10 International Legal Strategy 63 (1993); "Taxation and Legal Requirements of California Corporations," 16 International Business Law Journal (Kokusai Shoji Homu) 202 (1988). Associate, Yuasa & Hara, Tokyo, Japan, 1987-1989. Contract Administrator, Chemsult AG, Saudi Arabia, 1977-1980. *Member:* San Francisco and American (Member, Section on International Law) Bar Associations; State Bar of California; International Bar Association (Member, Section on Business Law); Japan Society of Northern California; California-Southeast Asia Business Association; American Chamber of Commerce in Japan (Member, Committee on Licensing, Patents & Trademarks, 1987-1989). (San Francisco Office).

DAVID S. KIM, born Seoul, South Korea, February 17, 1961; admitted, 1990, California and U.S. District Court, Northern and Central Districts of California. *Education:* Western Illinois University (B.B.A., 1983; M.B.A., 1985); Southwestern University School of Law, Los Angeles (J.D., 1989). Recipient, Bradley and Pollack Scholarship, 1990. *Member:* State Bar of California; California Trial Lawyers Association; Los Angeles Trial Lawyers Association; California Korean Bar Association. (Los Angeles Office). *LANGUAGES:* English and Korean. *PRACTICE AREAS:* Litigation; Real Estate.

DOUGLAS L. BRYAN, born Whittier, California, September 7, 1960; admitted, 1991, California and U.S. District Court, Central District of California; 1992, U.S. Court of Appeals, Ninth Circuit. *Education:* California Polytechnic State University (B.S., 1983); Southwestern University School of Law (J.D., 1991). *Member:* State Bar of California; American Bar Asso-

(This Listing Continued)

AS24B

ciation. (Los Angeles Office). *PRACTICE AREAS:* Tax Law; Corporate Law; Corporate Reorganizations; Constitutional Law; Insurance.

ROBERT W. MULCAHY, born Boston, Massachusetts, May 8, 1940; admitted, 1970, New York; 1971, District of Columbia; 1976, California; 1991, State Bar of Texas. *Education:* Boston College (B.S., Chemistry, 1963); George Washington University (J.D., 1968). *Member:* District of Columbia; State Bar of California; American Bar Association; The Licensing Executive Society. The Houston Volunteer Lawyers Association; Houston Intellectual Property Law Association. (Alhambra Office). *PRACTICE AREAS:* Intellectual Property; Patent Agent; Copyright Law; Trademark Law; Trade Secrets and Licensing.

OF COUNSEL

DEBORAH S. CHEW, born Singapore, May 27, 1964; admitted, 1988, Singapore; 1991, California. *Education:* National University of Singapore (LL.B., with honors, 1987). Associate, Arthur Loke & Partners, Singapore, 1988-1991. *Member:* State Bar of California; American Immigration Lawyers Association; Singapore American Business Association (Founding Member and Director); Hong Kong Association of California (Director); Asian Business Association; Law Society of Singapore and Academy of Law of Singapore. (San Francisco Office). *LANGUAGES:* English and Chinese (Mandarin, Cantonese, Taiwanese and Chiu-chow dialect).

CHRISTINA Y. CHEN, born Canton, China, May 2, 1943; admitted, 1983, California. *Education:* San Francisco State University (B.A., 1969); Hastings College of the Law, University of California (J.D., 1979). (Of Counsel, San Francisco, California Office). *LANGUAGES:* English and Chinese (Mandarin, Cantonese and Toisan dialect).

ROGER S. SAXTON, born Martins Ferry, Ohio, April 30, 1952; admitted, 1979, Sweden (as Jurist); 1980, Pennsylvania and U.S. District Court, Western District of Pennsylvania; 1992, New South Wales, Australia. *Education:* Case Western Reserve University (J.D., 1979); Studies in Japanese Law, Sophia University and University of Tokyo, Tokyo, Japan (1977-1980); Studies in Australian Law, University of Sydney (1989-1991). *Member:* Pennsylvania Bar Association; Law Society of New South Wales; Inter Pacific Bar Association. (Of Counsel, Sydney, Australia). *LANGUAGES:* English, Swedish and Japanese.

KAZUKO ITOH, born Tokyo, Japan, January 17, 1923; admitted, 1959, Japan (Not admitted in the U.S.). *Education:* Tsuda College; Tokyo Bunrika University. Legal Advisor to Her Britanic Majesty's Ambassador, Tokyo, 1976—. Legal Consultant to the American Embassy, Tokyo, 1976—. *Member:* Tokyo Bar Association; International Bar Association. (Of Counsel, Tokyo, Japan). *LANGUAGES:* Japanese, English, French and Spanish. *PRACTICE AREAS:* General Civil and Trial Practice; International Arbitration; Patent Litigation.

DUCK-SOON CHANG, born Korea, July 23, 1960; admitted, 1985, Korea and Korea Patent Bar; 1991, New York; 1992, California. *Education:* Judicial Training and Research Institute of the Supreme Court of Korea (198 3-1984); College of Law, Seoul National University (B.Jur,. 1983); Harvard Law School (LL.M., 1990). Author: "Technology Transfer, Cooperation and Joint Venture Agreements with Korea", Chapter 4 of Legal Aspects of Business Transactions and Investment in the Far East (Kluwer, 1988); "Arbitration Procedures in Korea," Vol. 1, Asia Law and Practice 7 (1989); "Arbitration in South Korea," Vol. 14 East Asian Executive Reports 1 (1992). Lecturer, International Patent Training and Research Institute of the Korean Industrial Property Office. Arbitrator, Korean Commercial Arbitration Board. *Member:* New York State and American Bar Associations; State Bar of California; Korean Bar Association; Korean Patent Bar Association; International Trademark Association. (Of Counsel, Seoul, Korea). *LANGUAGES:* Korean, English, Japanese (reads only). *PRACTICE AREAS:* Joint Venture; Licensing; Commercial Arbitration; Intellectual Property.

SENIOR PARTNER

MINGLIANG LAN, born Hainan Province, China, August 12, 1927; admitted, 1989 (Not admitted in the United States). *Education:* Beijing Zhengfa University of Politics and Law (1956). *LANGUAGES:* Chinese, English. *PRACTICE AREAS:* Public International Law; Intellectual Property.

ASSOCIATES

VINCENT I.S. HSIEH, born Taipei, Taiwan, January 15, 1964; admitted, 1993, New York. *Education:* National Taiwan University (LL.B., 1987) Boston University (LL.M., in International Banking, 1992). *Member:* American Bar Association; New York County Lawyers Association. (New York Office). *LANGUAGES:* Mandarin Chinese.

(This Listing Continued)

ZHOUGEN LI, born Shunde, Guangdong Province, PRC, October 1, 1935; (Not admitted in the United States). *Education:* Yue Xue Teachers Training College. 1985-1991, Judge (ret.) Guangzhou Middle People's Court, Civil Division and Director of Administration. Recipient, 1984, 1985 Guangzhou City Court Systems Advance Specialist of the Year; 1988, Guangdong Province Outstanding Judge of the year; 1989 Third Degree Honor awarded by the Guangdong Province High Court. *LANGUAGES:* Chinese (Mandarin and Cantonese). *PRACTICE AREAS:* Litigation; Contract; Intellectual Property.

YAOWU RONG, born Wei Chen County, Ji Bei, March 19, 1979; admitted, 1993, China; (Not admitted in the United States). *Education:* Xiamen University (B.A., 1992); (Now Mid. Graduated College of Xiamen University). (Xiamen Office). *LANGUAGES:* Chinese, English. *PRACTICE AREAS:* Civil Law; Commercial Law.

YUAN JIANG, born Fujian Province, China, April 15, 1956; admitted, 1983, China (Not admitted in the United States). *Education:* China University of Political Science and Law, 1979-1983; Part-time graduate student at China University of Political Science and Law, international private law, 1986-1989. Cadre at Research Department, China Lawyer Association, 1989-1990. Reporter, China Lawyer Magazine, 1990-1993. (Beijing Office). *LANGUAGES:* Chinese. *PRACTICE AREAS:* Labor Law; Leasing; Litigation.

XIAODONG HAO, born Inner Mongolia, China, March 9, 1965; admitted, 1990, China (Not admitted in the United States). *Education:* Inner Mongolia University (B.S.); China University of Political Science and Law (LL.B., 1991). (Beijing Office). *LANGUAGES:* Chinese, English, Japanese. *PRACTICE AREAS:* Litigation; Business Law; Intellectual Property.

SIYANG LIAO, born Shanghai Province, China, April 15, 1970. *Education:* China Political/Legal University (L.L.B., 1992). (Beijing Office). *LANGUAGES:* English, Chinese. *PRACTICE AREAS:* Contract Law; Joint Venture Law; Intellectual Property Law.

PEIZHONG GAN, born China, May 8, 1956; admitted, 1988, China (not admitted in the United States). *Education:* The Department of Law, Beijing University (LL.B., 1983; LL.M., 1989). Chief Editor, Encyclopedia of Commercial Law of China and the Encyclopedia of Corporate Law. Author: 21 articles and 3 books, e.g. "Legal Issues on Contracting Management in the Enterprises Owned by the Whole People," "Several Legal Issues on Corporate Reorganization in China". Lecturer, 1988. Associate Professor, 1994, Lectures on Corporate and Companies Law, 1984-1985. Assessor in the Beijing Intermediate Court. (Beijing Office). *LANGUAGES:* Chinese, English. *PRACTICE AREAS:* Corporate Law; Commercial Law; Litigation; Intellectual Property.

JIANXIN LI, born Jiangmen, China, October, 1966; admitted, 1988, China (Not admitted in the United States). *Education:* Guangzhou University (Law Department, 1984-1986); Zhongshan University (Economic Management Department, 1987-1990). Attorney, Guangzhou Second Foreign Economic Law Office, 1986-1990. (Guangzhou Office). *LANGUAGES:* English, Chinese (Mandarin and Cantonese). *PRACTICE AREAS:* Intellectual Property Litigation; Contracts; Real Estate; Trade; Insurance Law; Adoption Law.

YIKUN ZHU, born Sichuan Province, China, August 1967; admitted, 1993, China (Not admitted in the United States). *Education:* Southwest College of Politics & Law (L.L.M., 1991). [Chinese, Russian, French, and English]. (Guangzhou Office). *PRACTICE AREAS:* Foreign Investment; Securities Law; Company Law; Intellectual Property; Tax Law; International Trade Dispute; Contracts.

DACHTCEREN ENKHBOLD, born Ulaanbaatar, Mongolia, March 11, 1946; admitted, 1973, Mongolia; (Not admitted in the United States). *Education:* International Relations Institute of Moscow (expert of Western Countries - U.S.A., Canada); Mongolian State University (Teacher of English Language). (Mongolia Office). *LANGUAGES:* Russian, English. *PRACTICE AREAS:* Economic Entities and Foreign Investment, Civil Law.

BYAMBAA BAYARMAA, born Moscow, Russia, November 6, 1960; admitted, 1982, Mongolia; (Not Admitted in the United States). *Education:* Moldova State University, Law Faculty, 1982; Passed State Examination on Bar Practice, March, 1994. (Mongolia Office). *LANGUAGES:* Russian, German, Romania, English. *PRACTICE AREAS:* Commercial and Contract Law.

JIANXIONG HUANG, born Rongyan City, Fujian, January 15, 1964; admitted, 1987 (Not admitted in the United States). *Education:* South-West Politics & Law College (B.A., 1984); College of Xiamen University (Master

(This Listing Continued)

of Law, 1990). (Xiamen Office). *LANGUAGES:* Chinese, Taiwanese, English. *PRACTICE AREAS:* Civil Law; Commercial Law; Investment Law; Real Estate Law.

MINGLIANG LAN, born Hainan Province, China, August 12, 1927; admitted, 1989 (Not admitted in the United States). *Education:* Beijing Zhengfa University of Politics and Law (1956). Publications: Outline of Administrative Law; General Situation of International Organization; International Constitution (Teaching Material); Outline and Guidance on International Law. *Member:* Asian-Africa Development Committee, China International Legal Study Committee; National Lawyer Committee; China-Hong Kong Law Study Committee; China Investment Consultancy Experts Committee; China Political and Legal Management Leaders Institution; China Trade Committee; Foreign Economic and Trade Arbitration Committee (Arbitrator); National Overseas Federation Legal Consultant Committee. (Shenzhen Office). *LANGUAGES:* Chinese, English. *PRACTICE AREAS:* Public International Law; Intellectual Property.

ALFRED YONG LIN, born Fuzhou, China, October 10, 1969; admitted, 1993, China (not admitted in the United States). *Education:* Xiamen University Law Department (B.A., 1992). (Shanghai Office). *LANGUAGES:* Chinese, English and Fuzhou. *PRACTICE AREAS:* General Civil Law; International Investment; Corporation Law.

HONGLIANG WU, born Shanghai, China, 1935; admitted, 1985, China; registered patent agent (not admitted in the United States). *Education:* Beijing Iron and Steel Institute (B.S., 1960). (Shanghai Office). *LANGUAGES:* Chinese (Shanghai dialect) and English. *PRACTICE AREAS:* Patent and Trademark Law; Intellectual Property.

JIANG-XIONG HUANG, born Rongyan City, Fujian Province, China, January 15, 1946; admitted, 1987, China (Not admitted in the United States). *Education:* Institute of Political Science and Law in South-west China (B.A. in Law, 1984); Post-graduate Institute of Xiamen University (LL.M. in civil law, 1990). Author: An Introduction to Civil Law, published by house of Xiamen University; Examples of Lawsuits, published by house of Xiamen University; A Guide for Taiwan People to Invest in Mainland China, published by Beijing Huayi Publishing House. Lecturer: Civil Law; Law of Estate and Practice, Law Department, Xiamen University. *Member:* China Jurisprudence Society; Fujian Jurisprudence Society; Xiamen Jurisprudence Society; Fujian Society of Administrative; Association for Industry and Commerce; Xiamen Society of Administration for Industry and Commerce; Xiamen Bar Association. (Xiamen Office). *LANGUAGES:* Chinese, Taiwanese, English. *PRACTICE AREAS:* Economic; Commercial; Civil; Criminal; Investment Law, and Real Estate Law in China.

ZHOUGEN LI, born Shunde, Guangdong Province, China, October 1, 1935; (Not admitted in the United States). *Education:* Yue Xue Teachers Training College. 1985-1991, Judge (ret.) Guangzhou Middle People's Court, Civil Division and Director of Administration. Recipient, 1984, 1985 Guangzhou City Court Systems Advance Specialist of the Year; 1988, Guangdong Province Outstanding Judge of the year; 1989 Third Degree Honor awarded by the Guangdong Province High Court. (Hong Kong Office). *LANGUAGES:* Chinese (Mandarin and Cantonese). *PRACTICE AREAS:* Litigation; Contract; Intellectual Property.

JIA LIN, born China; admitted, 1989, China; 1991, California. *Education:* Zhongshan University, Guangzhou, China (LL.B.); People's University Beijing, China (LL.M.). Lecturer, People's University, 1989—. (Beijing Office).

LEGAL SUPPORT PERSONNEL

ZHANGQING WU, born Shantou Guangdong Province, PRC October 15, 1967. *Education:* Shenzhen University (LL.B., 1991).

SONG GAO, born Fujian Province, China, April 2, 1969. *Education:* Hau Qiao University (LL.B.).

SHIJIE CHEN, born Xiamen, Fujian Province, China, November 18, 1970. *Education:* Xiamen University (LL.B., 1992). (Xiamen Office). *LANGUAGES:* English, Chinese. *PRACTICE AREAS:* Adoption Law; Contracts; Insurance; Trade.

REVISER OF THE PEOPLE'S REPUBLIC OF CHINA AND MONGOLIA LAW DIGESTS FOR THIS DIRECTORY.

ARNBERGER, KIM, BUXBAUM & CHOY

FOREIGN TRADE CENTRE, SUITE 519
NO.15 HU BING NORTH ROAD
XIAMEN, PEOPLE'S REPUBLIC OF CHINA
Telephone: (592) 506-3059
Facsimile: (592) 511-1044

REVISER OF THE PEOPLE'S REPUBLIC OF CHINA AND MONGOLIA LAW DIGESTS FOR THIS DIRECTORY.

Hong Kong Office: 3201 Citibank Tower, 3 Garden Road, Central. Telephone: (852) 2523-7001. Fax: (852) 2845-0947.

Beijing (Peking), People's Republic of China Office: China World Trade Centre, Suite 2523, No. 1 Jian Guo Men Wai Avenue. Telephone: (86)(1) 505-2288 Ext: 2523. Fax: (86)(1) 505-2638.

Guangzhou (Canton), People's Republic of China Office: China Hotel Office Tower, Suite 512. Telephone: (86)(20) 666-3388. Ext. 2512. Fax: (86)(20) 669-1217.

Shenzhen, People's Republic of China Office: Shenzhen Development Center, Suite 2103, Renmin Nan Lu, Shenzhen. Telephone: (86)(755) 229-8009. Facsimile: (86)(755) 229-8011.

Shanghai, People's Republic of China Office: 7th Floor, Block 2, Jing Ming Building, No. 8 Zun Yi Road, Shanghai. Telephone: (86)(21) 219-4180. Facsimile: (86)(21) 219-7421.

Ulaanbaatar, Mongolia Office: Ulaanbaatar Supreme Court Building, Room 429, 432. Telephone: (976)(1) 31-0711. Fax: (976)(1) 32-5102.

New York Office: 100 Maiden Lane, 16th Floor, Suite 1600B, New York, New York 10038. Telephone: (212) 504-6109. Fax: (212) 412-7016.

San Francisco Office: 44 Montgomery Street, Suite 500, San Francisco 94104. Telephone: (415) 955-0553. Fax: (415) 753-1235.

Los Angeles Office: 3731 Wilshire Boulevard, Suite 910, West Tower, Los Angeles, California, 90010. Telephone: (213) 380-7780. Facsimile: (310) 358-0226; (213) 380-5798.

Alhambra Office: 320 South Garfield, Suite 206, Alhambra, California 91801. Telephone: (818) 281-9088. Fax: (818) 281-7189.

Corporate, Employment Law, Commodities, Securities, Complex Commercial Litigation, International Transactions, Intellectual Property, Aircraft and Equipment Leasing Financing and Taxation.

MEMBERS OF FIRM

DAVID C. BUXBAUM, born New York, N.Y., July 16, 1933; admitted, 1970, New York and U.S. District Court, Southern, Eastern, Northern and Western Districts of New York; 1971, U.S. Court of Appeals, Second Circuit; 1974, U.S. Supreme Court; 1975, U.S. Court of Appeals, Seventh and Fourth Circuits; 1978, U.S. Court of Appeals, Eighth Circuit; 1979, U.S. Court of Appeals, First Circuit; 1981, California; 1989, U.S. District Court, Central District of California; 1991, U.S. District Court, Northern District of California; U.S. Court of Appeals, Ninth Circuit. *Education:* New York University (B.A., 1954); University of Michigan (J.D., 1959) concurrent graduate studies, University of Michigan Graduate School; graduate study, Harvard University and University of Washington (M.A., 1963; Ph.D., 1968). Member, Far East Honor Society, University of Michigan. Author: *Articles:* "Preliminary Trends in the Development of the Legal Institutions of Communist China and the Nature of the Criminal Law," International and Comparative Law Quarterly, January, 1962, reprinted in *Government of Communist China,* Chandler, San Francisco, 1966; "Horizontal and Vertical Influences Upon the Substantive Criminal Law of Mainland Chinese, Some Preliminary Observations," Osteuropa Recht, No. 1, 1964; "Chinese Family Law in Common Law Setting: A Note on the Institutional Environment and the Substantive Family Law of the Chinese in Malaysia and Singapore," Journal of Asian Studies, August, 1966; "Some Aspects of Civil Procedure and Practice at the Trial Level in Tanshui and Hsinchu...," XXX Journal of Asian Studies, 1971; *Lawyer's Challenge in China Trade: New and Developing Legal System,* New York Law Journal, International Law Finance and Trade, February, 1979; *Commodities Trade with China,* New York Law Journal, December, 1978; *Regulation of Commodity Futures Exchanges in Japan,* New York Law Journal, October, 1978; *Commodities Transactions in China and Hong Kong,* New York Law Journal, June, 1978; *Jurisdiction Over Foreign Transactions and Foreign Nationals,* New York Law Journal, April, 1978; *Two Cases of Dispute Settlement,* U.S.-China Business Review, Vol. 1, No. 2, March/April, 1974; *Two Cases of Dispute Settlement,* Arbitration and Dispute Settlement in Trade with China, Special Report No. 4 for Members of the National Council for United States-China Trade, February, 1974; *Negotiation with the Chinese,* Trade with China, 1973; *American Trade with the People's Republic of China: Some Preliminary Perspectives,* Columbia Journal of Transnational Law, Vol. 12, No. 1, 1973; *Liability of Federal Officials in Damage for Acts Unconstitu-*

(This Listing Continued)

tional or in Excess of their Authority; Expanding the Concept of the Rule of Law, Capital University Law Review, Vol. 8, Issue 4, 1979; *Taking on the Government Alone; Sole Practitioner Battles Way to Supreme Court and Wins,* Legal Times of Washington, December, 1978; *Disclosure of Management Remuneration, Transaction, Litigation and Employment History,* Los Angeles Daily Journal, March, 1979; *Contracts in China,* China Trade, Praeger, 1982. Monthly Columnist, New York Law Journal on Commodities Law, 1976-1982; *Contract Law in China, The Dynamics of Statutory Development and Practice,* Doing Business in China, 1990, Streng et al, ed. Contracts in China during the Qing Dynasty: Key to the Civil Law, Journal of Oriental Studies, University of Hong Kong, 1993. Author: *The Commercial Laws of China,* and *Patents Law and Practice, Trademark Law and Practice, The People's Republic of China,* Digest of the Commercial Laws of the World, 1982-1993. *M.A. Dissertation:* "Legal Institutions of Contemporary Mainland China," University of Washington, 1962. *Ph.D. Dissertation:* Some Aspects of Substantive Family Law and Social Change in Rural China, 1896-1967," University of Washington, 1968. *Case Note:* "Freedom of Marriage in a Pluralistic Society," Malaya Law Review, 1963. Editor: *Traditional and Modern Legal Institutions in Asia and Africa, Journal of Asian and African Studies,* Supplement Edition, 1967; *Family Law and Customary Law in Asia: A Contemporary Legal Perspective,* 1968; *Law and Social Change: A Case Study of Family Law and Social Change in China and Other Developing Areas,* University of Washington Press, 1978; *Transition and Permanence: Chinese History and Culture, A Festschrift in Honor of Dr. Kung-Chan Hsiao,* 1971; *Chinese Family Law and Social Change in Historic and Comparative Perspective,* University of Washington Press, 1978; *China Trade: Prospects and Perspectives,* Prager, 1982; Sole Counsel for Successful Respondents, *Butz v. Economou,* 438 US 478, 1978. Associate Professor, Chinese Law, Comparative Law and Domestic Relations, University of Washington, 1968-1969. Assistant Lecturer, Chinese Law, Domestic Relations, Labor Law, Jurisprudence, Comparative Law, University of Singapore, 1963-1964. Adjunct Professor of Law: Touro Law School, 1980; Southwestern University School of Law, 1983-1988. Member, Commission on Labor Law, Singapore, 1963-1964. Member, Committee on Far Eastern Law, Section of International and Comparative Law, 1965-1971. Member, Panel of Arbitrators, American Arbitration Association. *Member:* New York Trial Lawyers Association (Member, Liaison Committee with Judicial Conference, 1971-1978). *LANGUAGES:* Chinese, French, German and Japanese (specialized reading). *PRACTICE AREAS:* International Law; Complex International Litigation; Complex International Contract; Joint Venture Contract; Investment Law; Trademark, Copyright and Patent Protection and Enforcement; Commodities and Securities.

KENNETH Y. CHOY, born Hong Kong, May 24, 1956; admitted, 1987, New York; U.S. District Court, Southern and Eastern Districts of New York; 1990, California; 1991, Central and Northern Districts of California and U.S. Court of Appeals, 9th Circuit (Not admitted in China). *Education:* San Francisco State University (B.A., 1977); Northeastern University (J.D., 1986). Judicial Intern to Hon. Dolores K. Sloviter, U.S. Court of Appeals for the Third Circuit, 1985-1986. *Member:* American Bar Association (Member, Section on Labor and Employment Law); American Immigration Lawyers Association. (New York Office). *LANGUAGES:* Chinese (Cantonese and Mandarin). *PRACTICE AREAS:* Litigation and Transactions in U.S. and People's Republic of China.

H. BENNETT ARNBERGER, born Globe, Arizona, July 8, 1953; admitted, 1983, California and U.S. District Court, Northern and Central Districts of California. *Education:* University of California at Berkeley (A.B., with honors and distinction, 1977); University of San Francisco (J.D., 1983). Phi Delta Phi. Author: "Ensuring Compliance Through Intellectual Property Audits," 5 International Legal Strategy 54 (1994); "Avoiding The Hidden Liabilities of Independent Contractors," I Foreign Assignments (Kaigai Chuzai) 99 (1994); "Proactive Prevention of Cross-Cultural Disputes," 6 International Legal Strategy 60 (1994); "Protecting Against Misappropriation of Trade Secrets," 10 International Legal Strategy 63 (1993); "Taxation and Legal Requirements of California Corporations," 16 International Business Law Journal (Kokusai Shoji Homu) 202 (1988). Associate, Yuasa & Hara, Tokyo, Japan, 1987-1989. Contract Administrator, Chemsult AG, Saudi Arabia, 1977-1980. *Member:* San Francisco and American (Member, Section on International Law) Bar Associations; State Bar of California; International Bar Association (Member, Section on Business Law); Japan Society of Northern California; California-Southeast Asia Business Association; American Chamber of Commerce in Japan (Member, Committee on Licensing, Patents & Trademarks, 1987-1989). (San Francisco Office).

DAVID S. KIM, born Seoul, South Korea, February 17, 1961; admitted, 1990, California and U.S. District Court, Northern and Central Districts of

(This Listing Continued)

California. *Education:* Western Illinois University (B.B.A., 1983; M.B.A., 1985); Southwestern University School of Law, Los Angeles (J.D., 1989). Recipient, Bradley and Pollack Scholarship, 1990. *Member:* State Bar of California; California Trial Lawyers Association; Los Angeles Trial Lawyers Association; California Korean Bar Association. (Los Angeles Office). *LANGUAGES:* English and Korean. *PRACTICE AREAS:* Litigation; Real Estate.

DOUGLAS L. BRYAN, born Whittier, California, September 7, 1960; admitted, 1991, California and U.S. District Court, Central District of California; 1992, U.S. Court of Appeals, Ninth Circuit. *Education:* California Polytechnic State University (B.S., 1983); Southwestern University School of Law (J.D., 1991). *Member:* State Bar of California; American Bar Association. (Los Angeles Office). *PRACTICE AREAS:* Tax Law; Corporate Law; Corporate Reorganizations; Constitutional Law; Insurance.

ROBERT W. MULCAHY, born Boston, Massachusetts, May 8, 1940; admitted, 1970, New York; 1971, District of Columbia; 1976, California; 1991, State Bar of Texas. *Education:* Boston College (B.S., Chemistry, 1963); George Washington University (J.D., 1968). *Member:* District of Columbia; State Bar of California; American Bar Association; The Licensing Executive Society. The Houston Volunteer Lawyers Association; Houston Intellectual Property Law Association. (Alhambra Office). *PRACTICE AREAS:* Intellectual Property; Patent Agent; Copyright Law; Trademark Law; Trade Secrets and Licensing.

OF COUNSEL

DEBORAH S. CHEW, born Singapore, May 27, 1964; admitted, 1988, Singapore; 1991, California. *Education:* National University of Singapore (LL.B., with honors, 1987). Associate, Arthur Loke & Partners, Singapore, 1988-1991. *Member:* State Bar of California; American Immigration Lawyers Association; Singapore American Business Association (Founding Member and Director); Hong Kong Association of California (Director); Asian Business Association; Law Society of Singapore and Academy of Law of Singapore. (San Francisco Office). *LANGUAGES:* English and Chinese (Mandarin, Cantonese, Taiwanese and Chiu-chow dialect).

CHRISTINA Y. CHEN, born Canton, China, May 2, 1943; admitted, 1983, California. *Education:* San Francisco State University (B.A., 1969); Hastings College of the Law, University of California (J.D., 1979). (Of Counsel, San Francisco, California Office). *LANGUAGES:* English and Chinese (Mandarin, Cantonese and Toisan dialect).

ROGER S. SAXTON, born Martins Ferry, Ohio, April 30, 1952; admitted, 1979, Sweden (as Jurist); 1980, Pennsylvania and U.S. District Court, Western District of Pennsylvania; 1992, New South Wales, Australia. *Education:* Case Western Reserve University (J.D., 1979); Studies in Japanese Law, Sophia University and University of Tokyo, Tokyo, Japan (1977-1980); Studies in Australian Law, University of Sydney (1989-1991). *Member:* Pennsylvania Bar Association; Law Society of New South Wales; Inter Pacific Bar Association. (Of Counsel, Sydney, Australia). *LANGUAGES:* English, Swedish and Japanese.

KAZUKO ITOH, born Tokyo, Japan, January 17, 1923; admitted, 1959, Japan (Not admitted in the U.S.). *Education:* Tsuda College; Tokyo Bunrika University. Legal Advisor to Her Britanic Majesty's Ambassador, Tokyo, 1976—. Legal Consultant to the American Embassy, Tokyo, 1976—. *Member:* Tokyo Bar Association; International Bar Association. (Of Counsel, Tokyo, Japan). *LANGUAGES:* Japanese, English, French and Spanish. *PRACTICE AREAS:* General Civil and Trial Practice; International Arbitration; Patent Litigation.

DUCK-SOON CHANG, born Korea, July 23, 1960; admitted, 1985, Korea and Korea Patent Bar; 1991, New York; 1992, California. *Education:* Judicial Training and Research Institute of the Supreme Court of Korea (198 3-1984); College of Law, Seoul National University (B.Jur,. 1983); Harvard Law School (LL.M., 1990). Author: "Technology Transfer, Cooperation and Joint Venture Agreements with Korea", Chapter 4 of Legal Aspects of Business Transactions and Investment in the Far East (Kluwer, 1988); "Arbitration Procedures in Korea," Vol. 1, Asia Law and Practice 7 (1989); "Arbitration in South Korea," Vol. 14 East Asian Executive Reports 1 (1992). Lecturer, International Patent Training and Research Institute of the Korean Industrial Property Office. Arbitrator, Korean Commercial Arbitration Board. *Member:* New York State and American Bar Associations; State Bar of California; Korean Bar Association; Korean Patent Bar Association; International Trademark Association. (Of Counsel, Seoul, Korea). *LANGUAGES:* Korean, English, Japanese (reads only). *PRACTICE AREAS:* Joint Venture; Licensing; Commercial Arbitration; Intellectual Property.

(This Listing Continued)

ASSOCIATES

JIANG-XIONG HUANG, born Rongyan City, Fujian Province, China, January 15, 1946; admitted, 1987, China. *Education:* Institute of Political Science and Law in South-west China (B.A. in Law, 1984); Post-graduate Institute of Xiamen University (LL.M. in civil law, 1990). Author: An Introduction to Civil Law, published by house of Xiamen University; Examples of Lawsuits, published by house of Xiamen University; A Guide for Taiwan People to Invest in Mainland China, published by Beijing Huayi Publishing House. Lecturer: Civil Law; Law of Estate and Practice, Law Department, Xiamen University. *Member:* China Jurisprudence Society; Fujian Jurisprudence Society; Xiamen Jurisprudence Society; Fujian Society of Administrative; Association for Industry and Commerce; Xiamen Society of Administration for Industry and Commerce; Xiamen Bar Association. *LANGUAGES:* Chinese, Taiwanese, English. *PRACTICE AREAS:* Economic; Commercial; Civil; Criminal; Investment Law, and Real Estate Law in China.

YAOWU RONG, born Wei Chen County, Ji Bei, March 19, 1979; admitted, 1993, China. *Education:* Xiamen University, B.A. of law, 1992 (Now Mid Graduated College of Xiamen University). *LANGUAGES:* English, Chinese. *PRACTICE AREAS:* Civil Law; Commercial Law.

VINCENT I.S. HSIEH, born Taipei, Taiwan, January 15, 1964; admitted, 1993, New York. *Education:* National Taiwan University (LL.B., 1987) Boston University (LL.M., in International Banking, 1992). *Member:* American Bar Association; New York County Lawyers Association. (New York Office). *LANGUAGES:* Mandarin Chinese.

ZHOUGEN LI, born Shunde, Guangdong Province, PRC, October 1, 1935; (Not admitted in the United States). *Education:* Yue Xue Teachers Training College. 1985-1991, Judge (ret.) Guangzhou Middle People's Court, Civil Division and Director of Administration. Recipient, 1984, 1985 Guangzhou City Court Systems Advance Specialist of the Year; 1988, Guangdong Province Outstanding Judge of the year; 1989 Third Degree Honor awarded by the Guangdong Province High Court. *LANGUAGES:* Chinese (Mandarin and Cantonese). *PRACTICE AREAS:* Litigation; Contract; Intellectual Property.

YUAN JIANG, born Fujian Province, China, April 15, 1956; admitted, 1983, China (Not admitted in the United States). *Education:* China University of Political Science and Law, 1979-1983; Part-time graduate student at China University of Political Science and Law, international private law, 1986-1989. Cadre at Research Department, China Lawyer Association, 1989-1990. Reporter, China Lawyer Magazine, 1990-1993. (Beijing Office). *LANGUAGES:* Chinese. *PRACTICE AREAS:* Labor Law; Leasing; Litigation.

XIAODONG HAO, born Inner Mongolia, China, March 9, 1965; admitted, 1990, China (Not admitted in the United States). *Education:* Inner Mongolia University (B.S.); China University of Political Science and Law (LL.B., 1991). (Beijing Office). *LANGUAGES:* Chinese, English, Japanese. *PRACTICE AREAS:* Litigation; Business Law; Intellectual Property.

SIYANG LIAO, born Shanghai Province, China, April 15, 1970. *Education:* China Political/Legal University (L.L.B., 1992). (Beijing Office). *LANGUAGES:* English, Chinese. *PRACTICE AREAS:* Contract Law; Joint Venture Law; Intellectual Property Law.

PEIZHONG GAN, born China, May 8, 1956; admitted, 1988, China (not admitted in the United States). *Education:* The Department of Law, Beijing University (LL.B., 1983; LL.M., 1989). Chief Editor, Encyclopedia of Commercial Law of China and the Encyclopedia of Corporate Law. Author: 21 articles and 3 books, e.g. "Legal Issues on Contracting Management in the Enterprises Owned by the Whole People," "Several Legal Issues on Corporate Reorganization in China". Lecturer, 1988. Associate Professor, 1994, Lectures on Corporate and Companies Law, 1984-1985. Assessor in the Beijing Intermediate Court. (Beijing Office). *LANGUAGES:* Chinese, English. *PRACTICE AREAS:* Corporate Law; Commercial Law; Litigation; Intellectual Property.

JIANXIN LI, born Jiangmen, China, October, 1966; admitted, 1988, China (Not admitted in the United States). *Education:* Guangzhou University (Law Department, 1984-1986); Zhongshan University (Economic Management Department, 1987-1990). Attorney, Guangzhou Second Foreign Economic Law Office, 1986-1990. (Guangzhou Office). *LANGUAGES:* English, Chinese (Mandarin and Cantonese). *PRACTICE AREAS:* Intellectual Property Litigation; Contracts; Real Estate; Trade; Insurance Law; Adoption Law.

YIKUN ZHU, born Sichuan Province, China, August 1967; admitted, 1993, China (Not admitted in the United States). *Education:* Southwest

(This Listing Continued)

ARNBERGER, KIM, BUXBAUM & CHOY, Xiamen—
Continued

College of Politics & Law (L.L.M., 1991). [Chinese, Russian, French, and English]. (Guangzhou Office). *PRACTICE AREAS:* Foreign Investment; Securities Law; Company Law; Intellectual Property; Tax Law; International Trade Dispute; Contracts.

DACHTCEREN ENKHBOLD, born Ulaanbaatar, Mongolia, March 11, 1946; admitted, 1973, Mongolia; (Not admitted in the United States). *Education:* International Relations Institute of Moscow (expert of Western Countries - U.S.A., Canada); Mongolian State University (Teacher of English Language). (Mongolia Office). *LANGUAGES:* Russian, English. *PRACTICE AREAS:* Economic Entities and Foreign Investment, Civil Law.

BYAMBAA BAYARMAA, born Moscow, Russia, November 6, 1960; admitted, 1982, Mongolia; (Not Admitted in the United States). *Education:* Moldova State University, Law Faculty, 1982; Passed State Examination on Bar Practice, March, 1994. (Mongolia Office). *LANGUAGES:* Russian, German, Romania, English. *PRACTICE AREAS:* Commercial and Contract Law.

MINGLIANG LAN, born Hainan Province, China, August 12, 1927; admitted, 1989 (Not admitted in the United States). *Education:* Beijing Zhengfa University of Politics and Law (1956). Publications: Outline of Administrative Law; General Situation of International Organization; International Constitution (Teaching Material); Outline and Guidance on International Law. *Member:* Asian-Africa Development Committee, China International Legal Study Committee; National Lawyer Committee; China-Hong Kong Law Study Committee; China Investment Consultancy Experts Committee; China Political and Legal Management Leaders Institution; China Trade Committee; Foreign Economic and Trade Arbitration Committee (Arbitrator); National Overseas Federation Legal Consultant Committee. (Shenzhen Office). *LANGUAGES:* Chinese, English. *PRACTICE AREAS:* Public International Law; Intellectual Property.

ALFRED YONG LIN, born Fuzhou, China, October 10, 1969; admitted, 1993, China (not admitted in the United States). *Education:* Xiamen University Law Department (B.A., 1992). (Shanghai Office). *LANGUAGES:* Chinese, English and Fuzhou. *PRACTICE AREAS:* General Civil Law; International Investment; Corporation Law.

HONGLIANG WU, born Shanghai, China, 1935; admitted, 1985, China; registered patent agent (not admitted in the United States). *Education:* Beijing Iron and Steel Institute (B.S., 1960). (Shanghai Office). *LANGUAGES:* Chinese (Shanghai dialect) and English. *PRACTICE AREAS:* Patent and Trademark Law; Intellectual Property.

JIANG-XIONG HUANG, born Rongyan City, Fujian Province, China, January 15, 1946; admitted, 1987, China (Not admitted in the United States). *Education:* Institute of Political Science and Law in South-west China (B.A. in Law, 1984); Post-graduate Institute of Xiamen University (LL.M. in civil law, 1990). Author: An Introduction to Civil Law, published by house of Xiamen University; Examples of Lawsuits, published by house of Xiamen University; A Guide for Taiwan People to Invest in Mainland China, published by Beijing Huayi Publishing House. Lecturer: Civil Law; Law of Estate and Practice, Law Department, Xiamen University. *Member:* China Jurisprudence Society; Fujian Jurisprudence Society; Xiamen Jurisprudence Society; Fujian Society of Administrative; Association for Industry and Commerce; Xiamen Society of Administration for Industry and Commerce; Xiamen Bar Association. (Xiamen Office). *LANGUAGES:* Chinese, Taiwanese, English. *PRACTICE AREAS:* Economic; Commercial; Civil; Criminal; Investment Law, and Real Estate Law in China.

ZHOUGEN LI, born Shunde, Guangdong Province, China, October 1, 1935; (Not admitted in the United States). *Education:* Yue Xue Teachers Training College. 1985-1991, Judge (ret.) Guangzhou Middle People's Court, Civil Division and Director of Administration. Recipient, 1984, 1985 Guangzhou City Court Systems Advance Specialist of the Year; 1988, Guangdong Province Outstanding Judge of the year; 1989 Third Degree Honor awarded by the Guangdong Province High Court. (Hong Kong Office). *LANGUAGES:* Chinese (Mandarin and Cantonese). *PRACTICE AREAS:* Litigation; Contract; Intellectual Property.

JIA LIN, born China; admitted, 1989, China; 1991, California. *Education:* Zhongshan University, Guangzhou, China (LL.B.); People's University Beijing, China (LL.M.). Lecturer, People's University, 1989—. (Beijing Office).

(This Listing Continued)

LEGAL SUPPORT PERSONNEL

ZHANGQUING WU, born Shantou Guangdong Province, PRC October 15, 1967. *Education:* Shenzhen University (LL.B., 1991). (Shenzhen Office).

SHIJIE CHEN, born Xiamen, Fujian Province, China, November 18, 1970. *Education:* Xiamen University (LL.B., 1992). (Xiamen Office). *LANGUAGES:* English, Chinese. *PRACTICE AREAS:* Adoption Law; Contracts; Insurance; Trade.

SONG GAO, born Fujian Province, China, April 2, 1969. *Education:* Hau Qiao University (LL.B.). (Shenzhen Office).

REVISER OF THE PEOPLE'S REPUBLIC OF CHINA AND MONGOLIA LAW DIGESTS FOR THIS DIRECTORY.

GUAM

ARRIOLA, COWAN & BORDALLO

C & A BUILDING
259 MARTYR STREET, SUITE 201
P.O. BOX X
AGANA, GUAM 96910
Telephone: 671-477-9730-3
Telecopier: 671-477-9734

General Civil and Trial Practice in Guam and Commonwealth of the Northern Marianas.

JOAQUIN C. ARRIOLA, born Agana, Guam, December 29, 1925; admitted to bar, 1953, Minnesota and District Court of Guam; 1957, U.S. Court of Appeals, Ninth Circuit; 1966, Trust Territory of the Pacific Islands; 1969, U.S. Supreme Court; 1978, District Court for the Northern Mariana Islands. *Education:* College of St. Thomas (A.B., cum laude, 1950); University of Minnesota (J.D., 1953). Gamma Eta Gamma. Chairman, Board of Regents, College of Guam, 1963-1966. Member, 3rd Guam Legislature, 1955-1956. Chairman, Judiciary Committee, 4th Guam Legislature, 1957-1958. Selective Service Government Appeal Agent, 1959-1971. Chairman, Territorial Planning Commission, 1962-1966 and Guam Housing & Urban Renewal Authority, 1963-1964. Small Business Administration Disaster Fee Counsel, 1962. Legislative Counsel, 5th, 6th, and 7th Guam Legislatures. Speaker, 9th and 10th Guam Legislatures (unicameral). *Member:* Guam (President, 1956-1957), American, International and Commonwealth of the Northern Mariana Islands Bar Associations.

MARK E. COWAN, born Ross, California, February 9, 1948; admitted to bar, 1972, California; 1973, District Court of Guam; 1975, Trust Territory of the Pacific Islands and U.S. Court of Appeals, Ninth Circuit; 1978, District Court of the Northern Mariana Islands; 1990, U.S. Claims Court; 1992, U.S. Supreme Court. *Education:* University of California at Berkeley (B.A., 1969); Boalt Hall School of Law, University of California (J.D., 1972). *Member:* Guam, American and Commonwealth of the Northern Mariana Islands Bar Associations; State Bar of California.

OLIVER WESTON BORDALLO, born Agana, Guam, January 24, 1956; admitted to bar, 1982, California; 1983, Guam; 1986, U.S. Court of Appeals, Ninth Circuit; 1992, District Court of the Northern Mariana Islands. *Education:* University of Santa Clara (B.S., 1977); University of California School of Law, Los Angeles (J.D., 1982). Member, Moot Court Honors Program, 1981. Summer Externship with Associate Justice Stanley Mosk, Supreme Court of California, 1982. Law Clerk, Superior Court of Guam, 1982-1983. *Member:* Guam (Member, Board of Governors, 1984-1986; Secretary, 1987-1991; Chairman, Ethics Committee, 1992—) and Commonwealth of the Northern Mariana Islands Bar Associations; State Bar of California.

ANITA PEREZ ARRIOLA, born Agana, Guam, October 2, 1957; admitted to bar, 1982, California; 1983, U.S. Court of Appeals, Ninth Circuit; 1989, Guam and Commonwealth of the Northern Mariana Islands; 1992, U.S. Supreme Court. *Education:* Smith College (A.B., cum laude, 1979); Georgetown University Law Center (J.D., 1982). Editor, American Criminal Law Review, 1981-1982. Former Partner, Public Advocates, Inc., San Francisco, California. *Member:* Guam and Commonwealth of the Northern Mariana Islands Bar Associations; State Bar of California; Berkeley Law Foundation (Member, Board of Directors 1988); National Women and the Law Association (Member, Board of Directors 1986-1988).

(This Listing Continued)

JOAQUIN C. ARRIOLA, JR., born Agana, Guam, U.S.A., May 3, 1964; admitted to bar, 1989, California and U.S. District Court, Northern District of California; 1990, Guam; 1991, U.S. District Court, District of Guam and U.S. Court of Appeals, Ninth Circuit; 1992, Commonwealth of the Northern Mariana Islands; U.S. District Court, District of the Northern Mariana Islands; 1993, U.S. Supreme Court. *Education:* Rutgers University (B.A., 1986); Santa Clara University (J. D., 1989). Phi Alpha Delta; Kappa Sigma. Editor in Chief, The Advocate. *Member:* Guam, American and Commonwealth of the Northern Mariana Islands Bar Associations; State Bar of California.

REPRESENTATIVE CLIENTS: Aetna Life Insurance Co.; American Express; Bank of Guam; Guam Savings & Loan Assn.; John Hancock Mutual Life Insurance Co.; Nissan Motor Corporation in Guam; Prudential Insurance Company of America; Royal-Globe Insurance Cos.; The Seven-Up Co.; Ticor Title Insurance; Title Guaranty of Guam, Inc.

CARLSMITH BALL WICHMAN MURRAY CASE & ICHIKI

A Partnership including Law Corporations

Established in 1857

4TH FLOOR BANK OF HAWAII BUILDING

P.O. BOX BF

AGANA, GUAM 96910-5027

Telephone: 671-472-6813

Telex: 721-6445 CWCMI GM

Telecopier: 671-477-4375

REVISERS OF THE HAWAII LAW DIGEST FOR THIS DIRECTORY

Honolulu, Hawaii Office: Suite 2200, Pacific Tower, 1001 Bishop Street. P.O. Box 656. Telephone: 808-523-2500.

Los Angeles, California Office: 555 South Flower Street, 25th Floor. Telephone: 213-955-1200.

Long Beach, California Office: 301 East Ocean Boulevard, 7th Floor. Telephone: 310-435-5631.

Washington, D.C. Office: 700 14th Street, N.W., 9th Floor. Telephone: 202-508-1025.

Mexico City, Mexico Office: Monte Pelvoux 111, Piso 1, Col. Lomas de Chapultepec, 11000 Mexico, D.F. Telephone: (011-52-5) 520-8514. Fax: (011-52-5) 540-1545.

Mexico, D.F. Office of Carlsmith Ball Garcia Cacho y Asociados, S.C. (Authorized to practice Mexican Law): Monte Pelvoux 111, Piso 1, Col. Lomas de Chapultepec, 11000 Mexico, D.F. Telephone: (011-52-5) 520-8514. Fax: (011-52-5) 540-1545.

Saipan, Commonwealth of the Northern Mariana Islands Office: Carlsmith Building, Capitol Hill, P.O. Box 5241. Telephone: 670-322-3455.

Wailuku, Maui, Hawaii Office: One Main Plaza, Suite 400, 2200 Main Street, P.O. Box 1086. Telephone: 808-242-4535.

Kailua-Kona, Hawaii Office: Second Floor, Bank of Hawaii Annex Building, P.O. Box 1720. Telephone: 808-329-6464.

Hilo, Hawaii Office: 121 Waianuenue Avenue, P.O. Box 686. Telephone: 808-935-6644.

Kapolei, Hawaii Office: Kapolei Building, Suite 318, 1001 Kamokila Boulevard. Telephone: 808-674-0850.

General Civil and Trial Practice in Guam and Micronesia. Admiralty, Fishery, Banking, Corporate, Insurance, Construction, Labor and Real Property Law.

MEMBERS OF FIRM

RUTH D. DAVIS, born Sussex, New Jersey, November 6, 1953; admitted to bar, 1982, Guam and U.S. District Court of Guam; 1985, Commonwealth of the Northern Mariana Islands. *Education:* College of William & Mary (B.A., 1976); University of Puget Sound (J.D., 1982). Member: Order of Barristers; Moot Court Board. *PRACTICE AREAS:* Banks and Banking; Loan Documentation.

PHILIP D. ISAAC, born Randolph, Massachusetts, February 21, 1935; admitted to bar, 1968, California and U.S. District Court, Southern District of California; 1978, U.S. Court of Appeals, Ninth Circuit; 1984, Republic of Palau; 1988, High Court, Trust Territory of the Pacific Islands; 1989, Guam and U.S. District Court of Guam. *Education:* United States Naval Academy (B.S., 1956); University of San Diego (J.D., 1967). Assistant Attorney General, Republic of Palau and Chief, Division of Criminal Law, 1984-1987. Attorney General, Republic of Palau, 1987-1989. Project Director, Chief Counsel, Legal Aid Society of San Diego, 1969-1973. *Member:*

(This Listing Continued)

State Bar of California; Bar Association of the Republic of Palau (President, 1985 and 1988). [Lt. U.S. Navy, 1956-1963; Designated Naval Aviator; President, Navy League of the United States (Guam Council), 1994]. *PRACTICE AREAS:* Public Utilities Regulation; Admiralty; Commercial Labor Litigation and Arbitration.

GARRY W. MORSE, born Kansas City, Kansas, October 26, 1955; admitted to bar; 1983, Virginia; 1984, U.S. District Court, Eastern District of Virginia; 1986, Virgin Islands and U.S. Court of Appeals, Third Circuit; 1990, Guam; 1991, U.S. District Court, District of Guam. *Education:* College of William & Mary (B.A., 1978); Marshall-Wythe School of Law (J.D., 1983). *Member:* Guam, Virgin Islands and Virginia Bar Associations. *PRACTICE AREAS:* Civil Litigation; Construction Litigation; Arbitration and Mediation; Corporate/Business Litigation; Insurance and Insurance Defense.

WILLIAM C. WILLIAMS, JR., born Tucson, Arizona, April 10, 1940; admitted to bar, 1969, New Mexico; 1970, Guam and Trust Territory of the Pacific Islands. *Education:* University of Arizona; California State University at Fullerton (B.A., 1966); University of New Mexico (J.D., 1969). Order of the Coif. Member, Board of Editors, New Mexico Law Review, 1968. *Member:* State Bar of New Mexico; Maritime Law Association of the United States. *PRACTICE AREAS:* Real Property; Corporate; Foreign Sales Corporation.

RESIDENT ASSOCIATES

KRISTEN S. ARMSTRONG, born Denver, Colorado, November 10, 1962; admitted to bar, 1989, California and U.S. District Court, Southern District of California; 1994, Guam. *Education:* University of Denver; Johns Hopkins University (B.A., summa cum laude, 1985); Stanford University (J.D., 1989). Tau Beta Pi. Editor, Stanford Environmental Law Journal. Author: "Regulating Toxics at the State Level: Proposition 65's Warning Requirement," Stanford Environmental Law Journal, Vol. 9, 1990. *Member:* San Diego County and American (Member, Sections on Environmental, Real Property and International Law) Bar Associations. *PRACTICE AREAS:* Real Property/Environmental; Corporate; Labor.

LISANNE M. BUTTERFIELD, born Brooklyn, New York, August 16, 1965; admitted to bar, 1991, Oregon and U.S. District of Oregon; 1993, District of Columbia; 1994, Guam. *Education:* University of Denver (B.A., 1987); Willamette University, College of Law (J.D., 1991). Contributing Editor, *"The Business Judgment Rule: Fiduciary Duties of Corporate Directors"* (Prentice Hall Law & Business (3 ed. 1989); Managing Editor, Willamette Int'l L.J. (1990-1991); Author: "Enforcing Foreign Judgments," Willamette Int'l. L.J. (May, 1991); Member, Moot Court Board (1989-1991). President, International Law Society (1989-1991). Judicial Law Clerk to Hon. Stephen B. Herrell, Circuit Court, State of Oregon, 1991-1992. *Member:* Multnomah County, Federal and American (Sections on: International Law; Litigation) Bar Associations; Oregon State Bar; Bar of the District of Columbia; Asia Pacific Lawyers Association. *PRACTICE AREAS:* Civil Litigation; Insurance Defense.

MEREDITH M. SAYRE, born The Dalles, Oregon, May 27, 1953; admitted to bar, 1981, Texas and U.S. District Court, Northern District of Texas; 1982, Oregon, U.S. District Court, District of Oregon and U.S. Court of Appeals, Ninth Circuit; 1983, Guam and District of Guam. *Education:* Linfield College (B.A., 1975); Gonzaga University (J.D., 1980). Phi Delta Phi. *Member:* State Bar of Texas; Oregon State Bar. *PRACTICE AREAS:* General Commercial Practice; Labor and Employment.

SINFOROSO M. TOLENTINO, born Agana, Guam, July 22, 1964; admitted to bar, 1989, Hawaii; 1990, Guam. *Education:* Georgetown University (B.S., 1986; J.D., 1989). Delta Theta Phi. Senior Notes and Comments Editor, Georgetown International Environmental Law Review, 1988-1989. *PRACTICE AREAS:* Estate Planning; Immigration; Employment Law; Corporate.

OF COUNSEL

ROGER P. CROUTHAMEL, born Riverside, California, August 8, 1948; admitted to bar, 1973, California; 1974, Trust Territory of the Pacific Islands; 1975, Guam; 1978, Commonwealth of the Northern Mariana Islands; 1981, Hawaii. *Education:* University of California at Santa Barbara (B.A., cum laude, 1970); University of California at Los Angeles (J.D., 1973). Delta Theta Phi. Law Clerk to Hon. Cristobal C. Duenas, District Court of Guam, 1974-1977. Secretary, Guam Bar Association, 1980-1982. Lawyer Delegate, Ninth Circuit Judicial Conference, 1985-1987.

All Partners and Associates are Members of the Guam and American Bar Associations.

(This Listing Continued)

CARLSMITH BALL WICHMAN MURRAY CASE &
ICHIKI, Agana—Continued

REVISERS OF THE HAWAII LAW DIGEST FOR THIS DIRECTORY

(For Complete Biographical Data on all Personnel, see Professional
Biographies at Honolulu, Hawaii)

CUNLIFFE, COOK, MAHER & KEELER

A PROFESSIONAL CORPORATION

SUITE 200, 210 ARCHBISHOP F.C. FLORES STREET
AGANA, GUAM 96910
Telephone: 671-472-1824
Telefax: 671-472-2422

General Civil, Criminal and Trial Practice, Corporate, Commercial, Real
Estate and Administrative Law.

F. RANDALL CUNLIFFE, born Tamuning, Guam, November 29,
1948; admitted to bar, 1976, California; 1978, Guam and U.S. District
Court, District of the Northern Mariana Islands; 1979, U.S. District Court,
Central District of California and U.S. District Court, District of Guam;
1980, U.S. Court of Appeals, Ninth Circuit; 1983, Commonwealth of the
Northern Mariana Islands; 1985, Republic of Belau; 1987, U.S. Supreme
Court; 1988, Trust Territory of the Pacific Islands. *Education:* California
State University at Northridge (B.S., 1972); Southwestern University
School of Law (J.D., 1976). *Member:* Guam and Commonwealth of the
Northern Mariana Islands Bar Associations; State Bar of California.

JEFFREY A. COOK, born Los Angeles, California, August 3, 1948;
admitted to bar, 1977, California; 1979, U.S. District Court, Central District of California; 1980, U.S. Court of Appeals, Ninth Circuit; 1981, Guam
and U.S. District Court, District of Guam. *Education:* University of California at Los Angeles (B.A., 1970); University of San Fernando Valley College of Law (J.D., 1976). *Member:* Guam Bar Association; State Bar of California; The Association of Trial Lawyers of America.

JOHN B. MAHER, born Kalamazoo, Michigan, September 10, 1952;
admitted to bar, 1980, Oregon; 1986, Guam, Trust Territory of the Pacific
Islands and U.S. District Court, District of Guam; 1987, U.S. Court of Appeals, Ninth Circuit. *Education:* University of Michigan (B.G.S., 1974);
Willamette University (J.D., 1980). *Member:* Guam Bar Association; Oregon State Bar.

THOMAS P. KEELER, born Bermuda, February 25, 1956; admitted to
bar, 1983, California, U.S. District Court, Central District of California and
U.S. Tax Court; 1985, Guam; 1986, Trust Territory of the Pacific Islands;
1987, Commonwealth of the Northern Mariana Islands and U.S. District
Court, District of Guam. *Education:* University of California at Irvine
(B.A., 1978); Golden Gate University (J.D., 1982). Regional Team Oralist,
Jessup International Law Moot Court Competition, 1980-1981. *Member:*
Guam, Commonwealth of the Northern Mariana Islands and American Bar
Associations; State Bar of California.

REPRESENTATIVE CLIENTS: Baba Corporation; Bank of Guam; Continental
Micronesia, Inc.; Guam Election Commission; Guam Visitors Bureau; Microne-
sian Hospitality, Inc.; Oceana Investment Group, Inc.; Seabridge Micronesia,
Inc.; Southern Pacific, Inc.; United Micronesia Development Association, Inc.

GAYLE & TEKER

A PROFESSIONAL CORPORATION

AGANA BAY BUILDING
220 EAST MARINE DRIVE
AGANA, GUAM 96910
Telephone: 671-477-9891; 477-9892; 477-9893; 477-9894
Facsimile: 671-472-2601

General Practice.

ANDREW M. GAYLE, born Peking, China, July 26, 1931; admitted to
bar, 1957, California and U.S. Court of Appeals, Ninth Circuit; 1958,
Guam; 1966, Trust Territory of the Pacific Islands and District Court for
the Northern Mariana Islands; 1971, U.S. Supreme Court. *Education:* Harvard University (A.B., 1952); Boalt Hall School of Law, University of California (J.D., 1957). Phi Alpha Delta. Member, Board of Trustees, Government of Guam Retirement Fund, 1965-1973. Member, Guam Election
Commission, 1966-1972. Legislative Counsel, Ninth, Tenth, Eleventh,

(This Listing Continued)

Twelfth, Nineteenth and Twentieth, Twenty-First and Twenty-Second
Guam Legislatures, 1967—. Counsel, First Guam Constitutional Conven-
tion, 1969-1970 and Second Guam Constitutional Convention, 1977-1978.
Member, Board of Regents, University of Guam, 1972-1974. Counsel to
Minority, Guam Legislature, 1975-1978. Chairman, Guam Parks and
Recreation Commission, 1979-1982. President, Board of Trustees, St.
John's School, 1989-1994. *Member:* Guam (President, 1963) and American
Bar Associations; State Bar of California.

LAWRENCE J. TEKER, born Seattle, Washington, December 14, 1940;
admitted to bar, 1967, North Dakota; 1968, District of Columbia; 1969,
Guam; 1970, Trust Territory of the Pacific Islands and District Court for
the Northern Mariana Islands; 1969, U.S. Court of Appeals, District of
Columbia Circuit; 1972, U.S. Court of Appeals, Ninth Circuit; 1992, U.S.
Supreme Court. *Education:* University of North Dakota (Ph.B., 1964); University of New Mexico (J.D., 1967). Attorney: Federal Trade Commission,
1967-1968; Corporation Counsel's Office, 1968-1969, Washington, D.C.
Assistant Attorney General, Government of Guam, 1969-1970. Commissioner, Guam Civil Service Commission, 1976-1978. Counsel, Port Authority of Guam, 1978-1982. *Member:* Guam and American Bar Associations;
The Association of Trial Lawyers of America.

MARTIN F. DEINHART, born Cleveland, Ohio, July 31, 1957; admitted to bar, 1983, Ohio; 1986, U.S. District Court, Northern District of Ohio
and U.S. Court of Appeals, Sixth Circuit; 1990, Guam; 1991, U.S. District
Court, District of Guam and U.S. Court of Appeals, Ninth Circuit. *Education:* Cleveland State University (B.A., 1979; J.D., 1983). *Member:* Guam
Bar Associations.

PHILLIP TORRES, born Palo Alto, California, January 22, 1951; admitted to bar, 1984, California; 1989, Guam; 1992, U.S. Supreme Court;
1994, U.S. District Court, Northern District of California; 1993, U.S. Court
of Appeals, Ninth Circuit. *Education:* Foothill College (A.A., 1977); University of California at Santa Barbara (B.A., 1979); University of San Francisco (J.D., 1982). *Attorney:* Legislative Counsel Bureau, State of California,
1982-1986; California State Department of Social Services, 1986-1989.
Member: Guam Bar Association; The State Bar of California.

ANA MARIA G. GABRIEL, born Tamuning, Guam, May 16, 1965;
admitted to bar, 1993, Guam. *Education:* University of California at San
Diego (B.A., 1987); Pepperdine University (J.D., 1990). Phi Alpha Delta.
Assistant Legislative Counsel, Twenty-Second Guam Legislature. *Member:*
Guam Bar and American Bar Associations.

REPRESENTATIVE CLIENTS: Aetna Life Insurance Co.; Guam Hilton Hotel;
Hotel Nikko Guam; Hyundai Construction Co.; Haseko; C. Itoh & Co. Ltd.;
Asahi Bank; Hanil Development Co. Ltd.; DAI-ICHI Hotels, Ltd.; Japan Cre-
ative Tours Ltd.; JDC; Caesars World.
COUNSEL FOR: Union Bank; Micronesia Industrial Corp.; Global Laundry,
Ltd.; Guam Dai-Ichi Hotel; Sagami Railway Co., Ltd.; Tumon Sands Plaza &
Hotel; Maeda Construction Co.; Cocos Lagoon Development Corp.; Creative
Tours Micronesia, Inc. ("JalPak"); Japan Development and Construction Corp.;
GMHP Associates; Tropicana Hotel; Hatsuho International Golf Course; Man-
gilao Golf Course; Lu Island Development, Inc.; Toyo Real Estate Co., Ltd.;
Holiday Inn Guam; Hotel Sun Route; 22nd Guam Legislature; InterPacific Re-
sorts Corporation; Sandcastle; Nippon Television Network Corporation; Televi-
sion Tokyo Channel 12 Ltd.; LSG Lufthansa Guam, Inc.

KEOGH AND BUTLER

C & A PROFESSIONAL BUILDING, SUITE 105
251 MARTYR STREET
P.O. BOX GZ
AGANA, GUAM 96910
Telephone: 671-472-6895
Telecopier: 671-472-6929

General Civil and Criminal Practice.

FIRM PROFILE: Keogh and Butler was formed in 1983 and conducts a
general civil and criminal practice on Guam, in the Commonwealth of the
Northern Mariana Islands and the Federated States of Micronesia.

MEMBERS OF FIRM

ROBERT L. KEOGH, born Orange, New Jersey, January 2, 1947; admitted to bar, 1973, Pennsylvania; 1977, Trust Territory of the Pacific Islands; 1978, Commonwealth Court of the Northern Mariana Islands; 1981,
Guam and Federated States of Micronesia. *Education:* Villanova University
(A.B., 1969; J.D., 1972); University of London, King's College (LL.M.,
1973). *PRACTICE AREAS:* Personal Injury; Wrongful Death; Medical
Malpractice; General Litigation.

GEORGE M. BUTLER, born Worthington, Minnesota, March 10,
1949; admitted to bar, 1978, Louisiana, 1979, Trust Territory of the Pacific

(This Listing Continued)

Islands; 1982, Federated States of Micronesia; 1983, Guam; 1984, Commonwealth of the Northern Mariana Islands. *Education:* Antioch College (B.A., 1972); Tulane University School of Law (J.D., 1978). **PRACTICE AREAS:** Bankruptcy; Corporate Law; Commercial Law; Real Estate; Immigration.

ASSOCIATES

SETH L. FORMAN, born Stamford, New York, October 6, 1954; admitted to bar, 1983, District of Columbia; 1985, Guam and Federated States of Micronesia. *Education:* Princeton University (A.B., 1975); Case Western Reserve University (M.S.A., 1977); Duke University (J.D., with high honors, 1983). Author: Comment, "Bravo's Fallout: International Law and Nuclear Pollution in the Pacific," 14 North Carolina Central Law Journal 172 (1983). *PRACTICE AREAS:* General Litigation; Appellate Advocacy.

MARVIN G. MCCOY, born Boulder, Colorado, March 10, 1948; admitted to bar, 1992, Washington State; 1993, U.S. Territory of Guam. *Education:* Portland State University (B.S., 1978); University of Puget Sound (J.D., 1992). **PRACTICE AREAS:** Immigration; Criminal Defense; Insurance Law.

LEGAL SUPPORT PERSONNEL

TERESA LEVISTE KEOGH, born Quezon City, Philippines, November 8, 1960; admitted to bar, 1988, Philippines; not admitted to Guam Bar due to admission restrictions regarding foreign legal education. *Education:* Colegio de la Purisima Concepcion (A.B., English, 1983); University of the Philippines (LL.B., 1987). *Member:* Integrated Bar of the Philippines. (Legal Assistant). *LANGUAGES:* English and Pilipino. *PRACTICE AREAS:* Specializing in Issues concerning Philippine Law..

REPRESENTATIVE CLIENTS: Continental Insurance Co.; Tower Development, Inc.; Hansen Helicopter; Americana Group, Inc.; Kloppenburg Enterprises: Triton Development, Inc.; Pacific Savings Bank (Palau); Truk Trading Corp.; Coral Sea Realty; Islan Supply; Alliance Air; Guam Air Terminal Services; Guam Economic Development Authority; Pacific Western Enterprises; L & W Equipment, Inc.

KLEMM, BLAIR, STERLING & JOHNSON

A PROFESSIONAL CORPORATION

Established in 1977

1008 PACIFIC NEWS BUILDING
238 ARCHBISHOP F.C. FLORES STREET
AGANA, GUAM 96910
Telephone: 671-477-7858; 477-7559
Facsimiles: 671-472-4290; 477-2904

General Civil and Trial Practice in Guam, Commonwealth of the Northern Mariana Islands, Federated States of Micronesia, Republic of Palau, and the Republic of the Marshall Islands, Insurance, Products Liability Defense, Banking, Commercial, Construction, Corporation, Real Property, Intellectual Property, Admiralty, Antitrust and Administrative Law.

J. BRADLEY KLEMM, born Waterloo, Iowa, November 27, 1941; admitted to bar, 1966, California and U.S. District Court, Northern District of California; 1970, U.S. Court of Appeals, Ninth Circuit; 1972, U.S. District Court, District of Guam and Trust Territory of the Pacific Islands; 1975, U.S. Supreme Court; 1978, U.S. District Court for the Northern Mariana Islands. *Education:* San Jose State College (B.S., with honors, 1963); Boalt Hall School of Law, University of California (LL.B., 1966). Law Clerk to William T. Sweigert, U.S. District Court, Northern District of California, 1966-1968. *Member:* Alameda County, Guam (President, 1977), Commonwealth of the Northern Mariana Islands and Federal Bar Associations; State Bar of California.

WILLIAM J. BLAIR, born Vallejo, California, December 13, 1947; admitted to bar, 1976, California and U.S. District Court, Northern District of California; 1977, U.S. Court of Appeals, Ninth Circuit; 1978, Guam, U.S. District Court, District of Guam, Trust Territory of the Pacific Islands, Commonwealth Trial Court for the Northern Mariana Islands and U.S. District Court for the Northern Mariana Islands; 1982, Supreme Court of the Federated States of Micronesia; 1985, Supreme Court of the Republic of Palau; 1989, Supreme Court of the Commonwealth of the Northern Mariana Islands. *Education:* University of California at Berkeley (A.B., with distinction, 1973); Hastings College of Law, University of California (J.D., 1976). Phi Beta Kappa; Order of the Coif. Member, Thurston Society. *Member:* Guam (President, 1986-1988), Commonwealth of the

(This Listing Continued)

Northern Mariana Islands and American Bar Associations; State Bar of California.

THOMAS C. STERLING, born Oxnard, California, February 27, 1951; admitted to bar, 1978, California, U.S. District Court, Central and Southern Districts of California and U.S. District Court for the Northern Mariana Islands; 1979, Guam; 1981, U.S. District Court, District of Guam and Superior Court for the Northern Mariana Islands; 1982, U.S. Court of Appeals, Ninth Circuit; 1 983, Trust Territory of the Pacific Islands; 1985, Supreme Court of The Republic of Palau. *Education:* University of California at Santa Cruz (B.A., 1973); University of California at Los Angeles (J.D., 1977). Member, Board of Trustees, Guam Territorial Law Library (President, 1986-1989). *Member:* State Bar of California; Guam and Commonwealth of the Northern Mariana Islands Bar Associations. **PRACTICE AREAS:** Insurance Law; Construction Law.

RICHARD L. JOHNSON, born Woburn, Massachusetts, August 2, 1952; admitted to bar, 1981, Hawaii, U.S. District Court, District of Hawaii and Trust Territory of the Pacific Islands; 1982, Supreme Court of the Federated States of Micronesia; 1983, Guam and U.S. District Court, District of Guam; 1984, U.S. Court of Appeals for the Ninth Circuit and Commonwealth Trial Court for the Northern Mariana Islands; 1985, U.S. District Court for the Northern Mariana Islands; Supreme Court of the Republic of Palau; 1987, U.S. Supreme Court. *Education:* Lafayette College (B.A., 1974); Suffolk University (J.D., cum laude, 1981). Member, Moot Court Board. Member, Suffolk University Law Review, 1980-1981. Counsel to the Senate, Republic of Palau National Congress, 1981-1983. *Member:* Guam, Commonwealth of the Northern Mariana Islands and American Bar Associations. *LANGUAGES:* Palaung.

ELIZABETH ROBERTSON, born Greer, South Carolina, June 18, 1961; admitted to bar, 1986, Guam and Trust Territory of the Pacific Islands; 1987, U.S. District Court, District of Guam, Commonwealth of the Northern Mariana Islands and U.S. District Court of Appeals, Ninth Circuit; 1989, Republic of Palau. *Education:* Newcomb College of Tulane University (B.A., cum laude, 1982); Tulane School of Law (J.D., 1986). Member, Panel of Arbitrators, American Arbitration Association. U.S. Legislative Internships, Senator Strom Thurmond, U.S. Senate and Honorable Carroll A. Campbell, Jr., U.S. House of Representatives, 1980. *Member:* Guam, Commonwealth of the Northern Mariana Islands and American Bar Associations; Maritime Law Association of the United States. **PRACTICE AREAS:** Admiralty; Trademark Enforcement.

VINCENT E. LEON GUERRERO, born Tamuning, Guam, April 10, 1958; admitted to bar, 1989, California, Guam and U.S. District Court, District of Guam; 1990, Supreme Court of the Commonwealth of the Northern Mariana Islands and U.S. District Court of the Northern Mariana Islands; 1993, U.S. District Court of Appeals, Ninth Circuit. *Education:* Regis College (B.A., 1979); California Western School of Law (J.D., 1988). *Member:* Guam and Commonwealth of the Northern Mariana Islands Bar Associations; State Bar of California.

KELLY O. CLARK, born Durango, Colorado, August 10, 1957; admitted to bar, 1989, Colorado, U.S. District Court, District of Colorado and U.S. Court of Appeals, Tenth Circuit; 1991, Guam. *Education:* Denver University (B.S.B.A., 1982); St. Mary's University of San Antonio (J.D., 1989). Recipient, American Jurisprudence Award in International Business Transactions. *Member:* Colorado, Guam and Inter-Pacific Bar Associations.

KRISTINA LYNN BAIRD, born Waukegan, Illinois; admitted to bar, 1992, Ohio; 1993, Guam and U.S. District Court, District of Guam. *Education:* Ohio University (B.A., 1989); Capital University (J.D., cum laude, 1992). Order of the Curia; Order of the Barristers. Recipient, American Jurisprudence Award in Criminal Law and Business Associations. Member: International Moot Court Team; Capital University Law Review. Author: "No More Excuses; Adopt the Circle of Poison Prevention Act of 1991." Assistant Attorney General, State of Ohio, 1991-1992. *Member:* Guam Bar Association.

THOMAS C. MOODY, born Monterey, California, January 18, 1962; admitted to bar, 1990, Texas; 1991, U.S. District Court, Western District of Texas and U.S. Court of Appeals, Fifth Circuit (Not admitted in Guam). *Education:* University of Texas at Austin (B.A., 1985); St. Mary's University of San Antonio (J.D., 1989). *Member:* American Bar Association; State Bar of Texas.

OF COUNSEL

WILLIAM B. CLEARY, born Van Nuys, California, September 17, 1953; admitted to bar, 1978, California; 1982, Guam and Federated States of Micronesia; 1991, New York and West Virginia. *Education:* United States International University (B.A., 1975); California Western School of

(This Listing Continued)

KLEMM, BLAIR, STERLING & JOHNSON, A
PROFESSIONAL CORPORATION, Agana—Continued

Law (J.D., 1978) Hokkaido University (LL.M., 1987; Ph.D., 1990). Legislative Counsel to Second Kosrae State Legislature, FSM, 1979-1980. Mombusho Scholar, 1983-1990. Member of the Faculty, University of Tsukuba, Tsukuba, Japan, 1993—. *Member:* Guam, New York State and American Bar Associations; The State Bar of California. (Also Of Counsel, Tokyo City Law & Tax Partner, Tokyo, Japan). *LANGUAGES:* Japanese.

REPRESENTATIVE CLIENTS: Asahi Bank (formerly known as Kyowa-Saitama Bank, Ltd.); Black Construction Co.; Cabras Marine Corp.; Casamar, Inc.; Chase Manhattan Bank; DFS Group L.P.; Dongwon Industries Co., Ltd.; First Hawaiian Bank; First Hawaiian Creditcorp.; Guam Palace Corporation; Hanjin Construction Co. (formerly known as Hanil Development Co., Ltd) Inchcape Shipping Services; International Bridge Corp.; Kawasho International (Guam) Inc.; Lucky Development Co., Ltd.; Marco Marine, Inc.; Mobil Oil Guam, Inc.; Mobil Oil Mariana Island, Inc.; Mobil Oil Micronesia, Inc.; Monsanto Co.; Nishimatsu Construction Co. Ltd.; Pacific International Co., Inc.; Palace Hotel Co., Ltd.; Reebok; R.J. Reynolds Tobacco Co.; Seventh-Day Adventist Clinic; Sumitomo Construction Co., Ltd.
INSURANCE CLIENTS: Associated Aviation Underwriters; Associated Marine Insurers Agents Pty. Ltd.; Chubb Group of Insurance Cos.; Chung Kuo Insurance Co., Ltd.; Commonwealth Land Title Insurance Co.; Design Professionals Insurance Co.; Korea Automobile Fire & Marine Insurance Co., Ltd.; Metropolitan Life Insurance Co.; The North of England Protecting and Indemnity Association Ltd.; Pacific Guardian Life Insurance Co., Ltd.; State Farm Insurance Co.

MAHER & THOMPSON, P.C.

SUITE 300
230 WEST SOLEDAD AVENUE
AGANA, GUAM 96910
Telephone: 671-477-7892
Fax: 671-477-7889

Civil Litigation, Immigration, Collection and Construction Law.

JAMES M. MAHER, born Newport, Oregon, October 23, 1955; admitted to bar, 1986, Guam, California, Republic of Palau and U.S. District Court, District of Guam; 1987, Commonwealth of Northern Mariana Islands. *Education:* Oregon State University (B.A., 1979); Golden Gate University (J.D., 1985). Author: Barusch v. Calvo-Right Result, Wrong Reason; U.S./Japan Arbitration: Practice, Problems, Prediction, Guam Bar Journal, Dry Season, 1989. Law Clerk, Judge Paul J. Abbate, Superior Court of Guam, 1985-1986. *Member:* Guam Bar Association; State Bar of California. *LANGUAGES:* German. *PRACTICE AREAS:* Civil Litigation; Construction Law; Immigration.

MITCHELL F. THOMPSON, born San Diego, California, February 14, 1959; admitted to bar, 1985, California; 1986, Guam, U.S. District Court, District of Guam and Republic of Palau; 1993, Commonwealth of the Northern Mariana Islands. *Education:* University of California at San Diego (B.A., 1981); University of California at Davis (J.D., 1985). Author: Guam's Bill of Rights-The Forgotten Shield, Guam Bar Journal, Dry Season, 1989. Law Clerk, Judge Peter C Siguenza, Jr., Superior Court of Guam, 1985-1986. *Member:* Guam and American Bar Associations; State Bar of California. *LANGUAGES:* Spanish. *PRACTICE AREAS:* Civil Litigation; Collection; Construction Law.

REPRESENTATIVE CLIENTS: Hamilton Tourist Development, Inc.; Yutenji Temple; Perez Acres Homeowners Association; Walters Wholesale Electric Co.; Hawaiian Rock Products; Apusento Garden (Guam), Inc.; National Pacific Insurance; Intercargo Insurance co.; Baba Corp.; Sin Guen Trading Co. (Guam), Inc.; Micronesian Brokers, Inc.; Sumitomo Marine & Fire Insurance Co.; Unitek Insulation, Inc.
REFERENCE: Union Bank, Agana, Guam.

MAIR, MAIR, SPADE & THOMPSON

A PROFESSIONAL CORPORATION

GCIC BUILDING, SUITE 807
AGANA, GUAM 96910
Telephone: 671-472-2089; 472-2090
Fax: 671-477-5206

General Civil Litigation and Trial Practice, Insurance and Institutional Defense, Commercial Litigation, Banking and Real Property Law.

DAVID A. MAIR, born Lucedale, Mississippi, April 24, 1954; admitted to bar, 1981, Alabama; 1982, Guam, District Court, District of Guam, U.S. Court of Appeals, Ninth Circuit; 1985, U.S. Supreme Court; 1988, Northern Mariana Islands and District Court for Northern Mariana Islands. *Education:* University of Alabama (B.A., 1978; J.D., honor graduate,

(This Listing Continued)

1980). Phi Beta Kappa. Assistant Attorney General, Territory of Guam, 1981-1982. *Member:* Guam and Northern Mariana Islands Bar Associations; Alabama State Bar.

JUNE S. MAIR, born Tuscaloosa, Alabama, June 5, 1956; admitted to bar, 1981, Alabama and U.S. District Court, Northern District of Alabama; 1982, Guam; 1984, District Court, District Court of Guam; 1988, U.S. Co urt of Appeals, Ninth Circuit; 1989, Northern Mariana Islands. *Education:* University of Alabama (B.A., 1978; J.D., 1980). *Member:* Guam (Member, Ethics Committee, 1988—), Northern Mariana Islands and American Bar Associations; Alabama State Bar. *LANGUAGES:* Spanish.

JOHN A. SPADE, born Juneau, Alaska, March 31, 1928; admitted to bar, 1979, Hawaii; 1981, Guam and District Court of Guam; 1982, U.S. Court of Appeals, Ninth Circuit. *Education:* University of Hawaii (Ed. B., 1963; M.A., 1964; J.D., 1979); Carnegie Mellon University (D.A., 1976). Phi Delta Kappa; Phi Kappa Phi. Founding Editor, University of Hawaii Law Review, 1978-1979. Author: "Nothing But the Truth: The Role of the Polygraph in the Judicial System," Polygraph Journal, 1978. Assistant Vice President, Academic Affairs, University of Guam, 1974-1976. Associate Dean and Adjunct Professor of Law, University of Hawaii Law School, 1979-1980. *Member:* Guam and Hawaii State Bar Associations.

RANDALL TODD THOMPSON, born San Diego, California, October 24, 1960; admitted to bar, 1989, Guam, District Court of Guam, Northern Mariana Islands and District Court of the Northern Mariana Islands; 1990, California and U.S. Court of Appeals, Ninth Circuit. *Education:* University of California, San Diego (B.A., 1984); University of California , Hastings College of the Law (J.D., 1988). *Member:* Guam, Northern Mariana Islands and American Bar Associations; State Bar of California.

SANDRA CRUZ, born Honolulu, Hawaii, December 2, 1963; admitted to bar, 1990, California and U.S. District Court, Northern District of California; 1991, Guam; 1992, District Court, District of Guam; 1993, Northern Mariana Islands and District Court of the Northern Mariana Islands, U.S. Court of Appeals, Ninth Circuit. *Education:* University of Guam (B.B.A., 1985); Santa Clara University (J.D., 1990). *Member:* Guam and Northern Mariana Islands Bar Associations; State Bar of California.

KEVIN A. SEELY, born Stanford, California, February 14, 1966; admitted to bar, 1992, Guam, District Court of Guam and U.S. Court of Appeals, Ninth Circuit; 1993, Northern Mariana Islands and District Court of Northern Mariana Islands. *Education:* University of California, Irvine (B.A., 1989); Northwestern School of Law of Lewis & Clark College (J.D., 1992). *Member:* Guam and Northern Mariana Islands Bar Associations.

PATRICIA F. FONSECA, born Hartford, New York, May 26, 1967; admitted to bar, 1993, Massachusetts and Guam. *Education:* Skidmore College (B.A., 1989) Valedictorian, Phi Beta Kappa; Boston University School of Law (J.D., 1992). *Member:* Guam, Massachusetts and American Bar Associations.

REPRESENTATIVE CLIENTS: FHP, Inc.; National Union Fire Insurance Co., Ltd.; American Home Assurance, Co.; The Tokio Marine & Fire Insurance Co., Ltd.; Continental Insurance Co.; Yasuda Fire & Marine Insurance Co., Ltd.; CIGNA Insurance Co.; Dai-Tokyo Fire & Marine Insurance Co.; National Pacific Insurance (Guam), Inc.; Mobil Oil (Guam), Inc.; Denny's of Guam, Inc.; Domino's Pizza (Guam), Inc.; Ambros, Inc.; Citizens Security Bank, Inc.; Carrier Corporation/Carrier International, Inc.; Guam Rock Products, Inc.

McCULLY, LANNEN, BEGGS & MELANÇON, P.C.

SUITE 1004 PACIFIC NEWS BUILDING
238 ARCHBISHOP FLORES STREET
AGANA, GUAM 96910
Telephone: 671-477-7418; 477-7283
Telefax: 671-472-1201

Commercial, Real Property Development, General Civil Litigation, Admiralty, Immigration, Bankruptcy and Debtor-Creditor.

DUNCAN G. MCCULLY, born Santa Monica, California, November 21, 1950; admitted to bar, 1976, Oregon; 1978, Guam and U.S. District Court, District of Guam; 1979, High Court of the Federated States of Micronesia, Commonwealth Trial Court and U.S. District Court, for the Commonwealth of the Northern Mariana Islands. *Education:* University of Oregon (B.A., 1972); Lewis and Clark College (J.D., 1976). *Member:* Guam Bar Association (Board of Governors, 1980-1982; Member, Ethics Com-

(This Listing Continued)

mittee, 1986-1990). *SPECIAL AGENCIES:* Counsel to Guam Economic Development Authority.

THOMAS J. LANNEN, born Los Angeles, California, July 22, 1953; admitted to bar, 1979, California, U.S. District Court, Central District of California and U.S. Court of Appeals, Ninth Circuit; 1984, Guam and U.S. District Court, District of Guam; 1985, High Court of the Trust Territory of the Pacific Islands; 1986, Supreme Court of the Republic of Belau. *Education:* University of California at Berkeley (B.A., 1976); Southwestern University School of Law (J.D., 1979). Deputy Federal Public Defender, Los Angeles, 1979-1982. Senior Deputy Federal Public Defender, 1982-1983. Chief Prosecutor for the Territory of Guam, 1984-1987 and Special Assistant, U.S. Attorney, 1984-1987. Member, Guam Bar Ethics Committee, 1990. *Member:* Guam Bar Association; State Bar of California.

MARK S. BEGGS, born Butte, Montana, September 12, 1953; admitted to bar, 1980, Oregon; 1981, U.S. District Court, District of Oregon; 1982, U.S. Court of Appeals, Ninth Circuit; 1983, Guam and District Court of Guam; 1985, Commonwealth of the Northern Mariana Islands and District Court for the Northern Mariana Islands. *Education:* University of Kansas; Willamette University (B.S., 1975); Gonzaga University (J.D., cum laude, 1980). *Member:* Guam and Northern Mariana (Inactive) Bar Associations; Oregon State Bar.

JEAN MELANÇON, born New Orleans, Louisiana, October 13, 1954; admitted to bar, 1980, Louisiana; 1987, Guam. *Education:* Tulane University (B.A., 1976; J.D., 1980). *Member:* Louisiana State and Guam Bar Associations; Maritime Law Association of the United States.

KEVIN J. FOWLER, born Kalamazoo, Michigan, February 24, 1960; admitted to bar, 1988, Oregon and Guam; 1990, U.S. District Court, District of Guam; 1992, Michigan and U.S. Court of Appeals, Ninth Circuit. *Education:* Western Michigan University (B.S., 1983); Northwestern School of Law of Lewis and Clark College (J.D., 1987). Law Clerk, Superior Court of Guam, 1987-1988. *Member:* Oregon State Bar; Guam Bar Association; State Bar of Michigan.

JOSEPH M. CONBOY, born Buffalo, New York, April 21, 1961; admitted to bar, 1989, New York; 1993, Guam and U.S. District Court, District of Guam. *Education:* Boston University (B.S., 1983); State University of New York at Buffalo (J.D., 1988). *Member:* Guam and New York State Bar Associations. *LANGUAGES:* Japanese.

OF COUNSEL

MELINDA C. SWAVELY, born Los Angeles, California, August 12, 1951; admitted to bar, 1978, California, Guam and U.S. District Court, District of Guam; 1980, U.S. Court of Appeals, Ninth Circuit. *Education:* University of California at Davis (B.A., 1973); McGeorge School of Law (J.D., 1977). *Member:* Guam Bar Association; State Bar of California (Inactive). *PRACTICE AREAS:* Immigration.

REPRESENTATIVE CLIENTS: American President Lines, Ltd.; Guam Economic Development Authority; Citibank, N.A.; Bank of Guam; Bank of Hawaii; MDI Guam Corporation; Nippon Steel Corp.; Allied Banking Corp.; Guam Plaza Hotel; OUG Development International Incorporated; Pacific Construction and Development Corp.; Century Bank; Guam AB Inc.; Guam Insurance Adjusters, Inc.

MOORE CHING BOERTZEL
CIVILLE DOOLEY & ROBERTS

A PROFESSIONAL CORPORATION

SUITE 400 GCIC BUILDING
414 WEST SOLEDAD AVENUE
AGANA, GUAM 96910
Telephone: 671-477-9708/472-8868
Facsimile: 671-477-0783/477-2511

General Civil and Trial Practice in Guam, the Commonwealth of the Northern Mariana Islands, the Federated States of Micronesia, the Republic of Palau and the Republic of the Marshall Islands, Insurance, Corporate, Finance, Real Estate, Commercial and Immigration Law.

JOHN E. MOORE, born Topeka, Kansas, July 24, 1935; admitted to bar, 1961, Oregon; 1962, U.S. District Court, District of Oregon; 1976, Guam and Trust Territory of the Pacific Islands; 1978, District Court for the Northern Mariana Islands and Superior Court of the Commonwealth of the Northern Mariana Islands. *Education:* University of Oregon (B.S., 1957); University of Oregon School of Law (J.D., 1961). Phi Alpha Delta. Deputy District Attorney, Lane County, Oregon, 1961-1966. Chief Deputy

(This Listing Continued)

District Attorney, Lane County, Oregon, 1967-1971. Chief Counsel, Oregon Department of Justice, Criminal Justice and Special Investigation Division and Counsel for Oregon State Police, 1972-1975. Counsel for Select Committee on Police Corruption, 14th Guam Legislature, 1977. *Member:* Guam and American Bar Associations; Oregon State Bar.

EDWIN K. W. CHING, born Honolulu, Hawaii, May 4, 1943; admitted to bar, 1969, Iowa and Hawaii; 1972, Guam, Trust Territory of the Pacific Islands and District Court for the Commonwealth of the Northern Mariana Islands; 1978, Superior Court of the Commonwealth of the Northern Mariana Islands; 1981, Federated States of Micronesia. *Education:* University of Hawaii (B.B.A., 1966); Drake University (J.D., 1969). Law Clerk to Justice Kazuhisa Abe, Hawaii Supreme Court, 1969-1970. *Member:* Iowa State, Hawaii State, Guam and American Bar Associations. *PRACTICE AREAS:* Real Estate; Commercial Transactions.

HARRY MASON BOERTZEL, born Philadelphia, Pennsylvania, October 9, 1944; admitted to bar, 1969, Virginia; 1974, Guam; 1982, Federated States of Micronesia. *Education:* College of William & Mary (A.B., 1966); University of Richmond (LL.B., 1969); George Washington University (LL.M., 1973). Phi Delta Phi. Associate Editor, University of Richmond Law Review, 1968-1969. Committee Counsel, Twelfth Guam Legislature, 1973-1975. Member, Judicial Council of Guam, 1978-1979. Member, Guam Board of Bar Examiners, 1978-1979. Founding Editor, Guam Bar Journal. Administrative Law Judge, Public Utilities Commission, 1988—. *Member:* Virginia State Bar; Guam (President, 1978-1979; Chairman, Ethics Committee, 1986-1987) and American Bar Associations. [With JAGC, U.S. Army, 1969-1973]

GEORGE PATRICK CIVILLE, born Dayton, Ohio, 1951; admitted to bar, 1977, Ohio and U.S. District Court, Southern District of Ohio; 1985, Guam and U.S. District Court, District of Guam; U.S. Court of Appeals, Ninth Circuit; 1986, Superior Court of Commonwealth of the Northern Mariana IsLands. *Education:* University of Dayton (B.A., 1973); University of Dayton School of Law (J.D., 1977). Member, Guam Supreme Court Rules Committee, 1993. *Member:* Guam (Vice President, 1986-1987; President, 1988-1990) and Saipan Bar Associations; American Immigration Lawyers Association. *PRACTICE AREAS:* Civil Litigation; Immigration Law.

DAVID W. DOOLEY, born Stockton, California, April 22, 1951; admitted to bar, 1976, California; 1977, U.S. Court of Appeals, Ninth Circuit; 1978, Guam, District Court of Guam and District Court for the Northern Mariana Islands. *Education:* University of California at Davis (B.A., with honors, 1973); University of California at Los Angeles (J.D., 1976). Phi Beta Kappa. Assistant Attorney General, Territory of Guam, 1977-1978.

THOMAS L. ROBERTS, born Pittsburgh, Pennsylvania, July 2, 1957; admitted to bar, 1984, Supreme Court of California; 1985, U.S. Court of Appeals for the Ninth Circuit; U.S. District Court for the Central District of California, Superior Court and U.S. District Court of Guam, Superior Court of the Commonwealth of the Northern Mariana Islands and U.S. District Court of the Commonwealth of the Northern Mariana Islands, Supreme Court of the Republic of Palau, High Court of the Trust Territory of the Pacific Islands; 1987, High Court and Supreme Court of the Republic of the Marshall Islands; 1990, U.S. Supreme Court. *Education:* University of California at Los Angeles (B.A., 1981); Loyola Law School, Los Angeles (J.D., 1984). *Member:* Guam, Saipan and American Bar Associations; State Bar of California.

TRAYLOR T. MERCER, born Honolulu, Hawaii, January 4, 1948; admitted to bar, 1974, North Carolina; 1976, U.S. District Court, Middle District of North Carolina; 1978, Trust Territory of the Pacific Islands; 1980, District Court for the Northern Mariana Islands; 1982, Federated States of Micronesia; 1983, U.S. Court of Appeals, Ninth Circuit and Republic of the Marshall Islands; 1985, Republic of Palau, Commonwealth of Northern Mariana Islands, Guam and District Court of Guam; 1990, U.S. Supreme Court. *Education:* Dartmouth College (B.A., Senior Fellow, 1970); Duke University (J.D., 1974). Staff Counsel, Marshall Islands Constitutional Convention, Nitijela and Political Status Commission, 1978. District Attorney, 1978-1979 and Attorney General, 1979-1980, Marshall Islands. Assistant Attorney General, 1980-1981 and Chief, Legal Division, Office of Attorney General, 1981-1984, Trust Territory of the Pacific Islands. *Member:* Guam and American Bar Associations; North Carolina State Bar.

JOSEPH A CALVO, born Oka, Tamuning, Guam, November 26, 1954; admitted to bar, 1991, Guam and U.S. District Court, District of Guam. *Education:* University of San Francisco (B.S., 1978); University of California, Hastings College of the Law (J.D., 1989). Law Clerk to the Hon. Peter C. Siguenza, Jr., Superior Court of Guam, 1989-1990. Ethics Committee Chairman, Guam Chamber of Commerce, 1992—. Assistant Administrative Law Judge, Guam Public Utilities Commission, 1991—. *Member:*

(This Listing Continued)

MOORE CHING BOERTZEL CIVILLE DOOLEY & ROBERTS, A PROFESSIONAL CORPORATION, Agana— Continued

Guam and American Bar Associations. **PRACTICE AREAS:** Commercial; Real Estate; Corporate Law.

JOYCE C. H. TANG, born Taipei, Taiwan, December 4, 1966; admitted to bar, 1993, Guam and U.S. District Court, District Court of Guam; 1993, California. Education: University of Southern California (B.S., 1989); Golden Gate University (J.D., 1993). Member: Guam and American Bar Associations; State Bar of California.

SCOTT W JOHANSEN, born Cleveland, Ohio, March 16, 1961; admitted to bar, 1988, Washington; 1993, Guam and U.S. District Court, District of Guam. Education: Lewis and Clark College (B.A., 1983); University of Oregon School of Law (J.D., 1987); University of San Diego School of Law (LL.M., in taxation, 1990). Member: Washington State Bar Association, Guam Bar Association.

REPRESENTATIVE CLIENTS: AIC International, Inc.; Aijour in Pacific Corp; Aijour in Pacific Corp. dba: Holiday Plaza Hotel; American International Group, Inc.; American Home Assurance Company of New York; American International Underwriters, Inc.; AOI Guam Corp.; Asahi Finance (Guam), Inc.; Columbus Development, Inc.; Commercial Sanitation Systems, Inc.; Cumberland Casualty & Surety Co.; D.B. Davis & Associates dba: Staywell Insurance; Dai-Tokyo Fire & Marine Insurance Co., Ltd.; Deloitte & Touche; Diamond Ko (Guam) Ltd.; First American Title Insurance Co.; First Hawaiian Bank; Fujiken Guam, Inc.; The General Conference of Seventh Day Adventists; General Electric Co.; Goodwind Development Corp.; Guam Airport Authority; Guam Capital Investment Corp.; Guam Hardwood, Inc.; Guam Insurance Adjusters, Inc.; Itasi Corporation; Johyo Sangyo (Guam) Ltd.; McDonald's Restaurants of Hawaii; Metro Bank; Micronesian Divers Assn.; MILICO (Massachusetts Indemnity and Life Insurance Co.); Mitsui Marine & Fire Insurance Co., Ltd. ; National Union Fire Insurance Company of Pittsburgh, Pa.; New Hampshire Insurance Co.; New Zealand Insurance Co., Ltd.; Orient Pacific Line; Owens-Corning Fiberglas Corp.; Pacific Indemnity Insurance Co.; Pacific Tyre, Ltd.; Primerica Financial Services; Primerica Life Insurance Co.; Public Utilities Commission of the Territory of Guam; Shell Guam, Inc.; Shell Company (Pacific Islands) Ltd.; Taiyo Fishery Co., Ltd.; The Asahi Bank, Ltd.; The General Conference of Seventh Day Adventists; The Long Term Credit Bank of Japan, Ltd.; Tokio Marine & Fire Insurance Co., Ltd.; Transico Liquidating Trust; United Overseas Investment Co.; United Seamen's Service Inc.; United Services Automobile Assn.; United States Aviation Underwriters; United States Department of Justice; Yasuda Fire & Marine Insurance Co., Ltd.; Yasuda Fire & Marine Insurance Co., Ltd; Zurich Insurance (Guam) Inc.

ROBERT J. TORRES

A PROFESSIONAL CORPORATION

SUITE 101

410 W. O'BRIEN DRIVE

AGANA, GUAM 96910

Telephone: 617-477-1075

Taxation, Business, Trust, Estate Planning and Real Estate Law.

ROBERT J. TORRES, JR., born Tamuning, Guam, July 6, 1958; admitted to bar, 1986, Massachusetts; 1987, U.S. Tax Court, U.S. District Court, District of Massachusetts, U.S. Court of Appeals, First and Ninth Circuits, Superior Court of Guam and U.S. District Court, District of Guam. Education: University of Notre Dame (B.B.A., Accounting, magna cum laude, 1980); Harvard University (J.D., 1985). Beta Gamma Sigma; Beta Alpha Psi. Member: Massachusetts and American Bar Associations. **PRACTICE AREAS:** Taxation Law; Business Law; Trust Law; Estate Planning; Real Estate Law.

ZAMSKY & COHEN

SUITE 501, BANK OF GUAM BUILDING

111 CHALAN SANTO PAPA

AGANA, GUAM 96910

Telephone: 671-477-3637/8/9

Facsimile: 671-472-1584

General Civil and Trial Practice, Maritime, Insurance, Corporation, Estate Planning, Finance, International, Probate, Real Estate, Taxation and Commercial Law.

(This Listing Continued)

MEMBERS OF FIRM

SAMUEL J. COHEN, born Brooklyn, New York, February 15, 1962; admitted to bar, 1987, Arizona; 1992, Guam; 1993, Commonwealth of the Northern Mariana Islands. Education: University of Arizona (B.A., 1984); University of Minnesota/University of London (J.D., cum laude, 1987); New York University (LL.M ., Taxation, 1992). Managing Editor, Minnesota Law Review. Foreign Legal Assistant, Showa Law Office, Tokyo, Japan (1989-1991). Author: "The Extension of U.S. Tax Treaties to U.S. Territories, as Illustrated By the Example of Guam," U.C.L.A. Pac. Basin L.J. (1992). Co-Authored with Nobutoshi Yamanouchi, "Understanding the Incidence of Litigation in Japan: A Structural Analysis," 25 Int'l Law. 443-454, (Summer 1991). Author: "The EEC Convention and U.S. Law Governing Choice of Law for Contracts, With Particular Emphasis on the Restatement Second: A Comparative Study," 13 Md. J. of Int'l Law and Trade 223-45 (1989); "The Deduction of Contingent Attorneys' Fees Owed to the Negligent Attorney From Legal Malpractice Damage Awards: The New Modern Rule," 24 Tort & Ins. L.J. 741-62 (1989); "The Regulation of Peremptory Challenges in the United States and England," 6 B.U. Int'l. L.J. 287-315 (1988). **LANGUAGES:** Japanese.

STEVEN A. ZAMSKY, born Portland, Oregon, February 5, 1947; admitted to bar, 1971, Oregon and U.S. Tax Court; 1972, U.S. District Court, District of Oregon; 1989, Guam; 1992, U.S. District Court, District of Guam and District Court of the Commonwealth of the Northern Mariana Islands; Supreme Court of the Commonwealth of the Northern Mariana Islands. Education: University of Oregon (B.S., Accounting, 1968; J.D., 1971). Order of the Coif; Phi Delta Phi (Exchequer, 1970-1971). Editor, Oregon Law Review, 1970-1971. Member: Oregon State Bar (Member, Legal Ethics Committee, 1984-1988); Guam Bar Association.

OF COUNSEL

JOHN A. BOHN, JR., born Oakland, California, October 31, 1937; admitted to bar, 1964, California; 1965, Guam, Trust Territory of the Pacific Islands. Education: Stanford University (A.B., cum laude, Phi Beta Kappa, 1959); London School of Economics (Fulbright Fellow, 1959-1960); Harvard Law School (J.D., 1963). Member: California and Guam Bar Associations.

REPRESENTATIVE CLIENTS: ACI Industrial Minerals; Goyo Boeki (Guam) Inc.; Guam Memorial Park, Inc.; Interbulk Shipping, Inc.; Island Imports, Inc.; KPMG Peat Marwick; K-Z Radio Inc.; Pacific American Title Insurance & Escrow Co.; Reeflink Pty., Ltd.; Shell Guam, Inc.; Shell Company (Pacific Islands) Ltd.; SGS (Guam), Inc.; Zurich Insurance (Guam), Inc.; Continental Micronesia, Inc.

CARBULLIDO & PIPES

A PROFESSIONAL CORPORATION

Established in 1983

YOUNG'S PROFESSIONAL BUILDING - FIRST FLOOR

788 NORTH MARINE DRIVE

UPPER TUMON, GUAM 96911

Telephone: 671-649-5297

Telecopier: 671-649-7848

General Civil and Trial Practice in Guam, Commonwealth of the Northern Marianas, Federated States of Micronesia and Republic of Palau. Commercial, Corporation, Construction, Real Estate, Administrative Law and Admiralty.

F. PHILIP CARBULLIDO, born Tamuning, Guam, February 5, 1953; admitted to bar, 1979, Guam, U.S. Court of Appeals, Ninth Circuit, District Court, Commonwealth of the Northern Mariana Islands and U.S. District Court, District of Guam; 1985, U.S. Supreme Court. Education: University of Oregon (B.S., 1975); University of California at Davis (J.D., 1978). Assistant Attorney General, Territory of Guam, 1978-1979. Legislative Counsel, 17th Guam Legislature, 1984-1985. Member, Guam Tax Code Commission, 1990. Member: Guam (Treasurer, 1980-1982) and American Bar Associations; The Association of Trial Lawyers of America.

RICHARD A. PIPES, (A LAW CORPORATION), born St. Louis, Missouri, March 14, 1952; admitted to bar, 1977, Missouri and U.S. District Court, Western District of Missouri; 1980, U.S. Court of Appeals, Ninth Circuit; 1981, Guam and U.S. District Court, District of Guam; 1983, U.S. Supreme Court and U.S. Court of Appeals, District of Columbia Circuit; 1986, U.S. District Court, District of the Northern Mariana Islands. Education: University of Missouri-Columbia (B.A., with honors, 1974); University of Missouri-Kansas City (J.D., 1977). Victor Wilson Memorial Scholar. Member, Governor's Task Force on Foreign Sales Corpora-

(This Listing Continued)

tions, 1984—. *Member:* Guam (Vice-President, 1984-1986) and American Bar Associations; The Missouri Bar; The Association of Trial Lawyers of America.

CYNTHIA V. ECUBE, born Manila, Philippines, July 31, 1962; admitted to bar, 1991, Guam; 1992, U.S. District Court, District of Guam. *Education:* University of Minnesota (B.A., 1985); Hamline University (J.D., 1990). Sigma Nu Phi. Assistant Attorney General, Territory of Guam, 1990-1992.

SANDRA D. LYNCH, born Huntington, West Virginia, March 4, 1954; admitted to bar, 1993, Guam, U.S. Court of Appeals, Ninth Circuit, U.S. District Court, District of Guam. *Education:* Marshall University (B.S., with honors, 1982); Capital University (J.D., 1990). *Member:* Guam Bar Association.

MILES J. DOLINGER, born Los Angeles, California, December 8, 1965; admitted to bar, 1993, California; 1994, Guam. *Education:* University of California at Santa Cruz (B.A., 1988); Golden Gate University School of Law (J.D., 1993). *Member:* State Bar of California.

REPRESENTATIVE CLIENTS: A.I. Marine Adjusters, Inc.; Bank of Nauru; Casamar Inc.; Continental Insurance Co.; First Commercial Bank, Ltd.; First Micronesian Trust Co.; Fuji Vending Group, Ltd.; Fukuya Shokai Co., Ltd.; Guam Financial Co., Ltd.; Guam Sunzen Co., Ltd.; Ingersoll-Rand Co.; Long Term Credit Bank of Japan, Ltd.; Matsuzato Hawaii, Inc.; Nansay (Guam) Inc.; Pacific Produce Corp.; Pacific Star Hotel; Republic of Nauru (Guam), Inc.; ROHR Industries, Inc.; Sammi Rock Products, Inc.; Sigallo-Pac Ltd.; Tuna Clipper Services, Inc.; University of Guam; Zee Fishing Co.; Zuiko International, Inc.
REFERENCES: Union Bank; The Asahi Bank, Ltd.

HONG KONG

ALEXANDER, HOLBURN, BEAUDIN & LANG

C/O 8TH FLOOR, CHEKIANG FIRST BANK CENTRE
1 DUDDELL STREET, CENTRAL
HONG KONG
Telephone: (852-2) 526-1171
Fax: (852-2) 845-0686

Vancouver, British Columbia Office: P.O. Box 10057. 2700 Toronto Dominion Bank Tower, 700 West Georgia Street. Telephone: 604-688-1351. Fax: 604-669-7642.
Taipei, Taiwan in Association with Perennial Law Office: 7F-2, No. 9. Roosevelt Road, Section 2. Telephone: (886-2) 395-6989. Fax: (886-2) 391-4235.

Corporate, Commercial, Real Estate and Immigration.

PARTNER

CALVIN KAM-WING CHUNG, born Hong Kong, November 2, 1946; admitted, 1981, Hong Kong; 1986, British Columbia. *Education:* University of Hong Kong (LL.B., 1978; P.C.L.L., 1979); University of Ottawa (Jt Committee on Foreign Accreditation Certificate, 1985). *Member:* Law Society of British Columbia, Canada. **PRACTICE AREAS:** Corporate/Commercial Law; Real Estate Law; Immigration Law.

(For complete biographical data on all personnel, see professional biographies at Vancouver, British Columbia, Canada)

ALLEN & OVERY

9TH FLOOR, THREE EXCHANGE SQUARE
8 CONNAUGHT PLACE
HONG KONG
Telephone: (852) 2840 1282
Telex: 68757
Facsimile: (852) 2840 0515

London, England Office: One New Change, EC4M 9QQ. Telephone: 0171 330 3000. Facsimile: 0171 330 9999.
Beijing, China Office: Suite 3204, Jing Guang Centre, Hu Jia Lou, Chaoyang District, 100020. Telephone: (86 1) 501 4681. Facsimile: (86 1) 501 4682.
Brussels, Belgium Office: Rue de la Loi 99, Box 8, 1040. Telephone: (32 2) 230 27 91. Facsimile (32 2) 230 66 13.

(This Listing Continued)

Budapest, Hungary Office: Mádach Trade Center, Mádach Imre utca 13-14, H-1075. Telephone: (361) 268 1511. Facsimile: (361) 268 1515.
Dubai, United Arab Emirates Office: 501 Al Futtaim Tower, P.O. Box 3251, Deira. Telephone: (971 4) 282296. Facsimile: (971 4) 212860.
Frankfurt, Germany Office: Taunusanlage 11, 11th Floor, 60329. Telephone: (49 69) 242 6120. Facsimile: (49 69) 242 61220.
Madrid, Spain Office: Antonio Maura 7, 6°, 28014. Telephone: (34 1) 521 2654. Facsimile: (34 1) 523 0458.
Moscow, Russia Office: 9 ul Tverskaya, Entrance No 5, 8th Floor, 103009. Telephone: (7 501) 940 4500. Facsimile: (7 501) 940 4501.
New York Office: Swiss Bank Tower, 10 East 50th Street, 10022. Telephone (1-212) 754 3340. Facsimile: (1-212) 754 7903.
Paris, France Office: 1 Avenue Franklin D. Roosevelt, 75008. Telephone (33-1) 49 53 06 37. Telex: 651079. Facsimile: (33-1) 49 53 91 52.
Prague, Czech Republic Office: Jindřišská 34, 110 00 Prague 1. Telephone: (42 2) 2410 3317. Facsimile: (42 2) 2410 3235.
Singapore Office: 20 Raffles Place #08-03, Ocean Towers, 0104. Telephone: (65) 533 0988. Facsimile: (65) 533 1322.
Tokyo, Japan Office: NSE Building, 5th Floor, 1-7-1 Kanda Jinbo-cho, Chiyoda-ku Tokyo 101. Telephone (81 3) 3259 9898. Facsimile (81 3) 3259 9888.
Warsaw, Poland Office: ul. Kopernika 17, IV Floor, 00-359. Telephone: (48 22) 262 226. Facsimile: (48 22) 262 360.

Firm engaged in International, Corporate, Commercial, Banking, Securities, Dispute Resolution and Property Law.

RESIDENT PARTNERS

Jonathan Gould	**Jonathan S.T. Mellor**
Jonathan L. F. Brayne	**Christopher K. Roberts**
David C. Hughes	**Kenneth Chan**
Guy Henderson	**Sidney A. Myers**
Christopher L. Rushton	**Michael Lui**
Simon A. Haddock	**Joseph Tse**

(For Complete List of Firm Personnel, see Professional Biographies at London, England).

ALSOP WILKINSON

4010 JARDINE HOUSE
ONE CONNAUGHT PLACE, CENTRAL
HONG KONG
Telephone: 852 524 2003
Facsimile: 852 810 1345

London, England Office: 6 Dowgate Hill, EC4R 2SS. Telephone 0171-248 4141. Telex: 885593. Fax: 0171-623 8286.
Liverpool, England Office: India Buildings, L2 ONH. Telephone: 0151-227 3060. Telex: 627369. Fax: 0151-236 9208.
Manchester, England Office: 11 St. James's Square, M2 6DR. Telephone: 0161-834 7760. Telex: 667965. Fax: 0161-831 7515.
Brussels, Belgium Office: Avenue de Cortenberg, 79-81, 1040. Telephone: 2-732-36-00. Fax: 2-734-87-93.
New York, New York Office: 230 Park Avenue, Suite 1150, New York, New York, 10169. Telephone: (212) 499-7500. Fax: (212) 499-7505.

Key Practice Areas: Banking, Commercial Litigation and Arbitration, Commercial Property, Commodities, Construction, Corporate and Commercial, Corporate Fraud and Investigations, Employment, Insolvency, Insurance and Reinsurance, Intellectual Property, Marine, Pensions, Private Client, Taxation.

RESIDENT PARTNERS

CAMILLE JOJO, born Manchester, England, April 18, 1956; admitted, 1980, England; 1982, Hong Kong; 1984, Victoria, Australia. *Education:* University College, Cardiff (LL.B., 1977); College of Law, Guildford (1978). *Member:* Law Society of Hong Kong, England and Wales. **LANGUAGES:** English. **PRACTICE AREAS:** Commercial; Corporate; Litigation.

STEWART J. CROWTHER, born England, December 2, 1948; admitted, 1974, England; 1979, Hong Kong. *Education:* Hertford College, Oxford (B.A., 1971; M.A., 1977). **LANGUAGES:** French. **PRACTICE AREAS:** Shipping; Aviation.

CLAUDIO DE BEDIN, born Hong Kong, September 10, 1955; admitted, 1985, Hong Kong; 1989, England and Wales. *Education:* Newcastle on Tyne Polytechnic (B.A. Hons.). *Member:* Hong Kong Law Society; Law

(This Listing Continued)

ALSOP WILKINSON, Hong Kong—Continued

Society of England and Wales. **LANGUAGES:** English, Italian, Cantonese. **PRACTICE AREAS:** Commercial; Corporate; Banking.

ASSOCIATES

James Griffiths	Seamus Donegan
Robert S. Pe	Heida Donegan
Nick Stone	Shandy Lili
John R. Edwards	Susanne Kwan

(For the Names of Partners Resident in Other Offices, see Listings for Those Offices)

APPLEBY, SPURLING & KEMPE

2217 JARDINE HOUSE
1 CONNAUGHT PLACE, CENTRAL
HONG KONG
Telephone: (852) 2 523 8123
Fax: (852) 2 524 5548
Telex: 70917 ACLHK HX

Hamilton, Bermuda Office: Cedar House, 41 Cedar Avenue, P.O. Box HM 1179, HM EX. Telephone: 809-2295-2244. Cable Address: "Appleby Bermuda" Telex: 3223 ASK BA. Telecopier: 809-292-8666.

The Firm is engaged in the practice of Bermuda corporate, commercial and trust law and other areas of Bermuda Law with the support of the Bermuda office. It is not authorized to practice Hong Kong Law.

RESIDENT PARTNER

MICHAEL J. SPURLING, born Bermuda, December 1, 1954; admitted, 1978, England; 1979, Bermuda (Not admitted in Hong Kong). *Education:* Bristol University, U.K. (LL.B., 1977); College of Law, London (Bar Finals, 1978). Author: "Bermuda Traits," Asian Law Journal, November 1992; "Bermuda's Company Law on the Move," Capital Asia, July 1992; "Redomiciliation," Asia Law Journal, December 1992; Asset Leasing & Finance Defense "Emerging Markers-Securitization and the Use of the Bermuda Purpose Trust," 1994; Asian Law and Practice, "Doing Business in Hong Kong-Bermuda and What it Has to Offer," 1994; The Practitioner Fuide to the Listing Rules (of Hong Kong)," Chapter 12 "Listing of a Bermuda Company," 1994 Edition, The International Services Institute (Hong Kong); Asian Law Journal "The Companies Law of Bermuda-What Does it Mean to Hong Kong Based Bermuda Companies?" Volume 2, No. 2, 1994; Asian Law Journal "The Why & Where Guide to Offshore Jurisdiction," 1994. Co-Author: Asian Law Journal "Sailing Offshore (Part II), 1993, with Philip Chresterman; "Hong Kong Companies on the Bermuda Trail," International Corporate Law, March 1991, pp. 20-22. Chairman, United Bermuda Party, 1987-1990. *Member:* England and Bermuda Bar Associations. **LANGUAGES:** German. **PRACTICE AREAS:** Company Law.

RESIDENT ASSOCIATES

FRANCES L. WOO, born Toronto, Canada, August 9, 1964; admitted, 1993, Ontario, Canada; 1994, England, Wales and Hong Kong. *Education:* University of Toronto (B.Sc. Hons., 1987); Osgoode Hall (LL.B., 1991). *Member:* Law Society Upper Canada; Law Society of England and Wales.

(For a complete list of firm personnel, see Professional Biographies in Hamilton, Bermuda).

ARNBERGER, KIM, BUXBAUM & CHOY

3201 CITIBANK TOWER
3 GARDEN ROAD, CENTRAL
HONG KONG
Telephone: (852) 2523-7001
Fax: (852) 2845-0947

REVISER OF THE PEOPLE'S REPUBLIC OF CHINA AND MONGOLIA LAW DIGESTS FOR THIS DIRECTORY.

Beijing (Peking), People's Republic of China Office: China World Trade Centre, Suite 2523, No. 1 Jian Guo Men Wai Avenue. Telephone: (86)(1) 505-2288 Ext: 2523. Fax: (86)(1) 505-2638.

Guangzhou (Canton), People's Republic of China Office: China Hotel Office Tower, Suite 512. Telephone: (86)(20) 666-3388. Ext. 2512. Fax: (86)(20) 669-1217.

(This Listing Continued)

Xiamen, People's Republic of China Office: Foreign Trade Centre, Suite 519, No. 15 Hu Bing North Road, Xiamen City. Telephone: (86)(592) 506-3059. Facsimile: (86)(592) 511-1044 Ext. 519.

Shenzhen, People's Republic of China Office: Shenzhen Development Center, Suite 2103, Renmin Nan Lu, Shenzhen. Telephone: (86)(755) 229-8009. Facsimile: (86)(755) 229-8011.

Shanghai, People's Republic of China Office: 7th Floor, Block 2, Jing Ming Building, No. 8 Zun Yi Road, Shanghai. Telephone: (86)(21) 219-4180. Facsimile: (86)(21) 219-7421.

Ulaanbaatar, Mongolia Office: Ulaanbaatar Supreme Court Building, Room 429, 432. Telephone: (976)(1) 31-0711. Fax: (976)(1) 32-5102.

New York Office: 100 Maiden Lane, 16th Floor, Suite 1600B, New York, New York 10038. Telephone: (212) 504-6109. Fax: (212) 412-7016.

San Francisco Office: 44 Montgomery Street, Suite 500, San Francisco 94104. Telephone: (415) 955-0553. Fax: (415) 753-1235.

Alhambra Office: 320 South Garfield, Suite 206, Alhambra, California 91801. Telephone: (818) 281-9088. Fax: (818) 281-7189.

Los Angeles Office: 3731 Wi; shire Boulevard, Suite 910, West Tower, Los Angeles, California, 90010. Telephone: (213) 380-7780. Facsimile: (310) 358-0226; (213) 380-5798.

Corporate, Employment Law, Commodities, Securities, Complex Commercial Litigation, International Transactions, Intellectual Property, Aircraft and Equipment Leasing Financing and Taxation.

MEMBERS OF FIRM

DAVID C. BUXBAUM, born New York, N.Y., July 16, 1933; admitted, 1970, New York and U.S. District Court, Southern, Eastern, Northern and Western Districts of New York; 1971, U.S. Court of Appeals, Second Circuit; 1974, U.S. Supreme Court; 1975, U.S. Court of Appeals, Seventh Circuit and Fourth Circuits; 1978, U.S. Court of Appeals, Eighth Circuit; 1979, U.S. Court of Appeals, First Circuit; 1981, California; 1989, U.S. District Court, Central District of California; 1991, U.S. District Court, Northern District of California; U.S. Court of Appeals, Ninth Circuit (Not admitted in Hong Kong). *Education:* New York University (B.A., 1954); University of Michigan (J.D., 1959) concurrent graduate studies, University of Michigan Graduate School; graduate study, Harvard University and University of Washington (M.A., 1963; Ph.D., 1968). Member, Far East Honor Society, University of Michigan. Author: *Articles:* "Preliminary Trends in the Development of the Legal Institutions of Communist China and the Nature of the Criminal Law," International and Comparative Law Quarterly, January, 1962, reprinted in *Government of Communist China,* Chandler, San Francisco, 1966; "Horizontal and Vertical Influences Upon the Substantive Criminal Law of Mainland Chinese, Some Preliminary Observations," Osteuropa Recht, No. 1, 1964; "Chinese Family Law in Common Law Setting: A Note on the Institutional Environment and the Substantive Family Law of the Chinese in Malaysia and Singapore," Journal of Asian Studies, August, 1966; "Some Aspects of Civil Procedure and Practice at the Trial Level in Tanshui and Hsinchu...," XXX Journal of Asian Studies, 1971; *Lawyer's Challenge in China Trade: New and Developing Legal System,* New York Law Journal, International Law Finance and Trade, February, 1979; *Commodities Trade with China,* New York Law Journal, December, 1978; *Regulation of Commodity Futures Exchanges in Japan,* New York Law Journal, October, 1978; *Commodities Transactions in China and Hong Kong,* New York Law Journal, June, 1978; *Jurisdiction Over Foreign Transactions and Foreign Nationals,* New York Law Journal, April, 1978; *Two Cases of Dispute Settlement,* U.S.-China Business Review, Vol. 1, No. 2, March/April, 1974; *Two Cases of Dispute Settlement,* Arbitration and Dispute Settlement in Trade with China, Special Report No. 4 for Members of the National Council for United States-China Trade, February, 1974; *Negotiation with the Chinese,* Trade with China, 1973; *American Trade with the People's Republic of China: Some Preliminary Perspectives,* Columbia Journal of Transnational Law, Vol. 12, No. 1, 1973; *Liability of Federal Officials in Damage for Acts Unconstitutional or in Excess of their Authority; Expanding the Concept of the Rule of Law,* Capital University Law Review, Vol. 8, Issue 4, 1979; *Taking on the Government Alone; Sole Practitioner Battles Way to Supreme Court and Wins,* Legal Times of Washington, December, 1978; *Disclosure of Management Remuneration, Transaction, Litigation and Employment History,* Los Angeles Daily Journal, March, 1979; *Contracts in China,* China Trade, Praeger, 1982. Monthly Columnist, New York Law Journal on Commodities Law, 1976-1982; *Contract Law in China, The Dynamics of Statutory Development and Practice,* Doing Business in China, 1990, Streng et al, ed. Contracts in China during the Qing Dynasty: Key to the Civil Law, Journal of Oriental Studies, University of Hong Kong, 1993. *The Commercial Laws of China,* and *Patents Law and Practice, Trademark Law and Practice, The People's Republic of China,* Digest of the Commercial Laws of the World, 1982-1993. *M.A. Dis-*

(This Listing Continued)

sertation: "Legal Institutions of Contemporary Mainland China," University of Washington, 1962. *Ph.D. Dissertation:* Some Aspects of Substantive Family Law and Social Change in Rural China, 1896-1967," University of Washington, 1968. *Case Note:* "Freedom of Marriage in a Pluralistic Society," Malaya Law Review, 1963. Editor: *Traditional and Modern Legal Institutions in Asia and Africa, Journal of Asian and African Studies,* Supplement Edition, 1967; *Family Law and Customary Law in Asia: A Contemporary Legal Perspective,* 1968; *Law and Social Change: A Case Study of Family Law and Social Change in China and Other Developing Areas,* University of Washington Press, 1978; *Transition and Permanence: Chinese History and Culture, A Festschrift in Honor of Dr. Kung-Chan Hsiao,* 1971; *Chinese Family Law and Social Change in Historic and Comparative Perspective,* University of Washington Press, 1978; *China Trade: Prospects and Perspectives,* Prager, 1982; Sole Counsel for Successful Respondents, *Butz v. Economou,* 438 US 478, 1978. Associate Professor, Chinese Law, Comparative Law and Domestic Relations, University of Washington, 1968-1969. Assistant Lecturer, Chinese Law, Domestic Relations, Labor Law, Jurisprudence, Comparative Law, University of Singapore, 1963-1964. Adjunct Professor of Law: Touro Law School, 1980; Southwestern University School of Law, 1983-1988. Member, Commission on Labor Law, Singapore, 1963-1964. Member, Panel of Arbitrators, American Arbitration Association. *Member:* American Bar Association (Member, Committee on Far Eastern Law, Section of International and Comparative Law, 1965-1971); New York Trial Lawyers Association (Member, Liaison Committee with Judicial Conference, 1971-1978). *LANGUAGES:* Chinese, French, German and Japanese (specialized reading). *PRACTICE AREAS:* International Law; Complex International Litigation; Complex International Contract; Joint Venture Contract; Investment Law; Trademark, Copyright and Patent Protection and Enforcement; Commodities and Securities.

KENNETH Y. CHOY, born Hong Kong, May 24, 1956; admitted, 1987, New York; U.S. District Court, Southern and Eastern Districts of New York; 1990, California; 1991, Central and Northern Districts of California and U.S. Court of Appeals, 9th Circuit (Not admitted in Hong Kong). *Education:* San Francisco State University (B.A., 1977); Northeastern University (J.D., 1986). Judicial Intern to Hon. Dolores K. Sloviter, U.S. Court of Appeals for the Third Circuit, 1985-1986. *Member:* American Bar Association (Member, Section on Labor and Employment Law); American Immigration Lawyers Association. (New York Office). *LANGUAGES:* Chinese (Cantonese and Mandarin). *PRACTICE AREAS:* Litigation and Transactions in U.S. and People's Republic of China.

H. BENNETT ARNBERGER, born Globe, Arizona, July 8, 1953; admitted, 1983, California and U.S. District Court, Northern and Central Districts of California. *Education:* University of California at Berkeley (A.B., with honors and distinction, 1977); University of San Francisco (J.D., 1983). Phi Delta Phi. Author: "Ensuring Compliance Through Intellectual Property Audits," 5 International Legal Strategy 54 (1994); "Avoiding The Hidden Liabilities of Independent Contractors," I Foreign Assignments (Kaigai Chuzai) 99 (1994); "Proactive Prevention of Cross-Cultural Disputes," 6 International Legal Strategy 60 (1994); "Protecting Against Misappropriation of Trade Secrets," 10 International Legal Strategy 63 (1993); "Taxation and Legal Requirements of California Corporations," 16 International Business Law Journal (Kokusai Shoji Homu) 202 (1988). Associate, Yuasa & Hara, Tokyo, Japan, 1987-1989. Contract Administrator, Chemsult AG, Saudi Arabia, 1977-1980. *Member:* San Francisco and American (Member, Section on International Law) Bar Associations; State Bar of California; International Bar Association (Member, Section on Business Law); Japan Society of Northern California; California-Southeast Asia Business Association; American Chamber of Commerce in Japan (Member, Committee on Licensing, Patents & Trademarks, 1987-1989). (San Francisco Office).

DAVID S. KIM, born Seoul, South Korea, February 17, 1961; admitted, 1990, California and U.S. District Court, Northern and Central Districts of California. *Education:* Western Illinois University (B.B.A., 1983; M.B.A., 1985); Southwestern University School of Law, Los Angeles (J.D., 1989). Recipient, Bradley and Pollack Scholarship, 1990. *Member:* State Bar of California; California Trial Lawyers Association; Los Angeles Trial Lawyers Association; California Korean Bar Association. (Los Angeles Office). *LANGUAGES:* English and Korean. *PRACTICE AREAS:* Litigation; Real Estate.

DOUGLAS L. BRYAN, born Whittier, California, September 7, 1960; admitted, 1991, California and U.S. District Court, Central District of California; 1992, U.S. Court of Appeals, Ninth Circuit. *Education:* California Polytechnic State University (B.S., 1983); Southwestern University School of Law (J.D., 1991). *Member:* State Bar of California; American Bar Asso-

(This Listing Continued)

ciation. (Los Angeles Office). *PRACTICE AREAS:* Tax Law; Corporate Law; Corporate Reorganizations; Constitutional Law; Insurance.

ROBERT W. MULCAHY, born Boston, Massachusetts, May 8, 1940; admitted, 1970, New York; 1971, District of Columbia; 1976, California; 1991, State Bar of Texas. *Education:* Boston College (B.S., Chemistry, 1963); George Washington University (J.D., 1968). *Member:* District of Columbia; State Bar of California; American Bar Association; The Licensing Executive Society. The Houston Volunteer Lawyers Association; Houston Intellectual Property Law Association. (Alhambra Office). *PRACTICE AREAS:* Intellectual Property; Patent Agent; Copyright Law; Trademark Law; Trade Secrets and Licensing.

OF COUNSEL

DEBORAH S. CHEW, born Singapore, May 27, 1964; admitted, 1988, Singapore; 1991, California. *Education:* National University of Singapore (LL.B., with honors, 1987). Associate, Arthur Loke & Partners, Singapore, 1988-1991. *Member:* State Bar of California; American Immigration Lawyers Association; Singapore American Business Association (Founding Member and Director); Hong Kong Association of California (Director); Asian Business Association; Law Society of Singapore and Academy of Law of Singapore. (San Francisco Office). *LANGUAGES:* English and Chinese (Mandarin, Cantonese, Taiwanese and Chiu-chow dialect).

CHRISTINA Y. CHEN, born Canton, China, May 2, 1943; admitted, 1983, California. *Education:* San Francisco State University (B.A., 1969); Hastings College of the Law, University of California (J.D., 1979). (Of Counsel, San Francisco, California Office). *LANGUAGES:* English and Chinese (Mandarin, Cantonese and Toisan dialect).

ROGER S. SAXTON, born Martins Ferry, Ohio, April 30, 1952; admitted, 1979, Sweden (as Jurist); 1980, Pennsylvania and U.S. District Court, Western District of Pennsylvania; 1992, New South Wales, Australia. *Education:* Case Western Reserve University (J.D., 1979); Studies in Japanese Law, Sophia University and University of Tokyo, Tokyo, Japan (1977-1980); Studies in Australian Law, University of Sydney (1989-1991). *Member:* Pennsylvania Bar Association; Law Society of New South Wales; Inter Pacific Bar Association. (Of Counsel, Sydney, Australia). *LANGUAGES:* English, Swedish and Japanese.

KAZUKO ITOH, born Tokyo, Japan, January 17, 1923; admitted, 1959, Japan (Not admitted in the U.S.). *Education:* Tsuda College; Tokyo Bunrika University. Legal Advisor to Her Britanic Majesty's Ambassador, Tokyo, 1976—. Legal Consultant to the American Embassy, Tokyo, 1976—. *Member:* Tokyo Bar Association; International Bar Association. (Of Counsel, Tokyo, Japan). *LANGUAGES:* Japanese, English, French and Spanish. *PRACTICE AREAS:* General Civil and Trial Practice; International Arbitration; Patent Litigation.

DUCK-SOON CHANG, born Korea, July 23, 1960; admitted, 1985, Korea and Korea Patent Bar; 1991, New York; 1992, California. *Education:* Judicial Training and Research Institute of the Supreme Court of Korea (198 3-1984); College of Law, Seoul National University (B.Jur,. 1983); Harvard Law School (LL.M., 1990). Author: "Technology Transfer, Cooperation and Joint Venture Agreements with Korea", Chapter 4 of Legal Aspects of Business Transactions and Investment in the Far East (Kluwer, 1988); "Arbitration Procedures in Korea," Vol. 1, Asia Law and Practice 7 (1989); "Arbitration in South Korea," Vol. 14 East Asian Executive Reports 1 (1992). Lecturer, International Patent Training and Research Institute of the Korean Industrial Property Office. Arbitrator, Korean Commercial Arbitration Board. *Member:* New York State and American Bar Associations; State Bar of California; Korean Bar Association; Korean Patent Bar Association; International Trademark Association. (Of Counsel, Seoul, Korea). *LANGUAGES:* Korean, English, Japanese (reads only). *PRACTICE AREAS:* Joint Venture; Licensing; Commercial Arbitration; Intellectual Property.

ASSOCIATES

VINCENT I.S. HSIEH, born Taipei, Taiwan, January 15, 1964; admitted, 1993, New York. *Education:* National Taiwan University (LL.B., 1987) Boston University (LL.M., in International Banking, 1992). *Member:* American Bar Association; New York County Lawyers Association. (New York Office). *LANGUAGES:* Mandarin Chinese.

ZHOUGEN LI, born Shunde, Guangdong Province, PRC, October 1, 1935; (Not admitted in the United States). *Education:* Yue Xue Teachers Training College. 1985-1991, Judge (ret.) Guangzhou Middle People's Court, Civil Division and Director of Administration. Recipient, 1984, 1985 Guangzhou City Court Systems Advance Specialist of the Year; 1988, Guangdong Province Outstanding Judge of the year; 1989 Third Degree

(This Listing Continued)

ARNBERGER, KIM, BUXBAUM & CHOY, Hong Kong—*Continued*

Honor awarded by the Guangdong Province High Court. *LANGUAGES:* Chinese (Mandarin and Cantonese). *PRACTICE AREAS:* Litigation; Contract; Intellectual Property.

YAOWU RONG, born Wei Chen County, Ji Bei, March 19, 1979; admitted, 1993, China; (Not admitted in the United States). *Education:* Xiamen University (B.A., 1992); (Now Mid. Graduated College of Xiamen University). (Xiamen Office). *LANGUAGES:* Chinese, English. *PRACTICE AREAS:* Civil Law; Commercial Law.

YUAN JIANG, born Fujian Province, China, April 15, 1956; admitted, 1983, China (Not admitted in the United States). *Education:* China University of Political Science and Law, 1979-1983; Part-time graduate student at China University of Political Science and Law, international private law, 1986-1989. Cadre at Research Department, China Lawyer Association, 1989-1990. Reporter, China Lawyer Magazine, 1990-1993. (Beijing Office). *LANGUAGES:* Chinese. *PRACTICE AREAS:* Labor Law; Leasing; Litigation.

XIAODONG HAO, born Inner Mongolia, China, March 9, 1965; admitted, 1990, China (Not admitted in the United States). *Education:* Inner Mongolia University (B.S.); China University of Political Science and Law (LL.B., 1991). (Beijing Office). *LANGUAGES:* Chinese, English, Japanese. *PRACTICE AREAS:* Litigation; Business Law; Intellectual Property.

SIYANG LIAO, born ShanghaiProvince, China, April 15, 1970. *Education:* China Political/Legal University (L.L.B., 1992). (Beijing Office). *LANGUAGES:* English, Chinese. *PRACTICE AREAS:* Contract Law; Joint Venture Law; Intellectual Property Law.

PEIZHONG GAN, born China, May 8, 1956; admitted, 1988, China (not admitted in the United States). *Education:* The Department of Law, Beijing University (LL.B., 1983; LL.M., 1989). Chief Editor, Encyclopedia of Commercial Law of China and the Encyclopedia of Corporate Law. Author: 21 articles and 3 books, e.g. "Legal Issues on Contracting Management in the Enterprises Owned by the Whole People," "Several Legal Issues on Corporate Reorganization in China". Lecturer, 1988. Associate Professor, 1994, Lectures on Corporate and Companies Law, 1984-1985. Assessor in the Beijing Intermediate Court. (Beijing Office). *LANGUAGES:* Chinese, English. *PRACTICE AREAS:* Corporate Law; Commercial Law; Litigation; Intellectual Property.

JIANXIN LI, born Jiangmen, China, October, 1966; admitted, 1988, China (Not admitted in the United States). *Education:* Guangzhou University (Law Department, 1984-1986); Zhongshan University (Economic Management Department, 1987-1990). Attorney, Guangzhou Second Foreign Economic Law Office, 1986-1990. (Guangzhou Office). *LANGUAGES:* English, Chinese (Mandarin and Cantonese). *PRACTICE AREAS:* Intellectual Property Litigation; Contracts; Real Estate; Trade; Insurance Law; Adoption Law.

YIKUN ZHU, born Sichuan Province, China, August 1967; admitted, 1993, China (Not admitted in the United States). *Education:* Southwest College of Politics & Law (L.L.M., 1991). [Chinese, Russian, French, and English]. (Guangzhou Office). *PRACTICE AREAS:* Foreign Investment; Securities Law; Company Law; Intellectual Property; Tax Law; International Trade Dispute; Contracts.

DACHTCEREN ENKHBOLD, born Ulaanbaatar, Mongolia, March 11, 1946; admitted, 1973, Mongolia; (Not admitted in the United States). *Education:* International Relations Institute of Moscow (expert of Western Countries - U.S.A., Canada); Mongolian State University (Teacher of English Language). (Mongolia Office). *LANGUAGES:* Russian, English. *PRACTICE AREAS:* Economic Entities and Foreign Investment, Civil Law.

BYAMBAA BAYARMAA, born Moscow, Russia, November 6, 1960; admitted, 1982, Mongolia; (Not Admitted in the United States). *Education:* Moldova State University, Law Faculty, 1982; Passed State Examination on Bar Practice, March, 1994. (Mongolia Office). *LANGUAGES:* Russian, German, Romania, English. *PRACTICE AREAS:* Commercial and Contract Law.

JIANXIONG HUANG, born Rongyan City, Fujian, January 15, 1964; admitted, 1987 (Not admitted in the United States). *Education:* South-West Politics & Law College (B.A., 1984); College of Xiamen University (Master of Law, 1990). (Xiamen Office). *LANGUAGES:* Chinese, Taiwanese, English. *PRACTICE AREAS:* Civil Law; Commercial Law; Investment Law; Real Estate Law.

(This Listing Continued)

AS38B

MINGLIANG LAN, born Hainan Province, China, August 12, 1927; admitted, 1989 (Not admitted in the United States). *Education:* Beijing Zhengfa University of Politics and Law (1956). Publications: Outline of Administrative Law; General Situation of International Organization; International Constitution (Teaching Material); Outline and Guidance on International Law. *Member:* Asian-Africa Development Committee, China International Legal Study Committee; National Lawyer Committee; China-Hong Kong Law Study Committee; China Investment Consultancy Experts Committee; China Political and Legal Management Leaders Institution; China Trade Committee; Foreign Economic and Trade Arbitration Committee (Arbitrator); National Overseas Federation Legal Consultant Committee. (Shenzhen Office). *LANGUAGES:* Chinese, English. *PRACTICE AREAS:* Public International Law; Intellectual Property.

ALFRED YONG LIN, born Fuzhou, China, October 10, 1969; admitted, 1993, China (not admitted in the United States). *Education:* Xiamen University Law Department (B.A., 1992). (Shanghai Office). *LANGUAGES:* Chinese, English and Fuzhou. *PRACTICE AREAS:* General Civil Law; International Investment; Corporation Law.

HONGLIANG WU, born Shanghai, China, 1935; admitted, 1985, China; registered patent agent (not admitted in the United States). *Education:* Beijing Iron and Steel Institute (B.S., 1960). (Shanghai Office). *LANGUAGES:* Chinese (Shanghai dialect) and English. *PRACTICE AREAS:* Patent and Trademark Law; Intellectual Property.

JIANG-XIONG HUANG, born Rongyan City, Fujian Province, China, January 15, 1946; admitted, 1987, China (Not admitted in the United States). *Education:* Institute of Political Science and Law in South-west China (B.A. in Law, 1984); Post-graduate Institute of Xiamen University (LL.M. in civil law, 1990). Author: An Introduction to Civil Law, published by house of Xiamen University; Examples of Lawsuits, published by house of Xiamen University; A Guide for Taiwan People to Invest in Mainland China, published by Beijing Huayi Publishing House. Lecturer: Civil Law; Law of Estate and Practice, Law Department, Xiamen University. *Member:* China Jurisprudence Society; Fujian Jurisprudence Society; Xiamen Jurisprudence Society; Fujian Society of Administrative; Association for Industry and Commerce; Xiamen Society of Administration for Industry and Commerce; Xiamen Bar Association. (Xiamen Office). *LANGUAGES:* Chinese, Taiwanese, English. *PRACTICE AREAS:* Economic; Commercial; Civil; Criminal; Investment Law, and Real Estate Law in China.

ZHOUGEN LI, born Shunde, Guangdong Province, China, October 1, 1935; (Not admitted in the United States). *Education:* Yue Xue Teachers Training College. 1985-1991, Judge (ret.) Guangzhou Middle People's Court, Civil Division and Director of Administration. Recipient, 1984, 1985 Guangzhou City Court Systems Advance Specialist of the Year; 1988, Guangdong Province Outstanding Judge of the year; 1989 Third Degree Honor awarded by the Guangdong Province High Court. (Hong Kong Office). *LANGUAGES:* Chinese (Mandarin and Cantonese). *PRACTICE AREAS:* Litigation; Contract; Intellectual Property.

JIA LIN, born China; admitted, 1989, China; 1991, California. *Education:* Zhongshan University, Guangzhou, China (LL.B.); People's University Beijing, China (LL.M.). Lecturer, People's University, 1989—. (Beijing Office).

LEGAL SUPPORT PERSONNEL

ZHANGQUING WU, born Shantou Guangdong Province, PRC October 15, 1967. *Education:* Shenzhen University (LL.B., 1991). (Shenzhen Office).

SHIJIE CHEN, born Xiamen, Fujian Province, China, November 18, 1970. *Education:* Xiamen University (LL.B., 1992). (Xiamen Office). *LANGUAGES:* English, Chinese. *PRACTICE AREAS:* Adoption Law; Contracts; Insurance; Trade.

SONG GAO, born Fujian Province, China, April 2, 1969. *Education:* Hau Qiao University (LL.B.). (Shenzhen Office).

REVISER OF THE PEOPLE'S REPUBLIC OF CHINA AND MONGOLIA LAW DIGESTS FOR THIS DIRECTORY.

BAKER & McKENZIE
14TH FLOOR, HUTCHISON HOUSE
10 HARCOURT ROAD
HONG KONG
Telephone: 2846-1888
Intn'l. Dialing: (852) 2846-1888
Cable Address: ABOGADO
Telex: 76416
Answer Back: 76416 ABOG HX
Facsimiles: (852) 2845-0476; 2845-0487; 2845-0490

Associated Offices of Baker & McKenzie in: Almaty, Amsterdam, Bangkok, Barcelona, Beijing, Berlin, Bogotá, Brasília, Brussels, Budapest, Buenos Aires, Cairo, Caracas, Chicago, Dallas, Frankfurt, Geneva, Hanoi, Ho Chi Minh City, Juárez, Kiev, London, Madrid, Manila, Melbourne, México City, Miami, Milan, Monterrey, Moscow, New York, Palo Alto, Paris, Prague, Rio de Janeiro, Riyadh, Rome, St. Petersburg, San Diego, San Francisco, São Paulo, Singapore, Stockholm, Sydney, Taipei, Tijuana, Tokyo, Toronto, Valencia, Warsaw, Washington, D.C. and Zürich.
Correspondent Law Firm: Hadiputranto, Hadinoto & Partners, Jakarta.

Banking, Commercial and Corporate Law, China, Industrial Property, International and Regional Investment, Litigation, Maritime, Real Estate, Tax, Trademark Registration.

ROBERT A. ARNOLD, born London, England; admitted, 1981, Solicitor of the Supreme Court of England and Wales; 1983, Solicitor of the Supreme Court of New South Wales, Australia; 1985, Solicitor of the Supreme Court of Hong Kong. *Education:* University of Warwick (LLB). *Member:* Law Society of New South Wales.

JOHN C. ATKINSON, born Melbourne, Australia; admitted, 1983, Western Australia; 1984, High Court of Australia; 1991, England and Hong Kong. *Education:* University of Western Australia (LL.B.). *LANGUAGES:* English.

PIUS K. W. CHENG, born Hong Kong; admitted, 1985, Hong Kong; 1989, England and Wales and A.C.T., Australia. *Education:* Chinese University of Hong Kong (B.B.A.); City of London Polytechnic; Cambridge University (LL.M.). *Member:* Law Society of Hong Kong; Law Society of England and Wales. *LANGUAGES:* English and Chinese.

YUK TONG CHEUNG, born Hong Kong; admitted, 1984, Hong Kong; 1988, New York, U.S.A.; 1991, England and Wales. *Education:* University of Hong Kong (LL.B. & P.C.LL.); London School of Economics (LL.M.). *Member:* Law Society of Hong Kong; New York State and American Bar Associations. *LANGUAGES:* English and Chinese (Putonghua and Cantonese).

PAUL S. ELLIOTT, born New Zealand; admitted 1979, New Zealand; 1983, England; 1984, Hong Kong. *Education:* University of Canterbury (LL.B., Hons.); London University (LL.M.). *LANGUAGES:* English.

STEPHEN R. ENO, born Manchester, England; admitted, 1980, Solicitor of Supreme Court of England; 1984, Hong Kong. *Education:* University of Kent at Canterbury (B.A., Hon.). *Member:* Law Society of England and Wales; Law Society of Hong Kong. *LANGUAGES:* English.

PATRICK B. FONTAINE, born England; admitted, 1985, England and Wales; 1987, Hong Kong. *Education:* University of College, London (LL.B. Hons.). *LANGUAGES:* English, French and Putonghua.

GEORGE FORRAI, born Budapest, Hungary; admitted, 1970, Solicitor of Supreme Court of New South Wales, Australia; 1973, Solicitor of Supreme Court of Victoria, Australia; 1974, Solicitor of High Court of Australia; 1975, Solicitor of Supreme Court of England and Wales; 1975, Solicitor of Supreme Court of Hong Kong, Barrister and Solicitor of Supreme Court of Papua, New Guinea; 1979, Advocate in the State of Brunei; 1987, New York, U.S.A. *Education:* University of Sydney (B.A., LL.B.); University of California at Berkeley (LL.M.). *Member:* Law Society of New South Wales; Law Society of England and Wales; Law Society of Hong Kong; American Bar Association.

MARK S. GOETZE, born Berlin, West Germany. admitted as Barrister and Solicitor, 1981, British Columbia; 1991, England and Wales and Hong Kong. *Education:* Simon Fraser University (B.A., 1976); University of Victoria (LL.B., 1980). *Member:* Law Society of British Columbia; Vancouver, Canadian and International Bar Associations; Law Society of England and Wales; Law Society of Hong Kong. *LANGUAGES:* English and German.

(This Listing Continued)

GRAEME ROSS HALFORD, born Lower Hutt, New Zealand; admitted, 1971, New Zealand; 1983, Victoria, Australia; 1988, England and Wales; 1989, Hong Kong. *Education:* Victoria University of Wellington (LL.B.). *Member:* Law Society of New Zealand. *LANGUAGES:* English.

WILLIAM KUO, born Hong Kong; admitted, 1980, Illinois, U.S.A.; 1984, U.S. Supreme Court and Solicitor of Supreme Court of New South Wales and Victoria, Australia; 1985, Solicitor of Supreme Court of Hong Kong; 1988, England and Wales; 1992, Singapore. *Education:* University of Illinois (B.Sc.); Northwestern University (J.D.); University of New South Wales (LL.B.); University of Hong Kong (P.C.LL.) *Member:* Illinois State Bar Association; Law Society of Hong Kong; Singapore Academy of Law.

ANGELA W. Y. LEE, born Hong Kong; admitted, 1983, Solicitor of Supreme Court of Hong Kong; 1987, England and Wales; 1989, A.C.T., Australia. *Education:* University of Hong Kong (B.A.); University of London (LL.B.); College of Law (London); University of East Asia (Macau) (Diploma in Chinese Law). *Member:* Law Society of Hong Kong.

LAWRENCE K. H. LEE, admitted, 1981, Solicitor of the Supreme Court of Hong Kong; 1984, New South Wales, Australia and Victoria; 1987, England and Wales. *Education:* University of Hong Kong (LL.B.; P.C.LL.).

CHEUK-YAN LEUNG, born Hong Kong; admitted, 1985, Hong Kong; 1988, England and Wales; 1989, A.C.T., Australia; 1991, Victoria, Australia. *Education:* Chinese University of Hong Kong (B.Soc.Sc.); University of Oxford (M.Phil.); College of Law, London (Common Professional Examination; Law Society's Final Examination). *Member:* Law Society of Hong Kong.

DAVID R. MARTIN, born Australia; admitted, 1983, Western Australia; 1988, England and Wales and Hong Kong. *Education:* University of Western Australia (B. Juris., 1981; LL.B., 1982). *Member:* Law Society of Hong Kong. *LANGUAGES:* English.

JOHN M. MORGANS, born Birmingham, England; admitted, 1965, Solicitor of Supreme Court of England & Wales; 1982, Solicitor of Supreme Court of Hong Kong; 1983, Barrister and Solicitor of Supreme Court of Victoria, Australia and Advocate in the State of Brunei. *Education:* University of Wales (LL.B.); Cambridge University (M.A.). *Member:* Law Society of England and Wales; Law Society of Hong Kong.

GRAHAM D. MORRISON, born Rinteln, West Germany; admitted, 1980, Solicitor of the Supreme Court of England and Wales; 1981, Solicitor of Supreme Court of Hong Kong. *Education:* Cambridge University (M.A., LL.B.). *Member:* Law Society of Hong Kong.

MICHAEL A. OLESNICKY, born South Australia, Australia; admitted, 1977, South Australia, Australia; 1981, New South Wales, Australia; 1991, England and Wales and Hong Kong. *Education:* Adelaide University (B.A.; LL.B., Hons.); Columbia University (LL.M., 1979).

DAVID R. SHANNON, born Sydney, Australia; admitted, 1972, Solicitor of Supreme Court of New South Wales, Australia; 1974, Barrister and Solicitor of Supreme Court of Victoria, Australia; 1980, Barrister and Solicitor of Supreme Court of A.C.T., Australia; 1983, Solicitor of Supreme Court of England and Wales; 1983, Solicitor of Supreme Court of Hong Kong. *Education:* University of Sydney (B.A., LL.B.); University of New South Wales (M.B.A.). *Member:* Law Institute of Victoria; Law Society of New South Wales; Law Society of England & Wales; Law Society of Hong Kong; International Bar Association (Member, Committee X - Franchising, 1983—).

PAUL CHUEN YAN TAN, born Hong Kong; admitted, 1982, Solicitor of the Supreme Court of New South Wales, Australia; 1985, England and Wales; 1986, Solicitor of the Supreme Court of Hong Kong. *Education:* University of Sydney (B.Ec.; LL.B.; LL.M.). *Member:* Law Society of New South Wales.

POH LEE TAN, born Malaysia; admitted, 1985, England and Wales; 1986, Solicitor of the Supreme Court of Hong Kong; 1990, A.C.T., Australia and High Court of Australia; 1991, Singapore. *Education:* London School of Economics and Political Science (Law Degree); Queens College, Cambridge (LL.M.).

CHRISTOPHER J. WILSON, admitted, 1983, New South Wales, Australia and High Court of Australia; 1987, England and Wales; 1988, Hong Kong. *Education:* Sydney University (B.Ec.; LL.B. Hons).

(This Listing Continued)

BAKER & McKENZIE, Hong Kong—Continued

COLE R. CAPENER, born Seattle, Washington, October 28, 1955; admitted, 1982, New York and District of Columbia, U.S.A.; 1984, Utah, U.S.A.; 1988, California, U.S.A. (Not admitted in Hong Kong). *Education:* University of Utah (B.A., magna cum laude, 1978); National Law Center, George Washington University (J.D., Hons., 1981). Phi Beta Kappa. Staff and Notes Editor, Journal of International Law and Economics, 1979-1981. *Member:* State Bar of California (International Law Section); American Bar Association. *LANGUAGES:* Chinese (Mandarin).

MITCHELL M. GITIN, born Brooklyn, N.Y., 1940; admitted, 1968, New York, U.S.A. (Not admitted in Hong Kong). *Education:* Cornell University (B.A., with distinction, 1960); Christ Church and Oxford University, Oxford, England (B.A., 1962; M.A., 1967); Harvard University (J.D., magna cum laude, 1967). Phi Beta Kappa. Editor, Harvard Law Review.

MICHAEL J. MOSER, born New York, N.Y.; admitted, 1981, New York, U.S.A.; 1989, District of Columbia, U.S.A. (Not admitted in Hong Kong). *Education:* School of Foreign Service, Georgetown University (B.S.F.S., magna cum laude,); Columbia University (Ph.D. with distinction); Harvard Law School (J.D.). Phi Beta Kappa. Appointments: Panel of Arbitrators: China International Economic and Trade Arbitration Commission, Beijing (one of five foreign nationals appointed); Singapore International Arbitration Centre; Hong Kong International Arbitration Centre; American Arbitration Association. Member, Governing Council and Management Committee, Hong Kong International Arbitration Centre. Fellow, Chartered Institute of Arbitrators, London (Member, Governing Committee, Hong Kong Branch). Member, United Nations Working Group on official translations of Chinese foreign investment legislation. *Member:* New York State and International Bar Associations; District of Columbia Bar; Harvard Alumni Association of China (Past Chairman). (Also at Beijing). *LANGUAGES:* English and Chinese (Mandarin).

RICHARD L. WEISMAN, born Norwich, Connecticut; admitted, 1982, Massachusetts, U.S.A. (Not admitted in Hong Kong). *Education:* Yale College (B.A.); Harvard Law School (J.D.).

WINSTON K. T. ZEE, born Hong Hong; admitted, 1981, District of Columbia, U.S.A. (Not admitted in Hong Kong). *Education:* Pacific Lutheran University (B.A., cum laude; M.B.A., 1978); Georgetown University (J.D., magna cum laude, 1981; LL.M. Tax, 1984). *Member:* District of Columbia Bar; American Bar Association.

LOCAL PARTNERS

PAUL JOHN CAROLAN, born London, England; admitted, 1984, England and Wales; 1985, Hong Kong; 1989, New South Wales, Australia. *Education:* University of Sussex (B.A.); Guildford College of Law. *Member:* Law Society of Hong Kong.

BARRY WAI-MAN CHENG, born Hong Kong; admitted, 1987, Hong Kong. *Education:* University College, Cardiff; The Law College, Guildford. *LANGUAGES:* English and Chinese (Cantonese and Mandarin).

BETTY MAN YEE CHOI, born Hong Kong; admitted, 1987, Hong Kong; 1991, England and Wales and A.C.T., Australia; 1992, Singapore. *Education:* University of Hong Kong (LL.B., 1984; P.C.LL., 1985). *LANGUAGES:* English, Cantonese and Putonghua.

NEIL M. DONOGHUE, born Caerleon, United Kingdom; admitted, 1984, England and Wales; 1989, Hong Kong. *Education:* University College, London (LL.B., Hons.); College of Law, Guildford. *Member:* Law Society of England and Wales. *LANGUAGES:* English.

DAVID J. FLEMING, born Sydney, Australia; admitted, 1983, New South Wales, Australia; 1991, Hong Kong and England and Wales. *Education:* University of New South Wales (B.A.; LL.B.). *Member:* Law Societies of New South Wales, England and Wales and Hong Kong.

JUNRI KONII, born Tokyo, Japan; admitted, 1986, Solicitor of Supreme Court of England and Wales; 1995, Hong Kong. *Education:* University of Cambridge (M.A.); College of Law, Lancaster Gate. *Member:* Law Society of England and Wales. *LANGUAGES:* English and Japanese.

ALAN H. LINNING, admitted, 1985, Scotland; 1988, Hong Kong; 1994, Tasmania, Australia. *Education:* University of Edinburgh (LL.B., Hons.). *Member:* Law Society of Scotland.

FIONA LOUGHREY, born Northern Ireland; admitted, 1985, England; 1987, Hong Kong; 1991, A.C.T., Australia. *Education:* University of

(This Listing Continued)

Manchester (LL.B., Hons., 1980); College of Law, Chester, England (Law Society Final Examination, 1981). *LANGUAGES:* English and French.

RODNEY J. McNEIL, born Sydney, Australia; admitted, 1989, New South Wales, Australia; 1992, Hong Kong and England and Wales. *Education:* Sydney University (B.A., 1980; LL.B., 1981); University of Newcastle (B.Med ., Hons, 1986). Instructor in Law, University of Newcastle, 1982-1985. *Member:* Law Society of New South Wales. *LANGUAGES:* Japanese, German and English.

F. JEANNIE SMITH, born Wolverhampton, England; admitted, 1988, England; 1992, Hong Kong; registered Trade Mark Agent, U.K. *Education:* Staffordsire University, England (LL.B., First Class Hons.); Polytechnic of Central London (Barrister). *Member:* Law Society of England and Wales; Law Society of Hong Kong; Institute of Trade Mark Agents; International Trademark Association, U.S.A.; Hong Kong Institute of Trade Mark Practitioners (President); Asian Patent Attorney Association, Hong Kong.

ERNEST KAM TOO WONG, born Hong Kong; admitted, 1986, Hong Kong. *Education:* University of Hong Kong (LL.B.). *Member:* Law Society of Hong Kong. *LANGUAGES:* English and Chinese.

FREDERICK R. BURKE, born San Francisco, California; admitted, 1988, New York and District of Columbia, U.S.A. (Not admitted in Hong Kong). *Education:* Stanford University (B.A., 1981); Columbia School of International Affairs (M.I.A., 1986); Columbia Law School (J.D., 1987). *Member:* The Association of the Bar of the City of New York; American Chamber of Commerce in Vietnam. *LANGUAGES:* English, Mandarin, Vietnamese, French, German and Italian.

STEPHEN M. NELSON, born Philadelphia, Pennsylvania; admitted, 1986, California, U.S.A. (Not admitted in Hong Kong). *Education:* University of Pennsylvania (B.A.); Columbia University (J.D.). *Member:* State Bar of California. *LANGUAGES:* English and Chinese.

ASSOCIATES

ANDREW J. L. AGLIONBY, born Bromley, England, 1962; admitted, 1990, England and Wales; 1994, Hong Kong. *Education:* University of East Anglia (LL.B., 1983); Inns of Court School of Law. *Member:* Law Societies of England and Wales and Hong Kong; Hong Kong Association of Environmental Law.

ANGELA C. S. ANG, born Kuala Lumpur, Malaysia, 1964; admitted, 1989, Supreme Court of Victoria and High Court of Australia; 1992, England and Wales; 1993, Hong Kong. *Education:* Monash University (B.Sc., 1986; LL.B., 1988). *Member:* Law Institute of Victoria, Melbourne. *LANGUAGES:* English, Malay, Cantonese and French.

JUDY BROWN, born Altrincham, England, 1962; admitted, 1989, England and Wales; 1994, Hong Kong. *Education:* Kings College, Cambridge (B.A., 1984; M.A., 1987); University of Newcastle-upon-Tyne, England (M.A., 1985); College of Law, Chancery Lane, London (Common Professional Examination, 1986; Solicitor's Finals Examination, 1987). *Member:* The Law Society of England and Wales.

EDMOND LAP YAN CHAN, born Hong Kong, 1966; admitted, 1991, Hong Kong. *Education:* University of Hong Kong (LL.B., 1988). *LANGUAGES:* English, Cantonese and Mandarin.

EDWARD P. CHAN, born Montreal, Quebec, Canada, 1965; admitted, 1993, Ontario, Canada; 1994, England and Wales and Hong Kong. *Education:* University of Toronto (B.Sc., Hons., 1988); Osgoode Hall Law School (LL.B., 1991). *Member:* Law Society of Upper Canada; Law Society of England and Wales; Law Society of Hong Kong; Canadian Bar Association. *LANGUAGES:* English and (Cantonese).

ELSA S. C. CHAN, born Hong Kong, 1961; admitted, 1992, Hong Kong. *Education:* University of Hong Kong (LL.B., 1989; P.C.LL., 1990). *Member:* Law Society of Hong Kong. *LANGUAGES:* Chinese and English.

RICO W. K. CHAN, born Hong Kong, 1964; admitted, 1991, Hong Kong. *Education:* University of Hong Kong (LL.B., 1988; Postgraduate Certificate in Law, 1989).

ANNE WAI YUI CHEN, born Hong Kong; admitted, 1987, Hong Kong. *Education:* University of Hong Kong (LL.B.; P.C.LL.). *Member:* Hong Kong Law Society; International Law Association. *LANGUAGES:* English and Chinese.

(This Listing Continued)

GERAMI KING HOI CHENG, born Hong Kong; admitted, 1985, New South Wales, Australia; 1992, Hong Kong. *Education:* University of New South Wales (B.Comm.; LL.B.); University of Hong Kong (P.C.LL.). *LANGUAGES:* English, Cantonese and Mandarin.

MILTON W. M. CHENG, born Singapore, 1965; admitted, 1992, England and Wales; 1993, Hong Kong. *Education:* King's College, University of London (LL.B., 1989). Barrister, Gray's Inn, London, 1990-1992. *Member:* Law Society of England and Wales, 1992—; Law Society of Hong Kong, 1993. *LANGUAGES:* English and Chinese.

DEBBIE FONG CHEUNG, born Hong Kong; admitted, 1985, Hong Kong. *Education:* University of Hong Kong (LL.B., 1982; P.C.LL., 1983). *Member:* Law Society of Hong Kong. *LANGUAGES:* English and Chinese.

ANNA CHONG, born Hong Kong, 1961; admitted, 1987, Hong Kong; 1991, England and Wales. *Education:* Keele University (B.Soc.Sc., 1984); The Law College, Lancaster Gate (1985). *LANGUAGES:* English and Cantonese.

LISA K. F. CHU, born Hong Kong, 1967; admitted, 1993, Hong Kong. *Education:* University of Hong Kong (LL.B., 1990; P.C.LL., 1991). *LANGUAGES:* Chinese and English.

YING WOO CHUNG, born Hong Kong; admitted, 1994, Hong Kong. *Education:* University of Hong Kong (B.Sc., 1978); University of London (LL.B., 1991); University of Hong Kong (P.C.LL., 1992). *LANGUAGES:* Chinese and English.

SALLY A. DURANT, born Plymouth, United Kingdom; admitted, 1983, England; 1990, Hong Kong. *Education:* Bristol University (LL.B. Hons., 1980); College of Law. *Member:* Law Society of England and Wales. *LANGUAGES:* English.

MARK G. FAIRBAIRN, born Sunderland, England, 1965; admitted, 1990, England and Wales; 1994, Hong Kong. *Education:* Nottingham University (LL.B., Hons., 1987); Nottingham Trent University (Law Society Finals, 1988). *Member:* Law Society of England and Wales. *LANGUAGES:* English.

DOW P. FAMULAK, born Trail, British Columbia, Canada, 1960; admitted, 1989, British Columbia, Canada; 1993, England and Wales and Hong Kong. *Education:* University of British Columbia (B.A., Hons., Economics, 1983); University of Saskatchewan (LL.B., 1988). *Member:* Law Society of British Columbia.

VERONICA K. S. FOK, born Hong Kong, 1966; admitted, 1991, England and Wales; 1994, Hong Kong. *Education:* Bristol University (LL.B., Hons., 1988); College of Law, London (Law Society Finals, 1989). *Member:* Law Society of England and Wales. *LANGUAGES:* English and Cantonese.

WENDY W. T. FUNG, born Hong Kong; admitted, 1994, Hong Kong. *Education:* Keele University (1990); Guildford Law College (1991). *Member:* Law Society of Hong Kong. *LANGUAGES:* English, Cantonese and Mandarin.

JOYCE K. W. HO, born Singapore, 1964; admitted, 1989, England and Wales; 1995, Hong Kong. *Education:* Brasenose College, Oxford University (B.A., Hons., 1986); College of Law, Guilford (Law Society Finals, 1987); Queen Mary and Westfield College, University of London (LL.M., with Merit, 1993). *Member:* Law Society of England and Wales. *LANGUAGES:* English, Mandarin, Cantonese and French.

THOMAS K. H. HO, born Hong Kong, 1965; admitted, 1991, New South Wales, Australia; 1993, Hong Kong and England and Wales. *Education:* University of New South Wales (LL.B./B.Juris., 1991). *Member:* The Law Society of Hong Kong; The New South Wales Law Society. *LANGUAGES:* Cantonese, Mandarin and English.

WILLIAM K. K. HO, born Hong Kong, 1961; admitted, 1990, England and Wales; 1991, Hong Kong. *Education:* University of Hong Kong (B.Soc. Sc., Hons., 1984); University College London (LL.B., Hons., 1987). *Member:* The Law Society of England and Wales; The Law Society of Hong Kong. *LANGUAGES:* English, Cantonese and Mandarin.

FREDERICK J. HORSEY, born Vancouver, Canada, 1962; admitted, 1988, British Columbia, Canada; 1992, England and Wales; 1994, Hong Kong. *Education:* University of British Columbia (B.A., Hons., 1984); Osgoode Hall Law School (LL.B., 1987); University of Cambridge (LL.M., 1989). *LANGUAGES:* English and French.

JAMES T. O. HUANG, born Singapore, 1964; admitted, 1991, Solicitor of Supreme Court of England and Wales; 1993, Hong Kong. *Education:*

(This Listing Continued)

University College London (LL.B., Hons., 1988); College of Law, Chester, England. *Member:* Law Society of England and Wales. *LANGUAGES:* English, Mandarin and Cantonese.

MARK C. INNIS, born Malaysia; admitted, 1987, New South Wales, Australia; 1991, England and Wales and Hong Kong. *Education:* University of Sydney (B.A.; LL.B., Hons.; LL.M.); Kurringai College of Advanced Education (Diploma, 1989); Securities Institute of Australia (ASIA). Associate to Mr. Justice Lockhart, Federal Court of Australia, 1986-1987. Deputy District Registrar, Federal Court of Australia, 1987. *Member:* Law Society of England and Wales; The Law Society of Hong Kong.

GRAEME S. M. JOHNSTON, born Hong Kong; admitted, 1990, Scotland; 1992, Hong Kong. *Education:* University of Aberdeen (LL.B.; Diploma Legal Practice). *Member:* Law Society of Scotland.

MOLLY KIAT, born Singapore, 1965; admitted, 1989, Singapore; 1994, England and Wales and Hong Kong. *Education:* National University of Singapore. *LANGUAGES:* English and Mandarin.

JOSEPH KWAN, born Hong Kong, 1967; admitted, 1992, Hong Kong; 1994, Solicitor of Supreme Court of England and Wales and Tasmania, Australia. *Education:* University of Birmingham, England (LL.B., 1989); University of Hong Kong (P.C.LL., 1990). *Member:* Law Society of Hong Kong. *LANGUAGES:* English, Cantonese and Mandarin.

VINNIE LAM, born Beijing, People's Republic of China, 1969; admitted, 1992, New South Wales, Australia; 1994, England and Wales and Hong Kong. *Education:* University of Sydney, Australia (B.Ec., 1989; LL.B., 1991). *Member:* Law Society of New South Wales. *LANGUAGES:* English, Cantonese and Mandarin.

HARVEY LAU, born Hong Kong, 1965; admitted, 1991, New York, U.S.A.; 1993, Hong Kong. *Education:* University of Hong Kong (LL.B., 1988; P.C.LL., 1989); New York University (LL.M., 1991). *Member:* Law Society of Hong Kong; New York State and American Bar Associations. *LANGUAGES:* Cantonese, Mandarin and English.

VIVIAN W. W. LAU, born Hong Kong, 1968; admitted, 1993, Hong Kong; 1994, England and Wales and Tasmania, Australia. *Education:* University of Hong Kong (LL.B., 1990; P.C.LL., 1991). *Member:* Law Society of Hong Kong. *LANGUAGES:* Cantonese, Mandarin and English.

BENNY LEE, born Singapore; admitted, 1988, Singapore; 1994, Hong Kong. *Education:* National University of Singapore (LL.B.). *Member:* Law Society of Singapore; Law Society of Hong Kong. *LANGUAGES:* English, Cantonese, Mandarin and Hakka.

ANITA P. F. LEUNG, born Hong Kong; admitted, 1989, Hong Kong; 1991, England and Wales and A.C.T., Australia. *Education:* University of Hong Kong (LL.B.; P.C.LL.). *Member:* Law Society of Hong Kong. *LANGUAGES:* English and Chinese (Cantonese and Mandarin).

FLORENCE C. H. LEUNG, born Hong Kong, 1964; admitted, 1994, Hong Kong. *Education:* University of Toronto (B.Sc., 1987); University of Hong Kong (P.C.L., 1992; C.P.E., 1991). *LANGUAGES:* Chinese and English.

KAREN L. LINKER, born London, England, 1966; admitted, 1991, England and Wales; 1994, Hong Kong. *Education:* Kingston University (LL.B., Hons., 1988); Guildford College of Law (Sols Finals, 1989). *Member:* Law Society of England and Wales; Law Society of Hong Kong. *LANGUAGES:* English.

ELAINE Y. L. LIU, born Hong Kong; admitted, 1992, Hong Kong; 1993, England and Wales. *Education:* University of Hong Kong (LL.B., 1987; P.C.LL., 1988); University of London (LL.M., 1989). *Member:* The Law Society of Hong Kong. *LANGUAGES:* Chinese (Mandarin and Cantonese) and English.

JACKIE F. K. LO, born Hong Kong, 1961; admitted, 1994, Hong Kong. *Education:* University of Hong Kong (LL.B., 1991; LL.M., 1994). *Member:* The Institute of Linguists, U.K. *LANGUAGES:* English and Chinese.

ANDREW W. LOCKHART, born New Zealand; admitted, 1986, New Zealand; 1992, England and Wales and Hong Kong. *Education:* Auckland University (LL.B., Hons.); Cambridge University (LL.M.). *Member:* Law Society of Hong Kong. *LANGUAGES:* English.

THESSA MAC, born Malaysia, 1964; admitted, 1993, New England and Wales; 1994, Hong Kong. *Education:* University College, Cardiff (LL.B., 1989); The College of Law, Guilford (The Solicitors Law Finals,

(This Listing Continued)

BAKER & McKENZIE, Hong Kong—Continued

1991). *Member:* Law Society of England and Wales; Law Society of Hong Kong. *LANGUAGES:* Cantonese, English, Malay and Japanese.

JOHN M. MAGUIRE, born England, 1963; admitted, 1988, England and Wales; 1991, Hong Kong. *Education:* College of St. Hild and St. Bede; Durham University (B.A., Hons., 1985); Guildford College of Law (Solicitors Finals Exams, 1986). *Member:* City of London Law Society; Freeman City of London Solicitors Company; Freeman City of London; Law Society of Hong Kong. *LANGUAGES:* English.

ALLAN J. MCCAY, born Stirling, Scotland, September 9, 1965; admitted, 1991, Scotland; 1993, Hong Kong. *Education:* Aberdeen University, Scotland (LL.B., Hons., 1988); Edinburgh University, Scotland (Diploma in Legal Practice, 1989). *Member:* Law Society of Scotland; Law Society of Hong Kong. *LANGUAGES:* English and French.

ELIZABETH WAI YIN MO, born Hong Kong; admitted, 1984, Hong Kong. *Education:* Chinese University of Hong Kong (B.A.); York University, Toronto, Canada (M.B.A.); Hong Kong University (LL.B.; P.C.LL.). *Member:* Hong Kong Law Society. *LANGUAGES:* English and Chinese (Cantonese and Mandarin).

JENNIFER NG, born Hong Kong, 1958; admitted, 1986, Hong Kong; 1989, England; 1991, Victoria, Australia. *Education:* University of Hong Kong (Bachelor of Social Science, 1980); Trent Polytechnic, England (C.P.E., 1982; College of Law (Solicitors Final Exam, 1983). *Member:* Law Society of Hong Kong. *LANGUAGES:* Chinese, English, French, German and Japanese.

HILARY M. NG-CORDELL, born Birmingham, England, 1960; admitted, 1985, England; 1987, Hong Kong. *Education:* Leicester University (LL.B., Hons., 1981); Guilford College of Law (Solicitors Final Examination, 1982). *Member:* Law Society of Hong Kong; Law Society of England. *LANGUAGES:* English and Mandarin.

GARY A. SEIB, born Sydney, Australia; admitted, 1986, New South Wales, Australia and High Court of Australia; 1991, England and Hong Kong. *Education:* University of Sydney (B.Ec., 1983; LL.B. Hons., 1985). *Member:* Law Societies of New South Wales, England and Wales, Hong Kong and Insol. International. *LANGUAGES:* English.

SUSAN SHYU, born Peng-Chen, Taiwan, July 22, 1966; admitted, 1992, Queensland, Australia; 1993, Hong Kong; 1994, England and Wales. *Education:* Queensland University of Technology (LL.B., 1988). *LANGUAGES:* Mandarin and English.

DOUGLAS C. T. SO, born Hong Kong, 1964; admitted, 1993, Hong Kong. *Education:* Seattle Pacific University (B.A., 1987); University of Hong Kong (LL.B., 1990; P.C.LL., 1991). *LANGUAGES:* Chinese and English.

CINDY SYNN-CHEE TAM, born Hong Kong, 1964; admitted, 1992, England and Wales; 1994, Hong Kong. *Education:* University of Cambridge, Clare College (B.A., 1986; M.A., 1990); College of Law, Guildford (Law Society's Final Examinations, 1988); University of British Columbia (M.B.A., 1990). *Member:* Law Society of England and Wales; Law Society of Hong Kong. *LANGUAGES:* English, Chinese and French.

LOKE KHOON TAN, born Singapore; admitted, 1988, Singapore; 1994, Hong Kong. *Education:* National University of Singapore (LL.B.). *Member:* Singapore Law Society; Academy of Law Singapore. *LANGUAGES:* English and Mandarin.

CYNTHIA Y. S. TANG, born Hong Kong, 1964; admitted, 1990, Hong Kong; 1991, England and Wales and A.C.T., Australia. *Education:* University of Nottingham (LL.B., 1987); College of Law, U.K. (Solicitors Final, 1988). *Member:* The Law Society of Hong Kong. *LANGUAGES:* English and Chinese.

RENOUKA TUCKER, born Bangkok, Thailand, 1968; admitted, 1994, Hong Kong. *Education:* S.O.A.S.-London University (LL.B., Upper Second Class Honours, 1990); Hong Kong University (P.C.LL., 1992).

PHILIP A. WALDEN, born England; admitted, 1986, Solicitor of Supreme Court of England; 1991, Hong Kong. *Education:* University of Sheffield (LL.B., Hons.); Kings College University of London (Msc.). *Member:* Law Society of England and Wales.

SIN YEE WONG, born Hong Kong, 1960; admitted, 1992, Hong Kong. *Education:* University of Hong Kong (V & II, 1982); Newcastle Polytechnic, Newcastle, England (Law Society Final, 1989). *Member:* Law Society of Hong Kong. *LANGUAGES:* Cantonese, Mandarin and English.

(This Listing Continued)

STEVE S. WOO, born Hong Kong, 1967; admitted, 1993, Hong Kong. *Education:* University of Hong Kong (LL.B., 1989). *LANGUAGES:* Chinese, English and Mandarin.

SHARON P. YAU, born Guangzhou, China, 1966; admitted, 1991, Hong Kong; 1992, England and Wales. *Education:* University of Hong Kong (LL.B., 1988; P.C.LL., 1989). *Member:* Law Society of Hong Kong. *LANGUAGES:* Chinese (Mandarin, Cantonese) and English.

CHLOROPHYLL W. Y. YIP, born Hong Kong, 1967; admitted, 1993, Hong Kong. *Education:* University of Hong Kong (LL.B., Hons., 1990; P.C.LL., 1991; LL.M., 1993). *LANGUAGES:* English, Cantonese and Mandarin.

RICKY C. W. YIU, born Hong Kong, 1964; admitted, 1992, Hong Kong. *Education:* The Chinese University of Hong Kong (B.Sc., 1986); Manchester Polytechnic, U.K. (Common Professional Exam., 1989; Law Society's Final, 1990). *Member:* Law Society of Hong Kong. *LANGUAGES:* English and Chinese.

CHRISTINA S. Y. YU, born Hong Kong, 1966; admitted, 1991, Hong Kong. *Education:* University of Hong Kong (LL.B., with honors, 1988; P.C.LL., 1989). *LANGUAGES:* English, Cantonese and Mandarin.

PRISCILLA H. S. YU, born Hong Kong, 1965; admitted, 1989, Hong Kong. *Education:* University of Hong Kong (LL.B., 1988). *Member:* Law Society of Hong Kong; Hong Kong Federation of Women Lawyers. *LANGUAGES:* English and Cantonese.

LAP YAN YUNG, born Hong Kong, 1965; admitted, 1993, Hong Kong. *Education:* University of Hong Kong (LL.B., 1988; P.C.LL., 1989); University of London (LL.M., 1991). *LANGUAGES:* Cantonese, English and Mandarin.

SARA YANG BOSCO, born South Bend, Indiana, 1958; admitted, 1984, New York, U.S.A. (Not admitted in Hong Kong). *Education:* University of Notre Dame, Notre Dame, Indiana (B.A., 1980); Indiana University School of Law, Bloomington, Indiana (J.D., 1983). *Member:* New York State and American Bar Associations. *LANGUAGES:* English and Mandarin-Chinese.

CHRISTOPHER M. BUCHAN, born Dundee, Scotland, 1966; admitted, 1990, Scotland; 1991, England and Wales (Not admitted in Hong Kong). *Education:* University of Dundee (LL.B., Hons., 1987; Diploma in Legal Practice, 1988). *Member:* Law Society of Scotland; Law Society of England and Wales; London Young Solicitors' Group; Solicitors' European Group. *LANGUAGES:* English.

ANDREW S. CASE, born Hartford, Connecticut, 1965; admitted, 1991, Connecticut, U.S.A.; 1992, New York, U.S.A. (Not admitted in Hong Kong). *Education:* Yale University (B.A., 1987); Columbia University (J.D., 1991). *Member:* Connecticut, New York State and American Bar Associations. *LANGUAGES:* English and Mandarin.

H. THEODORE CHANG, born New York, N.Y., 1962; admitted, 1993, New York, U.S.A. (Not admitted in Hong Kong). *Education:* Vassar College (A.B., 1984); Columbia University (M.A., 1991); Boston College Law School (J.D., 1991). *Member:* New York State Bar Association. *LANGUAGES:* Chinese (Cantonese and Mandarin), German and English.

ANNIE A. Y. CHEN, born Hong Kong, 1962; admitted, 1988, California, U.S.A. (Not admitted in Hong Kong). *Education:* University of Hong Kong; Brown University (B.A., magna cum laude, 1985); Columbia University (J.D., 1988). Harlan Fiske Stone Scholar. *Member:* State Bar of California; American Bar Association. *LANGUAGES:* English, Cantonese and Mandarin.

LANCE C. H. CHEN, born Taipei, Taiwan, 1962; admitted, 1991, California, U.S.A. (Not admitted in Hong Kong). *Education:* National Taiwan University (B.A., 1984); Santa Clara University (J.D., cum laude, 1991). *Member:* State Bar of California; American Bar Association. *LANGUAGES:* Mandarin and English.

MAGGIE C. F. CHENG, born Hong Kong, 1969; admitted, 1993, New South Wales, Australia (Not admitted in Hong Kong). *Education:* College of Law, Sydney, Australia (Graduate Diploma, 1993); University of New South Wales (Bachelor, 1993). *Member:* Associate of Australian Society of Accountants. *LANGUAGES:* Cantonese, English and Mandarin.

ELIZABETH A. CHIPPINDALE, born Toronto, Canada; admitted, 1992, Ontario, Canada (Not admitted in Hong Kong). *Education:* McMaster University; University of Ottawa (LL.B., 1990); Golden Gate University (LL.M., Tax, 1992). *Member:* Canadian Bar Association; International

(This Listing Continued)

Fiscal Association; Canadian Tax Foundation. *LANGUAGES:* English.

ALEXANDER G. CHRISTIE, born Australia, 1962; admitted, 1989, New South Wales, Australia (Not admitted in Hong Kong). *Education:* Macquarie University (B.A., Hons.; LL.B., 1987); Amsterdam University, The Netherlands (Post Grad Diploma EE.C., Law, 1989).

WEI HAN CHUNG, born Singapore, 1968; admitted, 1991, Singapore (Not admitted in Hong Kong). *Education:* National University of Singapore (LL.B., 1991). *LANGUAGES:* English and Chinese.

THAO H. CUNG, born Saigon, Vietnam, 1967; admitted, 1992, California, U.S.A. (Not admitted in Hong Kong). *Education:* University of California at Berkeley (B.A., 1989); Harvard Law School (J.D., 1992). *Member:* State Bar of California. *LANGUAGES:* English and Vietnamese.

LINDA A. DE SILVA, born Manama, Bahrain, 1962; admitted, 1989, New South Wales, Australia (Not admitted in Hong Kong). *Education:* University of Adelaide (B.A., 1982); University of Sydney (LL.B., 1987).

JOHN V. GROBOWSKI, born Cleveland, Ohio, 1947; admitted, 1988, District of Columbia, U.S.A. (Not admitted in Hong Kong). *Education:* Denison University (B.A., 1970); University of Chicago (M.A., 1979); Beijing University; George Washington University (J.D., 1988). *Member:* The District of Columbia Bar; American Bar Association (Member, International Law and Practice Section). *LANGUAGES:* English and Chinese.

VICTOR HO, born Boston, Massachusetts, 1967; admitted, 1992, California, U.S.A. (Not admitted in Hong Kong). *Education:* Amherst College (B.A., Comparative Religions, cum laude, 1988); International Institute for Human Rights and International Law, Strasbourg (Certificate, 1988); University of California School of Law (J.D., 1991). *LANGUAGES:* Cantonese and Mandarin.

STANLEY D. JIA, born China, 1962; admitted, 1989, New York. U.S.A. (Not admitted in Hong Kong). *Education:* Zhongshan University, Guangzhou, China (LL.B., 1984); University of California, Boalt Hall School of Law (LL.M., 1986); New York University School of Law (LL.M., 1987). *Member:* American Bar Association. *LANGUAGES:* English and Chinese.

ANDREAS W. LAUFFS, born Duesseldorf, Germany, 1958; admitted, 1991, New York, U.S.A.; 1992, Germany (Not admitted in Hong Kong). *Education:* Friedrich-Wilhelms University, Bonn (Dip. in Modern Chinese Language, 1983; First Legal State Exam., 1985; Ph.D., in Law, 1989; Second Legal State Exam, 1989); Cornell University (LL.M., 1991). Lecturer, Friedrich-Wilhelms University, Bonn, Chinese Law, 1988. *Member:* German-Chinese Lawyers Association; European Association for Chinese Law; German-Japanese Lawyers Association. *LANGUAGES:* English, German, Mandarin, Japanese and French.

HANH LE YOUNG, born My Tho, Vietnam, 1963; admitted, 1994, Washington, U.S.A. (Not admitted in Hong Kong). *Education:* Oberlin College (B.A., 1986); University of Washington (J.D., 1994). *Member:* Washington State and American Bar Associations; Hong Kong Vietnam Business Association. *LANGUAGES:* English, Vietnamese and French.

ROBERT D. LEWIS, born Bakersfield, California, 1957; admitted, 1985, California, U.S.A. (Not admitted in Hong Kong). *Education:* Brigham Young University (B.A., 1982; J.D., 1985). Guest Lecturer, Fudan University Department of Law, Shanghai, People's Republic of China, Winter Term, 1993. *LANGUAGES:* Mandarin Chinese.

CHIANG LING LI, born Guangzhou, China, 1966; admitted, 1994, Ontario, Canada (Not admitted in Hong Kong). *Education:* University of Toronto (B.Sc., 1989); Queen's University Law School (LL.B., 1992). *LANGUAGES:* Chinese and English.

MEI YIN LIM, born Singapore, 1967; admitted, 1991, Singapore; 1994, England and Wales (Not admitted in Hong Kong). *Education:* National University of Singapore (LL.B., Hons., 1990). *Member:* Singapore Academy of Law. *LANGUAGES:* English, Mandarin and Cantonese.

SEOK HUI LIM, born Singapore, 1967; admitted, 1990, England and Wales; 1991; Singapore (Not admitted in Hong Kong). *Education:* London School of Economics (LL.B., 1989). *Member:* Law Society of Singapore; English Bar Association; The Honourable Society of Gray's Inn. *LANGUAGES:* English, Chinese (Mandarin and Hokkien) and Japanese.

SHIH YANN LOO, born Thailand, 1964; admitted, 1989, England and Wales; 1991, Singapore (Not admitted in Hong Kong). *Education:* University of London (LL.B., 1988); Council of Legal Education (Barrister-at-Law, 1989). *Member:* English Bar Association; Singapore Law Society; Gray's Inn (England). *LANGUAGES:* English, Mandarin and Cantonese.

CHUN FAI LUI, born Singapore, 1963; admitted, 1989, Singapore (Not admitted in Hong Kong). *Education:* National University of Singapore (LL.B., Hons., 1988); Keio University (Japanese Language Studies, 1992); China University of Politics and Law (P.R.C. Law Course, 1994). *Member:* Law Society of Singapore; The Academy of Law, Singapore; Inter-Pacific Bar Association. *LANGUAGES:* English, Mandarin, Cantonese and Japanese.

DAVID E. NEUVILLE, born Queens, New York, 1960; admitted, 1986, New York, U.S.A. (Not admitted in Hong Kong). *Education:* Swarthmore College (B.A., 1982); Harvard Law School (J.D., 1985). *LANGUAGES:* English.

ANDREW W. PETRY, born Elsinore, Denmark, 1966; admitted, 1992, England and Wales (Not admitted in Hong Kong). *Education:* Pembroke, Oxford, England (1988); Willems Universität, Münster, Germany; College of Law, Chester (1989). *LANGUAGES:* English, German, Dutch and French.

PHILANA WAI-YIN POON, born Hong Kong, 1967; admitted, 1993, New York and New Jersey, U.S.A.; 1994, District of Columbia, U.S.A. (Not admitted in Hong Kong). *Education:* University of Toronto (B.Comm., 1989); Cornell University (J.D., 1992). *Member:* New York State and American (Student Category, 1989-1992) Bar Associations; District of Columbia Bar. *LANGUAGES:* English, Chinese (Cantonese) and French.

IAIN C. L. SEOW, born Singapore, 1966; 1991, Called to the Bar of England and Wales; admitted, 1993, Singapore (Not admitted in Hong Kong). *Education:* King's College, London (LL.B., 1990). *Member:* Law Society of Singapore; General Council of the Bar (U.K.). *LANGUAGES:* English and Mandarin.

JEFFREY R. SIMS, born Oakland, California; admitted, 1994, California, U.S.A. (Not admitted in Hong Kong). *Education:* Stanford University (B.A.); Columbia University (M.A.); Harvard University (J.D., 1994). *Member:* State Bar of California. *LANGUAGES:* English, Chinese (Mandarin), Japenese and Italian.

CHRISTOPHER W. SMITH, born Tunbridge Wells, England, 1966; admitted, 1994, England and Wales (Not admitted in Hong Kong). *Education:* Leeds University (B.A., 1988); Manchester Polytechnic (C.P.E., 1991; L.S.F., 1992). *LANGUAGES:* English, Mandarin and French.

PETER J. STIRLING, born Perth, Western Australia, 1966; admitted, 1991, Western Australia (Not admitted in Hong Kong). *Education:* University of Western Australia (B.A., 1989; B. of Juris., 1989; Bachelor of Laws, 1990).

RICHARD Y. SUNG, born Taipei, Taiwan, 1965; admitted, 1991, California and U.S. District Court, Central District of California, U.S.A. (Not admitted in Hong Kong). *Education:* Columbia University (B.A., 1987); University of California at Los Angeles School of Law (J.D., 1991); University of California at Los Angeles Graduate School of Management (M.B.A., 1991). Staff and Business Editor, Pacific Basin Law Journal, 1989-1991. *LANGUAGES:* English, Chinese (Mandarin and Cantonese) and Japanese.

ANDREW C. K. TAN, born Penang, Malaysia, 1965; admitted, 1989, Singapore; 1994, England and Wales (Not admitted in Hong Kong). *Education:* The National University of Singapore (LL.B., Hons., 1988). *Member:* Law Society of Singapore; The Academy of Law, Singapore. *LANGUAGES:* English, Mandarin, Malay and Hokkien.

GREGORY WOO HIN TAN, born Singapore, 1967; admitted, 1994, England and Wales (Not admitted in Hong Kong). *Education:* King's College, London (LL.B., 1992); College of Law, London, England (1993). *Member:* Law Society of England and Wales. *LANGUAGES:* English and Mandarin.

HUEY S. TAN, born Malaysia, 1966; admitted, 1991, England and Wales (Not admitted in Hong Kong). *Education:* University of London (LL.B., 1988); College of Law, Guildford (Solicitors Exam, 1991). *Member:* Law Society of England and Wales. *LANGUAGES:* English and Mandarin.

JEFFERSON P. VANDERWOLK, born Boston, Massachusetts, 1956; admitted, 1986, New York and New Hampshire, U.S.A. (Not admitted in Hong Kong). *Education:* Boston University (B.A., 1979); The American University, Cairo, Egypt (M.A., 1981); Columbia University (J.D., 1985). Lecturer, Faculty of Law, University of Hong Kong, 1991-1994. Senior Correspondent, Tax Notes International, 1991—. Hong Kong Correspondent, Bulletin for Fiscal Documentation, 1991—. *Member:* New York State, New Hampshire and American Bar Associations; International Fiscal As-

(This Listing Continued)   *(This Listing Continued)*

BAKER & McKENZIE, Hong Kong—Continued

sociation; Taxation Institute of Hong Kong (Council Member). *LAN-GUAGES:* English.

DANCHI WANG, born Beijing, China; admitted, 1990, New York, U.S.A. (Not admitted in Hong Kong). *Education:* Wellesley College (B.A., 1986); Harvard Law School (J.D., 1989). *LANGUAGES:* Chinese and English.

CORINNA M. WONG, born Toronto, Ontario, 1968; admitted, 1993, California, U.S.A. (Not admitted in Hong Kong). *Education:* University of California at Los Angeles (B.A., 1990); Boston University (J.D., 1993). *Member:* State Bar of California (Member, Taxation Section). *LAN-GUAGES:* English, Cantonese and Mandarin.

HELEN H. YEE, born Los Angeles, California, 1963; admitted, 1992, California, U.S.A. (Not admitted in Hong Kong). *Education:* California State University, Los Angeles (B.A., 1988); University of California, Hastings College of the Law (J.D., 1991). *Member:* San Francisco County (Immigration Committee, 1994—) and Alameda County (Immigration Council, 1994—) Bar Associations; State Bar of California; American Immigration Lawyers Association. *LANGUAGES:* English, Cantonese and Spanish.

DANIAN ZHANG, born Shanghai, China, 1958; admitted, 1990, Pennsylvania, U.S.A.; 1991, District of Columbia, U.S.A. (Not admitted in Hong Kong). *Education:* Fudan University School of Law (LL.B., 1986); Duke University School of Law (J.D., 1989); Fudan University, International Politics Department (LL.B., 1993). *Member:* American Bar Association. *LANGUAGES:* Chinese (Shanghai dialect and Mandarin).

YULIN ZHANG, born Zhejiang, China, 1963; admitted, 1988, People's Republic of China (Not admitted in Hong Kong). *Education:* Beijing University (B.A., 1987; LL.B., 1987; Graduate, 1989); University of British Columbia (LL.M., 1994). *Member:* American Society of International Law.

BARLOW LYDE & GILBERT

Established in 1986

4001 GLOUCESTER TOWER
THE LANDMARK, CENTRAL
HONG KONG
Telephone: 526 4202
Telex: 82205 BLG HK
Fax: 810 5994

London, England Office: Beaufort House, 15 St. Botolph Street, London EC3A 7NJ. Telephone: 0171-247 2277. Telex: 913281. Fax: 0171-782 8500.

Other London, England Office: Suite 893, Lloyd's, One Lime Street, London EC3M 7DQ. Telephone: 0171-782 8051. Fax: 0171-782 8053.

Insurance, Reinsurance, Professional Indemnity, Aerospace, Medico-Legal, Product Liability, Commercial and Technical Litigation, Shipping.

RESIDENT PARTNERS

CHRISTOPHER S.K. SHARROCK. LANGUAGES: English. *PRAC-TICE AREAS:* Arbitration; Litigation; Professional Indemnity; Insurance.

RODERICK WHITE. LANGUAGES: English. *PRACTICE AREAS:* Shipping; Arbitration; Litigation; Insurance; Commodities; International Trade; Aerospace.

PETER MILLS. LANGUAGES: English. *PRACTICE AREAS:* Shipping; Arbitration; Litigation; Commodities; Insurance.

JULIAN RANDALL. LANGUAGES: English. *PRACTICE AREAS:* Arbitration; Litigation; Professional Indemnity; Insurance; Defamation.

BEITEN BURKHARDT MITTL & WEGENER

Rechtsanwälte

605 B, SIXTH FLOOR, PEREGRINE TOWER
LIPPO CENTER
89 QUEENSWAY
HONG KONG
Telephone: (852) 2524 6468
Telefax: (852) 2524 7028

Munich, Germany Office: Leopoldstrasse 236, D-80807. Telephone: (089) 35065-00. Telefax: (089) 35065-123.

Berlin, Germany Office: Kurfürstenstrasse 72-74, D-10787 Berlin. Telephone: (0 30) 264 71-0. Telefax: (0 30) 264 71-123.

Frankfurt/Main, Germany Office: Arndtstrasse 28, D-60325 Frankfurt/Main. Telephone: (0 69) 75 60 95-0. Telefax: (0 69) 75 60 95-12.

Nürnberg, Germany Office: Obere Turnstrasse 8, D-90429 Nürnberg. Telephone: (09 11) 2 79 71-0. Telefax: (09 11) 2 79 71-99.

Leipzig, Germany Office: Käthe-Kollwitz-Strasse 54, D-04109 Leipzig. Telephone: (03 41) 4 77 25 97. Telefax: (03 41) 4 77 25 99.

Potsdam, Germany Office: Heinrich-Mann-Allee 105 B, D-14473 Potsdam. Telephone: (0331) 33 43 06. Telefax: (0331) 33 43 29.

Hof, Germany Office: Oberer Torplatz 1, D-95028 Hof. Telephone: (09281) 80 23. Telefax: (09281) 1 65 69.

Plauen, Germany Office: Lindenstrasse 5, D-08523 Plauen. Telephone: (03741) 22 35 11; 22 49 62. Telefax: (03741) 22 49 62.

New York, New York Office: 215 East 73rd Street, New York, NY 10021. Telephone: (212) 570-2141. Telefax: (212) 734-7011.

London, England Office: Swedenborg House, 21 Bloomsbury Way, London, WC1A 2TH. Telephone: (0171) 2 42 44 66. Telefax: (0171) 2 42 44 67.

Moscow, Russia Office: Ul. Alekseja Tolstovo D.30/1, 103001 Moscow. Telephone and Telefax: (095) 202 37 60; 290 05 56.

Prague, Czech Republic Office: Na Bojišti 24, 120 00 Prague 2. Telephone: (2) 24 91 5808. Telefax: (2) 24 91 5804.

Budapest, Hungary Office: József Nádor Tér 9, H-1051 Budapest. Telephone: (1) 2 66 18 10. Telefax: (1) 2 66 18 11.

Beijing, People's Republic of China Office: Unit 10, 29th Floor, Jing Guang Centre, Hu Jia Lou, Chao Yang Qu, 100020. Telephone: (86-1) 501 4569; 501 3388 Ext. 2910. Telefax: (86-1) 501 3034.

Commercial Law, Company Law, M & A, Joint Ventures, Finance, Banking, Leasing, Domestic and International Tax, Antitrust, EC Law, Real Property and Private Construction, Electronic Data Processing (Protection and Licensing), Media, Publishing, Unfair Competition, Trademarks, Copyright, Labour, General and Special Administrative Law Particularly Public Construction and Planning Regulations and Public International Law, Environmental Law, Agricultural Law, Privatization and Restitution (former GDR), Probate, Family and Estate Planning, Insolvency and Sports, Insurance, Automobile Accidents and Injuries.

FIRM PROFILE: BEITEN BURKHARDT MITTL & WEGENER is a nation-wide and international law firm with 108 lawyers. The firm's head office is in Munich. All the firm's offices provide a comprehensive range of services in the main areas of civil and commercial law.

ERNST-ULLRICH TSCHOEPKE, born Clausthal-Zellerfeld, 1955; admitted, 1985, Germany. *Education:* Universities of Marburg, Göttingen, Lausanne, Geneva and Bonn (law degree, 1981). Lecturer for Mining Legislation, Marketing, Fiscal and Legal Environment of Mining for UN and SADDCC. Draftsman for Legislation in Zambia, Swaziland and Angola. With, Tschoepke, Lietzmann, Bülthoff, Essen, 1985-1991; Pritchard Englefield & Wang, Hong Kong, 1991-1994. *Member:* German-Philippine Lawyers Association (Founder Member); German Society for Comparative Law. *LANGUAGES:* German, English and Portuguese. *PRACTICE AREAS:* International Mining Law; Expropriation and Restitution.

JÜRGEN BURKHARDT, born Konstanz, 1940; admitted, 1967, Germany. *Education:* Universities of Munich (law degree, 1963) and Zurich (Swiss law degree, 1966; Dr. jur., 1966). With Axel Springer Verlag, 1965-1968. In-house counsel with Gruner+Jahr, Munich, 1969-1971. Member: Advisory Board, Vogel Medien GmbH & Co. KG, Würzburg; Supervisory Board, rotring international, Hamburg; Legal Committee, German Association of Publishers (VDZ); German-American Chamber of Commerce. Lecturer, Cartel, Competition and Media Law, University of Erlangen-Nürnberg, 1990—. *LANGUAGES:* German, English and Italian. *PRAC-*

(This Listing Continued)

TICE AREAS: Company Law; Acquisitions and Sales; Restructuring; Press Law; Publishing and Radio; Cartels; Probate and Family Law.

DAVID JOHN RIMMER, born Suffolk, England, 1941; admitted, 1966, as Solicitor, England and Wales; 1987, Hong Kong. *Education:* College of Law, London (Law Society Finals Part I, 1961; Law Society Finals Part II, 1965). With, Redifon Flight Simulation Ltd., 1966-1970; In-house Counsel, British Aricraft Corporation, 1970-1973; Rimmers, England, 1973-1986; Private Practice, Hong Kong, 1987. Chairman of Europe Committee, Hong Kong General Chamber of Commerce. Legal Committee Member, Hong Kong Coalition of Service Industries. *Member:* Inter Pacific Bar Association (Council Member). *LANGUAGES:* English and French. *PRACTICE AREAS:* Financial Services; Insolvency; Liquidations.

JENNIFER M.Y. WU, born Hong Kong, 1966; admitted, 1990, as Solicitor, England and Wales; 1991, Hong Kong. *Education:* King's College London (LL.B., 1987); University of Hamburg (LL.M., 1993). With, Clyde & Co., Solicitors, London and Hong Kong, 1988-1991. *LANGUAGES:* Chinese (Cantonese), English and German. *PRACTICE AREAS:* Insolvency; Liquidations.

BLOOM & KRETEN

10/F VOGUE BUILDING
67 WYNDHAM STREET
CENTRAL
HONG KONG
Telephone: 011-85-28-77-80-11

Towson, Maryland Office: 401 Washington Avenue. Telephone: 410-337-2295. Facsimile: 410-337-2296.
Sacramento, California Office: 77 Cadillac Drive. Telephone: 916-921-6181. Fax: 916-921-9213.
European Office: Rue Frans Merjay, 21 B-1060, Brussels, Belgium.

Patent, Trademark and Copyright Law. Patent Litigation, Licensing and International Technology Transfers.

LEONARD BLOOM, born Wilmerding, Pennsylvania, March 2, 1929; admitted, 1957, Maryland and U.S. District Court, District of Maryland; 1981, U.S. Supreme Court; 1982, District of Columbia and U.S. Court of Appeals for the Federal Circuit; registered to practice before U.S. Patent and Trademark Office; registered to practice before Canadian Patent office (Not admitted in Hong Kong). *Education:* The Johns Hopkins University (B.E., 1951); University of Maryland (LL.B., 1957). Member, Order of the Coif. Member, Maryland Law Review, 1956-1957. Associate Professor, Law for Scientists and Engineers, Loyola College of Baltimore, 1980-1981. *Member:* District of Columbia Bar; Bar Association of the District of Columbia; Bar Association of Baltimore City; Baltimore County, Federal and American Bar Associations; American Intellectual Property Law Association; Licensing Executives Society; The Association of Corporate Patent Counsel; Maryland Patent Law Association; Institute of Electrical and Electronic Engineers; United States Trademark Association (Author, Maryland Section, State Trademark and Unfair Competition Law, 1988). [1st Lt., U.S. Air Force, 1951-1953]

BERNHARD KRETEN, born Elizabeth, New Jersey, December 9, 1946; admitted, 1989, California and U.S. District Court, Eastern District of California; 1990, U.S. Court of Appeals, Ninth and Federal Circuits; 1992, U.S. District Court, Central District of California. *Education:* University of Pennsylvania (B.S.M.E., 1970); McGeorge School of Law, University of the Pacific (J.D., cum laude, 1988). National Merit Scholar. Member, Traynor Honor Society, McGeorge School of Law, 1988. Author: Article on Intellectual Property Law, Docket, Sacramento County Bar Associations, April, 1991. *Member:* Sacramento County, Federal Circuit and American Bar Associations; State Bar of California. *LANGUAGES:* French and Latin.

(For complete biographical data on all personnel, see Professional Biographies at Towson, Maryland)

BOUGHTON PETERSON YANG ANDERSON

CITIBANK PLAZA
3602 CITIBANK TOWER
3 GARDEN ROAD CENTRAL
HONG KONG
Telephone: 011-852-877-3088
Fax: 011-852-525-1099

Hong Kong Office: 3602 Citibank Tower, Citibank Plaza, 3 Garden Road Central. Telephone: 852-877-3088. Fax: 852-525-1099.
Taipei, Taiwan Office: Room 605, Bank Tower 205, Tun Hua North Road. Telephone: 886-2-712-0006 Fax: 886-2-719-2145.
Shanghai Office: Flat E, 17th Floor, Block 2 Jin Ming Building, 8 Zun Yi Road South, Shanghai, China, PRC. Telephone: 8621-219-3118.
Affiliated Law Firm: Aird & Berlis, Suite 1800, BCE Place, P.O. Box 754, 181 Bay Street, Toronto, Ontario, M5J 2T9. Telephone: 416-364-1241. Cable Address: "Maxims". Telex: 06-22702. Fax: 416-364-4916.

General, Commercial and Corporate Practice, Intellectual Property, General Litigation (Civil and Criminal) including Trial and Appellate Courts. Administrative and Regulatory Tribunals, Banking, Securities Regulation, Immigration, Taxation, Estate Planning, Commercial and Residential, Real Estate, Bankruptcy and Receivership, Labor Relations, Personal Injury, General Insurance, Natural Resource, Municipal and Transportation Law.

FIRM PROFILE: Boughton Peterson Yang Anderson is a full service law firm committed to serving the needs of our international and domestic clients. We have an extensive Pacific Rim practice with offices in Hong Kong, Taipei and Shanghai.

Boughton Peterson Yang Anderson is affiliated nationally and internationally with the Ontario law firm of Aird & Berlis.

RESIDENT MEMBERS

VICTOR J. YANG, born Shanghai, China, August 19, 1945; admitted, 1974, British Columbia. *Education:* University of British Columbia (B.Comm., 1972; LL.B., 1970). *LANGUAGES:* Cantonese, Mandarin, Shanghainese. *PRACTICE AREAS:* International Practice; Mergers and Acquisitions.

KEVIN S. LEE, admitted, 1984, Nova Scotia; 1986, British Columbia. *Education:* University of British Columbia (B.A., 1980); Dalhousie University (LL.B., 1984). *LANGUAGES:* Cantonese. *PRACTICE AREAS:* Taxation (International); Immigration.

STANLEY CHOW, born Georgetown, Guyana, December 29, 1963; admitted, 1991, Ontario; 1994, England and Wales; British Columbia. *Education:* Queen's University (B.Comm., with honours, 1986); University of Toronto (LL.B., with honours, 1989). *Member:* Law Society of Upper Canada; Law Society of England and Wales. *LANGUAGES:* Cantonese. *PRACTICE AREAS:* Corporate and Commercial; Securities.

LESTER A. WONG, born Hong Kong, July 31, 1966; admitted, 1993, Ontario and British Columbia. *Education:* University of Western Ontario (B.S.C., 1988); University of British Columbia (LL.B., 1991). *LANGUAGES:* Cantonese. *PRACTICE AREAS:* Corporate.

All Members of the Firm are Members of the Vancouver and Canadian Bar Associations and the Law Society of British Columbia.

REPRESENTATIVE CLIENTS: ADI International Co., Ltd., AT & T Global Information Solutions Canada Ltd.; Arnold Brothers Transport Ltd.; Bank of Nova Scotia; B.C. Film; B.C. Utilities Commission; Better Business Bureau of B.C.; Bramalea Ltd.; Brown Bros. Ford Sales & Service Ltd.; Canaccord Capital Corporation; Canada Trustco.; China Resources Ltd.; CITIC Ningbo Inc.; Clearly Canadian Beverage Corporation; Crown Life Insurance Co.; Daewoo International (America) Corp.; Deloitte & Touche; Dun & Bradstreet Canada Ltd.; Federal Business Development Bank; Forest and Marine Financial Corp.; Golden Capital Securities Ltd.; Great West Life; Greater Vancouver Convention & Visitors Bureau; Henderson Land Group; Hong Kong Bank of Canada; Hyatt Hotel; Insurance Corporation of British Columbia; Iritech S.P.A.; Jardine Matheson & Co.; Korea Exchange Bank of Canada; Knowledge Network; Kubota Tractor Canada Ltd.; Lai Sun Group; Laurentian Bank of Canada; Lomak Transportation Corp.; Mutual Life of Canada; Nesbitt Thompson Inc.; N.R.S. Real Estate Service; Penfund Management Ltd.; Peter Kiewit & Sons Co. Ltd.; PHH Home Equity Inc.; Shun Tak Group; Singamas Container Group; Society of Composers, Authors & Music Publishers of Canada; Spelling Television Inc.; Trilea Centres Inc.; Tri-University Meson Facility (UBC); Trizec Corporation Group; Vancouver City Savings Credit Union; Van Waters & Rogers Ltd.; Yellow Freight Systems Inc.

(For Complete Biographical Data on all Personnel see Professional Biographies at Vancouver, British Columbia, Canada.)

ROBIN BRIDGE & JOHN LIU

Established in 1983

22ND FLOOR, LANE CRAWFORD HOUSE
70 QUEEN'S ROAD CENTRAL
HONG KONG
Telephone: (852) 2810-8728
Cable Address: INJUNCt
Fax: (852) 2521-5700

Intellectual Property, Litigation and General Practice.

FIRM PROFILE: *The firm was established in 1983 and offers a full range of legal services. It is well known for its Intellectual Property Law. This 5 partner firm has a legal support staff of 40 consisting of associates, paralegal personnel and office administrators.*

MEMBERS OF FIRM

ROBIN MOORE BRIDGE, born England, March 28, 1943; admitted, 1967, England and Hong Kong; 1981, Victoria, Australia; 1984, Hong Kong as Notary Public. *Education:* Radley College, England; College of Law, Lancaster Gate, London, England. *Member:* Past President, Hong Kong Group of Asian Patent Attorneys Association; Law Reform Commission of Hong Kong, Copyright Subcommittee; Law Society of Hong Kong; The Institute of Trade Mark Agents (UK); European Communities Trade Mark Association; Licensing Executive Society; International Trade Mark Association; International Association for the Protection of Industrial Property; Anti-Counterfeiting Group (UK); The Chartered Institute of Patent Agents (Overseas Member). *LANGUAGES:* English. *PRACTICE AREAS:* Intellectual Property Law; Civil Litigation.

JOHN YEE-MAN LIU, born Hong Kong, December 28, 1953; admitted, 1979, Hong Kong; 1983, England; 1984, Victoria, Australia; 1988, Hong Kong as Notary Public; 1989, Singapore. *Education:* University of Hong Kong (LL.B. Hons, 1976; P.C. LL., 1977). *Member:* Law Society of Hong Kong; Law Society of England and Wales; Asian Patent Attorneys Association. The Notaries' Society (U.K.), Society of Notaries (H.K., Council Member). *LANGUAGES:* English, Mandarin, Cantonese and Chiu Chow. *PRACTICE AREAS:* Corporate and Commercial Law; Civil Litigation; Matters Relating to the People's Republic of China.

TIMOTHY JOHN HANCOCK, born Surrey, England, March 29, 1953; admitted, 1980, England and Hong Kong. *Education:* Southampton University (LL.B., 1974); College of Law, Guildford, England, 1974-1975. *Member:* Law Society of England and Wales; Law Society of Hong Kong; Licensing Executive Society; International Association for the Protection of Industrial Property; International Trade Mark Association; Asian Patent Attorneys Association. *LANGUAGES:* English. *PRACTICE AREAS:* Intellectual Property Law; Civil Litigation.

ANTHONY CLINTON DUDLEY EVANS, born Wales, February 21, 1953; admitted, 1979, England; 1981, Hong Kong; 1982, Victoria, Australia. *Education:* King's College, London University (LL.B. Hons, 1975). *Member:* Law Society of England and Wales; Law Society of Hong Kong; International Bar Association; Common Law Institute of Intellectual Property; International Trade Mark Association; Asian Patent Attorneys Association; International Association for the Protection of Industrial Property; The Institute of Trade Mark Agents (Overseas Member); Hong Kong Law Society (Member, Standing Committee on Intellectual Property and Civil Litigation Committee). *LANGUAGES:* English. *PRACTICE AREAS:* Intellectual Property Law; Civil Litigation.

ANTHONY TAT-HAY TONG, born Hong Kong, September 14, 1963; admitted, 1990, Hong Kong; 1991, England & Wales, ACT of Australia. *Education:* University of Hong Kong (LL.B., 1987; PCLL, 1988). *Member:* Law Society of Hong Kong; International Trade Mark Association; Asian Patent Attorneys Association. *LANGUAGES:* English, Cantonese and Mandarin. *PRACTICE AREAS:* Civil Litigation; Intellectual Property Law.

ASSOCIATES

HELEN WAI-YEE CHAN, born Hong Kong, December 23, 1967; admitted, 1992, Hong Kong. *Education:* University of Hong Kong (LL.B., 1989; PCLL., 1990). *Member:* The Law Society of Hong Kong. *LANGUAGES:* Cantonese, English and Mandarin. *PRACTICE AREAS:* Conveyancing; Corporate and Commercial; Matrimonial.

LEO HUEN-MING CHENG, born Hong Kong, January 23, 1962; admitted, 1992, Hong Kong. *Education:* The Polytechnic Wolverhampton,
(This Listing Continued)

England (LL.B., 1988); College of Law, Lancaster Gate, England. *Member:* The Law Society of Hong Kong. *LANGUAGES:* Cantonese, English and Mandarin. *PRACTICE AREAS:* Litigation; Commercial.

DONNA MICHELLE NICHOLLS, born New Zealand, April 3, 1966; admitted, 1991, United Kingdom; 1992, Hong Kong. *Education:* Essex University, England (LL.B., 1987); College of Law, Guildford, England (1989); University of Hong Kong (LL.M., 1994). *Member:* Law Society of England and Wales; Law Society of Hong Kong. *LANGUAGES:* English. *PRACTICE AREAS:* Civil Litigation.

SELINA KA-PO WU, born Hong Kong, January 24, 1952; admitted, 1979, Hong Kong; 1982, England; 1983, Australia; 1990, Singapore. *Education:* University of Hong Kong (LL.B., Hons., 1974; P.C.L.L., 1977). *Member:* Law Society of Hong Kong; Law Society of England and Wales. *LANGUAGES:* English and Cantonese. *PRACTICE AREAS:* Conveyancing.

NANCY KEUNG MEI CHUEN, born Hong Kong, April 17, 1968; admitted, 1994, Hong Kong. *Education:* University of Hong Kong (LL.B., 1991; PCLL., 1992). *Member:* The Law Society of Hong Kong. *LANGUAGES:* Cantonese, English and Mandarin. *PRACTICE AREAS:* Conveyancing; Corporate and Commercial; Litigation.

BROWN & WOOD

SUITE 2606, ASIA PACIFIC FINANCE TOWER
CITIBANK PLAZA
3 GARDEN ROAD, CENTRAL
HONG KONG
Telephone: 011-852-2509-7888
Telecopier: 011-852-2509-3110

New York, New York Office: One World Trade Center, 10048-0557.
Telephone: 212-839-5300.
San Francisco, California Office: 555 California Street, 94101-1715.
Telephone: 415-772-1200.
Washington, D.C. Office: 815 Connecticut Avenue, N.W., Suite 701, 20006-4004.
Telephone: 202-973-0600.
Los Angeles, California Office: 10900 Wilshire Boulevard, 90024-3959.
Telephone: 310-443-0200.
London, England Office: Blackwell House, Guildhall Yard.
Telephone: 0171-606-1888.
Trenton, New Jersey Office: 172 West State Street, 08608-1104.
Telephone: 609-393-0303.
Tokyo, Japan Office: Shiroyama JT Mori Building, 3-1 Toranomon 4-chome, Minato-ku.
Telephone: 011-813-5472-5360.

General Practice.
Firm engaged in American and International Law Practice.

RESIDENT PARTNERS

E. MARK WALSH, born Dublin, Ireland, May 23, 1961; admitted, 1986, Ireland; 1987, New York (Not admitted in Hong Kong). *Education:* Trinity College, Dublin (B.A. (Mod), 1984; M. Litt., 1987); King's Inns, Dublin (B.L., 1986).

L. MARKUS WILTSHIRE, born Oklahoma City, Oklahoma, September 18, 1946; admitted, 1982, New York (Not admitted in Hong Kong). *Education:* Oklahoma City University (B.A., 1968); Rice University (Ph.D., 1977); Rutgers University-Newark (J.D., 1981).

RESIDENT ASSOCIATES

CEDRIC TIENWEI CHOU, born Taipei, Taiwan, China, December 14, 1953; admitted, 1991, California (Not admitted in Hong Kong). *Education:* National Chengchi University (B.L., 1976); University of California, Los Angeles (J.D., 1989).

MICHAEL MINXIANG DAI, born Fuzhou, China, October 2, 1963; admitted, 1992, Minnesota (Not admitted in Hong Kong). *Education:* Beijing Foreign Relations Institute (B.A., 1984); Chinese Academy of Social Sciences (Graduate Studies, 1984-1986); Cumberland School of Law (J.D., 1992).

JASON TZU-CHENG KUO, born Taipei, Taiwan, China, June 15, 1967; admitted, 1993, New Jersey; 1994, New York (Not admitted in Hong
(This Listing Continued)

Kong). *Education:* University of Minnesota (B.S., 1988); Georgetown University (J.D., 1993).

(For Complete Biographical Data on all Partners and Associates, see Professional Biographies at New York, New York)

BRYAN CAVE

A Partnership including a Professional Corporation

Established in 1873

SUITE 2106
LIPPO TOWER, 21/F
89 QUEENSWAY
HONG KONG
Telephone: 852-2522-2821
Facsimile: 852-2522-3930

St. Louis, Missouri Office: One Metropolitan Square, 211 North Broadway, Suite 3600, 63102-2750. Telephone: (314) 259-2000. Facsimile: (314) 259-2020.

Washington, D.C. Office: 700 Thirteenth Street, N.W., 20005-3960. Telephone: (202) 508-6000. Facsimile: (202) 508-6200.

New York, N.Y. Office: 245 Park Avenue, 10167-0034. Telephone: (212) 692-1800. Facsimile: (212) 692-1900 and Other New York, N.Y. Office: 575 Lexington Avenue, 10022. Telephone: (212) 371-1660. Facsimile: (212) 593-0243 and Other New York, N.Y. Office: 575 Lexington Avenue, 10022. Telephone: (212) 371-1660. Facsimile: (212) 593-0243.

Kansas City, Missouri Office: 3300 One Kansas City Place, 1200 Main Street, 64141-6914. Telephone: (816) 374-3200. Facsimile: (816) 374-3300.

Overland Park, Kansas Office: 7500 College Boulevard, Suite 1100, 66210-4035. Telephone: (913) 338-7700. Facsimile: (913) 338-7777.

Phoenix, Arizona Office: 2800 North Central Avenue, Twenty-First Floor, 85004-1098. Telephone: (602) 230-7000. Facsimile: (602) 266-5938.

Los Angeles, California Office: 777 South Figueroa Street, Suite 2700. 90017-5418. Telephone: (213) 243-4300. Facsimile: (213) 243-4343.

Santa Monica, California Office: 120 Broadway, Suite 500, 90401-2305. Telephone: (310) 576-2100. Facsimile: (310) 576-2200.

Irvine, California Office: 18881 Von Karman, Suite 250, 92715-1500. Telephone: (714) 757-8100. Facsimile: (714) 757-8106.

London SW1H 9BU England Office: 29 Queen Anne's Gate. Telephone: 011-44-71-222-0511. Facsimile: 011-44-71-222-1240.

Frankfurt, Federal Republic of Germany Office: In Cooperation with Rossbach & Partner, Stresemannallee 33, D-60596 Frankfurt am Main. Telephone: 011-49-69-631 50 24. Facsimile: 011-49-69-631 31 64.

Riyadh 11465 Saudi Arabia Office: In Cooperation with Kadasah Law Firm, P.O. Box 20883. Telephones: 011-966-1-465-1371 and 1165. Facsimile: 011-966-1-464-3789.

Dubai, U.A.E. Office: Al-Mehairi-Bryan Cave, Holiday Centre, Commercial Tower, Suite 1103, P.O. Box 13677, UAE. Telephone: 011-971-4-314-123. Facsimile: 011-971-4-318-287.

General Civil Practice. Administrative, Antitrust, Aviation, Banking, Bankruptcy, Coal, Communications, Computer, Corporate Financing, Corporation, Environmental, Estate Planning, Government Contract, Health Care, Immigration, Intellectual Property, International, Labor, Legislative, Mining, Patent and Trademark, Probate, Products Liability, Real Estate, Securities, Tax Exempt Financing, Taxation, Technology, Transportation, Trust and University Law. General Civil Trial and Appellate Practice.

PARTNERS

CLELLAND PEABODY HUTTON, born Guatemala, 1947; admitted, 1978, New York (Not admitted in Hong Kong). *Education:* University of Virginia (B.A., with honors, 1969; M.A., English, 1973; M.B.A., 1977; J.D., 1977). *Member:* The Association of the Bar of the City of New York; New York State and American Bar Associations. *LANGUAGES:* French and English.

MARY ELLEN MCCONNELL HUTTON, born Pennsylvania, 1947; admitted, 1980, New York (Not admitted in Hong Kong). *Education:* Hollins College (B.A., with honors, 1969); University of Virginia (J.D., 1979). *Member:* New York State and American (Member, Section on Real Property, Probate and Trust Law) Bar Associations; Society of Trust and Estate Practitioners. *LANGUAGES:* French.

(This Listing Continued)

MICHAEL MORGAN, born Ohio, 1950; admitted, 1979, Missouri; 1985, District of Columbia (Not admitted in Hong Kong). *Education:* Princeton University (B.A., 1972); Case Western Reserve University (J.D., 1979). Order of the Coif. *PRACTICE AREAS:* Acquisitions, Divestitures and Mergers Law; International Business Law; Securities Regulation Law.

OF COUNSEL

HUGH T. SCOGIN, JR., born 1950; admitted, 1983, California. *Education:* College of Charleston (B.S., 1981); Harvard University (J.D., 1983). (Also at Santa Monica, California Office).

CHADBOURNE & PARKE

SUITE 3704
PEREGRINE TOWER
LIPPO CENTRE
89 QUEENSWAY
HONG KONG
Telephone: (852) 2842-5400
Telecopier: (852) 2521-7527

New York, N.Y. Office: 30 Rockefeller Plaza, 10112. Telephone: 212-408-5100. Telecopier: 212-541-5369.

Washington, D.C. Office: Suite 900, 1101 Vermont Avenue, N.W., 20005. Telephone: 202-289-3000. Telecopier: 202-289-3002.

Los Angeles, California Office: 601 South Figueroa Street, 90017. Telephone: 213-892-1000. Telecopier: 213-622-9865.

London, England Office: 86 Jermyn Street, SW1 6JD. Telephone: 44-171-925-7400. Facsimile: 44-171-839-3393.

Moscow, Russia Office: 38 Maxim Gorky Naberezhnaya, 113035. Telephone: 7095-974-2424. Telecopier: 7095-974-2425. International satellite lines via U.S.: Telephone: 212-408-1190. Telecopier: 212-408-1199.

New Delhi, India Office: Chadbourne & Parke Associates, A16-B Anand Niketan, 110 021. Telephone: 91-11-301-7568/7581/7582. Telecopier: 91-11-301-7351.

RESIDENT PARTNERS

PETER D. CLEARY, born Calgary, Alberta, Canada, March 30, 1953; admitted, 1980, New York; 1990, California (Not admitted in Hong Kong). *Education:* Princeton University (A.B., 1974); Harvard University (J.D., 1977).

ROBERT J. BOHME, born Brooklyn, New York, September 20, 1957; admitted, 1982, New York and U.S. District Court, Southern District of New York; 1983, U.S. District Court, Eastern District of New York (Not admitted in Hong Kong). *Education:* Fordham College (B.A., summa cum laude, 1978); Fordham University School of Law (J.D., cum laude, 1981). Phi Beta Kappa. Member, Fordham Law Review, 1980-1981.

RESIDENT COUNSEL

MARTIN C.M. BASHALL, born Marlborough, United Kingdom, April 17, 1954; admitted, 1984, England (Not admitted in Hong Kong). *Education:* University of Rhodesia (B.L., 1975); College of Law, England (English Solicitor, 1982). Representative Member, American Business Council of Dubai and Northern Emirates, 1992. *Member:* Law Society of England and Wales; International Bar Association.

RESIDENT ASSOCIATES

KERIN CANTWELL, born September 9, 1963; admitted, 1989, California (Not admitted in Hong Kong). *Education:* Wellesley College (B.A., cum laude, 1985); Harvard University (J.D., 1989). Law Clerk to Hon. Laughlin E. Waters, 1989-1991.

MITCHELL A. SILK, born Chicago, Illinois, October 15, 1961; admitted, 1987, Pennsylvania (inactive); 1989, District of Columbia; 1990, New York (Not admitted in Hong Kong). *Education:* National Taiwan Normal University; Georgetown University (B.S.F.S., 1983); University of Maryland (J.D., 1986); Beijing University (cert. advanced studies in law, 1987). Associate Editor, 1984-1985 and Executive Editor, 1985-1986, Maryland Journal of International Law and Trade. Award for Best Brief in Mid-Atlantic Region of the Phillip C. Jessup International Moot Court Competition. Author: *Taiwan Trade and Investment Law* (Oxford University Press, 1994, 691 pp.); "China's Tax Treaty Relations," 1988 Proceedings of the American Society of International Law; "U.S. China Investment Opportunities Concerning Intellectual Property Transfer," 15 Syracuse Journal of International Law and Commerce 215, 1989; "Legal Efforts of the U.S. and the Republic of China on Taiwan in Controlling the Transnational Flow of

(This Listing Continued)

CHADBOURNE & PARKE, Hong Kong—Continued

Counterfeit Goods," 10 Maryland Journal of International Law and Trade 209, 1986. Co-Author: *Environmental Law and Policy in the People's Republic of China* (1987, 449 pp.); "Transnational Deposits, Government Succession, Frozen Assets and The Taiwan Relations Act: National Bank of Pakistan v. The International Bank of China," 8 International Tax and Business Lawyer 1, 1990. President, International Law Society, 1984-1985. Adjunct Professor of Law: Beijing University, 1986-1987; Shenzhen University, 1987; Shanghai Institute of Foreign Trade, 1987. *Member:* American Bar Association; American Society of International Law; International Association of Jewish Lawyers and Jurists (Member, American Section, Board of Governors, 1991—). *LANGUAGES:* Chinese (Mandarin and Cantonese).

GEORGE HE ZHU, born Shanghai, China, October 6, 1964; admitted, 1992, New York and Oregon (Not admitted in Hong Kong). *Education:* Peking University (LL.B., 1987); Columbia University (J.D., 1991). Member, Portland Chamber of Commerce, 1992, *Member:* Oregon State Bar; American Bar Association; Taiwan Chamber of Commerce; Japan American Society; Northwest Regional China Council. *LANGUAGES:* Mandarin Chinese, Shanghai Dialect.

(For Biographical Data of other Personnel, see Professional Biographies at New York, N.Y., Washington, D.C., Los Angeles, California, London, England, Moscow, Russia and New Delhi, India)

VIVIEN CHAN & CO.

Solicitor & Notaries

Agents for Trade Marks & Patents

15TH FLOOR, ONE EXCHANGE SQUARE
8 CONNAUGHT PLACE
HONG KONG
Telephone: (852) 2522-9183
Fax: (852) 2845-9160

Beijing, China Office: Unit 2706, Jing Guang Centre, Hu Jia Lou, Chao Yang Qu, 100020. Telephone: 501 3388 ext. 27065-7. Facsimile: 501 5127.

Banking, Corporate and Commercial, Tax, Property, Immigration, Intellectual Property, Insolvency, Insurance, Litigation, Family, Mergers and Acquisitions, China Practice, Regional Investment and Legal Expertise.

FIRM PROFILE: *We have an international practice and provide a comprehensive range of legal services to mainly corporate clients on a local and regional basis. The Firm has a substantial China practice, with extensive experience in PRC intellectual property litigation and foreign investment advice. We have an established branch office in Beijing. With the formal appointment and recognition by the Ministry of Justice, PRC to set up our law office in Beijing and appointment of our senior partner, Miss Vivien Chan by the Ministry of Justice, PRC to undertake attesting and notarial duties; we will be able to service our clients investing in China more expeditiously.*

The Firm acts as legal advisors to financial institutions, substantial privately held corporations, public companies and certain private family businesses. We have established affiliates in most countries in Asia.

The Firm currently has 12 lawyers and a paralegal support of over 40 members. The University of Hong Kong awards prizes in the Firm's name each year to students with the best achievement in company law for their undergraduate law course, and civil procedure and international commercial transactions for their graduate law course.

PARTNERS

VIVIEN CHAN, born 1954; admitted, 1981, England and Hong Kong; 1984, Victoria, Australia; 1990, Singapore. *Education:* Reading University (LL.B. Hons); Kings College, London University (LL.M. Hons). Notary Public, Notarial Attesting Officer appointed by Ministry of Justice of the People's Republic of China. Vice Chairman, Hong Kong Committee for UNICEF. Honorary Legal Adviser, Committee Member of Finance Committee and Chairman of Staff Provident Fund Committee, Hong Kong Arts Centre. Honorary Legal Adviser to the Hong Kong Artists' Guild. Honorary Legal Adviser to the Queen Mary Hospital Doctors' Association. Honorary Legal Adviser to the Soong Ching Ling Foundation, Hong Kong. Honorary Legal Adviser to the Direct Selling Association of Hong Kong Limited. Elected District Board Member of Wanchai, Tai Hang and So Kon Po, 1985-1988 and 1988-1991. *LANGUAGES:* English and Chinese (Cantonese and Mandarin). *PRACTICE AREAS:* Banking; Corporate;

(This Listing Continued)

Commercial; Tax; Property; Mergers and Acquisitions; China Practice; Regional Investment and Legal Expertise.

GEORGE A. RIBEIRO, born 1958; admitted, 1984, Hong Kong; 1989, England; 1990, Canberra, Australia. *Education:* Hong Kong University (LL.B. Hons.; P.C.LL.). Demonstrator, Hong Kong University, 1981-1982. *LANGUAGES:* English and Chinese (Cantonese). *PRACTICE AREAS:* Litigation; Commercial Insolvency; Immigration; Insurance; Family.

ADA LEE PIK YUE, born 1962; admitted, 1988, Hong Kong. *Education:* University of Nottingham, London (LL.B.). *LANGUAGES:* English and Chinese (Mandarin and Cantonese). *PRACTICE AREAS:* Conveyancing; Corporate; Commercial.

ASSOCIATES

JACKIE WAH WANG KEI, born 1966; admitted, 1992, Hong Kong. *Education:* University of Hong Kong (LL.B., Hons.; P.C.LL.). *LANGUAGES:* English and Chinese (Cantonese and Mandarin). *PRACTICE AREAS:* Litigation; Insolvency; Family.

GEORGE TUNG MAN KEUNG, born 1964; admitted, 1993, Hong Kong. *Education:* University of Wales Institute of Science and Technology, Cardiff; East London Polytechnic, London (LL.B.). *LANGUAGES:* English, Chinese (Mandarin, Cantonese and Shanghainese) and Malay. *PRACTICE AREAS:* Intellectual Property; Litigation.

JEFFREY MAK CHUN HING, born 1965; admitted, 1992, Hong Kong. *Education:* University of Hong Kong (LL.B., Hons.; P.C.LL.). *LANGUAGES:* English and Chinese (Cantonese and Mandarin). *PRACTICE AREAS:* Construction Arbitration; Property.

HOWARD TSANG HOW LEUNG, born 1956; admitted, 1989, Hong Kong. *Education:* University of Bath (B.Pharm); University of Hong Kong (LL.B., Hons.; P.C.LL.). *Member:* Royal Pharmaceutical Society of Great Britain. *LANGUAGES:* English and Chinese (Cantonese and Mandarin). *PRACTICE AREAS:* Commercial; Intellectual Property; Pharmaceutical Litigation.

CATHY WAN, born 1964; admitted, 1989, Hong Kong; 1991, England and Canberra, Australia. *Education:* University of Keele (B.Soc.S.); The College of Law, London. *LANGUAGES:* English and Chinese (Cantonese and Mandarin). *PRACTICE AREAS:* Banking; China Practice; Commercial; Property; Mergers and Acquisitions.

BONITA CHAN BOW YE, born 1969; admitted, 1994, Hong Kong. *Education:* City Polytechnic of Hong Kong (LL.B., Hons.; P.C.LL.). *LANGUAGES:* English and Chinese. *PRACTICE AREAS:* Litigation.

OF COUNSEL

XI ZHENG ZHENG, born 1967. *Education:* Peking University (B.A.; Degree in Law). *LANGUAGES:* English and Chinese (Mandarin). *PRACTICE AREAS:* Commercial Law.

SINDA GUO WEI, born 1970. *Education:* Beijing Foreign Language University (Graduate).

VINCENT TSO SHIU KEI, born 1966; admitted, 1992, Queensland, Australia. *Education:* University of Queensland (B.Com.; LL.B.). *LANGUAGES:* English and Chinese (Cantonese and Mandarin). *PRACTICE AREAS:* Corporate; Commercial; Australian Practice.

VICTOR CHU & CO.

Solicitors

19TH FLOOR, TOWER II
THE GATEWAY
25 CANTON ROAD
KOWLOON
HONG KONG
Telephone: (852) 29561818
Fax: (852) 29561161/29561162

Banking, Corporate, Commercial, Securities, Mergers and Acquisitions, Property, Litigation and China related matters.

FIRM PROFILE: *Victor Chu, a London-trained lawyer, returned to practise in Hong Kong in 1982 after spending ten years in England. He founded Victor Chu & Co. in 1985 with one specific ambition - to develop a dynamic Hong Kong-based practice with a strong international capability. This remains the Firms's philosophical objective.*

(This Listing Continued)

MEMBERS OF FIRM

VICTOR LAP-LIK CHU, born Guangzhou, China; admitted, 1982, England and Hong Kong; 1984, Victoria, Australia; 1994, Singapore. *Education:* University of London, University College (LL.B., Hons.). 1993, Ministry of Justice of China Appointed Attesting Officer. 1994, Arbitrator, China International Economic and Trade Arbitration Commission. Author: "The Practitioner's Guide to the Hong Kong Codes on Takeovers and Mergers and Share Repurchases," 1993; "Negotiating Contracts in China," French Journal of International Business Law, 1987. Council Member, Hong Kong Stock Exchange, 1988-1991. (Chairman, Membership Committee; Vice-Chairman, Listing Committee). Member, Hong Kong Panel on Takeovers and Mergers, 1988—(Member of Working Party for the revision of the Takeovers Code, 1990-1991), Securities and Futures Commission's Working Party for the revision of Hong Kong's Securities Laws, 1991; Member, Advisory Committee of the Hong Kong Securities & Futures Commission, 1992—; Part time Member, Central Policy Unit of Hong Kong Government, 1993—. *Member:* Law Society of England and Hong Kong; Bentham Club; International Bar Association (Executive Vice Chairman, Hong Kong Host Committee, Section on Business Law Conference in Hong Kong, October, 1991); International Bar Association (Country Representative for Hong Kong, and Council Member of Asia-Pacific Forum); Inter-Pacific Bar Association (Vice-Chairman, Financial Institutions and Transactions Committee). *LANGUAGES:* English and Chinese (Cantonese and Mandarin). *PRACTICE AREAS:* Corporate; Securities; Takeovers and Mergers; China-Related Transactions.

BARBARA WAI KUN MOK, born Hong Kong; admitted, 1983, Hong Kong; 1987, England; 1989, Australia; 1994, Singapore. *Education:* University of Hong Kong (LL.B., Hons., 1980; LL.M., 1988). *Member:* Law Society of Hong Kong; Law Society of England; International Bar Association; Inter-Pacific Bar Association. *LANGUAGES:* English and Chinese (Cantonese and Mandarin). *PRACTICE AREAS:* Corporate; Banking; Securities; China-Related Transactions.

LAWRENCE CHIK-YUEN CHEUNG, born Hong Kong; admitted, 1982, Hong Kong; 1985, England and Wales; 1986, Victoria, Australia. *Education:* University of Hong Kong (LL.B., Hons., 1979; P.C.L.L., 1980). *LANGUAGES:* Chinese (Cantonese, Chiu Chow and Mandarin) and English. *PRACTICE AREAS:* Real Estate Law.

DAVID ALEXANDER RICHARDSON, born Hong Kong; admitted, 1984, British Columbia, Canada; 1987, Hong Kong. *Education:* University of Hong Kong (LL.B., Hons., 1977; P.C.L.L. , 1978); University of British Columbia (LL.B., 1983). *Member:* Law Society of Hong Kong. *LANGUAGES:* English and Chinese (Cantonese). *PRACTICE AREAS:* Corporate; Securities; International Business Transactions.

CONSULTANTS

MARK ALEXANDER PIERREPONT, born Eastbourne, England; admitted, 1983, England; 1992, Hong Kong. *Education:* Eastbourne College Public School and City of London Polytechnic (B.A., Hons.); Guildford Law School, Guildford, England (Law Soc. Finals). *Member:* Law Society of England and Wales; Law Society of Hong Kong. *LANGUAGES:* English. *PRACTICE AREAS:* Commercial Litigation.

ARUN K. NIGAM, born London, England; admitted, 1972, England and Wales; 1980, Hong Kong; 1983, Victoria, Australia; 1984, India; 1985, Brunei; 1990, New South Wales, Australia; 1992, Singapore. *Education:* Gonville and Caius College, Cambridge University (M.A., Hons.). *LANGUAGES:* English, French and German. *PRACTICE AREAS:* Banking; Finance; Corporate; Commercial.

TONY LIONEL HUNTER-TILNEY, born Barrie, Ontario, Canada; admitted, 1972, Barrister, England and Wales; 1979, Solicitor, England and Wales; 1992, Solicitor, Hong Kong. *Education:* Magdalen College, Oxford (B.A., Natural Science, 1969); Inns of Court, School of Laws (Barrister, 1972; Solicitor, 1979). Co-Author: "The Lugano and San Sebastian Conventions," Butterworths, 1990. *Member:* Inner Temple, 1969-1979; Western Circuit, 1974-1978; Law Society of England and Wales, 1979. *LANGUAGES:* English, French and Italian. *PRACTICE AREAS:* Commercial Litigation; Intellectual Property; Administrative and Public Law; European Community Law.

SAMUEL KWUN CHARK YU, born Hong Kong; admitted, 1983, Hong Kong; 1987, England and Wales; 1988, Australian Capital Territory, Australia; 1994, Singapore. *Education:* University of Hong Kong (LL.B., 1980; P.C.L.L., 1981). *Member:* The Law Society of Hong Kong; Asian Patent Attorneys Association (APAA). *LANGUAGES:* Chinese and English. *PRACTICE AREAS:* Intellectual Property Matters.

(This Listing Continued)

ASSOCIATES

WINNIE WING-YAN LAM, born Hong Kong; admitted, 1987, Hong Kong. *Education:* Leicester Polytechnic; College of Law, England. *LANGUAGES:* English and Chinese. *PRACTICE AREAS:* Real Estate Law.

ANGELA MAN KAY HO, born Hong Kong; admitted, 1989, Hong Kong; 1991, England and Australia Capital Territory, Australia. *Education:* York University (M.B.A., 1987); University of Hong Kong (LL.B., 1984; P.C.L.L., 1985). *Member:* Law Society of Hong Kong. *LANGUAGES:* Chinese, English and Japanese. *PRACTICE AREAS:* Corporate and Commercial Transactions.

DAVID MICHAEL BROOKS, born England; admitted, 1989, England; 1992, Hong Kong; 1994, Tasmania, Australia. *Education:* Oriel College, Oxford University (B.A., Hons., 1985); Manchester Polytechnic (1985-1986). *Member:* The Law Society of England. *LANGUAGES:* English. *PRACTICE AREAS:* Corporate; Securities; Takeovers and Mergers.

SIMON JEFFREY MORRIS, born London, England; admitted, 1982, Victoria, Australia; 1993, Hong Kong. *Education:* University of Melbourne (LL.B., B.Comm., 1981). Author: Butterworths Capital Gains Tax Service (sections dealing with capital gains tax), 1989—; Practitioners Guide to the Codes on Takeovers and Mergers and Share Repurchases, 1993. *Member:* Associate, Securities Institute of Australia, 1987—. *LANGUAGES:* English. *PRACTICE AREAS:* Corporate Finance including public capital raisings and takeovers; Public Company Compliance and Legal Audits; Joint Ventures.

ANNABELLA YING LAI WONG, born Hong Kong; admitted, 1989, Hong Kong. *Education:* University of Hong Kong (LL.B., 1986; P.C.L.L., 1987). *LANGUAGES:* Cantonese, English and Mandarin. *PRACTICE AREAS:* Corporate, Commercial and China-Related Transactions.

FRANCES SHUN-LAN HAU, born Hong Kong; admitted, 1991, Hong Kong. *Education:* University of Hong Kong (LL.B., Hons., 1985; P.C.L.L., 1989). *Member:* The Law Society of Hong Kong. *LANGUAGES:* Chinese and English. *PRACTICE AREAS:* Commercial Litigation.

ANNE KO, born Hong Kong; admitted, 1991, Hong Kong. *Education:* Ealing College of Higher Education, England (LL.B., Hons., 1987); University of Hong Kong (P.C.L.L., 1989). *Member:* The Law Society of Hong Kong. *LANGUAGES:* English and Chinese (Mandarin and Cantonese). *PRACTICE AREAS:* Corporate and Commercial Transactions.

MARGUERITE ANNE WALKER, born Kingston, Jamaica; admitted, 1991, Hong Kong. *Education:* University of London, England (LL.B., Hons., 1985); University of Hong Kong (P.C.L.L., 1987). *Member:* The Law Society of Hong Kong. *LANGUAGES:* English and French. *PRACTICE AREAS:* Corporate, Commercial and Securities Law.

JEFFREY JIE WANG, born Shenyang, China; admitted, 1985, People's Republic of China; 1990, Virginia, U.S.A. *Education:* Jilin University (LL.B., 1981); Foreign Affairs Institute (LL.M., 1984); Duke University (LL.M., 1988). Associate Legal Advisor, Ministry of Foreign Affairs, P.R. China, 1985-1990. *Member:* American Bar Association; China Society of International Law; China Association of Lawyers. *LANGUAGES:* Chinese and English. *PRACTICE AREAS:* Corporate, Commercial and China-Related Transactions.

LOUISA S.M. LAM, born Hong Kong; admitted, 1990, Hong Kong. *Education:* University of Hong Kong (LL.B., 1987; P.C.L.L., 1988). *Member:* The Law Society of Hong Kong. *LANGUAGES:* Chinese (Cantonese), English and Japanese. *PRACTICE AREAS:* Real Estate Law.

NICOLA JANE WON, born Wellington, New Zealand; admitted, 1989, New Zealand; 1993, Hong Kong. *Education:* Victoria University of Wellington (LL.B., B.C.A., 1988). New Zealand Practicing Certificates, 1990-1992. Part-time tutor of Commercial Law, 1988-1989. *Member:* Wellington District Law Society; Auckland District Law Society. *LANGUAGES:* English. *PRACTICE AREAS:* Corporate, Commercial and Securities Law.

STANLEY WING LEUNG CHAN, born Hong Kong; admitted, 1994, Hong Kong. *Education:* The Chinese University of Hong Kong (B.S.Sc., 1985); University of Wales (LL.B., 1990); University of Hong Kong (P.C.L.L., 1992). *Member:* The Law Society of Hong Kong, Hong Kong (1994). *LANGUAGES:* English, Cantonese, Mandarin and Japanese. *PRACTICE AREAS:* Corporate and Commercial Law; China-related Transactions.

KELLY YIM MAN POON, born Hong Kong, February 1, 1962; admitted, 1994, Hong Kong. *Education:* Southern Illinois University (B.A., 1985; M.A., 1986); Manchester Polytechnic (C.P.E., 1991); University of Hong Kong (P.C.L.L., 1992). *Member:* The Law Society of Hong Kong (1994).

(This Listing Continued)

VICTOR CHU & CO., Hong Kong—Continued

LANGUAGES: English and Chinese (Cantonese and Mandarin). **PRACTICE AREAS:** Corporate and Commercial Law; Securities Law; China Related Transactions.

YING LI, born Changchun, People's Republic of China, March 28, 1962; admitted, 1994, Hong Kong. *Education:* Peking University (LL.B., 1984; LL.M., 1987); Harvard Law School (J.D., 1994). **LANGUAGES:** Chinese (Mandarin), English.

LEGAL SUPPORT PERSONNEL

ELIZABETH KA-YEE KAN, born Hong Kong; admitted, 1990, Certified Public Accountant. *Education:* American Institute of Certified Public Accountants; University of Minnesota, Minneapolis (B.A., Economics and B.S.B., Accounting, 1981). *Member:* Hong Kong Society of Accountants. **LANGUAGES:** English and Chinese.

ANGEL M.Y. HO, born Hong Kong; admitted, 1992, Certified Public Accountant, Hong Kong and United Kingdom. *Education:* Hong Kong Polytechnic. *Member:* The Chartered Association of Certified Accountants; The Hong Kong Society of Accountants. **LANGUAGES:** English and Chinese.

GRACE KAR-WAH LAM, born Hong Kong. *Education:* Hong Kong Polytechnic (1980-1983). (Office Management, Personnel and Administration). **LANGUAGES:** Cantonese, Mandarin and English.

ELLEN MO-YIN CHIU, born Hong Kong; admitted, 1986, Certified Public Accountant. *Education:* University of Illinois at Urbana-Champaign (B.S., Accountancy, Hons., 1983). *Member:* American Institute of Certified Public Accountants; Illinois CPA Society. **LANGUAGES:** Chinese and English.

IVAN HO YIN WONG, born Hong Kong. *Education:* Aston University (B.Sc., 1984). *Member:* AMIEE (1984). **LANGUAGES:** Cantonese and English. **PRACTICE AREAS:** Intellectual Property Matters.

CLEARY, GOTTLIEB, STEEN & HAMILTON

Established in 1946

56TH FLOOR
BANK OF CHINA TOWER
ONE GARDEN ROAD
HONG KONG
Telephone: 852-521-4122
Cable Address: "Cleargolaw, Hong Kong"
Telex: 60401 Clear HX
Fax: 852-845-9026

New York, New York Office: One Liberty Plaza, New York, N.Y. 10006. Telephone: 212-225-2000.

Washington, D.C. Office: 1752 N Street, N.W., Washington, D.C. 20036. Telephone: 202-728-2700.

Paris, France Office: 41, Avenue de Friedland, 75008 Paris, France. Telephone: 33-1-4074-6800.

Brussels, Belgium Office: Rue de la Loi 23, Bte 5, 1040 Brussels, Belgium. Telephone: 32-2-287-2000.

London, England Office: City Place House, 55 Basinghall Street, London, EC2V 5EH, England. Telephone: 44-71-614-2200.

Tokyo, Japan Office: Morgan Carroll Terai Gaikokuho Jimu Bengoshi Jimusho, 20th Floor, Shin Kasumigaseki Building, 3-2, Kasumigaseki 3-Chome, Chiyoda-Ku, Tokyo 100, Japan. Telephone: 81-3-3595-3911.

Frankfurt, Germany Office: Ulmenstrasse 37-39, 60325 Frankfurt am Main, Germany. Telephone: 49-69-971-03-0.

Firm engaged in American and International Practice, but not authorized to appear before the Hong Kong Courts or to act as Solicitors.

RESIDENT PARTNERS

ROBERT P. DAVIS, born Newark, New Jersey, February 16, 1953; admitted, 1979, New York (Not admitted in Hong Kong). *Education:* Yale University (B.A., 1975); Cornell Law School (J.D., magna cum laude, 1978). Note Editor, Cornell Law Review, 1977-1978. Resident at: New York Office, 1978-1993; Hong Kong Office, 1993—. *Member:* Association of the Bar of the City of New York; American Bar Association.

CHRISTOPHER E. AUSTIN, born Cincinnati, Ohio, September 23, 1958; admitted, 1984, New York (Not admitted in Hong Kong). *Education:*

(This Listing Continued)

Tulane University of Louisiana (B.A., 1980); New York University (J.D., cum laude, 1982). Phi Beta Kappa; Order of the Coif. Senior Note and Comment Editor, New York University Law Review, 1982-1983. Author: "Due Process, Court Access Fees and the Right to Litigate," 57 New York University Law Review 768, 1982. Resident at: New York Office, 1983-1993; Hong Kong Office, 1993—.

SPECIAL COUNSEL

MICHAEL M. HICKMAN, born Hillsboro, Illinois, October 30, 1957; admitted, 1986, New York (Not admitted in Hong Kong). *Education:* University of Washington (B.A., 1979); University of Washington Law School (J.D., 1985).

ASSOCIATES

JINDUK HAN, born Seoul, Korea, June 18, 1963; admitted, 1989, New York (Not admitted in Hong Kong). *Education:* Columbia University (B.A., 1985); Harvard Law School (J.D., cum laude, 1988).

DAVID W. HIRSCH, born Seattle, Washington, December 24, 1959; admitted, 1989, New York (Not admitted in Hong Kong). *Education:* Princeton University (A.B., 1982); Keio University (1983-1984, Rotary Graduate Scholarship); Harvard Law School (J.D., cum laude, 1988). Articles Editor, Harvard International Law Journal, 1987-1988. Legal Trainee, Nagashima & Ohno, Tokyo, Japan, 1988. Resident at: New York Office, 1989-1991; Tokyo Office, 1991-1994; Hong Kong, 1994—. *Member:* American Bar Association.

LAURIE A. SMILEY, born Seattle, Washington, August 23, 1959; admitted, 1990, Delaware; 1991, New York (Not admitted in Hong Kong). *Education:* Whitman College (B.A., 1981); Tulane Law School (J.D., magna cum laude, 1989).

DAVID F. JOHNSON, born Kingston, Jamaica, April 25, 1964; admitted, 1991, New York (Not admitted in Hong Kong). *Education:* University of the West Indies (LL.B., 1986); New York University (J.D., 1990). *Member:* Association of the Bar of the City of New York.

FABRICE BAUMGARTNER, born Vevey, Switzerland, August 13, 1965; admitted, 1990, Paris; 1992, New York (Not admitted in Hong Kong). *Education:* University of Paris IX Dauphine (Maîtrise en Sciences de Gestion, 1987); University of Paris II Assas (Maîtrise en Droit Privé, 1987, D.E.A. Droit Privé, 1989); University of Chicago (LL.M., 1991). Resident at: Paris Office, 1991-1994; Hong Kong Office, 1994—.

YONG G. LEE, born Seoul, Korea, May 11, 1964; admitted, 1992, New York (Not admitted in Hong Kong). *Education:* Princeton University (B.A., 1986); Harvard Law School (J.D., cum laude, 1989).

(For biographical data of the partners resident in other offices of the Firm, see Professional Biographies at New York, N.Y., Washington, D.C., Paris, France, Brussels, Belgium, London, England, Tokyo, Japan, Frankfurt, Germany).

CLIFFORD CHANCE

Established in 1980

30TH FLOOR, JARDINE HOUSE
ONE CONNAUGHT PLACE
HONG KONG
Telephone: (852) 2810 0229
Fax: (852) 2810 4708; 2810 4858; 2810 4743

Amsterdam, The Netherlands Office: Apollolaan 171, 1077 AS, P.O. Box 7301, 1007 JH. Telephone: (31 20) 577 71 11. Fax: (31 20) 676 93 26.

Bahrain, Manama Associated Office: Law Office of Shaikh Isa bin Mohammed Al Khalifa. P.O. Box 20717. Telephone: (973) 531535; 531073. Fax: (973) 536272; 530608.

Barcelona, Spain Office: Pau Claris 102, 08009. Telephone: (34 3) 318 68 64. Fax: (34 3) 317 73 23.

Brussels, Belgium Office: Avenue Louise 65, Box 2, 1050. Telephone: (32 2) 533 59 11. Fax: (32 2) 533 59 59.

Budapest, Hungary Office: Köves & Partners, Clifford Chance. Madách Trade Center, Madách Imre Út 14, 1075. Telephone: (36 1) 268 1600. Fax: (36 1) 268 1610.

Dubai, United Arab Emirates Office: 18th Floor, Dubai World Trade Centre, P.O. Box 9380. Telephone: (971 4) 314333. Fax: (971 4) 313990; 314565.

Frankfurt/Main, Germany Office: Friedrichstraße 2-6, 60323. Telephone: (49 69) 971 4090. Fax: (49 69) 971 40977.

Hanoi, Vietnam Office: 52 Nguyen Binh Khiem. Telephone: (844) 229 182/3/4/5/6. Fax: (844) 229 190.

(This Listing Continued)

London, England Office: 200 Aldersgate Street, EC1A 4JJ. Telephone: (44 171) 600 1000. Fax: (44 171) 600 5555.

Madrid, Spain Office: Paseo de la Castellana 110, 28046. Telephone: (34 1) 562 7674. Fax: (34 1) 562 49 93.

Milan, Italy Associated Office: Grimaldi e Clifford Chance. Via Gesú, 3, 20121. Telephone: (39 2) 7600 8040. Fax: (39 2) 7600 4950.

Moscow, Russia Office: Ul. Sadovaya - Samotechnaya 24/27, 2nd Floor, 103051. Telephone: (7 501) 258 50 50. Fax: (7 501) 258 50 51.

New York, New York Office: Swiss Bank Tower, 10 East 50th Street, 10022. Telephone: (1 212) 750 1440. Fax: (1 212) 758 6625.

Paris, France Office: 112 avenue Kléber, BP 163 Trocadéro, 75770 Paris Cedex 16. Telephone: (33 1) 44 05 52 52. Fax: (33 1) 44 05 52 00.

Riyadh, Saudi Arabia Associated Office: The Law Firm of Salah Al-Hejailan. P.O. Box 1454, 11431. Telephone: (966 1) 479 2200. Fax: (966 1) 479 1717.

Rome, Italy Associated Office: Grimaldi e Clifford Chance. Viale G. Rossini 7, 00198. Telephone: (39 6) 807 2251. Fax: (39 6) 807 8201.

Shanghai, People's Republic of China Office: Suite 898, Shanghai Centre, 1376 Nanjing Xi Lu, 200040. Telephone: (86 21) 279 8461. Fax: (86 21) 279 8462.

Singapore Office: 16 Collyer Quay #31-00, 0104. Telephone: (65) 535 1855. Fax: (65) 535 6855.

Tokyo, Japan Office: 6th Floor, South Hill Nagatacho Building, 11-30 Nagatacho 1-chome, Chiyoda-ku, 100. Telephone: (81 3) 3581 4311. Fax: (81 3) 3593 0651.

Warsaw, Poland Office: Warsaw Corporate Centre, ul. Emilii Plater 28, 00-688. Telephone: (48 2) 630 3344. Fax: (48 2) 630 3355.

International Banking and Finance including Asset-based, Acquisition, Project Finance, Securitization and Capital Markets, Public and Private Company, Commercial and Regulatory Work, Dispute Settlement and China-related Work.

Firm engaged in English, Hong Kong and General International Practice.

PARTNERS

JIM BAIRD. PRACTICE AREAS: Hostile Takeover; Mergers and Acquisitions; Corporate Law; Acquisitions, Divestitures, Mergers.

ROGER BEST. PRACTICE AREAS: Maritime; Complex Litigation; Banking Litigation; Arbitration; Insolvency.

JOHN EAST. PRACTICE AREAS: Ship Financing; Banking Law; Asian-Pacific; Asset Based Lending; Project Finance.

JOHN HOLMES. LANGUAGES: French. **PRACTICE AREAS:** Securities; Commercial Law; Corporate Law.

HUW JENKINS. PRACTICE AREAS: Asset Based Lending; Ship Financing; Securities Banking Regulation; Equipment Leasing.

TIMOTHY SOUTAR. PRACTICE AREAS: Export Credit Financing; Power Project Development; Banking Law; Asset Based Lending; Project Finance.

ANDREW D. TAYLOR. PRACTICE AREAS: Finance Law; Securities Banking Regulation; Securities; Banking Law.

RESIDENT LOCAL PARTNERS

STUART VALENTINE. PRACTICE AREAS: China Investment; General China Law.

PHILIP RAPP. PRACTICE AREAS: China Investment; General China Law.

WANG WAI LI. PRACTICE AREAS: Infrastructure Projects; Project Financing; China Banking Law; General Banking.

ROGER M. DENNY. PRACTICE AREAS: Hostile Takeover; Corporate Law; Acquisitions, Divestitures; Mergers and Acquisitions.

GAO PEIJI. PRACTICE AREAS: China Legal Practice Consultant.

(For the names of Partners resident in other offices, see the Professional Biographies for those offices)

CLYDE & CO.
15TH FLOOR
ASIA PACIFIC FINANCE TOWER
CITIBANK PLAZA
3 GARDEN ROAD
HONG KONG
Telephone: (852) 878 8600
Telex: 61972 Clyde HX
Fax: (852) 522 5907

London, England Office: 51 Eastcheap, EC3M 1JP. Telephone: (44) 171-623 1244. Telex: 884886 Clyde G. Fax: (44) 171-623 5427.

Also offices in: Guildford (England), Cardiff (Wales), Singapore, Dubai (United Arab Emirates), Sao Paulo (Brazil), Caracas (Venezuela). For full details of these offices, see entry under London, England.

International practice including shipping, aviation, insurance and reinsurance; commodity, trade and transport; company, commercial and intellectual property; energy; oil and gas; taxation; litigation; agent for trademarks and patents; joint ventures, countertrade and banking; debt collection, personal injury and employee's compensation.

RESIDENT PARTNERS

ALEC EMMERSON, admitted, 1979, England and Wales; 1984, Hong Kong. **PRACTICE AREAS:** Admiralty and Maritime Law; Marine and Non-Marine Litigation; Salvage and Collision Work; Arbitration; Trade and Transport Disputes; Insurance; Carriage of Goods by Air, Road and Sea.

CORINNA CRESSWELL, admitted, 1978, England and Wales; 1992, Hong Kong. **PRACTICE AREAS:** Marine and Non-Marine Litigation; Insurance; Carriage of Goods by Sea, Road and Air; Trade and Transportation Disputes; Defamation; Sale and Purchase Disputes; Arbitration.

RICHARD TANNER, admitted, 1978, England and Wales; 1985, Hong Kong. **PRACTICE AREAS:** Agency and Distributorships; Banks and Banking; Business Law; Company Law; Copyright Law; Corporate Law; Finance Law; Immigration; Intellectual Property; Leases.

JUDITH FRUIN-BALL, admitted, 1983, England and Wales; 1985, Hong Kong. **PRACTICE AREAS:** Litigation; Insurance; Personal Injury; Employee's Compensation; Trade; Transport Law.

MICHAEL RODERICK, admitted, 1986, England and Wales; 1990, Hong Kong. **PRACTICE AREAS:** Admiralty and Maritime Law; Alternative Dispute Resolution; Civil Law; Commercial Law; Transportation; Insurance; Litigation.

NICHOLAS GRAYDON, admitted, 1989, England and Wales; 1993, Hong Kong. **PRACTICE AREAS:** Admiralty and Maritime Law; Marine Insurance; Collision; Commercial Law; Fraud; Sale and Carriage of Goods; Negotiable Instruments; Litigation; Arbitration; Alternative Dispute Resolution.

CONSULTANT

BRENT KINNEY, admitted, 1970, Alberta, Canada as Barrister and Solicitor; 1994, England and Wales. **PRACTICE AREAS:** Banks and Banking; Business Law; Commercial Law; Company law; Contracts; Corporate Law; Energy; Oil and Gas; Finance and Securities.

Languages: English, French, Cantonese, Mandarin

CONYERS, DILL & PEARMAN
Established in 1985

SUITE 401, THREE EXCHANGE SQUARE
8 CONNAUGHT PLACE, CENTRAL
HONG KONG
Telephone: (852) 2524-7106
Facsimile: (852) 2845-9268

Hamilton, Bermuda Office: Clarendon House, 2 Church Street, P.O. Box HM 666, HM CX. Telephone: (809) 295-1422. Telex: 3213 CODAN BA. Facsimile: (809) 292-4720.

Guernsey, Channel Islands Office: P.O. Box 265, Suite 6, Tower Hill House, Le Bordage, St. Peter Port, GY1 3QU. Telephone: (44) 1481 727429. Facsimile: (44) 1481 711750.

British Virgin Islands Office: Todman Building No. 1, Main Street, P.O. Box 3140, Road Town, Tortola. Telephone: (809)494-2065/6. Facsimile: (809)494-4929.

(This Listing Continued)

CONYERS, DILL & PEARMAN, Hong Kong—Continued

Firm engaged in Bermuda and General International Law Practice, but not authorized to appear before the Hong Kong Courts or to act as Hong Kong Solicitors.

FIRM PROFILE: *Corporate & Tax Law & in particular, transactions involving Bermuda companies. Advice on and arrangement for the incorporation of companies in other low tax jurisdictions and for the administration of such companies.*

RESIDENT PARTNER

ROSEMARIE P.Y. CHEN, born Malaysia, August 12, 1960; admitted, 1983, England; 1985, High Court of Malaya; 1986, Supreme Court of Singapore; 1992, Bermuda (Not admitted in Hong Kong). *Education:* University of Bristol, England (LL.B. Hons., 1982); Council of Legal Education, London, England. *Member:* Gray's Inn, London, England, Malaysia, Singapore and Bermuda Bar Associations; Inter-Pacific Bar Association; International Bar Association. *LANGUAGES:* English, Cantonese, Bahasa Malaysia. *PRACTICE AREAS:* Company and Commercial Law.

RESIDENT ASSOCIATES

LILIAN S.C. WOO, born Hong Kong, June 1, 1965; admitted, 1990, Hong Kong as Solicitor; 1992, England and Wales. *Education:* University of Buckingham, England (LL.B. Hons., 1986); College of Law , Chester, England (1988). *Member:* Hong Kong Law Society. *LANGUAGES:* English, Cantonese, Mandarin. *PRACTICE AREAS:* Company and Commercial Law.

JULIE E. MCLEAN, born Bermuda, March 17, 1967; admitted, 1993, British Columbia, Canada and Bermuda. *Education:* University of Western Ontario (B.A., 1989); The Law Faculty of the University of British Columbia (LL.B., 1992). *Member:* West Coast Environmental Law Association (1990-1992); Bermuda Bar Association. *LANGUAGES:* English. *PRACTICE AREAS:* Corporate and Mutual Funds.

(For Complete Biographical Data on all Personnel, see Professional Biographies at Hamilton, Bermuda).

COUDERT BROTHERS

American Attorneys at Law

25TH FLOOR
NINE QUEEN'S ROAD CENTRAL
HONG KONG
Telephone: (852) 2810-4111
Cable Address: "Treduoc"
Telecopier: (852) 2845-9021
Telex: HX74073 "Amlaw"

REVISERS OF THE FRANCE LAW DIGEST FOR THIS DIRECTORY.

New York, N.Y. 10036-7794: 1114 Avenue of the Americas.
Washington, D.C. 20006: 1627 I Street, N.W.
Los Angeles, California 90017: 1055 West Seventh Street, Twentieth Floor.
San Francisco, California 94111: 4 Embarcadero Center, Suite 3300.
San Jose, California 95113: Suite 1250, Ten Almaden Boulevard.
Paris 75008, France: Coudert Frères, 52, Avenue des Champs-Elysees.
London, EC4V 5AA, England: 4 Dean's Court.
Brussels B-1050, Belgium: Tour Louise. 149 Avenue Louise-Box 8.
Beijing 100020, People's Republic of China: Suite 2708-09 Jing Guang Centre Hu Jia Lou, Chao Yang Qu.
Shanghai 200002, People's Republic of China: c/o Suite 1804, Union Building, 100 Yanan Road East.
Singapore 0104: Tung Centre, 20 Collyer Quay.
Sydney N.S.W. 2000, Australia: Suite 2202, State Bank Centre, 52 Martin Place.
Tokyo 107, Japan: 1355 West Tower, Aoyama Twin Towers, 1-1-1 Minami-Aoyama, Minato-ku.
Moscow, Russia: Ulitsa Staraya Basmannaya 14.
01301 Sao Paulo, SP, Brazil: Machado, Meyer, Sendacz, e Opice, Advogados, Rua da Consolacao, 247, 8 Andar.
Bangkok 10500, Thailand: Bubhajit Building, 20 North Sathorn Road, 10th Floor.
Ho Chi Minh City, Vietnam: c/o Saigon Business Centre, 49-57 Dong Du Street, District 1.

(This Listing Continued)

Firm engaged in American and International Law Practice but not authorized to appear before the Hong Kong Courts or to act as Hong Kong Solicitors.

RESIDENT PARTNERS

VIVIENNE BATH, born Murwillumbah, Australia, May 23, 1955; admitted, 1981, Australia Capital Territory and State of New South Wales, Australia; 1987, New York; 1992, England (Not Practicing) (Not admitted in Hong Kong). *Education:* Australian National University (B.A., Asian Studies, Honours, 1978; LL.B., Honours, 1981); Harvard University (LL.M., 1984). *Member:* New York State Bar Association; American Society of International Law; Law Society of New South Wales. *LANGUAGES:* English, Chinese (Mandarin) and German.

DAVID RICHARD HALPERIN, born Brooklyn, New York, 1944; admitted, 1975, New York (Not admitted in Hong Kong). *Education:* Columbia University (A.B., 1965); Harvard University (M.A.T., 1966; J.D., 1974); Hague Academy of International Law (1974); Europa Institute, University of Amsterdam (1974). Author: "The Regulation of Foreign Banking in the United States," The International Lawyer 1975. Personal Assistant to Dr. Henry Kissinger, Assistant to the President for National Security Affairs, 1970-1971. Special Assistant to Admiral E.R. Zumwalt, Chief of Naval Operations, 1968-1970. *Member:* American and International Bar Associations; International Institute for Strategic Studies (London). [With U.S. Navy, 1966-1970; LCDR, USNR, 1970—]

W. GAGE MCAFEE, born New York, N.Y., March 23, 1943; admitted, 1969, New York; 1973, U.S. Supreme Court; 1979, District of Columbia (Not admitted in Hong Kong). *Education:* Harvard University (A.B., 1965); Columbia Law School (J.D., 1968). Department of State, Agency for International Development, 1968-1969. Legal Adviser, Office Civil Operations and Revolutionary Development Support, Military Assistance Command, Vietnam, 1969-1971. Adjunct Professor, Saigon University Faculty of Law, 1970-1971. Member, Council of Foreign Relations. *Member:* New York State, American and International Bar Associations; The District of Columbia Bar; The International Institute for Strategic Studies. *LANGUAGES:* French, Vietnamese and Chinese.

OWEN D. NEE, JR., born Bronxville, New York, November 22, 1943; admitted, 1974, New York (Not admitted in Hong Kong). *Education:* Princeton University (B.A., 1965); Columbia University (J.D., 1973). Member, Board of Editors, 1971-1973 and Business Manager, 1973, Columbia Law Review. Editor, Commercial Business and Trade Laws of the Peoples Republic of China, 1991. Author: "China," Euromoney Publications, 1986. [With United States Army, 1969-1971]. (Managing Partner). *LANGUAGES:* Chinese and Vietnamese.

HENRY J. USCINSKI, born New York, N.Y., October 1, 1949; admitted, 1986, Connecticut; 1987, New York, U.S. District Court, Southern and Eastern Districts of New York and U.S. District Court, District of Connecticut; 1988, District of Columbia. *Education:* Wheeling College (B.A., 1970); Duquesne University (M.A., 1971); Washington College of Law of American University (J.D., 1985). Editor-in-Chief, American University Law Review. Law Clerk to Hon. Frank Q. Nebeker, District of Columbia Court of Appeals, 1985-1986. Author: "Arbitration in the PRC: Practice and Procedure of the China International Economic and Trade Arbitration Commission," 1994 Hong Kong Director's Law Yearbook; "Enforcement of Arbitral Awards and Foreign Judgments in the People's Republic of China," 1993 Hong Kong Director's Law Yearbook; "Commercial and Maritime Arbitration in the People's Republic of China," Law Journal of the Thai Bar Association (March 1993). *Member:* Association of the Bar of the City of New York; Connecticut and American Bar Associations; The District of Columbia Bar.

SOOK YOUNG YEU, born Bongae, South Korea, May 10, 1955; admitted, 1981, California; 1982, New York and U.S. District Court, Southern and Eastern Districts of New York (Not admitted in Hong Kong). *Education:* Yale University (B.A., 1977); University of California at Berkeley (J.D., 1980). Associate Editor, California Law Review, 1978-1980. *Member:* State Bar of California; American Bar Association. *LANGUAGES:* Korean.

(This Listing Continued)

RESIDENT ASSOCIATES

Elizabeth A. Bowler
(Not admitted in Hong Kong)

Rupert X. Li
(Not admitted in Hong Kong)

John C. Cole, Jr.
(Not admitted in Hong Kong)

Jeffrey J. Miller
(Not admitted in Hong Kong)

Cornelia S. Edelman
(Not admitted in Hong Kong)

Steven L. Toronto
(Not admitted in Hong Kong)

Jong-Dae Lee
(Not admitted in Hong Kong)

REVISERS OF THE FRANCE LAW DIGEST FOR THIS DIRECTORY.

(For biographical data of the New York personnel, see Professional Biographies at New York, N.Y.).
(For biographical data of the Washington personnel, see Professional Biographies at Washington, D.C.).
(For biographical data of the San Francisco personnel, see Professional Biographies at San Francisco, California).
(For biographical data of the Los Angeles personnel, see Professional Biographies at Los Angeles, California).
(For biographical data of the San Jose personnel, see Professional Biographies at San Jose, California).
(For biographical data of the Paris personnel, see Professional Biographies at Paris, France).
(For biographical data of the Brussels personnel, see Professional Biographies at Brussels, Belgium).
(For biographical data of the London personnel, see Professional Biographies at London, England).
(For biographical data of the Beijing personnel, see Professional Biographies at Beijing, People's Republic of China).
For biographical data of the Hong Kong personnel, see Professional Biographies at Hong Kong.
(For biographical data of the Tokyo personnel, see Professional Biographies at Tokyo, Japan).
(For biographical data of the Singapore personnel, see Professional Biographies at Singapore).
(For biographical data of the Sao Paulo personnel, see Professional Biographies at Sao Paulo, Brazil).
(For biographical data of the Shanghai personnel, see Professional Biographies at Shanghai, People's Republic of China).
(For biographical data of the Sydney personnel, see Professional Biographies at Sydney, Australia).
(For biographical data of the Moscow personnel, see Professional Biographies at Moscow, U.S.S.R.).
(For biographical data of the Ho Chi Minh City personnel, see Professional Biographies at Ho Chi Minh City, Vietnam).

CRAVATH, SWAINE & MOORE

SUITE 2609
ASIA PACIFIC FINANCE TOWER
CITIBANK PLAZA
3 GARDEN ROAD, CENTRAL

HONG KONG
Telephone: 852-509-7200
Facsimile: 852-509-7272

New York City Office: Worldwide Plaza, 825 Eighth Avenue, 10019. Telephone: 212-474-1000. Facsimile: 212-474-3700. Cable Address: "Cravath, New York". Telex: 1-25547.
London, England Office: 33 King William Street, 10th Floor, London, EC4R 9DU. Telephone: 071-606-1421. Facsimile: 071-860-1150.

General Practice.
Firm engaged in American and International Law Practice, but not authorized to appear before the Hong Kong courts or to act as Solicitors.

(This Listing Continued)

RESIDENT PARTNERS

RICHARD M. ALLEN, born Chicago, Illinois, September 26, 1940; admitted, 1967, New York (Not admitted in Hong Kong). *Education:* Purdue University (B.S., 1963); Duke University (LL.B., 1966). *Member:* The Association of the Bar of the City of New York; American Bar Association; College of American Investment Counsel.

W. CLAYTON JOHNSON, born Roanoke, Virginia, September 14, 1955; admitted, 1980, California; 1985, New York (Not admitted in Hong Kong). *Education:* University of Virginia (B.A., 1977); University of Virginia Law School (J.D., 1980). *Member:* The Association of the Bar of the City of New York; New York State Bar Association.

SPECIALIST ATTORNEY-HONG KONG

SU LIN HAN, born August 23, 1963; admitted, 1991, California; 1992, District of Columbia (Not admitted in Hong Kong). *Education:* Beijing Foreign Languages Institute at Bai Dui-Zi and Beijing University (B.A., 1985); University of Connecticut at Storrs (M.A., 1988); Boalt Hall School of Law (J.D., 1991). *Member:* American Bar Association.

(For biographical data of all Resident Partners and Specialist Attorney-Hong Kong, see Professional Biographies at New York, New York)

DAVIS POLK & WARDWELL

THE HONG KONG CLUB BUILDING
3A CHATER ROAD
HONG KONG
Telephone: 852 533 3300
Fax: 852 533 3388

New York, N.Y. Office: 450 Lexington Avenue, 10017. Telephone: 212-450-4000. Cable Address: "Davispolk New York." Telex: ITT-421341; ITT-423356. Telecopier: 212-450-4800.
Washington, D.C. Office: 1300 I Street, N.W. Telephone: 202-962-7000. Telecopier: 202-962-7111.
Paris, France Office: 4, Place de la Concorde, 75008. Telephone: 011-331-40.17.36.00 Telecopier: 011-331-42.65.22.34. Cable Address: "Davispolk Paris."
London, England Office: 1 Frederick's Place, EC2R 8AB. Telephone: 011-44-71-418-1300. Telex: 888238. Telecopier: 011-44-71-418-1400.
Tokyo, Japan Office: In Tokyo practicing as Reid Gaikokuho-Jimu-Bengoshi Jimusho. Tokio Kaijo Building Annex, 2-1, Marunouchi 1-Chome, Chiyoda-Ku, 100. Telephone: 011-81-3-201-8421. Telecopier: 011-81-3-201-8444. Telex: 2224472 DPWTOK.
Frankfurt, Germany Office: MesseTurm, 60308 Frankfurt am Main, Federal Republic of Germany. Telephone: 011-49-69-97-57-03-0. Telecopier: 011-49-69-74-77-44.

American and General International Practice.
Firm engaged in American and International Law Practice, but not authorized to appear before the Hong Kong courts or to act as Solicitors.

RESIDENT PARTNERS

ROBERT LEE HECKART, born Poplar Bluff, Missouri, June 11, 1948; admitted, 1974, New York. *Education:* Yale University (A.B., 1970); Harvard Law School (J.D., 1973). *Member:* The Association of the Bar of the City of New York; American and International Bar Associations.

JAMES DUNCAN PHYFE, born New York, N.Y., January 29, 1942; admitted, 1973, New York. *Education:* Harvard University (A.B., 1964; J.D., 1971); Princeton University (M.P.A., 1967). *Member:* The Association of the Bar of the City of New York; New York State and American Bar Associations.

RICHARD A. DRUCKER, born New York, N.Y., March 30, 1952; admitted, 1978, New York (Not admitted in Hong Kong). *Education:* University of Vermont (B.A., 1974); University of Virginia (J.D., 1977). *Member:* The Association of the Bar of the City of New York; American and International Bar Associations; First Tokyo Bar Association. Registered with the Nichibenren as Gaikokuho-Jimu-Bengoshi in Japan.

ASSOCIATES

John D. Anderson (Not admitted in Hong Kong); **William F. Barron** (Not admitted in Hong Kong); **Sandip C. Bhattacharji** (Not admitted in Hong Kong); **Catherina Celosse** (Not admitted in Hong Kong); **Show-Mao Chen** (Not admitted in Hong Kong); **James B. Gatehouse** (Not admitted in Hong Kong); **Yusing Ko** (Not admitted in Hong Kong); **Vivien Y. Liu** (Not

(This Listing Continued)

DAVIS POLK & WARDWELL, Hong Kong—Continued

admitted in Hong Kong); *Averill L. Powers* (Not admitted in Hong Kong); *Anthony Root* (Not admitted in Hong Kong); *Raymond J. Simon* (Not admitted in Hong Kong).

(For Complete Biographical Data on all Personnel see Professional Biographies at New York City)

DEACONS

in association with GRAHAM & JAMES/SLY & WEIGALL

Established in 1880

ALEXANDRA HOUSE, 3RD-6TH FLOORS
HONG KONG

Telephone: (852) 2825 9211
Cable Address: "Otery, Hong Kong"
Telex: 73475 OTERY HX
Fax: (852) 2810 0431

Bangkok, Thailand Associated Office: Deacons Graham & James. 16th Floor, Q House Sathorn, 11 Sathorn Road, Bangkok, 10120. Tel: 662 679-1844. Fax: 662 679-1864. Telex: 82981 HARVEY TH. Cable Address: HARVEY.

Beijing, People's Republic of China Office: Graham & James. Suite 1903, CITIC Building, 19 Jianguomenwai Dajie, 100004. Tel: 861-507-8557. Fax: 861-500-2557. Telex: 22969 GJJPEK CN.

Guangzhou, People's Republic of China Office: Deacons. Room 1405, 14/F, North Tower World Trade Centre, 371-375 East Huanshi Road. Tel: 8620-7781178/1278. Fax: 8620-7789618.

Hanoi, Vietnam Associated Office: Deacons Graham & James, 2A Nguyen Dinh Chieu. Tel: (84-4) 269222/227998. Fax: (84-4) 227284. Ho Chi Minh City (application licence pending) Deacons Graham & James.

Jakarta, Indonesia Associated Office: Hanafiah Soeharto Ponggawa. BNI Building, 24/F Jalan Jenderal Sudirman Kav No, 1, 10220. Tel: 6221-570-1837. Fax: 6221 570-2927.

Kowloon, Hong Kong Office: 930 Ocean Centre, Harbour City. Tel: 852-2738-1414. Cable Address: "Stmay, Hong Kong". Telex: 73475 OTERYHX. Fax: 852-2730-4379.

Taipei, Taiwan Associated Office: Deacons Graham & James, 7th Floor, 54 Chung Shan N. Road, Sec. 3, 10451. Tel: 886-2-597-4521. Fax: 886-2-592-6601.

Tokyo, Japan Associated Office: Kurosu Gaikokuho Jimu Bengoshi Jimusho (Graham & James) Shiroyama JT Mori Building 8/F, 3-1 Toranomon 4-chome, Minato-Ku, 105. Tel: 813-3459-5481 thru 3. Fax: 813-3459-0240.

Tokyo, Japan Associated Office: Haarmann, Hemmelrath & Partner. Shiroyama JT Mori Building, 3-1 Toranomon 4-chome, Minato-ku, 105. Tel: 813-3459-5485/0740. Fax: 813-3578-8956.

Brisbane, Australia Associated Office: Sly Weigall Cannan & Peterson. Riverside Centre, Level 20, 123 Eagle Street, 4000 Brisbane. Tel: 617-833-0444. Fax: 617-833-0555.

Canberra, Australia Associated Office: Sly & Weigall. 9th Floor, National Mutual Center, 15 London Circuit, Canberra Act, 2600. Tel: 616-249-7666. Fax: 616-257-2560.

Melbourne, Australia Associated Office: Sly & Weigall. 385 Bourke Street, Level 25, 3000. Tel: 613-608-0411. Fax: 613-608-0505.

Perth, Australia Associated Office: Sly & Weigall. R & I Bank Tower, 108 St. George's Terrace, 6000. Tel: 619-321-9379. Fax: 619-324-1334.

Sydney, New South Wales, Australia Associated Office: Sly & Weigall. Gold Fields House, Circular Quay, 2000. Tel: 612-330-8000. Fax: 612-330-8111.

Los Angeles, California Associated Office: Graham & James. 14th Floor, Citicorp Plaza, 801 South Figueroa Street, 90017-5434. Tel: 213-624-2500. Fax: 213-623-4581.

Newport Beach, California Associated Office: Graham & James. Suite 800, 4675 MacArthur Court, 92660-1836. Tel: 714-752-0550. Fax: 714-851-2497.

New York, New York Associated Office: Graham & James. 24th Floor, 885 Third Avenue, 10022-4802. Tel: 212-848-1000. Fax: 212-688-2449.

Palo Alto, California Associated Office: Graham & James. 5 Palo Alto Square, Suite 1000, 3000 El Camino Real, 94306-2119. Tel: 415-856-6500. Fax: 415-856-3619.

Sacramento, California Associated Office: Graham & James. 24th Floor, 400 Capitol Mall, 95814-4602. Tel: 916-558-6700. Fax: 915-441-6700.

(This Listing Continued)

San Francisco, California Associated Office: Graham & James. Suite 300, One Maritime Plaza, 94111-3942. Tel: 415-954-0200. Fax: 415-391-2493.

Washington, D.C. Associated Office: Graham & James. Suite 700, 2000 M Street, N.W., 20036-3113. Tel: 202-463-0800. Fax: 202-463-0823.

Berlin, Germany Associated Office: Haarmann, Hemmelrath & Partner. Budapester Strasse 40a, D-10787 Berlin. Tel: 49-30-26473-0. Fax: 49-30-26473-133.

Brussels, Belgium Associated Office: Taylor Joynson Garrett. EEC Office, 14 Rue Montoyer, 1040 Brussels. Tel: 32-2-514-0402/4672. Fax: 32-2-514-0088.

Bucharest, Romania Associated Office: Taylor Joynson Garrett. Piata Alexandru Sahia NR3, Apartment 1, Sector 2, Bucharest. Tel: 401-611-8798. Fax: 401-611-7898.

Düsseldorf, Germany Associated Office: Graham & James. Martin-Luther-Platz 26, 40212. Düsseldorf 1. Tel: 49-211-83-99-200. Fax: 49-211-83-99-209.

Düsseldorf, Germany Associated Office: Haarmann, Hemmelrath & Partner. Martin-Luther-Platz 26 40212, Düsseldorf 1. Tel: 49-211-8399-0. Fax: 49-211-8399-133.

Frankfurt, Germany Associated Office: Haarmann, Hemmelrath & Partner. Neue Mainzer Street 69-75, 60311. Tel: 49-69-920-590. Fax: 49-69-920-59-133.

Leipzig, Germany Associated Office: Haarmann, Hemmelrath & Partner. Neumarkt 24, D-04109 Leipzig. Tel: 49-341-211-3160. Fax: 49-341-295-196.

London, England Associated Office: Taylor Joynson Garrett. Carmelite, 50 Victoria Embankment, Blackfriars, London EC4Y 0DX. Tel: 44-171-353-1234. Fax: 44-171-936-2666.

London, England Associated Office: Graham & James. Carmelite, 50 Victoria Embankment, Blackfriars, London EC4Y 0DX. Tel. 44-171-353-1840. Fax: 44-171-353-1841.

Milan, Italy Associated Office: Graham & James. Via Visconti, Napoleone, 12, 20121. Tel: 392-7600-6484. Fax: 392-783091.

Munich, Germany Associated Office: Haarmann, Hemmelrath & Partner. Effnerstrasse 38, D-81925 München. Tel: 49-89-924-000. Fax: 49-89-910-2047.

Prague, Czechoslovakia Republic Associated Office: Haarman, Hemmelrath & Partner, Cermakova 7, 1200 Prague. Tel: 49-224-2390-36 to 40. Fax: 49-224-2388-42.

Jeddah, Saudi Arabia Associated Office: The Law Firm of Salah Al-Hejailan. P.O. Box 15141. Tel: 966-2-653-4422. Fax: 966-2-651-7241.

Kuwait, Kuwait Associated Office: Mishare M. Al-Ghazili & Partners, P.O. Box 4970, Safat, 13050. Tel: 965-242-2516. Fax: 965-242-2895.

Riyadh, Saudia Arabia Associated Office: Law Offices of Salah Al-Hejailan. P.O. Box 1454, 11431. Tel: 966-1-479-2200. Fax: 966-1-479-1717.

Mexico City, Mexico Associated Office: Gallastegui y Lozano, Bosque de Duraznos 69, Torre B, Despacho 503, 504, Bosques de las Lomas, 11709 Mexico, D.F. Tel: 525-596-0638. Fax: 525-596-8069.

General International and Hong Kong Practice including Corporate, Commercial, Banking, China Trade and Investment, Shipping, Real Property, Tax and Trust, Probate, Designs, Patents, Trademarks, Copyrights, Entertainment and Trade Law, Litigation, Insolvency, Immigration, Telecommunications, Trade Finance, Environmental Law, Vietnam Law and Construction and Development.

FIRM PROFILE: Deacons is a long established and prominent Hong Kong law firm, providing an extensive range of services, through 100 lawyers of different nationalities and support staff of 300 people. The firm has its origins in Hong Kong, and acts for many of the major local corporations and individual clients, as well as having a substantial overseas client base. We are proud of our ability to communicate with, and meet the expectations of, such a diverse range of clients.

Deacons in association with Graham & James; Sly & Weigal forms one of the largest legal networks in the Pacific Rim. Graham & James is a major American law firm and Sly & Weigall a leading Australian law firm. Through this network, offices are maintained across Asia in Tokyo, Beijing, Bangkok, Jakarta, Taipei and Hanoi. With the opening of a new office in Guangzhou, Deacons is well positioned to assist international clients with all their requirements for legal services in this dynamic and growing market.

The network also has a strong presence in Europe with affiliations in the United Kingdom, Hungary, Belgium, Germany and Italy, giving the firm

(This Listing Continued)

a worldwide network of 32 offices employing more than a thousand lawyers.

Clients:

In Hong Kong, Deacons' reputation is built upon its long service to many of the business community's most outstanding organizations. Domestic and international banks, financial houses, investment corporations, airlines, property firms, oil, shipping, manufacturing and trading companies, utilites, insurance companies as well as media and entertainment interests are all included amongst Deacons' clients. The on-going expansion of the firm's client base reflects the vibrancy of the territory's domestic economy, and the spectacular growth of business in and with China.

PARTNERS

JAMES BERTRAM, College of Law, Lancaster Gate, College of Commerce, Liverpool, admitted, 1970, England; 1971, Hong Kong. Notary Public. *PRACTICE AREAS:* General Corporate and Commercial.

ANNIE WONG, admitted, 1973, England and Hong Kong. Notary Public. *LANGUAGES:* Chinese (Cantonese and Mandarin). *PRACTICE AREAS:* General Commercial and Conveyancing; Probate and Trusts.

JOHN ROSE, admitted, 1972, England; 1974, Hong Kong; 1982, New South Wales, Australia. Notary Public. *PRACTICE AREAS:* Commercial Litigation; Media Related Litigation.

ANTHONY FOX, LL.B. (Hons) (Nottingham University) admitted, 1974, England and Hong Kong. *LANGUAGES:* French. *PRACTICE AREAS:* Banking and Finance.

DAVID LAWRENCE, LL.B. (University College, London), admitted, 1973, England; 1976, Hong Kong. Notary Public. *LANGUAGES:* French. *PRACTICE AREAS:* General Commercial; Private Company Work; Landlord and Tenant Work.

ALAN WELLS, LL.B. (Hons) (London University) admitted, 1976, England; 1977, Hong Kong; 1982, Victoria, Australia. *PRACTICE AREAS:* Intellectual Property; Anti-Counterfeiting Enforcement and Licensing Programmes.

JOHN RICHARDSON, M.A., LL.B. (International Law Cambridge University), admitted, 1977, England; 1978, Hong Kong; Notary Public. *PRACTICE AREAS:* General Corporate and Commercial.

MARK ROBERTS, B.A. (Hons) City of London Polytechnic, admitted, 1977, England and Hong Kong; 1982 Victoria, Australia. Notary Public. *PRACTICE AREAS:* Shipping Litigation; Debt Recovery.

RICHARD MORRIS, B.A. (Oxford University), admitted, 1976, England; 1977, Hong Kong. Notary Public. *PRACTICE AREAS:* General Commercial Litigation; International Trade and Trade Finance.

PETER WINTLE, College of Law, Guildford, admitted, 1976, England; 1978, Hong Kong. Notary Public. *PRACTICE AREAS:* General Commercial Litigation.

ROBERT LEE, B.A. (Cornell University), admitted, 1979, England; 1980, Hong Kong. Notary Public. (Also at Guangzhou, People's Republic of China Office). *LANGUAGES:* Chinese (Cantonese and Mandarin), German and French. *PRACTICE AREAS:* China Trade and Investment; Real Estate and Development in the P.R.C..

CATHERINE BACON, B.A. (Hons) (Durham University), admitted, 1978, England; 1981, Hong Kong. *PRACTICE AREAS:* Commercial Law; Trusts and Probate; Environmental Law.

DEAN YOUNG, LL.B. (Dundee University), admitted, 1979, England; 1982, Hong Kong. *PRACTICE AREAS:* Shipping and Aviation Finance; Environmental Law.

PHILIP SMITH, LL.B. (Victoria University of Wellington, N.Z.), admitted, 1970, New Zealand; 1979, England; 1984, Hong Kong. *PRACTICE AREAS:* General Civil and Commercial Litigation; Personal Injury and Insurance Related Matters.

TIMOTHY DOBSON, LL.B. (Hons) (Edinburgh University), admitted, 1979, Scotland; 1981, Hong Kong. *LANGUAGES:* French. *PRACTICE AREAS:* General Commercial and Corporate; Laws and Regulations of Vietnam.

PAUL SCHOLEFIELD, LL.B. (Reading University), admitted, 1981, England; 1982, Hong Kong. *LANGUAGES:* French. *PRACTICE AREAS:* Intellectual Property.

PETER AHERNE, admitted, 1980, England; 1982, Hong Kong. *PRACTICE AREAS:* General Commercial Conveyancing.

(This Listing Continued)

LAM WING-WO, LL.B., P.C.LL. (University of Hong Kong), admitted, 1981, Hong Kong; 1984, England; 1989, Singapore; 1990, New South Wales. *LANGUAGES:* Chinese (Cantonese and Mandarin). *PRACTICE AREAS:* Banking and Finance; Project Finance.

LILIAN CHIANG, LL.B., P.C.LL. (University of Hong Kong), admitted, 1981, Hong Kong; 1984, England; 1985, Victoria, Australia; 1990, New South Wales; 1990, Singapore. Notary Public. *LANGUAGES:* Chinese (Cantonese and Mandarin). *PRACTICE AREAS:* General Commercial Conveyancing.

JIMMY WU, LL.B., P.C.LL. (University of Hong Kong), admitted, 1981, Hong Kong; 1984, England; 1985, Victoria, Australia; 1988, New York, U.S.A.; 1990, Singapore. Notary Public. *LANGUAGES:* Chinese (Cantonese and Chiuchow). *PRACTICE AREAS:* General Commercial Conveyancing.

CHARLES COOK, B.A. (Hons), Preston Polytechnic, admitted, 1982, England; 1983, Hong Kong. *LANGUAGES:* French. *PRACTICE AREAS:* General Civil and Commercial Litigation; Criminal and Matrimonial Law.

MARK BRADLEY, LL.B. (Bristol University), admitted, 1981, England; 1983, Hong Kong. *LANGUAGES:* French. *PRACTICE AREAS:* Insolvency.

SIMON DEANE, LL.B. (Hons) (Exeter University), admitted, 1984, England; 1987, Hong Kong. *LANGUAGES:* German and French. *PRACTICE AREAS:* Banking and Finance.

CHRISTINA HUNG, LL.B., (Hons), P.C.LL. (University of Hong Kong); admitted, 1983, Hong Kong; 1987, England and Wales; 1989, Australian Capital Territory University. *LANGUAGES:* Chinese (Cantonese and Mandarin). *PRACTICE AREAS:* General Civil and Commercial Litigation.

RAYMOND HAYES, B.A. (London University), M.Litt (Oxford University); admitted, 1985, England; 1987, Hong Kong. *LANGUAGES:* French and Italian. *PRACTICE AREAS:* General Commercial Conveyancing.

KEITH COLE, LL.B. (Hons) (University of Southampton), admitted, 1986, England; 1988, Hong Kong. *PRACTICE AREAS:* General Commercial; Computer Law; Entertainment and Telecommunications Law.

JOSEPH LAM, B.A., University of Manitoba, Canada; LL.B., University of Sydney, Australia; admitted 1985, New South Wales; 1988, Australia, England, Wales and Hong Kong. *LANGUAGES:* Chinese (Cantonese). *PRACTICE AREAS:* Banking and Finance.

DAVID CHAN, B.S.Sc. (Chinese University of Hong Kong), admitted, 1986, England and Hong Kong; 1990, Australia; 1992, Singapore. *LANGUAGES:* Chinese (Mandarin and Cantonese). *PRACTICE AREAS:* General Commercial.

WILLIAM MACKESY, B.A. (Oxford University), admitted, 1985, England and Wales; 1988, Hong Kong. *PRACTICE AREAS:* Corporate Finance and Securities Law; Corporate and Commercial Law.

SIMON LAI, LL.B., P.C.LL., (University of Hong Kong), admitted, 1985, Hong Kong; 1989, England and Wales; 1990, Australian Capital Territory; 1992, New South Wales, Australia. *LANGUAGES:* Chinese (Cantonese and Mandarin). *PRACTICE AREAS:* Corporate Finance; Securities and Commercial Law.

FRANKI CHEUNG, B.A. (Hons.) (Univ. of Kent), admitted, 1985, Hong Kong; 1988, England and Wales; 1989, Attorney, State Bar of California. *LANGUAGES:* Chinese (Mandarin and Cantonese). *PRACTICE AREAS:* China Trade; Investment; Banking; Finance.

ALEX LAI, LL.B., P.C.LL. (Univ. of Hong Kong), Diploma in Chinese Law (Univ. of East Asia), admitted, 1987, Hong Kong. *LANGUAGES:* Chinese (Mandarin and Cantonese). *PRACTICE AREAS:* Construction; Litigation; Arbitration.

HANDA LAM, LL.B. (Hons), P.C.LL. (Univ. of Hong Kong), admitted, 1986, Hong Kong; 1990, England and Wales; 1990, Australian Capital Territory. *LANGUAGES:* Cantonese, Mandarin and Shanghaiese. *PRACTICE AREAS:* Conveyancing.

DAVID ZEE, LL.B. (Hons)., P.C.LL. (Univ. of Hong Kong), Chinese Law Diploma, East Asia Open Institute, admitted, 1990, Hong Kong; 1991, England and Wales; 1991, Australian Capital Territory, 1994, California, USA. *LANGUAGES:* Cantonese and Mandarin. *PRACTICE AREAS:* Corporate; Commercial; Employment Law.

(This Listing Continued)

DEACONS, Hong Kong—Continued

RAYNE CHAI, LL.B. (Hons), (Univ. of Hong Kong), admitted, 1989, Hong Kong; 1991, England and Wales; 1991, Australian Capital Territory; 1994, Singapore. *LANGUAGES:* Cantonese, Mandarin and French. *PRACTICE AREAS:* Conveyancing; Probate and Wills.

CONSULTANTS

WAI-PAT WONG, admitted, 1954, Hong Kong; 1975, England. Notary Public. *LANGUAGES:* Chinese (Cantonese). *PRACTICE AREAS:* General Commercial Conveyancing; Trusts and Probate.

ANDREW CHRISTIE, LL.B. (Edinburgh University), W.S., admitted, 1972, Scotland; 1973, Hong Kong. Notary Public. *LANGUAGES:* French. *PRACTICE AREAS:* General Corporate and Commercial; Employment Law.

BERNARD FLEMING, (Not admitted in Hong Kong). LL.B., (Hons) Canterbury, New Zealand; Barrister/Solicitor High Court of New Zealand, 1977. *PRACTICE AREAS:* Construction and Project Development.

CHRISTOPHER SHINE, (Not admitted in Hong Kong). B.A., LL.B., Australian National University; Barrister/Solicitor Australia Capital, 1980; New South Wales, 1980; Barrister High Court of Australia, 1989. *PRACTICE AREAS:* Telecommunications and Technology Transfer.

PETER WILLOUGHBY, LL.B., LL.M., London School of Economics, admitted, 1962, England, Wales and Nigeria; 1973, Hong Kong. *LANGUAGES:* French. *PRACTICE AREAS:* Tax Law; Stamp Duty; Estate Duty; Value Added Tax; Commercial Law; Property Law.

U.S. LAW CONSULTANTS

SALLY HARPOLE, (Not admitted in Hong Kong). Admitted, 1978, California. J.D. (U. Washington); A.B. (Hons., U.C., Berkeley) Arbitrator, China International Economic and Trade Arbitration Commission, Chartered Institute of Arbitrators. President, American Chamber of Commerce in the P.R. of China, 1985-1986. (Managing Partner, Graham & James, Beijing (Peking), People's Republic of China Office). *LANGUAGES:* Chinese (Cantonese and Mandarin), French and German. *PRACTICE AREAS:* China Trade and Investment; U.S. Corporate Law; Arbitration.

DAVID LIVDAHL, (Not admitted in Hong Kong). A.B. (Macalester College), M.A. (Columbia University), J.D. (Columbia University); admitted, 1977, California; 1988, Japan (Foreign Licensed Attorney). (Partner, Graham & James, American Attys). *LANGUAGES:* Japanese, Chinese (Mandarin). *PRACTICE AREAS:* Corporate; Joint Venture; Licensing.

SAMUEL ZHANG, (Not admitted in Hong Kong). admitted, 1987, New York (Partner, Graham & James), LL.M., Ann Arbour, Michigan, B.A., Zhongshan University, China, LL.M., Wuhan University, Diploma, The Hague Academy of International Law. *LANGUAGES:* Mandarin and Cantonese. *PRACTICE AREAS:* China Trade; Investment.

DEBEVOISE & PLIMPTON

Established in 1931

13/F ENTERTAINMENT BUILDING
30 QUEEN'S ROAD CENTRAL
HONG KONG
Telephone: 852-2810-7918
Fax: 852-2810-9828

New York, N.Y. Office: 875 Third Avenue, 10022. Telephone: 212-909-6000, Telex: (Domestic) 148377 DEBSTEVE NYK. Telecopier: 210-909-68363

Los Angeles, California Office: 601 South Figueroa Street, Suite 3700, 90017. Telephone: 213-680-8000. Telex: 401527 DPLA. Telecopier: 213-680-8100.

Washington, D.C. Office: 555 13th Street, N.W., 20004. Telephone: 202-383-8000. Telex: 405586 DPDC WUUD. Telecopier: (202) 383-8118.

Paris, France Office: 21 Avenue George V 75008. Telephone: (33-1) 40 73 12 12. Telecopier: (33-1) 47 20 50 82. Telex: 648141F DPPAR.

London, England Office: 1 Creed Court, 5 Ludgate Hill, EC4M 7AA. Telephone: (44-171) 329-0779. Telex: 88 4569 DPLON G. Facsimile: (44-171) 329-0860.

Budapest, Hungary Office: 1065 Budapest, Révay Köz 2.III/2. Telephone: (36-1) 131-0845. Telecopier: (36-1) 132-7995.

(This Listing Continued)

General Practice.
Firm engaged in American and International Practice, but not authorized to appear before the Hong Kong Courts or to act as Solicitors.
FIRM PROFILE: OFFICE PROFILE: The Hong Kong Office of Debevoise & Plimpton, opened in 1994, is staffed with lawyers experienced in joint venture, privatizations, project and equipment financings, direct foreign investments, financial services, anti-dumping proceedings and securities law. The Hong Kong office draws upon the resources of the firm's New York, Washington and Los Angeles offices in American-related transactions and the firm's Paris and London offices in European-oriented transactions.

RESIDENT PARTNER

JEFFREY S. WOOD, born December 14, 1941; admitted, 1969, District of Columbia; 1973, N.Y. (Not admitted in Hong Kong). *Education:* Princeton (A.B., 1963); Cambridge University, England (B.A., Trinity, 1965); Yale (LL.B., 1968). Phi Beta Kappa. Note and Comment Editor, Yale Law Journal, 1967-1968. *Member:* The Association of the Bar of the City of New York; American College of Investment Counsel; International Bar Association; Inter-Pacific Bar Association. *PRACTICE AREAS:* Project Financing; International Corporate Finance; Corporate and Commercial Law.

SPECIAL COUNSEL

NEIL KAPLAN, born September 1, 1942; admitted, 1965, England; 1983, Victoria, Australia (qualified as solicitor and barrister); 1986, New York (Not admitted in Hong Kong). *Education:* King's College, London (LL.B., 1964). Q.C., 1982. Deputy Principal Crown Counsel, Hong Kong, 1980-1982; Principal Crown Counsel, Hong Kong, 1982-1984. Chairman, Hong Kong International Arbitration Centre, 1991—. Convenor, Disputes Review Board, Hong Kong Provisional Airport Authority, 1994—. Co-Author: Arbitration in Hong Kong Butterworths, 1991), Arbitration in Hong Kong and China (Butterworths, 1994). Arbitration Panelist: China, Singapore, Hong Kong, London. Fellow, Chartered Institute of Arbitrators, 1979 (Vice President, 1992—). *PRACTICE AREAS:* Litigation; Complex International Commercial Arbitration; Constriction Arbitration; Other Alternate Dispute Resolution.

ASSOCIATES

GREGORY V. GOODING, born March 9, 1961; admitted, 1989, New York (Not admitted in Hong Kong). *Education:* Kenyon (A.B., 1983); Yale (J.D., 1987). Managing Editor, Journal International Law, 1986-1987. *Member:* American and International Bar Associations; Inter-Pacific Bar Association. *PRACTICE AREAS:* Corporate and Commercial Law; Project Financing; Securities Law; Mergers and Acquisitions.

XIAOMING LI, born February 22, 1957; admitted, 1991, N.Y. (Not admitted in Hong Kong). *Education:* Jilin University (B.A., 1982); Beijing Institute of International Relations (M.A., 1984); Duke (J.D., 1990). Assistant Professor, Beijing Institute of International Relations, 1983-1985. Assistant Secretary, China Council for the Promotion of the International Trade, Beijing, 1985-1986. Deputy Secretary General, China International Economic and Trade Arbitration Commission, Beijing, 1987-1988. *Member:* The Association of the Bar of the City of New York; International Bar Association; Inter-Pacific Bar Association. *LANGUAGES:* Mandarin Chinese. *PRACTICE AREAS:* Commercial Law; International Investments; Project Financings; Acquisitions.

LAW OFFICES OF
ROY IAN DELBYCK

(in Affiliation with Rode & Qualey)

SUITE 509, OCEAN CENTRE HARBOR CITY
5 CANTON ROAD, TSIMSHATSUI, KOWLOON
HONG KONG
Telephone: 852-810-5777
Telecopier: 852-810-5288

Affiliated New York, N.Y. Office: Rode & Qualey, 295 Madison Avenue. Telephone: 212-685-4437. Telecopier: 212-213-3206. Telex: 238790NYK-UR.

Affiliated Washington, D.C. Office: Rode & Qualey, Suite 400, 1825 I Street, N.W. Telephone: 202-223-0957. Telecopier: 202-429-9574.

U.S. Customs and International Trade Law. Firm engaged in American and International practice, but not authorized to appear before the Hong Kong Courts, or to act as Hong Kong Solicitors.

(This Listing Continued)

ROY IAN DELBYCK, born Brooklyn, New York; admitted, 1983, California. *Education:* Connecticut College (B.A., cum laude, 1974); University of California at Davis (J.D., 1983). Managing Editor, U.C. Davis Law Review, 1982-1983. Vice-President, 1992-1993, Governor, 1989-1991 and Chairman, Textile Committee of The American Chamber of Commerce in Hong Kong. Member, Softgoods Subcommittee, The Hong Kong Expanders' Association. Member, Textiles Committee, The Hong Kong Chamber of Commerce. *Member:* State Bar of California; American Bar Association. *LANGUAGES:* English, Chinese (Mandarin) and Russian.

(For Complete Biographical Data on all Personnel see Professional Biographies of Rode & Qualey, New York, N.Y.)

DENTON HALL

A Member of the Denton International Group of Law Firms

10/F HUTCHISON HOUSE
10 HARCOURT ROAD
CENTRAL
HONG KONG
Telephone: 852-820 6272
Telex: 65750 DHB HX
Fax: 852-810 6434

Other Offices: London, England; Milton Keynes, Buckinghamshire, England; Moscow, Russia; Beijing, People's Republic of China; Brussels, Belgium; Los Angeles, California; Singapore; Tokyo, Japan.
Associated Offices: Amsterdam, Berlin, Chemnitz, Copenhagen, Dusseldorf, Frankfurt, Hamburg, Rotterdam and Vienna.

Banking, Company and Commercial, Corporate Finance M & A, Construction, Litigation and Arbitration, Media/Entertainment, Telecommunications, Intellectual Property, Infrastructure Projects.

PARTNERS

CHRISTOPHER CLARKE. PRACTICE AREAS: Commercial Litigation; Corporate and Banking.

MARTIN DOWNEY. PRACTICE AREAS: Construction; Construction Litigation.

PETER JANSEN. PRACTICE AREAS: Construction; Construction Litigation.

BERNADINE LAM. LANGUAGES: Cantonese. **PRACTICE AREAS:** Commercial; Corporate Finance; Corporate Law.

RAYMOND KWOK. LANGUAGES: Cantonese. **PRACTICE AREAS:** Property.

OF COUNSEL

JOHN KUZMIK (Also at Beijing, People's Republic of China). *LANGUAGES:* Mandarin. *PRACTICE AREAS:* Commercial; Corporate.

CONSULTANTS

SHEENA BRAND. PRACTICE AREAS: Construction; Construction Litigation.

CHRIS BRITTON. PRACTICE AREAS: Intellectual Property.

MICHAEL GERTLER. PRACTICE AREAS: Communications; Media.

(For all Firm Personnel, see Professional Biographies at London, England).

DEWEY BALLANTINE

ASIA PACIFIC FINANCE TOWER
SUITE 3907
CITIBANK PLAZA
3 GARDEN ROAD, CENTRAL
HONG KONG
Telephone: 852-2509-7000
Fax: 852-2509-7088

New York, New York Office: 1301 Avenue of the Americas, 10019-6092. Telephone: 212-259-8000. Fax: 212-259-6333.
Washington, D.C. Office: 1775 Pennsylvania Avenue, N.W., 20006-4605. Telephone: 202-862-1000. Fax: 202-862-1093.
Los Angeles, California Office: 333 South Hope Street, 90071-1406. Telephone: 213-626-3399. Fax: 213-625-0562.

(This Listing Continued)

London, England Office: 150 Aldersgate Street, London EC1A 4EJ, England. Telephone: 011-44-71-606-6121. Fax: 011-44-71-600-3754.
Dewey Ballantine Theodore Goddard Offices:
Prague, Czech Republic Office: Revolucni 13, 110 00 Prague 1, Czech Republic. Telephone: (42-2) 2481-0283. Fax: (42-2) 231-0983.
Budapest, Hungary Office: Vadasz utca 31, H-1054 Budpaest Hungary. Telephone: (36-1) 111-9620. Fax: (36-1) 112-2272.
Warsaw, Poland Office: ul. Klonowa 8, 00-591, Warsaw, Poland. Telephone: 48-22-49-3288. Fax: 48-22-49-8023.
Kraków, Poland Office: Pl. Axentowicza 6. 30-034 Kraków Poland. Telephone: 48-12-340-339. Fax: 48-12-333-624.

General Practice.

RESIDENT PARTNERS

JOSEPH M. JUHAS, born Torrington, Connecticut, November 22, 1944; admitted, 1971, New York (Not admitted in Hong Kong). *Education:* Harvard University (A.B., 1966); University of Pennsylvania (LL.B., 1969). *PRACTICE AREAS:* Corporate; Leasing; Project Finance.

JOSEPHINE C. WANG-HO, born Yunan, China, January 19, 1942; admitted, 1976, New York (Not admitted in Hong Kong). *Education:* National Taiwan University (LL.B., 1964); Columbia University (M.C.L., 1965); New York University (LL.M., 1967); Harvard Law School, East Asian Legal Institute Research Fellow, (1967-1971). Adjunct Lecturer of Law, National Taiwan University, 1968, Soochow University, 1968, New York City College, 1975 and Hunter College, 1978-1979, University of Florida, 1989. Advisory Board, Overseas Chinese Association, 1993. Member, Women's Policy Group, Washington, D.C., 1993. Governor and Supervisor, American Chamber of Commerce, Taipei, 1988-1992. Country Representative, International Bar Association, 1988—; American Bar Association. *LANGUAGES:* Mandarin Chinese, Cantonese, Shanghainese and Szechuanese. *PRACTICE AREAS:* Corporate.

RESIDENT ASSOCIATES

HELEN KWOK-WAI HO, born Kowloon, Hong Kong, September 29, 1954; admitted, 1990, District of Columbia, New York and Maryland (Not admitted in Hong Kong). *Education:* University of Hong Kong (B.S., 1977; D.M.S., 1980; M.B.A., 1982); Georgetown University (J.D., magna cum laude, 1989). Order of the Coif. Member of Staff, Law and Policy in International Business, 1988-1989. *Member:* The District of Columbia Bar; Maryland State, New York State and American Bar Associations.

MICHAEL J. KUNZ, born Middle Village, New York, October 26, 1963; admitted, 1989, New York; 1991, District of Columbia (Not admitted in Hong Kong). *Education:* Georgetown University (B.S.B.A., magna cum laude, 1985; J.D., cum laude, 1988).

MAO TONG, born Beijing, China, May 12, 1957; admitted, 1988, New York; 1993, District of Columbia (Not admitted in Hong Kong). *Education:* Columbia University (J.D., 1986). President, China Business Association, 1988-1990. Member, Board of Directors, China Financial Forum and Foreign Trade Advisor to the Governor of Sichuan and the Mayor of Tianjin, 1990-1992.

DUNSTAN STYLES & CO

(in association with Allens Arthur Robinson)

SUITE 1504
ONE EXCHANGE SQUARE
8 CONNAUGHT PLACE
HONG KONG
Telephone: (852) 2840 1202
Rapifax: (852) 2840 0686

Allens Arthur Robinson is an international network of group and associated offices representing the Allens Arthur Robinson group in Australia.
Group and Associated Offices:
London, England: Allens Arthur Robinson, Level 5, Bucklersbury House, 3 Queen Victoria Street, EC4N 8EL. Telephone: (44 171) 248 6130. Rapifax: (44 171) 248 6334.
New York, NY: Allens Arthur Robinson, 280 Park Avenue, 10017. Telephone: (1 212) 867 1555. Rapifax: (1 212) 867 7979.
Singapore: Allens Arthur Robinson, 65 Chulia Street #42-05, OCBC Centre, 0104. Telephone: (65) 535 6622. Rapifax: (65) 535 4855.
Jakarta, Indonesia: Wiradinata & Widyawan, Niaga Tower, 26th Floor, Jl. Jend. Sudirman, Kav 58, 12190. Telephone: (62 21) 250 5175. Rapifax: (62 21) 250 5185.

(This Listing Continued)

DUNSTAN STYLES & CO, *Hong Kong—Continued*

Port Moresby, Papua New Guinea: Allens Arthur Robinson, Level 11, Pacific Place, Cnr Musgrave Street & Champion Parade. Telephone: (675) 202 000. Rapifax: (675) 200 588.

Shanghai, People's Republic of China: AAR China Limited, Fuxing Xi Lu 37 Long 6 Hao. 200031. Telephone: (86 21) 437 7582. Rapifax: (86 21) 473 7819.

Allens Arthur Robinson's international network of offices represents:

Sydney, New South Wales, Australia: Allen Allen & Hemsley, The Chifley Tower, 2 Chifley Square, 2000. Telephone: (61 2) 230 4000. Rapifax: (61 2) 233 7022.

Canberra, Australian Capital Territory, Australia: Allen Allen & Hemsley, 3rd Floor, 16 Moore Street, 2601. Telephone: (61 6) 247 5800. Rapifax: (61 6) 257 1369.

Melbourne, Victoria, Australia: Arthur Robinson & Hedderwicks, Levels 27-34, 530 Collins Street, 3000. Telephone: (61 3) 614 1011. Rapifax: (61 3) 614 4661.

Brisbane, Queensland, Australia: Feez Ruthning, Riverside Centre, 123 Eagle Street, 4000. Telephone: (61 7) 833 3333. Rapifax: (61 7) 832 4233.

Surfers Paradise, Queensland, Australia: Feez Ruthning, Level 14, 50 Cavill Avenue, 4217. Telephone: (61 75) 70 0200. Rapifax: (61 75) 92 2285.

Perth, Western Australia, Australia: Parker & Parker, AMP Building, 140 St George's Terrace, 6000. Telephone: (61 9) 322 0321. Rapifax: (61 9) 322 2243.

Adelaide, South Australia, Australia: Finlaysons, 81 Flinders Street, 5000. Telephone: (61 8) 235 7400. Rapifax: (61 8) 232 2944.

FIRM PROFILE: Allens Arthur Robinson is engaged in general Hong Kong, China and International practice.

RESIDENT PARTNER

ROBERT CORNISH, Admitted in Hong Kong; England and Wales; New South Wales, Australia; New Zealand. *LANGUAGES:* English, Mandarin and Cantonese. *PRACTICE AREAS:* China Trade and Investment; Corporate; Commercial; Banking; Securities; Litigation; Intellectual Property.

HEAD OF CHINA TEAM

Zili Shao

FAIRBAIRN CATLEY LOW & KONG

Solicitors & Notaries Public

Agents for Trade Mark & Patents

43RD FLOOR, GLOUCESTER TOWER
THE LANDMARK, CENTRAL
HONG KONG
Telephone: 2522-2041; 2525-9161
Telex: 69219 EFKAY HX
Fax: 2845-9282; 2845-2928
Interchange: DX-9113-IC

FIRM PROFILE: The firm is one of Hong Kong's larger practices involved in all major aspects of Hong Kong law whilst remaining international in outlook. Built upon strong local and international foundations the firm has a well balanced mix of Chinese and British professional staff, speaking English, Cantonese, Mandarin and French. Clients include substantial Hong Kong and overseas based public and private companies as well as private individuals drawn from a wide cross-section of industry and commerce. The firm engages in all aspects of commercial and company law including mergers and acquisitions, joint venture and partnership, securities law, taxation, corporate finance, company and group restructurings, general corporate affairs, general banking business including loan and security documentation. The firm has a specialist department for copyright, trademarks and patents work, including registration, protection and enforcement, licensing and franchising and associated litigation. The firm's property and real estate department undertakes all work in connection with residential, commercial and industrial property, tenancies, project development, mortgages and land use.

(This Listing Continued)

AS58B

Associate offices in London and Melbourne and a member of Multilaw.

PARTNERS

William M. Catley	*Li Nin Hong*
Robert E. Low	*Christopher R.J. Hooley*
Billy C.H. Kong	*Judith A. Garratt*
Anthony R. Eccles	*Grace H.W. Chu*
R.S. Fraser	*Ng Kwok Cheong*
Paul E. Firmin	*Johnny C.M. Fee*
Edward A. Waller	*Dorina W.M. Wu*
Celia F.N. Chung	*Susan C.A. Kendall*

ASSOCIATES

Tam Sau Hing	*Loretta W.M. Chan*
Kitty Y.W. Chan	*Ray S.W. Poon*
Michael S. Lee	*Tse Yuen Ming, Valent*
Cary K.C. Fung	*Patrick T.C. Hui*
Francis C.F. Chan	*Corrina L.Y. Kwan*
Terry C.W. Wong	

CONSULTANT

KAREN S.Y. CHAN

Member of Multilaw

FRESHFIELDS

24TH FLOOR
ONE EXCHANGE SQUARE
HONG KONG
Telephone: (852) 846 3400
Fax: (852) 810 6192; G4
Fax: 8525022009

Other Offices in: Bangkok, Barcelona, Brussels, Frankfurt, Hanoi, London, Madrid, Moscow, New York, Paris, Singapore and Tokyo.

International, Corporate, Commercial, Securities, Banking, Aircraft and Litigation Law.

RESIDENT PARTNERS

MARK FREEMAN, born Nassau, Bahamas, September 29, 1943; admitted, 1969, England as Solicitor; 1985, Hong Kong. *Education:* Emmanuel College, Cambridge (M.A., LL.B.). *Member:* Hong Kong Law Society; Company and Financial Law Committee. *LANGUAGES:* English. *PRACTICE AREAS:* Aviation Finance; Banking Law; International Capital Markets; Project Finance; Commercial Law; Energy Law.

THOMAS E. JONES, born Penn Yan, New York, August 11, 1949; admitted, 1980, California (Not admitted in Hong Kong). *Education:* Williams College (B.A., 1971); Harvard University (Ed.M., 1974); University of California at Berkeley (M.A., 1977); Harvard University and Boalt Hall School of Law, University of California (J.D., 1980). *Member:* State Bar of California. Board of Governors, American Chamber of Commerce, Beijing, 1990-1991. Author: Chapter: "Foreign Exchange Balancing Issues," The Life and Death of a Joint Venture in the People's Republic of China (Asia Law & Practice Ltd, 1993). *LANGUAGES:* English and Chinese. *PRACTICE AREAS:* Joint Ventures; Licensing; Commercial law; Banking Law.

ALASTAIR J. CRAWFORD, born England, June 22, 1959; admitted, 1984, England as Solicitor; 1990, Hong Kong. *Education:* St. John's College, Cambridge (M.A.). *PRACTICE AREAS:* Commercial Litigation; International Arbitration.

TERESA KO, born Hong Kong, August 23, 1960; admitted, 1986, England as Solicitor; 1986, Hong Kong. *Education:* University of Westminster (B.A., Hons., Law); Jesus College, Cambridge (LL.M., Law). *LANGUAGES:* English, Cantonese and Mandarin. *PRACTICE AREAS:* Aviation Finance; Joint Ventures; Corporate Law; Mergers and Acquisitions; Securities Offerings; Privatizations.

PATRICK S. GAYNOR, born England, 1954; admitted, 1981, Solicitor, England (Not admitted in Hong Kong). *Education:* St. Andrew's University, College of Law (M.A.). *Member:* Law Society. *PRACTICE AREAS:* Corporate Law; Mergers and Acquisitions; Securities Offerings; Corporate Restructuring.

(This Listing Continued)

KEVIN JULIAN, born Dartford, England, September 5, 1951; admitted, 1975, England and Wales as Solicitor; Singapore as Advocate and Solicitor; Hong Kong as Advocate and Solicitor. *Education:* Downing College, Cambridge (B.A. Hons.; 1974; M.A., 1977). *PRACTICE AREAS:* International Finance; Project Finance; Joint Ventures; Power Project Development; Property Development.

MARTIN TAYLOR, born England, November 29, 1960; admitted, 1986, Solicitor, England and Wales (Not admitted in Hong Kong). *Education:* University of Bristol (LL.B.). *PRACTICE AREAS:* Mergers and Acquisitions; Securities Offerings; International Capital Markets; Joint Ventures; Corporate and Commercial Law.

NICOLAS F. JOHNSTON, born Canberra, October 10, 1960; admitted, 1984, Solicitor, New South Wales; 1989, Solicitor, England and Wales (Not admitted in Hong Kong). *Education:* University of Sydney (B.A., LL.B.). *PRACTICE AREAS:* International Banking and Finance; Project Finance; Aviation Finance.

NORMAN P. GIVANT, born Oakland, California, September 1, 1943; admitted, 1980, California; 1982, New York (Not admitted in Hong Kong). *Education:* Dartmouth College and University of California (B.A., 1966); Boalt Hall School of Law (J.D., 1980). *Member:* New York State and American Bar Associations; State Bar of California; President, American Chamber of Commerce, Shanghai. *LANGUAGES:* English and Chinese. *PRACTICE AREAS:* Direct Investment in The People's Republic of China.

RESIDENT ASSOCIATES

CARL B. CHENG, born Rahway, New Jersey, May 1, 1960; admitted, 1985, California (Not admitted in Hong Kong). *Education:* Yale College (B.A., 1982); Boalt Hall School of Law, University of California at Berkeley (J.D., 1985); National Taiwan Normal University and Beijing University (Chinese Language Training, 1990-1992 and 1993); Keio University (Japanese Language Training, 1992-1993). Member, California Law Review, 1983-1985. Author: "Important Rights and the Private Attorney General Doctrine," 73 California Law Review, 1929 (1985). *Member:* State Bar of California. *LANGUAGES:* English, Chinese and Japanese. *PRACTICE AREAS:* Direct Investment in The People's Republic of China.

DOUGLAS C. MARKEL, born Buffalo, New York, June 14, 1962; admitted, 1991, New York (Not admitted in Hong Kong). *Education:* Yale University (B.A., 1984); Harvard University (J.D., 1990). Yale-China Teaching Fellow, Changsha, Hunan, People's Republic of China, 1984-1986. *LANGUAGES:* Mandarin and Cantonese Chinese, French and English. *PRACTICE AREAS:* Direct Investment in The People's Republic of China.

IVAN YI-FAN CHIANG, born Tapei, Taiwan, January 30, 1961; admitted, 1993, New York (Not admitted in Hong Kong). *Education:* National Taiwan University (B.A., 1983); Department of Political Science, Columbia University (M.A., 1987; M.Phil., 1989); School of Law, Columbia University (J.D., 1992). *Member:* New York State Bar Association. *LANGUAGES:* English, Chinese and Taiwanese. *PRACTICE AREAS:* Direct Investment in The People's Republic of China.

RANDALL P. PEERENBOOM, born Green Bay, Wisconsin, May 5, 1958; admitted, 1993, Hawaii (Not admitted in Hong Kong). *Education:* University of Wisconsin-Madison (B.A., Philosophy, 1980); University of Hawaii (M.A., Chinese Religions, 1987; Ph.D., Philosophy, 1990); Columbia University (J.D., 1993). Author of several works on: Chinese philosophy and law, including Law and Morality in Ancient China: The Silk Manuscripts of Huang-Lao. *LANGUAGES:* English, Mandarin and Japanese. *PRACTICE AREAS:* Direct Investment in The Prople's Republic of China.

MATTHEW COSANS, born London, England, July 26, 1960; admitted, 1985, England. *Education:* Cambridge University (M.A., Hons., 1982); College of Law (1983). *Member:* Law Society of England and Wales. *PRACTICE AREAS:* Direct Investment in The Prople's Republic of China.

MARK DAY, born Adelaide, South Australia, February 17, 1954; admitted, 1993, Melbourne, Victoria. *Education:* University of Queensland (B.A., 1979; M.A. Qual., 1982); Beijing Languages Institute (Chinese Language Training, 1980); Nanjing University, China (Certificate of Training in Economics, 1980-1982); University of Melbourne, Law School (LL.B.,

(This Listing Continued)

1992). *Member:* Law Institute of Victoria. *LANGUAGES:* English and Chinese. *PRACTICE AREAS:* Direct Investment in The People's Republic of China.

(For List of Partners see Professional Biographies at London, England).

FULBRIGHT & JAWORSKI L.L.P.

2901 CENTRAL PLAZA
18 HARBOUR ROAD
WANCHAI
HONG KONG
Telephone: 011-852-511-5100
Fax: 011-852-511-9515

Houston, Texas Office: 1301 McKinney, Suite 5100, 77010-3095. Telephone: 713-651-5151. Cable Address: "Fulbright." Telecopier: 713-651-5246. Telex: 76-2829.

Washington, D.C. Office: Market Square, 801 Pennsylvania Avenue, N.W., 20004-2604. Telephone: 202-662-0200. Telecopier: 202-662-4643. Telex: 89-2602.

Austin, Texas Office: 600 Congress Avenue, Suite 2400, 78701. Telephone: 512-474-5201. Telecopier: 512-320-4599.

San Antonio, Texas Office: 300 Convent Street, Suite 2200, 78205. Telephone: 210-224-5575. Telecopier: 210-223-6459.

Dallas, Texas Office: 2200 Ross Avenue, Suite 2800, 75201. Telephone: 214-855-8000. Telecopier: 214-855-8200.

New York, New York Office: 666 Fifth Avenue, 10103. Telephone: 212-318-3000. Telecopier: 212-318-3000. Telex: TWX 710-581-3676.

Los Angeles California Office: 865 South Figueroa Street, 29th Floor, 90017-2571. Telephone: 213-892-9200. Telecopier: 213-680-4518. Telex: 69-1208.

London, England Office: 2 St. James's Place, SW1A 1NP. Telephone: 011-44171-629-1207. Telecopier: 011-4471-493-8259.

General International Practice. Arbitration of Commercial Disputes, Commercial and Corporate, International Trade Transactions, Taxation.
Firm engaged in American and International Law Practice but not authorized to appear before the Hong Kong Courts or to act as Hong Kong Solicitors.

PARTNERS IN CHARGE

JEFFREY A. BLOUNT, born Alexandria, Virginia, November 24, 1957; admitted, 1983, District of Columbia (Not admitted in Hong Kong). *Education:* Princeton University (A.B., 1979); University of Virginia (J.D., 1983). *Member:* The District of Columbia Bar; American Bar Association. *PRACTICE AREAS:* Tax Law; Commercial Law.

GEORGE H. LIU, born Taiwan, September 14, 1945; admitted, 1975, Illinois; U.S. District Court, Northern District of Illinois; U.S. Supreme Court (Not admitted in Hong Kong). *Education:* Central University of Iowa (B.A., 1968); Western Illinois University; Valparaiso University (J.D., 1974). State of Illinois Director, Far East Office, 1978-1980. *Member:* Illinois State, International and American Bar Associations; Inter-Pacific Bar Association; Law Association for Asia Pacific. *PRACTICE AREAS:* International Transactions; Corporation Law.

SUSAN P. LIU, born Port Chester, New York, January 12, 1948; admitted, 1977, Illinois (Not admitted in Hong Kong). *Education:* Valparaiso University (B.A., 1974); University of Chicago (J.D., 1977). *Member:* Illinois State, International and American (Co-Chairman, Far East Law Committee, 1984-1985) Bar Associations; Inter-Pacific Bar Association; Law Association for Asia Pacific. *PRACTICE AREAS:* International Transactions; Corporation Law.

ASSOCIATES

PHEBE W. CHU, admitted, 1993, California (Not admitted in Hong Kong). *Education:* University of California at Davis (B.S., 1988; J.D., 1992); University of San Diego (M.B.A., 1993). *PRACTICE AREAS:* International.

DAVID K.W. CHUNG, admitted, 1988, California (Not admitted in Hong Kong). *Education:* Santa Clara University (B.S., 1983; M.B.A., 1985); University of San Francisco School of Law (J.D., 1988). *PRACTICE AREAS:* International.

P. LIEN DANG GALLOWAY, born Bien Hoa, Vietnam, February 17, 1959; admitted, 1989, Texas (Not admitted in Hong Kong). *Education:* Gonzaga University (B.Ed., 1982); University of Notre Dame (J.D., 1988). *PRACTICE AREAS:* International.

(This Listing Continued)

FULBRIGHT & JAWORSKI L.L.P., Hong Kong—
Continued

ROBERT B. MOY, admitted, 1988, New Jersey; 1989, New York (Not admitted in Hong Kong). *Education:* Wharton School, University of Pennsylvania (B.S., 1985); St. John's University (J.D.,1988); Georgetown University (Ll.M., 1993). *PRACTICE AREAS:* International.

(For Biographies of Houston, Texas Personnel, see Houston, Texas Professional Biographies).
(For Biographies of Austin, Texas Personnel, see Austin, Texas Professional Biographies).
(For Biographies of San Antonio, Texas Personnel, see San Antonio, Texas Professional Biographies).
(For Biographies of Dallas, Texas Personnel, see Dallas, Texas Professional Biographies). (For Biographies of Los Angeles, California Personnel, see Los Angeles, California Professional Biographies).
(For Biographies of New York, New York Personnel, see New York, New York Professional Biographies).
(For Biographies of London, England Personnel, see London, England Professional Biographies).

GIBSON, DUNN & CRUTCHER

Established in 1890

10TH FLOOR, TWO PACIFIC PLACE
88 QUEENSWAY
HONG KONG
Telephone: 011-2852-526-6816
Telex: 65665 GIBTK HX
Telecopier: 011-2852-845-9144

Los Angeles, California Office: 333 South Grand Avenue, 90071-3197. Telephone: 213-229-7000. Telex: 188171 GIBTRASK LSA (TRT), 674930 GIBTRASK LSA (WUT). Telecopier: 213-229-7520. Cable Address: GIBTRASK LOS ANGELES.

International Investments, International Tax, International Corporate Finance and Capital Markets Transactions, Trust and Estate Planning, Acquisitions, Banking and General Corporate and Commercial Law.
Firm engages in American and International Law Practice but is not authorized to appear before Hong Kong Courts or to act as Hong Kong Solicitors.

FIRM PROFILE: Gibson, Dunn & Crutcher, originating in Los Angeles, has been providing legal services to clients since 1890. Today, the firm has grown to one of the largest law firms in the world with approximately 650 attorneys in 17 offices situated in most of the world's important business centers. The firm has experts in virtually every area of the law, particularly those which relate to commercial transactions and disputes, and has more effective geographical coverage in the United States than any other major firm. The firm's lawyers and staff are dedicated to providing quality service on a timely and cost effective basis.

The Hong Kong office provides advice in connection with a broad range of areas, including financings, acquisitions, international tax planning, international corporate finance and capital markets transactions; trust and estate planning; banking, corporate and commercial investments; international matters; and matters relating to the People's Republic of China, including joint ventures and other investment vehicles for participation in China's growth.

RESIDENT PARTNERS

CHARLES R. COLLINS, born September 1, 1931; admitted, 1960, California; 1972, Tennessee (Not admitted in Hong Kong). *Education:* University of California at Los Angeles (B.A., 1953); Harvard University (LL.B., cum laude, 1959). *PRACTICE AREAS:* Real Estate Law; Securities Law; Bankruptcy Law; Mergers and Acquisitions Law; General Corporate Law; International Law.

JAMES EDWARD BASS, born January 3, 1959; admitted, 1987, California (Not admitted in Hong Kong). *Education:* Yale University (B.A., magna cum laude, 1982); Stanford University (J.D., 1987). Editor-in-Chief, Stanford Journal of International Law, 1986-1987. Judicial Clerk for the Hon. Thomas Gibbs Gee, U.S. Court of Appeals for the Fifth Circuit. Lecturer, College of Business and Management, Peking University, 1994. *LANGUAGES:* Chinese. *PRACTICE AREAS:* Corporations; Securities; International.

HSIAO-CHIUNG LI, born November 22, 1962; admitted, 1987, Pennsylvania; 1988, District of Columbia; 1994, New York (Not admitted in
(This Listing Continued)

Hong Kong). *Education:* Wesleyan University (B.A., 1984); Yale Law School (J.D., 1987). Phi Beta Kappa. Law Clerk to Hon. John M. Ferren, D.C. Court of Appeals, 1987-1988. *LANGUAGES:* Chinese. *PRACTICE AREAS:* Corporations; International.

OF COUNSELS

XUHUA HUANG, born November 29, 1964; admitted, 1989, People's Republic of China (Not admitted in Hong Kong). *Education:* People's University of China (B.L., 1986); People's University of China. Tutor, People's University of China, 1986-1987. Assistant Judge, Xiqu District People's Court of Changsha, China, 1986. Chief of the Commercial Department of China Global Law Office, 1993. *Member:* International Bar Association. (Hong Kong and New York City Offices).

FENGWEN JIANG, born February 1, 1959; admitted, 1989, Pennsylvania; 1990, Virginia; 1991, District of Columbia (Not admitted in Hong Kong). *Education:* Peking University School of Law, China (LL.B., 1984); University of California, Boalt Hall School of Law (LL.M., 1986; J.D., 1988). *LANGUAGES:* Chinese (Mandarin). *PRACTICE AREAS:* Corporations; International Trade and Investment.

ASSOCIATES

STELLA S. LEUNG, born February 3, 1968; admitted, 1992, Texas (Not admitted in Hong Kong). *Education:* University of Texas at Austin (B.A., 1989); University of Texas School of Law (J.D., with honors, 1992). Articles Editor, American Journal of Criminal Law, 1991-1992. *LANGUAGES:* Chinese.

DEBORAH M. ROSENBERG, born September 23, 1966; admitted, 1992, California (Inactive); 1993, District of Columbia (Not admitted in Hong Kong). *Education:* Harvard College (A.B., 1989); Harvard Law School (J.D., 1992). *LANGUAGES:* Chinese (Mandarin), Japanese.

STEPHEN B. DORROUGH, born January 2, 1967; admitted, 1994, Washington (Not admitted in Hong Kong). *Education:* Brigham Young University (B.A., 1991); East China University of Politics and Law, Shanghai, P.R.C.; University of Hong Kong Faculty of Law, Hong Kong; University of Utah (J.D., 1994). William H. Leary Scholar. *LANGUAGES:* Cantonese, Mandarin.

(For information on firm personnel, address and telephone information regarding the firm's offices located in Century City, Irvine, San Diego, Menlo Park and San Francisco, California; Denver, Colorado; Washington, D.C.; New York, N.Y.; Dallas, Texas; Seattle, Washington; London, England; Paris, France; Tokyo, Japan and Jeddah and Riyadh, Saudi Arabia (Affiliated Offices), see professional biographies at Los Angeles, California)

GOODMAN PHILLIPS & VINEBERG

30/F, PEREGRINE TOWER, LIPPO CENTRE
89 QUEENSWAY ROAD
G.P.O. 953
HONG KONG
Telephone: 852-522-1061
Facsimile Communications: 852-845-9089

Montreal Office: 5 Place Ville Marie, 17th Floor, Montreal, Quebec, Canada H3B 2G2. Telephone: 514-866-8541. Facsimile Communications: 514-875-0344.
Toronto Office: 250 Yonge Street, Suite 2400, P.O. Box 24, Toronto, Ontario, Canada M5H 2M6. Telephone: 416-979-2211. Facsimile Communications: 416-979-1234.
New York, New York Office: 430 Park Avenue, 10th Floor, New York, New York, 10022. Telephone: 212-308-8866. Facsimile Communications: 212-308-0132.

General Corporate, Mergers and Acquisitions, Securities, Joint Ventures, Tax, Banking, Financings and Financial Services, Competition and International Contracts.

RESIDENTS

ERMANNO PASCUTTO, born Italy, May 22, 1953; admitted, 1979, Ontario (Not admitted in Hong Kong). *Education:* University of Toronto (LL.B., 1977). Executive Director, Ontario Securities Commission, 1984-1989. Deputy Chairman, Vice-Chairman and Executive Director, Hong Kong Securities and Futures Commission, 1989-1994.

CALLY JORDAN, born Ottawa, Ontario, 1949; admitted, 1981, Ontario and Quebec; 1984, California; 1986, New York (Not admitted in Hong Kong). *Education:* Carleton University (B.A., 1970) University of
(This Listing Continued)

Toronto (M.A., 1973) McGill University (LL.B., 1977; B.C.L., 1980); University of Paris I (Sorbonne) (D.E.A., 1978). Author (Partial Listing): "Countervailing Duties: Softwood Products Revisited," Trade Law Topics, March 1986; "The Convention on Recognition of Trusts," 1 N.Y. Int'l Law Rev. 18, 1987; "U.S. Takeover Defences—In the Canadian Context," 2 Rev. Int'l Bus. Law 205, 1988; "The Canada-United States Free Trade Agreement," The Review of Banking & Financial Services, New York, February 1989; "Multijurisdictional Disclosure System," The Review of Commodities and Securities Regulation, New York, March 28, 1990; "Multijurisdictional Disclosure System," Securities and Corporate Regulation Review, 109, September 1990; "Cross-border Shopping for Securities Markets," The Financial Post, p. 9, June 19, 1991; "Benefits of Cross-border Security Law," The Financial Post, p. 30, September 9, 1991. Associate Professor, Faculty of Law McGill University, 1991—. *Member:* Canadian (Executive), New York State (Member, International Section) and American Bar Associations; Union Internationale des Avocats; Association International des Jeunes Avocats.

MARIE-JOSÉE TRÉPANIER, born Valleyfield, Québec, June 30, 1962; admitted, 1987, Québec (Not admitted in Hong Kong). *Education:* University of Montréal (LL.B., 1986); École du Barreau du Québec; Quebec Law School; London School of Economics, London, England (LL.M., 1989). Member, University of London Alumni Association, 1989—. *Member:* The National and International Commercial Arbitration Centre.

GRAHAM & JAMES
(IN ASSOCIATION WITH DEACONS)
HONG KONG
(See Deacons)

GRICE & CO., SOLICITORS

(In Association with White & Case)

3501 EDINBURGH TOWER, THE LANDMARK
15 QUEEN'S ROAD CENTRAL
HONG KONG
Telephone: (852) 826-0333
Facsimile: (852) 526-7166

New York, New York: Telephone: 212-819-8200. Facsimile: 212-354-8113.
Washington, D.C.: Telephone: 202-872-0013. Facsimile: 202-872-0210.
Los Angeles, California: Telephone: 213-620-7700. Facsimile: 213-687-0758; 213-617-2205.
Miami, Florida: Telephone: 305-371-2700. Facsimile: 305-358-5744.
Mexico City, Mexico: Telephone: (52-5) 207-9717. Facsimile: (52-5) 208-3628.
Tokyo, Japan: Telephone: (81-3) 3239-4300. Facsimile: (81-3) 3239-4330.
Hong Kong: Telephone: (852) 2822-8700. Facsimile: (852) 2845-9070.
Singapore, Republic of Singapore: Telephone: (65) 225-6000. Facsimile: (65) 225-6009.
Bangkok, Thailand: Pacific Legal Group Ltd., In Association With White & Case, Telephone: (662) 236-6154/7. Facsimile: (662) 237-6771.
Hanoi, Viet Nam: Representative Office, Telephone: (84-4) 227-575/6/7. Facsimile: (84-4) 227-297.
Bombay, India: Telephone: (91-22) 282-6300. Facsimile: (91-22) 282-6305.
London, England: Telephone: (44-171) 726-6361. Facsimile: (44-171) 726-4314; (44-171) 726-8558.
Paris, France: Telephone: (33-1) 42-60-34-05. Facsimile: (33-1) 42-60-82-46.
Brussels, Belgium: Telephone: (32-2) 647-05-89. Facsimile: (32-2) 647-16-75.
Stockholm, Sweden: Telephone: (46-8) 679-80-30. Facsimile: (46-8) 611-21-22.
Helsinki, Finland: Telephone: (358-0) 631-100. Facsimile: (358-0) 179-477.
Moscow, Russia: Telephone: (7-095) 201-9292/3/4/5. Facsimile: (7-095) 201-9284.
Budapest, Hungary: Telephone: (36-1) 269-0550; (36-1) 131-0933. Facsimile: (36-1) 269-1199.

(This Listing Continued)

Prague, Czech Republic: Telephone: (42-2) 2481-1796. Facsimile: (42-2) 232-5522.
Warsaw, Poland: Telephone/Facsimile: (48-22) 26-80-53; (48-22) 27-84-86. International Telephone/Facsimile: (48-39) 12-19-06.
Istanbul, Turkey: Telephone: (90-212) 275-68-98; (90-212) 275-75-33. Facsimile: (90-212) 275-75-43.
Ankara, Turkey: Telephone: (90-312) 446-2180. Facsimile: (90-312) 437-9677.
Jeddah, Saudi Arabia: Law Office of Hassan Mahassni, Telephone: (966-2) 651-3535. Facsimile: (966-2) 651-3636.
Riyadh, Saudi Arabia: Law Office of Hassan Mahassni, Telephone: (966-1) 476-7099. Facsimile: (966-1) 479-0110.
Almaty, Kazakhstan: Telephone: (7-3272) 50-7491/2. Facsimile: (7-3272) 61-0842.

General International Practice.

PARTNERS

R. GEOFFREY GRICE, born Perth, Western Australia, March 22, 1956; admitted, 1987, England and Wales; 1988, Hong Kong; 1993, Northern Territory of Australia. *Education:* University of Western Australia (B.A., 1981); Cambridge University (B.A., Hons., 1983; M.A., 1987); Nichibei Kaiwa Gakuin, Tokyo (Diploma in Advanced Japanese, 1979). *Member:* Law Society of England and Wales; Law Society of Hong Kong.

ASSOCIATES

STEVEN P. ALLEN, born Adelaide, Australia, March 14, 1962; admitted, 1986, South Australia; 1994, England and Wales (Not admitted in Hong Kong). *Education:* University of Adelaide (LL.B., 1986); South Australia Institute of Technology (G.D.L.P., 1987). (Also Associate, White & Case).

ANDREW HIN CHI CHAN, born Hong Kong, February 5, 1968; admitted, 1993, Scotland; 1994, Hong Kong. *Education:* University of Aberdeen (LL.B., 1991; D.L.P., 1992). (Also Associate, White & Case).

ANDREW P. MCLEAN, born Manchester, England, January 7, 1962; admitted, 1986, England and Wales; 1994, Hong Kong. *Education:* Birmingham University (LL.B., 1983). (Also Associate, White & Case).

KIM MARGARET ROONEY, born Sydney, Australia, 1957; admitted, 1980, West Australia; 1991, England; 1992, Hong Kong. *Education:* University of Western Australia Law School (B.Juris., 1979; LL.B., 1980).

ALEX Y. WONG, born Beijing, China, November 30, 1964; admitted, 1994, Hong Kong. *Education:* University of Hong Kong (LL.B., 1991). (Also Associate, White & Case).

(For biographical data as to other locations, see Professional Biographies at New York, New York; Washington, D.C.; Los Angeles, California; Miami, Florida; Mexico City, Mexico; Tokyo, Japan; Hong Kong; Singapore, Republic of Singapore; Bangkok, Thailand; Hanoi, Viet Nam; Bombay, India; London, England; Paris, France; Brussels, Belgium; Stockholm, Sweden; Helsinki, Finland; Moscow, Russia; Budapest, Hungary; Prague, Czech Republic; Warsaw, Poland; Istanbul and Ankara, Turkey; Jeddah and Riyadh, Saudi Arabia; Almaty, Kazakhstan).

HAMPTON, WINTER AND GLYNN

38TH FLOOR, ASIA PACIFIC FINANCE TOWER
CITIBANK PLAZA
3 GARDEN ROAD, CENTRAL
HONG KONG
Telephone: (852) 2847 2300
Telex: 83987 JUS HX
Fax: (852) 2845 9168

Associated Firm: Hill Taylor Dickinson, Irongate House, Duke's Place, London EC3A 7LP England. Telephone: 071 283 9033. Fax: 071 283 1144.

FIRM PROFILE: The firm was established in 1972 and has developed an international practice with special emphasis on the Asia Pacific region and China and is engaged in the following areas: company, corporate finance, commercial, tax, international transactions, commercial litigation and arbitration, family, shipping, intellectual property, probate, private client, immigration, commercial fraud and criminal litigation.

(This Listing Continued)

HAMPTON, WINTER AND GLYNN, Hong Kong—
Continued

PARTNERS

DAVID GLYNN, admitted, 1965, England; 1975, Hong Kong; 1980, Victoria, Australia. Notary Public. Fellow, International Academy of Matrimonial Lawyers. *Member:* Gibraltarian Bar (Honorary Member); Hong Kong Family Law Association; Committee of the Hong Kong Marriage and Personal Counselling Service. *PRACTICE AREAS:* Family Law; Matrimonial Law; Matrimonial Finance; Conflict of Jurisdictions.

DAVID COTTERILL, admitted, 1974, England; 1975, Hong Kong; 1982, Victoria, Australia. *Education:* London University (LL.B.). Associate, Chartered Institute of Arbitrators. *PRACTICE AREAS:* Commercial Litigation and Arbitration.

ROBIN EGERTON, admitted, 1984, England and Hong Kong. *Education:* Durham University (B.A.). Fellow, International Academy of Matrimonial Lawyers. *PRACTICE AREAS:* Family Law; Child Care; Matrimonial Law; Matrimonial Finance.

SHARON SER, admitted, 1983, England; 1987, Hong Kong. *Education:* London School of Economics, London University (LL.B.). *Member:* The Hong Kong Family Law Association (Chairman). *PRACTICE AREAS:* Family Law; Child Care; Matrimonial Law; Matrimonial Finance; Commercial Fraud; Criminal Litigation; Advocacy.

FRANCIS RODRIGUES, admitted, 1986, Hong Kong. *Education:* University of Hong Kong (LL.B.). *PRACTICE AREAS:* Conveyancing and Commercial Transactions; Probate and Administration of Estates.

NICHOLAS MALLARD, admitted, 1983, England; 1989, Hong Kong. *Education:* Liverpool University (LL.B.). *Member:* Hong Kong Insurers Club. (Also Partner, Hill Taylor Dickinson, London). *PRACTICE AREAS:* Shipping; Admiralty and International Trade Litigation; Dispute Resolution.

MARTIN LISTER, admitted, 1984, England and Hong Kong. *Education:* King's College, London University (LL.B.). *Member:* Hong Kong Insurers Club; The British Chamber of Commerce in Hong Kong. *PRACTICE AREAS:* Corporate and Commercial Transactions; Joint Ventures; Insurance and Securities Regulation; Retirement Schemes and Trusts; Intellectual Property; Tax.

NIGEL BINNERSLEY, admitted, 1984, England; 1985, Hong Kong. *Education:* University College of Wales (LL.B.). (Also Partner, Hill Taylor Dickinson, London). *PRACTICE AREAS:* Shipping; Admiralty and International Trade Litigation; Dispute Resolution.

MARTIN WALDRON, admitted, 1976, England; 1981, Hong Kong; 1985, Victoria, Australia. *Education:* School of Oriental and African Studies, London University (B.A.); University of East Asia (Diploma, Chinese Law); University of Hong Kong (LL.M.). Associate, The Chartered Institute of Arbitrators. External Examiner, Post Graduate Certificate in Laws, University of Hong Kong and City Polytechnic of Hong Kong. *PRACTICE AREAS:* Commercial Litigation and Arbitration.

CONSULTANTS

BRUCE FUNG NAI-LOK, admitted, 1984, Hong Kong. *Education:* Hong Kong Polytechnic (Higher Diploma, Accounting); London University (LL.B.). *Member:* Association of Certified Accountants. *PRACTICE AREAS:* Conveyancing; Corporate Affairs; Taxation and Accounting Matters.

ROBERT CHENEY, admitted, 1983, Canada; 1993, Hong Kong. *Education:* Simon Fraser University (B.A.); University of British Columbia (LL.B.). *Member:* The Canadian Chamber of Commerce in Hong Kong. *PRACTICE AREAS:* Corporate Law; Joint Ventures and Investments in Hong Kong, China, Thailand and South East Asia.

CHEN ZHINAN, admitted, 1984, China (Not admitted in Hong Kong). *Education:* Zhongshan University, Guangzhou, China (1965-1970); South Western University School of Law, Los Angeles (1983-1984); Chengdu University of Science and Technology, Chengdu, China (1986-1987); Cardiff University, Law Department, Wales (1988-1989). Author: Translation of "Encyclopedia of International Law" from English to Chinese. **LAN-**

(This Listing Continued)

GUAGES: English and Chinese (Cantonese, Mandarin). *PRACTICE AREAS:* Maritime Law.

ASSOCIATES

Michael Chik	James Knight
Caterina Chiu	Simmy Mak
Philippa Hewitt	Vanky Mak
	Jonathan Mok

HEALY & BAILLIE

Established in 1948

LUK HOI TONG BUILDING
SUITE 1301, 31 QUEEN'S ROAD CENTRAL
HONG KONG
Telephone: (852) 2537-8628
Telecopier: (852) 2521-9072
MCI E-MAIL: 641-2689

New York, New York Office: 29 Broadway, 10006-3293. Telephone: 212-943-3980. Telecopier: 212-425-0131. MCI E-MAIL: 566-4694. Telex: 422089. Cable "Mainbrace New York".

Admiralty, Corporate and General Practice.

RESIDENT PARTNER

GENRONG YU, born Shanghai, The People's Republic of China, March 17, 1949; admitted, 1990, New York. *Education:* Anhui Normal University (B.A., 1982); Shanghai Maritime Institute (LL.M., 1985); University of Maine (J.D., 1989). Instructor of Law, Shanghai Maritime Institute, China, 1985-1986. Assistant Lawyer, Shanghai Lawyers Office for Maritime Affairs, 1985-1986. *Member:* American Bar Association; Maritime Law Association of the United States. *PRACTICE AREAS:* Maritime Law; Commercial Law; International Practice.

(For Complete Biographical Data on all Personnel see Professional Biographies in New York, New York)

HELLER EHRMAN WHITE & McAULIFFE

A Partnership including Professional Corporations

2816-17 JARDINE HOUSE
1 CONNAUGHT PLACE, CENTRAL
HONG KONG
Telephone: (011) 852-2526-6381
Facsimile: (011) 852-2810-6242

Los Angeles, California Office: 601 S. Figueroa Street. Telephone: 213-689-0200. Facsimile: 213-614-1868.
Palo Alto, California Office: 525 University Avenue, Suite 1100. Telephone: 415-324-7000. Facsimile: 415-324-0638.
San Francisco, California Office: 333 Bush Street. Telephone: 415-772-6000. Facsimile: 415-772-6268. Cable Address: "Helpow". Telex: 340-895; 184-996.
Seattle, Washington Office: 6100 Columbia Center, 701 Fifth Avenue. Telephone: 206-447-0900. Facsimile: 206-447-0849.
Portland, Oregon Office: 1600 Koin Center, 222 S.W. Columbia Street. Telephone: 503-227-7400. Facsimile: 503-241-0950.
Anchorage, Alaska Office: 1900 Ensearch Center, 550 West 7th Avenue. Telephone: 907-277-1900. Facsimile: 907-277-1920.
Tacoma, Washington Office: 1400 First Interstate Plaza, 1201 Pacific Avenue. Telephone: 206-572-6666. Facsimile: 206-572-6743.
Washington, D.C. Office: The Southern Building, 805 15th Street, N.W., Suite 610, Telephone: 202-842-1700. Facsimile: 202-842-4080.
Singapore Office: 50 Raffles Place, 17-04 Shell Tower. Telephone: (011) 65 538-1756. Facsimile: (011) 65 538-1537.

General Practice.

SPECIAL COUNSEL

SIMON LUK, born Hong Kong, February 10, 1954; admitted, 1979, New York (Not admitted in Hong Kong). *Education:* Columbia University (A.B., 1975; J.D., 1978). Phi Beta Kappa. Harlan Fiske Stone Scholar. Member, Columbia Journal of Transnational Law, 1977-1978. Author: "Legal Institutions in China," The Association of the Bar of the City of New York, March, 1980; "China's New Breed of Lawyers," New York Law Journal, December, 1979.

(This Listing Continued)

ASSOCIATES

KRISTINE A. WONG, born Edmonton, Alberta, Canada, July 6, 1964; admitted, 1994, California (Not admitted in Hong Kong). *Education:* University of California at Davis (B.A., 1988); University of California, Hastings College of the Law (J.D., 1992). Omicron Delta Epsilon.

(For complete biographical data on Anchorage, Alaska, Los Angeles, California, Palo Alto, California, San Francisco, California, Washington, D.C., Portland, Oregon, Seattle, Washington, Tacoma, Washington and Singapore office personnel, see Professional Biographies at each of those cities)

HERBERT SMITH

17TH FLOOR, EDINBURGH TOWER
15 QUEEN'S ROAD CENTRAL
HONG KONG
Telephone: 852-845 6639
Telex: 72266
Fax: 852-845 9099

London, England Office: Exchange House, Primrose Street, EC2A 2HS. Telephone: 071-374-8000. Telex: 886633. Fax: 071-496-0043.
Paris, France Office: 41 Avenue George V., 75008. Telephone: 3314-723-9124. Telex: 219602. Fax: 3314-720-9213.
Brussels, Belgium Office: 15, Rue Guimard, 1040. Telephone: 322-511 7450. Fax: 322-511 7772.

RESIDENT PARTNERS

N.K. Bacon	*M. Lloyd-Williams*
T.C. Parkes	*Patricia Shih*
P.T. Bellis	*M.D. Johnson*
A.J. Calderwood	*J.C. Young*
D.N. Francis	*A.I. Alder*
	A. Tortoishell

(For List of Partners see Professional Biographies at London, England)

HILBORNE, HAWKIN & CO.

Legal Consultants, Advocates and Solicitors
Trademark, Copyright & Patent Agents
Established in 1965
M2-3, NEW HENRY HOUSE
10, ICE HOUSE STREET, CENTRAL
HONG KONG
Telephone: 852-869-0828
Facsimile: 852-810-1703

Orange, California Administrative Office: 2534 N. Santiago Blvd., 92667. Telephone: (714) 283-1155. Facsimile: (714) 283-1555; 532-2713.
Brunei Service Address for Trademark Registration: Suite 31, 3rd Floor, Britannia House, 38 Jalan Cator, Bandar Seri Begawan, 2085, Brunei Darussalem. Telephone: 6732-228382. Facsimile: 6732-228389.
Singapore Service Address for Trademark Registration: c/o Loke & Seah, 3 Shenton Way, #21-10, Shenton House, Singapore, 0106. Telephone: 65-223-7088. Facsimile: 65-223-7028.
Malaysia Service Address for Trademark Registration: Lots 1708/9, 17th Floor, Wisma Hla, Jalan Rajah Chulan, 50200, Kuala Lumpur, West Malaysia. Telephone: 03-2414823. Facsimile: 03-2414641.

FIRM PROFILE: The firm's clientele consists of multi-national corporations and select "private and entrenched" individuals. Founded in 1965, the firm offers a full range of legal services and is well known internationally in areas of intellectual property, licensing, franchising, joint ventures and international business transactions. Subject to local bar rules, the firm accepts instructions for representation in Singapore, Malaysia, Brunei, Hong Kong, England and Wales.

MEMBERS OF FIRM

VINI KUMAR, born 1935; admitted, 1965, Malaysia; 1966, Brunei; 1969, Singapore; 1961, England and Wales. Certified as a Legal Consultant by the State Bars of New York and California for these jurisdictions.

ALAN H. DAY, born 1943; admitted, 1971, England and Wales; 1972, Hong Kong.

(This Listing Continued)

OF COUNSEL

KEITH E. KLINE, born 1955; admitted, 1986, California. Registered Patent Attorney (USPTO).

Please direct all inquiries to our Administrative Office in California, USA.

HOLMAN, FENWICK & WILLAN

1418 TWO PACIFIC PLACE
88 QUEENSWAY
HONG KONG
Telephone: 2522 3006
Telex: 63536 HFWHK HX
Telefax: 2887 8110

London, England Office: Marlow House, Lloyds Avenue, EC3N 3AL. Telephone: 0171-488-2300. Telex: 8812247 HFWLON. Telefax: 0171 481 0316.
Paris, France Office: 3 Rue la Boëtie, 75008. Telephone: 44-94-40-50. Telex: 281699F HFWPA A. Telefax: 42-65-46-25.
Singapore Office: 10 Collyer Quay #08-02, Ocean Building, Singapore, 0104. Telephone: 534 0195. Telex: HFWSIN RS 26188. Telefax: 534 5864.
Piraeus, Greece Office: 6th Floor, 86 Filonos Street. Telephone: 429-3978. Telefax: 429-3118.
Rouen, France Office: 47 Avenue Gustave Flaubert, 76000. Telephone: 32.08.18.60. Telefax: 35.89.90.54.

Admiralty, all aspect of Maritime Law, International Trade, Commodities, Transportation, Insurance and Reinsurance, Corporate Litigation and Insolvency, Ship Finance, Company and Commercial Matters, Commercial Property, Aviation and Professional Negligence.

RESIDENT PARTNERS

PETER REES SMITH. PRACTICE AREAS: Admiralty Law; P and I Club; Casualties; Charter Parties and Bills of Lading; Marine Disasters.

MICHAEL T. STEVENS. PRACTICE AREAS: Admiralty and Maritime Law, International Maritime; Admiralty and Maritime Law, Shipping; Admiralty and Maritime Law, Marine and Inland Marine; Admiralty and Maritime Law, Salvage; Admiralty and Maritime, Seamen.

PHILIP W.Y. MO. PRACTICE AREAS: Ship Mortgage Reinforcement; Casualties; Maritime Law; Charter Parties and Bills of Lading; Marine Disasters.

GUY J.V. HARDAKER. PRACTICE AREAS: Commercial Law; Communications and Media Telecommunications; Energy-Utilities; Marine Insurance Law; Charter Parties and Bills of Lading.

ANTHONY J. JEX. PRACTICE AREAS: Business Law, Buying and Selling; Business Law, Joint Ventures; Company Law, Commercial; Ship Finance; Ship Registration.

PAUL J. HATZER. PRACTICE AREAS: Admiralty and Maritime Law, International Maritime; P and I Clubs; Charter Parties and Bills of Lading; Bankruptcy, Insolvency; Arbitration and Mediation, International Arbitration.

SIMON S. DAVIDSON. PRACTICE AREAS: Admiralty and Maritime Law; Arbitration; Commodities; Insurance; Contracts.

CONSULTANT

Andrew J. Sheppard

Languages: Cantonese, English, French and Mandarin

(For Complete List of Partners see Professional Biographies at London, England).

JOHNSON STOKES & MASTER

(In association with Norton Rose)

Established in 1863

17TH FLOOR, PRINCE'S BUILDING
10 CHATER ROAD
HONG KONG
Telephone: 28432211
Cable Address: "Retsam Hong Kong", "Nojon Hong Kong"
Telex: HX 73704, HX 75107
Kalle Infotec/Rapifax: 28451735; 28459121
Correspondence Address: G.P.O. Box 387, Hong Kong

Commercial Office: 16th Floor, Prince's Building, 10 Chater Road, Hong Kong. Telephone: 28432211. Cable Address: "Nojon Hong Kong". Telex: HX 73704. Kalle Infotec/Rapifax: 28451735; 28459121.

Conveyancing Office: 17th and 218th Floors, Prince's Building, 10 Chater Road, Hong Kong. Telephone: 28432211. Cable Address: "Retsam Hong Kong". Telex: HX 85326. Kalle Infotec/Rapifax: 28105562.

Litigation Office: 19th Floor, Prince's Building, 10 Chater Road, Hong Kong. Telephone: 28432211. Cable Address: "JisemHong Kong". Telex: HX 85242. Kalle Infotec/Rapifax: 28104719.

Kowloon, Hong Kong Office: 5th Floor, 673 Nathan Road. Telephone: 27897373. Cable Address: "Sekot Hong Kong". Telex: HX 43897. Kalle Infotec/Rapifax: 27898555; 27892672.

Bangkok Office; JSM (Thailand) Ltd., 19th floor, C.P. Tower, 313 Silom Road. Telephone: 231-0960-4 and 231-0585-8. Fax: 231-0965.

Beijing Office: Johnson Stokes & Master China Consultants Ltd., Level 21, Units 15-16, China World Tower, China World Trade Centre. Telephone: 505-2331. Fax: 505-2323. Telex: 222449 JSMBJ CN.

Guangzhou Office: Johnson Stokes & Master China Consultants Limited, Room 304, China Hotel Office Tower, Liu Hua Lu, Guangzhou, 510015. Telephone: 666-6888 (Ext. 304). Fax: 667-7014.

Hanoi, Vietnam Office: Johnson Stokes & Master. 4th Floor, 27 Ly Thai To Street Hanoi. Telephone: 844-244316/7/8. Facsimile: 844-244319.

General International and Hong Kong Practice, including Aviation, Banking, China and Indo-China Trade and Investment, Corporate and Commercial, Construction, Corporate Finance, Corporate Restructuring and Insolvency, Mergers and Acquisitions, Insurance, Intellectual Property, Litigation, Probate, Property, Securities, Shipping, Taxation, Trusts and Succession.

PARTNERS

RICHARD MARTIN RUSSELL, LL.B., LL.M. (Columbia), admitted 1972, England; 1974, Hong Kong. Notary Public.

SIMON SIK-ON IP, admitted 1971, Notary Public, England; 1972, Hong Kong. Justice of the Peace.

PETER STUART ALLENBY EDWARDS, B.A., M.A. (Oxon), admitted 1972, England; 1976, Hong Kong. Notary Public.

HUMPHREY KWOK-KEE HEUNG, B.A., admitted 1975, Hong Kong. Notary Public.

RIN CHING-KWOK LEE, LL.B., LL.M., admitted 1974, England; 1975, Hong Kong. Notary Public.

ROBERT SUI-YUEN LYNN, LL.B., admitted 1976, Hong Kong. Notary Public.

AMY SUET-FONG KO, admitted, 1971, England; 1972, Hong Kong. Notary Public.

AUGUSTO NORBERTO DA ROZA, LL.B., admitted 1976, Hong Kong. Notary Public.

KENG-YIP LIM, admitted 1976, England; 1977, Hong Kong. Notary Public.

ANSON KAM-CHOY KAN, admitted 1977, Hong Kong. Notary Public.

DANIEL ROCHFORT BRADSHAW, LL.B., LL.M., admitted 1970, New Zealand; 1976, England; 1979, Hong Kong.

DEREK HO-FAI CHEUNG, admitted 1979, Hong Kong.

WILLIAM JONATHAN CLAYDON LYNE, LL.B., admitted 1977, England; 1979, Hong Kong. Notary Public.

FUN-KUEN AU, LL.B., admitted 1979, Hong Kong. Notary Public.

(This Listing Continued)

WILLIAM RAE MURDIE, B.A., admitted 1975, England; 1977, Hong Kong.

RUPERT WILLIAM NICHOLL, LL.B., admitted 1979, England and Hong Kong.

IAN ROBERT DENZIL CHAPMAN, M.A. (Cantab), admitted 1980, England and Hong Kong.

SAMUEL YIN-SHUN WONG, LL.B., LL.M., admitted 1980, Hong Kong; 1983, England. Notary Public.

YUEN-MAN ELAINE LO, LL.B., admitted 1984, Hong Kong.

KEITH PO-KEUNG CHEUNG, LL.B., admitted 1981, Hong Kong.

ROSALINE OI-WAN CHEUNG, LL.B., admitted 1981, Hong Kong.

NICHOLAS DAVID HUNSWORTH, B.A. (Oxon), admitted 1982, England; 1984, Hong Kong.

CHRISTOPHER JOHN BONSALL, B.A., LL.B., M.A., LL.M., admitted 1977, England; 1979, Hong Kong; 1983, Australia and Brunei. Notary Public.

ANITA YUEN LEE, LL.B., admitted 1982, Hong Kong; 1985, England.

JACOB YUI-SUEN TSE, LL.B., admitted 1983, Hong Kong; 1986, England.

ELLEN TSAO, LL.B., admitted 1983, Hong Kong; 1987, England.

BILLY KUN LOK HO, B.Sc., admitted, 1985, Hong Kong.

LESLIE JOHN WITOLD KACZMAREK, LL.B., admitted 1982, Scotland; 1985, Hong Kong.

MABEL MAY-BO LEE, LL.B., admitted 1977, Hong Kong; 1981, England; 1983, Australia; 1986, Canada. Notary Public.

JAMES FRASER CHAPMAN, LL.B., admitted 1979, Scotland; 1986, Hong Kong.

PETER ANDREW KEMP, LL.B., admitted 1983, England; 1985, Hong Kong.

ROBERT TERENCE KWONG-SHIEN TUNG, LL.B., admitted 1984, Hong Kong.

PAUL KA-HONG YU, B.Soc.Sc., admitted 1985, Hong Kong.

ALASTAIR CRAIG MACAULAY, LL.B., admitted 1983, Scotland; 1984, Hong Kong.

PAUL KENDRICK WOOD, LL.B., admitted 1974, England; 1982, Hong Kong.

SIMON JAMES GRAHAM RAE, LL.B., admitted 1981, Scotland; 1985, Hong Kong.

TAMMY KWAI-FONG GOH, LL.B., admitted 1982, Hong Kong; 1987, England.

PETER GARY BIESTY, LL.B., admitted 1984, England; 1986, Hong Kong.

JOSEPHINE ANN PHILLIPS, LL.B., admitted 1984, England; 1987, Hong Kong.

DAVID JAMES PLUNKETT, B.Sc., LL.B., admitted 1982, New Zealand; 1986, England; 1987, Hong Kong.

ELIZABETH GOMERSALL, B.Phil. (Oxon), admitted 1984, England; 1985, Hong Kong.

RAYMOND TIM-YIU CHAN, LL.B., admitted 1985, Hong Kong; 1989, England.

GAVIN PAUL NESBITT, LL.B., admitted 1986, England; 1987, Hong Kong.

CAROL SUK-YI CHEN, LL.B., admitted 1985, Hong Kong; 1989, England.

PETER HING-CHOI HO, LL.B., LL.M. (Cantab), admitted 1986, Hong Kong.

SOPHIE MARINA JUNE WU, B.A., LL.B., admitted 1986, Hong Kong; 1990, England.

JANET MO-YIN HO, LL.B., admitted 1986, Hong Kong.

AUDREY OI-YEE AU, LL.B., admitted, 1986, Hong Kong.

ALLAN WANG-MAN YU, LL.M., admitted, 1985, Hong Kong.

(This Listing Continued)

JEANIE SIU-YU LAI, M.A., admitted, 1988, Hong Kong.

KENNY KAM SHAN WONG, LL.B., admitted, 1988, Hong Kong.

CONSULTANTS

ROBIN SOMERS PEARD, admitted 1964, England; 1965, Hong Kong. Notary Public.

JOHN FORTESCUE PAYNE, M.A. (Oxon), admitted 1964, England; 1967, Hong Kong. Notary Public.

ANTHONY ROBERT CHETTLE, M.A., LL.B., admitted 1966, England; 1968, Hong Kong. Notary Public.

KEVIN SAU HONG CHING, LL.M., admitted, 1983, Hong Kong.

NORTON ROSE RESIDENT PARTNERS

DAVID JOHN SHAW, M.A. (Cantab), admitted 1970, England; 1976, Hong Kong.

JEFFERY VERNON COURTNEY LEWIS BARRATT, LL.B., LL.M., admitted, 1973, Hong Kong.

DAVID PETER ROBERT STANNARD, LL.B., admitted 1981, England; 1983, Hong Kong.

PETER HASLAM, B.A. (Cantab), admitted 1981, England; 1983, Hong Kong.

MARTIN D.K. SCOTT, LL.B., admitted 1983, England and Hong Kong.

ROBERT JAMES JAMES, M.A., admitted, 1977, Hong Kong.

ASSISTANT SOLICITORS

MICHAEL ASHWORTH, (Not admitted in Hong Kong). LL.B., admitted 1987, England.

ANN ELIZABETH BANG, J.D., admitted 1992, United States. (Not Admitted in Hong Kong).

MICHAEL JOHN BARKER, B.A., admitted 1990, England; 1994, Hong Kong.

CAROLINE BARRANCO, (Not admitted in Hong Kong). M.Sc., 1993.

CAROLINE ELIZABETH BENNETT, LL.B., admitted 1986, England; 1992, Hong Kong.

DAVID JOHN ALEXANDER BOYLE, M.A., admitted 1985, England; 1991, Hong Kong.

ELIZABETH MICHELE BROWN, B.Sc., admitted 1990, England; 1993, Hong Kong.

KATHARINA ALICE BYRNE, LL.B., admitted 1994, Hong Kong; 1993, England.

LAURA LYNNE CAMPBELL, LL.B., admitted 1994, Hong Kong; 1993, England; 1987, Ontario, Canada.

ALAN CHIU-YUEN CHAN, LL.B., admitted 1992, Hong Kong.

AMY NGAR-MEI CHAN, LL.B., admitted 1992, Hong Kong.

FRANCIS WAN-KIT CHAN, LL.B., admitted 1993, Hong Kong.

SALLY PUI-BING CHAN, LL.B., admitted 1993, Hong Kong.

VIVIAN SOK-CHONG CHAN, LL.B., admitted 1989, Hong Kong.

ADA KIT-YI CHEN, LL.B., admitted 1992, Hong Kong.

MAGGIE MAN-CHE CHENG, LL.B., admitted 1991, Hong Kong.

ERIC TAT-MING CHEUNG, LL.B., admitted 1989, Hong Kong.

TERENCE CHIU-HANG CHEUNG, LL.B., admitted 1993, Hong Kong.

JACQUELINE SUNG-TAK CHIU, LL.B., admitted 1994, Hong Kong.

JOLETA MEI-MAN CHIU, LL.B., admitted 1993, Hong Kong.

AMY FUK-KWAN CHOW, LL.B., admitted 1986, Hong Kong; 1990, England.

LILLIAN CHOW, LL.B., admitted 1992, Hong Kong.

KHAI-MENG CHOY, M.A., admitted 1994, Hong Kong.

ERIC FREDERICK CURLEWIS, B.A., admitted 1988, Hong Kong.

GERALDINE DOWNEY, LL.B., admitted 1985, England; 1986, Hong Kong.

(This Listing Continued)

DAVID A. ELLIS, LL.B., admitted 1988, England; 1991, Hong Kong.

JULIA KA-YEE FUNG, LL.B., admitted 1991, Hong Kong.

ANDREW JOHN GRANT, LL.B., B.Com., admitted, 1987, New Zealand; 1992, Hong Kong.

CHENG HOO, LL.B., admitted 1990, Hong Kong.

JANET YUNG-YUNG HUI, LL.B., admitted 1990, Hong Kong.

PATRICK PO-ON HUI, LL.B., admitted 1989, Hong Kong.

HELEN JAMES, LL.B., admitted 1994, Hong Kong; 1990, England.

STEPHEN JAMIESON, LL.B., admitted 1991, England and Hong Kong.

MARIA JOANNIDES-SMITH, (Not admitted in Hong Kong). LL.B., admitted 1992, South Africa.

JASON WATSON KERR, (Not admitted in Hong Kong). LL.B., admitted 1990, England.

ATHENA SHUK WAI LAI, LL.B., admitted 1991, Hong Kong.

BILLY YICK-CHUNG LAM, LL.B., admitted 1989, Hong Kong.

LAI-FUNG LAM, LL.B., admitted 1992, Hong Kong.

LORETTA SUK-HAN LAM, LL.B., admitted 1993, Hong Kong.

PATRICIA LAM, LL.B., admitted 1986, Hong Kong; 1989, England.

PEARL CHUN-MING LAM, LL.B., admitted 1987, Hong Kong.

JEFFREY HAYDON LANE, LL.B., LL.M., admitted 1989, England; 1990, Hong Kong.

VINCENT HUNG KWONG LAU, LL.B., admitted 1991, Hong Kong.

ELSA TSZ KWAN LEE, LL.B., admitted 1991, Hong Kong.

PAUL LEE, (Not admitted in Hong Kong). LL.B., admitted 1991, England.

MADELINE FONG-UNG LEONG, LL.B., admitted 1992, Hong Kong.

EMMA SIU-YING LEUNG, LL.B., admitted 1991, Hong Kong.

NORMAN WAI-HUNG LEUNG, LL.B., admitted 1993, Hong Kong.

IAN KEITH LEWIS, LL.B., admitted 1988, England; 1991, Hong Kong.

ROSITA YEE-MAN LI, (Not admitted in Hong Kong). LL.B., admitted 1992, England.

WENDY WEN-YU LI, (Not admitted in Hong Kong). LL.M., admitted 1989, England.

LUCAS LU-KAR LIANG, LL.B., admitted 1993, Hong Kong.

AILEEN SUSAN LLOYD, LL.B., admitted 1989, Hong Kong.

ANDREW MACGEOCH, M.A., admitted 1993, England and Hong Kong.

JONATHAN JAMES EDWARD MAHONY, (Not admitted in Hong Kong). LL.B., admitted 1991, England.

CATHERINE ANN MCCAUSLAND, LL.B., admitted 1989, New Zealand; 1993, Hong Kong.

NG MEI-LING, (Not admitted in Hong Kong). LL.M., admitted 1992, England.

STEVEN MILLER, LL.B., admitted 1984, Australia; 1987, Hong Kong and England.

JACKLYN SUK-FUN NG, LL.B., admitted 1984, Hong Kong.

CAROLINE WENDY NICHOLAS, M.A., admitted 1990, England; 1993, Hong Kong.

SARA SIN-MAN OR, LL.B., admitted 1990, Hong Kong.

GLYN COLIN RYLAND, LL.B., admitted 1988, England; 1992, Hong Kong.

EDWARD JAMES SHEEN, LL.B., admitted, 1990, England; 1992, Hong Kong.

PETER ZHONGGUEN SHEN, (Not admitted in Hong Kong). B.A., admitted 1991, New Zealand.

(This Listing Continued)

JOHNSON STOKES & MASTER, Hong Kong—Continued

JOSEPH THOMAS SIMONE, B.A., admitted 1984, United States. (Not Admitted in Hong Kong).

JOHN HEARNE SLATER, B.A., admitted 1990, England; 1991, Hong Kong.

THOMAS SHIU-TSUNG SO, LL.B., admitted 1988, Hong Kong.

RICHARD JONATHAN STOCK, (Not admitted in Hong Kong). LL.B., admitted 1991, New Zealand.

ANNA YICK-MAN TAM, LL.M., admitted 1993, Hong Kong.

KEUNG TSANG, LL.B., admitted 1992, Hong Kong.

THOMAS PETER JOHN VAIZEY, B.A., admitted 1992, England and Hong Kong.

SIMON WALKER, LL.B., admitted 1989, England; 1993, Hong Kong.

STEPHANIE YUK-CHING WAN, LL.B., admitted 1993, Hong Kong.

KAY LOUISE WHARTON, B.A., admitted, 1991, England; 1992, Hong Kong.

PATRICK CHI-KWONG WONG, (Not admitted in Hong Kong). LL.B., admitted 1992, England.

ROSANA CHAN WONG, LL.B., admitted 1989, Hong Kong; 1991, England and Wales.

TERENCE TAI-CHEONG WONG, (Not admitted in Hong Kong). LL.B., admitted 1993, England.

ALLAN FREDERICK WOODLEY, (Not admitted in Hong Kong). LL.B., admitted 1986, Australia.

PATRICK YEUNG-WEI WU, M.B.A., B.Sc., admitted 1981, England; 1982, Hong Kong.

RICHARD WAI-SANG WU, LL.B., admitted 1987, Hong Kong.

JEREMY XIAO, (Not admitted in Hong Kong). admitted 1983, People's Republic of China.

ANGELA SOAT-YEE YIM, LL.B., admitted 1990, Hong Kong.

JONES, DAY, REAVIS & POGUE

1501 ONE EXCHANGE SQUARE
8 CONNAUGHT PLACE
HONG KONG
Telephone: 852-2526-6895
Telecopier: 852-2810-5787 or 852-2868-5871

In Atlanta, Georgia: 3500 One Peachtree Center, 303 Peachtree Street, N.E. Telephone: 404-521-3939. Cable Address: "Attorneys Atlanta". Telex: 54-2711. Telecopier: 404-581-8330.

In Brussels, Belgium: Avenue Louise 480, 7th Floor. B-1050 Brussels. Telephone: 32-2-645-14-11. Telecopier: 32-2-645-14-45.

In Chicago, Illinois: 77 West Wacker. Telephone: 312-782-3939. Telecopier: 312-782-8585.

In Cleveland, Ohio: North Point, 901 Lakeside Avenue. Telephone: 216-586-3939. Cable Address: "Attorneys Cleveland." Telex: 980389. Telecopier: 216-579-0212.

In Columbus, Ohio: 1900 Huntington Center. Telephone: 614-469-3939. Cable Address: "Attorneys Columbus." Telecopier: 614-461-4198.

In Dallas, Texas: 2300 Trammell Crow Center, 2001 Ross Avenue. Telephone: 214-220-3939. Cable Address: "Attorneys Dallas." Telex: 730852. Telecopier: 214-969-5100.

In Frankfurt, Germany: Triton Haus, Bockenheimer Landstrasse 42, 60323 Frankfurt am Main. Telephone: 49-69-9726-3939. Telecopier: 49-69-9726-3993.

In Geneva, Switzerland: 20, rue de Candolle. Telephone: 41-22-320-2339. Telecopier: 41-22-320-1232.

In Irvine, California: 2603 Main Street, Suite 900. Telephone: 714-851-3939. Telex: 194911 Lawyers LSA. Telecopier: 714-553-7539.

In London, England: One Mount Street. Telephone: 44-71-493-9361. Cable Address: "Surgoe London WI." Telecopier: 44-71-493-9666.

In Los Angeles, California: 555 West Fifth Street, Suite 4600. Telephone: 213-489-3939. Telex: 181439 UD. Telecopier: 213-243-2539.

In New York, New York: 599 Lexington Avenue. Telephone: 212-326-3939. Cable Address: "JONESDAY NEWYORK." Telex: 237013 JDRP UR. Telecopier: 212-755-7306.

(This Listing Continued)

In Paris, France: 62, rue du Faubourg Saint-Honore. Telephone: 33-1-44-71-3939. Cable Address: "Surgoe Paris." Telex: 290156 Surgoe. Telecopier: 33-1-49-24-0471.

In Pittsburgh, Pennsylvania: 500 Grant Street, 31st Floor. Telephone: 412-391-3939. Cable Address: "Attorneys Pittsburgh". Telecopier: 412-394-7959.

In Riyadh, Saudi Arabia: Law Office of Saud M.A. Shawwaf, P.O. Box 2700. Telephones: (966-1) 465-6543, (966-1) 464-8534 or (966-1) 464-8540. Telex: 401831 SAUCON SJ. Telecopier: (966-1) 464-8480.

In Taipei, Taiwan: 8th Floor, 2 Tun Hwa South Road, Section 2. Telephone: (886-2) 704-6808. Telecopier: (886-2) 704-6791.

In Tokyo, Japan: Toranomon MT Building, 4th Floor, 10-3, Toranomon 3-Chome, Minato-Ku, Tokyo 105, Japan. Telephone: 81-3-3433-3939. Telecopier: 81-3-5401-2725.

In Washington, D.C.: Metropolitan Square, 1450 G Street, N.W. Telephone: 202-879-3939. Cable Address: "Attorneys Washington." Telex: 89-2410 ATTORNEYS WASH. Telecopier: 202-737-2832.

Firm engaged in American and International law practice but not authorized to appear before the Hong Kong courts or to act as Hong Kong Solicitors.

MEMBER OF FIRM IN HONG KONG

WILLIAM ANTHONY STEWART, born Munich, Germany, August 22, 1954; admitted, 1979, New York, 1984, Texas (Not admitted in Hong Kong). *Education:* Reed College (B.A., 1975); Yale University (J.D., 1978). Phi Beta Kappa. Chairman, Legal Committee, American Chamber of Commerce in Hong Kong, 1993-1994. First American Member, Foreign Lawyers Committee, Law Society of Hong Kong, 1994—.

ASSOCIATES

MITCHELL DAVID DUDEK, born Sidney, Ohio, April 19, 1962; admitted, 1990, Texas (Not admitted in Hong Kong). *Education:* Texas A&M University (B.S., 1984; M.B.A., 1986); The Ohio State University (J.D., 1989).

XIANGYUAN Y. JIANG, born Shaanxi, China, May 30, 1956; admitted, 1984, China; 1990, Illinois (Not admitted in Hong Kong). *Education:* Central-South Institute of Political Science and Law, China (Bachelor of Law, 1984); ITT Chicago Kent College of Law (LL.M., 1987; J.D., 1989).

Languages: English, Mandarin

KAYE, SCHOLER, FIERMAN, HAYS & HANDLER

9 QUEEN ROAD CENTRE, 18TH FLOOR
HONG KONG
Telephone: 852-8458989
Telex: 62816 KAY HX
Facsimile: 852-8453682; 852-8452389

New York, N.Y.: 425 Park Avenue, 10022. Telephone: 212-836-8000. Telex: 234860 KAY UR. Facsimile: 212-836-8689.

Washington, D.C.: McPherson Building, 901 Fifteenth Street, N.W., Suite 1100, 20005. Telephone: 202-682-3500. Telex: 897458 KAYSCHOL WSH. Facsimile: 202-682-3580.

Los Angeles, California: 1999 Avenue of the Stars, Suite 1600, 90067. Telephone: 213-788-1000. Facsimile: 213-788-1200.

Beijing (Peking), People's Republic of China: Scite Tower, Suite 708, 22 Jianguomenwai Dajie, 100004. Telephone: 861-5124755. Telex: 222540 KAY CN. Facsimile: 861-5124760.

Firm Engaged in American and International Law Practice, but not authorized to appear before Hong Kong Courts or to act as Hong Kong Solicitors.

RESIDENT PARTNERS

FRANKLIN D. CHU, admitted, 1976, District of Columbia (Not admitted in Hong Kong). *Education:* Harvard College (A.B., magna cum laude, 1971); L'Institut de'Etudes Politiques, Paris, France, 1968-1969; Yale University (J.D., 1976). Member, Board of Editors, Yale Law Journal, 1975-1976. Panel of Arbitrators of American Arbitration Association. *Member:* The District of Columbia Bar; American and International Bar Associations; Asia-Pacific Lawyers Association; Zatee-Pacific Bar Association. *LANGUAGES:* Mandarin Chinese, French. *PRACTICE AREAS:* International Investment and Finance.

(This Listing Continued)

HONG KONG COUNSEL

FRANK L. GNIFFKE, admitted, 1969, District of Columbia; 1972, Hawaii; 1980, California; 1988, Japan (Gaikokuho-Jimu Bengoshi). *Education:* Carleton College (B.A., 1963); University of Hawaii (M.A., 1966); Harvard Law School (J.D., 1969). *Member:* State Bar of California; The District of Columbia Bar; Hawaii and American Bar Associations; First Tokyo Bar Association. *LANGUAGES:* Japanese, Chinese (Mandarin) and German. *PRACTICE AREAS:* International Investment and Trade Relating to Asia.

RESIDENT ASSOCIATES

RONGWEI CAI, admitted, 1990, Oregon (Not admitted in Hong Kong). *Education:* Xiamen University School of Law (LL.B., with honors, 1984; LL.M. Candidate, 1984-1986); Columbia University (LL.M., 1987); Lewis & Clark Law School (J.D., 1990). Recipient, University Scholarship, Xiamen University, 1980-1986. Member, Cornelius Honor Society, Lewis & Clark Law School. Author: "Tax Reform Under Way in China," Trade Winds, (January, 1994); "Legal Education and Practice of Law in China," International Lawyers' Newsletter (June/July 1993, Vol. XV, No. 3); "Legal Pitfalls That Foreign Investors Should Avoid When Doing Business in the United State," The World Journal (February 14, 1993); "PracticalTips on Doing Business With PRC," 48 Northwest China Council Quarterly 5-6 (October 1992); "Introduction to Investment Immigration in the United States," The World Journal (July 19 and 26, 1992); "Legal Methods for Civil Discovery Abroad," 4 International Legal Perspectives 38 (Fall 1988); "Formation of Contracts Under Chinese Foreign Economic Contract Law and Vienna Convention on Contracts for International Sale of Goods," Lewis and Clark Law School Third Annual International Business Law Seminar, 116-36 (October 28, 1988). Co-Author: Rongwei Cai, Cuanhua Han, Jiafang Ruan, *Admiralty Law,* Lujiang Publishing Co., 1987. Director, Taiwan COmmerce Association of Portland, 1993-1994. Secretary, Pacific Northwest International Trade Association China Business Center. *Member:* Multnomah County and American Bar Associations; Oregon State Bar; American Immigration Lawyers Association. *LANGUAGES:* Chinese (Mandarin and Taiwanese). *PRACTICE AREAS:* International Business; China Practice.

BRIDGET CHI, admitted, 1991, California (Not admitted in Hong Kong). *Education:* University of Texas at Austin (B.A., 1987); Georgetown University (J.D., 1990). *LANGUAGES:* Mandarin Chinese. *PRACTICE AREAS:* International Trade.

NEIL L. MEYERS, born Newark, New Jersey, U.S.A., June 23, 1961; admitted, 1991, Washington. *Education:* University of Washington (LL.M., East Asian Law, 1992); Rutgers University School of Law (J.D., 1991); Brandeis University (B.A., Philosophy, 1985). With: Reliance International Law Offices, Taipei, 1992—; Tsar & Tsai Law Offices, Taipei, 1990; Denton Hall Burgin & Warrens, Hong Kong, 1989; Intag International, Ltd., Taipei, 1987; Kuangchi Program Service, Taipei, 1986-1987. Author, various papers and articles: "Political Risk Insurance and Investment in the P.R.C."; "Venture Capital Investment in Taiwan"; "Taiwan's Six Year National Development Plan, Technology Transfer and Opportunities for American Businesses"; "Statutory Encouragement of Investment and Economic Development in Taiwan, R.O.C."; "Chinese (P.R.C.) Methods of Resolving Economic Disputes Involving Foreigners and their Legal Basis"; "The R.O.C. Fair Trade Law: A Brief Review of the Earliest Cases."; "The Legalization of Commodities Futures Trading in Taiwan, R.O.C.," University of British Columbia Law Review, Vol. 27:2 (1993); "Chinese Methods for Resolution of Economic Disputes Involving Foreigners and Their Legal Basis (Translation for Chinese), "University of Washington School of Law, Pacific Rim Law and Policy Journal, (1993). Research and Teaching Assistant, to Professor Paul C.B. Liu, University of Washington, School of Law, 1991-1992. Member, American Chamber of Commerce, Taipei. *Member:* Washington State Bar Association; Seattle-King County Bar Association. *LANGUAGES:* English and Chinese. *PRACTICE AREAS:* China Practice; International Business Transactions; Intellectual Property.

JUAN E. ZUNIGA, admitted, 1992, California and U.S. District Court, Central District of California (Not admitted in Hong Kong). *Education:* Harvard University (A.B., 1986; J.D., 1992). *Member:* Mexican American Bar Association of Los Angeles County; Hispanic National Bar Association; Los Angeles Center for Law and Justice (Member, Board of Directors). *LANGUAGES:* Spanish. *PRACTICE AREAS:* Litigation; Immigration; International.

(For complete biographical data on all personnel, see Professional Biographies at at New York, New York)

LATHAM & WATKINS
11TH FLOOR CENTRAL BUILDING
NUMBER ONE PEDDER STREET
HONG KONG
Telephone: 011-852-841-7779
Fax: 011-852-841-7749

Los Angeles, California Office: 633 West Fifth Street, Suite 4000, 90071. Telephone: 213-485-1234. Telecopier: 213-891-8763.

Costa Mesa, California Office: Suite 2000, 650 Town Center Drive, 92626-1918. Telephone: 714-540-1235. Telecopier: 714-755-8290.

San Diego, California Office: Suite 2100, 701 B Street, 92101-8197. Telephone: 619-236-1234. Telecopier: 619-696-7419.

San Francisco, California Office: 505 Montgomery Street, Suite 1900, 94111. Telephone: 415-391-0600. Fax: 415-395-8095.

Washington, D.C. Office: Suite 1300, 1001 Pennsylvania Avenue, N.W., 20004. Telephone: 202-637-2200. Telecopier: 202-637-2201.

Chicago, Illinois Office: Suite 5800 Sears Tower, 60606. Telephone: 312-876-7700. Telecopier: 312-993-9767.

Newark, New Jersey Office: One Newark Center, 07101-3174. Telephone: 201-639-1234. Fax: 201-639-7298.

New York, N.Y. Office: Suite 1000, 885 Third Avenue, 10022-4802. Telephone: 212-906-1200. Telecopier: 212-751-4864.

London, England Office: One Angel Court, EC2R 7HJ. Telephone: +-44-71-374 4444. Telecopier: +-44-71-374 4460.

Moscow, Russia Office: Suite C200, 113/1 Leninsky Prospeckt, 117198. Telephone: +-7 503 956-5555. Fax: +-7 503 956-5556.

Warsaw, Poland Office: St. Szpitalna 1, Suite 49, 9th Floor, 00-018. Telephone: +48-2-227-9610. Telecopier: +48-2-227-9610.

ASSOCIATES

JEFFREY L. HALLOS, born Youngstown, Ohio, July 18, 1963; admitted, 1989, California; 1991, District of Columbia (Not admitted in Hong Kong). *Education:* Bucknell University (B.A., Economics, magna cum laude, 1985) Phi Beta Kappa; Cornell Law School (J.D., cum laude, 1988). Note Editor, International Law Journal, 1987-1988. Judicial Clerkship with Honorable Joseph W. Hatchett, U.S. Court of Appeals, Eleventh Circuit, 1988-1989. *Member:* Los Angeles County and American Bar Associations; State Bar of California; District of Columbia Bar. (Also at Washington, D.C. Office).

(For biographical data on Los Angeles, California, Costa Mesa, California, San Diego, California, San Francisco, California, Washington, D.C., Chicago, Illinois, New York, New York, London, England, Moscow, Russia and Warsaw, Poland personnel, see Professional Biographies at each of those cities)

JOSÉ E. AND ASSOCIATES, LTD.
SUITE 1602 PARK IN COMMERCIAL CENTRE
56 DUNDAS STREET
HONG KONG
Telephone: 852-710-9880
Facsimile: 852-359-7542

Gainesville, Florida Office: Law Offices of José E. Latour & Associates, P.A., 500 E. University Ave., Suite "D". 32601. Telephone: 904-371-0067. Fax: 904-371-1457.

Miami, Florida Office: Law Offices of José E. Latour & Associates, P.A., 1101 Brickell Avenue, Suite 801. 33131. Telephone: 305-359-0300. Fax: 305-539-0490.

Immigration, Business and Investor Visas. International and Offshore Corporate Structuring. Music Industry Law.

JOSÉ E. LATOUR, born Havana, Cuba, July 20, 1961; admitted, 1990, Florida. *Education:* University of Florida (B.S., 1983; J.D., 1987). Co-Author: "AILA Guide to Visa Processing," American Immigration Lawyers Association, 1992, 1993. Lecturer, American Immigration Lawyers Association National Seminar, 1992-1994. U.S. Vice Consul: Mexico; Malabo, Equatorial Guinea, 1987-1990. *Member:* The Florida Bar (Member, International Law Section). *(Immigration and Nationality Law). *LANGUAGES:* Spanish. *PRACTICE AREAS:* Immigration and Nationality Law; International Law; Entertainment Law.

*Approved Areas of Practice under the Florida Designation Plan

(For complete Biographical data on all Personnel, see Professional Biographies at Gainesville, Florida)

LINKLATERS & PAINES

Established in 1976

14TH FLOOR, ALEXANDRA HOUSE
CHATER ROAD
HONG KONG
Telephone: 852 842 4888
Telex: 83695
Fax: 852 810 8133; 852 810 1695

London, England Office: Barrington House, 59-67 Gresham Street, EC2V 7JA. Telephone: 0171-606-7080. Cable Address: Linklaters, London, EC2V 7JA. Telegrams: Linklaters, London. Telex: 884349. Fax: 0171-606-5113.

General and International Law Practice.

RESIDENT PARTNERS

S. D. Boughton	Giles L. White
Alan M. Stevens	Michael J. Firth
Thomas W. Hope	David C. Mullarkey
Andrew Malcolm	Jeremy G. Parr
Raymond M. Cohen	Clive B. Ransome

(For full list of offices see entry at London, England)

LOVELL WHITE DURRANT

11TH FLOOR, PEREGRINE TOWER
LIPPO CENTRE, QUEENSWAY
HONG KONG
Telephone: 2810 4770
Fax: 2868 4051

London, England Office: 65 Holborn Viaduct, EC1A 2DY. Telephone: 0171 236 0066. Fax: 0171 248 4212; 236 0084; 248 7273. Telex: 887122 LWD G.

New York, New York Office: 527 Madison Avenue, 10th Floor, 10022. Telephone: (212) 758 3773. Fax: (212) 486 0367.

Paris, France Office: 37 Avenue Pierre 1er de Serbie, 75008. Telephone: (1) 49 52 04 26. Fax: (1) 47 23 96 12.

Brussels, Belgium Office: Avenue Louise 523, Bte 24, 1050. Telephone: (2) 647 0660. Fax: (2) 647 1124.

Prague, Czech Republic Office: U Prasne brany 3, State Mesto, 1. Telephone: (2) 2481 1672. Fax: (2) 2481 1608.

Ho Chi Minh City, Vietnam Office: 141 Vo Van Tan Street, District 3. Telephone: (848) 298 787. Fax: (848) 392 868.

Beijing, Republic of China Office: Office 5D, CITIC Building, 19 Jianguomenwai Dajie, 100004. Telephone: (861) 506 3588. Fax: (861) 500 1972.

Tokyo, Japan Office: Shin-Kasumigaseki Building, 20th Floor, 3-3-2 Kasumigaseki, Chiyoda-ku, 100. Telephone: (3) 3503 2571. Fax: (3) 3503 0699.

Shanghai, People's Republic of China Associated Office: Room 1703, Shanghai International Trade Centre, 2200 Yan An Road (W). Telephone: (21) 219 4419. Fax: (21) 219 5462.

Firm engaged in English and General International Practice.

RESIDENT PARTNERS

Gavin J. McQuater
Patrick P. Sherrington
Charles M. Picken
Anthony R. Marshall
Christopher G. E. Nightingale
D.S. Cheung
Stephen M.D. Hayward
Andrew W. Foyle
Robert O. Lee
Allan C.Y. Leung
Mark C. McGaw
Paul A. Oldman

(For List of Partners see Professional Biographies at London, England).

MARGOLIS & ASSOCIATES

1901 PACIFIC PLAZA
410 DES VOEUX ROAD WEST
HONG KONG
Telephone: 852-2517-3900
Fax: 852-2549-9600

Firm engaged in Hong Kong and international law practice. Also trademark, patent, copyright registration and co-ordination in Asia. Intellectual Property, Technology, Media and Entertainment Law; Joint Ventures; Licensing, Distribution and Franchising; Anti-counterfeiting and Public and Private International Law.

FIRM PROFILE: Established at the beginning of 1994 as an internationally oriented firm, including professional staff with major law firm experience focusing on intellectual property, technology and media law, including enforcement. The firm works closely with private investigators throughout the region.

LAWYERS

JARED R. MARGOLIS, admitted, 1984, New York, Ontario; 1988, Hong Kong. *Education:* McGill University (L.L.B., B.C.L., 1982). Author: Hong Kong chapter in "International Copyright Law and Practice" (Eds. Nimmer and Geller). Co-Author: "The Law of Intellectual and Industrial Property in Hong Kong" (Butterworths). General Editor: "IP Asia" (1988-1991). *Member:* Asian Patent Attorneys Association; American Bar Association (Sections on Intellectual Property and International Law); International Trademark Association; Union Internationale des Avocats. *LANGUAGES:* English, French, German and Chinese. *PRACTICE AREAS:* Intellectual Property; Technology; Entertainment; Media Law; Litigation.

SONJIA NORMAN, admitted, 1989, Hong Kong. *Education:* London School of Economics (L.L.B., 1984); Hong Kong University (P.C.LL., 1987). *Member:* International Bar Association; International Trademark Association. *LANGUAGES:* English, French, Spanish and Chinese. *PRACTICE AREAS:* Intellectual Property and Commercial Law; Media Law.

MIYAKO IKUTA, admitted, 1994, Paris. *Education:* Ritsumeikan (L.L.B., 1988); University of Paris II (D.E.A., 1992; D.E.S.S., 1993). *LANGUAGES:* English, French, Japanese and Chinese. *PRACTICE AREAS:* Intellectual Property Law; International Trade and Litigation.

MASONS

Established in 1983

1301-05, ONE PACIFIC PLACE
88 QUEENSWAY
HONG KONG
Telephone: 852-2521 5621
DX: 9103
Fax: 852-2845 2956
Telex: 78000

London, England Office: 30 Aylesbury Street, London EC1R 0ER. Telephone: 0171 490 4000. Fax: 0171 490 2545. Telex: 811117. DX: 53313 Clerkenwell.

Guangzhou, People's Republic of China Office: Room S1804 18th Floor, South Tower, Guangzhou World Trade Centre, 317-375 Huanshi Dong Lu, 5100060. Telephone: 86 20 766 0000. Fax: 86 20 777 1718.

Brussels, Belgium Office: Avenue Louise 391-Bte 1, B-1050. Telephone: (32) 2-646 0260. Fax: (32) 2-646 7323.

Cairo, Egypt Associated Office: Dr. Hatem Gabr. 5 Salah Salem Road, Heliopolis. Telephone: 2-669988/2-668245.

Bristol, England Office: Broad Street House, 5-8 Broad Street, BS1 2HW. Telephone: 0117-922 6622. Fax: 0117-922 6105. DX: 78154 Bristol.

Manchester, England Office: World Trade Centre, Exchange Quay, Manchester, M5 3EJ. Telephone: 0161-877 377. Fax: 0161-877 6869. DX: 25769 Old Trafford.

Leeds, England Office: Minerva House, 29 East Parade, LA1 5TN. Telephone: 0113 233 8905. Fax: 0113 245 4285. DX: 706955 Leeds Park Square.

FIRM PROFILE: Masons has offices in London, Bristol, Manchester, Leeds, Brussels, Hong Kong and Guangzhou and associated offices in the USA, across Scandinavia and in Cairo. The firm works regularly in continental Europe, the Middle East, the Pacific Rim, Africa and the Indian subcontinent.

Masons provides a broad range of legal services and is well known for ad-
(This Listing Continued)

vising the construction, engineering and computer industries. While the firm's main specialities include large-scale (often international) dispute resolution and advice on major projects generally, Masons also offers a full range of commercial, legal risk management and private client services.

RESIDENT PARTNERS

Iain Black
Jonathan Cheung
Dean Lewis
Robert Lewington
Timothy Hill

McKENNA & CO

5TH FLOOR, LIPPO TOWER
89 QUEENSWAY
HONG KONG
Telephone: (852) 2846 9100
Fax: (852) 2845 3575

London, England Office: Mitre House, 160 Aldersgate Street, EC1A 4DD. Telephone: 071 606 9000. Telex: 27251. Fax: 071-606 9100. CDE Box 724.

London Lloyd's Office: 908 Lloyd's, One Lime Street, London EC3M 7DQ. Telephone: 0171-929 1250. Fax: 0171-626 5749 DX Box 724.

Brussels, Belgium Office: Avenue de Cortenberg 66, Box 10, B-1040. Telephone: (32)(2)735.38.36. Telex: 27122. Fax: (32)(2)735.77.43.

Budapest, Hungary Office: H-1122. Maros utca 22, 1st Floor. Telephone: (36)(1) 202 6527; (36)(1) 202 6936; (36)(1) 201 9199; (36)(1) 156 5354. Fax: (36)(1) 156 5391.

Moscow, Russia Office: McKenna & Co, International, MosenkáPlaza, 24/27 Sadovaya-Samotyochnaya Street, Russian Federation, Moscow, 103051. Telephone: (7 501) 258 5000. Fax: (7 501)258 5100.

Prague, Czech Republic Office: Betlémský palác, First Floor, Husova 5, 110 00 Prague 1. Telephone: (42)(2) 2424 8518-22. Fax: 42(2) 2424 8524.

Warsaw, Poland Office: McKenna & Co Sp. zo.o., ul. Kopernika 30, Suite 213, 00-950, Warsaw. Telephone: (48) 22 26 69 88. Fax: (48) 22 26 41 93.

Hong Kong Office: 5th Floor, Lippo Tower, 89 Queensway, Hong Kong. Telephone: (852) 846 9100. Fax: (852) 845 3575.

Associated Firms:

Sigle Loose Schmidt-Diemitz and Partners: Stuttgart, Berlin, Leipzig, Frankfurt/Main, Chemnitz and Moscow. .

Minter Ellison: Sydney, Melbourne, Canberra, Brisbane and the Gold Coast.

General Practice in Hong Kong, including major projects, banking, commercial, company, insolvency, construction, conveyancing, corporate finance, intellectual property litigation and advice in relation to the PRC and throughout the South East Asia Region.

RESIDENT PARTNERS

Richard H. Earl
Trevor Butcher
Glenn R.A. Haley
Geoffrey J. Shaw
Raymond W. K. Lau
George H. Rosenberg

CONSULTANTS

David H. Renton
Peter Cashin
Michael Skrbic

ASSISTANT SOLICITORS

Thomas Chan
Dora W.M. Chow
John T.K. Yeap
George Tung

Languages: English, Cantonese and Mandarin

McMILLAN BULL CASGRAIN

Patent and Trade Mark Agents

17TH FLOOR, 9 QUEEN'S ROAD, CENTRAL
HONG KONG
Telephone: 852-843-7333
Fax: 852-845-5566

Vancouver, British Columbia Office: Bull, Housser & Tupper, Suite 3000, 1055 West Georgia Street, P.O. Box 11130. Telephone: 604-687-6575. Cable Address: "Tursid". Telex: 04-53395; 04-55121. Fax: 604-641-4949.

Surrey, British Columbia Office: Suite 201, 9648 - 128th Street, V3T 2X9. Telephone: 604-581-4677. Fax: 604-581-5947.

Taipei, Taiwan Office: 5F-1, No. 415, Sec. 4, Hsinyi Road. Telephone: (01) 720-0192. Fax: (02) 720-0219.

Banking, Corporate and Business Law, China investments and Trade, Corporate Finance, Immigration Law, International Business Transactions, Maritime and Shipping, Real Estate including Commercial Property Acquisitions, Securities Law and Stock Exchange practice, Taxation, Technology Law, Trade Law, but not authorized to practice in Hong Kong.

DOUGLAS HOWARD MOORE, born Calgary, Alberta, March 1, 1958; admitted, 1985, Ontario (Not admitted in Hong Kong). *Education:* Queen's University; Osgoode Hall (LL.B., 1983). (Consultant, Robert W.H. Wang & Company, Hong Kong).

(For complete biographical data on all personnel, see Professional Biographies at Vancouver, British Columbia, Canada)

MILBANK, TWEED, HADLEY & McCLOY

3007 ALEXANDRA HOUSE
16 CHATER ROAD
HONG KONG
Telephone: 852-2526-5281
Fax: 852-2840-0792, 852-2845-9046 ABA/net Milbank HK

New York, New York Office: 1 Chase Manhattan Plaza, 10005. Telephone: 212-530-5000. Cable Address: "Miltweed NYK" ITT: 422962; 423893. Fax: 212- 530-5219. ABA/net: Milbank NY; MCI Mail: Milbank Tweed.

Midtown Office: 50 Rockefeller Plaza, 10020. Telephone: 212-530-5800. Fax: 212-530-0158.

Los Angeles, California Office: 601 South Figueroa Street, 30th Floor, 90017. Telephone: 213-892-400. Fax: 213-629-5063. Telex: 678754. ABA/net: Milbank LA.

Washington, D.C. Office: Suite 1100, 1825 Eye Street, N.W., 20006. Telephone: 202-835-7500. Cable Address: "Miltweed Wsh". ITT 440667. Fax: 202-835-7586.

Tokyo, Japan Office: Nippon Press Center Building, 2-1, Uchisaiwai-cho 2-chome, Chiyoda-ku, Tokyo 100. Telephone: 81-3-3504-1050. Fax: 81-3-3595-2790, 81-3-3502-5192.

London, England Office: Ropemaker Place, 25 Ropemaker Street, EC2Y 9AS. Telephone: 44-171-374-0423. Cable Address: "Miltuk G." Fax: 44-171-374-0912.

Singapore Office: 14-02 Caltex House, 30 Raffles Place, 0104. Telephone: 65-534-1700. Fax: 65-534-2733. ABA/net: EDNANG.

Moscow, Russia Office: 24/27 Sadovaya-Samotyochnaya, Moscow, 103051. Telephone: 7-502-258-5015. Fax: 7-502-258-5014.

Jakarta, Indonesia Correspondent Office: Makarim & Taira S., 17th Floor, Summitmas Tower, Jl, Jend. Sudirman 61, Jakarta. Telephone: 62-211252-1272 or 2460. Fax: 62-21-252-2750 or 2751.

Firm engaged in New York and United States Federal and International Law Practice but not authorized to appear before Hong Kong Courts or Administrative Agencies or to act as Hong Kong Solicitors.

PARTNERS

GLENN S. GERSTELL, born New York, New York, 1951; admitted, 1977, New York; 1981, District of Columbia (Not admitted in Hong Kong). *Education:* New York University (B.A., 1974); Columbia (J.D., 1976). Adjunct Professor of Law, Georgetown University Law School, 1985-1987. Adjunct Assistant Professor, New York Law School, 1980. (Partner in Charge at Singapore Office).

DOUGLAS A. TANNER, born Palo Alto, California, 1953; admitted, 1978, California; 1987, New York (Not admitted in Hong Kong). *Education:* Stanford University (A.B., 1974; M.B.A., 1978; J.D., 1978). Senior

(This Listing Continued)

MILBANK, TWEED, HADLEY & McCLOY, Hong Kong—Continued

Note Editor, Stanford Law Review, 1977-1978. Law Clerk to Judge Joseph T. Sneed, U.S. Court of Appeals, 9th Circuit, 1978-1979. *Member:* Bar Association of San Francisco (Chair, Barristers Corporation Committee, 1981-1982); State Bar of California (Member, Corporations Committee, Business Law Section, 1990-1993); New York State Bar Association.

OF COUNSEL

YOUNG JOON KIM, born Seoul, Korea, 1957; admitted, 1984, New York (Not admitted in Hong Kong). *Education:* Yale University (B.A., 1980); Harvard University (J.D., 1983).

PETER JAMES THOMPSON, born Newcastle, England, 1936; admitted as Solicitor, 1962, England; 1964, Hong Kong; admitted to bar, 1988, New York. *Education:* University of Hull, England (LL.B., 1958). Recipient, Honorary Doctorate of Laws, University of Hull, England, 1985. Member, Hong Kong Port Development Board. Member, Hong Kong Public Service Commission. Justice of the Peace. *LANGUAGES:* French, Cantonese.

ASSOCIATES

J. NIXON FOX III, born Tulsa, Oklahoma, 1959; admitted, 1984, Texas; 1988, District of Columbia (Not admitted in Hong Kong). *Education:* Southern Methodist University (B.B.A., magna cum laude, 1981); University of Texas (J.D., 1984); New York University (LL.M. in Taxation, 1985). *Member:* State Bar of Texas; The District of Columbia Bar; American Bar Association (Member, Taxation Section).

JACQUELINE SEEN-MAN LEUNG, admitted, 1993, California (Not admitted in Hong Kong). *Education:* University of Pennsylvania; Stanford University (A.B., with honors and Distinction, 1989); New York University (J.D., 1992). Author: "Caveat Emptor or Caveat Broker: Alternatives to Judicial Allocation of Liability for Property Defects Discovered after the Closing," Real Estate Review v. 23 n. 2, 1993. *Member:* State Bar of California. *LANGUAGES:* Cantonese, Mandarin.

YIBING MAO, born Beijing, 1963; admitted, 1990, Virginia (Not admitted in Hong Kong). *Education:* Jilins University (LL.B., 1984); Beijing University (LL.M., 1986); Duke University (J.D., 1989). *Member:* Virginia State Bar. *LANGUAGES:* Mandarin, Japanese.

BRENT VARDEMAN WOODS, born Lubbock, Texas, May 26, 1961; admitted, 1988, California (Not admitted in Hong Kong). *Education:* Princeton University (B.A., 1983); Cambridge University (M.Phil, 1985); Harvard University (J.D., 1988). *Member:* State Bar of California.

ANTHONY CHAN WING YUEN, born Malaysia; admitted, 1989, England and Wales; 1993, Hong Kong. *Education:* University of London (LL.B., 1986); Chancery Lane College of Law. *LANGUAGES:* Chinese and English.

MORRISON & FOERSTER

Established in 1883

ENTERTAINMENT BUILDING, 23RD FLOOR
30 QUEEN'S ROAD CENTRAL
HONG KONG
Telephone: 011-585-0888
Facsimile: 011-585-0800

Other offices located in: San Francisco, Los Angeles, New York, Washington, D.C., London, Brussels, Tokyo, Sacramento, Palo Alto, Walnut Creek, Orange County, Denver and Seattle.

General International Financial and Commercial Practice, including Foreign Investment in the United States. Banking, Corporation, Real Estate, Securities and Tax Law. Firm engaged in American and International Law Practice, but not authorized to appear before the Hong Kong Courts or to act as Hong Kong Solicitors.

FIRM PROFILE: Morrison & Foerster is one of the world's largest international law firms with 500 lawyers located in 14 offices worldwide. The firm's legal practice encompasses every major area of commercial law, including corporate finance, institutional lending, financial services, real estate, environmental and land use planning, mining and natural resources, agriculture, intellectual property, energy, telecommunications and entertainment, insurance, alternative dispute resolution, products liability, bankruptcy and workouts, financial transactions, labor and employment,

(This Listing Continued)

civil, criminal and securities litigation, antitrust, international trade and tax.

MEMBERS OF FIRM

JOSEPH M. BARBEAU, born June 24, 1955; admitted, 1982, Minnesota; 1983, California (Not admitted in Hong Kong). *Education:* University of Minnesota (B.A., summa cum laude, 1977); University of Minnesota Law School (J.D., magna cum laude, 1981). Order of the Coif; Phi Beta Kappa. Articles Editor, Minnesota Law Review, 1980-1981. Law Clerk to Judge Gerald W. Heaney, U.S. Court of Appeals, Eighth Circuit, 1981-1982.

PHILIP J. MCCONNAUGHAY, born January 5, 1953; admitted, 1978, Illinois; 1979, California; 1984, District of Columbia; 1990, Japan as a Gaikokuho-Jimu-Bengoshi and member of the Japan Federation of Bar Associations (Not admitted in Hong Kong). *Education:* University of Illinois (B.A., cum laude, 1975); University of Illinois College of Law (J.D., summa cum laude, 1978). Phi Beta Kappa; Order of the Coif. Editor, University of Illinois Law Review. Law Clerk to Judge Alfred Y. Kirkland, U.S. District Court, Northern District, Illinois, 1978-1979. Special Deputy General Counsel, United States Equal Employment Opportunity Commission, 1983-1984.

JOHN A. OTOSHI, born July 12, 1954; admitted, 1985, New York (Not admitted in Hong Kong). *Education:* University of California, Berkeley (A.B., 1976); Columbia Graduate School of Arts and Sciences (M.A., 1979; M.Phil., 1981); Columbia University School of Law (J.D., 1984). Phi Beta Kappa. Harlan Fiske Stone Scholar. Articles and Book Reviews Editor, Columbia Law Review, 1983-1984.

OF COUNSEL

RICHARD H. LAWRENCE III, born January 20, 1953; admitted, 1979, New York (Not admitted in Hong Kong). *Education:* University of Massachusetts (B.A., summa cum laude, 1975); Columbia University School of Law (J.D., 1978). *LANGUAGES:* Mandarin.

XIAO HU MA, born July 1, 1962; (Not admitted in Hong Kong). qualified as a PRC lawyer, 1988; approved by the Ministry of Justice of the PRC as a senior PRC lawyer, 1989; approved by the Ministry of Justice of the PRC and the China Securities Regulatory Commission to be a qualified lawyer to practice law in the securities area, 1993. *Education:* Beijing University (LL.M., 1987; LL.B., 1984). *LANGUAGES:* Cantonese, English and Mandarin.

ASSOCIATES

JONATHAN H. LEMBERG, born September 8, 1959; admitted, 1987, New Jersey; 1988, New York (Not admitted in Hong Kong). *Education:* University of Chicago (B.A., 1982); Columbia University School of Law (J.D., 1987). Managing Editor, Columbia Journal of Transnational Law, 1986-1987. *LANGUAGES:* Mandarin and Japanese.

CHRISTOPHER YIN, born July 29, 1967; admitted, 1992, California (Not admitted in Hong Kong). *Education:* Princeton University (A.B., 1989); University of Michigan Law School (J.D., 1992). *LANGUAGES:* Mandarin and Cantonese.

(For biographical data on San Francisco, Los Angeles, Sacramento, Walnut Creek, Palo Alto and Irvine, CA, New York, NY, Washington, DC, Denver, CO, Seattle, WA, London, England, Brussels, Belgium and Tokyo, Japan see professional biographies at each of those cities).

NORTON ROSE

(in association with Johnson Stokes & Master)

17TH FLOOR, PRINCE'S BUILDING
10 CHATER ROAD
HONG KONG
Telephone: +852 28432211
Telex: NOJON HX 75107
Fax: +852 28459121

Other Offices: London, Bahrain, Brussels, Moscow, Paris, Piraeus, Prague and Singapore.

FIRM PROFILE: Norton Rose is a leading City and International law firm with its principal office in the City of London. The firm provides a wide range of legal services primarily to the business and financial communities as well as to a number of sovereign governments and state organizations. We are known particularly for our corporate and debt finance, banking, company and commercial law, natural resources, insurance, property development, aerospace and maritime practices and wide-ranging ex-

(This Listing Continued)

pertise on tax matters. Norton Rose has a major litigation department handling all forms of commercial dispute resolution.

In Hong Kong the firm's principal areas of practice are banking; capital markets; corporate finance; corporate; joint ventures; mergers and acquisitions; project finance; shipping litigation.

RESIDENT PARTNERS

DAVID P.R. STANNARD, admitted, 1981, England and Wales; 1983, Hong Kong. **PRACTICE AREAS:** Corporate Finance; Capital Markets; Mergers and Acquisitions; Corporate and Commercial.

JEFFERY V.C.L. BARRATT, admitted, 1976, England and Wales; 1984, Hong Kong. **PRACTICE AREAS:** Banking; Project Finance; Capital Markets.

PETER HASLAM, admitted, 1981, England and Wales; 1983, Hong Kong. **PRACTICE AREAS:** Banking; Project Finance; Capital Markets; Acquisitions Finance.

JAMES R. JAMES, admitted, 1977, England and Wales; 1983, Hong Kong. **PRACTICE AREAS:** Commercial; Shipping Litigation.

MARTIN D.K. SCOTT, admitted, 1983, England and Wales; 1986, Hong Kong. **PRACTICE AREAS:** Corporate Finance; Capital Markets; Mergers and Acquisitions; Corporate and Commercial.

DAVID J. SHAW, admitted, 1970, England and Wales; 1976, Hong Kong. M.A. (Cantab), admitted, 1970, England; 1976, Hong Kong. **PRACTICE AREAS:** Corporate Finance; Capital Markets; Mergers and Acquisitions; Corporate and Commercial.

Languages: English, Cantonese and Mandarin

(For Complete Biographical Data on all Personnel, see Biographical Card at London, England)

O'MELVENY & MYERS

Established in 1885

1104 LIPPO TOWER
LIPPO CENTRE
89 QUEENSWAY, CENTRAL
HONG KONG
Telephone: 011-852-523-8266
Facsimile: 011-852-522-1760

Los Angeles, California Office: 400 South Hope Street. Telephone: 213-669-6000. Cable Address: "Moms." Facsimile: 213-669-6407.
Century City, California Office: 1999 Avenue of the Stars, 7th Floor. Telephone: 310-553-6700. Facsimile: 310-246-6779.
Newport Beach, California Office: 610 Newport Center Drive, Suite 1700. Telephone: 714-760-9600. Cable Address: "Moms." Facsimile: 714-669-6994.
San Francisco, California Office: Embarcadero Center West Tower, 275 Battery Street, Suite 2600. Telephone: 415-984-8700. Facsimile: 415-984-8701.
New York, N.Y. Office: Citicorp Center. 153 53rd Street, 54th Floor. Telephone: 212-326-2000. Facsimile: 212-326-2061.
Washington, D.C. Office: 555 13th Street, N.W., Suite 500 West. Telephone: 202-383-5300. Cable Address: "Moms." Facsimile: 202-383-5414.
Newark, New Jersey Office: One Gateway Center, 7th Floor, 07102. Telephone: 201-639-8600. Facsimile: 201-639-8630.
London, England Office: 10 Finsbury Square, London, EC2A 1LA. Telephone: 011-44-171-256-8451. Facsimile: 011-44-171-638-8205.
Tokyo, Japan Office: Sanbancho KB-6 Building, 6 Sanbancho, Chiyoda-Ku. Telephone: 011-81-3-3239-2800. Facsimile: 011-81-3-3239-2432.
Hong Kong Office: 1104 Lippo Tower, Lippo Centre, 89 Queensway, Central Hong Kong. Telephone: 011-852-523-8266. Facsimile: 011-852-522-1760.

General and International Practice. Authorized to practice U.S. federal law and the laws of the District of Columbia and of all states with the exception of Louisiana.

FIRM PROFILE: Foreign direct investment, international capital markets, project finance, real estate projects and other transactional matters.

(This Listing Continued)

PARTNER

HOWARD CHAO, born Taipei, Taiwan, June 13, 1954; admitted, 1980, California and U.S. District Court, Central District of California. *Education:* Purdue University (B.S., 1976); Boalt Hall School of Law, University of California (J.D., 1980). Phi Beta Kappa; Phi Kappa Phi; Order of the Coif. International Rotary Fellow, 1979-1980. Associate Editor, California Law Review, 1977-1980. *LANGUAGES:* Mandarin Chinese, French.

SPECIAL COUNSEL

Fiona M. Connell

(For Complete Personnel and Biographical Data see Professional Biographies at Los Angeles, California)

OSLER RENAULT

Canadian Barristers and Solicitors
SUITE 1708, ONE PACIFIC PLACE
88 QUEENSWAY
HONG KONG
Telephone: 011-852-2877-3933
Fax: 011-852-2877-0866

London, England Office: Osler Renault* - 20 Little Britain, London, EC1A 7DH. Telephone: 071-606-0777. Fax: 071-606-0222.
Paris, France Office: Osler Renault* - 4, rue Bayard, 75008 Paris. Telephone: 33-1.42.89.00.54. Fax: 33-1.42.89.51.60.
New York, N.Y. Office: Osler Renault* - 200 Park Avenue, Suite 3217, 10166-0193. Telephone: 212-867-5800. Fax: 212-867-5802.
Singapore Office: Osler Renault* - 65 Chulia Street, #40-05 OCBC Centre, Singapore 0104. Telephone: (65) 538-2077. Fax: (65) 538-2977.
*Osler Renault is an international partnership of Osler, Hoskin & Harcourt and Ogilvy Renault.
Osler, Hoskin & Harcourt has offices at: P.O. Box 50, 1 First Canadian Place, Toronto, Ontario, Canada M5X 1B8. Telephone: 416-362-2111. Fax: 416-862-6666 and 50 O'Connor Street, Suite 1500, Ottawa, Ontario, Canada K1P 6L2. Telephone: 613-235-7234. Fax: 613-235-2867.
Ogilvy Renault has offices at: 1981 McGill College Avenue, Suite 1100, Montreal, Quebec, Canada H3A 3C1. Telephone: 514-847-4747. Fax: 514-286-5474 and Suite 1600, 45 O'Connor Street, Ottawa, Ontario, Canada K1P 1A4. Telephone: 613-780-8661. Fax: 613-230-5459 and 500 Grande-Allée Est, Suite 520, Quebec, Quebec G1R 2J7. Telephone: 418-640-5000. Fax: 418-640-1500.

RESIDENT IN HONG KONG

STEVEN J. TRUMPER, born London, Ontario, 1952; admitted, 1982, Ontario (Not admitted in Hong Kong). *Education:* University of Western Ontario (B.A., Honours, 1975); Queen's University (LL.B., 1980).

P. DOUGAL MACDONALD, born Toronto, Ontario, 1957; admitted, 1985, Ontario (Not admitted in Hong Kong). *Education:* Queen's University (B.A., 1980) Osgoode Hall (LL.B., 1983).

HARTLAND J. A. PATERSON, born Calgary, Alberta, 1959; admitted, 1987, Québec (Not admitted in Hong Kong). *Education:* Queen's University (B.A., 1982); McGill University (B.C.L., 1986; LL.B., 1986).

OLIVIA S. M. LEE, born Peking, China, 1963; admitted, 1991, British Columbia; 1993, Solicitor, High Court of Hong Kong and Solicitor, Supreme Court of England and Wales. *Education:* University of British Columbia (B.Comm., 1990; LL.B., 1990).

PAUL, WEISS, RIFKIND, WHARTON & GARRISON

13TH FLOOR, HONG KONG CLUB BUILDING
3A CHATER ROAD (CENTRAL)
HONG KONG
Telephone: (852) 2536-9933
Facsimile: (852) 2536-9622

New York, N.Y. Office: 1285 Avenue of the Americas, 10019-6064. Telephones: 212-373-3000, TDD 212-373-2000. Cable Address: "Longsight, New York". Facsimile: 212-757-3990.
Washington, D.C. Office: 1615 L Street, N.W., Suite 1300. Telephones: 202-223-7300. TDD 202-223-7490. Facsimile: 202-223-7420. Cable Address: "Longsight, Washington".

(This Listing Continued)

PAUL, WEISS, RIFKIND, WHARTON & GARRISON,
Hong Kong—Continued

Paris, France Office: 199, Boulevard Saint-Germain, 75007. Telephone: (33-1) 45.49.33.85. Cable Address: "Longsight, Paris". Telex: 203178F. Facsimile: (33-1) 42-22-64-38.

Tokyo, Japan Office: 11th Floor, Main Tower, Akasaka Twin Tower, 17-22, Akasaka 2-chome, Minato-ku, 107. Telephone: (81-3) 3505-0291. Facsimile: (81-3) 3505-4540. Telex: 02428120 PWRWGT.

Beijing, People's Republic of China Office: Suite 1910, Scite Tower, 22 Jianguomenwai Dajie, 100004. Telephones: (86-1) 5123628-30, (86-1) 5122288X.1910. Telex: 210169 PWRWG CN. Facsimile: (86-1) 5123631.

General Practice.

RESIDENT PARTNER

JOHN E. LANGE, born Ridgewood, New Jersey, June 28, 1955; admitted, 1981, District of Columbia; 1990, New York (Not admitted in Hong Kong). *Education:* Princeton University (A.B., summa cum laude, 1977); Harvard Law School (J.D., cum laude, 1981). Deputy General Counsel, Multinational Force and Observers, Rome, Italy and Sinai, Egypt, 1984-1986. Attorney Advisor, Office of the Legal Advisor, U.S. Department of State, 1981-1983. *Member:* The Association of the Bar of the City of New York; The District of Columbia Bar; American Bar Association. *PRACTICE AREAS:* International Joint Ventures and Project Finance; Corporate Finance; Mergers & Acquisitions.

ASIAN COUNSEL

JEANETTE K. CHAN, born Hong Kong; admitted, 1985, British Columbia; 1988, New York; 1993, United Kingdom and Hong Kong (Not admitted in Hong Kong). *Education:* University of Toronto (B.A., with distinction, 1980); University of British Columbia (LL.B., 1983); Harvard University (LL.M., 1986). *Member:* New York State Bar Association; Law Society of the United Kingdom; Law Society of Hong Kong. *LANGUAGES:* Mandarin, Cantonese, Shanghainese, English. *PRACTICE AREAS:* International; Corporate Commercial; Telecommunications; Corporate Finance.

RESIDENT ASSOCIATES

RORY A. BABICH, admitted, 1989, New Jersey; 1990, New York (Not admitted in Hong Kong). *Education:* Rutgers University (B.A., 1985); University of Pennsylvania (J.D., 1989).

CHARLES F. GOLDSMITH, born Salem, Massachusetts, May 5, 1965; admitted, 1991, New York (Not admitted in Hong Kong). *Education:* Harvard University (B.A., 1986; J.D., 1990). *LANGUAGES:* Mandarin.

ANITA CHU YELLAND, born Hong Kong, May 27, 1958; admitted, 1988, England and Wales (Not admitted in the United States). *Education:* The Chinese University of Hong Kong, Hong Kong (B.Soc.Sc., 1st hons., 1982); Cambridge University, Cambridge, England (B.A. (Hons), Law, 1985; M.A., Arts, 1990). Top Student in class in year of graduation, 1982. Holder of South China Morning Post Scholarship. University of California Exchange Program Tuition Waiver Scholarship, 1980. Rotary Foundation Scholarship. Student Ambassador to the USA, 1980. Assistant to Hong Kong Urban Councillor Miss Maria Wai Chu Tam, 1978-1981. Legal Advisor, Shell Hong Kong Limited. *Member:* The Law Society of the United Kingdom; American Chamber of Commerce. *LANGUAGES:* English, Chinese (Cantonese and Mandarin). *PRACTICE AREAS:* Foreign Investment (People's Republic of China); Banking Services; Financial Services; Mergers and Acquisitions; General Commercial; Corporate.

(For Biographical data of other Personnel, see Professional Biographies at New York, Washington, D.C., Paris, France, Tokyo, Japan and Beijing, China)

PERKINS COIE

23RD FLOOR, ASIA PACIFIC FINANCE TOWER
CITIBANK PLAZA, 3 GARDEN ROAD
HONG KONG
Telephone: (852) 2878-1177
Facsimile: (852) 2524-9988 DX-9230-IC

REVISERS OF THE WASHINGTON LAW DIGEST FOR THIS DIRECTORY

London, England Office: 36/38 Cornhill, EC3V 3ND. Telephone: 0171-369-9966. Facsimile: 0171-369-9968.

(This Listing Continued)

Taipei, Taiwan Office: 8/F, TFIT Tower, 85 Jen Ai Road, Section 4, Taipei 106, Taiwan, R.O.C. Telephone: 886-2-778-1177. Facsimile: 886-2-777-9898.

Seattle, Washington Office: 1201 Third Avenue, 40th Floor. Telephone: 1-(206) 583-8888. Facsimile: 1-(206) -583-8500.

Anchorage, Alaska Office: 1029 West Third Avenue, Suite 300, Anchorage, AK 99501. Telephone: 1-(907) 279-8561. Facsimile: 1-(907) 276-3108.

Bellevue, Washington Office: Suite 1800, One Bellevue Center, 411 - 108th Avenue N.E. Bellevue, WA 98004. Telephone: 1-(206) 453-6980. Facsimile: 1-(206) 453-7350.

Los Angeles, California Office: 1999 Avenue of the Stars, Ninth Floor, Los Angeles, CA 90067. Telephone: 1-(310) 788-9900. Facsimile: 1-(310) 788-3399.

Olympia, Washington Office: 1110 Capitol Way South, Suite 405, Olympia, WA 98501. Telephone: 1-(206) 956-3300. Facsimile: 1-(206) 956-1208.

Portland, Oregon Office: U.S. Bancorp Tower, Suite 2500, 111 Southwest Fifth Avenue, Portland, OR 97204. Telephone: 1-(503) 295-4400. Facsimile: 1-(503) 295-6793.

Spokane, Washington Office: N. 221 Wall Street, Suite 600, Spokane, WA 99201. Telephone: 1-(509) 624-2212. Facsimile: 1-(509) 458-3399.

Washington, D.C. Office: 607 Fourteenth Street, N.W., Washington, D.C. 20005-2011. Telephone: 1-(202) 628-6600. Facsimile: 1-(202) 434-1690.

Firm engaged in American and International Practice, but not authorized to appear before the Hong Kong courts or to act as Hong Kong solicitors.

RESIDENT PARTNER

ROBERT S. MUCKLESTONE, born Seattle, Washington, May 15, 1929; admitted, 1954, Washington (Not admitted in Hong Kong). *Education:* University of Washington (B.S., 1951; LL.B., 1954).

PARTNER

MICHAEL EDWARD MCGOWEN, born Fort Campbell, Kentucky, October 23, 1955; admitted, 1983, California (Not admitted in Hong Kong). *Education:* Chinese University of Hong Kong; University of California at Berkeley (B.A., Asian Studies, 1980); Hastings College of Law, University of California (J.D., 1983). Editor, Hastings International and Comparative Law Review, 1982-1983. *LANGUAGES:* English, Thai, Mandarin and Cantonese.

ASSOCIATE

JAMES S. TSANG, born Hong Kong, July 12, 1958; admitted, 1985, Texas; 1990, California (Not admitted in Hong Kong). *Education:* University of Texas at Austin (B.B.A., with honors, 1979; M.B.A., 1982); St. Edward's University; Southern Methodist University (J.D., 1985); Rutgers University. *LANGUAGES:* Mandarin, Cantonese and English.

REVISERS OF THE WASHINGTON LAW DIGEST FOR THIS DIRECTORY

(For biographical data of personnel resident in other offices of Perkins Coie, see Professional Biographies at London, England, Taipei, Taiwan, Bellevue, Olympia, Seattle and Spokane, Washington, Anchorage, Alaska, Los Angeles, California, Portland, Oregon and Washington, D.C.)

PILLSBURY MADISON & SUTRO

6/F ASIA PACIFIC FINANCE TOWER
CITIBANK PLAZA
3 GARDEN ROAD
CENTRAL
HONG KONG
Telephone: 011-852-509-7100
FAX: 011-852-509-7188

San Francisco, California Office: 225 Bush St. Telephone: 415-983-1000. Fax: 415-398-2096.

Costa Mesa, California Office: Plaza Tower, 600 Anton Boulevard, Suite 1100, Costa Mesa, California, 92626. Telephone: 714-436-6800. Fax: 714-662-6999.

Los Angeles, California Office: Citicorp Plaza, 725 South Figueroa Street, Suite 1200, 90017. Telephone: 213-488-7100. Fax: 213-629-1033.

New York, New York Office: One Liberty Plaza, 165 Broadway, 51st Floor. Telephone: 212-374-1890. Fax: 212-374-1852.

Menlo Park, California Office: 2700 Sand Hill Road, 94025. Telephone: 415-233-4500. FAX: 415-233-4545.

(This Listing Continued)

Sacramento, California Office: 400 Capitol Mall, Suite 1700, 95814.
   Telephone: 916-329-4700. Fax: 916-441-3583.
San Diego, California Office: 101 West Broadway, Suite 1800, 92101.
   Telephone: 619-234-5000. Fax: 619-236-1995.
San Jose, California Office: Ten Almaden Boulevard, 95113. Telephone:
   408-947-4000. Fax: 408-287-8341.
Washington, D. C. Office: 1667 K Street, N.W., Suite 1100, 20006.
   Telephone: 202-887-0300. Fax: 202-296-7605.
Tokyo, Japan Office: Churchill and Shimazaki,
   Gaikokuho-Jimu--Bengoshi-Jimusho, 11-12, Toranomon 5-chome,
   Minato-ku, Tokyo 105, Japan. Telephone: 800-729-9830;
   011-81-3-5472-6561. Fax: 011-81-3-5472-5761.

General Civil Practice and Litigation in all State and Federal Courts. Business: Bankruptcy and Creditors' Rights, Commercial Transactions/Energy, Corporate and Securities, Corporate/Technologies, Employee Benefits, Environment, Health and Safety, Estate Planning, Financial Institutions, Project Finance and Insurance, Labor, Political Law, Real Estate, Tax. Litigation: Alternative Dispute Resolution, Antitrust/Trade Regulation, Appellate, Banking/Financial Institutions, Class Action, Commercial Disputes, Construction/Real Estate Energy Matters, Environmental/Land Use, ERISA, Insurance, Intellectual Property, Labor/Equal Opportunity, Maritime/Admiralty, Media/Entertainment/Sports, Securities, Torts/-Product Liability, White Collar Crime. Specialty Practices: Health Care, International, Latin America, Mexico, The Pacific Rim, Multimedia and Food Labeling.

FIRM PROFILE: Founded in 1874, Pillsbury Madison & Sutro has grown to become one of the largest law firms in the United States, with more than 600 attorneys and expertise in virtually every area of the law. With offices in seven California cities, New York, Washington, D.C., and two offices in Asia, Hong Kong and Tokyo, the firm combines a strong domestic practice with a dynamic presence in the rapidly changing international markets. The firm's corporate expertise encompasses all aspects of business law and covers the full range of legal needs. Its litigation practice is conducted by trial lawyers who have handled landmark cases in the federal and state courts. The firm's clients range from large multinational corporations to start-up companies to individuals.

MEMBERS OF FIRM

DONALD J. HESS, born Melbourne, Australia, November 28, 1952; admitted, 1977, Victoria, Australia; 1987, New York; 1988, California. *Education:* Monash University, Melbourne, Australia (B.Sc., 1974; LL.B., Hons., 1976); Melbourne University (LL.M., 1979).

D. STANLEY ROWLAND, born Berkeley, California, January 31, 1953; admitted, 1981, California. *Education:* University of California at Berkeley (B.A., cum laude, 1975); Cornell University (J.D., cum laude, 1981). Phi Beta Kappa; Phi Delta Phi. (Managing Partner). **PRACTICE AREAS:** General Corporate Law; Finance Law; Securities Law; International Law.

ROBERT J. SPJUT, born San Francisco, California, September 1, 1948; admitted, 1972, California. *Education:* University of San Francisco (J.D., 1971); London School of Economics and Political Sciences, London, England (LL.M., 1972).

(For biographical data on San Francisco, San Diego, Los Angeles, Sacramento, San Jose, Costa Mesa and Menlo Park, CA, Washington, DC, Tokyo, Japan and New York, New York personnel, see Professional Biographies at each of those cities).

PRITCHARD ENGLEFIELD & WANG

HONG KONG

(See Robert W.H. Wang & Co.)

Corporate and Commercial Law, Intellectual Property including Trade Marks, Shipping Finance, Immigration, Probate, Conveyancing, Litigation.

RICHARDS BUTLER

ALEXANDRA HOUSE, TWENTIETH FLOOR
16-20 CHATER ROAD
HONG KONG
Telephone: 810 8008
Telex: 62554 RBLAW HX
Fax: 810 0664

London, England Office: Beaufort House, 15 St Botolph Street, EC3A 7EE. Telephone: 0171-247 6555. Telex: 949494 RBLAW G. Fax: 0171-247 5091.
Abu Dhabi, United Arab Emirates Office: Al-Sayegh Richards Butler. P.O. Box 46904, Saif Bin Ghobash Building, Zayed the Second Street. Telephone: 2-725561. Telex: 22261 RBLAW EM. Fax: 2-778630.
Brussels, Belgium Office: Avenue de la Renaissance 1, Bte 11, 1040. Telephone: 2-732 20 55. Fax: 2-735 46 91.
Paris, France Office: 134 rue du Faubourg Saint Honoré, 75008. Telephone: 1-44 13 63 53. Fax: 1-42 89 20 60.

Corporate, Commercial, Maritime and Admiralty Law.

RESIDENT PARTNERS

Christopher G. Howse
Andrew P. Biggs
Robin C. Nicholson
David M. Norman
John D. McGuinness
Andrew S. Hughes
A. David Morrison
David A. Stokes
Elizabeth Hardy
P.J. Fortune
Christopher J. Williams
David J. Coogans

(For Complete List of Partners, see Professional Biographies at London, England).

ROMULO

1203D TOWER 1
ADMIRALTY CENTRE
18 HARCOURT ROAD
HONG KONG
Telephone: (852) 28662292
Cable Address: "Derecho Hong Kong"
Telex: 86305 DROIT HX
Fax: (852) 28661601

Metro Manila, Republic of the Philippines Office: Romulo, Mabanta, Buenaventura, Sayoc & de los Angeles. Fourth Floor, King's Court, 2129 Chino Roches Avenue. Telephone: (632) 815-30-11. Telex: 45029 ORO PM; Eastern 63312 ORO PN. Cable Address: "Oro" Manila.

Firm engaged in Philippine and International Practice, but not authorized to appear before the Hong Kong Courts or to act as Solicitors.

RESIDENT PARTNERS

Jose F. Buenaventura (Not admitted in Hong Kong)

RESIDENT ASSOCIATES

Joseph Anthony M. Alejandro   **Jacqueline Therese J. Romero-Laurel**

(For Complete Biographical Data on all Personnel, see Professional Biographies at Manila, Republic of the Philippines).

SHEARMAN & STERLING

STANDARD CHARTERED BANK BUILDING
4 DES VOEUX ROAD CENTRAL
HONG KONG
Telephone: (852) 2978-8000
Fax: (852) 2978-8099

New York, N.Y. Office: 599 Lexington Avenue, New York, New York 10022-6069 and Citicorp Center, 153 East 53rd Street, New York, New York 10022-4676. Telephone: (212) 848-4000. Telex: 667290
(This Listing Continued)

SHEARMAN & STERLING, Hong Kong—Continued

Num Lau. Fax: 599 Lexington Avenue: (212) 848-7179. Citicorp Center: (212) 848-5252.

Abu Dhabi, United Arab Emirates Office: P.O. Box 2948. Telephone: (971-2) 324477. Fax: (971-2) 774533.

Beijing, People's Republic of China Office: Suite #2205, Capital Mansion, No. 6, Xin Yuan Nan Road. Chao Yang District Beijing, 100004. Telephone: (861) 465-4574. Fax: (861) 465-4578.

Budapest, Hungary Office: Szerb utca 17-19, 1056 Budapest. Telephone: (36-1) 266-3522. Fax: (36-1) 266-3523.

Düsseldorf, Federal Republic of Germany Office: Königsallee 46, D-40212 Düsseldorf. Telephone: (49-211) 13 62 80. Telex: 8 588 294 NYLO. Fax: (49-211) 13 33 09.

Frankfurt, Federal Republic of Germany Office: Bockenheimer Landstrasse 55, D-60325 Frankfurt am Main. Telephone: (49-69) 97-10-70. Fax: (49-69) 97-10-71-00.

London, England Office: 199 Bishopsgate, London EC2M 3TY. Telephone: (44-71) 920-9000. Fax: (44-71) 920-9020.

Los Angeles, California Office: 725 South Figueroa Street, 21st Floor, 90017-5421. Telephone: (213) 239-0300. Fax: (213) 239-0381, 614-0936.

Paris, France Office: 12 rue d'Astorg, 75008. Telephone: (33-1) 44-71-17-17. Telex: 282964 Royale. Fax: (33-1) 44-71-01-01.

San Francisco, California Office: 555 California Street, 94104-1522. Telephone: (415) 616-1100. Fax: (415) 616-1199.

Taipei, Taiwan Office: 7th Floor, Hung Kuo Building, 167 Tun Hwa North Road. Telephone: (886-2) 545-3300. Fax: (866-2) 545-3322.

Tokyo, Japan Office: Shearman & Sterling (Thomas Wilner Gaikokuho-Jimu-Bengoshi Jimusho), Fukoku Seimei Building, 5th Fl. 2-2-2,Uchisaiwaicho, Chiyoda-ku, Tokyo 100, Japan. Telephone: (81 3) 5251-1601. Fax: (81 3) 5251-1602.

Toronto, Ontario, Canada Office: Commerce Court West, Suite 4405, P.O. Box 247, M5L 1E8. Telephone: (416) 360-8484. Fax: (416) 360-2958.

Washington, D.C. Office: 801 Pennsylvania Avenue, N.W., Suite 900, 20004-2604. Telephone: (202) 508-8000. Fax: (202) 508-8100.

General Practice.
Firm engaged in American and International Law Practice, but not authorized to practice before Hong Kong Courts or act as Hong Kong Solicitors.

FIRM PROFILE: Shearman & Sterling, founded in 1873, has more than 500 lawyers in 15 offices throughout the world. The firm's practice encompasses most major areas of business law, including: Antitrust and Trade Regulation; Banking; Bankruptcy and Corporate Reorganization; Compensation and Benefits; Environmental; Finance (including Corporate Finance, Domestic Private Finance, Financial Institutions, International Private Finance and Project Finance); Individual Clients, Trusts and Estates; Insurance; International Trade and Government Relations; Litigation and Arbitration; Mergers and Acquisitions; Oil and Gas; Privatizations; Real Estate; and Tax. The Firm is also engaged in the practice of French, German and Hungarian law through its offices in France, Germany and Hungary.

RESIDENT PARTNERS

ALBERT THEODORE POWERS, born Norfolk, Nebraska, 1953; admitted, 1978, Colorado; 1982, New York; 1983, California (Not admitted in Hong Kong). *Education:* University of Denver (B.A., 1974); University of Pennsylvania (J.D., 1977); New York University (LL.M. in Taxation, 1979). Law Clerk to the Hon. Robert H. McWilliams, U.S. Court of Appeals, Tenth Circuit, 1977-1978. (Managing Partner).

ALAN F. DENENBERG, born Philadelphia, Pennsylvania, 1960; admitted, 1987, New York; 1988, California (Not admitted in Hong Kong). *Education:* McGill University, Canada (B.A., 1982); Osgoode Hall Law School, Toronto, Canada (LL.B., 1985); Columbia University (LL.M., 1986).

CLARK T. RANDT, JR., born Cleveland, Ohio, 1945; admitted, 1976, New York (Not admitted in Hong Kong). *Education:* Yale University (A.B., 1968); University of Michigan (J.D., 1975); University of East Asia, Macau (People's Republic of China Law Diploma, 1988); Harvard Law School (1974). First Secretary and Commercial Attache, U.S. Embassy, Beijing, People's Republic of China, 1982-1984. Governor, American Chamber of Commerce in Hong Kong, 1987-1990.

EDWARD L. TURNER III, born Montgomery, Alabama, 1944; admitted, 1971, New York; 1982, California (Not admitted in Hong Kong). *Education:* Vanderbilt University (B.A., 1966; J.D., 1970). (Managing Partner, Asia).

(This Listing Continued)

RESIDENT ASSOCIATES

SCOTT B. BOLLINGER, born Norfolk, Virginia, 1962; admitted, 1988, Georgia; 1989, District of Columbia (Not admitted in Hong Kong). *Education:* Cambridge University; University of Virginia (B.A., with high distinction, 1984; J.D., 1988). Phi Beta Kappa.

MARCELO A. COSMA, born Villa Nueva-Guaymallen, Mendoza, Argentina, March 25, 1964; admitted, 1992, New York (Not admitted in Hong Kong). *Education:* Princeton University (A.B., magna cum laude, 1986); National University of Singapore (Rotary Foundation Scholar, 1986-1987); University of Chicago (J.D., 1991; M.A., 1991). *Member:* American Bar Association. *PRACTICE AREAS:* Securities and Financial Products; Mergers and Acquisitions.

R. LEE EDWARDS, born Boston, Massachusetts, December 23, 1964; admitted, 1993, New York (Not admitted in Hong Kong). *Education:* Columbia College (A.B., 1986); Columbia University (J.D., 1992).

STEPHANIE S. L. WONG, born Hong Kong, 1965; admitted, 1990, New York and U.S. Tax Court (Not admitted in Hong Kong). *Education:* University of Hong Kong (LL.B., 1987); New York University (LL.M., 1990). *LANGUAGES:* English, Chinese (Cantonese and Mandarin).

JIA JONATHAN ZHU, born Shanghai, China, October 17, 1962; admitted, 1993, New York (Not admitted in Hong Kong). *Education:* Zhengzhou University (B.A., 1982); Nanjing University (M.A., 1984); Cornell Law School (J.D., 1992).

(For Biographical data of all Partners, see Professional Biographies at New York, New York)

SHUM & CO.

(Associated Office of Stikeman, Elliott)

29 QUEEN'S ROAD CENTRAL
SUITE 1103, CHINA BUILDING
HONG KONG
Telephone: 852-2526-5531
Fax: 852-2845-9076

Montreal, Quebec Office: 1155 René-Lévesque Boulevard West, 40th Floor, H3B 3V2. Telephone: 514-397-3000. Fax: 514-397-3222.

Toronto, Ontario Office: Commerce Court West, 53rd Floor, M5L 1B9. Telephone: 416-869-5500. Fax: 416-947-0866.

Ottawa, Ontario Office: 50 O'Connor Street, Suite 914, K1P 6L2. Telephone: 613-234-4555. Fax: 613-230-8877.

Calgary, Alberta Office: 855 - 2nd Street S.W., 1500 Bankers Hall, T2P 4J7. Telephone: 403-266-9000. Fax: 403-266-9034.

Vancouver, British Columbia Office: 666 Burrard Street, Suite 1700, Park Place, V6C 2X8. Telephone: 604-631-1300. Fax: 604-681-1825.

New York, New York Office: 126 East 56th Street, 11th Floor, Tower 56, 10022. Telephone: 212-371-8855. Fax: 212-371-7087.

Washington, D.C. Office: 1300 I Street, N.W., Suite 1210 West, 20005-3314. Telephone: 202-326-7555. Fax: 202-326-7557.

London, England Office: Cottons Centre, Cottons Lane, SE1 2QL. Telephone: 71-378-0880. Fax: 71-378-0344.

Paris, France Office: In Association with Société Juridique Internationale, 39, rue François Ier, 75008. Telephone: 33-1-40-73-82-00. Fax: 33-1-40-73-82-10.

Budapest, Hungary Office: Andrássy út 100, II Floor, H-1062. Telephone: 36-1-269-1790. Fax: 36-1-269-0655.

Hong Kong Office: 29 Queen's Road Central, Suite 1102, China Building. Telephone: 852-2868-9903. Fax: 852-2868-9912.

Taipei, Taiwan Office: 117 Sec. 3 Min Sheng East Road, 8th Floor. Telephone: 886-2-719-9573. Fax: 886-2-719-4540.

Firm engaged in Canadian and International Law Practice, but not authorized to appear before the Hong Kong Courts or to act as Hong Kong Solicitors.

CHING-WO NG, born China, September 4, 1950; admitted, 1981, Alberta; 1985, England and Wales; 1987, Hong Kong. *Education:* University of Alberta (B.Sc., with Hons., 1973; M.Sc., 1975; LL.B., 1980). *Member:* Edmonton Bar Association; Law Society of Alberta. *LANGUAGES:* English, Chinese (Mandarin, Cantonese and Taiwanese).

ERIC C. M. KONG, born Hong Kong, July 8, 1957; admitted, 1983, British Columbia; 1993, England and Wales and Hong Kong (Not admitted in Hong Kong). *Education:* University of British Columbia (1979); Os-

(This Listing Continued)

goode Hall Law School (LL.B., 1982). *Member:* Canadian Bar Association. *LANGUAGES:* English, Cantonese, Mandarin.

EDNA S. C. CHEUNG, born Hong Kong, March 2, 1966; admitted, 1992, British Columbia (Not admitted in Hong Kong). *Education:* University of Alberta (B.Comm., 1988); Osgoode Hall (LL.B., 1991). *Member:* Canadian Bar Association; Law Society of British Columbia; Canadian Chamber of Commerce in Hong Kong. *LANGUAGES:* English, Chinese.

JOANNA AN CHU Y. SHUM, born Hong Kong, November 5, 1956; admitted, 1981, Hong Kong; 1985, England and Wales; 1986, Victoria, Australia; 1991, New South Wales, Australia and Singapore. *Education:* University of Hong Kong (LL.B., Hon., 1978; P.C.LL., 1979). *Member:* The Law Society of Hong Kong. *LANGUAGES:* English, Cantonese.

KELVIN KEE FUNG SHUM, born Hong Kong, January 20, 1956; admitted, 1981, Hong Kong; 1985, England and Wales; 1986, Victoria, Australia; 1990, New South Wales, Australia; 1991, Singapore. *Education:* University of Hong Kong (LL.B., Hon., 1978; P.C.LL., 1979). *Member:* The Law Society of Hong Kong. *LANGUAGES:* English and Cantonese.

(For biographical data on other personnel, see Professional Biographies at Montreal, Quebec, Toronto, Ontario, Ottawa, Ontario, Calgary, Alberta, Vancouver, British Columbia, New York, New York, Washington, D.C., London, England, Paris, France, Budapest, Hungary, Hong Kong and Taipei, Taiwan)

SIMMONS & SIMMONS

Established in 1979

24TH FLOOR, JARDINE HOUSE
ONE CONNAUGHT PLACE, CENTRAL
HONG KONG
Telephone: 852-2868 1131
Telecopier: 852-2810 5040
Telex: 75888 SANDS HX

London, England Office: 21 Wilson Street, EC2M 2TQ. Telephone: 44-171-628 2020; 44-171-528 9292. Facsimile: 44-171-628 2070. Telex: 888562SIMMON G.

Paris, France Office: 2, Avenue Bugeaud, 75116. Telephone: 33-1-45016767. Telecopier: 33-1-45012232. Telex: TRANSAV 649381F.

Brussels, Belgium Office: Rue d'Arlon 118, 1040. Telephone: 32-2-280 16 70. Telecopier: 32-2-280 04 84.

Lisbon, Portugal Office: Rua Castilho, n° 32-9°, 1250. Telephone: 351-1-352 1318. Telecopier: 351-1-352 1418.

Milan, Italy Office in joint practice with Studio Avv. Eugenio Grippo: Via Dei Boschetti 1, 20121. Telephone: 39-2-76003012. Telecopier: 39-2-782770.

Abu Dhabi Office: The Blue Tower, Khalifa Street, P.O. Box 5931. Telephone: 971 2 347882. Telecopier: 971 2 347832.

New York, New York Office: 115 East 57th Street, 10022. Telephone: 1-212-688-6620. Telecopier: 1-212-355-3594.

Local Hong Kong, China and General International Business and Financial Law Practice.

RESIDENT PARTNERS

STEPHEN SCHOFIELD, born Prestwich, England, May 22, 1951; admitted, 1977, England and Wales; 1983, Hong Kong. *Education:* Liverpool University (LL.B.). *Member:* International Trade Mark Association; Inter Pacific Bar Association; Law Society of Hong Kong. *LANGUAGES:* English. *PRACTICE AREAS:* Commercial Law; Trade Law; Intellectual Property Law.

DAVID B. BARKER, born Cheltenham, England, November 24, 1951; admitted, 1978, England and Wales; 1991, Hong Kong. *Education:* Hertford College, Oxford (B.A.). *Member:* Law Society of Hong Kong. *LANGUAGES:* English. *PRACTICE AREAS:* Commercial Property Law.

COLIN E. LEAVER, born Cuckfield, England, May 25, 1958; admitted, 1982, England and Wales; 1990, Hong Kong. *Education:* Lincoln College, Oxford (M.A.). *Member:* Law Society of Hong Kong. *LANGUAGES:* English. *PRACTICE AREAS:* Corporate Finance; Company Law.

SIMON R. MORGAN, born Wales, June 16, 1955; admitted, 1980, England and Wales; 1988, Hong Kong. *Education:* Liverpool University (LL.B.). *Member:* Law Society of Hong Kong; Law Society of England and Wales; Fellow Chartered Institute of Arbitrators. *LANGUAGES:* English. *PRACTICE AREAS:* Litigation; Insolvency; Arbitration.

(This Listing Continued)

PHILIP T. NUNN, born England, November 3, 1949; admitted, 1974, England and Wales; 1981, Hong Kong. *Education:* Nottingham University (LL.B.). *Member:* Hong Kong Housing Authority Building Committee; Co-Chairman Buildings Appeal Committee; Associate of the Chartered Institute of Arbitrators. *LANGUAGES:* English. *PRACTICE AREAS:* Construction Law; Project Finance; Development Law.

LEONORA BARNES, born London, England, September 27, 1952; admitted, 1977, England and Wales; 1985, Hong Kong. *Education:* Bristol University (LL.B.). Honorary Lecturer, The Law Faculty of Law, University of Hong Kong. *Member:* Hong Kong Federation of Women Lawyers. *LANGUAGES:* English. *PRACTICE AREAS:* Conveyancing; Probate.

ANDREW N.B. WINGFIELD, born London, England, July 30, 1959; admitted, 1985, England and Wales; 1986, Hong Kong. *Education:* University of Bristol (B.Sc.). *Member:* Law Society of England and Wales; Law Society of Hong Kong; Hong Kong Society of Accountants (Legal Committee). *LANGUAGES:* English. *PRACTICE AREAS:* General Corporate Law; Banking; Securities.

WONG KWAI HUEN, born China, December 30, 1951; admitted, 1985, Hong Kong; 1989, England and Wales; 1990, Australia. *Education:* Chinese University of Hong Kong (B.A.); University of London (LL.B.); University of East Asia (Dipl. Chinese Law). *LANGUAGES:* English, Cantonese and Mandarin. *PRACTICE AREAS:* P.R.C. Law; Trade Law; Litigation and Arbitration.

TIMOTHY CONTI, born Amersham, England, March 13, 1958; admitted, 1983, England and Wales; 1988, Hong Kong. *Education:* King's College, Cambridge University (M.A.); University College, London University (LL.M.). Author: "Trade and Investment Law in Hong Kong," Chapter on China Trade. *Member:* Law Society of Hong Kong. *LANGUAGES:* English, French, Russian and Mandarin. *PRACTICE AREAS:* Commercial Law; Securities Law; P.R.C. Law.

CHRISTOPHER JOHN WOODS, born Wanelli, Wales, February 17, 1957; admitted, 1984, England and Wales; 1988, Hong Kong. *Education:* Nottingham, Polytechnic (B.A.). *Member:* Law Society of Hong Kong; International Trade Mark Association. *LANGUAGES:* English. *PRACTICE AREAS:* Intellectual Property.

JULIA CHARLTON, born Newcastle-upon-Tyne, October 9, 1959; admitted, 1985, England and Wales; 1987, Hong Kong. *Education:* King's College, University of London (LL.B., AKC). Member, Securities Law Committee, Law Society of Hong Kong. *LANGUAGES:* English, French, German and Mandarin. *PRACTICE AREAS:* Corporate Finance; Capital Markets.

(For List of other Partners, see Professional Biographies at London, England).

SIMPSON THACHER & BARTLETT

A Partnership which includes Professional Corporations

ASIA PACIFIC FINANCE TOWER - 32ND FLOOR
3 GARDEN ROAD, CENTRAL
HONG KONG
Telephone: 852-2514-7600
Telecopier: 852-2869-7694

New York, NY Office: 425 Lexington Avenue, 10017-3954. Telephone: 212-455-2000. Telecopier: 212-455-2502. ESL 62928462.

Columbus, Ohio Office: One Riverside Plaza, 43215. Telephone: 614-461-7799. Telecopier: 614-461-0040.

London Office: 100 New Bridge Street, London EC4V 6JE, England. Telephone: 0171 246 8000. Telecopier: 0171 329 3883.

Tokyo Office: Ark Mori Building, 29th Floor, 12-32, Akasaka 1-Chome, Minato-Ku, Tokyo 107, Japan. Telephone: 81-3-5562-8601. Telecopier: 81-3-5562-8606. ESL 62765846.

Firm engaged in American and International Practice in Hong Kong. Not authorized to appear before the Hong Kong Courts or to act as Solicitors.

PARTNERS

WALTER A. LOONEY, JR., born Rockville Centre, New York, August 13, 1950; admitted, 1978, New York (Not admitted in Hong Kong). *Education:* Boston College (A.B., 1972); University of Virginia (M.A., 1973); Harvard University (J.D., 1977). *Member:* The Association of the Bar of the City of New York; New York State and American Bar Associations.

(This Listing Continued)

SIMPSON THACHER & BARTLETT, Hong Kong— *Continued*

GEORGE KEITH MILLER, born Washington, D.C., March 6, 1954; admitted, 1979, District of Columbia; 1984, New York (Not admitted in Hong Kong). *Education:* Yale University (B.A., magna cum laude, 1975); Harvard University (M.P.A., J.D., 1979). *Member:* The Association of the Bar of the City of New York; New York State and American Bar Associations.

RESIDENT ASSOCIATES

Alan G. Brenner
(Not admitted in Hong Kong)

Philip M. J. Culhane
(Not admitted in Hong Kong)

Kuang-Hsiang (Chris) Lin
(Not admitted in Hong Kong)

Karen Mieko Sakanashi
(Not admitted in Hong Kong)

Elizabeth A. Shaghalian
(Not admitted in Hong Kong)

Anuradha M. Shastri
(Not admitted in Hong Kong)

Benedict Tai
(Not admitted in Hong Kong)

Lawrence A. Vranka, Jr.
(Not admitted in Hong Kong)

(For biographical data of the New York, N.Y. partners, see Professional Biographies at New York, N.Y.).

SINCLAIR ROCHE & TEMPERLEY

42ND FLOOR, BANK OF CHINA TOWER
1 GARDEN ROAD
HONG KONG
Telephone: (852) 28200200
Fax: (852) 28459244.
Telex: 63646 Snclrhx

Other Offices: London (England), Singapore, Shanghai (China), Vietnam and Bucharest, (Romania).

International Commerce Practice.

IAN J. GAUNT (Managing Partner).

(For Complete Biographical Data on all personnel, see Professional Biographies at London, England Office)

SKADDEN, ARPS, SLATE, MEAGHER & FLOM

30/F PEREGRINE TOWER, LIPPO CENTRE
89 QUEENSWAY
CENTRAL
HONG KONG
Telephone: 011-852-820-0700
Fax: 011-852-820-0727

New York, New York Office: 919 Third Avenue, 10022. Telephone: 212-735-3000. Fax: 212-735-2000; 212-735-2001. Telex: 645899 Skarslaw.

Boston, Massachusetts Office: One Beacon Street, 02108. Telephone: 617-573-4800. Fax: 617-573-4822.

Washington, D.C. Office: 1440 New York Avenue, N.W., 20005, Telephone: 202-371-7000. Fax: 202-393-5760.

Wilmington, Delaware Office: One Rodney Square, 19899. Telephone: 302-651-3000. Fax: 302-651-3001.

Los Angeles, California Office: 300 South Grand Avenue, 90071. Telephone: 213-687-5000. Fax: 213-687-5600.

Chicago, Illinois Office: 333 West Wacker Drive, 60606. Telephone: 312-407-0700. Fax: 312-407-0411.

San Francisco, California Office: Four Embarcadero Center, 94111. Telephone: 415-984-6400. Fax: 415-984-2698.

Houston, Texas Office: 1600 Smith Street, Suite 4460, 77002. Telephone: 713-655-5100. Fax: 713-655-5181.

Newark, New Jersey Office: One Riverfront Plaza, 07102. Telephone: 201-596-4440. Fax: 201-596-4444.

Tokyo, Japan Office: 12th Floor, The Fukoku Seimei Building, 2-2-2, Uchisaiwaicho, Chiyoda-ku, 100. Telephone: 011-81-3-3595-3850. Fax: 011-81-3-3504-2780.

London, England Office: 25 Bucklersbury EC4N 8DA. Telephone: 011-44-71-248-9929. Fax: 011-44-71-489-8533.

(This Listing Continued)

Sydney, New South Wales, Australia Office: Level 26-State Bank Centre, 52 Martin Place, 2000. Telephone: 011-61-2-224-6000. Fax: 011-61-2-224-6044.

Toronto, Ontario Office: Suite 1820, North Tower, P.O. Box 189, Royal Bank Plaza, M5J 2J4. Telephone: 416-777-4700. Fax: 416-777-4747.

Paris, France Office: 105 rue du Faubourg Saint-Honoré, 75008. Telephone: 011-33-1-40-75-44-44. Fax: 011-33-1-49-53-09-99.

Brussels, Belgium Office: 523 avenue Louise, Box 30, 1050. Telephone: 011-32-2-648-7666. Fax: 011-32-2-640-3032.

Frankfurt, Germany Office: MesseTurm, 27th Floor, 60308. Telephone: 011-49-69-9757-3000. Fax: 011-49-69-9757-3050.

Beijing, China Office: 1605 Capital Mansion Tower, No. 6 Xin Yuan Nan Road, Chao Yang District, 100004. Telephone: 011-86-1-466-8800. Fax: 011-86-1-466-8822.

Budapest, Hungary Office: Mahart Building, H-1025 Apáczai Csere János u.11, Vl.em. Telephone: 011-36-1-266-2145. Fax: 011-36-1-266-4033.

Prague, Czech Republic Office: Revolucni 16, 110 00. Telephone: 011-42-2-231-75-18. Fax: 011-42-2-231-47-33.

Moscow, Russia Office: Pleteshkovsky Pereulok 1, 107005. Telephone: 011-7-501-940-2304. Fax: 011-7-501-940-2511.

Firm engaged in American and International law practice, but not authorized to practice before Hong Kong Courts or act as Hong Kong Solicitors.

RAYMOND W. VICKERS, born Wilmington, N.C., 1943; admitted, 1969, New York (Not admitted in Hong Kong). *Education:* Harvard University (A.B., 1965; LL.B., 1968).

MICHAEL V. GISSER, born Scarsdale, N.Y., 1957; admitted, 1985, New York; 1987, California (Not admitted in Hong Kong). *Education:* Harvard University (A.B., cum laude, 1978); Stanford University (J.D., 1982). Order of the Coif. Member and Senior Articles Editor, Stanford Law Review. Law Clerk to Judge Dorothy W. Nelson, U.S. Court of Appeals, Ninth Circuit, 1982-1983.

JONATHAN F. PEDERSEN, born New York, N.Y., 1958; admitted, 1985, New York (Not admitted in Hong Kong). *Education:* Princeton University (B.A., 1980); Yale University (J.D., 1985).

GREGORY G.H. MIAO, born Guangzhou, China, 1954; admitted, 1988, New York (Not admitted in Hong Kong). *Education:* East China Normal University (LL.B., 1982); New York University (LL.M., 1985). (Also at Beijing, China, Office).

COUNSEL

JEFFREY S. CHRISTIE, born Philadelphia, Pa., 1954; admitted, 1979, District of Columbia (Not admitted in Hong Kong). *Education:* Bucknell University (B.A., 1976); George Washington University (J.D., with honors, 1979); Georgetown University (LL.M., 1985).

(For Biographical data on other Personnel, see New York, New York Professional Biographies).

SLAUGHTER AND MAY

27TH FLOOR, TWO EXCHANGE SQUARE
HONG KONG
Telephone: (852) 521 0551
Telex: HX 86230
Fax: (852) 845 2125; (852) 845 9079

London, England Office: 35 Basinghall Street, EC2V 5DB. Telephone: (0171) 600 1200. Telex: 883486; 888926. Fax: (0171) 726 0038; (0171) 600 0289; (0171) 600 1455 (G-4).

Paris, France Office: 112 Avenue Kléber, 75116. Telephone: (1) 44.05.60.00. Telex: 642514. Fax: (1) 44.05.60.60; (1) 44 05 60 99 (G-4).

Brussels, Belgium Office: Rue D'Arlon 69/71, 1040. Telephone: (2) 230 5631. Fax: (2) 230 7699.

Frankfurt am Main, Germany Office: Westend-Carree Grüneburgweg 16, D-60322 Frankfurt am Main. Telephone: (69) 9551370. Fax: (69) 5964126.

Tokyo, Japan Office: Mitsui Asahi Building, 1-1 Kanda Sudacho, Chiyoda-ku, 101. Telephone: (3) 3258 5700. Telex: 2227208. Fax: (3) 3258 5708.

New York, New York Office: 126 East 56th Street, 10022-3613. Telephone: (212) 888-1112. Fax: (212) 888-1170; (212) 832-2021; (212) 832 0075 (G-4).

International, Corporate, Commercial, Banking, Securities, Litigation and Property Law.

(This Listing Continued)

RESIDENT PARTNERS

R.J. Thornhill; St. J.A. Flaherty; C.M. Horton; P. Olney; C.W. Harvey-Kelly; N.G. Brown; W. Chow; M.P. Yeadon.

STEPHENSON HARWOOD & LO

Established in 1979

18TH FLOOR, EDINBURGH TOWER, THE LANDMARK
15 QUEEN'S ROAD CENTRAL
HONG KONG
Telephone: 852-2868 0789
Telex: 66278 SHL HX
Fax: 852-2868 1504

Other Associated Offices: Guangzhou, People's Republic of China, London, England, Brussels, Belgium, Kuwait, Kuwait, and Madrid, Spain.

Company/Commercial, including flotations, equity issues, international public offerings, takeovers, mutual funds and unit trusts, cross-border mergers and acquisitions and joint ventures. China trade and investment, employment, banking and capital markets, project finance, arbitration and litigation, insolvency, shipping, property, pensions, tax, trusts and estate planning law.

PARTNERS

MICHAEL HODDINOTT, born December 12, 1944; admitted, 1970, England and Wales; 1979, Hong Kong. Senior Partner, Stephenson Harwood & Lo. *LANGUAGES:* English and French. *PRACTICE AREAS:* Corporate; Commercial; Trusts and Asset Protection.

JOHN GALE, born February 1, 1958; admitted, 1982, England and Wales; 1983, Hong Kong. *LANGUAGES:* English. *PRACTICE AREAS:* Corporate Finance; Mutual Funds; Banking.

IAN DEVEREUX, born July 10, 1956; admitted, 1981, England and Wales; 1982, Hong Kong. *LANGUAGES:* English, Cantonese and Mandarin. *PRACTICE AREAS:* Property.

VICTORIA YOUNGHUSBAND, born July 14, 1954; admitted, 1984, England and Wales; 1991, Hong Kong. *LANGUAGES:* English and French. *PRACTICE AREAS:* Corporate Finance; Commercial; Financial Services.

MALCOLM KEMP, born March 13, 1954; admitted, 1980, England and Wales; 1982, Hong Kong. *LANGUAGES:* English and German. *PRACTICE AREAS:* Litigation; Shipping.

ANDREW HART, born September 18, 1961; admitted, 1987, England and Wales; 1988, Hong Kong. *LANGUAGES:* English. *PRACTICE AREAS:* Litigation.

PAUL WESTOVER, born October 14, 1960; admitted, 1987, England and Wales; 1991, Hong Kong. *LANGUAGES:* English. *PRACTICE AREAS:* Corporate Finance; Mergers and Acquisitions; Commercial.

PETER BRADLEY, born April 7, 1961; admitted, 1988, England and Wales; 1992, Hong Kong. *LANGUAGES:* English and French. *PRACTICE AREAS:* Corporate Finance; Commercial Law.

KENNETH LO, O.B.E., born October 13, 1922; admitted, 1951, Hong Kong; 1967, England and Wales. Senior Partner, Lo and Lo, Hong Kong. *LANGUAGES:* English and Cantonese. *PRACTICE AREAS:* Property.

T.S. LO, C.B.E., born January 23, 1935; admitted, 1961, Hong Kong, England and Wales. *LANGUAGES:* English, Mandarin and Cantonese. *PRACTICE AREAS:* People's Republic of China.

L.S.K. KO, born September 15, 1939; admitted, 1963, England and Wales; 1964, Hong Kong. *LANGUAGES:* English and Cantonese. *PRACTICE AREAS:* Litigation.

PHILIP KAN, born May 9, 1947; admitted, 1976, Hong Kong; 1984, England and Wales; 1992, Singapore. *LANGUAGES:* English, Cantonese and Mandarin. *PRACTICE AREAS:* Company; Commercial; Property.

ANTHONY ISAACS, born August 9, 1934; admitted, 1960, England and Wales; 1980, Hong Kong. Senior Partner of Stephenson Harwood. (Resident, at London, England Office). *LANGUAGES:* English, French and Italian. *PRACTICE AREAS:* Corporate; Corporate Finance.

(For Complete List of Stephenson Harwood's Overseas Offices, Please see London, England Office)

STIKEMAN, ELLIOTT

29 QUEEN'S ROAD CENTRAL
SUITE 1506, CHINA BUILDING
HONG KONG
Telephone: 852-2868-9903
Fax: 852-2868-9912

Montreal, Quebec Office: 1155 René-Lévesque Boulevard West, 40th Floor, H3B 3V2. Telephone: 514-397-3000. Fax: 514-397-3222.

Toronto, Ontario Office: Commerce Court West, 53rd Floor, M5L 1B9. Telephone: 416-869-5500. Fax: 416-947-0866.

Ottawa, Ontario Office: 50 O'Connor Street, Suite 914, K1P 6L2. Telephone: 613-234-4555. Fax: 613-230-8877.

Calgary, Alberta Office: 855 - 2nd Street S.W., 1500 Bankers Hall, T2P 4J7. Telephone: 403-266-9000. Fax: 403-266-9034.

Vancouver, British Columbia Office: 666 Burrard Street, Suite 1700, Park Place, V6C 2X8. Telephone: 604-631-1300. Fax: 604-681-1825.

New York, New York Office: 126 East 56th Street, 11th Floor, Tower 56, 10022. Telephone: 212-371-8855. Fax: 212-371-7087.

Washington, D.C. Office: 1300 I Street, N.W., Suite 1210 West, 20005-3314. Telephone: 202-326-7555. Fax: 202-326-7557.

London, England Office: Cottons Centre, Cottons Lane, SE1 2QL. Telephone: 71-378-0880. Fax: 71-378-0344.

Paris, France Office: In Association with Société Juridique Internationale, 39, rue François Ier, 75008. Telephone: 33-1-40-73-82-00. Fax: 33-1-40-73-82-10.

Budapest, Hungary Office: Andrássy út 100, II Floor, H-1062. Telephone: 36-1-269-1790. Fax: 36-1-269-0655.

Hong Kong: In Association with Shum & Co., 29 Queen's Road Central, Suite 1103, China Building. Telephone: 852-2526-5531. Fax: 852-2845-9076.

Taipei, Taiwan Office: 117 Sec. 3 Min Sheng East Road, 8th Floor. Telephone: 886-2-719-9573. Fax: 886-2-719-4540.

Firm engaged in Canadian and International Law Practice, but not authorized to appear before the Hong Kong Courts or to act as Hong Kong Solicitors.

RESIDENTS IN HONG KONG

BRIAN G. HANSEN, born New Zealand, September 10, 1950; admitted, 1980, Alberta; 1989, British Columbia (Not admitted in Hong Kong). *Education:* Victoria University, New Zealand (LL.B., Hon., 1972; LL.M., 1973); Dalhousie University (LL.M., 1973). Editor, Canadian Taxation and Alberta Corporation Manual, De Boo, 1981. Professor of Law: Dalhousie University, 1974-1977; Calgary University, 1977-1979. *Member:* Canadian Bar Association.

ANDES FU-MIN LIN, born Hong Kong, October 27, 1950; admitted, 1981, Ontario (Not admitted in Hong Kong). *Education:* York University (B.A., 1975; M.B.A., 1979); Osgoode Hall Law School (LL.B., 1979). *Member:* Canadian Bar Association; Law Society of Upper Canada; Canadian Tax Foundation. *LANGUAGES:* English, Cantonese, Mandarin.

(For biographical data on other personnel, see Professional Biographies at Montreal, Quebec, Toronto, Ontario, Ottawa, Ontario, Calgary, Alberta, Vancouver, British Columbia, New York, New York, Washington, D.C., London, England, Paris, France, Budapest, Hungary, Hong Kong and Taipei, Taiwan)

SULLIVAN & CROMWELL

28TH FLOOR, NINE QUEEN'S ROAD, CENTRAL
HONG KONG
Telephone: (011)(852)826-8688
Telecopier: (011)(852)522-2280

New York City Offices: 125 Broad Street. 10004-2498; Midtown Office: 250 Park Avenue, 10177-0021. Telephone: 212-558-4000. Telex: 62694 (International); 12-7816 (Domestic). Cable Address: "Ladycourt, New York". Telecopier: 125 Broad Street 212-558-3588; 250 Park Avenue 212-558-3792.

Washington, D.C. Office: 1701 Pennsylvania Avenue, N.W., 20006-5805. Telephone:202-956-7500. Telex: 89625. Telecopier: 202-293-6330.

Los Angeles, California Office: 444 South Flower Street, 90071-2901. Telephone: 213-955-8000. Telecopier: 213-683-0457.

Paris Office: 8, Place Vendôme, Paris 75001, France. Telephone: (011)(331)4450-6000. Telex: 240654. Telecopier: (011)(331)4450-6060.

(This Listing Continued)

SULLIVAN & CROMWELL, Hong Kong—Continued

London Office: St. Olave's House, 9a Ironmonger Lane, London EC2V 8EY, England. Telephone: (011)(44171)710-6500. Telecopier: (011)(44171)710-6565.

Melbourne, Australia Office: 101 Collins Street, Melbourne, Victoria 3000. Telephone: (011)(613)654-1500. Telecopier: (011)(613)654-2422.

Tokyo Office: Gaikokuho Jimu Bengoshi Office of Robert G. DeLaMater, a member of the firm of Sullivan & Cromwell, Tokio Kaijo Building Shinkan, 2-1, Marunouchi, 1-chome Chiyoda-ku, Tokyo 100, Japan. Telephone: (011)(813)3213-6140. Telecopier: (011)(813)3213-6470.

General Practice. Firm engaged in American and International law practice, but not authorized to practice before Hong Kong Courts or act as Hong Kong Solicitors.

PARTNERS IN HONG KONG

DONALD C. WALKOVIK, born Kenosha, WI., 1948; admitted, 1974, New York. *Education:* Univ. of Wisconsin (B.B.A., 1970); Harvard (J.D., 1973).

JOHN EVANGELAKOS, born Montreal, Quebec, Canada, 1960; admitted, 1987, New York. *Education:* Harvard (A.B., 1982); New York Univ. (J.D., 1985).

ASSOCIATES IN HONG KONG

JOHN NELSON CHRISMAN, born Akron, OH., 1964; admitted, 1988, California. *Education:* Southern Methodist (B.A. and B.S., 1985); Univ. of Texas (J.D., 1988).

SCOTT D. CLEMENS, born Bryn Mawr, PA., 1952; admitted, 1987, New York. *Education:* Brigham Young Univ. (B.A., 1976); Univ. of Michigan (M.A., magna cum laude, 1979); Yale Univ. (J.D., 1986). Chair, Asian Pacific Law Committee, 1993). *Member:* New York State Bar Association (Member, International Law and Practice Section).

SUNG JIN HWANG, born Taegu, Korea, 1960; admitted, 1991, California. *Education:* Johns Hopkins Univ. (B.S., 1984); Univ. of California, Los Angeles (J.D., 1991).

PETER P.H. LIN, born Hong Kong, 1965; admitted, 1991, New York. *Education:* McMaster Univ., Canada (B.A., summa cum laude, 1986); Univ. of Toronto, Canada (LL.B., 1989).

YOICHIRO TANIGUCHI, born Tokyo, Japan, 1964; admitted, 1990, New York. *Education:* Harvard Univ. (B.A., 1986); Columbia Univ. (J.D., 1989). *Member:* American Bar Association.

CHUN WEI, born Nanjing PRC, 1959; admitted, 1990, New York. *Education:* Beijing University (LL.B., 1983); Columbia University (LL.B., 1984).

JOHN D. YOUNG, JR., born Charleston, WV., 1961; admitted, 1991, New York. *Education:* Wake Forest Univ. (B.S., 1982; J.D., 1990); Univ. of Southwestern Louisiana (M.B.A., 1989).

(For Biographical Data on all Partners and Associates see Professional Biographies at New York, N.Y.).

THIEFFRY ET ASSOCIÉS

Established in 1977

BANK OF CHINA TOWER, 21ST FLOOR
1 GARDEN ROAD
HONG KONG
Telephone: (852) 25 23 4833
Telefax: (852) 25 24 6438

Paris, France Office: 23 avenue Hoche, 75008. Telephone: (1) 45.62.45.54. Telex: "THIEFRY 640 689 F". Telefax: (1) 42.25.80.07.

New York, N.Y. Office: 780 Third Avenue, 10017. Telephone: 212-750-0080. Telefax: 212-750-0054.

Brussels, Belgium Office: 100, Avenue de Tervueren, 1040. Telephone: (2) 733.97.15. Telefax: (2) 733.97.16.

Shanghai, People's Republic of China Office: Room 1406 Ruijin Building, 205 Maoming Nan Lu, 200020. Telephone: (86-21) 472 79 93; 472 70 96. Fax: (86-21) 472 43 92.

Associated Offices: Shenzhen, People's Republic of China; Beirut, Lebanon; Cairo, Egypt; Jeddah, Saudi Arabia.

(This Listing Continued)

Transnational Arbitration, Litigation and Transactions (Acquisitions, Transfers of Technology, Joint Ventures, General Corporate, Tax and Contractual Practice, Environmental and Intellectual Property Law).

VINCENT MERCIER, born Nice, France, May 24, 1960; admitted, 1988, Paris. *Education:* Paris II University (D.E.A. de Droit Privé Général, 1985); Paris I University (D.E.S.S. de Droit du Commerce Exterieur, 1987). *Member:* American Bar Association (Vice Chair, TIPS-International Torts and Insurance Practice Committee, 1991-1992). (Also at Shanghai, People's Republic of China Office). *LANGUAGES:* French and English.

XAVIER PORCHER, born Lille, France, April 7, 1964; admitted, 1993, Paris (Not admitted in Hong Kong). *Education:* Université de Paris V (Maîtrise en Droit Privé, 1988); Institut d'Etudes Politiques (Diploma, 1990). *LANGUAGES:* French and English.

TORY TORY DesLAURIERS & BINNINGTON

SUITE 1705, ONE EXCHANGE SQUARE
8 CONNAUGHT PLACE
HONG KONG
Telephone: 852-868-3099
Facsimile: 852-523-8140

Toronto, Ontario Office: P.O. Box 270, Suite 3000, Aetna Tower, M5K 1N2. Telephone: 416-865-0040. Facsimile: 416-865-7380.

London, England Office: 44/45 Chancery Lane, WC2A 1JB. Telephone: 071-831-8155. Facsimile: 071-831-1812.

Affiliated with:

Desjardins Ducharme Stein Monast:

Montreal, Quebec Office: Bureau 2400, 600 rue de la Gauchetiere West, H3B 4L8. Telephone: 514-878-9411. Facsimile: 514-878-9092.

Quebec City, Quebec Office: 1150 rue de Claire-Fontaine, Bureau 300, G1R 5G4. Telephone: 418-529-6531. Facsimile: 418-523-5391.

Lawson Lundell Lawson & McIntosh:

Vancouver, British Columbia Office: 1600 Cathedral Place, 925 W. Georgia Street, V6C 3L2. Telephone: 604-685-3456. Facsimile: 604-669-1620.

Yellowknife, Northwest Territories Office: Suite 204, 4817 49th Street, X1A 3S7. Telephone: 403-669-9990. Facsimile: 403-669-9991.

Administrative Law, Aircraft Finance, Banking, Bankruptcy, Commercial Law, Competition Law, Computer and Technology Law, Corporate Law, Corporate Finance, Criminal, Employment Law, Environmental, Estates, Euromarket, Foreign Investment, General Practice, Insolvency and Receivership, International, Labour, Litigation, Mergers and Acquisitions, Municipal, Negligence, Oil and Gas Law, Property Development and Financing, Real Property, Securities, Taxation.

LOUISE E. PEARSON, born Ottawa, Ontario, March 31, 1957; admitted, 1984, Ontario. *Education:* Queen's University (B.A., 1978; LL.B., 1982). (Resident Partner). *PRACTICE AREAS:* General Corporate; Securities; Mergers and Acquisitions.

ADVOKATFIRMAN VINGE KB

2003 HUTCHISON HOUSE
10 HARCOURT ROAD, CENTRAL
HONG KONG
Telephone: +852-2523 6149
Telefax: +852-2810 5343

For offices in: Stockholm, Malmö and Helsingborg, Sweden see those cities.

Gothenburg, Sweden Office: Nils Ericsonsgatan 17, P.O. Box 11025, S-404 21. Telephone: 31-80 51 00. Telex: 21119 VINGE S. Telefax: +76-31-15 8811.

London, England Office: 44/45 Chancery Lane, WC2A 1JB. Telephone: 71 404 4825. Telex: 25585 VINGE G. Telefax: +71-831 6860.

Paris, France Office: 21, Rue Jean Goujon, F-75008. Telephone: +33 1 4075 3737. Telefax: +33-1-75630549.

Brussels, Belgium Office: Avenue Louise 475/B 12, 1050. Telephone: +32-(2) 646 36 20; (2) 646 36 80. Telefax: (2) 646 41 46.

Admiralty, Transport, Corporate, Labor, Environmental, Tax, Contracting, Antitrust, Patent, Trademark, Bankruptcy, Entertainment and Finance Law.

(This Listing Continued)

RESIDENT PARTNER

THOMAS LAGERQVIST, born 1944; (Not admitted in Hong Kong). *Education:* University of Stockholm (LL.M., Jur. kand., 1971). *Member:* Swedish Bar Association (1976); International Bar Association; Licensing Executives Society; Swedish Association for Labour Law.

ASSOCIATES

NICLAS HÖGSTRÖM, born Vancouver, Canada, May 22, 1964. *Education:* University of Uppsala (jur.kand., LL.B., 1990); University of Oslo (Diploma in Shipping Law, 1988); London School of Economics and Political Science (Master of Law, LL.M., 1991). *LANGUAGES:* Swedish and English.

INTERNATIONAL COUNSEL

MARY L. RILEY, born 1950; admitted, New York and Massachusetts (Not admitted in Hong Kong). *Education:* University of California (B.A., 1974); Harvard University (G.S.A.S., M.A., 1974); Columbia University School of Law (J.D., 1987). *Member:* American Bar Association; New York Bar Association. *LANGUAGES:* English, Mandarin and Cantonese.

WALKER & CORSA

THE CENTRE MARK, 1603
287 QUEEN'S ROAD CENTRAL
HONG KONG
Telephone: 852-854-1718
Fax: 852-541-6189
Cable Address: "Naidshk Hong Kong"
Telex: 65117 NAIAD HX

New York, N.Y. Office: One Wall Street Court, 10005. Telephone: 212-344-4700. Cable Address: "Naiads New York". Telex: RCA 235725. Fax: 212-422-5299.
Hoboken, New Jersey Office: 96 Hudson Street, 07030. Telephone: 201-656-7450. Fax: 201-656-0920.
Stamford, Connecticut Office: 999 Summer Street, Suite 200, 06905. Telephone 203-978-1299. Fax: 203-327-9536.

Admiralty and International Law.
Firm engaged in American and International Practice, but not authorized to appear before the Hong Kong courts or to act as Solicitors.

RESIDENT PARTNER

JON W. ZINKE, born Mineola, New York, October 9, 1953; admitted, 1981, New York and U.S. District Court, Southern and Eastern Districts of New York (Not admitted in Hong Kong). *Education:* State University of New York Maritime College (B.S., 1975); Brooklyn Law School (J.D., 1980). *PRACTICE AREAS:* International Trade Law; Arbitration; Admiralty; Maritime Litigation.

(For Biographical data on New York, N.Y. personnel, see Professional Biographies at New York, N.Y.)

ROBERT W.H. WANG & COMPANY

Established in 1980

17TH & 18TH FLOORS
NINE QUEEN'S ROAD CENTRAL
HONG KONG (BRITISH CROWN COLONY)
Telephone: (852) 843 7333
Fax: (852) 845 2504; 845 5566

REVISERS OF THE HONG KONG LAW DIGEST FOR THIS DIRECTORY

Associated Offices: Pritchard Englefield & Wang, 17th & 18th Floors, Nine Queen's Road Central, Hong Kong. Telephone: (852) 843 7333. Fax: (852) 845 2504.
Robert W.H. Wang & Woo, 50 Raffles Place, 12-05 Shell Tower, Singapore, 0104. Telephone: 225 0123. Fax: 225 5065.
Pannone & Partners, 14 New Street, London EC2M 4TR. Telephone: 071-972-9720. Fax: 071-972-9722.

Corporate and Commercial Law, Intellectual Property including Trade Marks, Shipping Finance, Immigration, Probate, Conveyancing, Litigation.

RESIDENT PARTNERS

ROBERT WEI HAN WANG, born 1944; admitted, 1973, Hong Kong; 1978, England; 1982, Australia; 1985, Singapore. Notary Public.

(This Listing Continued)

ANNA HUNG YUK WU, born 1951; admitted, 1977, Hong Kong.

MICHAEL DALTON, born 1934; admitted, 1958, England; 1981, Hong Kong. Notary Public.

ANDREW WEI HUNG WANG, born 1955; admitted, 1982, Hong Kong. Notary Public.

KING WAI HUI, born 1950; admitted, 1982, Hong Kong; 1991, Singapore.

ROGER KWAI SANG WONG, born 1957; admitted, 1983, Hong Kong; 1987, England; 1991, Singapore.

TWIGGY MEI HO LIU, born 1955; admitted, 1984, Hong Kong; 1987, England; 1988, Australia.

CHRISTOPHER HING TAI CHAN, born 1951; admitted, 1984, Hong Kong; 1987, England; 1988, Australia; 1990, Singapore.

JEREMY DAVID LEVY, born 1954; admitted, 1981, England; 1985, Hong Kong.

ELLEN WAI LING CHAN, born 1961; admitted, 1986, Hong Kong; 1991, England.

STEPHEN KAI PING LO, born 1957; admitted, 1987, England; 1988, Hong Kong; 1990, Australia.

CONSULTANTS

MIMI MI MI HO, born 1954; admitted, 1980, Hong Kong; 1984, England; 1984, Australia; 1991, Singapore.

LESLIE ROBERT SIMON, born 1949; admitted, 1979, England; 1982, Hong Kong.

DAVID JOHN RIMMER, born 1941; admitted, 1966, England; 1987, Hong Kong.

ANTHONY FRANCIS HILL, born 1949; admitted, 1981, New South Wales, Australia; 1988, England; 1988, Hong Kong.

DENISE MACEDO NOVAES (HINGORANI), born 1961; admitted, 1986, Brazil (Not Admitted in Hong Kong).

GEORGE KIN BIAO YIP, born 1944; admitted, 1979, Australia; 1990, England and Hong Kong.

SUSIE SAU FUN CHEUNG, born 1952; admitted, 1981, England; 1994, Hong Kong.

Languages: English, Cantonese, Mandarin, German, French, Portuguese and Spanish

REVISERS OF THE HONG KONG LAW DIGEST FOR THIS DIRECTORY

WEIR & ASSOCIATES
SOLICITORS

Agents for Trademarks and Patents

Established in 1985

HUNG KEI BUILDING
5-8 QUEEN VICTORIA STREET
HONG KONG
Telephone: 852-2526-1767
Facsimile: 852-2868-3568

International Business, Banking and Finance, Corporate Commercial, Litigation, Securities, Business Immigration, International Transactions, Real Estate, Patent and Trademarks.

FIRM PROFILE: An international practice with its lawyers qualified in Hong Kong, Malaysia, Singapore, Australia, Canada, the United States and France who provide a comprehensive range of legal services to mainly corporate clients on a local and regional basis. The Firm has a substantial China/Asian practice, with extensive experience in PRC property, litigation and foreign investments advice. An established presence in Hong Kong, Beijing, Shanghai, Taipei and also enjoying associations with independent legal offices in Los Angeles, New York, Atlanta, London, Rome, Toronto and Vancouver. The Firm acts as a legal advisor to financial institutions, substantial privately held corporations, public companies and certain private family businesses. The Firm currently has five lawyers and a paralegal support staff of 25 members.

(This Listing Continued)

WEIR & ASSOCIATES SOLICITORS, Hong Kong—Continued

PRINCIPALS OF THE FIRM

SHANE F. WEIR, born Saskatchewan, Canada, June 8, 1954; admitted, 1978, Canada; 1992, England; 1992, Hong Kong. *Education:* University of Saskatchewan (B.A., LL.B., 1977). Registered Investment Advisor, pursuant to the Securities Ordinance and Protection of Investors Ordinance of Hong Kong. Lecturer: University of Saskatchewan; City Polytechnic of Hong Kong. *Member:* Law Societies of Canada, England, Wales and Hong Kong; Trademark Agents Association; Royal Hong Kong Yacht Club; Can-Am Ice Hockey (Hong Kong) Association.

CHEONGHAR WEIR, (WONG CHEONGHAR), born Manchester, England, April 30, 1961; admitted, 1985, Solicitor, England and Wales; 1987, Hong Kong; 1990, Australia; 1993, Singapore. *Education:* University of Leeds (LL.B., Hons., 1982); University of Hong Kong (LL.M., 1992). *Member:* Law Societies of England, Hong Kong; Commonwealth Society (Hong Kong).

ALFRED CHUNN HORNG CHAN, born Malaysia, January 25, 1966; admitted, 1991, qualified in United Kingdom as Barrister-at-Law; 1992, Advocate and Solicitor, Malaysia. *Education:* Birmingham University (UK) (LL.B. Hons.). *Member:* Middle Temple, London and Malaysian Bar.

SIMON WOO, born Hong Kong, August 1, 1950; admitted, 1993, Solicitor, Hong Kong. *Education:* B.D.S. (Hons.) University of Sydney (L.D.S); University of Victoria (LL.B. (Hons.). President of the Young Solicitors Group in Hong Kong. *Member:* Legal Education Committee of the Law Society of Hong Kong; Legal Advisor to Y.D.C.P. of the Hong Kong Dental Association; Member of the Ethics and Legislation Committee of the Hong Kong Dental Association.

Languages: English and Cantonese

WHITE & CASE

3503 EDINBURGH TOWER
15 QUEEN'S ROAD CENTRAL
HONG KONG
Telephone: (852) 822-8700
Facsimile: (852) 845-9070

New York, New York: Telephone: 212-819-8200. Facsimile: 212-354-8113.
Washington, D.C.: Telephone: 202-872-0013. Facsimile: 202-872-0210.
Los Angeles, California: Telephone: 213-620-7700. Facsimile: 213-687-0758; 213-617-2205.
Miami, Florida: Telephone: 305-371-2700. Facsimile: 305-358-5744.
Mexico City, Mexico: Telephone: (52-5) 207-9717. Facsimile: (52-5) 208-3628.
Tokyo, Japan: Telephone: (81-3) 3239-4300. Facsimile: (81-3) 3239-4330.
Singapore, Republic of Singapore: Telephone: (65) 225-6000. Facsimile: (65) 225-6009.
Bangkok, Thailand: Pacific Legal Group Ltd., In Association With White & Case, Telephone: (662) 236-6154/7. Facsimile: (662) 237-6771.
Hanoi, Viet Nam: Representative Office, Telephone: (84-4) 227-575/6/7. Facsimile: (84-4) 227-297.
Bombay, India: Telephone: (91-22) 282-6300. Facsimile: (91-22) 282-6305.
London, England: Telephone: (44-171) 726-6361. Facsimile: (44-171) 726-4314; (44-171) 726-8558.
Paris, France: Telephone: (33-1) 42-60-34-05. Facsimile: (33-1) 42-60-82-46.
Brussels, Belgium: Telephone: (32-2) 647-05-89. Facsimile: (32-2) 647-16-75.
Stockholm, Sweden: Telephone: (46-8) 679-80-30. Facsimile: (46-8) 611-21-22.
Helsinki, Finland: Telephone: (358-0) 631-100. Facsimile: (358-0) 179-477.
Moscow, Russia: Telephone: (7-095) 201-9292/3/4/5. Facsimile: (7-095) 201-9284.
Budapest, Hungary: Telephone: (36-1) 269-0550; (36-1) 131-0933. Facsimile: (36-1) 269-1199.
Prague, Czech Republic: Telephone: (42-2) 2481-1796. Facsimile: (42-2) 232-5522.
Warsaw, Poland: Telephone/Facsimile: (48-22) 26-80-53; (48-22) 27-84-86. International Telephone/Facsimile: (48-39) 12-19-06.

(This Listing Continued)

Istanbul, Turkey: Telephone: (90-212) 275-68-98; (90-212) 275-75-33. Facsimile: (90-212) 275-75-43.
Ankara, Turkey: Telephone: (90-312) 446-2180. Facsimile: (90-312) 437-9677.
Jeddah, Saudi Arabia: Law Office of Hassan Mahassni, Telephone: (966-2) 651-3535. Facsimile: (966-2) 651-3636.
Riyadh, Saudi Arabia: Law Office of Hassan Mahassni, Telephone: (966-1) 476-7099. Facsimile: (966-1) 479-0110.
Almaty, Kazakhstan: Telephone: (7-3272) 50-7491/2. Facsimile: (7-3272) 61-0842.

General International Practice.
Firm engaged in American and International Law Practice, but not authorized to appear before Hong Kong Courts or to act as Solicitors.

RESIDENT PARTNERS

GEORGE K. CROZER, IV, born Philadelphia, Pennsylvania, March 12, 1942; admitted, 1969, New York (Not admitted in Hong Kong). *Education:* Princeton University (A.B., 1965); University of Michigan (J.D., 1968).

LAWRENCE S. YEE, born New York, New York, October 30, 1947; admitted, 1978, New York; 1979, District of Columbia (Not admitted in Hong Kong). *Education:* Oberlin College (A.B., 1969); New York University (J.D., 1977). *Member:* The Association of the Bar of the City of New York; The District of Columbia Bar; American Bar Association.

RESIDENT ASSOCIATES

STEVEN P. ALLEN, born Adelaide, Australia, March 14, 1962; admitted, 1986, South Australia; 1994, England and Wales (Not admitted in Hong Kong). *Education:* University of Adelaide (LL.B., 1986); South Australia Institute of Technology (G.D.L.P., 1987). (Also Associate, Grice & Co., Solicitors).

ANDREW HIN CHI CHAN, born Hong Kong, February 5, 1968; admitted, 1993, Scotland; 1994, Hong Kong. *Education:* University of Aberdeen (LL.B., 1991; D.L.P., 1992). (Also Associate, Grice & Co., Solicitors).

ISABELLA DE LA HOUSSAYE, born New Orleans, Louisiana, February 2, 1964; admitted, 1991, New York (Not admitted in Hong Kong). *Education:* Princeton University (B.A., 1986); Columbia University (J.D., 1990).

MEI-YING HAO, born Hebei, China, November 14, 1956; admitted, 1993, Illinois (Not admitted in Hong Kong). *Education:* China University of Political Science (LL.M., 1988); Northwestern University (J.D., 1993).

SHARON E. HARTLINE, born Pottstown, Pennsylvania, October 17, 1960; admitted, 1986, New York; 1987, District of Columbia (Not admitted in Hong Kong). *Education:* Muhlenberg College (A.B., 1982); Columbia University (J.D., 1985).

ANDREW P. MCLEAN, born Manchester, England, January 7, 1962; admitted, 1986, England and Wales; 1994, Hong Kong. *Education:* Birmingham University (LL.B., 1983). (Also Associate, Grice & Co., Solicitors).

JACK H. SU, born Taipei, Taiwan, April 15, 1964; admitted, 1991, California (Not admitted in Hong Kong). *Education:* Indiana University (B.A., 1985); Washington University (J.D., 1990).

ALEX Y. WONG, born Beijing, China, November 30, 1964; admitted, 1994, Hong Kong. *Education:* University of Hong Kong (LL.B., 1991). (Also Associate, Grice & Co., Solicitors).

(For biographical data as to other locations, see Professional Biographies at New York, New York; Washington, D.C.; Los Angeles, California; Miami, Florida; Mexico City, Mexico; Tokyo, Japan; Singapore, Republic of Singapore; Bangkok, Thailand; Hanoi, Viet Nam; Bombay, India; London, England; Paris, France; Brussels, Belgium; Stockholm, Sweden; Helsinki, Finland; Moscow, Russia; Budapest, Hungary; Prague, Czech Republic; Warsaw, Poland; Istanbul and Ankara, Turkey; Jeddah and Riyadh, Saudi Arabia; Almaty, Kazakhstan).

WILDE SAPTE

31ST FLOOR
ONE EXCHANGE SQUARE
HONG KONG
Telephone: (852) 2810 5081
Facsimile: (852) 2810 1295

London, England Office: 1, Fleet Place, EC4M 7WS. Telephone: 0171-246 7000. Facsimile: 0171-246 7777. Telex: 887793 lde/cde 145.

(This Listing Continued)

Brussels, Belgium Office: 27 Avenue des Arts, 1040. Telephone: (32-2) 280 1404. Facsimile: (32-2) 280 1764.

New York, New York Office: 19th Floor, 450 Lexington Avenue, 10017. Telephone: (212) 867 4530. Facsimile: (212) 557 4451.

Paris, France Office: 217 rue du Faubourg St. Honoré, 75008. Telephone: (33-1) 44 95 02 70. Facsimile: (33-1) 42 89 62 25.

Tokyo, Japan Office: 2nd Floor, AIG Building, 1-1-3 Marunouchi, Chiyoda-ku 100. Telephone: (81-3) 3215 3801. Facsimile: (81-3) 3215 3868.

Lloyd's Office: 40 Lime Street, London, EC3M 5DG. Telephone: 0171 246 7000. Fax: 0171 246 7722.

Banking, Corporate Lending, Acquisition Finance, Aviation, Shipping, Leasing, Work-outs, Trade Finance, Structured Finance, Project Finance, Insolvency, Property, Insurance, Employment, Charities, EC Law and Company and Commercial.

FIRM PROFILE: *Wilde Sapte is a commercial City firm handling a wide range of work for our UK and international clients.*

The practice is centered around the company and commercial, banking, property, insolvency, insurance and transport expertise, though smaller specialist groups, such as an intellectual property group and a Japanese unit, have been formed to serve particular client needs. It is a progressive and much respected firm which has tripled in size over the last decade. In the last year, in response to increasing international demands from the business communities, offices have been opened in Hong Kong, Tokyo and at Lloyd's to complement those existing in New York, Paris and Brussels. In addition, the practice has extensive connections with law firms in jurisdictions throughout the world.

CONTACT PARTNERS

Ashley Burns

(For complete list of all personnel, see Professional Biographies at London, England)

WILKINSON & GRIST

Solicitors and Notaries Public,

Agents for Trademarks and Patents,

China Appointed Attesting Officer

Established in 1860

PRINCE'S BUILDING, 6TH FLOOR

CHATER ROAD

HONG KONG

Telephone: (852 2) 524 6011
Telecopier: (852) 2520 2090; (852) 2527 9041;
Telex: 75603 WILGR HX

Kowloon Office: 9th Floor, Shui Hing House 23-25 Nathan Road. Telephone: (852) 2369 9236. Telecopier: (852) 2369 4577.

Arbitration, Banking, Bankruptcy, China Trade, Company Formation, Competition, Copyright, Trade Secrets and Confidential Information, Construction, Consumer Protection, Conveyancing, Corporate and Commercial, Distributorship, Agency & Franchising, Employment and Industrial Relations, Family, Franchising and Technology Transfer, General Intellectual Property Practice, Landlord and Tenant, Civil Litigation, Maritime and Admiralty, Patents and Registered Designs, Personal Injuries, Private Client Work, Probate, Administration of Estates, Trusts and Wills, Product Liability, Property and Real Estate, Securities and Stock Exchange Listings, Tax and Estate Duty, Trade Regulations, General Domestic and International Legal Practice.

PARTNERS

ELLA SHUK-KI CHEONG, admitted, 1963, Hong Kong, England and Wales, Victoria, Australia and Singapore. Notary Public. *PRACTICE AREAS:* Intellectual Property.

PETER GEORGE BROWN, admitted, 1971, Hong Kong, England and Wales and Victoria, Australia. *Education:* LL.B. (London). *PRACTICE AREAS:* Company and Commercial.

NEIL JAMES, admitted, 1972, Hong Kong and England and Wales. Notary Public. *PRACTICE AREAS:* Company, Commercial and Insolvency.

LIT-ON LEUNG, admitted, 1975, Hong Kong, England and Wales and Australian Capital Territory. *Education:* B.A. (Hong Kong). Notary Public. *PRACTICE AREAS:* Company, Commercial and Conveyancing.

CATHERINE YUEN NGAI CHONG, admitted, 1976, Hong Kong, England and Wales, Victoria, Australia and Singapore. *Education:* LL.B. P.C.LL. (Hong Kong. Notary Public. China Appointed Attesting Officer. *PRACTICE AREAS:* Hong Kong and China Conveyancing, Landlord and Tenant and Property Finance.

MICHAEL WAH-TIP CHAN, admitted, 1978, Hong Kong, England and Wales, Victoria, Australia and Singapore. *Education:* LL.B. P.C.LL. (Hong Kong). *PRACTICE AREAS:* Company, Commercial and China Trade.

ANNE CHING YEE CHOI, admitted, 1978, Hong Kong, England and Wales, New South Wales and Victoria, Australia. *Education:* LL.B. P.C.LL. (Hong Kong). Notary Public. *PRACTICE AREAS:* Intellectual Property.

NICHOLAS JOHN BENNETT, admitted, 1979, Hong Kong, England and Wales and Nepal. *Education:* M.A. (Oxon). Notary Public. *PRACTICE AREAS:* Litigation and Insolvency.

YVONNE CHUA, admitted, 1980, Hong Kong, England and Wales, Victoria, Australia and Singapore. *Education:* LL.B. P.C.LL. (Hong Kong). Notary Public. *PRACTICE AREAS:* Intellectual Property, Administration of Estates and Probate.

JOHN ROBERTSON BUDGE, admitted, 1979, Hong Kong, England and Wales and Victoria, Australia. *Education:* J.P. FCI Arb. Notary Public. *PRACTICE AREAS:* Litigation.

CHI CHUEN TANG, admitted, 1981, Hong Kong, England and Wales, Australia and Singapore. *Education:* LL.B. P.C.LL. (Hong Kong). *PRACTICE AREAS:* Company, Commercial and Private Client.

CLERESA PIE YUE WONG, admitted, 1983, Hong Kong, England and Wales, Australia and Singapore. *Education:* LL.B. LL.M. P.C.LL. (Hong Kong). *PRACTICE AREAS:* Conveyancing, Landlord and Tenant and Property Finance.

KEITH MAN KEI HO, admitted, 1985, Hong Kong, England and Wales, Australia and Singapore. *Education:* B. Soc. Sc. (Hong Kong). *PRACTICE AREAS:* Litigation.

KENNETH KAI WING YU, admitted, 1985, Hong Kong, England and Wales and Australia. *Education:* B. Sc. (Hong Kong). *PRACTICE AREAS:* Conveyancing, Administration of Estates and Probate and Private Client.

JUDY LAU SAU YU, admitted, 1986, Hong Kong, England and Wales and Australia. *Education:* LL.B. P.C.LL. (Hong Kong). *PRACTICE AREAS:* Conveyancing and Landlord and Tenant.

RICHARD KAY WAH CHAN, admitted, 1987, Hong Kong, England and Wales and Australian Capital Territory. *Education:* LL.B. P.C.LL. (Hong Kong). *PRACTICE AREAS:* Conveyancing and Landlord and Tenant.

TIMOTHY JOHN SCOTT, admitted, 1985, Hong Kong and England and Wales. *PRACTICE AREAS:* Litigation.

LAI KING WONG, admitted, 1984, Hong Kong, England and Wales and Ontario, Canada. *Education:* B.A. (Hong Kong). *PRACTICE AREAS:* Labour Law, Commercial and Conveyancing.

SHIRLEY S.Y. KWOK, admitted, 1987, Hong Kong, England and Wales, Australian Capital Territoryand and Singapore. *Education:* LL.B. P.C.LL. LL.M. (Hong Kong). *PRACTICE AREAS:* Intellectual Property.

ANDREA SUI YI FONG, admitted, 1989, Hong Kong, England and Wales and Australian Capital Territory. *Education:* LL.B. P.C.LL. (Hong Kong). *PRACTICE AREAS:* Intellectual Property.

CONSULTANTS

EDWARD WILLIAM DUDLEY RADCLIFFE, admitted, 1976, Hong Kong and England and Wales. *PRACTICE AREAS:* Litigation.

ASSISTANTS

RAYMOND CHI-KIN CHAN, admitted, 1993, Hong Kong. *Education:* LL.B. P.C.LL. (Hong Kong). *PRACTICE AREAS:* Company, Commercial and China Trade.

(This Listing Continued)

(This Listing Continued)

WILKINSON & GRIST, Hong Kong—Continued

ESTHER WAI-LING HO, admitted, 1992, Hong Kong and England and Wales. *Education:* M.A. (Cantab). P.C.LL. (Hong Kong). *PRACTICE AREAS:* Intellectual Property.

ANITA MAN-YEE HUDSON, admitted, 1995, Hong Kong and England and Wales. *Education:* LL.B. M.Phil (Cantab). *PRACTICE AREAS:* Litigation.

ANITA MAN-YEE LEE, admitted, 1991, Hong Kong. *Education:* B. Soc. Sc. (Chinese University, Hong Kong). *PRACTICE AREAS:* Litigation.

FLEMY CHI-LAN LEE, admitted, 1990, Hong Kong and England and Wales. *Education:* LL.B. P.C.LL. (Hong Kong). *PRACTICE AREAS:* Intellectual Property.

MENA SHUK-MAN LO, admitted, 1990, Hong Kong. *Education:* LL.B. P.C.LL. (Hong Kong). *PRACTICE AREAS:* Intellectual Property.

FRANCIS SIU-KIN MOK, admitted, 1993, Hong Kong and England and Wales. *Education:* B.Soc. Sc. LL.B. P.C.LL. (Hong Kong). *PRACTICE AREAS:* Litigation.

ANDREW PHILIP OLSON, admitted, 1988, Hong Kong and England and Wales. *Education:* B.A. (Cantab). *PRACTICE AREAS:* Company and Commercial.

ROSA CHAU-SHEUNG PANG, admitted, 1994, Hong Kong. *Education:* LL.B. P.C.LL. (Hong Kong). *PRACTICE AREAS:* Intellectual Property.

KIN-HON THAM, admitted, 1995, Hong Kong, England and Wales and Singapore. *Education:* LL.B. (Singapore). *PRACTICE AREAS:* Company and Commercial.

Memberships: Law Society of Hong Kong; Law Society of England and Wales; International Bar Association (IBA); International Association for the Protection of Industrial Property (AIPPI); Federation Internationale des Conseils Propriete Industrielle (FICPI); Asian Patent Attorneys Association (APAA); International Trademark Association (INTA); Marques: European Community Trademark Association (ECTA); Institute of Trade Mark Agents (UK ITMA); Chartered Institute of Patent Agents (UK CIPA); Australian Institute of Patent Agents; Patent and Trademark Institute of Canada; Licensing Executive Society - (LES) U.K. and China; Hong Kong Franchise Association (HKFA); American Chamber of Commerce; Hong Kong General Chamber of Commerce.

Cantonese, English and Mandarin.

WINTHROP, STIMSON, PUTNAM & ROBERTS

2505 ASIA PACIFIC FINANCE TOWER
CITIBANK PLAZA
3 GARDEN ROAD, CENTRAL
HONG KONG
Telephone: 011-852-530-3400
Telefax: 011-852-530-3355

New York Main Office: One Battery Park Plaza, New York, N.Y. 10004-1490. Telephone: 212-858-1000.

Stamford, Connecticut Office: Financial Centre, 695 East Main Street, P.O. Box 6760, 06904-6760. Telephone: 203-348-2300.

Washington, D.C. Office: 1133 Connecticut Avenue, N.W., 20036. Telephone: 202-775-9800.

Palm Beach, Florida Office: 125 Worth Avenue, 33480. Telephone: 407-655-7297.

London Office: 2 Throgmorton Avenue, London EC2N 2AP, England. Telephone: 011-4471-628-4931.

Brussels Office: Rue du Taciturne 42, B-1040 Brussels, Belgium. Telephone: 011-322-230-1392.

Tokyo, Japan Office: 608 Atagoyama Bengoshi Building 6-7, Atago 1-chome, Minato-ku, Tokyo 105 Japan. Telephone: 011-813-3437-9740.

Firm engaged in American and International Law Practice but not authorized to appear before Hong Kong Courts or to act as Solicitors.

RESIDENT PARTNERS

WILLIAM C. F. KURZ, born Baton Rouge, Louisiana, August 26, 1942; admitted, 1968, New York (Not admitted in Hong Kong). *Education:* Harvard College (A.B., 1964); Harvard Law School (LL.B., 1967). Lecturer in Law, Columbia Law School, 1987—.

(This Listing Continued)

YEOW MING CHOO, born Malaysia, 1953; admitted, 1977, Malaysia; 1980, Illinois (Not admitted in Hong Kong). *Education:* University of Malaya Law School (B.L., 1977); Harvard Law School (J.D., 1980).

ROBERT L. LIN, born Taipei, Taiwan, March 3, 1960; admitted, 1986, New York (Not admitted in Hong Kong). *Education:* Yale University (B.A., summa cum laude, 1982); Boalt Hall School of Law, University of California at Berkeley (J.D., 1986). Phi Beta Kappa. Chinese Alumni Scholar. Recipient, Triffin Award. *Member:* American Bar Association. *LANGUAGES:* Mandarin Chinese.

RESIDENT ASSOCIATES

JENG-YANG CHEN, born Taipei, Taiwan, November 18, 1964; admitted, 1989, Taiwan; 1994, New York (Not admitted in Hong Kong). *Education:* National Taiwan University (LL.B., 1987); Cornell Law School (LL.M., 1990); Northwestern University (J.D., cum laude, 1993).

RICHARD R. J. DING, born Taipei, Taiwan, R.O.C., April 27, 1962; admitted, 1993, New York (Not admitted in Hong Kong). *Education:* University of California at Los Angeles (B.A., 1985); National Chengchi Graduate School of Business Administration, Taipei (M.B.A., 1987); Columbia University (J.D., 1992). [1st Lt., Army, 1987-1990]. *LANGUAGES:* Chinese and French.

LI LI, born People's Republic of China, December 3, 1953; admitted, 1991, New York (Not admitted in Hong Kong). *Education:* Beijing Normal College of Foreign Language, Beijing, People's Republic of China (B.A., 1984); Duke University (M.A., 1987); Emory University; Columbia University (J.D., 1991). *LANGUAGES:* Chinese.

JEFFREY M. MADDOX, born Denver, Colorado, September 27, 1963; admitted, 1991, New York (Not admitted in Hong Kong). *Education:* Middlebury College (B.A., 1985); University of Denver (J.D., 1990).

DAVID T. I. VONG, born Macau, September 8, 1961; admitted, 1987, New York (Not admitted in Hong Kong). *Education:* The Hague School of International Law, The Netherlands; The London School of Economics, England (LL.B., 1985); Yale University (LL.M., 1986).

ELLA BETSY WONG, born Hong Kong, August 12, 1967; admitted, 1993, New York (Not admitted in Hong Kong). *Education:* Oxford University, Oxford, United Kingdom (B.A. Hons., 1989); Columbia University (J.D., 1992). Harlan Fiske Stone Scholar. Recipient, Parker School Award for International & Comparative Law. *LANGUAGES:* Cantonese, Mandarin Chinese.

STEVENSON, WONG & CO. INCORPORATING HELEN A. LO & CO.

ROOM 2002-2009 20TH FLOOR
EDINBURGH TOWER, THE LANDMARK
15 QUEEN'S ROAD CENTRAL
VICTORIA, HONG KONG
Telephone: (852) 2526 6311
Cable Address: "Quadrant", "Wongo", Hong Kong
Telex: 65868 WONGO-HX

Fax: 852-2845 9184; 852-2845 0638; 852-2810 5868 (G2/G3/G4) E-Mail: stevwong @ hk.net

Acquisitions, Takeovers and Mergers, ·Company, Commercial, Banking, Copyright, Corporate Finance and Floatation, Joint Venture, Asset Leasing, Project Finance, Capital Markets, Regulatory work in the Banking, Securities and Futures Fields. Unit Trusts and Mutual Funds, Real Property Conveyancing, Real Estate, Rent and Lease, Copyright, Industrial Relations and Employment, Family Law, Distributorship, Agency and Franchising, Licensing, Insurance, International Trade, Migration, Partnership, General Civil Litigation, Arbitration and Alternate Dispute Resolution, Probate, Taxation, Trust and Provident Funds, Trademarks, Patents and General Intellectual Property Practice and Litigation, Trusts and Wills.
Intellectual Property: Copyright Law, Trademark Litigation, Trademark Prosecution, General Intellectual Property Practice.

FIRM PROFILE: The firm is an amalgamated one of the well established commercial and conveyancing practice Stevenson, Wong & Co. which originally commenced practice in 1978 incorporates Helen A. Lo & Co., which commenced practice in 1960. Since its foundation, Helen A. Lo & Co., has been the leading specialist practice in divorce and family law in Hong Kong.

Fluent French language skills in the partnership have developed a tradi-
(This Listing Continued)

tional, long established and ever growing connection with the French business and commercial community of Hong Kong. Further, members of the firm frequently act in cross border transactions involving either parties from different jurisdictions or transactions to be carried out in overseas jurisdictions.

Countries covered by the Firm: Hong Kong. Through being the Hong Kong founder member in 1982 of INTERLAW, an international association of law firms, the firm has reliable and immediate connections to legal advice and assistance from 37 firms practising in 37 different jurisdictions worldwide.

PARTNERS

ANGUS H. FORSYTH, born Bangalore, India, 1944. admitted, 1970, England; 1971, Hong Kong. *Education:* Guildford Law College Law Society, England (Part II Qualifying Examination, 1970). Member, Disciplinary Committee, Law Society of Hong Kong. *LANGUAGES:* English. *PRACTICE AREAS:* Commercial and Company Law; Insurance; Securities and Futures Regulatory Law; Immigration; Unit Trusts and Mutual Funds.

DAISY W.L. TONG, born Hong Kong, 1948. admitted, 1975, England and Hong Kong; 1983, Victoria, Australia; 1988, New York, U.S.A.; 1991, Singapore. *Education:* University of Hong Kong (LL.B., 1972). *LANGUAGES:* English, Cantonese and Mandarin. *PRACTICE AREAS:* Civil Litigation; Commercial and Company; Conveyancing; Trust.

BEBE P.Y. CHU, born Hong Kong, 1952. admitted, 1977, Hong Kong; 1983, England; 1986, New York, U.S.A.; 1991, Singapore. *Education:* University of Hong Kong (LL.B., 1974; P.C.LL., 1975). *LANGUAGES:* English, Cantonese, Mandarin, Shanghainese. *PRACTICE AREAS:* Divorce and Family Law; Civil Litigation; Conveyancing and Property Law.

ANTHONY S.Y. CHIANG, born Hong Kong, 1958; admitted, 1983, Hong Kong; 1988, England; 1990, Australia; 1991, Singapore. *Education:* University of Hong Kong (LL.B., 1980; P.C.LL., 1981). *LANGUAGES:* English, Cantonese, Mandarin. *PRACTICE AREAS:* Conveyancing and Property Law; Commercial and Company Law; China Property Law; Corporate Finance; Banking.

MIMMIE M.L. CHAN, born Brunei, 1956; admitted, 1983, Hong Kong; 1987, England; 1991, Singapore. *Education:* University of Hong Kong (LL.B., 1980; P.C.LL., 1981). *LANGUAGES:* English, Cantonese, Mandarin. *PRACTICE AREAS:* Civil Litigation; Intellectual Property Law.

WILLY Y.P. CHENG, born Hong Kong, 1958; admitted, 1983, Hong Kong. *Education:* University of Hong Kong (LL.B., 1980; P.C.LL., 1981; LL.M., 1992). *LANGUAGES:* English, Cantonese. *PRACTICE AREAS:* Conveyancing and Property Law; Company Law; Civil & Criminal Litigation.

BRUNO C. K. CHAN, born Hong Kong, 1952; admitted, 1982, Hong Kong. *Education:* Washington University, U.S.A. (B.A., 1975). *LANGUAGES:* English, Cantonese. *PRACTICE AREAS:* Divorce and Family Law; General Civil Litigation.

STEPHEN POWNER, born Nigeria, 1962; admitted, 1986, England; 1990, Hong Kong; 1991, Australia. *Education:* University of London, King's College (LL.B., 1983). *LANGUAGES:* English, French. *PRACTICE AREAS:* Commercial; Construction and Personal Injuries Litigation; Criminal; Matrimonial; Employment and Tenancy Law and Practice.

CONSULTANT

PAULETTE Y. TSOI, born Eu (Seine Maritime), France, 1939. admitted, 1971, Hong Kong. *Education:* Faculte des Lettres, Lille, France (Licenciee-es-Lettres, 1961); London University (LL.B., 1968). Member, Disciplinary Committee, Law Society of Hong Kong. *LANGUAGES:* English, French and Spanish. *PRACTICE AREAS:* Commercial and Company Law; Immigration; Conveyancing and Property Law.

ASSISTANT SOLICITORS

ANDREW G. ORR, born New Zealand, 1965; admitted, 1989, New Zealand; 1993, Hong Kong. *Education:* University of Auckland (B.Com (Economics/LL.B.)). *LANGUAGES:* English. *PRACTICE AREAS:* Banking Law; Commercial and Company Law.

CHAU CHAN PIU, born Hong Kong, 1956; admitted, 1988, Hong Kong. *Education:* University of Kent (B.A., 1983). *LANGUAGES:* English and Cantonese. *PRACTICE AREAS:* Conveyancing and Litigation.

HELEN M. BELSHAW, born England, 1966; admitted, 1991, England; 1993, Hong Kong. *Education:* The Nottingham Trent University (LL.B., 1987); Law Society College of Law, Chester (Law Society Finals, 1989).

(This Listing Continued)

LANGUAGES: English. *PRACTICE AREAS:* Commercial and Civil Litigation; Employment Law (both contentious and non-contentious); Aviation Law.

SARAH J. WARREN, born Singapore, 1963; admitted, 1987, England; 1989, Hong Kong. *Education:* University of Exeter (LL.B., 1984); College of Law, Guildford, Surry (Law Society Finals, 1985). *LANGUAGES:* English. *PRACTICE AREAS:* Divorce and Family Law.

ALVIN W.S. CHENG, born Hong Kong, 1968; admitted, 1994, Hong Kong. *Education:* University of Hong Kong (LL.B., 1991). *LANGUAGES:* English, Cantonese. *PRACTICE AREAS:* Divorce; Family Law; Civil Litigation; Criminal Litigation.

JENNY P.C. LEUNG, born Hong Kong, 1967; admitted, 1994, Hong Kong. *Education:* University of Hong Kong (LL.B., 1991). *LANGUAGES:* English, Cantonese. *PRACTICE AREAS:* Civil Litigation.

FLORRIE F.Y. CHENG, born Hong Kong, 1969; admitted, 1994, Hong Kong. *Education:* University of Newcastle upon Tyne (LL.B., 1991). *LANGUAGES:* English, Cantonese. *PRACTICE AREAS:* Commercial & Company.

JANE K.L. CHEUNG, born Hong Kong, 1967; admitted, 1994, England and Hong Kong. *Education:* Metropolitan University of Manchester (LL.B., 1989). *LANGUAGES:* English, Cantonese. *PRACTICE AREAS:* Divorce & Family Law.

OVERSEAS STAFF

PHILIPPE BOUTRON, (Not admitted in Hong Kong). *Education:* University of Paris (Doctorates of International Law and Intellectual Property, 1979). *LANGUAGES:* French and English. *PRACTICE AREAS:* International Law; Intellectual Property Law.

CAO SI TAO, born Guangdong, 1964; (Not admitted in Hong Kong). *Education:* Sun Yat-sen University, Canton, China (Bachelor of Law, 1985); University of Law, Economics & Social Sciences of Paris, France (Diplome d'Etudes Approfondies in Law, 1991). *LANGUAGES:* English, Mandarin, Cantonese, French and Japanese. *PRACTICE AREAS:* Foreign Investment; Joint Venture Law of the P.R.C..

GEOFFREY D. CAROLAN, born New Zealand, 1966. *LANGUAGES:* English. *PRACTICE AREAS:* Commercial and Company Law; Conveyancing; Litigation; Matrimonial; Estate Administration; Taxation.

STELLA SBERRO, born France, 1967; (Not admitted in Hong Kong). *Education:* University of Strasbourg Centre d'etude (Master of Business & Company Law, 1990); International de Propriete Industriel (DESS, Accords et Propriete Industrielle, 1991). *LANGUAGES:* French, English and Spanish. *PRACTICE AREAS:* Business Law; Intellectual Property Law.

Languages: Chinese (Cantonese, Mandarin). English, French, German, Spanish.

INDIA

AMARCHAND & MANGALDAS & HIRALAL SHROFF & CO.

Advocates, Solicitors & Notary

Established in 1990

APARTMENT NO. 4B, PREMCHAND HOUSE ANNEXE
HIGH COURT WAY, ASHRAM ROAD
AHMEDABAD 380 009, INDIA
Telephone: (91-79) 403147; 425310
Fax: (91-79) 427354

ASSOCIATE

Ketan Trivedi

(For Complete Biographical Data, see Professional Biographies at Bombay, India)

H.M. BHAGAT

Advocates, Solicitors & Notary

Established in 1961

INDUSTRY HOUSE, BEHIND NATRAJ CINEMA
ASHRAM ROAD
AHMEDABAD 380 009, INDIA
Telephone: 079 405034; 404334; 444343; 464343; 465222
Fax: 91-79-404334

Establishment engaged in India. Entitled to plead before any Court in India.
Administrative Law, Adoption, Advocacy, Commercial, Company, Constitutional and Contract Laws, Real Estate, Commercial and Domestic Conveyancing, Consumer Protection, Nationality, Foreign Exchange Laws, Customs, Excise, Partnership, Succession, Insurance, Litigation.
FIRM PROFILE: It is a leading establishment of the State of Gujarat, broadly based practice with a reputation for offering a full range of quality legal services. Five member-lawyers with a few more panel advocates.

H.M. BHAGAT, born July 18, 1939; admitted, 1961, Advocate, Bombay Bar Council. *Member:* Bombay Incorporated Law Society (1964—); Gujarat High Court Bar Association (1967—). *LANGUAGES:* English, Gujarati and Hindi. *PRACTICE AREAS:* Corporate Law; Administrative Law; Adoption; Nationality.

REPRESENTATIVE CLIENTS: Governments; Big Houses; Public and Private Sector Corporations; Financial Institutions; Multinational Companies.

AMARCHAND & MANGALDAS & HIRALAL SHROFF & CO.

Advocates, Solicitors & Notary

Established in 1990

201, MIDFORD HOUSE, MIDFORD GARDEN STREET
OPPOSITE TAJ RESIDENCY HOTEL, OFF. M.G. ROAD
BANGALORE 560 025, INDIA
Telephone: (91-80) 5584870
Fax: (91-80) 5584266

ASSOCIATES

Dhananjay Joshi   **Chitralekha Urs**
    Nayantara Urs

(For Complete Biographical data, see Professional Biographies at Bombay, India)

DAVE & GIRISH & CO.

FLAT NO.GB, GROUND FLOOR
SANGEETH APARTMENTS
NO. 13, 18TH CROSS
MALLESWARAM
BANGALORE 560 055, INDIA
Telephone: (91-80) 341508

Bombay, India Office: 41, Rajgir Chambers, Shahid Bhagat Singh Road, 400 023. Telephone: (91) 22-2084191; 2084190; 2860547; 251262. Telex: 011-86697 GMD IN. Fax: (22) 2624282.

FIRM PROFILE: Founded in 1978 By Mr. Mohanial Dave. Mr. Girish Dave associated with him in 1980. The firm has two offices: in Bombay and Bangalore with three partners in Bombay and three partners in Bangalore.

The firm mainly deals in international banking, financial and corporate legal services such as documentation, litigation, and arbitration, in corporate restructuring, technical know-how, joint ventures, domestic and offshore: loans, mutual funds, placement of securities (including Euro issues and domestic public issues), project finance, factoring, securitization, commercial contracts, shipping finance, computer and intellectual property laws and insolvency.

PARTNERS

MAYURA PADMANABHAN (Managing Partner). *LANGUAGES:* English, Hindi and Kannada. *PRACTICE AREAS:* Conveyancing; Banking and Financial Documentation; Investment Banking; Investments; Mutual Funds; Joint Ventures; Corporate and Commercial Matters.

(This Listing Continued)

GIRISH M. DAVE. *LANGUAGES:* English, Hindi and Gujarati. *PRACTICE AREAS:* Corporate and Investment Banking; General Litigation including Cross Border Litigation; Shipping Finance; Offshore Investments; Foreign Currency Loan Documentation; Joint Ventures; Technical Collaborations; Commercial Matters and General Banking Documents.

MONA BHIDE. *LANGUAGES:* English, Hindi and Gujarati. *PRACTICE AREAS:* General Litigation; Maritime Law; Banking and Financial Documentation.

REPRESENTATIVE CLIENTS: International Finance Corporation; Citibank N.A.; ANZ Grindlays' ABN Amro Bank; Hong Kong and Shanghai Banking Corporation Ltd.; BHF Bank; Dresdner Bank; Indian Rayon & Industries Ltd.; Grasim Industries Ltd.; Apple Industries Ltd.; Global Liquidators Bank of Credit and Commerce International (Overseas) Bank, Cayman Islands; Indbank Merchant Banking Services Limited; Canara Bank; Canbank Mutual Fund; Canbank Financial Services Limited; Discount & Finance House of India; Esanda Finance Ltd; SBI Factors Ltd.; Standard Chartered Bank; Atash Industries (India) Limited; Vysya Bank Ltd.; Lechler (India) Private Ltd.; Index Computing Pvt Ltd.; Floatglass India Ltd.

SINGHANIA & CO.

204-A MITTAL TOWERS
6/21 M.G. ROAD
BANGALORE 560 001, INDIA
Telephone: 91-80-558 8763
Telefax: 91-80-558 4593

New Delhi, India Office: B-92 Himalaya House, 23 Kasturba Gandhi Marg, 110 001. Telephone: 91-11-3318300/3731400. Telefax: 91-11-3314413/3713383. Telex: 31-62662 DCS IN. Mobile Car Tel: 91-11-4613334. Cable: SINGANIACO.
Branches also in: Bombay, Calcutta, delhi, Hyderabad, Madras, London and New York.

General Practice.

FIRM PROFILE: Founded in 1969 by Mr. D.C. Singhania provides comprehensive legal services primarily in Corporate and Business law practice. It is one of the leading law firms in India based in New Delhi but having branch offices at Bombay, Calcutta, Madras, Bangalore and Hyderabad in India and also representative offices at London and New York.

ASSOCIATES

Ravinder Singhania
A.G. Sirsi
R. Poornima
Ms. Anuradha

(For complete biographical data on all Personnel, see Professional Biographies at New Delhi, India)

ADVANI & CO.

Barristers-at-Law

NIRMAL, 14TH FLOOR
NARIMAN POINT
BOMBAY 400 021, INDIA
Telephone: (91-22) 202-4422; 202-4424; 204-6236
Fax: (91-22) 287-5671
Telex: 118 3557 BZIN IN

Pune, India Office: Nehru Memorial Hall, 4, Dr. Ambedkar Road, 411 001. Telephone: (91-212) 622 940; 625 805. Fax: (91-212) 622 948.
Dubai, United Arab Emirates Office: in association with Nabarro Nathanson of London and affiliated offices world wide: Dubai World Trade Centre, P.O. Box 9381. Telephone: (9714) 314 475. Fax: (9714) 313 514.
Bahrain Office: Manzoor Garden, House No. 6, E.N.T. No. 199, Road No. 503, Area No. 505. Telephone: (973) 695-5611. Fax: (973) 691-1129.
St Petersburg, Florida Affiliated Office: 5240C Coquina Key Drive SE, 33705. Telephone/Facsimile: (813) 823-4864. Internet: RASLaw@aol.com.

General Civil Practice, Joint Ventures, Construction Industry, Oil and Gas Industry, Arbitration and Litigation, Corporate Law, Technology Transfer, Shipping, Real Estate, Media and Communications, Banking, International Trade and Intellectual Property.

(This Listing Continued)

FIRM PROFILE: Advani & Co. provides a full range of legal services for companies and individuals with interests in India and the Gulf States. Through its joint office in Dubai with Britain's Nabarro Nathanson, Advani & Co. offers clients both local insight and global resources in a number of the world's fastest growing markets. Mr. Ashok Advani's activities as publisher of Business India, the sub-continent's leading business magazine, underscores Advani & Co.'s position as one of the few modern, full-service law firms in the region.

Members and associates are fluent in: English, Hindi and other Indian regional languages.

MEMBERS OF FIRM

HIROO H. ADVANI, born Hyderabad, March 25, 1947; admitted, Barrister at Law, Middle Temple, U.K. and India. *Education:* Cambridge University (M.A. in Law); Bombay University (Gold Medal in Law). *Member:* International Bar Association; Bombay Bar Association. **PRACTICE AREAS:** Litigation; Arbitration; Construction; Shipping; Media; Project Finance.

ASHOK H. ADVANI, born Hyderabad, September 14, 1945; admitted, India, Barrister-at-Law, U.K. *Education:* Oxford University (B.A.). Publisher, the Business India Group. **PRACTICE AREAS:** General Commercial Law; Civil Matters.

JAVED GAYA, born London, February 19, 1956; admitted, India and United Arab Emirates (Consultancy only). *Education:* Worcester College, Oxford University (B.A. Honors in Law). (Resident, Dubai Office). **PRACTICE AREAS:** International Litigation; Shipping.

ASSOCIATES

D.L. BHOJWANI, admitted, India. Former Judge, Bombay City Civil Court.

J.B. RAMCHANDANI, admitted, India.

ARVIND D. SABNIS, born November 2, 1934; admitted, India. *Education:* Bombay University (B.A., LL.B).

HABIB H. DATOOBHOY, born June 27, 1932; admitted, India, Barrister-at-Law, Lincoln's Inn, London. *Education:* Cambridge University (M.A., LL.B.).

K.N. VAISHNAV, born March 11, 1960; admitted, India. *Education:* Bombay University (B.Sc., LL.B.).

AMIN KHERADA, born August 16, 1958; admitted, India. *Education:* Bombay University (B.Comm., LL.B.).

MILAN BHISE, born September 28, 1961; admitted, India. *Education:* Bombay University (M.A., D.M.S., LL.B.).

ASIF LAMPWALLA, born August 18, 1968; admitted, India. *Education:* Bombay University (B.Com., LL.B.).

PUNE, INDIA OFFICE

NETRAPRAKASH BHOG, born May 21, 1947; admitted, India. *Education:* Pune University (B.A., B.Com., LL.B.).

MOHAN BARRETT, born October 2, 1963; admitted, India. *Education:* Pune University (B.Sc., LL.B.).

DILIP BHADLE, born June 1, 1953; admitted, India. *Education:* Pune University (B.A., LL.B.).

MANASI YANDE, born October 15, 1956; admitted, India. *Education:* Bombay University (B.A., LL.B.).

BAHRAIN OFFICE

RENA SETHI, admitted, India. *Education:* University of Bombay.

OF COUNSEL

MANOJ MENDA, admitted, India, Supreme Court Bar Association, registered Patent and Trademark Attorney. *Education:* University of Bombay (B.Com., LL.B.). **PRACTICE AREAS:** Intellectual Property Law.

RUSSELL A. STAMETS, born Oak Lawn, Illinois, March 14, 1963; admitted, 1994, Illinois and Pennsylvania. *Education:* DePauw University (B.M., 1985); Indiana University (M.A., 1990; J.D., 1993). born Oak Lawn, Illinois, March 14, 1963; admitted, Illinois and Pennsylvania. Education: DePauw University (B.M., 1985). Indiana University (M.A., 1990; J.D., 1993). **PRACTICE AREAS:** Corporate Law; International Trade and Investment.

(This Listing Continued)

REPRESENTATIVE CLIENTS: Rockwater (a division of Brown & Root); ETPM-McDermott; Saipem; Snamprogetti; Occidental Petroleum; Stolt Comex Seaway S.A.; Klockner Industrie-Anlagen Gmbh; Ottokumpu Group; Kone Corporation; Hyundai Corporation; Chellaram Group of Companies; Oy Sisu-Auto Ab; Dolphin Offshore Ltd.; Shaw Wallace Ltd.; Dunlop India Ltd.; Jashanmal Group of Companies; Mothercare.

AMARCHAND & MANGALDAS & HIRALAL SHROFF & CO.

Advocates, Solicitors and Notary

Established in 1918

LENTIN CHAMBERS, DALAL STREET
BOMBAY 400 023, INDIA
Telephone: (91-22) 2654866; 2650942; 2650500
Fax: (91-22) 2653891; 2653502; 4928163
Telex: 011-83612 AMCO IN
Cable: AMCO IN

Bombay Litigation Office: 20 New Bansilal Building. Homi Modi Street. 400023. Telephone: (91-22) 2621839; 2621840. Fax: (91-22) 2621838.

New Delhi, India Office: United India Life Building, Block F, Connaught Place, 110001. Telephone: (91-11) 3314637; 3315690; 3310179. Fax: (91-11) 3312586; 6438237. Telex: 031 61397 AMCO IN. Cable: LECAID.

Delhi Litigation Office: 13 Abul Fazl Road. Bengali Market. New Delhi. Telephone: (91-11) 3355148; 3355149. Fax: (91-11) 3355147.

Bangalore, India Office: 201, Midford House, Midford Garden Street, Opposite Taj Residency Hotel, Off. M.G. Road, 560 025. Telephone: (91-80) 5584870. Fax: (91-80) 5584266.

Ahmedabad, India Office: Apartment No. 4B, Premchand House, Annexe, High Court Way, Ashram Road, 380 009. Telephone: (91-79) 403147, 425310. Fax: (91-79) 427354.

Calcutta, India Office: No. 3 Anand Lok, 227 A.J.C. Bose Marg (Lower Circular Road). Telephone: (91-33) 2470508. FAX: (91-33) 2472349.

Associated Offices:

Suresh A. Shroff & Co.

Anand, Amarchand & Mangaldas

Arnold & Porter with offices in Washington, New York, Los Angeles, Denver and Tokyo.

General Practice in all Courts. Corporate Laws, Corporate Financing, Banking, Joint Ventures and Foreign Collaborations, Project Finance, Infrastructure Development and Finance. Utilities, Energy Law, Oil and Gas, Franchising, Restructuring of Business Organizations, Taxation, including Taxation of Foreign Corporations and Nationals, Foreign Exchange Laws, International Equity/ Debt Offerings, Shipping and Admiralty, Insurance, Litigation, Arbitration, Real Estate, Privatization, Conveyancing, International Loan and Financial Documentation, Company Formation and Acquisitions, Financial Services, Mergers and Takeovers, Intellectual Property, Monopolies Control, Consumer Protection and Product Liability.

MEMBERS OF FIRM

SURESH A. SHROFF, born Bombay, August 9, 1931; admitted, 1951, India; 1954, Solicitor, High Court Bombay; 1957, Advocate-on-Record, Supreme Court of India. *Education:* Science Bombay University; Government Law College Bombay (LL.B.). *Member:* International Bar Association; Supreme Court Bar Association.

BHARATI S. SHROFF, born Bombay, November 2, 1932; admitted, 1967, India. *Education:* Bombay University (B.A.); Government Law College Bombay (LL.B.).

SHARDUL S. SHROFF, born Bombay, October 1, 1955; admitted, 1980, India; 1985 Advocate-on-Record, Supreme Court, India. *Education:* Sydenham College Bombay University (B.Com.); Government Law College Bombay (LL.B.). Delivered papers on Counter trade, Arbitration (ICC and others); Export documentation at workshop organized by the International Trade Centre/UNCTAD/GATT and functioning of Capital Markets in India. Contributory Editor for India in "Capital Asia," published from Hong Kong. Delivered several papers at International Workshop of International Trade Centre. Member of Faculty of Management Development Institute (MDI), Gurgaon (India). Delivered papers on International Sales Contracts and Contract documentation. Faculty Member on Programme for Enforcement of Security and recovery of dues conducted by MDI. Member of the Core group of INDO-EC Business Forum, Secretary General SAARCLAW, (India Chapter). Member of Governing Board SAARCLAW (Colombo). Member of the Convention on Privatization and Orga-

(This Listing Continued)

AMARCHAND & MANGALDAS & HIRALAL SHROFF & CO., Bombay—Continued

nizer of Seminar on Decontrol and Marketization of Public Sector Undertakings. Co-contributor for India Chapter of Butterworths Publication "Joint Ventures with International Partners". Country Author on Chapter on "Custodial Service in India" for Capital Asia. Co-Author for book on "Sick Industrial Companies (Special Provisions) Act 1985." Speaker and Chairman of Session at Seminar on Liberalization and Euro-Equity and Debenture Issues for Indian Companies organized by the Federation of Chambers of Commerce in India at Bombay in 1993. *Member:* Delhi Bar Association; International Bar Association; Supreme Court Bar Association.

CYRIL S. SHROFF, born November 7, 1959; admitted, 1982, India; 1983, Solicitor, High Court Bombay; 1984, Advocate-on-Record, Supreme Court of India. *Education:* Sydenham College, Bombay University; Government Law College Bombay (LL.B.). Member of Legal Sub-Committee of Expert Group established by government of India on Infrastructure Development and Finance. Principal Contributor for India Chapter of Butterworths Publication "Joint Ventures with International Partners." Author of Chapter on "Recognition and Enforcement of Foreign Judgements in India," by Sweet & Maxwell. Author of Country Chapter on "International Franchising" by Matthew Bender. Co-Author of text on "Sick Industrial Companies (Special Provision) Act 1985." Author of detailed study on Legal Aspects of the Securities and Capital Markets in India for United States Agency for International Development (USAID). Country Author of Chapter on "Custodial Service in India" for Capital Asia. Contributory Editor for India to the Asia Edition of "International Corporate Law," called "ASIA LAW", published by Euromoney; Indian Contributor for "Project Finance Yearbook," 1993, published by Euromoney. Contributory Editor for: Euromoneys Securities and Capital Market Reporter; "Asian Law Journal". Delivered several papers on Structuring International Equity Offerings Lease Finance, Insurance Law In India. Speaker at Seminar on Legal and Regulatory Aspects of Doing Business in India LEXPO+93 organized by Embassy of the United States of America, 1993 - delivered paper for India held at Manila in June 1993 on "Legal Aspects of Documentation and Debt Recovery in India" organized by World Bank, Asian Development Bank and ADFIAP. Delivered paper on infrastructure development and project finance for the Centenary Celebration seminar of Bombay Law Society and several other seminars in India and abroad. *Member:* International Bar Association; Bombay Bar Association; Supreme Court Bar Association.

OF COUNSEL

P.N. BHAGWATI, born 1921; admitted, 1945, India. Retired Chief Justice, Supreme Court of India. Judge and Chief Justice of the Gujarat High Court, 1960-1973. Judge, Supreme Court of India, 1973-1986. Chief Justice of India, 1985-1986. Other public associations/Awards: International Labour Organization - Member, Committee of Experts on the Application on Conventions and Recommendations, 1978—. Chairman, Advisory Board, Centre for Independence of Judges and Lawyers, Geneva, 1989. Member, Executive Committee, International Society for Labour Law and Social Security, 1987—. Member, Executive Committee, Commonwealth Legal Education Association, London. Chairman, Committee for implementing legal aid schemes, Government of India, 1981-1985. Member, Human Rights Committee, International Law Association. Chairman, Editorial Board, Indian Council of Social Science Research for encyclopaedia of social legislation. Chairman, Indian Council for Enviro-legal action (ICELA), New Delhi. Member, Editorial Board, Law Reports of The Commonwealth. Member, Executive Committee, International Association of Lawyers Against Nuclear Arms (ILANA). Honorary Member, The Conference of Chief Justices of English speaking African countries. Recipient: Outstanding Contribution in the field of Legal Aid Award, International Bar Association; Shiromani Award; National Citizen's award 1987 for eminent contribution to jurisprudence. *Member:* Indian Arbitration Council; Federation of Indian Chamber of Commerce and Industry; International Arbitration.

ASSOCIATES

Pallavi Shroff	Anirudha Das
V.H. Chandaria	Dhananjay Joshi
Sharad Mathkar	Sumeeta Arora
Ritu Bhalla	Ajoy Roy
Seema Thakore	Monica Sharma
Vandana Shroff	L. Vishvanathan
Ketan Trivedi	M. Rajesh
Chitralekha Urs	Margaret D'Souza

(This Listing Continued)

Nayantara Urs	K.B.S. Manian
Neelina Chatterjee	Rashika Gupta
Radha Jayaraman	Abhijit Joshi
Rajesh Begur	Sameer Tapia

Languages: English and Hindi (including other Indian languages)

REPRESENTATIVE CLIENTS: International Finance Corporation, Washington; Asian Development Bank, Manila; Asian Financial & Investment Corporation, Manila; Asian Capital Partners, Goldman Sachs; Lehman Brothers; Bankers Trust; United States Agency for International Development (USAID); Overseas Private Investment Corporation (OPIC); US Exim Bank; J. Makowski & Co.; Thermo Energy; Klienwort Benson Ltd.; Bear Sterns Inc.; Industrial Development Bank of India; Industrial Credit & Investment Corporation of India, Limited; ICICI-Securities Limited (a joint venture between ICICI and J.P Morgan); Capital International, Fidelity Investments; Life Insurance Corporation of India; Unit Trust of India; General Insurance Corporation of India; State Bank of India; GIC Mutual Fund; SCICI Limited; Standard Chartered Bank; SRF Finance Group; Delhi Stock Exchange; National Stock Exchange of India Ltd.; The Coca-Cola Company; Cargill Inc.; Peugeot Automobiles; Imperial Chemical Industries (ICI) India Group; HCL Limited; HCL-Hewlett Packard Limited; Indian Oil Corporation; National Institute of Information Technology; BCE Telecom International, Canada; ABB Asea Brown Boveri Limited; Tata Chemicals Limited; Tata Group of Companies; Titan Watches Limited; ITC Group, Santa Fe; Gujarat Apar Polymers Limited; Kotak Mahindra Finance Limited; Industrial Bank of Japan; Digital Equipment (India) Limited; Delegation of the European Economic Communities (EEC); Asian Hotels Ltd.; Yak Yeti Hotels Ltd (Nepal); Stock Holding Corporation of India Ltd; Infrastructure Leasing & Financial Services Limited; Development Bank of Singapore (DBS); Union Bank of Switzerland (UBS); Singapore Airlines; Oppenheimer & Co.; ISPAT Group of Companies; Turner Broadcasting (CNN).

BHASIN & CO.

Advocates, Supreme Court of India

Established in 1982

116 MITTAL COURT, 'A' WING
BACKBAY RECLAMATION, NARIMAN POINT
BOMBAY 400 021, INDIA
Telephone: 2842050; 2042954
Telex: 118-5651 LAW IN
Fax: 91-22-2874332

New Delhi, India Office: 10th Floor, 10 Hailey Road, 110 001. Telephone: 3326968; 3329878. Cable Address: "Lawyerco", New Delhi. Telex: 31-66030 LAW IN. Fax: 91-11-3329273.

General Legal Practice, Litigation, Administrative, Antitrust, Arbitration, Aviation, Banking, Bankruptcy, Conveyancing, Competition, Constitutional, Corporate, Foreign Investments, Industrial Relations, Labour, International Contracts, Oil and Mining, Property, Real Estate, International Taxation, Taxation of Foreign Nationals, Exchange Control and International Private Law, Consumer Protection & Liability.

MEMBERS OF FIRM

Lalit Bhasin	R.C. Dhuru
Nina Gupta	Madhusumita Swami
B.N. Das	Vijay Barboza
K.B. Swami	Kalpane Kutty Krishnamurthy

(For Biographical Data on all Personnel, see Professional Biographies at New Delhi, India).

CONSULTA JURIS

1D. 3RD FLOOR, FINE MANSION
203, DR. D.N. ROAD
P.O. BOX 1042
BOMBAY 400 001, INDIA
Telephone: 2610794/5521099/5535448/8197181
FAX: 091-22-2624202/2024202.
TELEX: 0081-011-82800/82575/82546/82022/86524

Confidential Investigations, Foreign Collaboration, Intellectual Property, Courtwork (Civil, Criminal, Customs, Drugs, Narcotics etc.) and Company Matters), Petroleum, Power, Fertilizers and Chemicals, Shipping, Aviation and Banking, Agency, Arbitration and Recovery matters, Personnel Placement, Opinions on Indian Laws.

M. PRABHAKARAN, born 1948; admitted, 1974, India. *Education:* B.Sc.LL.B. (First Class and University Rank), Post Graduate Diploma in Business and Industrial Management, Post Graduate Diploma in Personnel Management and Industrial Relations, Doctoral Scholar in Management. Author: Judicial Reforms, 1979; Government Contracts, 1980. Visiting

(This Listing Continued)

Faculty, Institute of Cost Accountants of India. *Member:* International Bar Association; Indian Law Institute.

U.K. SRIVASTAVA, BA BL, admitted, 1985, India.

S. DASGUPTA, BA LL.B, admitted, 1983, India.

R.A. SAPKALE, MA LL.B, admitted, 1973, India.

CRAWFORD BAYLEY & CO.

Established in 1916

STATE BANK BUILDINGS
N.G.N. VAIDYA MARG
BOMBAY 400 023, INDIA
Telephone: 2663713; 2660277; 2661785
Cable Address: LEX BOMBAY
Telex: 118-4598 CBAC
Facsimile: 22-266 0355; 22-266 0986

Civil Litigation; Arbitration; Banking; and Financial Transactions; Corporate Law; Acquisitions; Mergers and Take Overs; Joint Venture and Foreign Collaborations, Exchange Control, Direct and Indirect Taxation, Antitrust, Shipping and Admiralty; Real Estate; Conveyancing; Insurance; Industrial Law; Patent; Trademark and Copyright; Testamentary and Succession Law.

FIRM PROFILE: The firm, in its present name, came into existence in 1916 as a result of the amalgamation of three separate firms, the earliest of which was founded in 1830, and offers a full range of legal services to clients both in India and abroad. This 11 partner firm has a legal support staff of over 37 consisting of 12 Solicitor Assistants and over 25 Advocate Assistants and Paralegal personnel.

MEMBERS OF FIRM

CAVAS HORMASJI PARDIWALA, born 1920; admitted, 1947, India. *Education:* LL.B. (Bombay). Notary. *LANGUAGES:* English. *PRACTICE AREAS:* Real Estate; Conveyancing; Trusts and Wills.

SHANTARAM YESHWANT REGE, born 1927; admitted, 1949, India. *Education:* LL.B. (Bombay). Notary. *LANGUAGES:* English. *PRACTICE AREAS:* Litigation; Admiralty; Aviation; Consumer Protection; Claims; Banking; Banking and Commercial Documentation.

RAJENDRA AMBALAL SHAH, born 1931; admitted, 1952, India. *Education:* LL.B. (Bombay). *LANGUAGES:* English. *PRACTICE AREAS:* Corporate Law; Foreign Investment; Joint Ventures; Intellectual Property Rights; Industrial and Financial Transactions; Taxation.

ARDESHAR RUTTONJI WADIA, born 1920; admitted, 1944, India. *Education:* B.A.; LL.B. (Bombay). *LANGUAGES:* English. *PRACTICE AREAS:* Corporate and Commercial Law; Foreign Collaborations; Joint Ventures; Taxation; Foreign Exchange Laws; Anti Trust Law.

DADI BEJONJI ENGINEER, born 1933; admitted, 1954, India. *Education:* B.A.; LL.B. (Bombay). *LANGUAGES:* English. *PRACTICE AREAS:* Corporate Law; Indirect Taxation; Foreign Exchange; Import Trade Control Regulations; Civil and Constitutional Law.

HEMRAJ CHATURBHUJ ASHER, born 1934; admitted, 1957, India. *Education:* M.A.; LL.B. (Bombay). *LANGUAGES:* English. *PRACTICE AREAS:* Corporate Law; Foreign Investment; Joint Ventures; Industrial; Financial and Commercial Transactions; Anti Trust Law; Taxation.

DILIP DWARKADAS UDESHI, born 1936; admitted, 1958, India. *Education:* LL.B. (Bombay). *LANGUAGES:* English. *PRACTICE AREAS:* Litigation; Commercial Arbitration; Banking; Commercial Documentation; Insurance.

DARIUS ERACHSHAW UDWADIA, born 1939; admitted, 1963, India; 1981, England. *Education:* M.A.; LLB. (Bombay). *LANGUAGES:* English. *PRACTICE AREAS:* Corporate and Commercial Law; Joint Ventures; Foreign Investment; Foreign Collaborations; Exchange Control; Taxation; Anti Trust; Conveyancing; International Loan and Financial Transactions and Instruments; Commercial Documentation.

CHAITAN MANBHAI MANIAR, born 1935; admitted, 1963, India. *Education:* M.A.; B.Com.; LL.B. (Bombay). *LANGUAGES:* English. *PRACTICE AREAS:* Corporate Law; Patent; Trademark; Copyright.

SURESH NARSAPPA TALWAR, born 1937; admitted, 1966, India. *Education:* B.Com.; LL.B. (Bombay). *LANGUAGES:* English. *PRACTICE AREAS:* Corporate Law; Taxation; Commercial Documentation; Anti Trust Laws.

(This Listing Continued)

DARIUS CAVASJI SHROFF, born 1944; admitted, 1965, India. *Education:* B.A.; LL.B. (Bombay). *LANGUAGES:* English. *PRACTICE AREAS:* Corporate and Commercial Law; Labour and Industrial Laws; Industrial Relations; Joint Ventures; Foreign Collaborations.

REPRESENTATIVE CLIENTS: General Motors; Ford Motor Co. Firestone Tyre & Rubber Co.; Boeing Co.; American Standard Inc.; Chevron Chemical Co.; USX Corp.; EKA Nobel; AB Astra; Sandvik AB; Phillip Morris Inc.; International Business Machines Corp.; Siemens; Honeywell Inc.; Eastman Kodak Co.; Pfizer Inc.; Park Davis Ltd.; Johnson & Johnson Ltd.; Merck & Co.; Ciba Geigy Ltd.; Sandoz; Basle; The Dow Chemical Company; Chase Manhattan Bank N.A.; Citibank N.A.; Chemical Bank N.A.; International Finance Corporation, USA; Bank of New York, USA; Morgan Guaranty Trust Company, USA; Bankers Trust Company, USA; The Hong Kong & Banking Corporation; Banque De Nationale Paris; Societe Generale; United Bank of Switzerland; Swiss Bank Corporation; Commerzbank A.G.; Deutsche Bank; Dresdnerbank A.G.; ABN-Amro Bank; Bank of Tokyo; Industrial Bank of Japan Ltd.; Reserve Bank of India.

DAVE & GIRISH & CO.

41, RAJGIR CHAMBERS
SHAHID BHAGAT SINGH ROAD
BOMBAY 400 023, INDIA
Telephone: (91-22) 2660880/2665191/2664262/2665190/2660547
Fax: (91-22) 2662282
Telex: 011-86697 GMD IN

Bangalore, India Office: 219, II Main Road, HIG Colony, RMV Extn. Stage II 560 094. Telephone: (91) 812 332911.

FIRM PROFILE: Founded in 1978 By Mr. Mohanial Dave. Mr. Girish Dave associated with him in 1980. The firm has two offices: in Bombay and Bangalore with three partners in Bombay and three partners in Bangalore.

The firm mainly deals in international banking, financial and corporate legal services such as documentation, litigation, and arbitration, in corporate restructuring, technical know-how, joint ventures, domestic and offshore: loans, mutual funds, placement of securities (including Euro issues and domestic public issues), project finance, factoring, securitization, commercial contracts, shipping finance, computer and intellectual property laws and insolvency.

PARTNERS

MOHANLAL M. DAVE (Senior Partner). *LANGUAGES:* English, Hindi, Gujarati and Sanskrit. *PRACTICE AREAS:* Property; Administrative and Constitutional Laws.

GIRISH DAVE (Managing Partner). *LANGUAGES:* English, Hindi and Gujarati. *PRACTICE AREAS:* Corporate and Investment; Banking; General Litigation including Cross Border Litigation; Shipping Finance; Offshore Investments; Foreign Currency Loan Documentation; Joint Ventures; Technical Collaborations; Commercial Matters and General Banking Documents.

MONA BHIDE. *LANGUAGES:* English, Hindi, Marathi and Gujarati. *PRACTICE AREAS:* General Litigation; Maritime Law; Banking and Financial Documentation.

REPRESENTATIVE CLIENTS: International Finance Corporation; Citibank N.A.; ANZ Grindlays Bank; ABN Amro Bank; Hong Kong and Shanhai Banking Corporation Ltd.; BHF Bank; Dresdner Bank; Indian Rayon & Industries Ltd.; Grasim Industries Ltd.; Apple Industries Ltd.; Global Liquidators Bank of Credit and Commerce International (Overseas) Bank, Cayman Islands; Indbank Merchant Banking Services Limited; Canara Bank; Canbank Mutual Fund; Canbank Financial Services Limited; Discount & Finance House of India; Esanda Finance Ltd.; SBI Factors Ltd.; Standard Chartered Bank; Atash Industries (India) Limited, Vysya Bank Ltd.; Lechler (India) Private Ltd.; Index Computing Pvt Ltd.; Floatglass India Ltd.

TYABJI DAYABHAI

LENTIN CHAMBERS
DALAL STREET
BOMBAY 400 023, INDIA
Telephone: (91-22) 2650247; 2650342; 2650625
Fax: (91-22) 2658209

Acquisitions and Mergers, Aviation, Banking, Collaborations, Conveyancing, Corporate Law, International Loans and Financial Documentation, Insurance, Litigation, Shipping.

JAYANT C. VAKIL, Advocate, Solicitor and Notary, Bombay.

(This Listing Continued)

TYABJI DAYABHAI, Bombay—Continued

GOOL M. KOTWAL, Advocate, Bombay.

NIMISH J. VAKIL, Advocate and Solicitor, Bombay. Solicitor, Supreme Court of England and Wales.

DESAI & DIWANJI

Advocates, Solicitors and Notaries

LENTIN CHAMBERS, DALAL STREET, FORT
BOMBAY 400 023, INDIA
Telephone: (22) 2651729/2651796/2651833/2656778/2651682
Telex: 11-85764 AMBU
Fax: (22) 2658245
Cable: 'REYWAL' Bombay

Admiralty and Shipping, Arbitration, Aviation, Banking and Finance, Corporate and Commercial, Collaborations and Joint Ventures, Computers and Software, Conveyancing and Real Property, Corporate Financing and Securities, Energy, Employment, Family Law, Financial Services, Issue Flotations and Offerings, Information Technology, International Financing, Insolvency, Insurance, Intellectual Property-Patents, Trade Marks, Copyrights and Designs, Investment, Litigation, Mergers and Acquisitions, Mining, Oil and Gas, Privatization, Taxation, Technology Transfers.

PARTNERS

Yeshwant M. Desai, Notary, B.A., LL.B.
Abbas E. Akikwala, Notary, B.A., LL.B.
Shishir K. Diwanji, Notary, B.A., LL.B.
Divya M. Shah, B.A., LL.B.
Vishwang Y. Desai, B.Sc., LL.B.
D.B. Negandhi, B.A., LL.B.
Ruzbeh Mistry, B.A., LL.B.
Abbas S. Chandurwala, B.A., LL.B.

NISHITH DESAI

Established in 1984

94-B MITTAL COURT
NARIMAN POINT
BOMBAY 400 021, INDIA
Telephone: 91 22 204 0068/282 0609/282 0610
Fax: 91 22 287 5792/284 5622
E-mail: S=Nishith%G=Desai%P=VSNBOM%VSNB@mcimail.com

Other Bombay, India Office: International Legal Research Center. A-201 Milton, Juhu Beach, Santacruz (W), 400 049. Telephone: 91 22 646 0254. Fax: 91 22 604 5993.

International Financial and Tax Law. International Business Strategy and Globalisation, International Structuring of Joint Ventures, Offshore and Domestic Funds, Institutional Investment, Project Finance, Intellectual Property Rights with Special Reference to Financial and Tax Aspects, Mergers and Acquisitions, Special Focus on Infrastructure, Leisure and Tourism Industry and Services Sector.

NISHITH M. DESAI, born Dohad, India, March 10, 1950; admitted, 1973, Bombay. *Education:* Government Law College, Bombay (LL.B., 1973); University of Bombay, Department of Law (LL.M., 1977); Euromoney School for International Financial Law, Hong Kong (1993). Author, "Non-resident: Investment Incentives and Tax-Planning," Taxmann, 1983 revised ed. 1986; Principal Contributor to Chapter on: "India's Laws and Policies on Foreign Investments," in Butterworths "Current Developments in International Investment Law," 1992; "Mauritius," International Bureau of Fiscal Documentation (IBFD), Netherlands, 1994. Lecturer: Foreign Investment and Taxation in India and Mauritius, 25th Biennial Conference, International Bar Association, Melbourne, 1994; Taxation and Foreign Investors: What You Should Expect To Pay, Assessing Opportunities in India Conference, Institute for International Research, Dubai, 1994; Investing in India, Asian Law Journal's Conference, Hong Kong, 1994; India - A Golden Opportunity For Mutual Funds, IBC Conference, Bangkok, 1994; Practical International Estate Planning, American Bar Associations Conference, Santa Barbara, California, 1994; Globalisation and International Business Strategies, Bombay, Management Association, Bombay, 1994; Indian Budget 1994-95. Institute of Chartered Accountants of India, Abu Dhabi, 1994; India's Economic Liberalisation: Emerging Opportuni-

(This Listing Continued)

---

ties, Overseas Indians Economic Forum, UAE, 1994; Tax and Investments Developments/Structuring Investment and Cross Border Transactions in the Asia-Pacific Region With Special Reference to India, IBFD's 11th Asian-Pacific Tax Conference, Singapore, 1994; Offshore India Funds: Structural Strategies, Institute for International Research's Offshore Funds Conference, New York, 1994. Member, Advisory Board, New York State Bar Associations International Law Review, 1992—. Senior Country Correspondent, Tax Notes International, U.S. Chairman/Country Representative, Law Asia Taxation Committee, Australia. *Member:* International Bar Association; International Tax Planning Association; Supreme Court Bar Association; Asia Pacific Tax and Investment Center. *LANGUAGES:* English, Hindi and Gujarati. *PRACTICE AREAS:* International Finance; International Taxation; International Business Strategy; Structuring of Joint Ventures; Institutional Investment and Offshore Funds; Infrastructure.

SHEFALI SHAH, born Bombay, India, April 22, 1968. *Education:* University of Bombay, Sydenham College of Commerce and Economics (B.Com., 1988); Institute of Chartered Accountants of India, Gold Medalist (C.A., 1991). *Member:* Institute of Chartered Accountants of India. *LANGUAGES:* English, Hindi, Gujarati, Marathi and French. *PRACTICE AREAS:* International Taxation; Structuring of Inbound/Outbound Investments; Joint Ventures and Foreign Collaborations; Structuring of Offshore Funds; Corporate Law; Exchange Control Regulations; Securities Regulations; Banking and Oil and Gas Industry; Mauritius Tax and Corporate Law.

RAVINA DALAMAL, born Kobe, Japan, June 17, 1970. *Education:* University of London (LL.B., with Honours, 1991). *Member:* The Chartered Institute of Bankers of England. *LANGUAGES:* English, Hindi, Indonesian/Malay and Japanese. *PRACTICE AREAS:* Corporate Law; Aircraft and Project Finance; Franchises.

BHARAT SHAH, born Jambusar, India, September 9, 1951; admitted, 1975, Bombay as Advocate and Solicitor. *Education:* Sardar Patel University (B.Sc., 1972); Government Law College, Bombay (LL.B., 1975). *Member:* Bar Council of Maharashtra; Incorporated Law Society of Bombay. *LANGUAGES:* English, Hindi and Gujarati. *PRACTICE AREAS:* Intellectual Property Rights; Conveyancing and Litigation.

KISHORE JOSHI, born Bombay, India, July 29, 1962; admitted, 1994, Bombay. *Education:* University of Bombay (B.A., 1990; LL.B., 1994). *LANGUAGES:* English, Hindi and Marathi. *PRACTICE AREAS:* Exchange Control Regulations; Taxation.

VAIBHAV PARIKH, born Dohad, India, June 4, 1970. *Education:* University of Bombay (B.E., in Electronics, 1991; Diploma in Software Technology, 1992. *LANGUAGES:* English, Hindi and Gujarati. *PRACTICE AREAS:* Computer and Multimedia Law; Intellectual Property Rights.

REPRESENTATIVE CLIENTS: Bechtel Corp., USA; The Clorox International, USA; Warner Bros., USA; Information Management Resources Inc., USA; AAP information Services Pty. Ltd, Australia; Scotts Holding Ltd., Singapore/ITC India; ANZ Grindlays Offshore Funds, Guernsey; Gaiacorp, UK; Industrial Technology (Far East) Ltd., UAE; Bear Stears Inc., USA; Carr Indosuez Asia, Hong Kong; Oppenheimer, Inc., USA; Alliance Capital, USA; Merrill Lynch; Citibank N.A.; George Soros Funds, USA; Dupont, USA; Unit Trust of India; Sterlite Industries, India; Duckworth Group, UK; Tilda Rice, UK; Jindal Group of Companies, India; Kamats' Fastfood Chain, India; Jhunjhnuwala Group of Companies, HK; Oceonics Group Plc., UK; Institute for International Research, UK; Guild Investment Management Co., USA; ARCO, USA; VST Industries, India; CRB Daewoo Capital; ECU Terminvest Plc., UK; Gujarat Machinery Ltd. Pfoudler; Club Corporation of America, USA; Peregrine, India/HK; Housing Development and Finance Corporation of India (HDFC).

DHRU & CO.

Solicitors, Advocates & Notary

NATWAR CHAMBERS
94, N.M. ROAD
BOMBAY 400 023, INDIA
Telephone: 270836, 270807, 270498
Fax: 91-22-276883

Antitrust Law, Arbitration (including International Arbitration), Administrative Law, Banking and Financial Transactions, Corporate Law, Foreign Collaborations and Joint Ventures, Acquisitions Mergers and Takeovers, Conveyancing, Real Estate, Intellectual Property, Personal Laws, Commercial Laws and General Practice in all Courts.

(This Listing Continued)

PARTNERS

D.B. DHRUV, B.Sc. LL.B. Solicitor, Advocate and Notary, State of Maharashtra.

K.M. PAREKH, LL.B. Solicitor and Advocate.

K.J. SHAH, B.Com. LL.B. Solicitor and Advocate.

MS. SHIRAZ A. CONTRACTOR, B.Com. LL.B. Solicitor and Advocate.

ASSISTANTS

MS. T. MEHTA, Solicitor.

MR. SHRIRAJ D. DHRUV, Solicitor.

MS. S. TANNA, Solicitor.

MS. M. MEHTA, Advocate.

GAGRAT & CO.

Advocates, Solicitors & Notaries

Established in 1934

ALLI CHAMBERS
NAGINDAS MASTER ROAD, FORT
BOMBAY 400 001, INDIA
Telephone: 2650057; 2650084; 2650158
Fax: 022-2657876
Telex: 011-83695
Cables: "Vigilant" Bombay

New Delhi, India Associated Office: Gagrat & Co., Supreme Court Advocates, Plaza Cinema Building, Connaught Circus, 110 001. Telephone: 3322311. Fax: 011-3713657.

London, England Associated Office: Gagrat Gardi & Co., Solicitors, Supreme Court of England, The Outer Temple, 222/225 Strand, WC2R 1BA. Telephone: 071-353 1266. Fax: 071-353 1255. Telex: 296454.

Dubai, United Arab Emirates Associated Office: Gagrat & Gardi, Legal Consultants, 201 Intercontinental Plaza, P.O. Box 8811. Telephone: 9714-275164. Fax: 9714-283829.

Antitrust Law, Arbitration, Aviation, Banking, Central Excise, Collaborations, Commercial Law, Constitutional Law, Conveyancing, Copyright Law, Corporate Law, Customs, Exchange Control, Foreign Investment, Joint Ventures, Labour Law, Litigation, Personal Law, Shipping, Taxation, Trademarks.

FIRM PROFILE: Gagrat & Co. is one of the largest Law Firms in India and has Associated Offices in New Delhi, London and Dubai. The Partners of the Firm are assisted by over 100 persons as Associates and supporting staff. The Firm acts for several large foreign and Indian Corporations, Corporate Groups, Banks, Hotels and Airlines in India. Several of the Partners are qualified to practice in more than one jurisdiction, are Directors of Companies and Banks and members on the Committees of Professional Bodies and Chambers of Commerce in India. The Firm provides a full and comprehensive legal service to its clients whether they operate on a national or international basis.

PARTNERS

R.A. GAGRAT, B.A., LL.B., Solicitor, Advocate, Supreme Court of India and Notary Union of India.

M.P. SHROFF, M.A., LL.B., Solicitor, Advocate, Supreme Court of India.

J.R. GAGRAT, LL.B., Solicitor, Advocate, Supreme Court of India, Solicitor, Supreme Court of England, and Notary, Union of India.

A.R. JANI, LL.B., Solicitor, Advocate and Notary, Greater Bombay.

M.D. DESAI, B.A., LL.B., Solicitor and Advocate.

H.D. PETIT, B.Com., LL.B., Solicitor, Advocate, Supreme Court of India and Solicitor, Supreme Court of England.

A.C. MEHTA, B.A., LL.B., Solicitor, Advocate, Supreme Court of India.

R.S. GODIWALA, B.A., LL.B., Solicitor and Advocate.

R.J. GAGRAT, M.A., (Cambridge), PIL (Harvard), Solicitor, Advocate, Supreme Court of India and Solicitor, Supreme Court of England.

(This Listing Continued)

V.B. AGARWALA, B.Sc., LL.B., Solicitor, Advocate, Supreme Court of India and Solicitor, Supreme Court of England.

P.N. KAPADIA, B.A., LL.B., Solicitor and Advocate.

M.M. JAYAKAR, B.A., (Hons), LL.B., Solicitor and Advocate Supreme Court of India.

C.A. JANI, B.Com., LL.B., Solicitor and Advocate.

P.A. JANI, B.Com., LL.B., Solicitor and Advocate.

Languages: English

JEHANGIR GULABBHAI & BILIMORIA & DARUWALLA

Solicitors, Advocates, Registered Trade Mark & Patent Agents; Trustees & Solicitors of reputed Public and Private Charitable Trust including Hospital.

Established in 1900

RAJABAHADUR MANSION, 20, AMBALAL DOSHI MARG
(HAMAM STREET)
BOMBAY 400 023, INDIA
Telephone: +91 (22) 2654743
Telex: 011-84070 JGBD IN
Fax: +91 (22) 2654252
Cable: HUMATA, Bombay - 1

General Litigations, Trademarks, Patents, Industrial Designs and Copyright Matters, Trade Secrets, Technical Know-how, Corporate Law, Testamentary Probate and Interstate Work, Conveyancing, Matrimonial Matters, Liaison Work with Trademark Registries, Patent Office, Industrial Designs and Copyright Offices and Central and State Governments, Criminal Prosecutions.

MR. TEHEMTAN NASSERWANJI DARUWALLA, BA, LL.B., Solicitor & Advocate; Registered Patent & Trade Mark Agent. (Partner). Professor, Teaching Trade Marks, Patents, Copyrights and Designs of the Faculty of Law, University of Bombay for Post Graduates, LL.M. 1976—; Professor, Government Law College, Bombay, 1979-1992. Honorary Solicitor and Executive Committee Member, B.D. Petit Parsee General Hospital. Lecturer: Training course on Law and Administration of Trade Marks, and WIPO Asian Regional Training course on the Law and Administration of Trade Marks, organized by WIPO (World Intellectual Property Organization) in collaboration with the Government of Australia with the assistance of United Nations Development Programme (UNDP), Canberra, November, 1985 and September, 1990; "Developments in National Law to Fight Commercial Counterfeiting," International Symposium on "Fighting" Counterfeiting in International Trade, organized by International Chamber of Commerce, Paris, May 30-31, 1989. Member of the Faculty of and numerous papers read at Seminars of ALL INDIA TRADE MARKS, PATENTS, DESIGNS & COPYRIGHT OWNERS ASSOCIATION OF INDIA; Delivered Lectures on numerous legal topics viz, Conveyancing, pleadings, partnership and on Intellectual Property Laws to Bar Council of Maharashtra & Goa; All India Company Secretaries Association and Bajaj Institute of Management. Contributor: "Intellectual Property in Asia and the Pacific," World Intellectual Property Organization (WIPO), Geneva; IP ASIA: Intellectual Property, Marketing and Communications Law published in Hong Kong. *Member:* IBA (International Bar Association); AIPPI (Association Internationale-pour la Protection de la Propriete Industrielle, Zurich); Bar Council of Maharashtra & Goa; Bombay Incorporated Law Society (Solicitors); High Court Bar Association, Bombay; Supreme Court Bar Association, New Delhi. *PRACTICE AREAS:* Registered Patent & Trade Mark Agent; Testamentary; Matrimonial; Criminal and Civil Litigation.

MRS. ALOO TEHEMTAN DARUWALLA, MA, LL.B., Advocate; Registered Patent & Trade Mark Agent. (Partner). *Education:* Certificat d'Etudes Francaises, (Grenoble); Diplome Superieur d'Etudes Francaises de l'Alliance Francaise (Paris). *PRACTICE AREAS:* Registered Patent & Trade Mark Agent; Testamentary and Intestate Matters; Civil Litigation.

MISS KATY BEHRAMJI BHARUCHA, BA, LL.B., Advocate; Registered Patent & Trade Mark Agent. *PRACTICE AREAS:* Registered Patent & Trade Mark Agent; Matrimonial & Commercial Litigations.

MRS. ROSHNI MEHRNOSH SIDHWA, B.A., LL.B., LL.M., Advocate. *PRACTICE AREAS:* Labour Laws and Trade Marks; Arbitration.

(This Listing Continued)

JEHANGIR GULABBHAI & BILIMORIA & DARUWALLA, Bombay—Continued

MR. NIKHILESH NATVARLAL PANCHAL, B. Com., LL.B., Advocate. *PRACTICE AREAS:* Intellectual Property Laws and General Litigation; Civil and Criminal.

MR. CHAKRAPANI BRAJESH MISRA, BA, LL.B., Advocate. *PRACTICE AREAS:* Litigation.

MISS BLOSSOM NORONHA, B.Sc., LL.B., Advocate. *PRACTICE AREAS:* Intellectual Property Laws; Rent Laws; General Litigation.

KANGA AND COMPANY

(Advocates, Solicitors and Notary)

READYMONEY MANSION
43, VEER NARIMAN ROAD
BOMBAY 400 023, INDIA
Telephone: 2042288; 2042289; 2042265; 2049238; 2873506; 2043726;
2851541; 2851542
Telex: 011-84727 KACO
Fax: 9122-2043726; 9122-2851540

Taxation, Company Law, Foreign Joint Venture, Conveyancing, Civil Litigation, Banking, Testamentary and Constitutional Matters.

MEMBERS OF FIRM

Damodar D. Damodar	Atul S. Dayal
Krishnaraj J. Merchant	Kishore M. Vussonji
Mansingh L. Bhakta	Bharat D. Damodar
Kandarp R. Modi	Sandeep H. Junnarkar
Jagdish S. Desai	Miss Kalpana V. Merchant
Subhash C. Kothari	Shailesh S. Vaidya
Atul M. Desai	Ashir R. Amin
	Ms. Preeti G. Mehta

ASSOCIATES

Miss Mumtaz M. Bandukwala	Ravi Gandhi
Miss Sonal N. Mehta	Miss. Priya Smart
Miss. Falgun Desai	Miss. Sunita Kurdukar

REPRESENTATIVE CLIENTS: Bank of America; Citibank, N.A.; Banque Nationale de Paris; Reliance Groups of Industries; Public Sector Banks like United Commercial Bank and Syndicate Bank; Reserve Bank of India.
REFERENCES: Bank of America, San Francisco, California; U.S.A. Citibank, Bombay.

LITTLE AND COMPANY

(Advocates, Solicitors & Notaries)

Established in 1885

CENTRAL BANK BUILDING
MAHATMA GANDHI ROAD
BOMBAY 400 023, INDIA
Telephone: 91-2652739, 2652665, 2652834, 2652930, 2653511, 2654922
Fax: 91-22-265-9918
Cable Address: "Legal Bombay"
Telex: 01183226 LEGL IN

General Practice, Arbitration, Banking, Commercial Disputes, Conveyancing, Copyright, Corporations, Energy, Exchange Control, Excise, Franchises, International Finance, Joint Ventures, Litigation, Mining, Oil, Partnership, Patents, Probate, Shipping, Taxation, Trademarks.

FIRM PROFILE: *Little & Co. established more than a hundred years ago, is one of the leading firms of advocates and solicitors based in Bombay with an extensive international and all India civil practice. The firm has acted as legal advisers to the East India Company, the Governments of India and of successively Bombay Presidency, Bombay State and the State of Maharashtra. With 35 lawyers including 18 partners supported by paralegal staff and sophisticated automation and communication technology, the firm practices in domestic and foreign banking, finance, venture capital, securities, international offerings, mutual funds, insurance, leasing, corporations, energy, intellectual property, shipping, air transportation, litigation, arbitration before all tribunals, taxation direct and indirect, leveraged lease or project finance for facilities and equipment including transportation, alternative energy and power plants. The firm advises many*

(This Listing Continued)

---

leading business groups, government companies and commercial banks in Bombay and has an extensive international clientele.

MEMBERS OF FIRM

CHARLES J.E. GRUNDY, LL.B. London. *LANGUAGES:* English and Portuguese. *PRACTICE AREAS:* Corporate Law; Conflict of Laws.

JAL J. VAKIL, LL.B. Bombay. *LANGUAGES:* English and Gujarati. *PRACTICE AREAS:* Admiralty Law; Shipping Law.

KANAIYALAL J. CHOKSHI, LL.B. Bombay. *LANGUAGES:* English and Gujarati. *PRACTICE AREAS:* Commercial Disputes; Litigation; Conveyancing.

SOHRAB E. MORRIS, B.A. Hons.; LL.B. Bombay. *LANGUAGES:* English and Gujarati. *PRACTICE AREAS:* Commercial Disputes; Banking Law; Probate Law.

SAIFUDDIN N. WAKHARIYA, B.A. Hons.; LL.B. Poona. *LANGUAGES:* English, Gujarati and Urdu. *PRACTICE AREAS:* Administrative Law; Energy Law; Litigation; Property Law.

DARA P. MEHTA, B.A.; LL.M. Harvard. *LANGUAGES:* English, Gujarati and French. *PRACTICE AREAS:* Corporate Law; Franchise Law; International Finance Law; Joint Ventures; Intellectual Property Law.

JAMSHED P.F. SHROFF, B.A.; LL.B. Bombay. *LANGUAGES:* English and Gujarati. *PRACTICE AREAS:* Litigation; Taxation Law; Probate Law.

GOVIND G. DESAI, B.A.; LL.M. Bombay. *LANGUAGES:* English and Marathi. *PRACTICE AREAS:* Corporate Law; Commercial Disputes; Litigation.

BALKRISHNA H. WANI, B.A.; LL.B. Bombay. *LANGUAGES:* English, Gujarati and Marathi. *PRACTICE AREAS:* Corporate Law; Litigation; Antitrust Law.

FARROKH J. SIDHWA, M.A.; LL.B. Bombay. *LANGUAGES:* English and Gujarati. *PRACTICE AREAS:* Banking Law; Commercial Disputes; Real Estate Law.

RAJNIKANT K. MEHTA, B.A.; LL.B. Bombay. *LANGUAGES:* English and Gujarati. *PRACTICE AREAS:* Arbitration; Oil Law; Litigation.

RAVINDRA K. KULKARNI, B.Sc.; LL.M. Bombay. *LANGUAGES:* English and Marathi. *PRACTICE AREAS:* Corporate Law; Excise and Customs Law; Energy Law; Project Finance; International Offerings.

JAYENDRA P. KAPADIA, B.Com., LL.B. Bombay. *LANGUAGES:* English and Gujarati. *PRACTICE AREAS:* Litigation; Commercial Disputes.

AJAY K. CHOKSHI, B.A., LL.B. Bombay. *LANGUAGES:* English and Gujarati. *PRACTICE AREAS:* Litigation; Commercial Disputes.

AJAY M. KHATLAWALA, B.Sc., LL.B. Bombay. *LANGUAGES:* English and Gujarati. *PRACTICE AREAS:* Arbitration; Litigation.

BAHRAM N. VAKIL, B.Com., LL.B. Bombay; LL.M. Columbia. Admitted New York bar 1985. *LANGUAGES:* English and Gujarati. *PRACTICE AREAS:* Corporate Law; Energy Law; Project Finance.

DINA K. WADIA, B.Com., LL.M. Cantab. *LANGUAGES:* English, German and Gujarati. *PRACTICE AREAS:* Corporate Law; Securities Law; Project Finance; Mutual Funds; International Offerings.

ANIL R. WANI, B.Com., LL.B. Bombay. *LANGUAGES:* English and Gujarati. *PRACTICE AREAS:* Excise Law; Customs Law; Monopolies; Litigation.

MAJMUDAR & CO.

Established in 1943

Law Firm: Advocates, Solicitors and Notaries

ISMAIL BUILDING
381, DR. D. N. ROAD
BOMBAY 400 001, INDIA
Telephone: 91-22-204 78 12 / 204 40 24
Fax: 91-22-202 49 92

General Practice in all Courts, Banking Law, Insurance Law, Financial and Mercantile Documentation, Contracts, Foreign Exchange Laws, Corporate Law, Joint Ventures, Arbitration, Real Estate and Property Consul-

(This Listing Continued)

tants, Conveyancing, Consumer Protection, Private International Law, Testamentary and Succession, Intellectual Property Rights.

MEMBERS OF FIRM

AHMAD HIRANI, Solicitor and Notary, Bombay. *Education:* B.Sc., LL.B.

AKIL HIRANI, Solicitor, Bombay and London; International Attorney, California, U.S.A. *Education:* B.A., LL.B.

Languages: English, Hindi, Gujarati, Marathi

REPRESENTATIVE CLIENTS: Industrial Development Bank of India; Industrial Finance Corporation of India Ltd.; Industrial Reconstruction Bank of India; Maharashtra State Financial Corporation; State Bank of India; United Commercial Bank; Securities and Exchange Board of India; Life Insurance Corporation of India; General Insurance Corporation of India; LIC Mutual Fund; S.R. Doshi Finance and Investment Ltd.; Bombay Paints Ltd.; Lok Housing and Construction Ltd.; Petrox Pvt. Ltd.

MULLA & MULLA & CRAIGIE BLUNT & CAROE

(Advocates, Solicitors and Notaries Public)

Established in 1895

JEHANGIR WADIA BUILDING
51 MAHATMA GANDHI ROAD
BOMBAY 400 001, INDIA
Telephone: 204 4960 / 2875121 (14 lines)
Fax: 9122-2040246 (INT'L)
Telex: 011-83967, 84250, 82471
After Hours Telephones: 4947153; 2020203; 3886655; 2022047
REVISERS OF THE INDIA LAW DIGEST FOR THIS DIRECTORY.

Corporate, Mergers and Acquisitions, Foreign Investments, Joint Ventures, Antitrusts Law, Banking and Securities Law, Air Law, Aircraft Finance, Maritime and Transport Law, Ship Finance, Marine & General Insurance Law, Product Liability, Litigation, Taxation, Trade and Customs Law, Environmental Law, Oil and Gas, Real Estate, Commodities, Labour, Arbitration, Bankruptcy, Intellectual Property and General Entertainment Law.

FIRM PROFILE: *The firm is India's largest law firm. Our origin dates back to the end of the last century when Sir Dinshaw Mulla and his brother, Rustomji Mulla established the firm in 1895. Sir Dinshaw Mulla was a Privy Counsellor and author of several legal works including Contract, Partnership, Sale of Goods, Insolvency, Civil Procedure Code etc., and which even today are leading authorities. The firm merged in 1952 with Messrs. Craigies Blunt & Caroe, that firm being solicitors in the East India Company. Since then the firm has grown to its current strength of over 150 lawyers, fee earners and administrative staff. Individual partners concentrate on different areas of the firm's practice enabling the providing of specialist legal, commercial and technical services to clients. The firm has built up very close working relationship with lawyers throughout the world. Many of the firm's lawyers are qualified Solicitors of the Supreme Courts of England and Hong Kong. Most of the firm's partners travel widely in the course of their work which enables them to make invaluable international contacts. Many of our partners have presented papers at International and Domestic Law Conferences. The firm's senior partner Mr. J.P. Thacker is the past President of the Solicitors' Law Society and past president of the Indian Merchants Chamber (he is the first and only Solicitor to occupy this position in the Chamber). Mr. D.M. Popat is Chairman, Indian Council of Arbitration (Western Region) as also Chairman Law Committee of Indian Merchants Chamber. The firm is the revisor of India Law Digest for Martindale-Hubbell International Law Directory and the India Correspondent for Euromoney Publications plc. Mr. H.D. Nanavati is the India correspondent for Shawcross & Beaumont-Air Law and Mr. S.J. Thacker is the India correspondent for Llyod's Maritime and Commercial Law Quarterly.*

PARTNERS

J.P. THACKER, LL.B. *PRACTICE AREAS:* Corporate and Commercial; Mergers and Acquisitions; Offshore Investments and Securities; Foreign Investments; Joint Ventures and Collaborations; Anti-Trust; Energy Law, Gas, Petroleum and Electricity.

S.K. WADIA, B.A., LL.B. *PRACTICE AREAS:* Litigation; Commercial; Corporate; Intellectual and Real Property; Transport and Accident; Insurance; Bankruptcy and Insolvency.

(This Listing Continued)

*E.B. DESAI, B.A., LL.B. *PRACTICE AREAS:* Corporate and Commercial; Mergers and Acquisitions; Offshore Investments and Securities; Foreign Investments; Joint Ventures and Collaborations; Anti-Trust; Arbitration; International, Commercial, Domestic; Enforcement of International Awards; Real Estate; Acquisitions, Disposals and Financing.

(MRS.) K.F. MEHTA, B.A., LL.B. *PRACTICE AREAS:* Real Estate; Acquisition, Disposals and Financing.

D.M. POPAT, B.A., B.Com., LL.B. *PRACTICE AREAS:* Corporate and Commercial; Mergers and Acquisitions; Offshore Investment and Securities; Foreign Investments; Joint Ventures and Collaborations; Anti-Trust; Arbitration; International, Commercial, Domestic; Enforcement of International Awards.

*E.A.K. FAIZULLABHOY, B.A., LL.B. *PRACTICE AREAS:* Corporate and Commercial; Mergers and Acquisitions; Offshore Investments and Securities; Foreign Investments; Joint Ventures and Collaborations; Anti-Trust; Real Estate; Acquisitions, Disposals and Financing.

H.D. NANAVATI, B.A., LL.B. (Bom.); LL.M. (Harward). *PRACTICE AREAS:* Air Law; Aircraft Finances; Aviation Disasters; Passenger; Baggage Claims; Purchase; Lease of Aircrafts.

*A.P. MAVANI, LL.B. *PRACTICE AREAS:* Industrial Relations; Labour and Welfare Legislation and Industrial Disputes; Litigation; Commercial; Corporate; Intellectual and Real Property; Transport and Accident; Bankruptcy and Insolvency.

*B.H. ANTIA, B.Sc., LL.B. *PRACTICE AREAS:* Banking; Documentation and Recovery; Excise and Customs Law; Real Estate; Acquisitions, Disposals and Financing.

**B.S. BHESANIA, B.Sc., LL.M. *PRACTICE AREAS:* Maritime Law, Marine Insurance and Salvage; Shipping Law; Collisions; Pollution; Charterparty Disputes; Maritime Claims/Marine Insurance; Real Estate; Acquisitions, Disposals and Financing.

*S.D. COLABAWALA, B.A., B.Com., LL.B. *PRACTICE AREAS:* Banking; Documentation and Recovery; Litigation; Commercial; Corporate; Intellectual and Real Property; Transport and Accident; Bankruptcy and Insolvency.

N.N. MULLA, LL.B. *PRACTICE AREAS:* Litigation; Commercial; Corporate; Intellectual and Real Property; Transport and Accident; Insurance; Bankruptcy and Insolvency.

**S.J. THACKER, B.Com., LL.B. *PRACTICE AREAS:* Maritime Law; Marine Insurance and Salvage; Shipping Law; Collisions; Pollution; Charterpary Disputes; Maritime Claims/Marine Insurance; Ship Building; Project Finance and Offshore Construction; Arbitration; International, Commercial, Domestic; Enforcement of International Awards.

*R.K. KRISHNAMURTHY, B.A., LL.B. *PRACTICE AREAS:* Banking; Documentation and Recovery; Excise and Customs Law; Intellectual Property Rights; Patents, Trade Marks, Copyrights; Communications; Franchising and General Entertainment.

**M.P. BHARUCHA, B.A., LL.B. *PRACTICE AREAS:* Corporate and Commercial; Mergers and Acquisitions; Offshore Investments and Securities; Foreign Investments; Joint Ventures and Collaborations; Anti-Trust; Environment & EHS; Product Liability and Consumer Protection; Pollution; Industrial Relations; Labour and Welfare Legislation and Industrial Disputes.

C.N. MISTRY, B.Com., LL.B. *PRACTICE AREAS:* Taxation; Income Tax and Planning.

Y.P. DANDIWALA, B.Sc., LL.B. *PRACTICE AREAS:* Corporate and Commercial; Mergers and Acquisitions; Offshore Investments and Securities; Foreign Investments; Joint Ventures and Collaborations; Anti-Trust.

**DARIUS J. KAKALIA, B.Com., LL.B. *PRACTICE AREAS:* Industrial Relations; Labour and Welfare Legislation and Industrial Disputes; Litigation; Commercial; Corporate; Intellectual and Real Property; Transport and Accident; Insurance; Bankruptcy and Insolvency.

*HORMAZDIYAR S. VAKIL, B.A., LL.B. *PRACTICE AREAS:* Excise and Customs Law; Litigation; Commercial; Corporate; Intellectual and Real Property; Transport and Accident; Insurance; Bankruptcy and Insolvency.

*JEHANGIR N. MISTRY, B.Com., LL.B. *PRACTICE AREAS:* Arbitration; International, Commercial, Domestic; Enforcement of International Awards; Real Estate; Acquisitions, Disposals and Financing; Litiga-

(This Listing Continued)

MULLA & MULLA & CRAIGIE BLUNT & CAROE,
Bombay—Continued

tion; Commercial; Corporate; Intellectual and Real Property; Transport and Accident; Insurance; Bankruptcy and Insolvency.

ASSISTANT SOLICITORS

M.R.S. Captain,
　I.O.M., B.A., LL.B.
S.B. Jijina, B.A., LL.B.
*Homiar Vakil
Khurshed J. Gandhi,
　B.Com., LL.B.
*(Mrs.) Alka M. Bharucha

*Hemant J. Shah
Tushar A. Mavani,
　B. Com., LL.B.
Rashna D. Zaiwalla, B.A., LL.B.
Rupa Bhatia, B.A., LL.B.
Abeezar E. Faizullabhoy,
　B.Com., LL.B.
Shiney Badlani, B.Com., LL.B.

*Solicitors Supreme Court of England
**Solicitors Supreme Courts of England and Hong Kong

REVISERS OF THE INDIA LAW DIGEST FOR THIS DIRECTORY.

ASHOK C. PRATAP & CO.

Barristers and Advocates
COOKS BUILDING
DR. D. N. ROAD
BOMBAY 400 001, INDIA
Telephone: 2048090; 2042532
Cable Address: "Indialaw"
Telex: 011-5109 LAW IN
FAX: 91-22-2871901

International Law, Joint Ventures, Technology Transfers, Foreign Trade, Corporation and Commercial Law, Taxation of Foreign Companies, Oil and Gas, International Arbitration.

ASHOK C. PRATAP, born October 2, 1940; admitted, 1962, England and all Courts and Tribunals in India. *Education:* University of Bombay (B.A., Economics and Politics, 1959); Lincoln's Inn, London (Barrister-at-Law, 1962); Council of Legal Education, London (Certificate in International Law, 1963). Prize winner, International Law, Council of Legal Education, 1963. Scholar, Conference on International and Comparative Law, Strasbourg, 1963. In Chambers of Sir Ivor Richards, Barrister-at-Law, London, 1962-1963. Associate, Rogers & Wells, New York City, 1963-1968. *Member:* International Law Association; American Society of International Law; British Institute of International and Comparative Law; Law Association for Asia and the Pacific.

ASSOCIATES

Sandhya Pratap
Dharmishta Tanna
Parul Nanabhai

Pratul D. Gandhi
Hutoxi Khan
Vaidehi Thacker

REPRESENTATIVE CLIENTS: Dresser Industries, Inc.; Monsanto Co.; Ingersoll Rand Inc.; Overseas Private Investment Corp. (OPIC); Ashton Tate Inc.; Hewlett Packard Co.; Foster Wheeler Energy Corp.; Piaggio & C.S. p. A.; United States Government (U.S.I.S., Department of State, Department of Justice); Global Marine Drilling Co.; J.C. Penney, Inc.; Lockheed Aircraft Co.; Tidewater, Inc.; Texas Instruments, Inc.; Rohm & Haas, Inc.; Honeywell, Inc.; Pepsico, Inc.; Cargill, Inc.; Italian Trade Commission in India; Mattel, Inc.; Olivetti & C.S.p.a.; Digital Equipment Corp; Owens Illinois, Inc.; Pacific Telesis; Raychem Corp; 3M; McDonnel Douglas Corp.; Beckman Instruments; Krebs Swiss; Millipore; Parker Hannifin, Inc.; Silicon Graphics; Sola International; General Electric; Walt Disney Company; Argyle Diamonds.

SHAH & SANGHAVI

Advocates, Solicitors & Notary
Established in 1966
114-A WING, 11TH FLOOR
MITTAL COURT, NARIMAN POINT
BOMBAY 400 021, INDIA
Telephone: 285 5755/285 5756/285 3592/285 3593
Facsimile: (091)(22)(245040)
Cable Address: JASHCHIM, BOMBAY

Civil Litigation, Arbitration, Corporate Law, Joint Ventures, Foreign Collaborations, Exchange Control, Conveyancing, Inheritance Law.

(This Listing Continued)

MEMBERS OF FIRM

J.C. SHAH, born 1932; admitted, 1957, India; Solicitor, U.K., 1961. *Education:* Bombay University (B.Sc.; LL.B.). *Member:* Supreme Court Bar Association; Incorporated Law Society; International Bar Association; Union Des Advocates Internationale; Chartered Institute of Arbitrators of U.K. & India; London Court of International Arbitration (Pacific Region). *PRACTICE AREAS:* Arbitration; Company Law; Conveyancing; Documents; Wills; Trust.

P.J. SHAH, born 1958; admitted, 1982, India; Solicitor, India & U.K, 1983. *Education:* Bombay University (B.Com.; LL.B.). *Member:* Incorporated Law Society; Supreme Court Bar Association; Chartered Institute of Arbitrators of U.K. & India. *PRACTICE AREAS:* Civil Litigation; Anti Trust Law; Bankruptcy; Contracts.

REPRESENTATIVE CLIENTS: The Minerals & Metal Trading Corporation Ltd.; State Bank of Mysore; Gujarat Industrial Investment Corporation; Gujarat State Finance Corporation.

SINGHANIA & CO.

83-C MITTAL TOWERS
NARIMAN POINT
BOMBAY 400 021, INDIA
Telephone: 91-22-2049773/2851011
OFF RES: 91-22-2188044/2180004
Telefax: 91-22-2045960/2851011
Telex: 11-82405 DCS IN

New Delhi, India Office: B-92 Himalaya House, 23 Kasturba Gandhi Marg, 110 001. Telephone: 91-11-3318300/3731400. Telefax: 91-11-3314413/3713383. Telex: 31-62662 DCS IN. Mobile Car Tel: 91-11-4613334. Cable: SINGANIACO.
Branches also in: Bangalore, Calcutta, Delhi, Hyderabad, Madras, London and New York.

General Practice.

FIRM PROFILE: *Founded in 1969 by Mr. D.C. Singhania provides comprehensive legal services primarily in Corporate and Business law practice. It is one of the leading law firms in India based in New Delhi but having branch offices at Bombay, Calcutta, Madras, Bangalore and Hyderabad in India and also representative offices at London and New York.*

MEMBER OF FIRM

K.G. SINGHANIA. LANGUAGES: English and Hindi. **PRACTICE AREAS:** Corporate Law; Arbitration; Joint Venture; Intellectual Property.

ASSOCIATES

S.N. Hassan

Bakhtawar N. Karbhari
Manjula N. Kulkarni

CONSULTANTS

M.N. Bhatkal

(For complete biographical data on all Personnel, see Professional Biographies at New Delhi, India).

WHITE & CASE

International Lawyers
THE TAJ MAHAL HOTEL
GROUND FLOOR, OLD WING
APOLLO BUNDER
BOMBAY 400 001, INDIA
Telephone: (91-22) 282-6300
Facsimile: (91-22) 282-6305

New York, New York: Telephone: 212-819-8200. Facsimile: 212-354-8113.
Washington, D.C.: Telephone: 202-872-0013. Facsimile: 202-872-0210.
Los Angeles, California: Telephone: 213-620-7700. Facsimile: 213-687-0758; 213-617-2205.
Miami, Florida: Telephone: 305-371-2700. Facsimile: 305-358-5744.
Mexico City, Mexico: Telephone: (52-5) 207-9717. Facsimile: (52-5) 208-3628.
Tokyo, Japan: Telephone: (81-3) 3239-4300. Facsimile: (81-3) 3239-4330.
Hong Kong: Telephone: (852) 2822-8700. Facsimile: (852) 2845-9070; Grice & Co., Solicitors, Telephone: (852) 2826-0333. Facsimile: (852) 2526-7166.

(This Listing Continued)

Singapore, Republic of Singapore: Telephone: (65) 225-6000. Facsimile: (65) 225-6009.

Bangkok, Thailand: Pacific Legal Group Ltd., In Association With White & Case, Telephone: (662) 236-6154/7. Facsimile: (662) 237-6771.

Hanoi, Viet Nam: Representative Office, Telephone: (84-4) 227-575/6/7. Facsimile: (84-4) 227-297.

London, England: Telephone: (44-171) 726-6361. Facsimile: (44-171) 726-4314; (44-171) 726-8558.

Paris, France: Telephone: (33-1) 42-60-34-05. Facsimile: (33-1) 42-60-82-46.

Brussels, Belgium: Telephone: (32-2) 647-05-89. Facsimile: (32-2) 647-16-75.

Stockholm, Sweden: Telephone: (46-8) 679-80-30. Facsimile: (46-8) 611-21-22.

Helsinki, Finland: Telephone: (358-0) 631-100. Facsimile: (358-0) 179-477.

Moscow, Russia: Telephone: (7-095) 201-9292/3/4/5. Facsimile: (7-095) 201-9284.

Budapest, Hungary: Telephone: (36-1) 269-0550; (36-1) 131-0933. Facsimile: (36-1) 269-1199.

Prague, Czech Republic: Telephone: (42-2) 2481-1796. Facsimile: (42-2) 232-5522.

Warsaw, Poland: Telephone/Facsimile: (48-22) 26-80-53; (48-22) 27-84-86. International Telephone/Facsimile: (48-39) 12-19-06.

Istanbul, Turkey: Telephone: (90-212) 275-68-98; (90-212) 275-75-33. Facsimile: (90-212) 275-75-43.

Ankara, Turkey: Telephone: (90-312) 446-2180. Facsimile: (90-312) 437-9677.

Jeddah, Saudi Arabia: Law Office of Hassan Mahassni, Telephone: (966-2) 651-3535. Facsimile: (966-2) 651-3636.

Riyadh, Saudi Arabia: Law Office of Hassan Mahassni, Telephone: (966-1) 476-7099. Facsimile: (966-1) 479-0110.

Almaty, Kazakhstan: Telephone: (7-3272) 50-7491/2. Facsimile: (7-3272) 61-0842.

General Practice.

RESIDENT MANAGING ATTORNEY

RAJ PANDE, born Poona, India, December 5, 1955; admitted, 1988, New York (Not admitted in India). *Education:* McGill University (B.Eng., 1979; LL.B., M.B.A./B.C.L., 1987).

(For biographical data as to other locations, see Professional Biographies at New York, New York; Washington, D.C.; Los Angeles, California; Miami, Florida; Mexico City, Mexico; Tokyo, Japan; Hong Kong; Singapore, Republic of Singapore; Bangkok, Thailand; Hanoi, Viet Nam; London, England; Paris, France; Brussels, Belgium; Stockholm, Sweden; Helsinki, Finland; Moscow, Russia; Budapest, Hungary; Prague, Czech Republic; Warsaw, Poland; Istanbul and Ankara, Turkey; Jeddah and Riyadh, Saudi Arabia; Almaty, Kazakhstan).

AMARCHAND & MANGALDAS & HIRALAL SHROFF & CO.

Advocates & Solicitors

Established in 1990

NO. 3 ANAND LOK, 227 A.J.C. BOSE MARG
(LOW CIRCULAR ROAD)
CALCUTTA, INDIA
Telephone: (91-33) 2470508
FAX: (91-33) 2472349

ASSOCIATE

Neelina Chatterjee

(For Complete Biographical Data, see Professional Biographies at Bombay, India)

T.P. DATTA & SONS

Established in 1950

Patents • TradeMarks • Designs • Copyright

**COMMERCE HOUSE • 2 GANESH CHANDRA AVENUE
CALCUTTA 700 013, INDIA**
Fax: (91-33) 27-9936 / 26-5800 / 28-5229

Washington D.C., USA Liaison Office: P.O. BOX 63, College Park, MD 20741, 0063, USA. Fax: (301) 699-0193

New York City, USA Liaison Office: 267 Fifth Avenue, Suite 801-118, 10016, USA. Telephone: (212) 560-7447 Fax: (212) 679-2310.

London, England, European Liaison Office: 213 Sirdar Road, N22 6QU.

Intellectual Property Law dealing with Patents, TradeMarks, Designs, and Copyright including Licensing and Technology Transfer in India. Associates in South/South-east Asia including Bangladesh, Bhutan, Burma, Indonesia, Nepal, Pakistan, Thailand & Sri Lanka.

D. Datta   **B.G. Ray**
P.K. Chakravorti   **A.K. Banerjee**

FOX & MANDAL

Solicitors & Advocates

Established in 1896

**12, OLD POST OFFICE STREET
CALCUTTA 700 001, INDIA**
*Telephone: 91 33 248 4843/8970/6681
Telex: 91 21 2793
Fax: 91 33 248 0832*

Bangalore, India Office: 3A & 3B Fernville, 4 Infantry Road Cross, 560 001. Telephone: 91 80 559 1949. Fax: 91 80 559 1949.

New Delhi, India Associated Office: Fox Mandal & Co., No. 1, Doctor's Lane, Gole Market, 110 001. Telephone: 91 11 34 4586/334 6872. Telex: 91 31 61 301. Fax: 91 11 373 2591.

Company, Property and Planning, Litigation, Joint Ventures and Collaborations, Shipping and Admiralty, Tax, Clientele, includes Indian and Foreign Companies and Banks.

FIRM PROFILE: Established in 1896, its affairs are being conducted by the following Solicitors and Advocates.

MEMBERS OF FIRM

D. Mandal	**K. Chunder**
R.N. Dhar	**Shuva Mandal**
A.K. Mandal	**K. Mandal**
S.K. Dhar	**D. Sen**
A.K. Dhar	**S. Mukherjee**
Anil Dhar	**P. Das**
Ms. J. Auddy	**P. Mandal**
A. Sarkar	**Ms. K. Mandal**
Ms. B. Mandal	**Shourya Mandal**
	D. Mukherjee

KHAITAN & CO.

Advocates and Notaries

Established in 1911

**9 OLD POST OFFICE STREET
CALCUTTA 700 001, INDIA**
*Telephone: (91) (33) 248 1249; 248 9787
Telefax: (91) (33) 248 7656; 220 7857
Telegram: KHAITANCO , CALCUTTA*

Bangalore, India Office: Sunrise Chambers, 22 Ulsoor Road, 560 042. Telephone: (91) (80) 559 7466. Telefax: (91) (80) 559 7452.

New Delhi, India Office: Himalaya House, 23 Kasturba Grandhi Marg, 110 001. Telephone: (91) (11) 331 3033. Telefax: (91) (11) 332 7314.

The firm is engaged in general legal practice in India with offices in Bangalore, Calcutta and New Delhi. Its areas of practice include Administrative Law, Antitrust Law, Arbitration Law, Banking Law, Bankruptcy Law, Business Litigation, Business Ownership and Succession, Constitutional Law, Conveyancing, Co-operative Law, Corporate Law, Criminal Law, Customs Law, Ecological and Environmental Law, Electricity and Energy

(This Listing Continued)

KHAITAN & CO., Calcutta—Continued

Law, Employment Law, Estate Planning, Excise Law, Family Law, Foreign Exchange and Investment Law, Franchising Law, Insurance Law, Intellectual Property, International Finance and Trade Law including Foreign Capital Issues, Joint Ventures and Collaboration Agreements, Labour Law, Maritime Law, Mergers and Acquisitions, Pensions and Profit Sharing, Personal Injury, Products Liability, Public Interest Litigation, Real Estate Law, Securities Law, Taxation Laws, Trust and Probate.

FIRM PROFILE: *Founded in 1911 by the late Debi Prasad Khaitan, a member of the Constituent Assembly that framed the Constitution of India in 1950. The firm has a broad based practice with a reputation of offering a full range of quality legal services. It is one of the leading commercial law firms in Bangalore, Calcutta and New Delhi. Clients include large business houses, multi national companies, banks, financial institutions, governmental bodies, educational and charitable institutions and individuals. The three offices of the firm have 12 partners and 55 full time associates.*

PARTNERS

RAM KISHORE CHOUDHURY, born 1936; admitted, 1960, India. *Education:* (B.Com., LL.B.). *Member:* Bar Association of Calcutta High Court; Income-tax Bar Association, Calcutta; Supreme Court of India Bar Association; Indian Council of Arbitration; International Bar Association, London; International Law Association, London.

PRADIP KUMAR KHAITAN, born 1941; admitted, 1965, India. *Education:* (B.Com., LL.B.). Attorney-at-Law. *Member:* Incorporated Law Society of Calcutta, Supreme Court of India Bar Association; Indian Council of Arbitration, International Court of Arbitration, Paris.

PURUSHOTTAM LAL AGARWAL, born 1942; admitted, 1966, India. *Education:* (B.Com., LL.B.). Attorney-at-Law. *Member:* Incorporated Law Society of Calcutta.

RAM NIRANJAN JHUNJHUNWALA, born 1941; admitted, 1966, India. *Education:* (B.Com., LL.B.). Notary Public and Attorney-at-Law. *Member:* Bar Association of Calcutta High Court; Incorporated Law Society of Calcutta; Supreme Court of India Bar Association; International Law Association, London; Honorary Organizing Secretary of International Law Association; Calcutta Centre of Regional Branch, India.

PRAMOD KHAITAN, born 1946; admitted, 1969, India. *Education:* (B.Com., LL.B.). Attorney-at-Law. *Member:* Incorporated Law Society of Calcutta; Supreme Court of India Bar Association.

UMESH KHAITAN, born 1948; admitted, 1972, India. *Education:* (B.A., Hons., LL.B.). *Member:* Delhi High Court Bar; Incorporated Law Society of Calcutta; Supreme Court of India Bar Association; Monopolies & Restrictive Trade Practices Bar; Indian Council of Arbitration; International Bar Association, London.

NAND GOPAL KHAITAN, born 1951; admitted, 1974, India. *Education:* (B.Com., LL.B.). Notary Public and Attorney-at-Law. *Member:* Incorporated Law Society of Calcutta; Supreme Court of India Bar Association; Public Grievance Committee; Collectorate of Customs; Government of India.

GAURI SANKAR ASOPA, born 1950; admitted, 1974, India. *Education:* (B.Com., LL.B.). Attorney-at-Law. *Member:* Incorporated Law Society of Calcutta.

PADAM KHAITAN, born 1953; admitted, 1976, India. *Education:* (B.Com.). Attorney-at-Law. *Member:* Incorporated Law Society of Calcutta.

ASSOCIATES

PURUSHOTTAM LAL KHAITAN, born 1928; admitted, 1957, India. *Education:* (B.Com., LL.B.). Attorney-at-Law. *Member:* Incorporated Law Society of Calcutta; Bar Association of Calcutta High Court; City Civil Court Calcutta Bar Association; Supreme Court Of India Bar Association.

RAMENDRA NATH MALLIK, born 1933; admitted, 1957, India. *Education:* (B.Com., LL.B.). Attorney-at-Law. *Member:* Incorporated Law Society of Calcutta.

NAGENDRA CHANDRA SHAH, born 1935; admitted, 1960, India. *Education:* (B.Com., LL.B.). Notary Public. *Member:* Bar Association of Calcutta High Court; Supreme Court of India Bar Association; International Bar Association, London.

(This Listing Continued)

SHREE KRISHNA LATH, born 1942; admitted, 1966, India. *Education:* (B.Com., LL.B.). Attorney-at-Law. *Member:* Incorporated Law Society of Calcutta.

RAMESH CHOUDHURY, born 1943; admitted, 1968, India. *Education:* (M.Com., LL.B.).

LALIT KUMAR PODDAR, born 1945; admitted, 1969, India. *Education:* (B.Sc., LL.B.). Attorney-at-Law. *Member:* Incorporated Law Society of Calcutta.

CHAND MAL GHORAWAT, born 1946; admitted, 1970, India. *Education:* (B.A., LL.B., LL.M.). *Member:* Incorporated Law Society of Calcutta, Bar Association; Customs, Excise & Gold (Control) Appellate Tribunal, New Delhi.

PURUSHOTTAM BALODIA, born 1946; admitted, 1973, India. *Education:* (B.Com., LL.B.).

ANGSHU MOHAN SEN, born 1947; admitted, 1974, India. *Education:* (B.A., LL.B.). *Member:* Baharampure Bar Association; City Civil Court Calcutta Bar Association.

AJOY KUMAR DEY, born 1948; admitted, 1975, India. *Education:* (B.Com., LL.B.). *Member:* Bar Association of Calcutta High Court.

OM PRAKASH AGARWAL, born 1952; admitted, 1975, India. *Education:* (B.Com.). Attorney-at-Law. *Member:* Incorporated Law Society of Calcutta.

OM PRAKASH JHUNJHUNWALA, born 1954; admitted, 1976, India. *Education:* (B.Com., Hons, LL.B.). Attorney-at-Law. *Member:* Incorporated Law Society of Calcutta.

TAPAS KUMAR CHOUDHURY, born 1953; admitted, 1977, India. *Education:* (B.A., LL.B.). *Member:* Bar Association of Calcutta High Court.

(MRS.) KUSUM DADOO, born 1953; admitted, 1978, India. *Education:* (B.Sc., LL.B.). Attorney-at-Law. *Member:* Incorporated Law Society.

DEBRAJ MUKHERJEE, born 1948; admitted, 1980, India. *Education:* (B.Com., LL.B.). *Member:* Incorporated Law Society of Calcutta.

(MRS.) ROOPA SHETH-MITRA, born 1958; admitted, 1983, India. *Education:* (B.A., LL.B.). *Member:* Incorporated Law Society of Calcutta; Supreme Court of India Bar Association; International Law Association, London.

RAJIV KHAITAN, born 1960; admitted, 1986, India. *Education:* (B.Com., LL.B.). *Member:* Incorporated Law Society of Calcutta.

ARVIND KUMAR JHUNJHUNWALA, born 1958; admitted, 1989, India. *Education:* (F.C.A., A.C.S., B.Com., Hons., LL.B.). *Member:* Incorporated Law Society of Calcutta; Institute of Chartered Accountants of India; Institute of Company Secretaries of India.

(MS.) SAROJ AGARWAL, born 1961; admitted, 1990, India. *Education:* (B.A., LL.B.).

RATNESH RAI, born 1966; admitted, 1990, India. *Education:* (B.A., LL.B.). *Member:* Incorporated Law Society of Calcutta.

AJAY CHOUDHURY, born 1965; admitted, 1993, India. *Education:* (B.Com., LL.B.).

VIVEK MURARKA, born 1965; admitted, 1993, India. *Education:* (B.Com., LL.B., C.A.).

ANIKET AGARWAL, born 1967; admitted, 1993, India. *Education:* (LL.B.).

SINGHANIA & CO.

E-1, 75-C PARK STREET
CALCUTTA 700 016, INDIA
Telephone: 91-33-292759/295088/295093/296042
Telefax: 91-33-292751
Telex: 21-2763 DCS IN

New Delhi, India Office: B-92 Himalaya House, 23 Kasturba Gandhi Marg, 110 001. Telephone: 91-11-3318300/3731400. Telefax: 91-11-3314413/3713383. Telex: 31-62662/DCS IN. Mobile Car Tel: 91-11-4613334. Cable: SINGANIACO.

Branches also in: Bangalow, Bombay, Delhi, Hyderabad, Madras, London and New York.

General Practice.
(This Listing Continued)

FIRM PROFILE: *Founded in 1969 by Mr. D.C. Singhania provides comprehensive legal services primarily in Corporate and Business law practice. It is one of the leading law firms in India based in New Delhi but having branch offices at Bombay, Calcutta, Madras, Bangalore and Hyderabad in India and also representative offices at London and New York.*

ASSOCIATES

Kunal Sarkar

CONSULTANT

Amal Dutta
K.K. Mukherjee

(For complete biographical data on all Personnel, see Professional Biographies at New Delhi, India)

SINGHANIA & CO.

614 BABU KHAN ESTATE
BASHIR BAGH
HYDERABAD 500 029, INDIA
Telephone: 91-40-236219
Telefax: 91-40-241779

New Delhi, India Office: B-92 Himalaya House, 23 Kasturba Gandhi Marg, 110 001. Telephone: 91-11-3318300/3731400. Telefax: 91-11-3314413/3713383. Telex: 31-62662 DCS IN. Mobile Car Tel: 91-11-4613334. Cable: SINGANIACO.
Branches also in: Bangalore, Bombay, Calcutta, Delhi, Madras, London and New York.

General Practice.

FIRM PROFILE: *Founded in 1969 by Mr. D.C. Singhania provides comprehensive legal services primarily in Corporate and Business law practice. It is one of the leading law firms in India based in New Delhi but having branch offices at Bombay, Calcutta, Madras, Bangalore and Hyderabad in India and also representative offices at London and New York.*

ASSOCIATES

Chundi Sai Kumar

(For complete biographical data on all Personnel, see Professional Biographies at New Delhi, India)

SINGHANIA & CO.

1 RAYALA TOWERS
781-785 ANNA SALAI
MADRAS 600 002, INDIA
Telephone: 91-44-835626
Telefax: 91-44-843110
Telex: 41-5287 DCS IN

New Delhi, India Office: B-92 Himalaya House, 23 Kasturba Gandhi Marg, 110 001. Telephone: 91-11-3318300/3731400. Telefax: 91-11-3314413/3713383. Telex: 31-62662 DCS IN. Mobile Car Tel: 91-11-4613334. Cable: SINGANIACO.
Branches also in: Bangalore, Bombay, Calcutta, Delhi, Hyderabad, London and New York.

General Practice.

FIRM PROFILE: *Founded in 1969 by Mr. D.C. Singhania provides comprehensive legal services primarily in Corporate and Business law practice. It is one of the leading law firms in India based in New Delhi but having branch offices at Bombay, Calcutta, Madras, Bangalore and Hyderabad in India and also representative offices at London and New York.*

ASSOCIATES

Raj Kishore   **S. Rajendran**

CONSULTANTS

T. Raghavan   **M.B. Gopalan**
Uttam Reddy

(For complete biographical data on all Personnel, see Professional Biographies at New Delhi, India)

SRIRAM & ASSOCIATES

6, II CROSS STREET
KARPAGAM GARDENS, ADYAR
MADRAS 600 020, INDIA
Telephone: (44) 4914451/4914452
Fax: (44) 4919083

General Civil, Commercial and Corporate Law, Customs and Excise duties, Trademarks, Arbitration, Conveyancing and Property Development, Litigation, Agreements, Collaborations, Mediation.

FIRM PROFILE: *The firm has eight associates with additional support staff. It offers a range of legal services. It has links with law firms in the main cities of India. The firm represents leading companies. Members of the firm also take up public interest causes pro bono.*

SENIOR PARTNER

PANCHU SRIRAM. *Education:* Elphinstone College, Bombay (B.A., Hons.); Government Law College, Bombay (LL.B.). Fellow, Salzburg Seminar. *Member:* International Bar Association; Lawasia. **LANGUAGES:** English and Indian.

SURANA & SURANA

Established in 1971

Attorneys-at-Law & Advocates
NATIONAL INSURANCE BUILDING
NO. 224, N.S.C. BOSE ROAD
MADRAS 600 001, INDIA
Telephone: 91-44-580387; 91-44-581616
Fax: 91-44-583339
Cable Address: "COURTWORK" Madras
Contact after Office hours: (7pm to 9pm I.S.T.) No. 164, Kutchery Road, Mylapore, Madras-600 004 (India)
Telephone: 91-44-845780; 91-44-842018

General practice and litigation in all Courts, conveyancing, International joint ventures/collaborations and Investments, Corporation and Commercial Laws, Copyright, Patents, Designs, Trade Marks, Admiralty, Aviation and Maritime Law, Banking and Investments, Insurance, National and International Commercial Arbitration, Time Shares, Human Rights, Privatization, Satellite and Computer Technology, Technology Transfers, Foreign Trade, International Law, Drafting and Negotiating Private and Public Sector Company Contracts, Environment Law, Constitutional Law, Administrative Law, Lobbying, Consumer Law, Entertainment Law.

FIRM PROFILE: *Surana & Surana (Established 1971; formerly known as P.S. Surana & Co.) is one of the largest Law firms in South India. Having its office opposite the Madras High Court. This partnership firm has a total of 18 attorneys including 4 Senior Counsel with an average experience at the bar of about 30 years. The capabilities of the firm's attorneys, paralegals, secretaries, stafff and infrastructure are being continuously upgraded and expanded to handle virtually any legal need and to provide quality legal service in all areas of law. This efficient dynamic and professionally managed firm values and enjoys long term relationships with its clients and has the reputation, the capabilities and the resources to handle particularly difficult and challenging matters including those involving multiple parties, legal ground breaking, and an immediate commitment of resources to achieve immediate relief. The firm has a flair for being innovative and a tradition for offering sound, economic and quick solutions to its clients. The firm is dedicated to the success of its clients and believes in being practical and result oriented.*

The firm is well know for its Civil, Commercial and Constitutional work and it expertise in negotiation and commercial arbitrations. The firm services clients across the globe and is retained by many business groups and companies.

SENIOR ADVOCATES

P.S. SURANA, born Rajasthan, India, October 26, 1950; admitted, 1971, India. *Education:* A.M. Jain College, Madras Law College (M.A.). Argued Cases in High Courts and Supreme Court of India; represents clients in Europe and U.S.A. Arbitrator for Tube Investments of India Group, Daraprakash Group and other leading business groups. Judge Philip C. Jessup International Law Moot Court Competition. Life Member, YMCA. Deputy District Governor, Lions Clubs International District 324-A. Member: South India Chamber of Commerce; Hindustan Chamber of Commerce; International Society For Krishna Consciousness (ISKON); Execu-

(This Listing Continued)

SURANA & SURANA, Madras—Continued

tive Committee, Tamilmadu Legal Aid Board. *Member:* Bar Association of Madras; Madras High Court Advocates Associations; Indian Council of Arbitration; S.S. Jain Medical Relief Society (Life Member); International Jurist Organisation (IJO), Asia Chapter; Punjab Association (Vice President); Management Committee of S.S. Jain Educational Society; Indian Vegetarian Congress. *LANGUAGES:* English, Hindi, Tamil and Rajasthani. *PRACTICE AREAS:* International and National Commercial Arbitration; Civil and Constitutional Litigation; Commercial Contracts.

G.V.S. IYER, born Kolar, May 8, 1926; admitted, 1952, High Court, Madras. *LANGUAGES:* English, Hindi, Tamil, Telugu and Canarese. *PRACTICE AREAS:* Civil Litigation; Real Estate Litigation.

C.S. GOPALAKRISHNAN, born Calicut, July 19, 1930; admitted, 1957, Kerala High Court. *Education:* Madras Christian College; Madras Law College. *LANGUAGES:* English, Malayalam and Tamil. *PRACTICE AREAS:* Civil Law; Arbitration; Corporate Trade Litigation.

MRS. LEELA SURANA, born Coonoor, March 26, 1955; admitted, 1980. *Education:* Providence College, Coonoor; Madras Law College. Member: Management Committee of G.S.S. College for Women; Pranic Healers Foundation, Tamil Nadu. President, Lioness Club of Nanganallur. *Member:* Bar Association of Madras; Madras High Court Advocates Association. *PRACTICE AREAS:* Arbitration; Trade Litigation; Real Estate.

The firm is a Member of Commercial Law Affiliates (CLA), a world wide affiliation of business and litigation law firms, Minneapolis, MN 55401 U.S.A.

REPRESENTATIVE CLIENTS: (A) (Government of India bodies) Rharal Petroleum Corporation; State Bank of India and Associate Banks; Punjab National Bank; Indian Bank, (B) (Foreign Collaboration Industries/Companico); Greaves Ltd; Carborundum Universal Ltd; E.I.D. Parry (India) Ltd; London Rubber Co., Ltd; Tube Investment of India Ltd; MTL Instruments Ltd; Enfield India Ltd; Nalli Group of Companies; Dasaprakash Group of Hotels and Restaurants; Federation of All India Hotels and Restaurants Association; All India Hire Purchase Associations; Shoppers and Investment Finance Co., Ltd; Devraj Nensee and Co Export House.

AMARCHAND & MANGALDAS & HIRALAL SHROFF & CO.

Advocates, Solicitors & Notary

Established in 1954

UNITED INDIA LIFE BUILDING, BLOCK F

CONNAUGHT PLACE

NEW DELHI 110 001, INDIA

Telephone: (91-11) 3314637; 3315690; 3310179

Fax: (91-11) 3312586; 6438237

Telex: 031-61397 AMCO IN

Cable: LEGAID

Delhi Litigation Office: 13, Abul Fazl Road. Near Bengali Market. New Delhi. 110001. Telephone: (91 11) 3355148; 3355149. Fax: (91 11) 3355147.

MEMBER

Shardul S. Shroff

ASSOCIATES

Pallavi Shroff	*Ajoy Roy*
Ritu Bhalla	*Monica Sharma*
Rashika Gupta	*Sumeeta Arora*
	Anirudha Das

OF COUNSEL

P.N. BHAGWATI Retired Chief Justice of Supreme Court of India.

(For Complete Biographical Data, see Professional Biographies at Bombay, India)

ANAND AND ANAND

ADVOCATES

Established in 1980

1, JAIPUR ESTATE

NIZAMUDDIN EAST

NEW DELHI 110 013, INDIA

Telephone: 4619639; 4615833; 4623148

Cable Address: "Trademark"

Telex: 031-65473 ACME IN

Fax: 011-4624243; 011-4632020; 011-3325045

Intellectual and Industrial Property Law including Prosecution and Litigation relating to Patents, Trademarks, Designs, Copyrights, Unfair Competition and related Antitrust Law and Criminal Matters before Courts and Expert Tribunals. Trade Secrets, Licensing and Franchising.

MEMBERS OF FIRM

RAJ K. ANAND (1938-1992).

N.K ANAND, born New Delhi, India, October 27, 1928; admitted, 1954, India. *Education:* Delhi University (B.A., 1951; LL.B., 1954). Author: "Counterfeiting and Piracy," read in 19th Biennial Conference IBA, October 1982; "Menace of Video Piracy," read at The National Seminar of Film and Video Piracy, Bombay, April 1987. *Member:* Bar Council of India; Supreme Court Bar Association; Delhi High Court Bar Association (Vice President, 1974-1976); International Bar Association; AIPPI (Founder President, Indian Group, 1985—); Patent and Trademark Bar Association. *LANGUAGES:* Indian and English.

AMARJIT SINGH MONGA, born Amritsar, India, January 26, 1953; admitted, 1976, India. *Education:* Delhi University (M.A.; LL.B., 1975). *Member:* Bar Council of India; Delhi High Court Bar Association (Member, Managing Committee, 1977-1978); District Court Bar Association. *LANGUAGES:* Indian and English.

PRAVIN ANAND, born New Delhi, India, May 5, 1955; admitted, 1979, India. *Education:* Delhi University (B.Sc. Chemistry, 1976; LL.B., 1979). Author: "Licensing of Technology and Intellectual Property Rights," read in 19th Biennial Conference IBA, October, 1982, published in International Business Lawyer, September, 1983; "Licensing of Technology," read at WIPO - UNDP - LAWASIA Conference, Bangkok, Thailand, March, 1983; "Criminal Provisions in Intellectual Property Right Legislation A Comparative Analysis," read in 20th Biennial Conference IBA, Vienna, September, 1984; "Doing Business in South Asia Legal Aspects (Trademarks)", Joint Regional Conference of IBA, LAWASIA and Bar Association of India, Bombay, February, 1986; "The Advantages to India in Acceding to the Paris Convention," National Seminar Organized by Faculty of Law and NISTADS, New Delhi, March, 1986; "North South Cooperation and Developing Countries," Vienna, June 1986; "Legal Protection of Computer Software and Integrated Circuits," Conference of Trademark Owners Association, Bombay, February 1987. Co-Author: "Regulatory Issues in Computer and Video Software," UNESCO, September 1987; Distinctiveness and Registrability of Marks; The Use, Assignment and Licensing of Marks-WIPO Training Course, Canberra, February 1988; Technology Transfer - Legal Guidelines and Contractual Practices, Les Conference, Sydney-April 1988. Franchising and Trade Mark Licensing-Paper read at Seminar on Licensing and Technology Transfer Arrangements, WIPO-FICCI, New Delhi, November 24 to 26, 1988. Speaker at WIPO Technology Transfer Seminar at Hanoi, Vietnam, April 1989; Industrial Property rights in developing Countries-AIPPI Congress, Amsterdam, June 1989. Contributor, Chapter on India in "Protecting Intellectual Property in Asia-Pacific," Longman Professional, 1989; "Arbitration in the Context of technology transfer agreement," New Delhi, 5th to 7th January, 1990, International Conference on arbitration organized by chartered Institute of Arbitrators, London and Hong Kong. Speaker: SAIC seminar on protection of trade names - Beijing, China, May, 1990; Symposium on Industrial Designs organized by WIPO at Amboise, France, October 4-5, 1990; SAARCLAW Conference in Colombo, Srilanka in 1991 and at the IPA Congress at New Delhi in January 1992. Speaker at APAA, Chiang Mai, Thailand (1992) AND Kuala Lumpur, Malaysia (1993); Speaker at Conference on "Doing Business with the New India," organized by the Institute of International Law & Business, New York (1994); Speaker at Conference on "Doing Business with the New India," organized by EURO Forum, London (1994). Contributor, Chapter on India in "Worldwide Trade Secrets Law," Clark Boardman Callaghan. Expert Witness before Parliamentary Committees for Trademark & Copyright Amendment Bills. Member, Committee on Paris Convention, Constituted by FICCI-May 1986; Reporter of ILR (Delhi

(This Listing Continued)

High Court), 1983-1984. Editorial Board of IP Asia, Entertainment Law, 1990—. Member, Expert Group on Foreign Collaboration and Arbitration Constituted by Department of Science and Technology, Government of India and Expert Group formed under the Auspices of Indo American Chamber of Commerce; Expert group appointed by WIPO for considering the applicability of arbitration to intellectual property. Expert Group to Consider Legislative Changes in Patents Act, Constituted by Government of India. *Member:* Bar Council of India; Delhi High Court Bar Association; International Bar Association; International Law Association; AIPPI (Member, Executive Committee, Indian Group, 1985—), APAA, APLA, American Intellectual Property Law Association, License Negotiation; Patent, Trademark and Copyright Litigation and Prosecution; Transfer of Technology. *LANGUAGES:* English and Indian.

ASSOCIATES

DEBJIT GUPTA, born Ranchi, India, April 1, 1965; admitted, 1989, India. *Education:* Ranchi University (B.Sc., Physics); Delhi University (LL.B., 1989). *Member:* Bar Council of India; Delhi High Court Bar Association. *LANGUAGES:* Indian and English.

BINNY KALRA, born Jalandhar, India, January 11, 1968; admitted, 1990, India. *Education:* Punjab University (B.A.); Delhi University (LL.B., 1990). *Member:* Bar Council of India; Delhi High Court Bar Association. *LANGUAGES:* Indian and English.

SHANTI KUMAR, born Dera Ismail Khan, Pakistan, August 24, 1934; admitted, 1992, India. *Education:* Allahabad University (B.Sc., Physics; M.Sc., 1956); Texas University, USA (M.S., 1987); Calcutta University (LL.B., 1963). Former Joint Controller of Patents and Designs, Patent Office, Govt. Retired as Director, Department of Science and Technology, Govt. of India. *Member:* Bar Council of India; Delhi High Court Bar Association. *LANGUAGES:* Indian and English.

VIVEK GROVER, born New Delhi, India, May 15, 1956; admitted, 1983, India. *Education:* Delhi University (B.A.); Delhi University (LL.B., 1983). *Member:* Bar Council of India; Delhi High Court Bar Association. *LANGUAGES:* Indian and English.

PRATHIBA KOTHA, born Bangalore, India, July 20, 1969; admitted, 1991, India. *Education:* Bangalore University (LL.B., 1991); Cambridge University, UK (LL.M., 1992). *Member:* Bar Council of India. *LANGUAGES:* Indian and English.

REPRESENTATIVE CLIENTS: IBM; General Electric; BAT; Cartier; Chanel Ltd.; Avis Inc., U.S.A.; Kellogg Co., U.S.A.; K Mart Corp., U.S.A.; De La Rue Giori, S.A., Switzerland; Glaxo Group, U.K.; N.V. Phillips' Gloeilampenfabrieken, Holland; BSN, France; Carrier International Corp.; Playboy Enterprises Inc.; Adidas; Ralston Purina; Varian Inc.; Blue Cross & Blue Shield Association; Citizen Watch Co.; Toshiba; Toyota; ITC Ltd.; Tata & Mody Groups.

ASHURST MORRIS CRISP

6 AURANGZEB ROAD D-202
NEW DELHI 110011, INDIA
Telephone: (91 11) 301 4054
Facsimile: (91 11) 301 4089

London, England Office: Broadwalk House, 5 Appold Street, EC2A, 2HA. Telephone: 0171-638-1111. Telex: 8807067. Fax: 0171-972-7990.
Brussels, Belgium Office: Avenue Louise 65, 1050. Telephone: (32-2) 537 6895. Fax: (32-2) 537 4353.
Paris, France Office: 8, Rue Clement Marot 75008. Telephone: (33-1) 47 20 0088. Fax: (33-1) 47 20 0093.
Tokyo, Japan Office: Kioicho Building, 8th Floor. 3-12 Kioicho. Chiyoda-ku. 102. Telephone (81-3) 5276 5900. Fax: (81-3) 5276 5922.

This is a representative office which provides support and co-ordination in the structuring and negotiation of major infrastructure projects and energy related transactions.

RESIDENT PARTNER

G. PICTON-TUBERVILL

BHASIN & CO.

Advocates, Supreme Court of India
Established in 1970

10TH FLOOR
10, HAILEY ROAD
NEW DELHI 110 001, INDIA
Telephone: 3326968; 3322601; 3329878; 3315024
Cable Address: "Lawyerco", New Delhi
Telex: 31-66030 LAW IN
Fax: 91-11-3329273

Bombay, India Office: 116, Mittal Court, 'A' Wing, Backbay Reclamation, Nariman Point, Bombay - 400 021. Telephone: 2842050; 2042954. Telex: 118-5651 LAW IN. Fax: 91-22-2874332.

General Legal Practice, Litigation, Administrative, Antitrust, Arbitration, Aviation, Banking, Bankruptcy, Conveyancing, Competition, Constitutional Corporate, Foreign Investments, Industrial Relations, Labour, International Contracts, Oil and Mining, Property, Real Estate, International Taxation, Taxation of Foreign Nationals, Exchange Control and International Private Law, Consumer Protection and Liability.

FIRM PROFILE: Established in 1970, Bhasin & Company has grown to become one of the leading Law Firms in India and one of the very few to have regular offices in Delhi, Bombay, Calcutta and Madras. There are approximately 30 Lawyers in the firm which has established a name for prompt and competent legal services of highest standards. The activities of the firm are broad-based - from civil aviation and tourism industry to general litigation and arbitration with specialized experience in international transactions, loan financing and joint ventures. The firm has close association with leading law firms in U.K., U.S.A., Singapore, Japan and Canada. The firm is well known in commercial and business circles as well as in the professional bodies like the International Bar Association, Lawasia, World Association of Lawyers, Union Internationale des Avocats, Inter-Pacific Bar Association, International Chamber of Commerce etc.

MEMBERS OF FIRM

LALIT BHASIN, born Rawalpindi, January 19, 1939; admitted, 1962, India. *Education:* Hindu College; Delhi University (B.A.); Faculty of Law, University of Delhi (LL.B.). Council Member, Section on: Business LawInternational Bar Association. Deputy Secretary General for Indian Sub-Continent, International Bar Association. General Secretary, Union Internationale des Avocates, India. Council Member, Inter-Pacific Bar Association. General Secretary, Bar Association of India. President, Indian Society for Afro-Asian Studies. Member, Governing Body, Society for Indian Ocean Studies. *LANGUAGES:* English, Hindi and French. *PRACTICE AREAS:* International Contract Law; Constitutional Law; Aviation Law; Business Law; Corporate Law; Arbitration; Commercial Law; Civil Law; Consumer Law; Protection Law; Liability Law.

MS. NINA GUPTA, admitted, 1979, India. *Member:* Delhi High Court Bar Association; Supreme Court Bar Association. *LANGUAGES:* English and Hindi. *PRACTICE AREAS:* Litigation; International Taxation Law; Corporate Law; Aviation Law; Commercial Law.

RAMESHWAR DAYAL, born Delhi, February 2, 1924; admitted, 1982, India. *Education:* Punjab University (M.A.); Delhi University (LL.B.). *LANGUAGES:* English, Hindi and Urdu. *PRACTICE AREAS:* Civil Law; Administrative Law; Constitutional Law; Family Law.

ASSOCIATES

R.C. DHURU. *LANGUAGES:* English and Hindi. *PRACTICE AREAS:* Conveyancing; Real Estate Law.

S.B. VERMA. *LANGUAGES:* English and Hindi. *PRACTICE AREAS:* Criminal Law.

VIJAY GUPTA. *LANGUAGES:* English and Hindi. *PRACTICE AREAS:* Commercial Law; Litigation.

MS. KIRAN KALRA. *LANGUAGES:* English and Hindi. *PRACTICE AREAS:* Banking Law; Consumer Protection.

K.B. SWAMI. *LANGUAGES:* English and Hindi. *PRACTICE AREAS:* Industrial Relations; Labour Law.

SHISHIR SHARMA. *LANGUAGES:* English and Hindi. *PRACTICE AREAS:* International Contract Law; Exchange Control Law.

MADHU SMITA SWAMI. *LANGUAGES:* English and Hindi. *PRACTICE AREAS:* Corporate Law; Company Law; Taxation Law.

(This Listing Continued)

BHASIN & CO., New Delhi—Continued

MS. RATNA DWIVEDI. LANGUAGES: English and Hindi. **PRACTICE AREAS:** Litigation.

PRAVIN SHARMA. LANGUAGES: English and Hindi. **PRACTICE AREAS:** Industrial Relations; Labour Law.

B.N. DAS. LANGUAGES: English and Hindi. **PRACTICE AREAS:** Constitutional Law; Oil and Mining Law.

VIPLAV SHARMA. LANGUAGES: English and Hindi. **PRACTICE AREAS:** Civil Litigation; Administrative Law; Consumer Protection.

VIKRANT DHAWAN. LANGUAGES: English and Hindi. **PRACTICE AREAS:** Litigation.

VIJAY BARBOZA. LANGUAGES: English and Hindi. **PRACTICE AREAS:** Banking Law.

MS. KALPANE KUTTY KRISHNAMURTHY. LANGUAGES: English and Hindi. **PRACTICE AREAS:** Labour Law.

MS. MRIDUL SHARMA. LANGUAGES: English and Hindi. **PRACTICE AREAS:** Litigation.

MONHIT DHINGRA. LANGUAGES: English and Hindi. **PRACTICE AREAS:** Litigation.

MS. RACHNA BHUTANI. LANGUAGES: English and Hindi. **PRACTICE AREAS:** Litigation.

REPRESENTATIVE CLIENTS: Oil & Natural Gas Commission (ONGC); Hotel Corporation of India (Centaur Hotels - HCI); India Tourism Development Corporation (ITDC Group of Hotels); Nationalized Banks; Insurance Corporations; International Airports Authority of India; National Thermal Power Corporation; Sports Authority of India; Oil India Ltd.; State Bank of India; Industrial Development Bank of India; Unit Trust of India; Air India; Indian Airlines; Alitalia Airlines; Eithiopian Airlines; Delta Airlines; Kuwait Airways; Gulfair; Thai Airways; Modiluft Airways; City Link Airways; Jet Airways; Tata Companies; Birla Companies; Modi Group; J.K. Group; Reliance Companies; Hinduja Bros.; Escorts Group; Oberoi Group of Hotels; Larsen & Toubro Ltd.; Hindustan Aeronautics Ltd.; Anglo French Drug Co.; Bombay Mercantile Bank Ltd.; WIMCO Ltd.; Mercury Travels India Ltd.; Indo Bosch Gems & Jewelry Ltd.; Castrol India Ltd.; Hero Honda Group; AIP - 9; Shew Wallace & Co. Ltd.; Elbee Couriers, Hindustan Motors Ltd.; Premier Automobile Ltd.; Maruti Udyog Ltd,; Standard Chartered Bank; United States of America (US Agency for International Development); Assurance Foreningen Gard-Norway; Fertichem-Geneva; J.M. Huber Corp.; Northern Engineering Industries-England; American Express Bank, Ltd.; American Express (TRS) Services; Falcon Holding Group L.P.; The Bank of Nova Scotia; Jordine Insurance Consultants Ltd.

CHADBOURNE & PARKE ASSOCIATES

A16-B ANAND NIKETAN
110 021 NEW DELHI, INDIA
Telephone: 91-11-301-7568/7581/7582
Telecopier: 91-11-301-7351

New York, N.Y. Office: Chadbourne & Parke, 30 Rockefeller Plaza, 10112. Telephone: 212-408-5100. Telecopier: 212-541-5369.

Washington, D.C. Office: Chadbourne & Parke, Suite 900, 1101 Vermont Avenue, N.W., 20005. Telephone: 202-289-3000. Telecopier: 202-289-3002.

Los Angeles, California Office: Chadbourne & Parke, 601 South Figueroa Street, 90017. Telephone: 213-892-1000. Telecopier: 213-622-9865.

London, England Office: Chadbourne & Parke, 86 Jermyn Street, SW1 6JD. Telephone: 44-171-925-7400. Facsimile: 44-171-839-3393.

Moscow, Russia Office: Chadbourne & Parke, 38 Maxim Gorky Naberezhnaya, 113035. Telephone: 7095-974-2424. Telecopier: 7095-974-2425. International satellite lines via U.S.: Telephone: 212-408-1190. Telecopier: 212-408-1199.

Hong Kong Office: Chadbourne & Parke, Suite 3704, Peregrine Tower, Lippo Centre, 89 Queensway. Telephone: (852) 2842-5400. Telecopier: (852) 2521-7527.

General Practice.

RESIDENT PARTNER

GREGORY N. ULLMAN, born Jacksonville, Florida, June 30, 1958; admitted, 1984, New York (Not admitted in India). *Education:* University of Florida (B.A., 1980); Columbia University (J.D., 1983). Phi Beta Kappa; Omicron Delta Kappa.

(This Listing Continued)

RESIDENT ASSOCIATES

ANAND S. DAYAL, born Jamshedpur, India, March 12, 1965; admitted, 1993, New York (Not admitted in India). *Education:* Indian Institute of Technology (B.Tech., 1977); Cornell University (M.S., 1 981; J.D., cum laude, 1992).

SADHANA KAUL, born Lucknow, India, April 10, 1964; admitted, 1991, New York (Not admitted in India). *Education:* St. Stephens College, New Delhi, India (B.A., 1985); Trinity College, Cambridge University (Law Tripos, 1988); Georgetown University (LL.M., 1989). Charles Wallace Trust Scholar.

MEAGHAN MCGRATH, born Denver, Colorado, October 7, 1967; admitted, 1993, New York (Not admitted in India). *Education:* Columbia College (B.A., cum laude, Phi Beta Kappa, 1989); Georgetown University (J.D., cum laude, 1992).

JEFFREY B.L. MELLER, born Chappaqua, New York, February 21, 1949; admitted, 1980, Vermont and U.S. District Court, District of Vermont; 1981, U.S. Court of Appeals, Second Circuit (Not admitted in India). *Education:* Tufts University (B.A., magna cum laude, 1971); Vermont Law School (J.D., 1979). *Member:* Vermont and American Bar Associations; Association of Trial Lawyers of America; Indian Council of Arbitration.

(For Biographical Data of other Personnel, see Professional Biographies at New York, N.Y., Washington, D.C., Los Angeles, California, London, England, Moscow, Russia and Hong Kong)

J.B. DADACHANJI AND CO.
(J.B. DADACHANJI RAVINDER NARAIN MATHUR AND COMPANY)

Advocates, Supreme Court of India and High Courts

Established in 1961

JEEVAN VIHAR BUILDING
3, PARLIAMENT STREET
NEW DELHI 110 001, INDIA
Telephone: 311013; 312628; 312573; 345906; 3732663; 3732641; 3732061
Cable: Justicia, New Delhi (India)
Telex: 031-66519 JBD IN
Fax: 3732505; 3746029

General Litigation Practice, including Constitutional, Antitrust, Labor and Industrial Laws, Oil and Mining, Property and Real Estate Law and Litigation in the Supreme Court of India and State High Courts. Tribunals including Central Excise and Customs Duty and Industrial Tribunals, Monopolies and Restrictive Trade Practices Commission, Consumer Forums, Arbitration including International Commercial Arbitrations.

General Corporate Practice, Formation of Joint Ventures, Collaboration and Licensing Agreements, International Contract, Formation of Companies including Joint Venture Companies, Foreign Investments, Corporate Law, Taxation including Taxation of Foreign Corporations and Nationals, Foreign Exchange Control Laws and Banking.

MEMBERS OF FIRM

J.B. DADACHANJI, born October 12, 1921; admitted, 1944, India. *Education:* Bombay University (B.A., Hons.; LL.B). India Member of the Expert Group of the U.N. Commission for International Trade Law. Formerly President of Indo-American Chamber of Commerce (Northern India Council) and Member Advisory Board (India), Citibank N.A.

RAVINDER NARAIN, born May 15, 1937; admitted, 1959, India. *Education:* Delhi University, India (B.Sc.; LL.B.); Harvard Law School (Course in Antitrust Laws).

O. C. MATHUR, born January 11, 1932; admitted, 1953, India. *Education:* Delhi University, India (B.A.; LL.B.). Honorary Secretary Bar Association of India.

MRS. A. K. VARMA, born April 24, 1938; admitted, 1963, India and Barrister-at-Law, London. (B.A. Econ.).

OF COUNSEL

P. A. S. RAO

DR. MRS. TAMALI SENGUPTA (J.S.D., Stanford University, U.S.A.).

(This Listing Continued)

P.K. GANGULY

ASSOCIATES

D. N. Mishra	Aditya Narain
Ashok Sagar	S. Sukumaran
Ms. Meera Harchandani	Madhuaudan Harau Harau
Amitabh Marwah	Ms. Amrita Mitra
Ms. Sayali Phatak	Ms. Gauri Advani
A. Singh Pasrich, M.A. (Oxon)	Ms. Punita Singh
Punit Tyagi	Ms. Ruohira Johrl
Mohit Kapoor	Ms. Dimple Sahl
Ms. Sonu Bhatnagar	Rajan Narain

REPRESENTATIVE CLIENTS: IBM World Trade Corporation; Westinghouse Electric Corporation; ITT Far East Inc.; Union Carbide Corporation Inc.; Du Pont Far East Inc.; Citibank NA; Bank of America; Rolls Royce India Ltd.; Coca-Cola Export Corporation; Estee Lauder Inc.; Great Lake Carbon Corporation; Combustion Engineering Inc.; Snam Progetti E.P.A.; Nestle (India) Ltd.; Ciba-Gelgy; Pfizers Ltd.; Cit-Alcatel; Sumitomo Shoji Kalsha; Halder Topsoe A.S.; Lurgi Private Ltd.; Dornier Aviation; DCM-Toyota; Godfrey Philips India Ltd. (India Associate of Philip Morris); Goodyear India Ltd.; Tata Group of Companies; Hindustan Lever (Indian Associate of Unilever); General Electric (USA); Kellogg Co.; Dassault (France); Allied Signals (USA); ITC Ltd. (Indian Associate of British American Tobacco Co. U.K.); Baush & Lomb.

DR. R.P. DHOKALIA & ASSOCIATES

C-31 D, GANGOTRI, ALAKNANDA
NEW DELHI 110 019, INDIA
Telephone: 6470074
Fax: 011-6424707

Patents, Designs, Trademarks, Copyright and Trade Secrets and Related Litigation, Civil and Criminal in all Forums, Licensing and Franchising.

MEMBERS OF FIRMS

DR. B.S. CHANHAN, admitted, 1974, India. Education: B.H.U. (B.Sc., LL.B.); Manchester University, England (Ph.D.).

VIVEK DHOKALIA, admitted, 1981, India. Education: Delhi University (B.A., Hons.); B.H.U. (LL.B.); Southern Methodist University, U.S.A. (M.C.I.); Yale University, U.S.A. (LL.M.).

NAVIN SINHA, admitted, 1974, India. Education: Allahabad University (B.Sc., LL.B.).

N.C. BEOHAR, admitted, 1968, India. Education: B.H.U. (B.Sc., LL.B.).

VIKRAM DHOKALIA, admitted, 1989, India. Education: (B.A., Hons.); Delhi University (LL.B.).

CONSULTANTS

DR. R.P. DHOKALIA. Education: Manchester University, England (LL.B., Ph.D.).

SURESH C. BEOHAR. Education: (B.E., Mechanical Engineer).

FOX MANDAL & CO

Solicitors & Advocates

NO. 1, DOCTOR'S LANE
GOLE MARKET
NEW DELHI 110 001, INDIA
Telephone: 91 11 34 4586/334 6872
Telex: 91 31 61 301
Fax: 91 11 373 2591

Calcutta, India Office: Fox & Mandal, 12, Old Post Office Street, 700 001. Telephone: 91 33 248 4843/8970/6681. Telex: 91 21 2793. Fax: 91 33 248 0832.

Bangalore, India Office: 3A & 3B Fernvillle, 4, Infantry Road Cross, 560 001. Telephone: 91 80 559 1949. Fax: 91 80 559 1949.

General Practice in all Courts. Banking Law, Joint Ventures and Foreign Collaborations, Taxation, Shipping and Admiralty, Corporate Laws, Insurance, Conveyancing, Documentation, Company Formation and Acquisition, Merger and Takeover, Service Law.

MEMBERS OF FIRM

D. Mandal	A.K. Dhar
A.K. Mandal	I. Ghosh
A.K. Ghose	Som Mandal

(This Listing Continued)

Ms. Sangeeta Mandal
Advocate on Record Supreme Court of India.

INTEL ADVOCARE

Advocates, Patent & Trade Mark Attorneys and Legal Consultants
C-27, GREATER KAILASH ENCLAVE-1
NEW DELHI 110048, INDIA
Telephone: (011-91-11) 6470971; 6462437
Telex: 031-71271 BECN-IN
Fax: (011-91-11) 6464000

Intellectual and Industrial Property Rights including undertaking Registration and Litigation arising from infringements of trade marks, copyright, patents and design. Franchising, Foreign Collaborations, Corporate Laws, Contracts, Recoveries, Banking, Industrial Relations, Labour Laws, Regulatory Legislation for Commercial and Industrial Establishments, National Security Laws, Recoveries, FERRA and Customs Matters, Monopolies and Restrictive Trade Practices, Banking and Foreign Investments.

HEMANT SINGH, born Varanasi, 1959; admitted, 1982, New Delhi. Education: Campus Law Center, Delhi University (B.A., Hons, 1979; LL.B., 1982). Author: "Impact of Dunkel Draft in SAARC Region," read in Third SAARC Law Conference, January 28-30, 1994, New Delhi, India. Member: Bar Council of India; Indian Law Institute; Supreme Court Bar Association of India; Delhi High Court Bar Association; South Asian Association for Regional Co-operation (SAARC LAW). LANGUAGES: Indian and English. PRACTICE AREAS: Intellectual and Industrial Property Rights; Franchising and Foreign Collaborations; Corporate Laws; Contracts; Recoveries; Banking; Foreign Investments; Monopolies and Restrictives Trade Practices..

ASSOCIATES

B.M. AGGARWAL, born 1932; admitted, 1954. Education: Punjab University (B.Sc., M.A.); Delhi University (LL.B.). Served in Provincial Civil Service (Judicial) at Delhi and Punjab, 1961-1964. Law and Commercial Manager, DCM (Delhi Cloth and General Mills Co. Ltd.). Rejoined Bar in 1990. Member: Supreme Court Bar Association of India; New Delhi High Court Bar Association. LANGUAGES: Indian and English. PRACTICE AREAS: Commercial Law; Industrial Law; Civil Litigations; Technical Knowhow and Foreign Collaborations; M.R.T.P.; Labour; Corporate Laws.

VINOD KUMAR KHANNA, born 1941; admitted, 1962. Education: B.Sc., M.A. (Eco), LL.B., A.C.S. LANGUAGES: Indian and English. PRACTICE AREAS: Employer and Employee Relationships; Labour Laws; Industrial Relations; Factory Legislations.

REKHA AGGARWAL, born 1961; admitted, 1987. Education: St. Stephens College (B.A. Hons., English) Delhi University (LL.B.). Member: Supreme Court Bar Association of India; Delhi High Court Bar Association; Indian Law Institute. LANGUAGES: Indian and English. PRACTICE AREAS: FERRA; Customs; Electricity; Banking; Recoveries; National Security Laws.

LALL LAHIRI & SALHOTRA

N-128, PANCHSHEEL PARK
NEW DELHI 110017, INDIA
Telephone: (011) 643-6436, (011) 642-9923
Fax: 91-11-646-0816

All services connected with Patents, Trade marks, Copyrights and Designs.

FIRM PROFILE: Established in 1983, Lall Lahiri & Salhotra is a leading firm in the field of intellectual property. It is the only firm in India which has access to a computerized data base of all registered and advertised trade marks in India and are able to give trade mark and proprietor name searches within 10 hours. The firm has attached with it a specialized investigation agency for the investigation of patent and trade mark infringements. Litigation work is undertaken in any part of the country. Specialists in Joint venture Agreements and Technology Licensing Agreements.

PARTNERS

AMAR RAJ LALL, born Amritsar, India, March 21, 1928; admitted, 1953, India. Education: Government College, Lahore; London School of Economics (BSC,; M.A., Economics). Barrister-at-Law, Middle Temple, London, United Kingdom. Member: Bar Council of India; Supreme Court

(This Listing Continued)

LALL LAHIRI & SALHOTRA, New Delhi—Continued

Bar Association; Delhi High Court Bar Association; International Trademark Association. Contributor to the International Annual Review, INTA.

ANURADHA SALHOTRA, born New Delhi, India, September 29, 1958; admitted, 1981, India. *Education:* Jawahar Lal Nehru University (B.A., Honors, Bachelor-of-Law, 1980). Faculty of Law, University of Delhi, India. *Member:* Bar Council of India; Delhi High Court Bar Association; American Intellectual Property Law Association.

ASSOCIATES

CHAMUPATI KUMAR VIRMANI, born Pakistan, November 18, 1928; admitted, 1952, India. *Education:* Benaras Hindu University, College of Science (B.Sc., 1948; Bachelor-of-Law, 1951). Faculty of Law, University of Delhi, India. *Member:* Bar Council of India; Delhi High Court Bar Association.

SANGEETA GOEL, born New Delhi, India, September 30, 1958; admitted, 1982, India. *Education:* Gargi College (B.Comm, 1979); University of Delhi, India (Bachelor-of-Law, 1982). Faculty of Law, University of Delhi, India. *Member:* Bar Council of India.

VIKRAM BHATIA, born Ambala, India, July 25, 1966; admitted, 1988, India. *Education:* M.D. University, Rohtak (B.A., Law; B.L., 1988). Faculty of Law, M.D. University, Rohtak, India. *Member:* Bar Council of India; Delhi High Court Bar Association. *LANGUAGES:* English and Hindi.

N. RAJANI, born Kabul, Afghanistan, August 25, 1971; admitted, 1994. *Education:* Dr. Ambedkar Government Law College (B.A., 1992; Bachelor-of-Law, 1994).

CONSULTANT

SHARAD VADEHRA, born Lucknow, India, August 24, 1967; admitted, 1994, India. *Education:* S.G.T.B. Khalsa College, Delhi University (B.Sc., Honors, 1987; M.Sc., 1989); Hansraj College, Delhi University (Bachelor-of-Law, 1994). Faculty of Law, Law Center, New Delhi, India. *Member:* Bar Council of India, Delhi High Court Bar Association.

RAJINDER NARAIN & CO.

14-F, CONNAUGHT PLACE
NEW DELHI 110 001, INDIA
Telephone: 331 32 32; 331 20 66; 332 53 01; 372 38 49; 371 32 87
373 96 27; 373 96 29; 335 28 31
Cable Address: "LEGAL"
Delhi Telex: (031) 61915
Fax: (+91 11) 332 83 19 OR 372 33 92 OR 371 32 86

General Corporate and Business Law Practice. Technology Transfers, Joint Ventures, Technical and Financial Collaborations with Indian and Foreign Companies, Power Projects, Telecom Laws, Licensing and Distribution Agency Law, International Franchising, Sale of Goods, Law relating to Turnkey Projects, International Tendering, Public and Private Sector Company Contracts, Formation of Companies, Exchange Control Laws including Foreign Investments, Banking Laws, Amalgamations, Mergers and Take Overs, International and National Arbitrations, Intellectual Property Law, Monopoly Law, Law relating to Restrictive Trade Practices, Shipping and Aircraft Laws, Construction Laws. General Law Practice: Law of Contracts, Personal Law, including Probate and Succession, Constitutional Law in the Supreme Court and High Courts, Industrial Labour Laws.

FIRM PROFILE: First Legal firm to be established in Delhi - soon after the Constitution of India was promulgated on the 26th of January, 1950 and the Supreme Court of India, in Chamber No. 1. The Firm counts amongst its Founder Partners: an Ex-Chief Justice of the High Court, a President of the Bar Association, an Honorary Secretary and a Sitting Judge. The Firm carries on work as Attorneys-at-Law with specialization in the areas mentioned above with its Main Office in the Central Business District of New Delhi and Office in the Supreme Court, Chamber No. 1.

MEMBERS AND ASSOCIATES OF FIRM

SURESH VOHRA, born Delhi, India, 1940; admitted, 1963, India. *Education:* University of Delhi (B.A.; LL.B.). *Member:* Supreme Court Bar Association; High Court and District Court Bar Associations. (Advocate on Record, Supreme Court of India).

RAVINDER NATH, born Delhi, India, 1944; admitted, 1967, India. *Education:* University of Delhi (B.Com., Hons; LL.B.); PIL (Harvard) King's College, London and University of San Diego (International and Comparative Laws). *Member:* International Bar Association; International

(This Listing Continued)

Law Association; Supreme Court Bar Association. (Advocate on Record, Supreme Court of India).

HON'BLE S.N. SHANKAR, Ex-Chief Justice, High Court of Orissa. Governor, State of Orissa. Ex-Member, Law Commission of India. *Member:* Supreme Court Bar Association. Senior Advocate.

RAMESHWAR NATH, *Member:* Supreme Court Bar Association (Former Hon. Secretary). Senior Advocate.

KESHAV DAYAL, Author: Commentary on the Delhi Development Act. Member: Indian Law Institute; Institute on Constitutional and Parliamentary Affairs; Indian Counsel of World Affairs. *Member:* Supreme Court Bar Association; Delhi Bar Association; Bar Association of India. (Senior Advocate).

P.K. JAIN, born 1943. *Education:* University of Delhi (B.A.; LL.B.). *Member:* Delhi Bar Council. (Advocate on Record, Supreme Court of India).

CH. AMARJIT SINGH, born 1940. *Education:* B.Sc., LL.B, Contracts and Civil Litigation. *Member:* High Court Bar Association, Delhi.

PRANAV ROACH, born 1965; admitted, 1989, India. *Education:* University of Punjab (B.A. Hons.); University of Delhi (LL.B.).

BHARAT DEEPAK

MS. NANDITA MUKHARJEE

SHARAD PURI

REPRESENTATIVE CLIENTS: The World Bank; The Agha Khan Foundation; Kodak International Development Research Center, Canada; Dana Corp. U.S.; BECHTEL INT'L; US Sea Container, U.K.; Aircraft Finance; (Fokker), Holland; Beechcraft; Swenska Handels Banken; Orell Fussli, Switzerland; Tetra-Pak Sweden, Switzerland and New Delhi; Mundipharma AG, Basle, Mathys, CH; Emag CH; Benke, Germany; SEG, Germany; State Bank of India; India Today Group; PLM International and Growth Funds, US; National Bank of Utah, NY; SONY; Export Credit Bank of Turkey, Skandinaviska Enskilda Banken, Sweden; Movenpick, Switzerland; Mastercard International; Lenox, US.; Zurich Reinsurance CH.; IKEA; CNN; International Monetary Fund (IMF), Washington; BMW, Germany; Orient Express, U.K.; Enron Houston, El Al, China N Coal; EC, Brussels & New Delhi.

NEW DELHI LAW OFFICES

Advocates & Solicitors
RAJENDRA BHAWAN (5TH FLOOR)
210 DEEN DAYAL UPADHYAY MARG.
NEW DELHI 110 002, INDIA
Telephone: (91-11) 332 7081; 373 9857; 373 9858
Fax: (91-11) 332 7101

General Practice Litigation, Structuring of Overseas Investment in India through Offshore Entities; Negotiation on behalf of Multinational Corporations with leading Industrial Houses in India in regard to Technical and Financial Collaboration. Transfer of Technology Licence Agreements, Franchising and Distribution Agreement; Advising and assisting in Transaction relating to loan syndications from international financial institutions and banks; Conveyancing and Documentation involved in Acquisition of Real Estate; Counselling in the Setting up of Liaison Offices, Branch Offices, Joint Venture Companies with Indian partners; Undertaking Company Research and Investigation on behalf of foreign investors, Due Diligence Audits; Corporate and Commercial Litigation including regular counselling on Structuring of the International Contracts with overseas parties; Domestic and International Arbitration; Identification of appropriate Providers of technology and investment overseas; Industrial Laws and Service Disputes; Anti Trust and Mercantile Laws; Foreign Exchange Laws and Exchange Control Regulations; Advising on issue of Bonds, Securities and private placements; Patent, Trademarks, Copyright, Design, Licensing and related litigation in all forums.

PARTNERS

V.S. YADAV, born 1939; admitted, 1963, India, Solicitor. *Education:* Bombay University (B.A., LL.B.). *Member:* Bombay Incorporated Law Society. *PRACTICE AREAS:* Corporate Law; Public Issues; Conveyancing and Documentation; Financial and Securities Arrangement; Succession; Property; Rent Matters; Domestic and International Arbitrations.

P.S. DASGUPTA, born 1955; admitted, 1978, India. *Education:* Delhi University (B.A., Hons., Ec.; LL.B.; Post Graduate Degree, Corporate Law and Labour Law). *PRACTICE AREAS:* Structuring and Negotiation of Joint Ventures; Foreign Collaboration; Corporate Law; Foreign Exchange;

(This Listing Continued)

Antitrust and Mercantile Laws; Project Contracts; Financing Contracts; Corporate Litigation; Mergers and Acquisitions.

R.C. DUBEY, born 1957; admitted, 1981, India. *Education:* Delhi University (B.A.; LL.B.). *PRACTICE AREAS:* General Practice Litigation; Corporate Law; Commercial Law; Commercial Litigation; Foreign Collaboration; Commercial Documentation; Domestic and International Arbitration.

A.M. DITTIA, born 1957; admitted, 1982, India. *Education:* Delhi University (B.A., Hons., LL.B.; Diploma in Journalism). *PRACTICE AREAS:* General Practice Litigation; Commercial and Mercantile Laws and Arbitration; Industrial Law; Service Disputes; Commercial Documentation.

VIVEK DHOKALIA, born 1958; admitted, 1981, India. *Education:* Banaras Hindu University (B.A.; LL.B.); Southern Methodist University, Texas (M.C.L.); Yale University (LL.M.). With Law Firm of Wolf, Arnold & Cardoso, Washington, D.C. *Member:* Indian Society of International Law. Patent and Trademark Attorney. *PRACTICE AREAS:* Corporate Law; Patent, Trademark, Copyright; Joint Venture; Technology Transfer; Banking; Licensing; Commercial Documentation.

OF COUNSEL

M.L. QAZI, born 1934; admitted, 1954, India. *Education:* Lucknow University, India (M.A., Ec.,; LL.B.). Was: Central Government Standing Counsel in senior capacity in Kashmir; Standing Counsel for Vigilance Anti Corruption Department; Panel Counsel, Forest Department, Banks, Insurance Companies, etc. Participated as Leader of a Delegation from J&K to AICC(I) Legal Cell National Convention at New Delhi and participated in International Conference under the auspices of Ladhak Ecological Development Group etc. *PRACTICE AREAS:* Civil Litigation; Constitutional Litigation; Criminal Litigation; Commercial Documentation.

T.V. SUBRAMANYAM, born 1939; admitted, 1991, India. *Education:* Bangalore University (B.Sc.; B.L.); Diploma in Industrial and Business Administration. Worked in Senior Executive position in leading Public Sector Companies. *PRACTICE AREAS:* Joint Venture; Foreign Collaborations; Corporate Foreign Exchange; Antitrust Laws; Mercantile Laws; Conveyancing; Commercial Litigation; Domestic and International Arbitrations.

ASSOCIATES

Ashok Mathur (Advocate on Record, Supreme Court of India)

Sunitha Narahari

Shireen Sethna

Benu Madan

Nisha Bonarji

Meera Singh

REPRESENTATIVE CLIENTS: Guardian Industries; Cummins Engines Ltd.; Heinz, Inc.; Hughes Network Systems; D'Arcy Masius Benton & Bowles Inc.; Stone and Webster; Carrier International; Pioneer Hi-Bred International Inc.; Voltarc Technologics Inc.; Nippon Steel Corporation; Fuji Bank; Astra Pharmaceuticals AB; Nutricia; Hoogovens; Groep BV; Hunter Douglas; Telectronics; Carlsberg; Reuters; GEC Marconi; Timken Company; Holderbank; Teledanmark International; Sinarmas Pulp & Paper; Kirloskar Cummins Ltd., Wimco Ltd.; Tata Timken Ltd.; Tata Metaliks Ltd.; Birla International Marketing Corporation; Willard India Ltd.; Bell Ceramics; Modi Overseas Ltd.; Carrier Aircon Ltd.; M.T.N.L.; Taj Group of Hotels; State Bank of India; Indian Overseas Bank; Indo-Lawenbrau Breweries Ltd.; Punjab Breweries Ltd.; Premier Breweries Ltd.

AMITABHA SEN & CO.

DBS EXECUTIVE CENTER, BARAKHAMBA LANE
WORLD TRADE TOWERS, 1ST FLOOR
NEW DELHI 110 001, INDIA
Telephone: (011-91-11) 331-4668; 331-2840; 60-0168
Telex: 031-62111-KTPL IN; 031-63421 DBSD IN
Fax: (011-91-11) 687-3305; 331-2830

Fremont, California Office: 4512 Enterprise Street, 94538. Telephone: (510) 490-8375. Fax: (510) 651-0906.

Palo Alto, California Correspondent Office: Fenwick & West. Two Palo Alto Square, 94306. Telephone: (510) 494-0600. Fax: (510) 494-8022.

Washington, D.C. Correspondent Office: Fenwick & West. 1920 N. Street, Suite 650, N.W., 20036. Telephone: (202)463-6300. Fax: (202) 463-6520.

London, England Correspondent Office: Hopkins & Wood. 2-3 Cursiter, EC4A 1NE. Telephone: (011-44-71) 404-0475. Fax: (011-44-71) 430-2358.

London, England Correspondent Office: Hammond Suddards, Moor House, 119 London Wall, EC2Y 5ET. Telephone: (011-44-71) 628-4767. Fax: (011-44-71) 628-6161.

(This Listing Continued)

General Practice of law with emphasis on all aspects of Doing Business in India; Indian Counsel for the American and the international business organizations; American counsel for the Indian companies doing or planning to do business in the United States and abroad; major areas of practice involve international and domestic corporate law, corporate taxation, corporate litigation and international arbitration; specialists in complex Indian laws involving FERA (Foreign Exchange Regulations Act), MRTP (Monopolies and Restrictive Trade Practices Act), NRI (Non-Resident Indians), RBI (Reserve Bank of India), banking, foreign investment and tax related matters, other areas of specialization include, but are not limited to, construction law, intellectual property rights relating to trademark, copyright, patent, designs and service mark, transfer of technology, licensing, joint venture, collaboration, incorporation, immigration, labor laws and constitutional questions.

AMITABHA SEN, born 1942; admitted, 1979, California; 1983, India. *Education:* Bengal Engineering College, University of Calcutta (Bachelor of Engineering, First Class, 1963); University of Saskatchewan, Canada (Master of Science, National Research Council Grant, 1966); Golden Gate University, San Francisco (MBA-Highest Scholastic Standing Awardee, 1974; Doctor of Jurisprudence, 1978). Registered Professional Engineer of the State of California. Professorial Lecturer of Operations Research at Golden Gate University, San Francisco. Senior Engineer, Project Engineer, Project Manager, Chief Engineer and Assistant to Vice President in Bechtel, International Engineering Company, L.K. Comstock Engineering and Construction Company. Extensive experience in U.S. and International Business and Corporate Litigation; Vice-Chairperson of the Dispute Resolution and Arbitration Committee of IPBA. *Member:* State Bar of California; Supreme Court Bar Association, India; Inter-Pacific Bar Association (IPBA); Association of Professional Engineers, California.

BUSHAN TILAK KAUL, born 1951; admitted, 1973, India. *Education:* Kashmir University (B.Sc., 1970); University of Delhi, LL.B., 1973; LL.M., 1975); Indian Law Institute, New Delhi (Post Graduate Diploma in Labor Law, 1975); London School of Economics (LL.M., with emphases on intellectual property law and international and comparative labor law, 1986). Recipient, Junior Research Fellowship in Law awarded by the Faculty of Law, Council, 1985-1986; Junior Research Fellowship in Law awarded by the Faculty of Law, University of Delhi, 1976-1977. Invitee of WIPO and UNDP Workshop on Teaching and Research in Intellectual Property Law, New Delhi jointly sponsored by WIPO and University of Delhi, October 1991. Assistant Professor of Law, Faculty of Law Himachal Pradesh University, Simla, India, 1977-1978. Senior Lecturer in Law, Faculty of Law, University of Delhi, 1980—. Guest Lecturer: in Labor Law at the Indian Law Institute, New Delhi, 1980—; in Law Internal Security Academy, Mount Abu, Rajasthan, 1988; in Law, Institute of Criminology and Forensic Science, Ministry of Home Affairs, Government of India, 1986. Author: Annual Survey of Industrial Relations Law in India, Indian Law Institute's yearly publication Annual Survey of Indian Law, 1989—. *Member:* Supreme Court Bar Association; High Court Bar Association.

PRADYUMNA ARORA, born 1936; admitted, 1978, India. *Education:* Punjab University (B.A.); Delhi University (LL.B. and LL.M.-Merit Scholar). Law Lecturer at Delhi University on Corporate, Criminal, Labor, Property and Family Law. Lecturer, Law, Indian Institute of Islamic Studies and at the Jamia Millia Islamia University, both in Delhi. Author: "The Personal Laws of India (Hindu Law, Christian Law and the Law of Civil Marriages)," Islamic & Comparative Law Quarterly, Series III, 1981-1982; "Judicial law making with a vengeance - some recent Indian decisions," Islamic and Comparative Law Quarterly. *Member:* Indian Law Institute; Indian Society of International Law.

V.K. SHALI, born 1954; admitted, 1976, India. *Education:* University of Delhi (LL.B., 1976; LL.M., 1981); Indian Law Institute, Administrative Law, 1986); Institute of Constitutional Law and Parliamentary Studies, (Post-Graduate Diploma in Constitutional Law and Parliamentary Studies, 1988); Institute of Criminology and Forensic Science (29th certificate course in Criminology and Forensic Science). Part Time Lecturer in Law, University of Delhi, September 1991—. Metropolitan Magistrate, Sub Judge Delhi. Deputy Registrar/Joint Registrar, Central Administrative Tribunal, Principal Bench, New Delhi. Executive Magistrate, Delhi Administration. Additional Rent Controller, Delhi, *Member:* High Court Bar Association.

SARUP SINGH

G-50 EAST OF KAILASH
NEW DELHI 110065, INDIA
Telephone: (91) (11) 636419
Fax: (91) (11) 6836838

Chandigarh, India Office: 69, Sector 8-A, Chandigarh, 160008.
Telephone: (91) (172) 29203.

Arbitration & Litigation, Corporate and Business Law, Intellectual Property, Energy and Power, Administrative and Constitutional Law, Criminal, Regulatory and Environmental Law, Joint Ventures & U.S. Immigration.

FIRM PROFILE: Firm engaged in Indian, United States and International Practice. Entitled to practice in all India Courts & Tribunals and Courts in California, U.S.A. The firm maintains close links with associates in India & United States.

Provides legal services at New Delhi and Chandigarh. Chandigarh is the focal point for the states of Punjab, Haryana and Himachal Pradesh.

SARUP SINGH, born Madras, India, September 2, 1947; admitted, 1971, India; 1990, California. Education: Punjab University (B.Sc., 1968, LL.B., 1971); The Fletcher School of Law & Diplomacy, Tufts University U.S.A. (M.A.,1988); Harvard Law School (Islamic Commercial Law, 1988). Participant, Conferences, Asia Pacific Lawyer's Association, "Arbitrability & Sovereign Immunity," Problems for Nations of Asia Pacific Region. Member: American Bar Association; Bar Association of India; Supreme Court Bar Association; Delhi High Court Bar Association; Punjab & Haryana High Court Bar Association; Indo-U.S. Chamber of Commerce; Asia Pacific Lawyer's Association; Indian Council of Arbitration. **LANGUAGES:** English, Punjabi and Hindi. **PRACTICE AREAS:** General Practice; International Law; U.S. Law.

ASSOCIATES

P.S. ARORA, born Karor, Pakistan, January 28, 1946; admitted, 1973. (Resident, Chandigarh, India Office).

GURPAL SINGH, born Ferozepur, India, December 18, 1968; admitted, 1992. (Resident, Chandigarh, India Office).

SINGHANIA & CO.

Established in 1969

Advocates and Solicitors

B-92 HIMALAYA HOUSE
23, KASTURBA GANDHI MARG
NEW DELHI 110 001, INDIA
Telephone: 91-11-3318300/3731400
Telefax: 91-11-3314413/3713383
Mobile Tel: 91-11-4613334
Cable: SINGANIACO

Bangalore, India Office: 204-A Mittal Towers, 6 Mahatma Gandhi Road, Banalore 560 001. Telephone: 91-80-5588763. Telefax: 91-80-5584593. After Office Hours Telephone: 91-80-553-376.

Bombay, India Office: 83-C Mittal Towers, Nariman Point, Bombay, 400 021. Telephone: 91-22-2049773/2851011. After Office Hours Telephone: 91-22-2188044/2180004. Telefax: 91-22-2045960/2851011. Telex: 11-82405 DCS IN.

Calcutta, India Office: E-1, 75-c, Prk Street, Calcutta 700 016. Telephone: 91-33-292759/295088/295093. Telefax: 91-33-292751. Telex: 21-2763 DCS IN.

Hyderabad, India Office: 614, Babu Khan Estate, Beshir Bagh, Hyderabad-500 029. Telephone: 91-40-236219. Telefax: 91-40-241779.

Madras, India Office: 1 Rayala Towers, 781-785 Anna salai, Madras 600 002. Telephone: 91-44-8522494/8522491/8521626. Telefax: 91-44-8520280. Telex: 41-5287 DCS IN.

South Delhi, India Office: P-24, Green Park Extension, New Delhi 110 016. Telephone: 91-11-6863841/6864700. Telefax: 91-11-6851218. Telex: 31-73281 SCPL In.

London, England Office: 2 Duke Street, St. James's SW1Y 6BJ. Telephone: 44-71-9252603/9302366. Telefax: 44-71-9250823/9302250. After Office Hours Telphone: 44-71-8283384. Telefax: 44-71-8280062. Mobile: (0850) 623736.

New York, U.S. Office: 40 West 57th Street, New York 10019. Telephone: 1-212-603-2441. Fax: 1-212-603-2298.

(This Listing Continued)

Corporate Practice Technology Transfers, Joint Ventures, Collaborations, Licensing, Distribution Agency and Franchise Law, Corporate Law, Drafting and Negotiating Government and Public Sector Company Contracts, Formation of Companies, Foreign Investments, Foreign Exchange Control Regulations, Banking, Private International Law, Aviation Law, International Tenders, Takeovers and Mergers, Import and Export, National and International Commercial Arbitration, Environmental Law, Immigration Law, Taxation of Foreign Companies and Nationals, Trademarks, Patents, Copyrights, Maritime and Shipping Law, Energy, Oil and Gas Laws, Construction Laws, Electricity Laws, Telecommunications Laws.

General Law Practice: General Law Practice in Supreme Court of India and State High Courts, Tribunals including Customs and Excise, Transportation Law, Industrial, Labour, Monopoly and Restrictive Trade Practice, Antitrust, Mining, Real Estate and Urban Laws, Arbitration, Administrative Procedures, Economic Regulations, Company Law, Conveyancing, Service Law.

Countries Covered by the Firm: Australia, Austria, Belgium, Brazil, Bulgsria, Canada, Denmark, France, Germany, Hungary, Hong Kong, India, Israel, Italy, Japan, Netherlands, New Zealand, Pakistan, Poland, Romania, S. Korea, Singapore, Sweden, Switzerland, U.S.A., U.S.S.R., United Kingdom.

FIRM PROFILE: Founded in 1969 by Mr. D.C. Singhania provides comprehensive legal services primarily in Corporate and Business Law Practice. It is one of the leading law firms in India having Head Office in New Delhi and branch offices at Bangalore, Bombay, Calcutta, Hyderaband and Madras, in India and also representative offices at London and New York.

MEMBERS OF FIRM

D.C. SINGHANIA, born Pacheri Bari, October 15, 1932; admitted, 1962, India. Education: Punjab University (B.A., LL.B). Two term Vice President, Governing Body, Indian Council of Arbitration. Chairman: Indian Society for Arbitrators. Awarded: World Lawyer Award by World Peace through Law Centre, Washington, DC; National Law Day Award. Member: International Bar Association; International Law Association; World Association of Lawyers; World Peace Through Law Center; International Associate of American Bar Association; Bar Association of India; Supreme Court Bar Association; Asia-Pacific Lawyers Association; International Fiscal Association. Fellow, Chartered Institute of Arbitrators, London. **LANGUAGES:** Hindi and English. **PRACTICE AREAS:** Commercial and Corporate Law; Investments; Commercial Arbitration; International Corporate Law; International Arbitration; Foreign Joint Ventures and Investments; Constitutional Law.

J.K. GUPTA, born Rewari, India, 1951; admitted, 1976, Delhi. Education: Punjab University (B.Sc.): University of Rajasthan (LL.M.). Member: Indian Council of Arbitration; Delhi Bar Association; International Bar Association. **LANGUAGES:** English and Hindi. **PRACTICE AREAS:** Arbitration; Personal Law; Commercial and Mercantile Law; Succession and Inheritance; Commercial and Mercantile Law.

K.G. SINGHANIA, born New Delhi, 1963; admitted, 1988, Bombay. Education: Delhi University (B.Com. Hons.; LL.B., 1988). Member: International Bar Association; American Bar Association; American Intellectual Property Law Association; Indian Council of Arbitration; Bombay High Court Bar Association. (Resident, Bombay Office). **LANGUAGES:** English and Hindi. **PRACTICE AREAS:** Corporate Law; Arbitration; Joint Venture; Intellectual Property.

RAVINDER SINGHANIA, born New Delhi, 1968; admitted, 1993, New Delhi. Education: Delhi University (B.Com., Hons., 1990; LL.B., 1993). Member: International Bar Association; Delhi High Court Bar Association; Advocates Association; Bangalore and Indian Law Institute. **LANGUAGES:** English and Hindi. **PRACTICE AREAS:** Arbitration; Commercial Litigation; Foreign Collaborations; Joint Ventures; Intellectual Property.

DILJEET TITUS, born Gorakhpur, 1966; admitted, 1989, India. Education: University of Delhi (B.A., 1986; LL.B., 1989). **LANGUAGES:** Hindi and English. **PRACTICE AREAS:** Corporate Law; Foreign Investments; Joint Ventures; Exchange Control.

VIBHU SHANKAR, born Lucknow, 1963; admitted, 1987, Lucknow. Education: Lucknow University (B.Com., 1984; LL.B., 1987). **LANGUAGES:** Hindi and English. **PRACTICE AREAS:** Civil Law; Corporate Law; Arbitration; Service Law; Labour Law.

(This Listing Continued)

ASSOCIATES

A.G. SIRSI, born 1927; admitted, 1948. *Education:* LL.B. A.C.S. Former Registrar of Companies. *LANGUAGES:* Hindi & English. *PRACTICE AREAS:* Arbitration and Company Law.

ANJANA BENIWAL, born Tura (Meghalaya), 1968; admitted, 1991, Jodhpur. *Education:* University of Rajsthan (LL.B., 1990). *Member:* High Court Bar Association, Delhi. *LANGUAGES:* Hindi, English and Punjabi. *PRACTICE AREAS:* Intellectual Property; Constitutional Law; Corporate Law and Foreign Collaboration; Anti-Trust Laws.

ANURADHA, born Hyderabad, 1967; admitted, 1991, Karnataka. *Education:* Bangalore University (LL.B., 1991); London University (LL.M., 1992). *Member:* Karnataka Bar Association. (Bangalore Office). *LANGUAGES:* English and Hindi. *PRACTICE AREAS:* Civil and Corporate Law.

BELA MAHESHWARI, born Wardha, 1968; admitted, 1990. *Education:* Nagpur University (LL.B., 1990). *Member:* Supreme Court Bar Association; Delhi High Court Bar Association; Indian Society of Arbitrators. *LANGUAGES:* Hindi, English and Marathi. *PRACTICE AREAS:* Civil Litigation and Arbitration; Consumer Protection; Monopolies and Restrictive Trade Practices.

BAKHTAWAR N. KARBHARI, born 1949; admitted, 1990, Bombay. *Education:* M. Comm LL.B. (Bombay Office). *LANGUAGES:* Hindi, English, Marathi & Gujrati. *PRACTICE AREAS:* Civil Litigation; Joint Ventures; Banking Matters.

CHUNDI SAI KUMAR, born 1962; admitted, 1988, Hyderabad, India. *Education:* Sri Venkateswara University (B.Com; B.L.). *Member:* Andhra Pradesh High Court Bar Association. *LANGUAGES:* English, Telugu and Hindi. *PRACTICE AREAS:* Arbitration; Constitutional Law; Labour Law.

K.G.S. MOORTHY, born Vishakhapatnam (AP), 1968; admitted, 1993. *Education:* Delhi University (B.A. History, M.A., History); Osmania University (B.L.). *Member:* Delhi High Court Bar Association. *LANGUAGES:* English, Hindi and Telugu. *PRACTICE AREAS:* Civil Law; Commercial Law.

KUNAL SARKAR, born Calcutta, 1952; admitted, 1979, Calcutta. *Education:* Ranchi University (B.A. Hons.); Calcutta University (M.A.; LL.B.). (Resident, Calcutta Office). *LANGUAGES:* Hindi, English and Bengali. *PRACTICE AREAS:* Arbitration; Corporate Law; Real Estate; Civil Law.

MANJULA N. KULKARNI, born 1961; admitted, 1993, Bombay. *Education:* B.A. LL.B. (Bombay Office). *LANGUAGES:* Hindi, English and Kannad. *PRACTICE AREAS:* Commercial and Labour Laws.

N.L. KAKKAR, born Meerut (U.P.), September 11, 1922; admitted, 1980, India. *Education:* Meerut College (B.A.); Law College Meerut (LL.B.). Lectured on Extradition Laws, National Academy of Mussoorie and Officers Training School, Delhi, 1971. Former District and Sessions Judge Delhi and Industrial Tribunal at Delhi, 1971-1980. *Member:* Supreme Court Bar Association; Delhi High Court Bar Association. *LANGUAGES:* Hindi, Urdu and English. *PRACTICE AREAS:* Civil and Criminal Law.

P.V. PATANKAR, admitted, 1969. *Education:* B.A. L.L.B. Member Bar Council of Maharashtra & Goa. (Bombay Office). *LANGUAGES:* Hindi, English & Marathi. *PRACTICE AREAS:* Litigation.

RAINU WALIA, born Bangkok, 1958; admitted, 1981, New Delhi. *Education:* Delhi University (LL.B.); Columbia University (LL.M.). *LANGUAGES:* English and Hindi. *PRACTICE AREAS:* Corporate Law; Intellectual Property; Trade Marks.

RAI SAHEB MITTAL, born Muzaffarnagar (U.P.), 1970; admitted, 1993, U.P. *Education:* Meerut University (B. Com., LL.B.); Lal Bahadur Shastri Institute of Management, Lucknow (P.G. Diploma in Personnel Management). *LANGUAGES:* Hindi and English. *PRACTICE AREAS:* Civil Law; Intellectual Property; Foreign Collaboration.

RAJESH BANATI, born New Delhi, 1965; admitted, 1989. *Education:* University of Delhi (B.Sc., LL.B.). *LANGUAGES:* Hindi and English. *PRACTICE AREAS:* Arbitration; Civil Law; Corporate Law.

RAJ KISHORE, born Madras, 1970; admitted, 1992, Madras. *Education:* University of Madras (B.L., 1992). *Member:* Madras High Court Advocate's Association. (Madras Office). *LANGUAGES:* English, Tamil and Hindi. *PRACTICE AREAS:* Civil Law; Corporate Law.

RAM NATH MADAAN, born Amritsar, Punjab, 1969; admitted, 1993, Delhi. *Education:* Guru Nanakdev University, Amritsar (B. Com.); Delhi

University (LL.B.). *LANGUAGES:* English, Hindi and Punjabi. *PRACTICE AREAS:* Foreign Collaboration; Joint Ventures; Corporate Law.

R. POORNIMA, born Bangalor, 1970; admitted, 1993, Bangalor. *Education:* N.L.S.I.U. (B.A. LL.B. Hons.). (Bangalore Office). *LANGUAGES:* Hindi, English & Kannadkak. *PRACTICE AREAS:* Commercial Laws and Litigation.

SHAHWAR GAUHAR, born 1964; admitted, 1992, Bar Council of Jammu and Kashmir. *Education:* Kashmir University (B.A., 1987); Lucknow University (LL.B., 1991). *Member:* Jammu and Kashmir Bar Association. *LANGUAGES:* English, Urdu and Kashmiri. *PRACTICE AREAS:* Civil Law.

SHALINI AGARWAL, born Delhi, 1965; admitted, 1990, Delhi. *Education:* University of Delhi (B.A. Hons., LL.B.); LL.M. (Cantab.). *LANGUAGES:* English and Hindi. *PRACTICE AREAS:* Intellectual Properties; Commercial Law.

S.N. HASSAN, admitted, 1993, Bombay. *Education:* B.A. LL.B. *Member:* Bar Council of Maharashtra and Goa. (Bombay Office). *LANGUAGES:* Hindi, English and Urdu. *PRACTICE AREAS:* Arbitration; General Practice.

S. RAJENDRAN, born Madras, 1970; admitted, 1993, Madras. *Education:* University of Madras (B.L., 1993). *LANGUAGES:* Tamil and Hindi. *PRACTICE AREAS:* Civil Law.

VIKRANT KHURANA, born New Delhi, 1969; admitted, 1992, Shimla, Himachal Pradesh. *Education:* H.P. University (B. Com., 1989; LL.B., 1992). *Member:* Himachal High Court Bar Association; New Delhi High Court Bar Association. *LANGUAGES:* Hindi, English and Punjabi. *PRACTICE AREAS:* Commercial and Corporate Law; Civil Law; Exchange Control; Foreign Investment; Joint Ventures; Imports and Exports; Intellectual Property Litigation.

V.P. MALIK, born Miranpur, 1933; admitted, 1965, India. *Education:* Punjab University (M.A.); Bhagalpur (LL.B.). *Member:* Delhi Bar Association; Delhi High Court Bar Association. *LANGUAGES:* Hindi, Urdu and English. *PRACTICE AREAS:* General Legal Practice.

CONSULTANTS

ALLAN E. KAY (U.S.A.).

AMAL DUTTA (Calcutta Office).

ARUN CHHABRA (Washington, D.C.).

B.S. MATHUR, born Bilaspur, 1925; admitted, 1983, India. *Education:* Delhi University (B.Sc., LL.B.); Aligarth University (B.Sc.Eng.). Retired Chief Engineer, Government of India, Approved Government Valuer. *Member:* Indian Council of Arbitration; Delhi High Court Bar Association. *LANGUAGES:* Hindi and English. *PRACTICE AREAS:* Arbitration; Construction Law; Valuation Law.

CHANDLER B. SHARMA, born 1939; admitted, 1979, India. *Education:* Delhi University (B.Sc.); Agra University (LL.B.); University of Minnesota (HBA); Woodrow Wilson College of Law (J.D.); Emory University (LL.M.). *Member:* State Bar of Georgia; American Bar Association. (U.S.A.). *LANGUAGES:* English, Hindi and Urdu.

E.C. AGARWALA

G.C. AGARWAL, born Haryana, 1935. *Education:* University of Rajasthan (M. Com.); Agra University (LL.B.); Jodhpur University (DCLL). Member and Former Acting Chairman, Central Board of Direct Taxes. *LANGUAGES:* Hindi, English, Urdu and Sanskrit. *PRACTICE AREAS:* Direct Taxes.

H.L. AGARWAL, Former Chief Justice, Orissa High Court. *LANGUAGES:* English and Hindi. *PRACTICE AREAS:* Civil and Corporate Law.

K.K. MUKHERJEE, born Burdwan, 1938; admitted, 1977, West Bengal. *Education:* Calcutta University (B.A. Hons., LL.B., M.B.A.); Chamber of Commerce, London (Cert-S-MNGT). *Member:* Bar Council of West Bengal; Supreme Court Bar Association; Chartered Institute of Arbitrators (Associate Member); Indian Council of Arbitrators; Institute of Administrative Management (Fellow Member); All India Management Association; National Institute of Personnel Management (Senor Member). (Calcutta Office). *LANGUAGES:* English and Bengali. *PRACTICE AREAS:* Corporate Laws; Intellectual Property; Arbitration; Shipping Law; Civil Litigation; Criminal Litigation.

M.A. RANGASWAMY, born 1921; admitted, 1944, Madras. *Education:* Madras University (M.A.; LL.B.). Guest Speaker, Institute of Criminology

(This Listing Continued)

SINGHANIA & CO., New Delhi—Continued

and Forensic Studies, New Delhi, 1975-1976. Imperial Customs Services of the Government of India, 1945-1980. Secretary to the Government of India, Department of Industrial Development. Member, Central Board of Excise and Customs. Member, Foreign Exchange Appellate Board. Textile Commissioner, Government of India. Chairman, Forward Markets Commission. Collector of Customs and Central Excise. *Member:* Supreme Court Bar Association; Delhi High Court Bar Association. *LANGUAGES:* Hindi, English and Tamil.

MARK REIDY (Washington, D.C.).

M.N. BHATKAL, admitted, 1963. *Education:* Bombay University (B.A. special and LL.B.). Senior Advocate, Bombay High Court. *Member:* Western India Advocates Association; Bangalore Bar Association; Indian Council of Arbitration; Chartered Institute of Arbitrators, London (Associate Member). *LANGUAGES:* English, Hindi, Kannad and Marathi. *PRACTICE AREAS:* Constitutional Law; Arbitration; Labour Law; Service Law.

M.B. GOPALAN (Madras Office).

MICHAEL PHULWANI, born Karachi (Pakistan), 1936; admitted, 1958, India; 1974, New York; 1976, New Jersey. *Education:* University of Rajasthan (B.A., 1955; LL.B., 1957). *Member:* Bar Association of India; Bergen County, New York State and New Jersey State Bar Associations; International Law Association; American Immigration Lawyers Association; Indo-American Lawyers Association; Asian Pacific Lawyers Association. (U.S.A.). *LANGUAGES:* Hindi, English, Urdu and Sindhi. *PRACTICE AREAS:* U.S. Immigration and Nationality Law.

R.R. MISRA, born Banda (U.P.), 1930; admitted, 1952. *Education:* Agra University (M. Com., LL.B., Ph.D.). Former Judge Allahabad High Court. *LANGUAGES:* English and Hindi. *PRACTICE AREAS:* Construction Law; Taxation; Civil Law; Criminal Law; Arbitration.

R. VENUGOPAL REDDY (Hyderabad).

S. RAJAGOPAL (New Delhi).

SURINDER SINGH BAGAI, born Montgomery (Pakistan), 1929; admitted, 1970, India. *Education:* Delhi University (B.A., M.A., LL.B.). *LANGUAGES:* Hindi, Punjabi and English. *PRACTICE AREAS:* Taxation.

T. RAGHAVAN (Madras Office).

UTTAM REDDY (Madras Office).

VIRENDER SOOD

V.P. ELHENCE, born 1935. *Education:* B.Sc. (1953); LL.B. (1955); Bachelor of Engineering (1958); Doctor of Engineering (1964, Germany). *Member:* Indian Council of Arbitrators; Fellow of Institution of Engineers; Fellow of Indian Society of Arbitrators. (South Delhi Office). *LANGUAGES:* English, Hindi and German.

REPRESENTATIVE CLIENTS: *U.S.A.:* Abercrombie & Kent Overseas Ltd.; Bank of America; General Binding Corp. (GBC); General Motors; Intergraph Corp.; J.C. Penney Co. Inc.; Martin Marietta, Microsoft Corporation; Northrop Corporation; Oceaneering International Inc.; Pillsbury Co.; Quality Inns.; Tandem Computers Inc.; TRW Inc.; The Singer Company; Associated Aviation Underwriters; Glenayre Electronics; Yale University; Cellular Communications International Inc.; Flint Electronics Inc.; Structural Dynamics Research Corporation; Sundstrand Corporation; The J. Peterman Co.; Bank of Boston; H.B. Fuller Co.; Island Pyrochemical; Albion Laboratories; Team Inc.; Arco; Universal Trading; Best Power; Agridyne Inc. *U.K.:* British Technology Group; British Telecom; Budget Rent A Car Inc.; Davy McKee (Stockton) Ltd.; National Westminster Bank; Vickers Shipbuilding & Engineering Ltd.; Land & Marine Engg Ltd. (Costain Group); British Gas; RCI Europe Ltd.; Standard Chartered Bank; Guinness Peat Aviation; Rolls Royce; Euro Alloys, Elders Exsud, British Airways; Aer Lingus; Humphreys & Glasgow Consultants; Lucas Industries; Sterling Publications; Smith Industries PLC. *France:* AIRBUS Industries; Banque Francaise Du Commerce Exterieur (BFCE); hospitex S.A.; I.N.A.O. (French Government Undertaking); Moulinex S.A.; Spie Capag; Generale Bank, Satelec. *Japan:* C. Itoh & Co. Ltd.; Chiyoda Corporation; Kobe Street Ltd.; Mitsubishi Bank; Mitsui & Co. Ltd.; Yokogawa Electric Corporation; Sanwa Bank; Bank of Tokyo; Toshiba Corporation; ITOCHU Ltd.; *Germany:* Class OHG; Degussa AG; Grundig AG; Norddeutsche Landesbank (NORD L/B); Thyssen Industrie AG; Elektrotechnik Export-Import; AEG Isolier; BMW; *Italy:* Montedison Group; Siemens Telecommunicazioni Spa; Saipem; ENI-Savio, Donna Elana; Alphapack; Promo-India; Arte Tapetti. *Netherlands:* Gist Brocades N.V.; GD Express Worldwide (TNT Express Worldwide (I) Private Limited). *Sweden:* Scandinavian Airlines System (SAS); Saab Aircraft AB. *Switzerland:* Banque Paribass (Suisse). *Hungary:* Taurus Hungarian Rubber Works; IKEA Trading Ltd. *Singapore:* Abacus Distribution Systems Pte. Ltd. *Others:* Ansett Airlines; Netafin, Singapore Airlines; Scientific Atlanta Inc.; Nationwide Nrws Pte Ltd.; Gulf Bank, Samsung Co. Ltd.; SPHC; Copca.

VAISH ASSOCIATES

Solicitors and Advocates

FLATS 5&7, 10 HAILEY ROAD
NEW DELHI 110 001, INDIA
Telephone: 332 9191; 332 9192; 332 9270
Telefax: 91-011-332 0484

General Corporate Practice, International Joint Venture, Collaboration, Licensing, Agency and Franchise, Agreements, Drafting and Negotiating, Formation of Companies, Advising on Foreign Exchange Regulations, Arbitration, Taxation of Foreign Corporations and Nationals, Labour, Energy, Maritime, Shipping, Construction and Intellectual Property Laws, Trade Marks, Patents, Copyrights, Environmental Laws and Regulations, General Law Practice in the Supreme Court, High Courts and Tribunals (including Income Tax, Customs, Excise, Industrial, Company Law Board, Labour and Administrative Tribunals, Monopolies and Restrictive Trade Practices Commission).

O.P. VAISH, born April 29, 1931; admitted, 1972, India. *Education:* Delhi University (M.A. Eco.; B.Com. Hons.); India (B.L., LL.M.). Designated as Senior Advocate, India, Served Indian Revenue Service, later Federation of Indian Chamber of Commerce and Industry as Corporate Laws and Tax Adviser. *Member:* Bank of America (Advisory Board); Associated Chambers of Commerce & Industry of India (ASSOCHAM) (Managing Committee); Indo-American Chamber of Commerce (North India Council); International Chamber of Commerce (Indian National Committee); Punjab, Haryana and Delhi (PHD) Chamber of Commerce and Industry; Indian Council of Arbitration; Asian Pacific Tax and Investment Centre, Singapore; International Fiscal Association (IFA) (Permanent Scientific Committee; Chairman, IFA-India Branch); International Bar Association; Asian Pacific Lawyers Association; Bar Association of India; Supreme Court Bar Association.

CONSULTANTS

K.C. Srivastava	*D.B. Ahuja*
Manju Vaish	*Bhargava Desai*
Kali Vohra	*S.K. Agarwal*
Vinay Vaish	*Bomi F. Daruwala*
Santosh Agarwal	*R. Parthasarathy*
N.S. Jain	*Rupesh Jain*
Ajay Vohra	*Savita Choudhary*
Ranjana Agarwal	*Sulekha Kaul*
T.R. Misra	*Gen. B.R. Parashar*
V.U. Eradi	*Ruby Gupta*

INDONESIA

AMIR INDAH PACHTA & PACHTA

Attorneys and Counsellors at Law

Established in 1989

MID PLAZA 2 BUILDING, 14TH FLOOR
JL. JEND. SUDIRMAN KAV. 10-11
JAKARTA 10220, INDONESIA
Telephone: (62-21) 570-6240 (Hunting); (62-21) 570-7713; 570-0550 ext. 6410
Fax: (62-21) 570-7710

Business Enterprises, Financial Institutions and Government Entities with specialization in the areas of Corporate Organization, Financial and Banking Transactions, Securities, International Business, Public Contract Law, General Construction Contract, International Copyright, Trademark Secret Protection and Patent, Environmental and Energy Law, Labour Law, Real Estate Transactions, Aviation and General Litigation.

FIRM PROFILE: The Law Firm Amir Indah Pachta & Pachta (AIPP) is committed to providing its clients with the highest caliber legal work, emphasizing thoroughness, promptness, efficiency and practicality. The firm's lawyers have outstanding records of achievement and come from diverse backgrounds. They are supported by energetic young associate lawyers. Computers, and facsimiles can be transmitted quickly to clients with compatible electronic equipment.

(This Listing Continued)

MEMBERS OF FIRM

RISNAWATY NASUTION, born Sipirok, South Tapanuli, North Sumatera, January 10, 1951. admitted to bar, 1987, Indonesia. *Education:* University of Indonesia, School of Law (S.H., 1977). Legal Officer, Bank Dagang Negara (Commercial State Bank), 1977-1989. *LANGUAGES:* Indonesian and English. *PRACTICE AREAS:* Banking Law.

ANDJAR P. WIRANA, born Danau-Ranau, South Sumatera, August 19, 1949. admitted to bar, 1981, Indonesia. *Education:* University of Indonesia, School of Law (S.H., 1981); University of Washington, School of Law, Seattle, USA, (LL.M., 1988). Visiting Scholar, University of Washington, School of Law, 1986-1987. Legal Counsel, United Nation High Commission on Refugees (UNHCR), 1990. Associate, Makarim & Taira.S., 1982-1987. Managing Editor, Law School Journal, "Hukum & Pembangunan," 1977-1986. Author: "The International Private Law Aspects in Oil and Gas Sales Contracts," Pertamina, 1980; "The Function of State Owned Enterprises," 1981; "A Fluctuation of Foreign Investment in Indonesia in Period 1967-1987," 1988. Lecturer, Indonesia Commercial Law and Law and Economics, University of Indonesia, School of Law, 1982—. *LANGUAGES:* Indonesian and English. *PRACTICE AREAS:* General Corporate Matters.

AMIR KARYATIN, born Semarang, Central Java, 1950. admitted to bar, 1984, Indonesia. *Education:* Krisnadwipayana University, School of Law (S.H., 1983). Associate, Makarim & Taira, 1984-1990. *LANGUAGES:* Indonesian and English. *PRACTICE AREAS:* Patents, Copyrights and Trademarks; General Litigation; Land Law.

INDAH WASONO, born Solo, Central Java, April 29, 1958. admitted to bar, 1983, Indonesia. *Education:* University of Indonesia, School of Law (S.H., 1983). *LANGUAGES:* Indonesian and English.

ASSOCIATES

SITI NURHATI A.H., born Jakarta, Indonesia, December 20, 1952. admitted to bar, 1980, Indonesia. *Education:* University of Indonesia, School of Law (S.H., 1980). *LANGUAGES:* Indonesian and English. *PRACTICE AREAS:* General Corporate Matters.

ZULKARNAIN MANULLANG, born Tanjung Karang, February 1, 1954. admitted to bar, 1986, Indonesia. *Education:* University of Indonesia, School of Law (S.H., 1986). Legal Officer, Lembaga Konsultasi dan Bantuan Hukum (Legal Aid and Consultant), Jakarta, 1986-1988. *LANGUAGES:* Indonesian and English. *PRACTICE AREAS:* Patents and Trademarks.

ARI DWIARI SARASWATI, born Jakarta, January 24, 1966. admitted to bar, 1989, Indonesia. *Education:* University of Trisakti, School of Law (S.H., 1989). *LANGUAGES:* Indonesian and English. *PRACTICE AREAS:* General Corporate Matters.

BAMBANG TRIATMANTO, born Godong, Semarang, Central Java, July 29, 1957. admitted to bar, 1985, Indonesia. *Education:* Krisnadwipayana University, School of Law (S.H., 1985). *LANGUAGES:* Indonesian and English. *PRACTICE AREAS:* General Litigation; Land Law.

KUKUH HARGIANTO, born Jakarta, November 15, 1968. admitted to bar, 1993, Indonesia. *Education:* University of Indonesia, School of Law (S.H., 1993). *LANGUAGES:* Indonesian and English. *PRACTICE AREAS:* General Litigation.

COUNSELLORS

ANTONIUS M. RAHMANATA, born Banjarmasin, South Borneo, November 17, 1926. admitted to bar, 1956, Indonesia. *Education:* University of Leyden, Holland (M.R., Master of Law, 1954); University of Columbia, New York, USA (M.A., 1965). Attorney, Makarim & Taira S., 1984-1988. Vice Dean, Faculty of Law, University of Lambung Mangkurat, 1958-1968. Lecturer, 1958-1970. Member: Board of Trustee, Lambung Mangkurat State University, 1972-1981; Parliament and People of Consultation Assembly (M.P.R.), 1977-1982. *LANGUAGES:* Indonesian, Dutch and English. *PRACTICE AREAS:* General Corporate Matters.

BAMBANG P. SOEDARSO, born Purwokerto, Central Java, 1945. admitted to bar, 1977, Indonesia. *Education:* University of Indonesia, School of Law (S.H., 1976); Dalhousie University, Canada (M.E.S., 1988). Lecturer, Land Law, University of Indonesia, School of Law, 1977—. *LANGUAGES:* Indonesian and English. *PRACTICE AREAS:* Land Law; Environment Law.

SUTOMO, born Blora, East Java, June 24, 1934. admitted to bar, 1960, Indonesia. *Education:* University of Indonesia, School of Law (S.H., 1959); Institute of State Finance (General Tax, 1963); University of Leiden, Neth-

erlands (International Taxation, 1976); Harvard Institute, Cambridge (Mining Taxation, 1978; Legal and Policy of Foreign Investment, Financing and Taxation, 1982). *Member:* International Fiscal Association (IFA). *LANGUAGES:* Indonesian and English. *PRACTICE AREAS:* Mining Law; General Tax Matters.

REPRESENTATIVE CLIENTS: South Australian Government Commercial Representative; Esco-Mobil Inc.; Stanvac Indonesia; Sapta Patra Wisesa-British Gas; Commercial and Industrial Credit Insurance Corp. Ltd. Hamilton 5, Bermuda; Baskin-Robbins International Corp.; Naryadelta Prarthana; United Nation High Commission on Refugees; Citicorp Credit Services, Inc.; First Pacific Bank Ltd.; Dae-Myung Overseas; Gabungan Koperasi Batik Indonesia (GKBI); Nichimen Corp.; Daiwabo; Jaido; Primatexco Indonesia; Garuda Indonesia; United Nations Development Programme (UNDP); International Labour Organization (ILO); Philip Morris Pariwara; PT. Astra International; AUTO 2000; Mercantile Club; Patra Nusa Lease; PT. Light Instrumenindo; PT. Rana Sankara; PT. Alrego; PT Sarutama Prima Perkasa; SETDCO Group; Airo Swadaya Stupa; PT. Bank Nusa International; PT. Bali Tunas Finance; PT. Bangun Tjipta Sarana; PT. Tunas Financindo Corp.; PT. Cosmopolitan Travelindo Int.; PT. ADI Boga Cipta; PT. Emdece; PT. Sukma Pradewa; PT. Aneka Barutama Tirta Chemie; Adelaide Ship Construction International Pty. Ltd.; PT. Sumberraya Maju; PT. Mitra Multi Miranco; PT. Rabo Finance Indonesia.

ALI BUDIARDJO, NUGROHO, REKSODIPUTRO

Counsellors at Law

Established in 1967

NIAGA TOWER, 24TH FLOOR
JALAN JENDERAL SUDIRMAN KAV. 58
JAKARTA 12190, INDONESIA
Telephone: 250-5125 (11 Lines); 250-5136
Telefax: 250-5001; 250-5121

Foreign and Domestic Commercial Transactions, Investment, Trade, Finance, Banking, Licensing, Leasing Transactions, Petroleum and Energy, Stock and Bond Issues on the Indonesian Stock Exchange, Mining, Forestry, Environment, Labor, Patent and Trademarks, Maritime and Shipping, Drafting, Negotiation and Review of Contracts.

PARTNERS

ALI BUDIARDJO, (FOUNDER), born Yogyakarta, Central Java, Indonesia, June 4, 1913. *Education:* Batavia School of Law (Meester in de Rechten, 1937); Massachusetts Institution of Technology, Cambridge (Master Degree Science, Industrial Management, 1961). Secretary General, Department of Defense, 1950-1953. Director General, State Planning Bureau, 1953-1959. Senior Adviser to the Prime Minister, 1959-1962. Founder: Legal Consultants Office "ALI BUDIARDJO", 1965; "ALI BUDIARDJO AND ASSOCIATES", 1967; "ALI BUDIARDJO, NUGROHO, REKSODIPUTRO", 1969—. Chairman, Indonesian Legal Consultants Association, 1988—. *LANGUAGES:* Indonesian, English and Dutch. *PRACTICE AREAS:* Mining.

NUGROHO (1919-1984).

MARDJONO REKSODIPUTRO, born Blitar, East Java, Indonesia, March 13, 1937. *Education:* Faculty of Law, University of Indonesia, Jakarta (S.H., 1961); University of Pennsylvania (Master Degree in Criminology, 1967). Dean, Faculty of Law, University of Indonesia, 1984-1990. Director of the Centre for Justice and the Rule of Law, University of Indonesia (Formerly known as Institute of Criminology), 1970—. Director, Legal Documentation Center, 1974-1984. Member, 1984—and Chairman, 1988—, National Drafting Committee of the Indonesian Criminal Code. *LANGUAGES:* Indonesian, English and Dutch. *PRACTICE AREAS:* Foreign and Domestic Commercial Transactions; Investment and Mining.

NETTY AMALUDIN SUTADIWIRIA, born Jakarta, Indonesia, December 30, 1928. *Education:* Faculty of Law, University of Indonesia, Jakarta (S.H., 1954). *LANGUAGES:* Indonesian, English and Dutch. *PRACTICE AREAS:* Investment Law; Mining; Real Estate Transaction; Coordinating and Supervision of Court Proceedings; Corporate Matters; Intellectual Property Rights; Copyright, Patent and Trademarks; Real Property; Licensing and Franchising.

BIENTARTI ABUBAKAR SALEH, born Kutoarjo, Central Java, Indonesia, July 14, 1930. *Education:* Faculty of Law, University of Indonesia, Jakarta (S.H., 1982). *LANGUAGES:* Indonesian, English and Dutch. *PRACTICE AREAS:* Corporate Matters; Investments; Commercial Transactions; Real Property; Labor and Employment.

SANITIOSO, born Tanjung Pinang, Riau, Indonesia, January 29, 1927. *Education:* Faculty of Law, University of Indonesia, Jakarta (S.H., 1955).

(This Listing Continued)   *(This Listing Continued)*

ALI BUDIARDJO, NUGROHO, REKSODIPUTRO, Jakarta—Continued

Head of the Bureau for Legal Affairs, Ministry of Sea Communication, 1956-1966. Head of the Bureau for Legal Affairs, Parliamentary and Foreign Cooperation of the Department of Communications, 1966-1983. *LANGUAGES:* Indonesian, English and Dutch. *PRACTICE AREAS:* Commercial Law; Investment Law and Corporate Management; Trademark.

MOHAMMAD NOOR SUMOWIDJOJO, born Jember, East Java, Indonesia, September 18, 1934. *Education:* Faculty of Law, University of Indonesia, Jakarta (S.H., 1960); London (Courses in Management Science (1971-1972). Lecturer, Indonesian Christian University, Jakarta, 1960-1966. *LANGUAGES:* Indonesian, English and Dutch. *PRACTICE AREAS:* Corporate, Loans, Investments, Labour, Natural Resources; International Business Transactions.

ACHMAD S. KARTOHADIPRODJO, born Garut, West Java, Indonesia, September 15, 1937. Licensed Advocate, 1969—. *Education:* Faculty of Law, Parahyangan Catholic University, Bandung, West Java (S.H., 1966); Boalt Hall School of Law, University of California, Berkeley (Foreign Investment and Administrative Law Program, 1973). Head of the Legal Bureau, Garuda Indonesian Airways, 1971-1984. *LANGUAGES:* Indonesian and English. *PRACTICE AREAS:* Aircraft Transactions; Banking, Leasing and Financing; Representative Office; Supervision of Litigation.

A. ZEN UMAR PURBA, born Tebing Tinggi, North Sumatra, Indonesia, July 18, 1942. *Education:* Faculty of Law, University of Indonesia, Jakarta (S.H., 1974); Harvard Law School (LL.M., 1979). Law Editor, *Tempo,* News Magazine, 1971-1979. Lecturer, Faculty of Law, University of Indonesia, 1974—. *Member:* The Indonesian Association of Counsellors at Law; Capital Market Lawyers Association. *LANGUAGES:* Indonesian and English. *PRACTICE AREAS:* Capital Market, Investment, Oil and Natural Resources; Environment and Corporate Legal Matters.

ARIFIN KADARISMAN, born Tegal, Indonesia, February 11, 1931. *Education:* Faculty of Law, University of Indonesia, Jakarta (S.H., 1958). *Member:* Association of Indonesian Insurance Lawyers; Association of Indonesian Legal Consultants. *LANGUAGES:* Indonesian, English and Dutch. *PRACTICE AREAS:* Corporate Law, Banking, Loan and Lease Financing; Investments, Commercial Transactions; Maritime and Insurance Law.

BRIGITTA IMAM RAHAYOE, born Solo, Central Java, Indonesia, March 23, 1950. *Education:* Faculty of Law, University of Indonesia, Jakarta (S.H., 1984). Member, Indonesian Legal Consultants Association. *LANGUAGES:* Indonesian and English. *PRACTICE AREAS:* Banking, Investments, Finance, Commercial Transactions; Corporate Matters.

TEUKU MUHAMMAD ZAHIRSJAH, born Idi, Aceh, Indonesia, June 9, 1930. *Education:* Faculty of Law, University of Indonesia, Jakarta (S.H., 1958). Managing Director of Bank Indonesia (Central Bank of Indonesia), 1981-1988. Ambassador to the Kingdom of Belgium and the Grand Duchy of Luxembourg (1990-1994). *LANGUAGES:* Indonesian, English and Dutch. *PRACTICE AREAS:* Banking and Investment.

MUHAMAD HUSSEYN UMAR, born Medan, Indonesia, January 21, 1931. *Education:* Faculty of Law, University of Indonesia, Jakarta (S.H., 1957); Maritime Law Training in U.S.A., U.K. and West Germany (1960-1961). Author: "Freight Forwarding Legislation," Pt Djambatan, 1962; "Sea-Transport In Deregulation," PT. Dian Rakyat, 1992. Lecturer, Maritime Law, Faculty for Post Graduate Studies, University of Indonesia, 1983. Director for State Maritime Enterprises, Directorate General of Sea-Communications, Jakarta, 1964-1969. Maritime Technical Attache, Indonesian Embassy, The Hague, 1964-1974. President Director, PANN Ship Financing Coy, Jakarta, 1974-1979 and PELNI National Shipping Lines, Jakarta, 1979-1983. Adviser, Shipping Ports, Multimodal Transport and Maritime Legislation, UNCTAD, Geneve, 1986-1988. Adviser, Indonesian Maritime Law Institute, 1984—. Chairman, Centre for Maritime Law Studies, University of Indonesia, 1987-1992. Member, Indonesian National Arbitration Board, 1984—. *LANGUAGES:* Indonesian, English and Dutch. *PRACTICE AREAS:* Commercial Transactions Law; Corporate; Investments; Ship Financing; Maritime Law and Transportation Law; Dispute Matters/Arbitration.

HAJATI SUROREDJO, born Tegal (Central-Java), Indonesia, October 4, 1929. *Education:* Faculty of Law, University of Indonesia, Jakarta (S.H., 1957); George Washington University, School of Law (Certificate of Achievement, 1964). Lecturer, Corporate Law, Faculty for Post Graduate Studies, University of Indonesia, 1983—. Director Civil Law, Department of Justice, Republic of Indonesia, 1966-1982. Expert Staff to the Minister of

(This Listing Continued)

Justice, Republic of Indonesia, 1982-1989. Consultant to the National Law Development Agency of the Department of Justice, 1988-1991. *Member:* Asian Law Association. *LANGUAGES:* Indonesian, English and Dutch. *PRACTICE AREAS:* Commercial Transaction, Investment; Corporate and Trademark Matters; Civil Law.

WURJATI MARTOSEWOJO, born Purbolinggo, Indonesia, February 10, 1931. *Education:* Faculty of Law, Pajajaran University, Bandung (S.H., 1964); State University of Leiden, The Netherlands (1969-1970). Director: Patent and Copyright, 1976-1982; Civil Law, 1982-1989, Department of Justice. *LANGUAGES:* Indonesian, English and Dutch. *PRACTICE AREAS:* Intellectual Property (Copyright, Patent and Trademarks); Licensing, Corporate Matters.

RICKY S. NAZIR, born Tondano, North Celebes, Indonesia, February 18, 1946. *Education:* Faculty of Law, University of Indonesia, Jakarta (S.H., 1982); qualified for appointment as a Notary (1989). *LANGUAGES:* Indonesian, English and Dutch. *PRACTICE AREAS:* Corporate Matters, Commercial Transactions; Real-Property, Investments, Labor and Employment.

FERRY P. MADIAN, born Hong Kong, December 13, 1962. *Education:* Faculty of Law, University of Indonesia, Jakarta (S.H., 1986); School of Law, University of Washington, Seattle (LL.M., 1993). *Member:* Indonesian Legal Consultants Association. *LANGUAGES:* Indonesian and English. *PRACTICE AREAS:* Investment Law; Stock and Bond issues on the Indonesian Stock Exchange; Mining and Corporate Law.

ERNST G. TEHUTERU, born UjungPandang, January 27, 1936. *Education:* Faculty of Law, University of Indonesia, Jakarta (S.H., 1963); Southern Methodist University, Dallas Texas (M.C.L., 1978). *LANGUAGES:* Indonesian, English and Dutch. *PRACTICE AREAS:* Mining; Investment; Environment; Labour; Business Transactions.

ASSOCIATES

EMIR NURMANSJAH, born Jakarta, Indonesia, September 26, 1966. *Education:* Faculty of Law, University of Indonesia (S.H., 1989); Bond Law School, Australia (LL.M., 1993). *LANGUAGES:* Indonesian and English. *PRACTICE AREAS:* Investment; Corporate Law; Commercial Transaction; Banking; Finance.

LOLANI K. IRDHAM-IDROES, born Jakarta, Indonesia, April 22, 1965. *Education:* Faculty of Law, University of Indonesia (S.H., 1988); Case Western Reserve University, School of Law, Cleveland (LL.M., 1993). *LANGUAGES:* Indonesian and English. *PRACTICE AREAS:* Investment, Corporate Law and Capital Market.

WAHYU NUGROHO, born Jakarta, Indonesia, April 7, 1965. *Education:* Faculty of Law, University of Indonesia (S.H., 1988). *LANGUAGES:* Indonesian and English. *PRACTICE AREAS:* Capital Market, Labor; Investment; Corporate Law; Banking Finance; Real Property; Litigation.

RITA TYASTUTI TAUFIK, born Malang, Indonesia, September 18, 1959. *Education:* Faculty of Law, University of Indonesia (S.H., 1984). *LANGUAGES:* Indonesian and English. *PRACTICE AREAS:* Corporate Matters and Investment.

NINI N. HALIM, born Jakarta, Indonesia, November 7, 1965. *Education:* Faculty of Law, University of Indonesia (S.H., 1990). *LANGUAGES:* Indonesian and English. *PRACTICE AREAS:* Intellectual Property, Corporate Law and Investment; Labor and Employment.

ANASTASIA HENDARIN, born Jakarta, Indonesia, October 20, 1964. *Education:* Faculty of Law, University of Indonesia (S.H., 1989). *LANGUAGES:* Indonesian and English. *PRACTICE AREAS:* Investment; Labor; Natural Resources; Real-Property and Corporate Law.

MAROJAHAN HUTABARAT, born Medan, Indonesia, January 30, 1966. *Education:* Faculty of Law, Parahyangan Catholic University (S.H., 1991). *LANGUAGES:* Indonesian and English. *PRACTICE AREAS:* Investment Law; Corporate Legal Matters; Capital Market Law.

NAFIS ADWANI, born Jakarta, Indonesia, March 17, 1958. *Education:* University of Indonesia (S.H., 1984). *LANGUAGES:* Indonesian and English. *PRACTICE AREAS:* Land Law; Corporate Law; Labour Law.

BANI WIRAWAN KUSNANDAR, born Rumbai, Indonesia, September 20, 1964. *Education:* University of Indonesia (S.H., 1990). *LANGUAGES:* Indonesian and English. *PRACTICE AREAS:* Investment Law; Corporate Law; Banking Law; Capital Market.

MOHAMAD ZAKY ACHTAR, born Jakarta, Indonesia, March 23, 1969. *Education:* University of Indonesia (S.H., 1993). *LANGUAGES:*

(This Listing Continued)

Indonesian and English. *PRACTICE AREAS:* Investment Law; Corporate Law; Mining; Banking Law.

LEVI LANA, born Ende-Flores-N.T.T., July 15, 1964. *Education:* Faculty of Law, University of Indonesia (S.H., 1993). *LANGUAGES:* Indonesian and English. *PRACTICE AREAS:* Intellectual Property; Investment; Land Law; Contract Law.

AUGUSTINE BAKUNGSANTI, born Togjakarta, July 5, 1967. *Education:* University of Indonesia (S.H., 1992). *LANGUAGES:* Indonesian and English. *PRACTICE AREAS:* Investment; Corporate Law; Shipping-/Maritime.

YANNY MEUTHIA SURYARETINA, born Banda Aceh, January 17, 1969. *Education:* University of Indonesia (S.H., 1993). *LANGUAGES:* Indonesian and English. *PRACTICE AREAS:* Shipping/Maritime; Trademark; Investment; Corporate Law.

OF COUNSEL

GREGORY CHURCHILL, born Niagara Falls, May 22, 1947; admitted, 1975, California (Not admitted in Indonesia). *Education:* Cornell University (B.A., magna cum laude Economics, 1969); Harvard Law School (J.D., 1975). Member, American-Indonesian B: - National Fulbright Commission, 1992—. Lecturer, Faculty of Law, University of Indonesia, 1976-1995. Lecturer on American Law, Post Graduate Faculty, University of Indonesia, 1981-1995. Research Assistant, Boalt Hall School of Law, University of California, 1975-1976. Peace Corps Volunteer, Malaysia, 1969-1971. Consultant to the Legal Documentation Center, University of Indonesia and National Law Development Agency of the Department of Justice, 1976-1995. With Graham & James, California, 1975-1976. *LANGUAGES:* Indonesian and English. *PRACTICE AREAS:* Investment Law, Corporate Law; Economic Regulations; Legal Information Systems; Development of Legal Institutions.

ERIK HAMMERSTEIN, born Rotterdam, The Netherlands, July 9, 1950; admitted, 1979, Amsterdam. *Education:* Trinity College Dublin BA (Hon); Nijmegen University MA, 1979. With Loeff Claeys Verbeke, Amsterdam 1979-1993, Partner. Member of IBA. *LANGUAGES:* Dutch, English, German, French and Indonesian. *PRACTICE AREAS:* Investment Law; Corporate Law; Banking and Capital Markets.

ALBERT P. PLOEGER, born Amsterdam, The Netherlands, May 4, 1962; admitted, 1989, Amsterdam. *Education:* Free University Amsterdam (Master of Law, 1988). Lecturer, Law Program, Post Graduate Faculty, University of Indonesia, 1994 - Associate, Loeff Claeys Verbeke the Netherlands, 1989-1993. *LANGUAGES:* English, Dutch, German and Indonesian. *PRACTICE AREAS:* Investment Law; Corporate Law; Banking Law; Commercial Law; Intellectual Property Rights.

LEGAL SUPPORT PERSONNEL

AZHAR HARIS, born Padang West Sumatera, Indonesia, September 21, 1950. *Education:* Accounting Academy of Indonesia (B.Sc., 1976). *LANGUAGES:* Indonesian and English. *PRACTICE AREAS:* Office Manager.

APRIYONO NUR DUMADI, born Klaten, Central Java, Indonesia, April 30, 1960. *Education:* Technical High School (Klaten, 1979). *LANGUAGES:* Indonesian and English. *PRACTICE AREAS:* Information Systems.

WINDRATI SELBY, born Salatiga, Central Java, Indonesia, July 16, 1949. *Education:* Department of English, Satya Wacana University, Salatiga (Dra., 1972). Authorized and Sworn Translator (1982). *LANGUAGES:* Indonesian and English. *PRACTICE AREAS:* English Language Editor.

BAMBANG GUNADI, born Purworejo, Central Java, Indonesia, June 16, 1950. *Education:* Akademi Pimpinan Perusahaan Indonesia, Jakarta (BBA., 1980). *LANGUAGES:* Indonesian and English. *PRACTICE AREAS:* Law Librarian.

WISHNU WIDJAJANTO BASUKI, born Samarinda, September 7, 1962. *Education:* Jember University (Drs., 1988); University of Indonesia (M.A., 1992). *LANGUAGES:* Indonesian and English. *PRACTICE AREAS:* Know-How and Research.

ANINDA PRIMAROSA LISTYARTO, born Jakarta, January 14, 1966. *Education:* University of Indonesia (S.H., 1990); Indiana University of Pennsylvania (M.B.A., 1993). *PRACTICE AREAS:* Corporate Law; Investment, Trademark and Banking Law.

BYA ONGKO SIDHARTA TADJOEDIN
WISMA KYOEI PRINCE 19TH FLOOR
JLAN JENDERAL SUDIRMAN KAV. 3
JAKARTA 10220, INDONESIA
Telephone: (021) 572-4225
Fax: (021) 572-4227

Corporate, Commercial and Financial Law Practice, Energy and Natural Resources, Maritime, Banking, Capital, Markets and Securities Law, Insurance, Intellectual Property, Investment, Labor, Franchising, Real Estate, Construction and Engineering, Mergers and Acquisitions, Tax Law, Arbitration, Hotel and Tourist Development, Environmental Law and Telecommunication Law.

FIRM PROFILE: The law firm BYA ONGKO SIDHARTA TADJOEDIN represents local and multinational corporations, private and publicly listed companies, offshore and local banks, financial institutions and insurance companies, manufacturers, traders, real estate developers, engineering and construction companies, telecommunication and shipping companies.

PARTNERS

ASFA DAVY BYA, born Palembang, Indonesia, 1960. *Education:* Faculty of Law, Christian University of Indonesia (S.H., 1983). *LANGUAGES:* Indonesian and English. *PRACTICE AREAS:* Business Law; Natural Resources Law; Maritime Law; Banking Law; Finance Law; Intellectual Property Law; Franchise Law; Mergers and Acquisitions; Resorts and Leisure Law; Corporate Law; Commercial Law.

HELEN THEORUPUN ONGKO, born Ambon, Indonesia, 1959. *Education:* Faculty of Law, University of Indonesia (S.H., 1986). *LANGUAGES:* Indonesian and English. *PRACTICE AREAS:* Banking Law; Business Law; Finance Law; Intellectual Property Law; Franchise Law; Mergers and Acquisitions; Resorts and Leisure Law; Corporate Law; Commercial Law; Telecommunication Law; Investment Law.

BOYKE ACHMAD SIDHARTA, born Jakarta, Indonesia, 1959. *Education:* Faculty of Law, University of Indonesia (S.H., 1988). *LANGUAGES:* Indonesian and English. *PRACTICE AREAS:* Corporate Law; Commercial Law; Capital Markets Law; Business Law; Environmental Law; Labour Law; Real Estate Law; Franchise Law; Intellectual Property Law; Natural Resources Law; Arbitration; Investment Law; Telecommunication Law.

FARINA TADJOEDIN, born Jakarta, Indonesia, 1965. *Education:* Faculty of Law, University of Indonesia (S.H., 1987). *LANGUAGES:* Indonesian and English. *PRACTICE AREAS:* Corporate Law; Commercial Law; Capital Markets Law; Banking Law; Finance Law; Taxation Law; Resort and Leisure Law; Mergers and Acquisitions; Intellectual Property Law; Labour Law; Real Estate and Construction Business.

YUDI ANGGRAITO SASTROWARDOJO, born Surabaya, Indonesia, 1962. *Education:* Faculty of Law, University of Airlangga, Surabaya (S.H., 1985)). *LANGUAGES:* Indonesian and English. *PRACTICE AREAS:* Corporate Law; Business Law; Commercial Law; Criminal Law; Consumer Law; Environmental Law; Press and Media Law and Litigation.

KANTOR PENGACARA PROF. MR. DR. S. GAUTAMA (GOUWGIOKSIONG)
NO. 9 MEDAN MERDEKA TIMUR
P.O. BOX 1341
JAKARTA 10013, INDONESIA
Telephone: 366529; 3809488; 3841358; 3847165
Cable Address: "Indolaw"
Telex: 46620 Indlaw IA
FAX: 62 (21) 374390

General Practice. Foreign Investments, Civil-Commercial Law, Patent and Trademarks and Private International Law.

SUDARGO GAUTAMA, born Jakarta, Indonesia, 1928; admitted, 1951, Indonesia. *Education:* Faculty of Law, University of Indonesia (LL.M., Meester in de Rechten 1950; Ph.D., Doctor of Law and Social Sciences 1955). Professor of Law, University of Indonesia, 1958. Visiting Professor: University of Amsterdam, 1967-1968; Sydney Law School, 1970. Delegate to the First Conference of the Law Association for Asia and the Western Pacific, Kualalumpur, 1968. Chairman, Indonesian Observers Delegation to Eleventh Session of the Hague Conference on Private International Law, 1968. *Member:* International Law Association (London); The

(This Listing Continued)

KANTOR PENGACARA PROF. MR. DR. S. GAUTAMA (GOUWGIOKSIONG), Jakarta—Continued

American Society of International Law (Washington); Association des Anciens Auditeurs de l'Academie de Droit International; Law Association for Asia and the Western Pacific; American Bar Association; International Bar Association.

T. TUEGEH-LONGDONG, born Balikpapan, Indonesia, 1936. *Education:* University of Indonesia (Meester in de Rechten, 1960). *Member:* Indonesia Bar Association. *LANGUAGES:* Indonesian, Dutch and English.

H. KOMALA LUMANAU, born Kuningan, Indonesia, 1934. *Education:* University of Indonesia (Meester in de Rechten, 1960). *LANGUAGES:* Indonesian, Dutch and English.

MOENARWATY SUKAJAT, born Malang, Indonesia, 1944. *Education:* University of Indonesia (S.H., 1970). *Member:* Indonesian Bar Association. *LANGUAGES:* Indonesian and English.

ELLYDA SOETIYARTO TANDJUNG, born Medan, Indonesia, 1947. *Education:* University of Indonesia (S.H., 1972). *LANGUAGES:* Indonesian and English.

LIZ ASNAHWATI, born Medan, Indonesia, 1950. *Education:* University of Indonesia (S.H., 1974). *LANGUAGES:* Indonesian and English.

ABIGAIL GAUTAMA, born Jakarta, Indonesia, 1951. *Education:* University of Indonesia (S.H., 1974). *LANGUAGES:* Indonesian, English and Dutch.

TETY IRAWATI, born Jakarta, Indonesia, 1951. *Education:* Trisakti University (S.H., 1975). *LANGUAGES:* Indonesian and English.

ELZA INDRARINI DEWI, born Blora, Indonesia, 1944. *Education:* Parahyangan University (S.H., 1968). *LANGUAGES:* Indonesian and English.

RIZAWANTO WINATA, born Ujungpandang, Indonesia, 1951. *Education:* University of Indonesia (S.H., 1982). *LANGUAGES:* Indonesian and English.

UDENG MULYAR, born Jakarta, Indonesia, 1942. *Education:* Krisnadwipayana University, Jakarta (S.H., 1985). *LANGUAGES:* Indonesian and English.

ROBBY WIDJAJA, born Bandung, Indonesia, 1938. *Education:* Parahyangan University, Bandung (S.H., 1970). *LANGUAGES:* Indonesian, English and Dutch.

JAMES SUDARGO, born Jakarta, Indonesia, 1956. *Education:* University of Indonesia (S.H., 1983). *LANGUAGES:* Indonesian and English.

WULAN P. AFIAT-PONDAAG, born Jakarta, Indonesia, 1959. *Education:* University of Indonesia (S.H., 1985). *LANGUAGES:* Indonesian and English.

REPRESENTATIVE CLIENTS: Japanese Embassy and Swiss Embassy, Jakarta; Freeport Indonesia, New York; Unilever London & Jakarta; Development Bank for Indonesia; Indonesia Overseas Bank (INDOVER); Bank Dagang Negara (State Commercial Bank); British American Tobacco; Pfizer Inc.; Richardson-Merrell; Toyo Menka; Sumitomo; Arnold Otto Meyer; Johs Larsen; Bank of America; Chase Manhattan Bank; C. Itoh; B.A.S.F.; A.B. Astra, Sweden, Toyota, Sony, Matsushieta Electric; Schering-Plough; Overseas Private Investment Corp. (OPIC), Washington, D.C.; Midland Bank Group International Trade Services; Citibank N.A.; Indonesian State Banks; Bank Negara Indonesia 1946; Bank Ekspor Impor Indonesia; Deutsche Bank (Asia); Singapore Airlines.
REFERENCES: Dr. Robert Delson, New York, N.Y.; Coudert Brothers, New York N.Y.; White and Case, Washington, D.C.

GIUNSENG MANULLANG PATENT & LAW OFFICE

Patent, Mark, Copyright & Related Causes

JALAN KAYU PUTIH TENGAH I A NO. 7
PULOMAS, JAKARTA 13210, INDONESIA
Telephone: (62) (021) 470-4185
Fax: (62) (021) 470-1450; 470-4184

Patent and Trademark Commercial and Banking Litigation and Corporate Practice and Translation Services.

GIUNSENG EP. MANULLANG, born Tarutung, North Sumatera, Indonesia, August 11, 1952; admitted, 1979, Jakarta, licensed Patent Consultant/Attorney, sworn Translator. *Education:* Faculty of Law, University of Indonesia (Master of Law, 1976); University of California Los Angeles (Business Law Program, 1986); Southern Methodist University, Dallas, Texas (LL.M., 1987). *Member:* Indonesian Bar Association. *LANGUAGES:* Indonesian and English.

ASSOCIATES

ROHANAPOS NAIBAHO. *Education:* Master of Law.

RONALD MANULLANG. *Education:* Bachelor of Art.

PRIA UTAMA TOBING. *Education:* Master of Law.

HARLY SIBARANI. *Education:* M.B.A., Engineering.

EDWINA TOBING. *Education:* Engineering.

EKAYANI TOBING. *Education:* Master of Art.

HADIPUTRANTO, HADINOTO & PARTNERS

THE LANDMARK CENTRE I, 24TH FLOOR
JALAN JENDERAL SUDIRMAN NO. 1
JAKARTA 12910, INDONESIA
Telephone: (21) 570-0396, 520-9424, 520-2444
Intn'l. Dialing: (62-21) 570-0396, 520-9424, 520-2444
Telex: 65347
Answer Back: 65347 ABOGAD IA
Facsimile: (62-21) 570-0399; 520-9434

International and General Practice. Corporation, Commercial, Foreign Investment. Tax and Labor Law, Banking and Finance, Capital Markets, Intellectual Property, Construction, Natural Resources. Telecommunications. Insurance.

MEMBERS OF FIRM

SRI INDRASTUTI HADIPUTRANTO, born Magelang, Central Java, Indonesia. *Education:* Faculty of Law and Social Sciences, University of Indonesia (S.H., 1970); Trisakti University, Tax Consultants Program, (1974); University of Washington (LL.M., 1981). *LANGUAGES:* Indonesian and English.

TUTI DEWI HADINOTO, born Jogyakarta, Indonesia. *Education:* Faculty of Law, University of Indonesia (S.H. 1981). *LANGUAGES:* Indonesian and English.

ERNA LETTY KUSOY, born Sukabumi, West Java, Indonesia. *Education:* University of Indonesia (S.H., 1967). Qualified as Notary Public, 1980. *LANGUAGES:* Indonesian, English and Dutch.

ENNY MELANITA, born Sukabumi, Indonesia. *Education:* Faculty of Law, University of Indonesia (S.H., 1981). *LANGUAGES:* Indonesian and English.

TIMUR SUKIRNO, born Jakarta, Indonesia. *Education:* Faculty of Law, University of Indonesia (S.H., 1988); Boston University (LL.M., 1991). *LANGUAGES:* Indonesian and English.

IKE ANDRIANI, born Bandung, Indonesia. *Education:* Parahiyangan Catholic University (S.H., 1994). *LANGUAGES:* Indonesian and English.

SALOMO RAHMATUAH DAMANIK, born Jakarta, Indonesia. *Education:* Faculty of Law, University of Indonesia (S.H., 1992). *LANGUAGES:* Indonesian and English.

SARINA SUTADISASTRA DANUNINGRAT, born Jakarta, Indonesia. *Education:* Faculty of Law, University of Krisnadwipayana (S.H., 1993). *LANGUAGES:* Indonesian and English.

DWI DARU HERDANI, born Jakarta, Indonesia. *Education:* Faculty of Law, University of Indonesia (S.H., 1992). *LANGUAGES:* Indonesian and English.

DANIEL GINTING, born Simalungun, Indonesia. *Education:* University of Indonesia (S.H., 1994). *LANGUAGES:* Indonesian, English and Dutch.

INDRI P. GURITNO. *Education:* Faculty of Law, University of Indonesia (S.H., 1994). *LANGUAGES:* English and Indonesian.

YANDRI HENDARTA, born Jambi, Indonesia. *Education:* Faculty of Law, Parahyangan Catholic University (S.H., 1992). *LANGUAGES:* Indonesian, English.

(This Listing Continued)

(This Listing Continued)

SRI WAHYU KARINI, born Bogor, West Java, Indonesia. *Education:* Faculty of Law, University of Indonesia (S.H., 1989). *LANGUAGES:* Indonesian and English.

TEGUH MARAMIS, born Jayapura, Indonesia. *Education:* Faculty of Law, University of Indonesia (S.H., 1988). *LANGUAGES:* Indonesian and English.

PARMAGITA MOERAD, born Bandung, Indonesia. *Education:* Faculty of Law, University of Parahyangan (S.H., 1991). *LANGUAGES:* Indonesian and English.

SIENDY KATIRACHMADIAH MUSMAR, born Bandung, Indonesia. *Education:* Faculty of Law, University of Parahyangan (S.H., 1991). *LANGUAGES:* Indonesian and English.

MOHAMAD KADRI NIZAROEDDIN, born Jakarta, Indonesia. *Education:* Faculty of Law, University of Indonesia (S.H., 1988). *LANGUAGES:* Indonesian and English.

ERIKA CHIKO NOVENI, born Jakarta, Indonesia. *Education:* Faculty of Law, University of Indonesia (S.H., 1987). *LANGUAGES:* Indonesian, English and Japanese.

INDRI PRAMITASWARI, born Jakarta, Indonesia. *Education:* Faculty of Law, University of Indonesia (S.H., 1994). *LANGUAGES:* Indonesian and English.

GRACE P. PRANATA, born Bandung, Indonesia. *Education:* Atmajaya Catholic University (S.H., 1993); Cornell University, Ithaca, New York, U.S.A. (LL.M., 1994). *LANGUAGES:* Indonesian and English.

AGUSDIN TRI RACHMANTO, born Jakarta, Indonesia. *Education:* Faculty of Law, University of Indonesia (S.H., 1990); Washington College of Law, American University, Washington, D.C. (LL.M., 1993). *LANGUAGES:* Indonesian and English.

HARUN ADMANA REKSODIPUTRO, born Jakarta, Indonesia. *Education:* Faculty of Law, University of Indonesia (S.H., 1993). *LANGUAGES:* Indonesian and English.

INDAH N. RESPATI, born Malang, Indonesia. *Education:* University of Indonesia (S.H., 1981). *LANGUAGES:* Indonesian and English.

NIA K. HARIMATARA SUJANI, born Cirebon, Indonesia. *Education:* Faculty of Law, University of Padjadjaran (S.H., 1991). *LANGUAGES:* Indonesian and English.

SRI IRMIATI SUMARYO, born Bogor, Indonesia. *Education:* University of Indonesia (S.H., 1982). *LANGUAGES:* Indonesian and English.

ZORAIDA SYARFUAN, born Jakarta, Indonesia. *Education:* University of Indonesia (S.H., 1992); University of Washington, Seattle, Washington, U.S.A. (LL.M., 1994). *LANGUAGES:* Indonesian and English.

CHRISTIAN BUDIANTO TEO, born Jakarta, Indonesia. *Education:* Faculty of Law, University of Indonesia (S.H., 1990). *LANGUAGES:* Indonesian and English.

ILYA UTAMA, born Jakarta, Indonesia. *Education:* Faculty of Law, University of Indonesia (S.H., 1993). *LANGUAGES:* Indonesian and English.

ALEX RASI WANGGE, born Ende, Indonesia. *Education:* Faculty of Law, University of Indonesia (S.H., 1982). *LANGUAGES:* Indonesian, English, Dutch, German and Latin.

BUDI UNGGUL W., born Palembang, Sumatera, Indonesia. *Education:* Faculty of Law, University of Indonesia (S.H., 1994). *LANGUAGES:* Indonesian and English.

WIMBANU WIDYATMOKO, born Jakarta, Indonesia. *Education:* University of Indonesia (S.H., 1989). *LANGUAGES:* Indonesian and English.

DOROTHEA NAWANG WULAN, born Jakarta, Indonesia. *Education:* University of Indonesia (S.H., 1992).

FOREIGN LEGAL CONSULTANT

CHARLES GAYLORD WATKINS, born Calgary, Alberta, Canada, 1941; admitted, 1976, Ontario; 1980, Alberta (Not admitted in Indonesia). *Education:* McGill University (B.Sc., 1962); Osgoode Hall Law School (LL.B., 1967); Yale Law School (LL.M., 1971). *LANGUAGES:* English and French.

HANAFIAH SOEHARTO PONGGAWA

in association with Deacons / Graham & James / Sly Weigall

GEDUNG BNI, 24TH FLOOR
JL. JENDERAL SUDIRMAN KAV. 1
JAKARTA 10220, INDONESIA
Telephone: 5701837 (Hunting)
Fax: HSP-JKT Ind (62-21) 5701835

Foreign Investment, Banking and Finance, General Corporate, Construction, Intellectual Property, Mining, Oil and Gas, Telecommunications, Real Property, Securities, Taxation.

FIRM PROFILE: This firm specializes in commercial and corporate work in connection with international and local transactions and intellectual property matters. It has three partners and ten associates and a foreign counsel. Its lawyers speak Indonesian, English, Mandarin, Dutch, German, French and Italian. This firm also has a litigation department to support its practice in the above areas.

PARTNERS

AL HAKIM HANAFIAH. *Education:* Faculty of Law, University of Indonesia (S.H., 1985); University of Washington, School of Law (LL.M., 1987). *LANGUAGES:* Indonesian, English and Dutch. *PRACTICE AREAS:* Foreign Investment Law; Banking Law; Securities; Mining Law; General Corporate and Commercial Law.

DEWI KAMARATIH SOEHARTO. *Education:* Faculty of Law, University of Indonesia (S.H., 1989). *LANGUAGES:* Indonesian and English. *PRACTICE AREAS:* Foreign Investment Law; Taxation Law; Intellectual Property Law; General Corporate and Commercial Law.

CONSTANT MARINO PONGGAWA. *Education:* Faculty of Law, Christian University of Indonesia (S.H., 1986); Southern Methodist University Law School (LL.M., 1989); Academy of American and International Law, International Comparative Law Center, Dallas, Texas (1989). *LANGUAGES:* Indonesian, English and Dutch. *PRACTICE AREAS:* Lease Law; Banking Law; Real Property Law; Shipping Law; General Corporate and Commercial Law.

ASSOCIATES

ISKANDAR NARO. *Education:* Faculty of Law, University of Indonesia (S.H., 1993). *LANGUAGES:* Indonesian and English. *PRACTICE AREAS:* Foreign and Domestic Investment Law; General Corporate and Commercial Law.

HELENA ADNAN. *Education:* Faculty of Law, University of Indonesia (S.H., 1991). *LANGUAGES:* Indonesian and English. *PRACTICE AREAS:* Intellectual Property Law; Trade Mark Enforcement Law; General Corporate and Commercial Law; Banking Law; Secured Transactions Law; Agency Law; Distributorship Law; Health Law; Food and Drug Registration.

EVA NOERDIN. *Education:* Faculty of Law, University of Indonesia (S.H., 1982). *LANGUAGES:* Indonesian and English. *PRACTICE AREAS:* Litigation; Intellectual Property Enforcement Law; General Corporate and Commercial Law.

MITA NURCAHYANTI DJAJADIREDJA. *Education:* Faculty of Law, University of Indonesia (S.H., 1991). *LANGUAGES:* Indonesian and English. *PRACTICE AREAS:* General Corporate and Commercial Law.

FERRY SISWOJO. *Education:* Faculty of Law, Tarumanegara University (S.H., 1993). *LANGUAGES:* Indonesian, English and Chinese (Mandarin, Tio Ciu, Hok Kian, Khek). *PRACTICE AREAS:* General Corporate and Commercial Law.

FABIAN BUDDY PASCOAL. *Education:* Faculty of Law, University of Indonesia (S.H., 1992). *LANGUAGES:* Indonesian and English. *PRACTICE AREAS:* Labour Law; Intellectual Property Enforcements Law.

IRAWATI HERMAWAN. *Education:* Faculty of Law, Padjadjaran University of Bandung, International Law Department (S.H., 1992). *LANGUAGES:* Indonesian and English. *PRACTICE AREAS:* Insurance Law; Intellectual Property Law.

ANTHONY L.P. HUTAPEA. *Education:* Faculty of Law, University of Indonesia (S.H., 1992). *LANGUAGES:* Indonesian and English. *PRACTICE AREAS:* Environmental Law; Litigation.

YONATHAN HERMANTO. *Education:* Faculty of Law, Satya Wacana Christian University (S.H., 1988). *LANGUAGES:* Indonesian and English. *PRACTICE AREAS:* Corporate and Commercial Law.

(This Listing Continued)

HANAFIAH SOEHARTO PONGGAWA, *Jakarta—Continued*

JONI ARIES BANGUN. *Education:* Faculty of Law, University of Indonesia (S.H., 1989). *LANGUAGES:* Indonesian and English. *PRACTICE AREAS:* Corporate Law; Commercial Law; Litigation; Securities Law.

ANDY KELANA. *Education:* Faculty of Law, Parahyangan Catholic University (S.H., 1989); Indiana University, Bloomington, School of Law (LL.M., 1992); University of Hawaii, College of Business Administration (M.B.A., 1994). *LANGUAGES:* Indonesian, English and Dutch. *PRACTICE AREAS:* Corporate Law; Commercial Law.

FOREIGN COUNSEL

WENDY PREEDY, admitted, 1985, Solicitor of the Supreme Court of England and Wales; 1987, Supreme Court of Hong Kong. *Education:* University of Surrey, Guildford, United Kingdom (B.Sc., Hons., 1982). *LANGUAGES:* Indonesian, English, German and French. *PRACTICE AREAS:* General Corporate and Commercial Law.

REPRESENTATIVE CLIENTS: Ashton Mining Ltd.; Autodesk, Inc.; P.T. Bakrie Investindo; Banque Paribas; Bintan Resort Corporation; Bostick Australia Pty. Ltd.; Chiyoda; Duty Free Shoppers Ltd.; Dyno Wes Farmers, Ltd.; Equitor Group; Gobel Group; The Government of the Special Capital Region of Jakarta; Hanil Bank; Hanil Synthetic Fiber; Hyosung Corporation; Itochu Corporation; PT Jan Darmadi Corporation; PT Jaya Obayashi; JGC Corporation; Kobayashi Pharmaceutical Co., Ltd.; LA Gear, Inc.; P.T. Makindo Securities; Mindo Group; Mees Pierson N.V.; Morgan Grenfell (Asia) Ltd.; The Nature Conservancy; Nissho Iwai Corporation; Omni Hotels Asia-Pacific; Normandy Anglo Asian Pty Ltd.; PT Orix Indonesia Finance; Samsung Corporation; Sanwa Indonesia Bank; S.C. Johnson & Son Inc.; Sharp Corporation; PT Styrindo Mono Indonesia; Sunrider Corporation; Tomen Corporation; U.S. Embassy; Yokogawa Electric Corporation; Zilog; Zurich Insurance Group; Genindo EPS Petroleum Ltd.

ALBERT HASIBUAN & REKAN

Established in 1972

JALAN MANGUNSARKORO 85, MENTENG
JAKARTA 10320, INDONESIA
Telephone: (62-21) 310-2656 (hunting)
Telefax: (62-21) 310-1586; 799-5418

In association with: P.T. Dharma Raksa, Consultants

International and General Practice, Banking and Financing, Business Relationships, Capital Market, Commercial and General Litigation, Construction, Corporate, Tax, Employment and Labour, Energy and Mining, Foreign Investment, Hotel Management, Insurance, Intellectual Property Rights, Joint Ventures, Maritime and Transportation.

FIRM PROFILE: *Member for Indonesia of Commercial Law Affiliates ("CLA"), the largest international network of independent law firms, the firm consists of some of Indonesia's most respected and experienced professionals, dedicated to providing prompt, attentive and cost effective service to local and international clients. Expertise covers most fields of commercial cross-border transactions while close local associations enable comprehensive coverage of all client requirements.*

MEMBERS OF FIRM

ALBERT HASIBUAN, born Bandung, West Java. *Education:* Faculty of Law, Christian University of Indonesia (S.H., 1967); Gajah Mada University (Ph.D., 1992). Member of Parliament; Member of Management Board, Indonesian National Board of Arbitration; Chairman, Indonesian Jurists' Association; Member, Indonesian Human Rights Commission. *LANGUAGES:* Indonesian, English and Dutch. *PRACTICE AREAS:* Commercial Litigation; Foreign Investment; Joint Ventures; Intellectual Property Rights.

JOHN KUSNADI, born Jakarta. *Education:* Faculty of Law, Christian University of Indonesia (S.H., 1969). *LANGUAGES:* Indonesian, English and Dutch. *PRACTICE AREAS:* Commercial Litigation; Employment and Labour; Intellectual Property Rights.

R.E.M. PATTIKAWA, born Jakarta. *Education:* Faculty of Law, Christian University of Indonesia (S.H., 1969). *LANGUAGES:* Indonesian, English and Dutch. *PRACTICE AREAS:* Commercial Litigation; Intellectual Property Rights; Criminal Law.

R.A. WIENDRATI ALIBAZAH-PRINGGODIGDO, born Jakarta. *Education:* Faculty of Law, University of Indonesia (S.H., 1957). *LANGUAGES:* Indonesian, English, Dutch and French. *PRACTICE AREAS:* Intellectual Property Rights; Joint Ventures; Hotel Management; Corpo-

(This Listing Continued)

---

rate Law; Real Estate Law; Business Organizations; Foreign Investment; Capital Market; Technical Assistance; Employment and Labour.

CONSULTANTS

UDAYA SASTRODIMEDJO, born Poerwokerto, Central Java; (Not admitted in Indonesia). *Education:* Rijksuniversiteit, Leiden (Masters, Taxation, 1955). Tax Consultant. President, P.T. Dharma Raksa. Former Chairman, Indonesian Tax Consultants' Association. Member, Supervisory Board, International Fiscal Association, Indonesia Branch. *LANGUAGES:* Indonesian, English and Dutch.

KAREN MILLS, born New York; admitted, 1968, New York (Not admitted in Indonesia). *Education:* New York University School of Law (J.D., 1968). Formerly associated with Haight, Gardner, Poor & Havens, New York, Maritime Financing. Senior Consultant, P.T. Dharma Raksa. Lecturer, Faculty of Law, Tarumanagara University. Member, Executive Committee, International Fiscal Association, Indonesia Branch. *Member:* International Bar Association. *LANGUAGES:* English, Indonesian and Italian. *PRACTICE AREAS:* International Business Transactions; Foreign Investment; Joint Ventures; Hotel Management; Mining and Energy; Tax; Insurance; Maritime and Transportation; Financing; ADR..

ASSOCIATES

ABDUL RACHIM. *Education:* Christian U. of Indonesia (S.H., 1969).

ODI CORNELIS. *Education:* Christian U. of Indonesia (S.H., 1969).

HENDRA GUNAWAN. *Education:* Faculty of Law, Tarumanagara University (S.H., 1983).

LAW OFFICES OF DEL JUZAR & WIRIANDINATA

JAKARTA, INDONESIA

(See Law Offices of Wiriadinata & Widyawan)

LUBIS, GANIE & SUROWIDJOJO

BUMI DAYA PLAZA, 28TH & 29TH FLOOR
JALAN IMAM BONJOL NO. 61
JAKARTA 10310, INDONESIA
Telephone: 335101; 3103195; 330013
Telecopier: LGS JKT Indonesia 0062-21-335328
Telex: 61588 LGS JKT

General Corporate and Commercial Law Practice.

FIRM PROFILE: *The firm is qualified to practice law in Indonesia and to provide legal services to and represent foreign and Indonesian clients on commercial and corporate law matters including: Acquisition & Corporate Reorganization (including Mergers); Agency & Distributorship; Banking; Arbitration; Capital Market; Commercial Litigation; Construction Contracts; Corporate Finance & Secured Transactions; Foreign and Domestic Investment; Commercial Litigation & Arbitration; International Trade; Labour; Lease Financing; Maritime/Shipping; Mining; Real Estate Transactions; Tax; Intellectual Proprietary Right (Trademark, Copyrights & Patents); Venture Capital; Insurance.*

SENIOR PARTNERS

TIMBUL THOMAS LUBIS, S.H., LL.M., born Tarutung, North Sumatra, Indonesia, January 27, 1948; admitted, 1977, Indonesia. *Education:* Faculty of Law, University of Indonesia (S.H., 1974); University of Washington (LL.M., 1981). Author: Thesis, "Personal Property Secured Transactions", Accounting for Management Program, Management Institution, University of Indonesia (1982). *Member:* Indonesia Bar Association (IKADIN, Jakarta Branch, 1986—); Secretary General of Indonesia Shorinji Kempo Self-Defense Association (PERKEMI) 1984-1992; Vice President of Indonesia Wushu Association (1992—); Vice Secretary General of Indonesia National Sport Committee (KONI)/Olympic Council of Indonesia (1986-1994). Secretary of Rules Committee of SEA Games Federation (1984—). Member, Rules Committee of the Olympic Council of Asia (1990-1994). (Founder & Senior Partner). *LANGUAGES:* Indonesian, English. *PRACTICE AREAS:* Capital Market; Commercial Transactions; Corporate Finance and Secured Transactions; Investment (including Foreign Investment); Labour; General Corporate; Property and Real Estate; Acquisition and Corporate Reorganization; Litigation (Including Maritime); Bank-

(This Listing Continued)

ruptcy/Liquidation; Contracts; Arbitration; Negotiation.

DR. MOHAMAD IDWAN GANIE, S.H., born Amsterdam, Holland, May 23, 1955. *Education:* Faculty of Law, University of Indonesia (S.H., 1977); University of Hamburg, Hamburg, West Germany (Doctor, 1983). Lecturer, Faculty of Law, University of Indonesia and Advocate Course of PERADIN (Association of Indonesian Advocates) 1984—. Chairman, Drafting of the National Maritime Law Code (Navigation Section) 1984—. *Member:* Indonesia Bar Association (IKADIN). (Founder & Senior Partner). *LANGUAGES:* Indonesian, German, English, Dutch, Latin. *PRACTICE AREAS:* Capital Market; General Corporate; Investment (including Foreign Investment); Corporate Finance and Secured Transactions (including Lease Financing & Vessel Financing); Mining Law (including gold and coal); Maritime/Shipping Law; Tax; Insurance (including Marine Insurance); Bankruptcy; Liquidation; Corporate Reorganization (including Mergers & Consolidation).

ARIEF TARUNAKARYA SUROWIDJOJO, S.H., LL.M., born Jogjakarta, Indonesia, April 9, 1953; admitted, 1980, Indonesia. *Education:* Faculty of Law, University of Indonesia (S.H., 1977); University of Washington (LL.M., International Business Transaction, 1984). Lecturer at the Faculty - University of Indonesia and Law Faculty - Pancasila University (Business Laws For Practitioners). *Member:* Indonesia Bar Association (Member, Board Supervisory of Jakarta Branch, 1989—). (Founder, Senior & Managing Partner). *LANGUAGES:* Indonesian, English. *PRACTICE AREAS:* General Corporate; Investment (including Foreign Investment); Capital Market; Commercial Transactions; Corporate Finance and Secured Transactions; Commercial Litigation; Labour; Agency & Distributorship; Venture Capital; Acquisition and Corporate Reorganization including Mergers; Liquidation; Intellectual Proprietary Rights; Trademark, Copyrights, Patent & Licensing.

PARTNERS

DJONI ZULKARNAIN ISHAK, S.H., born P.Pinang/Bangka, Indonesia, April 4, 1954. *Education:* Faculty of Law, University of Indonesia (S.H., 1980). (Partner). *LANGUAGES:* Indonesian, English. *PRACTICE AREAS:* Corporate Law; Financing and Secured Transactions; Contracts; Leasing; Foreign Investment; Reorganization including Mergers.

HIDAYAT ACHYAR, S.H., born Surabaya, Indonesia, July 22, 1954; admitted, 1978, Indonesia. *Education:* Faculty of Law, University of Indonesia (S.H., 1981). *Member:* Indonesia Bar Association. *LANGUAGES:* Indonesian, English. *PRACTICE AREAS:* General Corporate; Commercial Litigation; Financing and Secured Transaction; Islamic Banking; Commercial Litigation; Leasing; Real Estate Transactions; Labour; Insurance; Criminal Law.

ASSOCIATES

INDRA CAHYA, S.H., born Jakarta, Indonesia, July 28, 1952. *Education:* Faculty of Law, University of Indonesia (S.H., 1981). *LANGUAGES:* Indonesia, English. *PRACTICE AREAS:* General Corporate; Trademarks; Commercial Litigation; Labour; Secured Transactions; Contracts.

WILLIAM EDWARD DANIEL, S.H. S.E., born Kediri, Indonesia, January 1, 1962. *Education:* STEI Indonesia Institute of Economy (S.E., Economic and Accounting, 1987); Faculty of Law, University of Indonesia (S.H., 1989). *LANGUAGES:* Indonesian, English. *PRACTICE AREAS:* General Corporate; Reorganization including Mergers; Consolidation; Taxation; Finance and Accounting.

ARI AHMAD EFFENDI, S.H., born Jakarta, Indonesia, May 26, 1958. *Education:* Faculty of Law, University of Indonesia (S.H., 1984). *LANGUAGES:* Indonesian, English. *PRACTICE AREAS:* General Corporate and Contracts; Capital Market; Commercial Litigation; Criminal Law.

BASUKI DWI NUGROHO, S.H., M.B.A., born Jakarta, Indonesia, August 3, 1963. *Education:* Faculty of Law, University of Indonesia (S.H., 1987); Institut Manajemen Prasetya Mulya (M.B.A., 1990). *Capital Market, General Corporate, Investment.* . *LANGUAGES:* Indonesian, English. *PRACTICE AREAS:* Capital Market; General Corporate; Investment; Property.

ASTI SOEKANTO, S.H., born Jakarta, Indonesia, February 13, 1959. *Education:* Faculty of Law, University of Indonesia (S.H., 1984). *LANGUAGES:* Indonesian, English. *PRACTICE AREAS:* Real Estate Transactions; General Corporate; Agency; Intellectual Property Rights; Trademark, Patent and Copyright Registrations.

M.U. FACHRI ASAARI, S.H., born Jakarta, Indonesia, May 31, 1964. *Education:* Faculty of Law, University of Indonesia (S.H., 1988); Executive Development Program Bank Niaga (1989). *LANGUAGES:* Indonesian,

(This Listing Continued)

English. *PRACTICE AREAS:* General Corporate; Banking; Capital Market; Corporate Finance.

MOHAMMAD SYAH INDRA AMAN, S.H., LL.M., born Bonn, Germany, May 17, 1967. *Education:* Faculty of Law, University of Indonesia (S.H., 1990); University of Washington, School of Law (LL.M., 1992). *LANGUAGES:* Indonesian, English, German. *PRACTICE AREAS:* Corporate Law; Banking Law; Capital Market; Corporate Finance Law.

MUHAMMAD HUSNI THAMRIN, S.H., born Jakarta, Indonesia, September 8, 1965; admitted, 1989, Indonesia. *Education:* Faculty of Law, University of Indonesia (S.H., 1990). *LANGUAGES:* Indonesia, English. *PRACTICE AREAS:* General Corporate; Corporate Finance.

HIKMAHANTO JUWANA, S.H. LL.M., born Jakarta, Indonesia, November 23, 1965. *Education:* Faculty of Law, University of Indonesia (S.H., 1987); Faculty of Law, Keio University, Japan (LL.M., 1992); Law Department, University of Nottingham (Ph.D. candidate, 1993). Faculty Member, Faculty of Law, University of Indonesia. *LANGUAGES:* Indonesian, English, Japanese. *PRACTICE AREAS:* General Corporate; International Law.

AHMAD FIKRI ASSEGAF, S.H. LL.M., born Jakarta, Indonesia, June 14, 1968. *Education:* Faculty of Law, University of Indonesia (S.H., 1992); Cornell Law School (LL.M., International Trade, Corporate Law and Finance, 1994). Lecturer, University of Indonesia, Law School, 1992—. *LANGUAGES:* Indonesian, English. *PRACTICE AREAS:* General Corporate; International Trade; Commercial Transactions; Corporate Finance.

TEDDY TURANGGA, S.H., born Jakarta, Indonesia, November 27, 1966. *Education:* Faculty of Law, University of Indonesia (S.H., 1992). *LANGUAGES:* Indonesian, English. *PRACTICE AREAS:* General Corporate Law; Real Estate Transaction.

MOHAMMAD GAMAL RESMANTO, S.H., born Jakarta, Indonesia, June 14, 1966. *Education:* Faculty of Law, University of Indonesia (S.H., 1991). *LANGUAGES:* Indonesian, English. *PRACTICE AREAS:* General Corporate; Real Estate Transaction.

VYATI KARTIKA SARI ISKANDAR, S.H., born Jakarta, Indonesia, March 13, 1968. *Education:* Faculty of Law, University of Indonesia (S.H., 1991). *LANGUAGES:* Indonesian, English. *PRACTICE AREAS:* General Corporate; Real Estate Transaction.

SRI KUSDINARTI MARTOATMODJO, S.H., born Jakarta, Indonesia, June 20, 1968. *Education:* Faculty of Law, University of Indonesia (S.H., 1992). *LANGUAGES:* Indonesian, English. *PRACTICE AREAS:* General Corporate; Real Estate Transaction.

PANJI ACHMAD, S.H., born Jakarta, Indonesia, July 3, 1969. *Education:* Faculty of Law, University of Indonesia (S.H., 1993); Faculty of Economic, University of Riau (1988). *LANGUAGES:* Indonesian, English. *PRACTICE AREAS:* General Corporate; Corporate Finance.

HELEN MARSINTH, S.H., born Padang, Indonesia, October 8, 1969. *Education:* Faculty of Law, University of Indonesia S.H., 1992). *LANGUAGES:* Indonesian, English. *PRACTICE AREAS:* General Corporate; Corporate Finance.

DIAN SITA SARI KUSDIHARJO, S.H., born Jakarta, Indonesia, May 25, 1969. *Education:* Faculty of Law, University of Indonesia (S.H., 1994); Faculty of Economic, University of Triskti (1988-1994). *LANGUAGES:* Indonesian, English. *PRACTICE AREAS:* General Corporate; Corporate Finance; Capital Market.

CINDY AGGRAENI MULKAN, S.H., born Bandung, Indonesia, December 10, 1972. *Education:* Faculty of Law, University of Indonesia (S.H. 1994). Lecturer, Faculty of Law, University of Indonesia. *LANGUAGES:* Indonesian, English. *PRACTICE AREAS:* Infrastructure Law (toll road, port terminal); Investment.

All Attorneys are Members of: Indonesian Bar Association (IKADIN); American-Indonesia Chamber of Commerce; Indonesian-German Chamber of Commerce; Indonesian Mining Association; Indonesian Financial Executive Association (IFEA).
Firm is registered with the Indonesian Capital Market Supervisory Board and a wide range of business and investment consulting services are available through SVS Consultants Group.

MULYA LUBIS & PARTNERS

Established in 1991

WISMA BANK DHARMALA, 5TH FLOOR
JALAN JENDRAL SUDIRMAN, KAV. 28
JAKARTA 12920, INDONESIA
Telephone: (62-21) 521-1931; 521-1932; 522-7468
Facsimile: (62-21) 521-1930

Corporate, Banking, Securities, Financial Services, Foreign Investment, Real Estate, Trade, Tax, Environmental, Energy and Natural Resources, Labor, Intellectual Property, Litigation.

MEMBERS OF FIRM

DR. T. MULYA LUBIS, born Muara Botung, North Sumatra, Indonesia, July 4, 1949; admitted, 1975, Indonesia. *Education:* Faculty of Law, University of Indonesia (S.H., 1974); Harvard University (LL.M., 1987); University of California at Berkeley (LL.M., 1978; S.J.D., 1990). Columnist, Tempo Magazine and Forum Keadilan. Author: "Law and Economy," 1991; "The Role of Law in the Economies of Developing Countries," with Richard M. Buxbaum, 1986. Member: Jakarta Lawyers Club, Co-Founder; Legal Aid Institute of Indonesia (LBH), Co-Founder. *Member:* Indonesian Bar Association (IKADIN, Co-Founder); International Bar Association (IBA); Asian Law Association (ALA); The Law Association for Asia and the Western Pacific (LAWASIA). *LANGUAGES:* English. *PRACTICE AREAS:* International Business Transactions; Intellectual Property Law; Corporate Law.

LELYANA Y. SANTOSA, born Medan, North Sumatra, Indonesia, December 31, 1954; admitted, 1980, Indonesia. *Education:* Faculty of Law, University of Padjadjaran, Bandung (S.H., 1980); Osgoode Hall Law School, York University, Canada (Fall Course, Real Estate Transactions). Advocate, Legal Aid Institute (LBH), 1980-1983. Legal Consultant, Kusnander & Associates, 1983-1984. *LANGUAGES:* English. *PRACTICE AREAS:* Civil Litigation; Corporate Law.

INSAN BUDI MAULANA, born Jakarta, Indonesia, September 18, 1959; admitted, 1986, Indonesia. *Education:* Faculty of Law, University of Indonesia (S.H., 1986); Faculty of Law, Kobe University, Japan (LL.M., 1992). Research Student, Kagawa University, Japan, 1988-1990. Editor, Journal of Law and Development, 1980-1985. Assistant Lawyer, Institute of Legal Aid and Consultation, 1982-1986. *Member:* International Association for the Protection of Industrial Property (AIPPI). *LANGUAGES:* Japanese and English. *PRACTICE AREAS:* Intellectual Property Law.

SOENYOTO, born Boyolali, Central Java, Indonesia, August 8, 1958; admitted, 1984, Indonesia. *Education:* Faculty of Law, Gajah Mada University, Yogyakarta (S.H., 1984). General Manager: Human Resources and Legal Departments, PT Ubertraco, 1985-1986; Human Resources and Legal Departments, PT Sari Alam Sakti Manunggal, 1986-1989. *LANGUAGES:* English. *PRACTICE AREAS:* Civil Litigation.

DINI CAROLINA PANGGABEAN, born Jakarta, Indonesia, March 8, 1968; admitted, 1993, Indonesia. *Education:* Faculty of Law, University of Indonesia (S.H., 1993). *LANGUAGES:* English. *PRACTICE AREAS:* Intellectual Property Law.

A. TAVIP BUDISANTOSO, born Bandung, Indonesia, August 27, 1964; admitted, 1992, Indonesia. *Education:* Faculty of Law, University of Indonesia (S.H., 1992); Faculty of Economics, University of Trisakti (S.E., 1991). *LANGUAGES:* English. *PRACTICE AREAS:* Corporate Law.

IENNE KUSHARTINA, born Surabaya, October 15, 1962; admitted, 1985, Indonesia. *Education:* Faculty of Law, Airlangga University, Surabaya (S.N., 1985). *LANGUAGES:* English. *PRACTICE AREAS:* Intellectual Property Law.

JONATHAN M. STREIFER, born Rochester, New York, April 29, 1963; admitted, 1993, California (Not admitted in Indonesia). *Education:* University of California, Santa Barbara (B.A., with high honors, 1986); University of California, Berkeley (Boalt Hall) School of Law (J.D., 1992). Recipient: Moot Court Award for Excellence in Written Advocacy; American Jurisprudence Award: Private International Law. Author: "Deregulation and Development: Financial Services in Indonesia"; "Tax Planning for Business Combinations and Reorganizations"; "Safety and Soundness Regulations in Indonesia." Co-Author: "Competition Law in the European Community"; "United States Immigration Law: Constitutional Considerations"; "Federal Jurisdiction for Foreign Torts Under the Alien Tort Statute." *Member:* State Bar of California. *LANGUAGES:* English and Bahasa Indonesia. *PRACTICE AREAS:* Corporate Law.

(This Listing Continued)

QUITA AMEILIA LESTARI, born Jakarta, Indonesia, May 8, 1968; admitted, 1994, Indonesia. *Education:* Faculty of Law, University of Padjadjaran (S.H., 1992). *LANGUAGES:* English. *PRACTICE AREAS:* Corporate Law.

REPRESENTATIVE CLIENTS: Fisons Pharmaceuticals, Britain; Sankyo Rikagaku, Japan; PT Ballast Indonesia; Dharmala Group; Lippo Bank; PT Ramayana Asuransi; Kwangtung Provincial Bank, Singapore; Nissin Foods, Japan; PT Matahari; PT Union Carbide; PSP Group; Bisnis Indonesia; PT Ramako Gerbang Mas; Bank Bukopin; PT Palmolite Adhesive Industry; Dong Kook Pharmaceuticals, Korea; PT Adiguna Shipping and Engineering; K. Otsuki Pearl Co., Japan; Kobayashi Pharmaceutical Co., Japan; PT Danareksa Sekuritas; Megapolitan Group; PT Grahawita Santika; PT Saseka Leasing; UCC Ueshima Coffee Co., Ltd., Japan; JCB International Co., Ltd., Japan; Louis Vuitton Malletier, France; PT Realty 88; Bank of China; BRI Finance Limited, Hong Kong; Lion Jimuki K.K., Japan; Asia Pizza, A.V.V.; PT Bursa Efek Jakarta (Jakarta Stock Exchange); PT Metro Supermarket Realty; Bank SBU; Berjaya Group Berhad; Perdanacipta Multi Finance; Shinko Corp., Japan; Gemala Group.

MAKARIM & TAIRA S.

17TH FLOOR, SUMMITMAS TOWER
JL. JENDERAL SUDIRMAN KAV. 61-62
JAKARTA, INDONESIA
Telephone: 252 1272
Telex: 60772 JURESE IA
Telefax: 252 2750; 252 2751

Australia Associated Office: Minter Ellison Morris Fletcher. 40 Market Street, Melbourne, Victoria 3000. Telephone: 617 4617. Fax: 617 4666. Telex: AA 33007.

International and General Practice, Foreign Investment, Commercial, Capital Markets, Banking and Finance, Construction, Energy and Natural Resources, Intellectual Property, Commercial Litigation, Tax, Mergers and Acquisitions, Property Development.

PARTNERS

NONO ANWAR MAKARIM, born Pekalongan, Central Java, Indonesia, September 25, 1939; admitted, 1973, Indonesia. *Education:* University of Indonesia (S.H., 1973); Harvard University (LL.M., 1975; S.J.D., 1978). Fellow, Harvard Center for International Affairs, 1973-1974. Member of and Counsel, Indonesian Delegation to the Uruguay Round of the Multilateral Trade Negotiations, 1994. Member: Parliament, 1967-1971; Board of Governors of the Jakarta International School; American-Indonesia Chamber of Commerce. Co-founder and Member: Board of Trustees of the Indonesian Environmental Bamboo Foundation, 1993; Board of Trustees of the Indonesian Bio-Diversity Foundation, 1993. *Member:* American-Indonesia Chamber of Commerce. *LANGUAGES:* English and Dutch. *PRACTICE AREAS:* Government Contracts; International Law; Commercial Law; Investments; Communications and Media; Environmental Law.

HOTMAN PARIS HUTAPEA, born North Sumatra, Indonesia, October 20, 1959; admitted, 1981, Indonesia. *Education:* Parahyangan Catholic University (S.H., 1981); University of Technology, Sydney, Australia (Graduate Study in Comparative Law, 1990); Singapore Institute of Arbitrators and Chartered Institute of Arbitrators, Singapore (1993). Foreign Associate, International Law Firm, Sydney, Australia, 1987-1988. Director, Law Education and Training Centre. *Member:* Indonesian Bar Association (AAI). *LANGUAGES:* English. *PRACTICE AREAS:* Contracts; Litigation; Negligence; Torts; Alternative Dispute Resolution; Bankruptcy.

RAINI ALFIDA, born Jakarta, Indonesia, December 14, 1961; admitted, 1984, Jakarta. *Education:* University of Indonesia (S.H., 1984); University of Technology, Sydney, Australia (Graduate study in Comparative Law, 1990). Foreign Associate, International Law Firm, Sydney, Australia, 1988-1990. *Member:* International Bar Association (IBA); Inter-Pacific Bar Association (IPBA); Indonesia-Australia Business Council. *LANGUAGES:* English. *PRACTICE AREAS:* Commercial Law; Corporate Law; Agency and Distributorship; Franchises and Franchising; Investments; Trademarks; Natural Resources.

VICTOR FUNGKONG, born Sintang, West Kalimantan, Indonesia, August 6, 1961; admitted, 1987, Jakarta. *Education:* University of Indonesia (S.H., 1987); Columbia University School of Law, New York (LL.M., 1990). Foreign Associate, Kelley, Drye & Warren, New York, 1994. *Member:* Inter-Pacific Bar Association (IPBA). *LANGUAGES:* English and Chinese Dialects. *PRACTICE AREAS:* Banks and Banking; Corporate Law; Finance; Mergers; Acquisitions and Divestitures; Securities.

(This Listing Continued)

ASSOCIATES

PUDJI WAHYUNI PURBO, born Jakarta, Indonesia, September 27, 1959; admitted, 1984, Jakarta. *Education:* University of Indonesia (S.H., 1984). *LANGUAGES:* English, German and French. *PRACTICE AREAS:* Property; Real Estate; Resorts and Leisure; Commercial Law; Zoning; Planning and Land Use.

AULIA KEMALSJAH SIREGAR, born Makassar, South Sulawesi, Indonesia, October 16, 1959; admitted, 1986, Jakarta. *Education:* University of Indonesia (S.H., 1986); International Law Institute, Washington, D.C. (1993). *LANGUAGES:* English. *PRACTICE AREAS:* Commercial Law; Corporate Law; Investments; Litigation; Business Law; Labor and Employment.

HENNY PINGKAN MADIAN, born Sungai Gerong, South Sumatra, Indonesia, July 5, 1963; admitted, 1989, Indonesia. *Education:* University of Indonesia (S.H., 1989); Cornell University (LL.M., 1994). *LANGUAGES:* English and Dutch. *PRACTICE AREAS:* Commercial Law; Business Law; Corporate Law; Mergers; Acquisitions and Divestitures; Investments.

AVRILINE M. HUTAHAYAN, born Kathmandu, Nepal, April 21, 1966; admitted, 1990, Indonesia. *Education:* University of Indonesia (S.H., 1990); Academy of American and International Law, International and Comparative Law Center, Dallas, Texas (1992). *LANGUAGES:* English. *PRACTICE AREAS:* Commercial Law; Corporate Law; Banks and Banking; Finance; Securities.

GALINAR R. ADIWOSO KARTAKUSUMA, born Jakarta, Indonesia, December 12, 1952; admitted, 1988, Jakarta. *Education:* University of Indonesia (S.H., 1988). *Member:* International Bar Association. *LANGUAGES:* English and French. *PRACTICE AREAS:* Agency and Distributorships; Bankruptcy; Commercial Law; Investments; Entertainment and Arts.

RATNA ISKANDAR, born Palembang, South Sumatra, Indonesia, October 22, 1958; admitted, 1982, Indonesia. *Education:* University of Trisakti (S.H., 1982); University of Houston (LL.M., 1992). *LANGUAGES:* English. *PRACTICE AREAS:* Banks and Banking; Business Law; Commercial Law; Finance; Securities.

YOSIA CEMBY HUTAPEA, born Palembang, South Sumatra, Indonesia, December 22, 1964; admitted, 1987, Indonesia. *Education:* University of Indonesia (S.H., 1987); Singapore Institute of Arbitrators and Chartered Institute of Arbitrators, Singapore (1993). *LANGUAGES:* English. *PRACTICE AREAS:* Bankruptcy; Litigation; Corporate Law; Torts; Labor and Employment; Debtor and Creditor.

FAISAL TADJUDDIN, born Jakarta, Indonesia, July 15, 1956; admitted, 1984, Indonesia. *Education:* Indonesian Christian University (S.H., 1984); The Singapore Institute of Arbitrators and Chartered Institute of Arbitrators, Singapore (1994). *LANGUAGES:* English and German. *PRACTICE AREAS:* Bankruptcy; Litigation; Corporate Law; Torts; Labor and Employment; Debtor and Creditor.

CAROL M. POLUAN, born Rumbai, East Sumatra, Indonesia, May 19, 1964; admitted, 1989, Indonesia. *Education:* University of Indonesia (S.H., 1989). *LANGUAGES:* English and Dutch. *PRACTICE AREAS:* Corporate Law; Intellectual Property Law; Trademarks; Patents.

INGE RESDIANO, born Jakarta, Indonesia, August 24, 1961; admitted, 1986, Indonesia. *Education:* University of Jayabaya (S.H., 1986). *LANGUAGES:* English. *PRACTICE AREAS:* Business Law; Corporate Law; Contracts; Investments; Mergers; Acquisitions and Divestitures.

LUIS F.S.S. PEREIRA, born Turiscai, East Timor, Indonesia, September 20, 1958; admitted, 1987, Indonesia. *Education:* Atma Jaya Catholic University (S.H., 1987). *LANGUAGES:* Portuguese, English, French and Spanish. *PRACTICE AREAS:* Corporate Law; Intellectual Property Law; Trademarks; Patents; Environmental Law.

AGUS LOEKMAN, born Yogyakarta, Indonesia, June 28, 1967; admitted, 1991, Indonesia. *Education:* University of Diponegoro (S.H., 1991). *LANGUAGES:* English. *PRACTICE AREAS:* Commercial Law; Corporate Law; Banks and Banking; Finance; Securities.

TUTI SIMORANGKIR, born Jakarta, Indonesia, May 16, 1953; admitted, 1982, Indonesia. *Education:* University of Indonesia (S.H., 1982). *LANGUAGES:* English. *PRACTICE AREAS:* Commercial Law; Corporate Law; Banks and Banking; Finance; Securities.

IGNATIUS ANDY, born Jakarta, Indonesia, February 11, 1967; admitted, 1992, Indonesia. *Education:* Parahyangan Catholic University (S.H.,

(This Listing Continued)

1992); Singapore Institute of Arbitrators and Chartered Institute of Arbitrators, Singapore (1994). *LANGUAGES:* English. *PRACTICE AREAS:* Corporate Law; Bankruptcy; Litigation; Torts; Labor and Employment.

E.Y. HENDRA, born Pontianak, Indonesia, November 6, 1964; admitted, 1989, Indonesia. *Education:* University of Indonesia (S.H., 1989). *LANGUAGES:* English and Teochew. *PRACTICE AREAS:* Corporate Law; Commercial Law; Banks and Banking; Finance; Securities.

SONDANG SIMATUPANG, born Pematang, Siantar, Indonesia, May 5, 1962; admitted, 1989, Indonesia. *Education:* Gadjah Mada University (S.H., 1989). *LANGUAGES:* English. *PRACTICE AREAS:* Corporate Law; Intellectual Property; Litigation; Labor and Employment; Debtor and Creditor.

RUDY ELIEZER TIENDAS, born Jakarta, Indonesia, November 1, 1964; admitted, 1991, Indonesia. *Education:* University of Atmajaya (S.H., 1991). *LANGUAGES:* English. *PRACTICE AREAS:* Corporate Law; Commercial Law; Finance; Securities.

IWAN BUDIARTO NURJADIN, born Jakarta, Indonesia, May 10, 1969; admitted, 1993, Indonesia. *Education:* University of Indonesia (S.H., 1993). *LANGUAGES:* English. *PRACTICE AREAS:* Corporate Law; Contract Law; Commercial Law.

GIANITA DEWAYANTHI KADARISMAN, born Jakarta, Indonesia, April 12, 1971; admitted, 1993, Indonesia. *Education:* University of Indonesia (S.H., 1993). *LANGUAGES:* English. *PRACTICE AREAS:* Corporate Law; Contract Law; Commercial Law.

FLORA NOVIA, born Bandung, Indonesia, November 3, 1966; admitted, 1989, Indonesia. *Education:* University of Indonesia (S.H., 1989); University of Wisconsin-Stevens Point, Wisconsin (Associate Degree, 1992); George Washington University, Washington, D.C. (Legal Assistant Program, 1992). *LANGUAGES:* English. *PRACTICE AREAS:* Corporate Law; Contract Law; Commercial Law.

IMING MAKNAWAN TESALONIKA, born Bandung, Indonesia, May 23, 1967; admitted, 1993, Indonesia. *Education:* Polytechnic University of Indonesia (Diploma, Civil Engineering, 1988); University of Indonesia (S.H., 1993). *LANGUAGES:* English. *PRACTICE AREAS:* Corporate Law; Contract Law; Commercial Law.

LINA ANGGRAINI AMRAN, born Jakarta, Indonesia, May 23, 1967; admitted, 1990, Indonesia. *Education:* University of Indonesia (1990); University of Technology, Sydney (MBA, 1993). *LANGUAGES:* English. *PRACTICE AREAS:* Corporate Law; Commercial Law; Banks and Banking; Finance; Securities.

MIRA DIANTRI SUDIRO, born Jakarta, Indonesia, February 6, 1968; admitted, 1992, Indonesia. *Education:* University of Padjajaran (1992); Boston University School of Law, Boston (LL.M., 1994). *LANGUAGES:* English. *PRACTICE AREAS:* Corporate Law; Banks and Banking; Finance.

FOREIGN CONSULTANTS

HILTON ROMNEY KING, born Melbourne, Australia, April 8, 1962; admitted, 1985, Australia. *Education:* University of Melbourne (LL.B., B.Com, 1985). Barrister and Solicitor, Supreme Court of Victoria. Solicitor: High Court of Australia; Freehill Hollingdale & Page, Melbourne, 1986-1988; Freehill Hollingdale & Page (Associated with Makarim & Taira S.), 1989-1991. *LANGUAGES:* English and Indonesian. *PRACTICE AREAS:* Commercial Law; Corporate Law; International Law; Investments; Mergers; Acquisitions and Divestitures; Taxation.

RICHARD WYKEHAM CORNWALLIS, born Dhekelia, Cyprus, November 16, 1959; admitted, 1985, Solicitor, Scotland. *Education:* University of Edinburgh (LL.B., 1981; Dip. L.P., 1982). Solicitor: Supreme Court of Hong Kong, 1986; Johnson, Stokes & Master, Hong Kong, 1985-1989. Senior Associate, Baker & Mckenzie, Singapore, 1989-1993. *LANGUAGES:* English. *PRACTICE AREAS:* Commercial Law; Corporate Law; International Law; Investments; Mergers; Acquisitions and Divestitures; Taxation.

MICHAEL REGINALD LASCELLES HOOTON, born Surrey, England, October 17, 1959; admitted, 1986, New York. *Education:* Stanford University (A.B., 1982); McGill University (LL.B., 1985); McGill Law Review (1983-1985). Associate: Eaton & Van Winkle, New York, 1985-1987; Hughes Hubbard & Reed, New York, 1987-1989. Foreign Legal Advisor, Anderson Mori, Tokyo, 1991-1993. *LANGUAGES:* English, French and Japanese. *PRACTICE AREAS:* Corporate Law; Commercial Law; Finance Law; Communications and Media; Taxation.

(This Listing Continued)

MAKARIM & TAIRA S., Jakarta—Continued

PARALEGALS

RAHAYUNINGSIH H. HOED, born Jakarta, Indonesia, October 7, 1961; admitted, 1985, Indonesia. *Education:* Sl., French Literature, Faculty of Letters, University of Indonesia (S.S., 1985). *LANGUAGES:* English and French.

NADIMAN TJENDRAWIRA, born Pontianak, Indonesia, March 29, 1956; admitted, 1979, Indonesia. *Education:* Trisakti Hotel and Tourism Academy (1979). *LANGUAGES:* English.

MARDIANA, born Banjarmasin, Indonesia, March 14, 1955; admitted, 1980, Indonesia. *Education:* Trisakti University (S.H., 1980). *LANGUAGES:* English.

REPRESENTATIVE CLIENTS: ACI (Asia); Amoco Indonesia Petroleum Co.; ARCO; Ashton Mining Limited; Ausasean; Australian Embassy; Bank Sumitomo Niaga; Baillieu Knight Frank; Bankers Trust; Bank of America; Bank Negara Indonesia 1946; Bank Ekspor Impor Indonesia; Bank Pacific; Bank Sumitomo Niaga; BATA; Bausch & Lomb (HK) Ltd.; The Broken Hill Proprietary Company Ltd.; (BHP); P.T. Bimantara Eka Santosa; Black's Voatch International; The BOC Group; Bonauli Real Estate P.T.; Bovis International; BP Minerals; P.T. BRC Lysaght Indonesia; BTR Nylex; Bumi Raya Utama, PT.; P.T. Burroughs Wellcome (Indonesia); Century Park Hotels; Caltex Asia Singapore; C. Itoh & Co.; CRI Project Management Pty Ltd.; Cadbury Schweppes Ltd.; P.T. Cigna Asuransi Indonesia; Colgate-Palmolive Company; Commonwealth Industrial Gases Ltd.; Colliersutaba Indo/Penilai; Deutsche Bank AG; DG Bank; Dresser Industries, Inc.; Duke Energy Corporation; East Asiatic Companies; Enso Gutzeit Oy.; Esso ESAB A.B.; Excelsior Sport Ltd. (HK); FMC Corp.; Ford Motor Company; Foster, Frankipile Indonesia; Fuji Bank International Indonesia; W.R. Grace Co.; Glaxo Holdings PLC; General Electric Company; Government of Republic of Indonesia; P.T. Gudang Garam; Gulf Agency Co.; Hutama Takenaka Corporation Indonesia; Hilton Hotels Corporation; Holiday Inns Inc.; Hutama Takenaka Corporation Indonesia; ICI; Industriekreditbank A.G.; Islamic Development Bank, P.T.; Jaya Fuji Leasing Pratama; P.T. Jardine Fleming Nusantara; Jasa Marga; John Hancock Insurance Company; Kajima Overseas Asia Ltd.; Lippo Bank; Lippo Merchants Finance; Lippo Securities; Lucky Goldstar International Corp.; Morgan Carroll Terai Gaikokuho Jimu Bengashi Jimusho; P.T. Mantrust; Marubeni Corporation; Mobil Oil Indonesia Inc.; Mobil EHS Inc.; Morgan EHS Inc.; Morgan Grenfell; P.T. Mutual International Finance Corporation; P.T. Monier Indonesia; Mulia Group; New York Life Worldwide Holding, Inc.; PT Nomura Indonesia; Nippon Telegraph & Telephone Corporation; Nippon Paper Industries Co. Ltd.; Newmont Holdings Pty. Ltd.; NL Industries; Ometraco; Paragon Resources NL; P & O Australia Ltd.; Ponderosa Group; Peregrine Securities; Perrodo; Petrolite Corp; Placer Development; P.T. Procter & Gamble Indonesia; Qantas Airways Ltd.; P.T. Rig Tenders Indonesia; P.T. Rajawali Wira Bhakti Utama; Renison Goldfields Consolidated; Reuter News; Rhone Poulenc; Rothmans of Pall Mall; Sarinah Jaya; Schlumberger Overseas S.A.; Schroders International Merchant Bank Ltd.; Shell; PT. Sinar Sahabat; Societe Generale De Surveillance S.A. (SGS); Sony Corp.; Standard Chartered Bank; Standard Chartered Leasing; Summarecon Group; Sumitomo Corp.; P.T. Summitmas Property; Sumitomo Forestry; Sungai Budi; P.T. Taisho Pharmaceutical Co. Ltd.; The Wellcome Foundation Ltd.; Toda Corporation; Total Bangun Persada; Transfield Australia; Unggul Indah Corporation; P.T. Unilever Indonesia; United Parcel Service; Usaha Bersama Securities; Westland Group PLC.

MAKES & PARTNERS LAW FIRM

in Association with

SKADDEN, ARPS, SLATE, MEAGHER & FLOM

(New York, Los Angeles, Toronto, London, Hong Kong, Beijing,

Tokyo, Sydney)

THE LANDMARK CENTRE, TOWER A, 26TH FLOOR
JALAN JENDERAL SUDIRMAN NO. 1
JAKARTA 12910, INDONESIA
Telephone: (62-21) 5710170 (Hunting)
Facsimile: (62-21) 5710169

Corporate, Commercial and General Business Law including Restructurings and Reorganizations, Mergers and Acquisitions, Agency and Distributorship, Banking, Corporate Finance including establishing financial institutions such as venture capital companies and leasing companies, Capital Markets including the issuance and sale of public securities of Indonesian companies on the Indonesian Stock Exchanges and offerings in global markets, Energy and Natural Resources including oil and gas contracts and the development of power plants, Foreign and Domestic Capital Investment including Investment Reorganization, Intellectual Property, Litigation and Real Property Law.

FIRM PROFILE: The Firm, consisting of experienced lawyers and distinguished counsel, provides a wide range of legal services to both Indonesian and international clients and is registered as a legal consultant at the Indonesian Capital Market Supervisory Board (Bapepam).

(This Listing Continued)

PARTNERS

YOZUA MAKES, born Jakarta, Indonesia. *Education:* University of Indonesia, Faculty of Law (S.H.); University of California at Berkeley, School of Law (LL.M.); Asian Institute of Management, Manila (MM). Appointed by the Minister of Justice of the Republic of Indonesia to appear before the courts throughout Indonesia. *LANGUAGES:* Indonesian and English.

MSM. PANGGABEAN, born Rumbai, Indonesia. *Education:* University of Indonesia, Faculty of Law (S.H.); Harvard Law School (LL.M.). Senior Officer, Bank of Indonesia (Central Bank), 1986-1990. *LANGUAGES:* Indonesian and English.

MOCHTAR, KARUWIN & KOMAR

Established in 1971

WISMA METROPOLITAN II, 14TH FLOOR
JALAN JENDERAL SUDIRMAN KAV. 31
JAKARTA 12920, INDONESIA
Telephone: 5711130
Cable Address: "Karuwin," Jakarta
Telex: 65611 KARWIN IA
Facsimile: 571-1162; 570-1686

Mailing Address: P.O. Box 2844, Jakarta, Indonesia 10001

Singapore Office: Shell Tower, 22-06, 50 Raffles Place, 0104. Telephone: 2253311. Telex: RS 28322 Karwin. Facsimile: 223-2191.

Associated San Francisco, California Office: Anthony F. Granucci, 20th Floor, One Sansome Street, 94104. Telephone: 415-951-4609. Facsimile: 415-921-3993.

Foreign Investments, Corporate, Tax, Capital Markets, Energy and Oil and Gas, Labor, International and Financing Law.

JOHN KARUWIN (1911-1978).

MOCHTAR KUSUMA-ATMADJA, born Jakarta, Indonesia, 1929. *Education:* University of Indonesia (S.H., 1955); Padjadjaran University (S.J.D., 1962); Yale University, Law School (LL.M., 1966); Harvard Law School (Special Student, 1964-1965); University of Chicago, Law School, Trade and Development Research Fellowship (1965-1966). Private Practice, Jakarta, Indonesia, 1970-1974. Minister of Justice of the Republic of Indonesia, 1974-1978. Minister of Foreign Affairs of the Republic of Indonesia, 1978-1988. Member, Panel of Arbitrators and Conciliators, ICSID, 1989—. *LANGUAGES:* Indonesian, English and Dutch.

DR. KOMAR, born Bandung, Indonesia, 1938. *Education:* Faculty of Law and Social Sciences, Padjadjaran University (S.H., 1962); University of California at Berkeley (LL.M., 1969); Padjadjaran University (S.J.D., 1981). Member, Faculty of Law, Padjadjaran University. Secretary General, ASEAN Law Association, 1986-1989. Member, Panel of Arbitrators and Conciliators, ICSID, 1989—. Private Practice, Bandung, Indonesia, 1963-1968. *Member:* Indonesian Lawyers Association. *LANGUAGES:* Indonesian, English and Dutch.

FRANK B. MORGAN, born Sacramento, California, U.S.A., 1938; admitted, 1966, California (Not admitted in Indonesia). *Education:* Stanford University (B.A., 1960); Harvard Law School (J.D., 1963). Phi Beta Kappa. Assistant Secretary, Ministry of Development, Bechuanaland Protectorate (Botswana), 1963-1965. Law Clerk to Judges Warren A. Madden and William Orr, U.S. Court of Appeals, San Francisco, California, 1965-1966. Private practice with Thelen, Marrin, Johnson & Bridges, San Francisco, California, 1966-1970. *Member:* The State Bar of California.

K. SANTOSO, born Parakan, Indonesia, 1926. *Education:* University of Indonesia (S.H., 1953). Private practice, Jakarta, Indonesia, 1953-1970. *Member:* Indonesian Bar Association. *LANGUAGES:* Indonesian, English, Dutch and German.

SIDIK SURAPUTRA, born Jakarta, Indonesia, 1936. *Education:* Faculty of Law and Social Sciences, University of Indonesia (S.H., 1961); Institute of Social Study, The Hague, Holland (graduate study, 1966-1967); Faculty of Law, University of Leiden, Holland (1967-1968); University of Indonesia (S.J.D., 1988). Lecturer on International Law, University of Indonesia. *Member:* Indonesian Bar Association. *LANGUAGES:* Indonesian, English and Dutch.

ARIANI NUGRAHA, born Melbourne, Australia, 1946. *Education:* Faculty of Law and Social Sciences, University of Indonesia (S.H., 1970). Paul, Hastings, Janofsky and Walker, Los Angeles, California, 1973. Tax

(This Listing Continued)

Consultant Program, Trisakti University, Jakarta, 1974. *LANGUAGES:* Indonesian and English.

M. SUKRISMAN HUSEIN, born Tasikmalaya, Indonesia, 1942. *Education:* Faculty of Law, Padjadjaran University (S.H., 1975); Academy of American and International Law, International and Comparative Law Center, Dallas, Texas (1984). *LANGUAGES:* Indonesian and English.

EMIR KUSUMAATMADJA, born Jakarta, Indonesia, 1957. *Education:* Faculty of Law, Padjadjaran University (S.H., 1982); University of California at Berkeley (LL.M., 1986). *LANGUAGES:* Indonesian and English.

THOMAS R. GOIN, born Madison, Wisconsin, 1949; admitted, 1976, California (Not admitted in Indonesia). *Education:* Brown University (B.A., 1971); University of California at Davis (J.D., 1976). Private practice with Thelen, Marrin, Johnson and Bridges, San Francisco, California, 1977-1983. *Member:* The State Bar of California; American Bar Association.

ENNY P. WIDHYA B., born Jakarta, Indonesia, 1953. *Education:* Faculty of Law, University of Indonesia (S.H., 1977); Notorial Department, Faculty of Law, University of Indonesia (C.N., 1992); Comparative Study Program, Bond University, Gold Coast, Australia (1994). *LANGUAGES:* Indonesian and English.

REZA SYARIEF, born Bandung, Indonesia, 1964. *Education:* Faculty of Law, Parahyangan University (S.H., 1988). *LANGUAGES:* Indonesian and English.

CRAIG M. HEGGIE, born Lanark, Scotland, 1958; admitted, 1983, As a Solicitor, Scotland; 1990, England (Not admitted in Indonesia). *Education:* University of Glasgow (LL.B. Hons., 1980). Private Practice with Maclay Murray & Spens, Glasgow, 1982-1985; Sinclair Roche & Temperley, London and Singapore, 1985-1993.

GITA TIFFANY BOER, born Vienna, Austria, 1966. *Education:* Faculty of Law, University of Indonesia (S.H., 1989); American University, Washington College of Law (LL.M., 1993). *LANGUAGES:* Indonesian and English.

INDAJANI K. HALIM, born Semarang, Indonesia, 1945. *Education:* Faculty of Law, Parahyangan Catholic University, Bandung (S.H., 1969). *LANGUAGES:* Indonesian and English.

MIRANTI S. MALIKUS-RAMADHANI, born Rangoon, Burma, 1965. *Education:* Faculty of Law, University of Indonesia (S.H., 1990). *LANGUAGES:* Indonesian and English.

KORI EMZITA, born Jeddah, Saudi Arabia, 1967. *Education:* Faculty of Law, University of Indonesia (S.H., 1990). *LANGUAGES:* Indonesian and English.

FADJAR WIDJAKSANA KANDAR, born Jakarta, Indonesia, 1966. *Education:* Faculty of Law, Parahyangan University, Bandung, Indonesia (S.H., 1990). *LANGUAGES:* Indonesian and English.

MALA MUKTI, born Jakarta, Indonesia, 1964. *Education:* Faculty of Law, University of Indonesia (S.H., 1987); Graduate study in Comparative Law at the University of Technology, Sydney, Australia. *LANGUAGES:* Indonesian and English.

YANTI S. ABDURRACHMAN, born Melbourne, Australia, 1964; admitted, 1989, Victoria as Barrister and Solicitor of the Supreme Court (Not admitted in Indonesia). *Education:* Faculty of Law, Morash University (B.A., 1986); Faculty of Law, University of Melbourne (Graduate Diploma Asian Law, 1992). Private Practice with Freehill Hollingdale & Page, Melbourne, 1988-1991. *Member:* Law Institute of Victoria. *LANGUAGES:* Indonesian and English.

AHMAD S. DJOYOSUGITO, born Yogyakarta, Indonesian, 1964. *Education:* Faculty of Law, Padjadjaran University, Bandung (S.H., 1990); School of Law (LL.M., 1992); School of Business, Bond University, Gold Coast, Australia (MBA, 1994). *LANGUAGES:* Indonesian, English.

SETH C. PRAGER, born Mineola, New York, 1959; admitted, 1985, Minnesota; 1988, District of Columbia (Not admitted in Indonesia). *Education:* Western Maryland College (B.A., magna cum laude, 1981); Washington and Lee University (J.D., cum laude, 1985). Phi Beta Kappa. Articles Editor, Washington and Lee Law Review. Private Practice with Faegre & Benson, Minneapolis, Minnesota, 1985-1987; Squire, Sanders & Dempsey, Washington, D.C., 1987-1989; Dickstein, Shapiro & Morin, Washington, D.C., 1989-1994. *Member:* The District of Columbia Bar; Minnesota State and American Bar Associations.

M.G. JUNIE S. WIYOGO, born Madiun, East Java, Indonesia, 1955. *Education:* Faculty of Law, Tarumanagara University, Jakarta (S.H., 1991); *(This Listing Continued)*

Queensland University of Technology, School of Law, Brisbane, Australia (LL.M., 1994). *LANGUAGES:* Indonesian and English.

BAMBANG PRAMUJITO SAID, born Bandung, Indonesia, 1964. *Education:* Faculty of Law, Padjadjaran University, Bandung (S.H., 1988); Judicial Administration, School of Public Administration, University of Southern California (M.P.A., 1993); Banking Law, Morin Center, Boston University School of Law (LL.M., 1994). *Member:* International Bar Association. *LANGUAGES:* Indonesian and English.

ANANDA AVIATI, born Surabaya, East Java, Indonesia, 1972. *Education:* Faculty of Law, University of Indonesia, Jakarta (S.H., 1994). *LANGUAGES:* Indonesian, English and Dutch.

MULYANA, born 1963, Karawang, West Java, Indonesia. *Education:* Faculty of Law, Parahyangan Catholic University, Bandung (S.H., 1987); Columbia Law School, New York, New York (LL.M., 1994). Assistant Lecturer in Law at Tarumanagara University, Faculty of Law Since 1988. *LANGUAGES:* Indonesian and English.

OF COUNSEL

ANTHONY F. GRANUCCI, born San Francisco, California, 1944; admitted, 1969, California (Not admitted in Indonesia). *Education:* University of California at Berkeley (B.A., 1965); Harvard University (J.D., cum laude, 1968). Lecturer in Law, Indiana University, 1968-1969. Private practice with Thelen, Marrin, Johnson and Bridges, San Francisco, California, 1969-1972. Foreign Legal Advisor, Mochtar, Karuwin & Komar, 1972-1987. *Member:* The State Bar of California; International Bar Association. (Also Practicing Individually, One Sansome Street, 20th Floor, San Francisco, California, U.S.A.).

REPRESENTATIVE CLIENTS: Alcatel; American Express Company; Asian Development Bank; Atlantic Richfield Company; Bank of America; Bank of India; Bankers Trust Co.; Bangkok Bank; Banque Nationale de Paris; BASF Aktiengesellschaft; The Bechtel Group; Bell Atlantic; British Petroleum; Burmah Oil Co.; Chemical Bank; Combustion Engineering, Inc.; Commonwealth Development Corp. (C.D.C.); Conoco; Dai-Ichi Kangyo Bank; Dow Chemical; Dupont; Enron; Exxon; Fluor Corp.; The Gillette Company; Hilton International; Hudbay Group; Roy M. Huffington, Ins.; Hyatt International; I.B.M.; International Finance Corporation; International Nickel Indonesia (INCO); The Kellog Corp.; Lloyds Bank, Plc.; Magma Power; Merrill Lynch; Mission Energy; Morgan Guaranty Trust Co.; Pennzoil; Revlon; Santa Fe Corp.; Toyota Motor Corp.; Utah International Corp.; Union Texas Petroleum, Inc.; Walt Disney Company.

LAW FIRM KARTINI MULJADI SH & ASSOCIATES

Established in 1990

(Successor to Kantor Notaris Kartini Muljadi SH, established 1973)

BINA MULIA BUILDING, 5 & 6TH FLOOR
JALAN H.R. RASUNA SAID KAV. 10
JAKARTA 12950, INDONESIA
Telephone: 62-21-525 6968
Telefax: 62-21-525 5561
Telex: 62231 RSCO

International and General Practice. Banking, Finance, Capital Markets, Securities, Intellectual Property, Environmental Law, Mining and Oil and Gas, Real Property, Taxation, Foreign Capital Investment, General Corporate and Commercial Matters, Specialists in Mergers, Consolidations and Acquisitions, Leasing Transactions.

SENIOR PARTNER

KARTINI MULJADI, born Surabaya, Indonesia. *Education:* Faculty of Law, University of Indonesia (S.H., 1958). *LANGUAGES:* Indonesian, English and Dutch.

PARTNERS

ADHY DARMAWAN, born Jakarta, Indonesia. *Education:* Faculty of Law, Trisakti University (S.H., 1968). *LANGUAGES:* Indonesian and English.

MOSES FERNANDEZ DA SILVA, born Larantuka, East Flores, Indonesia. *Education:* Faculty of Law, Jayabaya University (S.H., 1985). *LANGUAGES:* Indonesian and English.

IRIANTO SHALIM, born Tangerang, Indonesia. *Education:* Faculty of Law, University of Gadjah Mada (S.H., 1987). *LANGUAGES:* Indonesian and English.

(This Listing Continued)

LAW FIRM KARTINI MULJADI SH & ASSOCIATES,
Jakarta—Continued

SRI MASTUTI SOETOWIDJOJO, born Semarang, Indonesia. *Education:* Faculty of Law, University of Indonesia (S.H., 1965). *LANGUAGES:* Indonesian, English and Dutch.

DIAN INDRAYANI TAMZIL, born Surabaya, Indonesia. *Education:* Faculty of Law, Trisakti University (S.H., 1975). *LANGUAGES:* Indonesian and English.

OF COUNSEL

Budiman Elkana S.H.   **Liman Sandjaja S.H.**
A. Bertus Rikin S.H.   **Setiawan S.H.**
        Prof. Ting Swan Tiong S.H.

In Association With: Mallesons Stephen Jaques.

LAW FIRM KARTINI MULJADI SH & ASSOCIATES

Established in 1990

IN ASSOCIATION WITH
MALLESONS STEPHEN JAQUES

(Successor to Kantor Notaris Kartini Muljadi SH, established 1973)

LEVEL 5, BINA MULIA I BUILDING
J1 H.R. RASUNA SAID KAV 10
JAKARTA 12950, INDONESIA

Telephone: 62-21-525 6968
Fax: 62-21-525 5561

Sydney, Australia Office: Level 60, Governor Phillip Tower, 1 Farrer Place, 2000. Telephone: (612) 250 3000. Fax: (612) 250 3133.
Melbourne, Australia Office: Level 28, Rialto, 525 Collins Street, 3000. Telephone: (613) 619 0619. Fax: (613) 614 1329.
Perth, Australia Office: Ground Floor, St. Georges Square, 225 St. George's Terrace, 6000. Telephone: (619) 324 8333. Telex: MLSJ AA92646. Fax: (619) 321 1017.
Brisbane, Australia Office: Level 30, Waterfront Place, 1 Eagle Street, 4000. Telephone: (617) 231 7500. Fax: (617) 221 1211.
Canberra, Australia Office: Level 10, Advance Bank Centre, 60 Marcus Clarke Street, 2601. Telephone: (616) 268 3900. Fax: (616) 257 3100.
Hong Kong Office: Bateson Starr in association with Mallesons Stephen Jaques, Suite 801, Asia Pacific Finance Tower, Citibank Plaza, 3 Garden Road, Central Hong Kong. Telephone: (852) 848 4600. Fax: (852) 868 0124.
Beijing, The Peoples Republic of China Office: Suite 701, Scite Tower, 22 Jianguomenwai Street, 100004. Telephone: (861) 5123565 ext. 701. Fax: (861) 5232018.
Taipei, Taiwan Office: 14th Floor, Mallesons Stephen Jaques, 138 Min Sheng East Road, Sec 3. Telephone: (886-2) 712 5808. Fax: (886-2) 712 9080.
Port Moresby, Papua New Guinea Office: Beresford Love, agents for Mallesons Stephen Jaques, Level 3, Hunter Building, Hunter Street. Telephone: (675) 211942. Fax: (675) 211586.
Singapore Office: Level 36, Hong Leong Building, 16 Raffles Quay, 0104. Telephone: (65) 3218930. Fax: (65) 2259060.
London, England Office: 2nd Floor, Aldermary House, 10-15 Queen Street, EC4N 1TX. Telephone: (44-171) 982 0982. Fax: (44-171) 982 9820.
New York, New York, U.S.A. Office: 9th Floor, Suite 911, 609 Fifth Avenue, 10017-1021. Telephone: (1-212) 319 9500. Fax: (1-212) 319 9506.

CONTACT PARTNER

Jeremy Wade

(For Complete Personnel, see Biographical Card at Sydney, Australia)

LAW OFFICE OF ALFONSO NAPITUPULU & ASSOCIATES

Legal Consultants
Patent & Trademark Attorneys
KOMPLEKS MANGGA DUA PLAZA, BLOCK E NO. 31
JALAN MANGGA DUA RAYA
JAKARTA 14430, INDONESIA
Telephone: (62-21) 612-0082; 612-1123
Fax: (62-21) 649-9254

Patent and Trademark, Commercial and Banking Litigation, Corporate, Investment, Finance.

FOUNDER

ALFONSO R.M. NAPITUPULU, born Balige, North Sumatera, Indonesia, December 3, 1950; admitted, 1979, Jakarta, licensed Patent Consultant/Attorney. *Education:* Faculty of Law, University of Indonesia, Jakarta (Master of Law, 1975). International Attorney, Bronson, Bronson & McKinnon, San Francisco, USA, 1984-1985. *Member:* Indonesian Bar Association. *LANGUAGES:* Indonesian and English.

ASSOCIATES

RUDI KURNIAWAN. *Education:* Master of Law.

ABRAHAM BM SIAHAAN. *Education:* Master of Law.

MUARA KARTA SIMATUPANG. *Education:* Master of Law.

MAWAR INVIOLITA NAPITUPULU. *Education:* Ec., MBA.

REPRESENTATIVE CLIENTS: PT. Bank Umum Nasional; Maersk Line Jakarta; PT. IPTN (Indonesian Air Craft Industry); PT. Arya Upaya Corporation (Member of Ongko Group); The Standard Steamship Owners Protection & Indemnity Association (Bermuda), Ltd., London, UK; Lytes Industries Co., Ltd., Hong Kong; Ithaca Acquisition, Inc., North Carolina, USA; PT Dianindah Reksawood Industri; PT Buana Talimas Textile; PT Eagle Indo Pharmaceutical Laboratories.

SURIA NATAADMADJA & ASSOCIATES

Established in 1982

JALAN MALAKA 19-D, 3RD FLOOR
JAKARTA 11230, INDONESIA
Telephone: (62-21) 6904403/6904791/6900579/6900580
Facsimile: (62-21) 6902792

Mailing Address: P.O. Box 43 JKRS, Jakarta 10570,, Indonesia

Jakarta Branch Office: Jalan Summagung III, Blok E3/2, Kelapa Gading Permai, Jakarta Utara 14240. Telephone: (62-21) 4896225.
Bandung, Indonesia Office: Jalan Jen, Sudirman 247, Bandung 40241, P.O. Box 77. Telephone: (62-22) 631668.
Associated U.S. Office: Law Office of Fredric D. Abramson, Chartered, 21155 Woodfield Road, Gaithersburg, Maryland, 20882. Telephone: (301) 840-9733. Fax: (301) 869-5636.

Foreign Investments, Corporate, Litigation, Family Law.

FIRM PROFILE: *The firm was established in 1982 and offers a full range of legal services. It is well known for its capability to solve difficult problems between foreign investors and its local partners.*

MEMBERS OF FIRM

SURIA NATAADMADJA, born Bandung, Indonesia, May 26, 1956; admitted, 1982, Indonesia. *Education:* Faculty of Economics, University of Indonesia (1979-1981); Faculty of Law, University of Indonesia (Master of Laws, S.H., 1981); Legal Continuing Education, Southern Methodist University (1986); Washington College of Law, American University (LL.M., 1987). *Member:* Indonesian Bar Association (IKADIN); International Bar Association (IBA); Asian Law Association (ALA); The Law Association for Asia and the Western Pacific (LAWASIA). *LANGUAGES:* Indonesian and English. *PRACTICE AREAS:* Foreign Investment; Corporate and Banking.

ROBBY P. SOESETYO, born Belawan, Indonesia, January 2, 1954; admitted, 1982, Indonesia. *Education:* Faculty of Law, University of Indonesia (Master of Laws, S.H., 1981). Legal Counsel: P.T. Sarimie Asli Jaya Industries, 1982-1984; P.T. Wicaksana Overseas Imports, 1984-1988; P.T. Sari Ayu, 1988—,.. *LANGUAGES:* Indonesian and English. *PRACTICE AREAS:* Corporate Legal Matters.

(This Listing Continued)

ASTRID SOETANTO AULIA, born Jakarta, Indonesia, April 27, 1954; admitted, 1982, Indonesia. *Education:* Faculty of Law, University of Indonesia (Master of Laws, S.H., 1981). Associated with Public Notary Office of Lilani Handajawati Tamzil S.H., 1981-1983. *LANGUAGES:* Indonesian and English. *PRACTICE AREAS:* Family Law.

PAULUS HERU TUMBELAKA, born Jakarta, Indonesia, October 18, 1955; admitted, 1984, Indonesia. *Education:* Faculty of Law, University of Indonesia (Master of Laws, S.H., 1981). Associate, Enny Poernomo & Associates, 1981-1983. *Member:* Indonesian Bar Association (Legal Assistant and Attorney Management Courses, (PERADIN), 1980). *LANGUAGES:* Indonesian and English. *PRACTICE AREAS:* Corporate Legal Matters.

GOENAWAN NATAADMADJA, born Bandung, Indonesia, September 3, 1957; admitted, 1984, Bandung; 1986, Indonesia. *Education:* Faculty of Dentistry, Trisakti University (1977); Faculty of Law, Parahyangan University (Master of Laws, S.H., 1986). Legal Counsel, P.T. Alpen Tile Industries, 1980-1983. *LANGUAGES:* Indonesian and English. *PRACTICE AREAS:* Corporate Legal Matters.

RETNO S. DARUSSALAM, born Jakarta, Indonesia, June 27, 1959; admitted, 1983. *Education:* Faculty of Law, University of Indonesia (Master of Laws, S.H., 1983). Senior Staff of Faculty of Law, University of Indonesia Law Review (HUKUM & PEMBANGUNAN), 1979-1983); Associate Editor, University of Indonesia Bulletin (WARTA U.I.), 1978-1980; Lecturer in Human and Civilization, Faculty of Law, University of Indonesia, 1986; Researcher in "Divorce Cause in Young Age", Faculty of Law, University of Indonesia; Researcher in "The Balinese Adat Law", Faculty of Law, University of Indonesia, 1983. *LANGUAGES:* Indonesian and English. *PRACTICE AREAS:* Family Law.

MIRZAIRULSYAH CHAIDIR, born Jakarta, Indonesia, May 4, 1954; admitted, 1990. *Education:* Faculty of Law, University of Indonesia (Master of Law, S.H., 1990). Indonesian Delegation to the United Nation Enforcement Force (UNEF) in Middle East, 1978-1979). *LANGUAGES:* Indonesian and English. *PRACTICE AREAS:* Civil and Criminal Litigation.

HALIM NATAADMADJA, born Bandung, Indonesia, May 15, 1961; admitted, 1986, Indonesia. *Education:* Faculty of Law, Trisakti University (Master of Law, S.H., 1986); Public Notary Education; Post Graduate Legal Program, Faculty of Law, University of Indonesia (1986). *LANGUAGES:* Indonesian and English. *PRACTICE AREAS:* Civil and Criminal Litigation.

ISAK JONATHAN, born Tobelo, Indonesia, April 29, 1954; (Not admitted in Indonesia). *Education:* Faculty of Law, University of Indonesia (1973-1981). *LANGUAGES:* Indonesian and English.

ADIYANTI, born Jakarta, Indonesia, December 18, 1967; (Not admitted in Indonesia). *Education:* Faculty of Law, University of Indonesia (Master of Laws, S.H., 1986). Legal Counsel, P.T. Nyonya Meneer, 1993. *LANGUAGES:* Indonesian and English.

NAUTA DUTILH

Attorneys, Civil Law Notaries, Tax Advisers

(Correspondent Office)

Soemadipradja & Taher

BANK BNI BUILDING, LEVEL 22
JL. JENDERAL SUDIRMAN KAV. 1
JAKARTA 10220, INDONESIA
Telephone: (62) 215702588
Telecopier: (62) 215702598

IMAN SJAHPUTRA & ASSOCIATES

Advocates & Solicitors & Patent & Trademark Attorneys

Established in 1988

JL. P. JAYAKARTA NO. 117, BLOK B-21
JAKARTA 10730, INDONESIA
Telephone: (62-21) 6599703; 6599704; 6490917; 6490919
Telex: 6 3 9 6 1 ia
Facsimile: (62-21) 6007471

Correspondent Offices:
Australia: H.R. HODGKINSON & Co.
Singapore: TAN KIM SENG & Partners
Japan: YAMAGAMI & YAMAGAMI
Singapore: GRACE KWEK & Co.

Intellectual Property Law, Copyright Law, Patent Litigation, Trademark Litigation, Trademark Prosecution, General Intellectual Property Practice, Corporate Law, Banking Law, Foreign Investment, Bankruptcy, Distributorships, Agency & Franchise Law, Industrial Relations, Arbitration, Family Law, Insurance Law, Litigation, General Legal Practice.

FIRM PROFILE: Countries covered by the firm: Asia and Australia.

IMAN SJAHPUTRA, born Pematang Siantar, Indonesia, October 27, 1958; admitted, 1989, Indonesia. *Education:* University of Gajah Mada, Yogyakarta (Law Degree, 1981; Candidate of Notary, 1989). *LANGUAGES:* Indonesian, English and Mandarin. *PRACTICE AREAS:* Intellectual Property Rights; International Business Transactions; Foreign Investment.

ASSOCIATES

HERI HERJANDONO, born Lamongan, Indonesia, May 12, 1944; admitted, 1986, Indonesia. *Education:* University of Gajah Mada, Yogyakarta (Law Degree, 1972). Senior Research Assistant: Law School of the University of Sydney, Australia, 1972; Law School of Macquarie University, Sydney, Australia, 1973. *LANGUAGES:* Indonesian and English. *PRACTICE AREAS:* Intellectual Property Rights; General Practice.

EDISON JINGGA, born Pematang Siantar, Indonesia, June 2, 1960. *Education:* University of Gadjah Mada, Yogyakrta (Law Degree, 1984). *LANGUAGES:* Indonesian, English and Mandarin. *PRACTICE AREAS:* Banking; Corporate; Foreign Investment.

HELMIAH BISYIR, born Jakarta, Indonesia, August 22, 1965. *Education:* University of Krisna Dwipayana, Jakarta (Law Degree, 1989). *LANGUAGES:* Indonesian, English and Arabic. *PRACTICE AREAS:* Banking; Corporate; Foreign Investment.

M.T. ENDAH MARTININGSIH, born Jakarta, Indonesia, March 2, 1963. *Education:* University of Kristen Indonesia, Jakarta (Law Degree, 1989). *LANGUAGES:* Indonesian and English. *PRACTICE AREAS:* Intellectual Property Rights; Corporate Law.

PHILIP JUSUF, born Jakarta, Indonesia, March 23, 1957. *Education:* University of Gadjah Mada, Yogyakarta (Law Degree, 1983). *LANGUAGES:* Indonesian and English. *PRACTICE AREAS:* General Practice.

HADI SETIA TUNGGAL, born Pematang Siantar, December 12, 1965. *Education:* University of Trisakti (Law Degree, 1991). *LANGUAGES:* Indonesian, English and Mandarin. *PRACTICE AREAS:* Intellectual Property Rights.

REPRESENTATIVE CLIENTS: Inchcape Berhad, Singapore; JK Micro (S) PTE, Ltd, Singapore; Murata Machinery Ltd., Japan; Slumberland Eastern Sdn. Bhd, Malaysia; Miror International Corp, Taipei, Taiwan; PT Bank Pasar Gunung Barisan, Indonesia; PT Medang Kerang Djaya, Indonesia; PT National Harvest Securities, Indonesia; PT Duta Fort Indonesia; Garuda Mas Group; PT Indotai Unifood Sejahtera; PT Delident Chemical Industries Indonesia Ltd; PT Nagata Indonesia Permai; PT Indocare Citra Pacific.

SOEBAGJO, ROOSDIONO, JATIM & DJAROT

CHASE PLAZA, 17TH FLOOR
JALAN JENDERAL SUDIRMAN KAV. 21
JAKARTA 12910, INDONESIA
Telephone: 62-021-5706436; 5700179; 5208120; 5208121; 5208122; 5208123
Facsimile: 62-021-5706437

Foreign Investment, Business Organization, Banking and Finance, Corporate Law, Contracts, Mining, Aviation, Property, Maritime, Construction and Development, Telecommunications, Taxation, Tourism, Technology Transfer, Mergers and Acquisitions, Restructurings, Insolvency, Arbitration and Mediation, Franchising, Leasing, Insurance, Employment, Trade Practices, Securities, Intellectual Property and Entertainment Law.

PARTNERS

FELIX OENTOENG SOEBAGJO, born Cilacap, Indonesia, March 13, 1948. *Education:* University of Indonesia (S.H., 1976); Boalt Hall School of Law, University of California at Berkeley (LL.M., 1980). Editor, *Hukum dan Pembangunan,* 1977-1979, Member, Center for Study of Law and Economy, 1976, and Vice Chairman, Center for Study of Multinational and Transfer of Technology, University of Indonesia, 1987. Expert, Law for Social Services at Sanggar Prativi, 1977-1979. Lecturer in Commercial Law, University of Pancasila, 1977-1979, 1993. Lecturer in Commercial Law, University of Indonesia, Faculty of Law, 1979— and in Law and Economy, Faculty of Economics, 1980-1985. *LANGUAGES:* English and Indonesian.

ANANGGA W. ROOSDIONO, born Jakarta, Indonesia, March 9, 1944. *Education:* University of Indonesia (S.H., 1966). *LANGUAGES:* English and Dutch.

FATMAH JATIM, born Teheran, Iran, September 3, 1952. *Education:* University of Indonesia (S.H., 1976); Harvard Law School (LL.M., 1984). Lecturer in Private International Law, Faculty of Law, University of Indonesia, 1979—. *LANGUAGES:* English and Indonesian.

DEWI DJAROT, born Jakarta, Indonesia, August 4, 1954. *Education:* University of Paris I, Pantheon, Sorbonne (Licence de Droit, 1977; Maîtrise de Droit, 1978; DEA, Diplome d'Etudes Approfondies, 1983; Doctorat de 3e Cycle, 1986). Lecturer in Private International Law, Faculty of Law, 1980-1990. *LANGUAGES:* French, English and Indonesian.

ASSOCIATES

BUDIONO KUSUMOHAMIDJOJO, born Bandung, Indonesia, January 7, 1949. *Education:* Parahyangan Catholic University (S.H., 1976); Doktor der Philosophie (Dr.phil.); Julius-Maximilians State University of Wuerzburg (Wuerzburg, Germany, 1982). Freelance Columnist, 1978—. Teaching and Research Positions, Parahyangan Catholic University, Bandung, 1982-1986. Legal Consultant, Jakarta, 1986—. With, Soebagjo, Roosdiono, Jatim & Djarot, 1994—. *LANGUAGES:* Indonesian, English, German and Dutch.

ZAINAL RAHMAN, born Banda Aceh, Indonesia, July 2, 1964. *Education:* University of Indonesia (S.H., 1988). *LANGUAGES:* English and Indonesian.

DAVE PURVIS, born Rumbai, Indonesia, September 4, 1965. *Education:* Christian University of Indonesia (UKI). *LANGUAGES:* English and Indonesian.

DUDI SUDIOTOMO KARTOHADIPRODJO, born Jakarta, Indonesia, November 15, 1968. *Education:* University of Indonesia (S.H., 1991). *LANGUAGES:* English and Indonesian.

RIEKE SAVITRI, born Palembang, Indonesia, April 8, 1969. *Education:* University of Indonesia (S.H., 1991). *LANGUAGES:* English and Indonesian.

CORNELIUS SIMANJUNTAK, born Rumbai, Indonesia, March 13, 1964. *Education:* Padjadjaran University (S.H., 1988). *LANGUAGES:* English and Indonesian.

YAUMI AZHAR, born Palembang, Indonesia, September 3, 1968. *Education:* University of Trisakti (S.H., 1991); Bond University, Gold Coast, Australia (Master of Law; LL.M., 1993). *LANGUAGES:* English and Indonesian.

LUKMAN NUR AZIS, born Subang, Indonesia, Mei 12, 1970. *Education:* University of Indonesia (S.H., 1993). *LANGUAGES:* English and Indonesian.

(This Listing Continued)

PIA ARIESTIANA RINANDA NASUTION, born Jakarta, Indonesia, March 23, 1969. *Education:* Catholic University of Atma Jaya (S.H., 1992). *LANGUAGES:* English and Indonesian.

ANTHONY C. KLOK, born Hobart, Australia, October 6, 1960. *Education:* University of Tasmania, Australia (Double Degree of Commerce and Law, B.Com., LL.B., A.A.S., T.I.A., 1982). Member: Dobson, Mitchell and Allport, 1983-1987; Arthur Andersen & Co., 1987-1988; Blake Dawson Waldron, 1988-1990. *LANGUAGES:* English.

ANTHONY J. HUDSON, born Melbourne, Australia, January 14, 1963. *Education:* University of Melbourne, Australia (B.Com., LL.B., 1985). With, Blake, Dawson Waldron, 1986-1993. *LANGUAGES:* English.

SOEWITO, SUHARDIMAN, EDDYMURTHY & KARDONO

Established in 1992

WISMA BANK DHARMALA, 14TH FLOOR, SUITE 1403
JL. JENDRAL SUDIRMAN KAV. 28
JAKARTA 12920, INDONESIA
Telephone: 021-521-2038
Facsimile: 021-521-2039

Mailing Address: P.O. Box 8314, Jakarta 12083, Indonesia

Corporate, Commercial and Financial Law Practice, Energy and Natural Resources, Maritime, Banking, Capital Markets and Securities Law, Insurance, Intellectual Property, Investment, Labor, Franchising, Real Estate, Construction and Engineering, Mergers and Acquisitions, Tax Law, Arbitration, Hotel and Tourist Development, Environmental Law.

FIRM PROFILE: The law firm Soewito, Suhardiman, Eddymurthy & Kardono represents local and multinational corporations, private and publicly listed companies, offshore and local banks, financial institutions and insurance companies, manufacturers, traders, real estate developers, engineering and construction companies and shipping companies.

PARTNERS OF THE FIRM

DYAH SOEWITO, born Jogyakarta, Indonesia, 1953. *Education:* Faculty of Law, University of Indonesia (S.H., 1977). Visiting Scholar Program, Boalt Hall School of Law, University of California, Berkeley, California, 1988; Academy of American and International Law, International and Comparative Law Center, Dallas, Texas, 1988. *Member:* Association of Indonesian Legal Consultants. *LANGUAGES:* Indonesian and English. *PRACTICE AREAS:* Business Law; Natural Resources Law; Maritime Law; Banking Law; Finance Law; Real Estate Law; Corporate Law; Commercial Law.

RETTY A. SUHARDIMAN, born Jakarta, Indonesia, 1953. *Education:* Faculty of Law, University of Indonesia (S.H., 1978); Academy of American and International Law, International and Comparative Law Center, Dallas, Texas (1989). *Member:* Association of Indonesian Legal Consultants. *LANGUAGES:* Indonesian and English. *PRACTICE AREAS:* Finance Law; Banking Law; Business Law; Intellectual Property Law; Franchise Law; Mergers and Acquisitions; Aviation Law; Corporate Law; Commercial Law.

IRA A. EDDYMURTHY, born Banda Aceh, Indonesia, 1959. *Education:* Faculty of Law, University of Indonesia (S.H., 1984). Visiting Scholar, Boalt Hall, University of California, Berkeley, 1990-1991. Academy of American and International Law, International and Comparative Law Center, Dallas, Texas, 1991. *Member:* International Bar Association; Inter-Pacific Bar Association; Association of Indonesian Capital Markets (Legal Consultant). *LANGUAGES:* Indonesian and English. *PRACTICE AREAS:* Corporate Law; Commercial Law; Capital Markets Law; Telecommunications; Finance Law; Taxation Law.

A. SUPRIYANI KARDONO, born Bandung, Indonesia, 1959. *Education:* Faculty of Law, University of Parahyangan (S.H., 1984); Academy of American and International Law, International and Comparative Law Center, Dallas, Texas (1993). *Member:* Association of Indonesian Legal Consultants. *LANGUAGES:* Indonesian and English. *PRACTICE AREAS:* Corporate Law; Commercial Law; Capital Markets Law; Business Law; Environmental Law; Labor Law; Franchise Law; Intellectual Property Law; Natural Resources Law; Arbitration.

(This Listing Continued)

ASSOCIATES

RUSMAINI LENGGOGENI, born Jakarta, Indonesia, 1968. *Education:* Faculty of Law, University of Indonesia (S.H., 1992); Academy of American and International Law, International and Comparative Law Center, Dallas, Texas, 1994. *LANGUAGES:* Indonesian and English. *PRACTICE AREAS:* Corporate Law; Banking Law; Commercial Law; Capital Market Law; Aviation Law; Intellectual Property Law.

RAHMAH L.W. PRASETYO, born Jakarta, Indonesia, 1967. *Education:* Faculty of Law, University of Trisakti (S.H., 1991). *LANGUAGES:* Indonesian and English. *PRACTICE AREAS:* Taxation Law; Commercial Law; Corporate Law; Immigration.

SUSANDARINI, born Jakarta, Indonesia, 1966. *Education:* Faculty of Law, University of Indonesia (S.H., 1989). *LANGUAGES:* Indonesian and English. *PRACTICE AREAS:* Financial Law; Banking Law; Commercial Law; Insurance; Capital Market Law; Maritime Law; Corporate Law.

FAJAR UTOMO, born Bandung, Indonesia, 1969. *Education:* Faculty of Law, University of Parahyangan (S.H., 1992). *LANGUAGES:* Indonesian and English. *PRACTICE AREAS:* Banking Law; Corporate Law; Labor Law; Commercial Law; Environmental Law.

DENI SRI ANJAYANI, born Cirebon, Indonesia, 1967. *Education:* Faculty of Law, University of Padjadjaran (S.H., 1991). *LANGUAGES:* Indonesian and English. *PRACTICE AREAS:* Corporate Law; Labor Law; Immigration; Intellectual Property Law; Environmental Law.

M.A. WIDJAKSONO, born Bandung, Indonesia, 1969. *Education:* Faculty of Law, University of Padjajaran (S.H., 1992). *LANGUAGES:* Indonesian and English. *PRACTICE AREAS:* Intellectual Property Law; Labour Law; Advertising; Marketing; Insurance.

ZACKY Z. HUSEIN, born Bandung, Indonesia, 1970. *Education:* Faculty of Law, University of Indonesia (S.H., 1992); Georgetown University Law Center, Washington, D.C., USA (LL.M., Common Law Studies, 1994). *LANGUAGES:* Indonesian and English. *PRACTICE AREAS:* Commercial Law; Business Law; International Trade Law; Government Contracts; Real Estate Law.

UTIEK R. ABDURACHMAN, born Blitar, Indonesia, 1961. *Education:* Faculty of Law, University of Indonesia (S.H., 1986); University of Wisconsin Law School, Madison, USA (M.L., East Asian Legal Studies, 1994). *LANGUAGES:* Indonesian and English. *PRACTICE AREAS:* Commercial Law; Business Law; Arbitration.

ADVISOR

MICHAEL D. TWOMEY, born New York City, 1958. *Education:* Yale University (B.A., magna cum laude, 1980); University of Virginia School of Law (J.D., 1986). *Member:* The Bar of the State of New York; American Bar Association (Sections of International Law and Practice, Business Law and Real Estate and Probate Law). *LANGUAGES:* English. *PRACTICE AREAS:* Corporate Law; Commercial Law; Finance Law; Business Law; Real Estate Law; Taxation Law.

LAW OFFICES OF
WIRIADINATA & WIDYAWAN

NIAGA TOWER, 26TH FLOOR
KAV. 58, JALAN JENDERAL SUDIRMAN
JAKARTA 12190, INDONESIA
Telephone: (6221) 2505175 (hunting)
Telecopier: (6221) 2505185, 2505186

Foreign Investment, Capital Markets and Securities, Banking and Finance, Oil and Gas, Resources and Energy, Telecommunications, Construction and Property, Intellectual Property, Corporate and Business Law, Arbitration.

FIRM PROFILE: The firm was established in 1972 under the name Del Juzar & Wiriadinata. In 1992 the firm changed its name to Wiriadinata & Widyawan. Throughout the 20 years of practice, the firm has consistently been working towards and maintaining its position as one of the leading corporate and commercial law firms in Indonesia. The firm has an association with the member firms of the Allens Arthur Robinson Group whose offices are in Sydney, Melbourne, Perth, Brisbane, Adelaide, Canberra, New York, London, Hong Kong, Singapore. The firm engages two Foreign Counsel.

HOESEIN WIRIADINATA, (SENIOR PARTNER), born Jakarta, Indonesia, December 29, 1941; admitted, 1970, Indonesia. *Education:* Pad-

(This Listing Continued)

jadjaran University (Master of Law Degree, 1968); Southern Methodist University, Law School (Master of Comparative Law, M.C.L., 1976). *Member:* International Law Society; Indonesian Legal Consultants Association; Indonesian Lawyers Association; LawAsia; Inter-Pacific Bar Association. *LANGUAGES:* Indonesian and English. *PRACTICE AREAS:* Natural Resources; Banks and Banking; Finance; Company and Corporate Law; Commercial Law; Finance; Arbitration and Mediation; Business Law; Telecommunications; Securities.

WIDYAWAN, (PARTNER), born Jakarta, Indonesia, September 13, 1954. *Education:* University of Indonesia (Master of Law Degree, 1977). *LANGUAGES:* Indonesian and English. *PRACTICE AREAS:* Energy and Natural Resources Law; Business Law; Commercial and Company Law; Construction Law; Banks and Banking Law; Securities.

TIO MINAR MANIK MANIHURUK, (PARTNER), born Medan, Indonesia, September 11, 1935; admitted, 1978, Indonesia. *Education:* University of North Sumatra (Master of Law Degree, 1978). *LANGUAGES:* Indonesian, English and Dutch. *PRACTICE AREAS:* Business Law; Company Law; Finance; Property; Securities; Capital Market Law.

SARNO ABDULAH. *LANGUAGES:* Indonesian and English. *PRACTICE AREAS:* Business Law; Construction Law; Property; Intellectual Property Law; Copyrights and Trademarks; Arbitration.

MIFTAHUL HUDA. *LANGUAGES:* Indonesian and English. *PRACTICE AREAS:* Banks and Banking Law; Business Law; Corporate Law; Finance; Securities.

SANTI ACHADIJATI DARMAWAN. *LANGUAGES:* Indonesian and English. *PRACTICE AREAS:* Business Law; Commercial Law; Securities; Mergers, Acquisitions; Foreign Investment.

PIPIEN UNIEKOWATI. *LANGUAGES:* Indonesian and English. *PRACTICE AREAS:* Business Law; Corporate; Commercial Law; Natural Resources; Construction Law; Contracts; Intellectual Property; Property.

ERY YUNASRI. *LANGUAGES:* Indonesian and English. *PRACTICE AREAS:* Banks and Banking Law; Business Law; Contracts; Finance; Securities.

TAMIZA SALEH. *LANGUAGES:* Indonesian and English. *PRACTICE AREAS:* Banks and Banking; Commercial Law; Securities.

ERNI ROHAINT. *LANGUAGES:* Indonesian and English. *PRACTICE AREAS:* Foreign Investment; Property; Commercial Law.

MIRA FADHYA. *LANGUAGES:* Indonesian and English. *PRACTICE AREAS:* Business Law; Commercial Law; Company Law; Intellectual Property; Natural Resources.

DHIRA DIANTARI JUZAR. *LANGUAGES:* Indonesian and English. *PRACTICE AREAS:* Business Law; Commercial Law; Company Law; Intellectual Property; Natural Resources.

IRMA SAVITRI. *LANGUAGES:* Indonesian and English. *PRACTICE AREAS:* Business Law; Commercial Law; Company Law; Intellectual Property; Natural Resources.

IRIL HISWARA. *LANGUAGES:* Indonesian and English. *PRACTICE AREAS:* Business Law; Commercial Law; Company Law; Intellectual Property; Natural Resources.

SARI NASUTION. *LANGUAGES:* Indonesian and English. *PRACTICE AREAS:* Business Law; Commercial Law; Company Law; Intellectual Property; Natural Resources.

ANDRI SENTANU. *LANGUAGES:* Indonesian and English. *PRACTICE AREAS:* Business Law; Commercial Law; Company Law; Intellectual Property; Natural Resources.

TJAHJADI BENJAMIN. *LANGUAGES:* Indonesian and English. *PRACTICE AREAS:* Business Law; Commercial Law; Intellectual Property; Natural Resources.

PROBORARAS. *LANGUAGES:* Indonesian and English. *PRACTICE AREAS:* Business Law; Commercial Law; Company Law; Intellectual Property; Natural Resources.

FOREIGN COUNSEL

DAVID JOHN SIMPSON, born Sydney, Australia, January 24, 1961. *Education:* University of Sydney (Bachelor of Economics, 1981; Bachelor of Laws, 1983); University of Cambridge (Master of Laws, 1985). *LANGUAGES:* English. *PRACTICE AREAS:* Corporate Law; Capital Market Law; Aviation Law; Corporate Finance; Banking Law; Project Finance; Foreign Investment.

(This Listing Continued)

LAW OFFICES OF WIRIADINATA & WIDYAWAN,
Jakarta—Continued

BARRY LEWIS IRWIN, born Belfast, Northern Ireland, September 21, 1960. *Education:* Australian National University (Bachelor of Arts, 1981; Bachelor of Law, 1983). *LANGUAGES:* English and German. *PRACTICE AREAS:* Resources and Energy Law; Corporate and Securities; Infrastructure Projects; Banking and Finance.

JAPAN

HOSOI LAW OFFICE

MOTOSHIRO-CHO 117-18
HAMAMATSU-SHI 430, JAPAN
Telephone: (053) 453-7760
Fax: (053)453-2120

Corporate Law, Real Estate, Shipping, Commerical, Litigation, General Practice, Licensing, Product Liability, Bankruptcy.

FIRM PROFILE: *Mr. Hosoi has Internationally practiced more than 20 years. Previously working for Braun, Moriya, Hoashi & Kubota, Hiratsuka & Partners, Aoki, Christensen & Nomoto in Tokyo.*

TAMEYUKI HOSOI, born Shizuoka Prefecture, Japan, April 5, 1943; admitted, 1972, Japan. *Education:* Chuo University (LL.B., 1966); University of London (U.C.L., Graduate School, Diploma in Shipping Law, 1977). Co-author: "Arrest of Ships", LLP, 1985. *Member:* Shizuoka Bar Associations; IBA. *LANGUAGES:* Japanese and English. *PRACTICE AREAS:* Securities; Finance; Corporate; Commercial; Shipping.

MOTOHARA & TANAKA

HOYU-KAIKAN BUILDING, 4TH FLOOR
1-7, TAMONDORI 2-CHOME, CHUO-KU
KOBE 650, JAPAN
Telephone: 078-341-3460
Fax: 078-341-3615

General Practice. International Business Transaction, Commercial, Corporation, Labour and Maritime Law.

MEMBERS OF FIRM

TOSHIFUMI MOTOHARA, born Taskasago, Hyogo Prefecture, Japan, April 22, 1931; admitted, 1955, Kobe. *Education:* Kyoto University (LL.B., 1953); Legal Training and Research Institute (Diploma, 1955). *Member:* Kobe Bar Association (President, 1974-1975); Japan Federation of Bar Associations (Vice-President, 1988-1989); International Bar Association (Councillor, 1987-1991); LAWASIA. *LANGUAGES:* Japanese and English.

HISAO TANAKA, born Kobe, Japan, September 27, 1953; admitted, 1983, Kobe. *Education:* Tokyo University (LL.B., 1978); Legal Training and Research Institute (Diploma, 1983). *Member:* Kobe Bar Association; Japan Federation of Bar Associations. *LANGUAGES:* Japanese and English.

KOHJI YONEDA, born Himeji, Hyogo Prefecture, Japan, February 17, 1957; admitted, 1990, Kobe. *Education:* Kyoto University (LL.B., 1988); Legal Training and Research Institute (Diploma, 1990). *Member:* Kobe Bar Association; Japan Federation of Bar Associations. *LANGUAGES:* Japanese and English.

JOLLY GAIKOKUHO JIMU BENGOSHI JIMUSHO

Established in 1988

MARUNOUCHI KS BUILDING 8TH FLOOR
18-25 MARUNOUCHI 2-CHOME, NAKA-KU
NAGOYA 460, JAPAN
Telephone: (052) 221-1751
Facsimile: (052) 221-1752

International Business Structures and Trade Documentation, US Litigation, Real Estate Transactions and Immigration.

(This Listing Continued)

FIRM PROFILE: *The firm was established in 1988 as first foreign law attorney outside Tokyo and offering a full range of legal services within limitations of the Special Law permitting such practice in Japan. The client base is primarily Japanese in matters dealing with U.S. legal questions or litigation. The Special Law prohibits advising on Japanese law or representing parties before Japanese authorities, but assistance to foreign persons in locating and maintaining liaison with competent Japanese counsel or in otherwise establishing contacts within Japan is offered.*

JAMES A. JOLLY, born Ariel, Washington, January 25, 1939; admitted, 1972, Hawaii; 1987, Washington; 1988, Japan. *Education:* Clark Junior College (A.A., 1959); Michigan State University (B.A., 1964); University of Hawaii; University of Texas at Austin (J.D., 1971); Japan-American Institute of Management Science (JMP certificate 1980). Delta Theta Phi. *Member:* Hawaii State, Washington State and American Bar Associations; Japan Federation of Bar Associations and Nagoya Bar Association; American Society of International Law; American Business Community of Nagoya; Japan-America Society. *LANGUAGES:* English and Japanese.

KAWAMITSU & EINSEL

Established in 1965

1-16-3 MAEJIMA
NAHA 900, JAPAN
Telephone: 098-862-1276; 098-862-4291; 098-867-4457
Cable Address: "Benlaw"
Facsimile: 098-869-2910

General Practice. Commercial and International Law. Patent and Trademark Law.

MEMBERS OF FIRM

SATOSHI KAWAMITSU, born April 3, 1936; admitted, 1965, Ryukyu Islands; 1972, Japan. *Education:* St. Marks School and the Brooks School, Massachusetts, 1953-1954; Waseda University Law School (LL.B., 1959); Indiana University, 1960-1961; International and Comparative Law Center, Southwestern Legal Foundation, Dallas, Texas, 1967. *Member:* Okinawa Bar Association (Vice-President, 1981-1982); Japan Federation of Bar Associations. *LANGUAGES:* Japanese and English. *PRACTICE AREAS:* Civil Litigation; Commercial Litigation; Family Law; Criminal Litigation; General Business Law.

REINHARD EINSEL, born March 13, 1927; admitted, 1956, Germany; 1965, Okinawa; 1972, Japan. *Education:* Georg Augusta University, Goettingen, Germany (Attorney-at-Law, 1956). Lecturer, Legal Training and Research Institute, Japanese Supreme Court, 1962—. *Member:* Deutscher Juristentag; International Law Association of Japan; Japanese Bar Association. *LANGUAGES:* German, English and Japanese. *PRACTICE AREAS:* Patent and Trademark Law.

AMIDA & HIROKAWA

202 OE BUILDING
8-1 NISHI-TEMMA, 2-CHOME, KITA-KU
OSAKA 530, JAPAN
Telephone: 06-361-9095/7
Cable Address: "Hiroatny"
Telex: J63030 HIROATNY
Facsimile: 06-361-1667; 06-361-9093

General Practice.

MEMBERS OF FIRM

KAKUICHI AMIDA (1902-1989).

KOJI HIROKAWA, born Hiroshima Prefecture, Japan, March 31, 1937; admitted, 1967, Japan. *Education:* Tokyo University (LL.B., 1961); University of Washington School of Law (M.C.L., 1970). *Member:* Osaka Bar Association; Japanese Federation of Bar Associations. *LANGUAGES:* Japanese, English, German and Korean. *PRACTICE AREAS:* Product Liability; International Transactions; General Practice.

ASSOCIATES

HIDEHIRO SUGAWARA, born Fukushima Prefecture, Japan, October 11, 1957; admitted, 1989, Japan. *Education:* Ritsumeikan University (LL.B., 1984). *Member:* Osaka Bar Association; Japanese Federation of Bar Associations. *LANGUAGES:* Japanese and English. *PRACTICE AREAS:* General Practice.

(This Listing Continued)

HITOSHI ASHIDA, born Kyoto Prefecture, Japan, June 26, 1957; admitted, 1993, Japan. *Education:* Kansai University (LL.B., 1981). *Member:* Osaka Bar Association; Japanese Federation of Bar Associations. *LANGUAGES:* Japanese and English. *PRACTICE AREAS:* General Practice.

KUMIKO SUENAGA, born Hiroshima Prefecture, Japan, April 1, 1969; admitted, 1993, Japan. *Education:* Osaka University (LL.B., 1991). *Member:* Osaka Bar Association; Japanese Federation of Bar Associations. *LANGUAGES:* Japanese and English. *PRACTICE AREAS:* International Transactions; General Practice.

ASAHI CHUO GENERAL LAW & ACCOUNTING OFFICE

Established in 1976

DAINI YURAKU BLDG. 8/F
1-7 HOMMACHI 4-CHOME, CHUO-KU
OSAKA 541, JAPAN
Telephone: 81-6-263-2130
Fax: 81-6-263-2137/2138

Hong Kong Office: Unit C2, 12/F, United Centre, 95 Queensway. Telephone: (852) 520-0626. Fax: (852) 528-4085.

Tax Law, Corporate Law, Banking and Finance, Bankruptcy, Real Estate, Civil and Commercial Litigation, Patent and Trademark Law, International Transactions.

FIRM PROFILE: *The Asahi Chuo General Law & Accounting Office was the first organization in Japan to offer a combined practice in legal and tax-related matters. Our firm has five lawyers and five certified public accountants and licensed tax accountants. Thus, we are able to offer not only legal services, but also accounting and tax-related services, including the preparation of tax returns. Our unique combination of expertise allows us to effectively handle cases where legal and accounting concerns overlap. Our firm's client base consists primarily of corporations but also includes individuals. Our corporate clients are engaged in industries ranging from finance, real estate and insurance to construction, transportation and the service sector. Firm members have authored various publications, including our ten-volume "Practical Real Estate Tax Law," "Practical Counselling for Stockholder's Representative Action," "Practical Counselling for Products Liability Law in Japan," and "Legal and Accounting Manual for Doing Business in Japan," and are currently working on manuscripts of future publications as well.*

PARTNERS

SHINICHI HAYASHI, born Hyogo Prefecture, Japan, March 8, 1948; admitted, 1973, Japan; registered as Licensed Tax Accountant, 1991, Japan. *Education:* Osaka University (LL.B., 1971); The Legal Training and Research Institute of the Supreme Court (1973). Author: "Acquisitions of Treasury Stock," 1970; "Problems Related to Joint Illegal Actions and Automobile Accidents Involving Damages to Fellow Passengers," 1973; "Encyclopedia of Problems in Real Estate Transactions," 1974; "Basics of Provisional Property Seizure and Disposition," 1977; "Basics of Real Estate Registration," 1977; "Practical Real Estate Tax Laws," 1990; "Manual of Inheritance Tax Measures for Owners of Rental Land and Rental Houses," 1991; "Practical Counselling for Stockholder's Representative Action," 1993; "Practical Counselling for Products Liability Law in Japan," 1994; "Legal and Accounting Manual for Doing Business in Japan," 1994. *Member:* Osaka Bar Association. *LANGUAGES:* Japanese and English. *PRACTICE AREAS:* Corporate Law; Tax Law; Real Estate Law; International Transactions.

KIYOTAKA JINNO, born Aichi Prefecture, Japan, January 15, 1949; registered as Certified Public Accountant, 1978; Licensed Tax Accountant, 1979, Japan. Author: "Practical Real Estate Tax Laws," 1990; "Manual of Inheritance Tax Measures for Owners of Rental Land and Rental Houses," 1991; "Practical Counselling for Stockholder's Representative Action," 1993; "Practical Counselling for Products Liability Law in Japan," 1994; "Legal and Accounting Manual for Doing Business in Japan," 1994. *LANGUAGES:* Japanese, English and Chinese. *PRACTICE AREAS:* Accounting; Taxation; Tax Returns.

SHIRO MATSUMOTO, born Kyoto Prefecture, Japan, January 10, 1951; admitted, 1978, Japan; appointed as judicial judge, 1978, Japan. *Education:* Kyoto University (LL.B., 1976); The Legal Training and Research Institute of the Supreme Court (1978). Author: "Practical Real Estate Tax Laws," 1990; "Practical Counselling for Stockholder's Representative Action," 1993; "Practical Counselling for Products Liability Law in Japan,"

(This Listing Continued)

1994; "Legal and Accounting Manual for Doing Business in Japan," 1994. *Member:* Osaka Bar Association. *LANGUAGES:* Japanese and English. *PRACTICE AREAS:* Civil and Commercial Law.

HARUO NAKAGAWA, born Fukui Prefecture, Japan, July 9, 1958; admitted, 1986, Japan. *Education:* Osaka University (LL.B., 1983); The Legal Training and Research Institute of the Supreme Court (1986). Author: "Practical Real Estate Tax Laws," 1990; "Practical Counselling for Stockholder's Representative Action," 1993; "Practical Counselling for Products Liability Law in Japan," 1994; "Legal and Accounting Manual for Doing Business in Japan," 1994. *Member:* Osaka Bar Association. *LANGUAGES:* Japanese and English. *PRACTICE AREAS:* Corporate Law; Real Estate Law.

KOICHI KAKEE, born Hiroshima Prefecture, Japan, January 1, 1951; registered as Licensed Tax Accountant, 1983, Japan. *Education:* Kwansei Gakuin University (B.A., 1974); Kwansei Gakuin University Graduate School (M.A., 1976). Author: "Practical Real Estate Tax Laws," 1990; "Practical Counselling for Stockholder's Representative Action," 1993. *LANGUAGES:* Japanese and English. *PRACTICE AREAS:* Taxation; Tax Returns.

SHUNSAKU NAKASHIMA, born Yamaguchi Prefecture, Japan, July 29, 1963; admitted, 1990, Japan. *Education:* Chuo University (LL.B., 1987); The Legal Training and Research Institute of the Supreme Court (1990). Author: "Practical Counselling for Stockholder's Representative Action," 1993; "Practical Counselling for Products Liability Law in Japan," 1994; "Legal and Accounting Manual for Doing Business in Japan," 1994. *Member:* Osaka Bar Association. *LANGUAGES:* Japanese and English. *PRACTICE AREAS:* Patent and Trademark Law; Real Estate Law.

JUNJI OKUDA, born Osaka Prefecture, Japan, May 21, 1962; admitted, 1991, Japan. *Education:* The University of Tokyo (LL.B., 1989); The Legal Training and Research Institute of the Supreme Court (1991). Author: "Practical Counselling for Stockholder's Representative Action," 1993; "Practical Counselling for Products Liability Law in Japan," 1994; "Legal and Accounting Manual for Doing Business in Japan," 1994. *Member:* Osaka Bar Association. *LANGUAGES:* Japanese and English. *PRACTICE AREAS:* Civil Law; Corporate Law.

ASSOCIATES

SOTARO NAGAMOTO, born Hiroshima Prefecture, January 1, 1947; registered as Certified Public Accountant, 1979; Licensed Tax Accountant, 1987, Japan. *Education:* Nagoya University (B.A., 1972). *LANGUAGES:* Japanese. *PRACTICE AREAS:* Accounting; Tax Returns.

CHUO LAW OFFICE

KOHDA BUILDING, 11TH FLOOR
2-10-2 NISHITEMMA, KITA-KU
OSAKA 530, JAPAN
Telephone: 06-365-8111
Facsimile: 06-365-8289

Antitrust, Banking and Finance, Bankruptcy, Civil and Commercial Litigation, Corporate Law, Domestic Relations, Employment Relations, Immigration, Intellectual Property, International, Labor, Municipal, Taxation, Real Estate, White-Collar Crime Defense.

MEMBERS OF FIRM

TSUGUJIRO NAKATSUKASA, born Osaka, Japan, 1936; admitted, 1964, Japan. *Education:* Osaka City University (LL.B., 1959); The Legal Training and Research Institute of the Supreme Court (1964). *Member:* Osaka Bar Association (Vice-President, 1982-1983); Japan Federation of Bar Associations (Director, 1991-1992). *LANGUAGES:* Japanese and English.

MOTOOMI IWAKI, born Wakayama, Japan, 1945; admitted, 1976, Japan. *Education:* Waseda University (LL.B., 1969); The Legal Training and Research Institute of the Supreme Court (1976). *Member:* Osaka Bar Association; Japan Federation of Bar Associations. *LANGUAGES:* Japanese.

JOJI MURANO, born Hyogo, Japan, 1951; admitted, 1979, Japan. *Education:* Osaka University (LL.B., 1976); The Legal Training and Research Institute of the Supreme Court (1979). *Member:* Osaka Bar Association; Japan Federation of Bar Associations. *LANGUAGES:* Japanese.

SHINJI MORI, born Kyoto, Japan, 1946; admitted, 1989, Japan. *Education:* Waseda University (LL.B., 1971); The Legal Training and Research Institute of the Supreme Court (1974). Judge, 1974-1989. *Member:* Osaka

(This Listing Continued)

CHUO LAW OFFICE, Osaka—Continued

Bar Association; Japan Federation of Bar Associations. *LANGUAGES:* Japanese.

SACHIE KATOH, born Chiba, Japan, 1946; admitted, 1974, Japan. *Education:* Waseda University (LL.B., 1969); The Legal Training and Research Institute of the Supreme Court (1971). Public Prosecutor, 1971-1974. *Member:* Osaka Bar Association; Japan Federation of Bar Associations. *LANGUAGES:* Japanese.

CHIYU ABO, born Miyagi, Japan, 1961; admitted, 1986, Japan; 1990, New York; 1991, Michigan. *Education:* Chuo University (LL.B., 1984); The Legal Training and Research Institute of the Supreme Court (1986); Cornell Law School (LL.M., 1990). Phi Kappa Phi. With Dickinson, Wright, Moon, Van Dusen & Freeman, Detroit, 1990-1992. *Member:* Osaka Bar Association; Japan Federation of Bar Associations; New York State Bar Association; State Bar of Michigan. *LANGUAGES:* Japanese and English.

TAKAHIKO ASAI, born Kyoto, Japan, 1959; admitted, 1988, Japan. *Education:* The University of Tokyo (LL.B., 1985); The Legal Training and Research Institute of the Supreme Court (1988). *Member:* Osaka Bar Association; Japan Federation of Bar Associations. *LANGUAGES:* Japanese and English.

TAKAHISA IGUCHI, born Osaka, Japan, 1959; admitted, 1992, Japan. *Education:* Osaka City University (LL.B., 1986); The Legal Training and Research Institute of the Supreme Court (1992). *Member:* Osaka Bar Association; Japan Federation of Bar Associations. *LANGUAGES:* Japanese and English.

HIROSHI NAKAMITSU, born Osaka, Japan, 1963; admitted, 1993, Japan. *Education:* Osaka University (LL.B., 1988); The Legal Training and Research Institute of the Supreme Court (1993). *Member:* Osaka Bar Association; Japan Federation of Bar Associations. *LANGUAGES:* Japanese.

MASAHIRO NAKATSUKASA, born Osaka, Japan, 1965; admitted, 1994, Japan. *Education:* Kyoto University (LL.B., 1992); The Legal Training and Research Institute of the Supreme Court (1994). *Member:* Osaka Bar Association; Japan Federation of Bar Associations. *LANGUAGES:* Japanese and English.

NAOKO NAKATSUKASA, born Aichi, Japan, 1965; admitted, 1994, Japan. *Education:* Kyoto University (LL.B., 1991); The Legal Training and Research Institute of the Supreme Court (1994). *Member:* Osaka Bar Association; Japan Federation of Bar Associations. *LANGUAGES:* Japanese and English.

CONSULTANTS

AKIRA OKAMURA, born Kyoto, Japan, 1921; admitted, 1991, Japan. *Education:* Kyoto University (LL.B., 1944); The Legal Training and Research Institute of the Supreme Court (1951). Judge, 1951-1983; Notary Public, 1983-1991. *Member:* Osaka Bar Association; Japan Federation of Bar Associations. *LANGUAGES:* Japanese.

NORIAKI FUKUYA, born Shimane, Japan, 1945; admitted, 1992, Japan. *Education:* Kansai University (LL.B., 1949); The Legal Training and Research Institute of the Supreme Court (1953). Public Prosecutor, 1953-1979. Notary, 1979-1992. *Member:* Osaka Bar Association; Japan Federation of Bar Associations. *LANGUAGES:* Japanese.

KITAHAMA LAW OFFICE

Established in 1973

KEIHAN YODOYABASHI BUILDING, 4TH FLOOR

3-2-25, KITAHAMA, CHUO-KU

OSAKA 541, JAPAN

Telephone: International Code (81) 6-202-1088

Telex: 522-2137 KITLAW J

Facsimile: International Code (81) 6-202-1080

International Transactions, Corporate Law, Litigation, Licenses, Patents and Trademarks

FIRM PROFILE: Established in 1973, the Kitahama Law Office offers a full range of domestic and international legal services. The client base is predominately Japanese, North American and European.

(This Listing Continued)

MEMBERS OF FIRM

NORIHIKO YASHIRO, born Himeji, Hyogo Prefecture, Japan, February 11, 1943; admitted, 1967, Osaka. *Education:* Tokyo University (LL.B., 1965); The Legal Training and Research Institute of the Supreme Court of Japan (1967). *Member:* Osaka Bar Association (Vice-President, 1988-1989); Japanese Federation of Bar Associations. *LANGUAGES:* Japanese.

TERUMICHI SAEKI, born Himeji, Hyogo Prefecture, Japan, December 28, 1942; admitted, 1968, Osaka. *Education:* Kyoto University (LL.B., 1965); The Legal Training and Research Institute of the Supreme Court of Japan (1968). *Member:* Osaka Bar Association (Vice-President, 1991-1992); Japanese Federation of Bar Associations. *LANGUAGES:* Japanese.

KATSUSUKE AMANO, born Himeji, Hyogo Prefecture, Japan, February 27, 1952; admitted, 1978, Osaka. *Education:* Kyoto University (LL.B., 1976); The Legal Training and Research Institute of the Supreme Court of Japan (1978). *Member:* Osaka Bar Association; Japanese Federation of Bar Associations. *LANGUAGES:* Japanese.

KENJI NAKASHIMA, born Nishinomiya, Hyogo Prefecture, Japan, June 8, 1955; admitted, 1984, Osaka. *Education:* Tokyo University (LL.B., 1980); The Legal Training and Research Institute of the Supreme Court of Japan (1984). Resident Japanese Law Consultant, Adams, Duque & Hazeltine, Los Angeles, California, 1991-1993. *Member:* Osaka Bar Association; Japanese Federation of Bar Associations. *LANGUAGES:* Japanese and English. *PRACTICE AREAS:* Bankruptcy; International Law; Litigation.

HIROSHI MORIMOTO, born Osaka City, Japan, July 13, 1960; admitted, 1987, Osaka. *Education:* Waseda University (LL.B., 1985); The Legal Training and Research Institute of the Supreme Court of Japan (1987). *Member:* Osaka Bar Association; Japanese Federation of Bar Associations. *LANGUAGES:* Japanese and English.

ASSOCIATES

NOBUKO ISHIBASHI, born Fukuoka City, Fukuoka Prefecture, Japan, June 12, 1961; admitted, 1989, Osaka. *Education:* Kyushu University (LL.B., 1985); The Legal Training and Research Institute of the Supreme Court of Japan (1989). *Member:* Osaka Bar Association; Japanese Federation of Bar Associations. *LANGUAGES:* Japanese.

HIDEFUMI NAITO, born Asaguchi Township, Okayama Prefecture, Japan, November 19, 1961; admitted, 1990, Osaka. *Education:* Kyoto University (LL.B., 1987); The Legal Training and Research Institute of the Supreme Court of Japan (1990). *Member:* Osaka Bar Association; Japanese Federation of Bar Associations. *LANGUAGES:* Japanese and English.

KENJI YAMAMOTO, born Ashiya City, Hyogo Prefecture, Japan, February 20, 1962; admitted, 1991, Osaka. *Education:* Osaka City University (LL.B., 1989); The Legal Training and Research Institute of the Supreme Court of Japan (1991). *Member:* Osaka Bar Association; Japanese Federation of Bar Associations. *LANGUAGES:* Japanese.

HIROKO TAKIGUCHI, born Osaka, Japan, December 24, 1963; admitted, 1992, Osaka, Japan. *Education:* Osaka University (LL.B., 1986); The Legal Training and Research Institute of the Supreme Court of Japan (1992). *Member:* Osaka Bar Association and Japanese Federation of Bar Associations. *LANGUAGES:* Japanese.

YUKIKO NARITA, born Osaka, Japan, September 30, 1964; admitted, 1993, Osaka. *Education:* Osaka Municipal University (LL.B., 1987); The Legal Training and Research Institute of the Supreme Court of Japan (1993). *Member:* Osaka Bar Association and Japanese Federation of Bar Associations. *LANGUAGES:* Japanese and English. *PRACTICE AREAS:* International General Practice; Litigation.

MASAFUMI KODAMA, born Kyoto, Japan, June 5, 1966; admitted, 1993, Osaka. *Education:* Tokyo University (LL.B., 1990); The Legal Training and Research Institute of the Supreme Court of Japan (1993). *Member:* Osaka Bar Association and Japanese Federation of Bar Associations. *LANGUAGES:* Japanese and English.

TORU WATANABE, born Ehime, Japan, February 2, 1966; admitted, 1993, Osaka. *Education:* Kyoto University (LL.B., 1991); The Legal Training and Research Institute of the Supreme Court of Japan (1993). *Member:* Osaka Bar Association and Japanese Federation of Bar Associations. *LANGUAGES:* Japanese.

TOSHIHIKO OINUMA, born Fukushima City, Fukushima Prefecture, Japan, May 13, 1966; admitted, 1994, Osaka. *Education:* Osaka City University (LL.B., 1992); The Legal Training and Research Institute of the Supreme Court of Japan (1994). *Member:* Osaka Bar Association; Japanese Federation of Bar Associations. *LANGUAGES:* Japanese and English.

(This Listing Continued)

AYUMU IIJIMA, born Kobe City, Hyogo Prefecture, Japan, December 14, 1966; admitted, 1994, Osaka. *Education:* Kyoto University (LL.B., 1992); The Legal Training and Research Institute of the Supreme Court of Japan (1994). *Member:* Osaka Bar Association; Japanese Federation of Bar Associations. *LANGUAGES:* Japanese.

LAW OFFICES OF H. MAEDA

ENOKI BUILDING, 2ND FLOOR
4 CHOME, 10-19 NISHITENMA, KITA-KU
OSAKA 536, JAPAN
Telephone: (06) 361-7956
Fax: (06) 361-7957

Business Transactions, Civil Litigation, Real Property, Patent and License, Criminal Law.

HARUKI MAEDA, born Osaka, Japan, January 2, 1948. *Education:* University of Tokyo (Master, 1971); Law School of University of Washington (Master, 1982). Author: "Legal Practices in the US Law Firms," Bulletin of Osaka Bar Association, 1974. *Member:* Japan Federal Bar Association.

REPRESENTATIVE CLIENTS: Far East Technology Co.; Osada Pacific Service Co.; Tohrin Co., Ltd.; Asaka Car Sales Co., Ltd.

MIDOSUJI LAW OFFICE

TOYOTA BUILDING, SUITE 208
4-3-11 MINAMI SEMBA, CHUOU
OSAKA, JAPAN
Telephone: 06-251-7266
Fax: 06-245-5520
Telex: MDLO J64929

General and International Practice, Corporate Law, Intellectual Property, Banking, Anti-trust, Real Estate, Bankruptcy and Litigation.

MEMBERS OF FIRM

HAJIME NITOH, born Sappolo, Hokkaido, October 5, 1925; admitted, 1954, Osaka. *Education:* Kansai University (LL.B.). *Member:* Japan Federation of Bar Associations. *LANGUAGES:* Japanese.

KATSUHIKO YONEHARA, born Osaka, Japan, January 30, 1928; admitted, 1954, Osaka. *Education:* Kyoto University (LL.B.). Instructor, Meiji University, 1954-1955. Assistant Judge, Tokyo District Court, 1954-1963. *Member:* Japan Federation of Bar Associations. *LANGUAGES:* Japanese and English.

TETSUZO FUYUSHIBA, born China, June 29, 1937; admitted, 1964, Osaka. *Education:* Kansai University (LL.B.). *Member:* Japan Federation of Bar Associations. *LANGUAGES:* Japanese.

TERUO TSUYUMINE, born Osaka, Japan, 1936; admitted, 1964, Osaka. *Education:* Osaka University. *Member:* Japan Federation of Bar Associations. *LANGUAGES:* Japanese and English.

YASUHITO TAMAKI, born Saijo, Ehime, October 4, 1938; admitted, 1964, Osaka. *Education:* Kyoto University (LL.B.). *Member:* Japan Federation of Bar Associations. *LANGUAGES:* Japanese and English.

FUMIO MOTOI, born Osaka, Japan, July 26, 1945; admitted, 1969, Osaka. *Education:* Kyoto University (LL.B.). Instructor, Senshu University, 1970-1972. Assistant Judge, Tokyo District Court, 1969-1975. *Member:* Japan Federation of Bar Associations. *LANGUAGES:* Japanese.

YOSHIHISA MANABE, born Shingu, Ehime, November 14, 1946; admitted, 1972, Osaka. *Education:* Kobe University (LL.B.). *Member:* Japan Federation of Bar Associations. *LANGUAGES:* Japanese and English.

SHOZO SEKI, born Marugame, Japan, January 1, 1948; admitted, 1978, Japan. *Education:* Boston University (LL.M., Master of Banking Law); Kyoto University (LL.B.). Instructor, Kinki University, 1976-1977. *Member:* Japan Federation of Bar Associations; Osaka Bar Association; Japan Association of the Law of Finance. *LANGUAGES:* Japanese and English.

TAKASHI YABUGUCHI, born Osaka, Japan, June 22, 1955; admitted, 1982, Osaka. *Education:* Kansai University (LL.B.). *Member:* Japan Federation of Bar Associations. *LANGUAGES:* Japanese.

KIMIHIKO UEMURA, born Osaka, November 15, 1958; admitted, 1987, Osaka. *Education:* Kyoto University (LL.B.). *Member:* Japan Federation of Bar Associations. *LANGUAGES:* Japanese.

(This Listing Continued)

ASSOCIATES

HIROAKI TSUGAWA, born Osaka, Japan, December 23, 1947; admitted, 1973, Osaka. *Education:* Kanazawa University (LL.B.). *Member:* Japan Federation of Bar Associations. *LANGUAGES:* Japanese.

MUNEKAZU KONTANI, born Osaka, Japan, April 14, 1953; admitted, 1982, Osaka; 1991, New York. *Education:* Tulane Law School (LL.M.); Kyoto University (LL.B.). *Member:* Japan Federation of Bar Associations; New York State Bar Association. *LANGUAGES:* Japanese and English.

MASANORI MASUDA, born Osaka, October 22, 1960; admitted, 1988, Osaka. *Education:* Kyoto University (LL.B.). *Member:* Japan Federation of Bar Associations. *LANGUAGES:* Japanese and English.

HITOSHI KUWAYAMA, born Tokyo, Japan, January 7, 1965; admitted, 1990, Osaka. *Education:* Kyoto University (LL.B.). *Member:* Japan Federation of Bar Associations. *LANGUAGES:* Japanese.

KIYOTAKA KAWASAKI, born Kyoto, November 26, 1965; admitted, 1991, Japan. *Education:* Tokyo University (LL.B., 1989). *Member:* Japan Federation of Bar Associations. *LANGUAGES:* Japanese and English.

SATORU NAKAMURA, born Kyoto, September 3, 1966; admitted, 1993, Japan. *Education:* Osaka University (LL.B., 1990). *Member:* Japan Federation of Bar Associations. *LANGUAGES:* Japanese and English.

HIROSHI AKIYAMA, born Kinosaki, Hyogo, August 6, 1969; admitted, 1994, Japan. *Education:* Kansai University (LL.B.). *Member:* Japan Federation of Bar Associations. *LANGUAGES:* Japanese.

KOICHI TAKAI, born Takatsuki, Osaka, October 1, 1965; admitted, 1994, Japan. *Education:* Kyoto University (LL.B.). *Member:* Japan Federation of Bar Associations. *LANGUAGES:* Japanese.

OF COUNSEL

YATAROU TAMURA, born Yamaguchi, April 6, 1923; admitted, 1950, Osaka. *Education:* Kyoto University (LL.B.). Public Prosecutor, 1950-1983. Superintendent Public Prosecutor, 1983-1986. *Member:* Japan Federation of Bar Associations. *LANGUAGES:* Japanese and English.

OH-EBASHI LAW OFFICE

SUITE 803, UMEDASHINMICHI BUILDING
1-5, DOJIMA 1-CHOME, KITA-KU
OSAKA 530, JAPAN
Telephone: 06-341-0461
Cable Address: "LAW IMT"
Telex: 523-7263 ISILAW J
Telefax: 06-347-0688; 06-347-0688

International Business Transactions, Japanese Domestic Civil and Commercial Law, Antitrust, Administrative Law, Bankruptcy and Litigation, Trade Regulation, Corporate Law, Insurance, Intellectual Property, Labor, Real Estate and Taxation.

TADASHI ISHIKAWA, born Okayama, Japan, August 24, 1943; admitted, 1973, Japan. *Education:* University of Tokyo College of Arts and Sciences (Diploma, 1965); University of Tokyo (LL.B., 1967) Legal Training and Research Institute (Diploma, 1973); Columbia University School of Law (LL.M., 1976); Harvard Law School (1976-1977). Research Fellow, University of Tokyo, Faculty of Law (1967-1970). *Member:* Osaka Bar Association; Japan Federation of Bar Associations; Japanese Association of Administrative Law; Japanese Private Law Association; Japanese Association of the Law of Civil Procedure. *LANGUAGES:* Japanese and English. *PRACTICE AREAS:* Administrative Law; Antitrust Law; Economic Regulations; Civil Law; International Transactions.

HIROAKI TSUKAMOTO, born Aichi, Japan, June 28, 1944; admitted, 1969, Japan. *Education:* Kyoto University (LL.B., 1967); Legal Training and Research Institute (Diploma, 1969). *Member:* Osaka Bar Association; Japan Federation of Bar Associations; Japanese Association of the Law of Civil Procedure. *LANGUAGES:* Japanese and French. *PRACTICE AREAS:* Civil Law; Product Liability; Corporations; Bankruptcy; Chinese Law.

MAKOTO MIYAZAKI, born Bangkok, Thailand, June 5, 1944; admitted, 1969, Japan. *Education:* Kyoto University (LL.B., 1967); Legal Training and Research Institute (Diploma, 1969). *Member:* Osaka Bar Association (Vice-President, 1992-1993); Japan Federation of Bar Associations; Japan Transportation Law Association. *LANGUAGES:* Japanese and English. *PRACTICE AREAS:* Civil Law; Bankruptcy; Taxation; Real Estate; Insurance.

(This Listing Continued)

OH-EBASHI LAW OFFICE, Osaka—Continued

HIROYASU UEDA, born Nara, Japan, June 6, 1956; admitted, 1981, Japan. *Education:* University of Tokyo College of Arts and Sciences (Diploma, 1977); University of Tokyo (LL.B., 1979); Legal Training and Research Institute (Diploma, 1981); University College London (Sept. 1989-June 1990). *Member:* Osaka Bar Association; Japan Federation of Bar Associations; Japanese Association of the Law of Civil Procedure. *LANGUAGES:* Japanese and English. *PRACTICE AREAS:* Civil Law; Labour Law; Bankruptcy; Corporations; International Transactions; Real Estate.

SHIRO KUNIYA, born Hyogo, Japan, February 22, 1957; admitted, 1982, Japan; 1987, New York. *Education:* Kyoto University (LL.B., 1980); Legal Training and Research Institute (Diploma, 1982); Georgetown University Law Center (LL.M., 1986). *Member:* Osaka Bar Association; Japan Federation of Bar Associations; American Bar Association; Japanese Association of the Law of Civil Procedure; Japan Association of International Economic Law. *LANGUAGES:* Japanese and English. *PRACTICE AREAS:* Civil Law; Corporations; International Transactions; Intellectual Property.

HIROHIKO IKEDA, born Osaka, Japan, June 21, 1960; admitted, 1987, Japan; 1992, New York. *Education:* Chuo University (LL.B., 1983); Legal Training and Research Institute (Diploma, 1987); University of Virginia School of Law (LL.M., 1991). *Member:* Osaka Bar Association; Japan Federation of Bar Associations; New York State Bar Association. *LANGUAGES:* Japanese and English. *PRACTICE AREAS:* Business Law; Corporate Law; Litigation.

CHIHIRO TANAKA, born Osaka, Japan, September 3, 1960; admitted, 1987, Japan; 1992, New York. *Education:* University of Tokyo College of Arts and Sciences (Diploma, 1983); Tokyo University (LL.B., 1985); Legal Training and Research Institute (Diploma, 1987); Harvard Law School (LL.M., 1991). *Member:* Osaka Bar Association; Japan Federation of Bar Associations. *LANGUAGES:* Japanese and English. *PRACTICE AREAS:* Business Law; Intellectual Property.

TEPPEI MOGI, born Hyogo, Japan, October 17, 1958; admitted, 1989, Japan. *Education:* University of Tokyo College of Arts and Sciences (Diploma, 1979); University of Tokyo (LL.B., 1983); Legal Training and Research Institute (Diploma, 1989); Katholieke Universiteit Leuven (LL.M., 1991). *Member:* Osaka Bar Association; Japan Federation of Bar Associations. *LANGUAGES:* Japanese and English. *PRACTICE AREAS:* Civil Law; Anti-Trust Law; International Arbitration; International Human Rights Law; EC Law.

MASAKO UENO, born Hyogo, Japan, April 27, 1932; admitted, 1964, Japan. *Education:* Kobe College (B.A., 1955); Kobe University (LL.B., 1964); Legal Training and Research Institute (Diploma, 1967). Former positions: The Japan Commercial Arbitration Association, 1955-1960; Judge, Kobe Summary Court, 1967-1972; Assistant Judge, Kobe District Court, 1972-1974; Coudert Brothers, New York, 1976-1977; IBM, Japan, 1977-1988. *Member:* Osaka Bar Association; Japan Federation of Bar Associations. *LANGUAGES:* Japanese and English.

MIYAKO TSUKAMOTO, born Hyogo, Japan, February 10, 1945; admitted, 1969, Japan. *Education:* Kyoto University (LL.B., 1967); Legal Training and Research Institute (Diploma, 1969). *Member:* Osaka Bar Association; Japan Federation of Bar Associations. *LANGUAGES:* Japanese and English.

SHIGETOSHI HIRANO, born Shiga, Japan, May 9, 1963; admitted, 1989, Japan. *Education:* Kyoto University (LL.B., 1987); Legal Training and Research Institute (Diploma, 1989); University of Pennsylvania (LL.M., 1993). *Member:* Osaka Bar Association; Japan Federation of Bar Associations. *LANGUAGES:* Japanese and English.

MICHIKO KANAI, born Miyazaki, Japan, June 16, 1955; admitted, 1990, Japan. *Education:* Kyoto University (B.A., 1979); Kobe University (LL.B., 1984); Harvard Law School (LL.M., 1986); Visiting Researcher at Harvard Law School (1986-1987); Legal Training and Research Institute (Diploma, 1990). *Member:* Osaka Bar Association; Japan Federation of Bar Associations. *LANGUAGES:* Japanese and English.

MASAMI KIRIYAMA, born Osaka, Japan, November 25, 1965; admitted, 1991, Japan. *Education:* Kyoto University (LL.B., 1989); Legal Training and Research Institute (Diploma, 1991). *Member:* Osaka Bar Association; Japan Federation of Bar Associations. *LANGUAGES:* Japanese and English.

AKIRA TABATA, born Wakayama, Japan, March 21, 1959; admitted, 1992, Japan. *Education:* Keio University (LL.B., 1981); Legal Training and

(This Listing Continued)

Research Institute (Diploma, 1992). *Member:* Osaka Bar Association; Japan Federation of Bar Associations. *LANGUAGES:* Japanese and English.

TORU MATSUMOTO, born Osaka, Japan, April 3, 1962; admitted, 1992, Japan. *Education:* Osaka City University (LL.B., 1987); Legal Training and Research Institute (Diploma, 1992). *Member:* Osaka Bar Association; Japan Federation of Bar Associations. *LANGUAGES:* Japanese and English.

YOUNG HWA YOON, born Hyogo, Japan, December 12, 1961; admitted, 1992, Japan. *Education:* Kyoto University (Phar.B., 1984); Legal Training and Research Institute (Diploma, 1992). *Member:* Osaka Bar Association; Japan Federation of Bar Associations. *LANGUAGES:* Japanese, English and Korean.

YASUHIRO UOZUMI, born Okayama, Japan, November 30, 1966; admitted, 1993, Japan. *Education:* Kyoto University (LL.B., 1991); Legal Training and Research Institute (Diploma, 1993). *Member:* Osaka Bar Association; Japan Federation of Bar Associations. *LANGUAGES:* Japanese and English.

MASAKI NOGAMI, born Mie, Japan, April 2, 1966; admitted, 1994, Japan. *Education:* Kyoto University (LL.B., 1992); Legal Training and Research Institute (Diploma, 1994). *Member:* Osaka Bar Association; Japan Federation of Bar Associations. *LANGUAGES:* Japanese and English.

YOICHI WAKASUGI, born Fukui, Japan, August 2, 1966; admitted, 1994, Japan. *Education:* Kyoto University (LL.B., 1992); Legal Training and Research Institute (Diploma, 1994). *Member:* Osaka Bar Association; Japan Federation of Bar Associations. *LANGUAGES:* Japanese and English.

RESIDENT FOREIGN LEGAL CONSULTANTS

HUA XIN GAO, born Shanghai, The People's Republic of China, March 12, 1954; admitted, 1982, People's Republic of China (Not admitted in Japan). *Education:* Fu Dan University (LL.B., 1979); Hua To Law School; Kansai University (LL.B., 1990). *LANGUAGES:* Chinese and Japanese. *PRACTICE AREAS:* Chinese Laws.

MOTONORI ARAKI, born Osaka, Japan, March 13, 1963; admitted, 1992, New York (Not admitted in Japan). *Education:* Chuo University, Tokyo (LL.B., 1986); Tulane University (LL.M., 1988); Georgetown University Law Center (J.D., 1991). Editor, Georgetown Immigration Law Journal, 1990-1991. Recipient, Tulane-Japan Friendship Award, 1989. Rotary Scholar, 1987-1988. *LANGUAGES:* Japanese and English.

OHARA & KANO

Established in 1980

 # 902 CITY COOP MINAMI-MORIMACHI
2-7, MINAMI-MORIMACHI 2-CHOME
KITA-KU
OSAKA 530, JAPAN
Telephone: (06) 313-1208
Telecopier: (06) 313-1209

FIRM PROFILE: Established in 1980, the Ohara & Kano Law firm offers a full range of domestic and international legal services. Areas of practice are general practice with particular emphasis upon international corporate and commercial transactions, litigation, foreign investments, intellectual property, bankruptcy, unfair competition, real estate, international arbitration, trust and wills and related works.

MEMBERS OF FIRM

NOZOMU OHARA, born 1942; admitted, 1969, Japan. *Education:* Kyoto University (LL.B., 1966; LL.M., 1973); The Legal Training and Research Institute of the Supreme Court of Japan (1969); Harvard Law School (LL.M., 1976). With Whitman & Ransom, New York, 1978-1979 and Fenwick, Stone, Davis & West, Palo Alto, California, Summer, 1979. *Member:* Osaka Bar Association; Japanese Federation of Bar Associations; Inter-Pacific Bar Association; LAW ASIA; Japan Commercial Arbitration Association; Japan Association of Industrial Property Law; Law & Computer Association of Japan; Osaka Chamber of Commerce & Industry; Fulbright Alumni Committee; Japan-American Society of Osaka. *LANGUAGES:* Japanese and English. *PRACTICE AREAS:* International Transactions; Intellectual Property; Unfair Competition; Litigation; International Arbitration.

CHIKARA KANO, born 1947; admitted, 1977, Japan. *Education:* Kyoto University (LL.B., 1970); The Legal Training and Research Institute of the Supreme Court of Japan (1977). *Member:* Osaka Bar Association; Japanese

(This Listing Continued)

Federation of Bar Associations. *LANGUAGES:* Japanese and English. *PRACTICE AREAS:* Litigation; Bankruptcy; Commercial Transactions.

HIROYUKI HIGASHITANI, born 1961; admitted, 1989, Japan. *Education:* Doshisha University (LL.B., 1985); The Legal Training and Research Institute of the Supreme Court of Japan (1989). *Member:* Osaka Bar Association; Japanese Federation of Bar Associations. *LANGUAGES:* Japanese and English. *PRACTICE AREAS:* Litigation; Unfair Competition; Intellectual Property; Commercial Transactions.

OHTA LAW OFFICE

TAKAHASHI BUILDING, 4TH FLOOR
9-3, NISHI-TENMA 5-CHOME, KITA-KU
OSAKA 530, JAPAN
Telephone: (06) 364-2418
Telecopier: (06) 364-6885

General Practice, Business Law, Corporate Law, Banking, Finance, Real Estate, Bankruptcy and Litigation.

TADAYOSHI OHTA, born Tottori, Japan, 1932; admitted, 1961, Japan. *Education:* Kyoto University (LL.B., 1955); The Legal Training and Research Institute of the Supreme Court of Japan (1961). *Member:* Osaka Bar Association; Japan Federation of Bar Association; Japan Association of the Law of Finance. *LANGUAGES:* Japanese.

ASSOCIATES

TATSUHIKO SHIBATA, born Osaka, Japan, 1958; admitted, 1986, Japan. *Education:* Kyoto University (LL.B., 1984); The Legal Training and Research Institute of the Supreme Court of Japan (1986); University of Pennsylvania Law School (LL.M., 1991). *Member:* Osaka Bar Association; Japan Federation of Bar Association; Japan Association of the Law of Finance. *LANGUAGES:* Japanese and English.

HIRONARI KISHIMOTO, born Osaka, Japan, 1960; admitted, 1990, Japan. *Education:* Kyoto University (LL.B., 1987); The Legal Training and Research Institute of the Supreme Court of Japan (1990). *Member:* Osaka Bar Association; Japan Federation of Bar Association. *LANGUAGES:* Japanese and English.

H. OKADA INTERNATIONAL LAW OFFICES

YODOGAWA ROKUBANKAN, 7TH FLOOR
1-22 TOYOSAKI, 3-CHOME, KITA-KU
OSAKA 531, JAPAN
Telephone: 06-374-6357
Telefax: 06-374-2456

Commercial, Corporate, and International Practice, Intellectual Property Law , Tax.

MEMBER OF FIRM

HARUO OKADA, born Toyama, Japan, March 2, 1954; admitted, 1982, Japan. *Education:* Tokyo University (Bachelor of Law (1978); Harvard Law School (Visiting Researcher) ; Michigan Law School (LL.M., 1986). *Member:* Osaka Bar Association.

Languages: Japanese and English.

SHIOMI & YAMAMOTO

KOAN-NISSEI BUILDING, 8TH FLOOR
2-20, IMABASHI 3-CHOME
CHUO-KU
OSAKA 541, JAPAN
Telephone: (06) 229-2441
Telex: TYAMALAW J63072
Fax: (06) 229-2442

General Practice, International Business Transactions and International Contracts Law, Admiralty, Anti-Monopoly and Corporate Reorganization Law. Intellectual Property Litigation.

TADAO YAMAMOTO, born 1941; admitted, 1968, Osaka. *Education:* Ritsumeikan University (1959-1963); Legal Training and Research Institute of the Supreme Court of Japan (1966-1968); University of Louisville School of Law (1970). The Ministry of Justice, Attorney General's Office, 1963-

(This Listing Continued)

1966. Visiting Scholar, East Asia Legal Studies, Harvard Law School, Summer, 1973, 1976 and 1979. Visiting Scholar, University of Santa Clara, 1982, University of Washington, 1983. Instructor, Patent Licensing Agreements for the Japan Patent Association, 1975—. *LANGUAGES:* Japanese and English.

FOSTER THORBJORNSEN, born Brooklyn, New York, June 24, 1960; admitted, 1985, Hawaii and U.S. District Court, District of Hawaii; 1986, U.S. Court of Appeals, Ninth Circuit (Not admitted in Japan). *Education:* University of Hawaii at Manoa (B.A., 1982); Tulane University (J.D., cum laude, 1985). Phi Alpha Delta. *Member:* Hawaii State and American Bar Associations.

Honorary Legal Advisor to British and Swiss Consulates

REPRESENTATIVE CLIENTS: ABN AMRO Bank N.V.; Daiei, Inc.; Daikin Clutch Mfg, Inc.; Deutsche Bank AG; Flouveil Cosmetics, Ltd.; Herman Miller, Inc.; Hosiden Electronics Inc.; Inaba Electric Co., Ltd.; Japan Swagelock K.K.; Mitsubishi Cable Industries, Ltd.; Morinaga Milk Co.; Morisawa & Co. Ltd.; Okamoto K.K.; Nippon Shoji Kaisha, Ltd.; Sumitomo Rubber Co., Ltd.; Tioxide Japan Co., Ltd.; Volcafe Ltd.; World Co., Ltd.; Yamazen K.K.; Yomiuri TV Co.

YAMAGAMI & YAMAGAMI

Established in 1947

5TH FLOOR, SEYAMA BUILDING
1-1 NISHI-TENMA, 5-CHOME, KITA-KU
OSAKA 530, JAPAN
Telephone: (81) 6-365-1800
Telex: J 63716
Facsimile: (81) 6-365-1801

General Practice. Corporation, Patent, Trademark and Licensing Law.

MAGOJIRO YAMAGAMI (1902-1976).

KAZUNORI YAMAGAMI, born Osaka, Japan, July 11, 1939; admitted, 1968, Japan. *Education:* Osaka University (Engineering in Metallurgy); Chuo University (LL.B., 1965); The Legal Training and Research Institute of the Supreme Court (1966-1968); University of Wisconsin Law School (Master of Legal Institutions, 1972). *Member:* Japan Federation of Bar Associations; Japan Patent Attorneys Association; Licensing Executives Society of Japan. *LANGUAGES:* Japanese and English. *PRACTICE AREAS:* International Transactions; Intellectual Property Right Litigation.

KATSUMI MATSUMOTO, born Tokushima, Japan, March 29, 1929; admitted, as a Judge by the Supreme Court of Japan, 1967 and became a Judge in the Osaka, Nara, Kobe and Yamaguchi District Courts (1967-1994) then on retirement as a Judge admitted to the Japanese Bar in 1994. *Education:* Kyoto University (LL.B., 1952); The Legal Training and Research Institute of the Supreme Court (1965-1967). *Member:* Japan Federation of Bar Associations. *LANGUAGES:* Japanese and English. *PRACTICE AREAS:* International Transactions; Intellectual Property Rights Litigation; General Practice.

YAMAGUCHI INTERNATIONAL LAW OFFICES

7TH FLOOR, HONMACHI-NISHII BUILDING
1-6-10, UTSUBO HONMACHI, NISHI-KU
OSAKA 550, JAPAN
Telephone: (Japan Country Code 81) 6-446-1123
Facsimile: (Japan Country Code 81) 6-446-1121

International and Domestic Commercial Transactions, Litigation, Corporate Matters, Licensing, Intellectual Property.

KOSHI YAMAGUCHI, born Kumano City, Mie Prefecture, Japan, September 27, 1949; admitted, 1977, Osaka. *Education:* Kyoto University (LL.B., 1975); The Legal Training and Research Institute of the Supreme Court of Japan (1977); Harvard Law School (LL.M., 1980). *Member:* Osaka Bar Association; Japanese Federation of Bar Associations; Danish Chamber of Commerce Western Japan (Director, 1990—). *LANGUAGES:* Japanese and English.

RESIDENT FOREIGN LEGAL CONSULTANT

THOMAS A. FLIPPEN, II, born San Jose, California, U.S.A., December 24, 1941; admitted, 1973, California; 1978, U.S. Supreme Court; 1982, Alaska (Not admitted in Japan). *Education:* University of California at Berkeley (B.A., 1969); Hastings College of The Law, University of California (J.D., 1972); University of Washington School of Law (LL.M., Japanese

(This Listing Continued)

YAMAGUCHI INTERNATIONAL LAW OFFICES,
Osaka—Continued

Law, 1988). Deputy District Attorney, Alameda County (Oakland), California, 1973-1977; Yanello & Flippen Law Offices, Oakland, California, 1977-1981; Boyko, Davis & Dennis, Anchorage, Alaska, 1982-1987; USMC, 1960-1964. *Member:* State Bar of California; Alaska Bar Association; American Chamber of Commerce Japan; Kansai George Washington Society (President, 1991-1993); Japan-American Society of Osaka (Director, 1993—). Resident Foreign Legal Consultant, Japan, 1989—. *LANGUAGES:* English, Japanese and Spanish.

SHUSAKU YAMAMOTO
PATENT LAW OFFICES

Established in 1979

FIFTEENTH FLOOR, CRYSTAL TOWER
1-2-27, SHIROMI, CHUO-KU
OSAKA 540, JAPAN
Telephone: 06-949-3910
Facsimile: 06-949-3915; 06-910-3056
Telex: 5233968 SHUPAT J

Industrial Property Law comprising Patents, Trademarks, Designs, Utility Models, Unfair Competition and related licensing.

FIRM PROFILE: *The firm has an international practice in the prosecution and enforcement of the full range of industrial property rights. The firm has particularly strong patent departments in biotechnology and electronics. Equipped with a fully English speaking staff, almost half of the firm's clients are foreign corporations.*

SHUSAKU YAMAMOTO, born Nara, Japan, 1943; admitted, 1973, Japan as Patent Attorney; registered to practise before the Japanese Patent Office and appear as Patent Counsel before the Courts. *Education:* Osaka University (B.Sc., 1966); Catholic University of America Law School (1978-1979); United States Patent Academy Training Course (1979). Author: "Reissue under the US Patent Law (1), (2) and (3)," Journal of Patent Management, Vol. 29, No. 9 & 11, 1979 and Vol. 30 No. 1, 1980; "Current Movement of the US Patent System," Journal of Patents, Vol. 34, No. 1, 1981; "Functional Descriptions in Claims and the Disclosure of Patent Specification," Journal of Patent Management, Vol. 34, No. 1, 1984. "Functional Descriptions of Claims and the Disclosure of Patent Specifications," Journal of Patent Management, Vol. 34, No. 1, 1984; "Japan: International Harmonization of the Patent and Utility Model Laws", IP Asia, November 18, 1992, "Amendments to Patent and Utility Model Law, a summary and comment", IP Asia, November 25, 1993; "Imitation of Product Configuration Prohibited under Unfair Competition Law", IP Asia, April 27, 1994; Impact on Japan of the United States-Japan Patent Law Harmonization Agreement", European Intellectual Property Review, Vol. 16, No. 5, May 5, 1994. *Member:* The Patent Attorneys Association of Japan; Osaka Chamber of Commerce. *LANGUAGES:* Japanese and English. *PRACTICE AREAS:* Biotechnology; Industrial Property Litigation.

ASSOCIATES

SEIJI OKUDA, born Kyoto, Japan, July 4, 1960; admitted, 1991, Japan as Patent Attorney; registered to practise before the Japanese Patent Office and appear as Patent Counsel before the Courts. *Education:* Kyoto University (B.E.Phys., 1984; M.E.Phys., 1986). *Member:* The Patent Attorneys Association of Japan. *LANGUAGES:* Japanese and English. *PRACTICE AREAS:* Electronics; Semi-Conductor Technology.

HIROMICHI NANJO, born Nagasaki, Japan, 1948; admitted, 1993, Japan as Patent Attorney; registered to practise before the Japanese Patent Office and appear as Patent Counsel before the courts. *Education:* Osaka University (B.T. Biochem., 1972; M.T. Biochem., 1974). *Member:* The Patent Attorneys Association of Japan. *LANGUAGES:* Japanese and English. *PRACTICE AREAS:* Biotechnology.

JOHN A. TESSENSOHN, born Singapore, October 28, 1967; admitted, 1993, Singapore as Advocate and Solicitor (not admitted in Japan). *Education:* National University of Singapore (LL.B., 1992). *Member:* The Law Society of Singapore; The Singapore Academy of Law. *LANGUAGES:* English and Chinese. *PRACTICE AREAS:* Industrial Property; Litigation; Trade Mark Prosecution and Enforcement; Intellectual Property Protection and Infringement.

(This Listing Continued)

CHUN LONG, born Zhejiang, China, October 4, 1957; admitted, 1987, China as Patent Attorney; registered to practise before China Patent Office and appear as Patent Counsel before the Courts (Not admitted in Japan). *Education:* Zhejiang Medical University, China (B.Sc., 1982); Kyoritsu Pharmaceutical College, Japan (Masters Degree in Pharmacy, 1993). *Member:* Pharmaceutical Association of China; Pharmaceutical Association of Japan. *LANGUAGES:* Chinese, Japanese and English. *PRACTICE AREAS:* Organic Chemistry; Pharmacy.

FOREIGN LEGAL ADVISOR

MARK D. SARALINO, born Akron, Ohio, March 5, 1961; admitted, 1989, Virginia; 1990, U.S. District Court, Northern District of Ohio; 1992, U.S. Court of Appeals for the Federal Circuit; registered to practise before the U.S. Patent and Trademark Office (Not admitted in Japan). *Education:* University of Akron (B.S.E.E., 1985; J.D., magna cum laude, 1989). *Member:* Virginia State and American Bar Associations; Cleveland Intellectual Property Law Association. (Also Associate, Renner, Otto, Boisselle and Sklar, Cleveland, Ohio).

TECHNICAL ASSISTANTS

REIKO KOMAKI (Master's degree in Pharmacy).

NOBUHIKO SUKENAGA (Master's degree in Synthetic Chemistry).

MINORU KATO (Master's degree in Agricultural Chemistry).

YOKO HAMAGUCHI (Doctorate in Pharmacy).

HAJIME NORISUE (Doctorate in Biochemistry).

MAKOTO ABE (Master's degree in Agronomy).

TETSUJI KAWAGUCHI (Master's degree in Organic Chemistry).

TAKAFUMI MOMII (Master's Degree in Polymer Science).

HIROAKI ZAIMA (Doctorate in Chemistry).

YOSHIHIRO NAKAMICHI (Master's Degree in Physical Chemistry).

TOYOKO KOZAI (Master's Degree in Chemistry).

HIROSHI URAMOTO (Doctorate in Chemical Engineering).

KAORI SAKURAI (Master's degree in Chemistry).

YOSHIMICHI KAJITANI (Master's degree in Chemistry).

MASAKO ANDO (Master's degree in Nuclear Physics).

SATOSHI TANAKA (Master's degree in Electrical Engineering).

SHUICHI KITA (Master's degree in Chemistry).

MAKOTO HASEGAWA (Doctorate in Electrical Engineering).

HARUO YAWATA (Master's degree in Electrical Engineering).

PARA LEGAL ASSISTANTS

Yoshiko Nakayama	Akiko Tsujio
Sakiko Hara	Mika Sakai
Makiyo Takagaki	Kuzuko Nishimoto
Kiyoko Kano	

REPRESENTATIVE CLIENTS: Bausch & Lomb Inc.; Biogen, Inc.; Chiron Corporation; ICI Americas, Inc.; Daikin Industries, Ltd.; La Jolla Cancer Research Foundation; PPG Industries, Inc.; Matsushita Electric Industrial Co., Ltd.; Mita Industrial Co., Ltd.; Scios Nova Inc.; Sekisui Chemical Co., Ltd.; Sharp Corporation; Shin-etsu Chemical Industrial Co., Ltd.; Shionogi & Co., Ltd.; The Lubrizol Corporation; Toyobo Co., Ltd.; Zeneca Ag Products

---

ABE SOGO LAW OFFICE

Established in 1989

SUITE 511, SHUWA KIOICHO TBR BLDG.
7, KOJIMACHI 5-CHOME, CHIYODA-KU
TOKYO 102, JAPAN
Telephone: 03-3288-9811
Fax: 03-3288-9812

International Business Transactions, Labor Law, Intellectual Property, Corporate Law, Antitrust, Real Estate Development and Financing and Civil and Commercial Litigation.

FIRM PROFILE: *The firm specializes in international practice, drawing on broad international expertise of the firm's members. The firm is a founding member of the International Lawyer's Network, an association of highly qualified legal practitioners with member offices throughout Asia, the Americas, Europe and Africa.*

(This Listing Continued)

PARTNERS

YOSHIKI ABE, born Akita Prefecture, Japan, 1943; admitted, 1975, Tokyo. *Education:* Tohoku University (LL.B., 1966); Tokyo University (LL.M., 1973); Legal Training and Research Institute (1973-1975); University of Washington (LL.M., 1978). Recipient: Kajima Scholarship, 1972; Fulbright Scholarship, 1977. Author: "The Utilization of Third Parties in the Development of Patentable Inventions," Master's Thesis, Tokyo University, 1973; "A Comparison of Dismissal Law in Japan and America," Master's Thesis, University of Washington, 1978; "Friction in Japan-America Trade Negotiations and Countermeasures Against It," Nihon Kokusai Mondai Kenkyusho, 1983; "Developing Key Foreign Personnel in Foreign-Backed Companies in Japan," Nihon Rodo Kyokai, 1989; "Create Yourself in Your Own Self-Image," K.K. Longseller, 1982; "Wisdom for a Good Life," Sangyo Noritsu University Press, 1986; "America: Where Good Faith Isn't Spoken," Nikkei Journal Press, 1988; "Art of Negotiation," Sangyo Noritsu University Press, 1990; "Learning the Art of Living," Mikasa Shobou, 1991; "Director's Handbook," Nikkei BP, 1994. Co-editor: "Business and Legal English-Japanese Dictionary," Nikkei Journal Press, 1991. Lecturer: International University of Japan, 1988-1991; Multinational Business Institute, McKinsey and Company Inc., Japan, 1986—. With: Patent Administration Department, Toyota Motor Co., Ltd., 1966-1971; Tokyo Aoyama Law Office, 1975-1981; Baker & McKenzie, London, 1978-1981. Founded: Nakamura & Abe Law Office, 1981; Abe Sogo Law Office, 1989. Of Counsel, Epstein Becker and Green, 1984. Director, Reuters Japan Company Limited. Statutory Auditor: Roland Berger Vaubel Company Limited; Dornier Medical Systems Company Limited. *Member:* Tokyo Bar Association; Patent Attorney's Association; Lawyer's Council for Management; American Bar Association (International Member); Inter-Pacific Bar Association; Asian Patent Attorney's Association; International Association for the Protection of Industrial Property; Japan America Society; Japan United Kingdom Society. *LANGUAGES:* Japanese and English. *PRACTICE AREAS:* Corporate; International Transactions; Intellectual Property; Labor; International Litigation.

KATSUAKI MATSUTOME, born Tokyo, 1955; admitted, 1985, Japan. *Education:* Sophia University (LL.B., 1979); Legal Training and Research Institute (1983-1985). With: Noriaki Matsuka Law Office, 1985-1991; Graham and James, Los Angeles, 1991-1992. *Member:* First Tokyo Bar Association. *LANGUAGES:* Japanese and English. *PRACTICE AREAS:* Corporate; Intellectual Property; International Transactions; Labor; International Litigation.

ASSOCIATES

NOBUHIRO WADA, born Kanagawa, Prefecture, 1958; admitted, 1988, Japan; 1994, New York. *Education:* Waseda University (LL.B., 1983); Legal Training and Research Institute (1986-1988); Southern Methodist University (LL.M., 1992). With: Gardere and Wynne, Dallas, 1991-1993; Epstein Becker & Green, New York, 1993-1994. *Member:* Tokyo Bar Association; New York Bar Association. *LANGUAGES:* Japanese and English. *PRACTICE AREAS:* Corporate; International Transactions; Intellectual Property; Labor; International Litigation.

HIROMI WATANABE, born Tokyo, 1961; admitted, 1990, Japan. *Education:* Chuo University (LL.B., 1985); Legal Training and Research Institute (1988-1990). *Member:* Tokyo Bar Association. *LANGUAGES:* Japanese and English. *PRACTICE AREAS:* Corporate; Intellectual Property; International Transactions; Labor; Anti-Monopoly Law.

SACHIKO SAITO, born Tokyo, 1961; admitted, 1992, Japan. *Education:* Waseda University (LL.B., 1984); Legal Training and Research Institute (1990-1992). *Member:* Tokyo Bar Association. *LANGUAGES:* Japanese and English. *PRACTICE AREAS:* Bankruptcy; Civil Litigation; Corporate; Intellectual Property.

OF COUNSEL

MASAYUKI OGATA, born Chiba Prefecture, 1950; admitted, 1984, Japan. *Education:* Hitotsubashi University (B.C.S., 1972); University College of London (Diploma in Law, 1986). Author: "Legal Aspects of Real Estate Investment and Joint Ventures in the U.K."; "Tax on Real Property Transactions in France"; "Real Estate Transactions and the VAT in the U.K."; "Regulation on the Development of Land in the U.K."; "Convertible Mortgages in the U.K."; "Group Financial Statement under U.K. Company Act," Kokusai Shoji Homu, 1991. With: Sumitomo Chemical Industry Co., Ltd, 1973-1976; Mochida Law Office, 1984-1985; Ohashi, Matsueda and Hasegawa Law Office, 1985-1988; Sinclair, Roche and Temperley, London, 1986-1987; White and Case, New York, 1987-1988; Tunematsu Yanase and Sekine Law Office, 1988-1991; MEC U.K. Limited, London, 1989-1991.

(This Listing Continued)

Member: The First Tokyo Bar Association. *LANGUAGES:* Japanese and English. *PRACTICE AREAS:* Finance; Tax; Real Estate; Investment.

SHARON DAY, born Buffalo, New York, 1963; admitted, 1993, New York (Not admitted in Japan). *Education:* Hawaii Loa College (B.A., 1985); Fordham University School of Law (J.D., 1992). *Member:* State Bar of New York. *LANGUAGES:* English and Japanese. *PRACTICE AREAS:* International Transactions.

ADACHI, HENDERSON, MIYATAKE & FUJITA

HALIFAX ONARIMON BUILDING, 3RD FLOOR
24-10, NISHI-SHINBASHI 3-CHOME, MINATO-KU
TOKYO 105, JAPAN
Telephone: (03) 5473-3970
Telefax: (03) 5473-3981
Telex: J28314
Cable Address: "Jamad Tokyo"

General Practice. International, Corporation, Commercial, Product Liability and Tax Law.

MEMBERS OF FIRM

JAMES S. ADACHI, born Wildwood, New Jersey, April 8, 1920; admitted, 1942, Wyoming; 1949, Japan. *Education:* University of Wyoming (B.A., cum laude, 1942); University of Wyoming Law School (J.D., 1942). President, American Chamber of Commerce in Japan, 1971. *Member:* Wyoming State Bar; The Dai-Ichi Tokyo Bar Association. *LANGUAGES:* Japanese and English.

DAN FENNO HENDERSON, born Chelan, Washington, May 24, 1921; admitted, 1949, Washington; 1954, Japan; 1955, Korea; 1956, California. *Education:* Whitman College (A.B., 1944); University of Michigan (B.A., 1945); Harvard Law School (J.D., 1949); University of California (Ph.D., in Political Science, 1955). Awarded LL.D., by Whitman College, 1983. Professor and Director, Asian Law Program, University of Washington, 1962-1983. Visiting Professor, Monash University, Australia, 1979. Law Faculty, University of Cambridge, England, 1980. Author: "Conciliation and Japanese Law," 2 Volumes, 1965; "The Constitution of Japan: First Twenty Years," 1969; "Foreign Enterprise in Japan," 1973; "Civil Procedure in Japan," 1983. *Member:* State Bar of California; Washington State Bar Association; The Dai-Ichi Tokyo Bar Association. *LANGUAGES:* Japanese and English.

TOSHIO MIYATAKE, born Japan, November 13, 1937; admitted, 1963, Japan. *Education:* Law Faculty, Kyoto University (LL.B., 1961); University of Washington School of Law (M.C.L., 1968). Visiting Assistant Professor, University of Washington Law School, 1970. Visiting Professor, Harvard Law School, 1983. Lecturer, Sophia University, 1989—. Chairman: Taxation and Legislation Committee, American Chamber of Commerce in Japan, 1984; Tax System Committee, The Federation of Japanese Bars, 1989-1990; Tax Law Committee, Inter-Pacific Bar Association, 1991-1993. *Member:* The Daini-Tokyo Bar Association; International Bar Association; International Fiscal Association; World Jurists Association; Inter-Pacific Bar Association; Japan Tax Association; The Japanese Society for Tax Law; The Air Law Institute of Japan. *LANGUAGES:* Japanese and English. *PRACTICE AREAS:* Tax Law; Contract Law; Corporate Law; Financial Transactions; Aircraft Accidents Law.

YASUHIRO FUJITA, born Fukushima, Japan, March 23, 1935; admitted, 1965, Japan; 1985, California. *Education:* Law Faculty, The University of Tokyo, Japan (LL.B., 1959); University of Washington School of Law (M.C.L., 1968). Order of the Coif. Engaged in General Practice of Law, Tokyo, 1965 and 1972—. Associate Professor, 1968-1972 and Visiting Professor, 1979, University of Washington School of Law. Lecturer in Law, University of Southern California, 1984—. Arbitrator, American Arbitration Association. *Member:* The Dai-Ichi Tokyo Bar Association; State Bar of California; Seattle-King County Bar Association, Washington (Associate Member). (Also Of Counsel, Irell and Manella, Los Angeles, California). *LANGUAGES:* Japanese and English.

YASUSHI MUROFUSHI, born Shizuoka, Japan, December 23, 1955; admitted, 1985, Japan. *Education:* Law Faculty, The University of Tokyo (LL.B., 1980 and 1981); The Legal Training and Research Institute of the Supreme Court (1985); Cornell Law School (LL.M., 1988). With Sullivan & Cromwell, New York, 1988-1989. *Member:* The Daini-Tokyo Bar Association; Inter-Pacific Bar Association. *LANGUAGES:* Japanese and English. *PRACTICE AREAS:* Finance Law; Corporate Law.

(This Listing Continued)

ADACHI, HENDERSON, MIYATAKE & FUJITA,
Tokyo—Continued

ASSOCIATES

SHUNJI SONOYAMA, born Shimane, Japan, June 30, 1949; admitted, 1989, Japan. *Education:* Law Faculty, Shimane University (LL.B., 1974); The Legal Training and Research Institute of the Supreme Court of Japan (1989). *Member:* The Daini-Tokyo Bar Association; International Association for the Protection of Industrial Property of Japan. *LANGUAGES:* Japanese and English. *PRACTICE AREAS:* Corporate Law; Intellectual Property Rights Law; Litigation.

SIMON TAKAGI, born Osaka, Japan, December 23, 1962; admitted, 1990, Japan. *Education:* Law Faculty, Osaka City University (LL.B., 1988); The Legal Training and Research Institute of the Supreme Court of Japan. *Member:* Tokyo Bar Association; International Fiscal Association. *LANGUAGES:* Japanese and English. *PRACTICE AREAS:* Tax.

MASAEI OKUDERA, born Iwate, Japan, December 30, 1949; admitted, 1992, Japan. *Education:* Law Faculty, Tohoku University (LL.B., 1972); The Institute for International Studies and Training of Japan (1974); The Legal Training and Research Institute of the Supreme Court of Japan (1992). *Member:* The Daini-Tokyo Bar Association. *LANGUAGES:* Japanese and English.

KIMIAKI MARUO, born Yamaguchi, Japan, September 9, 1958; admitted, 1994, Japan. *Education:* Law Faculty, Waseda University (LL.B., 1981); The Legal Training and Research Institute of the Supreme Court of Japan (1994). *Member:* The Daiichi-Tokyo Bar Association. *LANGUAGES:* Japanese and English.

RESIDENT FOREIGN LEGAL CONSULTANT

SANDER A. COHEN, born Boston, Massachusetts, February 4, 1966; admitted, 1994, New York (Not admitted in Japan). *Education:* University of Toronto (B.A., 1987); University of Toronto School of Graduate Studies (1987-1988); Georgetown University Law Center (J.D., 1991); Université de Montréal Law School (LL.B., 1993). *Member:* American Chamber of Commerce in Japan. *LANGUAGES:* Japanese, French and Italian.

AKASAKA INTERNATIONAL LAW, PATENT & ACCOUNTING OFFICE

IF, NISSANKEN KAIKAN BUILDING
3-14, TORANOMON 5-CHOME, MINATO-KU
TOKYO 105, JAPAN
Telephone: (03) 5472-4488
Fax: (03) 5472-4491/2
Telex: 2424519 SMDLAW J
Cable Address: SMDLAWPAT

International Commercial Transactions, Corporate Law, Patent Law, Industrial and Intellectual Property Rights, Contract Law, Real Estate, Immigration Law, Admiralty and Maritime Law, Bankruptcy Law, Insurance Law, Domestic and International Litigation and Arbitration.

MEMBERS OF FIRM

MASAHIKO SUMIDA, born Kobe, Japan, 1943; admitted, 1981, Japan; 1984, as Patent Attorney. *Education:* Waseda University (LL.B., 1967); Legal Training and Research Institute of the Supreme Court (1979-1981). Japanese diplomat in France and Madagascar, 1967-1972. *Member:* Committee on Anticounterfeiting, International Association for the Protection of Industrial Property; International Exchange Committee, Japan Federation of Bar Associations; International Relations Committee, Tokyo Bar Association. *LANGUAGES:* Japanese, French and English. *PRACTICE AREAS:* Intellectual Property; General Commercial Law; Corporate Law; Litigation and Arbitration.

KAZUO SATORI, born Atami, Japan, 1947; admitted, 1981, Japan; 1984, Marine Proctor. *Education:* Tokyo University (LL.B., 1969); Legal Training and Research Institute of the Supreme Court (1979-1981); University of London, England (Diploma in Shipping Law, 1985-1986). *Member:* Japan Maritime Association; Japan Shipping Exchange; Association of Average Adjusters of Japan; LAWASIA. *LANGUAGES:* Japanese and English. *PRACTICE AREAS:* Maritime Law; Insurance Law; Financial Law; Hotel Development and Bankruptcy.

(This Listing Continued)

MASAHIKO TSUNODA, born Nagoya, Japan, 1953; admitted, 1987, Japan. *Education:* Waseda University (LL.B., 1975); Legal Training and Research Institute of the Supreme Court (1979-1981). District Office Prosecuting Attorney, 1981-1987. *Member:* Tokyo Bar Association. *LANGUAGES:* Japanese. *PRACTICE AREAS:* Criminal Law; Debt Recovery.

YOSHIHIRO MAKISE, born Osaka, Japan, 1930; admitted, 1962, Japan. *Education:* Tokyo University (LL.B., 1955); Legal Training and Research Institute of the Supreme Court (1960-1962); Doctorat d'Université de Paris (1967-1975). Author: "The Legal Theory of Money." *Member:* British Academy of Experts. *LANGUAGES:* Japanese, French and English. *PRACTICE AREAS:* International Litigation and Arbitration.

RESIDENT FOREIGN LEGAL CONSULTANTS

STEPHEN J.E. HOCKLEY, born Sydney, Australia, 1952; admitted, 1981, New South Wales as a Solicitor (Not admitted in Japan). *Education:* University of Sydney (B.A., Political Science, 1973); University of New South Wales (LL.B., 1979). *LANGUAGES:* English. *PRACTICE AREAS:* Commercial; Company; Tax Law; Civil Litigation; Criminal Litigation; Intellectual Property Law.

OLIVER DAVID, born Geneva, Switzerland, 1964; admitted, 1990, Geneva (Not admitted in Japan). *Education:* Faculty of Law, University of Geneva, Switzerland. *LANGUAGES:* French, English and Japanese. *PRACTICE AREAS:* Civil Litigation; General Commercial Law; Intellectual Property.

The accounting and financial management component of AKASAKA INTERNATIONAL LAW, PATENT & ACCOUNTING OFFICE consists of five Certified Public Accountants.

ALLEN & OVERY

(A.M. Pease Gaikokuho Jimubengoshi Jimusho)

NSE BUILDING, 5TH FLOOR
1-7-1 KANDA JINBO-CHO, CHIYODA-KU
TOKYO 101, JAPAN
Telephone: (81 3) 3259 9898
Facsimile: (81 3) 3259 9888

London, England Office: One New Change, EC4M 9QQ. Telephone: 0171 330 3000. Facsimile: 0171 330 9999.

Beijing, China Office: Suite 3204, Jing Guang Centre, Hu Jia Lou, Chaoyang District, 100020. Telephone: (86 1) 501 4681. Facsimile: (86 1) 501 4682.

Brussels, Belgium Office: Rue de la Loi 99, Box 8, 1040. Telephone: (32 2) 230 27 91. Facsimile (32 2) 230 66 13.

Budapest, Hungary Office: Mádach Trade Center, Mádach Imre utca 13-14, H-1075. Telephone: (361) 268 1511. Facsimile: (361) 268 1515.

Dubai, United Arab Emirates Office: 501 Al Futtaim Tower, P.O. Box 3251, Deira. Telephone: (971 4)282296. Facsimile: (971 4) 212860.

Frankfurt, Germany Office: Taunusanlage 11, 11th Floor, 60329. Telephone: (49 69) 242 6120. Facsimile: (49 69) 242 61220.

Hong Kong Office: 9th Floor, Three Exchange Square, 8 Connaught Place. Telephone: (852) 2840 1282. Telex: 68757. Facsimile: (852) 2840 0515.

Madrid, Spain Office: Antonio Maura 7, 6°, 28014. Telephone: (34 1) 521 2654. Facsimile: (34 1) 523 0458.

Moscow, Russia Office: 9 ul Tverskaya, Entrance No 5, 8th Floor, 103009. Telephone: (7 501) 940 4500. Facsimile: (7 501) 940 4501.

New York Office: Swiss Bank Tower, 10 East 50th Street, 10022. Telephone (1-212) 754 3340. Facsimile: (1-212) 754 7903.

Paris, France Office: 1 Avenue Franklin D. Roosevelt, 75008. Telephone (33-1) 49 53 06 37. Telex: 651079. Facsimile: (33-1) 49 53 91 52.

Prague, Czech Republic Office: Jindřišská 34, 110 00 Prague 1. Telephone: (42 2) 2410 3317. Facsimile: (42 2) 2410 3235.

Singapore Office: 20 Raffles Place #08-03, Ocean Towers, 0104. Telephone: (65) 533 0988. Facsimile: (65) 533 1322.

Warsaw, Poland Office: ul. Kopernika 17, IV Floor, 00-359. Telephone: (48 22) 262 226. Facsimile: (48 22) 262 360.

Firm engaged in English and General International Practice but not authorized to appear before Japanese Courts or to act as Japanese Bengoshi.

RESIDENT PARTNERS

Alex M. Pease   Andrew M.H. Ballheimer

(For Complete List of Firm Personnel, see Professional Biographies at London, England).

ANDERSON MŌRI

Established in 1950

(Formerly Anderson, Mōri & Rabinowitz)

AIG BUILDING
1-3, MARUNOUCHI 1-CHOME, CHIYODA-KU
CENTRAL P.O. BOX 1195
TOKYO 100, JAPAN
Telephone: 03-3214-1371
Cable Address: "Bengoshi Tokyo"
Telex: J22558 Bengoshi
Facsimile: 03-3201-7334; 03-3201-7340 (Group 3); 03-5222-7821 (Group 4)

General Practice.

FIRM PROFILE: *The firm has been practicing since 1950 and offers a full range of legal services. Areas of practice are general practice with particular emphasis upon international corporate and international financing, including a variety of general corporate and commercial transactions, securities and related work, aircraft and film financing, leasing, foreign investment, tax, litigations, copyright, patents and trademarks.*

MEMBERS OF FIRM

TSUYOSHI NAGAHAMA, born Fukuoka, Japan, January 6, 1938; admitted, 1964, Japan. *Education:* Tokyo University (LL.B., 1961); Harvard Law School (LL.M., 1968). *Member:* Dai-ni Tokyo Bar Association. **LANGUAGES:** Japanese and English.

NORITAKA MORIUCHI, born Osaka, Japan, August 23, 1938; admitted, 1964, Japan. *Education:* Tokyo University (LL.B., 1962). *Member:* First Tokyo Bar Association. **LANGUAGES:** Japanese and English.

KOICHIRO NAKAMOTO, born Osaka, Japan, May 11, 1939; admitted, 1967, Japan. *Education:* Tokyo University (LL.B., 1962); Harvard Law School (LL.M., 1971). *Member:* Dai-ni Tokyo Bar Association. **LANGUAGES:** Japanese and English.

AKIRA KAWAMURA, born Kyoto, Japan, May 9, 1941; admitted, 1967, Japan. *Education:* Kyoto University (LL.B., 1965); University of Sydney (LL.M., 1979). *Member:* Dai-ni Tokyo Bar Association. **LANGUAGES:** Japanese and English.

KOTARO HAYASHI, born Yokohama, Japan, September 23, 1943; admitted, 1968, Japan. *Education:* Tokyo University (LL.B., 1966); Harvard Law School (LL.M., 1971). *Member:* Tokyo Bar Association. **LANGUAGES:** Japanese and English.

MITSUO SASAKI, born Tokyo, Japan, January 23, 1943; admitted, 1969, Japan. *Education:* Tokyo University (LL.B., 1967); Monash University (LL.M., 1978). *Member:* Dai-ni Tokyo Bar Association. **LANGUAGES:** Japanese and English.

SANEAKI ICHIJO, born Kanagawa, Japan, August 6, 1945; admitted, 1973, Japan. *Education:* Chuo University (LL.B., 1968); New York University (LL.M., 1980). *Member:* First Tokyo Bar Association. **LANGUAGES:** Japanese and English.

OSAMU HIRAKAWA, born Tokyo, Japan, September 22, 1947; admitted, 1973, Japan; 1979, New York. *Education:* Tokyo University (LL.B., 1976); University of Washington (LL.M., 1977). *Member:* Dai-ni Tokyo Bar Association; American Bar Association. **LANGUAGES:** Japanese and English.

TOMOO NISHIKAWA, born Shiga, Japan, December 17, 1948; admitted, 1977, Japan. *Education:* Tokyo University (LL.B., 1972); Harvard Law School (LL.M., 1979). *Member:* Dai-ni Tokyo Bar Association. **LANGUAGES:** Japanese and English.

HIDEYUKI KOBAYASHI, born Ishikawa, Japan, February 1, 1952; admitted, 1980, Japan. *Education:* Tokyo University (LL.B., 1974). Visiting Scholar, Yale Law School, 1982-1983. Professor of Law, Sophia University, 1989—. *Member:* Dai-ni Tokyo Bar Association. **LANGUAGES:** Japanese and English.

MASAAKIRA KITAZAWA, born Nagoya, Japan, November 3, 1952; admitted, 1978, Japan; 1982, New York. *Education:* Tokyo University (LL.B., 1976); Harvard Law School (LL.M., 1981). *Member:* Dai-ni Tokyo Bar Association; New York State Bar Association; American Bar Association. **LANGUAGES:** Japanese and English.

KENICHI NAKANO, born Fukuoka, Japan, July 14, 1952; admitted, 1980, Japan; 1985, New York. *Education:* Tokyo University (LL.B., 1977); New York University (M.C.J., 1984). *Member:* Dai-ni Tokyo, New York State and American Bar Associations. **LANGUAGES:** Japanese and English.

KAZUTOSHI KAKUYAMA, born Hiroshima, Japan, July 4, 1952; admitted, 1980, Japan; 1986, New York. *Education:* Chuo University (LL.B., 1975); Tulane Law School (LL.M. in Admiralty, 1984). *Member:* First Tokyo Bar Association; New York State Bar Association. **LANGUAGES:** Japanese and English.

HIDETO ISHIDA, born Hyogo, Japan, August 24, 1952; admitted, 1978, Japan; 1991, New York. *Education:* Tokyo University (LL.B., 1976); Harvard Law School (LL.M., 1989). *Member:* Dai-ni Tokyo Bar Association; New York State Bar Association. **LANGUAGES:** Japanese and English.

ISAO SHINDO, born Aichi, Japan, November 13, 1955; admitted, 1983, Japan; 1988, New York. *Education:* Tokyo University (LL.B., 1978); Harvard Law School (LL.M., 1987). *Member:* Dai-ni Tokyo Bar Association. **LANGUAGES:** Japanese and English.

ASSOCIATES

KUNIHIKO MORISHITA, born Okayama, Japan, February 20, 1957; admitted, 1986, Japan. *Education:* Tokyo University (LL.B., 1981; LL.M., 1993). *Member:* Dai-ni Tokyo Bar Association. **LANGUAGES:** Japanese and English.

KOJI FUJITA, born Hyogo, Japan, February 7, 1961; admitted, 1986, Japan; 1991, New York. *Education:* Tokyo University (LL.B., 1984); University of Michigan (LL.M., 1990). *Member:* Dai-ni Tokyo Bar Association. **LANGUAGES:** Japanese and English.

HARUYUKI HIRATA, born Okayama, Japan, March 20, 1961; admitted, 1986, Japan; 1991, New York. *Education:* Waseda University (LL.B., 1984); University of Washington (LL.M., 1990). *Member:* First Tokyo Bar Association. **LANGUAGES:** Japanese and English.

TATSU KATAYAMA, born Kyoto, Japan, August 23, 1960; admitted, 1987, Japan; 1992, New York. *Education:* Tokyo University (LL.B., 1985); University of Pennsylvania (LL.M., 1991). *Member:* Dai-ni Tokyo Bar Association. **LANGUAGES:** Japanese and English.

NAOSUKE FUJITA, born Tokyo, Japan, November 19, 1962; admitted, 1987, Japan. *Education:* Waseda University (LL.B., 1985); University of Michigan (LL.M., 1991). *Member:* Dai-ni Tokyo Bar Association. **LANGUAGES:** Japanese and English.

KANJI IWATO, born Fukushima, Japan, October 31, 1961; admitted, 1988, Japan; 1994, New York. *Education:* Waseda University (LL.B., 1985); New York University (M.C.J., 1992). *Member:* Dai-ni Tokyo Bar Association. **LANGUAGES:** Japanese and English.

TOSHIHIDE SHICHI, born Gifu, Japan, August 2, 1962; admitted, 1988, Japan; 1994, New York. *Education:* Tokyo University (LL.B., 1986); New York University (LL.M., 1993). *Member:* Dai-ni Tokyo Bar Association; American Bar Association. **LANGUAGES:** Japanese and English.

TAKASHI SUZUKI, born Tokyo, Japan, September 15, 1962; admitted, 1988, Japan. *Education:* Waseda University (LL.B., 1986); University of Cambridge, Queens' College (LL.M., 1992). *Member:* Dai-ni Tokyo Bar Association; International Bar Association. **LANGUAGES:** Japanese and English.

KENICHI MASUDA, born Hyogo, Japan, January 11, 1963; admitted, 1988, Japan; 1993, New York. *Education:* Tokyo University (LL.B., 1986); University of Chicago (LL.M., 1992). *Member:* Dai-ni Tokyo Bar Association. **LANGUAGES:** Japanese and English.

HIROHITO AKAGAMI, born Mito, Japan, January 24, 1963; admitted, 1988, Japan. *Education:* Tokyo University (LL.B., 1986); University of London, London School of Economics and Political Science (LL.M., 1993). *Member:* Dai-ni Tokyo Bar Association. **LANGUAGES:** Japanese and English.

YUKIHIKO SUGIURA, born Aichi, Japan, December 20, 1962; admitted, 1989, Japan. *Education:* Nagoya University (LL.B., 1985). *Member:* Dai-ni Tokyo Bar Association. **LANGUAGES:** Japanese and English.

TAKASHI AKAHANE, born Osaka, Japan, March 29, 1963; admitted, 1989, Japan. *Education:* Tokyo University (LL.B., 1987); Georgetown University Law Center (LL.M., 1994). *Member:* Dai-ni Tokyo Bar Association. **LANGUAGES:** Japanese and English.

HIROKI WAKABAYASHI, born Sapporo, Japan, January 17, 1964; admitted, 1989, Japan; 1994, New York. *Education:* Tokyo University (LL.B., 1987); University of Chicago (LL.M., 1993). *Member:* Dai-ni Tokyo

(This Listing Continued)

(This Listing Continued)

ANDERSON MŌRI, Tokyo—Continued

Bar Association; American Bar Association. *LANGUAGES:* Japanese and English.

KAZUO HIRAHATA, born Shizuoka, Japan, February 14, 1964; admitted, 1989, Japan; 1994, New York. *Education:* Waseda University (LL.B., 1987); New York University (LL.M., 1993). *Member:* Dai-ni Tokyo Bar Association. *LANGUAGES:* Japanese and English.

YOJI MAEDA, born Hiroshima, Japan, June 15, 1964; admitted, 1990, Japan. *Education:* Tokyo University (LL.B., 1988); University of Virginia (LL.M., 1994). *Member:* Dai-ni Tokyo Bar Association. *LANGUAGES:* Japanese and English.

FUMITAKA ESHIMA, born Fukuoka, Japan, August 28, 1964; admitted, 1990, Japan. *Education:* Tokyo University (LL.B., 1988). *Member:* Dai-ni Tokyo Bar Association. *LANGUAGES:* Japanese and English.

YUMIKO MATSUO, born Montreal, Canada, January 13, 1965; admitted, 1990, Japan. *Education:* Tokyo University (LL.B., 1988). *Member:* Dai-ni Tokyo Bar Association. *LANGUAGES:* Japanese and English.

RYUGO YOSHIMURA, born Osaka, Japan, February 17, 1965; admitted, 1990, Japan. *Education:* Tokyo University (LL.B., 1988). *Member:* Dai-ni Tokyo Bar Association. *LANGUAGES:* Japanese and English.

TAKASHI SOGA, born Kanagawa, Japan, June 8, 1965; admitted, 1990, Japan; 1994, New York. *Education:* Tokyo University (LL.B., 1988); University of Michigan (LL.M., 1993). *Member:* Tokyo Bar Association. *LANGUAGES:* Japanese and English.

RYU UMEZU, born Kanagawa, Japan, April 7, 1965; admitted, 1991, Japan. *Education:* Tokyo University (LL.B., 1989). *Member:* Dai-ni Tokyo Bar Association. *LANGUAGES:* Japanese and English.

SEIGO YAMASAKI, born Hyogo, Japan, September 12, 1965; admitted, 1991, Japan. *Education:* Tokyo University (LL.B., 1989). *Member:* Tokyo Bar Association. *LANGUAGES:* Japanese and English.

YOSHIMASA FURUTA, born Gifu, Japan, January 6, 1966; admitted, 1991, Japan. *Education:* Tokyo University (LL.B., 1988). *Member:* Dai-ni Tokyo Bar Association. *LANGUAGES:* Japanese and English.

KAZUAKI NAGAI, born Tochigi, Japan, March 1, 1966; admitted, 1992, Japan. *Education:* Tokyo University (LL.B., 1990). *Member:* Dai-ni Tokyo Bar Association. *LANGUAGES:* Japanese and English.

TAKESHI WATANABE, born Tokyo, Japan, February 17, 1967; admitted, 1992, Japan. *Education:* Tokyo University (LL.B., 1990). *Member:* Dai-ni Tokyo Bar Association. *LANGUAGES:* Japanese and English.

YOSHIKO NAKAYAMA, born Tokyo, Japan, February 23, 1967; admitted, 1992, Japan. *Education:* Tokyo University (LL.B., 1990). *Member:* Dai-ni Tokyo Bar Association. *LANGUAGES:* Japanese and English.

KENICHI SADAKA, born Gifu, Japan, April 6, 1967; admitted, 1992, Japan. *Education:* Tokyo University (LL.B., 1990). *Member:* Dai-ni Tokyo Bar Association. *LANGUAGES:* Japanese and English.

KANAKO MISHIKU, born Tokyo, Japan, April 26, 1965; admitted, 1993, Japan. *Education:* Tokyo University (LL.B., 1988). *Member:* Dai-ni Tokyo Bar Association. *LANGUAGES:* Japanese and English.

TETSUYA ITOH, born Okayama, Japan, April 18, 1967; admitted, 1993, Japan. *Education:* Tokyo University (LL.B., 1991). *Member:* Dai-ni Tokyo Bar Association. *LANGUAGES:* Japanese and English.

SHINGO MORIKAWA, born Nagoya, Japan, August 29, 1968; admitted, 1993, Japan. *Education:* Tokyo University (LL.B., 1991). *Member:* Tokyo Bar Association. *LANGUAGES:* Japanese, English and Mandarin.

SHIGEYOSHI EZAKI, born Tokyo, Japan, October 31, 1967; admitted, 1994, Japan. *Education:* Tokyo University (LL.B., 1992); Legal Research and Training Institute of Supreme Court of Japan (1994). *Member:* Dai-ni Tokyo Bar Association. *LANGUAGES:* Japanese and English.

JUNICHI KONDO, born Yokohama, Japan, March 4, 1969; admitted, 1994, Japan. *Education:* Tokyo University (LL.B., 1992); Legal Research and Training Institute of Supreme Court of Japan (1994). *Member:* Dai-ni Tokyo Bar Association. *LANGUAGES:* Japanese and English.

AOKI, CHRISTENSEN & NOMOTO

Established in 1897

SUITE 521, FUJI BUILDING
2-3, MARUNOUCHI 3-CHOME, CHIYODA-KU,
C.P.O. BOX 2107
TOKYO, JAPAN
Telephone: 03-3211-8871-3
Cable Address: "McIvor" Tokyo
Telex: J24809
Facsimile: 03-3213-2365; 03-3211-7054

Securities, Financial and Corporate Law.

FIRM PROFILE: The firm was established in 1897 and offers a full range of legal services, particularly in the securities and financial field. The client base is Japanese, North American and European in scope.

MEMBERS OF FIRM

KUNIO AOKI, born Kanagawa Pref., Japan, August 31, 1943; admitted, 1968, Japan. *Education:* Chuo University (LL.B., 1966); Law School of Columbia University (LL.M., 1973). *Member:* First Tokyo Bar Association. *LANGUAGES:* Japanese and English. *PRACTICE AREAS:* Securities; Finance; Corporate; Commercial.

AKIRA NOMOTO, born Kyoto, Japan, January 26, 1927; admitted, 1964, Japan. *Education:* Third Higher School, Kyoto (presently Department of Liberal Arts of Kyoto University, 1944). Personnel Advisor for U.S. Air Force Base in Japan, 1950-1959. *Member:* Tokyo Bar Association. *LANGUAGES:* Japanese and English. *PRACTICE AREAS:* Corporate; Civil; Commercial.

MIKIO IMAMURA, born Ehime Prefecture, Japan, October 5, 1927; admitted, 1971, Japan. *Education:* Tokyo University. *Member:* Second Tokyo Bar Association. *LANGUAGES:* Japanese and English. *PRACTICE AREAS:* Securities; Finance; Corporate; Commercial.

TOSHIHIKO OKEDA, born Changchun, People's Republic of China, April 6, 1945; admitted, 1978, Japan. *Education:* Chuo University (LL.B., 1968). *Member:* First Tokyo Bar Association. *LANGUAGES:* Japanese and English. *PRACTICE AREAS:* Securities; Finance; Corporate; Commercial.

FUSAKO OTSUKA, born Kanagawa Prefecture, Japan, October 28, 1947; admitted, 1983, Japan. *Education:* Keio University (LL.B., 1970; LL.M., 1973). *Member:* First Tokyo Bar Association. *LANGUAGES:* Japanese and English. *PRACTICE AREAS:* Securities; Finance; Corporate; Commercial.

HIROYOSHI KUROMARU, born Akita Prefecture, Japan, December 28, 1952; admitted, 1983, Japan. *Education:* Tokyo University (LL.B., 1980); University of Washington School of Law (LL.M., 1987). *Member:* First Tokyo Bar Association. *LANGUAGES:* Japanese and English. *PRACTICE AREAS:* Securities; Finance; Corporate; Commercial.

ASSOCIATES

HITOSHI SUMIYA, born Nagoya, Japan, April 16, 1958; admitted, 1987, Japan. *Education:* Waseda University (LL.B., 1983); New York University Law School (LL.M., 1991). *Member:* First Tokyo Bar Association. *LANGUAGES:* Japanese and English. *PRACTICE AREAS:* Securities; Finance; Corporate; Commercial.

KEN TAKAHASHI, born Tokyo, Japan, May 18, 1962; admitted, 1987, Japan. *Education:* Keio University (LL.B., 1985); University of London (U.C.L., 1990-1991). *Member:* Tokyo Bar Association. *LANGUAGES:* Japanese and English. *PRACTICE AREAS:* Securities; Finance; Corporate; Commercial.

NORIFUSA HASHIMOTO, born Kumamoto, Japan, September 5, 1958; admitted, 1988, Japan. *Education:* Waseda University (LL.B., 1983); Boston University (LL.M., 1992). The Daiwa Bank, Limited, 1983-1984. *Member:* First Tokyo Bar Association. *LANGUAGES:* Japanese and English. *PRACTICE AREAS:* Securities; Finance; Corporate; Commercial.

TAIZO NAMURA, born Tokyo, Japan, December 16, 1956; admitted, 1988, Japan. *Education:* Tokyo University (LL.B., 1982). *Member:* Tokyo Bar Association. *LANGUAGES:* Japanese and English. *PRACTICE AREAS:* Securities; Finance; Corporate; Commercial.

TADASHI ISHII, born Saitama Prefecture, Japan, January 30, 1960; admitted, 1988, Japan. *Education:* Sophia University (LL.B., 1982). *Member:* Tokyo Bar Association. *LANGUAGES:* Japanese and English. *PRACTICE AREAS:* Securities; Finance; Corporate; Commercial.

(This Listing Continued)

JAY A. SANCHEZ, born New York, New York, 1967; (Not admitted in Japan). *Education:* Harvard College (B.A., cum laude, 1989); Harvard Law School (J.D., cum laude, 1992). *LANGUAGES:* English and Spanish. *PRACTICE AREAS:* Securities; Corporate; Commercial.

REPRESENTATIVE CLIENTS: Alcan Aluminium, Ltd.; British Gas PLC; Chevron Corporation; Del Monte Corp.; Hoechst AG; General Motors Corp.; General Signal Corp.; Glaxo Holdings p.l.c.; Imperial Chemical Industries PLC (ICI); ITT; Minnesota Mining & Manufacturing Co.; Perkin-Elmer Corp.; Philip Morris Companies Inc.; Tetra Pak International AB.

ASAHI LAW OFFICES

(Masuda & Ejiri - Tokyo Yaesu)

NEW ATT BUILDING, 7TH & 8TH FLOORS
11-7, AKASAKA 2-CHOME, MINATO-KU
TOKYO 107, JAPAN
Telephone: (03) 3505-0003 (8th floor); (03) 3505-3031 (7th floor)
Fax: (03) 3505-1333 (8th floor); (03) 3505-3081 (7th floor)
Telex: 02223551 MAELAW
Cable Address: MAEINTLLAW

Member Lex Mundi, A Global Association of Independent Firms.
Corporate and General Practice, Mergers and Acquisitions, International Investments, Financing, Securities, Insurance, Antitrust, Construction, Taxation, Patents, Trademarks, Intellectual Properties, Entertainment and Labor Law, Maritime Law, Litigation and Criminal Law.

NOBUO YAMADA, born Tokyo, Japan, 1937; admitted, 1964, Japan. *Education:* Tokyo University (LL.B., 1962); Legal Training and Research Institute of The Supreme Court of Japan (1946). Author: "Questioning and Notification the Right to Refuse Answer to any Questions in the Tax Evasion Control Law," Law Journal of the Legal Training and Research Institute '77-1; "Regarding the Public Defender System," Bessatsu Hanrei Times No. 7. *Member:* Daini Tokyo Bar Association. *LANGUAGES:* Japanese. *PRACTICE AREAS:* Litigation; Criminal Law; Finance.

JUNJI MASUDA, born Tokyo, Japan, 1943; admitted, 1968, Japan. *Education:* Tokyo University (LL.B., 1966); Legal Training and Research Institute of The Supreme Court of Japan (1968); Columbia Law School (LL.M., 1971). Licensed Legal Consultant, State of New York, 1991. Author: "Expansion of In Personam Jurisdiction," 1972; "Dangers in No-Contest Clauses in Patent License Agreements," 1972; "Registration Requirements for Unlisted Companies and Foreign Companies," 1972; "Public Offering and Listing of Foreign Stock," Matthew Bender, 1981; "International Loan Agreement," Yuhikaku, 1983; "Legal Problems of Cross-Border M&A," 1988; "Acquisitions by Tender Offer of U.S. Companies by Japanese Companies," 1989; "Exxon-Florio Provisions and its Developments," 1989; "Proposed Regulations of Exxon-Florio Provisions," 1989; "M&A and Insider Trading," 1989; "Disclosure of M&A Information," 1990; "Guidelines for Treatment of M&A Information," 1990; "Acquisitions of Overseas Enterprises," Shojihomu Kenkyu-kai, 1992. Co-Author: "Export-Import Controls and Customs Duties of Various Foreign Countries," Seirin Shoin Shinsha, 1973; "Foreign Investments in the United States of America—Incentives and Restrictions" 1979; "An Overview of U.S. Bankruptcy Law," 1981; "Restriction on Acquisition of U.S. Companies for Reason of National Security," 1989; "Shareholders Derivative Lawsuits," 1993. *Member:* Daini Tokyo Bar Association; American Bar Association; New York City Bar Association; Columbia Law School Japanese Advisory Council; Columbia Law School Board of Visitors; American Foreign Law Association; Japanese American Society for Legal Studies (Councillors); International Legal Society; International Bar Association; Japanese Chamber of Commerce in New York; Nippon Club; Tokyo Club. *LANGUAGES:* Japanese and English. *PRACTICE AREAS:* Mergers, Acquisitions and Divestitures; Business Law; Company Law; International Law.

TAKASHI EJIRI, born Chiba, Japan, 1942; admitted, 1969, Japan. *Education:* Tokyo University (LL.B., 1967); Legal Training and Research Institute of The Supreme Court of Japan (1969); Harvard Law School (LL.M., 1970). Author: "Protection of Property under The U.S.-Japanese Treaty," 1970. Co-Author: "Commentaries on Conflict of Law Rules of Japan," Gakuyo Shobo, 1984; "Methods of Financing in Overseas Markets," 1986; "Japanese Securities Market," Euromoney Books, 1990; "Best Solution of International Disputes," Minjiho-Kenkyukai, 1992. *Member:* Tokyo Bar Association; Japan Federation of Bar Associations (Vice Chairman, International Relations Committee, 1986-1994); Inter-Pacific Bar Association (Chairperson of Financial Institutions and Transactions Committee,

(This Listing Continued)

1993—). *LANGUAGES:* Japanese and English. *PRACTICE AREAS:* Mergers, Acquisitions and Divestitures; Labor and Employment; Securities; Banking.

TERUHIKO ASAOKA, born Kanagawa, Japan, 1944; admitted, 1971, Japan. *Education:* Tokyo Metropolitan University (LL.B., 1969); Legal Training and Research Institute of the Supreme Court of Japan (1971). *Member:* Daini Tokyo Bar Association. *LANGUAGES:* Japanese. *PRACTICE AREAS:* Litigation; Trusts and Estates.

SHOICHIRO NIWAYAMA, born Hiroshima, Japan, 1946; admitted, 1971, Japan. *Education:* Tokyo University, Legal Training and Research Institute of The Supreme Court of Japan (1971). Author: "Lawyer and Business out of Courts," Hohgaku Seminer extra number - Lawyer; "Liberty and Prolonged Trial," Liberty & Justice Volume 32, No. 5; Co-Author: "Criminal Procedure (the first and second volumes)," Chikuma Shobo, 1988. *Member:* Daini Tokyo Bar Association. *LANGUAGES:* Japanese. *PRACTICE AREAS:* Litigation; Constitutional Law; Finance.

YOSHIKO KOIZUMI, born Mie, Japan, 1943; admitted, 1972, Japan. *Education:* Tokyo University of Education, now Tsukuba University (B.A. in Law, 1966); Legal Training and Research Institute of The Supreme Court of Japan (1972); University of London, The London School of Economics and Political Science (LL.M., 1977). Author: "Liquidated Damages and Consequential Damages under UK and US Law," JCA Journal, 1982; "Plant Construction Contract - From a Standpoint of Contractor's Risk Management," Shojihomu Kenkyu-kai, 1992. Supervisor: "Manual and Forms for Entry and Residence Procedures in Japan for Foreign Nationals," 1991. *Member:* Daini Tokyo Bar Association. *LANGUAGES:* Japanese and English. *PRACTICE AREAS:* Contracts; Construction Law; Immigration and Naturalization.

YOSHIKAZU YAMADA, born Kanagawa, Japan, 1944; admitted, 1972, Japan. *Education:* Tokyo University (LL.B., 1969); Legal Training and Research Institute of The Supreme Court of Japan (1972). *Member:* Daini Tokyo Bar Association. *LANGUAGES:* Japanese and English. *PRACTICE AREAS:* Litigation; Intellectual Property; Entertainment; Civil Law; Real Estate.

JUN NORISUGI, born Tokyo, Japan, 1947; admitted, 1974, Japan. *Education:* Waseda University (LL.B., 1971); Legal Training and Research Institute of The Supreme Court of Japan (1974); University of Michigan Law School (LL.M., 1976). Author: "Joint Venture Agreement Forms," JATEC, 1981. *Member:* Dai-ichi Tokyo Bar Association. *LANGUAGES:* Japanese and English. *PRACTICE AREAS:* Corporate Law; Entertainment and the Arts; Antitrust and Trade Regulation.

NORIHIKO HADANO, born Aichi, Japan, 1946; admitted, 1975, Japan. *Education:* Tokyo University (LL.B., Private Law, 1970; Public Law, 1972); Legal Training and Research Institute of The Supreme Court of Japan (1975); New York University School of Law (M.C.J., 1978). Co-Author: "Mortgage," Kin'yu Zaisei, 1984; "Legal Forms for Civil Litigation," Daiichi Hoki, 1984; "Practice in Civil Litigation, Vol. 3 & 4," Tokyo Nunoi, 1990 and 1993; "Law Reflected in Judgments," Gyosei, 1990. *Member:* Dai-ichi Tokyo Bar Association. *LANGUAGES:* Japanese and English. *PRACTICE AREAS:* Products Liability; Insurance; Labor and Employment.

AKINOBU MIYOSHI, born Fukuoka, Japan, 1952; admitted, 1978, Japan. *Education:* Waseda University (LL.B., 1974); Legal Training and Research Institute of The Supreme Court of Japan (1978); University of Pennsylvania Law School (LL.M., 1982). Author: "U.S. Real Estate Law and Transaction," Kokusai Shoji Homu, 1983. Co-Author: "Banking Practice III Collection," Kin'yu Zaisei, 1979. *Member:* Tokyo Bar Association. *LANGUAGES:* Japanese and English. *PRACTICE AREAS:* Real Estate; Bankruptcy.

TETSURO TORIUMI, born Tokyo, Japan, 1950; admitted, 1979, Japan; 1988, Japan as Patent Attorney. *Education:* Waseda University (LL.B., 1974); Legal Training and Research Institute of The Supreme Court of Japan (1979); University of British Columbia Law School (LL.M., 1983). *Member:* Daini Tokyo Bar Association. *LANGUAGES:* Japanese and English. *PRACTICE AREAS:* Corporate Law; Litigation; Intellectual Property.

MASAMI TOTANI, born Nagoya, Japan, 1951; admitted, 1981, Japan; 1986, New York. *Education:* Chuo University (LL.B., 1975); Legal Training and Research Institute of The Supreme Court of Japan (1980); Columbia Law School (LL.M., 1985). Author: "Commercial Court in France," Journal of the Japan Commercial Arbitration Association, 1983; "Securitization in France," Journal of the Japanese Institute of International Business Law, 1990. *Member:* Daini Tokyo Bar Association; New York State

(This Listing Continued)

ASAHI LAW OFFICES, Tokyo—Continued

Bar Association; Tokyo Fashion Forum (Chairman, 1993). *LANGUAGES:* Japanese, English and French. *PRACTICE AREAS:* Corporate Law; Finance; Litigation; European Community Law; Commodities.

OSAMU SUDOH, born Gifu, Japan, 1952; admitted, 1980, Japan. *Education:* Tokyo University (LL.B.); Legal Training and Research Institute of The Supreme Court of Japan (1980). Author: "Utilization of Trust in case of Merger and Capital Reduction," Junkan Shojihomu No. 1067 and No. 1069; "Practice of Dissolution and Liquidation Procedure of Subsidiary," Shojihomu Kenkyu-kai, 1988. *Member:* Daini Tokyo Bar Association; The Trust Law Society. *LANGUAGES:* Japanese. *PRACTICE AREAS:* Litigation; Business Law; Trusts and Estates; Bankruptcy.

NOBUO NAKATA, born Tokyo, Japan, 1957; admitted, 1985, Japan; 1991, New York. *Education:* Tokyo University (LL.B., Public Law, 1981; Private Law, 1982); Legal Training and Research Institute of The Supreme Court of Japan (1985); University of Pennsylvania Law School (LL.M., 1990). Author: "Practical Issues concerning the Shareholder's Proposal Right at the General Meeting of the Shareholders," Commercial Law Review No. 1182; "U.S. Practice in Debt Collection and Security Interest - UCC Filing," Gekkan Kaigai Chuzai, October, November, December, 1991 and February, March, 1992; "Recent Development of Asset Back Finance in Japan," M & A Review, November, 1993. *Member:* Tokyo Bar Association; New York State Bar Association. *LANGUAGES:* Japanese and English. *PRACTICE AREAS:* Banks and Banking; Structured Finance; Project Finance.

SOMUKU IIMURA, born Hokkaido, Japan, 1953; admitted, 1986, Japan. *Education:* Tokyo University (LL.B., 1981); Legal Training and Research Institute of The Supreme Court of Japan (1986). *Member:* Daini Tokyo Bar Association. *LANGUAGES:* Japanese and English. *PRACTICE AREAS:* Corporate Law; Mergers, Acquisitions and Divestitures; Securities.

JUNKO MORI, born Tokyo, Japan, 1956; admitted, 1987, Japan. *Education:* Chuo University (LL.B., 1981); Legal Training and Research Institute of The Supreme Court of Japan (1987); Columbia Law School (LL.M., 1991). *Member:* Tokyo Bar Association. *LANGUAGES:* Japanese and English. *PRACTICE AREAS:* Finance; Intellectual Property.

KEN HASHIMOTO, born Tokyo, Japan, 1958; admitted, 1987, Japan. *Education:* Chuo University (LL.B., 1981); Legal Training and Research Institute of the Supreme Court of Japan (1987). *Member:* Dai-ichi Tokyo Bar Association. *LANGUAGES:* Japanese and English. *PRACTICE AREAS:* Corporate Law; Litigation.

HIROYUKI UMEZONO, born Fukuoka, Japan, 1963; admitted, 1988, Japan; 1994, New York. *Education:* Waseda University (LL.B., 1986); Legal Training and Research Institute of The Supreme Court of Japan (1988); Columbia Law School (LL.M., 1992). *Member:* Dai-ichi Tokyo Bar Association; New York State Bar Association. *LANGUAGES:* Japanese and English. *PRACTICE AREAS:* Mergers and Acquisitions; Finance; Computer Law; Securities.

YUKIHIRO FUJIMOTO, born Tokyo, Japan, 1961; admitted, 1989, Japan; 1994, New York. *Education:* Waseda University (LL.B., 1986); Legal Training and Research Institute of The Supreme Court of Japan (1989); University of Chicago Law School (LL.M., 1993). *Member:* Tokyo Bar Association; New York State Bar Association. *LANGUAGES:* Japanese and English. *PRACTICE AREAS:* Mergers, Acquisitions and Divestitures.

TAKEMI HIRAMATSU, born Tokyo, Japan, 1963; admitted, 1989, Japan; 1994, New York. *Education:* Tokyo University (LL.B., 1987); Legal Training and Research Institute of The Supreme Court of Japan (1989); Columbia Law School (LL.M., 1993). Author: "Legal Problems in Commercial Use of Names and Likenesses," Merchandising Rights Reports, 1991. Co-Author: "Shareholders' Derivative Suits in the Future Anticipated to Increase Due to Successive Scandals of Japanese Major Corporations," International Legal Strategy, 1993. *Member:* Daini Tokyo Bar Association; New York State Bar Association. *LANGUAGES:* Japanese and English. *PRACTICE AREAS:* Corporate Law; Mergers and Acquisitions; Litigation; Intellectual Property.

SEIICHIRO UMENO, born Tokyo, Japan, 1961; admitted, 1989, Japan; 1994, New York. *Education:* Waseda University (Bachelor of Politics, 1985); Legal Training and Research Institute of The Supreme Court of Japan (1989); University of Pennsylvania Law School (LL.M., 1993). *Member:* Daini Tokyo Bar Association; American Bar Association; New York

(This Listing Continued)

State Bar Association. *LANGUAGES:* Japanese and English. *PRACTICE AREAS:* Litigation; Corporate Law; Intellectual Property; Criminal Law.

YUJI ONUKI, born Ibaraki, Japan, 1959; admitted, 1990, Japan. *Education:* Aoyama Gakuin University (LL.B., 1983); Legal Training and Research Institute of The Supreme Court of Japan (1990); The American University Law School (LL.M., 1994). *Member:* Daini Tokyo Bar Association. *LANGUAGES:* Japanese and English. *PRACTICE AREAS:* Wills; Family Law; Real Estate; Antitrust.

CHIKAKO KUROYANAGI, born Kanagawa, Japan, 1961; admitted, 1990, Japan. *Education:* Keio University (LL.B., 1984; LL.M., 1987); Legal Training and Research Institute of The Supreme Court of Japan (1990); Columbia University Law School (LL.M., 1994). *Member:* Tokyo Bar Association. *LANGUAGES:* Japanese and English. *PRACTICE AREAS:* Banks and Banking; Labor and Employment.

MASAHIKO KANAMURA, born Tokyo, Japan, 1962; admitted, 1990, Japan. *Education:* Hitotsubashi University (B.Com., 1985); Legal Training and Research Institute of The Supreme Court of Japan (1990). *Member:* Dai-ichi Tokyo Bar Association. *LANGUAGES:* Japanese and English. *PRACTICE AREAS:* Contracts; Insurance.

KIMI KOINUMA, born Aichi, Japan, 1965; admitted, 1991, Japan. *Education:* Keio University (LL.B., 1988); Legal Training and Research Institute of The Supreme Court of Japan (1991). *Member:* Daini Tokyo Bar Association. *LANGUAGES:* Japanese and English. *PRACTICE AREAS:* Commercial Law; Corporate Law.

YOSHINOBU FUJIMOTO, born Hyogo, Japan, 1965; admitted, 1991, Japan. *Education:* Waseda University (LL.B., 1989); Legal Training and Research Institute of the Supreme Court of Japan (1991). *Member:* Daini Tokyo Bar Association. *LANGUAGES:* Japanese and English. *PRACTICE AREAS:* Litigation; Antitrust and Trade Regulation.

HISASHI MENJO, born Kanagawa, Japan, 1961; admitted, 1991, Japan. *Education:* Tokyo Metropolitan University (LL.B., 1985); Legal Training and Research Institute of The Supreme Court of Japan (1991). *Member:* Daini Tokyo Bar Association. *LANGUAGES:* Japanese. *PRACTICE AREAS:* Litigation; Medical Malpractice; Immigration and Naturalization.

MASAFUMI OSHINO, born Kouchi, Japan, 1960; admitted, 1992, Japan. *Education:* Tokyo University (LL.B., 1984); Legal Training and Research Institute of The Supreme Court of Japan (1992). *Member:* Daini Tokyo Bar Association. *LANGUAGES:* Japanese and English. *PRACTICE AREAS:* Computers and Software; Telecommunications; Copyrights; Trademarks.

OSAMU ITO, born Saitama, Japan, 1965; admitted, 1992, Japan. *Education:* Hitotsubashi University (LL.B., 1989); Legal Training and Research Institute of The Supreme Court of Japan (1992). *Member:* Tokyo Bar Association. *LANGUAGES:* Japanese, English and Italian. *PRACTICE AREAS:* Immigration; Naturalization.

KEIKO TAMURA, born Aichi, Japan, 1963; admitted, 1992, Japan. *Education:* Kyoto University (LL.B., 1988); Legal Training and Research Institute of The Supreme Court of Japan (1992). *Member:* Daini Tokyo Bar Association. *LANGUAGES:* Japanese. *PRACTICE AREAS:* Medical Malpractice; Personal Injury; Leases and Leasing.

JUNKO KAI, born Tokyo, Japan, 1967; admitted, 1992, Japan. *Education:* Tokyo University (LL.B., 1990); Legal Training and Research Institute of The Supreme Court of Japan (1992). *Member:* Daini Tokyo Bar Association. *LANGUAGES:* Japanese. *PRACTICE AREAS:* Litigation; Trusts and Estates; Family Law.

HIROMASA SHIOZAKI, born Kumamoto, Japan, 1963; admitted, 1993, Japan. *Education:* Tokyo University (LL.B., 1989); Legal Training and Research Institute of The Supreme Court of Japan (1993). *Member:* Daini Tokyo Bar Association. *LANGUAGES:* Japanese and English. *PRACTICE AREAS:* Bankruptcy; Commercial Law.

TSUTOMU KURIBAYASHI, born Kagawa, Japan, 1964; admitted, 1993, Japan. *Education:* Waseda University (LL.B., 1989); Legal Training and Research Institute of The Supreme Court of Japan (1993). *Member:* Tokyo Bar Association. *LANGUAGES:* Japanese and English. *PRACTICE AREAS:* Civil Law; Debtor and Creditor; Bankruptcy.

YASUSHI TOYAMA, born Tokyo, Japan, 1965; admitted, 1993, Japan. *Education:* Waseda University (LL.B., 1988); Legal Training and Research Institute of The Supreme Court of Japan (1993). *Member:* Daini Tokyo Bar Association. *LANGUAGES:* Japanese. *PRACTICE AREAS:* Environmental Law; Admiralty and Maritime; Bankruptcy.

(This Listing Continued)

SATOSHI KARASHIMA, born Kumamoto, Japan, 1965; admitted, 1993, Japan. *Education:* Waseda University (LL.B., 1989); Legal Training and Research Institute of The Supreme Court of Japan (1993). *Member:* Daini Tokyo Bar Association. *LANGUAGES:* Japanese and English. *PRACTICE AREAS:* Administrative Law; Antitrust and Trade Regulation.

SATORU MITSUMORI, born Yamanashi, Japan, 1966; admitted, 1993, Japan. *Education:* Tokyo University (LL.B., 1991); Legal Training and Research Institute of The Supreme Court of Japan (1993). *Member:* Daini Tokyo Bar Association. *LANGUAGES:* Japanese. *PRACTICE AREAS:* Communications and Media; Product Liabilities; Bankruptcy.

HIROSHI SUGA, born Yamaguchi, Japan, 1967; admitted, 1993, Japan. *Education:* Tokyo University (LL.B., 1991); Legal Training and Research Institute of The Supreme Court of Japan (1993). *Member:* Daini Tokyo Bar Association. *LANGUAGES:* Japanese and English. *PRACTICE AREAS:* Labor and Employment.

RYUJI UWATOKO, born Osaka, Japan, 1967; admitted, 1994, Japan. *Education:* Tokyo University (LL.B., 1992); Legal Training and Research Institute of The Supreme Court of Japan (1994). *Member:* Daini Tokyo Bar Association. *LANGUAGES:* Japanese. *PRACTICE AREAS:* Antitrust and Trade Regulations; Product Liabilities.

KENJI INOUE, born Tokyo, Japan, 1968; admitted, 1994, Japan. *Education:* Tokyo University (LL.B., 1992); Legal Training and Research Institute of The Supreme Court of Japan (1994). *Member:* Daini Tokyo Bar Association. *LANGUAGES:* Japanese and English. *PRACTICE AREAS:* Litigation; Labor and Employment.

TAKASHI MICHISHITA, born Tokyo, Japan, 1969; admitted, 1994, Japan. *Education:* Tokyo University (LL.B., 1992); Legal Training and Research Institute of The Supreme Court of Japan (1994). *Member:* Tokyo Bar Association. *LANGUAGES:* Japanese and English. *PRACTICE AREAS:* Negotiable Instruments; Trademarks.

PATENT ATTORNEYS

YUZO AGATA, born Aichi, Japan, 1946; admitted, 1974, Japan as Patent Attorney. *Education:* Tokyo Institute of Technology (CE.B., 1969). Author: "Japanese Translation of Patents, Copyrights and Trademarks, John Wiley & Sons, 1989," Nihon Hyoron-sha, 1991. *LANGUAGES:* Japanese and English.

MASARU MURAYAMA, born Tokyo, Japan, 1925; admitted, 1979, Japan as Patent Attorney. *Education:* Nihon University (EE.B., 1950). Former Appeal Examiners-in-Chief of Department of Appeal of the Patent Office. *LANGUAGES:* Japanese.

TSUNENORI SASAKI, born Saitama, Japan, 1942; admitted, 1973, Japan as Patent Attorney. *Education:* Tokyo University of Education; Tsukuba University (B.A., Law, 1966). *LANGUAGES:* Japanese.

TAX ATTORNEY

YUICHI SUGIYAMA, born Tokyo, Japan, 1954; admitted, 1992, Japan as Tax Attorney. *Education:* Waseda University (CS.B., 1976). National Tax Auditor, 1982; National Tax Examiner, Tokyo Regional Taxation Bureau, 1985. *Member:* Association of Tokyo Certified Tax Accountants. *LANGUAGES:* Japanese and English.

JUDICIAL SCRIVENER

KAZUYOSHI TAKEDA, born Tokyo, Japan, 1950; admitted, 1985, Japan as Judicial Scrivener. *Education:* Waseda University (LL.B., 1975). *LANGUAGES:* Japanese.

ASAMURA PATENT OFFICE

Established in 1891

331 NEW OHTEMACHI BUILDING
2-2-1 OHTEMACHI, CHIYODA-KU
TOKYO 100, JAPAN
Telephone: (03)3211-3651/8
Facsimile: (03)3246-1239; (03)3270-5076
Cable Address: "Patentory" Tokyo
Telex: J22979 ASAMURA

Patent and Trademark Law.
(This Listing Continued)

MEMBERS OF FIRM

KIYOSHI ASAMURA, born Hyogo Prefecture, Japan, January 4, 1937. admitted, 1963, Japan as Patent Attorney. *Education:* Waseda University (B.S., 1959). President, Asian Patent Attorneys Association, 1994—. Councillor and Vice President, Asian Patent Attorneys Association, 1970-1972, 1974—. Councillor: The Japanese Association of FICPI, 1977—; The Licensing Executive Society of Japan, 1978—. Executive Committee Member, International Association for the Protection of Industrial Property, 1975—. Director, The United States Trademark Association, 1986-1988. *Member:* The Japan Patent Attorneys Association (Vice President, 1979-1980 and 1992-1993; President, 1993-1994). *LANGUAGES:* Japanese and English.

HAJIME ASAMURA, born Tokyo, Japan, April 13, 1940. admitted, 1968, Japan as Patent Attorney. *Education:* Nippon University (LL.M., 1966). *Member:* The Japan Patent Attorneys Association. *LANGUAGES:* Japanese and English.

TSUNEAKI KOIKE, born Tokyo, Japan, December 10, 1932. admitted, 1958, Japan as Patent Attorney; 1967, Japan as Attorney at Law. *Education:* Tohoku University (B.A., Econ., 1955; LL.B., 1957); Legal Training and Research Institute. *Member:* The Japan Patent Attorneys Association; Second Tokyo Bar Association. *LANGUAGES:* Japanese and English.

KENJI KANEKO, born Chiba Prefecture, Japan, June 25, 1928. admitted, 1967, Japan as Patent Attorney. *Education:* Tokyo Institute of Technology (M.E., 1953). Examiner, Japanese Patent Office, 1960-1965. *Member:* The Japan Patent Attorneys Association. *LANGUAGES:* Japanese and English.

TOSHICHIRO NITTA, born Chiba Prefecture, Japan, November 21, 1930. admitted, 1957, Japan as Patent Attorney. *Education:* Chuo University (LL.B., 1954). *Member:* The Japan Patent Attorneys Association. *LANGUAGES:* Japanese and English.

SONOKO OGATA, born Tokyo, Japan, October 12, 1931. admitted, 1962, Japan as Patent Attorney. *Education:* Saitama University (B.A., 1954). *Member:* The Japan Patent Attorneys Association. *LANGUAGES:* Japanese, English and French.

SHOJI KAMON, born Fukui Prefecture, Japan, September 20, 1930; admitted, 1984, Japan as Patent Attorney. *Education:* Waseda University (B.E., 1952). Examiner, Trial-Examiner and Trial-Examiner-in-Chief, Japanese Patent Office, 1957-1968, 1972-1984. Technical Counselor, Tokyo District Court, 1968-1972. *Member:* The Japan Patent Attorneys Association. *LANGUAGES:* Japanese and English.

TOSHIJI USAMI, born Tokyo, Japan, March 31, 1933; admitted, 1983, Japan as Patent Attorney. *Education:* Waseda University (LL.B., 1956). Examiner and Examiner-in-Chief, Japanese Patent Office, 1964-1983. *Member:* The Japan Patent Attorneys Association. *LANGUAGES:* Japanese and English.

SEKIZO HAYASHI, born Gifu Prefecture, Japan, September 5, 1933; admitted, 1987, Japan as Patent Attorney. *Education:* Shizuoka University (B.E., 1956). Examiner-in-chief and Trial Examiner-in-chief, Japanese Patent Office, 1972-1987. Counselor: WIPO, 1969-1970; Tokyo High Court, 1983-1986. *Member:* The Japan Patent Attorneys Association. *LANGUAGES:* Japanese and English.

KAZUO HOSHIKAWA, born Zenra Hokudo, May 2, 1936; admitted, 1988, Japan as Patent Attorney. *Education:* Tokyo Institute of Technology (M.E., 1959). Examiner, Examiner-in-Chief and Trial Examiner-in-Chief, 1959-1987. Counselor for PCT and TRT Affairs, 1975-1977. Director, Documentation Division, 1981-1983 and Director, Industrial Property Training Institute, 1987-1988, Japanese Patent Office. Councillor, Asian Patent Attorneys Association, 1994—. *Member:* The Japan Patent Attorneys Association. *LANGUAGES:* Japanese and English.

YUKIO IWAMOTO, born Toyama Prefecture, Japan, May 4, 1938. admitted, 1975, Japan as Patent Attorney. *Education:* Meiji University (B.S., 1962). *Member:* The Japan Patent Attorneys Association. *LANGUAGES:* Japanese and English.

KOJI KIKAWA, born Chiba Prefecture, Japan, September 10, 1938; admitted, 1977, Japan as Patent Attorney. *Education:* Chiba University (B.Agri., 1963). *Member:* The Japan Patent Attorneys Association. *LANGUAGES:* Japanese and English.

KUNIAKI SHIMIZU, born Aichi Prefecture, Japan, September 10, 1941; admitted, 1984, Japan as Patent Attorney. *Education:* Meiji University (B.E., 1964). *Member:* The Japan Patent Attorneys Association. *LANGUAGES:* Japanese and English.

(This Listing Continued)

ASAMURA PATENT OFFICE, Tokyo—Continued

TOHRU MORI, born Kanagawa Prefecture, Japan, January 25, 1943. admitted, 1969, Japan as Patent Attorney. *Education:* Keio University (B.E., 1965). *Member:* The Japan Patent Attorneys Association. *LANGUAGES:* Japanese and English.

TERUO NAGANUMA, born Saitama Prefecture, Japan, September 28, 1947; admitted, 1982, Japan as Patent Attorney. *Education:* Tokyo University (M.Agri., 1974). *Member:* The Japan Patent Attorneys Association. *LANGUAGES:* Japanese, English and German.

OF COUNSEL

HARUO GOTO, born Niigata Prefecture, Japan, March 3, 1935; admitted, 1992, Japan as Patent Attorney. *Education:* Nihon University (LL.B., 1957). Examiner, 1974-1982. Director, PCT Affairs Office, 1982-1987. Examiner-in-Chief, Trial Examiner-in-Chief, 1987-1992. Director, Litigation Office, Japanese Patent Office, 1989-1991. Professor, Nihon University, 1994—. *Member:* The Japan Patent Attorneys Association. *LANGUAGES:* Japanese and English.

KAZUMI KAGEYAMA, born Shizuoka Prefecture, Japan, February 18, 1915. admitted, 1967, Japan as Patent Attorney. *Education:* Tokyo University (M.T., 1940). *Member:* The Japan Patent Attorneys Association. *LANGUAGES:* Japanese, English and German.

SHIROU MURATA, born Yamaguchi Prefecture, Japan, December 19, 1918. admitted, 1967, Japan as Patent Attorney. *Education:* Ryojun Institute of Technology (M.E., 1941). *Member:* The Japan Patent Attorneys Association. *LANGUAGES:* Japanese and English.

TATSUTO NISHI, born Ibaragi Prefecture, Japan, January 1, 1919. admitted, 1964, Japan as Patent Attorney. *Education:* Tohoku University (M.T., 1943). *Member:* The Japan Patent Attorneys Association. *LANGUAGES:* Japanese, English and German.

SHUN EBINE, born Chiba Prefecture, Japan, April 28, 1908. admitted, 1952, Japan as Patent Attorney. *Education:* Tokyo University (LL.B., 1931). Director, First Examination Department, 1947-1949 and Director, Appeal and Trial Department, 1949-1952, Japanese Patent Office. *Member:* The Japan Patent Attorneys Association (Vice President, 1967-1968). *LANGUAGES:* Japanese, English and French.

YUKIHIRO TATEISHI, born Fukuoka Prefecture, Japan, November 27, 1920. admitted, 1959, Japan as Patent Attorney. *Education:* Kyushu University (LL.B., 1947). Examiner, Japanese Patent Office, 1952-1957. *Member:* The Japan Patent Attorneys Association. *LANGUAGES:* Japanese and English.

ASSOCIATES

YUTAKA YOSHIDA, born Kogendo, Korea, June 26, 1941; admitted, 1981, Japan as Patent Attorney. *Education:* Kyushu University (B.E., 1965). Examiner, Japanese Patent Office, 1968-1981. *Member:* The Japan Patent Attorneys Association. *LANGUAGES:* Japanese and English.

TAKAKAZU YAMAMOTO, born Miyazaki Prefecture, Japan, May 16, 1943; admitted, 1986, Japan as Patent Attorney. *Education:* Kumamoto University (M.E., 1969). Examiner and Trial Examiner, Japanese Patent Office, 1969-1986. *Member:* The Japan Patent Attorneys Association. *LANGUAGES:* Japanese and English.

HIDEO IWAI, born Tokyo, Japan, November 25, 1947; admitted, 1976, Japan as Patent Attorney. *Education:* Aoyama-Gakuin University (LL.B., 1970). *Member:* The Japan Patent Attorneys Association. *LANGUAGES:* Japanese and English.

TAKASHI JIBU, born Okayame Prefecture, Japan, March 19, 1948; admitted, 1989, Japan as Patent Attorney. *Education:* Shizuoka University (B.Sc., 1971); Tohoku University (M.Sc., 1973). *Member:* The Japan Patent Attorneys Association. *LANGUAGES:* Japanese and English.

NORIO TAKANASHI, born Chiba Prefecture, Japan, June 24, 1950. admitted, 1981, Japan as Patent Attorney. *Education:* Rikkyo University (LL.B., 1974). *Member:* The Japan Patent Attorneys Association. *LANGUAGES:* Japanese and English.

MASAHIRO MURAKAMI, born Akita Prefecture, Japan, February 11, 1931; admitted, 1989, Japan as Patent Attorney. *Education:* Chuo University (1961-1963). Examiner, Trial Examiner and Senior Examiner, 1971-1988, Japanese Patent Office. *Member:* The Japan Patent Attorneys Association. *LANGUAGES:* Japanese, English and French.

(This Listing Continued)

SADAFUMI KOBORI, born Kumamoto Prefecture, Japan, January 3, 1942; admitted, 1983, Japan as Patent Attorney. *Education:* Kyushu University (B.Chem., 1965). *Member:* The Japan Patent Attorneys Association. *LANGUAGES:* Japanese and English.

MASAHARU SEKI, born Niigata Prefecture, Japan, November 20, 1944; admitted, 1993, Japan as Patent Attorney. *Education:* Tokyo University (B.E., 1967). *Member:* The Japan Patent Attorneys Association. *LANGUAGES:* Japanese and English.

CHIZUKO TAKAHARA, born Gunma Prefecture, Japan, January 3, 1947; admitted, 1971, Japan as Patent Attorney. *Education:* Chuo University (LL.B., 1969). *Member:* The Japan Patent Attorneys Association. *LANGUAGES:* Japanese and English.

MITSUO OKANO, born Wakayama Prefecture, Japan, October 25, 1950; admitted, 1990, Japan as Patent Attorney. *Education:* Musashino Art University (B.A., 1974). *Member:* The Japan Patent Attorneys Association. *LANGUAGES:* Japanese and English.

REIJI SUZUKI, born Shizuoka Prefecture, Japan, April 4, 1953; admitted, 1992, Japan as Patent Attorney. *Education:* Gakushuin University (LL.B., 1976). *Member:* The Japan Patent Attorneys Association. *LANGUAGES:* Japanese and English.

ITSUKO KAJIWARA, born Osaka, Japan, April 1, 1957; admitted, 1988, Japan as Patent Attorney. *Education:* Osaka University of Foreign Studies (B.A., 1981); Kyoto University (B.E., 1985). *Member:* The Japan Patent Attorneys Association. *LANGUAGES:* Japanese and English.

YUKIHIRO IKEDA, born Tokyo, Japan, April 11, 1957; admitted, 1992, Japan as Patent Attorney. *Education:* Tokyo University (B.Pharm., 1981). *Member:* The Japan Patent Attorneys Association. *LANGUAGES:* Japanese and English.

KIMIKO YANO, born Tokyo, Japan, January 21, 1958; admitted, 1986, Japan as Patent Attorney. *Education:* Keio University (B.A., 1980). *Member:* The Japan Patent Attorneys Association. *LANGUAGES:* Japanese, English and French.

RYOJI MOCHIZUKI, born Yamanashi Prefecture, Japan, February 24, 1959; admitted, 1986, Japan as Patent Attorney. *Education:* Waseda University (B.C.S., 1982). *Member:* The Japan Patent Attorneys Association. *LANGUAGES:* Japanese and English.

TOMIMASA KONISHI, born Aichi Prefecture, Japan, April 16, 1959; admitted, 1987, Japan as Patent Attorney. *Education:* Nagoya University (B.Chem., 1982). *Member:* The Japan Patent Attorneys Association. *LANGUAGES:* Japanese and English.

KAZUHIRO MIYAGI, born Oita Prefecture, Japan March 13, 1960; admitted, 1994, Japan as Patent Attorney. *Education:* Chuo University (LL.B., 1982). *Member:* Japan Patent Attorneys Association. *LANGUAGES:* Japanese and English.

SADAHARU KATO, born Tokyo, Japan, March 4, 1961; admitted, 1992, Japan; 1994, Japan as Patent Attorney. *Education:* Tokyo University (LL.B., 1985); Legal Training and Research Institute (1992). *Member:* Daiichi Tokyo Bar Association; Japan Patent Attorneys Association. *LANGUAGES:* Japanese and English.

MAKOTO SHIOTANI, born Osaka, Japan, September 18, 1961; admitted, 1991, Japan as Patent Attorney. *Education:* Nihon University (LL.B., 1985). *Member:* The Japan Patent Attorneys Association. *LANGUAGES:* Japanese and English.

AKIKO YAMAGUCHI, born Tokyo, Japan, March 22, 1965; admitted, 1994, Japan as Patent Attorney. *Education:* Chiba University (B.Pharm., 1987). *LANGUAGES:* Japanese and English.

ASHURST MORRIS CRISP

KIOICHO BUILDING, 8TH FLOOR
3-12 KIOICHO
CHIYODA-KU
TOKYO 102, JAPAN
Telephone: (81-3) 5276 5900
Fax: (81-3) 5276 5922

London, England Office: Broadwalk House, 5 Appold Street, EC2A 2HA. Telephone: 0171-638-1111. Telex: 887067. Fax: 0171-972-7990.
Brussels, Belgium Office: Avenue Louise 65, 1050. Telephone: (32-2) 537 6895. Fax: (32-2) 537 4353.

(This Listing Continued)

Paris, France Office: 8, rue Clément Marot, 75008. Telephone: (33-1) 47 20 0088. Fax: (33-1) 47 20 0093.

New Delhi, India Office: 6 Aurangzeb Road D-202. 110011. Telephone: (91 11) 301 4054. Facsimile: (91 11) 301 4089.

General and International law practice engaged in Corporate, Banking, Mergers and Acquisitions, Employment, Tax, Immigration, Intellectual Property, Joint Ventures, Competition, Property Investment and Development Work under the Laws of England, France and the EC.

RESIDENT PARTNER

A.W.N. Kitchin

ATSUMI & USUI

614 SHUWA KIOICHO TBR BUILDING
5-7, KOJIMACHI, CHIYODA-KU
TOKYO 102, JAPAN
Telephone: (81) 3-5276-6131
Facsimile: (81) 3-5276-6235/6292

International and Cross-border Financial Transactions, Capital Markets, M&A, Corporate Law, Litigation, Martime, Taxation, Labor and Intellectual Property Matters.

FIRM PROFILE: Mr. Hiroo Atsumi and Mr. Yoshimasa Usui established "ATSUMI & USUI" on August 11, 1994.

MICHIAKI MAKINO, born 1930; admitted, 1967, Japan. *Education:* Graduated, Nagoya University (LL.B., 1954); The Legal Training and Research Institute of the Supreme Court of Japan. *Member:* Second Tokyo Bar Association. *LANGUAGES:* Japanese, English.

HIROO ATSUMI, born 1948; admitted, 1977, Japan; 1982, New York. *Education:* Graduated, The University of Tokyo (LL.B., 1973); The Legal Training and Research Institute of the Supreme Court of Japan; New York University School of Law (M.C.J., 1981). *Member:* Second Tokyo Bar Association; New York State Bar Association. *LANGUAGES:* Japanese and English.

YOSHIMASA USUI, born 1949; admitted, 1978, Japan; 1983, New York. *Education:* Graduated, The University of Tokyo (LL.B., 1973); The Legal Training and Research Institute of the Supreme Court of Japan; University of Pennsylvania Law School (LL.M., 1981). *Member:* The First Tokyo Bar Association; New York State Bar Association. *LANGUAGES:* Japanese and English.

YOSHIKO OHSHIMA, born 1956; admitted, 1988, Japan. *Education:* Graduated, Keio University (LL.B., 1980); The Legal Training and Research Institute of the Supreme Court of Japan. *First Tokyo Bar Association. LANGUAGES:* Japanese and English.

KAORU HARAGUCHI, born 1956; admitted, 1989, Japan. *Education:* Graduated, Chuo University (LL.B., 1979); The Legal Training and Research Institute of the Supreme Court of Japan; University of Chicago (LL.M., 1994). *Member:* Tokyo Bar Association. *LANGUAGES:* Japanese and English.

EIJI YAMAHARA, born 1962; admitted, 1992, Japan. *Education:* Graduated, Waseda University (LL.B., 1987); The Legal Training and Research Institute of the Supreme Court of Japan. *Member:* Tokyo Bar Association. *LANGUAGES:* Japanese and English.

HIROAKI TAKAHASHI, born 1961; admitted, 1992, Japan. *Education:* Graduated, The University of Tokyo (LL.B., 1987); The Legal Training and Research Institute of the Supreme Court of Japan (1992). *Member:* Second Tokyo Bar Association. *LANGUAGES:* Japanese and English.

MISAKO SUZUKI, born 1962; admitted, 1994, Japan. *Education:* Graduated, Waseda University (LL.B., 1984); The Legal Training and Research Institute of the Supreme Court of Japan. *Member:* Second Tokyo Bar Association. *LANGUAGES:* Japanese, English and Spanish.

THE BABA LAW OFFICE

Established in 1952

404 HIBIYA PARK BUILDING
8-1, YURAKUCHO 1-CHOME, CHIYODA-KU
TOKYO 100, JAPAN
Telephone: 03-3271-1857; 03-3271-1858
Fax: 03-3213-4857
Commercial, Civil, Labor and Antitrust Law.

TOSAKU BABA, born Kōbe, Japan, May 24, 1909; admitted, 1946, Japan. *Education:* Tokyo University; Tokyo University Law School (LL.B., 1927). Editor-in-Chief, "Hanrei-Times" (Journal of Jurisprudence), 1949-1960. Author: "Theory and Practice of American Government Contract," 1953; "Practical Problems in the Labor Law," 1962. Proctor, Japanese Prize-Courts, 1942-1944. Defence Counsel, War-Crimes Tribunals, Yokohama, Tokyo and Manus Island, 1945-1951. Member: International Private Law Section, 1963-1965 and Commercial Law Section, 1976-1978, Government Legislative Council. *Member:* First Tokyo (Vice Chairman of Council, 1956-1958; Vice President, 1960-1961; Chairman of Council, 1974-1975) and Japanese Federated Bar Associations. [Judge-Advocate of Japanese Navy (Commander), 1932-1945]. *LANGUAGES:* Japanese, English, French and German.

ASSOCIATES

FUMIHIKO MITSUDA, born Tokyo, Japan, February 25, 1911; admitted, 1981, Japan. *Education:* Tokyo University; Tokyo University Law School (LL.B., 1934). Judge of Tokyo District Court, 1937-1957. Judge of Tokyo High Court, 1957-1976. *Member:* First Tokyo and Japanese Federated Bar Associations.

KOICHI TAKATSU, born Tokyo, Japan, August 29, 1942; admitted, 1971, Japan. *Education:* Tokyo University; Tokyo University Law School. Assistant in Tokyo University Law School (Civil Law) 1965-1968. Tutor in Tokyo University Law School (Antitrust) 1968-1969. *Member:* First Tokyo and Japanese Federated Bar Associations. *LANGUAGES:* Japanese, English, German and French.

ICHIRO TAKAHASHI, born Yamagata, Japan, February 5, 1954; admitted, 1981, Japan. *Education:* Tōhoku University; Tōhoku University Law School. *Member:* First Tokyo and Japanese Federated Bar Associations. *LANGUAGES:* Japanese, English and German.

Languages: Japanese, English, German and French.

REPRESENTATIVE CLIENTS: Sony Corp.; The Tokyo Electric Power Inc.; Esso Sekiyu K.K.
REFERENCES: Volney F. Morin Law Offices, Los Angeles, California.

BLAKEMORE & MITSUKI

Established in 1950

912 IINO BUILDING
1-1, UCHISAIWAI-CHO 2-CHOME, CHIYODA-KU
TOKYO 100, JAPAN
Telephone: (03) 3503-5571
Cable Address: "Blakelaw Tokyo"
Telex: J25296 BANDM
Telefax: (03) 3503-4707; (03) 3591-7087

REVISERS OF THE JAPAN LAW DIGEST FOR THIS DIRECTORY.

Seattle, Washington Associated Office: Griffith Way, 1201 Third Avenue, 40th Floor, 98101-3099. Telephone: 206-583-8778. Telex: 320319 PERKINS SEA. Telefax: 206-583-8500.

San Francisco, California Associated Office: Rosser H. Brockman, Citicorp Center, One Sansome Street, Suite 1900, 94104-4405. Telephone: 415-362-4040. Telefax: 415-951-4660.

General Practice, Trial, Arbitration, Antitrust, Bankruptcy, Corporation, Corporate Reorganization, Finance, Foreign Investments, Intellectual Property, Securities and Taxation.

MEMBERS OF FIRM

THOMAS L. BLAKEMORE (1915-1994).

MASATSUGU MITSUKI, admitted, 1950, Japan. *Education:* Graduated, Tokyo Imperial University, 1947. *LANGUAGES:* Japanese, English.

TETSU TANAKA, admitted, 1957, Japan. *Education:* Graduated, Kyushu University, 1953. *LANGUAGES:* Japanese, English.

(This Listing Continued)

BLAKEMORE & MITSUKI, Tokyo—Continued

YOSHIHIRO TAKENOSHITA, admitted, 1973, Japan. *Education:* Graduated, The University of Tokyo (B.Agr., 1965; M.Agr., 1967; LL.B., 1970); Dickinson School of Law (M.C.L., 1988). *LANGUAGES:* Japanese, English.

HIDEYUKI SAKAI, admitted, 1976, Japan. *Education:* Graduated, The University of Tokyo, 1974; Duke University School of Law (LL.M., 1982). *LANGUAGES:* Japanese, English.

TAKAKI TOKUOKA, admitted, 1981, Japan. *Education:* Graduated, The University of Tokyo (LL.B., 1977; LL.M., 1979); Harvard Law School (LL.M., 1985). *LANGUAGES:* Japanese, English.

ICHIRO OTSUKA, admitted, 1981, Japan; 1988, New York. *Education:* Graduated, Kyoto University, 1979; Cornell Law School (LL.M., 1988). *LANGUAGES:* Japanese, English.

TAKASHI HIRANO, admitted, 1985, Japan. *Education:* Graduated, Chuo University, 1980. *LANGUAGES:* Japanese, English.

YUTAKA SAKAI, admitted, 1985, Japan. *Education:* Graduated, Keio University, 1980; University of London (LL.M., 1990). *LANGUAGES:* Japanese, English.

KAZUKO SUMITA, admitted, 1989, Japan. *Education:* Graduated, The University of Tokyo, 1980. *LANGUAGES:* Japanese, English.

FUMIE OMURA, admitted, 1994, Japan. *Education:* Graduated, Keio University, 1984. *LANGUAGES:* Japanese, English and Russian (reading only).

REVISERS OF THE JAPAN LAW DIGEST FOR THIS DIRECTORY.

BRAUN MORIYA HOASHI & KUBOTA

Established in 1955

911 IINO BUILDING
1-1, 2-CHOME, UCHISAIWAI-CHO, CHIYODA-KU
TOKYO 100, JAPAN
Telephone: 81-3-3504-0251
Cable Address: "Japanattorney"
Telex: 0 222-3753
Telefax: 81-3-3595-0985

International Matters, Corporation, Finance, Foreign Investments, Taxation, Admiralty Law and General Civil and Trial Practice.

MICHAEL A. BRAUN (1913-1992).

HIDETAKA MORIYA, born Kagawa, Japan, October 22, 1930; admitted, 1957, Japan. *Education:* Chuo University (LL.B., 1954); The Legal Institute of the Supreme Court. *Member:* Japan Commercial Arbitration Association (Panel of Arbitrators); The Japan Shipping Exchange, Inc. (Panel of Arbitrators); First Tokyo Bar Association; Japan Maritime Law Association (Councilor); Comité Maritime International (Titular Member). *LANGUAGES:* Japanese and English. *PRACTICE AREAS:* Admiralty and Maritime Law; Environmental Law.

AKIO HOASHI (1935-1993).

TAKEO KUBOTA, born Osaka, Japan, January 28, 1930; admitted, 1963, Japan. *Education:* Hokkaido University, fishery course; Chuo University (LL.B., 1960); The Legal Training and Research Institute of the Supreme Court. *Member:* Panel of Arbitrators; The Japan Shipping Exchange, Inc.; Tokyo Bar Association; The Japan Maritime Law Association (Councilor). *LANGUAGES:* Japanese and English. *PRACTICE AREAS:* Admiralty and Maritime Law.

HIDESHIGE HARUKI, born Gumma, Japan, July 29, 1940; admitted, 1966, Japan. *Education:* Waseda University (LL.B., 1964); The Legal Training and Research Institute of the Supreme Court; University of Pennsylvania Law School (LL.M., 1971). Associated with Mayer Brown & Platt, Chicago, Illinois, 1971-1972. *Member:* Second Tokyo Bar Association. *LANGUAGES:* Japanese and English. *PRACTICE AREAS:* Business Law; Corporate Law; Licensing; Finance; Mergers and Acquisitions; Real Estate; Securities.

CHISEKO FUKUDA, born Hyogo, Japan, January 10, 1946; admitted, 1972, Japan. *Education:* Keio University (LL.B., 1969); The Legal Training and Research Institute of the Supreme Court; New York University Law School (LL.M., 1977). Associated with Lovejoy, Wasson, Lundgren &

(This Listing Continued)

Ashton, New York, 1977 and with Merrill Lynch International & Co., New York, 1978. *Member:* First Tokyo Bar Association; Committee to the International Finance Bureau of the Ministry of Finance of Japan. *LANGUAGES:* Japanese and English. *PRACTICE AREAS:* Business Law; Corporate Law; Licensing; Finance; Securities; Mergers and Acquisitions.

NOBUTO YAMAGUCHI, born Tokyo, Japan, May 28, 1953; admitted, 1980, Japan. *Education:* Waseda University (LL.B., 1978); The Legal Training and Research Institute of the Supreme Court; University of Washington (LL.M., 1981). *Member:* First Tokyo Bar Association; The Law Association of Asia and Pacific; Japan-Korea Lawyers Council. *LANGUAGES:* Japanese and English. *PRACTICE AREAS:* Vessel Finance; Admiralty and Maritime Law; Bankruptcy; Business Law; Finance.

NORIKO SAWAI, born Tokyo, Japan, September 12, 1948; admitted, 1978, Japan. *Education:* Hitotsubashi University (LL.B., 1971); The Legal Training and Research Institute of the Supreme Court. Associated with Richards & O'Neil, New York, N.Y., 1981-1982. *Member:* Second Tokyo Bar Association. *LANGUAGES:* Japanese and English. *PRACTICE AREAS:* Business Law; Corporate Law.

SHOJI USHIJIMA, born Kumamoto, Japan, May 4, 1953; admitted, 1986, Japan. *Education:* Tokyo University (LL.B., 1978); The Legal Training and Research Institute of the Supreme Court; University of Illinois (LL.M., 1991). Associated with Richards & O'Neil, New York, N.Y., 1991-1992. *Member:* First Tokyo Bar Association. *LANGUAGES:* Japanese and English.

YASUMASA MASUMOTO, born Fukuoka, Japan, December 20, 1945; admitted, 1975, Japan; 1990 New York and California. *Education:* Tokyo University (LL.B., 1969); The Legal Training and Research Institute of the Supreme Court; Duke University School of Law (LL.M., 1989). Associated with Healy & Baillie, New York, 1989; Nixon Hargrave, Devans & Doyle, New York, 1990; Haight, Gardner, Poor & Havens, New York, 1990. *Member:* Tokyo Bar Association. *LANGUAGES:* Japanese and English. *PRACTICE AREAS:* Admiralty and Maritime Law.

JINYA YASHIGE, born Okayama, Japan, November 8, 1960; admitted, 1990, Japan. *Education:* Hitotsubashi University (LL.B., 1986); The Legal Training and Research Institute of the Supreme Court. *Member:* First Tokyo Bar Association. *LANGUAGES:* Japanese and English.

FUMIKO SOEJIMA, born Fukuoka, Japan, October 4, 1964; admitted, 1991, Japan. *Education:* Hitotsubashi University (LL.B., 1987); The Legal Training and Research Institute of the Supreme Court. *Member:* The Second Tokyo Bar Association. *LANGUAGES:* Japanese and English.

MASATOSHI IKEUCHI, born Tokyo, Japan, May 3, 1962; admitted, 1991, Japan. *Education:* Chuo University (LL.B., 1985); The Legal Training and Research Institute of the Supreme Court. *Member:* First Tokyo Bar Association. *LANGUAGES:* Japanese and English.

BROWN & WOOD

(Craig E. Chapman Gaikokuho-Jimu-Bengoshi Jimusho)

SHIROYAMA JT MORI BUILDING
15TH FLOOR
3-1 TORANOMON 4-CHOME, MINATO-KU
TOKYO 105, JAPAN
Telephone: 011-813-5472-5360
Facsimile: 011-813-5472-5058

New York, New York Office: One World Trade Center, 10048-0557. *Telephone:* 212-839-5300.
San Francisco, California Office: 555 California Street, 94101-1715. *Telephone:* 415-772-1200.
Washington, D.C. Office: 815 Connecticut Avenue, N.W., Suite 701, 20006-4004.
Telephone: 202-973-0600.
Los Angeles, California Office: 10900 Wilshire Boulevard, 90024-3959. *Telephone:* 310-443-0200.
London, England Office: Guildhall Yard. *Telephone:* 0171-606-1888.
Trenton, New Jersey Office: 172 West State Street, 08608-1104. *Telephone:* 609-393-0303.
Hong Kong Office: Suite 2606, Asia Pacific Finance Tower, Citibank Plaza, 3 Garden Road, Central. *Telephone:* 011-852-2509-7888.

Firm Engaged in American and International Law Practice but not authorized to appear before Japanese courts or to act as Japanese Bengoshi.

(This Listing Continued)

RESIDENT PARTNER

CRAIG E. CHAPMAN, born Norwich, Connecticut, June 5, 1954; admitted, 1981, New York; 1992, Japan (Gaikokuho-Jimu-Bengoshi). *Education:* Connecticut College (B.A., 1977); Case Western Reserve University (J.D., 1980).

RESIDENT ASSOCIATE

STEPHANIE M. OANA, born Port Huron, Michigan, May 25, 1965; admitted, 1993, New York (Not admitted in Japan). *Education:* Harvard-/Radcliffe (A.B., 1987); University of Michigan (J.D., 1991).

(For Complete Biographical Data on all Partners and Associates, see Professional Biographies at New York, New York)

BRUCKHAUS WESTRICK STEGEMANN

ARK MORI BUILDING, 22F
12-32, AKASAKA 1-CHOME
MINATO-KU TOKYO 107, JAPAN
Telephone: (81-3) 5561-0236
Telefax: (81-3) 5561-0238

Düsseldorf, Germany Office: Freiligrathstrasse 1, 40479 Düsseldorf. Telephone: (0211) 49 79-0. Telefax: (0211) 49 79-103. Telex: 858 7027 JUS D.

Frankfurt am Main, Germany Office: Taunusanlage 11, 60329 Frankfurt am Main. Telephone: (069) 27308-0. Telefax: (069) 232664. Telex: 41 49 17 WEST CD.

Hamburg, Germany Office: Alsterarkaden 27, 20354 Hamburg. Telephone: (040) 36 90 60. Telefax:(040) 36 906-155. Telex: 212 522 EURO D.

Berlin, Germany Office: Friedrichstrasse 95 (IHZ), 10117 Berlin. Telephone: (030) 26 43-3303. Telefax: (030) 26 43-3366.

Leipzig Office: Grimmaische Strasse 25, 04109, Leipzig. Telephone: (0341) 127230. Telefax: (0341) 1272333.

Brussels, Belgium Office: Rue de la Loi 99/101, B-1040 Brussels. Telephone: 32-2 2 87 26 11. Telefax: 32-2 2 30 39 03.

New York, New York Office: 767 Fifth Avenue, GM Building, New York 10153. Telephone: (212) 486-1100. Telefax: (212) 759-3151.

Moscow, Russia Office: Malyj Gnezknikovskij per. 9 No. 2, 103009 Moscow. Telephone: (7-503) 9562300; (7-501) 9401200. Telefax: (7-503) 9562301; (7-501) 9401211.

Corporate Law, Commercial Law, Mergers, Acquisitions and Divestitures, Joint Ventures, Banks and Banking, Finance, Securities, Capital Markets, Leases and Leasing, Equipment Finance, Aircraft Finance and Leasing, Antitrust and Trade Regulation, German and EC Cartel Law, Competition, Unfair Trade, Intellectual Property (trademarks, patents, copyrights), Taxation, Property, Real Estate, Energy, Natural Resources, Environmental Law, Administrative Law, Computers and Software, Food and Drug, Biotechnology, Labour and Employment, Products Liability, Insurance, Litigation, Arbitration, Broadcasting, Telecommunications, Aviation, Subsidies and State Aids, Construction Law, Zoning, Planning and Land Use, Customs and Foreign Trade Law, European Community Law, German-French Investments, Russian and Post Soviet Commerce.

MEMBER OF FIRM

Christian Bunsen, Licensed as Gaikokuho-Jimu-Bengoshi

BUNKYO SOGO LAW OFFICES

Established in 1971

3-18-11 HONGO, BUNKYO-KU
TOKYO 113, JAPAN
Telephone: 81-3-3813-6544
Fax: 81-3-3814-0252

General Practice. Civil, Criminal and International Litigation, Corporate, Real Estate, Personal Injury, Family Law, Consumer Protection, Environmental Law, Workers Compensation.

MEMBERS OF FIRM

TOSHIRO UEYANAGI, admitted, 1983, Japan; 1992, New York. *Education:* University of Tokyo, Legal Training and Research Institute (Diploma, 1983); University of Washington (LL.M., 1990). *Member:* Dai-ichi Tokyo Bar Association; Japan Federation of Bar Associations; New York State Bar.

(This Listing Continued)

NOBUO KOJIMA, admitted, 1984, Japan. *Education:* Waseda University; Legal Training and Research Institute (Diploma, 1984). *Member:* Tokyo Bar Association; Japan Federation of Bar Associations.

HIROSHI KAWAHITO, admitted, 1978, Japan. *Education:* The University of Tokyo; Legal Training and Research Institute (Diploma, 1978). *Member:* Tokyo Bar Association; Japan Federation of Bar Associations.

YOKO KUROIWA, admitted, 1981, Japan. *Education:* Chuo University; Legal Training and Research Institute (Diploma, 1981). *Member:* Tokyo Bar Association; Japan Federation of Bar Associations.

KAZUNARI TAMAKI, admitted, 1985, Japan. *Education:* Chuo University; Legal Training and Research Institute (Diploma, 1985). *Member:* Tokyo Bar Association; Japan Federation of Bar Associations.

MANABU SUNOSE, admitted, 1986, Japan. *Education:* The University of Tokyo; Legal Training and Research Institute (Diploma, 1986). *Member:* Tokyo Bar Association; Japan Federation of Bar Associations.

MASAYUKI SAKAMOTO, admitted, 1993, Japan. *Education:* Kyoto University; Legal Training and Research Institute (Diploma, 1993). *Member:* Daini Tokyo Bar Association; Japan Federation of Bar Associations.

Languages: Japanese and English.

RICHARD V. BURGUJIAN
GAIKOKUHO JIMU BENGOSHI JIMUSHO

TORANOMON NO. 45 MORI BUILDING, THIRD FLOOR
1-5, TORONOMON 5-CHOME MINATO-KU
TOKYO, JAPAN
Telephone: 0081-3-3431-6943
Facsimile: 0081-3-3431-6945

Washington, D.C. Office: Finnegan, Henderson, Farabow, Garrett & Dunner, Suite 700, 1300 I Street, N.W., 20005-3315. Telephone: 202-408-4000. Facsimile: 202-408-4400. ITT Telex: 440275 ITT; RCA Telex: 248740 FHFG. Cable Address: "Finderbow".

Brussels, Belgium Office: Finnegan, Henderson, Farabow, Garrett & Dunner, Avenue Louise 326, Box 37, 1050. Telephone: 011-322-646-0353. Facsimile: 011-322-646-2135.

Firm engaged in U.S. and International Intellectual Property Law Practice but not authorized to appear before Japanese Courts or to act as Japanese Attorneys.

RESIDENT ATTORNEY

RICHARD V. BURGUJIAN, born New York, New York, August 11, 1949; admitted, 1985, New Jersey and U.S. District Court, District of New Jersey; 1987, New York; 1989, District of Columbia; registered to practice before U.S. Patent and Trademark Office (Not admitted in Japan). *Education:* Stevens Institute of Technology (B.E., 1971); Rensselaer Polytechnic Institute (M.E., 1972); Fairleigh Dickinson University (M.S., 1975); Rutgers University School of Law (J.D., 1984). Licensed Professional Engineer, New Jersey. *Member:* The District of Columbia Bar; American Bar Association; Institute of Electrical and Electronic Engineers; American Intellectual Property Law Association.

CLEARY, GOTTLIEB, STEEN & HAMILTON

(Morgan Carroll Terai Gaikokuho Jimubengoshi Jimusho)

Established in 1946

SHIN KASUMIGASEKI BUILDING
20TH FLOOR, 3-2, KASUMIGASEKI 3-CHOME, CHIYODA-KU
TOKYO 100, JAPAN
Telephone: 81-3-3595-3911
Cable Address: "Cleargolaw, Tokyo"
Telex: 28546 CGSHTYO
Facsimile: (81) (3) 3595-3910

New York, New York Office: One Liberty Plaza, New York, N.Y. 10006. Telephone: 212-225-2000.

Washington, D.C. Office: 1752 N Street, N.W., Washington, D.C. 20036. Telephone: 202-728-2700.

Paris, France Office: 41, Avenue de Friedland, 75008 Paris, France. Telephone: 33-1-4074-6800.

(This Listing Continued)

CLEARY, GOTTLIEB, STEEN & HAMILTON, Tokyo—Continued

Brussels, Belgium Office: Rue de la Loi 23, Bte 5, 1040 Brussels, Belgium. Telephone: 32-2-287-2000.

London, England Office: City Place House, 55 Basinghall Street, London EC2V 5EH England. Telephone: 44-71-614-2200.

Hong Kong Office: 56th Floor, Bank of China Tower, One Garden Road, Hong Kong. Telephone: 852-521-4122.

Frankfurt, Germany Office: Ulmenstrasse 37-39, 60325 Frankfurt am Main, Germany. Telephone: 49-69-971-03-0.

American and International Practice as Morgan Carroll Terai Gaikokuho Jimubengoshi Jimusho. Not authorized to appear before the Japanese Courts or otherwise to act as Bengoshi.

RESIDENT PARTNERS

TSUNEMASA TERAI, born Tokyo, Japan, December 27, 1949; admitted, 1976, Japan (withdrew, 1991); 1982, New York; 1991, Japan as Gaikokuho-Jimu-Bengoshi. *Education:* Keio University (Bachelor of Arts in Law, 1972, Valedictorian; Master of Arts in Law, 1974); Institute of Legal Research and Training of the Supreme Court, Tokyo (1976); University of Michigan (LL.M., 1981). Resident in New York, 1982-1991. *Member:* Association of the Bar of the City of New York; American Bar Association; The First Tokyo Bar Association.

DONALD L. MORGAN, born Houston, Texas, January 21, 1934; admitted, 1962, District of Columbia; 1992, Japan as Gaikokuho Jimu Bengoshi. *Education:* Harvard College (A.B., magna cum laude, 1956); Harvard Law School (LL.B., magna cum laude, 1962). Articles Editor, Harvard Law Review, 1961-1962. *Member:* The District of Columbia Bar; American Bar Association; The First Tokyo Bar Association.

ASSOCIATES

THOMAS M. DOYLE II, born Lansing, Michigan, September 14, 1964; admitted, 1990, Michigan; 1991, District of Columbia (Not admitted in Japan). *Education:* Harvard University (B.A., magna cum laude, 1987); Stanford University (J.D.,1990). Member, Stanford Law Review, 1988-1990. Member, Stanford Journal of International Law, 1988-1990. Resident at: Washington Office, 1990-1994; Tokyo Office, 1994—. *Member:* The District of Columbia Bar; State Bar of Michigan.

JOSEPH M. TITLEBAUM, born Boston, Massachusetts, March 11, 1963; admitted, 1990, Massachusetts; 1991, New York (Not admitted in Japan). *Education:* Columbia University (A.B., cum laude, 1985); Harvard Law School (J.D., cum laude, 1989). Managing Editor, Harvard Human Rights Yearbook, 1988-1989. Legal Trainee, Tomotsune, Kimura & Mitomi, Tokyo, Japan, 1989-1990. Resident at New York Office, 1990-1992; Tokyo Office, 1992—. *Member:* American Bar Association.

PETER A. E. SWANGER, born Burea, Ohio, January 11, 1963; admitted, 1994, New York (Not admitted in Japan). *Education:* Earlham College (B.A., 1985); Harvard University (M.A., 1990); Harvard Law School (J.D., 1993). Managing Editor, International Law Journal. Resident at New York Office, 1993-1994; Tokyo Office, 1994—.

(For biographical data of the partners resident in other offices of the Firm, see Professional Biographies at New York, N.Y., Washington, D.C., Brussels, Belgium, London, England, Paris, France, Hong Kong and Frankfurt, Germany).

CLIFFORD CHANCE

Established in 1987

6TH FLOOR, SOUTH HILL NAGATACHO BUILDING
11-30 NAGATACHO 1-CHOME
CHIYODA-KU
TOKYO 100, JAPAN
Telephone: (81 3) 3581 4311
Fax: (81 3) 3593 0651

Amsterdam, The Netherlands Office: Apollolaan 171, 1077 AS, P.O. Box 7301, 1007 JH. Telephone: (31 20) 577 71 11. Fax: (31 20) 676 93 26.

Bahrain, Manama Associated Office: Law Office of Shaikh Isa bin Mohammed Al Khalifa. P.O. Box 20717. Telephone: (973) 531535; 531073. Fax: (973) 536272; 530608.

Barcelona, Spain Office: Pau Claris 102, 08009. Telephone: (34 3) 318 68 64. Fax: (34 3) 317 73 23.

Brussels, Belgium Office: Avenue Louise 65, Box 2, 1050. Telephone: (32 2) 533 59 11. Fax: (32 2) 533 59 59.

(This Listing Continued)

Budapest, Hungary Office: Köves & Partners, Clifford Chance. Madách Trade Center, Madách Imre Út 14, 1075. Telephone: (36 1) 268 1600. Fax: (36 1) 268 1610.

Dubai, United Arab Emirates Office: 18th Floor, Dubai World Trade Centre, P.O. Box 9380. Telephone: (971 4) 314333. Fax: (971 4) 313990; 314565.

Frankfurt/Main, Germany Office: Friedrichstraße 2-6, 60323. Telephone: (49 69) 971 4090. Fax: (49 69) 971 40977.

Hanoi, Vietnam Office: 52 Nguyen Binh Khiem. Telephone: (844) 229 182/3/4/5/6. Fax: (844) 229 190.

Hong Kong Office: 30th Floor, Jardine House, One Connaught Place. Telephone: (852) 2810 0229. Fax: (852) 2810 4708; 2810 4858; 2810 4743.

London, England Office: 200 Aldersgate Street, EC1A 4JJ. Telephone: (44 171) 600 1000. Fax: (44 171) 600 5555.

Madrid, Spain Office: Paseo de la Castellana 110, 28046. Telephone: (34 1) 562 7674. Fax: (34 1) 562 49 93.

Milan, Italy Associated Office: Grimaldi e Clifford Chance. Via Gesú, 3, 20121. Telephone: (39 2) 7600 8040. Fax: (39 2) 7600 4950.

Moscow, Russia Office: Ul. Sadovaya - Samotechnaya 24/27, 2nd Floor, 103051. Telephone: (7 501) 258 50 50. Fax: (7 501) 258 50 51.

New York, New York Office: Swiss Bank Tower, 10 East 50th Street, 10022. Telephone: (1 212) 750 1440. Fax: (1 212) 758 6625.

Paris, France Office: 112 avenue Kléber, BP 163 Trocadéro, 75770 Paris Cedex 16. Telephone: (33 1) 44 05 52 52. Fax: (33 1) 44 05 52 00.

Riyadh, Saudi Arabia Associated Office: The Law Firm of Salah Al-Hejailan. P.O. Box 1454, 11431. Telephone: (966 1) 479 2200. Fax: (966 1) 479 1717.

Rome, Italy Associated Office: Grimaldi e Clifford Chance. Viale G. Rossini 7, 00198. Telephone: (39 6) 807 2251. Fax: (39 6) 807 8201.

Shanghai, People's Republic of China Office: Suite 898, Shanghai Centre, 1376 Nanjing Xi Lu, 200040. Telephone: (86 21) 279 8461. Fax: (86 21) 279 8462.

Singapore Office: 16 Collyer Quay #31-00, 0104. Telephone: (65) 535 1855. Fax: (65) 535 6855.

Warsaw, Poland Office: Warsaw Corporate Centre, ul. Emilii Plater 28, 00-688. Telephone: (48 2) 630 3344. Fax: (48 2) 630 3355.

International Banking and Finance including Project Finance, Aircraft, Ship and Asset Based Finance and Capital Markets, Company Law, Commercial Law, Mergers and Acquisitions and EC related advice.
Firm engaged in English, Hong Kong and General International Practice.

RESIDENT PARTNERS

ROBERT BURLEY. PRACTICE AREAS: Asset Based Lending; Structured Finance; Bank Finance; Aircraft Finance and Leasing; Project Finance.

ANDREW GRENVILLE. PRACTICE AREAS: Power Projects; Project Finance; Mergers and Acquisitions; Commercial Law; Joint Ventures.

PHILLIP PALMER. PRACTICE AREAS: Capital Markets; Asset Based Finance; Bank Finance; Aircraft Finance and Leasing; Project Finance.

DAN REYNELL. PRACTICE AREAS: Structured Finance; Asset Based Finance; Capital Markets; Project Finance.

(For names of Partners resident in other offices, see Professional Biographies for those offices)

COUDERT BROTHERS

(Pickrell Gaikokuho-Jimu-Bengoshi Jimusho)

1355 WEST TOWER, AOYAMA TWIN TOWERS
1-1-1 MINAMI-AOYAMA, MINATO-KU
TOKYO 107, JAPAN
Telephone: (81) (3) 3423-0337
Facsimile: (81) (3) 3423-3550; 3423-0929

New York, New York 10036-7794: 1114 Avenue of the Americas.
Washington, D.C. 20006: 1627 I Street, N.W., 12th Floor.
Los Angeles, California 90017: 1055 West Seventh Street, Twentieth Floor.

(This Listing Continued)

San Francisco, California 94111: 4 Embarcadero Center, Suite 3300.

San Jose, California 95113: Suite 1250, Ten Almaden Boulevard.

Paris 75008, France: Coudert Frères, 52, Avenue des Champs-Elysées.

London, EC4M 7JP, England: 20 Old Bailey.

Brussels B-1050, Belgium: Tour Louise. 149 Avenue Louise-Box 8.

Beijing, People's Republic of China 100020: Suite 2708-09, Jing Guang Centre, Hu Jia Lou, Chao Yang Qu.

Shanghai, People's Republic of China 200002: c/o Suite 1804, Union Building, 100 Yanan Road East.

Hong Kong: Nine Queen's Road, 25th Floor.

Singapore 0104: Tung Centre, 20 Collyer Quay.

Sydney N.S.W. 2000, Australia: Suite 2202, State Bank Centre, 52 Martin Place.

01301 Sao Paulo, SP, Brazil: Machado, Meyer, Sendacz, e Opice, Advogados, Rua da Consolacao, 247, 8 Andar.

Moscow, Russia: Ulitsa Staraya Basmannaya 14.

Bangkok 10500, Thailand: Bubhajit Building, 20 North Sathorn Road, 10th Floor.

Ho Chi Minh City, Vietnam: c/o Saigon Business Centre, 49-57 Dong Du Street, District 1.

Firm Engaged in American and International Law Practice and International Arbitration but not authorized to appear before Japanese courts or to act as Japanese Bengoshi.

RESIDENT PARTNERS

GREG L. PICKRELL, born Spencer, Iowa, September 5, 1951; admitted, 1977, California; licensed as a foreign legal consultant, 1993, Japan. *Education:* Iowa State University (B.S., with distinction, 1973); University of Michigan (J.D., cum laude, 1977). Phi Kappa Phi. *Member:* State Bar of California; American Bar Association (Member, Sections on: Corporation, Banking and Business Law; International Law; Science and Technology); Southeast Asia Business Council; Silicon Valley World Forum. (Resident).

RESIDENT ASSOCIATES

Julie N. Mack
(Not admitted in Japan)

Marilyn Selby Okoshi
(Not admitted in Japan)

(For biographical data of the New York personnel, see Professional Biographies at New York, N.Y.).

(For biographical data of the Washington personnel, see Professional Biographies at Washington, D.C.).

(For biographical data of the San Francisco personnel, see Professional Biographies at San Francisco, California).

(For biographical data of the Los Angeles personnel, see Professional Biographies at Los Angeles, California).

(For biographical data of the San Jose personnel, see Professional Biographies at San Jose, California).

(For biographical data of the London personnel, see Professional Biographies at London, England).

(For biographical data of the Paris personnel, see Professional Biographies at Paris, France).

(For biographical data of the Brussels personnel, see Professional Biographies at Brussels, Belgium).

(For biographical data of the Beijing personnel, see Professional Biographies at Beijing, People's Republic of China).

(For biographical data of the Hong Kong personnel, see Professional Biographies at Hong Kong).

(For biographical data of the Singapore personnel, see Professional Biographies at Singapore).

(For biographical data of the Sao Paulo personnel, see Professional Biographies at Sao Paulo, Brazil).

(For biographical data of the Shanghai Personnel, see Professional Biographies at Shanghai, People's Republic of China).

(For biographical data of the Sydney personnel, see Professional Biographies at Sydney, Australia).

(For biographical data of the Moscow personnel, see Professional Biographies at Moscow, U.S.S.R.).

DAVIS POLK & WARDWELL

(Reid Gaikokuho-Jimu-Bengoshi Jimusho)

TENTH FLOOR TOKIO KAIJO BUILDING ANNEX
2-1, MARUNOUCHI 1-CHOME, CHIYODA-KU

TOKYO 100, JAPAN
Telephone: 011-81-3-201-8421
Telecopier: 011-81-3-201-8444
Telex: 2224472 DPWTOK

New York, N.Y. Office: 450 Lexington Avenue, 10017. Telephone: 212-450-4000. Cable Address: "Davispolk New York". Telex: ITT-421341; ITT-423356. Telecopier: 212-450-4800.

Washington, D.C. Office: 1300 I Street, N.W. 20005. Telephone: 202-962-7000. Telecopier: 202-962-7111.

Paris, France Office: 4, Place de la Concorde, 75008. Telephone: 011-331-40.17.36.00. Telecopier: 011-331-42.65.22.34. Cable Address: "Davispolk Paris".

London, England Office: 1 Frederick's Place, EC2R 8AB. Telephone: 011-44-71-418-1300. Telex: 888238. Telecopier: 011-44-71-418-1400.

Frankfurt, Germany Office: MesseTurm, 60308 Frankfurt am Main, Federal Republic of Germany. Telephone: 011-49-69-97-57-03-0. Telephone: 011-49-69-74-77-44.

Hong Kong Office: The Hong Kong Club Building, 3A Chater Road. Telephone: 852 533 3300. Fax: 852 533 3388.

Firm engaged in American and General International Law Practice but not authorized to appear before Japanese courts or to act as Bengoshi.

RESIDENT PARTNER

EDWARD S. REID, born Detroit, Michigan, March 24, 1930; admitted, 1957, Michigan; 1958, New York; 1982, District of Columbia; 1991, Japan as Gaikokuho-Jimu-Bengoshi. *Education:* Yale University (A.B., 1951); Harvard University (LL.B., 1956). *Member:* The Association of the Bar of the City of New York; New York State and American Bar Associations; American Law Institute.

RESIDENT ASSOCIATES

Theodore A. Paradise; Steven C. Susser (Not admitted in Japan); *Kaoru Umino* (Not admitted in Japan).

(For Complete Biographical Data on all Personnel see Professional Biographies at New York City)

DENTON HALL

A Member of the Denton International Group of Law Firms

Playle Miles

(Gaikokuho Jimu Bengoshi Jimusho)

2ND FLOOR, ICHIBANCHO 27 BUILDING
27 ICHIBANCHO
CHIYODA-KU

TOKYO 102, JAPAN
Telephone: 81-3 3222 5977
Fax: 81-3 3222 5980

Other Offices: London, England; Milton Keynes, Buckinghamshire, England; Beijing, People's Republic of China; Brussels, Belgium; Hong Kong; Los Angeles, California; Singapore; Moscow, Russia.

Associated Offices: Amsterdam, Berlin, Chemnitz, Copenhagen, Dusseldorf, Frankfurt, Hamburg, Rotterdam and Vienna.

RESIDENT PARTNERS

RICHARD PLAYLE. LANGUAGES: Japanese, French. **PRACTICE AREAS:** Commercial; Corporate Law.

(For all Firm Personnel, see Professional Biographies at London, England).

DOHKE & TERAMOTO

KIMURA BUILDING 3RD. FLOOR, HONGO
3-39-3, BUNKYO-KU
TOKYO 113, JAPAN
Telephone: 03-3818-0418
Fax: 03-3818-0429
E-Mail: PEC00422@niftyserve. or.jp

Venture Capital Finance, Intellectual Property Laws, Computer Business Laws.

MEMBERS OF FIRM

ATSUO DOHKE, born Gifu, Japan, February 7, 1959; admitted, 1984, Japan. *Education:* University of Tokyo (LL.B., 1982). *LANGUAGES:* Japanese and English. *PRACTICE AREAS:* Corporation Law; Real Estate Law; Bankruptcy Law; Litigations.

SHINTO TERAMOTO, born Wakayama, Japan, 1963; admitted, 1987, Japan. *Education:* University of Tokyo (LL.B., 1985). Visiting Scholar at College of Law of Arizona State University, 1993-1994. Co-Author: "Setting up Enterprises in Japan," published by JETRO, 1992. Member, Technological Committee of Software Information Center (SOFTIC). *LANGUAGES:* Japanese and English. *PRACTICE AREAS:* Venture Capital Finance; Intellectual Property Law; Partnership.

FRESHFIELDS

(J.L. McKeand Gaikokuho-Jimu-Bengoshi-Jimusho)

ARK MORI BUILDING, 8F
1-12-32 AKASAKA, MINATO-KU
TOKYO 107, JAPAN
Telephone: (813) 3583 3483
Fax: (813) 3583 1561/1571

Other Offices in: Bangkok, Barcelona, Brussels, Frankfurt, Hanoi, Hong Kong, London, Madrid, Moscow, New York, Paris, and Singapore.

General and International Practice.

RESIDENT PARTNERS

JAMES L. MCKEAND, born Warwickshire, England, March 5, 1954; admitted 1978 as a solicitor, and as a Gaikokuho-Jimu-Bengoshi, 1991. *Education:* University of Liverpool (LL.B., 1975). *Member:* First Tokyo Bar Association.

JAMES A.H. LAWDEN, born London, England, August 10, 1955; admitted 1981 as a solicitor and as a Gaikokuho-Jimu-Bengoshi, 1992. *Education:* University of Oxford, New College (B.A., Hons., 1978; M.A.). *Member:* First Tokyo Bar Association.

CHARLES R. STEVENS, born Philadelphia, Pennsylvania, December 17, 1941; admitted, 1967, New York; licensed as a Foreign Legal Consultant, 1987, Japan. *Education:* Princeton University (B.A., 1963); Harvard Law School (LL.B., cum laude, 1966). Fulbright Research Fellow in Japanese Commercial Law, University of Tokyo, 1967. Lecturer in Law, Parker School of Foreign and Comparative Law, Columbia University School of Law, 1969-1979. Lecturer in Law, Harvard Law School, 1972-1973; 1979-1981. Arbitrator, Japan Commercial Arbitration Association, 1991-1993. Member, Executive Committee, Asia-Pacific Council, London Court of International Arbitration. Member, Hong Kong Law Reform Commission Subcommittee, UNCITRAL Model Law on Arbitration, 1985-1987. Member, Council on Foreign Relations, Inc. *Member:* The Association of the Bar of the City of New York (Member, Committee on Foreign and Comparative Law, 1970-1973); American Bar Association (Chairman, Committee on Far Eastern Law, 1971-1975). *LANGUAGES:* Japanese.

(For List of Partners see Professional Biographies at London, England).

FUKUDA, NAKAGAWA & YAMAKAWA LAW OFFICE

SIXTH FLOOR, DAIWA BANK BUILDING
6-21, 1-CHOME, NISHI-SHIMBASHI, MINATO-KU
TOKYO 105, JAPAN
Telephone: (03) 3591-8161-5
Cable Address: "Fukudaoffice"
Telecopier: GII I, GII (03) 3508-8148

Corporate, Foreign Investment, Litigation, Patent, Copyright, General Practice.

MEMBERS OF FIRM

TSUYOSHI FUKUDA, born Kobe, Japan, September 29, 1928; admitted, 1953, Japan. *Education:* Tokyo University (B.Jur., 1951); Legal Training and Research Institute (1951-1953). *Member:* First Tokyo Attorneys Association. *LANGUAGES:* Japanese and English.

YASUO NAKAGAWA, born Tagawa, Japan, December 5, 1943; admitted, 1970, Japan. *Education:* Department of Law, Tokyo University (B.Jur., 1968); Legal Training and Research Institute (1968-1970). *Member:* First Tokyo Attorneys Association. *LANGUAGES:* Japanese and English.

HIROMITSU YAMAKAWA, born Shizuoka, Japan, June 18, 1944; admitted, 1972, Japan. *Education:* Department of Law, Tokyo University (B.Jur., 1969); Legal Training and Research Institute (1970-1972); School of Law, University of Illinois (M.C.L., 1978). *Member:* First Tokyo Attorneys Association. *LANGUAGES:* Japanese and English.

IZUMI SATO, born Tokyo, Japan, May 28, 1959; admitted, 1987, Japan. *Education:* Waseda University (B.A., 1982); Legal Training and Research Institute(1985-1987). *Member:* First Tokyo Attorneys Association. *LANGUAGES:* Japanese and English.

GIBSON, DUNN & CRUTCHER

(Givens, Gaikokuho Jimu Bengoshi Jimusho)

Established in 1890

TORANOMON 3-CHOME ANNEX BUILDING
3-7-12 TORANOMON, MINATO-KU
TOKYO 105, JAPAN
Telephone: 011-81-3-3431-6800
Telecopier: 011-81-3-3431-6892

Los Angeles, California Office: 333 South Grand Avenue, 90071-3197. Telephone: 213-229-7000. Telex: 188171 GIBTRASK LSA (TRT), 674930 GIBTRASK LSA (WUT). Telecopier: 213-229-7520. Cable Address: GIBTRASK LOS ANGELES.

Practice includes Corporate Finance, Mergers and Acquisitions, Tax, Industrial and Intellectual Property, Real Estate, Labor, Litigation, Trade Regulation, Securities, U.S. Regulatory Matters, Banking, Commercial and General Corporate Law.
Firm engaged in U.S. and International Corporate and Commercial Law Practice as a gaikokuho jimu bengoshi jimusho comprised of one or more of the firm's Lawyers, not authorized to appear before Japanese courts or otherwise to act as bengoshi.

FIRM PROFILE: Gibson, Dunn & Crutcher, originating in Los Angeles, has been providing legal services to clients since 1890. Today, the firm has grown to one of the largest law firms in the world with approximately 650 attorneys in 17 offices situated in most of the world's important business centers. The firm has experts in virtually every area of the law, particularly those which relate to commercial transactions and disputes, and has more effective geographical coverage in the United States than any other major firm. The firm's lawyers and staff are dedicated to providing quality service on a timely and cost effective basis.

Much of the work in the Tokyo office involves representation of Japanese companies investing or doing business outside Japan, including corporate, tax, real estate, acquisition, financing, licensing and regulatory matters. Our work also involves advising U.S. and other non-Japanese companies investing or doing business in Japan, including regulatory and government relations, joint venture, licensing and financing matters.

(This Listing Continued)

PARTNER

STEPHEN B. GIVENS, born July 18, 1954; admitted, 1983, New York; 1990, Japan (Gaikokuho Jimu Bengoshi). *Education:* University of North Carolina at Chapel Hill (A.B., History, 1976); Harvard University (J.D., 1982). *Member:* Second Tokyo Bar Association. (Los Angeles, California and Tokyo, Japan Offices). **LANGUAGES:** Japanese. **PRACTICE AREAS:** International Business; Corporate Law; Corporate Financing Law.

RESIDENT ASSOCIATE

NAOYUKI AGAWA, born April 14, 1951; admitted, 1985, New York; 1986, District of Columbia (Not admitted in Japan). *Education:* Georgetown University (B.S.F.S., magna cum laude, 1977; J.D., 1984). **LANGUAGES:** Japanese. **PRACTICE AREAS:** General Corporate; International Trade.

(For information on other firm personnel, see professional biographies at Los Angeles, Century City, Irvine, San Diego, Menlo Park and San Francisco, California; Denver, Colorado; Washington, D.C.; New York, N.Y.; Dallas, Texas; Seattle, Washington; Paris, France; Hong Kong and Jeddah and Riyadh, Saudi Arabia (Affiliated Offices), see professional biographies at Los Angeles, California)

GIDE LOYRETTE NOUEL

HOMEI BUILDING 3F
3-19 AKASAKA 1-CHOME, MINATO-KU
TOKYO 107, JAPAN
Telephone: (81.3) 55.62.03.01
Telecopier: (81.3) 55.62.03.06

Paris, France Office: 26 Cours Albert 1er, 75008. Telephone: (1) 40.75.60.00. Cable Address: "3 Avocagidva Paris 86." Telex: 651261F GILOY. Telecopier: (1) 43.59.37.79.

New York, New York Office: Swiss Bank Tower, 10 East 50th Street, 10022. Telephone: (1-212) 644-1201. Telex: 424353 GIDE. Telecopier: (1-212) 644-1205.

Brussels, Belgium Office: Rue de la Loi 99.101, B-1040. Telephone: (32.2) 231.11.40. Telecopier: (32.2) 231.11.77.

Warsaw, Poland Office: Ul. Kopernika 17, 00-359. Telephone: (48.22) 26.22.21. Telecopier: (48.22) 26.03.02.

Riyadh, Saudi Arabia Office: P.O. Box 4615, 11412. Telephone: (966.1) 476.60.39. Telex: 401677 NASHWA. Telecopier: (966.1) 476.18.96.

Beijing, People's Republic of China Office: Suite 3309 A, Jing Guang Centre, Hu Jia Lou, Chaoyang District, 100020. Telephone: (86.1) 501 4511. Telecopier: (86.1) 501 4551.

Prague, Czech Republic Office: 34 Jindrisska, 11207. Telephone: (42.2) 24.21.34.65;24.21.36.50. Telecopier: (42.2) 24.21.09.12;24.22.58.53.

St. Petersburg, Russia Office: 34 Souvorovsky Prospect, App 45, P.O. Box 172, 193015. Telephone by satellite: (7.812) 850.16.85. Telecopier by satellite: (7.812) 850.16.86.

Moscow, Russia Office: 9, Ulitsa Tverskaya - App 66, 103009. Telephone by satellite: (7.501) 940.45.00. Telecopier by satellite: (7.501) 940.45.01.

Budapest VII, Hungary Office: EMKE Building, Rákóczi út 42, BP 409, 1072. Telephone: (36.1) 268.1236; 268.1237; 268.1238. Telecopier: (36.1) 268.1239.

Madrid, Spain Office: Antonio Maura 7, 6°, 28014. Telephone: (34.1) 531.25.01. Telecopier: (34.1) 531.35.30.

Hanoi, Vietnam Office: Hanoi Business Centre, 51 Ly Thai To. Telephone: (84.42) 66.122.3. Telecopier: (84.42) 66.030.1.

French and International Law.

RESIDENT ASSOCIATES

LAURENT DUBOIS, born 1948; admitted, 1971, Paris; Licensed as Foreign Law Consultant, 1988, Japan. *Education:* University of Paris X (1971; Institut de Droit Comparé (Institute of Comparative Law); Institut de Droit des Affaires (Institute of Business Law). *Member:* Tokyo Bar Association. **LANGUAGES:** French, English and Japanese.

Philippe Dalpayrat   **Mathieu Geny**

(For Biographical Data on Personnel, see Professional Biographies at Paris, France).

H. GOTO & PARTNERS

Gyosei Shoshi
(Administrative Documentation Lawyer)
Established in 1988
VILLA HEIGHTS
SHINJUKU GYOEN 801
7-3, SHINJUKU 2 CHOME, SHINJUKU-KU
160 TOKYO, JAPAN
Telephone: 03-3255-4195
Fax: 03-3225-4385

Japanese laws relating to Administrative Procedure, International Relations, Pharmaceutical and other Product Relations, Construction Industry, Industrial Property, Incorporation, and other Government and Private Business.

FIRM PROFILE: The firm was established in 1988 and offers an extensive range of administrative documentation service required for doing business in Japan, with particular emphasis placed on government approval and license for manufacturing and importing drug, Quisi-drug, cosmetic, medical device and accessory, foodstuff including agricultural produces, cake and candy, etc.; construction business license, government and public bidding relating thereto; documentation for incorporating various kinds of corporations, patent and know-how agreements. This partner firm has a legal support staff of six paralegal and administrative personnel.

PARTNERS

HIROSHI GOTO, born Hokkaido, Japan, July 18, 1928; admitted, 1988, Japan. *Education:* Special Agricultural School, Hokkaido University (Bachelor of Agriculture, 1948); Law School, Hokkaido University (LL.B., 1952); Graduate Work (U.S. Constitutional Law), under Fulbright Program, (1954). Admitted as Gyosei Shoshi (Administrative Documentation Lawyer). Senior Partner. Author: "Patent and License Terminology Dictionary (Eng to Jap, Jap to Eng). Lecturer on American Government, University of Rio Grande, Japan; Attorney-Advisor, Staff Judge Advocate Office, U.S. Fifth Air Force, Japan, 1955-1964, Legal & Patent Counsel, Rohm and Haas Asia, 1964-1988, America-Japan Society (member). *Member:* Tokyo to Gosci Shoshi Association, Japan Association of International Economic Law, Japan Association of Industrial Property Law. **LANGUAGES:** Japanese, English, Chinese and Korean. **PRACTICE AREAS:** Patent Licensing; Product Registration.

YOSHIMASA KUBODERA, born Tokyo, Japan, September 5, 1954; admitted, 1988, Japan. *Education:* Law School, Nihon University (LL.B., 1979). Administrative Documentation Lawyer, Japan, 1988. *Member:* Toyko-to Goyosei Shoshi Association. **LANGUAGES:** Japanese and English. **PRACTICE AREAS:** Construction Industry License; Incorporation Procedure.

COUNSEL

MASAHIRO SHIOZAKI, born Chiba Prefecture, Japan, February 24, 1915; admitted, 1962, Japan. *Education:* Tohoku Imperial University (B.E., Chemistry, 1941). Chief Patent Counsel, Taisho Pharmaceutical Co., Ltd., 1955-1965. *Member:* The Patent Attorneys Association of Japan; A.I.P.P.I. **LANGUAGES:** Japanese and English. **PRACTICE AREAS:** Patent and Trademark Prosecution; Pharmaceutical Product Registration.

GRAHAM & JAMES

(Kuroso Gaikokuho-Jimu-Bengoshi Jimusho)
SHIROYAMA JT MORI BLDG. 8F
3-1 TORANOMON 4-CHOME MINATO-KU
TOKYO, JAPAN
Telephone: (011-81-3-3459-5481, 5482, 5483)
Telefacsimile: (011-81-3-3459-0240, 0242)

Other offices located in: San Francisco, Los Angeles, Newport Beach, Palo Alto, Sacramento and Fresno, California; Washington, D.C.; New York, New York; Milan, Italy; Beijing, China; London, England; Dusseldorf, Germany; Taipei, Taiwan.

Associated Offices: Deacons in Association with Graham & James, Hong Kong; Sly and Weigall, Sydney, Melbourne, Brisbane, Perth and Canberra, Australia.

(This Listing Continued)

GRAHAM & JAMES, Tokyo—Continued

Affiliated Offices: Graham & James in Affiliation with Taylor Joynson Garrett, London, England, Bucharest, Romania and Brussels, Belgium; Hanafiah Soeharto Ponggawa, Jakarta, Indonesia; Deacons and Graham & James, Bangkok, Thailand; Haarmann, Hemmelrath & Partner, Berlin, Munich, Leipzig, Frankfurt and Dusseldorf, Germany; Mishare M. Al-Ghazali & Partners, Kuwait; Sly & Weigall Deacons in Association with Graham & James, Hanoi, Vietnam and Guangzhou, China; Gallastegui y Lozano, S.C., Mexico City, Mexico; Law Firm of Salah Al-Hejailan, Jeddah and Riyadh, Saudi Arabia.

Firm engaged in American and International law practice but not authorized to appear before Japanese courts or administrative agencies or to act as Japanese Bengoshi.

MEMBERS OF FIRM

STEPHEN E. CHELBERG, born Urbana, Illinois, 1958; admitted, 1983, Illinois and U.S. Court of Appeals, Seventh Circuit; 1987, California and U.S. Court of Appeals, Ninth Circuit (Not admitted in Japan). *Education:* Stanford University (B.A., with honors and distinction , 1980); University of Michigan (J.D., cum laude, 1983). Phi Beta Kappa. Note Editor, Michigan Yearbook of International Legal Studies, 1982-1983. Author: "The Contours of Extraterritorial Jurisdiction in Drug Smuggling Cases," Michigan Yearbook of International Legal Studies 43, 1983. *Member:* Chicago, Illinois State and American Bar Associations; State Bar of California. *LANGUAGES:* French and Japanese. *PRACTICE AREAS:* International Business Law; Commercial Law.

PHILLIP DAVID CROWLEY, born Parks, New South Wales, Australia, 1960; admitted, 1986, New South Wales, Australia (Not admitted in Japan). *Education:* Sydney University (B.A., 1983; LL.B., 1986). *Member:* Law Society of New South Wales. *LANGUAGES:* French and Japanese.

STEVEN S. DOI, born Indio, California, 1962; admitted, 1987, California (Not admitted in Japan). *Education:* Pomona College (B.A., 1983); University of California at Los Angeles School of Law (J.D., 1986). (Also at Los Angeles, California Office). *PRACTICE AREAS:* Corporate Law.

KEN M. KUROSU, (Not admitted in Japan). A.B. (Stanford University); J.D., (University of Washington); admitted to bar, 1983, California; 1984, with distinction U.S. District Court, Central District of California and U.S. Court of Appeals, Ninth Circuit. (Partner, Graham & James, American Attys). *LANGUAGES:* Japanese. *PRACTICE AREAS:* General Corporate and Commercial.

JOHN MATHESON, born New Zealand, 1958; admitted, 1982, New Zealand; 1988, England and Hong Kong; 1992, New South Wales, Australia (Not admitted in Japan). *Education:* University of Canterbury (M.Sc., honors, 1983; LL.B., 1981). M.Sc., LL.B. (Canterbury), admitted, 1982, New Zealand; 1988, England and Hong Kong. (Resident in Tokyo, Japan). *PRACTICE AREAS:* General Commercial; Environmental and Planning; Litigation.

RESIDENT ASSOCIATES

Mitsuru Claire Chino (Not admitted in Japan); *John T. Murphy* (Not admitted in Japan).

HAARMANN, HEMMELRATH & PARTNER

SHIROYAMA JT MORI BUILDING, 8F
3-1 TORANOMON 4-CHOME
MINATO-KU
105 TOKYO, JAPAN
Telephone: 81-3-34 59 54 85
Fax: 81-3-35 78 89 56

Munich Office: Effnerstrasse 38, D-81925 München. Telephone: (089) 924 00-0. Telefax: (089) 92400-133. Telex: 523900 HUP D.

Düsseldorf Office: Martin-Luther-Platz 26, D-40212 Düsseldorf. Telephone: (0211) 8399-0. Telefax (0211) 8399-1333.

Berlin Office: Budapester Strasse 40a, D-10787 Berlin. Telephone: (030) 264 73-0. Telefax: (030) 264 73-133.

Frankfurt/Main Office: Neue Mainzer Strasse 75, D-60311 Frankfurt/Main. Telephone: (069) 920 59-0. Telefax: (069) 920 59-133.

Leipzig Office: Neumarkt 24, D-04109 Leipzig. Telephone: (0341) 1263-0. Telefax: (0341) 1263-133.

(This Listing Continued)

Prague Office: Cermàkova 7, CZ-1200 00 Prague 2, Czech Republic. Telephone: 42-2-24 23 90 36. Telefax: 42-2-24 23 88 42.

Corporate and Business Law, International and National Tax Law, Banking, Commercial Law, Labour Law, all Areas of Mergers and Acquisitions, Financial Transactions, International Law, Antitrust Law, Unfair Competition and Intellectual Property Rights Law, EEC Law, Real Estate Transactions, Management and Leveraged Buy-outs, National and Cross-border Leasing Transactions, Structuring of Funds, Accounting Services.

FIRM PROFILE: The firm, established in 1987, has strongly developed as a multi-disciplinary firm in Germany with seven offices. The firm is affiliated with Graham & James (US, Italy, Japan and China), Taylor Joynson Garrett (UK), Deacons (Hong Kong and Southeast Asia) and is a member of the international tax and audit network RSM International.

RESIDENT MEMBERS OF FIRM

ANDREAS DIETL, born Munich, Germany, November 26, 1959; admitted, 1988, Munich. *Education:* University of Munich (J.D., 1985); Northwestern University, Chicago (LL.M., 1989). *Member:* International Bar Association; German-American Lawyers Association; German-South African Lawyers Association. *LANGUAGES:* German, English and Spanish. *PRACTICE AREAS:* Corporate; Commercial; Mergers and Acquisitions; Finance; Equipment Finance and Leasing.

Languages: German, English, French, Japanese, Mandarin, Dutch, Spanish, Italian, Russian, Czech and Slovakian.

(For Biographical Data on other Members of Firm, See Professional Biographies at Munich, Düsseldorf, Berlin, Frankfurt and Leipzig, Germany and Prague, Czech Republic).

HAMADA & MATSUMOTO

SANKYU BUILDING
6-14, KASUMIGASEKI 3-CHOME, CHIYODA-KU
TOKYO 100, JAPAN
Telephone: 03-3580-3377 and 3370
Telex: J28844 "HYLAW"
Telefax: (G2/G3) 03-3581-4713/4715; 3592- 0912, 0916; (G4)
03-5251-7985

General Practice. Corporate, International Financing, Foreign Investments, Banking, Licensing and Intellectual Property Law and Litigation.

MEMBERS OF FIRM

KUNIO HAMADA, born Hyogo, Japan, May 24, 1936; admitted, 1962, Japan. *Education:* The University of Tokyo (LL.B., 1960); Harvard Law School (LL.M., 1966). *Member:* The Daini-Tokyo Bar Association; International Bar Association; Inter-Pacific Bar Association (President, 1991-1992). *LANGUAGES:* English and Japanese.

KEIJI MATSUMOTO, born Kyoto, Japan, September 27, 1940; admitted, 1965, Japan. *Education:* The University of Tokyo (LL.B., 1963); Columbia Law School (LL.M., 1971). *Member:* The Daini-Tokyo Bar Association. *LANGUAGES:* English and Japanese.

FUMIHIKO SAITO, born Fukui, Japan, June 9, 1945; admitted, 1973, Japan. *Education:* The University of Tokyo (LL.B., 1970); University of Washington School of Law (LL.M., 1976). *Member:* Tokyo Bar Association; Inter-Pacific Bar Association. *LANGUAGES:* English and Japanese.

OSAMU NAKAMOTO, born Dairen, Japan, April 8, 1942; admitted, 1974, Japan. *Education:* The University of Tokyo (B.S., 1966); University of Washington School of Law (LL.M., 1978). *Member:* The Daini-Tokyo Bar Association. *LANGUAGES:* English and Japanese.

GOTARO ICHIKI, born Fukuoka, Japan, December 4, 1949; admitted, 1975, Japan. *Education:* Hitotsubashi University (LL.B., 1973); University of Washington School of Law (LL.M., 1981); Comparative Law Research Fellow, University of Washington School of Law (1981-1982). *Member:* The Daini-Tokyo Bar Association; Inter-Pacific Bar Association. *LANGUAGES:* English and Japanese.

HIDEAKI TANAKA, born Tokyo, Japan, September 14, 1948; admitted, 1977, Japan. *Education:* Keio University (LL.B., 1972; LL.M., 1975); New York University School of Law (LL.M., 1981). *Member:* The Daini-Tokyo Bar Association. *LANGUAGES:* English and Japanese.

YOGO KIMURA, born Tokyo, Japan, September 16, 1943; admitted, 1977, Japan. *Education:* The University of Tokyo (LL.B., Political Science, 1970); The University of Michigan Law School (M.C.L., 1986). *Member:*

(This Listing Continued)

The Daini-Tokyo Bar Association; Inter-Pacific Bar Association. *LANGUAGES:* English and Japanese.

YUSAKU ONO, born Fukushima, Japan, July 1, 1949; admitted, 1978, Japan; 1986, New York, U.S.A. *Education:* Chuo University (LL.B., 1974); New York University School of Law (M.C.J., 1983). *Member:* The Daini-Tokyo and New York State Bar Associations. *LANGUAGES:* English and Japanese.

TORU ISHIGURO, born Tokyo, Japan, June 19, 1954; admitted, 1980, Japan; 1984, New York, U.S.A. *Education:* The University of Tokyo (LL.B., 1978); Columbia Law School (LL.M., 1983). *Member:* The Daini-Tokyo Bar Association; International Bar Association; Inter-Pacific Bar Association. *LANGUAGES:* English and Japanese.

HARUME NAKANO, born Hyogo, Japan, January 9, 1955; admitted, 1985, Japan. *Education:* Keio University (LL.B., 1977; LL.M., 1980); Cornell Law School (LL.M., 1990). *Member:* The Daini-Tokyo Bar Association. *LANGUAGES:* English and Japanese.

ASSOCIATES

AYAKO IKEDA, born Aichi, Japan, December 5, 1959; admitted, 1984, Japan; 1991, New York, U.S.A. *Education:* The University of Tokyo (LL.B., 1982); London School of Economics and Political Science, University of London (LL.M., 1985); Georgetown University Law Center (LL.M., 1991). *Member:* The Daini-Tokyo Bar Association. *LANGUAGES:* English and Japanese.

YASUZO TAKENO, born Tokyo, Japan, June 9, 1959; admitted, 1987, Japan. *Education:* Waseda University (LL.B., 1985); University of Oxford (M.Litt., 1993). *Member:* The Daini-Tokyo Bar Association. *LANGUAGES:* English and Japanese.

KEN MIURA, born Tokyo, Japan, September 15, 1960; admitted, 1990, Japan. *Education:* Keio University (B.A., 1984). *Member:* The Daini-Tokyo Bar Association. *LANGUAGES:* English and Japanese.

SHIRO YANAGI, born Fukuoka, Japan, April 2, 1961; admitted, 1990, Japan. *Education:* Waseda University (LL.B., 1985). *Member:* The Daini-Tokyo Bar Association. *LANGUAGES:* English and Japanese.

AKIMOTO KAWAMURA, born Nagasaki, Japan, January 17, 1964; admitted, 1991, Japan. *Education:* The University of Tokyo (LL.B., 1989). *Member:* The Daini-Tokyo Bar Association. *LANGUAGES:* English and Japanese.

SATOSHI NAKAMURA, born Tochigi, Japan, October 5, 1964; admitted, 1991, Japan. *Education:* The University of Tokyo (LL.B., 1989). *Member:* The Daini-Tokyo Bar Association. *LANGUAGES:* English and Japanese.

EIKO HAKODA, born Saitama, Japan, May 25, 1957; admitted, 1992, Japan. *Education:* The University of Tokyo (B.A., 1980). *Member:* The Daini-Tokyo Bar Association. *LANGUAGES:* English and Japanese.

HIKARU KAIEDA, born Kagoshima, Japan, October 17, 1962; admitted, 1993, Japan. *Education:* The University of Tokyo (LL.B., 1987 and 1989). *Member:* The Daini-Tokyo Bar Association. *LANGUAGES:* English and Japanese.

YUICHIRO KUWANO, born Tokyo, Japan, May 18, 1966; admitted, 1993, Japan. *Education:* Waseda University (LL.B., 1991). *Member:* The Daini-Tokyo Bar Association. *LANGUAGES:* English and Japanese.

KATSUHIKO KUWAYAMA, born Mie, Japan, October 19, 1963; admitted, 1994, Japan. *Education:* The University of Tokyo (LL.B., 1987). *Member:* The Daini-Tokyo Bar Association. *LANGUAGES:* English and Japanese.

HAMAYOTSU & HAMAYOTSU

2ND FLOOR, NAGATA-CHO PALACE SIDE BUILDING
11-4, NAGATA-CHO 1-CHOME
CHIYODA-KU
TOKYO 100, JAPAN
Telephone: (03) 3593-3351
Cable Address: HAMAJURIST
Telefax: (03) 3593-3399

FIRM PROFILE: The firm was established in 1980 and offers legal services in areas of Agency and Distributorships, Business, Commercial and Company Law, Civil Law, Communications and Media (Television), Computers and Software, Contracts, Debtor and Creditor, Energy, Entertainment and Arts, Criminal Law and Family Law.

(This Listing Continued)

MEMBERS OF FIRM

NAOFUMI HAMAYOTSU, born Nagoya, Japan, January 20, 1944; admitted, 1971, Japan. *Education:* Tokyo University (LL.B., 1969); Legal Training and Research Institute of The Supreme Court of Japan (1969-1971); graduate study, Southern Methodist University (M.C.L., 1975); Whitman & Ransom, New York (1975-1976). Recipient: AFS and Fulbright Scholarships; American Jurisprudence Award (Company Law). Co-Author: "Horei Kommentaru," (Commentaries on Japanese Private International Law), Gakuyo Shobo, 1983; "Shogai Torihiki no Kiso Chishiki," (Basic Knowledge of International Transactions), Japan Federation of Bar Associations, 1989. *Member:* Daini Tokyo Bar Association; Law Association for Asia and the Western Pacific; International Bar Association. *LANGUAGES:* Japanese and English. *PRACTICE AREAS:* Distributorships; Joint Ventures; Licensing; Computer Software; Television; Energy (LNG); Entertainment and Arts; Contracts.

TOSHIKO HAMAYOTSU, born Taipei, January 6, 1945; admitted, 1972, Japan. *Education:* Keio University (LL.B., 1967); Legal Training and Research Institute of The Supreme Court of Japan (1970-1972); Academy of American and International Law, Dallas (1979). Co-Author: "Tsuma Tachi no Horitsu plus Zeikin," (Law plus Tax for Wives), KK Gyosei, 1988; "Sozoku no Shikumi to Zeikin," (Inheritance and Tax), Hogaku Shoin, 1989. *Member:* Tokyo Bar Association; Japan Women's Bar Association; House of Councilors, National Parliament (1992—); Minister for Global Environmental Issues and Director-General of Environment Agency of Government of Japan (April, 1994—). *LANGUAGES:* Japanese and English. *PRACTICE AREAS:* Civil Law; Debtor and Creditor; Criminal Law; Family Law; Environmental Law.

ASSOCIATE

AKIO OTSUKA, born Tochigi, Japan, January 28, 1959; admitted, 1986, Japan. *Education:* Hitotsubashi University (LL.B., 1984); Legal Training and Research Institute of The Supreme Court of Japan, (1984-1986); Graduate study, Southern Methodist University (LL.M., 1990; M.B.A., 1991). *Member:* Dai-ichi Tokyo Bar Association. *LANGUAGES:* Japanese and English. *PRACTICE AREAS:* Business Law; Civil Law; Contracts; Criminal Law; Family Law.

Languages: English and Japanese.

HARADA, OZAKI & HATTORI

SUITE 450, MARUNOUCHI BUILDING
4-1, MARUNOUCHI 2-CHOME
CHIYODA-KU
TOKYO 100, JAPAN
Telephone: 03-3216-2828
Telecopier: 03-3287-1937

General Practice, International Transactions, Corporation, Commercial Transactions, Litigation, Bankruptcy, Trademark, Intellectual Property Rights, Copyright, Immigration, Arbitration, Antitrust and Estate.

MEMBERS OF FIRM

NOBUYASU HARADA, born Tokyo, Japan, July 12, 1943; admitted, 1972, Japan. *Education:* Tokyo University (LL.B., 1967); University of Illinois School of Law (M.C.L., 1975). *Member:* Dai Ichi Tokyo Bar Association; Japan Federation of Bar Associations. *LANGUAGES:* Japanese and English.

YUKIMASA OZAKI, born Tokyo, September 2, 1959; admitted, 1989, Japan. *Education:* Waseda University (LL.B., 1984); Legal Research and Training Institute (1987-1989); University of Wisconsin Law School (M.L.I., 1992). *Member:* Dai Ichi Tokyo Bar Association; Japan Federation of Bar Associations. *LANGUAGES:* Japanese and English.

AKITO HATTORI, born Tokyo, Japan, November 28, 1958; admitted, 1989, Japan. *Education:* Waseda University, Department of Political Science (B.A., Political Science, 1982) and Department of Law (LL.B., 1986). *Member:* Dai-Ichi Tokyo Bar Association and Japan Federation of Bar Association. *LANGUAGES:* Japanese and English.

SHIN-ICHIRO NOJIMA, born Tokyo, Japan, October 2, 1961; admitted, 1992, Japan. *Education:* Waseda University, Department of Law (LL.B., 1985). *Member:* Dai Ichi Tokyo Bar Association; Japan Federation of Bar Associations. *LANGUAGES:* Japanese and English.

(This Listing Continued)

HARADA, OZAKI & HATTORI, Tokyo—Continued

OF COUNSEL

TAKEO HAYAKAWA, born October 2, 1914; admitted, 1978, Japan. *Education:* Tokyo University (LL.B., 1947); Tokyo University, Faculty of Law, Graduate Studies, Ministry of Education Grant (1947-1949); University of Michigan, Graduate Studies, GARIOA Fellowship and University of Michigan Fellowship (LL.M., 1953); University of Chicago and Columbia University, Fulbright Research Scholar Grant (1963-1964); University of Hawaii, East-West Center, Senior Specialist (1965); Occidental College, Los Angeles, Fulbright Scholar (1986-1987). Visiting Professor, Jointly Appointed by Law School and Political Science Department, State University of New York at Buffalo and University of Iowa, 1970-1971. Professor, Senshu University, Faculty of Law, 1978-1985. *Member:* Dai Ichi Tokyo, American (International Associate) and International Bar Associations; Japan Federation of Bar Associations. *LANGUAGES:* Japanese and English.

Languages: Japanese and English.

HASHIDATE LAW OFFICE

7TH FLOOR, IMPERIAL TOWER
1-1, UCHISAIWAICHO, 1-CHOME
CHIYODA-KU
TOKYO 100, JAPAN
Telephone: (03) 3504-3800; (03) 3504-1007
Telex: 02-228108 HLOTYO
Telecopier: (03) 3504-1009

General Practice.

MEMBERS OF FIRM

KENJI HASHIDATE, born Chiba, Japan, June 22, 1947; admitted, 1973, Japan. *Education:* Waseda University, Tokyo (B.A., 1971); Japan Legal Training and Research Institute, Tokyo (1973); University of Washington (LL.M., 1975). Special Student at Columbia Graduate Law School, 1975-1976. Associated with the Law Offices of Sullivan & Cromwell, Debevoise Plimpton Lyons & Gates and Kelley Drye & Warren, New York City, 1976 and with Law Office of Coward Chance, London, 1977. Author: "Financing Corporations with Convertible Debentures in U.S.A. and Japan," Kinokuniya, 1976; "American Regulation of Foreign Banks," Toyo Economic Press, 1978; "Legal Aspects of International Loan Transactions," Financial Law Journal, 1983. Co-Author: "International Financial Transactions Practice," Financial Law Journal, 1985; "Security Aspects of International Finance," Treatise on Secured Transactions. *Member:* Japan Federation and First Tokyo Bar Association; American Bar Association (Associate Member). *LANGUAGES:* Japanese and English.

TOSHINAO NAKAMURA, born Saitama, Japan, November 25, 1947; (Not admitted in Japan). registered as Certified Public Accountant, 1980, Japan; registered as Licensed Tax Accountant, 1989, Japan. *Education:* Waseda University, Tokyo (B.A., 1971). *LANGUAGES:* Japanese and English.

TAKAHIRO HOSHINO, born Tokyo, Japan, November 22, 1955; admitted, 1981, Japan. *Education:* Waseda University, Tokyo (LL.B., 1979); Japan Legal Training and Research Institute, Tokyo (1981). Assistant Judge, Utsunomiya District Court, 1981-1984 and Tokyo District Court, 1984-1987. *Member:* Japan Federation of Bar Associations; First Tokyo Bar Association. *LANGUAGES:* Japanese and English.

SETSUKO YUFU, born Tokyo, Japan, March 28, 1952; admitted, 1981, Japan. *Education:* Waseda University, Tokyo (LL.B., 1974); Japan Legal Training and Research Institute, Tokyo (1981); University of Amsterdam, International Course in European Integration (Diploma, 1986). Associated with, Loeff Claeys Verbeke, Brussels, 1986-1987. Author: "Joint Ventures under EEC Competition Law," 642 Gendai Hō-Shakaigaku no Shomondai I, 1992. *Member:* Japan Federation of Bar Associations; Dai-ni Tokyo Bar Association; EC Studies Society of Japan; The Japan Association of International Economic Law. *LANGUAGES:* Japanese, English and German.

JUN MAMIYA, born Fukuoka, Japan, November 1, 1960; admitted, 1988, Japan. *Education:* Kyushu University, Fukuoka (LL.B., 1983); Japan Legal Training and Research Institute, Tokyo (1988). *Member:* Japan Federation of Bar Associations; First Tokyo Bar Association. *LANGUAGES:* Japanese and English.

KOUHEI YABUTA, born Fukuoka, Japan, December 24, 1961; admitted, 1991, Japan. *Education:* Chuo University, Tokyo (LL.B., 1984); Japan

(This Listing Continued)

Legal Training and Research Institute, Tokyo (1991). *Member:* Japan Federation of Bar Associations; First Tokyo Bar Association. *LANGUAGES:* Japanese and English.

ALISON ANGELA JONES, born Melbourne, Australia, February 23, 1965; admitted, 1991, Victoria (Not admitted in Japan). *Education:* Monash University, Australia (B.A., 1987; LL.B., 1990). *Member:* Victorian Law Institute; Australian and New Zealand Chamber of Commerce Legal Committee. *LANGUAGES:* English and French.

JOHN W. REED, JR., born San Francisco, California, November 5, 1964; admitted, 1994, New York (Not admitted in Japan). *Education:* University of California at Berkeley (B.A., 1987); University of California Regent's Scholar; Harvard Law School (J.D., 1993). Earl Warren Scholar. *LANGUAGES:* English.

HAYASHIDA, KASHIWAGI & TAZAWA

OZAWA BUILDING
21-18, TORANOMON 1-CHOME, MINATO-KU
TOKYO 105, JAPAN
Telephone: Tokyo 508-2271/3
Cable Address: "Sommylaw Tokyo"
Telex: J23738
Telecopier: (03) 595-2657

General Practice. International Business, Aviation, Corporation, Patent and Trademark Law.

MEMBERS OF FIRM

YASUOMI HAYASHIDA, born Kumamoto, Japan, March 19, 1927; admitted, 1956, Japan. *Education:* Chuo University (LL.B., 1953); Hastings College of Law, University of California, Research on Aviation Law, 1972. Public Procurator, 1955-1956. *Member:* Second Tokyo Bar Association (Vice-President, 1976-1977). *LANGUAGES:* Japanese and English.

TOSHIHIKO KASHIWAGI, born 1941; admitted, 1969, Japan. *Education:* Keio University (LL.B.); University of Washington (LL.M.). *Member:* Second Tokyo Bar Association. *LANGUAGES:* Japanese and English.

SHIGERU TAZAWA, born 1951; admitted, 1976, Japan; 1982, New York. *Education:* Kyoto University (LL.B., 1974); New York University School of Law (LL.M., 1981). With, Kaye, Scholer, Fierman, Hays & Handler, New York, 1981 and Reid & Priest, New York, 1981-1982. *Member:* Second Tokyo Bar Association. *LANGUAGES:* Japanese and English.

KENICHIRO HAYASHIDA, born 1958; admitted, 1984, Japan; 1989, New York. *Education:* Hitotsubashi University (LL.B., 1982); Legal Research and Training Institute of the Supreme Court of Japan (1982-1984); University of Pennsylvania Law School (LL.M., 1988). With, Perkins Coie, Seattle, 1988-1989 and Beaumont & Son, London, 1989. *Member:* Second Tokyo Bar Association; New York State Bar Association. *LANGUAGES:* Japanese and English.

Languages: Japanese and English.

HIRATSUKA & PARTNERS

1104 KIOI-TBR BUILDING
5-7, KOJIMACHI, CHIYODA-KU
TOKYO 102, JAPAN
Telephone: (03)-3230-0911
Telex: 2324418 MAKLAW J
Telecopier: GIII + GII (03)-3262-0944

Admiralty, Insurance, Litigation and Shipping Law.

FIRM PROFILE: This firm offers a full range of Maritime and General Legal Services (especially Litigation) including, but not limited to, Shipping, Commercial, Insurance, Ship Sale, Purchase and Maritime Disasters of every nature, to clients in Japan as well as those from abroad.

MEMBERS OF FIRM

MAKOTO HIRATSUKA, born Tokyo, Japan, December 22, 1939. admitted to bar, 1966, Japan. *Education:* Faculty of Law, Tokyo University (LL.B., Private Law Course, 1963; Public Law Course, 1964); Legal Training and Research Institute of the Supreme Court (1964-1966); University of London (U.C.L., Graduate School; Diploma in Shipping Law, 1972). Co-author: "International Litigation," Volume VI, Practical Civil Procedure Law Series, April 30, 1971. *Member:* First Tokyo Bar Association; Private International Law Association of Japan; International Law Association of

(This Listing Continued)

Japan; Japanese Maritime Law Association. *LANGUAGES:* Japanese and English. *PRACTICE AREAS:* Maritime; Admiralty; Insurance; International Litigation.

TORU NISHIKI, born Mie Prefecture, Japan, January 29, 1943. admitted to bar, 1968, Japan. *Education:* Faculty of Law, Tokyo University (LL.B., Private Law Course, 1966); Legal Training and Research Institute of the Supreme Court (1966-1968). Co-author: "Legal Advice on Labour Accidents", April, 1971; "Law to Help Aggrieved People", June, 1979. *Member:* Tokyo Bar Association; Japanese Maritime Law Association. *LANGUAGES:* Japanese and English. *PRACTICE AREAS:* Maritime; Litigation.

YUTAKA TSURUSAKI, born Nagasaki Prefecture, Japan, June 26, 1951. admitted to bar, 1978, Japan. *Education:* Faculty of Law, Tokyo University (LL.B., Private Law Course, 1976); Legal Training and Research Institute of the Supreme Court (1976-1978); University of London (U.C.L., Graduate School; Diploma in Shipping Law, 1982). Author: "For the Early Re-revision of the Revised International Carriage of Goods by Sea Act," Kaiun, 1993. Co-Author: "Arrest of Vessels in Japan", LMCLQ, 1981; "Significant Changes under New Japan COGSA 1992," International Maritime Law, 1994. *Member:* First Tokyo Bar Association. *LANGUAGES:* Japanese and English. *PRACTICE AREAS:* Maritime; Admiralty; International Litigation; Contract.

FUKASHI KOBAYASHI, born Chiba Prefecture, Japan, June 8, 1961. admitted to bar, 1988, Japan. *Education:* Faculty of Law, Waseda University (LL.B., 1985); Legal Training and Research Institute of the Supreme Court (1986-1988). *Member:* First Tokyo Bar Association. *LANGUAGES:* Japanese and English. *PRACTICE AREAS:* Maritime; Admiralty; International Litigation.

CONSULTANT

TORU ARIIZUMI, born Yamanashi Prefecture, Japan, June 10, 1906. admitted to bar, 1967, Japan. *Education:* Faculty of Law, Tokyo University (LL.B., 1932; LL.D., 1958); London School of Economics (1957). Professor of Law: Tokyo University , 1948-1967; Sophia University, 1967-1977. Professor Emeritus, Tokyo University, 1967—. Legislative Council of the Ministry of Justice (Sub Committee on Civil Code), 1955—. President, Social Insurance Council, 1966-1979. Chairman, Land Appraisal Committee, 1974-1981. *Member:* Japanese Labor Law Society (President, 1960-1962). *LANGUAGES:* Japanese.

ASSOCIATES

TORU YAMADA, born Kanagawa Prefecture, Japan, September 23, 1967; admitted, 1993, Japan. *Education:* Faculty of Law, Tokyo University (LL.B., Private Law Course, 1990); Legal Training and Research Institute of the Supreme Court (1990-1992). *Member:* First Tokyo Bar Association. *LANGUAGES:* Japanese, English and Russian. *PRACTICE AREAS:* Maritime; International Litigation.

INASAWA & KATAOKA

Established in 1922

SANNO GRAND BUILDING, ROOM 422
14-2, NAGATA-CHO 2-CHOME
CHIYODA-KU
TOKYO, JAPAN
Telephone: 81-3-3580-3451
Fax: 81-3-3581-3633

General practice with emphasis on matters involving commercial transactions, business planning, economic regulations, real estate, leasing, intellectual property rights, financing, merger and acquisition, litigation, negotiation, international transactions, technical licensing agreements, joint ventures, sales representation.

FIRM PROFILE: Established in 1922, Inasawa & Kataoka, one of the most reputable legal firms in Tokyo, offers a wide range of legal services to its Japanese and international client base. The legal staff includes two attorneys and two attorneys of counsel. The firm incorporates the services of a broad international network of lawyers.

MEMBERS OF FIRM

KOICHI INASAWA, born Tokyo, Japan, October 22, 1934; admitted, 1961, Japan. *Education:* Chuo University Law School (LL.B., 1957). Conducted legal research, University of California Law School, Berkeley, 1969. *Member:* Tokyo Bar Association. *LANGUAGES:* Japanese and English. *PRACTICE AREAS:* International Transactions; Corporate Law.

(This Listing Continued)

GO KATAOKA, born Tokyo, Japan, September 12, 1958; admitted, 1989, Japan. *Education:* Rikkyo University (LL.B., 1982). *Member:* Tokyo Bar Association. *PRACTICE AREAS:* Corporate Law; Family Law.

ISHII LAW OFFICE

623 FUJI BUILDING
2-3, MARUNOUCHI 3-CHOME, CHIYODA-KU
TOKYO 100, JAPAN
Telephone: 03-3214-4731
Telefax: (03) 3287-1327

General Corporate Practice, Civil, Commercial and Criminal Litigation, Antitrust and Trade Law, International Commercial Transactions.

SEIICHI ISHII, born Tokyo, Japan, 1923; admitted, 1950, Japan; private practice since 1954. *Education:* Tokyo University (LL.B., 1945); Foreign Ministry Training Institute, 1945-1946; Supreme Court Judicial Training Institute, 1947-1950. Author: "A Legal Criticism of Resale Price Maintenance Regulations by the FTC," 55 *Kokusai Shogyo,* 164 (in Japanese), 1973; "Symposium on Legal Ethics," 22 *Ho no Shihai,* 1 (in Japanese), 1972; "The Lawyer's Profession and Calling," *The Legal Profession: The Lawyer's Calling and Ethics,* 1-118, 1969; "For the Development of the Attorney's Profession," 19-1 *Jiyu to Seigi,* 14 (Journal of the Japan Federation of Bar Associations [in Japanese]), 1968; "The Present and Future of the Bar Association," *Gendai no Saiban,* (Special issue at 201 *Hanrei Times,* 45 [in Japanese]), 1967. Foreign Ministry Liaison with Supreme Allied Command, 1946-1947. Lecturer in Civil Law, Tokyo [National] Foreign Language University, 1954-1958. Chairman, International Law Study Committee, Japan International Commercial Arbitration Association, 1972-1973. Member: National Securities Council, 1986—; Legislative Council of the Ministry of Justice, 1976-1978. Leader, Japanese Lawyers Delegation to China, Japanese-Chinese Friendship Association, 1982. *Member:* Japan Federation of Bar Associations (President, 1984-1986; Vice-President, 1975-1976); Dai-ni Tokyo Bar Association (President, 1975-1976; Vice-President, 1964-1965); Kanto District Bar Association (Managing Director, 1965-1966); International Bar Association (Section on Business Law). *LANGUAGES:* Japanese and English. *PRACTICE AREAS:* Civil Litigation; Commercial; Corporate; Real Estate Law; Antitrust.

YUICHI OZAWA, born Tokyo, Japan, 1943; admitted, 1969, Japan; entered Ishii Law Office, 1969. *Education:* Tokyo University (LL.B., 1967); Supreme Court Judicial Training Institute, 1967-1969; University of Michigan, 1972-1973. Editor, "Legal Practice and Forms of Contract for Real Estate Transactions," (in Japanese), 1981. Author: "Internationalization of Business Activities and Foreign Law," (in Japanese), *Kaisha Homu Nyumon* , 1983; "On Amendment of the Anti-Monopoly Law," 140 *New Business Law* 11, (in Japanese), 1977. Co-Author: "The American Partnership: Fundamental Law for Joint Venture" (pts. 1-4, in Japanese), 3 *Kokusai Shoji Homu* (International Business Law) 1975. Managing Member, Legislative Council of the Ministry of Justice, Commercial Law Section, 1985-1991. Instructor, Supreme Court Judicial Training Institute, 1991—. *Member:* Dai-ni Tokyo Bar Association. *LANGUAGES:* Japanese and English. *PRACTICE AREAS:* Civil Litigation; Commercial; Corporate; Real Estate Law; Antitrust.

TAKESHI ODAGI, born Ibaragi, Japan, 1942; admitted, 1970, Japan; entered Ishii Law Office, 1970. *Education:* Tokyo University (LL.B., 1967), Supreme Court Judicial Training Institute, 1968-1970; Columbia Law School (LL.M., 1974). Author: "Precedents on Unlimited Guarantees: Theory and Practice," *New Business Law* (in Japanese), 1981; "Questions and Answers: Is It a Violation of the Antimonopoly Law to Offer One's Best Prices to a Trade Association?" 27 *New Business Law* (in Japanese), 1972. Co-Author: "The American Partnership: Fundamental Law on Joint Venture" (pts. 1-4, in Japanese), 3 *Kokusai Shoji Homu* (International Business Law) 1975. *Member:* Dai-ni Tokyo Bar Association. *LANGUAGES:* Japanese and English. *PRACTICE AREAS:* Civil Litigation; Commercial; Corporate Law; Joint Ventures; Licensing; Real Estate Planning Law.

SHUHEI SAKURAI, born Tottori, Japan, 1946; admitted, 1972, Japan; entered Ishii Law Office, 1972. *Education:* Tokyo University (LL.B., 1970); Boalt Hall School of Law, University of California (LL.M., 1977); Supreme Court Judicial Training Institute, 1970-1972. Author: "Problems with Reduction in Subcontract Prices," 397 *New Business Law,* 1988 *Member:* Dai-ni Tokyo Bar Association. *LANGUAGES:* Japanese and English. *PRACTICE AREAS:* Civil Litigation; Commercial; Corporate; Real Estate Law; Antitrust.

(This Listing Continued)

ISHII LAW OFFICE, Tokyo—Continued

SUMIO MORIWAKI, born Tokyo, Japan, 1957; admitted, 1981, Japan; entered Ishii Law Office, 1981. *Education:* Tokyo University (LL.B., 1979); Supreme Court Judicial Training Institute, 1979-1981; Harvard Law School (LL.M., 1985). Author: "Antitrust Law and Arbitration: the U.S. Precedents," 37 JCA Journal, 1990. With Arnold & Porter, Washington, D.C., 1985-1986. *Member:* Dai-ni Tokyo Bar Association. *LANGUAGES:* Japanese and English. *PRACTICE AREAS:* Civil Litigation; International Transactions; Commercial; Corporate Law.

ASSOCIATES

RIEKO SATO, born Saitama, Japan, 1956; admitted, 1984, Japan; entered Ishii Law Office, 1984. *Education:* Tokyo University (LL.B., 1981); Supreme Court Judicial Training Institute, 1982-1984; University of Illinois Law School (LL.M., 1989). With Shearman & Sterling, New York, N.Y., 1989-1990. *Member:* Dai-ni Tokyo Bar Association. *LANGUAGES:* Japanese and English.

MASAKI OKADA, born Kyoto, Japan, 1959; admitted, 1988, Japan; entered Ishii Law Office, 1988. *Education:* Tokyo University (LL.B., 1986); Supreme Court Judicial Training Institute, 1986-1988; University of Illinois Law School (LL.M., 1994—). With Pillsbury, Madison & Sutro, Los Angeles, California, 1994-1995. *Member:* Dai-ni Tokyo Bar Association. *LANGUAGES:* Japanese and English.

TOSHIAKI YAMADA, born Tokyo, Japan, 1961; admitted, 1988, Japan; 1994, New York; entered Ishii Law Office, 1988. *Education:* Tokyo University (LL.B., 1986); Supreme Court Judicial Training Institute, 1986-1988; Duke University Law School (LL.M., 1993). With, Hale and Dorr, Boston, Massachusetts, 1993-1994. *Member:* Dai-ni Tokyo Bar Association. *LANGUAGES:* Japanese and English.

JUN TAKEUCHI, born Osaka, Japan, 1961; admitted, 1989, Japan; entered Ishii Law Office, 1989. *Education:* Tokyo University (LL.B., 1987); Supreme Court Judicial Training Institute, 1987-1989. *Member:* Dai-ni Tokyo Bar Association. *LANGUAGES:* Japanese and English.

TAKETO TANIGAKI, born Kyoto, Japan, 1964; admitted, 1992, Japan; entered Ishii Law Office, 1992. *Education:* Kyoto University (LL.B., 1990). Supreme Court Judicial Training Institute, 1990-1992. *Member:* Dai-ni Tokyo Bar Association.

YAEKO HODAKA, born Kanagawa, Japan, 1966; admitted, 1992, Japan; entered Ishii Law Office, 1992. *Education:* Keio Gijuku University (LL.B., 1988). Supreme Court Judicial Training Institute, 1990-1992. *Member:* Dai-ni Tokyo Bar Association.

KOJI KATO, born Hukuoka, Japan, 1968; admitted, 1994, Japan; entered Ishii Law Office, 1994. *Education:* Tokyo University (LL.B., 1992). Supreme Court Judicial Training Institute, 1992-1994. *Member:* Dai-ni Tokyo Bar Association.

FOREIGN COUNSEL

THOMAS G. RUTHENBERG, born St. Clair Shores, Michigan, 1955; admitted, 1988, California; entered Ishii Law Office, 1988 (Not admitted in Japan). *Education:* University of Michigan (B.A., 19 84); Hastings College of the Law, University of California (J.D., 1988). Author: "Statutory Requirements for Investment in Japan," Pacific Rim Advisory Council Monograph Series, Auckland Conference, 1990. *Member:* The State Bar of California; American Bar Association.

ISHIZAWA, KÔ & SATO

FUKOKU SEIMEI BUILDING 17 F
2-2, UCHISAIWAICHO 2-CHOME, CHIYODA-KU
TOKYO 100, JAPAN
Telephone: 03-3508-0721
Telecopier: 03-3508-0725

General Practice. Corporation, Taxation, Securities, Antitrust, Intellectual Property, International Business Law. Arbitration and Litigation.

MEMBERS OF FIRM

YOSHIRO ISHIZAWA, born Fukushima, Japan, March 29, 1941; admitted, 1965, Japan. *Education:* Tokyo University (LL.B., 1963); Legal Training and Research Institute of Supreme Court of Japan; Graduate study, Southern Methodist University School of Law (M.C.L., 1972). With Debevoise & Plimpton, 1972. *Member:* First Tokyo Bar Association; Japan Federation of Bar Associations. *LANGUAGES:* Japanese and English.

(This Listing Continued)

PRACTICE AREAS: International Business; Corporate Law; Securities; Intellectual Property; Commercial Law.

YASUHIKO KÔ, born Oita, Japan, June 26, 1947; admitted, 1981, Japan; 1985, New York. *Education:* Tokyo University (LL.B., 1970); Legal Training and Research Institute of the Supreme Court of Japan (1981); Harvard Law School (LL.M., 1983). Author: "Copyright Protection and Video Tape Recorders", 1983; "United States International Trade Law,", 1985. With, Cleary, Gottlieb, Steen & Hamilton, New York Office, 1983-1984, Paris Office, 1984. Corporate Counsel, Pfizer Inc., New York, 1984-1985. Statutory Auditor, The Koa Fire & Marine Insurance Co., Ltd., 1994—. Lecturer, Nippon Bunri University, 1994—. *Member:* First Tokyo Bar Association; Japan Federation of Bar Associations; New York State Bar Association and American Bar Association. *LANGUAGES:* Japanese, English and French.

JUNYA SATO, born Tokyo, Japan, May 4, 1953; admitted, 1982, Japan; 1990, New York. *Education:* Tokyo University (LL.B., 1978); Legal Training and Research Institute of Supreme Court of Japan; Duke University School of Law (LL.M., 1987). With Hughes Hubbard & Reed, 1988-1989. *Member:* First Tokyo Bar Association; Japan Federation of Bar Associations; New York State Bar Association; The Association of the Bar of the City of New York. *LANGUAGES:* Japanese and English. *PRACTICE AREAS:* International Business Transactions; Corporation and Securities.

SHOICHIRO SATO, born Fukushima, Japan, February 16, 1924; admitted, 1950, Japan; Justice of Supreme Court of Japan, 1990-1994. *Education:* Tokyo University (LL.B., 1947); Legal Training and Research Institute of Supreme Court of Japan. *Member:* First Tokyo Bar Association (President, 1981-1982; Vice President, 1970-1971); Japan Federation of Bar Associations (Vice-President, 1981-1982). *LANGUAGES:* Japanese and English.

AKIHIRO SEKIGUCHI, born Tokyo, Japan, April 8, 1964; admitted, 1994, Japan. *Education:* Tokyo University (LL.B., 1989); Legal Training and Research Institute of Supreme Court of Japan. *LANGUAGES:* Japanese and English.

JONES, DAY, REAVIS & POGUE

(DeMarchi Gaikokuho Jimu Bengoshi Jimusho)

TORANOMON MT BUILDING
4TH FLOOR, 10-3, TORANOMON 3-CHOME
MINATO-KU, TOKYO 105, JAPAN
Telephone: 81-3-3433-3939
Telecopier: 81-3-5401-2725

In Atlanta, Georgia: 3500 One Peachtree Center, 303 Peachtree Street, N.E. Telephone: 404-521-3939. Cable Address: "Attorneys Atlanta". Telex: 54-2711. Telecopier: 404-581-8330.

In Brussels, Belgium: Avenue Louise 480, 7th Floor. B-1050 Brussels. Telephone: 32-2-645-14-11. Telecopier: 32-2-645-14-45.

In Chicago, Illinois: 77 West Wacker. Telephone: 312-782-3939. Telecopier: 312-782-8585.

In Cleveland, Ohio: North Point, 901 Lakeside Avenue. Telephone: 216-586-3939. Cable Address: "Attorneys Cleveland." Telex: 980389. Telecopier: 216-579-0212.

In Columbus, Ohio: 1900 Huntington Center. Telephone: 614-469-3939. Cable Address: "Attorneys Columbus." Telecopier: 614-461-4198.

In Dallas, Texas: 2300 Trammell Crow Center, 2001 Ross Avenue. Telephone: 214-220-3939. Cable Address: "Attorneys Dallas." Telex: 730852. Telecopier: 214-969-5100.

In Frankfurt, Germany: Triton Haus, Bockenheimer Landstrasse 42, 60323 Frankfurt am Main. Telephone: 49-69-9726-3939. Telecopier: 49-69-9726-3993.

In Geneva, Switzerland: 20, rue de Candolle. Telephone: 41-22-320-2339. Telecopier: 49-22-320-1232.

In Hong Kong: 1501 One Exchange Square, 8 Connaught Place. Telephone: 852-2526-6895. Telecopier: 852-2810-5787.

In Irvine, California: 2603 Main Street, Suite 900. Telephone: 714-851-3939. Telex: 194911 Lawyers LSA. Telecopier: 714-553-7539.

In London, England: One Mount Street. Telephone: 44-71-493-9361. Cable Address: "Surgoe London WI." Telecopier: 44-71-493-9666.

In Los Angeles, California: 555 West Fifth Street, Suite 4600. Telephone: 213-489-3939. Telex: 181439 UD. Telecopier: 213-243-2539.

In New York, New York: 599 Lexington Avenue. Telephone: 212-326-3939. Cable Address: "JONESDAY NEWYORK." Telex: 237013 JDRP UR. Telecopier: 212-755-7306.

(This Listing Continued)

In Paris, France: 62, rue du Faubourg Saint-Honore. Telephone: 33-1-44-71-3939. Cable Address: "Surgoe Paris." Telex: 290156 Surgoe. Telecopier: 33-1-49-24-0471.

In Pittsburgh, Pennsylvania: 500 Grant Street, 31st Floor. Telephone: 412-391-3939. Cable Address: "Attorneys Pittsburgh". Telecopier: 412-394-7959.

In Riyadh, Saudi Arabia: Law Offices of Saud M.A. Shawwaf, P.O. Box 2700. Telephones: (966-1) 465-6543, (966-1) 464-8534 or (966-1) 464-8540. Telex: 401831 SAUCON SJ. Telecopier: (966-1) 464-8480.

In Taipei, Taiwan: 8th Floor, 2 Tun Hwa South Road, Section 2. Telephone: (886-2) 704-6808. Telecopier: (886-2) 704-6791.

In Washington, D.C.: Metropolitan Square, 1450 G Street, N.W. Telephone: 202-879-3939. Cable Address: "Attorneys Washington." Telex: 89-2410 ATTORNEYS WASH. Telecopier: 202-737-2832.

Firm engaged in American and General International Law Practice as DeMarchi Gaikokuho Jimu Bengoshi Jimusho and not authorized to appear before the Japanese Courts or otherwise to act as Bengoshi.

PARTNERS

DARVIN DEMARCHI, JR., born Buffalo, New York, November 26, 1938; admitted, 1962, Ohio; 1992, Japan (Gaikokuho Jimu Bengoshi). *Education:* Yale University (B.A., 1959; LL.B., 1962). Order of the Coif.

ASSOCIATES

DAVID R. NELSON, born Hamamatsu, Japan, March 25, 1960; admitted, 1986, Washington; 1990, California (Not admitted in Japan). *Education:* St. Olaf College (B.A., 1983); Columbia University (J.D., 1986).

Languages: Japanese, Chinese (Mandarin).

KAJITANI LAW OFFICES

672 MARUNOUCHI BUILDING
2-4-1 MARUNOUCHI CHIYODA-KU
TOKYO 100, JAPAN
Telephone: 81-3-3212-1451
Cable Address: "Kajitani Law Tokyo"
Facsimile: 81-3-3201-5456

General and International Practice, Commercial, Corporation, Administrative, Antitrust, Bankruptcy, Insurance and Patent Laws, Litigation.

GEN KAJITANI, born Tokyo, Japan, January 15, 1935; admitted, 1959, Japan. *Education:* Tokyo University (LL.B., 1957); The Legal Training and Research Institute of the Supreme Court of Japan, University of Michigan Law School (M.C.L., 1963); Harvard Law School (1963-1964). Director, Japanese American Society for Legal Studies, 1983—. Member, Labor Relations Commission for Seafarers, 1985—. President, First Tokyo Bar Association, 1993-1994. Vice President, Japanese Federation of Bar Associations, 1993-1994. Councillor, International Bar Association. *Member:* First Tokyo Bar Association; Japanese Federation of Bar Associations. *LANGUAGES:* Japanese and English.

GO KAJITANI, born Tokyo, Japan, November 22, 1936; admitted, 1967, Japan. *Education:* Seikei University (LL.B., 1959); The Legal Training and Research Institute of the Supreme Court of Japan. *Member:* First Tokyo Bar Association; Japanese Federation of Bar Associations; Japan Bar Association. *LANGUAGES:* Japanese and English.

MASAAKI OKA, born Kagawa, Japan, February 2, 1956; admitted, 1982, Japan. *Education:* Tokyo University (LL.B., 1980); The Legal Training and Research Institute of the Supreme Court of Japan. *Member:* First Tokyo Bar Association; Japanese Federation of Bar Associations. *LANGUAGES:* Japanese and English.

ASSOCIATES

TORU NAGASAWA, born Tochigi, Japan, January 15, 1959; admitted, 1984, Japan. *Education:* Tokyo University (LL.B., 1982); The Legal Training and Research Institute of the Supreme Court of Japan. *Member:* First Tokyo Bar Association; Japanese Federation of Bar Associations. *LANGUAGES:* Japanese and English.

AKINORI WATANABE, born Osaka, Japan, September 25, 1960; admitted, 1986, Japan. *Education:* Tokyo University (LL.B., 1984); The Legal Research and Training Institute of the Supreme Court of Japan. *Member:* First Tokyo Bar Association; Japanese Federation of Bar Associations. *LANGUAGES:* Japanese and English.

YUJI TAKEDA, born Ehime, Japan, November 28, 1961; admitted, 1989, Japan. *Education:* Tokyo University (LL.B., 1986); The Legal Train-

(This Listing Continued)

ing and Research Institute of the Supreme Court of Japan. *Member:* First Tokyo Bar Association; Japanese Federation of Bar Associations. *LANGUAGES:* Japanese and English.

YOKO WACHI, born Kanagawa, Japan, April 29, 1960; admitted, 1989, Japan. *Education:* Waseda University (LL.B., 1984); The Legal Training and Research Institute of the Supreme Court of Japan. *Member:* First Tokyo Bar Association; Japanese Federation of Bar Associations. *LANGUAGES:* Japanese and English.

JO KAWAZOE, born Tokyo, Japan, June 21, 1958; admitted, 1991, Japan. *Education:* Chuo University (LL.B., 1982); The Legal Training and Research Institute of the Supreme Court of Japan. *Member:* First Tokyo Bar Association; Japanese Federation of Bar Associations. *LANGUAGES:* Japanese and English.

NOBUHIRO OKA, born Tokyo, Japan, April 5, 1963; admitted, 1993, Japan. *Education:* Keio University (LL.B., 1986); The Legal Training and Research Institute of the Supreme Court of Japan. *Member:* First Tokyo Bar Association; Japanese Federation of Bar Associations. *LANGUAGES:* Japanese and English.

KEIICHIRO ISHIKAWA, born Tokyo, Japan, November 29, 1964; admitted, 1994, Japan. *Education:* Keio University (LL.B., 1987); The Legal Training and Research Institute of the Supreme Court of Japan. *Member:* First Tokyo Bar Association; Japanese Federation of Bar Associations. *LANGUAGES:* Japanese and English.

KAMANO SOGO LAW OFFICES

AMERICAN INTERNATIONAL BUILDING
20-5 ICHIBANCHO, CHIYODA-KU
TOKYO 102, JAPAN
Telephone: (81) (3) 5276-0131
Fax: (81) (3) 5276-0132

International, General Corporate, Securities, Banking and Antitrust Law.

HIROYUKI KAMANO, born July 21, 1945; admitted, 1981, Japan; 1982, District of Columbia. *Education:* Kyoto University, Kyoto, Japan (LL.B., 1969); University of Tokyo. Tokyo, Japan (LL.M., 1971); Harvard University (LL.M., 1974). Author: "Development of Corporate Democracy in the United States," Civil Minimum (Written in Japanese), January, 1975; "The 15th Ministerial Meeting of OECD," Economy and Diplomacy No. 651 (Written in Japanese), 1976; "OECD Guidelines on Multinational Corporation," Economy and Diplomacy No. 651 (Written in Japanese), 1976; "The 16th Ministerial Meeting of OECD," Economy and Diplomacy No. 663 (Written in Japanese), 1977; "Conference Between Prime Minister Fukuda and President Carter," Economy and Diplomacy No. 673 (Written in Japanese), 1978; "Bilateral Exchange Between Japanese Dietmen and U.S. Congressmen," Economy and Diplomacy No. 680 (Written in Japanese), 1979; "Securities Investment Under the New Foreign Exchange and Foreign Trade Control Law," 3 East Asian Executive Reports No. 6, 3 (Written in English), 1981; "The Japanese and the American in the New Era," Yuai (Written in Japanese), December, 1983; "Japan As a World Leader -- Balancing East With West," 5 Speaking of Japan No. 40, at 14 (Written in English), 1984; "Benefiting From Japan's Liberalized Financial Market," 6 East Asian Executive Reports No. 9, at 9 (Written in English), 1984; "The Meeting-Competition-Defense Under the Robinson-Patman Act," 13 Kokusai Shoji Homu, No. 1, at 7 (Written in Japanese), 1985; "U.S. Ban on Technology Outflow to Communist Bloc Countries," 13 Kokusai Shoji Homu, No. 1, at 56 (Written in Japanese), 1985; "Trade Protectionism in the U.S.," Nihon Keizai Shimbun, April 14-May 7, 1986 (Written in Japanese); "Washington Hotline," Toyo Keizai, 1985-1989, bi-weekly (Written in Japanese); "New Angle," Nihon Kogyo Shimbun, 1987-1990, quarterly (Written in Japanese); "Trouble Outlook," Nihon Kugyo Shimbun, 1991—, monthly (Written in Japanese); "Patent Matia Attacks Japan, "1993 (Written in Japanese). Official and Assistant Director, The Japanese Ministry of Foreign Affairs, 1971-1979. Guest Lecturer: Smithsonian Institute, 1982; Georgetown University Law Center, 1984 and Foreign Service Institute, U.S. Department of State, 1984-1988 and Commentator, Harvard Law School, 1985. *Member:* The District of Columbia Bar; Tokyo Bar Association; American Society of International Law.

KENJI OKAMOTO, born April 1, 1959; admitted, 1993, Japan. *Education:* Kyoto University, Kyoto, Japan (LL.B., 1981). *LANGUAGES:* Japanese, French and English.

(This Listing Continued)

KAMANO SOGO LAW OFFICES, Tokyo—Continued

MIWA MAEFAWA, born January 21, 1967; admitted, 1993, New York. *Education:* Sophia University, Tokyo, Japan (LL.B., 1990); Georgetown Law Center (LL.M., 1992). *LANGUAGES:* Japanese and English.

KAMATA & MATAICHI

TSUKASA BUILDING
15-4 UCHIKANDA 2-CHOME, CHIYODA-KU
TOKYO 101, JAPAN
Telephone: Tokyo 3254-6733
Cable Address: "Attnykubota Tokyo"
Telex: J23955 KBOTALAW
Fax: Tokyo 3258-2867

General and International Law Practice. Corporation, Antitrust, Licensing, Arbitration, Patent, Trademark and Copyright Law.

MEMBERS OF FIRM

TAKASHI KAMATA, born 1935; admitted, 1967, Japan. *Education:* Tokyo University (LL.B., 1959). *Member:* Second Tokyo Bar Association. *LANGUAGES:* Japanese and English. *PRACTICE AREAS:* Civil Law; Commercial Litigation; Patent Law; Trademark Law.

YOSHIO MATAICHI, born 1949; admitted, 1974, Japan; 1987, New York. *Education:* Tokyo University (LL.B., 1972); University of New South Wales (LL.M., 1980); Columbia Law School (LL.M., 1987). *Member:* Second Tokyo and New York State Bar Associations. *LANGUAGES:* Japanese and English. *PRACTICE AREAS:* Patents; Trademarks; Copyright; Licensing; Corporations; Mergers and Acquisitions.

YUMIKO SHIBA, born 1957; admitted, 1983, Japan. *Education:* Tokyo University (LL.B., 1980). *Member:* Second Tokyo Bar Association. *LANGUAGES:* Japanese and English.

KAMORI SOGO

Attorneys at Law
KIOICHO BUILDING
3-12, KIOICHO, CHIYODA-KU
TOKYO 102, JAPAN
Telephone: (81-3) 3238-2920
Telecopier: (81-3) 3238-2631

General Practice. Corporate Finance and Intellectual Property Law. Litigation, Arbitration and Administrative Procedures.

FIRM PROFILE: Admitted in Japan and New York.

MEMBERS OF FIRM

AKIMITSU KAMORI, born Nobeoka, Japan, December 15, 1953; admitted, 1982, Japan; 1988, New York. *Education:* LaSalle H.S. and Oita-Uenogaoka H.S. (1972); Tokyo University, College of Arts and Sciences (1974); Tokyo University (LL.B., Private Law, 1978; LL.B., Public Law, 1980); Legal Training and Research Institute of Supreme Court of Japan (Degree in Law, 1982); Yale University (Diploma, American Law, 1986); Cornell Law School (LL.M., 1987). Law Clerk to Hon. Ryohei Kusaba, Kofu District Court, Kofu, Japan, 1980-1981. With:Nishimura & Sanada, Tokyo, Japan, 1982-1986; St. John, Oberdorf, Williams, Edington & Curtin (now Robinson, St. John & Wayne), New York, 1987-1988; Dewey Ballantine, New York, 1988-1994. *Member:* Japan Federation of Bar Associations; The Dai-Ichi Tokyo Bar Association; American Bar Association; New York State Bar Association; The Association of the Bar of the City of New York; AIPPI (International Intellectual Property Association).

KANEKO & IWAMATSU

Established in 1957
906 SHIN KOKUSAI BUILDING
4-1 MARUNOUCHI 3-CHOME, CHIYODA-KU
TOKYO 100, JAPAN
Telephone: 81-3-214-3631
Facsimile: 81-3-284-0814

Intellectual Property, Patent, Copyright, Trade Secret and Trademark. Medical, Pharmaceutical and Environmental Law, Corporation and Bankruptcy.

(This Listing Continued)

AS148B

MEMBERS OF FIRM

TATSUO KUROYANAGI, born Tokyo, Japan, February 20, 1932; admitted, 1957, Japan. *Education:* Tohoku University (LL.B., 1955). Author: "A Study on the Medical Malpractice Litigation," 1987. *Member:* Daini Tokyo Bar Association (Vice President, 1977).

IWAO HANAOKA, born Tokyo, Japan, January 5, 1934; admitted, 1959, Japan. *Education:* Tokyo University (LL.B., 1957). Former Instructor, Civil Practice, Legal Training and Research Institute, The Supreme Court of Japan. *Member:* Daini Tokyo Bar Association; AIPPI (Japan).

KAZUO TEZUKA, born Tokyo, Japan, April 7, 1941; admitted, 1967, Japan. *Education:* Tokyo University (LL.B., 1965); Columbia University (LL.M., 1972). *Member:* Daini Tokyo Bar Association (Vice President, 1991).

MASAYUKI ABE, born Hokkaido, Japan, November 29, 1950; admitted, 1979, Japan. *Education:* Tokyo University (LL.B., 1976). *Member:* Daini Tokyo Bar Association.

KATSUYOSHI SHIMBO, born Mie, Japan, April 8, 1955; admitted, 1984, Japan. *Education:* Tokyo University (LL.B., 1980). *Member:* Daini Tokyo Bar Association.

TAKAO KARASAWA, born Miyagi, Japan, September 29, 1959; admitted, 1990, Japan. *Education:* Keio Gijuku University (LL.B., 1982). *Member:* Daini Tokyo Bar Association.

TAKASHI KISAKI, born Hyogo, Japan, May 29, 1964; admitted, 1991, Japan. *Education:* Tokyo University (LL.B., 1989). *Member:* Daini Tokyo Bar Association.

Languages: Japanese, English, German and French.

KASHIWAGI SOGO LAW OFFICES

Established in 1959

Formerly known as

Kashiwagi & Yamashita.

7TH FLOOR, DAIWA BANK TORANOMON BUILDING
6-21, 1-CHOME, NISHI-SHIMBASHI, MINATO-KU
TOKYO 105, JAPAN
Telephone: 81-3-3503-5464
Cable Address: KASHIWAGILAW
Fax: 81-3-3581-0305/0320

General Domestic and International Practice, Administrative, Banking, Bankruptcy, Commercial, Construction, Copyright, Corporate, Foreign Investments, Labor and Employment, Litigation, Patent and Trademark Law, Real Estate and Trade Regulation.

FIRM PROFILE: Established in 1959, Kashiwagi Sogo Law Offices has long represented clients in international transactions in addition to maintaining a substantial domestic practice. The firm's combined expertise in domestic and multinational matters enables it to guide its overseas clients conducting business in Japan, as well as advise its Japanese clients with investments and businesses abroad.

Mr. Kaoru Kashiwagi, the firm's founding partner, and the other members of the firm are dedicated to providing their clients with excellent legal representation based on experience, continuing legal education, and active involvement in business and legal developments.

MEMBERS OF FIRM

KAORU KASHIWAGI, born Tokyo, Japan; admitted, 1952, Japan; 1989, Hawaii (Foreign Law Consultant). *Education:* Tokyo University (LL.B., 1950); Judicial Training and Research Institute of the Supreme Court of Japan (1950-1952); International and Comparative Law Center, Dallas, Texas (1977). Author: "Opening of Japan's Public Works Construction Market: Dramatic Changes in Japan's Bidding System," International Construction Law Review Summer, 1994. Member, Advisory Board, International and Comparative Law Center (1980—). Member, Mediation Committee, Tokyo Family Court (1970). Member, Sub-Committee for Compulsory Execution in Civil Affairs, Legislative Council, Ministry of Justice (1979-1980). Member, Consultation Committee for Enactment of the Rules of Civil Affairs, Supreme Court (1980). Member, Sub-Committee for Commercial Code, Legislative Council, Ministry of Justice (1983-1985). Of Counsel, Society for Prevention of Cruelty to Animals, (1975—). *Member:* Daini Tokyo Bar Association (Vice-President, 1965); Keizai Doyu Kai; U.S.-Japan Association; Tokyo American Club. *LANGUAGES:* Japanese and English. *PRACTICE AREAS:* Litigation; Arbitration; Antitrust; Cor-

(This Listing Continued)

porate-reorganization; Bankruptcy; Construction; Civil and Commercial Law.

KOJI MATSUURA, born Nagoya, Japan; admitted, 1979, Japan. *Education:* Tokyo University (LL.B., 1975; LL.B., 1977); Judicial Research and Training Institute of the Supreme Court of Japan (1977-1979); International and Comparative Law Center, Dallas, Texas (1979). Author: "Intellectual Property Rights," Japan Business Law Letter, Vol. 1, No. 9, 1989. Co Author: "Law and Technology of Machine Translation," SOFTIC, 1992; "Reverse Engineering," SOFTIC, 1991; "Violations of Intellectual Property Rights," Chukei Shuppan, 1988. *Member:* Daini Tokyo Bar Association. *LANGUAGES:* Japanese and English. *PRACTICE AREAS:* Litigation; Business Law; Patent; Copyright; Intellectual Property.

HIROSHI IMAI, born Tokyo, Japan; admitted, 1979, Japan. *Education:* Tokyo University (LL.B., 1977); Judicial Research and Training Institute of the Supreme Court of Japan (1977-1979); University of British Columbia (LL.M., 1983). *Member:* Daini Tokyo Bar Association. *LANGUAGES:* Japanese and English. *PRACTICE AREAS:* Foreign Investment; Corporate; Banking; Business Law.

SHUICHI KASHIWAGI, born Tokyo, Japan; admitted, 1980, Japan. *Education:* Waseda University (LL.B., 1977); Judicial Research and Training Institute of the Supreme Court of Japan (1978-1980); International and Comparative Law Center, Dallas, Texas (1982); Columbia University School of Law (LL.M., 1983). Associate, Skadden, Arps, Slate, Meagher & Flom, (1983-1984). Co-Author: "Doing Business in Japan," Japan Legal Publishers, 1990. *Member:* Daini Tokyo Bar Association. *LANGUAGES:* Japanese and English. *PRACTICE AREAS:* Administrative; Commercial; Corporate; Trade Regulation.

TAKU FUKUI, born Tokyo, Japan; admitted, 1987, Japan. *Education:* Keio University (LL.B., 1985); Judicial Research and Training Institute of the Supreme Court of Japan (1985-1987); International and Comparative Law Center, Dallas, Texas (1988). Co Author: "An Introduction to Antitrust Law for Bankers," 1992; "Unlawful Acts," Japan Business Law Letter, Oct. 1989. *Member:* Daini Tokyo Bar Association. *LANGUAGES:* Japanese and English. *PRACTICE AREAS:* Litigation; Arbitration; Antitrust; Banking; Commercial; Insurance.

MIKAKO NAGAO, born Tokyo, Japan; admitted, 1989, Japan. *Education:* Keio University (LL.B., 1984); Judicial Research and Training Institute of the Supreme Court of Japan (1987-1989); International and Comparative Law Center, Dallas, Texas (1990). Co-Author: "1993 Revised Commercial Code - Practice and Policy," Dai Ichi Houki, 1993. *Member:* Daini Tokyo Bar Association. *LANGUAGES:* Japanese and English. *PRACTICE AREAS:* Bankruptcy; Commercial; Construction; Real Estate.

NAOTO KASAI, born Kawasaki, Japan; admitted, 1990, Japan. *Education:* Chuo University (LL.B., 1985); Judicial Research and Training Institute of the Supreme Court of Japan (1988-1990); International and Comparative Law Center, Dallas, Texas (1991). Co-Author: "Housing Lending Law," Gyosei 1992. *Member:* Daini Tokyo Bar Association. *LANGUAGES:* Japanese and English. *PRACTICE AREAS:* Business Law; Litigation; Real Estate; Trade Regulation.

MITSUYOSHI SAITO, born Tokyo, Japan; admitted, 1992, Japan. *Education:* Hitotsubashi University (LL.B., 1990); Judicial Research and Training Institute of the Supreme Court of Japan (1990-1992); International and Comparative Law Center, Dallas, Texas (1993). *Member:* Daini Tokyo Bar Association. *LANGUAGES:* Japanese and English. *PRACTICE AREAS:* Administrative; Commercial; Labor; Bankruptcy.

MICHAEL J. YOSHII, born California; admitted, 1984, Hawaii; 1988, California; 1993, Japan as Foreign Licensed Attorney (Gaikokuho Jimu Bengoshi). *Education:* Dartmouth College, Hanover, New Hampshire (B.A., cum laude, 1978); University of California, Davis School of Law (J.D., 1982). Author: "Appellate Standards of Review in Hawaii," 7 Univ. of Hawaii Law Review, 277-300, 1985. Instructor, Vermont Law School, South Royalton, Vermont, 1982-1983. Law Clerk, Hawaii Supreme Court, 1983-1984. *Member:* Daini Tokyo Bar Association; Hawaii State Bar Association; California State Bar Association. *LANGUAGES:* English and Japanese. *PRACTICE AREAS:* International Litigation; Intellectual Property; Licensing; Real Estate Development; Antitrust.

AKIKO KUROKOCHI, born Tokyo, Japan; admitted, 1994, Japan. *Education:* Waseda University (LL.B., 1983); Judicial Research and Training Institute of the Supreme Court of Japan (1992-1994). *Member:* Daini Tokyo Bar Association. *LANGUAGES:* Japanese and English. *PRACTICE AREAS:* Litigation; Commercial; Antitrust; Trade Regulation; Criminal Law.

(This Listing Continued)

REPRESENTATIVE CLIENTS: Autodesk K.K.; ACT Financial Systems Ltd.; Air New Zealand; Bowater Corporation; COBE Laboratories, Inc.; Dai-Ichi Kangyo Bank; Fujita Corp.; Honshu Chemical; JGC Corporation; Kowa Real Estate Investment Co., Ltd.; Kyoduto Petroleum Industry Ltd.; Mitsui & Co.; Mitsui Kanko Development Co., Ltd.; Mitsui Leasing & Development, Ltd.; Mitsui Oil Exploration Co., Ltd.; Naigai Co., Ltd.; Nihon Unisys, Ltd.; Nippon Paint; Obayashi Corporation; SABIC; Satake Corporation; Shin-Etsu Chemical Co., Ltd.; Shin Nikkei Company, Ltd.; 3DO Japan; Toho Bussan Kaisha Ltd.; Tokyo Telemessage Inc.; Western Digital Corporation

---

KELLEY DRYE & WARREN

(Gaikokuho-Jimu Bengoshi-Jimusho)

A Partnership including Professional Associations

TORANOMON 37 BUILDING 5F

3-5-1, TORANOMON, MINATO-KU

TOKYO 105, JAPAN

Telephone: (3) 5472-6351

Fax: (3) 5472-6431

New York, N.Y. Office: 101 Park Avenue, 10178. Telephone: 212-808-7800. Telex: 12369. Fax: (212) 808-7897.

Los Angeles, California Office: 515 South Flower Street, 90071. Telephone: 213-689-1300. Fax: (213) 688-8150.

Washington, D.C. Office: 1200 19th Street, N.W., Suite 500. 20036. Telephone: 202-955-9600. Fax: (202) 955-9792.

Chicago, Illinois Office: Suite 1400, 303 West Madison Street, 60606. Telephone: 312-346-6350. Fax: (312) 346-8982.

Stamford, Connecticut Office: Two Stamford Plaza, 281 Tresser Boulevard, 06901-3229. Telephone: 203-324-1400. Fax: (203) 327-2669; (203) 964-3188.

Miami, Florida Office: 201 South Biscayne Boulevard, 2400 Miami Center, 33131. Telephone: 305-372-2400. Fax: (305) 372-2490.

Parsippany, New Jersey Office: 5 Sylvan Way, 07054. Telephone: 201-539-0099. Fax: (201) 539-3167.

Brussels, Belgium Office: 106 Avenue Louise, 1050. Telephone: (2) 646 1110. Fax: (2) 640-0589.

Firm engaged in American and General International Law Practice but not authorized to appear before Japanese Courts or to act as Bengoshi.

RESIDENT ASSOCIATES

TETSUYA OGAWA, born Osaka, Japan, 1960; admitted, 1987, California, U.S. District Court, Central District of California and U.S. Court of Appeals, Ninth Circuit; 1994, Japan (Gaikokuho Jimu Bengoshi). *Education:* University of California at Irvine (B.A., 1982); Pepperdine University (J.D., 1986). *Member:* State Bar of California; Tokyo Dai-Ichi Bar Association. *LANGUAGES:* Japanese.

(For Biographical data on all Personnel, see Professional Biographies at New York, N.Y.).

KOBAYASHI AND TODO

SUITE 403, SANNO GRAND BUILDING

14-2, NAGATA-CHO 2-CHOME, CHIYODA-KU

TOKYO 100, JAPAN

Telephone: (03) 3580-2036

Cable: "TOKOBALAW TOKYO"

Telex: J28810 KOBALAW

Fax: (03) 3580-0789

General and International Practice, Corporation, Patent, Trademark and Copyright Law, Licensing, Antitrust, Litigation.

MEMBERS OF FIRM

TOSHIO KOBAYASHI, admitted, 1961, Japan. *Education:* Tokyo Commercial College (Hitotsubashi University); Tokyo University (LL.B.); Legal Training and Research Institute of Supreme Court of Japan. Author: "Management of Trademark," Toyo Keizai Shinpo Sha; "Directory of Industrial Property Rights," Nikkan Kogyo Shinbun Sha. *Member:* Japan Federation of Bar Associations; Daini Tokyo Bar Association. *LANGUAGES:* Japanese and English.

YUTAKA TODO, admitted, 1970, Japan. *Education:* Keio University (LL.B.); Legal Training and Research Institute of Supreme Court of Japan. Prosecutor, Yokohama District Court. With Tokyo District Prosecutor's Office. Secretary and Referee, Federal Trade Commission. *Member:* Japan Federation of Bar Associations; Daini Tokyo Bar Association. *LANGUAGES:* Japanese and French.

(This Listing Continued)

KOBAYASHI AND TODO, Tokyo—Continued

YASUTERU TERAKAMI, admitted, 1975, Japan. *Education:* Keio University (LL.B.); Legal Training and Research Institute of Supreme Court of Japan. *Member:* Japan Federation of Bar Associations; Daini Tokyo Bar Association. *LANGUAGES:* Japanese and English.

KEIICHI IWASHITA, admitted, 1985, Japan. *Education:* Tokyo Commercial College (Hitotsubashi University - LL.B.); Legal Training and Research Institute of Supreme Court of Japan. *Member:* Japan Federation of Bar Associations; Daini Tokyo Bar Association. *LANGUAGES:* Japanese and English.

SHIN'ICHI OKAMURA, admitted, 1984 as registered Patent Attorney, Japan. *Education:* Chuo University (B.L.). *Member:* Japan Patent Attorney Association. *LANGUAGES:* Japanese and English.

GEN KANO, admitted, 1992, Japan. *Education:* Keio University (LL.B.); Legal Training and Research Institute of Supreme Court of Japan. *Member:* Japan Federation of Bar Association; Daini Tokyo Bar Association. *LANGUAGES:* Japanese and English.

KOGA & PARTNERS

Established in 1970

SUITE 401, SHUWA DAINI SHIBA-KOEN 3-CHOME BLDG.

22-1, TORANOMON 3 -CHOME, MINATO-KU

TOKYO 105, JAPAN

Telephone: 81-3-3578-8681

Telecopier: 81-3-3578-8682

General Practice. Corporation, International, Trade, Investment, Estate, Taxation, Product Liability, Copyright, Trademark, Labor, Criminal and Administrative Law. Litigation.

FIRM PROFILE: KOGA & PARTNERS has nine lawyers. The firm was founded by Masayoshi Koga in 1970. The other eight lawyers have subsequently joined the firm. Four lawyers have obtained M.C.L. from the Law Schools of the University of Washington, University of Michigan and University of California (Berkeley), respectively, and one has studied at the Cambridge University. The two junior partners are admitted to the New York bar.

Although the size of the firm is not large, its practices encompass broad areas of law, including corporate business, international business, litigation, industrial property rights, copyright and real estate investment.

MEMBERS OF FIRM

MASAYOSHI KOGA, born Saga Prefecture, Japan, March 20, 1927; admitted, 1957, Japan. *Education:* Tokyo University (LL.B., 1952). Author: "Court on Trial", by Jerome Frank (Translation), 1960; "Art of Advocacy", by L.D. Stryker (Translation), 1961; "Basic Problems on the History of The Japanese Bar", 1970. Lecturer, Aoyama Gakuin Women's Junior College, 1967-1970. Member, Legislative Council to the Ministry of Justice, 1979-1982. *Member:* Daini Tokyo Bar Association (President, 1972); Japan Federation of Bar Associations (Vice President, 1972); Japan Bar Association (Director, 1972-1977); Japanese-American Society for Legal Studies; Judicial Examination Management Committee (Ministry of Justice). *LANGUAGES:* Japanese, English, French and German (Reading only). *PRACTICE AREAS:* General Practice.

SEIICHI YOSHIKAWA, born Kanagawa Prefecture, Japan, March 31, 1941; admitted, 1965, Japan. *Education:* Tokyo University (LL.B., 1963); University of Washington Law School (M.C.L., 1969). Author: "The English Legal Profession", 1976. Co-author: "The Warren Court," by Archibold Cox (Translation), 1970; "Fair Trade Commission vs., MITI: History of the Conflict between the Antimonopoly Policy and the Industrial Policy in the Post War Period of Japan", Case Western Reserve Journal of International Law, Vol. 15, 1983. *Member:* Daini Tokyo Bar Association (President, 1993); Japan Federation of Bar Associations (Vice President, 1993); Japanese-American Society for Legal Studies; The Law Association for Asian and Western Pacific. *LANGUAGES:* Japanese, English and French (Reading only). *PRACTICE AREAS:* International; Corporation; Litigation.

YOICHIRO YAMAKAWA, born Ehime Prefecture, Japan, July 21, 1941; admitted, 1966, Japan. *Education:* Tokyo University (LL.B., 1964); University of Michigan Law School (M.C.L., 1969). Author: "Freedom of the Press and The Law of Libel", 1970. Co-author: "The Warren Court", by Archibold Cox (Translation), 1970. Lecturer, Hosei University Law Faculty, 1970-1972. Visiting Professor, University of Michigan Law School,

1991-1992. *Member:* Daini Tokyo Bar Association; Japan Federation of Bar Associations; International Bar Association (Member, Section on Business Law). *LANGUAGES:* Japanese and English. *PRACTICE AREAS:* Freedom of Expression; Joint Venture; Licensing; Distributorship; Intellectual Property Rights; Real Estate Investment; General Corporate Practice; Litigation.

AKIRA NAKAGAWA, born Niigata Prefecture, Japan, August 23, 1941; admitted, 1970, Japan. *Education:* Kyoto University (LL.B., 1964). *Member:* Daini Tokyo Bar Association; Japan Federation of Bar Associations. *LANGUAGES:* Japanese and English. *PRACTICE AREAS:* Litigation.

ISOMI SUZUKI, born Tokyo, Japan, April 17, 1950; admitted, 1975, Japan; 1981, New York. *Education:* Hitotsubashi University (LL.B., 1973); University of California at Berkeley (LL.M., 1979). Author: "Foreign Monetary Obligation and the Article 403 of the Civil Code", Jurist, June 1, 1976. Co-Author: "Commentary on Arbitration Law," 1988. Recipient, Fulbright Scholarship, 1978-1980. *Member:* Daini Tokyo Bar Association; Japan Federation of Bar Associations; Japan Private International Law Association; American Bar Association (Member, Section on Business Law, Antitrust and International Law). *LANGUAGES:* Japanese and English. *PRACTICE AREAS:* Private International Law; Mergers and Acquisitions; International Corporate Transaction; Transnational Litigation.

YOICHI KITAMURA, born Tokyo, Japan, November 9, 1950; admitted, 1977, Japan; 1983, New York. *Education:* Tokyo University (LL.B., 1975); University of Michigan Law School (M.C.L., 1981). Co-author: "Against the Law," by Leonard Levy (Translation), 1981. *Member:* Daini Tokyo Bar Associations; Japan Federation of Bar Associations. *LANGUAGES:* Japanese and English. *PRACTICE AREAS:* Intellectual Property Rights; Trademark; Criminal; Litigation.

ASSOCIATES

YOKO HAYASHI, born Ibaragi Prefecture, Japan, June 9, 1956; admitted, 1983, Japan. *Education:* Waseda University (LL.B., 1979); Newnham College, University of Cambridge (1987-1988). Author: "The Legal Profession in England," Jurist, November 1, 1988. *Member:* Daini Tokyo Bar Association. *LANGUAGES:* Japanese and English. *PRACTICE AREAS:* Litigation; Estate; Corporate.

AKIKO ONO, born Kanagawa Prefecture, Japan, February 21, 1963; admitted, 1993, Japan. *Education:* Waseda University (LL.B., 1985). *Member:* Daini Tokyo Bar Association. *LANGUAGES:* Japanese and English. *PRACTICE AREAS:* Copyright; Corporation; International; Litigation.

TATSUO NINOSEKI, born Tokyo, Japan, June 25, 1963; admitted, 1994, Japan. *Education:* Hitotsubashi University (LL.B., 1987). *Member:* Daini Tokyo Bar Association. *LANGUAGES:* Japanese and English. *PRACTICE AREAS:* Corporate; Copyright; Criminal; Litigation.

OF COUNSEL

HIDEO SHIMIZU, born Tokyo, Japan, October 21, 1922; admitted, 1988, Japan. *Education:* Faculty of Law, University of Tokyo (Bachelor). Author: "Freedom of Thought, Conscience and Speech," 1961; "Law and Mass Communication," 1970; "Communication Law," 1979; "Disclosure of Public Information," 1981; "Communication Law 2," 1987; "Ethics of Mass Media," 1990. Professor Emeritus, Aoyama Gakuin University. Commissioner, Administration Commission of Motion Picture Code of Japan, 1990—. Chairman, Council of Publishing Ethics of Japan, 1990—. *Member:* Japan Federation of Bar Association; The Japan Society for Studies in Mass Communication; The Japan Society for Publishing Studies; The Japan Society for Public Law Studies; Japan Civil Liberties Union. *LANGUAGES:* Japanese, English and German (Reading only). *PRACTICE AREAS:* Constitution; Media Law.

TSUYOSHI ABE, born Oita, Japan, March 30, 1926; admitted, 1991, Japan. *Education:* Tokyo University (LL.B., 1951). Judge: Fukuoka High Court, 1969-1975; Tokyo High Court, 1981-1985. Chief Judge, Kyoto Family Court, 1989-1991. *Member:* Daini Tokyo Bar Association; Japan Federation of Bar Associations. *LANGUAGES:* Japanese and English. *PRACTICE AREAS:* Family Law.

AKINOBU TANSO, born Saga Prefecture, Japan, June 3, 1927; admitted, 1979, Kyoto, Japan; 1993, Tokyo, Japan. *Education:* Tokyo University (LL.B., 1952); Special Fellow of Tokyo University (1952-1957); Kyushu University (Doctor of Law, 1962). Visiting Scholar (as Fulbrighter) at Law School of Pennsylvania University and Law School of Columbia University, 1961-1963. Visiting Professor (Fellowship of American Council of Learned Societies) at Law School of Columbia University, 1971-192. Law Department of Freiburg University and München University in Germany, 1972-

(This Listing Continued)

(This Listing Continued)

1973. Associate Professor, Kyushu University, 1958-1967. Professor, Hokkaido University, 1967-1969. Dean of the Faculty of Law, Ritsumeikan University, 1984-1985. Chairman of Graduate (Doctor) Course, Daitobunka University, 1993—. Books and Articles: several books concerning Japanese Antimonopoly Law and more than 60 papers on economic law and international economic law. *Member:* Daini Tokyo Bar Association. *LANGUAGES:* Japanese, English and German. *PRACTICE AREAS:* Antitrust; Joint Venture; Intellectual Property; Dumping; International Trade Conflicts.

TOSHIO YANAGIHARA, born Niigata, Japan, September 21, 1951; admitted, 1983, Japan. *Education:* Tokyo University (LL.B., 1977). *Member:* Tokyo Bar Association. *LANGUAGES:* Japanese. *PRACTICE AREAS:* Copyright.

REPRESENTATIVE CLIENTS: Bungei Shunju Sha; Celine; Club Corporation of Asia; Daiichi Life Insurance Co., Ltd; Electronic Industries Association of Japan; General Sekiyu K.K. (Exxon affiliate); Japan Tobacco Corporation; The Mitsubishi Bank; The Mitsui Bank & Trust Corporation; Nippon Soda Co., Ltd.; PFU Limited; Sears, Roebuck and Co.; Shuei Sha; Time Warner Inc.; The Toa Fire and Marine Re-Insurance Co., Ltd; Turner Broadcasting Systems, Inc.; The Walt Disney Company; The Yomiuri Shimbun-Sha ; Yomiuri Travel, Inc.

KOGO, MORI & FUJIMOTO

SUITE 402, SHUWA KIOI-CHO PARK BUILDING

3-6, KIOI-CHO, CHIYODA-KU

TOKYO 102, JAPAN

Telephone: 03-5275-5241

Facsimile: 03-5275-5259

Commercial, Corporate and International Practice. Admiralty.

MEMBERS OF FIRM

MOTOHIKO KOGO, born Chiba, Japan, February 11, 1941; admitted, 1967, Japan. Proctor in Admiralty, 1971. *Education:* Waseda University (LL.B., 1963; LL.M., 1965); Southern Methodist University Law School (M.C.L., 1971). *Member:* Tokyo Bar Association.

ITSUKO MORI, born Mie, Japan; admitted, 1967, Japan. *Education:* Tohoku University (LL.B., 1959); The Graduate School of Tohoku University (LL.M., 1962); Continuing Legal Education Program at Academy of American and International Law by the South Western Legal Foundation, Dallas, Texas (1972). *Member:* First Tokyo Bar Association.

EISUKE FUJIMOTO, born Kumamoto, Japan, October 26, 1950; admitted, 1980, Japan. *Education:* Chuo University (LL.B., 1976). *Member:* First Tokyo Bar Association.

YASUYUKI KURIBAYASHI, born Aichi, Japan, December 14, 1962; admitted, 1992, Japan. *Education:* Osaka University (LL.B., 1988). *Member:* Tokyo Bar Association.

LAW OFFICES OF HIDEKI KOJIMA

Established in 1984

GOBANCHO KATAOKA BUILDING

GOBANCHO 2-7 CHIYODA-KU

TOKYO 102, JAPAN

Telephone: (81-3) 3222-1401

Telefax: (81-3) 3222-1405

International, Commercial, Corporate, Banking, Property, Litigation, Finance and Corporate Law.

HIDEKI KOJIMA, born Kanagawa, Japan, February 17, 1947; admitted, 1973, Japan; 1981, New York. *Education:* Waseda University (LL.B., 1970); The Legal Training and Research Institute of the Supreme Court of Japan (1971-1973); Georgetown University Law Center (M.C.L., 1979); Southern Methodist University (M.C.L., 1978). Author: "Law of International Sales of Goods," (in Japanese), Roppo Shuppan, 1986. Lecturer, Law Department, Nippon University 1984-1993. *Member:* Daini-Tokyo and International Bar Associations; Japan Federation of Bar Associations; Association Internationale des Jeunes Avocats; American Bar Association; New York State Bar Association; Inter-Pacific Bar Association. *LANGUAGES:* Japanese and English. *PRACTICE AREAS:* International Business Law.

ASSOCIATES

NAOKI IDEI, born Kumamoto, Japan, October 31, 1960; admitted, 1988, Japan; 1994, New York. *Education:* Tokyo University (LL.B., 1985); The Legal Training and Research Institute of the Supreme Court of Japan (1986-1988); New York University School of Law (LL.M. in Trade Regulation, 1993). Co-Author: "On Referential Use of Copyrighted Work" (in Japanese), Research on Intellectual Property Rights Vol. I., Tokyo-Nunoi Shuppan, 1989. *Member:* Daini-Tokyo Bar Association; Japan Federation of Bar Associations. *LANGUAGES:* Japanese and English. *PRACTICE AREAS:* International Business Law; Corporate Law; Civil Litigation; Antitrust and Trade Regulation; Intellectual Property Law.

MACHIKO FUJIMURA, born Tokyo, Japan, September 1, 1949; admitted, 1978, Japan. *Education:* Tokyo Metropolitan University (LL.B., 1974). The Legal Training and Research Institute of the Supreme Court of Japan (1976-1978). Legal Professional: Assistant Judge of District Court (1978-1986). *Member:* Daini-Tokyo Bar Association; Japan Federation of Bar Associations. *LANGUAGES:* Japanese and English. *PRACTICE AREAS:* Litigation; Property Law.

YOSHITADA OGISO, born Tokyo, Japan, March 25, 1956; admitted, 1985, Japan; 1994, New York. *Education:* Waseda University, Faculty of Political Science and Economics (B.A., 1981); The Legal Training and Research Institute of the Supreme Court of Japan (1983-1985); New York University School of Law (LL.M., 1992). Author: "Employees Pension Law: Related Issues in Connection with Takeovers of Companies and Businesses." Legal Professional: Assistant Judge of Maebashi District and Family Court, 1987-1988 and Assistant Judge of Civil Division of Nagoya District Court, 1985-1987. *Member:* Daiichi-Tokyo Bar Association; Japan Federation of Bar Associations. *LANGUAGES:* Japanese and English. *PRACTICE AREAS:* International Business and Litigation; Corporate Law; Securities Regulation and Structured Finance.

TAKESHI KIKUCHI, born Tokyo, Japan, December 27, 1959; admitted, 1992, Japan. *Education:* Tokyo University (LL.B., 1985); The Legal Training and Research Institute of the Supreme Court of Japan (1990-1992). *Member:* Daini-Tokyo Bar Association; Japan Federation of Bar Associations. *LANGUAGES:* Japanese and English. *PRACTICE AREAS:* Intellectual Property; Litigation.

KAZUNORI KIRIHARA, born Nakamachi, Ibaraki Prefecture, Japan, September 3, 1959; admitted, 1992, Japan. *Education:* Chuo University (LL.B., 1984); The Legal Training and Research Institute of the Supreme Court of Japan (1990-1992). *Member:* Daini-Tokyo Bar Association; Japan Federation of Bar Associations. *LANGUAGES:* Japanese and English. *PRACTICE AREAS:* International Business; Intellectual Property.

HIROMASA OGAWA, born Shizuoka Prefecture, Japan, November 21, 1963; admitted, 1993, Japan. *Education:* Chuo University (LL.B., 1986); The Legal Training and Research Institute of the Supreme Court of Japan (1991-1993). *Member:* Daini-Tokyo Bar Association; Japan Federation of Bar Associations. *LANGUAGES:* Japanese and English. *PRACTICE AREAS:* International Business.

YUJI NANAMEKI, born Tokyo, Japan, December 12, 1958; admitted, 1994, Japan. *Education:* Gakushuin University (LL.B., 1982); The Legal Training and Research Institute of the Supreme Court of Japan (1992-1994). *Member:* Daini-Tokyo Bar Association; Japan Federation of Bar Associations. *LANGUAGES:* Japanese and English.

SAYURI UMEDA, born Hokkaido, Japan, December 27, 1963; admitted, 1994, Japan. *Education:* Chuo University (LL.B., 1986); The Legal Training and Research Institute of the Supreme Court of Japan (1992-1994). *Member:* Daini-Tokyo Bar Association; Japan Federation of Bar Associations. *LANGUAGES:* Japanese and English. *PRACTICE AREAS:* International Business; Intellectual Property.

YUMI JAMOCHI, born Hyogo Prefecture, Japan, June 4, 1968; admitted, 1994, Japan. *Education:* Osaka University (LL.B., 1992); The Legal Training and Research Institute of the Supreme Court of Japan (1992-1994). *Member:* Daini-Tokyo Bar Association; Japan Federation of Bar Associations. *LANGUAGES:* Japanese and English.

OF COUNSEL

LYNN F. PICKARD, born Syracuse, New York, May 4, 1941; admitted, 1972, New York (Not admitted in Japan). *Education:* Syracuse University (B.A. Philosophy, 1963); New York University, School of Law (J.D., 1971); Sophia University, Tokyo, Japan, Graduate School of International Business (1975). Author: "Japanese Law Concerning Product Liability," Yuasa and Hara Journal, 1977; "Service of Process on a Japanese Defendant to Commence a Foreign Lawsuit," The International Litigation Quarterly,

(This Listing Continued)

(This Listing Continued)

LAW OFFICES OF HIDEKI KOJIMA, Tokyo—Continued

March, 1989. (U.S. Navy Lieutenant, 1964-1968). With, Whitman & Ransom, Esqs., New York, U.S.A., 1971-1973; Yuasa and Hara, Esqs., Tokyo, Japan, 1976-1983; Central International Law Office, Seoul, Korea, 1983-1985. Member: American Chamber of Commerce in Japan; National Eagle Scout Association. *Member:* American Bar Association; New York State Bar Association; Inter-Pacific Bar Association; Asia-Pacific Lawyers Association; Roppongi Bar Association. *LANGUAGES:* English, Japanese and Korean. *PRACTICE AREAS:* International Business.

CHARLES OCHSNER, born Neuchatel, Switzerland, May 4, 1951; admitted, 1977, Switzerland (Not admitted in Japan). *Education:* University of Geneva, Faculty of Law (License en droit, 1974; Brevet d'avocat, 1977). Board Member, Swiss Chamber of Commerce and Industry in Japan, 1986-1992. (Also Member, Pirenne Python Schifferli Peter & Partners, Geneva, Switzerland). *LANGUAGES:* French, English, Japanese and German.

KAZUO MASUI, born Tokyo, Japan, May 7, 1944; admitted, 1976, Japan. *Education:* Tokyo University (B.Sc., Chemistry, 1967); Japanese Legal Training and Research Institute of the Supreme Court of Japan (1974-1976); Georgetown University Law Center (M.C.L., 1978). *Member:* Daini-Tokyo Bar Association; Japan Federation of Bar Associations. *LANGUAGES:* Japanese and English. *PRACTICE AREAS:* Intellectual Property.

ISAMU HASHIMOTO, born Nagano, Japan, July 16, 1945; admitted, 1986, Japan. *Education:* Tokyo University (LL.B., 1969). Legal Training and Research Institute of the Supreme Court of Japan (1984-1986). Professor, Local Autonomy College, 1982-1983; Assistant Director, Bureau of Finance, 1983-1984 and Assistant Director, Bureau of Administration, 1978-1979, Ministry of Home Affairs; First Secretary, Embassy of Japan in London, 1979-1982. *Member:* Daiichi-Tokyo Bar Association; Japan Federation of Bar Associations. *LANGUAGES:* Japanese and English. *PRACTICE AREAS:* Administrative Law; Advertising and Marketing; Agency and Distributorships; Antitrust and Trade Regulation; Business Law; Chemicals and Chemistry; Company Law; Environmental Law; Intellectual Property; Labor and Employment.

HIROSHI MIYAGAWA, born Tokyo, Japan, September 25, 1953; admitted, 1979, Japan. *Education:* Waseda University (LL.B., 1977); The Legal Training and Research Institute of the Supreme Court of Japan (1977-1979). Author: "Finding of Damages," Japan Federation of Bar Associations, 1988; "Conflicts Regarding Traffic Accidents and Medical Malpractice," Shinnihonhoki, 1989; "Lease Law Counseling," Yuhikaku, 1993 (in Japanese). Legal Professional: Assistant Judge: Fukuoka District Court, 1979-1982; Utsunomiya District and Family Court, 1982-1985; Tokyo District Court, 1985-1987; Yokohama District Court, 1987-1989. Judge of Yokohama District Court, 1989-1991. *Member:* Daiichi-Tokyo Bar Association; Japan Federation of Bar Associations. *LANGUAGES:* Japanese and English. *PRACTICE AREAS:* Litigation.

GREGORY F. BUHYOFF, born Lockport, New York, January 9, 1956; admitted, 1989, California (Not admitted in Japan). *Education:* University of Hawaii (B.A., 1985); University of the Pacific McGeorge School of Law (J.D. with Distinction, 1988). *Member:* California State Bar Association (International Law Section); International Bar Association; Lawasia. *LANGUAGES:* English, Chinese and Vietnamese. *PRACTICE AREAS:* Unfair Competition; Asia-Pacific Investment.

SHUHEI YOSHIDA, born Tokyo, Japan, June 19, 1952; admitted, 1982, Japan. *Education:* Waseda University (LL.B., 1977); The Legal Training and Research Institute of the Supreme Court of Japan (1980-1982). *Member:* Daiichi-Tokyo Bar Association; Japan Federation of Bar Associations. *LANGUAGES:* Japanese. *PRACTICE AREAS:* Property Lease; Domestic Relations; Will and Testament.

KOMATSU & KOMA

Established in 1967
SANNO GRAND BUILDING #815
14-2, NAGATA-CHO 2-CHOME, CHIYODA-KU
TOKYO 100, JAPAN
Telephone: 03-3580-0521
Telex: KOMLAW J33936
Telecopier: 03-3593-1026; 03-3593-3869

General and International Law. Corporation, Securities, Leasing and International Finance, Taxation, Intellectual Property, Administrative, Antitrust, Labor Law and Litigation.

YUSUKE KOMATSU, admitted, 1961, Japan. *Education:* Tokyo University (LL.B.); The Legal Training and Research Institute of the Supreme Court; graduate study, University of Chicago Law School and New York University Law School (LL.M., 1969). With Chicago offices of Baker and McKenzie, 1964-1966 and Whitman and Ransom, New York, 1967-1969. Author: "Legal Analysis of Sino-Japanese Trade", New York University Journal of International Law and Politics, Vol. 1, No. 2, 1968.

KEISUKE KOMATSU, admitted, 1972, Japan. *Education:* Chuo University (LL.B.); The Legal Training and Research Institute of the Supreme Court.

FUMIO KOMA, admitted, 1977, Japan; 1984, New York. *Education:* Waseda University School of Politics and Economics (B.A. in economics, 1971); The Legal Training and Research Institute of the Supreme Court; graduate study, University of Washington Law School (LL.M., 1982). Associated with Whitman and Ransom, New York, 1982-1984. Co-Author: "On Antihaven Tax Measures," 1981. Author: "Shareholders' Derivative Suite," 1994.

KUNICHIKA NAKANO, admitted, 1979, Japan; 1985, New York. *Education:* Osaka University (LL.B., 1972); The Legal Training and Research Institute of the Supreme Court; graduate study, University of Pennsylvania Law School (LL.M., 1985).

YASUNORI HASHIGUCHI, admitted, 1985, Japan. *Education:* Tokyo University (LL.B., 1981); The Legal Training and Research Institute of the Supreme Court; University of Washington (LL.M., 1991). Associated with Davis Wright Tremaine, Washington, 1991-1992.

SHINGO HISATA, admitted, 1986, Japan. *Education:* Tokyo University (LL.B., 1977); The Legal Training and Research Institute of the Supreme Court; University of Illinois at Urbana-Champaign (LL.M., 1991). Associated with Masuda, Funai, Eifert and Mitchell, Chicago, 1991-1992.

JUKO AKATSU, admitted, 1987, Japan. *Education:* Chuo University (LL.B., 1982); The Legal Training and Research Institute of the Supreme Court. Associated with Taylor Joynson Garrett, London, 1991-1992 and Linklaters & Paines, London, 1992-1993.

OSAMU TANAKA, admitted, 1988, Japan. *Education:* Tokyo University (LL.B., 1985); The Legal Training and Research Institute of the Supreme Court.

KEIKO IMAMURA, admitted, 1988, Japan; 1993, New York. *Education:* Keio University (B.A. in Economics, 1982; LL.B., 1984); The Legal Training and Research Institute of the Supreme Court; Harvard Law School (LL.M., 1992). Associated with Weil, Gotshal & Manges, New York, 1992-1993.

WAN-SIK LEE, admitted, 1988, Japan; 1992, New York. *Education:* Waseda University (B.A., 1981); The Legal Training and Research Institute of the Supreme Court; New York University Law School (LL.M., 1991). Associated with Whitman Breed Abbott & Morgan (formerly, Whitman & Ransom), New York, 1991-1992.

YOSHIHIKO AMAGAI, admitted, 1989, Japan. *Education:* Meiji University (LL.B., 1984); The Legal Training and Research Institute of the Supreme Court.

SHUNICHI TAKINO, admitted, 1989, Japan. *Education:* Waseda University (LL.B., 1982; LL.M., 1987); The Legal Training and Research Institute of the Supreme Court.

HIROKO YAMAMOTO, admitted, 1990, Japan. *Education:* Waseda University (LL.B., 1979); The Legal Training and Research Institute of the Supreme Court.

ETSUKO FUNABASHI, admitted, 1991, Japan. *Education:* Waseda University (LL.B., 1980); The Legal Training and Research Institute of the Supreme Court.

(This Listing Continued)

MINORU KOSUGE, admitted, 1991, Japan. *Education:* Waseda University (LL.B., 1986); The Legal Training and Research Institute of the Supreme Court.

KEISUKE MOCHIZUKI, admitted, 1991, Japan. *Education:* Waseda University (LL.B., 1984); The Legal Training and Research Institute of the Supreme Court.

TAKENARI SHIMIZU, admitted, 1992, Japan. *Education:* Waseda University (LL.B., 1990); The Legal Training and Research Institute of the Supreme Court.

TETSURO SATO, admitted, 1994, Japan. *Education:* Tokyo University (LL.B., 1991); The Legal Training and Research Institute of the Supreme Court.

TIBOR M. BARANSKI, JR., admitted, 1992, New York and Massachusetts; 1993, District of Columbia (Not admitted in Japan). *Education:* Kanazawa University, Faculty of Law and Letters, Japan (1977-1978); Princeton University (B.A., cum laude, 1980); Columbia University, Graduate Division (1980-1981); Peking University, Law School, PRC (Advanced Studies Degree, 1984); State University of New York, Buffalo (J.D., 1987). Advisor: Attorney General of the United States for the U.S./China Joint Session on Trade, Investment and Economic Law, Peking, PRC, 1987. Co-Author: "Chinese Commercial Dispute Resolution Methods: the State Commercial and Industrial Administration Bureau," The American Journal of Comparative Law, Vol. 35, No. 4, 1987. *LANGUAGES:* Hungarian, German, Chinese and Japanese.

HIROBUMI D. ABE, admitted, 1989, New York; 1991, District of Columbia (Not admitted in Japan). *Education:* Columbia University (B.A., 1984); Georgetown University Law Center (J.D., 1988). *LANGUAGES:* Japanese and Spanish.

JOHN Y. SASAKI, admitted, 1991, California (Not admitted in Japan). *Education:* Cornell University (A.B., with distinction); Boalt Hall, University of California at Berkeley (J.D., 1991).

KONAKA TOYAMA & HOSOYA

Established in 1972

MAIN TOWER, 16TH FLOOR
AKASAKA TWIN TOWERS
17-22, AKASAKA 2-CHOME, MINATO-KU
TOKYO 107, JAPAN
Telephone: 03-3585-8851
Cable Address: "Kontolawyer"
Telecopier: 03-3587-0101

International Investments, Civil and Commercial Litigation, Arbitration, Joint Ventures, Agency and Distributorship, Antitrust and Trade Regulations, Advertising, Banking, Bankruptcy, Commercial and Corporate Law, Computers and Software, Intellectual Property, Construction Law, Financing and Securities, Mergers and Acquisitions, Pharmaceutical Law, Telecommunications, International Taxation.

FIRM PROFILE: The firm was established in 1972 by its two founding partners and has steadily grown to its present size. It offers a variety of legal services in international transactions including, most commonly, those listed above.

NOBUYUKI KONAKA, born 1931; admitted, 1955, Japan. *Education:* Tokyo University (LL.B., 1953); Legal Training and Research Institute, 1955. Judge of Fukuoka, Tokyo, Tsu and Utsunomiya District Courts, 1955-1967. Anderson, Mori & Rabinowitz, Tokyo, 1967-1972. Member of the Panel of Arbitrators of the Japan Commercial Arbitration Association, 1972—. *Member:* First Tokyo Bar Association; Japanese American Society for Legal Studies. *LANGUAGES:* Japanese and English.

KOZO TOYAMA, born 1940; admitted, 1965, Japan. *Education:* Tokyo University (LL.B.); University of Illinois, College of Law (M.C.L.); Legal Training and Research Institute. Nagashima & Ohno, Tokyo, 1965-1968, 1969-1971; Arnold & Porter, Washington, D.C. and Cahill, Gordon & Reindel, New York, 1968-1969; Pavey, Wilson, Cohen & Carter, Melbourne, and Stephen, Jacques & Stephen, Sydney, 1971. *Member:* First Tokyo Bar Association (Vice President, 1979); Inter-Pacific Bar Association (Council, 1994—). *LANGUAGES:* Japanese and English.

YOSHINORI HOSOYA, born 1945; admitted, 1971, Japan. *Education:* Tokyo University (LL.B.); New York University, School of Law (LL.M.);
(This Listing Continued)

Legal Training and Research Institute. Graham & James, San Francisco, California, 1975-1976. *Member:* Second Tokyo Bar Association. *LANGUAGES:* Japanese and English.

SETSUKO UENO, born 1950; admitted, 1978, Japan. *Education:* Keio University (LL.B.); Legal Training and Research Institute; Zürich Universität. *Member:* First Tokyo Bar Association. *LANGUAGES:* Japanese, English and German.

EIICHIRO NAKATANI, born 1959; admitted, 1984, Japan. *Education:* Tokyo University (LL.B.); Legal Training and Research Institute. Allen & Overy, London, 1991-1992. *Member:* First Tokyo Bar Association. *LANGUAGES:* Japanese and English.

RYOYU NAITO, born 1953; admitted, 1985, Japan. *Education:* Waseda University (LL.B., LL.M.); University of Illinois, College of Law (LL.M.); Legal Training and Research Institute. Miyake, Imai & Ileda, Tokyo, 1985-1989; Whitman & Ransom, New York, 1989-1990; Morrison & Foerster, Los Angeles, 1991-1992. *Member:* Tokyo Bar Association. *LANGUAGES:* Japanese and English.

NORIKO HIGASHIZAWA, born 1959; admitted, 1988, Japan. *Education:* Keio University, Faculty of Law (LL.B.); Duke University Law School (LL.M); Legal Training and Research Institute. *Member:* Dai-ni Tokyo Bar Association. *LANGUAGES:* Japanese and English.

ASAHI YAMASHITA, born 1962; admitted, 1991, Japan. *Education:* Tokyo University (LL.B.); Legal Training and Research Institute. *Member:* Dai-ni Tokyo Bar Association. *LANGUAGES:* Japanese and English.

YOSHIHIRO TAKATORI, born 1963; admitted, 1992, Japan. *Education:* Waseda University (LL.B.); Legal Training and Research Institute. *Member:* First Tokyo Bar Association. *LANGUAGES:* Japanese and English.

SEISHI IKEDA, born 1965; admitted, 1994, Japan. *Education:* Tokyo University (LL.B.); Legal Training and Research Institute. *Member:* First Tokyo Bar Association. *LANGUAGES:* Japanese and English.

OF COUNSEL

KAZUO AKIYOSHI, born 1905; admitted, 1933, Japan. *Education:* Kyushu Imperial University (LL.B., 1930). *Member:* Dai-ni Tokyo Bar Association. *LANGUAGES:* Japanese and English.

KUBOTA & MASUI

Established in 1970

TSUKASA BUILDING
15-4 UCHIKANDA 2-CHOME, CHIYODA-KU
TOKYO 101, JAPAN
Telephone: (03) 3254-6731
Telex: J23955 KBOTALAW
Fax: (03) 3258-2867

General and International Law Practice. Patent and Trademark Law, Corporation, Antitrust, Licensing and Arbitration.

MEMBERS OF FIRM

YUTAKA KUBOTA, born 1926; admitted, 1952, Japan. *Education:* Tokyo University (LL.B., 1950); Harvard Law School (LL.M., 1961). Author: "Arbitration Agreements between Japanese and American Companies"; "Presumption of Manufacturing Process of Novel Substance"; "Remedies for Breach of License Agreements". *Member:* Second Tokyo Bar Association. *LANGUAGES:* Japanese and English.

KAZUO MASUI, born 1944; admitted, 1976, Japan. *Education:* Tokyo University (B.Sc., 1967); Georgetown University Law Center (M.C.L., 1978). Author: "Computer Program and Copyright"; "Rule of Evidence and Insufficient Examination". *Member:* Second Tokyo Bar Association. *LANGUAGES:* Japanese and English.

OF COUNSEL

TAKASHI YAMADA, born 1925; admitted, 1955, Japan. *Education:* Tokyo University (LL.B., 1949). Judge, Tokyo District Court, 1951-1955. *Member:* Second Tokyo Bar Association. *LANGUAGES:* Japanese.

REPRESENTATIVE CLIENTS: Nippon Steel Corporation; Asahi Breweries, Ltd.; Nippon Seiko K.K.; Sumitomo Electric Industries, Ltd.; Japan Satellite Broadcasting, Inc.; Sankyo Co., Ltd.

LINKLATERS & PAINES

Established in 1987

MITSUI ASAHI BUILDING 3F
1-1 KANDA SUDA-CHO
CHIYODA-KU
TOKYO 101, JAPAN
Telephone: (3) 3258 3691
Telex: 2227236
Fax: (3) 3258 3692; (3) 5295 8214

London, England Office: Barrington House, 59-67 Gresham Street, EC2V 7JA. Telephone: 0171-606-7080. Cable Address: Linklaters, London, EC2V 7JA. Telegrams: Linklaters, London. Telex: 884349. Fax: 0171-606-5113.

General and International Law Practice.

RESIDENT PARTNERS

Peter S. Gray   Andrew Roberts

(For full list of offices see entry at London, England)

LOEFF CLAEYS VERBEKE

NSE BUILDING, 5TH FLOOR
1-7-1 KANDA JINBO-CHO
CHIYODA-KU
TOKYO 101, JAPAN
Telephone: 81-3-32599831
Telecopier: 81-3-32599888

Amsterdam, The Netherlands Office: 15 Apollolaan, P.O. Box 75088, 1070 AB. Telephone: 31-20-5741200. Telex: 14292 LEX NL. Telecopier: 31-20-6718775.

Brussels, Belgium Office: 268 A Avenue de Tervueren, A-1150. Telephone: 02-778.22.11. Telecopier: 02-763.21.85.

Antwerp, Belgium Office: "De Hertoghe," 8th Floor, 92 Disguinlei, B.8, B-2018. Telephone: 32.3.2385656. Telex: 72748 (EURLAWB). Telecopier: 32.3.2387877.

Liege, Belgium Office: 13, Rue Simonon, (Place de Bronckart), B-4000. Telephone: 32-41-527722. Telecopier: 32-41-527511.

New York, New York Office: Swiss Bank Tower, 23rd Floor, 10 East 50th Street, 10022. Telephone: 212-759-9000. Fax: 212-759-9018.

Paris, France Office: 1, Avenue Franklin D. Roosevelt, 75008. Telephone: 33-1-49539125. Telecopier: 33-1-42891460.

Rotterdam, The Netherlands Office: 70 Weena, P.O. Box 74, 3000 AB. Telephone: 31-10-4034777. Telex: 23395 (LEX NL). Telecopier: 31-10-4149388.

Singapore Office: 20 Raffles Place, #08-03, Ocean Towers, Singapore, 0104. Telephone: 65-5335332. Fax: 65-5330313.

Barcelona, Spain Office: 550, 4° 1A, Av. Diagonal, 08021. Telephone: 34-3-2007117. Telecopier: 34-3-2023098.

Madrid, Spain Office: Balañá Eguía, Antonio Mauro 7, 5°, 28014. Telephone: 34-1-5312501. Telecopier: 34-1-5313530.

Jakarta, Indonesia Associated Office: Ali Budiardjo, Nugroho, Reksodiputro, Niaga Tower, 24th floor, Jalan Jenderal Sudirman Kav. 58, 12920. Telephone: 62.21.2505125/2505136, Telecopier: 62.21.2505121/2505001.

Luxembourg, Luxembourg Office: Zeyen Beghin Feider. 67, Rue Ermesinde, P.O. Box 5017, 1050. Telephone: 352.468946. Telecopier: 352.468947.

Dutch attorneys may represent clients before all Dutch Courts, before the European Court of Justice and the Benelux Court of Justice, and are admitted to plead before all Courts of the Memberstates of the Common Market (EEC).

RESIDENT PARTNER

CEES VELLEKOOP, born 1956; admitted, 1981, Rotterdam, The Netherlands; 1986, Amsterdam; licensed to practice in Japan as a foreign lawyer: Gaikokuho-Jimu-Bengoshi). *Education:* Erasmus University Rotterdam (1980);. *Member:* International Bar Association; Interpacific Bar Association; Netherlands Commercial Law Association. (Amsterdam Office).

(This Listing Continued)

Languages: Dutch, English, French, German, Italian, Japanese, Russian and Spanish.

(For Personnel and other data, see Professional Biographies at Amsterdam, Antwerp, Barcelona, Brussels, Liège, New York, Paris, Rotterdam, and Singapore).

LOGAN, TAKASHIMA & NEMOTO

Established in 1960

330 NEW OHTEMACHI BUILDING
2-1, OHTEMACHI 2-CHOME
CHIYODA-KU
TOKYO 100, JAPAN
Telephone: (03) 3242-6181/5
Cable Address: "Loganlaw Tokyo"
Telex: J22767
Telecopier: (03) 3246-0307

Administrative Law, Antitrust Law, Arbitration, Banking Law, Corporate Law, Copyright Law, License Negotiation, General Intellectual Property, Distributorship, Agency and Franchise Law, Foreign Investments, Insurance Law, International Contracts, International Private Law, Litigation, Maritime and Admiralty Law, Negligence Law, Personal Injury Law, Product Liability Law, Corporate Taxation, International Taxation, Taxation of Foreign Nationals, Exchange Control, Commercial Transactions, Trade Regulations and General Legal Practice.

FIRM PROFILE: The firm was established in 1960 and, as one of the oldest firms in Tokyo in the arena of international legal practice, offers a full range of legal services in international commercial transactions and admiralty. The client base is from North America, Europe and throughout the Far East.

MEMBERS OF FIRM

HIROMI NEMOTO, born Fukushima Prefecture, Japan, December 29, 1932; admitted, 1959, Japan. *Education:* Chuo University, 1957. *Member:* Tokyo Bar Association. *LANGUAGES:* Japanese and English. *PRACTICE AREAS:* Litigation; Maritime and Admiralty Law; Commercial Transactions.

HIROSHI KAWAKAMI, born Mukden, Manchuria, September 10, 1939; admitted, 1964, Japan. *Education:* Tokyo University, 1962; University of Washington (M.C.L., 1968); Harvard Law School (LL.M., 1969). *Member:* First Tokyo Bar Association. *LANGUAGES:* Japanese and English. *PRACTICE AREAS:* International Banking; Business; Licensing and Trade.

SOICHI KONDO, born Tokyo, Japan, May 18, 1939; admitted, 1968, Japan. *Education:* Tokyo University, 1966; University of Michigan Law School, 1971. *Member:* Tokyo Bar Association. *LANGUAGES:* Japanese and English. *PRACTICE AREAS:* Corporate Law; License Negotiation; Commercial Transactions.

YASUHIKO NISHIYAMA, born Tottori Prefecture, Japan, May 22, 1945; admitted, 1974, Japan. *Education:* Hitotsubashi University, 1969; The Graduate School of Hitotsubashi University (LL.M., 1975); University of Michigan Law School (LL.M., 1977). *Member:* First Tokyo Bar Association. *LANGUAGES:* Japanese and English. *PRACTICE AREAS:* Admiralty; Litigation; International Contracts; License Negotiation; Commercial Transactions; Financing Transactions.

KAZUYOSHI ENDO, born Osaka, Japan, January 20, 1948; admitted, 1977, Japan. *Education:* Chuo University, 1971; The Graduate School of Chuo University (LL.M., 1975); University of Illinois at Urbana-Champaign College of Law (M.C.L., 1980). *Member:* Tokyo Bar Association. *LANGUAGES:* Japanese and English. *PRACTICE AREAS:* International Business Transactions; Licensing; Admiralty; Litigation.

RYO OKUYAMA, born Shizuoka Prefecture, Japan, November 8, 1950; admitted, 1979, Japan. *Education:* Rikkyo University, 1974; University of Virginia Law School (LL.M., 1984). *Member:* First Tokyo Bar Association. *LANGUAGES:* Japanese and English. *PRACTICE AREAS:* International Business Transactions; Licensing; Venture Capital; Admiralty.

ASSOCIATE

YUKO CHIYODA, born Kyoto, Japan, January 14, 1961; admitted, 1994, Japan. *Education:* Sophia University (1983). *Member:* Tokyo Bar Association. *LANGUAGES:* Japanese and English. *PRACTICE AREAS:* Corporate Law; Civil Law.

(This Listing Continued)

OF COUNSEL

NOBUYUKI TAKASHIMA, born Tokyo, Japan, February 14, 1927; admitted, 1953, Japan. *Education:* Tokyo Imperial University, 1950. *Member:* First Tokyo Bar Association. **LANGUAGES:** Japanese and English. **PRACTICE AREAS:** Corporation; Finance; Contract; Antitrust.

LOVELL WHITE DURRANT

SHIN-KASUMIGASEKI BUILDING, 20TH FLOOR
3-3-2 KASUMIGASEKI, CHIYODA-KU
TOKYO 100, JAPAN
Telephone: (3) 3503 2571
Fax: (3) 3503 0699

London, England Office: 65 Holborn Viaduct, EC1A 2DY. Telephone: 0171 236 0066. Fax: 0171 248 4212; 236 0084; 248 7273. Telex: 887122 LWD G.
New York, New York Office: 527 Madison Avenue, 10th Floor, 10022. Telephone: (212) 758 3773. Fax: (212) 486 0367.
Paris, France Office: 37 Avenue Pierre 1er de Serbie, 75008. Telephone: (1) 49 52 04 26. Fax: (1) 47 23 96 12.
Brussels, Belgium Office: Avenue Louise 523, Bte 24, 1050. Telephone: (2) 647 0660. Fax: (2) 647 1124.
Prague, Czech Republic Office: U Prasne brany 3, State Mesto, 1. Telephone: (2) 2481 1672. Fax: (2) 2481 1608.
Ho Chi Minh City, Vietnam Office: 141 Vo Van Tan Street, District 3. Telephone: (848) 298 787. Fax: (848) 392 868.
Hong Kong Office: 11th Floor, Peregrine Tower, Lippo Centre, Queensway. Telephone: 2810 4770. Fax: 2868 4051.
Beijing, Republic of China Office: Office 5D, CITIC Building, 19 Jianguomenwai Dajie, 100004. Telephone: (861) 506 3588. Fax: (861) 500 1972.
Shanghai, People's Republic of China Associated Office: Room 1703, Shanghai International Trade Centre, 2200 Yan An Road (W). Telephone: (21) 219 4419. Fax: (21) 219 5462.

Arbitration, Aviation, Banking, Building and Engineering, China, Collective Investment Schemes, Commercial, Commodities, Competition and Trade Regulation, Computers, Construction, Corporate Finance, Corporate Law, East-West Trade, EEC, Employment, Energy, Environmental Law, Financial Services, Fraud and Asset Recovery, Insolvency, Insurance, Intellectual Property, Litigation, Management Buy-Outs and Venture Capital, Media Law, Mergers and Acquisitions, Pensions, Planning, Product Liability, Property, Rating, Shipping, Taxation, Trusts and Estate Planning.

RESIDENT PARTNER

David S. Baker

(For List of Partners see Professional Biographies at London, England)

MACFARLANES (HOWARD GAIKOKUHO JIMU-BENGOSHI JIMUSHO)

SANBANCHO KB-6 BUILDING
6 SANBANCHO, CHIYODA-KU
TOKYO 102, JAPAN
Telephone: (03) 3239 3661
Fax: (03) 3239 2884

London, England Office: 10 Norwich Street, EC4A 1BD. Telephone: (0171) 831 9222. Fax: (0171) 831 9607. Telex: 296361 MACFAR G.
Brussels, Belgium Office: Avenue Louise 106, 1050. Telephone: (02) 647 06 50. Fax: (02) 646 4729. Telefax: 20317 OMSSA.

Firm engaged in English and General International Practice including general corporate, commercial and banking work, mergers and acquisitions, divestitures, joint ventures, intellectual property and licensing, dispute resolution and European community law advice. Not authorized to appear before the Japanese courts or otherwise to act as Japanese bengoshi.

PARTNER

JULIAN FRANCIS HOWARD, born Bournemouth, England, September 2, 1961; admitted, 1986, Solicitor, Supreme Court of England and Wales. Licensed to practice in Japan as a Foreign Lawyer (Gaikokuho-jimi-bengoshi). Jurisdiction of Primary Qualification: United Kingdom.

MASUDA & EJIRI

TOKYO, JAPAN

(See Asahi Law Offices)

MATSUO & KOSUGI

Established in 1963

TAIYO GINZA BUILDING, 7&8F
7-14-16 GINZA CHUO-KU
TOKYO 104, JAPAN
Telephone: 81-3-3542-9141-6
Cable Address: "Lexjapan Tokyo"
Telex: J23741
Telefax: 81-3-3545-1016; 81-3-3546-1144
Answerback: LEXJAPAN

General Domestic and International Practice in Banking, Commercial and Corporate Law, Domestic and International Corporate Reorganization and Bankruptcy, Maritime Law, Ship and Aircraft Finances, International Finances, Criminal, Domestic and Transnational Litigation.

FIRM PROFILE: The firm was established in 1963 and serves as legal counsel to more than 100 Japanese banks and corporations. We also serve a number of large international clients as well as other international entities with interests in Japan.

TASUKU MATSUO, born Tokyo, Japan, 1931; admitted, 1960, Japan. *Education:* Waseda University (LL.B., 1953); University of Washington (M.C.L., 1969). Teaching Fellow, Columbia University Law School, New York, 1984. Visiting Professor: Katholieke Universiteit, Leuven, Belgium, 1989, 1993; University of Melbourne Law School, Melbourne, Australia, 1994. Author: *U.S. & Japan Bankruptcy Law,* 1971. Co-author: "Trade with Japan," in *Law and Politics in China's Foreign Trade,* V. L. Lee, editor, 1977; "Creditor's Rights Under Japanese Law," in *Current Legal Aspects of Doing Business in Japan and East Asia,* J.O. Haley, editor, 1978. Contributor, "Doing Business in Japan," Z. Kitagawa, General Editor, 1982 (Author of Vol. 7, Chapter 7, Bankruptcy and 8, Corporate Reorganization). Contributor, "Digest of the Commercial Laws of the World," *Oceana Publications, Inc.,* 1992 (Author of "The Commercial Laws of Japan"). Member, Advisory Board: International and Comparative Law Center of The Southwestern Legal Foundation, 1975—; Japan Immigration Association, 1987—. *Member:* Tokyo Bar Association. **LANGUAGES:** Japanese and English. **PRACTICE AREAS:** International and Domestic Practice; Bankruptcy; Corporate Litigation; Labor/Employment Disputes; International Commercial Matters and Acquisitions.

TAKEO KOSUGI, born Tokyo, Japan, 1942; admitted, 1974, Japan. *Education:* Tokyo University (LL.B., 1966); Harvard University (LL.M., 1972). Subsequent experience: Judge, Osaka District Court, 1968-1972 and Kushiro District Court, 1972-1974: Ropes & Gray, Boston, 1972; Visiting Scholar, Harvard University Law School, 1974-1975; Milbank, Tweed, Hadley & McCloy, New York, 1975-1976; Law Office of S.G. Archibald, Paris, 1976; Lecturer, Supreme Court Legal Training and Research Institute, 1979—; Tsukuba University Business Law Course, 1992—. Author: "Enforcement of Foreign Judgments in Japan," in *Lawasia: Proceedings of the Fifth Biennial Conference Seoul, 1977,* 1978; "Regulation of Practice by Foreign Lawyers," 27 Am. J. of Comp. Law 678, 1979. Translation D.G. Epstein "Debtor-Creditor Law in a nutshell". Member: Advisory Board for Law Reform, Ministry of Justice, 1986—; Advisory Board on Oversea Construction, Ministry of Construction, 1982-1984; Advisory Board on Oversea Oil Exploration, Agency of Natural Resources and Energy, Ministry of International Trade and Industry, 1982-1984, Japan's Representative to the LAWASIA. *Member:* Tokyo Bar Association. **LANGUAGES:** Japanese and English. **PRACTICE AREAS:** Banking; Finance; Plant Export; International Construction.

TAKASHI NAGAHAMA, born Toyohashi, Japan, 1945; admitted, 1975, Japan. *Education:* Tokyo University (LL.B., 1970); University of Washington (LL.M., 1979). Subsequent Experience: Milbank, Tweed, Hadley & McCloy, New York, 1979-1980. Translation, D.G. Epstein "Debtor-Creditor Law in a nutshell". *Member:* Tokyo Bar Association. **LANGUAGES:** Japanese and English. **PRACTICE AREAS:** General Corporate

(This Listing Continued)

MATSUO & KOSUGI, Tokyo—Continued

Law; International Trade and Finance; Bankruptcy; Antitrust; Trademark; Intellectual Property; Litigation.

TAEKO MIZUNO (TADA), born Nagoya, Japan, 1955; admitted, 1982, Japan; 1989, New York. *Education:* Tokyo University (LL.B., 1978); University of California at Berkeley (LL.M., 1987). Subsequent Experience: Skadden, Arps, Slate, Meagher & Flom, New York, 1987-1988. *Member:* Tokyo Bar Association; New York Bar Association. *LANGUAGES:* Japanese and English. *PRACTICE AREAS:* Mergers and Acquisitions (Domestic and International); Commercial Transactions (Domestic and International).

KEIICHIRO SUE, born Oita, Japan, January 27, 1957; admitted, 1984, Japan. *Education:* Tokyo University (LL.B., 1982); Japan Legal Training and Research Institute; Lueven Catholic University, Belgium (LL.M., 1992); Columbia University (LL.M., 1994). *Member:* First Tokyo Bar Association. *LANGUAGES:* Japanese and English. *PRACTICE AREAS:* Labor; Litigation.

YASUHISA OKUNO, born Hyogo, Japan, January 3, 1953; admitted, 1985, Japan. *Education:* Tokyo University (LL.B., 1978); Japan Legal Training and Research Institute. *Member:* Tokyo Bar Association. *LANGUAGES:* Japanese and English. *PRACTICE AREAS:* Corporate Law; Banking; Commercial Transactions; Litigation; Administrative Law.

MASAYOSHI TANIGUCHI, born Kyoto, Japan, July 26, 1957; admitted, 1986, Japan. *Education:* Waseda University (LL.B., 1982); University of Washington (LL.M., 1991). Member, Skadden, Arps, Slate, Meagher & Flom, Los Angeles, 1991-1992. *Member:* Tokyo Bar Association. *LANGUAGES:* Japanese and English. *PRACTICE AREAS:* Corporate; Litigation; Entertainment Law; International Transactions.

HIROSHI UCHIDA, born Tottori, Japan, November 22, 1958; admitted, 1986, Japan. *Education:* Kyoto University (LL.B., 1984). Japan Legal Training and Research Institute. *Member:* Tokyo Bar Association. *LANGUAGES:* Japanese and English. *PRACTICE AREAS:* Corporate Law; Anti-dumping; Intellectual Property; Litigation.

TOJIRO ISHII, born Saitama, Japan, December 1, 1958; admitted, 1987, Japan. *Education:* Rikkyo University (LL.B., 1981); Japan Legal Training and Research Institute. *Member:* Tokyo Bar Association. *LANGUAGES:* Japanese and English. *PRACTICE AREAS:* Corporate Law; Bankruptcy; Litigation.

MASAYUKI KITANOSONO, born Tokyo, Japan, August 24, 1959; admitted, 1988, Japan. *Education:* Rikkyo University (LL.B., 1983); Japan Legal Training and Research Institute. *Member:* Tokyo Bar Association. *LANGUAGES:* Japanese and English. *PRACTICE AREAS:* Corporate Law; Real Estate; Banking.

MASAMI SATO, born Aichi, Japan, August 1, 1963; admitted, 1989, Japan; 1992, New York. *Education:* Kyoto University (LL.B., 1987); Japan Legal Training and Research Institute; University of New York (M.C.J., 1992). Experience: Milbank, Tweed, Hadley & McCloy, New York, 1992-1993; Lillick & Charles, San Francisco, 1993. *Member:* Tokyo Bar Association; New York Bar Association. *LANGUAGES:* Japanese and English. *PRACTICE AREAS:* Corporate Law; Litigation; International Transaction.

KOICHI SHIGA, born Aichi, Japan, August 15, 1961; admitted, 1989, Japan. *Education:* Chuo University (LL.B., 1984); Japan Legal Training and Research Institute. *Member:* Tokyo Bar Association. *LANGUAGES:* Japanese and English. *PRACTICE AREAS:* Finance; Banking Transactions; Bankruptcy; Litigation.

YOSUKE MORISHIMA, born Osaka, Japan, January 31, 1961; admitted, 1990, Japan. *Education:* Chuo University (LL.B., 1985); Japan Legal Training and Research Institute. *Member:* Tokyo Bar Association. *LANGUAGES:* Japanese and English. *PRACTICE AREAS:* Commercial Transactions; Banking; Finance; Bankruptcy; Litigation.

MASAMICHI SAITO, born Sapporo, Japan, March 8, 1965; admitted, 1990, Japan. *Education:* Waseda University (LL.B., 1988); Japan Legal Training and Research Institute. *Member:* Tokyo Bar Association. *LANGUAGES:* Japanese and English. *PRACTICE AREAS:* Commercial Transactions; Litigation.

MARIKO OBANA, born Yamaguchi, Japan, April 3, 1961; admitted, 1990, Japan. *Education:* Waseda University (LL.B., 1985). Japan Legal Training and Research Institute, 1988-1990. *Member:* Dai-ni Tokyo Bar

(This Listing Continued)

Association. *LANGUAGES:* Japanese and English. *PRACTICE AREAS:* Transnational Commercial Transactions; Corporate Law; Litigation.

TAMOTSU TAKURA, born Aomori, Japan, April 5, 1955; admitted, 1991, Japan. *Education:* Tokyo University (LL.B., 1982); University of Washington School of Law (LL.M., 1993). Japan Legal Training and Research Institute, 1989-1991. Experience: Davis Wright Tremaine, Seattle, 1993. *Member:* Tokyo Bar Association; Copyright Law Association. *LANGUAGES:* Japanese, English, French and German. *PRACTICE AREAS:* Intellectual Property Law.

HIROSHI NISHIYAMA, born Yamanashi, Japan, November 11, 1963; admitted, 1991, Japan. *Education:* Tohoku University (LL.B., 1986). Japan Legal Training and Research Institute, 1988-1990. *Member:* Tokyo Bar Association. *LANGUAGES:* Japanese and English. *PRACTICE AREAS:* Corporate Law; Litigation.

TERUO SAITO, born Ibaraki, Japan, April 21, 1959; admitted, 1992, Japan. *Education:* Meiji University (LL.B., 1983); Japan Legal Training and Research Institute, 1990-1992. *Member:* Tokyo Bar Association. *LANGUAGES:* English. *PRACTICE AREAS:* Corporate Law; Litigation; Commercial Transactions.

KAZUYA SAWADA, born Osaka, Japan, January 18, 1961; admitted, 1992, Japan. *Education:* Keio University (LL.B., 1983); Japan Legal Training and Research Institute, 1990-1992. *Member:* Tokyo Bar Association. *LANGUAGES:* English. *PRACTICE AREAS:* Corporate Law; Litigation; Commercial Transactions.

FUJIO IIDA, born Tokyo, Japan, December 13, 1964; admitted, 1992, Japan. *Education:* Hitotsubashi University (LL.B., 1990); Japan Legal Training and Research Institute, 1990-1992. *Member:* Tokyo Bar Association. *LANGUAGES:* English. *PRACTICE AREAS:* Commercial Transactions; Contract Law.

KOJI NISHIMURA, born Tokyo, Japan, October 6, 1965; admitted, 1992, Japan. *Education:* Chuo University (LL.B., 1989); Japan Legal Training and Research Institute, 1990-1992. *Member:* Tokyo Bar Association. *LANGUAGES:* English. *PRACTICE AREAS:* Corporate Law; Litigation; Commercial Transactions.

YUTAKA MATSUNO, born Hokkaido, Japan, March 26, 1963; admitted, 1993, Japan. *Education:* Tokyo University (LL.B., 1987); Japan Legal Training and Research Institute, 1991-1993. *Member:* Tokyo Bar Association. *LANGUAGES:* Japanese and English. *PRACTICE AREAS:* Corporate Law; Contract Law.

ETSUO DOI, born Saitama, Japan, May 8, 1961; admitted, 1994, Japan. *Education:* Tokyo University (LL.B., 1988); Japan Legal Training and Research Institute, 1992-1994. *Member:* Tokyo Bar Association. *LANGUAGES:* Japanese and English. *PRACTICE AREAS:* Corporate; Litigation Law.

YUKO ONAGA, born Okinawa, Japan, October 13, 1964; admitted, 1994, Japan. *Education:* Tokyo University (LL.B., 1989); Japan Legal Training and Research Institute , 1992-1994. *Member:* Tokyo Bar Association. *LANGUAGES:* Japanese and English. *PRACTICE AREAS:* Corporate; Contract Law.

MAYER, BROWN & PLATT

(Kawachi Gaikokuho Jimu Bengoshi Jimusho)

URBANNET OTEMACHI BUILDING 13F
2-2, OTEMACHI 2-CHOME, CHIYODA-KU
TOKYO 100, JAPAN
Telephone: 011-81-3-5255-9700
Facsimile: 011-81-3-5255-9797

Chicago, Illinois Office: 190 South LaSalle Street, 60603-3441. Telephone: (312) 782-0600. Pitney Bowes: (312) 701-7711. Telex: 190404. Cable: LEMAY.

Washington, D.C. Office: 2000 Pennsylvania Avenue, N.W., 20006-1882. Telephone: (202) 463-2000. Pitney Bowes: (202) 861-0484, Pitney Bowes: (202) 861-0473. Telex: 892603. Cable: LEMAYDC.

New York, New York Office: 787 Seventh Avenue, Suite 2400, 10019-6018. Telephone: (212) 554-3000. Pitney Bowes: (212) 262-1910. Telex: 701842. Cable: LEMAYEN.

Houston, Texas Office: 700 Louisiana Street, Suite 3600, 77002-2730. Telephone: (713) 221-1651. Pitney Bowes: (713) 224-6410. Telex: 775809. Cable: LEMAYHOU.

(This Listing Continued)

Los Angeles, California Office: 350 South Grand Avenue, 25th Floor, 90071-1503. Telephone: (213) 229-9500. Pitney Bowes: (213) 625-0248. Telex: 188089. Cable: LEMAYLA.

London, England Office: 162 Queen Victoria Street, EC4V 4DB. Telephone: 011-44-71-248-1465. Fax: 011-44-71-329-4465. Telex: 8811095. Cable: LEMAYLDN.

Berlin, Germany Office: Spreeufer 5, 10178. Telephone: 011-49-30-240-7930. Facsimile: 011-49-30-240-79344.

Brussels, Belgium Office: Square de Meeûs 19/20, Bte. 4, 1040. Telephone: 011-32-2-512-9878. Fax: 011-32-2-511-3305. Telex: 20768 MBPBRU B.

Mexico City, Mexico, D.F. Correspondent: Jáuregui, Navarrete, Nader y Rojas, S.C., Abogados, Paseo de la Reforma 199, Pisos 15, 16 y 17, 06500. Telephone: 011-525-591-16-55. Fax: 011-525-535-80-62; 011-525-703-22-47. Cable: JANANE.

In Tokyo, engaged in American and International practice as "Kawachi Gaikokuho Jimu Bengoshi Jimusho", not authorized to appear before Japanese courts or otherwise to act as a Bengoshi.

PARTNERS

MICHAEL T. KAWACHI, born Los Angeles, California, March 26, 1955; admitted, 1978, California; admitted as foreign law consultant (Gaikokuho Jimu Bengoshi), Japan, 1989. *Education:* University of California, Los Angeles (A.B., magna cum laude, 1975); International Christian University, Tokyo, Japan (1974-1975); Columbia University (J.D., 1978). Graduate Research Associate, Faculty of Law and Political Science, Tokyo University, Tokyo, Japan, 1978-1980. Associate Editor, Columbia Journal of Transnational Law, 1977-1978. Rotary International Foundation Graduate Fellow, 1978-1980. Member, Board of Councillors, International Christian University, 1992—, Secretary, 1993—. *Member:* State Bar of California; American Bar Association (Member, Section on International Law and Practice); First Tokyo Bar Association. *LANGUAGES:* Japanese.

JOHN C. ROEBUCK, born Richmond, California, March 26, 1950; admitted, 1975, District of Columbia (Not admitted in Japan). *Education:* Princeton University (A.B., magna cum laude, 1972); University of Michigan (J.D., magna cum laude, 1975). Order of the Coif. Editor, University of Michigan Law Review, 1973-1975. *LANGUAGES:* Japanese.

ANDREW G. HARING, born Mansfield, Ohio, June 27, 1963; admitted, 1990, New York (Not admitted in Japan). *Education:* Washington & Lee University (B.A., 1985); University of Michigan (J.D., 1988; M.Jur., 1989). *Member:* New York State and American (Member, Section on International Law and Practice) Bar Associations.

MILBANK, TWEED, HADLEY & McCLOY

(Watanabe Tsugumichi Gaikokuho Jimu Bengoshi Jimusho)

NIPPON PRESS CENTER BUILDING
2-1, UCHISAIWAI-CHO 2 CHOME, CHIYODA-KU
TOKYO 100, JAPAN
Telephone: 81-3-3504-1050
Fax: 81-3-3595-2790; 81-3-3502-5192

New York, New York Office: 1 Chase Manhattan Plaza, 10005. Telephone: 212-530-5000. Cable Address: "Miltweed NYK" ITT: 422962; 423893. Fax: 212-530-5219. ABA/net: Milbank NY. MCI Mail: Milbank Tweed.

Midtown Office: 50 Rockefeller Plaza, 10020. Telephone: 212-530-5800. Fax: 212-530-0158.

Los Angeles, California Office: 601 South Figueroa Street, 30th Floor, 90017. Telephone: 213-892-4000. Fax: 213-629-5063. Telex: 678754. ABA/net: Milbank LA.

Washington, D.C. Office: Suite 1100, 1825 Eye Street, N.W., 20006. Telephone: 202-835-7500. Cable Address: "Miltweed Wsh". ITT 440667. Fax: 202-835-7586. ABA/net: Milbank DC.

London, England Office: Ropemaker Place, 25 Ropemaker Street, EC2Y 9AS. Telephone: 44-171-374-0423. Cable Address: "Miltuk G." Fax: 44-171-374-0912.

Hong Kong Office: 3007 Alexandra House, 16Chater Road. Telephone: 852-2526-5281. Fax: 852-2840-0792, 852-2845-9046. ABA/net: Milbank HK.

Singapore Office: 14-02 Caltex House, 30 Raffles Place, 0104. Telephone: 65-534-1700. Fax: 65-534-2733. ABA/net: EDNANG.

Moscow, Russia Office: 24/27 Sadivaya-Samotyochnaya, 103051. Telephone: 7-502-258-5015. Fax: 7-502-258-5014.

(This Listing Continued)

Jakarta, Indonesia Correspondent Office: Makarim & Taira S., 17th Floor, Summitmas Tower, Jl, Jend. Sudirman 61, Jakarta. Telephone: 62-211252-1272 or 2460. Fax: 62-21-252-2750 or 2751.

Firm engaged in American and International Law Practice but not authorized to appear before Japanese Courts to act as Japanese Bengoshi.

PARTNER

JAY D. GRUSHKIN, born New York, New York, 1957; admitted, 1982, District of Columbia; 1991, New York; 1993, Japan (Gaikokuho Jimu Bengoshi). *Education:* University of Pennsylvania (B.A., magna cum laude, 1979); Vanderbilt University (J.D., 1982). Member, Order of the Coif. Raymonde I. Paul Scholar in International Law. Executive Articles Editor, Vanderbilt Journal of Transnational Law, 1981-1982. *Member:* The District of Columbia Bar; New York State, Tokyo and American Bar Associations.

OF COUNSEL

HISAYO YASUDA, born Tokyo, Japan, 1953; admitted, 1982, New York; 1988, Japan (Gaikokuho Jimu Bengoshi). *Education:* Jochi (Sophia) University, Tokyo, Japan (B.A., 1975); University of Chicago (M.A., 1981); Chicago-Kent College of Law (J.D., 1981). *Member:* New York State, Tokyo and American Bar Associations. *LANGUAGES:* Japanese.

RESIDENT ASSOCIATES

CHIEKO EDA, born 1950; admitted, 1986, New York; 1990, California (Not admitted in Japan). *Education:* (Jochi (Sophia) University, Tokyo, Japan (B.A., 1973); Columbia University (J.D., 1975). *Member:* State Bar of California. *LANGUAGES:* Japanese.

DAO NGUYEN, born Saigon, Vietnam, 1965; admitted, 1991, California (Not admitted in Japan). *Education:* Harvard University (B.A., with honors, 1987); University of California at Los Angeles (J.D., 1991). *Member:* The State Bar of California (Member, Business Law and International Law Sections); American Bar Association (Member, Sections on: Business Law; International Law and Practice). *LANGUAGES:* Vietnamese, French.

DAVID J. IMPASTATO, born Chapel Hill, North Carolina, February 9, 1963; admitted, 1992, New York (Not admitted in Japan). *Education:* University of California at Berkeley (B.A., 1986); Columbia University (J.D., 1991).

MITSUI, YASUDA, WANI & MAEDA

Established in 1986

AKASAKA 2.14 PLAZA BUILDING
14-32, AKASAKA 2-CHOME
MINATO-KU
TOKYO 107, JAPAN
Telephone: 3-3224-0020
Facsimile: 3-3224-0030
Telex: J33276 MYWMTYO

General and International Law Practice. Corporation, Securities, Banking, Taxation, Administrative, Antitrust, Intellectual Property and Litigation.

FIRM PROFILE: The firm of Mitsui, Yasuda, Wani & Maeda was formed in 1986 by a group of attorneys experienced in handling financial, intellectual property and corporate transactions in Japan, the United States of America and the United Kingdom. Since its establishment, the firm has been commented as very much up-and-coming international firm in Japan.

The firm maintains close contact with major law firms in the United States, The United Kingdom, Continental Europe, Asia, Australia and other parts of the world. As there are foreign associates with the firm, it has been also to provide immediate preliminary advice on structuring cross-border arrangements of major focus for Japanese investment.

TAKUHIDE MITSUI, born Tokyo, Japan, March 5, 1948; admitted, 1977, Japan; 1984, New York and District of Columbia. *Education:* University of Tokyo (LL.B., 1974); Legal Training and Research Institute (Diploma, 1977); Columbia University Law School (LL.M., 1983). Author: "U.S. Tax Treatment of Interest Paid to Foreign Investors," Journal of The Japanese Institute of International Business Law, February 1985. *Member:* The Dai-ni Tokyo, New York State and District of Columbia Bar Associations; American Bar Association; International Bar Association; Japan Federation of Bar Associations. *LANGUAGES:* Japanese and English. *PRACTICE AREAS:* Banking; Securities; Corporate; Taxation.

(This Listing Continued)

MITSUI, YASUDA, WANI & MAEDA, Tokyo—Continued

MITSUHIRO YASUDA, born Miyazaki, Japan, January 11, 1949; admitted, 1977, Japan; 1983, New York. *Education:* University of Tokyo (LL.B., 1975); Legal Training and Research Institute (Diploma, 1977); New York University Law School (M.C.J., 1982). Co-Author: "International Securities Regulation - JAPAN," Oceana Publications Inc., 1986. *Member:* The Dai-ni Tokyo and New York State Bar Associations; Japan Federation of Bar Associations. *LANGUAGES:* Japanese and English. *PRACTICE AREAS:* Securities.

AKIHIRO WANI, born Kyoto, Japan, September 1, 1951; admitted, 1979, Japan; 1983, New York and U.S. District Court, Southern and Eastern Districts of New York. *Education:* University of Tokyo (LL.B., 1975; LL.M., 1977); Legal Training and Research Institute (Diploma, 1979); Columbia University School of Law (LL.M., 1981). Editorial Staff, Kitagawa Doing Business in Japan, Kyoto Comparative Law Center, Matthew Bender, 1979-1981. General Editor, CCH's Japan Business Law Guide, 1992—. Adjunct Professor of Law, The University of Tokyo, 1992-1993. *Member:* The Association of the Bar of the City of New York; The Dai-ni Tokyo, New York State and American Bar Associations; Japan Federation of Bar Associations; Maritime Law Association of the United States. *LANGUAGES:* Japanese and English. *PRACTICE AREAS:* General Corporate; Financing.

HIROSHI MAEDA, born May 10, 1954; admitted, 1981, Japan. *Education:* University of Tokyo (LL.B., 1979); Legal Training and Research Institute (Diploma, 1981); Cornell Law School (LL.M., 1986). *Member:* The Dai-ni Tokyo Bar Association; Japan Federation of Bar Associations. *LANGUAGES:* Japanese and English. *PRACTICE AREAS:* Structured Finance; Banking.

AKIHIKO HARA, born Saga, Japan, October 11, 1952; admitted, 1980, Japan; 1985, New York. *Education:* University of Tokyo (LL.B., 1978); Legal Training and Research Institute (Diploma, 1980); Columbia University School of Law (LL.M., 1984). With: Pennie & Edwards, New York, 1984-1985; Mori Sogo Law Offices, Tokyo, 1985-1992. Author: "Gray Market in the United States," NBL, 1986. Co-Author: "Licensing in Foreign and Domestic Operations - Joint Ventures," Clark Boardman, 1985. Vice Chairman, Committee on Foreign Law Consultants of The Dai-ni Tokyo Bar, 1991-1993. Member, Committee on Intellectual Property, 1990-1991 and Committee on International Issues of Intellectual Property, 1991-1992, of MITI. *Member:* Dai-ni Tokyo and New York State Bar Associations. *LANGUAGES:* Japanese and English. *PRACTICE AREAS:* Corporate; Intellectual Property; Litigation.

JUNKO YASUDA, born Tokyo, Japan, December 14, 1951; admitted, 1978, Japan. *Education:* University of Tokyo (LL.B., 1976); The Legal Training and Research Institute, Tokyo (1978); Duke University (LL.M., 1986). Associated with Phillips, Donkers & Giraud, Paris, 1988-1989. *Member:* Japan Federation of Bar Associations; Tokyo Bar Association. *LANGUAGES:* Japanese and English. *PRACTICE AREAS:* Corporate; Financing.

YASUNOBU SATO, born Tokyo, Japan, May 5, 1957; admitted, 1984, Japan; 1991, New York. *Education:* Waseda University (B.A., 1982); Legal Training and Research Institute (Diploma, 1984); Harvard Law School (LL.M., 1989). Author: "New EC Regulations on Merger & Acquisition," Journal of the Japanese Institute of International Business Law, 1991. United Nations High Commissioner for Refugees, Australia, New Zealand and the South Pacific, 1991-1992. United Nations Transitional Authority, Cambodia, 1992-1993. *Member:* Japan Federation of Bar Associations; Tokyo Bar Association. *LANGUAGES:* Japanese and English. *PRACTICE AREAS:* General Corporate; Litigation; Finance; Human Rights.

KAYOKO NAITO, born Kobe, Japan, May 2, 1949; admitted, 1985, Japan; 1992, New York. *Education:* Kyoto University (LL.B., 1972); Legal Training and Research Institute (Diploma, 1985); Columbia University Law School (LL.M., 1989). Associated with Davis Polk & Wardwell, New York, 1989-1990. *Member:* The Dai-ni Tokyo and New York State Bar Associations; Japan Federation of Bar Associations. *LANGUAGES:* Japanese and English. *PRACTICE AREAS:* Corporate; Financing; Securities.

MASANORI HAYASHI, born Hiroshima, Japan, May 19, 1958; admitted, 1989, Tokyo, Japan. *Education:* University of Tokyo (LL.B., 1984); Legal Training and Research Institute (Diploma, 1989). *Member:* Tokyo Bar Association; Japan Federation of Bar Associations. *LANGUAGES:* Japanese and English. *PRACTICE AREAS:* Copyright; Litigation.

OSAMU NOMOTO, born Niigata, Japan, September 22, 1961; admitted, 1990, Japan. *Education:* Keio University (LL.B., 1984; LL.M., 1988);

(This Listing Continued)

Legal Training and Research Institute (Diploma, 1990). *Member:* First Tokyo Bar Association; Japan Federation of Bar Associations. *LANGUAGES:* Japanese and English. *PRACTICE AREAS:* General Corporate; Litigation; Bankruptcy.

TATSUO TEZUKA, born Fukushima, Japan, September 13, 1964; admitted, 1993, Japan. *Education:* Waseda University (LL.B., 1988); Legal Training and Research Institute (Diploma, 1993). *Member:* The Dai-ni Tokyo Bar Association; Japan Federation of Bar Associations. *LANGUAGES:* Japanese and English. *PRACTICE AREAS:* General Corporate; Litigation.

JUN-ICHI SAKOMOTO, born Tokyo, Japan, April 2, 1953; admitted, 1993, Japan. *Education:* Keio University (Ec. B.A., 1976; LL.B., 1978); Legal Training and Research Institute (Diploma, 1993). *Member:* The Dai-ni Tokyo Bar Association; Japan Federation of Bar Associations. *LANGUAGES:* Japanese and English. *PRACTICE AREAS:* General Corporate; Financing; Copyright; Litigation.

AKEMI SAKAI, born Nagoya, Japan, December 22, 1961; admitted, 1991, New York (Not admitted in Japan). *Education:* Keio University (LL.B., 1987); The University of Chicago (LL.M., 1990). *Member:* American Bar Association; New York State Bar Association. *LANGUAGES:* English. *PRACTICE AREAS:* Securities; Financing; Corporate.

KUNSEN GEN, born Kobe, Japan, June 8, 1966; admitted, 1994, Japan. *Education:* University of Tokyo (LL.B., 1991); Legal Training and Research Institute (Diploma, 1994). *Member:* Japan Federation of Bar Associations; The Dai-ni Tokyo Bar Association. *LANGUAGES:* Japanese and English. *PRACTICE AREAS:* Corporate; Financing; Copyright.

YASUTAKA NUKINA, born Kobe, Japan, October 7, 1966; admitted, 1994, Japan. *Education:* Sophia University (LL.B., 1990; LL.M., 1992); Legal Training and Research Institute (Diploma, 1994). *Member:* Japan Federation of Bar Associations; The Dai-ni Tokyo Bar Association. *LANGUAGES:* Japanese and English. *PRACTICE AREAS:* Corporate; Litigation.

Languages: Japanese and English

MIYAKE & YAMAZAKI

Established in 1976

SOGO NAGATA-CHO BUILDING
11-28 NAGATA-CHO 1-CHOME, CHIYODA-KU
TOKYO 100, JAPAN
Telephone: 03-3580-5931
Facsimile: 03-3580-5400

Bangkok, Thailand Office: Suite 1903 Wall Street Tower, 33/96 Surawong Road, Bangrak, 10500. Telephone: (66-2) 266-2840. Facsimile: (66-2) 238-0858.

General Practice. International and Domestic Legal Practice.

MEMBERS OF FIRM

NOBUO MIYAKE, born Tokyo, Japan, August 25, 1939; admitted, 1966, Japan. *Education:* Tokyo University (LL.B.); New York University School of Law, Institute of Comparative Law. *Member:* Dai-ni Tokyo and Japanese Bar Associations; Inter-Pacific Bar Association (Secretary General, 1991—). *LANGUAGES:* Japanese and English.

JUNICHI YAMAZAKI, born Tokyo, Japan, September 5, 1943; admitted, 1978, Japan. *Education:* Tokyo University. *Member:* Dai-ni Tokyo and Japanese Bar Associations; Inter-Pacific Bar Association. *LANGUAGES:* Japanese, English and French.

KENICHI NAGAYA, born Nagoya, Japan, September 24, 1954; admitted, 1983, Japan. *Education:* Waseda University. *Member:* Dai-ni Tokyo and Japanese Bar Associations; Inter-Pacific Bar Association. *LANGUAGES:* Japanese and English.

AKIRA YAMADA, born Osaka, Japan, May 16, 1953; admitted, 1986, Japan; 1990, New York. *Education:* Kyoto University. *Member:* Dai-ni Tokyo and Japanese Bar Associations; Inter-Pacific Bar Association. (Resident Partner, Bangkok Office). *LANGUAGES:* Japanese and English.

ASSOCIATES

YOSHINORI ONO, born Tokyo, Japan, March 19, 1958; admitted, 1986, Japan. *Education:* Tokyo University (LL.B.). *Member:* Dai-ni Tokyo and Japanese Bar Associations; Inter-Pacific Bar Association. *LANGUAGES:* Japanese and English.

(This Listing Continued)

ATSUSHI FUJIOKA, born Osaka, Japan, August 26, 1963; admitted, 1990, Japan. *Education:* Hitotsubashi University. *Member:* Dai-ni Tokyo and Japanese Bar Associations; Inter-Pacific Bar Association. *LANGUAGES:* Japanese and English.

KYOKO OGURA, born Fukuoka, Japan, August 26, 1957; admitted, 1993, Japan. *Education:* Seijo University. *Member:* Dai-ni Tokyo and Japanese Bar Associations; Inter-Pacific Bar Association. *LANGUAGES:* Japanese and English.

YASUTAKA KENO, born Yokohama, Japan, February 9, 1961; admitted, 1994, Japan. *Education:* Keio University. *Member:* Dai-ni Tokyo and Japanese Bar Associations; Inter-Pacific Bar Association. *LANGUAGES:* Japanese and English.

MOMO-O, MATSUO & NAMBA

HAKUWA BUILDING 8F
2-1 KOJIMACHI 3-CHOME, CHIYODA-KU
TOKYO 102, JAPAN
Telephone: (03) 3288-2080
Telex: 3232-2040 MMNLAW
Telecopier: (03) 3288-2081

International Legal Practice.

SHIGEAKI MOMO-O, born Kobe, Japan, August 19, 1940; admitted, 1966, Japan. *Education:* Tokyo University (LL.B., 1964); Legal Research and Training Institute of the Supreme Court (1964-1966); University of Texas School of Law (M.C.J., 1969). *Member:* First Tokyo Bar Association. *LANGUAGES:* Japanese and English.

MAKOTO MATSUO, born Tokyo, Japan, May 28, 1949; admitted, 1975, Japan; 1979, New York. *Education:* Tokyo University (LL.B., 1973); Legal Research and Training Institute of the Supreme Court (1973-1975); Columbia University School of Law (LL.M., 1978). *Member:* First Tokyo Bar Association; New York State and American Bar Associations. *LANGUAGES:* Japanese and English.

SHUICHI NAMBA, born Tokyo, Japan, December 18, 1957; admitted, 1984, Japan; 1988, New York and California. *Education:* Tokyo University (LL.B., 1982); Legal Research and Training Institute of the Supreme Court (1982-1984); Colombia University School of Law (LL.M., 1987). *Member:* First Tokyo Bar Association; New York State and American Bar Associations. *LANGUAGES:* Japanese and English.

YURIKO KANEMATSU, born Tokyo, Japan, January 23, 1961; admitted, 1988, Japan. *Education:* Waseda University (LL.B., 1983; LL.M., 1986); Legal Research and Training Institute of the Supreme Court (1986-1988). University of Ottawa, School of Graduate Studies and Research, 1991—. *Member:* First Tokyo Bar Association. *LANGUAGES:* Japanese and English.

TATSUO UENO, born Tokyo, Japan, May 9, 1962; admitted, 1990, Japan. *Education:* Tokyo University (LL.B., 1987); Legal Research and Training Institute of the Supreme Court of Japan (1988-1990). *Member:* First Tokyo Bar Association. *LANGUAGES:* Japanese and English.

JUNYA NAITO, born Matsue, Japan, August 22, 1964; admitted, 1991, Japan. *Education:* Tokyo University (LL.B., 1989); Legal Research and Training Institute of the Supreme Court (1989-1991). *Member:* First Tokyo Bar Association. *LANGUAGES:* Japanese and English.

MASAO TORIKAI, born Chiba, Japan, January 7, 1963; admitted, 1994, Japan. *Education:* Tokyo University (LL.B., 1987); Legal Research and Training Institute of the Supreme Court (1992-1994). *Member:* First Tokyo Bar Association. *LANGUAGES:* Japanese and English.

A Member of Interlaw, An Association of Law Firms in Major World Centers.

MORGAN, LEWIS & BOCKIUS

(Gaikokuho-Jimu Bengoshi Jimusho)

CS TOWER
1-11-30 AKASAKA, MINATO-KU
TOKYO 107, JAPAN
Telephone: 011-81-3-587-2900
Telecopy: 011-81-3-587-2082

Philadelphia, Pennsylvania Office: 2000 One Logan Square, 19103-6993. Telephone: 215-963-5000.

(This Listing Continued)

Washington, D.C. Office: 1800 M Street, N.W., 20036. Telephone: 202-467-7000.

New York, New York Office: 101 Park Avenue, 10178. Telephone: 212-309-6000.

Los Angeles, California Office: 801 South Grand Avenue, 90017-3189. Telephone: 213-612-2500.

Miami, Florida Office: 5300 First Union Financial Center, 200 South Biscayne Boulevard, 33131-2339. Telephone: 305-579-0300.

Harrisburg, Pennsylvania Office: One Commerce Square, 417 Walnut Street, 17101-1904. Telephone: 717-237-4000.

Princeton, New Jersey Office: 100 Overlook Center, 08540. Telephone: 609-520-6600.

Newport Beach, California Office: 4675 MacArthur Court, Suite 740, 92660. Telephone: 714-851-6333.

London, England Office: 4 Carlton Gardens, Pall Mall. Telephone: 071-839-1677.

Brussels, Belgium Office: Rue Guimard 7, B-1040. Telephone: 32-2/512.55.01.

Frankfurt, Germany Office: Siesemayerstrasse 44,D-6000 Frankfurt/Main. Telephone: 069-72-3478.

Firm engaged in American and General International Law Practice but not authorized to appear before Japanese courts or to act as Benjashi.

FIRM PROFILE: Morgan, Lewis & Bockius is an international law firm with 750 lawyers and a diverse practice. Founded in 1873, the Firm was one of the first to develop an integrated, multicity practice.

The Firm's practice areas include antitrust; arbitration and ADR proceedings; banking, thrift and consumer financial services; bankruptcy and reorganization; business and corporate; construction; customs; energy regulation; environmental; executive compensation and employee benefits; food, drug and cosmetics regulation; foreign direct investment in the United States; government contracts; government regulation; immigration; insurance and reinsurance; intellectual property and technology, including patent, trademark and copyright; international financings; international trade; labor and employment; legislation and government relations; leveraged lease and project financings; litigation; mergers and acquisitions; municipal finance; personal law; productsliability; public utilities; real estate; securities; tax; and transportation law.

MEMBER OF FIRM IN TOKYO

WILLIAM R. HUSS, born April 23, 1949; admitted, 1975, Virginia; 1976, District of Columbia; 1983, New York; 1990, Japan (Gaikokuho-Jimu-Bengoshi). *Education:* Georgetown University (B.S.F.S., 1971); The National Law Center George Washington University (J.D., 1975). *Member:* The Virginia State Bar; The District of Columbia Bar; New York State and American Bar Associations; First Tokyo Bar Association. *LANGUAGES:* Japanese.

SPECIAL COUNSEL

ALVIN L. KASSEL, born December 15, 1917; admitted, 1941, New York (Not admitted in Japan). *Education:* New York University; New York Law School (LL.B., 1941). Co-Author: "Transfer Prices: United States Tax Treatment of Non-Arms Length Business Transactions Between Controlled Entities," Vol. 13, No. 3, March 1985 and Vol. 13, No. 4, April 1985, "U.S. International Trade Commission Investigations Under Section 337 of the Tariff Act of 1930," Vol. 13, No. 10, October 1985, Journal of the Japanese Institute of International Business Law (Kokusai Shoji Homu).

Members of the Firm, Counsel, Of Counsel and Associates in Philadelphia and Harrisburg, Pennsylvania, Washington, D.C., New York, New York, Los Angeles and Newport Beach, California, Miami, Florida, Princeton, New Jersey, London, England, Brussels, Belgium and Frankfurt/Main, Germany are listed in the Biographical Section respectively.

MORI SOGO LAW OFFICES

NKK BUILDING
1-1-2 MARUNOUCHI, CHIYODA-KU
TOKYO 100, JAPAN
Telephone: 81-3-5223-7700
Facsimile: 81-3-5223-7600

General Practice. Corporations, Litigation, Commercial Transactions, International Transactions, Real Estate, Merger and Acquisition, Banking, Financing, Securities, Insurance, Entertainment, Intellectual Property, Copyright, Antitrust, Taxation, Bankruptcy and Corporate Reorganization.

MEMBERS OF FIRM

RYOSAKU MORI (1900-1971).

(This Listing Continued)

MORI SOGO LAW OFFICES, Tokyo—Continued

HIROSHI FUKUDA, born 1929; admitted, 1962, Japan. *Education:* Tokyo University (LL.B.). With Legislative Bureau of House of Representatives, 1956-1960. Director, 1974-1975, Deputy Secretary General, 1981-1983 and Chairman, Committee on Lawyers Ethics, 1987-1988, Japan Federation of Bar Associations. *Member:* Daini-Tokyo Bar Association (Vice President, 1977-1978). *LANGUAGES:* Japanese, English and French.

TOHRU MOTOBAYASHI, born 1938; admitted, 1963, Japan. *Education:* Tokyo University (LL.B.); Harvard Law School (LL.M., 1969). Author: "Force Majeure Clause," 1985; "International Arbitration," 1988; Jurisdiction of Multi-national Litigations," 1993. Co-Author: "Distributorship Agreement—Legal Problems and Practice," 1972; "Bankrupt v.s. Creditors," 1978. With Mayer, Brown and Platt, Illinois, 1969-1970. Chairman, International Transaction Law Committee, 1987—. *Member:* Tokyo Bar Association (Vice President, 1986-1987); The Civil Procedure Law Association of Japan; International Bar Association. *LANGUAGES:* Japanese and English.

MASAO KOBIKI, born 1937; admitted, 1963, Japan. *Education:* Tokyo University (LL.B.). Author: "Civil Procedure Law Commentary," 1981; "Reduction of Corporate Capital," 1984; "Corporate Reorganization—Documentary," 1975; Reorganized Company v.s. Creditors," 1978. Legal Advisor to Trustee of Kojin Co., Ltd., 1975-1980. *Member:* Daini-Tokyo Bar Association; Kanto Federation of Bar Association (Managing Director, 1991-1992). *LANGUAGES:* Japanese and English.

HIDEAKI KUBORI, born 1944; admitted, 1971, Japan. *Education:* Tokyo University (LL.B.). Author: "Management of General Shareholders' Meeting," 1986; "Forefront of Corporate Reorganization," 1980; "Insider Tradings and Shareholders' Meetings," 1988; "Case Stories of General Shareholders' Meeting," 1987; "How to Manage General Shareholders' Meeting," 1986; "Scenario of Management-led General Shareholders' Meeting," 1987; "Managing Shareholders' Meetings," (Video Taped) 1992. Co-Author: "Practical Guide for Corporate Auditor," 1983; "Forefront of Copyright Business and Law," 1985; "Defense Tactics in M & A," 1990; "Handbook of How to Deal with Shareholders," 1989. *Member:* Daini-Tokyo Bar Association (Vice President, 1989-1990); The Copyright Law Association of Japan. *LANGUAGES:* Japanese and English.

HARUMICHI UCHIDA, born 1947; admitted, 1973, Japan; 1980, New York. *Education:* Tokyo University (LL.B.); New York University Law School (LL.M., 1979). With Donovan, Leisure, Newton & Irvine, New York, Los Angeles, 1979-1980. Author: "Investment in the US and Antitrust Law". Co-Author: "Practical Guide for Corporate Auditor," 1983; "Forefront of Copyright Business and Law," 1985; "Legal Strategy in Merger and Acquisition," 1987; "Practical Guide to Avoid Misappropriation of Trade Secret," 1990. Council Member, Fair Treatment of Personnel of Kamakura-City, 1991—. Member, Study Group of Security Interest in Mobile Equipment under UNIDROIT (International Institute for the Unification of Private Law), 1993—. *Member:* Daini-Tokyo Bar Association; American Bar Association; New York State Bar Association; International Bar Association; Inter-Pacific Bar Association (Vice-Chairman, Intellectual Property Committee, 1993—); Institute for Intellectual Property (Member, Committee of Trade Secret Protection and Civil Procedures, 1993—). *LANGUAGES:* Japanese and English.

TAKASHI IIDA, born 1946; admitted, 1974, Japan. *Education:* Tokyo University (LL.B.). Author: "Getting Defendant off by Making Use of Civil Litigation Technique," 1988. Co-Author: "Medical Malpractice Dictionary"; "Medical Malpractice Litigation Practice." *Member:* Daini-Tokyo Bar Association. *LANGUAGES:* Japanese and English.

YOSHIFUMI KOBAYASHI, born 1951; admitted, 1976, Japan. *Education:* Tokyo University (LL.B.). Co-Author: "Practical Guide for Corporate Auditor's Guide," 1983. *Member:* Tokyo Bar Association. *LANGUAGES:* Japanese and English.

RYOSUKE AIHARA, born 1952; admitted, 1977, Japan. *Education:* Tokyo University (LL.B.). Co-Author: "Practical Guide for Corporate Auditor's Guide," 1983. *Member:* Daini-Tokyo Bar Association. *LANGUAGES:* Japanese and English.

RYOTA YAMAGISHI, born 1953; admitted, 1980, Japan. *Education:* Tokyo University (LL.B.). Author: "Legal Problems in Pre-paid Cards," 1988; "Q & A on Credit Sale and Lease Cases," 1988; "Guarantor's Indemnification Right and Natural Deed"; "General Terms for Credit Companies"; "Legal Notarial of Prepaid Cards". Co-Author: "Legal Problems in Conditional Sale," 1985; "Handbook of How to Deal with Shareholders," 1989; "Practical Issues Concerning Finance and Retention of Ownership Title."

(This Listing Continued)

Member: Daini-Tokyo Bar Association. *LANGUAGES:* Japanese and English.

MASATAKE YONE, born 1954; admitted, 1981, Japan; 1987, New York. *Education:* Tokyo University (LL.B.); Cornell Law School (LL.M., 1985). With Sullivan & Cromwell, New York, 1985-1986; Freshfields, London, 1986-1987. Author: "Insider Trading Compliance Programs," 1988; "Dawn of Merger and Acquisition in Japan," 1987; "Due Diligence Review in Merger and Acquisition," 1989; "Insider Trading Regulations," 1989; "How to Deal with Insider Trading Regulations." Co-Author: "Defense Tactics in M & A," 1990. *Member:* Daini-Tokyo Bar Association; New York State Bar Association. *LANGUAGES:* Japanese and English.

SUSUMU MASUDA, born 1955; admitted, 1982, Japan; 1987, California. *Education:* Tokyo University (LL.B.); University of Washington, Law School (LL.M., 1986). With Lillick, McHose & Charles, Los Angeles, 1986-1987. Author: "Recent Developments in American Law Regulating Lock-Ups," 1988. Co-Author: "Legal Problems in Conditional Sale," 1985. *Member:* Daini-Tokyo Bar Association; State Bar of California; American Bar Association. *LANGUAGES:* Japanese and English.

WATARU SUEYOSHI, born 1956; admitted, 1983, Japan. *Education:* Tokyo University (LL.B.). Author: "Information Network Society and Law," 1988; "Biotechnology Study Group and its Role," 1988. *Member:* Daini-Tokyo Bar Association; Biotechnology Law Study Group. *LANGUAGES:* Japanese and English.

YOSHIO ITEYA, born 1956; admitted, 1983, Japan; 1989, New York. *Education:* Kyoto University (LL.B.); Harvard Law School (LL.M., 1988). With White & Case, New York, 1988-1990. Author: "Gaikokuho-Jimu Bengoshi (Foreign Business Lawyers) in Japan," 1988; "Suggested Approach to U.S. Intellectual Property for Japanese Corporations," 1990; "Legal Issues with Respect to Doing Business in Japan," 1990; "NAFTA and its Impact on Japanese Corporations," 1992. *Member:* Daini-Tokyo Bar Association; New York State Bar Association; American Bar Association. *LANGUAGES:* Japanese and English.

TOMOHISA TABUCHI, born 1957; admitted, 1984, Japan. *Education:* Tokyo University (LL.B.). Co-Author: "Law and Practice of Pre-paid Cards." *Member:* Tokyo Bar Association. *LANGUAGES:* Japanese and English.

TOMOHISA SHINAGAWA, born 1958; admitted, 1985, Japan; 1991, New York. *Education:* Tokyo University (LL.B.); Columbia University School of Law (LL.M., 1990). With Skadden Arps Slate Meagher & Flom, New York, 1990-1991. Author: "Defensive Measures in Hostile Takeovers and Directors' Liability in the United States," 1990; "Legal Problems on Mergers of Listed Companies," 1993. Co-Author: "Handbook of How to Deal with Shareholders," 1989; "The 1990 Amendments to the Securities and Exchange Law: Impact on M & A in Japan," 1990. *Member:* Daini-Tokyo Bar Association; New York State Bar Association; American Bar Association. *LANGUAGES:* Japanese and English.

NAOTO NAKAMURA, born 1960; admitted, 1985, Japan. *Education:* Hitotsubashi University (LL.B.). Author: Mori Sogo Law Offices Compilation: "Handbook on Legal Measures to Deal with Shareholders-Procedures and Strategy," 1989; "General Shareholders' Meeting White Paper of 1988," 1989; "Activation of Marketing Strategy." Co-Author: "Defense Tactics in M & A," 1990; "Legal Nature of Prepaid Cards"; "Handbook of How to Deal with Shareholders," 1989. *Member:* Daini-Tokyo Bar Association. *LANGUAGES:* Japanese and English.

ZEN TATSUMURA, born 1956; admitted, 1985, Japan. *Education:* Hitotsubashi University (LL.B.). Author: "Regulations of Acquisition of Capital Stock by Foreigners." Co-Author: "Handbook of How to Deal with Shareholders," 1989. *Member:* Daini-Tokyo Bar Association. *LANGUAGES:* Japanese, English and French.

YOICHI OKUDA, born 1960; admitted, 1986, Japan. *Education:* Tokyo University (LL.B.). Co-Author: "Handbook of How to Deal with Shareholders," 1989. *Member:* Daini-Tokyo Bar Association. *LANGUAGES:* Japanese and English.

NAOSUKE ICHIKAWA, born 1959; admitted, 1987, Japan. *Education:* Keio University (LL.B.). *Member:* Tokyo Bar Association. *LANGUAGES:* Japanese and English.

HAJIME WATANABE, born 1959; admitted, 1987, Japan; 1994, Illinois (as Foreign Legal Consultant). *Education:* Tokyo University (LL.B.); University of Illinois Law School (LL.M., 1993). Author: "Handling of Insider Trading Regulations," 1987; "Insider Trading Regulations and Legal Services," 1988. Co-Author: "Defense Tactics in M & A," 1990; "Handbook of How to Deal with Shareholders," 1989; "Intellectual Property Rights and

(This Listing Continued)

their Surroundings." *Member:* Daini-Tokyo Bar Association. (Also with Jenner & Block, Chicago, Illinois). *LANGUAGES:* Japanese and English.

MAKOTO IMAMURA, born 1961; admitted, 1988, Japan; 1994, New York. *Education:* Tokyo University (LL.B.); Harvard Law School. With Skadden, Arps, Slate, Meagher & Flom, New York, 1992-1993. *Member:* Daini-Tokyo Bar Association. *LANGUAGES:* Japanese and English.

KAZUHIRO KANAMARU, born 1960; admitted, 1988, Japan. *Education:* Tokyo University (LL.B.). Co-Author: "Defense Tactics in M & A," 1990. *Member:* Daini-Tokyo Bar Association. *LANGUAGES:* Japanese and English.

SHIN KIKUCHI, born 1960; admitted, 1989, Japan. *Education:* Tokyo University (LL.B.); Harvard Law School (LL.M., 1994). Ministry of the Interior, 1982-1987. With Paul, Weiss, Rifkind, Wharton & Garrison, New York, Sept., 1994. *Member:* Daini-Tokyo Bar Association. *LANGUAGES:* Japanese and English.

TAKUYA IIZUKA, born 1965; admitted, 1990, Japan. *Education:* Chuo University (LL.B.). *Member:* Tokyo Bar Association. *LANGUAGES:* Japanese and English.

SATOKO KUWABARA, born 1964; admitted, 1990, Japan. *Education:* Tokyo University (LL.B.); University of Oxford (1993-1994). With Freshfields, London, Sept., 1994. *Member:* Daini-Tokyo Bar Association. *LANGUAGES:* Japanese and English.

MASANORI SATO, born 1965; admitted, 1990, Japan; 1994, New York. *Education:* Tokyo University (LL.B.); University of Chicago Law School (LL.M., 1993). With: Cleary, Gottlieb, Steen & Hamilton, New York, 1993-1994; Linklaters & Paines, London, Sept., 1994. *Member:* Daini-Tokyo Bar Association. *LANGUAGES:* Japanese and English.

KO FUJITA, born 1964; admitted, 1990, Japan; 1994, New York. *Education:* Tokyo University (LL.B.); New York University School of Law (LL.M., 1993). With Kaye, Scholer, Fierman, Hays & Handler, New York, 1993-1994. *Member:* Daini-Tokyo Bar Association. *LANGUAGES:* Japanese and English.

HIDEKI MATSUI, born 1964; admitted, 1990, Japan. *Education:* Tokyo University (LL.B.). *Member:* Tokyo Bar Association. *LANGUAGES:* Japanese and English.

SOICHIRO FUJIWARA, born 1966; admitted, 1991, Japan. *Education:* Tokyo University (LL.B.). *Member:* Daini-Tokyo Bar Association. *LANGUAGES:* Japanese and English.

TAKASHI MIYATANI, born 1965; admitted, 1991, Japan. *Education:* Tokyo University (LL.B.). *Member:* Daini-Tokyo Bar Association. *LANGUAGES:* Japanese and English.

MAKOTO SHIMIZU, born 1963; admitted, 1992, Japan. *Education:* Tokyo University (LL.B.). The Bank of Japan, 1987-1989. *Member:* Daini-Tokyo Bar Association. *LANGUAGES:* Japanese and English.

NOBORU SUWA, born 1965; admitted, 1992, Japan. *Education:* Tokyo University (LL.B.). *Member:* Daini-Tokyo Bar Association. *LANGUAGES:* Japanese and English.

HAJIME TANAHASHI, born 1966; admitted, 1992, Japan. *Education:* Tokyo University (LL.B.). *Member:* Daini-Tokyo Bar Association. *LANGUAGES:* Japanese and English.

YOSHIYUKI NAKAMURA, born 1964; admitted, 1992, Japan. *Education:* Tokyo University (LL.B.); Harvard Law School (Sept., 1994). The Bank of Japan, 1987-1989. *Member:* Daini-Tokyo Bar Association. *LANGUAGES:* Japanese and English.

MINORU SAWAGUCHI, born 1966; admitted, 1993, Japan. *Education:* Tokyo University (LL.B.). *Member:* Daini-Tokyo Bar Association. *LANGUAGES:* Japanese and English.

YURIKO TAKANO, born 1968; admitted, 1993, Japan. *Education:* Tokyo University (LL.B.). *Member:* Daini-Tokyo Bar Association. *LANGUAGES:* Japanese and English.

AKIHITO NAKAMACHI, born 1968; admitted, 1993, Japan. *Education:* Kyoto University (LL.B.). *Member:* Tokyo Bar Association. *LANGUAGES:* Japanese and English.

AKIRA MARUMO, born 1966; admitted, 1993, Japan. *Education:* Tokyo University (LL.B.). *Member:* Tokyo Bar Association. *LANGUAGES:* Japanese and English.

TSUNEMICHI YOKOYAMA, born 1968; admitted, 1993, Japan. *Education:* Tokyo University (LL.B.). *Member:* Daini-Tokyo Bar Association. *LANGUAGES:* Japanese and English.

TOMIHIRO TSUCHIYA, born 1968; admitted, 1994, Japan. *Education:* Tokyo University (LL.B.). *Member:* Daini-Tokyo Bar Association. *LANGUAGES:* Japanese and English.

DAIKEN TSUNODA, born 1967; admitted, 1994, Japan. *Education:* Tokyo University (LL.B.). *Member:* Tokyo Bar Association. *LANGUAGES:* Japanese and English.

SATOKO NIIYA, born 1968; admitted, 1994, Japan. *Education:* Kyoto University (LL.B.). *Member:* Tokyo Bar Association. *LANGUAGES:* Japanese and English.

OF COUNSEL

KOJI SHINDO, born 1931; admitted, 1992, Japan. *Education:* Tokyo University (LL.B.); Yale Law School (LL.M., 1965). Professor of Law, Tokyo University, 1968-1992. Dean of Law Department, Tokyo University, 1989-1990. Professor Emeritus, Tokyo University, 1992—. Member, Legislative Council, 1980—. President, Civil Procedure Law Association, 1983-1986. Member and Deputy President, Tokyo Labor Relations Commission, 1977—. Author: "Civil Procedure Law," 1974; "Causes of Action and Res Judicata," 1986; "Bankruptcy and Attachment Law Issues Concerning the ISDA Master Agreement," 1993. Co-Author: "Commentary-Civil Procedure Law," 1986. *Member:* Daini-Tokyo Bar Association. *LANGUAGES:* Japanese, English and German.

MORRISON & FOERSTER

(Robert S. Townsend Gaikokuho-Jimu-Bengoshi-Jimusho)

Established in 1883

AIG BUILDING, 14TH FLOOR
1-1-3 MARUNOUCHI, CHIYODA-KU
TOKYO 100, JAPAN
Telephone: 011-81-3-3214-6522
Facsimile: 011-81-3-3214-6512

Other offices located in: San Francisco, Los Angeles, New York, Washington, D.C., London, Brussels, Hong Kong, Sacramento, Palo Alto, Walnut Creek, Orange County, Denver and Seattle.

In Tokyo, engaged in American and International Law practice as "Robert S. Townsend, Gaikokuho-Jimu-Bengoshi-Jimusho." Not authorized to appear before Japanese courts or otherwise to act as a Japanese Bengoshi.

FIRM PROFILE: *Morrison & Foerster is one of the world's largest international law firms with 500 lawyers located in 14 offices worldwide. The firm's legal practice encompasses every major area of commercial law, including corporate finance, institutional lending, financial services, real estate, environmental and land use planning, mining and natural resources, agriculture, intellectual property, energy, telecommunications and entertainment, insurance, alternative dispute resolution, products liability, bankruptcy and workouts, financial transactions, labor and employment, civil, criminal and securities litigation, antitrust, international trade and tax.*

MEMBERS OF FIRM

CHARLES S. BARQUIST, born September 22, 1953; admitted, 1979, New York; 1988, California; 1993, Japan as a Gaikokuho-Jimu-Bengoshi. *Education:* University of Michigan (A.B., with high distinction, 1975); Harvard Law School (J.D., cum laude, 1978). Phi Beta Kappa. Law Clerk to Judge Milton Pollack, U.S. District Court, Southern District of New York, 1978-1979. *Member:* Association of the Bar of the City of New York (Member, 1981-1986, Chairman, 1984-1986, Committee on State Legislation; Member, Committee on Professional Discipline, 1986-1988). (Tokyo and Los Angeles Offices).

VINCENT J. CHIARELLO, born February 18, 1957; admitted, 1981, California; 1983, New York (Not admitted in Japan). *Education:* The Bernard M. Baruch College of the City University of New York (B.B.A., summa cum laude, 1978); Yale Law School (J.D., 1981). Law Clerk to Judge Anthony M. Kennedy, U.S. Court of Appeals, Ninth Circuit, 1981-1982. (Tokyo and San Francisco Offices). *PRACTICE AREAS:* Litigation; Intellectual Property Litigation; Accounting Malpractice Litigation; Securities Litigation.

KENNETH SIEGEL, born October 11, 1958; admitted, 1986, California; 1994, Japan as a Gaikokuho-Jimu-Bengoshi. *Education:* Amherst Col-

MORRISON & FOERSTER, *Tokyo—Continued*

lege (A.B., magna cum laude, 1981); The Johns Hopkins University, School of Advanced International Studies; University of Chicago Law School (J.D., 1986). *LANGUAGES:* Japanese.

ROBERT S. TOWNSEND, born July 3, 1956; admitted, 1984, California; 1993, Japan as a Gaikokuho-Jimu-Bengoshi. *Education:* University of California, Berkeley (B.S., with highest honors, 1978); Stanford Law School (J.D., 1984). Phi Beta Kappa. Vice President: Stanford Public Interest Law Foundation, 1982-1983; Stanford International Law Society, 1982-1983. Extern, Legal Resources Centre, Johannesburg, South Africa, 1983. Visiting Attorney, Philippines, 1986-1988. (Managing Partner, Tokyo Office).

LISA CHRISTOFFERS YANO, born November 20, 1954; admitted, 1986, New York; 1991, California (Not admitted in Japan). *Education:* St. Lawrence University; Kean College of New Jersey (B.A., summa cum laude, 1980); Yale Law School (J.D., 1985). *LANGUAGES:* Japanese.

ASSOCIATES

MICHAEL C. GRAFFAGNA, born August 4, 1962; admitted, 1989, California (Not admitted in Japan). *Education:* University of Illinois (B.A., summa cum laude, 1984); Harvard Law School (J.D., cum laude, 1989). Phi Beta Kappa. *LANGUAGES:* Japanese.

G. JIYUN LEE, born January 26, 1967; admitted, 1992, California (Not admitted in Japan). *Education:* University of California, Santa Cruz (B.A., 1989); Harvard Law School (J.D., cum laude, 1992).

(For biographical data on San Francisco, Los Angeles, Sacramento, Walnut Creek, Palo Alto and Irvine, CA, New York, NY, Washington, DC, Denver, CO, Seattle, WA, London, England, Brussels, Belgium and Hong Kong see professional biographies at each of those cities).

MUDGE ROSE GUTHRIE ALEXANDER & FERDON

(Mudge, Stern, Baldwin & Todd)

(Caldwell, Trimble & Mitchell)

INFINI AKASAKA
8-7-15 AKASAKA, MINATO-KU
TOKYO 107, JAPAN
Telephone: (03) 3423-3970
Fax: (03) 3423-3971

New York City Office: 180 Maiden Lane, New York, N.Y., 10038. Telephone: 212-510-7000. Telecopier: 212-248-2655/57.
Los Angeles, California Office: 21st Floor, 333 South Grand Avenue, 90071. Telephone: 213-613-1112. Telecopier: 213-680-1358.
Washington, D.C. Office: 1200 19th Street, N.W., Suite 400, 20037. Telephone: 202-973-1200. Telecopier: 202-429-9367.
West Palm Beach, Florida Office: Suite 900, 515 North Flagler Drive, 33401. Telephone: 407-650-8100. Telecopier: 407-833-1722.
Parsippany, New Jersey Office: Morris Corporate Center Two, Building D, 1 Upper Pond Road. Telephone: 201-335-0004. Telecopier: 201-402-1593.
European Office: 12, Rue de la Paix, 75002 Paris, France, Telephone: 42.61.57.71. Telecopier: 42.61.79.21.

General Practice.

RESIDENT PARTNER

TAKASHI MATSUMOTO, born Dandong, Manchuria, October 8, 1943; admitted, 1986, New York (Not admitted in Japan). *Education:* Osaka University (B.A., 1964; LL.B., 1966); New York University (LL.M., 1990). *Member:* New York State and American Bar Associations; Inter Pacific Bar Association. *LANGUAGES:* Japanese. *PRACTICE AREAS:* Corporate; Banking; Bankruptcy; Employment; International Trade.

NAGASHIMA & HASHIMOTO

MAISON HIRAKAWA, 3RD FLOOR
2-5-2 HIRAKAWA-CHO
CHIYODA-KU
TOKYO 102, JAPAN
Telephone: 03-3239-5750
Telex: J 27765 BENCH
Fax: 03-3239-8538

General Practice. International Transactions.

MEMBERS OF FIRM

TAKAAKI NAGASHIMA, born Tokyo, Japan, April 1, 1943; admitted, 1973, Japan; 1978, District of Columbia; 1979, New York. *Education:* Chuo University (LL.B., 1968); Tokyo Metropolitan University (1969-1971); Legal Research and Training Institute, Supreme Court of Japan; George Washington University (LL.M., 1976). *Member:* The Japan Federation of Bar Association; Daini Tokyo, New York State and American Bar Associations; District of Columbia Bar. *LANGUAGES:* Japanese and English.

AKIRA HASHIMOTO, born Hiroshima-Ken, Japan, August 27, 1947; admitted, 1973, Japan; 1984, New York. *Education:* Tokyo University (LL.B., 1970); Legal Research and Training Institute, Supreme Court of Japan (1971-1973); University of Paris (D.S.U., Droit Commercial, 1974; Docteur en droit, 1980); Harvard Law School (LL.M., 1982). *Member:* Tokyo Bar Association; New York State Bar Association. *LANGUAGES:* Japanese, English and French.

ASSOCIATES

KENJI KURODA, born Tokyo, Japan, January 11, 1963; admitted, 1986, Japan; 1989, New York. *Education:* Waseda University; Legal Research and Training Institute, Supreme Court of Japan (1984-1986); Duke University (LL.M., 1989); Fudan University in Shanghai (Law, 1990). *Member:* The Japan Federation of Bar Association; Tokyo Bar Association. *LANGUAGES:* Japanese, English and Chinese.

GEORGE HIBBERT, born Tokyo, Japan, January 27, 1958; admitted, 1984, Oregon; 1985, U.S. District Court, District of Oregon (Not admitted in Japan). *Education:* Waseda University; University of Oregon (B.A., 1980); Northwestern School of Law of Lewis and Clark College (J.D., 1984). *Member:* Multnomah County and American Bar Associations; Oregon State Bar (Member, Sections on: Debtor-Creditor; Construction Law). *LANGUAGES:* English and Japanese.

OFER SHARONE, born Israel, September 10, 1967; admitted, 1994, California. *Education:* University of Illinois (B.S., summa cum laude, 1989); Harvard Law School (J.D., cum laude, 1992). Phi Beta Kappa. *LANGUAGES:* Hebrew.

NAGASHIMA & OHNO

Established in 1961

KIOICHO BUILDING
3-12 KIOICHO, CHIYODA-KU
TOKYO 102, JAPAN
Telephone: (81-3) 3288-7000
Facsimile: GIII & GIV (81-3) 5213-7800

General and International Law Practice. Civil, Commercial, Corporation, Banking, Securities, Antitrust, Labor, Tax and Intellectual Property Law. Litigation, Arbitration and Administrative Procedures.

MEMBERS OF FIRM

YASUHARU NAGASHIMA, born 1926; admitted, 1953, Japan. *Education:* Tokyo University (LL.B.); Legal Training and Research Institute of the Supreme Court of Japan; graduate study, Harvard Law School (LL.M., 1962). Hale & Dorr, Boston, Mass., Summer, 1963; Milbank, Tweed, Hadley & McCloy, New York, 1963-1964. Visiting Professor, Harvard Law School, Fall, 1978. Lecturer, Yale Law School, Fall, 1989. Director, Japanese American Society for Legal Studies, 1964—. Secretary, Harvard Law School Association of Japan, 1982-1992. Member, Private International Law Sub-Committee, Legislative Council of the Ministry of Justice, 1986-1989. Legal Staff, Mitsubishi Chemical Industries Limited, 1949-1950. *LANGUAGES:* Japanese, English and French (reads only).

YOSHIO OHNO, born 1926; admitted, 1954, Japan. *Education:* Tokyo University (B.A. in Economics, 1949; LL.B.); Legal Training and Research Institute of the Supreme Court of Japan; graduate study, Tulane University

(This Listing Continued)

School of Law (LL.M., 1967). Foley & Lardner, Milwaukee, Wisconsin, 1967-1968. *LANGUAGES:* Japanese and English.

TOMIO FUKUI, born 1924; admitted, 1958, Japan. *Education:* Keio University (LL.B.); Legal Training and Research Institute of the Supreme Court of Japan. O'Melveny and Myers, Los Angeles, California, 1971-1972. *LANGUAGES:* Japanese and English.

TADAO HOZUMI, born 1933; admitted, 1962, Japan. *Education:* Tokyo University (LL.B.); Legal Training and Research Institute of the Supreme Court of Japan; graduate study, Columbia University School of Law (M.C.L., 1965). Stitt & Hemmendinger, Washington, D.C., 1965-1966. Research Assistant, Faculty of Law, Tokyo University, 1957-1960. *LANGUAGES:* Japanese and English.

ISAO IJUIN, born 1939; admitted, 1964, Japan. *Education:* Tokyo University (LL.B.); Legal Training and Research Institute of the Supreme Court of Japan; graduate study, University of Illinois, College of Law (M.C.L., 1973). Cleary, Gottlieb, Steen & Hamilton, Brussels, 1974-1975. House Counsel, Shell Oil Company, Japan, 1966-1972. *LANGUAGES:* Japanese and English.

HIROTOMI KIMURA, born 1942; admitted, 1969, Japan. *Education:* Tokyo University (LL.B.); Legal Training and Research Institute of the Supreme Court of Japan; graduate study, University of Illinois, College of Law (1974). Milbank, Tweed, Hadley & McCloy, New York, 1974-1975; Paul, Hastings, Janofsky & Walker, Los Angeles, 1975. Lecturer, University of Illinois, College of Law, Fall, 1989. Lecturer, Tax Law, Faculty of Law, Sophia University, 1984-1994. *LANGUAGES:* Japanese and English.

AIJIRO TSUNODA, born 1939; admitted, 1971, Japan. *Education:* Tokyo University (LL.B.); Legal Training and Research Institute of the Supreme Court of Japan; graduate study, Harvard Law School (LL.M., 1976). Cleary, Gottlieb, Steen & Hamilton, New York, 1976-1977. *LANGUAGES:* Japanese and English.

MASAYUKI YOSHIDA, born 1944; admitted, 1972, Japan. *Education:* Tokyo University of Education (LL.B.); Legal Training and Research Institute of the Supreme Court of Japan; graduate study, University of Pennsylvania Law School (LL.M., 1978); Harvard Law School, Fall, 1978. Cleary, Gottlieb, Steen & Hamilton, New York, 1979; Morrison & Foerster, London, 1979; American Stock Exchange, New York, Winter, 1978; The Securities and Exchange Commission, Washington, D.C., Summer, 1978; Legislative Bureau of the Japanese National Diet, 1967-1970. *LANGUAGES:* Japanese and English.

HISASHI HARA, born 1947; admitted, 1975, Japan. *Education:* Tokyo University (LL.B.); Legal Training and Research Institute of the Supreme Court of Japan; graduate study, Harvard Law School (LL.M., 1980). Arnold & Porter, Washington, D.C., 1980-1981. *LANGUAGES:* Japanese and English.

KOICHI TAKEUCHI, born 1948; admitted, 1977, Japan. *Education:* Tokyo University (B.A. in Pedagogics, 1973); Legal Training and Research Institute of the Supreme Court of Japan; graduate study, Columbia University School of Law (LL.M., 1982). Cleary, Gottlieb, Steen & Hamilton, New York, 1982-1983; Morrison & Foerster, London, Summer, 1983. *LANGUAGES:* Japanese and English.

KAZUO OHTAKE, born 1952; admitted, 1978, Japan. *Education:* Tokyo University (LL.B.); Legal Training and Research Institute of the Supreme Court of Japan; graduate study, Harvard Law School (LL.M., 1983). Paul, Weiss, Rifkind, Wharton & Garrison, New York, 1983-1984; Freshfields, London, 1984-1985. *LANGUAGES:* Japanese and English.

YUKO MIYAZAKI, born 1951; admitted, 1979, Japan. *Education:* Tokyo University (LL.B.); Legal Training and Research Institute of the Supreme Court of Japan; graduate study, Harvard Law School (LL.M., 1984). The World Bank, Washington, D.C., 1984-1986. *LANGUAGES:* Japanese and English.

KENICHI FUJINAWA, born 1955; admitted, 1980, Japan. *Education:* Tokyo University (LL.B.); Legal Training and Research Institute of the Supreme Court of Japan; graduate study, Harvard Law School (LL.M., 1986). Shearman & Sterling, New York, 1986-1987. *LANGUAGES:* Japanese and English.

TOHRU NAKAJIMA, born 1954; admitted, 1980, Japan. *Education:* Tokyo University (LL.B.); Legal Training and Research Institute of the Supreme Court of Japan; graduate study, Harvard Law School (LL.M., 1985). Cleary, Gottlieb, Steen & Hamilton, New York, 1985-1986; Wilson, Sonsini, Goodrich & Rosati, Palo Alto, 1986-1987. *LANGUAGES:* Japanese and English.

(This Listing Continued)

ATSUSHI FUJIEDA, born 1955; admitted, 1982, Japan. *Education:* Tokyo University (LL.B.); Legal Training and Research Institute of the Supreme Court of Japan; graduate study, University of California, Los Angeles (LL.M., 1987). Paul, Hasting, Janofsky & Walker, Los Angeles, 1987-1988. Covington & Burling, Washington, D.C., 1988. *LANGUAGES:* Japanese and English.

JUN NAITOH, born 1956; admitted, 1982, Japan. *Education:* Waseda University (LL.B.); Legal Training and Research Institute of the Supreme Court of Japan. *LANGUAGES:* Japanese and English.

OF COUNSEL

RICHARD W. RABINOWITZ, born New Haven, Connecticut, May 14, 1924; admitted, 1950, Connecticut; 1951, U.S. District Court, District of Connecticut; 1953, Japan; 1966, Korea. *Education:* Yale University (B.A., 1945; A.M., 1951); Yale Law School (LL.B., 1950); Harvard University (Ph.D., 1956). Phi Beta Kappa. Author: "Historical Development of the Japanese Bar," 70 Harvard Law Review 61, 1956. Fellow, Social Science Research Council, 1952—. Overseas Research and Training Fellow, Ford Foundation, 1953-1955. Research Associate in Law, Harvard Law School, 1954-1955. Program Secretary, Japanese American Program for Cooperation in Legal Studies, 1954-1961. Visiting Professor from the Profession, Harvard Law School, Spring Semester, 1988. *Member:* Connecticut Bar Association; Second Tokyo Bar Association.

ASSOCIATES

MASATOSHI YASUNAGA, born 1952; admitted, 1984, Japan. *Education:* Tokyo University (B.S. in Mathematics, 1977); Legal Training and Research Institute of the Supreme Court of Japan; graduate study, University of Illinois, College of Law (LL.M., 1989). Davis Polk & Wardwell, New York, 1989-1990; Cleary, Gottlieb, Steen & Hamilton, Paris, 1990-1991. *LANGUAGES:* Japanese and English.

RYUJI SAKAI, born 1957; admitted, 1985, Japan. *Education:* Tokyo University (LL.B.); Legal Training and Research Institute of the Supreme Court of Japan; graduate study, University of Pennsylvania Law School (LL.M., 1990). Wilson, Sonsini, Goodrich & Rosati, Palo Alto, 1990-1992. *LANGUAGES:* Japanese and English.

KOJI MORITA, born 1959; admitted, 1986, Japan. *Education:* Tokyo University (LL.B.); Legal Training and Research Institute of the Supreme Court of Japan; graduate study, Columbia University School of Law (LL.M., 1992). Mitsui & Co., Ltd., 1983-1984; Jones, Day, Reavis & Pogue, New York, 1992-1993; McCorriston Miho & Miller, Hawaii, 1993. *LANGUAGES:* Japanese and English.

YASUHIDE WATANABE, born 1956; admitted, 1986, Japan. *Education:* Tokyo University (LL.B.); Legal Training and Research Institute of the Supreme Court of Japan; graduate study, Columbia University School of Law, (LL.M., 1991). Morrison & Foerster, New York and San Francisco, 1991-1992; Pünder, Volhard, Weber & Axster, Frankfurt, 1992-1993. *LANGUAGES:* Japanese and English.

KAZUNOBU NISHI, born 1962; admitted, 1987, Japan. *Education:* Tokyo University (LL.B.); Legal Training and Research Institute of the Supreme Court of Japan; graduate study, Harvard Law School (LL.M., 1990). Simpson, Thacher & Bartlett, New York, 1992-1993. *LANGUAGES:* Japanese and English.

KIMITOSHI YABUKI, born 1956; admitted, 1987, Japan. *Education:* Tokyo University (LL.B.); Legal Training and Research Institute of the Supreme Court of Japan; graduate study, Columbia University School of Law (LL.M., 1991). Covington & Burling, Washington, D.C., 1991-1992; Covington & Burling, Brussels, 1992-1993. *LANGUAGES:* Japanese and English.

HISAYA KIMURA, born 1958; admitted, 1985, Japan. *Education:* Waseda University (LL.B.); Legal Training and Research Institute of the Supreme Court of Japan; graduate study, Harvard Law School (LL.M., 1990). Visiting Researcher, Harvard Law School, 1990-1991; Milbank, Tweed, Hadley & McCloy, New York, 1991-1993. *LANGUAGES:* Japanese and English.

YUKAKO WAGATSUMA, born 1962; admitted, 1988, Japan. *Education:* Tokyo University (LL.B.); Legal Training and Research Institute of the Supreme Court of Japan; graduate study, New York University School of Law (LL.M., 1992). Cleary, Gottlieb, Steen & Hamilton, Washington, D.C., 1992-1993. *LANGUAGES:* Japanese and English.

SOICHIRO UNO, born 1963; admitted, 1988, Japan. *Education:* Hitotsubashi University (LL.B.); Legal Training and Research Institute of the Supreme Court of Japan; graduate study, Harvard Law School (LL.M.,

(This Listing Continued)

NAGASHIMA & OHNO, Tokyo—Continued

1993). Gibson, Dunn & Crutcher, Los Angeles, 1993-1994. *LANGUAGES:* Japanese and English.

ERIKO WATANABE, born 1958; admitted, 1988, Japan. *Education:* Tohoku University (LL.B.); Legal Training and Research Institute of the Supreme Court of Japan; graduate study, University of Washington, School of Law (LL.M., 1994). Kirkland & Ellis, Chicago, 1994—. *LANGUAGES:* Japanese and English.

KAZUMOCHI KOMETANI, born 1964; admitted, 1989, Japan. *Education:* Tokyo University (LL.B.,); Legal Training and Research Institute of the Supreme Court of Japan; graduate study, Michigan Law School (1994—). *LANGUAGES:* Japanese and English.

TAKAO HIGUCHI, born 1962; admitted, 1989, Japan. *Education:* Tokyo University (LL.B.); Legal Training and Research Institute of the Supreme Court of Japan; graduate study, Columbia University School of Law (1994—). *LANGUAGES:* Japanese and English.

SHUNPEI TANAKA, born 1959; admitted, 1989, Japan. *Education:* Tokyo University (LL.B.); Legal Training and Research Institute of the Supreme Court of Japan; graduate study, The University of Illinois, College of Law (1994—). *LANGUAGES:* Japanese and English.

YOSHIKAZU SUGINO, born 1957; admitted, 1989, Japan. *Education:* Tokyo University (LL.B.); Legal Training and Research Institute of the Supreme Court of Japan; graduate study, Columbia University, School of Law (LL.M., 1994). Winthrop, Stimson, Putnam & Roberts, New York, 1994—. *LANGUAGES:* Japanese and English.

KEITARO OSHIMO, born 1964; admitted, 1989, Japan. *Education:* Tokyo University (LL.B.); Legal Training and Research Institute of the Supreme Court of Japan; graduate study, Harvard Law School (LL.M., 1992). Bogle & Gates, Seattle, 1992-1993. *LANGUAGES:* Japanese and English.

MAKOTO TAKADA, born 1959; admitted, 1990, Japan. *Education:* Tokyo University (B.S. in Engineering, 1983); Legal Training and Research Institute of the Supreme Court of Japan; graduate study, University of Chicago Law School (1994—). Kumagai Gumi Co., Ltd., 1983-1985. *LANGUAGES:* Japanese and English.

SATOSHI INOUE, born 1965; admitted, 1990, Japan. *Education:* Tokyo University (LL.B.); Legal Training and Research Institute of the Supreme Court of Japan; graduate study, Harvard Law School (LL.M., 1994). Sullivan & Cromwell, New York, 1994—. *LANGUAGES:* Japanese and English.

KIYOSHI HIRASAWA, born 1960; admitted, 1990, Japan. *Education:* Tokyo University (LL.B.); Legal Training and Research Institute of the Supreme Court of Japan; graduate study, Stanford Business School (1992-1994). The Bank of Tokyo, Ltd., 1985-1988. *LANGUAGES:* Japanese and English.

NORIYUKI KATAYAMA, born 1964; admitted, 1990, Japan. *Education:* Waseda University (LL.B.); Legal Training and Research Institute of the Supreme Court of Japan; graduate study, University of Washington, School of Law (1994—). *LANGUAGES:* Japanese and English.

SHINICHI MATSUI, born 1962; admitted, 1990, Japan. *Education:* Tokyo University (LL.B.); Legal Training and Research Institute of the Supreme Court of Japan; graduate study, Chicago Law School (LL.M., 1993). Covington & Burling, Washington, D.C., 1993-1994. *LANGUAGES:* Japanese and English.

HIROKI INOUE, born 1963; admitted, 1990, Japan. *Education:* Tokyo University (LL.B.); Legal Training and Research Institute of the Supreme Court of Japan; graduate study, Harvard Law School (1994—). *LANGUAGES:* Japanese and English.

WAKABA HARA, born 1964; admitted, 1990, Japan. *Education:* Keio University (LL.B.); Legal Training and Research Institute of the Supreme Court of Japan; graduate study, Columbia University School of Law (LL.M., 1993). Paul Weiss Rifkind Wharton & Garrison, New York, 1994—. *LANGUAGES:* Japanese and English.

NOBUYUKI TAJI, born 1963; admitted, 1991, Japan. *Education:* Tokyo University (LL.B.); Legal Training and Research Institute of the Supreme Court of Japan. *LANGUAGES:* Japanese and English.

AKI SAITO, born 1966; admitted, 1991, Japan. *Education:* Tokyo University (LL.B.); Legal Training and Research Institute of the Supreme

(This Listing Continued)

AS164B

Court of Japan; College of Europe (1993). *LANGUAGES:* Japanese, English and French.

MASAHIRO MATSUOKA, born 1967; admitted, 1992, Japan. *Education:* Tokyo University (Bachelor of Liberal Arts); Legal Training and Research Institute of the Supreme Court of Japan. *LANGUAGES:* Japanese, English and Mandarin.

KENTA TSUJIMAKI, born 1966; admitted, 1992, Japan. *Education:* Tokyo University (LL.B.); Legal Training and Research Institute of the Supreme Court of Japan. *LANGUAGES:* Japanese and English.

YOSHIMI OHARA, born 1966; admitted, 1992, Japan. *Education:* Tokyo University (LL.B.); Legal Training and Research Institute of the Supreme Court of Japan. *LANGUAGES:* Japanese and English.

HIDENORI NAKAGAWA, born 1967; admitted, 1992, Japan. *Education:* Tokyo University (LL.B.); Legal Training and Research Institute of the Supreme Court of Japan. *LANGUAGES:* Japanese and English.

NAOHIRO NISHIMURA, born 1967; admitted, 1993, Japan. *Education:* Tokyo University (LL.B.); Legal Training and Research Institute of the Supreme Court of Japan. *LANGUAGES:* Japanese and English.

JUN KANDA, born 1963; admitted, 1993, Japan. *Education:* Tokyo University (LL.B.); Cambridge University (B.A.); Legal Training and Research Institute of the Supreme Court of Japan. Ministry of Foreign Affairs, 1986-1990. *LANGUAGES:* Japanese and English.

YUICHIRO MORI, born 1968; admitted, 1993, Japan. *Education:* Waseda University (LL.B.); Legal Training and Research Institute of the Supreme Court of Japan. *LANGUAGES:* Japanese and English.

HIROSHI MITOMA, born 1968; admitted, 1993, Japan. *Education:* Tokyo University (LL.B.); Legal Training and Research Institute of the Supreme Court of Japan. *LANGUAGES:* Japanese and English.

YUKO TAMAI, born 1965; admitted, 1994, Japan. *Education:* Tokyo University (LL.B.); Legal Training and Research Institute of the Supreme Court of Japan. *LANGUAGES:* Japanese and German.

KENJI UTSUMI, born 1969; admitted, 1994, Japan. *Education:* Tokyo University (LL.B.); Legal Training and Research Institute of the Supreme Court of Japan. *LANGUAGES:* Japanese and English.

HIROKO TANAKA, born 1963; admitted, 1994, Japan. *Education:* Tokyo University (LL.B.); Duke University School of Law (LL.M., 1991); Legal Training and Research Institute of the Supreme Court of Japan. The Nippon Credit Bank Ltd., International Securities Division, 1986-1987. *LANGUAGES:* Japanese and English.

NAKAGAWA & TAKASHINA

Established in 1976

6TH FLOOR, AKASAKA NAKAGAWA BUILDING
11-3, AKASAKA 3-CHOME
MINATO-KU
TOKYO 107, JAPAN
Telephone: 81-3 3589 2921
Fax: 81-3 3589 2926 (G4 & G3)

General International and Domestic Law Practice.

FIRM PROFILE: *The firm's practice is focused primarily on international and domestic finance, corporate and commercial law. The firm initially concentrates in the area of asset based, cross-border leasing and other types of financing originating in Japan, and still maintains a strong emphasis in this field. In addition, however, the firm also provides a full range of legal services related to international and domestic business transactions and investments. There are currently two partners and seven other lawyers, along with other paralegal and supporting staff.*

MEMBERS OF FIRM

NOBORU NAKAGAWA, born August 9, 1936; admitted, 1967, Japan. *Education:* Tokyo University (LL.B., 1960); Legal Training and Research Institute (1965-1967); Notre Dame Law School (1970-1971). Member: Yuasa and Hara, 1967-1976; Nakagawa & Takashina, 1976—. *Member:* Second Tokyo Bar Association. *LANGUAGES:* Japanese, English and French. *PRACTICE AREAS:* International Finance and Commercial Law; Taxation; Company Law; Intellectual Property; Antitrust; Real Property; Labor and Employment.

YUTAKA WATANABE (1946-1988).

(This Listing Continued)

MASAYOSHI TAKASHINA, born November 18, 1951; admitted, 1982, Japan. *Education:* Waseda University (LL.B., 1977); Legal Training and Research Institute (1980-1982). Member, Nakagawa & Takashina, 1982—, Partner, 1989. *Member:* Second Tokyo Bar Association. *LANGUAGES:* Japanese and English. *PRACTICE AREAS:* International Finance; Cross-Border Leasing; Securitization; Commercial Law; Company Law; Licensing and Dispute Settlement.

TAKASHI KANAI, born January 24, 1963; admitted, 1989, Japan. *Education:* Keio University (LL.B., 1985; LL.M. in Private Law, 1987); Legal Training and Research Institute (1987-1989); Cornell Law School (LL.M., 1992); Queen Mary and Westfield College, University of London (LL.M, Commercial and Corporate Law, 1993). Member, Nakagawa & Takashina, 1989—. *Member:* Second Tokyo Bar Association. *LANGUAGES:* Japanese and English. *PRACTICE AREAS:* International Finance; Company Law and Commercial Law; Franchising Law.

HIDEHIKO SUZUKI, born December 31, 1959; admitted, 1989, Japan. *Education:* Waseda University (LL.B., 1982; LL.M., 1985; Doctor of Law Course, 1985-1987); Legal Training and Research Institute (1987-1989). Member, Nakagawa & Takashina, 1989—. Staff Attorney, Legal Training and Research Institute of Supreme Court of Japan, 1993—. *Member:* Second Tokyo Bar Association. *LANGUAGES:* Japanese and English. *PRACTICE AREAS:* International Finance; Intellectual Property; Commercial Law; Litigation.

MINA OHNO, born December 12, 1962; admitted, 1990, Japan. *Education:* Keio University (LL.B., 1985); Legal Training and Research Institute (1988-1990). Member, Nakagawa & Takashina, 1990—. *Member:* Second Tokyo Bar Association. *LANGUAGES:* Japanese and English. *PRACTICE AREAS:* International Finance; Cross-Border Leasing; Company Law and Commercial Law.

MIHO MIZUGUCHI, born November 18, 1965; admitted, 1991, Japan. *Education:* Waseda University (LL.B., 1989); Legal Training and Research Institute (1989-1991). Member, Nakagawa & Takashina, 1991—. *Member:* Second Tokyo Bar Association. *LANGUAGES:* Japanese and English. *PRACTICE AREAS:* International Finance; Cross-Border Leasing; Licensing; Company Law and Dispute Settlement.

NAGAHIDE SATOH, born March 17, 1957; admitted, 1991, Japan. *Education:* Hitotsubashi University (LL.B., 1985); Legal Training and Research Institute (1989-1991). Member, Nakagawa & Takashina, 1991—. *Member:* Second Tokyo Bar Association. *LANGUAGES:* Japanese and English. *PRACTICE AREAS:* International Finance; Licensing; Company Law; Commercial Law and Dispute Settlement.

KEI AMEMIYA, born January 23, 1967; admitted, 1993, Japan. *Education:* Chuo University (LL.B., 1989); Legal Training and Research Institute (1991-1993). Member, Nakagawa & Takashina, 1993—. *Member:* Tokyo Bar Association. *LANGUAGES:* Japanese and English. *PRACTICE AREAS:* International Finance; Cross-border Leasing; Licensing; Company Law; Commercial Law and Dispute Settlement.

LAURENT DEVELLE, born France, August 14, 1966; admitted, 1993, France as Avocat. *Education:* University of Paris (Bachelor's degree in Law, 1990; Master's degree in Business Law, 1991); Institut d' Etudes Politiques de Paris (IEP, 1984-1987). (Also with Clifford Chance, Paris, France). *LANGUAGES:* French and English. *PRACTICE AREAS:* Commercial Law; Company Law; Taxation Law; Insurance Law and Environmental Law.

Languages: Japanese, English and French.

NAKAMURA LAW OFFICE

Established in 1969

SOGO NAGATA-CHO BUILDING
11-28 NAGATA-CHO 1-CHOME, CHIYODA-KU
TOKYO 100, JAPAN
Telephone: 03-581-6911-2
Telex: 2222935 SANDN J
Telecopier: 03-581-6913

Civil, Commercial and Maritime Law.

SEIICHI NAKAMURA, born Saitama Prefecture, Japan, March 13, 1937; admitted, 1966, Japan. *Education:* Waseda University (LL.B., 1959; LL.M., 1964); Legal Training and Research Institute of the Supreme Court of Japan; Boalt Hall School of Law, University of California (LL.M., 1970).

(This Listing Continued)

With Yonemura & Yasaki, Oakland, California, Summer, 1969 and Lillick & Charles, San Francisco and Lillick & McHose, Los Angeles, California, 1969-1970. Co-author: "Patent and Know-How Licensing in Japan and the United States," University of Washington Press. *Member:* The First Tokyo Bar Association. *LANGUAGES:* Japanese and English. *PRACTICE AREAS:* Maritime Law; International Ship Financing; Joint Venture; Patent and Know-How Licensing.

NAKAMURA & PARTNERS
(INTERNATIONAL PATENT AND LAW OFFICE)

Formerly Nakamatsu
NEW TOKYO BUILDING
3-1, MARUNOUCHI 3-CHOME, CHIYODA-KU
TOKYO 100, JAPAN
Telephone: 3211-8741-5
Cable Address: "Nakapatent"
Telex: 02225631
Answer Back Code: NAKPAT J
FAX: 03-3214-6358 (G2 & G3); 03-3214-6359 (G2 & G3)

Patent, Trademark and Copyright Law. Licensing, Joint Venture, Incorporation and Contracts. General Practice.

FIRM PROFILE: The firm was established in 1917 and has been generally known as a firm specializing in domestic and international intellectual property matters, and all the attorneys at law in the firm have long engaged in litigations, licensing contracts, negotiations, etc., relating to intellectual property matters as well as patent and trademark prosecutions before the Patent Office. But over the course of years, it has become more and more common for us to be consulted on general corporate matters and various international transactions such as joint venture, distributorship agreement, M & A, etc., by clients for whom we originally rendered services regarding intellectual property matters. Further, we have been consulted by, given advice to, and represented in litigation many of our clients in connection with general corporate matters and international transactions.

The firm consists of five sections: Electrical and Electronics Section, Mechanical Section, Chemical Section, Trademark Section and Legal Section. Each section has several partners who closely supervise the members in their section. The managing partners are not only involved in the management of the firm and the coordination of the partners but also play a leading role in the firm's practice.

MEMBERS OF FIRM

KANNOSUKE NAKAMATSU, President; Federation of Japanese Bar Association, 1966-1967; Japanese Patent Attorneys Association, 1955-1956; International Association for the Protection of Industrial Property, Japanese Group, 1964-1973. (1895-1973).

MINORU NAKAMURA, born Chiba Prefecture, Japan, January 17, 1927; admitted, 1952, Attorney at Law and Patent Attorney, Japan. *Education:* Faculty of Law, Tokyo University (LL.B., 1950). Chairman, Intellectual Property Committee, Federation of Japanese Bar Associations, 1979-1981. Registered Arbitrator, Japan Commercial Arbitration Association. *Member:* Second Tokyo Bar Association; Japan Patent Attorneys Association. *LANGUAGES:* Japanese and English. *PRACTICE AREAS:* Intellectual Property Law; International Business Law.

KAZUKO MATSUO, born Tokyo, Japan, October 31, 1929; admitted, 1958, Attorney at Law and Patent Attorney, Japan. *Education:* Faculty of Law, Tokyo University (LL.B., 1953); Graduate Study, 1953-1956; New York University, Institute of Comparative Law, 1963-1964; M.C.J., 1965; Research Fellow, University of Michigan Law School, 1964-1965. Lecturer, St. Paul University, 1971-1977. *Member:* Second Tokyo Bar Association; Japan Patent Attorneys Association. *LANGUAGES:* Japanese and English. *PRACTICE AREAS:* Intellectual Property Law; International Business Law.

FUMIAKI OHTSUKA, born Ohita Prefecture, Japan, September 28, 1932; admitted, Patent Attorney, Japan. *Education:* Kyushu University (graduated from Engineering School, 1956). Council Member of Asian Patent Attorneys Association. Committee Member of National Examination for Patent Attorneys, 1979-1980. *Member:* Japan Patent Attorneys Association. *LANGUAGES:* Japanese, English and German. *PRACTICE AREAS:* Electrical, Mechanical and Aeronautical Engineering.

(This Listing Continued)

NAKAMURA & PARTNERS (INTERNATIONAL PATENT AND LAW OFFICE), Tokyo—Continued

SADANAO AMEMIYA, born Yamanashi Prefecture, Japan, October 24, 1927; admitted, 1960, Attorney at Law and Patent Attorney, Japan. *Education:* Faculty of Law, Tokyo University (LL.B., 1956). *Member:* Second Tokyo Bar Association; Japan Patent Attorneys Association. Deputy Chairman of Committee of Intellectual Property and Member, Patent Committee, Federation of Japanese Bar Association, 1952-1953. *LANGUAGES:* Japanese and English. *PRACTICE AREAS:* Intellectual Property Law; International Business Law.

YOSHIO KUMAKURA, born Saitama Prefecture, Japan, January 19, 1940; admitted, 1969, Attorney at Law and Patent Attorney, Japan. *Education:* Faculty of Law, Tokyo University (LL.B., 1963); Harvard University, U.S.A. (LL.M., 1976). Lecturer, Dokkyo University, 1986—. *Member:* Second Tokyo Bar Association; Japan Patent Attorneys Association. *LANGUAGES:* Japanese and English. *PRACTICE AREAS:* Intellectual Property Law; International Business Law.

KAICHI SHISHIDO, born Tokyo, Japan, October, 1935; admitted, Patent Attorney, Japan. *Education:* Science University of Tokyo (graduated from Physical Department, 1959). *Member:* Japan Patent Attorneys Association. *LANGUAGES:* Japanese and English. *PRACTICE AREAS:* Physical and Mechanical Engineering.

MIDORI TANAKA, born Yokohama, Japan, September 26, 1932; admitted, 1961, Attorney at Law and Patent Attorney, Japan. *Education:* Faculty of Law, Chuo University (LL.B., 1955). *Member:* Second Tokyo Bar Association; Japan Patent Attorneys Association. *LANGUAGES:* Japanese, English and German. *PRACTICE AREAS:* Intellectual Property Law; International Business Law.

KUNIO IZAWA, born Matsuyama, Ehime Prefecture, Japan, September 25, 1936; admitted, 1966, Patent Attorney, Japan. *Education:* Faculty of Law and Commerce, Matsuyama Commerce College (LL.B., 1959). *Member:* Japan Patent Attorneys Association. *LANGUAGES:* Japanese and English. *PRACTICE AREAS:* Industrial Property Law and Practice.

KENJI KATO, born Saitama Prefecture, Japan, January 12, 1944; admitted, 1969, Patent Attorney, Japan. *Education:* Chuo University (Faculty of Law, 1966). *Member:* Japan Patent Attorneys Association. *LANGUAGES:* Japanese and English. *PRACTICE AREAS:* Trademark Law.

TOSHIO IMASHIRO, born Yokosuka, Kanagawa Prefecture, Japan, August 29, 1941; admitted, 1970, Patent Attorney, Japan. *Education:* Chuo University (Faculty of Technology, 1966). *Member:* Japan Patent Attorneys Association. *LANGUAGES:* Japanese and English. *PRACTICE AREAS:* Electronics, Electrical and Mechanical Engineering.

HIDETO TAKEUCHI, born Tokyo, Japan, July 4, 1934; admitted, 1988, Patent Attorney, Japan. *Education:* Electro-telecommunication University (Faculty of Electro-telecommunication, 1958). Examiner and Appeal Examiner, JPO, 1958-1985. Director General of Examination and Appeals Department, 1985-1987. *Member:* Japan Patent Attorneys Association. *LANGUAGES:* Japanese and English. *PRACTICE AREAS:* Electronics and Electro-Telecommunication Engineering.

HIROO MURAKOSO, born Saitama, Japan, July 2, 1941; admitted, 1977, Patent Attorney, Japan. *Education:* Science University of Tokyo (Faculty of Applied Physics, 1965). *Member:* Japan Patent Attorneys Association. *LANGUAGES:* Japanese and English. *PRACTICE AREAS:* Optical and Mechanical Engineering.

NOBUO OGAWA, born Saitama, Japan, October 3, 1945; admitted, 1978, Patent Attorney, Japan. *Education:* Tokyo Institute of Technology (Faculty of Chemistry, 1968). *Member:* Japan Patent Attorneys Association. *LANGUAGES:* Japanese and English. *PRACTICE AREAS:* Chemistry, Applied Chemistry and Microbiology.

KOICHI OISHI, born Tokyo, Japan, May 15, 1946; admitted, 1973, Patent Attorney, Japan. *Education:* Tokyo University (Faculty of Civil Engineering, 1970; Master of Chemical Engineering, 1972). *Member:* Japan Patent Attorneys Association. *LANGUAGES:* Japanese, English and German. *PRACTICE AREAS:* Optics, Chemical and Physical Engineering.

ATSUSHI HAKODA, born 1948; admitted, 1979, Patent Attorney, Japan. *Education:* Kanazawa University (Faculty of Chemistry, 1971). *LANGUAGES:* Japanese and English. *PRACTICE AREAS:* Chemistry and Applied Chemistry.

TAKAKI NISHIJIMA, born 1950; admitted, 1980, Patent Attorney, Japan. *Education:* Tokyo Institute of Technology (Faculty of Chemical En-

(This Listing Continued)

gineering, 1974). *LANGUAGES:* Japanese and English. *PRACTICE AREAS:* Chemical and Mechanical Engineering.

ATSUSHI OHSHIMA, born 1953; admitted, 1982, Patent Attorney, Japan. *Education:* St. Paul University (Faculty of Law, 1976). *LANGUAGES:* Japanese and English. *PRACTICE AREAS:* Trademark Law.

KOICHI TSUJII, born 1956; admitted, 1983, Attorney at Law and Patent Attorney, Japan; 1989, New York. *Education:* Chuo University (Faculty of Law, 1979); Cornell University Law School (LL.M., 1989). *Member:* Second Tokyo Bar Association; Japan Patent Attorneys Association. *LANGUAGES:* Japanese and English. *PRACTICE AREAS:* Intellectual Property Law; International Business Law.

ASSOCIATES

MAKOTO AIHARA, born 1967; admitted, 1993, Patent Attorney, Japan. *Education:* Tokyo University (Faculty of Agricultural Chemistry, 1991). *Member:* Japan Patent Attorneys Association. *LANGUAGES:* Japanese and English. *PRACTICE AREAS:* Chemistry and Agricultural Chemistry.

KENJI ASAI, born 1953; admitted, 1986, Patent Attorney, Japan. *Education:* Tokyo Metropolitan University (Faculty of Industrial Chemistry, 1976; Master of Industrial Chemistry, 1978). *Member:* Japan Patent Attorneys Association. *LANGUAGES:* Japanese and English. *PRACTICE AREAS:* Engineering Chemistry.

TAKESHI DESHIMARU, born 1952; admitted, 1982, Patent Attorney, Japan. *Education:* Kyoto Institute of Technology (Faculty of Mechanical Engineering, 1974; Master of Mechanical Engineering, 1976). *Member:* Japan Patent Attorneys Association. *LANGUAGES:* Japanese and English. *PRACTICE AREAS:* Electrical and Mechanical Engineering.

DAISAKU FUJIKURA, born 1960; admitted, 1987, Patent Attorney, Japan. *Education:* Chuo University (Faculty of Law, 1983). *LANGUAGES:* Japanese and English. *PRACTICE AREAS:* Trademark Law.

MASAJI HIRAI, born 1950; admitted, 1989, Patent Attorney, Japan. *Education:* Ritsumeikan University (Faculty of Chemistry, 1974). *Member:* Japan Patent Attorneys Association. *LANGUAGES:* Japanese and English. *PRACTICE AREAS:* Electro-Chemical and Mechanical Engineering.

MAKOTO HIRANO, born 1948; admitted, 1993, Patent Attorney, Japan. *Education:* Waseda University (Faculty of Applied Physics, 1972). *Member:* Japan Patent Attorneys Association. *LANGUAGES:* Japanese and English. *PRACTICE AREAS:* Physics and Mechanical Engineering.

SARI INO, born 1956; admitted, 1992, Patent Attorney, Japan. *Education:* Columbia University (Faculty of Mechanical Engineering, 1980; Engineering, Mechanics, 1985). *Member:* Japan Patent Attorneys Association. *LANGUAGES:* Japanese and English. *PRACTICE AREAS:* Mechanical Engineering.

TOHRU ISHIKAWA, born 1955; admitted, 1989, Patent Attorney, Japan. *Education:* Nihon University (Faculty of Agricultural Chemistry, 1980; Law, 1983). *Member:* Japan Patent Attorneys Association. *LANGUAGES:* Japanese and English. *PRACTICE AREAS:* Chemical Engineering.

HIROYUKI ITAKI, born 1958; admitted, 1984, Patent Attorney, Japan. *Education:* St. Paul University (Faculty of Law, 1982). *LANGUAGES:* Japanese and English. *PRACTICE AREAS:* Trademark Law.

TAKEHIKO KOBAYASHI, born 1967; admitted, 1994, Patent Attorney, Japan. *Education:* Waseda University (Faculty of Law, 1990). *Member:* Japan Patent Attorneys Association. *LANGUAGES:* Japanese and English. *PRACTICE AREAS:* Trademark Law.

EIICHIRO KUBOTA, born 1963; admitted, 1991, Attorney at Law, Japan. *Education:* Tokyo University (Faculty of Engineering). *Member:* Second Tokyo Bar Association. *LANGUAGES:* Japanese and English. *PRACTICE AREAS:* Intellectual Property Law; International Business Law.

ICHIRO KURASAWA, born 1961; admitted, 1989, Patent Attorney, Japan. *Education:* Jiyu-Gakuen. *Member:* Japan Patent Attorneys Association. *LANGUAGES:* Japanese and English. *PRACTICE AREAS:* Physical and Mechanical Engineering.

MITSURU MATSUSHITA, born 1962; admitted, 1987, Patent Attorney, Japan. *Education:* Nihon University (1984). *Member:* Japan Patent Attorneys Association. *LANGUAGES:* Japanese and English. *PRACTICE AREAS:* Mechanical Engineering.

(This Listing Continued)

SATOSHI MIYAGAKI, born 1961; admitted, 1989, Attorney at Law and Patent Attorney, Japan. *Education:* Chuo University (Faculty of Law, 1984). *Member:* Second Tokyo Bar Association. *LANGUAGES:* Japanese and English. *PRACTICE AREAS:* Intellectual Property Law; International Business Law.

KEIZO MIYAGAWA, born 1955; admitted, 1990, Patent Attorney, Japan. *Education:* Kyoto University (Faculty of Agricultural Science, 1979). *Member:* Japan Patent Attorneys Association. *LANGUAGES:* Japanese and English. *PRACTICE AREAS:* Chemistry and Agricultural Chemistry.

AKIHIKO NAKAZAWA, born 1963; admitted, 1987, Patent Attorney, Japan. *Education:* Shibaura Institute of Technology (Faculty of Industrial Engineering). *Member:* Japan Patent Attorneys Association. *LANGUAGES:* Japanese and English. *PRACTICE AREAS:* Mechanical Engineering.

KIYOSHI OKA, born 1957; admitted, 1992, Patent Attorney, Japan. *Education:* Tokyo University (Faculty of Mechanics). *Member:* Japan Patent Attorneys Association. *LANGUAGES:* Japanese and English. *PRACTICE AREAS:* Mechanical Engineering.

TADAHITO ORITA, born 1963; admitted, 1989, Attorney at Law, Japan. *Education:* Waseda University (Faculty of Law, 1986). *Member:* Second Tokyo Bar Association. *LANGUAGES:* Japanese and English. *PRACTICE AREAS:* Intellectual Property Law; International Business Law.

YOSHIHIKO SHIMAZOE, born 1954; admitted, 1987, Patent Attorney, Japan. *Education:* Yokohama National University (Faculty of Architecture, 1977). *LANGUAGES:* Japanese and English. *PRACTICE AREAS:* Architectural and Mechanical Engineering.

SEIJI SUGIYAMA, born 1951; admitted, 1993, Patent Attorney, Japan. *Education:* Hokkaido University (Faculty of Engineering, 1974). *Member:* Japan Patent Attorneys Association. *LANGUAGES:* Japanese and English. *PRACTICE AREAS:* Mechanical and Civil Engineerings.

IZUMI TADANO, born 1921; admitted, 1967, Patent Attorney, Japan. *Education:* Tainan Technical College (Faculty of Applied Chemistry, 1941). *LANGUAGES:* Japanese and English. *PRACTICE AREAS:* Chemistry and Applied Chemistry.

SHIN-ICHIRO TANAKA, born 1958; admitted, 1985, Attorney at Law and Patent Attorney, Japan. *Education:* Hitotsubashi University (Faculty of Law, 1983). *Member:* Second Tokyo Bar Association; Japan Patent Attorneys Association. *LANGUAGES:* Japanese and English. *PRACTICE AREAS:* Intellectual Property Law; International Business Law.

EIJI TOMIOKA, born 1951; admitted, 1993, Attorney at Law, Japan. *Education:* Tokyo University (Faculty of Economics, 1977). Judge, District Court, 1979-1993. *Member:* Second Tokyo Bar Association. *LANGUAGES:* Japanese and English. *PRACTICE AREAS:* Intellectual Property Law.

KAZUHIKO YOSHIDA, born 1963; admitted, 1990, Attorney at Law and Patent Attorney, Japan. *Education:* Tokyo University (Faculty of Law, 1988). *Member:* Second Tokyo Bar Association. *LANGUAGES:* Japanese and English. *PRACTICE AREAS:* Intellectual Property Law; International Business Law.

SATOSHI YOSHIDA, born 1963; admitted, 1990, Patent Attorney, Japan. *Education:* Tokyo Metropolitan University (Faculty of Mathematics, 1986). *LANGUAGES:* Japanese and English. *PRACTICE AREAS:* Computer Engineering; Electronics.

COUNSEL

KIKUO NISHIMOTO, born 1916; admitted to practice before Japanese Patent Office. *Education:* Keio University (Faculty of Law, 1961). *LANGUAGES:* Japanese and English. *PRACTICE AREAS:* Foreign Industrial Property Procedures.

REPRESENTATIVE CLIENTS: BP America; Bristol-Myers Squibb Co.; Digital Equipment Corp.; Emhart Corp.; Exxon Research and Engineering Co.; General Mills, Inc.; Kimberly-Clark Corp.; Lego A/S; Otis Elevator Company of United Technologies Corp.; PPG Industries, Inc.; Playboy Enterprises, Inc.; The Procter & Gamble Co.; Schlumberger Ltd.; Texas Instruments Inc.; TRW Inc., Walt Disney Productions; Xerox Corp.; Glaxo Group Ltd.; National Research Development Corp.; United Kingdom Atomic Energy Authority; Boehringer Ingelheim KG; AKZO Nederland BV; Gist-Brocades NV; Montecatini Edison S.p.A.; F. Hoffmann-La Roche & Co., AG; N.V. Phillips; Toray Industries, Inc.; Sony Corp.; Ajinomoto, Inc.; Mitsui & Co.; Fuji Photo Film Co., Ltd.; Fuji Electric Co., Ltd.; Mazda Motor Corp.; Rikagaku Research Institute; Kawasaki Heavey Industries, Ltd.; Nippon Flour Mills Co., Ltd.; Nippon Telegraph & Telephone Corp.; TDK Corp.

NARITOMI LAW OFFICE

13TH FLOOR, URBANNET OHTEMACHI BUILDING
OHTEMACHI 2-2-2, CHIYODA-KU
TOKYO 100, JAPAN
Telephone: (03) 3231-0101 (6 Lines)
Telecopier: (03) 3231-0102

General Practice. Corporations, International Trade, Finance, Securities, Admiralty, Litigation.

MEMBERS OF FIRM

NOBUO NARITOMI, (LL.D. Tokyo) *Member:* Japan Federation of Bar Associations, (President, 1970-1971); Honorary Life Council Member, International Bar Association (1896-1977).

NOBUKATA NARITOMI, born Tokyo, Japan, February 7, 1931; admitted, 1965, Japan. *Education:* Tokyo University (LL.B., 1957); Legal Training and Research Institute of the Supreme Court of Japan (1962); Inns of Court Law School, London (LL.M., 1968); Barrister-at-Law (England, 1972). *Member:* The Japan Federation of Bar Associations; First Tokyo Bar Association; Honourable Society of Lincoln's Inn; International Bar Association. *LANGUAGES:* Japanese and English.

SEIICHI TAKEDA, born Aomori Prefecture, November 2, 1932; admitted, 1967, Japan. *Education:* Tokyo University (LL.B., 1957); Legal Training and Research Institute of the Supreme Court of Japan (1965). Official of the International Revenue Service in the Ministry of Finance of Japan, 1957-1965. *Member:* The Japan Federation of Bar Associations; Second Tokyo Bar Association. *LANGUAGES:* Japanese and English.

KAKUICHI HARIMOTO, born Nagasaki, Japan, June 19, 1911; admitted, 1981, Japan. *Education:* Kyoto Imperial University (LL.B., 1936). Judge, District Courts of Japan, 1938-1972. Chief Judge, Shizuoka District and Family Court, 1972-1973. Notary Public, 1973-1981. *Member:* First Tokyo Bar Association.

SUSUMU YOSHIOKA, born Tokyo, Japan, December 26, 1915; admitted, 1980, Japan. *Education:* Tokyo Imperial University (LL.B., 1937). Judge, Tokyo District Court and Tokyo Appeal Court, 1937-1980. Professor, Daito-Bunka University, 1982—. Member of Commerical Law Sub Committee in the Law Reform Committee of the Ministry of Justice of Japan, 1984—. *Member:* First Tokyo Bar Association. *LANGUAGES:* Japanese, English and German.

NEW TOKYO SOGOH LAW OFFICES

NEW TOKYO BUILDING, SUITE 241
3-3-1 MARUNOUCHI, CHIYODA-KU
TOKYO 100, JAPAN
Telephone: (03) 3201-3232
Fax: (03) 3201-3231

General Practice, Corporations, International Trade, Bankruptcy, Financial Transactions and Litigation.

MEMBERS OF FIRM

MITSUE AIZAWA, admitted, 1979, Japan. *Education:* Keio University (M.A.); Legal Training and Research Institute of the Supreme Court of Japan; Howard Law School (M.C.J.). Co-Author/Editor: *A Guide through the Maze of Shareholder Derivative Actions* (1994). Author: *Guide Book on the Investment Environment for Entities in Asian Countries* (1991); *Textbook of Bankruptcy Law in Japan* (1988). *Member:* Tokyo Bar Association; Inter-Pacific Bar Association (Vice Chairperson, Environmental Law Committee). *LANGUAGES:* Japanese and English. *PRACTICE AREAS:* Corporate Law; Business Insolvency; Environmental Law; International Law; Intellectual Property.

YUTAKA KIMURA, admitted, 1981, Japan. *Education:* Chuo University (LL.B); Legal Training and Research Institute of the Supreme Court of Japan. *Member:* Tokyo Bar Association; Inter-Pacific Bar Association. *PRACTICE AREAS:* Lease Law; Corporate Law; Medical Malpractice.

YOSHIHIRO KITAZAWA, admitted, 1981, Japan. *Education:* Kyoto University (LL.B.); Legal Training and Research Institute of the Supreme Court of Japan; New York University (M.C.J.). Co-Author/Editor: *A Guide through the Maze of Shareholder Derivative Actions* (1994). *Member:* Daini Tokyo Bar Association; Inter-Pacific Bar Association. *LANGUAGES:* Japanese and English. *PRACTICE AREAS:* Corporate Law; Computers and Software; Securities; Consumer Law.

(This Listing Continued)

NEW TOKYO SOGOH LAW OFFICES, Tokyo—
Continued

MASAYOSHI MORIKAWA, admitted, 1991, Japan. *Education:* Hokkaido University (LL.B.); Legal Training and Research Institute of the Supreme Court of Japan. *Member:* Daini Tokyo Bar Association.

MIE FUJIMOTO, admitted, 1993, Japan. *Education:* Tokyo University (LL.B.); Legal Training and Research Institute of the Supreme Court of Japan. Co-Author: *A Guide through the Maze of Shareholder Derivative Actions* (1994). *Member:* Daini Tokyo Bar Association. *LANGUAGES:* Japanese and English.

FOREIGN LAW CONSULTANT

ROBERTA BEARY BLUSTEIN, admitted, 1979, New York; 1984, District of Columbia; 1984, United States Supreme Court (Not admitted in Japan). *Education:* Eisenhower College (B.A., 1974); St. John's University (J.D., 1978). Contributor, *A Guide through the Maze of Shareholder Derivative Actions* (1994). Former Senior Attorney, U.S. Government National Mortgage Association. *Member:* District of Columbia Bar, New York State and American Bar Associations. *PRACTICE AREAS:* Licensing and Distribution; Joint Ventures; Real Estate.

NISHIMURA & SANADA

Established in 1966

ARK MORI BUILDING, 29TH FLOOR
12-32, AKASAKA 1-CHOME, MINATO-KU
TOKYO 107, JAPAN
Telephone: (03) 5562-8500
Facsimile: (03) 5561-9711/4
Telex: J27691 JURISTS

General and International Law Practice. Corporation, Securities, Taxation, Administrative, Antitrust, Intellectual Property and Entertainment Law and Litigation.

FIRM PROFILE: Nishimura & Sanada, located in the Minato-ku district in the heart of Tokyo, is one of the largest law firms in Japan. The firm offers comprehensive legal services primarily to corporate clients, financial institutions, governments and government related entities both domestic and international. The firm currently includes 45 Japanese attorneys, many of whom have obtained graduate degrees from American law schools and have worked in major law firms in the United States and England. Some have been admitted to the bars of New York and California. A staff of over 100 assists and supports the firm's activities.

MEMBERS OF FIRM

TOSHIRO NISHIMURA, admitted, 1961, Japan. *Education:* The University of Tokyo (LL.B., 1959); Legal Training and Research Institute of Supreme Court of Japan; graduate study, Columbia University Law School (M.C.L., 1964). With Logan, Barnard & Okamoto, Tokyo, 1961-1963 and New York and Chicago offices of Baker & McKenzie, 1964-1965. Author: "Corporate Acquisitions in Japan: Evolving Business and Legal Environment," Legal Aspects of Doing Business with Japan, Practicing Law Institute, 1985; "New Issues for the Japanese Legal Profession in the Era of Internationalization," 42 Liberty and Justice No. 1, Japan Federation of Bar Associations, 1991. Co-Author: *"Dictionary of Industrial Proprietary Rights,"* Nikkan Kogyo Shimbun Sha, 1968. *Member:* Japan Federation of Bar Associations (Chairman, Committee on International Relations, 1986-1994); International Bar Association (Councillor, 1988—).

YUKIHIKO SANADA, admitted, 1969, Japan. *Education:* Waseda University (LL.B., 1965); Legal Training and Research Institute of Supreme Court of Japan; graduate study, University of Washington Law School (LL.M., 1975). With Sullivan & Cromwell, New York, 1976-1977.

MOTOHIKO AIBA, admitted, 1971, Japan. *Education:* Keio University (LL.B., 1965; LL.M., 1969); Legal Training and Research Institute of Supreme Court of Japan; graduate study, University of Michigan Law School (LL.M., 1977). With San Francisco and Los Angeles Offices of Graham & James, 1978. Author: "Reclamation of Goods from a Fraudulent Buyer under Uniform Commercial Code," Proceedings of Keio University Graduate School of Law, Vol. 1, 1968 and many case reviews in Keio University Law Review; "Doing Business in Japan: Overview of the Japanese Legal Considerations and Education Structures," The Continuing Legal Education Society of British Columbia, March, 1983. Co-Author: *"Anglo-American Commerical Law Dictionary,"* Commerical Law Centre, Inc., 1986.

(This Listing Continued)

MASAHIRO SHIMOJO, admitted, 1973, Japan; 1982, California. *Education:* The University of Tokyo (LL.B., 1966); Legal Training and Research Institute of Supreme Court of Japan; graduate study, University of Michigan Law School (M.C.L., 1980). With Manatt, Phelps, Rothenberg & Tunny, Los Angeles, 1980-1984. Author: "Japan's New Banking Law: Securities Business by Banks," 1 UCLA Pac. Basin L.J. 83 (1982).

AKIRA KOSUGI, admitted, 1974, Japan. *Education:* Keio University (LL.B., 1969; LL.M., 1971); Legal Training and Research Institute of Supreme Court of Japan; graduate study, New York University School of Law (M.C.J., 1977, LL.M., 1978). With Tokyo Kokusai Law Office, Tokyo, 1974-1976 and Rogers & Wells, New York, 1978-1979.

MASARU ONO, admitted, 1978, Japan; 1983, New York. *Education:* The University of Tokyo (LL.B., 1976); Legal Training and Research Institute of Supreme Court of Japan; graduate study, University of Michigan Law School (LL.M., 1982). With Yanagida & Nomura, 1978-1981, Morgan, Lewis & Bockius, Los Angeles, 1982 and Mudge Rose Guthrie Alexander & Ferdon, New York, 1983.

EIICHI KASHIKURA, admitted, 1979, Japan. *Education:* The University of Tokyo (LL.B., 1977); Legal Training and Research Institute of Supreme Court of Japan; graduate study, University of Washington Law School (LL.M., 1985). With Hill, Betts & Nash, New York, 1985 and Milbank, Tweed, Hadley & McCloy, New York, 1986.

EMIKO KASAHARA, admitted, 1979, Japan. *Education:* Keio University (LL.B., 1977); Legal Training and Research Institute of Supreme Court of Japan. With Linklaters & Paines, London, 1989. Lecturer of Kyorin University, 1992-1993.

KOICHI KUSANO, admitted, 1980, Japan; 1987, New York. *Education:* The University of Tokyo (LL.B., 1978); Legal Training and Research Institute of Supreme Court of Japan; graduate study, Harvard Law School (LL. M., 1986). With Debevoise & Plimpton, New York, 1986-1987. Author: "M&A's Legal Techniques and Impediments in Major Countries-Japan," Kinyu Homu Jijo, 1990; "Derivative Action by Shareholders," Jurist, 1992; *"Negotiation as a Game,"* Maruzen Library, 1994. Co-Author: *"International Economical Frictions and Corporate Acquisitions,"* Nihon Hyoron-sha, 1989; *"The Law of Commerce in Japan,"* Simon and Schuster (Asia) Pte Ltd., 1993.

TAKASHI YONEDA, admitted, 1980, Japan. *Education:* The University of Tokyo (LL.B., 1978); Legal Training and Research Institute of Supreme Court of Japan. With Linklaters & Paines, London, 1987-1988 and Davis Polk & Wardwell, New York, 1988-1989.

SATOSHI OGISHI, admitted, 1981, Japan. *Education:* The University of Tokyo (LL.B., 1979); Legal Training and Research Institute of Supreme Court of Japan; graduate study, Stanford University, Graduate School of Business (M.B.A., 1989). Author: "The Function and Role of Paralegal," Jurist No. 971, 1991;Co-Author: *"International Frictions in the Era of Mutual Interdependence,"* The Tokyo University Press, 1988.

KATSU SENGOKU, admitted, 1982, Japan. *Education:* Waseda University (LL.B., 1980; LL.M., 1987); Legal Training and Research Institute of Supreme Court of Japan; graduate study, Yale Law School (LL.M., 1984). Author: "Patent Infringement Law in the United States -- Some Comparisons with Japanese Law No. 1," 37 Patent Management 151, 1987; "Copyright Studies in U.S. Law Schools," 14 Copyright Law Journal 92, 1987. *Member:* The Copyright Law Association of Japan.

SHINICHI TAKAHASHI, admitted, 1984, Japan; 1991, New York. *Education:* The University of Tokyo (LL.B., 1982); Legal Training and Research Institute of Supreme Court of Japan; graduate study, Columbia University Law School (LL.M., 1990). With Simpson Thacher & Bartlett, New York, 1990-1991.

HIROYUKI TEZUKA, admitted, 1986, Japan; 1993, New York. *Education:* The University of Tokyo (LL.B., 1984); graduate study Harvard Law School (LL.M., 1992). Legal Training and Research Institute of Supreme Court of Japan. With Cleary, Gottlieb, Steen & Hamilton, New York, 1992-1993. Co-Author: "Legal Issues in Shareholders Derivative Actions Against Directors of Sankyo Manufacturing," Shoji Homu No. 1160, 1989. Author: "The Nature and Legal Functions of Punitive Damages Awards in Various States in the U.S. and Their Enforceability in Japan," Jurist No. 1020, 1993; "Recent Developments in U.S. Shareholders Derivative Suits and Detrivative Actions in Japan," Shoji Homu Nos. 1334 (I), 1336 (II), 1337 (III), 1993; "Excercise of Shareholders' Rights by Foreign Shareholders at Shareholders Meetings and Practical Reactions by Companies," Shoji Homu No. 1354, 1994. Co-Editor/Author: "Complete Legal Forms Annotated," Vol. 29 International Civil Litigation, Sanseido, 1994.

(This Listing Continued)

ASSOCIATES

HIDEAKI OZAWA, admitted, 1980, Japan; 1992, New York. *Education:* The University of Tokyo (LL.B., 1978; Master of Engineering, 1985); Legal Training and Research Institute of Supreme Court of Japan; graduate study, Columbia University Law School (LL.M., 1991). With Atago Law Office, 1980-1986; Hijiribashi Law Office, 1986-1987 and Dewey, Ballentine, New York, 1991-1992.

TAKANOBU TAKEHARA, admitted, 1987, Japan; 1992, New York. *Education:* The University of Tokyo (LL.B., 1981); Legal Training and Research Institute of Supreme Court of Japan; graduate study, University of Michigan Law School (LL.M., 1991). Attorney for the Japanese Government, 1983-1987. With Cleary, Gottlieb, Steen & Hamilton, New York, 1991-1992.

MASAHIRO UENO, admitted, 1986, Japan; 1992, New York. *Education:* The University of Tokyo (LL.B., 1984); Legal Training and Research Institute of Supreme Court of Japan; graduate study, Pennsylvania University Law School (LL.M., 1991). With Milbank, Tweed, Hadley & McCloy, New York, 1991-1992.

MASAKAZU IWAKURA, admitted, 1987, Japan; 1994, New York. *Education:* The University of Tokyo (LL.B., 1985); Legal Training and Research Institute of Supreme Court of Japan; graduate study, Harvard Law School (LL.M., 1993). Part-Time Lecturer (International Taxation), St. Paul's (Rikkyo) University, 1992—. Statutory Auditor, Sansui Electric Co., Ltd., 1990-1991. With Debevoise & Plimpton, New York, 1993-1994 and Arnold & Porter, Washington, 1994-1995. *Member:* The International Bar Association; Asia Pacific Forum Section on Business Law (Taxation Committee).

HIROTO TERASHIMA, admitted, 1987, Japan; 1993, New York. *Education:* The University of Tokyo (LL.B., 1985); Legal Training and Research Institute of Supreme Court of Japan; graduate study, University of Michigan Law School (LL.M., 1992). With Sullivan & Cromwell, New York, 1992-1993 and Linklaters & Paines, London, 1993-1994.

NOBUYUKI SAKURABA, admitted, 1987, Japan. *Education:* Waseda University (LL.B., 1985); Legal Training and Research Institute of Supreme Court of Japan. Judge, Hanjiho, 1987-1992.

KOZO KAWAI, admitted, 1988, Japan. *Education:* The University of Tokyo (LL.B., 1984); Legal Training and Research Institute of Supreme Court of Japan; graduate study, Columbia University Law School (LL.M., 1993); Katholieke Universiteit Leuven (LL.M. (EC Law), 1994). On leave with Cleary, Gottlieb, Steen & Hamilton, Brussels, 1994—. Research Associate of The University of Tokyo, 1984-1985. *Member:* The Japanese American Society for Legal Studies.

MITSUHIRO KAMIYA, admitted, 1988, Japan; 1995, New York. *Education:* The University of Tokyo (LL.B., 1986); Legal Training and Research Institute of Supreme Court of Japan; graduate study, Cambridge University (LL.M., 1993) and Columbia University Law School (LL.M., 1994). With Debevoise & Plimpton, New York, 1994-1995.

TOSHIHIRO MAEDA, admitted, 1988, Japan; 1995, New York. *Education:* The University of Tokyo (LL.B., 1986); Legal Training and Research Institute of Supreme Court of Japan; graduate study, Cornell University Law School (LL.M., 1994). On leave with Skadden, Arps, Slate, Meagher & Flom, New York, 1994—.

MAKOTO IGARASHI, admitted, 1989, Japan. *Education:* The University of Tokyo (LL.B., 1987); Legal Training and Research Institute of Supreme Court of Japan; graduate study, Harvard Law School (LL.M., 1994). On leave with Cravath, Swaine & Moore, New York, 1994—.

SATOSHI KAWAI, admitted, 1989, Japan. *Education:* The University of Tokyo (LL.B., 1987); Legal Training and Research Institute of Supreme Court of Japan; graduate study, Columbia University Law School (1994—).

MASAKI HOSAKA, admitted, 1989, Japan. *Education:* The University of Tokyo (LL.B., 1987); Legal Training and Research Institute of Supreme Court of Japan; graduate study, Harvard Law School (1994—).

YOSHIHIKO FUCHIBE, admitted, 1989, Japan. *Education:* The University of Tokyo (LL.B., 1987); Legal Training and Research Institute of Supreme Court of Japan; graduate study, University of London (1994—).

YOSHIHIKO KAWAKAMI, admitted, 1990, Japan. *Education:* The University of Tokyo (LL.B., 1988); Legal Training and Research Institute of Supreme Court of Japan; graduate study, Harvard Law School (1994—).

(This Listing Continued)

YOSHIHIKO YANO, admitted, 1990, Japan. *Education:* Waseda University (LL.B., 1987); Legal Training and Research Institute of Supreme Court of Japan.

KANAME MASUDA, admitted, 1990, Japan. *Education:* Chuo University (LL.B., 1987); Legal Training and Research Institute of Supreme Court of Japan.

ASA SHINKAWA, admitted, 1991, Japan. *Education:* The University of Tokyo (LL.B., 1989); Legal Training and Research Institute of Supreme Court of Japan.

KAZUHIRO TAKEI, admitted, 1991, Japan. *Education:* The University of Tokyo (LL.B., 1989); Legal Training and Research Institute of Supreme Court of Japan. Adjunct Professor to the Faculty of Law, Rikkyo University, International Taxation, 1994—. Author: *Corporate Legal Forms Annotated/Corporate V-Foreign Corporations,* Sanseido Co., Ltd., 1994. Co-Author: "Current Developments of Derivative Actions in Japan," International Bar Association, Asia Pacific Forum Newsletter, 1993.

KATSUYUKI YAMAGUCHI, admitted, 1991, Japan. *Education:* The University of Tokyo (LL.B., 1989); Legal Training and Research Institute of Supreme Court of Japan.

KEI ITO, admitted, 1992, Japan. *Education:* The University of Tokyo (LL.B., 1990); Legal Training and Research Institute of Supreme Court of Japan.

MUNEFUMI SONODA, admitted, 1992, Japan. *Education:* The University of Tokyo (LL.B., 1990); Legal Training and Research Institute of Supreme Court of Japan.

YOH OHTA, admitted, 1993, Japan. *Education:* The University of Tokyo (LL.B., 1991); Legal Training and Research Institute of Supreme Court of Japan.

KATSUMI NAKASHIMA, admitted, 1993, Japan. *Education:* Keio University (LL.B., 1988); Legal Training and Research Institute of Supreme Court of Japan.

MASAYA SUGITANI, admitted, 1993, Japan. *Education:* The University of Tokyo (B.A., 1991); Legal Training and Research Institute of Supreme Court of Japan.

HIROSHI UCHIMA, admitted, 1993, Japan. *Education:* The University of Tokyo (LL.B., 1991); Legal Training and Research Institute of Supreme Court of Japan.

TOMOKO SASHO, admitted, 1993, Japan. *Education:* The University of Tokyo (LL.B., 1991); Legal Training and Research Institute of Supreme Court of Japan.

HIDEKI EBATA, admitted, 1993, Japan. *Education:* Chou University (LL.B., 1991); Legal Training and Research Institute of Supreme Court of Japan.

NAOMI AOYAMA, admitted, 1994, Japan. *Education:* The University of Tokyo (LL.B., 1991); Legal Training and Research Institute of Supreme Court of Japan.

SHIGEHIKO ISHIMOTO, admitted, 1994, Japan. *Education:* The University of Tokyo (LL.B., 1992); Legal Training and Research Institute of Supreme Court of Japan.

MASAKO YAJIMA, admitted, 1994, Japan. *Education:* Keio University (LL.B., 1992); Legal Training and Research Institute of Supreme Court of Japan. *PRACTICE AREAS:* General Corporate.

YOSHIAKI IKEDA, admitted, 1994, Japan. *Education:* The University of Tokyo (LL.B., 1992); Legal Training and Research Institute of Supreme Court of Japan.

OF COUNSEL

MASATOMI KOMATSU, admitted, 1985, Japan. *Education:* The University of Tokyo (LL.B., 1941); Judicial Research Institute of Ministry of Justice in Japan; graduate study, Research Scholar at Columbia University Law School (1965-1966). Chief Judge of Fukushima District Court. Chief Justice of Takamatsu High Court. Professor of Toyo University (1985-1990).

ADVISORS ON FOREIGN LAW

BRENT J. THORN, admitted, 1981, New York (Not admitted in Japan). *Education:* Brigham Young University (B.A., 1977); University of Utah, College of Law (J.D., 1980). William O. Leary Scholar. Executive Editor, Utah Law Review. With Davis Polk & Wardwell, New York, 1980-1985.

(This Listing Continued)

NISHIMURA & SANADA, Tokyo—Continued

T. MARK HALPERN, admitted, 1989, Ontario, Canada (Not admitted in Japan). *Education:* University of Toronto (B.A., 1980; LL.B., 1986; M.B.A., 1991). With Government of Ontario, 1987-1989; Blake, Cassels & Graydon, 1989-1991; Government of Canada, 1991-1993.

DANIEL C. HOUNSLOW, admitted, 1988, England and Wales; 1993, Hong Kong (Not admitted in Japan). *Education:* Kingston Polytechnic School of Law (B.A., 1984); Trinity Hall, Cambridge University (LL.M., 1985); Chester Law College (1985-1986). With Norton Rose, London, 1986-1993; Norton Rose, Hong Kong, 1993-1994.

SETH L. HURWITZ, admitted, 1986, Illinois; 1987, District of Columbia (Not admitted in Japan). *Education:* Cornell University (B.A., 1982); University of Chicago Law School (J.D., 1986). With Fried, Frank, Harris, Shriver & Jacobson, Washington, D.C., 1986-1989; Counsel, President's Intelligence Oversight Board, The White House, 1989-1993.

JUN UEDA, admitted, 1989, California (Not admitted in Japan). *Education:* University of the Pacific (B.A., 1986); McGeorge School of Law, University of the Pacific (J.D., 1989). With Tardiff & Staton, California, 1991-1993.

ALAN R. SCHWARTZ, admitted, 1994, New York (Not admitted in Japan). *Education:* Princeton University (B.A., 1988); Harvard Law School (J.D., 1993).

OGAWA SOGO LAW OFFICES

Established in 1967

TORANOMON 11 MORI BUILDING 6TH FLOOR
2-6-4, TORANOMON, MINATO-KU
105 TOKYO, JAPAN
Telephone: 813-3591-2228
Telefax: 813-3503-6909

International Business Law, Corporation, Foreign Investments, Patent, Trademark, Copyright, Taxation, and Labor.

FIRM PROFILE: *The Firm was established in 1967 and offers a full range of legal services.*

PARTNERS

KAGEHITO OGAWA, born Niigata, Japan, December 29, 1923; admitted, 1965, Japan. *Education:* University of Tokyo (LL.B., 1949). *Member:* Daini-Tokyo Bar Association, Patent Attorneys Association of Japan and Inter-Pacific Bar Association. *LANGUAGES:* Japanese and English. *PRACTICE AREAS:* Civil Law; Commercial Law; Intellectual Property Law.

MITSUAKI ISAKA, born Tokyo, Japan, December 25, 1954; admitted, 1987, Japan. *Education:* University of Tokyo (M.Sc., 1979). *Member:* Daini-Tokyo bar Association and International Association of Young Lawyers. *LANGUAGES:* Japanese, English, French and Italian. *PRACTICE AREAS:* International Investment Law; Taxation Law; Patent Law; Trademark and Copyright Law.

HIROO MUKOOYAMA, born Tochigi, Japan, August 22, 1914; admitted, 1963, Japan. *Education:* University of Tokyo (LL.B., 1940); University of Kyushu (LL.D., 1961). *Member:* Daini-Tokyo Bar Association. *LANGUAGES:* Japanese, Chinese and English. *PRACTICE AREAS:* Labor Law.

ICHIRO IIKURA, born Ooita, Japan, October 21, 1931; admitted, 1972, Japan. *Education:* Hosei University (LL.B, 1960). *Member:* Daini-Tokyo Bar Association. *LANGUAGES:* Japanese and English. *PRACTICE AREAS:* Civil Law; Commercial Law.

OHHARA LAW OFFICE

Established in 1930

5TH FLOOR, URBANNET KOJIMACHI BUILDING
6-2, KOJIMACHI 1-CHOME, CHIYODA-KU
TOKYO 102, JAPAN
Telephone: (03) 3239-1311
Fax: (03) 3239-1811

General and International Law Practice, Corporation, Patent and Trademark Law, Real Estate Law, Family, Inheritance Law, Labor Law, Administrative Law.

(This Listing Continued)

MEMBERS OF FIRM

SEIZABURO OHHARA, born Niigata Prefecture, March 10, 1941; admitted, 1970, Japan. *Education:* Keio University (LL.B., 1963; LL.M., 1967). *LANGUAGES:* Japanese.

NOBORU ODAGIRI, born Yamagata Prefecture, February 24, 1933; admitted, 1965, Japan. *Education:* Waseda University (LL.B., 1958). *LANGUAGES:* Japanese.

TERUHIKO SAKAINO, born Tokyo, January 12, 1947; admitted, 1975, Japan. *Education:* Keio University (LL.B., 1969). *LANGUAGES:* Japanese.

MASASHI HIRAIWA, born Shizuoka Prefecture, December 4, 1952; admitted, 1981, Japan. *Education:* Keio University (LL.B., 1975; LL.M., 1978). Associated with Lillick & McHose, Los Angeles, 1989. *LANGUAGES:* Japanese and English.

HIROSHI HATTORI, born Tokyo, April 26, 1953; admitted, 1984, Japan. *Education:* Kyoto University (LL.B., 1982). *LANGUAGES:* Japanese.

KAZUO TANABE, born Tokyo, August 3, 1957; admitted, 1987, Japan. *Education:* Keio University (LL.B., 1980). *LANGUAGES:* Japanese.

TOSHIYA AKASAKA, born Ibaragi Prefecture, October 30, 1958; admitted, 1988, Japan. *Education:* Keio University (LL.B., 1982). *LANGUAGES:* Japanese.

MARUHITO KONDO, born Osaka Prefecture, March 6, 1962; admitted, 1988, Japan. *Education:* Keio University (LL.B., 1984; LL.M., 1988); Chinese University of Hong Kong (1988); People's University of China with Scholarship (1988). Associated with Robert Lee & Fong, Hong Kong, 1989. *LANGUAGES:* Japanese, English and Mandarin Chinese.

KAORU HIRUTA, born Gunma Prefecture, November 25, 1958; admitted, 1989, Japan. *Education:* Keio University (LL.B., 1981). *LANGUAGES:* Japanese.

KAZUYORI UKAI, born Kanagawa Prefecture, January 15, 1962; admitted, 1990, Japan. *Education:* Keio University (LL.B., 1985). *LANGUAGES:* Japanese.

TOSHIO TSUKAKOSHI, born Gunma Prefecture, March 6, 1948; admitted, 1988, Japan. *Education:* Keio University (LL.B., 1971). *LANGUAGES:* Japanese.

MITSUO BANNO, born Tokyo, November 13, 1932; admitted, 1993, Japan. *Education:* Keio University (LL.B., 1955; LL.M., 1957). *LANGUAGES:* Japanese, English and German.

TOMOO IHARA, born Saitama Prefecture, May 23, 1964; admitted, 1993, Japan. *Education:* Keio University (LL.B., 1987). *LANGUAGES:* Japanese.

MARIKO SUGAWARA, born Tochigi Prefecture, April 13, 1966; admitted, 1994, Japan. *Education:* Keio University (LL.B., 1989; LL.M., 1992). *LANGUAGES:* Japanese, French and English.

COUNSEL

NAOKO MIYAZAWA, born Nagano Prefecture, March 30, 1961. *Education:* Kyoto University (LL.B., 1984). Registered as Judicial Scrivener, Japan, 1991. *LANGUAGES:* Japanese.

OKABE INTERNATIONAL PATENT OFFICE

Established in 1961

602 FUJI BUILDING, 2-3, MARUNOUCHI 3-CHOME, CHIYODA-KU
TOKYO 100, JAPAN
Telephone: 03-3213-1561-5
Cable Address: "Ohasy, Tokyo"
Telex: J28428 OHASY
Telefax: 03-3214-0929

Patent, Trademarks and Designs.
(This Listing Continued)

MEMBERS OF FIRM

MASAO OKABE, born Tokyo, Japan, February 5, 1926; admitted, 1961, Japan as Patent Attorney. *Education:* Tokyo University (B.S., 1947). Executive Counselor, Japanese Group, AIPPI. President, Asian Patent Attorneys Association, 1982-1989. *Member:* Patent Attorneys Association of Japan (President, 1981-1982). *LANGUAGES:* Japanese and English.

YOSHIO INOUE, born Tochigi, Japan, June 4, 1942; admitted, 1973, Japan as Patent Attorney. *Education:* Saitama University (Bachelor of Physical Engineering, 1968). Japanese group of AIPPI and Asian Patent Attorneys Association. *Member:* Patent Attorneys Association of Japan (Counselor, 1981-1984). *LANGUAGES:* Japanese and English.

NOBUAKI KATO, born Nagano, Japan, March 26, 1944; admitted, 1976, Japan as Patent Attorney. *Education:* Shinshu University (Bachelor of Electrical Engineering). Japanese group of AIPPI and Asian Patent Attorneys Association. *Member:* Patent Attorneys Association of Japan. *LANGUAGES:* Japanese and English.

YUZURU OKABE, born Tokyo, Japan, November 21, 1953; admitted, 1986, Japan as Patent Attorney. *Education:* Yokohama University (Bachelor of Mechanical Engineering). Japanese group of AIPPI and Asian Patent Attorneys Association. *Member:* Patent Attorneys Association of Japan. *LANGUAGES:* Japanese and English.

SHINICHI USUI, born Saitama, Japan, February 25, 1953; admitted, 1989, Japan as Patent Attorney. *Education:* Tokyo University (Bachelor of Chemical Engineering). Japanese group of AIPPI and Asian Patent Attorneys Association. *Member:* Patent Attorneys Association of Japan. *LANGUAGES:* Japanese, English and German.

IKUO FUJINO, born Saitama, Japan, May 21, 1945; admitted, 1985, Japan as Patent Attorney. *Education:* Ibaraki University (Bachelor of Chemical Engineering). Japanese group of AIPPI and Asian Patent Attorneys Association. *Member:* Patent Attorneys Association of Japan. *LANGUAGES:* Japanese and English.

TAKAO OCHI, born Kanagawa, Japan, March 6, 1956; admitted, 1991, Japan as Patent Attorney. *Education:* Yokohama University (Bachelor of Mechanical Engineering). Japan group of AIPPI and Asian Patent Attorneys Association. *Member:* Patent Attorneys Association of Japan. *LANGUAGES:* Japanese and English.

TERUHISA MOTOMIYA, born Chiba, Japan, January 14, 1961; admitted, 1988, Japan as Patent Attorney. *Education:* Nihon University (Bachelor of Law). Japanese group of AIPPI and Asian Patent Attorneys Association. *Member:* Patent Attorneys Association of Japan. *LANGUAGES:* Japanese and English.

REFERENCE: Fitzpatrick, Cella, Harper & Scinto, New York, N.Y.

OKABE & YAMAGUCHI

9TH FLOOR, YOKOKAWA BLDG.
17-27, SHINKAWA 1-CHOME, CHUO-KU
TOKYO 104, JAPAN
Telephone: (03) 3555-7931
Facsimile: (03) 3555-7934
Telex: 252-3308 HOKLAW J

Maritime Law, Aviation Law and Insurance Law including Charterparties and Bills of Lading, Casualties, Offshore Pollution, Through Transport and Re-Insurance.

MEMBERS OF FIRM

HIROKI OKABE, born Fukuoka, Japan, January 17, 1950; admitted, 1979, Japan. *Education:* Tokyo Mercantile Marine Academy (Navigation Course, 1973). Contributor, Handbook for International Multimodal Transportation, published by JIFFA. *Member:* Tokyo Bar Association; International Bar Association; Association of Average Adjusters of Japan. *LANGUAGES:* Japanese and English.

SHUJI YAMAGUCHI, born Hyogo, Japan, December 27, 1956; admitted, 1982, Japan. *Education:* Kyoto University. Contributor, Handbook for International Multimodal Transportation, published by JIFFA. *Member:* First Tokyo Bar Association; International Bar Association; Japan Maritime Law Association; Association of Average Adjusters of Japan. *LANGUAGES:* Japanese and English.

TEISHI AIZAWA, born Miyagi, Japan, January 20, 1950; admitted, 1990, Japan. *Education:* Waseda University School of Politics and Econom-

(This Listing Continued)

ics. *Member:* Tokyo Bar Association; International Bar Association. *LANGUAGES:* Japanese and English.

TAKEHIKO TOZUKA, born Fukuoka, Japan, September 9, 1962; admitted, 1991, Japan. *Education:* Kyoto University. *Member:* Tokyo Bar Association. *LANGUAGES:* Japanese and English.

OKAMOTO, SUZUKI & TAKAMATSU

8TH FLOOR, AUTHENTIC HANZOMON
2, KOJIMACHI 2-CHOME, CHIYODA-KU
TOKYO 102, JAPAN
Telephone: 81 (3) 3264-0671
Telecopier: 81 (3) 3264-0675

Corporate, Securities, Finance, Anti-Trust, Commercial Litigation, Personal Injury Defense Action, Trademarks, Copyright, Unfair Competition, Employment Relations, Tax, Bankruptcy and Reorganization, Insurance, International Practice and Real Property.

MEMBERS OF FIRM

KOJI OKAMOTO, born Japan, December 4, 1948; admitted, 1978, Japan. *Education:* Meiji University (LL.B., 1972); Legal Training and Research Institute (1978). Author: "Manual for Traffic Accident Personal Injury Action," Shin Nippon Hoki, 1991. Co-Author: "Civil Action for Personal Injury from a Traffic Accident-Manual for Calculation of Damages," Tokyo Three Bar Associations, 1990. *LANGUAGES:* Japanese and English. *PRACTICE AREAS:* General Commercial Litigation; Insurance Litigation; Personal Injury Defense and Real Property.

GINJIRO SUZUKI, born Japan, September 25, 1951; admitted, 1978, Japan. *Education:* Meiji University (LL.B., 1975); Legal Training and Research Institute (1978). Author: "Practice of Bankruptcy Administration," Kinzai, 1992; "Bankruptcy Law," New Ed. Keizai Horei, 1990; "Union Negotiation and Confinements Ct. Decision of October 28, 1986," 8 Supreme Court Decisions on Employment Relations 298, Nikkeiren, 1988. *LANGUAGES:* Japanese and English. *PRACTICE AREAS:* Employment Relations; Bankruptcy and Reorganization and Corporate.

KAORU TAKAMATSU, born Japan, August 16, 1953; admitted, 1978, Japan. *Education:* Kyoto University (LL.B., 1976); Legal Training and Research Institute (1978); University of Washington School of Law (LL.M., Asian Law, 1981). With Adachi, Henderson, Miyatake & Fujita, Tokyo, 1978-1992; Sheppard, Mullin, Richter and Hampton, Los Angeles, 1981-1982. Author: "Parallel Importation of Trademarked Goods: A Comparative Analysis," 57 Washington Law Review 433, 1982; "International Litigation and Enforcement of Judgements in Japan," 10 International Trade Law and Practice 159, 1984. *Member:* Dai-ni Tokyo Bar Association. *LANGUAGES:* Japanese and English. *PRACTICE AREAS:* Corporate; Finance; Licensing; Intellectual Property Rights.

MICHIAKI NAKANO, born Japan, April 27, 1957; admitted, 1985, Japan. *Education:* Waseda University (LL.B., 1981); Legal Training and Research Institute (1985); Cornell Law School (LL.M., 1990). With Powell, Goldstein, Frazer & Murphy, Atlanta (1990-1991); Arnall Golden & Gregory, Atlanta (1991-1992). Author: "Recent Developments in Equal Employment Laws in the U.S./1991 Civil Rights Act," 20 Journal of International Business Law 623, 1992. Co-Author: "1990 Clean Air Act: Its Impact on Japan," 19 Journal of International Business Law 1, 1991. *LANGUAGES:* Japanese and English. *PRACTICE AREAS:* Corporate, Trademarks, Copyright, Unfair Competition; Employment Relations; International Transactions and International Litigation.

FOREIGN LAW CONSULTANT

PAUL CLARK, born Chelan, Washington, January 19, 1949; admitted, 1974, California; 1975, Washington. *Education:* Whitman College (A.B., 1971); Boalt Hall School of Law, University of California (J.D., 1974); University of Washington (LL.M., Asian Law, 1977). With Adachi, Henderson, Miyatake & Fujita, Tokyo (1978-1980); Legal Department, Marubeni Corporation, Tokyo (1980-1993). Associate Editor, California Law Review, 1973-1974. *LANGUAGES:* English and Japanese. *PRACTICE AREAS:* International Transactions and Finance.

OKAZAKI, OHASHI & MAEDA

Established in 1983

8TH FLOOR, ROKKEN BLDG.
1-8-8 KANDA-OGAWAMACHI, CHIYODA-KU
TOKYO 101, JAPAN
Telephone: 03-3252-6866
Facsimile: 03-3252-6865

Copyright, Entertainment, Computer Software, Litigation and General Corporate Practices.

MEMBERS OF FIRM

KANEKICHI ABIRU (1896-1986).

HIROSHI OKAZAKI, born Taegu, South Korea, July 20, 1943; admitted, 1971, Japan. *Education:* Waseda University (LL.B., 1967); The Legal Training and Research Institute of the Supreme Court of Japan; University of Virginia School of Law (M.C.L., 1977). *Member:* First Tokyo Bar Association; Japanese Federation of Bar Associations; The Copyright Law Association of Japan. *LANGUAGES:* Japanese and English. *PRACTICE AREAS:* Commercial Law; Litigation; Copyright Infringement.

MASAHARU OHASHI, born Tokyo, Japan, March 31, 1947; admitted, 1972, Japan. *Education:* Tokyo University (LL.B., 1969); The Legal Training and Research Institute of the Supreme Court of Japan; Harvard Law School (LL.M., 1976). *Member:* First Tokyo Bar Association; Japanese Federation of Bar Associations; The Copyright Law Association of Japan. *LANGUAGES:* Japanese and English. *PRACTICE AREAS:* Commercial Law; Litigation; Computer Law.

TOSHIFUSA MAEDA, born Tokyo, Japan, June 11, 1951; admitted, 1984, Japan. *Education:* Tokyo University (LL.B., 1978); The Legal Training and Research Institute of the Supreme Court of Japan (1984). *Member:* First Tokyo Bar Association; Japanese Federation of Bar Associations. *LANGUAGES:* Japanese. *PRACTICE AREAS:* Commercial Law; Litigation; Criminal Law.

O'MELVENY & MYERS

Established in 1885

SANBANCHO KB-6 BUILDING
6 SANBANCHO, CHIYODA-KU
TOKYO 102, JAPAN
Telephone: 011-81-3-3239-2800
Facsimile: 011-81-3-3239-2432

Los Angeles, California Office: 400 South Hope Street. Telephone: 213-669-6000. Cable Address: "Moms." Facsimile: 213-669-6407.

Century City, California Office: 1999 Avenue of the Stars, 7th Floor. Telephone: 310-553-6700. Facsimile: 310-246-6779.

Newport Beach, California Office: 610 Newport Center Drive, Suite 1700. Telephone: 714-760-9600. Cable Address: "Moms." Facsimile: 714-669-6994.

San Francisco, California Office: Embarcadero Center West Tower, 275 Battery Street, Suite 2600. Telephone: 415-984-8700. Facsimile: 415-984-8701.

New York, N.Y. Office: Citicorp Center. 153 53rd Street, 54th Floor. Telephone: 212-326-2000. Facsimile: 212-326-2061.

Washington, D.C. Office: 555 13th Street, N.W., Suite 500 West. Telephone: 202-383-5300. Cable Address: "Moms." Facsimile: 202-383-5414.

Newark, New Jersey Office: One Gateway Center, 7th Floor, 07102. Telephone: 201-639-8600. Facsimile: 201-639-8630.

London, England Office: 10 Finsbury Square, London, EC2A 1LA. Telephone: 011-44-171-256-8451. Facsimile: 011-44-171-638-8205.

Hong Kong Office: 1104 Lippo Tower, Lippo Centre, 89 Queensway, Central Hong Kong. Telephone: 011-852-523-8266. Facsimile: 011-852-522-1760.

General and International Practice. Authorized to practice U.S. federal law and the laws of the District of Columbia and of all states with the exception of Louisiana.

SPECIAL COUNSEL

DALE M. ARAKI, born Berkeley, California, March 23, 1960; admitted, 1986, California; 1994, Japan, Gaikokuho-JIMU Bengoshi. *Education:* University of Hawaii (B.A., 1982); Harvard University (J.D., 1986). Author: "Minority Investments in U.S. Companies," Journal of the Japanese Insti-

(This Listing Continued)

---

tute of International Business Law (Kokusai Shōji Hōmu) Vol. 18, No. 12 (1990). *Member:* Tokyo Dai-Ni Bar Association. *LANGUAGES:* Japanese.

ASSOCIATES

David G. Litt

(For Complete Personnel and Biographical Data see Professional Biographies at Los Angeles, California)

OZAWA AKIYAMA & FUJIHIRA

9TH FLOOR, NO. 5 MORI BUILDING
17-1, TORANOMON 1-CHOME
MINATO-KU
TOKYO 105, JAPAN
Telephone: (03) 3591-7488
Fax: (03) 3595-1827

Corporate and General Practice. Litigation. Banking and Finance Law. Workouts and Bankruptcy. Mergers and Acquisitions. Real Estate.

MEMBERS OF FIRM

MASAYUKI OZAWA, born 1941; admitted, 1973, Japan; 1982, Japan Patent Bar. *Education:* Tokyo University (LL.B., LL.M.); Legal Training and Research Institute of the Supreme Court of Japan. Sanwa Bank Limited, Tokyo, 1964-1971. *LANGUAGES:* Japanese and English.

YASUO AKIYAMA, born 1946; admitted, 1986, Japan. *Education:* Tokyo University (Bachelor of Economics); Legal Training and Research Institute of the Supreme Court of Japan. Nomura Securities, Tokyo, 1971-1972. Nisshin Trading, Tokyo, 1972-1984. *LANGUAGES:* Japanese and English.

KATSUHIKO FUJIHIRA, born 1958; admitted, 1985, Japan; 1990, New York. *Education:* Tokyo University (LL.B.); Legal Training and Research Institute of the Supreme Court of Japan; University of Pennsylvania (LL.M.). Sanwa Bank Limited, Tokyo, 1982-1983 and New York, 1990-1991. Shearman & Sterling, New York, 1989-1990. Cleary, Gottlieb, Steen & Hamilton, Brussels, 1990. *LANGUAGES:* Japanese and English.

YUJI KATSUKI, born 1958; admitted, 1990, Japan. *Education:* Meiji University (Bachelor of Economics); Legal Training and Research Institute of the Supreme Court of Japan. *LANGUAGES:* Japanese.

AKIHISA KAGAWA, born 1956; admitted, 1991, Japan. *Education:* Tokyo University of Foreign Studies (B.A.); Legal Training and Research Institute of the Supreme Court of Japan. *LANGUAGES:* Japanese, English and Spanish.

TAKUMA TSUYUKI, born 1961; admitted, 1994, Japan. *Education:* Keio Gijuku University (LL.B.); Legal Training and Research Institute of the Supreme Court of Japan. *LANGUAGES:* Japanese and English.

PAUL, HASTINGS, JANOFSKY & WALKER

A Partnership including Professional Corporations

(Futami Gaikokuho-Jimu-Bengoshi Jimusho)

Firm Established in 1951; Office in 1988

TORANOMON OHTORI BUILDING
EIGHTH FLOOR, 4-3 TORANOMON 1-CHOME, MINATO-KU
TOKYO 105, JAPAN
Telephone: (03) 3507-0730
Facsimile: (03) 3507-0734

Los Angeles, California Office: Twenty-Third Floor, 555 South Flower Street, 90071-2371. Telephone: 213-683-6000. Cable Address: "Paulhast." Twx: 910-321-4065.

Orange County, California Office: Seventeenth Floor, 695 Town Center Drive, Costa Mesa, 92626-1924. Telephone: 714-668-6200.

Washington, D.C. Office: Tenth Floor, 1299 Pennsylvania Avenue, N.W., 20036-5331. Telephone: 202-508-9500.

Atlanta, Georgia Office: 42nd Floor, Georgia Pacific Center, 133 Peachtree Street, N.E., 30303-1840. Telephone: 404-588-9900.

Santa Monica, California Office: Fifth Floor, 1299 Ocean Avenue, 90401-1078. Telephone: 310-319-3300.

Stamford, Connecticut Office: Ninth Floor, 1055 Washington Boulevard, 06901-2217. Telephone: 203-961-7400.

New York, New York Office: 31st Floor, 399 Park Avenue, 10022-4697. Telephone: 212-318-6000.

(This Listing Continued)

Firm engaged in American and General International Law Practice but not authorized to appear before Japanese courts or to act as Bengoshi.

MEMBERS OF FIRM

NORMAN A. FUTAMI, born Hermosa Beach, California, January 5, 1960; admitted, 1984, California; 1993, Japan (Gaikokuho Jimu Bengoshi). *Education:* Yale University (B.A., summa cum laude, 1981); Harvard University (J.D., 1984). Phi Beta Kappa. (Also at Los Angeles, California). *LANGUAGES:* English and Japanese.

KAORUHIKO SUZUKI, born Tokyo, Japan, June 5, 1947; admitted, 1975, California (Not admitted in Japan). *Education:* Harvard University (A.B., magna cum laude, 1971; J.D., 1975). Lecturer: Japanese Legal System, University of Southern California Law School, 1976-1979; Law and Information, Seikei University, Tokyo, Japan, 1988. (Also at Los Angeles, California). *LANGUAGES:* English and Japanese.

ASSOCIATES

STEPHEN A. YAMAGUCHI, born Long Beach, California, February 29, 1964; admitted, 1989, California (Not admitted in Japan). *Education:* Stanford University (B.A., 1986); International Christian University; Columbia University (J.D., 1989). *LANGUAGES:* English and Japanese.

(For Complete Biographical Data on all Personnel, see Los Angeles, California, Professional Biographies).

PAUL, WEISS, RIFKIND, WHARTON & GARRISON

(Lakhdhir Gaikokuho Jimu Bengoshi Jimusho)

11TH FLOOR MAIN TOWER, AKASAKA TWIN TOWER
17-22, AKASAKA 2-CHOME MINATO-KU
TOKYO 107, JAPAN
Telephone: (81-3) 3505-0291
Facsimile: (81-3) 3505-4540
Telex: 02428120 PWRWGT

New York, N.Y. Office: 1285 Avenue of the Americas, 10019-6064. Telephones: (212) 373-3000, TDD 212-373-2000. Cable Address: "Longsight, New York". Telex: WUI 666-843. Facsimile: 212-757-3990.
Washington, D.C. Office: 1615 L Street, N.W., Suite 1300, 20036-5694. Telephones: 202-223-7300, TDD 202-223-7490. Telex: 248237 PWA UR. Facsimile: 202-223-7420. Cable Address: "Longsight, Washington".
Paris, France Office: 199, Boulevard Saint Germain, 75007. Telephone:(33-1) 45.49.33.85. Telex: 269940 F. Facsimile: (33-1) 42-22-64-38.
Beijing, People's Republic of China: Suite 1910, Scite Tower, 22 Jianguomenwai Dajie, 100004. Telephones: (86-1) 5123628-30, (86-1) 5122288X.1910. Telex: 210169 PWRWG CN. Facsimile: (86-1) 5123631.
Hong Kong Office: 13th Floor, Hong Kong Club Building, 3A Chater Road, Central Hong Kong. Telephone: (011-852) 2536-9933. Facsimile: 011 (852) 2536-9622.

Firm engaged in American and International Practice in Tokyo as Lakhdhir Gaikokuho Jimu Bengoshi Jimusho and not authorized to appear before the Japanese Courts or otherwise to act as Bengoshi.

RESIDENT PARTNER

DAVID K. LAKHDHIR, born New York, N.Y., January 12, 1958; admitted, 1984, New York; qualified in Japan as a Gaikokuho-Jimu-Bengoshi, 1993; 1994, District of Columbia. *Education:* Harvard College (A.B., magna cum laude, 1980); Harvard Law School (J.D., cum laude, 1983). Visiting Scholar, Indian Law Institute, New Delhi, India, 1983-1984. *Member:* Japan Federation of Bar Associations; Second Tokyo Bar Association; The Association of the Bar of the City of New York (Committee on Foreign and Comparative Law, 1989-1993). *PRACTICE AREAS:* Mergers and Acquisitions; Securities; Finance; International Business Transactions.

ASSOCIATES

DARREL J. HOLSTEIN, born Christchurch, New Zealand, December 9, 1959; admitted, 1989, New York (Not admitted in Japan). *Education:* Canterbury University, New Zealand (1979-1981); Tohoku University, Japan (B.L., 1986); Harvard Law School (J.D., 1989). *LANGUAGES:* Japanese.

BRUCE E. NUSSBAUM, born Brooklyn, New York, February 21, 1963; admitted, 1989, New York (Not admitted in Japan). *Education:* Uni-

(This Listing Continued)

versity of Pennsylvania (B.A.B.S., magna cum laude, 1985); Harvard Law School (J.D., cum laude, 1988). *Member:* American Bar Association.

(For Biographical Data of other Personnel, see Professional Biographies at New York, Washington, D.C., Paris, France, Beijing, People's Republic of China, and Hong Kong)

PILLSBURY MADISON & SUTRO

TORANOMON ACT BUILDING, 6TH FLOOR
5-11-12, TORANOMON 5-CHOME
MINATO-KU
TOKYO 105, JAPAN
Telephone: 800-729-9830
Tel: 011-813-5472-6561
FAX: 011-81-3-5472-5761

Los Angeles, California Office: Citicorp Plaza, 725 South Figueroa Street, Suite 1200. Telephone: 213-488-7100. Fax: 213-629-1033.
Menlo Park, California Office: 2700 Sand Hill Road. Telephone: 415-233-4500. Fax: 415-233-4545.
Orange County Office: Plaza Tower, 600 Anton Boulevard, Costa Mesa. Telephone: 714-436-6800. Fax: 714-662-6999.
Sacramento, California Office: 400 Capitol Mall, Suite 1700. Telephone: 916-329-4700. Fax: 916-441-3583.
San Diego, California Office: 101 West Broadway, Suite 1800. Telephone: 619-234-5000. Fax: 619-236-1995.
San Francisco, California Office: 225 Bush Street. Telephone: 415-983-1000. Fax: 415-983-1200 (Russ), 415-983-1600 (Bush).
San Jose, California Office: Ten Almaden Boulevard. Telephone: 408-947-4000. Fax: 408-287-8341.
Washington, D. C. Office: 1667 K Street, N.W., Suite 1100. Telephone: 202-887-0300. Fax: 202-296-7605.
New York, New York Office: One Liberty Plaza, 165 Broadway, 51st Floor. Telephone: 212-374-1890. Fax: 212-374-1852.
Hong Kong Office: 6/F Asia Pacific Finance Tower, Citibank Plaza, 3 Garden Road, Central. Telephone: 011-852-509-7100. Fax: 011-852-509-7188.

General Practice.

FIRM PROFILE: *Founded in 1874, Pillsbury Madison & Sutro has grown to become one of the largest law firms in the United States, with more than 600 attorneys and expertise in virtually every area of the law. With offices in seven California cities, New York, Washington, D.C., and two Asia, Hong Kong and Tokyo, the firm combines a strong domestic practice with a dynamic presence in the rapidly changing international markets. The firm's corporate expertise encompasses all aspects of business law and covers the full range of legal needs. Its litigation practice is conducted by trial lawyers who have handled landmark cases in the federal and state courts. The firm's clients range from large multinational corporations to start-up companies to individuals.*

PARTNERS

JAMES A. CHURCHILL, born Kingsport, Tennessee, September 13, 1935; admitted, 1961, Louisiana; 1962, U.S. Court of Appeals, Fifth Circuit and U.S. District Court, Eastern District of Louisiana; 1989, California; 1992, Japan (Gaikokuho-Jimu-Bengoshi). *Education:* Princeton University (A.B., cum laude, 1957); Harvard Law School (LL.B., 1960); Tulane University School of Law (M.C.L., 1963). *Member:* Louisiana, Tokyo and American Bar Associations; State Bar of California; American Law Institute.

NAOKI SHIMAZAKI, born Tokyo, Japan, October 7, 1957; admitted, 1984, California and U.S. District Court, Central District of California; 1991, Japan (Gaikokuho Jimu Bengoshi). *Education:* University of California at Davis (A.B. with highest honors, 1980); University of California at Los Angeles (M.B.A., 1984; J.D., 1984). Phi Beta Kappa; Order of the Coif. Member, UCLA Pacific Basin Law Journal, 1983-1984. Author: "An American Lawyer in Tokyo: Problems of Establishing A Practice," UCLA Pacific Basin Law Journal, 1983. *Member:* State Bar of California; Daini Tokyo Bar Association. *LANGUAGES:* Japanese.

(For biographical data on Los Angeles, Menlo Park, Orange County, Sacramento, San Diego, San Francisco, San Jose, Washington, New York and Hong Kong personnel, see Professional Biographies in the listings for each of those cities).

SAITO LAW OFFICE

TOKYO GINZA BLDG., RM. 302
12-2, GINZA 6-CHOME, CHUO-KU
TOKYO 104, JAPAN
Telephone: 03-3574-9531
Fax: 03-3575-4530
Cable: "MSAITOLAW TOKYO"
Telex: 2523467 MSLAW J

MASAO SAITO, born Nakatsu City, Japan, September 23, 1937; admitted, 1967, Japan. *Education:* International Christian University (B.L.A., 1961). *Member:* Daini Tokyo Bar Association. *LANGUAGES:* Japanese and English. *PRACTICE AREAS:* Corporate Law; Labour Law.

SAKURA KYODO LAW OFFICES

(Formerly Kawai, Takeuchi, Nishimura & Inoue)

SUITE 814, SHUWA KIOICHO TBR BUILDING
5-7 KOJIMACHI CHIYODA-KU
TOKYO 102, JAPAN
Telephone: 03 (3230) 4400
Telecopier: 03 (3263) 7785

General and International Law Practice. International Transactions, Corporate, Bankruptcy, Reorganization and Criminal Law.

MEMBERS OF FIRM

KOJI TAKEUCHI, born Japan, September 3, 1944; admitted, 1970, Japan; 1986, New York with examination. *Education:* Tokyo University, Faculty of Law (LL.B., 1968); Columbia University School of Law (LL.M., 1983). Author: "International Bankruptcy: A Critique of Existing Notions of Territorialism and a Suggestion for the Development of International Bankruptcy," 76 Hogaku Shirin 45, 1978; "Creditors Rights and Bankruptcy in Japan," ABA National Institute, 1983. Lecturer, Hosei University, 1977-1982. *Member:* Tokyo Bar Association (Representative of the General Councillors, 1972-1973); Scholarly Society of Civil Procedure Law. *LANGUAGES:* Japanese and English.

HIROYUKI KAWAI, born Japan, April 18, 1944; admitted, 1970, Japan. *Education:* Law Faculty of Tokyo University (LL.B., 1968); International and Comparative Law Center, Dallas, Texas. Author: *The Vocation of a Lawyer,* 1982; "The Organization and Effectiveness of Compulsory Arrangement," Bankruptcy: Problems of Theory & Practice, 1983; "Relieving Anxiety over Legal Fees: A Re-examination of an Attorneys Duties," Freedom & Justice, 1985. *Member:* Tokyo Second Bar Association. *LANGUAGES:* Japanese and English.

KUNIHIKO NISHIMURA, born Japan, June 17, 1947; admitted, 1976, Japan. *Education:* Law Faculty of Tokyo University (LL.B., 1974); International and Comparative Law Center, Dallas, Texas (1980). Author: "Transactional Credit Protection," and "Transactional Debt Collection," Banking Transaction Procedures, 1979; "An Attorney's Perspective on Bankruptcy Procedures for Creditors," 295, 298 New Business Law, 1983-1984. *Member:* Tokyo Bar Association. *LANGUAGES:* Japanese and English.

TOMOHARU INOUE, born Japan, March 7, 1955; admitted, 1980, Japan. *Education:* Law Faculty of Tokyo University (LL.B., 1978). Co-Author: *Studies on The Legal Problems of Packaged Software for Personal Computers,* 1985. *Member:* Tokyo Second Bar Association; Copyright Law Society; Computers and the Law Society. *LANGUAGES:* Japanese.

HIDESHIGE AOKI, born Japan, August 22, 1952; admitted, 1984, Japan. *Education:* Law Faculty of Tokyo University (LL.B., 1979). *Member:* Tokyo Second Bar Association. *LANGUAGES:* Japanese.

OSAMU YASUDA, born Fukuoka, Japan, November 6, 1956; admitted, 1984, Japan. *Education:* Law Faculty of Waseda University (1979). *Member:* Tokyo Second Bar Association. *LANGUAGES:* Japanese.

JUNICHI ARATAKE, born Japan, October 1, 1956; admitted, 1986, Japan. *Education:* Law Faculty of Keio Gijyuku University (LL.B., 1980). *Member:* Tokyo Bar Association. *LANGUAGES:* Japanese and English.

NOBUTAKA NONAKA, born Japan, July 25, 1956; admitted, 1988, Japan. *Education:* Law Faculty of Waseda University (LL.B., 1981); Graduate School of Law (LL.M., Law of Corporations and Business Enterprises, 1986). *Member:* Tokyo Second Bar Association. *LANGUAGES:* Japanese and English.

(This Listing Continued)

YO CHIHARA, born Japan, December 12, 1961; admitted, 1988, Japan. *Education:* Law Faculty of Waseda University (LL.B., 1986). *Member:* Tokyo Second Bar Association. *LANGUAGES:* Japanese.

ASSOCIATES

SHOZABURO YOSHINO, born Niigata, Japan, March 12, 1951; admitted, 1990, Japan. *Education:* Law Faculty of Gakushuin University (LL.B., 1973); Graduate School of Law, Waseda University (J.D., 1981); Freiburg University, Germany (J.D., 1981). Professor of Law, Tokai University, 1989—. *Member:* Tokyo Bar Association. *LANGUAGES:* Japanese, German and English.

ETSUKO FUJIMOTO, born Saitama, Japan, September 3, 1945; admitted, 1974, Japan. *Education:* Law Faculty of Tokyo University (LL.B., 1970 and 1972); University of Washington (LL.M., 1985). *Member:* Tokyo Second Bar Association. *LANGUAGES:* Japanese and English.

RIKO KUBOTA, born Japan, September 21, 1960; admitted, 1989, Japan. *Education:* Law Faculty of Waseda University (LL.B., 1983); Graduate School of Law (LL.M., Law of Corporation and Business Enterprises, 1987). *Member:* Tokyo Bar Association. *LANGUAGES:* Japanese.

MINAO SHIMIZU, born Japan, March 7, 1961; admitted, 1990, Japan. *Education:* Law Faculty of Tokyo University (LL.B., 1985). *Member:* Tokyo Bar Association. *LANGUAGES:* Japanese.

KEN HARAGUCHI, born Tokyo, Japan, February 8, 1964; admitted, 1991, Japan. *Education:* Law Faculty of the University of Tokyo (LL.B., 1989). *Member:* Tokyo Bar Association. *LANGUAGES:* Japanese.

HIROKA KONO, born Tokushima, Japan, October 2, 1961; admitted, 1989, Japan. *Education:* Law Faculty of Waseda University (LL.B., 1984); University of Washington (LL.M., 1991). *Member:* Tokyo Bar Association. *LANGUAGES:* Japanese and English.

YORIKO NOMA, born Tokyo, Japan, May 27, 1959; admitted, 1986, Japan. *Education:* Law Faculty of Keio University (LL.B., 1982); University of Washington (LL.M., 1992). *Member:* Tokyo Bar Association. *LANGUAGES:* Japanese and English.

SHINJIRO MOTOYAMA, born Tokyo, Japan, December 8, 1966; admitted, 1993, Japan. *Education:* Law Faculty of Tokyo University (LL.B., 1991). *Member:* Tokyo Second Bar Association. *LANGUAGES:* Japanese.

SHIGEKI FUNAHASHI, born Kanagawa, Japan, May 27, 1965; admitted, 1993, Japan. *Education:* Law Faculty of Chuo University (LL.B., 1989); Graduate School of Law of Yokohama National University (LL.M., 1992). *Member:* Tokyo Bar Association. *LANGUAGES:* Japanese and English.

NAOKI KINOSHITA, born Tokyo, Japan, January 20, 1965; admitted, 1994, Japan. *Education:* Law Faculty of Keio University (LL.B., 1988). *Member:* Tokyo Bar Association. *LANGUAGES:* Japanese.

KIYOTAKA MATSUI, born Kobe, Japan, March 27, 1969; admitted, 1994, Japan. *Education:* Law Faculty of Kobe University (LL.B., 1992). *Member:* Tokyo Second Bar Association. *LANGUAGES:* Japanese.

REPRESENTATIVE CLIENTS: Itoman & Co., Ltd.; Kenwood Inc.; Sumitomo Marine, Inc.; Shuwa Corp.
REFERENCES: Hurt, Richardson, Garner, Todd & Cadenhead, Atlanta, Georgia; Axelrod & Kroll, Rochester, N.Y.

SANNO LAW OFFICES

Established in 1964

404 SANNO GRAND BUILDING
14-2 NAGATA-CHO 2 CHOME, CHIYODA-KU
TOKYO 100, JAPAN
Telephone: 3-3592-0812; 3-3581-9491
Fax: 3-3501-2276; 2359

General Practice. Litigation including International Transactions, Corporation, Arbitration and Foreign Investments.

FIRM PROFILE: The firm offers a full range of legal services. It is well known for its Corporation Law, Bankruptcy and Reconstruction Law.

MEMBERS OF FIRM

KAZUHIKO MATSUI, born Kurume-shi, Japan, November 2, 1924; admitted, 1957, Japan. *Education:* Tokyo University (LL.B., 1953). *Member:* First Tokyo Bar Association. *LANGUAGES:* Japanese and English. *PRACTICE AREAS:* Corporate Trade Litigation.

(This Listing Continued)

HIROSHI NAKANE, born Okazaki-shi, Japan, February 18, 1930; admitted, 1957, Japan. *Education:* Tokyo University (B.A., 1953); Harvard Law School (LL.M., 1959). *Member:* First Tokyo Bar Association; Japanese-American Law Association. *LANGUAGES:* Japanese and English. *PRACTICE AREAS:* International Litigation; Arbitration; Foreign Investments.

TETSUYA NAKAGAWA, born Tokyo, Japan, September 24, 1951; admitted, 1977, Japan. *Education:* Tokyo University (LL.B., 1975). *Member:* First Tokyo Bar Association. *LANGUAGES:* Japanese and English. *PRACTICE AREAS:* Bankruptcy; Corporation.

HITOSHI KANAMORI, born Tokyo, Japan, August 1, 1954; admitted, 1992, Japan. *Education:* Waseda University (LL.B., 1954). *Member:* Tokyo Bar Association. *LANGUAGES:* Japanese and English. *PRACTICE AREAS:* Domestic Litigation; Criminal Cases.

ASSOCIATES

MASATERU KAMEI, born Oita, Japan, January 24, 1963; admitted, 1994, Japan. *Education:* Chuo University (LL.B., 1985). *Member:* First Tokyo Bar Association. *LANGUAGES:* Japanese and English. *PRACTICE AREAS:* Domestic Litigation.

REPRESENTATIVE CLIENTS: The Tokai Bank; Mitsubishi Trust Co.; Nippon Denso Co.; Tomy Kogyo, Inc.; Far East Oil Trading Co.; Nitto Koei Co. (Administrator); Nihon Sangyo Kikai Co. (Receiver).

SATO & TSUDA

Established in 1971

SHIOZAKI BUILDING, 7-1 HIRAKAWACHO 2-CHOME,
CHIYODA-KU

TOKYO 102, JAPAN
Telephone: 03-3265-8401
Telefax: 03-3265-8405

New address effective April 1, 1995: AI Building, 20-5 Ichibancho, Chiyoda-Ku

International Private Law, Corporate and Contract Law, Administrative Law and Anti-Trust Law.

MEMBERS OF FIRM

TETSUO SATO, born Japan, October 22, 1924; admitted, 1950, Japan. *Education:* Tohoku University, 1948; Legal Training and Research Institute of the Supreme Court of Japan, 1950; Continuing Legal Education Program, Georgetown Law School, Washington, D.C., 1960-1961. Prosecuting Attorney in Tokyo and Yokohama Districts, 1950-1954. Attorney, Ministry of Justice, 1954-1957. Legal Attaché to the Japanese Embassy in Washington, D.C., 1958-1961. Attorney, Ministry of Justice, 1961-1962. *Member:* Daiichi Tokyo Bar Association; Japan-American Society for Legal Studies, Japan Branch; International Private Law Society in Japan; International Law Association of Japan. (Also Of Counsel, Layton Brooks & Hecht, New York, N.Y.). *LANGUAGES:* Japanese and English. *PRACTICE AREAS:* International Investment; Corporate Matters; Anti-Trust Law; International Taxation.

TOKYO OF COUNSEL

MINORU TSUDA, born Japan, August 5, 1909; admitted, 1934, Japan. *Education:* Kyoto Imperial University, 1933. District Court Judge, 1935-1945. Attorney, Ministry of Justice, 1945. Chief Secretary, General Secretariat of Ministry of Justice, 1955-1958. Director: Judicial System and Research Division, Ministry of Justice, 1958-1964; Criminal Affairs Bureau, Ministry of Justice, 1964-1968. Regional Prosecutor General at Sapporo High Prosecution Office, 1968-1969. Vice Minister of Justice, 1969-1972. Member: Legislative Council, Ministry of Justice, 1958-1972; Transport Council, Ministry of Transportation, 1972-1978. *Member:* Daiichi Tokyo Bar Association. *LANGUAGES:* Japanese and English. *PRACTICE AREAS:* Government Contracts; Construction Contracts; Anti-Trust Law.

NEW YORK OF COUNSEL

ROBERT LAYTON, born New York, N.Y., February 19, 1931; admitted, 1956, New York (Not admitted in Japan). *Education:* Yale University (LL.B., 1954). Diplomate, Hague Academy of International Law, 1959. Attorney, Adviser, Department of Justice, 1958-1961. (Also Partner, Layton Brooks & Hecht, New York, N.Y.). *LANGUAGES:* English, Spanish and Hungarian. *PRACTICE AREAS:* International Arbitration and Litigation.

SHEARMAN & STERLING

(Thomas Wilner Gaikokuho-Jimu-Bengoshi Jimusho)

FUKOKU SEIMEI BUILDING, 5TH FLOOR
2-2-2, UCHISAIWAICHO
CHIYODA-KU, TOKYO 100, JAPAN
Telephone: (81-3) 5251-1601
Fax: (81-3) 5251-1602

New York, N.Y. Office: 599 Lexington Avenue, New York, New York 10022-6069 and Citicorp Center, 153 East 53rd Street, New York, New York 10022-4676. Telephone: (212) 848-4000. Telex: 667290 Num Lau. Fax: 599 Lexington Avenue: (212) 848-7179. Citicorp Center: (212) 848-5252.

Abu Dhabi, United Arab Emirates Office: P.O. Box 2948. Telephone: (971-2) 324477. Fax: (971-2) 774533.

Beijing, People's Republic of China Office: Suite #2205, Capital Mansion, No. 6, Xin Yuan Nan Road. Chao Yang District Beijing, 100004. Telephone: (861) 465-4574. Fax: (861) 465-4578.

Budapest, Hungary Office: Szerb utca 17-19, 1056 Budapest. Telephone: (36-1) 266-3522. Fax: (36-1) 266-3523.

Düsseldorf, Federal Republic of Germany Office: Königsallee 46, D-40212 Düsseldorf. Telephone: (49-211) 13 62 80. Telex: 8 588 294 NYLO. Fax: (49-211) 13 33 09.

Frankfurt, Federal Republic of Germany Office: Bockenheimer Landstrasse 55, D-60325 Frankfurt am Main. Telephone: (49-69) 97-10-70. Fax: (49-69) 97-10-71-00.

Hong Kong, Hong Kong Office: Standard Chartered Bank Building, 4 Des Voeux Road Central, Hong Kong. Telephone: (852) 2978-8000. Fax: (852) 2978-8099.

London, England Office: 199Bishopsgate, London EC2M 3TY. Telephone: (44-71) 920-9000. Fax: (44-71) 920-9020.

Los Angeles, California Office: 725 South Figueroa Street, 21st Floor, 90017-5421. Telephone: (213) 239-0300. Fax: (213) 239-0381, 614-0936.

Paris, France Office: 12 rue d'Astorg, 75008. Telephone: (33-1) 44-71-17-17. Telex: 282964 Royale. Fax: (33-1) 44-71-01-01.

San Francisco, California Office: 555 California Street, 94104-1522. Telephone: (415) 616-1100. Fax: (415) 616-1199.

Taipei, Taiwan Office: 7th Floor, Hung Kuo Building, 167 Tun Hwa North Road. Telephone: (886-2) 545-3300. Fax: (866-2) 545-3322.

Toronto, Ontario, Canada Office: Commerce Court West, Suite 4405, P.O. Box 247, M5L 1E8. Telephone: (416) 360-8484. Fax: (416) 360-2958.

Washington, D.C. Office: 801 Pennsylvania Avenue, N.W., Suite 900, 20004-2604. Telephone: (202) 508-8000. Fax: (202) 508-8100.

General Practice.
Firm engaged in American and General International Law Practice, but not authorized to appear before Japanese courts.

FIRM PROFILE: Shearman & Sterling, founded in 1873, has more than 500 lawyers in 15 offices throughout the world. The firm's practice encompasses most major areas of business law, including: Antitrust and Trade Regulation; Banking; Bankruptcy and Corporate Reorganization; Compensation and Benefits; Environmental; Finance (including Corporate Finance, Domestic Private Finance, Financial Institutions, International Private Finance and Project Finance); Individual Clients, Trusts and Estates; Insurance; International Trade and Government Relations; Litigation and Arbitration; Mergers and Acquisitions; Oil and Gas; Privatizations; Real Estate; and Tax. The Firm is also engaged in the practice of French, German and Hungarian law through its offices in France, Germany and Hungary.

MANAGING PARTNER

THOMAS B. WILNER, born Toronto, Canada, 1944; admitted, 1969, Pennsylvania; 1971, New York; 1973, District of Columbia; 1975, U.S. Supreme Court; 1992, Tokyo, Japan. *Education:* Yale University (B.A., 1966); University of Pennsylvania (LL.B., 1969). Law Clerk to the Hon. William H. Hastie, Chief Judge, U.S. Court of Appeals for the Third Circuit, 1969-1970.

(For Biographical data of all partners, see Professional Biographies at New York, N.Y.).

SHIBA INTERNATIONAL LAW OFFICES

NISHI-SHINBASHI EXCEL BLDG. 8-9F
1-20-10 NISHI-SHINBASHI, MINATO-KU
TOKYO 105, JAPAN
Telephone: 81-3-3503-2921
Facsimile: 81-3-3503-2924; 2925

International Transactions, Corporations, Litigation, Banking, Finance, Trade Regulation, Real Estate, Merger and Acquisition, Securities, Intellectual Property, Copyright, Antitrust, Foreign Investment.

MEMBERS OF FIRM

SHINTARO HAGIWARA, born Osaka, Japan, January 1, 1952; admitted, 1978, Japan. *Education:* Tokyo University (1976); Supreme Court Legal Training and Research Institute (1976-1978); University of Cambridge (LL.M., 1983). Author: "Doing Business in Japan," 1991. *Member:* Daini-Tokyo Bar Association; International Bar Association; International Economic Law Academy. *LANGUAGES:* Japanese and English.

HIROSHI KINOSHITA, born Tachikawa, Tokyo, Japan, April 10, 1951; admitted, 1977, Japan; 1983, New York. *Education:* Law Faculty, Hitotsubashi University (LL.B., 1975); Supreme Court Legal Training and Research Institute (1975-1977); Columbia Law School (LL.M., 1981). International Partner, Baker & McKenzie, 1985-1991. *Member:* Tokyo Bar Association; New York State Bar Association. *LANGUAGES:* Japanese and English.

MORIHIKO TATSUNO, born Osaka, Japan, August 20, 1951; admitted, 1978, Japan; 1982, New York. *Education:* Law Faculty, Tokyo University (LL.B., 1976); Supreme Court Legal Training and Research Institute (1976-1978); Columbia Law School (LL.M., 1981). *Member:* Tokyo Bar Association; New York State Bar Association. *LANGUAGES:* Japanese and English.

ASSOCIATE

KENICHI SENKAWA, born Nishinomiya, Hyogo, Japan, November 28, 1961; admitted, 1992, Japan. *Education:* Law Faculty, Hitotsubashi University (LL.B., 1987); Supreme Court Legal Training and Research Institute (1990-1992). *Member:* Tokyo Bar Association. *LANGUAGES:* Japanese and English.

KEN KODAKA, born Yokohama, Japan, April 19, 1966; admitted, 1995, Japan. *Education:* Law Faculty, Keio University (LL.B., 1993); Supreme Court Legal Training and Research Institute (1993-1995). *Member:* Tokyo Bar Association. *LANGUAGES:* Japanese and English.

SHIMADA, SENO, AMITANI & HIRATA

Established in 1990

KANDA CHUO BUILDING 2 F
3-20, KANDA NISHIKI-CHO, CHIYODA-KU
TOKYO 101, JAPAN
Telephone: (03) 3291-2971
Fax: (03) 3291-2888
Telex: 222-3779SSAH J

Admiralty, Aircraft Finance, Arbitration, Banking and Finance, Competition and Trade Regulation, Corporate and Commercial, Insurance, Mergers and Acquisitions, Real Estate, Securities, Ship Finance, Tax, Technology Transfer, Wills, Estates and Trusts, Litigation, Intellectual Property.

FIRM PROFILE: The firm has links with other well-established law firms throughout Japan and around the world (in particular, countries in the Far East, Oceania, Western Europe and North America). The firm is also affiliated with leading accountancy firms in Tokyo.

PARTNERS

MAKOTO SHIMADA, born 1956; admitted, 1981, Japan. *Education:* Keio University (LL.B.); Legal Training and Research Institute of the Supreme Court of Japan; University of London (LL.M., 1986). Lecturer: Kyorin University, International Business Law, 1990-1992; Keio University, Civil and Commercial Law, 1992—. Visiting Professor, Pacific McGeorge School of Law, Asian Commercial Law, 1987. With: Ughi & Nunziante, Rome, Fall, 1986; Norton Rose, London, 1986-1988; Loeff Claeys Verbeke, Rotterdam, Winter, 1988. *LANGUAGES:* Japanese and English.

KATSUHISA SENO, born 1956; admitted, 1984, Japan. *Education:* Keio University (LL.B.); Legal Training and Research Institute of the Supreme Court of Japan. *LANGUAGES:* Japanese and English.

(This Listing Continued)

MITSUHIRO AMITANI, born 1956; admitted, 1985, Japan. *Education:* Keio University (B.A., 1981; LL.M., 1983); Legal Training and Research Institute of the Supreme Court of Japan; University of Washington (L.L.M., 1989). With: Fong Miho Okano & Wong, Honolulu, Spring, 1988; Davis Wright & Jones, Seattle, Summer, 1989. *LANGUAGES:* Japanese and English.

OHKI HIRATA, born 1956; admitted, 1983, Japan. *Education:* Nagoya University (LL.B.); Legal Training and Research Institute of the Supreme Court of Japan; University College, London (Diploma in Shipping Law, 1989). With, Clyde & Co., London, 1989. *LANGUAGES:* Japanese and English.

ASSOCIATES

TAMAMI MURATA, born 1960; admitted, 1988, Japan. *Education:* Keio University (LL.B.); Legal Training and Research Institute of the Supreme Court of Japan. *LANGUAGES:* Japanese and English.

MOTOKO MISUMI, born 1963; admitted, 1992, Japan. *Education:* Keio University (LL.B.); Legal and Research Institute of the Supreme Court of Japan. *LANGUAGES:* Japanese and English.

SHINBASHI INTERNATIONAL LAW OFFICE

MISU BLDG., NO. 1, 8TH FLOOR
34-7, NISHI-SHINBASHI 2-CHOME, MINATO-KU
TOKYO 105, JAPAN
Telephone: 03-3438-0303
Fax: 03-3433-8380; 03-5472-6210

Corporate and Commercial, Investment and Financing, Litigation, Trademark Registration and Tax.

FIRM PROFILE: Shinbashi International Law Office has a diversified general and international practice that includes handling of corporate, commercial, investment, financing, litigation, trademark and copyright matters. Among our clients, we work closely with a broad spectrum of foreign companies doing business with or investing in Japan. In turn, we also provide counsel to Japanese companies in their domestic and international dealings.

MEMBERS OF FIRM

TAKESHI KIKUCHI, born 1931; admitted, 1960, Japan. *Education:* Tokyo Metropolitan University (LL.B., 1955); The Legal Training and Research Institute, Supreme Court of Japan (1964-1966); U.C.L.A. (Copyright and U.S. Law, 1969-1970). Author: "International Transactions," Seirin Shoin, 1973 and Roppou Shuppan-sha; "Practice for Manufacturers on Exclusive Distributorship Agreement," Press-sha, 1968. Associated with Baker Ancel & Hruby, Los Angeles, 1975; Bristows Cooke & Carpmael, London, 1980. Lecturer, Intellectual Property Law, Aoyama Gakuin University, 1974—. *LANGUAGES:* Japanese and English.

YASUHIRO AKITA, born 1939; admitted, 1966, Japan. *Education:* Waseda University (LL.B., 1963); The Legal Training and Research Institute, Supreme Court of Japan (1964-1966); University of Washington (LL.M., 1974). Associated with Shearman & Sterling, New York, 1974-1976. *LANGUAGES:* Japanese and English.

NORIKO HAYASHI, born 1943; admitted, 1968, Japan. *Education:* Tokyo University (LL.B., 1966); The Legal Training and Research Institute, Supreme Court of Japan (1966-1968). *LANGUAGES:* Japanese and English.

ASSOCIATE

KOICHI KANEKO, born 1948; admitted, 1971, Japan (Tokyo Certified Tax Accountants Association). *Education:* Keio University (B.E., 1972). *LANGUAGES:* Japanese and English.

SHINMYO & PARTNERS

Established in 1969

DAIWA BANK TORANOMON BUILDING, 7TH FLOOR
6-21, NISHI-SHIMBASHI 1-CHOME
MINATO-KU

TOKYO, JAPAN
Telephone: 03-3502-2661
Cable Address: "SAPJ"
Telex: 02228481 SAP J
Facsimile: 03-3502-3843

Corporation Law, Commercial Transactions and Contract Law, International Financing and Investments, Ship and Aircraft Financing, Licensing and Joint Ventures, Real Estate and Construction Matters, Trademark and Copyright, Admiralty, Taxation, Entertainment, Immigration, Litigation and Arbitration and General Practice.

FIRM PROFILE: The firm was established in 1969 and offers a full range of legal services. Particularly, the firm is known for its extensive practice in international commercial transactions. It has a worldwide client base. Currently, there are six lawyers and a support staff of seven.

ICHIRO SHINMYO, born Hokkaido, Japan, July 13, 1938; admitted, 1965, Japan. *Education:* Chuo University (1962); Columbia University School of Law (1973). *Member:* First Tokyo Bar Association. *LANGUAGES:* Japanese and English.

AKIHIKO WATANABE, born Okayama, Japan, January 1, 1952; admitted, 1987, Japan. *Education:* Hitotsubashi University (1976); Kyoto University (LL.M., 1984; S.J.D. Candidate, 1990); University of Pennsylvania School of Law (LL.M., 1991). *Member:* First Tokyo Bar Association. *LANGUAGES:* Japanese and English.

YASUMI OCHI, born Osaka, Japan, September 18, 1960; admitted, 1987, Japan. *Education:* Waseda University (1985); Cornell Law School (1992). *Member:* First Tokyo Bar Association. *LANGUAGES:* Japanese and English.

SUSUMU KAMIYA, born Tokyo, Japan, June 27, 1961; admitted, 1990, Japan. *Education:* Waseda University (1985). *Member:* Tokyo Bar Association. *LANGUAGES:* Japanese and English.

SHOJIRO KANNO, born Kanagawa, Japan, June 27, 1958; admitted, 1991, Japan. *Education:* Keio University (1983). Member: First Tokyo Bar Association. *LANGUAGES:* Japanese and English.

SHOWA LAW OFFICE

Established in 1985

TSURUYA HACHIMAN BLDG. 5F
2-4, KOJIMACHI, CHIYODA-KU

TOKYO 102, JAPAN
Telephone: 81-3-5276-2727
Cable Address: EFNYLAW
Fax: 3-5276-2730; 3-5276-2735; 3-5276-2737

MEMBERS OF FIRM

EIICHI FUKUSHIMA, born Tokyo, Japan, 1946; admitted, 1970, Japan. *Education:* Tokyo University (LL.B., 1968); The Legal Training and Research Institute of The Supreme Court of Japan (1970); graduate study, Georgetown University Law Center (M.C.L., 1975). *Member:* Daini Tokyo Bar Association. *LANGUAGES:* Japanese and English.

NOBUTOSHI YAMANOUCHI, born Tokyo, Japan, 1947; admitted, 1972, Japan. *Education:* Tokyo University (LL.B., 1970); The Legal Training and Research Institute of The Supreme Court of Japan (1972); graduate study, The University of Michigan Law School (LL.M., 1975). *Member:* Daini Tokyo Bar Association. *LANGUAGES:* Japanese and English.

MASATOMO SUZUKI, born Shizuoka Prefecture, Japan, 1949; admitted, 1979, Japan. *Education:* Keio University (LL.B., 1973; LL.M., 1977); The Legal Training and Research Institute of the Supreme Court of Japan (1979); graduate study, The University of Pennsylvania Law School (LL.M., 1983). Lecturer, Civil Law, Keio University, 1991—. *Member:* Daini Tokyo Bar Association. *LANGUAGES:* Japanese and English.

SHINYA WATANABE, born Tokyo, Japan, 1949; admitted, 1979, Japan. *Education:* Keio University (B.A., 1973); The Legal Training and Research Institute of the Supreme Court of Japan (1979); graduate study, Cor-

(This Listing Continued)

nell University Law School (LL.M., 1984). *Member:* Daini Tokyo Bar Association. *LANGUAGES:* Japanese and English.

KOICHI INOUE, born Aichi Prefecture, Japan, 1957; admitted, 1984, Japan; 1989, New York. *Education:* Tokyo University (LL.B., 1982); The Legal Training and Research Institute of the Supreme Court of Japan (1984); Cornell University Law School (LL.M., 1988). *Member:* Daini Tokyo Bar Association; American Bar Association. *LANGUAGES:* Japanese and English.

YOSHIYUKI MIYASHITA, born Fukushima Prefecture, Japan, 1958; admitted, 1984, Japan; 1991, New York. *Education:* Tohoku University (LL.B., 1982); The Legal Training and Research Institute of the Supreme Court of Japan (1984); Cornell University Law School (LL.M., 1990). Author: "International Protection of Computer Software," 11 Computer/L.J. 1, 41, 1991. *Member:* Daini Tokyo Bar Association; American Bar Association; New York State Bar Association. *LANGUAGES:* Japanese and English.

KOSEI WATANABE, born Tokyo, Japan, 1957; admitted, 1984, Japan; 1990, New York. *Education:* Tokyo University (LL.B., 1982); The Legal Training and Research Institute of the Supreme Court of Japan (1984); graduate study, Harvard Law School (LL.M., 1989). *Member:* Daini Tokyo Bar Association; American Bar Association; New York State Bar Association; International Bar Association; Inter-Pacific Bar Association. *LANGUAGES:* Japanese and English.

ASSOCIATES

KAZUO KURASAWA, born Nagano Prefecture, Japan, 1958; admitted, 1988, Japan. *Education:* Tokyo University (LL.B., 1981); graduate study, Georgetown University Law Center (LL.M., 1992); The Legal Training and Research Institute of the Supreme Court of Japan (1988). *Member:* Daini Tokyo Bar Association. *LANGUAGES:* Japanese and English.

MICHIRU TAKAHASHI, born Tokyo, Japan, 1961; admitted, 1989, Japan. *Education:* Kyoto University (LL.B., 1985); The Legal Training and Research Institute of the Supreme Cour t of Japan (1989); graduate study, Cornell University Law School (LL.M., 1993). *Member:* Daini Tokyo Bar Association. *LANGUAGES:* Japanese and English.

YOSHIMICHI MAKIYAMA, born Saga Prefecture, Japan, 1958; admitted, 1990, Japan. *Education:* Tokyo University (LL.B., 1984); The Legal Training and Research Institute of the Supreme Court of Japan (1990). *Member:* Daini Tokyo Bar Association. *LANGUAGES:* Japanese and English.

IWAO HOSOKAI, born Niigata Prefecture, Japan, 1958; admitted, 1992, Japan. *Education:* Keio University (LL.B., 1981); The Legal Training and Research Institute of the Supreme Court of Japan (1992). *Member:* Daini Tokyo Bar Association. *LANGUAGES:* Japanese and English.

SIDLEY & AUSTIN

A Partnership including Professional Corporations
(John R. Box Gaikokuho-Jimu-Bengoshi)

Established in 1866

TAISHO SEIMEI HIBIYA BUILDING
7TH FLOOR, 9-1 YURAKUCHO, 1 CHOME
CHIYODA-KU

100 TOKYO, JAPAN
Telephone: 011-81-3-3218-5900
Facsimile: 011-81-3-3218-5922

Chicago, Illinois Office: One First National Plaza 60603. Telephone: 312-853-7000. Telecopier: 312-853-7036.

Los Angeles, California Office: 555 W. 5th Street, 40th Floor. 90013-1010. Telephone: 213-896-6000. Telecopier: 213-896-6600.

Washington, D.C. Office: 1722 Eye Street, N.W. 20006. Telephone: 202-736-8000. Telecopier: 202-736-8711.

New York, N.Y. Office: 875 Third Avenue 10022. Telephone: 212-906-2000. Telecopier: 212-906-2021.

London, England Office: Broadwalk House, 5 Appold Street, EC2A 2AA. Telephone: 011-44-71-621-1616. Telecopier: 011-44-71-626-7937.

Singapore Office: 36 Robinson Road, #18-01 City House, Singapore 0106. Telephone: 011-65-224-5000. Telecopier: 011-65-224-0530.

General Practice.
(This Listing Continued)

SIDLEY & AUSTIN, *Tokyo—Continued*

RESIDENT PARTNER

JOHN R. BOX, born East St. Louis, Illinois, September 22, 1956; admitted, 1981, Illinois; licensed to practice law in Japan (as a Gaikok uho-Jimu-Bengoshi). *Education:* University of Illinois (B.S., with highest honors, 1978); University of California-Berkeley (J.D., 1981). C.P.A., Illinois, 1978. *Member:* Chicago and American (Member, Sections on: Business Law; International Law and Practice) Bar Associations. **PRACTICE AREAS:** Corporate and Securities Law; Capital Markets.

(For Biographical Data of all Personnel, see Professional Biographies at Chicago, Illinois).

SIMPSON THACHER & BARTLETT

A Partnership which includes Professional Corporations

David Sneider Gaikokuho Jimu Bengoshi Jimusho

ARK MORI BUILDING, 29TH FLOOR
12-32, AKASAKA 1-CHOME, MINATO-KU
TOKYO 107, JAPAN
Telephone: 81-3-5562-8601
Telecopier: 81-3-5562-8606
ESL 62765846

New York, NY Office: 425 Lexington Avenue, 10017-3954. Telephone: 212-455-2000. Telecopier: 212-455-2502. ESL 62928462.

Columbus, Ohio Office: One Riverside Plaza, 43215. Telephone: 614-461-7799. Telecopier: 614-461-0040.

London Office: 100 New Bridge Street, London EC4V 6JE, England. Telephone: 0171 246 8000. Telecopier: 0171 329 3883.

Hong Kong Office: Asia Pacific Finance Tower - 32nd Floor, 3 Garden Road, Central, Hong Kong. Telephone: 852-2514-7600. Telecopier: 852-2869-7694.

Firm engaged in American and International Practice in Tokyo as David Sneider Gaikokuho Jimu Bengoshi Jimusho and not authorized to appear before the Japanese Courts or otherwise to act as Bengoshi.

PARTNER

DAVID A. SNEIDER, born Tokyo, Japan, July 25, 1957; admitted, 1985, New York; 1994, Japan as a Gaikokuho Jimu Bengoshi. *Education:* Yale University (B.A., summa cum laude, 1979); Tokyo University, Tokyo, Japan; Harvard University (J.D., cum laude, 1984). Phi Beta Kappa. *Member:* New York State and American Bar Associations; Inter-Pacific Bar Association. *LANGUAGES:* Japanese.

RESIDENT ASSOCIATES

Michael S. Bennett
(Not admitted in Japan)

Jay M. Ptashek
(Not admitted in Japan)

SKADDEN, ARPS, SLATE, MEAGHER & FLOM

(Zaloom Gaikokuho-Jimu-Bengoshi Jimusho)

12TH FLOOR, THE FUKOKU SEIMEI BUILDING
2-2-2, UCHISAIWAICHO, CHIYODA-KU
TOKYO 100, JAPAN
Telephone: 011-81-3-3595-3850
Fax: 011-81-3-3504-2780

New York, New York Office: 919 Third Avenue, 10022. Telephone: 212-735-3000. Fax: 212-735-2000; 212-735-2001. Telex: 645899 Skarslaw.

Boston, Massachusetts Office: One Beacon Street, 02108. Telephone: 617-573-4800. Fax: 617-573-4822.

Washington, D.C. Office: 1440 New York Avenue, N.W., 20005. Telephone: 202-371-7000. Fax: 202-393-5760.

Wilmington, Delaware Office: One Rodney Square, 19899. Telephone: 302-651-3000. Fax: 302-651-3001.

Los Angeles, California Office: 300 South Grand Avenue, 90071. Telephone: 213-687-5000. Fax: 213-687-5600.

Chicago, Illinois Office: 333 West Wacker Drive, 60606. Telephone: 312-407-0700. Fax: 312-407-0411.

San Francisco, California Office: Four Embarcadero Center, 94111. Telephone: 415-984-6400. Fax: 415-984-2698.

(This Listing Continued)

Houston, Texas Office: 1600 Smith Street, Suite 4460, 77002. Telephone: 713-655-5100. Fax: 713-655-5181.

Newark, New Jersey Office: One Riverfront Plaza, 07102. Telephone: 201-596-4440. Fax: 201-596-4444.

London, England Office: 25 Bucklersbury EC4N 8DA. Telephone: 011-44-71-248-9929. Fax: 011-44-71-489-8533.

Hong Kong Office: 30/F Peregrine Tower, Lippo Centre, 89 Queensway, Central. Telephone: 011-852-820-0700. Fax: 011-852-820-0727.

Sydney, New South Wales, Australia Office: Level 26-State Bank Centre, 52 Martin Place, 2000. Telephone: 011-61-2-224-6000. Fax: 011-61-2-224-6044.

Toronto, Ontario Office: Suite 1820, North Tower, P.O. Box 189, Royal Bank Plaza, M5J 2J4. Telephone: 416-777-4700. Fax: 416-777-4747.

Paris, France Office: 105 rue du Faubourg Saint-Honoré, 75008. Telephone: 011-33-1-40-75-44-44. Fax: 011-33-1-49-53-09-99.

Brussels, Belgium Office: 523 avenue Louise, Box 30, 1050. Telephone: 011-32-2-648-7666. Fax: 011-32-2-640-3032.

Frankfurt, Germany Office: MesseTurm, 27th Floor, 60308. Telephone: 011-49-69-9757-3000. Fax: 011-49-69-9757-3050.

Beijing, China Office: 1605 Capital Mansion Tower, No. 6 Xin Yuan Nan Road, Chao Yang District, 100004. Telephone: 011-86-1-466-8800. Fax: 011-86-1-466-8822.

Budapest, Hungary Office: Mahart Building, H-1052 Apáczai Csere János u.11, Vl.em. Telephone: 011-36-1-266-2145. Fax: 011-36-1-266-4033.

Prague, Czech Republic Office: Revolucni 16, 110 00. Telephone: 011-42-2-231-75-18. Fax: 011-42-2-231-47-33.

Moscow, Russia Office: Pleteshkovsky Pereulok 1, 107005. Telephone: 011-7-501-940-2304. Fax: 011-7-501-940-2511.

Firm engaged in general American and International law practice, but not authorized to appear before Japanese courts or to act as Bengoshi.

PARTNER

E. ANTHONY ZALOOM, born Chicago, Ill., 1943; admitted, 1970, California; 1983, New York; Admitted to Japan as a Gaikokuho Jimu Bengoshi, 1987 (Not admitted in Japan). *Education:* Princeton University (A.B., summa cum laude, 1966); Harvard Law School (J.D., 1969).

(For Biographical data on other Personnel, see New York, New York Professional Biographies).

SLAUGHTER AND MAY

Grindrod Keeler Gaikokuho Jimubengoshi Jimusho

MITSUI ASAHI BUILDING
1-1 KANDA SUDACHO, CHIYODA-KU
TOKYO 101, JAPAN
Telephone: (3) 3258 5700
Fax: (3) 3258 5708
Telex: 2227208

London, England Office: 35 Basinghall Street, EC2V 5DB. Telephone: (0171) 600 1200. Telex: 883486; 888926. Fax: (0171) 726 0038; (0171) 600 0289; (0171) 600 1455 (G-4).

Paris, France Office: 112 Avenue Kléber, 75116. Telephone: (1) 44.05.60.00. Telex: 642514. Fax: (1) 44.05.60.60; (1) 44 05 60 99 (G-4).

Brussels, Belgium Office: Rue D'Arlon 69/71, 1040. Telephone: (2) 230 5631. Fax: (2) 230 7699.

Frankfurt am Main, Germany Office: Westend-Carree Grüneburgweg 16, D-60322 Frankfurt am Main. Telephone: (69) 9551370. Fax: (69) 5964126.

Hong Kong Office: 27th Floor, Two Exchange Square. Telephone: (852) 521 0551. Telex: HX 86230. Fax: (852) 845 2125; (852) 845 9079.

New York, New York Office: 126 East 56th Street, 10022-3613. Telephone: (212) 888-1112. Fax: (212) 888-1170; (212) 832-2021; (212) 832 0075 (G-4).

Firm engaged in International, Corporate, Commercial, Banking and Securities practice under English law and Hong Kong law, but not authorized to appear before Japanese Courts or Administrative Agencies or to act as Japanese lawyers.

RESIDENT PARTNERS

P.A.S. Grindrod; M.S. Keeler.

SUGHRUE, MION, ZINN, MACPEAK & SEAS

A Partnership including Professional Corporations

Established in 1988

TOEI NISHI SHIMBASHI BUILDING 4F
13-5 NISHI SHIMBASHI 1-CHOME
MINATO-KU

TOKYO 105, JAPAN
Telephone: (03) 3 503-3760
Facsimile: (03) 3 503-3756

Washington, D.C. Office: Suite 800, 2100 Pennsylvania Avenue, NW. Telephone: 202-293-7060. Telex: 6491103. Facsimile: 202-293-7860.

Patent, Trademark, Copyright, Unfair Competition Law. Practice before the Federal Courts and Administrative Agencies. Antitrust, International Trade Regulation, International Patent and Trademark Law.

MEMBERS OF FIRM

JOHN R. INGE, born Cumberland, Maryland, September 17, 1946; admitted, 1974, Massachusetts; 1988, District of Columbia; registered to practice before U.S. Patent and Trademark Office (Not admitted in Japan). *Education:* Carnegie-Mellon University (B.S., with honors, 1968); Suffolk University (J.D., 1974). Eta Kappa Nu. Lecturer, "Basic U.S. Patent Practice," Japan, 1979-1988. *Member:* The District of Columbia Bar; Massachusetts and American Bar Associations; Licensing Executive Society; Foreign Lawyers Association of Japan; International Trade Commission Trial Lawyers Association. **PRACTICE AREAS:** Intellectual Property Law.

(For complete biographical data on all personnel, see Professional Biographies at Washington, D.C.)

SULLIVAN & CROMWELL

(Gaikokuho Jimu Bengoshi Office of Robert G. DeLaMater)

TOKIO KAIJO BUILDING SHINKAN
2-1, MARUNOUCHI, 1-CHOME CHIYODA-KU

TOKYO 100, JAPAN
Telephone: (011)(813)3213-6140
Telecopier: (011)(813)3213-6470

New York City Offices: 125 Broad Street, 10004-2498; Midtown Office: 250 Park Avenue, 10177-0021. Telephone: 212-558-4000. Telex: 62694 (International); 12-7816 (Domestic). Cable Address: "Ladycourt, New York". Telecopier: 125 Broad Street 212-558-3588; 250 Park Avenue 212-558-3792.
Washington, D.C. Office: 1701 Pennsylvania Avenue, N.W., 20006-5805. Telephone:202-956-7500. Telex: 89625. Telecopier: 202-293-6330.
Los Angeles, California Office: 444 South Flower Street, 90071-2901. Telephone: 213-955-8000. Telecopier: 213-683-0457.
Paris Office: 8, Place Vendôme, Paris 75001, France. Telephone: (011)(331)4450-6000. Telex: 240654. Telecopier: (011)(331)4450-6060.
London Office: St. Olave's House, 9a Ironmonger Lane, London EC2V 8EY, England. Telephone: (011)(44171)710-6500. Telecopier: (011)(44171)710-6565.
Melbourne, Australia Office: 101 Collins Street, Melbourne, Victoria 3000. Telephone: (011)(613)654-1500. Telecopier: (011)(613)654-2422.
Hong Kong Office: 28th Floor, Nine Queen's Road, Central, Hong Kong. Telephone: (011)(852)826-8688. Telecopier: (011)(852)522-2280.

Robert G. DeLaMater is a gaikokuho jimu bengoshi with primary qualification in the law of the State of New York and designation in the laws of the other States of the United States except Louisiana.

PARTNER IN TOKYO

ROBERT G. DELAMATER, born Morgantown, WV., 1959; admitted, 1986, New York (Not admitted in Japan). *Education:* Harvard (A.B., 1981); Columbia (J.D., 1984).

SPECIAL COUNSEL IN TOKYO

OSAMU WATANABE, born New York, NY., 1960; admitted, 1988, New York (Not admitted in Japan). *Education:* Antioch (B.A., 1982); Yale (J.D., 1985).

(This Listing Continued)

ASSOCIATE IN TOKYO

TANEKI ONO, born Hyogo, Japan, 1956; admitted, 1987, New York (Not admitted in Japan). *Education:* Tokyo University (LL.B., 1980); Cornell University (LL.M., 1985).

(For Biographical Data on all Partners and Associates of Sullivan & Cromwell, see Professional Biographies at New York, N.Y.).

SUYAMA LAW OFFICE

Established in 1985

631 NEW KOKUSAI BUILDING
4-1, MARUNOUCHI 3-CHOME, CHIYODA-KU

TOKYO 100, JAPAN
Telephone: (03) 3215-1271
Fax: (03) 3215-1273

International Practice in Banking, Commercial and Corporate Law.

SHINICHI SUYAMA, born Tokyo, Japan, February 2, 1949; admitted, 1978, Japan. *Education:* Hitotsubashi University (LL.B., 1973); Columbia University (LL.M., 1981). *Member:* First Tokyo Bar Association; International Bar Association; The Law Association for Asia and the Pacific; Inter-Pacific Bar Association. **LANGUAGES:** Japanese and English.

SUZUYE & SUZUYE

UBE BUILDING
3-7-2 KASUMIGASEKI
CHIYODA-KU

TOKYO 100, JAPAN
Telephone: 03-3502-3181
Cable Address: "Suzuyepat Tokyo"
Telex: 2223648
Facsimile: 03-3508-2140

Patent, Design, Trademark and Copyright Law. Prosecution.

SENIOR PARTNERS OF FIRM

TAKEHIKO SUZUYE, born Tokyo, Japan, March 30, 1928; admitted as Patent Attorney, 1949, Japan. *Education:* Tohoku University (B.E., Telecommunication Engineering, 1953); Nihon University (LL.B., 1957). Author: "The Patent Law," Japan, 1973; "Patent Opposition System in Japan," APLA Quarterly Journal, Vol. IV, 1976. Co-Author: "Industrial Designs & Overseas Design Laws," 1980; "A Study of Patent Infringement Cases," (Japanese) Nikko Forum, Vol. 2, No. 10, 1981; "Case Review-Industrial Property Laws," 1977. Professorial Lecturer, Patent Laws, Tohoku University, 1964-1979; Industrial Property Law, Tokai University, 1975. Awarded State Yellow Ribbon Medal, 1983. Director, 1966-1979 and Chairman, 1980—, The Suzuye Institute of International Industrial Property Rights. Presiding Examiner, Japan General Merchandise Center Examining Board under Export Designs Law, 1972—. Interim Member, Examining Section, 1970, Member, Examining Section, 1977 and Judgement Section, 1978, Qualification Examining Commission for Patent Attorneys. President, Japanese Patent Attorneys Association, 1987. *Member:* Japanese Patent Attorneys Association (Member, Journal Committee, 1954; Council Member, 1958; Chairman, Patent Work Study Committee, 1967; Member, Industrial Property Right System Special Committee, 1968; Vice President, 1969; Chairman, Internal Regulations Committee, 1972; Member: Patent Attorneys System Committee, 1977; Training Institute Managing Committee, 1978-1979; Executive Members System Committee, 1980; Executive Board System Special Committee, 1981; Deputy Chairman, Industrial Property System Counterplan Committee, 1983; Chairman, Planning Committee, 1984; Chairman, Association's New Building Special Committee, 1985; Member, Association's New Building Special Committee, 1986; Executive Board System Special Committee, 1988; Patent Attorneys Law Revision Special Committee, 1989; Council Member, 1990; Member, Council Member Activation Study Committee, 1990; Patent Attorneys Law Revision Special Committee, 1990; Chairman, Board of Council Members, 1991). Director, Patent Attorneys Cooperative Association, 1975-1977; Executive Members Special Committee, 1980, Patent Attorneys Political Union Treasury, 1976-1977. Director, The Invention Association, 1987; Member: Patent and Trademark Institute of Canada (Non-resident Associate); Chartered Institute of Patent Agents (U.K., Foreign Member); United States Trademark Association (Foreign Associate Member); AIPPI (Council Member, Japanese Group); Asian Patent Attorneys Association; FICPI, 1982—.

(This Listing Continued)

SUZUYE & SUZUYE, Tokyo—Continued

SADAO MURAMATSU, born Tokyo, Japan, April 13, 1927; admitted as Patent Attorney, 1979, Japan. *Education:* Tokyo University (B.E., Electrical Engineering, 1951). Professorial Lecturer, Patent Law, Tokyo University, 1977-1987. Author: "Matters Indispensable to The Construction of Invention" (Japanese), Nikko Forum, Vol. 3, No. 7, 1982; "Official Guidelines on Patent Applications for Computer-Applied Technology," Japan Patents & Trademarks, 1983. Experience at Japanese Patent Office (Examiner, 1956-1963; Trial Examiner, Board of Trials, 1963-1966; Director, Examining Division, 1966-1969; Trial Examiner-in-Chief, 1972-1975; Director-General, 5th Examination Dept., 1976-1979). Interim Member, 1966, Member, 1974-1977, Qualification Examining Commission for Patent Attorneys. Director, Examining Section, Qualification Examining Commission for Patent Attorneys, 1987—. *Member:* Japanese Patent Attorneys Association (Member, Patent Committee, 1981); AIPPI (Japanese Group); Asian Patent Attorneys Association.

ATSUSHI TSUBOI, born Yokohama, Japan, March 7, 1931; admitted as Patent Attorney, 1965, Japan. *Education:* Tokyo Suisan University (B.S., 1961). Author: "Identification of Allegedly Infringing Object," (Japanese), Nikko Forum, Vol. 3, No. 9, 1982. *Member:* Japanese Patent Attorneys Association (Member, Committees on: Material Equipment, 1976; Examining Standard Study, 1968; Design, 1975; Deputy Chairman, Examining Standard Study Committee, 1972; Chairman, Internal Regulations Revision Preparation Committee, 1979; Council Member, 1977-1978; Member, Patent System Working Deliberation Committee, 1981; Internal Regulations Committee, 1982; Foreign Lawyers Countermeasure Committee, 1984).

YOSHIRO HASHIMOTO, born Gifu-ken, Japan, May 14, 1933; admitted, as Patent Attorney, 1985, Japan. *Education:* Nagoya University (B.E., Applied Chemistry, 1956). Author: "Introduction to the French Patent System," (Japanese), J.I.I.I., 1972; "Commentary on the Patent Cooperation Treaty," (Japanese) under Preface of Dr. A. Bogsch, Director General of WIPO, J.I.I.I., 1978; "Patent Related Treaties," (Japanese), Yuhikaku, 1985; "Patent Law," (Japanese), Yuhikaku, 1986. Co-Author: "The Patent Law Commented," (Japanese), Two Volumes, Seirin Shoin Shinsha, 1983. Contributor: "About the PCT," (Essays Contributed to the Former Judge Hara); "The Patent Cooperation Treaty and National Laws," (Essays Contributed in Memory of Late Professor Toyosaki). Co-Translator: Japanese edition of "Guide to the Application of the Paris Convention for the Protection of Industrial Property," by Prof. G.H.C. Bodenhausen, Former Director of BIRPI, Japanese Group of AIPPI, 1968. Professorial Lecturer, Patent Law, Nagoya University, 1979-1982; Industrial Property Laws, Chuo University, 1983—. Experience at Japanese Patent Office (Examiner, 1960-1975; Trial Examiner, Board of Trials, 1967-1971; Director, Examining Division, 1971-1974; Trial Examiner-in-Chief, 1975-1985; Director, Office of Examining Standards, 2nd Examining Department, 1976-1978; Director, 2nd Division, Board of Trials, 1982-1985; Director General, Industrial Property Training Institute, 1983-1985). Consultant Seconded for Preparation and Drafting of Patent Cooperation Treaty, BIRPI, 1968-1969. Member, Japanese Delegation to Washington Diplomatic Conference on Patent Cooperation Treaty, 1970. Alternate Delegate to Diplomatic Geneva Conference on Revision of Paris Convention, 1984. Member, PCT Study Mission to the U.S. and Europe, 1976. Participant in PCT-, ICIREPAT. Interim Member, 1971-1978, 1981-1984 and Member, 1985, Qualification Examining Commission for Patent Attorneys. *Member:* Japanese Patent Attorneys Association; Chartered Institute of Patent Agents (UK, Foreign Member); AIPPI (Japanese Group); FICPI; Asian Patent Attorneys Association.

YOSHIO ISHIKAWA, born Hiroshima-ken, Japan, October 30, 1927; admitted as Patent Attorney, 1982, Japan. *Education:* Senshu University (LL.B.), 1956). Contributing Author: "Industrial Property Right Manual," Nikkan Kogyo Shimbunsha, May 1965; "Dictionary of Industrial Property Terminology," Nihon Kogyo Shimbunsha, December 1968; "Article by Article Commentary on Industrial Property Laws - Patent Office's Edition," Patent Association, December 1970. Co-Author: "New Detailed Commentary on Patent Law," Nihon Hatsumei Shimbunsha, 1970; "Challenge to Patents," Patent Association, April 1973. Editorial Supervisor: "Basic Knowledge of Formalities of Application Procedure" and "Practice on Formalities of Application Procedure," both, Patent Association, December 1981; "Use of Design Registration System and Several Points at Issue," Nikko Forum, Vol. 4, No. 7, 1983; Editor, "A Story of Service Marks," Toyo Hoki Shuppan, 1985. Experience at Japanese Patent Office (Examiner, Trademark Division, 1971-1973; Director, Trademark Division, 1973-1978; Director, Office of Merchandise Examining Standards, 1974 and

(This Listing Continued)

Trademark Examining Standards, 1974-1978; Trial Examiner, Board of Trials, 1978; Trial Examiner-in-Chief, 1978-1979; Director, Office of Litigation, 1980, 20th Division, 1981). Interim Member, 1973-1978 and Executive Secretary, 1978, National Council of Pharmacy. Interim Member, Qualification Examining Commission for Patent Attorneys, 1972-1981. *Member:* Japanese Patent Attorneys Association; AIPPI (Council Member, Japanese Group).

YOSHIO HANAWA, born Tokyo, Japan, March 7, 1927; admitted as Patent Attorney, 1969, Japan. *Education:* Tokyo Institute of Technology (B.E., Organic Chemistry, 1950). Author: "Mooted Points in Application of Provisions for Exception to Loss of Novelty," (Japanese), Nikko Forum, Vol. 3, No. 8, 1982. *Member:* Japanese Patent Attorneys Association (Member, Committees on: Patent System Promotion, 1971; Industrial Property System Special, 1972; Patent, 1973 and 1976; Training, 1978; Training Institute Working, 1978-1980; Patent Attorneys Training Institute, 1981; Patent System Working Deliberation, 1982; Deputy Chairman, Patent Committee, 1983); AIPPI (Japanese Group).

KOHEI SUZUYE, born Tokyo, Japan, October 16, 1907; admitted, as Patent Attorney, 1992, Japan. *Education:* Tokyo University (B.E., Mechanical Engineering, 1931); Tokyo University (LL.B., 1934). Professorial Lecturer, Tokyo University, 1947-1962. Decorated with Grand Cordon of the Merit of the Sacred Treasure, 1985. Division Director, General Affairs Div., Patent Office, 1945-1947; Division Director, Machinery Bureau, Ministry of Commerce & Industry, 1947-1954; Director, Scientific & Technical Administration committee, Prime Minister's Office, 1954-1956; Director, Planning & Adjustment Bureau, Science & Technology Agency, 1956-1961; Administrative Vice-Minister of Science & Technology, 1961-1964; Chief Director, Research Development Corporation of Japan, 1964-1975. *Member:* Civil Aeronautics Council, Ministry of Transportation, 1954; Foreign Investment Council, Ministry of Finance, 1961; Radio Technical Council, Ministry of Postal Services, 1961; Industrial Property Council, Patent Office, 1966; Industrial Science & Technology Council, Ministry of International Trade & Industry, 1973; Science & Technology Council, 1977. Chief Director: Japan Science & Technology Federation, 1973; Remote Sensing Technology Center, 1975; Ability Development Engineering Center, 1976—. Counselor/Consultant: Japan Science & Technology Information Center, 1975—; Research Development Corporation of Japan, 1975; Physics & Chemistry Laboratory, 1975; Nagaoka Technology & Science College, 1978—; Interim Administration Investigation Board, 1981; Science & Technology Agency, 1984—; Power Reactor, Nuclear Fuel Development Corporation, 1984—.

HIDEICHI ARAKI, born Kanagawa-ken, Japan, January 30, 1920; admitted, 1986, Japan. *Education:* Tokyo University (LL.B., 1941). Professor of Law, Akita Keizai University, 1985—. Judge, Maebashi District Court, 1957-1960, Tokyo District Court, 1961-1964, 1969-1974 and Tokyo High Court, 1964-1969, 1976-1985. Presiding Judge, Tokyo High Court, 1969-1974, 1976-1985. Acting Chief Judge, Tokyo High Court, 1976-1985. *Member:* First Tokyo Bar Association.

MITSUAKI HIRANO, born Tokyo, Japan, December 2, 1925; admitted, as Patent Attorney, 1949, Japan. *Education:* Tokyo University (B.E., Architectural Engineering, 1950). Manager, Takamatsu Branch of the Housing Loan Corporation, 1978-1980; Director, Housing Site Department, 1980-1981; Managing Director, Kinoshita Housing Construction Co., Ltd., 1981-1984; Senior Managing Director, Kinoshita Housing Construction Co., Ltd., 1984-1992; Counselor, Kinoshita Housing Construction Co., Ltd., 1992—. License: 1st Class Architect, 1959. *Member:* Japanese Patent Attorneys Association; Architectural Institute of Japan.

PARTNERS

TETSUYA KAZAMA, born Hokkai-Do, Japan, August 2, 1934; admitted, as Patent Attorney, 1991, Japan. *Education:* College of Tokyo Agriculture and Technology (B.E., Textile Machinery, 1963). Experience in Japanese Patent Office (Examiner, Textile Machinery, 1967-1975; Appeal Examiner, Polymer Processing Group, 1976-1978; Dispatched Staff Member, WIPO, Geneva, 1978-1980; Appeal Examiner, Chemical Engineering Group, 1981; Counsellor, International Affairs, General Administration Div., 1981-1982; Director, Civil Engineering Div., 1983; Director, Construction Div., 1983-1984; Appeal Examiner-in-Chief, Business Machinery Group, 1984; Principal Director, Heat Machinery Div., 1985; Superintending Director, Industrial Machinery Div., 1986; Superintending Appeal Examiner-in-Chief, Business Machinery Group, 1987; Superintending Appeal Examiner-in-Chief, General Machinery Group, 1989-1991). *Member:* Japanese Patent Attorneys Association; AIPPI (Japanese Group).

KAZUTOSHI NAKAMURA, born Kanagawa-ken, Japan, September 25, 1937; admitted, as Patent Attorney, 1989, Japan. *Education:* Nihon

(This Listing Continued)

University (B.E., Electrical Engineering, 1962). Experience at Japanese Patent Office (Examiner, 1962-1980; Trial Examiner, Board of Trials, 1980-1987; Trial Examiner-in-Chief, 1987-1989). *Member:* Japanese Patent Attorneys Association.

SHOJI KAWAI, born Tokyo, Japan, February 6, 1936; admitted as Patent Attorney, 1967, Japan. *Education:* Chuo University (LL.B., 1960). Author: "Inventive Step," (Japanese), Nikko Forum, Vol. 3, No. 4, 1982. *Member:* Japanese Patent Attorneys Association (Member, Committees on: Patent Attorney System's 70th Anniversary Commemorative Project Execution, 1974; Trademarks, 1975; Patent, 1979; Planning, 1980; Patent, 1981; Deputy Chairman, Patent System Working Deliberation Committee, 1978; Council Member, 1982).

TOSHIMI KOIDE, born Nagano-ken, Japan, September 11, 1945; admitted as Patent Attorney, 1975, Japan. *Education:* Chuo University (LL.B., 1969); Georgetown University, Washington D.C., The School of Languages and Linguistics, Division of English (1979); Tokyo Denki University (A.D., Electrical Engineering, 1986). Author: "Patent and Trademark Infringements in Export and Import," (Japanese), Nikko Forum, Vol. 3, No. 2, 1982. *Member:* Japanese Patent Attorneys Association (Member, 1981, 1983; Deputy Chairman, Trademark Committee, 1985); Asian Patent Attorneys Association; AIPPI (Japanese Group); International Trademark Association (Foreign Associate Member).

MAKOTO NAKAMURA, born Yokohama, Japan, January 23, 1949; admitted as Patent Attorney, 1982, Japan. *Education:* Waseda University (B.E., Metal Engineering, 1971; Metal Engineering, 1973). Author: "The Protection of Computer Software," (Japanese), Nikko Forum, Vol. 4, Nos. 8 and 9, 1983; "A Discussion: Trial Decision Cancellation Case on Light Oil Composition Having Fluidity at Low Temperature," Tokyo Kanri, Vol. 42, No. 10, 1992. *Member:* Japanese Patent Attorneys Association.

AKIRA KOHNO, born Shimane-ken, Japan, April 6, 1949; admitted, as Patent Attorney, 1984, Japan. *Education:* Osaka University (B.S., Physics, 1972). *Member:* Japanese Patent Attorneys Association.

MASANOBU TAKATORI, born Yamanashi-ken, Japan, April 29, 1949; admitted as Patent Attorney, 1980, Japan. *Education:* Nihon University (LL.B., 1974; Postgraduate Law course, 1976); Tokyo Denki University (B.E., Electronics Engineering, 1986). Professorial Lecturer, Industrial Property, Nihon University, 1981-1983; Author: "Tendency of EEC Intellectual Properties Systems to be unified by the end of 1992," Japan Patent Association, 1990; "Protection of Form of Merchandise," (Japanese), Nikko Forum, Vol. 3, No. 1, 1982; "Ex Parte Industrial Property Litigation and Current Status," Vol. 19, No. 2, Industrial Property News, 1984; "Criteria Now Adopted in Japan, the U.S. and South Korea to Determine the Distinctiveness of Trademarks," (Japanese), Vol. 44, No. 5, Patent, 1991 and (English), No. 68, May, 1991, Suzuye Report; "European Community Unified Design Laws," Vol. 44, No. 6, Patent, 1991. *Member:* Japanese Patent Attorneys Association; Licensing Executives Society (Working Member, Tradesecret Working Group, 1989-1991); Japan Trademark Association (Member, Committee on Foreign Trademarks Systems, 1990—); AIPPI (Japanese Group).

TOSHIO SHIRANE, born Tokyo, Japan, June 7, 1948; admitted, as Patent Attorney, 1987, Japan. *Education:* Meiji University (LL.B., 1972). *Member:* Japanese Patent Attorneys Association.

KATSUMASA FUSEDA, born Tokyo, Japan, May 26, 1926; admitted as Patent Attorney, 1984, Japan. *Education:* Tokyo Higher School of Technology (Electrical, 1944). Technical Official, Ministry of Commerce and Industry, 1946. Official, Agency of Science and Technology, 1956. Examiner, Patent Office, 1977-1980. Trial Examiner, Board of Trials, 1980-1983. *Member:* Japanese Patent Attorneys Association.

KAZUTO HASEGAWA, born Nagano-ken, Japan, February 23, 1924; admitted as Patent Attorney, 1979, Japan. *Education:* Waseda University (B.E., Mechanical Engineering, 1946). Author: "First Users Right," (Japanese), Nikko Forum, Vol. 4, No. 10, 1983. *Member:* Japanese Patent Attorneys Association (Member, Patent Attorneys Business Countermeasure Committee, 1985).

HIRONOBU SAITO, born Tokyo, Japan, October 13, 1936; admitted, as Patent Attorney, 1992, Japan. *Education:* Tokyo Agriculture and Technology University (B.E., Industrial Chemistry, 1966). Experience at Japanese Patent Office (Examiner, 1966-1990; Trial Examiner, Board of Trials, 1990-1992; Organic and Inorganic Chemistry, Metal Technology, and Electric Machinery and apparatus). *Member:* Japanese Patent Attorneys Association.

(This Listing Continued)

HIROSHI TAKAYAMA, born Hokkaido, Japan, June 15, 1956; admitted, as Patent Attorney, 1990, Japan. *Education:* Hokkaido University (B.E., Metalurgy, 1979). *Member:* Japanese Patent Attorneys Association.

TOSHIRO NAKAMURA, born Nagano-ken, Japan, July 25, 1960; admitted, as Patent Attorney, 1991, Japan. *Education:* Keio Gijuku University (LL.B., 1984). *Member:* Japanese Patent Attorneys Association.

KOJI MIZUNO, born Aichi-ken, Japan, January 22, 1963; admitted, as Patent Attorney, 1988, Japan. *Education:* Aoyama Gakuin University (B.E. Physics, 1987). *Member:* Japanese Patent Attorneys Association.

MASAKO NISHIMURA, born Tokyo, Japan, January 19, 1957; admitted, as Patent Attorney, 1992, Japan. *Education:* Tsuda College (B.A., 1979; M.A., International and Cultural Studies, 1981); Tokyo Metropolitan University (LL.B., 1984). *Member:* Japanese Patent Attorneys Association.

ATSUKO MATSUMI, born Shizuoka-ken, Japan, December 15, 1955; admitted, as Patent Attorney, 1986, Japan. *Education:* Meiji University (LL.B., 1978). *Member:* Japanese Patent Attorneys Association.

TARO YAGUCHI, born Kobe, Japan, September 4, 1967; admitted, as Patent Attorney, 1993, Japan. *Education:* Science University of Tokyo (B.E., Mechanical Engineering, 1990). *Member:* Japanese Patent Attorneys Association.

COUNSEL

TAKAYOSHI SAGAE, born Yamagata-ken, Japan, January 25, 1945; admitted, 1970, Japan. *Education:* Tokyo University (LL.B., 1968); Institute of Legal Search and Education, Supreme Court, 1969-1970. Author: "Attachment of Intangible Property Right," (Japanese), Patent, Vol. 34, No. 3, 1981. Co-Author: "You and Law," 1976, Japan, Tokyo Bar Association. Member, Industrial Property Committee, Japan Federation of Bar Associations, 1981. *Member:* Tokyo Bar Association (Assisting Clerk, Executive Board, 1976-1977; Member, Judicial Matter Deliberation Committee, 1978-1980; Council Member, 1982).

Languages: Japanese, English and German

TAKEDA LAW & PATENT OFFICE

THE IMPERIAL TOWER
1-1-1, UCHISAIWAI-CHO, CHIYODA-KU

TOKYO 100, JAPAN
Telephone: 03-3508-8050
Fax: 81-3-3591-1149
Telex: 2228475 MTAKED J
Cable Address: "Takelawpat"

Industrial Property, Joint Venture and Transfer of Technology, Antitrust, Domestic, Foreign Trademark and Design and Patent Law.

MEMBERS OF FIRM

MASAHIKO TAKEDA, born 1927; admitted, 1964, Japan and as Patent Attorney. *Education:* Tokyo University (LL.B., 1953); University of Michigan, Law School (M.C.L., 1961). Judge of Kobe and Fukuoka District Courts, 1956-1964. Chairman of Patents, Trademarks and Copyrights Committee of International Bar Association, 1971-1973. Executive President of AIPPI, Director of Japanese Branch of International Law Association. Registered Arbitrator, Japan Commercial Arbitration Association. With, Nakamura, Yamamoto, Takeda & Partners, 1964-1982. *Member:* Second Tokyo Bar Association; Japanese Patent Attorneys Association; American Intellectual Property Law Association; American Bar Association. *LANGUAGES:* Japanese and English.

MASAJI TAKIGUCHI, born 1935; admitted, as Patent Attorney. Examiner and Judge in the Patent Office, 1963-1983. Investigator, Technical Fields at the Tokyo District Court. *LANGUAGES:* Japanese and English.

KOUICHI NAKAZATO, born 1948; admitted, 1971 as Patent Attorney. *Member:* AIPPI; APAA. *LANGUAGES:* Japanese and English.

TANAKA & TAKAHASHI

NEW AOYAMA BUILDING W-1352
1-1, MINAMI AOYAMA 1-CHOME, MINATO-KU
TOKYO 107, JAPAN
Telephone: (81) 3-3475-1631
Telecopier: (81) 3-3403-8820; (81) 3-3403-8825
Telex: J26775 Tataniat

General Practice. Corporation Law, Tax, Foreign Investment, Aviation, Banking, Securities, Labor Law and Litigation.

ATTORNEYS

ISAO TAKAHASHI, born Niigata, Japan, 1939; admitted, 1964, Japan. *Education:* Tokyo University (LL.B., 1962); Legal Research and Training Institute of the Supreme Court (1962-1964); The University of Michigan Law School (M.C.L., 1970). *Member:* Second Tokyo Bar Association. *LANGUAGES:* Japanese and English.

AKIKO INOUE, born Yamanashi, Japan, 1943; admitted, 1971, Japan. *Education:* Tokyo University (LL.B., 1969); Legal Research and Training Institute of the Supreme Court (1969-1971); University of Washington School of Law (LL.M., 1975). *Member:* Tokyo Bar Association. *LANGUAGES:* Japanese and English.

NAOKI KINAMI, born Tokyo, Japan, 1948; admitted, 1975, Japan; 1980, New York. *Education:* Tokyo University (LL.B., 1973); Legal Research and Training Institute of the Supreme Court (1973-1975); Georgetown University (M.C.L., 1979). *Member:* Second Tokyo Bar Association. *LANGUAGES:* Japanese and English.

HIROYUKI KANAE, born Hyogo, Japan, 1954; admitted, 1979, Japan; 1988, New York. *Education:* Waseda University (LL.B., 1976); University of Illinois, College of Law (M.C.L., 1987). Legal Research and Training Institute of the Supreme Court (1977-1979). *Member:* Second Tokyo, New York State and American Bar Associations. *LANGUAGES:* Japanese and English.

KEIJI ISAJI, born Gifu, Japan, 1957; admitted, 1981, Japan. *Education:* Tokyo University (LL.B., 1979); Legal Research and Training Institute of the Supreme Court (1979-1981); The University of Michigan Law School (LL.M., 1989). *Member:* Second Tokyo Bar Association. *LANGUAGES:* Japanese and English.

IZURU GOTO, born Aichi, Japan, 1957; admitted, 1986, Japan; 1993, New York. *Education:* Tokyo University (LL.B., 1981); Duke University School of Law (LL.M., 1992). Legal Research and Training Institute of the Supreme Court of Japan, (1984-1986). *Member:* First Tokyo Bar Association. *LANGUAGES:* Japanese and English.

TAKASHI SUGAWARA, born Yamagata, Japan, 1954; admitted, 1988, Japan. *Education:* Tokyo University (B.A., 1979; LL.B., 1983); Legal Research and Training Institute of the Supreme Court (1986-1988); Cornell University Law School (LL.M., 1992). *Member:* Second Tokyo Bar Association. *LANGUAGES:* Japanese, English and French.

ATSUSHI YAMASHITA, born Kumamoto, Japan, 1958; admitted, 1988, Japan. *Education:* Tokyo University (LL.B., 1984); Legal Research and Training Institute of the Supreme Court (1986-1988). *Member:* Second Tokyo Bar Association. *LANGUAGES:* Japanese and English.

MASAYUKI OKAMOTO, born Hyogo, Japan, 1964; admitted, 1990, Japan. *Education:* Tokyo University (LL.B., 1988); Legal Research and Training Institute of the Supreme Court (1988-1990). *Member:* First Tokyo Bar Association. *LANGUAGES:* Japanese and English.

NAOKI WATANABE, born Hokkaido, Japan, 1963; admitted, 1991, Japan. *Education:* Keio University (LL.B., 1986). Legal Research and Training Institute of the Supreme Court (1989-91). *Member:* Second Tokyo Bar Association. *LANGUAGES:* Japanese and English.

DOUGLAS J. BARKER, born Oakland, California, 1961; admitted, 1987, Alaska; 1988, District of Columbia (Not admitted in Japan). *Education:* Stanford University (B.A., 1983); University of Oregon School of Law (J.D., 1986). *Member:* Alaska and American Bar Associations; The District of Columbia Bar.

TMI ASSOCIATES

Established in 1990

SUITE 803, 37 MORI BUILDING
5-1, TORANOMON 3-CHOME, MINATO-KU
TOKYO 105, JAPAN
Telephone: 03-5472-8511
Telecopier: 03-5472-0866

General International and Japanese Law Practice, Corporate Law, International Transactions, Intellectual Property Law, Entertainment Law, Antitrust Law, Civil Litigation, Banking and Finance Law, Securities Law, Mergers and Acquisitions.

MEMBERS OF FIRM

KATSURO TANAKA, admitted, 1970, Japan. *Education:* Chuo University (LL.B., 1968); Legal Training and Research Institute of Supreme Court of Japan; Graduate Study, Columbia University Law School (LL.M., 1979). With McIvor, Kauffman & Christensen, Tokyo, 1970-1971, Takahashi and Tanaka, Tokyo, 1971-1980 and Los Angeles Office of Graham & James, 1979, Nishimura & Sanada, 1981-1990. *LANGUAGES:* Japanese and English.

EIZO MATSUO, admitted, 1975, Japan; 1983, New York. *Education:* Chuo University (LL.B., 1973); Legal Training and Research Institute of Supreme Court of Japan; Graduate Study, New York University School of Law (LL.M., 1983). With: Goto Law Office, Tokyo, 1975-1976; Takahashi and Tanaka, Tokyo, 1976-1982; Graham & James, San Francisco, 1983; Nishimura & Sanada, 1984-1990. *LANGUAGES:* Japanese and English.

TOMOHIRO TOHYAMA, admitted, 1980, Japan. *Education:* Keio University (LL.B., 1973); Legal Training and Research Institute of Supreme Court of Japan, Graduate Study, University of California, Los Angeles, School of Law (LL.M., 1984). With Mason & Sloane, 1984-1985, Pollock, Bloom & Dekom, 1985 and Pryor, Cashman, Sherman & Flynn, 1985, Nishimura & Sanada, 1980-1990. *LANGUAGES:* Japanese and English.

YOSHIYUKI INABA, admitted, 1974, Japan as a Patent Attorney. *Education:* Sophia University (B.S. Mechanical Engineering, 1973); Patent Academy, U.S. Patent and Trademark Office. With Unuma & Associates, Tokyo, 1974-1985, Koda & Androlia, Los Angeles, 1978-1980, Stevens, Davis, Miller & Mosher, Washington, D.C., 1980 and Inaba & Associates, Tokyo, 1985-1990. *LANGUAGES:* Japanese and English.

KUNIO NAMEKATA, admitted, 1979, Japan. *Education:* Tokyo University (LL.B., 1977); Legal Training and Research Institute of Supreme Court of Japan; University of Michigan Law School (LL.M., 1994). With Tokyo Fuji Law Office (Formerly Kugisawa, Sudo & Ozawa), Tokyo, 1979-1991. *LANGUAGES:* Japanese and English.

RYOSUKE ITO, admitted, 1983, Japan; 1988, New York; 1990, California. *Education:* Tokyo University (LL.B., 1980); Legal Training and Research Institute of Supreme Court of Japan; Graduate Study, New York University, School of Law (M.C.J., 1988). With: Nishimura & Sanada, 1983-1987; De Bandt, van Hecke & Lagae, Brussels, Belgium, 1988; Graham & James, San Francisco, 1988-1991. *LANGUAGES:* Japanese and English.

MITSUKO MIYAGAWA, admitted, 1986, Japan; 1994, New York. *Education:* Tokyo University (LL.B., 1984); Legal Training and Research Institute of Supreme Court of Japan; Graduate Study, Harvard Law School (LL.M., 1993). With Nishimura & Sanada, 1986-1990; Proskauer Rose Goetz & Mendelsohn, New York, 1993-1994; Theodore Goddard, London, 1994. *LANGUAGES:* Japanese and English.

OSAMU ISHIHARA, admitted, 1987, Japan. *Education:* Waseda University (LL.B., 1985); Legal Training and Research Institute of Supreme Court of Japan. With Nishimura & Sanada, 1987-1990. *LANGUAGES:* Japanese and English.

SHINJI OHGA, admitted, 1986, Japan as a Patent Attorney. *Education:* Nippon University (B.S., Pharmacy, 1981; Research Course of Pharmacy, 1982). With: Unuma & Associates, Tokyo, 1982-1988; Mori & Company, Tokyo, 1988-1990. *LANGUAGES:* Japanese and English.

SHIGEYUKI MITO, admitted, 1989, Japan. *Education:* Keio University (LL.B., 1982); Undergraduate Study, New Paltz College, University of New York (1986); Undergraduate Study, New York University (1987). With Nishimura & Sanada, 1989-1990. *LANGUAGES:* Japanese and English.

(This Listing Continued)

SEIKO TAKAICHI, admitted, 1989, Japan. *Education:* Tokyo University (LL.B., 1983); Legal Training and Research Institute of Supreme Court of Japan. With Nishimura & Sanada, 1989-1990. *LANGUAGES:* Japanese and English.

NAOMICHI CHIBA, admitted, 1990, Japan. *Education:* Chuo University (LL.B., 1986); Legal Training and Research Institute of Supreme Court of Japan. With Nishimura & Sanada, 1990. *LANGUAGES:* Japanese and English.

YOSHIYASU YAMAGUCHI, admitted, 1991, Japan. *Education:* Tokyo University (LL.B., 1988); Legal Training and Research Institute of Supreme Court of Japan. *LANGUAGES:* Japanese and English.

YUKO KIMIJIMA, admitted, 1992, Japan. *Education:* Keio University (LL.B., 1989); Legal Training and Research Institute of Supreme Court of Japan. Assistant Lecturer, Intellectual Property Law, Keio University. Visiting Scholar, Max-Planck-Institut, Germany, 1993—. *LANGUAGES:* Japanese and English.

HIROYUKI MORISAKI, admitted, 1992, Japan. *Education:* Tokyo University (LL.B., 1989); Legal Training and Research Institute of Supreme Court of Japan. *LANGUAGES:* Japanese and English.

MASAHIKO NAKAMURA, admitted, 1992, Japan. *Education:* Tokyo University (LL.B., 1990); Legal Training and Research Institute of Supreme Court of Japan. *LANGUAGES:* Japanese and English.

YOSHIRO MASUMOTO, admitted, 1993, Japan. *Education:* Tokyo University (LL.B., 1987); Legal Training and Research Institute of Supreme Court of Japan. *LANGUAGES:* Japanese and English.

YUKIHIRO TERAZAWA, admitted, 1993, Japan. *Education:* Keio University (LL.B., 1989); Legal Training and Research Institute of Supreme Court of Japan. *LANGUAGES:* Japanese and English.

KAZUYA SENDA, admitted, 1992, Japan as a Patent Attorney. *Education:* Chuo University (B.S., Industrial Chemistry, 1992). *LANGUAGES:* Japanese and English.

YOSHIFUMI AKAZAWA, admitted, 1994, Japan. *Education:* Keio University (LL.B., 1990); Legal Training and Research Institute of Supreme Court of Japan. *LANGUAGES:* Japanese and English.

SATORU NAGASAKA, admitted, 1994, Japan. *Education:* Tokyo University (LL.B., 1990); Legal Training and Research Institute of Supreme Court of Japan. *LANGUAGES:* Japanese and English.

NOBUHISA HOSAKA, admitted, 1994, Japan as a Patent Attorney. *Education:* Chuo University (LL.B., 1993). *LANGUAGES:* Japanese and English.

JOHN M. KURIYAMA, admitted, 1992, Hawaii (Not admitted in Japan). *Education:* University of Hawaii (B.B.A., 1988); Stanford University (J.D., 1992). *LANGUAGES:* English and Japanese.

WILLIAM E. BARTHELL, admitted, 1993, Wisconsin (Not admitted in Japan). *Education:* University of Wisconsin, Madison, Wisconsin (B.B.A., 1986); University of Hawaii at Manoa (M.A., Asian Studies, 1991); University of Wisconsin (J.D., 1993). *LANGUAGES:* English and Japanese.

QIU FU GING, admitted, 1983, China (Not admitted in Japan). *Education:* Hwa Dong University, China (LL.B., 1981). Visiting Scholar at Yokohama National University, Japan, 1988-1994. With Shanghai Di-A Law Firm, Shanghai, 1983-1986; Shanghai Di-Ryu Law Firm (Shanghai Pouchisan Law Firm), Shanghai, 1986-1988; Shanghai Paiyuran Law Firm, Shanghai, 1988. *LANGUAGES:* Chinese and Japanese.

TOKYO AOYAMA LAW OFFICE

(Associated Office of Baker & McKenzie)

410 AOYAMA BUILDING, 2-3, KITA AOYAMA 1 CHOME
MINATO-KU, TOKYO 107, JAPAN
Telephone: (03) 3403-5281
Intn'l. Dialing: (81-3) 3403-5281
Cable Address: ABOGADO TOKYO
Telex: 28249
Answer Back: ABOGADO J28249
Facsimiles: (81-3) 3470-3152; 3470-3658; 3479-4224; 3479-4386

Postal Address: C.P.O Box 1576, Tokyo, 100-91, Japan

(This Listing Continued)

Associated Offices of Baker & McKenzie in: Almaty, Amsterdam, Bangkok, Barcelona, Beijing, Berlin, Bogotá, Brasília, Brussels, Budapest, Buenos Aires, Cairo, Caracas, Chicago, Dallas, Frankfurt, Geneva, Hanoi, Ho Chi Minh City, Hong Kong, Juárez, Kiev, London, Madrid, Manila, Melbourne, México City, Miami, Milan, Monterrey, Moscow, New York, Palo Alto, Paris, Prague, Rio de Janeiro, Riyadh, Rome, St. Petersburg, San Diego, San Francisco, São Paulo, Singapore, Stockholm, Sydney, Taipei, Tijuana, Toronto, Valencia, Warsaw, Washington, D.C. and Zürich.
Correspondent Law Firm: Hadiputranto, Hadinoto & Partners, Jakarta.

Corporate, Banking, Finance, Real Estate, Foreign Investment, Tax Law, Patent and Trademark, Litigation, General Practice.

MIKAKO FUJIKI, born Taipei, Taiwan, September 20, 1933; admitted, 1959, Japan. *Education:* Department of Law, Tokyo University (B.Jur.); Legal Training and Research Institute. *Member:* First Tokyo Bar Association. *LANGUAGES:* Japanese and English. *PRACTICE AREAS:* Health Care and Hospital Law; Intellectual Property Law; Franchise Law; Computers and Technology Law; Regulatory Law.

MORIHIRO MURATA, born Chiba, Japan, July 20, 1946; admitted, 1988, Japan. *Education:* Keio University (B.A., 1969). Certified Public Accountant, Japan, 1975. Licensed Tax Attorney, Japan, 1988. *Member:* Japan Tax Association; Tokyo Certified Tax Accountants Associations; JICPA. *LANGUAGES:* Japanese and English. *PRACTICE AREAS:* Taxation; Securities and Financial Products.

KIYOSHI ODAKA, born Sawara, Chiba Prefecture, Japan, October 29, 1945; admitted, 1975, Japan. *Education:* Department of Law, Chuo University (B.Jur., 1969); Legal Training and Research Institute (1973-1975); New South Wales University (1978-1979). *Member:* Tokyo Bar Association. *LANGUAGES:* Japanese and English.

HIDEO OHTA, born Zushi City, Kanagawa Prefecture, Japan, June 24, 1949; admitted, 1977, Japan. *Education:* Department of Law, Chuo University (B.Jur., 1972); Legal Training and Research Institute (1975-1977); Queen's University (LL.M., 1982). Research Assistant in Law, the Department of Law, Chuo University, 1972-1975. *Member:* Tokyo Bar Association. *LANGUAGES:* Japanese and English. *PRACTICE AREAS:* Corporate and Partnership Law; Labor and Employment Law; Commercial Litigation; Regulatory Law; Real Estate Law.

SHINICHI SAITO, born Tokyo, Japan, October 13, 1945; admitted, 1973, Japan. *Education:* Department of Law, Chuo University (B. Jur., 1968); Legal Training and Research Institute (1971-1973); Columbia Law School (LL.M., 1977). *Member:* First Tokyo Bar Association. *LANGUAGES:* Japanese and English.

HIDETAKA SEKINE, born Tokyo, Japan, February 7, 1938; admitted, 1973, Japan; registered as a Patent Attorney, 1977, Japan. *Education:* Department of Law, Tokyo University, Public Law (LL.B., 1962); Political Science (LL.B., 1965); Private Law (LL.B., 1968); Legal Training and Research Institute (1971-1973). *Member:* First Tokyo Bar Association; Japanese Patent Attorneys Association; International Association for the Protection of Industrial Property. *LANGUAGES:* Japanese and English. *PRACTICE AREAS:* Intellectual Property Law.

MASATSUGU SUZUKI, born Mukden, Manchuria, February 20, 1937; admitted, 1966, Japan; registered as a Patent Attorney, 1967, Japan. *Education:* Department of Law, Chuo University (B. Jur., 1969); Legal Training and Research Institute (1964-1966); Academy of American and International Law, Dallas, Texas, 1969 and Northwestern University Law School (LL.M., 1972). *Member:* Tokyo Bar Association (Chairman, Section of Anti-Monopoly Law of The Tokyo Bar Association); Japanese Patent Attorneys Association; Japan Bar Association; International Association for the Protection of Industrial Property (AIPPI); International Law Association; International Bar Association; Law Asia. *LANGUAGES:* Japanese and English.

YUKINORI WATANABE, born Chiba, Japan, May 2, 1933; admitted, 1988, Japan. *Education:* Department of Law Tokyo University (B.Jur.); Legal Research and Training Institute (1986-1988). Adviser, International Monetary Fund, 1975-1978. Director: Asian Development Bank, 1979-1983; World Bank, 1984-1986; General Income Tax Department, National Tax Administration. *Member:* First Tokyo Bar Association. *LANGUAGES:* Japanese, English and French.

(This Listing Continued)

TOKYO AOYAMA LAW OFFICE, Tokyo—Continued

LOCAL PARTNERS

HIROSHI KONDO, born Tokyo, Japan, February 7, 1957; admitted, 1987, Japan. *Education:* Chuo University (B.Jur.); Legal Research and Training Institute (1985-1987); Harvard University Law School (LL.M., 1991). *Member:* Tokyo Bar Association. *LANGUAGES:* Japanese and English. *PRACTICE AREAS:* Antitrust Law; Computers and Technology Law; Corporate and Partnership Law; Employee Benefits; Mergers and Acquisitions.

NOBUKO NARITA, born Tokyo, Japan, September 4, 1947; admitted, 1972, Japan. *Education:* Waseda University (B.Jur., 1970); Legal Training and Research Institute (1970-1972); University of California at Berkeley (LL.M., 1980). Attorney, Litigation Department of Justice Ministry, 1972-1981. *Member:* Tokyo Bar Association. *LANGUAGES:* Japanese and English.

OF COUNSEL

KOHJI MORI, born Tokyo, Japan, November 2, 1938; admitted, 1994, Japan. *Education:* Tokyo University, Cultural Department; Tokyo University, Law Department (Law). *Member:* First Tokyo Lawyers' Association. *LANGUAGES:* Japanese and English.

ATTORNEYS AT FOREIGN LAW

JOHN KAKINUKI, born San Francisco, California, June 20, 1956; admitted, 1985, California, U.S.A.; 1986, U.S. District Court, Northern District of California; 1988, District of Columbia, U.S.A.; 1990, U.S. Court of Appeals, Federal Circuit; 1991, U.S. District Court, Southern District of California; 1993, U.S. District Court, Central District of California; 1994, Japan as Attorney at Foreign Law. *Education:* University of California, Berkeley (1974-1977); International Christian University, Tokyo, Japan (B.A., 1979); University of California, Hastings College of the Law (J.D., 1984). *Member:* State Bar of California; The District of Columbia Bar; American Bar Association (Member, Sections on: Patent, Trademark and Copyright; International Law and Practice); American Intellectual Property Law Association; Tokyo Bar Association. *LANGUAGES:* English and Japanese. *PRACTICE AREAS:* Computers and Technology Law; Intellectual Property Law; Commercial Litigation; Regulatory Law.

JEREMY D. PITTS, born London, England, August 14, 1960; admitted, 1985, New South Wales, Australia; 1991, Victoria, Australia; 1993, Japan as Attorney at Foreign Law; 1994, England and Wales. *Education:* University of New South Wales (LL.B., B.Com., in Marketing). *Member:* Tokyo Bar Association; New South Wales Law Society. *PRACTICE AREAS:* Banking and Finance; Securities and Financial Products; Construction and Property Development; Australian Law.

ASSOCIATES

NAOAKI EGUCHI, born Tokyo, Japan, May 4, 1960; admitted, 1988, Japan. *Education:* Hitotsubashi University (LL.B.); Legal Research and Training Institute (1986-1988); University College London (LL.M., International Business Law, 1992). *Member:* Tokyo Bar Association. *LANGUAGES:* Japanese and English. *PRACTICE AREAS:* Banking and Finance; Securities and Financial Products; Insurance Law; Real Estate Law; Mergers and Acquisitions.

YASUYOSHI GOTO, born Akita, Japan, March 11, 1960; admitted, 1991, Japan. *Education:* Chuo University (B.Jur.); Legal Research Training Institute (1989-1991). *Member:* Tokyo Bar Association. *LANGUAGES:* Japanese and English.

YOSHIYA ISHIMURA, born Tokyo, Japan, November 6, 1959; admitted, 1993, Japan. *Education:* Keio University Law School (B.L., 1983); Legal Research and Training Institute (1991-1993). *Member:* Tokyo Bar Association. *LANGUAGES:* Japanese and English. *PRACTICE AREAS:* Antitrust Law; Corporate and Partnership Law; Labor and Employment Law; Commercial Litigation.

MASA MATSUSHITA, born Yokohama, Japan, 1960; admitted, 1989, Japan. *Education:* Chuo University (LL.B., 1983); Legal Research and Training Institute (1987-1989); Harvard University Law School (LL.M., 1993). *Member:* Tokyo Bar Association. *LANGUAGES:* Japanese, Chinese (Mandarin) and English.

SHOJI MIZUSHIMA, born Hyogo-ken, Japan, March 7, 1927; admitted, 1981, Japan. *Education:* Kyoto University, Department of Law (1950-1953). *Member:* Tokyo Tax Attorneys Association; Japan Tax Association. *LANGUAGES:* Japanese and English. *PRACTICE AREAS:* Taxation;

(This Listing Continued)

Mergers and Acquisitions; Employee Benefits; Securities and Financial Products.

YOSHIAKI MUTO, born Kawasaki City, Japan, December 13, 1964; admitted, 1992, Japan. *Education:* Tohoku University, Department of Law (B.Jur., 1988); Legal Training and Research Institute (1990-1992). *Member:* Tokyo Bar Association. *LANGUAGES:* Japanese and English.

MIHO NIUNOYA, born Tokyo, Japan, August 31, 1964; admitted, 1993, Japan. *Education:* Hitotsubashi University (LL.B., 1991); Legal Training and Research Institute (1991-1993). *Member:* Tokyo Bar Association. *LANGUAGES:* Japanese and English. *PRACTICE AREAS:* Antitrust Law; Corporate and Partnership Law; Intellectual Property Law; Immigration Law; Labor and Employment Law; Civil Litigation.

TAKESHI TAKAHASHI, born Tokyo, Japan, October 1, 1960; admitted, 1991, Japan. *Education:* Hitotsubashi University (LL.B.); Legal Research and Training Institute (1989-1991). *Member:* Toyko Bar Association. *LANGUAGES:* Japanese and English. *PRACTICE AREAS:* Construction and Property Development; Corporate and Partnership Law; Labor and Employment Law; Commercial Litigation; Mergers and Acquisitions.

SHINJI TOYOHARA, born Sasebo, Japan, January 26, 1961; admitted, 1994, Japan. *Education:* University of Tokyo. *Member:* Tokyo Bar Association.

HIDEYUKI YAMAMOTO, born Osaka, Japan, January 6, 1959; admitted, 1994, Japan. *Education:* Kyoto University (B.Ec., 1981); Legal Research and Training Institute (1992-1994). *Member:* Tokyo Bar Association; Japanese Institute of Certified Public Accountants. *PRACTICE AREAS:* Corporate and Partnership Law; Taxation.

ANNE KA TSE HUNG, born Hong Kong, January 12, 1964; admitted 1989, New South Wales, Australia; 1993, England and Wales (Not admitted in Japan). *Education:* University of New South Wales (B.Comm.; LL.B.). *Member:* Law Society of New South Wales; Law Society of England and Wales. *LANGUAGES:* English, Japanese, Cantonese and Mandarin. *PRACTICE AREAS:* Natural Resources Law; Corporate and Partnership Law; Employee Benefits.

W. TEMPLE JORDEN, born Tokyo, Japan, August 6, 1950; admitted, 1983, District of Columbia, U.S.A. (Not admitted in Japan). *Education:* Yale University (B.A., 1975); Cornell Law School (J.D., 1978); University of Nagoya, Nagoya, Japan; University of Washington (LL.M., 1983). U.S.-/Japan Friendship Commission Fellowship, 1982-1983. Charles A. Dana Fellowship, 1983-1984. Fulbright-Hays Graduate Research Fellowship, University of Tokyo, 1984-1985. Research Scholar, International Center for Comparative Law and Politics, University of Tokyo Faculty of Law, 1991-1992. *Member:* The District of Columbia Bar. *LANGUAGES:* English and Japanese.

BRUCE W. MACLENNAN, born Portland, Maine, June 19, 1952; admitted, 1993, Illinois, U.S.A. (Not admitted in Japan). *Education:* Antioch College (B.A., 1978); University of Washington (J.D., 1993). Articles Executive Editor, Pacific Rim Law & Policy Journal, 1992-1993. *Member:* Chicago, Illinois State and American (Member, International Section) Bar Associations. *LANGUAGES:* Japanese, Chinese and Spanish.

JEAN-DENIS MARX, born Strasbourg, France, July 18, 1963; admitted, 1993, France. (Not admitted in Japan). *LANGUAGES:* French, English, Japanese and German.

BERNHARD STEVES, born Hamburg, December 2, 1957; admitted, 1987, England (Not admitted in Japan). *Education:* School of Oriental and African Studies, London (B.A., 1984); City University London (Diploma in Law, 1985); Inns of Court School of Law (1985-1986). *Member:* The Bar of England and Wales (Lincoln's Inn). *LANGUAGES:* English, Japanese, Chinese, German and French. *PRACTICE AREAS:* Intellectual Property Law; Communications and Media Law; Trade; Computers and Technology Law; Litigation.

PAUL A. DAVIS, admitted, 1967, New Zealand; 1976, Victoria, Australia; 1977, New South Wales, Australia; 1983, England; 1988, Hong Kong (Not admitted in Japan). *Education:* Canterbury University (LL.M., Hons.); Nagoya University (postgraduate).

TOKYO CITY LAW & TAX PARTNERS

N.S. EXCEL BUILDING
22-45, NISHISHINJUKU 7-CHOME
SHINJUKU-KU
TOKYO 160, JAPAN
Telephone: (81) 3-3365-0911
Fax: (81) 3-3365-0958

General Practice, Commercial Transactions, Litigation, Real Estate, Inheritance, Leases, Corporation, Taxation, Comprehensive Legal and Tax Services by an International team of attorneys and licensed tax accountants.

MEMBERS OF FIRM

SHIGEAKI ITOH, born 1948; admitted, 1980, Japan. *Education:* Chuo University (LL.B., 1977); Legal Training and Research Institute of the Supreme Court (1980). *Member:* Tokyo Bar Association. **LANGUAGES:** Japanese and English.

KOHJI MATSUDA, born 1951; admitted, 1981, Japan. *Education:* Waseda University (LL.B., 1976); Legal Training and Research Institute of the Supreme Court (1981). *Member:* Tokyo Bar Association. **LANGUAGES:** Japanese, English, Korean and Chinese.

KEITO MIZOGUCHI, born 1956; admitted, 1983, Japan. *Education:* Chuo University (LL.B., 1979); Legal Training and Research Institute of the Supreme Court (1983). *Member:* Tokyo Bar Association. **LANGUAGES:** Japanese and English.

MASAAKI SAWANO, born 1954; admitted, 1985, Japan. *Education:* Waseda University (LL.B., 1978); Legal Training and Research Institute of the Supreme Court (1985); Columbia University School of Law (LL.M., 1992). *Member:* Tokyo Bar Association; Council of Legal Advisors of Management. **LANGUAGES:** Japanese and English.

ASSOCIATES

SHIGEMICHI HIRAMATSU, born 1950; admitted, 1987, Japan. *Education:* Keio University (LL.B., 1974); Legal Training and Research Institute of the Supreme Court (1987). *Member:* Tokyo Bar Association. **LANGUAGES:** Japanese and English.

KEISUKE IDE, born 1964; admitted, 1990, Japan. *Education:* Chuo University (LL.B., 1987); Legal Training and Research Institute of the Supreme Court (1990). *Member:* Tokyo Bar Association. **LANGUAGES:** Japanese and English.

MAKOTO MIYATA, born 1959; admitted, 1991, Japan. *Education:* Chuo University (LL.B., 1983); Legal Training and Research Institute of the Supreme Court (1991). *Member:* Tokyo Bar Association. **LANGUAGES:** Japanese and English.

HAJIME SHINJI, born 1964; admitted, 1993, Japan. *Education:* Tokyo University (LL.B., 1988); Legal Training and Research Institute of the Supreme Court (1993). *Member:* Tokyo Bar Association. **LANGUAGES:** Japanese and English.

SHINYA OKAUCHI, born 1966; admitted, 1994, Japan. *Education:* Chuo University (LL.B., 1989); Legal Training and Research Institute of the Supreme Court (1994). *Member:* Tokyo Bar Association. **LANGUAGES:** Japanese and English.

OF COUNSEL

WILLIAM B. CLEARY, born 1953; admitted, 1978, California; 1982, Guam and Federated States of Micronesia; 1990, New York and West Virginia (Not admitted in Japan). *Education:* United States International University (B.A., 1975); California Western School of Law (J.D., 1978) Hokkaido University, Faculty of Law-Monbusho Fellow (LL.M., 1987; LL.D., 1990). Legislative Counsel to Second Kosrae State Legislature, FSM, 1979-1980. Monbusho Scholar, 1983-1990. Member of the Faculty, University of Tsukuba, Tsukuba, Japan, 1993—. *Member:* Guam, New York State and American Bar Associations; The State Bar of California. **LANGUAGES:** English and Japanese.

TOKYO EIWA

Established in 1991
MAISON HIRAKAWA, 3RD FLOOR
2-5-2, HIRAKAWA-CHO
CHIYODA-KU
TOKYO 102, JAPAN
Telephone: 03-3239-8801
Telecopier: 03-3239-5277

General Practice, Anti-Monopoly Act, Intellectual Property Law, Computer Law, Advertising Law, Entertainment Law, Sports Law, Law Concerning Technology Transfer, Joint Venture Contracts, Acquisition, Foreign Investment Law, U.S. COCOM Regulations, Bankruptcy Law, Litigation and Arbitration.

MEMBERS OF FIRM

HIDETOSHI MASUNAGA, born Kagoshima-City, Japan, July 12, 1942; admitted, 1973, Japan; 1981, District of Columbia; 1984, New York. *Education:* Tokyo University (LL.B., 1965; Bachelor of Engineering, 1971); School of Law, Columbia University (LL.M., 1979). Legal Research and Training Institute, Supreme Court of Japan, 1971-1973. *Member:* Japan Federation of Bar Associations; Dai-ichi Tokyo Bar; District of Columbia Bar; New York State Bar Association. **LANGUAGES:** Japanese and English. **PRACTICE AREAS:** Intellectual Property Law; Entertainment Law; Licensing.

KEN OSANAI, born Aomori, Japan, October 10, 1943; admitted, 1971, Japan. *Education:* Chuo University, 1967; Graduate School of Law, Chuo University, 1968; New York University School of Law, 1977. Author: "Risk Management of International Trade," "Trade Secret (co-translation), "Note and Check" (co-author). *Member:* Japan Federal Bar Associations; First Tokyo Bar Association. **LANGUAGES:** Japanese, English.

ICHIRO TAKANO, born Tokyo, Japan, May 8, 1956; admitted, 1987, Japan. *Education:* Waseda University, 1980. Legal Training and Research Institute of the Supreme Court of Japan, 1987. *Member:* Japan Federal Bar Associations; First Tokyo Bar Association. **LANGUAGES:** Japanese, English.

TATSUO SHIGETA, born Tokyo, Japan, October 9, 1962; admitted, 1988, Japan; 1994, California. *Education:* Waseda University (LL.B., 1986); Legal Research and Training Institute, Supreme Court of Japan (1986-1988). *Member:* Japan Federation of Bar Associations; Dai-ni Tokyo Bar Association; State Bar of California. **LANGUAGES:** Japanese and English.

CHIKAYUKI OBARA, born Hokkaido, Japan, March 17, 1961; admitted, 1993, Japan. *Education:* Chuo University (LL.B., 1984); Legal Research and Training Institute, Supreme Court of Japan (1991-1993). *Member:* Japan Federation of Bar Associations; Dai-ichi Tokyo Bar Association. **LANGUAGES:** Japanese and English.

KENSAKU FUKUI, born Kumamoto, Japan, October 20, 1965; admitted, 1993, Japan. *Education:* Tokyo University (LL.B., 1991); Legal Research and Training Institute, Supreme Court of Japan (1991-1993). *Member:* Japan Federation of Bar Associations; Dai-ichi Tokyo Bar Association. **LANGUAGES:** Japanese and English.

HASASHI KUSAKABE, born Tokyo, Japan, January 28, 1961; admitted, 1994, Japan. *Education:* University of Tokyo (B.A., 1986); Legal Research and Training Institute, Supreme Court of Japan (1992-1994). *Member:* Japan Federation of Bar Associations; Dai-ichi Tokyo Bar Association. **LANGUAGES:** Japanese and English.

TOMOTSUNE KIMURA & MITOMI

SANNO GRAND BUILDING
14-2, NAGATACHO 2-CHOME, CHIYODA-KU
TOKYO, JAPAN
Telephone: 03-3580-0800
Telecopier: 03-3593-3336; 03-3581-6915
Telex: J28596 TKANDM

General International Practice. Corporation, Securities, Joint Venture, Licensing, Taxation, Administrative, Antitrust and Litigation.

NOBUYUKI TOMOTSUNE, admitted, 1967, Japan. *Education:* Tokyo University (LL.B., 1963); The Legal Training and Research Institute of the Supreme Court; graduate study, University of Washington Law School (LL.M., 1972). Associated with Cravath, Swaine & Moore, New York, 1973; Sullivan & Cromwell, New York, 1973-1974.

(This Listing Continued)

TOMOTSUNE KIMURA & MITOMI, Tokyo—Continued

AKIKO KIMURA, admitted, 1973, Japan. *Education:* Kyoto University (LL.B., 1971); The Legal Training and Research Institute of the Supreme Court; graduate study, Harvard Law School (LL.M., 1978). Associated with Cravath, Swaine & Moore, New York, 1979.

FUYUO MITOMI, admitted, 1974, Japan. *Education:* Tokyo University (LL.B., 1972); The Legal Training and Research Institute of the Supreme Court; graduate study, Harvard Law School (LL.M., 1978). Associated with Davis Polk & Wardwell, New York, 1978-1979; Morrison & Foerster, San Francisco, 1979.

MAKOTO KIMURA, admitted, 1975, Japan; 1980, New York. *Education:* Kyoto University (LL.B., 1973); The Legal Training and Research Institute of the Supreme Court; graduate study, School of Law, Columbia University (LL.M., 1979). Associated with Shearman & Sterling, New York, 1979-1980.

TSUTOMU MIYANO, admitted, 1988, Japan. *Education:* Tokyo University (LL.B., 1986); The Legal Training and Research Institute of the Supreme Court; graduate study, Harvard Law School (LL.M., 1993). Associated with Cravath, Swaine & Moore, New York, 1993-1994.

SAORI NAKAMURA, admitted, 1988, Japan; 1993, New York. *Education:* Kyoto University (LL.B., 1986); The Legal Training and Research Institute of the Supreme Court; graduate study, University of Michigan Law School (LL.M., 1992). Associated with Davis Polk & Wardwell, New York, 1992-1993.

FUMITOMO HITOKI, admitted, 1990, Japan. *Education:* Chuo University (LL.B., 1985); The Legal Training and Research Institute of the Supreme Court.

SHINJI ITOH, admitted, 1990, Japan. *Education:* Waseda University (LL.B., 1987); The Legal Training and Research Institute of the Supreme Court.

MASAFUMI KAWAMURA, admitted, 1991, Japan. *Education:* Kyoto University (LL.B., 1989); The Legal Training and Research Institute of the Supreme Court.

DAISUKE TAGA, admitted, 1991, Japan. *Education:* Tokyo University (LL.B., 1989); The Legal Training and Research Institute of the Supreme Court.

TOUGO DOUWAKI, admitted, 1992, Japan. *Education:* Tokyo University (LL.B., 1989); The Legal Training and Research Institute of the Supreme Court.

KEN KIYOHARA, admitted, 1992, Japan. *Education:* Tokyo University (LL.B., 1989); The Legal Training and Research Institute of the Supreme Court.

MASAHIKO MIYASHITA, admitted, 1992, Japan. *Education:* Tokyo University (LL.B., 1980); National Police Agency, Ministry of Home Affairs (1980-1990); The Legal Training and Research Institute of the Supreme Court.

HIRONORI SHIBATA, admitted, 1994, Japan. *Education:* Tokyo University (LL.B., 1992); The Legal Training and Research Institute of the Supreme Court.

WILLIAM LAWRENCE SEGAL, admitted, 1988, New York (Not admitted in Japan). *Education:* Oberlin College (B.A., History, 1982); Columbia University Law School (J.D., 1985).

MEMBERS OF FIRM

HIROSHI NAGAYASU, born Hyogo, Japan, December 20, 1947; admitted, 1974, Japan. *Education:* Tokyo University (LL.B., 1971). *Member:* Dai-ni Tokyo Bar Association. **LANGUAGES:** Japanese and English. **PRACTICE AREAS:** Corporate Law; International Commercial Transactions; Real Estate; Litigation/Arbitration.

NORIFUMI TATEISHI, born Kumamoto, Japan, September 21, 1953; admitted, 1979, Japan. *Education:* Tokyo University (LL.B., 1977); Harvard Law School (LL.M., 1985). *Member:* Tokyo Bar Association. **LANGUAGES:** Japanese and English. **PRACTICE AREAS:** Corporate Law; International Commercial Transactions; Financial Transactions; Securities Business; Litigation/Arbitration.

GAIKOKU-HO JIMU BENGOSHI

JEFFREY P. CLEMENTE, born Darby, Pennsylvania, October 21, 1948; admitted, 1978, New Jersey and U.S. District Court, District of New Jersey; 1988, District of Columbia and New York; 1989, U.S. Supreme Court; 1990, Japan as Gaikokuho Jimu Bengoshi. *Education:* Cornell University (B.S., 1970; M.B.A., 1972); Seton Hall University (J.D., cum laude, 1978). *Member:* New Jersey State Bar Association; The District of Columbia Bar; Dai-ni Tokyo Bar Association (Special Foreign Member). [LTC, USAR]. **LANGUAGES:** English and Japanese. **PRACTICE AREAS:** General Practice (U.S. Law); International Commercial Transactions; Financial Transactions; Trans-national Litigation.

TRENITÉ VAN DOORNE

AKASAKA WING BUILDING 5 F
6-6-15 AKASAKA
MINATO-KU
107 TOKYO, JAPAN
Telephone: 813-5563-2911
Telefax: 813-5563-2912

Associated Offices:

Amsterdam, Netherlands Office: De Lairessestraat 113. Mailing Address: P.O. Box 75265, 1070 AG AMSTERDAM. Telephone: 31 (0) 20-6789123. Telefax: 31 (0) 20-6789589.

Rotterdam, Netherlands Office: Weena 666. Mailing Address: P.O. Box 190, 3000 AD ROTTERDAM. Telephone: 31 (0) 10-404 2111. Telefax: 31 (0) 10-404 2333.

Rijswijk, Netherlands Office: Haagweg 175. Mailing address: P.O. Box 1073, 2280 CB RIJSWIJK. Telephone: 31 (0) 70-390 10 15. Telefax: 31 (0) 70-399 68 44.

The Hague, Netherlands Office: Churchillplein 5. Mailing address: P.O. Box 17207, 2502 CE THE HAGUE. Telephone: 31 (0) 70-338 3131. Telefax: 31 (0) 70-358 4798.

Brussels, Belgium Office: Avenue Louise 149, 1050 BRUSSELS. Telephone: 32-2-537 5159. Telefax: 32-2-537 6961.

Willemstad, Curaçao, Netherlands Antilles Office: Promes, Trenité Van Doorne, Julianaplein 22, P.O. Box 504. Telephone: 599-9-613400. Telefax: 599-9-612023.

RESIDENT PARTNER
ATTORNEY AT LAW

ELS M.A. VAN DER RIET, born 1958; admitted, 1986, Rotterdam; 1994, licensed to practice in Japan as a Foreign Lawyer (Gaikokuho Jimu Bengoshi). *Education:* Vrije Universiteit, Amsterdam (1984); University of Illinois, Champaign-Urbana, U.S.A. (M.C.L., 1985). **LANGUAGES:** English, French and German. **PRACTICE AREAS:** Corporate Law; Commercial Law.

(For complete biographical data on all personnel, see professional biographies at the Netherlands)

TOZAI SOGO LAW OFFICE

KIOICHO K BUILDING, 3-28 KIOICHO
CHIYODA-KU
TOKYO 102, JAPAN
Telephone: 81-3-3221-3691
Facsimile: 81-3-3221-3694

General Practice, International Commercial Transactions, Corporate Law, Financial Transactions, Securities Business, Real Estate, Litigation/Arbitration.

(This Listing Continued)

TSUNEMATSU YANASE & SEKINE

Established in 1987

SUMITOMO SARUGAKUCHO BUILDING
8-8, SARUGAKUCHO 2-CHOME, CHIYODA-KU
TOKYO 101, JAPAN
Telephone: (03) 5280-2711
Telex: J32723 HIBIYAX
Facsimile: (03) 5280-2731

Securities, Banking and Financial Services, Intellectual Property, Taxation, Entertainment, Corporate and International Business Law.

(This Listing Continued)

MEMBERS OF FIRM

KEN TSUNEMATSU, admitted, 1968, Japan. *Education:* The University of Tokyo (LL.B., 1955); Columbia University School of Law (M.C.L., 1963). *LANGUAGES:* Japanese and English. *PRACTICE AREAS:* General Corporate; Securities; Financial Law.

SHUJI YANASE, admitted, 1968, Japan. *Education:* The University of Tokyo (LL.B., 1966); Columbia University School of Law (LL.M., 1972). *LANGUAGES:* Japanese and English. *PRACTICE AREAS:* General Corporate; Securities; Financing; Mergers and Acquisitions.

OSAMU SEKINE, admitted, 1969, Japan. *Education:* The University of Tokyo (LL.B., 1967); Harvard Law School (LL.M., 1974). *LANGUAGES:* Japanese and English. *PRACTICE AREAS:* Banking; Futures Transaction; Securities and General Corporate.

TSUTOMU HASHIMOTO, admitted, 1976, Japan. *Education:* The University of Tokyo (LL.B., 1971); University of Pennsylvania Law School (LL.M., 1980). *LANGUAGES:* Japanese and English. *PRACTICE AREAS:* General Corporate; Securities; Banking and Lease.

TOSHIO KOBAYASHI, admitted, 1980, Japan; 1987, New York. *Education:* Kyoto University (LL.B., 1974); Waseda University (LL.M., 1978); Harvard Law School (LL.M., 1986). *LANGUAGES:* Japanese and English. *PRACTICE AREAS:* General Corporate; Securities; Financing; Mergers and Acquisitions; Intellectual Property.

HIDETAKA MIHARA, admitted, 1986, Japan. *Education:* Nihon University (LL.B., 1981); Cambridge University (LL.M., 1990). *LANGUAGES:* Japanese and English. *PRACTICE AREAS:* Securities; International Business Law.

ASSOCIATES

FUMIO NAKAJIMA, admitted, 1986, Japan; 1993, New York. *Education:* Waseda University (LL.B., 1984); University of Pennsylvania Law School (LL.M., 1992). *LANGUAGES:* Japanese and English. *PRACTICE AREAS:* General Corporate; Securities; Litigation.

MINORU OTA, admitted, 1987, Japan. *Education:* Hitotsubashi University (LL.B., 1985); University of Washington (LL.M., 1994). *LANGUAGES:* Japanese and English.

TOSHIKI SATO, admitted, 1989, Japan. *Education:* Waseda University (LL.B., 1986); The University of London (University College, London) (LL.M., 1993). *LANGUAGES:* Japanese and English.

FUMIHIDE SUGIMOTO, admitted, 1989, Japan. *Education:* Waseda University (LL.B., 1985); Columbia University School of Law (LL.M., 1993). *LANGUAGES:* Japanese and English.

HIDEYUKI SUNASAKA, admitted, 1990, Japan. *Education:* The University of Tokyo (LL.B., 1988). *LANGUAGES:* Japanese and English.

MIYUKI ISHIGURO, admitted, 1991, Japan. *Education:* Hitotsubashi University (LL.B., 1989). *LANGUAGES:* Japanese and English.

ICHIRO OYA, admitted, 1991, Japan. *Education:* Waseda University (LL.B., 1985). *LANGUAGES:* Japanese and English.

TAKASHI SOHMA, admitted, 1992, Japan. *Education:* Waseda University (LL.B., 1987). *LANGUAGES:* Japanese and English.

HIROYUKI ISHIZUKA, admitted, 1993, Japan. *Education:* Chuo University (LL.B., 1989). *LANGUAGES:* Japanese and English.

MASAKI KANEHYO, admitted, 1994, Japan. *Education:* The University of Tokyo (LL.B., 1989). *LANGUAGES:* Japanese and English.

USAMI LAW OFFICE

Established in 1945

ROOM 319 SANSHIN BUILDING
4-1, YURAKU-CHO 1-CHOME CHIYODA-KU
TOKYO, JAPAN
Telephone: 3591-4716, 7620, 3776

General Practice. International Law. Foreign Investments, Maritime and Labor Laws. Patents and Trademarks.

KAZUKO ITOH, born Tokyo, Japan, January 17, 1923; admitted, 1959, Japan. *Education:* Tsuda College; Tokyo Bunrika University. Legal Advisor to Her Britanic Majesty's Ambassador, Tokyo, 1976—. Legal Consultant to the American Embassy, Tokyo, 1976—. *Member:* Tokyo Bar Association; International Bar Association. *LANGUAGES:* Japanese, English,

(This Listing Continued)

French and Spanish. *PRACTICE AREAS:* General Civil and Trial Practice; International Arbitration; Patent Litigation.

SAKUJI HARADA. *LANGUAGES:* Japanese and English. *PRACTICE AREAS:* Insurance.

SAKUZO KANEKO. *LANGUAGES:* Japanese and English. *PRACTICE AREAS:* Real Estate.

KENJI AIZAWA. *LANGUAGES:* Japanese and English. *PRACTICE AREAS:* Corporation; Competition.

WAKAE IDA. *LANGUAGES:* Japanese and English. *PRACTICE AREAS:* Real Estate.

Languages: Japanese, English, French and Spanish.

USHIJIMA & ASSOCIATES

NEW AOYAMA BUILDING
1-1 MINAMI-AOYAMA 1-CHOME
MINATO-KU
TOKYO 107, JAPAN
Telephone: 03-3470-7000
Telex: J24567 USHILAW
Facsimile: 03-3470-7007 and 7063

International Investments, Mergers and Acquisitions, Banking and Finance, Securities, Real Estate Developments and Construction, Taxation, Patents, Trademarks, Administrative, Antitrust, Litigation, Arbitration, Corporate and General Practice.

SHIN USHIJIMA, born Miyazaki Prefecture, Japan, 1949; admitted, 1979, Japan; Prosecutor, 1977-1979. *Education:* Tokyo University (LL.B., 1975); The Legal Training and Research Institute of the Supreme Court of Japan (1977). Author: "Internationalization of Economy and Internationalization of Legal Proceedings," NBL, 1982; "Internationalization of Corporate Reorganization Proceedings," NBL, 1982; translated version also published in the U.S.A., 1985, Law in Japan; "Antitrust Laws in the United States of America," Business View, 1984; "The True Nature of the Laws of the United States of America," Business View, 1985; "One Aspect of a Foreign Creditor's Guarantee Against a Japanese Company Subject to Corporate Reorganization," Credit Management, 1988; Translator, Uniform Partnership Act of 1976, Uniform Limited Partnership Act of 1976. *Member:* Daini Tokyo Bar Association. *LANGUAGES:* Japanese and English.

YASUSHI WATANABE, born Tokyo, Japan, 1952; admitted, 1989, Japan; Prosecutor, 1977-1989 (1986-1989, Legal Counsel for the Ministry of Justice, Judicial System and Research Department). *Education:* Waseda University (LL.B., 1975); The Legal Training and Research Institute of the Supreme Court of Japan (1977). Author: "Sales of Goods/Commercial Law," The Law of Commerce in Japan, 1993, Prentice-Hall. *Member:* Daini Tokyo Bar Association. *LANGUAGES:* Japanese and English.

KOHTARO TAMURA, born Tokyo, Japan, 1957; admitted, 1983, Japan. *Education:* Tokyo University (LL.B., 1981). The Legal Training and Research Institute of the Supreme Court of Japan (1983). Author: "How Japan's New Land Value Tax Works," East Asian Executive Reports, 1991; "Investor/Protection in Japanese Real Estate Syndications," Nippon Fudosan Gakkai, 1992; "Basic Law on Real Estate Securitization," Keiso Shobo, 1994. *Member:* Daini Tokyo Bar Association. *LANGUAGES:* Japanese and English.

ASSOCIATES

TETSUYA ARASEKI, born Osaka, Japan, 1958; admitted, 1986, Japan. *Education:* Waseda University (LL.B., 1983); The Legal Training and Research Institute of the Supreme Court of Japan (1986). *Member:* Tokyo Bar Association. *LANGUAGES:* Japanese and English.

YOHICHIRO HAMABE, born Ishikawa Prefecture, Japan, 1961; admitted, 1987, Japan. *Education:* Keio University (LL.B., 1985); The Legal Training and Research Institute of the Supreme Court of Japan (1987). *Member:* Daini Tokyo Bar Association. *LANGUAGES:* Japanese and English.

AKIHITO KATAYAMA, born Tokushima Prefecture, Japan, 1961; admitted, 1990, Japan. *Education:* Tokyo University (LL.B., 1985); The Legal Training and Research Institute of the Supreme Court of Japan (1987). Judge, 1987-1990. *Member:* Daini Tokyo Bar Association. *LANGUAGES:* Japanese and English.

(This Listing Continued)

USHIJIMA & ASSOCIATES, Tokyo—Continued

MAMI IKEBUKURO, born Toyama Prefecture, Japan, 1961; admitted, 1988, Japan. *Education:* Tokyo University (LL.B., 1986); The Legal Training and Research Institute of the Supreme Court of Japan (1988). *Member:* Daini Tokyo Bar Association. *LANGUAGES:* Japanese and English.

MITSUHIRO GONDA, born Shizuoka Prefecture, Japan, 1963; admitted, 1989, Japan. *Education:* Sophia University (LL.B., 1987); The Legal Training and Research Institute of the Supreme Court of Japan (1989). *Member:* Daini Tokyo Bar Association. *LANGUAGES:* Japanese and English.

RYUNOSUKE USHIJIMA, born Tokyo, Japan, 1961; admitted, 1990, Japan. *Education:* Waseda University (LL.B., 1984); The Legal Training and Research Institute of the Supreme Court of Japan (1990). *Member:* Daini Tokyo Bar Association. *LANGUAGES:* Japanese and English.

OSAMU INOUE, born Fukuoka Prefecture, Japan, 1963; admitted, 1991, Japan. *Education:* Hokkaido University (LL.B., 1986); The Legal Training and Research Institute of the Supreme Court of Japan (1991). *Member:* Daini Tokyo Bar Association. *LANGUAGES:* Japanese and English.

HIROSHI NAGASE, born Tokyo, Japan, 1959; admitted, 1992, Japan. *Education:* Tokyo University (LL.B., 1984); The Legal Training and Research Institute of the Supreme Court of Japan (1992). *Member:* Daini Tokyo Bar Association. *LANGUAGES:* Japanese and English.

MASANORI INOUE, born Fukuoka Prefecture, Japan, 1963; admitted, 1993, Japan. *Education:* Tokyo University (LL.B., 1989); The Legal Training and Research Institute of the Supreme Court of Japan (1993). *Member:* Daini Tokyo Bar Association. *LANGUAGES:* Japanese and English.

MASAKAZU UEDA, born Kyoto Prefecture, Japan, 1963; admitted, 1994, Japan. *Education:* Keio University (LL.B., 1987; LL.M., 1991); The Legal Training and Research Institute of the Supreme Court of Japan (1994). *Member:* Daini Tokyo Bar Association. *LANGUAGES:* Japanese and English.

KENICHI KOJIMA, born Kanagawa Prefecture, Japan, 1966; admitted, 1994, Japan. *Education:* Tokyo University (LL.B., 1991); The Legal Training and Research Institute of the Supreme Court of Japan (1994). *Member:* Daini Tokyo Bar Association. *LANGUAGES:* Japanese and English.

GAIKOKU-HO JIMU BENGOSHI

RICHARD L. GALIN, born Brooklyn, New York, 1955; admitted, 1979, District of Columbia; 1983, California; 1989, Japan (Gaikokuho-Jimu-Bengoshi). *Education:* Long Island University (B.S., magna cum laude, 1975); Georgetown University (J.D., cum laude, 1979). Chairman, Business Law Section, Beverly Hills Bar Association, 1988-1989. Partner, Rosen, Wachtell & Gilbert, Los Angeles, California, 1988-1991 (on leave of absence, 1989-1991). Attorney, Office of the Comptroller of the Currency, Washington, D.C., 1980-1983. *Member:* State Bar of California; The District of Columbia Bar; Daini Tokyo Bar Association.

FOREIGN LEGAL ADVISOR

SUELY MORI, born São Paulo, Brazil, 1960; admitted, 1989, Pennsylvania; 1990, District of Columbia (Not admitted in Japan). *Education:* Pomona College (B.A., 1982); University of San Diego (J.D., 1986). *Member:* The District of Columbia Bar; Inter-Pacific Bar Association; Pennsylvania and American Bar Associations. *LANGUAGES:* Japanese, English and Portuguese.

WELTY, SHIMEALL & ASSOCIATES INTERNATIONAL LAW & PATENT OFFICE

ROOM 450 NEW OHTEMACHI BUILDING
2-1, 2-CHOME, OHTEMACHI, CHIYODA-KU
C.P.O. BOX 995
TOKYO, JAPAN
Telephone: 3241-1526-8, 3245-0428/0820, 3279-5826/4
Cable Address: "Elwel-Tokyo"
Telex: Elwel J26813
Fax: 81-3-3279-1662

Corporation Law, Investments, Patents, Trademarks, Copyrights and Unfair Competition.

ELMER E. WELTY (1906-1992).

WARREN G. SHIMEALL, born 1925; admitted, 1949, Oklahoma; 1950, U.S. District Court, Oklahoma; 1952, Korea; 1954, Japan; 1971, U.S. Customs Court. *Education:* University of Tulsa, George Washington University, Oklahoma City University and University of Oklahoma (J.D., 1949); Harvard PIL Summer Program for Practicing Lawyers (1979); Harvard Negotiation Workshop (1988). Phi Delta Phi. Adjunct Lecturer, Nihon University, Tokyo Seminar Lecturer, "International Commercial Arbitration," Seoul National University, 1979. Lecturer, "Real Estate Mortgage Law," Japanese Institute of International Business Law, 1980. Author, "Strategic Planning for the Protection of U.S. Technology and Intellectual Property in the Trade Relationship between the United States and Japan", Journal of International Law, Case Western Review, Vol. 15, No. 3, Summer, 1983. *Member:* Oklahoma and American (Member, International Copyright Treaties and Laws Committee, Patent, Trademark and Copyright Law Section) Bar Associations; Second Tokyo Bar Association; Japan Federation of Bar Associations; International Legal Society; American Society of International Law; Japanese-American Society for Legal Studies; American Chamber of Commerce in Japan (Member, Licenses, Patents and Trademark Committee; ACCJ, Madoguchi Representative to Japan Patent Office); American Trial Lawyers Association; American Intellectual Property Law Association. [Col., U.S. Army, Reserve]

ASSOCIATES

AKIO KANEKO, born Japan, March 1, 1927; admitted, 1966, Japan. *Education:* Chiba National University, Department of Industrial Science (Master Degree, 1949). Japan Patent Office, MITI, 1949, Chief The Laboratory of Chemical Products, MITI, 1953-1954. Examiner for Classification, Japan Patent Office, 1954-1957. Primary Examiner, Japan Patent Office, 1957-1964. Appeal Trial Judge, Appellate Trial Br., Japan Patent Office, 1964-1966. *Member:* Japan Patent Attorneys' Association. *LANGUAGES:* Japanese.

KAZUKI ASAKA, born Tokyo, Japan, November 18, 1947; admitted, 1974, Japan. *Education:* Chuo University (LL.B., 1970). Director of Industrial Property Right Laws Seminar, Chuo University, 1984—. *Member:* Japan Patent Attorneys' Association; Japan Patent Attorneys' Association (Special member of Patent System Utilization Council, 1983—). *LANGUAGES:* Japanese and English.

KAZUNORI SAITOH, born Hokkaido, Japan, 1951; admitted, 1980, Japan. *Education:* Hokkaido University (B.S., Geology, 1975). *Member:* Japan Patent Attorneys' Association; AIPPI of Japan.

CONSULTANTS

TERUO DOI, born Fukuoka, Japan, September 2, 1926. *Education:* Hosei University (LL.B., 1952); Waseda University (LL.M., 1954); Fulbright Scholar, 1954-1957, University of Mississippi Law School; Tulane University (M.C.L., 1956); Harvard Law School (1956-1957, graduate study program). Professor of Law, Waseda University, 1968—. Member, Copyright Council, Japanese Government, 1974—. Author: "Intellectual Property Law of Japan," 1980. Co-editor, "Patent and Knowhow Licensing in Japan and the United States," 1977. President, Japanese Copyright Society, 1981—. Chairman, LAWASIA Intellectual Property Standing Committee. Japan Contributor, European Intellectual Property Review, Oxford, U.K. Staff Consultant, Intellectual Property Law, Welty, Shimeall & Kasari, Tokyo, 1980—. *LANGUAGES:* Japanese and English.

ITTOKU MONMA, born Japan, June 5, 1928. *Education:* Chuo University (LL.B., 1955); Fulbright Scholar, Boalt Hall School of Law, University of California (1957-1958). Instructor, American Law, Chuo University, 1958-1960. Liaison Officer, Tokyo High and District Courts, 1958-1960.

(This Listing Continued)

Lecturer, Kobe Gakuin University Law School, 1973—. Executive, Matsushita Electric Co., 1960-1977. *Member:* Japan Lawyers Association (Hosokai); American Bar Association (International Member); Japan Law and Computers Association (Director). *LANGUAGES:* Japanese and English.

OF COUNSEL

SUSUMU KASARI, born November 25, 1924; admitted, 1955, Japan. *Education:* Doshisha University, Kyoto, Japan. Author: "Establishment of Joint Ventures," Joint Ventures and Japan, Chas Tuttle & Sophia U., 1967. Seminar Lecturer, International Financing and Patent Licensing, Sophia University, Tokyo, 1970-1976. *Member:* Tokyo Bar Association, Japan Patent Attorney's Association; Japan Federation of Bar Associations. *LANGUAGES:* English and Japanese.

REPRESENTATIVE CLIENTS: Amoco Chemical Corp.; Armstrong World Industries, Inc.; Aseeco Corp.; Beckman Instruments, Inc.; BS & B Engineering Co.; BS ' B Safety Systems; Cincinnati Inc.; Citibank, N.A.; Cosdel Inc.; Dart Industries; Dow Corning; Dunlop Ltd.; Farrell Lines Inc.; F.W. Woolworth; Harnischfeger Corp.; Ingersoll-Rand Co.; Kearney & Trecker Corp.; Martin Marietta Corp.; Masoneilan International Corp.; Massachusetts Institute of Technology; Mead Corp.; Midland International Ltd.; NCR Corp.; Oxy Metal Industries Inc.; Prentice-Hall Inc.; Scott Paper Co.; Sperry Corp.; Standard Oil Co. (Indiana); Sybron Corp.; The M.W. Kellogg Co.; Tymshare Inc.; United Airlines; Upjohn International Inc.; Western Union Co.; Wm. Wrigley Jr. Co.

WHITE & CASE

AMERICAN INTERNATIONAL BUILDING
20-5, ICHIBANCHO, CHIYODA-KU
TOKYO 102, JAPAN
Telephone: (81-3) 3239-4300
Facsimile: (81-3) 3239-4330

New York, New York: Telephone: 212-819-8200. Facsimile: 212-354-8113.

Washington, D.C.: Telephone: 202-872-0013. Facsimile: 202-872-0210.

Los Angeles, California: Telephone: 213-620-7700. Facsimile: 213-687-0758; 213-617-2205.

Miami, Florida: Telephone: 305-371-2700. Facsimile: 305-358-5744.

Mexico City, Mexico: Telephone: (52-5) 207-9717. Facsimile: (52-5) 208-3628.

Hong Kong: Telephone: (852) 2822-8700. Facsimile: (852) 2845-9070; Grice & Co., Solicitors, Telephone: (852) 2826-0333. Facsimile: (852) 2526-7166.

Singapore, Republic of Singapore: Telephone: (65) 225-6000. Facsimile: (65) 225-6009.

Bangkok, Thailand: Pacific Legal Group Ltd., In Association With White & Case, Telephone: (662) 236-6154/7. Facsimile: (662) 237-6771.

Hanoi, Viet Nam: Representative Office, Telephone: (84-4) 227-575/6/7. Facsimile: (84-4) 227-297.

Bombay, India: Telephone: (91-22) 282-6300. Facsimile: (91-22) 282-6305.

London, England: Telephone: (44-171) 726-6361. Facsimile: (44-171) 726-4314; (44-171) 726-8558.

Paris, France: Telephone: (33-1) 42-60-34-05. Facsimile: (33-1) 42-60-82-46.

Brussels, Belgium: Telephone: (32-2) 647-05-89. Facsimile: (32-2) 647-16-75.

Stockholm, Sweden: Telephone: (46-8) 679-80-30. Facsimile: (46-8) 611-21-22.

Helsinki, Finland: Telephone: (358-0) 631-100. Facsimile: (358-0) 179-477.

Moscow, Russia: Telephone: (7-095) 201-9292/3/4/5. Facsimile: (7-095) 201-9284.

Budapest, Hungary: Telephone: (36-1) 269-0550; (36-1) 131-0933. Facsimile: (36-1) 269-1199.

Prague, Czech Republic: Telephone: (42-2) 2481-1796. Facsimile: (42-2) 232-5522.

Warsaw, Poland: Telephone/Facsimile: (48-22) 26-80-53; (48-22) 27-84-86. International Telephone/Facsimile: (48-39) 12-19-06.

Istanbul, Turkey: Telephone: (90-212) 275-68-98; (90-212) 275-75-33. Facsimile: (90-212) 275-75-43.

Ankara, Turkey: Telephone: (90-312) 446-2180. Facsimile: (90-312) 437-9677.

Jeddah, Saudi Arabia: Law Office of Hassan Mahassni, Telephone: (966-2) 651-3535. Facsimile: (966-2) 651-3636.

Riyadh, Saudi Arabia: Law Office of Hassan Mahassni, Telephone: (966-1) 476-7099. Facsimile: (966-1) 479-0110.

Almaty, Kazakhstan: Telephone: (7-3272) 50-7491/2. Facsimile: (7-3272) 61-0842.

(This Listing Continued)

General Practice.

RESIDENT PARTNERS

ROBERT F. GRONDINE, born Milford, Massachusetts, January 29, 1952; admitted, 1981, New York and Massachusetts; 1990, California; 1991, District of Columbia; 1993, Registered in Japan as Foreign Legal Consultant (Not admitted in Japan). *Education:* Dartmouth College (A.B., 1974); Boston University (J.D., 1980). *Member:* The Association of the Bar of the City of New York; Los Angeles County, New York State, Daini Tokyo and American Bar Associations; State Bar of California; District of Columbia Bar; Japan Federation of Bar Associations.

GARY M. THOMAS, born Renton, Washington, March 1, 1951; admitted, 1977, California; 1978, Illinois; 1993, Japan as a Gaikokuho Jimu Bengoshi. *Education:* University of Washington (B.A., 1973); Harvard University (J.D., 1977); Asia University (LL.M., 1989; M.B.A., 1994). *Member:* State Bar of California; Second Tokyo, Illinois State, American and International Bar Associations.

CHRISTOPHER P. WELLS, born Washington, D.C., September 25, 1954; admitted, 1979, California; 1987, Japan as a Gaikokuho Jimu Bengoshi. *Education:* University of Rochester (B.A., 1975); University of California, Los Angeles (M.B.A., 1979; J.D., 1979). *Member:* Tokyo Bar Association; State Bar of California.

RESIDENT ASSOCIATES

JONATHAN M. HEIMER, born Oceanside, New York, May 26, 1963; admitted, 1991, California (Not admitted in Japan). *Education:* Union College (B.A., 1985); University of Michigan (J.D., 1990).

GLEN SUGIMOTO, born Yokohama, Japan, October 26, 1960; admitted, 1994, Washington. *Education:* Stanford University (B.S., 1982; M.S., 1984); University of Washington (J.D., 1993).

OSAMU UMEJIMA, born Maebashi, Gunma, Japan, November 5, 1959; admitted, 1989, New York (Not admitted in Japan). *Education:* Hokkaido (LL.B., 1982); New York University (LL.M., 1989).

(For biographical data as to other locations, see Professional Biographies at New York, New York; Washington, D.C.; Los Angeles, California; Miami, Florida; Mexico City, Mexico; Hong Kong; Singapore, Republic of Singapore; Bangkok, Thailand; Hanoi, Viet Nam; Bombay, India; London, England; Paris, France; Brussels, Belgium; Stockholm, Sweden; Helsinki, Finland; Moscow, Russia; Budapest, Hungary; Prague, Czech Republic; Warsaw, Poland; Istanbul and Ankara, Turkey; Jeddah and Riyadh, Saudi Arabia; Almaty, Kazakhstan).

WHITMAN BREED ABBOTT & MORGAN

(Richard A. Eastman Gaikokuho Jimu Bengoshi Jimusho)

SUITE 450, NEW OTEMACHI BUILDING
2-2-1 OTEMACHI
CHIYODA-KU
100 TOKYO, JAPAN
Telephone: 81-3-3242-1289
Telecopier: 81-3-3242-1290

New York, N.Y. Offices: 200 Park Avenue, 10166. Telephone: 212-351-3000.

Los Angeles, California Office: 633 West Fifth Street, 90071. Telephone: 213-896-2400.

Sacramento, California Office: Senator Hotel Building, 1121 L Street, 95814. Telephone: 916-441-4242.

Greenwich, Connecticut Office: 2 Greenwich Plaza, 06830. Telephone: 203-869-3800.

Washington, D.C. Offices: 1215 17th Street, N.W. Telephone: 202-887-0353; 1818 N Street, N.W. Telephone: 202-466-1100.

Newark, New Jersey Office: One Gateway Center, 07102-5398. Telephone: 201-621-2230.

Palm Beach, Florida Office: 220 Sunrise Avenue. Telephone: 407-832-5458.

London, England Office: 11 Waterloo Place. Telephone: 01-839-3226. Telex: 917881.

Associated with: Tyan & Associes, 22, La Sagesse Street, Beirut, Lebanon. Telephone 337968. Fax: 200969. Telex: 43928.

Firm engaged in American and International Practice, but not authorized to appear before Japanese Courts.

(This Listing Continued)

WHITMAN BREED ABBOTT & MORGAN, Tokyo—
Continued

RESIDENT PARTNER

RICHARD A. EASTMAN, born Quincy, Massachusetts, 1937; admitted, 1966, California; 1985, New York; 1987, Japan (as Gaikokuho Jimu Bengoshi (Foreign Legal Counsellor). *Education:* Harvard University (B.A., cum laude, 1959; LL.B., cum laude, 1965). Author: "Tax Aspects of Doing Business in Japan" in *Current Legal Aspects of Doing Business in the Far East* (ABA, 1972); "Allocation of Risk in Construction Contracts," *International Business Lawyer,* July/August, 1984; "The FIDIC Red Book Fourth Edition," *Construction Lawyer,* November, 1989; Chapter 4, "Joint Venturing In the Far East" in *Business Opportunities in the Far East* (Dow Jones-Irwin (1990). Member, Keizai Doyukai (Board of Managers, 1992—), American Chamber of Commerce in Japan. *Member:* State Bar of California; New York State and American Bar Associations; Second Tokyo Bar Association; Japan Federation of Bar Associations; American Arbitration Association; London Court of International Arbitration. Fellow, Chartered Institute of Arbitrators. *LANGUAGES:* Japanese, Russian. *PRACTICE AREAS:* International Law; International Joint Ventures; International Construction Law; Construction Arbitration; Japanese Trade.

WILDE SAPTE

2ND FLOOR, AIG BUILDING

1-1-3 MARUNOUCHI, CHIYODA-KU

TOKYO 100, JAPAN

Telephone: (81-3) 3215 3801

Facsimile: (81-3) 3215 3868

London, England Office: 1, Fleet Place, EC4M 7WS. Telephone: 0171-246 7000. Facsimile: 0171-246 7777. Telex: 887793 lde/cde 145.

Brussels, Belgium Office: 27 Avenue des Arts, 1040. Telephone: (32-2) 280 1404. Facsimile: (32-2) 280 1764.

Hong Kong Office: 31st Floor, One Exchange Square. Telephone: (852) 2810 5081. Facsimile: (852) 2810 1295.

New York, New York Office: 19th Floor, 450 Lexington Avenue, 10017. Telephone: (212) 867 4530. Facsimile: (212) 557 4451.

Paris, France Office: 217 rue du Faubourg St. Honoré, 75008. Telephone: (33-1) 44 95 02 70. Facsimile: (33-1) 42 89 62 25.

Lloyd's Office: 40 Lime Street, London, EC3M 5DG. Telephone: 0171 246 7000. Fax: 0171 246 7722.

Banking, Corporate Lending, Acquisition Finance, Aviation, Shipping, Leasing, Work-outs, Trade Finance, Structured Finance, Project Finance, Insolvency, Property, Insurance, Employment, Charities, EC Law and Company and Commercial.

FIRM PROFILE: *Wilde Sapte is a commercial City firm handling a wide range of work for our UK and international clients.*

The practice is centered around the company and commercial, banking, property, insolvency, insurance and transport expertise, though smaller specialist groups, such as an intellectual property group and a Japanese unit, have been formed to serve particular client needs. It is a progressive and much respected firm which has tripled in size over the last decade. In the last year, in response to increasing international demands from the business communities, offices have been opened in Hong Kong, Tokyo and at Lloyd's to complement those existing in New York, Paris and Brussels. In addition, the practice has extensive connections with law firms in jurisdictions throughout the world.

CONTACT PARTNERS

Philip Quirk

(For complete list of all personnel, see Professional Biographies at London, England)

WILSON, ELSER, MOSKOWITZ, EDELMAN & DICKER

AIU BUILDING

1-3 MARUNOUCHI 1-CHOME, CHIYODA-KU

TOKYO 100, JAPAN

Telephone: 011-813-216-6551

Telex: (781) 2227216

Facsimile: 011-813-216-6965

New York, N.Y. Office: 150 East 42nd Street, 10017-5639. Telephone: 212-490-3000. Telex: 177679. Facsimile: 212-490-3038; 212-557-7810.

Los Angeles, California Office: 1055 W. Seventh Street, Suite 2700, 90017. Telephone: 213-624-3044. Telex: 17-0722. Facsimile: 213-624-8060.

Washington, D.C. Office: The Colorado Building, Fifth Floor, 1341 "G" Street, N.W.20005. Telephone: 202-626-7660. Telex: 89453. Facsimile: 202-628-3606.

San Francisco, California Office: 555 Montgomery Street, 94111. Telephone: 415-433-0990. Telex: 16-0768. Facsimile: 415-434-1370.

Newark, New Jersey Office: One Gateway Center, 07102-5311. Telephone: 201-624-0800. Telex: 6853589. Facsimile: 201-624-0808.

Philadelphia, Pennsylvania Office: The Curtis Center, Independence Square West, 19106. Telephone: 215-627-6900. Telex: 6711203. Facsimile: 215-627-2665.

Baltimore, Maryland Office: 250 West Pratt Street, 21202. Telephone: 410-539-1800. Telex: 19-8280. Facsimile: 410-539-1820.

Miami, Florida Office: International Place, 100 Southeast Second Street, 33131. Telephone: 305-374-1811. Telex: 81045940. Facsimile: 305-579-0261.

Chicago, Illinois Office: 120 N. La Salle Street, 26th Floor, 60602. Telephone: 312-704-0550. Telex: 156590. Facsimile: 312-704-1522.

White Plains, N.Y. Office: 925 Westchester Avenue, 10604. Telephone: 914-946-7200. Facsimile: 914-946-7897.

Dallas, Texas Office: 5000 Renaissance Tower, 1201 Elm Street, 75270. Telephone: 214-698-8000. Facsimile: 214-698-1101.

London, England Office: 142 Fenchurch Street. Telephone: 01- 623-6723. Telex: 885741. Facsimile: 01-626-9774.

Albany, New York Office: One Steuben Place, 12207. Telephone: 518-449-8893. Fax: 518-449-8927.

Affiliate Office in Paris, France. Honig Buffat Mettetal. 21 Rue Clément Marot. Telephone: 33 (1) 44.43.88.88. Fax: 33 (1) 44.43.88.77.

FIRM PROFILE: *WILSON, ELSER, MOSKOWITZ, EDELMAN & DICKER is a full service international law firm, ranking among the largest law firms in the United States with offices in eleven major cities in the United States. We have provided our clients with a full range of expert and innovative legal services for more than a quarter of a century. Our dramatic growth during this period has been a response to the emerging needs of existing clients and addition of new ones. Initially, ours was an insurance-related practice and we maintain a preeminent position with regard to all aspects of insurance law and the insurance/reinsurance industry serving insureds, brokers, insurers and reinsurers. As our clients have matured and broadened in scope, so have our services and expertise and we have expanded into the general corporate law, including creditors' rights and bankruptcy, trusts and estates and real estate transactions and regulatory work.*

RESIDENT PARTNER

E. PAUL DOUGHERTY, JR., born Baltimore, Maryland, November 20, 1956; admitted, 1981, New Jersey and U.S. District Court, District of New Jersey; 1982, New York and U.S. District Court, Southern and Eastern Districts of New York (Not admitted in Japan). *Education:* Georgetown University (B.S.B.A., cum laude, 1978); Villanova University (J.D., 1981). *Member:* The Association of the Bar of the City of New York; American Bar Association (Member, Section on Tort and Insurance Practice).

(For additional Biographical data, see Professional Biographies at New York, New York).

WINTHROP, STIMSON, PUTNAM & ROBERTS

(Nathan-Pote Gaikokuho Jimu Bengoshi Jimusho)

608 ATAGOYAMA BENGOSHI BUILDING
6-7, ATAGO 1-CHOME, MINATO-KU
TOKYO 105, JAPAN
Telephone: 011-813-3437-9740
Telefax: 011-813-3437-9261

New York Main Office: One Battery Park Plaza, New York, N.Y. 10004-1490. Telephone: 212-858-1000.

Stamford, Connecticut Office: Financial Centre, 695 East Main Street, P.O. Box 6760, 06904-6760. Telephone: 203-348-2300.

Washington, D.C. Office: 1133 Connecticut Avenue, N.W., 20036. Telephone: 202-775-9800.

Palm Beach, Florida Office: 125 Worth Avenue, 33480. Telephone: 407-655-7297.

London Office: 2 Throgmorton Avenue, London EC2N 2AP, England. Telephone: 011-4471-628-4931.

Brussels Office: Rue du Taciturne 42, B-1040 Brussels, Belgium. Telephone: 011-322-230-1392.

Hong Kong Office: 2505 Asia Pacific Finance Tower, Citibank Plaza, 3 Garden Road, Central. Telephone: 011-852-530-3400.

Firm engaged in American and International Law Practice but not authorized to appear before Japanese courts or to act as Bengoshi.

RESIDENT PARTNER

JEFFREY L. POTE, born Melrose, Massachusetts, June 12, 1950; admitted, 1980, New York; 1990, Japan as Gaikokuho-Jimu-Bengoshi. *Education:* Brown University (A.B., 1972); Claremont Graduate School (M.A., 1974); Columbia Law School (J.D., 1979). Harlan Fiske Stone Scholar. *Member:* New York State Bar Association (Member, Sections on Banking; International Law); Tokyo Bar Association. *LANGUAGES:* Japanese and Mandarin.

RESIDENT ASSOCIATES

DANIEL A. SCHLESINGER, born New York, N.Y., June 10, 1955; admitted, 1987, New York (Not admitted in Japan). *Education:* Yale University (B.A., 1977); Oxford University, Oxford, England (M.A., 1980); Harvard University (J.D., 1986). Phi Beta Kappa. Marshall Scholarship. *LANGUAGES:* Japanese, Korean and French.

YAGI SŌGŌ LAW OFFICES

Established in 1972

NEW AOYAMA BUILDING
1-1, MINAMI-AOYAMA 1-CHOME, MINATO-KU
TOKYO 107, JAPAN
Telephone: 03-3475-1800
Cable Address: "Yagisogo"
Telex: 02422562 YASLAW J
Facsimile: 03-3475-1830

General Practice, Corporate, International, Mergers and Acquisitions, Real Estate, Taxation, Administrative, Regulatory, Government Contracts, Intellectual Property, Governmental Relations, Financing, Securities, Construction, Antitrust, Anti-dumping, Litigation and Arbitration.

YASUJI YAGI, born Chiba Prefecture, Japan, 1940; admitted, 1969, Japan. *Education:* Keio University (LL.B., 1963; LL.M., 1967); The Legal Training and Research Institute of The Supreme Court of Japan (1969). Author: "Torts in Private International Law," and "The Right of Third Parties to Intervene in Suits Under the Japanese Civil Procedure Code." *Member:* Daini Tokyo Bar Association; American Society of International Law; International Bar Association (Member, Committees on Antitrust, Commercial Banking, Taxes and Security); Japanese-American Society for Legal Studies. *LANGUAGES:* Japanese and English.

ASSOCIATES

MASARU EGAWA, born Tokyo, Japan, 1938; admitted, 1970, Japan. *Education:* Keio University (LL.M., 1967); The Legal Training and Research Institute of the Supreme Court of Japan (1970). *Member:* Dai-Ichi Tokyo Bar Association. *LANGUAGES:* Japanese and English.

NAOSHIGE KANZAKI, born Tokyo, Japan, 1950; admitted, 1978, Japan. *Education:* Keio University (LL.B., 1973); The Legal Training and

(This Listing Continued)

Research Institute of The Supreme Court of Japan (1978); graduate study, Tulane University School of Law, (LL.M., 1984). Manatt, Phelps, Rothenberg & Tunney, Los Angeles, 1984; Law Office of Kuoting Wang, Los Angeles, 1985; Graham & James (Los Angeles; Raleigh, North Carolina), 1986. *Member:* Dai-Ichi Tokyo Bar Association. *LANGUAGES:* Japanese and English.

TAKUYA NAKA, born Saitama Prefecture, Japan, 1953; admitted, 1982, Japan; 1986, New York. *Education:* Waseda University (LL.B., 1977); Columbia Law School (LL.M., 1986); The Legal Training and Research Institute of the Supreme Court of Japan (1982). *Member:* Daini Tokyo Bar Association. *LANGUAGES:* Japanese and English.

CHARLES LEROY DUPREE, IV, born San Antonio, Texas, November 26, 1965; admitted, 1991, California (Not admitted in Japan). *Education:* University of Michigan (B.A., with highest distinction, 1987); UCLA School of Law (J.D., 1991). Phi Beta Kappa. *Member:* State Bar of California. *LANGUAGES:* English and Japanese.

YAMASAKI LAW & PATENT OFFICE

SOGO NAGATACHO BUILDING 8F
11-28, NAGATA-CHO 1-CHOME, CHIYODA-KU
TOKYO 100, JAPAN
Telephone: 03-3581-9371
Cable Address: "Yamatorny"
Telex: 02226942 YAMLAW J
FAX No.: 03-3581-0240

International and Domestic Practice in Commercial, Corporate, Banking and Securities, Intellectual Property and Antitrust Law and Litigation.

YUKUZO YAMASAKI, born 1924; admitted, 1961, Japan; registered as Patent Attorney, 1967, Japan. *Education:* Tokyo University (LL.B.); Southern Methodist University School of Law (M.C.L., 1965). With Kaye, Scholer, Fierman, Hays & Handler, New York, 1965-1966. Author: *Digest of Japanese Infringement Cases 1966-1968,* 1970; "Japanese Case Law Report," A.I.P.P.I., Journal of the Japanese Group of AIPPI, 1981-1992. *Member:* Inter-Pacific Bar Association (Chairman, Intellectual Property Committee, 1991-1993); Japanese Bar Association (Member, 1977—; Chairman, Intellectual Property Rights Committee, 1989-1990); First Tokyo Bar Association (Chairman, Human Rights Committee, 1983-1984); The Patent Attorneys Association of Japan; Industrial Property Council of the Patent Office (Council Member, 1991—). *LANGUAGES:* Japanese, English, Chinese and German.

KANAKO ITOH, born 1953; admitted, 1983, Japan. *Education:* Kyoto University (LL.B.). *Member:* First Tokyo Bar Association. *LANGUAGES:* Japanese and English. *PRACTICE AREAS:* Intellectual Property Law; Business Law; Commercial Law.

HIROSHI KIMURA, born 1928; registered as Patent Attorney, 1972, Japan. *Education:* Chiba University. R & D worker, Japan Inorganic Color & Chemicals Company, Ltd., 1950-1984. *Member:* The Patent Attorneys Association of Japan. *LANGUAGES:* Japanese and English.

AKIHIRO MATSUNAMI, born 1951; admitted, 1988, Japan. *Education:* Keio University (LL.B.); Legal Training and Research Institute of the Supreme Court of Japan. *Member:* First Tokyo Bar Association. *LANGUAGES:* Japanese and English. *PRACTICE AREAS:* Intellectual Property Law; Civil Law; Commercial Law.

NOBUO HINO, born 1953; admitted, 1989, Japan, Registered as Patent Attorney. *Education:* Tokyo University (B.S.). *Member:* First Tokyo Bar Association (Board of Representatives, Intellectual Property Committee, Business Law Committee and Unfair Competition Prohibition Committee). *LANGUAGES:* Japanese and English. *PRACTICE AREAS:* Intellectual Property Law; Patent Infringement Litigation; Criminal Law; Inheritance Law.

EIKO AKAGI, born 1967; admitted, 1993, New York (Not admitted in Japan). *Education:* Keio University (LL.B.); Keio University Graduate School of Law (LL.M.); George Washington University National Law Center (LL.M., Patent and Trade Regulations Law). Recipient, Fulbright YKK Award for Graduate Studies, 1991. *LANGUAGES:* Japanese and English.

(This Listing Continued)

YAMASAKI LAW & PATENT OFFICE, Tokyo—Continued

FOREIGN LAW COUNSEL

STEPHEN G. HARRIS, born 1941; admitted, 1972, California, U.S. Court of Appeals 9th Circuit and U.S. District Court, Central District of California. *Education:* George Washington University (Alumni Scholar); University of California at Los Angeles (B.A., 1965); Whittier College, School of Law (J.D., 1972). Former Trial Attorney, NLRB, Los Angeles. Formerly with Law Firm of Richard D. Fraade, Beverly Hills and London. *Member:* State Bar of California. *LANGUAGES:* English, Japanese and Spanish.

Languages: Japanese, English, Chinese, German and Spanish.

YAMASHITA AND OHSHIMA

4TH FLOOR, SANKYU BUILDING
6-14, KASUMIGASEKI 3-CHOME, CHIYODA-KU
TOKYO 100, JAPAN
Telephone: 03-3580-3251
Fax: 03-3581-4854

General and International Practice. Corporation, Investment, Commercial, Litigation, Intellectual Property, Real Estate.

SHIGEO OHSHIMA, born 1924; admitted, 1960, Japan. *Education:* The University of Tokyo (LL.B., 1952); The Legal Training and Research Institute, Supreme Court of Japan (1958-1960). *Member:* First Tokyo Bar Association. *LANGUAGES:* Japanese, English and French.

TAKEYA YAMASHITA, born 1911; admitted, 1960, Japan. *Education:* College of Communication, Ministry of Communication and The Legal Training and Research Institute, Supreme Court of Japan (1958-1960). *Member:* Second Tokyo Bar Association. *LANGUAGES:* Japanese and English.

EIICHI KANDA, born 1961; admitted, 1987, Japan; 1992, New York. *Education:* Keio University (LL.B., 1984); The Legal Training and Research Institute, Supreme Court of Japan (1985-1987); University of Chicago Law School (LL.M., 1991). Associated with Winthrop, Stimson, Putnam & Roberts, New York, 1991-1992; Morrison & Foerster, Los Angeles, 1992. *Member:* First Tokyo Bar Association; American Bar Association. *LANGUAGES:* Japanese and English.

AKIO NOMA, born 1958; admitted, 1986, Japan; 1991, New York. *Education:* Tokyo University (LL.B., 1984); The Legal Training and Research Institute, Supreme Court of Japan; University of Pennsylvania Law School (LL.M., 1990). Associated with Christy & Viener, New York, 1990-1991. Worked at Mckinsey & Company, Inc., 1991-1993. *Member:* First Tokyo Bar Association; American Bar Association. *LANGUAGES:* Japanese and English.

AKIHIRO OHSAKU, born 1956; admitted, 1991, Japan. *Education:* The University of Tokyo (LL.B., 1982); The Legal Training and Research Institute, Supreme Court of Japan (1989-1991). *Member:* Second Tokyo Bar Association. *LANGUAGES:* Japanese and English.

ADVISORS ON FOREIGN LAW

KENNETH A. MAZZER, born 1947; admitted, 1977, New York (Not admitted in Japan). *Education:* Princeton University (A.B., 1974); Columbia Law School (J.D., 1977). *LANGUAGES:* English and Japanese.

MICHAEL R. OKADA, born 1964; admitted, 1989, California (Not admitted in Japan). *Education:* Columbia University (A.B., 1986); University of Southern California (J.D., 1989). *LANGUAGES:* English, German and Japanese.

OF COUNSEL

KAZUO IHARA, born 1937; admitted, 1963, Japan. *Education:* The University of Tokyo (LL.B., 1961); The Legal Training and Research Institute, Supreme Court of Japan (1961-1963); Special Student, School of Law, University of Washington (1964-1965). *Member:* First Tokyo Bar Association; Japan Commercial Arbitration Association (Panel of Arbitrators); Japan Federation of Bar Associations (Chairman, Education Committee). *LANGUAGES:* Japanese and English.

YANAGIDA, NOMURA & AKAI

1310 NORTH TOWER
YURAKUCHO DENKI BUILDING
7-1, YURAKUCHO 1-CHOME, CHIYODA-KU
TOKYO 100, JAPAN
Telephone: 03-3213-0034/8
Cable Address: "Yanagidalaw"
Telex: J25352 "Horitsu"
Facsimile: (GII/III) 03-3214-5234

General Practice. Corporate, International Financing, Foreign Investment, Patents and Intellectual Property, International and Domestic Litigation and Arbitration.

MEMBERS OF FIRM

YUKIO YANAGIDA, born Toyama, Japan, January 22, 1933; admitted, 1960, Japan. *Education:* Waseda University (LL.B., 1956; LL.M., 1958); Harvard Law School (LL.M., 1966). Visiting Professor, Harvard Law School, 1991. *Member:* Tokyo Bar Association; Japan Federation of Bar Associations (Executive Governor, 1988-1989); LAWASIA (The Law Association for Asia and the Pacific) (Vice-Chair of the Japan Committee, 1992—; Board of Overseers of Harvard College (Visiting Committee, 1993—); The International Section of the Harvard Law School Association (Vice Chair, 1993—); The American-Japan Society, Inc. (Council, 1994—). *LANGUAGES:* English and Japanese.

KUNIAKI NOMURA, born Tokyo, Japan, June 13, 1945; admitted, 1970, Japan. *Education:* Waseda University (LL.B., 1968); University of Michigan (LL.M., 1975). *Member:* Tokyo Bar Association; Japan Federation of Bar Associations. *LANGUAGES:* English and Japanese.

IZUMI AKAI, born Shimane, Japan, June 24, 1955; admitted, 1982, Japan; 1991, New York. *Education:* Tokyo University (LL.B., 1980); The University of Chicago Law School (LL.M., 1987). *Member:* Dai-Ichi Tokyo Bar Association; Japan Federation of Bar Associations. *LANGUAGES:* English and Japanese.

HIROSHI AKIYAMA, born Gunma, Japan, December 3, 1946; admitted, 1984, Japan. *Education:* Tokyo University (B.A., 1971). *Member:* Tokyo Bar Association; Japan Federation of Bar Associations. *LANGUAGES:* French, English and Japanese.

ASSOCIATES

TAKASHI SHIMOKADO, born Kumamoto, Japan, January 27, 1954; admitted, 1985, Japan. *Education:* Waseda University (LL.B., 1981); University of Washington School of Law (LL.M., 1990). *Member:* Tokyo Bar Association; Japan Federation of Bar Associations. *LANGUAGES:* English and Japanese.

MAKOTO OGO, born Yokohama, Japan, April 6, 1958; admitted, 1986, Japan. *Education:* Hitotsubashi University (LL.B., 1983); Harvard Law School (LL.M., 1993). *Member:* Tokyo Bar Association; Japan Federation of Bar Associations. *LANGUAGES:* English and Japanese.

TOSHIMASA TAKAHASHI, born Tochigi, Japan, August 4, 1959; admitted, 1987, Japan. *Education:* Tokyo University (LL.B., 1985); The University of Chicago Law School (LL.M., 1994). *Member:* Tokyo Bar Association; Japan Federation of Bar Associations. *LANGUAGES:* English and Japanese.

NAOKI YANAGIDA, born Toyama, Japan, February 27, 1960; admitted, 1987, Japan. *Education:* Waseda University (LL.B., 1985); Harvard Law School (LL.M., expected 1995). *Member:* Tokyo Bar Association; Japan Federation of Bar Associations. *LANGUAGES:* English and Japanese.

MICHIHIRO SATANI, born Gunma, Japan, December 18, 1964; admitted, 1991, Japan. *Education:* Waseda University (LL.B., 1987). *Member:* Tokyo Bar Association; Japan Federation of Bar Associations. *LANGUAGES:* English and Japanese.

TAKAHIRO TAGAWA, born Aichi, Japan, March 5, 1966; admitted, 1993, Japan. *Education:* Keio University (LL.B., 1989). *Member:* Tokyo Bar Association; Japan Federation of Bar Associations. *LANGUAGES:* English and Japanese.

TOSHIHIKO TSUCHIYA, born Yamanashi, Japan, July 7, 1965; admitted, 1993, Japan. *Education:* Keio University (LL.B., 1988). *Member:* Tokyo Bar Association; Japan Federation of Bar Associations. *LANGUAGES:* English and Japanese.

NAOKI SUGITA, born Shizuoka, Japan, September 4, 1965; admitted, 1994, Japan. *Education:* Tokyo University (LL.B., 1988). *Member:* Tokyo

(This Listing Continued)

Bar Association; Japan Federation of Bar Associations. *LANGUAGES:* English and Japanese.

RYUHEI MOGI, born Hyogo, Japan, January 16, 1967; admitted, 1994, Japan. *Education:* Tokyo University (LL.B., 1991). *Member:* Tokyo Bar Association; Japan Federation of Bar Associations. *LANGUAGES:* English and Japanese.

YOSHIDA & PARTNERS

Established in 1924 by Seizo Yoshida.

2ND FLOOR, ICHIBANCHO WEST BLDG.
10 ICHIBANCHO, CHIYODA-KU
TOKYO 102, JAPAN
Telephone: (03) 5210-5121
Telecopier: (03) 5210-3230
Telex: 252-3980 ADMLAW J

Maritime Law, including Admiralty, Insurance, Charter Party and Cargo Disputes, Commercial Law.

MEMBERS OF FIRM

YOICHI OGAWA, born Tokyo, Japan, August 20, 1934; admitted, 1969, Japan. *Education:* Tokyo Mercantile Marine Academy (Navigation Course, 1958). Contributor, Enforced Sales of Vessels, Maritime Law Vol. II, IBA, 1977. Master Mariner, with Y.S. Line, 1958-1965, 1967-1969. Member: Panel of Maritime and Salvage Arbitrators, The Japan Shipping Exchange Inc.; Panel of Arbitrators, International Commercial Arbitration Commission of the Chamber of Commerce. *Member:* Tokyo Bar Association; Japan Maritime Law Association; International Bar Association; Japan Institute of Navigation. *LANGUAGES:* Japanese and English. *PRACTICE AREAS:* Marine Casualty; Marine Insurance; Salvage; Oil Pollution.

SEIJIRO NINOMIYA, born Tokyo, Japan, May 22, 1942; admitted, 1969, Japan. *Education:* Waseda University (LL.B., 1967). Contributor, "Registration of Vessels Mortgages on Vessels," Handbook on Maritime Law Vol. III, IBA, 1983. *Member:* Tokyo Bar Association; International Bar Association. *LANGUAGES:* Japanese and English. *PRACTICE AREAS:* Vessel Finance; Cargo Recovery and Defense; Marine Casualty; Marine Insurance; Litigation.

SOTARO MORI, born Saga, Japan, January 20, 1951; admitted, 1977, Japan. *Education:* Waseda University School of Politics and Economics. *Member:* Tokyo Bar Association; Japan Maritime Law Association. *LANGUAGES:* Japanese and English. *PRACTICE AREAS:* Charter Parties; Cargo Defense; Marine Casualty; Shipping Law.

TAKAYUKI MATSUI, born Tokyo, Japan, October 15, 1961; admitted, 1993, Japan. *Education:* Hitotsubashi University Legal Department (LL.B., 1986). *Member:* Tokyo Bar Association. *LANGUAGES:* Japanese and English. *PRACTICE AREAS:* Marine Insurance; Marine Casualty; Shipping Law.

PROCTORS IN ADMIRALTY

MUNEHISA KISHIMOTO, born Asahikawa, Japan, January 29, 1937. Registered Proctor in Admiralty, 1971. *Education:* Tokyo Mercantile Marine Academy (Navigation Course, 1961); Meiji University (LL.B., 1974). Master Mariner, with Taiheiyo Kaiun Co., Ltd., 1961-1972. *LANGUAGES:* Japanese and English. *PRACTICE AREAS:* Marine Casualty.

MICHIO KIMISHIMA, born Ohtawara, Japan, September 29, 1925. Registered Proctor in Admiralty, 1991. *Education:* Tokyo Mercantile Marine Academy (Navigation Course, 1945). Master Mariner, with Yamashita Line, 1949-1963. Marine Court Judge, 1963-1983. High Marine Court Judge, 1983-1991. The Chief Judge of High Marine Court, 1990-1991. *LANGUAGES:* Japanese and English. *PRACTICE AREAS:* Marine Casualty.

YOSHIMOTO & SUMIMOTO

T.B.R. BUILDING, ROOM 314
NO. 10-2, 2-CHOME, NAGATA-CHO
CHIYODA-KU
TOKYO 100, JAPAN
Telephone: 813 3593-2407/9
Fax: 813 3595-0356
Telex: J24525 Lawhyrt

General and International Law Practice. Maritime, Corporation and Foreign Investments Trademark Law.

(This Listing Continued)

MEMBERS OF FIRM

HIDEO YOSHIMOTO, born Hiroshima, Japan, May 4, 1918; admitted, 1950, Japan. *Education:* Kansai College, Osaka, Japan; Chūō University, Tokyo, Japan (LL.B., 1949). Researched and Studied General Maritime Law, at Libraries of University of Columbia, New York Law Institute and University of London Institute of Advance Legal Studies, 1976. Author: "Present Aspect of Time Charter by Demise"; "Application of Theory of Implied Warrantee on Interpretation of Charter Party," appeared in magazine The Shipping, published by Japan Shipping Exchange Association, 1978 and 1979; "The Timecharter in Japan: A Comparison" appeared in The Transnational Lawyer: Volume 1, Number 2, Fall 1988 published by McGeorge School of Law, University of the Pacific; Books: "Basic Theory of Interpretation of Charterparty" published on April 17, 1986; "Law on Products Liability in the World" published on July 10, 1994. Partner: Logan, Bernhard & Okamoto, 1962-1963; Hill, Betts, Yamaoka, Freehill & Longcope, Tokyo Office, 1965-1970; Yamaoka & Yoshimoto, 1971-1980. Arbitrator, International Commercial Arbitration Association of Japan. *Member:* First Tokyo Bar Association (President, 1975-1976); Japan Federation of Bar Associations (Director, 1964; Vice President, 1967-1968; 1975-1976); American Society of International Law; Academy of Maritime Law of Japan; Academy of Japan International Economy Law; Academy of Motor Traffic Law of Japan (Law Reform Committee, Ministry of Justice). *LANGUAGES:* English and Japanese.

TOSHIMI SUMIMOTO, born Hiroshima, Japan, February 2, 1932; admitted, 1962, April. *Education:* Chuo University of Tokyo, Japan (LL.B., 1959). Auditor, First Tokyo Bar Association, 1982-1983. *LANGUAGES:* Japanese and English.

YUASA AND HARA

Established in 1902

NEW OHTEMACHI BUILDING, SECTION 206
2-1 OHTEMACHI 2-CHOME, CHIYODA-KU
C.P.O. BOX 714
TOKYO 100, JAPAN
Telephone: 813-3270-6641
Cable Address: "Yualawofce Tokyo"
Telex: J26431 YULAWPT
Telefax: 813-3246-0272

General and International Practice. Corporation, Banking and Investment, Patent and Trademark Law. Litigation.

FIRM PROFILE: Clients include major Japanese companies and leading foreign banks and companies doing business in Japan. Currently staffed with 200, including lawyers, patent attorneys, chartered accountants, paralegals, technical persons and other supporting staff.

MEMBERS OF FIRM

KYOZO YUASA, born 1899; admitted, 1924, Japan; 1927, England (Inner Temple, London). *Education:* The Third Higher School; Tokyo Imperial University (M.L.). Author of "Law on Bills of Exchange and Promissory Notes, 1932; Law on Cheques, 1933" Japanese translation of Sir Henry Slesser's book on "Law" and English translations of Japanese laws. Member, Inner Temple, London, 1924—. Awarded LL.D. by John Marshall Law School, U.S.A. Decorated with the Third Order of the Sacred Treasure of the Japanese Government, 1971. Vice President, Rotary International, 1972. President, Patent Attorneys Association of Japan, 1969-1979. Vice-President, Japanese Group of AIPPI, 1973—. President, Asian Patent Attorneys Association, 1969-1977. Honorary Member of AIPPI. Awarded Ph.D. by China Culture University, 1983. *Member:* First Tokyo Bar Association. *LANGUAGES:* Japanese and English. *PRACTICE AREAS:* Corporation and Business Law Practice; International Arbitration.

MASASHIGE OHBA, born 1925; admitted, 1957, Japan. *Education:* Chūō University (LL.B., 1953); Academy of Law, Southern Methodist University, 1966. *Member:* AIPPI (Member, Executive Committee and Managing Trustees of Japanese Group); LES (President of Japan, 1992); Japanese Trademark Association (Vice President, 1988-1991); LIDC, Japan Association of Industrial Property Law (Academy); Second Tokyo Bar Association. *LANGUAGES:* Japanese and English. *PRACTICE AREAS:* Intellectual Property Rights; Litigation; Licensing and Joint Venture Agreements.

SHIGERU OGISO, born 1922; admitted, 1970, Japan. *Education:* Waseda University (LL.B., 1950); Yale Law School (1961-1962). Judge: Sapporo, Yokohama, Hiroshima, Kobe and Utsunomiya District Courts, 1952-1970. Chief of 4th Section of Justice Minister's Secretariat, 1970.

(This Listing Continued)

YUASA AND HARA, Tokyo—Continued

Member: First Tokyo Bar Association. *LANGUAGES:* Japanese and English. *PRACTICE AREAS:* Corporation and Business Law Practice; International Arbitration.

CHIKAO FUKUDA, born 1942; admitted, 1971, Japan. *Education:* Chuo University Law School (LL.B., 1967); Legal Training & Research Institute, 1969-1971; New York University School of Law, Institute of Comparative Law (M.C.J., 1974-1975). *Member:* Second Tokyo Bar Association. *LANGUAGES:* Japanese and English. *PRACTICE AREAS:* Corporate; Investment; Intellectual Property and Licensing; Litigation.

KAZUHIKO NIWA, born 1945; admitted, 1971, Japan. *Education:* Tokyo University (LL.B., 1969; Legal Training & Research Institute, 1969-1971; City of London Polytechnic Business Law (M.A., 1973-1974). *Member:* First Tokyo Bar Association. *LANGUAGES:* Japanese and English. *PRACTICE AREAS:* Banking; Construction; Technology Transfer; Shipping; Commercial Transactions.

YUKUKAZU HANAMIZU, born 1945; admitted, 1973, Japan. *Education:* Chuo University (LL.B., 1969); Legal Training and Research Institute, 1973; University of London (Diploma in Shipping Law, 1979). *Member:* Tokyo Bar Association. *LANGUAGES:* Japanese and English. *PRACTICE AREAS:* Corporate; Technology Transfer.

(MS.) JUNKO HIRAKAWA, born 1947; admitted, 1973, Japan; 1979, New York. *Education:* Chuo University (LL.B., 1970); Legal Training and Research Institute, 1973; University of Washington (LL.M., 1977). *Member:* Second Tokyo Bar Association; American Bar Association. *LANGUAGES:* Japanese and English. *PRACTICE AREAS:* Banking; Finance; International Investment; Commercial Transactions.

TSUNEO SATO, born 1944; admitted, 1977, Japan. *Education:* Chuo University (LL.B., 1970); Legal Training and Research Institute (1977). *Member:* Daini Tokyo Bar Association. *LANGUAGES:* Japanese, English and German. *PRACTICE AREAS:* Corporate; Licensing; Franchise; Mergers and Acquisitions; Intellectual Property Law; Litigation.

OSAMU SUZUKI, born 1950; admitted, 1977, Japan. *Education:* Chuo University (LL.B., 1972); Legal Training and Research Institute, 1977. *Member:* Second Tokyo Bar Association. *LANGUAGES:* Japanese and English. *PRACTICE AREAS:* Intellectual Property Rights; Litigation; Licensing and Corporate.

HIDEO OZAKI, born 1950; admitted, 1982, Japan. *Education:* Kyoto University (M.S., 1975); Chuo University (LL.B., 1978); Legal Training and Research Institute (1982). *Member:* Tokyo Bar Association. *LANGUAGES:* Japanese and English. *PRACTICE AREAS:* Patent Litigation.

KEIJI KONDO, born 1951; admitted, 1984, Japan. *Education:* Tokyo University (D. Eng. in Mineral Development Engineering, 1982); Legal Training and Research Institute (1984). *Member:* Tokyo Bar Association. *LANGUAGES:* Japanese and English. *PRACTICE AREAS:* Intellectual Property; International Taxation; Litigation.

ATSUSHI TSUDA, born 1922; registered Patent Attorney, Japan, 1967. *Education:* Yokohama Technical College, Aeronautical Engineering Department. Formerly, engineer of Kawasaki Aircraft Company. (Patent Attorney). *LANGUAGES:* Japanese and English. *PRACTICE AREAS:* Mechanical.

ICHIO SHAMOTO, born 1930; registered Patent Attorney, 1983, Japan. *Education:* The Eighth Higher School; Faculty of Engineering, Nagoya University (B. Eng ., 1953). Examiner, Appeal Examiner, Examiner-in-Chief, Appeal Examiner-in-Chief, Director of Examination Standard Section, Director General of the Fourth Examination Department and Director General of Department of Appeals of Japanese Patent Office, 1953-1983. *Member:* JPAA; AIPPI; FICPI (Delegate, Executive Committee); APAA (Councillor, President of Japan Group); LES. (Patent Attorney). *LANGUAGES:* Japanese and English. *PRACTICE AREAS:* Chemistry.

KIYOSHI HASEGAWA, born 1920; registered Patent Attorney, 1964, Japan. *Education:* Keijo Imperial University (M.L., 1943). Trademark Examiner and Trial Judge, Japanese Patent Office, 1958-1962. Vice President, 1975 and President, 1988, The Patent Attorney's Association of Japan. (Patent Attorney). *LANGUAGES:* Japanese and English. *PRACTICE AREAS:* Trademark and Design.

YUKIO YAGYU, born 1940; registered Patent Attorney, 1965, Japan. *Education:* Chuo University (LL.B.). (Patent Attorney). *LANGUAGES:* Japanese and English. *PRACTICE AREAS:* Trademark.

(This Listing Continued)

RYOZO NOGUCHI, born 1929; registered Patent Attorney, 1960, Japan. *Education:* Nihon University, Faculty of Engineering. (Patent Attorney). *LANGUAGES:* Japanese and English. *PRACTICE AREAS:* Chemistry.

SHOSUKE IMAI, born 1931; registered Patent Attorney, 1967, Japan. *Education:* Technical Department, Nagoya University (B.Eng., 1954). (Patent Attorney). *LANGUAGES:* Japanese and English. *PRACTICE AREAS:* Mechanical.

CHUJI MASUI, born 1938; registered Patent Attorney, 1961; admitted, 1973, Japan. *Education:* Department of Applied Physics, Shizuoka University (B.Sc., 1963). Examiner, Japanese Patent Office, 1963-1972. *Member:* JPAA (Vice President, 1991). (Patent Attorney). *LANGUAGES:* Japanese and English. *PRACTICE AREAS:* Mechanical.

TADAHIKO KURITA, born 1943; registered Patent Attorney, 1971, Japan. *Education:* Faculty of Engineering, Chiba University (B.Eng., 1966). Staff of Nihon Hikaku K.K. Research Institute, 1966-1968. (Patent Attorney). *LANGUAGES:* Japanese and English. *PRACTICE AREAS:* Chemistry.

TATSUO TOMIZU, born 1936; registered Patent Attorney, 1973, Japan. *Education:* Faculty of Chemical Engineering, Kanazawa University (B.Eng., 1960). Staff, Patent Section of Research Laboratory, Toppan Printing Co., Ltd., 1960-1968. (Patent Attorney). *LANGUAGES:* Japanese and English. *PRACTICE AREAS:* Chemistry.

YASUSHI KOBAYASHI, born 1947; registered Patent Attorney, 1971, Japan. *Education:* Faculty of Science and Engineering, Chuo University (B.Eng., 1971). Staff, Dr. Takeda & Takeda, Patent Firm, 1971-1976. (Patent Attorney). *LANGUAGES:* Japanese and English. *PRACTICE AREAS:* Electrical.

MASAO HASHIMOTO, born 1945; registered Patent Attorney, 1974, Japan. *Education:* Faculty of Technology, Tokyo Metropolitan University (B.Eng., 1969). Staff Hitachi Powdered Metals Co., Ltd., 1969-1971. (Patent Attorney). *LANGUAGES:* Japanese and English. *PRACTICE AREAS:* Mechanical.

AKIO CHIBA, born 1944; registered Patent Attorney, 1975, Japan. *Education:* Faculty of Science & Technology, Waseda University (B.Eng., 1969). Staff, Toyo Kanetsu K.K., Waseda University, 1969-1971. (Patent Attorney). *LANGUAGES:* Japanese and English. *PRACTICE AREAS:* Mechanical.

TAKESHI KANOH, born 1936; registered Patent Attorney, 1978, Japan. *Education:* Faculty of Engineering, Gunma University (B.Eng., 1959). Staff, Nihon Bunka Roller Shutter Co., 1959-1970. (Patent Attorney). *LANGUAGES:* Japanese and English. *PRACTICE AREAS:* Chemistry.

SHIGERU ITOH, born 1947; registered Patent Attorney, 1978, Japan. *Education:* Faculty of Engineering, Ibaraki University (B.Eng., 1970). Staff, Saito and Onodera Patent Office, 1970-1972. (Patent Attorney). *LANGUAGES:* Japanese and English. *PRACTICE AREAS:* Mechanical.

KAZUHIRO NAKATA, born 1952; registered Patent Attorney, 1976, Japan. *Education:* Law School, Chuo University (LL.B., 1975). Staff, Ohtsuka Patent Office, 1975-1979. (Patent Attorney). *LANGUAGES:* Japanese and English. *PRACTICE AREAS:* Trademark and Design.

HIDEO TANAKA, born 1942; registered Patent Attorney, 1984, Japan. *Education:* Faculty of Science, Tokyo University of Education (B.Sc., 1966). Examiner and Trial Judge, Japanese Patent Office, 1966-1984. (Patent Attorney). *LANGUAGES:* Japanese and English. *PRACTICE AREAS:* Electrical.

(MS.) IZUMI ADACHI, born 1953; registered Patent Attorney, 1981, Japan. *Education:* Law School, Keio University (LL.B., 1977). Member of Professor N. Monya's Seminar on Intellectual Properties, 1977-1980. (Patent Attorney). *LANGUAGES:* Japanese and English. *PRACTICE AREAS:* Trademark and Design.

TAKAHIKO OHTSUKA, born 1947; registered Patent Attorney, 1981, Japan. *Education:* Faculty of Engineering, Utsunomiya University (B.Eng., 1970). Staff of Meisei Electric Co., Ltd., 1970-1977. (Patent Attorney). *LANGUAGES:* Japanese and English. *PRACTICE AREAS:* Electrical.

YOSHIO AKIMOTO, born 1949; registered Patent Attorney, 1978. *Education:* Faculty of Engineering, Nihon University (B. Eng., 1977). Staff, IDE Patent Office 1978-1982. (Patent Attorney). *LANGUAGES:* Japanese and English. *PRACTICE AREAS:* Electrical.

CHIKANORI SAKURAI, born 1937; registered Patent Attorney, 1985, Japan. *Education:* Department of Technology, Chiba University (B.Eng.,

(This Listing Continued)

1964). Examiner and Appeal Examiner, Japanese Patent Office, 1964-1985. (Patent Attorney). *LANGUAGES:* Japanese and English. *PRACTICE AREAS:* Chemistry.

FUJIHIRO KANDA, born 1943; registered Patent Attorney, 1986, Japan. *Education:* Department of Technology, Toyama University (B.Eng., 1966). Examiner and Appeal Examiner, Japanese Patent Office, 1966-1986. (Patent Attorney). *LANGUAGES:* Japanese and English. *PRACTICE AREAS:* Mechanical.

ASSOCIATES

MASATO KOBAYASHI, born 1960; admitted, 1986, Japan; 1991, New York. *Education:* Tokyo University (LL.B., 1984); Legal Training and Research Institute (1986); Columbia Law School (LL.M., 1990). *Member:* First Tokyo Bar Association. *LANGUAGES:* Japanese and English. *PRACTICE AREAS:* International Transactions; Computer Software Licensing; Bankruptcy.

(MS.) MICHIKO KAWAKAMI, born 1959; admitted, 1986, Japan. *Education:* Keio University (LL.B., 1982); Legal Training and Research Institute (1986); Oxford University (Diploma in Law, 1990). *Member:* First Tokyo Bar Association. *LANGUAGES:* Japanese and English. *PRACTICE AREAS:* International Practice.

KŌJIRO FURUSAWA, born 1960; admitted, 1987, Japan. *Education:* Sophia University (LL.B., 1983); Legal Training and Research Institute (1987). *Member:* Tokyo Bar Association. *LANGUAGES:* Japanese and English. *PRACTICE AREAS:* Corporate; Litigation.

SHIGERU OHIRA, born 1960; admitted, 1987, Japan; 1993, New York. *Education:* Chuo University (LL.B., 1984); Legal Training and Research Institute (1987); Cornell Law School (LL.M., 1992). *Member:* Tokyo Bar Association. *LANGUAGES:* Japanese and English. *PRACTICE AREAS:* Corporation; General Business.

KAZUHIDE SHIMASUE, born 1966; admitted, 1990, Japan. *Education:* Tokyo University (LL.B., 1988); Legal Training and Research Institute (1990). *Member:* First Tokyo Bar Association. *LANGUAGES:* Japanese and English. *PRACTICE AREAS:* Intellectual Property; Unfair Competition Law; Litigation.

SEIJI OHNO, born 1959; admitted, 1991, Japan. *Education:* Tokyo University (LL.B., 1985); Legal Training and Research Institute (1991). *Member:* First Tokyo Bar Association. *LANGUAGES:* Japanese and English. *PRACTICE AREAS:* General Practices; Litigation.

KOZO YABE, born 1962; admitted, 1991, Japan. *Education:* Chuo University (LL.B., 1985); Legal Training and Research Institute (1991); University of Illinois College of Law (LL.M., 1994). *Member:* First Tokyo Bar Association. *LANGUAGES:* Japanese and English. *PRACTICE AREAS:* Litigation; International Business Transactions; Trademark, Design and Copyright Laws.

TOSHIYUKI FUKAI, born 1964; admitted, 1992, Japan. *Education:* Waseda University (B.A. in Political Science, 1988); Legal Training and Research Institute (1992). *Member:* Tokyo Bar Association. *LANGUAGES:* Japanese and English. *PRACTICE AREAS:* General Practices; Litigation.

KATSUYUKI TANAKA, born 1964; admitted, 1993, Japan. *Education:* Tokyo University (LL.B., 1990); Legal Training and Research Institute (1993). *Member:* Tokyo Bar Association. *LANGUAGES:* Japanese and English. *PRACTICE AREAS:* General Practices; Litigation.

KENSUKE ISOBE, born 1967; admitted, 1993, Japan. *Education:* Tokyo University (LL.B., 1991); Legal Training and Research Institute (1993). *Member:* Tokyo Bar Association. *LANGUAGES:* Japanese and English. *PRACTICE AREAS:* General Practices; Litigation.

(MS.) AKI MARUHASHI, born 1968; admitted, 1993, Japan. *Education:* Tokyo University (LL.B., 1991); Legal Training and Research Institute (1993). *Member:* Tokyo Bar Association. *LANGUAGES:* Japanese and English. *PRACTICE AREAS:* General Practices; Litigation.

YASUFUMI SHIROYAMA, born 1968; admitted, 1994, Japan. *Education:* Tokyo University (LL.B., 1992); Legal Training and Research Institute (1994). *Member:* First Tokyo Bar Association. *LANGUAGES:* Japanese and English. *PRACTICE AREAS:* General Practices; Litigation.

KEN TAKII, born 1967; admitted, 1994, Japan. *Education:* Tokyo University (LL.B., 1992); Legal Training and Research Institute (1994). *Member:* First Tokyo Bar Association. *LANGUAGES:* Japanese and English. *PRACTICE AREAS:* General Practices; Litigation.

(This Listing Continued)

AKINORI YAMAKAWA, born 1968; admitted, 1994, Japan. *Education:* Tokyo University (LL.B., 1991); Legal Training and Research Institute (1994). *Member:* First Tokyo Bar Association. *LANGUAGES:* Japanese and English. *PRACTICE AREAS:* General Practices; Litigation.

TODD MARSHALL MCHENRY, born 1963; admitted, 1988, California (Not admitted in Japan). *Education:* Yale University (B.A. in Music, 1985); Hastings College of Law (J.D., 1988); Kansai Gaidai Center for International Education (1992-1993). Associate with: Barton, Klugman and Oetting, Los Angeles, California, 1988-1992. *Member:* California Bar Association; American Bar Association. *LANGUAGES:* English and Japanese. *PRACTICE AREAS:* International Practice.

HIROMICHI AOKI, born 1959; registered Patent Attorney, 1984, Japan. *Education:* Law School, Chuo University (LL.B., 1981). (Patent Attorney). *LANGUAGES:* Japanese and English. *PRACTICE AREAS:* Trademark and Design.

KUNIHIRO SANO, born 1950; registered Patent Attorney, 1985, Japan. *Education:* Faculty of Technology, Chiba University (B.Eng., 1974). (Patent Attorney). *LANGUAGES:* Japanese and English. *PRACTICE AREAS:* Mechanical.

KIYOSHI MURAKAMI, born 1944; registered Patent Attorney, 1985, Japan. *Education:* Faculty of Agriculture, Tokyo University (B.Agr., 1968). (Patent Attorney). *LANGUAGES:* Japanese and English. *PRACTICE AREAS:* Chemistry.

SHIGERU SAKUMA, born 1947; registered Patent Attorney, 1985, Japan. *Education:* Faculty of Engineering, Tokyo Institute of Technology (B.Eng., 1969). (Patent Attorney). *LANGUAGES:* Japanese and English. *PRACTICE AREAS:* Mechanical.

HIROSHI UCHIDA, born 1938; registered Patent Attorney, 1986, Japan. *Education:* Faculty of Science and Engineering, Nihon University (B.Eng., 1969). (Patent Attorney). *LANGUAGES:* Japanese and English. *PRACTICE AREAS:* Mechanical.

JUNJI KAMATA, born 1962; registered Patent Attorney, 1987, Japan. *Education:* Faculty of Engineering, Kyoto University (M.Eng., 1986). *LANGUAGES:* Japanese and English. *PRACTICE AREAS:* Chemistry.

(MS.) SUMIE OHTSUKA, born 1947; registered Patent Attorney, 1988, Japan. *Education:* Tokyo Science University (B.SC., 1971). *LANGUAGES:* Japanese and English. *PRACTICE AREAS:* Electrical.

HIROYUKI TOMITA, born 1948; registered Patent Attorney, 1988, Japan. *Education:* Faculty of Pharmaceutical Sciences, Tokyo University (B.Pharm., 1974). *LANGUAGES:* Japanese and English. *PRACTICE AREAS:* Chemistry.

(MS.) KEIKO HONDA, born 1958; registered Patent Attorney, 1987, Japan. *Education:* Aoyama Gakuin University (LL.B., 1981). *LANGUAGES:* Japanese and English. *PRACTICE AREAS:* Trademark and Design.

MASAHITO MORIKAWA, born 1956; registered Patent Attorney, 1988, Japan. *Education:* Aoyama Gakuin University (LL.M., 1981). *LANGUAGES:* Japanese and English. *PRACTICE AREAS:* Trademark and Design.

(MS.) AKIKO KITABORI, born 1962; registered Patent Attorney, 1989, Japan. *Education:* Waseda University (B.Eng., 1985). (Patent Attorney). *LANGUAGES:* Japanese and English. *PRACTICE AREAS:* Chemistry.

HITOSHI NAKAMURA, born 1965; registered Patent Attorney, 1990, Japan. *Education:* Chuo University (LL.B., 1990). *LANGUAGES:* Japanese and English. *PRACTICE AREAS:* Trademark and Design.

OSAMU HOSHINO, born 1960; registered Patent Attorney, 1985, Japan. *Education:* Hosei University (LL.B., 1983). *LANGUAGES:* Japanese and English. *PRACTICE AREAS:* Mechanical.

(MS.) MITSUE HASHIBA, born 1961; registered Patent Attorney, 1991, Japan. *Education:* Keio University (B.Eng., 1984). *LANGUAGES:* Japanese and English. *PRACTICE AREAS:* Mechanical.

YOSHIYUKI MATSUSHIMA, born 1964; registered Patent Attorney, 1991, Japan. *Education:* Tohoku University (M.Eng., 1988). *LANGUAGES:* Japanese and English. *PRACTICE AREAS:* Chemistry.

MASATOSHI ANZE, born 1946; registered Patent Attorney, 1992, Japan. *Education:* Tokyo Denki University (B.Eng., 1970). *LANGUAGES:* Japanese and English. *PRACTICE AREAS:* Mechanical.

(This Listing Continued)

YUASA AND HARA, Tokyo—Continued

(MS.) HIROKO EJIRI, born 1947; registered Patent Attorney, 1984, Japan. *Education:* Tokyo University (D.Pharm., 1975). *LANGUAGES:* Japanese and English. *PRACTICE AREAS:* Chemistry.

SHIGEO TAKEUCHI, born 1959; registered Patent Attorney, 1992, Japan. *Education:* Faculty of Engineering, Science University of Tokyo (B.Eng., 1982). Staff: SHIMIZU Pharmaceutical Co., Ltd., 1983-1988; Higashiyama Patent Office, 1988-1993. (Patent Attorney). *LANGUAGES:* Japanese and English. *PRACTICE AREAS:* Mechanical.

SHINYA HOSOKAWA, born 1958; registered Patent Attorney, 1992, Japan. *Education:* Faculty of Engineering, Hokkaido University (B.Eng., 1980). Staff, Tsukuni and Associates, 1986-1989. (Patent Attorney). *LANGUAGES:* Japanese and English. *PRACTICE AREAS:* Chemistry.

(MS.) KAORU SUZUKI, born 1959; registered Patent Attorney, 1992, Japan. *Education:* Chou University, Law School (LL.B., 1981). (Patent Attorney). *LANGUAGES:* Japanese and English. *PRACTICE AREAS:* Trademark and Design.

EIICHI YAMAGUCHI, born 1959; registered Patent Attorney, 1993, Japan. *Education:* Seikei University, Law School (LL.B., 1982). (Patent Attorney). *LANGUAGES:* Japanese and English. *PRACTICE AREAS:* Trademark and Design.

HIROAKI NOYA, born 1954; registered Patent Attorney, 1993, Japan. *Education:* Faculty of Engineering, Osaka University (B.Eng., 1978). Staff of Nihon Zoki Pharmaceutical Co., 1978-1991. (Patent Attorney). *LANGUAGES:* Japanese and English. *PRACTICE AREAS:* Chemistry.

(MS.) MAKIKO IWAMOTO, born 1970; registered Patent Attorney, 1993, Japan. *Education:* Law School, Nihon University (LL.B., 1993). (Patent Attorney). *LANGUAGES:* Japanese and English. *PRACTICE AREAS:* Trademark and Design.

YUMOTO & OTA

KIOI ROYAL HEIGHTS, 3-29, KIOI-CHO, CHIYODA-KU
TOKYO 102, JAPAN
Telephone: 3234-2441
Facsimile: 3262-2729

Commercial, Corporate and International Practice.

YASUMASA YUMOTO, admitted, 1965, Japan. *Education:* Tokyo University (LL.B., 1960); University of California at Berkeley (LL.M., 1968). *Member:* First Tokyo Bar Association.

KIYOSHI OTA, admitted, 1993, Japan. *Education:* Tokyo University (LL.B., 1961). The Mitsubishi Bank, Ltd., 1961-1990. Managing Director, Akai Electric Co., Ltd., 1991-1994. *Member:* First Tokyo Bar Association.

MASARU KANAZAWA, admitted, 1986, Japan; 1992, New York. *Education:* Chuo University (LL.B., 1980); University of Washington School of Law (LL.M., 1990). Kelley Drye & Warren Los Angeles, 1990-1991. *Member:* First Tokyo Bar Association; New York and American Bar Associations.

ERI FURUKAWA, admitted, 1988, Japan; 1993, New York. *Education:* Waseda University (LL.B., 1985); Duke University School of Law (LL.M., 1992). Alston & Bird, Atlanta, 1992-1994. *Member:* First Tokyo Bar Association.

MAKI MIYAZAKI, admitted, 1992, Japan. *Education:* Tokyo University (LL.B., 1988). *Member:* Tokyo Bar Association.

KAZAKHSTAN

BAKER & McKENZIE - CIS LIMITED

155 ABAI AVENUE #29/30
ALMATY 480009, KAZAKHSTAN
Telephone: (3272) 50-99-45
Intn'l. Dialing: (7-3272) 50-99-45
Facsimilè: (7-3272) 50-95-79

Associated Offices of Baker & McKenzie in: Amsterdam, Bangkok, Barcelona, Beijing, Berlin, Bogotá, Brasília, Brussels, Budapest, Buenos Aires, Cairo, Caracas, Chicago, Dallas, Frankfurt, Geneva,

(This Listing Continued)

Hanoi, Ho Chi Minh City, Hong Kong, Juárez, Kiev, London, Madrid, Manila, Melbourne, México City, Miami, Milan, Monterrey, Moscow, New York, Palo Alto, Paris, Prague, Rio de Janeiro, Riyadh, Rome, St. Petersburg, San Diego, San Francisco, São Paulo, Singapore, Stockholm, Sydney, Taipei, Tijuana, Tokyo, Toronto, Valencia, Warsaw, Washington, D.C. and Zürich.

Correspondent Law Firm: Hadiputranto, Hadinoto & Partners, Jakarta.

Arbitration, Aviation, Company and Commercial Joint Ventures, Construction and Engineering Projects, Criminal Law, Banking, General Commercial, Litigation, Oil and Gas/Mining, Property, Taxation.

PARTNER

MICHAEL E. WILSON, born Chesterfield, England, December 3, 1958; admitted, 1984, England; 1988, New South Wales, Australia; 1989, Victoria, Australia (Not admitted in Kazakhstan). *Education:* College of Law, Chester (Solicitor's Final Qualifying, 1981); Manchester University (LL.B., hons., 1980). *Member:* Major Projects Association; Society of Construction Law; Law Society of England and Wales. *LANGUAGES:* English and Japanese. *PRACTICE AREAS:* Construction and Engineering Projects; Oil and Gas/Mining; Company and Commercial Joint Ventures; Aviation.

ASSOCIATES

MARAT IBRAGIMOV, born Almaty, Kazakhstan, January 29, 1953; admitted, 1975, Kazakhstan. *Education:* Kazakh University (Law degree, 1975). Lecturer, Almaty Institute of National Economy, and Kazakh University, 1976-1990. Assistant Public Prosecutor, 1975-1976. *Member:* Almaty Collegium of Attorneys. *LANGUAGES:* Russian, English and Kazakh. *PRACTICE AREAS:* General Commercial; Oil and Gas/Mining; Taxation; Property; Litigation; Arbitration.

IGOR A. NOVIKOV, born Shemonaikha, Kazakhstan, September 17, 1960; admitted, 1982, Kazakhstan. *Education:* State University in Leiden, The Netherlands (Law degree, 1994); Kazakh University (Law degree, 1982). Prosecutor, Office of General Prosecutor of Republic of Kazakhstan, 1982-1994). *LANGUAGES:* Russian, English and Kazakh. *PRACTICE AREAS:* Criminal Law; Banking; Oil and Gas/Mining; General Commercial; Arbitration.

PHILLIP ROSENBLATT, born New York, U.S.A.; admitted, 1993, New York, U.S.A. (Not admitted in Kazakhstan). *Education:* Touro College (B.S., 1988); Fordham Law School (J.D., 1992). Certified Public Accountant, New York. *Member:* New York State (Member, International Law Section) and American (Member, Sections on: International Law and Practice; Natural Resources, Energy and Environmental Law) Bar Associations; New York State and American Societies of Certified Public Accountants; Central Asian and Trans-Caucasian Law Association. *LANGUAGES:* English, Russian, French, German, Turkish and Kazakh.

SALANS HERTZFELD & HEILBRONN

10A ABAYA PROSPECT
CORNER "FURMANOVA," 11TH FLOOR, SUITE 5
480013 ALMATY, KAZAKHSTAN
Telephone: 7 3272.634.053; 634.049

Other Almaty, Kazakhstan Office: SALANS HERTZFELD & HEILBRONN. 86 Gogol Street, 5th Floor, 480091. Office Move Planned for April 1, 1995.

Paris, France, Office: 9, Rue Boissy D'Anglas, 75008. Telephone: 42.68.48.00. Telex: 280990 PARILEX. Fax: 42.68.15.45; 42.68.15.46; 42.68.15.47.

New York, N.Y. Office: 750 Lexington Avenue, 10022. Telephone: 212.644.0800. Fax: 212.644.1003.

London, England Office: 103 Mount Street. W1Y-5HE. Telephone: 44.171.491.3735. Fax: 44.171.408 0843.

Moscow, Russia Office: Gazetnyi Pereulok, 17/9, (Ex. UL. Ogareva). 103009. Telephone: 7.501.940.2944. Fax: 7.501.940.2806.

Warsaw, Poland Office: ul. Podwale 7, 00-252. Telephone: 48.22 31.96.88; 31.25.72; 31.29.20. Fax: 48.22 31.39.32; 31.15.65.

St. Petersburg, Russia Office: Dom Zhurnalistov, 70 Nevskii Prospekt. 191 025. Telephone: 7.812.272.4572; 273.6844. Fax: 7.812.273.6844.

Other St. Petersburg, Russia Office: 6 Inzhenernaya Ulitsa, 191011. Telephone: 7.812.850.1504; 210.4040; 210.4447; 210.4008; 210.4032; 210.4005; 210.4348; 210.4812. Fax: 7.812.850.1505; 210.4114. Office move planned for March 15, 1995.

Kiev, Ukraine Office: Ukrainskii Dim, Vul. Kreshchatik 2 (4th Floor), 252601. Telephone: 7.044.228.5451. Fax: 7.044.228.6398.

(This Listing Continued)

AIGOUL KENJEBAYEVA, born Almaty, Kazakhstan, March 23, 1956. *Education:* Kazakh State University (J.D., 1978); Tashkent State University (Ph.D., 1988); Duke University Law School (LL.M., 1993). *LANGUAGES:* Russian, English and Kazakh. *PRACTICE AREAS:* Eastern Europe Commerce.

KAREN ANN WIDESS, born Los Angeles, California, December 26, 1956; admitted, 1985, California. *Education:* University of California at Berkeley (B.A., 1978); London School of Economics (Post-Graduate Diploma in International Law, 1984); University of Southern California (J.D., 1985). *LANGUAGES:* English, Russian, French, Spanish and German. *PRACTICE AREAS:* Eastern European Commerce.

ELSHAT T. SEKSEMBAYEVA, born Semipalatinsk, Kazakhstan, November 24, 1957. *Education:* Kazakh State University Law School (1979); Tashkent State University (Ph.D., 1988). Associate Professor of Law, Almaty State University (1992-1993). *LANGUAGES:* Russian, Kazakh and English.

OF COUNSEL

ANATOLY DIDENKO, born Ukraine, 1944. *Education:* Kazakh State University (Diploma, 1967; Cand.Jur.Sc., 1971); Kharkov Legal Institute (Dr.Jur.Sc., 1985);. Professor, Department of Civil Law, Faculty of Law, Kazakh State University, 1987—; Head of Department of Civil Law, Faculty of Law, Kazakh State University, 1990—. *LANGUAGES:* Russian and English. *PRACTICE AREAS:* Civil Law; Commercial Law; Legal Reform.

WHITE & CASE

33 VINOGRADOVA STREET NO. 3
ALMATY 480100, KAZAKHSTAN
Telephone: (7-3272) 50-7491/2
Facsimile: (7-3272) 61-0842

New York, New York: Telephone: 212-819-8200. Facsimile: 212-354-8113.
Washington, D.C.: Telephone: 202-872-0013. Facsimile: 202-872-0210.
Los Angeles, California: Telephone: 213-620-7700. Facsimile: 213-687-0758; 213-617-2205.
Miami, Florida: Telephone: 305-371-2700. Facsimile: 305-358-5744.
Mexico City, Mexico: Telephone: (52-5) 207-9717. Facsimile: (52-5) 208-3628.
Tokyo, Japan: Telephone: (81-3) 3239-4300. Facsimile: (81-3) 3239-4330.
Hong Kong: Telephone: (852) 2822-8700. Facsimile: (852) 2845-9070; Grice & Co., Solicitors, Telephone: (852) 2826-0333. Facsimile: (852) 2526-7166.
Singapore, Republic of Singapore: Telephone: (65) 225-6000. Facsimile: (65) 225-6009.
Bangkok, Thailand: Pacific Legal Group Ltd., In Association With White & Case, Telephone: (662) 236-6154/7. Facsimile: (662) 237-6771.
Hanoi, Viet Nam: Representative Office, Telephone: (84-4) 227-575/6/7. Facsimile: (84-4) 227-297.
Bombay, India: Telephone: (91-22) 282-6300. Facsimile: (91-22) 282-6305.
London, England: Telephone: (44-171) 726-6361. Facsimile: (44-171) 726-4314; (44-171) 726-8558.
Paris, France: Telephone: (33-1) 42-60-34-05. Facsimile: (33-1) 42-60-82-46.
Brussels, Belgium: Telephone: (32-2) 647-05-89. Facsimile: (32-2) 647-16-75.
Stockholm, Sweden: Telephone: (46-8) 679-80-30. Facsimile: (46-8) 611-21-22.
Helsinki, Finland: Telephone: (358-0) 631-100. Facsimile: (358-0) 179-477.
Moscow, Russia: Telephone: (7-095) 201-9292/3/4/5. Facsimile: (7-095) 201-9284.
Budapest, Hungary: Telephone: (36-1) 269-0550; (36-1) 131-0933. Facsimile: (36-1) 269-1199.
Prague, Czech Republic: Telephone: (42-2) 2481-1796. Facsimile: (42-2) 232-5522.
Warsaw, Poland: Telephone/Facsimile: (48-22) 26-80-53; (48-22) 27-84-86. International Telephone/Facsimile: (48-39) 12-19-06.
Istanbul, Turkey: Telephone: (90-212) 275-68-98; (90-212) 275-75-33. Facsimile: (90-212) 275-75-43.
Ankara, Turkey: Telephone: (90-312) 446-2180. Facsimile: (90-312) 437-9677.

(This Listing Continued)

Jeddah, Saudi Arabia: Law Office of Hassan Mahassni, Telephone: (966-2) 651-3535. Facsimile: (966-2) 651-3636.
Riyadh, Saudi Arabia: Law Office of Hassan Mahassni, Telephone: (966-1) 476-7099. Facsimile: (966-1) 479-0110.

General Practice.

RESIDENT ASSOCIATE

JAMES B. VARANESE, born Cleveland, Ohio, November 22, 1958; admitted, 1987, Ohio; 1989, District of Columbia (Not admitted in Kazakhstan). *Education:* Harvard University (A.B., 1983; M.P.P., 1987; J.D., 1987).

(For biographical data as to other locations, see Professional Biographies at New York, New York; Washington, D.C.; Los Angeles, California; Miami, Florida; Mexico City, Mexico; Tokyo, Japan; Hong Kong; Singapore, Republic of Singapore; Bangkok, Thailand; Hanoi, Viet Nam; Bombay, India; London, England; Paris, France; Brussels, Belgium; Stockholm, Sweden; Helsinki, Finland; Moscow, Russia; Budapest, Hungary; Prague, Czech Republic; Warsaw, Poland; Istanbul and Ankara, Turkey; Jeddah and Riyadh, Saudi Arabia).

KOREA

PUSAN INTERNATIONAL LAW OFFICES

4TH & 5TH FLOORS, YUSHIN BUILDING
7, 5-KA, CHUNGANG-DONG, CHUNG-KU
PUSAN, KOREA
Telephone: 011 82-51 463-7755
Fax: 011 82-51 463-7807-9

Admiralty, Maritime Law, International Trade, Finance, Banking and Business Law, Real Estate, Insurance, Intellectual Property, Foreign Investment, Labor Law, Arbitration, Corporate Matters, General Litigation.

MEMBERS OF FIRM

SEOK JOO KIM, born Namhae, Korea, February 5, 1930; admitted, 1956, Korea. *Education:* Pusan National University (LL.B., 1955). Judge: Pusan District Court, 1960-1961; Taegu District Court, 1961-1968; Taegu High Court, 1968-1973. Associate Judge, Pusan District Court, 1973-1978. Chief Judge, Pusan District Court Masan Branch, 1978-1979. Associate Judge, Taegu High Court, 1979-1982. Chief Judge, Cheju District Court, 1982-1983. Chief Judge, Masan District Court, 1983-1986. Chief Judge, Taegu District Court, 1986-1987. Chief Judge, Taegu High Court, 1987-1988. *Member:* Korean Bar Association. [JAG Officer, ROK Air Force, 1957-1960]. *LANGUAGES:* Korean, English, Japanese and Chinese (Written only).

WON CHUL LEE, born Heunghae, Korea, September 15, 1955; admitted, 1982, Korea. *Education:* Seoul National University (LL.B., 1977). Judge: Masan District Court, 1985-1988; Masan District Court Chungmu Branch, 1988-1989. *Member:* Korean Bar Association. [JAG Officer, ROK Army, 1982-1985]. *LANGUAGES:* Korean, English, Japanese and Chinese (Written only).

KWEON BYUNG PARK, born Pusan, Korea, December 7, 1953; admitted, 1983, Korea. *Education:* Pusan National University (LL.B., 1976). Judge: Pusan District Court, 1983-1987; Masan District Court Chungmu Branch, 1987-1989; Pusan District Court, 1989-1990. *Member:* Korean Bar Association. *LANGUAGES:* Korean, English, Japanese and Chinese (Written only).

KIJUNE YOO, born Puyeo, Korea, August 10, 1959; admitted, 1985, Korea; 1990, New York. *Education:* Seoul National University (LL.B., 1982); New York University (LL.M., 1989). Associate, Healy & Baillie, New York, 1989-1990. Lecturer in Law , Inje University, 1991—. Author: "The Chinese New Patent Law", Pusan Bar Association, 1988; "How to Invest in China", Pusan Bar Association, 1990; "Chinese Maritime Law", Korean Maritime Law Association, 1990; "Liability of Stand-On Vessels in Collisions" Human Rights and Justice, August, 1990. *Member:* Korean Bar Association; New York State Bar and American Chamber of Commerce in Korea. *LANGUAGES:* Korean, English, Chinese and Japanese.

HONG SU ROH, born Pusan, Korea, October 30, 1965; admitted, 1989, Korea. *Education:* Pusan National University (LL.B., 1987; LL.M., 1990). *Member:* Korean Bar Association. [JAG Officer, ROK Army, 1990-1993]. *LANGUAGES:* Korean, English and Chinese (Written only).

(This Listing Continued)

PUSAN INTERNATIONAL LAW OFFICES, Pusan—
Continued

FOREIGN LEGAL CONSULTANT

ROBERT B. HOLLEY, born Provo, Utah, November 14, 1958; admitted, 1985, West Virginia. *Education:* Yonsei University; Brigham Young University (B.A., cum laude, 1982); West Virginia University (J.D., 1985). Foreign Legal Consultant, Kim Chang & Lee, Seoul, 1985-1989; Foreign Legal Consultant, Yoo & Seok, Pusan, 1989-1990; Lecturer, Pusan University of Foreign Studies, 1989-1991. *Member:* West Virginia State Bar; American Bar Association; International Bar Association; American Chamber of Commerce in Korea (Chairman, Pusan Committee, 1991-1994). Pusan Tongbaek Rotary Club (Director, 1991—, current President); General Society of Mayflower Descendants, J. Reuben Clark Law Society. *LANGUAGES:* English, Korean and Chinese.

THE LAW OFFICES OF YOO & SEOK

Established in 1985

3/F, SEDONG BUILDING
65-25, 2-GA, NAM HANG-DONG, YOUNG DO-KU
PUSAN, KOREA
Telephone: 082-051-414-9697
Fax: 082-051-462-4484

Marine and Commercial fields with particular reference to Maritime Law, Marine Claims, Marine Insurance, Salvage, Collision at Sea, Pollution, Personal Injury, Employers and Public Liability Claims, Fishing Vessel Claims and Disputes.

FIRM PROFILE: Established in 1986. The law offices of YOO & SEOK has grown to become one of Korea's leading Maritime and Commercial Law firms.

The firm has a reputation for offering a full range of quality legal services, especially in Maritime and Commercial Law.

The client base is Korean, Japanese, East Asian in scope. The firm has two partners, one master mariner and six staffs.

MEMBERS OF FIRM

JUNG DONG YOO, born Pusan, Korea, July 19, 1957; admitted, 1985, Pusan. *Education:* University of Seongkyunkwan (1980; 1982); Korea Maritime University (1993). *Member:* Korea Bar Association. *LANGUAGES:* Korean and English. *PRACTICE AREAS:* Maritime and Commercial Law; International Trade and Insurance.

MAN KEE MIN, born Milyang, Korea; admitted, 1991. *Education:* University of Seongkyunkwan (1984); Seoul National University (1986). *Member:* Korea Bar Association. *LANGUAGES:* Korean and English. *PRACTICE AREAS:* International Business Law; Taxation.

ARAM INTERNATIONAL LAW OFFICES

Established in 1993

6TH FLOOR, DAEJEONG BUILDING
51-7 BANPO-DONG, SEOCHO-KU
SEOUL 137-040, KOREA
Telephone: (82-2) 592-0892
Telefax: (82-2) 596-6081

Mailing Address: Seocho P.O. Box 421, Seoul, Korea

Full-Service Firm, engaged primarily in an Internationally-Oriented Business, Civil, Administrative and Technology Law Practice. Representation in Relation to International Business Transactions with or Operations in Korea, of all sorts. Also: Litigation, Arbitration and Claims Dispute Resolution. Maritime and Transportation Practice. Patent/Trademark, Intellectual Property and Unfair Competition Practice. Computer, Biotech, Telecommunications and other High-Technology Practice.

FIRM PROFILE: The firm's attorneys have many years of experience in representing a worldwide clientele on various Korean legal matters, but especially ones arising in the fields listed above. Large-firm expertise without the large-firm overhead. Multilingual paralegal, technical and support staff are employed. Client base includes U.S., European, Japanese and Pacific Rim-based firms operating in manufacturing, service, commercial and technological fields. Aram International is a young law firm which seeks to provide vigorous and dynamic representation of its clients in a

(This Listing Continued)

timely manner, at reasonable and efficient cost, and taking into account carefully the specific desires and needs of its clients.

KYUNG-HAN SOHN, born Pusan, Korea, 1951; admitted, 1979, Korea; 1981, Korea Patent & Trademark Bar; 1986, New York. *Education:* Seoul National University, School of Law (LL.B., 1973; LL.M., 1983); Judicial Research and Training Institute, Supreme Court of Korea (1977-1979); University of Pennsylvania, Law School (LL.M., 1985); Max-Planck-Institut, Munich, Germany (Research Fellow, 1988). Visiting Attorney: Pillsbury, Madison & Sutro, 1986; Vinson & Elkins, 1987. Author: "Customs Duties in Korea on Royalty and Advertising Expenses," 1984; "Regulation of International Transfer of Technology: U.S. and Korean Perspectives," 1985; "Limitation of Liability Clause in Bills of Lading," 1987; "National Report on Korean Law Applicable to Marine Transport Claims," 1988; "Unfair Competition Law of Korea," 1988; "Avoidance of Contract under the U.N. Convention on Contracts for the International Sale of Goods," 1990; "Delivery of Cargo with Bank Guarantees," 1990; "Doing Business in the U.S.," 1990; "Recognition and Enforcement of Foreign Judgements and Arbitration Awards in Korea," 1991; "Protections and Current Trends in Intellectual Property Law in Korea," 1991; "Legal Aspects of the Korean Telecommunications Industry and Market," 1992; "Software Licensing in Korea," 1993; "Visa and Tax Issues under Korean Law, Relating to Transfer of Expatriate Management or Staff to Korea," 1994; "Licensing, Distribution and Franchise Agreements in Korea," 1994. Lecturer in Law, Hankuk University of Foreign Studies, 1983; Seoul City University, 1988; Seoul National University, 1990—. Senior Member, Bae, Kim & Lee, P.C., 1988-1993. Member, Central International Law Firm, 1979-1988. Arbitrator, Korean Commercial Arbitration Board. *Member:* Korean, Seoul, New York State and International Bar Associations; Korea (Vice-President, 1988-1990) and Asia (Vice-President, Korea National Group, 1982-1984) Patent Attorneys Associations; Korea International Trade Law Association (Executive Secretary, 1990—); Korea Maritime Law Association; Licensing Executives Society (Director, Korea Chapter, 1990—); International Association of Young Lawyers (AIJA); Unidroit; Asia-Pacific Lawyers Association; AIPPI (Vice-President, Korea National Group, 1990-1993); AIPLA; INTA; Korea Private International Law Association (Executive Secretary, 1993—); Korea-U.S. Business Council (Working Group); European Union Chamber of Commerce in Korea. Member-Advisor, Korean Commercial Arbitration Board Commission on Revision of the Arbitration Act 1994-1995; (Ministry of Information and Communications) and Commission on Internationalization of the Telecommunications Industry (1994—). *LANGUAGES:* Korean, English, Japanese, reads German. *PRACTICE AREAS:* International Business Transactions and Operations; Intellectual Property; Computers and Software; Communications and Media; Litigation and Arbitration.

WOO-SEOK CHOE, born Seoul, Korea, 1959; admitted, 1987, Korea; 1995, New York. *Education:* Seoul National University, School of Law (LL.B., 1983; LL.M., 1985); Judicial Research and Training Institute, Supreme Court of Korea (1985-1987); Columbia University School of Law, New York (LL.M., 1994). Author: "Delegation of Authority of Corporate Board of Directors," 1985; "Mergers & Acquisitions in Korea," 1992; "Principles of Business Taxation in Korea," 1992; "Software Licensing in Korea," 1993. Lecturer in Law, Kookmin University, 1993. Senior Associate, Bae, Kim & Lee, P.C., 1990-1993. Associate, Kim, Chang & Lee, 1988-1990. *Member:* Korean and Seoul Bar Associations; New York State Bar Association; Korea International Trade Law Association; Korea Private International Law Association. [Judge Advocate, Korean Army, 1986-1988]. *LANGUAGES:* Korean and English, reads German, Japanese and Chinese. *PRACTICE AREAS:* International Business and Commercial Law; Company and Corporate Law; International Finance and Taxation; Antitrust and Trade Regulation; Computers and Software.

JAE-CHANG OH, born Namweon, Korea, 1961; admitted, 1990, Korea. *Education:* Korea University, School of Law (LL.B., 1985; LL.M. Candidate, 1993—. Judicial Research and Training Institute, Supreme Court of Korea (1988-1990). Litigation Associate, Park, Kim and Jung, 1993-1994. *Member:* Korean and Seoul Bar Associations; Korea Private International Law Association. [Judge Advocate, Korean Army, 1990-1993]. *LANGUAGES:* Korean and English, reads French. *PRACTICE AREAS:* Litigation and Arbitration; Commercial Law; Franchises and Franchising; Taxation; Transportation.

BYEONG-OK SONG, born Cheonan, Korea, 1960; admitted, 1993, Korea Patent & Trademark Bar. *Education:* Seoul National University, School of Natural Sciences (B.S., 1984; M.S., 1986);. International Patent Training and Research Institute (1992-1993). Author: "Doctrine of Equivalents," 1992. Research Aide, Korea Industrial Property Office, 1992. Patent (Electronics, Mechanics, Optics, Computers and Telecommunications).

(This Listing Continued)

Law Clerk and Attorney, Kim & Chang, 1991-1994. *Member:* Korea Patent Attorneys Association. *LANGUAGES:* Korean and English, reads Japanese. *PRACTICE AREAS:* Patents; Industrial Property; Computers; Technology and Science; Unfair Competition.

(MS.) YOUNG-MI LEE, born Seoul, Korea, 1959; admitted, 1995, Korea Patent & Trademark Bar. *Education:* Ewha Women's University, School of Law (LL.B., 1982). International Patent Training and Research Institute, Trademark & Servicemark and Design Rights Divisions (1993-1994). *Member:* Korea Patent Attorneys Association. *LANGUAGES:* Korean and English. *PRACTICE AREAS:* Industrial Property Protection, Rights and Infringement; Trademarks; Designs and Design Rights; Anticounterfeiting; International Technology.

ICK-WHAN PARK, born Cheongju, Korea, 1960; admitted, 1993, Korea. *Education:* Seoul National University, School of Law (LL.B., 1985; LL.M., 1989); University of Mannheim (Germany), Law Division (1989); Judicial Research and Training Institute, Supreme Court of Korea (1991-1993). Author: "A Study on the Fair Use Doctrine under American Copyright Law," 1989. Associate, Lim, Chung & Suh, 1993-1995. Legal Researcher for International Affairs, Copyright Deliberation and Conciliation Committee, Ministry of Culture & Information of Republic of Korea, 1988-1989. *Member:* Korean and Seoul Bar Associations; Deutsche Vereinigung fuer Gewerblichen Rechtsschutz und Urheberrecht. *LANGUAGES:* Korean, English, German, reads Japanese. *PRACTICE AREAS:* Agency and Distributorships; International Joint Ventures and Establishment of Business; Business Law; Copyrights; Investments.

RESIDENT FOREIGN LEGAL CONSULTANTS

PAUL STEPHAN PENCZNER, born Memphis, Tennessee, U.S.A., 1955; admitted, 1982, District of Columbia; 1983, U.S. District Court for District of Columbia and U.S. Court of Appeals for District of Columbia Circuit; 1985, U.S. Court of Appeals for Federal Circuit; 1987, U.S. Court of International Trade (Not admitted in Korea). *Education:* University of Guanajuato, Mexico (1973); Memphis State University (B.A., summa cum laude, 1978); George Washington University, National Law Center (J.D., 1981); Franklin Pierce Law Center, Advanced Licensing Institute (1993). Phi Kappa Phi. Pi Delta Phi. Dobro Slovo. Author: "Enforcement of Korean Design Rights," 1988; "Regulations Governing Permissible Overseas Investments Revised," 1989; "Protections and Current Trends in Intellectual Property Law in Korea," 1991; "Introduction to Antidumping Law in Korea," 1991; "Comparing Western and Korean Approaches to Law and Business," 1994. Senior Resident Legal Consultant, Bae, Kim & Lee, P.C., 1987-1993. Senior Associate, Evans & Lowe, Washington, D.C., 1982-1987. Aide, U.S. Congress, Washington, D.C., 1980. Arbitrator, Korean Commercial Arbitration Board. *Member:* District of Columbia Bar; American (Korea Regional Coordinator, Asia-Pacific Law Committee, Section of International Law and Practice, 1992—), Inter-Pacific and International Bar Associations; AIPLA; George Washington Law Alumni Association; American Chamber of Commerce in Korea; Australian Business Group in Korea; Korean-German Chamber of Commerce and Industry; Swiss-Korean Business Council; European Union Chamber of Commerce in Korea. *LANGUAGES:* English, German, French and Spanish, reads Italian and Russian.

TAE-WON KIM, born Seoul, Korea, 1949; admitted, 1989, New York (not admitted in Korea). *Education:* Seoul National, University School of Law (LL.B., 1973); Choongang University, Graduate School of International Business Management (M.B.A., 1985); Southern Methodist University School of Law, Dallas, Texas (LL.M., 1986; J.D., 1989). Author: "Legal Aspects of International Project Financing," 1984; "U.S. Trade Regulation," 1988. Lecturer on Legal Aspects of International Business Contracts, Samsung Group of Companies, Institute of Continuing Education, 1989-1990. Senior Associate Attorney, Weiner Lesniak (New York Area Office, Roseland, N.J.), 1992-1994. Of Counsel, Epstein Becker & Green, P.C. (New York), 1990-1992. In-House Counsel, Office of General Counsel, Samsung Group of Companies, 1989-1990. Manager of Legal Department, Samsung Construction Co., Ltd., 1977-1985. *Member:* New York State Bar Association; Korea International Trade Law Association. *LANGUAGES:* Korean and English.

(MS.) SUSAN SOOK-JA YOON, born Seoul, Korea, 1953; admitted, 1992, New York. *Education:* University of Texas at Austin (B.S., 1977); Brooklyn Law School, New York (J.D., 1988). Business Consultant, Hong Kong (1991-1993). Pharmacist, New York (1979-1988). *Member:* New York State Bar Association; New York State Licensed Pharmacists Association. *LANGUAGES:* English and Korean.

(This Listing Continued)

COUNSEL

DR. HUN-JAE SUH, born Pusan, Korea, 1950. *Education:* Seoul National University, School of Law (LL.B., 1973; LL.M., 1982; S.J.D., 1986). Consultant, Maritime and Insurance Departments, Kim, Chang & Lee, 1980-1982. Chief of Insurance & Claims Department, Taebong Industries Co., Ltd., 1978-1980. Author: "Marine Insurance Abandonment," 1982; "Maritime Liens," 1983; "Warranties in Anglo-American Marine Insurance Contract Law," 1983; "A Study on Seaworthiness," 1985; "Expiration of Marine Cargo Insurance: 'Choongnam Bangjuk' Fire Case," 1985; "Combined-Transport Documentation," 1985; "Liabilities of Combined-Transport Operators," 1986; "Fishery Disaster Insurance Policies," 1988; "Recent U.S. Shipping Legislation, and Its Effects," 1989; "Delivery of Cargo under Letters of Indemnity, and Liabilities of Shipping Agents," 1989; "Reexamination of Special Characteristics of Letter of Credit Transactions," 1991; "Oil Pollution Compensation System," 1991. Professor: Pusan University, School of Law, 1982-1990; Choongang University, School of Law, 1990—. Member, Advisory Committee, for Commercial Code Reform, to Minister of Justice of Republic of Korea, 1990. *LANGUAGES:* Korean and English. *PRACTICE AREAS:* Admiralty and Maritime Law; Shipping and Transportation; International Law; International Trade; Contracts.

HYUNG-GUL KIM, born Seoul, Korea, 1962; admitted, 1994, New York. *Education:* Korea University, School of Law (LL.B., 1984; LL.M., 1986; Ph.D. Candidate, 1986—); University of Pennsylvania, Law School (LL.M., 1992; S.J.D., Candidate, 1992—). Senior Researcher, Korea Information Society Development Institute, 1988-1992. Author: "Electronic Data Interchange (EDI) and International Trade," 1992; "The Telecommunications Services Trade, and the GATT Uruguay Round," 1993. *Member:* New York State Bar Association; Korea International Trade Law Association; American Society of International Law; Federal Communications Bar Association. *LANGUAGES:* Korean and English. *PRACTICE AREAS:* Communications and Media (Telecommunications); Electronic Data Interchange; Data Protection; Information Technology; Video Law.

TAE-YEON CHO, born Buyeo, Korea, 1952; admitted, 1983, Korea; 1983, Korea Patent and Trademark Bar; 1990, New York. *Education:* Seoul National University, School of Law (LL.B., 1980); Judicial Research and Training Institute, Supreme Court of Korea (1981-1983); University of Chicago, Law School (LL.M., 1988); George Washington University, National Law Center (M.C.L., 1989). Author: "An Introduction to Korean Intellectual Property Law," 1987; "Trademark Licensing and Registration," 1985 & 1987; "Recent Developments in Korean Industrial Property Law," 1985; "Case Studies on International Trademark Disputes," 1990 & 1991; "Protection of BIOS under Korean Computer Program Protection Act," 1991; "Legal Aspects of, Governmental Regulation of, and Policy and Practice as to International Patent, Technology and Know-How Licensing Agreements," 1991; "How to Cope with a Patent Dispute," 1991. Senior Member, Lee International Patent & Law Offices, 1991-1995. Member, Central International Law Firm, 1983-1991. *Member:* Korean, Seoul, New York State and American Bar Associations; Korea Patent Attorneys Association; Korean Intellectual Property Research Society; AIPPI; INTA; Asia-Pacific Lawyers Association; Korea International Trade Law Association; Korea-U.S. Business Council (Working Group). *LANGUAGES:* Korean and English, reads Japanese. *PRACTICE AREAS:* Patents and Industrial Property; Intellectual Property; Computers and Software; Technology and Science; International Business Transactions.

JONG WAN SUH, born Seoul, Korea, 1961; admitted, 1990, Korea Patent Trademark Bar. *Education:* Seoul National University, School of Pharmacology (B.S., 1984); Seoul National University, Graduate School of Pharmacology (M.S., 1986); International Patent Training and Research Institute (1989). Senior Associate, Bae, Kim & Lee, P.C., 1991-1994. Pharmaceutical and Chemical Patent Specialist, Chong Kun Dang Corporation, 1986-1991. *Member:* Korea Patent Attorneys Association. *LANGUAGES:* Korean, English and Japanese. *PRACTICE AREAS:* Biological Patents; Chemistry Patents; Pharmaceutical Patents; Other Patent and Industrial Property Protection; (International, Infringement, Prosecution, Registration); Products Liability.

Languages: Korean, English, Japanese, German, French and Spanish. Reads: Italian, Russian and Chinese.

BAE, KIM & LEE

Established in 1980

SHIN-A BUILDING
39-1 SEOSOMUN-DONG, CHUNG-KU
SEOUL 100-752, KOREA
Telephone: 317-4114
Telex: LAWBKL K24960
Cable Address: "LAWBKL"
Telefax: 757-2267; 755-7676

Mailing Address: C.P.O. Box 4576, Seoul, Korea

Finance, Banking, Securities Offerings, International Trade and Investment, Joint Ventures, Technology Transfers/Licensing, Corporations, Franchises, Distributorships, Taxation, Labor, Maritime, Insurance, Telecommunications, Construction, Realty, Business Visas, Arbitration, Enforcement Actions and other Business Transactional, Civil and Administrative Litigation. Computer/High-Tech, Patent and Intellectual Property Law and Litigation.

FIRM PROFILE: Bae, Kim & Lee, one of the nation's largest and most renowned law firms, is a full-service firm with a practice emphasis in international business transactions and dispute resolution. Characterized by steady, consistent growth since its founding, it now ranks as one of the country's pre-eminent providers of legal services, both domestic and international. Highly experienced in serving the needs of its diverse client base, and having the added benefit of multi-lingual American and European foreign legal consultants, the firm is particularly well-equipped to meet the needs of foreign business entities seeking to do business in or with Korea. Among its specializations include international business transactions/joint ventures, trade regulation, securities, banking, corporate finance and intellectual property, in addition to which the firm enjoys a strong reputation in the fields of both international and domestic arbitration and litigation.

MYUNG IN BAE, born Changwon, Korea, 1932; admitted, 1957, Korea. Education: Seoul National University, Law School (LL.B., 1956). Author: "Certain Defenses to and Elements of Crimes of Negligence," 1969. Exchange Lecturer, Gaiyo University Law School, Tokyo, Japan, 1985-1986. Public Prosecutor, Seoul, Chungju and Pusan District Offices, 1958-1968. Senior Public Prosecutor, Ministry of Justice and Seoul District Office, 1968-1978. Assistant Chief Prosecutor, Daegu District Office, 1978-1979. Chief Prosecutor, Kwangju District Office, 1979-1980. Director of Bureau of Procurator Affairs, Ministry of Justice, 1980-1981. Assistant Prosecutor General, 1981. Chief of Kwangju High Prosecutor's Office, 1981-1982. Chief of Judicial Research Institute, 1982. Minister of Justice of the Republic of Korea, 1982-1985. Chief Director, Agency for National Security Planning of the Republic of Korea, 1988. Member: Seoul and Korean Bar Associations. LANGUAGES: Korean, English and Japanese.

IN SUB KIM, born Youngdong, Korea, 1936; admitted, 1962, Korea. Education: Korea University, Law School (LL.B., 1961); Seoul National University, Graduate School of Justice (LL.M., 1963). Author: "Interpretation of Articles 607 & 608 of the Civil Code," 1969; "Interested Parties in Administrative Litigation," 1974; "Elements of Suspension of Administrative Disposition," 1976; "Particular Issues in Patent Infringement Actions," 1986. Lecturer, Judicial Research and Training Institute, Supreme Court of the Republic of Korea, 1977—. Judge: Seoul District Civil Court, 1963-1966 and 1968-1969; Seoul District Criminal Court, 1967 and 1970-1971; Seoul High Court of Appeals, 1972-1974. Assistant Judge, Supreme Court of the Republic of Korea, 1974-1977. Presiding Judge, Seoul District Court, 1977-1980. Commissioner: Policy Advisory Commission, Board of Audit and Inspection, 1983-1988; Commission for Examination of Industrial Disasters, Ministry of Labor, 1985-1989; Bank Dispute Co-ordination Commission, Bank of Korea, 1991—; National Cable Broadcasting Commission; Special Counsel, Korean Securities and Exchange Commission, 1990—. Member: Seoul (Director, 1985-1991) and Korean (Director, 1983-1985) Bar Associations. LANGUAGES: Korean, English and Japanese.

WON IL KANG, born Euisung, Kyungsang-Bukdo, Korea, 1942; admitted, 1962, Korea. Education: Seoul National University Law School (LL.B., 1963); Seoul National University Graduate School of Law (LL.M., Candidate, 1963-1964); Seoul National University Graduate School of Administration (M.Admin.). Author: Review of Korean Legal Relief System (1986). Professional Experience: Judge Advocate, Korean Army (1964-1967); Public Prosecutor, Daeku, Andong, Inchon, Seoul and Pusan District Offices (1968-1979); Senior Public Prosecutor, Ministry of Justice, Daeku and Seoul District Offices (1979-1983); Assistant Chief Prosecutor, Seoul District Office (1983-1985); Vice Chief of Judicial Research and Training Center (1985-1986); Chief Prosecutor, Choonchun District Office (1986-1987);

(This Listing Continued)

Section Chief of Criminal Section 2, Supreme Public Prosecutors' Office (1987-1988); Probational Section Chief of Central Investigation Section, Supreme Prosecutors' Office (1988); Chief Prosecutor, Inchon District Office (1988-1991); Partner, Won Il Kang's Law Office (1991-1993). Member: Korean and Seoul Bar Associations. LANGUAGES: Korean and English.

JUNG HOON LEE, born Seoul, Korea, 1947; admitted, 1972, Korea; 1983, California; 1984, New York; 1987, Korea Patent Bar. Education: Seoul National University, Law School (LL.B., 1968); Seoul National University, Graduate School of Justice (1970); Judicial Research and Training Institute, Supreme Court of the Republic of Korea (1971-1972); Seoul National University, Graduate School of Law (LL.M., 1974); George Washington University, National Law Center (1979); University of Notre Dame, Law School (J.D., 1983). Judge Advocate, Korean Army, 1972-1975. Editor, "The Justice," Korean Legal Center, 1986— and Korean Bar Association Journal, 1988—. Author: "The Korean Anti-Dumping Law," 1985. Co-Author: "Enforcement of Korean Design Rights," 1988. Lecturer, Judicial Research and Training Institute, 1986—. Public Prosecutor, Seoul and Suwon District Offices, 1975-1978. Member, Shin & Kim, 1984-1986. Member: Seoul (Director of International Affairs, 1991-1992), Korean (Executive Secretary, International Affairs Committee, 1991—), New York State, American, Inter-Pacific and International Bar Associations; State Bar of California; Korea Patent Attorneys Association; GATT Uruguay Round Negotiations, Republic of Korea Delegation (Member-Advisor, 1990-1993); Ministry of Culture, Copyright Deliberation and Conciliation Committee (Member, 1993—); Korean Legal Center; Korea-U.S. Business Council Working Group. LANGUAGES: Korean and English; German and Japanese (reads only).

YONG SUK OH, born Muan, Korea, 1951; admitted, 1980, Korea; 1986, New York. Education: Korea University, Law School (LL.B., first in class, 1976); Judicial Research and Training Institute, Supreme Court of the Republic of Korea (1978-1980); Korea University, Graduate School of Law (1980-1982); Harvard Law School (LL.M., 1985). Member, Lee & Ko, 1980-1986. Visiting Attorney: Whitman & Ransom, New York City, 1985-1986. Member: Seoul, Korean, New York State, American Inter-Pacific and International Bar Associations. LANGUAGES: Korean and English; German and Japanese (reads only).

JAE SHIK LEE, born Chilgok, Korea, 1950; admitted, 1983, Korea. Education: Seoul National University, Law School (LL.B., 1974); Dongkuk University, Graduate School of Business Administration (M.B.A., 1975); Judicial Research and Training Institute, Supreme Court of the Republic of Korea (1981-1983); St. Mary's University, School of Law (1991-1992). Judge Advocate, Korean Army, 1978-1980. Member: Seoul and Korean Bar Associations. LANGUAGES: Korean and English; German and Japanese (reads only). PRACTICE AREAS: Civil Litigation; Commercial Litigation.

EUI IN HWANG, born Namwon, Korea, 1954; admitted, 1985, Korea; 1987, Korea Patent Bar. Education: Seoul National University, Law School (LL.B., 1978); Seoul National University, Graduate School of Law (LL.M., 1981); Judicial Research and Training Institute, Supreme Court of the Republic of Korea (1984-1985); University of California at Berkley, Boalt Hall School of Law (1992-1993). Visiting Researcher, Gaiyo University Law School, Tokyo, Japan (1993). Author: "Legal Aspects of Worker Participation in Company Management," 1981; "A Study on the Withholding of Individual Income Tax as to Bonuses other than Regular Wages and on the Levying of a Global Income Tax Thereon," 1990. Member: Seoul, Korean and Inter-Pacific Bar Associations; Korea Patent Attorneys Association. LANGUAGES: Korean and English; German and Japanese (reads only). PRACTICE AREAS: Taxation.

KEUN BYUNG LEE, born Taejon, Korea, 1960; admitted, 1984, Korea; 1992, New York. Education: Seoul National University, Law School (LL.B., 1983); Judicial Research and Training Institute, Supreme Court of the Republic of Korea (1983-1984); New York University, School of Law (LL.M., 1991). Author: "Subordinated Debt," 1992. Associate, Kim, Shin & Yu, 1985-1986. Visiting Attorney: Kelley Drye & Warren, New York City, 1991; International Institute for Securities Market Development of U.S. Securities and Exchange Commission, and National Association of Securities Dealers, Washington, D.C., 1992; Simmons & Simmons, London, England, 1992; Arendt & Medernach, Luxembourg, 1992. Member: Seoul, Korean and New York State Bar Associations; Korea International Trade Law Association. LANGUAGES: Korean and English; Japanese (reads only). PRACTICE AREAS: Securities; Banking; Corporate Finance.

SUK JIN CHON, born Seoul, Korea, 1958; admitted, 1987, Korea; 1993, California. Education: Seoul National University, Law School (LL.B., 1982); Seoul National University, Graduate School of Law (LL.M., 1984);

(This Listing Continued)

Judicial Research and Training Institute, Supreme Court of the Republic of Korea (1985-1987); University of California at Berkeley, Boalt Hall School of Law (LL.M., 1992). Case Review and Comment: Computer Associate v. Altair, 1992, Apple v. Microsoft, 1993, Article "Gigabit Telecommuting"; "Workflow Software"; "Vicko-on-Demand"; "Telecommuting," 1992-1993. Author: " Battle of the Forms - Seller v. Buyer," 1984; "Mergers and Acquisitions in Korea," 1991. Co-Author: "Enforcement of Korean Design Rights," 1988. Visiting Attorney: Ware & Freidenrich, Palo Alto, California, 1992; O'Melveny & Myers, Los Angeles, California, 1993. *Member:* Seoul and Korean Bar Associations; State Bar of California; Korea Intellectual Property Law Association (Director); Korean Commercial Law Association; M & A Study Association of Korea. *LANGUAGES:* Korean and English; German and Japanese (reads only). *PRACTICE AREAS:* Intellectual Property; Computer and Communications.

JONG KU KANG, born Daegu, Korea, 1959; admitted, 1985, Korea. *Education:* Seoul National University, Law School (LL.B., 1982); Judicial Research and Training Institute, Supreme Court of the Republic of Korea (1984-1985); Seoul National University, Graduate School of Law (LL.M., 1987); University of London (UCL Maritime Law Program, 1989-1990). Author: "Conditional Sale of Movables," 1987; "Delivery of Cargo under Letters of Guarantee in Korea," 1991. Associate, Central International Law Firm, 1987-1989. Visiting Attorney: Thomas, Cooper & Stibbard, Ince & Co. and Steamship Mutual Underwriting Association, London, England, 1990; Van Bael & Bellis, Brussels, Belgium, 1991. *Member:* Seoul, Korean and International Bar Associations; Asia-Pacific Lawyers Association; European Maritime Law Organization; Korean Maritime Law Association; Korean Competition Law Association. *LANGUAGES:* Korean and English; German and Japanese (reads only). *PRACTICE AREAS:* Maritime; Insurance; International Trade; Aviation.

SUNG JIN KIM, born Pusan, Korea, 1958; admitted, 1986, Korea. *Education:* Seoul National University, Law School (LL.B., 1981); Seoul National University, Graduate School of Law (1982-1984); Judicial Research and Training Institute, Supreme Court of the Republic of Korea (1984-1986); University of Washington (LL.M., 1994). *Member:* Seoul and Korean Bar Associations. *LANGUAGES:* Korean and English; German and Japanese (reads only).

YANG HO OH, born Cheonju, Korea, 1962; admitted, 1985, Korea. *Education:* Seoul National University, Law School (LL.B., 1984); Judicial Research and Training Institute, Supreme Court of the Republic of Korea (1984-1986); Harvard Law School (LL.M., 1994). Author: "Principles of Good Faith in Civil Procedure," 1985. *Member:* Seoul, Korean and International Bar Associations. *LANGUAGES:* Korean and English; Japanese (reads only).

DONG WOO SEO, born Daegu, Korea, 1963; admitted, 1987, Korea; 1992, New York. *Education:* Seoul National University, Law School (LL.B., magna cum laude, 1985); Judicial Research and Training Institute, Supreme Court of the Republic of Korea (1985-1987); National Laureate: National Bar Examination, Judicial Research and Training Institute; Korea University, Graduate School of Law, (1988-1991); Harvard Law School (LL.M., 1992). Author: "Standing of Parties in Litigation Over Realty Owned in Common," 1986; "Material Retardation Standard in U.S. Antidumping Law," 1992. Co-Author: "Overseas Bonds With Warrants Issued by Korean Corporations," 1989. Visiting Attorney: Rogers & Wells, Washington, D.C., 1992; Cleary, Gottlieb, Steen & Hamilton, New York City, 1993. *Member:* Seoul, Korean and New York State Bar Associations. *LANGUAGES:* Korean and English; German, Japanese and French (reads only). *PRACTICE AREAS:* Trade Regulation.

IN MAN KIM, born Seoul, Korea, 1961; admitted, 1988, Korea. *Education:* Seoul National University, Law School (LL.B., 1985); Judicial Research and Training Institute, Supreme Court of the Republic of Korea (1986-1988). *Member:* Seoul and Korean Bar Associations. *LANGUAGES:* Korean and English; German and Japanese (reads only).

JONG GIL KIM, born Kimcheon, Korea, 1962; admitted, 1988, Korea. *Education:* Seoul National University, Law School (LL.B., 1985); Judicial Research and Training Institute, Supreme Court of the Republic of Korea (1986-1988); Beijing University Law School (1994—). *Member:* Seoul, Korean and Inter-Pacific Bar Associations. *LANGUAGES:* Korean, English and Chinese; Japanese (reads only).

CHEONG HAN LEE, born Cheonju, Korea, 1963; admitted, 1988, Korea. *Education:* Seoul National University, Law School (LL.B., 1985); Judicial Research and Training Institute, Supreme Court of the Republic of Korea (1986-1988). *Member:* Seoul and Korean Bar Associations. *LANGUAGES:* Korean and English; German and Japanese (reads only).

PRACTICE AREAS: Maritime; Insurance; International Trade and Aviation.

HOO DONG LEE, born Daegu, Korea, 1964; admitted, 1988, Korea. *Education:* Seoul National University, Law School (LL.B., 1986); Seoul National University, Graduate School of Law (1986-1988; 1991—); Judicial Research and Training Institute, Supreme Court of the Republic of Korea (1986-1988). *Member:* Seoul and Korean Bar Associations. *LANGUAGES:* Korean, English and Japanese.

MS. BOH YOUNG HWANG, born Youngil, Korea, 1964; admitted, 1989, Korea. *Education:* Seoul National University, Law School (LL.B., 1987); Judicial Research and Training Institute, Supreme Court of the Republic of Korea (1987-1989); Harvard Law School (LL.M., 1993). Co-Author: "Arbitration of Private Intellectual Property Disputes," 1992. Visiting Attorney, Morgan & Finnegan, New York (1993). *Member:* Seoul, Korean and Korean Women's (Secretary General, 1991—) Bar Associations; New York State Bar Association; Korea Patent Attorneys Association; AIPPI; KITLA. *LANGUAGES:* Korean and English; Japanese (reads only). *PRACTICE AREAS:* Intellectual Property; Technology and Science.

BYUNG HA JEON, born Iri, Korea, 1964; admitted, 1989, Korea. *Education:* Seoul National University, Law School (LL.B., 1987); Judicial Research and Training Institute, Supreme Court of the Republic of Korea (1987-1989). Prosecutor, Korean Air Force, 1989-1992. *Member:* Seoul and Korean Bar Associations. *LANGUAGES:* Korean and English; Japanese (reads only).

BYUNG HO CHOI, born Pusan, Korea, 1964; admitted, 1989, Korea. *Education:* Seoul National University, Law School (LL.B., 1987); Judicial Research and Training Institute, Supreme Court of the Republic of Korea (1987-1989). *Member:* Seoul and Korean Bar Associations. *LANGUAGES:* Korean and English; Japanese (reads only).

RI BONG HAN, born Daegu, Korea, 1964; admitted, 1989, Korea. *Education:* Seoul National University, Law School (LL.B., cum laude, 1987); Seoul National University, Graduate School of Law (1990—); Judicial Research and Training Institute, Supreme Court of the Republic of Korea; National Laureate: National Bar Examination. *Member:* Seoul and Korean Bar Associations. *LANGUAGES:* Korean, English and Japanese; German (reads only). *PRACTICE AREAS:* International Arbitration and Litigation; International Business Transactions.

EUI JONG CHUNG, born Seoul, Korea, 1963; admitted, 1991, Korea. *Education:* Seoul National University, Law School (LL.B., 1986); Seoul National University, Graduate School of Law (LL.M., 1988); Judicial Research and Training Institute, Supreme Court of the Republic of Korea (1989-1991). Author: "The Constitutional Law System of the French Fifth Republic," 1988. *Member:* Seoul and Korean Bar Associations. *LANGUAGES:* Korean and English; French and Japanese (reads only).

WOOK YOO, born Seoul, Korea, 1963; admitted, 1990, Korea. *Education:* Seoul National University, Law School (LL.B., 1986); Seoul National University, Graduate School of Law (LL.M., 1988); Judicial Research and Training Institute, Supreme Court of the Republic of Korea (1988-1990). *Member:* Seoul and Korean Bar Associations. *LANGUAGES:* Korean, English and Japanese.

HYUNG YEON PARK, born Seoul, Korea, 1964; admitted, 1990, Korea. *Education:* Korea University, Law School (LL.B., 1987; LL.M., 1993) Judicial Research and Training Institute, Supreme Court of the Republic of Korea (1988-1990). Author: "Dumping Criteria under the International Anti-dumping Code: Particular Focus on the EC Council Regulation," 1992. *Member:* Seoul and Korean Bar Associations. *LANGUAGES:* Korean and English; German (reads only).

GUN CHUL DO, born Daegu, Korea, 1965; admitted, 1990, Korea. *Education:* Seoul National University, Law School (LL.B., 1988); Judicial Research and Training Institute, Supreme Court of the Republic of Korea (1988-1990). *Member:* Seoul and Korean Bar Associations. *LANGUAGES:* Korean and English; Japanese (reads only).

SIH KYOUNG YANG, born Chonju, Korea, 1965; admitted, 1990, Korea. *Education:* Seoul National University, Law School (LL.B., 1988); Judicial Research and Training Institute, Supreme Court of the Republic of Korea (1988-1990). *Member:* Seoul and Korean Bar Associations. *LANGUAGES:* Korean and English.

HYUNG SUK LEE, born Goheung, Korea, 1965; admitted, 1992, Korea. *Education:* Seoul National University Law School (LL.B., 1988); Judicial Research and Training Institute, Supreme Court of the Republic of Korea (1990-1992). *LANGUAGES:* Korean, English and Japanese.

(This Listing Continued)

(This Listing Continued)

BAE, KIM & LEE, Seoul—Continued

HYUN WOOK PARK, born Pusan, Korea, 1967; admitted, 1992, Korean. *Education:* Seoul National University Law School (LL.B., 1990); Judicial Research and Training Institute, Supreme Court of the Republic of Korea (1990-1992). *LANGUAGES:* Korean, English and Japanese.

HYEON KANG, born Keojae, Kyungnam Province, Korea, 1964; admitted, 1993, Korea. *Education:* Korea University Law School (LL.B., 1990); Judicial Research and Training Institute, Supreme Court of the Republic of Korea (1991-1993). *Member:* Seoul and Korean Bar Associations. *LANGUAGES:* Korean, English and German.

DO HYUNG KIM, born Pusan, Korea, 1964; admitted, 1993, Korea. *Education:* Seoul National University Law School (LL.B., 1987); Seoul National University Graduate School of Law (LL.M., 1991); Judicial Research and Training Institute, Supreme Court of the Republic of Korea (1991-1993). Public Prosecutor, Daegu District Office, 1993-1995. *LANGUAGES:* Korean, English and German.

SEUNG BOK NAH, born Hampyong, Korea, 1963; admitted, 1994, Korea. *Education:* Department of Chinese Language and Literature, Seoul National University (B.A., 1990; Minor: Jurisprudence); Judicial Research and Training Institute, Supreme Court of the Republic of Korea (1992-1994). *Member:* Korean and Seoul Bar Associations. *LANGUAGES:* Korean, English and Chinese.

KWANG HYUN RYOO, born Namwon, Korea, 1967; admitted, 1994, Korea. *Education:* Seoul National University Law School (LL.B., 1989); Judicial Research and Training Institute, Supreme Court of the Republic of Korea (1992-1994). Public Prosecutor, Pusan District Office, 1994-1995. *LANGUAGES:* Korean, English, German and Japanese.

HAN GIL JOO, born Seoul, Korea, 1964; admitted, 1995, Korea. *Education:* Seoul National University Law School (LL.B., 1987); Seoul National University Graduate School of Law (LL.M., 1989); Judicial Research and Training Institute, Supreme Court of the Republic of Korea (1993-1995). *LANGUAGES:* Korean, English and German.

KWON HEE LEE, born Chincheon, Korea, 1955; admitted, 1990, Korea Patent Bar. *Education:* Dankuk University, Law School (LL.B., 1979); International Patent Training Institute (1989). Author: "Parallel Importation into Korea," 1989. Trademark and Design Manager, Hwasung-Nike Co., Ltd., 1983-1984. Trademark and Design Specialist, Central International Law Firm, 1984-1988. *Member:* Korea and Asia Patent Attorneys Associations. *LANGUAGES:* Korean and English; Japanese (reads only). *PRACTICE AREAS:* Intellectual Property.

EUN KYUNG LEE, born Seoul, Korea, 1965; admitted, 1992, Korea Patent Bar. *Education:* Seoul National University (B.S., 1988); Seoul National University Graduate School of Pharmacy (M.S., 1990). Professional Experience: KINITI (1989-1991); Hansung International Patent & Law Offices (1992-1994). *Member:* Korea Patent Attorneys Association. *LANGUAGES:* Korean and English; Japanese (reading only).

FOREIGN LEGAL CONSULTANTS

MICHAEL A. HAY, DR., born Dunipace, Scotland, 1961 (dual British-French citizen); admitted, 1987, Scotland qualified for Solicitor Clerkship; 1989, New York and U.S. District Court, Southern and Eastern Districts of New York; 1990, U.S. District Court, Northern and Western Districts of New York (Not admitted in Korea). *Education:* University of Edinburgh, Scotland (LL.B., Hons., 1983; Dip.L.P., 1987; Ph.D., Comparative Law, England, Scotland and France, 1988); University of Paris, Institute of Comparative Law and French Supreme Court (Cour de Cassation) Research Studies, Paris, France (1984); Institute of Advanced Legal Studies, London, England (1984,1985); Northwestern University, Chicago, U.S.A., (LL.M., 1988). James Nelson Raymond International Fellowship; University of Edinburgh Faculty of Law Scholarship. Author: "The Antitrust Status of Territorial Restraints in Know-How Licenses" (European Community Law), 1988. Arbitrator, Korean Commercial Arbitration Board. Associate, Seward & Kissel, New York City, 1988-1991. *Member:* New York State, American and International Bar Associations; New York County Lawyers' Association; Scottish Lawyers' European Group; British Institute of International & Comparative Law; Union Internationale des Avocats; American, European and British Chambers of Commerce in Korea; French Chamber of Commerce & Industry in Korea. *LANGUAGES:* English, French and Korean; Italian (reads only). *PRACTICE AREAS:* International Arbitration and Litigation; Trademarks; International Business Transactions.

(This Listing Continued)

AS202B

ANNIE EUN-AH LEE, born Seoul, Korea, 1965; admitted, 1991, New York (Not admitted in Korea). *Education:* Ewha Woman's University (B.A., 1987); Boston College Law School (J.D., cum laude, 1990). Author: "Toward Institutionalization of Reciprocity in Transnational Legal Services: A Proposal for a Multilateral Convention under the Auspices of the GATT," 8 B.C. Int'l. and Comp. L. Rev. 91 (1990). Associate, White & Case, New York City (1990-1992). *Member:* New York State and American Bar Associations. *LANGUAGES:* Korean, English and French. *PRACTICE AREAS:* Banking and Corporate Finance.

SANG GOO LEE, born Seoul, Korea, 1964. *Education:* Harvard University (A.B., 1987); University of Chicago, Graduate history program (1989-1990); Brooklyn Law School (J.D., 1993). Research Assistant, Korea Development Institute, Seoul, 1987-1988; Legal Clerk, Bae, Kim & Lee, P.C. (1989). *LANGUAGES:* English and Korean.

WON HYONG LEE, born Seoul, Korea, 1968; admitted, 1994, CIS (Not admitted in Korea). *Education:* Dankook University Law School (LL.B., 1992); Moscow State University Law School (LL.M., 1994). *LANGUAGES:* Korean, Russian and English.

OF COUNSEL

BOK KEE MIN, DR., born Seoul, Korea, 1913; admitted, 1945, Korea. *Education:* Kyungsung National University, Law School (LL.B., 1938); Kyunghee University, Law School (J.S.D., 1965). Judge, Seoul High Court of Appeals, 1947-1949. Vice-Minister of Justice of the Republic of Korea, 1950. Chief Prosecutor, Seoul District Office, 1951. Public Prosecutor General, 1955. Justice, Supreme Court of the Republic of Korea, 1961. Minister of Justice of the Republic of Korea, 1963-1966. Chief Justice, Supreme Court of the Republic of Korea, 1968-1978. Commissioner, Advisory Commission to the President of the Republic for National Administration, 1980-1992. *Member:* Seoul and Korean Bar Associations. *LANGUAGES:* Korean and Japanese; English (reads only).

WOUN GIE KIM, born Dangjin, Korea, 1924; (Not admitted in Korea). *Education:* Korea University (B.A., 1949); George Washington University, School of Business (1958); University of London, School of Business (1964). Director of Bureau, Ministry of Finance, 1961-1967. Vice-Minister of Construction of the Republic of Korea, 1968-1970. President, Korea Development Bank, 1972-1978. Minister of Finance of the Republic of Korea, 1978-1980. Deputy Prime Minister and Minister, Economic Planning Board, 1980-1982. Chairman, Board of Directors, Korea Highway Corporation, 1982—. Advisor, Ssangyong Group, 1983—. *LANGUAGES:* Korean, English and Japanese.

LEE SIK CHAI, born Seoul, Korea, 1949; admitted, 1972, Korea; 1983, England and Wales (Barrister-at-Law, Middle Temple); 1985, Korea Patent Bar. *Education:* Korea University, Law School (LL.B., 1971); University of London (LL.M., 1980); City University, London (M.A., 1982). Author: "Treatise on Commercial Law," Bakyung-Sa Publishers, 1990. Visiting Professor, 1984-1987 and Professor, 1987—, of Commercial and Maritime Law, Korea University, Law School. Member, Central International Law Firm, 1984-1987. *Member:* Seoul and Korean Bar Associations; Korea Patent Attorneys Association; Honourable Society of the Middle Temple, England and Wales. *LANGUAGES:* Korean and English.

CENTRAL INTERNATIONAL LAW FIRM

Established in 1962

5TH FLOOR, KOREA REINSURANCE BUILDING
80, SOOSONG-DONG, CHONGRO-KU
KWANGWHAMOON P.O. BOX 356
SEOUL, KOREA
Telephone: 735-5621/6; 735-5072/4
Telex: CENTPAT 23250
Facsimile: 2-733-5206/7
Cable Address: CENTPAT

General Commercial Practice: General Legal Practice including Corporate Matters and Commercial Litigation, International Trade including Capital Investment and Technology and Know-how Licensing, Finance, Tax, Labor, International Litigation and Arbitration, Insurance. Intellectual Property (Prosecutions and Litigation): Patents, Trademarks, Unfair Trade Practices, Utility Models, Industrial Designs, Copyrights, Computer Programs.

(This Listing Continued)

MEMBERS OF FIRM

BYONG HO LEE, born Korea, March 17, 1926; admitted, 1954, Korea. *Education:* College of Law, Seoul National University (B.Jur., 1952); Southern Methodist University, School of Law, U.S.A. (M.C.L., 1962); Honorary Doctor of Laws (LL.D., Hon.), Marquis Giuseppe Scicluna International University Foundation U.S.A. (1987). Author: "Patent, Trademark and Licensing in Korea," published in 1968, second edition, 1978; "Comparative Study of Legal Systems in Various Countries," published in 1974. Judge Advocate of the ROK Army. Judge, 1956-1959. Chairman of the Public Relations Committee of the Korean Bar Association, 1966. President of the International Legal Center, 1993. President of the Korean Branch of the International Law Association, 1973. Instructor, Graduate School of Law, Seoul National University, 1977. Arbitrator of the Korean Commercial Arbitration Board, 1980. Advisor to the Central Committee for National Unification of Korea, 1982. Director of the Korean Youth Federation, 1982. Senior Partner of Central International Law Firm, 1962—. Legal Advisor to the Olympic Organizing Committee, 1986. President of World Deity Association for Eradication of Substance Abuse, 1990. *Member:* Seoul Bar Association (President, 1983-1984); Korean Bar Association; Korean Patent Attorneys Association (President, 1971-1972; 1973-1974); Asian Patent Attorneys Association (President, Korea branch, 1969-1984); Asia-Pacific Lawyers Association (President, 1984—); AIPPI; International Bar Association; American Bar Association. *LANGUAGES:* Korean, English, Japanese and Chinese. *PRACTICE AREAS:* Intellectual Property Law; General Litigation; Foreign Investment Law.

HYUNG KOO CHOI, born Korea, May 21, 1958; admitted, 1984, Korea. *Education:* College of Law, Seoul National University (B.Jur., 1982); Judicial Training and Research Institute of the Supreme Court of Korea (1982-1985); Columbia University, School of Law, U.S.A. (LL.M., 1993). Judge Advocate of the ROK Army, 1985-1988. *Member:* Korean Bar Association; Korean Patent Attorneys Association; Asia-Pacific Lawyers Association. *LANGUAGES:* Korean, English and Japanese. *PRACTICE AREAS:* Licensing; Intellectual Property Law; International Business Transactions.

JOON PYO HAHM, born June 11, 1958; admitted, 1989, Korea. *Education:* College of Economics, Seoul National University (B.Econ., 1986); Judicial Training and Research Institute of the Supreme Court of Korea (1987-1988). Researcher, The International Financing Department of Lucky Inc., 1986. Associated with: Kim, Chang & Lee Law Office, 1989; Judicial Development and Research Institute of the Seoul National University, 1990. Publication: "The Problem of the Korean Financing System & Laws," 1986. *Member:* Korean Bar Association; Asia-Pacific Lawyers Association. *LANGUAGES:* Korean, English, French (reads only) and Japanese (reads only). *PRACTICE AREAS:* Tax Law; Insurance Law; General Litigation.

SEUNG WOOK CHOI, born Korea, November 2, 1960; admitted, 1989, Korea. *Education:* College of Law, Seoul National University (B.Jur., 1983); Graduate School of Law, Seoul National University (1983-1986); Judicial Training and Research Institute of the Supreme Court of Korea (1987-1988). Managing Attorney, Labor-Management Relations Center, Asia-Pacific Lawyers Association, 1990—. Contributing Columnist, The Daily Economic Newspaper; "Wage-related Issues under the Korean Labor Standards Act," 1991; "Justifiable Termination," 1991. *Member:* Korean Bar Association; Asia-Pacific Lawyers Association. *LANGUAGES:* Korean, English, Japanese (reads only) and French (reads only). *PRACTICE AREAS:* Labor Law; International Business Transactions.

WOON GIL YEO, born Korea, July 31, 1961; admitted, 1989, Korea. *Education:* College of Law, Seoul National University (B.Jur., 1983); Graduate School of Law, Seoul National University (1983-1986); Judicial Training and Research Institute of the Supreme Court of Korea (1987-1988). *Member:* Korean Bar Association; Asia-Pacific Lawyers Association. *LANGUAGES:* Korean, English, Japanese and German (reads only). *PRACTICE AREAS:* International Business Transactions; Intellectual Property.

DAE SUNG KIM, born Korea, January 16, 1962; admitted, 1990, Korea. *Education:* College of Law, Seoul National University (B.Jur., 1985); Graduate School of Law, Seoul National University (M.Jur., 1987); Judicial Training and Research Institute of the Supreme Court of Korea (1988-1990). *Member:* Korean Bar Association; Asia-Pacific Lawyers Association. *LANGUAGES:* Korean, English, Japanese and German (reads only). *PRACTICE AREAS:* Maritime Law; Insurance Law.

SUNG HEE KWON, born Korea, October 2, 1963; admitted, 1990, Korea. *Education:* College of Law, Ewha Women's University (B.Jur., 1986); Judicial Training and Research Institute of the Supreme Court of Korea (1988-1990). *Member:* Korean Bar Association; Asia-Pacific Lawyers Asso-

ciation. *LANGUAGES:* Korean, English, German (reads only) and Japanese (reads only). *PRACTICE AREAS:* Intellectual Property Law; Family Law; Criminal Law; General Litigation.

SONG HO KIM, born Korea, October 25, 1961; admitted, 1989, California (Not admitted in Korea). *Education:* University of California, Los Angeles (B.A., Economics, 1985); Southwestern University School of Law (J.D., 1989). *Member:* State Bar of California; American Bar Association; Asia-Pacific Lawyers Association. *LANGUAGES:* English and Korean. *PRACTICE AREAS:* Licensing; International Business Transactions; Intellectual Property Law.

HEE IHN KIM, born Korea, November 7, 1958; admitted, 1991, New York (Not admitted in Korea). *Education:* College of Law, Yonsei University (LL.B., 1982); The Dickinson School of Law (LL.M., 1990); University of Pennsylvania Law School, U.S.A. (LL.M., 1991). Lecturer, Korea Air and Correspondence University Law School, 1993—. Associated with Pennie & Edmonds, N.Y., N.Y., U.S.A. (1991-1992). Publication: "Product Liability in Korea," (1989); "Extraterritorial Jurisdiction of U.S. Basic Antitrust Law-The Sherman Act," (1990); "Section 337 of the 1988 Omnibus Trade and Competitiveness Act," (1990); "How to Solve So-Called Prisoner's Dilemma in Tender Offer," (1991). *Member:* New York State and American Bar Associations; Asia-Pacific Lawyers Association. *LANGUAGES:* English and Korean. *PRACTICE AREAS:* Foreign Investment; Licensing; Intellectual Property Law; International Business Transactions; Computer Software Program Protection.

DANIEL KIM, born Philadelphia, Pennsylvania, February 11, 1966; admitted, 1994, California and U.S. District Court, Central District of California (Not admitted in Korea). *Education:* University of California, Los Angeles (B.A., Philosophy, 1990); University of California, Los Angeles School of Law (J.D., 1993). *LANGUAGES:* English and Korean.

DALL RYONG CHOI, born Korea, February 14, 1945; admitted, 1983, Licensed Patent Attorney. *Education:* Han Yang University (B.S., Electronic Engineering, 1974). Technical Training on Multicommunication System at Nippon Telegraph & Telephone Public Corporation, Japan, August-September, 1973. Central International Law Firm, 1974-1976, 1982—. Manager of Patent and Planning Department, Dong-Yang Precision Industrial Co., Ltd., 1976-1978. Manager of Han Kuk Microscope Co., Ltd., 1978-1980. *Member:* Korean Patent Attorneys Association; APAA; AIPPI. *LANGUAGES:* Korean, Japanese and English. *PRACTICE AREAS:* Electronic and Mechanical.

SANG HYUN CHOI, born Korea, November 26, 1934; admitted, 1985, Licensed Patent Attorney. *Education:* Seoul National University. Sam Sung Mool-San Company; Daihan Coal Corporation; Honam Oil Refinery Co., Ltd. Publications: "Worldwide Trademark Transfers" (Korean Chapter), Law and Practice, USTA, 1992. *Member:* Korean Patent Attorneys Association. *LANGUAGES:* Korean, English and Japanese. *PRACTICE AREAS:* Trademarks and Designs.

HO HYUN NAHM, born Korea, January 18, 1953; admitted, 1987, Licensed Patent Attorney. *Education:* College of Law, Chongju University (B. Jur., 1976); Graduate School of Public Administration, Seoul National University (M.Pa., 1985). Ministry of Culture and Information, 1980-1982; Law offices Lee & Ko, 1982-1987. Publication: "The Korean Government's Policy Regarding Technological Inducement: An Evaluation and a Recommendation," Treatise, 1985. *Member:* Korean Patent Attorneys Association; EC Trademark Association. *LANGUAGES:* Korean, English and Japanese. *PRACTICE AREAS:* Trademarks and Designs.

KYOUNG JIN MOON, born Korea, December 18, 1952; admitted, 1983, Licensed Patent Attorney. *Education:* Seoul National University (B.S. Nuclear Engineering, 1976); Korea Advanced Institute of Science and Technology (M.S. Mechanical Engineering, 1978); North Carolina State University (Ph.D. Mechanical Engineering, 1988). Experience: Research Assistant at Mechanical and Aerospace Engineering Department of North Carolina State University, U.S.A. (1984-1988); Training for Patent Examination: WIPO, German Patent Office (1979), Primary Patent Examiner at Korean Industrial Property Office (1978-1983). Publication: "Trends in Shipbuilding Technology as Reflected in Patent Associations," 1983. *Member:* Korean Patent Attorneys Association. *LANGUAGES:* Korean, English and Japanese. *PRACTICE AREAS:* Intellectual Property; Electronics and Mechanical Engineering.

SANG GOO JEONG, born Korea, October 11, 1953; admitted, 1989, Licensed Patent Attorney. *Education:* Seoul National University (B.S., Mechanics, 1977). Ministry of National Defense Arsenal, 1977-1982. Daewoo Precision Inc. Ltd., 1982. *Member:* Korean Patent Attorneys Association.

(This Listing Continued)

CENTRAL INTERNATIONAL LAW FIRM, Seoul—
Continued

LANGUAGES: Korean, English and Japanese. PRACTICE AREAS: Precision Mechanism.

BYUNG SEOK BARK, born Korea, May 13, 1960; admitted, 1990, Korean Patent Bar, Licensed Patent Attorney. Education: Kyung-pook National University (B.S., Agrochemistry, 1982); Korea Advanced Institute of Science and Technology (M.S., Biochemistry, 1985); Columbia University, School of Law (1990). Training for Patent Examination: Japanese Patent Office (1988); U.S. Patent and Trademark Office (1987). Experience: Primary Patent Examiner at Korean Industrial Property Office (Organic Chemistry, Genetic Engineering & Microbiology, 1985-1990). Member: Korean Patent Attorneys Association. LANGUAGES: Korean, English and Japanese. PRACTICE AREAS: Chemistry and Biotechnology.

JEONG SOON LEE, born October 10, 1962; admitted, 1990, Korean Patent Bar; Licensed Patent Attorney. Education: Ewha Women's University (B.S., Pharmacy, 1985; M.S., Pharmaceutics, 1987). Experience: Joon Koo Lee Patent Office (1987-1988); Central International Law Firm (1988—). Publication: "The Effect of Surfactants on the dissolution of Sulfanilamide granules." Other Qualification: Licensed Pharmacist. Member: Korean Patent Attorneys Association, Korean Pharmacists Association. LANGUAGES: Korean and English. PRACTICE AREAS: Pharmacy.

NAM KYUNG LEE, born Korea, May 1, 1968; admitted, 1992, Korean Patent Bar; Licensed Patent Attorney. Education: Seoul National University (B.S., Pharmacy, 1990). Experience: Central International Law Firm, 1991—. Other Qualifications: Licensed Pharmacist. Member: Korean Patent Attorneys Association; Korean Pharmacists Association. LANGUAGES: Korean and English. PRACTICE AREAS: Pharmacy.

JANG CHAN SUH, born Korea, July 17, 1956; admitted, 1992, Korean Patent Bar; Licensed Patent Attorney. Education: Yonsei University (B.S., Electric Engineering, 1980). Training for Patent Examination: Japanese Patent Office (1990). Experience: Korean Monopoly Office (1980-1987), Primary Patent Examiner at Korean Industrial Property Office (1987-1993). LANGUAGES: Korean, English and Japanese. PRACTICE AREAS: Electronic and Electric Engineering.

GEORGE T. BREITENSTEIN, born Wisconsin, U.S.A., October 5, 1943; admitted, 1974, Florida, U.S.A.; 1976-1982, U.S. Court of Customs and Patent Appeals; 1979, District of Columbia; 1982, U.S. Court of Appeals for the Federal Circuit and U.S. Patent and Trademark Office; 1988, Federal District Court, Middle District of Florida. (Not admitted in Korea). Education: University of Wisconsin, School of Pharmacy (B.S., Pharmacy, 1966); University of Miami, School of Law (J.D., 1974). Registered to practice Pharmacy: 1966, Wisconsin; 1968, Florida; 1982, Virginia. Examiner, U.S. Patent and Trademark Office, 1974-1982. Member: American Bar Association (Patent, Trademark and Copyright Sections; Law, Science and Technology Sections); American Intellectual Property Lawyers Association; The Florida Bar; District of Columbia Bar. LANGUAGES: English. PRACTICE AREAS: Intellectual Property.

YOUNG TAE SOHN, born Korea, December 5, 1948; admitted, 1990, Korean Patent Bar; Licensed Patent Attorney. Education: College of Law, Korea University (B.Jur., 1977). Member: Korean Patent Attorneys Association; Asian Pacific Patent Association. LANGUAGES: Korean, English and German (Reads only). PRACTICE AREAS: Trademarks and Designs.

CJ INTERNATIONAL
LAW OFFICES

Established in 1986

1712/14 KYOBO BUILDING

CHONG-RO 1-KA

SEOUL, KOREA

Telephone: 736-0145

Facsimile: (02) 736-2232; 723-8366

Admiralty, Anti-dumping, Arbitration, Banking, Business Consulting, Feasibility Study, Government Negotiation, Insurance, International Trade and Investment, Labor, Litigation, Offshore Financing, Securities, Tax and Transfer of Technology.

FIRM PROFILE: CJ International, a professional corporation, is jointly represented by Mr. Wu Dong Park, a former Justice of the Supreme Court, and Dr. Chan Jin Kim, former Assistant Minister for economic

(This Listing Continued)

affairs to the Prime Minister, 1980-1986. Mr. Hoi Chang Lee, a former Justice of the Supreme Court, 1986-1993, and Prime Minister, 1993-1994, serves as advisor to the firm. The firm is the premier Korean law firm in the field of government and regulatory representation.

MEMBERS OF FIRM

WU DONG PARK, born Ham An, Korea, September 30, 1934; admitted, 1957, Korea. Education: Seoul National University (LL.B., 1957). Author: "Commentary Civil Procedural Law," (co-author); "Commentary Compulsory Enforcement Law," (co-author); "Litigation for Bodily Injury." Justice, Supreme Court of the Republic of Korea, 1986-1993. Deputy Administrator, Office of Court Administration, 1983-1986. President, Seoul Family Court, 1981-1983. Judge, Seoul Court of Appeals, Daejon and Pusan District Courts. Chairman, Newspapers Ethics Committee, 1994—. Member: Korean Bar Association. LANGUAGES: Korean, Japanese. PRACTICE AREAS: Litigation; Arbitration.

CHAN JIN KIM, born Kwang Ju, Korea, February 24, 1941; admitted, 1964, Korea. Education: Seoul National University (LL.B., 1963; LL.M., 1967); University of Michigan Law School (M.C.L., 1969); University of Washington, School of Law (Ph.D. in Law, 1972). Editor: Business Laws in Korea, English, 2nd edition, 1988; Trade Law of the United States, Korean, 1990; Korean Journal of Comparative Law (KJCL), 1973-1990. Author: Foreign Investment in Korea: Law and Administration, English, 1972; Foreign Capital Inducement Theory, Korean, 1976; "Antimerger Laws of the United States, Japan and Korea," Volume XII KJCL, 1984; "New Antidumping Law of Korea," Volume XV KJCL, 1987. Commissioner, Korea Trade Commission, 1993—. Member, Foreign Capital Inducement Deliberation Committee, 1988—. Guest News Commentator, KBS TV and Radio, 1991—. Director-General, Office of Foreign Contract Review, Economic Planning Board, 1973-1978. Secretary to the President for Economic Affairs, 1978-1980. Assistant Minister for Economic Affairs and Senior Advisor to the Prime Minister, Republic of Korea, 1980-1986. Visiting Professor, University of Washington Law School, Fall Quarter, 1986. Counsel to the Korean Delegation for § 301 Negotiations with the United States Trade Representative on Cigarette and Wine, 1988-1990. Counsel to the Korean Delegation for Korea-USSR Trade Agreement, 1990. Special Counsel to the Green Round Strategy Committee, Ministry of Environment, 1994—. Member: Korean, American (Associate) and International Bar Associations; LAWASIA (Councillor); Korean Research Institute of Comparative Law (President, 1973—); Korean Competition Law Society (President, 1988—). LANGUAGES: Korean, English, Japanese and German. PRACTICE AREAS: Trade; Investment; Fair Trade Law; Anti-dumping Law; Government Negotiation.

KI CHANG LEE, born Seoul, Korea, June 23, 1935; naturalized as a U.S. Citizen in 1967; admitted, 1967, New York (Not admitted in Korea). Education: University of New Hampshire, N.H. (B.A., 1959); Columbia University, New York (M.A., 1962); Brooklyn Law School, Brooklyn, N.Y. (J.D., 1965); Parker School of Foreign and Comparative Law, Columbia University (1967). Attorney, Gulf Oil Corporation, New York, 1966-1969. Attorney Advisor, U.S. Department of Defense stationed in Korea, 1969-1978. Private law practice since 1978. Member: New York State Bar. LANGUAGES: Korean, English and Japanese. PRACTICE AREAS: Contracts Law; Banking Law.

YUN JAE BAEK, born Seoul, Korea, June 25, 1959; admitted, 1984, Korea. Education: Seoul National University (LL.B., 1982; LL.M., 1984); Judicial Training and Research Institute (1985); Harvard Law School (LL.M., 1993). Author: "International Arbitration and Dispute Resolution involving Estate Parties," thesis. Member: Korean and New York Bar Associations. LANGUAGES: Korean, English, Japanese and French. PRACTICE AREAS: Corporate, Banking & Securities Law; Insurance & Maritime Law.

SANG KIE LEE, born Kwang Ju, Korea, December 18, 1959; admitted, 1986, Korea. Education: Seoul National University (LL.B., 1981; LL.M., 1983); Judicial Training and Research Institute (1986). Member: Korean Bar Association. LANGUAGES: Korean, English and Japanese. PRACTICE AREAS: Tax Law; Administrative Law; Litigation.

KANG-HO JHE, born Seoul, Korea, October 22, 1961; admitted, 1987, Korea. Education: Seoul National University (LL.B., 1984); Judicial Training and Research Institute (1987). Member: Korean Bar Association. LANGUAGES: Korean, English, Japanese and German. PRACTICE AREAS: Securities Law; Corporate Banking Law; Issuance of Convertible Bond.

CHARLEY TSCHOY, born Seoul, Korea, February 6, 1960; admitted, 1988, Korea. Education: Seoul National University (LL.B., 1982; LL.M., 1988); Judicial Training and Research Institute (1988); Tuebingen Univer-

(This Listing Continued)

sity Law School (1989-1994). *Member:* Korean Bar Association. *LANGUAGES:* Korean, English and German. *PRACTICE AREAS:* Labor Law; Trade Law.

HYUNG JIN KIM, born Mok Po, Korea, September 17, 1961; admitted, 1989, Korea. *Education:* Seoul National University (LL.B., 1984); Judicial Training and Research Institute (1989). *Member:* Korean Bar Association. *LANGUAGES:* Korean, English and Japanese. *PRACTICE AREAS:* Antidumping Law; Foreign Exchange Control Law.

SUNG WOO LIM, born Pohang, Korea, September 30, 1966; admitted, 1989, Korea. *Education:* Seoul National University (LL.B., 1987); Judicial Training and Research Institute (1989). *Member:* Korean Bar Association. *LANGUAGES:* Korean, English, German and Japanese. *PRACTICE AREAS:* Litigation; Taxation Law; Copyright Law.

HYUNG DOO NAM, born Buan, Korea, July 6, 1964; admitted, 1989, Korea. *Education:* Seoul National University (LL.B., 1986); Judicial Training and Research Institute (1989). *Member:* Korean Bar Association. *LANGUAGES:* Korean, English and Japanese. *PRACTICE AREAS:* Administrative Law; Tax Law; Litigation.

HAE SUK LEE, born Seoul, Korea, November 14, 1953; admitted, 1988, California (Not admitted in Korea). *Education:* Ewha Woman's University, Seoul, Korea (B.A., 1976); Seoul National University (M.A., 1981); Santa Clara University (J.D., 1987). Attorney, Baker & McKenzie, 1988-1990. *Member:* State Bar of California. *LANGUAGES:* Korean and English. *PRACTICE AREAS:* Corporate Law; Commercial Law.

SUNG YONG KIM, born Young Kwang, Korea, March 16, 1966; admitted, 1990, Korea. *Education:* Seoul National University (LL.B., 1988); Judicial Training and Research Institute (1990). *Member:* Korean Bar Association. *LANGUAGES:* Korean, English and Chinese. *PRACTICE AREAS:* Corporate Reorganization Law; Mergers and Acquisitions.

JUN SUNG LEE, born Seoul, Korea, April 4, 1966; admitted, 1990, Korea. *Education:* Seoul National University (LL.B., 1989); Judicial Training and Research Institute (1991). *Member:* Korean Bar Association. *LANGUAGES:* Korean and Japanese. *PRACTICE AREAS:* Litigation.

JEONG-SUK LEE, born Haman, Korea, October 1, 1965; admitted, 1994, Korea. *Education:* Kunkook University (LL.B., 1988); Judicial Training and Research Institute (1994). *Member:* Korean Bar Association. *LANGUAGES:* Korean and Japanese. *PRACTICE AREAS:* Litigation.

ADVISORS

HOI-CHANG LEE, born Seoul, Korea, June 2, 1935; admitted, 1957, Korea. *Education:* Seoul National University (LL.B., 1957); University of California at Berkeley and Harvard University (Visiting Scholar of Law, 1969-1970). Chairman: Board of Audit and Inspection, 1993; Central Election Management Committee, 1988-1989. Justice, Supreme Court, 1988-1993, 1981-1986. Order of Service Merit, Blue Stripes, 1986. Assistant Minister for Planning and Coordination, Ministry of Court Adminstration, Supreme Court, 1980-1981. Senior Judge: Seoul High Court, 1976-1981; Seoul Civil District Court, 1971-1975. Judge: Seoul High Court, 1965-1970; Seoul Dstrict Court, 1960-1965. Judge Advocate, R.O.K. Air Force, 1957-1960. Author: "Commentary on Criminal Law." Professor, Judicial Research and Training Institute, 1971-1973. *Member:* Korean Bar Association. *LANGUAGES:* Korean and Japanese. *PRACTICE AREAS:* Litigation; Arbitration.

HA & HA

Established in 1961

formerly Ha Patent Office

*4F YOUNG HWA BUILDING
742-20, BANPO-DONG, SEOCHO-KU*
SEOUL 137-040, KOREA
*Telephone: (02) 548-1609; (02) 548-5229; (02) 548-2945; (02) 511-3156
(DIRECT)
Fax: (02) 548-9555; (02) 511-3405*

Mailing Address: Gwang Hwa Moon, P.O. Box 357, Seoul, Korea

Intellectual Property Prosecution, Litigation, Intellectual Property Auditing, and Evaluation.

FIRM PROFILE: *Established in 1961. Ha & Ha has been one of Korea's pioneering Intellectual Property law firms. The firm has maintained excellent reputation for offering the best quality service to the international clients including Japanese, European and North American companies. The*

(This Listing Continued)

firm has 2 partners and 40 staffs including PH.D.s and Masters in various technical and legal field.

MEMBERS OF FIRM

SANG KU HA, born Hapchun, Kyung Nam, Korea; admitted 1960, Korean Patent Bar. *Education:* Dankuk University (LL.B., 1948); Han Yang University (BSEE, 1950). Lecturer, Hanyang University. *Member:* Korean Patent Attorneys Association; AIPPI; APAA. *Languages:* Korean, Japanese and English. *PRACTICE AREAS:* International Patent and Trademark Law.

YOUNG WOOK HA, born Seoul, Korea, January 28, 1957; admitted 1989, Korean Patent Bar; 1993, Pennsylvania. *Education:* Franklin Pierce Law Center (Master of Intellectual Property, M.I.P., 1990; J.D., 1992); Universidad Iberoamericana, UNAM (1984-1985); Hankuk University of Foreign Studies (B.A., 1984). Adjunct Professor, Law, I.I.P.T.I. *Member:* Korean Patent Attorneys Association; American Bar Association; PBA; AIPPI; AIPLA; INTA. *Languages:* Korean, English and Spanish. *PRACTICE AREAS:* International Trade Law; International Patent Law; Trademark and Copyright Law.

HWANG MOK PARK & JIN

Established in 1993

*6TH FLOOR, PEERES BUILDING
222, 3-KA, CHUNGJUNG-RO, SEODAEMUN-KU*
SEOUL, KOREA
*Telephone: (02) 365-6251/5
Facsimile: (02) 365-3369/70
Telex: HMPNJ K23724*

General Practice, Maritime and Shipping Law, Insurance Law, Aviation Law, Foreign Investment, Financing, Corporate Law, Commercial and International Law, Litigation and Tax Litigation, Patent, Trademark and Copyright Law, Telecommunications Law, Tax Law.

FIRM PROFILE: *Hwang Mok Park & Jin provides superior, value-oriented legal services to its clients. The firm is a full service law firm, and it provides services to its international and Korean clients for matters both in Korea and overseas. The firm's clients include all sizes and types of companies doing business in diverse fields. The firm is the Korea representative for the Lex Mundi group of law firms.*

MEMBERS OF FIRM

JU MYUNG HWANG, born Seoul, Korea, April 15, 1939; admitted, 1963, Korea. *Education:* Seoul National University Law School (LL.B., 1962); George Washington University Law School (1974-1975). Judge: Busan District Court, 1965-1969; Seoul Civil District Court, 1969-1973; Seoul Criminal District Court, 1973-1974; Seoul High Court, 1975. Research Judge, The Supreme Court, 1975-1977. General Counsel, Korea Oil Corporation, 1977-1978. Executive Director and General Counsel, Daewoo Group, 1978-1980. *Member:* Seoul Bar Association. [Judge Advocate, Air Force, Republic of Korea, 1962-1965]. *LANGUAGES:* Korean, English and Japanese. *PRACTICE AREAS:* Insurance Law; Maritime Law; Taxation Law; Litigation; Patent and Trademark Law.

JUNG SYNN SUH, born Chungmu, Kyungsangnam-do, Korea, August 8, 1940; admitted, 1962, Korea. *Education:* Seoul National University Law School (LL.B., 1962). Public Prosecutor, 1965-1992. Assistant Director, Judicial Research and Training Institute, 1981-1983. Vice-Minister of Justice, 1988-1989. Director, Seoul High Public Prosecutor's Office, 1989-1992. *Member:* Seoul Bar Association. [Judge Advocate, Army, 1962-1965]. *LANGUAGES:* Korean and English. *PRACTICE AREAS:* Litigation; Criminal Law; Administrative Law; Corporate Law.

KUN SU MOK, born Busan, Korea, November 17, 1957; admitted, 1983, Korea; 1988, New York. *Education:* Seoul National University Law School (LL.B., 1980); Judicial Training Institute (1981-1983); George Washington University, National Law Center (M.C.L., 1986-1988). *Member:* Seoul and New York State Bar Associations. *LANGUAGES:* Korean, English and Japanese. *PRACTICE AREAS:* Finance Law; Foreign Investment Law; Corporate Law.

SANG IL PARK, born Seoul, Korea, July 23, 1958; admitted, 1983, Korea. *Education:* Seoul National University Law School (LL.B., 1981); Judicial Training Institute (1981-1983); The University of Chicago, Law School (LL.M., 1989-1990). Associated with, McGuire, Woods, Battle, & Boothe, Richmond, Virginia, U.S.A., 1990-1991. *Member:* Seoul Bar Association. *LANGUAGES:* Korean, English and Japanese (read only). *PRACTICE*

(This Listing Continued)

HWANG MOK PARK & JIN, Seoul—Continued

AREAS: Finance Law; Foreign Investment Law; Securities Law; Banking Law; Telecommunications Law; International Trade; Corporate Law.

MAN JAE JIN, born Wonju, Kangwondo, Korea, January 27, 1958; admitted, 1985, Korea. *Education:* Seoul National University, Department of French Language and Literature (B.A., 1981); Graduate School of Law, Seoul National University (1982); Judicial Training Institute (1983-1984). Associated with, Elborne, Mitchell & Co., London, England, 1988-1989. *Member:* Seoul Bar Association. **LANGUAGES:** Korean, English, French and Japanese. **PRACTICE AREAS:** Maritime Law; Shipping Law; Insurance Law.

YOUNG SEOK LEE, born Busan, Korea, November 30, 1962; admitted, 1987, Korea. *Education:* Seoul National University Law School (LL.B., 1985); Judicial Training Institute (1985-1987); University of Illinois at Urbana/Champaign Law School (LL.M., 1991-1992). Associated with Burke & Pansons, New York, 1992-1993. *Member:* Seoul Bar Association. **LANGUAGES:** Korean and English. **PRACTICE AREAS:** Maritime Law; Insurance Law; Computer Law; Antitrust Law.

DONG HA KIM, born Andong, Korea, March 5, 1961; admitted, 1989, Korea. *Education:* Seoul National University Law School (LL.B., 1984); Judicial Training Center (1984-1985). *Member:* Seoul Bar Association. **LANGUAGES:** Korean, English and Japanese. **PRACTICE AREAS:** Litigation.

WOO YOUNG CHOI, born Taegu, Korea, December 2, 1961; admitted, 1989, Korea. *Education:* College of Law, Seoul National University Law School (LL.B., 1984); Judicial Training Institute (1984-1985). *Member:* Seoul Bar Association. **LANGUAGES:** Korean, English and Japanese. **PRACTICE AREAS:** Taxation Law; Litigation.

KYUN JE PARK, born Kyungsangnam-do, Korea, November 16, 1963; admitted, 1991, Seoul, Korea. *Education:* Seoul National University Law School (LL.B., 1986); Judicial Training Institute (1986-1988). *Member:* Seoul Bar Association. **LANGUAGES:** Korean and English. **PRACTICE AREAS:** Foreign Investment Law; Corporate Law; Labor Law.

SUNG KEUK CHO, born Seoul, Korea, January 13, 1962; admitted, 1991, Korea. *Education:* Seoul National University Law School (LL.B., 1984); Graduate School of Law, Seoul National University (1984-1985); Judicial Training Institute (1986-1988). *Member:* Seoul Bar Association. **LANGUAGES:** Korean and English. **PRACTICE AREAS:** Maritime Law; Shipping Law; Insurance Law.

SEUNG SOON CHOI, born Seoul, Korea, June 27, 1960; admitted, 1990, Korea; 1993, New York. *Education:* Korea University School of Law (LL.B., 1983); Judicial Training Institute (1985-1987); Boston University Law School (LL.M., International Banking Law Studies, 1992); University of Pennsylvania Law School (LL.M., 1993). *Member:* Seoul and New York State Bar Associations. **LANGUAGES:** Korean and English. **PRACTICE AREAS:** Maritime Law; Shipping Law; Insurance Law; Finance Law; Corporate Law; Litigation; Foreign Investment Law.

DONG PYUNG JOO, born Euijongbu, Korea, May 5, 1964; admitted, 1992, Korea. *Education:* Korea University School of Law (LL.B., 1987); Judicial Training Institute (1987-1989). **LANGUAGES:** Korean and English. **PRACTICE AREAS:** Litigation; General International Business Transactions; Securities Law; Banking Law; Environmental Law.

YOUNG HWAN HAN, born Chang Nyung, Kyungsangnam-do, Korea, February 1, 1964; admitted, 1987, Korea. *Education:* Seoul National University Law School (LL.B., 1987); Judicial Training Institute (1989-1991). *Member:* Seoul Bar Association. **LANGUAGES:** Korean and English. **PRACTICE AREAS:** Litigation; Insurance Law; Maritime Law.

SEUG HEE YOON, born Nonsan, Korea, August 24, 1965; admitted, 1994, Korea. *Education:* Ewha Womens University Law School (LL.B., 1987); Judicial Training Institute (1992-1993). *Member:* Seoul Bar Association. **LANGUAGES:** Korean, English and Japanese. **PRACTICE AREAS:** Litigation.

TAX ATTORNEYS

HEUNG JU HWANG, born Onyang, Korea, June 20, 1954; admitted, 1979, Korea. *Education:* Korea University (B.A., 1977); Kyunghee University Business School (M.B.A., 1993); Passed U.S. Uniform C.P.A. Examination (1988). With, Seihwa Accounting Corporation (correspondent firm in Korea for Price Waterhouse) International Tax Service Group, 1980-1991; Price Waterhouse New York Office, International Tax Services Group, 1987-1989. Certified Tax Accountant, 1980—. Member: Korean

(This Listing Continued)

Institute of Certified Public Accountants, 1980—; American Chamber of Commerce in Korea, Taxation Committee, 1991—; European Communities Chamber of Commerce in Korea, Taxation Committee, 1992—. [Service: Finance Officer, 1977-1980]. **LANGUAGES:** Korean and English. **PRACTICE AREAS:** Corporate Taxation Law; Individual Taxation Law; International Taxation Law; Accounting; Business Consulting; Mergers and Acquisitions.

YOON HEE LEE, born Daegu, Korea, August 27, 1957; admitted, 1984, Korea. *Education:* Hankuk University of Foreign Studies (B.A., 1982); Seoul City University (M.A., 1988). With, Seihwa Accounting Corporation (correspondent firm in Korea for Price Waterhouse) International Tax Services Group, 1982-1991. Certified Public Accountant, 1982—. Member: Korean Institute of Certified Public Accountants. [Service: 1978-1980]. **LANGUAGES:** Korean, English and Japanese. **PRACTICE AREAS:** Corporate Taxation Law; Individual Taxation Law; Accounting; Mergers and Acquisitions; Business Consulting.

JOON SUNG KIM, born Kwangju, Korea, June 12, 1967; admitted, 1993, Korea. *Education:* Korea University (B.A., 1990; Graduate School, 1993). With San Tong Corporation, member firm in Korea for KPMG, 1990-1994. Member, Korean Institute of Certified Public Accountants. **LANGUAGES:** Korean and English. **PRACTICE AREAS:** Corporate Taxation Law; Taxation Law; International Taxation Law; Accounting; Business Consulting.

PATENT ATTORNEYS

HAK HYUN CHOI, born Kwangju, Korea, April 16, 1953; admitted, 1993, Korea. *Education:* Seoul National University (B.S., 1979). With, Il Yang Pharmaceutical Industrial Co. Teaching Position, Korea Advanced Institute of Science and Technology, 1980-1981. *Member:* Korean Patent Attorney Association. **LANGUAGES:** Korean, English and Japanese. **PRACTICE AREAS:** Patent; Utility Model, Design and Trademark; Copyright.

FOREIGN LEGAL CONSULTANTS

MARK A. WESEMAN, born Lansing, Michigan, February 5, 1959; admitted, 1991, Wisconsin and U.S. District Court, Eastern and Western Districts of Wisconsin (Not admitted in Korea). *Education:* Mankato State University (B.S., summa cum laude, 1988); Cornell Law School (J.D., 1991). *Member:* State Bar of Wisconsin; American Bar Association (Member, Sections on: International Law; Natural Resources, Energy and Environmental Law); Inter-Pacific Bar Association; American Chamber of Commerce in Korea (Chairman, Intellectual Property Rights Committee, 1993—). **LANGUAGES:** English and Spanish (read only). **PRACTICE AREAS:** Environmental Law; Intellectual Property Law; Trade Law; International Business Transactions; Foreign Investment Law; Shipping Law.

JOSEPH LEE SPRINGSTEEN, born San Antonio, Texas, November 4, 1965; admitted, 1992, Florida (Not admitted in Korea). *Education:* University of Florida (B.A., 1988); Walter F. George School of Law, Mercer University (J.D., 1992). Foreign Legal Advisor, For Former Minister of Legislation, Chong Keon Kim, Republic of Korea, 1992-1994. *Member:* The Florida Bar; American Bar Association (Member, Section on Business Law); American Chamber of Commerce in Korea (Member, Legal Affairs and Pharmaceuticals Committees). **LANGUAGES:** English and Korean (read only). **PRACTICE AREAS:** Commercial Transactions; Corporate Law; Trade Law; International Business Transactions; Foreign Investment Law.

OF COUNSEL

HEE JIN KIM, born Kimje, Korea, July 20, 1951; admitted, 1988, New York; 1989, District of Columbia (Not admitted in Korea). *Education:* Seoul National University (B.A., Economics, 1973); Harvard Business School (M.B.A., 1982); Georgetown University Law Center (J.D., 1988). Author: Publications: "Product Liability and Corporate Strategy," "Antidumping Laws, Investigations and Cases-United States and Canada". Lecturer, Hankuk University of Foreign Studies, 1982-1983. Senior Advisor, Kia Economic Research Institute, 1991—. General Counsel, Korean Trade Commission, 1991—. Legal Advisor, Korean Institute of Economics and Technology, 1991—. Associated with Winthrop, Stimson, Putnam & Roberts (Washington, D.C., New York and Brussels), 1988-1990. Arnold & Porter, 1988. General Manager, Korea Foreign Trade Association, Washington Office, 1984-1988. Deputy Director, Korean Ministry of Trade and Industry, 1982-1983, 1978-1980. Assistant Director, National Assembly Secretariat, 1976-1978. Research Fellow, Economic and Science Advisory Council, 1975-1976. Economist, The Bank of Korea, 1973-1975. United States Certified Public Accountant. **LANGUAGES:** Korean, English, Japanese and Spanish. **PRACTICE AREAS:** Trade Law; Corporate Law; Secu-

(This Listing Continued)

rities; Taxation Law; Banking Law; Finance Law; Commercial Transactions; Arbitration; Foreign Investment Law.

REPRESENTATIVE CLIENTS: Air Products & Chemicals; Bristol Myers Squibb Co.; BAeSEMA Group; British Telecom; Chevron Corp.; Corning Glass Works; Daewoo Electronics; Daewoo Group; Dow Chemical; Esso; Exxon; IBM; Johnson & Johnson; Korea Development Bank; Hanil Bank; Hüls AG; Korea First Bank; Commercial Bank of Korea; Kraft General Foods; Merck & Co., Inc.; Nike; Prudential; Saint-Gobain; UK P&I; Britannia P&I; Liverpool & London P&I; Southwestern Bell Corp.; Swedish Club; Skuld P&I; American Home Insurance Co.; Hyundai Marine & Fire Insurance Co.; Samsung; Korean Automobile Insurance Co.; Citibank; Cheil Food & Chemicals; Citibank Seoul Branch; Shell Pacific; East Asiatic Company; Bankers Trust-Seoul; Goodyear Tire & Rubber.

KIM & ASSOCIATES

Established in 1977

SALVATION ARMY OFFICE BUILDING
1-58, SHINMUN-RO, CHONGRO-KU
SEOUL 110-061, KOREA
Telephone: 732 - 5656/8
Telex: KIMLAW K24534
Facsimile: 733 - 0949

General Practice, Admiralty, Marine Insurance, Arbitration, International Trade, Finance and Banking, Foreign Investment, Corporate, Civil, Islamic, Company, Conveyancing, Debt Recovery Claims, Litigation.

FIRM PROFILE: The firm was established in 1977 and offers a full range of legal services. It is well known for its Civil and Admiralty Litigation. The client base is Korean and North American in scope. This 2 partner firm has a legal support staff of 10 consisting of paralegal personnel and office administrators.

BYONG JOON KIM, born Inchon, Korea, October 10, 1948; admitted, 1971, Korea; 1984, New York and Pennsylvania. Education: Seoul National University, Korea (B.A. in Law and LL.B., 1971); Tulane University of Louisiana (LL.M., 1983); New York University (M.C.L., 1984). Author: Korean Civil Procedure, Seyong Publication Company, 1976; "Korean Arbitration Procedure," Journal of Korean Bar Association, 1981. Chairman of Trustees, Trade and Management Institute of Korea, 1984—. Judge of Pusan District Court, 1971-1975 and of Cheonju District Court, 1975-1976. Member: Korean, New York State, Pennsylvania and American Bar Associations. LANGUAGES: Korean, English, Chinese and Japanese. PRACTICE AREAS: Civil Litigation; Admiralty; Corporate.

ASSOCIATE

JUNG SUP KIM, admitted, 1974, Korea. Education: Seoul National University (LL.B., 1971). Member: Korean Bar Association. LANGUAGES: Korean, English and Japanese. PRACTICE AREAS: Civil and Criminal Litigation.

FOREIGN LEGAL CONSULTANTS

A.M.M. SALMAN, born Colombo (Ceylon), Sri Lanka, September 15, 1932; admitted, 1956, Colombo, Sri Lanka; 1964, as Solicitor of the Supreme Court of England (Not admitted in Korea). Education: Council of Legal Education, Colombo (Attorney at Law, 1956). Member: Sri Lanka Bar Association. LANGUAGES: English, Sinhalese and Arabic. PRACTICE AREAS: International Business Law; Admiralty; Islamic Law.

NEIL ARLEN ROOT, born Audubon, Iowa, March 24, 1953; admitted, 1981, Iowa; 1983, Nebraska (Not admitted in Korea). Education: University of Iowa (B.B. Business Administration, 1975); University of Nebraska (J.D., 1981). Member: Iowa State, Nebraska State and American Bar Associations. LANGUAGES: English and Korean. PRACTICE AREAS: International Business Law.

LEGAL SUPPORT PERSONNEL

WOO GAP PARK, born Kyungsangnamdo, Korea, May 2, 1939. Education: University of Myungju, Department of Law (LL.B., 1971). Working at the Ministry of Justice, 1972; Judicial Administrations Society, 1977-1979. Paralegal, 1979—. Legal Research, Drafting, Legal Pleadings, Client Correspondence, Deposition Summaries and File Investigation.

Languages: Korean, English, Chinese, Japanese, Sinhalese and Arabic.

REPRESENTATIVE CLIENTS: Hyosung Corp.; Ssangyong Corp.; Shindong-A Corp.; Hyundai Merchant Marine Co., Ltd.; Daesung Energy Corporation; U.S. 8th Army; Accugraph Corp.; I.C.C. Steamship Corp.; S.T.C. Industries Corp.; Gyung Nam Enterprise Co.; Industrial Advancement Administration.

KIM & CHANG

Established in 1973

SEYANG BUILDING
223, NAEJA-DONG, CHONGRO-KU
SEOUL, KOREA
Telephone: 737-4455
Cable Address: "Lawkimchang"
Telex: LAWKIM K28588
Telefax: (02) 737-9091/3

COMPILERS OF THE KOREA LAW DIGEST FOR THIS DIRECTORY.

Los Angeles, California Associated Office: Hong & Chang, Suite 1010, 800 West Sixth Street, 90017. Telephone: 213-629-5611. Telecopier: 213-629-1170.

Corporate, Securities and Banking, Litigation and Arbitration, Real Estate, Labor, Employment, Intellectual Property, Tax, Overseas Investment, Trade and Foreign Exchange, Maritime, Insurance, Antitrust, Contracts, Project Financing, Technology Licensing, Franchising, Fair Trade, Telecommunications, Entertainment and Aviation.

FIRM PROFILE: Kim and Chang was established in 1973 and is the largest law firm in Korea. Kim and Chang has about 120 attorneys, including 20 resident expatriate foreign legal consultants and a support staff of over 350 people. Kim and Chang is the recognized leader in providing specialized legal services for international transactions involving Korea. The firm is a full service firm which has developed departmental specialization. Kim and Chang, as well as having major Korean clients, represents major multinational companies and also serves numerous medium and small foreign clients doing business in or with Korea.

MEMBERS OF FIRM

YOUNG MOO KIM, born Seoul, Korea, July 19, 1942; admitted, 1966, Korea; 1970, Illinois, U.S.A. Education: College of Law, Seoul National University (B.Jur., 1964); Graduate School of Justice, Seoul National University (M.Jur., 1966); University of Chicago Law School (M.C.L., 1967); Harvard Law School (J.D., 1970, Member of Board of Student Advisers). Special Legal Assistant to the Korean Prime Minister, 1970-1971. Commissioner Expert, Korean Legal Institutions Office, 1972. Member, Foreign Capital Deliberation Committee of the Ministry of Finance of Korea, 1981-1982. Member, Special Committee of Revision to the Commercial Code of the Ministry of Justice, 1981-1984. Member, Import Surveillance Committee of the Ministry of Trade & Industry, 1983-1985. Member, Trade Policy Advisory Committee of the Ministry of Trade and Industry, 1986—. Commissioner of the Korea Trade Commission, 1987-1990. Member of the Presidential Commission on the 21st Century 1989—. Director of the Korea Institute for International Economy Policy, 1990—. Nonstanding Commissioner of Securities and Exchange Commission, 1991—. Lecturer, Graduate School of Justice, Seoul National University, 1970-1971. Member: Korean Bar Association; Chicago, Illinois State and American Bar Associations; Korean Society for Law and Society; International Law Association (Korea); Harvard Club. LANGUAGES: Korean, English and Japanese.

SOO KIL CHANG, born Seoul, Korea, March 27, 1942; admitted, 1965, Korea. Education: College of Law, Seoul National University (B.Jur., 1964); Graduate School of Justice, Seoul National University (M.Jur., 1965). Judge Advocate, Republic of Korea Army, 1966-1969. Judge, Seoul District Civil Court and Seoul District Criminal Court, 1969-1973. Author: "On the Legal Nature of Presumptions," Seoul National University, 1966; "A Memorandum on the Korean Industrial Property Right," Korean Journal of Comparative Law, Vol. IV, Korean Research Institute of Comparative Law, 1976; "International Sales Contract in Model Contracts of International Commercial Transactions," Korean Bar Association, 1983; Chapter on "Present Attitude affecting Enforcement of Foreign Money Judgment," Survey of World Enforcement of Foreign Money Judgment, 1988. Arbitrator, Korean Commercial Arbitration Board, 1985—. Member, Administrative Trial Committee of the Ministry of Trade and Industry, 1986—. Member: Seoul Bar Association (Vice President, 1989-1991); Korean Bar Association (Executive Director, Public Relations, 1993—); Korean Patent Attorneys Association (Vice President, 1984-1985); Korea Intellectual Property Research Society (President, 1989-1991); International Association for the Protection of Industrial Property (Korean Chapter; Vice President, 1984-1989); Asian Patent Attorneys Association; Licensing Executives Society. LANGUAGES: Korean, English and Japanese.

JAE HOO LEE, born Seoul, Korea, August 25, 1940; admitted, 1963, Korea. Education: College of Law, Seoul National University (B.Jur.,

(This Listing Continued)

KIM & CHANG, Seoul—Continued

1962); Institute for International and Foreign Trade Law of Georgetown University Law Center (Special Student, 1975-1976). Lecturer of Judicial Research and Training Institute of the Supreme Court of Korea, 1985-1988. Judge Advocate, Republic of Korea Navy (1962-1965). Judge, Daejun District Court, Seoul District Civil Court, Seoul District Criminal Court and Seoul High Court, 1965-1976. Research Judge, Republic of Korea Supreme Court, 1977-1979. Executive Director, Korea Legal Center, 1983-1988. Commissioner of Fair Trade Commission, Korea, 1989—. *Member:* Seoul (Vice-President, 1985-1986, 1991-1992) and Korean Bar Associations (Executive Director, 1984). *LANGUAGES:* Korean, English and Japanese.

CHUN-PYO JHONG, born Pusan, Korea, February 7, 1931; admitted, 1954, Korea. *Education:* College of Law, Seoul National University (LL.B., 1953); Southern Methodist University Law School (LL.B., 1957); Yale Law School (LL.M., 1958; J.S.D., 1961). Phi Alpha Delta. Author: "The Settlement of Disputes Arising from International Trade and Investment," LAWASIA Journal, Vol. 1 (1969); "The Vital Role of Loan Covenants," ADB Quarterly Review, July 1978; "The Asian Development Bank," International Financial Law, Euromoney Publications (1983); "Development Financing and Law," Asian Development Review, Vol. 2 (1984); "The Role of International Financing Institutions in Promoting Trade and Investment in the Pacific Basin," Current Legal Aspects of Doing Business in the Pacific Basin, American Bar Association (1987); "State Immunity in Civil Proceedings Instituted in Foreign Courts," J.S.D. dissertation, Yale Law School (1961). Lecturer: UNITAR-UNESCO Regional Training Course on International Law (1969); Asian Productivity Organization (1973). Prosecutor, Seoul District Prosecutors Office, 1954. Legal Editor, 1961-1965 and Senior and Training Editor and Assistant Managing Editor, 1966-1968, Lawyers Cooperative Publishing Company, Rochester, New York. Legal Counsel, Assistant General Counsel and Deputy General Counsel, 1968-1969 and General Counsel, 1979-1990, Asian Development Bank, Manila, Philippines. Arbitrator: Korean Commercial Arbitration Board; International Center for Settlement of Investment Disputes (ICSID) of World Bank. *LANGUAGES:* Korean, English and Japanese.

HONG-CHOO HYUN, born Seoul, Korea, August 19, 1940; admitted, 1963, Korea. *Education:* College of Law, Seoul National University (LL.B., 1963); Graduate School of Law, Seoul National University (LL.M., 1967); School of Law, Columbia University, New York (LL.M., 1969). Awarded: Order of Public Service Merit, 1973, 1985 and 1993; Order of National Security Merit, 1979 and 1981; Medal for Excellence, Columbia Law School, 1993. Judge Advocate, ROK Army, 1964-1967; Prosecutor: Seoul District Public Prosecutor's Office, 1968-1969; Ministry of Justice and Seoul District Public Prosecutor's Office, 1969-1974; Senior Prosecutor, Ministry of Justice and Seoul High Public Prosecutor's Office, 1974-1980. First Deputy Director, Agency for National Security Planning, 1980-1985. Member, National Assembly, 1985-1988. Minister of Legislation, 1988-1990. Ambassador Extraordinary and Plenipotentiary of the Korean Permanent Observer Mission to the United Nations, New York, New York, USA, 1990-1991; Ambassador Extraordinary and Plenipotentiary to the United States of America, 1991-1993. *LANGUAGES:* Korean and English.

YOUNG-TAEK SUH, born Taegu, Korea, April 23, 1939. *Education:* Economics, College of Commerce, Seoul National University (1962); Graduate School of Economics, Seoul National University (M.A., 1967); Harvard Law School, International Tax Program (1968-1969); Harvard Law School (Visiting Scholar, 1993). Director: International Tax Affairs, Ministry of Finance, 1971; Direct Taxation, Ministry of Finance, 1973. Commissioner, Taejun and Taegu Regional Tax Office, 1975-1976. Director General: Indirect Tax, National Tax Administrations, 1977-1980; Taxation Bureau, Ministry of Finance, 1980-1983. Commissioner, National Tax Tribunal, 1983-1984. Chief Staff, Finance Committee, National Assembly, 1984-1985. Assistant Minister, Finance and Taxation, Ministry of Finance, 1985-1988. Commissioner, National Tax Administration, 1988-1991. Minister, Construction, 1991-1993. Member: National Policy Advisory Committee; Democratic Liberal Party, 1993—. *Member:* IFA, Harvard Club. *LANGUAGES:* Korean and English.

KYE SUNG CHUNG, born Kimje, Jeonbuk Province, Korea, January 15, 1951; admitted, 1976, Korea. *Education:* College of Law, Seoul National University (B.Jur., 1973); Judicial Research and Training Institute of Supreme Court of Korea (1976). Editorial Adviser for Korea to Capital Asia, Hong Kong, 1989—. Member of Industrial Deregulation Review Committee, Ministry of Trade, Industry & Energy, Korea, 1993—. With Shearman & Sterling, New York, New York, 1982-1983. Author: "The Internationalization of the Korean Securities Market: Legal and Economic Perspectives," Columbia Journal of Transnational Law, Vol. 27, Number 1,

(This Listing Continued)

The Columbia Journal of Transnational Law Association, Inc., 1988. Co-Author: "Law and Practice Concerning Overseas Issuance of Korean Securities," The Korea Economic Daily, 1989; "Insider Dealing Regulation Ineffective in Practice," Asia Law and Practice, November 1990; "Cracking Open Korea's Stock Exchange," International Financial Law Review, October 1991; "Problems relating to Systems of Securities Investment by Foreigners Sangjanghyup, Vol. 27., Korea Listed Companies Association, 1993. *Member:* Korean Bar Association. *LANGUAGES:* Korean, English and Japanese.

WOO TAIK KIM, born Seoul, Korea, September 1, 1947; admitted as Tax Attorney, 1973, Korea; Certified Public Accountant, 1973, Korea; 1976, New York, U.S.A. *Education:* Graduate School of Business, Columbia University, New York, U.S.A. (1972); College of Commerce, Seoul National University (1970). Author: "Assessment and Collection of Tax from Non-Residents," Cahiers De Droit Fiscal International, Volume LXXa, 1985. Co-Author: "Business Operations in the Republic of Korea," Tax Management Inc., 1984; "Transfer of Assets into and out of a Taxing Jurisdiction," Cahiers De Droit Fiscal International Volume LXXIa, 1986; "Currency Fluctuations and International Double Taxation," Cahiers De Droit Fiscal International, Volume LXXIb, 1986. *Member:* The Korean Institute of Tax Attorneys; The Korean Institute of Certified Public Accountants; American Institute of Certified Public Accountants; New York State Society of Certified Public Accountants; International Fiscal Association. *LANGUAGES:* Korean, Japanese and English.

DAE YUN CHO, born Seoul, Korea, October 25, 1950; admitted, 1979, Korea. *Education:* College of Law, Seoul National University (B.Jur., 1973); Graduate School of Law, Seoul National University, (1975); Yale Law School (LL.M., 1976); Judicial Research and Training Institute of Supreme Court of Korea, (1979). Lecturer, College of Law and Graduate School of Law, Soongjun University, 1977-1978. Author: "Foreign Banking in Korea in the 1980's," Korean Journal of Comparative Law, Vol. XI, Korean Research Institute of Comparative Law, 1983; "Some Observations on the US Trade and Tariff Act of 1984," Journal of Enterprise Management, 1985; "GATT Procedures for Settling Trade Disputes," KITLA Journal, 1991. Member, Task Force Committee for Trade Negotiation, 1984—; Korean Commercial Arbitration Board, 1989—; Advisor to Korea Trade Commission, 1990—; Director, Korea International Trade Law Academy. *Member:* Korean Bar Association. *LANGUAGES:* Korean, English and Japanese.

WONCHUL PARK, born Goheung, Jeonnam Province, Korea, June 24, 1950; admitted, 1978, Trade Attorney, Korea; 1985, New York, U.S.A. *Education:* College of Law, Seoul National University (B.Jur., 1976); Graduate School of Foreign Trade, Sung Gyun Kwan University (1982); Cornell Law School (LL.M., 1984); New York University Law School (1985). Lecturer, Kyong Hee University Law School, 1989. With: Korea Exchange Bank, 1976-1978; Debevoise & Plimpton, 1985-1986. *Member:* New York State Bar Association. *LANGUAGES:* Korean and English.

YONG KAP KIM, born Hapcheon, Kyungnam Province, Korea, March 3, 1952; admitted, 1976, Korea. *Education:* College of Law, Seoul National University (LL.B., 1976); Judicial Research and Training Institute of Supreme Court of Korea, (1976); University of Pennsylvania Law School (LL.M., 1984). Judge Advocate, Republic of Korea Army, 1976-1979. With: Covington & Burling, Washington, D.C., 1984; Matsuo & Kosugi, Tokyo, Japan, 1985. *Member:* Korean Bar Association. *LANGUAGES:* Korean, English and Japanese.

KYUNG TAEK JUNG, born Kwangjoo, Korea, January 16, 1952; admitted, 1977, Korea; 1987, New York, U.S.A. *Education:* College of Law, Seoul National University (B.Jur., 1974); Harvard Law School (LL.M., 1986); Judicial Research and Training Institute of the Supreme Court of Korea (1977). Judge Advocate, Republic of Korea Navy (1977-1980). With Skadden, Arps, Slate, Meagher & Flom, New York, N.Y., 1986-1987. Author: "Litigation Practice in Fair Trade Law," Korean Bar Association, 1989. *Member:* Korean and New York State Bar Associations. *LANGUAGES:* Korean and English.

HI-TAEK SHIN, born Seoul, Korea, August 6, 1952; admitted, 1977, Korea. *Education:* College of Law, Seoul National University (B.Jur., summa cum laude, 1975); Graduate School of Law, Seoul National University (M.Jur., 1981); Judicial Research and Training Institute of the Supreme Court of Korea (summa cum laude, 1977); Yale Law School (LL.M., 1983; J.S.D., 1990). Judge Advocate, Republic of Korea Army and Republic of Korea/United States Combined Forces Command (1977-1980). Kim & Chang (1980—). *Member:* Korean Bar Association. *LANGUAGES:* Korean and English.

(This Listing Continued)

YOUNG JUNE YANG, born Namwon, Jeonbuk Province, Korea, July 7, 1954; admitted, 1977, Korea; 1986, New York, U.S.A. *Education:* College of Law, Seoul National University (B.Jur., 1977); Judicial Research and Training Institute of the Supreme Court of Korea (1977); University of Michigan Law School (LL.M., 1985). Judge Advocate, Republic of Korea Army, 1977-1980. Kim & Chang, 1980—. With Paul, Weiss, Rifkind, Wharton & Garrison, New York, N.Y., 1985-1986. Auditor, Korea Copyright Deliberation & Mediation Committee, 1990—. Member, Korea Semi-Conductor Chip Deliberation & Mediation Committee. *Member:* Seoul, Korean and American Bar Associations; Korea Patent Attorneys Association; Korea Intellectual Property Research Society (Secretary General, 1988-1993). *LANGUAGES:* Korean, English and Japanese.

SUNG MIN CHU, born Pusan, Korea, August 27, 1949; admitted, 1978, Korea. *Education:* College of Law, Seoul National University (B.Jur., 1973); Graduate School of Law, Seoul National University (M.Jur., 1973-1975); Judicial Research and Training Institute, Supreme Court (1976-1978). Judge Advocate, Korean Army, 1978-1981. With, Kim, Chang and Lee, Seoul, 1981-1983 and Lee & Ko, Seoul, 1983-1986. *Member:* Korean Bar Association; Korean Patent Attorneys Association (Vice-President, 1990-1992); Asian Patent Attorneys Association; International Association for the Protection of Industrial Property (Korean National Group; Vice-President, 1993); Licensing Executives Society. *LANGUAGES:* Korean and English.

JAE HYUN SHIN, born Taegu, Korea, December 13, 1946; admitted, 1990, New York (Not admitted in Korea). *Education:* College of Law, Seoul National University (LL.B., 1970); Graduate School of Law, Seoul National University (LL.M., 1974; Post Graduate Studies in Public Law, 1981); New York University, School of Law (M.C.J., 1989). Lecturer: Kookmin College; Inha University; Seoul City College; Sookmyung Women's University. Consultant: Law Offices Kim, Chang & Lee, 1975-1982; Central International Law Firm, 1983-1984; Law Offices Lee & Ko, 1984-1990. *Member:* New York State Bar Association. *LANGUAGES:* Korean and English.

SUNG CHULL JUNN, born Taegu, Korea, June 15, 1949; admitted, 1983, New York (Not admitted in Korea). *Education:* College of Liberal Arts & Science, Seoul National University (B.A., 1973); University of Minnesota Business School (M.B.A., 1983); University of Minnesota Law School (J.D., 1983). Author: "Direction and Technics for Direct Investment in the U.S., 1987, Korea Foreign Trade Association;" Protection of Creditors' Rights under the U.S. Law 1989, Reid & Priest. Partner, Reid & Priest, New York and Washington, U.S.A., 1989-1991. General Counsel, Korean Trades Representative Club of New York, 1989-1990. Counsel, Korea Foreign Trade Association, 1989-1990. *LANGUAGES:* Korean and English.

BYUNG SUK CHUNG, born Seoul, Korea, October 9, 1954; admitted, 1980, Korea. *Education:* College of Law, Seoul National University (B.Jur., 1977); Graduate School of Law, Seoul National University (1980); University College London (LL.M., 1987); Judicial Research and Training Institute of the Supreme Court of Korea, (1980). Associated with Haight Gardner Poor & Havens, September, 1987-March, 1988. Author: "Public Auction Sale of the Vessels in Korea," Human Rights and Justice, December, 1992; "Shipowner's Lien on the Cargo," The Journal of the Korean Maritime Law Association, December, 1992. Co-Author: "Provisional Remedies in Arbitration-Korea." *Member:* Korean Bar Association; Korean Maritime Law Association; Korean Association of Shipping Studies. *LANGUAGES:* Korean, English and Japanese (reads only).

CHUN WOOK HYUN, born Cheju, Cheju Province, Korea, July 5, 1953; admitted, 1978, Korea; 1988, New York, U.S.A. *Education:* College of Law, Seoul National University (B.Jur., 1976); Harvard Law School (LL.M., 1987); Judicial Research and Training Institute of the Supreme Court of Korea (1978). Judge Advocate, Republic of Korea Navy, 1978-1981. Participant in the Foreign Lawyers' Program of Sullivan & Cromwell, New York, 1987-1988. Special Legal Counsel, Ministry of Labor. Public Member: Seoul District Labor Board, 1990—; Member of Special Committee for the Labor Law Changes, 1991—. *Member:* Korean, New York State and American Bar Associations. *LANGUAGES:* Korean, English, Japanese and French.

ICK RYOL HUH, born Andong, Kyungbuk Province, Korea, May 24, 1955; admitted, 1981, Korea; 1988, New York, U.S.A. *Education:* College of Law, Seoul National University (B.Jur., 1977); Graduate School of Law, Seoul National University (M.Jur., 1979); Judicial Research and Training Institute of Supreme Court of Korea (1981); Columbia University School of Law (LL.M., 1987). Participant in the Foreign Attorney Program of Milbank, Tweed, Hadley & McCloy, New York, 1987-1988. *Member:* Korean

(This Listing Continued)

and New York State Bar Associations. *LANGUAGES:* Korean and English.

KANG SEOK JEON, born Pusan, Korea, October 11, 1952; admitted, 1979, Korea; 1988, New York, U.S.A. *Education:* College of Law, Seoul National University (B.Jur., 1976); Graduate School of Law, Seoul National University (1978); Judicial Research and Training Institute of The Supreme Court of Korea (1979); Columbia Law School (LL.M., 1988). Judge Advocate, Republic of Korea Army and the Ministry of National Defense of Korea, 1979-1982. Editorial Advisor to the I.P. Asia Series, Hong Kong, 1987—. Associated with White and Case, New York, New York, 1988-1989. Awarded, Ministry of Finance Appreciation Award for foreign investment related public service, 1992. Member: Committee of Korean Industry Restructuring Policy, Ministry of Trade and Industry, 1992—; Government Advisory Group of International Economic Affairs, Economic Planning Board, 1993—; Business Globalization Support Group, Ministry of Trade, Industry and Energy, 1994—. Author: "High-tech Management, Mergers and Acquisitions," Joong-Ang Daily News, 1991. "Non-Judicial Dispute Resolution Procedures in the Republic of Korea, with an Emphasis on Arbitration," Korean Journal of Comparative Law, Volume XIV, Korean Research Institute of Comparative Law, 1986. *Member:* Association of the Bar of the City of New York; Korean, New York State and American Bar Associations. *LANGUAGES:* Korean and English.

JOON PARK, born Seoul, Korea, October 30, 1954; admitted, 1979, Korea. *Education:* College of Law, Seoul National University (B.Jur., 1977); Graduate School of Law, Seoul National University (1984); Harvard Law School (LL.M., 1988); Judicial Research and Training Institute of the Supreme Court of Korea (1979). Judge Advocate, Republic of Korea Army, 1979-1982. Sullivan & Cromwell, New York, New York, 1988-1989. Author: "Internationalization of the Korean Securities Market," International Tax and Business Lawyer, Volume 7, Number 1, Boalt Hall School of Law, University of California, Berkeley, 1989; "Liberalization of Capital Market and International Securities Enforcement," (written in Korean) Securities Vol. 63, March 1990, Korea Securities Dealers Association. *Member:* Korean Bar Association. *LANGUAGES:* Korean, English and Japanese.

JAE KYUNG CHOI, born Seoul, Korea, February 12, 1955; admitted, 1979, Korea; 1990, New York, U.S.A. *Education:* College of Law, Seoul National University (B.Jur., 1977); Graduate School of Law, Seoul National University (1984); Judicial Research and Training Institute of the Supreme Court of Korea (1979); University of Pennsylvania Law School (LL.M., 1989). Judge Advocate, Republic of Korea Navy, 1979-1982. Member, Kelley, Drye & Warren, New York, 1989-1990. *Member:* Korean Bar Association. *LANGUAGES:* Korean and English.

JONG YUL LEE, born Susan, Korea, May 10, 1949; admitted, Certified Public Accountant, Tax Attorney, 1972, Korea. *Education:* Business Administration, College of Commerce, Seoul National University (1973); Kyunghee University (M.B.A., Tax Administration, 1989). Certified Public Accountant, California, U.S.A., 1986. With: the Korea Development Bank, 1973-1976; Sunkyung Business Group of Companies, 1976-1977; Deloitte Haskins & Sells (Deloitte & Touche), Accounting Firm, Korea Office (Tax Partner), 1977-1991 and New York Office (Tax Manager), 1985-1987; KMG Hungerfords, Sydney Office (Tax Manager), 1984-1985. *Member:* The Korean Institute of Certified Public Accountants; The California State Society of Certified Public Accountants; The International Fiscal Association. Co-Chairman, Taxation Committee, The American Chamber of Commerce in Korea. *LANGUAGES:* Korean and English.

DOO BONG PARK, born Mokpo, Korea, December 24, 1948; admitted, Tax Attorney, 1981, Korea. *Education:* Myungji University (B.A., 1976). With: National Tax Administration, International Tax Division, 1968-1981; KPMG (Peat Marwick, 1982-1991. *Member:* The Korean Institute of Tax Attorneys. *LANGUAGES:* Korean and English.

WOO HYUN BAIK, born Koyang, Kyonggi Province, Korea, July 7, 1955; admitted, Certified Public Accountant, 1978, Korea. *Education:* College of Business Administration, Seoul National University (1978); The Wharton School of the University of Pennsylvania (1991). Passed the Uniform CPA Exam, California, U.S.A., 1991. With: Samil Accounting Corporation, 1981-1983. *Member:* The Korean Institute of Certified Public Accountants; International Fiscal Association. *LANGUAGES:* Korean and English.

WON KEE PAE, born Seoul, Korea, May 28, 1955; admitted, Certified Public Account, 1979, Korea; Registered, Tax Attorney, 1990, Korea. *Education:* College of Commerce, Sung Kyun Kwan University (1978); Graduate School of Sung Kyun Kwan University (M.B.A., 1985). With: the Bank of Korea; Coopers & Lybrand, 1978-1987; Korea-Japan Management Con-

(This Listing Continued)

KIM & CHANG, Seoul—Continued

sulting Co., Ltd. 1987-1989; KPMG-Sang Tong & Co., 1989-1990. *Member:* The Korean Institute of Certified Public Accountants; The Korean Institute of Tax Attorneys. *LANGUAGES:* Korean, Japanese and English.

MAN SOO HAN, born Kyungnam Province, Korea, October 5, 1958; admitted, 1983, Korea. *Education:* College of Law, Seoul National University (B.Jur., 1981); Graduate School of Law, Seoul National University (M.Jur., 1987); Judicial Research and Training Institute of the Supreme Court of Korea (1983); University of Washington Law School (LL.M., 1991). Lecturer of Law, Sungshin Women's University, 1989; Seoul City University, 1992—. *Member:* Korean Bar Association; International Fiscal Association. *LANGUAGES:* Korean, English and Japanese.

JONG HYEON CHOI, born Onyang, Chungnam Province, Korea, November 15, 1955; admitted, 1981, Korea; 1991, New York. *Education:* College of Law, Seoul National University (B.Jur., 1978); Judicial Research and Training Institute of the Supreme Court of Korea (1981); University of Michigan Law School (LL.M., 1990). Judge Advocate, Republic of Korea Air Force, 1981-1984. *Member:* Korean Bar and New York Bar Association; Korean Maritime Law Association; Korean Association of Shipping Studies. *LANGUAGES:* Korean, English and Japanese.

KWANG HYUN SUK, born Seoul, Korea, September 6, 1956; admitted, 1981, Korea. *Education:* College of Law, Seoul National University (B.Jur., 1979); Graduate School of Law, Seoul National University (1981); Judicial Research and Training Institute of the Supreme Court of Korea, (1981); Albert-Ludwigs-Universität, Freiburg i.Br. (LL.M., 1991). Judge Advocate, Republic of Korea Navy, 1981-1984. Participant in the Foreign Lawyers' Program, Linklaters & Paines, London, 1991. *Member:* Korean Bar Association. *LANGUAGES:* Korean and English.

SOO MAN PARK, born Mokpo, Jeonnam Province, Korea, February 17, 1957; admitted, 1981, Korea. *Education:* College of Law, Seoul National University (B.Jur., 1979); Judicial Research and Training Institute of the Supreme Court of Korea, (1981); Wolfson College, Oxford, U.K. (Diploma in Law, 1990). Judge Advocate, Republic of Korea Navy, 1981-1984. Associated with Clifford Chance, London, 1990-1991. *Member:* Korean Bar Association. *LANGUAGES:* Korean, English, Japanese and German.

SANG YEOL PARK, born Seoul, Korea, April 29, 1956 (lunar); admitted, 1981, Korea; 1991, New York, U.S.A. *Education:* College of Law, Seoul National University (B.Jur., 1979); Judicial Research and Training Institute of the Supreme Court of Korea, (1981); Columbia University School of Law (LL.M., 1990). Judge Advocate, Republic of Korea Army, 1981-1984. Associated with Skadden, Arps, Slate, Meagher & Flom, New York, 1990-1991. *Member:* Korean and New York Bar Association. *LANGUAGES:* Korean and English.

HEE CHUL KANG, born Jinhae, Kyungnam Province, Korea, October 5, 1958; admitted, 1981, Korea; 1992, New York, U.S.A. *Education:* College of Law, Seoul National University (B.Jur., 1979); Graduate School of Law, Seoul National University, (1981); Judicial Research and Training Institute of the Supreme Court of Korea, (1981); Harvard Law School (LL.M., 1990). Judge Advocate, Republic of Korea Army, 1981-1984. Editor, Korean Bar Association Journal, 1992—. *Member:* Korean and New York Bar Association. *LANGUAGES:* Korean and English.

JIN HONG LEE, born Seoul, Korea, October 12, 1957; admitted, 1982, Korea. *Education:* College of Law, Seoul National University (B. Jur., 1980); Graduate School of Law, Seoul National University (M.Jur., 1986); Judicial Research and Training Institute of the Supreme Court of Korea (1982); Graduate UCL, University of London (S.L. Diploma, 1992). Judge Advocate, Republic of Korea Army, 1982-1985. *Member:* Korean Bar Association. *LANGUAGES:* Korean and English.

DONG SHIK CHOI, born Sinan, Jeonnam Province, Korea, November 30, 1957; admitted, 1982, Korea; 1991, New York, U.S.A. *Education:* College of Law, Seoul National University (B.Jur., 1980); Graduate School of Law, Seoul National University (M.Jur., 1985); Judicial Research and Training Institute of the Supreme Court of Korea (1982); University of Michigan Law School (LL.M., 1991). Judge Advocate, Republic of Korea Army, 1982-1985. Publications: "A Study on the Accounting Period to which a Revenue or an Expense is Attributable in Korean Tax Law," Tax Attorney, 1985-1986; "Franchising in Korea," American Bar Association, 1989; "A Foreign Investor's Collection of Its Investment in a Foreign Invested Enterprise in Korea," Modern Tasks regarding Corporate Law, 1992; "Satellite and CATV Regulations in Korea," 1993. Participant, Foreign Lawyers' Program of Davis Polk and Wardwell, New York, 1991.

(This Listing Continued)

Member: Korean and New York State Bar Associations. *LANGUAGES:* Korean, English and Japanese.

KYUNG TAE KIM, born Sangju, Kyungbuk Province, Korea, April 21, 1958; admitted, 1982, Korea; 1992, New York, U.S.A. *Education:* College of Law, Seoul National University (B.Jur., 1980); Judicial Research and Training Institute of the Supreme Court of Korea (1982); Georgetown University Law School (LL.M., 1991). Judge Advocate, Republic of Korea Army, 1982-1985. *Member:* Korean and New York Bar Associations. *LANGUAGES:* Korean, English and Japanese.

YON KYUN OH, born Damyang, Jeonnam Province, Korea, October 22, 1958; admitted, 1982, Korea; 1992, New York. *Education:* College of Law, Seoul National University (B.Jur., 1980); Judicial Research and Training Institute of the Supreme Court of Korea (1982); Columbia University School of Law (LL.M., 1991). Judge Advocate, Republic of Korea Army, 1982-1985. *Member:* Korean and New York State Bar Associations. *LANGUAGES:* Korean, English and Japanese.

YOUNG HOON BYUN, born Hong Cheon, Kangwon Province, Korea, November 9, 1957; admitted, 1983, Korea. *Education:* College of Law, Seoul National University (B.Jur., 1981); Judicial Research and Training Institute of the Supreme Court of Korea (1983); Harvard Law School (LL.M., 1992). Judge Advocate, Republic of Korea Navy, 1983-1986. Visiting Attorney, Matsuo & Kosugi, Tokyo, Japan, 1987; Special Attorney, Morrison & Foerster, San Francisco, USA, 1992-1993. *Member:* Korean, New York State, and American Bar Associations. *LANGUAGES:* Korean, English and Japanese.

MIN HAN, born Kang Leung, Kangwon Province, Korea, December 15, 1958; admitted, 1983, Korea; 1993, New York. *Education:* College of Law, Seoul National University (B.Jur., 1981); Judicial Research and Training Institute of the Supreme Court of Korea (1983); Cornell Law School (LL.M., 1992). Judge Advocate, Republic of Korea Army, 1983-1986. Foreign Visiting Attorney, Cleary, Gottlieb, Steen & Hamilton, New York, 1992-1993. *Member:* Korean and New York Bar Associations. *LANGUAGES:* Korean, English and Japanese.

WEON JUNG KIM, born Andong, Kyungbuk Province, Korea, April 15, 1958; admitted, 1983, Korea. *Education:* College of Law, Seoul National University (B.Jur., 1981); Judicial Research and Training Institute of the Supreme Court of Korea (1983); Columbia University, School of Law (LL.M., 1992). Judge Advocate, Republic of Korea Army, 1983-1986. Law Office of Paul, Hastings, Janofsky and Walker, 1992-1993. *Member:* Korean Bar Association. *LANGUAGES:* Korean, English and Japanese.

CHANG YONG SHIN, born Pusan, Korea, August 4, 1957; Certified Public Accountant, 1983, Korea. *Education:* College of Business Administration, Seoul National University (1980); George Washington University (MBA, 1994). With San Tong Accounting Corporation, 1982-1985. *Member:* The Korean Institute of Certified Public Accountants. *LANGUAGES:* Korean and English.

DONG JUN YEO, born Seoul, Korea, October 2, 1957; admitted, Certified Public Accountant, 1983, Korea; 1991, Illinois. *Education:* College of Social Science, Seoul National University (International Economics, 1980); Graduate School, University of Illinois, Urbana-Champaign (M.A., Accounting, 1987). With: Samil Accounting Corporation, 1981-1985; Coopers & Lybrand, New York, 1987-1992. *Member:* The Korean Institute of Certified Public Accountants; The American Institute of Certified Public Accountants. *LANGUAGES:* Korean and English.

SANG HWAN LEE, born Euisung, Kyungbuk Province, Korea, June 14, 1959; admitted, 1984, Korea. *Education:* College of Law, Seoul National University (B.Jur., 1982); Judicial Research and Training Institute of the Supreme Court of Korea (1984); Cornell Law School (LL.M., 1993). Judge Advocate, Republic of Korea Air Force, 1985-1988. Visiting Attorney at Matsuo & Kosugi, Tokyo, 1990; Visiting Attorney at Cleary, Gottlieb, Steen & Hamilton, New York, 1993. *Member:* Korean Bar Association. *LANGUAGES:* Korean, English and Japanese.

SUNG KEUN YOON, born Chungwon, Choongbuk Province, Korea, July 15, 1959; admitted, 1984, Korea. *Education:* College of Law, Seoul National University (B.Jur., 1982); Judicial Research and Training Institute of the Supreme Court of Korea (1984); Graduate School of Law, Seoul National University (M.Jur., 1986); University of Michigan, Law School (LL.M., 1993); Peking University (Visiting Scholar, 1994). Judge Advocate, Republic of Korea Air Force, 1985-1988. Lecturer, Law Department of Sangji College, 1985-1987. Visiting Attorney, Johnson, Stokes and Master, Hong Kong, 1993-1994. *Member:* Korean Bar Association. *LANGUAGES:* Korean, English and Chinese..

(This Listing Continued)

YOUNG JAY RO, born Seoul, Korea, September 10, 1959; admitted, 1984, Korea; 1994, New York, U.S.A. *Education:* College of Law, Seoul National University (B.Jur., 1982); Judicial Research and Training Institute of the Supreme Court of Korea (1984); Yale Law School (LL.M., 1992). Judge Advocate, Republic of Korea Air Force, 1985-1988. Associated with Davis, Pork & Wardwell, New York, 1993-1994. *Member:* Korean Bar Association. *LANGUAGES:* Korean, English and Japanese.

KYONG HOON LEE, born Pusan, Korea, February 28, 1960; admitted, 1984, Korea; 1994, New York. *Education:* College of Law, Seoul National University (B.Jur., 1982); Judicial Research and Training Institute of the Supreme Court of Korea (1984); Harvard Law School (LL.M., 1992). Judge Advocate, Republic of Korea Air Force, 1985-1986. Legal Officer, Defense Logistics Agency of the Ministry of National Defense of Korea, 1986-1987. Visiting Attorney at Debevoise & Plimpton, 1993-1994. *Member:* Korean Bar Association; New York State Bar. *LANGUAGES:* Korean, English and French.

KI YOUNG KIM, born Pusan, Korea, December 11, 1961; admitted, 1988, Korea. *Education:* College of Law, Seoul National University (B.Jur., 1984); Graduate School of Law, Seoul National University (M.Jur., 1986); Judicial Research and Training Institute of the Supreme Court of Korea, 1988; UC Berkeley, U.S.A. (LL.M., 1993). Visiting Attorney at Shearman & Sterling, 1993. *Member:* Korean Bar Association. *LANGUAGES:* Korean, English and Japanese.

YOUNG KYUN CHO, born Kwangyang, Jeonnam Province, Korea, October 5, 1962; admitted, 1988, Korea. *Education:* College of Law, Seoul National University (B.Jur., 1985); Graduate School of Law, Seoul National University (1985-1987); Judicial Research and Training Institute of the Supreme Court of Korea (1988). *Member:* Korean Bar Association. *LANGUAGES:* Korean, English, Japanese and German.

YOUNG JOO HWANG, born Moon Kyung, Kyongbuk Province, Korea, January 9, 1957; admitted, 1984, Korea. *Education:* College of Law, Seoul National University (B.Jur., 1981); Judicial Research and Training Institute of the Supreme Court of Korea (1984). Judge Advocate, Republic of Korea Army, 1985-1987. *Member:* Korean Bar Association. *LANGUAGES:* Korean, English and Japanese.

SEON JIB CHOI, born Samchuk, Kangwon Province, Korea, January 7, 1956; admitted, 1987, Korea. *Education:* College of Education, Seoul National University (B.A., 1979); Judicial Research and Training Institute of the Supreme Court of Korea (1987); Graduate School of Law, Tokyo University, Japan (M.Jur., 1991). Officer, Ministry of Finance, Assistant Tax Judge of National Tax Tribunal; Assistant Director of the Bureau of Insurance, 1979-1992. Legal Counsel, National Tax Administration, 1992—. Lecturer, The Training Institute of Tax Officials, 1992—; College of Law, Yonsei University, 1994—; Non-standing Committee, the Insurance Supervisory Board (Non-Life Insurance). Publications: Overview of the Korean Tax System in Japanese Journal (University of Meiji Gakuin in 1990); Commentary on the Japanese Court decisions on the claims for seeing shareholders' list (Jurist in Japan, May-June 1991); On the Residence in Income Tax Treaties (A Collection of learned papers for Prof. Lee in College of Law, Seoul National University, 1992); On the Residence in IRC (Tax Attorney, Winter, 1991). *Member:* Korean Bar Association; Japanese Administrative Law Association; Japanese Tax Law Association; Korean International Trade Law Association. *LANGUAGES:* Korean, English, Japanese and German.

JIN YEONG CHUNG, born Yeong-ju, Kyungbuk Province, Korea, March 25, 1961; admitted, 1985, Korea. *Education:* College of Law, Seoul National University (B.Jur., 1984); Judicial Research and Training Institute of the Supreme Court of Korea (1985). Judge Advocate, Republic of Korea Air Force, 1986-1989. *Member:* Korean Bar Association. *LANGUAGES:* Korean, English, Japanese and German.

BYUNG MOO PARK, born Taegu, Kyungbuk Province, Korea, June 23, 1961; admitted, 1985, Korea. *Education:* College of Law, Seoul National University (B.Jur., 1984); Judicial Research and Training Institute of the Supreme Court of Korea (1985); Graduate School of Business Administration, Yonsei University (M.B.A., 1988); Graduate School of Law, Seoul National University (M. Jur., 1989). *Member:* Korean Bar Association. *LANGUAGES:* Korean, English, Japanese and German.

CHUNG HWAN CHOI, born Wonju, Kangwon Province, Korea, October 2, 1961; admitted, 1989, Korea. *Education:* College of Law, Seoul National University (B.Jur., 1984); Graduate School of Law, Seoul National University (M.Jur., 1990); Judicial Research and Training Institute of the Supreme Court of Korea (1989). *Member:* Korean Bar Association. *LANGUAGES:* Korean, English, Japanese and German.

SUNG EYUP PARK, born Jeonju, Jeonbuk Province, Korea, December 7, 1961; admitted, 1985, Korea. *Education:* College of Law, Seoul National University (B.Jur., 1984); Judicial Research and Training Institute of the Supreme Court of Korea (1985); Columbia Law School (LL.M., 1994). Judge Advocate, Republic of Korea Air Force, 1986-1989. *Member:* Korean Bar Association. *LANGUAGES:* Korean, English and Japanese.

JAE HONG AHN, born Seoul, Korea, March 3, 1962; admitted, 1985, Korea. *Education:* College of Law, Seoul National University (B.Jur., 1984); Judicial Research and Training Institute of the Supreme Court of Korea (1985). Judge Advocate, Republic of Korea Navy, 1986-1989. *Member:* Korean Bar Association. *LANGUAGES:* Korean, English, Japanese and German.

DONG HEE SUH, born Jeongup, Jeonbuk Province, Korea, August 18, 1960; admitted, 1985, Korea. *Education:* College of Law, Seoul National University (B.Jur., 1984); Judicial Research and Training Institute of the Supreme Court of Korea (1985). With, Law Offices of: Ko & Park, Seoul, 1987-1989; Lee & Ko, Seoul, 1989-1992. Kim & Chang, 1992—. *Member:* Korean Bar Association. *LANGUAGES:* Korean, English and Japanese (reads only).

YONG HO JO, born Seoul, Korea, December 7, 1961; admitted, Certified Public Accountant, 1988, Korea. *Education:* College of Business Administration, Seoul National University (B.S., 1985); Graduate School of Business Administration, Seoul National University (M.B.A., 1987); International Bureau of Fiscal Documentation, Netherlands (1993); University of Washington (MPA, 1994). Accountant, Samil Accounting Corporation, 1987-1989. *Member:* The Korean Institute of Certified Public Accountants. *LANGUAGES:* Korean and English.

MIN BAE PARK, born Seoul, Korea, August 13, 1962; admitted, 1987, Korea. *Education:* College of Law, Seoul National University (B.Jur., 1985); Judicial Research and Training Institute of the Supreme Court of Korea (1987). Judge Advocate, Republic of Korea Army, 1987-1990. *Member:* Korean Bar Association. *LANGUAGES:* Korean, English and Japanese.

BYUNG CHOL YOON, born Taegu, Korea, November 9, 1962; admitted, 1987, Korea. *Education:* College of Law, Seoul National University (B.Jur., 1985); Judicial Research and Training Institute of the Supreme Court of Korea (1987); Graduate School of Law, Seoul National University (LL.M., 1993). Judge Advocate, Republic of Korea Army, 1987-1990; Judge, Seoul District Court South Branch, 1990-1991; Judge, Seoul Criminal District Court, 1991-1992. *Member:* Korean Bar Association. *LANGUAGES:* Korean and English.

SUN HUN SONG, born Seoul, Korea, October 8, 1961; admitted, 1988, Korea. *Education:* College of Law, Seoul National University (B.Jur., 1984); Graduate School of Law, Seoul National University (1986); Judicial Research and Training Institute of the Supreme Court of Korea (1988). Judge Advocate, Republic of Korea Air Force, 1988-1990. *Member:* Korean Bar Association. *LANGUAGES:* Korean, English and Japanese.

YONG HO KIM, born Koryung, Kyungbuk Province, Korea, February 3, 1962; admitted, 1988, Korea. *Education:* College of Law, Seoul National University (B.Jur., 1985); Judicial Research and Training Institute of the Supreme Court of Korea (1988). Judge Advocate, Republic of Korea Navy, 1988-1991. *Member:* Korean Bar Association. *LANGUAGES:* Korean, English and Japanese.

SANG WOOK HAN, born Seoul, Korea, March 10, 1962; admitted, 1988, Korea. *Education:* College of Law, Seoul National University (B.Jur., 1984); Judicial Research and Training Institute of The Supreme Court of Korea (1988); Graduate School of Law, Seoul National University (LL.M., 1991). Judge Advocate, Republic of Korea Army, 1988-1991. *Member:* Korean Bar Association. *LANGUAGES:* Korean, English and Japanese.

HYUNG DOO KIM, born Tongyoung, Korea, March 14, 1962; admitted, 1988, Korea. *Education:* College of Law, Seoul National University (B.Jur., 1985); Graduate School of Law, Seoul National University (1988); Judicial Research and Training Institute of the Supreme Court of Korea (1988). Judge Advocate, Republic of Korea Air Force, 1988-1991. *Member:* Korean Bar Association. *LANGUAGES:* Korean and English.

CHANG SIK HWANG, born Taegu, Korea, March 31, 1962; admitted, 1988, Korea. *Education:* College of Law, Seoul National University (B.Jur., 1985); Judicial Research and Training Institute of the Supreme Court of Korea (1988); Graduate School of Law, Seoul National University (M.Jur., 1992). Judge Advocate, Republic of Korea Air Force, 1988-1991). *Member:* Korean Bar Association. *LANGUAGES:* Korean and English.

(This Listing Continued)

(This Listing Continued)

KIM & CHANG, Seoul—Continued

JONG KOO PARK, born Yangyang, Kangwon Province, Korea, February 4, 1963; admitted, 1988, Korea. *Education:* College of Law, Seoul National University (B.Jur., 1985); Judicial Research and Training Institute of the Supreme Court of Korea (1988). Judge Advocate, Republic of Korea Air Force, 1988-1991. *Member:* Korean Bar Association. *LANGUAGES:* Korean, English and Japanese.

YOUNG ICK CHOI, born Taegu, Kyungbuk Province, Korea June 4, 1963; admitted, 1988, Korea. *Education:* College of Law, Seoul National University (B.Jur., 1986); Judicial Research and Training Institute of the Supreme Court of Korea (1988). Judge Advocate, Republic of Korea Army, 1988-1991. *Member:* Korean Bar Association. *LANGUAGES:* Korean, English and Japanese.

KEUN HWA JUNG, born Seoul, Korea, June 21, 1964; admitted, 1988, Korea. *Education:* College of Law, Seoul National University (B.Jur., 1986); Judicial Research and Training Institute of the Supreme Court of Korea (1988). Judge Advocate, Republic of Korea Army, 1989-1991. *Member:* Korean Bar Association. *LANGUAGES:* Korean, English and Japanese.

PILL CHONG SHIN, born Seoul, Korea, March 22, 1963; admitted, 1988, Korea. *Education:* College of Law, Seoul National University (B.Jur., 1986); Judicial Research and Training Institute of the Supreme Court of Korea (1988). Judge: Seoul District Court South Branch, 1988-1990; Seoul Civil District Court, 1990-1992. *Member:* Korean Bar Association. *LANGUAGES:* Korean, English and Japanese.

YONG MOON YOON, born Taegu, Korea, September 18, 1963. became a certified public accountant, Korea, 1989. *Education:* Department of Economics, Seoul National University (B.S., 1986); Graduate School of Business Administration, Seoul National University (M.B.A., 1988). Samil Accounting Corporation, 1987-1989. *Member:* The Korean Institute of Certified Public Accountants. *LANGUAGES:* Korean, English and Japanese.

JEONG CHAN SEO, born Daegu, Korea, January 15, 1963; admitted, 1989, Korea. *Education:* College of Law, Seoul National University (B.Jur., 1986); Graduate School of Law, Seoul National University (1988); Judicial Research and Training Institute of the Supreme Court of Korea (1989). Judge Advocate, Republic of Korea Army, 1989-1992. *Member:* Korean Bar Association. *LANGUAGES:* Korean and English.

HI SUN YOON, born Kwangju, Jeonnam Province, Korea, May 25, 1963; admitted, 1989, Korea. *Education:* College of Law, Seoul National University (B.Jur., 1985); Graduate School of Law, Seoul National University (M.Jur., 1987); Judicial Research and Training Institute of the Supreme Court of Korea (1989). Judge Advocate, Republic of Korea Army, 1989-1992. *Member:* Korean Bar Association. *LANGUAGES:* Korean, English and Japanese.

CHUL YOUNG KIM, born Limsil, Jeonbuk Province, Korea, July 6, 1963; admitted, 1989, Korea. *Education:* College of Law, Korea University (B.Jur., 1985); Judicial Research and Training Institute of the Supreme Court of Korea (1989);. Judge Advocate, Republic of Korea Army, 1989-1992. *Member:* Korean Bar Association. *LANGUAGES:* Korean and English.

TAE GYUN ROH, born Euijungbu, Kyonggi Province, Korea, December 13, 1964; admitted, 1989, Korea. *Education:* College of Law, Seoul National University (B.Jur., 1987); Judicial Research and Training Institute of the Supreme Court of Korea (1989). Judge Advocate, Republic of Korea Navy, 1989-1992. *Member:* Korean Bar Association. *LANGUAGES:* Korean, English and Japanese.

JOO YOUNG KIM, born Seoul, Korea, February 19, 1965; admitted, 1989, Korea. *Education:* College of Law, Seoul National University (B.Jur., 1986); Judicial Research and Training Institute of the Supreme Court of Korea (1989). Judge Advocate, Republic of Korea Army, 1989-1992. *Member:* Korean Bar Association. *LANGUAGES:* Korean, Japanese and English.

CHANG HYEON KO, born Pusan, Korea, June 26, 1965; admitted, 1990, Korea. *Education:* College of Law, Seoul National University (B.Jur., 1988); Judicial Research and Training Institute of the Supreme Court of Korea (1990); School of Banking, Hanyang University, Korea (M.B.A., 1993). Judge Advocate, Republic of Korea Air Force, 1990-1993. *Member:* Korean Bar Association. *LANGUAGES:* Korean, English and Japanese.

YEONG MAN HEO, born Kyeongsan, Kyeongbuk Province, Korea, July 20, 1965; admitted, 1990, Korea. *Education:* College of Law, Seoul

(This Listing Continued)

National University (B.Jur., 1988); Judicial Research and Training Institute of the Supreme Court of Korea (1990). Judge Advocate, Republic of Korea Army, 1990-1993. *Member:* Korean Bar Association. *LANGUAGES:* Korean and English.

JISOO JANG, born Seoul, Korea, February 21, 1966; admitted, 1990, Korea. *Education:* College of Law, Seoul National University (B.Jur., 1988); Judicial Research and Training Institute of the Supreme Court of Korea (1990). Judge Advocate, Republic of Korea Navy, 1990-1993. *Member:* Korean Bar Association. *LANGUAGES:* Korean, English and Japanese.

JAE SOON JANG, born Andong, Kyungbuk Province, Korea, February 25, 1955; (Not admitted in Korea). *Education:* College of Liberal Arts and Sciences, Kyongbuk University (1981). With: The National Tax Administration, 1982-1983; International Tax Division of Ministry of Finance, 1984-1986; Samil Accounting Corporation, 1987-1990. Lecturer, National Tax Official Training Institute. *LANGUAGES:* Korean and English.

DONG SO KIM, born Hapcheon, Kyungnam Province, Korea, October 9, 1963; admitted, Certified Public Accountant, 1989, Korea. *Education:* College of Business Administration, Yonsei University (B.S., 1988). With: Samil Accounting Corporation, 1987-1991. *Member:* The Korean Institute of Certified Public Accountants. *LANGUAGES:* Korean and English.

YONG TAEK LIM, born Busan, Korea, January 23, 1965; admitted, Certified Public Accountant, 1992, Korea. *Education:* College of Business Administration, Seoul National University (B.S., 1988); Graduate School of Business Administration, Seoul National University (1990). With, Anjin Accounting Corporation, 1990-1993. *Member:* The Korean Institute of Certified Public Accountants. *LANGUAGES:* Korean and English.

SANG IK HAN, born Seoul, Korea, November 13, 1965; admitted, Certified Public Accountant, 1988, Korea. *Education:* College of Business and Economics, Yonsei University (1988); Graduate School of Seoul National University (M.B.A., 1990). With: Sandong Accounting Corporation, 1992-1993. *Member:* The Korean Institute of Certified Public Accountants. *LANGUAGES:* Korean, English and Japanese.

GENE SOON PARK, born Buffalo, N.Y., U.S.A., February 15, 1962; admitted, 1994, Korea. *Education:* College of Law, Seoul National University (B.Jur., 1984); Graduate School of Law, Seoul National University (LL.M., 1986); Ph.D., course Work (1990); Judicial Research and Training Institute of the Supreme Court of Korea (1994). Lecturer: Law, Hanshin University, 1988 & 1990; Korea Broadcast Correspondence University, 1987, 1989 & 1991. *Member:* Korean Bar Association. *LANGUAGES:* Korean, English, Japanese and German.

SUNG JOO YOON, born Seoul, Korea, April 5, 1965; admitted, 1991, Korea. *Education:* College of Law, Seoul National University (B.Jur., 1988); Judicial Research and Training Institute of the Supreme Court of Korea (1991). Judge Advocate, Republic of Korea Army, 1991-1994. *Member:* Korean Bar Association. *LANGUAGES:* Korean and English.

JIN SEOK LIM, born Yeongju, Kyeongbuk Province, Korea, April 20, 1966; admitted, 1991, Korea. *Education:* Seoul National University (B.A., Political Science, 1988); Judicial Research and Training Institute of the Supreme Court of Korea (1991). Judge Advocate, Republic of Korea Navy, 1991-1994. *Member:* Korean Bar Association. *LANGUAGES:* Korean, English and Japanese.

JUNG-KEOL SUH, born Andong, Kyungbuk, Korea, March 11, 1967; admitted, 1988, Korea. *Education:* College of Law, Seoul National University (B.Jur., 1989); Judicial Research and Training Institute of the Supreme Court of Korea (1991). Judge: Seoul Civil District Court, 1991-1993; Seoul Criminal District Court, 1993-1994. *Member:* Korean Bar Association. *LANGUAGES:* Korean, French and English.

YOUNG WOO CHANG, born Seoul, Korea, October 11, 1961; certified public accountant, New York, U.S.A., 1990; admitted, 1993, Korea. *Education:* Yonsei University (Business Administration, 1985); Graduate School of Business, George Washington University (1987). With, KPMG Peat Marwick, New York Office, 1987-1994. *Member:* The Korean Institute of Certified Public Accountants; The New York State Society of Certified Public Accountants; The Institute of Chartered Financial Analysts in U.S.A. *LANGUAGES:* Korean and English.

JAE HUN KIM, born Busan, Korea, September 17, 1965; admitted, 1994, Korea. *Education:* College of Law, Seoul National University (B.Jur., 1988); Graduate School of Law, Seoul National University (LL.M., 1991); Judicial and Training Institute of the Supreme Court of Korea (1994). *Member:* Korean Bar Association. *LANGUAGES:* Korean, English and Japanese.

(This Listing Continued)

SUNG JIN JOH, born Seoul, Korea, June 14, 1966; admitted, 1991, Korea. *Education:* College of Law, Seoul National University (B.Jur., 1989); Judicial Research and Training Institute of the Supreme Court of Korea (1991). Judge Advocate, Republic of Korea Army, 1991-1994. *Member:* Korean Bar Association. *LANGUAGES:* Korean and English.

HAN WOO PARK, born Seoul, Korea, July 2, 1966; admitted, 1991, Korea. *Education:* College of Law, Seoul National University (B.Jur., 1989); Judicial Research and Training Institute of the Supreme Court of Korea (1991). Judge Advocate, Republic of Korea Army, 1991-1994. *Member:* Korean Bar Association. *LANGUAGES:* Korean and English.

YOON SUN CHO, born Seoul, Korea, July 22, 1966; admitted, 1994, Korea. *Education:* Seoul National University (B.A., International Relations, 1988); Judicial Research and Training Institute of the Supreme Court of Korea (1994). *Member:* Korean Bar Association. *LANGUAGES:* Korean, English and Japanese.

SEONG TAIK KIM, born Cheju, Cheju Province, Korea, October 3, 1941. admitted as Patent and Trademark Attorney, Korea, 1979. *Education:* College of Science and Engineering, Korea University (B. Sc., 1966). Honam Fertilizer Company, Ltd., as a research chemist, 1966-1972. *Member:* Korean Patent Attorneys Association; Korea Intellectual Property Society; Asian Patent Attorneys Association; International Association for the Protection of Industrial Property. *LANGUAGES:* Korean, English, Japanese and German (read only).

YEONG-CHANG KOO, born Pusan, Korea, April 21, 1929; admitted to Patent and Trademark Attorney, Korea, 1972. *Education:* College of Engineering, Seoul National University (1952). With: The Korea Cement Manufacturing Co., 1957-1959; The Korea Electric Power Co., 1959-1961; The Ulsan Development Planning Authority, 1962; Bureau of Standard, Ministry of Commerce and Industry, 1963; Bureau of Utilities, Ministry of Commerce and Industry, 1964. Examiner, Korea Industrial Property Office ("KIPO"), 1969. Trial Examiner, KIPO, 1975. Appellate Trial Examiner, KIPO, 1981. Koo Patent Office, 1989. Kim & Chang, 1990—. *Member:* Korea Patent Attorneys Association; International Association for the Protection of Industrial Property; Asian Patent Attorneys Association. *LANGUAGES:* Korean, English and Japanese.

D.W. KIM, born Seoul, Korea, October 2, 1937. Registered to practice before the U.S. Patent and Trademark Office, 1973. *Education:* Western Michigan University (B.S., Chemistry, 1962); Wayne State University (M.S., Chemistry, 1965); University of Louisville (Graduate Studies in Pharmacology, 1971). With: Smith Kline & French Laboratories, Philadelphia, Pa., 1967-1969; Abbott Laboratories, North Chicago, Il.; Velsicol Chemical Corp., Chicago, Il., 1973-1977. Central International Law Firm, Seoul, Korea, 1978-1985. *Member:* New York International Patent Club. *LANGUAGES:* Korean and English. *PRACTICE AREAS:* Pharmaceuticals; Agrochemicals; Chemical Technology; Patent Practice.

YONGJIN JEON, born Seoul, Korea, March 15, 1956; admitted, 1991, New York. *Education:* College of Law, Korea University (B.Jur., 1979); Albany Law School (J.D., 1991). Kim & Chang, 1993—. Yangjae Law Office, 1991-1992; C.H. Hwang International Patent and Law Office, 1992-1993. *Member:* New York State Bar Association; American Bar Association; American Intellectual Property Law Association; Copyright Society of the U.S.A. *LANGUAGES:* Korean, English and Japanese. *PRACTICE AREAS:* Trademark Law; Copyright Law.

HYE SUK WEE, born Jangheung, Jeonnam Province, Korea, January 10, 1952; admitted, Patent and Trademark Attorney, 1991, Korea. *Education:* College of Pharmacy, Seoul National University (B.S., Pharmacy, 1975). With: Chong Kun Dang Pharmaceutical Company, 1975-1979; Central International Law Firm, 1979-1990. *Member:* Korean Patent Attorneys Association; Korea Pharmacists Association. Kim & Chang, 1990—. *LANGUAGES:* Korean, English and Japanese. *PRACTICE AREAS:* Pharmaceuticals; Agrochemistry; Biochemistry and Genetic Engineering.

KOOK-CHAN AN, born Wonju, Kangwon Province, Korea, July 2, 1959; admitted, Patent and Trademark Attorney, 1990, Korea. *Education:* College of Engineering, Seoul National University (B.Eng., 1981). With: Daewoo Motor Company, 1983-1988; Lee International Patent Office, 1988-1989. *Member:* Korean Patent Attorneys Association; AIPPI; Asian Patent Attorneys Association. *LANGUAGES:* Korean, English and Japanese. *PRACTICE AREAS:* Metallurgical Engineering; Mechanical Engineering; Automotive Engineering.

KUIY-DONG LEE, born Hong Sung, Chungnam Province, Korea, January 10, 1964; admitted, Patent and Trademark Attorney, 1992, Korea. *Education:* College of Natural Science, Seoul National University (B.Sc.,

(This Listing Continued)

1986); Graduate School of Natural Science, Seoul National University (M.Sc., 1988). *Member:* Korea Patent Attorneys Association; APAA; AIPPI. *LANGUAGES:* Korean and English. *PRACTICE AREAS:* Organic Chemistry Law; Biotechnology Law.

SEONG-KI KIM, born Kapyung, Kyungki Province, Korea, February 16, 1954; admitted, Patent and Trademark Attorney, 1987, Korea; 1991, New York; 1992, District of Columbia. *Education:* College of Education, Seoul National University (B.S., 1978); Korea Advanced Institute of Science (M.S., 1980); School of Public Administration, Seoul National University (MBA, 1984); Cornell Law School (J.D., 1990). Patent Examiner, Korean Industrial Property Office, 1980-1982 and 1985-1991. Deputy Director, Ministry of Trade and Industry, 1982-1985. With: First Law Offices of Korea, 1991-1992. *Member:* Committee for Revision of Patent Law, KIPO (1994—); Committee for Revision of Patent Attorney Law, KIPO (1994—); Adjunct Prof., International Intellectual Property Training Institute, KIPO (1992—); Korean Patent Attorneys Association (Standing Committee, 1992-1994; Member of Board of Directors, 1994-1996); New York State Bar Association; Asian Patent Attorneys Association; International Association for the Protection of Industrial Property. *LANGUAGES:* Korean and English.

NAM-YEON KWON, born Jinju, Kyungsangnam Province, Korea, September 10, 1965; admitted, Patent and Trademark Attorney, 1991, Korea. *Education:* College of Liberal Arts, Yonsei University (B. Lit., 1987). With: First Interstate Bank of California, 1987-1989. Kim & Chang, 1991—. *Member:* Korean Patent Attorneys Association. *LANGUAGES:* Korean, English and Japanese. *PRACTICE AREAS:* Trademark, Design Patent, Copyright.

JOO-MEE KIM, born Pusan, Korea, July 3, 1966; admitted, Patent and Trademark Attorney, 1991, Korea. *Education:* College of Pharmacy, Seoul National University (B. Pharm., 1989). Kim & Chang, 1991—. *Member:* Korean Patent Attorneys Association. *LANGUAGES:* Korean and English. *PRACTICE AREAS:* Pharmaceutics; Pharmacology; Microbiology.

MI-SUNG SHIM, born Kwangju, Chulla Province, Korea, October 13, 1966; admitted, Patent and Trademark Attorney, 1991, Korea. *Education:* College and Graduate School of Natural Sciences, Seoul National University (B.Sc., 1989; M.Sc., 1991). Kim & Chang, 1991—. *Member:* Korean Patent Attorneys Association. *LANGUAGES:* Korean and English. *PRACTICE AREAS:* Organic Synthetic Chemistry; Industrial Organic Chemistry.

JEE-HONG YOON, born Seoul, Korea, January 26, 1961; admitted, 1992, Patent and Trademark Attorney, Korea. *Education:* Yonsei University, College of Engineering (B.S., 1984); Korea Advanced Institute of Science and Technology (M.S., Electronics Engineering, 1988). Korea Telecom, 1988-1992; Kim & Chang, 1992—. *Member:* Korean Patent Attorneys Association. *LANGUAGES:* Korean and English. *PRACTICE AREAS:* Image Data Compression; Digital Signal Processing; Telecommunications.

KEUN-BOK SEO, born Kwangju, Korea, June 20, 1961; admitted, 1993, Patent and Trademark Attorney, Korea. *Education:* Seoul National University (B.S., Chemical Engineering, 1985). Research Chemist, Korea Research Institute of Chemical Technology, 4th Polymer Lab, 1985-1991. BASF Korea Ltd., 1991. Kim & Chang, 1991—. *Member:* Korean Patent Attorneys Association. *LANGUAGES:* Korean and English. *PRACTICE AREAS:* Polymer Chemistry; Membrane Technology; Polymer Alloys and Composite Materials.

SEOK-JAE LEE, born Gongju, Korea, December 9, 1964; admitted, 1992, Patent and Trademark Attorney, Korea. *Education:* Korea University, College of Agriculture (B.S., 1988). Mogam Biotechnology Research Institute, 1987-1989. Kim & Chang, 1992—. *Member:* Korean Patent Attorneys Association. *LANGUAGES:* Korean and English. *PRACTICE AREAS:* Biotechnology; Biochemistry.

RYANG-EUN KIM, born Seoul, Korea, May 20, 1963; admitted, 1992, Patent and Trademark Attorney, Korea. *Education:* Ewha Women's University, College of Law (B.Jur., 1985); Graduate School of Law, Ewha Women's University (LL.M., 1988). Central International Law Firm, 1985-1987. Kim & Chang, 1990-1992. Tsutada Patent Law Office, Osaka, Japan, 1992-1993. Kim & Chang, 1993—. *Member:* Korean Patent Attorneys Association; Japan Trademark Association. *LANGUAGES:* Korean, Japanese and English. *PRACTICE AREAS:* Trademarks; Designs.

DONG-HEE OH, born Seoul, Korea, February 2, 1957; admitted, 1992, Patent and Trademark Attorney, Korea. *Education:* College of Engineering, Seoul National University (B.S., 1979). Hyundai Electrical Engineering Co., Ltd., 1979-1990. Kim & Chang, 1992—. *Member:* Korean Patent At-

(This Listing Continued)

KIM & CHANG, Seoul—Continued

torneys Association. *LANGUAGES:* Korean, English and Japanese. *PRACTICE AREAS:* Electrical and Electronics Engineering.

IL-DO HAN, born Busan, Korea, March 12, 1962; admitted, 1990, Patent and Trademark Attorney, Korea. *Education:* University of California, Berkeley (B.S., Applied Mathematics/Electrical Engineering, 1986); University of Southern California (M.S., Electrical Engineering, 1988); Stanford University (M.S., Engineering Management, 1990). Hughes Aircraft Co., 1986-1989. Goldstar Information and Communications Inc., 1992—. Kim & Chang, 1993—. *LANGUAGES:* Korean and English. *PRACTICE AREAS:* Electrical and Electronics Engineering.

FOREIGN LEGAL CONSULTANTS

JEFFREY D. JONES, born Boise, Idaho, June 7, 1952; admitted, 1978, California; 1980, Illinois and U.S. District Court, Northern District of Illinois (Not admitted in Korea). *Education:* Brigham Young University (B.A., cum laude, 1975; J. Reuben Clark Law School, J.D., cum laude, 1978). Member, J. Reuben Clark Society of International Law. Associated with Baker & McKenzie (Tokyo Japan, 1978-1979; Chicago, Illinois, 1979-1980). Author: "Licensing Operations in Korea," an introduction to the Law and Legal System of Korea, 733 S.H. Song, ed. 1983. *Member:* American Society of International Law; American Bar Association; California State Bar Association; Illinois State Bar Association; J. Reuben Clark Law Society. *LANGUAGES:* English and Korean.

ROBERT L. GILBERT, born Reno, Nevada, April 2, 1950; admitted, 1980, California and U.S. District Court, Eastern District of California (Not admitted in Korea). *Education:* Pomona College (B.A., 1972); University of the Pacific, McGeorge School of Law (J.D., 1980). Member, Pacific Law Journal, 1979-1980. Assistant Editor, Owens Forms and Procedures, 1978-1979. Phi Alpha Delta. Intern, California State Lands Commission, 1978. With United States Army Judge Advocate General's Corps., 1981-1984. *Member:* State Bar of California. *LANGUAGES:* English and Korean.

KIRK V. GALE, born Tokyo, November 26, 1951; admitted, 1980, California (Not admitted in Korea). *Education:* Friends World College (B.A. in French Language; International Relations, 1973); Hastings College of Law, University of California (J.D., 1979). *LANGUAGES:* English and French.

HYO YOUNG (FRANK) KANG, born Seoul, Korea, December 28, 1955; admitted, 1985, Maryland and U.S. District Court, District of Maryland (Not admitted in Korea). *Education:* Duke University (B.S., 1978); Georgetown University Law Center (J.D., 1984). Peace Corps., Philippines, 1978-1980. U.S. Army Judge Advocate General's Corps, 1985-1988. Instructor, Business and Real Estate Law, Central Texas College, Pacific Far East Campus, 1988. *Member:* Maryland State Bar Association. *LANGUAGES:* English, Korean and Cebuano.

ROBERT M. DONALDSON, born Provo, Utah, June 24, 1959; admitted, 1988, California and U.S. District Court, Central District of California (Not admitted in Korea). *Education:* Brigham Young University (B.A., 1984); Brigham Young University, J. Reuben Clark Law School (J.D., 1987). Phi Delta Phi. Note and Comment Editor, B.Y.U. Law Review, 1986-1987. Author: "Mitsubishi and Antitrust Arbitration; It's All the Japanese You Need to Know," B.Y.U. Law Review 216, 1986. Judicial Clerk, Arizona Court of Appeals, 1987-1988. *Member:* California State and American (Member, International Law Section) Bar Associations. *LANGUAGES:* English and Korean.

ROSS D. MEADOR, born Mexico D.F., Mexico, August 23, 1954; admitted, 1987, California (Not admitted in Korea). *Education:* University of California, San Diego (B.A., 1980); University of California, Berkeley, Boalt Hall School of Law (J.D., 1986). S.K. Yee Scholarship Award. Executive Editor, International Tax and Business Lawyer. Vice President, International Law Society. *Member:* Ecology Law Quarterly; Moot Court, Outstanding Brief and Oral Argument Awards. Morrison & Foerster, San Francisco, California, 1986—; Kim & Chang, 1989—. *Member:* California State, San Francisco, American (Member, International Law and Business Law Sections) Bar Association. *LANGUAGES:* English.

MIN KYO LEE, born Seoul, Korea, January 29, 1957; admitted, 1987, Pennsylvania; 1988, District of Columbia (Not admitted in Korea). *Education:* Seoul National University (B.A., Political Science, 1979); Graduate School of Law, Seoul National University (LL.M., 1982); Duke University School of Law (LL.M., 1984; J.D., 1987; S.J.D., 1990). Member, Skadden, Arps, Slate, Meagher & Flom, Washington, D.C., 1987-1989. *LANGUAGES:* Korean and English.

(This Listing Continued)

AS214B

JUN S. CHO, born Pohang, Korea, February 28, 1960; admitted, 1989, New York; 1990, Washington, D.C. (Not admitted in Korea). *Education:* College of William and Mary (B.A., Economics, 1981); New York University Graduate School of Arts and Sciences (Economics, 1982-1983); New York University School of Law (J.D., 1988). N.Y.U. Journal of International Law and Politics, 1986-1988; Symposium Editor, 1987-1988; Arnold & Porter, Washington, D.C., 1988-1990. *LANGUAGES:* English and Korean.

SCOTT R. BALFOUR, born Battle Creek, Michigan, June 11, 1961; admitted, 1990, Michigan and U.S. District court, Eastern District of Michigan (Not admitted in Korea). *Education:* Michigan State University (B.S., 1983); University of Detroit (J.D., cum laude, 1990). With Timmis & Inman, 1990-1992. *Member:* State Bar of Michigan; American Bar Association; International Law Society. *LANGUAGES:* English and Spanish.

WAYNE A. BOATWRIGHT, born Los Angeles, California, April 10, 1962; admitted, 1990, California; 1991, U.S. District Court, Central District of California (Not admitted in Korea). *Education:* Brigham Young University (B.A., 1987); Cornell University School of Law (J.D., 1990). With Rogers & Wells, Los Angeles, 1990-1992. *Member:* State Bar of California; American Bar Association (International Law and Business Law). *LANGUAGES:* English and Spanish.

WILLIAM C. CHOI, born Seoul, Korea, June 15, 1959; admitted, 1985, California and U.S. District Court, Central District of California; 1986, U.S. Tax Court (Not admitted in Korea). *Education:* San Jose State University (B.S., Highest Honors, 1981); University of Southern California (J.D., 1985). Member, University of Southern California Law Review, 1983-1984. With: Latham & Watkins, Law Firm, Los Angeles, 1985-1992; Deloitte, Haskins & Sells, (Deloitte & Touche) Accounting Firm, San Jose, California, 1981-1982. Passed C.P.A. Examination, 1982. Intern, Chief Judge of U.S. Tax Court, 1984. Author: "California Fractures Certainty on Unitary Taxation," International Tax Review, December, 1991-January, 1992; Clifford Trusts: " Proposals For Resolution of the Gift-Leaseback Conflict," 58 Southern California Law Review 1409, Sept., 1985. *Member:* California and American Bar Associations (Section on Taxation; Subsection on International Taxation). *LANGUAGES:* English and Korean.

HWA SOO CHUNG, born Seoul, Korea, September 30, 1958; admitted, 1993, California (Not admitted in Korea). *Education:* Harvard University (A.B., 1980); Princeton University (M.P.A., 1982); University of California, Hastings College of Law (J.D., 1992). With: United Nations Conference on Trade and Development, 1983-1985; Economic Planning Board, 1985-1986; Ilhae Institute, 1986-1987. Co-Author: "The Multifibre Arrangement in Theory and Practice"; "Korea's Domestic Trade Politics and the Uruguay Round in Domestic Trade Politics and the Uruguay Round.". *LANGUAGES:* English, Korean, French and Spanish.

SUHN KYOUNG HONG, born Seoul, Korea, August 29, 1945; admitted, 1985, California (Not admitted in Korea). *Education:* Seoul National University (B.A., English Literature, 1967); Wellesley College (B.A., Sociology, 1969); Yale Law School (J.D., 1985). Phi Beta Kappa. With: Pettit & Martin, San Francisco, 1985-1989; Jones, Day, Reavis & Pogue, Los Angeles, 1989-1992. *LANGUAGES:* Korean and English.

ROBERT BYUNGIL LEE, born Seoul, Korea, December 5, 1956; admitted, 1982, New York; 1984, California (Not admitted in Korea). *Education:* Cornell University (B.A., 1978); Fordham University School of Law (J.D., 1982). With: Kim, Chang & Lee, Seoul, 1982-1984. Graham & James, Los Angeles, 1984-1985; Loeb & Loeb, Los Angeles, 1985-1992. *Member:* New York State Bar Association and State Bar of California. *LANGUAGES:* Korean and English.

TAM HEE KIM, born Seoul, Korea, April 10, 1961; admitted, 1992, Ontario, Canada (Not admitted in Korea). *Education:* Glendon College, York University (B.A., Honors, 1985); Osgoode Hall Law School, York University (LL.B., 1991). With: Owens, Wright, Articling Student; Law Research Institute, Seoul National University, Visiting Research Scholar. *Member:* Canadian Bar Association (International Law Section); Canada Business Club; Canada Korea Society. *LANGUAGES:* English, Korean and French.

JAEHA JASON SHIN, born Seoul, Korea, February 6, 1964; admitted, 1990, California and U.S. District Court, Central District of California (Not admitted in Korea). *Education:* Northwestern University (B.A., with honors, 1987); Boalt Hall School of Law, University of California, Berkeley (J.D., 1990). With: Baker & McKenzie, Los Angeles, California. *LANGUAGES:* English and Korean.

IL YOUNG BYUN, born Seoul, Korea, December 6, 1961; admitted, 1989, New York (Not admitted in Korea). *Education:* University of Chi-

(This Listing Continued)

cago (B.A., Honors, 1984); University of Michigan (J.D., 1987). Executive Editor, Michigan Journal of International Law, 1987. Fulbright Scholar, Ministry of Finance, Korea, 1988-1989. With: Seward & Kissel, New York , 1989-1991; Aoki, Christensen & Nomoto, Tokyo, 1991-1993. *Member:* International Bar Association. *LANGUAGES:* English, Korean and Japanese.

GLENN P. RICKARDS, born Glenn Cove, New York, May 2, 1950; admitted, 1978, Washington and U.S. District Court, Western District of Washington; registered to practice before the U.S. Patent and Trademark Office (Not admitted in Korea). *Education:* Brigham Young University (B.S., Chemistry, 1975); Brigham Young University, J. Reuben Clark Law School (J.D., cum laude, 1978). *Member:* Washington State Bar Association. *LANGUAGES:* English, Spanish and Mandarin.

THOMAS C. KIMBROUGH, born Memphis, Tennessee, December 13, 1963; admitted, 1988, California; 1988, Washington, D.C. (Not admitted in Korea). *Education:* Georgetown University (B.S.F.S., 1985); University of California, Berkeley, Boalt Hall School of Law (J.D., 1988). Associate Editor, International Tax and Business Lawyer. Cole Corette & Abrutyn, Washington, D.C., 1988-1991. *Member:* California State; District of Columbia; American Bar Association. *LANGUAGES:* English, Korean and Spanish.

SANG HYUK PARK, born Los Angeles, California, U.S.A., June 5, 1968; admitted, 1993, New York (Not admitted in Korea). *Education:* University of Chicago (B.A., with Honors in Economics, 1990); Cornell Law School (J.D., with Specialization in Business Law and Regulation, 1993). Akin, Gump, Hauer & Feld, Washington, D.C., 1992. *LANGUAGES:* Korean and English.

SANGHOON LEE, born Seoul, Korea, September 4, 1968; admitted, 1994, New York (Not admitted in Korea). *Education:* Brown University (A.B., 1990); Cornell Lw School (J.D., 1993). Corporate Associate: Proskauer Rose Goetz & Mendelsohn, New York, 1993-1994; Kim & Chang, 1994—. Author: "Reconsidering Limits on Foreign Investment in United States Airlines," Cornell Journal of Law and Public Policy, Spring 1992. *LANGUAGES:* English and Korean.

STEFAN L. MOLLER, born Goteborg, Sweden, May 6, 1953; admitted, 1987, California (Not admitted in Korea). *Education:* University of Stockholm, Sweden (J.D., 1980); Southern Methodist University (LL.M., 1980); Southern Methodist University (J.D., 1986). Law Clerk, District Court of Norrkoping, Sweden, 1980-1983. Associate: Latham & Watkins, Los Angeles, California, 1987-1991; Stefan L. Moller, Goteborg, Sweden, 1992-1994; Kim & Chang, 1994—. *Member:* California Bar Association. *LANGUAGES:* English, Swedish and German.

JUNG HAN, born Pusan, Korea, April 7, 1965; admitted, 1994, New York (Not admitted in Korea). *Education:* College of Law, Seoul National University (B.Jur., 1988); University of Washington School of Law (LL.M., 1989); Santa Clara University School of Law (J.D., 1994). With, Samsung Aerospace Industries, Ltd., Feb.-May 1988, Aug.-Nov., 1989, June 1991. *LANGUAGES:* English and Korean.

OF COUNSEL

SANG HYUN SONG, born Seoul, Korea, December 21, 1941; admitted, 1964, Korea. *Education:* College of Law, Seoul National University (LL.B., 1963); Judge Advocate, Republic of Korea Army, 1964-1967; Tulane University Law School (LL.M., 1968); University of Cambridge (Diploma, 1969); Cornell Law School (J.S.D., 1970). Associated with, Haight, Gardner, Poor & Havens, New York, N.Y., 1970-1972. Author: "A Comparative Study on Maritime Cargo Carrier's Liability in Anglo-American and French Law," (1970); "Introduction to the Law and Legal System of Korea," (1983); "The Intellectual Property Law Code," (1989); "A Commentary on the Computer Program Protection Law," (1989); "The Outlines of Korean Civil Procedures," (1990). Visiting Scholar to Hamburg University, 1974-1975 and Harvard Law School, 1978-1979. Visiting Professor, Harvard Law School, 1991 and University of Melbourne, 1990, 1992 and 1994, Inge Rennert Distinguished Professor of Law, NYU Law School, 1994. Professor of Law, Seoul National University, 1972—. Member: Advisory Committee to the Supreme Court, 1979—; Advisory Committee to the Ministry of Justice, 1980—; Copyright Deliberation and Conciliation Committee of the Ministry of Culture and Sports, 1987—; Computer Program Deliberation Committee of the Ministry of Science and Technology, 1987—; Arbitrator: The Korean Commercial Arbitration Board, 1980—; World Bank (ICSID), 1986—; Board of Directors, The Korea Stock Exchange, 1988-1994. *Member:* Korean Intellectual Property Research Society Inc. (President, 1986); Korean Maritime Law Association (Vice President, 1982—);

(This Listing Continued)

Korean International Trade Law Association (President, 1990—). *LANGUAGES:* Korean, English, German and French.

KIHWAN KIM, born Euisung, Kyungbuk Province, Korea, February 15, 1932. *Education:* Grinnell College (B.A., 1957); Yale University (M.A., 1959); University of California, Berkeley (Ph.D., Economics, 1971). Acting Assistant Professor, University of California, Berkeley and Davis (1965-1970); Associate Professor, Portland State University (1970-1976); Director of Research, Korea International Economic Institute (1976-1981); Senior Counselor to the Deputy Prime Minister and Minister of Economic Planning (1979-1981); President, Korea Development Institute (1982-1983); Vice Minister, Ministry of Trade and Industry (1983-1984); Secretary General, International Economic Policy Council (1984-1986); Chief Delegate, North-South Korean Economic Talks (1984-1986); Chairman and President, The Ilhae Foundation (1986-1987); President, The Sejong Institute (1987-1989); Consultant, The World Bank (1990); Visiting Scholar, University of Tokyo (1990-1991); Visiting Professor, University of California, Berkeley (1991-1992). Chairman, Korea National Committee for Pacific Economic Cooperation, 1993—; Korea Trade Promotion Corporation (KOTRA), 1993—. *Member:* Monetary Board (1981-1983); Commission for Banking and Financial Sector Reforms (1982-1983); Foreign Capital Deliberation Board (1982-1983); Pacific Board of Economists for *Time* magazine (1982-1983); Advisory Board Ministry of National Unification, 1994—. *LANGUAGES:* Korean, English and Japanese.

CHUNG-HAN LEE, born Seoul, Korea, July 11, 1923. *Education:* College of Engineering, Seoul National University (B. Eng., 1948); Graduate School, Seoul National University (M. Eng., 1950); Yale University (M. Eng., 1957); The University of Manchester Institute of Science and Technology, England (Ph.D., Solid-State Electronics, 1970). Professor Emeritus of Electronics Engineering, Seoul National University, 1988—. Lecturer, Instructor and Professor, College of Engineering, Seoul National University, 1949-1988. *Member:* IEEE (USA); IEICE (Japan); KITE (Korea; President, 1982); KIEE (Korea). *LANGUAGES:* Korean, English and Japanese. *PRACTICE AREAS:* Solid-State Electronics; Electronic Components and Materials.

COMPILERS OF THE KOREA LAW DIGEST FOR THIS DIRECTORY.

KIM, CHANG & LEE

Established in 1958

9TH FLOOR, DAEIL BUILDING
43-1 INSA-DONG, CHONGRO-KU
SEOUL, KOREA
Telephone: 397-9800
Cable Address: "ATTYKIM" Seoul
Telex: "LAWHL" K25009
Facsimile: 725-8727; 725-8728

Foreign Investment, International Commercial Transactions, Banking and Securities, Corporate Law, Maritime Law, Insurance, Real Estate, Environmental Law, Taxation, Litigation, Labor, Intellectual Property, Telecommunications and Family Law.

FIRM PROFILE: Founded in 1958 by Houng Han Kim and Dr. Tai-Young Lee, Kim, Chang & Lee is Korea's oldest law firm and the first firm in Korea to engage in international corporate law practice. The firm represents leading Korean and foreign corporations in their Korean and transnational operations.

MEMBERS OF FIRM

HOUNG HAN KIM, born Seoul, Korea, November 18, 1924; admitted, 1949, Korea. *Education:* College of Law, Seoul National University (LL.B., 1949); George Washington University Law School (M.C.L., 1954; LL.M., 1955). Lecturer of Law: Ewha Women's University, 1958-1959; College of Law, Seoul National University, 1959-1960; Graduate School of Law, Seoul National University, 1959-1960; Judicial Research and Training Institute of the Supreme Court of Korea, 1964-1967. Judge, Seoul District Court, 1950-1953. Private law practice since 1958. Chairman, Editorial Committee for Korean Legal Center's Laws of the Republic of Korea, 1983—. *Member:* USO Seoul Council (President, 1978-1979); Seoul Rotary Club (President, 1979-1980, Rotary International District 365, Governor for 1984-1985); National Committee on Women's Affairs, Ministry of Health & Social Affairs, Republic of Korea, 1983-1986. *Member:* Seoul and International Bar Associations; International Legal Society. *LANGUAGES:* Korean, English and Japanese. *PRACTICE AREAS:* Foreign Investment Law; International Commercial Transactions; Corporate Law; Labor Law.

(This Listing Continued)

KIM, CHANG & LEE, Seoul—Continued

EUI JAE KIM, born Seoul, Korea, October 26, 1937; admitted, 1960, Korea. *Education:* College of Law, Seoul National University (LL.B., 1960; LL.M., 1965); Southern Methodist University Law School (LL.M., 1969; J.D., 1971). Lecturer of Law, College of Commerce, Seoul National University, 1966-1967. Judge, Seoul Civil District Court and Seoul Criminal District Court, 1962-1968. *Member:* Seoul Bar Association. [Judge Advocate, Air Force, Republic of Korea, 1959-1962]. *LANGUAGES:* Korean and English. *PRACTICE AREAS:* Foreign Investment Law; International Commercial Transactions; Intellectual Property Law.

KYUNG-JOON CHOI, born Seoul, Korea, August 3, 1960; admitted, 1982, Korea; 1988, New York; 1991, Massachusetts; 1991, Illinois; 1992, District of Columbia and California. *Education:* College of Law, Seoul National University (LL.B., magna cum laude, 1983); Judicial Research and Training Institute of the Supreme Court of Korea (Chief Justice Award for Highest Scholastic Achievement, 1983-1984); Harvard Law School (LL.M., 1987); Boston University School of Law (LL.M., in Banking Law Studies, 1988); Boston University (M.A., in Economics, 1989); New York University School of Law (J.D., magna cum laude, 1991). Order of Coif. Member, New York University Law Review. Judge, Seoul Civil District Court, 1985-1986. Summer Associate: Morrison & Foerster, New York, 1989; Coudert Brothers, New York, 1990. With: Testa, Hurwitz & Thibeault, Boston, 1991-1992. *Member:* Seoul, New York State, Illinois State, Massachusetts and American Bar Associations; State Bar of California; District of Columbia Bar. *LANGUAGES:* Korean, English and Japanese. *PRACTICE AREAS:* Banking Law; Securities; International Commercial Transactions; Maritime Law; Litigation.

BAE KYUNG YOON, born Yosu, Chollanam Province, Korea, December 20, 1961; admitted, 1991, Korea. *Education:* College of Law, Seoul National University (LL.B., 1988); Graduate School of Law, Seoul National University (LL.M., in Taxation, 1988-1990); Judicial Research and Training Institute of the Supreme Court of Korea (1989-1991). Author: "Tax Treatment of Treasury Stock under Corporate Tax Law," Masters Thesis; "Prohibition of Ship Arrest," Maritime Korea, 1993; "Necessity of Provisional Remedies in Intellectual Property Cases," Human Rights and Justice, 1993; "Tax Aspects of Property Division in Dissolution," Tax Research Association Publication, 1993. *Member:* Seoul Bar Association. *LANGUAGES:* Korean, English and Japanese. *PRACTICE AREAS:* Taxation Law; Litigation; Insurance Law; Maritime Law.

JAE WOOK OH, born Taegu, Korea, April 14, 1968; admitted, 1991, Korea. *Education:* College of Law, Seoul National University (LL.B., 1985); Judicial Research and Training Institute of the Supreme Court of Korea (1989-1991). *Member:* Seoul Bar Association. [Judge Advocate, Korean Army, 1991-1993]. *LANGUAGES:* Korean, German, Japanese and English. *PRACTICE AREAS:* Litigation; Telecommunications.

CHANG SUP KIM, born Gwesan, Choeng Chungbuk Province, Korea, September 5, 1964; admitted, 1994, Korea. *Education:* College of Law, Korean University (LL.B., 1987); Judicial Research and Training Institute of the Supreme Court of Korea (1992-1994). *Member:* Seoul Bar Association. *LANGUAGES:* Korean, English and German. *PRACTICE AREAS:* Litigation.

DUK MIN LEE, born Hampyung, Chollenam Provence, Korea, May 4, 1965; admitted, 1994, Korea. *Education:* College of Social Science, Seoul National University (B.A., Political Science, 1988); Judicial Research and Training Institute of the Supreme Court of Korea, (1992-1994). *Member:* Seoul Bar Association. *LANGUAGES:* Korean, English and French. *PRACTICE AREAS:* Litigation.

BYONG WOOK KIM, born Pusan, Korea, March 12, 1956; admitted, 1986, Korea. *Education:* College of Law, Seoul National University (LL.B., 1984); Judicial Research and Training Institute of the Supreme Court of Korea (1984-1985); University of New South Wales, Australia (LL.M., 1991). Korean Law Consultant, Clayton Utz, Sydney, 1990-1994. *LANGUAGES:* Korean, English, Japanese, German and Latin. *PRACTICE AREAS:* Foreign Investment Law; International Commercial Transactions.

RESIDENT FOREIGN LEGAL CONSULTANTS

HAROLD Y. SHIM, born Tolsan, Chollanam Province, Korea, August 16, 1954; admitted, 1985, Washington; 1987, U.S. District Court, Western District of Washington (Not admitted in Korea). *Education:* University of Washington (B.A., 1980); University of California at Davis (J.D., 1984). Law Clerk, to the Honorable Warren Chan, King Country Superior Court, 1985. With: Helsell, Fetterman, Martin, Todd & Hokanson, Seattle, 1985-1988. Of Counsel, Bullivant, Houser, Bailey, Pendergrass & Hoffman, Seat-

(This Listing Continued)

tle, 1988-1990. Lecturer in Business Law, University of Maryland, Asian Division, 1994—. Chairman, Washington State Commission on Asian American Affairs, 1987-1988. Commissioner: Washington State Commission on Asian American Affairs, 1985-1988; Martin Luther King, Jr. State Holiday Commission, 1987-1989. Legal Advisor, Seattle Consulate General of the Republic of Korea, 1989-1991. Vice-President and Counsel, Seattle-Washington State Korean Association, 1988. *Member:* Washington State Bar Association. *LANGUAGES:* English, Korean and Mandarin Chinese. *PRACTICE AREAS:* Intellectual Property Law; Real Property Law; Environmental Law; Maritime Law.

OF COUNSEL

TAI YOUNG LEE, born Unsan, Pyonganbuk Province, Korea, August 10, 1914; admitted, 1952, Korea. *Education:* Ewha Women's University (B.A., 1936; LL.D., 1970); College of Law, Seoul National University (LL.B., 1949); Graduate School, Seoul National University (LL.M., 1957; J.S.D., 1969); Southern Methodist University (1957-1958); Drew University (LL.D., 1981). Founder and Director, Korea Legal Aid Center for Family Relations, 1956—. Conciliator, Seoul Family Court, 1963. Vice Chairman, Commission for Studying Family Laws, 1964. President, Women's Organizations United for Revision of the Family Law, 1984—. Korea Vice President, International Federation of Women Lawyers, 1964-1973. Author: "The Divorce System in Korea," 1957; "A Study on Divorce in Korea," 1969; "Common Sense in Law for Women," 1972; "The Morals of Contemporary Women," 1974; "Research on the Divorce Rate in Korea," 1981; "Research on Child Custody in Korea," 1982; "Women of North Korea," 1988; "37-Year History of the Movement to Revise Family Law," 1992. Professor and Dean, College of Law and Political Science, Ewha Women's University, 1963-1971. Member: Drafting Committee for Domestic Relations Adjudication Law, 1963; National Council of Women, Board Member, 1964-1967; National YWCA of Korea, Board Member, 1954—; International Commission of Jurists, 1981—, Vice-President, 1986—. *LANGUAGES:* Korean, English and Japanese. *PRACTICE AREAS:* Family Law.

HYUNG JOONG KANG, born Seoul, Korea, September 20, 1943; admitted, 1966, Korea. *Education:* College of Law, Seoul National University (LL.B., 1966); Graduate School of Justice, Seoul National University (LL.M., 1968); Columbia University School of Law (1984). Judge: Pusan District Court; Seoul Criminal District Court. Senior Judge: Suwon District Court; Kwangju District Court; Seoul Northern District Court; Seoul Civil District Court. Research Judge: Seoul High Court; Supreme Court. Publications: Approximately 60 articles published in legal periodicals in Korea, mostly on civil procedure, including, "Child Custody and Support," "Litigation Settlement," "Study of Practical Issues Concerning Joinder of Claims," "Study of Problems in the 1990 Amendment to the Code of Civil Procedure," and "Obtaining Judgement by Fraud." Lecturer of Law, Korea University College of Law and Soongjeon University College of Law and Political Science. *Member:* Seoul Bar Association. *LANGUAGES:* Korean, English and Japanese. *PRACTICE AREAS:* Litigation.

RESIDENT TAX CONSULTANT

KOOK-HEE LEE, born Mojun-ri, Choongcheongnam Province, Korea, November 30, 1934; admitted as Certified Public Accountant and Certified Tax Accountant, 1965, Korea. *Education:* College of Commerce, Seoul National University (B.Ec., 1963); University of Maryland (1977-1978); Graduate School, Sungkyoonkwan University (M.B.A., 1985); Graduate School, Hongik University (completed course work for Ph.D. in Accounting, 1985-1987). Managing Partner and Tax Specialist, Lee K. & Co. (a member firm of Jeffreys Henry International), 1989-1992. International Tax Partner, Anjin Accounting Corp. (a member firm of Ernst & Whinney International), 1986-1989. Senior Manager, Daewoo Accounting Corp., 1982-1986. Manager, Shinhan Accounting Corp., 1974-1982. Internal Auditor, Honam Oil Refinery, 1971-1974. Auditor, (self employed), 1969-1971. Senior Staff, Korea Electric Co., 1962-1968. *Member:* Korean Institute of Certified Public Accountants (Vice Chairman, International Accounting Committee, 1981-1983; Statutory Auditor, 1989-1991. *LANGUAGES:* Korean and English. *PRACTICE AREAS:* Taxation Law.

REPRESENTATIVE CLIENTS: Air Products & Chemicals; Alcoa; American Cyanamid; Allied Signal; Asahi Corporation; Bell Helicopter; Brown & Williamson; Canon, Inc.; Chase Manhattan Bank; Chemical Bank; Corning, Inc.; Daewoo Group; Delta Airlines; Dow Chemical; Exxon; First National Bank of Chicago; Ford Motor Co.; Goodyear Tire and Rubber Co.; Hankook Tire Manufacturing Co.; IBM; International Finance Corp.; Kimberly-Clark Corp.; Kohap Group; Korea Chemical Co.; Kraft General Foods; Lockhead; Mitsui & Co.; Manufacturers Hanover Trust Co.; MasterCard International; Minnesota Mining and Manufacturing Company; Kukdong Group; Litton Industries; Nestle; Nikon Corporation; Pfizer; Revlon; Sealand Service Inc.; Ralston Purina; Ssangyong Oil; Time, Inc.; Timex Corporation; Westinghouse Electric Corp.

KIM & KIM LAW OFFICES

Attorneys and Counsellors at Law

Established in 1982

KYOBO BUILDING, SUITE 1611
1-1, CHONGRO-1-KA, CHONGRO-KU
SEOUL, KOREA
Telephone: 735-2980, 3370
TLX: K23653
Telecopier: (02) 732-3370
Cable Address: "Sskimlaw"

Mailing Address: C.P.O. Box 6869, Seoul, Korea

General Practice. International Business Transactions, International Environmental, Corporate, Finance, Banking, Insurance, Foreign Investment, Tax, International Trade and Maritime Law. Litigation. Patent and Intellectual Properties, Energy, Oil and Gas.

FIRM PROFILE: KIM & KIM LAW OFFICES, is a law office named formerly as Law Offices Soung Soo Kim with affiliated offices in San Francisco, New York and Chicago, the United States. The firm is engaged in corporate practice with an emphasis on international business law, international patent registrations, international and domestic taxation, trade disputes, international financing and investment, and securities and litigation. The Law Office practices before the Korean Courts, the various Korean Government agencies and the Korean Commercial Arbitration Board and the relevant United States or California Courts and International Arbitration Associations.

International trade and export sales problems, including export licensing, actions relating to dumping, countervailing duties, unfair competition, injury and import relief, energy explorations and Maritime disputes are major areas of the firm's concern. The office has been involved in recent cases concerning Technology Transfer, Oil and Gas exploration and Joint Ventures of Oil and Gas industries between the United States or EEC countries and Korea along with Korea Energy Law Institute.

KIM & KIM LAW OFFICES are active in international financial matters, including investment financing and Venture Capital. It provides legal services, including the negotiation of loan agreements, relating to Domestic Bank and conventional international financing, and comprehensive planning both for foreign direct and portfolio investment in Korea and for Korean investment abroad including International Real Estate investments. It has also been involved in the settlement of investment disputes between foreign investors and host governments through Korean Commercial Arbitration Board and the Korean Courts.

Another major portion of the office's work relates to taxation and intellectual property laws. In addition to tax planning for the financial and investment transactions described above, the office represents individuals and corporations before the National Tax Office and the Korean High Courts on rulings, disputes and tax litigation, and before the Executive and Legislative Branches of the Korean Government on legislative proposals relating to international and domestic tax matters. Specialized expertise will be developed in "competent authority" and other matters governed by Korea bilateral tax treaties. The Office offers full tax and business planning for companies and individuals that invest in Korea.

The office was organized in September 1982, by Soung Soo Kim.

MEMBERS OF FIRM

SOUNG SOO KIM, born Korea, August 18, 1943; admitted, 1967, Korea; 1981, California. *Education:* Seoul National University (LL.B., 1965; LL.M., 1969); Boalt Hall School of Law, University of California at Berkeley (LL.M., 1977); Hastings College of Law, University of California (J.D., 1979); Visiting Scholar at Harvard Law School (1979-1980). Editor, Seoul National University Law Review, 1963-1964. Student Delegate to MRA World Assembly in Japan, 1962. Winner at International Court of Justice Moot Court Competition, 1964. Judge: Advocate General Office and Navy Ministry of National Defense, Korea, 1969-1971; Civil and Criminal District Court, Kwangju and Seoul, Korea, 1971-1976. Secretary General, Legal Aid office, S.N.U., 1968-1969. Arbitrator, Korean Commercial Arbitration Board, 1983—. Conciliator, International Centre for Settlement of Investment Disputes, 1986-1992. Arbitrator, International Chamber of Commerce, Court of Arbitration, 1985-1986. Executive Committee member of Energy Section, LAWASIA, 1988—. Council Member, Asia-Pacific Lawyers Association, 1989—. President, Korea Energy Law Institute, KELI, 1989—. Administrative Adjudicator, Ministry of Energy and Resources, 1991-1993. Managing Committee Member, Petroleum Fund, Ministry of Energy and Resources, 1992-1993. Legal Counsel, Overseas Korean

(This Listing Continued)

Traders Association , 1993—. Author: "Occupation Theory and Tokdo Island," Seoul National University Law Review, 1963; "Local Remedies Rule applied in Korea," Seoul National University, LL.M. Dissertation, 1969; "Judicial Remedies for Water Pollution," University of California, LL.M. Dissertation, 1977; "Institutional Balance and Doctrinal Development in Environmental Law," University of California, 1979; "Judicial Intervention in Environmental Disputes in Comparative Aspects-Based on Korean and United States' Responses," Korean Journal of Comparative Law, 1983; "Aviation Torts in Korea," Selected Problems on Contemporary Comparative Law, Seoul, 1987; "Impact of Multilateral Agreements in Energy," The World Peace Through Law Conference, Seoul, Korea, 1987; "International Cooperation and Bilateral Agreements in Energy Resources Development," The 1st International Energy Law Conference, Caracas, Venezuela, 1988; "Balancing Elements in Production Sharing Contracts," LAWASIA Energy Law Conference, Hong Kong, 1988; "Balancing Elements in Energy Agreements in Asia - Doctrinal Developments Based on Korean Experiences," Beijing, China, 1990; "Korean Response to Northern Region's Prosperity," Anchorage, Alaska, U.S.A., 1990; "The Development of Energy Laws for World Peace (on the basis of Korean Experiences)," The World Peace Through Law Conference, Barcelona, Spain, 1991; "China International Business Transactions Law," Korea Energy Law Institute. *Member:* Seoul Bar Association; Korean Bar Association; State Bar of California; American Bar Association. **LANGUAGES:** Korean, English, German and Japanese. **PRACTICE AREAS:** International Business Transactions Law; International Energy Law; International Environmental Law; Corporate Law; Finance Law; Banking Law; Insurance Law; Foreign Investment and Taxation Law; International Arbitration and Litigation.

TAE SIK MIN, born Korea, August 29, 1964; admitted, 1989, Korea. *Education:* Seoul National University, College of Law (LL.B., 1987); Judicial Research and Training Institute, The Supreme Court of Korea (1987-1988). *Member:* Seoul Bar Association; Korean Bar Association. [Judge Advocate Officer, Court Martial, Korean Army (1989-1992)]. **LANGUAGES:** Korean. **PRACTICE AREAS:** Criminal Law; Civil Law; Corporate Law; Copyright Law; Taxation Law.

SANG KI OH, born Korea, November 18, 1959; admitted, 1987, Korea; 1994, New York. *Education:* Korea University (LL.B., 1982); Judicial Research and Training Institute, Supreme Court of Korea (1985-1987); Georgetown University Law School (LL.M., 1992); Southern Methodist University Law School (LL.M., 1993). Author: "The Constitutional Status of the Alien in USA," Georgetown University Law School. *Member:* New York Bar Association; Seoul Bar Association; Korean Bar Association. **LANGUAGES:** Korean and English. **PRACTICE AREAS:** International Trade Law; Intellectual Property Law; Antitrust Law; Corporate Law; Commercial Law.

FOREIGN LEGAL CONSULTANT

CHARLES GEORGE ROWELL, born Milwaukee, Wisconsin, U.S.A., 1964; admitted, 1993, Illinois (Not admitted in Korea). *Education:* John Marshall Law School (J.D., 1993); Elmhurst College, Economics and Business (B.S., 1986); Harper College, Business Administration (A.A., 1984). Business Development Officer, Citibank, F.S.B., February 1989 - October 1993. Sales/Business Banking Officer, ABN/LaSalle National Bank, November 1987 - February 1989. Team Leader/Account Sales Representative, Continental Illinois National Bank, June 1986 - November 1987. *Member:* Illinois and Chicago Bar Association. **LANGUAGES:** English. **PRACTICE AREAS:** International Business Transactions Law; International Trade Law; International Litigation Law; International Banking Law.

OF COUNSEL

TAE GYUN CHOUNG, born Korea, March 21, 1924; admitted, 1951, Korea. *Education:* Seoul National University, College of Laws (LL.B., 1952). Prosecutor, Seoul District Prosecution Office, 1953. Chief Prosecutor, Pusan District Prosecution Office, 1979. Vice-Minister, Ministry of Justice, 1981. Justice, Korean Supreme Court, 1981. Author: "Research on Preventive Methods of Juvenile Delinquents." *Member:* Korean Bar Association. **LANGUAGES:** Korean and English.

JAMES JOONSOO KIM, born U.S.A.; admitted, 1981, California (Not admitted in Korea). *Education:* University of California, Berkeley (B.A., 1977); Hastings College of Law, University of California (J.D., 1980). With, San Francisco Neighborhood Legal Assistance Foundation, San Francisco, California, 1979-1980. Attorney, Legal Section, Hyundai Construction and Engineering Co., Seoul, Korea, 1981-1982. *Member:* State Bar of California; American Bar Association. (Resident, San Francisco, California, U.S.A.). **LANGUAGES:** Korean and English. **PRACTICE AREAS:** International Business Transactions Law; International Trade Law; International Litigation.

(This Listing Continued)

KIM & KIM LAW OFFICES, Seoul—Continued

JAY H. KIM, born U.S.A.; admitted, 1978, Illinois (Not admitted in Korea). *Education:* Korea University, Faculty of Law, Seoul, Korea (LL.B., 1960); Western Michigan University, Graduate School, Kalamazoo, Michigan (M.S.L., 1968); Illinois Institute of Technology, Chicago-Kent College of Law, Chicago, Illinois (J.D., 1976). Chairperson, Pacific Asian Coalition/Midwest Asians for Unity, 1977-1978. Member, Illinois Advisory Committee, U.S. Commission on Civil Rights, 1979-1982. Chairman, Board of Directors, The Korean American Association of Chicago, 1979-1980. Member Panel, American Arbitration Association, 1983—. Vice President, North River Commission, 1980—. *Member:* Chicago Bar Association. (Resident, Chicago, Illinois, U.S.A.). *LANGUAGES:* Korean and English. *PRACTICE AREAS:* International Business Transactions Law; International Trade Law; Litigation.

SUNG JOO HONG, born Korea, January 31, 1955; (Not admitted in Korea). *Education:* Korea University, School of Business (1983). Certified Public Accountant: Sam-Il Accounting Firm, 1987-1992; Sam-Kyeong Accounting Firm, 1992—. *Member:* Korean Certified Public Accountant Association. (Certified Public Accountant (CPA)). *LANGUAGES:* Korean and English. *PRACTICE AREAS:* Corporate Taxation Law; International Corporate Law; Individual Taxation Law.

STEWART D. RINE, born New Mexico, U.S.A., November 27, 1953; admitted, 1979, California (Not admitted in Korea). *Education:* University of California at Riverside (B.S., Cum Laude in Economics, 1976); Hastings College of Law, University of California at San Francisco (J.D., 1979). Legal Counsel, Manufacturers Hanover Trust Co., 1991-1993. Legal Counsel, Central Bank of California, 1987-1990. *Member:* State Bar of California. *LANGUAGES:* English and Korean. *PRACTICE AREAS:* International Financing Law; International Business Transactions Law.

REPRESENTATIVES CLIENTS: Hyundae Group; Daesung Group; Samwhan Group; Kohap Group; Lucky-Gold Star Group; Korea Electricity Power Co.; Korea Gas Co.
REFERENCES: First Interstate Bank; Bank of California in Seoul, Korea.

RYUL KIM & ASSOCIATES

SEOCHO-KU, SEOCHO-DONG
1575-9 SAMHWA BLD. NO. 430
SEOUL, KOREA
Telephone: (011) 822-522-3945
Fax: (011) 822-522-5048

Please direct all inquiries to the Long Beach, California Main Office:
Sumitomo Tower, Ninth Floor, 444 West Ocean Boulevard, Long Beach, California, 90802-4516. Telephone: (310) 495-9633. Fax: (310) 437-0903.

Criminal, Family, Immigration & Nationality, Inheritance, Trust, Medical, Pharmaceutical and other Product Liability, Marine Cargo Insurance Subrogation, Collection, Enforcement of Judgment, North Korean Law.

MEMBERS OF FIRM

RYUL (MIKHAIL) KIM, born 1955; admitted, 1984, California; (Not authorized to appear before the Korean Court). *Education:* Yonsei University (Civil Engineering, 1974); U.C.L.A. (B.A., Economics, 1980); Western State University (J.D., 1983). Recipient: Wiley Manuel Award; Jessup International Moot Court Award; The State Board of Governor's Award. Member, U.S. Court of International Trade. *Member:* Association of Trial Lawyers of America; California Trial Lawyers Association; College of Trial Advocacy. *LANGUAGES:* English, Korean and Mandarin Chinese (Semi-Fluent).

BONG GIL (HOWARD) KIM, born 1922; admitted, 1953, Korea. *Education:* Seoul National University (LL.B., 1949). Tried Numerous Landmark cases before the Korean Supreme Court. [Judge Advocate, Army, Republic of Korea]. *LANGUAGES:* Korean, English and Japanese.

KIM, SHIN & YU

Established in 1967
12TH FLOOR, LEEMA BUILDING
146-1, SUSONG-DONG, CHONGRO-KU
C.P.O. BOX 3238
SEOUL, KOREA
Telephone: (02) 735-5822
Cable Address: "Attksy Seoul"
Telex: K23168
Facsimile: (02) 739-6606/6182/6183; (02) 722-0951

International Trade & Investment, Corporate & Commercial Law, Banking & Institutional Lending, Licensing and Technology Transfer, Intellectual Property, Tax, Domestic & International Construction, Employment & Labor Relations, Admiralty & Shipbuilding, Environment, Telecommunication, Arbitration & Litigation, Coordination & Commitment.

FIRM PROFILE: Kim, Shin & Yu was founded in 1967 and offers a full range of legal services meeting virtually every client need. The firm represents clients not only on a national but also on an international level. The firm is comprised of a full staff of legal support personnel. Most of the staff are fluent in foreign languages, such as English, French, Japanese, Russian, Spanish and Italian. The firm serves a broad and diversified client base. Kim, Shin & Yu practices in all aspects of corporate, antitrust, securities, business and commercial law. We place particular emphasis on international trade and investment, banking, fair trade, securities and finance, taxation, admiralty, technology transfer, intellectual property, international construction, arbitration/litigation, employment and labor relations.

MEMBERS OF FIRM
GENERAL LAW DEPARTMENT

JIN OUK KIM, born Kyongsang Buk-Do, Korea, May 11, 1936; admitted, 1960, Korea. *Education:* Seoul National University (LL.B., 1960); University of Michigan (M.C.L., 1967). Judge, Seoul District Court, 1960-1966. Arbitrator, Korean Commercial Arbitration Board, 1970—. Member, Foreign Capital Inducement Deliberation Committee, Ministry of Finance. *Member:* Seoul Bar Association, Seoul, Korea; International Bar Association (Board Member); Seoul Club. *LANGUAGES:* English, Korean and Japanese.

ROK SANG YU, born Chulla Nam Do, Korea, March 2, 1944; admitted, 1970, Korea. *Education:* Chungang University (LL.B., 1967); Postgraduate Judicial School, Seoul National University (LL.M., 1970); The Southwestern Legal Foundation in University of Texas at Dallas; Postgraduate course for Shipping Law at University of Southhampton, England. Author: "Legal Issues on Collision of Ships," The Journal of Korean Association of Shipping Studies (1988); "The Legal Status of On-Deck Cargo under the Hague Rules," The Journal of the Korean Maritime Law Association (1988). Arbitrator, Korean Commercial Arbitration Board. *Member:* Seoul Bar Association, Seoul, Korea. *LANGUAGES:* English, Korean and Japanese.

JAY K. LEE, born Kyungsang Nam-Do, Korea, September 14, 1949; admitted, 1979, Korea; 1984, New Jersey. *Education:* Seoul National University (LL.B., 1974); Judicial Research and Training Institute (1979); Boston University (J.D., 1984); New York University (LL.M., 1986). Judge, Kwang Ju District Court, 1979-1980. Arbitrator, Korean Commercial Arbitration Board. Author: "Foreign Investment in Korea - Overview of the Liberalization Process," Law Asia Conference, 1991; "Guidance for Overseas Investment," Federation of Korean Industries, Conference, 1991. *Member:* Seoul, New York State and New Jersey State Bar Associations. *LANGUAGES:* Korean, English and Japanese.

HAE DUK JUNG, born Seoul, Korea, February 28, 1957; admitted, 1983, Korea; 1991, Hawaii as Foreign Law Consultant. *Education:* Seoul National University (LL.B., 1980); University of Hawaii, Center for Korean Studies in Hawaii (1990-1991). *Member:* Seoul and Hawaii Bar Associations. *LANGUAGES:* Korean, English, Japanese and German.

KI TAI PARK, born Kyungsang Buk-Do, Korea, February 5, 1958; admitted, 1985, Korea. *Education:* Seoul National University (LL.B., 1980); Passed the Civil Servants Exam (1980); Judicial Research and Training Institute (1984). Judge Advocate, Army of the Republic of Korea, 1985-1987. *Member:* Seoul Bar Association. *LANGUAGES:* English, Japanese and German.

SUNG YOUL KIM, born Kyungsang Buk-Do, Korea, February 9, 1961; admitted, 1984, Korea; 1992, New York. *Education:* Seoul National

(This Listing Continued)

University (LL.B., 1983); Judicial Research and Training Institute (1984); California Western School of Law (J.D., 1990); Boston University School of Law (LL.M., 1992). Judge Advocate, Army of the Republic of Korea, 1985-1988. Visiting Scholar, School of Law, University of California, Berkeley, 1990-1991. Legal Advisor, Korean Delegation, Moscow Meeting for KAL Incident, 1993. Lecturer: Sookmyung Women's University, 1992—; Korea University, 1993—. Co-Author: "The Impact of Trade Actions on Mergers and Acquisitions by Korean Companies," Transnational Law and Business Studies, Fall 1993. Author: "Private Rights of Action under Section 36 of the Investment Company Act," Transnational Law and Business Studies, Winter 1993. *Member:* Seoul and New York State Bar Association. *LANGUAGES:* English, Korean and Japanese.

SUNG WHAN LEE, born Busan, Korea, September 12, 1954; admitted, 1986, Korea. *Education:* Seoul National University (LL.B., 1978; LL.M., 1985); Judicial Research and Training Institute (1986); Doctoral Course at Seoul National University (1988); Visiting Scholar at the East and West Center, University of Hawaii (1989). *Member:* Seoul Bar Association. *LANGUAGES:* English, Korean and German.

SUNG CHUL LEE, born Chulla Nam-Do, Korea, November 2, 1957; admitted, 1987, Korea. *Education:* Yonsei University (LL.B., 1980; M.A., 1987); Judicial Research and Training Institute (1987); University of Wales, College of Cardiff, Doctoral Course (Maritime Law) at University of London (London School of Economic and Political Science, 1991-1993). Legal Advisor, Delegation of the Republic of Korea, 1992. *Member:* Seoul and International (London) Bar Associations. *LANGUAGES:* English, Korean and Japanese.

JOONG JAE LEE, born Daejon, Chungchung Nam-Do, Korea, May 19, 1963; admitted, 1987, Korea. *Education:* Korea University (LL.B., 1985); Judicial Research and Training Institute (1987); Southern Methodist University, School of Law (LL.M., 1991; J.D., 1994). *Member:* Seoul Bar Association. *LANGUAGES:* Korean, English and Japanese.

JOONG HEE PARK, born Kongju, Chungchung Nam-Do, Korea, February 7, 1960; admitted, 1988, Korea. *Education:* Seoul National University (LL.B., 1984); Judicial Research and Training Institute (1988). *Member:* Seoul Bar Association. *LANGUAGES:* Korean and English.

SUNG CHOL OH, born Nonsan, Korea, June 14, 1963; admitted, 1988, Korea. *Education:* Seoul National University (LL.B., 1985); Judicial Research and Training Institute (1988); Graduate School of S.N.U. (1988); Language training course in University of Paris III (1990). Attorney, Korea Legal Aid Corporation, 1988-1989. *Member:* Seoul Bar Association. *LANGUAGES:* Korean, French, English and Japanese.

JONG HOON LEE, born Seoul, Korea, August 11, 1961; admitted, 1989, Korea. *Education:* Seoul National University (LL.B., 1985; LL.M., 1993); Judicial Research and Training Institute (1988). Researcher, Case Research Committee of Supreme Court, 1985-1986. Author: "A Study concerning the Conversion of an Individual Enterprise into a Corporation," LL.M. Thesis, 1993. *Member:* Seoul Bar Association. *LANGUAGES:* Korean, English and German.

SEOK WON HA, born Jinju, Korea, December 15, 1962; admitted, 1989, Korea. *Education:* Seoul National University (LL.B., 1985); Judicial Research and Training Institute (1989). *Member:* Seoul Bar Association. *LANGUAGES:* Korean, English and German.

SOONG HEE LEE, born Seoul, Korea, April 23, 1964; admitted, 1990, Korea. *Education:* Seoul National University (LL.B., 1987); Judicial Research and Training Institute (1990). Judge Advocate, Army of the Republic of Korea, 1990-1992. *Member:* Seoul Bar Association. *LANGUAGES:* Korean and English.

KWON HOE KIM, born Jincheon Chungchung Buk-Do, Korea, May 26, 1965; admitted, 1991, Korea. *Education:* Seoul National University (LL.B., 1988); Judicial Research and Training Institute (1991). *Member:* Seoul Bar Association. *LANGUAGES:* Korean and English.

SUNG WOOK LEE, born Seoul, Korea, October 21, 1964; admitted, 1991, Korea. *Education:* Seoul National University (LL.B., 1987); Judicial Research and Training Institute (1991). *Member:* Seoul Bar Association. *LANGUAGES:* Korean and English.

SEUNG JOON LEE, born Seoul, Korea, February 9, 1965; admitted, 1991, Korea. *Education:* Yeonsei University (LL.B., 1987); Judicial Research and Training Institute (1991). Judge Advocate, Army of the Republic of Korea, 1991-1993. *Member:* Seoul Bar Association. *LANGUAGES:* Korean and English.

(This Listing Continued)

MOON SOO PARK, born Kochang, February 9, 1966; admitted, 1993, Korea. *Education:* Seoul National University (LL.B., 1989); Judicial Research and Training Institute (1993). *Member:* Seoul Bar Association. *LANGUAGES:* Korean and English.

FOREIGN TAX CONSULTANT

JOO YOUNG YI, born Seoul, Korea, September 10, 1959; admitted, 1988, District of Columbia. *Education:* Kyung Hee University (B.A., 1983); George Washington University (M.A., 1988). Certified Public Accountant, District of Columbia, 1988. *Member:* American Institute of Certified Public Accountants. *LANGUAGES:* Korean and English.

FOREIGN LAW CONSULTANTS

HIESUCK KIM, born Seoul, Korea, April 28, 1954; admitted, 1981, New York (Not admitted in Korea). *Education:* Brown University (A.B., 1977); Georgetown University Law Center (J.D., 1980). Member, Advisory Committee, Government Legislation Administration Agency, 1983. *LANGUAGES:* English and Korean.

CRAIG P. EHRLICH, born Chicago, Illinois, July 12, 1956; admitted, 1981, Illinois. *Education:* University of Illinois, Urbana (B.S., 1978; J.D., 1981). *Member:* Illinois and Chicago Bar Associations. *LANGUAGES:* English.

HYUN CHONG KIM, born Seoul, Korea, September 27, 1959; admitted, 1986, New York (Not admitted in Korea). *Education:* Columbia University (B.A., 1981; M.A., 1982; J.D., 1985). Formerly associated with Milbank, Tweed, Hadley & McCloy, 1985-1986; Skadden, Arps, Slate, Meagher & Flom, 1986-1988. Lecturer, Korea University, 1991—. *Member:* New York State Bar Association. *LANGUAGES:* Korean, English and French.

GWANG EUN LEE, born Jinju, Korea, November 3, 1960; admitted, 1989, Virginia (Not admitted in Korea). *Education:* University of Michigan at Ann Arbor (B.A., 1985); American University (LL.M., 1989); University of Southern California (J.D., 1988). *Member:* Virginia and American Bar Associations. *LANGUAGES:* English and Korean.

BYOUNG CHAN KIM, born Korea, April 11, 1955; admitted, 1989, New York (Not admitted in Korea). *Education:* Syracuse University (J.D., 1988); New York University (LL.M., 1989); Hankuk University of Foreign Studies (B.A., 1977); Indiana University (M.B.A., 1984). Certificate, CPA, Illinois. *Member:* New York State Bar Association. *LANGUAGES:* English and Korean.

JONGKWAN PECK, born Seoul, Korea, March 15, 1965; admitted, 1990, New York (Not admitted in Korea). *Education:* Boston College (B.S., 1986); Georgetown University Law Centre (J.D., 1989). Member, Law and Policy International Business Law Review, 1987-1988. Author: "Ramifications of the 1987 Labor Uprising in Korea," 20 Law and Policy International Business 331, 1988. *Member:* New York State Bar Association. *LANGUAGES:* English, Korean and French.

THOMAS P. PINANSKY, born Portland, Maine, December 10, 1958; admitted, 1985, Texas; 1988, District of Columbia. *Education:* Harvard University (A.B., magna cum laude, 1981); University of Pennsylvania (J.D., 1985). Author/Co-Author: "Korea's Travel Market: Establishing a Business Presence," Journal of the American Chamber of Commerce in Korea, 1991; "1991 Revisions to the Tax Laws of the Republic of Korea," CCH Journal of Asian Pacific Taxation, 1991; "International Agency and Distribution Agreements," Butterworth Group of London, 1991; "Legal Aspects of Establishing a Business Presence in Korea," Journal of the American Chamber of Commerce in Korea, 1990. *Member:* State Bar of Texas; The District of Columbia Bar; International Bar Association; American Chamber of Commerce in Korea (Governor, Board of Governors); Asia-Pacific Council of American Chambers of Commerce (Vice Chairman); Visit USA Committee. *LANGUAGES:* English, French and Korean.

GARY B. SULLIVAN, born El Paso, Texas, July 18, 1954; admitted, 1985, Texas and U.S. District Court, Northern District of Texas (Not admitted in Korea). *Education:* University of Texas (B.A. and B.B.A. summa cum laude, 1980; J.D., 1983). Phi Beta Kappa. Member, Jessup International Moot Court Team and Board of Advocates. Editor-in-Chief, Texas International Law Journal, Vol. 18. Author: "Implicit Waiver of Sovereign Immunity by Consent to Arbitration: Territorial Scope and Procedural Limits," Texas International Law Journal 1983; "Korean Investment in Eastern Europe," Eastern Europe Opportunities, Feb, 1991. Co-Author: "Recognition of Proprietary Interests in Software in Korea: Programming for Comprehensive Reform," Michigan Yearbook of International Legal Studies, Vol. 8. Of Counsel to Bentley & Malone, Dallas, Texas, 1985-1986. Foreign Legal Consultant, Min & Sohn, 1985-1988. *Member:* American Bar

(This Listing Continued)

KIM, SHIN & YU, Seoul—Continued

Association (Member, International Section); American Society of International Law; American Chamber of Commerce in Korea (Chair, Legal Services Committee); International Commission of Jurists. *LANGUAGES:* English, Russian, Spanish, Korean and French.

PHILIPPE LI, born Paris, France, May 26, 1965; admitted, 1988, Paris (Not admitted in Korea). *Education:* Universite Paris I Pantheon-Sorbonne (Maître en Droit, 1987; DEA Droit Privé , 1988). de Ricci, Selnet & Associes, 1989-1990. Deputy Director, French Chamber of Commerce & Industry in Korea, 1990-1991. Author: "Le régime juridique des investissements etrangers en Coree," 1989; "Investir et s'implanter en Coree," 1991; "La reforme de la reglementation des investissements etrangers en Coree," 1991; "Conseils pratiques pour la creation d'une joint-venture en Coree," 1992; "Coree: les transferts de technologie, une approche juridique," 1993; all in Les Cahiers Juridiques et Fiscaux de l'Exportation; "L'Ouverture de la Bourse de Seoul aux investisseurs etrangers," La Tribune de l'Expansion, 1991; "Presentation de l'avenant a la convention fiscale franco-coreenne," in "Revue de droit des affaires internationales," 1993. *Member:* Paris Bar Association. *LANGUAGES:* French, English and Korean.

SEUNG WOOK SHIN, born Seoul, Korea, October 19, 1963; admitted, 1992, Pennsylvania (Not admitted in Korea). *Education:* Korea University (B.A., 1987); Graduate School of Industrial Administration, Carnegie Mellon University (M.B.A., 1989); University of Pittsburgh (J.D., 1992). Managing Editor, Journal of Law and Commerce. Summer Associate, Reed Smith Shaw & McClay, 1990 and 1991. *LANGUAGES:* English, Korean and Italian.

PATENT/TRADEMARK DEPARTMENT

KYU HWAN HAN, born Chulla Nam Do, Korea, September 20, 1936; admitted, 1965, Korea as Patent Attorney. *Education:* Law School, Seoul National University (LL.B., 1962); The University of Tokyo (1983). Vice President, Korean Patent Attorneys Association, 1984-1986. Council Member, The Asian Patent Attorneys Association, 1984-1992. Member, Ad Hoc Committee for the Study of Trademark of APPA, 1982-1992. Member, Executive Committee of AIPPI, 1983—. Vice President AIPPI Korea, 1987-1989; President, AIPPI, Korea, 1990-1992. Author: "Corporation Law," "On Creativity." *Member:* KPAA; AIPPI; INTA; AIPLA; FICPI; APAA; The Institute of Industrial Property Law in Japan. *LANGUAGES:* Korean, English and Japanese.

JAE RYUN SONG, born Chulla-Buk-Do, Korea, December 7, 1937; admitted, 1978, Korea as Patent Attorney. *Education:* Chunbuk University (B.S. Mechanical Engineering, 1962). Mechanical Engineer, Ministry of Commerce and Industry, 1962-1972. Examiner, Machinery Examination Bureau, Trial Examiner and Chief, Senior Examiner, Korean Industrial Property Office (KIPO), 1973-1986. *Member:* KIPO (Industrial Property Administration Committee); KPAA; APAA; AIPPI. *LANGUAGES:* Korean, Japanese and English.

PATRICK YANGOH KIM, born Pusan, Korea, March 1, 1952; admitted, 1985, Korea as Patent Attorney. *Education:* Seoul National University (B.E. Textile Eng., 1975); Graduate School of Kunkook University (M.E. Polymer Sci., 1988); Franklin Pierce Law Center, Concord, New Hampshire (MIP, Patent, 1992). Military Officer, 1975-1977. Member: Mitsui & Co., Ltd., 1977-1985; Kang & Kang Patent Law Offices, 1986-1989; YOUME Patent Law Offices, 1989-1992. Director, APAA Korea, 1990—. *Member:* KPAA; APAA; AIPPI. *LANGUAGES:* Korean, Japanese and English.

S. TED KWON, born Korea, July 27, 1960; admitted, 1985, Korea as Patent Attorney. *Education:* Hong Ik University (B.A. Economics, 1984; LL.M., 1990). Lecturer, Industrial Property Law, Korean Industrial Property Academy, 1988-1990. Committee Member, Revision of the Examination Criteria, KIPO. Associate: Y.S. Chang & Associates, 1986-1988; S.Y. Cha Patent Office, Aug. 1988 - Jun. 1990. *Member:* KPAA; APAA; AIPPI; INTA. *LANGUAGES:* Korean, English and Japanese.

SUNG WON HUH, born Kyungsang Nam-Do, Korea, May 15, 1959; admitted, 1992, Korea as Patent Attorney. *Education:* Busan National University (B.E. Machine Design, 1984). Member: Hyosung Motors Technical R & D Center, 1984-1987; Korean Patent Law Office, 1987-1991; Euije Jo & Associates, 1991-1992. *LANGUAGES:* Korean, Japanese, English and German.

HYUN JOO LEE, born Chulla Nam-Do, Korea, October 5, 1968; admitted, 1992, Korea as Patent Attorney. *Education:* Seoul National Univer-

(This Listing Continued)

sity (B.S., Pharmaceutics, 1991). *LANGUAGES:* Korean, English and Japanese.

LEGAL SUPPORT PERSONNEL

BYUNG HO PARK, born Seoul, Korea, July 26, 1935. *Education:* Seoul National University (B.A., Law, 1959). Chief Secretary to the President, Korea Coal Corporation. *LANGUAGES:* Korean, English and Japanese.

YOO YIK KIM, born Seoul, Korea, March 10, 1935. *Education:* Seoul National University (1951). Foreign News Editor, Korea Herald Daily News. *LANGUAGES:* Korean, English and Japanese.

UNNY LAH, born Seoul, Korea, October 24, 1934. *Education:* Syracuse University, New York (B.S., Chemistry, 1961). Chemical Engineer, Ministry of Commerce and Industry, Seoul, Korea, 1962-1970. Manager, Research Section, Korea Petroleum Center, 1971-1974. Examiner and Technical Specialist, Chemistry and Pharmaceuticals, Korea Patent Office, 1978-1984. *LANGUAGES:* Korean, English and Japanese.

YONG KUN OH, born Chulla Buk-do, Korea, May 6, 1933. *Education:* Chun-Buk University (B.S., Electrical Engineering, 1956). Professor, Engineering Dept., Korea University, 1963-1978. Examiner and Technical Specialist, Electronics/Electrical Engineering, Korea Patent Office, 1978-1984. *LANGUAGES:* Korean, Japanese and English.

YEON-HO KIM INTERNATIONAL LAW OFFICE

SUITE 3701, KOREA WORLD TRADE TOWER
159-1 SAMSUNG-DONG, KANGNAM-KU
SEOUL 135-729, KOREA
Telephone: 82-2-551-1256
Fax: 82-2-551-5570

Trade Laws, Banking and Security Laws, Intellectual Property Laws, Tort Laws, General Commercial Litigation, Arbitration.

MEMBERS OF FIRM

YEON-HO KIM, born Taegu, Korea, April 9, 1958; admitted, Korea, 1989; New York, 1992. *Education:* Sungkyunkwan University (B.A., Law, 1982); Sungkyunkwan Graduate School (M.A., Law, 1984); Korea Judiciary Training and Research Institute (Apprentice, 1 986); Georgetown Law School (LL.M., General, 1991); Boston University Law School (LL.M., International Banking, 1992). Arbitrator, Korean Commercial Arbitration Board. *Member:* Seoul, New York, and American (Sections on Business Law, International Law and practice: Antitrust Law, Litigation, Patent, Trademark and Copyright Law, Tort and Insurance practice) Bar Associations; U.S. District Court of Hawaii.

BYUNG-KWON IN, born Hongsung, Korea, December 25, 1961. *Education:* Sungkyunkwan University (B.A., Law, 1984). Mediator, Korean Commercial Arbitration Board.

MOYOUNG-HOYUNG LEE, born Sooncheon, Korea, February 17, 1967. *Education:* Wonkwang University (B.A., Public Administration, 1989).

JIN-YOUNG SON, born Seoul, Korea, July 25, 1971. *Education:* Chungang University (B.A., English Linguistics, 1993).

LEE & KO

17TH & 18TH FLOORS, MARINE CENTER MAIN BUILDING
118, 2-KA NAMDAEMUN-RO, CHUNG-KU
C.P.O. BOX 8735
SEOUL, KOREA
Telephone: 753-2151
Cable Address: "Lawlee"
Telecopier: 82-2-753-0373/5
Telex: K22887

Corporate, Foreign Investment, Banking, Securities, Corporate and Project Finance, Maritime, Insurance, Intellectual Property, International Arbitration and Litigation, Tax and Tax Planning, Technology, Software and Copyright Licensing, Franchising, Unfair Competition and Antitrust, Telecommunications, Air, Rail and Other Transportation Matters, Real Estate, Energy, Construction, Labor, Aviation, Environment, International Trade and Distribution, Bankruptcy and Corporate Reorganization, Entertainment.

(This Listing Continued)

FIRM PROFILE: Lee & Ko, founded in 1977, offers the most highly professional and efficient legal services available in Korea through a system of attorney specialization and fully computer-integrated system for delivery of services. The firm provides a complete range of services for private international law matters to multinational and Korean clients. Lee & Ko has extensive professional experience related to establishment and operation of manufacturing industries and service businesses, including franchising, wholesaling and retailing, advertising, business consulting, entertainment, etc. Dedicated to excellence, we provide timely, efficient and accurate responses to clients as the overriding priority.

MEMBERS OF FIRM

TAE HEE LEE, born Pusan, Korea, May 9, 1940; admitted, 1963, Korea; 1976, California; 1977, U.S. Court of Appeals; 1980, U.S. Supreme Court. *Education:* College of Law, Seoul National University (LL.B., 1962); Graduate School of Law, Seoul National University (1962-1963); Harvard Law School (LL.M., 1971; J.D., 1974). Judge Advocate Officer, Korean Army, 1963-1966. Judge: Seoul District Civil Court, 1966-1968; Seoul District Criminal Court, 1969-1971. Foreign Associate, Graham & James, Los Angeles, 1974-1977. Arbitrator: Korean Commercial Arbitration Board, 1978—; Arbitrator, American Arbitration Association, 1986—. Arbitrator, China International Economic and Trade Arbitration Commission, 1993—. Conciliator, International Centre for Settlement of Investment Disputes, 1980—. Lecturer, Judicial Training and Research Institute, Korea Supreme Court, 1981—. Director, Korean Legal Center, 1981-1990. Vice Chairman, Editors Committee for English Translation of Laws of Republic of Korea, 1981—. Commissioner, Special Consideration Committee for Amendment of Civil and Commercial Code, Ministry of Justice, 1981-1982. Advisor, Policy Advisory Committee, Ministry of Justice, 1983-1989. Legal Counsel, Korea Foreign Trade Association, 1985—. Advisor, Trade Policy Advisory Committee, Ministry of Commerce and Industry, 1986-1991. Articles: "Foreign Exchange Controls in Korea and Their Impact upon International Commercial Transactions," Korean Journal of Comparative Law, Vol. 9, 1981; "Some Aspects of U.S. - Korean Trade Relations," Dickinson Journal of International Law, 1984; "Warranty by Uniform Commercial Code of U.S.A.," Korean Bar Association Journal, Vol. 15, Jan. 1985; "The U.S. Trade and Tariff Act of 1984," Journal of Commercial Arbitration, April 1985; "A Study of Civil Code Dispute in Meiji Japan," Korean Journal of Comparative Law, Vol. 13, 1985; "Koreans and the Eurobond Market," International Financial Law Review, Oct. 1985; Book: *International Contract Law-Theories and Practices*, Hackyunsa, 1985. *Member:* Korean Bar Association; Seoul Bar Association; State Bar of California; American Bar Association; International Bar Association; Inter-Pacific Bar Association; Korea-Japan Lawyers Association; International Law Association; International Fiscal Association; Licensing Executives Society; Korean Patent Attorneys Association; Asian Patent Attorneys Association; International Association for the Protection of Industrial Property; International Trademark Association. *LANGUAGES:* Korean, English and Japanese (read only). *PRACTICE AREAS:* International Commercial Law; Corporate Law; Business Law; International Franchising; Aviation; International Arbitration.

KEONG HEE RYU, born Soonchun, Korea, March 15, 1942; admitted, 1964, Korea. *Education:* College of Law, Seoul National University (LL.B., 1964); Graduate School of Law, Seoul National University (1964-1966). Judge Advocate Officer, Korean Air Force, 1966-1969. Judge: Seoul District Civil Court, 1969-1972; Seoul District Criminal Court, 1972-1974; Seoul District Civil Court, 1974; Cheju District Court, 1974-1977; Seoul District Criminal Court, 1977-1979; Seoul Family Court, 1979; Kwangju High Court, 1981-1982. Private Practice, 1979-1981. Presiding Judge: Chunjoo District Court, 1982-1983; Seoul Family Court, 1983-1985. *Member:* Korean Bar Association; Seoul Bar Association. *LANGUAGES:* Korean, English and Japanese (read only). *PRACTICE AREAS:* Litigation; Corporate Reorganization.

MOON SUNG LEE, born Choongju, Korea, April 15, 1954; admitted, 1978, Korea; 1988, New York. *Education:* College of Law, Seoul National University (LL.B., 1975); Judicial Training and Research Institute, Korea Supreme Court (1976-1978); George Washington University Law School (M.C.L., 1987). Judge Advocate Officer, Korean Army, 1978-1981. Judge, Soowon District Court, 1981-1982. Foreign Associate, Skadden, Arps, Slate Meagher & Flom, New York, 1987-1988. Arbitrator, Korean Commercial Arbitration Board, 1992—. *Member:* Korean Bar Association; Seoul Bar Association; Inter-Pacific Bar Association; New York Bar Association. *LANGUAGES:* Korean, English and Japanese (read only). *PRACTICE AREAS:* Joint Ventures; Telecommunications; Licensing; Software License; Copyright; Mergers and Acquisitions; International Arbitration.

(This Listing Continued)

HYUN PANG, born Seoul, Korea, May 31, 1954; admitted, 1978, Korea; 1990, New York. *Education:* College of Law, Seoul National University (LL.B., 1976); Graduate School of Law, Seoul National University (1976-1983); Judicial Training and Research Institute, Korea Supreme Court (1976-1978); University of Michigan Law School (LL.M., 1989). Judge Advocate Officer, Korean Army, 1978-1981. Public Prosecutor, Ministry of Justice, 1981-1982. Foreign Associate, Morrison & Foerster, San Francisco, 1989-1990. Arbitrator, Korean Commercial Arbitration Board, 1991—. *Member:* Korean Bar Association; Seoul Bar Association; Inter-Pacific Bar Association; New York Bar Association. *LANGUAGES:* Korean, English and Japanese (read only). *PRACTICE AREAS:* Taxation and Tax Planning; Real Estate; Energy Law.

YONG SUK YOON, born Pusan, Korea, October 12, 1954; admitted, 1980, Korea; 1991, New York. *Education:* College of Law, Seoul National University (LL.B., 1978); Judicial Training and Research Institute, Korea Supreme Court (1978-1980); University of Washington Law School (LL.M., 1990). Judge Advocate Officer, Korean Air Force, 1980-1983. Foreign Associate, Graham & James, San Francisco, 1990-1991. Arbitrator, Korean Commercial Arbitration Board, 1992—. *Member:* Korean Bar Association; Seoul Bar Association; Inter-Pacific Bar Association; International Bar Association; New York Bar Association. *LANGUAGES:* Korean, English and Japanese (read only). *PRACTICE AREAS:* Maritime and Insurance; Construction; Air, Rail and Other Transportation; Labor and Employment.

SOO CHANG KIM, born Seoul, Korea, March 15, 1955; admitted, 1981, Korea. *Education:* College of Law, Korea University (LL.B., 1977); Graduate School of Law, Korea University (1977-1979); Judicial Training and Research Institute, Korea Supreme Court (1979-1981). Judge Advocate Officer, Korean Army, 1981-1984. Foreign Associate, Milbank, Tweed, Hadley & McCloy, New York, 1986. Arbitrator, Korean Commercial Arbitration Board, 1992—. Commissioner on the OECD, Subcommittee of International Finance, Committee of Financial & Industrial Development, Ministry of Finance, 1994—. *Member:* Korean Bar Association; Seoul Bar Association; International Bar Association; Inter-Pacific Bar Association. *LANGUAGES:* Korean, English and Japanese (read only). *PRACTICE AREAS:* Securities and Banking; Project Finance; Corporate Finance; Mergers and Acquisitions.

CHANG JOON KIM, born Pusan, Korea, October 8, 1955; admitted, 1981, Korea; 1984, Korean Marine Enquiry Board. *Education:* College of Law, Seoul National University (LL.B., 1978); Graduate School of Law, Seoul National University (1978-1980); Judicial Training and Research Institute, Korea Supreme Court (1979-1981). Judge Advocate Officer, Korean Air Force, 1981-1984. Foreign Counsel, Sinclair Roche & Temperley, London, 1991-1992. Arbitrator, Korean Commercial Arbitration Board, 1993—. *Member:* Korean Bar Association; Seoul Bar Association; Inter-Pacific Bar Association. *LANGUAGES:* Korean, English and Japanese (read only). *PRACTICE AREAS:* Litigation; Maritime and Insurance.

JAE HOON KIM, born Kochang, Korea, February 25, 1956; admitted, 1983, Korea; 1992, New York. *Education:* College of Law, Seoul National University (LL.B., 1980); Graduate School of Law, Seoul National University (1980-1982); Judicial Training and Research Institute, Korea Supreme Court (1981-1983); Academy of American and International Law, Southwestern Legal Foundation, Dallas (1988); Cornell Law School (LL.M., 1992). Judge Advocate Officer, Korean Army, 1983-1986. Foreign Associate, Morgan Lewis & Bockius, Los Angeles, 1992; Morrison & Foerster, New York, 1993. Arbitrator, Korean Commercial Arbitration Board, 1994—. *Member:* Korean Bar Association; Seoul Bar Association; New York Bar Association. *LANGUAGES:* Korean, English and German (read only). *PRACTICE AREAS:* Intellectual Property (Trademark, Copyright, Software); Foreign Investment and Technology Licensing; Trade Regulation and Unfair Competition.

KYU WHA LEE, born Seoul, Korea, July 29, 1958; admitted, 1983, Korea; 1991, New York. *Education:* College of Law, Seoul National University (LL.B., 1981); Judicial Training and Research Institute, Korea Supreme Court (1981-1983); George Washington University Law School (M.C.L., 1988); Tulane Law School (J.D., 1990). Foreign Associate, Morrison & Foerster, New York, 1990-1991. Judge Advocate Officer, Korean Army, 1983-1986. *Member:* Korean Bar Association; Seoul Bar Association; New York Bar Association. *LANGUAGES:* Korean, English and Japanese (read only). *PRACTICE AREAS:* Franchise and Joint Venture; International Trade (GATT, Antidumping, Countervailing Duty, Tariff); International Sales and Distribution.

HYOUNG DON KIM, born Taegu, Korea, October 3, 1960; admitted, 1985, Korea. *Education:* College of Law, Seoul National University (LL.B.,

(This Listing Continued)

LEE & KO, Seoul—Continued

1983); Judicial Training and Research Institute, Korea Supreme Court (1983-1984). Judge Advocate Officer, Korean Army, 1985-1987. *Member:* Korean Bar Association; Seoul Bar Association. *LANGUAGES:* Korean, English and Japanese (read only). *PRACTICE AREAS:* Banking and Foreign Exchange Regulation; Corporate Finance and Project Finance; Securities.

YONG SEOK AHN, born Chungju, Korea, January 7, 1962; admitted, 1985, Korea. *Education:* College of Law, Seoul National University (LL.B., 1984); Judicial Training and Research Institute, Korea Supreme Court (1984-1985). Judge Advocate Officer, Korean Navy, 1986-1989. The Orientation in American Law Program, University of California, Davis and Berkeley, 1992. *Member:* Korean Bar Association; Seoul Bar Association. *LANGUAGES:* Korean, English and Japanese (read only). *PRACTICE AREAS:* Antitrust and Trade Regulation; Environmental Law; Foreign Investment.

SEUNG KYU LEE, born Seoul, Korea, May 24, 1957; admitted, 1985, Korea. *Education:* College of Law, Seoul National University (LL.B., 1981); Judicial Training and Research Institute, Korea Supreme Court (1983-1985). Judge Advocate Officer, Korean Army, 1986-1990. *Member:* Korean Bar Association; Seoul Bar Association. *LANGUAGES:* Korean, English and Japanese (read only). *PRACTICE AREAS:* Litigation; Personal Injury; Products Liability.

EUNJAI LEE, born Seoul, Korea, September 9, 1960; admitted, 1985, Korea; 1992, New York. *Education:* College of Law, Seoul National University (LL.B., 1983); Judicial Training and Research Institute, Supreme Court (1983-1985); Graduate School of Law, Seoul, Korea National University (LL.M., 1989); University of Chicago Law School (LL.M., 1990); University of Pennsylvania Law School (LL.M., 1991); Iowa College of Law (J.D., 1994). Judge Advocate Officer, Korean Army, 1986-1989. Foreign Associate, Winthrop, Stimson, Putnam & Roberts, New York, 1992. *Member:* Korean Bar Association; Seoul Bar Association; New York Bar Association. *LANGUAGES:* Korean and English. *PRACTICE AREAS:* Antitrust; International Trade; Intellectual Property.

MEE HYON LEE, born Seoul, Korea, January 20, 1961; admitted, 1987, Korea. *Education:* College of Law, Seoul National University (LL.B., 1983); Graduate School of Law, Seoul National University (LL.M., 1985); Judicial Training and Research Institute, Korea Supreme Court (1985-1987). Associate, Law Offices C.J. International, 1987-1990. Academy of American and International Law, Southwestern Legal Foundation, 1993. *Member:* Korean Bar Association; Seoul Bar Association. *LANGUAGES:* Korean, English and Japanese (read only). *PRACTICE AREAS:* Corporate Law; Labor and Employment; Securities and Finance.

KAP YOU KIM, born Taegu, Korea, July 19, 1962; admitted, 1988, Korea; 1994, New York. *Education:* College of Law, Seoul National University (LL.B., 1985); Graduate School of Law, Seoul National University (LL.M., 1988); Judicial Training and Research Institute, Korea Supreme Court (1986-1988); Harvard Law School (LL.M., 1994); Academy of American and International Law, Southwestern Legal Foundation, 1992. Foreign Associate, Haynes & Boone, Dallas, 1994; Healy & Baillie, New York, 1994; Ince & Co, London, 1995. *Member:* Korean Bar Association; Seoul Bar Association; New York Bar Association. *LANGUAGES:* Korean, English, German and Japanese (read only). *PRACTICE AREAS:* Environmental Law; Maritime and Insurance; Aviation.

KWANG BAE PARK, born Chungdo-kun, Korea, December 3, 1963; admitted, 1988, Korea. *Education:* College of Law, Seoul National University (LL.B., 1986); Judicial Training and Research Institute, Korea Supreme Court (1986-1988). Judge Advocate Officer, Korean Army, 1988-1991. *Member:* Korean Bar Association; Seoul Bar Association. *LANGUAGES:* Korean, English and Japanese. *PRACTICE AREAS:* Real Estate; Taxation; Immigration.

YEO KYOON YOON, born Seoul, Korea, March 1, 1964; admitted, 1988, Korea. *Education:* College of Law, Seoul National University (LL.B., 1986); Judicial Training and Research Institute, Korea Supreme Court (1986-1988). Judge Advocate Officer, Korean Army, 1988-1991. *Member:* Korean Bar Association; Seoul Bar Association. *LANGUAGES:* Korean, English and Japanese (read only). *PRACTICE AREAS:* Maritime and Insurance; Aviation; Labor and Employment.

WOO YUNG JUNG, born Seoul, Korea, August 19, 1959; admitted, 1989, Korea. *Education:* College of Law, Seoul National University (LL.B., 1983); Graduate School of Law, Seoul National University (LL.M., 1985); Judicial Training and Research Institute, Korea Supreme Court (1987-

1989). Judge Advocate Officer, Korean Army, 1989-1992. *Member:* Korean Bar Association; Seoul Bar Association. *LANGUAGES:* Korean, English and German (read only). *PRACTICE AREAS:* Corporate Reorganization; Banking and Finance.

BURM HUR, born Masan, Korea, December 31, 1963; admitted, 1989, Korea. *Education:* College of Law, Seoul National University (LL.B., 1986); Judicial Training and Research Institute, Korea Supreme Court (1987-1989); Graduate School of Banking, Hanyang University (M.B.A., 1992). Judge Advocate Officer, Korean Army, 1989-1992. *Member:* Korean Bar Association; Seoul Bar Association. *LANGUAGES:* Korean, English and Japanese (read only). *PRACTICE AREAS:* Entertainment (Music, TV Distribution); Commercial Finance.

CHUNG WOOK KIM, born Jinhae, Korea, April 29, 1963; admitted, 1990, Korea. *Education:* College of Law, Seoul National University (LL.B., 1986); Judicial Training and Research Institute, Korea Supreme Court (1988-1990). Judge Advocate Officer, Korean Army, 1990-1993. *Member:* Korean Bar Association; Seoul Bar Association. *LANGUAGES:* Korean, English and Japanese (read only). *PRACTICE AREAS:* Maritime; Insurance.

SEUNG HWAN TOH, born Seoul, Korea, September 4, 1964; admitted, 1990, Korea. *Education:* College of Law, Seoul National University (LL.B., 1987); Judicial Training and Research Institute, Korea Supreme Court (1988-1990). Judge Advocate Officer, Korean Army, 1990-1993. *Member:* Korean Bar Association; Seoul Bar Association. *LANGUAGES:* Korean, English and Japanese. *PRACTICE AREAS:* Foreign Investment; Corporate Law.

YOUNG JOON CHO, born Inchon, Korea, January 23, 1965; admitted, 1990, Korea. *Education:* College of Law, Seoul National University (LL.B., 1987); Judicial Training and Research Institute, Korea Supreme Court (1988-1990). Judge Advocate Officer, Korean Army, 1990-1993. *Member:* Korean Bar Association; Seoul Bar Association. *LANGUAGES:* Korean, English, Spanish and Japanese (read only). *PRACTICE AREAS:* Corporate Tax; Corporate Finance.

JAE HOON CHUNG, born Seoul, Korea, January 27, 1964; admitted, 1991, Korea. *Education:* College of Law, Seoul National University (LL.B., 1986); Graduate School of Law, Seoul National University (LL.M., 1988); Judicial Training and Research Institute, Korea Supreme Court (1989-1991). *Member:* Korean Bar Association; Seoul Bar Association. *LANGUAGES:* Korean, Japanese and German (read only). *PRACTICE AREAS:* Bankruptcy; Litigation.

SANG HOON LEE, born Taejeon, Korea, May 1, 1962; admitted, 1992, Korea. *Education:* College of Law, Seoul National University (LL.B., 1985); Graduate School of Law, Seoul National University (LL.M., 1987); Judicial Training and Research Institute, Korea Supreme Court (1990-1992). *Member:* Korean Bar Association; Seoul Bar Association. *LANGUAGES:* Korean, English, Japanese and German (read only). *PRACTICE AREAS:* Labor Law; Commercial Law; Antitrust.

CHUNG HAE KANG, born Hadong, Korea, May 20, 1964; admitted, 1992, Korea. *Education:* College of Law, Seoul National University (LL.B., 1986); Judicial Training and Research Institute, Korea Supreme Court (1990-1992). *Member:* Korean Bar Association; Seoul Bar Association. *LANGUAGES:* Korean, English, French and Japanese (read only). *PRACTICE AREAS:* Environmental Law; Litigation.

DUK KYU HYUN, born Cheju, Korea, April 20, 1964; admitted, 1993, Korea. *Education:* College of Law, Seoul National University (LL.B., 1987); Graduate School of Law, Seoul National University (LL.M., 1990); Judicial Training and Research Institute, Korea Supreme Court (1991-1993). *Member:* Korean Bar Association; Seoul Bar Association. *LANGUAGES:* Korean, English, German (read only) and Japanese (read only). *PRACTICE AREAS:* Computers and Software; Maritime and Insurance.

CHANG SEOK OH, born Taejeon, Korea, December 17, 1963; admitted, 1993, Korea. *Education:* College of Business Administration, Seoul National University (B.A. in Business Administration, 1986); College of Law, Seoul National University (LL.B., 1988); Graduate School of Law, Seoul National University (LL.M., 1991); Judicial Training and Research Institute, Korea Supreme Court (1991-1993). *Member:* Korean Bar Association; Seoul Bar Association. *LANGUAGES:* Korean, English and Japanese (read only). *PRACTICE AREAS:* Litigation; Insurance.

JIN SEOP LIM, born Pusan, Korea, June 10, 1965; admitted, 1993, Korea. *Education:* College of Law, Seoul National University (LL.B., 1988); Judicial Training and Research Institute, Korea Supreme Court (1991-1993). *Member:* Korean Bar Association; Seoul Bar Association.

(This Listing Continued)

(This Listing Continued)

LANGUAGES: Korean, English and French (read only). *PRACTICE AREAS:* Litigation; Personal Injury.

CHOON WON LEE, born Changwon, Korea, January 26, 1966; admitted, 1993, Korea. *Education:* College of Law, Seoul National University (LL.B., 1988); Judicial Training and Research Institute, Korea Supreme Court (1991-1993). *Member:* Korean Bar Association; Seoul Bar Association. *LANGUAGES:* Korean, English and German (read only). *PRACTICE AREAS:* Real Estate; Litigation.

MIN HEE KIM, born Inchon, Korea, July 24, 1964; admitted, 1993, Korea. *Education:* College of Law, Seoul National University (LL.B., 1987); Graduate School of Law, Seoul National University, 1987-1990. Judicial Training and Research Institute, Korea Supreme Court, 1991-1993. *Member:* Korean Bar Association; Seoul Bar Association. *LANGUAGES:* Korean, English and German (read only). *PRACTICE AREAS:* Trade Regulation; Litigation.

HEE JEU KANG, born Masan, Korea, February 22, 1963; admitted, 1994, Korea. *Education:* College of Law, Yonsei University (LL.B., 1985); Graduate School of Law, Seoul National University (LL.M., 1992); Judicial Training and Research Institute, Korea Supreme Court (1992-1994). *Member:* Korean Bar Association; Seoul Bar Association. *LANGUAGES:* Korean, English, Japanese and German (read only). *PRACTICE AREAS:* Litigation; Taxation.

DONG EUN KIM, born Pusan, Korea, December 14, 1964; admitted, 1994, Korea. *Education:* College of Law, Seoul National University (LL.B., 1987); Graduate School of Law, Seoul National University (LL.M., 1990); Judicial Training and Research Institute, Korea Supreme Court (1992-1994). *Member:* Korean Bar Association; Seoul Bar Association. *LANGUAGES:* Korean, English, German (read only) and Japanese (read only). *PRACTICE AREAS:* Project Finance; Environmental Law.

DAE SOON LEE, born Seoul, Korea, February 12, 1965; admitted, 1994, Korea. *Education:* College of Law, Seoul National University (LL.B., 1988); Judicial Training and Research Institute, Korea Supreme Court (1992-1994). *Member:* Korean Bar Association; Seoul Bar Association. *LANGUAGES:* Korean, English, German (read only) and Japanese (read only). *PRACTICE AREAS:* Maritime; Marine Casualty and Disasters; Oil Pollution.

SANG GON KIM, born Yanggu, Korea, October 3, 1968; admitted, 1994, Korea. *Education:* College of Law, Seoul National University (LL.B., 1992); Judicial Training and Research Institute, Korea Supreme Court (1992-1994). *Member:* Korean Bar Association; Seoul Bar Association. *LANGUAGES:* Korean, English, German (read only). *PRACTICE AREAS:* Labor Law; Antidumping.

HYEONG GUN LEE, born Kuchang, Korea, July 26, 1968; admitted, 1994, Korea. *Education:* College of Law, Seoul National University (LL.B., 1992); Judicial Training and Research Institute, Korea Supreme Court (1992-1994). *Member:* Korean Bar Association; Seoul Bar Association. *LANGUAGES:* Korean, English and Japanese (read only). *PRACTICE AREAS:* Copyright; Entertainment.

DUK YEUL BAEK, born Ahndong, Korea, May 7, 1948; admitted, 1983, Korea Patent Bar. *Education:* College of Law, Seoul National University (LL.B., 1971); Graduate School of Law, Pusan National University (1973-1975); Patent Attorney Training Course, Korean Patent Office (1982-1983). Il Shin Steel Co., Ltd., 1977-1980; Y.S. Chang & Associates, Patent Law Firm, 1981-1984. *Member:* Korean Patent Attorneys Association; Licensing Executives Society; International Association for the Protection of Industrial Property; Asian Patent Attorneys Association; International Trademark Association. *LANGUAGES:* Korean, English and Japanese. *PRACTICE AREAS:* Intellectual Property (T/Mark, Pat., Reg. & Lit. for Electronics & Mechanical Eng.); Technology Licensing.

BYUNG MOON LEE, born Chungmu, Korea, September 1, 1952; admitted, 1988, Korea Patent Bar. *Education:* College of Engineering, Seoul National University (B.S. in Applied Chemistry, 1975); Patent Attorney Training Course, Korean Patent Office (1986-1987). Ordnance Officer, Korean Navy, 1975-1978. Lotte Machinery Manufacturing Co., Ltd., 1978-1979; S.Y. Cha Patent Law Firm, 1986-1987; Nam & Nam Patent Law Firm, 1987-1988. *Member:* Korean Patent Attorneys Association. *LANGUAGES:* Korean, English and Japanese (read only). *PRACTICE AREAS:* Intellectual Property (Pat., Reg. & Lit., for Chem. Eng., Pharmaceutical & Biotechnology); Computers and Software.

(This Listing Continued)

CONSULTANTS

MUN KI CHOO, born Seoul, Korea, February 18, 1925; admitted, 1952, Korea. *Education:* College of Law, Seoul National University (LL.B., 1949); Graduate School of Law, Seoul National University (1949-1950). Public Prosecutor: Seoul District Public Prosecutor's Office, 1953-1973; Seoul Supreme Public Prosecutor's Office, 1973-1979; Chief Prosecutor: Chungju District Public Prosecutor's Office, 1979-1980; Taejun District Public Prosecutor's Office, 1980-1981. Commissioner: National Compensation Committee, 1974-1978; Korea Legal Aid Association, 1974-1978; Deliberation Committee for Korea Legal Cultural Prize, 1976. Lecturer: Dongkuk University; Kunkuk University; Ewha Womans University, 1954-1979. *Member:* Korean Bar Association; Seoul Bar Association; Korea Legal Law Institute; Korea Comparative Law Institute; Korea Legal Institute. *LANGUAGES:* Korean, English and Japanese (read only).

KEON KIM, born Mokpo, Korea, October 28, 1949; (Not admitted in Korea). *Education:* College of Science, Korea University (B.S. in Chemistry, 1974); Graduate School, Princeton University (Ph.D. in Chemistry, 1979). Assistant Professor, 1979-1981, Associate Professor, 1982-1985 and Professor, 1985, of Department of Chemistry, Korea University. *LANGUAGES:* Korean, English and Japanese (read only).

HO YOUNG KIM, born Chongju, Korea, December 17, 1949; (Not admitted in Korea). *Education:* College of Engineering, Korea University (B.S. in Engineering, 1972); Graduate School, Korea University (M.S. in Engineering, 1974); Graduate School, University of Illinois at Chicago (M.S. in Engineering, 1980; Ph.D. in Engineering, 1982). Associate Professor, Department of Mechanical Engineering, Korea University, 1982—. *LANGUAGES:* Korean, English and Japanese (read only).

*RESIDENT FOREIGN
LEGAL CONSULTANTS*

JAMES E. KITTELSEN, born Washington, D.C., July 31, 1945; admitted, 1974, Wisconsin; 1974, U.S. District Court, Western District of Wisconsin; 1980, Minnesota (Not admitted in Korea). *Education:* Sophia University, Tokyo, Japan (B.S. in International Economics, 1970); University of Wisconsin Law School (J.D., 1974); University of Washington (LL.M in Asian Law, 1985). Arbitrator, Korean Commercial Arbitration Board, 1989— . *LANGUAGES:* English and Japanese. *PRACTICE AREAS:* International Commercial Law; International Arbitration; International Trade.

TIMOTHY E. TRINKA, born Chicago, Illinois, October 20, 1956; admitted, 1983, Illinois (Not admitted in Korea). *Education:* University of Iowa (B.B.A., 1979); The John Marshall Law School (J.D., 1982); Salzburg University, Salzburg Austria, in Cooperation with University of the Pacific McGeorge School of Law (Diploma in International Legal Studies, 1981; Diploma in Advanced International Legal Studies, 1983). *Member:* American Bar Association; International Bar Association; Inter-Pacific Bar Association. *LANGUAGES:* English. *PRACTICE AREAS:* Corporate Finance; Banking; Securities.

IN BONG LYO, born Seoul, Korea, August 10, 1957; admitted, 1989, California (Not admitted in Korea). *Education:* University of Michigan (B.A. in Political Science, 1981; M.A. in Political Science, 1983); Hastings College of the Law, University of California (J.D., 1988). Director, Korean-American Bar Association of Northern California, 1986-1987. Associate, Law Offices Lillick & Charles, San Francisco, 1988-1989. *Member:* State Bar of California; International Association of Korean Lawyers. *LANGUAGES:* English and Korean. *PRACTICE AREAS:* Corporate Finance; Banking.

RICHARD D. EMMERSON, born Canada, June 15, 1957; admitted, 1985, the Roll of Barristers and Solicitors of the Supreme Court of Ontario (Not admitted in Korea). *Education:* Queen's University (B.A., Hons., 1980; LL.B., 1983). Arbitrator, Korean Commercial Arbitration Board, 1992—. Vice-Chairman, Canadian Business Club of Korea, 1993—. *Member:* Canadian Bar Association (International Trade Section); Law Society of Upper Canada. *LANGUAGES:* English and French. *PRACTICE AREAS:* Foreign Investment and Licensing; International Business Law.

JOHN TODA, born Seattle, Washington, June 15, 1960; admitted, 1992, Washington. *Education:* Washington University (B.A., Economics and Mathematics, 1982); University of Washington (M.B.A., Finance and Quantitative Methods, 1984); University of Puget Sound School of Law (J.D., 1992). Financial Analyst, Utilities and Transportation Commission, Olympia, Washington, 1986-1991. Associate, Bogle & Gates, Seattle, Washington, 1992-1994. *Member:* American Bar Association. *LANGUAGES:* English. *PRACTICE AREAS:* Securities; Corporate Finance.

(This Listing Continued)

LEE & KO, Seoul—Continued

TAE YOUNG KIM, born Seoul, Korea, May 3, 1963; admitted, 1990, Texas (Not admitted in Korea). *Education:* Southwest Texas State University (B.B., in Accounting, 1989); Southern Methodist University School of Law (J.D., 1990). Foreign Legal Counsel, Kim, Chang & Lee, Seoul, Korea, 1990-1994. *Member:* American Bar Association; State Bar of Texas. *LANGUAGES:* Korean and English. *PRACTICE AREAS:* Banking and Project Financing; Franchise; International Litigation and Arbitration.

JAMES K. CHANG, born Seoul, Korea, October 1, 1962; admitted, 1990, California. *Education:* University of Southern California (B.S. in Business Administration, 1985); Georgetown University (J.D. & M.B.A., 1989). International Tax Associate, Price Waterhouse, Long Beach, California, 1989-1990. Associate, Law Offices of Ibold & Anderson, Los Angeles, California, 1990-1994. *Member:* State Bar of California. *LANGUAGES:* English, Japanese and Korean. *PRACTICE AREAS:* Maritime and Insurance; Telecommunications; Taxation.

VERONICA K. LEE, born Seoul, Korea, May 2, 1965; admitted, 1989, Supreme Court of New South Wales, Australia (Not admitted in Korea). *Education:* University of Sydney (BEc., 1986 and LL.B., 1988). Associate, Rosenblum & Partners, Sydney, Australia, 1989-1991; Clayton Utz, Sydney, Australia, 1991. Foreign Legal Consultant, Kim, Chang & Lee, Seoul, Korea on Secondment from Clayton Utz 1992-1993, independently, 1994. *Member:* Law Society of New South Wales, Australia. *LANGUAGES:* Korean and English. *PRACTICE AREAS:* Banking and Finance; Foreign Investment.

MIN, SOHN & KIM

723-2, YOKSAM 2-DONG, KANGNAM-KU
SEOUL 135-082, KOREA
Telephone: 564-3320/6
Telecopier: 564-3327
Internet: jwestkor@soback.hana.nm.kr

General Practice, Corporate, Foreign Trade and Investment, Licensing, Intellectual Property, Insurance, Banking, Securities, Maritime, Taxation, Labor, Environment, Arbitration and Litigation.

FIRM PROFILE: The firm was founded by former Judge B.K. Min in 1971 as one of the first international law offices in Korea. A full range of legal services are provided for foreign clients active in the Korean market. Multinational clients are based mainly in North America, Europe and the Far East, and include advertising, cosmetics, manufacturing, telecommunications, insurance and food products firms. The Korean and joint venture clientele ranges from major banks to manufacturers in the pharmaceutical, textile, automotive and chemicals sectors.

MEMBERS OF FIRM

BYOUNG KOOK MIN, born Korea, September 27, 1938; admitted, 1964, Korea; 1980, New York. *Education:* Seoul National University (LL.B., 1963; LL.M., 1964); New York University Law School (M.C.J., 1970; LL.M., 1980). Author: "Corporate Election," 1 Korean Journal of Comparative Law, 1973; "Foreign Investment and Taxation in Korea," Law Asia, 1977; "Limitation of Shipowners' Liability under the Commercial Code of Korea," Journal of Maritime Law and Commerce, 1985; "Korean Regime on Intellectual Property," The International Lawyer, 1985; "Environmental Regulation in Korea," Asia Law & Practice, 1991. Judge, Seoul Civil District Court, 1964-1970. Arbitrator, Korean Commercial Arbitration Board, 1970—. *Member:* The Presidential Commission for the 21st Century, 1994—; Seoul Bar Association; New York Bar Association; American Bar Association; Korean Patent Attorneys Association; American Chamber of Commerce in Korea; International Association for the Protection of Industrial Property; Asian Patent Attorneys Association.

KUN UNG SOHN, born Korea, January 19, 1942; admitted, 1967, Korea. *Education:* Seoul National University (LL.B., 1965; LL.M., 1967; J.S.D., 1971). Editor, Law Newspaper, 1969. *Member:* Seoul Bar Association (Standing Committee, 1977, Auditor, 1980 and Director, Research Committee of Legal Practice, 1980). *PRACTICE AREAS:* Litigation.

BONG HEE HAN, born Korea, August 15, 1958; admitted, 1987, Korea; 1993, New York. *Education:* Seoul National University (LL.B., 1981; LL.M., 1983; J.S.D., Candidate, 1988); Judicial Research and Training Institute of the Supreme Court of Korea (1987); University of Chicago (LL.M., 1992). Foreign Associate, Whitman & Ransom, 1992-1993. Author: "A Comparative Study of Stock Dividends," 1983. *Member:* Seoul Bar

(This Listing Continued)

Association; New York Bar Association. *PRACTICE AREAS:* Foreign Investment; Intellectual Property Protection; Corporate Litigation.

CHANG HEE LEE, born Korea, May 1, 1960; admitted, 1984, Korea as Tax Attorney; 1991, New York. *Education:* Seoul National University (LL.B.); Dongkuk University; Harvard University (LL.M/ITP Certificate, 1991; S.J.D., 1994). Certified Public Accountant, Korea, 1984. Author: "Legal Aspects of Establishing a Business Presence in Korea," The Transnational Lawyer, 1990; "Korean Taxation of Technology Transfer," International Tax & Business Lawyer, 1992. Associated with Coopers & Lybrand, Seoul, 1983-1985. *Member:* Korean Institute of Certified Public Accountants. *PRACTICE AREAS:* International Tax Planning; Corporate Finance.

JUNG IL LEE, born Korea, June 22, 1961; admitted, 1985, Korea; 1994, New York. *Education:* Yonsei University (LL.B., 1983); Judicial Research and Training Institute of the Supreme Court of Korea, 1987; Seoul National University (Masters, 1989); University of Washington Law School (LL.M., 1990); Southwestern University Law School (J.D., 1992). Author: "Regulation of the Advertising Business in Korea," Asialaw, 1994; "Comparative Research on Unfair Trade Practices Between the United States and Korea," LL.M. Thesis, University of Washington, 1990. *Member:* Seoul and Korean Bar Associations; New York Bar Association. *PRACTICE AREAS:* International Trade and Investment; Corporate Litigation.

WONKYU HAN, born Korea, February 23, 1961; admitted, 1987, Korea. *Education:* Seoul National University (LL.B., 1983; LL.M., 1985); Judicial Research and Training Institute of the Supreme Court of Korea, 1987; New York University School of Law (LL.M., 1992); Columbia Business School (M.B.A., 1994). Author: "License as a Method of Technology Inducement," 1984. *Member:* Seoul Bar Association.

TAE KWON LEE, born Korea, September 25, 1961; admitted, 1988, Korea. *Education:* Seoul National University (LL.B., 1985); Judicial Research and Training Institute of the Supreme Court of Korea (1988). *Member:* Seoul Bar Association. *PRACTICE AREAS:* Commercial Litigation; Foreign Investment.

SEON HO KIM, born Korea, September 22, 1962; admitted, 1988, Korea; 1994, New York. *Education:* Seoul National University (LL.B., 1985); Judicial Research and Training Institute of the Supreme Court of Korea, 1988; Georgetown University Law Center (LL.M., 1993). *Member:* Seoul Bar Association; New York Bar Association. *PRACTICE AREAS:* Corporate; Intellectual Property; Litigation.

DON EOK CHOI, born Korea, November 17, 1965; admitted, 1990, Korea. *Education:* Sung Kyun Kwan University (LL.B., 1987); Judicial Research and Training Institute of the Supreme Court of Korea (1990). *Member:* Seoul Bar Association. *PRACTICE AREAS:* Corporate Litigation.

SANG BAE AHN, born Korea, February 18, 1959; admitted, 1988, Patent Bar. *Education:* Kyung Hee University (LL.B., 1982); Graduate School of Administration, Kyung Hee University (1985); International Patent Training Institute in Korea (1988). *Member:* Korea Intellectual Property Research Society, Inc. (KIPS); Korean Patent Attorneys Association; APAA; AIPPI. *PRACTICE AREAS:* Trademark, Patent and Copyright Registration and Litigation.

KYONG SOO CHOI, born Korea, April 20, 1961; admitted, 1988, Patent Bar. *Education:* Seoul National University (B.Sc., Naval Engineering and Architecture, Electronic Engineering). Patent Attorney, First Law Offices of Korea, 1988-1990. *Member:* Korean Patent Attorneys Association; APAA. *PRACTICE AREAS:* Patent Registration and Litigation (Electronics and Mechanical Engineering).

IN CHUL LEE, born Korea, January 1, 1960; admitted, 1986, Korea. *Education:* Seoul National University (B.Sc., 1982; LL.M., 1989); Yonsei University (M.B.A., 1992). Author: "Legal Research on Improved Patent," LL.M. Thesis, Seoul National University, 1989. *Member:* Seoul and Korean Bar Associations. *PRACTICE AREAS:* Patent Litigation.

YOON MIN LEE, born Korea, February 8, 1964; admitted, 1991, Patent Bar. *Education:* Seoul National University (M.Sc., Geophysics, 1986). *Member:* Korean Patent Attorneys Association. *PRACTICE AREAS:* Computer Software; Copyright, Patents and Trademarks.

FOREIGN LEGAL CONSULTANTS

JAMES M. WEST, born Akron, Ohio, July 20, 1955; admitted, 1982, Texas (Not admitted in Korea). *Education:* University of Texas at Austin (B.A., highest honors, 1976; J.D., honors, 1982); Harvard University (S.J.D., 1989). Phi Beta Kappa. Articles Editor, Texas International Law

(This Listing Continued)

Journal, 1981-1982. Author: "The Constitutional Court of the Republic of Korea," American Journal of Comparative Law, 1992; "The United States Embargo on Trade with North Korea," Korean Journal of Comparative Law, 1992. Instructor, Harvard Law School Graduate Division, 1987-1989. Lecturer on International Economic Law, Yonsei University and Korea University, 1990. *Member:* State Bar of Texas; American Society of International Law; American Chamber of Commerce in Korea (Co-Chairman, Telecommunications Committee). *PRACTICE AREAS:* International Commercial and Financial Transactions.

KYONG MOK KIM, born Korea, October 2, 1960; admitted, 1990, Pennsylvania (Not admitted in Korea). *Education:* Northeastern University (B.A., 1986); Case Western Reserve University (J.D., 1990). In-house counsel, Kia Motors Corp., 1990-1992. Co-Author: "Korea Toxic Chemical Substances Control Act: Overview and Implications for Foreign Suppliers," Asia Law & Practice, 1992. *Member:* Pennsylvania State and American (Member, International and Business Sections) Bar Associations. *PRACTICE AREAS:* Corporate; Product Liability; Foreign Investment.

MINWOON THOMAS YANG, born Pusan, Korea, October 30, 1965; admitted, 1993, New York (Not admitted in Korea). *Education:* University of Chicago (A.B., honors, 1988); Harvard Law School (J.D., 1992). Phi Beta Kappa. Associate, Whitman Breed Abbott & Morgan, New York, 1992-1994. *PRACTICE AREAS:* Joint Ventures; Licensing; Aircraft Finance; Intellectual Property.

MAOCHANG LI, born Harbin, China, October 23, 1959; (Not admitted in Korea). *Education:* Beijing University Law School (LL.B., 1983; LL.M., 1986); The Hague Institute of Social Studies (Post-Graduate Diploma, International Economic Law, 1988); Harvard Law School (LL.M., 1992). Visiting Scholar, Harvard Law School, 1990-1991. Clerk, Haidian District Court, Beijing, 1982. Assistant Professor, International Law, China School of Law & Diplomacy, 1986-1989. Research Associate, International Law Collaborative, Boston, 1990-1991. Author: "The Treaty Succession Problem of Hong Kong in International Law," 1983; "Settlement of Disputes involving Foreign Investment in the Framework of the Joint Venture Law of China," 1988; "Handling Crimes across the Taiwan Strait," 1992. *PRACTICE AREAS:* International Business Transactions; Dispute Resolution.

HWA JIN KIM, born Korea, 1960; (Not admitted in Korea). *Education:* Seoul National University (B.S., 1983); Sung Kyun Kwan University (LL.M., with honors, 1985); University of Munich, Germany (Dr. iur., magna cum laude, 1989); Harvard Law School (Research Fellow, 1989-1990; LL.M., 1994); Northwestern University, (LL.M., 1993; S.J.D. Candidate, 1993—). Economist, First Economic Research Institute, Korea Explosives Group, 1990-1992. Author: "Transnational Mergers and United States Antitrust Law," 1990; "European Community Law on Financial Services and Reciprocity," 1990; "The European Financial Common Market," 1991; "Mergers and Acquisitions Across the European Community," 1991; "Legal Aspects of the Private ECU," 1991; "European and German Economic and Monetary Union," 1991; "Legal Protection of Foreign Investments," 1991.

Languages: Korean, English, Chinese, German, Russian, Japanese (read only) and Spanish (read only)

MYUNG-SHIN & PARTNERS

12TH FLOOR, JINDO BUILDING
37, DOWHA-DONG, MAPO-GU
SEOUL, KOREA
Telephone: (2) 714-9922/32
Facsimile: (2) 714-9933/34

Mailing Address: P.O. Box 504, Gwang Wha Moon, Seoul, Korea

Industrial Property, Patent, Utility Model, Design, Trademark, Unfair Competition and Copyright Law.

FIRM PROFILE: *The firm was established in 1972 and offers various services regarding intellectual property. The client base is European, North American and Japanese in scope. This 4-partner firm is a mid-sized well-known patent law firm located in Seoul.*

MEMBERS OF FIRM

MYUNG-SHIN KIM, born Pohang, Korea, January 28, 1944; admitted, 1972, Korea. *Education:* Korea University (LL.B., 1966; LL.M., 1971). Author: "The Revised Korean Industrial Property Law and Practice," 1981; "Standards for Trademark Examination in Korea," 1985; "Recent Developments in Intellectual Property Field in Korea," 1987. Instructor: Aviation College of Korea, 1971-1974; Kang Won University, 1971-1972; Graduate

(This Listing Continued)

School of Korea University, 1979-1985. Vice President, Korean Patent Attorneys Association, 1990. President, Korean Group of Asian Patent Attorneys Association, 1991-1993. Vice-President, Asian Patent Attorneys Association, 1994—. Arbitrator, Korean Commercial Arbitration Board, 1982—. *Member:* Korean Patent Attorneys Association; Asian Patent Attorneys Association; A.I.P.P.I.; International Trademark Association; Licensing Executive Society; Korean Intellectual Property Research Society (Vice President, 1986—). *LANGUAGES:* Korean, English, Japanese and German. *PRACTICE AREAS:* Trademark Law; Patent Law; Copyright Law; Unfair Competition Law.

SEONG-KOO KANG, born Inchon, Korea, July 9, 1946; admitted, 1985, Korea. *Education:* Kyunghee University (LL.B., 1969). Head, Patent Section at Gold-Star Tele-Communication Company, Ltd., 1974-1984. *Member:* Korean Patent Attorneys Association; Asian Patent Attorneys Association; A.I.P.P.I.; Licensing Executive Society. *LANGUAGES:* Korean, English and Japanese. *PRACTICE AREAS:* Trademark Law; Design Law.

KEE-SUB KWON, born Andong, Korea, June 20, 1960; admitted, 1985, Korea. *Education:* Korea University (LL.B., 1982; LL.M., 1984). Judicial Research and Training Institute, Supreme Court of the Republic of Korea, 1984-1985. *Member:* Korean Bar Association. *LANGUAGES:* Korean, English, German and Japanese (read only). *PRACTICE AREAS:* Copyright Law; Trademark Law; Civil Procedure Law.

ASSOCIATES

SEOK-HEE WON, born Seoul, Korea, January 4, 1960; admitted, 1995, Korea. *Education:* Hankook Aviation University (B.S. in Mechanical Engineering, 1982). Daewoo Motors Co., 1985-1987. *LANGUAGES:* English, Japanese. *PRACTICE AREAS:* Patent Law.

WON-OH KIM, born Busan, Korea, March 25, 1964; admitted, 1995, Korea. *Education:* Korea University (LL.B. in Law, 1986); Graduate School at Korea University (LL.M. in International Law, 1988; Ph.D., 1991). Korea Development Bank, 1991-1993. *LANGUAGES:* English, German, Japanese. *PRACTICE AREAS:* Trademark Law; Design Law; Copyright Law.

MIN-CHEOL KIM, born Jinhae, Korea, October 25, 1966; admitted, 1995, Korea. *Education:* Seoul National University (B.S. in Chemistry, 1993). *LANGUAGES:* English, Japanese. *PRACTICE AREAS:* Patent Law.

CONSULTANT

HOON KIM, born Kwangyang, Chonranam-do, Korea, April 15, 1943; admitted, 1991, Korea. *Education:* Korea University (LL.B., 1966); Judicial Graduate School of Seoul National University (LL.M., 1970). Judge Advocate, 1970-1972, Judge, 1973-1979 and Chief Judge, 1985-1990, Seoul and Kwangjoo District Courts. Judge, Seoul High Court, 1981-1982. Secretary, Judge of Supreme Court, 1983-1984. *Member:* Korean Bar Association. *LANGUAGES:* Korean, English and German. *PRACTICE AREAS:* Civil Procedure Law.

SEOUL MARITIME LAW OFFICE

Established in 1992

303, HARIM BLDG. 1699-14
SEOCHO 4-DONG, SEOCHO-GU
SEOUL, KOREA
Telephone: 82-2-595-7121/2
Fax: 82-2-595-9626

Admiralty, Maritime, Insurance, Aviation, International Trade Law.

FIRM PROFILE: *The firm offers a full range of legal services and puts emphasis upon maritime law practice.*

MEMBERS OF FIRM

HYUN KIM, born Seoul, Korea, January 17, 1956; admitted, 1988, Korea; 1991, New York. *Education:* Seoul National University (LL.B., 1980; LL.M., 1983); Cornell Law School (LL.M., 1984); University of Washington (LL.M., 1985; Ph.D. in Law, 1990); Judicial Research and Training Institute of Korea Supreme Court (1986-1988). Foreign Legal Consultant: Bogle & Gates, Seattle, WA, 1985. Legal Adviser to Korea Maritime & Port Administration. Lecturer in Law: Chungnam University, 1992; Hollym University, 1993. Co-Author: Basic Text on Maritime Law in Korea, 1993. Author: "Limitation of Shipowners' Liability in Korea," University of Washington Ph.D. dissertation, 1990. *Member:* Korean Maritime Law Association; U.S. Maritime Law Association; Korean Air Law Association.

(This Listing Continued)

SEOUL MARITIME LAW OFFICE, Seoul—Continued

LANGUAGES: Korean, English, German and Japanese. *PRACTICE AREAS:* Maritime; Insurance; Aviation.

SEONG KANG, born Chonju, Korea, November 25, 1968; admitted, 1993, Korea. *Education:* Seoul National University (LL.B., 1990); Judicial Research and Training Institute of Korea Supreme Court (1991-1993). *LANGUAGES:* Korean, English, German and Japanese. *PRACTICE AREAS:* Maritime Law; Intellectual Property Law.

LEGAL SUPPORT PERSONNEL

YOUNG KUK KIM, born Milyang, Korea, May 25, 1966. *Education:* Kyongnam University (LL.B., 1993). *LANGUAGES:* Korean and English. *PRACTICE AREAS:* Maritime Law.

REPRESENTATIVE CLIENTS: U.K.P&I Club; London P&I Club; Steamship Mutual P & I Club; Pan Ocean Shipping Co.; Korea Special Shipping Co.; Samsung Fire & Marine Insurance Co.; Lucky Insurance Co.; Hyundai Marine Ins. Co.; Federation of Korea Seafarers' Unions; Sumitomo Marine Insurance Co.

SHIN & KIM

Established in 1981

SAMDO BUILDING
1-170, SOONWHA-DONG, CHUNG-KU
P.O. BOX 8261
SEOUL 100-130, KOREA
Telephone: (02) 316-4114
Telex: Justice K22375
Fax: (02) 756-0900/756-6226

Foreign Investment, Corporate, Maritime, International Finance, Banking, Trade, Patents, Copyrights, Trademarks, Securities, Litigation, Antitrust, Technology Transfer and Licensing, Taxation, Labor and Management Consulting.

MEMBERS OF FIRM

YOUNG MOO SHIN, born Chungchungnam-Do, Korea, 1944; admitted, 1970, Korea; 1980, New York. *Education:* Seoul National University, College of Law (LL.B., 1967); Seoul National University, Graduate School of Justice (LL.M., 1970); Yale Law School (LL.M., 1976; J.S.D., 1978). Author: Book, "Securities Regulations in Korea," University of Washington Press and Seoul National University Press, 1983; "Regulations of Proxy Solicitations in Korea," Business Law in Korea, Panmun Book Company, Ltd., Seoul, Korea, 1982; "Regulations of Disclosure and Insider Trading," 9 Korean Journal of Comparative Law, 1980; "Regulation of Takeover Bids," 10 Korean Journal of Comparative Law, 1981. Judge Advocate, Korean Army, 1970-1973. Judge, Daejon District Court, 1973-1975. Foreign Observer, The U.S. Securities and Exchange Commission, 1978 and The American Stock Exchange, 1978. Associate, Coudert Brothers, New York, 1978-1980. Lecturer on Law, Choongnam National University, 1973-1975. Adjunct Professor of Law, Korea University, 1982—. Commissioner, The External Audit Supervision Commission; The Insurance Supervisory Commission. Member: The Deliberation Committee for Capital Market Liberalization; Council on Financial Industry Development. Arbitrator, The Korean Commercial Arbitration Board, 1981—. Member, Board of Directors, Korean Research Institute of Comparative Law, 1981—. *Member:* Korean, Seoul (Director of External Relations), New York State and American Bar Associations; Korean Patent Lawyers Association. *LANGUAGES:* Korean, English, Japanese and German (read only).

SUNG WHAN OH, born Ansung-goon, Kyunggi, Korea, 1934; admitted, 1957, Korea. *Education:* Seoul National University, College of Law (LL.B., 1957). Judge Advocate, Korean Army, 1957-1960; Judge: Taegu District Court, 1960-1961; Seoul District Court, 1961-1963; Seoul District Civil Court, 1964-1966; Seoul District Criminal Court, 1964-1966; Seoul High Court, 1966-1967; Judgement Researcher, Supreme Court, 1967-1970; Chief Judge: Choonchun District Court, 1970-1971; Seoul District Criminal Court and Professor, Judicial Research and Training Institute, 1971-1973; Chief Judge: Seoul District Civil Court, 1973-1975; Seoul District Criminal Court, 1975-1977; Seoul High Court, 1977-1979; Head, Northern Division of Seoul District Court, 1979-1981; Assistant Chief, Office of Court Administration, 1981-1982; Justice, Supreme Court, 1982-1986. Partner, Law Office of Sung Whan Oh, 1987-1992. Member, Central Election Management Committee. *Member:* Korean and Seoul Bar Associations. *LANGUAGES:* Korean.

(This Listing Continued)

SUNG MIN CHOI, born Kyungsangbuk-Do, Korea, 1941; admitted, 1978, Korea. *Education:* Seoul National University, College of Law (LL.B., 1963). *Member:* Korean and Seoul Bar Associations; Korean Patent Lawyers Association. *LANGUAGES:* Korean, English, German and Japanese (read only).

DOO SIK KIM, born Choongchungbuk-Do, Korea, 1957; admitted, 1982, Korea; 1988, New York. *Education:* Seoul National University, College of Law (LL.B., 1980); Judicial Training Institute (1980-1982); University of Chicago Law School (LL.M., 1987). Associate, Wilson, Sonsini, Goodrich & Rosati, Palo Alto, California, 1987-1988. Consultant, Coudert Brothers, Brussels, Belgium, 1988. *Member:* Korean, Seoul, New York State and American Bar Associations. *LANGUAGES:* Korean, English, Japanese and German (read only).

CHANG BOK HUR, born Seoul, Korea, 1955; admitted, 1981, Korea; 1990, New York. *Education:* Seoul National University, College of Social Science (B.A., 1978); Seoul National University, Graduate School of Law (1980); Judicial Training Institute (1979-1981); University of Pennsylvania (LL.M., 1989). Judge Advocate, Korean Army, 1981-1984. Foreign Intern, Skadden Arps Slate Meagher & Flom, New York, 1989-1990. *Member:* Korean, Seoul, New York State and American Bar Associations. *LANGUAGES:* Korean, English and Japanese.

WOONG SOON SONG, born Chungchongnam-Do, Korea, 1953; admitted, 1984, Korea; 1993, New York. *Education:* Seoul National University, College of Law (LL.B., 1975); Graduate School of Justice, Seoul National University (1977); Judicial Training Institute (1983-1984); Columbia University (LL.M., 1990). Associate, White & Case, New York (Foreign Lawyers Program), 1990-1991; Resident, Linklaters and Paines, London, 1991. *Member:* Korean, Seoul and New York State Bar Associations. *LANGUAGES:* Korean, English and Japanese (read only).

SUNG GEUN KIM, born Ansung, Korea, 1958; admitted, 1983, Korea; 1992, New York. *Education:* Seoul National University, College of Law (LL.B., 1981); Judicial Training Institute (1981-1983); Georgetown University Law School (LL.M., 1991). Judge Advocate, Korean Army, 1983-1986. Foreign Associate, Arnold & Porter, Washington, D.C., 1991-1992; Foreign Associate, Wilkie Farr & Gallagher, Washington, D.C., 1992. *Member:* Korean, Seoul and New York State Bar Associations. *LANGUAGES:* Korean, English and Japanese (read only).

YONG SEOK PARK, born Seoul, Korea, 1960; admitted, 1984 Korea. *Education:* Seoul National University, College of Social Science (B.A., 1983); Judicial Training Institute (1983-1984). *Member:* Korean and Seoul Bar Associations. *LANGUAGES:* Korean, English and Japanese (read only).

YOUN TAEK CHOI, born Seoul, Korea, 1958; admitted, 1985, Korea; 1991, New York. *Education:* Seoul National University, College of Law (LL.B., 1980); Judicial Training Institute (1982-1984); Columbia Law School (LL.M., 1991). Associate, Coudert Brothers, New York, 1989-1990. *Member:* Korean, Seoul and New York State Bar Associations. *LANGUAGES:* Korean, English and Japanese (read only).

JAE DOO SHIM, born Seoul, Korea, 1955; admitted, 1985, Korea. *Education:* Seoul National University, College of Law (LL.B., 1977); Judicial Training and Research Institute (1984-1985); Seoul National University, Graduate School of Law (1986); University of Wales, College of Cardiff (LL.M., Maritime Law, 1992). *Member:* Korean and Seoul Bar Associations. *LANGUAGES:* Korean, English, French (read only) and Japanese (read only).

SE RYUL HONG, born Seoul, Korea, 1960; admitted, 1985, Korea. *Education:* Seoul National University, College of Law (LL.B., 1984); Judicial Training Institute (1984-1985). *Member:* Korean and Seoul Bar Associations. *LANGUAGES:* Korean, English and Japanese (read only).

BYOUNG SEON CHOE, born Inchon, Korea, 1959; admitted, 1987, Korea. *Education:* Seoul National University, College of Social Science (B.A., 1981); Seoul National University, College of Law (LL.M., 1984; Ph.D. Candidate); Judicial Training Institute (1985-1987); University of Washington, School of Law (LL.M., 1992). Foreign Legal Consultant, Field Fisher Waterhouse, London (1992-1993). *Member:* Korean and Seoul Bar Associations. *LANGUAGES:* Korean, English, Japanese (read only) and German (read only).

IN SUK SHIM, born Kangreung, Korea, 1964; admitted, 1989, Korea. *Education:* Seoul National University, College of Law (LL.B., 1986); Judicial Training Institute (1987-1989). *Member:* Korean and Seoul Bar Associations. *LANGUAGES:* Korean, English, Japanese and French (read only).

(This Listing Continued)

YOON & PARTNERS

Established in 1989

SUITE 831
KOREA CHAMBER OF COMMERCE & INDUSTRY BUILDING
45 NAMDAEMOONRO-4-KA, CHUNG-KU
C.P.O. BOX 4160
SEOUL, KOREA
Telephone: (02) 773-0161
Intn'l. Dialing: (82-2) 773-0161
Facsimiles: (82-2) 773-4947; 773-4948 Groups II & III

Corporate, Commercial, Foreign Investment, International Trade, Taxation, Intellectual Property and Licensing, Computer and High Technology, Telecommunications, Banking and Financing, Securities, Futures Trading, Insurance, Aerospace, Maritime, Labor and Employment, Administrative Proceedings and Government Relations, Arbitration and Litigation.

MEMBERS OF FIRM

HOIL YOON, born Tokyo, Japan, November 22, 1943; admitted, 1967, Korea; 1973, Illinois; 1977, U.S. Supreme Court and U.S. Court of Customs and Patent Appeals; 1981, District of Columbia; 1988, New York. *Education:* Seoul National University College of Law (LL.B., magna cum laude, 1965; Seoul National University Graduate School of Justice (LL.M., summa cum laude, 1967); University of Notre Dame Law School (J.D., magna cum laude, 1973). Visiting Lecturer, Columbia University School of Law, 1985-1987. Legal Officer, Republic of Korea Air Force, 1967-1970. Judge, Seoul Civil District Court, 1970. Associate, Baker & McKenzie, Chicago, 1973-1979. Partner, Baker & McKenzie, Chicago, 1979-1987, New York, 1987-1989. Recipient, Presidential Citation/Decoration of Republic of Korea, 1984. Chairman, Subcommittee on Korea of American Bar Association, Section on International Law and Practice, 1983-1984. Member: Panel of Arbitrators, American Arbitration Association, New York, 1982—; Korean Commercial Arbitration Board, 1991—. Panel of Conciliators, International Center for Settlement of Investment Disputes, 1992—. Director: U.S.-Korea Society, New York, 1984-1989; Korean American Community Services, 1982-1988. Commissioner, Administrative Adjudication Commission, Korean Ministry of Foreign Affairs, 1990-1994. Member: New Products Advisory Committee, Korea Stock Exchange, 1991-1994; Korea Futures Trading Association, 1990—; Board of Directors of the Korean Bar Association, 1991-1992. Vice Chairman, Section of International Law, Seoul Bar Association, 1991-1992. *Member:* The Association of the Bar of Seoul, Korean, The City of New York, New York State, Chicago, Illinois State, American and International Bar Associations; The District of Columbia Bar; American Intellectual Property Law Association; Inter-Pacific Bar Association; Korean International Trade Law Association; International Rotary Club.

SAI REE YUN, born Ahndong, Korea, November 20, 1953; admitted, 1980, Korea; 1986, Illinois; 1988, New York; 1990, District of Columbia. *Education:* Seoul National University College of Law (LL.B., 1976; LL.M., 1980); Judicial Research and Training Institute, Supreme Court of Korea (1978-1980); Harvard Law School (LL.M., 1982); Hastings College of the Law, University of California (J.D., 1986). Public Prosecutor, Pusan District Prosecutor's Office, Pusan, Korea, 1980-1981. Associate: Lee & Ko, Seoul, Korea, 1983-1984; Baker & McKenzie, Chicago, 1986-1987, New York, 1987-1989. *Member:* Seoul, Korean, Chicago, Illinois State, New York State and American Bar Associations; The District of Columbia Bar; American Society of International Law; International Fiscal Association; Korean International Trade Law Association; Antitrust Law Study Association; International Tax Study Association.

YOUNG-CHEOL JEONG, born Seoul, Korea, March 28, 1955; admitted, 1983, Korea; 1986, Illinois. *Education:* Seoul National University College of Law (LL.B., 1978); Seoul National University Graduate School of Law (LL.M., 1982); Judicial Research and Training Institute, Supreme Court of Korea (1981-1983); Columbia Law School (LL.M., 1984; J.D., 1986). Assistant Director, Ministry of Government Administration, 1981. Associate, Baker & McKenzie, Chicago, 1986-1989. *Member:* Seoul, Korean, Chicago, Illinois State, American and International Bar Associations; American International Property Law Association; American Society of International Law; International Trade Law Association; Competition Law Association; Korea Private International Law Association; Korea Telecommunications Law Study Group; AIPPI; Korea Commercial Law Association; Korea Securities Law Association.

KEECHANG KIM, born Daegu, Korea, January 23, 1963; admitted, 1990, Korea. *Education:* Seoul National University College of Law (LL.B.,

(This Listing Continued)

1985); The University of Chicago Law School (LL.M., 1986); Judicial Research and Training Institute, Supreme Court of Korea (1988-1990).

HEE-WOONG YOON, born Pusan, Korea, October 28, 1965; admitted, 1992, Korea. *Education:* Seoul National University College of Law (LL.B., 1987); Seoul National Graduate School of Law (LL.M., 1989); Judicial Research and Training Institute, Supreme Court of Korea (1990-1992). *Member:* Seoul and Korean Bar Associations.

KWANG HEE CHO, born Kyung-Buk, Korea, July 15, 1967; admitted, 1994, Korea. *Education:* Seoul National University College of Law (LL.B., 1989); Seoul National University Graduate School of Law, Law Faculty, 1992; Judicial Research and Training Institute, Supreme Court of Korea, 1992-1994. *Member:* Seoul and Korean Bar Associations.

YEON KEUM KO, born Kwangju, Korea, November 23, 1968; admitted, 1994, Korea. *Education:* Seoul National University College of Law (LL.B., 1989); Judicial Research and Training Institute, Supreme Court of Korea, 1992-1994. *Member:* Seoul and Korean Bar Associations.

JAE YOUNG KIM, born Pusan, Korea, July 29, 1965; admitted, 1995, Korea. *Education:* Seoul National University College of Law (LL.B., 1988); Seoul National University Graduate School of Law, Law Faculty, 1992; Judicial Research and Training Institute, Supreme Court of Korea, 1991-1995. *Member:* Seoul and Korean Bar Associations.

GYU GEUN CHA, born Kyung-Nam, Korea, April 11, 1968; admitted, 1995, Korea. *Education:* Seoul National University College of Law (LL.B., 1991); Seoul National University Graduate School of Law, Law Faculty, 1995; Judicial Research and Training Institute, Supreme Court of Korea, 1993-1995. *Member:* Seoul and Korean Bar Associations.

OF COUNSEL

JUNG CHUL SHIN, born Daejon, Korea, December 17, 1933; admitted, 1956, Korea. *Education:* Seoul National University College of Law (LL.B., 1956). Legal Officer, Republic of Korea Army, 1957-1960. Judge: Kwangju District Court, 1960; Seoul District Court, 1961-1963; Seoul Criminal District Court, 1963-1964; Seoul Civil District Court, 1964-1965; Seoul High Court, 1965-1966. Research Judge, the Supreme Court of the Republic of Korea, 1970. Presiding Judge, Seoul Criminal District Court, 1979-1980. Chief Judge: Chunchon District Court, 1970-1971; Seoul Civil District Court, 1971-1974; Seoul High Court, 1974-1978. Chief, Office of Planning and Coordination, Court Administration Bureau, The Supreme Court of the Republic of Korea, 1978-1979. Senior Presiding Judge, Chunchon District Court, 1980-1981. Chief Commissioner, Election Management Commission for the Kangwon Province, 1980-1981. Justice, The Supreme Court of the Republic of Korea, 1981-1986. *Member:* Seoul and Korean Bar Associations.

FOREIGN LEGAL CONSULTANTS

WOOJIN (EUGENE) CHANG, born Seoul, Korea, 1959; admitted, 1988, California (Not admitted in Korea). *Education:* Massachusetts Institute of Technology (B.S., 1980); Sloan School of Management, M.I.T. (M.S., 1983); Boalt Hall School of Law, University of California (J.D., 1988). Eta Kappa Nu; Tau Beta Pi. Recipient, American Jurisprudence Award for Corporate Tax Class. Associate Editor, International Tax and Business Lawyer, 1986-1988. Partner, Akre, Bryan & Chang, Los Angeles, 1992-1994. Associate, Mckittrick, Jackson, DeMarco and Peckenpaugh, Newport Beach, 1991-1992. Associate, Latham & Watkins, Los Angeles, 1988-1991. *Member:* State Bar of California; Korean Bar Association.

JISOO KIM, born Seoul, Korea, October 18, 1963; admitted, 1991, Connecticut; 1992, New York (Not admitted in Korea). *Education:* Brown University (B.A., 1986); Columbia University School of International Affairs (M.I.A., International Relations, 1988); Fordham University Law

(This Listing Continued)

YOON & PARTNERS, Seoul—Continued

School (J.D., 1991). Associate, Watson, Farley & Williams, New York, 1991-1993. *Member:* New York State and American Bar Associations; New York Korean Lawyers' Association.

LAOS

DIRKSEN FLIPSE DORAN & LE

Established in 1993

MEKONG COMMERCE BUILDING I
LUANG PRABANG ROAD
P.O. BOX 2920
VIENTIANE, LAOS
Telephone: (856-21) 216927-9
Fax: (856-21) 216919

Seattle, Washington U.S.A. Office: Le, Dirksen, Flipse & Doran. 1001 Fourth Avenue, Suite 3200, 98154. Telephone: 206-292-1650. Fax: 206-760-8041.

Ho Chi Minh City, Vietnam Office: Le, Dirksen, Flipse & Doran. 100 Nguyen Trai, District 1. Telephone: 84-8-390-102. Fax: 84-8-390-102.

FIRM PROFILE: *As the only officially licensed law firm in Laos, Dirksen Flipse Doran & Le provides a full range of legal services to foreign and local investors operating in Laos, Vietnam, Cambodia, and Myanmar (Burma). The firm advises clients on both international and local issues arising from the establishment and operation of their business ventures. Areas of concentration include Direct Foreign Investment, Corporate, Commercial, Hotels & Resorts, Transportation (Aviation), Power Generation (Hydropower), Privatization, Arbitration, Litigation, and Intellectual Property.*

MEMBERS OF FIRM

TODD E. DIRKSEN, born Green Bay, Wisconsin, 1964; admitted, 1994, New York (Not admitted in Laos). *Education:* Loma Linda University (B.A., 1989); Institut D'Etudes Francaises (Diplome, 1985); Georgetown University Law Center (J.D., 1992). Author: "Legal Perspectives on Doing Business in Vietnam," 2 Asia Bus. L. Rev. 8, 1993. *LANGUAGES:* English and French. *PRACTICE AREAS:* Foreign Investment; Construction; Hotels; Corporate; Intellectual Property.

MARY S. FLIPSE, born Chiang Mai, Thailand, 1967; admitted, 1994, New York (Not admitted in Laos). *Education:* Middle Tennessee State University (B.A., 1989); Georgetown University Law Center (J.D., 1992). Author: "Asia's Littlest Dragon: An Analysis of the Laos Foreign Investment Law and Decree," 23 Law & Pol. in Int'l Bus. 199, 1991-1992. *LANGUAGES:* English, Lao and Thai. *PRACTICE AREAS:* Foreign Investment; Corporate; Construction; Transportation; Labor; Litigation.

DAVID D. DORAN, born Bangkok, Thailand, 1964; admitted, 1992, California; 1995, Washington (Not admitted in Laos). *Education:* Loma Linda University (B.A., Summa Cum Laude, 1986); Institut D'Etudes Francaises/Alliances Francaises (1987); University of Washington School of Law (J.D., 1990). Associate Articles Editor, Washington Law Review; *L'Institut Universitaire de Hautes Etudes Internationales* (Certificat des Affaires Internationales, Droit et Economie, mention très bien, 1992), special emphasis in privatization and ownership reform in Eastern Europe. Author: "Equitable Tolling of Statutory Benefit Time Limitations: A Congressional Intent Approach," 64 Washington Law Review 681 (1989). *LANGUAGES:* English and French. *PRACTICE AREAS:* Privatization and Ownership Reform; Land Development; Property; Environment; Corporate.

TUYEN DINH LE, born Hue, Vietnam, October 2, 1957; admitted, 1990, Washington (Not admitted in Laos). *Education:* University of Portland (B.S.M.E., 1982); University of Saigon, School of Economics, Saigon Vietnam; Hastings College of Law, University of California (J. D., 1985); University of Hue, School of Law, Hue, Vietnam. Author: "Vietnam Moves Toward Market Economy," Pacific Economic Review, September 1993. Lecturer: "Negotiating in Vietnam/Asia" CLE Seminar Chairperson/-Faculty, November 1993, Seattle Washington. *Member:* Washington State and American Bar Associations (Member, International Section); International Bar Association; Asian Bar Association; Vietnamese Bar Association. (Resident, Seattle, Washington and Ho Chi Minh City, Vietnam Offices). *LANGUAGES:* Vietnamese, French, Chinese and English. *PRAC-*

(This Listing Continued)

TICE AREAS: International Business; Immigration; Intellectual Property Law; General Civil Practice.

LAWYERS

PHASITH PHOMMARAK, born Attopeu Province, Laos, 1937; admitted, 1972, Laos. *Education:* Georgetown University (Amercian Language Inst.) (Certificate, 1963); Institut Royal de Droit et Administration Publique (Diplome, 1969). *LANGUAGES:* Lao, English, French, Vietnamese, Khmer, Japanese, Thai, German, Swedish and Russian. *PRACTICE AREAS:* Arbitration; Litigation; Commercial Contracts.

MICHAEL D. POPKIN, born Montreal, Canada, 1966. *Education:* University of Toronto (B.A., 1989); University of British Columbia (LL.B., 1993). *LANGUAGES:* English and French. *PRACTICE AREAS:* International Corporate; Joint Ventures; Transportation (Aviation).

MINAMONE BONACORSI NORDTVEIT, born Vientiane, Laos, 1968. *Education:* Pantheon Sorbonne University (License de Droit des Affaires, 1991); Pantheon Sorbonne University (Maitrise de Droit Prive, 1992). *LANGUAGES:* French, Lao and English. *PRACTICE AREAS:* Judicial Administration.

REPRESENTATIVE CLIENTS: Shell Oil (Laos); Guthrie GTS Ltd. (Singapore); Telstra/OTC (Australia); ; Theiss Contractors (Australia); Columbia Helicopter (U.S.); Seattle Aerosky (U.S.); Seiyu Ltd. (Japan); CTAS Air Services (China/-Hong Kong); Fu Yee Corp. (Malaysia); Renown Corp. (Thailand); RNVA Company (Russia); Asian Development Bank (Philippines); International Monetary Fund (U.S.); AIRCOM Aircraft Leasing (Austria).

MALAYSIA

CHEONG KEE FONG & CO

Notary Public, Advocates & Solicitors

SUITE 1702, 17TH FLOOR, WISMA LIM FOO YONG
86 JALAN RAJA CHULAN
50200 KUALA LUMPUR, MALAYSIA
Telephone: (3) 2416977
Fax: (3) 2416984

Banking Law, Commercial Law, Company Law, Conveyancing-Commercial, Financial Services, Landlord & Tenant, Tax.

PARTNERS

Kee Fong Cheong　　　　　　　　**Miss Joo Lian Ee**

DAVID CHONG & CO.

SUITE 13A.01, 13A FLOOR
WISMA MCA, 163 JALAN AMPANG
50450 KUALA LUMPUR, MALAYSIA
Telephone: 2632277
Fax: 2632278

Singapore Office: 65 Chulia Street, OCBC Centre, #31-00 East Lobby, 0104. Telephone: 2240955. Fax: 5333570; 5386585; 5387559.

Johor Bahru, Malaysia Office: Suite 204-206, 2nd Floor. Pusat Professional, Jalan Syed Mohd Mufti, 80000. Telephone: 2249128. Fax: 2249386.

Labuan, Malaysia Office: Suite 114,1st Floor, Hotel Labuan, Jalan Merdeka, P.O. Box 80107, 87011. Telephone: 411697; 416604. Fax: 41936.

Sydney, Australia Office: Level 29 Governor Phillip Tower, 1 Farrer Place, NSW, 2000. Telephone: 2585811. Fax: 2585800.

Suzhou, People's Republic of China Office: Suzhou Economy and International Trade Law Firm. Telephone: 877101. Fax: 879121.

Company and Commercial, Company Secretarial Services, Banking, Finance and Securities, Tax Practice and Planning, Conveyancing and Property Building and Construction, Admiralty and Shipping, Insurance, Copyright, Trademark Patent and Registered Design, Civil and Commercial Litigation, Bankruptcy and Insolvency, Arbitration, Family, Probate and Administration of Estates, General Practice.

(This Listing Continued)

OF COUNSEL

n 1955; admitted, 1986, California. Registered

our Administrative Office in California, USA.

IBRAHIM & CO.

Established in 1987

MENARA BANK PEMBANGUNAN
AN SULTAN ISMAIL
LA LUMPUR, MALAYSIA
lephone: 60-3-2926688
Telefax: 60-3-2981632
Telex: MA 21542

l, Mergers and Acquisitions, Joint Ventures,
atization Projects, Banking and Financial Ser-
, Immigration, Telecommunications, Employ-
aw, Arbitration and Civil Litigation.

EMBERS OF FIRM

M, born 1951; admitted, 1975, England (Inner
ducation: University of London (LL.B., Hons.,
lish and Malay. *PRACTICE AREAS:* Project
rk; Construction Law.

963; admitted, 1985, England (Lincoln's Inn);
pore. *Education:* University of London (LL.B.,
S: English. *PRACTICE AREAS:* Arbitration;
rate Litigation.

rn 1960; admitted, 1984, New Zealand; 1985,
oria University of Wellington (LL.B., Hons.,
LANGUAGES: English and Chinese. *PRAC-*
and Privatisation; Privatisation; Mergers and

NIOR ASSOCIATES

rn 1962; admitted, 1985, Malaysia. *Education:*
(LL.B., Hons., 1984). *LANGUAGES:* English
AREAS: Banking Law; Conveyancing; Loan

60; admitted, 1985, New South Wales, Austra-
tion: University of Sydney (B. Econs., 1983;
S: English and Chinese. *PRACTICE AREAS:*
g; Property Development Law; Offshore Tax

CK KEONG, born 1963; admitted, 1987, Aus-
ucation: University of Sydney (LL.B., Hons.,
lish. *PRACTICE AREAS:* Banking Corporate
Project Finance.

n 1959; admitted, 1986, New Zealand. *Educa-*
ry, New Zealand (LL.B., Hons., 1985). *LAN-*
TICE AREAS: Corporate Law; Commercial

1962; admitted, 1986, England (Lincoln's Inn);
University of London (LL.B., Hons., 1986).
d Chinese. *PRACTICE AREAS:* Commercial
t Financing.

); admitted, 1984, Malaysia; 1989, Singapore.
sity of Singapore (LL.B., Hons., 1983). *LAN-*
nese. *PRACTICE AREAS:* Property Develop-
orporate Law.

n 1965; admitted, 1988, Malaysia. *Education:*
England (LL.B., Hons.). *LANGUAGES:* En-
E AREAS: Project Construction; Engineering.

n 1943; admitted, 1985, Malaysia. *Education:*
B., Hons.). *LANGUAGES:* English and Chi-
Banking and Property Law.

AN HJ. ABDULLAH, born 1957; admitted,
MARA Institute of Technology, Malaysia (Ad-
NGUAGES: English and Malay. *PRACTICE*
ty Law; Registered Patent Agent.
This Listing Continued)

LL.B. (Hons) I.I.U., Advocate and Solicitor
lish and Malay. *PRACTICE AREAS:* Liti-

HONG & KRAAL

cates & Solicitors

R, WISMA BUMI RAYA
LAN RAJA LAUT
LUMPUR, MALAYSIA
(603) 291-1511 (5 Lines)
ax: (603) 292-9105

loor, No. 10, Leboh Bishop, 10200.
ax: 613-1-33.

ng and Finance, Contracts, Conveyancing,
on, Insurance, Joint Ventures, Labour and

PARTNERS

ter-at-Law, Lincoln's Inn, London.

rister-at-Law, Inner Temple, London.

LL.B., (Hons.) (Malaya), Malaysia.

(Hons.) (U.I.A.), Malaysia.

Hons.), London.

AL ASSISTANTS

ons (Mal.), LL.B., London.

U, LL.B. (Hons.) (London) Barrister-at-

Hons.) London.

AH, (MS.), LL.B., (Hons.) London.

ns.) Wales, Barrister-at-Law.

LL.B., (Hons.) (NOHS).

) (Keele).

(London), Barrister-at-Law.

G, LL.B., (Hons.) (Newcastle).

ns.) (Durham).

aysia, English, Hindi and Chinese.

& COMPANY

blished in 1962

H-01, BANGUNAN MING
BUKIT NANAS
LUMPUR, MALAYSIA
) 3-2327344 (15 Lines)
) 3-2382915/2308708

Acquisitions, Property Law, Conveyancing,
ation, Insurance Law, Wills and Estate,
d Construction, Administration and Con-

as established in 1962 and there are 5 part-

PARTNERS

and Managing Partner). *LANGUAGES:*
Mandarin. *PRACTICE AREAS:* Banking

. LANGUAGES: Bahasa Malaysia and
ivil and Commercial Litigation.

GUAGES: Bahasa Malaysia and English.
aw; Corporate Law.
isting Continued)

AS231B

CHOOI & COMPANY, Kuala Lumpur—Continued

YAP LEE TENG, (MS). LANGUAGES: Bahasa Malaysia and English. **PRACTICE AREAS:** Banking Law; Corporate Law.

IRA BISWAS, (MS). LANGUAGES: Bahasa Malaysia, English and Hindi. **PRACTICE AREAS:** Civil and Commercial Litigation.

Languages: Bahasa Malaysia, English, Mandarin and Hindi.

CHOR PEE ANWARUL & CO.

SUITE 19.04 WISMA CYCLECARRI
288 JALAN RAJA LAUT
50350 KUALA LUMPUR, MALAYSIA
Telephone: 603-294-6878
Fax: 603-294-6879

Singapore Office: Chor Pee & Company, 50 Raffles Place, 18th. Floor Shell Tower. Telephone: (65) 2201911. Fax: (65) 2244118.

Hanoi, Vietnam Office: Chor Pee & Company, 96 Ba Trieu Street, Hoan Kiem District. Telephone: (844) 228 787/228 788. Fax: (844) 251 875.

Ho Chi Minh City, Vietnam Office: Chor Pee & Company, The Colonnade, 27 Nguyen Trung Truc, District 1. Telephone: (848) 224 986. Fax: (848) 225 441.

Johor Bahru, Malaysia Office: Unit 10.01 Wisma LKN, 49 Jalan Wong Ah Fook, 80000. Telephone: 607-223-4733. Fax: 607-223-4734.

Company and Commercial Law, Conveyancing and Property Law, Civil and Commercial Litigation, Corporate Law, Criminal Law, Banking, Finance and Securities, Intellectual Property, Building and Construction Law, Insurance Law, Vehicle and Industrial Accidents Claims, Probate and Administration of Estates, Arbitration, Admiralty and Shipping Law, Bankruptcy and Insolvency, Employment Law, Family Law, Immigration Matters. The Firm has particular experience in Law on Foreign Investment in Vietnam.

(For complete biographical data on all personnel, see Professional Biographies at Singapore)

HILBORNE, HAWKIN & CO.

Legal Consultants, Advocates and Solicitors

Trademark, Copyright & Patent Agents

Established in 1965

MALAYSIA SERVICE ADDRESS FOR TRADEMARK REGISTRATION:
LOTS 1708/9, 17TH FLOOR WISMA HLA
JALAN RAJAH CHULAN
KUALA LUMPUR 50200, MALAYSIA
Telephone: 03-2414823
Facsimile: 03-2414641

Orange, California Administrative Office: 2534 N. Santiago Blvd., 92667. Telephone: (714) 283-1155. Fax: (714) 283-1555; 532-2713.

Brunei Service Address for Trademark Registration: Suite 31, 3rd Floor, Brutannia House, 38 Jalan Cator, Bandar Seri Begawan, 2085, Brunei Darussalam. Telephone: 6732-228382. Facsimile: 6732-228389.

Hong Kong Office: M2-3, New Henry House, 10, Ice House Street, Central. Telephone: 852-869-0828. Facsimile: 852-810-1703.

Singapore Service Address for Trademark Registration: c/o Loke & Seah, 3 Shenton Way, #21-10, Shenton House, Singapore, 0106. Telephone: 65-223-7088. Facsimile: 65-223-7028.

FIRM PROFILE: *The firm's clientele consists of multi-national corporations and select "private and entrenched" individuals. Founded in 1965, the firm offers a full range of legal services and is well known internationally in areas of intellectual property, licensing, franchising, joint ventures and international business transactions. Subject to local bar rules, the firm accepts instructions for representation in Singapore, Malaysia, Brunei, Hong Kong, England and Wales.*

MEMBERS OF FIRM

VINI KUMAR, born 1935; admitted, 1965, Malaysia; 1966, Brunei; 1969, Singapore; 1961, England and Wales. Certified as a Legal Consultant by the State Bars of New York and California for these jurisdictions.

ALAN H. DAY, born 1943; admitted, 1971, England and Wales; 1972, Hong Kong.

(This Listing Continued)

KEITH E. KLINE, bc
Patent Attorney (USPTO)

Please direct all inquiries

ZAIL

12TH FLOOR,
JA
50250 KU
T

Corporate and Commerc
Construction, Property, Pr
vices, Intellectual Proper
ment Law, Administrative

MOHD ZAID IBRAH
Temple); 1976, Malaysia.
1974). **LANGUAGES:** En
Financing; Privatisation W

JULIAN DING, born
1986, Malaysia; 1992, Sing
Hons., 1984). **LANGUAG**
Construction Claims; Corp

CHEW SENG KOK, b
Malaysia. *Education:* Vic
1984; LL.M., Hons., 1989
TICE AREAS: Corporate
Acquisitions.

S

LEE HOOI CHENG, b
University of Buckingham
and Chinese. **PRACTICE**
Syndication.

LIM KAR HAN, born l
lia; 1986, Malaysia. *Educ*
LL.B., 1985). **LANGUAG**
Banking Law; Conveyanci
Matters.

ANDREW PHANG TU
tralia; 1992, Malaysia. *Ec*
1987). **LANGUAGES:** En
Finance law; Corporate and

KHEM THADANI, bo
tion: University of Canterb
GUAGES: English. **PRA**
Law.

LOH WEI LIAN, born
1987, Malaysia. *Education*
LANGUAGES: English a
Law; Corporate Law; Proje

JENNY LYE, born 19
Education: National Unive
GUAGES: English and Ch
ment Law; Banking Law; C

SHAHRIL LAMIN, bc
University of Buckingham
glish and Malay. **PRACTI**

MARGARET KAM, bc
University of London (LI
nese. **PRACTICE AREAS:**

MOHAMAD BUSTAN
1992, Malaysia. *Education:*
vance Diploma in Law). *L*
AREAS: Intellectual Prope

ASSOCIATES

SHARIFAH SAZITA SYED HAMZAH, born 1963; admitted, 1990, England (Lincoln's Inn); 1991, Malaysia. *Education:* University of London (LL.B., Hons., 1989). *LANGUAGES:* English and Malay. *PRACTICE AREAS:* Conveyancing; Banking Law.

SULIP R. MENON, born 1963; admitted, 1989, England (Lincoln's Inn); 1991, Malaysia. *Education:* University of London (LL.B., Hons., 1988). *LANGUAGES:* English. *PRACTICE AREAS:* Commercial Law; Corporate Litigation.

HWANG TENG HOOI, born 1962; admitted, 1991, England and Malaysia. *Education:* University of London (LL.B. Hons.; LL.M.). *LANGUAGES:* English and Chinese. *PRACTICE AREAS:* Civil Litigation; Commercial Litigation; Shipping Law.

FOONG CHEE MENG, born 1966; admitted, 1989, Australia. *Education:* University of Sydney (LL.B., Hons., LL.M.). *LANGUAGES:* English and Chinese. *PRACTICE AREAS:* Corporate Law; Privatisation; Project Financing.

FELICIA LING, born 1967; admitted, 1992, Malaysia. *Education:* University of Malaya (LL.B., Hons.). *LANGUAGES:* English and Chinese. *PRACTICE AREAS:* Construction Law; Corporate Litigation.

NORMA ISMAIL, born 1964; admitted, 1990, Malaysia. *Education:* International Islamic University, Malaysia (LL.B., Hons.). *LANGUAGES:* English and Malay. *PRACTICE AREAS:* Personal Injury Litigation; Commercial Law.

CHEONG PUI FAN, born 1964; admitted, 1991, Malaysia. *Education:* University of Bristol, England (LL.B., Hons.). *LANGUAGES:* English and Chinese. *PRACTICE AREAS:* Commercial Law; Conveyancing.

AMIR FAEZAL ZAKARIA, born 1967; admitted, 1993, Malaysia. *Education:* Leeds Polytechnic, London (LL.B., Hons.). *LANGUAGES:* English and Malay. *PRACTICE AREAS:* Civil Litigation; Corporate Law.

ANITA AWAT RAM ABDULLAH, born 1967; admitted, 1993, Malaysia. *Education:* University of Warwick, England; International Islamic University, Malaysia (LL.B., Hons). *LANGUAGES:* English and Malay. *PRACTICE AREAS:* Corporate Finance; Project Finance.

FARAH DEBA MOHD SOFIAN, born 1968; admitted, 1992, Malaysia. *Education:* University of London, England; International Islamic University (LL.B., Hons). *LANGUAGES:* English and Malay. *PRACTICE AREAS:* Intellectual Property Law.

NAZRI MD NAWAWI, born 1968; admitted, 1992, Malaysia. *Education:* Birmingham Polytechnic, United Kingdom (LL.B., Hons). *LANGUAGES:* English and Malay. *PRACTICE AREAS:* Commercial Litigation; Banking Law.

TEH CHIN MAY, born 1967; admitted, 1993, Malaysia. *Education:* University of Malaya (LL.B., Hons.). *LANGUAGES:* English and Chinese. *PRACTICE AREAS:* Banking Law; Commercial Law.

JAMES KHONG, born 1967; admitted, 1992, Malaysia. *Education:* University of Malaya (LL.B., Hons); University of Cambridge, United Kingdom (LL.M., First Class). *LANGUAGES:* English and Chinese. *PRACTICE AREAS:* Corporate Finance; Project Finance.

IDAYU ZAINUDDIN, born 1968; admitted, 1994, Malaysia. *Education:* Mara Institute of Technology, Malaysia (Advanced Diploma in Law). *LANGUAGES:* English and Malay. *PRACTICE AREAS:* Property; Banking; Intellectual Property.

JUNE KHOO, born 1966; admitted, 1992, Malaysia. *Education:* University of Monash (LL.B., Hons.; B.Ec.). *LANGUAGES:* English and Chinese. *PRACTICE AREAS:* Litigation; Construction Contracts.

JEYARATNAM & CHONG

16TH FLOOR, MENARA TAN & TAN
NO. 207, JALAN TUN RAZAK
50400 KUALA LUMPUR, MALAYSIA
Telephone: 603-2637077; 2647077
Facsimile: 603-2637149; 2637150

Ipoh, Perak Darul Ridzuan, Malaysia Office: No. 13, Jalan Tun Sambanthan, 30000. Telephone: 605-254 8866; 253 7581. Fax: 605-254 0244.

(This Listing Continued)

Corporate and Commercial, Mergers, Acquisitions, Joint Ventures, Construction Law, Property, Listing, Projects, Banking and Financial Services, Intellectual Property, Immigration, Employment Law and Civil Litigation.

FIRM PROFILE: *The firm is the final form of a series of mergers with its beginnings in 1932. Presently supported by 12 associates (legal assistants) and support staff of 60. The firm provides a comprehensive range of services specialising in corporate and property. It presently advises various multinationals within and outside Asia in these areas.*

MEMBERS OF FIRM

TAN SRI DATUK SERI V. JEYARATNAM, P.S.M., S.P.M.P., J.P., born 1925; admitted, 1953, England (Lincoln's Inn) and Malaysia. *Education:* London University (LL.B., Hons, 1953).

CHONG KIM WENG, born 1959; admitted, 1982, England (Gray's Inn); 1983, Malaysia. *Education:* University of East Anglia (LL.B. Hons., 1982). *PRACTICE AREAS:* Corporate Law; Conveyancing.

LEE POH KWEE, born 1958; admitted, 1982, Malaysia. *Education:* University of Malaya (LL.B., Hons., 1982). *PRACTICE AREAS:* Banking Law; Corporate Law; Conveyancing.

TEH SAW HOON, born 1959; admitted, 1984, Malaysia. *Education:* University of Malaya (LL.B., Hons., 1983). *PRACTICE AREAS:* Banking Law; Corporate Law; Conveyancing.

ALBERT TOONG YU LEONG, born 1955; admitted, 1982, Malaysia. *Education:* London Guild Hall University (B.A., Hons., Business Law); Lincolns Inn (Barrister-at-Law). *PRACTICE AREAS:* Corporate Law; Litigation.

FREDRICK INDRAN NICHOLAS, admitted, 1984, England; 1986, Malaysia. *Education:* London University (LL.B., Hons., 1984). *PRACTICE AREAS:* Criminal Law.

ASSOCIATES

LO KHIEN NGOH, admitted, 1990, Malaysia. *Education:* University of London (LL.B., Hons., 1989). *PRACTICE AREAS:* Corporate Law; Conveyancing.

RAJA SINGAM S/O DEVAPITCHAI, admitted, 1991, Malaysia. *Education:* University of London (Ext) (B.A., Hons., 1979; LL.B., Hons., 1989). *PRACTICE AREAS:* Civil and Commercial Litigation; Conveyancing.

LEE SIU KHENG, admitted, 1992, Malaysia. *Education:* University of Malaya (LL.B., Hons., 1991). *PRACTICE AREAS:* Banking Law; Conveyancing.

JAGJEET SINGH S/O RANJIT SINGH, admitted, 1992, Malaysia. *Education:* University of London (LL.B., Hons., 1991). *PRACTICE AREAS:* Civil Litigation.

INDRA RAMANATHAN, admitted, 1992, Malaysia. *Education:* London University (LL.B., Hons., 1991). *PRACTICE AREAS:* Civil Litigation; Banking Law; Conveyancing.

JAMES LEE WEE SOON, admitted, 1991, New Zealand; 1992, Malaysia. *Education:* University of Otago (LL.B., 1991). *PRACTICE AREAS:* Banking Law; Conveyancing.

WONG SHUK YEE, admitted, 1993, Malaysia. *Education:* University of New South Wales, Australia (B. Comm., in accounting; LL.B., 1991). *PRACTICE AREAS:* Banking Law; Conveyancing.

MELENI MERCY NICHOLAS, admitted, 1993, Malaysia. *Education:* Lincoln's Inn (LL.B., Hons., 1989). *PRACTICE AREAS:* Banking Law; Conveyancing.

CHIN POH YEEN, admitted, 1993, Malaysia. *Education:* University of East Anglis (LL.B., Hons., 1991). *PRACTICE AREAS:* Civil Litigation; Conveyancing.

LAM NAI JIT, admitted, 1992, Malaysia. *Education:* University of Kent, England (B.A., with honors, 1991). *PRACTICE AREAS:* Civil Litigation.

HEE KANG YOW, admitted, 1993, Malaysia. *Education:* University of King's College (LL.B., Hons., 1991). *PRACTICE AREAS:* Civil Litigation.

RAHIMAH BEE BTE MOHD YUSOF, admitted, 1994, Malaysia. *Education:* Mara Institute of Technology, Malaysia (LL.M., Advocate, Diploma in Law, 1993). *PRACTICE AREAS:* Civil Litigation.

KHAW & HUSSEIN

Advocates & Solicitors

Notary Public

6TH FLOOR, MENARA BOUSTEAD
NO. 69, JALAN RAJA CHULAN
50200 KUALA LUMPUR, MALAYSIA
Telephone: (603) 2417633
Telefax: (603) 2483904/2440078

Corporate, Company and Commercial Law, Finance, Contracts, Joint Ventures and Business Law, Agency and Distributorships, Real Estate, Construction Law, Arbitration and Professional Liability, Creditor Collections, Bankruptcy Law, Wills and Probate.

PARTNERS

YEW-MEI KHAW, admitted, 1967, Barrister-at-Law, Lincoln's Inn; 1968, Malaysia, Advocate and Solicitor; 1976, Singapore, Advocate and Solicitor; 1977, Commissioner for Oaths; 1979, Notary Public. *Education:* Liverpool (LL.B., Hons., 1966); Paris (Licence en Droit, 1971).

AZHAR AZIZAN HARUN, admitted, 1987, Malaysia, Advocate and Solicitor. *Education:* Malaysia (LL.B., Hons., 1986); London (LL.M., 1990).

SENIOR ASSOCIATES

AH KOK FONG, admitted, 1987, Malaysia, Advocate and Solicitor. *Education:* Malaysia (B.Sc., Hons., 1980); London (LL.B., Hons., 1985); Malaysia (C.L.P., 1986).

CHENG WEE TEO, admitted, 1989, Malaysia, Advocate & Solicitor. *Education:* Malaysia (LL.B., Hons., 1988); Malaysia (C.L.P., 1989).

KOK WAI NG, admitted, 1990, Malaysia, Advocate & Solicitor; 1989, Singapore, Advocate & Solicitor. *Education:* Singapore (LL.B., Hons, 1988).

BAN HUAT KWA, admitted, 1992, Malaysia, Advocate & Solicitor; 1990, New South Wales, Barrister; 1990, Australian Capital Territory, Barrister & Solicitor; 1991, High Court Australia, Barrister. *Education:* Australia (B. Com., 1987; LL.B., 1988; LL.M., 1991).

ASSOCIATES

SEE TING YON. *Education:* London (LL.B., Hons). Barrister-at-Law, Lincoln's Inn; Advocate & Solicitor, Malaysia.

SUI SANG WANG. *Education:* Liverpool (LL.B., Hons.). Barrister-at-Law, Lincoln's Inn; Advocate and Solicitor, Malaysia.

AISHA Z. ABDULLAH. *Education:* Norwich (LL.B., Hons.). Barrister-at-Law, Middle Temple; Advocate and Solicitor, Malaysia.

ANIMAH BT FUAD KOSAI. *Education:* Malaysia (LL.B., Hons.); Nottinghams (LL.M.). Advocate & Solicitor, Malaysia.

Languages: English, Bahasa Malaysia, French and Chinese.

K. SUKUMAR & CO.

LOT 1808, 18TH FLOOR
1GB PLAZA, JALAN KAMPAR, OFF JALAN TUN RAZAK
50400 KUALA LUMPUR, MALAYSIA
Telephone: 03-4411648
Telefax: 03-4411571

Trademarks, Copyright, Designs, Patents, Commercial and Corporate, Litigation and General Practice.

SUKUMAR KARUPPIAH, admitted, 1989, Singapore; 1993, Malaysia. *Education:* LL.B., Hons. (Singapore). *LANGUAGES:* English, Malay and Tamil.

LEGAL ASSISTANTS

PEGGY OOI CHEE CHOOI, admitted, 1994. *Education:* LL.B., Hons. (London), C.L.P. *LANGUAGES:* English. Malay and Chinese.

LEE BOON PENG & CO.

Advocates and Solicitors

Established in 1964

22ND FLOOR, WISMA LEE RUBBER
JALAN MELAKA
50100 KUALA LUMPUR, MALAYSIA
Telephone: (03) 2982622
Telefax: (03) 2983966

Investment and Trade, Corporate and Securities, Tax, Banking, Litigation, Intellectual Property and Real Estate.

MEMBERS OF FIRM

DATO' LEE BOON PENG, born Malaysia, December 20, 1921; admitted, 1964, Malaysia. *Education:* Barrister at Law (Middle Temple). Member of Parliament, 1974-1986. *LANGUAGES:* English, Malay and Chinese.

ALEX CHIN GUAN LEE, born Malaysia, November 24, 1958; admitted, 1982, England; 1985, Malaysia. *Education:* University of Manchester (B.Sc.); City University (Diploma at Law with distinction); Cambridge (LL.M.); Oxford (B.C.L.); Chicago-Kent (J.D.); Barrister at Law (Middle Temple). *LANGUAGES:* English and Malay.

LEE SIOW NYUK, born Malaysia, September 5, 1954; admitted, 1979, Malaysia. *Education:* Singapore (LL.B. Hons.). *LANGUAGES:* English, Malay and Chinese.

LEE TIAN LAY, born Malaysia, October 27, 1959; admitted, 1984, England; 1985, Malaysia. *Education:* Kent (B.A. Law Hons) (Lincoln's Inn). *LANGUAGES:* English, Malay and Chinese.

TAN MOH HUAT, born Malaysia, June 13, 1962; admitted, 1987, Malaysia. *Education:* Malaya (LL.B. Hons). *LANGUAGES:* English, Malay and Chinese.

TAN MUI TECK, born Malaysia, June 21, 1968; admitted, 1991, England; 1992, Malaysia. *Education:* Kingston Polytechnic (LL.B. Hons.); Barrister-at-Law (Lincoln's Inn). *LANGUAGES:* English, Malay and Chinese.

ANNA YEONG SUFERN, born Malaysia, October 11, 1967; admitted, 1992, Malaysia. *Education:* Malaya (LL.B. Hons.). *LANGUAGES:* English, Malay and Chinese.

JIMMY CHIN KEEM FEUNG, born Malaysia, August 20, 1965; admitted, 1992, Malaysia. *Education:* Essex (LL.B., Hons.); Barrister-at-Law (Inner Temple). *LANGUAGES:* English, Malay and Chinese.

RAJA, DARRYL & LOH

Advocates & Solicitors, Notary Public, Commissioner for Oaths, Registered Patent Agent & Trade Mark Agents

18TH FLOOR WISMA SIME DARBY JALAN RAJA LAUT
50350 KUALA LUMPUR, MALAYSIA
Telephone: 603-294 9999 (20 lines)
Facsimile: 603-298 4759; 603-293 8028; 603-293 3823

Mailing Address: P.O. Box 12625, 50784 KUALA LUMPUR, MALAYSIA

Corporate, Company and Commercial Law, Property Law and Conveyancing, Contract, Finance and Banking, Revenue Law, Foreign Investment, Building and Construction, Intellectual Property Law, Insurance Law, Administrative Law, Wills and Estate, Family Law, Labour Law, Civil Litigation, Arbitration.

PARTNERS

YOON KWAI LOH, admitted, 1965, Malaysia; 1967, Singapore. *Education:* University of Singapore (LL.B., Hons., 1965).

JENNIFER N.F. CHEONG, admitted, 1979, Malaysia; 1993, Singapore; Commissioner for Oaths & Notary Public. *Education:* University of Singapore (LL.B., Hons., 1978).

DARRYL S.C. GOON, admitted, 1980, England, Barrister-at-Law, Lincoln's Inn; 1982, Malaysia; 1993, Singapore; Registered Patent Agent and Trademark Agent. *Education:* University of London (LL.B., Hons., 1979; LL.M., 1980); London Institute of World Affairs (Diploma in Air & Space Law).

(This Listing Continued)

RAJASEKARAN MURUGAIAH, admitted, 1983, England, Barrister-at-Law, Middle Temple; 1984, Malaysia. *Education:* University of London (LL.B., Hons., 1982).

WEI MUN CHANG, admitted, 1985, New Zealand, Barrister & Solicitor; 1986, Malaysia. *Education:* University of Canterbury (LL.B., 1985).

PHYE KEAT CHEW, admitted, 1987, Malaysia. *Education:* University of Malaya (LL.B., Hons., 1986). Trademark Agent.

CHRISTOPHER K.F. FOO, admitted, 1981, Malaysia. *Education:* University of Malaya (LL.B., Hons., 1980).

LEGAL ASSISTANTS

MUN YEE CHAN, admitted, 1988, England, Barrister-at-Law, Middle Temple; 1989, Malaysia. *Education:* University of London (LL.B., Hons., 1986).

JIN NEE WONG, admitted, 1990, New South Wales, Australia, Barrister-at-Law; 1991, Malaysia. *Education:* University of Sydney (LL.B., 1989).

SAI YEANG NG, admitted, 1990, England, Barrister-at-Law, Inner Temple; 1991, Malaysia. *Education:* University of Keele (B.Soc.Sc., Hons., 1989).

SOOK YEE HO, admitted, 1990, Victoria, Australia, Barrister & Solicitor; 1991, Malaysia. *Education:* Monash University (B.Ec., 1987; LL.B., 1989).

SIAO HUI WONG, admitted, 1988, Australia, Barrister & Solicitor, Victoria; 1989, Malaysia. *Education:* University of Melbourne (LL.B., 1987).

EVELYN PEARL MALAYAPILLAY, admitted, 1991, England, Barrister-at-Law, Lincoln's Inn; 1992, Malaysia. *Education:* University of London (LL.B., Hons., 1989; LL.M., 1991).

RAVINDRA KUMAR G. RENGASAMY, admitted, 1987, Malaysia. *Education:* University of London (LL.B., Hons., 1985); Certificate of Legal Practice (1986).

BONG KWANG TEO, admitted, 1987, Malaysia. *Education:* University of Malaya (LL.B., Hons., 1986).

ANGELINE MOOI SEAN YEOH, admitted, 1990, Australia, Barrister and Solicitor; 1994, Malaysia. *Education:* Monash University (B.Ec., 1987; LL.B., 1989).

KUI PENG SOO, admitted, 1993, Malaysia. *Education:* University of Leicester (LL.B., Hons., 1991); Certificate of Legal Practice (1992).

AZNUL AFFENDI HASAN BASRI, admitted, 1991, England, Barrister-at-Law, Lincoln's Inn; 1994, Malaysia. *Education:* University of Cambridge (B.A., 1990; M.A., 1994).

SATHANANTHA KUMAR S., admitted, 1992, Malaysia. *Education:* University of London (LL.B., Hons., 1990); Certificate of Legal Practice (1991).

SABARINA SAMADI, admitted, 1993, England, Barrister-at-Law, Gray's Inn; 1994, Malaysia. *Education:* University of Liverpool (LL.B., Hons., 1992).

SHARADAMANI RUDRALINGAM, admitted, 1992, England, Barrister-at-Law, Inner Temple; 1994, Malaysia. *Education:* The London School of Economics and Political Science; University of London (LL.B., Hons., 1991).

LEONG CHEOK KENG, admitted, 1994, Malaysia. *Education:* National University of Singapore (B.Acc., Hons., 1990); University of Leeds (LL.B., Hons., 1992); Certificate of Legal Practice (1993).

IRENE LI MING NG, admitted, 1993, England, Barrister-at-Law, Middle Temple; 1994, Malaysia. *Education:* University of Lancaster (LL.B., Hons., 1992).

RAM RAIS & PARTNERS

Advocates & Solicitors

Registered Patent Agents

Notary Public

Commissioner for Oaths

Established in 1973

WISMA PACKER 195

JALAN TUANKU ABDUL RAHMAN

50100 KUALA LUMPUR, MALAYSIA

Telephone: (60-3) 2931125, 2935123, 2925266,

2925360, 2925016

Telefax: (60-3) 2930716

Telex: MA 32383

Trademarks, Patents, Copyright, Designs, Banking, Taxation, Commercial and Corporate, Conveyancing, Investment and Trade, Litigation and General Practice.

PARTNERS

HARIRAM JAYARAM, born Alor Setar, Malaysia, October 17, 1938; admitted, 1970, Malaysia. *Education:* LL.B. (Hons.) (S'pore); LL.M. (London). *LANGUAGES:* English, Malay and Tamil.

DATO' RAIS YATIM, born Jelebu, Malaysia, April 15, 1942; admitted, 1973, Malaysia. *Education:* LL.B. (Hons.) (S'pore); Ph.D. (London). *LANGUAGES:* English and Malay.

LEGAL ASSISTANTS

SRI DEV NAIR, born Kuala Lumpur, Malaysia, August 27, 1956; admitted, 1989, Malaysia. *Education:* LL.B. (Hons.) (London). *LANGUAGES:* English, Malay, Tamil and Malayalam.

YEOH SUAT GAIK, born Petaling Jaya, Malaysia, January 3, 1968; admitted, 1993, Malaysia. *Education:* B.Comm.; LL.B. (The Australian National University). *LANGUAGES:* English, Malay and Mandarin.

W.A. SHASHILA, born Penang, Malaysia, July 23, 1968; admitted, 1993, Malaysia. *Education:* LL.B. (Hons.) (London). *LANGUAGES:* English, Malay and Tamil.

A.S. CHANDRASEGARAM, born Melaka, Malaysia, July 29, 1936; admitted, 1992, Grays Inn; 1993, Malaysia. *Education:* B.A. (London University); LL.B. (Hons.) (London University); Barristers-at-Law (Grays Inn). Award A.M.N. *LANGUAGES:* English, Malay and Tamil.

NIK SAGHIR & ISMAIL

Established in 1978

28TH FLOOR, MENARA MAYBANK, JALAN TUN PERAK

50050 KUALA LUMPUR, MALAYSIA

Telephone: (603) 2325566

Facsimile: (603) 2388019

Mailing Address: P.O. Box 11680, Kuala Lumpur, Malaysia 50754

Kota Bharu, Kelantan Office: 2880-P, Taman Sri Setia, Jalan Mahmood, 15200. Telephone: (609) 7481078. Facsimile: (609) 7441922.

Shah Alam, Selangor Office: Lot 19, Level 1B, Plaza Perangsang, Persiaran Perbandaran, 4000. Telephone: (603) 5507700. Facsimile: (603) 5507600.

Johor Bahru, Johor Office: Unit 903, Level 9, Wisma LKN, 49 Jalan Wong Ah Fook, 80000. Telephone: (607) 2230889. Facsimile: (607) 2235998.

Privatization, Energy, Corporate, and Securities, Acquisitions and Take Overs, Taxation, Banking, Finance, Islamic Banking and Finance, Business and Commercial Law, Aviation, Shipping, Conveyancing, Property, Joint Ventures, Building Contracts, Legislative Practice, Trademarks, Railway Laws, Petroleum, Bankruptcy, Tax Appeals and Civil litigation.

MEMBERS OF FIRM

TAN SRI DATO' (DR.) ABDUL AZIZ BIN ABDUL RAHMAN, born 1933, Barrister-at-Law, Lincoln's Inn, London, 1967, admitted 1991, Malaysia. P.S.M., S.P.S.K., S.I.M.P., D.J.M.K., D.P.C.M., D.I.M.P., P.M.K., K.M.N., S.M.K., Hon. PhD (UUM), D.B.A. h/c (IMC), Hon. M.I.P.R., A.M.P. (Harvard), F.C.I.T. (United Kingdom), F.M.I.M., F.M.I.D.

NIK SAGHIR BIN MOHD NOOR, KMN, born 1933, Barrister-at-Law, Lincoln's Inn, London, 1964, admitted 1980, Malaysia.

(This Listing Continued)

NIK SAGHIR & ISMAIL, Kuala Lumpur—Continued

ISMAIL BIN IBRAHIM, born 1941, Barrister-at-Law, Lincoln's Inn, London, 1970, admitted 1974, Malaysia, Commissioner for Oaths, Notary Public.

NASIR ZIHNI BIN YUSOFF, born 1957, LL.B. (Hons) (London) Barrister-at-Law, Lincoln's Inn, London, 1983, admitted 1984, Malaysia, Diploma in Science (ITM).

MOHAMED BIN HAJI ABDUL HAMID, K.M.N., A.M.S., P.P.T., born 1936, LL.B. (Hons) Singapore, 1968, admitted 1991, Malaysia.

ASSOCIATES

ANG KIAN LENG, born 1934; admitted 1969, Malaysia.

MOHD. KASSIM BIN AHMED, born 1936; admitted 1975, Malaysia.

NOR HAMIAH ABD. HAMID HASANI, born 1964; admitted 1988, Malaysia.

ROGER TAN KOR MEE, born 1961; admitted 1989, Malaysia.

TAN WEE LI, born 1966; admitted 1991, Malaysia.

ROSMAWATI BT AB. WAHID, born 1967; admitted 1992, Malaysia.

TUAN ZUBAIDAH BT TUAN MUDA, born 1952; admitted 1992, Malaysia.

CINDY CHEW YOKE THING, born 1958; admitted 1992, Malaysia.

SITI ROSLINA BT MAT ARIS, born 1967; admitted 1992, Malaysia.

TAN SHEH-LYNN, born 1968; admitted 1992, Malaysia.

CHEE YIN MEI, born 1968; admitted 1992, Malaysia.

SHAMEER BIN OTHMAN, born 1969; admitted 1993, Malaysia.

ANG NYEE NYEE, born 1968; admitted 1993, Malaysia.

KHUAN WAI SHIR, born 1968; admitted 1993, Malaysia.

MAUREEN ONG SWEE KIN, born 1967; admitted 1993, Malaysia.

LIM GAY BIN, born 1969; admitted 1994, Malaysia.

SHEARN DELAMORE & CO.

Established in 1921

NO. 2, BENTENG
50050 KUALA LUMPUR, MALAYSIA
Telephone: (603) 2300644
Telex: JURES MA 30379
Fax: (603) 2385625; (603) 2382376

Civil Litigation, Arbitration, Building Contracts, Aviation Law, Shipping, Criminal Law, Insurance Law, Industrial Relations, Labour Law, Intellectual Property Patent and Trademark, Conveyancing, Banking, Corporate, Public Listing, Mergers and Acquisitions, Privatization, Joint Ventures, Immigration, Company Secretarial, Family Law, Income Tax, Sales Tax and Estate Duty.

FIRM PROFILE: *Shearn Delamore & Co. was first established as Ford & Delamore in 1921 and is one of the oldest and largest law firms in Malaysia. In 1938, it changed its name to Shearn Delamore & Co. The firm has 20 partners and 44 assistants practicing in two offices in Kuala Lumpur and Penang. Headed by senior partner, Dato' R.T.S. Khoo, the practice has seven departments: Conveyancing and Banking, Corporate Affairs, Intellectual Property Law, Labour and Industrial Relations, Taxation and Revenue Law, Litigation and Company Secretarial.*

PARTNERS

DATO R.T.S. KHOO, admitted, 1963, Malaysia, Barrister-at-Law, Lincoln's Inn. *LANGUAGES:* English and Malay. *PRACTICE AREAS:* Criminal Law; Civil Litigation.

DATO V.L. KANDAN, admitted, 1965, Malaysia, Barrister-at-Law, Lincoln's Inn. *LANGUAGES:* English and Malay. *PRACTICE AREAS:* Patent and Trademark Law.

S. WOODHULL, admitted, 1967, Malaysia, Barrister-at-Law, Inner Temple. *Education:* Malaya (B.A.). *LANGUAGES:* English and Malay. *PRACTICE AREAS:* Taxation Law.

(This Listing Continued)

V.T. NATHAN, admitted, 1969, Malaysia, Barrister-at-Law, Lincoln's Inn. *LANGUAGES:* English and Malay. *PRACTICE AREAS:* Industrial Relations.

CECIL W.M. ABRAHAM, admitted, 1970, Malaysia, Barrister-at-Law, Middle Temple. *Education:* London (LL.B., Hons.). *LANGUAGES:* English and Malay. *PRACTICE AREAS:* Civil Litigation; Arbitration; Shipping Law.

SANTHA B. MENON, admitted, 1965, Malaysia, Barrister-at-Law, Inner Temple. *LANGUAGES:* English and Malay. *PRACTICE AREAS:* Conveyancing; Banking Law.

RAHMAT JAMARI, admitted, 1976, Malaysia. *Education:* Singapore (LL.B.). *LANGUAGES:* English and Malay. *PRACTICE AREAS:* Corporate Law; Privatisation.

MICHAEL H.K. LIM, admitted, 1978, Malaysia. *Education:* Wellington (LL.B., LL.M). *LANGUAGES:* English and Malay. *PRACTICE AREAS:* Corporate Law; Mergers and Acquisitions.

WILFRED ABRAHAM, admitted, 1975, Malaysia, Barrister-at-Law, Middle Temple. *LANGUAGES:* English and Malay. *PRACTICE AREAS:* Building Contract Law; Arbitration; Civil Litigation.

S. RADHAKRISHNAN, admitted, 1979, Malaysia, Barrister-at-Law, Inner Temple. *LANGUAGES:* English and Malay. *PRACTICE AREAS:* Insurance Law; Civil Litigation.

WONG SAI FONG, admitted, 1980, Malaysia, Barrister-at-Law, Lincoln's Inn. *LANGUAGES:* English and Malay. *PRACTICE AREAS:* Patent and Trademark Law.

ROBERT LAZAR, admitted, 1980, Malaysia, Barrister-at-Law, Middle Temple. *Education:* London (LL.B., Hons.). *LANGUAGES:* English and Malay. *PRACTICE AREAS:* Civil Litigation; Aviation Law.

YEOH JIN AIK, admitted, 1980, Malaysia, Barrister-at-Law, Lincoln's Inn. *LANGUAGES:* English and Malay. *PRACTICE AREAS:* Civil Litigation.

LIM TEONG SIT, admitted, 1984, Malaysia. *Education:* Singapore (LL.B.). *LANGUAGES:* English and Malay. *PRACTICE AREAS:* Corporate Law; Banking Law.

TENG WEE MING, admitted, 1978, Malaysia, Barrister-at-Law, Lincoln's Inn. *LANGUAGES:* English and Malay. *PRACTICE AREAS:* Conveyancing; Banking Law.

PEH LEE KHENG, admitted, 1981, Malaysia, Barrister-at-Law, Gray's Inn. *Education:* Leicester (LL.B., Hons.). *LANGUAGES:* English and Malay. *PRACTICE AREAS:* Industrial Relations.

SAR SAU YEE, admitted, 1979, Malaysia, Barrister-at-Law, Lincoln's Inn. *LANGUAGES:* English and Malay. *PRACTICE AREAS:* Conveyancing; Banking Law.

FOO YET NGO, admitted, 1982, Malaysia, Barrister-at-Law, Gray's Inn. *Education:* Kent (B.A., Hons.). *LANGUAGES:* English and Malay. *PRACTICE AREAS:* Family Law; Civil Litigation.

N. SIVABALAH, admitted, 1984, Malaysia. *Education:* Malaya (LL.B., Hons.; U.M.). *LANGUAGES:* English and Malay. *PRACTICE AREAS:* Industrial Relations.

GRACE C.G. YEOH, admitted, 1985, Malaysia, Barrister-at-Law, Middle Temple. *Education:* London (LL.B., Hons.; LL.M. Hons.). *LANGUAGES:* English and Malay. *PRACTICE AREAS:* Corporate Law.

SENIOR LEGAL ASSISTANTS

P. JAYASINGAM, admitted, 1986, Malaysia, Barrister-at-Law, Gray's Inn. *Education:* London (LL.B., Hons; LL.M., Hons.). *LANGUAGES:* English and Malay. *PRACTICE AREAS:* Industrial Relations.

JEYANTHINI KANNAPERAN, admitted, 1986, Malaysia, Barrister-at-Law, Gray's Inn. *Education:* London (LL.B., Hons.). *LANGUAGES:* English and Malay. *PRACTICE AREAS:* Civil Litigation.

GOH KA IM, admitted, 1988, Malaysia, Barrister-at-Law, Gray's Inn. *Education:* Bristol (LL.B., Hons.). *LANGUAGES:* English and Malay. *PRACTICE AREAS:* Taxation Law.

RABINDRA S. NATHAN, admitted, 1987, Malaysia. *Education:* Cantuar, New Zealand (LL.B., Hons.); Cantab, England (LL.M., Hons.). *LANGUAGES:* English and Malay. *PRACTICE AREAS:* Civil Litigation.

LORRAINE CHEAH, admitted, 1988, Malaysia, Barrister-at-Law, Middle Temple. *Education:* Wales (LL.B., Hons.); New South Wales

(This Listing Continued)

(LL.M.). *LANGUAGES:* English and Malay. *PRACTICE AREAS:* Civil Litigation.

HARJEET SINGH, admitted, 1989, Malaysia, Barrister-at-Law, Lincoln's Inn. *Education:* Bucks (LL.B., Hons.). *LANGUAGES:* English and Malay. *PRACTICE AREAS:* Criminal Law; Civil Litigation.

CHRISTINA S.C. KOW, admitted, 1986, Malaysia. *Education:* Melbourne (LL.B.). *LANGUAGES:* English and Malay. *PRACTICE AREAS:* Corporate Law; Banking Law.

G. CHACKO VADAKETH, admitted, 1988, Malaysia, Barrister-at-Law, Lincoln's Inn. *Education:* Cantab, England (B.A., Hons.). *LANGUAGES:* English and Malay. *PRACTICE AREAS:* Civil Litigation; Medical Law; Negligence Law.

LEGAL ASSISTANTS

MEERA SAMANTHER, admitted, 1987, Malaysia, Barrister-at-Law, Middle Temple. *Education:* London (LL.B., Hons.; LL.M., Hons.). *LANGUAGES:* English and Malay. *PRACTICE AREAS:* Civil Litigation.

KAREN ABRAHAM, admitted, 1989, Malaysia. *Education:* Adelaide (LL.B.). *LANGUAGES:* English and Malay. *PRACTICE AREAS:* Patent and Trademark Law.

MAIDZUARA MOHAMMED, admitted, 1990, Malaysia, Barrister-at-Law, Gray's Inn. *Education:* London (LL.B., Hons.). *LANGUAGES:* English and Malay. *PRACTICE AREAS:* Civil Litigation.

RODNEY GOMEZ, admitted, 1990, Malaysia, Barrister-at-Law, Middle Temple. *Education:* London (LL.B., Hons.). *LANGUAGES:* English and Malay. *PRACTICE AREAS:* Building Contract Law; Arbitration.

FIONA SEQUERAH, admitted, 1990, Malaysia, Barrister-at-Law, Gray's Inn. *Education:* London (LL.B., Hons.). *LANGUAGES:* English and Malay. *PRACTICE AREAS:* Conveyancing; Banking Law.

THAVALINGAM THAVARAJAH, admitted, 1990, Malaysia, Barrister-at-Law, Gray's Inn. *Education:* London (LL.B., Hons.). *LANGUAGES:* English and Malay. *PRACTICE AREAS:* Industrial Relations.

KIRIN SHANTI MOGAN, admitted, 1990, Malaysia, Barrister-at-Law, Gray's Inn. *Education:* Bristol (LL.B., Hons.). *LANGUAGES:* English and Malay. *PRACTICE AREAS:* Civil Litigation.

SEE GUAT HAR, admitted, 1990, Malaysia, Barrister-at-Law, Middle Temple. *Education:* London (LL.B., Hons.). *LANGUAGES:* English and Malay. *PRACTICE AREAS:* Conveyancing; Banking Law.

WINSTON CHEN, admitted, 1990, Malaysia, Barrister-at-Law, Lincoln's Inn. *Education:* London (LL.B., Hons.). *LANGUAGES:* English and Malay. *PRACTICE AREAS:* Corporate Law.

ONG LEE LIAN, admitted, 1991, Malaysia, Barrister-at-Law, Inner Temple. *Education:* Essex (LL.B., Hons.). *LANGUAGES:* English and Malay. *PRACTICE AREAS:* Industrial Relations.

LINDA WANG, admitted, 1991, Malaysia, Barrister-at-Law, Gray's Inn. *Education:* Leeds (LL.B., Hons.). *PRACTICE AREAS:* Patent and Trademark Law.

AILEEN CHEW PENG LI, admitted, 1991, Malaysia, Barrister-at-Law, Gray's Inn. *Education:* London (LL.B., Hons.). *LANGUAGES:* English and Malay. *PRACTICE AREAS:* Conveyancing; Banking Law.

VICTOR LEAN, admitted, 1992, Malaysia, Barrister-at-Law, Middle Temple. *Education:* London (B.A., Hons.); Cantab (LL.M., Hons.). *LANGUAGES:* English and Malay. *PRACTICE AREAS:* Corporate Law.

DHINESH BHASKARAN, admitted, 1992, Malaysia, Barrister-at-Law, Gray's Inn. *Education:* Cantab (LL.B., Hons.; LL.M.). *LANGUAGES:* English and Malay. *PRACTICE AREAS:* Civil Litigation.

VICTOR PEH, admitted, 1992, Malaysia. *Education:* York (B.A., Hons.); Bucks (LL.B., Hons.). *LANGUAGES:* English and Malay. *PRACTICE AREAS:* Building Contract Law; Arbitration.

ARUN KRISHNALINGAM, admitted, 1992, Malaysia, Barrister-at-Law, Inner Temple. *Education:* London (LL.B., Hons.). *PRACTICE AREAS:* Civil Litigation; Shipping Law.

DAPHNE CHOY, admitted, 1993, Malaysia. *Education:* New South Wales, Australia (B.A., LL.B.). *LANGUAGES:* English and Malay. *PRACTICE AREAS:* Civil Litigation.

CHRISTINA C. W. SIEW, admitted, 1993, Malaysia. *Education:* Cantab (LL.B., Hons.). *LANGUAGES:* English and Malay. *PRACTICE AREAS:* Civil Litigation.

(This Listing Continued)

DOMINIC AW KIAN-WEE, admitted, 1993, Malaysia, Barrister-at-Law, Middle Temple. *Education:* University of Hull (LL.B., Hons). *LANGUAGES:* English and Malay. *PRACTICE AREAS:* Corporate Law.

PUTRI NOOR SHARIZA NOORDIN, admitted, 1993, Malaysia. *Education:* University of London (LL.B., 1990); University of Malaya (C.L.P., 1992). *LANGUAGES:* English and Malay. *PRACTICE AREAS:* Corporate Law.

ELISA CHONG SOO LEE, admitted, 1994, Malaysia. *Education:* Monash (LL.B). *LANGUAGES:* English and Malay. *PRACTICE AREAS:* Patent Law; Trademark Law.

SWEE-KEE NG, admitted, 1992, England and Wales; 1994, Malaysia. *Education:* Ohio Wesleyan University, Delaware, Ohio (B.A., 1975); University of Oxford (B.A., M.A., 1988-1991). *LANGUAGES:* English and Malay. *PRACTICE AREAS:* Conveyancing; Banking Law.

VIJAYAN VENUGOPAL, admitted, 1993, England; 1994, Malaysia. *Education:* University of London, London, England (LL.B, 1992); Middle Temple, London, England (1993). *LANGUAGES:* English and Malay. *PRACTICE AREAS:* Industrial Relations.

GURMEET KAUR SIDHU, admitted, 1992, England; 1994, Malaysia. *Education:* Hull University, London, England (LL.B., 1991); Gray's Inn, London, England (1992). *PRACTICE AREAS:* Civil Litigation.

LEE SEAN GOH, admitted, 1993, Malaysia. *Education:* University of Melbourne, Melbourne, Australia (B.Com., Accountancy; LL.B., Hons., 1992). *LANGUAGES:* English and Malay. *PRACTICE AREAS:* Corporate Law; Conveyancing.

CHUAH JERN ERIN, admitted, 1993, England and Wales; 1994, Malaysia. *Education:* Nottingham BPP Cadmus; Methodist College (A-Levels); University of Nottingham (LL.B., Hons.). *LANGUAGES:* English and Malay. *PRACTICE AREAS:* Trademark Law.

FELIX RAJ A/L AROKCASAMY, admitted, 1994, Malaysia. *Education:* University of London (LL.B., 1992). Lecturer, Banking Law, 1992-1993. *LANGUAGES:* English, Bahasa, Malay.

THAM KAM WAH, admitted, 1994, Malaysia. *Education:* Prime College (A-Levels, 1989); University of Hull (2nd Class Upper, 1992). *LANGUAGES:* English and Malay. *PRACTICE AREAS:* Corporate Law; Banking; Law; Conveyancing.

SIVAKUMARAN SUNITHA, born Ipoh, Malaysia. May 29, 1968; admitted, 1994, Malaysia. *Education:* Help College (LL.B., 1990); Poly of Wales (LL.B., 1992). *LANGUAGES:* English, Sahasa, Malaysia, Tamil. *PRACTICE AREAS:* Intellectual Property Law (Trademarks and Copyright).

MURALEEDHARAN T.N. NAIR, born Baham, Negeri Sembilan, Malaysia, June 23, 1953; admitted, 1995, Malaysia. *Education:* University of London, London, England (LL.B., with honors, 1992). *LANGUAGES:* English. *PRACTICE AREAS:* Litigation (Building Construction Arbitration).

Languages: Malay and English.

SHOOK LIN & BOK

20TH FLOOR, ARAB MALAYSIAN BUILDING
JALAN RAJA CHULAN
50200 KUALA LUMPUR, MALAYSIA
Telephone: (03) 2011788
Cable Address: Shobok
Telex: MA 30352
Facsimile: (603) 2011778; 2011779

Corporate, Acquisitions and Take Overs, Project Financing, Tax, Banking, Conveyancing, Joint Ventures, Insurance, Maritime and Shipping, Building Contracts, Trademarks, Copyrights, Patents, Designs, Civil Litigation, Labour and Industrial Litigation.

PARTNERS

DATO' PARAM CUMARASWAMY, (Barrister at Law, Inner Temple, London); admitted, 1967, Malaysia; 1971, Singapore.

HASHIM MAJID, (Barrister at Law, Lincoln's Inn, London); admitted, 1966, England; 1975, Malaysia.

TOO HING YEAP, (LL.B., Hons., Singapore, 1971); admitted, 1971, Malaysia.

(This Listing Continued)

SHOOK LIN & BOK, Kuala Lumpur—Continued

CYRUS V. DAS, (LL.B., Hons., Singapore); admitted, 1973, Malaysia.

PORRES P. ROYAN, (LL.B., Hons., Singapore, 1973); admitted, 1973, Malaysia.

LAI WING YONG, (LL.B., Hons., Singapore, 1975); admitted, 1975, Malaysia.

KATHERINE LIM SUI HONG, (MS), (LL.B., Hons., Singapore, 1965); admitted, 1966, Singapore; 1977, Malaysia.

PATRICIA SHARMILLA DAVID, (MS), (LL.B., Hons., Singapore, 1976); admitted, 1976, Malaysia.

NAGARAJAH MUTTIAH, (Barrister at Law, Lincoln's Inn, London); admitted, 1979, England; 1980, Malaysia.

ROMESH ABRAHAM, (LL.B., Hons., University of Southampton, 1982; Barrister at Law, Gray's Inn, London, 1983); admitted, 1984, Malaysia.

YOONG SIN MIN, (MS), (LL.B., Hons., Singapore); admitted, 1985, Malaysia.

YUEN KIT LEE, (MS), (LL.B., Hons., University of Malaya); admitted, 1985, Malaysia.

DR. ARJUNAN SUBRAMANIAM, (B.A. (Hons) (Malaya), LL.B., Hons., London, LL.M. (London). PH.D. Malaya, C.L.P. (Malaya); admitted 1992.

MICHAEL C.M. SOO, (LL.B., Hons., (London); Barrister at Law, Gray's Inn, London, Admitted 1985, Malaysia; 1993, Singapore.

JOHN MATHEW, (LL.B., Hons., University of Malaya); admitted, 1987, Malaysia.

HO YUE CHAN, (LL.B., Hons., Barrister at Law, Lincoln's Inn, London); admitted, 1987, Malaysia.

S. NANTHA BALAN, (LL.B., Hons., Buckingham, C.L.P.); admitted, 1988, Malaysia.

CONSULTANTS

MICHAEL KUAN LEE WONG, (LL.B., Hons., Singapore, 1962); admitted 1964, Malaysia.

ASSOCIATES

HOH KIAT CHING, (MS), (LL.B., Hons., Leeds; Barrister-at-Law, (Lincoln's Inn); LL.M., (Commercial & Corporate Law), King's College, London); admitted, 1989, Malaysia.

KHONG MEI LIN, (MS), (LL.B., Hons., University of Adelaide, G.D.L.P.); admitted, 1989, Malaysia.

CHONG SU-SAN, (MS), (LL.B., Hons., Bristol, Barrister at Law, London); admitted, 1990, Malaysia.

DEBORAH JASWINDER KAUR, (MS), (B.A., (Economics) LL.B., University of London, Barrister-at-Law, Lincoln's Inn) admitted, 1991, Malaysia.

HO PHUAY LING, (MS), (LL.B., Hons., University of Malaya); admitted, 1989, Malaysia.

KAREN KAUR, (MS), (LL.B., Hons., University of Malaya) admitted 1991, Malaysia.

DAVINDER KAUR, (MS), (B.A. Hons., M.A., University of Malaya; LL.B., Hons., University of London, C.L.P.); admitted, 1991, Malaysia.

LEE WOOI MEIN, (MS), (B.Sc., University of Melbourne, LL.B., Hons.; University of London, C.L.P.); admitted, 1991, Malaysia.

MOHANADASS KANAGASABAI, (LL.B., Hons., University of Buckingham, C.L.P.); admitted, 1991, Malaysia.

MICHAEL CHAI WOON CHEW, (B.Sc., Hons., University of Surrey, LL.B., Hons. (University of Buckingham, Barrister-at-Law, Lincoln's Inn)); admitted, 1991, Malaysia.

LAU MAY LING, (MS), (B.Ec, LL.B., University of Monash); admitted, 1990, Victoria; 1991, Malaysia.

LILIAN LIEW MAY SIM, (MS), (B.Ec, (Accounting), LL.B., Hons., University of Monash); admitted, 1992, Malaysia.

GEETHA SIVAPATHASUNDRAM, (MS), (LL.B., Hons., University of Wales., Barrister-at-Law, Lincoln's Inn); admitted, 1992, Malaysia.

(This Listing Continued)

KENNETH CHINSON ST. JAMES, (B. Comm (Finance), LL.B., University of New South Wales, Australia); admitted, 1991, New South Wales; 1992, Malaysia.

STEVEN THIRUNEELAKANDAN, (LL.B., Hons., University of Leicester., Barrister-at-Law, Middle Temple); admitted, 1992, Malaysia.

JALALULLAIL OTHMAN, (LL.B., Hons., University of London, C.L.P.); admitted 1992, Malaysia.

KONG PIK FOONG, (MS), B.A. (Keele), Barrister (Middle Temple); admitted 1992, Malaysia.

KINGTON TONG KUM LOONG, (LL.B., Hons., King's College London, Barrister at Law, Gray's Inn); admitted 1993, Malaysia.

LEONG YUE HONG, (LL.B., Hons., University of London, Barrister at Law, Lincoln's Inn); admitted, 1985, London, 1986, Malaysia.

SUSHEILA ANNE SREEDHARAN, (MS), (LL.B., Hons., University of Leicester, CLP), admitted 1993, Malaysia.

MICHELE K. LIM, (MS), (LL.B., Hons., University of Wales, Aberystwyth, Barrister at Law, Middle Temple); admitted, 1993, Malaysia.

LIM CHEE KHANG, (LL.B., Hons., LSE., University of London, Barrister at Law, Lincoln's Inn); admitted, 1993, Malaysia.

LIM AI LEEN, (MS), (LL.B., University of Birmingham, Barrister at Law, Middle Temple); admitted, 1993, Malaysia.

KATHLEEN KOH SIOK SIEN, (MS), (B.EC., LL.B., Monash University, Australia); admitted, 1993, Malaysia.

LAURA HO THANT THEANG, (MS), (LL.B., Hons. (Bristol), LL.M., University of Cambridge, Barrister at Law, Gray's Inn); admitted, 1993, Malaysia.

PUNITHAVATHY KANDIAH, (MS), (LL.B., Hons., University of Warwick); admitted, 1993, Malaysia.

TAN CHEE LING, (MS), (B.Ec., Accounting, LL.B., Monash University; Advocate and Solicitor of the Supreme Court of Victoria, Australia); admitted 1993, Malaysia.

GEETA GNANARAJAH, (MS), (LL.B., Hons., University of Warwick; C.L.P. Hons., University of Malaya); admitted, 1994, Malaysia.

SHANTHI C. SOMASKANTHAN, (MS), (LL.B., Hons., University Hull, C.L.P.); admitted 1994, Malaysia.

YAP JER YEE, (MS), (B.Sc., LL.B., Monash University, Australia); admitted 1992, Malaysia.

AZLINDA EZRINA ARIFFIN, (MS), (LL.B., Hons., University of Wales, Cardiff, Barrister at Law, Gray's Inn, London); admitted 1993, England and Wales; 1994, Malaysia.

TENG CHONG MOI, (MS), (LL.B., Hons., University of London, C.L.P.; B.B.A., Hons.; University Kebangsaan Malaysia); admitted, 1994, Malaysia.

RAMESH KUMAR KUMARAGURU, (LL.B., Hons., University of London, C.L.P.); admitted, 1994, Malaysia.

ENG TIONG MEI, (MS), (LL.B., Hons., University of Wolverhampton, C.L.P.); admitted, 1994, Malaysia.

MEERA BADMANARAN, (MS), (LL.B., Hons., LL.M., London School of Economics, C.L.P.); admitted, 1994, Malaysia.

WONG CHI KIT, (MS), (B.A., LL.B., University of Otago, Diploma in Shariah Law; International Islamic University, Diploma in Business Law; National University of Singapore); admitted, 1991, Malaysia.

CHAN KIM HONG AGNES, (MS), (Acis, LL.B., University of London, C.L.P.); admitted, 1994, Malaysia.

MICHAEL TOH HOON WOOI, (B.Comm, (Accounting), LL.B., University of New South Wales, Australia); admitted, 1992, New South Wales, Australia; 1995, Malaysia.

RABINDRAN THAVER, (LL.B., (Hons.), Wales, C.L.P.); admitted, 1995, Malaysia.

SKRINE & CO

STRAITS TRADING BUILDING
NO. 4, LEBOH PASAS BESAR
P.O. BOX 10987
50732 KUALA LUMPUR, MALAYSIA
Telephone: 03-2945111 (25 lines)
Telex: Skrine MA 30949
Facsimile: 03-2934327 (3 lines)
Tele gram: "SKRINCO"

Corporate, Acquisitions and Take-Overs, Tax, Banking, Conveyancing, Joint Ventures, Insurance, Shipping, Building Contracts, Trademarks, Copyrights, Patents, Designs, Civil Litigation, Labour and Industrial Litigation.

PARTNERS

CHIN YOONG CHONG

CHEN KAH LENG, LL.B. (S'pore).

WONG CHONG WAH, LL.B.

DATUK D.J. PUTHUCHEARY, LL.B. (Belfast).

BURHANUDDIN TAJUDIN

K. ANANTHAM, LL.B. (S'pore).

LEE TATT BOON

VINAYAK P. PRADHAN, LL.B. (S'pore).

TOMMY THOMAS

THERESA CHONG, LL.B. (S'pore).

SHAMSUL-BAHRAIN BIN IBRAHIM

KOK CHEE KHEONG, LL.B. (Malaya).

PHILIP T.N. KOH, LL.B. (Malaya); LL.M. (Lond.).

AMBIGA SREENEVASAN, LL.B. (Exxon).

WONG CHEE LIN, M.A. (Oxon).

LOOI LAI HENG, B.Ec., LL.B. (Monash).

NALLINI PATHMANATHAN, B.Sc. (Lond.).

CONSULTANTS

DATO DR PETER MOONEY, M.A., LL.B., LL.D. (Glas.).

KWOK YOKE HOW

ASSISTANTS

LIM SOO KENG, LL.B. (Lond.).

JEANNE LEE GAIK IM, LL.B. (Man.); LL.M. (Lond.).

CHARANJEET KAUR KANG, LL.B.

CHARMAYNE ONG POH YIN, LL.B.

KHOO GUAN HUAT, LL.B. (Malaya).

QUAY CHEW SOON, LL.B., LL.M. (S'pore).

PETER PEREIRA, LL.B. (Lond.).

CHOONG SHAW MEI, LL.B. (Malaya).

SAIDAH RASTAM, LL.B. (Essex).

LEONG WAI HONG, LL.B. (S'pore).

LIM BOON KONG, LL.B. (S'pore).

MUBASHIR BIN MANSOR, LL.B. (Essex).

LEE SIEW CHOO

CHUNG WAI SEE, B. Econ., LL.B. (Monash).

ANNA G. VADAKETH, LL.B. (Lond.).

CHENG KEE CHECK, LL.B. (S'pore).

VINAYAGA RAJ RAJARATHNAM, LL.B. (Man.).

SITPAH SELVARATNAM, LL.B. (Wales); LL.M. (Cantab.).

TIMOTHY Y.H. SIAW, B.Sc., LL.B. (Monash).

PANG TENG WAH, B.Ec., LL.B. (Monash).

NG KIT FONG, LL.B. (Melb.).

(This Listing Continued)

IVAN Y.F. LOO, LL.B. (Bristol).

SELVI NACHIAPPAN, LL.B. (Lond.).

ISHAR ISMAIL, LL.B. (Man.).

GANESA K. SINNADURAI

SAM CHOONG KHUAT YAU, LL.B. (Lond.).

TREVOR JASON MARK PADASIAN, B.A., LL.B. (ANU).

LIM CHEE WEE, B.Comm., LL.B. (UNSW).

LOO FOONG MENG, LL.B. (Malaya).

PEARL W.K. LIM, B.Ec. (Adel.); LL.B. (Melb.).

SUFIAN BIN JUSOH, LL.B. (UWCC).

DANIEL TAN CHUN HAO, B. Eng., LL.B.

YEW YEE TEE, LL.B. (Malaya).

CHENG MAI, LL.B. (Malaya).

SU PUAY LENG, LL.B. (Malaya).

FAIZAH JAMALUDIN, LL.B. (Brunel); LL.M. (Southampton).

JANINI RAJESWARAN, LL.B. (Hull); LL.M. (Bristol).

DOUGLAS W.L. YEE, LL.B. (Man.).

MEGAT NOOR ISHAK BIN MEGAT IBRAHIM, (AMN).

TAI FOONG LAM, LL.B. (Lond.).

SHANKAR GUNARATNAM, LL.B. (Lond.).

BELDEN PREMARAJ, LL.B. (Liverpool).

MONGOLIA

ARNBERGER, KIM, BUXBAUM & CHOY

ULAANBAATAR, SUPREME COURT BUILDING
ROOM 429, 431 & 432
ULAANBAATAR, MONGOLIA
Telephone: (976) (1) 310-711
Facsimile: (976) (1) 325-102

REVISER OF THE PEOPLE'S REPUBLIC OF CHINA AND MONGOLIA LAW DIGESTS FOR THIS DIRECTORY.

Hong Kong Office: 3201 Citibank Tower, 3 Garden Road, Central. Telephone: (852) 2523-7001. Fax: (852) 2845-0947.

Beijing (Peking), People's Republic of China Office: China World Trade Centre, Suite 2523, No. 1 Jian Guo Men Wai Avenue. Telephone: (86)(1) 505-2288 Ext: 2523. Fax: (86)(1) 505-2638.

Guangzhou (Canton), People's Republic of China Office: China Hotel Office Tower, Suite 512. Telephone: (86)(20) 666-3388. Ext. 2512. Fax: (86)(20) 669-1217.

Xiamen, People's Republic of China Office: Foreign Trade Centre, Suite 519, No. 15 Hu Bing North Road, Xiamen City. Telephone: (86)(592) 506-3059. Facsimile: (86)(592) 511-1044 Ext. 519.

Shenzhen, People's Republic of China Office: Shenzhen Development Center, Suite 2103, Renmin Nan Lu, Shenzhen. Telephone: (86)(755) 229-8009. Facsimile: (86)(755) 229-8011.

Shanghai, People's Republic of China Office: 7th Floor, Block 2, Jing Ming Building, No. 8 Zun Yi Road, Shanghai. Telephone: (86)(21) 219-4180. Facsimile: (86)(21) 219-7421.

New York Office: 100 Maiden Lane, 16th Floor, Suite 1600B, New York, New York 10038. Telephone: (212) 504-6109. Fax: (212) 412-7016.

San Francisco Office: 44 Montgomery Street, Suite 500, San Francisco 94104. Telephone: (415) 955-0553. Fax: (415) 753-1235.

Los Angeles Office: 3731 Wilshire Boulevard, Suite 910, West Tower, Los Angeles, California, 90010. Telephone: (213) 380-7780. Facsimile: (310) 358-7780; (213) 380-5798.

Alhambra Office: 320 South Garfield, Suite 206, Alhambra, California 91801. Telephone: (818) 281-9088. Fax: (818) 281-7189.

Corporate, Employment Law, Commodities, Securities, Complex Commercial Litigation, International Transactions, Intellectual Property, Aircraft and Equipment Leasing Financing and Taxation.

(This Listing Continued)

ARNBERGER, KIM, BUXBAUM & CHOY,
Ulaanbaatar—Continued

MEMBERS OF FIRM

DAVID C. BUXBAUM, born New York, N.Y., July 16, 1933; admitted, 1970, New York and U.S. District Court, Southern, Eastern, Northern and Western Districts of New York; 1971, U.S. Court of Appeals, Second Circuit; 1974, U.S. Supreme Court; 1975, U.S. Court of Appeals, Seventh Circuit and Fourth Circuits; 1978, U.S. Court of Appeals, Eighth Circuit; 1979, U.S. Court of Appeals, First Circuit; 1981, California; 1989, U.S. District Court, Central District of California; 1991, U.S. District Court, Northern District of California; U.S. Court of Appeals, Ninth Circuit (Not admitted in Mongolia). *Education:* New York University (B.A., 1954); University of Michigan (J.D., 1959) concurrent graduate studies, University of Michigan Graduate School; graduate study, Harvard University and University of Washington (M.A., 1963; Ph.D., 1968). Member, Far East Honor Society, University of Michigan. Author: *Articles:* "Preliminary Trends in the Development of the Legal Institutions of Communist China and the Nature of the Criminal Law," International and Comparative Law Quarterly, January, 1962, reprinted in *Government of Communist China,* Chandler, San Francisco, 1966; "Horizontal and Vertical Influences Upon the Substantive Criminal Law of Mainland Chinese, Some Preliminary Observations," Osteuropa Recht, No. 1, 1964; "Chinese Family Law in Common Law Setting: A Note on the Institutional Environment and the Substantive Family Law of the Chinese in Malaysia and Singapore," Journal of Asian Studies, August, 1966; "Some Aspects of Civil Procedure and Practice at the Trial Level in Tanshui and Hsinchu...," XXX Journal of Asian Studies, 1971; *Lawyer's Challenge in China Trade: New and Developing Legal System,* New York Law Journal, International Law Finance and Trade, February, 1979; *Commodities Trade with China,* New York Law Journal, December, 1978; *Regulation of Commodity Futures Exchanges in Japan,* New York Law Journal, October, 1978; *Commodities Transactions in China and Hong Kong,* New York Law Journal, June, 1978; *Jurisdiction Over Foreign Transactions and Foreign Nationals,* New York Law Journal, April, 1978; *Two Cases of Dispute Settlement,* U.S.-China Business Review, Vol. 1, No. 2, March/April, 1974; *Two Cases of Dispute Settlement,* Arbitration and Dispute Settlement in Trade with China, Special Report No. 4 for Members of the National Council for United States-China Trade, February, 1974; *Negotiation with the Chinese,* Trade with China, 1973; *American Trade with the People's Republic of China: Some Preliminary Perspectives,* Columbia Journal of Transnational Law, Vol. 12, No. 1, 1973; *Liability of Federal Officials in Damage for Acts Unconstitutional or in Excess of their Authority; Expanding the Concept of the Rule of Law,* Capital University Law Review, Vol. 8, Issue 4, 1979; *Taking on the Government Alone; Sole Practitioner Battles Way to Supreme Court and Wins,* Legal Times of Washington, December, 1978; *Disclosure of Management Remuneration, Transaction, Litigation and Employment History,* Los Angeles Daily Journal, March, 1979; *Contracts in China,* China Trade, Praeger, 1982. Monthly Columnist, New York Law Journal on Commodities Law, 1976-1982; *Contract Law in China, The Dynamics of Statutory Development and Practice,* Doing Business in China, 1990, Streng et al, ed. Contracts in China during the Qing Dynasty: Key to the Civil Law, Journal of Oriental Studies, University of Hong Kong, 1993. *The Commercial Laws of China,* and *Patents Law and Practice, Trademark Law and Practice, The People's Republic of China,* Digest of the Commercial Laws of the World, 1982-1993. *M.A. Dissertation:* "Legal Institutions of Contemporary Mainland China," University of Washington, 1962. *Ph.D. Dissertation:* Some Aspects of Substantive Family Law and Social Change in Rural China, 1896-1967," University of Washington, 1968. *Case Note:* "Freedom of Marriage in a Pluralistic Society," Malaya Law Review, 1963. Editor: *Traditional and Modern Legal Institutions in Asia and Africa, Journal of Asian and African Studies,* Supplement Edition, 1967; *Family Law and Customary Law in Asia: A Contemporary Legal Perspective,* 1968; *Law and Social Change: A Case Study of Family Law and Social Change in China and Other Developing Areas,* University of Washington Press, 1978; *Transition and Permanence: Chinese History and Culture, A Festschrift in Honor of Dr. Kung-Chan Hsiao,* 1971; *Chinese Family Law and Social Change in Historic and Comparative Perspective,* University of Washington Press, 1978; *China Trade: Prospects and Perspectives,* Prager, 1982; Sole Counsel for Successful Respondents, *Butz v. Economou,* 438 US 478, 1978. Associate Professor, Chinese Law, Comparative Law and Domestic Relations, University of Washington, 1968-1969. Assistant Lecturer, Chinese Law, Domestic Relations, Labor Law, Jurisprudence, Comparative Law, University of Singapore, 1963-1964. Adjunct Professor of Law: Touro Law School, 1980; Southwestern University School of Law, 1983-1988. Member, Commission on Labor Law, Singapore, 1963-1964. Member, Panel of Arbitrators, American Arbitration Association. *Member:* American Bar Association

(This Listing Continued)

(Member, Committee on Far Eastern Law, Section of International and Comparative Law, 1965-1971); New York Trial Lawyers Association (Member, Liaison Committee with Judicial Conference, 1971-1978). *LANGUAGES:* Chinese, French, German and Japanese (specialized reading). *PRACTICE AREAS:* International Law; Complex International Litigation; Complex International Contract; Joint Venture Contract; Investment Law; Trademark, Copyright and Patent Protection and Enforcement; Commodities and Securities.

KENNETH Y. CHOY, born Hong Kong, May 24, 1956; admitted, 1987, New York; U.S. District Court, Southern and Eastern Districts of New York; 1990, California; 1991, Central and Northern Districts of California and U.S. Court of Appeals, 9th Circuit (Not admitted in Mongolia). *Education:* San Francisco State University (B.A., 1977); Northeastern University (J.D., 1986). Judicial Intern to Hon. Dolores K. Sloviter, U.S. Court of Appeals for the Third Circuit, 1985-1986. *Member:* American Bar Association (Member, Section on Labor and Employment Law); American Immigration Lawyers Association. (New York Office). *LANGUAGES:* Chinese (Cantonese and Mandarin). *PRACTICE AREAS:* Litigation and Transactions in U.S. and People's Republic of China.

H. BENNETT ARNBERGER, born Globe, Arizona, July 8, 1953; admitted, 1983, California and U.S. District Court, Northern and Central Districts of California. *Education:* University of California at Berkeley (A.B., with honors and distinction, 1977); University of San Francisco (J.D., 1983). Phi Delta Phi. Author: "Ensuring Compliance Through Intellectual Property Audits," 5 International Legal Strategy 54 (1994); "Avoiding The Hidden Liabilities of Independent Contractors," I Foreign Assignments (Kaigai Chuzai) 99 (1994); "Proactive Prevention of Cross-Cultural Disputes," 6 International Legal Strategy 60 (1994); "Protecting Against Misappropriation of Trade Secrets," 10 International Legal Strategy 63 (1993); "Taxation and Legal Requirements of California Corporations," 16 International Business Law Journal (Kokusai Shoji Homu) 202 (1988). Associate, Yuasa & Hara, Tokyo, Japan, 1987-1989. Contract Administrator, Chemsult AG, Saudi Arabia, 1977-1980. *Member:* San Francisco and American (Member, Section on International Law) Bar Associations; State Bar of California; International Bar Association (Member, Section on Business Law); Japan Society of Northern California; California-Southeast Asia Business Association; American Chamber of Commerce in Japan (Member, Committee on Licensing, Patents & Trademarks, 1987-1989). (San Francisco Office).

DAVID S. KIM, born Seoul, South Korea, February 17, 1961; admitted, 1990, California and U.S. District Court, Northern and Central Districts of California. *Education:* Western Illinois University (B.B.A., 1983; M.B.A., 1985); Southwestern University School of Law, Los Angeles (J.D., 1989). Recipient, Bradley and Pollack Scholarship, 1990. *Member:* State Bar of California; California Trial Lawyers Association; Los Angeles Trial Lawyers Association; California Korean Bar Association. (Los Angeles Office). *LANGUAGES:* English and Korean. *PRACTICE AREAS:* Litigation; Real Estate.

DOUGLAS L. BRYAN, born Whittier, California, September 7, 1960; admitted, 1991, California and U.S. District Court, Central District of California; 1992, U.S. Court of Appeals, Ninth Circuit. *Education:* California Polytechnic State University (B.S., 1983); Southwestern University School of Law (J.D., 1991). *Member:* State Bar of California; American Bar Association. (Los Angeles Office). *PRACTICE AREAS:* Tax Law; Corporate Law; Corporate Reorganizations; Constitutional Law; Insurance.

ROBERT W. MULCAHY, born Boston, Massachusetts, May 8, 1940; admitted, 1970, New York; 1971, District of Columbia; 1976, California; 1991, State Bar of Texas. *Education:* Boston College (B.S., Chemistry, 1963); George Washington University (J.D., 1968). *Member:* District of Columbia; State Bar of California; American Bar Association; The Licensing Executive Society. The Houston Volunteer Lawyers Association; Houston Intellectual Property Law Association. (Alhambra Office). *PRACTICE AREAS:* Intellectual Property; Patent Agent; Copyright Law; Trademark Law; Trade Secrets and Licensing.

OF COUNSEL

DEBORAH S. CHEW, born Singapore, May 27, 1964; admitted, 1988, Singapore; 1991, California. *Education:* National University of Singapore (LL.B., with honors, 1987). Associate, Arthur Loke & Partners, Singapore, 1988-1991. *Member:* State Bar of California; American Immigration Lawyers Association; Singapore American Business Association (Founding Member and Director); Hong Kong Association of California (Director); Asian Business Association; Law Society of Singapore and Academy of Law of Singapore. (San Francisco Office). *LANGUAGES:* English and Chinese (Mandarin, Cantonese, Taiwanese and Chiu-chow dialect).

(This Listing Continued)

CHRISTINA Y. CHEN, born Canton, China, May 2, 1943; admitted, 1983, California. *Education:* San Francisco State University (B.A., 1969); Hastings College of the Law, University of California (J.D., 1979). (Of Counsel, San Francisco, California Office). *LANGUAGES:* English and Chinese (Mandarin, Cantonese and Toisan dialect).

ROGER S. SAXTON, born Martins Ferry, Ohio, April 30, 1952; admitted, 1979, Sweden (as Jurist); 1980, Pennsylvania and U.S. District Court, Western District of Pennsylvania; 1992, New South Wales, Australia. *Education:* Case Western Reserve University (J.D., 1979); Studies in Japanese Law, Sophia University and University of Tokyo, Tokyo, Japan (1977-1980); Studies in Australian Law, University of Sydney (1989-1991). *Member:* Pennsylvania Bar Association; Law Society of New South Wales; Inter Pacific Bar Association. (Of Counsel, Sydney, Australia). *LANGUAGES:* English, Swedish and Japanese.

KAZUKO ITOH, born Tokyo, Japan, January 17, 1923; admitted, 1959, Japan (Not admitted in the U.S.). *Education:* Tsuda College; Tokyo Bunrika University. Legal Advisor to Her Britanic Majesty's Ambassador, Tokyo, 1976—. Legal Consultant to the American Embassy, Tokyo, 1976—. *Member:* Tokyo Bar Association; International Bar Association. (Of Counsel, Tokyo, Japan). *LANGUAGES:* Japanese, English, French and Spanish. *PRACTICE AREAS:* General Civil and Trial Practice; International Arbitration; Patent Litigation.

DUCK-SOON CHANG, born Korea, July 23, 1960; admitted, 1985, Korea and Korea Patent Bar; 1991, New York; 1992, California. *Education:* Judicial Training and Research Institute of the Supreme Court of Korea (198 3-1984); College of Law, Seoul National University (B.Jur,. 1983); Harvard Law School (LL.M., 1990). Author: "Technology Transfer, Cooperation and Joint Venture Agreements with Korea", Chapter 4 of Legal Aspects of Business Transactions and Investment in the Far East (Kluwer, 1988); "Arbitration Procedures in Korea," Vol. 1, Asia Law and Practice 7 (1989); "Arbitration in South Korea," Vol. 14 East Asian Executive Reports 1 (1992). Lecturer, International Patent Training and Research Institute of the Korean Industrial Property Office. Arbitrator, Korean Commercial Arbitration Board. *Member:* New York State and American Bar Associations; State Bar of California; Korean Bar Association; Korean Patent Bar Association; International Trademark Association. (Of Counsel, Seoul, Korea). *LANGUAGES:* Korean, English, Japanese (reads only). *PRACTICE AREAS:* Joint Venture; Licensing; Commercial Arbitration; Intellectual Property.

ASSOCIATES

DR. GALDANGIIN SOVD, born Mongolia, July 13, 1930; admitted, 1963, Mongolia. *Education:* Sverdlovsk Law Institute, USSR (B.A.,1963); Moscow State University, Law Department (J.D., 1973). Lecturer, Mongolian State University. Author: Books, Criminal Law Textbook, 1966; Criminal Law Textbook, 1975; Criminal Law Courts, 1973; Criminal Law (Part I, 1978); Criminal Law (Part II, 1983); Criminal Law Commentary, 1982; Commentary, 1989. Investigator and Judge, 1954-1959. Head of the Law Department of the Mongolia State University, 1963-1973. First Deputy Chairman of the Mongolian Supreme Court, 1973-1979. Head of the Department, Presidium of the Great People's Khural (Parliament, 1979-1984). Head of the Law Department of the Mongolian State University, 1984-1989. Director, Institute of State and Law, Academy of Sciences, 1989—. (Mongolia Office). *LANGUAGES:* Russian. *PRACTICE AREAS:* Russian Law.

DACHTCEREN ENKHBOLD, born Ulaanbaatar, Mongolia, March 11, 1946; admitted, 1973, Mongolia;. *Education:* International Relations Institute of Moscow (expert of Western Countries - U.S.A., Canada); Mongolian State University (Teacher of English Language). *LANGUAGES:* Russian, English. *PRACTICE AREAS:* Economic Entities and Foreign Investment, Civil Law.

BYAMBAA BAYARMAA, born Moscow, Russia, November 6, 1960; admitted, 1982, Mongolia; (Not Admitted in the United States). *Education:* Moldova State University, Law Faculty, 1982; Passed State Examination on Bar Practice, March, 1994. *LANGUAGES:* Russian, German, Romania, English. *PRACTICE AREAS:* Commercial and Contract Law.

VINCENT I.S. HSIEH, born Taipei, Taiwan, January 15, 1964; admitted, 1993, New York. *Education:* National Taiwan University (LL.B.) 1987) Boston University (LL.M., in International Banking, 1992). *Member:* American Bar Association; New York County Lawyers Association. (New York Office). *LANGUAGES:* Mandarin Chinese.

ZHOUGEN LI, born Shunde, Guangdong Province, PRC, October 1, 1935; (Not admitted in the United States). *Education:* Yue Xue Teachers

Training College. 1985-1991, Judge (ret.) Guangzhou Middle People's Court, Civil Division and Director of Administration. Recipient, 1984, 1985 Guangzhou City Court Systems Advance Specialist of the Year; 1988, Guangdong Province Outstanding Judge of the year; 1989 Third Degree Honor awarded by the Guangdong Province High Court. *LANGUAGES:* Chinese (Mandarin and Cantonese). *PRACTICE AREAS:* Litigation; Contract; Intellectual Property.

YAOWU RONG, born Wei Chen County, Ji Bei, March 19, 1979; admitted, 1993, China; (Not admitted in the United States). *Education:* Xiamen University (B.A., 1992); (Now Mid. Graduated College of Xiamen University). (Xiamen Office). *LANGUAGES:* Chinese, English. *PRACTICE AREAS:* Civil Law; Commercial Law.

YUAN JIANG, born Fujian Province, China, April 15, 1956; admitted, 1983, China (Not admitted in the United States). *Education:* China University of Political Science and Law, 1979-1983; Part-time graduate student at China University of Political Science and Law, international private law, 1986-1989. Cadre at Research Department, China Lawyer Association, 1989-1990. Reporter, China Lawyer Magazine, 1990-1993. (Beijing Office). *LANGUAGES:* Chinese. *PRACTICE AREAS:* Labor Law; Leasing; Litigation.

XIAODONG HAO, born Inner Mongolia, China, March 9, 1965; admitted, 1990, China (Not admitted in the United States). *Education:* Inner Mongolia University (B.S.); China University of Political Science and Law (LL.B., 1991). (Beijing Office). *LANGUAGES:* Chinese, English, Japanese. *PRACTICE AREAS:* Litigation; Business Law; Intellectual Property.

SIYANG LIAO, born Shanghai Province, China, April 15, 1970. *Education:* China Political/Legal University (L.L.B., 1992). (Beijing Office). *LANGUAGES:* English, Chinese. *PRACTICE AREAS:* Contract Law; Joint Venture Law; Intellectual Property Law.

PEIZHONG GAN, born China, May 8, 1956; admitted, 1988, China (not admitted in the United States). *Education:* The Department of Law, Beijing University (LL.B., 1983; LL.M., 1989). Chief Editor, Encyclopedia of Commercial Law of China and the Encyclopedia of Corporate Law. Author: 21 articles and 3 books, e.g. "Legal Issues on Contracting Management in the Enterprises Owned by the Whole People," "Several Legal Issues on Corporate Reorganization in China". Lecturer, 1988. Associate Professor, 1994. Lectures on Corporate and Companies Law, 1984-1985. Assessor in the Beijing Intermediate Court. (Beijing Office). *LANGUAGES:* Chinese, English. *PRACTICE AREAS:* Corporate Law; Commercial Law; Litigation; Intellectual Property.

JIANXIN LI, born Jiangmen, China, October, 1966; admitted, 1988, China (Not admitted in the United States). *Education:* Guangzhou University (Law Department, 1984-1986); Zhongshan University (Economic Management Department, 1987-1990). Attorney, Guangzhou Second Foreign Economic Law Office, 1986-1990. (Guangzhou Office). *LANGUAGES:* English, Chinese (Mandarin and Cantonese). *PRACTICE AREAS:* Intellectual Property Litigation; Contracts; Real Estate; Trade; Insurance Law; Adoption Law.

YIKUN ZHU, born Sichuan Province, China, August 1967; admitted, 1993, China (Not admitted in the United States). *Education:* Southwest College of Politics & Law (L.L.M., 1991). [Chinese, Russian, French, and English]. (Guangzhou Office). *PRACTICE AREAS:* Foreign Investment; Securities Law; Company Law; Intellectual Property; Tax Law; International Trade Dispute; Contracts.

JIANXIONG HUANG, born Rongyan City, Fujian, January 15, 1964; admitted, 1987 (Not admitted in the United States). *Education:* South-West Politics & Law College (B.A., 1984); College of Xiamen University (Master of Law, 1990). (Xiamen Office). *LANGUAGES:* Chinese, Taiwanese, English. *PRACTICE AREAS:* Civil Law; Commercial Law; Investment Law; Real Estate Law.

MINGLIANG LAN, born Hainan Province, China, August 12, 1927; admitted, 1989 (Not admitted in the United States). *Education:* Beijing Zhengfa University of Politics and Law (1956). Publications: Outline of Administrative Law; General Situation of International Organization; International Constitution (Teaching Material); Outline and Guidance on International Law. *Member:* Asian-Africa Development Committee, China International Legal Study Committee; National Lawyer Committee; China-Hong Kong Law Study Committee; China Investment Consultancy Experts Committee; China Political and Legal Management Leaders Institution; China Trade Committee; Foreign Economic and Trade Arbitration Committee (Arbitrator); National Overseas Federation Legal Consultant Committee. (Shenzhen Office). *LANGUAGES:* Chinese, English. *PRACTICE AREAS:* Public International Law; Intellectual Property.

(This Listing Continued)

(This Listing Continued)

ARNBERGER, KIM, BUXBAUM & CHOY,
Ulaanbaatar—Continued

ALFRED YONG LIN, born Fuzhou, China, October 10, 1969; admitted, 1993, China (not admitted in the United States). *Education:* Xiamen University Law Department (B.A., 1992). (Shanghai Office). *LANGUAGES:* Chinese, English and Fuzhou. *PRACTICE AREAS:* General Civil Law; International Investment; Corporation Law.

HONGLIANG WU, born Shanghai, China, 1935; admitted, 1985, China; registered patent agent (not admitted in the United States). *Education:* Beijing Iron and Steel Institute (B.S., 1960). (Shanghai Office). *LANGUAGES:* Chinese (Shanghai dialect) and English. *PRACTICE AREAS:* Patent and Trademark Law; Intellectual Property.

JIANG-XIONG HUANG, born Rongyan City, Fujian Province, China, January 15, 1946; admitted, 1987, China (Not admitted in the United States). *Education:* Institute of Political Science and Law in South-west China (B.A. in Law, 1984); Post-graduate Institute of Xiamen University (LL.M. in civil law, 1990). Author: An Introduction to Civil Law, published by house of Xiamen University; Examples of Lawsuits, published by house of Xiamen University; A Guide for Taiwan People to Invest in Mainland China, published by Beijing Huayi Publishing House. Lecturer: Civil Law; Law of Estate and Practice, Law Department, Xiamen University. *Member:* China Jurisprudence Society; Fujian Jurisprudence Society; Xiamen Jurisprudence Society; Fujian Society of Administrative; Association for Industry and Commerce; Xiamen Society of Administration for Industry and Commerce; Xiamen Bar Association. (Xiamen Office). *LANGUAGES:* Chinese, Taiwanese, English. *PRACTICE AREAS:* Economic; Commercial; Civil; Criminal; Investment Law, and Real Estate Law in China.

ZHOUGEN LI, born Shunde, Guangdong Province, China, October 1, 1935; (Not admitted in the United States). *Education:* Yue Xue Teachers Training College. 1985-1991, Judge (ret.) Guangzhou Middle People's Court, Civil Division and Director of Administration. Recipient, 1984, 1985 Guangzhou City Court Systems Advance Specialist of the Year; 1988, Guangdong Province Outstanding Judge of the year; 1989 Third Degree Honor awarded by the Guangdong Province High Court. (Hong Kong Office). *LANGUAGES:* Chinese (Mandarin and Cantonese). *PRACTICE AREAS:* Litigation; Contract; Intellectual Property.

JIA LIN, born China; admitted, 1989, China; 1991, California. *Education:* Zhongshan University, Guangzhou, China (LL.B.); People's University Beijing, China (LL.M.). Lecturer, People's University, 1989—. (Beijing Office).

LEGAL SUPPORT PERSONNEL

ZHANGQUING WU, born Shantou Guangdong Province, PRC October 15, 1967. *Education:* Shenzhen University (LL.B., 1991). (Shenzhen Office).

SHIJIE CHEN, born Xiamen, Fujian Province, China, November 18, 1970. *Education:* Xiamen University (LL.B., 1992). (Xiamen Office). *LANGUAGES:* English, Chinese. *PRACTICE AREAS:* Adoption Law; Contracts; Insurance; Trade.

SONG GAO, born Fujian Province, China, April 2, 1969. *Education:* Hau Qiao University (LL.B.). (Shenzhen Office).

REVISER OF THE PEOPLE'S REPUBLIC OF CHINA AND MONGOLIA LAW DIGESTS FOR THIS DIRECTORY.

MYANMAR

DELANEY & CO. INDOCHINA LIMITED

THE LIBERTY HOTEL
343, PYAY (PROME) ROAD
SAN CHAUNG TOWNSHIP
YANGON, MYANMAR
Telecopy: (951) 34144

Thailand Office: 28/11 Soi Ruamrudee, Wireless Road, Bangkok 10330. Telephone: (662) 253-8528. Telecopy: (662) 253-4256. Mobile GSM: (661) 811-1787. Phonelink: (151, 152) 441069. Mailing Address: MBE Asoke Suite #347, 44/1-3 Asoke Road, Bangkok 10110.

(This Listing Continued)

Cambodia Office: The Allson Star, 138, Monivong Boulevard, Phnom Penh.
New York Office: 167 East 67th Street, Suite 5A, New York, New York 10021, United States of America.
Washington, D.C. Office: 2916 Fessenden Street, N.W., Washington, D.C. 20008 Unites States of America. Telephone: (202) 364-6742. Fax: (202) 364-6749.

Direct Co-Investment, General Corporate, Mergers and Acquisitions, Securities, Corporate Finance, Structured Finance, Public Finance, Leasing, Banking, Restructuring, Private Investment Funds, Futures and Options, Interest Rate and Currency Swaps, Labor, Immigration, Joint Ventures, Venture Capital, Legislative, Lobbying, Government Bidding, Privatizations, Public Concessions, Energy, Environmental, Media and Telecommunications, Oil and Gas, Utilities, Real Estate, Construction, Tax, Trust and Estates, Intellectual Property, General Litigation, Criminal Litigation, Arbitration and Mediation.

(For complete biographical data on all personnel, see Professional Biographies at Bangkok, Thailand)

MAW HTOON & PARTNERS

Advocates and Notary Public
Affiliated with
Kanung & Partners Law Offices, Bangkok
Arndt & Van Patten Law Office, Los Angeles
Michael Nyunt Law Office, Sydney

49/51, 31ST STREET
YANGON, MYANMAR
Telephone: (951) 71919/76595/36869/64171
Facsimile: (951) 34586
Telex: 21201 BM Attn: 727

Bangkok, Thailand Affiliated Office: Kanung & Partners Law Offices, 12th Floor, Nai Lert Park, 2/4 Wireless Road, Bangkok 10330. Telephone: (662) 267-8931. Facsimile: (662) 267-8941/2.
Los Angeles, California, USA Affiliated Office: Arndt & Van Patten Law Office, 523 West Sixth Street, 90014. Telephone: (213) 622-7174. Facsimile: (213) 622-8026. Telex: 494-2100.
Sydney, Australia Affiliated Office: Michael Nyunt Law Office, Suite 701, The Cliveden, 4 Bridge Street, Sydney, N.S.W. 2000. Telephone: (612) 247-6838. Facsimile: (612) 247-7024.

General Practice, Commercial and Corporate, Joint Ventures and Investment, Intellectual Property, Taxation, Commercial Arbitration and Litigation, Privatisation.

MEMBERS OF FIRM

U ZALI MAW, admitted, 1957, England, Barrister-at-Law of Gray's Inn; 1958, Myanmar. *Education:* Cambridge (B.A., Hons.; M.A.); Yale (M.A.). Fellow, Rotary Foundation, 1953-1954. Lecturer, Faculty of Law, Rangoon University, 1960-1962. *PRACTICE AREAS:* Corporate; Commercial; Arbitration.

U YE HTOON, admitted, 1966, Myanmar. *Education:* Bucknell University (B.A.); Rangoon University (B.L.). Chairman: Shambhala Co., Ltd.; Ye Htoon Group Consultants. *PRACTICE AREAS:* Commercial; Joint Ventures; Investment.

U THAN SEIN, admitted, 1960, Myanmar; Notary Public. *Education:* Yangon University (B.A.; B.L.). *PRACTICE AREAS:* Commercial; Intellectual Property; Privatisation.

U MAUNG MAUNG, admitted, 1971, Myanmar. *Education:* Yangon University (B.A., Law; LL.B.). *PRACTICE AREAS:* Litigation; Taxation and Revenue; Banking Law; Finance.

U SAN LWIN, admitted, 1983, Myanmar. *Education:* Yangon University (B.A.; R.L.). *PRACTICE AREAS:* Litigation; Corporate; Commercial.

U THAN TUN AUNG, admitted, 1985, Myanmar. *Education:* Yangon University (B.A.; R.L.). *PRACTICE AREAS:* Corporate; Commercial; Civil Litigation; Commercial Litigation.

U AUNG KYWE, admitted, 1986, Myanmar. *Education:* Yangon University (B.A.; R.L.). *PRACTICE AREAS:* Litigation; Revenue Appellate Courts.

(This Listing Continued)

U AUNG MYINT OO, admitted, 1987, Myanmar. *Education:* Yangon University (LL.B.). *PRACTICE AREAS:* Litigation; Taxation Appellate Court.

OF COUNSEL

MICHAEL M. NYUNT, admitted, 1965, Myanmar. *Education:* Yangon University (B.Comm.; LL.B.); Australia (A.A.I.I.; A.C.I.I.). *PRACTICE AREAS:* International Business.

Languages: Burmese, English, Japanese and Hindi

NEPAL

SINHA-VERMA LAW CONCERN

"SINHA SADAN", CHA 2/207, GAIRIDHARA

KATHMANDU, NEPAL

Telephone: (977-1) 415773

Fax: (977-1) 415774

Telex: 2487 Suhrid NP

Foreign Investment, Joint Ventures, Contracts, Company Law, Taxation, Arbitration, Trade Marks, Patents and other Business Laws.

Sushil Kumar Sinha,   **Navin Kumar Verma,** Advocate
Sr. Advocate   **Anil Kumar Sinha,** Advocate

Mukesh Kumar Singh, Advocate

DHRUBA BAR SINGH THAPA & ASSOCIATES

Advocates & Consultants

Established in 1987

BALAJU RING ROAD

P.O. BOX 828

KATHMANDU, NEPAL

Telephone: (977) (1) 272 534

Telefax: (977) (1) 272-866

PROF. DHRUBA BAR SINGH THAPA, born Kathmandu, Nepal, September 19, 1937; admitted, 1987, Kathmandu. *Education:* Nepal Law College, Kathmandu (B.L., 1961); Tribhuvan University, Kathmandu (M.A., 1963); McGill University, Montreal (LL.M., 1968). Dean and Professor, International Law and Human Rights, Institute (Faculty) of Law, Tribhuvan University, Kathmandu, 1973-1979. Secretary to His Majesty's Government of Nepal, Ministry of Law and Justice, 1979-1987. Judge, Zonal Appellate Courts of Nepal, 1972-1973. *Member:* Nepal Bar Association; Supreme Court of Nepal (Advocate); Supreme Court Bar Association; Nepal Law Society; LAWASIA; International Council of Environmental Law; International Law Association; Member of Executive Committee, International Society for Labour Laws and Social Security; Chairman, Nepal Society for Labour Law and Social Security. *LANGUAGES:* English, French and Nepali (Native). *PRACTICE AREAS:* International; Constitutional; Commercial; Environmental; Aviation; Corporation; Banking; Joint Ventures; Contracts; International Financing; Taxation; Copyright; Patents and Trademarks; International Arbitration; Conveyancing Law; Labour Law; Government Law.

(This Listing Continued)

ASSOCIATES

DR. L.K. UPADHYAYA, LL.M. (Patna); Ph.D. (Calcutta).

SAJJAN BAR SINGH THAPA, B.L. (Tribhuvan).

PAKISTAN

AFRIDI, ANGELL & KHAN

(In Association with Ayub Khan Kundi & Co.)

8, STREET 31, 8TH AVENUE F-7/1

ISLAMABAD 44000, PAKISTAN

Telephone: 92-51-217-031

Fax: 92-51-217-032

Abu Dhabi, United Arab Emirates Office: Bin Hamoodah Building, P.O. Box 3961. Telephone: 9712-329-134. Fax: 9712-326-905. Telex: 23632 Ordig Em. Cable Address: "Dignior Abu Dhabi".

Dubai, United Arab Emirates Office: City Tower, Level 8, Dubai-Abu Dhabi Road, P.O. Box 9371. Telephone: 9714-310-900. Fax: 9714-310-800. Telex: 46145 Ordig Em. Cable Address: "Dignior Dubai".

Sharjah, United Arab Emirates Office: Al-Boorj Avenue, P.O. Box 5925. Telephone: 9716-544-062. Fax: 9716-547-336. Telex: 68331 Ordig Em. Cable Address: "Dignior Sharjah".

Jebel Ali, United Arab Emirates Office: Jebel Ali Free Trade Zone, P.O. Box 16894. Telephone: 9714-816-010. Fax: 9714-816-774. Telex: 46145 Ordig Em.

New York, N.Y. Office: 230 Park Avenue, 10169. Telephone: 212-697-0300. Fax: 212-697-0385.

General International, Regional and Pakistan practice including representation of Clients in Administrative, Corporate, Banking, Private Power Generation Project and other Energy, Maritime, Commercial, Financial, Real Estate, Petroleum, Arbitration and Litigation Matters; also Commercial Agency, Governmental Licensing and Registration, Employment, Islamic Law, Construction and Project Development.

FIRM PROFILE: This office was established to provide a specialized Pakistan capability to Afridi & Angell and is licensed to practice as Advocates and Legal Consultants. The Firm has two partners and two associates.

PARTNERS

M.A.K. AFRIDI, born Karachi, Pakistan, February 2, 1936; admitted, 1958, Pakistan; 1974 admitted as a legal consultant (not admitted as Advocate) in the United Arab Emirates. *Education:* Peshawar University (LL.B., 1958). Author: "The Emirates Lay Down the Law on Interest-Free Banking," International Financial Law Review, 1985; "Construction Contracting in the United Arab Emirates," International Construction Law Review, 1985. Co-Author: with Amjad Ali Khan, "The Effect of Islamic Principles on the Conduct of Business in the Gulf," paper presented at GulfAmerica conference Houston, Texas, 1988; with Nicholas B. Angell, "Recent Developments in the United Arab Emirates," paper delivered at International Bar Association Conference, Singapore, 1985. Correspondent: International Construction Law Review. Partner, Orr Dignam & Co., Pakistan, 1964-1974. Resident Partner, Orr Dignam & Co., Middle East Office, Sharjah, United Arab Emirates, 1974-1980. Partner, Chadbourne, Parke & Afridi, Middle East Offices, United Arab Emirates, 1980-1991. *Member:* The ICC International Court of Arbitration (Pakistan Representative); International Bar Association. *LANGUAGES:* English, Urdu and Pushtu.

AMJAD ALI KHAN, born Peshawar, Pakistan, August 27, 1955. Admitted to bar, 1980, Punjab; 1983, New York; 1991, admitted as a legal consultant in the United Arab Emirates (Not admitted as an advocate in the United Arab Emirates). *Education:* Government College Lahore (B.A., 1976); Punjab University (LL.B., 1979); University of California, Berkeley (LL.M., 1981). Author: "The Courts and the Legal System in the U.A.E.," - Middle East Executive Reports, August 1983; "Agency and Distributorship in the U.A.E.," - Middle East Executive Reports, August 1985; "U.A.E. Draft Regulations for Financial Institutions," Middle East Executive Reports, December 1988; "Establishing a Business Presence in the United Arab Emirates," - Outlook, February 1991; "United Arab Emirates, - General Questions on Banking and Securities Law," - International Financial Law Practice Files, 1991; "Commercial Agencies and Distributorships: An International Guide," - Prentice Hall, 1992. Co-Author: with Gary R. Feulner, "Dispute Resolution in the Emirates," - Middle East Executive Reports, July 1985; with M.A.K. Afridi, "The Effect of Islamic Legal Principles on

(This Listing Continued)

AFRIDI, ANGELL & KHAN, Islamabad—Continued

the Conduct of Business in the Gulf," paper presented at the Gulf America conference, Houston, Texas, 1988; with Gary R. Feulner, "U.A.E. Brokerage Regulations," - Middle East Executive Reports, April 1988; with Charles Laubach, "Recent Legal and Business Developments in the U.A.E.," - Middle East Executive Reports, August 1988; Special Report on Arbitration," published as a special supplement of the International Financial Law Review, May 1993. *Member:* New York State Bar Association. *LANGUAGES:* English and Urdu.

ASSOCIATES

MASOOD K. AFRIDI, born Kohat, Pakistan, September 28, 1965; admitted, 1991, New York; 1993, Pakistan. *Education:* University of Bristol (LL.B., 1987); Fordham University (LL.M., 1990). Recipient, Edward J. Hawke Prize. Co-author: with C. Chakadaran, "Arrest of Vessels in the United Arab Emirates," Chapter in Maritime Law Handbook published by the International Bar Association, 1987. *LANGUAGES:* English, Urdu and French.

SAMI U. ZAFAR, born Rawalpindi, Pakistan, November 2, 1948; (admission pending). *Education:* Government College Lahore (B.A., 1968); Punjab University (LL.B., 1970); University of London (LL.M., 1975); Harvard Law School (LL.M., 1988). Author: "Judicial Treatment of Forum Clauses in Pakistan," Pakistan Legal Decisions, 1990; "Judicial Treatment of Choice of Forum Clauses in U. S. A. - A Historical Perspective," Punjab University Law Journal, 1988; "Judicial Treatment of Choice of Forum Clauses in England," Punjab University Law Journal, 1987; "Freedom of the High Seas - A Rule of Convenience?," Punjab University Law Journal, 1982. Co-Author: with Naeem Butt, "Islamic Banking in Pakistan: Where It Is - Where Is It Going?," Punjab University Law Journal, 1988; with Bashir Ahmed, "Foreign Investment Laws of Pakistan," Punjab University Law Journal, 1987; with Bashir Ahmed, "International Contracts: The Judicial Treatment of Ouster of Jurisdiction Clauses in Pakistan," Punjab University Law Journal, 1986. Associate Professor of Law at the University of Punjab, teaching there since 1976.

(For Biographical data on other firm personnel, see Professional Biographies at Abu Dhabi, Dubai and Sharjah, United Arab Emirates and New York, N.Y.)

QAMAR ABBAS & CO.

Barristers, Advocates

66, ST "A", PH. V DEFENCE

KARACHI 75500, PAKISTAN

Telephone: (92 + 21) 214595; 219651

Telex: 24669

Cable: "Winning, Karachi"

Fax: Int. (92 + 21) 262-7913; 585-4461

Mailing Address: G.P.O. Box 3710, Karachi-74200, Pakistan

Government Relations, Government Permissions, Arbitration, Admiralty, Aviation, Shipping, Banking, Energy, Company Law, International Agreements, Litigation, Commercial, Corporate, Damages, Recoveries, International Business, General Practice, Oil and Energy.

A. HAQ KHAN, Barrister-at-Law, of Lincoln's Inn, London, Advocate, Lahore High Court.

Q.I. ABBAS, Barrister-at-Law, of Inner Temple, London, Advocate, Supreme Court Pakistan, All High Courts.

SHAIK RIAZ, Advocate, Sind High Court.

A.R. BUTT, Advocate, Sind High Court.

RIAZ AHMED, LL.B., Advocate, Lahore and Islamabad.

MZ. FARAH NAZ, Advocate, Sind High Court.

S. ALI, Advocate, Sind High Court.

MZ. GULAB SAEED, Advocate, Sind High Court.

G.B. MALIK, Advocate, District Courts.

CH. IFTIKHAR AHMED, Advocate, District Courts.

SARFARAZ SULEHRI, Advocate, Sind High Court.

Languages: English, Urdu, Arabic, German, French, Japanese, Chinese

---

ABRAHAM & SARWANA

Established in 1969

MEZZANINE FLOOR, PIDC HOUSE

DR ZIAUDDIN ROAD

KARACHI 75530, PAKISTAN

Telephone: 568 7360; 568 7370; 212 378

Fax: 568 7364; 587 1102; 263 5770

Telex: 21374 LEXIS PK

Cable: LEXIS, Karachi

General and International Law Practice. Admiralty, Banking, Energy, Oil and Gas, Insurance, Contracts, Corporate Law, International Investment and Establishment of Projects and Branches in Pakistan, Work Permits, Employment and Labor Law, Taxation, Patent and Trademark, Trial and Appellate Advocacy. Arbitration, Aviation, Shipping.

FIRM PROFILE: The firm was established in 1969 and offers a full range of legal services.

MEMBERS OF FIRM

S. AHMED SARWANA, admitted, 1963, Senior Advocate, Supreme Court and High Courts of Pakistan. *Education:* (B.A., LL.B., Karachi); (LL.M., Pennsylvania). Professor of Law, S.M. Law College, Karachi. Author: "Commercial Laws of Pakistan". Former Associate of Morgan, Lewis & Bockius, New York and Philadelphia. Karachi High Court Bar Association (Hon. Secretary, 1979-1980; Vice-President, 1986-1987). *Member:* Supreme Court Bar Association (Vice-President, Pakistan, 1993-1995).

B. MUHAMMEDALLY, admitted, 1965, Advocate, High Court of Sindh. *Education:* (B.A.; LL.B., Karachi).

S. ASHRAF ALI, admitted, 1964, Advocate, High Court of Sind. *Education:* (M.A., LL.B., Karachi); (MITMA, London). *Member:* A.P.A.A. (Japan).

SHUJAAT ALI, admitted, 1952, Advocate, High Court of Sind. *Education:* (LL.B., Karachi).

ASSOCIATES

Wigar Hasan   Tahir Lughmani

Ms. Nasira Hamid   Khalid Habibulla

SENIOR COUNSEL

ZAHOORUL HAQ, Formerly Justice, High Court of Sind.

A.A. KADEER. *Education:* Usmania (M.A.); University of Paris, Sorbonne (Docteur en Droit).

Languages: English, French and Urdu

REPRESENTATIVE CLIENTS: American Express; Caltex Oil; Grindlays Bank; Guardian-Royal Exchange Assurance; Banque IndoSuez; Pakistan International Airlines; Philips Electric; Aerospatiale; Karachi Dock Labor Board; Dar Al-Maal Al-Islami; Gould, Inc. AIG Life Insurance Co.; Deutsche Bank; British Electricity International; Air Lanka; State Cement Corp.; Sui Southern Gas; Pakistan Steel Mills; Mackinon Mackenzie; Emirates Bank; Neptune Orient Lines; Yemen Airways; Karachi Stevedores Conference; Organon Pakistan Ltd.; National Power International; Volkart Pakistan Ltd.; Lockheed Corpn.

HAIDERMOTA & CO.

Barristers at Law & Advocates

305 KASHIF CENTRE

SHAREA FAISAL

KARACHI 75530, PAKISTAN

Telephone: (92) (21) 513235; 529231

Facsimile: (92) (21) 513119

Commercial Matters including Banking, Corporate Law, Domestic and International Arbitration, Mudaraba and Musharaqa Financing, Shipping, Conveyancing, Insurance, Foreign Investment, International Trade, Project Finance, Aircraft Leasing, Aviation Law, Power Generation Projects, Privatizations, Environmental Law, Customs, Excise and Taxation.

MEMBERS OF FIRM

A.M. HAIDERMOTA, born 1931. Barrister-at-Law. Advocate: High Court, 1956; Supreme Court of Pakistan, 1964. *Education:* called to the English Bar from Lincoln's Inn, London, 1955; St. Xavier's College, Calcutta University (B.A., Honours). Professor, S.M. Law College. District Governor, Lions International, District 305 E. Leader, Pakistan delegation, UNCTAD's Conference on Shipping Legislation.

(This Listing Continued)

KAZIM HASAN, born 1951. Barrister-at-Law. Advocate: High Court, 1979; Supreme Court of Pakistan, 1993. *Education:* called to the English Bar from Middle Temple, London, 1979; St. John's College, Cambridge University, England (Law Tripos, 1975). Associate: Sidley & Austin, London, 1977; Rodinet & Hogan (Attorneys), Cannes, France, 1976.

KHOZEM A. HAIDERMOTA, born 1962. Attorney-at-Law. New York Bar 1990. Advocate, Sindh High Court, 1993. *Education:* Georgetown University (Juris Doctor/Master of Science in Foreign Service, May, 1988); The Wharton School, University of Pennsylvania (B.Sc., Econ., concentration in Finance, Cum Laude, May, 1984). Associate: Carter, Ledyard & Milburn, New York, February, 1989 - May, 1992 and Summers 1986/1987. Author: "Insider Trading Laws in Pakistan: A Critique," Journal of Pakistan Tax and Corporate Laws, May 1993.

Languages: English, French, Urdu and Gujrati.

REFERENCES: State Bank of Pakistan (central bank); Taseer Hadi Khalid & Co. (member of Klynveld Peat Marwick Goerdeler); Ghandhara Nissan Ltd; Hashwani Hotels Limited (owners of Marriott Hotels at Karachi and Islamabad).

ORR, DIGNAM & CO.

3RD FLOOR, 1-B, STATE LIFE SQUARE
I.I. CHUNDRIGAR ROAD
KARACHI 74000, PAKISTAN
Telephone: (92-21) 241-5384; 241-6003; 241-5086
Telex: 29529 MJLAW PK
Cable Address: DIGNIOR, KARACHI
Fax: (95-21) 241-6571

Islamabad, Pakistan Office: 3-A, Street No. 32, Sector F-8/1. Telephone: (92-51) 253-086; 260-517; 260-518. Fax: (92-51) 260-653.

FIRM PROFILE: The firm was established in Pakistan in 1972. It specializes in civil law and has an extensive practice in corporate and banking work, Commercial law, International Joint Ventures, Maritime law, Construction Law, International and local Arbitration, Insurance, Mergers and Acquisitions, Petroleum Law, Aviation Law, Civil Litigation, Shipping Law, Admiralty Jurisdiction, Foreign Investments, Government Licensing of Foreign Investments, Agency, Distributor, Energy, Oil and Mining Laws, Exchange Control Laws and Trade Regulations, Public Flotations, Customs and Excise Laws, Drug Regulations, and International Contracts.

MAHOMED J. JAFFER, born Karachi, Pakistan, September 1, 1930; admitted, 1956, East Pakistan High Court; 1962, Pakistan Supreme Court. *Education:* University of Dublin, Trinity College (B.A. (Mod) LL.B., 1952; Barrister at Law, 1954). Author: "Islamic Banking in Pakistan," Euromoney, 1988-1989; "Enforcement of Islamic Laws, Corporate Law and Related Topics," ICAP, 1986, 1988, 1990-1991. Member, Advisory Board, Hong Kong Bank Branch. Chairman, H.H. Prince Aga Khan Shia Imami Ismaili International Conciliation and Arbitration Board, 1986-1993. Former Member, East Pakistan Bar Council. *Member:* Sindh High Court Bar Association; International Bar Association; LAWASIA. *PRACTICE AREAS:* Corporate Law; Banking; Insurance Law; International Law; Arbitration; Construction Law; International Trade Law; Mergers and Acquisitions.

RAFIUD DEEN AHMAD, born Bolaram, India, March 9, 1939; admitted, 1963, Lahore High Court; 1964, Dacca High Court; 1971, Karachi High Court. *Education:* Dacca University (B.A., 1958); Punjab University (M.A., 1960); Lincoln's Inn (Barrister at Law, 1963). Member: International Court of Arbitration, 1986-1988; International Chamber of Commerce. *Member:* Karachi High Court Bar Association; Sindh Bar Council. *PRACTICE AREAS:* Corporate Law; International Investments; Arbitration; Insurance Law; Technology Transfer; Oil and Gas Law; Energy Law.

MAUDOOD A. KHAN, born Quadian, India, April 12, 1941; admitted, 1966, Lahore District Court; 1977, Karachi High Court. *Education:* University of Punjab (LL.B., 1964). *Member:* Karachi and Sindh High Court Bar Associations. *PRACTICE AREAS:* Corporate Law; Banking Law; Foreign Investment; Loan Syndication; Energy Law; Joint Ventures; Public Flotations (local and international); Securities and Exchange Laws; Mergers and Acquisitions; Conveyancing; International Contracts; Exchange Control Laws; Transfer of Technology; Intellectual Property.

M.H. KAZMI, born Allahabad, India, August 1, 1932; admitted, 1964, Sindh High Court; 1985, Pakistan Supreme Court. *Education:* University of Sindh; University of Punjab (B.A., 1952); University of Karachi (LL.B., 1957). Author: "Arrest of Ships - 7," Lloyds of London Press, 1988. *Member:* Karachi and Sindh High Court Bar Associations; Bar Council of Pakistan.

(This Listing Continued)

stan. *PRACTICE AREAS:* Admiralty; Banking Law; Insurance Law; Civil Litigation.

SAJID ZAHID, born Coimbatore, India, November 14, 1949; admitted, 1977, Sindh High Court; 1988, Pakistan Supreme Court. *Education:* Lincoln's Inn (Barrister at Law, 1972). Member, Rotary Club of Karachi (President, 1988-1989). Member, Executive Committee of Management Association of Pakistan. *Member:* Karachi and Sindh High Court Bar Associations. *PRACTICE AREAS:* Banking Law; Construction Law; Joint Ventures; Technology Transfer; Petroleum and Gas Contracts; Corporate Law; Commercial Law; Arbitration; Civil Litigation.

ZAHIR RIAZ, born Lahore, Pakistan, April 19, 1957; (admission pending); admitted, 1994. *Education:* University of London (LL.B., 1980); University of Cambridge (LL.B., 1982); Gray's Inn (Barrister at Law, 1982). *Member:* Honourable Society of Gray's Inn. *PRACTICE AREAS:* Company Law; Construction Law; Engineering Law; Banking and Finance; International Arbitration Law; Energy Law.

ASSOCIATES

FAKHRUDDIN FAROOQI, born Agra, India, July 1, 1928; admitted, 1962, Sindh High Court; 1989, Pakistan Supreme Court. *Education:* Karachi University (B.A., 1954; LL.B., 1956); Sindh Muslim Law College (LL.B., 1956). *Member:* Karachi and Sindh High Court Bar Associations. *PRACTICE AREAS:* Civil Law; Banking Law; Insurance Law; Shipping; Industrial Law; Labour Law; Property Law.

NADEEM AHMAD, born Karachi, Pakistan, September 10, 1950; admitted, 1975, Karachi. *Education:* Karachi University (B.A., 1971; M.A., Political Science, 1976); Sindh Muslim Law College (LL.B., 1974). *Member:* Karachi and Sindh High Court Bar Associations; Sindh Bar Council. *PRACTICE AREAS:* Corporate Law; Conveyancing; Banking Law.

YUSUF KASSIM, born Edinburgh, Scotland, February 17, 1940; admitted, 1974, Karachi District Court; 1976, Karachi High Court. *Education:* St. Patrick's College and University of Karachi (B.A., 1962); Sindh Muslim Law College, University of Karachi (LL.B., 1972). Author: "Administrative Tribunals - Ground for Challenging Tribunal and Agency Actions," Pakistan Law Journal, 1976. *Member:* Karachi and High Court of Sindh Bar Associations. *PRACTICE AREAS:* Maritime Law; Construction Law; Conveyancing; Banking Law; Insurance Law; Probate and Succession; Rent and Property Law; Contracts; Tort.

ALIYA KHAN, born Tokyo, Japan, July 8, 1958; admitted, 1982, England (pending admission in Pakistan). *Education:* Cambridge University (B.A. (Hons), 1980); Inns of Court, School of Law (Barrister at Law, 1981). Co-Author: "Aircraft Finance, Registration, Security and Enforcement," Longman, 1989; "International Banking Secrecy," Sweet & Maxwell, 1992. *Member:* Honourable Society of Gray's Inn. *PRACTICE AREAS:* Corporate Law; Banking Law; Aviation; Foreign Investment; Mergers and Acquisitions; International Loan Syndication.

ZAHID HUSSAIN BORHANI, born Amravati, Maharashtra, India, June 4, 1938; admitted, 1971, Sindh High Court. *Education:* S.M. Arts College (B.A., 1958); University of Karachi (LL.B., 1962). *Member:* Sindh Bar Council; Sindh High Court Bar Association; Karachi Bar Association; Income Tax Bar Association, Karachi. *PRACTICE AREAS:* Civil Litigation; Conveyancing; Maritime Law; Landlord and Tenant Law; Labor Law; Corporate Law.

RIZWAN NAVEED AKHUND, born Karachi, Pakistan, February 9, 1966; admitted, 1991, England; 1993, Advocate, High Courts of Pakistan. *Education:* University of Karachi (B.Com., 1986); University College London (LL.B., Hons., 1990; LL.M., 1992); Middle Temple (Barrister-at-Law, 1991). Member, Punjab Bar Council, 1993. *PRACTICE AREAS:* Banking Law; Corporate Law; Foreign Investment Law; Mergers and Acquisitions; International Trade Law; International Syndicated Loans; Project Finance; Arbitration.

AYSHA QADIR, born Peshawar, Pakistan, April 4, 1968. *Education:* International Islamic University, Islamabad, Pakistan (LL.B., 1989); Punjab University (B.A., 1989); Cambridge University, United Kingdom (LL.M., 1992). Advocate in apprenticeship, District Courts, Islamabad. *Member:* Women's Legal Aid Committee, Ministry of Women's Development, Government of Pakistan; Islamabad Bar Association.

ALY ABBAS SHAH, born Karachi, Pakistan, November 20, 1969; admitted, (Pending admission). *Education:* University of Buckingham (LL.B., Honours; LL.M., 1992). Lincoln's Inn (Barrister-at-Law, 1993). *Member:* English and Sindh Bar Council, Pakistan. *PRACTICE AREAS:* Civil Litigation; Construction Law; Arbitration Law; Banking and Corporate Law.

(This Listing Continued)

ORR, DIGNAM & CO., Karachi—Continued

AHMAD ATTAUR REHMAN, born Lahore, Pakistan, October 28, 1964; admitted, 1993, England; 1994, Advocate, High Courts of Pakistan. *Education:* University of Buckingham (LL.B., Hons., 1991; LL.M., 1992). Lincoln's Inn (Barrister-at-Law, 1993). *Member:* Lahore High Court Bar Association. **PRACTICE AREAS:** Banking Law; Construction Law; Insurance Law; International Contracts.

ASIM NASIM, born Karachi, Pakistan, September 6, 1972; (admission pending). *Education:* University of London (LL.B., Hons., 1993). Lincoln's Inn (Barrister-at-Law, 1994). **PRACTICE AREAS:** Corporate Law; Commercial Law.

ADVISOR

IRTIZA HUSAIN, born January 1, 1933. Ex-Officio Secretary to the Government of Pakistan; Chairman, Corporate Law Authority and Monopoly Control Authority, 1981-1989. *Member:* Institute of Chartered Accountants of Scotland; Institute of Chartered Accountants of Pakistan (Fellow and Former Chairman; Past President). **PRACTICE AREAS:** Corporate Law; Mergers and Acquisitions; Monopoly; Antitrust Law.

REPRESENTATIVE CLIENTS: American Express Banking Corporation; Cyanamid (Pakistan), Ltd.; Hughes Aircraft Co.; Rothmans International Tobacco (UK) Ltd.; Engro Chemical Pakistan Ltd.; Citibank, N.A.; Hong Kong & Shanghai Banking Corp.; ICI Pakistan Ltd.; Sterling Winthrop; Wellcome Pakistan, Ltd.; Siemens (Pakistan) Engineering Co. Ltd.; Fauji Fertilizer Co. Ltd.; Fauji Foundation; Burmah Castrol plc; ANZ Grindlays Bank plc; Societe Generale; Crescent International Petroleum Co. Ltd.; Sharjah; IFU, Denmark; New Hampshire Insurance Co., U.S.A.; Commercial Union Assurance plc; Allied Dunbar Assurance plc; IBM Semea Srl; Alcatel CIT; Clough Engineering Ltd (Australia); Singapore Telecom International.

SATTAR & SATTAR, ATTORNEYS-AT-LAW

Established in 1972

UNITED BANK BUILDING
MCLEOD ROAD
P.O. BOX 6699
KARACHI, PAKISTAN
Telephone: (92-21) 2415001; 2415229; 2414376
Fax: (92-21) 2414728
Telex: 21451 SATAR PK.
Cable: Lawstar, Karachi (Pakistan)

Rawalpindi, Pakistan Representative Office: 65-D Kashmir Road.
Telephones: 567983; 864461.

Foreign Investments, Government Licensing of Foreign Investment, Agency, Distributor, Franchise, Representative Arrangements, Joint-Ventures, Acquisitions & Mergers, Corporate Law, Commercial Law, Oil and Mining Laws, Exchange Control Laws and Trade Regulations, Customs & Excise Laws, Property Laws, Industrial Relations, Employers Liability, Social Security and Labour Laws, Food and Drug Regulations, International Contracts, Product Liability & Insurance Laws, Maritime and Admiralty Law, Litigation, Intellectual Property, (Patent, Trademarks and Copyrights); Taxation Laws (Corporate and Personal Income Taxations), Securities Law including private and public placements.

MEMBERS OF FIRM

Abdul R. Sattar	*M.Saif Malik*
Kader Sattar	*A.R. Adam*
Mohd Aslam	*Habib Bawany*

REPRESENTATIVE CLIENTS: IBM; 3M Corporation; Pepsi Cola; Chrysler Corporation; Procter & Gamble; Walt Disney; Eastman Kodak; Honda Motors; Alcatel; Gillette; Mobil Chemicals; Occidental Petroleum; Lufthansa German Airlines; FMC Corp; Chase Manhattan Bank; Union Carbide; Monsanto; Philips Petroleum; Bayer; Lasmo Oil; Snamprogetti (ENI Group); Singapore Telecom; Mitsui & Co.; Rohm & Hass; Daewoo Corp; Eli Lilly; Commercial Union Assurance; Litton Industries; Dresser Industries; Time Warner; Petrofina; Mazda Motors; Midland Bank; Moulinex; Smithkline Beecham; Fiat, McCann Erickson, Thompshon CSF; Sealand Corp; Upjohn Pharmaceuticals; CMB Shipping; Sumitomo Corp; Samsung Company; Total (France); Schlumberger Group; Nestle; Bankers Trust; Raytheon Corporation; Marubeni Corporation; Deutsche Bank; Roussel UCLAF; Rexnord Corporation; AT&T; Basf; General Electric Corp; D. Swarovski & Co; Emirates Bank; Houston Industries; Barring Securities; Crosby Securities; Case Poclain S.A.

M.L. SHAHANI

51-D-1, BLOCK-6
NURSERY, P.E.C.H.S.
KARACHI 75400, PAKISTAN
Telephone: (92-21) 4556186-444865
Fax: (92-21) 4553913

Banking Litigation, Retail Banking, Industrial Law, Privatization, Civil Appeals, Civil Litigation, Press Law, Constitutional Law, Breach of Contract, Divorce, Matrimonial Law, Separation Agreements, Election Law, Legislative Practice, Local Government, Municipal Finance, Municipal Law, Government Contracts, Human and Civil Rights, Social Security, Guardianship, Inheritance, Trusts, Wills, Successions, International Successions, Collective Bargaining, Employment Compensation, Employment Discrimination, Industrial Relations, International Labor, Labor Legislation, Labor Relations, Labor Unions, Management Labor and Employment, Libel and Defamation, Medical Liability, Land Registration, Land Titles, Personal Property, Property Conveyancing.

MOHAN LAL A. SHAHANI, born Dadu, Pakistan, March 18, 1949; admitted, 1974, Advocate; 1976, High Court; 1982, Supreme Court. *Education:* University of Sindh (B.Com., 1969; M.A. (Econ), 1971; LL.B., 1973); Pakistan Institute of Management, Karachi (Certificate, Labour Laws, 1973). Recipient: Award Winner of Essays on Administration of Justice, Sindh High Court Bar Association, 1985-1986; Human Rights Award by Lawyers for Human Rights and Legal Aid and for protection of Rights of Religious Minorities in Pakistan, 1994. Author: "Multinational Corporation and Their Role on Economy Trade," Brotherhood of Asian Trade Unions, Manila, Philippines, 1977; "Human Rights and the Church," Men's Department of Baptist World Alliance, Singapore, 1986. Fellow, Salzburg Seminar, American Law and Legal Institutions, 1988. Debator, Colleges and University of Sindh. Speaker, International Seminars on Labour Laws of Asia/Pacific Region, Bangkok, Manila, Singapore, Los Angeles and Colombo, 1977-1986. First Secretary General, Pakistan Trade Union Congress, 1977-1982. Council, Men's Department of Baptist World Alliance, Los Angeles, 1985-1990. Director, Karachi Young Men's Christian Association, 1972-1986. Attended Presidential Prayer Breakfast, Washington, D.C., 1990. *Member:* Karachi Bar Association; Sindh High Court Bar Association; Supreme Court Bar Association of Pakistan, Islamabad (Executive Committee Member); American Bar Association; Lawyers Christian Fellowship, U.K.; Law Asia Australia; Union Advocates International, Paris.

SURRIDGE & BEECHENO

FINLAY HOUSE
I.I. CHUNDRIGAR ROAD
KARACHI 74000, PAKISTAN
Telephone: +92 (21) 242 7292 to 94; 242 7297; 242 5790
Telex: 20310 ESENB PK
Telegrams: "Litigation Karachi"
Telefax: +92 (21) 241 6830

REVISERS OF THE PAKISTAN LAW DIGEST FOR THIS DIRECTORY.

Lahore, Pakistan Office: Ghulam Rasool Building, 60, Shahrah-e-Quaid-e-Azam. Telephones: +92 (42) 305 178; 636 7390. Telegrams: "Litigation Lahore". Telex: 44987 ESENB PK. Telefax: +92 (42) 636 7390.

All branches of Civil Law, both Contentious and Non-Contentious including Foreign Investment and Joint Ventures, Corporate Law, Banking and Finance, Admiralty and Shipping, Aviation, Building and Engineering Contracts including BOT Projects and Trademarks and Patents.

MEMBERS OF FIRM

ABDULRAHIM ABDULLA BHOJANI, born 1928; admitted, 1953, England; Barrister-at-Law of Lincoln's Inn; B.A. (London); Advocate, High Court of Sindh.

EHSAN AHMAD NOMANI, born 1932; admitted, 1957, Pakistan; 1964, England; Barrister-at-Law of Gray's Inn; M.A., LL.B. (Allahabad); Advocate of the Supreme Court of Pakistan.

AFTAB AHMED KHAN, born 1932; Advocate of the Supreme Court of Pakistan; B.A., LL.B. (Partner resident in Lahore).

ANWAR ALY SHAREEF, born 1933; Advocate of the Supreme Court of Pakistan; B.A., LL.B.

(This Listing Continued)

KAIRAS NADER KABRAJI, born 1951; M.A., LL.B. (Cantab); Advocate, High Court of Sindh.

ASSOCIATES

Mohammed Naeem, Advocate	Seena Mohammed Ali, Advocate
Khalid Rahman, Advocate	Mohammed Sabir, Advocate
Nasimuddin Sheikh, Advocate	Syed Mohammed Saleem,
Salman Talibuddin, Advocate	Advocate
S.N. Murtuza, Advocate	S. Munawwar Ali
Sabiha Hassan, Advocate	Ashfaq Husain Quraishi,
Hassan Mahmood, Advocate	Advocate
Shahana Ahmed Ali, Advocate	M. Zakaria Shamim, Advocate
Zarmina Dastur, Advocate	Khalid Saleem Ansari, Advocate
Zainab Suleman, Advocate	Mohammed Iqbal Shaikh,
Farah A. Japanwalla, Solicitor	Advocate
Mohammed Rehan Aqeel,	Syed Asad Ali Zaidi, Advocate
Advocate	

REPRESENTATIVE CLIENTS: The World Bank; International Finance Corporation; Asian Development Bank; Citicorp Group; Standard Chartered Group; Shell; Pepsico Inc.; Corn Products (CPC) Group; Philip Morris; Sandoz; Ciba-Geigy; Glaxo; Abbott Laboratories; Johnson & Johnson; British Airways; K.L.M.; Toyota; Sheraton; Taylor Woodrow; Mitsubishi; General Electric; London Protection & Indemnity Clubs; The Hub Power Co., Ltd.
REFERENCES: Shearman & Sterling, New York; Baker & Mackenzie, Chicago; Milbank, Tweed, Hadley & McCloy, New York; Haight, Gardner, Poor & Havens, New York; Linklaters & Paines, London; Slaughter & May, London Hong Kong; Norton, Rose, London; Clifford Chance, London; Beaumont & Son, London; Barlow Lyde & Gilbert, London.
LEGAL ADVISERS TO: British High Commission; Swiss Embassy.

REVISERS OF THE PAKISTAN LAW DIGEST FOR THIS DIRECTORY.

VELLANI & VELLANI

810-820 MUHAMMADI HOUSE, 8TH FLOOR
I. I. CHUNDRIGAR ROAD
KARACHI 74000, PAKISTAN
Telephone: 241-4021; 241-3066
Cable Address: "VELLANY" Karachi
Telex: 29355 VLANI PK
Fax: 92-21-241-9874

Commercial Matters including Corporation Work. Arbitration, Shipping and Banking. Patents, Designs and Trademarks.

FATEHALI W. VELLANI, born Zanzibar, Tanzania, 1932; admitted, 1956, Advocate, Supreme Court of Pakistan and Barrister-at-Law, Middle Temple (London). *Education:* University College of Wales, Aberystwyth (B.A., Economics, 1953). *Member:* Karachi Bar Association; High Court Bar Association (Karachi); Supreme Court Bar Association; American Society of International Law; General Council of the Bar (England); Chartered Institute of Patent Agents; Institute of Trade Marks Agents. (Also Partner of Fatehali W. Vellani & Co. at this address). *LANGUAGES:* Urdu and English.

BADARUDDIN F. VELLANI, born Karachi, Pakistan, 1958; admitted, 1982, Barrister-at-Law, Middle Temple (London); 1983, Advocate, High Court of Sind. *Education:* Lourghborogh University of Technology (B.Sc., Chemical Engineering, Hons., 1980); The City University, London (Diploma in Law, 1981). *Member:* Karachi Bar Association; High Court Bar Association (Karachi); General Council of the Bar (England); The Institution of Chemical Engineers (England); Sarclaw. (Also Partner of Fatehali W. Vellani & Co. at this address). *LANGUAGES:* Urdu and English.

ASSOCIATES

KHAWJA MANSOOR, born Calcutta, India, 1941; admitted, 1967, Advocate in the East Pakistan Bar Council. *Education:* University of Dhaka (B.A., History, Hons., 1961; M.A., History, 1963; LL.B., 1967). *Member:* Karachi Bar Association; High Court Bar Association (Karachi). *LANGUAGES:* Urdu and English. *PRACTICE AREAS:* Trademark Law; Copyright Law; Litigation.

MOHAMMED ALI ZAHED, born Bangladesh, Pakistan, 1958; admitted, 1988, Advocate. *Education:* University of Karachi (B.Sc., Geology with Mathematics and Physics, Hons. 1979; M.Sc., Petroleum Geology and Sedimetation, 1980; LL.B., 1984). *Member:* Karachi Bar Association. *LANGUAGES:* Urdu, Bengali and English. *PRACTICE AREAS:* Trademark Law; Copyright Law.

DJALEH AKBAR, born Karachi, Pakistan, 1964; admitted, 1990, Advocate. *Education:* University of Karachi (B.A., 1986; LL.B., 1988). *Mem-*

(This Listing Continued)

---

ber: Karachi Bar Association. *LANGUAGES:* Urdu and English. *PRACTICE AREAS:* Trademark Law; Copyright Law; Commercial Law; Corporate Law.

JAVED SAFDAR TANWIRI, born Karachi, Pakistan, 1953; admitted, 1979, Advocate. *Education:* University of Karachi (B.Com., 1973; LL.B., 1977). *Member:* Karachi Bar Association; High Court Bar Association (Karachi). *LANGUAGES:* Urdu, Sindhi and English. *PRACTICE AREAS:* Trademark Law; Copyright Law.

Languages: English and Urdu

CORNELIUS, LANE & MUFTI

Established in 1975

NAWAI WAQT HOUSE
4 SHARAE FATMA JINNAH
LAHORE, PAKISTAN
Telephone: 92-42-6306301/6360824/6360868
Fax: 92-42-6303301

London, England Office: Lane & Partners, 46/47 Bloomsbury Square, WC1A 2RL. Telephone: 01-242-2626; 01-831-6911. Fax: 01-242-0367.
Cable Address: Lanelaw London WC1.

Business Law, Commercial Transactions, Copyright Law, Civil Litigation, Arbitration and Banking Matters.

MEMBERS OF FIRM

AFZAL H. MUFTI, Advocate, Supreme and High Courts of Pakistan, 1967. *Education:* Punjab (B.A., LL.B.); Oxon (B.A., Hons. in Jurisprudence; M.A.) Pakistan Rhodes Scholar (1966). *LANGUAGES:* English and Urdu. *PRACTICE AREAS:* International Commercial Transactions; Commercial Credits; Project Finance; Development Lending; Contracts; Procurement; International Organizations.

HAMID KHAN, Advocate, Supreme and High Courts of Pakistan, 1968. *Education:* Punjab (M.A., LL.B.); University of California at Berkeley (LL.M.). *LANGUAGES:* English and Urdu. *PRACTICE AREAS:* Civil Litigation; Administrative Law; Employment Law; Banking Commercial Transactions.

JAWWAD S. KHAWAJA, Advocate, Supreme and High Courts of Pakistan, 1975. *Education:* Punjab (B.A., LL.B.); University of California at Berkeley (LL.M.). *LANGUAGES:* English and Urdu. *PRACTICE AREAS:* Commercial; Corporate; Banking Law; Constitutional Law; Litigation; Contracts; Conflicts; International Business Transactions; Contract Negotiations.

SALMAN ASLAM BUTT, Advocate, Supreme and High Courts of Pakistan, 1982. *Education:* Punjab (LL.B.); London (LL.M.). *LANGUAGES:* English and Urdu. *PRACTICE AREAS:* Corporate Law; Banking Law; International Trade; Financial Matters; Property; Contracts.

ASSOCIATES

M. IQBAL AKHTAR. *Education:* Punjab (LL.B.). *LANGUAGES:* English and Urdu. *PRACTICE AREAS:* General Litigation; Revenue Disputes; Land Disputes.

IJAZ-UL-AHSAN. *Education:* Punjab (LL.B.); Cornell (LL.M.). *LANGUAGES:* English and Urdu. *PRACTICE AREAS:* Corporate Law; Commercial Law; Banking Law; Civil Litigation; Trademarks; Patents; Copyright Law; Contracts; International Business Transactions.

KHAWAJA ASIF MAHMOOD. *Education:* Punjab (LL.B.). *LANGUAGES:* English and Urdu. *PRACTICE AREAS:* Civil Litigation; Labour Law; Banking Law; Property and Transactions Law.

MEHBOOB AHMAD. *Education:* Punjab (LL.B.). *LANGUAGES:* English and Urdu. *PRACTICE AREAS:* Corporate Law; Commercial Law; Banking Law; Trademarks; Patents; Copyright Law; Property; Contracts.

KARIM NAWAZ MALIK. *Education:* Punjab (LL.B.). *LANGUAGES:* English and Urdu. *PRACTICE AREAS:* Civil Litigation; Labour Law.

GEOFFREY AND KHITRAN
Counsellors at Law
Established in 1959

Solicitors, Notaries Public, English Barristers, Advocates, Legislative

Counsels and American Attorneys at Law

SUL SABEEL
128-E-1 GULBERG MAIN BOULEVARD
LAHORE 54660, PAKISTAN
Telephone: +(92-42) 724-8518; 636-2036; 878544
Fax: +(92-42) 636-9430/724-8518
Emergency Fax: + (92-21) 262-7913

Other Lahore Office: One Justice Mohammed Akram Road, Lahore High Court, Geoffrey Square, Lahore, 54000.

General Law Practice, Trademarks, Arbitration, Intellectual Property and Service of Documents, Execution of Decrees, Foreign Investments, Collection of Debts owed in Pakistan, India, Nepal and Bangladesh, Family Law.

FIRM PROFILE: The Firm has Offices and Associates in all important Cities in Pakistan. Assignments of Legal Work accepted from Overseas concerning practically all Legal and Corporate Matters in the Indo-Pakistan Subcontinent.

The firm has Affiliates and Correspondents Worldwide.

CHAIRMAN OF THE FIRM

M.J. IQBAL JAFREE OF SLARPORE, B.A., LL.B., summa cum laude, Punjab; M.A., Sangamon State, 1972; LL.M., with Honor Paper, Harvard Law School, 1966; Hon LL.D., Read U.; Postgrad Studies in Business Administration. Bradford University Management Centre (Queen Elizabeth II Tops Fellowship, 1975). Counsellor-at-Law, United States Federal Courts, US Tax Court; Advocate, Pakistan High Courts and entitled to practice in the United Arab Emirates. Pupillage under Mr. Justice Malik Mohammed Akram (Later Chief Justice of Pakistan) 1959-1960. Recipient: Gold Medal in Jurisprudence (Punjab Univ. Law College), 1958; Paris Biennale Award, 1965; Sir Herbert Read Medal, 1992. Listed in the *Debrett's People of Today, 1994. Who's Who in the World, Who's Who in America (under Geoffrey) and Who's Who in American Law,* First Edition. Formerly Assistant Attorney-General of the State of Illinois (USA), Legal Counsel (Human Rights), United Nations Secretariat, NY 1966-1967 and Special Advisor to the President of Pakistan, 1980-1984. Drafted the Establishment of the Office of Ombudsman (Presidential Executive) Order, 1983, a law designed to diagnose and exorcise bureaucratic maladministration; and Article 164 of the Law of Evidence and other legal reforms. Co-Author: *"International Recognition and Enforcement of Money Judgments,"* American Bar Association/BLI, Ohio, 1994. *PRACTICE AREAS:* Trial Advocacy; Arbitration; Commercial Transactions; Art Law; Civil Liberties; International Law.

ASSOCIATES

HAMID SHARIF, LL.M. (Cantab). Barrister at Law (admitted in England, Lincoln's Inn).

MALIK MOHAMMED NAZEER, LL.B., Honours, South Bank University, London. Non-practising Barrister in England (Lincoln's Inn).

AFTAB IQBAL CHAUDHAREE, B.A., LL.B. Deputy Attorney General, Pakistan, 1990-1995; Advocate, Pakistan Supreme Court.

NASEER AHMAD SHAIKH, B.A., LL.B., Advocate, Supreme Court.

RAO MOHAMMED SALEEM KHAN, B.A., LL.B., Advocate.

SAFINA CHOUDHARY, LL.B., London School of Economics (admitted in England, of the Lincoln's Inn, Barrister at Law).

ZULQARNAIN SAEED, LL.B. (Birmingham Polytechnic). Passed Solicitor's Final Exam (England). Law Pupil under Distinguished Professor-Laureate M.J.I. Jafree (1995).

YASMEEN AMANULLAH, B.A., LL.B. Law Pupil under M.J.I. Jafree (1995).

OF COUNSELS

QAMARUL ISLAM ABBAS, Barrister at Law (Inner Temple).

SHELLY WAXMAN, J.D., Attorney-at-Law (Illinois and Michigan).

DEBORAH PURCELL, J.D., Attorney-at-Law (Ohio).

(This Listing Continued)

KHALID RANJHA, LL.B., (Punjab), LL.M., Ph.D., (London) Advocate, Supreme Court. Advocate-General, Government of the Punjab (1993).

HASNAIN ALMAKKY, B.A., LL.B., (Punjab), LL.M., (Boalt Hall).

HAMEEDA JAFFERJI, Solicitor (enrolled in England).

(All Associates and most of the Consultants are admitted in Pakistan)

Languages: English, French and Urdu.

HASSAN & HASSAN

(Advocates)

PAAF BUILDING
7-D KASHMIR-EGERTON ROAD
LAHORE, PAKISTAN
Telephone: (92-42) 6360800-03
Cable Address: "Lawconsult", Lahore/Rawalpindi
Telex: 44805 HASAN PK
Telefax: (92-42) 6360811-12

Rawalpindi, Pakistan Office: Room No. 38, First Floor, Al-Abbas Market, Adamjee Road. Telephone: (92-51) 568906-564233.

Civil Law both contentious and non-contentious, Corporate and Commercial Law, Air, International and Local Arbitration, Banking and Finance, Foreign Investment, International Business, International Joint Ventures, Mergers and Acquisitions, Oil and Gas Law, Contracts, Construction Law, Labour Law, Intellectual and Real Property Law.

MEMBERS OF FIRM

DR. PARVEZ HASSAN, born 1941. Advocate: Supreme Court of Pakistan, 1975—; Lahore High Court, 1969—. *Education:* Punjab University (LL.B., 1961); Yale University (LL.M., 1963); Harvard University (S.J.D., 1969). Visiting Lecturer, 1969—, Civil Services Academy, Lahore, National Institute of Public Administration, Lahore, Pakistan Administrative Staff College, Lahore, National Defence College, Rawalpindi. Associate: Sullivan & Cromwell, New York, N.Y., 1965-1966; Covington & Burling, Washington, D.C., Summer, 1965; Satterlee & Warfield, New York, N.Y., Summer, 1963. Consultant: U.N. Projects on (I) Environmental Protection Legislation in the ESCAP Region, 1977-1978, and (II) Forest Legislation in the ESCAP Region, 1985. Deputy Chairman, 1989-1990 and became Chairman of the I.U.C.N. Commission on Environmental Law 1990—. Member, Pakistan Environmental Protection Council, 1989—. President, Environmental Protection Society of Pakistan, 1989—.

DR. TARIQ HASSAN, born 1952. (presently on leave of absence with World Bank, Washington, D.C.). Advocate, Lahore High Court, 1976—. *Education:* Punjab University (LL.B., 1972); Harvard University (LL.M., 1976; S.J.D., 1980). Lecturer, Punjab University Law College, 1984—. Associate: Shearman & Sterling, New York, N.Y., 1980-1981; Hale & Dorr, Boston, Massachusetts, Winter, 1976. Consultant, International Fund for Agricultural Development, Rome, 1986. Senior Counsel, World Bank, Washington, D.C., 1989—.

ASSOCIATES

Fakhar Mahmud	Fayyaz Mahmood
Saqlain Haider Malik	Rahat Kaunain
Faisal Islam	Syed Ahmad Hassan
Asim Nazir	Ibrar Gul Niazi

REPRESENTATIVE CLIENTS: Government of Pakistan; Government of Punjab; Government of North West Frontier Province; General Tire & Rubber Co.; Dawood Hercules Chemicals Ltd.; Occidental Petroleum Corporation; China National Machinery & Equipment Import and Export Corporation; Cargill, Inc.; FMC International AG; American Express International Banking Corp.; International Finance Corp.; Commonwealth Development Corporation; Bank of America; Deutsche Bank; Hong Kong Shanghai Bank; Pakistan Industrial Credit and Investment Corporation Limited; Lahore Stock Exchange; Islamabad Stock Exchange; Noon Group of Companies; Packages Group of Companies; Crescent Group of Companies; Habibullah Group of Companies; Ayesha Group of Companies; Saifullah Group of Companies; Premier Sugar Group of Companies; F.L. Smidth, Denmark; Morgan Stanley, Hong Kong.

SURRIDGE & BEECHENO

GHULAM RASOOL BUILDING

60, SHAHRAH-E-QUAID-E-AZAM

LAHORE, PAKISTAN

Telephone: +92 (42) 305 178; 636 7390

Telex: 44987 ESENB PK Telegrams: "Litigation, Lahore"

Telefax: +92 (42) 636 7390

REVISERS OF THE PAKISTAN LAW DIGEST FOR THIS
DIRECTORY.

Karachi, Pakistan Office: Finlay House, I.I. Chundrigar Road, 74000.
Telephones: +92 (21) 242 7292 to 94; 242 7297; 242 5790. Telex:
20310 ESENB PK. Telegrams: "Litigation Karachi." Telefax: +92 (21)
241 6830.

RESIDENT MEMBER

AFTAB AHMED KHAN, born 1932. Advocate of the Supreme Court of
Pakistan, B.A., LL.B.

RESIDENT ASSOCIATES

Mian Abdul Rashid, Advocate   Mamoon Rashid Shaikh,

Advocate

REVISERS OF THE PAKISTAN LAW DIGEST FOR THIS
DIRECTORY.

(For biographical data of the Karachi office personnel, see Professional
Biographies at Karachi, Pakistan).

BILAL LAW ASSOCIATES

Advocates, Legal Consultants and Solicitors

100-A, SATELLITE TOWN

RAWALPINDI 46300, PAKISTAN

Telephone: 92-51-424000; 424001; 842024; 842095

Fax: 92-51-424002; 841174

Cable Address: "LEGALAID" Rawalpindi

All branches of Civil Law, Environment Law, Arbitration, Banking, Corporate, International Trade & Business, Foreign Investment and Joint Ventures, General Legal Practice.

MEMBERS OF FIRM

MOHAMMAD BILAL, Senior Advocate, Supreme Court of Pakistan.
Member, Pakistan Bar Council, 1990-1995. Member, Provincial Bar Council, 1973-1978. Ex-Deputy Attorney General for Pakistan, 1988-1989. President, High Court Bar Association, Rawalpindi, 1982-1983 and 1987-1988.
President, Bar Association, Rawalpindi, 1978-1979.

TARIQ BILAL, Advocate High Court; LL.M. (Georgetown).

ASAD IQBAL SIDDIQUI, Advocate.

ASSOCIATES

INAYAT ULLAH KHAN, LL.B. (Leeds University, Barrister-at-Law
(Lincoln's Inn). Advocate High Court.

KHALID WAHEED, Advocate High Court, Income Tax Advisor.

MOHAMMAD MUNIR PIRACHA, Advocate Supreme Court.

Language: English, Urdu, Arabic and French.

COUNSEL FOR: National and International Companies besides General Practice.

REPUBLIC OF THE PHILIPPINES

ABIERA & SAN JOSE

Established in 1993

13TH FLOOR, ROYAL MATCH BLDG.

6780 AYALA AVENUE, MAKATI

METRO MANILA 1200, REPUBLIC OF THE
PHILIPPINES

Telephone: 815-40-35 (D.L.), 810-1701 (Loc. 548)

Telefax: (632) 816-09-01

Cable: ASLAW MANILA

Mailing Address: P.O. Box 3444 MCPO, Philippines, Makati, Metro
Manila 1274

Corporation, Taxation, Mining, Aviation, Contracts, Labor and Commercial Law, General Civil and Trial Practice, Patents and Trademarks, Immigration.

MEMBERS OF FIRM

RAFAEL D. ABIERA, JR., born Silay City, Philippines, March 31,
1927; admitted, 1954, Philippines. Education: University of Sto. Tomas
(A.A., 1949); Ateneo de Manila (LL.B., 1953). Lex Aquila Legis, Fraternity. Lecturer, Institute on Intellectual and Property Rights, U.P. Law Center, February, 1975. Member, Legal Staff, Perkins, Ponce Enrile, Siguion
Reyna, Montecillo & Bello, 1964-1972. Partner, Belo Abiera & Associates,
June, 1972 - June, 1993. Member: Integrated Bar of the Philippines; Philippine Bar Association (Director, 1987-1988); Legal Management Council of
the Philippines (President, 1987); Asian Patent Attorney Association; Intellectual Property Association of the Philippines (Director, 1977—; President, 1993-1994); LAWASIA; International Law Association (Philippine
Chapter); Ateneo Alumni Association; Ateneo Law Alumni Foundation.
LANGUAGES: English. PRACTICE AREAS: Corporate and Business
Law; Intellectual Property Rights; Immigration Law; Labor Law.

GALICANO E. SAN JOSE, born Teresa, Rizal, Philippines, June 25,
1928; admitted, 1954, Philippines. Education: University of Sto. Tomas
(A.A., 1949; LL.B., 1953). Member: Integrated Bar of the Philippines
(Rizal Chapter). LANGUAGES: English. PRACTICE AREAS: Civil Law;
Criminal Law; Trial Practice.

REPRESENTATIVE CLIENTS: Hong Kong & Shanghai Banking Corporation
Limited; United Associates, Inc.; Philippine Packings & Seals Corporation;
Industrial Chemical Phils., Inc.; Merck & Co., Inc.; Warner Music Philippines,
Inc.; Munichre Service Limited; Screen Grafix, Inc.; Merck, Sharp & Dohme
(Phil.), Inc.; Clupak, Inc.; The Sanforized Co.; Sunshine Biscuits, Inc.; Phelps
Dodge Phils., Inc.; Raychem Corporation; Marion Merrell Dow, Inc.; Wendy's
International, Inc.; Japan Medical Supply Co., Inc.; The Pillsbury Company;
Miwon Co., Ltd.; Orion Corporation, Ltd.; Gruppo Lepetit S.p.A.; Raychem
Limited; Calgon Corporation; Upson Industries Corporation; Bevan Supplies;
AIG Construction Company; Southwind Trading and Marketing Corporation;
American Environmental Systems Corporation; Global Manufacturing Corpo-
ration.
REFERENCES: Hong Kong & Shanghai Banking Corporation; Bank of the
Philippine Island.
CORRESPONDENTS: Robert V. Wilder, 17452 Avenue Drive, Morgan Hill,
CA 95037; Sandler, Greenblum & Bernstein, 2920 South Glebe Road, Arling-
ton, VA 22206, U.S.A.

AGCAOILI & ASSOCIATES

7TH FLOOR, CITIBANK CENTER

PASEO DE ROXAS, MAKATI

METRO MANILA, REPUBLIC OF THE PHILIPPINES

Telephone: 818-8549

Cable Address: "Avasslaw"

Telex: RCAGLOBCOM 22630 AVA PH

Facsimile: (632) 819-1868

General Practice. Corporate, Domestic and International Banking and
Finance, Civil, Insurance, Labor, Maritime, Mining, Estate, Taxation,
Patents, Trademarks, Copyrights and Unfair Competition Law.

MEMBERS OF FIRM

ALFONSO V. AGCAOILI, born Tuguegarao, Cagayan, Philippines,
August 2, 1916; admitted, 1939, Philippines. Education: University of Philippines (A.A., 1935; LL.B., 1939). Professor, University of The East, 1949-
1961. Investigator, Bureau of Immigration, 1940-1941. Solicitor, Solicitor

(This Listing Continued)

AGCAOILI & ASSOCIATES, Metro Manila—Continued

General's Office, 1945. Attorney, Government Corporate Counsel's Office, 1946-1949. Bar Examiner in Labor Law, Bar Examinations, 1971. *Member:* Integrated Bar of the Philippines; Philippine Bar Association (Director, 1976). *LANGUAGES:* English and Pilipino.

ANTONIO V. AGCAOILI, born Lukban, Quezon, Philippines, October 1, 1935; admitted, 1960, Philippines. *Education:* University of Philippines (A.A., 1956; LL.B., 1960; M.B.A., 1964). *Member:* Integrated Bar of the Philippines (Director); Philippine Bar Association; Legal Management Council. *LANGUAGES:* English and Pilipino.

EVENER J. VILLASANTA, born Lopez, Quezon, Philippines, November 8, 1931; admitted, 1959, Philippines. *Education:* Manuel L. Quezon University (Associate in Arts, 1954; Bachelor of Laws, 1958). *Member:* Integrated Bar of the Philippines; Philippine Bar Association; Asian Patent Attorneys Association; American Society of International Law. *LANGUAGES:* English and Pilipino.

ASSOCIATES

JOHN T. LAVADIA, born Bacon, Sorsogon, August 29, 1953; admitted, 1982, Philippines. *Education:* University of the East (BSBA, 1976); Ateneo de Manila University (LL.B., 1981. Attorney, Office of Justice Venicio Escolin of the Supreme Court of the Philippines, 1981-1982. *Member:* Integrated Bar of the Philippines. *LANGUAGES:* English, Chinese and Pilipino.

JOSE LUIS V. AGCAOILI, born Manila, Philippines, April 10, 1960; admitted, 1988, Philippines. *Education:* Dela Salle University (Bachelor of Science in Business Administration, 1981); Ateneo de Manila University (Bachelor of Laws, 1987). *Member:* Integrated Bar of the Philippines. *LANGUAGES:* English and Pilipino.

ENRIQUE A. PARUNGO, born Manila, Philippines, November 8, 1959; admitted, 1987, Philippines. *Education:* San Beda College (Bachelor of Arts in Political Science, 1982); Ateneo de Manila University (Bachelor of Laws, 1986). Bill Drafter/Legislative Counsellor, House of Representatives, Philippine Congress, September 1987-January 1988. *Member:* Integrated Bar of the Philippines. *LANGUAGES:* English and Pilipino.

OSCAR TOLETE ZALDIVAR, born Allacapan, Cagayan, Philippines, September 6, 1957; admitted, 1983, Philippines. *Education:* University of the East (B.A., 1978); Ateneo de Manila University (Bachelor of Laws, 1982). Hearing Officer, Housing and Land Use Regulatory Board, 1981-1985. Legal Officer, Department of Trade and Industry, 1985-1987. Public Attorneys Office, Department of Justice, 1987-1990. *Member:* Integrated Bar of the Philippines. *LANGUAGES:* English and Pilipino.

MARIA CARMEN AGCAOILI-OREÑA, born Metro Manila, Philippines, July 12, 1966; admitted, 1991, Philippines. *Education:* De La Salle University (A.B. Political Science, 1986); Ateneo de Manila University (LL.B., 1990). *Member:* Integrated Bar of the Philippines. *LANGUAGES:* Pilipino and English.

FRANCIS ESPIRITU ORENA, born Baguio City, Philippines, December 3, 1963; admitted, 1991, Philippines. *Education:* Ateneo de Manila University (A.B., 1985; LL.B., 1990). *Member:* Integrated Bar of the Philippines. *LANGUAGES:* Pilipino and English.

REPRESENTATIVE CLIENTS: Citibank, N.A.; Bank of America, NT&SA; Banque Nationale de Paris; Bank of Montreal; Bank of Hawaii; Dresdner Bank, A.G.; Kuwait Asia Bank; Economic Development Corporation of Canada; Asian Development Bank; Home Oil (Phil.), Inc.; Citicorp Investment Philippines; Citicorp Overseas Investment Corp.; Lucas Industries, Ltd.; Sumitomo Heavy Industries, Inc.; Telerate; United Philippine Lines, Inc.; Manila Jockey Club, Inc.; Bechtel Overseas Corp.; East Asiatic Company, Ltd.; Philippine Coconut Oil Producers Association, Inc.; BF Home, Inc.; Vacu-Lug Philippines, Inc.; Luzon Mahogany Corp.; Ekman & Company; Eli Lilly and Company; Sandoz, Inc.; First Quezon City Insurance Co., Inc.; Mobil Oil Corp.; Union Special Corp.; Reichhold Chemicals, Inc.

REFERENCES: Shearman & Sterling, and White & Case, New York, N.Y., U.S.A.; Coudert Brothers, Alexandra House, Hong Kong; Clifford Chance, London; Gowling & Henderson, Ontario.

ANGARA ABELLO CONCEPCION REGALA & CRUZ

5TH FLOOR, ACCRA BUILDING
122 GAMBOA STREET
LEGASPI VILLAGE, MAKATI 1200
METRO MANILA, REPUBLIC OF THE PHILIPPINES
Telephone: (632) 817-0966
Fax: (632) 816-01-19
Cable Address: "Acralaw, Philippines"
Telex: RCA (722) 22374 Eastern 63622 PN
PT&T: 4375

Mailing Address: MCC P.O. Box 1425, Makati, Metro Manila

Cebu City, Philippines Office: 2nd Floor, Aniceta Building, Osmena Boulevard. Telephones: (032) 76439; (032) 90675. Fax: (032) 53894.

General Practice. Foreign Investments. Civil and Commercial Law. Corporations. International Franchising. Banking and Finance. Patents, Trademarks and Copyrights. Insurance. Taxation. Securities. Insolvency and Reorganizations. Estates and Trusts. Oil and Mining. Commercial and Banking Litigation. Arbitration. Labor Law.

MEMBERS OF FIRM

EDGARDO J. ANGARA, born Baler, Quezon, Philippines, September 24, 1934; admitted, 1959, Philippines. *Education:* University of the Philippines (LL.B.); University of Michigan (LL.M.). Senator of the Republic of the Philippines. Delegate, Philippine Constitutional Convention 1971. President, University of the Philippines, 1981-1987. *Member:* Integrated Bar of the Philippines (President, 1979-1981; Executive Vice President, 1977-1979); Philippine Bar Association (President, 1975-1976); Philippine Constitution Association; Philippine Society of International Law; Asean Law Association (President, 1981); American Bar Association (Associate Member). *LANGUAGES:* English and Pilipino.

MANUEL G. ABELLO, born Manila, Philippines, October 14, 1934; admitted, 1959, Philippines. *Education:* Georgetown University (B.A.); University of the Philippines (B.S.J., cum laude; LL.B., cum laude); Harvard University (LL.M.). Chairman, Securities and Exchange Commission, 1981-1986. *Member:* Integrated Bar of the Philippines; Patent Attorneys Association of the Philippines (Founding Chairman, 1978); Legal Management Council of the Philippines (Director, 1972); Asean Law Association. *LANGUAGES:* English and Pilipino. *PRACTICE AREAS:* Banks and Banking; Bankruptcy; Business Law; Corporate Law; Securities.

JOSE C. CONCEPCION, born Davao City, Philippines, July 6, 1934; admitted, 1959, Philippines. *Education:* University of the Philippines (LL.B., cum laude); University of Pennsylvania (LL.M.). *Member:* Integrated Bar of the Philippines; Philippine Society of International Law. Sigma Rho Fraternity. *LANGUAGES:* English and Pilipino. *PRACTICE AREAS:* Litigation; Arbitration.

TEODORO D. REGALA, born Manila, Philippines, December 27, 1933; admitted, 1962, Philippines. *Education:* University of Sydney (B.A.); University of the Philippines (B.S.J., cum laude, LL.B., cum laude); Harvard University (LL.M.). Assistant Professor of Law, Far Eastern University, 1963-1964. Professorial Lecturer in International Business Transactions, Graduate Studies, College of Law, University of the Philippines. Special Lecturer, Seminar on Corporation Code of the Philippines, 1980; 2nd Seminar on Corporation, University of the Philippines Law Center, 1982. Examiner in Mercantile Law, 1984 Bar Examinations. *Member:* Integrated Bar of the Philippines; Philippine Society of International Law; Asean Law Association; International Bar Association (Member, Section on Business Law); Inter Pacific Bar Association (Jurisdictional Council Member for the Philippines). Phi Kappa Phi and Phi Gamma Mu International Honor Societies. *LANGUAGES:* English and Pilipino. *PRACTICE AREAS:* Banks and Banking; Corporate Law; Investments; Mergers, Acquisitions and Divestitures; Corporate.

AVELINO V. CRUZ, born Pasig, Rizal, Philippines, December 17, 1940; admitted, 1962, Philippines. *Education:* San Beda College (A.A., LL.B., magna cum laude); University of Michigan (LL.M.). Professor, San Beda College of Law, 1965-1973. Special Lecturer, University of the Philippines Law Center. Professorial Lecturer, College of Law, University of the Philippines. *Member:* Integrated Bar of the Philippines (Member, Board of Governors; Vice President for Southern Luzon Region, 1977-1979; President, Rizal Chapter, 1977-1979); Legal Management Council of the Philippines (President, 1972-1973); Philippine Society of International Law; Asean Law Association (Secretary General; President, 1985-1987); Citizens

(This Listing Continued)

Legal Aid Society of the Philippines (President, 1989); American Bar Association (Associate Member). *LANGUAGES:* English and Pilipino. *PRACTICE AREAS:* Business Law; Public Utilities; Asian Law; Business Litigation; International Business Litigation.

ROGELIO A. VINLUAN, born Manila, Philippines, April 12, 1937; admitted, 1961, Philippines. *Education:* University of the Philippines (B.S.J., LL.B., cum laude); Yale University (LL.M.). Author, "International Aspects of Intellectual Property Protection," IBP Journal, 1985; Intellectual Property Law: Towards Global Standards (Philippines), Intellectual Corporate Law Supplement, June, 1992. *Member:* Integrated Bar of the Philippines (President, Makati-Pasay Chapter, 1983-1985); Intellectual Property Association of the Philippines (President, 1985-1987; Chairman, 1987-1989; Member, Council of Presidents); Philippine Society of International Law; Asian Patent Attorneys Association (Council Member, 1985-1992; Chairman, Anti-Counterfeiting Committee); Licensing Executive Society (Director, International Trademark Association, Member, Education Committee). *LANGUAGES:* English and Filipino. *PRACTICE AREAS:* Litigation; Intellectual Property; Copyrights; Franchises and Franchising.

VICTOR P. LAZATIN, born Mabalacat, Pampanga, Philippines, August 16, 1947; admitted, 1972, Philippines. *Education:* University of the Philippines (A.B.; LL.B., cum laude); University of Michigan, Clyde Alton Dewitt Fellow (LL.M.). Faculty and Construction Arbitrator, Philippine Institute of Construction Arbitrators. Lecturer, Construction Contracts and Commercial Arbitration, Professional Lecturer, University of the Philippines, 1972-1973. *Member:* Integrated Bar of the Philippines; Maritime Law Association of the Philippines; American Chamber of Commerce in the Philippines; Asia-Pacific Lawyers Association. (Managing Partner). *LANGUAGES:* English and Pilipino. *PRACTICE AREAS:* Litigation; Alternative Dispute Resolution; Construction; Civil Law.

VIOLETA CALVO-DRILON, born Sta. Ana, Manila, Philippines, August 20, 1943; admitted, 1968, Philippines. *Education:* St. Theresa's College (B.A., magna cum laude); University of the Philippines (LL.B.). Panel Speaker, Reports on Recent Corporate Legal Developments, Committee on Business Organizations (Committee G) at the IBA SBL 8th Conference at London, September 15, 1987. Speaker on "Legal Aspects of Joint Venture" at the Seminar on International Business Law and Practices, Sponsored by the International Chamber of Commerce (ICC), Confederation of Asia-Pacific Chamber of Commerce and Industry (CACCI) and the Philippine Chamber of Commerce (PCCI), June 30, 1987. Speaker on International Joint Ventures in the Philippine Setting at the 8th Law Asia Conference on International Law Practice in the LAWASIA Region, September 13, 1983. Rapporteur, International Conference on the "Consequence of the Enforcement of the U.N. Convention on the Elimination of all forms of Discrimination as regards Women," July 12-15, 1981, Vienna. *Member:* Integrated Bar of the Philippines; University of the Philippines Women Lawyers Circle (President, 1978-1980); Legal Management Council of the Philippines; International Law Association; Philippine Association of Multinational Companies; Regional Headquarters, Inc. (Legal Adviser, 1981); Asean Law Association; International Bar Association (Member, Section on Business Law). *LANGUAGES:* English and Pilipino. *PRACTICE AREAS:* Investments; Corporate Law; Family Law; Charitable Organizations.

FLAVIO P. GUTIERREZ, born Bacolor, Pampanga, Philippines, February 7, 1943; admitted, 1972, Philippines. *Education:* University of the Philippines (B.S.B.A.); University of Santo Tomas (LL.B.). Certified Public Accountant. Delegate, 12th Joint Meeting of Philippines-Japan Economic Cooperation Committee, Tokyo, Japan, March 14 and 15, 1989. *Member:* Integrated Bar of the Philippines; Philippine Institute of Certified Public Accountants; Asean Law Association; Philippine Association of Management Accountants; Tax Management Association of the Philippines. *LANGUAGES:* English and Pilipino. *PRACTICE AREAS:* Taxation; Natural Resources; Mortgages; Litigation; Property.

LUIS A. VERA CRUZ, JR., born Tuguegarao, Cagayan, Philippines, June 27, 1950; admitted, 1975, Philippines. *Education:* University of the Philippines (B.S.B.A.; LL.B.); Cornell University (LL.M.). *Member:* Integrated Bar of the Philippines. *LANGUAGES:* English and Pilipino. *PRACTICE AREAS:* Litigation; Commercial Law; Civil Law; Contracts; Torts; Criminal Law; Family Law.

MARCIAL G. DE LA FUENTE, born Manila, Philippines, November 3, 1947; admitted, 1975, Philippines. *Education:* San Beda College (A.B. Philosophy); University of the Philippines (LL.B.). Division Chief, Department of Labor and Employment, Field Services Division, 1976-1977. Section Chief, Labor Regulations Office, 1975. Executive Assistant, Office of the Undersecretary of Labor, 1976. Task Force Head, Labor Inspection of Clark Air Base and Subic Naval Base, 1975. *Member:* Integrated Bar of the

(This Listing Continued)

Philippines; Personnel Management Association of the Philippines; Employers Confederation of the Philippines. *LANGUAGES:* English and Pilipino. *PRACTICE AREAS:* Labor and Employment; Employee Benefits.

DANILO R. DEEN, born 1935; admitted, 1960, Philippines. *Education:* University of San Carlos (A.A.; LL.B.). Regional Chairman, People's Economic Council, Region VII, 1988-1989. *Member:* Integrated Bar of the Philippines (Delegate, House of Delegates, 1981; President, IBP Cebu City Chapter; Vice-President, Eastern Visayan Region, 1984; Member, Board of Governors, 1985); Asean Law Association; Maritime Law Association of the Philippines; American Chamber of Commerce (Director, Cebu City Chapter, 1989—); Cebu Chamber of Commerce and Industry (Vice President, 1989—). (Resident Partner, Cebu Branch Office). *LANGUAGES:* English, Pilipino and Spanish. *PRACTICE AREAS:* Labor and Employment; Business Law; Corporate Law; General Practice; Commercial Law.

TERESITA J. HERBOSA, born Manila, Philippines, October 28, 1950; admitted, 1978, Philippines. *Education:* University of the Philippines (A.B. cum laude; LL.B. cum laude); University of Michigan (M.C.L.). Participant, EEC-Asean Seminar on Transfer of Technology and Socio-Economic Development, Kuala Lumpur, 1985. *Member:* Integrated Bar of the Philippines; Aviation Lawyers Association of the Philippines; Asean Law Association. *LANGUAGES:* English and Pilipino. *PRACTICE AREAS:* Contracts; Communications and Media; Environmental Law; Transportation.

TADEO F. HILADO, born Iloilo City, Philippines, June 30, 1952; admitted, 1978, Philippines. *Education:* De La Salle University (A.B. summa cum laude); University of the Philippines (LL.B.); University of Michigan (LL.M.). Participant, EEC-Asean Seminar on Transfer of Technology and Socio-Economic Development, Jakarta, Indonesia, 1984. Visiting Lawyer, Graham & James, San Francisco, California, 1981-1982. *Member:* Integrated Bar of the Philippines; Legal Management Council of the Philippines; International Bar Association (Section on Business Law). *LANGUAGES:* English and Pilipino. *PRACTICE AREAS:* Business Law; Mergers, Acquisitions and Divestitures; Investments; Securities; Environmental Law.

EUSEBIO V. TAN, born Manila, Philippines, February 6, 1951; admitted, 1976, Philippines. *Education:* De La Salle College (B.A. summa cum laude); Ateneo de Manila University (LL.B.); Columbia University (LL.M.). Participant, EC-ASEAN Seminar on Joint Venture Management and Industrial Cooperation, Kuala Lumpur, Malaysia, 1989, conducted by the Euro-Asia Centre of INSEAD. Special Lecturer on "Philippine Agricultural Investments " to the Overseas Study Team to the Philippines from the Republic of China, 1990; Speaker at the Committee X (International Franchising) Seminar on the "Latest Developments in International Franchising in the Philippines" and at the Committee G (Business Organizations) Seminar on the "Legal Aspects of Joint Ventures in the Philippines" at the 10th Biennial Conference of the Section on Business Law of the International Bar Association held in Hong Kong in October 1991. Speaker on "Transfer Pricing in the Philippines" at the Inter Pacific Bar Association's (IPBA) Tax Law Committee Program, and Contributor of the article on the Philippines in the booklet on the "Current Developments Affecting Foreign Investors" prepared by the IPBA's Cross Border Investment Committee, for the IPBA's Third Annual Meeting and Conference in Taipei, Taiwan, in May 1993. *Member:* Integrated Bar of the Philippines (Treasurer, Pasay City-Makati-Mandaluyong-San Juan del Monte Chapter, 1987-1989; Director, 1989-1991; Vice President, Makati Chapter, 1991-1993; President, Makati Chapter, 1993—; Member, National Committee in Legal Aid, 1991-1993); Philippine Bar Association; International Bar Association (Section on Business Law); Inter-Pacific Bar Association (Charter Member); Financial Executives Institute of the Philippines (Chairman, Tax and Legal Committee; Member, Business Education Committee and Professional Development Committee). *LANGUAGES:* English and Filipino. *PRACTICE AREAS:* Investments; Business Law; Mergers, Acquisitions and Divestitures; Franchises and Franchising; Construction Law; Leases and Leasing; Banks and Banking.

SENEN Y. GLINOGA, born Pitogo, Quezon, Philippines, October 19, 1938; admitted, 1946, Philippines. *Education:* De La Salle College (B.S.C.); Ateneo de Manila University (LL.B.). *Member:* Integrated Bar of the Philippines; Tax Management Association of the Philippines. *LANGUAGES:* English and Pilipino. *PRACTICE AREAS:* Taxation; Employee Benefits; Corporate Law; Insurance; Banks and Banking.

ANTONIO M. LLORENTE, born March 24, 1955; admitted, 1980, Philippines; 1990, New York. *Education:* Ateneo de Manila University (B.S.; LL.B.). Professor, Ateneo de Manila University College of Law. *Member:* Integrated Bar of the Philippines. *LANGUAGES:* English and

(This Listing Continued)

ANGARA ABELLO CONCEPCION REGALA & CRUZ, Metro Manila—Continued

Pilipino. **PRACTICE AREAS:** Contracts; Criminal Law; Entertainment and the Arts; Property; Real Estate; Litigation; Torts.

EMITERIO C. MANIBOG, JR., born October 28. 1950; admitted, 1977, Philippines. *Education:* Far Eastern University (B.A.); Ateneo de Manila University (LL.B.). *Member:* Integrated Bar of the Philippines. **LANGUAGES:** English and Pilipino. **PRACTICE AREAS:** Labor and Employment; Employee Benefits; Social Law.

ROLANDO F. DEL CASTILLO, born Manila, Philippines, November 15, 1941; admitted, 1968, Philippines. *Education:* Ateneo de Manila University (A.B.; LL.B.); Harvard Law School (LL.M.). Lecturer, Philippine Trust Institute. Professor: Arellano University Law Foundation; Ateneo de Manila University College of Law. *Member:* Integrated Bar of the Philippines (Board of Editors, Law Journal, 1982-1983). **LANGUAGES:** English and Pilipino. **PRACTICE AREAS:** Corporate Law; Taxation; Debtor and Creditor; Property; Agency and Distributorship.

FRANCISCO EDRALIN LIM, born Manila, Philippines, February 9, 1955; admitted, 1981, Philippines; 1988, New York. *Education:* University of Santo Tomas (A.B. cum laude; Ph.B. magna cum laude); Ateneo de Manila University (LL.B.); University of Pennsylvania (LL.M.). Associate, Morgan, Lewis & Bockius, Washington, D.C., 1987-1989. Professor, Ateneo de Manila University College of Law; Holder, Justice Jose C. Colayco Professorial Chair in Remedial Law, 1993-1994. Author: "Determining The Reach and Content of Summary Decisions," The Review of Litigation, University of Texas, 1987. *Member:* Integrated Bar of the Philippines (Vice Chairman, Editorial Board, Journal, 1990-1992); New York State Bar Associations; ASEAN Law Association; Foreign Lawyers Forum (Washington, D.C.); American Society of International Law; Maritime Law Association of the Philippines; American Bar Association (Section of International Law and Practice). **LANGUAGES:** English and Pilipino. **PRACTICE AREAS:** Commercial Law; Civil Law; Debtor and Creditor; Litigation; White Collar Crime.

ROMULO ASISTORES ESPALDON, JR., born Manila, Philippines, July 12, 1956; admitted, 1982, Philippines. *Education:* University of the Philippines (B.S.; LL.B.). *Member:* Integrated Bar of the Philippines. **LANGUAGES:** English and Pilipino. **PRACTICE AREAS:** Commercial Law; Civil Law; Contracts; Torts; Family Law.

EMERICO O. DE GUZMAN, born Manila, Philippines, November 10, 1956; admitted, 1983, Philippines. *Education:* University of the Philippines (B.S.; LL.B.). *Member:* Integrated Bar of the Philippines. **LANGUAGES:** English and Pilipino. **PRACTICE AREAS:** Labor and Employment; Litigation; Employee Benefits.

REGINA P. PADILLA-GERALDEZ, born Manila, Philippines, September 16, 1953; admitted, 1979, Philippines. *Education:* University of the Philippines (A.B.,cum laude; LL.B. cum laude); University of Michigan (LL.M.). Associate Commissioner, Commission on Immigration and Deportation, 1988-1989; Acting Undersecretary for Legal Affairs, Department of Agrarian Reforms, 1989-1990. Visiting Lawyer, Baker & McKenzie, San Francisco, California, 1981-1983. *Member:* Integrated Bar of the Philippines; University of the Philippines Women Lawyers' Circle (President, 1993-1994; Vice President and Director, 1992-1993); Asean Law Association (Assistant Secretary). **LANGUAGES:** English and Pilipino. **PRACTICE AREAS:** Appellate Practice; Real Estate; Immigrations & Naturalization; Civil Law; Property.

ANA TERESA A. ARNALDO-ORACION, born Manila, Philippines, June 7, 1956; admitted, 1982, Philippines. *Education:* University of the Philippines (B.S.; LL.B.); Cambridge University (LL.M.). *Member:* Integrated Bar of the Philippines; Maritime Law Association of the Philippines (Director, 1983—); U.P. Women Lawyers' Circle (Director and Corporate Secretary, 1989—). **LANGUAGES:** English and Pilipino. **PRACTICE AREAS:** Litigation; Insurance; Admiralty and Maritime Law.

ALELI ANGELA G. QUIRINO, born Manila, Philippines, May 13, 1944; admitted, 1985, Philippines. *Education:* Assumption College (A.B.; B.S.E. magna cum laude); Ateneo de Manila University (LL.B.). Co-Author: Towards Standards (Philippines), Intellectual Corporate Law Supplement, June, 1992. Delegate, OMPI/WIPO Preparatory Meeting for the Diplomatic Conference for the Conclusion of the Trademark Law Treaty, Geneva, December, 1993. *Member:* Integrated Bar of the Philippines (Director, Makati Chapter; Assistant Treasurer, 1993-1995); Ateneo Law Alumni Foundation (Director and Board Secretary, 1991-1995); Asean Law Association; Intellectual Property Association of the Philip-

(This Listing Continued)

pines (Director and Treasurer, 1993-1995); Asian Patent Attorneys Association (Member, Committee on Trademarks); Association Internationale pour la Protection de Propiete Industrielle (Member, Executive Committee). **LANGUAGES:** English, Filipino, Spanish and French. **PRACTICE AREAS:** Intellectual Property; Trademarks; Copyrights; Franchises and Franchising; Energy; Antitrust and Trade Regulation; Business Law.

ERNESTO R. AÑASCO, born Manila, Philippines, November 26, 1952; admitted, 1985, Philippines. *Education:* Philippine School of Business Administration and Philippine Christian University (B.A.); San Beda College of Law (LL.B.). *Member:* Integrated Bar of the Philippines. **LANGUAGES:** English and Filipino. **PRACTICE AREAS:** Labor and Employment; Social Law; Employee Benefits.

SENIOR ASSOCIATES

ROBERTO CECILIO O. LIM, born 1958; admitted, 1984, Philippines. *Education:* De La Salle University (A.B.); University of the Philippines (LL.B.). Law Clerk, Justice H. Concepcion, Supreme Court of the Philippines, 1983. Technical Assistant to the President of the 1986 Constitution Commission of the Republic of the Philippines. Visiting Lawyer: Ince & Co., The Streamship Mutual and Underwriting Association Ltd., 1989; Shaw and Croft, Holman Fenwick & Willan, 1990. *Member:* Integrated Bar of the Philippines; Maritime Law Association of the Philippines.

GUILLERMO P. DABBAY, JR., born 1959; admitted, 1984, Philippines. *Education:* University of the Philippines (A.B.; LL.B.). *Member:* Integrated Bar of the Philippines.

ALBERT DENNIS NOCON AÑOVER, born 1961; admitted, 1987, Philippines. *Education:* University of the Philippines (A.B. Economics); Ateneo de Manila University (LL.B.). *Member:* Integrated Bar of the Philippines.

ALEX FERDINAND S. FIDER, born 1961; admitted, 1987, Philippines. *Education:* University of the Philippines (A.B.; LL.B.); University of London (LL.M.). Law Clerk, Justice Abdulwahid Bidin, Supreme Court of the Philippines, 1987. *Member:* Integrated Bar of the Philippines; Intellectual Property Association of the Philippines.

GODOFREDO L. LABAY, born 1950; admitted, 1983, Philippines. *Education:* Sacred Heart College (A.B.); University of the East (LL.B.). *Member:* Integrated Bar of the Philippines.

VICTORIA V. LOANZON, born 1954; admitted, 1988, Philippines. *Education:* Maryknoll College (A.B.); University of the Philippines (LL.B.; M.A. in Urban-Regional Planning). Certificate, International Course in Planning, Housing and Building (Bouncentrus, The Netherlands). *Member:* Integrated Bar of the Philippines; Immigration Lawyers Association of the Philippines (Secretary); Citizens Legal Aid Society of the Philippines (Deputy Secretary General); Philippine Institute of Environmental Planners; ASEAN Association for Planning and Housing; ASEAN Law Association; University of the Philippines Women Lawyers' Circle; Intellectual Property Association of the Philippines.

JOSABETH A. ANTONIO, born 1963; admitted, 1988, Philippines. *Education:* University of the Philippines (A.B.; LL.B.). *Member:* Integrated Bar of the Philippines.

SALVADOR L. PEÑA, born 1961; admitted, 1988, Philippines. *Education:* University of the Philippines (A.B.); Ateneo de Manila University (LL.B.). *Member:* Integrated Bar of the Philippines.

JOSEPHINE ALESSANDRA G. COCHICO, born 1964; admitted, 1990, Philippines. *Education:* University of the Philippines (A.B.; LL.B.). *Member:* Integrated Bar of the Philippines.

ROWENA L. GARCIA, born 1963; admitted, 1990, Philippines. *Education:* University of the Philippines (B.A.); San Beda College (LL.B.). *Member:* Integrated Bar of the Philippines.

ERNESTO B. FRANCISCO, JR., born 1962; admitted, 1990, Philippines. *Education:* University of Santo Tomas (B.A.); Ateneo de Manila University (LL.B.). Special Assistant, Legal and Legislative Affairs, Office of Senator Herrera, 1987-1989. *Member:* Integrated Bar of the Philippines.

JEFFERSON M. MARQUEZ, born 1964; admitted, 1990, Philippines. *Education:* University of Santo Tomas (B.S.C.); San Beda College (LL.B.). *Member:* Integrated Bar of the Philippines.

LELAND R. VILLADOLID, JR., born 1963; admitted, 1990, Philippines. *Education:* University of the Philippines (B.S.); Ateneo de Manila University (LL.B.). *Member:* Integrated Bar of the Philippines,.

(This Listing Continued)

ASSOCIATES

BRIGIDA S. ALDEGUER, born 1952; admitted, 1992, Philippines. *Education:* University of the Philippines (A.B.; LL.B.); Ateneo de Manila University (J.D.).

REDENTOR A. BONBOLAN, born 1969; admitted, 1994, Philippines. *Education:* Ateneo de Manila University (A.B.); University of the Philippines (LL.B.).

GERARDO T. BUAN, born 1963; admitted, 1992, Philippines. *Education:* De La Salle University (A.B.); San Beda College (LL.B.).

J. MARIA EMMANUEL A. CARAL, born 1965; admitted, 1992, Philippines. *Education:* Ateneo de Manila University (A.B.; J.D.).

GILBERTO GALLOS, born 1965; admitted, 1994, Philippines. *Education:* University of the Philippines (B.A.); Ateneo de Manila University (J.D.).

CARLOS P. BATMAYTAN, III, born 1969; admitted, 1994, Philippines. *Education:* Ateneo de Manila University (A.B.; J.D.).

VINCENTE D. GEROCHI, III, born 1967; admitted, 1994, Philippines. *Education:* Ateneo de Manila University (A.B.; J.D.).

MARIBETH A. LIPARDO, born 1966; admitted, 1992, Philippines. *Education:* University of the Philippines (A.B.); Ateneo de Manila University (J.D.).

CIPRIANO J. MERCADO, born 1964; admitted, 1994, Philippines. *Education:* University of Nueva Caceres (B.A.); Ateneo de Manila University (J.D.).

RODRIGO H. NEPOMUCENO, born 1967; admitted, 1993, Philippines. *Education:* Ateneo de Manila University (B.S., J.D.).

LOURDES A. PASCUAL, born 1968; admitted, 1994, Philippines. *Education:* Ateneo de Manila University (B.S.; J.D.).

MIRIAN KATHERINE T. RECINTO, born 1965; admitted, 1994, Philippines. *Education:* De La Salle University (A.B.; B.S.C.); Ateneo de Manila University (J.D.). Certified Public Accountant.

TEODORO L. REGALA, JR., born 1966; admitted, 1994, Philippines. *Education:* Ateneo de Manila University (A.B.); San Beda College of Law (LL.B.).

TORIBIO U. REYES, III, born 1968; admitted, 1993, Philippines. *Education:* Ateneo de Manila University (B.S., J.D.).

ANTONINO B. ROMAN, III, born 1968; admitted, 1994, Philippines. *Education:* Ateneo de Manila University (A.B.; J.D.).

JUDE JOSHUE L. SABIO, born 1965; admitted, 1994, Philippines. *Education:* Ateneo de Manila University (A.B.); University of the Philippines (LL.B.).

AILEEN MAY P. SANTOS, born 1967; admitted, 1994, Philippines. *Education:* University of the Philippines - Iloilo (B.A.); De La Salle University (M.B.A.); Ateneo de Manila University (J.D.). Certified Public Accountant.

MA. DOLORES T. SYQUIA, born 1964; admitted, 1993, Philippines. *Education:* University of the Philippines (B.S., LL.B.).

ERNESTO A. TABUJARA III, born 1965; admitted, 1992, Philippines. *Education:* University of the Philippines (A.B.; LL.B.). *Member:* Integrated Bar of the Philippines. **LANGUAGES:** English and Filipino.

NORIANNE KATHERINE R. TAN, born 1966; admitted, 1993, Philippines. *Education:* University of Philippines (B.S.); Ateneo de Manila University (J.D.).

GIOVANNI F. VALLENTE, born 1966; admitted, 1993, Philippines. *Education:* Ateneo de Manila University (A.B., J.D.).

LEANDRO B. VERCELES, JR., born 1957; admitted, 1988, Philippines. *Education:* University of the Philippines (B.S.); Ateneo de Manila University (LL.B.). Congressman, Virac, Catanduanes.

ANGELA C. YLAGAN, born 1967; admitted, 1993, Philippines. *Education:* Assumption College (B.S.C.); University of Philippines (LL.B.). Certified Public Accountant.

JOSE R. ZULUETA, born 1957; admitted, 1990, Philippines. *Education:* University of the Philippines (A.B.; LL.B.).

(This Listing Continued)

OF COUNSEL

EFREN IRA PLANA, born San Juan, Metro Manila, Philippines, June 28, 1928; admitted, 1955, Philippines. *Education:* University of the Philippines (A.B.; LL.B. cum laude). Phi Kappa Phi and Phi Gamma Mu International Honor Societies. Author: "Investment Incentives in the Philippines," 1969; "Tax Law Innovations," 1978. Professorial Lecturer, College of Law, University of the Philippines. Associate Justice, Supreme Court, 1981-1986. Commissioner of Internal Revenue, 1975-1980. Deputy Minister of Finance, 1980-1981. Associate Justice, Court of Appeals, 1973-1975. Deputy Minister of Justice, 1972-1973. Undersecretary of National Defense, 1970-1972. Director and Chief Legal Counsel, Board of Investments, 1968-1970. Deputy Chief Legal Counsel, Department of Justice, 1964-1968. *Member:* Integrated Bar of the Philippines; Philippine Society of International Law; American Society of International Law. **LANGUAGES:** English and Pilipino.

ROBERTO REGALA (1972-1979).

CONSULTANT

ARMANDO Q. ONGSIOCO, born Pasay City, Philippines, July 2, 1928; admitted, 1960, Philippines. *Education:* Far Eastern University (A.A.; LL.B.). *Member:* Integrated Bar of the Philippines; Patent Attorneys Association of the Philippines (Treasurer, 1978-1982); Asian Patent Attorneys Association; Asean Law Association; Aviation Lawyers Association of the Philippines; Immigration Lawyers Association of the Philippines. **LANGUAGES:** English and Pilipino.

CEBU CITY BRANCH OFFICE
SENIOR ASSOCIATES

SERECIO MATHEW B. JO, born 1963; admitted, 1988, Philippines. *Education:* University of San Carlos (B.Sc.; LL.B.).

JOSEPH S. TANCO, born 1962; admitted, 1988, Philippines. *Education:* University of San Carlos (A.B.,; LL.B.).

ASSOCIATES

IOLANDA B. ABELLA, born 1967; admitted, 1990, Philippines. *Education:* University of San Carlos (B.S.; LL.B.).

ENRIQUE MELCHOR O. DIOLA, JR., born 1963; admitted, 1990, Philippines. *Education:* University of the Philippines-Cebu (A.B.); Ateneo de Manila University (LL.B.).

JOSELITO M. YBAÑEZ, born 1961; admitted, 1990, Philippines. *Education:* Ateneo de Manila University (B.S.; LL.B.).

REPRESENTATIVE CLIENTS: The Philippine Long Distance Telephone Co.; San Miguel Corp.; Manila Electric Co.; Atlas Consolidated Mining & Development Corp.; Compania General de Tabacos de Filipinas; Philex Mining Corp.; Metropolitan Bank & Trust Co.; China Banking Corp.; Bank of Tokyo; Deutsche Bank A.G.; First Chicago Leasing & Equipment Credit Corp.; Citibank, N.A.; Korea Exchange Bank; Pilipinas Bank; Prudential Bank & Trust Co.; Rizal Commercial Banking Corporation; The Hongkong & Shanghai Banking Corporation; Far East Bank & Trust Company; First Philippine International Bank; Mandarin Oriental Hotel; Manila Peninsula Hotel; Hotel Nikko Manila Garden; Asiaworld International Group; Pilipinas Shell Petroleum Corp.; Caltex Philippines, Inc.; Westinghouse Electric, S.A.; Eveready Battery Co. Phils., Inc.; Matsushita Electronics Philippines, Inc.; Philips Electronics and Lighting, Inc.; Uniden Electronic Components Corp. of the Phils.; Motorola Philippines, Inc.; Texas Instruments (Phils.), Inc.; NEC Corp.; S.C. Johnson & Sons, Inc.; DOLE Philippines, Inc.; Bayer Philippines, Inc.; Astra Pharmaceuticals Philippines, Inc.; Wyeth Philippines, Inc.; Pepsi-Cola Bottling Group of the Philippines, Inc.; Coca Cola Bottlers Phils., Inc.; Jardine Davies, Inc.; Goldilocks Bake Shop; Marubeni Corporation; Itochu Corporation; Procter and Gamble Philippines, Inc.; McDonalds Corporation; Tetra Pak Philippines, Inc.; FIAB Finanziaria Maglificio Biellese Fratelli Fila, S.P.A.; Philippine Association of the Recording Industry; Philippine American Life Insurance Co.; Philippine Airlines, Inc.; Korean Airlines; Magsaysay Lines, Inc.; Toyota Motor Philippines Corp.; DHL (Philippines) Services Corp.; SGS Far East Limited; Yamamura Glass Company Ltd.; Asahi Glass Co. Ltd.; The Embassy of Japan; The Embassy of the Federal Republic of Germany; The Embassy of Israel.

BALGOS & PEREZ

Established in 1946

5TH FLOOR, CORINTHIAN PLAZA
PASEO DE ROXAS, MAKATI
METRO MANILA, REPUBLIC OF THE PHILIPPINES
Telephone: 2-8191021
Fax: 632-8100792

FIRM PROFILE: The Law Firm of Balgos & Perez is a professional partnership duly organized as such pursuant to the laws of the Philippines and is based in Makati, Metro Manila. It is engaged in the general practice of law and is known for its expertise in pleadings and litigation. It is involved

(This Listing Continued)

BALGOS & PEREZ, Metro Manila—Continued

in corporate law, especially in corporate rehabilitation, take-overs, mergers and acquisitions, banking, insurance, transportation and labor.

The Firm was founded in 1946 when Alejandro F. de Santos joined his Law classmates, Jose B. Herrera and Artemio G. Delfino and formed De Santos Herrera and Delfino. Its first clients were Manila Surety & Fidelity Co., Inc. and Paramount Surety & Insurance Co., Inc. When Jose B. Herrera joined the judiciary in the late 1950's and Artemio G. Delfino became the in-house counsel of the Makati Medical Center, the Law Firm was reorganized and in 1971 became De Santos, Balgos & Perez.

Alejandro F. de Santos died in July 1985 and the remaining partners, Marcial O.T. Balgos and Hernando B. Perez, formed what is now known as Balgos & Perez Law Offices since 1985. The Firm has held offices at 5th Floor, Corinthian Plaza, Paseo de Roxas, Makati, Metro Manila.

It has for its present clientele entities which number not less than a hundred and fifty and are representative of Philippine business activities like banking, finance, securities, insurance, transportation, media, etc. At present, the Law Firm is composed of the following:

MEMBERS OF FIRM

MARCIAL O.T. BALGOS, born June 30, 1932. *Education:* University of Manila (A.A., high honors, 1952; LL.B., 1956). Among the top twenty in the 1956 Philippine Bar Examination. Authored various articles on procedure, corporate rehabilitation and sequestration published in the Integrated Bar Journal and The Philippine Law Gazette, noted legal publications in the Philippines. Author: "The Motor Vehicles Insurance Law" and "Handbook on the Law on Pleadings". Corporate Secretary, Philippine Commercial International Bank. Chairman, First Provincial Development Bank. (Senior Partner).

HERNANDO B. PEREZ, born September 27, 1939. *Education:* Ateneo de Manila University (LL.B., 1961; M.A., Business Administration, 1975); and among the top twenty in the Bar Examinations. Author: "The Insurance Code and Insolvency Law". Secretary, Philippine Department of Transportation and Communications. Minority Floor Leader, House of Representatives, Philippine Congress. (Of Counsel).

EDGARDO M. MAGTALAS, born March 16, 1939. *Education:* University of Manila, College of Law (LL.B., cum laude, 1961). Assistant Vice-President and Assistant Chief Legal Counsel, Philippine National Bank, 1978. Senior Vice-President and General Counsel, Republic Planters Bank, 1978-1987. (Finance Officer).

JUNIOR MEMBERS

RAFAEL S. DOMINGO, born June 3, 1952. *Education:* Marquette University of Wisconsin, U.S.A. (B.A., 1976); University of The Philippines (LL.B., 1980). *PRACTICE AREAS:* Labor Law; Civil and Criminal Litigation; Aviation Law; Transportation Law; Insurance Law.

ENRICO G. VELASCO, born March 10, 1953. *Education:* San Beda College (B.A., 1974); University of The Philippines (LL.B., 1978). *PRACTICE AREAS:* Real Property Law; Civil and Criminal Litigation; Family Law; Labor Law.

RAMON P. GUTIERREZ, born December 5, 1953. *Education:* University of Santo Tomas (B.A., 1974; LL.B., 1978). *PRACTICE AREAS:* Corporate Law; Civil and Criminal Litigation; Maritime and Admiralty Law; Labor; Intellectual Property.

EDGAR A. PACIS, born December 17, 1952. *Education:* University of the Philippines (B.A., 1973; LL.B., 1978). *PRACTICE AREAS:* Land Titles and Deeds; Civil and Criminal Litigation; Banking Law; Taxation; Finance.

ASSOCIATES

MA. ROSARIO M. ENAGE-ARANGUREN, born September 17, 1965. *Education:* University of the Philippines (B.A., 1987); Ateneo de Manila University (J.D., 1991). *PRACTICE AREAS:* Real Property Law; Civil and Criminal Litigation; Corporate Law; Labor Law.

MICHAEL Z. UNTALAN, born May 20, 1965. *Education:* University of the Philippines (B.A., 1987); Ateneo de Manila University (J.D., 1992). *PRACTICE AREAS:* Banking Law; Finance; Civil and Criminal Litigation; Corporate Law; Aviation Law.

VINCENT JASON T. VILLANUEVA, born February 11, 1966. *Education:* Ateneo de Manila University (B.S., Business Management, 1986; LL.B., 1991). *PRACTICE AREAS:* Civil and Criminal Litigation; Banking Law; Technology Transfer Law; Corporate Law.

(This Listing Continued)

ISAGANI A. CORTES, born July 1, 1967. *Education:* University of the East (A.B., 1987); University of the Philippines (LL.B., 1991). *PRACTICE AREAS:* Banking Law; Civil and Criminal Litigation; Maritime and Admiralty Law.

EDWARD P. MARTINEZ, born January 27, 1968. *Education:* Ateneo de Manila University (B.S.L.M., 1989; J.D., 1993). *PRACTICE AREAS:* Civil and Criminal Litigation; Family Law; Labor Law; Banking Law.

RAMON C. CHINGCUANGCO, born November 27, 1964. *Education:* University of the Philippines (B.A., 1987; LL.B., 1993). *PRACTICE AREAS:* Civil and Criminal Litigation; Transportation Law; Telecommunications Law; Insurance Law; Corporate Law.

PAUL JOMAR S. ALCUDIA, born July 21, 1966. *Education:* University of the Philippines (B.S., Economics, 1988; LL.B., 1993). *PRACTICE AREAS:* Civil and Criminal Litigation; Insurance Law; Taxation Law; Transportation Law.

GEORGINA M. YAMBAO, born September 9, 1966. *Education:* Assumption College (B.A., 1987); Ateneo de Manila University (J.D., 1992). *PRACTICE AREAS:* Corporate Law; Franchising and Technology Transfer.

BALMEO, BAUTISTA & PEÑASALES

Established in 1994

ROOM 314, CITYLAND III
HERRERA STREET, LEGASPI VILLAGE, MAKATI
METRO MANILA 1200, REPUBLIC OF THE PHILIPPINES
Telephone: (632) 895-65-69; (632) 893-2972-74; 897-6916
Fax: (632) 895-6529; (632) 893-2975

General Practice, Taxation, Customs Law, Corporation Law and Finance, Banking, Administrative Law, Labor Law, Transnational Transactions, Admiralty, Litigation, Patents, Trademarks and Immigration Law.

MEMBERS OF FIRM

LEONIDES F. BALMEO, born Baliwag, Bulacan, Philippines, July 3, 1944; admitted, 1970, Philippines. *Education:* University of Santo Tomas (B.A., 1964); Ateneo de Manila University (LL.B., 1969); New York University (LL.M., 1976). Participant, Price Waterhouse & Company's Continuing Education Program in Illinois and Texas, U.S.A., 1974-1976. Former Senior Partner and Tax Department Head, Castillo, Laman, Tan & Pantaleon. Former Senior Tax Staff Member, International Tax Service, Price Waterhouse & Co., N.Y., N.Y. Professor of Taxation, Ateneo de Manila University. Lecturer, University of the Philippines Law Center Institute of Tax Law. *Member:* Integrated Bar of the Philippines; Tax Management Association of the Philippines. *LANGUAGES:* English and Pilipino. *PRACTICE AREAS:* Taxation Law; Customs Law; Corporation Law and Finance.

LOVELL R. BAUTISTA, born Initao, Misamis Oriental, Philippines, August 14, 1948; admitted, 1983, Philippines; 1985, State Bar of New York, U.S.A. *Education:* Liceo de Cagayan (B.S.C., Major in Accounting, 1969); Passed CPA Board 1974; Ateneo de Manila (LL.B., 1982); University of Pennsylvania, U.S.A. (LL.M., 1984). Former Tax Partner, KPMG Fernandez Santos and Lopez. Professor, Taxation, San Sebastian College of Law. *Member:* New York State Bar Association; Integrated Bar of the Philippines; Philippine Institute of Certified Public Accountants; Tax Management Association of the Philippines; Rotary Club of Makati North; American Chamber of Commerce in the Philippines. *LANGUAGES:* English, Spanish and Pilipino. *PRACTICE AREAS:* Corporate Organization and Restructuring; Taxation; Administrative Law.

ANTERO A. PEÑASALES, born Iloilo City, Philippines, October 28, 1951; admitted, 1978, Philippines. *Education:* University of the Philippines (B.A., 1973; LL.B, 1977); Tulane University, New Orleans, Louisiana (LL.M., Admiralty, 1985). Former Law Clerk, Walker and Corsa, N.Y., N.Y. Co-Author: "Philippine Admiralty and Maritime Law," 1987 ed. Former Visiting Attorney, Phelps, Dumble, Claverie & Sims, New Orleans, LA. Former Partner, Teves, Campos & Hernandez. *Member:* Integrated Bar of the Philippines; Maritime Law Association of the Philippines. *LANGUAGES:* English and Pilipino. *PRACTICE AREAS:* Admiralty; Litigation; Corporation Law.

KATHRYN A. GO-PEREZ, born Cebu City, Philippines, October 3, 1965; admitted, 1991, Philippines. *Education:* University of the Philippines (B.A, 1986); Ateneo de Manila University (LL.B., 1990). *Member:* Inte-

(This Listing Continued)

grated Bar of the Philippines; Tax Management Association of the Philippines, Federacion Internacional de Abogadas. *LANGUAGES:* English and Pilipino. *PRACTICE AREAS:* Taxation; Corporation Law; Real Estate Transactions; Admiralty.

ASSOCIATES

GRACIELA M. BARLETA, born San Pablo City, Laguna, Philippines, August 8, 1965; admitted, 1993, Philippines. *Education:* College of the Holy Spirit (B.Sc., Major in Accounting, 1986); Passed CPA Board, 1987; Ateneo de Manila University (J.D., 1992). *Member:* Philippine Institute of Accountants; Integrated Bar of the Philippines. *LANGUAGES:* English and Pilipino. *PRACTICE AREAS:* Taxation Law; Corporation Law.

FRANCISCO B. GONZALEZ V., born City of Manila, October 20, 1967; admitted, 1994, Philippines. *Education:* De la Salle University (B.S.C., Major in Accounting, 1989); Passed CPA Board, 1989; Ateneo de Manila University (J.D., 1993). *Member:* Integrated Bar of the Philippines; Philippine Institute of Certified Public Accountants; Tax Management Association of the Philippines. *LANGUAGES:* English and Pilipino. *PRACTICE AREAS:* Taxation; Corporate Law.

REPRESENTATIVE CLIENTS: Aboitiz and Co.; Aboitiz Air Transport Corporation; Aboitiz Jebsen Bulk Transport Corporation; Aboitiz Shipping Corporation; Association of International Shipping Lines; Batey Ads; Burger Machine, Inc.; Consolidated Industrial Gases, Inc.; Cebu Oxygen and Acetylene Corporation; Conference of Interisland Shipowners and Operators (CISO); Cotabato Light and Power Company; Davao Light and Power Company; Electric Power Development Company; Gaisano Metro; Lucky Tableware Factory, Inc.; Malabon Zoo Foundation, Inc.; Metropolitan Club, Inc.; Morning Star Milling Corporation; National Development Corporation; New London Food Products, Inc.; New Zealand Milk Products; Paramount Insurance Corporation; Pepsi-Cola Products Philippines, Inc.; Philippine Dairy Products Corporation; Pillsbury Flour Milling Corporation; Reefer Van Specialists, Inc.; Refrigerated Transport Services, Inc.; Rhone-Poulenc Rorer Philippines, Inc.; Royal Oil Products, Inc.; Satelec Pierre Rolland Philippines Corporation; Solid Circuits, Inc.; Visayan Glass Factory; Vita Realty Corporation.

LAW OFFICES
BAUTISTA PICAZO BUYCO TAN & FIDER

Established in 1987

8TH FLOOR, SINGAPORE AIRLINES BUILDING
138 H.V. DE LA COSTA STREET, SALCEDO VILLAGE, MAKATI
METRO MANILA, REPUBLIC OF THE PHILIPPINES
Telephone: (632) 810-47-66 to 67; (632) 812-91-81 to 90
Fax: (632) 810-47-68; (632) 865-391

Extension Office (Litigation Department):
Bautista Law Building, 30 Scout Albano Street, Diliman, Quezon City.
Telephone: (632) 99-15-11 to 12; (632) 924-1248. Fax: (632) 924-1669.

Commercial and Civil Law, Banking and Finance, Securities, Corporations, Mergers and Acquisitions, Foreign Investments, Taxation, Labor, Immigration, Civil, Criminal and Administrative Litigation, Public Utilities, Trademarks, Copyrights and Patents.

MEMBERS OF FIRM

ANTONIO A. PICAZO, born 1941; admitted, 1964. *Education:* University of the Philippines (LL.B.); University of Pennsylvania (LL.M.).

ANTONIO R. BAUTISTA, born 1938; admitted, 1959. *Education:* University of the Philippines (B.S. Jur.; LL.B.); University of Michigan (LL.M.; J.D., cum laude).

SILVERIO BENNY J. TAN, born 1956; admitted, 1983. *Education:* University of the Philippines (A.B., Political Science, cum laude; LL.B., cum laude).

PURISIMO S. BUYCO, born 1955; admitted, 1981. *Education:* Central Philippines University (A.B., History, magna cum laude); University of the Philippines (LL.B., cum laude).

ALEX ERLITO S. FIDER, born 1953; admitted, 1985. *Education:* University of the Philippines (A.B., Economics; LL.B.).

ENCARNACION GEMMA M. SANTOS, born 1962; admitted, 1986. *Education:* University of the Philippines (A.B., History, cum laude; LL.B.).

AMELIA P. BAUTISTA, born 1939; admitted, 1982. *Education:* Guagua National Colleges (A.B., cum laude); University of Santo Tomas (LL.B).

VICTORIA R. TAMAYAO, born 1959; admitted, 1988. *Education:* University of the Philippines (B.S., Business Economics, cum laude; LL.B.).

(This Listing Continued)

YSIDRO J. PEREZ, born 1932; admitted, 1955. *Education:* University of the Philippines (LL.B.).

MARIO C. LORENZO, born 1940; admitted, 1963. *Education:* University of the Philippines (LL.B.); Asian Institute of Management (M.A., Management).

ASSOCIATES

GABRIEL A. DEE, born 1964; admitted, 1989. *Education:* University of the Philippines (A.B., History; LL.B.).

CYNTHIA Y. LIGERALDE-DE LA PAZ, born 1962; admitted, 1987. *Education:* University of the Philippines (A.B., Psychology, cum laude; LL.B).

MA. ADELINA S. GATDULA, born 1962; admitted, 1988. *Education:* University of the Philippines (A.B., Economics, cum laude; LL.B.).

CARLO MAGNO J. VERZO, born 1961; admitted, 1989. *Education:* University of the Philippines (A.B., Anthropology; LL.B).

EUGENIO H. VILLAREAL, born 1964; admitted, 1988. *Education:* Ateneo de Manila (B.S., Legal Management; LL.B.).

ESTRELITA G. GACUTAN, born 1963; admitted, 1989. *Education:* University of the Philippines (A.B., Political Science, cum laude; LL.B.).

FRANCIS A. VER, born 1955; admitted, 1989. *Education:* University of the Philippines (A.B., Communication Arts; B.S., Foreign Service; LL.B).

MAXIMO J.L.C. ABAD, born 1967; admitted, 1993. *Education:* University of the Philippines (A.B., Anthropology); Ateneo de Manila University (LL.B.).

PETER PAUL A. BERMEJO, born 1965; admitted, 1992. *Education:* Ateneo de Manila University (B.S., Biology; LL.B).

EVANGELINE B. CABIGAO-DESCALLAR, born 1963; admitted, 1990. *Education:* Ateneo de Manila University (B.S. Legal Management; LL.B.).

FRANCIS JOSEPH G. ESCUDERO, born 1969; admitted, 1994. *Education:* University of the Philippines (A.B., Political Science; LL.B.).

LUIS MANUEL L. GATMAITAN, born 1965; admitted, 1992. *Education:* University of the Philippines (A.B., Economics); Ateneo de Manila University (LL.B).

EDELINE G. GONZALES-RAMOS, born 1966; admitted, 1992. *Education:* University of the Philippines (A.B., Economics; LL.B.).

MANUEL ANTONIO Z. GONZALEZ, born 1965; admitted, 1994. *Education:* New York University (B.S., Political Science, Hons.); University of the Philippines (LL.B.).

DIOSDADO B. MARASIGAN, born 1964; admitted, 1992. *Education:* University of San Jose Recoletos (B.S., Commerce, cum laude); Ateneo de Manila University (LL.B). Certified Public Accountant, 1985.

BERNARD P. OLALIA, born 1965; admitted, 1992. *Education:* Ateneo de Manila University (B.S., Legal Management); University of the Philippines (LL.B.).

JONAS KARL V. PEREZ, born 1962; admitted, 1990. *Education:* University of the Philippines (A.B., Philosophy); Ateneo de Manila University (LL.B.).

LOURDES MARIVIC K. PUNZALAN-ESPIRITU, born 1968; admitted, 1994. *Education:* De La Salle University (B.S.C., Accounting, Hons.); University of the Philippines (LL.B.). Certified Public Accountant, 1989.

CELINA L. SALCEDO, born 1965; admitted, 1992. *Education:* University of Santo Tomas (A.B., Journalism); University of the Philippines (LL.B.).

MARY LINDA E. SALVADOR, born 1965; admitted, 1992, New York; 1993, Philippines. *Education:* Ateneo de Manila University (A.B., Interdisciplinary Studies; LL.B.).

MA. LEAH J. SEBASTIAN, born 1967; admitted, 1994. *Education:* University of the Philippines (B.A., History; LL.B.).

MA. THERESA S. VELOSO, born 1967; admitted, 1994. *Education:* University of the Philippines (B.A., Comparative Literature; LL.B.).

MARK O. VERGARA, born 1966; admitted, 1993. *Education:* Ateneo de Manila University (B.S., Legal Management; LL.B.).

(This Listing Continued)

LAW OFFICES BAUTISTA PICAZO BUYCO TAN & FIDER, Metro Manila—Continued

CHARLIE C. YALUNG, born 1967; admitted, 1994. *Education:* University of the Philippines (B.A., Economics; LL.B.).

REPRESENTATIVE CLIENTS: AB Capital Corp.; ACI Insulation Phils. Inc.; Adamson & Adamson, Inc.; Alen Group of Companies; A&A Development Corp.; Asian Bank Corp.; A. Soriano Group; Asiatrust Bank; Atlas Consolidated Mining; Citytrust Investment Phils.; Coca-Cola Bottlers Phils.; Development Bank of the Phils.; Dizon Copper Silver Mines; Electro-Systems Industries Engineering Corp.; Far East Bank; First Pacific Limited; Fridays Holdings Inc.; Gateway Property Group; Hayakawa Electronics Limited (Phils.); Insular Investment and Trust Corp.; Insular Savings Bank; International Container Terminal Services; Lopez Sugar Corp.; Kroll Associati (Phils.); Manila Standard; Mariwasa Manufacturing Inc.; Metro Pacific Group; Metro Bank Group; Nissan Car Lease Phils. Inc.; Paramount Vinyl Products Inc.; PDCP Bank; Peregrine Capital Phils.; Philippine Long Distance Telephone Co.; Philippine Long-Term Equity Fund; Phinma Group of Companies; Prudentialife Group; Puratos Phils.; RCBC Capital Corp.; San Miguel Corp.; Security Diners Corp.; SMART Information Technologies Inc.; South Sea Textile Group; Toyota Motors; UBP Capital Corp.; Universal Food Corp.

BELO GOZON ELMA
PAREL ASUNCION & LUCILA

Established in 1993

15TH FLOOR, SAGITTARIUS CONDOMINIUMS
H.V. DE LA COSTA STREET
SALCEDO VILLAGE, MAKATI 1227
METRO MANILA, REPUBLIC OF THE PHILIPPINES
Telephone: 816-3716 to 19; 812-4496 to 97
Cable Address: BGE Law
Fax: (632) 817-0696; 812-0008

Mailing Address: P.O. Box 2346 Makati Central Post Office

Correspondent Offices: Bufete M. Trigo Chacon, Vada del Generalisimo, 53, 5", 8. Madrid (16), P;20 de la Castellana, 123; Qualley, Larson & Jones, 220 Badgerow Building, 422 Fourth Street, Sioux City, Iowa 51101.

General Practice, Corporation, Taxation, Contracts, Natural Resources, Aviation, Patents and Trademarks, Copyright, Labor, Insurance, Foreign Investments, Telecommunications, Banking and Immigration Law, Administrative Law, Litigation.

FOUNDING PARTNERS

ENRIQUE M. BELO, born Roxas City, Philippines, September 8, 1922; admitted, 1950, Philippines. *Education:* University of the Philippines (A.A., 1946; LL.B., cum laude, Valedictorian, 1949); Bar Topnotcher (1949); Harvard Law School (LL.M., 1951). Phi Kappa Phi. Recipient, Order of the Chevalier First Class of St. Olav, Norway. Senior Partner, Ponce Enrile, Siguion Reyna, Montecillo & Belo, 1956-1972. Vice Consul (a.h.), Thailand in the Philippines, 1956-1992. Delegate, Constitutional Convention, 1971. Knight of the Order, White Elephant granted by the King of Thailand. Member, Parliament representing the Province of Capiz, 1984-1986. *Member:* Philippine Bar Association (President, 1974-1975; Director, 1962-1967, 1973-1986); Integrated Bar of the Philippines; Philippine Constitution Association; Harvard Law Alumni Association.

FELIPE L. GOZON, born Manila, Philippines, December 8, 1939; admitted, 1963, 13th place, Philippines; 1984, New York. *Education:* University of the Philippines (A.A., 1958; LL.B., 1962); Yale Law School (LL.M., 1965). Phi Kappa Phi. Order of the Purple Feather. Recipient: Most Distinguished Service Award, Leadership Award, Presidential Award of Merit, Philippine Bar Association 1986, 1989, 1990; Certificate of Appreciation, Supreme Court, July 6, 1989; Chief Justice Special Award, Chief Justice of the Philippines, June 11, 1991. Vice-President-Legal, Philippine Airlines, Inc., 1971-1972. Advisor and Consultant, Philippine Air Panel, 1971-1993. Author: "The Civil Aeronautics Board: Powers, Procedures and Regulation", 1993. Special Lecturer: Taxation, Economic Development Foundation, 1969; Current Issues Affecting Airlines in the Philippines, U.P., Law Center, 1985. Lecturer: Seminar on Carriage of Goods by Air, Institute of Advanced Studies, 1984. Special Lecturer, 16th World Law Conference "Legal Issues in International Civil Aviation Arising from Deregulation," Manila, 1993. Promoting Ethical Behavior Among Sheriffs, Sheriffs' Conference, 1989; Monopoly and Press Censorship: Some Lessons from the Philippine Experience, 14th Conference on the law of the World at Beijing, 1990. *Member:* Integrated Bar of the Philippines (Director, Pasay, Makati, Mandaluyong & San Juan Chapter, 1973-1974); Philippine Bar Association

(This Listing Continued)

(President, 1988-1989; Director, 1983-1993); Telecommunications and Broadcasting Attorneys of the Philippines (Chairman, 1993); Philippine Society of International Law; Tax Management Association; Aviation Lawyers Association of the Philippines (President, 1982-1983; Director, 1984—); American and International Bar Associations.

MAGDANGAL B. ELMA, born Lucban, Quezon, Philippines, January 2, 1939; admitted, 1967, Philippines. *Education:* University of the Philippines (B.S.J., cum laude, 1961; LL.B., cum laude, 1961); Yale Law School (LL.M., 1962). Phi Kappa Phi., Pi Gamma Mu. Contributing Editor, American Jurisprudence and American Law Reports, 1962-1967. Editor, Lawyers Cooperative Publishing Company, Rochester, New York. Associate Justice, Court of Appeals, 1987. Undersecretary, Department of Environment and Natural Resources, 1987. Deputy/Acting Executive Secretary, Office of the President of the Philippines, 1988-1991. Presidential Assistant II, Legal and Judicial Affairs, Office of the President of the Philippines, 1990-1992. Author: "The Aquino Presidency and the Constitution," 1993. Special Lecturer, U.P. Law Center. Professor, U.P. College of Law. Member, Board of Editorial Consultants, Supreme Court Reports Annotated. *Member:* Integrated Bar of the Philippines; Legal Management Council of the Philippines; Philippine Bar Association (Director, 1994-1995); Philippine Society of International Law; Asia Pacific Lawyers Association; Philippine Constitution Association.

ROBERTO O. PAREL, born Manila, Philippines, February 19, 1956; admitted, 1981, Philippines. *Education:* University of the Philippines (A.B., Philosophy, 1976; LL.B., 1980). Professor, Law, San Sebastian College of Law, Manila Alumnus, 1989 Academy of American and International Law, The Southwestern Legal Foundation, Dallas, Texas. Member, Alumni Association of the Academy of American and International Law (Philippines). *Member:* Intergrated Bar of the Philippines; Philippine Bar Association; Philippine Society of International Law.

MEMBERS

LUCIDO A. GUINTO, born Bacoor, Cavite, November 23, 1921; admitted, 1950, Philippines. *Education:* University of the Philippines (A.A., 1940; LL.B., 1949). Attorney, Board of Liquidators, 1952-1957. Corporate Auditor, 1958-1979. *Member:* Integrated Bar of the Philippines.

GENER E. ASUNCION, born Tarlac, Tarlac, Philippines, September 12, 1945; admitted, 1972, Philippines. *Education:* University of Santo Tomas (B.A., cum laude; LL.B., cum laude). Recipient, Academic Award for Academic Excellence from the Rector Magnificus, University of Santo Tomas, 1971. Editor-in-Chief, UST Law Review, 1971. Judicial Assistant of Associate Justice Ruperto G. Martin, Supreme Court of the Philippines, 1975-1977. Professor, Civil Law, Civil Law Review, Ortañez University, 1975-1984. *Member:* Integrated Bar of the Philippines.

ROBERTO RAFAEL V. LUCILA, born Camalig, Albay, Philippines, June 7, 1956; admitted, 1981, Philippines. *Education:* University of the Philippines (A.B., Psychology, 1976; LL.B., 1980). Phi Kappa Phi. Scholar, First National City Bank, CITIBANK. Accredited Tax Law Specialist, US Internal Revenue Service Special Examining Unit, Office of Personnel Management, 1982. Assistant Executive Secretary, Legislation, Office of the President of the Philippines, 1990-1992. Chairman: Philippine Retirement Authority, 1991-1992; South China Sea Fishery Disputes Committee, 1991-1992. Seminars on Taxation, Foundation for Accounting Education, New York City, 1982; 29th Academy of American and International Law, International and Comparative Law Center, The Southwestern Legal Foundation, Dallas, Texas, 1992. Lecturer, College of Business Administration, University of the Philippines, 1993. Professor, College of Law, San Sebastian College. Legal Counsel, University of the Philippines, 1981. Member, Philippine National Railways, Board of Directors, 1989-1990; Civil Aeronautics Board, 1990-1991. *Member:* Integrated Bar of the Philippines; Association of Philippine Barristers (Member, Board of Trustees, 1991); Philippine Bar Association; Philippine Constitution Association; Legal Management Association of the Philippines.

ANTONIO A. MERELOS, born Capoocan, Leyte, Philippines, December 7, 1939; admitted, 1969, Philippines. *Education:* Lyceum of the Philippines (A.B., 1963; B.S.J., Journalism, 1964; LL.B., 1968). Resident Scholar, Advanced Management Program, Session 75, Australian Administrative Staff College, Mount Eliza, Victoria, Australia, 1982. Legal Office, Office of the President, Malacañang, Manila, 1976-1988. Director, Office of the President, 1988-1993. *Member:* Integrated Bar of the Philippines; Philippine Bar Association; Philippine Constitution Association.

CHARLTON JULES P. ROMERO, born Quezon City, Philippines, February 25, 1963; admitted, 1989, Philippines. *Education:* University of the Philippines (A.B., Broadcast Communication, 1983; LL.B., 1988). In-

(This Listing Continued)

structor, Broadcast Communication, University of the Philippines, 1983-1984. *Member:* Integrated Bar of the Philippines; Philippine Bar Association; Philippine Constitution Association.

ERIC VINCENT A. ESTOESTA, born Manila, Philippines, July 18, 1965; admitted, 1991, Philippines. *Education:* San Beda College (A.B., Economics, 1986); Ateneo de Manila University (LL.B., 1990). *Member:* Integrated Bar of the Philippines; Ateneo de Manila Alumni Association; Fraternal Order of Utopia, Ateneo de Manila University.

ALVIN AGUSTIN T. IGNACIO, born Manila, Philippines, May 28, 1965; admitted, 1991, Philippines. *Education:* University of Santo Tomas (A.B., Philosophy, 1986); Ateneo de Manila University (LL.B., 1990). *Member:* Integrated Bar of the Philippines; Ateneo de Manila Alumni Association; Fraternal Order of Utopia, Ateneo de Manila University.

BERNARD RAYMOND T. SAULOG, born Manila, Philippines, February 18, 1965; admitted, 1991, Philippines. *Education:* University of the Philippines (A.B., Political Science, 1986); Ateneo de Manila University (LL.B., 1990). *Member:* Integrated Bar of the Philippines; Ateneo de Manila Alumni Association.

MA. RHODORA L. POLICARPIO, born Manila, Philippines, February 1, 1966; admitted, 1993, Philippines. *Education:* University of the Philippines (B.S., Business Administration, 1987; LL.B., 1992). Portia Sorority, Inc. *Member:* Integrated Bar of the Philippines.

REGINO A. MORENO, born Caloocan City, Philippines, March 21, 1963; admitted, 1993, Philippines. *Education:* University of Pangasinan (A.B., Political Science); University of Santo Tomas (LL.B., 1987). *Member:* Integrated Bar of the Philippines; Aegis Juris Fraternity.

RAUL C. VILLANUEVA, born Butuan, Agusan del Norte, Philippines, April 21, 1967; admitted, 1994, Philippines. *Education:* University of the Philippines (B.A., Economics, 1987; LL.B., 1992). *Member:* Integrated Bar of the Philippines; Grand Lodge of the Philippines of Free and Accepted Masons, 1989.

MA. C. ELEANOR M. MONTENEGRO, born Cagayan de Oro City, Misamis Oriental, Philippines, September 17, 1968; admitted, 1994, Philippines. *Education:* Ateneo de Manila (A.B., Social Sciences, 1989); University of the Philippines (LL.B., 1993). *Member:* Integrated Bar of the Philippines; Portia Sorority, Inc.

REU LAWRENCE D. AGUSTIN, born Quezon City, Philippines, January 18, 1967; admitted, 1994, Philippines. *Education:* University of the Philippines (B.S., Economics, 1988; LL.B., 1992). *Member:* Integrated Bar of the Philippines; Alpha Phi Beta Fraternity, University of the Philippines.

REPRESENTATIVE CLIENTS: San Miguel Corp.; Andres Soriano Corp.; Hong Kong and Shanghai Banking Corp.; Atlas Consolidated Mining & Development Corp.; Rohm & Haas (Philippines), Inc.; Merck, Sharp & Dohme (Phils.) Inc.; Cluett Peabody & Co. Inc.; The Sanforized Co.; Global Marine, Inc.; Brinkerhoff Maritime Drilling Corp.; Munichre Services Ltd.; Woodward & Dickerson; ConAgra, Inc.; U-Bix Corp.; Screen Grafix, Inc.; General Milling Corp.; G.F. Equity, Inc.; National Contracting Co. Ltd.; Classic Chemical (Arlington, Texas); United Biscuits (U.K.) Ltd.; Amsterdam Ballast Dredging Corp. (Holland); Achelis Philippines, Inc.; The Manufacturer's Life Insurance Co.; Schering Plough Corp.; Paper Corporation Industries of the Phil. (Inc.) (PICOP); Sandre Int'l.; Sandre Phil.; Cardinal Ceramic, Inc.; Westmont Holdings, Inc.; Westmont Asia Motors; Express Telecommunications Co., Inc.; Astro Air, Inc.; Marcopper Mining Corporation; Placer Dome, Ltd.; Republic Broadcasting System, Inc.; Selenga Mining Corporation; International Air Transport Association (IATA); BSP Philippines, Inc.; Mar Fishing Co.; DHL Philippines Corp.; Associated Freight Consolidators, Inc.; Lawyers Cooperative Publishing Comimpany (Phil.), Inc.; Justitia Realty & Management Corp.; Sagittarius Condominium Corp.; Gozon Development Corp.; Gozon Foundation, Inc.; Starmin Mining Inc.; Lex Realty Corp.; Balaque Realty Co., Inc.; Intelleciron Co. Mngt. Sol Planners, Inc.; Ortigas & Co.; Phil. Veterans Bank; Ribo-Tuba Nickel Mining Corp.; Security Bank & Trust Co.
REFERENCES: Harry Johnston of Time, Inc.; John Carey of Coudert Bros.; Cravath Swaine & Moore; The Hong Kong and Shanghai Banking Corp.; Russell Prince of Seward & Kissel, Quentin H. Smith; Morris Garfinkle of Galland, Kharasch, Morse & Garfinkle, P.C.; Gerard A. Sumida of Carlsmith, Wichman, Case, Mukai and Tchiki.

BENGZON, ZARRAGA, NARCISO, CUDALA, PECSON, BENGSON & JIMENEZ

Established in 1951

SIXTH FLOOR, SOL BUILDING
112 AMORSOLO STREET, LEGASPI VILLAGE
1229 MAKATI
METRO MANILA, REPUBLIC OF THE PHILIPPINES
Telephone: 815-9071 to 78; 810-8235; 810-8581; 810-9801; 810-9803
Fax: (632) 817-3251; 813-0081
Cable Address: "Bengzonlex"

Dagupan City Office: 2nd Floor, Meneses Bldg. Telephone: 21-48.

General Practice. Patents, Trademarks, Corporation, Labor, Taxation, Insurance, Commercial and Civil Law. Public Utility and Mining Law.

FIRM PROFILE: *Ours is a middle-sized firm. For more than forty years, we have been providing timely, efficient, results-oriented and cost-effective professional legal services to a diversified roster of national and international clients. Cases and business transactions are aggressively handled by lawyers with a mind to achieving the clients' objectives swiftly and efficiently.*

FOUNDER

JOSE P. BENGZON, born Lingayen, Pangasinan, Philippines, May 5, 1898; admitted, 1921, Philippines. *Education:* Ateneo de Manila (A.B.); University of the Philippines (LL.B.). Served in three Branches of the Government: in the Executive, as City Fiscal of Manila, 1946-1948; Undersecretary of Justice, 1948-1950; Acting Commissioner of the Bureau of Immigration, 1949-1950; Secretary of Justice, 1950-1951; Chief of the Reparations Mission, Tokyo, Japan, 1962; in the Legislative, as Member of Congress, 1941; Member of the Interim Batasan Pambansa, Philippine Parliament, 1978; in the Judiciary, as Presiding Justice of the Court of Appeals, 1962-1964; Associate Justice of the Supreme Court, 1964-1968; Consultant to the Supreme Court on Judicial Administration and Supervision of all Courts, 1973-1975. (Deceased, 1990).

MEMBERS OF FIRM

JOSE F.S. BENGZON, JR., born Lingayen, Pangasinan, December 3, 1932; admitted, 1957, Philippines. *Education:* Ateneo de Manila (A.B.; LL.B.); Harvard Law School. Qualified Legal Consultant, Philippine Investment Laws, State of California, USA. Philippine Constitutional Commission, 1971. Philippine Constitutional Convention, 1986. *Member:* Philippine Bar Association (President, 1977-1978); World Law Center; The Law Association for Asia and the Western Pacific (LAWASIA); International Bar Association; ASEAN Law Association; Asia Pacific Council; London Court of International Arbitration; International Court of Arbitration (Arbitrator); International Chamber of Commerce (Arbitrator) International Academy of Estate and Trust Law; American Arbitration Association; Harvard Law Club of the Philippines. *LANGUAGES:* Filipino, English and Spanish. *PRACTICE AREAS:* Business Law; International Transactions.

ISIDRO C. ZARRAGA, born Loay, Bohol, May 28, 1925; admitted, 1952, Philippines. *Education:* University of San Carlos (A.A.); University of Santo Tomas (A.B.); University of the Philippines (LL.B.). Author: "Natural Children—Complex Action for Recognition and Partition," Philippine Law Journal, U.P., 1951. Representative, 3rd District of Bohol, Philippine Congress, 1987—. *Member:* Philippine Bar Association; New York State Bar Association; American Bar Association; ASEAN Law Association; World Jurist Association; American Judicature Society; American Studies Association of the Philippines; Integrated Bar of the Philippines; International Law Association (Philippine Branch). *LANGUAGES:* Filipino, English and Spanish. *PRACTICE AREAS:* Litigation.

EDILBERTO S. NARCISO, JR., born Manila, May 25, 1934; admitted, 1958, Philippines. *Education:* University of Santo Tomas (A.A.); Ateneo de Manila (LL.B.); Universidad de Madrid (Doctor of Laws). Author: "Obligaciones Naturales." *Member:* Philippine Bar Association; Intellectual Property Association of the Philippines; Asian Patent Attorneys Association; Association Internationale pour la Protection de la Propriete Industrielle; The Philippine-Japan Society, Inc.; International Trademark Association; Integrated Bar of the Philippines. *LANGUAGES:* Filipino, English and Spanish. *PRACTICE AREAS:* Patents, Trademarks and Copyrights; Business Law; International Transactions.

(This Listing Continued)

BENGZON, ZARRAGA, NARCISO, CUDALA, PECSON, BENGSON & JIMENEZ, *Metro Manila—Continued*

EDUARDO B. CUDALA, born Lingayen, Pangasinan, September 26, 1930; admitted, 1956, Philippines. *Education:* Ateneo de Manila (Litt.B.; LL.B.). Senior Attorney, 1961-1969 and Deputy Clerk of Court, 1969-1970, Court of Appeals. *Member:* Philippine Bar Association; Integrated Bar of the Philippines. *LANGUAGES:* Filipino and English. *PRACTICE AREAS:* Business Law; Litigation.

ARTURO E. PECSON, born Santa Cruz, Zambales, November 22, 1934; admitted, 1961, Philippines. *Education:* Ateneo de Manila University (Litt.B.; LL.B.). *Member:* Philippine Bar Association; Integrated Bar of the Philippines; Legal Management Council of the Philippines. *LANGUAGES:* Filipino and English. *PRACTICE AREAS:* Litigation.

ANTONIO E. BENGSON, III, born Lingayen, Pangasinan, March 31, 1941; admitted, 1966, Philippines. *Education:* Ateneo de Manila University (B.S.; LL.B.); Georgetown University Law Center. Ateneo Law Journal, 1963-1965. Representative, 2nd District of Pangasinan, Philippine Congress, 1987. *Member:* Integrated Bar of the Philippines; Legal Management Council of the Philippines (Director); Ateneo Law Alumni Association (Director); Aviation Lawyers Association of the Philippines (Director). *LANGUAGES:* Filipino and English. *PRACTICE AREAS:* Aviation; Business Law.

JOSE VICENTE E. JIMENEZ, born Dagupan City, Philippines, April 4, 1949; admitted, 1974, Philippines. *Education:* San Beda College (A.B. magna cum laude; LL.B. with honors). Staff Member, The Bedan Barrister, 1970-1973. Member, Legal Management Council of the Philippines, 1988. *Member:* Philippine Bar Association; Inter-Pacific Bar Association; Integrated Bar of the Philippines. *LANGUAGES:* Filipino and English. *PRACTICE AREAS:* Business Law; International Transactions; Intellectual Property.

PONCIANO C. GONZALES, JR., born Manila, Philippines, November 16, 1948; admitted, 1974, Philippines. *Education:* University of the Philippines (A.B.; LL.B.). *Member:* Integrated Bar of the Philippines; Aviation Lawyers Association of the Philippines; Asia-Pacific Lawyers Association. *LANGUAGES:* Filipino and English. *PRACTICE AREAS:* Litigation; Aviation Law.

HERMINIO A. LIWANAG, born Mandaluyong, Metro Manila, December 24, 1950; admitted, 1975, Philippines. *Education:* Far Eastern University (A.B.); Ateneo de Manila University (LL.B.). Member, Employers Confederation of the Philippines, 1987. *Member:* Philippine Bar Association; Integrated Bar of the Philippines. *LANGUAGES:* Filipino and English. *PRACTICE AREAS:* Labor; Industrial Relations.

ELOY E. BELLO, IV, born Dagupan City, Pangasinan, September 13, 1958; admitted, 1985, Philippines. *Education:* Ateneo de Manila University (A.B., Political Science; LL.B.). *Member:* Philippine Bar Association; Integrated Bar of the Philippines. *LANGUAGES:* Filipino and English. *PRACTICE AREAS:* Litigation; Licensing/Registration of Food, Drugs and Cosmetics.

ERNESTO T. CALUYA, JR., born Batac, Ilocos Norte, November 24, 1954; admitted, 1980, Philippines. *Education:* Ateneo de Manila University (A.B., Philosophy; LL.B.). *Member:* Philippine Bar Association; Integrated Bar of the Philippines. *LANGUAGES:* Filipino and English. *PRACTICE AREAS:* Litigation; Labor and Industrial Relations.

AGERICO M. UNGSON, born Mandaluyong, Metro Manila, July 20, 1954; admitted, 1980, Philippines. *Education:* De La Salle University (A.B., Philosophy); San Beda College (LL.B.). *Member:* Integrated Bar of the Philippines. *LANGUAGES:* Filipino and English. *PRACTICE AREAS:* Litigation.

ENRICO G. VALDEZ, born Manila, February 15, 1961; admitted, 1988, Philippines. *Education:* Philippine School of Business Administration (B.S. Accounting); Ateneo de Manila University (LL.B.). *Member:* Integrated Bar of the Philippines. *LANGUAGES:* Filipino and English. *PRACTICE AREAS:* Taxation.

ASSOCIATES

MA. ROMELA M. BENGZON, born Iloilo City, September 14, 1960; admitted, 1986, Philippines; 1994, New York. *Education:* University of the Philippines (A.B., Political Science); Ateneo de Manila University (LL.B.). *LANGUAGES:* Filipino, English and French. *PRACTICE AREAS:* Business Law; International Transactions; Trademarks.

(This Listing Continued)

AGNES LEONOR L. CASABAR-OXALES, born Cotabato City, June 19, 1965; admitted, 1990, Philippines. *Education:* University of the Philippines (A.B., Sociology; LL.B.). *Member:* Philippine Bar Association; Integrated Bar of the Philippines. *LANGUAGES:* Filipino and English. *PRACTICE AREAS:* Intellectual Property Law; Immigration.

STEPHANIE G. DY, born Sta. Cruz, Manila, September 27, 1963; admitted, 1990, Philippines. *Education:* U.P. Diliman (A.B. Political Science; LL.B.). *Member:* Philippine Bar Association; Integrated Bar of the Philippines; U.P. Women Lawyer Circle; FIDA. *LANGUAGES:* English, Filipino, Fukienese and Mandarin. *PRACTICE AREAS:* Labor; Litigation.

AISSA V. ENCARNACION, born Quezon City, October 22, 1964; admitted, 1993, Philippines. *Education:* University of the Philippines (B.S., Business Administration; LL.B.). *Member:* U.P. Women Lawyers Circle; Integrated Bar of the Philippines; Federacion Internationale de Abogados. *LANGUAGES:* Filipino and English. *PRACTICE AREAS:* Business Law.

MA. MELVA M. EVANGELISTA-VALDEZ, born Binmaley, Pangasinan, November 11, 1959; admitted, 1985, Philippines. *Education:* University of the Philippines (A.B., Political Science; LL.B.). *Member:* Philippine Bar Association; Integrated Bar of the Philippines; U.P. Women Lawyer Circle. *LANGUAGES:* Filipino and English. *PRACTICE AREAS:* Business Law.

PACIANO F. FALLAR, JR., born Romblon, January 17, 1968; admitted, 1994, Philippines. *Education:* Ateneo de Mannila University (A.B., Philosophy); University of the Philippines (LL.B.). *Member:* Integrated Bar of the Philippines. *LANGUAGES:* Filipino and English. *PRACTICE AREAS:* Labor; Business Law.

IMELDA B. MABANDOS, born Davao City, December 24, 1961; admitted, 1989, Philippines. *Education:* San Pedro College (B.S., Biology); Ateneo de Davao University (LL.B.). *Member:* Integrated Bar of the Philippines. *LANGUAGES:* Filipino and English. *PRACTICE AREAS:* Litigation; Patents and Trademarks.

ALAN DAVID L. MATUTINA, born Manila, November 2, 1964; admitted, 1994, Philippines. *Education:* University of the Philippines (B.S., Statistics); Ateneo de Manila University (LL.B.). *Member:* Integrated Bar of the Philippines. *LANGUAGES:* Filipino and English. *PRACTICE AREAS:* Business Law; Taxation.

GERALDINE MARIE C. PALOMA, born Tondo, Manila, January 30, 1965; admitted, 1991, Philippines. *Education:* U.P. Diliman (A.B. Philippine Studies); Ateneo de Manila (LL.B.). *Member:* Philippine Bar Association; Integrated Bar of the Philippines; FIDA; WLAP. *LANGUAGES:* Filipino and English. *PRACTICE AREAS:* Business Law.

DENNIS C. PAÑGAN, born Sta. Ana Pampanga, 1968; admitted, 1994. *Education:* University of the Assumption (A.B., Political Science); San Beda College (LL.B.). *Member:* Integrated Bar of the Philippines. *LANGUAGES:* Filipino and English. *PRACTICE AREAS:* Labor; Litigation.

TEODORO A. PASTRANA, born Unisan, Quezon, May 20, 1968; admitted, 1992, Philippines. *Education:* De La Salle University (A.B., Economics); San Beda College (LL.B.). *Member:* Integrated Bar of the Philippines. *LANGUAGES:* Filipino and English. *PRACTICE AREAS:* Labor; Litigation.

BERNARDO KARLO M. PONFERRADA, born Tacloban City, October 24, 1966; admitted, 1993, Philippines. *Education:* University of the Philippines (BSC, Marketing Management); Ateneo de Manila University (LL.B.). *Member:* Integrated Bar of the Philippines. *LANGUAGES:* Filipino and English. *PRACTICE AREAS:* Litigation.

ROSARIO P. RODRIGUEZ, born Manila, Philippines, 1966; admitted, 1992, Philippines. *Education:* San Beda College (LL.B.). *Member:* Integrated Bar of the Philippines. *LANGUAGES:* Filipino, English and Spanish. *PRACTICE AREAS:* Litigation.

PHIO L. VIOVICENTE, born Matag-ob, Leyte, September 3, 1963; admitted, 1990, Philippines. *Education:* University of the Philippines (A.B., Political Science); San Beda College (LL.B.). *Member:* Philippine Bar Association; Integrated Bar of the Philippines. *LANGUAGES:* Filipino and English. *PRACTICE AREAS:* Labor; Litigation.

DAGUPAN CITY OFFICE

MEL MARIANO T. RAMOS, born San Carlos City, Pangasinan, December 10, 1955; admitted, 1983, Philippines. *Education:* University of the East (A.B.; LL.B.). *Member:* Integrated Bar of the Philippines. *LANGUAGES:* Filipino and English. *PRACTICE AREAS:* Litigation.

BITO, LOZADA, ORTEGA & CASTILLO

Established in 1901

(Formerly Ross, Selph & Carrascoso)

**5TH AND 6TH FLOORS, ALPAP I BUILDING
140 ALFARO STREET
SALCEDO VILLAGE, MAKATI
METRO MANILA, REPUBLIC OF THE PHILIPPINES**
*Telephone: (632) 818-23-21 to 25; 810-43-90
Cable Address: "Sevans, Manila"
Telex: EASTERN-64376 RCA-23201, ITT (GMCR)-45554
Fax: (63-2) 810-3153*

Mailing Address: P.O. Box 781, Manila, 1099

REVISERS OF THE PHILIPPINE REPUBLIC LAW DIGEST FOR THIS DIRECTORY.

General Practice, Foreign Investments, Corporation, Taxation, Patents, Trademarks, Copyrights and Technology Transfers, Civil and Criminal Litigation, Insurance, Securities, Labor Law, Admiralty, Estates and Trusts, Aviation, Immigration, Banking and Finance, Oil and Mining.

FIRM PROFILE: The firm's beginnings can be traced to Pillsbury & Sutro which was founded in 1901 by partners from the San Francisco, U.S.A. firm of Pillsbury, Madison and Sutro. While the firm name has undergone changes, Ross, Selph & Carrascoso was the firm name for many years and the present name was adopted in 1988. All partners were American until 1936 when the first Filipino partner was admitted. The firm carries an extensive and diversified domestic and international practice from Manila and corresponds with leading law firms in major cities of the world. It acts as legal adviser to the British Embassy and Swedish Embassy in the Philippines. It is also the Philippine Republic Law Digest Reviser of Martindale-Hubbell Law Directory.

MEMBERS OF FIRM

JAMES ROSS (1910-1946).

EWALD E. SELPH (1923-1966).

JAMES MADISON ROSS (1927-1968).

ANTONIO T. CARRASCOSO, JR. (1918-1965).

JESUS B. BITO (1955-1991).

MARIANO M. LOZADA (1951-1991).

GREGORIO F. ORTEGA, born Batangas, Batangas, Philippines, March 5, 1932; admitted, 1958, Republic of the Philippines. *Education:* University of the Philippines (A.A., 1953; LL.B., 1957). *LANGUAGES:* English and Pilipino. *PRACTICE AREAS:* Admiralty; Civil and Criminal Litigation; Estates and Trusts; Finance; Banking; Aviation Law.

TOMAS O. DEL CASTILLO, JR., born San Quintin, Pangasinan, Philippines, February 27, 1941; admitted, 1963, Republic of the Philippines. *Education:* University of the Philippines (A.A., 1958; LL.B., 1962). *LANGUAGES:* English and Pilipino. *PRACTICE AREAS:* Civil and Criminal Litigation; Intellectual Property Law and Litigation; Admiralty; Taxation; Aviation Law.

BENJAMIN T. BACORRO, born Manaoag, Pangasinan, Philippines, November 22, 1945; admitted, 1970, Republic of the Philippines. *Education:* University of the Philippines (A.B., 1965; LL.B., 1969). *LANGUAGES:* English and Pilipino. *PRACTICE AREAS:* Admiralty; Civil and Criminal Litigation; Labor Law; Intellectual Property Law.

ELIZER A. ODULIO, born Manila, Philippines, June 24, 1950; admitted, 1976, Republic of the Philippines. *Education:* Ateneo de Manila University (A.B., 1971); University of the Philippines (LL.B., 1975). *LANGUAGES:* English and Pilipino. *PRACTICE AREAS:* Labor Law; Admiralty; Civil and Criminal Litigation; Immigration Law.

RENATO G. CALMA, born Manila, Philippines, October 21, 1950; admitted, 1976, Republic of the Philippines. *Education:* De La Salle College (A.B., 1971); Ateneo de Manila University (LL.B., 1975). *LANGUAGES:* English and Pilipino. *PRACTICE AREAS:* Corporate Law; Taxation; Intellectual Property Law; Technology Transfers; Finance; Banking; Foreign Investments.

PEDRO M. CARBONELL, II, born Bacnotan, La Union, Philippines, May 16, 1949; admitted, 1974, Republic of the Philippines. *Education:* Ateneo de Manila University (A.B., 1969; LL.B., 1973). *LANGUAGES:* English and Pilipino. *PRACTICE AREAS:* Admiralty; Civil and Criminal Litigation; Labor Law.

(This Listing Continued)

ASSOCIATES

LENITO T. SERRANO, born San Nicolas, Ilocos Norte, Philippines, September 22, 1953; admitted, 1978, Republic of the Philippines. *Education:* Ateneo de Manila University (A.B., 1973); University of the Philippines (LL.B., 1977). *LANGUAGES:* English and Pilipino. *PRACTICE AREAS:* Immigration Law; Civil and Criminal Litigation; Labor Law; Admiralty.

ROANE ALFREDO P. LOPEZ, III, born Manila, Philippines, January 29, 1964; admitted, 1990, Republic of the Philippines. *Education:* University of the Philippines (A.B., 1984; LL.B., 1989). *LANGUAGES:* English and Pilipino. *PRACTICE AREAS:* Intellectual Property Law; Technology Transfers; Civil and Criminal Litigation.

RAMSEY DOMINGO G. PICHAY, born Bauang, La Union, Philippines, August 4, 1961; admitted, 1991, Republic of the Philippines. *Education:* University of the Philippines (A.B., 1985; LL.B., 1990). *LANGUAGES:* English and Pilipino. *PRACTICE AREAS:* Immigration Law; Civil and Criminal Litigation; Admiralty; Labor Law.

PAULINE DOLOR A. ADVINCULA, born Quezon City, Philippines, November 30, 1963; admitted, 1989, Republic of the Philippines. *Education:* St. Paul College (B.S.S.A., 1984); Ateneo de Manila University (LL.B., 1988). *LANGUAGES:* English and Pilipino. *PRACTICE AREAS:* Intellectual Property Law; Technology Transfers.

CONRADO S. GOZOS, JR., born Batangas City, Philippines, January 17, 1967; admitted, 1992, Republic of the Philippines. *Education:* University of the Philippines (A.B., 1987; LL.B., 1991). *LANGUAGES:* English and Pilipino. *PRACTICE AREAS:* Civil and Criminal Litigation; Admiralty; Taxation; Labor Law.

EDMOND EDWARD M. FLAMINIANO, born Manila, Philippines, September 16, 1965; admitted, 1992, Republic of the Philippines. *Education:* University of Sto. Tomas (B.S., 1987); Ateneo de Manila University (J.D., 1991). *LANGUAGES:* English and Pilipino. *PRACTICE AREAS:* Intellectual Property Law; Technology Transfers; Civil and Commercial Litigation.

FIORELLO R. JOSE, born Manila, Philippines, September 29, 1965; admitted, 1992, Republic of the Philippines. *Education:* University of the Philippines (A.B., 1987; LL.B., 1991). *LANGUAGES:* English and Pilipino. *PRACTICE AREAS:* Civil and Commercial Litigation; Taxation; Labor Law; Admiralty.

DOMINADOR E. ALMEDA, born Manila, Philippines, September 16, 1962; admitted, 1992, Republic of the Philippines. *Education:* Fordham University (B.S., 1984); Ateneo de Manila University (LL.B., 1990). *LANGUAGES:* English and Pilipino. *PRACTICE AREAS:* Corporate Law; Labor Law; Taxation; Civil and Criminal Litigation; Admiralty.

TEODORO C. BAROQUE, JR., born Manila, Philippines, March 24, 1968; admitted, 1994, Republic of the Philippines. *Education:* University of Santo Tomas (A.B., 1989); Ateneo de Manila University (J.D., 1993). *LANGUAGES:* English and Pilipino. *PRACTICE AREAS:* Corporate Law; Civil and Criminal Litigation; Labor Law; Taxation.

ANA LIZA A. PERALTA-NAZARENO, born San Marcelino, Zambales, Philippines, June 7, 1968; admitted, 1994, Republic of the Philippines. *Education:* Ateneo de Manila University (B.S.L.M. 1988; J.D., 1993). *LANGUAGES:* English and Pilipino. *PRACTICE AREAS:* Corporate Law; Civil and Criminal Litigation; Labor Law; Admiralty.

REPRESENTATIVE CLIENTS: General Motors Corporation; E.I. Du Pont de Nemours & Co.; Kraft General Foods, Inc.; Texas Instruments; Imperial Chemicals Corporation; Schering A.G.; British Petroleum; Del Monte Corporation; IBM Japan Ltd.; Pfizer, Inc.; 3M Company Inc.; Caltex (Philippines) Inc.; Protection and Indemnity (P & I) Clubs (Europe Based)

REVISERS OF THE PHILIPPINE REPUBLIC LAW DIGEST FOR THIS DIRECTORY.

CARAG, CABALLES, JAMORA & SOMERA

*2ND FLOOR, THE PLAZA ROYALE
120 ALFARO STREET, SALCEDO VILLAGE, MAKATI*
METRO MANILA, REPUBLIC OF THE PHILIPPINES
*Telephone: 812 52 46; 812 52 47; 812 52 48
Telex: 64716 ROTA PN
Fax: 8188971; 8151436*

Mailing Address: P.O. Box 7172, Domestic Airport Post Office, Lock Box, 1300 Domestic Road, Pasay City, Philippines.

(This Listing Continued)

CARAG, CABALLES, JAMORA & SOMERA, Metro Manila—Continued

General Practice, Civil and Commercial Law, Corporations, Banking, Finance, Insolvency, Insurance, Taxation, Patents, Trademarks, Copyrights, Technology Transfer, Oil and Mining, Foreign Investments, Probate, Estate Planning and Administration, Telecommunications, Computer Law, Immigration, Labor, Admiralty, Criminal and Election Law.

MEMBERS OF FIRM

CARLO A. CARAG, born Tuguegarao, Cagayan, October 14, 1957; admitted, 1983, Philippines; Registered Trademark and Patent Attorney. Education: University of the Philippines (Bachelor of Arts, cum laude, 1978; Bachelor of Laws, cum laude, 1982); London School of Economics, University of London (Master of Laws, 1985). Grantee, British Foreign and Commonwealth Office Scholarship, 1984-1985. Member, Philippine Team, Philip C. Jessup International Law Moot Court Competition, Washington, D.C., 1980-1981. Vice-Chairman, Editorial Board, Philippine Law Journal, 1980-1981. Formerly Graduate School Professorial Lecturer, De La Salle University, 1987; Formerly Associate, Sycip, Salazar Hernandez and Gatmaitan; Formerly Visiting Foreign Lawyer, Linklaters and Paines, London, 1985-1986. Member, Committee to Formulate Guidelines on Financial and Technical Assistance Agreements with the Government of the Philippines in connection with Large Scale Exploration, Development and Utilization of Mineral Resources, 1990. Resource Person, Seminars on Mining Investment Opportunities in the Philippines held in Toronto, London and Manila sponsored by the United Nations, 1992. Philippine Correspondent, Asian Law Journal, a Hong Kong based publication, 1992—. Member, Editorial Board, I. P. Asia, a Hong Kong-based publication and Trademark World, a London based publication, 1987—. Editor-in-Chief, LES Philippines Update, 1994. Contributor: Patent World, a London based publication, 1989—; Copyright World, a London based publication, 1989—. Technical Expert, Stanford Research Institute (SRI) International, Project on Intellectual Property Rights Adjudication Study in the Philippines, 1993. Member: International Bar Association; The Law Association for Asia and the Pacific (LAWASIA); Inter-Pacific Bar Association; Asia-Pacific Lawyers Association (Vice-Chairman, Philippine National Group); Maritime Law Association of the Philippines; United Kingdom Institute of Trademark Agents (Oversea Member); European Communities Trade Mark Association (Associate Member); International Trademark Association International Trademark Committee (Formerly National Reporter for the Philippines, Asia-Pacific Region Sub-Committee, 1991-1994); MARQUES (Firm Representative, Association of European Trademark Proprietors); Licensing Executives Society of the Philippines (Treasurer); Intellectual Property Association of the Philippines (Member of the Board of Directors); Asian Patent Attorneys Association; Association Internationale pour la Protection de la Propriete Industrielle; Chamber of International Trade; Philippine Chamber of Commerce and Industry; Council to Combat Counterfeiting and Piracy of Patents, Copyright and Trademarks (COMPACT); Philippine-British Society. PRACTICE AREAS: Corporate Law; Securities Law; International Business Transactions; Banking and Finance; Oil and Mining Law; Computer Law; Labor Law; Maritime Law; Insurance Law; Aviation Law; Intellectual Property Law; Technology Transfer; Taxation Law; Telecommunication Law.

MANUELITO O. CABALLES, born Boac, Marinduque, Philippines, July 6, 1957; admitted, 1983, Philippines. Education: University of the Philippines (Bachelor of Arts, 1978; Bachelor of Laws, 1982). Director, Integrated Bar of the Philippines, Makati Chapter. Member, Philippine Team, Philip C. Jessup International Law Moot Court Competition, Washington, D.C., 1981. Member, Editorial Board, Philippine Law Journal, 1981. Formerly Senior Associate, Castillo, Laman, Tan and Pantaleon. Member: Maritime Law Association of the Philippines; The Law Association for Asia and the Pacific (LAWASIA); Inter-Pacific Bar Association; Asia-Pacific Lawyers Association. PRACTICE AREAS: Corporate Law; Litigation; Labor Law; Immigration; Oil and Mining Law; Admiralty; Telecommunications Law.

ELPIDIO C. JAMORA, JR., born Sapian, Capiz, Philippines, November 23, 1953; admitted, 1983, Philippines. Education: Lyceum of the Philippines (Bachelor of Arts, 1977); University of the Philippines (Bachelor of Laws, 1982). Formerly Associate, Ledesma, Saludo & Associates. Formerly Senior Associate, Castillo, Laman, Tan and Pantaleon. Member: Maritime Law Association of the Philippines; The Law Association for Asia and the Pacific (LAWASIA); Inter-Pacific Bar Association; Asia-Pacific Lawyers Association. PRACTICE AREAS: Corporate Law; Litigation; Admiralty; Labor Law; Banking and Finance; Insolvency.

(This Listing Continued)

BENJAMIN A. SOMERA, JR., born Quezon City, Philippines, March 11, 1957; admitted, 1983, Philippines. Education: University of the Philippines (Bachelor of Arts, 1978; Bachelor of Laws, 1982). Formerly Senior Partner, Somera Law Office. Member: Metro Manila Trial Lawyers Association, Inc. (Member, Board of Directors, 1987); Maritime Law Association of the Philippines (Trustee, 1992—); The Law Association for Asia and the Pacific (LAWASIA); Inter-Pacific Bar Association; Asia-Pacific Lawyers Association. PRACTICE AREAS: Administrative Law; Litigation; Labor Law; Insurance Law; Admiralty; Probate Law.

ASSOCIATES

REYNILDA T. CABAHUG-DE LEON, born Cebu City, Philippines, June 10, 1966; admitted, 1994, Philippines. Education: University of the Philippines (Bachelor of Arts, Political Science, 1987); Ateneo de Manila University (Juris Doctor, 1992). Legal Apprentice, Ongkiko Buyco Dizon and Associates, summer 1990-1991. Member: Ateneo Human Rights Center; Student Council, Ateneo de Manila School of Law. Member: Integrated Bar of the Philippines, Pasig Chapter.

CHESELDEN GEORGE V. CARMONA, born Socorro, Or. Mindoro, April 23, 1968; admitted, 1994, Philippines. Education: de la Salle University (Bachelor of Arts, 1988); University of the Philippines (Bachelor of Laws, 1993). President, Society of Law Students (1990). Presiding Officer, UP Paralegal Volunteer Organization (1991), Secretary General, Students Right and Welfare (STRAW) Alliance (1991). Member, Editorial Board, Philippines Law Journal (1991). National Chairman, Committee on Paralegal Education, Association of Law Students of the Philippines (1991). Member, Board of Trustees, Developmental Legal Assistance Center (1991). Organizer/Lecturer, various paralegal seminars for students, farmers, urban poor, laborer, medical doctors. Chairman, Law Student Government;s Quick Reaction Team (1989), Committee on Foreign Interventin (1990). Consultant, Office of the Vice President of the Republic of the Philippines (1993). Lecturer, De La Salle University, Department of Political Science (1988). Legal Researcher, Free Legal Assistance Group, Sentro ng Batas Pangtao, Loyola House of Studies, House of Representatives (1989-1992).

PERICLES J. C. R. CASUELA, born Manila, March 22, 1967; admitted, 1993, Philippines. Education: Ateneo de Manila University (Bachelor of Arts, 1987; Juris Doctor, 1992). Legal Apprentice, Office of the Solicitor General, 1990.

FRANCIS PENA DIGNADICE, born Manila, April 24, 1966; admitted, 1993, Philippines. Education: University of the Philippines (Bachelor of Arts, major in Political Science, 1988; Bachelor of Laws, 1992). Volunteer, National Citizens' Movement for Free Elections (NAMFREL). Law Intern, Office of Legal Aid, UP College of Law. Legal Assistant, Bermillo Law Office. Member: Student Editorial Board, Philippine Law Journal, 1988-1991; Lex Scripta, Inc., 1990-1992; UP Law Christian Fellowship; UP Diliman Debating Team; Lawyers in Christ (LINC).

MA. ELOISA V. REYES, born Manila, Philippines, December 17, 1969. Education: University of the Philippines (Bachelor of Arts, magna cum laude, 1990); Ateneo de Manila University (Juris Doctor, Second Honors, 1994). Associate Editor, Philippine Human Rights Monitor, 1993. Legal Apprentice, De Borja Medialdea Ata Bello Guevarra & Serapio Law Offices, summer 1993. Member, Ateneo Human Rights Center.

MARIA TRINIDAD P. VILLAREAL, born Manila, April 24, 1965; admitted, 1991, Philippines. Education: University of the Philippines (Bachelor of Arts, 1986; Bachelor of Laws, 1990). Member, Philippine Team that placed 3rd in the 1989 Philip C. Jessup International Law Moot Court Competition. Oralist, Regional Finals (Philippine Round) of the 1989 Philip C. Jessup International Law Moot Court Competition. Champion, Evelio Javier Oratorical Contest (1988). Chairperson, University of the Philippines College of Law Office of Legal Aid Interns' Committee for the Nomination of the Most Outstanding Office of Legal Aid Intern (1989-1990). President, Demosthenes Circle (UP Law Oratorical and Debating Society (1988). Contributor, Philippine Law Register, Special Issue on the Ratification of the 1987 Philippine Constitution. Member: Maritime Law Association of the Philippines.

REPRESENTATIVE CLIENTS: Louis Vuitton Malletier (of France); International Resort Corporation (of Korea); Merill Lynch International, Inc.; MINORCO (of Luxembourg); Western Mining Corporation Limited (of Australia); The World Wrestling Federation (U.S.A.); Azupharma GmbH (Germany); Credit Lyonnais; Dow Jones & Company, Inc. (U.S.A.); Guccio Gucci S.p.A. (Italy); Ferrero, S.p.A. (Italy); Inui Steamship Co., Ltd. (Japan); Buenamar Compania Naviera S.A. (Panama); Pandiman (Phils.), Inc. (local commercial correspondent of various shipowners' mutual protection and indemnity clubs around the world); Citibank N.A.; Finance One Limited (Thailand); McGraw Hill, Inc. (U.S.A.); Internet Systems Corp. (U.S.A.); Just Japan Co. Ltd. (Ja-

(This Listing Continued)

pan); Shakey's International Limited (Hong Kong); Motion Picture Anti Film Piracy Council of the Philippines; Shangri-La International Hotel Management Ltd. (Hong Kong); Benquet Corp.; Petrofields Exploration and Development Co., Inc.; Banashaw Mining and Development Corporation; Chase Resources (Philippines) Croration; Chase Minerals (Philippines) Corporation; Delta Minerals (Philippines) Corporation; Telecommunications Technologies Philippines, Inc.; Marina Properties Corporations (flagship company in the Philippines of the Tan Yu Group); Review Publishing Co., Ltd. (Hong Kong) (publisher of Far Eastern Economic Review); Holiday Inn (Phils.), Inc.; Hyundai Motor Co. (Korea); Ben Franks International (U.S.A.); Lorenzana Food Corp.; Tri-Chefs Food Corp.; Lahi Crafts, Inc.; Bell International, Inc.; Euro-C.B. Phils., Inc; International Noble Metals Exploration Ltd. (Australia); Hong Jeen Co. (Korea); Pico Art Exhibition Contractors Phils., Inc.; Onapal Phil. Commodities, Inc.; Dakila Shipping Corp.; Bio-Strata Pharmaceuticals, Inc.; Covertek International Phils., Inc.; Mega Airconditioning and Refrigeration Specialists, Inc.; Asia-Apollo Development Corp.; Indo Phil Textile Mills, Inc.; Horizon Travel and Tours, Inc.; Pentaking Multicrafts Corp.; Francisco V. del Rosario Group of Companies; Intercon Garments, Inc.; Central Vegetable Oil Manufacturing Co., Inc.; Ho-Jin Phils., Inc.; Dae San Philippines Corporation; Olympian Riding Co., Inc.; Boo Young Phil. Ind. Corp.; Sam Bang Philippines, Inc,; Shin Heung Philippines, Inc.; Gold Leaf Electronic Industry Co., Inc.; Phoenix Property Management, Inc.; Binondo Properties, Inc.; Fiestapack, Inc.; Swed-Phil., Inc.; Peregrine Real Estate Co., Inc.; Kum Kang Ceramic Phil. Co., Inc.; Justpark Asian Corp; Jin-San Phils., Inc.; Solar Wide Phils., Inc.; Fee-Fil Mag Phils., Inc.; Y.S. Glove Phil. Co., Inc.

CASTILLO LAMAN TAN PANTALEON & SAN JOSE

Established in 1981

SECOND, THIRD AND FOURTH FLOORS
VALERO TOWER, 122 VALERO STREET
SALCEDO VILLAGE, MAKATI
METRO MANILA 1227, REPUBLIC OF THE PHILIPPINES
Telephone: 8176791; 8104371
Cable Address: "Counsel Manila"
Telecopier: (632) 819-2725; (632) 817-5938

Mailing Address: P.O. Box 2028 MCPO, Makati, Metro Manila 1260, Rep. of the Philippines

General Practice. Civil and Commercial Law. Corporations, Banking, Finance, Bankruptcy, Insurance, Taxation, Patents, Trademarks, Copyrights, Oil and Mining, Foreign Investments, Probate, Estate Planning and Administration, Trade Disputes, Telecommunications, Immigration, Labor, Admiralty, Criminal, Election and Deportation Cases. Real Property Law.

FIRM PROFILE: Castillo Laman Tan & Pantaleon was established on January 2, 1981 as a full-service law firm by the late Gregorio R. Castillo and 16 other partners and associates. After ten years in practice, the firm has grown into an organization of more than 40 lawyers and paralegals, providing legal advice and assistance in such areas as corporate and finance, foreign investments, intellectual property, civil, commercial and criminal litigation, tax and customs, estate planning, employment and immigration, telecommunications, civil aeronautics, shipping, real estate, mining and energy, and insurance. In October, 1991, the firm was cited by the London-based International Corporate Lawyer as one of only two most favored law firms in the Philippines. In January 1995, Mr. Roberto V. San Jose, an outstanding and respected lawyer with a reputation for a brilliant legal mind and professional integrity, joined the firm.

MEMBERS OF FIRM

GREGORIO R. CASTILLO Founding Partner (January, 1981 - October 24, 1992).

NOEL A. LAMAN, born Isabela, Negros Occidental, Philippines, July 10, 1939; admitted, 1961, Philippines. *Education:* University of the Philippines (B.S.J.; LL.B.); University of Michigan (LL.M.). Chapter Director and Officer, Integrated Bar of the Philippines, 1972-1978. Professor of Law, Jose Rizal College, 1968-1969. Special Lecturer on Industrial Property Laws, 1982 and International Arbitration, 1981, U.P. Law Center Seminars. *Member:* Intellectual Property Association of the Philippines (IPAP); Asian Patent Attorneys Association (APAA); International Bar Association (IBA); Licensing Executives Society of the Philippines (LESP). *LANGUAGES:* English and Filipino. *PRACTICE AREAS:* Corporate Law; Administrative and Regulatory Law; Intellectual Property and Related Litigation; Franchising and Technology Transfer.

ANCHETA K. TAN, born Siasi, Sulu, Philippines, May 8, 1941; admitted, 1967, Philippines. *Education:* Silliman University (B.A., magna cum laude); University of the Philippines (LL.B.). Editor-in-Chief, The Philippine Collegian, 1966. Vice Chairman of the Editorial Board, Philippine Law Journal, 1964. General Counsel, Philippine Chamber of Commerce and

(This Listing Continued)

Industry. President, Employers Confederation of the Philippines (1991-1995). Participant, 11th Program of Instruction for Lawyers, Harvard Law School. Substitute Member, International Labor Organization Governing Body. *LANGUAGES:* English and Filipino. *PRACTICE AREAS:* Labor Law; Civil Law; Criminal Litigation.

POLO S. PANTALEON, born San Jose, Nueva Ecija, Philippines, January 23, 1942; admitted, 1971, Philippines. *Education:* De La Salle University (B.A., cum laude); University of the Philippines (LL.B., cum laude). *Member:* Petroleum Club of the Philippines; Aviation Lawyers Association of the Philippines; Phi Kappa Phi and Pi Gamma Mu (international honor societies). Participant, 16th Program of Instruction for Lawyers, Harvard Law School. *LANGUAGES:* English and Filipino. *PRACTICE AREAS:* International Loan Transactions; Administrative Law; Conveyancing; Corporate Law and Strategy; Distributorship, Agency & Franchise Law; Foreign Investments; Property and Real Estate Law; Oil and Mining Law; General Legal Practice.

ROBERTO V. SAN JOSE, born Manila, Philippines, November 7, 1941; admitted, 1967, Philippines. *Education:* De La Salle University (A.B., summa cum laude); University of the Philippines (LL.B., magna cum laude). *LANGUAGES:* English and Filipino. *PRACTICE AREAS:* Litigation; Corporate Law.

FELIPE T. CUISON, born Dagupan City, Philippines, April 11, 1932; admitted, 1956, Philippines. *Education:* University of the Philippines (A.A.; LL.B.). *Member:* Maritime Lawyers Association of the Philippines. *LANGUAGES:* English and Filipino. *PRACTICE AREAS:* Admiralty Law; Civil Law; Criminal Litigation.

EVA POLICAR-BAUTISTA, born Naic, Cavite, Philippines, September 13, 1939; admitted, 1962, Philippines. *Education:* University of the Philippines (A.A., with honors; LL.B.); Yale Law School (LL.M.). Phi Kappa Phi and Pi Gamma Mu (international honor societies). Director for Finance and Administration and Board Secretary, Philippine Board of Investments, 1979-1980. Member, Technical Staff of the Inter-Agency Committee on Domestic Borrowings of Foreign Firms, 1978-1980. *Member:* President, Legal Management Council of the Philippines, 1992-1993; Tax Management Association of the Philippines (TMAP); Chairperson, Publications Committee of the Inter-Pacific Bar Association (IPBA). Vice President, U.P. Women Lawyers Circle. *LANGUAGES:* English and Filipino. *PRACTICE AREAS:* Administrative Law; Foreign Investments Law; Corporate Law; Taxation Law.

PAULINO C. PETRALBA, born Lal-lo, Cagayan, Philippines, September 13, 1948; admitted, 1974, Philippines. *Education:* University of Santo Tomas (B.A. magna cum laude); University of the Philippines (LL.B.). *LANGUAGES:* English and Filipino. *PRACTICE AREAS:* Administrative Law; Corporate Law.

YOLANDA MENDOZA-ELEAZAR, born Quezon City, Philippines, October 17, 1955; admitted, 1984, Philippines. *Education:* University of the Philippines (B.S., cum laude; LL.B.). *LANGUAGES:* English and Filipino. *PRACTICE AREAS:* Corporate Law; Conveyancing; Foreign Investments Law; Bankruptcy; General Legal Practice.

ROBERTO N. DIO, born Lucena, Quezon, Philippines, October 30, 1958; admitted, 1985, Philippines. *Education:* University of the Philippines (B.A., cum laude; LL.B.). Editor, Philippine Law Register, 1980. Member, Editorial Board, Philippine Law Journal, 1982-1984. Member, Movement of Attorneys for Brotherhood, Integrity and Nationalism, Inc.; Reporter, International Trademark Association. Trustee, Law Foundation of Makati, Inc. *Member:* Maritime Lawyers Association of the Philippines; Coalition for Human Rights, Issues and Struggles. *LANGUAGES:* English and Filipino. *PRACTICE AREAS:* Litigation; Corporate Law; Industrial and Intellectual Property Law; Admiralty Law; Administrative Law; Insurance Law; Real Estate Law; Garments and Textile Law.

MEL A. MACARAIG, born Pasay City, Philippines, February 28, 1959; admitted, 1986, Philippines. *Education:* University of the Philippines (B.S.; LL.B.). Counsel, General Electric Asia Pacific, 1990. Member, Editorial Board, Philippine Law Journal, 1985. *LANGUAGES:* English and Filipino. *PRACTICE AREAS:* Corporate Law; Litigation; Industrial and Intellectual Property Law.

MARIA VICTORIA D. SARMIENTO, born Pampanga, Philippines, June 1, 1959; admitted, 1985, Philippines. *Education:* University of the Philippines (B.A., magna cum laude; LL.B.). *LANGUAGES:* English and Filipino. *PRACTICE AREAS:* Taxation Law.

(This Listing Continued)

CASTILLO LAMAN TAN PANTALEON & SAN JOSE,
Metro Manila—Continued

SENIOR ASSOCIATES

ZENAIDA L. SALIPSIP, born Manila, Philippines, July 5, 1941; admitted, 1968, Philippines. *Education:* Far Eastern University (B.S.C.; LL.B.); National Defense College of the Philippines (M.N.S.A.). *Member:* Federacion Internationale de Abogadas. *LANGUAGES:* English and Filipino. *PRACTICE AREAS:* Corporate Law.

ROLANDO S. SANTOS, born Manila, Philippines, February 7, 1943; admitted, 1968, Philippines. *Education:* San Beda College (A.B.; LL.B.). Professor of Law, San Beda College. *LANGUAGES:* English and Filipino. *PRACTICE AREAS:* Litigation.

ERIC S. SANTOS, born Bulacan, Philippines, September 1, 1959; admitted, 1985, Philippines. *Education:* University of the Philippines (B.S., cum laude; M.B.A.; LL.B.). *LANGUAGES:* English and Filipino. *PRACTICE AREAS:* Litigation.

DINA D. LUCENARIO, born Manila, Philippines, December 20, 1962; admitted, 1989, Philippines. *Education:* University of the Philippines (B.S., cum laude; LL.B.). *LANGUAGES:* English and Filipino. *PRACTICE AREAS:* Corporate Law.

MARIANNE M. GUERRERO, born Manila, Philippines, March 1, 1965; admitted, 1989, Philippines. *Education:* De La Salle University (B.A.); Ateneo de Manila University (LL.B.). Assistant Managing Editor, Ateneo Law Journal, 1988. *Member:* Federacion Internationale de Abogadas. *LANGUAGES:* English and Filipino. *PRACTICE AREAS:* Corporate Law; Litigation.

ASSOCIATES

DELFIN P. ANGCAO, born Manila, Philippines, October 25, 1957; admitted, 1988, Philippines. *Education:* Divine Word College (B.S.); University of the East (LL.B.). *LANGUAGES:* English and Filipino. *PRACTICE AREAS:* Corporate Law; Litigation.

TEODORO L. BONIFACIO, JR., born Manila, Philippines, August 12, 1960; admitted, 1989, Philippines. *Education:* University of the Philippines (B.S.; LL.B.). *LANGUAGES:* English and Filipino. *PRACTICE AREAS:* Industrial Relations Law; Immigration Law; Litigation; Property Law; Real Estate Law.

JOSEPH GREGSON A. CASTILLO, born Manila, Philippines, March 7, 1966; admitted, 1992, Philippines. *Education:* University of the Philippines (B.A.; LL.B.). *LANGUAGES:* English and Filipino. *PRACTICE AREAS:* Corporate Law; Taxation; Litigation.

PILAR JULIANA S. CAYETANO, born Mi., U.S.A., March 22, 1966; admitted, 1992, Philippines. *Education:* University of the Philippines (B.A., cum laude; LL.B). *LANGUAGES:* English and Filipino. *PRACTICE AREAS:* Commercial Law; Litigation; Intellectual Property Law.

ENRIQUE W. GALANG, born Angeles City, Philippines, September 7, 1967; admitted, 1993, Philippines. *Education:* University of the Philippines (B.A., LL.B). *LANGUAGES:* English and Filipino. *PRACTICE AREAS:* Litigation; Corporate Law.

REGINA JULIETA G. PIMENTEL, born Manila, Philippines, September 24, 1966; admitted, 1992, Philippines. *Education:* Ateneo de Manila University (B.S.; J.D., second honors). *Member:* Federacion Internationale de Abogadas. *LANGUAGES:* English and Filipino. *PRACTICE AREAS:* Labor Law; Corporate Law.

RAUL G. QUIROZ, born Manila, Philippines, December 5, 1964; admitted, 1993, Philippines. *Education:* University of the Philippines (B.S.; LL.B.). *LANGUAGES:* English and Filipino. *PRACTICE AREAS:* Corporate Law; Litigation.

DUANE A. X. SANTOS, born Manila, Philippines, December 14, 1966; admitted, 1993, Philippines. *Education:* University of Pennsylvania (B.A., with distinction), Ateneo de Manila University (J.D.). *LANGUAGES:* English and Filipino. *PRACTICE AREAS:* Corporate Law; Taxation; Litigation.

JESUS M. DISINI, JR., born Manila, Philippines, April 27, 1968; admitted, 1994, Philippines. *Education:* University of the Philippines (B.S., cum laude; LL.B.). Technical Editor, Philippine Law Journal, 1992. Phi Kappa Phi and Pi Gamma Mu (International Honor Societies). *LANGUAGES:* English and Filipino. *PRACTICE AREAS:* Corporate Law; Litigation.

(This Listing Continued)

ROBERTO L. FIGUEROA, born Rosario, Cavite, Philippines, April 27, 1970; admitted, 1994, Philippines. *Education:* University of the Philippines (B.A., magna cum laude; LL.B). Phi Kappa Phi and Pi Gamma Mu (International Honor Societies). Member, Philippine Team, ASEAN Varsities Debate II. Member, Philippine Team, Philip C. Jessup International Moot Court Competition. *LANGUAGES:* English and Filipino. *PRACTICE AREAS:* Corporate Law; Litigation; Intellectual Property Law; Real Property Law.

JOSE MARIA CLINT B. FABIOSA, born Tagbilaran, Bohol, Philippines, October 10, 1968; admitted, 1994, Philippines. *Education:* University of the Philippines (B.A., cum laude; LL.B.). *LANGUAGES:* English and Filipino. *PRACTICE AREAS:* Corporate Law; Litigation.

CECILIA FARIDA M. GOROSPE, born Manila, Philippines, November 21, 1966; admitted, 1994, Philippines. *Education:* University of the Philippines (B.S.); Ateneo de Manila University (J.D.). *LANGUAGES:* English and Filipino. *PRACTICE AREAS:* Corporate Law; Real Property Law; Litigation.

MARC RENE A. MIRANDA, born Manila, Philippines, December 7, 1967; admitted, 1994, Philippines. *Education:* Ateneo de Manila University (B.S.; J.D.). *LANGUAGES:* English and Filipino. *PRACTICE AREAS:* Labor Law; Litigation.

REPRESENTATIVE CLIENTS: Ajinomoto Co., Inc.; American Home Products Corp.; Alchemco Philippines, Inc.; Ansaldo Energia SPA; Asian Development Bank; Ayala Corp.; Barbizon Corp.; Becton Dickinson & Co.; Boehringer Ingelheim Zentrale GmbH; Boehringer Mannheim (Philippines), Inc.; The Boots Co. (Philippines), Inc.; Bristol-Myers Co.; BMW AG; C. Palanca Group of Companies; California Energy Co., Inc.; Carrier International; Chamber of Mines of the Phils.; Clarion Manufacturing Corp. of the Philippines; Commission of the European Communities; The Connel Company-Philippines; Consolidated Orix Leasing & Finance Corp.; Credit Suisse; D.M. Consunji, Inc.; Delifrance Asia Pte. Ltd.; Dentsu, Young, Rubicam & Alcantara, Inc.; Duncan Pharmaceuticals Philippines, Inc.; Elan Pharma, Inc.; Eli Lilly (Phils.) Inc.; Escobal Japan Limited; Euro-Pacific Resorts, Inc.; F. Jacinto Group, Inc.; Far East IX Charter Entertainment Co., Inc.; Farmitalia Carlo Erba; Fil-Estate Golf and Development, Inc.; Firestone Tire & Rubber Co.; Foundation Specialist-Torno SpA Joint Venture; French Oil Mill & Machinery Co.; GEC Alsthom International; General Electric Company (USA); Gillette Phils., Inc.; Glaxo Group Ltd.; GMCR, Inc.; Greenfield Development Corp.; Guoco Holdings (Phils.), Inc.; Inter-Continental Hotels; International Finance Corporation; Jardine Fleming Exchange Capital Securities, Inc.; Jardine Mathieson, Ltd.; Jollibee Foods Corp.; Kewalram Phils., Inc.; Kodak Philippines Ltd.; Kumagai Gumi, Ltd.; Kuok Philippine Properties, Inc.; La Chemise Lacoste SA; LKG Investment and Finance Corp.; Marsman & Co.; Mead Johnson & Co.; Med-Asia, Inc.; Merck, Inc.; Mrs. Fields Development Corp.; Nedlloyd Lines, Inc.; NBD Bank, N.A.; Nihon Garter Phils., Inc.; Nippon Koei Co., Ltd.; Nobile, Inc.; Nomura/Jafco Investments (Asia) Ltd.; Nonwoven Fabrics Philippines, Inc.; Overseas Private Investment Corporation; Oxbow Power Corp.; Parke Davis and Co.; Pepsi Co., Inc.; Philippine Associated Smelting & Refining Corp.; Philippine Carpet Manufacturing Corp.; PPI Del Monte Philippines, Inc.; The Philodrill Corp.; The Philippine Village Hotel, Inc.; Puerto Azul Land, Inc.; Rohm Electronics Phils., Inc.; Rhone-Poulenc Rorer Philippines, Inc.; Silahis International Hotel, Inc.; Solid Development Corp.; Solid Mills, Inc.; Sony Corporation; Sterling Paper Products Ent., Inc.; Sterling Products International Inc.; Stiefel Phils., Inc.; Suzuki Philippines, Inc.; U-Freight Phils., Inc.; United Nations Development Program; Urban Bank, Inc.; Voyager Entertainment Co.; Warner-Lambert Philippines, Inc.; William Lines, Inc.; Zuellig Corporation.

CESAR C. CRUZ & PARTNERS

Established in 1958

26TH FLOOR, RUFINO PACIFIC TOWER
AYALA AVENUE CORNER HERRERA STREET, MAKATI
METRO MANILA, REPUBLIC OF THE PHILIPPINES
Telephone: (632) 810-6267
Fax: (632) 811-0208; 811-0209

General Practice: Corporate, Patent, Trademark, Copyright, Foreign Investment, International Financial Agreements, Labour-Management Relations, Civil, Criminal, Admiralty, and Immigration laws and related litigations.

FIRM PROFILE: The firm was established in 1958 and offers a full range of legal services. It is well known for its Corporate, Labor, Patent, Trademark and Copyright Law departments. The managing partner of the firm is Judge Cesar C. Cruz who is supported by six associates, three paralegals, an office manager, secretarial and clerical pools with up-to-date office computers.

MEMBERS OF THE FIRM

CESAR C. CRUZ, (Founder), born Metro Manila, Philippines, December 26, 1933; admitted to bar, 1958, Philippines. *Education:* University of Philippines (Pre-Law, 1953; Bachelor of Laws, LL.B., 1957). Attended Program of Instruction for Lawyers at Harvard University, 1979. Former Municipal Judge-Mandaluyong, Metro Manila. *Member:* Integrated Bar of the

(This Listing Continued)

Philippines; Philippine Bar Association; Asian Patent Attorney's Association; USTA; AIPPI; Licensing Executive Society; Intellectual Property Association of the Philippines; Legal Management Council of the Philippines. *LANGUAGES:* Filipino, English and Spanish. *PRACTICE AREAS:* Corporate Law; International Law; Civil Law; Technology Transfer; Patent, Trademark and Copyright Laws and related litigations.

JAIME M. PADILLA, born February 1, 1962; admitted, 1987, Philippines. *Education:* University of Philippines (Bachelor of Arts, Cum Laude, 1982; Bachelor of Laws, LL.B., 1986). Law Clerk, Justice Vicenie V. Mendoza, Court of Appeals, 1988. Lifetime Member, Phi Kappa Phi International Honors Society. Member, Pi Gamma Mu Honors Society. *Member:* Integrated Bar of the Philippines; Philippine Bar Association; Legal Management Council of the Philippines; Maritime Law Association of the Philippines. *LANGUAGES:* Filipino, English and Cebuano. *PRACTICE AREAS:* Labor Relations Law; Commercial Law; Civil Law; Administrative Law; Admiralty Law and related litigations.

JOSE UY COCHINGYAN, III, born Quezon City, Metro Manila, September 10, 1960; admitted, 1987, Philippines. *Education:* University of the Philippines (Bachelor of Arts, 1982; Bachelor of Laws, LL.B.). *Member:* Integrated Bar of the Philippines; Philippine Bar Association; Legal Management Council of the Philippines. *LANGUAGES:* Filipino, English and Chinese (Mandarin and Fookien). *PRACTICE AREAS:* Corporation Law; Commercial Law; Civil Law; Labor Relations Law; Foreign Investment Law; Immigration Law and related litigations.

RAYMUND NONATO SL. AQUINO, born Manila, Philippines, September 4, 1968; admitted, 1994, Philippines. *Education:* Ateneo de Manila University (Bachelor of Science, 1989; Juris Doctor, 1993). *Member:* Integrated Bar of the Philippines; Philippine Bar Association; Legal Management Council of the Philippines. *LANGUAGES:* Filipino and English. *PRACTICE AREAS:* Corporate Law; Civil Law; Labor Relations Law; Intellectual Property Law; Litigation.

MARY JANE VALERIE C. DEL VALLE, born July 29, 1967; admitted, 1994, Philippines. *Education:* University of the Philippines (Bachelor of Arts, 1989; Bachelor of Laws, 1993). *Member:* Integrated Bar of the Philippines; Women Lawyer's Circle; UP Law Alumni Association; Philippine Bar Association; Legal Management Council of the Philippines. *LANGUAGES:* Filipino, English and Waray. *PRACTICE AREAS:* Civil Law; Intellectual Property Law; Taxation; Labor Law; Corporate Law; Litigation.

REPRESENTATIVE CLIENTS: Hoechst Aktiengesellschaft; Hoechst Philippines, Inc.; Hoechst Far East Marketing Corporation; Nichimen Corporation; China Airlines, Ltd.; Mobil Philippines, Inc.; Tambunting Group of Companies; Planters Development Bank; European Chamber of Commerce of the Philippines; Nissan Diesel Philippines Corporation; Playtex International,; Victoria Manufacturing Corporation; Ansons Group of Companies; Zahnfabrik (Philippines), Inc.; MTU Maintenance GmbH; Aris (Philippines), Inc.; Uniden Corporation of Philippines; Tsukiden Kogyo (Philippines), Inc.; Peetrobras S.A.; Hoechst-Roussel Pharmaceuticals, Inc.; A.W. Metz & Co. AG; Cassella Aktiengesellschaft; Joh.A. Benckiser GmbH; Marion-Merrill Dow, Inc.; Outokumpu Oy; Chemie Linz AG.

DEGUZMAN FLORENTINO CELIS
MONCUPA & TORIO

Established in 1984

SUITE C, 15TH FLOOR, STRATA 200 BUILDING
EMERALD AVENUE, ORTIGAS CENTER, 1600 PASIG
METRO MANILA, REPUBLIC OF THE PHILIPPINES
Telephone: 631-8621
Cable Address: NOVOLEX, MANILA
Fax: (632) 631-7685

Mailing Address: P.O. Box 12021 Ortigas Center, Emerald Avenue, Pasig, Metro Manila, Philippines

Corporate, Taxation, Litigation, Patents and Trademark.

MEMBERS OF FIRM

FRANCISCO G. DE GUZMAN, born Cuyapo, Nueva Ecija, Philippines, June 4, 1932; admitted, 1956, Philippines. *Education:* Manuel L. Quezon University (A.B.; LL.B.); Harvard Law School (LL.M.). Instructor, Manuel L. Quezon University, 1965-1967. Guest Lecturer, Philippine Law Center. *Member:* Intergrated Bar of the Philippines; Philippine Bar Association; Tax Management Association of the Philippines; Legal Management Council of the Philippines. Asian Patent Attorneys Association; Licensing Executive Society Philippines; Rotary Club of Pasig. *LANGUAGES:* Pilipino and English. *PRACTICE AREAS:* Taxation; Corporate Law.

(This Listing Continued)

LOURDES F. FLORENTINO, born Manila, Philippines, February 14, 1931; admitted, 1956, Philippines. *Education:* Manuel L. Quezon University (LL.B. cum laude). Deputy Clerk of Court and Chief of Legal Research Office of the Supreme Court of the Philippines, 1974-1977. Law Professor, Manuel L. Quezon University. *Member:* Integrated Bar of the Philippines. *LANGUAGES:* Pilipino and English. *PRACTICE AREAS:* Litigation; Civil Law; Family Law.

MARIANO L. CELIS, II, born Manila, Philippines, July 29, 1946; admitted, 1976, Manila. *Education:* University of Santo Tomas (B.S.C. Accounting, 1966); Ateneo De Manila University (LL.B., 1975). *Member:* Integrated Bar of the Philippines; UTOPIA (Ateneo) Foundation, Inc. (Trustee). *LANGUAGES:* Pilipino and English. *PRACTICE AREAS:* International Transactions; Corporate Law; Patents and Trademark.

EFREN C. MONCUPA, born Dinalupihan, Bataan, Philippines, January 14, 1951; admitted, 1976, Philippines. *Education:* University of Sto. Tomas (A.B., Political Science, 1971); Ateneo de Manila University (LL.B., 1975). *Member:* Integrated Bar of the Philippines; Free Legal Assistance Group (FLAG). *LANGUAGES:* Pilipino, English and Pampango. *PRACTICE AREAS:* Litigation; Charitable Organizations; Human and Civil Rights Law.

NESTOR L. TORIO, JR., born Aparri Cagayan, September 22, 1950; admitted, 1976, Philippines. *Education:* San Beda College (A.B., Economics, 1971); Ateneo de Manila University (LL.B., 1975). *Member:* Integrated Bar of the Philippines; Fraternitas Aquilae Legis (Ateneo). *LANGUAGES:* Pilipino and English. *PRACTICE AREAS:* Litigation; Customs Law.

ASSOCIATES

BIENVENIDO A. SALINAS, JR., born Calbayog City, Western Samar, March 9, 1955; admitted, 1986, Philippines. *Education:* Ateneo de Manila University (A.B., Philosophy, 1976); Loyola School of Theology (1976-1978); Ateneo Law School (1980-1984); UST Faculty of Civil Law (LL.B., 1985). Roll of Attorneys, Supreme Court, June 2, 1986. *Member:* Integrated Bar of the Philippines; UTOPIA (Ateneo) Foundation, Inc.; Liberati Fratres, Inc. *LANGUAGES:* Pilipino and English. *PRACTICE AREAS:* Litigation; Labor Law; Criminal Law; Foundations.

AMALIA ESPIRITU DIONISIO, born Pulilan, Bulacan, Philippines, June 1, 1961; admitted, 1991, Philippines. *Education:* Jose Rizal College (Mgt., 1986; LL.B., 1990). *Member:* Integrated Bar of the Philippines-Bulacan Chapter. *LANGUAGES:* Pilipino and English. *PRACTICE AREAS:* Corporate Law; Patents and Trademark; Litigation.

Languages: English and Pilipino.

REPRESENTATIVE CLIENTS: Philippine Electric Corp.; Ferro-Chrome Philippines, Inc. (Austria); Vulcan Mining & Industrial Corp.; United Laboratories, Inc.; Greenfield Development Corp.; Sunny Farms Corp. (USA); Philippine Long Distance Telephone Co.; Northern Gas Corp.; Leisure Sleep Far East, Inc.; Leisure Sleep Australia PTY. LTD.; Manila Electric Co.; Filbrid Livestock Agricultural Corp.; Hooven Philippines, Inc.; First Philippine Industrial Corp.; Corporate Investment Philippines, Inc.; Don Senen Gabaldon Foundation, Inc.; South East Asia Food, Inc.; Genpacco, Inc.; International Freeport Traders, Inc.; Integrated Microelectronics, Inc.; Asian Institute of Journalism; Philippines Rural Reconstruction Movement; Cooperative Foundation of the Phils., Inc.; 3M Phils., Inc.; Asian Petroleum Corp.; First Asian Industrial Equities, Inc.; Ancar Motors, Inc.; Cash Management & Lending Investors, Corp.; Tireking & Rubber Products, Inc.; Association of Foundation, Inc.; Topsite Tours and Travel, Inc.; F.B. Ladao, Sales Inc.

DE LA ROSA TEJERO & NOGRALES

THE PENTHOUSE, ALPAP I BUILDING
140 ALFARO STREET, SALCEDO VILLAGE, MAKATI
METRO MANILA 3117, REPUBLIC OF THE
PHILIPPINES
Telephone: 812-43-81; 812-43-92; 812-43-93; 812-43-94
Fax: (832) 816-03-04

General Practice, Litigation, Corporation Laws, Taxation, Tele-Communications, Technology Transfer, Patents, Trademarks, Copyrights, Environmental Laws, Food and Drug Laws, Product Liability, Labor and Commercial Laws.

MEMBERS OF FIRM

JACINTO R. DE LA ROSA, JR., born Candelaria, Quezon, Philippines, March 23, 1941; admitted, 1967, Republic of the Philippines. *Education:* University of Sto. Tomas (A.B., cum laude); San Beda College (LL.B.). Senior Partner, Siguion Reyna, Montecillo & Ongsiako Law Offices up to 1991. Delegate, Employer's Group, International Labor Organization. Professor, Labor Laws, Arellano University College of Law. *Member:* Inte-

(This Listing Continued)

DE LA ROSA TEJERO & NOGRALES, Metro Manila—Continued

greted Bar of the Philippines; Philippine Bar Association. **LANGUAGES:** Pilipino and English. **PRACTICE AREAS:** General Practice; Litigation; Food and Drug Law; Product Liability Law; Labor Law.

DIONISIO A. TEJERO, born Dolores, Abra, Philippines, February 8, 1942; admitted, 1988, Republic of the Philippines. *Education:* University of the Philippines (A.B.; LL.B.); Asian Institute of Management (Management Development Program, 1979). Vice President and Associate General Counsel, San Miguel Corporation until 1990. Instructor, Taxation, Philippine School of Business Administration, 1970-1973. Resource Speaker: Technology Transfer and Intellectual Property seminars; University of the Philippines; Licensing Executive Society International meetings and conferences; Labor Laws and Labor Relations lectures. Founding President, Licensing Executive Society of the Philippines, an affiliate of Licensing Executive Society International. *Member:* Intellectual Property Association of the Philippines; ASIAN Patent Attorney's Association; LAWASTA; Asia Pacific Lawyers Association; Association Internationals pour la Protection de la Propriete Industrielle; Integrated Bar of the Philippines; Philippine Bar Association. **LANGUAGES:** Pilipino and English. **PRACTICE AREAS:** Intellectual Property; Labor Law; Technology Transfer; Environmental Law; Food and Drug Law; Product Liability; Corporation.

GEORGE C. NOGRALES, born Davao City, Philippines, July 15, 1953; admitted, 1980, Republic of the Philippines. *Education:* Ateneo de Manila University (A.B.; LL.B., with Honors). Partner, Siguion Reyna Montecillo & Ongsiako Law Offices up to March 1991. *Member:* Integrated Bar of the Philippines; Philippine Bar Association. **LANGUAGES:** Pilipino and English. **PRACTICE AREAS:** General Practice; Litigation; Environmental Law; Food and Drug Law; Product Liability; Corporation; Labor Law.

SENIOR ASSOCIATES

LUIS R. LADRERA, born Manila, Philippines, October 17, 1958; admitted, 1988, Republic of the Philippines. *Education:* University of the Philippines (A.B.; LL.B.). Assistant Solicitor General, Office of the Solicitor General, 1988-1992. *Member:* Integrated Bar of the Philippines. **LANGUAGES:** Pilipino and English. **PRACTICE AREAS:** Labor Law; Litigation; Technology Transfer; Food and Drug Law; Product Liability; Telecommunications.

ELISA O. ABALAJON, born Mandaluyong City, Philippines, December 18, 1967; admitted, 1993, Republic of the Philippines. *Education:* University of Sto. Tomas (A.B., cum laude); Ateneo de Manila University, School of Law (J.D., with Honors). *Member:* Integrated Bar of the Philippines. **LANGUAGES:** Pilipino and English. **PRACTICE AREAS:** Labor Law; Litigation; Environmental Law; Food and Drug Law; Product Liability; Intellectual Property.

ASSOCIATES

ROWENA G. ROMEY-WILWAYCO, born Manila, Philippines, August 2, 1986; admitted, 1993, Republic of the Philippines. *Education:* University of the Philippines (A.B.); Ateneo de Manila University (J.D., with Honors). Law Clerk, Office of the Associate Justice of the Supreme Court, 1992-1993. *Member:* Integrated Bar of the Philippines. **LANGUAGES:** Pilipino and English. **PRACTICE AREAS:** Labor Law; Intellectual Property; Food and Drug Law; Product Liability; Corporations.

PETER G. SANCHEZ, born Manila, Philippines, May 18, 1967; admitted, 1983, Republic of the Philippines. *Education:* University of the Philippines (A.B.); Ateneo de Manila University (J.D.). *Member:* Integrated Bar of the Philippines. **LANGUAGES:** English and Pilipino. **PRACTICE AREAS:** General Practice; Labor Law; Litigation.

ARNEL P. ALAMBRA, born Quezon City, Philippines, October 1, 1965; admitted, 1994, Republic of the Philippines. *Education:* University of the Philippines (A.B., LL.B.). *Member:* Integrated Bar of the Philippines. **LANGUAGES:** English and Pilipino. **PRACTICE AREAS:** General Practice; Labor Law; Litigation.

PARALEGALS

CRISANTO C. SARUCA, born Manila, Philippines, November 15, 1967. passed, 1983, Republic of the Philippines. *Education:* University of the Philipines (B.S.); Lyceum of the Philippines College of Law (LL.B.). **LANGUAGES:** English and Pilipino.

(This Listing Continued)

NELSON S. VICTORINO, born Tariao, Philippines, January 4, 1967. passed, 1984, Republic of the Philippines. *Education :* University of the Philippines (A.B.) Arellano Law Foundation (LL.B., Valedictorian). **LANGUAGES:** English and Pilipino.

V.E. DEL ROSARIO & PARTNERS

ROSADEL BUILDING
1011 METROPOLITAN AVENUE, MAKATI
METRO MANILA, REPUBLIC OF THE PHILIPPINES
Telephone: 818-6011 to 13, 87-78-76 to 77
Fax: (632) 818-0194 Groups 2 & 3
Telex: 45352 PM; 23211 ROSDL PH

FIRM PROFILE: *The firm was established in 1949 and offers a full range of legal services that include Intellectual Property, Copyrights, Patents, Design, Admiralty and Shipping, Ship Finance, Ship Mortgage Registration, Labor and Employment, Civil Litigation, Corporation Law, Foreign Investment, Taxation, and Immigration. The Firm has an international law practice with clients mostly from North America, Japan and the EEC. This four (4) partner firm has thirteen (13) lawyers and a legal support staff of twenty seven (27) consisting of paralegal personnel, CPAs and office administrators.*

VICENTE E. DEL ROSARIO, admitted, 1940, Philippines. *Education:* Ateneo de Manila University (LL.B., summa cum laude). Former Law Professor, University of St. Thomas and University of the East; Member, 1957 and 1966, Committee in Philippine Bar Examination and Integration of the Philippine Bar. *Member:* Institute of Trade Mark Agents; Registered Philippine Patent Attorney. **LANGUAGES:** English, Tagalog and Spanish. **PRACTICE AREAS:** Patents and Trademarks; General Litigation.

VIRGILIO MA DEL ROSARIO, admitted, 1971, Philippines. *Education:* Ateneo de Manila University (LL.B., 2nd Honors, 1971); Harvard Law School (LL.M., 1973); Harvard International Tax Program (1974). 5th Placer, 1971 Philippine Bar Examination. *Member:* United States Trademark Association; European Communities Trademark Practitioners' Association; Association International Pour La Protection de La Propriete Industrielle; Licensing Executives Society; Asia Pacific Lawyers Association; Institute of Trademark Agents; Harvard Club of New York City. Registered Phil. Patent Attorney. **LANGUAGES:** English and Tagalog. **PRACTICE AREAS:** Taxation Law; Corporation Law; Foreign Investment Law.

VALERIANO DEL ROSARIO, admitted, 1982, Philippines. *Education:* Ateneo de Manila University (LL.B., 2nd Honors, 1981); University of Wales, United Kingdom (LL.M. in Maritime law and Policy, 1983). Legal Assistant, Sindair, Roche and Tamperley, London, England, 1983-1986. Lecturer, Transportation Law, Ateneo de Manila University, School of Law. **LANGUAGES:** English and Tagalog. **PRACTICE AREAS:** Maritime/Admiralty Law; General Litigation.

FRANCISCO L. ESTRELLA, admitted, 1955, Philippines. *Education:* Far Eastern University (LL.B., 1954). Special Assistant to Secretary of Labor, 1974; Acting Director of Labor Relations and Bureau of Employment Services, 1975; Chief Labor Appeals Review Staff, 1977; Director, National Capital Ministry of Labor and Employment, 1982; Assistant Minister for Regional Operations of Department of Labor and Employment, 1987; Member, Phil. Delegation to International Labor Conference, 1974, 1980, 1982; Phil. Panel RP-US Joint Labor Advisory Committee on U.S. Bases, 1975 to 1986; Labor Law Committee Integrated Bar of the Phils., 1987-1989. **LANGUAGES:** English and Tagalog. **PRACTICE AREAS:** Labor Law; Employment Law.

Languages: English and Tagalog

ERMITAÑO, MANZANO & ASSOCIATES

Established in 1986

SUITE 1403, PACIFIC BUILDING
6776 AYALA AVENUE, MAKATI
METRO MANILA, REPUBLIC OF THE PHILIPPINES
Telephone: 8189891 to 93
Fax: (632) 8177690

Litigation, Labor, Corporate, Business and Immigration Law, Taxation, Investments, Securities.

(This Listing Continued)

FIRM PROFILE: *The firm was established in 1986 by Mr. L.M. Ermitaño after his withdrawal as partner of a prestigious firm, and offers to clients a full range of legal services. The firm represents both domestic and international clients.*

MEMBERS OF FIRM

LUIS M. ERMITAÑO, born Daraga, Albay, Philippines, October 12, 1938; admitted, 1962, Philippines. *Education:* Ateneo de Manila (LL.B., 1962). Lecturer, Continuing Legal Education, University of the Philippines Law Center, 1973—. *Member:* Philippine Bar Association; Integrated Bar of the Philippines; Employers Confederation of the Philippines; Legal Management Council of the Philippines. *LANGUAGES:* Filipino, English and Spanish. *PRACTICE AREAS:* Litigation; Labor and Corporate Law.

NORBERTO P. MANZANO, born Tago, Surigao del Sur, Philippines, June 6, 1949; admitted, 1974, Philippines. *Education:* Far Eastern University (A.B., 1969); San Beda College (LL.B. Silver Medal, 1973). Member, Lex Leonum, San Beda College of Law. *Member:* Integrated Bar of the Philippines. *LANGUAGES:* Filipino and English. *PRACTICE AREAS:* Litigation; Labor and Corporate Law.

ROMEO C. DIMAYUGA, born Lipa City, Philippines, September 15, 1926; admitted, 1951, Philippines. *Education:* University of Sto. Tomas (LL.B., 1951); Universidad Central de Madrid (D.C.L., 1954). *Member:* Integrated Bar of the Philippines. *LANGUAGES:* Filipino, English and Spanish. *PRACTICE AREAS:* Corporate Law; Business Law.

JOHN AGERICO B. ROSARIO, born Dagupan City, Philippines, March 16, 1964; admitted, 1992, Philippines. *Education:* University of the Philippines (B.S.B.E., 1985; LL.B., 1991). *Member:* Integrated Bar of the Philippines. *LANGUAGES:* Filipino and English. *PRACTICE AREAS:* Litigation; Business Law; Immigration Law.

LUIS MANUEL D. ERMITANO, born Manila, Philippines, May 1, 1965; admitted, 1992, Philippines. *Education:* Ateneo de Manila University (B.S., Legal Management, 1987); Ateneo de Manila College of Law (J.D., Second Honors, 1988, 1989, 1991). *Member:* Integrated Bar of the Philippines. *LANGUAGES:* Filipino and English. *PRACTICE AREAS:* Corporate Law; Tax Law; Investments Law; Securities Law.

EDUARDO I. ALAJAR, JR., born Roxas City, Capiz, Philippines, July 12, 1966; admitted, 1992, Philippines. *Education:* University of the Philippines-Visayas (B.S.B.A., Accounting, 1986); Ateneo de Manila University (J.D., Silver Medalist, Second Honors, 1988, 1989, 1991). Pi Gamma Mu International Honors Society. University Scholar, 1984-1986; College Scholar, 1986. Certified Public Accountant, Philippines, 1987. *Member:* Integrated Bar of the Philippines; Philippines Institute of Certified Public Accountants. *LANGUAGES:* Filipino and English. *PRACTICE AREAS:* Corporate Law; Tax Law; Investments Law; Securities Law.

REPRESENTATIVE CLIENTS: Hilton International Corp.; Asia Industries; Radio Communication of the Philippines; Philippine Amusement and Gaming Corp.; A. Soriano Corp.; Phelps Dodge Phils. Inc.; Atlas Mining and Development Corp.; Paper Industries Corporation of the Philippines; First Philippine Industrial Corp.; Philippine Airlines; Egypt Air; Columbian Carbon Phils., Inc.; Ateneo de Manila; De La Salle University; De La Salle-Zobel School; St. Paul College (Pasig); Allied Banking Corp.; Hyatt Hotel; Acesite (Phils.), Inc.; Holiday Inn; Manila Pavilion Hotel; Asia Brewery, Inc.; Industrial Gases Company; Central Azucarera deBais; Binalbagan Isabela Sugar Co.; Makati Commercial Estate Association, Inc.; Parsons International Ltd.; Electrolux General Services, Inc.

FORTUN & NARVASA

Established in 1993

SUITE 407, CITYLAND 10 TOWER 1
6815 AYALA AVENUE, 1226 MAKATI
METRO MANILA, REPUBLIC OF THE PHILIPPINES
Telephone: 813-2005; 812-8670
Fax: 812-7199

Philippine and International Law Practice. Admiralty and Maritime Law, Banking and Business Law, Children and Marital Law, Commercial Law, Civil, Criminal and Administrative Litigation, Intellectual and Industrial Property Law, Labour and Employment Law, Taxation and Real Estate Law.

FIRM PROFILE: *In a short span of time (having been established in June 1993), Fortun & Narvasa has metamorphosed into one of the hottest litigation law firms in the Philippines. The firm presently has 3 partners and 5 associates. The firm is a member of several lawyers' associations, and has actively promoted various endeavors towards the improvement of the Philippine judicial system.*

(This Listing Continued)

MEMBERS

PHILIP SIGFRID ALFARO FORTUN, born Manila, Philippines, April 11, 1958; admitted, 1983, Philippines. *Education:* University of the Philippines (A.B., 1978; LL.B., 1984). *Member:* International Bar Association; Maritime Law Association of the Philippines. *LANGUAGES:* English and Pilipino. *PRACTICE AREAS:* Commercial Arbitration; Criminal Litigation; Family Law; Intellectual Property Litigation; Agrarian Law; Admiralty and Maritime Law.

GREGORIO YUSECO NARVASA, II, born Manila, Philippines, October 30, 1959; admitted, 1986, Philippines. *Education:* Ateneo de Manila University (B.S. BMH, 1959); University of the Philippines (LL.B., 1985). *LANGUAGES:* English, Pilipino. *PRACTICE AREAS:* Criminal and Civil Litigation; Corporate Law; Family Law; Intellectual Property Law.

RODERICK R. CRISOL SALAZAR, III, born Legazpi City, Philippines, September 4, 1962; admitted, 1988, Philippines. *Education:* University of the Philippines (A.B., Economics, 1983; LL.B., 1987). *Member:* Maritime Law Association of the Philippines. *LANGUAGES:* English and Pilipino. *PRACTICE AREAS:* Corporate Law; Litigation; Maritime Law; Immigration; Securities.

ASSOCIATES

RAYMOND PARSIFAL ALFARO FORTUN, born Manila, Philippines, July 31, 1964; admitted, 1989, Philippines. *Education:* University of the Philippines (B.S.F., 1984; LL.B., 1988). *Member:* Maritime Law Association of the Philippines. *LANGUAGES:* English and Pilipino. *PRACTICE AREAS:* Labor and Employment; Litigation; Maritime Law; Property and Real Estate; Intellectual Property; Industrial Property.

MYLENE TUPAZ MARCIA, born Manila, Philippines, June 12, 1967; admitted, 1993, Philippines. *Education:* University of Santo Tomas (B.A., Pol.Sci., 1988); San Beda College of Law (LL.B., 1992). *LANGUAGES:* English and Pilipino. *PRACTICE AREAS:* Litigation; Civil Law; Criminal Law; Commercial Law.

JOHANN CECILIO AQUINO IBARRA, born Camiling, Tarlac, Philippines, November 22, 1966; admitted, 1994, Philippines. *Education:* Far Eastern University (B.Sc., Accounting, 1987); San Beda College of Law (LL.B., 1993). Member: Philippine Institute of Certified Public Accountants. *LANGUAGES:* English and Pilipino. *PRACTICE AREAS:* Corporate Law; Litigation; Taxation; Property and Real Estate; Commercial Law.

RICARDO ANTE SANTOS, born Cotabato City, Philippines, February 2, 1962; admitted, 1994, Philippines. *Education:* University of the Philippines (A.B., Philosophy, 1986; LL.B., 1992). *LANGUAGES:* English and Pilipino. *PRACTICE AREAS:* Litigation; Criminal Law; Commercial Law.

DEVI-KATERINA S. MARTINEZ-NEGRE, born Manila, Philippines, September 25, 1963; admitted, 1991, Philippines. *Education:* University of the Philippines (A.B., 1984); Ateneo de Manila University (J.D., 1991). *LANGUAGES:* English and Pilipino. *PRACTICE AREAS:* Intellectual and Industrial Property; Labor and Employment; Corporate Law; Property and Real Estate Law; Litigation.

LEDESMA SALUDO & AGPALO

Established in 1963

FOURTH FLOOR, PARKVIEW BUILDING
112 GAMBOA STREET
LEGASPI VILLAGE, 1229 MAKATI
M.C.P.O. BOX 3703
METRO MANILA, REPUBLIC OF THE PHILIPPINES
Telephone: (632) 8921596-98; (632) 8920059-60 & 69
Telex: 23624 dalesal ph
Facsimile: (632) 810 73 79
Cable Address: DALESAL MAKATI

Mailing Address: P.O. Box 4068, Manila, Philippines

Corporation and Banking, Insurance, Taxation, Civil, Criminal and Commercial Law, Labor, Immigration, Maritime, Mining, Estate, Patents, Trademarks, Copyrights and Unfair Competition Law. General Practice.

FIRM PROFILE: *Since its formation in 1963 and continuously until to present, the Firm has not only engaged in the general practice of law but has likewise specialized in the fields of Corporate, Tax, Banking and Patents and Trademark Law among others. It counts, as its clients, local as well as foreign corporate entities and maintain correspondent relations with*

(This Listing Continued)

LEDESMA SALUDO & AGPALO, Metro Manila— Continued

a number of lawyers in America, Europe and all of Asia. The law firm is one of the more established firms in the country today based on the compliment of lawyers and number of its clientele and cases being handled.

PARTNERS

RAMON L. LEDESMA (1961-1993).

ANICETO G. SALUDO, JR., born Maasin, Southern Leyte, Philippines, November 1, 1935; admitted, 1961, Philippines. *Education:* University of the Philippines (Associate in Arts, 1956; Bachelor of Science in Jurisprudence, 1959; Bachelor of Laws, 1960). Professor, University of the Philippines, Legal Consultant, Ministry of Budget and Management, Republic of the Philippines, 1981. Consultant to the Governor, Central Bank of the Philippines, 1983. President, U.P. Law Alumni Association, 1985-1986. Founding President Patent Attorneys Association of the Philippines, 1977-1979. Founding Chairman Intellectual Property Association of the Philippines, 1980-1982. Association Internationals Pour La Protection De La Propriate Industrialla (AIPPI); United States Trademark Association (USTA); Licensing Executives Society; Philippine Society of International Law; Vice President Asian Patent Attorneys Associations. *LANGUAGES:* Pilipino and English. *PRACTICE AREAS:* Corporate Law and Finance; Intellectual Property Law.

RUBEN E. AGPALO, born Mamburao, Occidental Mindoro, Philippines, March 23, 1934; admitted, 1960, Philippines. *Education:* University of the Philippines (Associate of Arts, cum laude; Bachelor of Science in Jurisprudence, 1959; Bachelor of Laws, 1960). Author: Books, *Legal Ethics*, University of the Philippines Law Center, 1985; *Statutory Construction*, University of the Philippines Law Center, 1986; *The Law on Election*, Trademark Law and Practice, 1987. Assistant Solicitor General, Ministry of Justice, 1977-1986. Commissioner, Commission on Elections, February-July, 1986. *LANGUAGES:* Pilipino and English. *PRACTICE AREAS:* Patent and Trademark Laws; Appellate Practice.

FIDEL M. MANALO, born Batangas City, Philippines, April, 27, 1921; admitted, 1948, Philippines. *Education:* University of the Philippines (Associate of Arts, 1939; Bachelor of Laws, 1947). Recipient: Most Outstanding Alphan Award, Alpha Phi Beta Fraternity, University of the Philippines, 1965-1971; Award for, Outstanding Performance in defense of the Right Media to Criticize Acts of Public Officials, Robert La Rue Deportation Case, 1955. Professorial Lecturer, Abad Santos Law School, 1952-1954 and College of Law, Lyceum of the Philippines, 1954-1965. Special Lecturer, University of the Philippines Law Center Institute on Trial Technique and Procedure, 1969. *Member:* American Society of International Law; Integrated Bar of the Philippines. *LANGUAGES:* Pilipino and English. *PRACTICE AREAS:* Trial Practice.

JUNIOR PARTNERS

DANTE H. CORTEZ, born 1940; admitted, 1962, Philippines. *Education:* San Beda College (A.B.; LL.B.). *LANGUAGES:* Pilipino, English and Spanish. *PRACTICE AREAS:* Litigation.

PABLO M. GANCAYCO, born 1957; admitted, 1986, Philippines. *Education:* University of the Philippines (A.B., LL.B.). *LANGUAGES:* Pilipino and English. *PRACTICE AREAS:* Corporate Law; Patent and Trademark and Copyright Laws.

AMADO D. ACQUINO, born 1925; admitted, 1953, Philippines. *Education:* Manuel Luis Quezon University (LL.B.). *LANGUAGES:* Pilipino and English. *PRACTICE AREAS:* Law on Land Registration and Titles; Constitutional and Political Law; Administrative Law; Legal Research.

FE L. CONCEPCION, born 1961; admitted, 1987, Philippines. *Education:* Polytechnic University of the Philippines (B.S.C.); University of the Philippines (LL.B.). *LANGUAGES:* Pilipino and English. *PRACTICE AREAS:* Corporation and Commercial Laws; Patents and Trademark Laws.

LIONEL A. TITONG, born 1961; admitted, 1987, Philippines. *Education:* Far Eastern University (LL.B.). *LANGUAGES:* Pilipino and English. *PRACTICE AREAS:* Litigation.

ASSOCIATES

ROLAND B. BELTRAN, born 1964; admitted, 1990, Philippines. *Education:* San Sebastian College (A.B.); San Beda College (LL.B.). *LANGUAGES:* Pilipino, Visayan and English. *PRACTICE AREAS:* Criminal Law; Civil Law; Immigration Law.

(This Listing Continued)

MAXIMO H. SIMBULAN IV, born 1964; admitted, 1989, Philippines. *Education:* San Beda College (LL.B.). *LANGUAGES:* Pilipino and English. *PRACTICE AREAS:* Corporate and Litigation.

CLARISA RISEL G. CASTILLO, born 1967; admitted, 1992, Philippines. *Education:* University of Sto, Tomas (A.B); San Beda College (LL.B.). *LANGUAGES:* Pilipino, Ilocano and English. *PRACTICE AREAS:* Trademarks and Patents; Corporation.

TERENCIO F. TALOMA, JR., born 1968; admitted, 1992, Philippines. *Education:* University of Sto. Tomas (A.B.); San Beda College (LL.B). *LANGUAGES:* Pilipino and English. *PRACTICE AREAS:* Corporate and Litigation.

DIOSDADO V. CALONGE, born 1949; admitted, 1980, Philippines. *Education:* University of the East (B.B.A.; LL.B.). *LANGUAGES:* Pilipino and English. *PRACTICE AREAS:* Corporate; Litigation.

VINCENTE FROILAN M. CASTELO, born 1964; admitted, 1991, Philippines. *Education:* Colegio de San Juan de Letran (A.B.); San Beda College (LL.B.). *LANGUAGES:* Pilipino and English. *PRACTICE AREAS:* Corporate; Telecommunications; Litigation.

JOSE RENY T. ALBARICO, born 1957; admitted, 1988, Philippines. *Education:* Seminario Mayor-Recoletos (A.B.) San Sebastian College (LL.B.); Universidad de Navarra, Spain (STB). *LANGUAGES:* Pilipino and English. *PRACTICE AREAS:* Corporate Law and Litigation.

BILLIE SUE A. GO-LIM, born 1961; admitted, 1988, Philippines. *Education:* University of the Philippines (A.B.; LL.B.). *LANGUAGES:* Pilipino, English and Chinese. *PRACTICE AREAS:* Corporate Law and Litigation.

RONALD B. ARIETE, born 1960; admitted, 1989, Philippines. *Education:* University of the Philippines (A.B.; LL.B). *LANGUAGES:* Pilipino and English. *PRACTICE AREAS:* Litigation; Commercial Law.

RANULFO M. OCAMPO, born 1959; admitted, 1986, Philippines. *Education:* University of Santo Tomas (A.B., LL.B.). *LANGUAGES:* Pilipino and English. *PRACTICE AREAS:* Litigation.

CELESTINO S. ABLAS, JR., admitted, 1979, Philippines. *Education:* University of the Philippines (LL.B.). *LANGUAGES:* Pilipino and English. *PRACTICE AREAS:* Criminal and Civil Law.

TOMAS A. OPPUS, admitted, 1954, Philippines. *Education:* San Beda College (LL.B.). *LANGUAGES:* Pilipino and English. *PRACTICE AREAS:* Corporate and Commercial Law.

OSCAR B. MATURAN, born 1951; admitted, 1977, Philippines. *Education:* University of San Carlos (A.B.); Ateneo de Manila University (LL.B.). *LANGUAGES:* Pilipino and English. *PRACTICE AREAS:* Litigation.

CONSULTANT

TROADIO T. QUIAZON, JR., born City of Manila, Philippines, June 13, 1921; admitted, 1948, Philippines. *Education:* University of the Philippines (A.A., 1940; LL.B., 1947). Chairman, Philippine Retirement Authority Association (PRAMAI), Minister of Trade (1971-1979). Assemblyman, Interim Batasang Pambansa (Parliament), 1978-1979. Minister of Commerce and Industry, (1970-1973), Minister of Trade and Tourism (1975-1979). Solicitor, Office of the Solicitor General, 1954-1958. Professor of Public Law, University of the Philippines. Bar Examiner in Commercial Law, 1950-1971. Acting Commissioner, Securities and Exchange Commission, 1970-1971. Legal Counsel, Joint Legislative - Executive Tax Commission, 1959-1969. *LANGUAGES:* Pilipino and English. *PRACTICE AREAS:* Preparation of Briefs; Opinions and Consultation on Legal and Business Matters.

REPRESENTATIVE CLIENTS: San Miguel Corporation; Philippine Long Distance Telephone Company, Inc.; Pilipino Telephone Corporation; Republic of Nauru Consular Office in the Philippines; Jewellmer, Inc.; Toyota Motor Corporation; Toyota Auto Parts; Mikado Philippines; Hitachi Zosen, Inc.; Allied Guarantee Insurance Co. Inc.; Asian Heavy Equipment Center, Inc.; Sicogon Resorts, Inc.; Planters Products, Inc.; Traders Royal Bank; Metropolitan Banking Corporation; Security Bank & Trust Company; Carpetmasters Philippines, Inc.; Sanofi, International; Fila Philippines, Inc.; Moanrch Insurance Co., Inc.; Hamana Auto-Body-Works Co., Ltd; Intercity Cable Systems, Inc.; Jevarps Manufacturing Corp.; Wellington Investment and Manufacturing Corp.; Veterans Electronics Communications, Inc.; Vegoil Philippines, Inc.; Basilan Lines, Inc.

MAKALINTAL BAROT TORRES & IBARRA

Established in 1974

2ND FLOOR, BENPRES BUILDING, EXCHANGE ROAD
CORNER MERALCO AVENUE, ORTIGAS CENTER 1600 PASIG
METRO MANILA, REPUBLIC OF THE PHILIPPINES
Telephone: 631-0981 to 0985
Cable Address: "Quiasonlaw Manila"
Fax: (632) 631-3847

Mailing Address: P.O. Box 274, 1502 Greenhills Post Office, 1502 Greenhills, Republic of the Philippines

Philippine Correspondent Interjurist Ltd., 8, rue de la Rotisserie, CH-1204 Geneva, Switzerland.

General Practice, Litigation, Banking Law, Business and Corporate Law, Civil Law, Criminal Law, Estate Planning & Taxation, Immigration Law, Insurance, Labor Law, Maritime & Admiralty Law, Patents, Trademark and Copyright Law, Public Utility Law, Telecommunications Law, Securities Law and Litigation.

MEMBERS OF FIRM

EDUARDO G. MAKALINTAL, born May 28, 1940; admitted, 1966, Philippines. *Education:* Ateneo de Manila University (LL.B., 1965). *LANGUAGES:* Pilipino, English and Spanish. *PRACTICE AREAS:* Corporate Law; Business Law; Contracts Law; Foreign Investments Law.

RODOLFO M. BAROT, born August 17, 1934; admitted, 1957, Philippines. *Education:* University of the Philippines (LL.B., 1956). *LANGUAGES:* Pilipino and English. *PRACTICE AREAS:* Civil Law; Criminal Law; Litigation.

MANUEL L.M. TORRES, born June 16, 1945; admitted, 1974, Philippines. *Education:* San Beda College (LL.B., 1973). *LANGUAGES:* Pilipino and English. *PRACTICE AREAS:* Corporate Law; Bankruptcy & Insolvency Law; Public Utility; Energy Law.

ORENCIO F. IBARRA, JR., born June 4, 1949; admitted, 1974, Philippines. *Education:* San Beda College (LL.B., 1973). *LANGUAGES:* Pilipino and English. *PRACTICE AREAS:* Civil Law; Criminal Law; Labor Law; Maritime Law; Litigation.

MIGUEL G. DAMASO, born September 29, 1952; admitted, 1979, Philippines. *Education:* Ateneo de Manila University (LL.B., 1978). *LANGUAGES:* Pilipino and English. *PRACTICE AREAS:* Immigration Law; Maritime and Admiralty Law; Telecommunications Law; Labor Law; Trademark, Patents and Copyright Law.

CRISOSTOMO A. QUIZON, born March 26, 1927; admitted, 1955, Philippines. *Education:* Manuel L. Quezon University (LL.B., 1954). *LANGUAGES:* Pilipino and English. *PRACTICE AREAS:* Civil Law; Real Property Law; Litigation.

ENRIQUE I. QUIASON, born October 10, 1960; admitted, 1986, Philippines. *Education:* University of the Philippines (LL.B., 1985); Georgetown University (LL.M., 1991). *LANGUAGES:* Pilipino and English. *PRACTICE AREAS:* Foreign Investments Law; Securities Law; Corporate Mergers & Acquisitions; Banking Law; Business Law; Litigation.

ASSOCIATES

ANTHONY B. PERALTA, born December 30, 1960; admitted, 1989, Philippines. *Education:* University of the Philippines (LL.B., 1986). *LANGUAGES:* Pilipino and English. *PRACTICE AREAS:* Corporate Law; Trademarks, Patents and Copyright Law; Securities Law; Litigation.

ARECIO R. RENDOR, JR., born April 15, 1963; admitted, 1989, Philippines. *Education:* University of Santo Tomas (LL.B., 1987). *LANGUAGES:* Pilipino and English. *PRACTICE AREAS:* Family Law; Civil Law; Litigation.

JOEL L. ESPINUEVA, born December 11, 1962; admitted, 1988, Philippines. *Education:* University of Santo Tomas (LL.B., 1987). *LANGUAGES:* Pilipino and English. *PRACTICE AREAS:* Copyright, Trademarks and Patents Law; Litigation.

RUELITO Q. SORIANO, born August 18, 1965; admitted, 1990, Philippines. *Education:* Ateneo de Manila University (LL.B., 1989). *LANGUAGES:* Pilipino and English. *PRACTICE AREAS:* Corporate Law; Contracts Law; Telecommunications Law; Public Utility Law.

(This Listing Continued)

ALBERT S. PABILONA, born September 17, 1967; admitted, 1993, Philippines. *Education:* Ateneo de Manila University (J.D., 1992). *LANGUAGES:* Pilipino, English and Chinese. *PRACTICE AREAS:* Civil Law; Litigation.

FERDINAND D. TOLENTINO, born October 8, 1963; admitted, 1994, Phlipines. *Education:* Ateneo de Manila University (J.D., 1992). *LANGUAGES:* Pilipino and English. *PRACTICE AREAS:* Corporate Law; Taxation; Investment Law; Labor Law; Litigation.

OF COUNSEL

QUERUBE C. MAKALINTAL, born December 22, 1910; admitted, 1933, Philippines. *Education:* University of the Philippines (LL.B., 1933). Chief Justice, Supreme Court of the Philippines, 1973-1975. Speaker, National Assembly of the Philippines, 1978-1984. *LANGUAGES:* Pilipino, English and Spanish. *PRACTICE AREAS:* Civil Law; Constitutional and Political Law.

COUNSEL

RUPERTO G. MARTIN, born March 27, 1913; admitted, 1938, Philippines. *Education:* University of Manila (LL.B., 1938; LL.M., 1948). Associate Justice, Court of Appeals, 1966-1975. Associate Justice of the Supreme Court, 1975-1978. *LANGUAGES:* Pilipino and English. *PRACTICE AREAS:* Civil Law; Constitutional and Political Law.

JULIO A. SULIT, born June 14, 1923; admitted, 1952, Philippines. *Education:* Far Eastern University (LL.B., 1951). Chairman, Securities & Exchange Commission, 1986-1988. *LANGUAGES:* Pilipino and English. *PRACTICE AREAS:* Corporate Law; Securities; Litigation.

PONCIANO G.A. MATHAY, born December 11, 1930; admitted, 1954, Philippines. *Education:* University of the Philippines (LL.B., 1953); Yale University (LL.M., 1954). Assistant Executive Secretary for Legal Affairs, Office of the President, 1969-1971. Chairman: Oil Industry Commission, 1971-1979; Board of Energy, 1979-1987; Energy Regulatory Board, 1987-1988; National Power Corporation, 1988-1991. *LANGUAGES:* Pilipino and English. *PRACTICE AREAS:* Public Utility; Energy Law.

WILFRIDO E. SANCHEZ, born January 9, 1937; admitted, 1962, Philippines. *Education:* Ateneo de Manila University (LL.B., 1961); Yale University (LL.M., 1963). Chairman, Tax and Tariff Committee, American Chamber of Commerce, 1989-1993. Co-Chairman, Tax Committee, Philippine Chamber of Commerce, 1976—. *LANGUAGES:* Pilipino and English. *PRACTICE AREAS:* Corporate Tax; Individual Tax; Business Tax; Estate Planning.

REPRESENTATIVE CLIENTS: Benpres Holdings; Lopez, Inc.; First Philippine Holdings Corporation; Manila Electric Corporation; ABS-CBN, Broadcasting Corporation Inc.; San Miguel Corporation; Metropolitan Bank & Trust Company; Philippine Commercial and Industrial Bank; Cagayan Electric Corporation; Royal Cargo Corporation; Kimberly-Clark Philippines, Inc.; Sky Vision Corporation; Central CATV, Inc.; Chronicle Securities Corporation; First Philippine Industrial Corporation; Philippine Petroleum Corporation; Philippine Electric Corporation; International Communications Corporation; Radio Communications of the Philippines, Inc.; Chemoil Lighterage Corporation; Hongkong Shanghai Bank; Philippine Steel Coating Corporation; ASB Realty Corporation; BA Finance Corporation; Ayala Corporation; Allied Bank & Trust Company; Transnational Diversified Corporation; Carmelray Development Corporation; Tiffany Tower Realty Corporation.

POBLADOR AZADA & BUCOY

7TH FLOOR, STATE CONDOMINIUM I
186 SALCEDO STREET, LEGASPI VILLAGE
MAKATI
METRO MANILA 1229, REPUBLIC OF THE PHILIPPINES
Telephone: (632) 892-07-86
Cable Address: "POBLAW" Manila
Telex: (632) 63207
Telefax: (632) 818 3858; (632) 761 0311

Mailing Address: P.O. Box 7340 & 7384, Airmail Distribution Center, Manila International Airport, Philippines

Phnom Pehn, Cambodia Office: House No. 223, Rue No. 1 Khand Donpenh, Sangkat Thsar Kandal 1, Alang Makang, Phnom Penh, Cambodia. Telefax: + 855 (23) 27434.

Patents, Trademarks and Copyrights.

MEMBERS OF FIRM

HONORIO U. POBLADOR, JR. (1917-1985).

(This Listing Continued)

POBLADOR AZADA & BUCOY, Metro Manila— *Continued*

CIPRIANO AZADA, born Manila, Philippines, October 12, 1923; admitted, 1951, Philippines. *Education:* Manuel L. Quezon University (LL.B.). *Member:* Philippine Bar Association; Integrated Bar of the Philippines; International Trademark Association (INTA Formerly USTA); Intellectual Property Association of the Philippines (IPAP); Asian Patent Attorneys Association (APAA); Association International Pour la Protection de la Propriete Industrielle (AIPPI); American Intellectual Property Law Association (AIPLA). *LANGUAGES:* English and Pilipino. *PRACTICE AREAS:* Legislative Representation; Trial and Appellate Litigation; Intellectual Property.

MANUEL A. POBLADOR, SR., born Manila, Philippines, May 23, 1953; admitted, 1981, Patent Agent. *Education:* University of the Philippines (LL.B.). *Member:* International Trademark Association (INTA Formerly USTA); Asian Patent Attorneys Association (APAA); Association International Pour la Protection de la Propriete Industrielle (AIPPI); Intellectual Property Association of the Philippines (IPAP); European Community Trademark Association (ECTA). *LANGUAGES:* English and Pilipino. *PRACTICE AREAS:* Intellectual Property; Legislative Representation.

ANTONIO AUDIE Z. BUCOY, born Manila, Philippines, April 28, 1959; admitted, 1985, Philippines. *Education:* University of the Philippines (A.B., Political Science; LL.B.). General Counsel and Trustee, National Executive Board, Boy Scouts of the Philippines. *Member:* Philippine Bar Association; Integrated Bar of the Philippines; Legal Management Council of the Philippines; Intellectual Property Association of the Philippines (IPAP); Asian Patent Attorneys Association (APAA); Association International Pour la Protection de la Propriete Industrielle (AIPPI). *LANGUAGES:* English and Pilipino. *PRACTICE AREAS:* Corporate and Tax Practice; Litigation.

ASSOCIATES

SUSANNA CRUZ-PINGOL, born Sta. Rosa, Nueva Ecija, Philippines, May 24, 1918; admitted, 1952, Philippines. *Education:* San Juan de Letran College (A.B.); Manila Law College (LL.B.). Professor, Spanish Taxation, Land Reform, National University Inc., 1963—. *Member:* Integrated Bar of the Philippines; Philippine Lawyers Association of the Philippines; Intellectual Property Association of the Philippines; Asian Patent Attorneys Association (APAA); Association International Pour la Protection de la Propriete Industrielle (AIPPI). *LANGUAGES:* English, Spanish and Pilipino. *PRACTICE AREAS:* Securities and Exchange Commission; Intellectual Property; Trial and Appellate Litigation.

LUIS M. DUKA, JR., born Sorsogon, Philippines, July 13, 1926; admitted, 1959, Philippines. *Education:* Bicol Colleges (A.A., 1950); University of the East (LL.B., 1958); U.S. Department of Agriculture Graduate School (Computer Programming, 1968); National Defense College (Master of National Security Administration, 1976). Member: Import Control Commission, 1952-1953; Government Survey and Reorganization Commission, 1956; National Economic Council, 1958. Legal Officer, Bureau of Census and Statistics, 1970. Chief, Legal Service, Ministry of Trade and Industry, 1983. Assistant Director, Bureau of Patents, Trademarks and Technology Transfer, 1991. *LANGUAGES:* English and Pilipino. *PRACTICE AREAS:* Legislative Representation; Trademarks.

AUGUSTO YPARRAGUIRRE ARREZA, JR., born Madrid, Surigao del Sur, May 18, 1957; admitted, 1986, Philippines. *Education:* University of the Philippines (LL.B., 1984). *Member:* Integrated Bar of the Philippines; Intellectual Property Association of the Philippines (IPAP); Asian Patent Attorneys Association (APPA); Association International Pour la Protection de la Propriete Industrielle (AIPPI). *LANGUAGES:* English and Pilipino. *PRACTICE AREAS:* Technical/Legal Assistance for Senate Committees; Legislative Representation.

AMELITA H. PURUGGANAN, born Solana, Cagayan, July 21, 1935; admitted, 1983, Patent Agent. *Education:* University of Santo Tomas (B.S. in Chemistry). Patent Examiner, Philippine Patent Office, 1972-1979. *Member:* Intellectual Property Association of the Philippines (IPAP); Asian Patent Attorneys Association (APAA); Association International Pour la Protection de la Propriete Industrielle (AIPPI). *LANGUAGES:* English and Pilipino. *PRACTICE AREAS:* Invention Patents; Technology Transfer Agreements.

LORETO ALANO MADARANG, born Manila, Philippines, September 19, 1955; admitted, 1988, Patent Agent. *Education:* Adamson University (Bachelor of Science in Chemical Engineering). Patent Examiner, 1982-

(This Listing Continued)

1987. *Member:* Intellectual Property Association of the Philippines (IPAP); Asian Patent Attorneys Association (APAA); Association International Pour la Protection de la Propriete Industrielle (AIPPI). *LANGUAGES:* English and Pilipino. *PRACTICE AREAS:* Patent Applications; Invention Patents.

LUZ B. BUENSUCESO, born Pasig, Metro Manila, Philippines, August 8, 1948; admitted, 1985, Patent Agent. *Education:* Mapua Institute of Technology (B.S., Ch.E., 1972). Patent Examiner, 1975-1987. Special Patent/Trademark Information Officer, 1987-1989. *Member:* Intellectual Property Association of the Philippines (IPAP); Asian Patent Attorneys Association (APAA); Association International Pour la Protection de la Propriete Industrielle (AIPPI). *LANGUAGES:* Pilipino and English. *PRACTICE AREAS:* Patent Application Prosecution.

GILBERT MARIO ABRIL DE LA CRUZ, born Manila, Philippines, January 19, 1965; admitted, 1986, Philippines, Certified Public Accountant; 1992, Philippines. *Education:* San Beda College of Law (BSC, Accounting, 1981-1985; LL.B., 1987-1991). Auditor, SyCip Gorres & Velayo, 1985-1987. *Member:* Integrated Bar of the Philippines; Philippine Institute of Certified Public Accountants; Intellectual Property Association of the Philippines (IPAP); Asian Patent Attorneys Association (APAA); American Intellectual Property Law Association (AIPLA); Association International Pour la Protection de la Propriete Industrielle (AIPPI). *LANGUAGES:* English and Pilipino. *PRACTICE AREAS:* Intellectual Property Law; Technology Transfers; Corporate Law; Taxation; Labor Law; Civil and Criminal Litigation.

ENRIQUE SAHAGUN MADARANG, born San Antonio, Zambales, May 12, 1948; admitted, 1977, Philippines. *Education:* University of the Philippines (B.S.B.A., 1969); University of the East (M.B.A., 1972); Far Eastern University (LL.B., 1975). Chief, Trademark Examining Division, Bureau of Patents, Trademarks & Technology Transfer, 1982-1995. *Member:* Intergrated Bar of the Philippines; Intellectual Property Association of the Philippines (IPAP). *LANGUAGES:* English, Pilipino. *PRACTICE AREAS:* Patents; Trademarks; Copyrights; Corporate; Litigation; Banking Laws.

ERWIN B. FERNANDEZ, born Manila, Philippines, November 21, 1959; admitted, 1985, Philippines. *Education:* University of the Philippines (B.S., Business Economics, 1980; LL.B., 1984). *Member:* Integrated Bar of the Philippines; Intellectual Property Association of the Philippines (IPAP); Asian Patent Attorneys Association (APAA); Association International Pour la Protection de la Propriete Industrielle (AIPPI). *LANGUAGES:* Pilipino and English. *PRACTICE AREAS:* Intellectual Property Law; Banking and Finance; Corporate Law; Litigation.

HORACIO UMALI POBLADOR, born Manila, Philippines, April 4, 1922; admitted, 1952, Philippines. *Education:* Ateneo de Manila University; Far Eastern University (Bachelor of Science in Commerce, 1947; Bachelor of Laws, 1951); American Institute of Banking (Special Studies), 1952. Professor, Business and Banking Laws, Assumption College and Mapua Institute of Technology, 1956-1964. President, Paramount Finance Corp. (JV with General Motors Acceptance Corp.). President, Paramount Insurance Corp. Past President, Bank Administration Institute. Past President, Rotary Club of Pasay. *Member:* Intellectual Property Association of the Philippines. *LANGUAGES:* English and Pilipino. *PRACTICE AREAS:* Banking; Trademarks; Patents; Copyrights.

TECHNOLOGY/MARKETING

JEAN-MARIE BERTIN, born Rety, France, April 12, 1944. *Education:* Brevet Professional en Metallurgie Syndicat General des Fondeurs de France, Paris; Ancien Eleve de la Faculte de Droit et des Sciences Politiques de Strasbourg; Ancien Eleve de l'Ecole Polytechnique des Ventes, Paris; Ancien Eleve de l'Ecole Universelle, Paris; Lycee Technique de Soissons and Ecole d'Ingenieuns de l'EGF a cuffies Soissons (Bachelors in: Electricite; Mechanical; Automatic). *LANGUAGES:* French and English. *PRACTICE AREAS:* Indochina Operations.

ELMER M. SOLOMON, born Batangas City, Philippines, November 29, 1965; admitted, 1989, Philippines. *Education:* Colegio de San Juan de Letran (B.S.M.E., 1988); Systems Technology Institute (Computer Programming, 1990). Registered Mechanical Engineer, Philippines, 1989. *Member:* Philippine Society of Mechanical Engineers (PSME). *LANGUAGES:* English and Pilipino. *PRACTICE AREAS:* Programming; Maintenance of Issued Patents and Registered Trademarks.

(This Listing Continued)

FINANCE/ADMINISTRATION

JUAN BALDONADO DIOCALES, born Cuyapo, Nueva Ecija, Philippines, June 12, 1931. *Education:* University of the East (Bachelor of Science in Commerce, Major in Accounting, 1958). Certified Public Accountant. *LANGUAGES:* English and Pilipino. *PRACTICE AREAS:* Public Accounting Practice.

DINA A. QUISEL, born Cavite City, Cavite, Philippines, August 26, 1956. *Education:* Philippine College of Commerce, now Polytechnic University of the Philippines (B.S.C., 1977). Certified Public Accountant. *LANGUAGES:* English and Pilipino. *PRACTICE AREAS:* Accounting.

CORAZON O. CALIPAY, born Capul, Northern Samar, Philippines, November 20, 1968. *Education:* University of San Carlos (B.S.C., Accounting). Certified Public Accountant. *Member:* Philippine Institute of Certified Public Accountants. *LANGUAGES:* English and Pilipino. *PRACTICE AREAS:* Accounting.

HAYDEE O. SOLOMON, born Binondo, Manila, Philippines, May 12, 1965. *Education:* University of Santo Tomas (B.S.I.E., 1987); Systems Technology Institute (Computer Programming, 1990). *LANGUAGES:* Chinese, English and Pilipino. *PRACTICE AREAS:* Administration.

POBLADOR BAUTISTA & REYES

Law Offices

5TH FLOOR, SEDCCO 1 BUILDING
RADA CORNER LEGASPI STREETS
LEGASPI VILLAGE, MAKATI
METRO MANILA, REPUBLIC OF THE PHILIPPINES
Telephone: 893-7623; 817-8061 to 67 Locals 306, 307, 308, 309, 311
Fax: (632) 893-7622

General Practice, Civil, Commercial & Criminal Litigation, Corporations, Bankruptcy, Banking & Finance, Insurance, Industrial & Intellectual Property, Probate, Family, Commercial Arbitration, Telecommunications, Immigration, Labor, Admiralty and Real Property Laws, Taxation.

MEMBERS OF FIRM

ALEXANDER J. POBLADOR, born Iloilo City, September 1, 1953. *Education:* University of the Philippines (Bachelor of Arts, cum laude, 1974; Bachelor of Laws, cum laude and Valedictorian, 1978). University of Michigan, 1982 DeWitt Fellow. Third Place, 1978 Bar Examinations. Editor-in-Chief, The Philippine Collegian, 1978. Chairman, Editorial Board, Philippine Law Journal, 1978. Professorial Lecturer in Criminal Law, College of Law, University of the Philippines. Bar Examiner in Criminal Law, 1986 Bar Examinations. Chapter Director, Integrated Bar of the Philippines, 1988-1989. *Member:* Phi Kappa Phi and Pi Gamma Mu (international honor societies). *PRACTICE AREAS:* Civil; Commercial; Criminal Litigation; Bankruptcy Law; Corporate Law; Real Property Law; Commercial Arbitration; Banking & Finance.

MARIO LUZA BAUTISTA, born Manila, February 2, 1954. *Education:* Ateneo de Manila University (Bachelor of Arts, 1975); University of the Philippines (Bachelor of Laws, 1979). *Member:* Pi Gamma Mu (international honor society); Order of the Purple Feather. Sixth Place, 1979 Bar Examinations. Chapter Director, Integrated Bar of the Philippines, 1990. *PRACTICE AREAS:* Civil, Commercial and Criminal Litigation; Labor Law; Telecommunications; Corporate Law; Family Law; Probate; Immigration; Insurance & Banking.

GILBERT RAYMUND T. REYES, born Manila, April 16, 1958. *Education:* University of the Philippines (Bachelor of Science, 1979; Bachelor of Laws, magna cum laude, 1983). Member, Phi Kappa Phi and Pi Gamma Mu (international honor societies). Chapter Director, Integrated Bar of the Philippines, 1991-1993. Director, Intellectual Property Association of the Philippines (IPAP), 1991. *PRACTICE AREAS:* Civil; Commercial; Criminal Litigation; Industrial and Intellectual Property Law; Real Property Law; Labor Law; Corporate Law; Family Law; Commercial Arbitration; Admiralty; Insurance.

SENIOR ASSOCIATES

JAIME G. HOFILEÑA, born Manila, September 25, 1960. *Education:* Ateneo de Manila University (Bachelor of Arts, magna cum laude and Valedictorian, 1982); University of the Philippines (Bachelor of Laws, Salutatorian, 1989). Member, Order of the Purple Feather. *PRACTICE AREAS:* Civil; Commercial; Criminal Litigation; Industrial and Intellectual Property Law; Real Property Law; Corporate Law; Commercial Arbitration.

DINO VIVENCIO A.A. TAMAYO, born Manila, August 11, 1964. *Education:* University of the Philippines (Bachelor of Arts, 1985); Ateneo de Manila University (Bachelor of Laws, second honors, 1989). *PRACTICE AREAS:* Industrial and Intellectual Property Law; Civil, Commercial and Criminal Litigation; Real Property Law; Corporate Law; Family Law; Banking & Finance.

ASSOCIATES

ROMEO JOHANN I. FERNANDEZ, born Manila, May 25, 1965. *Education:* University of the Philippines (Bachelor of Arts, Dean's Medal, 1986); Ateneo de Manila University (Bachelor of Laws, second honors, 1990). Sixth Place, 1990 Bar Examinations. *PRACTICE AREAS:* Corporate Law; Civil, Commercial and Criminal Litigation; Labor Law; Industrial and Intellectual Property Law; Banking & Finance.

MARIA FILOMENA SINGH-PAULITE, born Quezon City, June 25, 1966. *Education:* University of the Philippines (Bachelor of Arts, 1987); Ateneo de Manila University (Juris Doctor, second honors, 1991). *PRACTICE AREAS:* Civil, Commercial and Criminal Litigation; Corporate Law; Admiralty; Real Property Law; Industrial and Intellectual Property Law; Family Law.

MARIE CECILE ROQUE-QUINTOS, born Manila, November 23, 1966. *Education:* University of the Philippines (Bachelor of Arts, cum laude, 1988; Bachelor of Laws, Dean's Medal, 1992). Member: Pi Gamma Mu (international honor society); Order of the Purple Feather; Editorial Board, Philippine Law Journal, 1991. *Member:* Federacion International de Abogadas; UP Women Lawyer's Circle. *PRACTICE AREAS:* Corporate Law; Family Law; Labor Law; Real Property Law; Insurance; Immigration; Industrial and Intellectual Property Law.

RAYMUND MARTIN C. RODRIGUEZ, born Manila, April 29, 1966. *Education:* University of the Philippines (Bachelor of Science, cum laude, 1986; Bachelor of Laws, 1990). Member: Phi Kappa Phi and Pi Gamma Mu (international honor societies). *PRACTICE AREAS:* Corporate Law; Banking & Finance; Insurance; Taxation.

NICK EMMANUEL C. VILLALUZ, born Cainta, Rizal, July 7, 1967. *Education:* University of the Philippines (Bachelor of Science, 1988; Bachelor of Laws, Dean's Medal, 1992). Member: Order of the Purple Feather; Philippine Team, Philip Jessup International Law Moot Court Competition, Dean's Medal, Washington D.C., 1991. Editorial Board, Philippine Law Journal (1990);. *PRACTICE AREAS:* Corporate Law; Civil; Commercial; Criminal Litigation; Real Property Law; Industrial and Intellectual Property Law; Commercial Arbitration; Labor; Telecommunications.

LEGAL SUPPORT PERSONNEL

PARALEGAL

JOSEPH V. LUY, born Manila, January 26, 1965. *Education:* University of the East (Bachelor of Science, Electronics and Communications, 1989). *PRACTICE AREAS:* Patent; Trademark and Copyright Registration & Prosecution.

REPRESENTATIVE CLIENTS: Aboitiz Transport Group of Companies; Ayala Corp.; Ayala Land; Ayala Hotels Inc.; Ayala Life Insurance, Co.; Ballast Nedam International B.V.; Banco Filipino; BAP Credit Guaranty Corp.; Citicorp Vickers; Cojuangco and Sons; Consolidated Orix Leasing and Finance; Fil-Estate Management, Inc.; Frandel Investments Holdings & Mgt. Corp.; GMCR Inc.; Greenfield Development Corp.; Hay Management Consultants Hong Kong Ltd.; International Capital Corporation; ISA Industries and Construction, Inc.; Kentucky Fried Chicken International Holdings, Inc.; Levi Strauss & Co.; Maruka Enterprises, Inc.; MBF Card International Ltd.; Mobil Phils., Inc.; New Image International Far East (Phil.), Inc.; Nippondenso; PCCI Finance Corp.; Pepsico, Inc.; Philippine Commercial & Capital Inc.; Philippine Fuji Xerox; Pizza Hut, Inc.; Purefoods, Inc.; Shoemart, Inc.; SCI Systems, Inc.; Sta. Lucia Realty & Development Corp.; Unisol Industries & Mfg Corp.; WD Scott Phils., Inc.; YKK Zipper Phils. Inc.

PONCE ENRILE CAYETANO REYES & MANALASTAS

Established in 1983

3RD FLOOR, VERNIDA IV BUILDING
ALFARO STREET, SALCEDO VILLAGE, MAKATI
METRO MANILA, REPUBLIC OF THE PHILIPPINES
Telephone: 815-9571 to 80
Cable Address: PECABAR PHILIPPINES
Facsimile: 632-8187355
Telex: PHILCOM 23732; EASTERN 66697

Mailing Address: P.O. Box 1333 MCPO, Makati, Philippines

(This Listing Continued)

(This Listing Continued)

PONCE ENRILE CAYETANO REYES & MANALASTAS, Metro Manila—Continued

FIRM PROFILE: *The Firm was established in 1983 and is engaged in all areas of law practice including Litigation, Corporation, Tax, Customs, Labor, Banking, Insurance, Patents, Trademarks, Copyright, Mining, Immigration, Transportation, Public Utilities, Energy and Environment. It is composed of five (5) Senior Partners; five (5) Junior Partners; six (6) Senior Associates and twenty-two (22) Junior Associates.*

MEMBERS OF FIRM

JUAN PONCE ENRILE, born 1924; admitted, 1954, Philippines. *Education:* Ateneo de Manila (Associate in Arts, cum laude); University of the Philippines (LL.B., cum laude); Harvard Law School (LL.M.). Elected. Congressman, Province of Cagayan, District I, House of Representatives, Republic of the Philippines, 1992—; Senator, Senate, Congress of the Republic of the Philippines, 1987-1992; Member of Parliament, Batasan Pambansa, 1978-1984; Minister of National Defense, 1970-1986; Secretary of Justice, 1968-1970; Chairman, Philippine National Bank, 1968-1978. Professor of Law, Far Eastern University, 1955-1962. Received Mahaputra Adipranada Medal Award from the Government of Indonesia, 1975; Legion of Honor, Degree of Commander, 1974; Philippine Legion of Honor, Degree of Commander-With First Bronze Anahaw Leaf, 1986. *LANGUAGES:* English and Pilipino.

RENATO L. CAYETANO, born 1934; admitted, 1960, Philippines. *Education:* University of the Philippines (B.A.; LL.B.); University of Michigan (M.P.A.; LL.M.; S.J.D.). Elected Member of Parliament, Batasan Pambansa, 1984-1986. Deputy Minister of Trade and Industry, 1984-1986. Administrator Processing Zone Authority (EPZA), 1984-1986. Professional Lecturer, Lyceum of the Philippines, 1970-1971. President, Rotary Club of Parañaque, 1976-1981. Member, European Chamber of Commerce. *Member:* Integrated Bar of the Philippines (Chairman of the House of Delegates and Governor, 1981-1983). *LANGUAGES:* English and Pilipino.

ELEAZAR B. REYES, born 1947; admitted, 1972, Philippines. *Education:* University of Sto. Tomas (B.A., summa cum laude); University of the Philippines (LL.B., cum laude). Member, Philippine Chamber of Commerce and Industry. *Member:* Integrated Bar of the Philippines. *LANGUAGES:* English and Pilipino.

JESUS M. MANALASTAS, born 1947; admitted, 1973, Philippines. *Education:* De la Salle University (B.A., summa cum laude); University of the Philippines (LL.B., cum laude); University of Pennsylvania (LL.M.). Member, Tax Management Association of the Philippines. *Member:* International Bar Association (Member, Section on Business Law). *LANGUAGES:* English and Pilipino.

ARMANDO M. MARCELO, born 1940; admitted, 1962, Philippines. *Education:* University of the Philippines (LL.B.). Vice President, Legal Affairs and Corporate Secretary, First Malayan Leasing and Finance Corporation, 1981-1983. Member, Rotary Club of Rizal West (President/Director, 1988-1989). *Member:* Integrated Bar of the Philippines (Chapter Secretary, 1987-1989). *LANGUAGES:* English and Pilipino.

REGULUS E. CABOTE, born 1940; admitted, 1964, Philippines. *Education:* University of the Philippines (A.A.; LL.B.); St. John's University (MBA); New York University School of Law (LL.M., Taxation). Lecturer, Ateneo University College of Law; Colegio de San Juan de Letran, Graduate School; Second Asian Tax Seminar. *Member:* Integrated Bar of the Philippines; Tax Management Association of the Philippines; Monthly Business and Tax Bulletin (Advisory Board). *LANGUAGES:* English and Pilipino.

JANETTE PEÑA-PIO DE RODA, born 1959; admitted, 1986, Philippines. *Education:* University of the Philippines (B.S. Business Economics, cum laude; LL.B., cum laude); Harvard Law School (LL.M.). *Member:* Integrated Bar of the Philippines; Canadian Chamber of Commerce. *LANGUAGES:* English and Pilipino.

DENIS B. HABAWEL, born 1957; admitted, 1982, Philippines. *Education:* De la Salle University (A.B. Economics); University of the Philippines (LL.B.). *Member:* Integrated Bar of the Philippines (President, Ifugao Chapter, 1989-1993); Intellectual Property Association of the Philippines. *LANGUAGES:* English and Pilipino.

EDWIN B. GASTANES, born 1958; admitted, 1987, Philippines. *Education:* Manuel L. Quezon University (A.B. Economics, magna cum laude); University of the Philippines (LL.B.). *Member:* Employers Confederation of the Philippines; Integrated Bar of the Philippines. *LANGUAGES:* English and Pilipino.

(This Listing Continued)

VALENTINO V. DIONELA, born 1959; admitted, 1985, Philippines. *Education:* National College of Business and Arts (A.B.); San Beda College (LL.B.). Research Attorney II, Legal Officer IV, Senior Legal Officer and Executive Assistant, 1985 and as Med-Arbiter, 1986-1987 with the Department of Labor and Employment. *Member:* Integrated Bar of the Philippines. *LANGUAGES:* English and Pilipino.

OF COUNSEL

JUSTICE FELIX O. ANTONIO (1983-1991).

SENIOR ASSOCIATES

ROSANNO P. NISCE, born 1963; admitted, 1988, Philippines. *Education:* Ateneo de Manila University (A.B., Economics; LL.B.). *LANGUAGES:* English and Pilipino.

JESUS E. BIGORNIA, JR., born 1946; admitted, 1975, Philippines. *Education:* Ateneo de Manila University (A.B., Political Science; LL.B.). *LANGUAGES:* English and Pilipino.

JESSE HERMOGENES T. ANDRES, born 1964; admitted, 1991, Philippines. *Education:* University of the Philippines (A.B., Economics; LL.B.). *LANGUAGES:* English and Pilipino.

MA. GABRIELLA P. ROLDAN-CONCEPCION, born 1964; admitted, 1991, Philippines. *Education:* University of the Philippines (A.B., Political Science, magna cum laude; LL.B.). *LANGUAGES:* English and Pilipino.

MA. RHODA REGINA M. REYES-RARA, born 1966; admitted, 1991, Philippines. *Education:* Ateneo de Manila University (B.S., Legal Management; LL.B.). *LANGUAGES:* English and Pilipino.

ASSOCIATES

CRISOSTOMO M. AKOL, born 1958; admitted, 1994, Philippines. *Education:* University of the Philippines in the Visayas (B.S., Management); San Beda College of Law (LL.B.). *LANGUAGES:* English and Pilipino.

MARIA LARRIE B. ALINSUNURIN, born 1966; admitted, 1993, Philippines. *Education:* University of the Philippines (B.A., Philosophy; LL.B.). *LANGUAGES:* English and Pilipino.

NELLIE JO P. AUJERO, born 1967; admitted, 1993, Philippines. *Education:* University of the Philippines in the Visayas (B.S. in Business Administration); University of the Philippines (LL.B.). *LANGUAGES:* English and Pilipino.

VENEPI R. CANTA, born 1963; admitted, 1990, Philippines. *Education:* University of the Philippines (A.B., Economics; LL.B.). *LANGUAGES:* English and Pilipino.

PERICLES C. CONSUNJI, born 1964; admitted, 1991, Philippines. *Education:* University of the Philippines (A.B. Political Science; LL.B.). *LANGUAGES:* English and Pilipino.

MARIE EMELYN CORPUS-MARTINEZ, born 1964; admitted, 1990, Philippines. *Education:* University of the Philippines (B.S. Economics, LL.B.). *LANGUAGES:* English and Pilipino.

JAIME M. FORTES, JR., born 1961; admitted, 1992, Philippines. *Education:* University of the Philippines (A.B., Political Science; LL.B.). *LANGUAGES:* English and Pilipino.

PABLO JOHN F. GARCIA, JR., born 1967; admitted, 1994, Philippines. *Education:* Ateneo de Manila University (A.B., Philosophy); University of the Philippines (LL.B.). *LANGUAGES:* English and Pilipino.

RAMON JOSE F.L. GUERRERO, born 1966; admitted, 1994, Philippines. *Education:* University of the Philippines (A.B., Philosophy); Ateneo de Manila University (J.D.). *LANGUAGES:* English and Pilipino.

ALFRED S. JACINTO, born 1968; admitted, 1994, Philippines. *Education:* University of the Philippines (B.S. Mathematics; LL.B.). *LANGUAGES:* English and Pilipino.

BENJIE PERFECTO L. LOPEZ, born 1967; admitted, 1993, Philippines. *Education:* University of the Philippines (B.S., Economics; LL.B.). *LANGUAGES:* English and Pilipino.

ANTONIO F.L. MALLARE, III, born 1963; admitted, 1993, Philippines. *Education:* Ateneo de Manila (B.S. Legal Management); University of the Philippines (LL.B.). Former agent, National Bureau of Investigation (NBI). *LANGUAGES:* English and Pilipino.

JOSE ROBERTO L. MAMURIC, born 1966; admitted, 1992, Philippines. *Education:* Loyola College, Maryland (B.S. in Accounting); Ateneo de Manila College of Law (J.D.). *LANGUAGES:* English and Pilipino.

(This Listing Continued)

LIBERATO DEOGRACIAS I. MANGALI, born 1964; admitted, 1992, Philippines. *Education:* University of the Philippines (A.B. Political Science, LL.B.). Elected, Municipal Councilor, Malabon, Metro Manila, 1992-1995. **LANGUAGES:** English and Pilipino.

ESTEBAN Y. MENDOZA, born 1966; admitted, 1993, Philippines. *Education:* University of the Philippines (A.B., Economics); Ateneo de Manila University (LL.B.). **LANGUAGES:** English, Pilipino and Fookien.

JOSE LUIS G. MONTALES, born 1968; admitted, 1994, Philippines. *Education:* Ateneo de Manila University (A.B. Philosophy); University of the Philippines (LL.B.). **LANGUAGES:** English and Pilipino.

KATRINA YSABEL M. PLATON, born 1966; admitted, 1993, Philippines. *Education:* University of the Philippines (B.S. in Business Administration); Ateneo de Manila School of Law (J.D.). **LANGUAGES:** English and Pilipino.

MARITES FILOMENA B. RANA, born 1964; admitted, 1992, Philippines. *Education:* University of the Philippines (B.S. Political Science; LL.B.). **LANGUAGES:** English and Pilipino.

REGINA MARIA S. RIEL, born 1963; admitted, 1992, Philippines. *Education:* University of the Philippines (B.S. in Economics, Cum Laude; LL.B.). **LANGUAGES:** English and Pilipino.

PETER H. SANTIAGO, born 1964; admitted, 1991, Philippines. *Education:* University of the Philippines (B.S. English; LL.B.). **LANGUAGES:** English and Pilipino.

REPRESENTATIVE CLIENTS: Aboitiz & Co.; Allied Banking Corp.; Amtrust Holdings, Inc.; Asian Savings Bank; A. Soriano Corp.; Atlas Consolidated Mining Corp.; Ayala Development Corp.; Bank of Credit and Commerce International Limited; Bank of America NT & SA.; Boehringer Ingelheim Zentrate GmbH; Citytrust Banking Corporation; Citibank; DHL Philippines Corp.; Dole Philippines, Inc.; Elizalde & Co.; Far East Bank and Trust Company; International Copra Export Corp.; Itochu & Company; Jaka Investment Corp.; Jardine Davies, Inc.; La Tondeña, Inc.; Manila Peninsula Hotel; Manila Broadcasting Corp.; Metropolitan Bank & Trust Co.; Pepsi Cola, Philippines; Phelps Dodge Phil., Inc.; Philippine Global Communications, Inc.; Philippine Stock Exchange Inc.; Pilipino Telephone Company; Shoemart, Inc.; Republic Glass Corp.; Rizal Commercial Banking Corp.; San Miguel Corporation; Telefunken Semicombustors (Phils.) Inc.; Uesugi Philippines; United Coconut Planters Bank; United Laboratories, Inc.; Westin Philippine Plaza Holdings, Inc.

PUNO & PUNO LAW OFFICES

Established in 1984

5TH FLOOR, HONGKONG BANK CENTRE
SAN MIGUEL AVENUE COR. TEKTITE ROAD, PASIG
METRO MANILA, REPUBLIC OF THE PHILIPPINES
Telephone: 631-1261 to 64; 631-1741 to 44
Telecopier: (632) 631-2517
Cable Address: "PUNOLAW MANILA"
Telex: EASTERN 63045 PUNO PN

Mailing Address: P.O. Box 12034, Ortigas, Center, Pasig, Philippines

Civil, Court and Agency Litigation, Corporations, Public Utilities, Aviation, Admiralty and Maritime, International Trade, Taxation, Banking, Real Estate, Labor and Industrial Relations, Intellectual Property, Insurance, Immigration, Naturalization, Commercial Arbitration and Family Law.

MEMBERS OF FIRM

RICARDO C. PUNO, born Guagua, Pampanga, January 4, 1923; admitted, 1949, Republic of the Philippines. *Education:* Ateneo de Manila University (B.A., summa cum laude, 1947); Manuel L. Quezon University (LL.B., magna cum laude, 1948). Author: "An Outline of Philippine Civil Law," Central Book Supply, 1954, 1958, 1964, 1967; "Cases and Comments on the Law on Succession in the Philippines," PCB Publishing, 1953, 1957, 1959, 1964; "The New Parameters of Registration in the Family Code," The Lawyers Review, 1987. District Judge, 1962-1973. Associate Justice, Court of Appeals, 1973-1978. Assemblyman, 1978-1984. Minister of Justice, Republic of the Philippines, 1979-1984. Bar Reviewer in Civil Law; Professor of Civil Law, Political Law and Remedial Law; Ateneo de Manila University, San Beda College, Manuel L. Quezon University; University of Santo Tomas; San Sebastian College; Adamson University; University of the Philippines Law Center, 1949-1991. *Member:* Integrated Bar of the Philippines; Philippine Bar Association; Philippine Society of International Law; American Chamber of Commerce; World Law Association; ASEAN Law Association (Vice President, 1983-1985; Chairman, Philippine National Committee, 1983-1985).

RICARDO V. PUNO, JR., born Manila, January 20, 1946; admitted, 1970, Republic of the Philippines. *Education:* Ateneo de Manila University

(This Listing Continued)

(B.A., cum laude, 1965); Ateneo College of Law (LL.B., cum laude, 1969); Harvard Law School (LL.M., 1971, S.J.D. Cand., 1973-1974). Author: Case Note, "Multinational Enterprises," Harvard International Law Journal, 1974; "Securities Regulation in Japan and the Philippines - A Comparative Analysis of Registration Systems," Ateneo Law Journal, 1975; "Aviation Law Reform: Haven't You Read the Fine Print in Your Ticket?" Philippine Law Gazette, 1982; "Korean Air Lines Flight 007: Did the Soviet Union Violate International Law," Journal of the Integrated Bar of the Philippines, 1984. Legal Officer and Personnel Director, United States Regional Headquarters, San Francisco, California, Philippine Airlines, Inc., 1977-1978. Vice President, General Counsel and Corporate Secretary, Philippine Airlines, Inc., 1979-1983, 1986-1990. Member, Philippine Panel on International Air Negotiations, 1979. Professor of Law, Corporations and Wills and Succession, Ateneo College of Law, 1974-1976. *Member:* Integrated Bar of the Philippines; Philippine Bar Association; American Bar Association; International Bar Association; The Law Association for Asia and the Western Pacific; Aviation Lawyers Association of the Philippines (President, 1986-1988); Ateneo Law Alumni Association (President, 1990-1992).

RENATO V. PUNO, born 1955; admitted, 1984, Republic of the Philippines. *Education:* University of Sto. Tomas (B.A., 1976); Ateneo de Manila University (LL.B., 1983). *Member:* Integrated Bar of the Philippines.

MELVIN V. MENDOZA, born 1956; admitted, 1982, Philippines. *Education:* Colegio de San Juan de Letran (A.B., 1976); University of the Philippines (LL.B., 1981). Senior Executive Assistant, Department of Local Government and Community Development, 1978-1982. Counsel, Philippine Airlines, Inc., 1982-1984. *Member:* Integrated Bar of the Philippines.

REGIS V. PUNO, born 1958; admitted, 1986, Philippines. *Education:* University of the Philippines (A.B., 1981); Ateneo de Manila (LL.B., with honors, 1985); Georgetown University Law Center (LL.M., 1987). Associate, Galland, Kharasch, Morse & Garfinkle, Washington, D.C., U.S.A. (1987-1988). *Member:* Integrated Bar of the Philippines.

ROSELLA PUNO MAPA, born 1961; admitted, 1987, Philippines. *Education:* Ateneo de Manila University (A.B., 1982; LL.B., with honors, 1986). *Member:* Integrated Bar of the Philippines; Federacion Internationale de Abogadas.

JOSE EMMANUEL M. EALA, born 1963; admitted, 1989, Philippines. *Education:* Ateneo de Manila University (A.B., 1984; LL.B., 1988). *Member:* Integrated Bar of the Philippines.

ASSOCIATES

ELVIN O. REYES, born 1959; admitted, 1987, Philippines. *Education:* PATS School of Aeronautics (B.S., 1981); Ateneo de Manila University (LL.B., 1986). *Member:* Integrated Bar of the Philippines.

RODERICO V. PUNO, born 1963; admitted, 1990, Philippines. *Education:* Ateneo de Manila University (A.B., 1985; LL.B., 1989). *Member:* Integrated Bar of the Philippines.

JOSEPH C. TAN, born 1957; admitted, 1986, Philippines. *Education:* University of San Francisco (B.S.B.A., 1978); Ateneo de Manila University (LL.B., 1985). *Member:* Integrated Bar of the Philippines.

JOSELITO U. CONTI, born 1966; admitted, 1992, Philippines. *Education:* University of the Philippines (B.A., 1987); Ateneo de Manila University (J.D., 1991). *Member:* Integrated Bar of the Philippines.

HELENA R. CALO, born 1966; admitted, 1992, Philippines. *Education:* University of the Philippines (B.A., 1987); Ateneo de Manila University (J.D., 1991). *Member:* Integrated Bar of the Philippines.

CELSO RAYMUNDO L. MAGSINO, JR., born 1962; admitted, 1992, Philippines. *Education:* University of the Philippines (B.S.; M.E., 1984); San Beda College of Law (LL.B., 1991). *Member:* Integrated Bar of the Philippines.

MARIA CRISTINA MAGDALENA F. VILLANUEVA, born 1969; admitted, 1994, Philippines. *Education:* Ateneo de Manila University (B.S.L.M., 1989); Ateneo de Manila University (J.D., 1993). *Member:* Integrated Bar of the Philippines.

REAGAN F. DE GUZMAN, born 1968; admitted, 1994, Philippines. *Education:* Ateneo de Manila University (B.S.; L.M., 1989); Ateneo de Manila University (J.D., 1993). *Member:* Integrated Bar of the Philippines.

REPRESENTATIVE CLIENTS: EMIRATES (The International Airline of the United Arab Emirates); Air France; Kuwait Airways; Gulf Air; Metropolitan Bank and Trust Co.; Traders Royal Bank; Philippine Savings Bank; Philippine Long Distance Telephone Co.; First Philippine Holdings Corp.; Manila Electric Co.; The PhilAm Life Insurance Co.; University of the East; Dolphin Ship Management; Phil. Pacific Ocean Lines; Bulletin Publishing Corp.; Philippine Trust

(This Listing Continued)

PUNO & PUNO LAW OFFICES, Metro Manila—
Continued

Co.; Ortigas & Co., Limited Partnership; Association of Philippine Coconut Dessicators; Blue Bar Coconut (Phils.), Inc.; Pampanga Sugar Development Corp.; Fiesta Brands, Inc.; Sunripe Coconut Products, Inc.; Peter Paul Phil. Corp.; Plastic Group (Phils.), Inc.; Automotive Manufacturers Institute, Inc.; Colombo Plan Staff College for Technician Education; Sports RBK Philippines (Distributor of "REEBOK" Products); Pasay Hongkong Realty Devt. Corp.; United Philippine Realty Corp.; Toyota Motors Phils.; UDC Aluminum Packaging; Benpres Holdings Corp.; Citadel Holdings Corp.; Isla Communications Co., Inc.

QUASHA ASPERILLA ANCHETA PEÑA & NOLASCO

DON PABLO BUILDING
114 AMORSOLO STREET, MAKATI
METRO MANILA 3117, REPUBLIC OF THE PHILIPPINES
Telephone: 892-3011; 892-5736
Fax: (632) 817-6423

International Mailing Address: P.O. Box 7345, Airmail Exchange Office, Ninoy Aquino International Airport 3120, Philippines.
Local Mailing Address: CCPO 210, Makati, Metro Manila 3117, Philippines.

Angeles City, Philippines Office: Lachica Building, Marlim Avenue, Diamond Subdivision, Balibago, 2017.

General Practice, Trial in all courts, Appellate, Administrative, Foreign Investments, Banking, Corporate, Mining, Insurance, Maritime, Probate, Trademarks, Patents, Unfair Competition Causes, Labor, Utilities, Taxation, Admiralty, Immigration, and Family Law.

FIRM PROFILE: The law firm of Quasha Asperilla Ancheta Peña & Nolasco is one of the oldest law firms in the Philippines. While it was only registered with the Securities and Exchange Commission as a formal partnership in 1978, the firm has been in actual practice as early as 1946 under the original name of William H. Quasha and Associates.

The firm's practice involves all areas of Law, with emphasis on Commercial, Corporate and Securities Law, Banking, Insurance, Civil and Criminal Law, Licensing, Trademark, Patent and Copyright Law, Labor, Litigation, Bankruptcy and Reorganizations, Immigration, Mining, Real Estate, and Admiralty. Administratively, the firm's practice is divided into the following areas: corporate, commercial, taxation, estates and trusts, labor law, litigation, intellectual property and family law.

The firm's corporate and commercial lawyers are well versed in securities law, mergers and acquisitions, foreign investments, joint ventures, franchising and distributorship. In addition, the firm is one of the leading firms in the Philippines in the Intellectual Property field.

MEMBERS OF FIRM

WILLIAM H. QUASHA, born N.Y., New York, May 19, 1912; admitted, 1936, New York; 1938, Federal Court, Southern District of New York; 1945, Philippines; 1947, U.S. Supreme Court; 1974, U.S. Court of Claims. Education: New York University (B.S. in M.E., 1933; M.A., 1935); St. John's University, New York (LL.B., 1936). Member, Faculty: New York University, 1933-1935; Sto. Tomas University, 1946-1947. Adjunct Professor, C.W. Post College, Long Island University, 1966. Lecturer: Harvard Law School, 1976; University of the Philippines, College of Law Graduate Program, 1979. President, Army and Navy Club of Manila, 1951. Director, Rotary Club of Manila, 1970-1975. Vice-President, U.S. Reserve Officer's Association, 1951. Department Commander, The American Legion, Philippine Department, 1954-1955. Member, Manila and National Executive Board Boy Scouts of the Philippines, 1949-1974. Chairman, Elks Cerebral Palsy Project, 1958-1960. Recipient: U.S. Bronze Star with Oak Leaf Cluster, 1945 and Philippine Legion of Honor (Officer's Rank), 1953. Grand Master, Grand Lodge of the Philippines, F. & A.M., 1962-1963. Chancellor, Philippine Episcopal Church, 1965—. President, St. Luke's Hospital, 1975—. Chairman, Republicans Abroad, Asia Pacific Region, 1985. Member, National Executive Board and Far East Council Executive Board, Boy Scouts of America, 1974—. Awardee: Philippine Women's University, Conrado Benitez Heritage Award, 1983; U.S. State Department's Tribute of Appreciation, 1983. Member: Intergrated Bar of the Philippines; Philippine, American, Federal, International Bar Associations; Lawasia (Life Member); Philippine Constitution Association. [Lt. Col., 1942-1946, AUS (Pacific Theater); USAR, 1946-1965; Ret. Res. AUS 1965—]. *LANGUAGES:*

(This Listing Continued)

English. *PRACTICE AREAS:* Foreign Investment Law; Corporate Law; Mining Law; Insurance Law; Family Law; Commercial Litigation; General Matters.

CIRILO F. ASPERILLA (1917-1993).

ALONZO Q. ANCHETA, born Sta. Maria, Ilocos Sur, Philippines, October 30, 1932; admitted, 1958, Philippines. Education: University of Manila (A.B., magna cum laude, 1953; LL.B., cum laude, 1957). Member, Legal Management Council of the Philippines (Director, 1976-1977, 1977-1978 and 1992-1995). *Member:* Integrated Bar of the Philippines; Philippine Bar Association; Aviation Lawyers Association (Vice-President, 1987); Intellectual Property Association of the Philippines (President, 1984 and 1985; Chairman, 1985-1987); Associacion Internationale pour la Proteccion de la Propriete Industrielle (AIPPI); Asian Patent Attorneys Association (Council Member, 1983-1989; Vice President, 1992-1995); Lawasia; Licensing Executives Society (LES); International Law Association; Asean Law Association (Philippine National Committee, 1986-1996); International Trademark Association; U.K. Anti-Counterfeiting Group; American Chamber of Commerce of the Philippines; Rotary Club of Marikina (President, 1979-1980); Jaycees International (Senator). *LANGUAGES:* English and Filipino. *PRACTICE AREAS:* Trademarks; Patents; Copyright and Unfair Competition; Licensing; Foreign Investments; Civil Law; Taxation; Corporate and General Matters.

NILO B. PEÑA, born Sarrat, Ilocos Norte, Philippines, January 25, 1937; admitted, 1960, Philippines. Education: University of the Philippines (A.A., 1955; LL.B., 1959). *Member:* Integrated Bar of the Philippines (IBP); National Committee on Legal Aid (Two years); University of the Philippines Law Alumni Association (President and Director, 1990, 1991, 1992, 1993, 1994); Philippine-Australian Business Council (Director). *LANGUAGES:* English and Filipino. *PRACTICE AREAS:* Mining; Foreign Investment; Family Laws; Commercial Litigation; General Matters.

POMPEYO C. NOLASCO, born Cagayan de Oro City, Philippines, February 2, 1936; admitted, 1961, Philippines. Education: Xavier University (A.B., 1956); Ateneo de Manila University (LL.B., 1960). Instructor in Law, School of Business Administration, Philippine Women's University, 1961-1965 and 1966-1967. Professor of Law: J. Abad Santos Law School, 1963-1964; University of Manila, 1967. *Member:* Integrated Bar of the Philippines. *LANGUAGES:* English, Spanish and Filipino. *PRACTICE AREAS:* Maritime Law; Seamen's Rights; Labor; Mining Laws; Banking; Litigation; General Matters.

FELISA B. BAGUILAT, born Salegseg, Kalinga, Mountain Province, Philippines, December 21, 1938; admitted, 1962, Philippines. Education: University of the Philippines (A.A., 1957; LL.B., 1961). Chief, Legal Research Section, Legal Division, Securities and Exchange Commission, Philippine Government, 1963-1974. *Member:* Integrated Bar of the Philippines. *LANGUAGES:* English and Filipino. *PRACTICE AREAS:* Corporate Law; Foreign Investment Law; General Matters.

FERNANDO F. VILORIA, born Castillejos, Zambales, Philippines, August 8, 1932; admitted, 1959, Philippines. Education: Manuel L. Quezon University (A.A., 1953; LL.B., 1958). Master in National Security Administration (MNSA), National Defense College of the Philippines, 1970. Supervising Agent, National Bureau of Investigation, Philippine Government, 1962-1971. *Member:* Integrated Bar of the Philippines. *LANGUAGES:* English and Filipino. *PRACTICE AREAS:* Criminal Law; Investigation; General Matters.

CONSTANTINE G. AGAGAN, born Sabtang, Batanes, Philippines, July 6, 1937; admitted, 1961, Philippines. Education: University of the Philippines (A.A., 1956; B.S.J., 1959; LL.B., 1960). *Member:* Integrated Bar of the Philippines. *LANGUAGES:* English and Filipino. *PRACTICE AREAS:* Criminal Law and Civil Litigation.

DELFIN A. MANUEL, JR., born Solano, Nueva Vizcaya, Philippines, March 2, 1948; admitted, 1973, Philippines. Education: Far Eastern University (A.B., 1967); University of the Philippines (LL.B., 1972). *Member:* Integrated Bar of the Philippines. *LANGUAGES:* English and Filipino. *PRACTICE AREAS:* Civil Litigation; Banking Law; General Matters.

DAISY P. ARCE, born Leyte, Philippines, November 14, 1947; admitted, 1973, Philippines. Education: University of Santo Tomas (B.S., Psychology, 1966); Ateneo de Manila University (LL.B., 1972). *Member:* Integrated Bar of the Philippines. *LANGUAGES:* English and Filipino. *PRACTICE AREAS:* Commercial; Banking Law.

CIRILO E. DORONILA, born Dumangas, Iloilo, Philippines, March 18, 1939; admitted, 1963, Philippines. Education: University of San Agustin (A.A., 1958); San Beda College (LL.B., 1962). *Member:* Integrated Bar of

(This Listing Continued)

the Philippines; Philippine Bar Association; International Bar Association. *LANGUAGES:* English and Filipino. *PRACTICE AREAS:* Research; Appellate; Constitutional; Corporate Laws; Civil Litigation; General Matters.

ILDEFONSO F. BAGASAO, born Cabanatuan City, Philippines, March 28, 1946; admitted, 1971, Philippines. *Education:* Ateneo de Manila University (B.S.B.A., Management, 1966); Ateneo Law School (LL.B., 1970). Chief of Investigation and Research, Commission on Immigration and Deportation, Philippine Government, 1975-1981. President, Immigration Lawyers Association of the Philippines, 1985-1987. *Member:* Integrated Bar of the Philippines. *LANGUAGES:* English and Filipino. *PRACTICE AREAS:* Immigration Law; Customs Law.

CONRADO S. DAR SANTOS, born Navotas, Metro Manila, Philippines, November 5, 1953; admitted, 1980, Philippines. *Education:* San Juan de Letran (A.B., 1974); University of the Philippines (LL.B., 1979). *Member:* Integrated Bar of the Philippines. *LANGUAGES:* English and Filipino. *PRACTICE AREAS:* Labor Laws; Seamen's Rights; Civil Litigation; General Matters.

DENNIS G. DIMAGIBA, born Tanauan, Batangas, Philippines, October 20, 1958; admitted, 1985, Philippines. *Education:* De La Salle University (A.B., B.S.C., 1979); Ateneo de Manila University (LL.B., 1984). Certified Public Accountant, Philippines, 1980. *Member:* Integrated Bar of the Philippines. *LANGUAGES:* English and Filipino. *PRACTICE AREAS:* Taxation Laws; Corporate Laws; General Matters.

HECTOR B. ALMEYDA, born Pagsanjan, Laguna, Philippines, June 3, 1940; admitted, 1966, Philippines. *Education:* University of the Philippines (A.B., 1961; LL.B., 1965). Instructor, Philippine Women's University, 1970-1972. *Member:* Integrated Bar of the Philippines. *LANGUAGES:* English and Filipino. *PRACTICE AREAS:* Litigation; General Matters.

ABEL C. COLOMA, born Davao City, Philippines, June 23, 1960; admitted, 1986, Philippines. *Education:* University of the Philippines (B.S.B.A., 1981; LL.B., 1985). *Member:* Integrated Bar of the Philippines. *LANGUAGES:* English and Filipino. *PRACTICE AREAS:* Insurance Law; Civil Law; General Matters.

ASSOCIATES

REDENTOR C. ZAPATA, born Quezon City, Philippines, December 17, 1958; admitted, 1987, Philippines. *Education:* Ateneo de Manila University (A.B., 1979); University of the Philippines (LL.B., 1986). *Member:* Integrated Bar of the Philippines. *LANGUAGES:* English and Filipino. *PRACTICE AREAS:* Contracts; Litigation; General Matters.

DANILO O. CORTINA, born Manila, Philippines, March 17, 1962; admitted, 1988, Philippines. *Education:* De La Salle University (B.S.C. Business Management, 1982); Ateneo de Manila (LL.B., 1987). *Member:* Integrated Bar of the Philippines. *LANGUAGES:* English and Filipino. *PRACTICE AREAS:* Mining; Litigation; General Matters.

PEDRO E. DELA CRUZ, born Pateros, Rizal, Philippines, May 3, 1925; admitted, 1966, Philippines. *Education:* University of Manila (B.S. Foreign Service, 1952; M.A. Political Science, 1953; LL.B., 1965). Legal Officer of the Agrarian Counsel. Legal Researcher, Court of Appeals. Senior Attorney, Court of Appeals. Attorney III, Supreme Court. *Member:* Integrated Bar of the Philippines. *LANGUAGES:* English and Filipino. *PRACTICE AREAS:* Research.

JOEL RAYMOND R. AYSON, born Cebu City, Philippines, April 4, 1964; admitted, 1989, Philippines. *Education:* University of the Philippines (A.B. Political Science, 1983; LL.B., 1988). *Member:* Integrated Bar of the Philippines. *LANGUAGES:* English and Filipino. *PRACTICE AREAS:* Administrative; Civil Litigation; Immigration; General Matters.

TEOFILO C. ABEJO II, born Manila, Philippines, March 22, 1962; admitted, 1989, Philippines. *Education:* University of the Philippines (A.B., 1983; LL.B., 1988). *Member:* Integrated Bar of the Philippines; Rotary Club of Quezon City. *LANGUAGES:* English and Filipino. *PRACTICE AREAS:* Labor Law; Litigation; General Matters.

MA. LUISA L. DELFIN, born Manila, Philippines, December 4, 1962; admitted, 1989, Philippines. *Education:* University of the Philippines (A.B. Philosophy, 1984; LL.B., 1988). *Member:* Integrated Bar of the Philippines; UP Women Lawyers' Circle. *LANGUAGES:* English and Filipino. *PRACTICE AREAS:* Corporate; Aviation; General Matters.

JUAN ORENDAIN P. BUTED, born Quezon City, Philippines, February 23, 1962; admitted, 1990, Philippines. *Education:* University of the Philippines (A.B. English, 1985; LL.B., 1989). *Member:* Integrated Bar of the

(This Listing Continued)

Philippines. *LANGUAGES:* English and Filipino. *PRACTICE AREAS:* Civil Litigation; Aviation; General Matters.

MELANIE ANN L. ZERRUDO, born Manila, Philippines, January 2, 1964; admitted, 1990, Philippines. *Education:* University of the Philippines (B.A. Communications, 1985); Ateneo de Manila University (LL.B., 1989). *Member:* Intergrated Bar of the Philippines. *LANGUAGES:* English and Filipino. *PRACTICE AREAS:* Family Law; General Matters.

LEONARDO P. SALVADOR, born Hagonoy, Bulacan, Philippines, April 11, 1965; admitted, 1991, Philippines. *Education:* University of the Philippines (A.B. Political Science, 1986; LL.B., 1990). *Member:* Integrated Bar of the Philippines. *LANGUAGES:* English and Filipino. *PRACTICE AREAS:* Civil Litigation; General Matters.

ANTONIO T. KHO, JR., born Jolo, Sulu, Philippines, June 29, 1966; admitted, 1992, Philippines. *Education:* De La Salle University (BS Commerce major in Business Management and Applied Economics, 1982-1987); San Beda College of Law (LL.B., 1991). 10th placer. *Member:* Integrated Bar of the Philippines. *LANGUAGES:* English and Filipino. *PRACTICE AREAS:* Civil Litigation; General Matters.

EVELYN C. GARCIA-CANTRE, born Manila, Philippines, February 10, 1962; admitted, 1993, Philippines. *Education:* St. Paul College (Bachelor of Science in Commerce, 1984); Ateneo de Manila University (LL.B., 1992). *Member:* Integrated Bar of the Philippines; Philippine Institute of Certified Public Accountants; Ateneo de Manila University Alumni Association. *LANGUAGES:* English and Filipino. *PRACTICE AREAS:* Licensing; Corporate Law; Foreign Investment; General Matters.

TRADEMARK AND PATENT ASSOCIATES

JAIME L. MARIO, born San Vicente, Ilocos Sur, Philippines, December 9, 1939; admitted, 1963, Philippines. *Education:* University of Santo Tomas (A.A., 1956); Far Eastern University (LL.B., 1962). Legal Officer, Philippine Patent Office, 1968-1973. *Member:* Integrated Bar of the Philippines. *LANGUAGES:* English and Filipino. *PRACTICE AREAS:* Patents, Trademarks and Copyright; Intellectual Property Litigation.

FELINO L. PADLAN, born Matalan, North Cotabato, Philippines, November 28, 1958; admitted, 1984, Philippines. *Education:* Rizal Memorial Colleges (A.B. Political Science, 1979); Ateneo de Davao University (LL.B., 1983). Manpower Development, Officer-NMYC, 1979-1984. Legal Officer, Bureau of Patents Trademark and Technology Transfer, 1985 to February, 1989. *Member:* Integrated Bar of the Philippines; St. Thomas More (Fraternal Member). *LANGUAGES:* English and Filipino. *PRACTICE AREAS:* Patents, Trademarks and Copyright; Intellectual Property Litigation.

JOCELYN S. SANTOS, born Obando, Bulacan, Philippines, September 19, 1954; (Not admitted in Philippines). *Education:* University of Santo Tomas (B.S., Ch.E., 1976). Patent Examiner II, Bureau of Patents, Trademarks and Technology Transfer, 1977-1979. *LANGUAGES:* English and Filipino. *PRACTICE AREAS:* Patents, Trademarks and Copyrights.

ONOFRE A. FRANCISCO, JR., born Davao City, Philippines, November 18, 1958. *Education:* Ateneo de Davao University (B.S., Biology, 1979). Assistant to the Director, Bureau of Patents, Trademarks and Technology Transfer, 1984-1987. Liason Officer, Presidential Legislative Liaison Office, Office of the President of the Philippines, 1987-1991. *Member:* Integrated Bar of the Philippines. *LANGUAGES:* English and Filipino. *PRACTICE AREAS:* Patents, Trademarks, Copyrights; Intellectual Property Litigation.

SPECIAL COUNSEL

AGAPITO I. CRUZ, born Orani, Bataan, Philippines, May 15, 1914; admitted, 1954, Philippines. *Education:* University of Sto. Tomas (B.S.E., 1946; M.A., 1947, Meritissimus); Centro Escolar University (Ph.D., 1953); Manila Law College (LL.B., 1954, Valedictorian). Professor of Philosophy and Psychology, Centro Escolar University and Philippine College of Criminology, 1947-1976. Professor of Law and Civil Law Reviewer, Manila Law College, 1954-1976. Chief, Translation Division, Filipino Language, Jose Rizal National Centennial Commission, 1957-1962. Technical Assistant, Presidential Electoral Tribunal, House of Representatives, 1962. Member, Committee on the Revision of Ballots, Electoral Tribunal. Attorney, Research Attorney and Rapporteur, Supreme Court, 1962-1973. Supervising Attorney, Acting Chief, Special Studies Division, Supreme Court, 1974-1976. Member, Screening Committee and Panel to Ease Docket Rapporteur; Committee to Study the Feasibility of Transferring the Supervision and Accreditation of Law Schools from the Department of Education and Culture to the Supreme Court, 1974-1976. Vice Chairman, Presidential Commission that drafted the Code of Muslim Personal Laws, 1976. Rap-

(This Listing Continued)

QUASHA ASPERILLA ANCHETA PEÑA & NOLASCO,
Metro Manila—Continued

porteur, International Conference of Associate Magistrates, Manila, 1977. Executive Judge, Court of First Instance of Mambusao, Capiz, 1976-1979. Recipient, Certificate of Merit and Recognition, University of the Philippines, 1979. *Member:* Integrated Bar of the Philippines. *LANGUAGES:* English, Spanish and Filipino. *PRACTICE AREAS:* Appellate Practice; General Matters.

SOFRONIO A. ONA, born San Jose, Batangas, Philippines, December 8, 1934; admitted, 1963, Philippines. *Education:* Ateneo de Manila University (A.A., 1954; LL.B., 1958); Indian Institute of Labor Studies, Ministry of Labor, New Delhi, India (Industrial Relations-Personnel Management Course, 1968). Member, Board of Trustees, Court of Industrial Relations-Hearing Commissioner and Senior Executive Assistant, 1964-1973. National Labor Relations Commission Labor Arbiter, 1973-1986. *Member:* Philippine Constitution Association (PHILCONSA); Integrated Bar of the Philippines; Philippine British Society; Philippine Columbian Association; Personnel Officers Association of the Philippines; Labor Arbiters Association of the Philippines; Rotary Club of Valle Verde (President, 1993-1994). *LANGUAGES:* English and Filipino. *PRACTICE AREAS:* Labor Litigation.

ENRIQUE D. TAYAG, born Angeles, Pampanga, Philippines, July 15, 1924; admitted, 1951, Philippines. *Education:* University of the Philippines (Associate in Arts, 1947; LL.B., 1951); University of Madrid (D.C.L., 1953). Civilian Attorney, Office of the Staff Judge Advocate, Hq. 13th AF (U.S.A.F.), 1954-1957. *Member:* Integrated Bar of the Philippines; Philippine Society of International Laws. *LANGUAGES:* English, Spanish and Filipino. *PRACTICE AREAS:* Corporate; Administrative Law; Election Law; General Matters.

EUFEMIA L. PARAYNO, born Orion, Bataan, Philippines, September 16, 1939; admitted, 1962, Philippines. *Education:* University of Philippines (Associate in Arts, 1957; LL.B., 1961). *LANGUAGES:* English and Filipino. *PRACTICE AREAS:* Garment and Textile Laws.

WAYNE G. QUASHA, born Manila, Philippines, December 1, 1947; admitted, 1975, District of Columbia and Virginia, Not Authorized to Appear Before the Philippine Courts or to act as Philippine Attorney. *Education:* Harvard College (B.A., cum laude, Classics, 1970); Harvard Business School (M.B.A., 1972); University of Virginia (J.D., 1975). Editor-in-Chief, Virginia Journal of International Law, 1974-1975. *Member:* District of Columbia Bar; Virginia State Bar; American Bar Association. *LANGUAGES:* English.

ANGELES CITY OFFICE

AUGUSTO G. PANLILIO, born Angeles City, Philippines, October 7, 1948; admitted, 1975, Philippines. *Education:* University of the East, Manila, Philippines (B.B.A., cum laude, 1968); Ateneo de Manila University (LL.B., Salutatorian, 1975). Certified Public Accountant, Philippines. *Member:* Integrated Bar of the Philippines. *LANGUAGES:* English and Filipino. *PRACTICE AREAS:* General Matters.

A member of INTERLAW, an International Association Independent of Law Firms, in major World Centers.

REPRESENTATIVE CLIENTS: The Standard Chartered Bank; New Zealand Insurance Co.; British Airways; Philip Morris, Inc.; Marcopper Mining Corp.; Philex Mining Corp.; Taysan Gold Mining Corp.; Balete Mining Corp.; Filgold Mining Corp.; Valley Gold Mining Corp.; Fuji-Xerox, Ltd.; Universal Foods Corp.; St. Luke's Medical Center; Imperial Chemical Industries Plc; The Inchcape Group; Sunlife Assurance Company of Canada; Philippine Episcopal Church; Nike International, Inc.; The Lego Foundation; Ogilvy & Mather Worldwide, Rohm & Haas Co.; Northern Strip Mining; King Features Syndicate; Pali Trevisani; International Transport Workers Federation (ITF); Mitsubishi Motors Corp.; Sea LAnd Service, Inc.; Guinness Plc; Sanrio Co., Ltd.; Puma Sportschuhfabriken Rudolf Dassler KG.; Philipp Brothers; SmithKline Beecham Plc; British Petroleum Southeast Asia Ltd.; P&O Australia, Ltd.; Ssangyong Corporation; Nippon Sanso Corporation; Hughes Aircraft Company.
REFERENCES: *Official Legal Advisors to:* His Excellency, The Australian Ambassador to the Philippines; His Excellency, The Canadian Ambassador to the Philippines; His Excellency, The New Zealand Ambassador to the Philippines; His Excellency, The German Ambassador to the Philippines; His Excellency, The Finnish Ambassador to the Philippines; His Excellency, The Brazilian Ambassador to the Philippines.

QUIJANO, ARROYO & PADILLA

Established in 1931

320 NATIVIDAD BUILDING, ESCOLTA
P.O. BOX 2495, MANILA
METRO MANILA, REPUBLIC OF THE PHILIPPINES
Telephone: (63-2) 241-4960; (63-2) 241-5078
Telefax: (63-2) 241-4972
Cable Address: "QUIARRO, Manila"

General Practice.

FIRM PROFILE: *The Law Firm of Quijano, Arroyo & Padilla is one of the oldest law offices in Manila. It is a professional partnership that started in 1931 under the name of Quijano & Roy (ex-Senate President); In 1936, it became Quijano & Liwag (former Secretary of Justice); in 1941, Quijano & Azores & Ezpeleta (Ambassador Extraordinary & Plenipotentiary); in 1958, Quijano & Arroyo (President Aquino's Executive Secretary) until 1978 when onwards, it took the name Quijano, Arroyo & Padilla.*

The Firm's practice involves almost all areas of law -- with emphasis on Labor and Civil cases. The lawyers of the Firm are, without exception, trained litigation lawyers.

J.G. QUIJANO (1931-1987).

JOKER P. ARROYO, born 1927; admitted, 1953, Republic of the Philippines; 1983, New York. *Education:* University of the Philippines (A.B., LL.B., 1952). Executive Secretary of the Republic of the Philippines, 1986-1987. Chairman, Philippine National Bank, 1986-1990. Executive/Alternate Director, Asian Development Bank, 1986-1990. Chairman, First Philippine Fund, Inc., N.Y., 1989-1994. Congressman for Makati, Metro-Manila. *Member:* Integrated Bar of the Philippines; Philippine Bar Association; New York State Bar Association; American Bar Association; The Association of Trial Lawyers of America; International Bar Association; Union Internationale des Avocats; Philippine Society of Internal Law; Civil Liberties Union of the Philippines (CLUP); Free Legal Assistance Group (FLAG); Movement of Attorneys for Brotherhood, Integrity & Nationalism, Inc. (MABINI). (On leave). *LANGUAGES:* English and Pilipino. *PRACTICE AREAS:* Corporation Law.

ROGELIO B. PADILLA, born 1938; admitted, 1964, Republic of the Philippines. *Education:* University of the Philippines (LL.B., 1963). Director: Hyatt Regency Hotel, Manila, 1986-1988; Commercial Bank of Manila, 1986-1988. *Member:* Integrated Bar of the Philippines; Philippine Society of International Law; American Society of International Law. *LANGUAGES:* English and Pilipino. *PRACTICE AREAS:* Probate and Estates; Land Registration and Recovery.

MACARIO D. CARPIO, born 1938; admitted, 1965, Republic of the Philippines. *Education:* University of the East (A.A., 1960; LL.B., 1964). *Member:* Integrated Bar of the Philippines. *LANGUAGES:* English and Pilipino. *PRACTICE AREAS:* Labor Law; Criminal Law; Civil Law.

SAMUEL B. MARQUEZ, born 1961; admitted, 1987, Republic of the Philippines. *Education:* University of the East (B.S.B.A., 1981; LL.B., 1986). *Member:* Integrated Bar of the Philippines; National Citizens Movement For Free Elections (NAMFREL). *LANGUAGES:* English and Pilipino. *PRACTICE AREAS:* Civil Law; Labor Law; Corporation Law.

HUMBERTO A. JAMBORA, born 1927; admitted, 1953, Republic of the Philippines. *Education:* Manuel L. Quezon University (LL.B., 1952). *Member:* Integrated Bar of the Philippines. *LANGUAGES:* English and Pilipino. *PRACTICE AREAS:* Land Registration and Recovery; General Practice.

REPRESENTATIVE CLIENTS: Associated Press; Chinese Commercial News; Jose "Pitoy" Moreno; New Yorker; Wellex Group; Gregg Shoes; Himmel Industries; Allied Bankers Corp.; Extraeo; FMC Manufacturing Corp.; Sterling Industrial Corp.; Vicar Mining Corp.; Mindow Farming, Inc.
REFERENCES: Peter Galliner, Director, International Press Institute, City University, London; Roderick K. Daane, General Counsel, University of Michigan, Ann Arbor, Michigan; Bernard Ladon of Lang, Cross, Ladon, Borick & Green, San Antonio, Texas; Franklin C. Latcham of Morrison & Foerster, San Francisco, California; Barry Bingham, Sr., Chairman of the Board, The Courier Journal, Louisville, Kentucky.

QUISUMBING TORRES & EVANGELISTA

(Associated with Baker & McKenzie)

11TH FLOOR, PACIFIC STAR BUILDING
MAKATI AVE. CORNER SEN GIL. J. PUYAT AVE. MAKATI 1200
METRO MANILA, REPUBLIC OF THE PHILIPPINES
Telephone: 817-3016 to 20; 817-0940 to 42; 817-1292; 817-1275
Intn'l. Dialing: (63-2) 817-3016 to 20; 817-0940 to 42; 817-1292; 817-1275
Cable Address: ABOGADO MANILA
Telex: 63726; 66848
Answer Back: 63726 JCL PN; 66848 JCL PN
Facsimiles: (63-2) 817-4432; 817-5416

· *Mailing Address:* MCPO Box 327, Makati 1299, Metro Manila, Philippines

Associated Offices of Baker & McKenzie in: Almaty, Amsterdam, Bangkok, Barcelona, Beijing, Berlin, Bogotá, Brasília, Brussels, Budapest, Buenos Aires, Cairo, Caracas, Chicago, Dallas, Frankfurt, Geneva, Hanoi, Ho Chi Minh City, Hong Kong, Juárez, Kiev, London, Madrid, Melbourne, México City, Miami, Milan, Monterrey, Moscow, New York, Palo Alto, Paris, Prague, Rio de Janeiro, Riyadh, Rome, St. Petersburg, San Diego, San Francisco, São Paulo, Singapore, Stockholm, Sydney, Taipei, Tijuana, Tokyo, Toronto, Valencia, Warsaw, Washington, D.C. and Zürich.

Correspondent Law Firm: Hadiputranto, Hadinoto & Partners, Jakarta.

General Practice. International Trade, Banking and Finance, Foreign Investments, Trusts, Corporate Law. International and Local Tax Law, Commercial and Civil Law, Technology Transfers and Licensing, Labor Law. Copyrights, Patents and Trademarks, Insurance Law, Admiralty, Immigration, Litigation, Petroleum and Natural Resources, Probate, Telecommunications, Securities.

LEO G. DOMINGUEZ, born Davao City, Philippines, May 28, 1955; admitted, 1981, Republic of Philippines. *Education:* Ateneo De Manila University (B.A. in Philosophy, 1975; LL.B., 1980). *Member:* Integrated Bar of the Philippines (Member, Special Committee on Environmental Studies and Concerns); Australia-New Zealand Chamber of Commerce; Philippine-Australia Business Council; Licensing Executives Society of the Philippines.

RAFAEL E. EVANGELISTA, JR., born Manila, Philippines, December 11, 1940; admitted, 1965, Republic of the Philippines; 1985, New York, U.S.A. *Education:* Ateneo de Manila University (A.B., 1960; LL.B., 1964); Georgetown University (LL.M., 1968). *Member:* Integrated Bar of the Philippines; New York State and American Bar Associations.

NATIVIDAD B. KWAN, born Dumaguete City, Negros Oriental, Philippines, October 5, 1949; admitted, 1976, Republic of the Philippines; 1985, New York, U.S.A. *Education:* Colegio de San Jose-Recoletos (B.S.C., Accounting, 1969); Ateneo de Manila University (LL.B., 1975). *Member:* Integrated Bar of the Philippines; New York State Bar Association; Tax Management Association of the Philippines.

LUCAS M. NUNAG, born Antequera, Bohol, Philippines, October 27, 1948; admitted, 1974, Republic of the Philippines. *Education:* University of Santo Tomas (A.B., 1969; LL.B., 1973). *Member:* Integrated Bar of the Philippines; Immigration Lawyers Association of the Philippines.

RAMON J. QUISUMBING, born Manila, Philippines, December 19, 1953; admitted, 1979, District of Columbia, U.S.A.; 1980, Virginia, U.S.A.; 1986, New York, U.S.A.; 1991, Republic of the Philippines. *Education:* University of South Florida (B.S., 1976); Georgetown University Law Center (J.D., 1979). *Member:* Integrated Bar of the Philippines; New York State and American Bar Associations.

FRANCISCO E. RODRIGO, JR., born Manila, Philippines, June 14, 1939; admitted, 1965, Republic of the Philippines; 1980, New York, U.S.A. *Education:* Ateneo University (B.S., 1960; LL.B., 1964). *Member:* Integrated Bar of the Philippines; New York State Bar Association.

ROMEO L. SALONGA, born San Miguel, Bulacan, Philippines, March 20, 1940; admitted, 1967, Republic of the Philippines; 1987, New York, U.S.A. *Education:* University of the Philippines (A.B., 1961; LL.B., 1966). *Member:* Integrated Bar of the Philippines; New York State and American Bar Associations.

JOSE R. SANDEJAS, born Manila, Philippines, December 9, 1937; admitted, 1964, Republic of the Philippines. *Education:* De La Salle College (B.S.C., 1958); Manuel Luis Quezon University (LL.B., 1963). *Member:*

(This Listing Continued)

Integrated Bar of the Philippines; Tax Management Association of the Philippines.

OF COUNSEL

VICENTE A. TORRES, born Pasay City, Philippines, July 30, 1927; admitted, 1956, Republic of the Philippines. *Education:* Fordham University (A.B., 1950); University of Santo Tomas (LL.B., 1955). *Member:* Integrated Bar of the Philippines; Legal Management Council of the Philippines; Aviation Lawyers Association of the Philippines; Philippine Bar Association.

LOCAL PARTNERS

RICARDO P. C. CASTRO, JR., born Iloilo City, Philippines, July 11, 1952; admitted, 1975, Republic of the Philippines. *Education:* University of San Agustin (A.B., 1970; LL.B., 1974); University of the Philippines in the Visayas (M.M., 1983). *Member:* Integrated Bar of the Philippines; Alumni Association of the Academy of American and International Law.

EDGARDO M. DE VERA, born Pandi, Bulacan, Philippines, April 9, 1954; admitted, 1982, Republic of the Philippines. *Education:* De La Salle College (B.S.C., 1975); Ateneo de Manila University (LL.B., 1981). *Member:* Integrated Bar of the Philippines; Tax Management Association of the Philippines.

CHRISTOPHER L. LIM, born Pasay City, Philippines, June 13, 1957; admitted, 1983, Republic of the Philippines. *Education:* De La Salle University (A.B., Economics, 1978); Ateneo de Manila University (LL.B., 1982). *Member:* Integrated Bar of the Philippines; Asian Patents Attorneys Association; Intellectual Property Association of the Philippines.

PEARL T. LIU, born Davao City, Philippines, September 29, 1955; admitted, 1983, Republic of the Philippines. *Education:* Assumption Convent (A.B., English, 1976; B.S.C. Accounting, 1977); Ateneo de Manila (LL.B., 1982). *Member:* Integrated Bar of the Philippines; Licensing Executives Society of the Philippines.

CORNELIO B. ABUDA, born Guinan E. Samar, Philippines, September 16, 1963; admitted, 1991, Republic of the Philippines. *Education:* Visayas State College of Agriculture (B.S.A.E., 1984); University of the Philippines (LL.B., 1990). *Member:* Integrated Bar of the Philippines; University of the Philippines Law Alumni Association; Philippine Society of Agricultural Engineers.

ARTHUR P. AUTEA, born Manila, Philippines, July 16, 1961; admitted, 1987, Republic of the Philippines. *Education:* University of the Philippines (A.B., 1981; LL.B., 1986). Confidential Lawyer, Court of Appeals, 1987. *Member:* Integrated Bar of the Philippines; University of the Philippines Law Alumni Association.

ANTHONY D. BENGZON, born Manila, Philippines, May 1, 1967; admitted, 1994, Republic of the Philippines. *Education:* Ateneo de Manila University (A.B., Management Economics, 1989); University of the Philippines (LL.B., 1993). *Member:* Integrated Bar of the Philippines.

ANDRÉ PHILIPPE G. BETITA, born San Juan, Metro Manila, Philippines, September 22, 1967; admitted, 1993, Republic of the Philippines. *Education:* Ateneo de Manila University (B.S., Management Engineering, 1988; J.D., 1992). *Member:* Integrated Bar of the Philippines.

EMMANUEL S. BUENAVENTURA, born Manila, Philippines, December 28, 1961; admitted, 1988, Republic of the Philippines. *Education:* Ateneo de Manila University (A.B., Economics, 1982); University of the Philippines (LL.B., 1987). *Member:* Integrated Bar of the Philippines.

SOLOMON RICARDO B. CASTRO, born Manila, Philippines, April 3, 1968; admitted, 1994, Republic of the Philippines. *Education:* University of the Philippines (B.S., Business Administration, cum laude, 1989; LL.B., 1993). *Member:* Integrated Bar of the Philippines.

DOUGLAS P. DEFENSOR, born Iloilo City, Philippines, May 13, 1951; admitted, 1976, Republic of the Philippines. *Education:* Trinity College of Quezon City (A.B., 1971); University of the Philippines (LL.B., 1975). *Member:* Integrated Bar of the Philippines.

BENJAMIN B. DEL ROSARIO, born Manila, Philippines, June 8, 1932; admitted, 1959, Republic of the Philippines. *Education:* University of the Philippines (A.B., 1953; LL.B., 1959). *Member:* Integrated Bar of the Philippines.

GEORGE GILBERT G. DELA CUESTA, born Quezon City, Philippines, January 2, 1968; admitted, 1994, Republic of the Philippines. *Educa-*

(This Listing Continued)

QUISUMBING TORRES & EVANGELISTA, Metro Manila—Continued

tion: University of the Philippines (Bachelor of Arts in Political Science, 1988; LL.B., 1992). *Member:* Integrated Bar of the Philippines.

ANGEL M. ESGUERRA, III, born Manila, Philippines, August 30, 1961; admitted, 1987, Republic of the Philippines. *Education:* University of the Philippines School of Economics (A.B., 1982); University of the Philippines (LL.B., 1986). *Member:* Integrated Bar of the Philippines.

MANUEL C. FAUSTO, JR., born Manila, Philippines, January 17, 1966; admitted, 1994, Republic of the Philippines. *Education:* University of the Philippines School of Economics (B.A., Economics, 1987); University of the Philippines College of Law (LL.B., 1993). *Member:* Integrated Bar of the Philippines.

RACHEL P. FOLLOSCO, born Tarlac, Tarlac, Philippines, September 25, 1966; admitted, 1994, Republic of the Philippines. *Education:* University of the Philippines (B.S., Business Administration and Accountancy, 1988; LL.B., 1993). *Member:* Integrated Bar of the Philippines; Philippine Institute of Certified Public Accountants.

VIRGILIO C. HERCE, born Manila, Philippines, March 13, 1965; admitted, 1993, Republic of the Philippines. *Education:* Ateneo de Manila University (B.S., 1985; J.D., 1992). *Member:* Integrated Bar of the Philippines.

RENE K. LIMCAOCO, born Manila, Philippines, November 3, 1964; admitted, 1991, Republic of the Philippines. *Education:* Stanford University (B.A., Economics, 1986); Ateneo de Manila University (LL.B., 1990). *Member:* Integrated Bar of the Philippines.

NARCISO A. MANANTAN, born Bacnotan, La Union, Philippines, January 2, 1938; admitted, 1965, Republic of the Philippines. *Education:* University of Santo Tomas (A.A., 1956; LL.B., 1962). *Member:* Integrated Bar of the Philippines; Intellectual Property Association of the Philippines; Asean Patent Attorneys Association; Association Internationale pour la Protection de la Propriete Industrielle.

MA. RUBY SARAH S. NITORREDA, born Davao City, Philippines, September 12, 1963; admitted, 1990, Republic of the Philippines. *Education:* University of the Philippines (A.B., Economics, 1983; LL.B., 1989). *Member:* Integrated Bar of the Philippines; Licensed Executives Society of the Philippines.

EDUARDO M. PAÑGAN, born Davao City, Philippines, March, 1, 1962; admitted, 1992, Republic of the Philippines. *Education:* Ateneo de Manila University (A.B., 1982); Ateneo Law School (LL.B., 1991). *Member:* Integrated Bar of the Philippines.

ANNA REGINA LEGASPI PANTALEON, born Manila, Philippines, February 28, 1967; admitted, 1992, Republic of the Philippines. *Education:* De La Salle University (A.B., Economics, 1987); University of the Philippines (LL.B., 1991). *Member:* Integrated Bar of the Philippines; Federacion Internationale de Abogadas.

MARIVIC K. PUNZALAN-ESPIRITU, born Roxas Quintal Mindoro, Philippines, February 26, 1968; admitted, 1994, Republic of the Philippines. *Education:* De La Salle University (Political Science & Accounting, 1988); University of the Philippines (LL.B., 1993). *Member:* Integrated Bar of the Philippines; Philippine Institute of Certified Public Accountants.

RODRIGO LOPE S. QUIMBO, born Catbalogan, Samar, November 20, 1962; admitted, 1990, Republic of the Philippines. *Education:* University of Santo Tomas (B.A., 1983); University of the Philippines (LL.B., 1989). *Member:* Integrated Bar of the Philippines.

KENNEDY B. SARMIENTO, born Manila, Philippines, December 29, 1963; admitted, 1990, Republic of the Philippines. *Education:* University of the Philippines (A.B., Economics, 1984; LL.B., 1989). *Member:* Integrated Bar of the Philippines; Intellectual Property Association of the Philippines; Asian Patent Attorney's Association; Association Internationale pour la Protection de la Prospriete Industrial Licensing Executive Society of the Philippines.

ULFREDO A. TUYAC, born Mabini, Bohol, Philippines, January 14, 1948; admitted, 1975, Republic of the Philippines. *Education:* Divine Word College of Tagbilaran (B.A., 1968; LL.B., 1974). *Member:* Integrated Bar of the Philippines.

CEAZAR LORENZO T. VENERACION, III, born Quezon City, Philippines, February 6, 1968; admitted, 1993, Republic of the Philippines. *Education:* University of the Philippines, College of Social Sciences and Philos-

(This Listing Continued)

AS276B

ophy (A.B., Political Science, 1988); University of the Philippines, College of Law (LL.B., 1992). *Member:* Integrated Bar of the Philippines; American Bar Association.

JOSEPHINE V. TAÑADA YAM-NARCISO, born Manila, Philippines, November 21, 1965; admitted, 1993, Republic of the Philippines. *Education:* Ateneo de Manila University (B.S., Management Honors Program, 1987); Ateneo College of Law (J.D., 1992). *Member:* Integrated Bar of the Philippines.

GIL ROBERTO L. ZERRUDO, born Quezon City, Philippines, October 12, 1963; admitted, 1989, Republic of the Philippines. *Education:* Ateneo de Manila University (A.B., 1984; LL.B., 1988). *Member:* Integrated Bar of the Philippines.

REYES SANTAYANA TAYAO MOLO & ALEGRE

3RD FLOOR, ZARAGOZA BUILDING
102 GAMBOA STREET, LEGASPI VILLAGE, MAKATI, METRO MANILA
METRO MANILA, REPUBLIC OF THE PHILIPPINES
Telephone: 843-39-76
Cable Address: "Marlich", Manila
Fax: (632) 843-39-77

General Practice and Litigation. Corporation, Taxation, Labor, Banking and Finance. Civil and Commercial Laws. Foreign Investments. Patents, Trademarks and Copyrights.

MEMBERS OF FIRM

MARCIAL P. LICHAUCO (1936-1971).

E.A. PICAZO (1938-1978).

LEOPOLDO PICAZO (1948-1977).

SALOMON F. REYES, born Manila, Philippines, January 29, 1933; admitted, 1956, Philippines. *Education:* University of the Philippines (A.A., with honors; LL.B., A.B., Cum laude); University of Manila (completed all academic requirements leading to LL.M). International Honor Societies of Phi Kappa Phi and Pi Gamma Mu. Recipient, University of the Philippines Presidential Pin. *Member:* Integrated Bar of the Philippines; Philippine Bar Association (Director, 1980-1982; Vice President, 1981-1982). *LANGUAGES:* English and Tagalog. *PRACTICE AREAS:* Corporate; Banking and Finance; Foreign Investments.

RAFAEL S. SANTAYANA, born Mauban, Tayabas, February 3, 1917; admitted, 1939, Philippines. *Education:* National University (A.A.); Philippine Law School (LL.B.). Secretary to the Undersecretary of National Defense, 1939-1940. Secretary to the Secretary of Labor, 1940. Public Defender, 1941. Legal Assistant Office of the Manila City Mayor, 1942. Chief, House Rentals Division, Office of the Manila City Mayor, 1943-1944. *LANGUAGES:* English and Tagalog. *PRACTICE AREAS:* Banking and Finance; Aviation; Patents; Trademarks and Copyrights.

SILVERIO S. TAYAO, born Bacolor, Pampanga, Philippines, February 17, 1931; admitted, 1955, Philippines. *Education:* University of the Philippines (A.A.; LL.B.); Harvard Law School (LL.M., 1960). Phi Kappa Phi. Special Attorney, Commission on Elections Philippines, 1955 and 1957. Professorial Lecturer, College of Law, University of the Philippines, 1982-1992. Judge, Regional Trial Court, 1990-1993. *Member:* Integrated Bar of the Philippines; Philippine Bar Association. *LANGUAGES:* English and Tagalog. *PRACTICE AREAS:* Litigation; Taxation; Nationalization Statutes.

PEDRO T. MOLO, born Legaspi City, Philippines, February 5, 1934; admitted, 1968, Philippines. *Education:* Far Eastern University (B.S.); San Beda College (LL.B.). *LANGUAGES:* Pilipino and English. *PRACTICE AREAS:* Corporate; Labor; Admiralty; Litigation.

ZOSIMO G. ALEGRE, born Borongan, Eastern Samar, Philippines, January 10, 1941; admitted, 1970, Philippines. *Education:* Lyceum of the Philippines (A.B.); University of the East (LL.B.). Trial Lawyer, Social Security System, 1970-1973. *Member:* Integrated Bar of the Philippines,. *LANGUAGES:* English, Pilipino (Tagalog), Visayan and Pampango. *PRACTICE AREAS:* Corporate; Labor; Litigation.

(This Listing Continued)

ASSOCIATES

GENE B. MACALAGUING, born Alubijid, Misamis Oriental, Philippines, July 14, 1949; admitted, 1978, Philippines. *Education:* Liceo de Cagayan (A.B.); Silliman University (LL.B.). *Member:* Integrated Bar of the Philippines. *LANGUAGES:* English, Pilipino and Cebuano. *PRACTICE AREAS:* Patents; Trademarks and Copyrights; Immigration.

LEGAL SUPPORT PERSONNEL

DOMINADOR S. MALAGUENO, born Camalig, Albay, Philippines, August 15, 1952. *Education:* Adamson University (B.S.C., 1982; LL.B., 1987). (Paralegal). *LANGUAGES:* English, Tagalog and Bicol.

REPRESENTATIVE CLIENTS: Adams Brands, Inc.; Army & Navy Club; A. Soriano Corp.; BASF Aktiengesellschaft; Bechtel International Corp.; CBI (Philippines) Inc.; Dillingham Construction International, Inc.; Everett Steamship Corp.; KLM Royal Dutch Airlines; MCPI Corporation; Parke, Davis & Co., Inc.; Pepsico, Inc.; Philippine Racing Club, Inc.; Peggy Mills, Inc.; Philarca Corp.; Reading & Bates Corporation; Saatchi & Saatchi DFS/Compton Inc.; San Miguel Corp.; Shell Oil; The Dow Chemical Co., Inc.; Union Bank of the Philippines; Uniroyal Chemical Co., Inc.; Universal Textile Mills, Inc.; Warner-Lambert Philippines, Inc.; W. D. Scott & Co., Inc.; Wire Rope Corporation of the Phils.

ROCO BUÑAG KAPUNAN MIGALLOS & JARDELEZA
LAW OFFICES

16TH FLOOR, STRATA 200 BUILDING
EMERALD AVENUE, PASIG
METRO MANILA, REPUBLIC OF THE PHILIPPINES
Telephone: 631-6171 to 76; 631-6191; 631-6192; 631-6193; 631-6194
Fax: (632) 631-6194; (632) 631-9530
Telex: 63539 ANSCOR PN; 45014 ANSCOR PM

General Practice, Foreign Investments, Franchising, Patents, Trademarks and Copyrights, Civil and Commercial Law, Banking and Finance, Taxation, Securities, Estates and Trusts, Mining, Commercial Litigation and Arbitration.

MEMBERS OF FIRM

RAUL S. ROCO, born Naga City, Philippines, October 26, 1941; admitted, 1965, Philippines. *Education:* San Beda College (A.B., magna cum laude, 1960; LL.B., 1964, Abbotts Award); University of Pennsylvania (LL.M., candidate). Delegate, Philippine Constitutional Convention, 1971. Examiner in Constitutional and International Law, 1985 Bar Examinations. Panel Speaker on Investment Companies, IBA-SBL Conference, 1985. Senior Partner, Accra Law Offices, 1975-1986. Director: Intellectual Property Association of the Philippines; Philippine Chamber of Commerce and Industry; Employers Confederation of the Philippines. Governor, Manila Overseas Press Club, 1989-1991. Correspondent, Asia Law and Practice, 1989—. President, Integrated Bar of the Philippines, 1983-1985; Executive Vice President, IBP, 1981-1983; Council Participant, Global Forum on Environment and Development for Survival, Moscow, January, 1990. Representative, 2nd District of Camarines Sur, House of Representatives, 1987-1992. Member, Senate of the Philippines, 1992—. Chairman: Committee on Justice and Human Rights; Committee on Banks, Financial Institutions and Currencies. *Member:* Asean Law Association; American Society of International Law; Asian Patent Attorney's Association; Association Internationale Pour La Protection de La Propriete Industrielle. *LANGUAGES:* English, Pilipino and Spanish. *PRACTICE AREAS:* Business Law; Litigation; Constitutional and Administrative Law.

JOSE MARIO C. BUÑAG, born Manila, Philippines, March 9, 1944; admitted, 1969, Philippines; 1989, New York. *Education:* Ateneo de Manila University (A.B., cum laude; LL.B., Valedictorian, cum laude); New York University School of Law (M.C.J.). Professorial Lecturer, Taxation: Ateneo de Manila School of Law; University of the Philippines Law Center. Partner, Accra Law Offices, 1975-1986. Tax Management Association of the Philippines, Director, 1984-1985, 1987-1990; President, 1991. Member, Legal Management Council of the Philippines. Chairman, IBP Committee on Unauthorized Practice of Law, 1990. *Member:* Integrated Bar of the Philippines; Asean Law Association; International Bar Association; Philippine Bar Association. *LANGUAGES:* English and Pilipino. *PRACTICE AREAS:* Corporate Practice; Joint Ventures Law; Foreign Investments Law; Taxation Law.

LORNA PATAJO-KAPUNAN, born Manila, Philippines, April 1, 1952; admitted, 1979, Philippines. *Education:* University of the Philippines (A.B.; LL.B.). Author: Paper on Intellectual Property Protection of Com-

(This Listing Continued)

puter Work Product Under Philippine Law for Asean Law Association, 1986. Examiner, Mercantile Law, Bar Examinations, 1988. Participant, Australian Congress, Association Internationale Pour La Protection de La Propriete Industrielle, October 1986, Singapore, October 1987, Kobe, 1989. Senior Associate, Accra Law Offices, 1979-1986. Member, IBP Journal Board of Editors. *Member:* Integrated Bar of the Philippines (Assistant Secretary, 1983-1986); Intellectual Property Association of the Philippines (Director, 1988—; Treasurer, 1985-1986; 1988—); Licensing Executives Society, Philippines (Director, 1988—); Philippine Bar Association; Federacion Internacional De Abogadas, Inc.; International Bar Association; Asian Patent Attorney's Association; Association Internationale Pour La Protection de la Propriete Industrielle. *LANGUAGES:* English and Pilipino. *PRACTICE AREAS:* Trademarks Law; Patents Law; Licensing Law; Joint Ventures Law; Franchises Law; General Corporate Practice; Litigation.

BARBARA ANNE C. MIGALLOS, born Manila, Philippines, August 8, 1954; admitted, 1980, Philippines. *Education:* University of the Philippines (A.B., cum laude; LL.B., cum laude). Senior Associate, Accra Law Offices, 1980-1986. Director, Federacion Internationale De Abogadas, 1989—; Chairperson, FIDA Free Legal Aid Clinic, 1989-1991. Correspondent, Asia Law and Practice, 1989—. *Member:* Integrated Bar of the Philippines; Philippine Bar Association; Asean Law Association; International Bar Association. *LANGUAGES:* English and Pilipino. *PRACTICE AREAS:* General Corporate Practice; Litigation; Joint Ventures Law.

FRANCIS HUISING JARDELEZA, born Iloilo City, Philippines, September 26, 1949; admitted, 1975, Philippines. *Education:* University of the Philippines (A.B., Political Science, 1970; LL.B., cum laude, 1974); Harvard Law School (LL.M., 1977). Foreign Associate, Sullivan and Cromwel, 1980-1981. Partner, Accra Law Offices, 1981-1986. Professional Lecturer, University of the Philippines College of Law. *Member:* Integrated Bar of the Philippines; Rotary Club of Makati. *LANGUAGES:* English and Pilipino. *PRACTICE AREAS:* Litigation; Labor Law; General Corporate Practice.

PABLITO ALHAMBRA PEREZ, born San Pablo City, Philippines, January 15, 1957; admitted, 1984, Philippines. *Education:* Ateneo de Manila University (A.B., cum laude); San Beda College (LL.B., Valedictorian). Associate, Accra Law Offices, 1984-1986. Lecturer, Civil Law on Obligation and Contracts, Partnership and Transportation Laws, San Beda College of Law, Trustee and Secretary, San Beda Law Alumni Association Inc. *Member:* Integrated Bar of the Philippines. *LANGUAGES:* English and Pilipino. *PRACTICE AREAS:* Litigation; Labor Law; General Corporate Practice.

TROY ANG LUNA, born Manila, Philippines, May 2, 1962; admitted, 1987, Philippines. *Education:* De La Salle University (A.B. Economics); Ateneo de Manila University (LL.B.). Editor-in-Chief, Ateneo Law Journal and Ateneo Law Bulletin, 1985-1986. *Member:* IBP Journal Board of Editorial Consultants, 1990—; IBP Committee on Unauthorized Practice of Law, 1990. *Member:* Integrated Bar of the Philippines. *LANGUAGES:* English and Pilipino. *PRACTICE AREAS:* Patent, Trademark and Copyright; Labor Law; General Corporate Practice; Litigation.

SOLOMON M. HERMOSURA, born Sta. Lucia, Ilocos Sur, Philippines, April 17, 1962; admitted, 1987, Philippines. *Education:* Adamson University (A.B. Political Science, With distinction; George Lucas Adamson Leadership Awardee); San Beda College (LL.B. Valedictorian, 1986 Most Outstanding Law Graduate). Professor, Civil Law, Corporation Laws, San Beda College of Law. *Member:* Integrated Bar of the Philippines. *LANGUAGES:* English and Pilipino. *PRACTICE AREAS:* Litigation; General Corporate Practice; Patent, Trademark and Copyright.

ASSOCIATES

MARTIN TIRADOR MEÑEZ, born Manila, Philippines, November 1, 1964; admitted, 1990, Philippines. *Education:* University of Santo Tomas (A.B., Philosophy, 1985); San Beda College (LL.B., 1989). Executive Assistant III, Justice Isagani A. Cruz, Supreme Court of the Philippines. Professor, Labor Law, Legal Forms, Arellano Law Foundation. *Member:* Integrated Bar of the Philippines. *LANGUAGES:* Pilipino and English. *PRACTICE AREAS:* Litigation; Labor Law.

FEDERICO GARCIA NOEL, JR., born Tacloban City, Leyte, Philippines, February 8, 1962; admitted, 1992, Philippines. *Education:* Mindanao State University-Iligan Institute of Technology (B.S.; B.A., Marketing, 1987); Ateneo de Manila University (Juris Doctor, 1991). Legal Staff, BPI-/Family Bank Legal Department, 1989. Transcript Legal Editor, Davide Fact Finding Commission, 1990. *Member:* Integrated Bar of the Philippines. *LANGUAGES:* English and Pilipino. *PRACTICE AREAS:* Litigation; Labor Law; Taxation; General Corporate Practice.

(This Listing Continued)

ROCO BUÑAG KAPUNAN MIGALLOS & JARDELEZA LAW OFFICES, Metro Manila—Continued

ROSABEL SOCORRO TESTON-BALAN, born Manila, Philippines, June 25, 1963; admitted, 1992, Philippines. *Education:* University of the Philippines (A.B., Economics, 1983); Ateneo de Manila University (Juris Doctor, 1991). Legal Officer II, Bureau of Internal Revenue, 1991. *Member:* Integrated Bar of the Philippines; Federacion Internacional de Abogadas, Inc. *LANGUAGES:* English and Pilipino. *PRACTICE AREAS:* Taxation; Litigation; General Corporate Practice.

ROBERTO TEOTICO ONGSIAKO, born Manila, Philippines, October 15, 1964; admitted, 1991, Philippines. *Education:* University of the Philippines (A.B., Philosophy, 1986); San Beda College (LL.B., 1990). Court Attorney, Office of Associate Justice Isagani A. Cruz, Supreme Court of the Philippines; Associate, Jardeleza Law Offices. *Member:* Integrated Bar of the Philippines. *LANGUAGES:* English and Pilipino. *PRACTICE AREAS:* Labor Law; Litigation.

CRESENCIO GONZALEZ RAMOS, JR., born Manila, Philippines, June 18, 1962; admitted, 1990, Philippines. *Education:* San Beda College (A.B., Economics; LL.B.). Clerk, Court V, National Capital Judicial Region, Makati, Metro Manila. *Member:* Integrated Bar of the Philippines. *LANGUAGES:* Pilipino and English. *PRACTICE AREAS:* Labor Law; Litigation.

ROMEO ARIAS BISON, JR., born Cebu City, Philippines, July 31, 1962; admitted, 1993, Philippines. *Education:* Philippine Christian University (A.B., Political Science, 1986); University of the East (LL.B., 1991). Administrative Staff, FEBTC, 1987. *Member:* Integrated Bar of the Philippines. *LANGUAGES:* English and Pilipino. *PRACTICE AREAS:* General Corporate Practice; Labor Law; Litigation.

IMELDA MENDOZA ABADILLA, born Lallo, Cagayan, Philippines, May 8, 1967; admitted, 1993, Philippines. *Education:* University of Santo Tomas (A.B. Political Science, magna cum laude, Rectors Awardee, 1988); San Beda College (LL.B., Valedictorian, 1992). Executive Assistant IV, Court of Appeals, 1992. Professor, Legal Bibliography, Legal Writing, San Beda College of Law. *Member:* Integrated Bar of the Philippines; Federacion Internationale De Abogadas. *LANGUAGES:* English and Pilipino. *PRACTICE AREAS:* General Corporate Practice; Labor Law; Litigation.

IMELDA RIZA P. DEL ROSARIO, born Davao City, Philippines, June 19, 1967; admitted, 1994, Philippines. *Education:* University of the Philippines (A.B., English, cum laude, 1988; LL.B., 1993). Editor, Philippine Law Journal, 1992-1993. *Member:* Integrated Bar of the Philippines. *LANGUAGES:* English and Pilipino. *PRACTICE AREAS:* General Corporate Practice; Labor Law; Litigation; Taxation.

REPRESENTATIVE CLIENTS: A. Soriano Corp.; San Miguel Corp.; Coca-Cola Bottlers Philippines, Inc.; Philex Mining Corp.; American Wire and Cable Co.; Pilipinas Shell Petroleum Corp.; Playknits, Inc.; San Miguel Brewery Hong Kong; Atlas Consolidated Mining and Development Corp.; Philippine Dairy Products Corp.; Phelps Dodge Philippines, Inc.; San Miguel Fabricas de Cerveza y Malta, SA (Spain); M. Greenfield, Inc. (B); AB Capital Investment Corp.; Asian Bank Corp.; Anchor Insurance and Brokerage Corp.; Atlas Fertilizer Corp.; Hitachi (Phils.); Union Industries, Inc.; La Tondeña Distillers Inc.; National Westminister Bank; Advanced Hair Studio, Pty. Ltd.; Roxas y Cia; State Investment Trust, Inc.; Anscor Hagedorn Securities, Inc.; Dharmala Capital Investment and Trust Co., Inc.

ROMULO, MABANTA, BUENAVENTURA, SAYOC & DE LOS ANGELES

FOURTH FLOOR, KING'S COURT
2129 CHINO ROCES AVENUE
P.O. BOX 2089, MAKATI
METRO MANILA 3117, REPUBLIC OF THE PHILIPPINES
Telephone: (632) 815-30-11
Telex: 45029 ORO PM; 63312 ORO PN
Fax: (632) 815-31-72; 810-31-10 ; 811-22-06;
Cable Address: "Oro" Manila

Hong Kong Office: Romulo. 1203D Tower 1 Admiralty Centre 18 Harcourt Road Hong Kong. Telephone: (852) 28662292. Cable Address: "Derecho Hong Kong". Telex: 86305 DROIT HX. Fax: (852) 28661601.

(This Listing Continued)

AS278B

General Practice, Foreign Investments, Corporation, Banking, Securities, Insurance, Commercial Laws, Maritime and Admiralty Practice, Copyrights, Patents and Trademarks, Probate, Taxation, Mining, Litigation and Labor.

FIRM PROFILE: Romulo, Mabanta, Buenaventura, Sayoc & De Los Angeles is one of the largest and oldest firms in the Philippines. It is the sole Philippine member of LEX MUNDI, a worldwide network of about 116 independent law firms. It has an office in Hong Kong.

The firm engages in the general practice of law but its fifty lawyers - all of whom speak English fluently and the majority of whom have received training and graduate degrees from universities abroad - individually specialize in particular areas of the law.

Legal expertise is available on: Admiralty Laws; Banking and Finance Laws, including foreign exchange transactions and loan syndications; Commercial Laws; Contract Laws; Corporate Laws including mergers and acquisitions; Employee Benefit Trusts; Energy and Infrastructure, including build-operate-transfer (BOT) agreements; Estate Planning; Foreign Investments Law and joint ventures; Intellectual Property Laws; Labor Laws; Litigation - civil, criminal and administrative; Securities Law, particularly public offerings; Privatization; and Tax Laws, corporate and personal.

The firm has substantial experience in assisting both foreign and local investors establish and pursue their business presence in the country in such industry sectors as manufacturing, power plants, oil and gas, telecommunications, computers and semi-conductors, banking, franchising, food processing, pharmaceutical, agribusiness, property development, travel and tourism. The firm also has a significant tax, labor and litigation practice, and has actively participated as counsel to the various players in initial public offerings (IPO's), privatization and project finance transactions.

MEMBERS OF FIRM

ROMAN OZAETA (1921-1972).

HERMINIO OZAETA (1955-1976).

RICARDO J. ROMULO, born Manila, January 8, 1933; admitted, 1959, Republic of the Philippines. *Education:* Georgetown University (A.B., cum laude, 1955); Harvard Law School (J.D., 1958). Phi Alpha Theta (American National Honor Society in History). Recipient: Harvard Book Award, 1950; Civitan Award, 1951. President: BASF Inc., Philippines; Federal Phoenix Assurance Co. Inc. Vice Chairman, Equitable Banking Corporation. Member of the Board of Directors: IBM Philippines; SM Fund Inc.; Sime Darby Pilipinas Inc.; Honda Philippines Inc. Member of the Board of Trustees: IBM Philippines Inc. Pension Plan; The Coca-Cola Export Corporation Retirement Plan Fund; Cyanamid Agricultural Research Foundation Inc. Member: Advisory Council to Commissioner of Internal Revenue, 1965-1969; Judiciary Reorganizing Committee, 1986; RP-US Business Council, 1987- ; Constitutional Commission, 1986; Fact Finding Commission, 1990. *Member:* Integrated Bar of the Philippines; Philippine Bar Association; The Philippine Society of International Law; Philippine Judicature Society. *LANGUAGES:* Pilipino and English. *PRACTICE AREAS:* Foreign Investments; Commercial Law; Taxation; Commercial Banking.

ROMAN MABANTA, JR., born Manila, May 23, 1925; admitted, 1949, Republic of the Philippines. *Education:* University of Philippines (A.A., 1944); University of Santo Tomas (LL.B., 1949); Columbia Law School (Post Graduate studies, 1950-1951); Harvard Law School (Post Graduate studies, 1951-1952). Professor and Bar Reviewer, Commercial Law, Francisco Law School, 1955-1965. Associate Professorial Lecturer and Bar Reviewer, Commercial Law, Faculty of Civil Law, University of Santo Tomas, 1983—. Member of the Board of Directors: Goulds Pumps Inc., Philippines; The Coca-Cola Export Corporation. *Member:* Integrated Bar of the Philippines; Philippine Bar Association; International Law Association; Law Association of Asia and Western Pacific (LAWASIA); American Bar Association (ABA); Management Association of the Philippines; Philippine Association of Law Professors. *LANGUAGES:* Pilipino and English. *PRACTICE AREAS:* Commercial Law; Insurance Law; Corporate Law; Litigation; Investments.

JOSE F. BUENAVENTURA, born San Fernando, La Union, Philippines, November 22, 1934; admitted, 1959, Republic of the Philippines. *Education:* Ateneo de Manila University (A.B., 1956; LL.B., 1959); Georgetown University Law Center (LL.M., 1964). Legal Editor, Prentice-Hall, Englewood Cliffs, New Jersey, USA, 1962. Associate Attorney: Fischer & Willis, Washington, D.C., USA, 1936-1966; Monzon Law Office, 1966-1967. President: Consolidated Coconut Corporation; La Concha Land Investment Corporation. Vice President, Pomelo Realty & Development Corporation. Member of the Board of Directors: Sanitary Wares Manufactur-

(This Listing Continued)

ing Corporation, Chairman; Agrotex Commodities Inc.; Cargill Philippines Inc.; Peter Paul Corporation, Philippines; Insular Investment and Trust Corporation; Insular Life Savings & Trust Co.; United Technologies Automotive Inc., Philippines. Member of the Board of Trustees: The Insular Life Assurance Co. Ltd. *Member:* Integrated Bar of the Philippines; Philippine Bar Association. (Resident Partner, Hong Kong Office). *LANGUAGES:* Pilipino and English. *PRACTICE AREAS:* Taxation; Foreign Investments; Commercial Banking; Corporate.

JESUS S.J. SAYOC, born Manila, October 15, 1919; admitted, 1948, Republic of the Philippines. *Education:* Far Eastern University (A.A., magna cum laude, 1939; LL.B., cum laude, 1947; LL.M., 1959). Assistant Attorney: Gibbs Law Office, 1948-1953; Chuidian Law Office, 1954-1960; Ross, Selph and Carrascoso, 1960-1963. Associate: Ozaeta, Gibbs and Ozaeta, 1963-1969; Ozaeta, Ozaeta, Romulo and de Leon, 1969-1972; Ozaeta, Romulo, de Leon, Mabanta & Reyes, 1972-1976. Associate Professor, Far Eastern University, 1959-1970. *Member:* Integrated Bar of the Philippines; Philippine Bar Association; Intellectual Property Association of the Philippines (Director); Law Association of Asia and Western Pacific (LAWASIA); International Association for the Protection of Industrial Property (AIPPI); Asian Patent Attorneys Association; Maritime Law Association of the Philippines (MARLAW); International Bar Association. *LANGUAGES:* Pilipino and English. *PRACTICE AREAS:* Ship Cargo Claims (Admiralty & Maritime Law); Intellectual Property; Copyright, Patents and Trademarks.

EDUARDO DE LOS ANGELES, born Manila, Philippines, May 25, 1942; admitted, 1967, Republic of the Philippines. *Education:* Ateneo de Manila University (A.B., 1962; M.A.-Cand.; LL.B., 1966); Columbia University (LL.M., 1970). Recipient, Thomas Fitzpatrick Professorial Chair for Management. Director, San Miguel Corporation, 1986-1992. Chairman, Philippine Education Trust Plans Inc. Consultant: Presidential Blue Ribbon Commission; Revision of Rules of Court Committee of the Supreme Court. Chairman: Technical Committee of the Bureau of Higher Education of the Department of Education; Legal Aid Committee, Philippine Judicature Society. Vice Chairman, Committee on Legal Education. Professorial Lecturer, Ateneo de Manila School of Law, 1971—. Bar Reviewer, Ateneo de Manila School of Law. Dean, Ateneo de Manila School of Law, 1984-1989. *Member:* Philippine Association of Law Professors (President, 1986); Philippine Association of Law Schools; Philippine Bar Association (President, 1992); ASEAN Law Association; Integrated Bar of the Philippines; American Bar Association (ABA). *LANGUAGES:* Pilipino and English. *PRACTICE AREAS:* Litigation; Administrative Law; Energy and Natural Resources; Securities; Telecommunications.

MA. ASUNCION R. TIÑGA, born Manila, September 1, 1939; admitted, 1961, Republic of the Philippines. *Education:* University of the East (A.A., 1956; LL.B., 1960). Secretary: Allen Arthur Inc., Manila; American Chamber of Commerce of the Philippines; Cyanamid Philippines Inc.; Hijo Plantation Inc.; Universal Food Corporation. Director: BASF Inc., Philippines; Kraft General Foods Inc., Philippines. *Member:* Integrated Bar of the Philippines; Philippine Bar Association. *LANGUAGES:* Pilipino and English. *PRACTICE AREAS:* Corporate Law.

TERESITA A.M. VILLARUZ, born Cebu City, Philippines, January 3, 1943; admitted, 1968, Republic of the Philippines. *Education:* University of the Philippines (A.B., 1962; LL.B., 1966). Iota Tautau International Legal Sorority. Vice President, Twentieth Century Fox Inc., Philippines. Director: Turner Entertainment Inc., Manila; Cargill Philippines Inc.; Simian Conservation Breeding and Research Center; Beverage Industries Inc. Member: UP Women Lawyer's Circle; Federacion Internacional de Abogadas. *Member:* Integrated Bar of the Philippines; Philippine Bar Association; Philippine Society of International Law; Law Association of Asia and Western Pacific (LAWASIA). *LANGUAGES:* Pilipino and English. *PRACTICE AREAS:* Incorporation; Distribution Agreements; Joint Ventures; Loans-/International Loans; Corporate Real Estate/Contracts.

EXEQUIEL B. JAVIER, born Hamtic, Antique, Philippines, October 16, 1946; admitted, 1972, Republic of the Philippines. *Education:* Ateneo de Manila University (A.B., 1967; LL.B., 1971); New York University (LL.M., 1975). Congressman, Lone District of Antique, June 30, 1987—. Professor, Political Law, Constitutional Law, and Taxation, Ateneo de Manila University School of Law, 1978—. Lecturer, UP Law Center, 1985. Member, Philippine Chamber of Commerce and Industry, PCCI. *Member:* Philippine Bar Association; Integrated Bar of the Philippines; Tax Management Association of the Philippines (TMAP) (Member, Taxation Committee). *LANGUAGES:* Pilipino and English. *PRACTICE AREAS:* Taxation; Banks and Banking; Constitutional Law.

(This Listing Continued)

ROGELIO NICANDRO, born Manila, Philippines, October 16, 1942; admitted, 1967, Republic of the Philippines. *Education:* San Beda College (A.B., 1962); Ateneo de Manila University (LL.B., 1966). President, Genesis Printing Corporation. Director, Legal Management Council of the Philippines. Trustee, Law Foundation of Makati Inc. Legal Consultant, Asian Development Bank, 1987—. Professorial Lecturer, Ateneo de Manila School of Law. *Member:* Integrated Bar of the Philippines; Philippine Bar Association; Association International Pour La Protection de la Propriete Industrielle; Asian Patent Attorneys Association; Intellectual Property Association of the Philippines. *LANGUAGES:* Pilipino and English. *PRACTICE AREAS:* Intellectual Property; Litigation; Contracts; Construction Law; Hotels and Resort Development.

JACINTO D. JIMENEZ, born Manila, Philippines, August 16, 1944; admitted, 1969, Republic of the Philippines. *Education:* Ateneo de Manila University (A.B., cum laude, 1964; LL.B., cum laude, 1968). Recipient: Alexander Sycip Professorial Chair; Chief Justice Claudio Teehankee Professorial Chair. Editor, Current Issues and Problems in Local Education. Director, Philippine Association of Law Professors, 1986-1991. Professorial Lecturer, Ateneo de Manila University, 1970—. Bar Reviewer: Ateneo de Manila University, 1979; University of the Philippines Law Center, 1982—; Far Eastern University, 1987—; University of Sto. Tomas, 1989—. *Member:* Integrated Bar of the Philippines; Philippine Bar Association; ASEAN Law Association; Philippine Society of International Law; Aviation Lawyers Association of the Philippines. *LANGUAGES:* Pilipino, English and Spanish. *PRACTICE AREAS:* Licensing; Banking; Civil Litigation; Commercial Litigation; Constitutional Law.

ENRIQUITO J. MENDOZA, born Malolos, Bulacan, Philippines, July 15, 1947; admitted, 1974, Republic of the Philippines. *Education:* University of the Philippines (A.B., 1968; LL.B., 1973). Corporate Secretary: Reader's Digest Inc., Philippines; Amerop Philippines Inc.; Filzucar Trading Inc. Director and Corporate Secretary: Beverage Industries Inc; Allen Arthur Inc., Manila. Director and Treasurer, Tradepower Inc., Philippines. Director, Simpcor Inc. President, Belami Corporation. *Member:* Integrated Bar of the Philippines; Philippine Bar Association. *LANGUAGES:* Pilipino and English. *PRACTICE AREAS:* Labor and Employment; Employee Benefits; Alternative Dispute Resolution; Copyrights, Patents and Trademarks; Intellectual Property; Corporate Law; Social Law.

WILMA M. VALDEMORO-CUA, born Manila, Philippines, June 28, 1949; admitted, 1974, Republic of the Philippines. *Education:* University of Santo Tomas (A.B., magna cum laude, 1969); University of the Philippines (LL.B., 1973). Corporate Secretary: Philippine Document Exchange Inc.; Philippine Indochem Corporation; Polymer Products Inc; Trust International Paper Corporation. Member, Women Lawyers Circle. Member of the Board of Directors: Tuscan Solar Development Corporation; GBC Clinical Laboratory Inc. *Member:* Integrated Bar of the Philippines; Philippine Bar Association; Law Association of Asia and the Western Pacific (LAWASIA); Asia-Pacific Lawyers Association (APLA). *LANGUAGES:* Pilipino and English. *PRACTICE AREAS:* Corporate Law (Incorporation, Restructuring, Takeovers, Contracts, Real Estate); Intellectual Property; Licensing; Franchise Requirements and Licensing; Mergers and Acquisitions; Reorganizations; Joint Ventures; Foreign Investments.

CYNTHIA ROXAS-DEL CASTILLO, born Manila, Philippines, October 14, 1952; admitted, 1977, Republic of the Philippines. *Education:* University of Santo Tomas (A.B., 1972); Ateneo de Manila University (LL.B., Class Valedictorian, 1976). Corporate Secretary and Director: Sanitary Wares Manufacturing Corporation; Four Winds Inc., Philippines. Corporate Secretary: Easy Call Telecommunications Inc., Philippines; American Standard Holdings Inc.; The Wyatt Co., Philippines. Consultant, Student Affairs, Ateneo de Manila University School of Law, 1987-1990. Dean, Ateneo de Manila University School of Law, 1990—. Lecturer and Pre-Bar Reviewer, Ateneo de Manila University School of Law, 1979—. *Member:* Integrated Bar of the Philippines; Federacion Internacional de Abogadas (FIDA). *LANGUAGES:* Pilipino and English. *PRACTICE AREAS:* Corporate Law; Securities; Offerings; Family Law.

GIZELA M. GONZALEZ, born 1957; admitted, 1986, Republic of the Philippines. *Education:* Harvard University (A.B., cum laude, 1979; LL.M., 1987); University of the Philippines College of Law (LL.B., cum laude, Class Valedictorian, 1985). Member of the Board of Directors: Solidbank Corporation; Solid Cement Corporation; Alabang Commercial Corporation. *Member:* Integrated Bar of the Philippines; ASEAN Law Association; Intellectual Property Association of the Philippines. *LANGUAGES:* Pilipino and English. *PRACTICE AREAS:* Intellectual Property; Banks and Banking; Corporate Law.

(This Listing Continued)

ROMULO, MABANTA, BUENAVENTURA, SAYOC & DE LOS ANGELES, Metro Manila—Continued

CARLOS G. BANIQUED, born San Carlos City, Pangasinan, April 5, 1957; admitted, 1982, Republic of the Philippines. *Education:* San Beda College (A.B., magna cum laude, 1977); University of the Philippines (LL.B., 1981); University of Pennsylvania Law School (LL.M., 1985). Legal Consultant: Asian Development Bank; International Tax and Business Law, Kaplan, Russin, Vecchi, Eytan & Collins, San Francisco, California, 1985-1986. Headed, Philippine Team, 1980 Philip C. Jessup International Law Moot Competition, Washington, D.C. Professional Lecturer, Ateneo de Manila University School of Law, 1990—. Special Lecturer, University of the Philippines Law Center Institute on Tax Law. Member: Philippine Society of International Law; American Chamber of Commerce of the Philippines, Taxes and Tariff Committee. *Member:* Integrated Bar of the Philippines; Philippine Bar Association; Tax Management Association of the Philippines; American Bar Association. *LANGUAGES:* Pilipino and English. *PRACTICE AREAS:* Taxation; Corporate Law.

MANUEL M. COSICO, born Kalayaan, Laguna, Philippines, June 15, 1941; admitted, 1968, Republic of the Philippines. *Education:* Laguna College (Bachelor of Arts); Ateneo de Manila University (LL.B., 1967); California Maritime Institute (Course on U.S. Maritime Laws and Practice, 1982). Judge, Regional Trial Court, National Capital Region, Makati, Philippines, 1986-1991. Professor, Evidence, Trial Technique and Special Proceedings, Ateneo de Manila University. *Member:* Maritime Law Association of the Philippines (MARLAW); Integrated Bar of the Philippines. *LANGUAGES:* Pilipino and English. *PRACTICE AREAS:* Probate/Estate Cases; Criminal Law; Civil Law; Labor Law; Litigation.

BENJAMIN Z. DE LEON, JR., born Taytay, Rizal, Philippines, September 17, 1946; admitted, 1971, Republic of the Philippines. *Education:* University of the Philippines (A.B., 1967; LL.B., 1971). *Member:* Integrated Bar of the Philippines; Philippine Bar Association. *LANGUAGES:* Pilipino and English. *PRACTICE AREAS:* Litigation; Intellectual Property; Copyrights and Patents; Immigration and Naturalization; Children's Adoption, Care, Custody; Negligence/Physical Injury.

REYNALDO G. GERONIMO, born Manila, Philippines, July 10, 1944; admitted, 1969, Republic of the Philippines. *Education:* Ateneo de Manila University (A.B., cum laude, 1964; LL.B., 1968); University of Pennsylvania Law School (LL.M., 1972; S.J.D.-Cand, 1973—). *Member:* Integrated Bar of the Philippines. *LANGUAGES:* Pilipino, English and Spanish. *PRACTICE AREAS:* Banking; Estate Planning; Taxation; Corporate; Litigation.

OF COUNSEL

JOSE T. TALE, born Iligan City, Philippines, February 23, 1951; admitted, 1980, Republic of the Philippines. *Education:* Ateneo de Manila University (A.B., 1972); Ateneo de Manila University College of Law (LL.B., 1979). Undersecretary, Presidential Management Staff, Office of the President of the Philippines, 1990-1992. Professorial Lecturer, Ateneo de Manila University College of Law, 1981—. *Member:* Philippine Bar Association; Integrated Bar of the Philippines. *LANGUAGES:* English and Pilipino. *PRACTICE AREAS:* Energy; Investments; Business Law; Corporate Law; Administrative Law.

SPECIAL COUNSEL

FORTUNATO I. GUPIT, JR., born Manila, Philippines, June 7, 1936; admitted, 1958, Philippines. *Education:* University of the Philippines (LL.B. 1957, B.A., 1958); Far Eastern University (L L.M., 1961) Universidad de Madrid (D.C.L., 1964). Philippines Association of Law Schools, 1986; Association of Law Professors, 1985; Legal Writing Association of the Philippines, 1977; Philippine Society of International Law, 1975. Author: "A Guide to Philippine Legal Materials," Rex Publishing, 1993; "Rules of Evidence," Rex Publishing, 1990; "Rules of Criminal Procedure, Rex Publishing, 1986. Dean and Professor of Law, Abad Santos Law School, 1977-1989. Professorial Lecturer, U.P. College of Law and Graduate School of Law, 1975-1977. Adjunct Professor, Far Eastern University, 1960-1974. Chief Counsel, Government Service Insurance System, 1976-1986. General Counsel, Philippine Airlines, 1990-1993. Consultant, Revision of the Rules Committee, Supreme Court of the Philippines, 1986—; Member, Civil Code Revision Committee, 1972-1990; Special Counsel, 1994. *Member:* Integrated Bar of the Philippines; Philippine Bar Association. *LANGUAGES:* English, Spanish, Filipino. *PRACTICE AREAS:* Appellate Practice; Air Law; Privatization; International Arbitration; Mortgage Foreclosures.

(This Listing Continued)

ASSOCIATES

FERNANDO R. ARGUELLES, JR., born Manila, Philippines, May 13, 1936; admitted, 1960, Republic of the Philippines. *Education:* Ateneo de Manila (A.B., 1956; LL.B., 1959). *Member:* Integrated Bar of the Philippines; Philippine Bar Association; Aviation Lawyers Association of the Philippines. *LANGUAGES:* Pilipino and English. *PRACTICE AREAS:* Litigation; Customs and Tariff Law; Aviation Licensing and Resolution; Civil Appeals; Civil Litigation.

MARIA TERESITA C. SISON GO, born Manila, Philippines, September 20, 1953; admitted, 1982, Republic of the Philippines. *Education:* University of the Philippines (A.B., 1975; LL.B., 1980). *Member:* Women's Lawyers' Circle (WILOCI); Federacion Internacional de Abogadas (FIDA); Integrated Bar of the Philippines; Philippine Bar Association; Immigration Lawyers Association of the Philippines. *LANGUAGES:* Pilipino and English. *PRACTICE AREAS:* Immigration and Naturalization (a. visas; b. work permits); Corporate Law (Incorporation).

PERRY L. PE, born Pasay City, June 30, 1961; admitted, 1986, Republic of the Philippines. *Education:* De La Salle University (A.B., 1981); Ateneo de Manila University (LL.B., 1985); Columbia University (LL.M., 1991). *Member:* Columbia Society of International Law; Integrated Bar of the Philippines; Philippine Bar Association; Maritime Law Association of the Philippines (MARLAW); Tax Management Association of the Philippines. *LANGUAGES:* Pilipino, English and Chinese. *PRACTICE AREAS:* Finance; Mergers and Acquisitions; Divestitures; Energy and Natural Resources; International Law; Communications and Media.

JOSE GABRIEL GERARDO R. BENEDICTO, born Bacolod City, Philippines, February 27, 1961; admitted, 1987, Republic of the Philippines. *Education:* Ateneo de Manila University (B.S., Management Major in Legal Management, 1982; LL.B., 1986). *Member:* Integrated Bar of the Philippines; Philippine Bar Association; Intellectual Property Association of the Philippines (Charter Member). *LANGUAGES:* Pilipino and English. *PRACTICE AREAS:* Litigation (Civil, Criminal, Administrative, Family Law); Labor; Intellectual Property (Patents, Trademarks, Copyrights).

JOAQUIN V. SAYOC, born Pasay City, Philippines, November 29, 1958; admitted, 1986, Republic of the Philippines. *Education:* De La Salle University (A.B., 1979); Ateneo de Manila University (LL.B., 1985). *Member:* Integrated Bar of the Philippines; Philippine Bar Association. *LANGUAGES:* Pilipino and English. *PRACTICE AREAS:* Agricultural Law; Antitrust and Trade Regulation; Appellate Practice; Copyrights; Intellectual Property.

MA. ELENA P. HERNANDEZ-CUEVA, born Manila, Philippines, March 11, 1958; admitted, 1984, Republic of the Philippines. *Education:* Ateneo de Manila University (A.B., Philosophy, 1979; LL.B., 1983). *Member:* Federacion Internacional de Abogadas, FIDA; Integrated Bar of the Philippines. *LANGUAGES:* Pilipino and English. *PRACTICE AREAS:* Agricultural Property; Distributorship Agreements; General Practice; Corporate Contracts and Incorporation; Contracts/Breach of Contracts.

LEO DELANO C. PASCUA, born Manila, Philippines, December 3, 1955; admitted, 1986, Republic of the Philippines. *Education:* University of the Philippines (A.B., Political Science, 1978); Ateneo de Manila (LL.B., 1984). *Member:* Integrated Bar of the Philippines; Philippine Bar Association. *LANGUAGES:* Pilipino and English. *PRACTICE AREAS:* Civil Law (Civil Appeals/Litigation); Criminal Law; Immigration and Naturalization; Labor and Employment.

JOSE SALVADOR Y. MIRASOL, born August 5, 1959; admitted, 1989, Republic of the Philippines. *Education:* University of the Philippines (LL.B., cum laude, Class Valedictorian, 1988); Ateneo de Manila University (A.B., Philosophy, cum laude and Departmental Awardee, 1980; B.S., Mathematics, cum laude, 1981; M.A., Philosophy, cand.). *Member:* Integrated Bar of the Philippines; Philippine Bar Association. *LANGUAGES:* Pilipino and English. *PRACTICE AREAS:* Real Estate; Property; Banks and Banking; Construction Law; Finance; Litigation.

JACQUELINE THERESE J. ROMERO-LAUREL, born Manila, Philippines, April 22, 1963; admitted, 1989, Republic of the Philippines. *Education:* De La Salle University (B.S., Commerce, Accounting, 1983); Ateneo de Manila University (LL.B., 1988). Certified Public Accountant, 1984. Member: Federacion Internacional de Abogadas; Philippine Institute of Certified Public Accountants. *Member:* Intergrated Bar of the Philippines. *LANGUAGES:* Pilipino and English. *PRACTICE AREAS:* Corporate Law; Taxation.

ROMEO M. MENDOZA, JR., born Manila, Philippines, November 21, 1963; admitted, 1990, Republic of the Philippines. *Education:* Ateneo de

(This Listing Continued)

Manila University (B.S., Business Management, 1985); University of the Philippines (LL.B., 1989). *Member:* Integrated Bar of the Philippines. *LANGUAGES:* Pilipino and English. *PRACTICE AREAS:* Litigation (Civil & Criminal); Telecommunications; Corporate Law.

MARIO RENATO A. NAVAS, born Manila, Philippines, November 12, 1963; admitted, 1990, Republic of the Philippines. *Education:* Ateneo de Manila University (B.S., Management Engineering, 1984; LL.B., Second Honors, 1989). *Member:* Integrated Bar of the Philippines. *LANGUAGES:* Pilipino and English. *PRACTICE AREAS:* Computers and Software; Corporate Law; Government; Construction Law including Resorts and Leisure; Family Law.

KIM S. JACINTO, born Cebu City, Philippines, August 5, 1960; admitted, 1981, Board of Accountancy (CPA); 1988, Republic of the Philippines. *Education:* De La Salle University (B.S., Commerce, Accounting, 1980); Ateneo de Manila University (LL.B., 1985); Georgetown University (LL.M., International and Comparative Law, 1987). *Member:* Federacion Internacional de Abogadas; Philippine Institute of Certified Public Accountants (PICPA); Integrated Bar of the Philippines. *LANGUAGES:* Pilipino, English, Mandarin and Fukienese. *PRACTICE AREAS:* Business Law; Securities; Taxation; Energy; Banks and Banking.

HERMINIO SARAYBA OZAETA, JR., born Manila, February 15, 1964; admitted, 1991, Manila, Philippines. *Education:* Ateneo de Manila University (Bachelor of Science, Major in Business Management (Hon)); Ateneo de Manila School of Law (LL.B., 1990). *Member:* Integrated Bar of the Philippines; Philippine Bar Association. *LANGUAGES:* Pilipino and English.

TRANQUIL G. SUAVERDEZ SALVADOR, III, born Quezon City, Philippines, May 19, 1967; admitted, 1992, Republic of the Philippines. *Education:* University of Santo Tomas (A.B., Bachelor of Arts in Economics, 1987); Ateneo de Manila School of Law (LL.B., 1991). *Member:* Integrated Bar of the Philippines. *LANGUAGES:* Pilipino and English. *PRACTICE AREAS:* Labor; Energy; Litigation; Consumer Protection; General Corporate.

BI YONG SO CHUNGUNCO, born 1962; admitted, 1989, Republic of the Philippines. *Education:* Ateneo de Manila University (B.S., Legal Management, 1983); Ateneo de Manila University School of Law (LL.B., Second Honor, 1988). *Member:* Integrated Bar of the Philippines. *LANGUAGES:* Pilipino, English and Chinese. *PRACTICE AREAS:* Banks and Banking (Currency Regulations, Loans); Business Law (Business Organizations, Joint Ventures); Corporate Law; Securities; Taxation (Capital Gains Tax, Estate and Gift Taxation, Stamp Duties).

LUIS G. DE DIOS, born 1962; admitted, 1990, Republic of the Philippines. *Education:* University of the Philippines (B.A., Economics, 1985); Ateneo de Manila (LL.B., 1989). *Member:* Integrated Bar of the Philippines. *LANGUAGES:* Pilipino and English. *PRACTICE AREAS:* Securities; Corporate Law; Company Law; Energy; Banks and Banking.

RAYMOND PAOLO AGUILAR ALIKPALA, born Manila, Philippines, February 21, 1966; admitted, 1993, Republic of the Philippines. *Education:* Ateneo de Manila University (A.B., 1988; J.D., 1992). *Member:* Integrated Bar of the Philippines. *LANGUAGES:* Pilipino and English. *PRACTICE AREAS:* Litigation; Corporate Law; Taxation; Alternative Dispute Resolution.

SUSANA C. FONG, born Manila, Philippines, February 10, 1960; admitted, 1985, Philippines. *Education:* De La Salle University (A.B.Z., B.S.c., 1981); Ateneo College (LL.B., 1985). *Member:* Integrated Bar of the Philippines; Federacion Internacional De Abogadas. *LANGUAGES:* English, Filipino, Mandarin, Cantonese, Fukienese, Japanese. *PRACTICE AREAS:* Banks and Banking; Securities; Investments; Commercial Law; Corporate Law.

OWEN SOCORRO CARSI CRUZ, born Manila, Philippines, February 13, 1962; admitted, 1993, Republic of the Philippines. *Education:* Ateneo De Manila University (A.B., Economics, 1983; J.D., Second Honors, 1992). *Member:* American Society of International Law; Philippine Society of International Law; Integrated Bar of the Philippines. *LANGUAGES:* Pilipino, English and Spanish. *PRACTICE AREAS:* Securities; Environmental Law; Corporate Finance; Investments; Property; Real Estate.

ANNA LEAH FIDELIS TESORO CASTAÑEDA, born Manila, Philippines, April 7, 1968; admitted, 1994, Philippines. *Education:* Ateneo De Manila University (A.B., 1989, J.D., 1993). Author: "Manual for Filipino Notaries, 37 Atenio L.J., Vol. 2 (1993); From Pre rogative to Prohibition: Int'l 2 (4) & Cust. Int'l Law in Nicaragua v. U.S., 38 Ateneo L.J. (Vol. 1) 1 (1994). Lecturer, Ateneo de Manila University School of Law, 1993—.

(This Listing Continued)

Member: Integrated Bar of the Philippines; American Society of International Law; Zonta Club of Manila; FIDA. *LANGUAGES:* English, Filipino. *PRACTICE AREAS:* Securities; Corporate Law; International Law - GATT; International Human Rights.

MARIA CRISTINA AZANA SINJIAN, born Manila, Philippines, January 24, 1966; admitted, 1994, Philippines. *Education:* University of Santo Tomas (B.S.c., B.A., 1987); Ateneo de Manila Law School (J.D., 1993). *Member:* Integrated Bar of the Philippines; Federacion Internaionale de Abogadas. *LANGUAGES:* English, Filipino. *PRACTICE AREAS:* Corporate Law; Establishment & Business; Incorporation; Foreign Investments; Franchise Agreements & Licensing.

PRISCILLA BALANE VALER, born Legaspi City, Philippines, January 16, 1965; admitted, 1993, Philippines. *Education:* University of Santo Tomas (B.S., accounting, 1985); Ateneo de Manila University (J.D., 1992). Author: "Tax Arbitrage in the Philippine Setting," Ateneo Law Journal, Vol. XXXVII, No. 1, December 1992. Philippine Institute of Certified Public Accountants; Certified Public Accountant. *Member:* Integrated Bar of the Philippines; Tax Management Association of the Philippines. *PRACTICE AREAS:* Taxation; Corporate Law; Litigation of Civil Cases.

MARKUS CHRISTIAN STEHMEIER HERNANDEZ, born Cagayan Deoro City, Philippines, September 14, 1966; admitted, 1994, Philippines. *Education:* U.P. Diliman (B.A., 1989); U.P. College of Law (LL.B., 1993). *Member:* Integrated Bar of the Philippines. *LANGUAGES:* English, Filipino, Cantonese. *PRACTICE AREAS:* General Practice.

EDMUNDO PEREZ GUEVARA, born Lucena City, Quezon, Philippines, May 17, 1963; admitted, 1988, Philippines. *Education:* University of the Philippines (A.B., 1984; LL.B., 1988). *Member:* Integrated Bar of the Philippines. *LANGUAGES:* English and German. *PRACTICE AREAS:* Taxation.

J. VICTOR EMMANUEL DE DIOS, born Manila, Philippines, November 6, 1964; admitted, 1990, Philippines. *Education:* University of the Philippines (B.S., Bus. Adm., 1986); Ateneo School of Law (LL.B., 1990); Harvard Law School (LL.M., 1994). Author: "Of Arrests and Preliminary Investigations: A Closer Look at Go v. Court Appeals," Ateneo Law Journal, Vol. 37, No. 2, June, 1993. Professorial Lecturer, Ateneo School of Law, 1992. Professor, Lyceum Law School, 1992; Senior Instructor, University of the Philippines College of Business, 1992. *Member:* Integrated Bar of the Philippines; Philippine Bar Association. *LANGUAGES:* English and Filipino. *PRACTICE AREAS:* Securities; Power and Infrastructure; Corporate Law.

JUAN RICARDO BUAN TAN, born Philippines, October 26, 1966; admitted, 1993, Philippines. *Education:* Ateneo de Manila (B.S.L.M., 1988; J.D., 1992). *Member:* Integrated Bar of the Philippines; Philippines Bar Association. *LANGUAGES:* Filipino and English. *PRACTICE AREAS:* Banking; Securities; Power and Infrastructure.

RONALDO MODESTO JAPIT VENTURA, born Manila, Philippines, April 30, 1966; admitted, 1993, Philippines. *Education:* Ateneo De Manila (B.S., 1988; J.D., 1992). *Member:* Integrated Bar of the Philippines. *LANGUAGES:* English and Tagalog. *PRACTICE AREAS:* Litigation; Corporate; Securities; Immigration; Intellectual Property; Property.

MICHAEL GALICIA AGUINALDO, born Manila, Philippines, August 2, 1967; admitted, 1993, Philippines. *Education:* De La Salle University (A.B., Philosophy, 1987); Ateneo De Manila University (J.D., 1992). Instructor, Labor Relations, Ateneo de Manila, College of the Law, 1994—. *Member:* Integrated Bar of the Philippines. *LANGUAGES:* English and Pilipino. *PRACTICE AREAS:* Labor Law; Corporate/Special Projects; Litigation; Contract Law; Sports Law.

SIGUION REYNA, MONTECILLO & ONGSIAKO

8755 PHILCOM BUILDING, PASEO DE ROXAS
MAKATI
P.O. BOX 760
METRO MANILA 3117, REPUBLIC OF THE PHILIPPINES
Telephone: 810-02-81
810-04-09
Telex: 22055 OPE PH
Fax: (632) 819-14-98

Mailing Address: P.O. Box 7567, A.D.C. - N.A.I.A., Philippines 3120

(This Listing Continued)

SIGUION REYNA, MONTECILLO & ONGSIAKO, Metro Manila—Continued

General Practice. Corporate, Labor, Intellectual Property Laws, Insurance, Investments, Banking, Taxation.

FIRM PROFILE: Our firm is the oldest in the Philippines, having been established in 1899 as The Philippine Branch of Coudert Brothers, a Wall Street law firm whose representatives came to the country at the turn of the century with the first wave of American Educators and administrators. The firm's cable addres, which our firm uses to this day, was "TRE-DUOC," the reverse of COUDERT. In 1902, the Coudert Brothers dissolved its Philippine office and its resident partners, John W. Hausserman & Charles C. Cohn, continued the practice with a firm bearing their names until sometime in 1910, when the firm merged with the firm of Ortigas and Fisher and became Hausserman, Ortigas, Cohn & Fisher. Hausserman would later establish Benguet Consolidated and become the leading pioneer in gold production in the country, while Fisher would become a justice of the Philippine Supreme Court. In 1923, the firm merged with another law firm, Kincaid, Perkins Kincaid, and from this merger emerged the firm Fisher, Dewitt, Perkins & Brady. When Don Alfonso Ponce Enrile, one of the most noted trial lawyers of this time, became partner of the firm in 1936, the hiring of American lawyers ceased and the Fipinization of the firm began.

Today, our firm has a complement of widely experienced lawyers and a large support staff, servicing hundreds of domestic and foreign clients in different areas of business activity. If a law firm's expertise is equal to the sum of total of the varied experiences of its active partners, our firm is proud of the fact that our present partners have an average of more than 35 years each of actual practice in various fields of law, each partner complementing the expertise of the others to give our clients a complete and multi-disciplinary solution to their problems.

MEMBERS OF FIRM

LEONARDO T. SIGUION REYNA, born Dagupan City, Philippines, April 18, 1921; admitted, 1948, Republic of the Philippines. *Education:* Ateneo de Manila (H.S., 1937); University of the Philippines (A.A., 1939); University of Santo Tomas (LL.B., 1947). Professor of Labor Laws, Institute of Law, Far Eastern University, 1950-1954. Vice Consul, Ad Honorem, Thailand in the Philippines, 1960. Delegate to the Philippine Constitutional Convention, 1971-1972. *Member:* Philippine Bar Association. *LANGUAGES:* English, Spanish, Filipino. *PRACTICE AREAS:* Labor Laws; Corporation Law; Investments; Banking.

MANUEL G. MONTECILLO, born Liliw, Laguna, Philippines, March 25, 1920; admitted, 1949, Republic of the Philippines. *Education:* University of the Philippines (A.A., 1941); Far Eastern University (LL.B., 1948); Columbia University (LL.M., 1952). Associate Professor of Law, Institute of Law, Far Eastern University, 1952. Vice President, Philippine Bar Association, 1984-1985. *Member:* Philippine Bar Association. *LANGUAGES:* English and Filipino. *PRACTICE AREAS:* Corporation Law; Taxation.

OSCAR R. ONGSIAKO, born Manila, Philippines, April 3, 1922; admitted, 1948, Republic of the Philippines. *Education:* Ateneo de Manila (A.B., 1942); Arellano University (LL.B., 1947). *Member:* Philippine Bar Association. *LANGUAGES:* English and Spanish. *PRACTICE AREAS:* Corporation Law; Labor Relations Law.

JOSE PACIS FLORES, born Manila, Philippines, September 18, 1930; admitted, 1955, Republic of the Philippines. *Education:* St. William's College (1950); University of the East (LL.B., 1954). Lecturer on Banking Laws, Citibank, N.A., 1986—. *Member:* Maritime Law Association of the Philippines (Legal Management Council of the Philippines); Philippine Bar Association; Immigration Lawyers Association. *LANGUAGES:* English, Spanish, Filipino. *PRACTICE AREAS:* Corporation Law; Insurance; Banking; Immigration.

AUGUSTO S. SAN PEDRO, born Lucena City, Philippines, August 31, 1933; admitted, 1958, Republic of the Philippines. *Education:* University of the Philippines (LL.B., 1957; B.S.B.A., 1963). Member, Phi Kappa Phi International Honor Society. *Member:* Philippine Bar Association (Director); Licensing Executive Society of the Philippines (Member, Board of Directors); Asean Patent Attorneys Association; Association Internationale Pour la Protection de la Propriete Industrielle. *LANGUAGES:* English and Filipino. *PRACTICE AREAS:* Industrial Property Law; Utilities.

SAKLOLO A. LEAÑO, born Manila, Philippines, March 18, 1929; admitted, 1954, Republic of the Philippines. *Education:* Silliman University; M.L.Q. School of Law (LL.B., 1953). Lecturer on Pleadings, University of the Philippines Law Center. Participant in Mock Trial Court, University of

(This Listing Continued)

the Philippines Law Center, 1975. Former Director, Philippine Bar Association, 1988-1989. Secretary General, Citizen Legal Aid Society of the Philippines. Former Member, Integrated Bar of the Philippines For Free Legal Aid Fund Raising Campaign, 1985-1986. *Member:* Licensing Executive Society of the Philippines; Aviation Lawyers Association of the Philippines; Attended Seminar on Aviation Law by Lloyd's Press in London in 1983; Integrated Bar of the Philippines. *LANGUAGES:* English and Filipino. *PRACTICE AREAS:* Litigation; Aviation; Labor.

CARLOS G. PLATON, born Romblon, Philippines, June 5, 1940; admitted, 1964, Republic of the Philippines. *Education:* University of the Philippines (A.B., 1959; LL.B., 1963). Technical Assistant to the Chief Justice, Supreme Court, 1963-1964. Panel Speaker on Transnational Corporations, Eleventh Conference on the Law of the World, Cairo Conference, September 25-30, 1983. *Member:* Integrated Bar of the Philippines; Philippine Bar Association (Board Member, 1993-1995); Management Association of the Philippines. *LANGUAGES:* English and Filipino. *PRACTICE AREAS:* Corporation Law; Labor.

HECTOR A. MARTINEZ, born Manila, Philippines, November 12, 1940; admitted, 1964, Republic of the Philippines. *Education:* University of the Philippines (A.A., 1959; LL.B., cum laude, 1963); Harvard Law School (LL.M., 1965). With Law Offices of Winthrop, Stimson, Putnam and Roberts, New York, N.Y., 1965-1966. *Member:* Philippine Bar Association; Licensing Executive Society of the Philippines. *LANGUAGES:* English and Filipino. *PRACTICE AREAS:* Tax; Corporation; Banking; Foreign Investments.

VICTOR N. ALIMURUNG, born Manila, Philippines, April 12, 1943; admitted, 1969, Republic of the Philippines. *Education:* Ateneo de Manila University (A.B., 1964; LL.B., 1968); Harvard Law School (LL.M., 1970). With Law Offices of Donald T. Sterling, Beverly Hills, California, 1970-1971. Professor of Law, Ateneo de Manila University, 1972—. *Member:* Philippine Bar Association. *LANGUAGES:* English and Filipino. *PRACTICE AREAS:* Civil Litigation.

CESAR P. MANALAYSAY, born Manila, Philippines, June 11, 1948; admitted, 1974, Republic of the Philippines. *Education:* Ateneo de Manila University (A.B., 1969; LL.B., 1973); Boalt Hall School of Law, University of California at Berkeley (LL.M., 1976). Instructor of Law, Ateneo de Manila University, 1984-1985. *Member:* Philippine Bar Association; Integrated Bar Association of the Philippines. *LANGUAGES:* English and Filipino. *PRACTICE AREAS:* Corporation Law; Litigation.

MARIO V. ANDRES, born San Mateo, Isabela, Philippines, March 26, 1948; admitted, 1972, Republic of the Philippines. *Education:* University of the Philippines (A.B., 1967; LL.B., 1971). Journal Editor, Minutes Secretary, 1971, Constitutional Convention, 1971-1973. Legal Officer, Metro Manila Councilors' Assembly (MMCA), 1973-1974. Trial Attorney, Office of the Solicitor General, 1974-1975. *Member:* Integrated Bar of the Philippines; Philippine Bar Association; Maritime Association of the Philippines. *LANGUAGES:* English and Filipino. *PRACTICE AREAS:* Litigation; Labor.

JOSE LIS C. LEAGOGO, born Makati, Metro Manila, Philippines, July 15, 1950; admitted, 1972, Republic of the Philippines. *Education:* University of the Philippines (A.B., 1971; LL.B., 1975). *Member:* Tax Management Association of the Philippines, Inc.; Philippine Bar Association. *LANGUAGES:* English and Filipino. *PRACTICE AREAS:* Tax.

EDGARDO G. BALOIS, born Llorente, Eastern Samar, Philippines, August 10, 1949; admitted, 1976, Republic of the Philippines. *Education:* Divine Word University, Tacloban City, Philippines (A.B., magna cum laude); University of the Philippines (LL.B., 1975). Member: Phi Gamma Mu; Phi Kappa Phi, International Honor Society. *Member:* Philippine Bar Association; Integrated Bar of the Philippines (Director, Makati Chapter). *LANGUAGES:* English, Filipino. *PRACTICE AREAS:* Corporate, Tax.

LUISITO M. LANTIN, born Lipa City, Batangas, Philippines, August 25, 1948; admitted, 1975, Republic of the Philippines. *Education:* University of the Philippines; Ateneo de Manila University. Professorial Lecturer, Polytechnic University of the Philippines (PUP). *Member:* Philippine Bar Association. *LANGUAGES:* English and Filipino. *PRACTICE AREAS:* Labor Laws.

ROMARIE G. VILLONCO, born Manila, Philippines, September 22, 1951; admitted, 1978, Republic of the Philippines. *Education:* Ateneo de Manila University. *Member:* Philippine Bar Association. *LANGUAGES:* English and Filipino. *PRACTICE AREAS:* Labor Laws.

REYNALDO D. GATMAITAN, born Pasig, Metro Manila, Philippines, June 16, 1950; admitted, 1976, Republic of the Philippines. *Education:* Uni-

(This Listing Continued)

versity of Santo Tomas (1967); University of the Philippines (A.B., 1971; LL.B., 1975). *Member:* Philippine Bar Association; Immigration Lawyers Association of the Philippines. *LANGUAGES:* English and Filipino. *PRACTICE AREAS:* Litigation; Immigration Practices.

JOSE P. CRISOSTOMO, JR., born Pasay City, Philippines, November 13, 1956; admitted, 1982, Republic of the Philippines. *Education:* University of the Philippines (B.S.B.E., 1976; LL.B., 1981). *Member:* Philippine Bar Association. *LANGUAGES:* English and Filipino. *PRACTICE AREAS:* Litigation; Tax; Product Liability.

LEONARDO SIGUION REYNA, JR., born Manila, Philippines, February 14, 1955; admitted, 1983, Republic of the Philippines. *Education:* Ateneo de Manila University. *Member:* Philippine Bar Association; Integrated Bar of the Philippines. *LANGUAGES:* English and Tagalog. *PRACTICE AREAS:* Labor.

CELSO L. CRUZ, born Manila, Philippines, February 3, 1956; admitted, 1983, Republic of the Philippines. *Education:* University of the Philippines (A.B.; LL.B.). Member: Order of the Purple Feather; Pi Gamma Mu International Society. *Member:* Integrated Bar of the Philippines; Philippine Bar Association. *LANGUAGES:* English and Filipino. *PRACTICE AREAS:* Product Liability; Litigation in Civil Cases, Trademarks, Patents, Copyright, Labor.

CARLOS M. NATIVIDAD, born Zamboanga, Philippines, November 26, 1957; admitted, 1983, Republic of the Philippines. *Education:* De La Salle University; University of the Philippines (LL.B., cum laude, 1982). *Member:* Philippine Bar Association. *LANGUAGES:* English, Filipino. *PRACTICE AREAS:* Litigation and Labor.

ANTONIO CANO PIDO, born Oebu City, Philippines, January 30, 1955; admitted, 1983, Republic of the Philippines. *Education:* Colegio de San Jose (B.S.C., 1976); University of the Philippines (LL.B., 1982). Executive Labor Arbiter, National Labor Relations Commission, June 1986 to May 1991. *Member:* Integrated Bar of the Philippines. *LANGUAGES:* English and Pilipino. *PRACTICE AREAS:* Labor Law; Telecommunications Law; Civil Law; Criminal Law.

CEASAR J. POBLADOR, born Iloilo City, Philippines, September 1, 1959; admitted, 1986, Republic of the Philippines. *Education:* University of the Philippines, College of Arts and Sciences (A.B. in Political Science); University of the Philippines, College of Law (LL.B.). Member, Phi Kappa Phi, International Honor Society. Author: "Questions on the Legal Treatment of Unregistered Foreign Trademarks in the Philippines," Philippine Law Journal, Vol. LIX, Second Quarter, June, 1984. *Member:* Integrated Bar of the Philippines. *LANGUAGES:* English and Filipino. *PRACTICE AREAS:* Litigation in Labor and Patent, Civil and Criminal Cases.

ASSOCIATES

ARI-BEN C. SEBASTIAN, born Manila, Philippines, February 23, 1961; admitted, 1987, Republic of the Philippines. *Education:* University of the Philippines (A.B., 1982; LL.B., 1986). *Member:* Integrated Bar of the Philippines. *LANGUAGES:* English and Filippino. *PRACTICE AREAS:* Litigation; Banking; Labor.

ERNESTINE CARMEN JO D. VILLAREAL-FERNANDO, born Manila, Philippines, March 4, 1961; admitted, 1988, Republic of the Philippines. *Education:* University of the Philippines College of Arts and Sciences (College Scholar; A.B. Economics-Dean's Medal); Computer Center, Michigan State University (Certificate, 1978); University of the Philippines, College of Law (LL.B., 1987). Philippine Senate Committee Secretary, Committee on Agriculture and Food, 1988. *Member:* Federacion Internationale des Abogadas (FIDA); Integrated Bar of the Philippines; U.P. Women Lawyers Circle; U.P. Delta Lambda Sigma Society; U.P. Economics Society Alumni Association. *LANGUAGES:* English, Tagalog, Ilonggo. *PRACTICE AREAS:* Labor; Litigation; Corporation.

GRACE P. QUEVEDO-PANAGSAGAN, born Isabela, Philippines, March 3, 1962; admitted, 1987, Republic of the Philippines. *Education:* University of the Philippines (A.B., Economics, cum laude, 1982; LL.B., Dean's Medal, 1986). Member, Phi Kappa Phi, International Honor Society. Legal Assistant to Justice Irene R. Cortes, Supreme Court, 1987-1988. *Member:* Integrated Bar of the Philippines; U.P. Women Lawyers Circle; Federacion Internacionale des Abogadas (FIDA). *LANGUAGES:* English, Tagalog, Ilocano. *PRACTICE AREAS:* Labor; Litigation; Corporation.

ROSEMARIE R. RIBO-ESGUERRA, born Fort Bonifacio, Philippines, June 19, 1962; admitted, 1989, Republic of the Philippines. *Education:* University of the Philippines (A.B., Political Science; LL.B., 1987). Member, U.P. Delta Lambda Sigma Sorority. Member, Presidential Management Staff, Office of the President of the Philippines, 1982-1983. Techni-

cal Research Analyst, Batasang Pambansa, Office of MP Antonio C. Carag, 1984-1985. *Member:* Integrated Bar of the Philippines; Philippine Society of International Law; Federacion Internationale des Abogadas (FIDA). *LANGUAGES:* English and Filipino. *PRACTICE AREAS:* Labor; Litigation; Corporate Competition.

VLADIMIR M. PLATON, born Manila, Philippines, December 9, 1962; admitted, 1989, Republic of the Philippines. *Education:* University of the Philippines (A.B., Political Science, 1984; LL.B., 1988). Member, Upsilon Sigma Phi. Research Assistant, University of the Philippines, College of Law, 1987-1988. *Member:* Integrated Bar of the Philippines. *LANGUAGES:* English, Filipino. *PRACTICE AREAS:* Litigation; Labor; Corporate Law.

NICANOR N. PADILLA, born Hong Kong, September 16, 1964; admitted, 1989, Republic of the Philippines. *Education:* University of the Philippines (A.B., Political Science, magna cum laude, 1984; LL.B., 1988, Dean's Medal). Research Assistant, University of the Philippines, College of Law, 1987-1988. Order of the Purple Feather; Pi Gamma Mu International Honor Society. Senior Lecturer in Business Law, U.P., College of Business Administration, 1990. *Member:* Integrated Bar of the Philippines. *LANGUAGES:* English, Tagalog, Spanish. *PRACTICE AREAS:* Litigation; Real Estate; Corporate; Agrarian.

FERDINAND M. HIDALGO, born Marinduque, May 29, 1962; admitted, 1989, Republic of the Philippines. *Education:* San Beda College, College of Arts and Sciences (B.S.C., Accounting, 1983); Ateneo de Manila University (LL.B., 1988). Human Rights Program Intern, Harvard Law School, 1988. Legal Assistant, Office of Justice Florentino Feliciano, Supreme Court of the Philippines, Nov. 1988-August 1989. *Member:* Integrated Bar of the Philippines; Fraternal Order of Utopia. *LANGUAGES:* English and Filipino. *PRACTICE AREAS:* Labor; Tax; Corporate.

MARIA CRISTINA A. DE LEON, born Quezon City, Philippines, December 6, 1964; admitted, 1990, Republic of the Philippines. *Education:* University of the Philippines (A.B., English, cum laude, 1985); Ateneo de Manila University (LL.B., 1989). Member, Phi Kappa Phi International Honor Society. Researcher/Private Secretary, Office of Justice Limcaoco, Court of Appeals, 1989-1990. *Member:* Integrated Bar of the Philippines. *LANGUAGES:* English and Filipino. *PRACTICE AREAS:* Labor; Litigation.

ALVIN C. BATALLA, born Manila, Philippines, October 2, 1959; admitted, 1990, Republic of the Philippines. *Education:* University of the Philippines (A.B., Political Science, 1982; LL.B., 1988). Researcher, Office of Executive Secretary, Office of the President of the Philippines, 1986. Researcher, Office of Justice Ricardo Pronove, Court of Appeals, 1987-1988. Technical Assistant, Office of Senator Rasul, Senate of the Philippines, 1988-1990. *Member:* Integrated Bar of the Philippines. *LANGUAGES:* English and Filipino. *PRACTICE AREAS:* Labor Law; Litigation.

ALMA D. FERNANDEZ-MALLONGA, born Quezon City, Philippines, September 30, 1960; admitted, 1987, Republic of the Philippines. *Education:* University of the Philippines (A.B., Sociology, summa cum laude, 1981; LL.B., 1987, cum laude, 1986). Associate, Castillo, Laman, Tan and Pantaleon Law Offices, 1986-1987. Senior Technical Assistant/Head, Technical Staff, Office of Senator Santanina T. Rasul, Senate of the Philippines, 1987-1991. Member, Pi Gamma Mu International Honor Society. *Member:* Integrated Bar Association of the Philippines, U.P. Women Lawyers Circle, Federacion Internationale des Abogadas (FIDA); Women's Legal Bureau, Inc. (Board Member). *LANGUAGES:* English and Filipino. *PRACTICE AREAS:* Labor; Litigation; Corporation.

LORENZO B. ZIGA, born Naga City, Philippines, July 21, 1961; admitted, 1992, Republic of the Philippines. *Education:* University of the Philippines (B.A., Communications-Journalism, 1984; LL.B., 1991). Vice Chairman, Philippine Law Journal, 1989-1990. Qualified in the 1990 Foreign Service Officers Examinations. Chief Planning Officer, Bureau of Communications Services, Office of the Press Secretary, 1987-1992. On detail to the Office of the Cabinet Secretary, Office of the President, 1988-1989. Liaison Officer, Presidential Task Force on the Improvement of Administration of Justice, 1988. Senior Lecturer, University of the Philippines. Reporter, *Veritas* Newsmagazine, 1986-1987. Technical Assistant to Justice Minister and Solicitor General Estelito P. Mendoza, 1985-1986. Consultant, Office of Senator Victor S. Ziga, Senate of the Philippines, Albay. *LANGUAGES:* English, Filipino, Bicol. *PRACTICE AREAS:* Litigation; Labor.

PETER M. BANTILAN, born Manila, Philippines, December 29, 1966; admitted, 1992, Republic of the Philippines. *Education:* University of Santo Tomas (A.B. Political Science , 1987); University of the Philippines (LL.B., 1991). Former Associate, Bito, Lozada, Ortega & Castillo, 1992. *Member:*

(This Listing Continued)

(This Listing Continued)

SIGUION REYNA, MONTECILLO & ONGSIAKO, *Metro Manila—Continued*

Integrated Bar of the Philippines (Quezon City Chapter). *LANGUAGES:* English and Filipino. *PRACTICE AREAS:* Litigation; Labor.

GERMAN QUINTOS LICHAUCO, born Manila, Philippines, October 11, 1963; admitted, 1992, Republic of the Philippines. *Education:* de la Salle University, (A.B., History & Political Science, 1987); Ateneo (J.D., 1992). Aquilae Legis Fraternitas. *Member Integrated Bar of the Philippines (Makati Chapter).* *LANGUAGES:* English and Filipino. *PRACTICE AREAS:* Corporate; Litigation; Labor; Tax.

EDMUNDO O. REYES, born Pasay City, Philippines, May 23, 1962; admitted, 1993, Republic of the Philippines. *Education:* University of San Francisco, San Francisco, California (B.A., Economics, 1984); Ateneo de Manila (LL.B., 1992). *Member:* Integrated Bar of the Philippines. *LANGUAGES:* English and Filipino. *PRACTICE AREAS:* General Practice.

REPRESENTATIVE CLIENTS: Air France; Asean (Philippines), Inc.; Atlantic Gulf & Pacific Company of Manila, Inc.; Atlas Consolidated Mining & Development Corp.; BA Finance Corp.; Bank of America NT & SA; Bulletin Publishing Corp.; Caltex (Philippines), Inc.; Cathay Pacific Airways, Ltd.; Central Azucarera de Tarlac; Citibank N.A.; Compania General de Tabacos de Filipinas; Continental Illinois National Bank & Trust Company of Chicago; Data General Philippines, Inc.; Dole (Philippines), Inc.; Dow Chemical Pacific, Ltd.; Electrolux Philippines; Franklin Baker Company of the Philippines, Inc.; Goodyear Tire & Rubber Company of the Philippines, Ltd.; Hong Kong & Shanghai Banking Corp.; Irving Trust Co.; Kawasaki Steel Corp.; KLM Royal Dutch Airlines; Marubeni Corp.; Mobil Oil Philippines, Inc.; Motion Picture Export Association of America; Motorola Philippines, Inc.; National Steel Corp.; Paper Industries Corporation of the Philippines, Inc.; Philippine Bank of Communications, Inc.; Philippine Global Communications, Inc. (RCA); Phimco Industries, Inc.; (Swedish Match Co.); Philippine Refining Co., Inc.; (Unilever); Philippine Sinter Corp.; Pilipinas Shell Petroleum Corp.; Rizal Commercial Banking Corp.; San Miguel Corp.; A. Soriano Corp.

SYCIP SALAZAR HERNANDEZ & GATMAITAN

Established in 1945

SYCIP LAW-ALL ASIA CENTER
105 PASEO DE ROXAS
1200 MAKATI
METRO MANILA, REPUBLIC OF THE PHILIPPINES
Telephone: (2) 817-9811 to 20; (2) 817-2001 to 09
Cable Address: "SYCIPLAW MANILA"
Telex: 63580 SSHG PN; 45117; 45800 SYCIPLW PM; 22135 SSL PH
Fax: (2) 817-3896; (2) 818-7562 (G II & III)

Mailing Address: P.O. Box 4223 CPO, 1099 Manila

General Practice. Litigation, International Law. Corporations, Securities, Taxation, Banking, Insurance, Admiralty, Aviation, Estate Planning, Probate, Telecommunications, Technology Transfer, Patents, Trademarks, Copyrights, Trusts, Labor, Immigration and Mining Law.

FIRM PROFILE: *The firm is the largest in the Philippines and offers a full range of legal services.*

MEMBERS OF FIRM

ALEXANDER SYCIP (Founding Partner; Deceased, 1975).

ANDRES G. GATMAITAN, born Manila, Philippines, June 30, 1940; admitted, 1965, Philippines. *Education:* University of the Philippines (B.S.J., cum laude; LL.B., cum laude); Yale University (LL.M.; J.S.D.). Foreign Attorney: Winthrop, Stimson, Putnam and Roberts, Summer, 1962; Cahill, Gordon, Reindel & Ohl, New York, New York, U.S.A., 1964-1965. Director, Tax Management Association of the Philippines, 1985-1986. *Member:* The International Bar Association; Asia-Pacific Lawyers Association; Inter-Pacific Bar Association. *LANGUAGES:* Filipino and English. *PRACTICE AREAS:* Corporations; Banking; Taxation; International Law.

JUAN C. REYES, JR., born Domalandan, Lingayen, Pangasinan, Philippines, November 26, 1930; admitted, 1955, Philippines; 1987, New York, New York, U.S.A.; Registered Patent and Trademark Attorney, Philippines. *Education:* University of the Philippines (A.A.; LL.B.). *Member:* Philippine Lawyers' Association; Philippine Society of International Law. *LANGUAGES:* Filipino and English. *PRACTICE AREAS:* Immigration; Probate; General Practice.

JUSTINO H. CACANINDIN, born Aringay, La Union, Philippines, November 2, 1935; admitted, 1960, Philippines. *Education:* San Sebastian

(This Listing Continued)

College (LL.B., summa cum laude); University of Michigan (LL.M.); Georgetown University (1964-1965). Instructor in Law, San Sebastian College, 1961-1962. Past President, Personnel Management Association of the Philippines, 1976. *LANGUAGES:* Filipino and English. *PRACTICE AREAS:* Labor.

ANGELITO C. IMPERIO, born Rizal, Nueva Ecija, Philippines, October 1, 1939; admitted, 1966, Philippines. *Education:* University of Santo Tomas (Ph.B., summa cum laude); University of the Philippines (LL.B.). Technical Assistant, Office of the Chief Justice, Supreme Court, 1964-1966. Fellow in Law, Development Academy of the Philippines, 1974. Editorial Adviser for the Philippines, CAPITAL ASIA, 1989—. *Member:* Philippine Bar Association; Financial Executives Institute of the Philippines. *LANGUAGES:* Filipino and English. *PRACTICE AREAS:* Banking; Securities; Corporations; Insurance; Telecommunications; Trusts; General Practice.

EDUARDO R. CENIZA, born Manila, Philippines, October 29, 1934; admitted, 1961, Philippines. *Education:* Lyceum of the Philippines (A.A., with high honors; LL.B., summa cum laude). Professor of Law, Lyceum of the Philippines, 1970-1972. *Member:* Citizens Legal Aid Society of the Philippines. *LANGUAGES:* Filipino, English and Spanish. *PRACTICE AREAS:* Litigation.

LLEWELLYN L. LLANILLO, born Piddig, Ilocos Norte, Philippines, August 17, 1944; admitted, 1969, Philippines; 1987, New York, New York, U.S.A.; Registered Trademark and Patent Attorney, Philippines. *Education:* Ateneo de Davao University (B.A.); University of the Philippines (LL.B.). Foreign Attorney, Anderson, Mori & Rabinowitz, Tokyo, Japan, 1975-1977. Editorial Adviser for the Philippines, IP Asia; Country Correspondent, Asia Law and Practice. *Member:* Integrated Bar of the Philippines (Director, 1985-1986; President, 1989-1991, Makati Chapter); The International Bar Association; United States Trademark Association; Asian Patent Attorneys Association; Association Internationale pour la Protection de la Propriete Industrielle; Licensing Executives Society of the Philippines (Director, 1982—; President, 1985—); Intellectual Property Association of the Philippines (Director, 1982—; Vice President, 1987—); Licensing Executive Society, Australia and New Zealand; Asia-Pacific Lawyers Association Philippine National Group (President, 1991—). *LANGUAGES:* Filipino, English and Japanese. *PRACTICE AREAS:* Technology Transfer; Patents; Trademarks; Copyrights; General Practice.

CIRILO T. TOLOSA, born Isabela, Negros Occidental, Philippines, December 18, 1939; admitted, 1963, Philippines. *Education:* University of San Agustin (A.A.); Ateneo de Manila University (LL.B., cum laude); University of Michigan (LL.M.). Professor of Law, Ateneo de Manila University, 1968-1972. *Member:* Legal Management Council of the Philippines (President, 1989; Director, 1986-1989); Philippine-Michigan Club; Philippine Bar Association. *LANGUAGES:* Filipino and English. *PRACTICE AREAS:* Taxation; Banking; Securities; Corporations; Estate Planning.

ROBERTO C. SAN JUAN, born Manila, Philippines, November 25, 1945; admitted, 1971, Philippines. *Education:* University of the Philippines (B.A.; LL.B.). *LANGUAGES:* Filipino and English. *PRACTICE AREAS:* Litigation.

ANDRES B. STA. MARIA, JR., born Manila, Philippines, September 17, 1948; admitted, 1974, Philippines. *Education:* University of the Philippines (B.S.B.A.; LL.B.); New York University (LL.M.); Cornell University. Legal Assistant: Cleary, Gottlieb, Steen and Hamilton, New York, New York, U.S.A., 1977; Coudert Brothers, New York, New York, U.S.A., 1977. *LANGUAGES:* Filipino and English. *PRACTICE AREAS:* Banking; Securities; Corporations; Aviation; General Practice.

RENE Y. SORIANO, born Balasan, Iloilo, Philippines, May 22, 1945; admitted, 1972, Philippines. *Education:* University of the Philippines (A.B.; LL.B.). *LANGUAGES:* Filipino and English. *PRACTICE AREAS:* Labor.

RAFAEL A. MORALES, born Calbayog City, Philippines, March 3, 1951; admitted, 1975, Philippines; 1986, New York, U.S.A. *Education:* University of the Philippines (A.B., cum laude; LL.B., cum laude); University of Michigan (LL.M.). Foreign Attorney: Rosenman & Colin, New York, New York, U.S.A., 1978-1979; Anderson, Mori & Rabinowitz, Tokyo, Japan, 1984-1986. Country Correspondent, Asia Law and Practice; Lexpress Limited; International Financial Law Review. *Member:* Philippine Bar Association; Asia-Pacific Lawyers Association; Inter-Pacific Bar Association; American Bar Association; Financial Executives Institute of the Philippines. *LANGUAGES:* Filipino and English. *PRACTICE AREAS:* Banking; Securities; Corporations; International Law; Insurance; Telecommunications; Trusts; General Practice.

VICENTE B. AMADOR, born Candelaria, Quezon, Philippines, December 18, 1949; admitted, 1976, Philippines; Registered Trademark and

(This Listing Continued)

Patent Attorney. *Education:* University of Santo Tomas (Ph.B., magna cum laude); University of the Philippines (LL.B.). *Member:* Legal Management Council of the Philippines; Philippine Bar Association. *LANGUAGES:* Filipino and English. *PRACTICE AREAS:* Patents; Trademarks; Copyrights; Labor.

NELSON T. ANTOLIN, born Manaoag, Pangasinan, Philippines, May 4, 1947; admitted, 1972, Philippines. *Education:* University of the Philippines (A.B.; LL.B.). *Member:* Philippine Bar Association. *LANGUAGES:* Filipino and English. *PRACTICE AREAS:* Litigation.

MIA G. GENTUGAYA, born Iloilo City, Philippines, May 31, 1951; admitted, 1978, Philippines. *Education:* University of the Philippines (A.B.; LL.B.). *Member:* Maritime Law Association of the Philippines (Charter Member); Philippine Bar Association. *LANGUAGES:* Filipino and English. *PRACTICE AREAS:* Banking; Securities; Corporations; Admiralty; Aviation.

AGNES MAMON-CACANINDIN, born Manila, Philippines, October 7, 1934; admitted, 1959, Philippines; 1984, New York, U.S.A.; Registered Trademark and Patent Attorney. *Education:* University of the Philippines (A.A. with highest honors; B.S.J. magna cum laude; LL.B., cum laude); Harvard Law School (LL.M.). Research Associate, University of Michigan Law School, 1962-1966. Associate, Vom Baur, Coburn, Simmons and Turtle, Washington, D.C., U.S.A., 1962-1966. *Member:* Intellectual Property Association of the Philippines; Asian Patent Attorneys Association; Association Internacionale pour la Protection de la Propriete Industrielle; United States Trademark Association; American Intellectual Property Law Association; New York State Bar Association; Philippine Bar Association. *LANGUAGES:* Filipino and English. *PRACTICE AREAS:* Patents; Trademarks; Copyrights.

EMMANUEL C. PARAS, born Manila, Philippines, November 28, 1949; admitted, 1977, Philippines. *Education:* De La Salle University (A.B.; B.S.C.); Ateneo de Manila University (LL.B.). *LANGUAGES:* Filipino and English. *PRACTICE AREAS:* Corporations; Securities.

LOZANO A. TAN, born Narvacan, Ilocos Sur, Philippines, November 1, 1949; admitted, 1976, Philippines. *Education:* University of Sto. Tomas (B.S.C.; LL.B.). *Member:* Philippine Bar Association. *LANGUAGES:* Filipino and English. *PRACTICE AREAS:* Labor.

EMMANUEL M. LOMBOS, born Manila, Philippines, December 26, 1954; admitted, 1980, Philippines. *Education:* Ateneo de Manila University (A.B.); University of the Philippines (LL.B.). *Member:* Philippine Bar Association. *LANGUAGES:* Filipino and English. *PRACTICE AREAS:* Litigation; Corporations; General Practice.

ROLANDO V. MEDALLA, JR., born Mambusao, Capiz, Philippines, March 20, 1955; admitted, 1980, Philippines. *Education:* De La Salle University (A.B., summa cum laude); University of the Philippines (LL.B., cum laude); University of Michigan (LL.M.). Professorial Lecturer: College of Law, University of the Philippines, 1980—; School of Economics, De La Salle University, 1980-1981. Foreign Attorney, Paul, Weiss, Rifkind, Wharton & Garrison, New York, New York, U.S.A., 1982-1983. *Member:* Tax Management Association of the Philippines (Director, 1986—); Philippine Bar Association. *LANGUAGES:* Filipino and English. *PRACTICE AREAS:* Taxation; Corporations; Estate Planning; General Practice.

DOMINGO G. CASTILLO, born Manila, Philippines, May 12, 1952; admitted, 1978, Philippines. *Education:* University of the Philippines (B.S.B.A.; LL.B.); New York University (LL.M.); City of London Polytechnic (Certificate in Maritime Law, with distinction). Foreign Attorney: Heller, Ehrman, White and McAuliffe, San Francisco, California, U.S.A., 1981; Sinclair, Roche and Temperley, London, United Kingdom, 1982. *Member:* Maritime Law Association of the Philippines (Charter Member); Philippine Bar Association. *LANGUAGES:* Filipino and English. *PRACTICE AREAS:* Admiralty; Litigation.

JOSE PERPETUO M. LOTILLA, born Sibalom, Antique, Philippines, June 3, 1956; admitted, 1981, Philippines. *Education:* Ateneo de Manila University (A.B.); University of the Philippines (LL.B.,). *Member:* Philippine Bar Association. *LANGUAGES:* Filipino and English. *PRACTICE AREAS:* Banking; Securities; Corporations; General Practice.

MARILYN A. VICTORIO-AQUINO, born Polillo, Quezon, Philippines, December 29, 1955; admitted, 1981, Philippines. *Education:* University of Santo. Tomas (A.B.); University of the Philippines (LL.B., cum laude). *Member:* Women Lawyers Circle; Federacion International de Abogadas (Philippines); Philippine Bar Association. *LANGUAGES:* Filipino and English. *PRACTICE AREAS:* Corporations; Taxation; Estate Planning; Banking; General Practice.

(This Listing Continued)

DANILO V. ORTIZ, born Cebu City, Philippines, December 20, 1952; admitted, 1978, Philippines. *Education:* Ateneo de Manila University (A.B.); University of the Philippines (LL.B.). *Member:* Philippine Bar Association. *LANGUAGES:* Filipino and English. *PRACTICE AREAS:* General Practice.

LUISITO V. LIBAN, born Quezon City, Philippines, April 26, 1954; admitted, 1983, Philippines. *Education:* National College of Business and Arts (B.S.B.A.); University of the Philippines (LL.B., cum laude). *LANGUAGES:* Filipino and English. *PRACTICE AREAS:* Labor.

RAY C. ESPINOSA, born Manila, Philippines, April 27, 1956; admitted, 1983, Philippines. *Education:* University of Santo. Tomas (B.S.); Ateneo de Manila University (LL.B., Second Honors); University of Michigan (LL.M.). Foreign Attorney, Covington & Burling, Washington, D.C., U.S.A., 1987-1988. Law Lecturer, Ateneo de Manila University. *LANGUAGES:* Filipino and English. *PRACTICE AREAS:* Banking; Securities; Corporations; Mining Law; General Practice.

MARIEVIC G. RAMOS-AÑONUEVO, born Malolos, Bulacan, Philippines, August 23, 1957; admitted, 1983, Philippines. *Education:* University of the Philippines (B.S.B.E.; LL.B.). *Member:* Philippine Bar Association; Women in Law Organization; Women Lawyer's Circle. *LANGUAGES:* Filipino and English. *PRACTICE AREAS:* Banking; Securities; Corporations; General Practice.

SIMEON KEN R. FERRER, born Manila, Philippines, May 28, 1956; admitted, 1983, Philippines. *Education:* University of the Philippines (B.S.B.E.; LL.B.); University of Michigan (LL.M.). *Member:* Philippine Bar Association. *LANGUAGES:* Filipino and English. *PRACTICE AREAS:* Banking; Securities; Corporations; General Practice.

ROCKY ALEJANDRO L. REYES, born Manila, Philippines, August 1, 1959; admitted, 1984, Philippines. *Education:* University of the Philippines (A.B.; LL.B., magna cum laude); Columbia University (LL.M.). Foreign Attorney: Anderson, Mori & Rabinowitz, Tokyo, Japan, 1988-1990. Registered Trademark and Patent Attorney. *LANGUAGES:* Filipino and English. *PRACTICE AREAS:* Banking; Securities; Corporations; General Practice.

ALFREDO BENJAMIN S. CAGUIOA, born Manila, Philippines, September 30, 1959; admitted, 1986, Philippines. *Education:* Ateneo de Manila University (A.B., LL.B., Second Honors). *Member:* Makati Law Foundation. *LANGUAGES:* Filipino and English. *PRACTICE AREAS:* Litigation.

OF COUNSEL

BENILDO G. HERNANDEZ, born Bongabong, Oriental Mindoro, Philippines, May 24, 1923; admitted, 1952, Philippines. *Education:* University of the Philippines and Far Eastern University (A.A.); Manuel L. Quezon University (LL.B., cum laude). Professor of Law, Manuel L. Quezon University, 1968. Governor and Vice President, Employers' Confederation of the Philippines, 1977—. Director, Labor and Management Lawyers of the Philippines, 1968—. Employers Adviser and Alternate Delegate, International Labor Conference (Geneva), 1974—. Delegate, ASEAN Confederation of Employers, 1979—. *Member:* International Law Association (Philippine Branch). Integrated Bar of the Philippines (President, 1975-1976; Director, 1977-1978, Oriental Mindoro Chapter); Personnel Management Association of the Philippines (Director, 1968-1974; President, 1975-1976). *LANGUAGES:* Filipino and English. *PRACTICE AREAS:* Labor.

ETHELWOLDO E. FERNANDEZ, born Zamboanga City, Philippines, January 15, 1928; admitted, 1954, Philippines. *Education:* University of the Philippines (A.A.); University of the Philippines and Manuel L. Quezon University (LL.B.). Senior Special Attorney, Department of Justice, 1960-1968. Judge, City Court of Manila, 1966. *Member:* Philippine Bar Association (Director, 1987-1988); LAWASIA (Member, Executive Committee, Energy Section). *LANGUAGES:* Filipino and English. *PRACTICE AREAS:* Mining Law; Corporations.

SENIOR ASSOCIATES

TEODORO C. FERNANDO, born 1954; admitted, 1982, Philippines. *Education:* University of the Philippines (A.B.; LL.B.). *LANGUAGES:* English and Filipino. *PRACTICE AREAS:* Litigation.

JOSE F. JUSTINIANO, born 1949; admitted, 1976, Philippines. *Education:* University of Santo Tomas (B.S.C.); Ateneo de Manila University (LL.B.). *LANGUAGES:* Filipino and English. *PRACTICE AREAS:* Litigation.

(This Listing Continued)

SyCIP SALAZAR HERNANDEZ & GATMAITAN, Metro Manila—Continued

ROBERTO J. LANDAS, born 1950; admitted, 1975, Philippines. *Education:* Far Eastern University (A.B.); Lyceum of the Philippines (LL.B.). *LANGUAGES:* Filipino and English. *PRACTICE AREAS:* Labor.

DANTE T. PAMINTUAN, born 1959; admitted, 1985, Philippines. *Education:* University of the Philippines (A.B.; LL.B.). *LANGUAGES:* Filipino and English. *PRACTICE AREAS:* Labor; Litigation.

MA. LUISA R. ALDECOA, born 1952; admitted, 1985, Philippines. *Education:* Maryknoll College (A.B.); Ateneo de Manila University (LL.B.). *LANGUAGES:* Filipino and English. *PRACTICE AREAS:* Labor.

ENRIQUE T. MANUEL, born 1953; admitted, 1981, Philippines; Registered Trademark and Patent Attorney. *Education:* University of the Philippines (A.B.; LL.B.). *LANGUAGES:* Filipino and English. *PRACTICE AREAS:* Patents; Trademarks; Copyrights.

MA. MELINA C. BAGADION-SALDAJENO, born 1960; admitted, 1986, Philippines. *Education:* University of the Philippines (A.B.; LL.B.). *LANGUAGES:* Filipino and English. *PRACTICE AREAS:* Taxation; Corporations.

VAL ANTONIO B. SUAREZ, born 1959; admitted, 1986, Philippines; 1989, New York. *Education:* University of the Philippines (A.B.); Ateneo de Manila University (LL.B.); Georgetown University (LL.M.). *LANGUAGES:* Filipino and English. *PRACTICE AREAS:* Corporations; Securities.

ERNESTO S. TAINO, JR., born 1939; admitted, 1963, Philippines. *Education:* San Beda College (A.A.; LL.B.). *LANGUAGES:* Filipino and English. *PRACTICE AREAS:* Taxation; Estate Planning.

JOSE MA. G. HOFILEÑA, born 1961; admitted, 1988, Philippines. *Education:* Ateneo de Manila University (A.B.; LL.B.); Harvard University (LL.M.). *LANGUAGES:* Filipino and English. *PRACTICE AREAS:* Corporations; General Practice.

ANTONETTE L. MANIAUL, born 1962; admitted, 1988, Philippines. *Education:* College of the Holy Spirit (A.B.); Ateneo de Manila University (LL.B.). *LANGUAGES:* Filipino and English. *PRACTICE AREAS:* Litigation; General Practice.

JOCELYN I. SANCHEZ-SALAZAR, born 1962; admitted, 1988, Philippines. *Education:* University of the Philippines (B.S.B.E., magna cum laude; LL.B.). *LANGUAGES:* Filipino and English. *PRACTICE AREAS:* Litigation; Mining Law.

ARTURO A.V.P. BALBASTRO, JR., born 1964; admitted, 1989, Philippines. *Education:* University of the Philippines (B.S.B.E., magna cum laude; LL.B.). *LANGUAGES:* Filipino and English. *PRACTICE AREAS:* Labor; Litigation.

HECTOR M. DE LEON, JR., born 1964; admitted, 1989, Philippines. *Education:* University of the Philippines (A.B. cum laude; LL.B); University of Michigan (LL.M.). *LANGUAGES:* Filipino and English. *PRACTICE AREAS:* Taxation; General Practice.

ALAN C. FONTANOSA, born 1959; admitted, 1990, Philippines. *Education:* University of San Carlos (A.B. cum laude; LL.B. magna cum laude). *LANGUAGES:* Filipino and English. *PRACTICE AREAS:* General Practice.

ROSE MARIE M. KING, born 1963; admitted, 1989, Philippines. *Education:* University of the Philippines (A.B. cum laude; LL.B.). *LANGUAGES:* Filipino and English. *PRACTICE AREAS:* General Practice.

IMELDA A. MANGUIAT, born 1961; admitted, 1988, Philippines. *Education:* University of the Philippines (B.S.B.E., cum laude; LL.B.). *LANGUAGES:* Filipino and English. *PRACTICE AREAS:* General Practice.

RICARDO MA. P.G. ONGKIKO, born 1963; admitted, 1989, Philippines. *Education:* University of the Philippines (A.B. magna cum laude; LL.B. cum laude); University of Michigan (LL.M.). *LANGUAGES:* Filipino and English. *PRACTICE AREAS:* Corporations; General Practice.

MA. JASMINE S. OPORTO, born 1959; admitted, 1989, Philippines. *Education:* University of the Philippines (B Landscape Architecture, cum laude; LL.B.). *LANGUAGES:* Filipino and English. *PRACTICE AREAS:* Corporations; General Practice.

TERESA R. TAM-YAP, born 1963; admitted, 1989, Philippines. *Education:* Assumption College (B.S.C.); Ateneo de Manila University (LL.B.

(This Listing Continued)

second honors). *LANGUAGES:* Filipino and English. *PRACTICE AREAS:* Corporations.

ASSOCIATES

THADDEUS R. ALVIZO, born 1964; admitted, 1990, Philippines. *Education:* University of the Philippines (B.S.B.A., cum laude; LL.B.). *LANGUAGES:* Filipino and English. *PRACTICE AREAS:* General Practice.

MARIA DELIA R. ANGELES, born 1964; admitted, 1991, Philippines. *Education:* Barnard College of Columbia University (A.B., magna cum laude); Ateneo de Manila University (LL.B., Second Honors). *LANGUAGES:* Filipino and English. *PRACTICE AREAS:* Banking; General Practice.

ELSIE LOUISE A. PFLEIDER ARANETA, born 1964; admitted, 1991, Philippines. *Education:* Ateneo de Manila University (A.B.; LL.B.). *LANGUAGES:* Filipino and English. *PRACTICE AREAS:* General Practice.

MARIA ESPERANZA L. BAGO, born 1967; admitted, 1993, Republic of the Philippines. *Education:* de la Salle University (A.B.); University of the Philippines (LL.B.). *LANGUAGES:* Filipino and English. *PRACTICE AREAS:* General Practice.

ARISTOTLE B. BATUHAN, born 1966; admitted, 1993, Philippines. *Education:* University of San Carlos (A.B., magna cum laude); University of the Philippines (LL.B.). *LANGUAGES:* Filipino and English. *PRACTICE AREAS:* General Practice.

JOSELITO JOHN G. BLANDO, born 1968; admitted, 1993, Philippines. *Education:* University of the Philippines (A.B.; LL.B.). *LANGUAGES:* Filipino and English. *PRACTICE AREAS:* General Practice.

VINCENT Z. BOLIVAR, born 1968; admitted, 1994, Philippines. *Education:* Seminary of St. Plus X (A.B., magna cum laude); University of Sto. Tomas (LL.B., cum laude). *LANGUAGES:* Filipino and English. *PRACTICE AREAS:* General Practice.

MINERVA Y. CHUA, born 1964; admitted, 1990, Philippines. *Education:* University of the Philippines (A.B., cum laude; LL.B.). *LANGUAGES:* Filipino and English. *PRACTICE AREAS:* Banking; Corporations; General Practice.

MILDRED C. DUERO, born 1961; admitted, 1986, Philippines. *Education:* College of the Holy Spirit (B.S.C. Economics, 1981); Ateneo de Manila University (LL.B., 1985). *LANGUAGES:* Filipino and English. *PRACTICE AREAS:* General Practice.

LESLIE C. DY, born 1963; admitted, 1990, Philippines. *Education:* De La Salle University (A.B., cum laude); Ateneo de Manila University (LL.B., Second Honors). *LANGUAGES:* Filipino and English. *PRACTICE AREAS:* Litigation.

RAFAEL L. ENCARNACION, born 1959; admitted, 1990, Philippines. *Education:* Ateneo de Manila University (A.B.; LL.B.). *LANGUAGES:* Filipino and English. *PRACTICE AREAS:* Labor; General Practice.

JAIME RENATO DANIEL B. GATMAYTAN, born 1965; admitted, 1991, Philippines. *Education:* University of the Philippines (A.B., cum laude, LL.B.). *LANGUAGES:* Filipino and English. *PRACTICE AREAS:* General Practice.

JOSEPH TRILLANA T. GONZALES, born 1967; admitted, 1992, Philippines. *Education:* University of the Philippines (A.B.; LL.B.). *LANGUAGES:* Filipino and English. *PRACTICE AREAS:* General Practice.

PRIMA LIZA J. TUMBOCON-GUEVARA, born 1963; admitted, 1990, Philippines. *Education:* University of the Philippines (B.S.B.A.; LL.B.). *LANGUAGES:* Filipino and English. *PRACTICE AREAS:* General Practice.

CARINA C. LAFORTEZA, born 1966; admitted, 1993, Philippines. *Education:* University of the Philippines (B.S.B.A., cum laude; LL.B., cum laude). *LANGUAGES:* Filipino and English. *PRACTICE AREAS:* General Practice.

CARLOS ROBERTO Z. LOPEZ, born 1965; admitted, 1991, Philippines. *Education:* University of the Philippines (A.B., cum laude; LL.B.). *LANGUAGES:* Filipino and English. *PRACTICE AREAS:* Corporations; Litigation; General Practice.

JOSE ALLAN N. MAGLASANG, born 1962; admitted, 1990, Philippines. *Education:* Mindanao State University (B.S.B.A., cum laude); University of the Philippines (LL.B.). *LANGUAGES:* Filipino and English. *PRACTICE AREAS:* General Practice.

(This Listing Continued)

AMER HUSSEIN N. MAMBUAY, born 1967; admitted, 1994, Philippines. *Education:* University of the Philippines (A.B.; LL.B.). *LANGUAGES:* Filipino and English. *PRACTICE AREAS:* General Practice.

ANGELIQUE A. SANTOS MANGASER, born 1967; admitted, 1993, Philippines. *Education:* University of the Philippines (A.B., cum laude); Ateneo de Manila University (J.D., Second Honors). *LANGUAGES:* Filipino and English. *PRACTICE AREAS:* General Practice.

MA. SOCORRO L. MANGUIAT, born 1968; admitted, 1994, Philippines. *Education:* Ateneo de Manila University (A.B., cum laude; J.D.). *LANGUAGES:* Filipino and English. *PRACTICE AREAS:* General Practice.

EUNEY MARIE J. MATA, born 1964; admitted, 1993, Philippines. *Education:* University of San Carlos (B.S.B.A., summa cum laude); Ateneo de Manila University (J.D., Second Honors). *LANGUAGES:* Filipino and English. *PRACTICE AREAS:* General Practice.

ROSEMARIE P. MEDINA, born 1968; admitted, 1994, Philippines. *Education:* University of the Sto Tomas (B.S.; LL.B., cum laude). *LANGUAGES:* Filipino and English. *PRACTICE AREAS:* General Practice.

MARIA TERESA D. MERCADO, born 1964; admitted, 1990, Philippines. *Education:* University of the Philippines (A.B., cum laude; LL.B.). *LANGUAGES:* Filipino and English. *PRACTICE AREAS:* Patents; Trademarks; Copyrights; General Practice.

ROWENA V. DAROY-MORALES, born 1952; admitted, 1994, Philippines. *Education:* University of the Philippines (A.B.; LL.B.). *LANGUAGES:* Filipino and English. *PRACTICE AREAS:* General Practice.

EMMANUEL L. PEÑA, JR., born 1962; admitted, 1990, Philippines. *Education:* De La Salle University (B.S.C.); Ateneo de Manila University (LL.B., Second Honors). *LANGUAGES:* Filipino and English. *PRACTICE AREAS:* Litigation; General Practice.

ZAYBER JOHN B. PROTACIO, born 1965; admitted, 1992, Philippines. *Education:* Atenio de Manila University (B.S.L.M.; LL.B.); University of Pennsylvania (LL.M.). *LANGUAGES:* Filipino and English. *PRACTICE AREAS:* General Practice.

RAMONCITA V. REYES, born 1961; admitted, 1991, Philippines. *Education:* Bennington College (A.B.); Ateneo de manila University (LL.B). *LANGUAGES:* Filipino and English. *PRACTICE AREAS:* Corporations; General Practice.

DENNIS LORENZO G. SOLIVEN, born 1962; admitted, 1989, Philippines. *Education:* Ateneo de Manila University (B.S.L.M.; LL.B. second honors). *LANGUAGES:* Filipino and English. *PRACTICE AREAS:* Banking; Corporations.

RAMON G. SONGCO, born 1965; admitted, 1991, Philippines. *Education:* University of St. La Salle (A.B., B.S.C.); Ateneo de Manila University (LL.B.). *LANGUAGES:* Filipino and English. *PRACTICE AREAS:* Corporations.

SHEILA MARIE L. URIARTE, born 1967; admitted, 1993, Philippines. *Education:* University of the Philippines (B.S.E.A., cum laude; LL.B.). *LANGUAGES:* Filipino and English. *PRACTICE AREAS:* General Practice.

PATENT AGENTS

PURIFICACION U. GALANG, born 1937; Registered Patent Agent. *Education:* University of Santo Tomas (B.S. Chem.). Licensed Chemist. Patent Examiner, 1972-1978 and Senior Patent Examiner, 1978-1981, Philippine Patent Office. *LANGUAGES:* Filipino and English. *PRACTICE AREAS:* Patents; Trademarks; Copyrights.

MILAGROS S. DICHOSO, born 1936; Registered Patent Agent. *Education:* University of Santo Tomas (B.S. Chem.). Licensed Chemist. Patent Examiner, 1970-1974, Senior Patent Examiner, 1974-1978 and Supervising Patent Examiner, 1978-1984, Philippine Patent Office. *LANGUAGES:* Filipino and English. *PRACTICE AREAS:* Patents; Trademarks; Copyrights.

Languages: English, Japanese, Spanish and Filipino.

REPRESENTATIVE CLIENTS: International Finance Corp.; American Express Co.; The Chase Manhattan Bank N.A.; Manufacturers Hanover Trust Co.; Chemical Bank; The First National Bank of Chicago; Citibank, N.A.; Morgan Guaranty Trust Co.; Bank of Montreal; Lloyds Bank; Bank of America NT & SA.; The Fuji Bank, Ltd.; Northwest Orient Airlines; Mitsubishi Metal Corp.; C. Itoh & Co., Ltd.; F. Hoffman-La Roche & Co., Ltd.; American Home Products Corp.; Abbott Laboratories; Carnation Co.; Colgate-Palmolive Co.; Atlantic Richfield Co.; Phillips Petroleum International, Inc.; Ciba-Geigy Ltd.; American

(This Listing Continued)

Standard; Timex Corp.; McDonald's Corp.; Merrill Lynch Pierce Fenner & Smith, Inc.; Broken Hill Proprietary Ltd.; Benguet Corporation ; A. H. Robins Co.; American Cyanamid Co.; G.D. Searle Co.; The Wander Co.; The Welcome Foundation.

TAN, MANZANO & VELEZ

Established in 1976

11TH FLOOR, PACIFIC BANK MAKATI BUILDING
6776 AYALA AVENUE, MAKATI
METRO MANILA 1200, REPUBLIC OF THE PHILIPPINES
Telephone: 818-32-49; 818-67-01/02; 818-67-26; 818-51-30
Cable Address: "Tanlaw, Manila"
Telex: RCA 22565 TSL PH; ITT 45920 TSL PM
Facsimile: (632) 817-73-58

Mailing Address: P.O. Box 3256, MCPO, Makati, Metro Manila 1272, Rep. of the Philippines

Patents, Trademarks, Copyrights, Infringement, Unfair Competition Causes, Inter Partes Cases, Admiralty, General Practice, Contracts, Corporation, Taxation, Immigration, Banking, Probate, Securities, Estate Planning, Trusts, Mining, Forestry Law, Insurance, Torts, Labor and International Law.

FIRM PROFILE: *Established in 1976, the firm's fields of specialization are Patents, Trademarks, Copyrights, Infringement, Unfair Competition Causes, Inter Partes Cases, Admiralty, Contracts, Corporation, Taxation, Immigration, Banking, Probate, Securities, Estate Planning, Trusts, Mining, Forestry Law, Insurance, Torts, Labor and International Law for which it has established a client based locally and world-wide, particularly in Asia, Western Europe and the United States. This 3 partner firm has a legal support staff of 30 consisting of lawyers, paralegal personnel, CPA's and consultants.*

MEMBERS OF FIRM

EUGENE A. TAN, born Philippines, March 27, 1943; admitted, 1968, Philippines. *Education:* Ateneo de Manila University (LL.B., Valedictorian). Author: "The Philippine Law on Agency," 1979 ed.; "The Philippine Chapter on Computer Software Protection Law" in 2 - Volume Treatise on Computer Software Protection Law published in the United States by BNA Books and authored by Cary H. Sherman, Hamish R. Sandison and Marc D. Guren; "Primer on Industrial and Intellectual Property Laws of the Philippines," 1987 ed.; "National Summary for Philippine Law" in William Tetley's Marine Cargo Claims, 1,448-page hard cover volume, Third ed., 1988. Professor of Law, College of Law, Ateneo de Manila University, 1973—. The Outstanding Young Men (TOYM) of the Philippines Awardee in Law, 1983. Ten Outstanding Young Persons (TOYP) of the World Meritorious Awardee in Law, 1983. National President, Integrated Bar of the Philippines, 1990-1991, the largest and the official association of lawyers in the Philippines. Deputy Secretary-General for Asia, International Bar Association (IBA), 1990-1992. Member: Philippine Bar Association (Director, 1982-1990; President, 1987-1988); Maritime Law Association of the Philippines (President, 1986-1987; Trustee, 1982-1990; Chairman, 1987-1988); Intellectual Property Association of the Philippines; Association of Patent Attorneys and Agents of the Philippines; The Law Association for Asia and the Pacific (LAWASIA); American Bar Association; BNA International Inc. (Member, Advisory Board); International and Comparative Law Center of The Southwestern Legal Foundation, University of Texas, Dallas, U.S.A. (Member, Advisory Board, 1987-1994); Asia/Pacific Center Advisory Council, Asia/Pacific Center for the Resolution of International Business Disputes, American Arbitration Association, San Francisco, California, U.S.A.; Presidential Advisor to the President, Union Internationale Des Avocats (UIA). *LANGUAGES:* English and Pilipino. *PRACTICE AREAS:* Patents; Trademarks; Copyrights; Infringement; Unfair Competition Causes; Inter Partes Cases; Admiralty; General Practice; Contracts; Insurance; Torts; International Law.

JAIME G. MANZANO, born Philippines, December 14, 1913; admitted, 1940, Philippines. *Education:* Philippine Law School (LL.B.). *Member:* Patent Attorneys Association of the Philippines (Vice-President, 1979); Intellectual Property Association of the Philippines (Vice-President, 1981); Association of Patent Attorneys and Agents of the Philippines. *LANGUAGES:* English and Pilipino. *PRACTICE AREAS:* Patents; Trademarks; Copyrights; Infringement; Unfair Competition Causes; Inter Partes Cases.

TERESITA C. VELEZ, born Philippines, January 31, 1926; admitted, 1954, Philippines. *Education:* University of Sto. Tomas (A.B.; LL.B.).

(This Listing Continued)

TAN, MANZANO & VELEZ, Metro Manila—Continued

Member: Philippine Bar Association (Treasurer, 1992-1995; Director, 1991-1995); Intellectual Property Association of the Philippines; Association of Patent Attorneys and Agents of the Philippines. *LANGUAGES:* English, Pilipino and Spanish. *PRACTICE AREAS:* Patents; Trademarks; Copyrights; Infringement; Unfair Competition Causes; Inter Partes Cases.

ASSOCIATES

BASILIO H. ALO, born Philippines, June 28, 1942; admitted, 1968, Philippines. *Education:* University of Sto. Tomas (A.B., Philosophy, 1962); University of the East (LL.B., 1967); University College, London, United Kingdom (LL.M., 1975). *LANGUAGES:* English, Pilipino and Spanish. *PRACTICE AREAS:* Trademarks; Patents; Copyrights; Infringement; Immigration; Labor; Criminal Law; Family Relations.

NONNATUS P. CHUA, born Philippines, September 11, 1961; admitted, 1989, Philippines. *Education:* University of the Philippines (B.S.B.A. in Accounting); Ateneo de Manila University (LL.B.). *LANGUAGES:* English and Pilipino. *PRACTICE AREAS:* Contracts; Corporation; Taxation; Immigration; Banking; Securities; Estate Planning; Trusts; Mining; Forestry Law.

AUGUSTO R. BUNDANG, born Philippines, August 14, 1964; admitted, 1990, Philippines. *Education:* Ateneo de Manila University (A.B., Economics, 1985; LL.B., 1989). *LANGUAGES:* English and Pilipino. *PRACTICE AREAS:* Patents; Trademarks; Copyrights; Infringement; Unfair Competition Causes; Inter Partes Cases; Labor; Criminal Law.

JOHN G. BONGAT, born Philippines, June 24, 1964; admitted, 1990, Philippines. *Education:* Ateneo de Manila University (A.B., Political Science, 1985); University of the Philippines (LL.B., 1989). *LANGUAGES:* English and Pilipino. *PRACTICE AREAS:* General Practice; Admiralty; Labor; Infringement; Unfair Competition.

RUDOLFO D. ALBA, born Philippines, October 10, 1945; admitted, 1976, Philippines. *Education:* San Beda College (C.P.A.; B.S.B.A. in Business Administration; LL.B.). *LANGUAGES:* English and Pilipino. *PRACTICE AREAS:* Taxation; Banking.

CARMEN F. MANZANO, born Philippines, July 16, 1947; (Not admitted in Philippines). *Education:* University of the East (LL.B.); Chemical Engineer and Master of Business Administration. *LANGUAGES:* English and Pilipino. *PRACTICE AREAS:* Patents; Trademarks; Copyrights.

REPRESENTATIVE CLIENTS: Monsanto Co.; Premark International, Inc.; The Dow Chemical Co.; Smith Kline & French Labs., Ltd.; Smith Kline & French Overseas Co.; Unilever Plc.; Unilever N.V.; Philippine Refining Co., Inc.; Nestle Philippines, Inc.; Societe Des Produits Nestle S.A.; Borden, Inc.; Rohm & Haas Co.; Federal Mogul Corp.; Caterpillar Tractor Co.; Twentieth Century Fox Corp.; Lucas Film, Ltd.; Trade Mark Owners Association, Ltd. (London); American President Lines, Ltd.; Microsoft Corp.; Griffith Hack & Co.; Chesebrough-Pond's, Inc.; Bugnion S.A.; Fidia S.p.A.; Soprintel S.A.; Beecham Group PLC; Orion Pharmaceutica; Rexall Corp.; Universal City Studios, Inc.; Carlton and United Breweries Ltd.; Akzo N.V.; Philip Morris, Inc.; World Federation of the Sporting Goods Industry; MCA, Inc.; Wella Ag.; Abbott Laboratories; Dow Corning Corp.; Cadbury Beverages, Inc.; Uni-Charm Corporation; CL Pharma Ag and Synergen, Inc.

VILLARAZA & CRUZ
LAW OFFICES

5TH FLOOR, LTA BUILDING
118 PEREA STREET
LEGASPI VILLAGE, 1229 MAKATI
P.O. BOX 5140 MAKATI CENTRAL
METRO MANILA, REPUBLIC OF THE PHILIPPINES
Telephone: 818-98-36
Telecopier: (63) (2) 816-7057; (63) (2) 817-1324

Foreign Investments, Corporate, Taxation, Intellectual Property, Communications, Banking, Estate Planning, International Transactions, Admiralty and Maritime, Transportation, Litigation, Labor and Bankruptcy.

FIRM PROFILE: *The Firm was established on May 1, 1980. From the start, the range of legal services it offered was already broad. The Firm's early practice in the fields of litigation and corporate law catered largely to the requirements of commercial banks, financing institutions and commercial corporations in general. It also provided services in the fields of taxation, investments and trade, intellectual property and bankruptcy law.*

By the middle of the decade, the Firm experienced phenomenal growth. With the invitation and addition of new partners and associates into the

(This Listing Continued)

Firm, its practice expanded into the fields of labor, immigration and customs, citizenship, transportation, family law, commercial law and communications. The rapid influx of a wide variety of clientele necessitated a physical expansion of the Firm's facilities. This move has made the firm one of the first law offices to fully exploit the use of computers, along with the facsimile machine, the laser printer and the cellular phone.

Thus, after only a decade of existence, the Firm has a battery of lawyers capable of providing a full array of services to its clientele. The Firm now owns and occupies two whole floors of a Makati building to contain its entire staff. Having firmly established itself in the domestic market, the Firm now seeks to formalize sufficient international linkages for the purpose of offering its services to more foreign clients. To this end, the Firm continues to experiment on new methods with which to provide its clients with more efficient, effective and economical services.

The Firm was formerly the Carpio Villaraza & Cruz Law Offices. Mr. Antonio Tirol Carpio, the Firm's former Managing Partner, has joined the National Government as Chief Presidential Legal Adviser (with Cabinet rank). Mr. F. Arthur L. Villaraza is now the Managing Partner of the Firm.

MEMBERS OF FIRM

F. ARTHUR L. VILLARAZA, born Manila, Philippines, December 3, 1949; admitted, 1975, Philippines. *Education:* University of the Philippines (B.A., 1971; LL.B., 1975). Phi Kappa Pi; Pi Gamma Mu. Author: "Money Market and the Usury Law," Philippine Law Journal, 1974. President, University of the Philippines Law Student Council, Columnist, Philippine Collegina; President, Handgunners Association of the Philippines, 1988—. *Member:* Integrated Bar of the Philippines; American Chamber of Commerce; Chamber of Filipino Entrepreneurs; Philippine Bar Association; Licensing Executives Society of the Philippines; German Club, Inc. *LANGUAGES:* Filipino and English.

AVELINO J. CRUZ, JR., born Philippines, April 26, 1953; admitted, 1977, Philippines. *Education:* Ateneo de Manila University (B.S., Mathematics, 1973); University of the Philippines (LL.B., cum laude, 1977). Phi Kappa Phi; Pi Gamma Mu. President, Law Student Government, 1975. President, Ateneo Student Council, 1972. Senior Editor, Philippine Collegian, 1976. Member, Editorial Board, The Guidon, 1972. Vice-Chairman, Student Editorial Board, Philippine Law Journal, 1976. *Member:* Integrated Bar of the Philippines (Director); Philippine Bar Association (Director); Asean Law Association (Membership Committee). *LANGUAGES:* Filipino and English.

SIMEON V. MARCELO, born Cabanatuan City, Philippines, October 21, 1954; admitted, 1980, Philippines. *Education:* Ateneo de Manila University (A.B., with honors, 1974); University of the Philippines (LL.B., 1979). Pi Gamma Mu. Member, Order of the Purple Feather, Honor Society of the U.P. College of Law. Member, Student Editorial Board, Philippine Law Journal, 1978-1979. Recipient, Crispin Llamado Scholarship Award, University of the Philippines College of Law. Professorial Lecturer in Ethics, Nueva Ecija Doctors Colleges, 1974. *Member:* Integrated Bar of the Philippines. *LANGUAGES:* Filipino, English and Spanish.

RAOUL R. ANGANGCO, born Manila, Philippines, May 15, 1954; admitted, 1981, Philippines. *Education:* Ateneo de Manila University (A.B., Economics, cum laude, 1976); University of the Philippines (LL.B., cum laude, Valedictorian, 1980). Phi Kappa Phi; Pi Gamma Mu. Most Outstanding University Graduate, 1980. Most Outstanding Law Graduate, 1980. President, Law Student Government, 1979-1980. Member, Student Editorial Board, Philippine Law Journal, 1978-1980. Member, Working Committee, Maritime Code Project, U.P. Law Center, 1983-1984. *Member:* Integrated Bar of the Philippines (National Executive Vice President, 1993-1995); Philippine Bar Association; Philippine Constitution Association; Aviation Lawyers Association of the Philippines; Maritime Law Association of the Philippines (Trustee, 1989-1994); International Bar Association; Inter-Pacific Bar Association; Law Association for Asia and the Pacific (LAWASIA); Manila Jaycees (EPP, 1990-1994). *LANGUAGES:* Filipino and English.

INOCENCIO P. FERRER, JR., born Bacolod City, Philippines, December 5, 1956; admitted, 1982, Philippines. *Education:* Ateneo de Manila University (B.S., Business Management, 1977); University of the Philippines (LL.B., 1981). Visiting Researcher, Harvard Law School, 1986-1987. Member, Editorial Board, Journal of the Integrated Bar. Executive Editor, Intellectual Property Journal, 1988. Member, Council to Combat Counterfeiting and Piracy of Patents, Copyright and Trademarks (COMPACT). *Member:* Integrated Bar of the Philippines; Licensing Executives Society of the Philippines (Director, 1988-1990); Asian Patent Attorneys Association;

(This Listing Continued)

A.I.P.P.I. Intellectual Property Association of the Philippines (Director, 1988-1990). *LANGUAGES:* Filipino and English.

FELICIANO A. ASPI, born Mabini, Batangas, Philippines, July 21, 1949; admitted, 1976, Philippines. *Education:* University of the East (A.B., cum laude, 1970); University of the Philippines (LL.B., 1975). Member, Student Editorial Board, Philippine Law Journal, 1973. Author: *Bar Examination Questions and Answers in Taxation.* Lecturer: in Law, University of Manila, College of Law, 1976-1980; in Taxation, Manila Central University, 1976-1980; in Business Laws, U.P. Institute of Small-Scale Industries, 1976-1978. Technical Assistant, 1971 Constitutional Convention, 1971-1973. *Member:* Integrated Bar of the Philippines; American Society of International Law. *LANGUAGES:* Filipino and English.

CELIA C. LIBREA-LEAGOGO, born San Pablo City, Philippines, December 15, 1950; admitted, 1982, Philippines. *Education:* Laguna College (A.B., magna cum laude, 1971); University of the Philippines (Certificate in Governmental Management, 1975; Master of Public Administration, 1975; LL.B., 1981). Pi Gamma Mu. Member: Alpha Phi Omega Auxiliary Sorority; Order of the Purple Feather, Honor Society of the U.P. College of Law. Senior Executive Assistant II, Commission on Audit, 1977-1979. *Member:* Integrated Bar of the Philippines; Federacion Internacional de Abogadas (Director); Women Lawyers' Circle (Assistant Pro); Women in Law; Philippine Bar Association (Vice-Chairperson, Committee on Human Rights); International Bar Association; Inter-Pacific Bar Association; The Law Association for Asia and the Pacific; Women Lawyers' Association of the Philippines, Inc.; Philippine Trial Lawyers Association, Inc.; ZONTA Club (MLPE); Iota Tau Tau International Legal Sorority. *LANGUAGES:* Filipino and English.

SYLVETTE Y. TANKIANG-FERRER, born Manila, Philippines, January 26, 1957; admitted, 1981, Philippines. *Education:* De La Salle University (A.B., Economics, summa cum laude, 1977); University of the Philippines (LL.B., cum laude, 1981); Harvard University (LL.M., 1986). *Member:* Integrated Bar of the Philippines; Philippine Bar Association; U.P. Women Lawyers' Circle. *LANGUAGES:* Filipino, English and Fukienese.

ELMA CHRISTINE F. ROMERO-LEOGARDO, born Manila, Philippines, October 26, 1958; admitted, 1985, Philippines. *Education:* University of the Philippines (A.B., cum laude, 1980; LL.B., 1984). Phi Kappa Phi. Pi Gamma Mu. *Member:* Integrated Bar of the Philippines; Philippine Bar Association; Immigration Lawyers Association of the Philippines (Treasurer, 1993-1995); Maritime Lawyers Association of the Philippines; U.P. Women Lawyers' Circle. *LANGUAGES:* Filipino and English.

RAFAEL ANTONIO M. SANTOS, born San Fernando, Pampanga, Philippines, February 16, 1960; admitted, 1988, Philippines. *Education:* University of the Philippines (B.S., Industrial Engineering , 1981; LL.B., 1988). *Member:* Integrated Bar of the Philippines; Philippine Bar Association; U.P. Law Alumni Association; U.P. Alumni Association. *LANGUAGES:* Filipino and English.

BIENVENIDO I. SOMERA, JR., born Quezon City, Philippines, September 30, 1960; admitted, 1986, Philippines. *Education:* University of the Philippines (B.S., Industrial Engineering, 1981; LL.B., 1985). *Member:* Integrated Bar of the Philippines; Philippine Bar Association; Intellectual Property Association of the Philippines; Association Internationale pour la Protection de la Propierte Industrialle (AIPPI); Asian Patent Attorneys Association; Licensing Executives Society of the Philippines; Council to Combat Counterfeiting and Piracy of Patents, Copyright and Trademarks (COMPACT). *LANGUAGES:* Filipino and English.

SENIOR ASSOCIATES

LUCITO A. TAN, born Kalookan City, Philippines, October 5, 1953; admitted, 1986, Philippines. *Education:* Philippine School of Business Administration (B.S.B.A., Accounting, 1975); University of the Philippines (LL.B., 1985).

J CONRADO P. CASTRO, born Laoag City, Ilocos Norte, Philippines, February 19, 1958; admitted, 1986, Philippines. *Education:* University of the Philippines (B.A., Philosophy, 1980; LL.B., 1985).

JOSE M. JOSE, born Pasay City, Philippines, March 3, 1964; admitted, 1989, Philippines. *Education:* University of the Philippines (A.B., Economics, 1984; LL.B., 1988).

EDUARDO V. DE MESA, born Guagua, Pampanga, March 20, 1953; admitted, 1986, Philippines. *Education:* Don Bosco Seminary College; University of Santo Tomas; University of the Philippines (LL.B., 1985).

(This Listing Continued)

ALEJANDRO ALFONSO E. NAVARRO, born Tarlac, Philippines, September 10, 1962; admitted, 1990, Philippines. *Education:* University of the Philippines (A.B., 1984; LL.B., 1990).

AUGUSTO A. SAN PEDRO, JR., born Metro Manila, Philippines, January 6, 1965; admitted, 1991, Philippines. *Education:* University of the Philippines (B.A., 1986; LL.B., 1990).

JOENATHAN P. TENEFRANCIA, born Baguio City, Philippines, August 2, 1962; admitted, 1991, Philippines. *Education:* University of the Philippines (B.S.E.M., 1985; LL.B., 1990).

OTHELO C. CARAG, born Solana, Cagayan, Philippines, January 21, 1963; admitted, 1990, Philippines. *Education:* University of the Philippines (A.B., Political Science, 1984; LL.B., 1990) Philippine School of Business Administration (B.S.B.A., Accounting, 1987).

JANNETTE V. SEVILLA, born Manila, Philippines, March 9, 1962; admitted, 1988, Philippines. *Education:* University of the Philippines (A.B., Political Science, 1987; LL.B., 1988).

CYNTHIA D. NUVAL AMBROSIO, born Quezon City, Philippines, December 17, 1966; admitted, 1992, Philippines. *Education:* University of the Philippines (B.A., Mass Communication, cum laude, 1987; LL.B., 1991).

MAXIMILIAN T. UY, born Manila, Philippines, September 4, 1964; admitted, 1991, Philippines. *Education:* University of the Philippines (B.S.B.A., 1986; LL.B., 1990).

ELVIRA C. OQUENDO, born Quezon City, Philippines, May 24, 1966; admitted, 1993, Philippines. *Education:* Ateneo de Manila University (B.S., Physics and Computer Engineering, 1988; J.D., 1992).

SUSAN D. VILLANUEVA, born Bacolod City, Philippines, November 11, 1966; admitted, 1992, Philippines. *Education:* University of the Philippines (A.B., History, 1987; LL.B., 1991).

BIENVENIDO BRAULIO M. AMORA, JR., born Davao City, Philippines, March 30, 1968; admitted, 1994, Philippines. *Education:* University of the Philippines (B.S., Economics, 1988; LL.B., 1993).

PATRICIA ANGELA O. BUNYE, born Manila, Philippines, December 9, 1968; admitted, 1994, Philippines. *Education:* Ateneo de Manila University (B.S., Legal Management, 1988; J.D., 1993).

MARJORIE ANN G. SAGMIT, born Manila, Philippines, January 17, 1968; admitted, 1994, Philippines. *Education:* University of the Philippines (A.B., Psychology, cum laude, 1988; LL.B., 1993).

NOEL T. CANLAS, born San Fernando Pampanga, Philippines, March 6, 1968; admitted, 1993, Philippines. *Education:* University of the Philippines (B.S., Psychology, 1988; LL.B., 1993).

MA. VIRGINIA P.G. ONGKIKO, born Quezon City, Philippines, April 30, 1966; admitted, 1994, Philippines. *Education:* University of the Philippines (A.B., Psychology, 1989; LL.B., 1993).

ANGELICA PIA F. PENA, born Manila, Philippines, December 31, 1968; admitted, 1994, Philippines. *Education:* University of the Philippines (B.S., Economics, magna cum laude, 1989; LL.B., cum laude, 1993).

RODEL A. CRUZ, born Manila, Philippines, February 11, 1969; admitted, 1994, Philippines. *Education:* University of the Philippines (A.B., Philosophy, cum laude, 1987; LL.B., 1993).

JOSE ANTONIO J. HERNANDEZ, born Manila, Philippines, August 16, 1965; admitted, 1994, Philippines. *Education:* University of the Philippines (B.S., Business Economics, 1986; LL.B., 1993).

CLARENCE MOSES M. TROCIO, born Cebu City, Philippines, November 25, 1967; admitted, 1994, Philippines. *Education:* University of the Philippines (A.B., Political Science, 1988; LL.B., 1993).

SHEILAH P. GALVEZ, born Manila, Philippines, July 20, 1964; admitted, 1992, Philippines. *Education:* University of the Philippines (B.A., Humanities, 1986; LL.B., 1991).

REPRESENTATIVE CLIENTS: Quaker Oats Co., Chicago, USA; Hambrecht & Quist of San Francisco, U.S.A.; Home Box Office, New York, USA; The Timberland Company, New Hampshire, USA; Sunkist Growers, Inc., California, USA; TNT Express Worldwide Ltd., United Kingdom; Japan Radio Co.; Matsushita Electric Works; Matsushita Electric Industrial Co., Ltd.; Sun East International Corporation, Japan; Kawada Industries, Inc., Japan; Davidoff Comercio E. Industria Ltda., Brazil; Citibank, N.A.; Chemical Bank, Manila Offshore Branch; ING Bank (Manila Offshore Branch); Caltop Philippines, Inc.; Dole Philippeans, Inc.; Philippine Commercial International Bank; Union Bank of the Philippines; Rizal Commercial Banking Corporation; China Banking Corporation; Filinvest Development Corporation; Insular Savings Bank; SM Invest-

(This Listing Continued)

VILLARAZA & CRUZ LAW OFFICES, Metro Manila—
Continued

ments, Inc.; Liberty Broadcasting Network Inc.; Radionet, Inc.; Kramer Pharmaceutical Corp.
REFERENCES: Robert Alan Evers, Pettite and Martin, Wash., D.C.; Thomas A. Wadden, Jr., Wash., D.C.; William Taggart, San Francisco; Denis Oyakawa, Graham & James, Los Angeles; Mark T. Shklov, Honolulu, Hawaii; Gordon Chang, Baker & McKenzie, Hong Kong.

YULO, ALILING & ASSOCIATES

GROUND FLOOR, C.J. YULO & SONS BUILDING
PASONG TAMO CORNER DON BOSCO ROAD
MAKATI
METRO MANILA, REPUBLIC OF THE PHILIPPINES
Telephone: (63-2) 816-6687; (63-2) 817-9861
Fax: (63-2) 817-9956
Telex: ITT 45085 CANLUBG

General Practice, Patents, Trademarks, Copyrights, Infringement and Unfair Competition Cases, Trade and Licensing Agreements, Litigation, Corporation, Labor, Taxation, Insurance, Banking, Immigration, Aviation, Admiralty and Maritime, Civil, Criminal, Commercial, and Family and Human Relations Law, Deposition Taking, Data/Evidence Gathering.

MEMBERS OF FIRM

JOSE ENRIQUE J. YULO, born Manila, Philippines, April 4, 1958; admitted, 1984, Republic of the Philippines. Education: Ateneo de Manila University (A.B., 1979; LL.B., 1983).

JOSE P.O. ALILING, IV, born Taal, Batangas, Philippines, May 7, 1950; admitted, 1976, Republic of the Philippines. Education: University of the Philippines (A.B., 1971; LL.B., 1975).

SINGAPORE

ALBAN TAY MAHTANI & DE SILVA

Advocates and Solicitors

Commissioner for Oaths

Trademark and Patents Agents

21 COLLYER QUAY #11-02
HONGKONG BANK BUILDING
SINGAPORE 0104
Telephone: (65)534-5266
Facsimile: (65)223-8762

Kuala Lumpur, Malaysia Associated Firm: Tay & Partners, Suite 6.01 6th Floor, Plaza See Hoy Chan, Jalan Raja Chulan, 50200 Kuala Lumpur, Malaysia. Telephone: (60-3)201-8628. Facsimile: (60-3)201-8618.

Johor Bahru, Malaysia Associated Firm: Tay & Partners, Site 3A-05/06, 3A Floor, Holiday Plaza, Jalan Dato Sulaiman, 80250. Telephone: (60-7)331-6136. Facsimile: (60-7)332-2898.

Investment Laws, Mergers and Acquisitions, Corporate, Securities, Tax, International Trade, Employment, Banking, Real Estate, Intellectual Property, Construction, Leisure and Entertainment, Litigation and Arbitration.

FIRM PROFILE: The Firm was established by four senior partners from an established law firm. The founding partners were heads of their respective departments in their previous firms and, together with their respective practices and experience, have set up the Firm.

The Firm is engaged in all areas of corporate and commercial law, banking and finance, employment, immigration and environment law, intellectual property law, construction law, property law and conveyancing and all aspects of litigation.

The Firm has a regional practice and works closely with other professional firms. The Firm is associated with Tay & Partners in Malaysia, which is headed by a partner of the Firm and staffed by Malaysian Lawyers.

All lawyers in the firm speak and write English, and many lawyers communicate effectively in Chinese and Malay.

(This Listing Continued)

PARTNERS

SUSAN DE SILVA, LL.B. (Hons.) (Singapore). **PRACTICE AREAS:** Corporate and Commercial Transactions; Tax.

ALBAN KANG, LL.B. (Hons.) (Singapore), LL.M. (Tr. Reg.) (NYU); also admitted in New York. **PRACTICE AREAS:** Intellectual Property; Corporate and Commercial Transactions; Entertainment Law.

NARESH MAHTANI, LL.B. (Hons.) (Singapore). Commissioner for Oaths, Singapore. **PRACTICE AREAS:** Construction Law; General Litigation; Arbitration.

TAY BENG CHAI, LL.B. (Hons.) (Singapore); also admitted to the Malaysian Bar. **PRACTICE AREAS:** Corporate and Commercial Transactions; Malaysian Practice.

LAU LEE JAN, LL.B. (Hons.) (Singapore); also admitted to the Malaysian Bar. **PRACTICE AREAS:** Corporate and Commercial Transactions; Conveyancing; Real Estate.

SHERYLENE WANG, LL.B. (Hons.) (Singapore). **PRACTICE AREAS:** Corporate and Commercial Transactions.

ASSOCIATES

SHEENA R. JACOB, LL.B. (Hons.) (Singapore), LL.M. (Tr.Reg.) (NYU); also admitted in New York. **PRACTICE AREAS:** Intellectual Property.

SUSANNA KHO, LL.B. (Hons.) (Singapore). **PRACTICE AREAS:** Conveyancing; Real Estate.

ANTHONY SOH, LL.B. (Hons.) (Singapore). **PRACTICE AREAS:** Construction Law; General Litigation.

AZMAN HISHAM JAAFAR, LL.B. (Hons.) (Singapore). **PRACTICE AREAS:** Corporate and Commercial Transactions.

EDMUND CHIN, LL.B. (London); LL.M. (London); M.B.A. (Imperial); Barrister-at-law, England. **PRACTICE AREAS:** Banking; Finance; Corporate and Commercial Transactions.

L. KUPPANCHETTI, LL.B. (Hons.) (Hull), Barrister-at-Law, Middle Temple, England. **PRACTICE AREAS:** Construction Law; General Litigation.

EDWARD LAM, LL.B. (Hons) (East Anglia), Barrister-at-law, Middle Temple, England. **PRACTICE AREAS:** General Litigation.

ALLEN & GLEDHILL

Advocates and Solicitors, Notaries Public and Commissioners for Oaths

36 ROBINSON ROAD, #18-01 CITY HOUSE
SINGAPORE 0106
Telephone: (65) 2251611 (General Line)
(65) 3204319 (Trademarks & Patents)
Telex: GLEDHIL RS 21600.
Telecopier: (65) 2248210.

General and International Practice, including Admiralty and Shipping, Asean Trade, Capital Markets, China Law Practice, Company and Corporate (including Venture Capital and Joint Ventures), Banking and Finance (including Project Financing), Commercial, Commodities and Futures Trading, Computer, Construction, Corporate Secretarial, Criminal, Environmental, Family and Matrimonial, Immigration, Insolvency, Insurance and Reinsurance, Intellectual Property (including Trademarks, Copyright, Patents and Designs), Labour, Litigation and Arbitration, Mergers and Acquisitions, Privatization, Probate and Administration, Real Estate and Conveyancing, Revenue, Securities and Trusts.

FIRM PROFILE: Established in 1902, Allen & Gledhill is one of the largest law firms in Singapore with 36 partners and a total of over 130 lawyers. It is a full service firm practising in a wide range of legal fields and maintains contacts with numerous firms of international repute in jurisdictions all over the world.

PARTNERS

MICHAEL HWANG, B.C.L.; M.A. (Oxon), Gray's Inn, Barrister-at-Law. **PRACTICE AREAS:** Litigation; Corporate Insolvency; Commercial Arbitration; Professional Negligence; Family Law.

C.J. CHEN, LL.B. (Hons.) (S'pore), Commissioner of Oaths & Notary Public. **PRACTICE AREAS:** Corporate Law; Commercial Law; Taxation; Commodities; Commodities Futures Trading.

(This Listing Continued)

MISS V. RAJAMANICKAM, LL.B. (Hons.) (S'pore). *PRACTICE AREAS:* Company Law; Business Law; Labour and Employment; Agency and Distributorships; Trusts and Estates.

K.S. LO, Middle Temple, Barrister-at-Law. *PRACTICE AREAS:* Appellate Practice; Civil Law; Commercial Law; Chancery and Equity; Trusts and Estates.

CHOR KOK PHUA, LL.B. (Hons.) (S'pore). *PRACTICE AREAS:* Property; Property Finance; Banking; Commercial Law; Probate.

HIANG CHYE GAN, LL.B. (Hons.) (S'pore); LL.M. (S'pore). *PRACTICE AREAS:* Real Estate; Landlord and Tenant Law; Banking; Construction Law; Receivership.

MRS. CHRISTINA ONG, LL.B. (Hons.) (S'pore). *PRACTICE AREAS:* Banks and Banking; Corporate Law; Finance; Investments; Securities.

MRS. PENNY GOH, LL.B. (Hons.) (S'pore). *PRACTICE AREAS:* Real Estate; Property Development; Property Joint Ventures; Property Finance; Banking.

LUCIEN WONG, LL.B. (Hons.) (S'pore). *PRACTICE AREAS:* Banks and Banking; Corporate Law; Finance; Investments; Securities.

MISS CHRISTINE CHAN, LL.B. (Hons.) (S'pore). *PRACTICE AREAS:* Corporate Law; Commercial Law; Contracts; Company Administration; Immigration and Naturalization.

TEE JIM TAN, LL.B. (Hons.) (S'pore), Commissioner of Oaths. *PRACTICE AREAS:* Intellectual Property; Biotechnology; Computers and Software; Franchises and Franchising; Construction Law.

CHRISTOPHER LAU, Gray's Inn, Barrister-at-Law, Commissioner for Oaths. *PRACTICE AREAS:* Admiralty and Maritime Law; Construction Law; Company Commercial Law; Insurance; Arbitration.

A. CHANDRAN, LL.B. (Hons.) (S'pore). *PRACTICE AREAS:* Property; Real Estate; Banking; Property Conveyancing; Property Finance.

MISS S. CHITRAN, LL.B. (Hons.) (S'pore). *PRACTICE AREAS:* Corporate Law; Commercial Law; Joint Ventures; Company Acquisitions and Sales; Company Secretarial Law.

MISS VIVIAN ANG, LL.B. (Hons.) (S'pore). *PRACTICE AREAS:* Admiralty and Maritime Law; Marine Insurance; Sale of Goods; Arbitration; Air Law.

EUGENE OOI, LL.B. (Hons.) (Lond.), Middle Temple, Barrister-at-Law. *PRACTICE AREAS:* Banks and Banking; Finance; Syndications; International Loans; Shipping Finance.

MISS MARGARET SOH, LL.B. (Hons.) (S'pore). *PRACTICE AREAS:* Banking; Real Estate; Commercial Law; Property Finance; Property Conveyancing.

RONNIE QUEK, LL.B. (Hons.) (S'pore). *PRACTICE AREAS:* Insolvency; Banking; Corporate Law; Commercial Litigation; Receiverships.

K. SHANMUGAM, LL.B. (Hons.) (S'pore). *PRACTICE AREAS:* Commercial Litigation; Banking; Insolvency; White Collar Crime; Libel and Defamation.

MISS JO-ANN SEE, LL.B. (Hons.) (S'pore). *PRACTICE AREAS:* Intellectual Property; Copyright; Trademarks; Patents; Licensing.

MISS WAI HONG CHOO, LL.B. (Hons.) (Lond.) Middle Temple, Barrister-at-Law. *PRACTICE AREAS:* Unit Trusts; Financial Services Regulation; Mergers and Acquisitions and Divestitures; Venture Capital; Corporate Law.

MISS WAI LIN YING, LL.B. (Hons.) (S'pore). *PRACTICE AREAS:* Property; Land Registration; Residential Property; Commercial Property; Property Finance.

MISS KATHY YONG, LL.B. (Hons.) (S'pore). *PRACTICE AREAS:* Property Development; Property Finance; Secured Transactions; Commercial Property; Banking.

DAVID YEOW, LL.B. (Hons.) (S'pore). *PRACTICE AREAS:* Corporate Law; Commodities Futures; Futures; Securities; Entertainment and the Arts.

MISS PATRICIA SEET, LL.B. (Hons.) (S'pore); LL.M. (S'pore). *PRACTICE AREAS:* Company Law; Taxation; Company Secretarial Law; Immigration and Naturalization; Labour and Employment.

(This Listing Continued)

KIM SHIN LEE, LL.B. (Hons.) (S'pore). *PRACTICE AREAS:* Corporate Law; Commercial Law; Environmental Law; Agency and Distributorships; Joint Ventures.

MISS ANJALI IYER, LL.B. (Hons.) (S'pore). *PRACTICE AREAS:* Ship Finance; Aircraft Finance and Leasing; Ship Building; Admiralty and Maritime Law; Corporate Finance.

ANDREW M. LIM, LL.B. (Hons.) (S'pore). *PRACTICE AREAS:* Corporate Law; Securities; Capital Markets; Finance; Mergers, Acquisitions and Divestitures.

MISS V. NALINA, LL.B. (Hons.) (S'pore). *PRACTICE AREAS:* Real Estate; Property; Property Finance; Property Conveyancing; Landlord and Tenant Law.

ANDRE YEAP, LL.B. (Hons.) (S'pore). *PRACTICE AREAS:* Commercial Litigation; Banking Litigation; Construction Law; Insolvency; Reinsurance.

MISS MELISSA ANNE TEO, B.A. (Hons.) LL.M. (Cantab). *PRACTICE AREAS:* Corporate Law; Commercial Law; Immigration and Naturalization; Probate; Communications and Media.

MISS TZE GAY TAN, LL.B. (Hons.) (S'pore). *PRACTICE AREAS:* Banks and Banking; Corporate Law; Finance; Investments; Securities.

Languages: English, Chinese, Malay and French.

ALLEN & OVERY

20 RAFFLES PLACE #08-03
OCEAN TOWERS
SINGAPORE 0104
Telephone: (65) 533 0988
Facsimile: (65) 533 1322

London, England Office: One New Change, EC4M 9QQ. Telephone: 0171 330 3000. Facsimile: 0171 330 9999.

Beijing, China Office: Suite 3204, Jing Guang Centre, Hu Jia Lou, Chaoyang District, 100020. Telephone: (86 1) 501 4681. Facsimile: (86 1) 501 4682.

Brussels, Belgium Office: Rue de la Loi 99, Box 8, 1040. Telephone: (32 2) 230 27 91. Facsimile: (32 2) 230 66 13.

Budapest, Hungary Office: Mádach Trade Center, Mádach Imre utca 13-14, H-1075. Telephone: (361) 268 1511. Facsimile: (361) 268 1515.

Dubai, United Arab Emirates Office: 501 Al Futtaim Tower, P.O. Box 3251, Deira. Telephone: (971 4) 282296. Facsimile: (971 4) 212860.

Frankfurt, Germany Office: Taunusanlage 11, 11th Floor, 60329. Telephone: (49 69) 242 6120. Facsimile: (49 69) 242 61220.

Hong Kong Office: 9th Floor, Three Exchange Square, 8 Connaught Place. Telephone: (852) 2840 1282. Telex: 68757. Facsimile: (852) 2840 0515.

Madrid, Spain Office: Antonio Maura 7, 6°, 28014. Telephone: (34 1) 521 2654. Facsimile: (34 1) 523 0458.

Moscow, Russia Office: 9 ul Tverskaya, Entrance No 5, 8th Floor, 103009. Telephone: (7 501) 940 4500. Facsimile: (7 501) 940 4501.

New York Office: Swiss Bank Tower, 10 East 50th Street, 10022. Telephone (1-212) 754 3340. Facsimile: (1-212) 754 7903.

Paris, France Office: 1 Avenue Franklin D. Roosevelt, 75008. Telephone (33-1) 49 53 06 37. Telex: 651079. Facsimile: (33-1) 49 53 91 52.

Prague, Czech Republic Office: Jindřišská 34, 110 00 Prague 1. Telephone: (42 2) 2410 3317. Facsimile: (42 2) 2410 3235.

Tokyo, Japan Office: NSE Building, 5th Floor, 1-7-1 Kanda Jinbo-cho, Chiyoda-ku Tokyo 101. Telephone (81 3) 3259 9898. Facsimile (81 3) 3259 9888.

Warsaw, Poland Office: ul. Kopernika 17, IV Floor, 00-359. Telephone: (48 22) 262 226. Facsimile: (48 22) 262 360.

Firm engaged in English and General International Practice but not authorized to appear before Singapore Courts or to advise Singapore law.

CONTACT PARTNERS

Christopher Rushton (Also at Hong Kong)

RESIDENT LAWYERS

Simon Citron

(For Complete Biographical Data on all Personnel, see Professional Biographies at London, England)

ALLENS ARTHUR ROBINSON

65 CHULIA STREET #42-05
OCBC CENTER
SINGAPORE 0104
Telephone: (65) 535 6622
Telex: RS 20978
Rapifax: (65) 535 4855

Allens Arthur Robinson is an international network of group and associated offices representing the Allens Arthur Robinson group in Australia. The firm is engaged in International Law practices, but not admitted as Solicitors in Singapore.

Group and Associated Offices:

London, England: Allens Arthur Robinson, Level 5, Bucklersbury House, 3 Queen Victoria Street, EC4N 8EL. Telephone: (44 171) 248 6130. Rapifax: (44 171) 248 6334.

New York, NY: Allens Arthur Robinson, 280 Park Avenue, 10017. Telephone: (1 212) 867 1555. Rapifax: (1 212) 867 7979.

Hong Kong: Dunstan Styles & Co., Suite 1504, One Exchange Square, 8 Connaught Place, Central. Telephone: (852) 2840 1202. Rapifax: (852) 2840 0686.

Jakarta, Indonesia: Wiriadinata & Widyawan, Niaga Tower, 26th Floor, Jl. Jend. Sudirman, Kav 58, 12190. Telephone: (62 21) 250 5175. Rapifax: (62 21) 250 5185.

Port Moresby, Papua New Guinea: Allens Arthur Robinson, Level 11, Pacific Place, Cnr Musgrave Street & Champion Parade. Telephone: (675) 202 000. Rapifax: (675) 200 588.

Shanghai, People's Republic of China: AAR China Limited, Fuxing Xi Lù 37 Long 6 Hao. 200031. Telephone: (86 21) 437 7582. Rapifax: (86 21) 473 7819.

Allens Arthur Robinson's international network of offices represents:

Sydney, New South Wales, Australia: Allen Allen & Hemsley, The Chifley Tower, 2 Chifley Square, 2000. Telephone: (61 2) 230 4000. Rapifax: (61 2) 233 7022.

Canberra, Australian Capital Territory, Australia: Allen Allen & Hemsley, 3rd Floor, 16 Moore Street, 2601. Telephone: (61 6) 247 5800. Rapifax: (61 6) 257 1369.

Melbourne, Victoria, Australia: Arthur Robinson & Hedderwicks, Levels 27-34, 530 Collins Street, 3000. Telephone: (61 3) 614 1011. Rapifax: (61 3) 614 4661.

Brisbane, Queensland, Australia: Feez Ruthning, Riverside Centre, 123 Eagle Street, 4000. Telephone: (61 7) 833 3333. Rapifax: (61 7) 832 4233.

Surfers Paradise, Queensland Australia: Feez Ruthning, Level 14, 50 Cavill Avenue, 4217. Telephone: (61 75) 70 0200. Rapifax: (61 75) 92 2285.

Perth, Western Australia, Australia: Parker & Parker, AMP Building, 140 St George's Terrace, 6000. Telephone: (61 9) 322 0321. Rapifax: (61 9) 322 2243.

Adelaide, South Australia, Australia: Finlaysons, 81 Flinders Street, 5000. Telephone: (61 8) 235 7400. Rapifax: (61 8) 232 2944.

FIRM PROFILE: Allens Arthur Robinson in Singapore provides regional legal services on a range of commercial transactions, including international loan and capital markets transactions, project financing, cross-border leasing and asset financing, and regional investment transactions.

RESIDENT PARTNERS

JOHN RICHARD HARRY, admitted, Victoria, New South Wales and UK. (Not admitted in Singapore). *LANGUAGES:* English. *PRACTICE AREAS:* Commercial; Resources.

(For complete personnel and biographical data, see Professional Biographies at Sydney, Australia).

BAKER & McKENZIE

21 COLLYER QUAY #16-01
HONGKONG BANK BUILDING
SINGAPORE 0104
Telephone: 2248066
Intn'l. Dialing: (65) 2248066
Cable Address: ABOGADO
Telex: 20852
Answer Back: ABOSIN RS20852
Facsimile: (65) 2243872; 2241038

Associated Offices of Baker & McKenzie in: Almaty, Amsterdam, Bangkok, Barcelona, Beijing, Berlin, Bogotá, Brasília, Brussels, Budapest, Buenos Aires, Cairo, Caracas, Chicago, Dallas, Frankfurt, Geneva, Hanoi, Ho Chi Minh City, Hong Kong, Juárez, Kiev, London, Madrid, Manila, Melbourne, México City, Miami, Milan, Monterrey, Moscow, New York, Palo Alto, Paris, Prague, Rio de Janeiro, Riyadh, Rome, St. Petersburg, San Diego, San Francisco, São Paulo, Stockholm, Sydney, Taipei, Tijuana, Tokyo, Toronto, Valencia, Warsaw, Washington, D.C. and Zürich.

Correspondent Law Firm: Hadiputranto, Hadinoto & Partners, Jakarta.

Firm engaged in International Law Practice, but not authorized to appear before the Singapore Courts or to act as Singapore Advocates and Solicitors.

DAVID J. HOWELL, born England; admitted, 1977, England and Wales; 1989, Hong Kong (Not admitted in Singapore). *Education:* Oxford University (M.A.); Inns of Court School of Law. *Member:* Law Society of England. *LANGUAGES:* English.

KIEN KEONG WONG, born Kuala Lumpur, Malaysia; admitted, 1985, England and Wales; 1986, Malaysia; 1994, Singapore. *Education:* Massachusetts Institute of Technology (S.B. and S.M.); University of London (Ph.D.); Oxford University (B.A.). *Member:* Lincoln Inn, London; Bar of Malaysia. *LANGUAGES:* English, Malay and Chinese.

LOCAL PARTNER

DEBORAH L. BLUM, born Calgary, Alberta, Canada, 1957; admitted, 1984, Alberta, Canada; 1988, England (Not admitted in Singapore). *Education:* University of Alberta (B.A., 1978; LL.B., 1981); University of London (LL.M., 1982). *LANGUAGES:* English and German.

OF COUNSEL

JOHN K. CONNOR, admitted, 1961, Victoria, Australia; 1963, Virginia, U.S.A.; 1964, New South Wales, Australia; 1974, England and Hong Kong; 1980, U.S. Supreme Court (Not admitted in Singapore). *Education:* University of Melbourne (LL.B.); University of Chicago (J.D.).

NEAL A. BIEKER, born Oregon, U.S.A., 1958; admitted, 1987, Victoria, Australia (Not admitted in Singapore). *Education:* Simon Fraser University (B.A., 1982); Monash University (LL.B., 1986). *Member:* Associate of the Securities Institute of Australia. *LANGUAGES:* English.

EDMUND H. M. LEOW, born Singapore, 1962; admitted, 1990, England and Wales; 1991, Hong Kong (Not admitted in Singapore). *Education:* Cambridge University (B.A., 1986; M.A., 1990). *LANGUAGES:* English and Chinese.

CHIU-ING NGOOI, born Malaysia, 1953; admitted, 1991, England and Wales and A.C.T., Australia; 1992, Malaya (Not admitted in Singapore). *Education:* Massachusetts Institute of Technology (B.S.; M.S.); University of Oxford (B.A.). *LANGUAGES:* English, Malay and Indonesian.

ANGUS T. S. PHANG, born Malaysia, 1961; admitted, 1986, England and Wales; 1989, Singapore; 1992, Hong Kong. *Education:* University of Surrey (B.Sc., Hons.); Polytechnic of Central London (Dipolma-in-Law). *LANGUAGES:* English.

RACHEL S. H. TAN, born Singapore, 1966; admitted, 1991, A.C.T. and Queensland, Australia; 1993, New South Wales, Australia (Not admitted in Singapore). *Education:* Australian National University (B.A., 1990; LL.B., 1991); Oxford University (B.C.L., 1992). *Member:* Queensland Law Society; New South Wales Law Society. *LANGUAGES:* English and Mandarin.

MICHAEL G. VELTEN, born Melbourne, Australia, 1964; admitted, 1989, Victoria, Australia (Not admitted in Singapore). *Education:* University of Melbourne (B.Comm., 1987; LL.B., 1988; M.A., Tax, 1992). *Mem-*
(This Listing Continued)

ber: Law Institute of Victoria, Australia. Fellow, Taxation Institute of Australia. *LANGUAGES:* English and Malay.

ADELINE M. K. WONG, born Kuching, Malaysia, May 30, 1966; admitted, 1990, New South Wales, Australia; 1992, Sarawak, Malaysia (Not admitted in Singapore). *Education:* University of New South Wales, Australia (Bachelor of Commerce, 1988; LL.B., 1990); Australian National University (Practical Legal Training in Law, 1990). *Member:* Law Society of New South Wales, Australia. *LANGUAGES:* English, Chinese and Malay.

BEAUMONT AND SON

Established in 1992

101 THOMSON ROAD
#29-02 UNITED SQUARE
SINGAPORE 1130
Telephone: (65) 352 2363
Fax: (65) 352 4282

London, England Office: Lloyds Chambers, 1 Portsoken Street, E1 8AW. Telephone: 0171.481.3100. Telex: 889018 Bosun G. Fax: 0171.481.3353.

Rio de Janeiro, Brazil Office: Rua Anfilófio de Carvalho, 29/518, CEP 20015-900. Telephone: (5521) 532 1445. Fax: (5521) 240 8541.

Paris, France Associated Office: Cabinet Garnault, 17 Avenue de Lamballe, 75016. Telephone: (1) 44.14.53.70. Telex: 645.858 ALORM PARIS. Fax: (1) 44.14.53.99.

Firm engaged in General and International Law Practice, but is not authorized to appear before the Singapore courts or to act as Singapore Advocates and Solicitors.

RESIDENT MEMBER

PHILIP M. BASS, born Wegberg, Germany, October 12, 1956; admitted, 1981, England and Wales (Not admitted in Singapore). *Education:* Exeter University (LL.B. Hons., 1978); College of Law (Solicitors Qualifying Examinations, 1979); University College London (Diploma in Air Space Law). *Member:* International Bar Association; Royal Aeronautical Society; Guild of Pilots and Air Navigators; West London Aero Club. *LANGUAGES:* French and Spanish.

BURKE & PARSONS

6 BATTERY ROAD #13-01
SINGAPORE 0104
Telephone: (65) 227-8168
Telefax: (65) 227-1218

New York, N.Y. Office: 1114 Avenue of the Americas, 10036. Telephone: 212-354-3800. Telefax: 212-221-1432. RCA Telex 232560 BURK UR. Cable Address: Azimuth.

Admiralty and International Law. Firm engaged in American and International Law Practice, but not authorized to appear before the Singapore courts or to act as Solicitors.

PARTNER IN CHARGE

RAYMOND J. BURKE, JR. (Not admitted in Singapore; Also at New York, New York Office).

(For biographical data on all personnel, see Professional Biographies at New York, New York)

DAVID CHONG & CO.

65 CHULIA STREET
OCBC CENTRE, #3100 EAST LOBBY
SINGAPORE 0104
Telephone: 2240955
Fax: 5333570; 5386585; 5387559

Kuala Lumpur, Malaysia Office: Suite 13A.01, 13A Floor, Wisma MCA, 163 Jalan Ampang, 50450. Telephone: 2632277. Fax: 2632278.

Johor Bahru, Malaysia Office: Suite 204-206, 2nd Floor, Pusat Professional, Jalan Syed Mohd Mufti, 80000. Telephone: 2249128. Fax: 2249386.

Labuan, Malaysia Office: Suite 114, 1st Floor, Hotel Labuan, Jalan Merdeka, P.O. Box 80107, 87011. Telephone: 411697; 416604. Fax: 411936.

(This Listing Continued)

Sydney, Australia Office: Level 29, Governor Phillip Tower, 1 Farrer Place, 2000. Telephone: 2585811. Fax: 2585800.

Suzhou, People's Republic of China Office: Suzhou Economy and International Trade Law Firm. Telephone: 877101. Fax: 879121.

Company and Commercial, Company Secretarial Services, Banking, Finance and Securities, Tax Practice and Planning, Conveyancing and Property Building and Construction, Admiralty and Shipping, Insurance, Copyright, Trademark Patent and Registered Design, Civil and Commercial Litigation, Bankruptcy and Insolvency, Arbitration, Family, Probate and Administration of Estates, Commissioner for Oaths and Notary Public, General Practice.

MEMBERS OF FIRM

DAVID CHONG KOK KONG, Barrister, Lincoln's Inn (England & Wales); M.Sc. (London), LL.M. (Singapore); Advocate and Solicitor (Singapore); Advocate and Solicitor (Malaya); Barrister and Solicitor (British Virgin Islands); Solicitor (NSW, Australia); Barrister and Solicitor (Australian Capital Territory); Advocate and Solicitor (Brunei). *LANGUAGES:* English. *PRACTICE AREAS:* Corporate and Commercial; Joint Ventures; Tax Planning; Corporate Restructuring; Banking and International Finance; Intellectual Property; Corporate Litigation; Conveyancing and Land Law.

KIM BOO, Barrister, Lincoln's Inn (England and Wales); Barrister (Hong Kong); Advocate and Solicitor (Singapore). *LANGUAGES:* English. *PRACTICE AREAS:* Trade Marks and General Practice.

DANIEL FONG TS'OI NUNG, B.A. (Hons) (London); LL.M. (Cantab); Barrister, Inner Temple (England and Wales); Advocate and Solicitor (Singapore). *LANGUAGES:* English. *PRACTICE AREAS:* Corporate; Conveyancing.

EUGENE LAI, LL.B. (London; LL.M. (Harvard); Advocate and Solicitor (Singapore); Solicitor (England and Wales); Attorney (New York). *LANGUAGES:* English. *PRACTICE AREAS:* Banking; Finance and Securities.

LAU CHIN WEE, B. Acc (Hons) (Malaya); Registered Accountant (Malaya); LL.B. (Hons) (Singapore); Advocate and Solicitor (Singapore); Advocate and Solicitor (Malaya). *LANGUAGES:* English and Malay. *PRACTICE AREAS:* Corporate; Commercial; Tax Planning; Corporate Restructuring.

PHILIP CHEW WENG FAH, LL.B. (Hons) (London); Barrister, Middle Temple (England and Wales); Advocate and Solicitor (Singapore); Advocate and Solicitor (Malaya). *LANGUAGES:* English and Malay. *PRACTICE AREAS:* Banking; Corporate and Commercial; Intellectual Property.

CELINE TAN SZE LIAN, Barrister, Gray's Inn (England and Wales); LL.M. (Singapore); Advocate and Solicitor (Singapore). *LANGUAGES:* English. *PRACTICE AREAS:* Corporate Secretarial.

CATHERINE HANAM, LL.B. (Hons) (London); Barrister, Middle Temple (England and Wales); Advocate and Solicitor (Singapore). *LANGUAGES:* English. *PRACTICE AREAS:* Corporate and Commercial; Corporate Restructuring; Intellectual Property.

MARY LYNNE TAN, LL.B. (Hons) (London); LL.M. (London); Barrister, Gray's Inn (England and Wales); Advocate and Solicitor (Singapore). *LANGUAGES:* English and Mandarin. *PRACTICE AREAS:* Conveyancing; Corporate Banking.

GILLIAN KANG, LL.B. (Hons) (Singapore); M.B.A. (London). *LANGUAGES:* English and French. *PRACTICE AREAS:* Tax Planning; Corporate and Commercial.

LORRAINE ANNE NONIS, LL.B. (Hons) (Singapore); Advocate and Solicitor (Singapore). *LANGUAGES:* English. *PRACTICE AREAS:* Conveyancing.

ONG BENG LAY, LL.B. (Hons) (Singapore); Advocate and Solicitor (Singapore). *LANGUAGES:* English and Mandarin. *PRACTICE AREAS:* Banking.

LATHA D. PILLAY, LL.B. (Hons) (Singapore); Advocate and Solicitor (Singapore). *LANGUAGES:* English and Malay. *PRACTICE AREAS:* Litigation.

MOLLINA SENGUPTA, LL.B. (Hons) (Singapore); Advocate and Solicitor (Singapore). *LANGUAGES:* English and Malay. *PRACTICE AREAS:* Banking.

(This Listing Continued)

DAVID CHONG & CO., Singapore—Continued

LIM PING PING, LL.B. (Hons) (Singapore); Advocate and Solicitor (Singapore). *LANGUAGES:* English and Mandarin. *PRACTICE AREAS:* Corporate; Commercial; Shipping; General Litigation.

PHILIP TEOH OON TEONG, LL.B. (Hons) (Singapore); Advocate and Solicitor (Singapore); Advocate and Solicitor (Malaya). *LANGUAGES:* English and Malay. *PRACTICE AREAS:* Shipping; Marine Insurance.

CATHERINE HO PENG HONG, LL.B. (Hons) (Singapore); Advocate and Solicitor (Singapore). *LANGUAGES:* English and Malay. *PRACTICE AREAS:* Conveyancing.

LAWRENCE LEE MUN KONG, LL.B. (Hons) (Singapore) LL.M. (London; Advocate and Solicitor (Singapore). *LANGUAGES:* English and Malay. *PRACTICE AREAS:* Litigation.

RAYMOND OOI OON PIN, LL.B. (Hons) (London); Barrister, Middle Temple (England and Wales); Barrister and Solicitor (Australian Capital Territory); Advocate and Solicitor (Singapore). *LANGUAGES:* English and Malay. *PRACTICE AREAS:* Banking; Corporate and Commercial.

ROHANA SAHAROM, LL.B. (Hons) (Singapore); Advocate and Solicitor (Singapore). *LANGUAGES:* English and Malay. *PRACTICE AREAS:* General Litigation; Probate.

LIEW SIOK FANG, LL.B. (Hons) (Singapore); Advocate and Solicitor (Singapore). *LANGUAGES:* English and Mandarin. *PRACTICE AREAS:* Corporate; General Commercial.

DANIEL SUN KOK MENG, LL.B. (Hons) (Singapore); LL.M. (Bristol); Advocate and Solicitor (Singapore). *LANGUAGES:* English and Mandarin. *PRACTICE AREAS:* Intellectual Property; General Litigation.

ATTLEE HUE KUAN YEW, LL.B. (Hons) (Singapore); Advocate and Solicitor (Singapore). *LANGUAGES:* English and Malay. *PRACTICE AREAS:* Corporate; Commercial; General Litigation.

LINDA TEOH SU-LING, LL.B. (Hons) (Singapore); Advocate and Solicitor (Singapore). *LANGUAGES:* English, Mandarin and French. *PRACTICE AREAS:* Banking.

PETER TAN KAH HUAN, LL.B. (Hons) (Singapore); Advocate and Solicitor (Singapore). *LANGUAGES:* English and Malay. *PRACTICE AREAS:* General Litigation.

ANGELINA YEO SOK HUANG, LL.B. (Hons) (Bristol); Barrister-at-Law; Advocate & Solicitor (Singapore). *LANGUAGES:* English and Mandarin. *PRACTICE AREAS:* Corporate; General Commercial.

RAPHAEL SOLOMON, LL.B. (Hons) (Singapore); Advocate and Solicitor (Singapore). *LANGUAGES:* English. *PRACTICE AREAS:* General Litigation.

HEE HWAN SENG, LL.B. (Hons) (London); Barrister-at-Law (Middle Temple); Advocate and Solicitor (Singapore). *LANGUAGES:* English and Mandarin. *PRACTICE AREAS:* Intellectual Property.

KAREN MARY CHAY WEI-MIN, LL.B. (Hons) (Singapore); Advocate and Solicitor (Singapore). *LANGUAGES:* English and Mandarin. *PRACTICE AREAS:* Conveyancing; Corporate Secretarial.

LAM WING HONG, LL.B. (Hons) (Singapore); Advocate and Solicitor (Singapore). *LANGUAGES:* English and Mandarin. *PRACTICE AREAS:* Corporate; General Commercial.

SUNIL GILL, LL.B. (Hons.) (Singapore); Advocate and Solicitor (Singapore). *LANGUAGES:* English, Malay and Hindi. *PRACTICE AREAS:* General Litigation.

CHOR PEE & COMPANY

Advocates & Solicitors

Commissioners for Oaths

Agents for Trade Marks, Designs & Patents

Established in 1964

50 RAFFLES PLACE
18TH FLOOR SHELL TOWER
SINGAPORE 0104
Telephone: 65-2201911
Fax: 65-2244118; 2240183
Telex: RS 21570 CPHH

Hanoi, Vietnam Office: 96, Ba Trieu Streett, Hoan Kiem District. Telephone: (844) 228 787/228 788. Fax: (844) 251 875.

Ho Chi Minh City, Vietnam Office: The Colonnade, 27 Nguyen Trung Truc, District 1. Telephone: (848) 224 986. Fax: (848) 225 441.

Kuala Lumpur, Malaysia Office: Chor Pee Anwarul & Company, Suite 19.04 Wisma Cyclecarri, 288 Jalan Raja Laut, 50350. Telephone: 603-294-6878. Fax: 603-294-6879.

Johor Bahru, Malaysia Office: Chor Pee Anwarul & Company, Unit 10.01 Wisma LKN, 49 Jalan Wong Ah Fook, 80000. Telephone: 607-223-4733. Fax: 607-223-4734.

PARTNERS

LIM CHOR PEE, BA (Cantab), Barrister-at-law, Inner Temple, England; Panel Member, Singapore International Arbitration Centre.

SIA MOON JOON, LL.B. (Hons) (S'pore).

KELVIN H. K. CHIA, LL.B. (Hons.) (S'pore).

MARY JUDITH DE SOUZA, LL.B. (Hons.) (S'pore).

CHEONG MIN LEE, LL.B. (Hons.) (S'pore).

LOW TIANG HOCK, Articleship B.L. Ed (S'pore).

CHEAH SWEE GIM, LL.B. (Hons.) (S'pore); LL.M. (TR REG) New York University.

AUDREY YANG, LL.B. (Hons.) (S'pore).

HARISH KUMAR, LL.B. (Hons.) (S'pore).

THIO YING YING, LL.B. (Hons.) (S'pore).

PATRICIA Y. S. LEE, LL.B. (Hons.) (S'pore).

TEK HENG, Barrister-at-law, Lincoln's Inn.

THOMAS C.K. LEI, LL.B. (Hons.) (S'pore).

CONSULTANT

SANT SINGH, Barrister-at-law, Middle Temple.

LEGAL ASSISTANTS/ASSOCIATES

RITA C.L. GOH, LL.B. (Hons.) (S'pore).

JOHN T.S. LOOI, LL.B. (Hons.) (S'pore).

NG ENG LENG, LL.B. (Hons.) (S'pore).

RAMOLA KANDIAH, LL.B. (Hons.) (S'pore).

KHOO KAH HO, LL.B. (Hons.) (S'pore).

ARIVA NANTHAM K., LL.B. (Hons.) (S'pore).

FABIAN C.T. TEO, LL.B. (Hons.) (S'pore).

NG MIN YEE, Barrister-at-law, Gray's Inn.

LEE TSE MEI, LL.B. (Hons.) (S'pore).

MILVI P.W. CHOK, LL.B. (Hons.) (S'pore).

WILLY B.C. TAY, LL.B. (Hons.) (S'pore).

LIM TANGUY YUTECK, Barrister-at-Law, Middle Temple.

CLIFFORD CHANCE

Established in 1981

16 COLLYER QUAY #31-00
SINGAPORE 0104
Telephone: (65) 535 1855
Fax: (65) 535 6855

Amsterdam, The Netherlands Office: Apollolaan 171, 1077 AS, P.O. Box 7301, 1007 JH. Telephone: (31 20) 577 71 11. Fax: (31 20) 676 93 26.

Bahrain, Manama Associated Office: Law Office of Shaikh Isa bin Mohammed Al Khalifa. P.O. Box 20717. Telephone: (973) 531535; 531073. Fax: (973) 536272; 530608.

Barcelona, Spain Office: Pau Claris 102, 08009. Telephone: (34 3) 318 68 64. Fax: (34 3) 317 73 23.

Brussels, Belgium Office: Avenue Louise 65, Box 2, 1050. Telephone: (32 2) 533 59 11. Fax: (32 2) 533 59 59.

Budapest, Hungary Office: Köves & Partners, Clifford Chance. Madách Trade Center, Madách Imre Út 14, 1075. Telephone: (36 1) 268 1600. Fax: (36 1) 268 1610.

Dubai, United Arab Emirates Office: 18th Floor, Dubai World Trade Centre, P.O. Box 9380. Telephone: (971 4) 314333. Fax: (971 4) 313990; 314565.

Frankfurt/Main, Germany Office: Friedrichstraße 2-6, 60323. Telephone: (49 69) 971 4090. Fax: (49 69) 971 40977.

Hanoi, Vietnam Office: 52 Nguyen Binh Khiem. Telephone: (844) 229 182/3/4/5/6. Fax: (844) 229 190.

Hong Kong Office: 30th Floor, Jardine House, One Connaught Place. Telephone: (852) 2810 0229. Fax: (852) 2810 4708; 2810 4858; 2810 4743.

London, England Office: 200 Aldersgate Street, EC1A 4JJ. Telephone: (44 171) 600 1000. Fax: (44 171) 600 5555.

Madrid, Spain Office: Paseo de la Castellana 110, 28046. Telephone: (34 1) 562 7674. Fax: (34 1) 562 49 93.

Milan, Italy Associated Office: Grimaldi e Clifford Chance. Via Gesú, 3, 20121. Telephone: (39 2) 7600 8040. Fax: (39 2) 7600 4950.

Moscow, Russia Office: Ul. Sadovaya - Samotechnaya 24/27, 2nd Floor, 103051. Telephone: (7 501) 258 50 50. Fax: (7 501) 258 50 51.

New York, New York Office: Swiss Bank Tower, 10 East 50th Street, 10022. Telephone: (1 212) 750 1440. Fax: (1 212) 758 6625.

Paris, France Office: 112 avenue Kléber, BP 163 Trocadéro, 75770 Paris Cedex 16. Telephone: (33 1) 44 05 52 52. Fax: (33 1) 44 05 52 00.

Riyadh, Saudi Arabia Associated Office: The Law Firm of Salah Al-Hejailan. P.O. Box 1454, 11431. Telephone: (966 1) 479 2200. Fax: (966 1) 479 1717.

Rome, Italy Associated Office: Grimaldi e Clifford Chance. Viale G. Rossini 7, 00198. Telephone: (39 6) 807 2251. Fax: (39 6) 807 8201.

Shanghai, People's Republic of China Office: Suite 898, Shanghai Centre, 1376 Nanjing Xi Lu, 200040. Telephone: (86 21) 279 8461. Fax: (86 21) 279 8462.

Tokyo, Japan Office: 6th Floor, South Hill Nagatacho Building, 11-30 Nagatacho 1-chome, Chiyoda-ku, 100. Telephone: (81 3) 3581 4311. Fax: (81 3) 3593 0651.

Warsaw, Poland Office: Warsaw Corporate Centre, ul. Emilii Plater 28, 00-688. Telephone: (48 2) 630 3344. Fax: (48 2) 630 3355.

International Banking and Finance, Project Finance, Corporate Finance, Company and Commercial Law.
Firm engaged in English and General International Practice with specific emphasis on Southeast Asia.

RESIDENT PARTNERS

SAM BONIFANT, (Not admitted in Singapore). Partner, University of Canterbury (LL.B. Hons., 1972); Barrister and Solicitor of the Supreme Court of New Zealand, 1974; Solicitor of the Supreme Court of England and Wales, 1981. **PRACTICE AREAS:** Project Finance; Banking Law; Asset Based Lending; Finance Law.

ANTHONY C. CANNELL, (Not admitted in Singapore). Partner, 1976 LL.B. (Hons); Solicitor of the Supreme Court of England and Wales 1976; Solicitor of the Supreme Court of Hong Kong 1988. **PRACTICE AREAS:** Project Finance; Ship Financing; Banking Law; Equipment Leasing.

(This Listing Continued)

RESIDENT LOCAL PARTNER

CAROL ROBERTS, (Not admitted in Singapore). Partner, University of Toronto B.A., Solicitor of the Supreme Court of England and Wales 1979. **PRACTICE AREAS:** Banking and Finance Law; General Bank Financing; Project Finance; Aircraft Financing.

(For the names of Partners resident in other offices, see Professional Biographies for those Offices).

CLYDE & CO.

SOUTH EAST ASIA OFFICE
10 COLLYER QUAY #13-06
OCEAN BUILDING
SINGAPORE 0104
Telephone: (65) 538 7696
Fax: (65) 538 7661

London, England Office: 51 Eastcheap, EC3M 1JP. Telephone: (44) 171-623 1244. Telex: 884886 CLYDE G. Fax: (44) 171-623 5427.

Also offices in Guildford (England), Cardiff (Wales), Hong Kong, Dubai (United Arab Emirates), Sao Paulo (Brazil), Caracas, Venezuela. For full details of these offices, see entry under London, England.

International practice including arbitration, aviation, commercial, joint venture work, finance, European Community, insurance, oil and gas, energy, shipping, admiralty and transport.

RESIDENT LAWYERS

John Whittaker
Andrew Bicknell
Russell Rawlings (Mariner)

Languages: English, French, German

COOMA, LAU & LOH

Advocates and Solicitors, Notary Public and Commissioners for Oath

STRAITS TRADING BUILDING
9 BATTERY ROAD, #17-08
SINGAPORE 0104
Telephone: (65) 5351822
Telex: COOMA RS 25430
Telefax: 5357409; 5357126; 5357782

General and International Practice including Admiralty and Shipping, Ship Finance, Building Contracts, Civil Engineering Disputes, Litigation, Arbitration, Insurance, Reinsurance, Banking and Finance (including Project Financing), Copyright, Patents, Trademarks, Corporate and Corporate Finance (including Venture Capital and Joint Ventures), Tax, Insolvency, Property and Conveyancing Law, Land Acquisition, Debt Collection, Family and Matrimonial Law, Wills, Probate, Trust and Estate Administration.

PARTNERS

QUENTIN LOH. Education: LL.B. (Hons) (Singapore).

TAT KUN SOO. Education: LL.B. (Hons) (Singapore).

K. JAYABALAN. Education: LL.B. (Hons) (London). Barrister-at-Law (England).

SWEE LENG CHEW. Education: LL.B. (Hons) (Singapore).

GERTRUDE CHAN. Education: LL.B. (Hons) (Singapore).

RABI DORAISAMY. Education: LL.B. (Hons) (Singapore).

HAU YIN HOO. Education: LL.B. (Hons) (Singapore).

YUEN CHEW LYE. Education: B.A. (Hons) (Malaya); A.C.I.I.; LL.B. (Hons) (England). Barrister-at-Law (England).

ROSALIND TAN. Education: LL.B. (Hons) (Singapore); LL.M. (Singapore).

RAVI CHELLIAH. Education: LL.B. (Hons) (Singapore).

DAVID KHOR. Education: LL.B. (Hons) (Singapore).

YONG NGEE HONG. Education: LL.B. (Hons) (Singapore).

HOPE WEE. Education: LL.B. (Hons) (Singapore).

LI CHOO QUEK. Education: LL.B. (Hons) (Singapore).

(This Listing Continued)

COOMA, LAU & LOH, Singapore—Continued

LEE KIAN LIM. *Education:* LL.B. (Hons) (Singapore).

LEGAL ASSISTANTS

IAN NG. *Education:* LL.B. (Hons) (Singapore); LL.M. (London).

ENG CHIANG CHUA. *Education:* LL.B. (Hons) (Singapore).

ALLAN TAN. *Education:* LL.B. (Hons) (Singapore).

JANICE OH. *Education:* LL.B. (Hons) (Singapore).

HILDA LEE. *Education:* LL.B. (Hons) (Singapore).

MICHAEL EU. *Education:* LL.B. (Hons) (Singapore); LL.M. (Singapore).

LI SUAN CHUA. *Education:* LL.B. (Hons) (Singapore).

VINCENT LIM. *Education:* LL.B. (Hons) (England). Barrister-at-Law (England).

GAVIN OOI. *Education:* LL.B. (Hons) (Singapore), Barrister-at-Law (England).

WEN-NA WUN. *Education:* LL.B. (Hons) (Singapore).

LIP KHOON ER. *Education:* LL.B. (Hons) (Singapore).

ALLAN PC TAN. *Education:* LL.B. (Hons) (England); M.A. (England) Barrister-at-Law.

JACQUELINE CHIM. *Education:* LL.B. (Hons) (Singapore).

ASSOCIATES

ALAN THAMBIAYAH. *Education:* LL.B. (Hons) (Singapore).

COUDERT BROTHERS

TUNG CENTRE

20 COLLYER QUAY

SINGAPORE 0104

Telephone: (65) 2229973

Telex: 21466 Coudert RS

Telecopier: (65) 2241756

Cable Address: "Treduoc"

REVISERS OF THE FRANCE LAW DIGEST FOR THIS DIRECTORY.

New York, New York 10036-7794: 1114 Avenue of the Americas.

Washington, D.C. 20006: 1627 I Street, N.W.

Los Angeles, California 90017: 1055 West Seventh Street, Twentieth Floor.

San Francisco, California 94111: 4 Embarcadero Center, Suite 3300.

San Jose, California 95113: Suite 1250, Ten Almaden Boulevard.

Paris 75008, France: Coudert Frères, 52, Avenue des Champs-Elysees.

London, EC4M 7JP, England: 20 Old Bailey.

Brussels B-1050, Belgium: Tour Louise. 149 Avenue Louise-Box 8.

Beijing, People's Republic of China 100020: Suite 2708-09 Jing Guang Centre, Hu Jia Lou Chao Yang Qu.

Shanghai, People's Republic of China 200002: c/o Suite 1804, Union Building, 100 Yanan Road East.

Hong Kong: 25th Floor, Nine Queen's Road Central.

Sydney N.S.W. 2000, Australia: Suite 2202, State Bank Centre, 52 Martin Place.

Tokyo 107, Japan: 1355 West Tower, Aoyama Twin Towers, 1-1-1 Minami-Aoyama, Minato-ku.

Moscow, Russia: Ulitsa Staraya Basmannaya 14.

01301 Sao Paulo, SP, Brazil: Machado, Meyer, Sendacz, e Opice, Advogados, Rua da Consolacao, 8 Andar.

Bangkok 10500, Thailand: Bubhajit Building, 20 North Sathorn Road, 10th Floor.

Ho Chi Minh City, Vietnam: c/o Saigon Business Centre, 49-57 Dong Du Street, District 1.

Firm engaged in American and International Law Practice but not authorized to appear before the Singapore Courts or to act as Singapore Advocates and Solicitors.

(This Listing Continued)

RESIDENT PARTNERS

IRWIN L. GUBMAN, born St. Paul, Minnesota, March 2, 1942; admitted, 1968, District of California; 1973, California. *Education:* University of Minnesota (B.A., summa cum laude, 1964); University of Chicago (J.D., 1967); Harvard University. Phi Beta Kappa. Author: "Dispute Avoidance and Resolution Through Use of Arbitration Clauses," ALI-ABA Resource Materials, Banking and Commercial Lending Law, Vol. X (1989); "Bank Counsel: The Working Relationship," ALI-ABA Resource Materials, Banking and Commercial Lending Law, Vol. VIII (1987). Co-Author with J. Keller, "Supervision of Foreign Banks in the United States," *ALI-ABA Resource Materials, Banking and Commercial Lending Law,* Volume XIV (1993); with R. Nassberg, "On the Role of Outside Counsel," *ALI-ABA Resource Materials, Banking and Commercial Lending Law,* Volume XIII (1992). Attorney Advisor, U.A., Arms Control and Disarmament Agency, Department of State, Washington, D.C., 1968-1970. Member, Public Policy Committee, California Bankers Clearing House Association, 1982-1986. *Member:* Bar Association of San Francisco; State Bar of California; American Bar Association (Member: Banking Law Committee, Section of Business Law; Law Practice Management Section); American Bankers Association (Member: Banking Leadership Conference, 1982-1984; Government Relations Council, 1985-1986); California Bankers Association (Member, Board of Directors, 1983-1986; Chairman: Government Relations Committee, 1983-1984 and Government and Public Affairs Group, 1985-1986).

JEFFREY LEOW, born Singapore, May 15, 1951; admitted, 1981, New York and California (Not admitted in Singapore). *Education:* University of California at Los Angeles (B.S., 1972); University of California at Berkeley (M.B.A., 1974); University of California School of Law at Los Angeles (J.D., 1980). *Member:* New York State and American Bar Associations; State Bar of California.

SENIOR ATTORNEY

RICHARD L. CASSIN, JR., born Keene, New Hampshire, February 13, 1953; admitted, 1978, Virginia (Not admitted in Singapore). *Education:* University of Vienna; Nasson College (B.A., 1975); Boston College (J.D., 1978). Editor (Articles) and Staff Member, Boston College Law Review. Legal Counsel Forum, American Consulting Engineers Council. *Member:* American Bar Association (Member, International Law and Practice Section).

RESIDENT ASSOCIATES

M. Tamara Box	**Efi Kremetis**
(Not admitted in Singapore)	(Not admitted in Singapore)
Michael S. Horn	**Mark A. Nelson**
(Not admitted in Singapore)	(Not admitted in Singapore)
Eleanor Siew-Yin Wong	

REVISERS OF THE FRANCE LAW DIGEST FOR THIS DIRECTORY.

(For biographical data of the New York personnel, see Professional Biographies at New York, N.Y.).

(For biographical data of the Washington personnel, see Professional Biographies at Washington, D.C.).

(For biographical data of the San Francisco personnel, see Professional Biographies at San Francisco, California).

(For biographical data of the Los Angeles personnel, see Professional Biographies at Los Angeles, California).

(For biographical data of the San Jose personnel, see Professional Biographies at San Jose, California) .

(For biographical data of the Paris personnel, see Professional Biographies at Paris, France).

(For biographical data of the Brussels personnel, see Professional Biographies at Brussels, Belgium).

(For biographical data of the London personnel, see Professional Biographies at London, England).

(For biographical data of the Tokyo personnel, see Professional Biographies at Tokyo, Japan).

(For biographical data of the Hong Kong personnel, see Professional Biographies at Hong Kong).

(For biographical data of the Beijing personnel, see Professional Biographies at Beijing, People's Republic of China).

(For biographical data of the Sao Paulo personnel, see Professional Biographies at Sao Paulo, Brazil).

(For biographical data of the Shanghai personnel, see Professional Biographies at Shanghai, People's Republic of China).

(For biographical data of the Sydney personnel, see Professional Biographies at Sydney, Australia).

(For biographical data of Moscow personnel, see Professional Biographies at Moscow, U.S.S.R.).

(For biographical data of the Ho Chi Minh City Personnel, see Professional Biographies at Ho Chi Minh City, Vietnam).

DENTON HALL

A Member of the Denton International Group of Law Firms

152 BEACH ROAD
#08-05 GATEWAY EAST
SINGAPORE 0718
Telephone: 65-2911219
Cable Address: "Burginhal Singapore"
Telex: 22803 DHBW
Fax: 65- 2938102

Other Offices: London, England; Beijing, People's Republic of China; Milton Keynes, Buckinghamshire, England; Brussels, Belgium; Hong Kong; Los Angeles, California; Tokyo, Japan; Moscow, Russia.
Associated Offices: Amsterdam, Berlin, Chemnitz, Copenhagen, Dusseldorf, Frankfurt, Hamburg, Rotterdam and Vienna.

RESIDENT PARTNER

MICHAEL DOBLE. PRACTICE AREAS: Energy and Natural Resources.

(For all Firm Personnel, see Professional Biographies at London, England).

DONALDSON & BURKINSHAW

Advocates and Solicitors, Notaries Public, Commissioner for Oaths,

Agents for Trademarks and Patents

Established in 1874

24 RAFFLES PLACE
#15-00, CLIFFORD CENTRE
SINGAPORE 0104
Telephone: 5339422 (10 Lines)
Telex: RS 21556; RS 21674 DONBURK
Telefax: (65) 5337806; 5333590 ; 5343905; 5350809
Cable Address: DENOTATION

Mailing Address: P.O. Box 3667, Singapore, 9056

Intellectual Property (Trade Marks, Service Marks, Copyright and Patent Law), Building and Construction Law, Arbitration Practice, Company and Commercial Law, Banking, Finance and Securities, Bankruptcy and Insolvency, Conveyancing and Property Law, Insurance (General and Marine Insurance), Admiralty and Shipping, Family Law, Probate and Administrative of Estates, Employment Law and Immigration Matters, Civil and Commercial Litigation, Medical Negligence and Malpractice.

FIRM PROFILE: *Founded in 1874 the firm is the oldest established partnership law practice and one of the leading law firms in Singapore. The firm comprises of 26 professional members (10 partners, 1 consultant and 14 associates) supported by a team of 116 support staff, including specialized paralegals.*

PARTNERS

CHANG-SHENG WU, LL.B. (Cantab); Barrister-at-law of Middle Temple; Notary Public and Commissioner for Oaths. **PRACTICE AREAS:** Construction Contracts; Arbitration Practice.

BOK HOAY TAN, LL.B. (Hons) (Singapore). **PRACTICE AREAS:** Intellectual Property; Insurance; Corporate Practice; Litigation.

DAVID P.K. WEE, Barrister-at-Law of the Inner Temple; Commissioner for Oaths. **PRACTICE AREAS:** Shipping; Corporate Practice; Medical Negligence and Malpractice.

ANGELA YAP, (MRS), LL.B. (Hons) (Singapore). **PRACTICE AREAS:** Real Estate; Banking Practice.

EUGENE OON TEIK LIM, LL.B. (Hons) (London); LL.M. (Cantab); Barrister-at-Law of the Middle Temple; Barrister of the High Court of Australia. **PRACTICE AREAS:** Corporate Banking; Commercial Litigation; Construction Contracts.

PEK GAN LEONG, (MS), LL.B. (Hons) (Singapore). **PRACTICE AREAS:** Real Estate; Banking Practice.

DAVID ARTHUR MITCHELL, LL.B. (Hons) (London); LL.M. (Singapore); Barrister-at-Law of the Lincoln's Inn. Fellow of the Singapore Institute of Arbitrators. **PRACTICE AREAS:** Banking; General Litigation; Medical Negligence and Malpractice.

(This Listing Continued)

JIMMY YAP NENG BOO, (Articleship) (B.L. Ed.) (Singapore). **PRACTICE AREAS:** Medical Negligence and Malpractice; Bankruptcy and Insolvency; General Litigation.

TENG LEONG LIM, LL.B. (Hons) (Singapore). **PRACTICE AREAS:** Banking; General Litigation; Intellectual Property; Medical Negligence and Malpractice.

ANGELA LEONG, (MRS.), LL.B. (Hons) (Singapore). **PRACTICE AREAS:** Intellectual Property.

CONSULTANT

HENRY MOSLEY DYNE, Solicitor, Member of the Law Society (England). Notary Public & Commissioner for Oaths. **PRACTICE AREAS:** Real Estate; Trust; Probate; Banking; Corporate Practice.

ASSOCIATES

PAUL LEE YAN CHEN, LL.B. (Hons) (London); LL.M. (London). Barrister-at-Law of the Lincoln's Inn.

CHARLES MING KHIN LIN, LL.B. (Hons) Barrister-at-Law of the Middle Temple.

LAY BEE LOH, (MS), LL.B. (Hons) Barrister-at-Law of the Middle Temple.

SYED FARIS ALSAGOFF, LL.M. (Cantab); Dip. of Buss.S. Barrister-at-Law of Grey's Inn.

CHOON KIAT TAN, LL.B. (Hons) (Singapore).

GER EAN ANG, (MS), LL.B. (Hons) (Singapore).

E-LAINE CHIAM, (MS.), LL.B. (Hons) (Singapore).

JOHN KHOON LEONG CHUNG, LL.B. (Hons) (London) B. Arch. (Singapore); Barrister-at-Law Lincoln's Inn; Member Singapore Inst. of Architects.

TERENCE EK LOON TAN, LL.B. (Hons) (Lond); LL.M. (Lond). Barrister-at-Law of Inner Temple.

SIMONE SIN YI LAI, (MS), LL.B. (Hons) (Lond) Barrister-at-law Middle Temple.

TENG TENG TAN, (MS), LL.B. (Hons) (Lond); Barrister-at-law Middle Temple.

JEFFREY K.S. CHAN, B.A. (Hons) (Law); Barrister at Law, Middle Temple.

SIMON HUNG MING SEOW, LL.B. (Hons) (S'pore).

Global Affiliation of independent law firms:
Selected to represent Singapore for internationally renowned legal-professional network such as LEX-MUNDI, INTERLEX and MULTI-LAW and member of the Association of Asian Patent Attorneys and Asia Pacific Lawyers Association.
With Correspondent and Associate Offices in: Washington, D.C., New York, Chicago, Philadelphia, Wilmington, Dallas, Atlanta, Boston, Los Angeles, San Francisco, Vancouver, Toronto, Montreal, London, Dublin, Paris, Moscow, Brussels, Amsterdam, Frankfurt, Helsinki, Milan, Rome, Zurich, Geneva, Madrid, Lisbon and Porto Jersey Tokyo, Seoul, Taipei, Hong Kong, Beijing, Manila, Bangkok, Kuala Lumpur, Jakarta, Brunei, Melbourne, Sydney, Perth, Canberra, Brisbane, Auckland, Wellington, New Delhi, Bombay and other major cities worldwide.

Languages: English, Chinese, Malay, Indonesian and Tamil

DREW & NAPIER

Solicitors, Notaries Public, Commissioners for Oaths, Trademarks and Patents Agents

Established in 1889

20 RAFFLES PLACE
17-00, OCEAN TOWERS
SINGAPORE 0104
Telephone: (65) 5350733 (main line)
Telex: Jures RS 21361
Fax: 5354906 (General Line); 5354864 (Banking/Corporate/Tax); 5353829 (Conveyancing); 5330694 (Intellectual Property) 5327149/5330693 (Litigation)

General Practice, Corporate, Commercial, Banking, Property and Real Estate, Insurance, Finance, Taxation, Shipping and Carriage, Trademarks and Patents, Labour Law and General Matters.

(This Listing Continued)

DREW & NAPIER, Singapore—Continued

FIRM PROFILE: *Established in 1889, Drew & Napier is one of the oldest law firms in Singapore. It is also one of the largest with 96 lawyers comprising 45 partners, 5 consultants, 9 senior legal assistants, 37 legal assistants and supporting non-legal staff of 34 executives and more than 300 general staff.*

The Firm has nine departments covering Corporate Finance, Banking, Taxation, Conveyancing, Intellectual Property, Secretarial Company Work, General and Commercial Litigation, Shipping, Debt Collection and Insolvency Practice.

The firm also has dedicated teams for Hong Kong, China, Vietnam and Indonesia. It also has representative office in Hanoi, Vietnam and associate firms in Hong Kong, Malaysia and Indonesia.

PARTNERS

SU MIEN THIO, LL.B. (Hons) (Malaya), LL.M. (Singapore), PH.D. (London). *PRACTICE AREAS:* Banking; Corporate Finance; Conveyancing; General Commercial Practice.

R. RAJ SINGAM, Barrister-at-Law, England, Commissioner for Oaths, Singapore. *PRACTICE AREAS:* Trial and Appellate Litigation in Civil Conflicts on Company; Banking, Industry and Partnership Law; Arbitration; Building Contracts; Property Rights; Injunctions; Mortgagees' Actions; Receivership; Matrimony; Crime.

MURGIANA HAQ, LL.B. (Hons) (Singapore). *PRACTICE AREAS:* Intellectual Property (litigation and non-contentious matters).

LOY JIN TAN, LL.B. (Hons) (Singapore), Commissioner for Oaths, Singapore. *PRACTICE AREAS:* Conveyancing; Banking; Probate and Administration; Company Law.

BEE LIAN TAN, LL.B. (Hons.) (Singapore). *PRACTICE AREAS:* Conveyancing; Banking; Probate and Administration; Company Law.

BEE LAN CHUA, LL.B. (Hons.) (Singapore). *PRACTICE AREAS:* Conveyancing; Banking; Probate and Administration; Company Law.

DAVINDER SINGH, LL.B. (Hons) (Singapore). *PRACTICE AREAS:* Banking; Corporate and General Litigation; Insolvency Practice Particularly for Financial Institutions.

STEVEN CHONG, LL.B. (Hons) (Singapore). *PRACTICE AREAS:* Shipping; Marine Insurance; Salvage; Collision; Shipping Frauds; Letters of Credit; Charterparty Arbitrations.

LEENA SANKARAN, LL.B. (Hons) (Singapore), LL.M. (Cantab). *PRACTICE AREAS:* Banking; Corporate Finance; Company Law.

MORRIS JOHN, LL.B. (Hons) (London), Barrister-at-Law, England. *PRACTICE AREAS:* General Litigation; Collection for Financial Institutions; Insurance; Insolvency Practices.

DAVID ANG, LL.B. (Hons) (Singapore). *PRACTICE AREAS:* Corporate Law Mergers and Acquisitions; Joint Ventures; Reconstructions; Employment Matters; Building Contracts and Commerical Transactions.

LIAN EE TEOH, LL.B. (Hons) (Singapore), ACIS, LL.M. (Singapore). *PRACTICE AREAS:* Revenue Matters including Income Tax; Estate Duty; Stamp Duty and Property Tax; Trusts; Estate Planning.

JIMMY YIM, LL.B. (Hons) (Singapore), LL.M. (Singapore). *PRACTICE AREAS:* Advocacy; General Litigation; Commercial Transactions.

WEE KIONG YEO, LL.B. (Hons) (London), Barrister-at-Law, England, B. Engineering (Mech), MBA (Singapore). *PRACTICE AREAS:* Banking; Corporate Finance; Venture Capital; Company Law.

DEDAR SINGH GILL, LL.B. (Hons) (Singapore). *PRACTICE AREAS:* General Litigation; Insolvency Practice Particularly for Financial Institutions; Commercial Transactions.

MUTHU ARUSU, LL.B. (Hons) (Singapore). *PRACTICE AREAS:* Shipping; Marine Insurance; Salvage; Collision; Shipping Frauds; Letters of Credit; Charterparty Arbitrations.

DAVID CHIN, LL.B. (Hons) (Singapore). *PRACTICE AREAS:* Conveyancing; Banking and Company Law.

ANDREW C.L. ONG, LL.B. (Hons) (London), Barrister-at-Law, England. *PRACTICE AREAS:* Corporate Law-Mergers and Acquisitions; Joint Ventures; Reconstructions; Employment Matters; Building Contracts and Commercial Transactions.

(This Listing Continued)

GARY A. PRYKE, B.A. (Wits), LL.B. (Hons) (Reading), LL.B. (UNISA), Solicitor, England. *PRACTICE AREAS:* Banking; Corporate Finance; Company Law.

INDRANEE RAJAH, LL.B. (Hons) (Singapore). *PRACTICE AREAS:* General Litigation and Insurance.

SHIRLEY CHUA-LIM, LL.B. (Hons) (Ext) (London), Barrister-at-Law, England. *PRACTICE AREAS:* Banking; Corporate Finance; Company Law.

GERALD TO, LL.B. (Hons) (Hong Kong), Solicitor.

CHRISTOPHER CHUAH, LL.B. (Hons.) (London), Barrister-at-Law, England. *PRACTICE AREAS:* General Litigation and Insolvency Practice.

AI LIN TEOH, LL.B. (Hons.) (Singapore), LL.M. (Cantab). *PRACTICE AREAS:* Banking; Corporate Finance; Company Law.

CHEN YEE CHAN, LL.B. (Hons.) (Singapore). *PRACTICE AREAS:* Conveyancing; Banking; Company Law.

LYE KUEN SIN, LL.B. (Hons.) (Singapore). *PRACTICE AREAS:* General Litigation; Shipping.

SHANG-YING WHANG, B.A. (Oxon), Barrister-at-Law, Lincoln's Inn. *PRACTICE AREAS:* Banking, Finance and Securities; Company and Commercial Law; Corporate Law; Employment Law; Immigration Matters.

BOON ANN SIN, LL.B. (Hons.) (Singapore), LL.M. (London). *PRACTICE AREAS:* Corporate Law-Mergers and Acquisitions; Joint Ventures; Reconstructions; Employment Matters; Building Contracts and Commercial Transactions.

CHENG HAN TAN, LL.B. (Hons.) (Singapore), LL.M. (Cantab). *PRACTICE AREAS:* General Litigation; Insolvency Practice Particularly for Financial Institutions and Commerical Transactions.

ROSALIND A. LAZAR, LL.B. (Hons.) (Singapore). *PRACTICE AREAS:* General Litigation; Insolvency; Commercial Transactions.

STEVEN H. H. SEOW, LL.B. (Hons.) (Singapore). *PRACTICE AREAS:* Corporate Law-Mergers and Acquisitions; Joint Ventures; Reconstructions; Employment Matters; Building Contracts and Commerical Transactions.

LENA GAN, LL.B. (Hons.) (Singapore), LL.M. (Singapore). *PRACTICE AREAS:* Banking; Corporate Finance; Company Law.

CATHERINE MAH, LL.B. (Hons.) (Bris.), Barrister-at-Law (Gray's Inn). *PRACTICE AREAS:* Corporate Law-Mergers and Acquisitions; Joint Ventures; Reconstructions; Employment Matters; Building Contracts and Commercial Transactions.

JOAN FRANCIS, LL.B. (Hons.) (Singapore), LL.M. (England). *PRACTICE AREAS:* Banking; Corporate Finance; Company Law.

CHING IAN KOH, B.A. (Hons.) (Cambridge), Barrister-at-Law, England. *PRACTICE AREAS:* General Litigation; Shipping.

CHRISTINA CHUA, LL.B. (Hons.) (Singapore). *PRACTICE AREAS:* Revenue Matters; Income Tax; Estate Duty; Stamp Duty; Property Tax.

PHILIP LAM, LL.B. (Hons.) (Singapore). *PRACTICE AREAS:* General Litigation; Debt Collection for Financial Institutions; Insolvency Practice.

KOK KENG LAU, LL.B. (Hons.) (Singapore). *PRACTICE AREAS:* General Litigation; Debt Collection for Financial Institutions; Insolvency Practice.

ABEL LEE, LL.B. (Hons.) (Singapore). *PRACTICE AREAS:* Conveyancing; Banking; Company Law.

RANDOLPH KHOO, LL.B. (Hons.) (Singapore). *PRACTICE AREAS:* General Litigation; Debt Collection for Financial Institutions; Insolvency Practice.

SUSHIL NAIR, LL.B. (Hons.) (Singapore). *PRACTICE AREAS:* General Litigation; Debt Collection for Financial Institutions; Insolvency Practice.

KOK HOE WONG, LL.B. (Hons.) (Singapore). *PRACTICE AREAS:* Banking; Corporate Finance; Company Law.

JOSEPH YEO, LL.B. (Hons.) (Singapore). *PRACTICE AREAS:* General Litigation; Debt Collection for Financial Institutions; Insolvency Practice.

(This Listing Continued)

EVELYN WEE, LL.B. (Hons.) (Singapore). *PRACTICE AREAS:* Banking; Corporate Finance; Company Law.

STEVEN S. L. SEAH, LL.B. (Hons.) (Singapore). *PRACTICE AREAS:* Intellectual Property (Litigation and Non-Contentious matters).

ANDREW H.S. ONG, LL.B. (Hons.) (Singapore). *PRACTICE AREAS:* General Litigation; Shipping.

SENIOR ASSISTANT SOLICITORS

PIH PENG LEE, LL.B. (Hons.) (Singapore). *PRACTICE AREAS:* Banking; Corporate Finance; Company Law.

WEE JIN TOH, LL.B. (Hons.) (Singapore). *PRACTICE AREAS:* Conveyancing; Banking; Company Law.

ANDRE F. MANIAM, LL.B. (Hons.) (Singapore). *PRACTICE AREAS:* General Litigation; Commerical Transactions.

WEE HANN LIM, LL.B. (Hons.) (Singapore). *PRACTICE AREAS:* Banking; Corporate Finance; Company Law.

TEAN LIM, LL.B. (Hons.) (Reading), LL.M. (Cambridge). *PRACTICE AREAS:* General Litigation; Shipping.

BONAVENTURE LO, B.A. (Hons.) Soc.Sc., M.Sc. Industrial Relations, LL.B. (Hons.) (London), Barrister-at-Law, England. *PRACTICE AREAS:* General Litigation; Debt Collection for Financial Institutions; Insolvency Practice.

JOSEPH KAN, LL.B. (Hons.) (Manchester), Barrister-at-Law, England. *PRACTICE AREAS:* General Litigation; Commercial Transactions.

LIAM BENG TAN, B.Engineering (Hons), LL.M. (London), LL.B. (Hons) (England), Barrister-at-Law (Lincoln's Inn).

ASSISTANT SOLICITORS

EVELYN FANG, LL.B. (Hons.) (Singapore). *PRACTICE AREAS:* Banking; corporate Finance; Company Law.

HRI KUMAR, LL.B. (Hons.) (Singapore). *PRACTICE AREAS:* General Litigation; Commercial Transactions.

TONY YEO, LL.B. (Hons.) (Singapore). *PRACTICE AREAS:* Intellectual Property (Litigation and Non-Contentious).

ADRIAN TAN, LL.B. (Hons.) (Singapore). *PRACTICE AREAS:* Intellectual Property (Litigation and Non-Contentious).

HAN YANG YAP, LL.B. (Hons.) (Singapore). *PRACTICE AREAS:* Banking; Corporate Finance; Company Law.

MARINA WASANTACHAT, LL.B. (Hons.) (Bris.), Barrister-at-Law, England. *PRACTICE AREAS:* Banking; Corporate Finance; Company Law.

HARPREET SINGH NEHAL, LL.B. (Hons.) (Singapore), LL.M. (London). *PRACTICE AREAS:* General Litigation; Commercial Transactions.

RICHARD CHOONG, LL.B. (Hons) (Singapore). *PRACTICE AREAS:* Intellectual Property (Litigation and Non-Contentious).

YEE MING LIM, LL.B. (Hons) (Singapore). *PRACTICE AREAS:* General Litigation; Commercial Transactions.

COLLIN SEAH, LL.B. (Hons) (Singapore). *PRACTICE AREAS:* General Litigation; Shipping.

PHILIP TAY, LL.B. (Hons) (Singapore). *PRACTICE AREAS:* General Litigation; Commercial Transactions.

BAN LEONG OO, Barrister-at-Law, Middle Temple. *PRACTICE AREAS:* Banking; Corporate Finance; Company Law.

GREGORY VIJAYENDRAN, LL.B. (Hons) (Singapore). *PRACTICE AREAS:* General Litigation; Commercial Transactions.

THYAPARAN KATHIRAVEL, LL.B. (Hons) (Liverpool), Barrister-at-Law, England. *PRACTICE AREAS:* General Litigation; Shipping.

ANDY LECK, LL.B. (Hons) (Bris.), Barrister-at-Law, England. *PRACTICE AREAS:* General Litigation; Commercial Transactions.

SHEN YI THIO, B.A. (Hons) (Cantab), Barrister-at-Law, England. *PRACTICE AREAS:* General Litigation; Commercial Transactions.

JENNIFER TAN, B.A. (Hons.) (U.K.), Barrister-at-Law, Gray's Inn. *PRACTICE AREAS:* Conveyancing; Banking; Company Law.

(This Listing Continued)

S. SIVANANTHAN, LL.B. (Hons) (London), Barrister-at-Law. *PRACTICE AREAS:* Intellectual Property (Litigation and Non-Contentious).

CONRAD LIM, LL.B., (Hons) (Bris), Solicitor, England and Wales. *PRACTICE AREAS:* Banking; Corporate Finance; Venture Capital; Company Law.

TING KWOK IU, B.A. (Hons), Solicitor, England and Wales, Solicitor, Hong Kong. *PRACTICE AREAS:* Banking; Corporate Finance; Venture Capital; Company Law.

TRUDY ONG, LL.B. (Hons) (London), Barrister-at-Law (Gray's Inn). *PRACTICE AREAS:* Conveyancing; Banking; Company Law.

RACHEL YAP, LL.B. (Hons)(Ext)(London), Barrister-at-Law (Middle Temple). *PRACTICE AREAS:* Conveyancing; Banking; Company Law.

ANIL SACHDEV, LL.B. (Hons) (Singapore). *PRACTICE AREAS:* Intellectual Property (Litigation and Non-Contentious).

EUGENE LEE, LL.B. (Hons) (Singapore). *PRACTICE AREAS:* Banking; Corporate Finance; Company Law.

SONIA LIM, LL.B. (Hons) (Singapore). *PRACTICE AREAS:* Banking; Corporate Finance; Company Law.

PENNY LO, LL.B. (Hons) (Singapore). *PRACTICE AREAS:* Banking; Corporate Finance; Venture Capital; Company Law.

KAREEN LOOI, LL.B. (Hons) (Singapore). *PRACTICE AREAS:* General Litigation; Commercial Transactions.

ROSABEL NG, LL.B. (Hons) (Singapore). *PRACTICE AREAS:* Banking; Corporate Finance; Venture Capital; Company Law.

MANOJ SANDRASEGARA, LL.B. (Hons) (Singapore). *PRACTICE AREAS:* General Litigation; Commercial Transactions.

CHERYL TAN, LL.B. (Hons) (Singapore). *PRACTICE AREAS:* General Litigation; Commercial Transactions.

CAVINDER BULL, B.A. (Hons.) (Oxon), Barrister-at-Law, Gray's Inn. *PRACTICE AREAS:* General Litigation; Commercial Transactions.

JOYCE SIA, LL.B. (Hons) (Singapore). *PRACTICE AREAS:* Conveyancing; Banking; Company Law.

SOO EE, JOSEPH TAY, LL.B. (Hons) (Singapore). *PRACTICE AREAS:* Conveyancing; Banking; Company Law.

CLARINDA CHIA, LL.B. (Hons) (London), Barrister-at-Law (Inner Temple). *PRACTICE AREAS:* Conveyancing; Banking; Company Law.

SIEW LIN KHOO, LL.B. (Hons) (Nottingham), Barrister-at-Law (Lincoln's Inn). *PRACTICE AREAS:* Intellectual Property (Litigation and Non-Contentious).

CONSTANCE LOH, LL.B. (Hons) (Bristol), Barrister-at-Law, (Middle Temple). *PRACTICE AREAS:* Intellectual Property (Litigation and Non-Contentious).

JOANNA TI, B.A. (Hons), Barrister-at-Law (Middle Temple), LL.B. (Hons) (Nottingham), Barrister-at-Law, (Lincoln's Inn). *PRACTICE AREAS:* Conveyancing; Banking; Probate and Administration; Company Law.

CONSULTANTS

DAVID MARSHALL, Barrister-at-Law, England. *PRACTICE AREAS:* Criminal Law and Arbitration; Civil and Commercial Litigation; Bankruptcy and Insolvency.

J. GRIMBERG, M.A. (Cantab), Barrister, England, Notary Public and Commissioner for Oaths. *PRACTICE AREAS:* Arbitration; Civil and Commercial Litigation; Bankruptcy and Insolvency.

S. C. LIM, Barrister, England, Notary Public and Commissioner for Oaths. *PRACTICE AREAS:* Conveyancing and Property Law.

S. SAURAJEN, LL.B. (Hons.) (Malaya). *PRACTICE AREAS:* Company Matters; Incorporation; Joint Ventures; Negotiations; Mergers; Acquisitions; Takeovers; Reconstructions; Amalgamations; Commercial Transactions.

SUZANNE LIAU, Solicitor, England, Attorney at Law, California. *PRACTICE AREAS:* Company Matters; Incorporation; Joint Ventures; Negotiations; Mergers; Acquisitions; Takeovers; Reconstructions; Amalgamations; Commercial Transactions.

ELLA CHEONG & G. MIRANDAH

(In Association with K. Sukumar & Co., W. Malaysia)

111 NORTH BRIDGE ROAD
#22-01/02 PENINSULA PLAZA
SINGAPORE 0617
Telephone: (65) 3394040
Telefax: (65) 3370031
Telex: RS 42619 ELLACO

General Practice, General Litigation, Patents, Copyrights, Design and Trade Marks, Licensing and Franchising, Banking, Corporate, Conveyancing and Tax.

PARTNERS

ELLA CHEONG, School of Law (England). Also admitted to practice in Hong Kong. *PRACTICE AREAS:* Intellectual Property; Agency and Distributorship; Copyrights; Franchises and Franchising.

GLADYS MIRANDAH, LL.B., (Hons.) (Singapore). *PRACTICE AREAS:* Intellectual Property; Patents, Agency and Distributorship; Copyrights; Franchises and Franchising; Products Liability; Commercial Law.

SUKUMAR KARUPPIAH, LL.B., (Hons.) (Singapore). (Also admitted to practice in W. Malaysia). *PRACTICE AREAS:* Business Law; Company Law; Taxation, Alternative Dispute Resolution; Litigation, Antitrust and Trade Regulation.

ASSOCIATES

PONNAMPALAM SIVAKUMAR, LL.B., (Hons.) (Singapore). *PRACTICE AREAS:* Computers and Software; Consumer Law; Contracts; Negligence, Torts.

SOH KAR LIANG, LL.B., (Hons.) (Singapore). *PRACTICE AREAS:* Banks and Financing.

MICHAEL S. KRAAL, LL.B., (Hons.) (Singapore). *PRACTICE AREAS:* Immigration and Naturalization.

FREEHILL HOLLINGDALE & PAGE

Established in 1852

6 BATTERY ROAD, #13-01
SINGAPORE 0104
Telephone: (65) 225 1288
Telex: (RS) 42674
Fax: (65) 225 3314

Sydney, New South Wales, Australia Office: Level 38, MLC Centre, 19-29 Martin Place, 2000. Telephone: (02) 225 5000. International: +(612) 225 5000. Telex AA 121885. Fax: (02) 322 4000.

Canberra City, Australian Capital Territory, Australia Office: London Court, 13 London Circuit, 2601. Telephone:(06) 240 6100. International: +(616) 240 6100. Telex: AA121885. Fax: (06) 240 6222.

Melbourne, Victoria, Australia Office: 101 Collins Street, 3000. Telephone: (03) 288 1234. International: +(613) 288 1234. Telex: AA33004. Fax: (03) 288 1567.

Perth, Western Australia Office: Australia Place, 15-17 William Street, 6000. Telephone: (09) 327 5777. International: +(619) 327 5777. Telex: AA92937. Fax: (09) 322 5954.

Brisbane, Queensland, Australia Office: Central Plaza II, 66 Eagle Street, 4000. Telephone: (07) 258 6666. International: +(617) 258 6666. Fax: (07) 258 6444.

London, England Office: Birchin Court, 20 Birchin Lane, EC3V 9DJ. Telephone: (0171) 283 9006. International: +(44 171) 283 9006. Fax: (0171) 454 9650.

Hanoi, Vietnam Office: 34A Quang Trung Street. Telephone: (844) 227 839. Fax: (844) 227 909.

Ho Chi Minh City, Vietnam Office: 203 Dong Khoi Street, #3-05. Telephone: (848) 242 630; (848) 242 733. Fax: (848) 242 736.

Firm engaged in Australian and International Law Practice but not authorized to appear before the Singapore Courts or to act as Singapore Advocates and Solicitors.

MEMBERS OF FIRM IN SINGAPORE

BARRY RICHARD JOHNSTON, admitted, 1967. *Education:* University of Hobart (LL.B., Hons.). *PRACTICE AREAS:* Litigation; Funds Management; Product Liability; Trade Law; Customs Law.

(This Listing Continued)

DOUGLAS MICHAEL FRANC, admitted, 1971. *Education:* University of Birmingham (LL.B.). *LANGUAGES:* German and French. *PRACTICE AREAS:* Banking; Finance; Energy; Resources; Engineering; Construction; Mergers and Acquisitions; Taxation; Revenue.

WILLIAM GEORGE FALCONAR NAPIER, admitted, 1981. *Education:* University of Wellington (B.A., LL.B. Hons.; LL.M. Hons.); Harvard University (LL.M.). *PRACTICE AREAS:* Banking; Finance; Funds Management; Privatisation; Infrastructure.

(For Biographical data on all Firm Personnel, see Professional Biographies at Brisbane, Canberra, Melbourne, Perth and Sydney, Australia)

FRESHFIELDS

16 COLLYER QUAY #33-01
HITACHI TOWER
SINGAPORE 0104
Telephone: (65) 5356211
Fax: (65) 5335007/5338007/5339007

Other Offices in: Bangkok, Barcelona, Brussels, Frankfurt, Hanoi, Hong Kong, London, Madrid, Moscow, New York, Paris, and Tokyo.

General and International Law Practice.

RESIDENT PARTNERS

CHARLES L.A. JULY, born England, February 17, 1957; admitted, 1981, England and Wales as Solicitor (Not admitted in Singapore). *Education:* Wadham College, Oxford (B.A., Hons, 1978). *LANGUAGES:* English and French. *PRACTICE AREAS:* International Finance; Project Finance; Asset Finance; Aviation Regulation.

ROGER J. DYER, born England, 1957; admitted, 1982, England and Wales as Solicitor; Hong Kong as Advocate and Solicitor (Not admitted in Singapore). *Education:* St. Peter's College, Oxford. *Member:* Law Society; The City of London Solicitors' Company. *LANGUAGES:* English. *PRACTICE AREAS:* International Finance; Project Finance; Asset Based Lending; Corporate Restructuring Law.

(For List of Partners see Professional Biographies at London, England).

HARIDASS HO & PARTNERS

Advocates and Solicitors, Notary Public and Commissioners for Oaths

24 RAFFLES PLACES
18-00 CLIFFORD CENTRE
SINGAPORE 0104
Telephone: 533-2323
Telex: RS 42091 JUSTIS
Fax: 533-1579

Company and Commercial, Corporate, Conveyancing and Property, Computer, Banking, Finance and Securities, Arbitration/Civil and Commercial Litigation, Bankruptcy and Insolvency, Admiralty and Shipping, Insurance and Intellectual Property Law.

PARTNERS

HARIDASS AJAIB, born Singapore, September 26, 1949; admitted, 1976, Singapore. *Education:* University of London (LL.B., Hons., 1974). Barrister (Middle Temple) Comm for Oaths. *LANGUAGES:* English, Tamil and Malay. *PRACTICE AREAS:* Admiralty & Maritime Law; Banks & Banking; Commercial Law; Litigation; Transportation.

WAH ONN HO, born Singapore, December 28, 1949; admitted, 1977, Singapore. *Education:* University of Singapore (LL.B., Hons., 1973). Commissioner for Oaths. *LANGUAGES:* English, Mandarin. *PRACTICE AREAS:* Banks & Banking Corporate Law; Finance; Investments; Property; Securities.

ANWARUL HAQUE, born Singapore, December 3, 1939; admitted, 1968, Singapore. *Education:* University of Singapore (LL.B., Hons., 1964); University of London (LL.M., 1981). Notary Public. *LANGUAGES:* English, Malay. *PRACTICE AREAS:* Admiralty & Maritime; Alternative Dispute Resolution; Insurance; Litigation; Transportation.

KWOK JEN FONG, born Singapore, May 21, 1949; admitted, 1975, Singapore. *Education:* University of Singapore (LL.B., Hons, 1974). *LANGUAGES:* English and Mandarin. *PRACTICE AREAS:* Banks and Banking; Corporate Law; Finance; Investments; Property; Securities.

(This Listing Continued)

GINA LEE-WAN, born Penang, Malaysia, October 4, 1956; admitted, 1981, Singapore. *Education:* University of Kent at Canterbury (B.A., Laws, Hons., 1974). Barrister (Gray's Inn). *LANGUAGES:* English, Cantonese, Italian. *PRACTICE AREAS:* Admiralty & Maritime Law; Alternative Dispute Resolution; Litigation; Insurance; Transportation.

PATRICIA CHEE, born Singapore, August, 1949; admitted, 1985, Singapore. *Education:* University of Singapore (B.B.A., 1972); University of London (LL.B., Hons., 1982). Barrister (Lincoln's Inn). *LANGUAGES:* English. *PRACTICE AREAS:* Banks & Banking Law; Business Law; Finance; Investment; Securities.

RANDHIR RAM CHANDRA, born Singapore, January 20, 1957; admitted, 1987, Singapore. *Education:* National University of Singapore (B.Soc.Sci., Hons., 1981); Victoria University of Manchester (LL.B., Hons., 1984). Barrister (Gray's Inn). *LANGUAGES:* English & Malay. *PRACTICE AREAS:* Alternative Dispute Resolution; Business Law; Commercial Law; Intellectual Property; Litigation.

AUDREY C.E. WONG, born Singapore, May 6, 1960; admitted, 1987, Singapore. *Education:* National University of Singapore (B.B.A., 1982); University of London, London School of Economics (LL.B., Hons., 1985). Barrister (Gray's Inn). *LANGUAGES:* English & Mandarin. *PRACTICE AREAS:* Business Law; Commercial Law; Corporate; Property; Real Estate.

HEE TEAN LEONG, born Singapore. December 7, 1959; admitted, 1987, Singapore. *Education:* National University of Singapore (LL.B., Hons., 1984; LL. M., 1988). *LANGUAGES:* English, Mandarin. *PRACTICE AREAS:* Bankruptcy; Business Law; Commercial Law; Criminal Law; Insurance.

HERMAN JEREMIAH, born Singapore, September 26, 1962; admitted, 1988, Singapore. *Education:* National University of Singapore (LL.B., Hons., 1987). *LANGUAGES:* English. *PRACTICE AREAS:* Alternative Dispute Resolution; Bankruptcy; Banks & Banking; Construction Law; Litigation.

THOMAS TAN, born Singapore, September 26, 1962; admitted, 1988, Singapore. *Education:* National University of Singapore (LL.B., Hons. 1987). *LANGUAGES:* English. *PRACTICE AREAS:* Admiralty & Maritime Law; Alternative Dispute Resolution; Insurance; Litigation; Transportation.

AUGUSTINE LIEW, born Singapore, May 28, 1955; admitted, 1986, Singapore. *Education:* University of Wales (LL.B., Hons., 1983). Barrister (Inner Temple). *LANGUAGES:* English. *PRACTICE AREAS:* Admiralty & Maritime Law; Alternative Dispute Resolution; Insurance; Litigation; Transportation.

KIEN THYE LIM, born Singapore, June 2, 1960; admitted, 1986, Singapore. *Education:* National University of Singapore (LL.B., Hons., 1985; LL.M., 1989). *LANGUAGES:* English, Mandarin. *PRACTICE AREAS:* Bank & Banking; Company Law; Computers & Software; Intellectual Property; Property.

VENKITESWARAN HARIHARAN, born Singapore, July 3, 1963; admitted, 1989, Singapore. *Education:* National University of Singapore (LL.B., Hons., 1988). *LANGUAGES:* English, Tamil & Malay. *PRACTICE AREAS:* Admiralty & Maritime Law; Agency & Distributorship; Insurance; Probate; Trusts & Estates.

ASSISTANTS

LUCY B.L. KHOO, admitted, 1973. *Education:* L.L.B. (Hons). Barrister (Gray's Inn).

SURESH DAMODARA, admitted, 1990. *Education:* L.L.B. (Hons).

JEYA PUTRA PANCHARATNAM, admitted, 1990. *Education:* L.L.B. (Hons).

YOGA SHARMINI YOGARAJAH, admitted, 1990. *Education:* B.A. L.L.B. (Hons) Barrister (Middle Temple).

R. SRIVATHSAN, admitted, 1991. *Education:* B.A. L.L.B. (Hons) Barrister (Lincoln's Inn).

HUI MEI KUOK, admitted, 1991. *Education:* L.L.B. (Hons) Barrister (Lincoln's Inn).

SHING JIT YUNG, admitted, 1991. *Education:* L.L.B. (Hons) Barrister (Middle Temple).

B.J. PRAKASH, admitted, 1992. *Education:* L.L.B. (Hons).

(This Listing Continued)

BOCK HOH NG, admitted, 1993. *Education:* L.L.B. (Hons), Barrister (Gray's Inn).

RAJA BOSE, admitted, 1993. *Education:* L.L.B. (Hons).

CORINA SONG, admitted, 1993. *Education:* L.L.B. (Hons); L.L.M.

SU MIN KHOO, admitted, 1993. *Education:* B.A. (Hons); Barrister (Lincoln's Inn).

BEE HOON NG, admitted, 1993. *Education:* L.L.B. (Hons); Barrister (Middle Temple).

ERIC A.H. CHERN, admitted, 1993. *Education:* L.L.B. (Hons); Barrister (Lincoln's Inn).

PATRICK TIAN HUAT EE, admitted, 1994. *Education:* L.L.B. (Hons); Barrister (Inner Temple).

KATHERINE KIT LIN CHAN, admitted, 1993. *Education:* B.A. (Hons); Barrister (Middle Temple).

PAUL WEI HAN NG, admitted, 1994. *Education:* L.L.B. (Hons); Barrister (Inner Temple).

HELLER EHRMAN WHITE & McAULIFFE

A Partnership including Professional Corporations

50 RAFFLES PLACE
17-04 SHELL TOWER
SINGAPORE 0104
Telephone: (011) 65 538-1756
Facsimile: (011) 65 538-1737

Los Angeles, California Office: 601 S. Figueroa Street. Telephone: 213-689-0200. Facsimile: 213-614-1868.

Palo Alto, California Office: 525 University Avenue, Suite 1100. Telephone: 415-324-7000. Facsimile: 415-324-0638.

San Francisco, California Office: 333 Bush Street. Telephone: 415-772-6000. Facsimile: 415-772-6268. Cable Address: "Helpow". Telex: 340-895; 184-996.

Seattle, Washington Office: 6100 Columbia Center, 701 Fifth Avenue. Telephone: 206-447-0900. Facsimile: 206-447-0849.

Portland, Oregon Office: 1600 Koin Center, 222 S.W. Columbia Street. Telephone: 503-227-7400. Facsimile: 503-241-0950.

Anchorage, Alaska Office: 1900 Ensearch Center, 550 West 7th Avenue. Telephone: 907-277-1900. Facsimile: 907-277-1920.

Tacoma, Washington Office: 1400 First Interstate Plaza, 1201 Pacific Avenue. Telephone: 206-572-6666. Facsimile: 206-572-6743.

Washington, D.C. Office: The Southern Building, 805 15th Street, N.W., Suite 610. Telephone: 202-842-1700. Facsimile: 202-842-4080.

Hong Kong Office: 2816-17 Jardine House, 1 Connaught Place, Central, Hong Kong. Telephone: (011) 852-2526-6381. Facsimile: (011) 852-2810-6242.

General Practice.

SPECIAL COUNSEL

M. KATHRYN MARIETTA, born Casa Grande, Arizona, November 27, 1958; admitted, 1985, California (Not admitted in Singapore). *Education:* California Polytechnic State University (B.S., 1981); Southern California Institute of Law (J.D., 1985).

FREDERICK W. TAYLOR, JR., born Cleveland, Ohio, October 21, 1933; admitted, 1968, New York; 1969, California (Not admitted in Singapore). *Education:* University of Florida (B.A., in History, 1957); University of Michigan (M.A., in Near Eastern Studies, 1959); New York University School of Law (J.D., cum laude, 1967); Harvard Business School (A.M.P., 1974). Publications: Who's Who in American Law; Who's Who in the World; Who's Who in the Asian Pacific Rim. *LANGUAGES:* Arabic. *PRACTICE AREAS:* International Commercial Transactions; Banking Law; Arbitration.

(For complete biographical data on Anchorage, Alaska, Los Angeles, California, Palo Alto, California, San Francisco, California, Washington, D.C., Portland, Oregon, Seattle, Washington, Tacoma, Washington and Hong Kong office personnel, see Professional Biographies at each of those cities)

HILBORNE, HAWKIN & CO.

Legal Consultants, Advocates and Solicitors

Trademark, Copyright & Patent Agents

Established in 1965

*SINGAPORE SERVICE ADDRESS FOR TRADEMARK
REGISTRATION:*

*C/O LOKE & SEAH, 3 SHENTON WAY, # 21-10, SHENTON
HOUSE*

SINGAPORE 0106

Telephone: 65-223-7088

Facsimile: 65-223-7028

Orange, California Administrative Office: 2534 N. Santiago Blvd., 92667. Telephone: (714) 283-1155. Fax: (714) 283-1555; 532-2713.

Brunei Service Address for Trademark Registration: Room 31, 3rd Floor, Britannia House, 38 Jalan Cator, Bandar Seri Begawan 2085, Brunei Darussalam. Telephone: 6732-228382. Facsimile: 6732-228389.

Malaysia Service Address for Trademark Registration: Lots 1708/9, 17th Floor Wisma Hla, Jalan Rajah Chulan, 50200, Kuala Lumpur, West Malaysia. Telephone: 03-2414823. Facsimile: 03-241-4641.

Hong Kong Office : M2-3 New Henry House, 10, Ice House Street, Central, Hong Kong. Telephone: 852-869-0828. Facsimile: 852-810-1703.

FIRM PROFILE: *The firm's clientele consists of multi-national corporations and select "private and entrenched" individuals. Founded in 1965, the firm offers a full range of legal services and is well known internationally in areas of intellectual property, licensing, franchising, joint ventures and international business transactions. Subject to local bar rules, the firm accepts instructions for representation in Singapore, Malaysia, Brunei, Hong Kong, England and Wales.*

MEMBERS OF FIRM

VINI KUMAR, born 1935; admitted, 1965, Malaysia; 1966, Brunei; 1969, Singapore; 1961, England and Wales. Certified as a Legal Consultant by the State Bars of New York and California for these jurisdictions.

ALAN H. DAY, born 1943; admitted, 1971, England and Wales; 1972, Hong Kong.

OF COUNSEL

KEITH E. KLINE, born 1955; admitted, 1986, California. Registered Patent Attorney (USPTO).

Please direct all inquiries to our Administrative Office in California, USA.

HOLMAN, FENWICK & WILLAN

10 COLLYER QUAY

#08-02 OCEAN BUILDING

SINGAPORE 0104

Telephone: 534-0195

Telex: HFWSIN RS 26188;

Telefax: 534 5864

London, England Office: Marlow House, Lloyds Avenue, EC3N 3AL. Telephone: 0171-488-2300. Telex: 8812247 HFWLON. Telefax: 0171-481-0316.

Paris, France Office: 3 Rue la Boëtie, 75008. Telephone: 44-94-40-50. Telex: 281699F HFWPA A. Telefax: 42-65-46-25.

Hong Kong Office: 1418 Two Pacific Place, 88 Queensway. Telephone: 2522 3006. Telex: 63536 HFWHK HX. Telefax: 2887 8110.

Piraeus, Greece Office: 6th Floor, 86 Filonos Street. Telephone: 429-3978. Telefax: 429-3118.

Rouen, France Office: 47 Avenue Gustave Flaubert, 76000. Telephone: 32.08.18.60. Telefax: 35.89.90.54.

English solicitors: Advice on English Law, International Maritime and Commercial law firm providing legal advice on Admiralty, all aspects of Maritime Law, International Trade, Insurance and Reinsurance, Ship Finance, General Corporate and Banking.

RESIDENT PARTNERS

PAUL T. ASTON. PRACTICE AREAS: Admiralty and Maritime Law; P and I Clubs; International Trade; Offshore Pollution.

(This Listing Continued)

PAUL A.J. SUPRAMANIAM. PRACTICE AREAS: Ship Finance; Corporate Law, International Finance; Corporate Law, International Corporate; Corporate Law, Privatization; Corporate Law, Securitization.

Languages: English, Malay and Tamil

(For Complete List of Partners, see Professional Biographies at London, England)

KHATTAR WONG & PARTNERS

Established in 1975

80 RAFFLES PLACE #25-01

UOB PLAZA 1

SINGAPORE 0104

*Telephone: (65) 535 6844; Telefax: Banking: (65) 534 4892;
Building/Engineering: (65) 538 8196; Conveyancing: (65) 533 0585;
Corporate: (65) 534 1909;
Litigation: (65) 535 1030; Intellectual Property: (65) 533 0283;
Shipping: (65) 535 1606; Tax: (65) 534 1090
Telex: RS 24896 KHAWONG*

FIRM PROFILE: *The firm was established in 1975. The firm offers services in virtually every facet of the law. The main areas of legal practice serviced by the firm are as follows: Arbitration, Banking and Finance, China Practice, Civil and Commercial Litigation, Commercial Tenancies, Construction and Engineering, Conveyancing and Property Law, Corporate and Securities Law, Estates and Succession, Family Law, Immigration, Industrial Relations and Employment, Insolvency and Bankruptcy, Insurance, Intellectual Property and Technology, International Business Transactions, International Finance and Capital Markets, Joint Ventures, Medical Law, Privatisation, Project Development and Project Finance, Shipping, Admiralty and Ship Finance, Tax and Tax Planning.*

MEMBERS OF FIRM

SAT PAL KHATTAR. PRACTICE AREAS: Tax Law; Tax Planning.

DR. DAVID S.Y. WONG. PRACTICE AREAS: Banking; Finance.

ABDUL RASHID GANI. PRACTICE AREAS: Insurance.

RAJAN MENON. PRACTICE AREAS: Banking and Finance.

LEE KIM SAN. PRACTICE AREAS: Conveyancing; Property Law.

KONG SENG CHOU. PRACTICE AREAS: Conveyancing; Property Law.

CHANG SEE HIANG. PRACTICE AREAS: Corporate; Securities Law.

LIM YEN LAN. PRACTICE AREAS: Family; Matrimonial Law.

ANNABEL ESS. PRACTICE AREAS: International Business Transactions.

DEBORAH BARKER. PRACTICE AREAS: Insolvency; Bankruptcy.

SCOTT THILLAGARATNAM. PRACTICE AREAS: Civil and Commercial Litigation.

CERINTHA CHIA. PRACTICE AREAS: Banking and Finance.

K. JAYA PRAKASH. PRACTICE AREAS: Shipping Admiralty; Ship Finance.

SIA SUAT HWA. PRACTICE AREAS: China Practice.

YANG LIH SHYNG. PRACTICE AREAS: Arbitration.

SIMON YUEN. PRACTICE AREAS: Industrial Relations; Employment.

MARGARET HAUW. PRACTICE AREAS: International Business Transactions.

LEONG KUM KWOK. PRACTICE AREAS: Project Development; Project Finance.

MAJ. LESLIE CHEW. PRACTICE AREAS: Arbitration; Civil and Commercial Litigation; Medical Law.

ANNE CHUA. PRACTICE AREAS: Commercial Tenancies.

LOUISE TAN. PRACTICE AREAS: Project Development; Project Finance.

CHRISTINA YEO

RAYMOND GWEE. PRACTICE AREAS: Privatisation.

(This Listing Continued)

CLAIRE LIM. PRACTICE AREAS: Capital Markets; International Finance.

SABINA SOH. PRACTICE AREAS: Joint Ventures.

JAMES POLYCARP LOW. PRACTICE AREAS: Joint Ventures.

GURBACHAN SINGH. PRACTICE AREAS: Estates; Succession; Immigration.

ROBERT WONG. PRACTICE AREAS: Corporate; Securities Law.

JOYCE A. TAN. PRACTICE AREAS: Intellectual Property; Technology.

CHAN SWEE CHIN. PRACTICE AREAS: Commercial Tenancies.

GWENDOLINE ONG

WANG YI SHING. PRACTICE AREAS: China Practice.

DANNY CHUA

AXEL CHAN

PARMINDER KAUR

TIM OEI

ADRIAN HUANG

RACHEL LEONG

CHYE KIT MIN

LATIFF IBRAHIM. PRACTICE AREAS: Construction; Engineering.

ERIC LOW

TAN WOON TIANG

TAN ENG SOON

JACQUELINE WOO

DEBORAH LI

CHARLES EZEKIEL

JOHNNY CHEO

ANITA FAM

LAU LI-CHOO

JEFF LEONG

LINDA T.C. CHEE

PRITHIPAL SINGH

YOW LOCK SEN

SENIOR ASSISTANTS

Madelene Sng	Valerie Ong
June L. M. Low	Jainil Bhandari
Serena Lim	Dennis Heng
Victor Sim	Gerard J.H. Seah
Timothy Tan	Steven Fung
Jacqueline Yih	Wong Chiang Hon
Wilson Tan	Zaid Hamzah

ASSISTANTS

Choo Li Li	Angeline Poon
Chang Mun Loong	Chia Kim Huat
Stuart Ong	James Lau Oon Beng
Malcolm K.L. Lim	Eudora Tan
Nambi J. Viswalingam	Ng Phay Chim
Grace Ooi	Kenny Poon
Sim Sze Kuan	Valerie Cheah
Moira Khaw	Elaine Chan
Guai Siew Ping	Amanda J. Foo
Marian W.M. Ho	Preetha Pillai
Kuah Boon Theng	Ranitha Chandran
Tan Lay Pheng	Janice Ngeow
Teo Weng Kie	Elvin Wan
Leong Kah Wah	Wang Tiak Kweng
Eunice Phua	Shashi Nathan
Yeong Wai Cheong	Ronnie C.L. Wai
Yong Po Wer	Dorothy Yeo
Rema Sreedharan	Lina Lau
Isoo Tan	Thong Huey Yann
Tan Li Lee	Martin Chee

(This Listing Continued)

Amita Dutt	Gwendolyn Lee
Michael Tan	Matthias Lee
Koh Chu Li	Terence Lim
Yap Chew Fern	Nor Azman Hamid
Bernard Ang	Shyami Rajalingam
Kenny Chooi	Jill Saddique
Pearl Lim	Wee Meng Seng
Tan Sui Lin	Angelina Wong
Shantini Tharmanason	Stefanie Yuen Thio
Boon Chin Aun	Ho Soo Lih
Lee Yueh Fang	Eric Tan Poh Lee
Lionel Tay Yew Jin	Surene Virabhak
Ooi Siew Pheng	Christopher Da Costa

Languages: English, Mandarin, Malay and Japanese.

LINKLATERS & PAINES

Established in 1992

6 BATTERY ROAD #36-01
SINGAPORE 0104
Telephone: (65) 221 1110
Telex: 33320
Fax: (65) 221 3334

London, England Office: Barrington House, 59-67 Gresham Street, EC2V 7JA. Telephone: 0171-606-7080. Cable Address: Linklaters, London, EC2V 7JA. Telegrams: Linklaters, London. Telex: 884349. Fax: 0171-606 5113.

General Practice.

RESIDENT PARTNERS

Christopher W. McFadzean

Ian Arstall

(For full list of offices see entry at London, England)

LOEFF CLAEYS VERBEKE

20 RAFFLES PLACE, #08-03
OCEAN TOWERS
SINGAPORE 0104
Telephone: 64-5335332
Fax: 65-5330313

Amsterdam, The Netherlands Office: 15 Apollolaan, P.O. Box 75088, 1070 AB. Telephone: 31-20-5741200. Telex: 14292 LEX NL. Telecopier: 31-20-6718775.

Brussels, Belgium Office: 268 A Avenue de Tervueren, A-1150. Telephone: 02-778.22.11. Telecopier: 02-763.21.85.

Antwerp, Belgium Office: "De Hertoghe," 8th Floor, 92 Disguinlei, B.8, B-2018. Telephone: 32.3.2385656. Telex: 72748 (EURLAWB). Telecopier: 32.3.2387877.

Liege, Belgium Office: 13, Rue Simonon, (Place de Bronckart), B-4000. Telephone: 32-41-527722. Telecopier: 32-41-527511.

New York, New York Office: Swiss Bank Tower, 23rd Floor, 10 East 50th Street, 10022. Telephone: 212-759-9000. Fax: 212-759-9018.

Paris, France Office: 1, Avenue Franklin D. Roosevelt, 75008. Telephone: 33-1-49539125. Telecopier: 33-1-42891460.

Rotterdam, The Netherlands Office: 70 Weena, P.O. Box 74, 3000 AB. Telephone: 31-10-4034777. Telex: 23395 (LEX NL). Telecopier: 31-10-4149388.

Tokyo, Japan Office: NSE Building, 5th Floor, 1-7-1 Kanda Jinbo-cho, Chiyoda-ku, Tokyo 101, Japan. Telephone: 81-3-32599831. Fax: 81-3-32599888.

Barcelona, Spain Office: 550, 4° 1A, Av. Diagonal, 08021. Telephone: 34-3-2007117. Telecopier: 34-3-2023098.

Madrid, Spain Office: Balañá Eguía, Antonio Mauro 7, 5°, 28014. Telephone: 34-1-5312501. Telecopier: 34-1-5313530.

Jakarta, Indonesia Associated Office: Ali Budiardjo, Nugroho, Reksodiputro, Niaga Tower, 24th floor, Jalan Jenderal Sudirman Kav. 58, 12920. Telephone: 62.21.2505125/2505136, Telecopier: 62.21.2505121/2505001.

Luxembourg, Luxembourg Correspondent Office: Zeyen Beghin Feider. 67, Rue Ermesinde, P.O. Box 5017, 1050. Telephone: 352.468946. Telecopier: 352.468947.

(This Listing Continued)

LOEFF CLAEYS VERBEKE, Singapore—*Continued*

Dutch attorneys may represent clients before all Dutch Courts, before the European Court of Justice and the Benelux Court of Justice, and are admitted to plead before all Courts of the member states of the Common Market (EEC).

ASSOCIATES

ALEXANDER G.F.M. ALTING VON GEUSAU, born 1962; admitted, 1986, Rotterdam. *Education:* University of Steubenville, Ohio (School of Economics, 1981-1982); Leyden University (1986). New York Office, 1986-1989; Rotterdam Office, 1989-1993. *Member:* The Association of the Bar of the City of New York.

Languages: Dutch, English, French, German, Italian, Japanese, Russian and Spanish.

(For Personnel and other data, see Professional Biographies at Amsterdam, Antwerp, Barcelona, Brussels, Liège, New York, Paris, Rotterdam and Tokyo)

ARTHUR LOKE & PARTNERS

Advocates and Solicitors, Notary Public and Commissioner for Oath,

Trademark and Patent Agents

Established in 1981

21 COLLYER QUAY #15-01
HONGKONG BANK BUILDING
SINGAPORE 0104
Telephone: (65) 224-7166
Fax: (65) 2226842

Investment Laws, Mergers and Acquisitions, Corporate, Securities, Tax, International Trade, Employment, Banking, Real Estate, Intellectual Property, Construction, Leisure and Entertainment, Litigation and Arbitration.

FIRM PROFILE: *The firm was founded in 1981 by Arthur Loke.*

Our clients range from significant Singapore public companies and multinational companies and their privately held counterparts to small businesses and individual investors. Our clients consult us on Singapore matters and also on regional transactions originating from South East Asia, Hong Kong and China. We work closely with other professional service firms including accounting firms, management consultancies and both local and foreign law firms.

All lawyers in the firm speak and write excellent English, and many lawyers communicate effectively in Chinese and Malay.

PARTNERS

ARTHUR LOKE, LL.B. (Hons.) (Singapore); Notary Public and Commissioner for Oaths, Singapore, also admitted in Western Australia. *PRACTICE AREAS:* Corporate and Commercial Transactions; Leisure and Entertainment.

TERESA HANGCHI, LL.B. (Hons.) (Singapore), LL.M. (London). *PRACTICE AREAS:* Intellectual Property.

STANLEY JEREMIAH, LL.B. (Hons) (London), LL.M. (London), Barrister-at-Law, England. ACI Arb, ACII. *PRACTICE AREAS:* Insurance Law; Conveyancing; Real Estate; Commercial Law.

JASMINE TAN CHIN CHWEE, LL.B. (Hons) (Singapore). *PRACTICE AREAS:* Conveyancing; Real Estate.

TAN SEI BEE, LL.B. (Hons.) (London), Barrister-at-Law, England. *PRACTICE AREAS:* Corporate and Commercial Litigation.

THAM KIT WAN, LL.B. (Hons) (Singapore). *PRACTICE AREAS:* Commercial Law.

JANET WEE, LL.B. (Hons.) (Singapore). *PRACTICE AREAS:* Conveyancing; Real Estate.

WONG YU CHIEN, LL.B. (Hons) (Singapore). *PRACTICE AREAS:* General Litigation; Family Law.

ASSOCIATES

PAMELA CHONG, LL.B. (Hons) (Birmingham); Barrister-at-law, England. *PRACTICE AREAS:* General Litigation; Conveyancing; Real Estate.

SHARON KHONG, LL.B. (Hons) (Singapore). *PRACTICE AREAS:* Conveyancing; Real Estate.

(This Listing Continued)

JAYNE LIM, LL.B. (Hons) (Singapore). *PRACTICE AREAS:* Conveyancing; Real Estate.

DENNIS LUI, LL.B. (Hons) (London), LL.M. (London). *PRACTICE AREAS:* Corporate; Banking; Commercial Law.

SHANTI JAWHARILAL, LL.B. (Hons) (Singapore). *PRACTICE AREAS:* Civil Litigation; Insurance Law; Family Law.

YUEN MEI SUM, LL.B. (Hons.) (Singapore). *PRACTICE AREAS:* Conveyancing; Real Estate.

CONSULTANT

MS. CAROL ANNE MEI LING TAN, LL.B. (Hons) (National University of Singapore); admitted, 1987, Singapore. *PRACTICE AREAS:* Consumer Property Financing; Conveyancing; Property Transactions; Probate; Administration of Estates; Succession; Project Financing.

MALLESONS STEPHEN JAQUES

LEVEL 36, 16 RAFFLES QUAY
HONG LEONG BUILDING
SINGAPORE 0104
Telephone: (65) 321 8930
Fax: (65) 225 9060

Sydney, Australia Office: Level 60, Governor Phillip Tower, 1 Farrer Place, 2000. Telephone: (612) 250 3000. Fax: (612) 250 3133.

Melbourne, Australia Office: Level 28, Rialto, 525 Collins Street, 3000. Telephone: (613) 619 0619. Fax: (613) 614 1329.

Perth, Australia Office: Ground Floor, St. Georges Square, 225 St. George's Terrace, 6000. Telephone: (619) 324 8333. Fax: (619) 3211017.

Brisbane, Australia Office: Level 30, Waterfront Place, 1 Eagle Street, 4000. Telephone: (617) 231 7500. Fax: (617) 221 1211.

Canberra, Australia Office: Level 10, Advance Bank Centre, 60 Marcus Clarke Street, 2601. Telephone: (616) 268 3900. Fax: (616) 257 3100.

Hong Kong Office: Bateson Starr in association with Mallesons Stephen Jaques, Suite 801, Asia Pacific Finance Tower, Citibank Plaza, 3 Garden Road, Central Hong Kong. Telephone: (852) 848 4600. Fax: (852) 868-0124.

Beijing, The Peoples Republic of China Office: Suite 701, Scite Tower, 22 Jianguomenwai Street, 100004. Telephone: (861) 5123565 ext. 701. Fax: (861) 5232018.

Taipei, Taiwan Office: 14th Floor, Mallesons Stephen Jaques, 138 Min Sheng East Road, Sec 3. Telephone: (8862) 712 5808. Fax: (8862) 712 9080.

Jakarta, Indonesia Associated Office: Law Firm Kartini Muljadi S.H. & Associates, in association with Mallesons Stephen Jaques, Level 5, Bina Mulia I Building, J1 J.R. Rasuna Said Kav 10, 12950. Telephone: (6221) 5256968. Fax: (6221) 5255561.

Port Moresby, Papua New Guinea Office: Beresford Love, agents for Mallesons Stephen Jaques, Level 3, Hunter Building, Hunter Street. Telephone: (675) 211942. Fax: (675) 211586.

London, England Office: 2nd Floor, Aldermary House, 10-15 Queen Street, EC4N 1TX. Telephone: (44 171) 9820982. Fax: (44 171) 9829820.

New York, New York, U.S.A. Office: 9th floor, Suite 911, 609 Fifth Avenue, 10017-1021. Telephone: (1-212) 319-9500. Fax: (1-212) 319-9506.

CONTACT PARTNER

David Olsson

(For Complete Personnel, see Biographical Card at Sydney, Australia).

MILBANK, TWEED, HADLEY & McCLOY

14-02 CALTEX HOUSE
30 RAFFLES PLACE
SINGAPORE 0104
Telephone: 65-534-1700
Fax: 65-534-2733
ABA/net: EDNANG

New York, New York Office: 1 Chase Manhattan Plaza, 10005. Telephone: 212-530-5000. Cable Address: "Miltweed NYK" ITT: 422962; 423893. Fax: 212- 530-5219. ABA/net: Milbank NY.

(This Listing Continued)

Midtown Office: 50 Rockefeller Plaza, 10020. Telephone: 212-530-5800. Fax: 212-530-0158.

Los Angeles, California Office: 601 South Figueroa Street, 30th Floor, 90017. Telephone: 213-892-4000. Fax: 213-629-5063. Telex: 678754. ABA/net: Milbank LA.

Washington, D.C. Office: Suite 1100, 1825 Eye Street, N.W., 20006. Telephone: 202-835-7500. Cable Address: "Miltweed Wsh". ITT 440667. Fax: 202-835-7586. ABA/net: Milbank DC.

Tokyo, Japan Office: Nippon Press Center Building, 2-1 Uchisaiwai-cho 2-chome, Chiyoda-ku, Tokyo 100. Telephone: 81-3-3504-1050. Fax: 81-3-3595-2790, 81-3-3502-5192.

London, England Office: Ropemaker Place, 25 Ropemaker Street, EC2Y 9AS. Telephone: 44-171-374-0423. Cable Address: Miltuk G." Fax: 44-171-374-0912.

Hong Kong Office: 3007 Alexandra House, 16 Chater Road. Telephone: 8522-526-5281. Fax: 852-2840-0792, 852-2845-9046. ABA/net: Milbank HK.

Moscow, Russia Office: 28 Pokrovka Street, 1st Floor, Moscow, 103062. International Telephone: 7-502-220-4776. International Fax: 7-502-220-4617. Local Telephone: 7-095-956-37507. Local Telephone/Fax: 7-095-956-3991.

Jakarta, Indonesia Correspondent Office: Makarim & Tiara S., 17th Floor, Summitmas Tower, Jl, Jend. Sudirman 61, Jakarta. Telephone: 62-211252-1272 or 2460. Fax: 62-21-252-2750 or 2751.

General Practice. Firm engaged in American and International Law Practice, but not authorized to appear before the Singapore Courts or to act as Singapore Advocates and Solicitors.

PARTNERS

GLENN S. GERSTELL, born New York, New York, 1951; admitted, 1977, New York; 1981, District of Columbia (Not admitted in Singapore). *Education:* New York University (B.A., 1974); Columbia (J.D., 1976). Adjunct Professor of Law, Georgetown University Law School, 1985-1987. Adjunct Assistant Professor, New York Law School, 1980. (Resident in Hong Kong Office).

THOMAS B. SIEBENS, born Bonn, Germany, 1951; admitted, 1977, District of Columbia; 1979, Pennsylvania; 1981, New York (Not admitted in Singapore). *Education:* Yale (B.A., 1973); George Washington University (J.D., 1976). *Member:* The District of Columbia Bar; International Bar Association.

GARY S. WIGMORE, born St. Louis, Missouri, January 26, 1952; admitted, 1983, New York (Not admitted in Singapore). *Education:* Oneonta State College (B.A., 1974); Carnegie-Mellon University (M.S., 1977); Fordham University (J.D., 1982). *Member:* New York State Bar Association.

ASSOCIATES

CAROLINE G. ANGOORLY, born Iraq, 1964; admitted, 1988, Victoria, Australia (Not admitted in Singapore). *Education:* Monash University (B.Sc., 1985; LL.B. Hons., 1987). *Member:* International Bar Association (Member, Section on Energy and Natural resources Law).

RENISHA BHARVANI, born Hong Kong, 1968; admitted, 1993, United Kingdom; 1994, Singapore. *Education:* University of Bristol, Bristol, England (LL.B., Honours, 1991). *LANGUAGES:* French, Cantonese.

SABURABI NILA IBRAHIM, born Singapore, 1956; admitted, 1988, New York (Not admitted in Singapore). *Education:* University of Singapore (LL.B., 1980); New York University (LL.M., 1986). *Member:* New York State Bar Association. *LANGUAGES:* Malay, Indonesia and Spanish.

MOCHTAR, KARUWIN & KOMAR

SHELL TOWER, 22-06
50 RAFFLES PLACE
SINGAPORE 0104
Telephone: 2253311
Telex: RS 28322 Karwin
Facsimile: 223-2191

Jakarta, Indonesia Office: Wisma Metropolitan II, 14th Floor, Jalan Jenderal Sudirman Kav. 31, P.O. Box 2844. Telephone: 5711130. Cable Address: "Karuwin," Jakarta. Telex: 65611 KARWIN IA. Facsimile: 571-1162; 570-1686.

Associated San Francisco, California Office: Anthony F. Granucci, 20th Floor, One Sansome Street, 94104. Telephone: 415-951-4609. Facsimile: 415-921-3993.

(This Listing Continued)

Practice Limited to Matters of Indonesian, Comparative and International Law.

Firm not authorized to appear before Singapore Courts or to act as Singapore Advocates and Solicitors.

DR. KOMAR, born Bandung, Indonesia, 1938. *Education:* Faculty of Law and Social Sciences, Padjadjaran University (S.H., 1962); University of California at Berkeley (LL.M., 1969); Padjadjaran University (S.J.D., 1981). Member, Faculty of Law, Padjadjaran University. Secretary General, ASEAN Law Association, 1986-1989. Member, Panel of Arbitrators and Conciliators, ICSID, 1989—. Private Practice, Bandung, Indonesia, 1963-1968. *Member:* Indonesian Lawyers Association. *LANGUAGES:* Indonesian, English and Dutch.

SIDIK SURAPUTRA, born Jakarta, Indonesia, 1936. *Education:* Faculty of Law and Social Sciences, University of Indonesia (S.H., 1961); Institute of Social Study, The Hague, Holland (graduate study, 1966-1967); Faculty of Law, University of Leiden, Holland (1967-1968); University of Indonesia (S.J.D., 1988). Lecturer on International Law, University of Indonesia. *Member:* Indonesian Bar Association. *LANGUAGES:* Indonesian, English and Dutch.

CRAIG M. HEGGIE, born Lanark, Scotland, 1958; admitted, 1983, As a Solicitor, Scotland; 1990, England (Not admitted in Singapore). *Education:* University of Glasgow (LL.B. Hons., 1980). Private Practice with Maclay Murray & Spens, Glasgow, 1982-1985; Sinclair Roche & Temperley, London and Singapore, 1985-1993.

GITA TIFFANY BOER, born Vienna, Austria, 1966. *Education:* Faculty of Law, University of Indonesia (S.H., 1989); American University, Washington College of Law (LL.M., 1993). *LANGUAGES:* Indonesian and English.

NAUTA DUTILH

Attorneys, Civil Law Notaries, Tax Advisers
CITY HOUSE #07-06
36, ROBINSON ROAD
SINGAPORE 0106
Telephone: (65) 2241932
Telecopier: (65) 2224724

ASSOCIATES ATTORNEYS AT LAW

JAAP J. TROMMEL, born 1958; admitted, 1986, The Netherlands (Not admitted in Singapore). *Education:* Utrecht University.

AUKJE A. VAN AMERONGEN-NIJDAM, born 1943; admitted, 1989, The Netherlands (Not admitted in Singapore). *Education:* Amsterdam University.

(For Complete Biographical Data on all Personnel, see Professional Biographies at Rotterdam, The Netherlands)

NORTON ROSE

(In Association with Lee & Lee)
5 SHENTON WAY
#33-08 UIC BUILDING
33RD FLOOR
SINGAPORE 0106
Telephone: +65 2237311
Telex: NOPURA RS 28880
Fax: +65 2245758

Other Offices: London, Bahrain, Brussels, Hong Kong, Moscow, Paris, Piraeus and Prague.

FIRM PROFILE: Norton Rose is a leading City and International law firm with its principal office in the City of London. The firm provides a wide range of legal services primarily to the business and financial communities as well as to a number of sovereign governments and state organizations. We are known particularly for our corporate and debt finance, banking, company and commercial law, natural resources, insurance, property development, aerospace and maritime practices and wide-ranging expertise on tax matters. Norton Rose has a major litigation department handling all forms of commercial dispute resolution.

In Singapore the firm specialises in aerospace finance; banking; capital markets; construction and engineering; corporate finance; joint ventures privatisation; project finance; ship finance.

(This Listing Continued)

NORTON ROSE, *Singapore—Continued*

RESIDENT PARTNERS

JAMIESON J. LOGIE, admitted, 1984, England and Wales. *PRACTICE AREAS:* Banking; Capital Markets; Project Finance; Assets Finance; Aerospace Finance; Ship Finance.

Languages: English and French

(For Complete Biographical Data on all Personnel, see Professional Biographies at London, England).

OSLER RENAULT

Canadian Advocates and Solicitors.

65 CHULIA STREET
#40-05 OCBC CENTRE
SINGAPORE 0104
Telephone: (65) 538-2077
Fax: (65) 538-2977

London, England Office: Osler Renault* - 20 Little Britain, London, EC1A 7DH. Telephone: 071-606-0777. Fax: 071-606-0222.
Paris, France Office: Osler Renault* - 4, rue Bayard, 75008 Paris. Telephone: 33-1.42.89.00.54. Fax: 33-1.42.89.51.60.
New York, N.Y. Office: Olser Renault* - 200 Park Avenue, Suite 3217, 10166-0193. Telephone: 212-867-5800. Fax: 212-867-5802.
Hong Kong Office: Osler Renault* - Suite 1708, One Pacific Place, 88 Queensway, Hong Kong. Telephone: 011-852-2877-3933. Fax: 011-852-2877-0866.
*Osler Renault is an international partnership of Osler, Hoskin & Harcourt and Ogilvy Renault.
Osler, Hoskin & Harcourt has offices at: P.O. Box 50, 1 First Canadian Place, Toronto, Ontario, Canada M5X 1B8. Telephone: 416-362-2111. Fax: 416-862-6666 and 50 O'Connor Street, Suite 1500, Ottawa, Ontario, Canada K1P 6L2. Telephone: 613-235-7234. Fax: 613-235-2867.
Ogilvy Renault has offices at: 1981 McGill College Avenue, Suite 1100, Montreal, Quebec, Canada H3A 3C1. Telephone: 514-847-4747. Fax: 514-286-5474 and Suite 1600, 45 O'Connor Street, Ottawa, Ontario, Canada K1P 1A4. Telephone: 613-780-8661. Fax: 613-230-5459 and 500 Grande-Allée Est, Suite 520, Quebec, Quebec G1R 2J7. Telephone: 418-640-5000. Fax: 418-640-1500.

General Canadian and International Practice but not authorized to appear before the Singapore Courts or to act as Singapore Advocates and Solicitors.

RESIDENT IN SINGAPORE

FRANCA CIAMBELLA, born Montreal, Quebec, 1962; admitted, 1990, Quebec (Not admitted in Singapore). *Education:* McGill University (B.Com., 1984; Common Law, 1989); University of Ottawa (L.L.L., 1987).

RAJAH & TANN

NO 4 BATTERY ROAD #15-00 & #16-00
BANK OF CHINA BUILDING
SINGAPORE 0104
Telephone: 5353600
Telex: TEETEE RS 20026
Fax: 5331183 & 5330827

FIRM PROFILE: The firm traces its roots to 1953 and has, in the course of a practice spanning over four decades, established a firm foundation in all major commercial disciplines. The litigation arm of the practice engages in an extensive range of contentious civil matters which include banking, insurance, building and construction disputes, tort, shipping, insolvency, arbitration, corporate litigation and other contract-based disputes. The conveyancing and corporate departments together cover property related transactions, incorporations and corporate secretarial work, preparation of joint-venture and other commercial agreements (with both a domestic and cross-border flavour) and also render advice and services in relation to other corporate, securities, trusts, intellectual property and tax matters, and in relation to financing (including ship-financing) arrangements. The practice presently comprises 25 lawyers and includes major banks, insurance companies, and statutory boards among its clients.

(This Listing Continued)

The contact partners are V K Rajah and Lee Law See.

PARTNERS

T.T. Rajah	Brij Raj Rai
V.K. Rajah	Ong Hway Cheng
Lee Lay See	Margaret Chin
Kee Lay Lian	Ng Hwee Chong

ASSISTANTS

Ng Puay Joo	Eric Chan
Vathani Y	Veronica Lai
Raymond Clement	Patricia Ong
Rebecca Chew	Lee Yean-Lin
Maureen Ann	Benjamin Ang
Grace Khor	Catherine Yeo
Aurill Kam	Ho Seng Chee
Koh Li Hia	Steven Lim
Loh Hsiu Lien	

RODYK & DAVIDSON

Advocates and Solicitors, Notaries Public, Commissioners for Oaths,

Trade Mark and Patent Agents

6 BATTERY ROAD, #38-01
SINGAPORE 0104
Telephone: (65) 2252626 (15 lines); 2206554
Telex: "ROANDA" RS 24295
Cable: "KYDOR" Singapore
Telefax: (G2/G3) (65) 2251838; 2257511; 2216308

Admiralty and Shipping Law, Arbitration, Banking and Finance, Building and Construction Practice, Civil Litigation Practice, Conveyancing and Property Law, Commercial Law, Computer Law, Corporate including Company Incorporation, Corporate Secretarial Work, Mergers and Acquisitions, Flotations, Joint-Venture Agreements and Restructuring, Entertainment Law, Intellectual Property Law including Copyright, Trademark and Patent Registration, International Business Transactions and Financing, Probate and Administration of Estates, Public and Private International Law, Tax Practice and Planning, Trust Structuring and the Administration of Trusts.

PARTNERS

YONG WHEE CHOO, LL.B. (Hons) Singapore (Sr. Managing Partner). *PRACTICE AREAS:* Banking and International Transactions; Real Property; Conveyancing.

DENNIS MAHENDRAN SINGHAM, LL.B. (Hons) (Lond) LL.M. A.K.C. (Lond) Barr-at-Law (Inner Temple, Eng). *PRACTICE AREAS:* Litigation and Arbitration; Family Law; Probate and Administration; Tax Planning and Practice; China, India & Myanmar Investment.

WOON LAI KENG, LL.B. (Hons) Singapore. *PRACTICE AREAS:* Real Property and Conveyancing/Projects Development.

LEE AI MING, LL.B. (Hons) Singapore. *PRACTICE AREAS:* Information Technology; Intellectual Property.

NORMAN HO KOK BENG, LL.B. (Hons) Singapore LL.M. (Lond). *PRACTICE AREAS:* Banking; International Transactions; Real Property and Conveyancing.

GOVINDARAJALU ASOKAN, LL.B. (Hons) Singapore LL.M. (Southampton). *PRACTICE AREAS:* Admiralty and Shipping/Insurance; Litigation and Arbitration; Ship Mortgage and Financing.

DIANE NG LEE MENG, LL.B. (Hons) Singapore LL.M. (Lond). *PRACTICE AREAS:* Real Property and Conveyancing; Ship Mortgage and Financing.

LOK VI MING, LL.B. (Hons) Singapore. *PRACTICE AREAS:* Litigation and Arbitration; Admiralty and Shipping.

LOW CHAI CHONG, LL.B. (Hons) Singapore. *PRACTICE AREAS:* Litigation and Arbitration; Admiralty and Shipping/Insurance; Family Law; Probate and Administration.

SIVAGNANARATNAM SIVANESAN, LL.B. (Hons) Singapore. *PRACTICE AREAS:* Company and Corporate Finance; China, India and Myanmar Investment.

(This Listing Continued)

GERALD BALENDRAN SINGHAM, LL.B. (Hons) (Lond) LL.M. (Corp/Comm) (Lond) Barr-at-Law (Lincoln's Inn, England). *PRACTICE AREAS:* Company and Corporate Finance; Joint Ventures; Indian Investment.

JACQUELINE LOKE MUN-TZE, LL.B. (Hons) (Buckingham) Barr-at-Law (Gray's Inn, England). *PRACTICE AREAS:* Company, Unit Trusts and Corporate Finance.

LEE CHENG, LL.B. (Hons) (Lond) LL.M. (Lond) Barr-at-Law (Lincoln's Inn, England). *PRACTICE AREAS:* Intellectual Property.

DIANE CECILIA FLETCHER, LL.B. (Hons) Singapore. *PRACTICE AREAS:* Company, Corporate Restructuring and Mergers.

GILBERT LEONG CHENG LOONG, LL.B. (Hons) Singapore LL.M. (Corp/Comm) (Lond). *PRACTICE AREAS:* Intellectual Property.

TAN JOO THYE, LL.B. (Hons) Singapore. *PRACTICE AREAS:* Litigation.

GLEN GOH CHOO KHENG, LL.B. (Hons) Singapore, M.B.A. (Boston). *PRACTICE AREAS:* Conveyancing.

ASSISTANTS

VIVIAN CHOO AI LEEN, LL.B. (Hons) Singapore.

GEOFFREY MAH JIN TEE, LL.B. (Hons) Singapore.

JESSIE THONG, B.A. (Law) (Hons) (Cantab) LL.M. (Cantab) Barr-at-Law (Gray's Inn, England).

GODWIN GILBERT CAMPOS, LL.B. (Hons) Singapore LL.M. (Monash. Aust).

JEFFREY CHAU SIANG HWEE, LL.B. (Hons) Singapore.

LEE LIAT YEANG, LL.B. (Hons) Singapore.

TEO NING NING, LL.B. (Hons) (Essex) Barr-at-Law (Gray's Inn, Eng).

WEE JEE PIN, LL.B. (Hons) (Hull) Barr-at-Law (Middle Temple, England).

JULIAN CHIN YE-PUNG, LL.B. (Hons) (Leicester) Barr-at-Law (Middle Temple, England).

LAWRENCE TEH KEE WEE, LL.B. (Hons) (Lond), Barr-at-Law (Inner Temple, England).

EILEEN TAY PUI LING, LL.B. (Hons) Singapore.

SANDRA CHOY LIN QUE, LL.B. (Hons) Singapore.

KOH TIEN HUA, LL.B. (Hons) (Lond). Barr-at-Law (Middle Temple, England).

LEE YUEN WAI, (LL.B. (Hons) (Sheffield), Barr-at-Law (Lincoln's Inn, England).

CHARISSA NG SIEW FONG, LL.B., (Hons) (Norringham) Barr-at-Law (Inner Temple, England).

CINDA SIM TECK AI, LL.B. (Hons) (Singapore).

NGIAM MING, B.A. (Hons) (Keele) Barr-at-Law (Middle Temple, England).

LYNETTE CHAN WEN EE, LL.B. (Hons) Singapore.

AMANDA TAN PHECK CHOO, LL.B. (Hons) Singapore.

PARALEGALS

ROGER SYN JUEN MING, B. England. (Monash) A.I.P.A.

ZHANG XUAN, LL.B. (UPSL, Beijing).

CONSULTANTS

GRAHAM STARFORTH HILL, M.A. (Oxon).

PATHMANABAN SELVADURAI, LL.B. (Hons) (Lond) Barr-at-Law (Middle Temple, England).

Languages: English, Mandarin, Malay and Tamil.

SHOOK LIN & BOK

Established in 1918

Advocates & Solicitors

Notary Public

Trademark & Patent Agent

1 ROBINSON ROAD, #18-00 AIA TOWER
SINGAPORE 0104
Telephone: (65) 535-1944
Fax: (65) 535-8577; (65) 534-1765; (65) 5 32-6148; (65) 532-5108

Other Offices: Messrs. Shook Lin & Bok, Kuala Lumpur, Malaysia (Associated Firm).

Arbitration, Banking, Finance & Securities, Civil & Commercial Litigation, Corporate, Company & Commercial Law, Conveyancing & Property Law, Criminal Law, Employment Law, Family Law, Insolvency, Insurance Law, Probate & Administration of Estates, Shipping & Admiralty, Tax.

FIRM PROFILE: Shook, Lin & Bok, established in 1918, is a full-service law firm in Singapore with an Asian regional capacity. We provide practical and effective solutions to the business and legal problems of our clients in Singapore and the Asia Pacific region.

PARTNERS

DR. PHILIP N. PILLAI, LL.B. (Hons) (Singapore), LL.M. (Harvard), S.J.D. (Harvard); admitted, 1972, Singapore. (Managing Partner). *PRACTICE AREAS:* Corporate Finance; International Finance; International Trade & Regulation; Privatisation; Securities; Collective Investment Schemes; Futures & Derivatives.

MRS. PAULINE PO LIN CHEN, Barrister-at-Law (Middle Temple); admitted, 1973, Singapore. *PRACTICE AREAS:* Conveyancing & Property Transactions; Project Financing; Property Development; Property Financing.

MRS. MEERA MANIAR, LL.B. (Hons) (Singapore); admitted, 1978, Singapore. *PRACTICE AREAS:* Banking & Finance; Company Administration & Secretarial Services; Corporate & Commercial (Domestic & International); General Commercial Practice; Intellectual Property; Property Financing.

SARJIT SINGH GILL, LL.B. (Hons) (Singapore); admitted, 1977, Singapore. *PRACTICE AREAS:* Admiralty & Shipping; Banking & Commercial Disputes; Building & Construction Disputes; Commercial Arbitration; Insolvencies & Receiverships.

KIM TECK KIM SEAH, LL.B. (Hons) (Singapore), LL.M. (Harvard); admitted, 1979, Singapore. *PRACTICE AREAS:* Banking & Finance; Corporate & Commercial (Domestic & International); Employment & Labour Law; General Commercial Practice.

KIANG KOK TEO, LL.B. (Hons) (Hull), Barrister-at-Law (Lincoln's Inn); admitted, 1983, Singapore. *PRACTICE AREAS:* Corporate Finance; International Finance; Securities; Collective Investment Schemes; Futures & Derivatives; Banking & Finance.

ALFONSO CHENG ANN ANG, LL.B. (Hons.) (Singapore), LL.M. (Vrije University, Brussels); admitted, 1981, Singapore. *PRACTICE AREAS:* Banking & Commercial Disputes; Building & Construction Disputes; Insolvencies & Receiverships.

KENNETH WEE KHENG TAN, LL.B. (Hons) (National University of Singapore); admitted, 1984, Singapore. *PRACTICE AREAS:* Admiralty and Shipping; Banking and Commercial Disputes; Commercial Arbitration; Insolvencies and Receiverships.

MS. SUSAN YIM PUI KONG, LL.B. (Hons) (National University of Singapore); admitted, 1985, Singapore. *PRACTICE AREAS:* Banking and Commercial Disputes; Banking and Finance; Corporate and Commercial (Domestic and International); Insolvencies and Receivership; Property Development.

LAI HUAT TAN, LL.B. (Hons) (National University of Singapore), LL.M. (London); admitted, 1985, Singapore. *PRACTICE AREAS:* Banking & Finance; Corporate Finance; Corporate & Commercial (Domestic & International); General Commercial Practice; Tax.

MS. JANE YUMIKO ITTOGI, LL.B. (Hons) (London), LL.M. (London), Barrister-at-Law (Middle Temple); admitted, 1988, Singapore. *PRACTICE AREAS:* Admiralty & Shipping; Banking & Commercial Disputes; Family & Matrimonial; Insolvencies & Receiverships.

(This Listing Continued)

SHOOK LIN & BOK, Singapore—Continued

RICHARD MING KIRK TAN, LL.B. (Hons) (National University of Singapore); admitted, 1985, Singapore. *PRACTICE AREAS:* Company Administration & Secretarial Services; Consumer Property Financing; Conveyancing & Property Transactions.

JIM KHENG HUAT LIM, LL.B. (Hons) (National University of Singapore); admitted, 1985, Singapore. *PRACTICE AREAS:* Intellectual Property and Computer Law; Company Administration and Secretarial Services; Corporate and Commercial (Domestic and International).

MS. CAROL ANNE MEI LING TAN, LL.B. (Hons) (National University of Singapore); admitted, 1987, Singapore. *PRACTICE AREAS:* Consumer Property Financing; Conveyancing; Property Transactions; Probate; Administration of Estates; Succession; Project Financing.

MS. SWEE FONG KOK, LL.B. (Hons) (Singapore); admitted, 1980, Singapore. *PRACTICE AREAS:* Conveyancing and Property Transactions; Property Development; Consumer Property Financing.

VICTOR CHONG PHANG TAN, LL.B. (Hons) (National University of Singapore); admitted, 1986. *PRACTICE AREAS:* Consumer Property Financing; Conveyancing and Property Transactions; Probate; Administration of Estates and Succession; Property Financing.

PETER KIAN HUAT LEE, LL.B. (Hons) (National University of Singapore); admitted, 1988, Singapore. *PRACTICE AREAS:* Corporate Finance; International Finance; Securities; Collective Investment Schemes; Futures and Derivatives.

S. THULASIDAS, LL.B. (Hons) (National University of Singapore); admitted, 1988, Singapore. *PRACTICE AREAS:* Banking and Commercial Disputes; Building and Construction Disputes; Commercial Arbitration; Insolvencies and Receiverships.

YUEN NG, LL.B. (Hons) (National University of Singapore); admitted, 1989, Singapore. *PRACTICE AREAS:* Banking and Commercial Disputes; Building and Construction Disputes; Insolvencies and Receiverships.

DENNIS SIANG BOK LIM, LL.B. (Hons) (National University of Singapore); admitted, 1988, Singapore. *PRACTICE AREAS:* Banking and Commercial Disputes; Building and Construction Disputes; Commercial Arbitration; Insolvencies and Receiverships.

KIAN MIN ONG, LL.B. (Hons) (London), Barrister-at-Law (Gray's Inn); B.Sc. (Hons) (Imperial College), A.R.C.S.; admitted, 1989, Singapore. *PRACTICE AREAS:* Banking and Finance; Company Administration and Secretarial Services; Corporate and Commercial (Domestic and International); General Commercial Practice.

CONSULTANT

MRS. NOELINE CORA YOONG, Barrister-at-Law (Inner Temple); admitted, 1956, Singapore. *PRACTICE AREAS:* Property Development.

PETER SOON KWANG KOH, LL.B. (Hons) (Singapore), LL.M. (London), admitted, 1977, Singapore. *PRACTICE AREAS:* Admiralty and Shipping; Marine Insurance; Maritime Arbitration.

FOREIGN LEGAL COUNSEL (CHINESE LAW COUNSEL)

QING SONG, (Not admitted in Singapore). LL.B. (Beijing University School of Law); LL.M. (Beijing University School of Law) (Admitted to practice in the PRC). *PRACTICE AREAS:* China Practice.

DAO FU WANG, (Not admitted in Singapore). LL.B. (Beijing University School of Law); (admitted to practice in the PRC, and in the field of Securities Law in PRC). *PRACTICE AREAS:* China Practice.

ASSOCIATES

MS. CHENG HAN GIAM, LL.B. (Hons) (National University of Singapore); admitted, 1985, Singapore.

MS. CECILIA LEE THOMAS, LL.B. (Hons) (National University of Singapore); admitted, 1987, Singapore.

AUDREY LIANG TEE WEE, LL.B. (Hons) (National University of Singapore); admitted, 1987, Singapore.

GERALD LU TSENG LEE, LL.B. (Hons) (National University of Singapore); admitted, 1989, Singapore.

MS. YING YING TUNG, LL.B. (Hons) (National University of Singapore); admitted, 1989, Singapore.

JOO KHIN NG, LL.B. (Hons) (National University of Singapore); admitted, 1990, Singapore.

(This Listing Continued)

SUHAIMI BIN LAZIM, LL.B. (Hons) (National University of Singapore); admitted, 1990, Singapore.

MS. WAI YIN CHEONG, LL.B. (Hons) (National University of Singapore); admitted, 1991, Singapore.

MS. SUZANNE YI LENG YING, LL.B. (Hons) (National University of Singapore); admitted, 1991, Singapore.

JANET TAN, LL.B. (Hons) (National University of Singapore); admitted, 1991, Singapore.

VINODH SABESAN COOMARASWAMY, LL.B. (Hons) (Nott), Barrister-at-Law (Inner Temple); admitted, 1992, Singapore.

MS. RACHEL PAO HWA CHEN, LL.B. (Hons) (Buckingham), Barrister-at-Law (Gray's Inn); admitted, 1992, Singapore.

NICHOLAS FOO NAM CHONG, LL.B. (Hons) (National University of Singapore); admitted, 1992, Singapore.

SIEW QUN KONG, LL.B. (Hons) (University of London), Barrister-at-law (Gray's Inn); admitted, 1992, Singapore.

KEAN SENG U, LL.B. (Hons) (Monash), Barrister & Solicitor (Supreme Court Victoria, Australia); admitted, 1991, Australia; admitted, 1993, Singapore.

MS. JACQUELIN GEK POH TAY, LL.B. (Hons) (National University of Singapore); admitted, 1993, Singapore.

MS. BOON YEAN LOW, LL.B. (Hons) (National University of Singapore); admitted, 1993, Singapore.

MS. HUEY CHING CHEW, LL.B. (Hons) (National University of Singapore); admitted, 1993, Singapore.

MS. CHRISTINA YOKE YEE THAM, LL.B. (Hons) (University of Leicester), Barrister-at-Law (Middle Temple); admitted, 1993, Singapore.

MS. WEI SIM HO, LL.B. (Hons) (National University of Singapore); admitted, 1993, Singapore.

MS. TANSY WING YUE TANG, B.A. (Hons) (Cantab), Barrister-at-Law (Gray's Inn); admitted, 1993, Singapore.

BERNARD CHONG WEE TAN, LL.B. (Hons) (National University of Singapore); admitted, 1994, Singapore.

HAROLD WAI KEONG OR, LL.B. (Hons) (University of London), Barrister-at-Law (Inner Temple); admitted, 1994, Singapore.

MS. CHERYL WAN SIM LIM, LL.B. (Hons) (National University of Singapore); admitted, 1994, Singapore.

NICHOLAS KUM YEW LOH, LL.B. (Hons) (University of London), Barrister-at-Law (Middle Temple); admitted, 1994, Singapore.

ROBSON TECK LENG LEE, LL.B. (Hons) (National University of Singapore); admitted, 1994, Singapore.

Languages: English, Chinese, Malay.

SINCLAIR ROCHE & TEMPERLEY

16 COLLYER QUAY

#12-02

SINGAPORE 0104

Telephone: (65) 533 1181

Fax: (65) 532 5454

Telex: 20433 Snclr

Other Offices: London (England), Hong Kong, Shanghai (China), Vietnam and Bucharest (Romania).

International Commerce Practice.

(For Complete Biographical Data on all personnel, see Professional Biographies at London, England Office)

THÜMMEL, SCHÜTZE & PARTNER

Established in 1981

STRAITS TRADING BUILDING
9 BATTERY ROAD #16-01
SINGAPORE 0104
Telephone: (00 65) 53 53 112
Telefax: (00 65) 53 43 100

Stuttgart, Germany Office: Landhausstraße 90, 70190 Stuttgart.
   Telephone: (0711) 1667-0, Telefax: (0711) 286 44 66, 2 62 69 10.
Paris, France Office: 46, Rue de Bassano, F-75008 Paris. Telephone:
   (0033) 1-53 67 50 00. Telefax: (0033) 1-47 20 78 76.
Dresden, Germany Office: Friedrichstraße 33, 01067 Dresden. Telephone:
   (0351) 496 5302. Telefax: (0351) 496 5346.
Berlin, Germany Office: Lützowstraße 33/36, 10785 Berlin. Telephone:
   (030) 2 61 11 31. Telefax: (030) 2 61 90 49. Telex: 3 01304.
Frankfurt, Germany Office: Eschersheimer Landshraße 10 60322
   Frankfurt. Telephone: (069) 9591350. Telefax: (069) 95913530.
Brussels Office: Avenue des Arts, 41 B-1040 Brussels. Telephone: (0032)
   2-512 7846. Telefax: (0032) 2-512 7023.

Firm engaged in International Law Practice, but not authorized to appear before the Singapore Courts or to act as Singapore Advocates and Solicitors.

RESIDENT ASSOCIATES

DR. JUR. TORSTEN OETTING, born Bremen, Germany, January 27, 1961; admitted, 1992, Germany (Not admitted in Singapore). *Education:* University of Mannheim (1983-1985); Ludwig-Maximilian University, Munich (1985-1988; Referendar in Berlin, 1989; Assessor, 1991). *LANGUAGES:* German, English, French.

DR. JUR. RENÉ-ALEXANDER HIRTH, born Stuttgart, Germany, February 27, 1963; admitted, 1993, Germany. *Education:* University of Tübingen (Referendar 1989, Assessor 1993). Assistant, University of Tübingen, 1989-1991. Doctor of Jurisprudence, 1991. Author: "Die Entwicklung der Rechtsprechung zum Vertrag mit Schutzwirkung zugunsten Dritter in ihrer Bedeutung für den Ausgleich von Drittschäden im Zahlungsverkehr" (The Development of Case law in regard to the Contract with protective effect for the benefit of third parties in view of its importance for compensation of third parties' damages in payment transactions), 1991. *Member:* German Bar Association. *LANGUAGES:* German, English.

(For Complete Biographical Data on all Personnel, see Professional Biographies at Stuttgart, Germany).

VINSON & ELKINS L.L.P.

50 RAFFLES PLACE
#19-05 SHELL TOWER
SINGAPORE 0104
Telephone: (65) 536-8300
U.S. Voice Mailbox: 713-758-3500
Fax: (65) 536-8311

London, England Office: 47 Charles Street, Berkeley Square, London
   W1X 7PB, England. Telephone: (44-171) 491-7236. Fax: (44-171)
   499-5320.
Moscow, Russian Federation Office: 16 Alexey Tolstoy Street, Second
   Floor, Moscow, 103001 Russian Federation. Telephone: 011- (70-95)
   956-1995. Telecopy: 011 (70-95) 956-1996.
Mexico City, Mexico Office: Aristóteles 77, 5°Piso, Colonia Chapultepec
   Polanco, 11560 Mexico, D.F. Telephone: (52-5) 280-7828. Fax: (52-5)
   280-9223.
Houston, Texas Office: 2300 First City Tower, 1001 Fannin, 77002-6760.
   Telephone: 713-758-2222. Fax: 713-758-2346.
Washington, D.C. Office: The Willard Office Building, 1455 Pennsylvania
   Avenue, N.W. Telephone: 202-639-6500. Fax: 202-639-6604.
Dallas, Texas Office: 3700 Trammell Crow Center, 2001 Ross Avenue.
   Telephone: 214-220-7700. Fax: 214-220-7716.
Austin, Texas Office: One American Center, 600 Congress Avenue.
   Telephone: 512-495-8400. Fax: 512-495-8612.

General International Practice including Joint Ventures, Project Finance, Corporate Securities and other Capital Markets Transactions, Infrastructure, Privatizations, Oil and Gas, Petrochemicals, Power, Pipeline and other Energy Projects and Airplane Finance.

(This Listing Continued)

Firm engaged in American, English and International Law Practice, but not authorized to appear before Singapore courts or to act as Singapore Advocates and Solicitors.

RESIDENT PARTNERS

STEPHEN D. DAVIS, born Andrews, Texas, January 17, 1957; admitted, 1982, Texas. *Education:* Louisiana State University (B.S.Ch.E., 1979); University of Texas (J.D., with honors, 1981). Phi Kappa Phi; Phi Lambda Upsilon; Tau Beta Pi. *PRACTICE AREAS:* Project Finance Law; International Corporate Finance Law; Natural Resources Law; Corporate and Joint Venture Law; Privatizations.

KEVIN P. LEWIS, born Houston, Texas, July 20, 1961; admitted, 1986, Texas; 1988, New York. *Education:* Yale University (B.A., 1983); Harvard University (J.D., 1986). Law Clerk to the Hon. Jerre S. Williams, U.S. Court of Appeals (Fifth Circuit), 1986-1987. *PRACTICE AREAS:* Project and Structured Finance Law; International Corporate Finance Law; Mergers and Acquisitions Law; Securities Offerings Law.

U.S. LIAISON PARTNER

MARK STEPHEN BERG, born Dallas, Texas, May 1, 1958; admitted, 1983, Texas. *Education:* Tulane University (B.A., 1980); University of Texas (J.D., 1983). Phi Delta Phi; Phi Beta Kappa; Omicron Delta Kappa. (Resident, Houston, Texas Office). *PRACTICE AREAS:* Project Finance and Structured Finance Law; Business Law; International Law.

WEE, RAMAYAH & PARTNERS

1 COLOMBO COURT #09-05
SINGAPORE 0617
Telephone: (65) 336-2626
Facsimile: (65) 338-8001

Maritime and Shipping Practice, Arbitration Aviation Law, Banking Law, Commercial and Corporate Law, Family Law, Trusts and Succession, Property Law and Conveyancing, Intellectual Property, Trade Mark and Copyrights, General and Marine Insurance, General Civil and Trial Practice.

FIRM PROFILE: Firm was founded in 1984. Currently there are 5 partners and 1 consultant.

MEMBERS OF FIRM

VINO GOPAL RAMAYAH, admitted, 1979, Singapore and Negeri Brunei Darussalam. *Education:* University of Singapore (LL.B., Hons, 1978); University of London (LL.M.); London Institute of World Affairs (Diploma, Air and Space Law). Appointed Commissioner for Oaths, Singapore, 1986. Appointed Town Councillor, 1989. *Member:* Singapore Maritime Law Association (Vice-President, 1990). *LANGUAGES:* English and Malay (Indonesian) Tamil. *PRACTICE AREAS:* Commercial Law; Corporate Litigation; Banking; Conveyancing; Shipping and Aviation.

LAURENCE JOHN WEE, admitted, 1983, Singapore; Barrister-at-Law; Middle Temple. *Education:* University of Buckingham, England (LL.B., Hons.). *LANGUAGES:* English. *PRACTICE AREAS:* Banking; Property Law; Conveyancing; Commercial and Corporate Law.

VANGAT RAMAYAH, admitted, 1980, Barrister-at-Law, Lincoln's Inn; 1982, Singapore. *Education:* University of London (LL.B., Hons, 1979; LL.M.); City of London College (M.A., Business Law). Appointed Commissioner for Oaths, Singapore. Formerly, Magistrate, Singapore. President, General Court Martial. *LANGUAGES:* English, Malay and Tamil. *PRACTICE AREAS:* Commercial Law; Conveyancing; Shipping Law; Transnational Joint Ventures.

RAJARAM RAMIAH, admitted, 1983, Barrister-at-Law, Middle Temple; 1986, Singapore. *Education:* University of London (LL.B., Hons.); University of Cambridge, Hughes Hall (LL.M.). Former District Judge, Magistrate, Coroner, Deputy Registrar of the Subordinate Courts of Singapore. President, General Court Martial. *LANGUAGES:* English, Tamil and Malay. *PRACTICE AREAS:* Civil Litigation; Corporate and Banking Law; Aviation.

SHANTINI RAMACHANDRA, admitted, 1986, Singapore. *Education:* National University of Singapore (LL.B., Hons); University of London, King's College (LL.M.). *LANGUAGES:* English, Tamil and Malay. *PRACTICE AREAS:* Intellectual Property Litigation.

PATRICK JOHN WEE, admitted, 1990, Singapore. *Education:* National University of Singapore (LL.B., Hons.). *LANGUAGES:* English and

(This Listing Continued)

WEE, RAMAYAH & PARTNERS, Singapore—Continued

Mandarin. *PRACTICE AREAS:* Banking Law; Conveyancing; Property Law.

LEE POH CHUN JANE, admitted, 1990, Singapore. *Education:* National University of Singapore (LL.B., Hons). *LANGUAGES:* English and Mandarin. *PRACTICE AREAS:* Property Law; Banking Law; Conveyancing.

CHIANG WEN-SHAN, admitted, 1990, Barrister-at-law, Gray's Inn; 1993, Singapore. *Education:* University of Leicester (LL.B., Hons.). *LANGUAGES:* English and Mandarin. *PRACTICE AREAS:* Insurance Law; Family Law.

JOYCE CHEW BEE POH, admitted, 1993, Singapore. *Education:* National University of Singapore (LL.B., Hons.). *LANGUAGES:* English and Mandarin. *PRACTICE AREAS:* Banking Law; Conveyancing.

G.B. VASU, admitted, 1994, Advocate and Solicitor of the Supreme Court of Singapore. *Education:* University of London (LL.B., Hons., 1988-1991); Middle Temple (Barrister-at-Law, 1991-1992). *LANGUAGES:* English, French, Tamil and Malay. *PRACTICE AREAS:* Civil and Criminal Litigation; Corporate and Banking Law.

JERRY LOO KAH KEONG, admitted, 1992, Barrister-at-Law, Middle Temple; 1994, Singapore. *Education:* University Leicester (LL.B., Hons); Columbia University (LL.M.). *LANGUAGES:* English and Mandarin. *PRACTICE AREAS:* General Litigation; Maritime Law; Corporate Law; Intellectual Property Law.

TAN CHING CHERN, admitted, 1993, Singapore. *Education:* National University of Singapore (LL.B., Hons.). *LANGUAGES:* English and Mandarin. *PRACTICE AREAS:* Banking Law; Conveyancing.

TENG HWEE KOON, admitted, 1995, Singapore. *Education:* National University of Singapore (LL.B., Hons.). *LANGUAGES:* English and Mandarin. *PRACTICE AREAS:* Banking Law; Conveyancing.

SHIREEN ABDULLAH, admitted, 1995, Singapore. *Education:* National University of Singapore (LL.B., Hons.). *LANGUAGES:* English and Malay. *PRACTICE AREAS:* General Litigation; Corporate Law; Banking Law.

CONSULTANT

DR. WEE CHONG JIN, DCL (Oxon). Chief Justice, Singapore, 1963-1990. Fellow, Singapore Academy of Law. *LANGUAGES:* English and Mandarin.

WHITE & CASE
50 RAFFLES PLACE #22-01, SHELL TOWER
SINGAPORE 0104
Telephone: (65) 225-6000
Facsimile: (65) 225-6009

New York, New York: Telephone: 212-819-8200. Facsimile: 212-354-8113.
Washington, D.C.: Telephone: 202-872-0013. Facsimile: 202-872-0210.
Los Angeles, California: Telephone: 213-620-7700. Facsimile: 213-687-0758; 213-617-2205.
Miami, Florida: Telephone: 305-371-2700. Facsimile: 305-358-5744.
Mexico City, Mexico: Telephone: (52-5) 207-9717. Facsimile: (52-5) 208-3628.
Tokyo, Japan: Telephone: (81-3) 3239-4300. Facsimile: (81-3) 3239-4330.
Hong Kong: Telephone: (852) 2822-8700. Facsimile: (852) 2845-9070; Grice & Co., Solicitors, Telephone: (852) 2826-0333. Facsimile: (852) 2526-7166.
Bangkok, Thailand: Pacific Legal Group Ltd., In Association With White & Case, Telephone: (662) 236-6154/7. Facsimile: (662) 237-6771.
Hanoi, Viet Nam: Representative Office, Telephone: (84-4) 227-575/6/7. Facsimile: (84-4) 227-297.
Bombay, India: Telephone: (91-22) 282-6300. Facsimile: (91-22) 282-6305.
London, England: Telephone: (44-171) 726-6361. Facsimile: (44-171) 726-4314; (44-171) 726-8558.
Paris, France: Telephone: (33-1) 42-60-34-05. Facsimile: (33-1) 42-60-82-46.
Brussels, Belgium: Telephone: (32-2) 647-05-89. Facsimile: (32-2) 647-16-75.

(This Listing Continued)

Stockholm, Sweden: Telephone: (46-8) 679-80-30. Facsimile: (46-8) 611-21-22.
Helsinki, Finland: Telephone: (358-0) 631-100. Facsimile: (358-0) 179-477.
Moscow, Russia: Telephone: (7-095) 201-9292/3/4/5. Facsimile: (7-095) 201-9284.
Budapest, Hungary: Telephone: (36-1) 269-0550; (36-1) 131-0933. Facsimile: (36-1) 269-1199.
Prague, Czech Republic: Telephone: (42-2) 2481-1796. Facsimile: (42-2) 232-5522.
Warsaw, Poland: Telephone/Facsimile: (48-22) 26-80-53; (48-22) 27-84-86. International Telephone/Facsimile: (48-39) 12-19-06.
Istanbul, Turkey: Telephone: (90-212) 275-68-98; (90-212) 275-75-33. Facsimile: (90-212) 275-75-43.
Ankara, Turkey: Telephone: (90-312) 446-2180. Facsimile: (90-312) 437-9677.
Jeddah, Saudi Arabia: Law Office of Hassan Mahassni, Telephone: (966-2) 651-3535. Facsimile: (966-2) 651-3636.
Riyadh, Saudi Arabia: Law Office of Hassan Mahassni, Telephone: (966-1) 476-7099. Facsimile: (966-1) 479-0110.
Almaty, Kazakhstan: Telephone: (7-3272) 50-7491/2. Facsimile: (7-3272) 61-0842.

General International Practice.
Firm engaged in American and International Law Practice, but not authorized to appear before Singapore courts or to act as Singapore Advocates and Solicitors.

RESIDENT PARTNERS

J. HAYWOOD BLAKEMORE, IV, born Roanoke, Virginia, February 2, 1950; admitted, 1979, Virginia; 1980, New York and District of Columbia (Not admitted in Singapore). *Education:* Randolph-Macon College (B.A., 1971); College of William & Mary (M.A., 1975); University of Virginia (J.D., 1979). *Member:* New York State, American, Inter-Pacific and International Bar Associations; American Society of International Law.

KENNETH C. ELLIS, born Leesburg, Florida, November 11, 1948; admitted, 1974, Florida (Not admitted in Singapore). *Education:* University of Florida (B.A., 1970; J.D., 1973). *Member:* The Florida Bar.

WENDELL C. MADDREY, born Birmingham, Alabama, April 25, 1956; admitted, 1983, New York (Not admitted in Singapore). *Education:* University of North Carolina (B.A., 1978); University of Virginia (J.D., 1982). *Member:* American Bar Association; American Society of International Law.

RESIDENT COUNSEL

KIMBERLEY R. LANDON, born Los Angeles, California, December 15, 1954; admitted, 1980, Texas (Not admitted in Singapore). *Education:* Southern Methodist University (B.S., 1975; J.D., 1979); University of Cardiff, Wales (LL.B., 1977).

RESIDENT ASSOCIATES

MICHAEL R. BARZ, born New York, New York, June 1, 1962; admitted, 1990, New York (Not admitted in Singapore). *Education:* Columbia University (B.S., 1984); Fordham University (J.D., 1990).

ALISTAIR A. DUFFIELD, born Belfast, Northern Ireland, May 27, 1955; admitted, 1980, England and Wales; 1988, New South Wales, Australia (Not admitted in Singapore). *Education:* Leeds University (LL.B., 1975); College of Law (1976).

JOHN-MICHAEL LIND, born New York, New York, February 11, 1965; admitted, 1990, New York (Not admitted in Singapore). *Education:* Claremont McKenna College (B.A., 1986); Hastings College of the Law, University of California (J.D., 1989). Member, Hastings International Comparative Law Review.

BRIAN M. MILLER, born Columbia, South Carolina, September 14, 1951; admitted, 1980, Massachusetts (Not admitted in Singapore). *Education:* New York University (A.B., 1974); University of Massachusetts (M.A., 1977; Ph.D., 1982); Harvard University (J.D., 1980).

KEVIN J. MURPHY, born Bronxville, New York, May 3, 1963; admitted, 1989, New York (Not admitted in Singapore). *Education:* University of Notre Dame (B.A., 1985); University of Michigan (J.D., 1988).

MADHURANI POWAR GARG, born Bombay, India, December 20, 1959; admitted, 1983, Maharashta, Bombay, India; 1987, New York; 1992, California (Not admitted in Singapore). *Education:* Institute of Science, University of Bambay (B.S., 1979); Government Law College, University of Bombay (LL.B., 1982); Yale University (LL.M., 1984; J.S.D., 1991).

(This Listing Continued)

NEELA RAMANATHAN, born May 5, 1965; admitted, 1988, Tamil Nadu, Madras, India (Not admitted in Singapore). *Education:* Government Law College, Madras University (LL.B., 1988); Fletcher School of Law and Diplomacy (M.A., 1991).

MICHAEL R. READING, born Ridgewood, New Jersey, December 28, 1968; admitted, 1994, New York (Not admitted in Singapore). *Education:* Purdue University (B.A., 1990); Duke University (J.D./LL.M., 1993); National University of Singapore (LL.M., 1994).

S. M. EDWIN THAM, born Kuala Lumpur, Malaysia, December 10, 1964; admitted, 1989, England and Wales (Middle Temple); 1991, New York (Not admitted in Singapore). *Education:* University of Nottingham (LL.B., 1988). *Member:* Honorable Society of the Middle Temple; New York State Bar Association; Maritime Law Association of Singapore.

BRIAN J. WESOL, born Oak Park, Illinois March 1, 1964; admitted, 1992, New York (Not admitted in Singapore). *Education:* Georgetown University (B.S.F.S., 1986); Jochi (Sophia) University, Tokyo, Japan; Columbia University (J.D., 1991).

(For biographical data as to other locations, see Professional Biographies at New York, New York; Washington, D.C.; Los Angeles, California; Miami, Florida; Mexico City, Mexico; Tokyo, Japan; Hong Kong; Bangkok, Thailand; Hanoi, Viet Nam; Bombay, India; London, England; Paris, France; Brussels, Belgium; Stockholm, Sweden; Helsinki, Finland; Moscow, Russia; Budapest, Hungary; Prague, Czech Republic; Warsaw, Poland; Istanbul and Ankara, Turkey; Jeddah and Riyadh, Saudi Arabia; Almaty, Kazakhstan).

WINSTON CHEN & CO.

(A Merger with David Ong & Lim)

Advocates & Solicitors; Commissioners for Oaths

36 ROBINSON ROAD
#07-01 CITY HOUSE
SINGAPORE 0106
Telephone: (65) 2239009
Fax: (65) 2256914; 2223396

Corporate and Conveyancing Department: 36 Robinson Road, #07-01 City House, 0106. Telephone: (65) 2239009. Fax: (65) 2256914; 2223396.

Corporate and Litigation Department: 4 Shenton Way, #15-07/10 Sing Kwan House, 0106. Telephone: (65) 2206888. Fax: (65) 2231736; 2254164.

General and International Practice, Corporate (Venture Capitol, including China, Burma, Hong Kong, Thailand, Taiwan, and Vietnam), Mergers and Acquisitions, Hotel Management, Banking and Finance, Construction, Family and Matrimonial, Immigration, Insolvency, Insurance, Intellectual Property, Civil and Commercial Litigation, Arbitration, Probate and Administration, Real Estate and Conveyancing, Securities and Trusts.

FIRM PROFILE: *Founded in 1983 and merged with David Ong & Lim in 1994. The firm has 11 professional members (5 partners and 6 legal assistants).*

PARTNERS

WINSTON CHEN, Barrister-at-Law; Advocate and Solicitor (Singapore), 1965.

DAVID ONG MUNG PANG, LLM (London); Barrister-at-Law; Advocate and Solicitor (Singapore), 1982. Commissioner for Oaths.

TEO GUAN TECK, LLB (Hons) Singapore; Advocate and Solicitor (Singapore), 1971; Commissioner for Oaths.

JASON LIM CHEN THOR, LLM (London); Barrister-at-Law; Advocate and Solicitor (Singapore), 1983.

LIM SIEW KUAN, Barrister-at-Law; Advocate and Solicitor ("Singapore) 1982. Commissioner for Oaths.

Languages: English, Mandarin, Japanese, Malay and Indonesian.

WONG MENG MENG & PARTNERS

SINGAPORE, SINGAPORE

(See Wong Partnership)

P.K. WONG & ADVANI

Advocatesa & Solicitors

Commissioner for Oaths

Established in 1987

OCEAN TOWERS
20 RAFFLES PLACE #12-03
SINGAPORE 0104
Telephone: 65-538-1822
Fax: 65-538-1838

Arbitration, Banking, Finance, Securities, Building and Construction Law, Corporate, Criminal, Family Law, Insurance, Intellectual Property, Litigation, Property and Conveyancing, Tax, Trust and Estate Planning.

FIRM PROFILE: *The basic philosophy of PKWA is to provide full and cost effective legal services and to advise clients of their legal rights in the light of commercial realities. PKWA emphasises a high degree of partner involvement to ensure quality and experienced advice.*

PKWA represents and continues to serve clients (public listed companies, private companies as well as individuals) in Singapore, Thailand, Indonesia, Philippines, Vietnam, Hong Kong, China and other countries in the Asia Pacific region. PKWA's lawyers travel regularly to these countries and their constant contact with such clients and local lawyers enable PKWA to update its clients on the latest legal and regulatory changes in these territories. PKWA has also assisted clients in making contracts, setting up business and negotiating joint ventures and other commercial transactions in these countries.

PARTNERS

PENG KOON WONG, admitted, 1965. *Education:* LL.B. (Hons) Singapore; Commissioner for Oaths. **PRACTICE AREAS:** Conveyancing; Corporate Banking and Finance; Trust and Estate Planning; Securities Regulation.

J.G. ADVANI, admitted, 1962. *Education:* LL.B. (Hons) Malaya; Commissioner for Oaths. **PRACTICE AREAS:** Corporate Banking and Finance; Commercial Crime and Criminal Law; Litigation; Probate and Administration; Securities Regulation.

GOH SOON HOCK, admitted, 1965. *Education:* LL.B. (Hons) Singapore; Commissioner for Oaths. **PRACTICE AREAS:** Arbitration; Alternative Dispute Resolution and Conciliation; Conveyancing.

LEE-WAN FOOK FANG, admitted, 1980. *Education:* LL.B. (Hons) Singapore; LL.M. (Vrije Universiteit) Brussels; Commissioner for Oaths. **PRACTICE AREAS:** Conveyancing; Corporate Banking and Finance.

KEH KEE GUAN, admitted, 1974. *Education:* LL.B. (Hons) Singapore; Commissioner for Oaths. **PRACTICE AREAS:** Corporate; Banking and Finance; Commercial Crime and Criminal Law; Intellectual Property; Litigation; Tax and Estate Planning.

ESTHER LIM SYN POH, admitted, 1974. *Education:* LL.B. (Hons) Singapore. **PRACTICE AREAS:** Conveyancing; Corporate Banking and Finance.

NG KAI MING, admitted, 1986. *Education:* LL.B. (Hons) Singapore. **PRACTICE AREAS:** Arbitration; Alternative Dispute Resolution; Conciliation and Litigation.

CHEE WEI LIN, admitted, 1987. *Education:* LL.B. (Hons) Singapore. **PRACTICE AREAS:** Commercial Crime and Criminal Law; Litigation; Securities Regulation.

ANTHONY TAN LAY TIONG, admitted, 1990. *Education:* LL.B. (Hons) Singapore. **PRACTICE AREAS:** Conveyancing; Probate and Administration.

MERLENE TOH-EMERSON, admitted, 1987, England and Wales; 1993, Singapore. *Education:* LL.B. (Hons) London; LL.M. Cambridge.

(This Listing Continued)

P.K. WONG & ADVANI, Singapore—Continued

PRACTICE AREAS: Corporate Banking and Finance; Securities Regulation.

ASSOCIATES

Christopher Song Hwee Tiong	Lynn Chua Sze Hwi
Serena Fah	Winston Quek Seng Soon
Janice Wu	Lana Ng-Rosenberger
Mark Wong Kuan Meng	Sebastian Quek Jwee Pang
	Patrick Ong Kok Seng

WONG PARTNERSHIP

Established in 1992

80 RAFFLES PLACE

UOB PLAZA 1 #58-01

SINGAPORE 0104

Telephone: (65) 532 7488

Facsimile: (65) 532 5711; (65) 532 5722

Other Singapore Office: 298 Tiong Bahru Road, #18-01/06 Tiong Bahru Plaza, 0316. Telephone: (65) 222 2000. Facsimile: (65) 439-9200.

General Commercial Practice, Banking and Finance, Corporate Finance and Securities, Mergers and Acquisitions, Project and Infrastructure Financing, Cross-Borders Corporate Transactions, Real Estate and Real Estate Finance, Commercial and Corporate Litigation and Arbitration, Bankruptcy and Insolvency, Building and Construction Law, Defamation, Employment and Labour Law, Professional Negligence, Commercial Crime, Energy and Telecommunications; Intellectual Property, Trademarks and Patents.

FIRM PROFILE: *Wong Partnership has a broad-based commercial law practice offering a full range of legal services. The client base is largely institutional in profile, and covers domestic as well as multinational corporations. The firm has 15 partners and 34 associates practising in a variety of areas of law, with a particular emphasis on corporate transactions and commercial and construction law litigation. The firm is actively involved in corporate transactions regionally in China, South-East Asia (including Myanmar and Vietnam) and the Indian sub-Continent. In addition, the firm has a close association with leading United States law firm Seyfarth, Shaw, Fairweather & Geraldson, both of whom are equal partners in the international firm of Seyfarth, Shaw & Wong. Seyfarth, Shaw & Wong is based in Singapore and has an off-shore practice covering South-East Asia and East Asia.*

PARTNERS

MENG MENG WONG, admitted, 1972, Singapore; 1978, Brunei. *Education:* National University of Singapore (LL.B. Hons).

SUET-FERN LEE, admitted, 1982, Singapore; 1981, England and Wales. *Education:* Girton College, Cambridge University (B.A. Hons., 1980; M.A., 1984); Gray's Inn (Barrister-at-Law).

NIM CHOR YOONG, admitted, 1982, Singapore; 1994, Malaysia. *Education:* National University of Singapore (LL.B. Hons., 1981).

ALVIN YEO, admitted, 1988, Singapore; 1987, England and Wales. *Education:* University of London (LL.B. Hons); Gray's Inn (Barrister-at-Law). Barrister-at-Law (Gray's Inn).

CHRISTOPHER CASSIM, admitted, 1985, Singapore. *Education:* National University of Singapore (B.L. Ed., Articleship).

MOHAN R. PILLAY, admitted, 1986, Singapore. *Education:* National University of Singapore (LL.B. Hons., 1985); University of London (LL.M., 1994). Associate of the Chartered Institute of Arbitrators.

FRANCES HONG PHENG NG, admitted, 1988, Singapore. *Education:* National University of Singapore (LL.B. Hons., 1987).

DILHAN PILLAY SANDRASEGARA, admitted, 1989, Singapore. *Education:* National University of Singapore (LL.B. (Hons., 1988); University of Cambridge (LL.M., 1990).

PEI FONG TAN, admitted, 1990, Singapore. *Education:* National University of Singapore (LL.B. Hons., 1989) (Singapore).

WAI KING NG, admitted, 1991, Singapore. *Education:* National University of Singapore (LL.B. Hons., 1990).

(This Listing Continued)

ASSOCIATES

ANGELA LIM, admitted, 1990, Singapore. *Education:* National University of Singapore (LL.B. Hons., 1989); University of London (LL.M.).

STEPHEN SOH, admitted, 1990, Singapore. *Education:* National University of Singapore (LL.B. Hons., 1989).

KAY KHENG TAN, admitted, 1990, Singapore. *Education:* National University of Singapore (LL.B. Hons., 1989).

MONICA YIP, admitted, 1990, Singapore. *Education:* National University of Singapore (LL.B. Hons., 1989).

VANESSA CHAN, admitted, 1991, Singapore; 1990, England and Wales. *Education:* New Hall Cambridge (B.A. Hons., 1989); Middle Temple (Barrister-st-Law).

MONIQUE CHING CHING CHONG, admitted, 1991, Singapore. *Education:* National University of Singapore (LL.B. Hons., 1990).

ANITA DORETT, admitted, 1991, Singapore. *Education:* National University of Singapore (LL.B. Hons., 1990).

CHARMAINE KIT MEI LYE, admitted, 1991, Singapore; 1989, England and Wales. *Education:* Pembroke College, Cambridge (B.A. Hons., 1988); Innter Temple (Barrister-at-Law).

BOCK ENG SIM, admitted, 1991, Singapore. *Education:* National University of Singapore (LL.B. Hons., 1990).

RACHEL YAAG NGEE ENG, admitted, 1992, Singapore. *Education:* National University of Singapore (LL.B., Hons., 1991).

YIN MEI LOCK, admitted, 1992, Singapore. *Education:* National University of Singapore (LL.B. Hons., 1991); University of Cambridge (LL.M., 1994).

CHI MENG CHEE, admitted, 1993, Singapore. *Education:* National University of Singapore (LL.B. Hons., 1992).

JOANNE DESILVA, admitted, 1993, Singapore; 1992, England and Wales. *Education:* Oxford University (B.A. Hons., 1991); Gray's Inn (Barrister-at-Law). Barrister-at-Law, Gray's Inn.

SERENA CHOOI LI LEE, admitted, 1993, Singapore; 1991, England and Wales. *Education:* University of Sheffield (LL.B. Hon's., 1988); Solicitor of the Supreme Court of England and Wales.

MERNG PHANG LIM, admitted, 1993, Singapore. *Education:* National University of Singapore (LL.B. Hons., 1992).

JOY WHEI MIEN TAN, admitted, 1993, Singapore; 1992, England and Wales. *Education:* Cambridge University (B.A. Hons., 1991); Middle Temple (Barrister-at-Law).

GEORGINA THEN, admitted, 1993, Singapore. *Education:* National University of Singapore (LL.B. Hons., 1992).

NICHOLAS CHAN, admitted, 1994, Singapore; 1993, England and Wales. *Education:* University of Cambridge (B.A. Hons., 1992); Innter-Temple (Barrister-at Law). Barrister-at-Law (Inner Temple).

MONICA CHONG, admitted, 1994, Singapore; 1993, England and Wales. *Education:* University of Leicester (LL.B. Hons., 1989); Solicitor of England and Wales.

KAREN PHEK-INN GUI, admitted, 1994, Singapore; 1993, England and Wales. *Education:* University of Wales, Aberystwyth (LL.B. Hons., 1992); Gray's Inn (Barrister-at-Law).

KAH HUI HO, admitted, 1994, Singapore. *Education:* National University of Singapore (LL.B. Hons., 1993).

EDWIN LEE, admitted, 1994, Singapore. *Education:* National University of Singapore (LL.B. Hons., 1993).

LORRAINE LEE, admitted, 1994, Singapore; 1993, England and Wales. *Education:* University of Kent (LL.B. Hons., 1992); Middle-Temple (Barrister-at-Law).

JANICE SOO SIM LIM, admitted, 1994, Singapore. *Education:* National University of Singapore (LL.B. Hons., 1993).

MONICA POH, admitted, 1994, Singapore; 1993, England and Wales. *Education:* University of Hull (B.A. Hons., 1992); Middle-Temple (Barrister-at-Law).

LAWRENCE TAN, admitted, 1994, Singapore; 1993, England and Wales. *Education:* University of Buckingham (LL.B. Hons., 1992); Middle-Temple (Barrister-at-Law).

(This Listing Continued)

LIAN SENG YAP, admitted, 1994, Singapore; 1993, England and Wales. *Education:* King's College, London (LL.B. Hons., 1992); Lincoln's Inn (Barrister-at-Law).

NIGEL LIAN CHUAN YEOH, admitted, 1994, Singapore; 1993, England and Wales. *Education:* King's College, London (LL.B. Hons., 1992); Lincoln's Inn (Barrister-at-Law).

CHRIS WONG WAI CHONG, admitted, 1995, Singapore; 1993, England and Wales. *Education:* University of Sheffield, U.K. (LL.B. Hons., 1990); Solicitor of England and Wales.

Languages: English, Chinese (Mandarin and dialects), Malay, Indonesian, French and German

---

HELEN YEO & PARTNERS

11 COLLYER QUAY #12-01
THE ARCADE
SINGAPORE 0104
Telephone: 2251400
Telefax: 2250020

We provide comprehensive legal services to domestic and international clients. Areas of practice include Corporate, Banking and Finance, Property and Real Estate, Litigation, Insolvency, Insurance, Trademarks, Patents, Copyright and other Intellectual Property. We also provide advice and assistance to and draft documents for companies investing or doing business in China, Vietnam, Indonesia, Myanmar and Cambodia. We have 13 partners and 16 associates.

PARTNERS

HELEN YEO, admitted, 1975, Singapore. *Education:* LL.B. (Hons). *PRACTICE AREAS:* Corporate; Banking; Vietnam.

CHOO HAN TECK, admitted, 1980, Singapore. *Education:* LL.B. (Hons); Master of Laws (Cambridge). *PRACTICE AREAS:* Litigation.

DOROTHY CHIA, admitted, 1979, Singapore. *Education:* LL.B. (Hons). *PRACTICE AREAS:* Property.

CHAN YOUNG YOUNG, admitted, 1984, Singapore. *Education:* FIrst Class (Hons) in Economics, London School of Economics & Political Science; Master of Laws (Cambridge). *PRACTICE AREAS:* Corporate; China.

CARRIE SEOW, admitted, 1984, Singapore. *Education:* LL.B. (Hons). *PRACTICE AREAS:* Corporate; Indonesia; Cambodia.

LEE HO WAH, admitted, 1987, Singapore. *PRACTICE AREAS:* Property; Banking.

PHILIP JEYARETNAM, admitted, 1988, Singapore. *Education:* First Class (Hons) in Law (Cambridge). *PRACTICE AREAS:* Litigation; Intellectual Property.

LEK SIANG PHENG, admitted, 1989, Singapore. *Education:* LL.B. (Hons). *PRACTICE AREAS:* Litigation.

ANTONY LEE, admitted, 1985, Singapore. *Education:* LL.B. (Hons); Master of Laws (Corporate and Commercial Law, London). *PRACTICE AREAS:* Litigation.

FRANCES CLARE LEE, admitted, 1987, Singapore. *Education:* LL.B. (Hons.). *PRACTICE AREAS:* Property.

YEW WOON CHOOL, admitted, 1989, Singapore. *Education:* LL.B. (Hons). *PRACTICE AREAS:* Intellectual Property.

CLAIRE WONG, admitted, 1989, Singapore. *Education:* LL.B (Hons). *PRACTICE AREAS:* Corporate.

TAN HENG THYE, admitted, 1990, Singapore. *Education:* LL.B. (Hons). *PRACTICE AREAS:* Vietnam; Corporate.

ASSOCIATES

ALAN LEE, admitted, 1990, Singapore.

FLORENCE GOH, admitted, 1990, Singapore.

DANIEL CHIA, admitted, 1989, Singapore.

SHIREENA WOON, admitted, 1991, Singapore.

TEO JUN LENG, admitted, 1991, Singapore.

PAUL WONG, admitted, 1992, Singapore.

DANIEL TAN, admitted, 1992, Singapore.

(This Listing Continued)

NEOH SUE LYNN, admitted, 1993, Singapore.

ALVIN CHIA, admitted, 1993, Singapore.

LAM CHAI HAR, admitted, 1993, Singapore.

CECILIA LIM, admitted, 1991, Singapore.

PETER TAN, admitted, 1992, Singapore.

WILSON HUE, admitted, 1992, Singapore.

LEONG PAT LYNN, admitted, 1994, Singapore.

CHRISTOPHER CHONG, admitted, 1994, Singapore.

YVONNE TAN, admitted, 1994, Singapore.

CONSULTANT

VERONICA LIM, admitted, 1979, Singapore. *Education:* LL.B. (Hons). *PRACTICE AREAS:* Property; Banking.

YEO-LEONG & PEH

Established in 1987

20 MCCALLUM STREET
#12-03 ASIA CHAMBERS
SINGAPORE 0106
Telephone: 2238168
Facsimile: (65) 2207888 (Litigation and General)
Facsimile: (65) 2211238 (Corporate and Conveyancing)
Facsimile: (65) 5453505 (Partner's Residence) (after office hours)

Banking and Finance, Commercial and Corporate Law, Corporate Finance, Investments, Real Estate, Property Law and Conveyancing, Intellectual Property, Marine Law, Debt Recovery, Incorporation and Company Secretarial Work, Immigration, Family Law, General Practice and Litigation, Probate, Wills, Trusts and Estates, Foreign Projects.

MEMBERS OF FIRM

JENNIFER YEO LAI-PENG, (MRS.), LL.M. in Banking Law Studies (Boston University); LL.B. (Hons) Singapore. Commissioner for Oaths. Advocate and Solicitor, Singapore.

ADRIAN PEH NAM CHUAN, LL.B. (Hons) Singapore. Advocate and Solicitor, Singapore.

SUSAN LEONG LAI ONN, LL.B. (Hons) Singapore. Advocate and Solicitor, Singapore.

CYNTHIA LIM AI MING, LL.B. (Hons) Singapore. Advocate and Solicitor, Singapore.

SOON KAH HWEE, LL.M. (London), LL.B. (Hons) Singapore, Advocate and Solicitor, Singapore.

IGNATIUS HO WOON CHOON, LL.B. (Hons) Singapore. Advocate and Solicitor, Singapore.

MARK HAN MENG KUAN, LL.B. (Hons) Singapore. Advocate and Solicitor, Singapore.

PHYLLIS LIM SOCK NGEE, LL.B. (Hons) Singapore. Advocate and Solicitor, Singapore.

TAN KEH WHOO, LL.B. (Hons) Singapore. Advocate and Solicitor, Singapore.

CHEN PERON, LL.B. (Hons) Singapore. Advocate and Solicitor, Singapore.

CHUA LIK TENG, LL.B. (Hons.), LSE. Barrister-at-Law, Middle Temple. Advocate and Solicitor, Singapore.

LOW WAI CHEONG, LL.B. (Hons) Singapore, Advocate and Solicitor, Singapore.

LIM MIEN CHIEH, LL.B. (Hons) Singapore, Advocate and Solicitor, Singapore.

ANG SEOW WEI, LL.B. (Hons.) Singapore. Advocate and Solicitor, Singapore.

DAPHNE ONG SU LIN, LL.B. (Hons.) Singapore. Advocate and Solicitor, Singapore.

(This Listing Continued)

YEO-LEONG & PEH, Singapore—Continued

FOREIGN LEGAL COUNSEL

LI YI, LL.B. (Hua Chao University), Quanzhou, Fujian, Peoples' Republic of China.

English, Mandarin, Malay, Indonesian, French; Chinese Dialects: Cantonese; Hokkien; Teochew; Hakka.

SRI LANKA

DESMOND FERNANDO, P.C.

26 CHARLES PLACE
COLOMBO 3, SRI LANKA
Telephone: 94 1 574900, 574901, 576280
Fax: 94 1 574901

DESMOND FERNANDO, admitted, 1958, Colombo. *Education:* University of Oxford (B.A., 1955; M.A., 1964). Examiner, Mercantile Law, Sri Lanka Law College, 1962-1965. Author: Chapter on Sri Lanka in IBA handbook on Admiralty Law. Member, International Commission of Jurist, 1988; Member, Executive Committee, 1992; President, Bar Association of Sri Lanka, 1989-1991; President's Counsel, 1990; Deputy Secretary General, International Bar Association, 1988-1992; Secretary General, 1992. Distinguished Counsellor, LAWASIA Council. Honorary Life Member, Bar Association of Sri Lanka, 1994—. Vice President, International Bar Association. *LANGUAGES:* English and French. *PRACTICE AREAS:* Admiralty and Commercial.

JULIUS & CREASY

Solicitors Attorneys-at-Law

Notaries Public and Patent and Trade Mark Agents

Established in 1879

NO. 22 3/1 22 3/2 SIR BARON JAYATILAKA MAWATHA
HONG KONG & SHANGHAI BANK BUILDING
P.O. BOX 154
COLOMBO, SRI LANKA
Telephone: 422601-5
Telex: 21458 JACEY CE
Facsimile: 446663; 435451

Sub-Office: Third Floor, State Bank Building, Colombo 1.
Litigation Office: 142, Hulttadorp Street, Colombo 12. Gooneahghepura Diac Place, Colombo 12.
Service Office: Goonesinghepura, Dias Place, Colombo 12.

Company and Corporate Law, Investment Law, Taxation, Mergers and Acquisitions, Shipping and Maritime Law, Shipping Finance and Mortgages, Real Estate, Intellectual Property Law, Conveyancing and Property Law, Arbitration, Civil Litigation, Insurance Banking, Domestic Law, Commercial Contracts and Joint Ventures, Wills, Probate, Trusts, Employment and Industrial Labour Law.

FIRM PROFILE: The Firm was established according to recorded history in 1879. The Firm was founded by two British Solicitors and tradition-bound it has maintained close links with and worked in close association with the United Kingdom, United States of America and E.E.C. Countries and since the emergence of the South Eastern Region Singapore, Hong Kong, India, Pakistan, Malaysia Australia etc.

PARTNERS

Mr. B.M. Amarasekera	Mr. N.H. Gunaratna
Mr. N. Ratnasabapathy	Mr. J.M. Swaminathan
(LL.B.) London	(LL.B.; LL.M.; M.Phil)
Mr. R. Senathi Rajah	Mr. G.R.M. Bandara (LL.B.)
Mr. J.M. CanagaRetna	Mr. J.A.R. Weerasinghe
Mr. H.A. Fernando	Mr. S.A. Cader
	Ms. C.R. Ranasinghe

CONSULTANT

T.G. Gaoneratne Litigation.

MURUGESU & NEELAKANDAN

Established in 1962

75 3/1 HEMAS BUILDING (3RD FLOOR)
YORK STREET
COLOMBO 1, SRI LANKA
Telephone: (94-1) 445254; 334949
Telex: CE 21494 (Murugesu 1114)
Fax: (94-1) 445255
Cables: Emanden, Colombo

Admiralty and Shipping, Arbitration, Banking Law, Civil Litigation, Company Law, Commercial Law, Debt Collection, Foreign Investment, Intellectual Property and Insurance.

FIRM PROFILE: Member of the International Group of Law Firms - A Law Firm Member of Lawasia,

PARTNERS

VELUPILLAI MURUGESU, admitted, 1948, Sri Lanka. Solicitor, Member of the Institute of Trade Marks. Attorney-at-Law and Notary Public. (Senior Partner). *LANGUAGES:* English. *PRACTICE AREAS:* Company Law; Commercial Law; Intellectual Property; Insurance.

KANDIAH NEELAKANDAN, admitted, 1970, Sri Lanka. Attorney-at-Law and Notary Public. *LANGUAGES:* English. *PRACTICE AREAS:* Admiralty and Shipping; Banking Law; Civil Litigation; Company Law; Commercial Law; Debt Collection; Foreign Investment; Insurance.

SIVANANTHAVALLI THURAIRAJA, admitted, 1969, Sri Lanka. Solicitor, Attorney-at-Law and Notary Public. *LANGUAGES:* English. *PRACTICE AREAS:* Banking Law; Intellectual Property.

SASHIDEVI NEELAKANDAN, admitted, 1980, Sri Lanka. Attorney-at-Law and Notary Public. *LANGUAGES:* English. *PRACTICE AREAS:* Arbitration; Banking Law; Commercial Law; Foreign Investment.

NITHIANANDAN MURUGESU, admitted, 1985, Sri Lanka. Attorney-at-Law and Notary Public. *LANGUAGES:* English. *PRACTICE AREAS:* Arbitration; Civil Litigation; Debt Collection; Intellectual Property and Insurance.

Languages: English.

JOHN WILSON & ASSISTANTS

Solicitors, Attorneys at Law, Notaries, and Patent and Trade Mark

Agents

Established in 1915

365 DAM STREET
COLOMBO 12, SRI LANKA
Telephone: 324579; 699165 (Residence)
Cable Address: WILSON COLOMBO 12
Telex: 21155 NESTLE CE
Fax: 94-1-699165

Commercial, Company and Banking, Debt Recovery, Intellectual Property, Conveyancing, Admiralty, Joint Ventures, Litigation.

JOHN WILSON, born January 1, 1924; admitted, 1946, Colombo; 1950, England as Solicitor. Notary Public. *Education:* St. Joseph's College North Point Darjeeling, India, Senior Cambridge (1940); Colombo Law College. Member of the Law Commission, 1977-91. *Member:* Sri Lanka Bar Association; Ceylon Law Society. *LANGUAGES:* English.

TAIWAN

ARESTY INTERNATIONAL LAW OFFICES

SUITE 2, FOURTH FLOOR
143 TA-TUNG SECOND ROAD
KAOHSIUNG, TAIWAN
Telephone: 07-291-3051
Fax: 08-732-7500

Boston, Massachusetts Office: Bay 107, Union Wharf. Telephone: 617-367-8393. Fax: 617-742-6452.

(This Listing Continued)

Private International Law emphasizing International Business Transactions, including Strategic Alliances, Technology Transfer, Financing, International Taxation, U.S. Customs, Immigration. United States Legal Practice emphasizes Banking Law, Securities, Corporate, Business Law, Real Estate, Estate Planning, and Litigation.

JEFFREY M. ARESTY, born Framingham, Massachusetts, December 31, 1951; admitted, 1976, Massachusetts; 1982, U.S. District Court, District of Massachusetts; 1982, District of Columbia; 1983, U.S. Supreme Court. *Education:* Johns Hopkins University (B.A., 1973); Boston University (J.D., 1976; LL.M., in Taxation, 1979; LL.M. in International Banking, 1993). Awarded Academic Achievement Award for Achieving Highest Cumulative Average in the Class. Co-Editor, *ABA Guide to International Business Negotiations,* 1994. *Member:* Massachusetts (Member: Executive Committee, 1981-1983; Taxation Section Council, 1980-1982; Vice Chairman, 1982-1983 and Chairman, 1983-1984, Law Practice Section Council) and American (Vice Chairman, 1981-1983 and Chairman, 1983-1984, Membership Committee; Vice Chairman, Computer Division, 1986-1991; Council, 1985-1991; Section of Economics of Law Practice; Member, Sections on International Law and Business Law; Massachusetts State Membership Chairman, 1986—; Co-Chairman, International Negotiations Task Force, 1992—) Bar Associations. *LANGUAGES:* Spanish. *PRACTICE AREAS:* International Law; Business; Taxation; Real Estate; Securities.

ASSOCIATES

ANDREW S. BREINES, born Englewood, New Jersey, October 2, 1966; admitted, 1991, Massachusetts. *Education:* Franklin & Marshall College (B.A., 1988); Pepperdine University (J.D., 1991). Phi Alpha Delta. *Member:* Boston (Member, Young Lawyers' Division), Massachusetts (Member, Young Lawyers' Section) and American (Member, Sections on: International Law and Practice; Young Lawyers Division; Business Law) Bar Associations. *PRACTICE AREAS:* General Practice.

INTERNATIONAL LAW CONSULTANT

YI-FU (EVE) SUN. *Education:* Soochow University Law School, Taiwan (LL.B., 1980); Bond University Law School, Australia (LL.M., in International Law, 1992). Legal Consultant in Immigration and Transnational Business Transactions. *LANGUAGES:* Chinese and English.

LEGAL SUPPORT PERSONNEL

INTERNATIONAL BUSINESS CONSULTANTS

VICTOR J. ARESTY. PRACTICE AREAS: Foreign direct real estate investment ventures; Matching foreign investors with U.S. investment opportunities as limited partners; Transnational business including overseas manufacturing and distribution; Export of goods from Taiwan, Korea, Italy, Spain and South America.

YEICHUN WANG. *Education:* Utah State University (M.S., in Economics, 1982); Georgia State University (M.S., in Computer and Information Systems, 1985). (Resident, Kaohsiung, Taiwan). *LANGUAGES:* Chinese and English. *PRACTICE AREAS:* Cross-cultural training; Negotiation skills in both Chinese and U.S. contexts; U.S. and Taiwanese business networks.

ALEXANDER, HOLBURN, BEAUDIN & LANG

C/O 7F-2, NO. 9, ROOSEVELT ROAD, SECTION 2
TAIPEI, TAIWAN
Telephone: (886-2) 395-6989
Fax: (886-2) 391-4235

Vancouver, Canada Office: P.O. Box 10057. 2700 Toronto Dominion Bank Tower, 700 West Georgia Street. Telephone: 604-688-1351. Fax: 604-669-7642.

Hong Kong Office, In Association with Lawrence Ong & Chung: c/o 8th Floor, Chekiang First Bank Centre, 1 Duddell Street, Central. Telephone: (852-2) 526-1171 Fax: (852-2) 845-0686.

Firm engaged in Canadian and International law practice. Corporate, Commercial, International Trade, Technology Transfer, Real Estate and Immigration. Not authorized to appear before R.O.C. courts.

(This Listing Continued)

RESIDENT ASSOCIATES

RICHARD P. HARNETTY, born Vancouver, British Columbia, April 5, 1960; admitted, 1991, British Columbia; 1994, England. *Education:* University of British Columbia (B.A., 1982; LL.B., 1990). *Member:* Canadian Bar Association; Law Society of British Columbia; Law Society of England and Wales; Canadian Society in Taiwan (Director, 1993—).

All Members of the Firm Are Members of the Vancouver and Canadian Bar Associations and The Law Society of British Columbia.

English, Chinese and French.

(For complete biographical data on all personnel, see professional biographies at Vancouver, British Columbia, Canada)

ALLIANCE INTERNATIONAL LAW OFFICES

(Legal Advisor to the Taiwan Stock Exchange Corporation)

Established in 1987

7TH FLOOR, ENTERPRISE BUILDING
54, CHUNG SHAN N. ROAD, SEC. 3
TAIPEI, TAIWAN
Telephone: (02) 597-4521
Telex: 25119 YBDTPE
Facsimile: (02) 592-6601

International Business Transactions, Foreign Investment, Corporate Law, Representations before Governmental Agencies, Administrative Agencies, Administrative Appeals and Litigations, Taxation, Estate Planning, Banking, Corporate Finance, Trademarks, Patents, Copyrights, Negotiable Instruments and Civil and Criminal Cases.

FIRM PROFILE: Alliance International Law Office was formed in June, 1987 by Mr. Jen-Kong Loh. Mr. Loh was the Minister of Finance from 1984 to 1985. Before that, he had held various senior government positions, such as Commissioner of the National Tax Administration of Taipei, Director-General of Customs, President of the Central Trust of China, and Vice Minister of Finance. When Mr. Loh was the Finance Minister, he was also a member of the Council for Economic Planning and Development, as well as a Managing Director of the Central Bank of China.

JEN-KONG LOH, born Wusih, Kiangsu, June 19, 1927; admitted, 1987, Taipei. *Education:* Soochow University School of Law (LL.B., 1956); Southern Methodist University (M.C.L., 1959). Author: "Federal Constitution of the United States," Carat Publishing Company, 1964; "Credit and Security in the Republic of China," University of Queensland Press, Australia, 1974. Lecturer, Graduate School of Law, Soochow University, 1986—. Vice Minister for Policy, 1981-1984 and Minister, 1984-1985, Ministry of Finance. Managing Director, Central Bank of China, 1984-1985. *Member:* Taipei Bar Association. (Founder). *LANGUAGES:* Chinese and English. *PRACTICE AREAS:* Tax Planning.

WAN-JYE CHANG, born Chang I, Shan Tung Province, December 4, 1928; admitted, 1986, Taipei; Licensed, Certified Public Accountant, R.O.C., 1984. *Education:* Taiwan Administration College (1951); Soochow University School of Law (LL.B., 1957); Institute for the Training of Judicial Officials (Class of Lawyers, 1987). Author: "Research for Commodity Tax," 1969 and "General Introduction of Tax Law," 1975, Jwei-Ming Printing Company, Ltd.; "Research on Tax System and Practice," Yung-Hsin Publishing Company, 1981. Research Fellow, Institute of Tax Administration, University of Southern California, 1978. Professor of Law, TamKang University, 1971-1989. Head of the Audit Department and Chief, Tax Administration of Taipei Hsien, 1965-1974. Chief Secretary, Tax Administration of Keelung City, 1972. Assistant Director, Finance Ministry's Law Review Committee, 1982-1988. Head of the Legal Department, National Tax Administration of Taipei, 1974-1982. *Member:* Taipei Bar Association; Certified Public Accountant Association. *LANGUAGES:* Chinese and English. *PRACTICE AREAS:* Tax Law.

SHIN-SHING LEE, born Hsinchu, November 10, 1949; admitted, 1981, Taipei. *Education:* Soochow University School of Law (LL.B., 1978); Summer Program, United States Law and Legal Institution, University of Wisconsin, 1986. With: National Tax Administration of Taipei, 1977-1978; National Tax Administration of Kaohsiung, 1978-1979; National Bureau of Standards, MOEA, 1979-1980; Lee and Li, 1980-1989. *Member:* Taipei Bar Association; Kaohsiung Bar Association. *LANGUAGES:* Mandarin, Taiwanese and English. *PRACTICE AREAS:* Litigation.

(This Listing Continued)

ALLIANCE INTERNATIONAL LAW OFFICES, Taipei—Continued

SUSAN HSING SHYY, born Tainan, Taiwan, Republic of China; admitted, 1983, Taipei. *Education:* Cheng-Chi University School of Law (LL.B., 1979); University of Pennsylvania (LL.M., 1985), Lee and Li, 1979-1987. Legal Counsel to Digital Equipment Corp. Taiwan, 1988-1992. *LANGUAGES:* Mandarin and English. *PRACTICE AREAS:* International Trade and Computer Law.

DAVID TA-WEI LU, born Taipei, Taiwan, Republic of China, October 8, 1952; admitted, 1990, Taipei. *Education:* Soochow University Law School, Taipei, Republic of China (LL.B., 1981); Tulane University (LL.M., 1984); Southern Methodist University (J.D., 1986). Teaching Assistant, Soochow University Law School, 1981-1983. Associate Professor of Law, Soochow University, 1986—. Lee and Li, 1986-1989. Associate. *LANGUAGES:* Mandarin and English. *PRACTICE AREAS:* Corporate; Commercial; Banking; Securities.

ZOË CHOU YUN YANG, born Taipei, September 27, 1957; (Not admitted in Taiwan). *Education:* National Taiwan University School of Law (LL.B., 1980). Associate, Cathy Law Firm, 1980-1982. Senior Associate, Lee and Li, 1982-1990. *LANGUAGES:* Mandarin, English and Taiwanese. *PRACTICE AREAS:* Corporate and Commercial Law; Foreign Investment.

YUAN SHYANG LIN, born Taipei, Taiwan, November 12, 1961; admitted, 1988, Taipei. *Education:* Fu Jen Catholic University School of Law (LL.B., 1985; LL.M., 1991). Associate, Taiwan International Patent & Law Office, 1989-1991. *LANGUAGES:* Chinese, Japanese and Taiwanese. *PRACTICE AREAS:* Intellectual Property Law.

HUEI-FEN LIEN, born Taipei, Taiwan, January 6, 1964; (Not admitted in Taiwan). *Education:* Soochow University School of Law (LL.B., 1987). *LANGUAGES:* Chinese and English. *PRACTICE AREAS:* Company Law; Civil Law and Litigation.

JENNY LEE, born Taipei, Taiwan, May 24, 1963; (Not admitted in Taiwan). *Education:* Soochow University School of Law (LL.B., 1987). Associate: Ding & Ding Attorneys-at-Law, 1987-1988; Lee and Li, 1988-1993. *LANGUAGES:* Mandarin and English. *PRACTICE AREAS:* Trademark Law.

CONSULTANTS

JEN YANG, born Nanking, China, January 10, 1939; (Not admitted in Taiwan). *Education:* Soochow University Law School (LL.B., 1965); Monash University Law School, Australia (LL.M., 1972). Author: "Outlines of Anglo-American Law of Contracts," Bookworld Company, 1965; "Laytime and Demurrage," Maritime Foundation, 1968; "Law of Contract of the R.O.C.," Academia Sinica, 1985; "Remedies in Contract for Defective Consent, A Comparative Study between Australia and the Republic of China," The National Chung Hsing Law Review, Vol. 22, 1986. Associate Professor, Soochow University Law School, 1985—. Specialist, Foreign Investment Commission, The Ministry of Economic Affairs, 1972-1973. (Investment Consultant). *LANGUAGES:* Chinese and English. *PRACTICE AREAS:* Anglo-American Contract Law.

MARTIN CHIA-PING TSAI, born Calcutta, India, December 7, 1948; (Not admitted in Taiwan). *Education:* National Taiwan University (B.S.E.E., 1972); Sloan School of Management, M.I.T. (S.M. Finance, 1976); Wharton School, University of Pennsylvania (M.A. Risk and Insurance, 1981). Assistant Director, Monetary Affairs Department, Ministry of Finance, The Republic of China, 1979-1980. (Financial Consultant). *LANGUAGES:* Chinese and English. *PRACTICE AREAS:* Financial and Strategy Consulting.

CHAI-BAN TSAI, born Taichung, Taiwan, October 17, 1941; (Not admitted in Taiwan). Licensed, Certified Public Accountant, R.O.C. *Education:* National Cheng-Chi University (B.A., 1966; M.A., 1970). Lecturer, Accounting Department, Soochow University, 1975— and Public Finance Department, National Cheng-Chi University, 1975—. Auditor, Audit Department of the Central Bank, 1967-1971; Audit Department of the Ministry of Finance, 1971-1974. *Member:* Certified Public Accountant Association. (Tax Consultant). *LANGUAGES:* Chinese and English. *PRACTICE AREAS:* Financial analysis and Auditing.

Languages: Chinese, English, Mandarin and Taiwanese.

BAKER & McKENZIE
15TH FLOOR, HUNG TAI CENTER
NO. 168, TUN HWA NORTH ROAD
TAIPEI 105, TAIWAN
Telephone: (02) 712-6151
Intn'l. Dialing: (886-2) 712-6151
Facsimiles: (886-2) 716-9250; 712-8292

Associated Offices of Baker & McKenzie in: Almaty, Amsterdam, Bangkok, Barcelona, Beijing, Berlin, Bogotá, Brasília, Brussels, Budapest, Buenos Aires, Cairo, Caracas, Chicago, Dallas, Frankfurt, Geneva, Hanoi, Ho Chi Minh City, Hong Kong, Juárez, Kiev, London, Madrid, Manila, Melbourne, México City, Miami, Milan, Monterrey, Moscow, New York, Palo Alto, Paris, Prague, Rio de Janeiro, Riyadh, Rome, St. Petersburg, San Diego, San Francisco, São Paulo, Singapore, Stockholm, Sydney, Tijuana, Tokyo, Toronto, Valencia, Warsaw, Washington, D.C. and Zürich.
Correspondent Law Firm: Hadiputranto, Hadinoto & Partners, Jakarta.

Litigation, Banking and Securities, Intellectual Property, Corporate, Mergers and Acquisitions, Investment, Tax, Visas and Registrations, Real Estate and Construction, Maritime and Aviation, and Labor.

LINDY L. Y. CHERN, born Taipei, Taiwan, January 25, 1951; admitted, 1975, Taipei, Taiwan, ROC. *Education:* National Taiwan University Law School (LL.B., 1973; LL.M., 1979). *Member:* Taipei Bar Association. *LANGUAGES:* Mandarin, Taiwanese and English. *PRACTICE AREAS:* Corporate and Partnership Law; Intellectual Property Law; Construction and Property Development; Computers and Technology Law; Communications and Media Law.

REMINGTON HUANG, born Nan-Tou, Taiwan, October 23, 1955; admitted, 1978, Taipei, Taiwan, ROC; 1993, Panchiao, Taiwan, ROC. *Education:* National Taiwan University (LL.B., 1977; LL.M.; 1980). *Member:* Taipei Bar Association. *LANGUAGES:* Mandarin, Taiwanese, English and German. *PRACTICE AREAS:* Commercial Litigation; Civil Litigation; Transportation Law; Bankruptcy, Insolvency and Reorganization; Antitrust Law.

JOHN S. LEE, born Taipei, Taiwan, January 2, 1941; admitted, 1967, Taipei, Taiwan, ROC; 1991, Keelung, Taiwan, ROC. *Education:* National Taiwan University (LL.B., 1963); Cheng Chi University (LL.M., 1970). Assistant Professor of Civil Law, Military Finance and Management College, 1971-1973. *Member:* Taipei Bar Association (Director, 1972-1974; Supervisor, 1975-1977); The Chinese Association of Comparative Law; The Patent Association of Asia and Western Pacific. *LANGUAGES:* Mandarin, Taiwanese, English and Japanese. *PRACTICE AREAS:* Commercial Litigation; Intellectual Property Law; Banking and Finance; Maritime Law; Insurance Law.

JAMES T. T. TSENG, born Taiwan, October 31, 1933; admitted, 1959, Tainan, Taiwan, ROC; 1971, Taipei, Taiwan, ROC. *Education:* National Taiwan University Law School (LL.B., 1957). President, National Bar Association of ROC, 1993—. *Member:* Taipei Bar Association; Asian Patent Attorney's Association (Standing Director, National Group of the Republic of China, 1975—); Comparative Law Society of China. *LANGUAGES:* Mandarin, English, Japanese and Taiwanese. *PRACTICE AREAS:* Corporate and Partnership Law; Intellectual Property Law; Banking and Finance; Real Estate Law; Arbitration and Dispute Resolution.

DAVID H. J. YANG, born Tainan, Taiwan, January 2, 1940; admitted, 1980, Taipei, Taiwan, ROC. *Education:* Soochow University Law School (LL.B., 1963); Graduate School of Law, University of Chinese Culture (LL.M., 1967); Faculty of Laws, University College, London University (LL.M. program, 1969-1970); London Institute of World Affairs (Diploma in Air and Space Law); College of Law, Florida State University (Jur.D.). *Member:* Taipei Bar Association; The Comparative Law Society of China. *LANGUAGES:* Mandarin, English and Taiwanese. *PRACTICE AREAS:* Aviation and Aerospace Technology; Intellectual Property Law; Communications and Media Law; Commercial Litigation; Maritime Law.

KENNETH W. GRAY, admitted, 1982, New South Wales, Australia; 1987, England and Hong Kong; 1988, Victoria, Australia (Not admitted in Taiwan, ROC). *Education:* University of New South Wales (B.Com., LLB.). *LANGUAGES:* English.

DOLLY TAI-LAN LO, born Taipei, Taiwan, March 9, 1955; admitted, 1980, Massachusetts, U.S.A. (Not admitted in Taiwan, ROC). *Education:* Wellesley College (B.A., 1977); Harvard Law School (J.D., 1980). Phi Beta

(This Listing Continued)

Kappa. *LANGUAGES:* English, Mandarin and Taiwanese. *PRACTICE AREAS:* Mergers and Acquisitions; Taxation; Corporate and Partnership Law; Government Relations.

TIFFANY T. F. HUANG, born Taipei, Taiwan, October 18, 1957; admitted, 1985, Taipei and Taoyuan, Taiwan, ROC; 1993, Panchiao, Taiwan, ROC. *Education:* National Chengchi University Law School (LL.B., 1979; LL.M., 1988); University of Washington in Seattle (LL.M., 1989). *LANGUAGES:* Mandarin, Taiwanese and English. *PRACTICE AREAS:* Arbitration and Dispute Resolution; Construction and Property Development; Commercial Litigation; Civil Litigation; Public Contracts and Utilities.

KEYE S. WU, born Canton, China, July 3, 1947; admitted, 1973, Taipei, Taiwan, ROC. *Education:* Cheng-Kung University (B.A.). *LANGUAGES:* Mandarin and English. *PRACTICE AREAS:* Corporate and Partnership Law; Franchise Law; Labor and Employment Law; Taxation.

WILLIAM E. BRYSON, JR., born Japan, June 27, 1958; admitted, 1984, Illinois, U.S.A.; 1988, New York, U.S.A. (Not admitted in Taiwan, ROC). *Education:* Duke University (B.A., 1980); Tulane University School of Law (J.D., 1984). *LANGUAGES:* English.

MICHELLE YA-LING GON, born Taipei, Taiwan, July 10, 1954; admitted, 1986, Illinois, U.S.A. (Not admitted in Taiwan, ROC). *Education:* National Taiwan University (LL.B., 1976); University of Illinois (M.C.L., 1982); Case Western Reserve University (J.D., 1985). Associate Law Professor, Schoow University, School of Law, 1989—. *Member:* Illinois State and American Bar Associations. *LANGUAGES:* Mandarin, Taiwanese and English. *PRACTICE AREAS:* Intellectual Property Law; Corporate and Partnership Law; Trade (China); Immigration Law; Labor and Employment Law.

MICHAEL WONG, born China, August 1, 1959; admitted, 1985, California, U.S.A. (Not admitted in Taiwan, ROC). *Education:* University of California at Los Angeles (B.A., 1981); Hastings College of the Law, University of California (J.D., 1985). *Member:* State Bar of California; Asian American and American Bar Associations. *LANGUAGES:* Mandarin and English. *PRACTICE AREAS:* Corporate and Partnership Law; Taiwan Law; Mergers and Acquisitions; Taxation; Entertainment, the Arts and Sports Law.

NANCY NAI-WEN CHANG, born Taipei, Taiwan, ROC, April 11, 1967; admitted, 1994, Taipei, Taiwan, ROC. *Education:* National Taiwan University (LL.B., 1990); China Culture University (LL.M.).

VICTOR C. M. CHANG, born Chia-Yi, Taiwan, September 22, 1963; admitted, 1988, Taipei, Taiwan, ROC. *Education:* National Taiwan University (LL.B., 1985); Columbia School of Law (LL.M., 1993). *Member:* Taipei Bar Association; Comparative Law Association. *LANGUAGES:* Mandarin, English and Taiwanese. *PRACTICE AREAS:* Commercial Litigation; Civil Litigation; Securities and Financial Products; Intellectual Property Law; Mergers and Acquisitions.

JUSTIN SHI-JENG DING, born Taipei, Taiwan, November 28, 1965; admitted, 1991, Taipei, Taiwan, ROC. *Education:* National Taiwan University (LL.B., 1990); University of Wisconsin (M.L.I., 1993). *LANGUAGES:* Mandarin, English and Taiwanese. *PRACTICE AREAS:* Securities and Financial Products; Banking and Finance; Civil Litigation; Taxation.

ERION YA-LI LEE, born Taipei, Taiwan, ROC, June 16, 1970; admitted, 1994, Taipei, Taiwan, ROC. *Education:* National Taiwan University (LL.B., 1992; LL.M., 1994).

STACEY GUEMIN LEE, born Taipei, Taiwan, December 11, 1959; admitted, 1983, Taipei, Taiwan, ROC; 1990, California, U.S.A.; 1993, Hsinchu and Kaohsiang, Taiwan, ROC. *Education:* National Cheng-Chi University (LL.B., 1982; LL.M., 1986); McGeorge School of Law, University of the Pacific (LL.M., 1988; J.D., 1992). *Member:* Taipei Bar Association; State Bar of California; American Bar Association. *LANGUAGES:* Chinese, English and Taiwanese. *PRACTICE AREAS:* Corporate and Partnership Law; Trade (Taiwan); Intellectual Property Law; Antitrust Law; Civil Litigation.

JUSTIN C. LIANG, born Chiayi, ROC, December 2, 1960; admitted, 1990, Taipei, ROC. *Education:* National Taiwan University (LL.B., 1984); Soochow University, Graduate School (LL.M., 1986). *Member:* Taipei Bar Association. *LANGUAGES:* Mandarin and English. *PRACTICE AREAS:*

(This Listing Continued)

Banking and Finance; Securities and Financial Products; Corporate and Partnership Law.

IVAN LEE-EN LIU, born Taichung, Taiwan, ROC, February 19, 1968; admitted, 1995, Taipei, Taiwan, ROC. *Education:* National Taiwan University (LL.B., 1990). *LANGUAGES:* Mandarin and English.

VITA WEI-CHI LIU, born Taipei, Taiwan, September 29, 1965; admitted, 1988, Taipei, Taiwan, ROC. *Education:* National Taiwan University Law School (LL.B., 1987); Harvard Law School (LL.M., 1991). *Member:* Taipei Bar Association. *LANGUAGES:* Mandarin, English and Taiwanese. *PRACTICE AREAS:* Commercial Litigation; Banking and Finance.

SERAPHIM G. R. MAR, born Tainan, Taiwan, ROC, November 23, 1961; admitted, 1990, Taipei, Taiwan, ROC. *Education:* National Taiwan University (LL.B., 1985); University of California, Boalt Hall School of Law Berkeley (LL.M., 1994). *Member:* Taipei and Hsinchu Bar Associations. *LANGUAGES:* Mandarin, Taiwanese and English.

GRACE SHAO, born Taipei, Taiwan, R.O.C., April 30, 1966; admitted, 1990, Taipei, Taiwan, ROC. *Education:* National Taiwan University (LL.B., 1988). *Member:* Taipei Bar Association. *LANGUAGES:* Mandarin, Taiwanese and English.

VINCENT LI-CHENG SHIH, born Tainan, Taiwan, July 15, 1967; admitted, 1993, Taipei, Taiwan. *Education:* National Taiwan University (LL.M., 1989). Patent Agent, 1993. Member, Society of Comparative Law, 1993. *Member:* Taipei Bar Association. *LANGUAGES:* Mandarin, Taiwanese and English. *PRACTICE AREAS:* Commercial Litigation; Civil Litigation; Intellectual Property Law.

H. HENRY CHANG, admitted, 1988, California, U.S.A., U.S. District Court, Central, Northern, Eastern and Southern Districts of California and U.S. Court of Appeals, Ninth Circuit; 1990, New York, U.S.A. and U.S. District Court, Southern District of New York (Not admitted in Taiwan, ROC). *Education:* Universitat Regensburg, West Germany; Cornell University (B.A., 1984); Tulane University School of Law (J.D., 1987). President, Mortar Board. Intern: Lt. Governor of Delaware, 1985; U.S. Attorneys Office, New Orleans, LA, 1986-1987. Consultant to The Shanghai Financial Law Firms. Member: Governing Board of Alhambra Hospital; National Association of Cornell Officers. Contributor, Business Asia Report. *Member:* Beverly Hills, Federal and American (Member, Patents, Trademarks and Copyrights Section) Bar Associations; National Health Lawyers Association. *LANGUAGES:* German, English and Chinese. *PRACTICE AREAS:* Corporate and Partnership Law; Intellectual Property Law; Arbitration and Dispute Resolution; Entertainment, the Arts and Sports Law; Communications and Media Law.

TING-TING CHU, born Taipei, Taiwan, December 9, 1967; admitted, 1993, New York, U.S.A. (Not admitted in Taiwan, ROC). *Education:* National Cheng-Chi University (LL.B., 1989); Boston University School of Law, Graduate Program in Banking Law Studies (LL.M., 1991). *LANGUAGES:* Mandarin and English. *PRACTICE AREAS:* Banking and Finance; Trade (Taiwan); Regulatory Law; Corporate and Partnership Law.

YUAN-SAN LU, born Taipei, Taiwan, September 18, 1957; admitted, 1989, New York, U.S.A.; 1991, District of Columbia, U.S.A. (Not admitted in Taiwan, ROC). *Education:* Soochow University (L.B., 1981); Chengchi University (M.A., 1984); Cornell University (LL.M., 1987); The American University (J.D., 1990). *LANGUAGES:* Mandarin and English.

KEVIN YUEH-HSIEN WANG, born Taipei, Taiwan, April 7, 1963; admitted, 1992, New York, U.S.A. (Not admitted in Taiwan, ROC). *Education:* National Chunghsing University (LL.B., 1985); The American University, Washington College of Law (LL.M., 1989); New York University School of Law (M.C.J., 1991). *Member:* New York State Bar Association. *LANGUAGES:* English and Mandarin. *PRACTICE AREAS:* Corporate and Partnership Law; Trade (China); China Law.

WAI B. ZEE, born Hong Kong, November 12, 1962; admitted, 1988, New York, U.S.A. (Not admitted in Taiwan, ROC). *Education:* Cornell University (A.B., 1984); Albany Law School of Union College (J.D., 1987); New York University School of Law (LL.M., 1992). *Member:* American Bar Association; Asian Bar Association of New York; International Trademark Association. *LANGUAGES:* English and Chinese. *PRACTICE AREAS:* Intellectual Property Law; Trade (China); Antitrust Law; Computers and Technology Law; Entertainment, the Arts and Sports Law.

CHA & PAN

11TH FLOOR, NO. 50
SING SHENG SOUTH ROAD
SECTION 1
TAIPEI, TAIWAN
Telephone: 02-356-3288
Fax: 02-356-7058

New York, New York Office: 36 West 44th Street. Telephone: 212-391-1888. Fax: 212-575-1830.

General and International Practice, Corporate, Foreign Investment, Trademark, Litigation, Patent, Copyright.

SHAW-YU LIU, born Miaoli, Taiwan, November 16, 1931; admitted, 1983, Taiwan. *Education:* National Taiwan University (LL.B., 1954); University of Meiji of Japan (LL.M., 1964);. Section Chief, Ministry of Justice, 1964-1971. Expert, Taiwan Supply Bureau, 1971-1983. Law Professor: Fu-Jen Catholic University, 1966—; Chinese Culture University, 1972—. *Member:* Taipei and Keelung Bar Associations. *LANGUAGES:* Chinese (Mandarin, Hakkaese and Taiwanese). *PRACTICE AREAS:* Commercial Litigation; Civil Litigation.

SPENSER Y. HOR, born Hualien, Taiwan, November 8, 1960; admitted, 1990, New York, New Jersey and District of Columbia. *Education:* National Taiwan University (LL.B., 1983); Eastern Illinois University School of Business (M.B.A., 1985); Southern Methodist University School of Law (LL.M., 1987; J.D., 1989). *LANGUAGES:* Chinese (Mandarin and Taiwanese). *PRACTICE AREAS:* International Trade; Finance; Banking; Corporate; Securities.

OF COUNSEL

LON SJUE CHEN, born Taipei, Taiwan, December 2, 1952; admitted, 1990, Taiwan. *Education:* Fu-Jen Catholic University (LL.B., 1975); London School of Economics and Political Science (LL.M., 1979; Ph.D., 1982). Research Fellow, University of Michigan School of Law, 1981. Associate Professor, 1983-1987, Professor, 1987—, and Chairman, Tunghai University Law School, 1988—. Director, Tunghai Graduate Legal Studies, 1988—. *Member:* Taichung Bar Association. *LANGUAGES:* Chinese (Mandarin and Taiwanese). *PRACTICE AREAS:* Private International Law.

REPRESENTATIVE CLIENTS: Mainland Affairs Committee, Republic of China; Ministry of Transportation and Communication, Republic of China; World Financial Services, Inc.; L.K.K. Developers, Inc.; Pedrini, SPA; Nautica Apparel, Inc.; Taiwan Security Daily News; Trustee of Princeton University; American Cyanamid Company; Castrol Taiwan Limited; The Procter & Gamble Company.

(For Biographical Data on Other Personnel of New York Office, see Professional Biographies at New York, New York)

CHEN SHYUU & PUN LAW OFFICES

Established in 1980

7TH FLOOR, ROSE MANSION
NO. 162, SEC. 3, SHIN-YI ROAD
TAIPEI, TAIWAN
Telephone: 886-2-7034488
Fax: 886-2-7047866

Antitrust and Unfair Competition, Banking and Business Law, Corporate, Environmental, General International Trade, Insurance, Litigation, Labor, Intellectual Property, Real Estate and Construction, Securities and Taxation.

MEMBERS OF FIRM

JIN-FANG PUN, born Kaoshung, 1960; admitted, 1983, Taiwan. *Education:* National Taiwan University (LL.B., 1982); University of California, Los Angeles, Law School (LL.M., 1989); Harvard University, Law School (LL.M., 1990). Editor, Law Journal of Wurzel & Root, 1985—. Author: "Internationalization of Securities Markets in Taiwan, the Republic of China," 1990; "Some Remedies for Squeezeouts and Freezeouts of Minority Shareholders in Close Corporations," 1989. Co-Author: "Labor Conditions and Labor Welfare," The Chinese National Federation of Industries, R.O.C., 1988; "Don't Lose Your Rights I," Legal Service Association, National Taiwan University, 1984. Formerly associated with: Powell, Goldstein, Frazer & Murphy, 1990-1991; Arnall, Golden & Gregory, 1991-1992. *Member:* Taipei and Tao-Yuan Bar Association; Chinese Comparative Law Society; Legal Aid, R.O.C. (Committee Chair, 1993—), National Federation of Bar Association. *LANGUAGES:* Chinese and English.

(This Listing Continued)

CHING-HSIOU CHEN, born Changhua, Taiwan, 1959; admitted, 1981, Taiwan. *Education:* National Taiwan University (LL.B., 1981; LL.M., 1984; Dr. of Law, 1991). Editor, Law Journal of Wurzel & Root, 1985—. Author: "Theory and Practice in Administrative Litigation," Public Law Series II, 1994; "Basic Principal on Taxation," Public Law Series III, 1993; "Subject Matter of Tax Actions," Public Law Series, I, 1991. Co-Author: "Legal Relation on Fair Trade Law and Intellectual Property Rights," Fair Trade Commission, Administrative Yuan, 1993; "Reducing and Recycling Wastes," Environmental Protection Agency, Administrative Yuan, 1992; "Study on Tax Penalties," Ministry of Finance, 1992; "Study on Legislation for Radioactive Wastes," Atomic Energy Committee, Administrative Yuan, 1992; "Study in Labor Standards and Labor Welfare," Chinese National Federation of Industries, R.O.C., 1987. Associate Professor, Soochow University School of Law, 1993—. Lecturer for Taxation, Public Finance Training Institute, Ministry of Finance, 1993—. Legal Advisor, Industrial Development Bureau, Ministry of Economic Affairs, 1992. Commissioner, Committee on Administrative Appeal, Taipei City Government, 1995—. Committee Member, Environmental Protection, Consumer Protection Foundation, 1992—. Director, R.O.C. Association of Taxpayer Protection, 1993. *Member:* Taipei and Kaoshung Bar Associations; Chinese Comparative Law Society. *LANGUAGES:* Chinese, English and Japanese.

SHU-HUAN SHYUU, born Nantou, Taiwan, 1958; admitted, 1981, Taiwan. *Education:* National Taiwan University (LL.B., 1981; LL.M., 1984). Editor, Law Journal of Wurzel & Root, 1985—. Author: "Collection and Presentation of the Merits in Civil Actions," 1984. Co-Author: "Study in the Relation between Fair Trade Law and Intellectual Property Rights," Fair Trade Commission, R.O.C., 1993; "Study in Labor Standards and Labor Welfare," Chinese National Federation of Industries, R.O.C., 1987; "How to Protect Your Rights I?," Legal Service Association, National Taiwan University R.O.C., 1985. Lecturer: in Law, Chung-Yuan University, 1994—; Tung-Hai University, 1991—. *Member:* Taipei and Taichung Bar Associations; Chinese Comparative Law Society; R.O.C. National Federation of Bar Association (Committee Chair, Civil Law Practice, 1993—). *LANGUAGES:* Chinese and Japanese.

SONG-MAW LIN, born Chia-Yi, Taiwan, 1935; admitted, 1991, Taiwan. *Education:* National Taiwan University (LL.B., 1957); National Kyushu University, Fukuoka, Japan (LL.M., 1966). Author: "Study on the Law of Cooperative Society"; "Study on Legislative Procedure in Japan". Assistant Professor, Civil Law, Tamsui Junior College of Business Administration, 1976-1991. Lecturer: Labor Law, Law School, National Chunshin University, 1986—; Commercial Law, Tatung College of Industry, 1966-1970; History of Chinese Law, West Japan College of Law, 1965. Committee Member, Law and Regulations, Ministry of Transportation and Communication, 1991—. Senior Advisor, Overseas Commerce Agency, Ministry of Economic Affairs (MOEA), 1990. Secretary General, Central Standard Bureau, MOEA, 1989. Executive Secretary, Anti-Counterfeiting Committee, MOEA, 1986. Secretary, Hong Kong Team, Executive Yuan, 1985. Deputy Director General: Department of Small and Medium Enterprises, MOEA, 1981; Export Processing Zone Administration (EPZA), MOEA, 1979. Director, Economic Section, Taipei Headquarters, East Asia Relation Association, 1977. Committee Member on Appeals, Laws and Regulations and Senior Advisor, Department of Investment, MOEA, 1976. Deputy Executive Secretary, Foreign Investment Commission, MOEA, 1970. *Member:* Taipei Bar Association. *LANGUAGES:* Japanese, Taiwanese and Mandarin Chinese.

WANG-MIN LIN, born Yun-Lin, Taiwan, 1963; admitted, 1991, Taiwan. *Education:* National Taiwan University (LL.B., 1985; LL.M., 1991). Author, "Study on the Service Procedure in Civil Action," 1991. Co-Author: "Don't Lose Your Rights II". Legal Service Association, National Taiwan University, 1986. *Member:* Taipei Bar Association. *LANGUAGES:* Chinese and Japanese.

KUAN-LING SHEN, born Pin-Tung, Taiwan, 1968; admitted, 1992, Taiwan. *Education:* National Taiwan University School of Law (LL.M., 1991; LL.M., 1994). Author, "Die einstweilige verfuegung im Rahmen der Unwelebaftung," 1993. *Member:* Taipei Bar Association. *LANGUAGES:* Chinese, English and German.

CHIA-MING CHAI, born Taipei, Taiwan, 1970; admitted, 1993, Taiwan. *Education:* National Taiwan University (LL.M., 1992). *Member:* Taipei Bar Association. *LANGUAGES:* Chinese and English.

CHING-HUI HUANG, born Taipei, Taiwan, 1968; admitted, 1994, Taiwan. *Education:* National Cheng-Chi University (LL.B., 1991). *Member:* Taipei Bar Association. *LANGUAGES:* Chinese and English.

(This Listing Continued)

DER-CHIANN TENG, born Taipei, Taiwan, 1968; admitted, 1994, Taiwan. *Education:* National Chunghsing University (LL.B., 1991). Clerk, Taipei District Court, Si-Lin Branch, 1994. *LANGUAGES:* Chinese and English.

SHIN LIAN LEI, born Chang Hua, Taiwan, 1969; admitted, 1994, Taiwan. *Education:* National Chunghsing University (LL.B., 1991). Legal Assistant, Tsar & Tsai Law Office, 1990. *LANGUAGES:* Chinese, English, Japanese and German.

VINCENT HWANG, born Taipei, Taiwan, 1963; admitted, 1994, Taiwan. *Education:* National Taiwan University (LL.B., 1990). *LANGUAGES:* Chinese and English.

DAVID CHEN, born Mau Li, Taiwan, 1963; admitted, 1994, Taiwan. *Education:* FU-JEN University (LL.B., 1990). Clerk and Editor, Committee on Laws and Regulations of Government Information Office, Administrative Yuan, 1991-1994. *LANGUAGES:* Chinese and English.

CHINA-PACIFIC LAW OFFICES

RM. 1503, FL. 15, NO. 88
SEC. 2 CHUNG HSIAO E. RD.
TAIPEI, TAIWAN
Telephone: (02) 395-6273; (02) 357-0177
Fax: (02) 395-6275

General Practice, International Trade, Computer Law, China Investment, Corporation, Environmental, Patent, Trademark & Copyrights, Maritime, Securities, Banking & Financing, Litigation, Taxation, Insurance, Real Estate, Labor Law.

MEMBERS OF FIRM

ANDREA Y.H. CHEN, born Tai Nan, Taiwan, October 25, 1957; admitted, 1980, Taiwan. *Education:* National Taiwan University, School of Law (LL.B., 1979); University of Pennsylvania Law School (LL.M., 1983); Harvard Law School (LL.M., 1984). Attorney-at-Law: Huang, Chang & Associates Law Offices, 1980-1981; Tsar & Tsai Law Offices, 1985-1986; The Legal Department, Multitech Industrial Corp., 1986-1987; Chen, Shyuu & Wang Law Offices, 1987-1993. Arbitrator, Commercial Arbitration Association of the R.O.C., 1987—. Author: "Legal Aspects of Offshore Banking in Taiwan," 1984. Co-Author: "Study in Labor Standards and Labor Welfare," 1987; "Laws and Regulations of Electronic Funds Transfer," 1991; "Establishment of Legal Protection for Industrial Design Products and Integrated Circuit Layout in the R.O.C.," 1993; "The Relationship between Unfair Competition & Antitrust Laws and the Laws of Intellectual Property Rights," 1993. Associate Professor, Law, Soochow University Law School, Taipei, Taiwan, R.O.C., 1987—. *Member:* Taipei, Panchiao & Taoyuan Bar Associations. *LANGUAGES:* Chinese (Mandarin and Taiwanese) and English. *PRACTICE AREAS:* International Trade Law; Computer Law; Environmental Law; Corporate Law; Investment Law; Banking Law; Finance Law; Securities; Patent, Trademark and Copyright Law; Maritime Law.

KEVIN K.S. CHEN, born Taipei, Taiwan, May 17, 1962; admitted, 1992, Taiwan. *Education:* National Chunghsing University, School of Law (LL.B., 1986); National Taiwan University, School of Law (LL.M., 1991). Specialist, Bureau of Environmental Dispute Resolution, 1987-1988. Special Secretary, Deputy Administrator, Office of Environmental Protection Administration, 1988-1992. Arbitrator, Commercial Arbitration Association of the R.O.C., 1991—. Author: "Study on System of Environmental Dispute Settlement in Japan," 1989. *Member:* Taipei, Panchiao & Keelung Bar Associations. *LANGUAGES:* Chinese and English. *PRACTICE AREAS:* Environmental Law; China Investment Law; Securities; Real Estate Law.

KAI-HSIUNG YU, born Taipei, Taiwan, April 19, 1965; admitted, 1993, Taiwan. *Education:* National Chunghsing University, School of Law (LL.B., 1987). *LANGUAGES:* Chinese (Mandarin and Taiwanese), Japanese and English. *PRACTICE AREAS:* General Practice; Litigation.

TZU-SU HUANG, born Taipei, Taiwan, October 21, 1966; admitted, 1993, Taiwan. *Education:* Soochow University, School of Law (LL.B., 1990). *LANGUAGES:* Chinese (Mandarin and Taiwanese) and English. *PRACTICE AREAS:* General Practice; Litigation; International Law.

CONCORDIA CONSULTING, LTD.

Established in 1987

SECTION 1, SUITE 704
432 KEELUNG ROAD
TAIPEI, TAIWAN
Telephone: 886 2 729-0268; 886 2 729-8976
Fax: 886 2 729-9837

Shanghai, People's Republic of China Office: Shanghai Fudan V & L Business Consultation Co., Ltd., 158 Yu Ping South Road, Hongqiao District, 200051. Telephone: 86 21 233-1281. Fax: 86 21 241-4095.
Hong Kong Liaison Office: Concordia Consulting, Ltd., 6F, Bank of America Tower, 12 Harcourt Road, Central, Hong Kong. Fax: 852 810-0502.

U.S. Immigration and Naturalization Law, Commercial Trade Law, Consultation and Franchising, Business Agreements, Joint-Venture Business and Commercial Law.

FIRM PROFILE: Concordia Consulting is a Hong-Kong based company, established in 1987 with its branch office in Taipei, Taiwan established in 1994. Shanghai Fudan V & L Business Consultation Co., Ltd. was licensed in Mainland China in 1994 and is a joint venture between Concordia Consulting and Shanghai Fudan University Law School, a well respected and recognized institution of higher learning in Shanghai. The President of Concordia Consulting, Fredrick N. Voigtmann, has practiced U.S. Immigration Law, Business and Commercial Law and Family Law in Taipei, Taiwan for fifteen years. Concordia Consulting is a well respected member of the Taipei community, known for providing pro bono and legal aid to the expatriate community. Concordia is an active, motivating force behind the first formal legal assistance program offered by foreign legal counsel in Taiwan which will begin in early 1995. The firm is also a member of the American Chamber of Commerce in Taiwan and in Shanghai, China.

MEMBERS OF FIRM

FREDRICK N. VOIGTMANN, born Iowa, July 14, 1940; admitted, 1965, Iowa Supreme Court (Not admitted in Taiwan). *Education:* Valparaiso University (B.A., 1962); Valparaiso University Law School (J.D., 1965). U.S. Air Force intensive Mandarin language training, Monterey, California, 1970. With: United States Air Force Office of Special Investigations, Special Agent, Active Duty, 1967-1981; United States Air Force Reserves, Manila, Republic of the Philippines, 1981-1992. Lt. Col. U.S.A.F. Retired. Graduated Squadron Officer's School, Air Command and Staff College. *Member:* Iowa Bar Association; American Bar Association; International Law Division; American Immigration Lawyers Association. (Also Member, Shangai Fudan V & L Business Consultation Co.). *LANGUAGES:* English and Chinese (Mandarin). *PRACTICE AREAS:* U.S. Immigration Law; Business Law; Commercial Law; Family Law; General Practice.

FREDRICK W. VOIGTMANN, born Texas, April 27, 1967; admitted, 1993, Ohio Supreme Court (Not admitted in Taiwan). *Education:* Ohio State University (B.A., 1990); Capital Law School (J.D., Order of the Curia, 1993). Internship, Ohio State Bar Association, Ethics and Professional Responsibility Section, 1991. *Member:* Ohio State Bar Association; Columbus Bar Association; American Bar Association, International Law Division; American Immigration Lawyers Association. (Also Member, Shanghai Fudan V& L Business Consultation Co.). *LANGUAGES:* English and Chinese (Mandarin). *PRACTICE AREAS:* U.S. Immigration Law; Business Law; Commercial Law; Family Law.

BRIAN J. GROSSMAN, born Canton, Ohio, November 20, 1965; admitted, 1993, Oregon Supreme Court (Not admitted in Taiwan). *Education:* Colorado College (B.A., 1988); Willamette University (J.D., 1993; Certification in Dispute Resolution, 1993). *Member:* Oregon State Bar Association; American Bar Association, International Law Division; American Immigration Lawyers Association; American Chamber of Commerce, Shanghai, China. (Also Member, Shanghai Fundan V & L Business Consultation Co.). *LANGUAGES:* English and Chinese (Mandarin). *PRACTICE AREAS:* U.S. Immigration Law; International Business Law; International Commercial Law; Joint Venture Law.

DEACONS GRAHAM & JAMES

(In Association with Sly & Weigall)

54 CHUNG SHAN N. ROAD, SECTION 3

7TH FLOOR

TAIPEI 10451, TAIWAN

Telephone: 886-2-597-4521

Telecopier: 886-2-592-6601

Other offices located in: San Francisco, Los Angeles, Newport Beach, Palo Alto, Sacramento and Fresno, California; Washington, D.C.; New York, New York; Milan, Italy; Beijing, China; Tokyo, Japan; London, England; Dusseldorf, Germany.

Associated Offices: Deacons in Association with Graham & James, Hong Kong; Sly and Weigall, Sydney, Melbourne, Brisbane, Perth and Canberra, Australia.

Affiliated Offices: Graham & James in Affiliation with Law Offices of Ahmed Zaki Yamani, Riyadh, Jeddah, Saudi Arabia and Manama, Bahrain; Taylor Joynson Garrett, London, England, Bucharest, Romania and Brussels, Belgium; Hanafiah Soeharto Ponggawa, Jakarta, Indonesia; Deacons and Graham & James, Bangkok, Thailand; Haarmann, Hemmelrath & Partner, Berlin, Munich, Leipzig, Frankfurt and Dusseldorf, Germany; Mishare M. Al-Ghazali & Partners, Kuwait; Sly & Weigall Deacons in Association with Graham & James, Hanoi, Vietnam and Guangzhou, China; Gallastegui y Lozano, S.C., Mexico City, Mexico; Law Firm of Salah Al-Hejailan, Jeddah and Riyadh, Saudi Arabia.

Firm engaged in American and International law practice but not authorized to appear before Taiwanese courts or administrative agencies. Specializes in international joint ventures, technology transfer, trade and investment financing and commercial transactions.

RESIDENT ASSOCIATE

DEREK G. WICKS, born England, 1942; admitted, 1981, England and Wales; 1985, Hong Kong (Not admitted in Taiwan). *Education:* University of Bristol (B.A., 1964; LL.B., 1978); Law Society of England and Wales (Part II Exam, 1979). Author: "Across the Wall, Taiwan Investment in the PRC," Asian Law Journal, 1993. Director, European Council, Commerce and Trade, Taiwan, 1993. Executive Director, European Council, Commerce and Trade, Taiwan, 1994. *Member:* The Law Society of England and Wales; The Law Society of Hong Kong.

EQUITABLE LAW OFFICES

(LEE AND ASSOCIATES)

2, 2ND FLOOR, LANE 27, LIN-YI STREET

P.O. BOX 734, TAIPEI

TAIPEI, TAIWAN

Telephone: 886-2-321 8079/321 6539

Fax: 886-2-397-1046

Copyright, Patent and Trademark Law (including assignment, license and anticounterfeit); Investment and Corporation Law (including technical cooperation, establishment of liaison office, branch office, subsidiary; arrangement of exclusive agency, distributorship, joint venture and corporate merger; application for tax privilege); International Trade and Financial Law (including preparation and review of contracts and other necessary documents); Antitrust Law (including unfair competition and consumer protection); Civil and Criminal Litigation in general (including negotiation and settlement).

DR. JOSEPH K. TWANMOH (1903-1987).

DR. WINFRED W.Y. LEE, born Taiwan, 1944; admitted, 1985, Taipei and Patent Office. *Education:* School of Law, Soochow University, Taipei (LL.B., 1968); Graduate Institute of Law, National Chunghsing University, Taipei (LL.M., 1971); Georgetown University Law Center, Washington, D.C., U.S.A. (M.C.L., 1975); School of Law, University of Washington, Seattle, U.S.A. (Ph.D., 1980). Associate Professor of Law, School of Law and Graduate Institute of Law, Soochow University, 1981—. Member, The Phi Tau Phi Scholastic Honor Society. *Member:* The Chinese Association of Comparative Law; Chinese Marketing Association; Taipei Bar Association; The Asian Patent Attorneys Association. Consulting Member to Enterprise Development Committee of Ministry of Economic Affairs; Arbitrator of the Commercial Arbitration Association of the Republic of China (R.O.C.). Fellow: United Board for Christian Higher Education in Asia. *LANGUAGES:* Chinese, Taiwanese and English.

(This Listing Continued)

SHENG-CHIEN LO, born Taiwan, 1959; admitted, 1990, R.O.C. *Education:* School of Law, Soochow University, Taipei (LL.B., 1988). *Member:* Taipei Bar Association. *LANGUAGES:* Chinese, Taiwanese and English.

ANDREW W.H. CHANG, born Taiwan, 1964. *Education:* University of Minnesota, U.S.A. (B.A., 1986); Soochow University, School of Law, Taipei (LL.B., 1994). *LANGUAGES:* Chinese, Taiwanese and English.

REPRESENTATIVE CLIENTS: *U.S.A.:* Abbott Laboratories; G.D. Searle & Co.; Cluett, Peabody & Co., Inc.; CITIBANK, N.A.; Honeywell, Inc.; Combustion Engineering, Inc.; The NutraSweet Co.; The Proctor & Gamble Co.; Micro-Age Computer Centers, Inc. *UK:* UK Government, ECGD; The Boots Company PLC. *GERMANY:* A. Nattermann & Cie. GmbH; H. Bahlsens Keksfabrik KG; TCHIBO Firsch-Röst-Kaffee GmbH; Dr. Babor GmbH & Co. *AUSTRALIA:* Gerard Industries Pty Ltd. *HONG KONG:* Le Saunda Licensing Ltd. *JAPAN:* M Retailing Systems. *R.O.C.:* China Steel Corp. and its Subsidiaries; S.I.T.A. Taipei Office; Yeh's Construction and Investment Corp.; Department of Taipei Mass Rapid Transit; Department of Kaohsiung Mass Rapid Transit.

FAR EAST LAW OFFICES

4TH FLOOR, CHIEN TAI BUILDING

176 CHUNG HSIAO EAST ROAD, SECTION 1

TAIPEI 10023, TAIWAN

Telephone: (02) 392-8811-3; 393-4839

Cable Address: "FELAW" TAIPEI

Facsimile: (02) 321-4414

International Trade Disputes, Foreign Investment, Corporate Financing, International Financing, Customs, Taxation, Corporation, Trademark, Admiralty, Banking, Insurance and General Practice.

MEMBERS OF FIRM

CHARLES YA-WEN CHIU, born Taiwan, 1945; admitted, 1979, District of Columbia; 1980, Taipei, Taiwan; 1991, United States Court of International Trade. *Education:* National Taiwan University (LL.B., 1967); Southern Methodist University (M.C.L., 1970); University of Washington (J.D., 1975); University of Cambridge (LL.B., 1981). Author: "Land Reform in Taiwan," Thesis, 1975. Associate Professor of Law, Soochow University and Chung Hsing University. Professor, National Chiao Tung University, 1981-1987. Visiting Foreign Scholar, University of Tokyo, Japan. Senior Research Fellow, Taxation Commission, Ministry of Finance, 1975-1976. Key Speaker, Doing Business in the Pacific Basin, American Bar Association Annual Convention, 1980. Member of the Drafting Board for Law of Trust, Sponsored by the Ministry of Finance. *Member:* American Bar Association; LAWASIA. *PRACTICE AREAS:* Banking Law; Corporation Law; Maritime Law; Antidumping Law and Other Trade Law; International Trade Dispute Litigation and Arbitration.

JEFFREY C. J. CHEN, born Taiwan, 1947; admitted, 1979, Taipei and Kaohsiung. *Education:* National Chunghsing University (LL.B., 1970); National Taiwan University (LL.M., 1975); The London School of Economics and Political Science, Universityo f London (LL.M. Course Sep., 1976). Author: "Legal Study on International Monetary Fund," Thesis, 1976; "Legal Study on American and Canadian Antidumping Systems," 1979 (Received Highest Award from Ministry of Economic Affairs and Executive Yuan). Lecturer, International Trade Law, National Chung Hsing University, 1977-1986 and Law and Regulations on Trade, Soochow University, 1978-1986. Legal Counsel and Secretary of Republic of China, Delegation for Sino-USA Non-rubber Footwear Negotiation, May 1977 and Delegation for Sino-USA Bilateral Trade Negotiation May, July, October and December, 1978. Specialist, Board of Foreign Trade, 1976-1979. Research Fellow, Commission of Taxation and Customs, Ministry of Finance, 1974-1975 and Department of Monetary Affairs, 1974-1975. Taxation Officer, Legal Department of National Taxation Bureau of Taipei, Ministry of Finance, 1973-1974. *Member:* Chinese Society of Comparative Law (Secretary General, 1983-1985; Treasurer, 1985-1987). *PRACTICE AREAS:* International Trade Law; Economic Law.

Languages: Taiwanese, Mandarin, English and Japanese

REPRESENTATIVE CLIENTS: Chinese Petroleum Corporation; Taiwan Textile Federation; Taiwan Sweaters Industry Association; China Development Corporation; Taiwan Electric Appliance Manufactures' Association; China Investment & Development Co., Ltd.; Yang Ming Line; Central Investment Holding Co., Ltd. Yeu Tyan Machinery Manufacturing Co., Ltd.; CPC Shell Lubricants Company Ltd.; Chinese Maritime Transport, Ltd.; Lilly Coating (Far East) Ltd.; H.B. Fuller Taiwan Co., Ltd.; National Bank of Canada; Berliner Handles-Und Frankfurt Bank; Nederlandsche Middenstandsbank nv; Credit Commercial de France; The Hongkong and Shanghai Banking Corp.; Sekin & Co.; Team Transport International; Oversea Chinese Commercial Bank; Taiwan Association of Shipbuilding Manufacturers; China Shipbuilding Corp.; KB International (Hong Kong) Ltd.; IBI Asia Ltd.; Credit Lyonnais; China Development Co.; Taipei City Bank; CIC-Union Europeenne, International; Fu I Industrial Co., Ltd.;

(This Listing Continued)

Dalvey Products Supply, Ltd.; TTET Union Corp.; New Northern Knitting Co., Ltd.; Gold Peak Industries (Taiwan) Ltd.
REFERENCES: Ince & Co.; Nagashima & Ohno; Simmons & Simmons; Grunfeld, Desiderio; Lebowitz & Silverman; Shearman & Sterling ASIA, L.C., Taiwan Branch; Chinese Petroleum Corporation; Taiwan Textile Federation; China Development Corporation.

FORMOSA TRANSNATIONAL ATTORNEYS AT LAW

Established in 1974

15TH FLOOR, LOTUS BUILDING
136 JEN-AI ROAD, SECTION 3
TAIPEI, TAIWAN
Telephone: 886-2-755-7366
Telex: 19031 FTLAW
Fax: 886-2-755-6486; 707-2299

Corporate, Banking, Investment, Security, Admiralty, Marine Insurance, International Trade, Patent and Trademark Law, General Civil Practice and Criminal Trial.

FIRM PROFILE: *Formosa Transnational ("FT") was established in 1974 by John C. Chen, K.C. Fan, Paiff Huang, and Henry H.M. Rai, for the purpose of providing specialized, professional service to the business community. Since its establishment, it has become one of the largest and best-known law firms in Taiwan. The firm acts on behalf of numerous clients in North America, Europe, Japan and the Asia-Pacific region. We also advise Chinese clients in their international transactions.*

MEMBERS OF FIRM

JOHN C. CHEN, born Tainan, Taiwan, August 10, 1939; admitted, 1973, Taiwan. *Education:* National Taiwan University Law School (LL.B., 1962); Judge Training Institute (1963-1964); Southern Methodist University Law School, U.S.A. (M.C.L., 1970); Academy of American and International Law, Southwestern Legal Foundation, U.S.A. (1980). *Member:* Taipei Bar Association; Taichung Bar Association; Chinese Society of Comparative Law; Chinese Society of International Law; Inter-Pacific Bar Association; LAWASIA; I.B.A.; Asia-Pacific Lawyers Association; Institute of International Affairs of R.O.C.; Commercial Arbitration Association of R.O.C.; A.B.A.; Asia Patent Attorneys Association; United States Trademark Association; American Chamber of Commerce in Taipei; Notarial Society of R.O.C.; Taipei Overseas Lions Club; NTU Law Foundation. *LANGUAGES:* Chinese (Mandarin and Taiwanese), English. *PRACTICE AREAS:* Banking; Finance; Foreign Investment; Intellectual Property; Corporate Law; Litigation.

K. C. FAN, born Hsinchu, Taiwan, March 16, 1939; admitted, 1973, Taiwan. *Education:* National Taiwan University Law School (LL.B., 1961); Judge Training Institute (1963-1964); Academy of American and International Law, Southwestern Legal Foundation, U.S.A. (1971); Columbia University Law School (LL.M., 1972). *Member:* Taipei Bar Association; Panchiao Bar Association; Taichung Bar Association; Chinese Society of Comparative Law; Chinese Society of International Law; LAWASIA; I.B.A.; Inter-Pacific Bar Association; Asia-Pacific Lawyers Association; Commercial Arbitration Association of R.O.C.; A.B.A.; Asia Patent Attorneys Association; Notarial Society of R.O.C.; Chinese Commercial and Industrial Coordination Society; Taipei Downtown Lions Club. *LANGUAGES:* Chinese (Mandarin, Hakka and Taiwanese), English. *PRACTICE AREAS:* Corporate Law; Business Transactions; International Trade; Litigation; Commercial Arbitration.

PAIFF HUANG, born Changhwa, Taiwan, May 24, 1938; admitted, 1974, Taiwan. *Education:* National Taiwan University Law School (LL.B., 1961); Judge Training Institute (1963-1964); Maritime Development Institute (1968); Academy of American and International Law, Southwestern Legal Foundation, U.S.A. (1973); University of Texas, School of Law (M.C.J., 1974). *Member:* Taipei Bar Association; Kaohsiung Bar Association; Chinese Society of Comparative Law; LAWASIA; I.B.A.; Asia-Pacific Lawyers Association; Inter-Pacific Bar Association; Commercial Arbitration Association of R.O.C.; A.B.A.; Asia Patent Attorneys Association; Notarial Society of R.O.C.; Advisory Board of International and Comparative Law Center, The Southwestern Legal Foundation; International Management Council Taipei Chapter; Chinese Society of International Law; Economic Trade Development Association of the R.O.C.; Sino-Soviet Economic Development Association; Chinese National Association of Industry and Commerce; China Maritime Institute; Chinese Association for Advancement of Management; ROC-USA Economic Council; Chinese Maritime Research Institute; Rotary Club of Taipei New East. *LANGUAGES:*

(This Listing Continued)

Chinese (Mandarin and Taiwanese), English. *PRACTICE AREAS:* Banking; Finance; Corporate Law; Business Transactions; Admiralty; Aviation; Insurance; Litigation; Intellectual Property; Commercial Arbitration.

HENRY H. M. RAI, born Miaoli, Taiwan, January 2, 1939; admitted, 1962, Taiwan. *Education:* National Taiwan University Law School (LL.B., 1961); Tokyo University (LL.M., 1969). *Member:* Taipei Bar Association; Hsinchu Bar Association; Chinese Society of Comparative Law; LAWASIA; Asia-Pacific Lawyers Association; Inter-Pacific Bar Association; Asia Patent Attorneys Association; Commercial Arbitration Association of R.O.C.; A.B.A.; Notarial Society of R.O.C.; Rotary Club of Taipei Yenping. *LANGUAGES:* Chinese (Mandarin, Hakka and Taiwanese), Japanese, English. *PRACTICE AREAS:* Corporate Law; Banking; Finance; Labor Law; Litigation; Taxation; Property Law.

HORNG-SHYA HUANG, born Taipei, Taiwan, July 15, 1954; admitted, 1980, Taiwan. *Education:* National Taiwan University Law School (LL.B., 1976); Academy of American and International Law, Southwestern Legal Foundation, U.S.A. (1989). *Member:* Taipei Bar Association; Panchiao Bar Association; Taoyuan Bar Association; Taichung Bar Association; Kaohsiung Bar Association; Chinese Society of Comparative Law; Advisory Board of International and Comparative Law Center, The Southwestern Legal Foundation. *LANGUAGES:* Chinese (Mandarin and Taiwanese), English. *PRACTICE AREAS:* Banking; Finance; Labor Law; Property Law; Fair Trade Law; Intellectual Property; Litigation; Corporate Law.

TSAI-SHYA CHEN, born Taiwan, October 7, 1936; admitted, 1976, Taiwan. *Education:* National Taiwan University Law School (LL.B., 1959); Chuo University, Japan (LL.M., 1965). *Member:* Taipei Bar Association; Chinese Society of Comparative Law. *LANGUAGES:* Chinese (Mandarin and Taiwanese), Japanese. *PRACTICE AREAS:* Banking; Finance; Corporate Law; Labor Law.

YU-LAN KUO, born Taiwan, February, 1960; admitted, 1988, Taiwan. *Education:* National Taiwan University Law School (LL.B., 1983). *Member:* Taipei Bar Association; Panchiao Bar Association; Hsinchu Bar Association; Chinese Society of Comparative Law; Inter-Pacific Bar Association; New Environment Foundation. *LANGUAGES:* Chinese (Mandarin and Taiwanese), English. *PRACTICE AREAS:* International Trade; Litigation; Environmental and Urban Planning; Economic and Commercial Regulation; Intellectual Property.

CHUN-YIH CHENG, born Taiwan, August 1, 1963; admitted, 1990, Taiwan. *Education:* National Chengchi University Law School (LL.B., 1985); National Chengchi University Graduate Institute of Law (LL.M., 1988). *Member:* Taipei Bar Association; Keelung Bar Association; Chinese Society of Constitutional Law; Chinese Society of Comparative Law. *LANGUAGES:* Chinese (Mandarin and Taiwanese), English. *PRACTICE AREAS:* Banking; Finance; Corporate Law; Foreign Investment; International Trade.

GEORGIA CHANG, born Taichung, Taiwan, December 23, 1966; admitted, 1989, Taiwan. *Education:* National Taiwan University Law School (LL.B., 1989). *Member:* Taipei Bar Association; Taoyuan Bar Association; Chinese Society of Comparative Law; International Federation of Women Lawyers, R.O.C. *LANGUAGES:* Chinese (Mandarin and Taiwanese), English. *PRACTICE AREAS:* Corporate Law; Fair Trade Law; International Trade; Litigation; Property Law.

YA-FAN LIN, born Yangho, Taiwan, December, 1966; admitted, 1990, Taiwan. *Education:* National Taiwan University Law School (LL.B., 1989). *Member:* Taipei Bar Association; Taichung Bar Association; Chinese Society of Comparative Law. *LANGUAGES:* Chinese (Mandarin and Taiwanese), English. *PRACTICE AREAS:* Labor Law; Litigation; Mainland Investment; Property Law.

SUE J. CHANG, born Chiai, Taiwan, February 2, 1953; admitted, 1982, Illinois; 1983, Texas; 1991, Washington. *Education:* National Taiwan University Law School (LL.B., 1975); Northwestern University School of Law (J.D., 1981). *Member:* Taipei Bar Association. *PRACTICE AREAS:* Foreign Investment; Intellectual Property. *LANGUAGES:* Chinese (Mandarin and Taiwanese), English.

JAU-YUAN HWANG, born Taiwan, September 28, 1962; admitted, 1986, Taiwan. *Education:* National Taiwan University Law School (LL.B., 1984); National Taiwan University Graduate Institute of Law (LL.M., 1989); Harvard Law School (Ph.D., 1991). *Member:* Taipei Bar Association; Chinese Society of Comparative Law. *LANGUAGES:* Chinese (Mandarin and Taiwanese), English. *PRACTICE AREAS:* Administrative Law; Corporate Law; Environmental Law; International Trade; Foreign Investment; Litigation.

(This Listing Continued)

FORMOSA TRANSNATIONAL ATTORNEYS AT LAW,
Taipei—Continued

VICTORIA S.Y. LIN, born Taiwan, August, 1964; admitted, 1992, Taiwan. *Education:* National Taiwan University Law School (LL.B., 1986); Soochow University Graduate Institute of Law. *Member:* Taipei Bar Association; Chinese Society of Comparative Law. *LANGUAGES:* Chinese (Mandarin and Taiwanese), English. *PRACTICE AREAS:* Maritime Law; Litigation; Fair Trade Law; International Trade; Consumer's Protection Law.

LI-MO LIN, born Chang-Huw, Taiwan, January, 1964; admitted, 1991, Taiwan. *Education:* National Taiwan University Law School (LL.B., 1986). *Member:* Taipei Bar Association; Panchiao Bar Association; Hsinchu Bar Association; Chinese Society of Comparative Law. *LANGUAGES:* Chinese (Mandarin and Taiwanese), English. *PRACTICE AREAS:* Banking; Finance; International Trade; Litigation; Property Law.

MICHAEL M.K. YANG, born Taiwan, December, 1964; admitted, 1994, Taiwan. *Education:* National Taiwan University Law School (LL.B., 1988). *Member:* Taipei Bar Association; Notarial Society of R.O.C. *LANGUAGES:* Chinese (Mandarin and Taiwanese), English. *PRACTICE AREAS:* Maritime Law; Litigation; Notarial Law; Property Law.

JASSY Y.C. HUNG, born Taiwan, March, 1968; admitted, 1992, Taiwan. *Education:* National Taiwan University Law School (LL.B., 1991); Soochow University Graduate Institute of Law. *Member:* Taipei Bar Association; Kaohsiung Bar Association; Chinese Society of Comparative Law. *LANGUAGES:* Chinese (Mandarin and Taiwanese), English. *PRACTICE AREAS:* Intellectual Property; Corporate Law; Trade Regulation; Antitrust Law; Security Law.

CHRISTINA S.H. YU, born Taiwan, July, 1970; admitted, 1994, Taiwan. *Education:* National Taiwan University Law School (LL.B., 1992). *Member:* Taipei Bar Association. *LANGUAGES:* Chinese (Mandarin and Taiwanese), English. *PRACTICE AREAS:* Intellectual Property; Corporate Law; International Trade; Litigation.

FA-LI LIN, born Taiwan, December, 1969; admitted, 1993, Taiwan. *Education:* National Chung-Shing University Law School (LL.B., 1993). *Member:* Taipei Bar Association. *LANGUAGES:* Chinese (Mandarin and Taiwanese), English. *PRACTICE AREAS:* Corporate Law; Engineering Contract; Consumer Protection Law; Fair Trade Law; Trade Regulation.

RESIDENT CONSULTANT

JINYUAN CHEN, born Taiwan, March 7, 1964; admitted, 1993, New York (Not admitted in Taiwan). *Education:* Georgetown University Law Center (LL.M., 1991); University of Wisconsin School of Law (LL.M., 1990); National Chengchi University Law School (LL.B., 1986). *Member:* American Bar Association; New York State Bar Association. *LANGUAGES:* Chinese (Mandarin and Taiwanese), English. *PRACTICE AREAS:* International Trade and Investment; International Business Transactions; Labor Management and Relations; Corporate Law.

RICK K. LEE, born Taiwan, October, 1951; admitted, 1993, New York; 1994, California (Not admitted in Taiwan). *Education:* Golden Gate University School of Law (J.D., 1993); Tulane University School of Law (LL.M., 1990); Tokyo University of Foreign Studies (Auditor, 1981); Takushoku University, Japanese Language Course (Diploma, 1980); National Taiwan University Law School (LL.B., 1974). *Member:* New York State Bar Association; California Bar Association. *LANGUAGES:* Chinese (Mandarin and Taiwanese), Japanese, English. *PRACTICE AREAS:* International Business Transactions; Intellectual Property; Corporate Law; International Trade and Investment.

REPRESENTATIVE CLIENTS: Department of Health, Executive Yuan; Energy Committee, Ministry of Economic Affairs; Taiwan Area National Expressway Engineering Bureau, Ministry of Transportation and Communications; Interchange Association, Taipei Office; Ret-Ser Engineering Agency, VACRS; Bank of Taiwan; Taiwan Power Company; Tang En Iron Works Co., Ltd.; Bankers Trust Company, Taipei Branch; Central Trust of China; China Securities Investment Trust Corp.; Taipei Architects Association; Chung Shing Textile Co., Ltd.; C. Itoh & Co., Ltd.; The Dai-Ichi Kangyo Bank Ltd.; IBM Corporation; Hitachi Electronic Components (Asia) Ltd., Taipei Branch; The International Commercial Bank of China; International Investment Trust Ltd.; Kajima Corp.; Kobe Steel Ltd.; Marubeni Corp.; Microtek International Inc.; Twinhead International Corp.; D-Link Corporation; The Mitsui Warehouse Co., Ltd.; AMP Incorporated; Nissho Iwai Corp.; Orient Leasing Co.; Russ Berrie and Company Inc., Taipei Branch; S.E.I.T.A. Public Co.; Shiseido Co., Ltd.; Stephenson & Turner Asia; Sumitomo Electric Industries Ltd.; Tomy Kogyo Company Inc.; Toyota Motor Corp.; Tuntex Distinct Corp.; Yamaha Nippon Gakka Co., Ltd.; The Yokohama Rubber Co., Ltd.; W.I. Carr Limited; Kao (Taiwan) Corp.; Samsung America Inc.; CSB Battery Co., Ltd.; City Chain (Taiwan) Co., Ltd., Taiwan Branch (H.K.); Jardine Freight Services (Taiwan) Ltd.; Through Transport

(This Listing Continued)

Mutual Services (TT Club); Chung Hwa Pulp Corp.; Hanjin Shipping Co., Ltd.; Lite-On Technology Corp.; UK P&I Club; Comapl Electronics, Inc.; Discovision Association; Dresdner Bank AG, Taipei Representative Office; American Express International Inc.; Korean Air; Takashimaya Co., Ltd.; Isetan Company Ltd.; Toshiba Corp.; Japan Asia Airways; Kajima Corp.; Mitsubishi Electric Corp.; Sankyo Company, Ltd.

HSU & HSU

Established in 1930

(Formerly Hsu Chieh Law Offices)

10TH FL., 10 LING SEN S. ROAD
TAIPEI 10042, TAIWAN
Telephone: 886-2-356-9955
Fax: 886-2-341-7074

General Practice, China Investment, Foreign Investment, Admiralty, Corporate Representation, Insurance, China International Arbitration.

MEMBERS OF FIRM

CHIEH HSU (1905-1989).

HWA-MIN HSU, born Shanghai, China, March 6, 1944; admitted, 1980, New York and U.S. District Court, Eastern and Southern Districts of New York (Not admitted in Taiwan). *Education:* College of Law, Fu-Jen Catholic University Taipei (LL.B., 1967); University of Miami Coral Gables, Florida (M.C.L., 1970). Associate Professor, Fu-Jen Catholic University, "China Investment Laws and Practice." Lecturer: International Arbitration and Litigation, United Nations Development Program, Jiangxi, Nanjiang, China. Associate: Hsu Chieh Law Offices, Taipei, 1967-1968; Dunn & Zuckerman Admiralty, New York, 1971-1973. Legal Advisor: Palace Museum, Beijing, China; Wuxi City Museum, Wuxi, China; Qiantang Investment Project, Hongzhou, China. *Member:* American Bar Association; American Immigration Lawyers Association. *LANGUAGES:* Chinese and English. *PRACTICE AREAS:* Law and Foreign Investment in People's Republic of China Law; China Arbitration; U.S. Law.

HO SHAN-LIN, born Ho Nan, China, May 20, 1948; admitted, 1979, Taiwan. *Education:* Political Law College. *Member:* Taiwan Bar Association. *LANGUAGES:* Chinese, English and Taiwanese. *PRACTICE AREAS:* Military Laws and Procedures for the R.O.C.; General Practice; Laws of the Republic of China.

WALTER C. F. CHANG, born Chia-I Hsien, Taiwan, December 4, 1962; admitted, 1991, Taiwan. *Education:* Fu-Jen University, Taiwan. *LANGUAGES:* Chinese, English and Taiwanese.

JENNIE Y. CHENG, born Taipei, Taiwan, March 6, 1970; admitted, 1992, Taiwan. *Education:* National Taiwan University (LL.B., 1992); National Chunghsing University (LL.M.-Pending). Former Associate, Chen & Lin Attorneys at Law. *LANGUAGES:* Chinese, English and Taiwanese. *PRACTICE AREAS:* Civil Law; Criminal Law; Negotiable Instruments.

REPRESENTATIVE CLIENTS: Taiwan Navigation Corp.; Orient Overseas Lines; China Merchant Steamship Co., Ltd. (Taiwan); Toddy Shipyard (U.S.A.); Gulf Oil Co., Ltd.; United World Chinese Commercial Bank; Malaysia Marine Corp. (Malaysia); Glafki Shipping Co. S.A. (Greek); Prima International Shipping (PTE) Ltd. (Singapore); Eastern Shipping Lines Inc. (Phil.); Argo Maritime Co. Ltd.; Paneios Ship Corp. (Guam); H.J. Burmester & Co.; Hermann Peelchau Versicherungen; Condor Transport Und Ruckversicherungs; Prudential Assurance Co. (West Germany); United Kingdom Mutual Ship Assurance Association Ltd. (Bermuda); Lloyd's Underwriters Assn. (England); The Britannia Steam Ship Insurance Association Ltd.

HUANG & PARTNERS

Attorneys-at-Law

(Founded in 1970 as T.C. Huang & Associates)

9TH FLOOR, NO. 563
CHUNG HSIAO EAST ROAD, SEC. 4
TAIPEI, TAIWAN
Telephone: (02) 7460868 (17 Lines)
Facsimile: (02) 7642448
Telex: 11509 UNILAW

General Corporate and Commercial Law, International Trade Disputes, Cross-Boarder Investment, Banking, Admiralty and Maritime Law, Public Works, Taxation, Insurance, Securities, Aircraft and Ship Financing, Customs, Automotive Law, Trademark, Patent and Copyright Law, Technology Licensing, Exports and Imports, General Civil and Criminal Litigation, Arbitration, Fair Trade Law and Labor and Employment Law.

(This Listing Continued)

MEMBERS OF FIRM

T.C. (TSING-CHIA) HUANG, born Chekiang, China, July 14, 1924; admitted, 1964, Republic of China. *Education:* National Cheng Chih University (B.A.; M.A.); Soochow University School of Law (LL.B.); Southern Methodist University Law School (LL.M.). Phi Delta Phi. Research Scholar in Residence, Southern Methodist University Law School, 1961-1962. Research Fellow in East Asian Studies, Harvard University, 1968-1969. Associate Professor of Corporate and Insurance Law and Associate Dean, Soochow University School of Law, 1961-1964. Guest Lecturer in International Law, National Naval War College, 1963-1966. Associate Professor of Admiralty, National Cheng Chih University Law College and Professor of Angelo-American Law, The Institute for the Judiciary, 1964-1966. Advisor to the Bank of Taiwan, 1978-1985 and Taiwan Bureau of Mines, 1970-1984. Legal Advisor on PRC Law, Ministry of Economic Affairs, 1992. Nominated as the Leading International Lawyer from Taiwan, International Financial Law Review, September, 1986. Listed in the Who's Who of Chinese Jurists, PRC's Zhong Guo Lao Dong Publishing Co. *LANGUAGES:* Mandarin, English and Taiwanese. *PRACTICE AREAS:* General Legal Practice; General Tax Practice; Administrative Law; Antitrust Law; Arbitration.

DELPHINE D.L. CHEN, born Taipei, Taiwan, March 1, 1960; admitted, 1993, Republic of China. *Education:* National Taiwan University School of Law (LL.B., 1982). Associated with the firm since 1982. *LANGUAGES:* Mandarin, Taiwanese and English. *PRACTICE AREAS:* Arbitration; Banking Law; Employer's Liability; Industrial Relations and Labour Law; Insurance Law; Maritime and Admiralty Law.

JAMIE C.M. HUANG, born Taipei, Taiwan, January 11, 1961; admitted, 1990, California (Not admitted in Taiwan). *Education:* University of California at Los Angeles (B.A., 1984); University of Santa Clara Law School (J.D., 1989). Associated with the firm since 1990. *LANGUAGES:* Mandarin, Taiwanese and English. *PRACTICE AREAS:* Banking Law; Corporate Law; Foreign Investments; Corporate Taxation; Mergers and Acquisitions; Securities and Exchange Law.

LANNY C.F. YEH, born Shanghai, China, November 26, 1947; (Not admitted in Taiwan). *Education:* National Chunghsing University School of Law (LL.B., 1971). Associated with T.C. Huang & Associates, 1971-1981. In-house Counsel, Raymond International Taiwan Ltd., 1981-1987. Manager of Legal Affairs, An Mau Steel Co., Ltd., 1987-1991. *LANGUAGES:* Mandarin, Shanghainese, English and Taiwanese. *PRACTICE AREAS:* Cross Boarder Investments; Investment in the PRC; Corporate Law; Fair Trade Law; Copyright Law.

AI-ER CHEN, born Sun-Shan, Taipei Hsien, Taiwan, June 25, 1962; admitted, 1986, Republic of China. *Education:* National Chung Hsing University (LL.B., 1984; LL.M., 1987). *LANGUAGES:* Mandarin, Taiwanese, German and English. *PRACTICE AREAS:* Arbitration; Banking Law; International Contracts; Taxation.

SUSAN C.C. HUANG, born Ping-Tong, Taiwan, January 8, 1963; admitted, 1988, Republic of China. *Education:* National Taiwan University (LL.B., 1985; LL.M., 1992). Associated with the firm since 1988. *LANGUAGES:* Mandarin, Taiwanese and English. *PRACTICE AREAS:* Arbitration; Criminal Law; Maritime and Admiralty Law; Product Liability Law; Patent and Trademark Prosecution and Litigation.

KATHLEEN Y.W. KU, born Changhua, Taiwan, August 20, 1968; admitted, 1991, Republic of China. *Education:* National Cheng Chih University (LL.B., 1990). Associated with the firm since 1991. *LANGUAGES:* Mandarin, Taiwanese and English. *PRACTICE AREAS:* Public Works; Property and Real Estate Law; Litigation; Bills Exchange Law; Securities and Exchange Law.

AN-CHI CHANG, born Kaohsiung, Taiwan, February 26, 1966; admitted, 1992, Republic of China. *Education:* National Taiwan University (LL.B., 1989); University of Washington, Seattle (LL.M., 1991). Associated with the firm since 1992. *LANGUAGES:* Mandarin, English and Taiwanese. *PRACTICE AREAS:* Litigation; State Compensation Law; Property and Real Estate Law; Public Works.

MING-SHI SUN, born Taipei, Taiwan, October 11, 1964; admitted, 1992, Republic of China. *Education:* National Taiwan University (LL.B., 1991). Associated with the firm since 1992. *LANGUAGES:* Mandarin, English and Taiwanese. *PRACTICE AREAS:* Bills Exchange Law; Insurance Law; Maritime and Admiralty Law; Property and Real Estate Law; Patent and Trademark Prosecution and Litigation.

SONYA S.Y. HSU, born Taipei, Taiwan, February 10, 1969; admitted, 1992, Republic of China. *Education:* National Chunghsing University

(This Listing Continued)

School of Law (LL.B., 1991). Associated with the firm since 1992. *LANGUAGES:* Mandarin, English and Taiwanese. *PRACTICE AREAS:* Securities and Exchange Law; Insurance Law; Bills Exchange Law; Rent and Lease; Patent and Trademark Litigation and Prosecution.

EUGENE C. HU, born Taipei, Taiwan, May 18, 1959; admitted, 1987, California (Not admitted in Taiwan). *Education:* University of California, Santa Cruz (B.A., 1982); University of California, Hastings College of Law (J.D., 1987). Associated with the firm since 1993. *LANGUAGES:* Mandarin and English. *PRACTICE AREAS:* Construction and Insurance Litigation; Securities and Exchange Law; Copyright Law; License Negotiation; Transfer of Technology.

PAUL C.T. CHEN, born Win-lin, Taiwan, August 22, 1960; (Not admitted in Taiwan). *Education:* Soochow University School of Law (LL.B., 1988). Legal Assistant, Guang Tai International Patent and Law Office, 1983-1989. Associated with the firm since 1990. *LANGUAGES:* Mandarin, Taiwanese and English. *PRACTICE AREAS:* Copyright Law; License Negotiation; Transfer of Technology,

REPRESENTATIVE CLIENTS: Advantest Corp.; Air Products & Chemicals, Inc.; American President Lines; American Club in China (Taipei); Asian Development Bank; Banker's Club Taiwan; Bankers Trust Company; Barclays Bank; Baxter Healthcare Ltd.; Belgian Bank; Bank of Taiwan; BOT Leasing Co., Ltd.; Central Reinsurance Corp.; CIGNA Worldwide Inc.; Club Corporation of Asia Ltd.; Dao Heng Bank; Ebasco Industries, Inc.; Evergreen Marine Corp.; Dr. Pepper Company; Fujitsu Ltd.; Fuji Xerox Co., Ltd.; Generation 2000 (Sportswear) Limited; Genstar Container Corporation; Hercules Inc.; Insurance Company of North America; International Paint (Taiwan) Ltd.; Jean Patou Parfumeur; Johnson & Higgins, Inc.; Kimberly-Clark Corp.; Kuehne & Nagel (Taiwan) Ltd.; Lloyds Bank; Maersk Taiwan Ltd.; Marine Midland Bank, N.A.; McGraw-Hill, Inc.; Mentor Graphics Corp.; Merck & Co., Inc.; Mitsui Marine & Fire Insurance Co., Ltd.; Philip Wain International; Proctor & Gamble Corp.; Schering (Taiwan) Ltd.; Shell Taiwan Ltd.; Sincere Navigation Corp.; Stolt-Nielsen; Taiwan Swire Ltd.; Tokio Marine & Fire Insurance Co., Ltd.; Toyo Electronic Mfg. Co., Ltd.; United Metals Enterprise Co., Ltd.; United Machinery Group Ltd.; United States Surgical Corp.; Warner Communications Inc.

JONES, DAY, REAVIS & POGUE

8TH FLOOR
2 TUN HWA SOUTH ROAD
SECTION 2
TAIPEI 10654, TAIWAN
Telephone: (886-2) 704-6808
Telecopier: (886-2) 704-6791

In Atlanta, Georgia: 3500 One Peachtree Center, 303 Peachtree Street, N.E. Telephone: 404-521-3939. Cable Address: "Attorneys Atlanta". Telex: 54-2711. Telecopier: 404-581-8330.

In Brussels, Belgium: Avenue Louise 480, 7th Floor, B-1050 Brussels. Telephone: 32-2-645-14-11. Telecopier: 32-2-645-14-45.

In Chicago, Illinois: 77 West Wacker. Telephone: 312-782-3939. Telecopier: 312-782-8585.

In Cleveland, Ohio: North Point, 901 Lakeside Avenue. Telephone: 216-586-3939. Cable Address: "Attorneys Cleveland." Telex: 980389. Telecopier: 216-579-0212.

In Columbus, Ohio: 1900 Huntington Center. Telephone: 614-469-3939. Cable Address: "Attorneys Columbus." Telecopier: 614-461-4198.

In Dallas, Texas: 2300 Trammell Crow Center, 2001 Ross Avenue. Telephone: 214-220-3939. Cable Address: "Attorneys Dallas." Telex: 730852. Telecopier: 214-969-5100.

In Frankfurt, Germany: Triton Haus, Bockenheimer Landstrasse 42, 60323. Frankfurt am Main. Telephone: 49-69-9726-3939. Telecopier: 49-69-9726-3993.

In Geneva, Switzerland: 20, rue de Candolle. Telephone: 41-22-320-2339. Telecopier: 41-22-320-1232.

In Hong Kong: 1501 One Exchange Square, 8 Connaught Place. Telephone: 852-2526-3939. Telecopier: 852-2810-5787.

In Irvine, California: 2603 Main Street, Suite 900. Telephone: 714-851-3939. Telex: 194911 Lawyers LSA. Telecopier: 714-553-7539.

In London, England: One Mount Street. Telephone: 44-71-493-9361. Cable Address: "Surgoe London WI". Telecopier: 44-71-493-9666.

In Los Angeles, California: 555 West Fifth Street, Suite 4600. Telephone: 213-489-3939. Telex: 181439 UD. Telecopier: 213-243-2539.

In New York, New York: 599 Lexington Avenue. Telephone: 212-326-3939. Cable Address: "JONESDAY NEWYORK." Telex: 237013 JDRP UR. Telecopier: 212-755-7306.

In Paris, France: 62, rue du Faubourg Saint-Honore. Telephone: 33-1-44-71-3939. Cable Address: "Surgoe Paris." Telex: 290156 Surgoe. Telecopier: 33-1-49-24-0471.

(This Listing Continued)

JONES, DAY, REAVIS & POGUE, Taipei—Continued

In Pittsburgh, Pennsylvania: 500 Grant Street, 31st Floor. Telephone: 412-391-3939. Cable Address: "Attorneys Pittsburgh". Telecopier: 412-394-7959.

In Riyadh, Saudi Arabia: Law Offices of Saud M.A. Shawwaf, P.O. Box 2700. Telephones: (966-1) 465-6543, (966-1) 464-8534 or (966-1) 464-8540. Telex: 401831 SAUCON SJ. Telecopier: (966-1) 464-8480.

In Tokyo, Japan: Toranomon MT Building, 4th Floor, 10-3, Toranomon 3-Chome, Minato-Ku, Tokyo 105, Japan. Telephone: 81-3-3433-3939. Telecopier: 81-3-5401-2725.

In Washington, D.C.: Metropolitan Square, 1450 G Street, N.W. Telephone: 202-879-3939. Cable Address: "Attorneys Washington." Telex: 89-2410 ATTORNEYS WASH. Telecopier: 202-737-2832.

General and International Practice, Corporate, Mergers and Acquisitions, Securities, Investment (Inbound and Outbound), Banking and Finance, Real Estate, Intellectual Property, Tax and Trade.

MEMBER OF FIRM IN TAIPEI

JACK JIH-TSAN HUANG, born Taipei, Taiwan, October 11, 1952; admitted, 1976, Taiwan; 1983, New York. *Education:* National Taiwan University (LL.B., 1975); Northwestern University (LL.M., 1979); Harvard University (S.J.D., 1983).

ASSOCIATES

KE-WEI WILLIAM HSU, born Taipei, Taiwan, November 17, 1957; admitted, 1991, New York (Not admitted in Taiwan). *Education:* National Taiwan University (LL.B., 1981); University of Pennsylvania (LL.M., 1984; M.B.A., 1994).

JEFFREY H. CHEN, born Wilkinsburg, Pennsylvania, July 2, 1955; admitted, 1989, Michigan; 1990, District of Columbia (Not admitted in Taiwan). *Education:* University of Michigan (B.A., 1977; M.A., 1984); George Washington University (J.D., 1988).

MICHAEL E. MANGELSON, born Provo, Utah, September 9, 1963; admitted, 1991, California (Not admitted in Taiwan). *Education:* Brigham Young University (B.A., 1988; J.D., 1991).

LOUIS FANG-LIN MENG, born Taipei, Taiwan, May 6, 1965. *Education:* Soochow University (LL.B., 1990); Southern Methodist University (LL.M., 1991; J.D., 1994).

ANDREW D. RUFF, born Detroit, Michigan, February 14, 1964. *Education:* Harvard University (A.B., 1988); University of California, Los Angeles (J.D., 1994).

STAFF ATTORNEYS

THOMAS TAI-MING CHEN, born Nan Tou, Taiwan, October 15, 1965; admitted, 1993, New York (Not admitted in Taiwan). *Education:* National Taiwan University (LL.B., 1989); Boston University (LL.M., 1992).

ERIC C.A. TSAI, born Taipei, Taiwan, October 6, 1967; admitted, 1992, Taiwan. *Education:* National Taiwan University (LL.B., 1990).

SARIA HSIN-HSIEN TSENG, born Taipei, Taiwan, June 6, 1970; admitted, 1993, Republic of China (Not admitted in Taiwan). *Education:* Chinese Culture University (B.A., 1992).

Languages: English, Mandarin, Taiwanese, Japanese.

KAO & KAO

Established in 1956

12TH FLOOR, NO. 183
SECTION 2, CHUNG-KING NORTH ROAD
P.O. BOX 61-115
TAIPEI 103, TAIWAN
Telephone: (02) 5539940
Facsimile: (02) 5535850

Patent, Trademark, Copyright, Investment, Litigation.

MEMBERS OF FIRM

CHIN-FU KAO, born Taipei, Taiwan, February 24, 1930; admitted, 1955, Taiwan, Republic of China; 1970, admitted to patent office. *Education:* National Taiwan University (LL.B., 1950). *Member:* Taipei Bar Association; Inter-Pacific Bar Association; Asian Patent Attorneys Association; United States Trademark Association; Licensing Executives Society; Inter-

(This Listing Continued)

---

national Association for the Protection of Industrial Property (AIPPI). *LANGUAGES:* Mandarin, Taiwanese, English and Japanese. *PRACTICE AREAS:* Civil Litigation; International Trade Law.

YUNG-YUAN KAO, born Taipei, Taiwan, 1958; admitted, 1991, Taiwan, Republic of China; 1992, admitted to patent office. *Education:* Soochow University Law School (LL.B., 1982); Franklin Pierce Law Center (Master of Intellectual Property, 1990). Visiting Scholars: United States Patent and Trademark Office and Copyright Office, 1990. *Member:* Licensing Executive Society (LES); American Intellectual Property Law Association; Taipei Bar Association; Asian Patent Attorneys Association; United States Trademark Association; International Association for the Protection of Industrial Property (AIPPI); Inter-Pacific Bar Association. *LANGUAGES:* Mandarin, Taiwanese and English. *PRACTICE AREAS:* Intellectual Property Law; Intellectual Property Litigation.

L. L. KUO, born Kaohsiung, Taiwan, 1960; (Not admitted in Taiwan). *Education:* Foreign Languages, Soochow University (B.S., 1983). *LANGUAGES:* Mandarin, Taiwanese, English and Japanese.

Y. C. KAO, born Taipei, Taiwan, 1965; (Not admitted in Taiwan). *Education:* Agriculture Extension, National Taiwan University (B.S., 1988). *LANGUAGES:* Mandarin, Taiwanese and English. *PRACTICE AREAS:* Trademark Law; Copyright Law.

CONSULTANT

YUNG-CHUAN KAO, born Taipei, Taiwan, 1956; (Not admitted in Taiwan). *Education:* Physics National Taiwan University (B.S., 1978); University of California at Berkeley (Ph.D., 1985); National Taiwan University. Experience: Professor of National Taiwan University. *LANGUAGES:* Mandarin, Taiwanese and English.

LEE AND LI

Established in 1953

7TH FLOOR, FORMOSA PLASTICS BUILDING
201, TUN HUA NORTH ROAD
P.O. BOX 619
TAIPEI, TAIWAN
Telephone: (02) 715-3300
Cable Address: "Leeandli" Taipei
Telex: 11651 Leeandli Taipei
Fax: CCITT Group III 2-713-3966

REVISERS OF THE TAIWAN (REPUBLIC OF CHINA) LAW DIGEST FOR THIS DIRECTORY.

Kaohsiung, Taiwan, R.O.C. *Office:* 251, 8th Fl., Min Hwa Rd., Ku-Shan District, P.O. Box 899. Telephone: 07-585-0230.

FIRM PROFILE: History: Lee and Li began as the law office of Mr. James Lee. Mr. Lee began his law practice in Shanghai and formed his own firm in Taipei in 1953. He was joined by Dr. C.N. Li in 1965. In 1970, in memory of Mr. James Lee who passed away that year, Dr. Li named the office "Lee and Li", thus marking the formal establishment of the firm.

Growth and Areas of Emphasis: Keeping pace with the rapid economic development of the Republic of China (R.O.C.), the firm has expanded steadily since its establishment. It is now the largest law firm in the R.O.C. and its scope of practice encompasses all areas of commercial law, with an emphasis on serving clientele of transnational nature. In addition to the legal services, Lee and Li is often called upon by the R.O.C. government to provide advice on various legislative and policy matters.

Structure: Lee and Li's main office in Taipei has more than 300 employees, with a legal and professional staff of 166. It also maintains an office in Kaohsiung, R.O.C. Lee and Li has established correspondent relationships with foreign law firms throughout America, Europe, Asia and Africa to facilitate matters involving the legal systems of the other countries. Lee and Li also has well-established working relationships with major business consulting firms, accounting firms and banking facilities. These connections have proven to be valuable resource to clients, particularly for those who are less familiar with the R.O.C. business community.

Client Base: Among approximately 20,000 clients, most of them are multi-national businesses. The leaders of modern industries including electronic, computer, petro-chemical, pharmaceutical, publication, trading, securities, insurance and banking industries, etc., of North America, Europe, Asia and other areas are mostly on Lee & Li's client list.

Scope of Practice: Lee and Li provides a full range of civil and commer-

(This Listing Continued)

cial legal services. The specialization includes corporate and investment, banking, securities, insurance, international contracts, litigation, patent, trademark, copyright and industrial and intellectual property right planning and enforcement. The Corporate and Investment Department handles incorporation procedures, tax planning, foreign investment, technical cooperation, know-how licensing, merger and acquisition, securities offerings, labor, management relations and other corporate matters. The Banking and Financial Services Department handles legal matters in establishing on-shore and off-shore banking entities, commercial and investment banking, private banking, international financing, trade finance, foreign exchange, securities and related services. The Patent and Trademark and Copyright Departments handle all aspects of intellectual property rights including patent, trademark and copyright registration, licensing and transfer for domestic and international clients. These Departments also support the other departments of the firm on the intellectual property protection aspects of corporate projects and enforcement action, where necessary. The Litigation Department handles a variety of civil and commercial litigation, ranging from contract litigation, admiralty and trade disputes, to infringement litigation. The litigators not only attend to the substantial and procedural details in each case, but also bring an overall strategy into the dispute resolution setting. The Industrial and Intellectual Property Right Planning and Enforcement Department assists domestic and international clients in their intensifying efforts to tackle patent, trademark, copyright, trade secret infringement in R.O.C. Together with the Litigation Department, it has handled several of the landmark cases in this area. The Special Contracts Section assists clients not only in drafting and negotiating of contracts, but also actively participates in overall planning of the projects, including government procurement projects and bids of international contractors.

Case Handling Procedure: Lee and Li employs a unique team-work approach that provides the most comprehensive, efficient and cost-saving legal services to its clients. Moreover, a Data and Information Center is established to ensure quick access to up-to-date information on laws and related matters, so that services may be rendered in the most efficient manner.

MEMBERS OF FIRM

JAMES M. LEE (1908-1970).

CHAO-NIEN LI (1909-1973).

FRANK C.S. WANG (1922-1982).

SENIOR PARTNERS

C.V. CHEN, born Yunnan, China, October 25, 1944; admitted, 1975, Republic of China; Patent Agent. *Education:* National Taiwan University School of Law (LL.B., 1967); Faculty of Law, University of British Columbia (LL.M., 1969); Harvard Law School (LL.M., 1970; S.J.D., 1972). Formerly associated with Underwood, Wright, White & Lord, Attorneys-at-Law, New York, Summer 1969. Author: "Contemporary International Law," (textbook); "Conflict of Laws and the Unification of Law Concerning Civil Liability of International Air Carriers." Republic of China Contributor to Pinner's World Unfair Competition Law—An Encyclopedia, Sijthoff & Noordhoff, 1978; Methodology in Conflicts of Law, A Re-visit, 1984. Associate Professor of Law, National Chengchi University and Soochow University, 1972—. Advisor to the Cabinet, Republic of China, 1989—. Legal Consultant to Central Bank of China, 1988—. Chief Legal Consultant to Ministry of National Defence, 1983—. Legal Consultant to Ministry of Foreign Affairs, 1984—. Presidential Appointee of the 25-Member Committee for Preparation of National Affairs Conference, 1990. Member of the 15-member Committee on Review and Drafting of Economic-Social Laws/-Regulations, the Council for Economic Development of the Executive Yuan, Republic of China, 1985—. Governor of the Commercial Arbitration Association of the Republic of China, 1989. Vice President, The Red Cross Society of the Republic of China. Director, Straits Exchange Foundation. *Member:* Taipei Bar Association; Kaohsiung Bar Association. *LANGUAGES:* Chinese, English. *PRACTICE AREAS:* Transnational Legal Problems (Corporate Law, Litigation, Intellectual Property).

PAUL S.P. HSU, born Hong Kong, British Crown Colony, March 25, 1939; admitted, 1993, Republic of China. *Education:* National Taiwan University School of Law (LL.B., 1962); Fletcher School of Law and Diplomacy, Tufts University (M.A., 1965); New York University Law School (LL.M., 1969). Author: Recent Government Policy and Incentive Measure Regarding Foreign Investment in the R.O.C.; Licensing in the R.O.C.; A Study of Capital Market Development in the Republic of China from a Legal Perspective; A Study of the Legal Issues Relating to Joint Venture Enterprises; A Practical Legal Guide for Conducting Business in the Republic of China; Co-Author: Joint Ventures in the Republic of China: A Study in

International Business Cooperation; Transformation of the Capital Market in Taiwan, The Republic of China--The Past, Present and Prospects, Columbia Journal Transactional Law; Business Operations in the Republic of China (Taiwan), published by Tax Management Inc. Contributor: Licensing of Technology in Taiwan, published by Tax Management International Journal; Trade and Investment in Taiwan-The Legal and Economic Environment in the R.O.C., published by Institute of American Culture, Academic Sinica; Incentives for Setting up Venture Capital Investment Enterprises, published by East Asian Executive Reports; National Correspondent, Investment Laws of the World, published by Oceana Publication Inc. Formerly associated with Underwood, Wright, White and Lord, Attorneys-at-Law, New York, 1968-1969. Lecturer in Law, Soochow University Law School, Taipei, China, 1969-1971. Professor of Law, National Taiwan University Law School, Taipei, China, 1969—. *LANGUAGES:* Chinese, English. *PRACTICE AREAS:* Corporate Law; Investments; Banks and International Banking; Finance; Securities; Licensing; Intellectual Property; Corporate Strategy.

CONSULTANTS

KWAN-TAO LI, born Shanghai, China, February 27, 1945; (Not admitted in Republic of China); admitted, New York. *Education:* National Taiwan University School of Law (LL.B., 1966); New York University Law School (LL.M., 1969). Co-author, "Joint-Ventures in the Republic of China," 1971; "A Study on Economic Contract Law of Mainland China," 1993. Lecturer in Law, Soochow University Law School, Taipei, China, 1969—; Catholic University of Fu-Jen Law School, Taipei, China, 1969-1971. Associate Professor of Law, Chinese Culture University, 1985—. Director: Far Eastern Medical Foundation, Yen Tjing Ling Medical Foundation, Yuan-Tze Memorial College of Engineering, Asia Cement Corporation, Tai Yuen Textile Co., Ltd. *LANGUAGES:* Chinese, English. *PRACTICE AREAS:* Corporate Law; Investments; Intellectual Property; Corporate Strategy.

DEAN T. CHIANG, born Sian, China, June 30, 1944; admitted, 1975, New Jersey; (Not admitted in Republic of China). *Education:* National Cheng-Chi University (LL.B., 1966); George Washington University (M.C.L.-A.P., 1969; Post-Graduate Diploma in Business Administration, 1970. Adjunct Lecturer in Insurance Law, National Cheng Chi University, 1985-1991. Administrative Resident, Holy Cross Hospital, Silver Springs, Maryland, 1970-1971. Private Law Practice in New Jersey, 1975-1980. Manager: New Jersey Blue Cross, 1971-1974; Prudential Insurance Company of America, 1975-1978; International Department, Prudential Reinsurance Company, 1978-1980; Asia Regional Office (Hong Kong), Prudential Reinsurance Company, 1980-1981. Director, Asia Regional Office (Hong Kong), Prudential Reinsurance Company, 1981-1982. Lee and Li, 1982—. *LANGUAGES:* Chinese, English. *PRACTICE AREAS:* Corporate Law; Mergers & Acquisitions; Construction and Engineering Law; Securities; Insurance.

NIGEL NIEN-TSU LI, born Taipei, November 3, 1954; admitted, 1980, Republic of China; 1986, California; Patent Agent. *Education:* Soochow University (LL.B., 1977); National Taiwan University (LL.M., 1980); Harvard Law School (LL.M., 1983). Recipient of ITT International Fellowship, 1982. Author: "The Legal Status of Transnational Commercial Arbitration in the R.O.C.," 1983; "Labor Law Developments in Taiwan," 1985; "Transnational Commercial Arbitration and Provisional Remedies in Taiwan," 1986; "The Less-Restrictive-Means Principle - A More or a Less Restrictive Methodology?" 1988; "Can Petition for Enforcement of Foreign Arbitral Award Toll Legal Time Bar in the Republic of China?," 1990; "Constitutionalism and National Affairs," 1991; "To Recognize Or Not To Recognize? Why Not? -- A Study of the Taiwan's Approach of Recognition and Enforcement of Mainland China and Hong Kong Arbitral Awards," 1993. Co-Author: "Law in the Social Living," textbook, 1988; " An Uncommon Bigamy and An Uncommon Constitutional Interpretation," 1990; "Copyright and Modern Life," 1992; "It's Your Consumer Protection Law," 1994. Instructor/Lecturer, Ministry of National Defense, 1981-1982. Foreign Attorney, Paul, Weiss, Rifkin, Wharton & Garrison, New York, Summer, 1983. Associate Professor, Soochow University, School of Law, 1994—. Lee and Li, 1986—. Arbitrator, R.O.C. Commercial Arbitration Association, 1986—. Board Member, R.O.C. Commercial Arbitration Association, 1990—. Vice President, Republic of China Harvard Club, 1990—. *Member:* National Assembly; Taipei Bar Association; State Bar of California; Chinese Society of Constitutional Law. *LANGUAGES:* Chinese, English. *PRACTICE AREAS:* Commercial Litigation/Arbitration; Constitutional Law.

LAWRENCE SHAO-LIANG LIU, born Taiwan, July 19, 1955; admitted, 1982, California; 1990, Republic of China. *Education:* National Taiwan

(This Listing Continued)

(This Listing Continued)

LEE AND LI, Taipei—Continued

University (LL.B., 1977); University of Pennsylvania (LL.M., 1980); University of Chicago (J.D., 1982). Editor of Chinese Yearbook of International Law and Affairs, 1987—. Contributor: Competition Law of the Pacific Countries, Matthew Bender & Company, Inc., 1986. Author: "Judicial Review and Emerging Constitutionalism: The Uneasy Case for the Republic of China on Taiwan," American Journal of Comparative Law, 1991; "Survey of Major Commercial Law Developments in the Republic of China: 1987-1988," Chinese Yearbook of International Law and Affairs; "Judicial Review and the Constitution: A Tale of Two Institutions," Institute of America, Academia Sinica; "Brave New World of Financial Reforms . . . Three Waves of Internationalization and Liberalization and Beyond," Chinese Yearbook of International Law and Affairs; "Experimenting with Competition Law: A Preliminary Analysis of the Draft Fair Trade Law of Taiwan, the Republic of China," World Competition Law and Economic Review; "Legal and Policy Perspectives on United States Trade Initiatives and Economic Liberalization in the Republic of China," Michigan Journal of International Law; "Financial Developments and Foreign Investment Strategies in Taiwan... A Legal and Policy Perspective," International Lawyer; "In the Name of Fair Trade: A Commentary on the New Competition Law and Policy of Taiwan, the Republic of China," The International Lawyer of ABA, Spring 1993. Co-Author: "The Transformation of the Securities Market in Taiwan, The Republic of China," Columbia Journal of Transportation Law, 1988. Baker & McKenzie, Attorneys at Law, Chicago, Illinois, Summer, 1981. Associate, Gibson, Dunn & Crutcher, Attorneys at Law, Los Angeles, California, 1982-1985. Associate Professor of Law: Chinese Culture University, 1985—; Soochow University, 1990—. Lee and Li, 1985—. Arbitrator and Supervisor, R.O.C. Commercial Arbitration Association, 1991—. Member: State Bar of California; American Bar Association; International Bar Association; Taipei Bar Association; Inter-Pacific Bar Association; Committee of Consumer Relations, Chinese National Chamber of Industries, R.O.C.; Industrial Policy Advisory Council, Ministry of Economic Affairs, R.O.C.; Visiting Committee, University of Chicago Law School, U.S.A. LANGUAGES: Chinese, English. PRACTICE AREAS: Securities; Banks and International Banking; Competition and Consumer Laws.

CHRISTOPHER L.C. CHANG, born Taiwan, February 11, 1951; (Not admitted in Republic of China). Education: National Cheng Chi University (LL.B., 1975). Lee and Li, 1976—. LANGUAGES: Chinese, English. PRACTICE AREAS: Corporate Law; Real Estate; Acquisitions.

JUDY YU-CHUNG CHANG, born Taipei, October 16, 1950; (Not admitted in Republic of China). Education: Fu Jen Catholic University (LL.B., 1973); The American University (LL.M., 1986). Lee and Li, 1974—. LANGUAGES: Chinese, English. PRACTICE AREAS: Trademarks and Copyrights.

ERIC CHEN, born Taiwan, May 15, 1950; (Not admitted in Republic of China). Education: National Tsing Hwa University (B.S., in Chemistry, 1971). Senior Engineer, General Instrument Company of Taiwan, 1973-1975. Lee and Li, 1975—. LANGUAGES: Chinese, English. PRACTICE AREAS: Intellectual Property.

GRACE J. Y. CHEN, born Taipei, July 31, 1949; (Not admitted in Republic of China). Education: National Taiwan University (B.A., 1973). Editor, Tung Hua Book Co., Ltd., 1968-1971. Lee and Li, 1971—. LANGUAGES: Chinese, English. PRACTICE AREAS: Trademarks.

DEREK NING-SUN CHENG, born Nanking, China, October 26, 1948; (Not admitted in Republic of China). Education: Soochow University Law School (LL.B., 1972); Southern Methodist University Law School (LL.M., 1980). Lecturer of Central Police Academy, 1985-1987. Lee and Li, 1974—. LANGUAGES: Chinese, English. PRACTICE AREAS: Sales & Licensing Contracts; Intellectual Property Management and Enforcement.

LIH-CHU CHOU, born Taipei, November 18, 1953; (Not admitted in Republic of China). Education: National Chung Shing University Law School (LL.B., 1976). Legal Assistant to Mr. Shun-Jui Chen Attorney at Law, 1976-1977. Lee and Li, 1977—. LANGUAGES: Chinese, English. PRACTICE AREAS: Real Estate; Ship Finance; Debt Collections.

SHIRLEY SHIOU-HUI HSU, born Taipei, November 11, 1946; (Not admitted in Republic of China). Education: Soochow University Law School (LL.B., 1970); Academy of American and International Law, International and Comparative Law Center, The Southwestern Legal Foundation (Certificate, 1980). Legal Assistant: Hsu Chieh Law Offices, 1970-1971 and to Mr. Francis S.F. Liu, Attorney-at-Law, 1972-1974; Lee and Li,

(This Listing Continued)

AS326B

1974—. LANGUAGES: Chinese, English. PRACTICE AREAS: Trademarks.

CHIH-KANG JEN, born Shensi, China, December 21, 1940; (Not admitted in Republic of China). Education: National Taiwan University Law School (LL.B., 1965); Georgetown University Law Center (Orientation in United States Legal System, 1988). Clerk of Taipei District Court, 1967-1969. Senior Special Assistant of Secretary Division, 1969-1972 and Section Chief of the Operation Division, 1973-1974, Investment Commission of MOEA, Lee and Li, 1974—. LANGUAGES: Chinese, English. PRACTICE AREAS: Corporate Law; Investments; Taxation.

SHAN-TEH LAN, born Taipei, July 27, 1948; (Not admitted in Republic of China). Education: National Cheng Chi University (LL.B., 1971). Summer Program, Orientation of American Law, University of California in Davis, 1991. Senior Assistant of the Investment Commission, Ministry of Economic Affairs, 1973-1977. Lee and Li, 1977—. LANGUAGES: Chinese, English. PRACTICE AREAS: Foreign Investments; Corporate Law; Technical Cooperation; Acquisitions; Franchises; Contracts; Labor & Employment; Taxation.

JANICE YUNG-FEN LEE, born Taipei, January 26, 1952; (Not admitted in Republic of China). Education: Soochow University Law School (LL.B., 1975); Completed Summer Program in United States Law and Legal Institutions, University of Wisconsin (1987). Clerk to District Court, Taipei, 1978. Lee and Li, 1978—. LANGUAGES: Chinese, English. PRACTICE AREAS: International Contracts; Government Procurement.

SHERRY SHIOU-LING LIN, born Taipei, July 20, 1949; (Not admitted in Republic of China). Education: National Taiwan University (LL.B., 1971). Lee and Li, 1976—. LANGUAGES: Chinese, English. PRACTICE AREAS: Banks and International Banking; Corporate Finance; Project Finance; Derivative Financial Products; Futures; Capital Markets (Debt and Equity); Mergers and Acquisitions; Mutual Funds; Unit Trusts; Cross-Boarder Fund Raising; Investments.

NANCY MEI-HSIANG PAI, born Taipei, September 13, 1949; (Not admitted in Republic of China). Education: Soochow University Law School, (LL.B., 1973); Completed Summer Program in United States Law and Legal Institutions, University of Wisconsin (1985). Lee and Li, 1974—. LANGUAGES: Chinese, English. PRACTICE AREAS: Corporate Law; Investments; Commercial Law; Labor & Employment; Environment Law; Maritime Law.

MING-LEI YEH, born Taiwan, December 27, 1949; (Not admitted in Republic of China). Education: Soochow University Law School (LL.B., 1973); University of Illinois Law School, U.S.A. (M.C.L., 1982). Co-writer of Tax Management, Foreign Income, Business Operations in Republic of China (1992, Tax Management Inc.). Lee and Li, 1976—. LANGUAGES: Chinese, English. PRACTICE AREAS: Investments; Licensing; Labor & Employment; Contracts; Taxation.

ASSOCIATES

JULIET CHAN, born Taiwan, January 25, 1969; admitted, 1994, Republic of China. Education: National Taiwan University (LL.B., 1992). Lee and Li, 1994—. LANGUAGES: Chinese and English. PRACTICE AREAS: Banking.

CHAO-TUNG CHANG, born Taiwan, December 26, 1960; admitted, 1990, Republic of China; Patent Agent. Education: National Cheng Chi University (LL.B., 1983); Soochow University (LL.M., 1994). Legal Clerk, Cathay Investment & Trust Co., Ltd., 1986-1987. Legal Specialist, Mictek Inc., 1987. Legal Staff, International Federation of Phonogram Institution (IFPI), 1988. Lee and Li, 1990—. Arbitrator, R.O.C. Commercial Arbitration Association. Member: Taipei Bar Association. LANGUAGES: Chinese, English. PRACTICE AREAS: Banks and International Banking; Corporate Finance; Capital Markets; Securities.

CHRISTINA MEI HSUAN CHAO, born Taipei, October 16, 1957; admitted, 1986, California; (Not admitted in Republic of China). Education: National Taiwan University Law School (LL.B., 1980); University of Pennsylvania (LL.M., 1983). Lee and Li, 1980-1982 and 1983-1989; Law offices of Peter Fei Pan, 1989-1992; Lee and Li, 1992—. Member: State Bar of California; American Bar Association; Inter-Pacific Bar Association. LANGUAGES: Chinese, English. PRACTICE AREAS: Technology Transfer; Licensing; Entertainment Law; Intellectual Property Management and Enforcement.

JAMES MIN-CHIANG CHEN, born Taipei, January 21, 1962; admitted, 1989, Republic of China; Patent Agent. Education: National Taiwan University Law School (LL.B., 1984); Soochow University Graduate Law School, Taipei, Taiwan, Republic of China (LL.M., 1986). Lee and Li,

(This Listing Continued)

1989—. Arbitrator, R.O.C. Commercial Arbitration Association. *Member:* Taipei Bar Association; Taichung Bar Association. *LANGUAGES:* Chinese, English. *PRACTICE AREAS:* Investment; Taxation; Litigation.

JESSICA JIA-CHIE CHEN, born Taipei, August 11, 1969; admitted, 1992, Republic of China; Patent Agent. *Education:* National Taiwan University (LL.B., 1991). Lee and Li. 1994—. *Member:* Taipei Bar Association. *LANGUAGES:* Chinese and English. *PRACTICE AREAS:* Litigation.

JUDY SHIH-CHUAN CHEN, born Taipei, October 1, 1963; (Not admitted in Republic of China); admitted, 1991, Texas. *Education:* University of California, Irvine (B.A., Economics, 1981-1984); American Graduate School of International Management (M.I.M., 1985-1986); Indiana University (J.D., 1987-1990). Legal Intern, Student Legal Services, Indiana, 1988-1990. Associate, Frazin Law Offices, Texas, 1992-1994; Lee and Li, 1994—. *Member:* Texas Bar Association. *LANGUAGES:* Chinese and English. *PRACTICE AREAS:* Corporate Law; Foreign Investment; Contracts.

PIIN-SHIOW CHEN, born Taiwan, March 10, 1965; admitted, 1990, Republic of China. *Education:* National Taiwan University (LL.B., 1987). Senior Clerk, Head Office of Hua Nan Commercial Bank, Ltd., 1990-1991. Lee and Li, 1991—. Arbitrator, R.O.C. Commercial Arbitration Association. R.O.C. Patent Agent. *Member:* Taipei Bar Association; Taichung Bar Association; Panchiao Bar Association. *LANGUAGES:* Chinese, English. *PRACTICE AREAS:* Litigation; Arbitration.

TA-CHUNG CHIANG, born Taiwan, May 9, 1961; admitted, 1986, Republic of China; Patent Agent. *Education:* National Taiwan University (LL.B., 1983); Soochow University Law School (LL.M., 1989). Formosa Transnational Attorneys-at-Law, 1987-1988; Lee and Li, 1988—. Arbitrator, ROC Commercial Arbitration Association. *Member:* Taipei Bar Association; Hsin Chu Bar Association; Tao-Yuan Bar Association. *LANGUAGES:* Chinese, English. *PRACTICE AREAS:* Litigation; Arbitration; Intellectual Property; Fair Trade Law; Consumer Protection Law; Securities; Corporate Law.

HELEN I. C. CHOU, born Taichung, January 11, 1965; admitted, 1992, Republic of China; Patent Agent. *Education:* National Taiwan University (LL.B., 1987); Soochow University Law School (LL.M., 1993). Lee and Li, 1992—. *Member:* Taipei Bar Association. *LANGUAGES:* Chinese, English. *PRACTICE AREAS:* Civil and Criminal Litigation.

JOYCE C. FAN, born Taipei, October 30, 1964; admitted, 1989, Republic of China; 1991, New York; Patent Agent. *Education:* National Taiwan University (LL.B., 1986); University of Washington (LL.M., 1988). Lee and Li, 1989—. *Member:* Taipei Bar Association; Keelung Bar Association; New York Bar Association. *LANGUAGES:* Chinese, English. *PRACTICE AREAS:* Trade Law; Government Procurement; Cross-Boarder Transactions.

JEAN CHEN-YI HSU, born Taipei, August 29, 1967; admitted, 1990, Republic of China. *Education:* National Taiwan University (LL.B., 1989). Baker & Mckenzie, Attorneys-at-Law, 1990-1991; Lee and Li, 1991—. *Member:* Taipei Bar Association; Keelung Bar Association; Hualien Bar Association. *LANGUAGES:* Chinese, English. *PRACTICE AREAS:* Commerical Law; Antidumping; Securities; International Banking; Litigation.

DENNIS JANG-DEAN HUANG, born Taiwan, July 24, 1966; admitted, 1992, Republic of China; Patent Agent. *Education:* National Cheng Chi University (LL.B., 1989); National Cheng Chi University Graduate Law School (1992—). Lee and Li, 1994—. *Member:* Taipei Bar Association; Keelung Bar Association; Taoyuan Bar Association. *LANGUAGES:* Chinese, English and Japanese. *PRACTICE AREAS:* Intellectual Property Management and Enforcement.

WEN-YEN KANG, born Taipei, July 4, 1963; admitted, 1992, Republic of China; Patent Agent. *Education:* National Taiwan University (LL.B., 1985); Harvard University (LL.M., 1991); New York University (LL.M., 1992). Assistant to Legislator Yuan, R.O.C., 1987-1989. Hsu Wen Pin Law Office, 1993. Lee and Li, 1994—. Arbitrator, R.O.C. Commercial Arbitration Association. *Member:* Taipei Bar Association. *LANGUAGES:* Chinese and English. *PRACTICE AREAS:* Litigation; Securities; Investment; Banking.

CATHERINE I.C. KEN, born Taiwan, June 15, 1964; admitted, 1987, Republic of China. *Education:* National Taiwan University Law School (LL.B., 1986); Harvard Law School (LL.M., 1991). Hsu Wen Pin Law Office, 1987-1989. Ding and Ding, 1989-1990. Say and Say, 1991-1993. Lee and Li, 1994—. *Member:* Taipei Bar Association. *LANGUAGES:* Chinese and English. *PRACTICE AREAS:* International Trade; Securities; Banking; Civil and Criminal Litigation.

(This Listing Continued)

PORTIA CHING-YU KU, born Taipei, September 28, 1966; admitted, 1993, New York and Republic of China. *Education:* National Taiwan University (LL.B., 1989); Yale University, School of Law (LL.M., 1992). Lee and Li, 1993—. *LANGUAGES:* Chinese, English. *PRACTICE AREAS:* Environment Law; Corporate Law; Construction Contracts; Fair Trade Law.

CHIA-CHING LEE, born Taipei, January 23, 1960; admitted, 1985, Republic of China; Patent Agent. *Education:* National Cheng Chi University (LL.B., 1982; LL.M., 1986). Lee and Li, 1988—. Lecturer, National Taipei College of Business, 1992—. *Member:* Taipei Bar Association; Kaohsiung Bar Association; The Commercial Arbitration Association of the Republic of China. *LANGUAGES:* Chinese, English. *PRACTICE AREAS:* Arbitration; Litigation.

ANGELA YAO LIN, born Taiwan, April 15, 1970; admitted, 1993, Republic of China; Patent Agent. *Education:* National Taiwan University Law School (LL.B., 1992); Soochow University Graduate Law School (1992—). Lee and Li, 1993—. *Member:* Taipei Bar Association. *LANGUAGES:* Chinese and English. *PRACTICE AREAS:* Civil and Criminal Litigation; Consumer Protection Law; Commercial Arbitration.

CALVIN LING, born Shanghai, China, August 23, 1931; admitted, 1957, Republic of China; Patent Agent. *Education:* National Taiwan University (LL.B., 1954). Lee and Li, 1990—. *Member:* Kaohsiung Bar Association; Tainan Bar Association. *LANGUAGES:* Chinese, English. *PRACTICE AREAS:* Civil Law; Commerical Law.

ALEX JUI-LIN LIU, born Taipei, April 12, 1954; admitted, 1991, New York (Not admitted in Republic of China). *Education:* Soochow University Law School (LL.B., 1977); Soochow University Graduate Law School (LL.M., 1982); University of Michigan (LL.M., 1988); University of Utah (J.D., 1991). Associate Professor of Law, Soochow University, 1992—. Associate Professor of Law, Chinese Culture University , 1992-1993. Legal Associate, Tsar & Tsar Law Offices, 1979-1982. Senior Associate, Lee and Li, 1983-1987. Summer Associate, Rogers & Wells, New York, 1989. Lee and Li, 1991—. *LANGUAGES:* Chinese, English. *PRACTICE AREAS:* Corporate and Investment; Banks and International Banking; Securities.

CHENG-YU LIU, born Kaohsiung, November 11, 1965; admitted, 1992, Republic of China. *Education:* National Taiwan University Medical Technology School (B.S., 1987); National Taiwan University Law School (LL.B., 1992). Medical Technologist, 1987, Republic of China. Lee and Li, 1992—. *Member:* Taipei Bar Association; Kaohsiung Medical Technologist Association. *LANGUAGES:* Chinese, English. *PRACTICE AREAS:* Banks and International Banking; Biotechnology; Finance.

J. C. LIU, born Keelung, October 30, 1956; admitted, 1991, New York; 1992, Washington, D.C.; (Not admitted in Republic of China). *Education:* National Chen-Chi University (LL.B., 1979); University of Washington Law School (LL.M., 1986); State University of New York at Buffalo Law School (J.D., 1989). Summer Associate, Baker & Mckenzie, Taipei, 1988; Associate, Damon & Morey, Buffalo, 1989-1992; Lee and Li, 1992—. *Member:* New York State Bar Association; District of Columbia Bar; American Bar Association. *LANGUAGES:* Chinese, English, Japanese. *PRACTICE AREAS:* Foreign Investments; General Corporate; Finance; Securities.

TENG-YUAN LIU, born Taipei, March 7, 1966; admitted, 1993, Republic of China; patent agent. *Education:* National Cheng Chih University (LL.B., 1988). Lee and Li, 1994—. *Member:* Taipei Bar Association; Taichung Bar Association; Changhua Bar Association. *LANGUAGES:* Chinese and English.

PETER FEI PAN, born Taipei, June 25, 1958; admitted, 1986, California; (Not admitted in Republic of China). *Education:* National Taiwan University (LL.B., 1980); University of Pennsylvania (LL.M., 1983). Special Program, Hastings College of the Law, University of California, 1984-1985. Associate, Lee and Li, 1983-1987. Law Office of Peter Fei Pan, 1987-1992. Lecturer, Tamkong University, 1993—. Co-Author: "Know Your Consumer Protection Law." Lee and Li, 1992—. *Member:* State Bar of California; San Francisco Bar Association. *LANGUAGES:* Chinese, English. *PRACTICE AREAS:* Corporate Law; Contracts; International Transaction; Telecommunications.

CECILE M. Y. SHAH, born Washington, D.C., United States, June 3, 1959; admitted, 1987, Massachusetts; 1988, New York; (Not admitted in Republic of China). *Education:* Mount Holyoke College (B.A., 1979); Boston College Law School (J.D., 1987). Lee and Li, 1990—. *Member:* Massachusetts, New York State and American Bar Associations; Inter-Pacific Bar Association. *LANGUAGES:* Chinese, English. *PRACTICE AREAS:* Corporate Law; Securities; Capital Markets.

(This Listing Continued)

AS327B

LEE AND LI, Taipei—Continued

DANIEL TUNG-HSIEN TSAI, born Tainan, August 24, 1962; admitted, 1987, Republic of China; Patent Agent. *Education:* National Taiwan University Law School (LL.B., 1984); Soochow University Graduate Law School (LL.M., 1987). Legal Staff, General Legal Counsel Office of Ministry of National Defense, 1988-1989. Attorney, Huang & Partners, Attorneys-at-Law, 1989-1992. Lee and Li, 1992—. *Member:* Taipei Bar Association; Kaohsiung Bar Association; Hsinchu Bar Association; Keelung Bar Association; R.O.C. Commercial Arbitration Association; Inter-Pacific Bar Association. *LANGUAGES:* Chinese, English. *PRACTICE AREAS:* Admiralty Law; International Trade; Insurance; Intellectual Property; Litigation.

RUEY-SEN TSAI, born Taipei, January 17, 1965; admitted, 1992, Republic of China; Patent Agent. *Education:* National Taiwan University (LL.B., 1987); Cornell University (LL.M., 1991). Lee and Li, 1993—. *Member:* Taipei Bar Association; Hsin-Chu Bar Association; Tainan Bar Association. *LANGUAGES:* Chinese, English, Japanese. *PRACTICE AREAS:* Intellectual Property.

AMY H.S. TSAO, born Taipei, January 30, 1967; admitted, 1993, New York; (Not admitted in Republic of China). *Education:* Soochow University School of Law (LL.B., 1990); Boston University (LL.M., 1992). Lee and Li, 1992—. *LANGUAGES:* Chinese, English. *PRACTICE AREAS:* Banks and International Banking; Corporate Finance; Capital Markets; Securities.

BO-SEN VON, born Taiwan, May 2, 1961; admitted, 1987, Republic of China; Patent Agent. *Education:* National Taiwan University (LL.B., 1984). Taiwan International Patent and Law Office, 1987-1989. Lee and Li, 1989—. *Member:* Taipei Bar Association; Taoyuan Bar Association; Asian Patent Attorneys Association. *LANGUAGES:* Chinese, English. *PRACTICE AREAS:* Litigation; Product Liability; Intellectual Property; Environment Law.

GRACE YA-HSIEN WANG, born Taipei, November 20, 1956; admitted, 1990, Republic of China; Patent Agent. *Education:* National Taiwan University (LL.B., 1979). Legal Assistant, Ta Li Law Offices, 1980. Legal Assistant, Baker & McKenzie, 1980-1982. Legal Assistant, Tseng Tsai Chern & Yang Law Offices, 1982-1985. Lee and Li, 1985—. Arbitrator, R.O.C. Commercial Arbitration Association. *Member:* Taipei Bar Association. *LANGUAGES:* Chinese, English. *PRACTICE AREAS:* Civil Law; Commerical Law; Litigation.

JONG WANG, born Taiwan, October 1, 1963; admitted, 1989, Republic of China and Judges Bench; Patent Agent. *Education:* National Cheng Chi University (LL.B., 1985); Soochow University Graduate Law School (LL.M., 1994). Lee and Li, 1985—. Arbitrator of the ROC Commerical Arbitration Association. *Member:* Taipei Bar Association (Vice Chairman, Committee on Environmental Laws); Chia Yi Bar Association; Inter-Pacific Bar Association. *LANGUAGES:* Chinese, English. *PRACTICE AREAS:* Antidumping; Countervailing and Trade Laws; Intellectual Property; Government Procurement; Environment Law; International Transactions.

MARGARET H.L. YANG, born Taiwan, January 24, 1963; admitted, 1987, Republic of China. *Education:* National Cheng Chi University Law School (LL.B., 1985; LL.M., 1990); Cornell Law School (LL.M., 1991). Lee and Li, 1994—. *Member:* Kaohsiung Bar Association; Pingtung Bar Association. *LANGUAGES:* Chinese and English. *PRACTICE AREAS:* Civil Law; Commercial Law; Medical and Health Law.

JULIAN C.C. YEN, born Changhua, August 21, 1965; admitted, 1993, Republic of China; Patent Agent. *Education:* Soochow University Law School (LL.B., 1990); Soochow University Graduate Law School (1992—). Lee and Li, 1994—. *Member:* Taipei Bar Association; Tainan Bar Association. *LANGUAGES:* Chinese and English. *PRACTICE AREAS:* Civil and Criminal Litigation.

TAYLOR H.C. CHEN, born Taipei, November 18, 1947 (Not admitted in Republic of China). *Education:* Tatung Institute of Technology (B.E., 1970). Lee and Li, 1985—. *LANGUAGES:* Chinese, English, Japanese. *PRACTICE AREAS:* Patents (Electronic).

FRANCIS L.C. CHOU, born Kaohsiung, November 20, 1953; (Not Admitted in Republic of China). *Education:* St. John's & St. Mary's Institute of Technology (Mechanical Engineering, 1974); Soochow University Law School (LL.B., 1984). Patent Engineer, Tai E International Patent and Trademark Office, 1981-1982. Associate, Stephen & Associates, 1982-1983. Lee and Li, 1983-1989. Trademark Chief, Louis International Patent Office, 1989-1990. Lee and Li, 1990—. *LANGUAGES:* Chinese, English, Japanese, German. *PRACTICE AREAS:* Patents; Trademarks.

(This Listing Continued)

YANN-DUN DENG, born Taiwan, February 21, 1958; (Not admitted in Republic of China). *Education:* National Taiwan University Law School (LL.B., 1980). Associate, Ding & Ding Law Offices, 1980-1983. Lee and Li, 1983—. *LANGUAGES:* Chinese, English. *PRACTICE AREAS:* Banks and International Banking; Capital Markets; Corporate Law.

LIANG-HSIN HO, born Taipei, May 16, 1951; (Not admitted in Republic of China). *Education:* National Chunghsing University (LL.B., 1974). Specialist, Great International Corporation, 1982-1984. Section Manager Investment Business Division, Tatung Company, 1985-1986. Lee and Li, 1986—. *LANGUAGES:* Chinese, English, Japanese. *PRACTICE AREAS:* Corporate Law.

RUSSELL RUEY-CHANG HORNG, born Taiwan, April 26, 1956; (Not admitted in Republic of China). *Education:* National Taipei Institute of Technology (Mechanical Engineering, 1979). Lee and Li, 1987—. *LANGUAGES:* Chinese, English. *PRACTICE AREAS:* Patents; Administrative Appeals; Administrative Court Proceedings.

ECHO HSU, born Tainan, December 31, 1961; (Not admitted in Republic of China). *Education:* Soochow University Law School (LL.B., 1985). Associate, Formosa Transnational Attorneys at Law, 1986-1989. Lee and Li, 1989—. *LANGUAGES:* Chinese, English. *PRACTICE AREAS:* Corporate Finance; Securities.

SHEAU-LING LEE, born Taipei, November 1, 1960; (Not admitted in Republic of China). *Education:* Fu-Jen University (B.S.). Lee and Li, 1984—. *LANGUAGES:* Chinese, English. *PRACTICE AREAS:* Patents (Chemical).

WENDY WEN-CHIN LEE, born Taipei, December 13, 1959; (Not admitted in Republic of China). *Education:* National Taiwan University (LL.B., 1982). Legal Assistant, Huang & Associates, 1983-1986. Lee and Li, 1986—. *LANGUAGES:* Chinese, English. *PRACTICE AREAS:* Trademarks.

TSUNG-HUNG LIN, born Taiwan, September 10, 1961; (Not admitted in Republic of China). *Education:* National Taiwan University (B.S., 1983); Tokyo Institute of Technology (M.S., 1993). Lee and Li, 1986-1990, 1993—. *LANGUAGES:* Chinese, English and Japanese. *PRACTICE AREAS:* Patents; Intellectual Property.

WEI-YUAN LIN, born Taipei, December 18, 1957; (Not admitted in Republic of China). *Education:* Tamkang University (B.S.). Lee and Li, 1982—. *LANGUAGES:* Chinese, English. *PRACTICE AREAS:* Patents.

DAISY F. LIU, born Hunan, China, April 23, 1947; (Not admitted in Republic of China). *Education:* Taichung Providence College of Arts and Science (1960). Lee and Li, 1971—. *LANGUAGES:* Chinese, English. *PRACTICE AREAS:* Loan; Securities; Banking Regulations.

DAVID B.H. LIU, born Kaohsiung, January 13, 1956; (Not admitted in Republic of China). *Education:* National Chunghsing University (LL.B., 1984). Lee and Li, 1979—. *LANGUAGES:* Chinese, English. *PRACTICE AREAS:* Immigration; Work Permits; Corporate Law; Investments.

HSIANG-HO LIU, born Taiwan, February 14, 1958; (Not admitted in Republic of China). *Education:* Soochow University Law School (LL.B., 1981); Franklin Pierce Law Center (Master of Intellectual Property, 1991). Lee and Li, 1983—. *LANGUAGES:* Chinese, English. *PRACTICE AREAS:* Copyrights; Infringement; Intellectual Property; Patents; Trademarks.

JINQ-CHEWN LIU, born Taipei, February 8, 1962; (Not admitted in Republic of China). *Education:* Soochow University Law School (LL.B., 1985). Lee and Li, 1985—. *LANGUAGES:* Chinese, English. *PRACTICE AREAS:* Litigation; Notarization; Compulsory Execution.

SIMON C.S. LIU, born Kaohsiung, January 19, 1954; (Not admitted in Republic of China). *Education:* Soochow University Law School (LL.B., 1978). Lee and Li, 1979—. *LANGUAGES:* Chinese, English. *PRACTICE AREAS:* Intellectual Property; Labor & Employment; Maritime Law; Investments; Contracts.

CAROL J. H. LO, born Taiwan, October 27, 1962; (Not admitted in Republic of China). *Education:* Fu-Jen University (LL.B., 1985). Lee and Li, 1985—. *LANGUAGES:* Chinese, English. *PRACTICE AREAS:* Trademarks.

ANNA C.H. LU, born Taipei, December 12, 1962; (Not admitted in Republic of China). *Education:* National Taiwan University (LL.B., 1985). Lee and Li, 1985—. *LANGUAGES:* Chinese and English. *PRACTICE AREAS:* Corporate Law; Taxation; Construction.

(This Listing Continued)

JILL C.M. PENG, born Taipei, June 1, 1963; (Not admitted in Republic of China). *Education:* National Taiwan University Taipei (LL.B., 1985). Lee and Li, 1985—. *LANGUAGES:* Chinese, English. *PRACTICE AREAS:* Corporate Law; Technical Cooperation; Liquidation; Acquisition; Contracts; Foundation & Association Reorganization and Taxation; Mergers; Visas; Work Permits; Corporate Taxation.

VIC C.Y. SHEN, born Taipei, November 2, 1958; (Not admitted in Republic of China). *Education:* Soochow University Law School (LL.B., 1984). Lee and Li, 1985—. *LANGUAGES:* Chinese, English. *PRACTICE AREAS:* Trademarks.

ALEX SENG NGEE TAN, born Malaysia, February 6, 1955; (Not admitted in Republic of China). *Education:* National Taiwan University (B.S., Chemical Engineering, 1983); Franklin Pierce Law Center (Master in Intellectual Property Law, 1994). Process Engineer, Chung Shing Textile Co.; Assistant Manager, Tai E International Patent, Trade Mark and Law Office, 1985-1988. Lee and Li, 1988—. *LANGUAGES:* Chinese, English. *PRACTICE AREAS:* Patents.

CATHY CHING-WEN TING, born Taiwan, October 13, 1960; (Not admitted in Republic of China). *Education:* Soochow University Law School (LL.B., 1984). Legal Assistant, Ta Li Law Office, 1984. Lee and Li, 1985—. *LANGUAGES:* Chinese, English. *PRACTICE AREAS:* Copyrights; Trademarks.

JIANG-CHERNG TSAO, born Taipei, October 22, 1957 (Not admitted in Republic of China). *Education:* Tamkang University (B.S., 1981). Technical Engineer, China Chemical and Pharmaceutical Company, 1983-1984. Lee and Li, 1984—. *LANGUAGES:* Chinese, English. *PRACTICE AREAS:* Patents (Chemistry and Pharmacy).

DAISY YE-RUNG WANG, born Taipei, December 15, 1956; (Not admitted in Republic of China). *Education:* National Taiwan University Law School (LL.B., 1980); University of Illinois Law School, USA (M.C.L., 1982). Staff, Patent Section, National Bureau of Standards, Ministry of Economic Affairs, 1977-1979. Lee and Li, 1979—. *LANGUAGES:* Chinese, English. *PRACTICE AREAS:* Intellectual Property; Technology Transfer.

JOLENE H.L. WANG, born Taiwan, May 3, 1963; (Not admitted in Republic of China). *Education:* National Taiwan University (B.S., 1985; M.S., 1987 in Animal Science). Lee and Li, 1987—. *LANGUAGES:* Chinese and English. *PRACTICE AREAS:* Patents (Biotechnology); Pharmacy and Chemistry.

LING-LING WANG, born Taipei, May 16, 1955; (Not admitted in Republic of China). *Education:* National Taiwan University (B.S., 1977). Lee and Li, 1979-1982, 1988—. *LANGUAGES:* Chinese, English. *PRACTICE AREAS:* Patents.

ROSE ANNE RU RU WANG, born Chungking, China, November 21, 1949; (Not admitted in Republic of China). *Education:* Soochow University Law School (LL.B., 1973). Lee and Li, 1973—. *LANGUAGES:* Chinese, English. *PRACTICE AREAS:* Corporate Law; Investments; Lease; Real Estate; Technical Cooperation.

WEN-SHEN WANG, born Taiwan, December 23, 1958; (Not admitted in Republic of China). *Education:* National Taiwan Institute of Technology (B.S., Mechanical Engineering, 1983). Consulting Engineer, Co-Tech R&D Consulting Co., Ltd., 1984-1987. Lee and Li, 1987—. *LANGUAGES:* Chinese, English. *PRACTICE AREAS:* Patents.

PATRICK YUE-MAN WONG, born Hong Kong, June 1, 1959; (Not admitted in Republic of China). *Education:* Soochow University Law School (LL.B., 1984). Lee and Li, 1984—. *LANGUAGES:* Chinese, English. *PRACTICE AREAS:* Investments; Corporate Law; Food & Drugs; Cosmetic Hygiene.

BETTY S.T. YANG, born Taiwan, September 18, 1956; (Not admitted in Republic of China). *Education:* National Taiwan University Law School (LL.B., 1978). Lee and Li, 1978—. *LANGUAGES:* Chinese, English. *PRACTICE AREAS:* Trademarks.

IRENE Y.L. YANG, born Kaohsiung, July 21, 1958; (Not admitted in Republic of China). *Education:* National Chunghsing University (LL.B., 1982). Lee and Li, 1988—. *LANGUAGES:* Chinese, English. *PRACTICE AREAS:* Litigation.

JOSEPH S. YANG, born Taiwan, October 20, 1956; (Not admitted in Republic of China). *Education:* National Taiwan University Law School (LL.B., 1979); University of San Diego Law School (M.C.L., 1992). Legal Assistant, Tai-E International Patent & Law Office, 1981-1982. Lee and Li, *(This Listing Continued)*

1982—. *LANGUAGES:* Chinese, English. *PRACTICE AREAS:* Trademarks.

ECHO CHIOU-ING YEH, born Taiwan, August 23, 1962; (Not admitted in Republic of China). *Education:* National Taiwan University Law School (LL.B., 1984). Legal Assistant, Chow & Lou, Attorneys-at-Law, 1984-1985. Lee and Li, 1985—. *LANGUAGES:* Chinese, English. *PRACTICE AREAS:* Investments; Corporate Law; Securities; Futures; Real Estate; Construction.

SOPHIA H.H. YEH, born Taipei, January 5, 1957; (Not admitted in Republic of China). *Education:* National Taiwan University (LL.B., 1980); University of Pennsylvania Law School (LL.M., 1986-1987). Lee and Li, 1981—. *LANGUAGES:* Chinese, English. *PRACTICE AREAS:* Corporate Law; Investments; Technology Transfer; Taxation; Securities.

ANNIE YUN-AN YU, born Taipei, March 20, 1963; (Not admitted in Republic of China). *Education:* National Taiwan University Law School (LL.B., 1985); Cornell University (LL.M., 1990). Lee and Li, 1985—. *LANGUAGES:* Chinese, English. *PRACTICE AREAS:* Commercial Law; Contracts; Competition Law; Trade Law.

CHENG-HUAN YU, born Chekiang, China, June 4, 1947; (Not admitted in Republic of China). *Education:* Soochow University Law School (LL.B., 1970). Lee and Li, 1977—. *LANGUAGES:* Chinese, English. *PRACTICE AREAS:* Trademarks.

Languages: English, Chinese (Mandarin, Shanghai, Canton, Hupei, Szechuan and Taiwan dialects), Japanese, French.

REPRESENTATIVE CLIENTS: Montres Rolex S.A.; Cathcan Equipment Asia Ltd.; Cathay Life Insurance Co., Ltd.; United Air Lines, Inc.; Zurich Insurance Company; Riedel Environment Technologies Ltd.; The Hong Kong and Shanghai Banking Corp.; Du Pont; Wang Laboratories, Inc.; Wyse Technology Taiwan Ltd.; Regent International; Ford Lio Ho Motor Company Ltd.; Alfred Dunhill Limited; Philips; AT&T; Carpenter Technology Corporation; General Instrument; Chanel; ICI Taiwan Ltd.; Cartier International B.V.; General Electric; Lehman-Global Financial Services Co., Ltd.; Hyatt International; Elders Finance Asia Limited; IBM Taiwan Corporation; 3M Taiwan Ltd.; Siemens Telecommunication Systems Limited; Citibank, N.A.; Unilever Plc; Merrill Lynch; Ciba-Geigy; Bristol-Myers Squibb; NBA Properties, Inc.; Unisys; Lockheed; Toshiba Corporation; Credit Lyonnais; Allied Signal; Nomura International H.K. Ltd.; Australian Guarantee; Barclays Bank Plc; Daiwa Securities Co.; Rohm and Hass; Societe Generale; Haagen-Dazs; Reader's Digest; Prudential Securities Inc.; Metropolitan Life Insurance Company.

REVISERS OF THE TAIWAN (REPUBLIC OF CHINA) LAW DIGEST FOR THIS DIRECTORY.

LI & ASSOCIATES

11TH FLOOR, SUITE ONE
NO. 163 KEELUNG ROAD, SECTION 1
TAIPEI, TAIWAN
Telephone: (02) 763-8630
Facsimile: (02) 763-9049

Administrative Appeals and Litigation, Civil Litigation, Copyrights, Patents and Trademarks, Fair Trade, Intellectual Property Rights, International Business Transactions, International Trade, Loan Documentation, Negotiable Instruments and Securities Law.

FIRM PROFILE: *Chun Li, one of the firm's partners, formerly practiced law in Taipei under the firm name Li & Associates. Dr. Li went to the United States in 1978 and was Legal Advisor to the Coordination Council for North American Affairs, Office in U.S.A., from 1984 through 1990. He returned to Taiwan in 1991 and in early 1993 reactivated Li & Associates, joined by his son, Fred K. Li, member of the New York and D.C. Bars, and currently an ROC National Assemblyman. The firm offers a wide range of legal services, including international trade, contracts, corporate and investment law, taxation, administrative appeals and litigation, etc.*

MEMBERS OF FIRM

CHUN LI, born Shanghai, China, December 3, 1919; admitted, 1963, Republic of China; 1981, Hawaii; 1987, District of Columbia; 1991, U.S. Military Court of Appeals. *Education:* Soochow University College of Law (LL.B., 1954); Southern Methodist University (LL.M., magna cum laude, 1956); Yale University (LL.M., 1959; J.S.D., 1960); Harvard University (J.D., 1973). President, Yale Alumni Club of Taipei, 1969-1970. Secretary, Harvard Alumni Club of Taipei, 1976-1977. Legal Consultant, Executive Yuan, Government of the Republic of China, 1957-1958. Senior Secretary, Executive Yuan, Government of the Republic of China, 1960-1964. Deputy Director-General, Government Information Office, Government of the Republic of China, 1973-1974. Ministry of National Defense, Government of the Republic of China, 1974-1977. Deputy Secretary-General, National Bar *(This Listing Continued)*

LI & ASSOCIATES, Taipei—Continued

Association of the Republic of China, 1976-1978. Legal Advisor, The Coordination Council for North American Affairs, Office in U.S.A., 1984-1990. Lecturer, Law, Soochow University College of Law, Taipei, Taiwan, China, 1956-1958. Professor: Law, Soochow University College of Law, Taipei, Taiwan, China, 1960-1963; International Law, National Chenghi University Graduate Institute of Diplomacy and International Law, Taipei, Taiwan, China, 1963-1970; Law, Soochow University Graduate Institute of Law, Taipei, Taiwan, China, 1976-1978. *Member:* Chinese Society of International Law (Member, Board of Directors, 1969-1970); Taipei Bar Association (Member, Board of Directors, 1966-1968; Member, Board of Overseers, 1968-1970). *LANGUAGES:* Chinese and English. *PRACTICE AREAS:* Contract Law; International Trade Law; Taxation Law; Administrative Appeals Law; Litigation.

FRED K. LI, born Keelung, Taiwan, China, January 4, 1952; admitted, 1985, New York and U.S. Tax Court; 1986, District of Columbia and U.S. Court of International Trade. *Education:* National Taiwan University (B.S., Chem. Eng., 1973); Harvard University (M.B.A., 1977; J.D., 1984). Associate, Roberts & Holland, New York, New York, 1984-1986. Translator, English version of The Fair Trade Law, published by the Industrial Development & Investment Center, Ministry of Economic Affairs, May 1991. Arbitrator, Commercial Arbitration Association of R.O.C., 1993—. Associate Professor, Law, Soochow University Graduate Institute of Law, Taipei, Taiwan, China, 1988-1991. Lecturer, Banking Institute of R.O.C., Taipei, Taiwan, China, 1988—. Member, National Assembly of R.O.C., 1992—. *Member:* American Bar Association; Inter-Pacific Bar Association. *LANGUAGES:* Chinese and English. *PRACTICE AREAS:* Finance Law; Business Law; Commercial Law.

LO & PARTNERS
INTELLECTUAL PROPERTY AND LAW
OFFICE

Established in 1991

6TH FLOOR-1 NO. 81
CHANG AN EAST ROAD, SEC. 2
TAIPEI, TAIWAN
Telephone: 886-2-5095579
Fax: 886-2-5094564

General and International Practice, Computer Law, Trademark, Patent, Copyright, Litigation, Foreign Investment, Corporate, Administrative Law.

FIRM PROFILE: The firm was established in 1991 and offers a full range of legal services. It is well known for its computer and intellectual property law. The firm has published two books in Chinese regarding computer law. The first book, "The Introduction of EDI Law," was written by Kevin J.F. Lin. The book is the first book of EDI Law in Taiwan. The second book, "The Computer Law," was written by Anthony M.T. Lo, Kevin J.F. Lin, Jennie C.W. Lee, Robin R.B. Hong and Moncia L.L. Chen. This is also the first complete computer law book in Taiwan.

MEMBERS OF FIRM

ANTHONY M.T. LO, born I-Lan, Taiwan, November 3, 1949; admitted, 1990, Taiwan. *Education:* National Taiwan University (LL.B., 1972); Chinese Culture University (LL.M., 1983); The University of Liverpool, England (Ph.D., 1988). Director, Taipei Prosecutors' Office of District Court. Editor, Major Laws of the Republic of China on Taiwan, Taiwan: Magnificent, English Translation, 1992. Recent Publication: Some Aspects of Non-Contractual State Liability in Public Law; A Comparative Study of the Law in Taiwan and England, Thesis for Ph.D. degree, University of Liverpool, 1988. Lecturer, Judge Training Institute. Associate Professor, Graduate School of National Central Police University and National Cheng Chi University.

JENNIE C.W. LEE, born Tauyuan, Taiwan, January 1, 1964; admitted, 1990, Taiwan. *Education:* National Taiwan University (LL.B., 1986; LL.M., 1990). Associate Lawyer, Central International Law Firm. Recent Publication: A Study of "Nortwendige Streitgenossen schaft aus materielle rechtlichen Gruden.". *LANGUAGES:* Chinese and English.

ROBIN R.B. HONG, born Tainan, Taiwan, November 14, 1964; admitted, 1992, Taiwan. *Education:* National Taiwan University (LL.B., 1987); Fu-Jen Catholic University (LL.M., 1993). Assistant Research Fellow, Administrative Court. Recent Publication: "Data Processing and Protection in

(This Listing Continued)

the Age of Information - Focus on German Federal Individual Data Protection Act of 1990," Thesis for LL.M., Fu-Jen Catholic University. *LANGUAGES:* Chinese, English and German.

KEVIN J.F. LIN, born Taipei, Taiwan, February 18, 1965; admitted, 1990, Taiwan. *Education:* National Taiwan University (LL.B., 1987; LL.M., 1993). Legal Research Fellow, Institute for Information Industry. Associate Lawyer, Tsar & Tsai Law Firm. Recent Publications: "An Introduction of EDI Contract," Institute for Information Industry, 1993; "Legal Issues of EDI," Thesis for LL.M., National Taiwan University, 1992; "Introduction of VAN Agreement," Information Law Analysis, March 1992; "The Liability for Defective Software Provider," Information Law Analysis, April 1991. *LANGUAGES:* Chinese and English.

NICOLE T.I. CHAN, born Taipei, Taiwan, August 12, 1968; admitted, 1992, Taiwan. *Education:* National Taiwan University (LL.B., 1990). Associate Lawyer, Meridian Law Office & Ding & Ding Law Office. *LANGUAGES:* Chinese and English.

STEVEN J.I. TSENG, born Kaohsiung, Taiwan, May 22, 1962. *Education:* Central Police University (LL.B., 1985; LL.M., 1991). Recent Publications: "A Study of Exclusionary Rule of Evidence - The Fruit of Poisonous Tree Doctrine," Thesis for LL.M., Central Police University, 1991; "The Exception of Exclusionary Rule of Evidence," Public Security Annual Report, 1993. Lecturer, Central Police University. *LANGUAGES:* Chinese, English and Japanese.

JANNY C.N. WANG, born Tai-Chung, Taiwan, September 21, 1965. *Education:* World College of Journalism; New York Institute of Technology (Master of Science in Communication Arts). MDK PR Consultant Inc.; U.S. Pristine Law Offices (U.S.); Benecresc International Inc. (U.S.). *LANGUAGES:* Chinese and English.

MALLESONS STEPHEN JAQUES

14TH FLOOR, 138 MIN SHENG EAST ROAD, SEC 3
TAIPEI, TAIWAN
Telephone: (886-2) 712 5808
Fax: (886-2) 712 9080

Sydney, Australia Office: Level 60, Governor Phillip Tower, 1 Farrer Place, 2000. Telephone: (612) 250 3000. Fax: (612) 250 3133.

Melbourne, Australia Office: Level 28, Rialto, 525 Collins Street, 3000. Telephone: (613) 619 0619. Fax: (613) 614 1329.

Perth, Australia Office: Ground Floor, St. Georges Square, 225 St. George's Terrace, 6000. Telephone: (619) 324 8333. Fax: (619) 3211017.

Brisbane, Australia Office: Level 30, Waterfront Place, 1 Eagle Street, 4000. Telephone: (617) 231 7500. Fax: (617) 221 1211.

Canberra, Australia Office: Level 10, Advance Bank Centre, 60 Marcus Clarke Street, 2601. Telephone: (616) 268 3900. Fax: (616) 257 3100.

Hong Kong Office: Bateson Starr in association with Mallesons Stephen Jaques, Suite 801, Asia Pacific Finance Tower, Citibank Plaza, 3 Garden Road, Central Hong Kong. Telephone: (852) 848 4600. Fax: (852) 868-0124.

Beijing, The Peoples Republic of China Office: Suite 701, Scite Tower, 22 Jianguomenwai Street, 100004. Telephone: (861) 512 3565 ext 701. Fax: (861) 523 2018.

Jakarta, Indonesia Associated Office: Law Firm Kartini Muljadi S.H. & Associates, in association with Mallesons Stephen Jaques, Level 5, Bina Mulia I Building, J.1. H.R. Rasuna Said Kav 10, 12950. Telephone: (6221) 525 6968. Fax: (6221) 525 5561.

Port Moresby, Papua New Guinea Office: Beresford Love, agents for Mallesons Stephen Jaques, Level 3, Hunter Building, Hunter Street. Telephone: (675) 211942. Fax: (675) 211586.

Singapore Office: Level 36, Hong Leong Building, 16 Raffles Quay, 0104. Telephone: (65) 321 8930. Fax: (65) 225 9060.

London, England Office: 2nd Floor, Aldermary House, 10-15 Queen Street, EC4N 1TX. Telephone: (44 171) 982 0982. Fax: (44 171) 982 9820.

New York, New York, U.S.A. Office: 9th floor, Suite 911, 609 Fifth Avenue, 10017-1021. Telephone: (1-212) 319-9500. Fax: (1-212) 319-9506.

RESIDENT PARTNER

Paul M. Hayden

(For Complete Personnel, see Biographical Card at Sydney, Australia).

McCUTCHEN, DOYLE, BROWN & ENERSEN

INTERNATIONAL TRADE BUILDING, TENTH FLOOR
333 KEELUNG ROAD, SECTION 1
TAIPEI 110, TAIWAN
Telephone: 886-2-723-5000
Facsimile: 886-2-757-6070

San Francisco, California Office: Three Embarcadero Center, 94111-4066. Telephone: 415-393-2000. Facsimile: 415-393-2286. Telex: 340817 MACPAG SFO.

Los Angeles, California Office: 355 South Grand Avenue, Suite 4400, 90071-1560. Telephone: 213-680-6400. Facsimile: 213-680-6499.

San Jose, California Office: Market Post Tower, Suite 1500, 55 South Market Street, 95113-2327. Telephone: 408-947-8400. Facsimile: 408-947-4750. Telex: 9102502931 MACPAG SJ.

Walnut Creek, California Office: 1331 North California Boulevard. Post Office Box V, 94596-4502. Telephone: 510-937-8000. Facsimile: 510-975-5390.

Menlo Park, California Office: 2740 Sand Hill Road, 94025-7020. Telephone: 415-233-4000. Facsimile: 415-233-4086.

Washington, D.C. Office: The Evening Star Building, Suite 800, 1101 Pennsylvania Avenue, N.W., 20004-2514. Telephone: 202-628-4900. Facsimile: 202-628-4912.

Affiliated Offices In: Bangkok, Thailand; Beijing, China; Shanghai, China.

FIRM PROFILE: Environmental Law, Franchising, Foreign Investment (Inbound and Outbound), Government Contracts, Products Procurement and Distribution, Labor, Real Estate, Construction, Transportation, Banking and Finance, Intellectual Property Rights, Technology Transfers and Trade.

ROBERT P. PARKER, born Longview, Texas, August 9, 1941; admitted to bar 1967, Texas; 1968, District of Columbia; 1975, U.S. Tax Court; 1976, U.S. Claims Court and U.S. Supreme Court; 1987, California (Not admitted in Taiwan). *Education:* University of Texas (B.A., 1963; J.D., with honors, 1967); University of Sydney, Australia. Phi Delta Phi. Rotary International Fellow, University of Sydney, Australia, 1964. Championship, Jessup International Law Moot Court Competition, 1966. Author: "Trade and Investment Under the New Legal Relationship," 1979; "Law and the American Corporation in Taiwan," 1980; "Trends in ROC Regulation of U.S. Economic Relations with the ROC," Council for Economic Planning and Development, Taipei, 1981; "Laws Affecting Franchise Operations in Taiwan," American Bar Association, 1982, revised 1989; "Transferring and Protecting Technology in Taiwan," 1983; "Terminating Franchise or Distribution Agreements in Taiwan," Journal of International Franchising and Distribution Law, 1993. Participated in Formulation of Taiwan Relations Act, 1979. President, American Chamber of Commerce, 1979, 1980. Member, Board of Governors and Supervisors, American Chamber of Commerce, 1978-1991. Chairman, Investment and Trade Committee, American Chamber of Commerce, 1980-1991. Executive Committee, USA-ROC Economic Council, 1981—. Vice Chairman, Asia-Pacific Council of American Chambers of Commerce, 1981-1983. Founder, 1979 and Vice-Chairman, 1981—, ICRT Radio Network, Taiwan. Director, U.S.-Taiwan Fulbright Commission, 1987-1991. Director, Tunghai University, 1981-1991. Executive Committee, USA-ROC Economic Council, 1981—. *PRACTICE AREAS:* International Business Transactions.

ROBERT E. COX, born Cedar Rapids, Iowa, 1954; admitted to bar, 1986, California (not admitted in Taiwan). *Education:* Wesleyan University (B.A., magna cum laude, 1976); Johns Hopkins/SAIS (M.A., 1978); Boalt Hall School of Law, University of California, Berkeley (J.D., 1986). Editor in Chief, International Tax and Business Lawyer, 1985-1986. Author: "The U.S.-China Double Taxation Treaty," 5 International Tax and Business Lawyer 111, 1987. International Economist, U.S. Department of Treasury, 1978-1979. Special Assistant to U.S. Director, World Bank, 1979-1980. Member, U.S. Delegation, Asian Development Bank, 1980-1983. Chairman, Investment and Trade Committee, American Chamber of Commerce, 1991—. Member, Board of Governors and First Vice-President, American Chamber of Commerce, 1992—. *Member:* American Bar Association; International Bar Association; American Society of International Law. *PRACTICE AREAS:* International Business Law.

JOAN C. Y. CHEN, born Taipei, Taiwan, R.O.C., April 3, 1958; admitted, 1983, Taiwan. *Education:* National Taiwan University (LL.B., with highest honors, 1980; LL.M., 1985). Author: "Maritime Litigation in the Absence of Pre-Trial Discovery," 1992. Co-Author: with Robert P. Parker:

(This Listing Continued)

"Terminating Franchise or Distributorship in Taiwan" Journal of International Franchising and Distribution Law, 1993. Legal Specialist, Committee on Laws and Regulations, ROC Ministry of Economic Affairs, 1981-1983. *Member:* Taipei Bar Association. *LANGUAGES:* Mandarin, Taiwanese and English.

JACQUELINE C. FU, born Keelung, Taiwan, January 9, 1966; admitted, 1990, Taiwan; 1994, New York. *Education:* National Taiwan University, Taiwan (LL.B., with highest honors, 1988); Harvard University (LL.M., 1992). *LANGUAGES:* Mandarin, Taiwanese and English.

DAVID C. GETZINGER, born Los Alamos, New Mexico, April 15, 1965; admitted, 1991, California (Not admitted in Taiwan). *Education:* Stanford University (B.A., 1987); University of California Berkeley (J.D., 1991).

KEATING H.S. HSU, born Taipei, Taiwan, October 18, 1965; admitted, 1989, Taiwan. *Education:* Soochow University (LL.B., 1989). *LANGUAGES:* Mandarin, Taiwanese and English.

FLORA M. HSU, born Taipei, Taiwan, January 10, 1967; admitted, 1990, Taiwan; 1994, New York. *Education:* National Taiwan University (LL.B., 1989; LL.M., 1992); Duke University (LL.M., 1993). *LANGUAGES:* Mandarin, Taiwanese and English.

JULIE H. SHU, born Taipei, Taiwan, September 1, 1967; admitted, 1991, Taiwan; 1994, New York. *Education:* National Taiwan University (LL.B., 1989); New York University (M.C.J., 1993). *LANGUAGES:* Mandarin, Taiwanese and English.

(For Complete Biographical data on all Personnel, see San Francisco, California Professional Biographies).

McMILLAN BULL CASGRAIN

Patent and Trade Mark Agents

5F-1, NO. 415, SEC. 4, HSINYI ROAD
TAIPEI, TAIWAN
Telephone: (02) 720-0192
Fax: (02) 720-0219

Vancouver, British Columbia Office: Bull, Housser & Tupper, Suite 3000, 1055 West Georgia Street, P.O. Box 11130. Telephone: 604-687-6575. Cable Address: "Tursid". Telex: 04-53395; 04-55121. Fax: 604-641-4949.

Surrey, British Columbia Office: Suite 201, 9648 - 128th Street, V3T 2X9. Telephone: 604-581-4677. Fax: 604-581-5947.

Hong Kong Office: 17th Floor, 9 Queen's Road, Central. Telephone: 852-843-7333. Fax: 852-845-5566.

Corporate and Business Law, Corporate Finance, Banking, Immigration Law, International Business Transactions, Maritime and Shipping, Real Estate including Commercial Property Acquisitions and Development, Taxation, Technology Law, but not authorized to practice in Taiwan.

RESIDENT ASSOCIATE

CLIVE M. ANSLEY, born Medicine Hat, Alberta, May 26, 1941; admitted, 1983, British Columbia (Not admitted in Taiwan). *Education:* University of British Columbia (B.A., 1966; M.A., 1968); University of Windsor (LL.B., 1980); University of London (LL.M., 1981).

(For complete biographical data on all personnel, see Professional Biographies at Vancouver, British Columbia, Canada)

PERENNIAL LAW OFFICE

7F-2. NO. 9 ROOSEVELT RD. SEC.2
TAIPEI, TAIWAN
Telephone: (886-2) 395-6989; 395-6979-87
Fax: (886-2) 391-4235

General Practice specializing in Litigation both Civil and Criminal, Real Estate Law, Foreign Investment, International Law, Bankruptcy, Labor Law and Commercial Law.

YUNG-RAN LEE, born Taipei, Taiwan, August 2, 1955; admitted, 1979, Taiwan. *Education:* National Taiwan University School of Law (LL.B., 1977; LL.M., 1981). Editor-in-Chief: Collections of Civil Case Judgments/Decisions with Legislative Grounds and Interpretations, June, 1987; Collections of Criminal Procedure Cases Judgments/Decisions with Legislative Grounds and Interpretations, June, 1987; Collections of Criminal Cases Judgments/Decisions with Legislative Grounds and Interpreta-

(This Listing Continued)

PERENNIAL LAW OFFICE, Taipei—Continued

tions, June, 1987; Collections of Civil Procedure Case Judgments/Decisions with Legislative Grounds and Interpretations, June, 1987; Collections of Commercial Laws Judgments/Decisions with Legislative Grounds and Interpretations, June, 1987; Collections of Judgments/Decisions related to Real Estate Mortgage, Easement, and Right of Cultivation and Raising Livestock, August, 1989; Collections of Judgments/Decisions related to Lease of Real Estate, (I, II), June, 1989; Collections of Income Tax Judgments/Decisions, (I, II, III), January, 1986; Form Book Used for Civil and Criminal Litigation, May, 1985. Author: Articles concerning Election and Recall Law, May, 1982; Articles concerning R.O.C. Constitutions and Temporary Provisions Effective During the Period of Communist Rebellion, February, 1984; Analysis of Election and Recall Law for Government Employee During the Period of Communist Rebellion, October, 1989; Collections of Articles on Laws concerning Real Estate (I, II, III), April, 1989 till February, 1990; Analysis of Disputed Real Estate Cases, October, 1989; Real Estate Litigation Practice, March, 1989. Lecturer in Law, Ming Chua College. Member, Ad Hoc Committee of the Nationwide Land Use Policy Convention, 1990. Adviser to the Ministry of Interior Regarding the Revision of National Property Law. Director of the Board, Medication Law Association. Arbitrator, Commercial Arbitration Association, 1985—. *Member:* Taipei Bar Association (Director of the Board, 1985-1989); American Bar Association (Member, Real Estate and International Law Sections). *PRACTICE AREAS:* Civil and Criminal Litigation; Real Estate Law; Law of Mainland China.

HSU-HUA YU, born Taiwan, December 19, 1962; admitted, 1992, Taiwan. *Education:* National Taiwan University (LL.B., 1990). *LANGUAGES:* Chinese and English. *PRACTICE AREAS:* Real Estate Law; Civil and Criminal Litigation; Military Law.

LIN YUNG SHENG, born November 12, 1966; (Not admitted in Taiwan). *Education:* National Cheng University (LL.B., 1990). *LANGUAGES:* Chinese and English. *PRACTICE AREAS:* Criminal Law.

MORRIS J.C. LIU, born Taiwan, August 30, 1965; admitted, 1992, Taiwan. *Education:* Bachelor of Tunhai University (LL.B., 1988). *LANGUAGES:* Chinese and English. *PRACTICE AREAS:* Real Estate Law; Intellectual Property Law.

DENISE TSENG HUI-CHING, born Taiwan, December 20, 1967; (Not admitted in Taiwan). *Education:* National Taiwan University (LL.B., 1990).

LOUIS CHEN BOR JING, born Taiwan, December 27, 1969; (Not admitted in Taiwan). *Education:* National Chunghsing University (LL.B., 1993). *LANGUAGES:* Chinese and English. *PRACTICE AREAS:* Real Estate Law.

CHANG SHIH-CHU, born Taiwan, November 27, 1964; admitted, 1992, Taiwan. *Education:* Cheng-Chi University (LL.B., 1991). Author: "Law of Administrative Appeals and Administrative Proceedings," 1993. *LANGUAGES:* Chinese, English and German. *PRACTICE AREAS:* Criminal Law; Civil Law; Military Law; Commercial Law.

JOSEPHINE HUANG, born Taiwan, April 21, 1965; admitted, 1992, Taiwan. *Education:* National Taiwan University (LL.B., 1987). *LANGUAGES:* Chinese, English and Japanese. *PRACTICE AREAS:* Real Estate Law; Civil and Criminal Litigation.

CHING-HUNG CHEN, born Taiwan, April 21, 1962; admitted, 1992, Taiwan. *Education:* National Taiwan University (LL.B., 1991). *LANGUAGES:* Chinese and Taiwanese. *PRACTICE AREAS:* Real Estate Law; Law of Mainland China.

SHIOU-FEN LEE, born Taiwan, December 14, 1968; admitted, 1993, Taiwan. *Education:* National Cheng-Chi University (LL.B., 1993). *LANGUAGES:* Chinese and Taiwanese. *PRACTICE AREAS:* Real Estate Law; Civil and Criminal Litigation.

YI-TING YEH, born Taiwan, March 18, 1968; (Not admitted in Taiwan). *Education:* Soochow University (LL.B., 1992). *LANGUAGES:* Chinese. *PRACTICE AREAS:* Enforcement and Execution of Judgements; Civil Litigation; Criminal Litigation.

WUN-TJER LIN, born Taiwan, October 8, 1955; admitted, 1990, Taiwan. *Education:* China Junior Municipal College (Civil Engineering, 1975). *LANGUAGES:* Chinese and Taiwanese. *PRACTICE AREAS:* Engineering Law; Real Estate Law; Civil Litigation.

JANET C.Y. LIU, born Taiwan, February 20, 1967; admitted, 1994, Taiwan. *Education:* National Cheng-Chi University (LL.B., 1989). *LAN-*

(This Listing Continued)

GUAGES: Chinese, Taiwanese and English. *PRACTICE AREAS:* Real Estate Law; Civil Litigation; Criminal Litigation.

PENG CHUAN YEH, born Taiwan, March 20, 1962; admitted, 1994, Taiwan. *Education:* National Chunghsing University (LL.B., 1984). *LANGUAGES:* Chinese and Taiwanese. *PRACTICE AREAS:* Real Estate Law; Civil Litigation.

CHEN CHIEN HUNG, born Taiwan, December 16, 1969; (Not admitted in Taiwan). *Education:* Chinese Culture University (LL.B., 1992). *LANGUAGES:* Chinese and English. *PRACTICE AREAS:* Real Estate Law.

SHEENA SHIN YU, born Taiwan, October 29, 1971; (Not admitted in Taiwan). *Education:* National Taiwan University (LL.B., 1993). *LANGUAGES:* Chinese and English. *PRACTICE AREAS:* International Trade Law; Investment Law.

DAPHNE K.J. LIAO, born Taiwan, September 3, 1964; (Not admitted in Taiwan). *Education:* Fu-Jen University (LL.B., 1987). *LANGUAGES:* Chinese and English. *PRACTICE AREAS:* Intellectual Property Law; International Law.

WANG FANG MING, born Taiwan, January 8, 1963; admitted, 1992, Taiwan. *Education:* National Chengchi University (LL.B., 1985; LL.M., 1993). *LANGUAGES:* Chinese, Japanese and English. *PRACTICE AREAS:* Criminal Law.

REPRESENTATIVE CLIENTS: Chinese Taipei Olympic Committee; China Youth Corps; China Broadcasting Corp.; Employee Association of Taiwan Television Co., Ltd.; New Asia Construction and Development Co., Ltd.; Li Ming Cultural Enterprise Co., Ltd.

PERKINS COIE

Perkins Coie Commercial Finance Limited Liability Company

Perkins Coie Corporate Finance Limited Liability Company

8/F, TFIT TOWER
85 JEN AI ROAD, SECTION 4
TAIPEI 106, TAIWAN
Telephone: 886-2-778-1177
Facsimile: 886-2-777-9898

REVISERS OF THE WASHINGTON LAW DIGEST FOR THIS DIRECTORY

London, England Office: 36/38 Cornhill. EC3V 3ND. Telephone: 0171-369-9966. Facsimile: 0171-369-9968.

Hong Kong Office: 23rd Floor, Asia Pacific Finance Tower, Citibank Plaza, 3 Garden Road, Hong Kong. Telephone: 852-2878-1177. Facsimile: 852-2524-9988.

Seattle, Washington Office: 1201 Third Avenue, 40th Floor, Seattle, WA 98101-3099. Telephone: 1-(206) 583-8888. Facsimile: 1-(206) 583-8500.

Anchorage, Alaska Office: 1029 West Third Avenue, Suite 300, Anchorage, AK 99501. Telephone: 1-(907) 279-8561. Facsimile: 1-(907) 276-3108.

Bellevue, Washington Office: Suite 1800, One Bellevue Center, 411-108th Avenue N.E. Bellevue, WA 98004. Telephone: 1-(206) 453-6980. Facsimile: 1-(206) 453-7350.

Los Angeles, California Office: 1999 Avenue of the Stars, Ninth Floor, Los Angeles, CA 90067. Telephone: 1-(310) 788-9900. Facsimile: 1-(310) 788-3399.

Olympia, Washington Office: 1110 Capitol Way South, Suite 405, Olympia, WA 98501. Telephone: 1-(206) 956-3300. Facsimile: 1-(206) 956-1208.

Portland, Oregon Office: U.S. Bancorp Tower, Suite 2500, 111 Southwest Fifth Avenue, Portland, OR 97204. Telephone: 1-(503) 295-4400. Facsimile: 1-(503) 295-6793.

Spokane, Washington Office: N. 221 Wall Street, Suite 600, Spokane, WA 99201. Telephone: 1-(509) 624-2212. Facsimile: 1-(509) 458-3399.

Washington, D.C. Office: 607 Fourteenth Street, N.W., Washington, D.C. 20005-2011. Telephone: 1-(202) 628-6600. Facsimile: 1-(202) 434-1690.

Litigation, Foreign Investment, Banking and Finance, Cross-Border Investments, Mergers and Acquisitions, Tax, Securities, Government Contracts, Intellectual Property Rights, Technology Transfer.

PETER C. CHEN, born Tainan, Taiwan, August 26, 1949; admitted, 1977, Taiwan. *Education:* National Chunghsing University (LL.B., 1971); National Taiwan University (LL.M., 1974). *Member:* Taipei Bar Association; Chinese Society of Comparative Law (Director, Legal Aid Centre, 1984-1987). *LANGUAGES:* Mandarin, Taiwanese and English. *PRAC-*

(This Listing Continued)

TICE AREAS: Business Transactions; Bankruptcy; Banking; General Corporate; Commercial Litigation.

T.S. CHANG, born Taipei, Taiwan, February 6, 1955 (Not admitted in Republic of China). *Education:* National Taiwan University (LL.B., 1977); University of Illinois at Urbana-Champaign, Illinois (M.C.L., 1983; LL.M. course completed, 1985). *LANGUAGES:* Mandarin and English. *PRACTICE AREAS:* Securities; Banking; Corporate Finance; General Corporate and Commercial Law.

JANE Y.J. TSENG, born Taipei, Taiwan, September 18, 1960; admitted, 1991, Taiwan. *Education:* National Taiwan University (LL.B., 1984). *Member:* Taipei Bar Association. *LANGUAGES:* Mandarin, Taiwanese and English. *PRACTICE AREAS:* Securities; Banking; Corporate Finance; General Commercial Law.

DANIEL L. LIN, born Taichung, Taiwan, September 28, 1963; admitted, 1991, Taiwan. *Education:* Soochow University (LL.B., 1987); Fu-Jen University (LL.M., 1991). *Member:* Taipei, Tauyuan and Taichung Bar Associations. *LANGUAGES:* Mandarin, Taiwanese, Hakka and English. *PRACTICE AREAS:* Business Transactions; General Corporate; General Commercial Law; Commercial Litigation.

LING Y. WU, born Taipei, Taiwan, October 10, 1953; admitted, 1988, Taiwan; 1989, California. *Education:* National Taiwan University (LL.B., 1975); Southern Methodist University (LL.M., 1980; J.D., 1984). *Member:* Taipei Bar Association; State Bar of California. *LANGUAGES:* Mandarin, Taiwanese and English. *PRACTICE AREAS:* Banking; General Corporate and Commercial Law.

SILVIA W. LEE, born Keelung, Taiwan, July 13, 1969; admitted, 1994, New York (Not admitted in Taiwan). *Education:* National Taiwan University (LL.B., 1991); Harvard Law School (LL.M., 1993). *Member:* New York State Bar Association. *LANGUAGES:* Mandarin, Taiwanese and English. *PRACTICE AREAS:* Securities; Banking; Foreign Investment; General Corporate Matters.

IVY Y. CHEN, born Taipei, Taiwan, February 1, 1968; (Not admitted in Taiwan). *Education:* Soochow University (LL.B., 1992). *Member:* Taipei Bar Association. *LANGUAGES:* Mandarin, Taiwanese and English. *PRACTICE AREAS:* Trademark.

LEGAL ASSISTANT

JULIE CHU, born Taipei, Taiwan, July 22, 1956 (Not admitted in Republic of China). *Education:* Soochow University (B.A, 1979); Chinese Culture University (M.A., 1981). *LANGUAGES:* Mandarin, Taiwanese, Hakka and English. *PRACTICE AREAS:* Corporate Registrations; Employment/Work Permits; Visas; Foreign Investment; Expatriate Taxation; Trademark Registrations.

PERKINS COIE COMMERCIAL FINANCE LIMITED LIABILITY COMPANY

PAUL J. CASSINGHAM, born Joliet, Illinois, July 13, 1955; admitted, 1982, Illinois (Not admitted in Republic of China). *Education:* Harvard University; Northwestern University (B.A., with distinction, 1976); University of Michigan (J.D., magna cum laude, 1980). *LANGUAGES:* English and Mandarin. *PRACTICE AREAS:* Advisory services relating to commercial finance; banking; securities; mergers and acquisitions; cross-border investments and general corporate and commercial matters.

PERKINS COIE CORPORATE FINANCE LIMITED LIABILITY COMPANY

NICHOLAS V. G. CHEN, born New York, New York, May 9, 1957; admitted, 1983, District of Columbia (Not admitted in Republic of China). *Education:* Yale University (B.A., 1979); New York University (J.D., 1982). *LANGUAGES:* English and Mandarin. *PRACTICE AREAS:* Advisory services relating to general corporate; securities; mergers and acquisitions; corporate finance; cross-border investment; mainland China; joint ventures; government procurement contracts; defense matters and international trade.

MARCUS J. WOO, born San Rafael, California, July 13, 1957; admitted, 1987, New Jersey, New York and U.S. District Court, District of New Jersey (Not admitted in Taiwan, ROC). *Education:* Oberlin College (B.A., 1979); Indiana University-Bloomington (J.D., 1986). Assistant District Attorney, Queens County, New York, 1987-1989. *Member:* American Bar Association; The Maritime Law Association of the United States; American Chamber of Commerce in Taipei; American Chamber of Commerce in Beijing. *LANGUAGES:* English, Mandarin and Cantonese. *PRACTICE AREAS:* Advisory services relating to general corporate; mergers and ac-

(This Listing Continued)

quisitions; cross-border investment; mainland China; joint ventures; government procurement contracts and international trade.

REVISERS OF THE WASHINGTON LAW DIGEST FOR THIS DIRECTORY

(For biographical data of personnel resident in other offices of Perkins Coie, see Professional Biographies at Hong Kong; London, England; Bellevue, Olympia, Seattle and Spokane Washington, Anchorage, Alaska, Los Angeles, California, Portland, Oregon and Washington, D.C.)

QI LIN INTERNATIONAL LAW OFFICES

Established in 1994

4TH FLOOR, SUITE C
245 TUN HUA SOUTH ROAD, SECTION 1
TAIPEI, TAIWAN
Telephone: 886-2-775-5533
Fax: 886-2-778-4658

Intellectual Property, Telecommunications, Foreign Investment, Licensing, Corporate, Insurance, International Trade, Competition Law, Civil Litigation, Immigration.

ARTHUR C.W. HSIEH, born Keelung, Taiwan, October 21, 1964; admitted, 1992, Taiwan. *Education:* National Chengchi University Law School (LL.B., 1986). Taiwan Patent Agent. Author, "Effects of the Modification of the Copyright Law on the Television Industry," 1994. *Member:* Taipei Bar Association; Keelung Bar Association. *LANGUAGES:* Mandarin, Taiwanese and English. *PRACTICE AREAS:* Civil Litigation; Intellectual Property Law; Construction Law; Franchise Law.

CHARLES HUANG, born Nantou County, Taiwan, August 29, 1960; admitted, 1991, Taiwan. *Education:* Soochow University Law School (LL.B., 1984); Fu Jen Catholic University Graduate School of Law (LL.M., 1991). Taiwan Patent Agent. Member, Ch'eng Ta Business Manager's Association. *Member:* Taipei Bar Association. *LANGUAGES:* Taiwanese, Mandarin and English. *PRACTICE AREAS:* Civil Law; Commercial Law; Banking Law; Property Law; Intellectual Property.

ROBERT C. LEE, born Ilan, Taiwan, September 29, 1963; (Not admitted in Taiwan). *Education:* National Chengchi University (LL.B., 1986). Author: "Telecommunications: Taiwan Ready to Open its Domestic Value-Added Services Market," IP Asia, May 1992. *Member:* American Chamber of Commerce in Taipei (Telecommunications, Tax, and Insurance Committees). *LANGUAGES:* Mandarin, Taiwanese and English. *PRACTICE AREAS:* Foreign Investment Law; Technical Cooperation; Telecommunication Law; Corporate Law.

GLORIA LIN, born Taipei, Taiwan, September 12, 1963; (Not admitted in Taiwan). *Education:* Soochow University (LL.B., 1986). *LANGUAGES:* Mandarin, Taiwanese and English. *PRACTICE AREAS:* Intellectual Property Law; Fair Trade Law; Civil Law.

FRANCIS KUO, born Hsinchu, Taiwan, May 24, 1969; (Not admitted in Taiwan). *Education:* National Taiwan University Law School (LL.B., 1991). *LANGUAGES:* Mandarin, Taiwanese and English. *PRACTICE AREAS:* Intellectual Property Law; Foreign Investment Law; Commercial Law.

MING-YIN TSAI, born Changhua, Taiwan, July 20, 1970; (Not admitted in Taiwan). *Education:* Chunghsing University Law School (LL.B., 1992); Tulane University Law School (LL.M., 1994). *LANGUAGES:* Mandarin, Taiwanese and English. *PRACTICE AREAS:* International Commercial Law; Foreign Investment; Fair Trade.

VINCENT Y.P. CHANG, born Miaoli, Taiwan, February 24, 1964; (Not admitted in Taiwan). *Education:* National Taiwan University Law Department (LL.B., 1986). *LANGUAGES:* Mandarin, Taiwanese and English. *PRACTICE AREAS:* Commercial Law; Foreign Investment Law; Insurance Law.

ERICH HOU, born Taipei, Taiwan, August 18, 1970; (Not admitted in Taiwan). *Education:* Chinese Cultural University Law School (LL.B., 1992). *LANGUAGES:* Mandarin and English. *PRACTICE AREAS:* Intellectual Property.

AURORA TSAI, born Taipei, Taiwan, October 1, 1962; (Not admitted in Taiwan). *Education:* Tan Chiang University (B.A., Accounting). *LANGUAGES:* Mandarin, Taiwanese and English. *PRACTICE AREAS:* Corporate; Taxation; Administrative Appeals.

(This Listing Continued)

QI LIN INTERNATIONAL LAW OFFICES, Taipei— Continued

QI LIN INTERNATIONAL CONSULTANTS LTD.

ROBIN J. WINKLER, born Madison, Wisconsin, July 7, 1954; admitted, 1983, Arizona (Not admitted in Taiwan). *Education:* New York University (B.A., 1976); University of Denver (J.D., 1982). Taiwan Trademark Agent. Arbitrator, Commercial Arbitration Association of the Republic of China. Taiwan Editor, IP Asia, 1988—. *Member:* American Chamber of Commerce in Taiwan, Intellectual Property and Licensing Committee (Chairman, 1992—); Asian Pacific Council of American Chambers of Commerce (Vice-chairman, Intellectual Property, 1992-1993). *LANGUAGES:* Mandarin and English. *PRACTICE AREAS:* Intellectual Property Law; Telecommunication Law; Competition Law; Foreign Investment Law.

RICHARD B. MAHONEY, born Framingham, Massachusetts, April29, 1960; admitted, 1992, Massachusetts (Not admitted in Taiwan). *Education:* New England School of Law (J.D., 1991); Hong Kong University School of Law (LL. M., 1993). *Member:* Massachusetts Bar Association. *LANGUAGES:* English, Spanish and Mandarin. *PRACTICE AREAS:* International Commercial Law; Foreign Investment; Intellectual Property; U.S. Immigration.

RELIANCE INTERNATIONAL LAW OFFICES

3RD FL., 21, CHANG-AN EAST ROAD, SECTION 1
TAIPEI, TAIWAN
Telephone: (02) 565-1888; (02) 551-8305
Telecopier: (02) 543-5331

Administrative Appeals, Admiralty and Maritime, Arbitration, Banking and Financing, China Practice, Civil and Criminal Litigation, Computer and Information Technology Law, Construction Law, Consumer Protection, Copyright, Corporate Finance, Estate Planning, Fair Trade and Competition Law, Futures, General Corporate and Commercial Practice, Immigration, Insurance, Intellectual Properties, International Business Transactions, International Trade and Investment, Labor, Mergers and Acquisitions, Patent, Real Estate, Securities, Taxation, Technology Licensing, Trade Secret, Trademark.

MEMBERS OF FIRM

JERRY P. YU, born Taipei, Taiwan, Republic of China, July 14, 1950; admitted, 1985, Republic of China; Patent Agent. *Education:* National Taiwan University School of Law (LL.B., 1973); New York University School of Law (LL.M., 1977); University of California Hastings College of Law (J.D., 1981). Associate Professor: Law, Chinese Culture University School of Law, 1982-1988; Law, Soochow University, 1984-1994. Arbitrator, Commercial Arbitration Association of the R.O.C. *Member:* Taipei Bar Association; Keelung Bar Association; International Bar Association; Asia-Pacific Lawyers Association; Inter-Pacific Bar Association; Chinese Society of Comparative Law Association; Chinese Society of International Law Association. *LANGUAGES:* Chinese and English.

LAWRENCE C. S. HSU, born Kaohsiung, Taiwan, Republic of China, March 6, 1952; admitted, 1986, Pennsylvania; 1987, District of Columbia and U.S. District Court for the Northern District of California; 1988, District of Columbia (Not admitted in Taiwan). *Education:* Chinese Culture University (LL.B., 1980); Southern Methodist University (M.C.L., 1982; J.D., 1984). Associate Professor: Law, Tunghai University, Graduate School of Law, Taichung, Taiwan, 1988—; Law, Tamkang University School of Business, Department of International Trade, Taipei, Taiwan, 1988-1991; Chinese Culture University School of Business, Taipei, Taiwan, 1991-1993. Member: Law Offices of Edward C.Y. Lau, San Francisco, California, 1986-1987; Alliance International Law Offices, Taipei, Taiwan, 1988-1989. Member, Committee on Review and Drafting of Commodity Futures Trading Laws and Regulations, the Securities Exchange Commission of the Ministry of Finance, Republic of China, 1993—. *Member:* Pennsylvania Bar Association; District of Columbia Bar Association; Chinese Society of Comparative Law Association. *LANGUAGES:* Chinese and English.

GEORGE C.C. CHEN, born Taipei, Taiwan, Republic of China, July 21, 1956; admitted, 1981, Judge, Republic of China; 1982, Taiwan. *Education:* National Taiwan University School of Law (LL.B., 1978); University of Washington School of Law (LL.M., 1985). Patent Agent, 1982. Assistant General Secretary, New Environment Foundation, 1989-1991. Legal Con-

(This Listing Continued)

sultant: Taipei City Computer Association, 1988—; Institute for Information Industries, 1987—; Chinese Information Software Association, 1990—; Financial Information Service Center, 1990—. Legal Advisor: Taipei County Computer Association, 1989; U.S. R.O.C. Trade Negotiations on Intellectual Property, 1992. Arbitrator, R.O.C. Commercial Arbitration Association, 1988—. Partner, Huang and Partners, Taipei, Taiwan, 1987-1988. Co-Author: "Copyright and Right of Publications"; "Review and Comment on the Copyright Law"; "Copyright Law Practice"; "Copyright Contracts"; "Copyright of Computer Software"; "Sixty Lectures on Trade Secrets"; "Research into Legal Protection of Trade Secrets"; "Research into Legal Protection of Inventions Relating to Computer Software"; "U.S. Laws regarding the Export of Computer Telecommunications and Electronics Products to the U.S.A." Author: "Computer Intellectual Property Law." Speaker, Judicial Yuan Ninth Professional Research Meeting, 1986. Lecturer, International Trade Law and Computer Law, Tunghai University, 1986—. Member: Baker and McKenzie, Taipei, Toronto and Sidney, 1982-1987. *Member:* Taipei Bar Association; Chinese Society of Comparative Law Association; Asian Patent Agents Association. *LANGUAGES:* Chinese and English.

JERRY G. FONG, born Hsinchu, Taiwan, Republic of China, October 17, 1957; admitted, 1990, Pennsylvania; New Jersey; District of Columbia (Not admitted in Taiwan). *Education:* National Taiwan University School of Law (LL.B., 1979; LL.M., 1986); University of Pennsylvania Law School (LL.M., 1987); Cornell University School of Law (LL.M., 1988; J.D., 1990). Law Clerk: Chinese Air Force Military Tribunal, 1979-1981. News Reporter, Commercial Times, 1983-1985. Vice Executive Secretary, Chinese National Federation of Industries, 1985-1986. Formerly associated with, Stradley, Ronon, Stevens & Young Law Offices, 1990-1992. Associate Professor, Chung Yuan Christian University, Department of Financial and Economic Law, 1992—. Author: "The Intellectual Property Negotiations between Taiwan and the United States: Its Influence and Impact," 1987; "A Comprehensive Handbook of Intellectual Property Rights and their Protection in the R.O.C.," 1987; "Understanding Trademark Law," 1994. Co-Author: "The Analysis of R.O.C.'s Copyright Law," 1992; "Business Law -- A Primer," 1992; "Copyright and Computer Forms of the R.O.C.," 1992; "Review and Comment on: Consumer Protection Law," 1994. *Member:* American Bar Association; District of Columbia Bar Association; Pennsylvania Bar Association; New Jersey Bar Association. *LANGUAGES:* Chinese and English.

LLOYD E. LOH, born Taipei, Taiwan, Republic of China, August 28, 1959; admitted, 1988, New York (Not admitted in Taiwan). *Education:* National Chunghsing University School of Law (LL.B., 1982); Southern Methodist University School of Law (LL.M., 1985; J.D., 1987). Taipei Representative, Asiamerica Law & Consultant Group, 1987-1989. Associate Professor: Law, Fu-Jen Catholic University, Taipei, Taiwan, 1987—; Law, National Defense Administration College, Graduate Institute of Law, Taipei, Taiwan, 1989—. Author: "Study on Insider Trading"; "Mergers and Acquisition"; "Limited Partnership Law of the U.S." *Member:* New York Bar Association; American Bar Association; Chinese Society of Comparative Law Association. *LANGUAGES:* Chinese and English.

HENRY K.N. SHIEH, born Taipei, Taiwan, Republic of China, October 24, 1960; admitted, 1990, Republic of China. *Education:* National Taiwan University School of Law (LL.B., 1984); Fu-Jen Catholic University School of Law (LL.M., 1994). Formerly associated with Chu & Chu Law Offices, 1990-1991. Author: "The Regulation of Futures Industry under U.S. Commodity Exchange Act," 1994. *Member:* Taipei Bar Association; Taichung Bar Association. *LANGUAGES:* Chinese and English.

VICTOR S.C. LEE, born Pingtung, Taiwan, Republic of China, April 20, 1961; admitted, 1990, Republic of China; 1994, Patent Office. *Education:* Fu-Jen Catholic University School of Law (LL.B., 1983). Law Clerk, Supreme Court of the Republic of China, 1987-1993. *Member:* Taipei Bar Association. *LANGUAGES:* Chinese and English.

JESSE C.H. CHEN, born Pingtung, Taiwan, Republic of China, January 10, 1962; (Not admitted in Taiwan). *Education:* Tulane University (B.A., 1986); Loyola School of Law (J.D., 1989). Formerly associated with: Gold Key International, Ltd., U.S.A., 1980-1988; Golden Bay Popeyes, Inc., U.S.A., 1989-1992; Ko Lin and Wei Law Offices, 1993-1994. *LANGUAGES:* Chinese and English.

GRACE Y.Y. LEI, born Taipei, Taiwan, Republic of China, August 31, 1968; admitted, 1991, Republic of China; 1994, Patent Office. *Education:* National Taiwan University School of Law (LL.B., 1991; LL.M., expected 1995). Formerly associated with, Chou-Chun Law Offices, 1992-1994. *Member:* Taipei Bar Association. *LANGUAGES:* Chinese and English.

(This Listing Continued)

JOHN C.Y. WU, born Taoyuan, Taiwan, Republic of China, February 8, 1969; admitted, 1992, Republic of China. *Education:* National Taiwan University School of Law (LL.B., 1992; LL.M., expected 1995). *Member:* Taipei Bar Association. *LANGUAGES:* Chinese and English.

ROCKY C.T. LIN, born Tainan, Taiwan, Republic of China, April 1, 1954; (Not admitted in Taiwan). *Education:* National Chunghsing University School of Law (LL.B., 1977). Formerly associated with: Wang Law Offices, 1980-1984; Che Heng Sun Law Offices, 1985-1986. *LANGUAGES:* Chinese and English.

JENNY H.C. HUANG, born Hualien, Taiwan, Republic of China, July 12, 1959; (Not admitted in Taiwan). *Education:* Chinese Culture University School of Law (LL.B., 1981). Formerly associated with: Johnson S.Y. Hu Law Offices, 1981-1985; Cheng & Cheng Law Offices, 1987-1990. *LANGUAGES:* Chinese and English.

ANNE M.Y. KUO, born Taipei, Taiwan, Republic of China, May 7, 1968; admitted, 1990, Republic of China; 1994, Patent Office. *Education:* National Taiwan University School of Law (LL.B., 1990; LL.M., expected 1995); Columbia University School of Law (LL.M., 1994). *Member:* Taipei Bar Association. *LANGUAGES:* Chinese and English.

OF COUNSEL

H.F. YU, born Chekiang, China, September 30, 1914; admitted, 1946, Republic of China. *Education:* Da-Hsia University (B.A., 1936); Shanghai College of Law (LL.B., 1941). Publisher, "The Law Monthly," 1950—. Author: "General Introduction of Corporation Law," 1978; "General Rules of Civil Law," 1978. Professor, Law, Chinese Culture University, Taipei, Taiwan, China, Republic of China, 1972-1986. Commissioner, Commission for Judicial Examination, 1986-1987. *Member:* National Bar Association of the Republic of China (Standing Member, Board of Directors, 1968-1970); Taipei Bar Association (Standing Member, Board of Directors, 1953-1960; Member: Board of Directors, 1949-1951, 1963-1967; Board of Overseers, 1951-1953, 1968-1973); Taipei Certified Public Accountant Association (Standing Member: Board of Directors, 1952-1958; Board of Overseers, 1958-1977). *LANGUAGES:* Chinese.

RUSSIN & VECCHI

International Legal Counsellors

In Affiliation with Walter, Conston, Alexander & Green, P.C. and

Adduci, Mastriani, Schaumberg & Schill

9TH FLOOR, 205 TUN HWA N. ROAD
TAIPEI, TAIWAN
Telephone: (886-2) 712-8956
Fax: (886-2) 713-4711

Bangkok, Thailand Office: Russin & Vecchi, International Legal Counsellors Thailand, Ltd., Sathorn City Tower, 175 South Sathorn Road, 18th Floor, 10120. Telephone: 662-679-6005, 662-679-6015. Fax: 662-679-6041, 662-679-6042.

Hanoi, Vietnam Office: Russin & Vecchi, 25 Ly Thuong Kiet Street. Telephone: (84-4) 251-699/251-700. Fax: (84-4) 251-742.

Ho Chi Minh City, Vietnam Office: Russin & Vecchi, OSIC Building, 6/F, 8 Nguyen Hue Street. Telephone: (84-8) 243-026/243-114. Fax: (84-8) 243-113.

Moscow, Russia Office: Russin & Vecchi, Danilovsky Hotel Complex, Bolshoy Starodanilovsky, Pereulok No. 5, Moscow 113191. Telephone: (7-095) 954-0652. Telex: 612506 RV MOS SU. Fax: (7-095) 954-0653.

New York, New York Office: Russin & Vecchi, 15th Floor, 90 Park Avenue, 10016-1387. Telephone: 212-210-9543. Fax: 212-210-9493.

Puerto Plata, Dominican Republic Office: Russin Vecchi & Heredia Bonetti, Plaza Turisol Local #11A. Telephone: 809-586-5535. Fax: 809-586-5861.

San Francisco, California Office: Russin & Vecchi, 16th Floor, 580 California Street, 94104. Telephone: 415-421-1100. Fax: 415-421-1103.

Santo Domingo, Dominican Republic Office: Russin Vecchi & Heredia Bonetti, Edificio Monte Mirador, Calle El Recodo No 2, Esquina Winston Churchill, Bella Vista, Apartado Postal 425. Telephone: 809-535-9511. Cable Address: "RUSVEC SANTO DOMINGO." Telex: 3264199 RUSVEC. Fax: 809-535-6649.

Washington, D.C. Office: Russin & Vecchi, Second Floor, 1140 Connecticut Avenue, N.W., 20036. Telephone: 202-223-4793. Fax: 202-223-4810.

General Commercial Practice. Corporate, Foreign Investment, Banking and Finance, Competition, Mergers and Acquisitions, Technology Transfer, Securities, Insurance, Venture Capital, Government Contracts, Trade, Transportation, Tax, Labor, Licensing, Franchising, Intellectual Property and Commercial Litigation.

T.Y. LEE, born Kaohsiung, Taiwan, Republic of China, 1947; admitted, 1974, Taipei, Taiwan. *Education:* National Taiwan University School of Law (LL.B., 1970 and LL.M., 1973); Southern Methodist University (M.C.L., 1978). Author: "The Legal Status of Foreign Juristic Persons in the Republic of China," 1973, with "New Trademark Law in Line with Commercial Practice," (Taiwan), Asia Law, March 1994. *Member:* Taipei Bar Association. *LANGUAGES:* Mandarin, Taiwanese, English.

THOMAS H. MCGOWAN, born Fairmont, Minnesota, 1950; admitted, 1975, District of Columbia (Not admitted in Taiwan). *Education:* University of Notre Dame (B.B.A., 1972); Georgetown University Law Center (J.D., 1975). Business Editor and Member of Executive Board, Law and Policy in International Business, International Law Journal of Georgetown University Law Center, 1974-1975. Author: "Banking, Credit, and Finance: The Transactional Aspects," Taiwan and International Trade and Investment: Law and Practice (Oxford University Press), 1994. Co-author: "Full Faith & Credit and Government Owned Banking Institutions in Korea," Korean Journal of Comparative Law, Volume VI, Korean Research Institute of Comparative Law, 1978; "Chattel Security in Korea," Korean Journal of Comparative Law, Volume VII, Korean Research Institute of Comparative Law, 1979. Director, U.S.A.-R.O.C. Economic Counsel, 1988—. *Member:* The District of Columbia Bar; American Bar Association.

SU-HWA WU, born Taipei, Taiwan, Republic of China, March 7, 1947; admitted, 1982, Taiwan. *Education:* National Taiwan University School of Law (LL.B. 1969); University of Illinois (M.C.L., 1974). *Member:* Taipei Bar Association; Tao Yuan Bar Association. *LANGUAGES:* English, Mandarin, Taiwanese.

HWEI-YU CHO, born Kaohsiung, Taiwan, Republic of China, 1953; (Not admitted in Taiwan). *Education:* National Taiwan University School of Law (LL.B., 1975). *LANGUAGES:* Mandarin, Taiwanese, English.

JONATHAN J. UCHIMA, born Memphis, Tennessee, 1962; admitted, 1987, California, U.S. District Court, Northern District of California and U.S. Court of Appeals, Ninth Circuit; 1989, District of Columbia and U.S. Court of Appeals for the Federal Circuit; 1990, U.S. Court of International Trade (Not admitted in Taiwan). *Education:* University of California at Los Angeles (B.A., 1984); University of San Francisco (J.D., with honors, 1987). University of London, Summer Seminar in London on Legal Aspects of International Finance (July, 1994). Recipient, American Jurisprudence Awards in: Constitutional Law, 1986; Wills and Trusts, 1987. Member, 1985-1986 and Comments Editor, 1986-1987, University of San Francisco Law Review. Associate, Russin & Vecchi, San Francisco, 1988-1991. *Member:* The District of Columbia Bar; State Bar of California; American Bar Association.

SHIRLIE CHI-YUN PAI, born Taipei, Taiwan, Republic of China, 1962; admitted, 1990, New York (Not admitted in Taiwan). *Education:* National Cheng-Chi University (LL.B., 1984); American University, Washington College of Law (LL.M., 1987 and J.D., 1991). Dickinson School of Law, Summer Seminar in Vienna and Strasbourg (Courses in European Integration and Comparative Commercial Law, Summer 1991). *Member:* New York State and American Bar Associations; National Asian Pacific American Bar Association. *LANGUAGES:* Mandarin, Taiwanese, English.

MARGARET Y.F. LAM, born Mauritius, 1963; admitted, 1991, Quebec (Not admitted in Taiwan). *Education:* McGill University (B.Sc., 1987); Universite de Sherbrooke (LL.B., 1990). Law Clerk to Madame Justice L'Heureux-Dube, Supreme Court of Canada, 1991. *Member:* Quebec and Canadian Bar Associations; The Federalist Society; Federaion of Canadian Bar Associations, French Secretary, Quebec Chapter (1993—); American Chamber of Commerce in Taiwan. *LANGUAGES:* English, French, Creole and Chinese (Hakka).

NAOMI LEE, born Kaoshiung, Taiwan, Republic of China, 1970; admitted, 1993, Taiwan. *Education:* National Taiwan University Law School (LL.B., 1992). *LANGUAGES:* Mandarin, Taiwanese, English.

AMY Y. M. CHIANG, born Kaohsiung, Taiwan, Republic of China, 1951; (Not admitted in Taiwan). *Education:* Soochow University Law School (LL.B., 1974). *LANGUAGES:* Mandarin, Taiwanese and English.

SUE-MEI HUANG, born Taoyuan, Taiwan, Republic of China, 1951; (Not admitted in Taiwan). *Education:* Soochow University School of Law (LL.B., 1974). *LANGUAGES:* Mandarin, Taiwanese, English.

(This Listing Continued)

(This Listing Continued)

RUSSIN & VECCHI, Taipei—Continued

MIAO-ER HSIUNG, born Chia-yi, Taiwan, Republic of China, 1969; (Not admitted in Taiwan). *Education:* Soochow University Law School (LL.B., 1992). *LANGUAGES:* Mandarin, Taiwanese and English.

VIVIAN YANG, born Taipei, Taiwan, Republic of China, 1969; (Not admitted in Taiwan). *Education:* Soochow University Law School (LL.B., 1992). *LANGUAGES:* Mandarin, Taiwanese, English and French.

REPRESENTATIVE CLIENTS: ABN AMRO Bank, N.V.; American International Assurance Co., Ltd.; am/pm International; Amway Corp.; ARCO Chemical Co.; Armstrong World Industries, Inc.; Bank of America; Bank of California; Banque Nationale de Paris; Bertelsmann Music Group; Capital Group; Carrier International Corp.; The Chase Manhattan Bank; Citibank, N.A.; Chemical Leasing Corp.; China Securities Investment Trust Corp.; Corestates Bank, N.A.; The Export-Import Bank of the Republic of China; The First National Bank of Boston; Formica Corp.; GE-RCA Licensing; Intel Semiconductor; Lotus Development; Nan Shan Life Insurance Co.; Northwest Airlines; Promodes, S.A.; San Miguel Brewery; Sumitomo Trust; Takugin International Asia, Ltd.; Tidewater Marine Int'l Inc.; Trans Asia Airways.

(For Biographical Data on other Personnel, see Professional Biographies at: Washington, D.C., U.S.A.; San Francisco, California, U.S.A.; New York, N.Y., U.S.A.; Bangkok, Thailand; Santo Domingo, Dominican Republic; Ho Chi Minh City, Hanoi, S.R. Vietnam; Moscow, Russia).

SAINT ISLAND INTERNATIONAL PATENT & LAW OFFICES

Established in 1974

7TH FLOOR, NO. 248, NANKING EAST ROAD, SEC. 3
TAIPEI, TAIWAN
Telephone: (02) 7751823-7; 7751832
Telex: 23533 SANTAPAT
Facsimile: (02) 7316376; 7316377

Mailing Address: P.O. Box 81-974, Taipei

Specializing in Patent, Trademark, Copyright and Related Practice.

MEMBERS OF FIRM

PATRICK I. C. YUN, born Nan-Tou, Taiwan, August 13, 1951. Patent Attorney, admitted to the Patent Office, 1973. *Education:* Taipei Institute of Technology (1971). Experience: Chartered Metallurgical Engineer and Lecturer, Patent Law of R.O.C., Tung-Nan Institute of Technology, 1975. Author: "Trademark and Enterprise," June 1977. *Member:* APAA; AIPPI; INTA; CIPA; FICPI. *LANGUAGES:* Chinese and English. *PRACTICE AREAS:* Patent and Trademark; Prosecution.

THOMAS Q. T. TSAI, born Taichung, Taiwan, December 25, 1950. Patent Attorney, admitted to the Patent Office, 1975. *Education:* Taipei Institute of Technology (1971); Ottawa University (B.A., 1987); Oklahoma City University (M.B.A., 1988); Franklin Pierce Law Center (M.I.P., 1989; J.D., 1991). Experience: Chartered HVAC & R Engineer and Lecturer of Ming-Tzu Institute of Technology, 1976-1979. Author: "Helical Rotary Compressor," 1977; "Trademarks in Taiwan, R.O.C.," 1983. *Member:* APAA (Director, Taiwan Group), INTA, ECTA, AIPPI and AIPLA. *LANGUAGES:* Chinese and English. *PRACTICE AREAS:* Patent and Trademark; Prosecution.

WILLIAM W. L. CHEN, born Taiwan, May 22, 1953; admitted, 1978, Republic of China. *Education:* Soochow University Law School (LL.B., 1976); Soochow University Graduate School of Law (1976-1978). *Member:* Taipei Bar Association; Inter-Pacific Bar Association; APAA; INTA; World Computer Law. *LANGUAGES:* Chinese and English. *PRACTICE AREAS:* I.P. Litigation; Licensing; Unfair Competition; Transnational Legal Problems; General Legal Practice.

HUAN-TENG YU, born Taiwan, November 14, 1932; (Not admitted in Taiwan). *Education:* Iwate University (B.S., 1965); Kyoto University (M.S., 1968). Experience: Technical Consultant of Industrial Bureau, Ministry of Economic Affairs, 1971-1974 and Professor of Tamkang College of Arts and Sciences, August 1975— and Taipei Institute of Technology, August 1973—. *Member:* Chinese Institute of Engineers, Chinese Electric Institute; Japanese Institute of Metal. *LANGUAGES:* Chinese, English and Japanese. *PRACTICE AREAS:* Patent Prosecution.

CHI-I WANG, born Taipei, Taiwan, August 15, 1933; (Not admitted in Taiwan). *Education:* Waseda University (B.E., 1966); Tokyo University (M.E., 1969). Experience: Technician of Department of Coal Mine Exploration, Ministry of Economic Affairs, 1955-1958, Superintendent of Entsen Heat Treatment Co., 1976 and Lecturer of Tapei Institute of Technology,

(This Listing Continued)

February 1977—. *Member:* Chinese Mineralogical and Metallurgical Institute; Japanese Institute of Metal. *LANGUAGES:* Chinese, English and Japanese. *PRACTICE AREAS:* Patent Prosecution.

JOHN J. N. CHYI, born Taipei, Taiwan, April 6, 1949; (Not admitted in Taiwan). *Education:* National Cheng-Kung University (B.S., 1971; M.S., 1973). Experience: Lecturer of Nan-Jen Institute of Technology, 1973. Editor: Fundamentals of Electronics, April 1972. *LANGUAGES:* Chinese and English. *PRACTICE AREAS:* Patent Prosecution.

JANE Y. C. YANG, born Taipei, Taiwan, December 9, 1952; admitted to the Patent Office, 1979. *Education:* Fu Jen University Law School (LL.B., 1974); American University (LL.M., 1989). *Member:* Institute of Trademark Agents (U.K.). *LANGUAGES:* Chinese and English. *PRACTICE AREAS:* Trademark Prosecution.

CHIEN-WAN LIU, born Kaohsiung, Taiwan, November 29, 1949; admitted to the Patent Office, 1980. *Education:* Chinese Culture University Law School (LL.B., 1973). *LANGUAGES:* Chinese and English. *PRACTICE AREAS:* Trademark Prosecution.

SEN-LIEH CHANG, born Taiwan, November 23, 1949; (Not admitted in Taiwan). *Education:* Taipei Institute of Technology. Experience: Electrical Engineer, Sanyo Electric Co., Taiwan. *LANGUAGES:* Chinese, English and Japanese. *PRACTICE AREAS:* Patent Prosecution.

HONG YUE DU, born Taiwan, January 5, 1948; (Not admitted in Taiwan). *Education:* Fu Jen University (B.S., 1970); Bonn University, West Germany (Pharmacology, 1978-1979). *LANGUAGES:* Chinese, German and English. *PRACTICE AREAS:* Patent Prosecution.

YUN-CHERNG SONG, born Taipei, Taiwan, March 17, 1951; (Not admitted in Taiwan). *Education:* Ming-Chi Institute of Technology and Tamkang University (B.S., 1979). Experience: Technician of Formosa Plastic Company, 1973-1976; Superintendent of TAI-HO Transportation Company, 1976-1978. *LANGUAGES:* Chinese, English and Japanese. *PRACTICE AREAS:* Patent Prosecution.

FRANK F.J. LIU, born Taipei, Taiwan, August 10, 1961; admitted, 1988, Republic of China. *Education:* Fu-Jen Catholic University Law School (LL.B., 1984). *Member:* Taipei Bar Association; Taoyuan Bar Association. *LANGUAGES:* Chinese and English. *PRACTICE AREAS:* I.P. Litigation; Licensing; Unfair Competition; General Legal Practice.

QUENTIN C. S. YANG, born Nantou, Taiwan, November 22, 1961; admitted, 1990, Republic of China. *Education:* Fu-Jen Catholic University Law School (LL.B., 1984). *Member:* Taipei Bar Association; Tainan Bar Association. *LANGUAGES:* Chinese and English. *PRACTICE AREAS:* I.P. Litigation; Licensing; Unfair Competition; General Legal Practice.

ANATASIA L. C. LAI, born Taichung, Taiwan, October 30, 1963; admitted, 1990, Republic of China; 1991, Taipei. *Education:* Fu-Jen Catholic University Law School (LL.B., 1985; LL.M., 1991). Author: "A Study On The Effects of Foreign Bankruptcy," 1991. *Member:* Taichung Bar Association; Taipei Bar Association. *LANGUAGES:* Chinese, English and Japanese. *PRACTICE AREAS:* I.P. Litigation; Licensing; Unfair Competition; General Legal Practice.

JACK W.Y. KONG, born Taipei, Taiwan, July 30, 1956. Patent Attorney; admitted, 1985, Patent Office. *Education:* National Chiao Tung University College of Engineering (B.S., 1978); National Taiwan University, Graduate School of Engineering (M.S., 1984). Chartered Electrical Engineer; Technical Engineer, Taipei Telecommunication Office, 1980-1982; Electrical Specialist, Consultative Department, Bureau of Commodity Inspection & Quarantine, 1982-1984. *Member:* APAA, AIPPI. *LANGUAGES:* Chinese and English. *PRACTICE AREAS:* Patent Prosecution.

SERKO & SIMON

3RD FLOOR ROSE MANSION
NO. 162 SHIN-YI ROAD, SECTION 3
TAIPEI 10632, TAIWAN
Telephone: 866-2-707-2847

New York, N.Y. Office: Suite 3371, 1 World Trade Center. Telephone: 212-775-0055. Telex: 426816 TRADE. Cable Address: "Trade Attys". Facsimile: 212-839-9103.

Washington, D.C. Office: Metropolitan Square, Suite 300, 655 15th Street, N.W. Telephone: 202-639-4017. Facsimile: 202-347-1945.

Atlanta, Georgia Office: Suite 1400 Bank South Building. Telephone: 404-659-4488.

(This Listing Continued)

San Juan, Puerto Rico Office: Banco de San Juan Building, Suite 302, P.O. Box 3222. Telephone: 809-723-3672. Facsimile: 809-725-4133.

Customs and International Trade Law. Export Law, Trade Regulations and Transportation Law. Administrative Federal Practice. Civil and Criminal Practice.

(For Complete Biographical Data on all Personnel see Professional Biographies at New York, New York)

SHEARMAN & STERLING

7TH FLOOR, HUNG KUO BUILDING
167 TUN HWA NORTH ROAD
TAIPEI, TAIWAN
Telephone: (886-2) 545-3300
Fax: (886-2) 545-3322

New York, N.Y. Office: 599 Lexington Avenue, New York, New York 10022-6069 and Citicorp Center, 153 East 53rd Street, New York, New York 10022-4676. Telephone: (212) 848-4000. Telex: 667290 Num Lau. Fax: 599 Lexington Avenue: (212) 848-7179. Citicorp Center: (212) 848-5252.

Abu Dhabi, United Arab Emirates Office: P.O. Box 2948. Telephone: (971-2) 324477. Fax: (971-2) 774533.

Beijing, People's Republic of China Office: Suite #2205, Capital Mansion, No. 6, Xin Yuan Nan Road. Chao Yang District Beijing, 100004. Telephone: (861) 465-4574. Fax: (861) 465-4578.

Budapest, Hungary Office: Szerb utca 17-19, 1056 Budapest. Telephone: (36-1) 266-3522. Fax: (36-1) 266-3523.

Düsseldorf, Federal Republic of Germany Office: Königsallee 46, D-40212 Düsseldorf. Telephone: (49-211) 13 62 80. Telex: 8 588 294 NYLO. Fax: (49-211) 13 33 09.

Frankfurt, Federal Republic of Germany Office: Bockenheimer Landstrasse 55, D-60325 Frankfurt am Main. Telephone: (49-69) 97-10-70. Fax: (49-69) 97-10-71-00.

Hong Kong, Hong Kong Office: Standard Chartered Bank Building, 4 Des Voeux Road Central, Hong Kong. Telephone: (852) 2978-8000. Fax: (852) 2978-8099.

London, England Office: 199Bishopsgate, London EC2M 3TY. Telephone: (44-71) 920-9000. Fax: (44-71) 920-9020.

Los Angeles, California Office: 725 South Figueroa Street, 21st Floor, 90017-5421. Telephone: (213) 239-0300. Fax: (213) 239-0381, 614-0936.

Paris, France Office: 12 rue d'Astorg, 75008. Telephone: (33-1) 44-71-17-17. Telex: 282964 Royale. Fax: (33-1) 44-71-01-01.

San Francisco, California Office: 555 California Street, 94104-1522. Telephone: (415) 616-1100. Fax: (415) 616-1199.

Tokyo, Japan Office: Shearman & Sterling (Thomas Wilner Gaikokuho-Jimu-Bengoshi Jimusho), Fukoku Seimei Building, 5th Fl. 2-2-2, Uchisaiwaicho, Chiyoda-ku, Tokyo 100, Japan. Telephone: (81 3) 5251-1601. Fax: (81 3) 5251-1602.

Toronto, Ontario, Canada Office: Commerce Court West, Suite 4405, P.O. Box 247, M5L 1E8. Telephone: (416) 360-8484. Fax: (416) 360-2958.

Washington, D.C. Office: 801 Pennsylvania Avenue, N.W., Suite 900, 20004-2604. Telephone: (202) 508-8000. Fax: (202) 508-8100.

Firm engages in General American and International Financial and Commercial Practice. Not authorized to appear before R.O.C. courts or to act as R.O.C. lawyers.

FIRM PROFILE: Shearman & Sterling, founded in 1873, has more than 500 lawyers in 15 offices throughout the world. The firm's practice encompasses most major areas of business law, including: Antitrust and Trade Regulation; Banking; Bankruptcy and Corporate Reorganization; Compensation and Benefits; Environmental; Finance (including Corporate Finance, Domestic Private Finance, Financial Institutions, International Private Finance and Project Finance); Individual Clients, Trusts and Estates; Insurance; International Trade and Government Relations; Litigation and Arbitration; Mergers and Acquisitions; Oil and Gas; Privatizations; Real Estate; and Tax. The Firm is also engaged in the practice of French, German and Hungarian law through its offices in France, Germany and Hungary.

(This Listing Continued)

ASIAN COUNSEL

MARK J. HARTY, born Memphis, Tennessee, 1956; admitted, 1983, New York (Not admitted in Taiwan). Education: Harvard University (A.B., 1978; J.D., 1982). LANGUAGES: English, Mandarin and Spanish.

(For Biographical data of all Partners, see Professional Biographies at New York, New York).

SHIEH & SHIEH

A PROFESSIONAL CORPORATION
Established in 1972

9TH FL., 112, SEC. 1, CHUNG HSIAO E. ROAD
P.O. BOX 84-861
TAIPEI, TAIWAN
Telephone: (02) 3939-400; (02) 3939-508
Telecopier: (02) 3939-411; (02) 3939-413

Los Angeles, California Office: P.O. Box 972, Pasadena, CA 91102. Telephone: (818) 405-0345. Facsimile: (818) 405-1180.

Tainan, Taiwan Office: 23, Lane 394, Kai-Yuan Rd., Tainan. Telephone: (06) 237-4849. Facsimile: (06) 275-2316.

FIRM PROFILE: The Firm was established in Taiwan in 1972 by Dr. Liang-Houh Shieh. The Firm also established an office in the USA in 1983. The attorneys at the firms are licensed to practice law in California, Florida, Illinois, New York, Washington D.C., Taiwan and Mainland China. The Firm is one of the most prestigious and qualified firms in the nation and in the world--its attorneys possess one of the best education and quality in handling complex litigation and transaction involving two or more countries. The Firm provides a full range of administrative, civil, commercial and criminal legal services.

Structure: Shieh & Shieh maintains an office in California and another office in Tainan City, Taiwan and establishes correspondent relationships with foreign law firms throughout America and Asia to facilitate legal matters involving foreign laws. The Firm has well established working relationships with major business consulting firms, accounting firms and banking facilities.

Client Base: The major clients of the Firm are the leaders of airlines, banks, bicycles, computers, construction, department stores, electronic, furnitures, hotels, industries, insurance, machinery, maritime, pharmaceutical, papers, plastics, publication, securities, steel, telecommunications, TV, textile, trading, travel agents, trust, tobacco & wine, wire & cable, etc.

The International Department handles the multinational and multistate transactions and litigation. The Firm possess the unique skills in handling the conflict of law and international litigation technique.

The Corporate Department handles incorporation, tax planning, labor, foreign investment, government contracts, licensing, technology transfer, mergers and acquisitions, securities, labor and other corporate matters.

The Banking and Financing Department handles establishment of wholesale branches, on-shore and off-shore banking entities, commercial and investment banking, private banking, international financing and other regulatory and documentary services.

The Intellectual Property Department handles all aspects of intellectual property rights including servicemark, trademark, patent and copyright registration, licensing and transfer for domestic and international clients.

The Litigation Department handles a variety of administrative, commercial, civil and criminal litigation and has created several landmark cases.

International Team Work: Through the E-mail system and other international modern technique, the Taipei office obtains the cases, statutes and relevant material from the Los Angeles office in a few minutes. Attorneys in Taipei are able to handle the litigation and transaction in the United States. The same is true with respect to the Los Angeles office. The time difference between the U.S. and Taiwan and the availability of the information and materials in both countries have become advantages to the Firm's clients where the Firm's American offices and Taiwan offices are working 24 hours per day and providing the most comprehensive, efficient and cost saving legal services to the Firm's clients worldwide.

MANAGING ATTORNEYS

LIANG-HOUH SHIEH, born China, October 17, 1947; admitted, 1972, Taiwan; 1974, Patent and Trademark Office of R.O.C.; 1983, New York and U.S. District Courts; 1984, Oregon, U.S. Court of International Trade and U.S. Tax Court; 1987, California, U.S. District Court and U.S. Court of

(This Listing Continued)

AS337B

SHIEH & SHIEH, A PROFESSIONAL CORPORATION,
Taipei—Continued

Appeal (9th Circuit); 1988, District of Columbia and U.S. Supreme Court. *Education:* Yale Law School (LL.M., 1980; J.S.D., Doctor of the Science of Law, 1981; J.D., 1984). Editor, Yale Law Journal, 1983-1984. *Member:* State Bar of California; The District of Columbia Bar; New York State Bar and Taipei Bar Associations. *LANGUAGES:* English, Mandarin (Chinese) and Fujianese (Taiwanese).

COUNSELS

FU-CHENG CHIN, born Taiwan, December 23, 1942; admitted, 1966, Taiwan; 1986, New York. *Education:* National Taiwan University (LL.B., 1965); Boston University (LL.M., 1985). *LANGUAGES:* English, Mandarin (Chinese) and Fujianese (Taiwanese).

KA-JUNG CHUNG, born Taiwan, August 7, 1957; admitted, 1988, Taiwan. *Education:* Fu-Jen University (LL.B., 1985).

HON. HENRY LIN, born Taiwan, March 1, 1953; admitted, 1985, Taiwan, Prosecutor. *Education:* National Taiwan University (LL.B., 1975).

GRACE WANG, born Taiwan, January 17, 1966; admitted, 1992, Taiwan. *Education:* National Taiwan University (LL.B., 1989).

STIKEMAN, ELLIOTT

117 SEC. 3 MIN SHENG EAST ROAD
8TH FLOOR
TAIPEI, TAIWAN
Telephone: 886-2-719-9573
Fax: 886-2-719-4540

Montreal, Quebec Office: 1155 René-Lévesque Boulevard West, 40th Floor, H3B 3V2. Telephone: 514-397-3000. Fax: 514-397-3222.

Toronto, Ontario Office: Commerce Court West, 53rd Floor, M5L 1B9. Telephone: 416-869-5500. Fax: 416-947-0866.

Ottawa, Ontario Office: 50 O'Connor Street, Suite 914, K1P 6L2. Telephone: 613-234-4555. Fax: 613-230-8877.

Calgary, Alberta Office: 855 - 2nd Street S.W., 1500 Bankers Hall, T2P 4J7. Telephone: 403-266-9000. Fax: 403-266-9034.

Vancouver, British Columbia Office: 666 Burrard Street, Suite 1700, Park Place, V6C 2X8. Telephone: 604-631-1300. Fax: 604-681-1825.

New York, New York Office: 126 East 56th Street, 11th Floor, Tower 56, 10022. Telephone: 212-371-8855. Fax: 212-371-7087.

Washington, D.C. Office: 1300 I Street, N.W., Suite 1210 West, 20005-3314. Telephone: 202-326-7555. Fax: 202-326-7557.

London, England Office: Cottons Centre, Cottons Lane, SE1 2QL. Telephone: 71-378-0880. Fax: 71-378-0344.

Paris, France Office: In Association with Société Juridique Internationale, 39, rue François Ier, 75008. Telephone: 33-1-40-73-82-00. Fax: 33-1-40-73-82-10.

Budapest, Hungary Office: Andrássy út 100, II Floor, H-1062. Telephone: 36-1-269-1790. Fax: 36-1-269-0655.

Hong Kong Office: 29 Queen's Road Central, Suite 1506, China Building. Telephone: 852-2868-9903. Fax: 852-2868-9912.

Hong Kong: In Association with Shum & Co., 29 Queen's Road Central, Suite 1103, China Building. Telephone: 852-2526-5531. Fax: 852-2845-9076.

Firm engaged in Canadian and International Law Practice, but not authorized to appear before the Taiwan Courts or act as Taiwan Solicitors.

Ching-Wo Ng
(Not admitted in Taiwan)

Andes Fu-Min Lin
(Not admitted in Taiwan)

(For biographical data on other personnel, see Professional Biographies at Montreal, Quebec, Toronto, Ontario, Ottawa, Ontario, Vancouver, British Columbia, Calgary, Alberta, New York, New York, Washington, D.C., London, England, Hong Kong, Paris, France and Budapest, Hungary)

TAI E INTERNATIONAL PATENT & LAW OFFICE

Established in 1952

9TH FL., 112 CHANG-AN EAST ROAD, SEC. 2
TAIPEI, TAIWAN
Telephone: (02) 508-1531; 506-1023
Facsimile: (02) 506-8147; 509-0804
Telex: 27777 TAIEPAT

Intellectual Property Practice: Patent, Trademark, Copyright, Prosecution and Enforcement; License Arrangement; Transfer of Technology.
Law: Administrative Law; Corporate Law; Criminal Law; Distributorship, Agency and Franchise Law; Foreign Investments; International Contracts; Litigations; General Legal Practice.

FIRM PROFILE: Tai E was established in 1952 as a law firm specialized in intellectual property matters in view of the increasing importance of that field of law to the rapidly developing society. Now, Tai E is one of the best-established and most resource-rich law firms in Taiwan specializing in intellectual property causes.

A professional corporation of over 190 personnel deployed in four offices have helped Tai E to become one of the top three largest firms in Taiwan. The leading position of this firm can be further evidenced by the fact that it usually ranks first or second in the number of patent and trademark applications granted and published in the official Gazette of the Taiwan Patent & Trademark Office.

PARTNERS

I-CHU LIN. *Education:* National Taiwan University Law School (LL.B.). *Member:* Taipei Bar Association; Taichung Bar Association; APAA; FICPI; AIPPI; USTA. (Patent Attorney). *LANGUAGES:* Chinese, English and Japanese. *PRACTICE AREAS:* Administrative Law; Agency and Distributorship Law; Antitrust Law; Trade Regulation Law; Business Law; Company Law; Copyright Law; Criminal Law; Family Law; Franchise Law; Intellectual Property Law; Patent and Trademark Law; Technology Law; Science Law; General Practice.

CHING-JANG LIN. *Education:* National Cheng Chi University, School of Law (LL.B.). Author: "Strategies to Prevent Counterfeiting Patents and Trademarks in Taiwan," Republic of China, 1984. Former Examiner, Patent & Trademark Office. Councilor, Taipei City. *Member:* Chinese Society of Comparative Law; LAWASIA; Taipei Inventors' Association (Honorable President). (Trademark Agent). *LANGUAGES:* Chinese and English.

CHIUNG-YAO CHI. *Education:* National Taiwan University Law School (LL.B.). *Member:* Taipei Bar Association; Chang Hwa Bar Association; APAA; Taipei Inventors' Association; USTA. (Patent Attorney). *LANGUAGES:* Chinese, English and Japanese.

TA-SHE LIN. *Education:* Marshall University, U.S.A. (M.A.). *Member:* Taipei Inventors' Association. (Trademark Agent, Office Manager). *LANGUAGES:* Chinese and English.

KEVIN W.C. CHANG. *Education:* Taiwan University Law School (LL.B.). *Member:* Kao-Hsiung Bar Association; Tainan Bar Association. (Patent Attorney). *LANGUAGES:* Chinese and English.

HENRY C.H. GUEI. *Education:* Cheng Chi University Law School (LL.B.). Former Examiner, Patent & Trademark Office. *Member:* Taipei Bar Association; Hsin Chu Bar Association; USTA; APAA. (Patent Attorney). *LANGUAGES:* Chinese and English.

W.C. CHIANG. *Education:* Chinese Culture University Law School (LL.B.). Taichung Bar Association; Chang Hua Bar Association. (Patent Attorney). *LANGUAGES:* Chinese and English.

ASSOCIATES

PI-CHUN CHIANG. *Education:* National Cheng Chi University (LL.B.). *Member:* Taipei Inventors' Association. (Trademark Agent, Office Manager). *LANGUAGES:* English and Chinese.

KUO-AN SU. *Education:* Chinese Culture University (B.A.; Law Programs). (Trademark Agent, Office Manager). *LANGUAGES:* English and Chinese.

PERKIN J.Y. LIAW. *Education:* Soochow University Law School (LL.B.). (Trademark Agent, Legal Assistant). *LANGUAGES:* Chinese and English.

(This Listing Continued)

FRANCES F.Y. CHEN. *Education:* Soochow University Law School (LL.B.). (Trademark Agent, Legal Assistant). *LANGUAGES:* Chinese and English.

DORA LING-JU TSAO. *Education:* Chinese Culture University (M.A.). (Trademark Agent). *LANGUAGES:* Chinese, German and English.

JACK Y.M. PAUNG. *Education:* Tokyo Institute of Technology (M.S.). (Engineering Consultant, Chemistry). *LANGUAGES:* Chinese, Japanese and English.

FRANK HSIN-TSANG LIN. *Education:* National Taiwan University (B.S.). (Engineering Consultant, Chemistry). *LANGUAGES:* Chinese, English, Japanese and German.

JOSEPH S.W. LEUNG. *Education:* Chinese University (M.S.). Author: "Role of Lipid of Endotoxin in the Production of Tumor Necrosis Factor"; "Advanced Level Biology-cell and Molecular Biology." *Member:* The Institute of Biology, United Kingdom. (Engineering Consultant, Biology). *LANGUAGES:* Chinese and English.

PETER M.J. CHANG. *Education:* Chiao Tung University (B.S.). (Engineering Consultant, Mechanics). *LANGUAGES:* Chinese and English.

KAREN K.L. CHEN. *Education:* Taiwan University (M.S.). (Engineering Consultant, Agricultural Mechanics). *LANGUAGES:* Chinese and English.

EAGLE S.L. LIN. *Education:* Manhattan College, U.S.A. (M.S.). (Engineering Consultant, Computer). *LANGUAGES:* Chinese and English.

LI-YEH CHAN. *Education:* Chengchi University Law School (LL.B.). Former Examiner, Patent & Trademark Office. *Member:* Taipei Bar Association. (Patent Attorney). *LANGUAGES:* Chinese and English.

FRED YEN. *Education:* Taiwan University (M.Sc., Micro-Organism). The Expression of Epstein-Barr Virus DNA Fragments ECORI-Dhet and BamHI-YH in Human Epithelial Cell Line RHEK-1.

BAO-JANE LUH. *Education:* University of Witwatersrand (M.Sc., Chemistry). Addition and Cycloaddition Reaction of 3H-1, 2-dithiole-3-one Oximes.

TAIWAN INTERNATIONAL PATENT & LAW OFFICE
(TIPLO ATTORNEYS-AT-LAW)

Established in 1965

7TH FLOOR, WE SHENG FIRST BUILDING
NO. 125, NANKING EAST ROAD, SECTION 2
P.O. BOX NO. 39-243
TAIPEI 10409, TAIWAN
Telephone: 02-507-2811
Facsimile: 02-508-3711

Intellectual Property and Unfair Competition, Corporate and Investment, Licensing, International Trade and Commerce, Civil and Criminal Litigation, General Legal Practice.

FIRM PROFILE: *TIPLO has been specializing in intellectual property law for the past three decades. The firm is now staffed with more than 150 full time members, including attorneys, technical specialists and professional personnel, all of whom are fluent in the Japanese and/or English language. The firm maintains the IBM S/38 and AS/400 computer system as well as various databases, such as registered Taiwan patents and trademarks. In addition, the firm is actively involved with international licensing of technology and intellectual property rights.*

MEMBERS OF FIRM

MING-SHEN LIN, (Founder of the firm), born Taipei, Taiwan, August 9, 1934; admitted to bar, 1958, Taiwan, Republic of China; admitted to patent office, 1959. *Education:* National Taiwan University (LL.B., 1956). Author: "Legal Aspects of doing Business in Taiwan," 1984; "Patent and Trademark Practice in Taiwan." Publisher of TIPLO Review. Chairman of Board of Trustees, NTU Law Foundation, 1990—. *Member:* Taipei Bar Association (President, 1990-1993); International Bar Association of the R.O.C. (President, 1993-1996); Chinese Society of Comparative Law; International Association for the Protection of Industrial Property (AIPPI); Asian Patent Attorneys Association (APAA) (President, Taiwan Group); United States Trademark Association (Foreign Member); American Bar Association (Foreign Member); Inter-Pacific Bar Association (IPBA) (Pres-

(This Listing Continued)

ident, 1993). *LANGUAGES:* Chinese (Mandarin and Taiwanese), English and Japanese. *PRACTICE AREAS:* Intellectual Property Law; Corporate Law and Licensing.

T.L. CHANG, born Taichung, Taiwan, 1932; (Not admitted in Taiwan). *Education:* National Taiwan University Law School (LL.B., 1955). Author: "Introduction for the System of Taiwan Intellectual Property (Japanese)." Experience: Research Assistant, Law Revision Planning Group, Council for U.S. Aid. *Member:* International Association for the Protection of Industrial Property (AIPPI). *LANGUAGES:* Chinese (Mandarin and Taiwanese) Japanese and English. *PRACTICE AREAS:* Intellectual Property Law; Corporate Law.

C.Y. CHEN, born Hsin-tsu, Taiwan, 1932; (Not admitted in Taiwan). *Education:* National Taiwan University Law School (LL.B., 1956). Co-Author: "Patent Practice in Taiwan". *LANGUAGES:* Chinese (Mandarin and Taiwanese) Japanese and English. *PRACTICE AREAS:* Intellectual Property Law.

H.G. CHEN, born Taichung, Taiwan, 1954; admitted to bar, 1982, Taiwan, Republic of China; admitted to patent office, 1983. *Education:* National Taiwan University (LL.B., 1981); Franklin Pierce Law Center (MIP, 1990). *Member:* Taipei and Taichung Bar Associations; Chinese Society of Comparative Law; Asian Patent Attorneys Association; American Intellectual Property Law Association. *LANGUAGES:* Chinese (Mandarin and Taiwanese) and English. *PRACTICE AREAS:* Intellectual Property Law; Litigation and Unfair Competition.

DAVID T. LIOU, born Yuan-Lin, Taiwan, 1954; admitted to bar, 1986, Taiwan, Republic of China. *Education:* National Taiwan University (LL.B., 1977); Tulane University, School of Law (LL.M., 1980); University of Florida, College of Law (J.D., 1982). Author: "The Development of Proportional Damages Rule in Both-to-Blame Collision Cases at Sea," Hwa Kang Law Review, 1984. Experience: Chairman, Legal Practice R&D Committee, Taipei Bar Association, 1990-1993. Deputy Chairman, International Relations Committee, Taipei Bar Association, 1990-1993; Finance Director, NTU Law Foundation, 1990-1993; Deputy Secretary General, Institute for Research & Development of Corporate Organizations of ROC, 1991; Associate Professor of Law, Soochow University and Chinese Culture University (Company Law & Law of Contracts, 1983—; Associate Attorney, Tsar & Tsai. *Member:* Taipei Bar Association; Inter-Pacific Bar Association (IPBA); Asian Patent Attorneys Association (APAA). *LANGUAGES:* Chinese (Mandarin and Taiwanese) and English. *PRACTICE AREAS:* Corporate; Foreign Investment; Joint Venture; Licensing; Contract; Taxation; Securities and Insurance.

EDWARD C.F. HUANG, born Taipei, Taiwan, 1957; admitted to bar, 1980, Taiwan, Republic of China; admitted to patent office, 1980. *Education:* National Taiwan University (LL.B., 1979); Tokyo University (LL.M., 1987; J.D. Candidate, 1990). *Member:* Taipei Bar Association (Secretary General, 1993—); Chinese Society of Constitutional Law; Japan Public Law Society. *LANGUAGES:* Chinese (Mandarin and Taiwanese) and Japanese. *PRACTICE AREAS:* Intellectual Property Law; Civil Law and Company Law.

J.K. LIN, born Taipei, Taiwan, 1965; admitted, 1993, Taiwan, Republic of China; admitted to patent office, 1993. *Education:* Law Department, Fujin University (LL.B., 1987). *LANGUAGES:* Chinese (Mandarin and Taiwanese) English and Japanese. *PRACTICE AREAS:* Intellectual Property Law.

C.F. CHEN, born Taipei, Taiwan, 1932; (Not admitted in Taiwan). *Education:* Taipei Institute of Technology Mechanical Engineering. *LANGUAGES:* Chinese (Mandarin and Taiwanese) and Japanese. *PRACTICE AREAS:* Patent Law; Aircraft; Automobile; Rolling Stock; Knitting Machine and Mechanical.

Y. CHUANG, born Keelung, Taiwan, 1932; (Not admitted in Taiwan). *Education:* Taipei Municipal First Girls' Senior High School. *LANGUAGES:* Chinese (Mandarin and Taiwanese) and Japanese. *PRACTICE AREAS:* Trademark Law; International Filing.

S.Y. FANG, born Hsin-Tsu, Taiwan, 1941; (Not admitted in Taiwan). *Education:* Chung Yuan Christian College of Science and Engineering (B.S., 1968); Franklin Pierce Law Center (IPSI., 1994). *LANGUAGES:* Chinese (Mandarin and Taiwanese) and English. *PRACTICE AREAS:* Patent Law - Refrigeration and Acoustics.

JANE HSIAO, born Taoyuan, Taiwan, 1954; (Not admitted in Taiwan). *Education:* Computer Science, Ming Chuan College (1976); Franklin Pierce Law Center (IPSI., 1994). *LANGUAGES:* Mandarin and English. *PRACTICE AREAS:* Patent Law-International Filing.

(This Listing Continued)

TAIWAN INTERNATIONAL PATENT & LAW OFFICE (TIPLO ATTORNEYS-AT-LAW), Taipei—Continued

CHARLES S.F. KAO, born Tainan, Taiwan, 1934; admitted to patent office, 1982. *Education:* National Taiwan University (LL.B., 1961). Specialist, Ministry of Economic Affairs, Investment Commission, 1974-1977. Chief, Patent Department, Ministry of Economic Affairs, National Bureau of Standards, 1978-1982. *Member:* Asian Patent Attorneys Association. *LANGUAGES:* Chinese (Mandarin and Taiwanese) and English. *PRACTICE AREAS:* Patent Law; Appeal Law; Administrative Suit Law.

C.Y. LIN, born Taipei, Taiwan, 1940; (Not admitted in Taiwan). *Education:* Taipei Medical College (B.P., 1964); Franklin Pierce Law Center (IPSI., 1994). *LANGUAGES:* Chinese (Mandarin and Taiwanese) and English. *PRACTICE AREAS:* Patent Law; Organic Chemistry; Pharmacology; Physical Pharmacy; Pharmaceutical Compounding; Chemical Analysis and Biotechnology.

P.Y. LIN, born Taichung, Taiwan, 1934; (Not admitted in Taiwan). *Education:* National Chunghsing University (B.A., 1958); Osaka Prefecture University Graduated School of Economic, Japan (M.S., 1962); Ph.D. Course Postgraduate in Osaka Prefecture University (1962-1968). *LANGUAGES:* Chinese (Mandarin and Taiwanese) and English. *PRACTICE AREAS:* Patent Law; Pharmaceutical Compounding; Organic Chemistry; Pharmacology; Physical Pharmacy.

Y.S. LIN, born Taipei, Taiwan, 1938; (Not admitted in Taiwan). *Education:* National Chen Kung University (B.C., 1960). *LANGUAGES:* Chinese (Mandarin and Taiwanese) and Japanese. *PRACTICE AREAS:* Accounting and Management.

W.J. LI, born Taipei, Taiwan, 1959; admitted, 1995, Taiwan, Republic of China. *Education:* National Taiwan University Law School (LL.B., 1981). *LANGUAGES:* Chinese (Mandarin and Taiwanese) and Japanese. *PRACTICE AREAS:* Trademark Law.

C.C. YANG, born I-Lan, Taiwan, 1927; (Not admitted in Taiwan). *Education:* Japan Nagasaki High Technical School. *LANGUAGES:* Chinese (Mandarin and Taiwanese) and Japanese. *PRACTICE AREAS:* Patent Law-International Filing.

JOHNNY H.J. YANG, born I-Lan, Taiwan, 1949; (Not admitted in Taiwan). *Education:* Soochow University Law School (LL.B., 1972). *LANGUAGES:* Chinese (Mandarin and Taiwanese) and Japanese. *PRACTICE AREAS:* Trademark Law.

S.T. YANG, born Hsin-Tsu, Taiwan, 1954; admitted, 1993, Taiwan, Republic of China. *Education:* National Taiwan University Law School (LL.B., 1976). *LANGUAGES:* Mandarin and English. *PRACTICE AREAS:* Trademark Law; Copyright Law.

SHARON CHANG, born Taiwan, 1963; (Not admitted in Taiwan). *Education:* National Sun Yat-Sen University, Foreign Language and Literature (1985). *LANGUAGES:* Chinese (Mandarin and Taiwanese) and English. *PRACTICE AREAS:* Patent Law-International Filing.

VIVIEN C.C. CHANG, born Kaoshiung, Taiwan, 1963; (Not admitted in Taiwan). *Education:* Soochow University (LL.B., 1988). *LANGUAGES:* Chinese (Mandarin and Taiwanese) and English. *PRACTICE AREAS:* Intellectual Property Law.

L.Y. CHANG, born Taiwan, 1966; (Not admitted in Taiwan). *Education:* National Taiwan University (B.S., Environment Engineering, 1988). *LANGUAGES:* Chinese (Mandarin and Taiwanese) and English. *PRACTICE AREAS:* Patent Law-Agricultural Chemistry; Food Chemistry; Polymer Chemistry.

L.C. CHANG, born Taiwan, 1964; (Not admitted in Taiwan). *Education:* National Taiwan University. *LANGUAGES:* Chinese (Mandarin and Taiwanese) and English. *PRACTICE AREAS:* Patent Law-Organoanalysis Chemistry; Natural Product Chemistry; Polymer Chemistry.

J.S. CHEN, born Taipei, Taiwan, 1962; (Not admitted in Taiwan). *Education:* Agriculture Mechanic Engineering, National Taiwan University (B.S., 1985). *LANGUAGES:* Chinese (Mandarin and Taiwanese) Japanese and English. *PRACTICE AREAS:* Patent Law-Mechanical.

P. CHEN, born Taipei, Taiwan, 1960; (Not admitted in Taiwan). *Education:* Transportation Engineering and Management, National Chaio Tung University (B.M., 1982). *LANGUAGES:* Chinese (Mandarin and Taiwanese) and English. *PRACTICE AREAS:* Patent Law; Softwares and Mechanics.

(This Listing Continued)

AS340B

CHUN-TZU CHEN, born 1963; admitted, 1988, Taiwan, Republic of China. *Education:* National Taiwan University (LL.B., 1984). Exchange student with Vienna University, Austria. Author: "Type of Contract for Utilizing Computer Software and Remedies for Failure in Achieving the Purpose.". *LANGUAGES:* Chinese (Mandarin and Taiwanese) German and English. *PRACTICE AREAS:* Copyright Law; Litigation.

L.C. CHENG, born Jiayi, Taiwan, 1961; (Not admitted in Taiwan). *Education:* Science in Chemistry, Tamkang University (B.S., 1983). *LANGUAGES:* Chinese (Mandarin and Taiwanese) and English. *PRACTICE AREAS:* Patent Law-Organosynthesis Chemistry; Adhesives; Dyes, Paintings, Coating and Resins; Liquid Crystals; Petroleum and Coal Chemistry.

L.Y. CHOU, born Taipei, Taiwan, 1963; (Not admitted in Taiwan). *Education:* National Taiwan University Law School (LL.B., 1985). *LANGUAGES:* Mandarin and English. *PRACTICE AREAS:* Foreign Investment; Corporate; Visa and Employment; Taxation.

JERRY CHIOU, born Taiwan, 1963; (Not admitted in Taiwan). *Education:* National Taiwan University (B.S., Electrical Engineering, 1984); University of California, Santa Barbara (M.S., 1988). Experience: Engineer, Honeywell (1988-1989). *LANGUAGES:* Chinese (Mandarin and Taiwanese) and English. *PRACTICE AREAS:* Patent Law-Optical Electronics and Solid State.

SILVIA FANG, born Taipei, Taiwan, 1964; (Not admitted in Taiwan). *Education:* National Taiwan University (LL.B., 1986); University of Iowa (M.C.L., 1991). *LANGUAGES:* Chinese (Mandarin and Taiwanese) and English. *PRACTICE AREAS:* Commercial Contract; Corporate; Taxation and Real Estate.

SCOTT GAU, born Taiwan, 1959; (Not admitted in Taiwan). *Education:* Taipei Institute of Technology (Mining Engineering, 1980); National Akita University Graduate School of Mining, Japan (M.S., 1988). *LANGUAGES:* Chinese (Mandarin and Taiwanese) and Japanese. *PRACTICE AREAS:* Patent Law- Mechanical.

ROBER HO, born Taipei, Taiwan, 1962; (Not admitted in Taiwan). *Education:* National Taiwan University (B.S., Electrical Engineering, 1984). *LANGUAGES:* Chinese (Mandarin and Taiwanese) and English. *PRACTICE AREAS:* Patent Law-Circuits and Networks.

JANICE C. LIAW, born Ying-ko, Taiwan, 1957; admitted to bar, 1992, Taiwan, Republic of China. *Education:* National Taiwan University (LL.B., 1979); University of Pennsylvania (LL.M., 1982); University of Washington (M.B.A., 1986). Experience: Accounts Controller, CAP Industry Ltd., U.K., 1988-1989; Associate Attorney, McCutchen, Doyle, Brown & Enerson, Taipei Office, 1989-1990. *LANGUAGES:* Chinese (Mandarin and Taiwanese) and English. *PRACTICE AREAS:* Foreign Investment; Corporate; Trademark and Admiralty.

JER-PING CHANG, born Taipei, Taiwan, 1966; admitted, 1992, Taiwan, Republic of China. *Education:* National Taiwan University (LL.B., 1988); National Chunghsing University Graduate School of Law (LL.M., 1991). Author: "Passing Off and Fair Trade Law". Experience: In Charge of Contract Review in R.O.C. Air Force. *Member:* Taipei, Taichung, Taiwan Bar Associations. *LANGUAGES:* Chinese (Mandarin and Taiwanese) English and German. *PRACTICE AREAS:* Unfair Competition Law; Litigation.

CHUNG-CHENG LIU, born Keelung, Taiwan, 1968; admitted, 1994, Taiwan, Republic of China. *Education:* National Taiwan University (LL.B., 1991). *Member:* Taipei Bar Association. *LANGUAGES:* Chinese (Mandarin and Taiwanese) Japanese and English. *PRACTICE AREAS:* Intellectual Property Law; Criminal Law.

C.F. TING, born Yuin-Lin, Taiwan, 1967; admitted, 1993, Taiwan, Republic of China. *Education:* Law Department, Fu-Jin University (LL.B., 1990). *LANGUAGES:* Chinese (Mandarin and Taiwanese) English and Japanese. *PRACTICE AREAS:* Intellectual Property Law; Civil Law.

MIN-HUI LI, born Taipei, Taiwan, 1964; admitted, 1991, New York; 1995, Taiwan. *Education:* National Taiwan University (LL.B., 1987); Duke University School of Law (LL.M., 1989). *LANGUAGES:* Chinese (Mandarin and Taiwanese) and English. *PRACTICE AREAS:* Commercial Contract; Corporate; Licensing; Litigation.

D.C. LIN, born Taipei, Taiwan, 1962; (Not admitted in Taiwan). *Education:* Electrical Engineering, National Taiwan University (B.S., 1984). *LANGUAGES:* Mandarin and English. *PRACTICE AREAS:* Patent Law-Hardwares.

C.C. LIN, born Hsin-Tsu, Taiwan, 1957; admitted, 1995, Taiwan, Republic of China. *Education:* Fu-Jen Catholic University Law School (LL.B.,

(This Listing Continued)

1980); Franklin Pierce Law Center (IPSI., 1994). *LANGUAGES:* Chinese (Mandarin and Taiwanese) and English. *PRACTICE AREAS:* Intellectual Property Law.

PAMELA P.W. LIOU, born Miao-li, Taiwan, 1962; (Not admitted in Taiwan). *Education:* National Taiwan University Law School (LL.B., 1984); University of Iowa (M.C.L., 1986). Author: "Comparison Study on Divorce Laws between the R.O.C. and U.S.A.," 1986; "Planning and Management of Foreign Direct Investment in the R.O.C.," 1988. *LANGUAGES:* Chinese (Mandarin and Taiwanese) and English. *PRACTICE AREAS:* Intellectual Property Law.

BETTY KO, born Taipei, Taiwan, 1952; (Not admitted in Taiwan). *Education:* Fu-Jen Catholic University. *LANGUAGES:* Chinese (Mandarin and Taiwanese) and English. *PRACTICE AREAS:* Trademark Law.

ANGELA SHEN, born Taiwan, 1960; (Not admitted in Taiwan). *Education:* Soochow University (LL.B., 1985); Franklin Pierce Law Center (IPSI., 1994). *LANGUAGES:* Chinese (Mandarin and Taiwanese) and English. *PRACTICE AREAS:* Trademark Law.

CHEN-PONG LIOU, born Taiwan, 1934; (Not admitted in Taiwan). *Education:* Taipei Institute of Technology Mining Engineering. *LANGUAGES:* Chinese (Mandarin and Taiwanese) and Japanese. *PRACTICE AREAS:* Patent Law-Mechanical.

SHIRLEY LIU, born Taiwan, 1966; (Not admitted in Taiwan). *Education:* National Taiwan University (B.S., Chemical Engineering, 1988). *LANGUAGES:* Chinese (Mandarin and Taiwanese) and English. *PRACTICE AREAS:* Patent Law-Polymer Chemistry; Textile and Paper; Environmental Science.

ZONG-YEU KUO, born Taiwan, 1965; (Not admitted in Taiwan). *Education:* Tunghai University (B.S., 1989). *LANGUAGES:* Chinese (Mandarin and Taiwanese) and Japanese. *PRACTICE AREAS:* Patent Law-Instrumental Analysis; Coordination Chemistry; Electrochemistry.

N.C. TSAO, born Taiwan, 1963; (Not admitted in Taiwan). *Education:* National Taiwan University (B.S., Veterinary Medicine, 1985); Institute of Veterinary Medicine, National Taiwan University (M.S., 1988). *LANGUAGES:* Chinese (Mandarin and Taiwanese) and English. *PRACTICE AREAS:* Patent Law; Biotechnology; Microbiology; Immunology; Enzymology.

T.S. YANG, born Taipei, Taiwan, 1932; (Not admitted in Taiwan). *Education:* Electrical Engineering, National Taiwan University (B.S., 1956). *LANGUAGES:* Chinese (Mandarin and Taiwanese) and Japanese. *PRACTICE AREAS:* Patent Law-Electrical.

NELSON YU, born Taiwan, 1961; (Not admitted in Taiwan). *Education:* National Taiwan University (B.S., Electrical Engineering, 1984). *LANGUAGES:* Chinese (Mandarin and Taiwanese) and English. *PRACTICE AREAS:* Patent Law-Personal Computer and Optical Fiber Communication.

KUANG-CHING FAN, born Taiwan, 1961; (Not admitted in Taiwan). *Education:* National Akita University Graduate School of Mining, Japan (M.S., 1988). *LANGUAGES:* Chinese (Mandarin and Taiwanese) and Japanese. *PRACTICE AREAS:* Patent Law-Electronic.

J.Y. LIN, born Taipei, Taiwan, 1968; (Not admitted in Taiwan). *Education:* Electrical Engineering Syracuse University (M.S., 1993). *LANGUAGES:* Chinese (Mandarin and Taiwanese) and English. *PRACTICE AREAS:* Patent Law-Electrical.

C.H. LI, born Taipei, Taiwan, 1962; (Not admitted in Taiwan). *Education:* University of Minnesota (M.S., Mechanical Engineering, 1992). *LANGUAGES:* Chinese (Mandarin and Taiwanese) and English. *PRACTICE AREAS:* Patent Law-Mechanical.

HARRY HSIAO, born Taiwan, 1959; (Not admitted in Taiwan). *Education:* Nihon University, Japan (B.S., Chemical Engineering, 1987). *LANGUAGES:* Chinese (Mandarin and Taiwanese) and Japanese. *PRACTICE AREAS:* Patent Law-Paintings; Metal Surface Treatment; Cosmetics.

C.Y. WANG, born Taiwan, 1962; (Not admitted in Taiwan). *Education:* National Cheng Kung University (B.S., Chemistry, 1985). *LANGUAGES:* Chinese (Mandarin and Taiwanese) and English. *PRACTICE AREAS:* Patent Law-Polymer Chemistry; Plastics Processing; Coatings; Synthetic Chemistry.

(This Listing Continued)

OF COUNSEL

CHI-EN LIANG, born Tainan, Taiwan, 1935; admitted, 1976, District of Columbia; 1978, New York; 1979, Taipei, Taiwan. *Education:* National Taiwan University (LL.B., 1957); Kyoto University, Japan (LL.M., 1967; Completed LL.D. Courses, 1970); University of Michigan (M.C.L., 1971); George Washington University (M.C.L.A.P., 1976). Experience: Legal Research Assistant, Council for International Economic Cooperation and Development, Executive Yuen, R.O.C. Judge, Taiwan Kaohsiong District Court. Associate, International Law Firms in New York City; Practicing Law in New York (since 1979) and in Taipei, Taiwan (since 1988). *LANGUAGES:* Chinese (Mandarin, Taiwanese), Japanese and English. *PRACTICE AREAS:* Taxation; Corporate Law; Foreign Investment.

TOP TEAM INTERNATIONAL PATENT & TRADEMARK OFFICE

2ND FLOOR, NO. 188, SECTION 3, HSIN-YI ROAD
P.O. BOX 26-947 TAIPEI
TAIPEI, TAIWAN
Telephone: (02)-703-9911
Facsimile: 886-2-755-2737, 886-2-704-1388 (GII or GIII)

Patent, Trademark and Copyright.

FIRM PROFILE: The TOP TEAM in Taiwan is a law office with services primarily in intellectual properties, including patents, trademarks, and copyrights. The office provides a full range of services within this area of law and they include:

(A) Patents, Trademark, and Copyrights: The office helps clients in the procurement of legal protections on the proprietary rights of their intellectual properties. This service includes the practices of preliminary investigations, preparations of specifications (in Chinese for domestic filing and in English or in Japanese for international filing), and the subsequent prosecutions after filing the applications.

(B) Infringement Investigations: The office provides investigations and counseling works for clients who are developing new products but are unaware of the patent restrictions thereto.

(C) Licensing: This service includes the licensing of all forms of intellectual properties, particularly in the cases of domestic or international technology transfers. The office participates in the evaluation, negotiating, and drafting of licensing agreements as well as in the subsequent application for an approval of technical cooperation to the R.O.C. government and enforcement of the license terms.

(D) Litigation: The office represents clients, both plaintiffs or defendants, in the suits concerning intellectual properties before the court of Taiwan. In the matter of patent infringements, the lawyer of the office is supported by a patent attorney and a patent professional of concerned technical fields to prosecute the civil and criminal litigation procedures in the court or administrative authorities including the customs for the inhibition of the accused products.

The office is especially renowned for its service in patent applications, both national and international. Besides representing clients before the Taiwanese Patent Office, the office has also extensive experiences in handling patent applications for domestic clients to the patent offices of the United States, Japan, Korea, European, German, United Kingdom, Australia, and so on.

The staffs of the office responsible for patent applications mostly possess advanced science degrees including electrical engineering, mechanical engineering, chemistry, and physics as well as direct related industrial experiences. Fields of inventions the office's staffs have practical patent prosecution experiences related mainly to high-technology inventions, including computer-related inventions, imaging technologies, optical instruments, digital communication systems, automated manufacturing machineries, aeronautical technologies, superconductive materials, new medicines, biotechnology-related disciplines, polymer chemistry, etc.

With its highly professional expertises, the domestic clients the office represents today are mostly large research institutes in Taiwan such as National Science Council which sponsors all research projects conducted by university faculties, Development Center of Biotechnology, Industrial Technology and Research Institute which conducts all forms of research projects for industrial applications, China Steel Co., Taiwan Electric Power Co., and Macronix International Co. Ltd. which is a large semiconductor chip manufacturer etc.

(This Listing Continued)

TOP TEAM INTERNATIONAL PATENT & TRADEMARK OFFICE, Taipei—Continued

MEMBERS OF FIRM

HENRY C.W. HONG, born Taipei, Taiwan, July 25, 1951; admitted, 1988, Taiwan Patent Office. *Education:* National Taiwan University (B.E., 1974); The University of Tokyo, Japan (M.E., 1982). Licensed Professional Engineer, Industrial Department of Taiwan R.O.C. *Member:* Asian Patent Attorneys Association (APAA). *LANGUAGES:* Chinese (Mandarin and Taiwanese), English and Japanese. *PRACTICE AREAS:* Mechanics; Automation Engineering.

T.C. SHIAU, born Taipei, Taiwan, April 4, 1954; (Not admitted in Taiwan). *Education:* Chemical Engineering, Tatung Institute of Technology (B.E., 1976). Not Admitted to Taiwan Patent Office, 1988. Experience: Chemical Engineer, Tatung Co., 1976-1982; Patent Engineer, Saint Island International Patent & Trademark Office, 1983-1985; Taiwan International Patent & Law Office, 1986-1987. *LANGUAGES:* Chinese (Mandarin and Taiwanese), English and Japanese. *PRACTICE AREAS:* Biotechnology; Polymer Science.

WILSON H.L. LEE, born Tainan, Taiwan, May 1, 1957; (Not admitted in Taiwan). *Education:* Feng Chia University (B.S., 1981). Not Admitted to Taiwan Patent Office, 1988. Experience: Saint Island International Patent & Trademark Office, 1984-1986. *LANGUAGES:* Chinese (Mandarin and Taiwanese) and English. *PRACTICE AREAS:* Trademark Practice; Litigation; Copyright Practice.

YEN-PONG JOU, born Kinmen, Fukien, March 11, 1960; admitted, 1990, Republic of China; 1991, Taiwan Patent Office. *Education:* Catholic Fu Jen University (LL.B., 1984). Experience: Special Assistant to Chairman, Hon Hai Precision Industry Co., Ltd. (Taiwan) and Foxconn International, Inc. (U.S.A.), 1985-1990. Author: " Legal Considerations on Distribution of High Technology Products", 1988; "Legal Analysis of the Environment of Investment and Trade in Hong Kong", 1989; A Study of "Regulations Governing the Indirect Investment and Technical Cooperation in Mainland", 1990; On the Review of Administrative Act on Holdings Companies from Tax Haven", 1991; "The Effect of Administrative Act on Holdings Companies from Tax Haven", 1991. *Member:* Taipei and Inter-Pacific Bar Associations. *LANGUAGES:* Chinese (Mandarin and Taiwanese) and English. *PRACTICE AREAS:* Intellectual Property Rights; Designation; Negotiable Instrument.

WEN-HONG YEH, born 1960; (Not admitted in Taiwan). *Education:* Electrical Engineering, Tatung Institute of Technology (B.E.). Not admitted to Taiwan Patent Office, 1988. *LANGUAGES:* English and Chinese. *PRACTICE AREAS:* Electrical Engineering; Computer Softwares; Patent Protection.

SEN-TAU WANG, born Taipei, February 21, 1960; (Not admitted in Taiwan). *Education:* Physics, Tam Kang University (B.S., 1988). Not admitted to Taiwan Patent Office, 1988. Experience: Mechanical Engineer; Hon Hai Precision Industry Co., Ltd. *LANGUAGES:* Chinese (Mandarin and Taiwanese), English, Japanese, German and French. *PRACTICE AREAS:* Mechanics; Electrical Engineering; Physics; Patent Protection.

RAY-RU SHYU, born 1961; (Not admitted in Taiwan). *Education:* National Taiwan Institute of Technology (B.S.M.E.); University of Huston, U.S.A. (M.S.M.E.). Not admitted to Taiwan Patent Office, 1988. *LANGUAGES:* Chinese and English. *PRACTICE AREAS:* Mechanical Engineering; Automatic Control Engineering.

HER-EA CHICH, born Taipei, November 18, 1960; (Not admitted in Taiwan). *Education:* Electronical Engineering, Taipei Institute of Technology. Not admitted to Taiwan Patent Office, 1988. *LANGUAGES:* Chinese and English. *PRACTICE AREAS:* Electrical Engineering; Patent Protection.

CHYI-CHYI SHIAU, born December 12, 1955; (Not admitted in Taiwan). *Education:* National Tsing-Hua University (BS; MS); Temple University (Ph.D.). Not admitted to Taiwan Patent Office. Analytical Chemist, Union Industry Institute of Industry Technology Research Institute. *LANGUAGES:* Chinese and English. *PRACTICE AREAS:* Physical Chemistry.

CHANG CHI-CHONG, born January 2, 1965; (Not admitted in Taiwan). *Education:* Tatung Institute of Technology (B.S.; M.S. Chemical Engineering). Not Admitted to Taiwan Patent Office. Experience: R & D of Lee Dai Chemical Ltd. *LANGUAGES:* English and Japanese. *PRACTICE AREAS:* Polymer Science.

(This Listing Continued)

TSENG KUO-KAI, born September 16, 1968; (Not admitted in Taiwan). *Education:* National Tsing-Hua University (B.S.; Power Mechanical Engineering). Not Admitted to Taiwan Patent Office. *LANGUAGES:* Chinese and English. *PRACTICE AREAS:* Mechanical Engineering.

LIN PO-YANG, born April 1, 1967; (Not admitted in Taiwan). *Education:* National Chiao-Tung University (B.S., Communication Engineering). Not Admitted to Taiwan Patent Office. *LANGUAGES:* Chinese and English. *PRACTICE AREAS:* Communication Engineering.

TRANSPAC INTERNATIONAL LAW OFFICES
FLOOR 11-2, NO. 5, LANE 116
AI-KWO E. ROAD
TAIPEI, TAIWAN
Telephone: 886-2-321-3207
Fax: 886-2-351-4371; 886-2-627-9533

General Business Law, Company Law, Joint Venture Formation, Technology Transfer or Technical Cooperation, Industrial Cooperation Program/-Offset, Export and Import Laws and Regulations, Dumping and Countervailing Duty, Franchising, International and Chinese Contract Formation and Administration, Intellectual Property Regulation, Government Procurement Law, Negotiation, Litigation and Arbitration.

FIRM PROFILE: TRANSPAC International Law Offices, formerly the Min-Fu Law Office, a well established with more than 12 years commercial trade experience when it incorporated an international spirit into its practice philosophy in 1992. The firm's headquarters is located in Taipei, Taiwan, ROC with a branch office in Taichung, Taiwan, ROC. Currently, TRANSPAC has established associations with several law firms in the U.S., Japan, Korea, Mainland China, Italy, Belgium and Switzerland. TRANSPAC also directly services companies and/or Government agencies outside ROC concerning legal matters in Taiwan.

TRANSPAC prides itself in being a full service legal consultancy. Most importantly, Transpac's multilingual (Chinese, Japanese and English) attorneys are uniquely qualified to assist our domestic and international clients in the area of ROC's Government procurement regulations and procedures. In addition, we can assist our clients in financial and marketing matters relating to the above areas.

MEMBERS OF THE FIRM

GRANT N.C. KUANG, born Tsingtao, China, March 1, 1947; admitted, 1992, Taipei. *Education:* Cornell University (LL.M., International Business Transactions, 1985); U.S. Army Judge Advocates General School (Government Contract-Procurement Law, 1978). Former Deputy Director and General Counsel, Defense Procurement Division, Coordination Counsel for North American Affairs, U.S.A. (DPD/CCNAA); General Counsel and International Contract Negotiator for Chun Shan Institute of Science and Technology (CSIST), Aero Industries Development Center (AIDC) and Indigenous Defense Fighter (IDF) Program. Lecturer: China External Trade Development Council (CETRA); Importers and Exporters Association of Taipei. *Member:* Taipei, Taoyuan, Taichung and Inter-Pacific Bar Associations. *LANGUAGES:* Chinese and English. *PRACTICE AREAS:* International Business Transactions.

TANG JAW-HAU, born Kao-Yao, Canton Province, China, October 12, 1937; admitted, 1982, Taipei. Former Chief Trial Judge, Court of Review for CAF. *Member:* Taipei Bar Association; World Cantonese Bar Association. *LANGUAGES:* Chinese and Cantonese. *PRACTICE AREAS:* Criminal Litigation.

SHEN LING, born Chia-shan, Cheliang Province, China, February 29, 1937; admitted, 1982, Taipei. Former Trial Judge, Court of Review for CN. *Member:* Taipei and Taichung Bar Associations. *LANGUAGES:* Chinese and English. *PRACTICE AREAS:* Civil; Maritime; Litigation.

CHIANG TSUNG HU, born Li-ling, Hu-Nan Province, China, April 9, 1937; admitted, 1994, Taipei. Chief Editor, Legal Voice Journal. Chief Lecturer, "The Legal World" for Fu Shing Radio Station. Retired Major General, Judge Advocates General Corps, ROC Armed Forces. Member, Taiwan Environmental Protection Association. *Member:* Taipei Bar Association. *LANGUAGES:* Chinese and English. *PRACTICE AREAS:* Environmental Law; Government Procurement Law.

ERIC S.R. LAY, born Nan-tou, Taiwan, November 2, 1954. *Education:* National Chen-Kung University (B.S., 1977); Cornell University (M.E., 1985). Patent Attorney, Patent Office, National Bureau of Standards,

(This Listing Continued)

MOEA. Licensed Patent Engineer, Chinese Society of Inventions, 1993. Licensed Professional Engineer, Industrial Department, MOEA. Former Deputy Director, Environmental Protection Bureau, Nan-tou County. Member, Taiwan Environmental Engineering Association. *LANGUAGES:* Chinese, Taiwanese, Japanese and English. *PRACTICE AREAS:* Intellectual Property Protection.

KUEI CHIH AN, born Chiang-Si Province, China, February 16, 1948; (Not admitted in Taiwan). *Education:* National Cheng-Chih University (LL.B., Public Finance, 1971). Financial and Tax Specialist. Former Section Leader of Profit-Seeking Enterprises Income Tax, Department of Taxation, Ministry of Finance. Staff Officer, Division of Tax Auditing & Investigation, Department of Finance. *LANGUAGES:* Chinese and English. *PRACTICE AREAS:* Tax Planning.

OF COUNSEL

LIN HUAN, born Jau-ling, Canton Province, China, February 28, 1950; admitted, 1993, New York (Not admitted in Taiwan). *Education:* Chung-Shin University, Taipei (LL.B., 1981); Su-Chou University, Taipei (LL.M., 1985); University of Virginia (LL.M., 1990); New York University (LL.M., 1991); Widener University, Delaware Law School (J.D., 1994). Former Legal Counsel to DPD/CCNAA, U.S.A., 1987-1989. Assistant Legal Counsel, General Counsel Office, MND/ROC, 1986-1987. *LANGUAGES:* Chinese, Cantonese, Taiwanese and English. *PRACTICE AREAS:* Corporate Law; Tax Law; Anti-Trust.

TSAR & TSAI LAW FIRM

Established in 1965

9TH FLOOR, OVERSEAS TRUST BUILDING

249 TUN HWA S. ROAD, SEC. 1

TAIPEI 106, TAIWAN

Telephone: 7814111; 7729555

FAX: 7213834 or 7315581

General Practice. Foreign Investment, Trade and Arbitration, Litigation, Contract, Corporation, Taxation, Banking, Insurance, Securities, Trademark, Patent and Copyright Law.

FIRM PROFILE: Founded in 1965, the firm has over 45 qualified attorneys and consultants and is one of the largest law firms in Taiwan employing over 120 persons. The firm plays a leading role in such areas of practice as foreign investment, merger and acquisition, insurance, securities, banking, taxation, labor, intellectual property and international dispute resolution. Major clients are multinational corporations and institutions from North America, Japan, European Community, Taiwan and Asia Pacific.

MEMBERS OF FIRM

RUCHIN TSAR (1903-1993).

PAUL C. TSAI, born Shanghai, China, September 26, 1931; admitted, 1965, Taiwan. *Education:* National Taiwan University Law School (LL.B., 1952); Yale Law School (LL.M., 1954; J.S.D., 1957). Responsible for the draft of the Statute for Encouragement of Investment, 1960 as amended and the Chattel Secured Transactions Act of 1965, The Republic of China. Associate Professor of Law, Soochow University Law School, 1957-1959; 1961-1963. Research Professor, China Cultural Institute, 1964. General Counsel, Foreign Exchange & Trade Commission (cabinet organ) and Secretary of its Administrative Appeal Committee, 1958-1963. General Counsel, Council for United States Aid (cabinet organ) and Director of its Law Revision Planning Group, 1960-1963. Counsellor, Council for International Economic Cooperation and Development (cabinet organ), 1963-1965, Republic of China. Awarded Special prize by the President of the Nation for outstanding performance in government service for the year, 1963. Member, Panels of Arbitrators, International Center for Settlement of Investment Disputes under the International Bank for Reconstruction and Development, 1966-1980. *LANGUAGES:* Chinese and English. *PRACTICE AREAS:* Corporate; Strategic Alliance.

C. Y. HUANG, born Changhua, Taiwan, Republic of China, 1948; admitted, 1977, New York; 1980, Taipei. *Education:* National Taiwan University School of Law (LL.B., 1970; LL.M., 1973); University of Michigan Law School (M.C.L., 1974); Harvard Law School (S.J.D., 1976). Author: "Multinationals in the Republic of China—Laws and Policies," Asia and the World Forum, 1978; "Legal Aspects of IFC's Investment in the Republic of China," 11 The Journal of International Law and Economics 465 (The George Washington University, 1977); "U.S. Trade Law—How to Defend ROC Against U.S. Trademark Protectionism," published by the Author,

(This Listing Continued)

January 1981; "International Commercial Law," published by the Author, July 1984. Professor of Law, National Chung Hsing University, 1977-1986. Member, Ad Hoc Committee of the Board of Foreign Trade, Advisor of Ministry of Economic Affairs, responsible for the drafting of the Proposed Trade Act, May, 1982-1986. Advisor to Ministry of Communications. Member, Trade Subcommittee of the Economic Reform Committee (cabinet organ), May-November, 1985. Advisor to the Committee on Improvement of Laws and Regulations Governing Economic and Social Affairs, Council for Economic Planning and Development (Cabinet organ), 1986—. Associated, Hale and Door, Boston, Massachusetts, U.S.A., 1974-1975. *Member:* Taipei, New York State (U.S.A.) and American Bar Associations; American Society of International Law. *LANGUAGES:* Chinese and English. *PRACTICE AREAS:* Corporate; Insurance; Financial Service.

JENNIFER LIN, born Taipei, Taiwan, China, October 6, 1956; admitted, 1980, Taipei and Taiwan. *Education:* National Taiwan University Law School (LL.B., 1979); Harvard Law School (LL.M., 1982). Publications: Taiwan's Copyright Law: New Concepts, Remaining Questions, A Review of the New Cable TV Law, The Protection of Computer Software in Taiwan. *Member:* Taipei and Taiwan Bar Associations; The Chinese Society of Comparative Law; Asia Patent Attorneys Association (International Councillor); International Trademark Association. *LANGUAGES:* Chinese and English. *PRACTICE AREAS:* Intellectual Property; Corporate; Litigation.

CHUNG-TEH LEE, born Taiwan, China, August 11, 1955; admitted, 1986, Taiwan. *Education:* National Taiwan University Law School (LL.B., 1977); University of California Berkeley Law School, Boalt Hall (LL.M., 1981; J.S.D., 1986). Member of Phi Tau Phi Scholastic Honor Society, 1977—. Author: "A Reexamination of the Nature of the Private International Law - The Concept of Universal Law," Law Monthly, 1983. "Legal Problems of Industrial Targeting and Its Impact on International Economic Relations," 1986. Associate Professor of Law, Fu-Jen Catholic University, 1986—. Judge, District Court of Yulin, 1982-1983. District Court of Changhwa, 1983-1985. *LANGUAGES:* Chinese and English. *PRACTICE AREAS:* Corporate; Litigation.

LILLIAN L.Y. CHU, born Tainan, Taiwan, China, March 19, 1959; admitted, 1981, Taiwan. *Education:* National Chengchi University Law Department (LL.B., 1981); National Taiwan University Graduate School of Law (LL.M., 1984). *LANGUAGES:* Chinese and English. *PRACTICE AREAS:* Corporate; Admiralty; Litigation.

DANIEL S.L. SHEN, born Taipei, Taiwan, China, October 27, 1955; admitted, 1988, Taiwan. *Education:* Fu-Jen Catholic University School of Law (LL.B., 1977); New York University School of Law (LL.M., 1982). Experience: Judge, District Court of Tainan, 1983-1985, District Court of Taoyuan, 1985-1987, The Ban-Chiao Branch of the District of Taipei, 1987-1988. *LANGUAGES:* Chinese and English. *PRACTICE AREAS:* Litigation; Intellectual Property.

JASON T. SU, born Taipei, Taiwan, China, July 29, 1931; (Not admitted in Taiwan). *Education:* Soochow University Law School (LL.B., 1960); Southern Methodist University Law School (M.C.L., 1968); National Chengchi University Graduate School of Public Administration (M.P.A., 1970). Experience: Research Assistant, Law Revision Planning Group, Council for United States Aid, (cabinet organ), 1961-1962; Specialist, Senior Specialist in charge of legal affairs, Council for International Economic Cooperation and Development, (cabinet organ), 1963-1973. Advisor, Office of International Financing, Ministry of Finance, 1973-1974. *LANGUAGES:* Chinese, English and Japanese. *PRACTICE AREAS:* Corporate.

JIM J.M. HWANG, born Taiwan, China, March 15, 1952; admitted, 1978, Pennsylvania (Not admitted in Taiwan). *Education:* Soochow University Law School (LL.B., 1975); George Washington University Law School (M.C.L., American Practice, 1977). *Member:* Pennsylvania Bar Association; American Bar Association (Member, Section on Corporation, Banking and Business Law and Section on International Law and Practice); International Bar Association (Member, Section on Business Law). *LANGUAGES:* Chinese and English. *PRACTICE AREAS:* Corporate; Taxation.

CHARLES V. WU, born Shanghai, China, January 11, 1948; (Not admitted in Taiwan). *Education:* Soochow University Law School (LL.B., 1971); University of Miami Law School (M.C.L., 1974). Experience: Banking and Real Estate. *LANGUAGES:* Chinese and English. *PRACTICE AREAS:* Corporate; Foreign Investment; Contracts.

RICHARD Y.C. CHUANG, born Taipei, Taiwan, China, December 1, 1948; admitted, 1983, California (Not admitted in Taiwan). *Education:* National Taiwan University School of Law (LL.B., 1971); University of Cali-

(This Listing Continued)

TSAR & TSAI LAW FIRM, Taipei—Continued

fornia at Berkeley, Boalt Hall School of Law (LL.M., 1980; J.S.D., 1986). Recipient Award: Fellowship, Social and Culture Center for Asian Pacific Region, Seoul, Korea, 1978. Author: "A Comparative Study on Policies and Regulations Governing the Operation of Foreign Banks in the Republic of China (Taiwan) and the Republic of Korea"; "Legal Aspects of Loan Agreements between US Lenders and ROC Borrowers in Taiwan after US Derecognition of ROC Government"; "A Study on Legal Problems Arising from the Relationship of Enterprise Groups in Taiwan". Associated Professor of Law, Soochow University Law School, 1986—. Financial Reporter, Economic Daily News and China Economic News, 1974-1979. San Francisco Correspondent, Economic Daily News, 1979-1983. *Member:* State Bar of California. Member, Committee for Screening Applications for Securities Listing, Taiwan Stock Exchange (1990-1992); Member, Committee for Screening Applications for Securities Traded on the Over-the-Counter Market, Taipei Securities Dealers Association (1990-1993). Adviser, Taipei Securities Dealers Association (1992-1993). *LANGUAGES:* Chinese, English and Japanese. *PRACTICE AREAS:* Corporate; Securities.

WELLINGTON Y. LIU, born Kaohsiung, Taiwan, China, September 27, 1950; admitted, 1982, Texas; 1977, Texas CPA; 1990, Taiwan, CPA. *Education:* National Taiwan University (B.B.A., 1973); University of Texas (M.B.A., 1977); University of Houston (J.D., 1982). *Member:* State Bar of Texas; American Bar Association; Taipei CPA Association; Texas CPA Society. *LANGUAGES:* Chinese and English. *PRACTICE AREAS:* Corporate; Tax.

MICHAEL S. HALLOCK, born Lake Charles, Louisiana, August 4, 1959; admitted, 1984, New Jersey (Not admitted in Taiwan). *Education:* Manhattanville College (B.A., 1981); George Washington University (J.D., with honors, 1984). Author: "Legal Aspects of Franchising in Taiwan"; "New Business Opportunities and Challenges in Taiwan After the Lifting of Foreign Exchange Controls and Other Liberalization Measures-a Legal Prospecture." *Member:* New Jersey State and American Bar Associations. *LANGUAGES:* English. *PRACTICE AREAS:* Corporate.

STEVEN S.K. CHEN, born Taiwan, China, October 1, 1960; admitted, 1987, Taiwan; joined the firm, 1988. *Education:* National Taiwan University Graduate School of Law (LL.M., 1987). *LANGUAGES:* Chinese, Japanese and English. *PRACTICE AREAS:* Litigation.

PEGGY L. LIN, born Taiwan, China, October 31, 1956; joined the firm, 1982; admitted, 1992, Taiwan. *Education:* National Chunghsing University Law School (LL.B., 1981). Author: "Resolving Major Public Construction Disputes," "Major Government Constructions Disputes: Assessment and Proposal." *Member:* Taipei and Taiwan Bar Associations. *LANGUAGES:* Chinese and English. *PRACTICE AREAS:* Corporate; Construction; Securities; Arbitration.

AMY LIN, born Taipei, Taiwan, China, July 11, 1946; associated with the firm, 1968; (Not admitted in Taiwan). *Education:* National Taiwan University Law School (LL.B., 1968). *LANGUAGES:* Chinese and English. *PRACTICE AREAS:* Corporate; Commercial Registrations.

SHAWN S.H. TENG, born Taiwan, China, December 22, 1958; admitted, 1991, California. *Education:* National Chunghsing University School of Law (LL.B., 1980); The George Washington University Law School (M.C.L., 1986). *Member:* California State Bar Association; American Bar Association; Los Angeles County Bar Association; American Immigration Lawyer Association. *LANGUAGES:* Chinese and English. *PRACTICE AREAS:* Corporate; Insurance.

BOB PAN, born Taiwan, China; September 28, 1955; associated with the firm, 1983; (Not admitted in Taiwan). *Education:* National Chunghsing University School of Law (LL.B., 1979). *LANGUAGES:* Chinese and English. *PRACTICE AREAS:* Intellectual Property.

RUBY HUANG, born Taipei, Taiwan, China, December 5, 1955; (Not admitted in Taiwan). *Education:* Fu-Jen Catholic University School of Law (LL.B., 1980). *LANGUAGES:* Chinese and English. *PRACTICE AREAS:* Intellectual Property.

FRANK S. F. CHEN, born Taiwan, China, April 24, 1954; joined the firm, 1991; (Not admitted in Taiwan). *Education:* National Chunghsing University School of Law (LL.B., 1976). Experience: Wenping & Co., 1980-1990. *LANGUAGES:* Chinese and English. *PRACTICE AREAS:* Intellectual Property.

NICOLE Y.L. LEE, born Taiwan, China, September 21, 1967; admitted, 1991, Taiwan. *Education:* National Taiwan University Law School (LL.B.,

(This Listing Continued)

1990). associated with the firm, 1991. *LANGUAGES:* Chinese and English. *PRACTICE AREAS:* Litigation.

PAULINE WANG, born Tainan, Taiwan, China, August 17, 1967; admitted, 1990, Taiwan. *Education:* National Taiwan University, College of Law (LL.B., 1989); Columbia University School of Law (LL.M., 1993). *LANGUAGES:* Chinese and English. *PRACTICE AREAS:* Corporate; Litigation.

JACKIE S.J. LIN, born Taiwan, China, January 6, 1965; admitted, 1991, New York; 1994, Taiwan. *Education:* The American University, Washington College of Law, International Legal Studies (LL.M., 1991); National Cheng-Chi University, School of Law (LL.B., 1987). *LANGUAGES:* Chinese and English. *PRACTICE AREAS:* Corporate; Securities.

MARGARET HUANG, born Taiwan, China, November 2, 1967; admitted, 1992, Taiwan. *Education:* National Taiwan University Law School (LL.B., 1990). Associated with the firm, 1992. *LANGUAGES:* Chinese and English. *PRACTICE AREAS:* Litigation; Corporate.

RITA CHEN, born Taichung, Taiwan, China, January 22, 1966; admitted, 1991, Taiwan. *Education:* National Taiwan University Law School (LL.B., 1989); George Washington University (LL.M., 1994). *LANGUAGES:* Chinese and English. *PRACTICE AREAS:* Intellectual Property.

JAMES S.J. CHENG, born Taiwan, China, May 27, 1965; admitted, 1992, Taiwan. *Education:* National Chunghsing University Law School (LL.B., 1987). Associated with the firm, 1992. *LANGUAGES:* Chinese and English. *PRACTICE AREAS:* Litigation; Corporate.

VIVIAN F.W. CHUANG, born Taiwan, China, September 17, 1966; admitted, 1992, Taiwan. *Education:* National Taiwan University Law School (LL.B., 1990). Experience: Central Weather Bureau of the Ministry of Transportation and Communications, 1992-1993; Associated with the firm, 1993. *LANGUAGES:* Chinese and English. *PRACTICE AREAS:* Litigation; Corporate.

JOYCE I-WEN HO, born Taichung, Taiwan, May 10, 1969; admitted, 1993, Taiwan. *Education:* National Taiwan University Law School (LL.B., 1991; LL.M., 1994). Publication: A Study on Earmarked Taxes - The New Revenue of Modern Welfare State. *LANGUAGES:* Chinese and English. *PRACTICE AREAS:* Corporate; Litigation.

DAVID K.W. CHUANG, born Singapore, February 20, 1970; admitted, 1992, Taiwan. *Education:* National Taiwan University Law School (LL.B., 1992). associated with the firm, 1994. *LANGUAGES:* Chinese and English. *PRACTICE AREAS:* Litigation; Corporate.

WINNIE CHERN, born April 9, 1967; admitted, 1994, Taiwan. *Education:* Southern Methodist University School of Law (LL.M., 1991); National Taiwan University Law School (LL.B., 1989). Experience: Banking Joint Credit Center, Chinese Bank, and Bank of Taiwan. *LANGUAGES:* Chinese and English. *PRACTICE AREAS:* Corporate; Litigation.

LUCIA C.H. YIOU, born October 17, 1968; admitted, 1994, Taiwan. *Education:* National Taiwan University Law School (LL.B., 1991). Experience: Department of Patents of National Bureau of Standards, Ministry of Economic Affairs, 1992-1994. *LANGUAGES:* Chinese and English. *PRACTICE AREAS:* Intellectual Property; Litigation.

AMY CHIN, born Taipei, Taiwan, November 25, 1964; admitted, 1992, New York. *Education:* National Cheng-chi University (LL.B., 1987); Soochow University School of Law (LL.M., 1990); Duke University School of Law (LL.M., 1991). Publication: "Legal Issues Concerning Standardized Consumer Credit Contracts in Taiwan." *Member:* American Bar Association; New York State Bar Association; Asian American Bar Association in the State of New York. *LANGUAGES:* Chinese and English. *PRACTICE AREAS:* Securities; Corporate.

JAY YOU, born Taiwan, China, December 6, 1958, associated with firm, 1989; (Not admitted in Taiwan). *Education:* Fu-Jen Catholic University Law School (LL.B., 1982). Experience: Department of Trademarks of National Bureau of Standards, Ministry of Economic Affairs, 1985-1988. *LANGUAGES:* Chinese and English. *PRACTICE AREAS:* Intellectual Property.

JOANNE CHEN, born Kaohsiung, Taiwan, China, November 6, 1960, associated with firm, 1989; (Not admitted in Taiwan). *Education:* National Cheng-Chi University Law Department (LL.B., 1983). Experience: Department of Trademarks of National Bureau of Standards, Ministry of Economic Affairs, 1987-1989. *LANGUAGES:* Chinese and English. *PRACTICE AREAS:* Intellectual Property.

(This Listing Continued)

TAMMY WU, born Taiwan, China, May 28, 1967; (Not admitted in Taiwan). *Education:* Soochow University Law School (LL.B., 1990). Associated with the firm, 1992. *LANGUAGES:* Chinese and English. *PRACTICE AREAS:* Commercial Registration.

MONICA M. LEE, born Taipei, Taiwan, China, November 19, 1963; joined the firm, 1993; (Not admitted in Taiwan). *Education:* Fu-Jen Catholic University School of Law (LL.B., 1986). *LANGUAGES:* Chinese and English. *PRACTICE AREAS:* Commercial Registration.

LUCY CHUANG, born August 6, 1961. *Education:* National Taiwan University (Majored in Agricultural Chemistry, B.S., 1983). associated with the firm, 1983. *LANGUAGES:* Chinese and English. *PRACTICE AREAS:* Patents; Biotechnology; Chemicals and Chemistry; Agricultural Law.

RAYMOND WANG, born March 15, 1967. *Education:* National Chiao Tung University (Majored in Industrial Engineering, B.S., 1985-1988); National Chiao Tung University Graduate School of Engineering (M.S., 1988-1990). associated with the firm, 1992. Qualified as professional engineer, 1993. Patent Attorney, Taiwan. Software Engineer, San-Hwai Computer Co., 1988-1990. Author: "The real-time Inference Engine in Flight Control System," 1992. [ARMY Headquarters, Ordnance Service (1990-1992)]. *LANGUAGES:* Chinese and English. *PRACTICE AREAS:* Patents; Computers and Software; Technology and Science; Communications and Media.

EVA CHIU, born June 11, 1961. *Education:* National Taiwan University (Majored in Agricultural Chemistry, B.S., 1984). associated with the firm, 1984. *LANGUAGES:* Chinese and English. *PRACTICE AREAS:* Patents; Biotechnology; Chemicals and Chemistry; Agriculture Law.

TIM LEE, born January 26, 1958. *Education:* National Taiwan Normal University (B.E., Industrial Education, 1980). associated with the firm, 1990. Taipei Dah Cherng High School, Electronic Teacher, 1986. Experience: South Rich Trade Company, Engineering Division, Computer Training & Service Center, 1990. *LANGUAGES:* Chinese and English. *PRACTICE AREAS:* Patents; Communications and Media; Technology and Science.

ARTHUR LAI, born March 16, 1960. *Education:* Chiao Tung University (Majored in Mechanical Engineering, B.S., 1983). Experience: Taiwan International Patent Law Offices, 1989-1992. *LANGUAGES:* Chinese and English. *PRACTICE AREAS:* Patents; Mechanical Engineering.

CHARLES HSU, born June 1, 1964. *Education:* National Chunghsing University (Majored in Chemistry, B.S., 1986). associated with the firm, 1992. Experience: Saint Island P&T Office, 1988-1989; Taiwan International Patent Law Offices, 1989-1992. *LANGUAGES:* Chinese and English. *PRACTICE AREAS:* Patents; Chemicals and Chemistry.

REMI HUANG, born December 9, 1968. *Education:* National Taiwan University (Majored in Chemical Engineering, B.S., 1991). associated with the firm, 1992. *LANGUAGES:* Chinese and English. *PRACTICE AREAS:* Patents; Chemical and Chemistry; Biotechnology.

WANG & WANG

146 SUNG CHIANG ROAD
FIFTH FLOOR
TAIPEI, TAIWAN
Telephone: (02) 541-0424
Fax: (02) 543-4803

San Francisco, California Office: Suite 800, 180 Montgomery Street. Telephone: 415-788-8008. Fax: 415-986-2241.

General Practice specializing in Patent, Trademark and Copyright, Litigation, Corporate, Foreign Investment and Commercial Law.

PARTNER

PROFESSOR KENNETH WANG, born China, 1914; admitted, 1938, China; 1958, New York; 1987, Taiwan; registered to practice before R.O.C. Patent and Trademark Office. *Education:* Soochow University Law School (LL.B., 1938); Harvard University (LL.M., 1947); St. John's University (LL.B., 1957; LL.D., 1986). Awarded President's Medal, 1984; Awarded Medal of Honor, St. Johns University, 1992. Professor of Law, Aurora University, 1941-1945, Soochow University. 1943-1944 and 1948-1950, Kwang-Hwa University, 1945-1947 and St. John's University, School of Law, 1952-1984. Visiting Professor of Law, University of Michigan Law School, 1962-1963. Private Practice (Ping Kung Law Offices), 1938-1945. Judge, Court of Appeals, Shanghai, China, 1945-1947. President, Aurora College, 1949-1951. Participant in the White House Conference on International Cooperation and Member of its Citizens' Committee on Develop-

(This Listing Continued)

ment of International Law, 1964. Member, Panel of Arbitrators, American Arbitration Association, 1984—. *Member:* American Society of International Law; Association of American Law Schools. Panel of Arbitrators, American Arbitration Association. *LANGUAGES:* English, Chinese and French.

FRANCIS S. L. WANG, born Shanghai, China, January 25, 1947; admitted, 1973, New York; 1975, U.S. District Court, Southern District of New York; 1976, California and U.S. District Court, Northern District of California; 1981, U.S. Tax Court; 1984, U.S. District Court, Central District of California; 1985, U.S. Court of Appeals, Ninth Circuit; 1992, U.S. Supreme Court. *Education:* Queens College (B.A., 1968); Cornell Law School (J.D., 1972). Co-Author: "Joint Ventures in the Republic of China," 1971; "Tax Liability of Foreign Bank Branches," 1982; "Impact of Company Law Revisions on Foreign Investment," 1980; "Tax Consideration of Technology Licensing," 1981; "Taiwan's Struggle with Counterfeiting," East Asian Executive Report, 1985; "Company Law of the Republic of China," Trade and Investment in Taiwan: The Legal and Economic Environment in the Republic of China, 1985; "The Role of Law in Taiwan's Evolving Economic and Social Agenda," Laws of International Trade, 1988. "Taiwan Copyright Protection For Foreign Works", 1P Asia, 1991; "Intellectual Property Developments in Taiwan and China," The Journal of Proprietary Rights, 1991; "Taiwan's New Copyright Law," ABA's International Lawyer (with Laura Young); "Taming the Tigers," National Law Journal. Lecturer: Chinese Society of Comparative Law Conference, ABA-Law and Development Seminar, 1980; Trade and Investment Law, U.S. Department of Commerce, 1980; International Tax, American Management Association, 1981; Banking Law, San Francisco Bankers Association, 1980; Intellectual Property in ROC, International Anticounterfeiting Coalition, 1983-1984; International Anticounterfeiting Coalition-Taiwan Task Force, 1985; Intellectual Property Infringement in the Developing World, United States Trademark Association, 1985; Syndicated Loans, 1978 and Banking, 1979, U.S.A.-ROC Economic Council; Technology Licensing, 1983 and Intellectual Property Protection, 1984, Institute for International Research and the United States Trademark Association; Trading with the Four Tigers, American Bar Association and the Commonwealth Club of California, Small Business Administration, 1988. Trading with Taiwan, U.S. Department of Commerce, 1988. Lecturer, "The Adequacy of Protection of Intellectual Property in Taiwan; and Civil Litigation in Taiwan as viewed from an American Lawyer's Perspective," International Business Law Conference, 1989; "Economic Development and Intellectual Property Protection in Taiwan," Venezuelan-American Chamber of Commerce, 1989; "Copyrights in the Pacific Rim: An International Perspective," Western Oregon State College, 1990. Panel Moderator, Intellectual Property Protection in Taiwan, International Anticounterfeiting Coalition, 1991; Panelist, Crosscultture Communication U.S. and Asia, U.S. Trademark Law Throughout The World," A Forum on Trademark Basics, U.S. Trademark Association, 1991; Business Responses to Global Change, Committee for Economic Development, CED Bay Area Forum on International Trade and Investment, 1991; Reporter, Trademarks in 2017; Enforcement/Dispute Resolution, World Trademark Symposium, U.S. Trademark Association, 1992; "The Role of I.P. in Economic Development," Venezuelan Chamber of Commerce, 1993; "Trade Policy's Role in Foreign Policy," International Anti-Counterfeiting Coalition, 1993. Testified before U.S. Senate International Trade Sub-committee, 1984 and International Trade Commission, 1983. Testified before United States Trade Representatives Office, 1985. Assisted Congressional Investigations conducted by U.S. House of Representatives Energy and Commerce Committee, 1983. Delegate and Counsel, AIT-CCNAA Consultation on Intellectual Property Protection, 1983-1984. *Member:* Bar Association of San Francisco; State Bar of California (Member, Executive Committee, Intellectual Property Section); New York State and American (Member, Sections on: International Law; Corporation, Banking and Business Law; Economics of Law Practice; Patent, Trademark and Copyright Law; Chair, PRC-ROC Copyright Sub-Section) Bar Associations; International Anticounterfeiting Coalition (Member, Board of Directors, 1990—); United States Trademark Association (Member: Board of Directors, 1992—; Board of Directors, Alliance for Promotion of Software Innovation, 1993) ; American Arbitration Association (Member, National Panel of Arbitrators). *LANGUAGES:* English and Chinese. *REPORTED CASES:* Banco do Brasil v. Latian, Inc.; New York Chinese TV Programs, Inc. vs. U.E. Enterprises Inc. et al, and Computer Associates vs. Altai. *PRACTICE AREAS:* Banking; Finance; Litigation; Intellectual Property.

(This Listing Continued)

WANG & WANG, Taipei—Continued

ASSOCIATES

LAURA W. YOUNG, born San Francisco, California, 1962; admitted, 1988, California and U.S. District Court, Northern District of California. *Education:* University of California at Berkeley (A.B., cum laude, 1984); Boalt Hall School of Law, University of California (J.D., 1987). Phi Alpha Theta. Co-Author, with Francis S.L. Wang: "Taiwan's New Copyright Law," ABA's International Lawyer. Author, "Taiwan's New Patent Law," East Asian Executive Reports, 1994. Author and Speaker, "Review of Current Developments in Taiwan," International Law and Technology Conference, State Bar of California, 1992. Speaker, "Enforcing Intellectual Property Rights in Taiwan, "International Anticounterfeiting Coalition, 1993; "Tawian Intellectual Property Protection," United States Trademark Association's Pacific Forum, 1992. Lecturer: "Protection of Computer Software in Taiwan," Intellectual Property Management Seminar, Beijing, 1992; Bar Association of San Francisco Seminar on China, Taiwan and Hong Kong, 1990; "Protecting American Electronics in Taiwan," American Electronics Association, 1990. *Member:* Bar Association of San Francisco; State Bar of California; Asian-American Bar Association; Taipei-American Chamber of Commerce; Commonwealth Club; United States Trademark Association; University Club of Taipei. (Resident). *LANGUAGES:* English, Chinese and French.

ARTHUR HSIEH, born Taipei City, Taiwan, R.O.C., January 29, 1962; admitted, 1988, Taiwan; registered to practice before R.O.C. Patent and Trademark Office. *Education:* National Chunghsing University (LL.B., 1984). *Member:* Taipei Bar Association. *LANGUAGES:* English and Chinese.

WEI YU-YING, born Tainan, Taiwan, October 12, 1955; admitted, 1991, Taiwan; registered to practice before R.O.C. Patent and Trademark Office. *Education:* National Chunghsing University (LL.B., 1978); George Washington University(LL.M., 1983). *Member:* Taipei Bar Association. *LANGUAGES:* Chinese, Taiwanese and English.

DELIA D. H. TANG, born Taipei City, R.O.C., October 28, 1966; admitted, 1993, Taiwan; registered to practice before R.O.C. Patent and Trademark Office. *Education:* National Chang Chi University (LL.B., 1989). *Member:* Taipei Bar Association. *LANGUAGES:* English and Chinese.

REPRESENTATIVE CLIENTS: American Film Marketing Assn.; Association of American Publishers; American Amusement Manufacturers Association; American Brands; Banco del Estado de Sao Paulo; Banco do Brasil; Business Software Association; Computer Associates International, Inc.; Commodore Computers; Cotia Exportacao & Importacao S.A.; Encyclopedia Britannica; Microsoft Corp.; Samsonite Corp.; Sears, Roebuck and Co.; Simon & Schuster; United Feature Syndicate; Universal, MCA.

WESTON PAN PACIFIC LAW OFFICES

(formerly, Bennett Jones Verchere/Weston)

SUITE 1466, 144 MIN CHUAN EAST ROAD, SECTION 3
TAIPEI, TAIWAN
Telephone: 886-2-719-5008
Fax: 886-2-717-6088

Correspondent Offices: Beijing, Shanghai, Hanoi, Ho Chi Minh City, Hong Kong, Kuala Lumpur, Singapore, Calgary, Toronto, Seattle.

Pan Pacific Business Development, including International Business, Corporate Structuring, Commercial Law and Employment Law, Dispute Resolution and Canadian and U.S. Immigration.

MARIE F. CHAN, born Port-Louis, Mauritius, August 3, 1964; admitted, 1993, Ontario (Not admitted in Taiwan). *Education:* University of Montreal (B.A., 1987); University of Ottawa (LL.B., 1990; LL.L., 1991). Tax Court of Canada Clerk (1993-1994).

ERIC B. DREWRY, born Ames, Iowa, February 16, 1948; admitted, 1975, Georgia (Not admitted in Taiwan). *Education:* Princeton University (B.A., 1970); Duke University (J.D., 1975). Assistant Professor, Tunghai University, 1989—.

OLIVER HUNG, born Hxinchu, Taiwan, January 10, 1968; admitted, 1992, Taipei. *Education:* National Taiwan University (LL.B., 1990). Legal Affairs Co-Editor, *China News* and *This Month in Taiwan.* .

JOHN D. WESTON, born Vancouver, British Columbia, April 19, 1958; admitted, 1983, New York and British Columbia; 1994, England (Not admitted in Taiwan). *Education:* Harvard University (B.A., 1980);

(This Listing Continued)

Osgoode Hall Law School (LL.B., 1983). Legal Affairs Co-Editor, *China News* and *This Month in Taiwan.* Past President, Canadian Society of Taiwan. Past Chairman, Kaohsiung American School. Committee Chairman, American Chamber Independent Business Committee. Deacon, Calvary International Baptist Church.

SPECIAL IMMIGRATION CONSULTANT

JENNY FENG, born Taipei, Taiwan, December 28, 1955. *Education:* Min Chuan College (1976). Immigrated to Canada as an Entrepreneur in 1989 and returned to Taiwan in 1993 to work in the immigration consulting area.

CORPORATE REGISTRATIONS/WORK PERMITS

SHIRLEY HSIEH, born Keelung, Taiwan, February 9, 1960. *Education:* Feng Chia University (LL.B., 1984).

Mandarin, Taiwanese, Hakka, English, French, German, Dutch, Spanish

WISDOM ATTORNEYS-AT-LAW

23RD FLOOR, NO. 95
ROOSEVELT ROAD, SECTION 2
TAIPEI, TAIWAN
Telephone: 2-366-1929
Facsimile: 2-366-1928

Intellectual Property and International Licensing, Unfair Competition, International Trade, Corporate and Investment, Securities, Litigation.

MEMBERS OF FIRM

LUCIUS J.C. SHEU, born Taiwan, September 2, 1957; admitted, 1991, Republic of China; Patent Attorney. *Education:* National Chunghsing University School of Law (LL.B., cum laude, 1980); Soochow University (LL.M., with highest honors, 1982); Georgetown University (1987). Research Fellow, Patent Office, Ministry of Economic Affairs, 1985-1986. Associate Research Fellow, Council for Economic Planning and Development, Executive Yuan, 1986-1990. Delegate, Sino-U.S. Intellectual Property Consultative Talks, 1987-1988. Associate Director, Research Project on Copyright Law, Copyright Committee, Ministry of the Interior, 1989. Director, Research Project on Trade Secret Law, Science and Technology Advisory Group, Executive Yuan, 1990. Legal Consultant, Taipei Computer Association, 1992—. Author: "Protection of Corporate Inventions under American Laws-Patent or Trade Secret?," 1990; "The Draft Agreement for the Protection of Copyright between the American Institute in Taiwan and the Coordination Council for North American Affairs: A Critical Appraisal," 1988; "The Impact of New Copyright Law on Computer Enterprises," 1992; "The Legal Status of Trade Secret and Its Protection," 1988; "Legislative Trend and Policy Issues on Trade Secrets," 1989; "Prospects of Trade Secret Legislation of Canada," 1990; "The Legal Protection on Trade Secrets-A Review on the Laws and Practices of the U.S.A., Canada, West Germany, Japan and R.O.C.," 1991; "Trade Secrets Protection in Taiwan," 1991; "The Legal Problem of Unsolicited Disclosures," 1992; "The Protection of Trade Secret in Asia," 1992; "The Impact of Fair Trade Law on Enterprises," 1992; "Vertical Price Fixing (Resale Price Maintenance)," 1992; "False, Untrue or Misleading Advertising," 1992; "Comparative Advertising and Disparagement," 1992; "Precautions and Compulsory Execution Regarding Tax Collection in Taiwan," 1986; "Environmental Protection and Economic Development," 1992. Co-Author: "An Elaboration of Compulsory Patent Licensing Systems," 1989; "Model Contract on Copyright," 1992; "The Legal Protection of Trade Secret," 1991; "Sixty Q & A on Trade Secret," 1992. Lecturer: International Trade Law, Chinese Culture University, 1989-1991; Patent, Trademark and International Trade Law, Tunghai University, 1990-1991; Copyright Law, Taiwan Police College, 1990—; Trade Secret Law, Professional Training Center, Ministry of Economic Affairs, 1991; Contract Law and Practice, Advanced Class on Sino-Japan Trade Practice, Board of Foreign Trade in cooperation with Tamkang University, 1991—. Member, The Phi Tau Phi Scholastic Honor Society. *Member:* Taipei Bar Association; The Chinese Society of International Law; Asian Patent Attorneys Association; Commercial Arbitration Association of the R.O.C. *LANGUAGES:* Mandarin, Taiwanese and English. *PRACTICE AREAS:* Intellectual Property Law; Competition Law; International Trade Law; Litigation.

JAMES C.Y. SHEU, born Taiwan, October 18, 1931; admitted, 1986, Patent Office of R.O.C. *Education:* National Taiwan University (B.S., 1955). Associate Director, Planning Department, Taiwan Highway Bureau, 1975-1976. Chairman of the Board and General Manager, Ding Shing Securities Co., Ltd., 1990—. *Member:* Engineer Association of the R.O.C. *LAN-*

(This Listing Continued)

GUAGES: Mandarin, Taiwanese, Japanese and English. *PRACTICE AREAS:* Patent Law; Securities; Investment Law.

JENNY S.J. HUANG, born Taiwan, October 1, 1942; admitted, 1970, Republic of China; Patent Attorney. *Education:* National Chunghsing University, School of Law (LL.B., 1967). Supervisor: National Bar Association of the R.O.C., 1978; Taitung Bar Association, 1993. President, Taitung Bar Association, 1977-1978. *Member:* Taitung Bar Association. *LANGUAGES:* Mandarin, Taiwanese and English. *PRACTICE AREAS:* Commercial Law; Litigation; Civil Law; Criminal Law.

THAILAND

ANEK & ASSOCIATES

International Legal Consultants

Established in 1982

SUITE 1901-1902 WALL STREET TOWER
33/96 SURAWONG ROAD, BANGRAK
BANGKOK 10500, THAILAND
Telephone: 234-6900 (7 lines)
Fax: 236-5835; 238-0858

Commercial, Litigation, Corporate Company and Immigration, Property and Development, Labour Relations and Employment, Intellectual Property, Taxation, Banking and Finance.

FIRM PROFILE: Anek and Associates is one of Thailand's leading and most widely recognized law firms. Founded in 1982 by Anek Srisanit, the firm has been providing a professional legal service to a wide base of international and national clients. Over the decade, Anek and Associates has expanded significantly with services being offered in all substantive areas of law by a team of lawyers whose combined experience and legal expertise continue to ensure that the requirements of clients will be met with maximum efficiency.

1992 Marks the 10th anniversary of the firm which prides itself on the highest ethical integrity and respect for the Kingdom's laws. With ten years of steady progress, Anek and Associates looks confidently into the future that the firm will continue to grow to meet the increasing need for a sophisticated legal service required by its clients.

MEMBERS OF FIRM

ANEK SRISANIT, born Samut Sakhon, Thailand, November 10, 1946; admitted, 1967, Thailand. *Education:* Thammasat University (LL.B., 1967). *Member:* Thai Bar Association; The Law Association for Asia and The Pacific; Asia Patent Attorney Association; International Bar Association; Asia-Pacific Lawyers Association; ASEAN Law Association; The Law Society of Thailand; The Lawyers Association of Thailand. *LANGUAGES:* Thai and English.

SANOH SRISANIT, born Samut Sakhon, Thailand, March 31, 1940; admitted, 1989, Thailand. *Education:* Srinakharinwirot University (B.Ed.); National Institute of Development Administration (M.P.A.). *Member:* NIDA Association. *LANGUAGES:* Thai and English.

GUN SOPAPAN, born Nakhon Ratchasima, Thailand, October 11, 1954; admitted, 1977, Thailand. *Education:* Ramkhamhaeng University (LL.B., 1977). Barrister-at-Law, 1982. *Member:* Thai Bar Association; The Law Association for Asia and Pacific. *LANGUAGES:* Thai and English.

APICHART PHUNKEASORN, born Bangkok, Thailand, July 9, 1961; admitted, 1984, Thailand. *Education:* Thammasat University (LL.B., 1983). Barrister-at-Law, 1987. Member, Thammasat University Student Alumni Association. *Member:* Thai Bar Association; The Lawyers Association of Thailand; The Law Association for Asia and Pacific. *LANGUAGES:* Thai and English.

PATAMA RAWANGPAI, born Bangkok, Thailand, July 1, 1962; admitted, 1985, Thailand. *Education:* Ramkhamhaeng University (LL.B., 1985); Australian Business College (Cert. Business Practice, 1988). *Member:* The Law Society of Thailand; The Lawyers Association of Thailand; Thai Bar Association. *LANGUAGES:* Thai and English.

CHATCHAWARL SORNSURARSDR, born Sakon Nakhon, Thailand, May 23, 1968; admitted, 1991, Thailand. *Education:* Thammasat University (LL.B., 1991); Chulalongkorn University (Candidate, LL.M.). *Member:* Thai Bar Association. *LANGUAGES:* Thai and English.

(This Listing Continued)

ADISAK PRAPAIKORNKIET, born Bangkok, Thailand, November, 1957; admitted, 1981, Thailand. *Education:* Ramkhamhaeng University (LL.B., 1981); Australia (Diploma, Business Management). *Member:* Thai Bar Association; The Law Society of Thailand. *LANGUAGES:* Thai and English.

THANAPORN NUNTEE, born Mae Hong Sorn, Thailand, May 14, 1962; admitted, 1985, Thailand. *Education:* Thammasat University (LL.B., Hons., 1985); Southern Methodist University (LL.M., 1992). Barrister-at-Law, 1986. *Member:* Thai Bar Association; The Law Society of Thailand; The Lawyers Association of Thailand. *LANGUAGES:* Thai and English.

RAPEEPHUN CHARUBHA, born Bangkok, Thailand, July 3, 1958; admitted, 1982, Thailand. *Education:* Ramkhamhaeng University (LL.B., 1980). Barrister-at-Law, 1991. *Member:* Thai Bar Association. *LANGUAGES:* Thai and English.

CHAYATAWATCH ATIBAEDYA, born Nong Khai, Thailand, May 20, 1963; admitted, 1994, Thailand. *Education:* Ramkhamhaeng University (LL.B., 1985; Barrister-at-Law, 1988); Nova Southeastern University (Master, International Business Administration, 1994). *Member:* Thai Bar Association; The Lawyers Association of Thailand. *LANGUAGES:* Thai and English.

ELIZABETH LUSH, born United Kingdom, January 25, 1969. *Education:* University College London (LL.B., 1992). *Member:* The Law Society, London. *LANGUAGES:* English.

PORNPIMON CHINPATTANAWANICH, born Petchaburi, Thailand, November 30, 1971; admitted, 1994, Thailand. *Education:* Thammasat University (LL.B., 1994). *Member:* Thai Bar Association; The Law Society of Thailand. *LANGUAGES:* Thai and English.

REPRESENTATIVE CLIENTS: Jim Thompson Thai Silk Co. Ltd.; Fuji Xerox Co.; Hilton International Corp.; Triton Oil Company of Thailand; Silco Garments Co. Ltd.; Thai Printers and Finishers Co. Ltd.; City Properties Co. Ltd.; Placid Oil Company, Swire & Maclaine Ltd.; Arabian-Thai Group of Companies; Cathay Pacific Airways Co. Ltd.; Thai Shimizu Co., Ltd.; Standard Chartered Bank; Japan Air Lines; Thai Military Bank Limited; Louis Vuitton Pacific Ltd.; Sukosol & Mazda Motor Industry Co.; United Malayan Bank Corporation; Reuters Limited; Ban Pu (Public) Co., Ltd.; Takeda Chemie Thai Ltd.

ARNDT & VAN PATTEN

A Law Partnership of Professional Corporations

4TH FLOOR PANUNEE BUILDING
518/3 PLOENCHIT ROAD
BANGKOK 10330, THAILAND
Telephone: 662-252-0177; 251-9832
Fax: 662-251-2323

Los Angeles, California Office: 315 West Sixth Street, Suite 502. Telephone: 2 13-622-7174. Telex: 213-494-2100. Fax: 213-622-8026.

General Commercial and Corporate Law. International Law.

CRAIG R. ARNDT, (P.C.), born Ashtabula, Ohio, 1937; admitted, 1963, California. *Education:* Yale University (B.A., magna cum laude, 1959); Yale Law School (LL.B., 1962). *Member:* Los Angeles County Bar Association; State Bar of California. *LANGUAGES:* French. *PRACTICE AREAS:* Commercial Law; Corporate Law; International Law.

BAKER & McKENZIE

SATHORN THANI II BUILDING, 19TH FLOOR
92/54-57 NORTH SATHORN ROAD, BANGRAK
BANGKOK 10500, THAILAND
Telephone: 236-6060; 266-8282; 266-8490; 267-5800
Intn'l. Dialing: (66-2) 236-6060; 266-8282; 266-8490; 267-5800
Cable Address: ABOGADO
Telex: 82129
Answer Back: 82129 ABOGADO TH
Facsimiles: (66-2) 236-6071 to 73
Postal Address: G.P.O. Box 2815, Bangkok 10501, Thailand

Associated Offices of Baker & McKenzie in: Almaty, Amsterdam, Barcelona, Beijing, Berlin, Bogotá, Brasília, Brussels, Budapest, Buenos Aires, Cairo, Caracas, Chicago, Dallas, Frankfurt, Geneva, Hanoi, Ho Chi Minh City, Hong Kong, Juárez, Kiev, London, Madrid, Manila, Melbourne, México City, Miami, Milan, Monterrey, Moscow, New York, Palo Alto, Paris, Prague, Rio de Janeiro, Riyadh, Rome, St. Petersburg, San Diego, San Francisco, São Paulo,

(This Listing Continued)

BAKER & McKENZIE, Bangkok—Continued

Singapore, Stockholm, Sydney, Taipei, Tijuana, Tokyo, Toronto, Valencia, Warsaw, Washington, D.C. and Zürich.
Correspondent Law Firm: Hadiputranto, Hadinoto & Partners, Jakarta.

General and International Law Practice. Commercial, Corporate, Litigation and Taxation Law.

MEMBERS OF FIRM

ATHUECK ASVANUND, born Bangkok, Thailand, January 29, 1951; admitted, 1976, Thailand. *Education:* Thammasat University (LL.B., Hons.); New York University (LL.M. in International Law, Hons). *Member:* Thai Bar Association. *LANGUAGES:* Thai, English and Chinese.

SUCHINT CHAIMUNGKALANONT, born Bangkok, Thailand, February 26, 1943; admitted, 1968, Thailand. *Education:* Chulalongkorn University (LL.B., Hons; LL.M.); Institute of Legal Education (Diploma). *Member:* Thai Bar Association; The Law Society of Thailand. *LANGUAGES:* Thai, English and Chinese.

JOHN W. HANCOCK, born Adelaide, South Australia. admitted, 1970, Adelaide, South Australia; 1982, Victoria, Australia (Not admitted in Thailand). *Education:* University of Adelaide, St. Marks College (LL.B.). *Member:* Law Society of South Australia; Law Institute of Victoria; Law Society for Asia and the South Pacific.

PORNAPA LUENGWATTANAKIT, born Bangkok, Thailand, December 7, 1959; admitted, 1982, Thailand. *Education:* Thammasat University (LL.B. Hons.); Harvard University (LL.M.). *Member:* Thai Bar Association. *LANGUAGES:* Thai and English.

HATASAKDI NA POMBEJRA, born Bangkok, Thailand, February 4, 1957; admitted, 1984, Thailand. *Education:* Thammasat University (LL.B., Hons); New York University (LL.M., Int'l. Legal Studies); University of Miami (M.C.L.). *Member:* Thai Bar Association. *LANGUAGES:* Thai and English.

SAWANEE AMORADHAT SETHSATHIRA, born Bangkok, Thailand; admitted, 1983, Thailand. *Education:* Chulalongkorn University (LL.B.); Cornell Law School (LL.M.); The Institute of Legal Education (Barrister-at-Law). *Member:* Thai Bar Association. *LANGUAGES:* Thai and English.

SIRIPONG SILPAKUL, born Bangkok, Thailand, June 9, 1950; admitted, 1978, Thailand. *Education:* Thammasat University (LL.B.); New York University (LL.M.). *Member:* Thai Bar Association. *LANGUAGES:* Thai and English.

ANURAT TIYAPHORN, born Bangkok, Thailand, October 8, 1952; admitted, 1980, Thailand. *Education:* Chulalongkorn University (LL.B., Hons); New York University (LL.M. in Corporations). *Member:* Thai Bar Association. *LANGUAGES:* Thai and English.

KITIPONG URAPEEPATANAPONG, born Betong, Yala, Thailand, September 28, 1955; admitted, 1978, Thailand. *Education:* Chulalongkorn University (LL.B., Hons., LL.M.); The Institute of Legal Education (Barrister-at-Law); University of British Columbia (LL.M.). *Member:* Thai Bar Association. *LANGUAGES:* Thai and English.

LOCAL PARTNERS

WEERAWONG CHITTMITTRAPAP, born Bangkok, Thailand, February 15, 1958; admitted, 1981, Thailand; 1992, New York, U.S.A. *Education:* Chulalongkorn University (LL.B., 1980); Temple University School of Law (LL.M., 1985); University of Pennsylvania Law School (LL.M., 1992). Adjunct Lecturer, Private International Law, Bangkok University School of Law, 1988-1990. *Member:* Thai Bar Association; New York State Bar Association. *LANGUAGES:* Thai and English.

CHAIPAT KAMCHADDUSKORN, born Bangkok, Thailand, March 28, 1961; admitted, 1984, Thailand. *Education:* Chulalongkorn University, Faculty of Laws (LL.B.); Columbia Law School (LL.M.). *Member:* Thai Bar Association; Trademark, Patent and Copyright Association of Thailand; The Law Society of Thailand. *LANGUAGES:* Thai and English.

CHIRACHAI OKANURAK, born Chainat Province, Thailand, October 12, 1958; admitted, 1980, Thailand. *Education:* Chulalongkorn University (LL.B., 1980); The American University (LL.M., 1985). *LANGUAGES:* Thai and English.

WIROT POONSUWAN, born Nakhon Nayok, Thailand, March 20, 1958; admitted, 1984, Thailand. *Education:* Chulalongkorn University (LL.B., 1981); Georgetown University Law Center (LL.M., 1984). *Member:*

(This Listing Continued)

Thai Bar Association; The Law Society of Thailand. *LANGUAGES:* Thai and English.

DHIRAPHOL SUWANPRATEEP, born Bangkok, Thailand, May 15, 1957; admitted, 1980, Thailand. *Education:* Thammasat University (LL.B.); Institute of Legal Education (Barrister-at-Law); Howard University (M.C.J.). *Member:* Thai Bar Association; Trademark, Patent and Copyright Association of Thailand. *LANGUAGES:* English and Thai.

SURIYONG TUNGSUWAN, born Nakhon Sawan, Thailand, May 27, 1960; admitted, 1982, Thailand. *Education:* Thammasat University (LL.B.); The Institute of Legal Education (Barrister-at-law); Columbia University (LL.M.). *Member:* Thai Bar Association. *LANGUAGES:* Thai and English.

KANIT VALLAYAPET, born Suphanburi, Thailand, May 11, 1955; admitted, 1978, Thailand. *Education:* Ramkhamhaeng University (LL.B.); The Institute of Legal Education (Barrister-at-Law). *Member:* Thai Bar Association. *LANGUAGES:* Thai and English.

SUPPARUT ALLAPACH, born Bangkok, Thailand, April 15, 1960; admitted, 1986, Thailand. *Education:* Ramkhamhaeng University (LL.B.). *Member:* The Law Society of Thailand. *LANGUAGES:* Thai and English.

SOMCHITT ATTAPICH, born Ayutthaya, Thailand, May 28, 1928; admitted, 1940, Thailand. *Education:* Thammasat University (LL.B.). *Member:* Thai Bar Association. *LANGUAGES:* Thai and English.

JAKKARIN BANTATHONG, born Bangkok, Thailand, April 7, 1963; admitted, 1986, Thailand. *Education:* Thammasat University (LL.B.); University of Bristol (Dip. in English Legal Studies); University of Southampton (LL.M. in Maritime Law). *Member:* Thai Bar Association. *LANGUAGES:* Thai and English.

MANANYA BENJAKUL, born Yala, Thailand, April 24, 1963; admitted, 1986, Thailand. *Education:* Chulalongkorn University (LL.B., 1985); Youngstown State University (M.S., 1988). Lecturer, Criminology, Police Cadet Academy, Summer, 1990. *Member:* Thai Bar Association. *LANGUAGES:* Thai and English.

LAKKANASIRI BHUSATHONG, born Nakhon Sawan Province, Thailand, December 13, 1961; admitted, 1985, Thailand. *Education:* Ramkhamhaeng University (LL.B., 1985); The Institute of Legal Education (Barrister-at-Law, 1987); Washington College of Law, The American University (LL.M., 1993). *Member:* Thai Bar Association; The Law Society of Thailand. *LANGUAGES:* Thai and English.

THINAWAT BUKHAMANA, born Bangkok, Thailand, September 14, 1963; admitted, 1985, Thailand. *Education:* Chulalongkorn University (LL.B.); Southern Methodist University (LL.M.). *Member:* Thai Bar Association; The Law Society of Thailand. *LANGUAGES:* Thai and English.

MONTIEN BUNJARNONDHA, born Bangkok, Thailand, August 29, 1968; admitted, 1991, Thailand. *Education:* Thammasat University (LL.B., 1989); University of Bristol (Dip. in English Legal Studies, 1990; LL.M., 1991). *Member:* Thai Bar Association. *LANGUAGES:* Thai and English.

CHOOPUN CHAIPRABHA, born Bangkok, Thailand, February 9, 1951; admitted, 1983, Thailand. *Education:* Thammasat University (LL.B.). *Member:* Thai Bar Association. *LANGUAGES:* Thai and English.

PATTARASUPANG CHALERMNON, born Phangnga, Thailand, May 8, 1965; admitted, 1989, Thailand. *Education:* Chulalongkorn University (LL.B., 1987); University of Houston (LL.M., 1992). *LANGUAGES:* Thai and English.

MANOON CHANGCHUMNI, born Chaiyaphum Province, Thailand, November 21, 1963; admitted, 1991, Thailand. *Education:* Ramkhamhaeng University (LL.B., 1988). *Member:* Thai Bar Association; The Law Society of Thailand. *LANGUAGES:* Thai and English.

THANASAK CHANYAPOON, born Bangkok, Thailand, February 10, 1968; admitted, 1993, Thailand. *Education:* Chulalongkorn University (LL.B., 1991). *Member:* Thai Bar Association; The Law Society of Thailand. *LANGUAGES:* Thai, English and Chinese.

PICHITPHON EAMMONGKOLCHAI, born Bangkok, Thailand, May 23, 1970; admitted, 1993, Thailand. *Education:* Chulalongkorn University (LL.B., 1991). *Member:* Thai Bar Association; The Law Society of Thailand. *LANGUAGES:* Thai and English.

PRECHAYA EBRAHIM, born Bangkok, Thailand, May 6, 1961; admitted, 1984, Thailand. *Education:* Chulalongkorn University (LL.B.,

(This Listing Continued)

Hons., 1983). *Member:* Thai Bar Association; Thai Law Society of Thailand. *LANGUAGES:* Thai and English.

WISIT KANJANOPAS, born Chon Buri Province, Thailand, April 6, 1963; admitted, 1985, Thailand. *Education:* Thammasat University (LL.B., Hons., 1985); The Institute of Legal Education (Barrister-at-Law, 1986); Chulalongkorn University (LL.M., 1992); Monash University (LL.M., 1993). *Member:* Thai Bar Association; The Law Society of Thailand. *LANGUAGES:* Thai, English and Chinese.

SASIWIMOL KASEMSRI, born Bangkok, Thailand, June 12, 1964; admitted, 1986, Thailand. *Education:* Chulalongkorn University (LL.B., 1986; LL.M., 1991); Franklin Pierce Law Center (M.I.P., 1993). *Member:* Thai Bar Association; The Law Society of Thailand. *LANGUAGES:* Thai and English.

KULKANIST KHAMSIRIVATCHARA, born Bangkok, Thailand, April 22, 1963; admitted, 1986, Thailand. *Education:* Thammasat University (LL.B., Barrister-at-Law); Southern Methodist University (LL.M., in International and Comparative Law); Texas and IIT Chicago-Kent College (M.A.L.S.). *Member:* Thai Bar Association. *LANGUAGES:* Thai and English.

SUTTIPHAT KHAMSIRIVATCHARA, born Bangkok, Thailand, January 18, 1961; admitted, 1984, Thailand. *Education:* Thammasat University (LL.B., 1983); Institute of Legal Education Thai Barrister, 1984; Southern Methodist University (LL.M., 1987); IIT Chicago-Kent College of Law (LL.M., 1989). *Member:* Thai Bar Association. *LANGUAGES:* Thai and English.

THITI KUMNERDDEE, born Bangkok, Thailand, December 3, 1967; admitted, 1993, Thailand. *Education:* Thammasat University (LL.B., 1988); Indiana University (LL.M., 1993). *Member:* Thai Bar Association; The Law Society of Thailand. *LANGUAGES:* Thai and English.

WITTAYA LUENGSUKCHAROEN, born Chachoengsao Province, Thailand, January 1, 1964; admitted, 1988, Thailand. *Education:* Chulalongkorn University (LL.B., 1987). *Member:* Thai Bar Association. *LANGUAGES:* Thai and English.

PRAVITH MANGKLATANAKUL, born Bangkok, Thailand, September 13, 1963; admitted, 1985, Thailand. *Education:* The University of Exeter (LL.M., 1990); University of Bristol (Dip. in English Legal Studies); Thammasat University (LL.B., 1985). *Member:* Thai Law Society. *LANGUAGES:* Thai and English.

PILAIPAN MEKARATANA, born Bangkok, Thailand, April 20, 1954; admitted, 1978, Thailand. *Education:* Ramkhamhaeng University (LL.B., 1977); Keio University (LL.M., 1986; Ph.D. Candidate, 1991). *Member:* Thai Bar Association. *LANGUAGES:* Thai, Japanese and English.

ANGELA NOBTHAI, born Lop Buri, Thailand, February 3, 1965; admitted, 1990, Thailand. *Education:* Chulalongkorn University (LL.B., 1987). *Member:* Thai Bar Association. *LANGUAGES:* Thai and English.

DUANGJAI SAE-UNG, born Surin Province, Thailand, December 11, 1965; admitted, 1988, Thailand. *Education:* Thammasat University (LL.B., 1987); The Institute of Legal Education (Barrister-at-Law, 1989). *Member:* Thai Bar Association; The Law Society of Thailand. *LANGUAGES:* Thai and English.

ASAWIN SANGCHAY, born Bangkok, Thailand, April 19, 1962; admitted, 1991, Thailand. *Education:* Thammasat University (LL.B., 1984). *Member:* Thai Bar Association. *LANGUAGES:* Thai, English and German.

TAJ SINGUSAHA, born Chainat Province, Thailand, September 22, 1956; admitted, 1993, Thailand. *Education:* University of Brussels, Belgium (LL.M., 1982); Thammasat University (LL.B., 1978). *Member:* Thai Law Society. *LANGUAGES:* Thai and English.

SURACHAI SUKSRIWONG, born Bangkok, Thailand, May 20, 1966; admitted, 1990, Thailand. *Education:* Thammasat University (LL.B., 1989); Washington College of Law, The American University (LL.M., 1992). *Member:* Thai Bar Association; The Law Society of Thailand. *LANGUAGES:* Thai and English.

SUNPASIRI SUNPA-A-SA, born Bangkok, Thailand, September 9, 1961; admitted, 1986, Thailand. *Education:* Chulalongkorn University (LL.B.); DePaul University, Chicago, U.S.A. (LL.M.). *Member:* Thai Bar Association. *LANGUAGES:* Thai and English.

NATTAYA TECHAROCHANARIT, born Bangkok, Thailand, April 20, 1967; admitted, 1990, Thailand. *Education:* Thammasat University (LL.B., 1984). *LANGUAGES:* Thai and English.

(This Listing Continued)

ORNANONG TESABAMROONG, born Srisakate Province, Thailand, December 19, 1958; admitted, 1986, Thailand. *Education:* Ramkhamhaeng University (LL.B., 1981); Institute of Legal Education (Barrister-at-Law, 1982). *Member:* Thai Bar Association. *LANGUAGES:* Thai and English.

TANG THONGPAKDEE, born Chanthaburi, Thailand, February 16, 1922; admitted, 1947, Thailand. *Education:* Thammasat University (LL.B.). *Member:* Thai Bar Association. *LANGUAGES:* Thai and English.

PRACHERN TIYAPUNJANIT, born Bangkok, Thailand, September 2, 1964; admitted, 1987, Thailand. *Education:* Thammasat University (LL.B. Hons.); University of Monash (LL.M., 1994). *Member:* Thai Bar Association; The Law Society of Thailand. *LANGUAGES:* Thai and English.

PEERAPAN TUNGSUWAN, born Chiang Rai, Thailand, October 28, 1960; admitted, 1984, Thailand. *Education:* Chulalongkorn University (LL.B.); University of London (London School of Economics and Political Science) (LL.M., 1993). *Member:* Thai Bar Association. *LANGUAGES:* Thai and English.

VIT VATANAYOTHIN, born Bangkok, Thailand, December 5, 1967; admitted, 1991, Thailand. *Education:* Chulalongkorn University (LL.B.); Southern Methodist University (LL.M.). *Member:* Thai Bar Association. *LANGUAGES:* Thai and English.

PIPHOB VERAPHONG, born Bangkok, Thailand, June 5, 1962; admitted, 1986, Thailand. *Education:* Chulalongkorn University (LL.B.); Institute of Legal Education (Thai Barrister, 1984); Boston University (LL.M.); Harvard University (LL.M.). *Member:* Thai Bar Association; The Law Society of Thailand. *LANGUAGES:* Thai and English.

WANEE VISITVUDHIKUL, born Bangkok, Thailand, July 14, 1964; admitted, 1990, Thailand. *Education:* Ramkhamhaeng University (LL.B., 1988). *LANGUAGES:* Thai and English.

NITAT WATTANAKUL, born Lop Buri, Thailand, March 31, 1965; admitted, 1986, Thailand. *Education:* Chulalongkorn University (LL.B., Hons., 1985; LL.M., 1990); Keio University (Ph.D. Candidate, 1993); University of Washington (LL.M., 1994). *Member:* Thai Bar Association. *LANGUAGES:* Thai, English and Japanese.

YOH WIWATTHANOPAS, born Nakhon Sawan, Thailand, June 18, 1961; admitted, 1988, Thailand. *Education:* Faculty of Law, Ramkhamhaeng University (LL.B.). *Member:* Thai Bar Association; The Law Society of Thailand. *LANGUAGES:* Thai and English.

WANCHAI YIAMSAMATHA, born Bangkok, Thailand, April 25, 1963; admitted, 1990, Thailand. *Education:* Thammasat University (LL.B., 1985); Southern Methodist University (LL.M., 1990). *Member:* Thai Bar Association; The Law Society of Thailand. *LANGUAGES:* Thai and English.

BANGKOK ATTORNEY CO., LTD.

(BACO)

17TH-18TH FLOOR WALL STREET TOWER
33/85 SURAWONGSE ROAD
BANGKOK 10500, THAILAND
Telephone: (662) 237-6806-8; 233-2902-5
Fax: (662) 236-3125; 237-0750

Corporate, Tax, Project Finance, Construction, Insurance, Banking and Finance, International Business Transactions, Real Estate, Immigration, Litigation, Commercial, Criminal and Labor.

MEMBERS OF FIRM

MANOP NAGADATTA, born Thailand, 1950; admitted, 1974, Thailand. *Education:* Thammasat University (LL.B., Hons., 1973; Barrister-at-Law, 1974); Tulane University (LL.M., 1975). Author of Law Textbooks: Insurance Law, International Sales Agreement, Hire of Work Hire of Service, Bills of Exchange. Lecturer, Law, Thammasat University and Sukhothai University. *Member:* Thai Bar Association; Law Society of Thailand; LAWASIA Association; Inter-Pacific Bar Association. *LANGUAGES:* Thai and English.

PRAKIAT NASIMMA, born Thailand, 1946; admitted, 1972, Thailand. *Education:* Thammasat University (LL.B., 1971). *Member:* Law Society of Thailand; LAWASIA Association. *LANGUAGES:* Thai and English.

(This Listing Continued)

BANGKOK ATTORNEY CO., LTD., Bangkok—Continued

ASSOCIATES

KANCHIT WANNASIRI, born Thailand, 1959; admitted, 1985, Thailand. *Education:* Ramkhamhaeng University (LL.B., 1985). *Member:* Law Society of Thailand. *LANGUAGES:* Thai and English.

NITTAYA PIPATKHEMAKORN, born Thailand, 1967; admitted, 1992, Thailand. *Education:* Thammasat University (LL.B., 1989; Diploma, Business Law). *Member:* Law Society of Thailand. *LANGUAGES:* Thai and English.

NUGOOL KHONGROD, born Thailand, 1963; admitted, 1988, Thailand. *Education:* Thammasat University (LL.B., 1987); Strayer College Graduate School of Business (M.B.A., 1991). *Member:* Law Society of Thailand. *LANGUAGES:* Thai and English.

SUCHIN JANSRITHONG, born Thailand, 1960; admitted, 1984, Thailand. *Education:* Ramkhamhaeng University (LL.B., 1984). *Member:* Law Society of Thailand. *LANGUAGES:* Thai.

SUTHAMMA VORAGANON, born Thailand, 1970; admitted, 1993, Thailand. *Education:* Thammasat University (LL.B., Hons., 1992). *Member:* Law Society of Thailand. *LANGUAGES:* Thai and English.

SUTHEE CHUAYBANRUNG, born Thailand, 1953; admitted, 1993, Thailand. *Education:* Nakorn-si-thammasat Technical College (B.S., Electrical Engineering, 1981); Ramkhamhaeng University (LL.B., 1991). *Member:* Law Society of Thailand. *LANGUAGES:* Thai and English.

TANOM PANGPA, born Thailand, 1965; admitted, 1986, Thailand. *Education:* Ramkhamhaeng University (LL.B., 1985; Barrister-at-Law, 1987). *Member:* Thai Bar Association; Law Society of Thailand. *LANGUAGES:* Thai.

THONGCHAI GAWBANSIRI, born Thailand, 1965; admitted, 1990, Thailand. *Education:* Thammasat University (LL.B., 1987; Diploma, Business Law). *Member:* Law Society of Thailand. *LANGUAGES:* Thai and English.

CONSULTANT

JOHN VIVERITO, born United States of America, 1966; admitted, 1993, California (Not admitted in Thailand). *Education:* Michigan State University (B.A., 1989); University of Miami (J.D., 1992); American Graduate School of International Management (Certificate of Advanced Study). *Member:* American Bar Association; State Bar of California. *LANGUAGES:* English.

BOONCHOO & PAD LTD.

Established in 1976

104 PANAVONGS BLDG., SUITE NO. 603
SURAVONGS ROAD
G.P.O. BOX 62
BANGKOK 10500, THAILAND
Telephone: (662) 237-0748; 235-3560; 235-0200 Ext. 25
Fax: (662) 237-1580

FIRM PROFILE: *The firm was established in 1976 as Boonchoo International and Associates and in 1989 it was changed to a three partner firm to offer a full range of legal services. General and International Law Practice specializing in Commercial and Corporate Law, Joint Ventures, Banking and Securities Law, Intellectual Property, Taxation, Arbitration and Litigation.*

MEMBERS OF FIRM

BOONCHOO YENSABAI, born Chanthaburi Province, Thailand, 1940; admitted, 1970, Thailand. *Education:* Chulalongkorn University (LL.B., 1967). In-House Counsel, Chase Manhattan Bank, N.A., Bangkok Branch, 1974-1980. Founder, Boonchoo International and Associates Ltd., 1976. *Member:* Thai Bar Association; The Law Society of Thailand. *LANGUAGES:* Thai and English. *PRACTICE AREAS:* Corporate; Commercial; Joint Ventures; Labour; Taxation.

PAD THANESWONGSAKUL, born Nakorn Sri Thammasat Province, Thailand, 1965; admitted, 1989, Thailand. *Education:* Chulalongkorn University (LL.B., Honours, 1988; LL.M., 1993). *Member:* Thai Bar Association; Law Society of Thailand. *LANGUAGES:* Thai and English. *PRACTICE AREAS:* Commercial Litigation; Arbitration; Tax Litigation; Intellectual Property.

(This Listing Continued)

SUMET MINGMONGKOLMITR, born Bangkok, Thailand, 1968; admitted, 1991, Thailand. *Education:* Chulalongkorn University (LL.B., 1990). *Member:* Thai Bar Association; Law Society of Thailand. *LANGUAGES:* Thai and English. *PRACTICE AREAS:* Corporate Law; Immigration Law; Government Registrations.

ANDREAS C. RICHTER, born Pfullendorf, Germany, 1964; (Not admitted in Thailand). *Education:* University of Hamburg (1993). *LANGUAGES:* German and English. *PRACTICE AREAS:* Corporate Law; Commercial Law; Bank and Monetary Law; International Finance and Securities; Joint Ventures.

OF COUNSEL

SAMRIENG MEKKRIENGKRAI, born Nakorn Sri Thammarat, Thailand, March 17, 1953; admitted, 1975, Thailand. *Education:* Chulalongkorn University (LL.B., 1975); Institute of Advanced Legal Education (Barrister-at-Law); University of Miami, U.S.A. (M.C.L., 1979). Associate Professor of Law, Chulalongkorn University, Thailand, 1975. *Member:* Thai Bar Association. (Also Of Counsel, Business Lawyers & Consultants Co., Ltd.). *LANGUAGES:* Thai and English. *PRACTICE AREAS:* Corporate; Government Contracts; Tax Matters.

RASAMEE SAWAMIPAK, born Lampang, Thailand, 1946; admitted, 1971, Thailand. *Education:* Chulalongkorn University (LL.B., 1968); Institute of Advanced Legal Education (Barrister-at-Law, 1971). *Member:* Thai Bar Association; The Law Society of Thailand. *LANGUAGES:* Thai and English. *PRACTICE AREAS:* Civil Litigation; Commercial Litigation.

LEGAL SUPPORT PERSONNEL

KWANKAMON YENSABAI, born Bangkok, Thailand, 1972. *Education:* Chulalongkorn University (Candidate of Bachelor of Communication Arts). (Paralegal). *LANGUAGES:* Thai and English. *PRACTICE AREAS:* Government Contacts; Filing Papers; File Investigation; Information Assistant and Documentary Research.

RATTHAPHOL SRIBOON, born Loei, Thailand, 1965. *Education:* Loei Teachers College (Diploma of Education, 1989). *LANGUAGES:* Thai. *PRACTICE AREAS:* Government Contacts; Filing Papers; File Investigation; Information Assistant and Documentary Research.

BOONSOM & MANOCH
INTERLAW LIMITED

PANAWONGSE BUILDING, 9TH FLOOR
104 SURAWONGSE ROAD
BANGKOK 10500, THAILAND
Telephone: 2354625; 2354626; 2336520; 2336522
Fax: (662) 2369268
Telex: 20427 Boonsom TH
Cable: Beeslaw

General Practice, Corporation, Mineral, Petroleum, Banking, Finance and Securities Transaction, Investment, Trademark, Patent, Copyright, Taxation, Labor, International Business Law, Litigation, Trials and Appeals.

FIRM PROFILE: *Boonsom & Manoch Interlaw Limited, formerly known as Boonsom Interlaw Limited, was established in 1981 by Boonsom Butrahongse who had worked as a senior lawyer in international law firms in Bangkok for more than 10 years. The firm provides and handles complete range of legal advice and services for its local and foreign clients and emphasizes litigation works and matters relating to Corporate Law, Property Law, Mining and Petroleum Law, Finance and Securities Laws and Regulations, Intellectual Property Law, Labour Law, Trademarks, Work Permits.*

BOONSOM BUTRAHONGSE, born Rajburi, Thailand, 1941; admitted, 1971, Thailand. *Education:* Chulalongkorn University (LL.B., 1968). *Member:* Thai Bar Association; The Law Association for Asia and the Western Pacific (Member, Energy Law Section); Thai Lawyers Association; Thai Lawyers Council. *LANGUAGES:* Thai and English.

MANOCH SUNGSUWAN, born Suphan Buri, Thailand, 1956; admitted, 1979, Thailand. *Education:* Chulalongkorn University (LL.B. with honors, 1978). *Member:* Thai Bar Association; Thai Lawyers Association; Thai Lawyers Council. *LANGUAGES:* Thai and English.

WANNEE PORNSOMBOONSIRI, born Bangkok, Thailand, 1958; admitted, 1982, Thailand. *Education:* Chulalongkorn University (LL.B. with honors, 1980). *Member:* Thai Bar Association; Thai Lawyers Association; Thai Lawyers Council. *LANGUAGES:* Thai and English.

(This Listing Continued)

OF COUNSEL

WEERA SUBPAISARN, born Ayudhya, Thailand, March 5, 1928; admitted, 1950, Thailand. *Education:* Thammasat University (LL.B., 1949). Lawyer, Seni Pramoj Law Office, 1950-1955. Judge, Senior Judge of Provincial Courts, Bangkok Civil and Criminal Courts, Appellate Court and Supreme Court of Thailand during 1955-1989, Retired as Chief Justice of Thonburi Civil Court in 1989. *Member:* Thai Bar Association. *LANGUAGES:* Thai and English.

CHULATHAI SALIGUPTA, born Bangkok, Thailand, 1965; admitted, 1988, Thailand. *Education:* Thammasat University (LL.B., 1988). *Member:* Thai Bar Association; Thai Lawyers Council. *LANGUAGES:* Thai and English.

SUWATCHAI SUTEPAKUL, born Bangkok, Thailand, 1965; admitted, 1988, Thailand. *Education:* Thammasat University (LL.B., 1988). *Member:* Thai Bar Association; Thai Lawyers Council. *LANGUAGES:* Thai and English.

SANYA SRIPINYO, born Chumphon, Thailand, December 30, 1967; admitted, 1990, Thailand. *Education:* Chulalongkorn University (LL.B., 1990). *Member:* Thai Bar Association; Thai Lawyers Council. *LANGUAGES:* Thai and English.

SOMPORN SAMUDTHRAKUN, born Chon Buri, Thailand, July 6, 1968; admitted, 1990, Thailand. *Education:* Chulalongkorn University (LL.B., 1990). *Member:* Thai Bar Association; Thai Lawyers Council. *LANGUAGES:* Thai and English.

PIPUT BOOTHONG, born Prachuap Khiri Khan, Thailand, June 8, 1966; admitted, 1990, Thailand. *Education:* Ramkhamhaeng University (LL.B., 1990). *Member:* Thai Bar Association; Thai Lawyers Council. *LANGUAGES:* Thai and English.

CHAKRAPONG BOONCHAN, born Bangkok, Thailand, 1971; admitted, 1994, Thailand. *Education:* Chulalongkorn University (LL.B., 1993). *LANGUAGES:* Thai and English.

MARUT BUNNAG INTERNATIONAL LAW OFFICE

Established in 1950

CENTRAL CHIDLOM TOWER, 9TH FLOOR
22 SOI SOMKID, PLOENCHIT ROAD
BANGKOK 10330, THAILAND
Telephone: 254-0860 to 254-0864
Telex: 82153 MARUT TH
Fax: (66-2) 254-0865

As from January 1996 the address will be: Ratchada Tower, 19th Floor, Ratchadaphisek Road, Kwaeng Huaykwang, Khet Huaykwang, Bangkok 10310. Mobilephone (Local) 01-911-3926. (International) (66-1) 911-3926. Fax: (66-2) 226-3321.

Practising in Domestic and Foreign Commercial Law, Intellectual Property Law, including Copyright, Corporation, Patent & Trademark Laws, Investment & Taxation Law, Joint venture Registrations, Negotiations with The Board of Investment, all Government Departments including Customs, Immigration & Labour, Ministries relating to Business, Maritime Law, Criminal Law, Insurance Law, Factory Licensing, Litigation & Work Permits.

FIRM PROFILE: *Prof. Marut Bunnag founded the original firm in 1950, expanding it in 1971 to embrace international legal matters and serve the interests of foreign companies and investors. He sponsors the Marut Bunnag International Law Journal. Since Prof. Marut Bunnag became involved in parliamentary affairs, holding various ministerial protfolios and currently President of the National Assembly, and Speaker of the House of Representatives, the firm of 15 lawyers/counsellors and 15 paralegals has been headed by his son Mr. Rujira Bunnag, a lawyer of 15 years experience.*

MEMBERS OF FIRM

PROF. MARUT BUNNAG, born Bangkok, Thailand, 1925; admitted, 1947, Thailand. *Education:* Thammasat University (LL.B., 1947). Senator, 1975-1976. Minister of Justice, 1981-1983. Minister of Public Health, 1983-1986, 1988-1990. Minister of Education, 1986-1988. Deputy Leader of Democrat Party, 1985—. Author: "Art of Advocacy," Law Text book, 1970. Law Lecturer, Art of Advocacy, Thammasat and Ramkhamhang Universi-

(This Listing Continued)

ties and Institute of Legal Education of Thailand (Bar Association of Thailand) 1972—. Member, Parliament, 1983-1991. President of Parliament, Speaker of the House of Representatives, 1992—. *Member:* Thai Bar Association; Law Society of Thailand; Lawyers Association of Thailand; World Peace Through Law Association; LAW ASIA Association; Asian Patent Attorneys Association; The Law Association for Asia and Western Pacific. *LANGUAGES:* Thai, English and French. *PRACTICE AREAS:* Litigation.

RUJIRA BUNNAG, born Bangkok, Thailand, 1957; admitted, 1979, Thailand. *Education:* Thammasat University (LL.B., 1977); The Institute of Legal Education of Thailand (Barrister-at-Law, 1980); Tulane University (LL.M. in Admiralty, 1984); University of Pennsylvania (LL.M., Business Law, 1985). Lecturer: Insurance Law and Business Liability Insurance, Faculty of Insurance, Assumption University; Insurance Law, Faculty of Law, Assumption University; Business Law, Faculty of Commerce and Accountary, Thammsat University; Admiralty Law, Master Degree of Law Program, Faculty of Law, Ramkhamhang University. Editor, Law journal of Marut Bunnag Thailand Law Office. Member, Committee of Lawyers Association of Thailand in Charge of Foreign Affairs, 1987-1992. *Member:* Thai Bar Association; Law Society of Thailand; Lawyers Association of Thailand; LAW ASIA Association; Asian Patent Attorneys Association; The Law Association for Asia and Western Pacific. *LANGUAGES:* Thai and English. *PRACTICE AREAS:* Commercial Law; Litigation.

ROONGNAPHA BUNNAG, born Bangkok, Thailand, 1958. *Education:* Chulalongkorn University (LL.B., 1980). *Member:* Asian Patent Attorneys Association. *LANGUAGES:* Thai and English. *PRACTICE AREAS:* Immigration Law; Investment Law; Intellectual Property Law.

CHUSAK KHUNAMORNLERT, born Chonburi, Thailand, 1956. *Education:* Thammasat University (LL.B., 1979). *LANGUAGES:* Thai and English. *PRACTICE AREAS:* Intellectual Property Law.

WARAWAT CHAIMANO, born Bangkok, Thailand, 1963. *Education:* Faculty in Law, Ramkhamhaeng University (Graduate, 1984). *LANGUAGES:* Thai and English. *PRACTICE AREAS:* Agreement Law; Thai Labour Law.

SUTHILERT CHANTARANGSU, born Bangkok, Thailand, 1966. *Education:* Ramkhamhaeng University (LL.B., 1989). *Member:* Thai Bar Association; Law Society of Thailand. *LANGUAGES:* Thai and English. *PRACTICE AREAS:* Agreement Law; Thai Labour Law.

RATTIKORN CHIARAKUL, born Bangkok, Thailand, 1965. *Education:* Chulalongkorn University (LL.B., 1987); Dickinson School of Law, USA (Master of Comparative Law, 1990). *LANGUAGES:* Thai and English. *PRACTICE AREAS:* U.S. & International Civil & Trade Law; Thai Business Law.

SUPREEYA CHUNSANIT, born Petchburi, Thailand, 1970. *Education:* Chulalongkorn University (LL.B., 1991). *Member:* Thai Bar Association; Law Society of Thailand. *LANGUAGES:* Thai and English. *PRACTICE AREAS:* U.S. & International Civil & Trade Law; Thai Agreement Law.

VICHIEN VORAVONG, born Bangkok, Thailand, 1962. *Education:* Ramkhamhaeng University (LL.B., 1984). *Member:* Thai Bar Association; Law Society of Thailand. *LANGUAGES:* Thai and English. *PRACTICE AREAS:* Agreement Law; Commercial Law.

WEERACHAI ARTHONMITR, born Rachburi, Thailand, 1960. *Education:* Dhurakijpundit University (LL.B., 1984). *Member:* Thai Bar Association; Law Society of Asia. *LANGUAGES:* Thai and English. *PRACTICE AREAS:* Commercial Law; Criminal Law.

REPRESENTATIVE CLIENTS: Austrian Embassy; Thai Military Bank; Triton Oil & Gas Co.; Berlitz Co.; General Telephone & Electronics Co.; Ice & Cold Storage Co., Ltd.; Okura Trading Co.; Okaya Co.; Sylvania; Hamilton Brothers Oil Co.; Weeks Petroleum; Tupperware of Australia; Diethelm Co.; Central Group; Central Department Stores & Central Plaza Hotel; Central Pattana Co, Ltd.; Associated Lapidaries Ltd.; Singapore Airlines; Lufthansa German Airlines; Finnair; Commercial Union Assurance Co., Ltd.; Hanover Insurance Co. Ltd.; Asia Trust Insurance Co. Ltd.; The Ayudhya Insurance Co.; Ltd.; Tour Royal Air Cargo Co., Ltd.; Erawan Hotel; The H.D. Lee Inc.; B.P. Home Product Co., Ltd.; The Regent (Thailand) Co., Ltd.; Hoechst Thai Ltd.; Stenhouse Jenkid Co., Ltd.; United Shoes Azur Co., Ltd.; Sandoz Chemicals (Thailand) Ltd.; Don Muang Tollway Co., Ltd.; Sears Roebuck; Asko Oy; Air Lanka; Banque Paribas; Babich Thailand; Cathay Trust; Elin Energieversorgung GES m.b.H.; L.A. GEAR; Kao Corporation; UMM Co., Ltd. New Man; Zotos International Inc; Pilecon Thai Co., Ltd.; Advanced Ground Systems Engineering Inc.; A.G.S.E. (Thailand) Ltd.; The Ayudhya Leasing Co.; The Ayudhya Factors Co.; Thames Water International (Thailand) Limited; SmithKline Beecham; Eastern Polymer Industry; Barapha Golf Co., Ltd.; Hi Tech Medical Hospital.

BUSINESS LAWYERS & CONSULTANTS CO., LTD.

109 CCT BUILDING, 4TH FLOOR
SURAWONGSE ROAD, KWAENG SURIYAWONGSE, KHET
BANGRAK
BANGKOK 10500, THAILAND
Telephone: (662) 237-6897, 98; 235-4700
Facsimile: (662) 237-6898

General Practice, Corporation Law, Investment Law, Joint Venture/-Shareholders Agreement, Mergers and Acquisitions, Labor Law, Taxation Law, International Loan Syndication, Banking, Finance and Securities, Intellectual Property, Real Estate and Litigation.

MEMBERS OF FIRM

PHORNTHEP PIYAWATTANAMETHA, born Bangkok, Thailand, 1949; admitted, 1979, Thailand. *Education:* Chulalongkorn University (LL.B., 1979); Thammasat University (LL.M., 1987; M.B.A., 1989); International & Comparative Law Center, Southwestern Legal Foundation, University of Texas, Dallas (1990). Associate and Senior Associate, International Legal Counsellors Thailand Ltd., 1985-1991; Founder and Managing Partner, Business Lawyers and Consultants Co., Ltd., Bangkok. *Member:* Thai Bar Association. *LANGUAGES:* English, Chinese and Thai.

THEWIN SAENTHAMPHOL, born Bangkok, Thailand, 1940; admitted, 1968, Thailand. *Education:* Thammasat University (LL.B., 1968); Institute of Legal Education, Thailand (Barrister-at-Law). *Member:* Thai Bar Association. *LANGUAGES:* English and Thai.

VIROJ PIYAWATTANAMETHA, born Bangkok, Thailand, 1974. *Education:* Thammasat University (LL.B., with honors, 1995). *LANGUAGES:* English, French and Thai.

OF COUNSEL

PRASIT KOVILAIKOOL, born Bangkok, Thailand, 1943; admitted, 1970, Thailand. *Education:* Chulalongkorn University (LL.B., 1968); Institute of Legal Education, Thailand (Barrister-at-Law, 1970); Columbia University (LL.M., 1974). Former Vice-President and Former Dean, Faculty of Law, Chulalongkorn University. Associate Professor of Law, Chulalongkorn University, 1994—. Member: Sri-Prathum University Council; Former legal drafting member, Juridical Council of Thailand. *Member:* Thai Bar Association; ASEAN Law Association (Governing Council); Public Law Association of Thailand (Vice- President); Legal Research Council of Thailand (Committee Member). *LANGUAGES:* English and Thai.

SAMRIENG MEKKRIENGKRAI, born Nakhon Si Thammarat, Thailand, 1953; admitted, 1975, Thailand. *Education:* Chulalongkorn University (LL.B., 1975); Institute of Legal Education (Barrister-at-Law); University of Miami (M.C.L., 1979). Associate Professor of Law, Chulalongkorn University, 1994—. *Member:* Thai Bar Association. (Also Of Counsel, Boonchoo & Partners Ltd., Lawyers). *LANGUAGES:* English and Thai.

PRANIT BHUMITTHAVARA, born Bangkok, Thailand, 1955. *Education:* Thammasat University (LL.B., 1978); L'Universite Robert Schuman de Strasbourg III (Doctorat d'Universite Droit Prive, Mention Tres Bien avec Eloges). Lecturer of Law, Thammasat University, 1994—. *LANGUAGES:* English, French and Thai.

CHANDLER & THONG-EK LAW OFFICES LIMITED

Established in 1974
7TH FLOOR
BUBHAJIT BUILDING
20 NORTH SATHORN ROAD
BANGKOK 10500, THAILAND
Telephone: (662) 266-6485 thru 6510
Fax: (662) 266-6483-4

Rayong, Thailand Office: 79/45-46 Chanta Udom Road, Rayong City, Rayong Province, Thailand. Telephone and Fax: (038) 614-700.

General Business Law Practice. Corporate, Taxation, Mineral, Banking and International Business Transactions.

OF COUNSEL

THONG-EK ANUDHIRA, born Ang Thong, Thailand, 1939; admitted, 1970, Thailand. *Education:* Assumption College; Chulalongkorn University (LL.B., 1968). Department of Public Prosecution, 1972-1974. *Member:* Thai Bar Association. *LANGUAGES:* Thai and English.

MEMBERS OF FIRM

ALBERT T. CHANDLER, born Oakland, California, 1936; admitted, 1965, California and District of Columbia; 1969, U.S. Supreme Court (Not admitted in Thailand). *Education:* University of California at Berkeley (B.S. Mining Engineering, 1958); Harvard University (LL.B., 1964). Sigma Xi. *Member:* State Bar of California; American Bar Association; International Bar Association (Section on Energy and Natural Resources Law); Society of Mining Engineers AIME; Society of Petroleum Engineers AIME; Engineering Institute of Thailand. *LANGUAGES:* English.

NIWES PHANCHAROENWORAKUL, born Ayudhya, Thailand, 1950; admitted, 1975, Thailand. *Education:* Bangkok Commercial College (B.A., with honors, 1972); Thammasat University (LL.B., with honors, 1975); New York University (LL.M. in Labor Law, 1979; LL.M., 1980). *Member:* Thai Bar Association. *LANGUAGES:* Thai and English.

SURASAK VAJASIT, born Rayong, Thailand, 1953; admitted, 1975, Thailand; 1979, England and Wales. *Education:* Thammasat University (LL.B., with honors, 1975); King's College, University of London (LL.B, with honors, 1978). *Member:* Thai Bar Association. *LANGUAGES:* Thai and English.

SUMIT MASRUNGSON, born Nakhon Sawan, Thailand, 1955. *Education:* Ramkhamhaeng University (LL.B., 1979); Dallas-Fort Worth School of Law (1990-1991). *Member:* Thai Bar Association. *LANGUAGES:* Thai and English.

RATANA POONSOMBUDLERT, born Bangkok, Thailand, 1961; admitted, 1984, Thailand. *Education:* Chulalongkorn University (LL.B. with honors, 1983); Eastern Michigan University (M.A. in Language and International Trade, 1986). *Member:* Thai Bar Association; International Bar Association (Energy Law Section). *LANGUAGES:* Thai and English.

JESSADA SAWATDIPONG, born Chiang Mai, Thailand, 1961; admitted, 1984, Thailand. *Education:* Chulalongkorn University (LL.B., 1983); Illinois Institute of Technology (MALS, 1987); University of Miami (LL.M., 1988). *Member:* Thai Bar Association. *LANGUAGES:* Thai and English.

WILAILUK OKANURAK, born Chumphon, Thailand, 1966; admitted, 1988, Thailand. *Education:* Chulalongkorn University (LL.B., 1987); American University (LL.M., 1990); Oxford Institute on International and Comparative Law, University of San Diego (Certificate of Summer Program 1990). *LANGUAGES:* Thai and English.

ASSOCIATES

CHADAPORN RUANGTOOWAGOON, born Chiang Mai, Thailand, 1965. *Education:* Thammasat University (LL.B., 1988). *Member:* Thai Bar Association. *LANGUAGES:* Thai, English and Chinese.

CHARONCHAI SALYAPONG, born Bangkok, Thailand, 1958. *Education:* Chulalongkorn University (LL.B., with honors, 1980; LL. M., 1985)); Tulane University (LL.M., 1983). *LANGUAGES:* Thai and English.

KANJANA SUTHIPRAPA, born Khon Kaen, Thailand, 1963; admitted, 1988, Thailand. *Education:* Ramkhamhaeng University (LL.B., 1985). *Member:* Thai Bar Association. *LANGUAGES:* Thai and English.

(This Listing Continued)

KOWIT SOMWAIYA, born Ubon Ratchathani, Thailand, 1957. *Education:* Thammasat University (LL.B., 1990); University of Illinois (LL.M., 1991). *LANGUAGES:* Thai and English.

MANOROM SUPPRASIT, born Bangkok, Thailand, 1969. *Education:* Thammasat University (LL.B., 1992). *LANGUAGES:* Thai and English.

PEANGNATE SAWATDIPONG, born Bangkok, Thailand, 1962. *Education:* Chulalongkorn University (LL.B., 1985). *Member:* Thai Bar Association. *LANGUAGES:* Thai and English.

PRAKASIT ITHART, born Bangkok, Thailand; admitted, 1988, Thailand. *Education:* Thammasat University (LL.B., with honors, 1987); Harvard University (LL.M., 1991); American University (LL.M. in International Legal Studies, 1992); Georgetown University (LL.M., 1991). *LANGUAGES:* Thai and English.

PRISNA SUNGWANNA, born Bangkok, Thailand, 1964. *Education:* Ramkhamhaeng University (LL.B., 1989). *LANGUAGES:* Thai and English.

UTHIT VISESSINLAPANOND, born Rayong, Thailand, 1967. *Education:* Ramkhamhaeng University (LL.B., 1990). *Member:* Thai Bar Association. *LANGUAGES:* Thai and English.

WICHAI NIMMANSOMBOON, born Petchburi, Thailand, 1957. *Education:* Thammasat University (LL.B., 1984); Southern Methodist (LL.M., 1994). *Member:* Thai Bar Association. *LANGUAGES:* Thai, English and Chinese.

WISAID ONTA, born Rayong, Thailand, 1962; admitted, 1992, Thailand. *Education:* Ramkhamhaeng University (LL.B., 1983). *LANGUAGES:* Thai and English.

CONSULTANTS

E. T. HUNT TALMAGE, III, born New York, N.Y., May 10, 1944; admitted, 1972, District of Columbia; 1976, U.S. Supreme Court (Not admitted in Thailand). *Education:* Sorbonne, University of Paris and University of Colorado (B.A., 1968); Georgetown University Law Center (J.D., 1971). *Member:* The District of Columbia Bar; American and International Bar Associations; American Society of International Law; International Law Association (American Branch). *LANGUAGES:* English and French.

COUDERT BROTHERS

Established in 1853

BUBHAJIT BUILDING
20 NORTH SATHORN ROAD, 10TH FLOOR
BANGKOK 10500, THAILAND
Telephone: (662) 266-6511
Fax: (662) 266-6521

REVISERS OF THE FRANCE LAW DIGEST FOR THIS DIRECTORY.

New York, New York 10036: 1114 Avenue of the Americas.
Washington, D.C. 20006: 1627 I Street, N.W.
Los Angeles, California 90017: 1055 West Seventh Street, Twentieth Floor.
San Francisco, California 94111: 4 Embarcadero Center, Suite 3300.
San Jose, California 95113: Suite 1250, Ten Almaden Boulevard.
Paris 75008, France: 52 Avenue des Champs-Elysees.
London, EC4M 7JP, England: 20 Old Bailey.
Brussels B-1050, Belgium: Tour Louise. 149 Avenue Louise, Box 8.
Beijing, People's Republic of China 100020: Suite 2708-09, Jing Guang Centre, Hu Jia Lou, Choa Yang Qu.
Shanghai, People's Republic of China 200002: c/o Suite 1804, Union Building, 100 Yanan Road East.
Hong Kong: 25th Floor, Nine Queen's Road Central.
Singapore 0104: Tung Centre, 20 Collyer Quay.
Sydney N.S.W. 2000, Australia: Suite 2202 State Bank Centre, 52 Martin Place.
Tokyo 107, Japan: 1355 West Tower, Aoyama Twin Towers, 1-1-1 Minami-Aoyama, Minato-ku.
Moscow, Russia: Ulitsa Staraya Basmannaya 14.
01301 Sao Paulo, SP, Brazil: Machado, Meyer, Sendacz, e Opice, Advogados, Rua da Consolacao, 247, 8 Andar.
Ho Chi Minh City, Vietnam: c/o Saigon Business Centre, 49-57 Dong Du Street, District 1.

General Practice.
(This Listing Continued)

RESIDENT PARTNERS

LANCE J. MILLER, born Los Angeles, California, August 10, 1954; admitted, 1980, California. *Education:* University of California at Berkeley (A.B., 1976); University of Southern California (J.D., 1980). Articles Editor, Southern California Law Review, 1979-1980. Author: "Licensing of Foreign Law Firms in Vietnam," (International Law Firm Management, 1993); "Selected Problems in the Representation of Japanese Investors in United States Real Estate," (ABA, 1989); Co-Author: "Non-Real Property Security in Real Property Financing," (CEB, 1987). *Member:* State Bar of California. *LANGUAGES:* English, French and Japanese.

RESIDENT ASSOCIATES

Vilaiporn Chalermlapasadorn   Dr. Chanvitaya Suvarnapunya
Chatchai Inthasuwan   Narissara Udomvongsa
Yongsith Kosawititkul   Chayut Vichuprapa
Orasa Leelataweewud   Kamonmit Vudhijumnonk
                Craig Alan Wilson

REVISERS OF THE FRANCE LAW DIGEST FOR THIS DIRECTORY.

(For biographical data of the New York personnel, see Professional Biographies at New York, N.Y.).
(For biographical data of the Washington personnel, see Professional Biographies at Washington, D.C.).
(For biographical data of the San Francisco personnel, see Professional Biographies at San Francisco, California).
(For biographical data of the Los Angeles personnel, see Professional Biographies at Los Angles, California).
(For biographical data of the San Jose personnel, see Professional Biographies at San Jose, California).
(For biographical data of the Paris personnel, see Professional Biographies at Paris, France).
(For biographical data of the Brussels personnel, see Professional Biographies at Brussels, Belgium).
(For biographical data of the London personnel, see Professional Biographies at London, England).
(For biographical data of the Hong Kong personnel, see Professional Biographies at Hong Kong).
(For biographical data of the Beijing personnel, see Professional Biographies at Beijing, People's Republic of China).
(For biographical data of the Tokyo personnel, see Professional Biographies at Tokyo, Japan).
(For biographical data of the Singapore personnel, see Professional Biographies at Singapore).
(For biographical data of the Sao Paulo personnel, see Professional Biographies at Sao Paulo, Brazil).
(For biographical data of the Shanghai personnel, see Professional Biographies at Shanghai, People's Republic of China).
(For biographical data of the Sydney personnel, see Professional Biographies at Sydney, Australia).
(For biographical data of the Moscow personnel, see Professional Biographies at Moscow, U.S.S.R.).
(For biographical data of the Ho Chi Minh personnel, see Professional Biographies at Ho Chi Minh, Vietnam).

DEACONS GRAHAM & JAMES

Established in 1969

(In Association With Sly & Weigall)

(Formerly Price Sanond Prabhas & Wynne)

16TH FLOOR, Q HOUSE SATHORN
11 SOUTH SATHORN ROAD
BANGKOK 10120, THAILAND
Telephone: (662) 679-1844
Fax: (662) 679-1864 Internet: DEACONS.BANGKOK@com.wov

General Practice. Corporate, Tax, Mining, Banking and International Law. Intellectual Property. Trial and Appeals.

FIRM PROFILE: Price Sanond Prabhas & Wynne, now known as Deacons Graham & James, was established over twenty-five years ago and is now a six partner firm with more than associate lawyers. The Firm's clientele consists primarily of multi-national corporations from Europe, America and Asia. The Firm's practice emphasizes matters relating to foreign companies investing in Thailand, such as joint venture agreements, corporate law, taxation, property law, mining and petroleum laws, license and technical assistance agreements, finance and securities regulations, litigation, intellectual property, visas, work permits, etc. The Firm handles the complete range of legal advice and services required for its clients to do business in Thailand.

(This Listing Continued)

DEACONS GRAHAM & JAMES, Bangkok—Continued

MEMBERS OF FIRM

HARVEY PRICE, born Detroit, Michigan, April 25, 1934; admitted, 1960, Michigan; 1961, California (Not admitted in Thailand). *Education:* Wayne State University (B.S., J.D.). Member, Board of Editors, Wayne Law Review, 1957-1958. Certified Public Accountant, Michigan, 1959. Lecturer in Law, Chulalongkorn University, 1962-1963. *Member:* State Bar of Michigan; The State Bar of California. *LANGUAGES:* Thai and English. *PRACTICE AREAS:* Commercial Law; Joint Ventures; Acquisitions; Licensing; Taxation; Corporate Law.

PRABHAS SAKUNWADHNA, born Bangkok, Thailand, May 8, 1947; admitted, 1972, Thailand. *Education:* Chulalongkorn University (LL.B.). *Member:* Thai Bar Association. *LANGUAGES:* Thai and English. *PRACTICE AREAS:* Commercial Law; Real Estate Transactions; Corporate Law.

ANDREW RODERICK WALTER WYNNE, born Birmingham, England, September 15, 1946; admitted, as Solicitor, 1970, England (Not admitted in Thailand). *Education:* University of Paris; Law Society's College of Law. *Member:* Law Society of London. *LANGUAGES:* English and French. *PRACTICE AREAS:* Commercial Law; Joint Ventures; Acquisitions; Licensing; Banking and Finance; Securities; Petroleum; Taxation; Corporate Law.

PORNLERT SINTHUVALEE, born Bangkok, Thailand, August 1, 1947; admitted, 1983, Thailand. *Education:* Thammasat University (LL.B., Hons.). *Member:* Thai Bar Association. *LANGUAGES:* English, Thai and Chinese. *PRACTICE AREAS:* Taxation; Banking and Finance; Securities; Commercial Law; Corporate Law.

CHULAPONG YUKATE, born Bangkok, Thailand, September 6, 1956; admitted, 1981, Thailand. *Education:* Chulalongkorn University (LL.B.); The University of Washington (LL.M., 1985). *Member:* Thai Bar Association. *LANGUAGES:* Thai, English and Chinese. *PRACTICE AREAS:* Litigation; Intellectual Property; Commercial Law.

CONSULTANT

ANDREW M. TANIGUCHI, born Honolulu, Hawaii, 1960; admitted, 1985, California; 1992, New York (Not admitted in Thailand). *Education:* Yale (B.A., 1982); Harvard (J.D., 1985). *LANGUAGES:* Japanese and English. *PRACTICE AREAS:* Corporate Law; Finance Law; Securities; Joint Venture Law; Japan Practice.

ASSOCIATES

CHOKECHAI SUNTHORNKAN, born Pattani, Thailand, April 29, 1945; admitted, 1971, Thailand. *Education:* Thammasat University (LL.B.). Thai Barrister at Law. *Member:* Thai Bar Association. *LANGUAGES:* Thai and English. *PRACTICE AREAS:* Commercial Law.

PEERANAND POOLSAWASDI, born Bangkok, Thailand, 1947; admitted, 1988, Thailand. *Education:* Ramkhamhaeng University (LL.B., 1988). *Member:* Thai Bar Association. *LANGUAGES:* Thai and English. *PRACTICE AREAS:* Commercial Law.

CHAMNIAN PINYODOONYACHET, born Nakhon Phanom, Thailand, 1957; admitted, 1981, Thailand. *Education:* Chulalongkorn University (LL.B., 1979). *Member:* Thai Bar Association. *LANGUAGES:* Thai and English. *PRACTICE AREAS:* Litigation; Commercial Law.

PRAMOTE SRISAMAI, born Nakhon Si Thammarat, December 16, 1962; admitted, 1985, Thailand. *Education:* Chulalongkorn University (LL.B., 1986). *LANGUAGES:* English and Thai. *PRACTICE AREAS:* Commercial Law.

AUSANEE THONGLIM, born Phangnga, Thailand, February 21, 1963; admitted, 1986, Thailand. *Education:* Ramkhamhaeng University (LL.B., 1986); Washington College of Law, The American University (LL.M., 1989). *Member:* The Law Society of Thailand. *LANGUAGES:* Thai and English. *PRACTICE AREAS:* Commercial Law.

SARANA CHAROENCHITR, born Bangkok, Thailand, July 18, 1968. *Education:* Chulalongkorn University (LL.B., Honours, 1990). *LANGUAGES:* English and Thai. *PRACTICE AREAS:* Commercial Law.

BURAT LUENGTHADA, born Bangkok, Thailand, April 16, 1968; admitted, 1991, Thailand. *Education:* Ramkhamhaeng University (LL.B., 1989). *Member:* Thai Bar Association. *LANGUAGES:* Thai and English. *PRACTICE AREAS:* Trademark and Patent Registration; Commercial Law.

(This Listing Continued)

AS354B

SANTI COOPAKANCHITKUL, born Bangkok, Thailand, March 28, 1956; admitted, 1979, Thailand. *Education:* Ramkhamhaeng University (LL.B., 1979). *Member:* Thai Bar Association. *LANGUAGES:* Thai, English, Chinese and Japanese. *PRACTICE AREAS:* Commercial Law.

ALISA YAMNARM, born New York, New York, April 12, 1969; admitted, 1995, New York and New Jersey (Not admitted in Thailand). *Education:* Benjamin N. Cardozo School of Law (J.D., 1994); New York University Graduate School of Arts & Science (M.A., Liberal Studies, 1991); Oberlin College (B.A., Chemistry, 1990). Author: "The Crisis of Unemployment and the Future of Reform in Central and Eastern Europe: Hungary as a Model," New Europe Law Review, 1994. Production Editor, New Europe Law Review, 1993-1994. Member, New Europe Law Review, 1992-1993. *LANGUAGES:* English, Thai and Spanish. *PRACTICE AREAS:* Commercial Law.

PRAKIT BOONPIPATANA, born Bangkok, Thailand, August 9, 1945. *Education:* Chulalongkorn University (LL.B., 1967). *Member:* Thai Bar Association. *LANGUAGES:* Thai and English. *PRACTICE AREAS:* Litigation.

SIRIKUL SRIWITCHUPONG, born Bangkok, Thailand, February 15, 1968; admitted, 1991, Thailand. *Education:* Chulalongkorn University (LL.B., 1991). *Member:* Thai Bar Association. *LANGUAGES:* Thai and English. *PRACTICE AREAS:* Commercial Law.

SIRIRAT KASEMSUWAN, born Bangkok, Thailand, October 18, 1969. *Education:* Chulalongkorn University (LL.B., 1991). *Member:* Thai Bar Association. *LANGUAGES:* Thai and English. *PRACTICE AREAS:* Commercial Law.

EIICHIRO KIMURA, born Kanagawa, Japan, 1963. *Education:* Soka University (LL.B., 1987); Chulalongkorn University (LL.M., 1993). *LANGUAGES:* Japanese, English and Thai. *PRACTICE AREAS:* Commercial Law.

PRIYANUCH TOSETTHEE, born Surin, Thailand, September 10, 1966. *Education:* Ramkhamhaeng University (LL.B., 1990). *Member:* Thai Bar Association. *LANGUAGES:* Thai and English. *PRACTICE AREAS:* Commercial Law.

ITHIPHON SAENGSAWANG, born Bangkok, Thailand, October 30, 1968. *Education:* Chulalongkorn University (LL.B., 1989). *Member:* Thai Bar Association. *LANGUAGES:* Thai and English. *PRACTICE AREAS:* Commercial Law.

RAWADEE CHAISUKSANT, born Bangkok, Thailand, July 23, 1965. *Education:* Thammasat University (LL.B., 1988). *Member:* Thai Bar Association. *LANGUAGES:* Thai and English. *PRACTICE AREAS:* Commercial Law.

Languages: Thai, English, French, Japanese, Chinese and Spanish.

DEJ-UDOM & ASSOCIATES

Attorneys-At-Law

CHARN ISSARA TOWER 9TH FLOOR
942/142-3 RAMA IV ROAD
BANGKOK 10500, THAILAND
Telephone: (662) 2330055, 2330068, 2330089, 2330097, 2330206, 2330154
Cable: COUNSEL TH
Fax: (662) 2366681, 2330227

General Practice, Business Start-ups, Investment in Thailand, Burma and Indo-China, Joint-Venture Projects, Corporate Matters, Finance and Banking, Government and International Commercial Contracts, Taxation, International and Local Securities Transactions, Intellectual Property, Immigration and Work Permits, Labor, Real Estate, Litigation and Arbitration.

(This Listing Continued)

FIRM PROFILE: The practice of Dej-Udom & Associates provides legal services to a wide range of clients from leading multinational corporations to local Thai companies. A member of the International Lawyers Network, a worldwide confederation of lawyers, the firm has access to contacts and information for legal services and business counseling around the world through over 50 leading law firms.

The office is also associated with a Vietnamese affiliate, the Scientific and Technological Cooperation for Developing Countries Corp. Ltd., Hanoi, Vietnam. Services and information concerning investment and Intellectual Property in Vietnam are available.

Dej-Udom & Associates can also provide a wide range of legal services for the Union of Myanmar (Burma) through its Rangoon-based Representative Office. Government permits, trademark registration, joint ventures, registration of companies and immigration and work permit services are available.

MEMBERS OF FIRM

DEJ-UDOM KRAIRIT, born Nakhon Sawan, Thailand, June 25, 1946; admitted, 1969, Bangkok. Education: Thammasat University, Faculty of Law (LL.B., 1968). Barrister-at-Law, 1969. Publications: Investment in Thailand; Royalty is Dutiable Value (Thai Version); Tax Exposure on Business Contracts (Thai Version); Patent System in Thailand (Thai and English); Tax Exposure on Contract of Employment (Thai Version); Off-Shore (Syndicate) Loan Analysis (Thai Version); Value Added Tax in Thailand (English); Thailand Trade Secret Laws and Practice (English). Visiting Lecturer, Law, Thammasat University and Chulalongkorn University. Member: Thai Bar Association; Lawyers Association of Thailand; Trademark, Patent and Copyright Association of Thailand; Asian Patent Attorneys Association; United States Trademark Association; World Peace Through Law Association for Asia and Western Pacific; Law Society of Thailand. LANGUAGES: Thai and English. PRACTICE AREAS: Tax Law; Corporate Law; Banking Law; Intellectual Property Law; Litigation.

WORAWUT KRAIRIT, born Nakhon Sawan, Thailand, April 25, 1951; admitted, 1976, Bangkok. Education: Thammasat University (LL.B., 1975). Visiting Lecturer, MBA Program, Thammasat University. Member: Thai Bar Association; Law Society of Thailand. LANGUAGES: Thai and English. PRACTICE AREAS: Corporate Law; Taxation Law; Government Licensing Law; Government Contract Law; Industrial Estates; Real Estate Investment Law.

PUNJAPORN KOSOLKITIWONG, born Bangkok, Thailand, September 12, 1961; admitted, 1980, Bangkok. Education: Thammasat University (LL.B., 1983). Thai Barrister-at-Law, 1988. Lecturer, Asia Foundation Program, Thammasat University. Member: Thai Bar Association; Law Society of Thailand. LANGUAGES: Thai and English. PRACTICE AREAS: Litigation; Arbitration; Commercial Contract Law.

NIPA WONGYEEKUL, born Bangkok, Thailand, February 14, 1964; admitted, 1990, Bangkok. Education: Thammasat University, Faculty of Law (LL.B., 1987; Business Law Diploma, 1988). Member: Thai Bar Association; Law Society of Thailand. LANGUAGES: Thai and English. PRACTICE AREAS: Securities; Investment Law; Joint Venture Projects; Commercial Law.

AIM-ON LARPISAL, born Bangkok, Thailand, December 23, 1964; admitted, 1990, Bangkok. Education: Chulalongkorn University, Faculty of Law (LL.B., 1986; LL.M., 1991). Member: Thai Bar Association; Law Society of Thailand; Asia Patent Attorney Association; Trademark, Patent, Copyright Association of Thailand. LANGUAGES: Thai and English. PRACTICE AREAS: Corporate Law; Labor Law; Intellectual Property Law.

PINRUCK INDRASUT, born Bangkok, Thailand, April 3, 1964; admitted, 1986, Bangkok. Education: Chulalongkorn University (LL.B., 1985). Barrister-at-Law, 1988. Member: Thai Bar Association; Law Society of Thailand. LANGUAGES: Thai and English. PRACTICE AREAS: Commercial Law; Taxation.

ASSOCIATES

PANADDA SANGDOUNG, born Phrae, Thailand, April 4, 1967; admitted, 1990, Bangkok. Education: Ramkhamheang University, 1989. Member: Lawyers Association of Thailand; Trademark, Patent and Copyright Association of Thailand; Asian Patent Association. LANGUAGES: Thai and English. PRACTICE AREAS: Trademark, Patent and Copyright Law.

ADIRACH MONANONT, born Bangkok, Thailand, October 15, 1967. Education: Thammasat University, Faculty of Law (LL.B., 1989). Member: Thai Bar Association. LANGUAGES: Thai and English. PRACTICE AREAS: Conveyancing; Property Law; Real Estate Development Law.

(This Listing Continued)

COUNSEL

JANE-LOUISE NIVEN, born Plymouth, England, September 30, 1962; admitted, 1987, High Court of New Zealand; 1990, Supreme Court of Victoria, Australia (Not admitted in Thailand). Education: Auckland University (B.A., 1986; Bachelor of Law, 1987). Member: Auckland District Law Society, New Zealand; Law Institute of Victoria, Australia. LANGUAGES: English. PRACTICE AREAS: Environmental Law; Construction Law; Leasing.

DAVID MORTON MANUEL, born Auckland, New Zealand, June 25, 1965; admitted, 1990, High Court of New Zealand (Not admitted in Thailand). Education: Otago University (B.A., Political Studies, 1989; Bachelor of Law, 1989). Member: Auckland District Law Society. LANGUAGES: English. PRACTICE AREAS: Commercial Law; Contracts.

REPRESENTATIVE CLIENTS: Almond Jewelry; American Standard; AMP; BP Oil; Bank Brussels Lambert; Blue Cross Insurance; Boots Pharmaceuticals; Chrysler; Citibank, N.A. (PBG); C.I. Property Co.; CPC/AJI Thailand; Courtaulds Coatings; Cosmic Oil Co.; Cussons; Danfoss Industries Ltd.; Delta Electronic; Deutsche Bank; Electrolux Thailand; Elf Petroleum; Exxon; First Asia Securities; Fuji Bank; Fuji-Serina Valve Co.; Hana Micro Electronics; Hammer Thai Co.; Heath Huding Langeveldt Group; Kodak; IBM; Interface Corp.; Merck; Michelin; Miki Corp.; Mitsubishi; Netzch; Nippon Senso Co.; NSK Bearing; Noris International Trading; Peterson Manufacturing Co.; Petrothai Co.; Procter & Gamble Manufacturing; Quelle; Samart Co.; Sanofi, Sarome, Schering; S.C. Johnson & Son; Sino-Thai Engineering and Construction; Standard Chartered Bank; Statoil; Sunroute Hotel; Siam Makro; Tokyu Department Store; Tomy; Thai Danu Bank; Union Bank of Switzerland; UCB Pharma; Union Carbide Thailand; Ueno Fine Chemicals Industry; Volvo Truck; WKK; Wakachiku Construction; Warner-Lambert.

DELANEY & CO. INDOCHINA LIMITED

28/11 SOI RUAMRUDEE, WIRELESS ROAD
BANGKOK 10330, THAILAND
Telephone: (662) 253-8528
Telecopy: (662) 253-4256 Mobile GSM: (661) 811-1787
Phonelink: (151,152) 441069

Mailing Address: MBE Asoke Suite #347, 44/1-3 Asoke Road, Bangkok 10110, Thailand

Cambodia Office: The Allson Star, 138, Monivong Boulevard, Phnom Penh.

Myanmar Office: The Liberty Hotel, 343, Pyay (Prome) Road, San Chaung Township, Yangon, Union of Myanmar. Telecopy: (951) 34144.

New York City Office: 167 East 67th Street, Suite 5A, New York, New York 10021, United States of America.

Washington, D.C. Office: 2916 Fessenden Street, N.W., Washington, D.C. 20008, Unites States of America. Telephone: (202) 364-6742. Fax: (202) 364-6749.

Direct Co-Investment, General Corporate, Mergers and Acquisitions, Securities, Corporate Finance, Structured Finance, Public Finance, Leasing, Banking, Restructuring, Private Investment Funds, Futures and Options, Interest Rate and Currency Swaps, Labor, Immigration, Joint Ventures, Venture Capital, Legislative, Lobbying, Government Bidding, Privatizations, Public Concessions, Energy, Environmental, Media and Telecommunications, Oil and Gas, Utilities, Real Estate, Construction, Tax, Trust and Estates, Intellectual Property, General Litigation, Criminal Litigation, Arbitration and Mediation.

FIRM PROFILE: Based in Bangkok and with satellite offices in Kuala Lumpur, Malaysia; Yangon, Myanmar; New York, New York and Washington, D.C. Delaney & Co. is a commercial firm which is engaged in transnational practice and direct investment activities. Firm engaged in Burmese, Cambodian, Lao, Thai and United States law.

JERRY W. NEELY, (Executive Chairman), born Torrence, California, 1936. Education: University of Southern California (B.S., Industrial Management/Business Administration, 1960). Beta Gamma Sigma (U.S.C. Chapter). Recipient, U.S.C. School of Business Outstanding Alumni Achievement Award. Chairman of the Board, President, and Chief Executive Officer, 1966-1988. Director and Chairman, Executive Committee, Smith International Inc., 1988—. Director: Smith International Inc.; Norris Cancer Hospital; All Coast Forest Products. Past Director: Security Pacific National Bank; Avery Products Inc.; Pertec Computer Corp.; American Petroleum Institute. Trustee, University of Southern California. Member: Young Presidents Organization (Former Chairman). (Resident, San Juan Capistrano, California). LANGUAGES: English and Spanish. PRACTICE AREAS: Venture Capital; Direct Investment; Energy; Agriculture; Timber; High Technology.

(This Listing Continued)

DELANEY & CO. INDOCHINA LIMITED, Bangkok—
Continued

JESDAPON WATSA, born Bangkok, Thailand, 1960. *Education:* Ramkhamhaeng University (LL.B., 1983); The Institute of Legal Education (Barrister-at-Law, 1985). Attorney, Yuthang-Surut-Suk Law Office, 1985-1990. Partner, Jesdaporn-Thaveechai Law Office, 1990-1992. Law Department Manager, Advanced Communications Co., Ltd., 1992-1993. *Member:* Thai Bar Association. *LANGUAGES:* Thai and English. *PRACTICE AREAS:* Litigation.

SUPOTE CHUNYAVONGCHOT, born Chiang Mai, Thailand, 1970. *Education:* Montfort College (Diploma, 1988); Chulalongkorn University (LL.B., 1992). (Director, Thailand). *LANGUAGES:* Thai, Japanese, and English.

PRANEENART NAYANETRA, born Lampang, Thailand, 1971. *Education:* Montfort College (Diploma, 1989); Chulalongkorn University (LL.B., 1993). Trainee, Bangkok Bank Public Company Limited, 1992. Legal Division, Citibank, N.A., Bangkok Branch, 1993. Credit Officer, American Express (Thailand) Co., Ltd., 1993-1994. *LANGUAGES:* Thai and English.

RAWEE BOAYEN, born Chiang Mai, Thailand, 1972. *Education:* Thammasat University (LL.B., 1995). *LANGUAGES:* Thai and English.

NUDTINEE SUWANPANITCH, born Phuket, Thailand 1973. *Education:* Thammasat University (LL.B., 1995). *LANGUAGES:* Thai and English.

KRISANA BUTAYOTEE, (Firm Manager), born Maha Sarakam, Thailand, 1970. *LANGUAGES:* Thai, English and Vietnamese.

OF COUNSEL

MARSHA A. COHAN, born Paterson, New Jersey, 1955; admitted, 1983, Appellate Division (First Department), New York; 1983, U.S. Federal District Courts for the Southern and Eastern Districts of New York; 1985, Court of Appeals, District of Columbia (Not admitted in Thailand). *Education:* Brown University (A.B., magna cum laude, 1977); Harvard University (A.M., 1979); Harvard University (J.D., cum laude, 1981); Stanford University Inter-University Program for Chinese Language Studies in Taipei (1976). Phi Beta Kappa. Adjunct Professor of Law, New York University School of Law. Lecturer, Harvard Law School. Fellowship, Committee on Scholarly Communications with the People's Republic of China, Beijing University, Beijing, People's Republic of China, 1981-1982. (Resident, Washington, D.C.). *LANGUAGES:* Chinese (Mandarin and Cantonese dialects), Spanish, and English. *PRACTICE AREAS:* General Corporate; Project Finance.

KANNAN MENON, born Kuala Lumpur, Malaysia, 1951; admitted, 1990, Appellate Division (First Department), New York (Not admitted in Thailand). *Education:* St. John's Institution, Kuala Lumpur (1969); Catawba College (B.A., 1974); New York University (M.F.A., 1976); New York Law School (J.D., magna cum laude, 1989). Recipient, Joseph Solomon Award for Excellence in Character and Fitness, 1989. First Place: Froessel Moot Court Competition, 1987-1988; National Moot Court Competition, 1988-1989. First Place Team, U.S. Competition, Jessup International Law Moot Court Competition, 1989. Member, New York Law School Law Review, 1986-1987. Associate, Skadden, Arps, Slate, Meagher & Flom, 1989-1994. Visiting Counsel, General Electric International (GE Malaysia), 1994-1995. *Member:* American Bar Association. (Resident, Kuala Lumpur, Malaysia). *LANGUAGES:* Malay, Bahasa Indonesian, Malayalan, Hindi, Tamil, and English. *PRACTICE AREAS:* General Corporate.

ANDREW RUBICAM DELANEY, born New York, New York, 1962; admitted, 1989, Appellate Division (First Department), New York; 1990, U.S. Federal District Courts for the Southern and Eastern Districts of New York (Not admitted in Thailand). *Education:* Amherst College (B.A., summa cum laude, 1984); Harvard University (J.D., 1988); Stanford University Inter-University Program for Chinese Language Studies in Taipei (1989). Phi Beta Kappa (Early Election). Henry R. Luce Scholar, Bangkok, Thailand, 1984-1985. Fellowship, Committee on Legal Education Exchange with China, 1988. Foreign Intern, Kanung-Prok & Associates International Law Offices Co., Ltd., Bangkok, Thailand, 1989-1990. Associate, Skadden, Arps, Slate, Meagher & Flom, New York, New York, and Hong Kong, 1989-1993. Fulbright Scholar attached to Associate Professor Tongthong Chandransu, Faculty of Law, Chulalongkorn University, 1991-1992. Consultant, Sin Poh Group of Companies and "Sing Sian Yit Pao Daily News," 1990—. *Member:* Council on Foreign Relations; American Bar Association; Association of the Bar of the City of New York. *LANGUAGES:* Thai, Chinese (Mandarin dialect), Vietnamese and English. *PRACTICE AREAS:* General Corporate; Securities Regulation; U.S. and International Litigation; Criminal Law.

DOMNERN SOMGIAT & BOONMA

(Formerly Jorgensen & Co.)

719 SI PHYA ROAD
BANGKOK 10500, THAILAND
Telephone: (66 2) 237 18 82 (5 lines)
Fax: (66 2) 236 34 79; 237 18 86
Cable: Tramark Bangkok
Telex: 84165 jorsen th

Mailing Address: GPO 203, Bangkok, Thailand 10501

Copyright Law, Patent Litigation, Patent Prosecution, Trademark Litigation, Trademark Prosecution, General Intellectual Property Practice.

PARTNERS

GARDEN DOMNERN, born New York, New York, November 3, 1928; admitted, 1954, Thailand; Registered Patent Agent. *Education:* Kenyon College (A.B.); Harvard University (J.D.). *Member:* Thai Bar Association; The Law Society of Thailand; Intellectual Property Association of Thailand (IPAT); LAWASIA; AIPPI; APAA; AIPLA; FICPI; INTA; ITMA. *LANGUAGES:* English, French and Thai.

TEJAVANIJA BOONMA, born Bangkok, Thailand, October 20, 1951; admitted, 1977, Thailand. *Education:* Chulalongkorn University (LL.B.); Columbia University (LL.M). *Member:* Thai Bar Association; The Law Society of Thailand; IPAT (Vice-President); APAA (Vice-President); AIPLA; INTA; AIPPI; ECTA; IPBA; ITMA. *LANGUAGES:* English and Thai.

WARNCKE NETTAYA, born Hat Yai, Thailand, March 1, 1958; admitted, 1978, Thailand. *Education:* Thammasat University (LL.B.); University of Hamburg (Sprachdiplom). *Member:* Thai Bar Association; The Law Society of Thailand; IPAT; APAA; AIPLA; INTA; AIPPI; ECTA. *LANGUAGES:* English, French, German and Thai.

NOPAKUN RUTORN, born Bangkok, Thailand, March 14, 1961; admitted, 1982, Thailand. *Education:* Chulalongkorn University (LL.B.); Southern Methodist University, Dallas, Texas (M.C.L.); North Texas State University (M.S.). *Member:* Thai Bar Association; The Law Society of Thailand; IPAT; APAA; INTA; ECTA. *LANGUAGES:* English and Thai.

OF COUNSEL

SITTHISIRI SOMGIAT (Retired Partner, Former Registrar of Trademarks).

ASSOCIATES

DONAVANIK TORBONGS, born April 1, 1926; Registered Patent Agent. *Education:* Chulalongkorn University (B.Sc.); Liverpool University (Ph.D.). Former Head of the Department of Chemistry, Chulalongkorn University, 1975-1976. Chief, Research Division, Royal Thai Naval Science Department, 1955-1961. *LANGUAGES:* English and Thai.

SRIANEKRATHA VIRAT, born Bangkok, Thailand, May 15, 1941; admitted, 1985, Thailand. *Education:* Ramkhamhaeng University (LL.B.). *Member:* Thai Bar Association; The Law Society of Thailand; IPAT; APAA. *LANGUAGES:* English, Chinese and Thai.

CHUAATHIGAWONGS JESADA, born Bangkok, Thailand, July 1, 1956; admitted, 1981, Thailand. *Education:* Chulalongkorn University (LL.B.). *Member:* Thai Bar Association; The Law Society of Thailand; IPAT; APAA. *LANGUAGES:* English, Chinese and Thai.

JITKANTIWONG CHALERMPHONG, born Bangkok, Thailand, April 10, 1960; admitted, 1983, Thailand. *Education:* Chulalongkorn University (LL.B., Hons.). *Member:* Thai Bar Association; The Law Society of Thailand; IPAT; APAA. *LANGUAGES:* English and Thai.

POONSOMBUDLERT KIAT, born Bangkok, Thailand, June 10, 1960; admitted, 1982, Thailand. *Education:* Chulalongkorn University (LL.B., Hons.); University of Michigan (M.C.L.); New York University (LL.M.); Copenhagen University (Research on Labor Laws). *Member:* Thai Bar Association; The Law Society of Thailand; IPAT; APAA. *LANGUAGES:* English and Thai.

MONGKOLSIT CHAKRAPAT, born Chon Buri, Thailand, June 14, 1958; Registered Patent Agent. *Education:* Ramkhamhaeng University

(This Listing Continued)

(This Listing Continued)

(LL.B.); Franklin Pierce Law Center (M.I.P.). *Member:* IPAT; APAA. *LANGUAGES:* English and Thai.

JADNAWK ANURAT, born Nakhon Ratchasima, Thailand, January 10, 1948; admitted, 1982, Thailand. *Education:* Ramkhamhaeng University (LL.B.). *Member:* Thai Bar Association; The Law Society of Thailand; IPAT. *LANGUAGES:* English and Thai.

NASAREE RUENGYOT, born Yasothon, Thailand, September 30, 1955; admitted, 1983, Thailand. *Education:* Thammasat University (LL.B.; Graduate Diploma in Business Law). *Member:* Thai Bar Association; The Law Society of Thailand; IPAT; APAA. *LANGUAGES:* English and Thai.

MUANGMANEE AMARIN, born Bangkok, Thailand, February 18, 1968. *Education:* Thammasat University (LL.B.; Graduate Diploma in Business Law). *Member:* Thai Bar Association; The Law Society of Thailand; IPAT. *LANGUAGES:* English and Thai.

Languages: English, French, German and Thai

FRESHFIELDS

Established in 1994

SATHORN CITY TOWER, 11TH FLOOR
175 SOUTH SATHORN ROAD
KHET SATHORN
BANGKOK 10120, THAILAND
Telephone: (662) 679 6123
Fax: (662) 679 6133/6134

Other Offices in: Barcelona, Brussels, Frankfurt, Hanoi, Hong Kong, London, Madrid, Moscow, New York, Paris, Singapore and Tokyo.

RESIDENT PARTNERS

ALEX SANFORD, born June 12, 1959; admitted, 1986, New York (Not admitted in Thailand). *Education:* Princeton University (Philosophy); Taiwan University; New York University School of Law (Juris Doctor). *Member:* New York State Bar Association. *LANGUAGES:* Mandarin, Thai, Russian and Chinese. *PRACTICE AREAS:* Investment; Business Law.

INTER CONSULTANTS LAW & ACCOUNTING ASSOCIATES

Established in 1988

399/48 THONGLOR 21 LANE
SUKHUMVIT 55 ROAD, KLONGTOEY
BANGKOK 10110, THAILAND
Telephone: 391-2077; 381-2869; 381-0679-80
Fax: (662) 381-2687

FIRM PROFILE: *The firm was first established in 1982 under the name of Inter Consultants Law Association - a legal firm specialising in civil and criminal laws investigation. To fully meet the growing demands of foreign clients the firm was changed to Inter Consultants Law and Accounting Associates and registered as a limited company in 1988. It was also registered with the Ministry of Finance as a Thai consultant firm. It has since grown both in terms of size and services. Its activities range from Civil and Criminal Litigation to Commercial Law, Tax and Accounting services to International Investment, Trade related services and Business Consultancy services.*

MEMBERS OF FIRM

SOMCHAI PRAYOONRAT, born Bangkok, Thailand, 1928. *Education:* Police Cadet Academy (B.A., 1952). Retired, Police Colonel. Member: Federal Bureau of Investigation National Academy (F.B.I.), U.S.A.; Association of Police Veterans. (Senior Legal Consultant). *LANGUAGES:* Thai and English. *PRACTICE AREAS:* Criminal Law; Real Estate; Transportation; Business Consultation; Commercial Law.

CHATWADEE PRAYOONRAT, born Bangkok, Thailand, 1964. *Education:* Thai Chamber of Commerce University (Bachelor of Accounting, 1985). *Member:* The Institute of Certified Accountants and Auditors of Thailand. (Executive Accountant, Managing Director). *LANGUAGES:* Thai and English. *PRACTICE AREAS:* Tax Law and Planning; Accounting Law and Auditing.

PIPAT SRIDHANASKULCHAI, born Bangkok, Thailand, 1942; admitted, 1965, Thailand. *Education:* Thammasat University (LL.B., 1965); Thai Bar Association (Barrister at Law, 1967). *Member:* Thai Bar Associa-

(This Listing Continued)

tion; Law Society of Thailand. (Lawyer). *LANGUAGES:* Thai and English. *PRACTICE AREAS:* Civil Law; Criminal Law; General Practice; Copyrights, Patents and Trademarks; Business Consultation.

PRACHYA PANTHONG, born Singhaburi, Thailand, 1959; admitted, 1983, Thailand. *Education:* Ramkhamhaeng University (LL.B., 1983). *Member:* Thai Bar Association; Law Society of Thailand. (Lawyer). *LANGUAGES:* Thai and English. *PRACTICE AREAS:* Civil Law; Criminal Law; Immigration Law; Labour Law; Family Law; General Practice.

Members: Thai Bar Association; Law Society of Thailand; Law Association for Asia and the Pacific; Thai Chamber of Commerce.

KANUNG & PARTNERS LAW OFFICES

Affiliated with Lewis, D'Amato, Brisbois & Bisgaard

12TH FLOOR, NAI LERT TOWER
NAI LERT PARK
2/4 WIRELESS ROAD
BANGKOK 10330, THAILAND
Telephone: 267-8931-41 (11 lines)
Fax: 267-8942

Los Angeles, California Office: Suite 221, North Figueroa Street, 90012. Telephone: (213) 250-1800. Telex: 194508. Facsimile: (213) 250-7900.

General Practice, Investment, Corporation, Banking and Securities, Tax, Maritime and International Business Law, Immigration and Naturalization, Labor Law, Civil and Criminal Trials, Patent and Trademark Law, Administrative Law.

FIRM PROFILE: *Established in 1991, the partnership is a successor firm to Kanung-Prok & Associates International Law Offices which was founded in 1983. Kanung and Partners Law Offices provide a complete range of high quality legal and consultancy services to business companies, government agencies and individuals, both Thai and foreign. These services are provided by a staff of 27 Thai lawyers, including 12 partners, having background experience in company, commercial and international business transactions as well as litigation and international arbitration. The firm maintains excellent relationship with government authorities and international organizations regulating business and trade and it has those contacts with the public and private sectors (including banking) which are indispensable for the effective representation and protection of its clients in Thailand. Partners have served at high levels in the government, the judiciary and the leading universities and most of the legal staff has government as well as business backgrounds. English and Thai are the main working languages but the firm also has some capability in French. The firm is well versed in all aspects of the laws and procedures relating to foreign investment, international trade and licensing, company finance, mergers and acquisitions, patents and trademarks, labour and environmental law. Senior partners drafted and pioneered the adoption of Thailand's labour, social security and environment laws and the firm continues to serve the public interest in these fields. It has helped to establish the Environmental Law Center of Thailand (ELCT). Ties are being established with law firms in other countries including the USA and Kanung and Partners are examining possibilities for doing business in IndoChina and other neighbouring countries.*

SENIOR PARTNERS

KANUNG LUCHAI, born Uttaradit, Thailand; admitted, 1947, Thailand; 1959, England. *Education:* Thammasat University (LL.B., 1946); Gray's Inn (Barrister-at-Law, 1959); Cambridge University (B.A. Hons.; LL.B., 1960); Chulalongkorn University (Doctorate Degree in Law, 1993).

SANSERN KRAICHITTI, born Bangkok, Thailand; admitted, 1946, Thailand; 1952, England. *Education:* Thammasat University (LL.B., 1946); Lincoln Inn Barrister-at-Law, London (1952); Columbia University (Legal Specialist, 1956); Chulalongkorn University (Honorary Doctor of Law, 1985); Ramkhamhaeng University (Honorary Doctor of Law, 1988).

NIKOM CHANDRAVITHUN, born Phrae, Thailand; admitted, 1948, Thailand. *Education:* Thammasat University (LL.B., 1948); University of Chicago (M.A., SSA, 1953); University of Wisconsin (M.A., Labour, Social Service Administration, 1983); Ramkhamhaeng University (Honorary Doctorate Degree in Law, 1991); National Institute of Administration (Honorary Doctorate Degree in Social Development, 1993).

DR. ARUN PANUPONG, born Phatthalung, Thailand; admitted, 1981, Thailand. *Education:* Thammasat University (LL.B., 1946); Diplome des Etudes Superieur, Droit International Public, University de Paris (Docteur en Droit, Universite de Paris, 1972); Docteur en Droit, Universite de Paris,

(This Listing Continued)

KANUNG & PARTNERS LAW OFFICES, Bangkok— Continued

1953; Diplome des Etudes Superieure, Sciences Economiques, Universite de Paris, 1954; Diplome des Etudes Superieur, Droit International Public, 1972); National Defense College, Thailand (1979).

VID TANTAYAKUL, born Phatthalung, Thailand. *Education:* Thammasat University, (LL.B., 1949); Bachelor of Science in Economics, (B.Sc. Econ., 1955).

TIEBTHAM SRINOBNIKOM, born Ang-Thong, Thailand; admitted, 1944, Thailand. *Education:* Thammasat University (LL.B., 1944).

BAMRUNG DISPANDHU, born Trad, Thailand; admitted, 1950, Thailand. *Education:* Thammasat University (LL.B., 1950).

PARTNERS

PANAT TASNEEYANOND, born Maesod, Thailand; admitted, 1964, Thailand. *Education:* Thammasat University (LL.B., 1963); University of California School of Law, Berkeley, (LL.B., 1976); University of Washington School of Law, Seattle, Washington (LL.M, Law and Marine Affairs, 1977).

THAVISAK NA TAKUATHUNG, born May 8, 1944. *Education:* Chulalongkorn University (Bachelor of Law, 1967); Legal Training Institute of the Bar Association of Thailand (Barrister-at-Law, 1969); University of Miami (Master of Comparative Law, 1971); College of Government Administration, Ministry of Interior (Certificate of High Level Administration, 1980); United Nations Asia and Far East Institute for Legal Affairs Tokyo, Japan (Certificate of Judicial Administration, 1982).

KANOK PHUSATHONG, born Bangkok, Thailand; admitted, 1953, Thailand. *Education:* Thammasat University (LL.B., 1952).

SUTHEP NIRUNDORN, born Bangkok, Thailand. *Education:* Thammasat University (LL.B., 1963); University of West Los Angeles, California (LL.M., 1971).

LYNN M. VEJHURAI, born Aklan, Philippines. *Education:* Aklan College (A.A. Pre-Law, 1957); Abad Santos Law School (LL.B., 1961).

ASSOCIATES

SAWAT CHAIMONGKOL, born Phayao, Thailand; admitted, 1954, Thailand. *Education:* Thammasat University (LL.B., 1952). *Member:* Thai Bar Association; Thai Lawyers Council.

PISAN RASMIBHUTI, born Lampang, Thailand; admitted, 1977, Thailand. *Education:* Ramkhamhaeng University (LL.B., 1977).

SUWAT WIRACHSAKUL, born Loei, Thailand; admitted, 1988, Thailand. *Education:* Ramkhamhaeng University (LL.B., 1987).

MITCHAI PRASITSANHA, born Bangkok, Thailand; admitted, 1988, Thailand. *Education:* Ramkhamhaeng University (LL.B., 1987).

DARAT CHINDASRI, born Bangkok, Thailand; admitted, 1982, Thailand. *Education:* Ramkhamhaeng University (LL.B., 1980).

YOUNGJAROON PHOOTRAKUL, born Bangkok, Thailand; admitted, 1986, Thailand. *Education:* Ramkhamhaeng University (LL.B., 1985).

PONGSAWAT AKSORNSAWADDI, born Tak, Thailand; admitted, 1986, Thailand. *Education:* Thammasat University (LL.B., 1984; M.A., Political Science, 1991). *Member:* Thai Bar Association; Thai Lawyers Council. *LANGUAGES:* Thai and English. *PRACTICE AREAS:* Commercial Law.

NITITHORN WONGYEUN, born Bangkok, Thailand; admitted, 1995, Thailand. *Education:* Thammasat University (LL.B., 1992). *Member:* Thai Bar Association; Thai Lawyers Council. *LANGUAGES:* Thai and English. *PRACTICE AREAS:* Commercial Law.

SANTISUK THIPSUK, born Prachin Buri, Thailand; admitted, 1994, Thailand. *Education:* Ramkhamhaeng University (LL.B., 1991). *Member:* Thai Bar Association; Thai Lawyers Council. *LANGUAGES:* Thai and English. *PRACTICE AREAS:* Commercial Law.

OF COUNSEL

Art Punyadilok   **Arkabuth Krairiksh**
         Kraimedh Varasarin

DR. MANA INTERNATIONAL LAW AND TAX OFFICE

Established in 1976

16/7 NORTH SATHORN ROAD (NEAR WIRELESS SQUARE)
BANGKOK 10500, THAILAND
Telephone: 2351010; 2348640-3
Fax: 66-2-2371159; 66-2-2371160

General Practice, Corporate, Taxation, Mining, Banking, Trademark, Patent, Copyright, Maritime, Insurance, Labour, Contract and Litigation.

FIRM PROFILE: Established in 1976, Dr. Mana International Law and Tax Office has grown to become one of Thailand's leading international law firms. The founder of the firm, Dr. Mana Pitayaporn is one of the most respected authorities on civil, commercial and tax law of Thailand. The firm has a broadly-based practice with a reputation for offering a full range of quality legal services. It is staffed by 5 attorneys, 4 legal advisors, 1 legal trainee, 2 accountants. Together with Thailand's thriving business Dr. Mana's burgeoning Law Office is on its progressive pace. Having been retained by multibillion international enterprises, the firm has rendered humendons services to its clients over a decade.

DR. MANA PITAYAPORN, born 1926; admitted, 1948, Thailand. *Education:* Thammasat University (LL.B., Honours; Barrister-at-law; LL.M.; LL.D.; Dip. in Taxation); Houston University (Corporate Income Tax, 1972). Dean, Law School, Thammasat University, 1977-1978. Author: "The Law of Personal Income Tax," 5th Ed., Krung Siam Printing, 1990; "Corporate Income Tax," in English, 1985; "Corporate Income Tax and Personal Income Tax," in Thai, 1985; "Trademark Law," in Thai, 1985. "The Company Income Tax Law," 8th Ed., Krung Siam Printing, 1990; "The Law on Hire of Property, Hire-purchase, Hire of Service, Hire of Work and Carriage," 15th Ed., Krung Siam Printing, 1990; "Trademark Law," 5th Ed., Krung Siam Printing, 1990; "Copyright Patent and Trademark Law," Ramkhamhaeng University Press, 1980. Professor, Tax and Civil Law. Member, Patent Law Scrutiny Committee, House of Parliament, 1975. *Member:* Trademark, Patent and Copyright Association of Thailand (President, 1978); Law Society of Thailand (Vice President, 1989-1992); Tax Association of Thailand (President, 1989—). *LANGUAGES:* Thai, English and Chinese.

WASANCHAI WATTANAWONGWISUT, born 1957; admitted, 1984, Thailand. *Education:* Ramkhamhaeng University (LL.B., Honours); Thammasat University (LL.M.); Chulalongkorn University (Certificate of Shipping Business). *Member:* Tax Association of Thailand (President); Law Society of Thailand (Member, Foreign Committee). *LANGUAGES:* Thai and English. *PRACTICE AREAS:* Civil Law; Commercial Law; Maritime Law; Intellectual Property Law.

ADUL TRAKULDIT, born 1934; admitted, 1994, Thailand. *Education:* Thammasat University (LL.B.; Barrister-at-Law). Public Prosecutor for 18 years. *LANGUAGES:* Thai and English. *PRACTICE AREAS:* Criminal Law.

SUKIT KHUNPHAPRUKSA, born 1962; admitted, 1992, Thailand. *Education:* Ramkhamhaeng University (LL.B.). *LANGUAGES:* Thai and English. *PRACTICE AREAS:* Civil Law; Commercial Law.

KIRATI PITAYAPORN, born 1969; admitted, 1989, Thailand. *Education:* Thammasat University (LL.B.); Boston University (M.S., Business and Administration); Tulane University (LL.B.). *LANGUAGES:* Thai and English.

CHAIWAT KOSATANAKOM, born 1968; admitted, 1994, Thailand. *Education:* Thammasat University (LL.B.). *LANGUAGES:* Thai, English and French.

MONTIEN TIRAARUNSIRI, born 1971; admitted, 1994, Thailand. *Education:* Thammasat University (LL.B., Honours; Barrister-at-Law). *LANGUAGES:* Thai and English. *PRACTICE AREAS:* Civil Law; Commercial Law; Criminal Law; Administrative Law.

WASIT KRAEWPRANG, born 1967; admitted, 1994, Thailand. *Education:* Ramkhamhaeng University (LL.B.). *LANGUAGES:* Thai and English.

REPRESENTATIVE CLIENTS: Allied Newspapers Ltd.; Asian Honda Motor Co., Ltd.; Automated System (HK) Ltd.; B. Grimm & Co. R.O.P.; Bangkok Post Publishing Co., Ltd.; BASF (Thai) Ltd.; The British Council; Bayer Thai Co., Ltd.; Castrol (Thailand) Ltd.; The Coca-Cola Export Corp.; Colgate-Palmolive (Thailand) Ltd.; Commercial Union Assurance Co., Ltd.; Diethelm & Co., Ltd.; Dusit Thani Hotel; East Asiatic Co. (Thailand) Ltd.; Ericsson Telephone Corp.; Foremost Dairies Co. (Bangkok) Ltd.; Gestetner (Thailand) Ltd.; Hoechst Thai

(This Listing Continued)

Ltd.; Honda Cars (Thailand) Ltd.; The Hong Kong & Shanghai Banking Corp.; Hyatt International Co., Ltd.; IBM (Thailand) Ltd.; Johnson & Johnson (Thailand) Ltd.; Jurong Shipyard Co., Ltd.; Lever Brothers (Thailand) Ltd.; Loxley (Bangkok) Co., Ltd.; 3M Thailand Ltd.; McDonald's Corp.; Mitsui Bank Ltd.; Montien Hotel; Narai Hotel; Nestle; Philips Electrical Company of Thailand Ltd.; Scandinavian Airline System; Swissotel; Toyota Motor Thailand Co., Ltd.

MIYAKE & YAMAZAKI

SUITE 1903 WALL STREET TOWER
33/96 SURAWONG ROAD, BANGRAK
BANGKOK 10500, THAILAND
Telephone: (66-2) 266-2840
Facsimile: (66-2) 238-0858

Tokyo, Japan Office: Sogo Nagata-cho Building, 11-28, Nagata-cho 1-chome, Chiyoda-ku, 100. Telephone: 03-3580-5931. Facsimile: 03-3580-5400.

RESIDENT PARTNER

Akira Yamada

(For Complete Biographical Data on all Personnel, see Professional Biographies at Tokyo, Japan)

UKRIT MONGKOLNAVIN LAW OFFICE

Established in 1970

10 SUKHUMVIT 5
BANGKOK 10110, THAILAND
Telephone: 255-4015
Telecopier: (662) 253 5529; 253 5530

General Practice, Trials and Appeals, Taxation, Corporation Law, Business Law, Banking, Securities and Investment Law, Maritime and International Law, Commercial Arbitration, Patent and Trademarks.

MEMBERS OF FIRM

DR. UKRIT MONGKOLNAVIN, born Bangkok, Thailand, March 10, 1933; admitted, 1959, Thailand. *Education:* Thammasat University (LL.B., 1958; B.A. in Social Science, 1959); University of Paris (Docteur en Droit, 1966). Professor of Law, President and Founder of the Firm. Member of Parliament 1972, 1973, 1976 (Vice-President) and 1977. Advisor to the Prime Minister, 1974-1975. Dean, Faculty of Law, Chulalongkorn University, 1972-1978. Member, National Research Council, Legal Section, 1973-1979. Member, Board of Trustees, The Thai Red Cross Society, 1985—. President, Pierra Maternity Foundation, Bangkok, 1985—. President of the Senate and of the Thai National Parliament, May 1984-May 1989. President, Thai National Legislative Assembly, April 1991-March 1992; President of the Senate, May 1992—. *Member:* ASEAN Law Association (Chairman, Thai National Committee, 1987-1989).

SUWIT SUWAN, born Sing Buri, Thailand, February 28, 1948; admitted, 1971, Thailand. *Education:* Chulalongkorn University (LL.B., 1970). Barrister-at-Law, Thailand, 1976. Member, Thailand Committee for the International Chamber of Commerce, 1983-1990. Assistant Counselor to the National Parliament, 1984-1989. *Member:* Law Society of Thailand (Member, Executive Council, 1986-1989); ASEAN Law Association (Secretary, Thai National Committee, 1987-1990).

PIYATAT CHUDHABUDDHI, born Rajburi, Thailand, December 18, 1935; admitted, 1966, Thailand. *Education:* Thammasat University (LL.B., 1959). Barrister-at-Law, Thailand, 1960. Legal Officer, Office of the Prime Minister, 1962-1965. Legal Advisor to U.S. Air Force, Korat, Thailand, 1965-1970. Assistant Counselor to the National Parliament, 1987-1989.

SURADESH TANCHAROEN, born Prachin Buri, Thailand, March 19, 1949; admitted, 1972, Thailand. *Education:* Thammasat University (LL.B., 1971).

BANPOT CHAIYANANDHA, born Bangkok, Thailand, March 26, 1952; admitted, 1973, Thailand. *Education:* Chulalongkorn University (LL.B., 1972); University of Miami (M.C.L., 1977).

KRISDA TANKULRAT, born Bangkok, Thailand, August 6, 1953; admitted, 1976, Thailand. *Education:* Chulalongkorn University (LL.B., with honours, 1975). Barrister-at-Law, Thailand, 1979.

SUTHIN THITIVORN, born Chon Buri, Thailand, October 14, 1947; admitted, 1978, Thailand. *Education:* Ramkhamhaeng University (LL.B., 1978).

(This Listing Continued)

KHACHORNRIT T. VONGS, born Bangkok, Thailand, August 22, 1948; admitted, 1971, Thailand. *Education:* Thammasat University (LL.B., 1971); University of Miami (M.C.L., 1975).

DR. ABHIJAI CHANDRASEN, born Bangkok, Thailand, May 8, 1948; admitted, 1970, Thailand. *Education:* Chulalongkorn University (LL.B., 1969); Barrister-at-Law, Thailand, 1971; University of Paris (Docteur en Droit, 1977). Assistant Counselor to the National Parliament, 1989-1990.

POLAPEE TULYASUWAN, born Bangkok, Thailand, October 17, 1958; admitted, 1981, Thailand. *Education:* Thammasat University (LL.B., 1978). Barrister-at-Law, Thailand, 1979.

WATTANA MONGKOLNAVIN, born Bangkok, Thailand, August 24, 1956; admitted, 1982, Thailand. *Education:* Ramkhamhaeng University (LL.B., 1981).

PRAWEEN KHAMPARAT, born Bangkok, Thailand, August 9, 1959; admitted, 1981, Thailand. *Education:* Ramkhamhaeng University (LL.B., 1980). Barrister-at-Law, Thailand, 1981.

CHATTIP TANTHAPRASAS, born Bangkok, Thailand, September 22, 1953; admitted, 1976, Thailand. *Education:* Thammasat University (LL.B., 1975); Chulalongkorn University (LL.M., 1981).

SUTESAK VATTANAVINID, born Bangkok, Thailand, July 24, 1959; admitted, 1985, Thailand. *Education:* Ramkhamhaeng University (LL.B., 1984).

SANONT CHOMPRADIST, born Bangkok, Thailand, January 3, 1960; admitted, 1985, Thailand. *Education:* Ramkhamhaeng University (LL.B., 1981). Barrister-at-Law, Thailand, 1983.

VIROJ LIMPANYAKUL, born Bangkok, Thailand, October 7, 1951; admitted, 1981, Thailand. *Education:* Thammasat University (LL.B., 1975); Georgetown University Law Center (M.C.L., 1980).

CHARAN BOONTHAN, born Bangkok, Thailand, October 6, 1964; admitted, 1988, Thailand. *Education:* Ramkhamhaeng University (LL.B., 1986); Professional Training Institute, The Law Society of Thailand (Certificate of Aptitude, 1987).

KINGKMON SINMA, born Samut Sakhon, Thailand, August 23, 1966; admitted, 1989, Thailand. *Education:* Chulalongkorn University (LL.B., 1st class honors, 1988); Harvard University (LL.M., 1993).

TAWATCHAI CHONGDARAKUL, born Bangkok, Thailand, June 19, 1961; admitted, 1987, Thailand. *Education:* Ramkhamhaeng University (LL.B., 1985).

WORAPOTE THANOMKUL, born Trad, Thailand, February 6, 1962; admitted, 1985, Thailand. *Education:* Chulalongkorn University (LL.B., 1985); Barrister-at-Law, Thailand, 1986; University of the Pacific McGeorge School of Law, Sacramento, CA (LL.M., 1993).

ARCHAVA SMUTHRANOND, born Bangkok, Thailand, December 8, 1961; admitted, 1985, Thailand. *Education:* Thammasat University (LL.B., 1984); Barrister-of-Law, Thailand (1986); Howard University, Washington, D.C., (M.C.L., 1988); Southeastern University (M.B.A., 1989); Southern Methodist University, Dallas (LL.M., 1990).

THAEVAN UTHAIVATHNA, born Bangkok, Thailand, November 14, 1960; admitted, 1982, Thailand. *Education:* Thammasat University (LL.B., 1981); Mid Western State University, Wichita Falls, Texas (M.A., 1987); London Institute on International and Comparative Law (a summer program of the University of San Diego, 1993); Hague Academy of International Law, The Hague, The Netherlands (1993).

CHONCHANUM SOONTHORNSARATOON, born Bangkok, Thailand, July 1, 1968; admitted, 1990, Thailand. *Education:* Chulalongkorn University (LL.B., 1989); Sukhothai Thammathirat University (M.A., Political Science, 1989); Mississippi State University (M.A., Political Science, 1991); Tulane University, Louisiana (LL.M., 1994).

KANITNOY PRANEECHIT, born Songkhla, Thailand, October 1, 1964; admitted, 1988, Thailand. *Education:* Ramkhamhaeng University (LL.B., 1987); University of the Pacific, McGeorge School of Law, California (LL.M., Transnational Legal Practice, 1994). *LANGUAGES:* Thai, English, Mandarin and Cantonese.

OF COUNSEL

WILLIAM J. KLAUSNER, born New York City, N.Y., U.S.A., July 10, 1929; admitted, 1953, Connecticut, U.S.A. (Not admitted in Thailand). *Education:* Yale University (B.A., 1950; J.D., 1953; M.A., 1955). Phi Beta Kappa. Advisor to the Asia Foundation, Thailand Office, 1956-1971. Rep-

(This Listing Continued)

UKRIT MONGKOLNAVIN LAW OFFICE, Bangkok—
Continued

resentative of the Asia Foundation, 1971-1973. Consultant to the Ford Foundation, Thailand, 1976—. Special Instructor, Faculty of Law, Chulalongkorn University, Bangkok, 1974—. Adjunct Professor, Political Science, Chulalongkorn University, 1989.

MOORATA WATANASHEEVAKUL, born Sakon Nakhon, Thailand, January 16, 1942; admitted, 1969, Thailand. *Education:* Chulalongkorn University (LL.B. with honours, 1966); New York University (LL.M., 1977). Barrister-at-Law, Thailand, 1967. Assistant Professor of Law, Chulalongkorn University, Bangkok, 1978—.

RANDY CHAMBERLAIN, born Atlanta, Georgia, April 22, 1969; admitted, 1993, California (Not admitted in Thailand). *Education:* Brown University (A.B., Public Policy and American Institutions, 1990); University of California, Hastings College of Law (J.D., 1993).

(All Members are admitted to practice in all Courts of Law within the jurisdiction of Thailand).

Languages: Thai, English and French

NATEE INTERNATIONAL LAW OFFICE, LTD.

16TH FLOOR, ALMA LINK BLDG.
25 SOI CHIDLOM, PLOENCHIT ROAD
BANGKOK 10330, THAILAND
Telephone: (662) 251-6624-5; 253-5157; 253-5369; 251-6617; 251-6619
Facsimile: (662) 253-6994

General Civil Practice with an emphasis on service to foreign companies doing business in Thailand. Corporation and Corporate Finance, Banking, Securities, Taxation, Real Estate, Labor, Construction, Trade, Government Contracts, Joint Venture Agreements, Intellectual Property, and Immigration.

NATEE THONGDEE, born Ratchaburi Province, Thailand, 1944; admitted, 1972, Thailand. *Education:* Chulalongkorn University (LL.B., 1969); Institute of Thai Legal Education (Diploma, 1970); Temple University, U.S.A. (LL.M., 1980). Lecturer and Assistant Professor of Corporation and Tax Law, Chulalongkorn University, 1977-1985. *Member:* Bar Association of Thailand (Barrister-at-Law); International Law Association of Thailand (Director, 1985—); Executive Committee of the Thai-Canadian Chamber of Commerce (1991—). *LANGUAGES:* Thai and English.

KOSOL SURIYAPORN, born Bangkok, Thailand, 1963; admitted, 1987, Thailand. *Education:* Chulalongkorn University (LL.B., with Honors, 1986); Institute of Thai Legal Education (Diploma, 1987). *Member:* Bar Association of Thailand (Barrister-at-Law). *LANGUAGES:* Thai and English.

RONNAVIT SIMASATHIRA, born Bangkok, Thailand, 1960. *Education:* Thammasat University (LL.B., 1981); California Western School of Law (LL.M., 1992). *LANGUAGES:* Thai and English.

SOMPORN MANODAMRONGTHAM, born Bangkok, Thailand, 1968. *Education:* Chulalongkorn University, (LL.B., with Honors, 1991). *Member:* Thai Lawyers Association. *LANGUAGES:* Thai and English.

WILAIWAN LUETRAKULPRAWAT, born Bangkok, Thailand, 1963; admitted, 1989, Thailand. *Education:* Chulalongkorn University (LL.B., 1985); Institute of Thai Legal Education (Diploma, 1989); The University of New South Wales, Australia (Master of Commerce in Information Systems, 1992). *Member:* Bar Association of Thailand (Barrister-at-Law). *LANGUAGES:* Thai and English.

ACHARA PORNKASEMSUK, born Bangkok, Thailand, 1969. *Education:* Chulalongkorn University (LL.B., 1992). *Member:* Thai Law Association. *LANGUAGES:* Thai and English.

NALINTHORN CHARTSIRI, born Bangkok, Thailand, 1969. *Education:* Thammasat University (LL.B., 1992). *LANGUAGES:* Thai and English.

THAWATCHAI SAENGCHAEM, born Chiang Rai, Thailand, 1971. *Education:* Chulalongkorn University (LL.B., 1994). *LANGUAGES:* Thai, Chinese and English.

(This Listing Continued)

KANOKLUCK BOONSAKULKIT, born Nakhon Ratchasima, Thailand, 1971. *Education:* Chulalongkorn University (LL.B., 1994). *LANGUAGES:* Thai and English.

OF COUNSEL

PHILIP PATRICK SHERIDAN, born Dublin, Ireland, 1963; admitted, 1994, New York. *Education:* Columbia College, Columbia University (B.A., 1986); Boston University School of Law (J.D., 1993). *Member:* New York State Bar Association. *LANGUAGES:* English and Spanish.

CONSULTANT

RATIYA RUANGSUWANA, born Bangkok, Thailand, 1971. *Education:* Connecticut College (B.A., 1994). *LANGUAGES:* English, Thai and French.

TAX COUNSEL

ARPORN NARTDILOK, born Bangkok, Thailand, 1931; (Not admitted in Thailand). *Education:* Thammasat University (LL.B., 1954). Director, Taxation and Legal Division of the Thai Revenue Department, 1986-1991. Professor of Taxation and Commercial Law, Thammasat University, 1979—.

REPRESENTATIVE CLIENTS: Asia Business Forum (Thailand) Co. Ltd.; Belgian/Luxembourg - Thai Chamber of Commerce; Canadian Airlines; Canadian Embassy in Thailand; Citibank, N.A.; Bangkok Branch; Citicorp Securities and Finance (Thailand) Ltd.; Citicorp Leasing (Thailand), Ltd.; Compagnie Generale de Geophysique; Daelim Industrial Co., Ltd.; Diners Club (Thailand) Ltd.; Eaton Corporation; Elf Atochem, Ltd.; Eridania Beghin-Say (Belgium); Gerber Products Co., Ltd.; H.A. Simons, Inc.; Kawasho Corporation, Inc.; Mechim S.A.; SNC-Lavalin International Group; (The) Nippon Road Co., Ltd.; Padaeng Industry Co., Ltd.; (The) Pead S. Buck Foundation, Inc.; Royal Time Citi Co. Ltd. (subsidiary of Citizen Trading Co.); Sanofi (Thailand) Ltd.; Shinko Industry Ltd.; Sprint International Communications Corporation; Thai-Canadian Chamber of Commerce; Thai-Singaporean Chamber of Commerce; Yamato Scientific Co., Ltd.

NOPADOL & KHAISRI LAW OFFICE LIMITED

In Association with

McCutchen, Doyle, Brown & Enersen

PACIFIC PLACE, 9TH FLOOR # 909, 10TH FLOOR # 1005
140 SUKHUMVIT ROAD
BANGKOK 10110, THAILAND
Telephone: (662) 254-3335/9; 254-3341/2
Facsimile: (662) 254-3330/1

San Francisco, California Affiliated Office: 3 Embarcadero Center. Telephone: 415-393-2000. Facsimile: 415-393-2286. Telex: 340817 MACPAG SFO.

San Jose, California Affiliated Office: Market Post Tower, Suite 1500, 55 South Market Street. Telephone: 408-947-8400. Facsimile: 408-947-8500. Telex: 910 250 2931 MACPAG SJ.

Walnut Creek, California Affiliated Office: 1855 Olympic Boulevard, Third Floor, P.O. Box V. Telephone: 415-937-8000. Facsimile: 415-930-2390.

Costa Mesa, California Affiliated Office: The Center Tower, Suite 1110, 650 Town Center Drive. Telephone: 714-668-1060. Facsimile: 714-668-1069.

Washington, D. C. Affiliated Office: The Willard Office Building, Suite 650, 1455 Pennsylvania Avenue, N.W. Telephone: 202-628-4900. Facsimile: 202-628-4912.

Shanghai, People's Republic of China Affiliated Office: Rui Jin Building, Suite 2001, 205 Mao Ming South Road. Telephone: 336201. Facsimile: 336461. Telex: 33919 BTHRD CN.

Taipei, Taiwan, Republic of China Affiliated Office: International Trade Building, Tenth Floor, 333 Keelung Road, Section 1. Telephone: 886-2-723-5000. Facsimile: 886-2-757-6070.

General Practice. Government Contracts. Investment, Banking and Finance, Petroleum, Customs, Corporate and Taxation Law.

NOPADOL INTRALIB, born Bangkok, Thailand, 1949; admitted, 1972, Thailand; 1976, England. *Education:* Chulalongkorn University (LL.B., Honors, 1971); Honorable Society of Gray's Inn, London, England (Barrister-at-Law, 1976). Visiting Lecturer, Police Cadet Academy, 1977-1980. Faculties of Law, Business Administration University and Chulalongkorn University, 1977-1989. Faculty of Law, Thammasat University, 1984-1992. *Member:* Thai Bar Association; Thai Lawyers Association; The Law Association for Asia and the Western Pacific (LAWASIA); The Asian Pa-

(This Listing Continued)

tent Attorneys Association; The ASEAN Law Association. *LAN-GUAGES:* Thai and English. *PRACTICE AREAS:* Banking and Finance; Government Contracts; International Trade; Joint Ventures; Natural Resources Law.

KHAISRI UTAIWAN, born Bangkok, Thailand, 1956; admitted, 1978, Thailand. *Education:* Chulalongkorn University, Faculty of Law (LL.B., lst Class Hons.); Temple University School of Law (LL.M., 1984). Visiting Lecturer, Chulalongkorn University, Master of Business Administrative Program, 1985-1988. *Member:* Thai Bar Association; International Law Association of Thailand. *LANGUAGES:* Thai and English. *PRACTICE AREAS:* Taxation; General Practice; Corporate and Investment Law.

NUTHAVUTH CHATLERTPIPAT, born Bangkok, Thailand, 1967. *Education:* Chulalongkorn University (LL.B., 1990). *LANGUAGES:* Thai and English. *PRACTICE AREAS:* Corporate Law; General Practice.

AREE JOUNGMAHAKOON, born Songkhla, Thailand, 1964; admitted, 1991, Thailand. *Education:* Ramkhamhaeng University (LL.B.). *Member:* Thai Bar Association. *LANGUAGES:* Thai and English. *PRACTICE AREAS:* Mergers and Acquisitions; Corporate Law.

TASSANEE MANEESORN, born Bangkok, Thailand, 1965; admitted, 1988, Thailand. *Education:* Thammasat University (LL.B.). *Member:* Thai Bar Association. *LANGUAGES:* Thai and English. *PRACTICE AREAS:* Labor Law; Corporate Law; Litigation.

RATCHADAPORN NIMPONGSAK, born Udon Thani, Thailand, 1968. *Education:* Thammasat University (LL.B., 1991). *Member:* Thai Bar Association. *LANGUAGES:* Thai and English. *PRACTICE AREAS:* International Business Transactions; Customs Law; Investment Law.

PROMYOS SNITWONGSE, born Bangkok, Thailand, 1965; admitted, 1991, Thailand. *Education:* Thammasat University (LL.B., 1987; Business Law, 1988); The American University, Washington, D.C., U.S.A. (LL.M., 1991). *LANGUAGES:* Thai and English. *PRACTICE AREAS:* General Business Law; International Law.

SAWITREE TREENAWARUT, born Bangkok, Thailand, 1965; admitted, 1988, Thailand. *Education:* Thammasat University (LL.B.). *Member:* Thai Bar Association. *LANGUAGES:* Thai and English. *PRACTICE AREAS:* Immigration Law; Labor Law.

KAMOL WATCHARAMANEE, born Bangkok, Thailand, 1961; admitted, 1989, Thailand. *Education:* Ramkhamhseng University (LL.B., 1989). *Member:* Thai Bar Association. *LANGUAGES:* Thai and English. *PRACTICE AREAS:* Real Estate; Acquisition; Corporate Law.

BENJAMIN SUKANJANAJTEE, born Seattle, Washington, U.S.A., 1967. *Education:* Chulalongkorn University (LL.B., 1989); University of Warwick (LL.M., International Economic Law, 1992). *LANGUAGES:* Thai, English and Japanese. *PRACTICE AREAS:* International Economic Law; Taxation Law; Corporate Law.

NAPAPHAN PETCHNINBUT, born Bangkok, Thailand, 1971; admitted, 1994, Thailand. *Education:* Chulalongkorn University (LL.B.). *Member:* Thai Bar Association. *LANGUAGES:* Thai and English. *PRACTICE AREAS:* Securities Law.

PICHAI PATWICHAICHOAT, born Bangkok, Thailand, 1961; admitted, 1985, Thailand. *Education:* Thammasat University (LL.B., 1985); J. Reuben Clark Law School, Brigham Young University, Provo, Utah (LL.M., 1993). Assistant Editor, Thammasat Law Journal, 1986-1987. Member: BYU Law Alumni Association; J. Reuben Clark Law Society. Foreign Legal Intern, Ater Wynne Hewitt Dodson & Skerritt, Portland, Oregon, Summer, 1991. Volunteer: United States Senator Mark O. Hatfield, Oregon, 1990-1991; Thailand Campus Crusade for Christ. Member: Thai Lawyers Association. *LANGUAGES:* Thai and English. *PRACTICE AREAS:* Business Law.

REPRESENTATIVE CLIENTS: Aermacchi S.p.A.; Alberto-Culver Co.; ANT Nachrichtentechnik GmbH; APAC Holdings, Ltd.; Asia Porcelain Industry Co., Ltd.; AT&T Asia/Pacific Inc.; Avibras Industrial Aeroespacial S.A.; Bangkok Expressway Co., Ltd.; Bangkok Metropolitan Bank, Ltd.; Banque Indosuez; Bell Helicopter Textron Inc.; Black & Decker, Inc.; Boeing Aerospace & Electronics Co.; Bumble Bee Seafoods, Inc.; TelecomAsia Corporation Ltd.; Cadillac Gage Textron, Inc.; Caltex Oil (Thailand), Ltd.; Central States Can Co.; The Chase Manhattan Bank, N.A.; The Church of Jesus Christ of Latter-Day Saints; Citibank, N.A.; Degussa AG; DEG - Deutsche Investitions - und Entwicklungsgesellschaft mbH; Diners Club (Thailand), Ltd.; Fokker Aircraft B.V.; Gaastra Investment Ltd.; Hawker Pacific Ltd.; Helikopter Service A-S; Hewlett Packard (Thailand), Ltd.; International School Association; Israel Aircraft Industries, Ltd.; Kumagai Gumi Co., Ltd.; Leo Burnett, Ltd.; The Mall Group Co., Ltd; Marconi Radar Projects, Ltd.; Mitsubishi Heavy Industries, Ltd.; Nippon Kokan Koji, K.K.; Park Lane Radisson; Phatara-Euromill Co., Ltd.; Potters Industries Inc.; Powell Duffryn plc; The PQ Corp.; Quality Inn Co., Ltd.; Robert Bosch GmbH; Sanwa International Finance, Ltd.; Schmidt International Hold-

(This Listing Continued)

ings Establishment; Shearson Lehman, S.p.A.; SICPA S.A.; Skandinaviska Enskilda Banken; Sony Magnetic Products (Thailand), Ltd.; Standard Elektrik Lorenz AG; Swarovski International Holding AG; Swiss Fund S.A.; Svenson Hair Center (Thailand), Ltd., Telefunken System Technik GmbH; Texaco, Inc.; Textron Financial Corporation; Thomson-CSF; Unisys Corp.; Van Dorn Co.

PACIFIC LEGAL GROUP LTD.

In Association with White & Case

SATHORN THANI II BUILDING, 14TH FLOOR
92/37 SATHORN NUA ROAD
BANGKOK 10500, THAILAND
Telephone: (66-2) 236-6154-7
Fax: (66-2) 237-6771

New York, New York: Telephone: 212-819-8200. Facsimile: 212-354-8113.
Washington, D.C.: Telephone: 202-872-0013. Facsimile: 202-872-0210.
Los Angeles, California: Telephone: 213-620-7700. Facsimile: 213-687-0758; 213-617-2205.
Miami, Florida: Telephone: 305-371-2700. Facsimile: 305-358-5744.
Mexico City, Mexico: Telephone: (52-5) 207-9717. Facsimile: (52-5) 208-3628.
Tokyo, Japan: Telephone: (81-3) 3239-4300. Facsimile: (81-3) 3239-4330.
Hong Kong: Telephone: (852) 2822-8700. Facsimile: (852) 2845-9070; Grice & Co., Solicitors, Telephone: (852) 2826-0333. Facsimile: (852) 2526-7166.
Singapore, Republic of Singapore: Telephone: (65) 225-6000. Facsimile: (65) 225-6009.
Hanoi, Viet Nam: Representative Office, Telephone: (84-4) 227-575/6/7. Facsimile: (84-4) 227-297.
Bombay, India: Telephone: (91-22) 282-6300. Facsimile: (91-22) 282-6305.
London, England: Telephone: (44-171) 726-6361. Facsimile: (44-171) 726-4314; (44-171) 726-8558.
Paris, France: Telephone: (33-1) 42-60-34-05. Facsimile: (33-1) 42-60-82-46.
Brussels, Belgium: Telephone: (32-2) 647-05-89. Facsimile: (32-2) 647-16-75.
Stockholm, Sweden: Telephone: (46-8) 679-80-30. Facsimile: (46-8) 611-21-22.
Helsinki, Finland: Telephone: (358-0) 631-100. Facsimile: (358-0) 179-477.
Moscow, Russia: Telephone: (7-095) 201-9292/3/4/5. Facsimile: (7-095) 201-9284.
Budapest, Hungary: Telephone: (36-1) 269-0550; (36-1) 131-0933. Facsimile: (36-1) 269-1199.
Prague, Czech Republic: Telephone: (42-2) 2481-1796. Facsimile: (42-2) 232-5522.
Warsaw, Poland: Telephone/Facsimile: (48-22) 26-80-53; (48-22) 27-84-86. International Telephone/Facsimile: (48-39) 12-19-06.
Istanbul, Turkey: Telephone: (90-212) 275-68-98; (90-212) 275-75-33. Facsimile: (90-212) 275-75-43.
Ankara, Turkey: Telephone: (90-312) 446-2180. Facsimile: (90-312) 437-9677.
Jeddah, Saudi Arabia: Law Office of Hassan Mahassni, Telephone: (966-2) 651-3535. Facsimile: (966-2) 651-3636.
Riyadh, Saudi Arabia: Law Office of Hassan Mahassni, Telephone: (966-1) 476-7099. Facsimile: (966-1) 479-0110.
Almaty, Kazakhstan: Telephone: (7-3272) 50-7491/2. Facsimile: (7-3272) 61-0842.

General and International Law Practice. Corporate, Financial and Foreign Investment, Environmental, Taxation and Customs, Litigation, Government Contracts, Immigration, Maritime, Infrastructure Projects and Real Estate Law.
Advisory services on China, Vietnam and Indochina matters.

FIRM PROFILE: The firm was established in 1992 and offers a full range of legal and consulting services. The firm is associated with White & Case and constitutes the White & Case office in Bangkok. The firm has a particular interest in environmental and large infrastructure project law. The client base consists, primarily, of North American, Japanese and European companies which are engaged in business transactions in Thailand. The firm also has a practice which concerns investment matters in China and Vietnam and Indochina. The firm has two directors and seven associate lawyers and consultants and a support staff of ten administrative personnel.

(This Listing Continued)

PACIFIC LEGAL GROUP LTD., Bangkok—Continued

DIRECTOR

PAUL G. RUSSELL, born Akron, Ohio, February 23, 1929; admitted, 1958, New York (Not admitted in Thailand). *Education:* Kenyon College (A.B., Hons., 1950); Harvard University (LL.B., 1957). *Member:* The Association of the Bar of the City of New York; New York State, American and International Bar Associations; Law Association for Asia and the Pacific. *LANGUAGES:* English.

ASSOCIATES

PEANGPANOR BOONKLUM, born Phitsanulok, Thailand, March 4, 1966; admitted, 1986, Thailand. *Education:* Chulalongkorn University (LL.B.; LL.M., Business Laws). *Member:* The Law Society of Thailand; Thai Bar Association.

PONGPITAK SAWETNANT, born Bangkok, Thailand, January 13, 1961; admitted, 1982, Thailand. *Education:* Thammasat University (LL.B., Hons.); University of California, Los Angeles (LL.M.). *Member:* Thai Bar Association; The Law Society of Thailand; American Bar Association; American Immigration Lawyers Association.

DOL BUNNAG, born Bangkok, Thailand, September 28, 1964; admitted, 1987, Thailand. *Education:* Chulalongkorn University (LL.B.); University of Texas at Austin (M.C.J.); University of Notre Dame (LL.M.). *Member:* The Law Society of Thailand; Thai Bar Association.

SUPARERK AUYCHAI, born Bangkok, Thailand, May 28, 1969; admitted, 1992, Thailand. *Education:* Chulalongkorn University (LL.B.); University of Michigan (LL.M.); New York University (LL.M.). *Member:* The Law Society of Thailand; Thailand Bar Association.

THERDTHAM PIANPICHARN, born Bangkok, Thailand, October 26, 1954; admitted, 1982, Thailand. *Education:* Thammasat University (LL.B.). *Member:* Thai Bar Association; The Law Society of Thailand.

WANNEE ARTTAVITWORAKARN, born Petchburi, Thailand, June 2, 1965; admitted, 1991, Thailand. *Education:* Ramkhamhaeng University (LL.M.). *Member:* The Law Society of Thailand; Thai Bar Association.

CONSULTANTS

JOSEPH E. STUMPF, born Minneapolis, Minnesota, September 4, 1965; admitted, 1993, California (Not admitted in Thailand). *Education:* San Diego State University (B.S., 1988); University of Southern California, Los Angeles (J.D., 1993).

POLLAK & CO., LTD.

Established in 1991

DIAMOND TOWER, 13TH FLOOR
427/162 SILOM ROAD, BANGRAK
BANGKOK 10500, THAILAND
Telephone: 231 5005; 231 5614 (DIRECT); 231 5228-9 ext. 162
Fax: 231 5535

Paris, France Associated Office: D.S. Paris, 46 rue de Bassano, 75008 Paris. Telephone: 33-1-53675000. Fax: 33-1-47207876.

Hanoi, Vietnam Office: D.S. Pollak & Partners - a Representative Office of Pollak & Co., Ltd., 76 Hang Trong. Telephone: (844) 254971; (844) 250218. Fax: (844) 260260.

Corporate Mergers, Acquisitions, Tax, Banking, Commercial Contracts, Property, General Practice, Arbitration, Litigation, Patents and Trademarks, Foreign Investment, Market Survey, Property and Real Estate.

FIRM PROFILE: Pollak & Co was established in 1991 by Dan A. Pollak, member of the Paris Bar (avocat a la Cour d'Appel de Paris).

When advising the firm's client in specific fields related to local law, local highly specialized legal consultants are hired on a case by case basis.

The firm has a supporting staff of five under the supervision of Mr. Pollak's assistant and office manager, Mrs. Sarivalee Greco.

DAN POLLAK, born Bucharest, Rumania, February 16, 1945; admitted, 1972, Paris; 1982, Bangkok. *Education:* University of Paris (D.E.S. Droit Prive, Doctorate, 1972); International Law Institute (Diploma, 1972). Member, Lawasia Commercial Arbitration Standing Committee, 1982. *Member:* International Bar Association; International Law Association (French Branch); Franco-British Chamber of Commerce (Vice-President, 1978-1981); Franco-Thai Chamber of Commerce; British Chamber of Commerce of Thailand; The Netherlands-Thai Chamber of Commerce. *LAN-*

(This Listing Continued)

GUAGES: English, French, Italian, Rumanian, Thai and Vietnamese. *PRACTICE AREAS:* Foreign Investment Law; International Trade Law; Commercial Contracts; Arbitration.

THANA BENJATHIKUL, born Songkhla, Thailand, April 16, 1957; admitted, 1981, Thailand. *Education:* Ramkhamhaeng University (LL.B., 1980). Barrister-at-Law, 1983. *Member:* Thai Bar Association; The Law Society of Thailand; The Law Association of Thailand; Board of Institute of Law Practice Training. *LANGUAGES:* Thai and English. *PRACTICE AREAS:* Commercial Law; Real Estate Law; Labour Law.

SASITHORN TANANUKUL, born Nakhon Sawan, Thailand, July 9, 1960; admitted, 1983, Thailand. *Education:* Ramkhamhaeng University (LL.B., 1982). *Member:* Thai Bar Association; The Law Association of Thailand. *LANGUAGES:* Thai and English. *PRACTICE AREAS:* Commercial Law; Real Estate Law; Civil Law; Criminal Law; Labour Law.

CHRISTOPHER J. SELINE, admitted, 1991, Illinois (Not admitted in Thailand). *Education:* McGeorge School of Law (LL.M., 1993); Case Western Reserve University (J.D., 1991); Oberlin College (B.A., 1987). *Member:* Inter-Pacific Bar Association; Roppongi Bar Association (Japan); American Bar Association; Illinois State Bar Association; District of Columbia Bar; Chicago Council of Lawyers; Japan Society for Security Management; Association for Computing Machinery. *LANGUAGES:* English. *PRACTICE AREAS:* Computer and High-Tech Law; International Licensing and Intellectual Property Law; International Litigation and Arbitration; International Commercial Law.

REPRESENTATIVE CLIENTS: Sci-Tech Intertrade; Group Paribas; Societe Generale, B.N.P.; Pansea Group of Companies; Foraid; Thai Present; Franco-Pacific; Group Alsthom; Group Guy Degrennes; Genest Enterprises; Freyssinet S.A.; Soletanche; Sanofi; Finance One Ltd.; Five Cail Babcock; Franco-Thai Chamber of Commerce (Bangkok); S.I.F. Enterprise Bachy; Group G.T.M. Pranda Group of Companies; Central Departmental Stores Ltd; Group Asia; Snecma; Thainox; Charles Chevignon; Ideal Loisirs; Euromill Group; International Mobile Machines Corp.; Credit Lyonnais; Group Lyonnaise de Eaux; Embassy of the Czech Republic; Matra Group.

RUSSIN & VECCHI

International Legal Counsellors Thailand, Ltd.

In Affiliation with Walter, Conston, Alexander & Green, P.C. and

Adduci, Mastriani, Schaumberg & Schill

SATHORN CITY TOWER
175 SOUTH SATHORN ROAD, 18TH FLOOR
BANGKOK 10120, THAILAND
Telephone: (662) 679-6005; (662) 679-6015
Fax: (662) 679-6041; (662) 679-6042

Hanoi, Vietnam Office: Russin & Vecchi, 25 Ly Thuong Kiet Street. Telephone: (84-4) 251-699/251-700. Fax: (84-4) 251-742.

Ho Chi Minh City, Vietnam Office: Russin & Vecchi, OSIC Building, 6/F, 8 Nguyen Hue Street. Telephone: (84-8) 243-026/243-114. Fax: (84-8) 243-113.

Moscow, Russia Office: Russin & Vecchi, Danilovsky Hotel Complex, Bolshoy Starodanilovsky, Pereulok No. 5, Moscow 113191. Telephone: (7-095) 954-0652. Telex: 612506 RV MOS SU. Fax: (7-095) 954-0653.

New York, New York Office: Russin & Vecchi, 15th Floor, 90 Park Avenue, 10016-1387. Telephone: 212-210-9543. Fax: 212-210-9493.

Puerto Plata, Dominican Republic Office: Russin Vecchi & Heredia Bonetti, Plaza Turisol Local #11A. Telephone: 809-586-5535. Fax: 809-586-5861.

San Francisco, California Office: Russin & Vecchi, 16th Floor, 580 California Street, 94104. Telephone: 415-421-1100. Fax: 415-421-1103.

Santo Domingo, Dominican Republic Office: Russin Vecchi & Heredia Bonetti, Edificio Monte Mirador, Calle El Recodo No 2, Esquina Winston Churchill, Bella Vista, Apartado Postal 425. Telephone: 809-535-9511. Cable Address: "RUSVEC SANTO DOMINGO." Telex: 3264199 RUSVEC. Fax: 809-535-6649.

Taipei, Taiwan Office: Russin & Vecchi, 9th Floor, 205 Tun Hwa N. Road. Telephone: (886-2) 712-8956. Fax: (886-2) 713-4711.

Washington, D.C. Office: Russin & Vecchi, Second Floor, 1140 Connecticut Avenue, N.W., 20036. Telephone: 202-223-4793. Fax: 202-223-4810.

General Practice. Investment, Banking, Trademark, Copyright, Patent, Mining, Petroleum, Customs, Corporate and Tax Law. Litigation.

(This Listing Continued)

RESIDENT PARTNERS

JAYAVADH BUNNAG, born Bangkok, Thailand, 1943; admitted, 1968, Thailand. *Education:* Chulalongkorn University (LL.B., 1968); Harvard Law School (LL.M., 1972). Lecturer, Thammasat and Chulolongkorn Universities Law School. Past President, Thai-German Chamber of Commerce, 1987-1988. *Member:* Thai Bar Association; Rapporteaur for Committee on Energy and Natural Resources, International Bar Association Hon. Treasurer, Energy Law Section, Law Association for Asia and the Western Pacific. *LANGUAGES:* Thai, English and French.

LEONARD A. CHINITZ, born Jersey City, New Jersey, 1942; admitted, 1967, Missouri and U.S. District Court, Eastern District of Missouri; 1969, Connecticut (Not admitted in Thailand). *Education:* University of Connecticut (B.A., 1964); University of Michigan (J.D., 1967). Visiting Professor of Law, Saigon University Faculty of Law, 1974. Member, Presidential Commission for Revision of the Foreign Investment Laws of the Dominican Republic, 1978. *Member:* The Bar Association of Metropolitan St. Louis; Connecticut Bar Association; The Missouri Bar. *LANGUAGES:* English and Spanish.

CHRISTOPHER J. KING, born Birmingham, England, 1944; admitted, 1968, England and Wales, as a Solicitor of the Supreme Court; 1979, California; 1983, Hong Kong, as a Solicitor of the Supreme Court (Not admitted in Thailand). *Education:* University of Bristol (LL.B., Honours, 1965); University of Singapore (Postgraduate Practical Certificate in Law, 1973). *Member:* State Bar of California; The Law Society, London; Law Society of Hong Kong; International Bar Association. *LANGUAGES:* English, French and German.

SURAPAN THIMKRAJANG, born Bangkok, Thailand, 1946; admitted, 1968, Thailand. *Education:* Thammasat University (LL.B., Honours, 1967); Bar Institute of Legal Education (Diploma, 1968). Vice-President, Law Association for Asia and the Western Pacific (LAWASIA), 1979-1981. *Member:* Thai Lawyers Association (Secretary-General); Thai Bar Association (Member, Board of Directors, 1979—); Law Association for Asia and the Western Pacific (LAWASIA; Member, Lawyers Ethical Committee, 1982—). *LANGUAGES:* Thai and English.

CHAVALIT UTTASART, born Bangkok, Thailand, 1948; admitted, 1971, Thailand; 1976, England. *Education:* Chulalongkorn University (LL.B., Honours, 1970); Bar Institute of Legal Education (Diploma, 1971); The Honorable Society of Gray's Inn, London, England (Barrister-at-Law, 1976). Part-time Lecturer: Ramkhamhaeng University, 1979—; Thammasat University, 1981—; Chulalongkorn University, 1981—. *Member:* Thai Bar Association; The Asian Patent Attorneys Association; The Trademark, Patent and Copyright Association of Thailand (President, 1989—); The Law Association for Asia and the Western Pacific (LAWASIA); ASEAN Law Association; International Trademark Association. *LANGUAGES:* Thai and English.

SUTHARM VALAISATHIEN, born Bangkok, Thailand, 1942; admitted, 1976, Thailand. *Education:* Thammasat University (B.A. in Political Science, 1965; LL.B., 1976); Certificate Institut International d'Administration Publique, Paris, 1969; Docteur en Droit, University of Paris, 1970. Author: "Privileges et immunities des fonctionnaires internationaux dans le systeme des Nations Unies."; "Doctoral Thesis, Paris, 1970." Law of International Institutions, Bangkok, 1976. Visiting Lecturer, Faculty of Law, Ramkhamhaeng University, Chulalongkorn University. Member, American Chamber of Commerce, French Chamber of Commerce, Australian - Thai Chamber of Commerce. Appointed Honorary Consul of Chile for Bangkok, Thailand, April, 1977—. *Member:* Thai Bar Association; Thai Lawyers Association; International Bar Association. *LANGUAGES:* Thai, English, French, Spanish, Italian and Chinese.

SUPOJ BOONYAVANICH, born Rajaburi, Thailand, 1947; admitted, 1971, Thailand. *Education:* Thammasat University (LL.B., 1970); Bar Institute of Legal Education (Diplo ma, 1971); University of Illinois College of Law (M.C.L., 1977; LL.M., 1979). *Member:* Thai Bar Association; Thai Lawyers Association; Law Association for Asia and the Western Pacific (LAWASIA); Association Internationale pour la Protection de la Propriete Industrielle; Asian Patent Attorneys Association; American University Alumni Association. *LANGUAGES:* Thai and English.

VIRA KAMMEE, born Phitsanulok, Thailand, 1953; admitted, 1980, Thailand. *Education:* Putney College for Further Education, London, England (Cert. in Commerce, 1973); Thammasat University (LL.B., 1979); Bar Institute of Legal Education (Diploma, 1981). *Member:* Thai Bar Association; Lawyer Association of Thailand; Trademark, Copyright and Patent Association of Thailand; Law Association for Asia and the Western Pacific

(This Listing Continued)

(LAWASIA); The Institute of Legal Education; Academy of American and International Law Alumni Association. *LANGUAGES:* Thai and English.

PRADIT SAHACHAIYUNTA, born Pathumthani, Thailand, 1952; admitted, 1985, Thailand. *Education:* Ramkhamhaeng University (LL.B., 1974); Institute of Legal Education, Thailand (Barrister-at-Law, 1975); University of London, England (LL.B. , with honors, 1984); Institute of Legal Education, London, England (Barrister-At-Law, with honors, Gray's Inn, 1985). *Member:* Thai Bar Association; Trademark, Patent and Copyright Association of Thailand; Thai Lawyers Association; Honorable Society of Gray's Inn. *LANGUAGES:* Thai and English.

TADA SASTARASATIT, born Petchburi, Thailand, May 28, 1950; admitted, 1973, Thailand. *Education:* Thammasat University, Bangkok, Thailand (LL.B., 1971); Institute of Legal Studies, Bangkok, Thailand; Gray's Inn, London, England. Member, The Honourable Society of Gray's Inn, 1976—. Assistant Editor, Labor Court Journal, 1985. Editorial Staff, Thai Bar Association Law Journal, 1988-1990. Visiting Lecturer, Sukothai-Thammatirat University, 1982-1986. Special Lecturer, Dhurakit Pundit University, 1985-1986. Lecturer: Thammasart University, Labour Law, 1989—; Chulalongkorn University, Labour Law, 1986-1988; Bangkok University, Law of International Trade, 1989—; Ramkhamhaeng University, Law of International Trade, 1992—, Kasetsart University, Mini MBA Course, Commercial Law, 1990—. Judge, Ministry of Justice, 1981-1985. *Member:* Thailand Bar Association; Labour Law Society of Thailand; Lawyers Society of Thailand. *LANGUAGES:* Thai and English.

DUMNERN SUBPAISARN, born 1956; admitted, 1979, Thailand. *Education:* Thammasat University (LL.B., 1979); Harvard Law School (LL.M., 1986). *Member:* Thai Lawyers Association of Thailand; Thai Bar Association.

ASSOCIATES

KITTISAK BUNYARATTAGANON, born Bangkok, Thailand, 1948; admitted, 1975, Thailand. *Education:* Chulalongkorn University (LL.B., 1975). *Member:* Thai Bar Association; Thai Lawyers Association. *LANGUAGES:* Thai and English.

KITJA NGANTHAVEE, born Phuket, Thailand, February 24, 1957; admitted, 1980, Thailand. *Education:* Thammasat University (LL.B., 1979); University College of Wales, Aberystwyt h (LL.B., 1984). Member, Gray's Inn, London. *Member:* Thai Bar Association. *LANGUAGES:* Thai and English.

NILOBON TANGPRASIT, born Lupburi Province, Thailand, 1959; admitted, 1982, Thailand. *Education:* Chulalongkorn University (LL.B., Hons, 1981); Thai Bar Association (Barrister-at-Law, 1983). *Member:* Thai Bar Association; Law Society of Thailand. *LANGUAGES:* Thai and English.

THANAPAT PUPAT, born Bangkok, Thailand, 1959; admitted, 1982, Thailand. *Education:* Chulalongkorn University (LL.B., 1982); University of Southern California (1986); New York University School of Law (M.C.J., 1987); The Institute of Legal Education (Barrister at Law, 1983). *Member:* Thai Bar Association. *LANGUAGES:* Thai and English.

ORNJIRA TANGWONGYODYING, born Bangkok, Thailand, 1961; admitted, 1986, Thailand. *Education:* Thammasat University (LL.B., Second Class Honor, 1983; LL.M., 1991). Lecturer: Kasetsart University, Mini MBA Course, Taxation Law, 1992-1993. *Member:* Law Society of Thailand. *LANGUAGES:* Thai and English.

THANARAK NAOWARAAT, born Bangkok, Thailand, 1964; admitted, 1988, Thailand. *Education:* Thammasat University (LL.B., Hons, 1987); Institute of Legal Education, Thai Bar Association (Barrister-at-Law, 1989). *Member:* Thai Bar Association; Law Society of Thailand. *LANGUAGES:* Thai, English and French.

SUWIT PIPATTANACHAIYAPONG, born Bangkok, Thailand, 1964; admitted, 1988, Thailand. *Education:* Chulalongkorn University (LL.B., 1st Class Hons, 1988); Institute of Legal Education, Thai Bar Association (Barrister-at-Law, 1989). *Member:* Thai Bar Association. *LANGUAGES:* Thai, English and Chinese (Mandarin).

CHANMANU SUMAWONG, born Bangkok, Thailand, May 20, 1956; admitted, 1978, Thailand. *Education:* Thammasat University (LL.B., 2nd class honour, 1978); George Washington University (M.C.L., 1981; LL.M., 1982). Judge: Ministry of Justice; Nakornratsrima Provincial Court, The Secretary of the Central Labour Court, Thailand, 1988-1989. *Member:* Thai Bar Association. *LANGUAGES:* Thai and English.

VARAVUDH MEESAIYATI, born Bangkok, Thailand, 1962; admitted, 1983, Thailand. *Education:* Stipatum University (LL.B., 1983); Thai

(This Listing Continued)

RUSSIN & VECCHI, Bangkok—Continued

Barrister (1984). *Member:* Thai Bar Association; Thai Lawyer Association. *LANGUAGES:* Thai and English.

ORAWAN TEJAPAIBUL, born Bangkok, Thailand, 1957; admitted, 1985, Massachusetts; 1987, California (Not admitted in Thailand). *Education:* Occidental College (B.A., 1980); Pace University (J.D., 1984); Boston University (LL.M., 1988). *LANGUAGES:* Thai and English.

UMAWADEE RATTANA-UDOM, born Bangkok, Thailand, 1963; admitted, 1989, Thailand. *Education:* Thammasat University (LL.B., 1984). *Member:* Thai Bar Association; Law Society of Thailand. *LANGUAGES:* Thai and English.

NETIPONG WICHITWECHKARN, born Bangkok, Thailand, 1963; admitted, 1986, Thailand. *Education:* Thammasat University (LL.B., 1985); Harvard University (LL.M., 1987); University of Chicago Law School (LL.M., 1988). Lecturer at Bangkok University, 2nd Special Lecturer at Ramkhamhaeng University. *Member:* Thai Bar Association. *LANGUAGES:* Thai and English.

PICHARN SUKPARANGSEE, born Chon Buri Province, Thailand, 1961; admitted, 1987, Thailand. *Education:* Thammasat University (LL.B., 1983). Registrar, Lawyers Association of Thailand (1990-1992). *Member:* Thai Bar Association; Law Society of Thailand; Lawyers Association of Thailand. *LANGUAGES:* Thai, English and French.

PORNCHAI WIWATPATTARAKUL, born Bangkok, Thailand, March 31, 1960; admitted, 1989, England; 1994, Thailand. *Education:* Thammasat University (LL.B., 1980); Oxford University (B.A., 1986); Dundee University (LL.M., 1989); Middle Temple (Barrister-at-Law). Author: "Forward Trading in Brent Crude," Lloyd's Maritime & Commercial Law Quarterly, pp. 143-145, May 1989. Junior Law Officer, Judicial Council, Bangkok, Thailand, 1982-1983. *LANGUAGES:* Thai and English.

ORAPIN SREESANGKOM, born Bangkok, Thailand, December 22, 1963; admitted, 1984, Thailand. *Education:* Thammasat University (LL.B., 1984); Institute of Legal Education (Barrister-at-Law, 1986); Harvard University (LL.M., 1989); Boston University (LL.M., 1990). Member, Thammasat Law School Alumni Association, 1991. Member, Lawyers Society of Thailand, 1986. Special Lecturer at Kasetsart University, Faculty of Business Administration. *Member:* Thai Bar Association. *LANGUAGES:* Thai and English.

SUPASAK CHIRASAVINUPRAPAND, born Bangkok, Thailand, August 24, 1964; admitted, 1990, Thailand. *Education:* Thammasat University (LL.B., 1985); Institute of Legal Education (Barrister-at-Law, 1986); Northeastern University (M.S., Economics, 1988); California Western School of Law (M.C.L., 1989); Arizona State University (LL.M., 1990). Lecturer at Bangkok University and Special Lecturer at Ramkhamhaeng University. *Member:* Thai Bar Association; Thai Lawyers Association; The Trademark, Patent and Copyright Association of Thailand; The Asian Patent Attorneys Association; International Association For the Protection of Industrial Property. *LANGUAGES:* Thai and English.

ARUNEE M. TAEPAISITPHONGSE, born Bangkok, Thailand, November 12, 1964; admitted, 1987, Thailand. *Education:* Thammasat University (LL.B., 1986); Institute of Legal Education (Barrister-at-Law, 1987); Western Michigan University (M.A., 1989); Tulane University (LL.M., 1990). *Member:* Thai Bar Association; Thai Lawyer Association. *LANGUAGES:* Thai and English.

SURAPOL ONOORA, born Samut Songkhram Province, Thailand, June 4, 1957; admitted, 1991, Thailand. *Education:* Thammasat University (LL.B., 1979); McGill University (LL.M., 1991). Part-time Lecturer: Ramkhamhaeng University, 1993—; Kasetsart University, 1993—; Bangkok University, 1993—. *Member:* Thai Lawyers Association. *LANGUAGES:* Thai and English.

SIRIPEN VONGSNARA, born Bangkok, Thailand, December 16, 1965; admitted, 1993, Thailand. *Education:* Ramkamhaeng University (LL.B., 1993). *LANGUAGES:* Thai, English.

THANATHIP PICHEDVANICHOK, born Bangkok, Thailand, January 12, 1965; admitted, 1993, Thailand. *Education:* Thammasat University (LL.B., 1986); Institute of Legal Education, Bangkok (Barrister-at-Law, 1988); Southern Methodist University (LL.M., 1989); University of Pennsylvania (LL.M., 1990). Thai Bar Association; Law Society of Thailand. *LANGUAGES:* Thai, English.

(This Listing Continued)

(For Biographical Data of other Personnel, see Professional Biographies at: Washington, D.C., U.S.A.; San Francisco, California, U.S.A.; New York, N.Y., U.S.A.; Taipei, Taiwan; Santo Domingo, Dominican Republic; Ho Chi Minh City, Hanoi, S.R. Vietnam; Moscow, Russia).

SIAM PREMIER INTERNATIONAL LAW OFFICE

9TH FLOOR, KIAN GWAN BUILDING I
140 WIRELESS ROAD
BANGKOK 10330, THAILAND
Telephone: (66) 2-255 1030-6; 251-8287; 251-8319
Telefax: (66) 2-253-4732; 253-9482

In Association with Victor Chu & Co. and Woo, Kwan, Lee & Lo.

General Practice, Corporation and Corporate Financing, Banking, Domestic and Foreign Investment, Taxation, Immigration, Mergers and Acquisitions, Litigation, Real Estate, Telecommunications, Industry and Infrastructure and Indo-China Practice.

MEMBERS OF FIRM

PHISUD DEJAKAISAYA, born Bangkok, Thailand, January 15, 1955; admitted, 1984, Thailand. *Education:* Thammasat University (LL.B., 1980); Southern Methodist University, U.S.A., (M.C.L., Scholarship, 1983-1984); Cornell University (Special Student, 1982); Academy of International and Comparative Law (Southwestern Legal Foundation's Scholarship, 1984). *Member:* Thai Bar Association; Thai Lawyers Association. *LANGUAGES:* Thai and English.

PIYAMARN PONGTORNPIPAT, born Bangkok, Thailand, 1958; admitted, 1981, Thailand. *Education:* Chulalongkorn University (LL.B., Honors, 1981); Sukhothai Thammathirat Open University, Faculty of Arts (Cert. of English for Lawyers, 1985); American University (LL.M., Fulbright Scholarship, 1988-1990); Academy of International and Comparative Law, Southwestern Legal Foundation's Scholarship, 1986. *Member:* Thai Bar Association; Thai Lawyers Association. *LANGUAGES:* Thai and English.

SURAPOL SRANGSOMWONG, born Bangkok, Thailand, 1958; admitted, 1981, Thailand. *Education:* Chulalongkorn University (LL.B., Honors, 1980). Thai Barrister at Law. *Member:* Thai Bar Association. *LANGUAGES:* Thai and English.

PADUNGSAK LAOHASURAYODHIN, born Bangkok, Thailand, November 5, 1955; admitted, 1980, Thailand. *Education:* Thammasat University (LL.B., 1979). *Member:* Thai Bar Association. *LANGUAGES:* Thai and English.

APICHART CHIRABANDHU, born Bangkok, Thailand, 1958; admitted, 1981, Thailand. *Education:* Ramkhamhaeng University (LL.B., 1980). *Member:* Thai Bar Association; Thai Lawyers Association. *LANGUAGES:* Thai and English.

ASSOCIATES

AMARA BHUWANAWAT, born Bangkok, Thailand, 1958; admitted, 1981, Thailand. *Education:* Chulalongkorn University (LL.B., 1980). Thai Barrister at Law. *Member:* Thai Bar Association. *LANGUAGES:* Thai and English.

ADUL KHOKITCHALERT, born Bangkok, Thailand, April 11, 1961; admitted, 1984, Thailand. *Education:* Thammasat University (LL.B., 1983). Thai Barrister at Law, 1987. *Member:* Thai Bar Association. *LANGUAGES:* Thai and English.

PHASUNSOOK AYANAPUTRA, born Bangkok, Thailand, 1959; admitted, 1986, Thailand. *Education:* Chulalongkorn University (LL.B., 1983); University of Iowa (M.C.L., 1987). Thai Barrister at Law. *Member:*

(This Listing Continued)

Thai Bar Association; Thai Lawyers Association. *LANGUAGES:* Thai and English.

SIRIRAT CHANGKASIRI, born Bangkok, Thailand, 1964; admitted, 1990, Thailand. *Education:* Thammasat University (LL.B., 1985); American University (LL.M., 1989). Thai Barrister at Law. *Member:* Thai Bar Association; Thai Lawyers Association. *LANGUAGES:* Thai and English.

PHOJ KHOMANANT, born Ang Thong Province, Thailand, 1963; admitted, 1986, Thailand. *Education:* Thammasat University (LL.B., 1985). *LANGUAGES:* Thai and English.

LINDA OSATHAWORANAN, born Bangkok, Thailand, 1969; admitted, 1992, Thailand. *Education:* Chulalongkorn University (LL.B., Honors, 1991). *LANGUAGES:* Thai and English.

SUCHART MEESOMBOONPOONSUK, born Bangkok, Thailand, 1967; admitted, 1992, Thailand. *Education:* Chulalongkorn University (LL.B., 1991). *Member:* Thai Bar Association. *LANGUAGES:* Thai, English, Japanese and Cantonese.

RAWAT CHOMSRI, born Bangkok, Thailand, 1969; admitted, 1991, Thailand. *Education:* Thammasat University (LL.B., 1991). *Member:* Thai Bar Association; Thai Lawyers Association. *LANGUAGES:* Thai and English.

KOSOL PATTAMA, born Nakhon Ratchasima Province, Thailand, 1967. *Education:* Ramkhamhaeng University (LL.B., 1992). *LANGUAGES:* Thai and English.

ORAWAN TIRAVEERAKAJORN, born Nakhon Ratchasima Province, Thailand, 1969. *Education:* Thammasat University (LL.B., 1991). *LANGUAGES:* Thai and English.

RUNGTIP VIBOONKIAT, admitted, 1992, Thailand. *Education:* Chulalongkorn University (LL.B., 1991). *LANGUAGES:* Thai and English.

TAWEE KHOSITJIRANUN, admitted, 1992, Thailand. *Education:* Chulalongkorn University (LL.B, 1st Honors, 1991). *LANGUAGES:* Thai and English.

WISON PRUMKACHANG, admitted, 1992, Thailand. *Education:* Chulalongkorn University (LL.B., 1991). *LANGUAGES:* Thai and English.

KASEM PUMPUANG, admitted, 1992, Thailand. *Education:* Chulalongkorn University (LL.B., Honors, 1991). *LANGUAGES:* Thai and English.

JIRASAWAT SURARIDDHIDHAMRONG, admitted, 1993, Thailand. *Education:* Howard University (M.C.J., 1993). *LANGUAGES:* Thai and English.

TREEPONG NA NONGKAI, admitted, 1993, Thailand. *Education:* Ramkhamhaeng University (LL.B., 1992). *LANGUAGES:* Thai and English.

PLUTTIPONG KLEESUWAN, admitted, 1984, Thailand. *Education:* Chulalongkorn University (LL.B., 1983); De Paul University, Chicago (LL.M., 1988). *LANGUAGES:* Thai and English.

SUPASIRI NAKARAT, admitted, 1993, Thailand. *Education:* Thammasat University (LL.B., 1992). *LANGUAGES:* Thai and English.

NITHI SOOMSWASDI, admitted, 1989, Thailand. *Education:* Thammasat University (LL.B., 1988; Thai Barrister-at-Law, 1990); Boston University (LL.M., 1994). *Member:* Thai Bar Association; The Law Society of Thailand. *LANGUAGES:* Thai and English.

KONG SURIYAMONTOL, admitted, 1994, Thailand. *Education:* Chulalongkorn University (LL.B., 1993). *LANGUAGES:* Thai and English.

OF COUNSEL

DR. SURAKIART SATHIRATHAI. *Education:* Chulalongkorn University (LL.B., Honors, 1979); Fletcher School of Law and Diplomacy, Tufts University (M.A.L.D., 1981); Harvard Law School (LL.M., 1982; S.J.D., 1985). Former Policy Adviser to the Prime Ministers of Thailand. Member, Board of Investment, Office of the Prime Minister, Thailand. Dean and Associate Professor of Law Faculty, Chulalongkorn University.

POL.LT.GEN. SUPAS CHIRABUNDHU. *Education:* Police Academic Diplomat, Thammasat University (LL.B.). Thai Barrister at Law. Former Associate Judge, 1973-1987. Acting Head Academic Affaire Office.

(This Listing Continued)

SUDHARMA YOONAIDHARMA. *Education:* Chulalongkorn University (Honors, LL.B.); George Washington University (M.C.L.); Harvard Law School (LL.M.); New York University (Post LL.M.). Researcher, Former Prime Minister's Policy Advisory Council, 1990-1991. Assistant Director at Sukhothai Thammathirat Open University, 1989-1990. Assistant to Senator, President of the National Assembly, 1990-1991.

SAKDA THANITCUL. *Education:* Chulalongkorn University (Honors, LL.B.); Kyoto University (LL.M.);. *LANGUAGES:* Thai, Japanese, English.

WEERASAK KOWSURAT. *Education:* Chulalongkorn University (Honors, LL.B.); Harvard Law School (LL.M.). Former Secretary to the President of Parliament of Thailand. Secretary: to the President of the Senate of Thailand; to the Chairman of the Constitutional Tribunal. Managing Director of Match Cross International Co., Ltd. Professor of Law Ramkhamhaeng University.

MICHAEL D. POPKIN, (Not admitted in Thailand). *Education:* University of Toronto (B.A., 1989); University of British Columbia (LL.B., 1993). *LANGUAGES:* English and French.

MARK E. SAFERITE, (Not admitted in Thailand). *Education:* Northern Arizona University (B.S., 1977; M.A., 1979); Santa Clara University School of Law (J.D., 1987). *LANGUAGES:* English.

THOMAS JAMES MILLER, (Not admitted in Thailand). *Education:* Melbourne University (B.A.; LL.B., Honors, 1986); Keio University, 1984. *LANGUAGES:* English and Japanese.

CONSULTANT

SUI LIN TEOH, (Not admitted in Thailand). *Education:* Queen Mary College, University of London (LL.B., Honors, 1988). *LANGUAGES:* English.

TILLEKE & GIBBINS

(Registered Ordinary Partnership)

Advocates & Solicitors

Established in 1893

TILLEKE & GIBBINS BUILDING
64/1 SOI TON SON, PLOENCHIT ROAD
BANGKOK 10330, THAILAND
Telephone: (International Dialing Area Code 66-2) 254-2640-58
Telefax: (International Dialing Area Code 66-2) 254-4304; (66-8)
621-0173
Telex: 82978 LYMAN TH
Cable Address: Lyman Bangkok

REVISERS OF THE BANGKOK LAW DIGEST FOR THIS DIRECTORY

Ho Chi Minh, Vietnam Office: Tilleke & Gibbins Consultants Ltd., 2nd Floor, The Vietnam National Gold-Silver and Gemstones Corporation Building, 3-5 Ho Tung Mau, District 1. Telephone: (84-8) 251-645, 251-695, 251-700. Fax: (84-8) 242-226.

Hanoi, Vietnam Office: Boss Hotel, Suite 207, 60 Nguyen Du Street. Telephone: (84-4) 227-895/6. Telefax: (84-4) 227-897.

Practice Groups: Banking and Finance, Commercial and International Trade, Corporate, Securities and Investment, Dispute Resolution, Environment, Food and Drugs, Intellectual Property, Japanese Client Services, Labor, Maritime, Aviation and Insurance, Private Client Services, Property and Construction, Taxation and Telecommunications.

FIRM PROFILE: Tilleke & Gibbins, established in 1893, is the largest independent law firm in Thailand as well as the oldest. The firm has also expanded to Vietnam, with offices in Hanoi and Ho Chi Minh City. The original and succeeding partners have served the royal family, the government and both the Thai and foreign business communities with distinction. The firm is the Thailand member of several international associations of independent law firms including Lex Mundi, Multilaw, and Legal Resources Group, an international association in the U.K. The firm is also the designated "Revisor for the Martindale-Hubbell Law Digest" for Thailand and co-authors the leading investors manual in Thailand, Thailand Business Basics.

(This Listing Continued)

TILLEKE & GIBBINS, Bangkok—Continued

SENIOR PARTNERS

ROJVIT B. PERIERA, born Bangkok, Thailand, 1921; admitted, 1946, Thailand. *Education:* Thammasat University (LL.B., 1946). Managing Partner, Tilleke & Gibbins T&G Trustee. President, Rotary Club of Bangkok South, 1971-1972. District Governor, Rotary International District 335, 1985-1986. Vice President, Franco-Thai Chamber of Commerce, 1986-1987. *Member:* Thai Bar Association; Law Society of Thailand; Asian Patent Attorneys Association; The Law Association for Asia and the Western Pacific (LAWASIA). *LANGUAGES:* Thai and English. *PRACTICE AREAS:* Litigation; Commercial Law.

DAVID LYMAN, born Washington, D.C., U.S.A., 1936; admitted, 1966, California (Not admitted in Thailand). *Education:* Duke University (B.S.E.E., 1958); Hastings College of the Law, University of California (J.D., 1965); Parker School of Foreign and Comparative Law, Columbia University (Certificate, 1974). Legal Consultant, Thailand, 1967—. Governor, 1974—, Honorary Secretary, Vice President, 1974, 1983-1985 and President, 1975, 1986, American Chamber of Commerce in Thailand. Director, Thai Board of Trade, 1975, 1986 and Vice Chairman, 1975-1977 (Taxation), 1985-1989 (Americans Abroad) and 1992—(Environmental Affairs) Asia Pacific Council of American Chambers of Commerce (APCAC), 1985-1989 and 1991—; Delegate to APCAC from Thailand, 1975—. Appointed as Founding Member of Thai Prime Minister's Foreign Investment Advisory Council, 1975. Chairman, 1988-1990 and Secretary, 1982-1987, Foreign Chambers of Commerce Working Group. Founder, Executive Board Member, Lex Mundi, 1989-1991; Designate to World Economic Forum, 1988—. *Member:* State Bar of California; American Bar Association; Law Association for Asia and the Western Pacific (LAWASIA); International Bar Association; Asian Patent Attorneys Association; International Bar Association; American Society of International Law. *LANGUAGES:* English. *PRACTICE AREAS:* Commercial Law; Corporate Law; Investment Law; Client Relations and Development; Management.

ALBERT LYMAN (1905-1984).

FREDA RING LYMAN, (MRS.) (1900-1986).

SENIOR ATTORNEYS

ANONGPORN THANACHAIARY, born Nakhon Nayok, Thailand, 1950; admitted, 1977, Thailand. *Education:* Thammasat University (LL.B. Honors, 1972); Bar Institute of Legal Education (Barrister-at-Law, 1983). Harvard University, Program of Instruction for Lawyers. *Member:* Thai Bar Association; Law Society of Thailand; Law Association for Asia and the Pacific (LAWASIA); Lawyers' Association of Thailand; Women Lawyers Association of Thailand; International Bar Association (IBA); Inter-Pacific Bar Association; Board of Institute of Law Practice Training; The Real Estate Association. *LANGUAGES:* Thai and English. *PRACTICE AREAS:* Commercial and International Trade; Communications; Property (Real Estate); Estate; Family Law.

SUNTORN CHANTARASAK, born Lop Buri Province, Thailand, 1929; admitted, 1953, Thailand. *Education:* Thammasat University (LL.B., 1950); Bar Institute of Legal Education (Barrister-at-Law, 1956). Officer, Department of Taxation, Ministry of Finance, 1950-1960. Judge and Chief Judge, Provincial Court, 1961-1980. Judge, Civil and Criminal Courts, 1974-1981. Judge and Senior Judge, Court of Appeals, 1980-1985, Judge and Senior Judge, Supreme Court, 1985-1989, Ministry of Justice; Judge Examination Committee, 1984-1986. *Member:* Thai Bar Association. *LANGUAGES:* Thai. *PRACTICE AREAS:* Litigation.

THANES PERIERA, born Bangkok, Thailand, 1951; admitted, 1982, Thailand. *Education:* Thammasat University (LL.B., 1974); University College of Wales, Aberystwyth (LL.B., 1978). Article: IP ASIA. *Member:* Thai Bar Association; Law Society of Thailand; Thai Recognized Group of Asian Patent Attorneys Association (Councillor); Licensing Executive Society (LES) Australia and New Zealand; Lawyers Association of Thailand; Trademark, Patent and Copyright Association of Thailand (Committee Member); United States Trademark Association. *LANGUAGES:* Thai and English. *PRACTICE AREAS:* Intellectual Property; Real Estate; Environmental Law.

CHINACHART VATANASUCHART, born Bangkok, Thailand, 1958; admitted, 1985, Thailand. *Education:* Ramkhamhaeng University (LL.B., 1979); Bar Institute of Legal Education (Barrister-at-Law, 1981); Tulane University, Louisiana (M.C.L., 1985; LL.M., 1986). *Member:* Thai Bar Association; Law Society of Thailand; Lawyers Association of Thailand; In-

(This Listing Continued)

ter-Pacific Bar Association. *LANGUAGES:* Thai and English. *PRACTICE AREAS:* Maritime; Customs; Labor Law.

DUSADEE TACHASINKUL, born Bangkok, Thailand, 1951; admitted, 1975, Thailand. *Education:* Thammasat University (LL.B., 1974); McGeorge School of Law, University of the Pacific (Certificate) International Business and Commercial Law. *Member:* Thai Bar Association; Law Society of Thailand; Lawyers Association of Thailand; Women Lawyers Association of Thailand. *LANGUAGES:* Thai, English and Cantonese. *PRACTICE AREAS:* Corporate; Securities; Investment Law.

SAY SUJINTAYA JENSEN, born Bangkok, Thailand, 1961; admitted, 1986, California (Not admitted in Thailand). *Education:* University of Southern California (B.A., 1983); University of Santa Clara (Summer Abroad Program); University of Hong Kong (1985); Loyola Marymount University, Los Angeles (J.D., 1986). *Member:* California Bar Association; International Trademark Association; Asian Patent Attorneys Association; Intellectual Property Association of Thailand. *LANGUAGES:* Thai and English. *PRACTICE AREAS:* Intellectual Property; Commercial Law.

ATTORNEYS

CHAKORN PICHAIWONGSE, born Songkhla, Thailand, 1962; admitted, 1982, Thailand. *Education:* Thammasat University (LL.B., 1982); Georgetown University (Certificate of Advanced English Studies, 1987); American University (LL.M., 1988). *Member:* Law Society of Thailand; Thai Bar Association; American Political Science Association (Congressional Fellow, 1992-1993). *LANGUAGES:* Thai and English. *PRACTICE AREAS:* Taxation; Commercial and International Trade; Telecommunications; Arbitration.

CHAOVAI SAPAYAPRAPA, born Bangkok, Thailand, 1945; admitted, 1980, Thailand. *Education:* Naval Rating School (Certificate, Navigation, 1966); Naval Communication School (Certificate, Radio & Telecommunications, 1967); Civil Aviation Training Centre (Certificate, Air Traffic Service, 1968); Sq. Comm., 1985, United States Air Force in Thailand (Diploma, Air Traffic Control, 1976); Ramkhamhaeng University (LL.B., 1980). *Member:* Thai Bar Association; The Law Society of Thailand; Law Association for Asia and the Pacific (LAWASIA); International Bar Association. *LANGUAGES:* Thai and English. *PRACTICE AREAS:* Litigation.

CHATBAUDEE CHARUSAKUL, born Yala, Thailand, 1953; admitted, 1975, Thailand. *Education:* Ramkhamhaeng University (LL.B., 1973); Bar Institute of Legal Education (Barrister-at-Law, 1983); Araneta University, Philippines (M.P.A., Silver Medal (Benemeritus), 1985). *Member:* Thai Bar Association; The Law Society of Thailand. *LANGUAGES:* Thai and English. *PRACTICE AREAS:* Litigation.

CHINTANA WIRASATHIEN, born Bangkok, Thailand, 1942; admitted, 1982, Thailand. *Education:* Chulalongkorn University (B.A., 1964); Ramkhamhaeng University (LL.B., 1981). *Member:* Thai Bar Association. *LANGUAGES:* Thai and English. *PRACTICE AREAS:* Translations.

DUSADEE JITTASAIYAPAN, born Bangkok, Thailand, 1959; admitted, 1981, Thailand. *Education:* Ramkhamhaeng University (LL.B., 1981); George Washington University (M.C.L., 1987); American University, Washington College of Law (LL.M., 1987). *Member:* Thai Bar Association; Law Society of Thailand; Inter-Pacific Bar Association. *LANGUAGES:* Thai and English. *PRACTICE AREAS:* Commercial and International Trade; Real Estate; Government Procurement; Labor; Telecommunications Law.

KITTI THAISOMBOON, born Bangkok, Thailand, 1965; admitted, 1988, Thailand. *Education:* Chulalongkorn University (LL.B.). *Member:* Thai Bar Association. *LANGUAGES:* Thai and English. *PRACTICE AREAS:* Commercial and International Trade; Estate; Family Law.

LADDA PHENPOL, born Bangkok, Thailand, 1937; admitted, 1989, Thailand. *Education:* Ramkhamhaeng University (LL.B.). *Member:* Law Society of Thailand; Thai Bar Association. *LANGUAGES:* Thai and English. *PRACTICE AREAS:* Corporate Law.

MANEERAT SAKRANONDA, born Nakhon, Pratom, Thailand, 1950; admitted, 1978, Thailand. *Education:* Ramkhamhaeng University (LL.B). *Member:* Thai Bar Association; Law Association for Asia and the Pacific (LAWASIA); Law Society of Thailand; Lawyers Association of Thailand; Women Lawyers Association of Thailand. *LANGUAGES:* Thai and English. *PRACTICE AREAS:* Litigation.

PIMVIMOL VIPAMANEERUT, born Bangkok, Thailand, 1965; (Not admitted in Thailand). *Education:* Chulalongkorn University (LL.B.); University of Southampton (LL.M., 1994); London Institute of Shipping and

(This Listing Continued)

Transport, London City College (Dipl. and Higher Cert. in Shipping Management, 1992-1993). *Member:* Law Society of Thailand. *LANGUAGES:* Thai and English. *PRACTICE AREAS:* Maritime Law.

PIYANUJ RATPRASTAPORN, born Bangkok, Thailand, 1962; admitted, 1990, Thailand (Not admitted in Thailand). *Education:* Thammasat University (LL.B., Honors, 1984); American University, Washington, D.C. (LL.M., 1987). *Member:* Law Society of Thailand; Thai Bar Association; Women Lawyers Association of Thailand. *LANGUAGES:* Thai and English. *PRACTICE AREAS:* Corporate; Securities; Investment Law.

PORNCHAI SRISAWANG, born Bangkok, Thailand, 1958; admitted, 1981, Thailand. *Education:* Ramkhamhaeng University (LL.B., 1979). *Member:* Thai Bar Association; Law Association for Asia and the Pacific (LAWASIA); Lawyers Association of Thailand; Thai Contractors Association. *LANGUAGES:* Thai and English. *PRACTICE AREAS:* Litigation; Land Law.

PRABJOTE SRIKIJJAPORN, born Bangkok, Thailand, 1958; (Not admitted in Thailand). *Education:* Sukhothai Thammathirat University (LL.B., 1992). *Member:* Intellectual Property Association of Thailand; Asian Patent Attorneys Association. *LANGUAGES:* Thai and English. *PRACTICE AREAS:* Patent Law.

SAMACK SANGWORNRAJASAP, born Maha Sarakham, Thailand, 1926; admitted, 1947, Thailand. *Education:* Thammasat University (LL.B., 1947). Public Prosecutor, 1948-1959. Judge, Court of Appeals, 1960-1980. Member, Examination Committee and Assistant to General Secretary, Bar Institute of Legal Education, 1968-1971 and 1974-1980. *Member:* Thai Bar Association; Law Society of Thailand; Lawyers Association of Thailand; Law Association for Asia and the Pacific (LAWASIA). *LANGUAGES:* Thai and English. *PRACTICE AREAS:* Litigation.

SANTHAPAT PERIERA, born Bangkok, Thailand, 1965; admitted, 1984, Thailand. *Education:* Thammasat University (LL.B.); University of Florida at Gainesville (Diploma); University of Miami (M.C.L.); Boston University (LL.M.) International Banking Law Studies. *Member:* Thai Bar Association; Law Society of Thailand. *LANGUAGES:* Thai and English. *PRACTICE AREAS:* Banking and Finance; Environmental Law.

SAWANG KUNANURUGSPONG, born Bangkok, Thailand, 1952; admitted, 1977, Thailand. *Education:* Ramkhamhaeng University (LL.B., 1976); Bar Institute of Legal Education (Barrister-at-Law, 1985); Thammasat University (Grad. Dip. Business Law, 1989). *Member:* Thai Bar Association; Law Society of Thailand; Lawyers Association of Thailand. *LANGUAGES:* Thai, English and Tae Chew. *PRACTICE AREAS:* Litigation.

SRILA THONGKLANG, born Lumpoon, Thailand, 1957; admitted, 1986, Thailand. *Education:* Ramkhamhaeng University (LL.B.); Bar Institute of Legal Education (Certificate) Intellectual Property Law. *Member:* Thai Bar Association; Law Society of Thailand; Trademark, Patent and Copyright Association of Thailand. *LANGUAGES:* Thai and English. *PRACTICE AREAS:* Litigation.

VALLOP SAKRANONDA, born Bangkok, Thailand, 1945; admitted, 1971, Thailand. *Education:* Thammasat University (LL.B., 1970). *Member:* Thai Bar Association; Law Society of Thailand; Lawyers Association of Thailand; Law Association for Asia and the Pacific (LAWASIA). *LANGUAGES:* Thai and English. *PRACTICE AREAS:* Litigation.

WORANUCH PERIERA, born Bangkok, Thailand, 1961; admitted, 1983, Thailand. *Education:* Chulalongkorn University (LL.B., LL.M. and Certificate, Negotiation Techniques and Contract Drafting); Office of the Judicial Affairs (Certificate) Intellectual Property Law. *Member:* Thai Bar Association; Law Society of Thailand; Asian Patent Attorneys Association; Trademark, Patent and Copyright Association of Thailand; Lawyers Association of Thailand. *LANGUAGES:* Thai and English. *PRACTICE AREAS:* Copyright Law.

OF COUNSEL

JUNJIRO J. NISHINO, born Japan, 1917; (Not admitted in Thailand). *Education:* Kanagawa University (B.A. Economics and Commerce); Thammasat University (LL.B., 1941); Foreign Service Institute, Ministry of Foreign Affairs, Tokyo (Diploma, 1947). Vice-Consul, Japanese Embassy, Thailand, 1937-1951. President, 1945-1950 and Chairman, 1950-1989, Tomen (Thailand) Co. Ltd. President, Tomen Enterprise (Bangkok) Ltd., 1987. Vice President, Thai Toray Textile Mills Co., Ltd., 1985-1989. President, Rotary Club of Dhonburi, 1981-1982. Vice-President, Thai-Japanese Association, 1971—. President, Japanese Association, 1971-1979; Director, 1970-1985, Advisor, 1985-1991, Japanese Chamber of Commerce in Bangkok. Chairman, Japanese School in Thailand, 1979—; Executive Committee

(This Listing Continued)

of East Asian Institute of Thommasat University, 1984-1989. *LANGUAGES:* Japanese, Thai, English and Mandarin. *PRACTICE AREAS:* Japanese Client Relations.

DR. CHAROEN KANTHAWONGS, born Bangkok, Thailand, 1933; admitted, 1957, Thailand. *Education:* Chulalongkorn University (LL.B., Honors); Syracuse University (M.A. International Relations; Ph.D., Higher Educational Administration). President, Bangkok University, 1962-1988. Law Lecturer, Chulalongkorn University, 1961-1962. Appointed Member of Parliament, 1973. Elected Member of Parliament, 1974, 1975, 1986, 1988-1990. Deputy Secretary to the Prime Minister, 1980-1983. Deputy Minister of Agriculture, 1988-1990. Deputy Secretary General to the Prime Minister, 1980-1983. Deputy Minister of Agriculture, 1988-1900. Minister of Science, Technology and Energy, 1990. President, Thai-Korean Chamber of Commerce, 1982-1985. Secretary General, International Association of University President, 1984-1987. Chairman, Commission of Science, Technology and Energy, House of Representatives, 1987. *Member:* Thai Bar Association; Law Society of Thailand; Lawyers Association of Thailand (Life Member); International Bar Association (IBA). *LANGUAGES:* Thai and English. *PRACTICE AREAS:* Government Relations.

Languages: Thai, English, Japanese, French, Chinese, German and Vietnamese.

REPRESENTATIVE CLIENTS: American Express Co.; Export Development Corp. Ltd.; Credit Agricole (HK); British, Chinese, Greek, Japanese, P & I Clubs; Bangkok Shipowners and Agents Association; Freeport-McMoran Oil and Gas; Maersk Oile og Gas AS; Unocal Corporation; All Nippon Airways Co. Ltd.; United Parcel Service of America, Inc.; The Coca-Cola Export Corporation; F. Hoffmann-La Roche & Co.; Kimberley-Clark Corp.; Ciba Geigy AG; Pfizer Corp.; Norsk Hydro; Wella AG; Data General Corp.; National Semiconductor Inc.; Nokia Cellular Systems Corp.; Telecom Corporation of New Zealand; Ohbayashi Corp.; COGEI SPA; GE & RCA Licensing Management; The Coca-Cola Company; Goodyear Thailand Ltd.; Phillip Morris Inc.; Phillips Electrical Co.; Seikosha Co. Ltd.; Asamura Patent Office; Tomen (Thailand) Ltd.; TMX (Thailand) Ltd.; Duty Free Shoppers/DFS Ltd.; Galeries Lafayette (Thailand) Ltd.; Sogo (Thailand) Co. Ltd.; LaChemise Lacoste; Triumph International.

REVISERS OF THE BANGKOK LAW DIGEST FOR THIS DIRECTORY

UDOM-PROK & ASSOCIATES

Established in 1983

THARINEE MANSION
105/36 BOROM-RAJ-CHANANEE ROAD, BANGKOKNOI
BANGKOK 10700, THAILAND
Telephone: (662) 435-4146; 435-4147
Fax: (662) 434-3318; 434-3364

General Practice. Investment, Corporate, Banking, Real Estate, Mining, Tax, Immigration and Naturalization, Civil and Criminal Trials, Patent and Trademark Law, Administrative Laws.

FIRM PROFILE: The firm comprises senior members who have considerable experience in legal, business and international matters, with profound knowledge in and intimate connection with government and business sectors.

PROK AMRANAND, born Thailand; admitted, 1947, Thailand. *Education:* Thammasat University (LL.B., 1946); Columbia University (M.B.A., 1949). Special Lecturer, Thammasat University, Chulalongkorn University and Kasetsat University, Bangkok, 1951-1961. Senior Officer, United Nations Economic and Social Commission for Asia and the Pacific (ESCAP), 1959-1977. Cabinet Member, Royal Thai Government, 1977-1980. Ambassador Extraordinary and Plenipotentiary to the United States, 1980-1982. Co-founder, Thailand-United States Trade Council, 1983. Participant, major part in the formulation of the Rules for International Commercial Arbitration and Conciliation for the Asian and Pacific Region, the Agreement Establishing the Asian Development Bank (Manila), the Agreement Establishing an Asian Clearing Union (Tehran) and the Agreement Establishing the Asian Reinsurance Corporation (Bangkok). *Member:* Thai Lawyers Association; Thai Bar Association. *LANGUAGES:* Thai, English. *PRACTICE AREAS:* Business Law.

PHAIBULYA MAOLANON. *Education:* Law Faculty, Paris University, France (1954-1956); Thammasat University, Bangkok, Thailand (LL.B., 1947); Assumption College, Bangkok. Foreign Service, Royal Government of Thailand. Ambassador Extra-ordinary and Plenipotentiary to Iran, 1982-1987. Ambassador-designate Phnom-Penh, 1978. Postings in Copenhagen, 1972; Hong Kong and Macao, 1965; Paris, 1954-1960; Saigon, 1947. Legal Staff, Thai Defence Team, territorial dispute case against Cambodian Government, International Court of Justice, The Hague, 1961-

(This Listing Continued)

UDOM-PROK & ASSOCIATES, Bangkok—Continued

1963. Advisor, Thai delegation to Special Political Committee, United Nations General Assembly (17th session), 1964. Special Lecturer, International Law, Thammasat University, 1972-1973. *LANGUAGES:* French, English and Thai. *PRACTICE AREAS:* International Law.

AMNUAY PLENGWIDHAYA, born Chon Buri, Thailand. *Education:* Thammasat University (LL.B., 1947);. Judge of Bangkok and provinces, 1960-1969; Chief Judge of Loey, 1969-1977; Judge of Appellate Court, 1977-1985; Judge of Supreme Court, 1985-1987. *LANGUAGES:* Thai, English. *PRACTICE AREAS:* Civil and Criminal Laws.

MANOCH KONGMONT, born Nakornsridhamaraj, Thailand; admitted, 1970, Thailand. *Education:* LL.B., 1957. Judge of Bangkok and provinces, 1975-1988; Chief Judge of Provincial Courts, 1988-1992. *LANGUAGES:* Thai, English. *PRACTICE AREAS:* Civil and Criminal Laws.

UDOMSAK SUKARAWAN, born Bangkok, Thailand; admitted, 1979, Thailand. *Education:* Ramkhamhaeng University (LL.B., 1977). With Bangkok International Law Office, 1979-1983. *Member:* Thai Bar Association; Thai Lawyers Association. *LANGUAGES:* Thai. *PRACTICE AREAS:* Litigation; Civil and Criminal Law.

M.L. PATANACHATRA SVASTI, born Bangkok, Thailand; admitted, 1987, Thailand. *Education:* Chulalongkorn University (LL.B. Hons., 1983). *Member:* Thai Bar Association; Thai Lawyers Association. *LANGUAGES:* English and Thai. *PRACTICE AREAS:* Business Law; Civil and Criminal Law.

TEERAPAN BUNLUESIN, born Lampang, Thailand. *Education:* Ramkhamhaeng University (LL.B., 1980); Technological University of the Philippines (M.M., 1993). Loan Officer, Bangkok Bank Ltd., 1981-1983. Attorney, Bangkok International Law Office, 1983-1991. *Member:* Thai Lawyers Association; Thai Bar Association. *LANGUAGES:* Thai and English. *PRACTICE AREAS:* Business Law; Civil and Criminal Law.

ASSOCIATES

CHATURON CHANTRASAP, born Bangkok, Thailand; admitted, 1992, Thailand. *Education:* Ramkhamhaeng University (LL.B., 1990). *LANGUAGES:* Thai and English. *PRACTICE AREAS:* Intellectual Property Law.

WATANA KHUNNARK, born Trad, Thailand; admitted, 1989, Thailand. *Education:* Ramkhamhaeng University (LL.B., 1986). *LANGUAGES:* Thai. *PRACTICE AREAS:* Business Law.

SUPANAT IMTHONG, born Bangkok, Thailand; admitted, 1992, Thailand. *Education:* Ramkhamhaeng University (LL.B., 1991). *LANGUAGES:* Thai and English. *PRACTICE AREAS:* Commercial Law; Real Estate Law.

SAMARN KONACHARAEN, born Phitsanulok, Thailand. *Education:* Ramkhamhaeng University (LL.B., 1983). Attorney, Bangkok International Law Office, 1984-1990. *Member:* Thai Lawyers Association; Thai Bar Association. *LANGUAGES:* Thai. *PRACTICE AREAS:* Labor; Civil and Criminal Law.

THONGPUND HANGSUKSA, born Samut Prakan, Thailand. *Education:* Sukhothai Thammathirat University (LL.B., 1989). *Member:* Thai Lawyers Association; Thai Bar Association. *LANGUAGES:* Thai. *PRACTICE AREAS:* Judgement Enforcement.

REPRESENTATIVE CLIENTS: Bangkok Bank, Ltd.; National Bank of Pakistan; Daichi Kangyo Bank; American Express (Thai) Co., Ltd.; Petroleum Authority of Thailand; Thai Wah Group of Companies; The Nation Publishing Group Co., Ltd.; Tosin Co., Ltd.; Empross Systems; Wang Petchaboon Co., Ltd. (World Trade Centre); Ban-Pu Coal Co., Ltd.; Pranda Jewelry Co., Ltd.

VICKERY & WORACHAI LTD.

Established in 1975

16TH FLOOR, DIETHELM TOWER A
93/1 WIRELESS ROAD
BANGKOK 10330, THAILAND
Telephone: (66-2) 256-6311 through 256-6314, 256-6316 and 256-7750
through 256-7754
Fax: (66-2) 256-6317 and 256-6318

General Practice. Corporation, Taxation, Banking, Finance and Securities, Investment, Arbitration, Government Contracting, Real Estate, Insurance, Customs, Maritime, Mining and Petroleum Law, Utilities, Energy and

(This Listing Continued)

Power Generation, Aviation and Aircraft Leasing and Finance, Trademarks, Patents, Intellectual Property, Litigation in all Courts.

FIRM PROFILE: Established in 1975, Vickery & Worachai Ltd. is a broad-based commercial and business practice acting primarily for multinational corporations conducting operations in Thailand. Many client relationships begin with a potential investor's initial enquiries about the legal and tax aspects of doing business in Thailand and continue through development and conduct of a project or venture. The firm also advises financial institutions and borrowers on project financing and takes an active role in assisting clients in contract and concession negotiations with Thai government entities. The firm handles substantial civil litigation, which is usually commercially related. The firm is a member of the International Lawyers' Group, with member firms in 36 countries.

PRAPONE SATAMAN (1917-1989).

HAROLD K. VICKERY, JR., born Worcester, Massachusetts, July 4, 1941; admitted, 1967, Massachusetts; 1970, U.S. Supreme Court (Not admitted in Thailand). *Education:* Trinity College, Hartford, Connecticut (B.A., 1963); University of Pennsylvania (J.D., 1966). U.S. Air Force Foreign Claims Commissioner for Thailand, 1968-1970. Member, Board of Governors, 1981-1984, 1986-1987, 1989-1992, 1994-1995 and President, 1984, The American Chamber Of Commerce In Thailand; Asia-Pacific Council of American Chambers of Commerce (Vice-Chairman, Intellectual Property, 1992-1994). *Member:* American Bar Association. [Lieutenant Colonel, U.S. Air Force Judge Advocate General's Department Reserve, Retired]

WORACHAI BHICHARNCHITR, born Bangkok, Thailand, September 3, 1954; admitted, 1979, Thailand. *Education:* Thammasat University (LL.B., 1976); New York University (LL.M., 1979). Lecturer in Law, Thammasat University, 1988—. Vice-President, Thai Swedish Chamber of Commerce, 1989—. Board Member, Law Association of Thammasat University, 1992—. *Member:* Thai Bar Association. *LANGUAGES:* Thai and English.

KIDKOM PHUMIRUK, born Lop Buri, Thailand, February 19, 1951; admitted, 1979, Thailand. *Education:* Ramkhamhaeng University (LL.B., 1979). *Member:* Thai Bar Association. *LANGUAGES:* Thai and English.

WICHIEN HARNPRAWEEN, born Bangkok, Thailand, June 2, 1963; admitted, 1986, Thailand. *Education:* Thammasat University (LL.B., with second class honors, 1986); Magdalene College, University of Cambridge (LL.M., 1990). *Member:* Thai Bar Association. *LANGUAGES:* Thai and English.

ADISAK PUNITES, born Bangkok, Thailand, May 8, 1964; admitted, 1986, Thailand. *Education:* Thammasat University (LL.B., 1986). *Member:* Thai Bar Association. *LANGUAGES:* Thai and English.

SATIT SENSUPA, born Lamphun, Thailand, February 1, 1957; admitted, 1984, Thailand. *Education:* Thammasat University (LL.B., 1984); Chulalongkorn University (LL.M., 1993); Barrister at Law, 1989. *Member:* Thai Bar Association. *LANGUAGES:* Thai and English.

KASEM RATANASONTI, born Hua Hin, Thailand, August 30, 1969; admitted, 1991, Thailand. *Education:* Chulalongkorn University (LL.B., 1991). *LANGUAGES:* Thai and English.

NUTCHARAT LEARTPAIBOON, born Nakhon Si Thammarat, Thailand, September 19, 1965; admitted, 1987, Thailand. *Education:* Thammasat University (LL.B., 1987); Southern Methodist University (LL.M., 1991). *LANGUAGES:* Thai and English.

ANAWAT MALAWAN, born Bangkok, Thailand, September 24, 1970; admitted, 1993, Thailand. *Education:* Chulalongkorn University (LL.B., 1992). *Member:* Thai Bar Association. *LANGUAGES:* Thai and English.

DUSIT ALI-ISHAK, born Yala, Thailand, September 21, 1953; admitted, 1977, Thailand. *Education:* Thammasat University (LL.B., with second class honors, 1976). Barrister-at-Law, 1977. *Member:* Thai Bar Association. *LANGUAGES:* Thai and English.

THITIKA LIMPAVATANAYU, born Bangkok, Thailand, April 19, 1970; admitted, 1991, Thailand. *Education:* Chulalongkorn University (LL.B., 1991). *Member:* Thai Bar Association. *LANGUAGES:* Thai and English.

JANTANA KEETANITINAN, born Samut Prakan, Thailand, June 30, 1969; admitted, 1992, Thailand. *Education:* Chulalongkorn University (LL.B., 1992). *Member:* Thai Bar Association. *LANGUAGES:* Thai and English.

(This Listing Continued)

Languages: Thai and English.

REPRESENTATIVE CLIENTS: Alfa-Laval (Thailand) Ltd.; Asea Brown Boveri; Associated Swedish Steels AB; Atlantic Richfield Co.; Bangkok Patana School; British Gas plc; Brown & Root, Inc.; Bureau Veritas SA; Central Department Store Group; Chicago Bridge & Iron Company; Connell Bros. Co. (Thailand), Ltd.; Dhana Siam Finance and Securities Public Co., Ltd.; Diethelm & Co., Ltd.; Digital Equipment Corp.; Telefonaktiebolaget L M Ericsson; Finnish Fund for Industrial Cooperation Ltd.; Fluor Daniel Corp.; Foot-Joy, Inc.; General Electric Co.; Hasbro Far East Ltd.; International Finance Corp.; Italthai Holding Co., Ltd.; Japan Airlines Development Co., Ltd.; Johnson & Johnson; Kodak Far East Purchasing Co., Inc.; Meridien SA; Minebea Co., Ltd.; Moscow Narodny Bank Ltd.; Nalco Chemical Company; NKK Corp.; Philip Morris Asia Inc.; The Post Publishing Public Co., Ltd.; SAAB-Scania A.B.; The Siam Sanwa Industrial Credit Co., Ltd.; Skandinaviska Enskilda Banken; Aktiebolaget SKF; Smith and Nephew Associated Companies plc; Stora Kopparbergs Bergslags AB; Sun Alliance and London Insurance plc; AB Tetra Pak; Tiger Medicals Limited; Tractebel; Thasos Shipping Co., Ltd.; Unocal Corp.; United Industrial Corp. Ltd.; United Malayan Banking Corporation Berhad; Wearne Brothers, Ltd.; Wilk & Hoeglund Ltd.

U.S. PACIFIC TERRITORIES

CARLSMITH BALL WICHMAN MURRAY CASE & ICHIKI

A Partnership including Law Corporations

Established in 1857

CARLSMITH BUILDING
CAPITOL HILL
P.O. BOX 5241
SAIPAN, U. S. PACIFIC TERRITORIES 96950
Telephone: 670-322-3455
Telecopier: 670-322-3368

REVISERS OF THE HAWAII LAW DIGEST FOR THIS DIRECTORY

Honolulu, Hawaii Office: Suite 2200, Pacific Tower, 1001 Bishop Street. P.O. Box 656. Telephone: 808-523-2500.

Los Angeles, California Office: 555 South Flower Street, 25th Floor. Telephone: 213-955-1200.

Long Beach, California Office: 301 East Ocean Boulevard, 7th Floor. Telephone: 310-435-5631.

Washington, D.C. Office: 700 14th Street, N.W., 9th Floor. Telephone: 202-508-1025.

Mexico City, Mexico Office: Monte Pelvoux 111, Piso 1, Col. Lomas de Chapultepec, 11000 Mexico, D.F. Telephone: (011-52-5) 520-8514. Fax: (011-52-5) 540 1545.

Mexico, D.F. Office of Carlsmith Ball Garcia Cacho y Asociados, S.C. (Authorized to practice Mexican Law): Monte Pelvoux 111, Piso 1, Col. Lomas de Chapultepec, 11000 Mexico, D.F. Telephone: (011-52-5) 520-8514. Fax: (011-52-5) 540-1545.

Agana, Guam Office: 4th Floor, Bank of Hawaii Building, P.O. Box BF. Telephone: 671-472-6813.

Wailuku, Maui, Hawaii Office: One Main Plaza, Suite 400, 2200 Main Street, P.O. Box 1086. Telephone: 808-242-4535.

Kailua-Kona, Hawaii Office: Second Floor, Bank of Hawaii Annex Building, P.O. Box 1720. Telephone: 808-329-6464.

Hilo, Hawaii Office: 121 Waianuenue Avenue, P.O. Box 686. Telephone: 808-935-6644.

Kapolei, Hawaii Office: Kapolei Building, Suite 318, 1001 Kamokila Boulevard. Telephone: 808-674-0850.

General Civil and Trial Practice. Admiralty, Fishery, Banking, Corporate, Insurance, Construction, Labor and Real Property Law.

RESIDENT PARTNERS

JOHN F. BIEHL, born Seattle, Washington, January 21, 1939; admitted to bar, 1966, California, U.S. Court of Appeals, Ninth Circuit and U.S. District Court, Central District of California; 1967, Washington and U.S. District Court, Western District of Washington; 1971, U.S. Supreme Court; 1981, Trust Territory of the Pacific Islands; 1982, Federated States of Micronesia; 1984, Northern Marianas Federal District Court; 1986, Commonwealth of the Northern Mariana Islands. *Education:* University of Washington (B.A., 1961; J.D., 1967). Delta Theta Phi. Member, Washington Law Review, 1964-1966. *Member:* Commonwealth of the Northern Mariana Islands Bar and Hawaii Bar Associations; District of Columbia Bar (inactive); Washington Bar Association (inactive); State Bar of California (inactive).

(This Listing Continued)

DAVID R. NEVITT, born Seattle, Washington, February 9, 1945; admitted to bar, 1975, Washington; 1979, U.S. District Court, Western District of Washington; 1983, Federated States of Micronesia; 1986, U.S. District Court for the Northern Mariana Islands and Commonwealth of the Northern Mariana Islands. *Education:* University of Washington (B.A., cum laude, 1972); Boalt Hall School of Law, University of California (J.D., 1975). Chief, Division of Litigation, Attorney General Office, Federated States of Micronesia, 1982-1983. Attorney General, Federated States of Micronesia, 1983-1985. *Member:* Washington State and Commonwealth of the Northern Marianas Bar Associations. [With U.S. Army, 1966-1969, 1st Lt., Infantry, Vietnam, 1968]

JOHN D. OSBORN, born Ponca City, Oklahoma, December 6, 1942; admitted to bar, 1969, Kansas and U.S. District Court, District of Kansas; 1990, U.S. District Court, Northern Mariana Island; 1990, Supreme Court of the Commonwealth of the Northern Mariana Islands. *Education:* University of Kansas (B.S., 1966; J.D., 1969). Phi Delta Phi. Member, Board of Directors, 1973-1977 and President, 1974-1976. Garden City Library Board. Member, 1975-1983, Vice-Chairman, 1978-1980 and Chairman, 1980-1983, Board of Trustees, Garden City Community Junior College. Member: Board of Governors, Kansas University Law Society, 1978-1980; State of Kansas Corrections Ombudsman Board, 1980-1984; Vice Chairman, 1982-1984. Special Workers' Compensation Administrative Judge, 1988-1990. Assistant Attorney General and Chief of Civil Litigation Division, Commonwealth of the Northern Mariana Islands, 1990-1993. *PRACTICE AREAS:* Commercial Litigation; Workers' Compensation; Insurance.

MARCIA K. SCHULTZ, born Iowa, August 24, 1953; admitted to bar, 1978, Iowa and Oregon; 1984, Republic of Palau; 1986, Trust Territory of the Pacific Islands; 1989, Commonwealth of Northern Mariana Islands; 1991, U.S. Court of Appeals, 9th Circuit. *Education:* Luther College; University of Iowa (B.A., with honors, 1975); University of Oregon (J.D., 1978). *Member:* Iowa State Bar Association; Oregon State Bar (inactive); Republic of Palau Bar; Commonwealth of the Northern Mariana Islands Bar. *PRACTICE AREAS:* Business; Litigation.

RESIDENT ASSOCIATES

LAWRENCE C. KING, born Merced, California, December 10, 1962; (admission pending); admitted to bar, 1992, California, Commonwealth of the Northern Mariana Islands and U.S. District Court for the Northern Mariana Islands. *Education:* University of California at Berkeley (B.A., 1985); Hastings College of Law, University of California (J.D., 1991). *Member:* State Bar of California; Bar Association of the Commonwealth of the Northern Mariana Islands. *PRACTICE AREAS:* Civil Litigation; General Corporate.

REVISERS OF THE HAWAII LAW DIGEST FOR THIS DIRECTORY

(For Complete Biographical Data on all Personnel, see Professional Biographies at Honolulu, Hawaii)

DOUGLAS F. CUSHNIE

SAN JOSE VILLAGE
P.O. BOX 949
SAIPAN, MARIANA ISLANDS 96950
Telephone: 670-234-6830 or 6843
Cable Address: "ABOGADOS MN"
Fax: 670-234-9723

General Civil Practice, Litigation and Business Law in Guam, Federated States of Micronesia, Republic of Palau, Republic of the Marshall Islands and Commonwealth of the Northern Mariana Islands.

DOUGLAS F. CUSHNIE, born Chicago, Illinois, November 23, 1937; admitted to bar, 1964, Texas; 1965, Hawaii and U.S. District Court for Hawaii; 1968, Trust Territory of the Pacific Islands; 1970, District Court of Guam; District Court for CNMI, Supreme Court of Palau; Supreme Court of Federated States of Micronesia; Supreme Court of Republic of Marshall Islands; Supreme Court of Commonwealth of Northern Mariana Islands. *Education:* Southern Methodist University (B.A., 1961); University of Texas (LL.B., 1964). Phi Alpha Delta. *Member:* Guam and American Bar Associations; State Bar of Texas; Bar Association of Hawaii; CNMI Bar Association.

ROBERT W. JONES, born Tulsa, Oklahoma, February 14, 1959; admitted to bar, 1988, Arizona and U.S. District Court, District of Arizona; 1993, Commonwealth of the Northern Mariana Islands and U.S. District

(This Listing Continued)

DOUGLAS F. CUSHNIE, Saipan—Continued

Court, District of the Northern Mariana Islands. *Education:* University of Oklahoma (B.A., 1984; J.D., 1988). *Member:* State Bar of Arizona; CNMI Bar Association. *LANGUAGES:* Japanese.

LAW OFFICE OF
ROBERT J. O'CONNOR

2ND FLOOR, NAURU BUILDING
P.O. BOX 1969
SAIPAN, MARIANA ISLANDS 96950
Telephone: 670-234-5684
Fax: 670-234-5683

General Trial and Appellate Practice in all courts of the Northern Mariana Islands, Guam, Federated States of Micronesia and Republic of Palau. Corporate, Taxation, Construction, Real Estate, Banking, Commercial, Labor and International Law.

FIRM PROFILE: The firm is a fast growing locally-based firm in private practice representing many prominant international businesses.

ROBERT J. O'CONNOR, JR., born Detroit, Michigan, June 15, 1949; admitted to bar, 1974, California; 1985, Commonwealth of Northern Mariana Islands; 1988, Republic of Palau; 1988, Territory of Guam; 1987, U.S. Court of Appeals, Ninth Circuit; U.S. District Court, Districts of Northern Mariana Islands and Guam. *Education:* Tulane University; University of Michigan (B.G.S., 1971); University of San Francisco Law School (J.D., 1974). Deputy District Attorney, Riverside, California, 1975-1979; Ventura County, California, 1979-1983. Deputy Attorney General and Acting Attorney General, Commonwealth of the Northern Mariana Islands, 1983-1985. Instructor, Civil Procedure, Santa Barbara College of Law, 1980-1983. *Member:* Commonwealth of Northern Marianas and Territory of Guam Bar Associations; State Bar of California; Republic of Palau Bar. *PRACTICE AREAS:* International; Construction; Complex Litigation.

DAVID G. BANES, born Sellersville, Pennsylvania, September 20, 1961; admitted to bar, 1987, New York; 1988, U.S. District Court, Southern and Eastern Districts of New York; 1992, Commonwealth of Northern Mariana Islands and U.S. District Court, District of Northern Mariana Islands; 1993, Republic of Palau. *Education:* University of Maryland (B.A., 1982); University of Pennsylvania (J.D., 1986); King's College, London. *Member:* New York State, Commonwealth of Northern Mariana Islands and American Bar Associations; Republic of Palau Bar. *LANGUAGES:* French. *PRACTICE AREAS:* General Civil Litigation.

GREGORY J. KOEBEL, born Montclair, New Jersey, August 4, 1961; admitted to bar, 1989, New York; 1993, California, Commonwealth of Northern Mariana Islands and Republic of Palau. *Education:* Montclair State College (B.A., 1984); Brooklyn Law School (J.D., 1988); New York University School of Law (LL.M., Taxation, 1992). Member, Brooklyn Journal of International Law. *Member:* Commonwealth of Northern Marianas Islands, New York State and American Bar Associations; State Bar of California; Republic of Palau Bar. *PRACTICE AREAS:* Taxation; Corporate Law; Commercial Transactions.

MICHAEL W DOTTS, born Oxnard, California, February 28, 1961; admitted to bar, 1987, California and U.S. Court of Appeals, Ninth Circuit; 1989, Commonwealth of Northern Mariana Islands; 1990, Republic of Palau. *Education:* University of California (A.B., 1984); Golden Gate University Law School (J.D., 1987). Director, Bank of Saipan, Inc. *PRACTICE AREAS:* Banking Law; International Finances.

STEVEN P. PIXLEY, born Williamsburg, Virginia, October 3, 1952; admitted to bar, 1978, North Carolina; 1980, U.S. District Court, Western District of North Carolina; 1983, U.S Court of Federal Claims; 1987, Virginia and U.S. District Court, Eastern District of Virginia; 1988, Federated States of Micronesia; 1994, Commonwealth of Northern Mariana Islands. *Education:* Virginia Polytechnic Institute (B.A., 1974); Haitian-American Institute; Wake Forest University (J.D., 1978). President, Political Science Honor Society, 1974. Author: "A Summary of Recent Fisheries Prosecutions in the Federated States of Micronesia," Forum Fisheries Agency, Honiara, Solomon Islands, 1989. Instructor, Torts, Corporate Law, Contracts and Procedure, Central Piedmont Community College, Charlotte, NC, 1980-1983. Assistant Attorney General, 1987-1988, Chief, Division of Litigation, 1987-1990 and Acting Attorney General, 1989-1990, Federated States of Micronesia. Representative, Federated States of Micronesia, 5th Annual Forum Fisheries Agency Surveillance Meeting, Solomon Islands,

(This Listing Continued)

1989. *Member:* North Carolina State Bar; Virginia State Bar. *PRACTICE AREAS:* Civil Law; Criminal Trial Practice.

IMELDA MANALAYSAY, born Bulacan, Philippines, January 22, 1966; admitted to bar, 1990, Philippines (Not admitted in the Commonwealth of Northern Mariana Islands). *Education:* University of Philippines (A.B., 1986); Ateno De Manila (LL.B., 1990). *Member:* Integrated Bar of the Philippines. *LANGUAGES:* English and Tagalog.

COUNSEL FOR: Bank of Saipan; L&T International, Inc.
REPRESENTATIVE CLIENTS: Mitsubishi Heavy Industries Co., Ltd.; Mitsubishi Corporation; DHL, Inc.; Bank of Saipan, Hyatt Hotel, Saipan; Dai-ichi Hotels; Philippine Airlines, OCK Construction, Ltd.; Lucky Development Co.; Winzler & Kelly, Inc.; Saipan Garment Industry Association; Hazama-Gumi, Inc.; Dai Nippon, Inc.; Caesar's World, Inc.; United Micronesian Development Association (UMDA); Marianas Cable Vision, Inc.; Air Micronesia, Inc.; Windjammer Cruises; Radua Pacific Corp.

WHITE, PIERCE, MAILMAN & NUTTING

P.O. BOX 5222
SAIPAN, MARIANA ISLANDS 96950
Telephone: 670-234-6547
Telecopier: 670-234-9537

General Trial and Appellate Practice in all Courts of the Northern Mariana Islands, Federated States of Micronesia and Republic of Palau. Corporate, Commercial, Real Estate, Construction, Family, Probate, Personal Injury, Criminal Defense Law.

FIRM PROFILE: The firm was founded in 1975, and is the oldest and largest locally-based firm in private practice in the Northern Mariana Islands

MICHAEL A. WHITE, born Philadelphia, Pennsylvania, January 12, 1945; admitted to bar, 1969, Pennsylvania; 1970, Trust Territory of the Pacific Islands; 1976, U.S. Supreme Court; 1978, Northern Mariana Islands; 1979, U.S. Court of Appeals, Ninth Circuit; 1981, Federated States of Micronesia and Palau. *Education:* Pennsylvania State University (B.A., 1966); Temple University (J.D., 1969). Member, Board of Trustees, Northern Marianas Retirement Fund, 1980—. Member, Northern Marianas Law Revision Commission, 1980-1993. Lawyer Representative, Ninth Circuit Judicial Conference, 1980-1982, 1985-1988, and 1991-1993. Member, District Court CJRA Committee, 1992-1993. Chairman, Advisory Committee on Rules on Civil Procedure, CNMI Supreme Court, 1993—. *Member:* Northern Marianas (President, 1980-1982, 1990-1991 and 1994—), Philadelphia and American (Member, House of Delegates, 1995) Bar Associations. *LANGUAGES:* English and Chamorro.

BRUCE L. MAILMAN, born Bakersfield, California, August 22, 1945; admitted to bar, 1988, California, U.S. District Court, Northern District of California and U.S. Court of Appeals, Ninth Circuit; 1989, Commonwealth of the Northern Mariana Islands and U.S. District Court, Northern Mariana Islands. *Education:* University of California at Berkeley (B.A., 1967); Hastings College of the Law (J.D., 1988). Student Extern, Supreme Court of California. Staff Member, Hastings Law Journal, 1986-1988. Member, 1993— and Secretary, 1994—, CNMI Vocational Rehabilitation Advisory Council. *Member:* Northern Mariana Islands (Director, 1992-1993) and American Bar Associations; State Bar of California (Inactive); The Association of Trial Lawyers of America.

STEPHEN J. NUTTING, born Waterloo, Iowa, June 6, 1953; admitted to bar, 1984, Iowa; 1985, Washington; 1990, Northern Mariana Islands, U.S. Court of Appeals, Ninth Circuit and U.S. District Court, Northern Mariana Islands. *Education:* University of Iowa (B.A., 1978); Creighton University, College of Law (J.D., 1984). Assistant Attorney General, Commonwealth of the Northern Mariana Islands, 1989-1990. *Member:* Iowa (Inactive), Washington State and Northern Mariana Islands Bar Associations.

RICHARD W. PIERCE, born Atlanta, Georgia, December 26, 1945; admitted to bar, 1978, Georgia; 1984, Virginia; 1989, U.S. Court of Appeals, Fourth and Ninth Circuits; 1990, Commonwealth of the Northern Mariana Islands. *Education:* University of the South; University of Georgia (B.A., 1973); Mercer University (J.D., 1978). Editor-in-Chief, Mercer Law Review, 1977-1978. Trial Attorney, U.S. Department of Justice, Antitrust Division, 1978-1983. Assistant U.S. Attorney for the Western District of Virginia, 1983-1988 and for the Districts of the Northern Mariana Islands and Guam, 1988-1991. *Member:* Northern Mariana Islands (Chairman, Disciplinary Committee, 1993—) Georgia and Virginia (inactive) Bar Associations.

(This Listing Continued)

S. JOSHUA BERGER, born Brooklyn, New York, July 11, 1953; admitted to bar, 1979, California; 1980, U.S. District Court, Northern District of California and U.S. Court of Appeals, 9th Circuit; 1981, Alaska and U.S. District Court, District of Alaska; 1993, Commonwealth of the Northern Mariana Islands. *Education:* University of California at Irvine (B.A., cum laude, 1975); University of California, Hastings College of Law (J.D., 1979). Phi Beta Kappa. Law Clerk, Superior Court, Alaska, 1979-1980. Assistant District Attorney, State of Alaska, 1980, 1983-1984. Deputy City Attorney, Fairbanks, Alaska, 1981-1983. Defender of the Fund, Republic of the Marshall Islands Nuclear Claims Tribunal, 1990-1993. *Member:* Northern Mariana Islands and Alaska (inactive) Bar Associations; State Bar of California (inactive).

JENNIFER GRIFFIN SKINNER, born Evanston, Illinois, February 18, 1963; admitted to bar, 1992, Hawaii; 1993, Commonwealth of the Northern Mariana Islands. *Education:* University of Colorado at Boulder (B.A., 1987); John Marshall Law School (J.D., 1992). Publications Editor, The Software Law Journal, 1991-1992. Fellow, Office of Management and Budget, Executive Office of the President, 1991. Law Clerk, 1992-1994 and Chief Law Clerk, 1993-1994, Superior Court for the Commonwealth of the Northern Mariana Islands. *Member:* Northern Mariana Islands, The Hawaii State (inactive) and American Bar Associations.

OF COUNSEL

CHARLES K. NOVO-GRADAC, born Kansas City, Kansas, September 8, 1950; admitted to bar, 1976, Kansas; 1977, Missouri; 1978, Trust Territory of the Pacific Islands; 1979, Commonwealth of the Northern Mariana Islands; 1982, Marshall Islands, Federated States of Micronesia; 1983, U.S. Court of Appeals, Ninth Circuit. *Education:* University of Kansas (B.A., with distinction, 1972; J.D., 1976). Phi Beta Kappa. Staff Member, Kansas Law Review, 1975-1976. *Member:* Northern Marianas Islands (President, 1986-1987, Director, 1986-1990, Chairman, Disciplinary Committee, 1989-1990), Kansas (Inactive) and American Bar Associations; The Missouri Bar (Inactive).

REPRESENTATIVE CLIENTS: Anshin Sogo Finance Corp.; Bank of America, NT&SA; Bank of Guam; Bank of Hawaii; Bank of Saipan; CIGNA; Commonwealth Ports Authority; Commonwealth Utilities Corp.; First American Title Insurance Co.; Guam Memorial Hospital; Guam Savings & Loan Assn.; Hartford Specialty Co.; Island Bottling Co., Inc. (Coca-Cola franchisee); Itochu Corp. (C. Itoh Corp.); J.C. Tenorio Enterprises, Inc.; Jones & Guerrero Co., Inc.; Kan Pacific Saipan, Inc.; Kobe Portopia (Hyatt Regency Hotel); McDonalds Corp.; Mirage Fashion, Ltd.; Nansay Micronesia Corporation; Nippon Trust & Banking Co., Ltd.; Pacific Development, Inc.; Pacific Resort Development, Inc.; Saipan Credit Union; Shimizu Construction Co., Ltd.; Sumitomo Trust & Banking Co., Ltd.; Turner Pacific, Inc.; Union Bank; United Micronesia Development Assn.; Western Equipment Co., Inc.

R. BARRIE MICHELSEN

P.O. BOX 1450
KOLONIA, POHNPEI
FEDERATED STATES OF MICRONESIA 96941
Telephone: 691-320-2871
Facsimile: 691-320-5502

General Practice of Law. Commercial Law, Corporate Representation, Civil and Criminal Litigation, Representation of Foreign Investment Business and Personal Injury Litigation.

R. BARRIE MICHELSEN, born Waterville, Maine, July 31, 1948; admitted to bar, 1976, Maine; 1979, Guam and U.S. Court of Appeals, Ninth Circuit; 1982, U.S. District Court, District of Maine; 1982, Supreme Court, Federated States of Micronesia; 1984, Supreme Court, Republic of Palau; 1985, High Court of the U.S. Trust Territories and Supreme Courts of Pohnpei and Chuuk States, Federated States ok States; 1986, Hawaii; 1987, High Court Republic of The Marshall Islands. *Education:* University of Maine (B.A., 1971; J.D., 1976). Assistant District Attorney, Maine, 1976-1979. Assistant Attorney General, Guam, 1979-1981. Litigation Chief, Federated States of Micronesia, 1981-1982. *Member:* Maine, Hawaii, Guam and American Bar Associations.

REPRESENTATIVE CLIENTS: College of Micronesia; Ambros Enterprises, Inc.; Federated Shipping Co., Inc.; Truk Transportation Co., Inc.; Bank of the Marshall Islands; Truk Continental Hotel; Bernard's Enterprises; Bank of Federated States of Micronesia; Bank of Hawaii; Pacific Islands Insurance Underwriters.

VIETNAM

BAKER & McKENZIE

Hanoi Representative Office
41 LY THAI TO STREET
. *HOAN KIEM DISTRICT*
HANOI, VIETNAM
Telephone: (4) 251428; 251429; 251430
Intn'l Dialing: (84-4) 251428; 251429; 251430
Facsimile: (84-4) 251432

Associated Offices of Baker & McKenzie in: Almaty, Amsterdam, Bangkok, Barcelona, Beijing, Berlin, Bogotá, Brasília, Brussels, Budapest, Buenos Aires, Cairo, Caracas, Chicago, Dallas, Frankfurt, Geneva, Ho Chi Minh City, Hong Kong, Juárez, Kiev, London, Madrid, Manila, Melbourne, México City, Miami, Milan, Monterrey, Moscow, New York, Palo Alto, Paris, Prague, Rio de Janeiro, Riyadh, Rome, St. Petersburg, San Diego, San Francisco, São Paulo, Singapore, Stockholm, Sydney, Taipei, Tijuana, Tokyo, Toronto, Valencia, Warsaw, Washington, D.C. and Zürich.
Correspondent Law Firm: Hadiputranto, Hadinoto & Partners, Jakarta.

LOCAL PARTNERS

NGUYEN TAN HAI, born Ha Nam, Vietnam, 1948; admitted, 1971, Vietnam; 1990, Victoria, Australia. *Education:* University of Saigon (LL.B., Economics, 1971); Chisholm Institute of Technology (Graduate Diploma in Data Processing, 1983); University of Melbourne (LL.B., 1988). Visiting Lecturer, Vietnamese Laws, The Constitutional & Administrative Law Centre, University of Melbourne, 1992-1993. Member: Victoria Council Against Violence, 1990-1991; Advisory Board, Asia Link Centre, University of Melbourne, 1993—. *Member:* Law Institute of Victoria, Australian Law Council; International Bar Association. *LANGUAGES:* English and Vietnamese. *PRACTICE AREAS:* Banking and Finance; Insurance Law; Oil and Gas/Mining; Real Estate Law; Taxation.

MARK ANDREW LOCKWOOD, born Melbourne, Australia; admitted, 1986, Victoria, Australia; 1992, Hong Kong and England and Wales (Not admitted in Vietnam). *Education:* Monash University (B.A.; LL.B. Hons.). *Member:* Law Institute of Victoria; Law Society of Hong Kong. *LANGUAGES:* English. *PRACTICE AREAS:* Banking and Finance; Communications and Media Law; Construction and Property Development; Taxation; Trade (Vietnam).

CHOR PEE & CO.

International Lawyers
96, BA TRIEU STREET
HOAN KIEM DISTRICT
HANOI, VIETNAM
Telephone: (844) 228 787/228 788
Fax: (844) 251 875

Singapore Office: 50 Raffles Place, 18th Floor, Shell Tower, 0104. Telephone: 65-2201911. Fax: 65-2244118; 2240183. Telex: RS 21570 CPHH.
Ho Chi Minh City, Vietnam Office: The Colonnade, 27 Nguyen Trung Truc, District 1. Telephone: (848) 224 986. Fax: (848) 225 441.
Branch Offices at Chor Pee Anwarul & Company, Kuala Lumpur and Jahor Bahru, Malaysia.

Law on Foreign Investment in Vietnam including preparation of all investment documentation and advice on setting up representative offices; establishing joint ventures and wholly-owned foreign enterprises; project financing; construction and project management; trading, distributorship and agency agreements; transfer of technology and technical assistance; trademark and other forms of licensing as well as identifying suitable projects and Vietnamese partners; handling all negotiations and lobbying for investment approvals at the highest level of government.

KELVIN H. K. CHIA, LL.B. (Hons.) (S'pore) Partner-in-charge.

CHEAH SWEE GIM, LL.B. (Hons.) (S'pore), LL.M. (TRREG) New York University Partner.

(This Listing Continued)

CHOR PEE & CO., Hanoi—Continued

LE THI HOA, Corporate Affairs Manager.

HUAN NGUYEN DINH, Corporate Affairs Manager.

(For Complete Biographical Data on all Personnel, see Professional Biographies at Singapore)

CLIFFORD CHANCE

52 NGUYEN BINH KHIEM
HANOI, VIETNAM
Telephone: (844) 229 182/3/4/5/6
Fax: (844) 229 190

Other Offices: Amsterdam, Bahrain, Barcelona, Brussels, Budapest, Dubai, Frankfurt, Hong Kong, London, Madrid, Milan, Moscow, New York, Paris, Riyadh, Rome, Shanghai, Singapore, Tokyo, Warsaw. (See London for full address details).

RESIDENT LOCAL PARTNER

FRASER WHITE, admitted, 1986.

DEACONS GRAHAM & JAMES

2A NGUYEN DINH CHIEU
HANOI, VIETNAM
Telephone: (84-4) 269222; (84-4) 227998
Facsimile: (84-4) 227284

Associated Offices: Asia: Bangkok, Beijing, Guangzhou, Hong Kong, Jakarta, Taipei, Tokyo. Australia: Brisbane, Canberra, Melbourne, Perth, Sydney. USA: Los Angeles, Newport Beach, New York, Palo Alto, Sacramento, San Francisco, Washington DC. North America: Mexico City. Europe: Berlin, Brussels, Düsseldorf, Frankfurt, Leipzig, London, Milan, Munich. Eastern Europe: Bucharest. Middle East: Jeddah, Kuwait, Riyadh.

FIRM PROFILE: Deacons Graham & James established its office (originally Sly & Weigall/Deacons) in 1992. Sly & Weigall/Deacons was the first international law firm with a permanent presence in Vietnam. The office has worked with over one hundred clients from the United States, Japan, Australia and Europe on all aspects of the foreign investment licensing process, as well as on intellectual property registration and enforcement secured transactions and technology transfers.

PARTNERS

CAMERON MCCULLOUGH, admitted, 1985, Supreme Court of Queensland; 1987, High Court of Australia. *Education:* University of Queensland (B.A.;B.L.). *PRACTICE AREAS:* Company Law; Joint Ventures; International Transactions; Shipping and Resources Law.

ERIC W. SEDLAK, admitted, 1984, Illinois and Northern District of Illinois; 1986, California, Northern District of California and Ninth Circuit Court of Appeals (Not admitted in Vietnam). *Education:* Haverford College (B.A., Economics, 1980); New York University (J.D., 1984). Articles Editor, New York University Journal of International Law and Politics, 1983-1984. Supervising Editor, Law Review of Developing Nations, 1983-1984. Graham & James, San Francisco, 1985-1988 and Tokyo, 1988-1994. *LANGUAGES:* German and Japanese. *PRACTICE AREAS:* Corporate Law; Commercial Law; Financial Transactions; Joint Ventures; Intellectual Property.

ASSOCIATES

SIMON JENSEN, admitted, 1989, Supreme Court of Queensland. *Education:* University of Queensland (B.Com., LL.B.). *PRACTICE AREAS:* Commercial Law; Corporate Law; Banking and Finance; Intellectual Property.

FREEHILL HOLLINGDALE & PAGE

Established in 1852
34A QUANG TRUNG STREET
HANOI, VIETNAM
Telephone: (844) 227 839
Fax: (844) 227 909

Sydney, New South Wales, Australia Office: Level 38, MLC Centre, 19-29 Martin Place, 2000. Telephone: (02) 225 5000. International: +(612) 225 5000. Telex AA 121885. Fax: (02) 322 4000.

Canberra City, Australian Capital Territory, Australia Office: London Court, 13 London Circuit, 2601. Telephone:(06) 240 6100. International: +(616) 240 6100. Telex: AA121885. Fax: (06) 240 6222.

Melbourne, Victoria, Australia Office: 101 Collins Street, 3000. Telephone: (03) 288 1234. International: +(613) 288 1234. Telex: AA33004. Fax: (03) 288 1567.

Perth, Western Australia Office: Australia Place, 15-17 William Street, 6000. Telephone: (09) 327 5777. International: +(619) 327 5777. Telex: AA92937. Fax: (09) 322 5954.

Brisbane, Queensland, Australia Office: Central Plaza II, 66 Eagle Street, 4000. Telephone: (07) 258 6666. International: +(617) 258 6666. Fax: (07) 258 6444.

Singapore Office: 6 Battery Road, #13-01, 0104. Telephone: (65) 225 1288. Telex: (RS) 42674. Fax: (65) 225 3314.

London, England Office: Birchin Court, 20 Birchin Lane, EC3V 9DJ. Telephone: (0171) 283 9006. International: +(44 171) 283 9006. Fax: (0171) 454 9650.

Ho Chi Minh City, Vietnam Office: 203 Dong Khoi Street, #3-05. Telephone: (848) 242 630; (848) 242 733. Fax: (848) 242 736.

JOHN ALEXANDER CAMPBELL DICK, admitted, 1985. *Education:* University of Western Australia (B.Com, LL.B.; B.Juris). *PRACTICE AREAS:* Corporate Law; Banking and Finance; Energy; Resources.

(For biographical data on all other Firm Personnel, see Professional Biographies at Brisbane, Canberra, Melbourne and Perth, Australia and Singapore)

FRESHFIELDS

50 LY THUONG KIET
HANOI, VIETNAM
Telephone: (84 4) 247 422/3/4
Fax: (84 4) 268 300

Other Offices: Bangkok, Barcelona, Brussels, Frankfurt, Hong Kong, London, Madrid, Moscow, New York, Paris, Singapore, Tokyo.

RESIDENT PARTNERS

ANTHONY P. FOSTER, born 1958; admitted, 1986, California. *Education:* St. John's College, Cambridge; University of California (J.D., 1984). *Member:* State Bar of California. *LANGUAGES:* English, French and German.

ASSOCIATES

ERIC MAUDE, born 1968. *Education:* University of Essex (LL.B.). *LANGUAGES:* French and English.

PATRICK PERTEGNAZZA, born Nice, France, 1965; admitted, Avocat à la Cour. *Education:* Paris University (Maîtrise de Droit des Affaires, DESS Droit et Commerce Extérieur). (Also at Paris Office). *LANGUAGES:* French, English and Italian. *PRACTICE AREAS:* Litigation.

CATHERINE POTTER, born 1969. *Education:* King's College, London; Université de Paris I, Panthéon-Sorbonne. *Member:* Ordre des Avocats à la Cour de Paris. *LANGUAGES:* English, French and German.

LE SONG LAI. *Education:* Hanoi National University, Vietnam (Bachelor Degree in Law, 1994). Recipient, Scholarships: Marubeni Corporation; World University Organization; South Korea. *LANGUAGES:* English and Russian. *PRACTICE AREAS:* Public International Law; Boundary Delimitation; Territorial Acquisition.

GIDE LOYRETTE NOUEL

HANOI BUSINESS CENTRE
51 LY THAI TO
HANOI, VIETNAM
Telephone: (84.42) 66.122.3
(84.42) 66.030.1

Paris, France Office: 26 Cours Albert 1er, 75008. Telephone: (1) 40.75.60.00. Cable Address: "3 Avocagidva Paris 86." Telex: 651261F GILOY. Telecopier: (1) 43.59.37.79.

New York, New York Office: Swiss Bank Tower, 10 East 50th Street, 10022. Telephone: (1-212) 644-1201. Telex: 424353 GIDE. Telecopier: (1-212) 644-1205.

Brussels, Belgium Office: Rue de la Loi 99.101, B-1040. Telephone: (32.2) 231.11.40. Telecopier: (32.2) 231.11.77.

Warsaw, Poland Office: Ul. Kopernika 17, 00-359. Telephone: (48.22) 26.22.21. Telecopier: (48.22) 26.03.02.

Riyadh, Saudi Arabia Office: P.O. Box 4615, 11412. Telephone: (966.1) 476.60.39. Telex: 401677 NASHWA. Telecopier: (966.1) 476.18.96.

Tokyo, Japan Office: Homei Building 3F, 3-19 Akasaka 1-Chome, Minato-Ku, 107. Telephone: (81.3) 55.62.03.01. Telecopier: (81.3) 55.62.03.06.

Beijing, People's Republic of China Office: Suite 3309 A, Jing Guang Centre, Hu Jia Lou, Chaoyang District, 100020. Telephone: (86.1) 501 4511. Telecopier: (86.1) 501 4551.

Prague, Czech Republic Office: 34 Jindrisska, 11207. Telephone: (42.2) 24.21.34.65;24.21.36.50. Telecopier: (42.2) 24.21.09.12;24.22.58.53.

St. Petersburg, Russia Office: 34 Souvorovsky Prospect, App 45, P.O. Box 172, 193015. Telephone by satellite: (7.812) 850.16.85. Telecopier by satellite: (7.812) 850.16.86.

Moscow, Russia Office: 9, Ulitsa Tverskaya - App 66, 103009. Telephone by satellite: (7.501) 940.45.00. Telecopier by satellite: (7.501) 940.45.01.

Budapest VII, Hungary Office: EMKE Building, Rákóczi út 42, BP 409, 1072. Telephone: (36.1) 268.1236; 268.1237; 268.1238. Telecopier: (36.1) 268.1239.

Madrid, Spain Office: Antonio Maura 7, 6°, 28014. Telephone: (34.1) 531.25.01. Telecopier: (34.1) 531.35.30.

French and International Law.

PARTNER IN CHARGE

Michel Pitron

(For Biographical Data on Personnel, see Professional Biographies at Paris, France).

MANDEL, NGO & PARTNERS

BUSINESS CENTER
HOTEL PULLMAN METROPOLE
15, NGO QUYEN STREET
HANOI, VIETNAM
Telephone: (84.4).269.975; (84.4).266.919
Fax: (84.4).244.809

Paris, France Office: 45, Avenue Montaigne. Telephone: (33-1) 4720 92 92. Telecopier: 47.23.91.55 (1st Floor) and 47.23.53.21 (3rd Floor).

General Business Practice including Litigation. International Arbitration, Corporate, Tax, Foreign Investments, Labor, Estate, Intellectual Property and EC Law, Immigration.

FIRM PROFILE: Advice to foreign clients investing in Vietnam.

RESIDENT

PIERRE JUNG, born Chartres, France, May 24, 1959 (Swiss national); admitted, 1988, Paris (Not admitted in Vietnam). *Education:* University of Paris (Licence, 1983; Maîtrise, 1984). *Member:* Paris Bar. **LANGUAGES:** English and German.

EMMANUEL MOULIN, born Montpellier, December 3, 1966; admitted, 1994, Paris. *Education:* University of Montpellier (Maîtrise en Droit des Affaires, 1990); Institut Supérieur de Gestion, Paris (M.B.A., 1992). **LANGUAGES:** French and English.

NICOLAS AUDIER, born Boulogne-Billancourt, France, October 24, 1961; admitted, 1992, Paris. *Education:* University of Paris X, Faculté de Droit et de Sciences Politiques (Maîtrise en Droit des Affaires, 1984; D.E.S.S. en Droit des Affaires Internationales, 1986, high honors); New York University School of Law (M.C.J., 1989).

(This Listing Continued)

OF COUNSEL

DUONG VAN DAM, born Hanoi, November 11, 1915; admitted, 1938 as Attorney at Law (Vietnamese Bar Association 1938-1945). *Education:* University of Hanoi and Paris (Licence en Droit et diplôme d'Etudes Supérieures de Droit indochinois, 1938). District Attorney of Hanoi City, 1954-1962. President of the Vietnamese delegation of economic and cultural relations with the French general delegation in Vietnam, 1955-1965. Founder and Chairman of the Catholic Association. Legal Adviser of the Vietnamese Chamber of Commerce. *Member:* U.I.A. *LANGUAGES:* Vietnamese, French and English.

(For Complete Biographical Data on all Personnel, see Professional Biographies at Paris, France).

PHILLIPS FOX

50 TRIEU VIET VUONG
HANOI, VIETNAM
Telephone: +84-4-26 8745/ 22 6497
Fax: +84-4-22 6058

Head Office: Melbourne, Victoria 3000, Australia. Telephone: +61-3 274 5000. Fax: +61-3 274 5111.

Other Australian Offices: Adelaide, Brisbane, Cairns, Canberra, Perth and Sydney.

New Zealand Offices: Auckland and Wellington.

FIRM PROFILE: Full service assistance to foreign investors in Vietnam, including advice on Vietnamese law, drafting legal documentation in Vietnamese and English, identification of business partners, negotiations with Vietnamese partners and authorities, presentation of seminars, workshops and lectures to government authorities and visiting delegations.

Phillips Fox, a major Australian law firm, was the first foreign law firm to be granted a licence by the Government of Vietnam to operate an official representative office in Hanoi. Phillips Fox has a contract with the State Committee for Co-operation and Investment (SCCI) for the production of the official English language translations of the Foreign Investment Laws of Vietnam and other publications.

RESIDENT PARTNER

William G. Magennis

SENIOR ASSOCIATES

Debra Counsell

ASSOCIATES

Maureen McLaughlin   **Le Hoai Nam**

CONSULTANTS

Nguyen Qui Binh

(For Complete list of firm personnel see Melbourne, Australia)

POLLAK & CO., LTD.

(D.S. Pollak & Partners)

Established in 1992

76 HANG TRONG
HANOI, VIETNAM
Telephone: (844) 254971; 250218
Fax: (844) 260260

Paris, France Associated Office: D.S. Paris, 46 rue de Bassano, 75008. Telephone: 33-1-53675000. Fax: 33-1-47207876.

Bangkok, Thailand Office: Pollak & Co., Ltd., Diamond Tower, 13th Floor, 427/162 Silom Road, 10500. Telephone: (662) 231 5005; 231 5614 (Direct); 231 5228-9 ext. 162. Fax: (662) 231 5535.

Taipei, Taiwan Associated Office: Denis Forman & Associated, 6th Floor, TFIT Tower, 85, Jen Ai Road, Sec. 4, Taipei, Taiwan, R.O.C.

Beijing, China Associated Office: D.S. Meyer & Partners, Kim Kun Hotel, Suite 317-321 Maijing 10004, P.R.C. Telephone/Fax: 86-1-50050-73.

Seoul, Korea Associated Office: Kim Shin & Yu, Philippe Li, CPO Box 3238, Seoul, Korea. Telephone: 02-735-5822. Fax: 02-739-6606.

Foreign Investment Law, Acquisitions, Tax, Commercial Contracts, Property, General Practice, Arbitration, Industrial and Intellectual Property, Market Survey, Real Estate.

(This Listing Continued)

AS373B

POLLAK & CO., LTD., Hanoi—Continued

FIRM PROFILE: Pollak & Co., Ltd. has established its office in Vietnam since September 1992 in collaboration with the Lawyers' Association of Hanoi (Hanoi Bar).

The firm enjoys the collaboration of two senior lawyers and two project consultants with the support of an administrative staff of four, all under the supervision of Mr. Eric Le Dreau, resident consultant.

For the purpose of advising the firm's clients in specific fields related to local law, local highly specialized legal consultants are hired on a case by case basis following the recommendation of the Lawyer's Association of Hanoi.

DAN POLLAK, born Bucharest, Rumania, February 16, 1945; admitted, 1972, Paris; 1982, Bangkok (Not admitted in Vietnam). *Education:* University of Paris (D.E.S. Droit Prive, Doctorate, 1972); International Law Institute (Diploma, 1972). Member, Lawasia Commercial Arbitration Standing Committee, 1982. *Member:* International Bar Association; International Law Association (French Branch); Franco-British Chamber of Commerce (Vice-President, 1978-1981); Franco-Thai Chamber of Commerce; British Chamber of Commerce of Thailand; The Netherlands-Thai Chamber of Commerce. *LANGUAGES:* English, French, Italian, Rumanian, Thai and Vietnamese. *PRACTICE AREAS:* Foreign Investment Law; International Trade Law; Commercial Contracts; Arbitration.

ERIC LE DREAU, born Saint Avold, Moselle, France, February 3, 1962; admitted, 1989, Paris (Not admitted in Vietnam). *Education:* University of Paris, D.E.S.S. (International Contracts Law, 1986; Licence Droit prive and Political Sciences, Toulouse, 1983; Maitrise International Law, 1984). *LANGUAGES:* French, English and Vietnamese. *PRACTICE AREAS:* Foreign Investment Law; Commercial Contracts; Intellectual Property Law.

MARK BRADY, born 1963; admitted, 1988, London (Not admitted in Vietnam). *Education:* University of Kent England (B.A. Hons in Law); Chancery Lane College of Law, England. *PRACTICE AREAS:* Banking; Stock Exchange Regulation; Restructuring and Refinancing; Joint-Ventures; Consultancy Agreements.

OF COUNSEL

NGUYEN THANH VINH, born Hanoi, Vietnam, 1925. *Education:* University of Hanoi (Licence Droit, Diploma of Indochina Law). Member: Deputy of Hanoi Council; Central Committee of Vietnam Fatherland's Front. *Member:* Hanoi Bar (Vice-Chairman). *LANGUAGES:* French, Russian and Vietnamese. *PRACTICE AREAS:* Foreign Investment Law in Vietnam; Intellectual Property Law; Commercial Law; Administrative Law; Civil Law; Penal Law; Commercial Litigation; Arbitration.

SIMÉON & ASSOCIÉS

13 TRAN HUNG DAO
HANOI, VIETNAM
Telephone: (84 4) 251 558; (84 4) 244 345
Fax: (84) 4 251 514

Paris, France Office: 5, Avenue Percier, 75008. Telephone: (1) 40 75 08 08. Fax: (1) 40 75 04 50.

Brussels, Belgium Office: Avenue de Tervuren 13, B-1040. Telephone: (2) 732 69 69. Fax: (2) 732 70 71.

Ho Chi Minh Ville, Vietnam Office: IBC Centre, 1A Me Linh Square. Telephone: (84) 4294 890. Fax: (84) 4 294 876.

Warsaw, Poland Office: Siméon Karniol Malecki, Aleje Jerozolimskie 30. 00024. Telephone: (48) 22 27 04 64. Fax: (48) 22 27 48 08; 39 12 32 01.

Domestic and International Corporate, Commercial and Trade Law Practice.

PARTNER

JACQUES WANTZ, born Talence, France, June 24, 1955; admitted, 1977, Paris. *Education:* University of Bordeaux (Maître en Droit, 1977); University of Pennsylvania Law School (LL.M., 1980). *LANGUAGES:* French and English.

(This Listing Continued)

CHRISTOPHER EDWARD POTTER, born Geneva, Switzerland, May 21, 1970; admitted, 1993, Paris. *Education:* King's College, London (LL.B., 1989); University of Paris I (Maîtrise en Droits français et anglais, 1992; DEA Droit Fiscal, 1993). *LANGUAGES:* English and French.

(For Complete Biographical Data on all Personnel, see Professional Biographies at Paris, France).

SINCLAIR ROCHE & TEMPERLEY

16 NGUYEN TRUONG TO
BA DINH DISTRICT
HANOI, VIETNAM
Telephone: (84 42) 50002
Fax: (84 42) 60770

Other Offices: London (England), Hong Kong, Singapore, Shanghai (China) and Bucharest (Romania).

FIRM PROFILE: *International Commercial Practice.*

(For Complete Biographical Data on all personnel, see Professional Biographies at London, England Office)

WHITE & CASE
REPRESENTATIVE OFFICE

57 NGUYEN DU STREET
HAI BA TRUNG DISTRICT
HANOI, VIETNAM
Telephone: (84-4) 227-575/6/7
Facsimile: (84-4) 227-297

New York, New York: Telephone: 212-819-8200. Facsimile: 212-354-8113.

Washington, D.C.: Telephone: 202-872-0013. Facsimile: 202-872-0210.

Los Angeles, California: Telephone: 213-620-7700. Facsimile: 213-687-0758; 213-617-2205.

Miami, Florida: Telephone: 305-371-2700. Facsimile: 305-358-5744.

Mexico City, Mexico: Telephone: (52-5) 207-9717. Facsimile: (52-5) 208-3628.

Tokyo, Japan: Telephone: (81-3) 3239-4300. Facsimile: (81-3) 3239-4330.

Hong Kong: Telephone: (852) 2822-8700. Facsimile: (852) 2845-9070; Grice & Co., Solicitors, Telephone: (852) 2826-0333. Facsimile: (852) 2526-7166.

Singapore, Republic of Singapore: Telephone: (65) 225-6000. Facsimile: (65) 225-6009.

Bangkok, Thailand: Pacific Legal Group Ltd., In Association With White & Case, Telephone: (662) 236-6154/7. Facsimile: (662) 237-6771.

Bombay, India: Telephone: (91-22) 282-6300. Facsimile: (91-22) 282-6305.

London, England: Telephone: (44-171) 726-6361. Facsimile: (44-171) 726-4314; (44-171) 726-8558.

Paris, France: Telephone: (33-1) 42-60-34-05. Facsimile: (33-1) 42-60-82-46.

Brussels, Belgium: Telephone: (32-2) 647-05-89. Facsimile: (32-2) 647-16-75.

Stockholm, Sweden: Telephone: (46-8) 679-80-30. Facsimile: (46-8) 611-21-22.

Helsinki, Finland: Telephone: (358-0) 631-100. Facsimile: (358-0) 179-477.

Moscow, Russia: Telephone: (7-095) 201-9292/3/4/5. Facsimile: (7-095) 201-9284.

Budapest, Hungary: Telephone: (36-1) 269-0550; (36-1) 131-0933. Facsimile: (36-1) 269-1199.

Prague, Czech Republic: Telephone: (42-2) 2481-1796. Facsimile: (42-2) 232-5522.

Warsaw, Poland: Telephone/Facsimile: (48-22) 26-80-53; (48-22) 27-84-86. International Telephone/Facsimile: (48-39) 12-19-06.

Istanbul, Turkey: Telephone: (90-212) 275-68-98; (90-212) 275-75-33. Facsimile: (90-212) 275-75-43.

Ankara, Turkey: Telephone: (90-312) 446-2180. Facsimile: (90-312) 437-9677.

Jeddah, Saudi Arabia: Law Office of Hassan Mahassni, Telephone: (966-2) 651-3535. Facsimile: (966-2) 651-3636.

Riyadh, Saudi Arabia: Law Office of Hassan Mahassni, Telephone: (966-1) 476-7099. Facsimile: (966-1) 479-0110.

(This Listing Continued)

Almaty, Kazakhstan: Telephone: (7-3272) 50-7491/2. Facsimile: (7-3272) 61-0842.

General Practice.

RESIDENT PARTNER

K. MINH DANG, born Saigon, Vietnam, December 10, 1954; admitted, 1982, California (Not admitted in Vietnam). *Education:* University of California, Los Angeles (B.A., 1978); Boalt Hall School of Law, University of California, Berkeley (J.D., 1981). *Member:* Los Angeles County and American Bar Associations; State Bar of California.

RESIDENT ASSOCIATE

TANYA G. PULLIN, born Portsmouth, Kentucky, September 15, 1957; admitted, 1986, Kentucky (Not admitted in Vietnam). *Education:* University of Kentucky (B.S., 1980; J.D., 1986); Duke University (M.A., 1985).

(For biographical data as to other locations, see Professional Biographies at New York, New York; Washington, D.C.; Los Angeles, California; Miami, Florida; Mexico City, Mexico; Tokyo, Japan; Hong Kong; Singapore, Republic of Singapore; Bangkok, Thailand; Bombay, India; London, England; Paris, France; Brussels, Belgium; Stockholm, Sweden; Helsinki, Finland; Moscow, Russia; Budapest, Hungary; Prague, Czech Republic; Warsaw, Poland; Istanbul and Ankara, Turkey; Jeddah and Riyadh, Saudi Arabia; Almaty, Kazakhstan).

BAKER & McKENZIE

Ho Chi Minh City Branch Representative Office

4TH FLOOR
58 DONG KHOI STREET
DISTRICT 1
HO CHI MINH CITY, VIETNAM
Telephone: (8) 295 585; 295 601; 295 602; 295 613
Intn'l Dialing: (84-8) 295-585; 295 601; 295 602; 295 613
Facsimile: (84-8) 295 618

Associated Offices of Baker & McKenzie in: Almaty, Amsterdam, Bangkok, Barcelona, Beijing, Berlin, Bogotá, Brasília, Brussels, Budapest, Buenos Aires, Cairo, Caracas, Chicago, Dallas, Frankfurt, Geneva, Hanoi, Hong Kong, Juárez, Kiev, London, Madrid, Manila, Melbourne, México City, Miami, Milan, Monterrey, Moscow, New York, Palo Alto, Paris, Prague, Rio de Janeiro, Riyadh, Rome, St. Petersburg, San Diego, San Francisco, São Paulo, Singapore, Stockholm, Sydney, Taipei, Tijuana, Tokyo, Toronto, Valencia, Warsaw, Washington, D.C. and Zürich.
Correspondent Law Firm: Hadiputranto, Hadinoto & Partners, Jakarta.

LOCAL PARTNERS

MARK ANDREW LOCKWOOD, born Melbourne, Australia; admitted, 1986, Victoria, Australia; 1992, Hong Kong and England and Wales (Not admitted in Vietnam). *Education:* Monash University (B.A.; LL.B. Hons.). *Member:* Law Institute of Victoria; Law Society of Hong Kong. *LANGUAGES:* English. *PRACTICE AREAS:* Banking and Finance; Communications and Media Law; Construction and Property Development; Taxation; Trade (Vietnam).

NGUYEN TAN HAI, born Ha Nam, Vietnam, 1948; admitted, 1971, Vietnam; 1990, Victoria, Australia. *Education:* University of Saigon (LL.B., Economics, 1971); Chisholm Institute of Technology (Graduate Diploma in Data Processing, 1983); University of Melbourne (LL.B., 1988). Visiting Lecturer, Vietnamese Laws, The Constitutional & Administrative Law Centre, University of Melbourne, 1992-1993. Member: Victoria Council Against Violence, 1990-1991; Advisory Board, Asia Link Centre, University of Melbourne, 1993—. *Member:* Law Institute of Victoria, Australian Law Council; International Bar Association. *LANGUAGES:* English and Vietnamese. *PRACTICE AREAS:* Banking and Finance; Insurance Law; Oil and Gas/Mining; Real Estate Law; Taxation.

COUDERT BROTHERS

Established in 1853

C/O SAIGON BUSINESS CENTRE
49-57 DONG DU STREET
DISTRICT 1
HO CHI MINH CITY, VIETNAM
Telephone: 84-8-298-777
Telecopier: 84-8-298-155

New York, New York 10036-7794: 1114 Avenue of the Americas.
Washington, D.C. 20006: 1627 I Street, N.W.
Los Angeles, California 90017: 1055 West Seventh Street, Twentieth Floor.
San Francisco, California 94111: 4 Embarcadero Center, Suite 3300.
San Jose, California 95113: Suite 1250, Ten Almaden Boulevard.
Paris 75008, France: 52 Avenue des Champs-Elysees.
London, EC4M 7JP, England: 20 Old Bailey.
Brussels B-1050, Belgium: Tour Louise. 149 Avenue Louise, Box 8.
Beijing, People's Republic of China 100020: Suite 2708-09, Jing Guang Centre, Hu Jia Lou, Choa Yang Qu.
Shanghai, People's Republic of China 200002: c/o Suite 1804, Union Building, 100 Yanan Road East.
Hong Kong: 25th Floor, Nine Queen's Road Central.
Singapore 0104: Tung Centre, 20 Collyer Quay.
Sydney N.S.W. 2000, Australia: Suite 2202 State Bank Centre, 52 Martin Place.
Tokyo 107, Japan: 1355 West Tower, Aoyama Twin Towers, 1-1-1 Minami-Aoyama, Minato-ku.
Moscow, Russia: Ulitsa Staraya Basmannaya 14.
01301 Sao Paulo, SP, Brazil: Machado, Meyer, Sendacz, e Opice, Advogados, Rua da Consolacao, 247, 8 Andar.
Bangkok 10500, Thailand: Bubhajit Building, 20 North Sathorn Road, 10th Floor.

General and International Practice.

PARTNERS

MICHAEL J. HAGAN, born Queens, New York, February 7, 1951; (Not admitted in Vietnam). admitted to bar, 1983, New York. *Education:* Providence College (B.A., 1972); Georgetown University Law Center (J.D., cum laude, 1982). Author: "The Restructuring of the Chinese Banking System," 2 China Law Reporter, 153, 1983. *Member:* The Association of the Bar of the City of New York; American Society of International Law. *LANGUAGES:* French.

(For biographical data of the New York personnel, see Professional Biographies at New York, N.Y.).
(For biographical data of the Washington personnel, see Professional Biographies at Washington, D.C.).
(For biographical data of the San Francisco personnel, see Professional Biographies at San Francisco, California).
(For biographical data of the Los Angeles personnel, see Professional Biographies at Los Angeles, California).
(For biographical data of the San Jose personnel, see Professional Biographies at San Jose, California).
(For biographical data of the London personnel, see Professional Biographies at London, England).
(For biographical data of the Paris personnel, see Professional Biographies at Paris, France).
(For biographical data of the Brussels personnel, see Professional Biographies at Brussels, Belgium).
(For biographical data of the Beijing personnel, see Professional Biographies at Beijing, People's Republic of China).
(For biographical data of the Hong Kong personnel, see Professional Biographies at Hong Kong).
(For biographical data of the Singapore personnel, see Professional Biographies at Singapore).
(For biographical data of the Tokyo Personnel, see Professional Biographies at Tokyo, Japan).
(For biographical data of the Sao Paulo personnel, see Professional Biographies at Sao Paulo, Brazil).
(For biographical data of the Shanghai Personnel, see Professional Biographies at Shanghai, People's Republic of China).
(For biographical data of the Sydney personnel, see Professional Biographies at Sydney, Australia).
(For biographical data of the Moscow personnel, see Professional Biographies at Moscow, U.S.S.R.).
(For biographical data of the Ho Chi Minh personnel, see Professional Biographies at Ho Chi Minh, Vietnam).

FREEHILL HOLLINGDALE & PAGE

Established in 1852

203 DONG KHOI STREET #3-05
HO CHI MINH CITY, VIETNAM
Telephone: (848) 242 630; (848) 242 733
Facsimile: (848) 242 736

Sydney, New South Wales, Australia Office: Level 38, MLC Centre, 19-29 Martin Place, 2000. Telephone: (02) 225 5000. International: +(612) 225 5000. Telex AA 121885. Fax: (02) 322 4000.

Canberra City, Australian Capital Territory, Australia Office: London Court, 13 London Circuit, 2601. Telephone:(06) 240 6100. International: +(616) 240 6100. Telex: AA121885. Fax: (06) 240 6222.

Melbourne, Victoria, Australia Office: 101 Collins Street, 3000. Telephone: (03) 288 1234. International: +(613) 288 1234. Telex: AA33004. Fax: (03) 288 1567.

Perth, Western Australia Office: Australia Place, 15-17 William Street, 6000. Telephone: (09) 327 5777. International: +(619) 327 5777. Telex: AA92937. Fax: (09) 322 5954.

Brisbane, Queensland, Australia Office: Central Plaza II, 66 Eagle Street, 4000. Telephone: (07) 258 6666. International: +(617) 258 6666. Fax: (07) 258 6444.

Singapore Office: 6 Battery Road, #13-01, 0104. Telephone: (65) 225 1288. Telex: (RS) 42674. Fax: (65) 225 3314.

London, England Office: Birchin Court, 20 Birchin Lane, EC3V 9DJ. Telephone: (0171) 283 9006. International: +(44 171) 283 9006. Fax: (0171) 454 9650.

Hanoi, Vietnam Office: 34A Quang Trung Street. Telephone: (844) 227 839. Fax: (844) 227 909.

ANDREW MESSENGER, admitted, 1985. *Education:* University of Melbourne (B.Com.; LL.B.). **PRACTICE AREAS:** Capital Raisings; Infrastructure; Telecommunications; Mergers and Acquisitions.

(For biographical data on all other Firm Personnel, see Professional Biographies at Brisbane, Canberra, Melbourne and Perth, Australia and Singapore)

LE, DIRKSEN, FLIPSE & DORAN

100 NGUYEN TRAI, DISTRICT 1
HO CHI MINH CITY, VIETNAM
Telephone: 84-8-390-102
Fax: 84-8-390-102

Seattle, Washington, USA Office: 1001 Fourth Avenue, Suite 3200. 98154. Telephone: 206-292-1650. Fax: 206-760-8041.

Vietiane, Laos Office: Dirksen Flipse Doran & Le. Mekong Commerce Building 1. Luang Prabang Road. P.O. Box 2929. Telephone: 856-21 216927-9. Fax: 856-21 216919.

Civil Practice, International Trade, Foreign Investment, Immigration Law.

FIRM PROFILE: *Our practice focuses on international business transactions between the US and East Asia, especially Viet Nam and Indochina. Our firm has corresponding relationships with law firms in San Francisco, California, Seoul, Korea, and Bangkok, Thailand.*

MEMBERS OF FIRM

TUYEN DINH LE, born Hue, Vietnam, October 2, 1957; admitted, 1990, Washington. *Education:* University of Portland (B.S.M.E., 1982); University of Saigon, School of Economics, Saigon Vietnam; Hastings College of Law, University of California (J. D., 1985); University of Hue, School of Law, Hue, Vietnam. Author: "Vietnam Moves Toward Market Economy," Pacific Economic Review, September 1993. Lecturer: "Negotiating in Vietnam/Asia" CLE Seminar Chairperson/Faculty, November 1993, Seattle Washington. *Member:* Washington State and American Bar Associations (Member, International Section); International Bar Association; Asian Bar Association; Vietnamese Bar Association. **LANGUAGES:** Vietnamese, French, Chinese and English. **PRACTICE AREAS:** International Business; Immigration; Intellectual Property Law; General Civil Practice.

TODD E. DIRKSEN (Not admitted in Vietnam).

MARY S. FLIPSE (Not admitted in Vietnam).

DAVID D. DORAN

(For Complete Biographical Data, see Professional Biographies at Vientane, Laos)

POLLAK & CO., LTD.

(D.S. Pollak & Partners)

Established in 1994

180 HAI BA TRONG
DISTRICT 1
HO CHI MINH CITY S.R., VIETNAM
Telephone: (848) 242155
Fax: (848) 241432

Paris, France Associated Office: D.S. Paris, 46 rue de Bassano, 75008. Telephone: 33-1-53675000. Fax: 33-1-47207876.

Bangkok, Thailand Office: Pollak & Co., Ltd., Diamond Tower, 13th Floor, 427/162 Silom Road, 10500. Telephone: (662) 231 5005; 231 5614 (Direct); 231 5228-9 ext. 162. Fax: (662) 231 5535.

Hanoi, S.R. Vietnam Office: D.S. Pollak & Partners, 76 Hang Trong. Telephone: (844) 254 971; 250 218. Fax: (844) 260 260.

Taipei, Taiwan Associated Office: Denis Forman & Associated, 6th Floor, TFIT Tower, 85, Jen Ai Road, Sec. 4, Taipei, Taiwan, R.O.C.

Beijing, China Associated Office: D.S. Meyer & Partners, Kim Kun Hotel, Suite 317-321 Maijing 10004, P.R.C. Telephone/Fax: 86-1-50050-73.

Seoul, Korea Associated Office: Kim Shin & Yu, Philippe Li, CPO Box 3238, Seoul, Korea. Telephone: 02-735-5822. Fax: 02-739-6606.

Foreign Investment Law, Acquisitions, Tax, Commercial Contracts, Property, General Practice, Arbitration, Industrial and Intellectual Property, Market Survey, Real Estate.

FIRM PROFILE: *Pollak & Co., Ltd. has established its office in Vietnam since September 1992 in collaboration with the Lawyers' Association of Hanoi (Hanoi Bar) and subsequently in Ho Chi Minh City in September 1994.*

DAN POLLAK, born Bucharest, Rumania, February 16, 1945; admitted, 1972, Paris; 1982, Bangkok (Not admitted in Vietnam). *Education:* University of Paris (D.E.S. Droit Prive, Doctorate, 1972); International Law Institute (Diploma, 1972). Member, Lawasia Commercial Arbitration Standing Committee, 1982. *Member:* International Bar Association; International Law Association (French Branch); Franco-British Chamber of Commerce (Vice-President, 1978-1981); Franco-Thai Chamber of Commerce; British Chamber of Commerce of Thailand; The Netherlands-Thai Chamber of Commerce. **LANGUAGES:** English, French, Italian, Rumanian, Thai and Vietnamese. **PRACTICE AREAS:** Foreign Investment Law; International Trade Law; Commercial Contracts; Arbitration.

ERIC LE DREAU, born Saint Avold, Moselle, France, February 3, 1962; admitted, 1989, Paris (Not admitted in Vietnam). *Education:* University of Paris, D.E.S.S. (International Contracts Law, 1986; Licence Droit prive and Political Sciences, Toulouse, 1983; Maitrise International Law, 1984). **LANGUAGES:** French, English and Vietnamese. **PRACTICE AREAS:** Foreign Investment Law; Commercial Contracts; Intellectual Property Law.

MARK BRADY, born 1963; admitted, 1988, London (Not admitted in Vietnam). *Education:* University of Kent England (B.A. Hons in Law); Chancery Lane College of Law, England. **PRACTICE AREAS:** Banking; Stock Exchange Regulation; Restructuring and Refinancing; Joint-Ventures; Consultancy Agreements.

RUSSIN & VECCHI

International Legal Counsellors.

In Affiliation with Walter, Conston, Alexander & Green, P.C. and
Adduci, Mastriani, Schaumberg & Schill

OSIC BUILDING, 6/F
8 NGUYEN HUE STREET
HO CHI MINH CITY, VIETNAM
Telephone: (84-8) 243-026/243-114
Fax: (84-8) 243-113

Bangkok, Thailand Office: Russin & Vecchi, International Legal Counsellors Thailand, Ltd., Sathorn City Tower, 175 South Sathorn Road, 18th Floor, 10120. Telephone: 662-679-6005, 662-679-6015. Fax: 662-679-6041, 662-679-6042.

Hanoi, Vietnam Office: Russin & Vecchi, 25 Ly Thuong Kiet Street. Telephone: (84-4) 251-699/251-700. Fax: (84-4) 251-742.

(This Listing Continued)

Moscow, Russia Office: Russin & Vecchi, Danilovsky Hotel Complex, Bolshoy Starodanilovsky, Pereulok No. 5, Moscow 113191. Telephone: (7-095) 954-0652. Telex: 612506 RV MOS SU. Fax: (7-095) 954-0653.

New York, New York Office: Russin & Vecchi, 15th Floor, 90 Park Avenue, 10016-1387. Telephone: 212-210-9543. Fax: 212-210-9493.

Puerto Plata, Dominican Republic Office: Russin Vecchi & Heredia Bonetti, Plaza Turisol Local #11A. Telephone: 809-586-5535. Fax: 809-586-5861.

San Francisco, California Office: Russin & Vecchi, 16th Floor, 580 California Street, 94104. Telephone: 415-421-1100. Fax: 415-421-1103.

Santo Domingo, Dominican Republic Office: Russin Vecchi & Heredia Bonetti, Edificio Monte Mirador, Calle El Recodo No 2, Esquina Winston Churchill, Bella Vista, Apartado Postal 425. Telephone: 809-535-9511. Cable Address: "RUSVEC SANTO DOMINGO." Telex: 3264199 RUSVEC. Fax: 809-535-6649.

Taipei, Taiwan Office: Russin & Vecchi, 9th Floor, 205 Tun Hwa N. Road. Telephone: (886-2) 712-8956. Fax: (886-2) 713-4711.

Washington, D.C. Office: Russin & Vecchi, Second Floor, 1140 Connecticut Avenue, N.W., 20036. Telephone: 202-223-4793. Fax: 202-223-4810.

Foreign Investment in Vietnam, Corporate, Tax, Intellectual Property, Real Property, Banking and Finance.

MEMBERS OF FIRM

SESTO E. VECCHI, born Canandaigua, New York, 1936; admitted, 1962, Pennsylvania; 1970, District of Columbia; 1981, New York (Not admitted in Vietnam). *Education:* Wharton School of Finance and Commerce, University of Pennsylvania (B.S. in Econ., 1958); Temple University (LL.B., 1961); University of Rome (Certificate in International Commercial Law, 1962). Associate Editor, Temple Law Quarterly. *Member:* Association of the Bar of the City of New York; New York State and Pennsylvania Bar Associations; District of Columbia Bar. (Also at Hanoi, Vietnam and New York, NY Offices). *LANGUAGES:* English and French.

MICHAEL J. SCOWN, born Glen Ellyn, Illinois, 1959; admitted, 1985, California. *Education:* University of California at Berkeley (A.B., 1981); University of San Francisco (J.D., 1985). Articles Editor, 1984-1985, University of San Francisco Law Review. Author: Note, "A Vote on Th' Talley-sheet Is Worth Two in the Box: Peterson v. City of San Diego," 18 University of San Francisco Law Review 635, 1984. Author: "Vietnam's Opening Door: U.S. Embargo Shuts Out Only American Firms," (with Sesto E. Vecchi), East Asian Executive Reports, December 1989; "The Vietnam Embargo - No End in Sight," CEB California Business Law Reporter, December 1989; "Representing Foreign Investors in California," (with Nicholas S. Freud), CEB California Business Law Reporter, July 1990; "An Introduction to the Emerging Equities Markets of Asia," East Asian Executive Reports (Two Part Series), November 1990; January 1991; "Renewing Trade with Vietnam," S.F. Chronicle, February 6, 1991; "Vietnam: Trading with the Enemy?" Export Today, September, 1991; "Vietnam's Evolving Framework For Oil and Gas Exploration," (Two-part series) East Asian Executive Reports Vol. XIV, no. 4,5; "Intellectual Property Rights in Vietnam," (with Sesto E. Vecchi) 11 UCLA Pacific Basin Law Journal 67, 1992; "As The Embargo Crumbles, Vietnam Prepares For U.S. Investors," The Journal of International Taxation, Jan. 1993, Vol. 4, No. 1; "Manager's Journal—Bucking The Wiles of Vietnam's Pirates," Asian Wall Street Journal, January 7, 1993; "Manager's Journal-Barstool Advice For the Vietnam Investor," Asian Wall Street Journal, July 15, 1993. Contributing Editor, CEB, California Business Law Reporter, 1989-1993. Correspondent, Vietnam, The Journal of International Taxation, 1993—. Foreign Service Officer, U.S. Department of State, 1985-1988. *Member:* State Bar of California; American Bar Association (Member, Sections of: International Law and Practice; Business Law); The Washington Foreign Law Society; U.S.-Vietnam Trade Council, 1992-1994; California Southeast Asia Business Council (Chair, Indochina Committee). (Also at Hanoi, S.R. Vietnam Office). *LANGUAGES:* English and Spanish.

NGO VAN LAN, born Quang-Binh Province, August 7, 1963. *Education:* Hue University, Vietnam (Licencie-en-Droit, 1964); National Institute of Public Administration, Saigon (M.A. Public Administration, 1969). Lecturer in Management, Open University of Ho Chi Minh City, 1992-1993. *Member:* Lawyers Association of Ho Chi Minh City. *LANGUAGES:* Vietnamese, English and French.

PHAN NGUYEN TOAN, born Hanoi, Vietnam, 1957; admitted, 1988, Vietnam. *Education:* Hanoi Law College (B.A., 1979); Institute for National Economics, B.A., 1987); Georgetown University in Vietnam (Business Management, 1989); Institute of International Development Law, Italy, 1991; Institute of Social Studies, Holland, 1992-1993; Yale Law School

(This Listing Continued)

(Visiting Scholar, 1993-1994). Member, Legal Finance Policy Department Ministry of Finance, 1982-1986. *Member, Vietnamese Lawyers Association, Hanoi.*

HAROLD P. FISKE, born New York, N.Y., 1962; admitted, 1992, California. *Education:* Brown University (B.A., International Relations, 1985); The Chinese University of Hong Kong (1985); Boston College Law School (J.D., 1992). *Member:* State Bar of California; American Bar Association. *LANGUAGES:* Mandarin Chinese, French and English.

TRAN TRUC, born Thua Thien, Vietnam, 1938. *Education:* Hue University (LL.B., 1964). District Attorney, Qui Nhon, 1970-1971 and Hue, 1971-1975.

(For Biographical Data on other Personnel, see Professional Biographies at: Washington, D.C., U.S.A.; San Francisco, California, U.S.A.; New York, N.Y., U.S.A.; Bangkok, Thailand; Taipei, Taiwan; Santo Domingo, Dominican Republic; Moscow, Russia).

SIMÉON & ASSOCIÉS
IBC CENTRE
1A ME LINH SQUARE
HO CHI MINH CITY, VIETNAM
Telephone: (84) 8 294 890
Fax: (84) 4 294 876

Paris, France Office: 5, Avenue Percier, 75008. Telephone: (1) 40 75 08 08. Fax: (1) 40 75 04 50.

Brussels, Belgium Office: Avenue de Tervuren 13, B-1040. Telephone: (2) 732 69 69. Fax: (2) 732 70 71.

Hanoi, Vietnam Office: 13 Tran Hung Dao. Telephone: 84 4 251 558; (84) 4 244 345. Fax: (84) 4 251 514.

Warsaw, Poland Office: Siméon Karniol Malecki, Aleje Jerozolimskie 30. 00024. Telephone: (48) 22 27 04 64. Fax: (48) 22 27 48 08; 39 12 32 01.

Domestic and International Corporate, Commercial and Trade Law Practice.

PARTNER

JACQUES WANTZ, born Talence, France, June 24, 1955; admitted, 1977, Paris. *Education:* University of Bordeaux (Maîtrise en Droit, 1977); University of Pennsylvania Law School (LL.M., 1980). *LANGUAGES:* French and English.

RESIDENT ASSOCIATES

LUC LEJEUNE, born Brest, France, November 3, 1965. *Education:* University of Aix-Marseille III (Maîtrise en Droit, 1987); University of Paris V (DESS, 1989); Institut d'Etudes Politiques de Paris (1990). *LANGUAGES:* French, English, German, Italian and Vietnamese.

French, English, German, Italian and Vietnamese

(For Complete Biographical Data on all Personnel, see Professional Biographies at Siméon & Associés, Paris, France)

TILLEKE & GIBBINS CONSULTANTS LTD.
2ND FLOOR, THE VIETNAM NATIONAL GOLD-SILVER AND GEMSTONES CORPORATION BUILDING
3-5 HO TUNG MAU
District 1 HO CHI MINH CITY, VIETNAM
Telephone: (84-8) 251-645, 251-695, 251-700
Fax: (84-8) 242-226

Bangkok, Thailand Office: Tilleke & Gibbins, R.O.P., Tilleke & Gibbins Building, 64/1 Soi Ton Son, Ploenchit Road. Telephone: (66-2) 254-2640-58. Telefax: (66-2) 254-4304; (66-8) 621-0173. Telex: 82978 LYMAN TH.

Hanoi, Vietnam Office: Boss Hotel, Suite 207, 60 Nguyen Du Street. Telephone: (84-4) 227-895/6. Telefax: (84-4) 277-897.

The firm provides investment, liaison and legal consulting services related to international commercial transactions, including intellectual property.

FIRM PROFILE: Tilleke & Gibbins Consultants Ltd., was established in 1989 as an affiliate of Tilleke & Gibbins R.O.P., Bangkok, Thailand. In July, 1992, they became the first foreign law firm to be granted a license to open an office in Vietnam. A license to open a branch of the representative office in Hanoi was issued in January, 1994.

(This Listing Continued)

AUSTRALIA

FINLAYSONS
81 FLINDERS STREET
ADELAIDE, SOUTH AUSTRALIA 5000, AUSTRALIA
Telephone: 618 235 7400
Facsimile: 618 232 2944

A member of the Allens Arthur Robinson Group comprising Allen Allen & Hemsley, Sydney & Canberra; Arthur Robinson & Hedderwicks, Melbourne; Parker & Parker, Perth; Feez Ruthning, Brisbane; Finlaysons, Adelaide.

Group and Associated Offices:
London, England; New York, NY; Singapore; Port Moresby, Papua New Guinea; Hong Kong; Jakarta, Indonesia; Shanghai, People's Republic of China.

Administrative Law, Advertising Law, Aeronautical Law, Antitrust Law, Arbitration, Banking Law, Bankruptcy, Competition Law, Constitutional Law, Construction Law, Consumer Protection Law, Conveyancing Law, Corporate Law, Distributorship, Agency and Franchise Law, Employer's Liability, Entertainment Law, Environmental Law, Foreign Investments, Immigration Law, Insurance Law, International Contracts, International Private Law, Litigation, Maritime and Admiralty Law, Negligence Law, Oil and Mining Law, Personal Injury Law, Product Liability Law, Property and Real Estate Law, Rent and Lease, Trade Regulations, Transportation Law, General Practice, Intellectual Property, Copyright Law, Licence Negotiation, Patent Litigation, Trademark Litigation, Trademark Prosecution, Transfer of Technology, Capital Taxation, Corporate Taxation, Customs Duties, Deferred Taxation, Indirect Taxation, Inheritance, Estate and Gift Taxation, International Taxation, International Taxation, Personal Income Taxation, Sales, Turnover, Value Added Taxes, Taxation of Foreign Nationals, Taxation of Oil and Mining Companies, Transfer Pricing, Exchange Control, General Tax Practice.

FIRM PROFILE: Finlaysons is an internationally based firm in terms of the clients it represents and the transactions in which it has been involved. In addition, the background of its lawyers and its links with law firms in major and financial and commercial centres of the world assist with the international nature of the practice. Total number of partners for Finlaysons is 19, total legal staff is approximately 100 and for the Allens Arthur Robinson Group total legal staff is over 700. The firm's areas of specialization include: Corporate and Commercial; Finance and Banking; Litigation; Intellectual Property; Tax; Resources; Environment and Planning; Construction and Property; Government Liaison; Technology; Media and Communications; Wine and Beverage; Health Care and Education.

PARTNERS

JON TORE GREGERSON, admitted, 1968, South Australia. *LANGUAGES:* English. *PRACTICE AREAS:* Commercial Law; Company Law; Securities; Mining Law; Resources; Trade Practices.

GERRICK WILLIAM GEORGE MCQUADE, admitted, 1972, South Australia. *LANGUAGES:* English. *PRACTICE AREAS:* Banking Law; Finance Law; Commercial Law; Company Law; Securities.

JOHN MAXWELL HARLEY, admitted, 1969, South Australia. *LANGUAGES:* English. *PRACTICE AREAS:* Health Industry Law; Local Government Law; Property Law; Wills; Estate Administration.

IAN LEWIS MAITLAND, admitted, 1974, South Australia. *LANGUAGES:* English. *PRACTICE AREAS:* Employment Law; Insurance Law; International Trade Law; Shipping Law; Aviation Law.

ALAN ROBERT MCARTHUR, admitted, 1978, Australian Capital Territory. *LANGUAGES:* English. *PRACTICE AREAS:* Communications Law; Media Law; Entertainment Law; Defamation; Insurance Law.

ANDREW GIFFIN HODGE, admitted, 1978, South Australia. *LANGUAGES:* English. *PRACTICE AREAS:* Insurance Law; Workers Compensation Law.

JEREMY GRAHAM SCHULTZ, admitted, 1980, South Australia. *LANGUAGES:* English. *PRACTICE AREAS:* Banking Law; Finance Law; Commercial Law; Environmental Law; Planning Law; Development Law; International Trade Law; Japan and Asia Business Law; Sports Law.

(This Listing Continued)

MARK FREDERICK RALPH BIELECKI, admitted, 1980, South Australia. *LANGUAGES:* English. *PRACTICE AREAS:* Commercial Law; Litigation; Product Liability Law; Trade Practices.

ERICA EBELING SIMES, admitted, 1982, New South Wales. *LANGUAGES:* English. *PRACTICE AREAS:* Banking Law; Finance Law; International Trade Law.

RODNEY WILLIAM DUNNE, admitted, 1982, South Australia. *LANGUAGES:* English. *PRACTICE AREAS:* Superannuation Law; Taxation Law.

WILLIAM THOMAS CAMPBELL TAYLOR, admitted, 1986, South Australia. *LANGUAGES:* English. *PRACTICE AREAS:* Company Law; Securities; Japan and Asia Business Law; Mining Law; Resources.

LEE SCOTT DEWHIRST, admitted, 1978, South Australia. *LANGUAGES:* English. *PRACTICE AREAS:* Communications Law; Media Law; Entertainment Law; Defamation; Intellectual Property Law; Taxation Law.

BRIAN FRANCIS AUSTIN, admitted, 1979, South Australia. *LANGUAGES:* English. *PRACTICE AREAS:* Insurance Law; Workers Compensation Law.

GEORGE COMYN MC KENZIE, admitted, 1982, Republic of South Africa. *LANGUAGES:* English, Afrikaans, Flemish and Dutch. *PRACTICE AREAS:* Commercial Law; Construction Law; International Trade Law.

STEFAN MARK JURY, admitted, 1981, South Australia. *LANGUAGES:* English. *PRACTICE AREAS:* Banking Law; Finance Law; Commercial Law; International Trade Law.

JOHN MATTHEW MARSDEN, admitted, 1987, South Australia. *LANGUAGES:* English. *PRACTICE AREAS:* Commercial Law; Litigation.

VIRGINIA SUE HICKEY, admitted, 1983, Victoria. *LANGUAGES:* English and Italian. *PRACTICE AREAS:* Commercial Law; Litigation; Malpractice Law; Insurance Law.

JOHN ANTHONY SHORTT-SMITH, admitted, 1982, Republic of South Africa. *LANGUAGES:* English and Dutch. *PRACTICE AREAS:* Commercial Law; Litigation; Product Liability Law; Trade Practices; Administrative Law.

MINTER ELLISON BAKER O'LOUGHLIN
Established in 1988

15TH FLOOR, AMP BUILDING
1 KING WILLIAM STREET
ADELAIDE, SOUTH AUSTRALIA 5000, AUSTRALIA
Telephone: (08) 233 5555
International: +61 8 233 5555
Facsimile: (08) 212 7518 G2 and G3 3

A member of the Minter Ellison Legal Group comprising Minter Ellison, Sydney, Melbourne, Canberra, Brisbane, Gold Coast; Minter Ellison Baker O'Loughlin, Adelaide; Minter Ellison Northmore Hale, Perth; Rudd Watts & Stone, (New Zealand), Auckland, Wellington, New Plymouth. Overseas Offices: Minter Ellison, London; McKenna & Co, Hong Kong; Khattar Wong, Singapore; Interjura Consultancy Services, Beijing; Makarim & Taira S., Jakarta.

Alternative Dispute Resolution, Arbitration, Banking, Finance and Securities, Building and Construction, Commercial Litigation, Corporate and Business, Government and Public Authorities, Industrial Relations, Insolvency, Insurance, Intellectual Property and Licensing, International Trade and Investment, Media, Mining and Resources, Planning, Local Government and Environment, Probate and Estates, Property Development and Contracting, Taxation and Revenue.

PARTNERS

Dean C. Davies	John K. Wellington
Anthony B. Fuller	Robyn M. Pak-Poy
Charles C.A. Binks	Andrew D. Short
Terence C. Evans	Neil L. Strawbridge
Richard J. Pash	Peter G. Chester
Neville W. Martin	Rosemary J. Batt
Ewan J. Vickery	Peter A. Campbell
Larry J. Opie	Raymond L. Beven
Paul D. Bear	Neil Gordon

(This Listing Continued)

MINTER ELLISON BAKER O'LOUGHLIN, Adelaide, South Australia—Continued

Peter J. Myhill	Gregory M. May
Denys O. Simpson	Michael R. Burnett
Peter C. Heinrich	Sybella G.M. Blencowe
	Richard J. Manuel

SENIOR ASSOCIATES

Penelope A. Eldridge	Clayton D. Wohling
David W. Fidler	Graham D. Edmonds-Wilson
John A. Homburg	John Levy
Jane Ekin-Smyth	Jennifer F. Tobin
Stephen B. Williams	Michael B. Manetta
Guy C. Biddle	Margaret E Ross
F. Adrian Swale	Casey Lau
	William A. Marryat

PIPER ALDERMAN

Established in 1988

167 FLINDERS STREET
ADELAIDE, SOUTH AUSTRALIA 5000, AUSTRALIA
Telephone: 618 205 3333
Facsimile: 618 205 3300

Corporate and Commercial Advice, Commercial Litigation, Banking, Finance and Securities, Government Liaison, Trade and Foreign Investment, Environmental Law, Intellectual Property, Liquor Licensing and Administrative Law, Insurance Law, Media Law, General, Public and Professional Liability, Defense of Compensation Claims, Health Law, Industrial Law, Building and Construction Law, Taxation Law and Insolvency Law and Mining Law, Property Law.

FIRM PROFILE: The firm is the product of the merger of a commercial and banking practice founded in the 1840's and a litigious and insurance practice founded in 1928. It offers a full range of effective legal services and acts for many of Australia's leading companies as well as government and private clients. This 26 partner firm employees some 30 additional lawyers and also has a legal support staff of 70 including paralegals, office administrators, computer specialists and accountants.

PARTNERS

ROBERT W. PIPER. LANGUAGES: English. **PRACTICE AREAS:** Trust and Estates; Corporate and Commercial Advice.

NIGEL D. WALLWORK. LANGUAGES: English. **PRACTICE AREAS:** Compensation; Industrial Law.

ANDREW A. BURDETT. LANGUAGES: English. **PRACTICE AREAS:** Corporate and Commercial Advice; Banking and Finance.

ANTHONY N. ABBOTT, Managing Partner. **LANGUAGES:** English. **PRACTICE AREAS:** Corporate and Commercial Advice; Commercial Litigation; Intellectual Property.

JOHN McC. HIATT. LANGUAGES: English. **PRACTICE AREAS:** Insurance Law; Defense of Compensation Claims; General Public and Professional Liability.

CHARLES N.H. BAGOT. LANGUAGES: English. **PRACTICE AREAS:** Commercial Litigation; Corporate Law; Mining Law.

ASHLEY H. WATSON. LANGUAGES: English. **PRACTICE AREAS:** Environmental Law; Licensing and Administrative; Corporate and Commercial Advice; Mining Law; Trade and Foreign Investment.

OWEN M. KEEN. LANGUAGES: English. **PRACTICE AREAS:** Corporate and Commercial Advice; Banking and Finance.

SIMON H. WARD. LANGUAGES: English. **PRACTICE AREAS:** Media Law; Insurance Law; Building and Construction; General Public and Professional Liability.

RAMSEY ANDARY. LANGUAGES: English and Arabic. **PRACTICE AREAS:** Franchising Law; Corporate and Commercial Advice; Property Law.

MARK A. GORDON. LANGUAGES: English. **PRACTICE AREAS:** Banking and Finance; Corporate and Commercial Advice.

DAVID G. EY. LANGUAGES: English. **PRACTICE AREAS:** Industrial Law; Defense of Compensation Claims; Insurance Law.

(This Listing Continued)

SIMON J. HANUS. LANGUAGES: English. **PRACTICE AREAS:** Insurance Law; Defense of Compensation Claim; Health Law.

GORDON T. GRIEVE. LANGUAGES: English. **PRACTICE AREAS:** Corporate Law; Commercial Litigation.

ALISON F. ADAIR. LANGUAGES: English. **PRACTICE AREAS:** Commercial Litigation.

RAYMOND M. MANSUETO. LANGUAGES: English and Maltese. **PRACTICE AREAS:** Insolvency; Liquidation; Commercial Litigation.

MICHAEL ST. J.R. BUTLER. LANGUAGES: English. **PRACTICE AREAS:** Taxation.

PETER S. LODGE. LANGUAGES: English. **PRACTICE AREAS:** Banking and Finance; Corporate and Commercial Advice.

MARK R. KEAM. LANGUAGES: English. **PRACTICE AREAS:** Defense of Compensation Claims.

TIMOTHY J.P. O'CALLAGHAN. LANGUAGES: English. **PRACTICE AREAS:** Defense of Compensation Claims; Insurance Law.

NICHOLAS J. ILES. LANGUAGES: English. **PRACTICE AREAS:** Commercial Litigation; Government Liason; Constitutional Law.

GLENN S. DAVIS. LANGUAGES: English. **PRACTICE AREAS:** Commercial Litigation; Insurance Law; Corporate Law.

IAN C. ROBERTSON. LANGUAGES: English. **PRACTICE AREAS:** Commercial Litigation.

ANTHONY K. PHELPS. LANGUAGES: English. **PRACTICE AREAS:** Insurance Law; Media Law.

LEO G. WALSH. LANGUAGES: English. **PRACTICE AREAS:** Commercial Litigation.

ALISTER G. MCFARLANE. LANGUAGES: English. **PRACTICE AREAS:** Commercial Litigation.

TRACEY A. KERRIGAN. LANGUAGES: English. **PRACTICE AREAS:** Defense of Compensation Claims.

CONSULTANTS

RONALD L. JOHNSON. LANGUAGES: English. **PRACTICE AREAS:** Corporate and Commercial Advice; Trusts and Estates.

JAMES R. PORTER. LANGUAGES: English. **PRACTICE AREAS:** Government Liaison.

BERYL E. LINN AM. LANGUAGES: English. **PRACTICE AREAS:** Trusts and Estates.

JAMES F. CORKERY, Professor. **LANGUAGES:** English. **PRACTICE AREAS:** Corporate and Commercial Advice; Director, Liability; Taxation.

SENIOR ASSOCIATES

GRANT K. FEARY. LANGUAGES: English. **PRACTICE AREAS:** Commercial Litigation.

MARK A. POCZMAN. LANGUAGES: English and Polish. **PRACTICE AREAS:** Corporate and Commercial Law; Taxation Law.

JOSEPHINE M. KING. LANGUAGES: English. **PRACTICE AREAS:** Franchising Law; Corporate and Commercial Advice; Property Law.

ELIZABETH C. OLSSON. LANGUAGES: English. **PRACTICE AREAS:** Family Law; Compensation Claims.

CATHERINE L. OSTER. LANGUAGES: English. **PRACTICE AREAS:** Corporate and Commercial Advice; Banking and Finance.

CARMEL J. PREECE. LANGUAGES: English. **PRACTICE AREAS:** Defence of Compensation Claims.

MATTHEW SELLEY. LANGUAGES: English. **PRACTICE AREAS:** Commercial Litigation.

BARKER GOSLING LEGAL GROUP

4TH FLOOR, 307 QUEEN STREET
BRISBANE, QUEENSLAND 4000, AUSTRALIA
Telephone: (07) 221 1244
Fax: (07) 221 1219 Dx: 166 Brisbane

Mailing Address: GPO Box 67, Brisbane, Queensland, 4001

(This Listing Continued)

A member of Barker Gosling Legal Group comprised the Practices of Barker Gosling in Sydney (NSW), Melbourne (VIC) and Brisbane (QLD), Barker Gosling in Perth (WA), Crossin Barker Gosling in Canberra (ACT).

FIRM PROFILE: *Barker Gosling Group comprises five long established Practices in the leading commercial centres of Australia. The Group provides a comprehensive range of legal services, both domestic and international, to a wide variety of companies, institutions and individuals. Partners of the Group are active members of the business and legal communities, serving on the Boards of many private and public companies and Committees of Government and Law Societies. All Partners and Senior Associates are admitted in the High Court and all Federal jurisdictions.*

PARTNERS

PETER ALCORN LILLEY, born November 27, 1937; admitted, 1960, Queensland.

WILLIAM GEORGE KIRBY, born December 12, 1938; admitted, 1965, Queensland.

JAMES THOMAS NOBLE, born December 16, 1945; admitted, 1973, Queensland.

KEITH JAMES CARL, born May 31, 1952; admitted, 1975, Queensland; 1991, Victoria.

STEVEN HUGH ROBSON MORRIS, born August 1, 1958; admitted, 1981, Queensland.

ROBERT JOHN BRUCE WINTER, born October 28, 1957; admitted, 1981, Queensland; 1991, Victoria.

LAWRENCE DIERCKE, born August 30, 1949; admitted, 1983, Queensland; 1991, New South Wales.

LESLEY MAY KING, born August 27, 1953; admitted, 1984, Queensland; 1988, New South Wales.

KELLI STALLARD, born March 20, 1960; admitted, 1984, Queensland; 1990, New South Wales.

ANTHONY NEIL BOGE, born October 3, 1964; admitted, 1987, Queensland.

PETER JAMES SCANLAN, born March 4, 1960; admitted, 1984, Queensland; 1988, New South Wales.

PETER ERIC BURDEN, born August 2, 1944; admitted, 1969, Victoria; 1990, Queensland.

SENIOR ASSOCIATES

GREGORY JAMES COX, born January 9, 1959; admitted, 1983, Queensland.

ANDREW IVO CHARLES, born August 19, 1966; admitted, 1991, Queensland.

JENNIFER MARGARET BOULTON, born September 21, 1957; admitted, 1980, Queensland; 1985, New South Wales.

Languages: German, French, Italian, Japanese.

BLAKE DAWSON WALDRON
RIVERSIDE CENTRE
123 EAGLE STREET
BRISBANE, QUEENSLAND 4000, AUSTRALIA
Telephone: (07) 259-7000
Facsimile: (07) 259-7111
Telex: AA22867DWN

Sydney, New South Wales, Australia Office: Grosvenor Place 225 George Street 2000. Telephone: (02) 2586000. Facsimile: (02) 2586999. Telex: AA22867DWN.

Melbourne, Victoria, Australia Office: 101 Collins Street 3000. Telephone: (03) 679-3000. Facsimile: (03) 679-3111. Telex: AA31033.

Perth, Western Australia, Australia Office: Forrest Centre, 221 St. George's Terrace, 6000. Telephone: (09) 366-8000. Facsimile: (09) 366-8111. Telex: AA22867DWN.

Canberra, Australian Capital Territory, Australia Office: 12 Moore Street, 2601. Telephone: (06) 234-4000. Facsimile: (06) 234-4111. Telex: AA22867DWN.

Port Moresby, Papua New Guinea Office: Mogoru Moto Building, Champion Parade. Telephone: (675) 21 1977. Facsimile: (675) 212630. Telex: NE 22223.

(This Listing Continued)

London, England Office: 66 Gresham Street, EC2V 7BB. Telephone: (071) 600 3030. Facsimile: (071) 600 3392.

Jakarta, Indonesia Associated Office: Soebagjo, Roosdiono, Jatim & Djarot. Chase Plaza, Jalan Jendral Sudirman Kav 21, 12910. Telephone: (6221) 570 6436. Fax: (6221) 570 6437. Telex: 62 941 SRJDIA.

Port Vila, Vanuatu Associated Office: Hudson & Co. Lo Lam House, Kumul Highway. Telephone: (678) 22166. Fax: (678) 24260.

FIRM PROFILE: *One of Australia's largest national law firms providing legal services in all areas required by commerce, finance and government. The firm has offices in all the major Australian commercial centres. Our practice also has international offices in London, Port Moresby and associated offices in Jakarta and Port Vila.*

BRISBANE PARTNERS

DONALD R. MAGAREY. PRACTICE AREAS: Corporate; Securities.

BRUCE M. CARROLL. PRACTICE AREAS: Commercial Property.

JOHN LOBBAN. PRACTICE AREAS: Commercial Litigation; Insolvencies.

DOUGLAS M. YOUNG. PRACTICE AREAS: Commercial Law; Resources Law; Native Title Issues.

M.SHANE MCNAMARA. PRACTICE AREAS: Resources; Trade Agreements.

MICHAEL W. FITZGERALD. PRACTICE AREAS: Banking; Project Finance.

JOHN C. WOOD. PRACTICE AREAS: Banking; Finance.

JEREMY R. COOPER. PRACTICE AREAS: Corporate; Commercial.

(For complete personnel and biographical data, see professional biographies at Sydney, Australia).

CLAYTON UTZ

Solicitors and Attorneys

Established in 1833

LEVELS 18, 19, 23-28 SANTOS HOUSE
215 ADELAIDE STREET
BRISBANE, QUEENSLAND 4000, AUSTRALIA
Telephone: (07) 228 5811
Fax: (07) 229 7566

Sydney, New South Wales, Australia Office: Levels 27-35, No 1 O'Connell Street, 2000. Telephone: (02) 353 4000. Fax: (02) 251 7832.

Melbourne, Victoria, Australia Office: Level 18, 333 Collins Street, 3000. Telephone: (03) 286 6000. Fax: (03) 629 8488.

Perth, Western Australia Office: BankWest Tower, 108 St. George's Terrace, 6000. Telephone: (09) 426 8444. Fax: (09) 481 3095. Telex: AA 93232.

Canberra, Australian Capital Territory, Australia Office: 9th Floor, Canberra House, 40 Marcus Clarke Street, 2601. Telephone: (06) 274 0999. Fax: (06) 274 0888.

Clayton Utz operates through national practice groups which focus on banking and financial services; commercial litigation and dispute resolution; competition law; construction; corporate law; corporatization and privatization; energy and natural resources; environment and planning law; insurance law; mergers and acquisitions; product liability; property; taxation and superannuation; technology, computer and intellectual property law; workout, recovery and insolvency; workplace relations and employment law.

(For complete biographical data on all personnel, see Professional Biographies at Sydney, Australia)

CORRS CHAMBERS WESTGARTH

COMALCO PLACE
12 CREEK STREET, QLD
BRISBANE, QUEENSLAND 4000, AUSTRALIA
Telephone: (07) 228 9333
International: +617 228 9333
Fax: (07) 229 2844.

Melbourne, Victoria, Australia Office: 600 Bourke Street, Vic. 3000. Telephone: (03) 672 3000. International: +613 672 3000. Fax: (03) 602 5544.

Sydney, New South Wales, Australia Office: Level 32, Governor Phillip Tower, 1 Farrer Place, 2001. International: (02) 210 6500. Fax: (02) 210 6611.

Canberra, Australia Office: Level 5, Advance Bank Centre. 60 Marcus Clarke Street, ACT, 2601. Telephone: (06) 257 7566. International: +616 257 7566. Fax: (06) 257 7563.

Gold Coast, Queensland, Australia Office: Level 4, Corporate Centre One, 2 Corporate Court, Bundal, QDL, 4217. International Telephone: (075) 77 7777. Fax: (075) 74 0478.

Perth, Western Australia, Australia Office: Commonwealth Bank Building, 150 St. George's Terrace, W.A. 6000. Telephone: (09) 321 8531. International: +619 321 8531. Fax: (09) 322 6953.

London, England Office: 2nd Floor, 103 Cannon Street, EC4N 5AD. Telephone: (171) 929 4955. International: +44171 929 4955.Fax: (171) 929 4164.

Commercial and Corporate Law including:
Banking & Finance, Computer & Communications, Corporate Reconstruction & Insolvency, Corporatisation, Customs & International Trade, Energy & Resources, Family Law, Franchising, Funds Management, Industrial Relations, Insurance & Product Liability, Intellectual Property, International Law, Joint Ventures, Litigation in all areas of practice, Mergers & Acquisitions, Planning, Pollution & Environment Law, Privatization, Professional Liability, Property Development & Construction, Securitisation, Stamp Duty, Superannuation, Taxation, Telecommunications.

PARTNERS

David J. Abernethy	Christine M Maher
Brian D. Bartley	Graham J Moore
Gregory R. Chapman	Ross H. Mortimer
Daryl S. Clifford	James P. O'Callaghan
Rodney M Dann	John S.P. O'Keeffe
Brian W. Ernst	Henry Prokuda
James W. Forrest	Eddie Scuderi
Teresa G. Handicott	Jonathan Shaw (Gold Coast)
Greg Hassall	Glen T. Smith
John S. Humphrey	John D. Story
John P. Kelly	(Managing Partner)
Harry G. Lakis	Susan D. Timbs
Raymond R. Lindwall	Ian L. Wright
Ian C. Young	

CONSULTANTS

John McGregor Florence	Roger A. North

SENIOR ASSOCIATES

Kim Broadfoot	Joanna Jenkins
Martin Byres	Michael G. MacGinley
Susan J. Campbell	Lisa MacLachlan (Gold Coast)
Paul Careless	Annette O'Hara
Alison Chappell	Chris O'Shea
Rhonda Chesmond	Vince Rogers
Bill M. Dixon	Cameron Seymour
Joanne Dwyer	Jayne Steele
Lisa Harris	Felicity Walsh

(For list of Personnel at London, England, Melbourne, Perth, Sydney, Bundall and Canberra, Australia see Professional Biographies at those locations).

FEEZ RUTHNING

LEVEL 32
RIVERSIDE CENTRE
123 EAGLE STREET
BRISBANE, QUEENSLAND 4000, AUSTRALIA
Telephone: (07) 833 3333
Rapifax: (07) 832-4233

Mailing Address: P.O. Box 7082, Riverside Centre, Brisbane 4001

A member of the Allens Arthur Robinson Group, comprising:

Sydney, New South Wales, Australia Office: Allen Allen & Hemsley, Level 23, The Chifley Tower, 2 Chifley Square, 2000. Telephone: (61 2) 230 4000. Rapifax: (61 2) 233 7022.

Melbourne, Victoria, Australia Office: Arthur Robinson & Hedderwicks, Levels 27-34, 530 Collins Street, 3000. Telephone: (61 3) 614 1011. Rapifax: (61 3) 614 4661.

Perth, Western Australia, Australia Office: Parker & Parker, AMP Building, 140 St George's Terrace, 6000. Telephone: (61 9) 322 0321. Rapifax: (61 9) 322 2243.

Adelaide, South Australia, Australia Office: Finlaysons, 81 Flinders Street, 5000. Telephone: (61 8) 235 7400. Rapifax: (61 8) 232 2944.

Canberra, Australian Capital Territory, Australia Office: Allen Allen & Hemsley, 3rd Floor, 16 Moore Street, 2601. Telephone: (61 6) 247 5800. Rapifax: (61 6) 257 1369.

Surfers Paradise, Queensland, Australia Office: Feez Ruthning, Level 14, 50 Cavil Avenue, 4217. Telephone: (61 75) 70 0200. Rapifax: (61 75) 92 2285.

Group and Associated Offices:

London, England Office: Allens Arthur Robinson, Level 5, Bucklersbury House, 3 Queen Victoria Street, EC4N 8EL. Telephone: (44 71) 248 6130. Rapifax: (44 71) 248 6334.

New York, New York Office: Allens Arthur Robinson, 280 Park Avenue, 10017. Telephone: (1 212) 867 1555. Rapifax: (1 212) 867 7979.

Singapore, Singapore Office: Allens Arthur Robinson, 65 Chulla Street #42-05, OCBC Centre, 0104. Telephone: (65) 535 6622. Rapifax: (65) 535 4855.

Hong Kong, Hong Kong Office: Dunstan Styles & Co., Suite 1504, One Exchange Square, 8 Connaught Place, Central. Telephone: (852) 840 1202. Rapifax: (852) 840 0686.

Jakarta, Indonesia Office: Wiriadinata & Widyawan, Niaga Tower, 26th Floor, Jl. Jend Sudirman, Kav 58, 12190. Telephone: (62 21) 250 5175. Rapifax: (62 21) 250 5185.

Port Moresby, Papua New Guinea Office: Allens Arthur Robinson, Level 11, Pacific Place, Cnr Musgrave Street & Champion Parade. Telephone: (675) 202 000. Rapifax: (675) 200 588.

Shanghai, People's Republic of China Office: AAR China Limited, Fuxing XI Lu 37 Long 6 Hao, 200031. Telephone: (86 21) 437 7582. Rapifax: (86 21) 473 7819.

Administrative Law, Advertising Law, Aeronautical Law, Antitrust Law, Arbitration, Banking Law, Bankruptcy, Competition Law, Constitutional Law, Construction Law, Consumer Protection Law, Conveyancing Law, Corporate Law, Distributorship, Agency and Franchise Law, Employer's Liability, Sports and Entertainment Law, Environmental Law, Foreign Investments, Immigration Law, Insurance Law, International Contracts, International Private Law, Litigation, Maritime and Admiralty Law, Media and Defamation, Negligence Law, Oil and Mining Law, Personal Injury Law, Product Liability Law, Property and Real Estate Law, Rent and Lease, Trade Regulations, Transportation Law, General Legal Practice, Intellectual Property, Copyright Law, Licence Negotiation, Transfer of Technology, General Intellectual Property Practice, Capital Taxation, Corporate Taxation, Customs Duties, Indirect Taxation, Inheritance, Estate and Gift Taxation, International Taxation, Personal Income Taxation, Turnover, Value Added Taxes, Taxation of Foreign Nationals, Taxation of Oil and Mining Companies, Transfer Pricing, Exchange Control, General Tax Practice.

FIRM PROFILE: *Feez Ruthning is an internationally based firm in terms of the clients it represents and the transactions in which it has been involved. In addition, the background of its lawyers and its links with law firms in major and financial and commercial centres of the world assist with the international nature of the practice. Total number of partners for Feez Ruthning is 30, total legal staff is over 105, and for the Allens Arthur Robinson Group total legal staff is over 700. The firm's areas of specialisation include: Corporate and Commercial; Finance and Banking; Litigation; Intellectual Property; Tax; Resources; Environment and Planning; Construction and Property; Government Liaison; Media and Communications.*

(This Listing Continued)

MEMBERS OF FIRM

HOWARD LEIGH STACK, admitted, 1968, Queensland and Western Australia. *Education:* University of Queensland (B.A., LL.B.). *PRACTICE AREAS:* Property and Construction; Corporate and Commercial; Media.

PETER JOHN SHORT, admitted, 1969, Queensland and Western Australia. *Education:* University of Queensland (LL.B). Notary Public. *PRACTICE AREAS:* Banking and Finance; Receiverships.

KENNETH DUNCAN MACDONALD, admitted, 1973, Queensland. *Education:* University of Queensland (B.A., Hons., LL.B., Hons.). *PRACTICE AREAS:* Mining and Petroleum; Corporate and Commercial.

MARTIN DOUGLAS EBERLEIN KRIEWALDT, admitted, 1974, Queensland. *Education:* University of Queensland (B.A., LL.B., Hons.). *PRACTICE AREAS:* Commercial Litigation; Banking; Professional Negligence and High Technology.

IAN ALLAN HODGETTS, admitted, 1972, Queensland. *Education:* University of Queensland (B.Com., LL.B.). *PRACTICE AREAS:* Property and Tourism Development; Planning and Environment Litigation; Resumptions; Compensation and Valuation Litigation; Business Acquisitions.

WILLIAM FRANCIS MANNING, admitted, 1970, Queensland; 1976, England and Wales; 1989, Hong Kong. *Education:* University of Queensland (B.A., LL.B.). *PRACTICE AREAS:* Mining and Petroleum; Corporate and Commercial.

ALAN MICHAEL MILLHOUSE, admitted, 1977, Queensland. *Education:* University of Queensland (B.Com., LL.B., Hons.); London (LL.M.). *PRACTICE AREAS:* Banking and Finance; Property; Commercial.

JOHN NORMAN GALLIMORE, admitted, 1978, Queensland. *Education:* University of Queensland (B.A., LL.B., Hons.). Notary Public. *PRACTICE AREAS:* Banking and Finance.

LARRY MARK LAZARIDES, admitted, 1977, Australian Capital Territory; 1978, Queensland and Western Australia. *Education:* Australian National University (B.Ec., LL.B., Hons.). *PRACTICE AREAS:* Property and Tourism Development; Town Planning.

PAUL GEOFFREY NEWMAN, admitted, 1979, Queensland. *Education:* University of Queensland (LL.M.). *PRACTICE AREAS:* Property; Town Planning.

PETER JEFFREY ALLEN, admitted, 1981, Queensland. *Education:* University of Queensland (B.A., LL.B., Hons.). *PRACTICE AREAS:* Taxation and Revenue; Corporate and Commercial; Superannuation.

MARIAN FRANCES GIBNEY, admitted, 1983, Queensland. *Education:* University of Queensland (B.A., LL.B. Hons.). *PRACTICE AREAS:* Professional Indemnity; Public Liability Insurance; Commercial Litigation.

ANDREW BUCHANAN, admitted, 1983, Queensland. *Education:* Australian National University (B.A.); University of Queensland (LL.B. Hons). *PRACTICE AREAS:* Intellectual Property; Maritime Law; Insurance Law.

ANDREW EDWARD KNOX, admitted, 1983, Queensland. *Education:* Australian National University (B.Ec., LL.B.). *PRACTICE AREAS:* Corporate and Commercial; Mining and Petroleum.

ALEXANDER JOHN WILSON, admitted, 1983, Queensland. *Education:* University of Queensland (B.Com. Hons., LL.B. Hons.). *PRACTICE AREAS:* Insolvency; Banking and Finance Litigation; Commercial Litigation.

DAVID ROGER MILLER, admitted, 1974, England and Wales; 1978, Queensland. *PRACTICE AREAS:* Industrial and Employment Law; Insurance; Personal Injuries.

GRANT RICHARD HIGGINS, admitted, 1974, New Zealand; 1982, Queensland. *Education:* University of Canterbury (LL.B. Hons.). *PRACTICE AREAS:* Property and Tourism Development.

LESLIE ANTHONY DAVIES, admitted, 1977, Victoria; 1982, Queensland. *Education:* Haileybury College, Melbourne (B.Ec., LL.B.). *PRACTICE AREAS:* Property.

JENNIFER CECILIA ENGLISH, admitted, 1984, Queensland. *Education:* University of Queensland (B.A., LL.B.). *PRACTICE AREAS:* Property; Banking and Finance; Commercial.

RICHARD THOMAS GAVEN, admitted, 1979, Queensland; 1981, Australian Capital Territory. *Education:* University of Queensland (LL.B.). *PRACTICE AREAS:* Commercial Litigation.

(This Listing Continued)

ERIN FEROS, admitted, 1985, Queensland. *Education:* University of Queensland (B.A., LL.B., Hons.). *PRACTICE AREAS:* Superannuation; Corporate and Commercial.

ADAM SCOTT THATCHER, admitted, 1986, Queensland. *Education:* University of Queensland (B.Comm., LL.B. Hons.). *PRACTICE AREAS:* Commercial; Banking and Finance; Property.

GEOFFREY NEIL RANKIN, admitted, 1986, Queensland. *Education:* University of Queensland (B.Comm., LL.B., Hons.). *PRACTICE AREAS:* Commercial Litigation; Insolvency.

JOHN ALOYSIUS GREIG, admitted, 1986, Queensland; 1988, England and Wales and Hong Kong. *Education:* University of Queensland (B.Comm., LL.B., Hons.). *PRACTICE AREAS:* Banking; Finance; Capital Markets and Insolvency; Australian and Hong Kong Investment.

ANTHONY CHARLES COTTER, admitted, 1983, Queensland. *Education:* University of Queensland (B.A., LL.B., Hons.). *PRACTICE AREAS:* Insurance; Commercial Litigation.

TRACEY ELLEN HARRIP, admitted, 1983, Queensland. *Education:* University of Queensland (LL.B., Hons.). *PRACTICE AREAS:* Commercial Litigation.

JOHN BARRY COOPER, admitted, 1989, Queensland. *Education:* University of Queensland (B.Comm., Hons., LL.B.). *PRACTICE AREAS:* Construction; Media Litigation.

GUY DAVID ALEXANDER, admitted, 1988, Queensland. *Education:* University of Queensland (B.A., LL.B., Hons.). *PRACTICE AREAS:* Corporate and Commercial.

LIONEL PAUL KER HOGG, admitted, 1989, Queensland. *Education:* University of Queensland (B.C.L., Oxon, LL.B., Hons.). *PRACTICE AREAS:* Banking and Finance; Sports Law.

MARK JOHN STUBBINGS, admitted, 1987, Queensland. *Education:* University of Queensland (B.Comm., LL.B.). *PRACTICE AREAS:* Property and Construction.

SENIOR ASSOCIATES

ANTHONY JAMES RITCHIE, admitted, 1985, Queensland. *Education:* QIT, Queensland (LL.B., Hons.).

DAVID MICHAEL HILL, admitted, 1979, Queensland.

DANIEL EDWARD YOUNG, admitted, 1987, Queensland. *Education:* University of Queensland (B.Comm., LL.B., Hons.).

KOTARO MATSUDA, admitted, 1989, Australian Capital Territory; 1990, Queensland. *Education:* Meiji University, Tokyo (LL.B., Hons.); Keio University, Tokyo (LL.M.). *LANGUAGES:* Japanese and English.

MARGARET PATRICIA STEWART, admitted, 1988, Queensland. *Education:* University of Queensland (B.A., LL.B., Hons.).

PETER ANTHONY SCHMIDT, admitted, 1986, Queensland. *Education:* University of Queensland (LL.B., B.Comm., Hons.).

PHILIP LEIGH MURRAY, admitted, 1987, Queensland. *Education:* University of Queensland (B.A., LL.B., Hons.). *LANGUAGES:* German.

JUSTIN ANTHONY MCDONNELL, admitted, 1986, Queensland, 1990, England and Wales. *Education:* University of Queensland (LL.B., Hons., B.Comm); Cambridge (LL.M.).

PETER CHARLES JOHN JAMES, admitted, 1990, Queensland. *Education:* Queensland University of Technology (LL.B., Hons.); University of Queensland (B.A.).

JOHN JOSEPH BAARTZ, Admitted, 1989, Queensland; 1991, England and Wales. *Education:* University of Queensland (LL.B., Hons).

ALEXANDER DAVID MONAGHAN, admitted, 1990, Queensland. *Education:* University of Queensland (B.Comm., Hons and LL.M.).

PETER ANDREW SMITH, admitted, 1991, Queensland. *Education:* University of Queensland (B.Comm., LL.B., Hons).

DAVID WILLIAM MARKS, admitted, 1992, Queensland. *Education:* University of Queensland (B.Comm. Hons.; LL.B., Hons).

CONSULTANTS

PETER RONALD ROWLAND, admitted, 1955, Queensland. *Education:* University of Queensland (B.A., LL.B.).

(This Listing Continued)

FEEZ RUTHNING, Brisbane, Queensland—Continued

GRAEME ORIEL MORRIS, admitted, 1954, Queensland. *Education:* University of Queensland (B.A., LL.B., Hons.). *PRACTICE AREAS:* Corporate and Commercial; Mining and Petroleum; Government Liaison.

PROF. WILLIAM DAVID DUNCAN, admitted, 1970, Queensland. *Education:* University of Queensland (LL.B.); London (LL.M.).

DR. BRYAN TERENCE HORRIGAN, admitted, 1991, Queensland. *Education:* University of Queensland (B.A., LL.B., Hons.); Oxford (D.Phil.).

FREEHILL HOLLINGDALE & PAGE

Established in 1852

CENTRAL PLAZA II
66 EAGLE STREET
BRISBANE, QUEENSLAND 4000, AUSTRALIA
Telephone: (07) 258 6666
International: +(617) 258 6666
Fax: (07) 258 6444

Sydney, New South Wales, Australia Office: Level 38, MLC Centre, 19-29 Martin Place, 2000. Telephone: (02) 225 5000. International: +(612) 225 5000. Telex AA 121885. Fax: (02) 322 4000.

Canberra City, Australian Capital Territory, Australia Office: London Court, 13 London Circuit, 2601. Telephone:(06) 240 6100. International: +(616) 240 6100. Telex: AA121885. Fax: (06) 240 6222.

Melbourne, Victoria, Australia Office: 101 Collins Street, 3000. Telephone: (03) 288 1234. International: +(613) 288 1234. Telex: AA33004. Fax: (03) 288 1567.

Perth, Western Australia Office: Australia Place, 15-17 William Street, 6000. Telephone: (09) 327 5777. International: +(619) 327 5777. Telex: AA92937. Fax: (09) 322 5954.

Singapore Office: 6 Battery Road, #13-01, 0104. Telephone: (65) 225 1288. Telex: (RS) 42674. Fax: (65) 225 3314.

London, England Office: Birchin Court, 20 Birchin Lane, EC3V 9DJ. Telephone: (0171) 283 9006. International: +(44 171) 283 9006. Fax: (0171) 454 9650.

Hanoi, Vietnam Office: 34A Quang Trung Street. Telephone: (844) 227 839. Fax: (844) 227 909.

Ho Chi Minh City, Vietnam Office: 203 Dong Khoi Street, #3-05. Telephone: (848) 242 630; (848) 242 733. Fax: (848) 242 736.

BRISBANE PARTNERS

DENIS MARK BYRNE, admitted, 1970. *Education:* University of Queensland (LL.B.). *PRACTICE AREAS:* Banking; Finance; Energy; Resources; Funds Management; Privatisation; Infrastructure; Trade Practices.

ELIZABETH ANN NOSWORTHY, admitted, 1970. *Education:* University of Queensland (B.A.; LL.B.); University of London (LL.M.). *PRACTICE AREAS:* Banking; Finance; Privatisation; Infrastructure; Stamp Duty; Telecommunications.

JOHN CHARLES GARLAND, admitted, 1970. *Education:* University of Queensland (LL.B.). *PRACTICE AREAS:* Employee Relations; Intellectual Property; Litigation; Product Liability; Media Law.

KEN FREDERICK WATSON, admitted, 1973. *Education:* University of Queensland (B. Com; LL.B.). *PRACTICE AREAS:* Industrial and Employment Law.

CORNELIUS DANIEL NEIL GRIFFIN, admitted, 1970. *Education:* University of Melbourne (LL.B.). *PRACTICE AREAS:* Engineering; Construction; Procurement Contracts.

ROBERT ANDREW CHANNON, admitted, 1970. *Education:* Cambridge University (M.A.). *PRACTICE AREAS:* Commercial Litigation; Product Liability; Trade; Customs Law.

MICHAEL JOHN BACK, admitted, 1982. *Education:* University of Sydney (B.A. Hons.; LL.B. Hons.). *PRACTICE AREAS:* Commercial Property; Environmental Law; Telecommunications.

(This Listing Continued)

PAUL DAMIAN JARDINE, admitted, 1985. *Education:* University of Queensland (LL.B.). *PRACTICE AREAS:* Commercial Property.

CONSULTANTS

Leo Williams

(For Biographical data on all other Firm Personnel, see Professional Biographies at Canberra, Melbourne, Perth and Sydney, Australia and Singapore)

GADENS RIDGEWAY

LEVELS 39-40, CENTRAL PLAZA ONE
345 QUEEN STREET
BRISBANE, QUEENSLAND 4000, AUSTRALIA
Telephone: (617) 231-1666
Fax: (617) 229-5850

Mailing Address: GPO Box 129, Brisbane 4001

Sydney, New South Wales, Australia Office: Levels 12-15, Skygarden Building, 77 Castlereagh Street, 2000. Telephone: (612) 232-5566. Fax: (612) 931-4888.

Melbourne, Victoria, Australia Office: Levels 20-23, AMP Tower, 535 Bourke Street, 3000. Telephone: (613) 614-4844. Fax: (613) 614-3770.

Cairns, Queensland, Australia Office: 95 Sheridan Street, 4870, P.O. Box 6001. Telephone: (6170) 31-1622. Fax: (6170) 51-7828.

Port Moresby, Papua New Guinea Office: Pacific Place, Cnr Musgrave Street & Champion Parade, P.O. Box 1042. Telephone: (675) 21-1033. Fax: (675) 21-1885.

Banking and Finance, Capital Raisings, Commercial Litigation, Dispute Resolution and Arbitration, Computer Law, Construction and Engineering, Corporate Law, Corporate Reconstructions, Employment Law, Entertainment Law, Export Grants, Foreign Investment, Hotel and Liquor Licensing, Insolvency, Insurance Law, Intellectual Property, Local Government, Manufacturing, Marine and Shipping Law, Media Law, Mergers, Acquisitions and Takeovers, Mining and Resources, Planning and Environmental Law, Private Client (Wills, Probate and Conveyancing), Property Development, Retailing, Sports Law, Taxation and Revenue, Tourism and Leisure, Trade, Export and Business Transactions, Trade Practices Legislation, Transport, Trusts and Funds Management.

RESIDENT PARTNERS

Robert Kelly
Ken Rose
Phillip Heraghty
Michael Woolmer
Paul Spiro
Roger Quick
Brian McPherson
Quentin Lanyon-Owen
John Davies
Richard Lukin
David Shirley

SENIOR ASSOCIATES

Bradley Russell
Adrian McCullagh
Ian Commins
Michael MacGinley

CONSULTANTS

Jane Seawright

(For list of Personnel at Cairns, Sydney and Melbourne, Australia and Port Moresby, New Guinea, see Professional Biographies at those locations)

MALLESONS STEPHEN JAQUES

LEVEL 30, WATERFRONT PLACE
1 EAGLE STREET
BRISBANE, QUEENSLAND 4000, AUSTRALIA
Telephone: (617) 231 7500
Fax: (617) 2211211

Sydney, Australia Office: Level 60, Governor Phillip Tower, 1 Farrer Place, 2000. Telephone: (612) 250 3000. Fax: (612) 250 3133.

(This Listing Continued)

Melbourne, Australia Office: Level 28, Rialto, 525 Collins Street, 3000. Telephone: (613) 619 0619. Fax: (613) 614 1329.

Perth, Australia Office: Ground floor, St. Georges Square, 225 St. George's Terrace, 6000. Telephone: (619) 324 8333. Fax: (619) 3211017.

Canberra, Australia Office: Level 10, Advance Bank Centre, 60 Marcus Clarke Street, 2601. Telephone: (616) 268 3900. Fax: (616) 257 3100.

Hong Kong Office: Bateson Starr in association with Mallesons Stephen Jaques, Suite 801, Asia Pacific Finance Tower, Citibank Plaza, 3 Garden Road, Central Hong Kong. Telephone: (852) 848 4600. Fax: (852) 868-0124.

Beijing, The Peoples Republic of China Office: Suite 701, Scite Tower, 22 Jianguomenwai Street, 100004. Telephone: 861 512 3565 ext. 701. Fax: 861 523 2018.

Taipei, Taiwan Office: Mallesons Stephen Jaques, 14th Floor, 138 Min Sheng East Road, Sec 3. Telephone: (886-2) 712 5808. Fax: (886-2) 712 9080.

Jakarta, Indonesia Office: Law Firm Kartini Muljadi SH & Associates, in association with Mallesons Stephen Jaques, Level 5, Bina Mulia I Building, J1 HR Rasuna Said Kav 10, 12950. Telephone: (62 21) 5256968. Fax: (62 21) 5255561.

Port Moresby, Papua, New Guinea Office: Beresford Love, agents for Mallesons Stephen Jaques, Level 3, Hunter Building, Hunter Street. Telephone: (675) 211 942. Fax: (675) 211 586.

Singapore Office: Level 36, Hong Leong Building, 16 Raffles Quay, 0104. Telephone: (65) 321 8930. Fax: (65) 225 9060.

London, England Office: 2nd Floor, Aldermary House, 10-15 Queen Street, EC4N 1TX. Telephone: (44 171) 982 0982. Fax: (44 171) 982 9820.

New York, New York, U.S.A. Office: 9th floor, Suite 911, 609 Fifth Avenue, 10017-1021. Telephone: (1-212) 319 9500. Fax: (1-212) 319 9506.

RESIDENT PARTNERS

Gary Bugden	**Michael McCafferty**
Richard Hart	**Simon Milne**
Jeff Mann	**John Samaha**
	Hugh Scott-MacKenzie

(For Complete Personnel, see Biographical Card at Sydney, Australia).

MIDDLETONS MOORE & BEVINS

Established in 1987

14TH FLOOR, 241 ADELAIDE STREET, QLD
BRISBANE, QUEENSLAND 4000, AUSTRALIA
Telephone: 07 231 1777
International: 61 7 231 1777
Facsimile: 07 231 1782

Sydney, New South Wales, Australia Office: 6th Floor, 7 Macquarie Place, 2000. Telephone: 02 390 8100. International: 61 2 390 8100. Facsimile: 02 247 2866.

Melbourne, Australia Office: 29th Floor, 200 Queen Street, 3000. Telephone: 03 602 2000. International: 61 3 602 2000. Facsimile: 03 602 5564. Telex: AA 31453.

Aviation, Banking and Finance, Commercial and General Litigation, Commercial Property, Companies and Securities, Computer and High Technology, Construction and Development Dispute Resolution, Environmental and Pollution Law, Foreign Investment, Government Liaison, Industrial Relations and Labour, Insolvency and Receivership, Insurance, Intellectual Property, International Business and Trade, Licensing and Trade Regulation, Media, Advertising and Entertainment, Mergers and Acquisitions Planning, Product Liability, Resources and Energy, Taxation and Revenue, Trade Practices, Transport and Trading.

FIRM PROFILE: *Middletons Moore & Bevins in Brisbane (formerly Holmans) is the product of an amalgamation in 1992 between three prominent firms, namely: Holmans, Middletons in Melbourne and Moore & Bevins in Sydney.*

The firm's key practice area is financial services, including banking and finance, commercial law, property and litigation, for both public and private sector clients.

PARTNERS

HAROLD SHAND. *Education:* (B.A., LL.B.). **PRACTICE AREAS:** Commercial; Resources; Mining; Rural Property; Commercial Property.

(This Listing Continued)

MICHAEL JOHN SPARKSMAN. *Education:* (B.A., LL.B). **PRACTICE AREAS:** Property; Local Government; Planning; Building; Construction; Retirement Villages.

PETER KENNEDY. *Education:* (LL.B.). **PRACTICE AREAS:** Banking; Finance; Commercial; Commercial Property; Insolvency; Liquidations and Workouts.

GUY HUMBLE. *Education:* (B.Comm., LL.B.). **PRACTICE AREAS:** Commercial Litigation; Insolvency; Liquidations and Workouts; Insurance; Alternative Dispute Resolution.

PETER JOHN MCLEOD. *Education:* (B.Com.; LL.B., Hons.). **PRACTICE AREAS:** Banking and Finance; Conveyancing; Commercial and Retail Leasing.

SENIOR ASSOCIATES

ANNA BURNETT. *Education:* (B.Econ., LL.B., Hons.). **PRACTICE AREAS:** Commercial Property; Liquor Licensing; Rural Sales; Leasing and Acquisitions.

CAMERON SPENCELEY. *Education:* (LL.B., Hons., LL.M.). **PRACTICE AREAS:** Commercial Litigation; Insurance Litigation; Insolvency.

ELIZABETH JAMESON. *Education:* (B.A., LL.B., Hons.). **LANGUAGES:** Japanese. **PRACTICE AREAS:** Commercial; Property; Business Structures; Intellectual Property.

Languages: English, Japanese, Finnish and German

MINTER ELLISON

WATERFRONT PLACE
1 EAGLE STREET
BRISBANE, QUEENSLAND 4000, AUSTRALIA
Telephone: +61 7 226 6333
Fax: +61 7 229 1066

Melbourne, Victoria, Australia Office: 40 Market Street, 3000. Telephone +61 3 617 4617. Facsimile: +61 3 617 4666.

Sydney, New South Wales, Australia Office: 44 Martin Place, 2000. Telephone: +61 2 210 4444. Facsimile: +61 2 235 2711.

Canberra, Australian Capital Territory, Australia Office: 8-10 Hobart Place, 2600. Telephone: +61 6 248 7533. Facsmilie: +61 6 249 8202.

Gold Coast, Queensland, Australia Office: Surfers Paradise, Level 7, 50 Cavill Avenue, 4217. Telephone: +61 75 708 444. Facsimile: +61 75 922 640.

London, England Office: 20 Lincoln's Inn Fields, WC2A 3ED. Telephone: +44 171 831 7871. Facsimile: +44 171 404 6722.

Hong Kong Associated Office: McKenna & Co. in association with Minter Ellison, Lippo Tower, 5th Floor, 89 Queensway. Telephone: +852 2846 9100. Facsimile: +852 2845 3575.

Adelaide, Australia Associated Office: Minter Ellison Baker O'Loughlin, 1 King William Street, 5000. Telephone: +61 8 233 5555. Facsimile: +61 8 212 7518.

Perth, Australia Associated office: Minter Ellison Northmore Hale, 152-158 St. George's Tce, 6000. Telephone: (09) 429 7444. Fax: (09) 429 7666.

Auckland, New Zealand Associated Office: Rudd Watts & Stone. United Bank Tower, 125 Queen Street. Telephone: +64 9 309 4863. Facsimile: +64 9 379 3326.

Wellington, New Zealand Associated Office: Rudd Watts & Stone. Trust Bank Centre, 125 The Terrace. Telephone: +64 4 472 4899. Facsimile: +64 4 473 8232.

Singapore Associated Office: Khattar Wong & Partners, 80 Raffles Place, #25-01 UOB Plaza, 0104. Telephone: +65 535 6844. Facsimile: +65 534 4892.

Jakarta, Indonesia Associated Office: Makarim & Taira S., Level 17, Summitmas Tower, Jl. Jend. Sudirman 61-62, 12069. Telephone: +62 21 252 1272. Fax: +62 21 252 2750.

Beijing, People's Republic of China Representative Office: Oxford Associates, Inc., 205 International Club, 21 Jianguomenwai Dajie, 100020. Telephone: +86 1 501 4681. Facsimile: +86 1 501 4682.

International law firm practising in all areas of commercial and corporate law. The firm is organized into specialist practice groups: Alternative Dispute Resolution, Banking and Finance, Commercial Litigation, Corporate, Insolvency, Insurance, International Business and Trade Law, Labour Law, Major Projects and Construction, Media Law, Planning and Environment, Property, Government and Public Administration, Resources, Securi-

(This Listing Continued)

MINTER ELLISON, *Brisbane, Queensland—Continued*

ties, Industry, Superannuation, Taxation and Revenue, Technology and Trade Protection.

PARTNERS OF FIRM

P.W. LEE, B.A., LL.B. *PRACTICE AREAS:* Company/Commercial; Resources.

N.B. ROBERTS, B.A., LL.B. *PRACTICE AREAS:* Litigation; Corporate Reconstruction; Insolvency.

A.W. WATT, LL.B. *PRACTICE AREAS:* Major Property Developments.

A.E. THORPE. *PRACTICE AREAS:* Property Development; Commercial Conveyancing.

R.P. CLARKE, B.A., LL.B. *PRACTICE AREAS:* Commercial/Retail Property Developments.

R.S. ASHTON, LL.B. LL.M. *PRACTICE AREAS:* Insurance; Professional Indemnity; Product Liability.

A.P. GREENWOOD, B.A., LL.B. *PRACTICE AREAS:* Intellectual Property; Trade Practices.

D.G. THOMAS, B. Com., LL.B. (Hons.). *PRACTICE AREAS:* Commercial Dispute Resolution; Administrative Law.

K. McCORMICK, B.A., LL.B. (Hons.), LL.M. *PRACTICE AREAS:* Labour Relations; Government/Constitutional Law.

W.D. THOMPSON, B.Com., LL.B. (Hons.), LL.M. *PRACTICE AREAS:* Taxation; Revenue Law.

P.A. KASMER, LL.B. (Hons.). *PRACTICE AREAS:* Banking; Finance.

D.J. GATELY, B.A., LL.B. *PRACTICE AREAS:* Insurance; Resources.

R.P. LANDSBERG, LL.B. (Hons.), B.Sc. (Hons.). *PRACTICE AREAS:* Major Property Development; Infrastructure Projects.

R.R. BOWIE. *PRACTICE AREAS:* Environment; Planning.

B.C. COWLEY, B.Com., LL.B. (Hons.). *PRACTICE AREAS:* Company/Commercial; Retirement Villages.

P.J. THOMAS, B.A., LL.B. (Hons.). *PRACTICE AREAS:* Banking; Finance.

J.W. BROADLEY, B.A., LL.B. *PRACTICE AREAS:* Commercial Litigation.

G.J. HAMILTON, B.Com., B.Econ., LL.B. *PRACTICE AREAS:* Insolvency; Corporate Reconstruction.

G.R.A. HALEY, LL.B. (Hons.). (Resident Partner, Hong Kong Office). *PRACTICE AREAS:* Construction Litigation.

M.L. CARKEET, B.A., LL.B. (Hons.). *PRACTICE AREAS:* Franchising; Computers.

N.P. WITHNALL, B.A., LL.B. *PRACTICE AREAS:* Corporate Trusts; Securities Industry.

S.C. SHERIDAN, B.A., LL.B. (Hons.). *PRACTICE AREAS:* Administrative Law; Construction/Insurance Dispute Resolution.

D.T. O'BRIEN, B.Econ. (Hons.), LL.B. (Hons.). *PRACTICE AREAS:* Corporate/Commercial Litigation.

C. CHARLTON, B.Com., LL.B. (Hons.). (Resident Partner, Gold Coast Office). *PRACTICE AREAS:* Resort Development; Foreign Investment.

G. BROWN, LL.B. (Hons.). *PRACTICE AREAS:* Banking and Finance.

D.S. RATHIE. *PRACTICE AREAS:* Insurance.

(For List of Partners in Sydney, Melbourne, Canberra and London Offices, see Professional Biographies at those locations)

SLY & WEIGALL

In association with Deacons/Graham & James

RIVERSIDE CENTRE
123 EAGLE STREET
BRISBANE, QUEENSLAND 4000, AUSTRALIA
Telephone: (07) 833 0444 International: +61 7 833 0444
Facsimile: (07) 833 0555

Canberra City, Australia Office: GPO Box 2013, 2601. Telephone: (06) 249 7666. International: +61 6 249 7666. Facsimile: (06) 257 2560.
Melbourne, Australia Office: 385 Bourke Street, 3000. Telephone: (03) 608 0411. International: +61 3 608 0411. Facsimile: (03) 608 0505.
Perth, Australia Office: 108 St. George's Terrace, 6000. Telephone: (09) 321 9379. International: +61 9 321 9379. Facsimile: (09) 324 1334.
Sydney, Australia Office: Gold Fields House, 1 Alfred Street, Circular Quay, 2000. Telephone: (02) 330 8000. International: +61 2 330 8000. Facsimile: (02) 330 8111.

RESIDENT PARTNERS

Brian John Burke	Helen Therese Ryan
Gregory John Vickery	James Kristen Peterson
Donald Robert Boyd	Peter James Kenny
David Leslie Nicholls	Gregory John Litster
William Rainsford Loughnan	Gregory Leighton Mann
Richard Geoffrey Hancock	Cameron Douglas McCullough
Ian Bradley Walker	John David Biddle
David Anthony Colenso	

CONSULTANTS

Richard John Silver	Howarth Edkins Peterson, C.B.E.
Andrew Neil Dutney	

SENIOR ASSOCIATES

Brett St. Clair Bolton	Bruce Hollas
Phillip Anthony Hourigan	Robert Douglas Backstrom

CORRS CHAMBERS WESTGARTH

LEVEL 4, CORPORATE CENTRE ONE
2 CORPORATE COURT
BUNDALL (GOLD COAST), QUEENSLAND 4217, AUSTRALIA
Telephone: +6175 77 7777
Fax: +6175 74 0478

Melbourne, Victoria, Australia Office: 600 Bourke Street, Vic. 3000. Telephone: (03) 672 3000. International: +613 672 3000. Fax: (03) 602 5544.
Sydney, New South Wales, Australia Office: Level 32, Governor Phillip Tower, 1 Farrer Place, 2001. International:02 612 210 6500. Fax: 02 612 210 6611.
Brisbane, Queensland, Australia Office: Comalco Place. 12 Creek Street, QLD, 4000. Telephone: (07) 228 9333. International: +(617) 228 9333. Fax: (07) 229 2844.
Canberra, Australia Office: Level 5, Advance Bank Centre. 60 Marcus Clarke Street, ACT, 2601. Telephone: (06) 257 7566. International: +616 257 7566. Fax: (06) 257 7563.
Perth, Western Australia, Australia Office: Commonwealth Bank Building, 150 St. Georges Terrace, W.A. 6000. Telephone: (09) 321 8531. International: +619 321 8531. Fax: (09) 322 6953.
London, England Office: 2nd Floor, 103 Cannon Street, EC4N 5AD. Telephone: (071) 929 4955. International: +4471 929 4955. Fax: (071) 929 4164.

Commercial and Corporate Law including:
Banking & Finance, Computer & Communications, Corporate Reconstruction & Insolvency, Corporatisation, Customs & International Trade, Energy & Resources, Family Law, Franchising, Funds Management, Industrial Relations, Insurance & Product Liability, Intellectual Property, International Law, Joint Ventures, Litigation in all areas of practice, Mergers & Acquisitions, Planning, Pollution & Environment Law, Privatization,

(This Listing Continued)

Professional Liability, Property Development & Construction, Securitisation, Stamp Duty, Superannuation, Taxation, Telecommunications.

PARTNER IN CHARGE

Jonathan Shaw

SENIOR ASSOCIATE

Lisa MacLachlan

(For list of Personnel at London, England, Melbourne, Perth, Sydney, Brisbane and Canberra, Australia see Professional Biographies at those locations).

GADENS RIDGEWAY

95 SHERIDAN STREET
P.O. BOX 6001
CAIRNS, QUEENSLAND 4870, AUSTRALIA
Telephone: (6170) 31-1622
FAX: (6170) 51-7828

Sydney, New South Wales, Australia Office: Levels 12-15, Skygarden Building, 77 Castlereagh Street, 2000. Telephone: (612) 232-5566. Fax: (612) 931-4888.

Melbourne, Victoria, Australia Office: Levels 20-23, AMP Tower, 535 Bourke Street, 3000. Telephone: (613) 614-4844. Fax: (613) 614-3770.

Brisbane, Queensland, Australia Office: Levels 39-40, Central Plaza One, 345 Queen Street, 4000, GPO Box 129, Brisbane 4001. Telephone: (617) 231-1666. Fax: (617) 229-5850.

Port Moresby, Papua New Guinea Office: Pacific Place, Cnr Musgrave Street & Champion Parade, P.O. Box 1042. Telephone: (675) 21-1033. Fax: (675) 21-1885.

Banking and Finance, Capital Raisings, Commercial Litigation, Dispute Resolution and Arbitration, Computer Law, Construction and Engineering, Corporate Law, Corporate Reconstructions, Employment Law, Entertainment Law, Export Grants, Foreign Investment, Hotel and Liquor Licensing, Insolvency, Insurance Law, Intellectual Property, Local Government, Manufacturing, Media Law, Mergers, Acquisitions and Takeovers, Mining and Resources, Planning and Environmental Law, Private Client (Wills, Probate and Conveyancing), Property Development, Retailing, Sports Law, Taxation and Revenue, Tourism and Leisure, Trade, Export and Business Transactions, Trade Practices Legislation, Transport, Trusts and Funds Management.

RESIDENT PARTNERS

Glen Morrow
Brian Willis

SENIOR ASSOCIATES

Mark Valente
Sandra Deane

(For list of Personnel at Brisbane, Sydney and Melbourne, Australia and Port Moresby, New Guinea, see Professional Biographies at those locations)

BLAKE DAWSON WALDRON

12 MOORE STREET
CANBERRA, AUSTRALIAN CAPITAL TERRITORY 2601, AUSTRALIA
Telephone: (06) 234 4000
Facsimile: (06) 234 4111
Telex: AA22867DWN

Sydney, New South Wales, Australia Office: Grosvenor Place 225 George Street 2000. Telephone: (02) 2586000. Facsimile: (02) 2586999. Telex: AA22867DWN.

Melbourne, Victoria, Australia Office: 101 Collins Street, 3000. Telephone: (03) 679 3000. Facsimile: (03) 679 3111. Telex: AA31033.

Brisbane, Queensland, Australia Office: Riverside Centre, 123 Eagle Street, 4000. Telephone: (07) 259 7000. Facsimile: (07) 259 7111. Telex: AA22867DWN.

Perth, Western Australia, Australia Office: Forrest Centre, 221 St. George's Terrace, 6000. Telephone: (09) 366 8000. Facsimile: (09) 366 8111. Telex: AA22867DWN.

(This Listing Continued)

Port Moresby, Papua New Guinea Office: Mogoru Moto Building, Champion Parade. Telephone: (675) 21 1977. Facsimile: (675) 212630. Telex: NE 22223.

London, England Office: 66 Gresham Street, EC2V 7BB. Telephone: (071) 600 3030. Facsimile: (071) 600 3392.

Jakarta, Indonesia Associated Office: Soebagjo, Roosdiono, Jatim & Djarot. Chase Plaza, Jalan Jendral Sudirman Kav 21, 12910. Telephone: (6221) 570 6436. Fax: (6221) 570 6437. Telex: 62 941 SRJDIA.

Port Vila, Vanuatu Associated Office: Hudson & Co. Lo Lam House, Kumul Highway. Telephone: (678) 22166. Fax: (678) 24260.

FIRM PROFILE: One of Australia's largest national law firms providing legal services in all areas required by commerce, finance and government. The firm has offices in all the major Australian commercial centres. Our practice also has international offices in London, Port Moresby and associated offices in Jakarta and Port Vila.

CANBERRA PARTNERS

BAYFIELD COLLISON. PRACTICE AREAS: Commercial; Taxation.

WILLIAM C. CONLEY. PRACTICE AREAS: Corporate and Securities.

IAN J. NICOL. PRACTICE AREAS: Commercial Litigation.

GARY A. RUMBLE. PRACTICE AREAS: Commercial Law; Administrative Law.

(For complete personnel and biographical data, see professional biographies at Sydney, Australia).

CLAYTON UTZ

Barristers and Solicitors

Established in 1833

9TH FLOOR, CANBERRA HOUSE
40 MARCUS CLARKE STREET
CANBERRA, AUSTRALIAN CAPITAL TERRITORY 2601, AUSTRALIA
Telephone: (06) 274 0999
Fax: (06) 274 0888

Sydney, New South Wales, Australia Office: Levels 27-35, No. 1 O'Connell Street, 2000. Telephone: (02) 353 4000. Fax: (02) 251 7832.

Melbourne, Victoria, Australia Office: Level 18, 333 Collins Street, 3000. Telephone: (03) 286 6000. Fax: (03) 629 8488.

Perth, Western Australia Office: BankWest Tower, 108 St. George's Terrace, 6000. Telephone: (09) 426 8444. Fax: (09) 481 3095. Telex: AA 93232.

Brisbane, Queensland, Australia Office: Levels 18, 19, 23-28 Santos House, 215 Adelaide Street, 4000. Telephone: (07) 228 5811. Fax: (07) 229 7566.

Clayton Utz operates through national practice groups which focus on banking and financial services; commercial litigation and dispute resolution; competition law; construction; corporate law; corporatization and privatization; energy and natural resources; environment and planning law; insurance law; mergers and acquisitions; product liability; property; taxation and superannuation; technology, computer and intellectual property law; workout, recovery and insolvency; workplace relations and employment law.

(For complete biographical data on all personnel, see Professional Biographies at Sydney, Australia)

CORRS CHAMBERS WESTGARTH

LEVEL 5, ADVANCE BANK CENTRE
60 MARCUS CLARKE STREET, ACT
CANBERRA, AUSTRALIAN CAPITAL TERRITORY 2601, AUSTRALIA
Telephone: (06) 257 7566
International: +616 257 7566;
Fax: (06) 257 7563

Melbourne, Victoria, Australia Office: 600 Bourke Street, 3000. Telephone: (03) 672 3000. International: +613 672 3000. Fax: (03) 602 5544.

(This Listing Continued)

CORRS CHAMBERS WESTGARTH, *Canberra,
Australian Capital Territory—Continued*

Sydney, New South Wales, Australia Office: Level 32, Governor Phillip Tower, 1 Farrer Place, 2001. International: (02) 210 6500. Fax: (02) 210 6611.

Brisbane, Queensland, Australia Office: Comalco Place. 12 Creek Street, QLD, 4000. Telephone: (07) 228 9333. International: +(61 7) 228 9333. Fax: (07) 229 2844.

Gold Coast, Queensland, Australia Office: Level 4, Corporate Centre One, 2 Corporate Court, Bundall, QDL, 4217. International Telephone: (075) 777777. Fax: (075) 74 0478.

Perth, Western Australia, Australia Office: Commonwealth Banks Building, 150 St. George's Terrace, W.A. 6000. Telephone: (09) 321 8531. International : +619 321 8531. Fax: (09) 322 6953.

London, England Office: 2nd Floor, 103 Cannon Street, EC4N 5AD. Telephone: (1071) 929 4955. International: +44171 929 4955. Fax: (171) 929 4164.

Commercial and Corporate Law including:
Banking & Finance, Computer & Communications, Corporate Reconstruction & Insolvency, Corporatisation, Customs & International Trade, Energy & Resources, Family Law, Franchising, Funds Management, Industrial Relations, Insurance & Product Liability, Intellectual Property, International Law, Joint Ventures, Litigation in all areas of practice, Mergers & Acquisitions, Planning, Pollution & Environment Law, Privatization, Professional Liability, Property Development & Construction, Securitisation, Stamp Duty, Superannuation, Taxation, Telecommunications.

PARTNERS

Grant B. Carolan	**P. Bill Williams**
Mark Love	(Partner In Charge)

(For list of Personnel at London, England, Melbourne, Perth, Sydney, Brisbane and Bundall, Australia see Professional Biographies at those locations).

FREEHILL HOLLINGDALE & PAGE

Established in 1852

LONDON COURT
13 LONDON CIRCUIT
CANBERRA, AUSTRALIAN CAPITAL TERRITORY 2601,
AUSTRALIA
Telephone: (06) 240 6100
International: +(616) 240 6100
Telex: AA 121885
Fax: (06) 240 6222

Sydney, New South Wales, Australia Office: Level 38, MLC Centre, 19-29 Martin Place, 2000. Telephone: (02) 225 5000. International: +(612) 225 5000. Telex AA 121885. Fax: (02) 322 4000.

Melbourne, Victoria, Australia Office: 101 Collins Street, 3000. Telephone: (03) 288 1234. International: +(613) 288 1234. Telex: AA33004. Fax: (03) 288 1567.

Perth, Western Australia Office: Australia Place, 15-17 William Street, 6000. Telephone: (09) 327 5777. International: +(619) 327 5777. Telex: AA92937. Fax: (09) 322 5954.

Brisbane, Queensland, Australia Office: Central Plaza II, 66 Eagle Street, 4000. Telephone: (07) 258 6666. International: +(617) 258 6666. Fax: (07) 258 6444.

Singapore Office: 6 Battery Road, #13-01, 0104. Telephone: (65) 225 1288. Telex: (RS) 42674. Fax: (65) 225 3314.

London, England Office: Birchin Court, 20 Birchin Lane, EC3V 9DJ. Telephone: (0171) 283 9006. International: +(44 171) 283 9006. Fax: (0171) 454 9650.

Hanoi, Vietnam Office: 34A Quang Trung Street. Telephone: (844) 227 839. Fax: (844) 227 909.

Ho Chi Minh City, Vietnam Office: 203 Dong Khoi Street, #3-05. Telephone: (848) 242 630; (848) 242 7333. Fax: (848) 242 736.

Freehill Hollingdale & Page, Canberra specialises in the following areas: Business Law, Commonwealth, Constitutional and Administrative Law, Customs Law, Food and Drug Law, Foreign Investment Law, Government Purchasing, Immigration Law, Information Technology Law, Legislative Drafting, Privatisation, Property Law, Statutory Interpretation, Telecommunications Law and Trade Law.

(This Listing Continued)

CANBERRA PARTNERS

BETTIE ANNE MCNEE, admitted, 1984. *Education:* Australian National University (LL.B.). **PRACTICE AREAS:** Corporate Law; Commercial Law; Foreign Investment; Federal Law; Federal Government Policy; Funds Management; Privatisation; Infrastructure; Telecommunications.

DANIEL MOULIS, admitted, 1983. *Education:* University of Sydney (LL.B.). **LANGUAGES:** Greek. **PRACTICE AREAS:** Environmental Law; Property; Trade; Customs Law.

CONSULTANT

Geoffrey Kolterman Kolts, O.B.E., Q.C.

(For Biographical data on all other Firm Personnel, see Professional Biographies at Brisbane, Melbourne, Perth and Sydney, Australia and Singapore)

MALLESONS STEPHEN JAQUES

LEVEL 10, ADVANCE BANK CENTRE
60 MARCUS CLARKE STREET
CANBERRA, AUSTRALIAN CAPITAL TERRITORY 2601,
AUSTRALIA
Telephone: (06) 268 3900
Fax: (06) 257 3100

Sydney, Australia Office: Level 60, Governor Phillip Tower, 1 Farrer Place, 2000. Telephone: (02) 250 3000. Fax: (02) 250 3133.

Melbourne, Australia Office: Level 28, Rialto, 525 Collins Street, 3000. Telephone: (03) 619 0619. Fax: (03) 614 1329.

Perth, Australia Office: Ground Floor, St. George Square, 225 St. Georges Terrace, 6000. Telephone: (09) 324 8333. Fax: (09) 321 1017.

Brisbane, Australia Office: Level 30, Waterfront Place, 1 Eagle Street, 4000. Telephone: (07) 231 7500. Fax: (07) 221 1211.

Hong Kong Office: Bateson Starr in association with Mallesons Stephen Jaques, Suite 801, Asia Pacific Finance Tower, Citibank Plaza, 3 Garden Road, Central Hong Kong. Telephone: (852) 848 4600. Fax: (852) 868-0124.

Beijing, The Peoples Republic of China Office: Suite 701, Scite Tower, 22 Jianguomenwai Street, 100004. Telephone: (861) 5122288 ext 701. Fax: (861) 5232018.

Taipei, Taiwan Office: 14th Floor, Mallesons Stephen Jaques, 138 Min Sheng East Road, Sec 3. Telephone: (886-2) 712 5808. Fax: (886-2) 712 9080.

Jakarta, Indonesia Associated Office: Law Firm Kartini Muljadi S.H. & Associates, in association with Mallesons Stephen Jaques, Level 5, Bina Mulia I Building, J1 H.R. Rasuna Said Kav 10, 12950. Telephone: (62 21) 525 6968. Fax: (62 21) 525 5561.

Port Moresby, Papua, New Guinea Office: Beresford Love, agents for Mallesons Stephen Jaques, Level 3, Hunter Building, Hunter Street. Telephone: (675) 211 942. Fax: (675) 211 586.

Singapore Office: Level 36, Hong Leong Building, 16 Raffles Quay, 0104. Telephone: (65) 321 8930. Fax: (65) 225 9060.

London, England Office: 2nd Floor, Aldermary House, 10-15 Queen Street, EC4N 1TX. Telephone: (44-171) 982 0982. Fax: (44-171) 982 9820.

New York, New York, U.S.A. Office: 9th floor, Suite 911, 609 Fifth Avenue, 10017-1021. Telephone: (1-212) 319 9500. Fax: (1-212) 319 9506.

RESIDENT PARTNERS

David Briggs	**Richard Kemp**
Christopher Chenoweth	**Justin Stanwix**
Ian Johnson	**John Topfer**

CONSULTANT

Noel Tanzer

(For Complete Personnel, see Biographical Card at Sydney, Australia)

MINTER ELLISON
8-10 HOBART PLACE
CANBERRA, AUSTRALIAN CAPITAL TERRITORY 2600, AUSTRALIA
Telephone: (06) 248 7533

Fax: (06) 249 8208

Melbourne, Victoria, Australia Office: 40 Market Street, 3000. Telephone: 617 4617. Fax: 617 4666.

Sydney, New South Wales, Australia Office: 44 Martin Place, 2000. Telephone: (02) 210 4444. Fax: (02) 235 2711.

Brisbane, Queensland, Australia Office: Waterfront Place, 1 Eagle Street, 4000. Telephone: (07) 226 6333. Fax: (07) 229 1066.

Gold Coast, Queensland, Australia Office: Surfers Paradise, Level 7, 50 Cavill Avenue, 4217. Telephone: (075) 708 444. Fax: (075) 922 640.

London, England Office: 20 Lincoln's Inn Fields, WC2A 3ED. Telephone: 0171-831 7871. Fax: 0171-404 6722.

Adelaide, Australia Associated Office: Minter Ellison Baker O'Loughlin. 1 King William Street, 5000. Telephone: (08) 233 5555. Fax: (08) 212 7518.

Auckland, New Zealand Associated Office: Rudd Watts & Stone. BNZ Tower, 125 Queen Street, P.O. Box 3798. Telephone: (09) 309 4863. Fax: NZ (09) 379 3326.

Wellingon, New Zealand Associated Office: Rudd Watts & Stone. Trust Bank Centre, 125 The Terrace, 1. Telephone: (04) 472 4899. Fax: (04) 473 8232.

Singapore Associated Office: Khattar Wong & Partners. 80 Raffles Place, #25-01 UOB Plaza, 0104. Telephone: 535 6844. Fax: 534 4892.

Jakarta, Indonesia Associated Office: Makarim & Taira S., Level 17, Summitmas Tower, Jl. Jend. Sudirman 61-62, 12069. Telephone: +62 21 252 1272. Fax: +62 21 252 2750.

Beijing, People's Republic of China Associated Office: Oxford Associates, Inc., 205 International Club, 21 Jianguomenwai Dajie, 100020. Telephone: +86 1 501 4681. Fax: +86 1 501 4682.

Perth, Western Australia, Australia Associated Office: Minter Ellison Northmore Hale. 152-158 St. George's Tce, 6000. Telephone: (09) 429 7444. Fax: (09) 429 7666.

Hong Kong Associated Office: McKenna & Co. in association with Minter Ellison. Lippo Tower, 5th Floor, 89 Queensway. Telephone: 2846 9100. Fax: 2845 3575.

International law firm practising in all areas of commercial and corporate law. The firm is organized into specialist practice groups: Alternative Dispute Resolution, Banking and Finance, Commercial Litigation, Corporate, Insolvency, Insurance, International Business and Trade Law, Labour Law, Major Projects and Construction, Media Law, Planning and Environment, Property, Government and Public Administration, Resources, Securities, Industry, Superannuation, Taxation and Revenue, Technology and Trade Protection.

RESIDENT PARTNERS

ROBERT P. CLYNES, LL.B. *PRACTICE AREAS:* Construction Law; Litigation.

DENIS P. O'BRIEN, B.A., LL.M. *PRACTICE AREAS:* Corporate Law; Commercial Law.

(For List of Partners in Sydney, Melbourne, Brisbane and London Offices, see Professional Biographies at those locations)

SLY & WEIGALL

In association with Deacons/Graham & James

GPO BOX 2013
CANBERRA, AUSTRALIAN CAPITAL TERRITORY 2601, AUSTRALIA
Telephone: (06) 249 7666 International: +61 6 249 7666

Facsimile: (06) 257 2560

Brisbane, Australia Office: Riverside Centre, 123 Eagle Street, 4000. Telephone: (07) 833 0444. International: +61 7 833 0444. Facsimile: (07) 833 0555.

Melbourne, Australia Office: 385 Bourke Street, 3000. Telephone: (03) 608 0411. International: +61 3 608 0411. Facsimile: (03) 608 0505.

Perth, Australia Office: 108 St. George's Terrace, 6000. Telephone: (09) 321 9379. International: +61 9 321 9379. Facsimile: (09) 324 1334.

(This Listing Continued)

Sydney, Australia Office: Gold Fields House, 1 Alfred Street, Circular Quay, 2000. Telephone: (02) 330 8000. International: +61 2 330 8000. Facsimile: (02) 330 8111.

RESIDENT PARTNERS

John Bede Weber	*Richard Christopher Refshauge*
Russell Victor Miller	*David Thomas Toole*
Neal Findlay Shirras Parkinson	*Anne Lorraine Trimmer*
Mark Ferdinand Treffers	*Ross Edward Watch*
Alan Anthony Bradbury	*Elizabeth Anne Whitelaw*

CONSULTANTS

Michael David Coper	*Maurice Prosper Cummins*
Philip Adrian Hawke	*Peter Anthony Hohnen*
Peter George Seaman	

SENIOR ASSOCIATE

Kikuji Ohe

Nevin Rupert Agnew

William James Dunn

Olivia Francesca Gesini

Graham Hryce

ANDERSON RICE

A Member of The Australasian Legal Alliance

Established in 1934

LEVEL 10
555 LONSDALE STREET
P.O. BOX 14099
MELBOURNE, VICTORIA 3000, AUSTRALIA
Telephone: (03) 672 2666

International Dialing: (61 3) 672 2666

Fax: (61 3) 642 0271

Insurance Law and Litigation, Corporate, Commercial and Banking Law, Commercial Litigation, Property and Probate Law.

MEMBERS OF FIRM

DONALD ERNEST BROOKES, born Australia; admitted, 1975, Victoria, Australia. *Education:* Monash University (LL.B., 1974). *Member:* Legal Practice Management; Insurance Law Association; Law Council of Australia. *PRACTICE AREAS:* Insurance Law.

CAREY JAMES NICHOL, born Australia; admitted, 1981, Victoria, Australia. *Education:* Monash University (LL.B., 1980). *Member:* Law Institute of Victoria (Executive Committee, Litigation Lawyers Section). *PRACTICE AREAS:* Commercial Litigation; Directors' Liabilities.

ALAN DAVID KORNHAUSER, born Australia; admitted, 1983, Victoria, Australia and High Court of Australia. *Education:* Monash University (LL.B., 1982). *Member:* Committees on Product Liability and Law Reform, Law Institute of Victoria; Australian Insurance Law Association. *PRACTICE AREAS:* Insurance Law and Litigation.

RONALD ANDREW FRANK WINCHESTER, born Scotland; admitted, 1963, Transvaal, South Africa; 1977, Maseru, Lesotho and Victoria, Australia. *Education:* University of Witwatersrand (Diploma of Law, 1962; Higher Diploma in Tax Law, 1975; Higher Diploma in Company Law, 1983). *Member:* Institute of Company Directors; International Bar Association; German Chamber of Industry and Commerce; German Australian Association. *LANGUAGES:* German. *PRACTICE AREAS:* Corporate Law; Commercial Law.

RICHARD JOHN WILLIAMS, born England; admitted, 1979, Victoria, Australia. *Education:* University of Melbourne (LL.B., 1978). *Member:* Australian Banking Lawyers Association; Australian Corporate Lawyers Association; Institute of Financial Services, Vic/Tas Division; Australian Association of Permanent Building Societies (Associate). *PRACTICE AREAS:* Banking and Finance Law.

JOANNA NICOLE DEVROME, born Australia; admitted, 1980, Victoria, Australia. *Education:* Monash University (LL.B., Hons, 1979). *Member:* Committees on Litigation and Accident Compensation, Law Institute of Victoria; Insurance Law Association. *PRACTICE AREAS:* Insurance and General Litigation; Medical Negligence; Work Cover.

BARRY JOHN JOSEPHS, born Australia; admitted, 1979, Victoria, Australia. *Education:* Monash University (LL.B., 1978). *Member:* Insur-

(This Listing Continued)

ANDERSON RICE, *Melbourne, Victoria—Continued*

ance Law Association. *PRACTICE AREAS:* Insurance and General Litigation.

ASSOCIATES

STEPHEN VINCENT CURTAIN, born Australia; admitted, 1976, Victoria, Australia. *Education:* Royal Melbourne Institute Technology. *Member:* Industrial Relations Society; Australian Institute of Management; Australian Institute of Credit Managers. *PRACTICE AREAS:* Commercial Litigation; Employment Law; Industrial Relations Law.

IAN LESLIE BEATTIE, born Australia; admitted, 1981, Tasmania, Australia; 1990, Victoria, Australia. *Education:* University of Tasmania (LL.B., 1979). *Member:* Mortgage Industry Association of Australia. *PRACTICE AREAS:* Banking Law; Finance Law; Property Law.

MARK LAURENCE WORSNOP, born Australia; admitted, 1988, Victoria, Australia. *Education:* University of Melbourne (B.A., 1985; LL.B., 1987). *Member:* Law Institute of Victoria, Litigation Lawyers Section and Education Sub-Committee. *PRACTICE AREAS:* Litigation and Estate Litigation; Insolvency and Bankruptcy; Trade Practices.

ARNOLD BLOCH LEIBLER

Established in 1952

21/333 COLLINS STREET

MELBOURNE, VICTORIA 3000, AUSTRALIA

Telephone: (03) 629 7444

Fax: (03) 629 7700; 629 3690

Mailing Address: G.P.O. Box 5071Y, Melbourne, Victoria, Australia 3001

PARTNERS

MARK M. LEIBLER A.O., LL.B. (Hons.) (Melb.), LL.M. (Yale). *LANGUAGES:* English. *PRACTICE AREAS:* Commercial.

JOHN C. FAST B.Ec. (Hons.), LL.B. (Hons.). *LANGUAGES:* English. *PRACTICE AREAS:* Commercial.

ROBERT J. HEATHCOTE LL.B. *LANGUAGES:* English. *PRACTICE AREAS:* Litigation.

JOSEPH I. GERSH B.Com., LL.B. (Hons.). *LANGUAGES:* English. *PRACTICE AREAS:* Commercial.

HENRY D. LANZER B.Com., LL.B. *LANGUAGES:* English. *PRACTICE AREAS:* Commercial.

STEVEN M. SKALA B.A., LL.B. (Hons.) (Qld.), B.C.L. (Oxon.). *LANGUAGES:* English. *PRACTICE AREAS:* Commercial.

SUSAN J. HERBERT. *LANGUAGES:* English. *PRACTICE AREAS:* Commercial Property.

JOSEPH BORENSZTAJN B.Ec. LL.B. *LANGUAGES:* English. *PRACTICE AREAS:* Commercial.

LEON ZWIER LL.B. *LANGUAGES:* English. *PRACTICE AREAS:* Litigation.

PHILIP CHESTER B.Ec., LL.B. *LANGUAGES:* English. *PRACTICE AREAS:* Commercial.

ROSS A. PATERSON B.Com., LL.B. (Hons.). *LANGUAGES:* English. *PRACTICE AREAS:* Commercial.

HUGH NORTHAM LL.B. *LANGUAGES:* English. *PRACTICE AREAS:* Litigation.

KENNETH A. GRAY LL.B. *LANGUAGES:* English. *PRACTICE AREAS:* Commercial Property.

JOHN P. MANETTA LL.B. (Hons.) (Adel.) LL.M. (Harv.). *LANGUAGES:* English. *PRACTICE AREAS:* Litigation.

STEPHEN L. SHARP B.Ec., LL.B. *LANGUAGES:* English. *PRACTICE AREAS:* Commercial.

KEVIN F. FRAWLEY B.Com., LL.B. *LANGUAGES:* English. *PRACTICE AREAS:* Litigation.

PAUL CHIAPPI B.Sc., LL.B. *LANGUAGES:* English. *PRACTICE AREAS:* Litigation.

(This Listing Continued)

SENIOR ASSOCIATES

PAULINE GRODSKI B.A., LL.B. *LANGUAGES:* English. *PRACTICE AREAS:* Commercial.

MICHAEL N. DODGE B.Sc., LL.B. *LANGUAGES:* English. *PRACTICE AREAS:* Commercial.

STEVEN KLEIN B. Com., LL.B. *LANGUAGES:* English. *PRACTICE AREAS:* Commercial.

JANE C. SHERIDAN, B.Sc., LL.B. (Hons.). *LANGUAGES:* English. *PRACTICE AREAS:* Litigation.

ZAVEN MARDIROSSIAN, B.A., LL.B. (Hons.). *LANGUAGES:* English and Armenian. *PRACTICE AREAS:* Litigation.

PAUL BASSAT, B.Com., LL.B. *LANGUAGES:* English. *PRACTICE AREAS:* Commercial.

BAKER & ARMSTRONG

Administrative Lawyers

224 QUEEN STREET

MELBOURNE, VICTORIA 3000, AUSTRALIA

Telephone: (03) 602-1922; International: +61 3 602-1922

Facsimile: (03) 602-1640; International: +61 3 602-1640

Administrative, Alternative Dispute Resolution, Anti-dumping, Citizenship, Commercial Foreign Investment, Competition, Constitutional, Customs, Government Liaison, Human Resources, Industrial and Immigration, International Trade, Litigation Commercial and Civil, Shipping and Transport.

FIRM PROFILE: The Firm offers a full range of services in relation to advising on all types of decisions made by government in Australia and related applications. Our clients include many from Europe, North America and Asia, including freight forwarders, customs brokers, insurers, manufacturers, universities, public and private companies, resources. Our concern is to provide practical cost-effective advice. Members of the Firm appear regularly before Federal and State Courts, Agencies and Tribunals. The firm is able to advise on all business issues affecting investment and trade with Australia.

PAUL D.B. BAKER, born Melbourne, Australia, May 17, 1956; admitted, 1981, Australia. *Education:* University of Melbourne (B.A., Hons, 1977; LL.B., 1980; LL.M., 1989). Accredited Immigration Law Specialist, 1992—. *Member:* Law Institute of Victoria (Chairman, Migration Committee, 1988-1992; Chairman, Customs and Excise Committee, 1986-1991; Chairman, Administrative Law Section, 1992-1994; Deputy Chairman, 1994—); Law Council of Australia (Chairman and Deputy Chairman, Customs Committee, 1988-1991; Member, Executive Committee, International Law Section, 1990— and Federal Litigation Section, 1992—; Member, International Trade and Business Committee, 1988—; Chairman, Nationality and Residence Committee, 1994—). *LANGUAGES:* French. *PRACTICE AREAS:* International Trade; Customs; Immigration; Anti-dumping.

R. MICHELE ARMSTRONG, born Melbourne, Australia, March 18, 1960; admitted, 1993, Australia. *Education:* Melbourne University (B.A., 1988; LL.B., 1988). Programme Manager, Research and Graduate Studies, Law School, Melbourne University. *Member:* Law Institute of Victoria; Law Council of Australia; International Bar Association. *LANGUAGES:* Swedish. *PRACTICE AREAS:* Commercial Litigation; Alternative Dispute Resolution; Competition.

PHILIP FRIEDE, born Germany, November 28, 1951; admitted, 1976, Australia. *Education:* Monash University (LL.B., 1974; B.Juris, 1976; Dip. Comm. Law, 1980). Lecturer, Commercial Law, Victorian University of Technology, 1980-1994. *Member:* Law Institute of Victoria; Law Council of Australia; International Bar Association. *PRACTICE AREAS:* Corporate; Industrial Human Resources; Taxation.

The firm is a member of the Immigration Lawyers Club.

Languages: French, Italian, Mandarin Chinese, Swedish

BAKER & McKENZIE

LEVEL 39 RIALTO
525 COLLINS STREET
MELBOURNE, VICTORIA 3000, AUSTRALIA
Telephone: (03) 617-4200
Intn'l. Dialing: (61-3) 617-4200
Telex: AA21618
Answer Back: ABOGADO AA21618
Facsimile: (61-3) 614-2103

Postal Address: P.O. Box 2119T, G.P.O., Melbourne, Victoria 3001

Associated Offices of Baker & McKenzie in: Almaty, Amsterdam, Bangkok, Barcelona, Beijing, Berlin, Bogotá, Brasília, Brussels, Budapest, Buenos Aires, Cairo, Caracas, Chicago, Dallas, Frankfurt, Geneva, Hanoi, Ho Chi Minh City, Hong Kong, Juárez, Kiev, London, Madrid, Manila, México City, Miami, Milan, Monterrey, Moscow, New York, Palo Alto, Paris, Prague, Rio de Janeiro, Riyadh, Rome, St. Petersburg, San Diego, San Francisco, São Paulo, Singapore, Stockholm, Sydney, Taipei, Tijuana, Tokyo, Toronto, Valencia, Warsaw, Washington, D.C. and Zürich.

Correspondent Law Firm: Hadiputranto, Hadinoto & Partners, Jakarta.

MEMBERS OF FIRM

TIMOTHY C. GARROOD, born Adelaide, Australia; admitted, 1977, South Australia; 1987, New South Wales, Australia; 1990, Victoria, Australia. *Education:* Adelaide University (LL.B.). *PRACTICE AREAS:* Construction and Property Development; Commercial Litigation.

PAUL D. MCSWEENEY, admitted, 1974, New South Wales, Australia; 1974, Victoria, Australia; 1988, Supreme Court of England and Wales and Supreme Court of Hong Kong. *Education:* University of Melbourne (B.A., LL.B., Hons.); University of Sydney (LL.M., Hons.). *PRACTICE AREAS:* Mergers and Acquisitions; Trade (Japan); Corporate and Partnership Law.

CHRISTOPHER B. PENMAN, born Sydney, Australia; admitted, 1973, New South Wales, Australia; 1979, England and Wales; 1979, Hong Kong; 1985, Victoria, Australia. *Education:* University of Sydney (LL.B. Hons.I.); University of London (LL.M.); University of Melbourne (Grad. Dip. Natural Resources Law). *PRACTICE AREAS:* Corporate and Partnership Law; Mergers and Acquisitions.

GRAHAM V. SHERRY, admitted, 1975, Victoria, Australia; 1984, New South Wales, Australia. *Education:* Melbourne University (LL.B., Hons.; B. Comm.). *PRACTICE AREAS:* Real Estate Law; Construction and Property Development.

LOCAL PARTNERS

IAN M. DIXON, born Mildura, Australia; admitted, 1976, Victoria, Australia; 1985, New South Wales, Australia. *Education:* Melbourne University (LL.B., Hons., B. Comm.). *Member:* Law Institute of Victoria; Law Society of New South Wales; Industrial Law Society, Victoria; Australian Sports Law Association. *LANGUAGES:* English. *PRACTICE AREAS:* Labor and Employment Law; Commercial Litigation; Insurance Law.

LEIGH W. DUTHIE, born Canberra, Australia; admitted, 1984, A.C.T. and New South Wales, Australia; 1988, Victoria, Australia. *Education:* Australian National University (LL.B., Hons.; B.Ec.); Sydney University (LL.M.). *PRACTICE AREAS:* Commercial Litigation; Intellectual Property Law; Arbitration and Dispute Resolution.

THEO KINDYNIS, born Sydney, Australia; admitted, 1983, Victoria and New South Wales, Australia. *Education:* University of New South Wales (B.A.; LL.B.). *PRACTICE AREAS:* Banking and Finance; Securities and Financial Products; Bankruptcy, Insolvency and Reorganization.

BRUCE C. WEBB, born United Kingdom; admitted, 1986, Victoria, Australia and High Court of Australia. *Education:* Monash University (B.A.; LL.B.); Accredited Property Law Specialist by Law Institute of Victoria. *PRACTICE AREAS:* Real Estate Law; Construction and Property Development.

ASSOCIATES

GILLAD DALAL, born Israel; admitted, 1988, Victoria, Australia. *Education:* Monash University (B.Ec.; LL.B.). *PRACTICE AREAS:* Banking and Finance; Bankruptcy, Insolvency and Reorganization; Mergers and Acquisitions.

DANIELLE T. GALVIN, born Melbourne, Australia; admitted, 1989, Victoria, Australia and High Court of Australia. *Education:* University of

(This Listing Continued)

Melbourne (B.A.; LL.B.). *PRACTICE AREAS:* Commercial Litigation; Labor and Employment Law; Construction and Property Development.

DARREN S. OLNEY, born Upper Hutt, New Zealand; admitted, 1991, Victoria, Australia. *Education:* Monash University (B.Sc.; LL.B.). *PRACTICE AREAS:* Corporate and Partnership Law; Government Relations; Insurance Law.

MICHAEL J. PABST, born Melbourne, Australia; admitted, 1993, Victoria, Australia. *Education:* Bond University (LL.B.). *PRACTICE AREAS:* Banking and Finance; Bankruptcy, Insolvency and Reorganization; Real Estate Law.

DONNA O. PELKA, born Nottingham, England; admitted, 1988, Victoria, Australia and High Court of Australia. *Education:* Monash University (B.A., LL.B.). *PRACTICE AREAS:* Commercial Litigation; Civil Litigation.

SIMON PHILLIPSON, born Sale, Australia; admitted, 1988, Victoria, Australia; 1992, England and Wales. *Education:* Melbourne University (B.Comm.; LL.B.). *PRACTICE AREAS:* Mergers and Acquisitions; Corporate and Partnership Law; Taxation.

G. MATTHEW SHERIDAN, born Montgomery, Alabama; admitted, 1988, Victoria, Australia; 1993, New York, U.S.A. *Education:* Hamilton College (B.A.); Monash University (LL.B., Hons.). *PRACTICE AREAS:* Banking and Finance; Bankruptcy, Insolvency and Reorganization; Securities and Financial Products.

JULIAN SPEED, born Swan Hill, Victoria; admitted, 1992, Victoria, Australia. *Education:* University of Melbourne (B.A., LL.B.). *LANGUAGES:* English, Spanish. *PRACTICE AREAS:* Corporate and Partnership Law; Mergers and Acquisitions; Intellectual Property Law.

PETER G. VITALE, born Korumburra, Australia; admitted, 1994, Victoria, Australia and High Court of Australia. *Education:* Monash University (B.Ec., LL.B.). *PRACTICE AREAS:* Labor and Employment Law; Real Estate Law; Government Relations.

ANTONY J. WYATT, born Melbourne, Australia; admitted, 1991, Victoria, Australia. *Education:* Monash University (B.Ec., LL.B., Hons.). *PRACTICE AREAS:* Corporate and Partnership Law; Mergers and Acquisitions; Commercial Litigation.

BEHAN & SPEED

Solicitors & Consultants
MELBOURNE PORT BUSINESS CENTRE
270 BAY STREET
(P.O. BOX 188)
MELBOURNE (PORT MELBOURNE), VICTORIA, 3207, AUSTRALIA
Telephone: (61.3) 646 3334
Facsimile: (61.3) 646 3946

Prominent areas of practise include: Company Law; Commercial Litigation; Mergers, Acquisitions & Divestitures; Entertainment & Arts Law; Sports Law; Debtor & Creditor Law; Business Law; Corporate Law; Litigation; Insurance Law; Franchises & Franchising; Construction Law; Real Estate; Leases & Leasing; Business & Management Consulting; Contracts; Immigration & Naturalisation; Labor & Employment Law; Property; Alternative Dispute Resolution; Bankruptcy; Intellectual Property; Trade Marks; Mortgages; Taxation; Health Care Law; Alcoholic Beverages Law (Liquor Licensing); Agency & Distributorships Matters; Zoning, Planning & Land Use; Wills; Probate; Trusts & Estates; Family Law; Personal Injury Law and Investments Law.

FIRM PROFILE: Behan & Speed is a long established legal practice. As a medium sized boutique practice, Behan & Speed's emphasis is on effective, learned, timely professional services. Personalised attention is a major emphasis of the practice, in addition to the provision of a diverse - highly understood - services range (of raised profile or otherwise) at commercially accepted rates.

The firm's clientele principally comprise both international and locally based corporations and private clients.

(This Listing Continued)

BEHAN & SPEED, *Melbourne, Victoria—Continued*

MEMBERS OF FIRM

MARK D. WHITE, *Credentials:* B.EC., LL.B., A.S.A., Registered Migration Agent. Member: Law Institute of Victoria; Australian Society of Certified Practising Accountants; Law Council of Australia. *PRACTICE AREAS:* Company Law; Corporate Law; Entertainment and Arts Law; Franchises and Franchising; Property.

FRANCIS J. RUGGIERO, *Credentials:* F.A.I.C.D., Registered Migration Agent. Member: Law Institute of Victoria; Law Council of Australia; Australian Insurance Law Group. Member, Inaugural Mediation Panel, Law Institute of Victoria. Past Executive Member, Courts Practice Committee, Litigation Lawyer's Section, Law Institute of Victoria. *PRACTICE AREAS:* Commercial Litigation; Debtor and Creditor Law; Litigation; Insurance Law; Bankruptcy.

CONSULTANTS

PATRICK G. LYNCH, *Credentials:* B.A., LL.B. Member: Law Institute of Victoria; Queensland Law Society. Past Executive Member, Liquor Law Committee, Property Law Section, Law Institute of Victoria. *PRACTICE AREAS:* Resorts and Leisure Law; Business Law; Trade Marks; Gaming; Alcoholic Beverages Matters.

BUSINESS CONSULTANTS

DEAN C. SADDINGTON, *Credentials:* DIP. C.D., DIP. O.H.& S., DIP. P.R., CERT. D.M., F.A.I.C.D., A.INST.ARB.A., A.I.P.C., A.I.M.M., A.A.M.I. Executive Member: Law Office Management Section, Law Institute of Victoria. Associate Member: General Practice Section, Law Council of Australia. *PRACTICE AREAS:* Business Reorganisations; Labor and Employment Matters; Alternative Dispute Resolution; Advertising and Marketing; Commercial Dispute Resolution.

BLAKE DAWSON WALDRON

101 COLLINS STREET
MELBOURNE, VICTORIA 3000, AUSTRALIA
Telephone: (03) 679 3000
Facsimile: (03) 679 3111
Telex: AA31033

Sydney, New South Wales, Australia Office: Grosvenor Place 225 George Street 2000. Telephone: (02) 2586000. Facsimile: (02) 2586999. Telex: AA22867DWN.

Brisbane, Queensland, Australia Office: Riverside Centre, 123 Eagle Street, 4000. Telephone: (07) 259 7000. Facsimile: (07) 259 7111. Telex: AA22867DWN.

Perth, Western Australia, Australia Office: Forrest Centre, 221 St. George's Terrace, 6000. Telephone: (09) 366 8000. Facsimile: (09) 366 8111. Telex: AA22867DWN.

Canberra, Australian Capital Territory, Australia Office: 12 Moore Street, 2601. Telephone: (06) 234 4000. Facsimile: (06) 234 4111. Telex: AA22867DWN.

Port Moresby, Papua New Guinea Office: Mogoru Moto Building, Champion Parade. Telephone: (675) 21 1977. Facsimile: (675) 212630. Telex: NE 22223.

London, England Office: 66 Gresham Street, EC2V 7BB. Telephone: (071) 600 3030. Facsimile: (071) 600 3392.

Jakarta, Indonesia Associated Office: Soebagjo, Roosdiono, Jatim & Djarot. Chase Plaza, Jalan Jendral Sudirman Kav 21, 12910. Telephone: (6221) 570 6436. Fax: (6221) 570 6437. Telex: 62 941 SRJDIA.

Port Vila, Vanuatu Associated Office: Hudson & Co. Lo Lam House, Kumul Highway. Telephone: (678) 22166. Fax: (678) 24260.

FIRM PROFILE: One of Australia's largest national law firms providing legal services in all areas required by commerce, finance and government. The firm has offices in all the major Australian commercial centres. Our practice also has international offices in London, Port Moresby and associated offices in Jakarta and Port Vila.

MELBOURNE PARTNERS

ALAN K. CORNELL. PRACTICE AREAS: Overseas Investment; Corporate Law.

WILLIAM R. MACKINNON. PRACTICE AREAS: Corporate; Commercial.

GEOFFREY W. HONE. PRACTICE AREAS: Corporate; Commercial.

(This Listing Continued)

GAVIN J.R. FORREST. PRACTICE AREAS: Commercial Litigation; Antitrust.

T. CAMPBELL JOHNSTON. PRACTICE AREAS: Corporate and Project Finance.

GARY G. TROLLOPE. PRACTICE AREAS: Insurance; Accident Compensation.

J.W. LOGAN ARMSTRONG. PRACTICE AREAS: Corporate; Commercial.

DOUGLAS A. PATRICK. PRACTICE AREAS: Commercial Property.

MARK J. BREHENY. PRACTICE AREAS: Banking; Finance.

PHILIP G. TRINCA. PRACTICE AREAS: Commercial Litigation.

DAVID J. DUNN. PRACTICE AREAS: Corporate; Securities.

RICHARD A.J. BUNTING. PRACTICE AREAS: Industrial Relations; Employment Law.

JOHN H. CARMEL. PRACTICE AREAS: Banking; Finance.

GEOFFREY GIBSON. PRACTICE AREAS: Commercial Litigation.

JAMES F. MURRAY. PRACTICE AREAS: Medical Defense; Professional Negligence.

RONALD HARMER. PRACTICE AREAS: Insolvencies; Receiverships.

RICHARD J.C. BROOKS. PRACTICE AREAS: Commercial Property.

RODNEY BUSH. PRACTICE AREAS: Environmental Planning; Tourism.

GAIL A. OWEN. PRACTICE AREAS: Resources; Industrial Relations.

GEORGE D. RAITT. PRACTICE AREAS: Antitrust; Intellectual Property.

CHRISTOPHER G. EVES. PRACTICE AREAS: Engineering; Infrastructure Projects.

CHRISTOPHER J. GODDARD. PRACTICE AREAS: Commercial Litigation; Insolvencies.

MARY L. PADBURY. PRACTICE AREAS: Intellectual Property; Antitrust.

JONATHAN LETTEN. PRACTICE AREAS: Commercial Litigation.

ASHLEY WHARTON. PRACTICE AREAS: Commercial Litigation.

ANTONY B. GREENWOOD. PRACTICE AREAS: Corporate; Commercial.

FRANCIS G.S. MACINDOE. PRACTICE AREAS: Corporate; Finance.

GRAEME J. HARRIS. PRACTICE AREAS: Resources; Antitrust.

ANDREW T. KINCAID. PRACTICE AREAS: Commercial Litigation.

ROBERT W. JAMIESON. PRACTICE AREAS: Environmental Planning; Town Planning.

MARIE E. MCDONALD. PRACTICE AREAS: Corporate Work; Information Technology.

BRUCE G. WHITTAKER. PRACTICE AREAS: Banking and Finance.

IAN G. CUNLIFFE. PRACTICE AREAS: Telecommunications; Broadcasting.

ELSPETH J.M. ARNOLD. PRACTICE AREAS: Corporate; Commercial.

PAUL HOBSON. PRACTICE AREAS: Banking; Finance.

DONALD J. MALONEY. PRACTICE AREAS: Corporate; Commercial.

PETER ARMITAGE. PRACTICE AREAS: Antitrust; Intellectual Property.

RODNEY G. RICHARD. PRACTICE AREAS: Corporate; Commercial.

(For complete personnel and biographical data, see professional biographies at Sydney, Australia)

CHAMBERS & COMPANY

LEVEL 43, ANZ TOWER
55 COLLINS STREET
MELBOURNE, VICTORIA 3000, AUSTRALIA
Telephone: 613 654 1988
Facsimile: 613 650 3958

Beijing, People's Republic of China Office: Suite 643, Kunlun Hotel, 2 Xinyuannanlu, Chaoyang District, Beijing 100004 China. Telephone: (861) 500 3388 ext. 643. Fax: (861) 508 1067.

International Trade Law, Mining and Oil & Gas Law, International and Domestic Joint Ventures, Mergers and Acquisitions, Civil Litigation and General Corporate Law.

FIRM PROFILE: *The firm's principal focus is directed towards the Asia-Pacific Region and the firm is actively involved in acquisitions and joint ventures involving international parties in Australia, China, Indonesia, Philippines, Japan and other countries in the Region.*

MEMBERS OF FIRM

ROBIN HAMILTON CHAMBERS, born Melbourne, Australia, September 13, 1940; admitted, 1966, Victoria; 1989, New South Wales, South Australia and Western Australia. *Education:* University of Melbourne (B.A., 1964; LL.B., with honours, 1965); Duke University (LL.M., 1968). Formerly General Counsel, CRA Limited, 1972-1984. Author: "Government Regulation of Foreign Investment in the Australian Mining Industry," Australian Mining & Petroleum Law Journal, 221, 1978; "Joint Ventures - Breakdowns and Repairs," AMPLA Journal 235, 1983; "Negotiating Joint Ventures in Australia - A Legal and Practical Analysis," Australia-China Trade and Investment Law Conference, 1985 (Australian Government Publishing Service); "Some Legal Aspects of Doing Business in China," International Trade Law Conference, Canberra, Australia, November 1993; "Joint Venturing on Construction Projects in East Asia," International Bar Association Conference, Melbourne, Australia, November 1994. *Member:* Law Institute of Victoria; American Society of International Law; International Bar Association; Australian Mining & Petroleum Law Association (Founder, President, 1980-1981); Law Council of Australia (Member, International Trade & Business Law Committee); Australia China Business Council (Executive Member); Australian German Association. *PRACTICE AREAS:* Natural Resources; Asia-Pacific Investment (China); International Joint Ventures; International Business Law.

RICHARD GLENN UDOVENYA, born Geelong, Victoria, Australia, May 26, 1961; admitted, 1984, New Zealand; 1985, Victoria. *Education:* University of Auckland (B.Com., 1984; LL.B., 1985). Associate, Securities Institute of Australia. *Member:* Law Institute of Victoria; Australian Mining and Petroleum Law Association; Australia-Russia Business Council; German-Australian Chamber of Industry and Commerce; New Zealand Law Society; Australia-New Zealand Chamber of Commerce and Industry (Executive Member); Defence Manufacturers Association of Australia. *PRACTICE AREAS:* Corporate Contracts; Company Investment; Mining & Minerals; Securities; Mergers, Acquisitions and Divestitures.

YONG PENG, born Tianjin, China, November 5, 1955; admitted, 1985, China; 1994, Victoria, Australia. *Education:* Beijing Institute of International Studies (B.A., 1982); China University of Political Science and Law (LL.M., 1985); University of California, Los Angeles (LL.M., 1986); University of Melbourne (LL.B., 1992). Formerly Associate: Sidley & Austin, 1986-1987; Deacons Solicitors & Notaries, Hong Kong, 1987-1989. *LANGUAGES:* English and Chinese (Mandarin). *PRACTICE AREAS:* Commercial and Company Law; Asia-Pacific Investment; China-related practice.

ELIZABETH A. MICHAEL, born Boynton Beach, Florida, June 19, 1964; admitted, 1989, Connecticut; 1992, Victoria, Australia. *Education:* Florida State University (B.A., Summa Cum Laude, 1986); Duke University (J.D., With Honors, 1989). Member: Institute of Corporate Managers, Secretaries and Administrators; American Businesswomen's Association of Melbourne. *Member:* American Bar Association; Connecticut Bar Association; Law Institute of Victoria. *LANGUAGES:* English and Spanish. *PRACTICE AREAS:* Commercial and Company Law; Commercial Litigation.

LINDA L. LONG, born Malacca, Malaysia, August 29, 1971; admitted, 1995, Victoria, Australia. *Education:* Australian National University (1990); Monash University (B.A., 1993; LL.B., 1994). *Member:* Law Institute of Victoria. *LANGUAGES:* English, Malay, Chinese (Hokkien and Mandarin), Indonesian, Japanese and Korean.

(This Listing Continued)

ASSOCIATE IN BEIJING, PEOPLE'S REPUBLIC OF CHINA

YANLI LIU, admitted, 1988, China (Not admitted in Australia). *Education:* Second Beijing Foreign Language Institute (B.A., 1978); Correspondent Legal Course, Ministry of Justice of PRC (1988); Columbia University School of Law, Program in Comparative Law (Certificate of Completion, 1989). Author: "Worldwide Trade Secrets Law," Chapter C9 China, by Clark Boardman Callaghan, 1993. Formerly with: China Patent Agent (HK) Ltd., 1986-1988; Gibson Dunn & Crutcher, 1988-1989; China Legal Service (HK) Ltd., 1990-1991; China Global Law Office, 1991-1992; Johnson Stokes & Master, 1992-1993. *LANGUAGES:* English and Chinese (Mandarin, Cantonese and Chaozhou). *PRACTICE AREAS:* Asia-Pacific Investment; Joint Ventures.

CLAYTON UTZ

Solicitors and Attorneys
Established in 1833

LEVEL 18
333 COLLINS STREET
MELBOURNE, VICTORIA 3000, AUSTRALIA
Telephone: (03) 286-6000
Fax: (03) 629-8488

Sydney, New South Wales, Australia Office: Levels 27-35, No 1 O'Connell Street, 2000. Telephone: (02) 353 4000. Fax: (02) 251 7832.
Perth, Western Australia Office: BankWest Tower, 108 St. George's Terrace, 6000. Telephone: (09) 426 8444. Fax: (09) 481 3095. Telex: AA 93232.
Brisbane, Queensland, Australia Office: Levels 18, 19, 23-28 Santos House, 215 Adelaide Street, 4000. Telephone: (07) 228 5811. Fax: (07) 229 7566.
Canberra, Australian Capital Territory, Australia Office: 9th Floor, Canberra House, 40 Marcus Clarke Street, 2601. Telephone: (06) 274 0999. Fax: (06) 274 0888.

Clayton Utz operates through national practice groups which focus on banking and financial services; commercial litigation and dispute resolution; competition law; construction; corporate law; corporatization and privatization; energy and natural resources; environment and planning law; insurance law; mergers and acquisitions; product liability; property; taxation and superannuation; technology, computer and intellectual property law; workout, recovery and insolvency; workplace relations and employment law.

(For complete biographical data on all personnel, see Professional Biographies at Sydney, Australia)

CORRS CHAMBERS WESTGARTH

600 BOURKE STREET
MELBOURNE, VICTORIA 3000, AUSTRALIA
Telephone: (03) 672 3000
International: +613 672 3000
Fax: (03) 602 5544

Sydney, New South Wales, Australia Office: Level 32, Governor Phillip Tower, 1 Farrer Place, 2001. International; (02) 210 6500. Fax: (02) 210 6611.
Brisbane, Queensland, Australia Office: Comalco Place. 12 Creek Street, QLD, 4000. Telephone: (07) 228 9333. International: +(61 7) 228 9333. Fax: (07) 229 2844.
Canberra, Australia Office: Level 5, Advance Bank Centre. 60 Marcus Clarke Street, ACT, 2601. Telephone: (06) 257 7566. International: +616 257 7566. Fax: (06) 257 7563.
Gold Coast, Queensland, Australia Office: Level 4, Corporate Centre One, 2 Corporate Court, Bundall, QLD, 4217. International Telephone: (075) 77 7777. Fax: (075) 74 0478.
Perth, Western Australia, Australia Office: Commonwealth Bank Building, 150 St. George's Terrace, W.A. 6000. Telephone: (09) 321 8531. International: +619 321 8531. Fax: (09) 322 6953.
London, England Office: 2nd Floor, 103 Cannon Street, EC4N 5AD. Telephone: (171) 929 4955. International: +44171 929 4955. Fax: (171) 929 4164.

Commercial and Corporate Law including:
Banking & Finance, Computer & Communications, Corporate Reconstruction & Insolvency, Corporatisation, Customs & International Trade, Energy & Resources, Family Law, Franchising, Funds Management, Indus-

(This Listing Continued)

CORRS CHAMBERS WESTGARTH, Melbourne, Victoria—Continued

trial Relations, Insurance & Product Liability, Intellectual Property, International Law, Joint Ventures, Litigation in all areas of practice, Mergers & Acquisitions, Planning, Pollution & Environment Law, Privatization, Professional Liability, Property Development & Construction, Securitisation, Stamp Duty, Superannuation, Taxation, Telecommunications.

PARTNERS

Simon W. Begg	Elizabeth M. McCallum
Delcho A. Bobeff	John W. McGuire
Jan P. Boxall	David Miles (Chief Executive and
Robert Buchanan	National Managing Partner)
Peter J. Carroll	Jan A. Moffatt
Philip A. Catania	Robert H. Mott
Anthony W. Le P. Darvall	Dennis R.H. Nettlefold
John W. H. Denton	(Managing Partner)
Ian S. Goddard	Barry D. O'Callaghan
Andrew J. Green	Frank D. O'Loughlin
Alan J. Hall	Michael J. Owen
Peter G. Hammond	Michael K.H. Pryse
Grant L. Hattam	Paul R. Rainey
Michael C.H. Hoyle	John M. S. Slattery
Edward A.K. Irving	James H.Y. Syme
Stephen R. Kerr	Michael G. Syme
W. David King	Carl D. Thompson
Stephen C. Kroker	David A. Todd
Steven D. Kunstler	Michael K. Trumble
Michael F. Macnamara	John F. Wardle
Ian M. Macphee	Janet M. Whiting

CONSULTANTS

William M. Carr	Anthony J. Duggan
Hongfei Chen	Douglas L. Goodman
Sir Edward Cohen	Bryan J. Gurry
Breen Creighton	Christopher S. Hacking
John C. Dahlsen	Frank L. Nelson
Shayne Daley	Jude Wallace
Derry C. Davine	John G. Wilkin

SENIOR ASSOCIATES

Gavin R. Bath	Richard A. Lustig
Ben B. D. Burtie	Daniel J. Marquet
Brendan J. Charles	Elizabeth J. Matthews
Peter M. Drake	Claire D. Miller
David J. Freedman	Alan J. Mitchell
Susanna Y. Gold	Michael McDonald
Stewart J. Grieve	James B. McDougall
Michael A. Herskope	Lisa A. Musgrave
Alistair M. Hillier	David A. Opperman
Elisa A. Interligi	Janie R. Perrott
Jeremy C. Johnson	Susan M. Phillips
Antony J. Kiburg	Joanne Richards
Marie-Clare Latour	Armando C. W. Scenna
David M. Lawson	Dianne Scott-Young
Richard A. Leder	Anne M. Thorek

(For list of Personnel at London, England, Perth, Sydney, Brisbane, Bundall and Canberra, Australia see Professional Biographies at those locations).

DAVIES COLLISON CAVE

Patent and Trade Mark Attorneys

Established in 1877

1 LITTLE COLLINS STREET
MELBOURNE, VICTORIA, AUSTRALIA
Telephone: 61 +3 +254 2777
Facsimile: 61 +3 +254 2770
Telex: AA31787

Mailing Address: P.O. Box 4387QQ, Melbourne Victoria, Australia 3001

Sydney, New South Wales Office: G.P.O. Box 3876, 2001. Telephone: 61 +2 +262 2611. Facsimile: 61 +2 +262 1080.

(This Listing Continued)

FIRM PROFILE: *Davies Collison Cave is a leading Australian Patent Attorney firm, specialising in patent, trademark and design protection and advice for Australia and overseas. The firm was formed by the merger between Davies and Collison and Arthur S. Cave & Co., both of which were established over one hundred years ago.*

In addition to their specialist patent attorney qualifications, the partners and professional staff of the firm are graduates in science or engineering with expertise in chemistry, biochemistry, genetic engineering, mechanical engineering, physics, electronics and computer science. Advice concerning trademark negotiation and protection is provided by graduates in law or those having legal qualifications and experience in this area.

MEMBERS OF FIRM

DESMOND JAMES RYAN, born April 25, 1931, Registered Patent Attorney, Barrister & Solicitor of the Supreme Court of Victoria and the High Court of Australia, LL.B. (Hons), Dip. Mech. Eng. *LANGUAGES:* English and French. *PRACTICE AREAS:* Patents (Engineering).

KEITH LESLIE, born August 23, 1943, Registered Patent Attorney, Dip. Elec. Eng. *LANGUAGES:* English. *PRACTICE AREAS:* Patents (Engineering).

JOHN MICHAEL SLATTERY, born September 9, 1942, Registered Patent Attorney, Barrister & Solicitor of the Supreme Court of Victoria, LL.B., B.Sc. *LANGUAGES:* English. *PRACTICE AREAS:* Patents (Chemistry, Biotechnology).

TERENCE GUY CORBETT, born March 6, 1935, Registered Patent Attorney, B.Sc., M.Sc., Ph.D. *LANGUAGES:* English. *PRACTICE AREAS:* Patents (Chemistry, Biotechnology).

GEOFFREY CHARLES PRYOR, born May 15, 1948, Registered Patent Attorney, Barrister & Solicitor of the Supreme Court of Victoria, LL.B., B.E. (Hons.). *LANGUAGES:* English. *PRACTICE AREAS:* Patents (Engineering, Electronics); Litigation.

GREGORY JOSEPH NOONAN, born June 21, 1951, Registered Patent Attorney, LL.B., B.Sc. (Hons.). *LANGUAGES:* English. *PRACTICE AREAS:* Patent Law.

ALAN DAVID DUNCAN, born January 11, 1939, Registered Patent Attorney, B.Sc. (Hons.), Assoc. Royal College of Science (Hons.), M.Sc., Grad., Dip., Legal studies. *LANGUAGES:* English. *PRACTICE AREAS:* Patents (Physics, Engineering, Materials Science); Licensing.

RAYMOND STENTON HIND, born May 17, 1945, Registered Patent Attorney, European Patent Attorney, B.Sc. (Eng.). *LANGUAGES:* English. *PRACTICE AREAS:* Patents (Engineering, Designs); Trademarks.

ANTHONY RICHARD SMEETON, born February 18, 1946, Registered Patent Attorney, B.E. *LANGUAGES:* English. *PRACTICE AREAS:* Patents (Engineering).

PETER HAROLD HUNTSMAN, born May 14, 1951, Registered Patent Attorney, European Patent Attorney, B.Tech. (Tech. (Hons.). *LANGUAGES:* English and French. *PRACTICE AREAS:* Patent Law.

TREVOR KEITH MICHAEL STEVENS, born March 21, 1948, Barrister & Solicitor of the Supreme Court of Victoria, Attorney of the Supreme Court of South Africa, Member of the Institute of Trade Mark Agents (UK), LL.B., LL.M. *LANGUAGES:* English. *PRACTICE AREAS:* Trade Marks; Litigation.

CHRISTINE FAYE LOWE, born December 24, 1957, Barrister & Solicitor of the Supreme Court of Victoria, B.Juris., LL.B. *LANGUAGES:* English. *PRACTICE AREAS:* Trade Marks; Litigation.

PETER ANDREW STEARNE, born May 28, 1960, Registered Patent Attorney, B.Sc. Hons.), Ph.D. *LANGUAGES:* English. *PRACTICE AREAS:* Patents (Chemistry, Biotechnology).

DAVID BRIAN WEBBER, born September 13, 1963, Registered Patent Attorney, B.E. (Hons.). *LANGUAGES:* English. *PRACTICE AREAS:* Patents (Electronics, Computer Science).

DAVIES RYAN DE BOOS
1 LITTLE COLLINS STREET
MELBOURNE, VICTORIA 3000, AUSTRALIA
Telephone: 61 +3 +2542888
Cable Address: Collimator
Telex: 31787
Facsimile: 61 +3 +2542880

Intellectual Property, Patents, Trademarks, Copyright, Licensing, Technology Law, Antitrust, Commercial Agreements, Commercial Litigation.

FIRM PROFILE: *Davies Ryan DeBoos is a leading Australian law firm in the field of commercial law and particularly intellectual property advice, litigation and licensing with a strong practical and academic base in both technology and the law. The firm has a unique association with Davies Collison Cave, a Patent Attorney firm, resulting in a special combination of a legal practice with extensive intellectual property trial and licensing experience and a patent attorney practice specialising in technology matters.*

Lawyers of the firm are experienced in technology licensing, litigation, general commercial law including trade practices law and the negotiation and drafting of commercial and related agreements.

MEMBERS OF FIRM

DESMOND JAMES RYAN, born Echuca, Victoria, Australia, April 25, 1931; admitted, 1981, Victoria. *Education:* Royal Melbourne Institute of Technology (Dip. Mech. Eng., 1954); Melbourne University (LL.B., Hons, 1974). Author: "Trademarks: Registered Users and the Customs Provisions," Pat. & Tm. Rev., 1978; "Limiting Liability of Industrial Property Agents," WIPO, 1983; "Obvious in the Light of What," IIC, 1981; "Protection of Geographical Indications in Australia under the EC/Australia Wine Agreement," EIPR, 1994. Visiting Fellow Lecturer in Patent Law, Melbourne University, 1989—. Member: Australian Government Industrial Property Advisory Committee, 1978-1985; Australian Government Trade Negotiations Advisory Group, 1990—. Chairman, Intellectual Property Committee, Law Council of Australia, 1989- 1991. President: Institute of Patent Attorneys of Australia, 1975-1976; Australian Group AIPPI, 1977-1984; LES: Australia/New Zealand, 1984-1985; LES International, 1988-1989; LES Gold Medal, 1992. *Member:* Law Institute of Victoria; Intellectual and Industrial Property Society; Asian Patent Attorneys Association; Federation Internationale des Counseils en Propriété Industrielle; United States Trade Mark Association; International Anti-Counterfeiting Coalition; American Intellectual Property Law Association; Chartered Institute of Patent Agents (London); Institute of Trade Mark Agents (London); International Bar Association; Competition Law Association; International Wine Law Association. *LANGUAGES:* English and French. *PRACTICE AREAS:* Industrial Property; Litigation; Advice; Technology Transfer and Licensing; Wine Law.

RODNEY MALCOLM DE BOOS, born Hastings, Victoria, Australia, June 18, 1949; admitted, 1972, Victoria. *Education:* Melbourne University (LL.B., 1971). Author: "Laws of Australia-Patents-Ownership, Devolution and Assignment", Chapter, publication due 1995. Lecturer in Patent and Know How Licensing, Melbourne University, 1990—. *Member:* Licensing Executives Society Australia and New Zealand, Inc. (Secretary, 1980-1983; President, 1985-1986); Licensing Executives Society International (Secretary, 1993—); International Bar Association (Member, Antitrust and Trade Law Committee); Law Council of Australia (Member, Trade Practices Committee; Deputy Chairman, 1984-1987; Member, Intellectual Property Committee); Inter-Pacific Bar Association; Law Institute of Victoria (Member, Trade Practices and Intellectual Property Committee); Intellectual and Industrial Property Society; Institute of Directors. *LANGUAGES:* English. *PRACTICE AREAS:* Commercial Law; Intellectual Property Licensing; Anti-Trust Trade Practices; Construction Contracts; Commercial Contracts; Research and Development Contracts.

RICHARD BARRY JARVIS, born North Adelaide, South Australia, October 4, 1944; admitted, 1976, Victoria; 1984, New South Wales; 1989, South Australia and Western Australia. *Education:* Melbourne University (B.Sc., 1969; LL.B., 1975). *Member:* Law Institute of Victoria; New South Wales Law Society; South Australian Law Society; Western Australian Law Society; Law Council of Australia (Member, Committees on: Intellectual Property; International Trade and Business); International Association for the Protection of Industrial Property (Australian Group) Inc.; Licensing Executives Australia and New Zealand, Inc.; Intellectual and Industrial Property Society. *PRACTICE AREAS:* Intellectual Property Litigation in State and Federal Courts; Licensing; Registration and Regulation of Pharmaceuticals.

(This Listing Continued)

JOHN MICHAEL SLATTERY, born Melbourne, Australia, September 9, 1942; admitted, 1982, Victoria. *Education:* Melbourne University (B.Sc., 1963); Australian National University (LL.B., 1978). *Member:* Law Institute of Victoria; Institute of Patent Attorney of Australia (Council Member, 1988—); Licensing Executives Society/Australia/New Zealand; Asian Patent Attorneys Association. *PRACTICE AREAS:* Chemistry and Biotechnology Patents; Trade Marks; Licensing; Litigation.

GEOFFREY CHARLES PRYOR, born Australia, May 15, 1948; admitted, 1975, Melbourne. *Education:* University of Melbourne (B. Elec. Eng., 1970; LL.B., 1982). *Member:* Institute of Patent Attorneys of Australia; Law Institute of Victoria; LES Australia and New Zealand; AIPPI; Asian Patent Attorneys Association. *PRACTICE AREAS:* Engineering and Electronics Patents; Litigation.

TREVOR KEITH MICHAEL STEVENS, born March 21, 1948; admitted, 1976, South Africa; 1983, Melbourne. *Education:* University of London (LL.M., 1974); University of Melbourne (LL.B., 1981). *Member:* Law Institute of Victoria; Law Council of Australia; United States Trademark Association; Institute of Trade Mark Agents. *PRACTICE AREAS:* Trade Marks; Litigation; Trade Practices; Copyright.

CHRISTINE FAYE LOWE, born Nhill, Australia, December 24, 1957; admitted, 1983, Victoria. *Education:* Monash University (Bachelor of Jurisprudence, 1982; LL.B., 1982). *Member:* Law Institute of Victoria; Law Council of Australia; United States Trade Mark Association; Overseas Member of Institute of Trade Mark Agents; AIPPI; Licensing Executives Society Australia & New Zealand; Intellectual and Industrial Property Society. *PRACTICE AREAS:* Trade Mark Law; Copyright Law; Trade Practices.

ASSOCIATES

DARRON SAMUEL SALTZMAN, born Melbourne, Australia, November 5, 1963; admitted, 1987, Victoria, High Court and Federal Court of Australia. *Education:* Monash University (B.Sc., 1984; LLB., Hons, 1986). *Member:* Law Institute of Victoria; Law Council of Australia; Industrial and Intellectual Property Society. *LANGUAGES:* English and Hebrew. *PRACTICE AREAS:* Intellectual Property and Commercial Litigation; Commercial Law; Franchising and Licensing.

ATTORNIES

SUSAN MARILYN SPICER, born Australia, October 9, 1948; admitted, 1972, Melbourne. *LANGUAGES:* English and Italian. *PRACTICE AREAS:* Real Property; Wills and Deceased Estates; Commercial Leasing.

CHRISTOPHER FRANCIS JORDAN, born Melbourne, Australia, April 25, 1965; admitted, 1989, Victoria; Federal and High Court, Australia. *Education:* Melbourne University (B.A., 1988; LL.B., 1988). *Member:* Law Institute of Victoria; Law Council of Australia; Industrial and Intellectual Property Society; Victorian Young Lawyers (Deputy Chairman). *LANGUAGES:* English. *PRACTICE AREAS:* Intellectual Property; Commercial Litigation.

JANICE MARGARET LUCK, born Australia, October 8, 1947; admitted, 1971, Tasmania; 1987, Victoria. *Education:* University of Tasmania (LL.B., Hons., 1970; LL.M., 1972). Senior Lecturer, Intellectual and Industrial Property, Monash University, Victoria, 1973-1987. Academic Associate, Lecturer in Trademark Law, Melbourne University, 1990. *LANGUAGES:* English. *PRACTICE AREAS:* Copyright; Trade Marks and Patent Law Advice and Research.

REBECCA ANNE BORDEN, born Bryn Mawr, Pennsylvania, USA, August 16, 1960; admitted, 1986, Pennsylvania; 1991, Victoria. *Education:* Rutgers University (B.A., 1982; M.A., 1985; J.D., 1986); Monash University (LL.M., 1993). *Member:* Law Institute of Victoria; American Bar Association; Industrial and Intellectual Property Society. *LANGUAGES:* English. *PRACTICE AREAS:* Intellectual Property Law.

JOHN ARTHUR HANNEBERY, born Melbourne, Australia, 1959. *Education:* University of Melbourne (B.Sc., 1983; LL.B., 1988). *Member:* Law Institute Speakers Bureau. *PRACTICE AREAS:* Intellectual Property Law; Commercial Litigation.

NICOLA JANE ADAMS, born Melbourne, Australia, March 31, 1971; admitted, 1995, Australia. *Education:* Monash University (B.Sc., 1993; LL.B., 1995). *Member:* Intellectual Property Society of Australia. *PRACTICE AREAS:* Intellectual Property; Licensing and Commercial Law.

DAVID JOHN BRENNAN, born Melbourne, Australia, June 3, 1969; admitted, 1993, Australia. *Education:* University of Melbourne (B.Comm,

(This Listing Continued)

DAVIES RYAN DE BOOS, *Melbourne, Victoria—Continued*

1992; LL.B., Hons., 1992). Author: "The Defence of Truth and Defamation," Law Reform, 1994 20 Monash University Law Review 151. *LANGUAGES:* English and French.

FREEHILL HOLLINGDALE & PAGE

Established in 1852

101 COLLINS STREET

MELBOURNE, VICTORIA 3000, AUSTRALIA

Telephone: (03) 288 1234

International: +(613) 288 1234

Telex: AA33004

Fax: (03) 288 1567

Sydney, New South Wales, Australia Office: Level 38, MLC Centre, 19-29 Martin Place, 2000. Telephone: (02) 225 5000. International: +(612) 225 5000. Telex AA 121885. Fax: (02) 322 4000.

Canberra City, Australian Capital Territory, Australia Office: London Court, 13 London Circuit, 2601. Telephone: (06) 240 6100. International: +(616) 240 6100. Telex: AA121885. Fax: (06) 240 6222.

Perth, Western Australia Office: Australia Place, 15-17 William Street, 6000. Telephone: (09) 327 5777. International: +(619) 327 5777. Telex: AA92937. Fax: (09) 322 5954.

Brisbane, Queensland, Australia Office: Central Plaza II, 66 Eagle Street, 4000. Telephone: (07) 258 6666. International: +(617) 258 6666. Fax: (07) 258 6444.

Singapore Office: 6 Battery Road, #13-01, 0104. Telephone: (65) 225 1288. Telex: (RS) 42674. Fax: (65) 225 3314.

London, England Office: Birchin Court, 20 Birchin Lane, EC3V 9DJ. Telephone: (0171) 283 9006. International: +(44 171) 283 9006. Fax: (0171) 454 9650.

Hanoi, Vietnam Office: 34A Quang Trung Street. Telephone: (844) 227 839. Fax: (844) 227 909.

Ho Chi Minh City, Vietnam Office: 203 Dong Khoi Street, #3-05. Telephone: (848) 242 630; (848) 242 733. Fax: (848) 242 736.

FIRM PROFILE: Freehill Hollingdale & Page is an Australian based international law firm with a strong and growing presence in Asia and Europe. Established over 140 years ago, we have expanded to become one of the largest commercial law firms in Australia and South-East Asia.

We specialise in the following areas: Asia, Aviation, Banking and Finance, Commercial Contracts, Constitutional, Corporate, Corporate Trusts, Employee Relations, Energy and Resources, Engineering and Construction, Environment, Foreign Investment, Funds Management, Government, Infrastructure, Insolvency, Insurance, Intellectual Property, Joint Ventures, Litigation, Media, Mergers and Acquisitions, Occupational Health and Safety, Privatisation, Product Liability, Property, Superannuation, Taxation and Revenue, Telecommunications, Trade and Customs, Trade Practices and Trademarks.

MEMBERS OF FIRM IN MELBOURNE

KEITH ALFRED ROBERT SKINNER, admitted, 1956. *Education:* University of Melbourne (LL.B.). *PRACTICE AREAS:* Corporate; Revenue; Funds Management.

DENIS JAMES DAVIES, admitted, 1966. *Education:* University of Melbourne (B.A.; LL.B.). *PRACTICE AREAS:* Engineering; Construction; Litigation; Media Law.

DAVID LEONARD BAILEY, admitted, 1966. *Education:* University of Melbourne (LL.B.; Hons.) Southern Methodist University (M.C.L.). *PRACTICE AREAS:* Banking; Finance; International Trade and Investment; Arbitration and Dispute Management.

MARCUS KIRKLAND FAIRBAIRN, admitted, 1967. *Education:* University of Cambridge, England (B.A.; M.A.). *LANGUAGES:* French. *PRACTICE AREAS:* Corporate; Revenue.

JOHN ALFRED EMERSON, admitted, 1971. *Education:* Monash University, Melbourne (B.Jurs.; LL.B.). *PRACTICE AREAS:* Revenue; Taxation.

JAMES MACKLIN PFEIFFER, admitted, 1971. *Education:* University of Melbourne (B.A.; LL.B.). *PRACTICE AREAS:* Corporate; Funds Raising; Securities Trading; Funds Management.

(This Listing Continued)

PETER ALGERNON FRANC HAY, admitted, 1975. *Education:* University of Melbourne (LL.B.). *PRACTICE AREAS:* Funds Raising; Energy; Resources; Mergers and Acquisitions; Privatisation; Infrastructure; Trade Practices.

PAUL MONTGOMERY, admitted, 1974. *Education:* Australian National University (B.A.; LL.B.). *PRACTICE AREAS:* Banking; Finance; Funds Management.

JOHN GERALD GRACE, admitted, 1971. *Education:* Victorian University of Wellington, New Zealand (LL.B.); Royal Melbourne Institute of Technology (Grad. Dip Mgt). *PRACTICE AREAS:* Energy; Resources; Privatisation; Infrastructure; International Law; Joint Ventures.

JOHN BALFOUR BLANCH, admitted, 1971. *Education:* Monash University, Melbourne (B.Juris.; LL.B.). *PRACTICE AREAS:* Property.

PETER FARLEY MITCHELL, admitted, 1975. *Education:* Monash University, Melbourne (B.Ec.; LL.B.). *PRACTICE AREAS:* Environmental Law; Property.

PETER MARK BUTLER, admitted, 1977. *Education:* University of Melbourne (LL.B.). *LANGUAGES:* French and Italian. *PRACTICE AREAS:* Litigation; Media Law; Trade; Customs Law; Trade Practices.

PAUL ASHLEY COOPER, admitted, 1979. *Education:* University of New South Wales (B.A.; LL.B.). *PRACTICE AREAS:* Banking; Finance; Funds Management; Privatisation; Infrastructure.

PETER WILLIAM STAWELL, admitted, 1975. *Education:* University of Melbourne (B.A.; LL.B.). *PRACTICE AREAS:* Banking; Finance.

STEPHEN MARCUS STERN, admitted, 1980. *Education:* Monash University, Melbourne (B.A.; LL.B., Hons.; LL.M.). *LANGUAGES:* French. *PRACTICE AREAS:* Intellectual Property; Litigation; Trade Practices.

JOHN LINDSAY COOPER, admitted, 1978. *Education:* Monash University, Melbourne (B.Ec.; LL.B.). *PRACTICE AREAS:* Industrial Relations; Employment Law.

GRAEME JAMES SMITH, admitted, 1981. *Education:* Melbourne University (B.A.; LL.B.). *PRACTICE AREAS:* Industrial Relations; Employment Law.

WAYNE MCMASTER, admitted, 1987. *Education:* University of Melbourne (LL.B.); Royal Melbourne Institute of Technology (Diploma of Metallurgy). Registered Patent Attorney. *PRACTICE AREAS:* Intellectual Property.

GRAEME ROSS WATSON, admitted, 1984. *Education:* University of Sydney (B.A.); University of Tasmania (LL.B.). *PRACTICE AREAS:* Industrial Relations; Employment Law.

MAXWELL DOUGLAS RALPH CAMERON, admitted, 1983. *Education:* Melbourne University (B.A.; LL.B.). *LANGUAGES:* French and Japanese. *PRACTICE AREAS:* Property.

IRENE HELEN ZEITLER, admitted, 1983. *Education:* University of Melbourne (B.A., Hons.; LL.B., Hons.). *LANGUAGES:* German. *PRACTICE AREAS:* Intellectual Property; Litigation; Computer Law; Trade Practices.

MICHAEL PETERS, admitted, 1987. *Education:* University of The Witwatersrand (B.Comm.; LL.B.). *LANGUAGES:* Afrikaans. *PRACTICE AREAS:* Funds Management; Superannuation.

RODD ASHTON LEVY, admitted, 1985. *Education:* University of Melbourne (B.A.; LL.B. Hons.). *PRACTICE AREAS:* Corporate; Mergers and Acquisitions; Stamp Duty.

DAVID HAROLD REICHENBERG, admitted, 1987. *Education:* University of The Witwatersrand (LL.B.). *LANGUAGES:* Afrikaans and Yiddish. *PRACTICE AREAS:* Banking; Finance.

ADRIAN JOHN ROBERTSON, admitted, 1976. *Education:* University of Melbourne (B.A.; LL.B.). *LANGUAGES:* Russian. *PRACTICE AREAS:* Funds Management; Superannuation.

JONATHAN DOUGLAS FORBES, admitted, 1985. *Education:* Monash University (B.Ec.; LL.B.). *PRACTICE AREAS:* Industrial Relations; Employment Law.

PETER JOHN HOLLOWAY, admitted, 1985. *Education:* University of Melbourne (B.Comm; LL.B.). *PRACTICE AREAS:* Litigation; Product Liability; Trade Practices; Occupational Health and Safety; Insurance.

(This Listing Continued)

STEPHEN FRANCIS MITCHELL, admitted, 1985. *Education:* Monash University (B.Ec.; LL.B.). *PRACTICE AREAS:* Corporate Finance; Government Finance; Funds Raisings; Privatisation.

PENELOPE ALICE PENGILLEY, admitted, 1983. *Education:* University of Melbourne (B.Sc., LL.B. Hons); Osgoode Hall, Canada (LL.M.). *PRACTICE AREAS:* Litigation; Product Liability; Trade Practices; Defamation; Insolvency.

ANTHONY BERNARD COBURN, admitted, 1979. *Education:* University of Auckland (LL.B.). *PRACTICE AREAS:* Banking and Finance; Funds Management; Stamp Duty; Telecommunications.

DOUGLAS OCHILTREE ROBERTSON, admitted, 1978. *Education:* University of Melbourne (B.A.; LL.B.). *PRACTICE AREAS:* Corporate; Funds Raisings; Energy; Resources; Funds Management; Telecommunications; Agribusiness.

PETER JAMES ROSE, admitted, 1984. *Education:* Australian National University of Melbourne (B.A.; LL.B.; LL.M.). *LANGUAGES:* Japanese. *PRACTICE AREAS:* Funds Raisings; Energy; Resources; Privatisation; Infrastructure; Trade Practices; Joint Ventures.

NICHOLAS JOHN WORMALD, admitted, 1983. *Education:* University of Cambridge (B.A. Hons.). *LANGUAGES:* French and German. *PRACTICE AREAS:* Corporate; Mergers and Acquisitions; Trade Practices.

JOHN MCDONALD CURTIS, admitted, 1974. *Education:* University of Melbourne (LL.B.). *PRACTICE AREAS:* Energy; Resources; Engineering; Construction; Privatisation; Infrastructure; Property.

ROBERT WILLIAM NICHOLSON, admitted, 1983. *Education:* Monash University (B.Sc.; LL.B.; LL.M.); University of Melbourne (MBA). *PRACTICE AREAS:* Funds Raisings; Energy; Resources; Mergers and Acquisitions; Privatisation; Infrastructure.

ALISON LEGGE, admitted, 1987. *Education:* Australian National University (B.A., Hons.; LL.B., Hons.). *PRACTICE AREAS:* Energy; Resources; Litigation; Trade Practices.

RUSSELL ANDREW BERRY, admitted, 1975. *Education:* Monash University (B.Juris.; LL.B., Hons.). *PRACTICE AREAS:* Intellectual Property; Litigation; Media Law; Telecommunications; Trade Practices.

WAYNE MAURICE CONDON, admitted, 1986. *Education:* Auckland University (LL.B.). *PRACTICE AREAS:* Intellectual Property; Litigation; Media Law; Product Liability; Telecommunications; Trade Practices.

DAMIEN LAURENCE LOCKIE, admitted, 1982. *Education:* Monash University (LL.B., LL.M.). *PRACTICE AREAS:* Stamp Duty; Taxation; Revenue.

ALAN STEWART MACLEAN, admitted, 1985. *Education:* Monash University (B.A., Hons., LL.B., Dip. Commercial Law). *LANGUAGES:* German. *PRACTICE AREAS:* Banking; Finance; Funds Raisings; Privatization; Infrastructure.

STEVEN STEVENS, admitted, 1988. *Education:* University of Melbourne (M.B., Hons.); Monash University (B.Ec., Hons., M.Ec.). *PRACTICE AREAS:* Funds Management; State Taxes.

QUENTIN DIGBY, admitted, 1984. *Education:* Australian National University (B.Ec.; LL.B., Hons.); University of Sydney (LL.M.). *PRACTICE AREAS:* Corporate; Funds Raisings; Funds Management; Mergers and Acquisitions; Securities Trading.

MICHAEL PETER FERRARO, admitted, 1984. *Education:* University of Melbourne (LL.B., Hons.). *PRACTICE AREAS:* Mergers and Acquisitions; Funds Raisings; Reconstructions; Securities Trading.

JOHN HUTCHINSON, admitted, 1985. *Education:* Oxford University (B.A., Hons.). *PRACTICE AREAS:* Corporate; Funds Management; Insurance.

JIM THEODORE, admitted, 1988. *Education:* University of Melbourne (B.Com.; LL.B.). *PRACTICE AREAS:* Property; Projects and Structured Finance; Construction; Engineering.

MALCOLM GEORGE TYLER, admitted, 1986. *Education:* University of Melbourne (B.Com., Hons.; LL.B.). *PRACTICE AREAS:* Funds Management; Corporate.

FRANK DI GIANTOMASSO, admitted, 1984. *Education:* Monash University (B.Sc., Honours in Pharmacology, LL.B.). Registered Patent Attorney. *LANGUAGES:* Italian. *PRACTICE AREAS:* Intellectual Property; Intellectual Property Litigation; Pharmaceuticals.

(This Listing Continued)

CONSULTANTS

JEFFREY STEPHEN KIDDLE, admitted, 1955. *Education:* University of Melbourne (LL.B.).

BRIAN DAVID KEWLEY, admitted, 1956. *Education:* University of Melbourne (LL.B.).

(For Biographical data on all other Personnel, see Professional Biographies at Brisbane, Canberra, Perth and Sydney, Australia and Singapore)

GADENS RIDGEWAY

AMP TOWER
535 BOURKE STREET
MELBOURNE, VICTORIA 3000, AUSTRALIA
Telephone: (613) 614-4844
Fax: (613) 614-3770

Sydney, New South Wales, Australia Office: Levels 12-15, Skygarden Building, 77 Castlereagh Street, 2000. Telephone: (612) 232-5566. Fax: (612) 931-4888.

Brisbane, Queensland, Australia Office: Levels 39-40, Central Plaza One, 345 Queen Street, 4000, GPO Box 129, Brisbane 4001. Telephone: (617) 231-1666. Fax: (617) 229-5850.

Cairns, Queensland, Australia Office: 95 Sheridan Street, 4870, P.O. Box 6001. Telephone: (6170) 31-1622. Fax: (6170) 51 7828.

Port Moresby, Papua New Guinea Office: Pacific Place, Cnr Musgrave Street & Champion Parade, P.O. Box 1042. Telephone: (675) 21-1033. Fax: (675) 21-1885.

Banking and Finance, Capital Raisings, Commercial Litigation, Dispute Resolution and Arbitration, Computer Law, Construction and Engineering, Corporate Law, Corporate Reconstructions, Employment Law, Entertainment Law, Export Grants, Family Law, Foreign Investment, Bloodstock Breeding and Racing, Hotel and Liquor Licensing, Insolvency, Insurance Law, Intellectual Property, Local Government, Manufacturing, Media Law, Mergers, Acquisitions and Takeovers, Mining and Resources, Planning and Environmental Law, Private Client (Wills, Probate and Conveyancing), Property Development, Retailing, Sports Law, Superannuation, Taxation and Revenue, Tourism and Leisure, Trade and Business Transactions, Trade Practices Legislation, Transport, Trusts and Funds Management.

RESIDENT PARTNERS

Warwick Teasdale
Jonathan Mott
James Davies
Robert Bett
David Coombes
Philip Turner
Stephen Curtain
Nicholas Wallace
Simon O'Hanlon
Simon Rofe
Timothy Watkin
Genevieve Overell
David Fogarty
Philip Bisset

SENIOR ASSOCIATES

Robert Warnock
Andrew Carnegie
Evelyn David
Alexandra Fogarty
Barbara Watson
Sebastian Saccuzzo
Andrew Chalet

CONSULTANTS

Robin Clements
Courtney Dyer
Hon. Harry Emery, Q.C.
Philip E. Fox

(For list of Personnel at Sydney, Brisbane and Cairns, Australia and Port Moresby, New Guinea, see Professional Biographies at those locations)

MALLESONS

MELBOURNE, VICTORIA, AUSTRALIA

(See Mallesons Stephen Jaques)

Banking and Finance, Mergers and Acquisitions, Issues and Underwriting, Corporate and Commercial Foreign Investment, Federal and State Government Liaison, Property Development, Mining, Resources and Energy, Technology, Trade Practices, Intellectual Property, Tourism and Leisure, Aviation, Telecommunications, Environment, Litigation and Alternative Dispute Resolution.

MALLESONS STEPHEN JAQUES

LEVEL 28, RIALTO
525 COLLINS STREET
MELBOURNE, VICTORIA 3000, AUSTRALIA
Telephone: (613) 619 0619
Fax: (613) 614 1329

Sydney, Australia Office: Level 60, Governor Phillip Tower, 1 Farrer Place, 2000. Telephone: (612) 250 3000. Fax: (612) 250 3133.

Perth, Australia Office: Ground Floor, St. Georges Square, 225 St. George's Terrace, 6000. Telephone: (619) 324 8333. Fax: (619) 321 1017.

Brisbane, Australia Office: Level 30, Waterfront Place, 1 Eagle Street, 4000. Telephone: (617) 231 7500. Fax: (617) 221 1211.

Canberra, Australia Office: Level 10, Advance Bank Centre, 60 Marcus Clarke Street, 2601. Telephone: (616) 268 3900. Fax: (616) 2573100.

Hong Kong Office: Bateson Starr in association with Mallesons Stephen Jaques, Suite 801, Asia Pacific Finance Tower, Citibank Plaza, 3 Garden Road, Central Hong Kong. Telephone: (852) 848 4600. Fax: (852) 868-0124.

Beijing, The Peoples Republic of China Office: Suite 701, Scite Tower, 22 Jianguomenwai Street, 100004. Telephone: (861) 5123565 ext 701. Fax: (861) 5232018.

Taipei, Taiwan Office: 14th Floor, Mallesons Stephen Jaques, 138 Min Sheng East Road, Sec 3. Telephone: (8862) 712 5808. Fax: (8862) 712 9080.

Jakarta, Indonesia Office: Law Firm Kartini Muljadi S.H. & Associates, in association with Mallesons Stephen Jaques, Level 5, Bina Mulia I Building, J1 H.R. Rasuna Said Kav 10, 12950. Telephone: (62 21) 5256968. Fax: (62 21) 5255561.

Port Moresby, Papua, New Guinea Office: Beresford Love, agents for Mallesons Stephen Jaques, Level 3, Hunter Building, Hunter Street. Telephone: (675) 211942. Fax: (675) 211586.

Singapore Office: Level 36, Hong Leong Building, 16 Raffles Quay, 0104. Telephone: (65) 321 8930. Fax: (65) 225 9060.

London, England Office: 2nd Floor, Aldermary House, 10-15 Queen Street, EC4N 1TX. Telephone: (44-171) 982 0982. Fax: (44-171) 982 9820.

New York, New York, U.S.A. Office: 9th floor, Suite 911, 609 Fifth Avenue, 10017-1021. Telephone: (1-212) 319 9500. Fax: (1-212) 319 9506.

RESIDENT PARTNERS

Bruce Akhurst	Emilios Kyrou
Ilana Atlas	Jim Lahore
Chris Beeny	Alison Lansley
Tony Border	Davyd Lewis
Tom Bostock	Cheng Lim
David Bretherton	Elizabeth Lomas
Frank Brody	John Malon
Donald Brooker	Eric Mayne
Neil Carabine	Robert Milliner
Andrew Clements	Stephen Minns
Michael Clough	Andrew Monotti
Tony D'Aloisio	Bruce Moore
Mark Darian-Smith	Ian Murray
Graham Dent	Richard Nelson
Peter Doyle	Frank O'Brien
Ann Dufty	Rowan Russell
Andrew Erikson	Gerald Ryan
Roger Forbes	Trevor Sheehan
Randall Gerkens	Bernie Shinners
John Hambly	Graham Thomson
Jonathan Hamer	Paula Tuckfield

(This Listing Continued)

Stephen Harper	Julie Turner
Jim Higgins	Robin Vague
Susan Hilliard	David Walsh
Tony Holland	Matt Walsh
Peter Kelly	John Waters
Rowan Kennedy	David Wells
Michael Kingston	Peter Willis
	David Wood

CONSULTANTS

Maxwell Ham	Roy Ernest Ricker
Frank Kenna	William Shmith
The Hon. Keith Marks, Q.C.	Colin Trumble

(For Complete Personnel, see Professional Biographies at Sydney, Australia).

MIDDLETONS MOORE & BEVINS

29TH FLOOR
200 QUEEN STREET
MELBOURNE, VICTORIA 3000, AUSTRALIA
Telephone: 03 602 2000
International: 61 3 602 2000
Facsimile: 03 602 5564
Telex: AA 31453

Sydney, New South Wales, Australia Office: 6th Floor, 7 Macquarie Place, 2000. Telephone: 02 390 8100. International: 61 2 390 8100. Facsimile: 02 247 2866.

Brisbane, Australia Office: 14th Floor, 241 Adelaide Street, QLD, 4000. Telephone: 07 231 1777. International: 61 7 231 1777. Facsimile: 07 231 1782.

Aviation, Banking and Finance, Commercial and General Litigation, Commercial Property, Companies and Securities, Computer and High Technology, Construction and Development Dispute Resolution, Environmental and Pollution Law, Foreign Investment, Government Liaison, Industrial Relations and Labour, Insolvency and Receivership, Insurance, Intellectual Property, International Business and Trade, Licensing and Trade Regulation, Media, Advertising and Entertainment, Mergers and Acquisitions Planning, Product Liability, Resources and Energy, Taxation and Revenue, Trade Practices, Transport and Trading.

FIRM PROFILE: Middletons Moore & Bevins can trace its history back to the 1800's to a practice which traded under the name of Cuthbert Hamilton & Wynn. The name "Middleton" first appeared on the firm's letterhead in 1935 when the firm became known as Green Dobson & Middleton. After several mergers with firms in Melbourne the firm became known as Middletons in 1970. The firm merged with Moore & Bevins of Sydney in 1992.

As one of Victoria's longest established commercial law firms, MMB Melbourne is very active in the resources area and the maritime insurance market. The firm is also well known in Banking and Finance and General Insurance Litigation and represents several major international clients.

PARTNERS

PETER MORPHETT TAYLOR, admitted, 1957, Victoria. *Education:* University of Melbourne (LL.B.). *LANGUAGES:* English. *PRACTICE AREAS:* Commercial Property; Local Government & Planning; Mortgage & Securities; Petroleum; Real Estate Agency Law & Practice; Trusts & Funds Management.

LAWRENCE WILLIAM QUINN, admitted, 1967, Victoria. *LANGUAGES:* English. *PRACTICE AREAS:* Banking & Finance; Commercial Property; Domestic Property & Conveyancing; Mergers, Acquisitions & Takeovers; Mortgages & Securities; Trust & Fund Management; Wills & Probate.

DAVID ROYLANCE, admitted, 1974, Victoria. *Education:* University of Melbourne (LL.B.). *LANGUAGES:* English. *PRACTICE AREAS:* Transportation Law; Trade Practices.

PETER HANCOCK BRAMWELL, admitted, 1978, Victoria. *Education:* University of Melbourne (B.Comm., LL.B.). *LANGUAGES:* English. *PRACTICE AREAS:* Commercial Law; Commercial Litigation; Foreign Investment; Mergers, Acquisitions & Takeovers; Mining; Petroleum; Superannuation.

ROBERT JOHN DESMOND, admitted, 1978, Victoria. *Education:* Monash University (B.Juris., LL.B.). *LANGUAGES:* English. *PRACTICE*

(This Listing Continued)

AREAS: Banking & Finance; Commercial Law; Income Tax; Insolvency, Liquidation & Workouts; Intellectual Property; Mergers, Acquisitions & Takeovers; Petroleum; Trade Practices.

PETER EWEN LESLIE, admitted, 1977, Victoria. *Education:* University of Melbourne (LL.B. Hons.). *LANGUAGES:* English. *PRACTICE AREAS:* Insurance; Occupational Health & Safety.

ELIZABETH MARGARET MCCRAE, admitted, 1974, Victoria. *Education:* University of Melbourne (B.Comm., LL.B.). *LANGUAGES:* English. *PRACTICE AREAS:* Commercial Property; Domestic Property and Conveyancing; Wills & Probate.

ROBERT CLIVE SPRINGALL, admitted, 1977, Victoria. *Education:* University of Melbourne (B.A. Hons., LL.B. Hons.). *LANGUAGES:* English and German. *PRACTICE AREAS:* Transportation Law; Immigration.

MARK MONTEITH DOBBIE, admitted, 1978, Victoria. *Education:* Monash University (B.Ec., LL.B., Dip. Com. L.). *LANGUAGES:* English. *PRACTICE AREAS:* Alternative Dispute Resolution; Commercial Litigation; Insurance; Local Government & Planning.

WARWICK JOHN STEWART ISHERWOOD, admitted, 1974, Victoria. *Education:* University of Melbourne (LL.B.). *LANGUAGES:* English. *PRACTICE AREAS:* Banking & Finance; Commercial Law; Computer Law; Insolvency, Liquidation & Workouts; Mergers, Acquisitions & Takeovers; Telecommunications; Trade Practices.

JOHN EDWARD KELLY, admitted, 1987, Victoria. *Education:* Monash University (B.Ec., LL.B.). *LANGUAGES:* English. *PRACTICE AREAS:* Alternative Dispute Resolution; Commercial Litigation; Petroleum.

ROSE GLORIA LOCKIE, admitted, 1984, Victoria. *Education:* Monash University (B.Juris, LL.B.). *LANGUAGES:* English. *PRACTICE AREAS:* Family Law.

PAUL FILDES, admitted, 1983, Victoria. *Education:* Monash University (B.Ec., LL.B.). *LANGUAGES:* English. *PRACTICE AREAS:* Family Law.

SCOTT JAMES STAUNTON, admitted, 1976, Victoria. *Education:* Monash University (B.Juris; LL.B.). *PRACTICE AREAS:* Insurance Law; Insurance Claims Management and Resolution; Personal Injury Law.

RICHARD GEOFFREY EAGER, admitted, 1974, Victoria. *Education:* University of Melbourne (LL.B.). *PRACTICE AREAS:* Commercial Law; Commercial Litigation; Mergers, Acquisitions & Takeovers; Superannuation and Funds Management; Commercial Property.

SENIOR ASSOCIATES

JOHN FRANCIS ZACHARIAH, admitted, 1975, Victoria. *Education:* Monash University (B.Juris., LL.B.). *LANGUAGES:* English. *PRACTICE AREAS:* Commercial Litigation; Insurance; Occupational Health & Safety.

CATHRYN LOUISE WHEELAHAN, admitted, 1989, Victoria. *Education:* University of Melbourne (B.A., LL.B.). *LANGUAGES:* English. *PRACTICE AREAS:* Commercial Litigation; Industrial & Labour Law; Insolvency, Liquidation & Workouts; Transportation Law; Trade Practices; Wills & Probate Litigation.

JOHN WARREN MANN, admitted, 1989, Victoria. *Education:* University of Melbourne (B.Comm., LL.B.). *LANGUAGES:* English. *PRACTICE AREAS:* Banking & Finance; Commercial Law; Foreign Investment; Insolvency, Liquidation & Workouts; Intellectual Property; Mergers, Acquisitions & Takeovers; Mortgages & Securities; Stamp Duties; Telecommunications; Trade Practices.

MARK PATRICK HOWARD, admitted, 1984, Victoria. *Education:* Monash University (B.Juris., LL.B.). *LANGUAGES:* English. *PRACTICE AREAS:* Alternative Dispute Resolution; Banking & Finance; Building & Construction; Commercial Litigation; Environmental Law; Insolvency, Liquidation & Workouts.

KEN ALEXANDER ADAMS, admitted, 1990, Victoria. *Education:* Monash University (B.A., LL.B.). *LANGUAGES:* English. *PRACTICE AREAS:* Banking & Finance; Commercial Litigation; Insurance.

DIANA HARDING, admitted, 1987, Victoria. *Education:* Monash University (B.Ec., LL.B.). *LANGUAGES:* English. *PRACTICE AREAS:* Income Tax.

GAVIN JAMES VALLELY, admitted, 1988, High Court of Australia. *Education:* University of Queensland (LL.B.). *PRACTICE AREAS:* Transport; Marine Insurance; Sale of Goods.

(This Listing Continued)

CONSULTANTS

RUSSELL MCDONALD BROWN, admitted, 1954, Victoria. *Education:* University of Melbourne (LL.B.). *LANGUAGES:* English. *PRACTICE AREAS:* Commercial Law; Computer Law; Foreign Investment; Mergers, Acquisitions & Takeovers; Trade Practices; Trusts & Fund Management.

BRYAN O'CONNELL, admitted, 1978, Victoria. *Education:* Monash University (B.Ec., LL.B., Graduate Diploma International & Comparative Law). *LANGUAGES:* English. *PRACTICE AREAS:* Banking & Finance; Banking Securities; International Banking; Banking Litigation; Disposition Resolution.

Languages: English and German

MINTER ELLISON
40 MARKET STREET
MELBOURNE, VICTORIA 3000, AUSTRALIA
Telephone: 617 4617

Fax: 617 4666

Sydney, New South Wales, Australia Office: 44 Martin Place, 2000. Telephone: (02) 210 4444. Fax: (02) 235 2711.

Brisbane, Queensland, Australia Office: Waterfront Place, 1 Eagle Street, 4000. Telephone: (07) 226 6333. Fax: (07) 229 1066.

Gold Coast, Queensland, Australia Office: Surfers Paradise, Level 7, 50 Cavill Avenue, 4217. Telephone: (075) 708 444. Fax: (075) 922 640.

Canberra, Australian Capital Territory, Australia Office: 8-10 Hobart Place, 2600. Telephone: (06) 248 7533. Fax: (06) 249 8208.

London, England Office: 20 Lincoln's Inn Fields, WC2A 3ED. Telephone: 0171-831 7871. Fax: 0171-404 6722.

Adelaide, Australia Associated Office: Minter Ellison Baker O'Loughlin. 1 King William Street. Telephone: (08) 233 5555. Fax: (08) 212 7518.

Auckland, New Zealand Associated Office: Rudd Watts & Stone. BNZ Tower, 125 Queen Street, P.O. Box 3798. Telephone: (09) 309 4863. Fax: NZ (09) 379 3326.

Wellington, New Zealand Associated Office: Rudd Watts & Stone. Trust Bank Centre, 125 The Terrace, 1. Telephone: (04) 472 4899. Fax: (04) 473 8232.

Singapore Associated Office: Khattar Wong & Partners. 80 Raffles Place, #25-01 UOB Plaza, 0104. Telephone: 535 6844. Fax: 534 4892.

Jakarta, Indonesia Associated Office: Makarim & Taira S., Level 17, Summitmas Tower, Jl. Jend. Sudirman 61-62, 12069. Telephone: +62 21 252 1272. Fax: +62 21 252 2750.

Beijing, People's Republic of China Associated Office: Oxford Associates, Inc., 205 International Club, 21 Jianguomenwai Dajie, 100020. Telephone: +86 1 501 4681. Fax: +86 1 501 4682.

Perth, Western Australia, Australia Associated Office: Minter Ellison Northmore Hale. 152-158 St. George's Tce, 6000. Telephone: (09) 429 7444. Fax: (09) 429 7666.

Hong Kong Associated Office: McKenna & Co. in association with Minter Ellison, Lippo Tower, 5th Floor, 89 Queensway. Telephone: 2846 9100. Fax: 2845 3575.

International law firm practising in all areas of commercial and corporate law. The firm is organized into specialist practice groups: Alternative Dispute Resolution, Banking and Finance, Commercial Litigation, Corporate, Insolvency, Insurance, International Business and Trade Law, Labour Law, Major Projects and Construction, Media Law, Planning and Environment, Property, Government and Public Administration, Resources, Securities, Industry, Superannuation, Taxation and Revenue, Technology and Trade Protection.

MEMBERS OF FIRM

KERRY C.H. DUNCAN, LL.B. *PRACTICE AREAS:* Banking Law; Commercial Finance Law; Company Law; Commercial Law.

IAN R. DAVIS, LL.B. (Hons). *PRACTICE AREAS:* Company Law; Commercial Law; Resources Law.

JANE H. WHITE, LL.B. *PRACTICE AREAS:* Property Law.

IAN G. LEWIS, LL.B. *PRACTICE AREAS:* Company Law; Commercial Law; Insolvency Law.

RICHARD H. EARL, B. Comm., LL.B. (Resident Partner, Hong Kong Office). *PRACTICE AREAS:* Banking Law; Commercial Finance Law; Insolvency Law.

(This Listing Continued)

MINTER ELLISON, *Melbourne, Victoria—Continued*

IAN S. PASCARL, LL.B. *PRACTICE AREAS:* Trade Practices Law; Intellectual Property Law.

KENNETH W. ANDERSON, B.Juris., LL.B. *PRACTICE AREAS:* Litigation.

RICHARD F. MCQUEEN, B.A., LL.B. *PRACTICE AREAS:* Litigation.

PETER L. BARTLETT, B.Juris., LL.B. *PRACTICE AREAS:* Litigation; Media Law.

DONALD J. MACCALLUM, LL.B. *PRACTICE AREAS:* Banking Law; Commercial Finance Law; Property Law.

ROBERT J. STEWART, LL.B. (Hons.), B.Comm., M.B.A. (National Managing Partner).

DAVID V. SHARPE, Barrister and Solicitor. *PRACTICE AREAS:* Property Law.

DONALD CLARKE, LL.B. (Hons.). *PRACTICE AREAS:* Company Law; Commercial Law.

IAN L. WALKER, B.Comm., LL.B. *PRACTICE AREAS:* Litigation.

DAVID G. INGLIS, B.A., LL.B. *PRACTICE AREAS:* Company Law; Commercial Law; Trade Practices Law; Intellectual Property Law.

JEFFREY E. FAURE, LL.B. (Hons.), A.A.S.A. *PRACTICE AREAS:* Company Law; Commercial Law; Revenue Law.

JOHN J. STEVEN, B.Econ., LL.B., Dip. Comm. Law. *PRACTICE AREAS:* Company Law; Commercial Law; Trade Practices Law; Intellectual Property Law.

FRED J. TINSLEY, LL.B. (Hons.). *PRACTICE AREAS:* Banking Law; Commercial Finance Law.

PETER D.S. COATS, B.A., LL.B. (Managing Partner, Melbourne). *PRACTICE AREAS:* Labor Law; Litigation.

WILLIAM L. FAZIO, B.Sc., LL.B. *PRACTICE AREAS:* Company Law; Commercial Law; Resources Law.

SCOTT C. CHESTERMAN, B.Comm., LL.B. *PRACTICE AREAS:* Litigation.

RICHARD D. MURPHY, B.Sc. (Hons.), LL.B. *PRACTICE AREAS:* Labor Law; Litigation.

BART F. OUDE-VRIELINK, B.Comm., LL.B. (Hons.). *PRACTICE AREAS:* Company Law; Commercial Law; Securities.

OLIVER J. BARRETT, Dip. Law. *PRACTICE AREAS:* Computers and Software; Intellectual Property.

RUSSELL D. KEEN, B.Comm., LL.B. (Hons.). *PRACTICE AREAS:* Insolvency Law; Commercial Litigation.

ELIZABETH M. FLYNN, LL.B. *PRACTICE AREAS:* Banking Law; Commercial Finance Law.

DAVID S. POULTON, B.A., LL.B. *PRACTICE AREAS:* Litigation; Maritime Law.

PHILLIP C. GREENHAM, B.Sc., LL.B. *PRACTICE AREAS:* Alternative Dispute Resolution Law; Building Law; Construction Law.

MICHAEL C. PRYLES, LL.B., LL.M., LL.D., S.J.D. *PRACTICE AREAS:* Alternative Dispute Resolution Law; Company Law; Commercial Law; International Trade Law; Government Law.

MARK E. ELLIOTT, B.Comm., LL.B. *PRACTICE AREAS:* Company Law; Commercial Law.

RICHARD A. WEST, B.App.Sc., LL.B. (Hons). *PRACTICE AREAS:* Administrative Law; Industrial Law; Employment Law; General Litigation.

PETER MEGENS, B.Comm., LL.B. *PRACTICE AREAS:* Building & Construction Law.

DAVID A. ETEROVIC, B.A., LL.B. *PRACTICE AREAS:* Banking Law; Finance Law.

MICHAEL H. O'BRYAN, LL.B. (Hons.), B.Sc. *PRACTICE AREAS:* Company Law; Commercial Law.

MICHAEL W. TEHAN, B.A., LL.B. *PRACTICE AREAS:* Industrial Law; Employment Law; Administrative Law; General Litigation.

(This Listing Continued)

AU22B

GLENYS A. FRASER, B.A., LL.B. (Hons.). *PRACTICE AREAS:* Trade Practices Law; Intellectual Property Law.

JUSTIN F. FAHEY, B.Comm., LL.B. *PRACTICE AREAS:* Company Law; Commercial Law; Revenue Law.

LINDA BERRY, B.A., LL.B. (Hons.). *PRACTICE AREAS:* Banking Law; Finance Law.

LLOYD BAGGOTT, B. Comm., LL.B. *PRACTICE AREAS:* Commercial Development and Property.

CONSULTANT

ANTHONY J. PYNE, B.A., LL.B., LL.M.,. *PRACTICE AREAS:* Aviation Law.

PHILLIPS FOX

120 COLLINS STREET
MELBOURNE, VICTORIA 3000, AUSTRALIA
Telephone: +61-3 274 5000
Fax: +61-3 274 5111

Other Australian Offices: Adelaide, Brisbane, Cairns, Canberra, Perth, Sydney.
New Zealand Offices: Auckland and Wellington.
Vietnam Office: Hanoi.

Administrative and Constitutional Law, Alternative Dispute Resolution, Aviation, Banking and Finance, Business and Corporate, Commercial Litigation, Construction, Electricity, Employment and Industrial Relations, Energy and Natural Resources, Entertainment, Environment, Financial Services, Franchising, Government Relations, Grants and Government Assistance, Health, Insolvency, Insurance, Intellectual Property, International Business, Managed Funds, Maritime, Media, Privatisation, Property, Sports, Superannuation, Tax and Revenue, Tourism, Trade Practices, Transport and Trade, Trusts and Estate Planning.

PARTNERS

Norman Abrams	Murray McCutcheon
Robert Allen	Aine Magee
Charles Anzarut	William Magennis
Julie Armstrong	Don Mazzone
Gregory Banks	Pamela Morey-Nase
Peter Black	John Morgan
John Boland	Keith Nathan
John Bolitho	Campbell Paine
Richard Burn	Michael Proud
Michael Cain	Peter Rashleigh
Christopher Charles	Alan Rassaby
Gregory Clayton	Gary Rothville
Paul Duggan	Michael Salter
Judith Earls	Ronald Salter
Christopher Edquist	Stephen Sawer
Mary Anne Hartley	Michael Serong
Colin Hiles	Jaginder Singh-Pasricha
Peter Kenny	Steven Smith
Michele Kramer	John Snowdon
Ronald Laird	Ian Sutherland
	Andrew Tulloch

CONSULTANTS

Graeme Henry	William Lasica
David Kelly	Geoffrey Masel
Elizabeth Kennedy	Alan Norster
	Peter Shattock

ARTHUR ROBINSON & HEDDERWICKS

530 COLLINS STREET
POSTAL ADDRESS: G.P.O. BOX 1776Q, MELBOURNE, 3001
MELBOURNE, VICTORIA 3000, AUSTRALIA
Telephone: (03) 614 1011
From Overseas: 61 (3) 614 1011
Fax: (03) 614 4661
Telex: AA31541 Telegraphic and
Cable Address: "Mandamus" Melbourne
Telex: AA 31541
Fax: Group 3: (03) 614 4661; 614 4161

REVISERS OF THE AUSTRALIA LAW DIGEST FOR THIS
DIRECTORY.

A member of the Allens Arthur Robinson Group, comprising:
Sydney, New South Wales, Australia: Allen Allen & Hemsley, The Chifley Tower, 2 Chifley Tower, 2000. Telephone: (61 2) 230 4000. Rapifax: (61 2) 233 7022.
Canberra, Australian Capital Territory, Australia: Allen Allen & Hemsley, 3rd Floor, 16 Moore Street, 2601. Telephone: (61 6) 247 5800. Rapifax: (61 6) 257 1369.
Perth, Western Australia, Australia: Parker & Parker, AMP Building, 140 St George's Terrace, 6000. Telephone: (61 9) 322 0321. Rapifax: (61 9) 322 2243.
Brisbane, Queensland, Australia: Feez Ruthning, Riverside Centre, 123 Eagle Street, 4000. Telephone: (61 7) 833 3333. Rapifax: (61 7) 832 4233.
Surfers Paradise, Queensland, Australia: Feez Ruthning, Level 14, 50 Cavill Avenue, 4217. Telephone: (61 75) 70 0200. Rapifax: (61 75) 92 2285.
Adelaide, South Australia, Australia: Finlaysons, 81 Flinders Street, 5000. Telephone: (618) 235 7400. Rapifax: (61 8) 232 2944.
Group and Associated Offices:
London, England: Allens Arthur Robinson, Level 5, Bucklersbury House, 3 Queen Victoria Street, EC4N 8EL. Telephone: (44 71) 248 6130. Rapifax: (44 71) 248 6334.
New York, NY: Allens Arthur Robinson, Bankers Trust Building, 280 Park Avenue, 10017. Telephone: (1 212) 867 1555. Rapifax: (1 212) 867 7979.
Singapore: Allens Arthur Robinson, 65 Chulia Street, #42-05, OCBC Centre, 0104. Telephone: (65) 535 8622. Rapifax: (65) 535 4855.
Port Moresby, Papua New Guinea: Allens Arthur Robinson, Level 11, Pacific Place, Cnr. Musgrave Street & Champion Parade. Telephone: (675) 202 000. Rapifax: (675) 200 588.
Hong Kong: Dunstan & Styles & Co, Suite 1504, One Exchange Square, 8 Connaught Place, Central. Telephone: (852) 840 1202. Rapifax: (852) 840 0686.
Jakarta, Indonesia: Wiriadinata & Widyawan, Niaga Tower, 26th Floor, Jl. Jend Sudirman, Kav 58, 12190. Telephone: (62 21) 250 5175. Rapifax: (62 21) 250 5185.
Shanghai, People's Republic of China: AAR China Limited, Fuxing Xi 37 Long 6 Hao, 200031. Telephone: (86 21) 437 7582. Rapifax: (86 21) 473 7819.

Administrative Law, Advertising Law, Aeronautical Law, Antitrust Law, Arbitration, Banking Law, Bankruptcy, Competition Law, Constitutional Law, Construction Law, Consumer Protection Law, Conveyancing Law, Corporate Law, Distributorship, Agency and Franchise Law, Employer's Liability, Entertainment Law, Environmental Law, Foreign Investments, Immigration Law, Insurance Law, International Contracts, International Private Law, Litigation, Maritime and Admiralty Law, Negligence Law, Oil and Mining Law, Product Liability Law, Property and Real Estate Law, Rent and Lease, Trade Regulations, Transportation Law, General Legal Practice, Intellectual Property, Copyright Law, Licence Negotiation, Patent Litigation, Trademark Litigation, Trademark Prosecution, Transfer of Technology, General Intellectual Property Practice, Capital Taxation, Corporate Taxation, Customs Duties, Deferred Taxation, Indirect Taxation, Inheritance, Estate and Gift Taxation, International Taxation, Personal Income Taxation, Sales, Turnover, Value Added Taxes, Taxation of Foreign Nationals, Taxation of Oil and Mining Companies, Transfer Pricing, Exchange Control, General Tax Practice.

FIRM PROFILE: Arthur Robinson & Hedderwicks is an internationally based firm in terms of the clients it represents and the transactions in which it has been involved. In addition, the background of its lawyers and its links with law firms in major and financial and commercial centres of the world assist with the international nature of the practice. Total number

(This Listing Continued)

of partners for Arthur Robinson & Hedderwicks is 56, total legal staff is over 155, and for the Allens Arthur Robinson Group total legal staff is over 700. The firm's areas of specialization include: Corporate and Commercial; Finance and Banking; Litigation; Intellectual Property; Tax; Resources; Environment and Planning; Construction and Property; Government Liaison; Media and Communications.

PARTNERS

ROBIN HAMILTON YORK SYME, LL.B., admitted, 1958, Victoria, Australia; 1987, New South Wales, Australia. *PRACTICE AREAS:* Corporate Law; Commercial Law; Mergers and Acquisitions.

JOHN HAROLD WAITE, LL.B., admitted, 1958, Victoria, Australia; 1987, New South Wales, Australia. *PRACTICE AREAS:* Natural Resources; International Law; Corporate Law.

ANTHONY GRENVILLE HISCOCK, M.A. (Oxon), LL.B., admitted, 1962, Victoria, Australia; 1987, New South Wales, Australia. *PRACTICE AREAS:* Trusts; Estate Planning.

ANTHONY ARTHUR BROWNE, B.A., LL.B., admitted, 1962, Victoria, Australia; 1987, New South Wales, Australia. *PRACTICE AREAS:* Finance; Corporate Finance; Project Finance.

MICHAEL BENNETT ROBINSON, LL.B., admitted, 1961, Victoria, Australia; 1987, New South Wales, Australia. *PRACTICE AREAS:* Taxation; Revenue Law.

PETER MITCHELL HOBDAY, LL.B., admitted, 1968, Victoria, Australia; 1987, New South Wales, Australia. *PRACTICE AREAS:* Negligence; Products Liability; Insurance.

GRAEME DEAN JOHN HENSHAW, LL.B., admitted, 1967, Victoria, Australia; 1987, New South Wales, Australia. *PRACTICE AREAS:* Commercial Property; Real Estate.

JOHN MICHAEL DOWLING, LL.B., admitted, 1967, Victoria, Australia; 1979, New South Wales, Australia. *PRACTICE AREAS:* Patent Law; Intellectual Property.

ROBERT BAXT, LL.B., B.A., LL.M., admitted, 1958, Victoria, Australia; 1962, New South Wales, Australia. *PRACTICE AREAS:* Antitrust; Mergers and Acquisitions; Taxation.

ANTHONY HARRIE ASHMORE PYMAN, B.Com., LL.B., admitted, 1971, Victoria, Australia; 1987, New South Wales, Australia. *PRACTICE AREAS:* Company Law; Commercial Law; Privatisation.

RICHARD TOM POULTON, LL.B., admitted, 1972, Victoria, Australia; 1979, Australian Capital Territory, Australia; 1987, New South Wales, Australia. *PRACTICE AREAS:* Banks and Banking; Finance; Natural Resources.

GEORGE GERALD MACCALLUM SWINBURNE, LL.B., admitted, 1970, Victoria, Australia; 1987, New South Wales, Australia. *PRACTICE AREAS:* Real Estate; Commercial Property.

GRAEME ALEXANDER REECE JOHNSON, B.A., LL.B., admitted, 1974, Victoria, Australia; 1987, New South Wales, Australia. *PRACTICE AREAS:* Sports and Entertainment Law; Advertising and Marketing; Construction Law.

MARK NICHOLAS CERCHÉ, B.Juris., LL.B., admitted, 1973, Victoria, Australia; 1987, New South Wales, Australia. *PRACTICE AREAS:* Superannuation; Employment Law.

COLIN ROBERT GALBRAITH, LL.M., admitted, 1973, Victoria, Australia; 1987, New South Wales, Australia. *PRACTICE AREAS:* Company Law; Commercial Law.

ANDREW FRANK GUY, LL.B., M.B.A. (Imede, Lausanne), admitted, 1971, Victoria, Australia. *PRACTICE AREAS:* Securities; Corporate Law.

IAN ANDREW RENARD, B.A., LL.M., admitted, 1973, Victoria, Australia; 1987, New South Wales, Australia. *PRACTICE AREAS:* Mergers and Acquisitions; Privatisations.

ANDREW MORRIS ROBSON, LL.B., B.Com., admitted, 1972, Victoria, Australia; 1987, New South Wales, Australia. *PRACTICE AREAS:* Libel and Defamation; Professional Liability; Contract Law.

LACHLAN KIRWAN DONALDSON, LL.B., admitted, 1973, Victoria, Australia; 1987, New South Wales, Australia. *PRACTICE AREAS:* Commercial Property; Alcoholic Beverages; Immigration and Naturalization.

(This Listing Continued)

ARTHUR ROBINSON & HEDDERWICKS, *Melbourne, Victoria—Continued*

THOMAS FITZGERALD YUNCKEN, B.A., LL.B., admitted, 1973, Victoria, Australia; 1987, New South Wales, Australia. *PRACTICE AREAS:* Construction Law; Property Insurance; Environmental Law.

WILLIAM JOHN FORREST, LL.B., M.B.A. (Harvard), admitted, 1968, Victoria, Australia; 1980, New York, U.S.A.; 1987, New South Wales, Australia. *PRACTICE AREAS:* Aviations Law; Corporate Law.

JOHN RICHARD HARRY, LL.B., LL.M. (Virginia), admitted, 1971, Victoria, Australia; 1987, New South Wales, Australia. *PRACTICE AREAS:* Natural Resources; Joint Ventures.

KEVIN SOL POSE, B.Juris., LL.B., B.C.L. (Oxon), admitted, 1971, Victoria, Australia; 1987, New South Wales, Australia. *PRACTICE AREAS:* Taxation; Revenue Law.

STEPHEN CHARLES SPARGO, LL.M., admitted, 1975, Victoria, Australia; 1987, New South Wales, Australia. *PRACTICE AREAS:* Corporate Finance; Banks and Banking.

IAN FREDERICK PYMAN, B.Juris., LL.B., admitted, 1976, Victoria, Australia; 1987, New South Wales, Australia. *PRACTICE AREAS:* Insolvency; Corporate Finance; Corporate Law.

JONATHAN JAMES WEBSTER, B.Com., LL.M., admitted, 1980, Victoria, Australia; 1987, New South Wales, Australia. *PRACTICE AREAS:* Securities; Corporate Law; Commercial Law.

ALAN PETERSON FREES, admitted, 1976, Victoria, Australia; 1987, New South Wales, Australia. *PRACTICE AREAS:* Corporate Law; Mergers and Acquisitions; Commercial Law.

PATRICK JAMES RYAN, B. Juris., LL.B., admitted, 1974, Victoria, Australia; 1974, Australian Capital Territory, Australia; 1987, New South Wales, Australia. *PRACTICE AREAS:* Antitrust; Mergers and Acquisitions.

CRAIG WILLIAM OWEN PHILLIPS, admitted, 1980, Victoria; 1992, Queensland. *Education:* (B.A., LL.B). *PRACTICE AREAS:* Resources Litigation; Arbitration; Commercial Litigation; Defamation.

CHRISTOPH ERNST SCHULZ, B.Com., LL.B., admitted, 1979, Victoria, Australia; 1987, New South Wales, Australia. *LANGUAGES:* German. *PRACTICE AREAS:* Environmental Law; Commercial Property.

RICHARD BARTHOLOMEW SANTAMARIA, B.Com., LL.B., admitted, 1977, Victoria, Australia; 1987, New South Wales, Australia. *PRACTICE AREAS:* Corporate Law; Takeovers; Restructuring; Employee Stock Ownership Plans.

MICHAEL THOMAS SCHOENBERG, B.A., LL.B., admitted, 1978, Victoria, Australia; 1987, New South Wales, Australia. *PRACTICE AREAS:* Commercial Law; Litigation.

CLINTON CHARLES HINCHEN, LL.B., admitted, 1981, Victoria, Australia. *PRACTICE AREAS:* Insolvency; Corporate Finance.

LOUISE MARY JENKINS, LL.B., B.A., admitted, 1981, Victoria, Australia. *PRACTICE AREAS:* Professional Liability; Insurance; Customs Law.

DALE WILLIAM POLLARD NICHOLLS, B.A., LL.B., M.B.A. (Harvard), J.D., admitted, 1975, Michigan, U.S.A.; 1975, District of Columbia, U.S.A.; 1985, Victoria, Australia. *PRACTICE AREAS:* Natural Resources; Oil and Gas; Project Finance; Mineral Joint Ventures.

RICHARD WILLIAM HAMER, B.Sc., LL.B., admitted, 1982, Victoria, Australia. *PRACTICE AREAS:* Intellectual Property.

BRUCE WILLIAM JOHNSTON, B.A., LL.B., admitted, 1976, New South Wales, Australia; 1985, Victoria, Australia. *PRACTICE AREAS:* International Law; Investments; Natural Resources.

PAUL MANVERS MEADOWS, B.A., LL.B., admitted, 1981, Victoria, Australia. *PRACTICE AREAS:* Commercial Law; Banks and Banking.

NICOLAS ALEXANDER TOLÉ, LL.B., B.A., admitted, 1982, Victoria, Australia. *PRACTICE AREAS:* Natural Resources; Corporate Finance.

PAUL JOSEPH KENNY, B.A., LL.B., admitted, 1984, Victoria, Australia; 1987, New York, U.S.A. *PRACTICE AREAS:* Corporate Finance; Privatisation; Energy.

(This Listing Continued)

ANTHONY LAWRENCE KUHN, B.Ec., LL.B., admitted, 1983, Victoria, Australia. *PRACTICE AREAS:* Commercial Law; Litigation; Libel and Defamation; Administrative Law.

WENDY WILSON PETER, B.Juris., LL.B., LL.M. (Cantab.), admitted, 1983, Victoria, Australia. *PRACTICE AREAS:* Antitrust; Corporate Law.

TIMOTHY JOHN GOLDER, B.Com., LL.B., admitted, 1984, Victoria, Australia. *PRACTICE AREAS:* Trademarks; Copyright; Computers and Software.

IAN PETER SCOTT O'DONAHOO, B.Ec., LL.B., admitted, 1984, Victoria, Australia. *PRACTICE AREAS:* Commercial Litigation; Products Liability; Constitutional Law; Consumer Law.

STEPHEN WAYNE CLIFFORD, B.Com., LL.B., admitted, 1983, Victoria, Australia. *PRACTICE AREAS:* Corporate Law; Mergers and Acquisitions.

HEATHER JANE GRAY, B.A., LL.B., admitted, 1985, Victoria, Australia. *PRACTICE AREAS:* Superannuation; Trusts and Estates.

JULIAN GRAHM RIEKERT, B.A., LL.B., LL.M, M.A., admitted, 1991, Victoria, Australia. *PRACTICE AREAS:* Labour and Employment; Discrimination.

EDWARD WINSLOW WOODWARD, LL.B., admitted, 1984, Victoria, Australia. *PRACTICE AREAS:* Insolvency; Commercial Law; Government.

SIMON PETER LYNCH, B.A., LL.B., admitted 1986, New South Wales, Australia; 1991, Victoria, Australia. *PRACTICE AREAS:* Corporate Finance; Banks and Banking.

STEVEN PEMBERTON, LL.B., admitted, 1986, Victoria, Australia. *PRACTICE AREAS:* Banking; Corporate Finance.

PAUL ANTHONY QUINN, LL.B., B.Com., admitted 1986, Victoria, Australia; 1991, England. *PRACTICE AREAS:* Commercial Law; Securities; Mergers and Acquisitions.

PETER STEWART, B.Ec., LL.M., admitted, 1987, Victoria, Australia. *PRACTICE AREAS:* Government; Finance.

MARYJANE CRABTREE, B.A., LL.B., admitted 1987, Victoria, Australia. *PRACTICE AREAS:* Products Liability; Insurance; Occupational Health and Safety.

CRAIG HENDERSON, B.A., LL.M., admitted 1987, Victoria, Australia; 1992, London, United Kingdom. *PRACTICE AREAS:* Corporate Law; Commercial Law.

CAMERON JOHN RIDER, B.A., LL.B., admitted, 1987, Victoria, Australia. *PRACTICE AREAS:* Taxation; Revenue Law.

SUSAN KAY WILLIAMSON, B.Com., LL.B., admitted 1983, Victoria, Australia. *PRACTICE AREAS:* Taxation; Revenue Law.

SENIOR ASSOCIATES

PRUDENCE LOUISE CAMPTON, B.Juris., LL.B., admitted, 1980, Victoria, Australia. *PRACTICE AREAS:* Medical Liability.

DIANA ENNIS, LL.B., admitted, 1984, Victoria, Australia. *PRACTICE AREAS:* Commercial Law.

MICHAEL ROBERT PATTISON, B.Sc., LL.B., admitted, 1986, Victoria, Australia. *PRACTICE AREAS:* Intellectual Property; Information Technology.

STUART JOHN BROWN, B.Ec., LL.B., admitted, 1988, Victoria, Australia. *PRACTICE AREAS:* Taxation; Commercial Law.

CATHERINE DOROTHY HEELEY, B.Ec., LL.B., admitted 1988, Victoria, Australia. *PRACTICE AREAS:* Commercial Law; Finance.

SHARON HUNT-SMITH, admitted, 1988, Victoria. *Education:* (B.A., LL.B.). *PRACTICE AREAS:* Utilities; General Commercial; Consumer Credit.

SCOTT LANGFORD, B.Sc., LL.B., admitted, 1988, Victoria, Australia. *PRACTICE AREAS:* Mergers and Acquisitions; Natural Resources.

MERREN ELIZABETH MCARTHUR, B.A., LL.B., admitted 1988, Victoria, Australia. *PRACTICE AREAS:* Commercial Law; Banking; Finance.

PENELOPE ASSELINEAU, D.E.A., Diplome De Droit Compare, admitted, 1986, Victoria, Australia and New South Wales, Australia. *LANGUAGES:* French. *PRACTICE AREAS:* Banks and Banking; Finance.

(This Listing Continued)

TANIA CINI, LL.B., Admitted 1989, Victoria, Australia. *PRACTICE AREAS:* Commercial Litigation; Insolvency.

DAVID KENNETH DAWBORN, LL.B., B.A., admitted 1989, Victoria, Australia. *PRACTICE AREAS:* Corporate Law; Commercial Law.

ANTHEA CLARE NOLAN, LL.B., admitted, 1989, Victoria, Australia. *PRACTICE AREAS:* Trusts and Estates; Superannuation.

NATALINA VELARDI, B.Ec., LL.B., admitted 1989, Victoria, Australia. *PRACTICE AREAS:* Commercial Law; Litigation.

STEPHEN GRANT ANDERSON, LL.B., B.Com., admitted, 1990, Victoria, Australia. *PRACTICE AREAS:* Mergers and Acquisitions; Corporate Law.

PHILIP MARTIN KUDNIG, LL.B., B.Sc., admitted, 1988, Victoria, Australia. *PRACTICE AREAS:* Commercial Law; Corporate Finance; Natural Resources.

NIK YEO, B.A., LL.B., admitted, 1989, Victoria, Australia. *PRACTICE AREAS:* Equity Pensions; Banking.

CAMERON BRUCE PRICE, B.Ec., LL.B., admitted, 1990, Victoria, Australia. *PRACTICE AREAS:* Corporate Law; Banking; Finance.

CONSULTANTS

PATRICK BRAZIL, A.O., B.A., LL.B.

DAVID WILLIAM ROGERS, LL.B., admitted, 1950, Victoria, Australia; 1987, New South Wales, Australia.

HENRY FRANCIS HOWDEN SELLECK, B.A., LL.M., admitted, 1944, Victoria, Australia; 1982, Australian Capital Territory.

REVISERS OF THE AUSTRALIA LAW DIGEST FOR THIS DIRECTORY.

SLY & WEIGALL

In association with Deacons/Graham & James

385 BOURKE STREET
MELBOURNE, VICTORIA 3000, AUSTRALIA
Telephone: (03) 608 0411 International: +61 3 608 0411
Facsimile: (03) 608 0505

Brisbane, Australia Office: Riverside Centre, 123 Eagle Street, 4000. Telephone: (07) 833 0444. International: +61 7 833 0444. Facsimile: (07) 833 0555.

Canberra City, Australia Office: GPO Box 2013, 2601. Telephone: (06) 249 7666. International: +61 6 249 7666. Facsimile: (06) 257 2560.

Perth, Australia Office: 108 St. George's Terrace, 6000. Telephone: (09) 321 9379. International: +61 9 321 9379. Facsimile: (09) 324 1334.

Sydney, Australia Office: Gold Fields House, 1 Alfred Street, Circular Quay, 2000. Telephone: (02) 330 8000. International: +61 2 330 8000. Facsimile: (02) 330 8111.

RESIDENT PARTNERS

Kenneth David James Barry	*Peter Stanley Barber*
Martin John O'Dell Armstrong	*Ross Kenneth Millen*
John Joseph Andrew Sharkey	*Robert William Sultan*
Robert Henry Neil Symons	*Peter James Watson*
Robert Ian Arthur Hando	*Jeffrey Robert Wilson*
Frank Watson Paton	*James Sage Ferry*
Nigel Lawson Watson	*Grant James John Ahearn*
Mary Elizabeth Hallett	*Richard Bruce Lewis*
Stewart Francis Sturrock Peters	*John Peter Young*
Patrick Gordon Alan Montgomery	*Bruce Akiva Goldman*

CONSULTANTS

E. Colquit Kennon	*The Hon. Alan Hunt, A.M.*
John David Claringbould	*Donald Ledingham Cooper*
	Dr. Maura B. McGill

SENIOR ASSOCIATES

Kirstin J.A. Mann	*Matthew John Hicks*
Susan Joy Sweeney	*Rowena Kathleen Hart*
Hedy L. Warren	*Geoffrey M. Emmett*
Andrew Hamlyn-Harris	*Anthony B. Whelan*
	Louise Ellen Sherry

SULLIVAN & CROMWELL

101 COLLINS STREET
MELBOURNE, VICTORIA 3000, AUSTRALIA
Telephone: (011)(613)654-1500
Telecopier: (011)(613)654-2422

New York City Offices: 125 Broad Street, 10004-2498; Midtown Office: 250 Park Avenue, 10177-0021. Telephone: 212-558-4000. Telex: 62694 (International); 12-7816 (Domestic). Cable Address: "Ladycourt, New York". Telecopier: 125 Broad Street 212-558-3588; 250 Park Avenue 212-558-3792.

Washington, D.C. Office: 1701 Pennsylvania Avenue, N.W., 20006-5805. Telephone: 202-956-7500. Telex: 89625. Telecopier: 202-293-6330.

Los Angeles, California Office: 444 South Flower Street, 90071-2901. Telephone: 213-955-8000. Telecopier: 213-683-0457.

Paris Office: 8, Place Vendôme, Paris 75001, France. Telephone: (011)(331)4450-6000. Telex: 240654. Telecopier: (011)(331)4450-6060.

London Office: St. Olave's House, 9a Ironmonger Lane, London EC2V 8EY, England. Telephone: (011)(44171)710-6500. Telecopier: (011)(44171)710-6565.

Tokyo Office: Gaikokuho Jimu Bengoshi Office of Robert G. DeLaMater, a member of the firm of Sullivan & Cromwell, Tokio Kaijo Building Shinkan, 2-1, Marunouchi, 1-chome Chiyoda-ku, Tokyo 100, Japan. Telephone: (011)(813)3213-6140. Telecopier: (011)(813)3213-6470.

Hong Kong Office: 28th Floor, Nine Queen's Road, Central, Hong Kong. Telephone:(011)(852)826-8688. Telecopier: (011)(852)522-2280.

PARTNERS IN MELBOURNE

JEFFREY F. BROWNE, born Clare, South Australia, 1944; admitted, 1969, South Australia; 1974, Australian Capital Territory; 1978, New York; 1982, Victoria; 1983, Western Australia and New South Wales. *Education:* Adelaide University (LL.B., 1966); Sydney University (LL.M., 1968); Harvard (LL.M., 1976). Australian Diplomatic Service, 1969-1974, including service in Malaysia, London, Ghana and Geneva, in the International Law Branch of the Department of Foreign Affairs and as Counsel to the Australian Legal Team, Nuclear Test Cases, International Court of Justice.

DUNCAN C. MCCURRACH, born Rochester, N.Y., 1959; admitted, 1985, New York (Not admitted in Australia). *Education:* Cornell (A.B., 1981); Univ. of Chicago (J.D., 1984).

ASSOCIATES IN MELBOURNE

GARY W. COBBLEDICK, born Johannesburg, South Africa, 1967; admitted, 1993, New York (Not admitted in Australia). *Education:* Univ. of Natal (B.A., 1988; LL.B., 1990); Harvard (LL.M., 1992).

MICHAEL D. SCHECTER, born New York, NY., 1964; admitted, 1994, New York (Not admitted in Australia). *Education:* Bates College (B.A., 1986); Cornell Law School (J.D., 1990).

RICHARD H. SIEGEL, born Norristown, PA., 1965; admitted, 1992, New York and Maryland (Not admitted in Australia). *Education:* Univ. of Maryland (B.S., 1988); Georgetown (J.D., 1991).

(For Biographical Data on all Partners and Associates see Professional Biographies at New York, N.Y.).

WESTGARTH MIDDLETONS

MELBOURNE, VICTORIA, AUSTRALIA

(See Middletons Moore & Bevins)

BLAKE DAWSON WALDRON

FORREST CENTRE
221 ST. GEORGE'S TERRACE
PERTH, WESTERN AUSTRALIA 6000, AUSTRALIA
Telephone: (09) 366-8000
Facsimile: (09) 366-8111
Telex: AA22867DWN

Sydney, New South Wales, Australia Office: Grosvenor Place 225 George Street 2000. Telephone: (02) 2586000. Facsimile: (02) 2586999. Telex: AA22867DWN.

Melbourne, Victoria, Australia Office: 101 Colins Street, 3000. Telephone: (03) 679 3000. Facsimile: (03) 679 3111. Telex: AA31033.

Brisbane, Queensland, Australia Office: Riverside Centre, 123 Eagle Street, 4000. Telephone: (07) 259 7000. Facsimile: (07) 259 7111. Telex: AA22867DWN.

Canberra, Australian Capital Territory, Australia Office: 12 Moore Street, 2601. Telephone: (06) 234 4000. Facsimile: (06) 234 4111. Telex: AA22867DWN.

Port Moresby, Papua New Guinea Office: Mogoru Moto Building, Champion Parade. Telephone: (675) 21 1977. Facsimile: (675) 212630. Telex: NE 22223.

London, England Office: 66 Gresham Street, EC2V 7BB. Telephone: (071) 600 3030. Facsimile: (071) 600 3392.

Jakarta, Indonesia Associated Office: Soebagjo, Roosdiono, Jatim & Djarot. Chase Plaza, Jalan Jendral Sudirman Kav 21, 12910. Telephone: (6221) 570 6436. Fax: (6221) 570 6437. Telex: 62 941 SRJDIA.

Port Vila, Vanuatu Associated Office: Hudson & Co. Lo Lam House, Kumul Highway. Telephone: (678) 22166. Fax: (678) 24260.

FIRM PROFILE: *One of Australia's largest national law firms providing legal services in all areas required by commerce, finance and government. The firm has offices in all the major Australian commercial centres. Our practice also has international offices in London, Port Moresby and associated offices in Jakarta and Port Vila.*

PERTH PARTNERS

MICHAEL W. HUNT. PRACTICE AREAS: Resources; Environmental Planning.

IAN F. CRAWFORD. PRACTICE AREAS: Intellectual Property.

IAN ADRIAN. PRACTICE AREAS: Commercial Litigation; Trade Practices.

NEIL C. FEARIS. PRACTICE AREAS: Corporate; Commercial.

JOHN G. CARRINGTON. PRACTICE AREAS: Insolvencies; Receiverships.

MICHAEL B. WOOD. PRACTICE AREAS: Banking; Finance.

PETER VOSS. PRACTICE AREAS: Commercial Litigation; Insurance Law.

MICHAEL LURIE. PRACTICE AREAS: Commercial Banking Law.

(For complete personnel and biographical data, see professional biographies at Sydney, Australia).

CLAYTON UTZ

Barristers and Solicitors
Established in 1833
BANKWEST TOWER
108 ST. GEORGE'S TERRACE
PERTH, WESTERN AUSTRALIA 6000, AUSTRALIA
Telephone: (09) 426 8444
Fax: (09) 481 3095
Telex: AA 93232

Sydney, New South Wales, Australia Office: Levels 27-35, No 1 O'Connell Street, 2000. Telephone: (02) 353 4000. Fax: (02) 251 7832.

Melbourne, Victoria, Australia Office: Level 18, 333 Collins Street, 3000. Telephone: (03) 286 6000. Fax: (03) 629 8488.

Brisbane, Queensland, Australia Office: Levels 18, 19, 23-28 Santos House, 215 Adelaide Street, 4000. Telephone: (07) 228 5811. Fax: (07) 229 7566.

(This Listing Continued)

Canberra, Australian Capital Territory, Australia Office: 9th Floor, Canberra House, 40 Marcus Clarke Street, 2601. Telephone: (06) 274 0999. Fax: (06) 274 0888.

Clayton Utz operates through national practice groups which focus on banking and financial services; commercial litigation and dispute resolution; competition law; construction; corporate law; corporatization and privatization; energy and natural resources; environment and planning law; Insurance Law; mergers and acquisitions; product liability; property; taxation and superannuation; technology, computer and intellectual property law; workout, recovery and insolvency; workplace relations and employment law.

(For complete biographical data on all personnel, see Professional Biographies at Sydney, Australia)

CORRS CHAMBERS WESTGARTH

COMMONWEALTH BANK BUILDING
150 ST. GEORGE'S TERRACE
PERTH, WESTERN AUSTRALIA 6000, AUSTRALIA
Telephone: (09) 321 8531
International: +619 321 8531
Fax: (09) 322 6953

Melbourne, Victoria, Australia Office: 600 Bourke Street, Vic. 3000. Telephone: (03) 672 3000. International: +613 672 3000. Fax: (03) 602 5544.

Sydney, New South Wales, Australia Office: Level 32, Governor Phillip Tower, 1 Farrer Place, 2001. International: (02) 210 6500. Fax: (02) 210 6611.

Brisbane, Australia Office: Comalco Place, 12 Creek Street, QLD, 4000. Telephone: (07) 228 9333. International: +617 228 9333. Fax: (07) 229 2844.

Gold Coast, Queensland, Australia: Level 4, Corporate Centre One, 2 Corporate Court, Bundall, QDL, 4217. International Telephone: (075) 77 7777. Fax: (075) 74 0478.

Canberra, Australia Office: Level 5, Advance Bank Centre, 60 Marcus Clarke Street, ACT, 2601. Telephone: (06) 257 7566. International: +616 257 7566. Fax: (06) 257 7563.

London, England Office: 2nd Floor, 103 Cannon Street, EC4N 5AD. Telephone: (171) 929 4955. International: +44171 929 4955. Fax: (171) 929 4164.

Commercial and Corporate Law including:
Banking & Finance, Computer & Communications, Corporate Reconstruction & Insolvency, Corporatisation, Customs & International Trade, Energy & Resources, Family Law, Franchising, Funds Management, Industrial Relations, Insurance & Product Liability, Intellectual Property, International Law, Joint Ventures, Litigation in all areas of practice, Mergers & Acquisitions, Planning, Pollution & Environment Law, Privatization, Professional Liability, Property Development & Construction, Securitisation, Stamp Duty, Superannuation, Taxation, Telecommunications.

PARTNERS

Brian G. Beresford	David H. Nadebaum
Alan H. Churley	Julian L. Sher
Ian H. Cochrane	Philip R. Wilson
Gavin D. Crocket	(Managing Partner)
Carmel J. McLure	Nicholas D.C. Dillon

SENIOR ASSOCIATES

Cameron Belyea	Rachael Offer
Kanaga Dharmananda	Andrew Roberts
Michael Kennedy	Kirsty Sutherland
	Ian Tait

(For list of Personnel at London, England, Brisbane, Canberra, Bundall, Melbourne and Sydney, Australia see Professional Biographies at those locations).

FREEHILL HOLLINGDALE & PAGE

Established in 1852

AUSTRALIA PLACE, 15-17 WILLIAM STREET
G.P.O. BOX U1942

PERTH, WESTERN AUSTRALIA 6000, AUSTRALIA
Telephone: (09) 327 5777, International: +619 327 5777
Cable Address: "MUIRWIL", "FREEHILLS, PERTH"
Telex: AA 92937
Fax: (09) 322 5954

Sydney, New South Wales, Australia Office: Level 38, MLC Centre, 19-29 Martin Place, 2000. Telephone: (02) 225 5000. International: +(612) 225 5000. Telex AA 121885. Fax: (02) 322 4000.

Canberra City, Australian Capital Territory, Australia Office: London Court, 13 London Circuit, 2601. Telephone:(06) 240 6100. International: +(616) 240 6100. Telex: AA121885. Fax: (06) 240 6222.

Melbourne, Victoria, Australia Office: 101 Collins Street, 3000. Telephone: (03) 288 1234. International: +(613) 288 1234. Telex: AA33004. Fax: (03) 288 1567.

Brisbane, Queensland, Australia Office: Central Plaza II, 66 Eagle Street, 4000. Telephone: (07) 258 6666. International: +(617) 258 6666. Fax: (07) 258 6444.

Singapore Office: 6 Battery Road, #13-01, 0104. Telephone: (65) 225 1288. Telex: (RS) 42674. Fax: (65) 225 3314.

London, England Office: Birchin Court, 20 Birchin Lane, EC3V 9DJ. Telephone: (0171) 283 9006. International: +(44 171) 283 9006. Fax: (0171) 454 9650.

Hanoi, Vietnam Office: 34A Quang Trung Street. Telephone: (844) 227 839. Fax: (844) 227 909.

Ho Chi Minh City, Vietnam Office: 203 Dong Khoi Street, #3-05. Telephone: (848) 242 630; (848) 242 733. Fax: (848) 242 736.

Barristers, Solicitors and Notaries.

MEMBERS OF FIRM IN PERTH

ROBERT JOHN MEADOWS, admitted, 1966. *Education:* University of Western Australia (LL.B.). *PRACTICE AREAS:* Litigation; Trade Practices.

JOHN ROBIN HAYWARD, admitted, 1967. *Education:* University of Western Australia (LL.B.). *LANGUAGES:* French. *PRACTICE AREAS:* Corporate; Funds Raisings; Funds Management; Privatisation; Infrastructure; Taxation; Revenue.

BRUNO GIOVANNI CAMARRI, admitted, 1970. *Education:* University of Western Australia (LL.B.). *LANGUAGES:* Italian. *PRACTICE AREAS:* Energy; Resources.

JOHN GEORGE SYMINTON, admitted, 1964. *Education:* Cape Town University (B.A.; LL.B.). *PRACTICE AREAS:* Property; Stamp Duty.

JOHN ROBERT BRODERICK LEY, admitted, 1975. *Education:* University of Western Australia (LL.B.). *PRACTICE AREAS:* Litigation; Media Law; Product Liability.

TIMOTHY HUBERT REINOLD, admitted, 1970. *Education:* England/Wales. *PRACTICE AREAS:* Banking; Finance; Environmental Law; Property.

RUSSELL DAVID ALLEN, admitted, 1974. *Education:* University of Melbourne (LL.B.). *PRACTICE AREAS:* Employee Relations.

ALEXANDER PHILIP SALVARIS, admitted, 1979. *Education:* University of Western Australia (B. Juris, Hons.; LL.B. Hons.). *LANGUAGES:* French. *PRACTICE AREAS:* Property.

PAUL ANTHONY HOPPER WRIGHT, admitted, 1977. *Education:* England/Wales. *PRACTICE AREAS:* Banking; Finance; Corporate; Funds Raisings.

PHILIP GEORGE CLIFFORD, admitted, 1979. *Education:* University of Western Australia (B.Juris; LL.B.; B.A.). *PRACTICE AREAS:* Engineering; Construction; Litigation.

JOHN CHRISTOPHER VAUGHAN, admitted, 1977. *Education:* Kingston-on-Thames Polytechnic (B.A.). *PRACTICE AREAS:* Insurance; Insolvency.

PETER CHARLES SUPET VAN HATTEM, admitted, 1980. *Education:* University of Western Australia (B.Juris, Hons.; LL.B. Hons.). *PRACTICE AREAS:* Government Trade; Resources.

(This Listing Continued)

DAVID ALEXANDER WALTON, admitted, 1980. *Education:* University of Western Australia (B.Juris, Hons.; LL.B.). *PRACTICE AREAS:* Banking; Finance; Stamp Duty.

PAUL DOMINIC EVANS, admitted, 1984. *Education:* University of Western Australia (B.Juris, Hons.; LL.B. Hons.). *PRACTICE AREAS:* Corporate; Litigation; Mergers and Acquisitions; Trade Practices.

STEVEN PENGLIS, admitted, 1982. *Education:* University of New South Wales (B.Juris; LL.B.). *PRACTICE AREAS:* Corporate; Litigation; Trade Practices.

PETER JOHN MANSELL, admitted, 1972. *Education:* University of The Witwatersrand (B.Com.; LL.B.; H.Dip.Tax). *LANGUAGES:* Afrikaans. *PRACTICE AREAS:* Corporate; Funds Raisings; Securities Trading; Privatisation; Infrastructure; Telecommunications.

PETER JOHN PATRIKEOS, admitted, 1976. *Education:* University of Melbourne. *PRACTICE AREAS:* Corporate; Energy; Resources; Funds Raisings; Funds Management; Mergers and Acquisitions; Privatisation; Infrastructure.

PETER SANDOR JAROSEK, admitted, 1983. *Education:* University of Western Australia (B.Juris; LL.B.). *PRACTICE AREAS:* Energy; Resources; Intellectual Property.

MICHAEL PETER HOLLINGDALE, admitted, 1982. *Education:* (SAB Dip Law). *PRACTICE AREAS:* Engineering; Construction; Litigation.

KONRAD JACQUES MONY DE KERLOY, admitted, 1983. *Education:* University of Western Australia (B.Juris; LL.B.). *LANGUAGES:* Polish. *PRACTICE AREAS:* Litigation; Funds Management; Product Liability.

DOUGLAS ROY STIPANICEV, admitted, 1984. *Education:* University of Western Australia (B.Juris; LL.B.). *PRACTICE AREAS:* Banking; Finance; Environmental Law; Property.

PAUL GWYN EVANS, admitted, 1985. *Education:* University of Western Australia (B.Juris; LL.B.). *PRACTICE AREAS:* Corporate; Funds Raisings; Stamp Duty.

MICHAEL FILAN ASHFORTH, admitted, 1986. *Education:* University of Western Australia (B.Juris, Hons.; LL.B. Hons.). *PRACTICE AREAS:* Corporate; Funds Raisings; Mergers and Acquisitions.

RICK JOSEPH MALONE, admitted, 1978. *Education:* University of Western Australia (B.Juris, LL.B.). *PRACTICE AREAS:* Corporate; Energy; Resources; Trade; Customs; Trade Practices.

SCOTT ELLIS, admitted, 1983. *Education:* University of Western Australia (B.Juris, LL.B.). *PRACTICE AREAS:* Intellectual Property; Litigation; Telecommunications; Trade Practices.

MICHELLE HULLETT, admitted, 1983. *Education:* University of Western Australia (B.Juris.; LL.B.). *PRACTICE AREAS:* Litigation; Telecommunications; Trade Practices.

DEBORAH MILTON, admitted, 1984. *Education:* University of Western Australia (B.Juris.; LL.B.). *PRACTICE AREAS:* Energy; Resources; Engineering; Construction; Environmental Law; Litigation.

TONI LUCEV, admitted, 1989. *Education:* University of Western Australia (B.Juris., Hons.; LL.B.). *PRACTICE AREAS:* Employee Relations; Litigation; Trade Practices.

JOHN PICKERING, admitted, 1989. *Education:* Western Australia Institute of Technology (B.Bus.); University of Western Australia (B.Juris; LL.B.; LL.M.). *PRACTICE AREAS:* Litigation; Stamp Duty; Taxation; Revenue.

PETER GEOFFREY LARK, admitted, 1994. *Education:* University of Cape Town (B.Com., Hons.); University of Western Australia (LL.B.). *LANGUAGES:* Afrikaans. *PRACTICE AREAS:* Taxation; Capital Gains; Mining and International Tax; Stamp Duty.

(For Biographical data on all other Personnel, see Professional Biographies at Brisbane, Canberra, Melbourne and Sydney, Australia and Singapore)

MALLESONS STEPHEN JAQUES

GROUND FLOOR, ST. GEORGES SQUARE
225 ST. GEORGE'S TERRACE
PERTH, WESTERN AUSTRALIA 6000, AUSTRALIA
Telephone: (619) 324 8333
Fax: (619) 321 1017

Sydney, Australia Office: Level 60, Governor Phillip Tower, 1 Farrer Place. Telephone: (612) 250 3000. Fax: (612) 250 3133.

Melbourne, Australia Office: Level 28, Rialto, 525 Collins Street, 3000. Telephone: (613) 619 0619. Fax: (613) 614 1329.

Brisbane, Australia Office: Level 30, Waterfront Place, 1 Eagle Street, 4000. Telephone: (617) 231 7500. Fax: (617) 221 1211.

Canberra, Australia Office: Level 10, Advance Bank Centre, 60 Marcus Clarke Street, 2601. Telephone: (616) 268 3900. Fax: (616) 257 3100.

Hong Kong Office: Bateson Starr in association with Mallesons Stephen Jaques, Suite 801, Asia Pacific Finance Tower, Citibank Plaza, 3 Garden Road, Central Hong Kong. Telephone: (852) 848 4600. Fax: (852) 868-0124.

Beijing, The Peoples Republic of China Office: Suite 701, Scite Tower, 22 Jianguomenwai Street, 100004. Telephone: (86 1) 512 3565 ext 701. Fax: (86 1) 523 2018.

Taipei, Taiwan Office: 14th Floor, Mallesons Stephen Jaques, 138 Min Sheng East Road, Sec 3. Telephone: (8862) 712 5808. Fax: (8862) 712 9080.

Jakarta, Indonesia Associated Office: Law Firm Kartini Muljadi S.H. & Associates, in association with Mallesons Stephen Jaques, Level 5, Bina Mulia I Building, J1 H.R. Rasuna Said Kav 10, 12950. Telephone: (6221) 525-6968. Fax: (6221) 525-5561.

Port Moresby, Papua, New Guinea Office: Beresford Love, agents for Mallesons Stephen Jaques, Level 3, Hunter Building, Hunter Street. Telephone: (675) 211 942. Fax: (675) 211 586.

Singapore Office: Level 36, Hong Leong Building, 16 Raffles Quay, 0104. Telephone: (65) 321 8930. Fax: (65) 225 9060.

London, England Office: 2nd. Floor, Aldermary House, 10-15 Queen Street, EC4N 1TX. Telephone: (44 171) 982 0982. Fax: (44 171) 982 9820.

New York, New York, U.S.A. Office: 9th floor, Suite 911, 609 Fifth Avenue, 10017-1021. Telephone: (1-212) 319-9500. Fax: (1-212) 319-9506.

RESIDENT PARTNERS

Rob Ainslie	**Michael Lishman**
Andrew Barclay	**Ben Luscombe**
Rob Cole	**John Naughton**
Michael Corboy	**Greg Pynt**
Brahma Dharmananda	**Geoff Rogers**
Bruce Dodd	**Tim Sharp**
Grant Donaldson	**Chris Stevenson**
John Garvey	**Gary Thomas**
Chris Humphry	**Leigh Warnick**
Laurence Iffla	**Michael Wright**

(For Complete Personnel, see Professional Biographies at Sydney, Australia).

PARKER & PARKER

Barristers, Solicitors & Notaries

LEVELS 21-26 AMP BUILDING
140 ST. GEORGE'S TERRACE
PERTH, WESTERN AUSTRALIA 6000, AUSTRALIA
Telephone: (09) 322 0321
Rapifax: (09) 322 2243

Mailing Address: GPO Box D151, Perth, Western Australia, 6001, Australia

A Member of the Allens Arthur Robinson Group, comprising:

Sydney, New South Wales, Australia Office: Allen Allen & Hemsley, Level 23, The Chifley Tower, 2 Chifley Square, 2000. Telephone: (61 2) 230 4000. Rapifax: (61 2) 233 7022.

Canberra, Australian Capital Territory, Australia Office: Allen Allen & Hemsley, 3rd Floor, 16 Moore Street, 2601. Telephone: (61 6) 247 5800. Rapifax: (61 6) 257 1369.

(This Listing Continued)

Melbourne, Victoria, Australia Office: Arthur Robinsons & Hedderwicks, Levels 27-34, 530 Collins Street, 3000. Telephone: (61 3) 614 1011. Rapifax: (61 3) 614 4661.

Brisbane, Queensland, Australia Office: Feez Ruthning, Riverside Centre, 123 Eagle Street, 4000. Telephone: (61 7) 833 3333. Rapifax: (61 7) 832 4233.

Surfers Paradise, Queensland, Australia Office: Feez Ruthning, Level 14, 50 Cavill Avenue, 4217. Telephone: (61 75) 70 0200. Rapifax: (61 75) 92 2285.

Adelaide, South Australia, Australia Office: Finlaysons, 81 Flinders Street, 5000. Telephone: (61 8) 235 7400. Rapifax: (61 8) 232 2944.

Group and Associated Offices:

London, England Office: Allens Arthur Robinson, Level 5, Bucklersbury House, 3 Queen Victoria Street, EC4N 8EL. Telephone: (44 171) 248 6130. Rapifax: (44 171) 248 6334.

New York, NY Office: Allens Arthur Robinson, 280 Park Avenue, 10017. Telephone: (1 212) 867 1555. Rapifax: (1 212) 867 7979.

Singapore Office: Allens Arthur Robinson, 65 Chulla Street #42-05, OCBC Centre 0104. Telephone: (65) 535 6622. Rapifax: (65) 535 4855.

Port Moresby, Papua New Guinea Office: Allens Arthur Robinson, Level 11, Pacific Place, Cnr. Musgrave Street & Champion Parade. Telephone: (675) 202 000. Rapifax: (675) 200 588.

Hong Kong Office: Dunstan Styles & Co., Suite 1504, One Exchange Square, 8 Connaught Place, Central. Telephone: (852) 840 1202. Rapifax: (852) 840 0686.

Jakarta, Indonesia Office: Wiriadinata & Widyawan, Niaga Tower, 26th Floor, Jl. Jend. Sudirman, Kav 58, 12190. Telephone: (62 21) 250 5175. Rapifax: (62 21) 250 5185.

Shanghai, People's Republic of China Office: AAR China Limited, Fuxing Xi Lu 37 Long 6 Hao., 200031. Telephone: (86 21) 437 7582. Rapifax: (86 21) 473 7819.

Administrative Law, Advertising Law, Aeronautical Law, Antitrust Law, Arbitration, Banking Law, Bankruptcy, Competition Law, Constitutional Law, Construction Law, Consumer Protection Law, Conveyancing Law, Corporate Law, Distributorship, Agency and Franchise Law, Employer's Liability, Entertainment Law, Environmental Law, Foreign Investments, Immigration Law, Insurance Law, International Contracts, International Private Law, Litigation, Maritime and Admiralty Law, Negligence Law, Oil and Mining Law, Personal Injury Law, Product Liability Law, Property and Real Estate Law, Rent and Lease, Trade Regulations, Transportation Law, General Legal Practice, Intellectual Property, Copyright Law, Licence Negotiation, Patent Litigation, Trademark Litigation, Trademark Prosecution, Transfer of Technology, General Intellectual Property Practice, Capital Taxation, Corporate Taxation, Customs Duties, Deferred Taxation, Indirect Taxation, Inheritance, Estate and Gift Taxation, International Taxation, Personal Income Taxation, Sales, Turnover, Value Added Taxes, Taxation of Foreign Nationals, Taxation of Oil and Mining Companies, Transfer Pricing, Exchange Control, General Tax Practice.

FIRM PROFILE: Parker & Parker is an internationally based firm in terms of the clients it represents and the transactions in which it has been involved. In addition, the background of its lawyers and its links with law firms in major and financial and commercial centres of the world assist with the international nature of the practice. Total number of partners for Parker & Parker is 29, total legal and support staff is over 200 and for the Allens Arthur Robinson Group total legal staff is over 700. The firm's areas of specialization include: Banking and Finance; Commercial Litigation; Construction; Corporate; Insurance; Licensing and Media; Intellectual and Industrial Property; Insolvency; Mergers and Acquisitions; Resources; Property; Business; Taxation and Superannuation.

PARTNERS

Rory E. Argyle	*Andrew A. Shearwood*
Jeremy N. Knowles	*Anthony S. Parker*
Dudley R. Stow	*Oscar Shub*
William G. Groves	*Joseph P. Longo*
Steven Cole	*Stuart J. Barrymore*
Ted Sharp	*Rosemary H. Peek*
Craig L. Readhead	*Geoffrey Walker*
Ian G. Peek	*Steven Paterniti*
Daniel Blue	*Susan A. Wilson*
John A. Chandler	*Tracy Caspersz*
John K. Atkins	*Jennifer A. Thornton*
Tony Joyner	*Rob Hay*
Peter de Zwart	*Richard J. Price*

(This Listing Continued)

Geoffrey M. Abbott

COUNSEL

Antony N. Siopis   Anthony V. McCarthy

CORPORATE COUNSEL

Peter I. Jooste

SLY & WEIGALL

In association with Deacons/Graham & James

108 ST. GEORGES TERRACE
PERTH, WESTERN AUSTRALIA 6000, AUSTRALIA
Telephone: (09) 321 9379 International: +61 9 321 9379
Facsimile: (09) 324 1334

Brisbane, Australia Office: Riverside Centre, 123 Eagle Street, 4000. Telephone: (07) 833 0444. International: +61 7 833 0444. Facsimile: (07) 833 0555.

Canberra City, Australia Office: GPO Box 2013, 2601. Telephone: (06) 249 7666. International: +61 6 249 7666. Facsimile: (06) 257 2560.

Melbourne, Australia Office: 385 Bourke Street, 3000. Telephone: (03) 608 0411. International: +61 3 608 0411. Facsimile: (03) 608 0505.

Sydney, Australia Office: Gold Fields House, 1 Alfred Street, Circular Quay, 2000. Telephone: (02) 330 8000. International: +61 2 330 8000. Facsimile: (02) 330 8111.

RESIDENT PARTNERS

Warwick Max Bradney	Ross George Stuart Harrison
Rodney Darold Warren	Ashley Temple Macknay
John Francis Hewett	Giovanni Groppoli
Johan Maritz Willers	Michael Norman Arnett
Colin John Munro	Patrick Brian O'Neal

SENIOR ASSOCIATES

Mark Benet Ashforth	Ronald Athol Doig
Estelle Louise Blewett	John Cameron Vaughan
Sonia Siham Newby	

CONSULTANT

Ian Andrew Morrison

ALLEN ALLEN & HEMSLEY

LEVEL 23
THE CHIFLEY TOWER
2 CHIFLEY SQUARE
SYDNEY, NEW SOUTH WALES 2000, AUSTRALIA
Telephone: (02) 230 4000
Cable Address: "Allens" Sydney
Telex: AA 121641
Rapifax: (02) 233 7022

Mailing Address: G.P.O. Box 50, Sydney, 2001

A member of the Allens Arthur Robinson group, comprising:

Canberra, Australian Capital Territory, Australia: Allen Allen & Hemsley, 3rd Floor, 16 Moore Street, 2601. Telephone: (61 6) 247 5800. Rapifax: (61 6) 257 1369.

Melbourne, Victoria, Australia: Arthur Robinson & Hedderwicks, Levels 27-34, 530 Collins Street, 3000. Telephone: (61 3) 614 1011. Rapifax: (61 3) 614 4661.

Brisbane, Queensland, Australia: Feez Ruthning, Riverside Centre, 123 Eagle Street, 4000. Telephone: (61 7) 833 3333. Rapifax: (61 7) 832 4233.

Surfers Paradise, Queensland, Australia: Feez Ruthning, Level 14, 50 Cavill Avenue, 4217. Telephone: (61 75) 70 0200. Rapifax: (61 75) 92 2285.

Perth, Western Australia, Australia: Parker & Parker, AMP Building, 140 St George's Terrace, 6000. Telephone: (61 9) 322 0321. Rapifax: (61 9) 322 2243.

Adelaide, South Australia, Australia: Finlaysons, 81 Flinders Street, 5000. Telephone: (61 8) 235 7400. Rapifax: (61 8) 232 2944.

Group and Associated Offices:

London, England: Allens Arthur Robinson, Level 5, Bucklersbury House, 3 Queen Victoria Street, EC4N 8EL. Telephone: (44 171) 248 6130. Rapifax: (44 171) 248 6334.

(This Listing Continued)

New York, NY: Allens Arthur Robinson, 280 Park Avenue, 10017. Telephone: (1 212) 867 1555. Rapifax: (1 212) 867 7979.

Singapore: Allens Arthur Robinson, 65 Chulia Street #42-05, OCBC Centre, 0104. Telephone: (65) 535 6622. Rapifax: (65) 535 4855.

Hong Kong: Dunstan Styles & Co., Suite 1504, One Exchange Square, 8 Connaught Place, Central. Telephone: (852) 2840 1202. Rapifax: (852) 2840 0686.

Jakarta, Indonesia: Wiriadinata &Widyawan, Niaga Tower, 26th Floor, Jl. Jend. Sudirman, Kav 58, 12190. Telephone: (62 21) 250 5175. Rapifax: (62 21) 250 5185.

Port Moresby, Papua New Guinea: Allens Arthur Robinson, Level 11, Pacific Place, Cnr. Musgrave Street & Champion Parade. Telephone: (675) 202 000. Rapifax: (675) 200 588.

Shanghai, People's Republic of China: AAR China Limited, Fuxing Xi Lu 37 Long 6 Hao. 200031. Telephone: (86 21) 437 7582. Rapifax: (86 21) 473 7819.

Administrative Law, Advertising Law, Aeronautical Law, Antitrust Law, Arbitration, Banking Law, Bankruptcy, Competition Law, Constitutional Law, Construction Law, Consumer Protection Law, Conveyancing Law, Corporate Law, Distributorship, Agency and Franchise Law, Employer's Liability, Entertainment Law, Environmental Law, Foreign Investments, Immigration Law, Insurance Law, International Contracts, International Private Law, Litigation, Maritime and Admiralty Law, Negligence Law, Oil and Mining Law, Personal Injury Law, Product Liability Law, Property and Real Estate Law, Rent and Lease, Trade Regulations, Transportation Law, General Legal Practice, Intellectual Property, Copyright Law, Licence Negotiation, Patent Litigation, Trademark Litigation, Trademark Prosecution, Transfer of Technology, General Intellectual Property Practice, Capital Taxation, Corporate Taxation, Customs Duties, Deferred Taxation, Indirect Taxation, Inheritance, Estate and Gift Taxation, International Taxation, Personal Income Taxation, Sales, Turnover, Value Added Taxes, Taxation of Foreign Nationals, Taxation of Oil and Mining Companies, Transfer Pricing, Exchange Control, General Tax Practice.

FIRM PROFILE: *Allen Allen & Hemsley is an internationally based firm in terms of the clients it represents and the transactions in which it has been involved. In addition, the background of its lawyers and its links with law firms in major financial and commercial centres of the world assist with the international nature of the practice. Total number of partners for Allen Allen & Hemsley is 62, total legal staff is over 200, and for the Allens Arthur Robinson group total staff is over 700. The firm's areas of specialization include: Corporate and Commercial; Finance and Banking; Litigation; Intellectual Property; Tax; Resources; Environment and Planning; Construction and Property; Government Liaison; Media and Communications.*

MEMBERS OF FIRM

HUGH HUNTER JAMIESON, admitted, 1954, New South Wales; 1985, Western Australia; 1989, Victoria. *Education:* University of Sydney (B.A.; LL.B.). *LANGUAGES:* English. *PRACTICE AREAS:* Intellectual Property; Commercial Litigation.

IAN RAINY LANCE HARPER, admitted, 1955, New South Wales; 1981, Western Australia; 1989, Victoria. *Education:* University of Sydney (B.A.; LL.B.). *LANGUAGES:* English. *PRACTICE AREAS:* Corporate Law; Entertainment Law.

FREDERICK PAUL LIND, admitted, 1961, New South Wales; 1982, Australian Capital Territory; 1985, Western Australia; 1989, Victoria. *Education:* University of Sydney (B.A.; LL.B.). *LANGUAGES:* English. *PRACTICE AREAS:* Litigation.

EZEKIEL SOLOMON, admitted, 1959, New South Wales; 1974, Papua, New Guinea; 1975, United Kingdom; 1976, Hong Kong; 1981, Western Australia; Licensed as Legal Consultant in New York; 1989, Victoria. *Education:* University of Sydney (LL.B. Hons.); Harvard Law School (LL.M.). *LANGUAGES:* English. *PRACTICE AREAS:* Corporate Law; Oil and Mining Law; Foreign Investments.

JOHN BERESFORD DORTER, admitted, 1965, New South Wales; 1971, Australian Capital Territory; 1972, Victoria; 1985, Western Australia; 1989, Northern Territory; 1991, South Australia and High Court of Australia. *Education:* University of Sydney (B.A.; LL.B.). *LANGUAGES:* English. *PRACTICE AREAS:* Arbitration; Construction Law.

JORGEN LOCKE NIELSEN, admitted, 1965, New South Wales; 1985, Western Australia; 1989, Victoria. *Education:* University of Sydney (B.A.; LL.B.). *LANGUAGES:* English. *PRACTICE AREAS:* Corporate Law.

(This Listing Continued)

ALLEN ALLEN & HEMSLEY, Sydney, New South Wales—Continued

NEIL MATHESON CAMERON, admitted, 1962, New South Wales; 1985, Western Australia; 1989, Victoria. *Education:* University of Sydney (LL.M.). *LANGUAGES:* English. *PRACTICE AREAS:* Property and Real Estate; General Taxation.

HARRY KEVIN MCCANN, admitted, 1964, New South Wales; 1981, Western Australia. *Education:* University of Sydney (B.A.; LL.B. Hons.); Harvard University (LL.M.). *LANGUAGES:* English. *PRACTICE AREAS:* Corporate Law; Oil and Mining; Foreign Investments.

ROGER GAIRE BLUNT, admitted, 1960, New Zealand; 1968, New South Wales; 1985, Western Australia; 1989, Victoria. *Education:* Canterbury University, New Zealand (LL.B.). *LANGUAGES:* English. *PRACTICE AREAS:* Intellectual Property; Trade Regulation; Product Liability.

JOHN ROBERT FELIX LEHANE, admitted, 1969, New South Wales; 1985, Western Australia; 1989, Victoria. *Education:* University of Sydney (B.A.; LL.M.). *LANGUAGES:* English. *PRACTICE AREAS:* Banking Law; Foreign Investments.

NOEL ALAN HEMMINGS, QC, admitted, 1974, Australian Capital Territory and Northern Territory; 1985, Tasmania; 1986, Victoria; 1991, New South Wales. *LANGUAGES:* English. *PRACTICE AREAS:* Environmental Law.

AMBROSE ANTHONY DUNNE, admitted, 1970, New South Wales; 1982, United Kingdom; 1985, Western Australia; 1989, Victoria. *Education:* University of Sydney (B.A.; LL.B.). *LANGUAGES:* English. *PRACTICE AREAS:* Banking Law.

JAMES WILLIAM DWYER, admitted, 1971, New South Wales; 1989, Victoria. *Education:* University of Sydney (B.A.; LL.B.). *LANGUAGES:* English. *PRACTICE AREAS:* Intellectual Property; Patent and Trademark; Copyright.

JAMES BERNARD THYNNE, admitted, 1968, Victoria; 1974, New South Wales; 1985, Western Australia. *Education:* Australian National University (B.A.; LL.B. Hons); University of London (LL.M.); Institute of Advance Legal Studies, London (Diploma Air-Space Law). *LANGUAGES:* French and English. *PRACTICE AREAS:* Corporate Law; Banking Law; Mining Law.

ALWYN IAN TONKING, admitted, 1971, New South Wales; 1985, Western Australia; 1989, Victoria. *Education:* University of Sydney (B.A.; LL.B.); University of London (LL.M.). *LANGUAGES:* English. *PRACTICE AREAS:* Mining Law; Product Liability; Intellectual Property; Trade Regulation.

*JAMES ANTHONY DUNSTAN, admitted, 1972, New South Wales; 1981, England; 1985, Western Australia; 1987, Hong Kong; 1989, Victoria; 1990, South Australia, Queensland. *Education:* University of Sydney (B.A.; LL.M.). *LANGUAGES:* English. *PRACTICE AREAS:* Banking Law; Foreign Investments.

JOHN ALAN CADELL, admitted, 1972, New South Wales; 1985, Western Australia; 1989, Victoria. *Education:* University of Sydney (B.A.; LL.M.). *LANGUAGES:* English. *PRACTICE AREAS:* Banking Law.

PETER CHRISTIAN GREEN, admitted, 1974, New South Wales; 1981, Western Australia; 1989, Victoria. *Education:* University of Sydney (LL.M. Hons.). *LANGUAGES:* English. *PRACTICE AREAS:* International Tax; Taxation of Oil and Mining Companies.

FREDERICK JOHN CHILTON, admitted, 1974, New South Wales; 1985, Western Australia. *Education:* University of Sydney (B.A.; LL.B. Hons.); Harvard University (LL.M.). *LANGUAGES:* English. *PRACTICE AREAS:* Corporate Law; Mining Law; Transfer of Technology.

PHILIP JOHN KERR, admitted, 1975, New South Wales; 1985, Western Australia. *Education:* University of Sydney (B.A. Hons.; LL.B.). *LANGUAGES:* English. *PRACTICE AREAS:* Patent and Trademark Litigation; Copyright; Intellectual Property.

ANTHONY CECIL BARNETT, admitted, 1969, England; 1971, New South Wales; 1985, Western Australia. *Education:* Cambridge University (M.A. Law). *LANGUAGES:* English. *PRACTICE AREAS:* Conveyancing; Property and Real Estate; Rent and Lease.

JOHN JACQUES ALLEN, admitted, 1975, New South Wales; 1985, Western Australia; 1989, Victoria. *Education:* University of Sydney (B.A.; LL.B.); Harvard University (LL.M.). *LANGUAGES:* English. *PRACTICE AREAS:* Corporate Law; Oil and Mining; Transfer of Technology.

(This Listing Continued)

PETER STEWART CAMERON, admitted, 1977, New South Wales; 1985, Western Australia; 1989, Victoria. *Education:* University of Sydney (B.A.; LL.B.). *LANGUAGES:* English. *PRACTICE AREAS:* Corporate Law.

LAWRENCE MARK MAGID, admitted, 1977, New York; 1981, U.S. Tax Court; 1983, New South Wales; 1985, Western Australia; 1989, Victoria. *Education:* Boston University (B.A.; J.D.); New York University (LL.M. in Taxation). *LANGUAGES:* English. *PRACTICE AREAS:* International Tax; Corporate Taxation.

PHILLIP JAMES CORNWELL, admitted, 1980, New South Wales; 1981, High Court; 1985, Western Australia; 1989, Victoria. *Education:* University of Sydney (B.A.; LL.B. 1st Class Hons.). *LANGUAGES:* English. *PRACTICE AREAS:* Banking Law.

DICCON JOHN ROBERTSON LOXTON, admitted, 1978, New South Wales; 1985, Western Australia; 1989, Victoria. *Education:* University of Sydney (B.A.; LL.B.). *LANGUAGES:* English. *PRACTICE AREAS:* Banking Law.

DAVID ALLAN WILSON MALONEY, admitted, 1971, Western Australia; 1981, New South Wales; 1989, Victoria. *Education:* University of Western Australia (LL.B.). *LANGUAGES:* English. *PRACTICE AREAS:* Oil and Mining; Corporate.

JUDITH PATRICIA MUTTON, admitted, 1958, New South Wales; 1985, Western Australia; 1989; Victoria. *Education:* University of Sydney (B.A.; LL.B.). *LANGUAGES:* English. *PRACTICE AREAS:* Conveyancing; Property and Real Estate; Rent and Lease.

STEPHEN JOHN WALKER, admitted, 1977, New South Wales; 1985, Western Australia. *Education:* Australian National University (LL.B. Hons.); University of Virginia (LL.M.). *LANGUAGES:* English. *PRACTICE AREAS:* Corporate Law.

ANDREW ROSS BOXALL, admitted, 1978, New South Wales; 1985, England and Wales; 1987, Western Australia; 1989, Victoria and Hong Kong. *Education:* University of Sydney (B.A. Hons.; LL.B.); Universite de Paris II (D.S.U.). *LANGUAGES:* French and English. *PRACTICE AREAS:* Banking Law; Foreign Investments.

JOHN KERIN MORGAN, admitted, 1973, New South Wales; 1989, Victoria. *Education:* University of Sydney (B.A.; LL.M.). *LANGUAGES:* English. *PRACTICE AREAS:* Corporate Law; Insurance Law.

TIMOTHY IGNATIUS L'ESTRANGE, admitted, 1980, New South Wales; 1989, Victoria. *Education:* University of New South Wales (B.Com.; LL.B.). *LANGUAGES:* English. *PRACTICE AREAS:* Litigation; Produce Liability; Intellectual Property.

RICHARD JAMES ALCOCK, admitted, 1981, New South Wales; 1989, Victoria. *Education:* University of New South Wales (B.com; LL.B.). *LANGUAGES:* English. *PRACTICE AREAS:* Corporate and Commercial Law; Investment in Asia.

MARK RICHMOND, admitted, 1981, New South Wales; 1989, Victoria. *Education:* University of Sydney (B.Ec.; LL.B. Hons.). *LANGUAGES:* English. *PRACTICE AREAS:* Taxation.

MICHAEL LEE BALL, admitted, 1980, South Australia; 1983, New South Wales; 1989, Victoria. *Education:* University of Adelaide (B.A. Hons.; LL.B. Hons.). *LANGUAGES:* English. *PRACTICE AREAS:* Litigation; Negligence Law.

STEPHEN JOHN MENZIES, admitted, 1983, Victoria; 1985, New South Wales. *Education:* University of Sydney (B.Ec.; LL.B.); University of London (LL.M.). *LANGUAGES:* English. *PRACTICE AREAS:* Corporate Law; Foreign Investments.

STEPHEN ARTHUR HIBBERT, admitted, 1984, New South Wales; 1989, Victoria. *Education:* University of Sydney (BE. Civil; LL.M.). *LANGUAGES:* English. *PRACTICE AREAS:* Construction Law; Arbitration.

EWEN GRAHAM WOLSELEY CROUCH, admitted, 1980, New South Wales; 1989; Victoria. *Education:* University of Sydney (B.Ec. Hons.; LL.B.). *LANGUAGES:* English. *PRACTICE AREAS:* Corporate Law.

CATHERINE PATRICIA PARR, admitted, 1982, New South Wales; 1989, Victoria. *Education:* University of New South Wales (B.Com.; LL.B.). *LANGUAGES:* English. *PRACTICE AREAS:* Banking Law.

DAVID HUGH CLIFFORD, admitted, 1976, South Australia; 1982, New South Wales; 1989, Victoria. *Education:* University of Adelaide (LL.B. Hons.). *LANGUAGES:* English. *PRACTICE AREAS:* Banking Law.

(This Listing Continued)

ALEC LEOPOLD, admitted, 1981, Australian Capital Territory; 1982, New South Wales; 1989, Victoria. *Education:* Australian National University (LL.B. Hons.). *LANGUAGES:* English. *PRACTICE AREAS:* Copyright; Intellectual Property Litigation.

MARK WORMELL, admitted, 1982, New South Wales. *Education:* Macquarie University (B.A.; LL.B.). *LANGUAGES:* English. *PRACTICE AREAS:* Banking Law.

IAN ROBERT WALLACE, admitted, 1981, New South Wales. *Education:* University of Sydney (B.Ec.; LL.B.). *LANGUAGES:* English. *PRACTICE AREAS:* Banking Law.

ROBERT DAVID JEREMY, admitted, 1982, New South Wales. *Education:* University of Sydney (B.A. Hons.; LL.B.). *LANGUAGES:* English. *PRACTICE AREAS:* Corporate Law; Admiralty and Maritime Law.

ANTONY ENORE MOLINO, admitted, 1980, New South Wales; 1990, South Australia. *Education:* University of New South Wales (B.A.; LL.B.). *LANGUAGES:* English. *PRACTICE AREAS:* Construction Law; Arbitration.

TONY JOSEPH WASSAF, admitted, 1980, New South Wales. *Education:* University of New South Wales (B.Comm.; LL.B.). *LANGUAGES:* English. *PRACTICE AREAS:* Oil and Mining Law.

IAN GARTH MCGILL, admitted, 1981, New South Wales. *Education:* University of New South Wales (B.Sc.; LL.B.); University of Virginia (LL.M.). *LANGUAGES:* English. *PRACTICE AREAS:* Entertainment Law; Intellectual Property.

LYNNE MAREE HARMAN, admitted, 1982, New South Wales. *Education:* University of Sydney (B.A.; LL.M.). *LANGUAGES:* English. *PRACTICE AREAS:* Litigation.

IAN HUNTLY PHILIP, admitted, 1983, New South Wales. *Education:* Australian National University (B.A., Hons. 1st Class); University of New South Wales (LL.B.). *LANGUAGES:* English. *PRACTICE AREAS:* Entertainment Law; Intellectual Property.

MICHAEL JOHN GREIG, admitted, 1985, New South Wales; 1989, England. *Education:* University of New South Wales (B.A.; LL.B.). *LANGUAGES:* French and English. *PRACTICE AREAS:* Corporate Law; Foreign Investments.

ROBERT HAVELOCK CORNISH, admitted, 1981, New Zealand; 1989, England, Wales and New South Wales. *Education:* University of Auckland (LL.B. Hons.). *LANGUAGES:* English. *PRACTICE AREAS:* Banking Law.

PETER JOHN ELLIOT ARTHUR, admitted, 1980, South Australia; 1987, New South Wales. *Education:* University of Adelaide (B.A.; LL.B.); Oxford University (BCL). *LANGUAGES:* English. *PRACTICE AREAS:* Litigation.

***ANDREW CAMPBELL CLARKE, admitted, 1984, New South Wales; 1987, New York. *Education:* University of Sydney (B. Ec.; LL.B., Hons.). *LANGUAGES:* English. *PRACTICE AREAS:* Corporate Law.

DAVID ANTONY COHEN, admitted, 1984, New South Wales. *Education:* University of Sydney (B.A.; LL.B.). *LANGUAGES:* Japanese and English. *PRACTICE AREAS:* Property and Real Estate; Foreign Investments; Corporate Law.

NEIL VINCENT RADFORD, admitted, 1985, England; 1989, New South Wales. *Education:* Oxford (M.A.). *LANGUAGES:* French and English. *PRACTICE AREAS:* Corporate Law.

MATTHEW JOHN CRAMER MCCANN, admitted, 1984, New South Wales. *Education:* Macquarie University (B.Ec; LL.B). *LANGUAGES:* English. *PRACTICE AREAS:* Commercial; Property; Corporate and Resources; Technology Law.

ANDREW ROSS BEATTY, admitted, 1985, New South Wales. *Education:* Sydney University (B.A.; LL.B.). *LANGUAGES:* English. *PRACTICE AREAS:* Environmental; Town Planning; Commercial Litigation.

TIMOTHY GORDON BEDNALL, admitted, 1984, South Australia; 1993, New South Wales. *Education:* Adelaide University (LL.B., Hons) (1st Class Hons.). *LANGUAGES:* English. *PRACTICE AREAS:* Corporate.

JOHN DOMINIC MARTIN, admitted, 1985, New South Wales. *Education:* Macquarie University (B.A.; LL.B. Hons.). *LANGUAGES:* English. *PRACTICE AREAS:* Corporate; Securities.

(This Listing Continued)

ALAN GEORGE GRAHAM MAXTON, admitted, 1985, New South Wales. *Education:* University of Sydney (B.Ec., LL.B. Hons.). *LANGUAGES:* English and Hebrew. *PRACTICE AREAS:* Banking; Finance.

LESLEY RONDA MINNS, admitted, 1990, New South Wales; 1986, Victoria. *Education:* University of Melbourne (B.A.; LL.B.). *LANGUAGES:* English. *PRACTICE AREAS:* Procurement Construction and Engineering related Contract Drafting and Disputes Work.

MICHAEL BRUCE ROSE, admitted, 1985, New South Wales; 1990, High Court and Federal Court of Australia; 1991, Queensland; 1994, England and Wales. *Education:* University of New South Wales (B.A.; LL.B.). *LANGUAGES:* English. *PRACTICE AREAS:* Commercial Litigation; Intellectual Property; Media.

CONSULTANTS

GRAHAM GEORGE COOKE, admitted, 1954, New South Wales; 1989, Victoria. *Education:* University of Sydney (B.A.; LL.B.). *LANGUAGES:* English. *PRACTICE AREAS:* Corporate Law.

PATRICK BRAZIL, admitted, 1953, Barrister, Supreme Court of Queensland; Australian Capital Territory; New South Wales; Victoria; Western Australia; South Australia. *Education:* University of Queensland (B.A., LL.B. Hons.). Member, Roll of Practitioners, High Court of Australia. *LANGUAGES:* English. *PRACTICE AREAS:* Administrative Law.

THOMAS WAYMOUTH MAGNEY, admitted, 1954, New South Wales; 1981, Western Australia; 1989, Victoria. *Education:* University of Sydney (LL.M. 1st Class Hons.). *LANGUAGES:* English. *PRACTICE AREAS:* Capital Taxation; Corporate Taxation; International Taxation.

JOHN JOSEPH MCGLINCHEY, admitted, 1950, New South Wales; 1981, Western Australia; 1989, Victoria. *LANGUAGES:* English. *PRACTICE AREAS:* Corporate Law; Oil and Mining Law.

PHILIP JOHN LETHBRIDGE KING, admitted, 1962, New South Wales; 1981, Western Australia; 1989, Victoria. *Education:* University of Sydney (B.A.; LL.B.). *LANGUAGES:* English. *PRACTICE AREAS:* Property and Real Estate Law; Conveyancing Law; Rent and Lease.

JILLIAN SHIRLEY SEGAL, admitted, 1979, New South Wales; 1987, Western Australia. *Education:* University of New South Wales (B.A. Hons., LL.B.); Harvard University (LL.M.). *LANGUAGES:* English. *PRACTICE AREAS:* Environmental Law; Corporate Law.

FRANK JOHN CONROY. *Education:* University of Western Australia (B.Com.); Macquarie University (M.B.A.). *LANGUAGES:* English.

DIANE ROSS, admitted, 1981, New South Wales. *Education:* ANU (B.Ec.; LL.B.); Sydney (LL.M.). *LANGUAGES:* English. *PRACTICE AREAS:* Superannuation and Tax.

JERROLD CRIPPS, admitted, 1956, New South Wales. *Education:* University of Sydney (LL.B.; LL.M.). *LANGUAGES:* English. *PRACTICE AREAS:* Environmental Law; Commercial Litigation; Local Government.

*Resident Partner, Allens Arthur Robinson, London, England
***Resident Partner, Allens Arthur Robinsonn, New York, U.S.A.

Languages: English, Cantonese, French, German, Indonesian, Italian, Japanese, Mandarin, Spanish.

BAKER & McKENZIE

A.M.P. CENTRE
50 BRIDGE STREET
SYDNEY, NEW SOUTH WALES 2000, AUSTRALIA
Telephone: (02) 225-0200
Intn'l. Dialing: (61-2) 225-0200
Cable Address: ABOGADO
Telex: AA21618
Answer Back: ABOGADO AA21618
Facsimile: (61-2) 223-7711

Postal Address: Box R126, Royal Exchange P.O.

Associated Offices of Baker & McKenzie in: Almaty, Amsterdam, Bangkok, Barcelona, Beijing, Berlin, Bogotá, Brasília, Brussels, Budapest, Buenos Aires, Cairo, Caracas, Chicago, Dallas, Frankfurt, Geneva, Hanoi, Ho Chi Minh City, Hong Kong, Juárez, Kiev, London, Madrid, Manila, Melbourne, México City, Miami, Milan, Monterrey, Moscow, New York, Palo Alto, Paris, Prague, Rio de Janeiro, Riyadh, Rome, St. Petersburg, San Diego, San Francisco, São

(This Listing Continued)

BAKER & McKENZIE, Sydney, New South Wales—
Continued

Paulo, Singapore, Stockholm, Taipei, Tijuana, Tokyo, Toronto,
Valencia, Warsaw, Washington, D.C. and Zürich.
Correspondent Law Firm: Hadiputranto, Hadinoto & Partners, Jakarta.

MEMBERS OF FIRM

MICHAEL C. AHRENS, admitted, 1960, New South Wales, Australia;
1969, Victoria, Australia and England; 1972, Hong, Kong; 1975, A.C.T.,
Australia. *Education:* University of Sydney (LL.B.); Harvard University
(LL.M.).

FRANK CAHILL, born Broken Hill, Australia; admitted, 1984, New
South Wales, Australia; 1987, Victoria, Australia. *Education:* University of
New South Wales (B.Sc.; M.G); University of Sydney (Dip. Law; B.A.B.).

MARK D. CHAPPLE, born Sydney, Australia; admitted, 1981, New
South Wales, Australia; 1988, Victoria, Australia. *Education:* University of
Sydney (B.E., LL.B.).

JOHN A. CONNORS, admitted, 1975 Victoria, Australia; 1978, New
South Wales, Australia; 1981, England and Wales; 1984, Hong Kong. *Education:* University of Melbourne (B.A., LL.B. (Hons), Dip., Crim.); University of London (LL.M.).

GRAEME J. DICKSON, born Sydney, Australia; admitted, 1978, New
South Wales, Australia; 1988, Victoria, Australia; 1992, Queensland, Aus-
tralia. *Education:* University of New South Wales (B.Comm., Accountancy;
LL.B.); University of Sydney (LL.M.). *Member:* Law Society of New South
Wales.

PETER T. DWIGHT, admitted, 1971, New South Wales, Australia;
1976, Victoria, Australia; 1977, A.C.T., Australia; U.S. Court of Appeals
for the District of Columbia Circuit and U.S. Court of Appeals, Seventh
Circuit; 1980, England; 1981, Hong Kong; 1982, Northern Territory, Australia. *Education:* University of Sydney (B.A., LL.B., Hons.); University of
Michigan (LL.M.).

STEVEN M. GLANZ, admitted, 1978, New South Wales, Australia;
1984, Victoria, Australia. *Education:* University of New South Wales
(B.Comm., LL.B.); Columbia University, New York, USA (LL.M.).

RICHARD T. GOUGH, born Woking Surrey, United Kingdom; admit-
ted, 1985, Solicitor of Supreme Court of England and Wales; 1989, New
South Wales, Australia; 1990, Victoria, Australia. *Education:* University of
Leeds (B.A. Hons.); University of Hull; College of Law, Chester. *Member:*
Law Society of England and Wales.

GEORGE C. HARRIS, admitted, 1979, New South Wales, Australia;
1985, Victoria, Australia. *Education:* University of Sydney (B.A., LL.B.,
LL.M.).

DAVID L. JACOBS, born Australia; admitted, 1976, New South Wales,
Australia; 1988, Victoria and Western Australia. *Education:* University of
Sydney (B.A.; LL.B.; LL.M.). *Member:* New Council of Australia; Law
Society of New South Wales. *LANGUAGES:* English.

MICHAEL J. KUNSTLER, admitted, 1982, New South Wales, Australia; 1988, Victoria, Australia. *Education:* Sydney University (B.EC.; LL.B.).
Member: New South Wales Law Society.

ROSS G. MCLEAN, born, London, England; admitted, 1980, New
South Wales, Australia; 1988, Victoria, Australia. *Education:* University of
New South Wales (B.A.); Sydney University (LL.B., Hons); London University (LL.M., Dist). Tutor in Law, Department of Accounting, University
of Sydney, 1983.

ROY E. MELICK, born Sydney, Australia; admitted, 1975, New South
Wales and Victoria, Australia. *Education:* University of New South Wales
(B.A.); University of Sydney (LL.B.). *Member:* Law Society of New South
Wales; Law Council of Australia (Member, Business Law Section).

TIMOTHY P. O'DOHERTY, born Newcastle, Australia; admitted,
1983, New South Wales, Australia; 1990, Victoria, Australia. *Education:*
University of Sydney (B.E.; LL.B.). *Member:* Law Society of New South
Wales.

RALPH B. PLINER, admitted, 1976, South Africa (Transvaal) and
Lesotho; 1980, Victoria and New South Wales, Australia. *Education:* University of Witwatersrand (B.Comm., LL.B.); University of Cambridge
(postgraduate, LL.B.).

(This Listing Continued)

ROBERT I. RICHARDS, admitted 1974, New South Wales, Australia;
1989, Victoria; 1991, High Court of Australia. *Education:* University of
New South Wales (B.Comm.); University of Sydney (LL.B.).

ANDREW M. SALGO, admitted, 1978, New South Wales, Australia;
1984, Victoria; 1986, High Court of Australia. *Education:* University of
New South Wales (B.A., LL.B.).

CHRISTOPHER J. SAXON, born, Australia; admitted, 1982, New
South Wales, Australia; 1987, England and Wales; 1988, Victoria, Australia. *Education:* University of Sydney (B.Ec.; LL.B.).

RODNEY STONE, admitted, 1978, New South Wales, Australia; 1985,
Victoria, Australia and England and Wales. *Education:* Sydney University
(B.A.; LL.B.); Columbia University (LL.M.).

TIMOTHY A. WOODHOUSE, admitted, 1974, New Zealand; 1980,
New South Wales, Australia and Victoria, Australia; 1987, England. *Edu-
cation:* University of Auckland (B.A., LL.B., Hons.); University of Virginia
(LL.M.).

EDWIN J. ZEMANCHEFF, admitted, 1984, New South Wales; 1985,
High Court of Australia; 1987, Victoria. *Education:* Sydney University (Diploma of Law). *Member:* Law Society of New South Wales.

LOCAL PARTNERS

FRANK J. CASTIGLIA, born, Sydney, Australia; admitted, 1986, New
South Wales, Australia. *Education:* University of New South Wales
(B.Comm.; LL.B.).

CHRISTOPHER J. CONNOR, born, Hobart, Tasmania; admitted,
1985, Tasmania and High Court of Australia; 1987, New South Wales,
Australia. *Education:* University of Tasmania (B.Com.; LL.B.). *Member:*
Taxation Institute of Australia.

JOHN R. FABBRO, admitted, 1983, New South Wales, Australia;
1990, Victoria, Australia. *Education:* University of New South Wales
(B.Comm.; LL.B.); London School of Economic and Political Science; University of London (LL.M.). *Member:* Law Society of New South Wales.

JOAN T. FITZHENRY, born Casino, New South Wales, Australia;
admitted, 1978, New South Wales, Australia; 1990, Victoria, Australia.
Education: University of Sydney (LL.B.). *Member:* Law Society of New
South Wales.

ANTHONY J. FOLEY, born Narrandera, Australia; admitted, 1983,
New South Wales, Australia. *Education:* Sydney University (LL.B.); Lon-
don School of Economics, University of London (LL.M.). *Member:* Law
Society of New South Wales.

JAMES A. HAMILTON, born Sydney, Australia; admitted 1982, New
South Wales, Australia; 1984, A.C.T., Australia. *Education:* University of
New South Wales (B.Comm; LL.B.).

FIONA J. INVERARITY, born Australia; admitted, 1985, New South
Wales, Australia; 1986, High Court of Australia; 1992, Victoria, Australia.
Education: University of Sydney (B.E.; LL.B.).

CAROLYN D. MALL, born Sydney, Australia; admitted, 1989, New
South Wales, Australia. *Education:* University of Sydney (B.A.; LL.B.).

BENJAMIN T. MCLAUGHLIN, born Queensland, Australia, 1960;
admitted, 1987, Queensland, Australia. *Education:* University of Queensland (B.Conn.; LL.B., Hons., 1986).

MICHAEL J. REED, born Sydney, Australia; admitted, 1979, Solicitor
of Supreme Court of New South Wales, Australia; 1983, Barrister and So-
licitor of Supreme Court of Victoria, Australia; 1984, Solicitor of Supreme
Court of England and Wales and Hong Kong. *Education:* University of
New South Wales (B.Comm., LL.B.); Sydney University (LL.M.). *Member:*
Law Society of New South Wales; Law Institute of Victoria.

TIMOTHY J. REED, born Australia; admitted 1982, New South Wales,
Australia; 1990, Victoria, Australia. *Education:* University of New South
Wales (B.A.; LL.B.).

GEOFFREY J. SHORT, born Toowoomba, Queensland; admitted,
1978, A.C.T., Australia; 1990, New South Wales, Australia; 1993, Victoria,
Australia. *Education:* Australian National University (B.Ec.; LL.B.); University of Technology, Sydney (LL.M.).

PENELOPE J. WARD, born Australia; admitted, 1984, New South
Wales and Victoria, Australia. *Education:* Monash University (B.A., Hons.;
LL.B.).

(This Listing Continued)

TIMOTHY H. WEEKES, born Sydney, Australia; admitted, 1976, New South Wales, Australia; 1977, A.C.T., Australia; 1979, Victoria, Australia. *Education:* University of New South Wales (B.Comm.; LL.B.).

ASSOCIATES

ANNE-MARIE L. ALLGROVE, born Taipei, Taiwan; admitted, 1992, New South Wales and A.C.T., Australia. *Education:* Australia National University (B.A.,; LL.B.). *LANGUAGES:* French.

SUSAN P. BAINES, born Melbourne, Australia; admitted, 1992, New South Wales, Australia. *Education:* University of Queensland (B.A.; LL.B.). *LANGUAGES:* English, French, Italian.

ANDREW J. D. BARCLAY, born Auckland, New Zealand; admitted 1981, New Zealand; 1986, Victoria, Australia. *Education:* Auckland University (LL.B., Hons); Monash University (Dip. Com. Law, LL.M.).

LIBBIE J. BIGGIN, born Melbourne, Australia; admitted 1989, Victoria, Australia. *Education:* Monash University (B.Ec., LL.B.).

STEPHANIE M. BRONK, born Gisbarne, New Zealand, 1955; admitted, 1990, News South Wales, Australia. *Education:* University of Technology (LL.B., 1989).

PAUL G. BROWN, born Sydney, Australia, 1963; admitted, 1991, New South Wales, Australia. *Education:* University of Sydney (B.A., 1984); Solicitors Admissions Board (Dip. Law, 1989).

DORA S. Y. CHAN, born Hong Kong; admitted, 1991, Hong Kong (Not admitted in Australia). *Education:* University of Hong Kong (LL.B., 1988; Postgraduate Certificate in Laws, 1989).

LESLIE J. CHRISTY, born Victoria, Australia; admitted, 1993, New South Wales, Australia. *Education:* Monash University (B.Sc.); University of Melbourne (B.Sc.); University of Cambridge (M.Phil.); University of Sydney (LL.B.); University of Technology, Sydney (G.D.Leg.Practice).

JULIEANNE E. COX, born Mudgee, New South Wales, Australia, February 23, 1966; admitted, 1990, New South Wales, Australia. *Education:* University of New South Wales (B.A., 1984; LL.B., 1989). *Member:* Law Society of New South Wales.

JOHN A. ELLIS, born, Sydney, Australia, 1961; admitted, 1992, New South Wales, Australia. *Education:* Sydney University (B.Ec., 1990); Sydney University Law School (LL.B., Hons., 1992).

PRISCA SHING LAN FAI, born, Kota, Kinabalu, 1964; admitted, 1989, New South Wales, Australia. *Education:* University of New South Wales (M.Comm., 1991); Australian National University (LL.B., 1989). *Member:* New South Wales Law Society. *LANGUAGES:* Chinese (Mandarin, Cantonese, Hakka), Malay.

HOWARD H. FRASER, born San Francisco, California; admitted, 1987, New South Wales, Australia. *Education:* University of Sydney (B.A.; LL.B.); Kings College, University of London (LL.M.).

SANDRA K. GIBBONS, born Sydney, Australia,; admitted, 1990, New South Wales, Australia. *Education:* University of Sydney (B.A., Hons., 1977); University of New South Wales (LL.B., 1989). *Member:* Law Society of New South Wales.

MICHAEL G. GIBSON, born Australia; admitted, 1987, New South Wales, Australia. *Education:* Macquarie University (B.A.; LL.B.); Macquarie University Law School (LL.B.).

STEVEN M. GOODMAN, born South Africa, 1967; admitted, 1991, New South Wales, Australia. *Education:* University of Australia (B.Comm., 1991; LL.B., 1991).

CHRISTINE E. GRAY, born, Sydney, Australia, 1969; admitted, 1992, New South Wales, Australia. *Education:* Macquarie University (LL.B., 1992).

PHILIP G. GRAY, born Sydney, Australia; admitted, 1992, New South Wales, Australia. *Education:* University of Sydney (B.A.; LL.B., Hons.). *LANGUAGES:* German.

PAULINE J. GULLEFORD, admitted, 1986, England (Not admitted in Australia). *Education:* Kingston Polytechnic (LL.B., Hons.); Council of Legal Education (Barrister at Law).

MICHAEL R. HALL, born Alsagier, United Kingdom; admitted, 1988, Massachusetts, U.S.A.; 1991, New South Wales, Australia. *Education:* Oxford University (B.A., 1986; B.C.L., 1987); Harvard University. *LANGUAGES:* French.

KAREN HANIGAN, born Sydney, Australia, 1966; admitted, 1989, New South Wales, Australia. *Education:* Sydney University (B.A., 1987; LL.B., 1989). *Member:* Law Society of New South Wales. *LANGUAGES:* German.

SALLY A. HANSON, born Sydney, New South Wales, Australia; admitted, 1984, New South Wales, Australia; 1985, South Australia, Australia. *Education:* University of Sydney (B.A. Hons., LL.B.).

WILLIAM HARA, born Istanbul, 1966; admitted, 1989, New South Wales, Australia. *Education:* University of New South Wales (LL.B., 1989).

DIANE E. HOUGHTON, born Horace, Zimbabwe; admitted, 1993, New South Wales, Australia. *Education:* University of the Witwatersrand (B.A.; Higher Diploma in Education); University of Cape Town (LL.B.); University of Tasmania (LL.B., Hons.).

TERESA M. LENTILE, born Sydney, Australia, 1961; admitted, 1984, New South Wales, Australia; 1990, England. *Education:* University of Sydney (B.Economics, 1982; B.Laws, Hons., 1984). *Member:* Law Society of England. *LANGUAGES:* Italian.

BRONWYN M. JAMES, born Sydney, Australia, 1966; admitted, 1989, New South Wales, Australia. *Education:* University of Sydney (B.A.; LL.B., 1989). *LANGUAGES:* English, French.

ANDREW W. JONES, born Sydney, Australia; admitted, 1993, New South Wales, Australia. *Education:* Bond University (B.Comm.; LL.B.).

FRANCES A. KYRIKOS, born Parramatta, Australia, 1966; admitted, 1989, New South Wales, Australia. *Education:* Sydney University (Economics, 1986; LL.B., 1988). *LANGUAGES:* Greek, French.

SCOTT LAYCOCK, born Sydney, Australia, 1964; admitted, 1989, New South Wales, Australia; 1991, England and Wales. *Education:* Sydney University (B.A., 1987; Dip. Law, 1989). *Member:* Law Society of New South Wales; Law Society of England.

CINDY J. LAZARUS, born Sydney, Australia; admitted, 1994, New South Wales, Australia. *Education:* University of Wollongong (B.Comm.); University of Technology, Sydney (LL.B.).

RHONDA LEE QUAN, born Australia, 1966; admitted, 1990, New South Wales, Australia. *Education:* University of Sydney (B.Ec., LL.B., 1990).

KELLI S. LONGWORTH, born, Sydney, Australia, 1967; admitted, 1992, New South Wales, Australia. *Education:* University of Queensland (B.A., Hons., 1989; LL.B., 1991). *LANGUAGES:* Japanese.

SARAH A. L. MADEW, born Queanbeyan, Australia, 1964; admitted, 1988, New South Wales, Australia; 1992, England and Wales. *Education:* University of Sydney (B.A., 1984; LL.B., 1987); University of Tübingen (LL.M., 1989). *LANGUAGES:* English, German and French.

JONATHAN M. MARQUARD, born Hillbrow, 1967; admitted, 1991, New South Wales, Australia. *Education:* University of New South Wales (B.A., 1987); University of Tasmania (B.A., LL.B., Hons., 1990). *Member:* Law Society of New South Wales. Fellow, University of Tasmania Council, 1990.

DAVID C. MCCREDIE, born, Sydney, Australia, 1967; admitted, 1993, New South Wales, Australia. *Education:* University of Sydney (B.A., 1990; LL.B., 1992). *Member:* Law Society of New South Wales. *LANGUAGES:* French, German and Italian.

ANNA L. MCHUGH, born Caterham, England; admitted, 1994, New South Wales, Australia. *Education:* University of Technology, Sydney (LL.B.).

KERRY E. MEDD, born Armidale, New South Wales, Australia; admitted, 1994, Sydney, Australia. *Education:* University of Sydney (B.A.; LL.B.). *LANGUAGES:* French.

DEREK A. NEVE, born Amsford, England; admitted 1991, New South Wales, Australia. *Education:* University of Sydney (LL.B., 1991); University of Freiburg (LL.M., 1993). *LANGUAGES:* German.

C. MARY NIXON, born Sydney, Australia; admitted, 1986, New South Wales, Australia. *Education:* New South Wales Institute of Technology (LL.B., Hons.).

NICHOLAS J. O'DAY, born Australia, 1962; admitted, 1989, Queensland, Australia; 1990, New South Wales, Australia; 1993, Hong Kong. *Education:* University of Queensland (B.Comm., 1983; LL.B., 1986). *LANGUAGES:* English.

(This Listing Continued)

(This Listing Continued)

BAKER & McKENZIE, *Sydney, New South Wales—
Continued*

NICHOLAS B. PAPPAS, born Sydney, Australia; admitted, 1982, New South Wales, Australia. *Education:* Sydney University Law School (LL.B.; LL.M.).

STEVEN M. PATEMAN, born Sydney, Australia, 1967; admitted, 1992, New South Wales, Australia. *Education:* University of New South Wales (B.Comm., 1991; LL.B., 1991). *Member:* Law Society of New South Wales.

JEFFREY V. RODWELL, born Brisbane, Australia; admitted, 1991, New South Wales, Australia. *Education:* University of New South Wales (B.S.W., 1978; LL.B., 1991).

MARK A. RUSSELL, born Cronulla, Australia, 1959; admitted, 1989, New South Wales. *Education:* Macquarie University (B.A., 1981); University of New South Wales (LL.B., 1985); Sydney University.

LYNNE M. SAUNDER, born Victoria, Australia; admitted, 1986, Victoria, Australia and High Court of Australia; 1988, New South Wales; 1992, England and Wales. *Education:* Melbourne University (B.A.; LL.B. Hons.).

CHERYL L. SLUSARCHUK, born Halifax, Nova Scotia, 1964; admitted, 1993, New South Wales, Australia. *Education:* University of Calgary (B.Comm., 1986); McGill University (LL.B., 1992).

ROGER D. SOO, born Bankstown, Australia, 1970; admitted, 1993, New South Wales, Australia. *Education:* University of Sydney (B.A.; LL.B., 1993). *LANGUAGES:* Italian, French and Chinese.

CHIAKI SUGISHITA-MAHNKEN, born Japan, 1963; admitted, 1992, New South Wales, Australia. *Education:* University of Tasmania (B.A., LL.B., 1991). *Member:* New South Wales Law Society. *LANGUAGES:* Japanese.

ANNETTE TECKEMEIER, born Bov, Denmark, 1962; admitted, 1989, Denmark (Not admitted in Australia). *Education:* Aarhus University (LL.M., 1989); University of Chicago (LL.M., 1990). *LANGUAGES:* Danish, Swedish, Norwegian, German, French.

MARTYN P. TIER, born New Zealand, 1966; admitted, 1990, New South Wales, Australia and A.C.T., Australia. *Education:* Australian National University (B.Ec., 1988; LL.B., 1990). *Member:* Law Society of New South Wales.

THOMAS D. WAIT, born Christchurch, New Zealand, 1967; admitted, 1990, New Zealand (Not admitted in Australia). *Education:* University of Canterbury, Christchurch, New Zealand (B.Comm.; LL.B., 1990).

LESLEY A. WATERS, born Leeton, New South Wales, Australia, 1964; admitted, 1987, New South Wales, Australia. *Education:* Macquarie University (B.A., LL.B., 1987); University of Pennsylvania (LL.M., 1991).

STEPHEN J. WATTS, born Sydney, Australia; admitted, 1988, New South Wales, Australia. *Education:* University of Sydney (B.A.); University of Technology (LL.B.). *Member:* Law Society of New South Wales.

ROBERT J. WILCHER, born Melbourne, Australia, March 8, 1961; admitted, 1986, New South Wales. *Education:* University of Sydney (B.A., 1982; LL.B., 1986).

D. JASON WILLIAMS, born Perth, Australia, December 1, 1967; admitted, 1991, Western Australia; 1994, New South Wales. *Education:* University of Western Australia (B.J., 1988; LL.B., 1989). *Member:* Law Society of Western Australia - Young Lawyers' (Committee Member, 1991-1993).

BARKER GOSLING LEGAL GROUP

28TH FLOOR, 135 KING STREET
SYDNEY, NEW SOUTH WALES 2000, AUSTRALIA
Telephone: (02) 391 3333
Fax: (02) 391 3456 Dx: 366 Sydney

Mailing Address: GPO Box 983, Sydney, New South Wales NSW, 2001

A member of Barker Gosling Legal Group comprised the Practices of Barker Gosling in Sydney (NSW), Melbourne (VIC) and Brisbane (QLD), Barker Gosling in Perth (WA), Crossin Barker Gosling in Canberra (ACT).

(This Listing Continued)

FIRM PROFILE: *Barker Gosling Group comprises six long established Practices in the leading commercial centres of Australia. The Group provides a comprehensive range of legal services, both domestic and international, to a wide variety of companies, institutions and individuals. Partners of the Group are active members of the business and legal communities, serving on the Boards of many private and public companies and Committees of Government and Law Societies. All Partners and Senior Associates are admitted in the High Court and all Federal jurisdictions.*

PARTNERS

PETER HUMFREY HENCHMAN, born August 24, 1937; admitted, 1963, New South Wales; 1987, Victoria.

PETER C. B. LARCOMBE, born November 2, 1934; admitted, 1957, New South Wales.

DAVID FRANK CASTLE, born April 23, 1937; admitted, 1961, New South Wales; 1987, Victoria.

DENNIS NEVILLE VUARAN, born January 6, 1948; admitted, 1971, New South Wales; 1987, Victoria.

COLIN JOHN DUNSTON, born August 28, 1948; admitted, 1972, New South Wales; 1988, Victoria.

JULIAN KENT PETERS, born December 10, 1943; admitted, 1971, New South Wales; 1987, Victoria.

ROBERT GEORGE SAUER, born January 5, 1950; admitted, 1974, New South Wales; 1987, Victoria.

RAYMOND AUSTIN NEWTON, born March 24, 1946; admitted, 1973, New South Wales; 1987, Victoria.

DAVID ALEXANDER TURNER, born September 16, 1952; admitted, 1978, New South Wales.

PHILIP ALLAN STEVENS, born February 17, 1949; admitted, 1974, New South Wales.

DEBORAH ANNE SMITHERS, born August 27, 1955; admitted, 1979, New South Wales; 1988, Victoria and Australian Capital Territory.

SUZANNE GAE WILLIAMS, born October 18, 1949; admitted, 1981, New South Wales.

SCOTT ROBERT JAMES SLOAN, born February 24, 1962; admitted, 1985, New South Wales.

KIM ADELE FORD, born October 12, 1959; admitted, 1983, New South Wales.

RICHARD DAVID FOGL, born September 27, 1960; admitted, 1984, New South Wales.

ASSOCIATES

GARRY MICHAEL BLAKE, born October 27, 1961; admitted, 1985, New South Wales; 1989, Vanuatu; 1991, England and Wales.

JENNIFER ANNE FINLAY-JONES, born February 16, 1962; admitted, 1986, New South Wales.

CHARLES WILLIAM BURROUGH, born September 25, 1953; admitted, 1978, England; 1988, New South Wales.

JENNIFER ANNE TALLIS, born June 17, 1962; admitted, 1985, South Australia; 1987, New South Wales.

ELISABETH AMANDA BOYCE, born October 2, 1963; admitted, 1987, New South Wales.

WILLIAM MARK ADDISON, born December 1, 1964; admitted, 1988, New South Wales.

LAURA ELIZABETH HARTLEY, born August 15, 1964; admitted, 1989, New South Wales.

ELIZABETH RUTH CAMPBELL, born January 8, 1966; admitted, 1989, New South Wales.

TIMOTHY JAMES FLAHVIN, born March 15, 1964; admitted, 1992, New South Wales.

CONSULTANTS

Edward Gosling
Peter Thompson

Languages: German, French, Italian, Japanese, Greek and Chinese.

BLAKE DAWSON WALDRON

GROSVENOR PLACE
225 GEORGE STREET
SYDNEY, NEW SOUTH WALES 2000, AUSTRALIA
Telephone: (02) 258 6000
Facsimile: (02) 258 6999
Telex: AA22867 DWN

Melbourne, Victoria, Australia Office: 101 Collins Street, 3000. Telephone: (03) 679 3000. Facsimile: (03) 679 3111. Telex: AA31033.

Brisbane, Queensland, Australia Office: Riverside Centre, 123 Eagle Street, 4000. Telephone: (07) 259 7000. Facsimile: (07) 259-7111. Telex: AA22867DWN.

Perth, Western Australia, Australia Office: Forrest Centre, 221 St. George's Terrace, 6000. Telephone: (09) 366-8000. Facsimile: (09) 366-8111. Telex: AA22867DWN.

Canberra, Australian Capital Territory, Australia Office: 12 Moore Street, 2601. Telephone: (06) 234-4000. Facsimile: (06) 234-4111. Telex: AA22867DWN.

Port Moresby, Papua New Guinea Office: Mogoru Moto Building, Champion Parade. Telephone: (675) 21 1977. Facsimile: (675) 212630. Telex: NE 22223.

London, England Office: 66 Gresham Street, EC2V 7BB. Telephone: (071) 600 3030. Facsimile: (071) 600 3392.

Jakarta, Indonesia Associated Office: Soebagjo, Roosdiono, Jatim & Djarot. Chase Plaza, Jalan Jendral Sudirman Kav. 21, 12910. Telephone: (6221) 570 6436. Fax: (6221) 570 6437. Telex: 62 941 SRJDIA.

Port Vila, Vanuatu Associated Office: Hudson & Co. Lo Lam House, Kumul Highway. Telephone: (678) 22166. Fax: (678) 24260.

FIRM PROFILE: One of Australia's largest national law firms providing legal services in all areas required by commerce, finance and government. The firm has offices in all the major Australian commercial centres. Our practice also has international offices in London, Port Moresby and associated offices in Jakarta and Port Vila.

PARTNERS

JAMES K. ARMITAGE. PRACTICE AREAS: Corporate and Securities.

NICHOLAS CARSON. PRACTICE AREAS: Commercial Litigation; Insurance.

JOHN D. ODBERT. PRACTICE AREAS: Local Government; Commercial Property.

A. JOHN STAMMERS. PRACTICE AREAS: Commercial Property.

HUGH D.H. KELLER. PRACTICE AREAS: Commercial Litigation.

PETER L. JOHNSTONE. PRACTICE AREAS: Commercial Litigation; Insurance.

PHILIP SIMONS. PRACTICE AREAS: Commercial Property.

DAVID R. SOMERVAILLE. PRACTICE AREAS: Corporate and Commercial.

ADRIAN G.H. MORRIS. PRACTICE AREAS: Industrial Relations; Employment.

GRAHAM J. BRADLEY (National Managing Partner).

WILLIAM D.M. CANNON. PRACTICE AREAS: Taxation.

JOHN P. FIELD. PRACTICE AREAS: Banking and Finance Law; Aircraft Financing; Corporate Finance.

PETER J. STAPLETON. PRACTICE AREAS: Corporate; Commercial.

JOHN G. KENCH. PRACTICE AREAS: Antitrust; Business Regulation.

ADAM M. S. BISITS. PRACTICE AREAS: Town and Environmental Planning; Property.

CHRISTOPHER A. GREINER. PRACTICE AREAS: Corporate; Commercial.

RICHARD H. FISHER. PRACTICE AREAS: Insolvencies; Receiverships; Corporate Reconstructions.

C. JOHN GORDON. PRACTICE AREAS: Commercial Property; Retail Banking.

(This Listing Continued)

JOHN V. O'HALLORAN. PRACTICE AREAS: Corporate and Commercial.

RICHARD F. FAWCETT. PRACTICE AREAS: International Capital Markets.

CHRISTOPHER DAVIDSON. PRACTICE AREAS: Commercial Litigation; Construction Litigation.

JOHN P. PAVLAKIS. PRACTICE AREAS: Professional Negligence; Medical Defense.

NICHOLAS KORNER. PRACTICE AREAS: Commercial Litigation.

DAVID J. McGUINNESS. PRACTICE AREAS: Insurance; Professional Negligence.

RICHARD A. ROLFE. PRACTICE AREAS: Banking; Finance.

MARK BRENNAN. PRACTICE AREAS: Environmental Planning; Pollution.

TREVOR E. DANOS. PRACTICE AREAS: Banking; Finance.

MEREDITH K. BEATTIE. PRACTICE AREAS: Commercial Litigation.

ROBERT J. TODD. PRACTICE AREAS: Commercial Litigation; Defamation.

GEOFFREY P. WOOD. PRACTICE AREAS: Infrastructure Projects.

ROBERT N. UPFOLD. PRACTICE AREAS: Income Tax Law.

CRAIG MURRAY. PRACTICE AREAS: Commercial Litigation.

MARK C. BUCHANAN. PRACTICE AREAS: Commercial Litigation; Insurance.

LUCY M. BYLHOUWER. PRACTICE AREAS: Commercial Litigation; Medical Defense.

JEREMY KRIEWALDT. PRACTICE AREAS: Corporate; Commercial.

DAVID S. EAST. PRACTICE AREAS: Corporate and Project Finance.

LISA M. RITSON. PRACTICE AREAS: Information Technology; Antitrust.

HELEN McKENZIE. PRACTICE AREAS: Industrial Relations; Employment Law; Occupational Health and Safety.

DAMIAN REICHEL. PRACTICE AREAS: Corporate; Commercial.

MICHAEL J. ASTILL. PRACTICE AREAS: Environmental Planning; Pollution.

RAYMON E. MAINSBRIDGE. PRACTICE AREAS: Insolvency Law; Receiverships; Liquidations.

DAVID MASON. PRACTICE AREAS: Corporate Finance.

ANTHONY W. RYAN. PRACTICE AREAS: Commercial Litigation; Tourism.

ALDO NICOTRA. PRACTICE AREAS: Intellectual Property; Competition and Trade.

PAUL R. MALLAM. PRACTICE AREAS: Communications; Government Regulation; Trade.

JOHN B. OWENS. PRACTICE AREAS: Regulated Financial Products.

STEPHEN N. NETTLETON. PRACTICE AREAS: Industrial Relations.

LAWRENCE JACKSON. PRACTICE AREAS: Construction Projects; Plain English document drafting.

DAVID A. WILLIAMSON. PRACTICE AREAS: Corporate; Commercial.

CLAYTON UTZ

Solicitors and Attorneys

Established in 1833

LEVELS 27-35
NO. 1 O'CONNELL STREET
SYDNEY, NEW SOUTH WALES 2000, AUSTRALIA
Telephone: (02) 353 4000
Fax: (02) 251 7832

Melbourne, Victoria, Australia Office: Level 18, 333 Collins Street, 3000. Telephone: (03) 286 6000. Fax: (03) 629 8488.

Perth, Western Australia Office: BankWest Tower, 108 St. George's Terrace, 6000. Telephone: (09) 426 8444. Fax: (09) 481 3095. Telex: AA 93232.

Brisbane, Queensland, Australia Office: Levels 18, 19, 23-28 Santos House, 215 Adelaide Street, 4000. Telephone: (07) 228 5811. Fax: (07) 229 7566.

Canberra, Australian Capital Territory, Australia Office: 9th Floor Canberra House, 40 Marcus Clarke Street, 2601. Telephone: (06) 274 0999. Fax: (06) 274 0888.

Clayton Utz operates through national practice groups which focus on banking and financial services; commercial litigation and dispute resolution; competition law; construction; corporate law; corporatization and privatization; energy and natural resources; environment and planning law; insurance law; mergers and acquisitions; product liability; property; taxation and superannuation; technology, computer and intellectual property law; workout, recovery and insolvency; workplace relations and employment law.

FIRM PROFILE: *Clayton Utz is one of Australia's largest and most successful national law firms. Our practice covers the full range of legal, tax and business issues likely to affect investment in and trade with Australia.*

Our clients include public and private corporations, including many from Asia, Europe and the United States; banks, merchant banks and other financial institutions; governments; resource companies; stockbrokers; accounting and other professional firms.

Fundamental to Clayton Utz is its hands-on approach to client needs and a thorough understanding of clients' businesses. The firm's primary aim is to provide commercially sound and practical advice.

SYDNEY PARTNERS

JULIEANN PATRICIA AHERN, admitted, 1980. *Education:* B.A.; LL.B. (NSW). *PRACTICE AREAS:* Product Liability.

MATTHEW ALLCHURCH, admitted, 1985. *Education:* LL.B., (Hons) (Manchester, UK). *LANGUAGES:* French. *PRACTICE AREAS:* Banking and Finance.

DEBORAH BAILEY, admitted, 1981. *Education:* B.Ec.; LL.B. (Syd). *PRACTICE AREAS:* Property Development.

ROBERT CHARLES BARNES, admitted, 1972. *Education:* B.A.; LL.B. (Syd). *PRACTICE AREAS:* Property.

KERRY VINCENT BENNETT, admitted, 1964. *Education:* LL.B. (Syd). Manager, Korea Services Group. *PRACTICE AREAS:* Corporate Law.

ALLAN WILLIAM BLAIKIE, admitted, 1991. *Education:* LL.B. (Qld). *PRACTICE AREAS:* Taxation; Superannuation.

GEOFFREY SPENCER BROWN, admitted, 1968. *Education:* B.A., LL.B. (Syd). *PRACTICE AREAS:* Corporatisation; Privatisation.

SERGIO PETER CAPELLI, admitted, 1984. *Education:* LL.B. (Hons) (Qld). *PRACTICE AREAS:* Construction Law.

IAN CLIFTON CARROLL, admitted, 1971. *Education:* B.A., LL.B., LL.M. (Syd). *PRACTICE AREAS:* Corporate Law.

JOSEPH JOHN CATANZARITI, admitted, 1980. *Education:* B.A., LL.B. (Syd). *LANGUAGES:* Italian. *PRACTICE AREAS:* Employment; Industrial Relations.

SAMUEL STUART CLARK, admitted, 1980. *Education:* B.A., LL.B. (Hons.) (Macquarie). *PRACTICE AREAS:* Product Liability.

MICHAEL THOMAS CORRIGAN, admitted, 1983. *Education:* B.A., LL.B. (Hons.) (ANU). *PRACTICE AREAS:* Trade Practices advice; Litigation.

(This Listing Continued)

DAVID PETER COWLING, admitted, 1982. *Education:* LL.B. (Syd). *PRACTICE AREAS:* Commercial Litigation; Securities Enforcement.

MICHAEL PATRICK COYLE, admitted, 1967. *Education:* Dip. Law (Syd). *PRACTICE AREAS:* Energy and Natural Resources.

CLIVE HORACE CRAVEN, admitted, 1972. *Education:* LL.B. (Hons.) (Syd). *PRACTICE AREAS:* Banking; Finance; Infrastructure.

NOEL ALBERT DAVIS, admitted, 1975. *Education:* LL.B. (Syd). *PRACTICE AREAS:* Taxation; Superannuation.

PHILIP MARK DAWSON, admitted, 1982. *Education:* B.Sc., LL.B. (NSW). *PRACTICE AREAS:* Commercial; Construction; Engineering Litigation.

GLENN DAVID EGGLETON, admitted, 1974. *Education:* B.A., LL.B., LL.M. (Syd). *PRACTICE AREAS:* Product Liability.

GEORGINA JOAN ELLIOTT, admitted, 1983. *Education:* B.A., LL.B. (NSW). *PRACTICE AREAS:* General Commercial Litigation.

JOHN FRANK ELLIOTT, admitted, 1983. *Education:* B.Ec., LL.B. (Syd). *PRACTICE AREAS:* Corporate Law.

JAMES MCHARG FITZSIMONS, admitted, 1982. *Education:* B.A., LL.B. (Syd). *PRACTICE AREAS:* Technology Computer Law; Intellectual Property.

STEPHEN JOHN GATES, admitted, 1970. *Education:* B.A., LL.B., LL.M. (Syd); M.Comp.L. (George Washington). *PRACTICE AREAS:* Taxation; Superannuation.

GLYNN ALLEN GILL, admitted, 1981. *Education:* B.Ec., LL.B., LL.M (Syd); M.B.A. (Deakin, ACT). *PRACTICE AREAS:* Banking; Finance.

ANTHONY MCDONALD GREGG, admitted, 1975. *Education:* B.A., LL.B. (Syd). *PRACTICE AREAS:* Banking; Finance.

GRAEME REDINGTON GEORGE GURNEY, admitted, 1979. *Education:* B.A., LL.B. (Syd). *PRACTICE AREAS:* Banking; Finance.

RODNEY TURNER HALSTEAD, admitted, 1966. *Education:* LL.B. (Syd); LL.M. (London). *PRACTICE AREAS:* Mergers and Acquisitions.

MICHAEL MURRAY HORNIBROOK, admitted, 1961. *Education:* B.A., LL.B. (Syd). *PRACTICE AREAS:* Banking; Finance.

GREGORY RAYMOND JAMES, admitted, 1981. *Education:* B.Com, LL.B. (NSW). *PRACTICE AREAS:* Public Company Takeovers; Corporate Reconstructions.

DOUGLAS SAMUEL JONES, admitted, 1985. *Education:* LL.B.; B.A.; LL.M. (Qld). *PRACTICE AREAS:* Construction Law.

DEAN BERNARD JORDAN, admitted, 1984. *Education:* B.Econ (Portsmouth); Dip.Ed., LL.B., LL.M. (Syd). *PRACTICE AREAS:* Commercial Litigation; Administrative Law.

PETER JOHN KEEL, admitted, 1980. *Education:* B.A., LL.B. (Macquarie); LL.M. (Syd). *PRACTICE AREAS:* Commercial Litigation.

J. RODON KING, admitted, 1966. *Education:* LL.B., LL.M., (Syd). Notary Public (NSW). *PRACTICE AREAS:* Corporate Law; Transport; Tourism.

STEVEN GARRY KLIMT, admitted, 1985. *Education:* B.A.; LL.BB. (Syd). *PRACTICE AREAS:* Credit Act Litigation.

(WILLIAM) PETER KNIGHT, admitted, 1978. *Education:* B.A., LL.B. (Syd); LL.M. (London). *PRACTICE AREAS:* Technology Computer Law; Intellectual Property.

SIBYLLE IRMGARD KRIEGER, admitted, 1980. *Education:* LL.B., (Hons.) (Adelaide); LL.M. (Columbia, NY). *LANGUAGES:* German. *PRACTICE AREAS:* Commercial Litigation.

JOHN WILLIAM LEES, admitted, 1974. *Education:* LL.B. (Syd). *PRACTICE AREAS:* Insurance Law.

JULIE MARION LEVIS, admitted, 1980. *Education:* B.A., LL.B. (NSW). *PRACTICE AREAS:* Commercial Law; Property Law.

GEORGE LIVANES, admitted, 1975. *Education:* B.A., M.A., LL.B. (Syd). *PRACTICE AREAS:* Property; Construction.

COLIN BRUCE LOVEDAY, admitted, 1980. *Education:* B.A., LL.B. (Macquarie). *PRACTICE AREAS:* Product Liability.

JOHN LOXTON, admitted, 1984. *Education:* B.A. (Hons.), LL.B. (Syd). *PRACTICE AREAS:* Banking; Finance.

(This Listing Continued)

MICHAEL BRIAN LYONS, admitted, 1969. *Education:* B.Com, LL.B. (Natal, Sth. Africa); H.Dip. Tax Law, H.Dip Company Law (Witwatersrand, Sth. Africa). *PRACTICE AREAS:* Corporate Law; International Law.

(WILLIAM) ROBERT MCCOMAS, admitted, 1953. *Education:* LL.B. (Syd). *PRACTICE AREAS:* Competition Law.

WALTER LEONARD MCDONALD, admitted, 1981. *Education:* B.Ec., LL.B. (Syd). *PRACTICE AREAS:* Technology R & D Syndications.

PETER CHANEL MCMAHON, admitted, 1979. *Education:* B.A., LL.B. (Syd). *PRACTICE AREAS:* Commercial Property.

ANDREW GEORGE POULOS, admitted, 1979. *Education:* B.A., LL.B. (NSW). *PRACTICE AREAS:* Environment Law; Planning; Local Government Law.

CRAIG PAUL PUDIG, admitted, 1981. *Education:* Diploma of Law (Sydney). *PRACTICE AREAS:* Construction Law.

ANTHONY LAWRENCE REIN, admitted, 1986. *Education:* B.Com, LL.B. (NSW). *PRACTICE AREAS:* Corporate Law.

TREVOR THOMAS ROBINSON, admitted, 1981. *Education:* B.Com, LL.B. (NSW). *PRACTICE AREAS:* Consumer Credit.

PETER ANDREW RUSSELL, admitted, 1984. *Education:* B.Ec., LL.B. (Hons.) (Syd). *PRACTICE AREAS:* Property Law.

BRIAN EDWARD SALTER, admitted, 1981. *Education:* B.A., LL.B. (ANU); LL.M. (Hons.) (Syd). *PRACTICE AREAS:* Securitisation; Banking; Finance.

RONALD WILLIAM SCHAFFER, admitted, 1988. *Education:* B.Ec., LL.B., (Hons.) (Syd). *PRACTICE AREAS:* Commercial and Banking Litigation.

JOHN MARTIN SHIRBIN, admitted, 1975. *Education:* B.A., LL.B. (Syd). *PRACTICE AREAS:* Banking; Finance.

(CATHERINE) MARY STILL, admitted, 1977. *Education:* B.A., LL.B. (Syd). *PRACTICE AREAS:* Intellectual Property.

GRAHAM GREGORY LAWTON TAYLOR, admitted, 1981. *Education:* B.Econ., LL.B. (Syd). *PRACTICE AREAS:* Property Development.

RICHARD MARCUS TOLTZ, admitted, 1963. *Education:* Dip. Law (SAB). *PRACTICE AREAS:* Corporate Law.

RICHARD CLAYTON TRAVERS, admitted, 1977. *Education:* B.A., LL.B. (Syd). *PRACTICE AREAS:* Environment Law; Product Liability.

TONY RAYMOND VERO, admitted, 1982. *Education:* B.Com., LL.B. (NSW). *PRACTICE AREAS:* Commercial Litigation; Insolvency.

SIDNEY WANG, admitted, 1976. *Education:* B.A., LL.B. (Syd). *PRACTICE AREAS:* Commercial Litigation.

MURRAY ALAN WEST, admitted, 1980. *Education:* LL.B. (Qld). *PRACTICE AREAS:* Banking; Finance.

BRIAN THOMAS WILSON, admitted, 1971. *Education:* LL.B., LL.M. (Syd). *PRACTICE AREAS:* Commercial Litigation; Insolvency.

MELBOURNE PARTNERS

VINCENT ANNETTA, admitted, 1986. *Education:* B.Ec., LL.B., LL.M., (Monash). *LANGUAGES:* Italian. *PRACTICE AREAS:* Commercial Litigation.

MAX CASEN, admitted, 1966. *Education:* LL.B. (Melbourne), LL.M. (Monash). *PRACTICE AREAS:* Corporate Law; Mergers and Acquisitions.

GREGORY CLIFTON, admitted, 1991. *Education:* LL.B. (Hons.) (First); B.Ec. (Adelaide). *PRACTICE AREAS:* Corporate Law; Taxation.

CHRISTOPHER ANTHONY DALE, admitted, 1979. *Education:* B.Juris., LL.B. (Monash). *PRACTICE AREAS:* Insolvency; Recovery; Workouts.

CHRISTOPHER ROBERT DAVIE, admitted, 1973. *Education:* B.A., LL.B. (Melb). *PRACTICE AREAS:* Corporate Law; Resources.

BRIAN JOHN DOYLE, admitted, 1961. *Education:* LL.B. (Tasmania); LL.B. Civil (Oxford, UK). *PRACTICE AREAS:* Corporate Law.

PAUL LAWRENCE EHRLICH, admitted, 1986. *Education:* LL.B. (Adelaide); LL.M. (Melb). *PRACTICE AREAS:* Corporate Law.

(This Listing Continued)

DAVID GRAHAM FAGAN, admitted, 1980. *Education:* LL.B., LL.M. (Melb). *PRACTICE AREAS:* Banking; Finance.

CHRISTOPHER JOHN FURNELL, admitted, 1982. *Education:* B.Comm, LL.B., LL.M. (Melb). *PRACTICE AREAS:* Banking; Finance.

IAN LONTE, admitted, 1964. *Education:* LL.B. (Melb). *PRACTICE AREAS:* Environmental; Planning; Local Government.

RODERICK LEWIS LYLE, admitted, 1979. *Education:* B.Comm, LL.B. (Melb); LL.M. (London). *PRACTICE AREAS:* Corporate Law.

JOHN MCMULLAN, admitted, 1983. *Education:* B.E., Civil (Melb); LL.B. (Monash). *PRACTICE AREAS:* Construction.

RICHARD ALLAN MEREINE, admitted, 1976. *Education:* B.Com. (Rhodes, Sth Africa); LL.B. (Witts, Sth. Africa). *PRACTICE AREAS:* Commercial and Corporate Law.

ANTONIO NICOLA PANE, admitted, 1985. *Education:* B.A., LL.B. (Monash). *PRACTICE AREAS:* Taxation; Superannuation.

CHARLES EDWARD ROSEDALE, admitted, 1977. *Education:* B.Ec., LL.B. (Monash). *PRACTICE AREAS:* Corporate Law.

BRADLEY GEORGE ROSS, admitted, 1980. *Education:* LL.B. (Melb). *PRACTICE AREAS:* Commercial Litigation.

MICHAEL CLIVE SARKIN, admitted, 1976. *Education:* LL.B. (Witwatersrand, Sth. Africa). *PRACTICE AREAS:* Competition Law.

ANNA SHARPE, admitted, 1982. *Education:* LL.B. (Hons), LL.M. (Qld). *PRACTICE AREAS:* Technology Computer Law; Intellectual Property.

GRAHAM FLOYD SMITH, admitted, 1981. *Education:* LL.B., B.A., Ph.D. (Law) (Monash). *PRACTICE AREAS:* Industrial Relations.

QUENTIN MICHAEL SOLOMON, admitted, 1985. *Education:* LL.B. (Tas). *PRACTICE AREAS:* Banking; Finance.

ANDREW JON STEPHENSON, admitted, 1983. *Education:* B.A.; LL.B. (Qld). *PRACTICE AREAS:* Construction Law.

MICHAEL PETER TUCKFIELD, admitted, 1981. *Education:* B.Com, LL.B. (Melb). *PRACTICE AREAS:* Banking; Finance.

(ARTHUR) BRADLEY VANN, admitted, 1987. *Education:* B.Com, LL.B. (Hons.) (Qld) ; BCL (Oxford). *PRACTICE AREAS:* Banking; Finance.

JOHN MCINTOSH WALTER, admitted, 1971. *Education:* LL.B. (Melb). *PRACTICE AREAS:* Banking; Finance.

PERTH PARTNERS

PETER LACHLAN WIESE, admitted, 1974. *Education:* LL.B. (Hons.) (W.A.). *PRACTICE AREAS:* Energy and Natural Resources; Commercial Projects.

DOMINIC JOHN BOURKE, admitted, 1974. *Education:* LL.B. (W.A.). *PRACTICE AREAS:* Insurance Law; Medico-Legal; Product Liability.

JOHN WALTER SALEEBA, admitted, 1977. *Education:* B.Com., LL.B. (W.A.). *PRACTICE AREAS:* General Commercial Law; Wills and Probate.

CHRISTIAN RICHARD WILLING, admitted, 1975. *Education:* LL.B. (Tas). *PRACTICE AREAS:* Property Law.

MARK JOHN BAHEN, admitted, 1975. *Education:* LL.B. (W.A.). *PRACTICE AREAS:* Commercial Law; Business Law.

GRAHAME BRETT NELSON, admitted, 1976. *Education:* LLB. (Hons.) (Liverpool, UK). *PRACTICE AREAS:* General Commercial and Technology Law.

PAUL CHARLES BLACKMAN, admitted, 1977. *Education:* LL.B. (Hons.) (Canterbury). *PRACTICE AREAS:* Commercial Litigation.

MICHAEL JOHN HARDY, admitted, 1977. *Education:* B.A., LL.B. (W.A.). *PRACTICE AREAS:* Administrative and Planning Law; Banking and Finance.

BARBARA ELIZABETH WHITTLE, admitted, 1975. *Education:* LL.B. (W.A.). *PRACTICE AREAS:* Banking; Finance.

DAVID JOHN MARTINO, admitted, 1979. *Education:* B.Juris, LL.B. (W.A.). *PRACTICE AREAS:* Commercial Litigation.

(This Listing Continued)

CLAYTON UTZ, Sydney, New South Wales—Continued

ROBERT LESLIE MCKENZIE, admitted, 1976. *Education:* B.Juris, LL.B. (W.A.). *PRACTICE AREAS:* Workout; Recovery; Insolvency.

TREVOR GEORGE O'SULLIVAN, admitted, 1972. *Education:* LL.B. (W.A.). *PRACTICE AREAS:* Financial and Property Disputes; Family Law.

PAUL STEPHEN FITZPATRICK, admitted, 1981. *Education:* B.Juris (Hons.), LL.B. (Hons.) (W.A.). *PRACTICE AREAS:* Corporate Litigation; Commercial Litigation.

STEPHEN RICHARD BOYLE, admitted, 1979. *Education:* B.Juris, LL.B. (W.A.). *PRACTICE AREAS:* Building and Construction.

JULIE ISABEL BISHOP, admitted, 1980. *Education:* LL.B. (Adelaide). *PRACTICE AREAS:* Commercial Litigation.

MICHAEL PHILLIP BOWEN, admitted, 1979. *Education:* LL.B.; B.Juris; B.Comm. (W.A.). *PRACTICE AREAS:* Corporate Law.

PETER JAMES YOUNG, admitted, 1981. *Education:* LL.B. (W.A.). *PRACTICE AREAS:* Commercial and Business Law.

GARY EDGAR BERSON, admitted, 1983. *Education:* LL.B. (W.A.). *PRACTICE AREAS:* Product Liability; Litigation.

PAUL ALLAN TOTTLE, admitted, 1981. *PRACTICE AREAS:* Technology Computer Law; Intellectual Property; Commercial Litigation.

RODERICK JOHN HAGER, admitted, 1979. *Education:* B.A., LL.B., LL.M. (Melb). *PRACTICE AREAS:* Property Law; Resources Law.

ROHAN G. SKEA, admitted, 1979. *Education:* B.Juris, LL.B. (Hons.) (Monash). *PRACTICE AREAS:* Corporatisation; Privatisation.

KEVIN ANTHONY DUNDO, admitted, 1983. *Education:* B.Comm (W.A.); LL.B. (ANU). *PRACTICE AREAS:* Commercial Law; Workout, Recovery and Insolvency.

IAN HENNESSY, admitted, 1981. *Education:* B.A. (Hons.); B.Juris (Hons.); LL.B. (W.A.). *PRACTICE AREAS:* Insurance Law.

DOUGLAS BISHOP, admitted, 1985. *Education:* LL.B. (Adelaide). *PRACTICE AREAS:* Commercial Litigation.

MARK PENDLEBURY, admitted, 1986. *Education:* B.Juris, LL.B. (W.A.). *PRACTICE AREAS:* Commercial Litigation.

MARK ANTHONY PAGANIN, admitted, 1984. *Education:* B. Juris; LL.B.; B.Comm. (Asia). *PRACTICE AREAS:* Corporate Law.

DAVID SIGLER, admitted, 1989, California, USA; 1991, Western Australia. *Education:* B.A. Political Science (Hons.) (Ca); J.D. (Ca). *PRACTICE AREAS:* Intellectual Property; Immigration; Commercial Law.

MICHELLE D'ADAMO, admitted, 1987. *Education:* B.Juris; LL.B. *PRACTICE AREAS:* Corporate Law; Takeovers; Commerical Advice.

LINDA CATHERINE EVANS, admitted, 1987. *Education:* B.Juris; LL.B. *PRACTICE AREAS:* Commerical Litigation; Trade Practices; Taxation; Corporate Disputes.

GEOFFREY JOHN SIMPSON, admitted, 1989. *Education:* B.Juris; LL.B. *PRACTICE AREAS:* Resources Law; Corporate Law.

BRISBANE PARTNERS

GEORGE WILLIAM DEEB, admitted, 1958. *Education:* B.A., LL.B. *PRACTICE AREAS:* Property Law.

MICHAEL JOHN MORROW, admitted, 1965. *Education:* LL.B. Notary Public. *PRACTICE AREAS:* Property Development; Corporate Law; Corporatisation.

GEOFFREY NICOLL HARLEY, admitted, 1967. *Education:* LL.B. *PRACTICE AREAS:* Industrial Relations; Employment Law; Commercial Litigation.

JEREMY CHARLES CHARLSTON, admitted, 1970. *PRACTICE AREAS:* Corporate Law; Intellectual Property; Technology; Computers.

PAUL HERMAN HENRI CORBIERE, admitted, 1972. *Education:* B.A.; LL.B. *LANGUAGES:* English, German and Italian. *PRACTICE AREAS:* Banking; Finance.

MICHAEL OSCAR KLUG, admitted, 1973. *Education:* LL.B. *LANGUAGES:* English and German. *PRACTICE AREAS:* Product Liability; Competition Law; Alternative Dispute Resolution; Commercial Litigation.

(This Listing Continued)

JOHN DAVID ELLIOTT, admitted, 1967. *Education:* LL.B. *PRACTICE AREAS:* Banking; Finance.

DAVID GEORGE COMINOS, admitted, 1974. *Education:* B.Comm., LL.M.(Hons). *PRACTICE AREAS:* Taxation; Company Structures; Trusts.

RALPH DOUGLAS PRAEGER, admitted, 1977. *Education:* LL.B. *PRACTICE AREAS:* Property Law.

ROSS GRAHAM PERRETT, admitted, 1981. *Education:* B.Com.; LL.B.(Hons). *PRACTICE AREAS:* Commercial Litigation.

TIMOTHY DAVID FERRIER, admitted, 1978. *Education:* LL.B. *PRACTICE AREAS:* Property Law; Foreign Investment.

CHRISTOPHER TERENCE COYNE, admitted, 1979. *PRACTICE AREAS:* Insurance Law; Professional Indemnity.

ROGER JOHN BURRELL, admitted, 1981. *Education:* B.Com., LL.B. *PRACTICE AREAS:* Corporate Law.

RANDAL JON DENNINGS, admitted, 1981. *Education:* B.A.; LL.B. *PRACTICE AREAS:* Banking; Finance; Consumer Credit.

ALAN HENRY MAGUIRE, admitted, 1981. *PRACTICE AREAS:* Banking; Finance.

ARCHIBALD FLETCHER, admitted, 1982. *Education:* LL.B.(Hons). *PRACTICE AREAS:* Construction Law.

LLOYD SIDNEY NASH, admitted, 1984. *Education:* LL.M. *PRACTICE AREAS:* Workout; Business Recovery; Insolvency.

BRIAN CORMACK NOBLE, admitted, 1984. *Education:* B.Com.; LL.B. *PRACTICE AREAS:* Property Law; Property Leasing.

SIMON WEBSTER LANG, admitted, 1984. *Education:* B.A.; LL.B.(Hons). *PRACTICE AREAS:* Insurance Law; Personal Injuries; Accident Compensation.

PAUL GERARD CALLAGHAN, admitted, 1984. *Education:* B.A.; LL.M. *PRACTICE AREAS:* Superannuation; Company Law; Taxation.

SALLY ANNE PITKIN, admitted, 1984. *Education:* LL.B. *PRACTICE AREAS:* Banking; Finance.

BRIAN JAMES CONRICK, admitted, 1972. *Education:* LL.M.; F.C.I. Arb.(U.K.); A.I.A.A. *PRACTICE AREAS:* Commercial Law; Construction Law; Arbitration.

KAREN MAREE TRAINOR, admitted, 1986. *Education:* Bsc.(Hons); LL.B.(Hons). *PRACTICE AREAS:* Environment Law; Planning Law.

ROGER VINCENT BYRNE, admitted, 1985. *Education:* LL.B. *PRACTICE AREAS:* Banking and Finance; Workout, Recovery and Insolvency.

RUTH ANN COPELIN, admitted, 1984. *Education:* LL.B. *PRACTICE AREAS:* Family Law.

MARK WILLIAM WALLER, admitted, 1987. *Education:* LL.B. (QUT). *PRACTICE AREAS:* Insurance Law; Professional Indemnity.

DALE STUART BRACKIN, admitted, 1986. *Education:* B.Ec., LL.B. (Hons.) (Qld). *PRACTICE AREAS:* Construction Law.

DARRYL DENIS MCDONOUGH, admitted, 1983. *Education:* LL.B. (Hons); B.Bus.Accy (Qld). *PRACTICE AREAS:* Corporate Law; Mergers and Acquisitions.

JOHN DAVID POWELL, admitted, 1982. *Education:* LL.B. (Qld). *PRACTICE AREAS:* Commercial Litigation.

CANBERRA PARTNERS

WILLIAM JOHN ALLEN, admitted, 1987. *Education:* B.Ec. (Hons.); LL.B. (Hons.) (Canberra). *PRACTICE AREAS:* Commercial Services.

JOHN DAVID BRADLEY, admitted, 1974. *Education:* B.Ec.; LL.B. (Canberra). *PRACTICE AREAS:* Commercial Law; Company Law; Taxation; Property; Leasing; Finance.

KEITH ARTHUR BRADLEY, admitted, 1978. *Education:* B.A.; LL.B. (Canberra). *PRACTICE AREAS:* Personal Injury.

CHRISTOPHER JAMES CROWLEY, admitted, 1971. *Education:* LL.B. (Melbourne). *PRACTICE AREAS:* Family Law.

PETER LAWRENCE CROWLEY, admitted, 1968. *Education:* LL.B. (Melbourne). *PRACTICE AREAS:* Commercial Property; Corporate Services Law; Banking; Finance.

(This Listing Continued)

ALFONSO DEL RIO, admitted, 1968. *Education:* LL.B.; B.Sc. (Canberra). *LANGUAGES:* Spanish. *PRACTICE AREAS:* Property Law; Environmental Law; Information Technology.

W. BRIAN LOFTUS, admitted, 1971. *PRACTICE AREAS:* Commercial Litigation.

WILLIAM JOHN GERARD MCCARTHY, admitted, 1982. *Education:* LL.B. (Tasmania). *PRACTICE AREAS:* Personal Injury.

THOMAS FRANCIS MEAGHER, admitted, 1967. *Education:* LL.B. (Syd). *PRACTICE AREAS:* Wills; Probate; Estate Administration.

ANNE MARIE PROCTOR, admitted, 1980. *Education:* B.A.; LL.B. (Canberra). *PRACTICE AREAS:* Family Law.

SALLY JOAN SHEPPARD, admitted, 1984. *Education:* LL.B. (Sydney). *PRACTICE AREAS:* Commercial Litigation.

PHILIP RAYMOND SMITH, admitted, 1976. *Education:* LL.B. (Canberra). *PRACTICE AREAS:* Commercial Litigation; Defamation.

JOHN SIDNEY SNELL, admitted, 1977. *Education:* B.Ec.; LL.B. (Canberra). *PRACTICE AREAS:* Conveyancing; Environmental Law; Local Government.

NICHOLAS JOHN SYMONS, admitted, 1976. *Education:* LL.B. (Canberra). *PRACTICE AREAS:* Property Law.

ROSEMARY ELIZABETH TOWNSEND, admitted, 1976. *Education:* LL.B. (Hons.) (Tasmania). *PRACTICE AREAS:* Banking; Finance.

CONSULTANTS

IAN D. ALFREDSON, (BRISBANE), admitted, 1960. *Education:* LL.B. *PRACTICE AREAS:* Mining and Resources.

SHENAGH BARNES, (SYDNEY), admitted, 1973. *Education:* LL.B., LL.M. *PRACTICE AREAS:* Corporate Law.

CATHERINE RUTH CAMERON, (BRISBANE), admitted, 1984. *Education:* B.A., LL.B. (Hons). *PRACTICE AREAS:* Property Law.

JULIANNA DEEB, (SYDNEY), admitted, 1984. *Education:* B.A., LL.B. (NSW). *PRACTICE AREAS:* Banking; Finance.

**PROFESSOR HAROLD A.J. FORD, (MELBOURNE). *PRACTICE AREAS:* Corporate Law; Trusts; Company Law.

ALEXANDER CHRISTY FREELEAGUS, (BRISBANE), admitted, 1953. *Education:* B.A., LL.B. *LANGUAGES:* English and Greek. *PRACTICE AREAS:* Mining and Resources.

PROF. CHRISTOPHER D. GILBERT, (BRISBANE), admitted, 1971. *Education:* B.A., LL.M., D. Jur. *PRACTICE AREAS:* Constitutional and Administrative Law; Commercial Law.

DEREK GRAHAM, (SYDNEY). *Education:* B.A. *PRACTICE AREAS:* Industrial Relations.

ROSS GRAINGER-SMITH, (BRISBANE), admitted, 1966. (Brisbane). *PRACTICE AREAS:* Insurance Law.

NEVILLE R. HEAD, (SYDNEY), admitted, 1957. *Education:* B.A., LL.B. *PRACTICE AREAS:* Corporate Law.

BYONG WOOK KIM, (SYDNEY), admitted, 1986 (Korea). *Education:* Master of Law (NSW). (Also Member, Kim, Chang & Lee, Seoul, Korea). *PRACTICE AREAS:* Korean Practice.

MICHAEL AWSTUN LEWIS, (PERTH), admitted, 1965. Notary Public. *PRACTICE AREAS:* Commercial Law; Resources Law.

IAN G. MEDCALF, (PERTH). *Education:* A.O., E.D., Q.C. *PRACTICE AREAS:* Government Relations; Constitutional Law; State and Federal Trusts; Property, Wills and Administration.

PROF. JAMES O'DONOVAN, (PERTH). *Education:* B.A., LL.B., Ph.D. *PRACTICE AREAS:* Insolvency and Reconstruction; Banking Law; Trusts and Equity.

MARILYN JANE PITTARD, (MELBOURNE), admitted, 1977. *Education:* LL.B., B.Ec. *PRACTICE AREAS:* Employment; Industrial Relations; Industrial Arbitration; Administrative Law.

THE HON ANDREW JOHN ROGERS, Q.C. (SYDNEY), admitted, 1956; appointed Queen's Counsel, 1973. *Education:* LL.B. (Hons) (Syd). Former Chief Justice of the Commercial Division of the Supreme Court of NSW. *PRACTICE AREAS:* Commercial Litigation Advice.

(This Listing Continued)

MICHAEL J. THOMPSON, (SYDNEY), admitted, 1985. *Education:* LL.B.; B.Com. (Economics) (NSW). *PRACTICE AREAS:* Construction; Work Practices.

COLLIER, SHANNON, RILL & SCOTT
LEVEL 12, 10 BARRACK STREET
SYDNEY, NEW SOUTH WALES 2000, AUSTRALIA
Telephone: 61-2-262-6700
Fax: 61-2-262-3263

Washington, D.C. Office: Suite 400, 3050 K Street, N.W., 20007. Telephone: 202-342-8400. Facsimile: 202-338-5534.

General Commercial and Administrative Law, International Trade, International Litigation, Intellectual Property, Joint Ventures, Energy and Natural Resources, Corporate, Environmental, Telecommunications, United States Immigration Law, Project and Trade Finance.

RESIDENT PARTNER

PATRICK B. FAZZONE, born Fairfield, Connecticut, December 12, 1953; admitted, 1981, District of Columbia (Not admitted in Australia). *Education:* Université de Rouen, Rouen, France; University of Connecticut (B.A., magna cum laude, with distinction in Pol. Sc., 1975); Duke University (J.D., 1981). Note and Comment Editor, Duke Law Journal, 1980-1981. Officer, Moot Court Board, Duke University Law School, 1979-1981. Fulbright Scholar in International Law, Graduate Institute for International Studies, Geneva, Switzerland, 1981. Author: "Analysis of the Trade and Tariff Act of 1984," Revue des Affaires Internationales (Paris, France), Tome 6, 1985; "Business Effects of the Extraterritorial Reach of the U.S. Export Control Laws," Droit et Pratique de Commerce International (Paris, France), Tome 8, 1982 also printed in New York University Journal of International Law, Spring, 1983; "Implied Rights of Action; Harmonization Within the Statutory Scheme," Duke Law Journal, Vol. 5, 1980. Lecturer in Law, University of Sydney Law School, 1989-1992. *Member:* The District of Columbia Bar (Member, Sections on: Litigation; International Law). *LANGUAGES:* English, French, Italian. *PRACTICE AREAS:* International Commercial Transactions; International Trade Law; Intellectual Property Law.

RESIDENT ASSOCIATE

ERNEST SCHWARTZ, born Montreal, Quebec, October 4, 1962; admitted, 1988, Victoria, Australia, Supreme Court of Victoria. *Education:* University of Melbourne, Australia (B.A., 1985; LL.B., 1987). Co-Author: International Contract Manual (Australia Section), 1992. Licensing Australian Technology Overseas, 1994 (in Conjunction with Australian Trade Commission). *Member:* Licensing Executives Society. *PRACTICE AREAS:* International Commercial Transactions; Intellectual Property Law.

REFERENCE: National Australia Bank, N.S.W.

(For complete biographical data on all personnel, see professional biographies at Washington, D.C.)

CORRS CHAMBERS WESTGARTH
LEVEL 32, GOVERNOR PHILLIP TOWER
1 FARRER PLACE
SYDNEY, NEW SOUTH WALES NSW 2001, AUSTRALIA
Telephone: (02) 210 6500
Fax: (02) 210 6611

Melbourne, Victoria, Australia Office: 600 Bourke Street, Vic. 3000. Telephone: (03) 672 3000. International: +613 672 3000. Fax: (03) 602 5544.

Brisbane, Queensland, Australia Office: Comalco Place, 12 Creek Street, QLD, 4000. Telephone: (07) 228 9333. International: +617 228 9333. Fax: (07) 229 2844.

Gold Coast, Queensland, Australia Office: Level 4, Corporate Centre One, 2 Corporate Court, Bundall, QDL, 4217. International Telephone: (075) 77 7777. Fax: (075) 74 0478.

Canberra, Australia Office: Level 5, Advance Bank Centre, 60 Marcus Clarke Street, ACT, 2601. Telephone: (06) 257 7566. International: +616 257 7566. Fax: (06) 257 7563.

Perth, Western Australia Office: Commonwealth Bank Building. 150 St. George's Terrace, W.A. 6000. Telephone: (09) 321 8531. International: +619 321 8531. Fax: (09) 322 6953.

(This Listing Continued)

CORRS CHAMBERS WESTGARTH, Sydney, New South Wales—Continued

London, England Office: 2nd Floor, 103 Cannon Street, EC4N 5AD. Telephone: (171) 929 4955. International: +44171 929 4955. Fax: (171) 929 4164.

Commercial and Corporate Law including:
Banking & Finance, Computer & Communications, Corporate Reconstruction & Insolvency, Corporatisation, Customs & International Trade, Energy & Resources, Family Lawa, Franchising, Funds Management, Industrial Relations, Insurance & Product Liability, Intellectual Property, International Law, Joint Ventures, Litigation in all areas of practice, Mergers & Acquisitions, Planning, Pollution & Environment Law, Privatization, Professional Liability, Property Development & Construction, Securitisation, Stamp Duty, Superannuation, Taxation, Telecommunications.

PARTNERS

Adrian Batterby	Andrew J. Lumsden
Jennifer M. Boland	Paul R. McCann
Carmen Champion	John G. McCombe
Richard Chivell	Roderick H. McGeoch
Edward B. Cowpe	Alan J. Macdonald
Charles M. Cowper	A. John Munton
Graeme J. Dennis	Peter T. Pether
Michael J. Ellis	Geoffrey H. Pike
Michael J. Falk	Andrew L. Price
Ronald A. Finlay	Stephen B. Price
Julian M. Gregory	Alan Rich (Managing Partner)
J. Henry Herron	Erica J. Robinson
Paul H. Hughes	Anthony J. Sheehan
F. John Kehoe	Peter W. Smith
William J. Koeck	Andrew W. Stevenson
Francis R. Lawson	Robert H. Tomlinson
Richard K. Liebmann	Peter G. West
Stuart D. Westgarth	

SENIOR ASSOCIATES

Sharon L. Bodell	David R. Hodges
Philip L. Breen	Alexandra Kagis
Paul A. Brown	Michael Lee
Michelle Carr	Sally McNamara
Nicholas S. G. Christian	Christopher P. Mitchell
John Coorey	Michael F. O'Neill
Michael P. Donovan	Robert J. Regan
Maurice A. Doria	Jacquie A. Shanahan
Richard Flitcroft	Lisa J. Simmons
Alan M. Friedlander	Petar Vladeta

(For list of Personnel at London, England, Brisbane, Canberra, Bundall, Melbourne and Perth, Australia see Professional Biographies at those locations).

COUDERT BROTHERS

SUITE 2202, STATE BANK CENTRE
52 MARTIN PLACE
SYDNEY, NEW SOUTH WALES N.S.W.2000, AUSTRALIA
Telephone: 612-223-1488
Facsimile: 612-235-3877 (NEFAX 4500)
Cable Address: "Treduoc" Sydney International
Telex: 25273 AMLAW AA

REVISERS OF THE FRANCE LAW DIGEST FOR THIS DIRECTORY

New York, New York 10036-7794: 1114 Avenue of the Americas.
Washington, D.C. 20006: 1627 I Street, N.W.
Los Angeles, California 90017: 1055 Seventh Street, Twentieth Floor.
San Francisco, California 94111: 4 Embarcadero Center, Suite 3300.
San Jose, California 95113: Suite 1250, Ten Almaden Boulevard.
Paris 75008, France: Coudert Frères, 52 Avenue des Champs-Elysees.
London, EC4M 7JP, England: 20 Old Bailey.
Brussels B-1050, Belgium: Tour Louise. 149 Avenue Louise, Box 8.
Beijing, People's Republic of China 100020: Suite 2708-09 Jing Guang Centre, Hu Jia Lou Chao Yang Qu.
Shanghai, People's Republic of China 200002: c/o Suite 1804, Union Building, 100 Yanan Road East.

(This Listing Continued)

Hong Kong: 25th Floor, Nine Queen's Road Central.
Singapore 0104: Tung Centre, 20 Collyer Quay.
Tokyo 107, Japan: 1355 West Tower, Aoyama Twin Towers, 1-1-1 Minami-Aoyama, Minato-ku.
Moscow, Russia: Ulitsa Staraya Basmannaya 14.
01301 Sao Paulo, SP, Brazil: Machado, Meyer, Sendacz, e Opice, Advogados, Rua da Consolacao, 247, 8 Andar.
Bangkok 10500, Thailand: Bubhajit Building, 20 North Sathorn Road, 10th Floor.
Ho Chi Minh City, Vietnam: c/o Saigon Business Centre, 49-57 Dong Du Street, District 1.

General and International Law Practice.
Firm engaged in American and International Law Practice, authorized to appear before the Australian Courts.

RESIDENT PARTNERS

PETER GREGORY NOBLE, born Sydney, New South Wales, Australia, January 13, 1952; admitted, 1976, New South Wales; 1982, Victoria; 1986, England and Wales. *Education:* University of New South Wales (B.Com; LL.B., 1976). Member: Banking Finance and Consumer Credit Committee of Law Council of Australia, 1983; Australia-Indonesia Business Council, 1993; Australia and Singapore Chamber of Commerce and Industry Ltd. 1994. Contributing Editor, Butterworths Australian Consumer Credit Law Reporter. *Member:* Law Society of New South Wales.

PETER J. NORMAN, born Sydney, Australia, August 13, 1956; admitted, 1980, New South Wales; 1983, High Court of Australia; 1985, Australian Capital Territory. *Education:* Macquarie University, New South Wales (B.A., LL.B., Hons., 1980); University of Virginia (LL.M., 1982). Fulbright Scholar. Lecturer in Banking Law and Taxation Law, Australian National University Law School, 1984-1986. Examiner in Taxation for the Supreme Court of New South Wales. Lecturer in Taxation Law, Sydney University Law Extension Committee, 1987—. *Member:* Law Society of New South Wales; Taxation Institute of Australia; International Fiscal Association.

RESIDENT ASSOCIATES

Maria Theresa Polczynski	Mark S. Williamson

RESIDENT CONSULTANT

W. WARREN SCOTT, III, born Wurzburg, West Germany, October 19, 1952; admitted, 1978, California; 1980, New York (Not admitted in Australia). *Education:* Georgetown University (B.A., with honors, 1974); University of Chicago (J.D., 1978). *Member:* Association of the Bar of the City of New York; State Bar of California; American Bar Association.

REVISERS OF THE FRANCE LAW DIGEST FOR THIS DIRECTORY

(For biographical data of the New York personnel, see Professional Biographies at New York, N.Y.).
(For biographical data of the Washington personnel, see Professional Biographies at Washington, D.C.).
(For biographical data of the San Francisco personnel, see Professional Biographies at San Francisco, California).
(For biographical data of the Los Angeles personnel, see Professional Biographies at Los Angeles, California).
(For biographical data of the San Jose personnel, see Professional Biographies at San Jose, California).
(For biographical data of the Paris personnel, see Professional Biographies at Paris, France).
(For biographical data of the London personnel, see Professional Biographies at London, England).
(for biographical data of the Brussels personnel, see Professional Biographies at Brussels, Belgium).
(For biographical data of the Beijing personnel, see Professional Biographies at Beijing, People's Republic of China).
(For biographical data of the Hong Kong personnel, see Professional Biographies at Hong Kong).
(For biographical data of the Singapore personnel, see Professional Biographies at Singapore).
(For biographical data of the Tokyo personnel, see Professional Biographies at Tokyo, Japan).
(For biographical data of the Sao Paulo personnel, see Professional Biographies at Sao Paulo, Brazil).
(For biographical data of the Shanghai personnel, see Professional Biographies at Shanghai, People's Republic of China).
(For biographical data of the Moscow personnel, see Professional Biographies at Moscow, U.S.S.R.).
(For biographical data of the Ho Chi Minh City personnel, see Professional Biographies at Ho Chi Minh City, Vietnam).

DIBBS, CROWTHER & OSBORNE

Established in 1883

50 CARRINGTON STREET
SYDNEY, NEW SOUTH WALES 2000, AUSTRALIA
Telephone: 2908200
Fax: 2902964

FIRM PROFILE: *Dibbs Crowther and Osborne has operated as a commercial law firm in Sydney for over 100 years. The principal areas of expertise are in banking and finance, commercial litigation, insolvency law, property and general commercial law and entertainment law, prospectuses, intellectual property, trusts, diligence, foreign banking.*

MEMBERS OF FIRM

PETER ROBERT EVERETT, admitted, 1965, New South Wales; 1991, Victoria. *Education:* University of Sydney (LL.B.). Author, Chapter on Banking for the Australian and New Zealand Commentary on Halsbury's Laws of England, published by Butterworths, 1974. Member/ Director: Banking Law Association of Australia (Member, Executive Committee). Director: Australian Chamber Orchestra: Australian Archaeological Institute in Athens. *Member:* Law Asia. **PRACTICE AREAS:** Banking Law; Commercial Law; Securities Law; Insolvency.

GEOFFREY HUGH SUTHERLAND, admitted, 1976, New South Wales. *Education:* University of New South Wales (Bachelor of Commerce and LL.B.). *Member:* Law Council of Australia (Member, Insolvency Committee); Commercial Law Association of Australia (President); Inter Pacific Bar Association (Vice Chairman, Financial Institutions and Transaction Committee); Australian Institute of Company Directors,; Australian Indonesian Business Council; Australia Taiwan Business Council; Law Asia. **PRACTICE AREAS:** Banking Law; Commercial Law; Securities Law; Insolvency.

PETER EDWARD SURGEON, admitted, 1976, New South Wales. *Education:* University of New South Wales (Bachelor of Commerce and LL.B.). *Member:* Inter Pacific Bar Association; Law Asia; Society for Computers and the Law; Business Law Committee Law Society of New South Wales. **PRACTICE AREAS:** Banking Law; Commercial Law; Securities Law; Computers; Insolvency; Intellectual Property.

DAVID JAMES SHARPE, admitted, 1980, New South Wales. *Education:* University of Sydney (LL.B.). *Member:* Law Council of Australia; Property Committee, Law Society of New South Wales. **PRACTICE AREAS:** Property Law; Banking Law; Securities Law; Trusts Law.

DALE JAMES KEMP, admitted, 1981, New South Wales. *Education:* Macquarie University (B.A., LL.B.). Notary Public. *Member:* Inter Pacific Bar Association; Australia Japan Chamber of Commerce. **PRACTICE AREAS:** Litigation; Banking Law; Administrative Law; Insolvency.

IAN DAVID OSBORNE, admitted, 1981, New South Wales; 1991, Victoria. *Education:* University New South Wales (Bachelor of Commerce; LL.B.). Notary Public. *Member:* Banking Law Association of Australia. **PRACTICE AREAS:** Banking Law; Commercial Law; Securities Law; Insolvency.

LYNETTE RUTH GERATHY, admitted, 1981, New South Wales. *Education:* University of Sydney (Bachelor of Economics; LL.B.). *Member:* Banking Law Association of Australia; Legislation Review Committee City of Sydney Chamber of Commerce. **PRACTICE AREAS:** Litigation; Banking Law; Property Law.

JUSTIN LIAN SIN KANG, admitted, 1985, New South Wales. *Education:* Macquarie University (B.A., LL.B.). **PRACTICE AREAS:** Litigation; Insolvency; Banking; Finance; Securities.

LEONARD PAUL LOZINA, admitted, 1985. New South Wales. *Education:* University of Sydney (LL.B.). *LANGUAGES:* Croatian. **PRACTICE AREAS:** Insolvency; Banking Law; Litigation.

CONSULTANTS

WILLIAM JAMES SINCLAIR, admitted, 1944, New South Wales. Notary Public.

BARON A. BROOKE, admitted, 1946, New South Wales.

DAVID RONALD OSBORNE, admitted, 1948, New South Wales. Notary Public.

(This Listing Continued)

GARTH JUSTIN SYMONDS, admitted, 1973, New South Wales. *Education:* University of Sydney (LL.B.); University of Oxford (M.A.). **PRACTICE AREAS:** Finance Law; Litigation; Insolvency; Entertainment; Prospectuses.

GARRY DOWNES, Q.C., F.C.I. ARB.

Barrister

Established in 1970

7 WENTWORTH CHAMBERS
180 PHILLIP STREET
SYDNEY, NEW SOUTH WALES 2000, AUSTRALIA
Telephone: + 61-2-232 1450
Facsimile: + 61-2-233 1849

Paris, France Office: Maison de la Porte, 25 rue du Jour, 75001. Telephone: + 33 1 45 08 82 34. Fax: + 33 1 45 08 82 31.
London, England Office: Essex Court Chambers, 24 Lincoln's Inn Fields, WC2A 3Ed. Telephone: + 44 71 813 8000. Fax: + 44 71 813 8080.

Litigation, Appellate, Administrative, Commercial/Equity, Constitutional, Insurance, Intellectual Property, Maritime, Trade Practices.

GARRY DOWNES, Q.C., born January 7, 1944; admitted, 1968, Australia. Queens Counsel, since 1983. High Court of Australia and Federal Jurisdictions, New South Wales, Victoria, Queensland, South Australia, Western Australia, Australian Capital Territory and Northern Territory. President, International Association of Lawyers (Union Internationale des Avocats). Chairman, New South Wales Council of Law Reporting. Immediate Past Chairman, Federal Litigation Section, Law Council of Australia. Fellow, Chartered Institute of Arbitrators. Former Member: New South Wales Barristers Admission Board; Faculty of Law, Sydney University; Council of New South Wales Bar Association. *LANGUAGES:* English and French.

DUNHILL MADDEN BUTLER

16 BARRACK STREET
SYDNEY, NEW SOUTH WALES 2000, AUSTRALIA
Telephone: (02) 233.3622
International Telephone: (612) 233.3622
DX: 254 Sydney
Fax: (02) 235.3099

Mailing Address: GPO Box 427, Sydney, 2001

Melbourne Office: 575 Bourke Street, Melbourne, Victoria 3000, Australia. Telephone: (03) 617.5711. International Telephone: (613) 617.5711. DX: 102 Melbourne. Fax: (03) 614.5577. Mailing Address: GPO Box 4592, Melbourne, Victoria, 3001.

General Practice, Administrative Law, Aviation, Banking and Finance, Biotechnology, Business Dispute Resolution, Capital Raisings, Commercial Property Planning and Construction, Computers, Commercial Litigation, Employment and Industrial Relations, Federal and State Taxation, Formation and Reconstruction of Business Structures, General Commercial and Corporate Advice, Franchising, Estate Planning, Insolvency, Insurance Advising, Insurance Litigation, Intellectual Property, Media and Defamation, Mining and Resources, Occupational Health and Safety, Products Liability, Professional Indemnity, Real Estate, Securities, Superannuation, Trade Practices and Consumer Law, Shipping, Transport, Telecommunications and Environmental and Planning Law.

SYDNEY PARTNERS

CEDRIC B. VASS, admitted, 1959, New South Wales; 1989, Victoria. Solicitors Admission Board. **PRACTICE AREAS:** General Insurance.

PETER G. MORGAN, admitted, 1965, New South Wales; 1989, Victoria. B.A., LL.B. **PRACTICE AREAS:** Business Structure; International Investment Structures.

DOUGLAS J. HAMILTON, admitted, 1970, New South Wales; 1989, Victoria. B.A., LL.B. **PRACTICE AREAS:** Company Business Law; Acquisitions; Restructuring and Securities.

JOHN M. CHURCHILL, admitted, 1977, New South Wales; 1989, Victoria. Solicitors Admission Board., LL.M. Managing Partner, Sydney. **PRACTICE AREAS:** Industrial Law; Occupational Health and Safety.

(This Listing Continued)

DUNHILL MADDEN BUTLER, *Sydney, New South Wales—Continued*

DAVID L. FABIAN, admitted, 1972, New South Wales; 1975, High Court of Australia; 1989, Victoria. LL.B. *PRACTICE AREAS:* Construction and Engineering.

ROBERT C. JORDAN, admitted, 1974, New South Wales; 1987, Australian Capital Territory; 1989, Victoria. B.A., LL.B. *PRACTICE AREAS:* Intellectual Property; Technology; Trade Practices (Anti Trust).

MICHAEL T.R. BINETTER, admitted, 1979, New South Wales; 1980, High Court of Australia; 1989, Victoria. B.Ec., LL.M. *PRACTICE AREAS:* Revenue Law; Superannuation.

HAROLD WERKSMAN, admitted, 1972, South Africa; 1982, New South Wales. B.A., LL.B. *PRACTICE AREAS:* Alternative Dispute Resolution; Directors and Officers Insurance.

PHILIP S.D. PURCELL, admitted, 1974, New South Wales; 1989, Victoria. B.A., LL.B. *PRACTICE AREAS:* Insurance.

GRAHAM A. FRANCIS, admitted, 1968, New South Wales; 1972, Papua New Guinea; 1989, Victoria. Solicitors Admission Board. *PRACTICE AREAS:* Commercial Property.

JOHN N. MILLER, admitted, 1972, New South Wales. B.A., LLB. *PRACTICE AREAS:* Commercial Property; Hospitality and Tourism.

MALCOLM DAVIES, admitted, 1975, New South Wales; 1977, Australian Capital Territory; 1989, Victoria; 1990, Northern Territory. LL.B. *PRACTICE AREAS:* Insurance; Aviation; Defamation.

IAN G. JOHNSTON, admitted, 1973, Victoria; 1984, New South Wales. B.A., LL.B. *PRACTICE AREAS:* Finance and Banking.

DAVID P. SELIG, admitted, 1978, New South Wales; 1984, England; 1989, Victoria. B.Comm., LL.B. *PRACTICE AREAS:* Corporate Reconstruction; Mergers and Acquisitions; Public Offerings.

BRUCE N. MCLEAN, admitted, 1979, New South Wales; 1989, Victoria. Solicitors Admission Board. *PRACTICE AREAS:* Insurance; Workers' Compensation Law.

CHRISTOPHER B. BRIERLEY, admitted, 1980, New South Wales; 1991, Victoria. LL.M. *PRACTICE AREAS:* Insurance; Professional Indemnity; General Insurance.

JOHN F. WHITEHOUSE, admitted, 1992, New South Wales. LL.B., B.A., B.Sc. *PRACTICE AREAS:* Planning; Environmental and Government.

PENNY A. EVANS, admitted, 1982, New South Wales; 1989, Victoria. B.A., LL.B. *PRACTICE AREAS:* Commercial Property.

ANDREW SPEARRITT, admitted, 1984, New South Wales; 1989, Victoria. B.A., LL.B. *PRACTICE AREAS:* Insurance; Workers' Compensation; Asbestos related Claims.

PETER H. STACEY, admitted, 1981, New South Wales; 1991, High Court of Australia. B.A., LL.B. *PRACTICE AREAS:* Construction and Engineering.

LOU L. DE BIASI, admitted, 1982, New South Wales; 1989, Victoria. B.Econ., LL.B., LL.M. *PRACTICE AREAS:* Banking and Finance.

ANASTASIA TSEKOURAS, admitted, 1984, New South Wales. B.A., LL.B., LL.M. *PRACTICE AREAS:* Finance and Revenue Law.

MICHAEL DANIEL, admitted, 1985, New South Wales; 1988, England and Wales. B Com., LL.B. *PRACTICE AREAS:* Insolvency; Commercial Litigation; Trade Practice (Anti Trust).

STEPHEN H. KLOTZ, admitted, 1987, Victoria; 1989, New South Wales. B.A., LL.B. *PRACTICE AREAS:* Intellectual Property; Trade Practices; Commercial Litigation; Alternative Dispute Resolution.

MICHAEL B. YATES, admitted, 1977, New South Wales, B. Comm, LL.B. *PRACTICE AREAS:* Company Flotations; Corporate Reconstruction; Mergers and Acquisitions.

MELBOURNE PARTNERS

BILL T. MCKAY, admitted, 1969, Victoria; 1989, New South Wales. LL.B. *PRACTICE AREAS:* Commercial Law.

PETER M. BEAUMONT, admitted, 1972, Victoria; 1989, New South Wales. LL.B., DIP TRP (Town and Regional Planning). *PRACTICE AREAS:* Planning Law.

(This Listing Continued)

PATRICK W.T. MCCABE, admitted, 1970, Victoria; 1989, New South Wales. LL.B. *PRACTICE AREAS:* Personal Injury.

ANDREW R. BRETHERTON, admitted, 1972, Victoria; 1989, New South Wales. LL.B. *PRACTICE AREAS:* Banking and Finance.

ANTHONY ELDER, admitted, 1976, Victoria; 1989, New South Wales. Council of Legal Education. *PRACTICE AREAS:* Commercial Litigation.

E.R. HUAN WALKER, admitted, 1962, Victoria; 1989, New South Wales. Dip. Sports Science, LL.B. *PRACTICE AREAS:* Personal Injury.

PETER M. NADALIN, admitted, 1981, Victoria; 1989, New South Wales. LL.B. *PRACTICE AREAS:* Banking and Finance.

STEVEN AMENDOLA, admitted, 1982, Victoria; 1989, New South Wales. LL.B. (Hons.). *PRACTICE AREAS:* Industrial Law.

DAVID E. NATHAN, admitted, 1984, Victoria; 1989, New South Wales. B.Sc., LL.B. *PRACTICE AREAS:* Product Liability.

BERNARD J. O'SHEA, admitted, 1985, Victoria; 1989, New South Wales. *PRACTICE AREAS:* Pharmaceutical Law.

BELINDA H.M. LIM, admitted, 1983, Victoria; 1989, New South Wales. B.A., LL.B. (Hons.). *PRACTICE AREAS:* Banking and Finance Litigation.

PETER MERRYLEES, admitted, 1978, Victoria; 1990, New South Wales. LL.B. (Hons.). *PRACTICE AREAS:* Environmental Law.

PAUL D. GAMBLE, admitted, 1983, Victoria; 1990, New South Wales. B.Juris., LL.B. *PRACTICE AREAS:* Insurance Litigation.

BRENDON R. WATKINS, admitted, 1986, Victoria; 1989, New South Wales. B.Ec., LL.B. *PRACTICE AREAS:* Banking and Finance Litigation.

PETER E. CASH, admitted, 1986, Victoria; 1989, New South Wales. B. Comm, LL.B. *PRACTICE AREAS:* Banking and Finance Litigation.

CRAIG PENN-TONKIN, admitted, 1979, Victoria. B.Ec., LL.B. *PRACTICE AREAS:* Property Law.

DAN M.Z. HOGAN, admitted, 1987, Victoria. LL.B. *PRACTICE AREAS:* Commercial Law.

JONATHAN S. SANDLER, admitted, 1982, South Africa; 1990, Victoria. B.A., LL.B. *PRACTICE AREAS:* Industrial Law; Alternative Dispute Resolution.

STEPHEN G. WALTERS, admitted, 1983, Victoria. B.Juris, LL.B. *PRACTICE AREAS:* Personal Injury.

RICHARD L. HORSLEY, admitted, 1979, Victoria. B.A., LL.B. *PRACTICE AREAS:* Insurance Litigation.

MICHAEL E. WILTON, admitted, 1982, Victoria, New South Wales, Western Australia and Australian Capital Territory. B.A., LL.B. *PRACTICE AREAS:* Corporate Law; Commercial Law.

SENIOR ASSOCIATES SYDNEY

Margaret Rodgers	Gail Chalmers
Simon Taylor	Ian Fox
Catherine Gilbert	Prue Mitchell
Jamie Nettleton	Eleny Tzioumis
Brian Williamson	Damyon Lill

SENIOR ASSOCIATES MELBOURNE

J.E. Boyall	D.V. Darzins
A.D. Bruce	I.F.K. Fullagar
V.J. Bennets	M.F. Levy
M.J. Casey	P. Linsdell

SYDNEY CONSULTANTS

Leslie Winter	Moira Rayner
Ian Palmer (Risk Management)	(Industrial Relations)

MELBOURNE CONSULTANTS

A.J. Fenton	C.K. McMillan
	H.M. Graham

FREEHILL HOLLINGDALE & PAGE

Established in 1852
LEVEL 38, THE MLC CENTRE
19-29 MARTIN PLACE
SYDNEY, NEW SOUTH WALES 2000, AUSTRALIA
Telephone: (02) 225 5000
International: +(612) 225 5000
Telegraphic and Cable Address: "Freehills, Sydney"
Telex: AA121885
Fax: (02) 322 4000

Canberra City, Australian Capital Territory, Australia Office: London Court, 13 London Circuit, 2601. Telephone:(06) 240 6100. International: +(616) 240 6100. Telex: AA121885. Fax: (06) 240 6222.

Melbourne, Victoria, Australia Office: 101 Collins Street, 3000. Telephone: (03) 288 1234. International: +(613) 288 1234. Telex: AA33004. Fax: (03) 288 1567.

Perth, Western Australia Office: Australia Place, 15-17 William Street, 6000. Telephone: (09) 327 5777. International: +(619) 327 5777. Telex: AA92937. Fax: (09) 322 5954.

Brisbane, Queensland, Australia Office: Central Plaza II, 66 Eagle Street, 4000. Telephone: (07) 258 6666. International: +(617) 258 6666. Fax: (07) 258 6444.

Singapore Office: 6 Battery Road, #13-01, 0104. Telephone: (65) 225 1288. Telex: (RS) 42674. Fax: (65) 225 3314.

London, England Office: Birchin Court, 20 Birchin Lane, EC3V 9DJ. Telephone: (0171) 283 9006. International: +(44 171) 283 9006. Fax: (0171) 454 9650.

Hanoi, Vietnam Office: 34A Quang Trung Street. Telephone: (844) 227 839. Fax: (844) 227 909.

Ho Chi Minh City, Vietnam Office: 203 Dong Khoi Street, #3-05. Telephone: (848) 242 630; (848) 242 733. Fax: (848) 242 736.

FIRM PROFILE: Freehill Hollingdale & Page is an Australian based international law firm with a strong and growing presence in Asia and Europe. Established over 140 years ago, we have expanded to become one of the largest commercial law firms in Australia and South-East Asia.

We provide advice in the following areas: Asia, Aviation, Banking & Finance, Construction Projects, Corporate, Corporatisation and Privatisation, Commercial Litigation, Employment Law and Industrial Relations, Energy and Natural Resources, Environment, Europe, Foreign Investment, Government, Immigration, Insolvency, Insurance, Intellectual Property, International Trade, Media, Mergers and Acquisitions, Occupational Health and Safety, Product Liability, Property, Superannuation, Taxation, Telecommunications, Trade and Customs, Trade Practices and Trademarks.

MEMBERS OF FIRM IN SYDNEY

JAMES HENRY GRAHAM, admitted, 1969. *Education:* University of Sydney (LL.B.). *PRACTICE AREAS:* Corporate; Funds Raisings; Funds Management; Superannuation; Insurance; Telecommunications.

PHILLIP THORNTON TAYLOR, admitted 1966. *Education:* University of Sydney (B.A.; LL.B.). *PRACTICE AREAS:* Banking; Finance; Funds Raisings; Funds Management; Stamp Duty.

BRUCE KELVIN CUTLER, admitted 1973. *Education:* University of New South Wales (B.Com.); University of Sydney (LL.B.). *PRACTICE AREAS:* Banking; Finance; Corporate; Mergers and Acquisitions; Privatisation; Infrastructure.

DAVID MYLES BENNETT, (Q.C.), admitted, 1961. *Education:* University of Tasmania (LL.B.). *PRACTICE AREAS:* Engineering; Construction; Litigation; Media Law; Product Liability.

KEVIN WILLIAM BROADLEY, admitted 1972. *Education:* N.S.W. Solicitors Admission Board of Study. *PRACTICE AREAS:* Energy; Resources; Environmental Law; Litigation; Media Law.

JAMES MICHAEL PAGE, admitted 1975. *Education:* University of Sydney (LL.B.). *PRACTICE AREAS:* Funds Management; Property; Trade Practices.

PETER JOHN ARTHUR CARNEY, admitted 1963. *Education:* University of Sydney (LL.B.). *PRACTICE AREAS:* Environmental Law; Property.

PATRICIA HELEN BROWN, admitted 1971. *Education:* University of Queensland (B.A., Hons.). *PRACTICE AREAS:* Banking; Finance; Corporate; Funds Raisings; Energy; Resources; Funds Management.

(This Listing Continued)

BRIAN JOHN MCFADYEN, admitted 1974. *Education:* University of Sydney (B.A.; LL.B.). *PRACTICE AREAS:* Commercial Property.

PETER JOHN PERRY, admitted 1969. *Education:* University of Western Australia (LL.B.); W.A. Solicitors Admission Board of Study. *PRACTICE AREAS:* Litigation; Trade Practices.

PETER STANLEY RIDOUT, admitted 1976. *Education:* University of Sydney (B.A.; LL.B.). *PRACTICE AREAS:* Engineering; Construction; Litigation; Privatisation; Infrastructure.

MICHAEL JOHN GRAY, admitted 1977. *Education:* University of New South Wales (B.Com.; LL.B.). *PRACTICE AREAS:* Corporate; Intellectual Property; Funds Management; Trade Practices.

HOWARD KEITH CHILLINGWORTH STEELE, admitted 1975. *Education:* Cambridge University (M.A.). *LANGUAGES:* Kiwi. *PRACTICE AREAS:* Litigation; Customs Law; Trade Practices.

JULIAN BLOCK, admitted 1957. *Education:* University of Witwatersrand (Dip. Law; H.Dip. Tax). Notary Public. *LANGUAGES:* Afrikaans. *PRACTICE AREAS:* Banking; Finance; Funds Raisings; Securities Trading; Funds Management.

CLAIRE GROSE, admitted 1968. *Education:* University of Adelaide (LL.B.). *PRACTICE AREAS:* Funds Raisings; Litigation; Funds Management.

JOHN HUGH CLIFFORD COLVIN, admitted 1979. *Education:* University of Sydney (B.Ec., Hons.); University of London (M.Sc., Econ.); University of Oxford (M.A.); N.S.W. Solicitors Admission Board of Study (Dip. Law). *PRACTICE AREAS:* Employee Relations; Funds Management; Trade Practices.

BRYAN DAVID WEIR, admitted, 1978. *Education:* University of New South Wales (B.Com.; LL.B.). *PRACTICE AREAS:* Corporate; Engineering; Construction; Mergers and Acquisitions; Privatisation; Infrastructure; Telecommunications.

ROY MERRILL RANDALL, admitted 1959. *Education:* University of Witwatersrand (B.Com.; LL.B.). *PRACTICE AREAS:* Funds Raisings; Energy; Resources; Privatisation; Infrastructure; Telecommunications.

ANTHONY JOSEPH MURATORE, admitted 1978. *Education:* University of New South Wales (B.A.; LL.B.). *PRACTICE AREAS:* Intellectual Property; Litigation.

RICHARD STUART GRAY, admitted 1978. *Education:* University of New South Wales (B.Com.; LL.B.); London School of Economics (LL.M.). *PRACTICE AREAS:* Banking; Finance; Funds Management.

JOHN KEVIN O'SULLIVAN, admitted 1978. *Education:* University of Sydney (B.A.; LL.B.); London School of Economics (LL.M.). *PRACTICE AREAS:* Banking; Finance; Funds Raisings; Funds Management; Securities Trading; Mergers and Acquisitions; Privatisation; Infrastructure.

GREGORY STEPHEN PEARCE, admitted 1978. *Education:* University of Sydney (B.A.; LL.B.). *PRACTICE AREAS:* Environmental Law; Funds Management; Property.

REBECCA ANNE DAVIES, admitted 1980. *Education:* Australian National University (B.Ec.; LL.B., Hons.). *PRACTICE AREAS:* Litigation; Funds Management.

GARY KENNETH LAWLER, admitted 1975. *Education:* University of Sydney (B.A.; LL.B.; LL.M. Hons.). *PRACTICE AREAS:* Mergers and Acquisitions.

GARRY CHARLES BESSON, admitted 1977. *Education:* University of Sydney (LL.B.; LL.M.). *PRACTICE AREAS:* Mergers and Acquisitions.

GORDON DAVID COOPER, admitted 1978. *Education:* University of New South Wales (B.Comm.; LL.B.). Notary Public. *PRACTICE AREAS:* Banking; Finance; Funds Management.

STEPHEN DAVID CHIPKIN, admitted, 1978. *Education:* University of Cambridge (B.Com.; B.A., Hons.; LL.B.). *PRACTICE AREAS:* Corporate; Funds Raisings; Funds Management.

YUKIO HAYASHI, admitted, 1978. *Education:* University of New South Wales (B.Juris.; LL.B.). *PRACTICE AREAS:* Corporate.

GRAHAM JOHN KELLY, admitted, 1971. *Education:* Australian National University (LL.B., Hons.). *PRACTICE AREAS:* Privatisation; Infrastructure; Trade Practices.

(This Listing Continued)

FREEHILL HOLLINGDALE & PAGE, Sydney, New South Wales—Continued

BARRY LEON BARKER, admitted, 1979. *Education:* University of New South Wales (B.Com.; LL.B.). *PRACTICE AREAS:* Environmental Law; Stamp Duty.

PHILIP JOHN CHRISTENSEN, admitted, 1980. *Education:* University of New South Wales (B.Com.; LL.B.). *LANGUAGES:* Bahasa Indonesian. *PRACTICE AREAS:* Corporate; Energy; Resources.

HELEN IRWIN WRIGHT, admitted, 1980. *Education:* University of New South Wales (LL.B.). *PRACTICE AREAS:* Funds Management; Property.

SHAUN GERARD MCGUSHIN, admitted, 1980. *Education:* University of Tasmania (LL.B.); University of Sydney (M.B.A.). *PRACTICE AREAS:* Banking; Finance; Funds Raisings; Securities Trading.

MARK RUSSELL COHEN, admitted, 1980. *Education:* University of New South Wales (B.Com.; LL.B.). *PRACTICE AREAS:* Corporate; Funds Raisings; Funds Management.

JOHN PEIRCE ANGUS, admitted, 1982. *Education:* University of Melbourne (B.A.; LL.B., Hons.). *PRACTICE AREAS:* Banking; Finance; Funds Management; Stamp Duty.

MURRAY JOHN DEARBERG, admitted, 1978. *Education:* University of Sydney (B.A.; LL.B.). *PRACTICE AREAS:* Property.

TIMOTHY MARK HIRSHMAN, admitted, 1981. *Education:* University of Sydney (LL.B.). *PRACTICE AREAS:* Corporate; Funds Raisings; Funds Management; Securities Trading; Mergers and Acquisitions; Trade Practices.

LEON PASTERNAK, admitted, 1981. *Education:* University of Sydney (B.Ec., Hons.; LL.B.); A.A.S.A. *PRACTICE AREAS:* Corporate; Funds Raisings; Funds Management; Securities Trading; Mergers and Acquisitions; Trade Practices.

DONALD BRUCE ROBERTSON, admitted, 1982. *Education:* University of Sydney (B.Ec., Hons.; LL.B., Hons.); Columbia University (LL.M.). *PRACTICE AREAS:* Litigation; Trade Practices.

GEOFFREY ALAN MCCLELLAN, admitted, 1979. *Education:* University of Sydney (B.Ec.; LL.B.). *PRACTICE AREAS:* Litigation; Media Law; Product Liability; Trade Practices.

GAVIN TERENCE BELL, admitted, 1982. *Education:* University of Sydney (LL.B.). *PRACTICE AREAS:* Engineering; Construction; Litigation.

JOHN GILBERT TABERNER, admitted, 1982. *Education:* University of Sydney (M.A. Hons.; LL.B.); George Washington University (M.Comp.L.). *PRACTICE AREAS:* Environmental Law; Property.

GEORGINA MARGARET GRAY, admitted, 1982. *Education:* University of New South Wales (B.A.; LL.B.). *PRACTICE AREAS:* Litigation; Funds Management; Trade Practices.

PHILLIPA JANE STONE, admitted, 1984. *Education:* University of Sydney (B.A. Hons.; LL.B. Hons.). *PRACTICE AREAS:* Corporate; Funds Raisings; Funds Management; Securities Trading; Mergers and Acquisitions; Privatisation; Infrastructure.

HEAN-LAY GAN, admitted, 1979. *Education:* University of Durham (B.A. Hons.). *LANGUAGES:* Malay and Hokkien. *PRACTICE AREAS:* Engineering; Construction; Litigation; Privatisation; Infrastructure; Telecommunications.

PETER JOSEPH SEYMOUR ROWE, admitted, 1980. *Education:* Solicitors Admission Board. *PRACTICE AREAS:* Banking; Finance; Funds Raisings; Funds Management; Privatisation; Infrastructure.

JOHN CHRISTOPHER WILLIAMSON-NOBLE, admitted, 1988. *Education:* Exeter University (LL.B.); University of Dundee (Dip. Petroleum Law). *PRACTICE AREAS:* Corporate; Funds Raisings; Energy; Resources; Privatisations; Infrastructure.

BRUCE JOHN RAMSAY, admitted, 1983. *Education:* University of Sydney (B.A.; LL.B. Hons.). *PRACTICE AREAS:* Intellectual Property; Litigation; Trade Practices.

MICHAEL DAVID HARMER, admitted, 1983. *Education:* University of Sydney (B.Ec.; LL.B.). *PRACTICE AREAS:* Employee Relations; Funds Management.

(This Listing Continued)

RONALD L. SPACKMAN, admitted, 1969. *Education:* University of Sydney (LL.B., Dip. Ed.). *PRACTICE AREAS:* Banking; Finance; Funds Management.

FREDERICK BRADDON JOLLEY, admitted, 1983. *Education:* Australian National University (B.Ec.; LL.B. Hons). *PRACTICE AREAS:* Corporate; Funds Raisings; Securities Trading; Mergers and Acquisitions.

STEPHANIE JOAN PURSLEY, admitted, 1983. *Education:* New South Wales Solicitors Admission Board (B.A.). *LANGUAGES:* French and German. *PRACTICE AREAS:* Funds Management; Property.

SHEILA CLARE MCGREGOR, admitted, 1984. *Education:* University of Sydney (B.A. Hons; LL.B.). *PRACTICE AREAS:* Intellectual Property; Telecommunications; Trade Practices.

DAVID LESLIE GORDON, admitted, 1985. *Education:* University of New South Wales (B.Comm.; LL.B.). *PRACTICE AREAS:* Corporate; Funds Raisings; Funds Management; Mergers and Acquisitions.

DON E. HARDING, admitted, 1963. *Education:* University of Sydney (B.A.; LL.B); University of California (LL.M.). *PRACTICE AREAS:* Corporate; Funds Management; Funds Raisings; Securities Trading; Mergers and Acquisitions; Trade Practices.

CATHERINE MARY MURPHY, admitted, 1982. *Education:* University of Sydney (B.S.; LL.B. Hons). *PRACTICE AREAS:* Property.

MARK BERNARD JOSEPH CREAN, admitted, 1980. *Education:* Leeds University (LLB. Hons.). *PRACTICE AREAS:* Corporate; Funds Raisings; Funds Management; Mergers and Acquisitions; Telecommunications; Trade Practices.

ALISTAIR JAMES MCLEAN DONALD, admitted, 1982. *Education:* University of Western Australia (B.Juris.; LL.B.). *PRACTICE AREAS:* Banking; Finance; Funds Raisings; Securities Trading.

HAROLD JOHN ANDREWS, admitted, 1980. *Education:* Solicitors Admission Board (Dip. Law). *PRACTICE AREAS:* Corporate; Funds Management; Property.

SEUNG KYU BANG, admitted, 1984. *Education:* University of Sydney (B.A.; LL.B.). *LANGUAGES:* Korean. *PRACTICE AREAS:* Corporate; Energy; Resources.

CHRISTOPHER PAUL BARTON, admitted, 1984. *Education:* London University (M.Sc.), Solicitors Admission Board. *PRACTICE AREAS:* Corporate; Employee Relations; Intellectual Property; Funds Management; Trade Practices.

ELIZABETH JOAN GRINSTON, admitted, 1986. *Education:* University of Sydney (B.A.; LL.B., Hons.). *LANGUAGES:* Japanese. *PRACTICE AREAS:* Intellectual Property; Litigation.

GRAEME EDWARD JAMES JOHNSON, admitted, 1987. *Education:* Australian National University (B.A.; LL.B., Hons.). *PRACTICE AREAS:* Litigation; Funds Management; Product Liability.

MICHAEL ALEXANDER VRISAKIS, admitted, 1985. *Education:* University of New South Wales (LL.B.). *LANGUAGES:* French and German. *PRACTICE AREAS:* Funds Management.

ADAM LIBERMAN, admitted, 1976. *Education:* University of New South Wales (B.Com.; LL.B.). *PRACTICE AREAS:* Corporate; Intellectual Property; Mergers and Acquisitions.

JULIANA WARNER, admitted, 1980. *Education:* University of New South Wales (B.A.; LL.B.). *PRACTICE AREAS:* Litigation.

LEANNE NORMAN, admitted, 1983. *Education:* Australian National University (B.A.; LL.B., Hons.). *PRACTICE AREAS:* Litigation; Media Law.

JUSTIN PELLY, admitted, 1986. *Education:* University of New South Wales (B.Com.; LL.B.). *PRACTICE AREAS:* Banking; Finance.

MARGARET STONE, admitted, 1991. *Education:* Australian National University (B.A., Hons.; LL.B., Hons.); Yale University (LL.M.). *PRACTICE AREAS:* Property.

CONSULTANTS

Ian F. Hutchinson	Roderick McLeod
Peter E. Hollingdale	Edmund A. O'Halloran
Warren F. Asprey	The Hon. John T. Ludeke
Brian E. Thornton	Assoc. Prof. Greg McGarry
Thomas O. Jones	Professor John Carter

(This Listing Continued)

(For biographical data on all other Firm Personnel, see Professional Biographies at Brisbane, Canberra, Melbourne and Perth, Australia and Singapore)

GADENS RIDGEWAY

LEVELS 12-15
SKYGARDEN BUILDING
77 CASTLEREAGH STREET
SYDNEY, NEW SOUTH WALES 2000, AUSTRALIA
Telephone: (612) 232-5566
Fax: (612) 931-4888

Melbourne, Victoria, Australia Office: Levels 20-23, AMP Tower, 535 Bourke Street, 3000. Telephone: (613) 614-4844. Fax: (613) 614-3770.

Brisbane, Queensland, Australia Office: Levels 39-40, Central Plaza One, 345 Queen Street, 4000, GPO Box 129, Brisbane 4001. Telephone: (617) 231-1666. Fax: (617) 229-5850.

Cairns, Queensland, Australia Office: 95 Sheridan Street, 4870, P.O. Box 6001. Telephone: (6170) 31-1622. Fax: (6170) 51-7828.

Port Moresby, Papua New Guinea Office: Pacific Place, Cnr. Musgrave Street & Champion Parade, P.O. Box 1042. Telephone: (675) 21-1033. Fax: (675) 21-1885.

Banking and Finance, Capital Raisings, Commercial Litigation, Dispute Resolution and Arbitration, Computer Law, Construction and Engineering, Corporate Law, Corporate Reconstructions, Employment Law, Entertainment Law, Export Grants, Family Law, Foreign Investment, Bloodstock Breeding and Racing, Hotel and Liquor Licensing, Industrial Relations, Insolvency, Insurance Law, Intellectual Property, Local Government, Manufacturing, Media Law, Mergers, Acquisitions and Takeovers, Mining and Resources, Planning and Environmental Law, Private Client (Wills, Probate and Conveyancing), Property Development, Retailing, Sports Law, Superannuation, Taxation and Revenue, Tourism and Leisure, Trade and Business Transactions, Trade Practices Legislation, Transport, Trusts and Funds Management.

RESIDENT PARTNERS

Peter Bowen
John Nelson
Gary Traill
Jon Denovan
David Snedden
John Rollason
Kevin Munro
John Fuller
Ian Clarke
Ivan Haege
David Baird
Neil Milne
Stuart Fowler
John McDonell
John Gibson
Ian Chipchase
James Green
Martin Hirst
Chris Coudounaris
Suzanne Stanton
Mark Skinner
Joanne Kelly
Doreen Toltz

SENIOR ASSOCIATES

Andrew Petersen
Frances Richards
Mark Robinson
Carol Berliner
Michael Bradley
Robert Riddell
Roslyn Forrest
Arthur Koumoukelis
Lydia Dowse
Maree Henshaw
Michael Hodgson
Kelly Levy

(This Listing Continued)

CONSULTANTS

Gordon Stewart

(For list of Personnel at Brisbane, Melbourne and Cairns, Australia and Port Moresby, New Guinea, see Professional Biographies at those locations)

JOHN GARNSEY, Q.C.

Senior Counsel and Advocate

Blackstone Chambers Barristers

LEVEL 62, MLC CENTRE
19 MARTIN PLACE
SYDNEY, NEW SOUTH WALES 2000, AUSTRALIA
Telephone: (+61 2) 220 9870; (+61 2) 960 1520; (+61) 041 11 91389
Fax: (+61 2) 233 4209

Commercial Law with emphasis on Corporations and Securities Law, Trade Practices and Competition Law, Trusts, Equity and Property Law and Alternative Dispute Resolution, Intellectual Property, Patents, Designs, Trade Marks, Confidential Information, Unfair Trade Practices, Arts and Information Technology and Defamation and Media Law.

JOHN GARNSEY, Q.C., born Sydney, Australia, November 23, 1945. admitted: Australia, Federal Register of Legal Practitioners for Australian High Court, Federal Court and other Commonwealth Courts; New South Wales: 1973, Solicitor and Barrister, 1989, Queen's Counsel; Australian Capital Territory: 1976, Barrister and Solicitor, 1990, Queen's Counsel; Victoria: 1977, Barrister and Solicitor and Bar Roll, 1990, Queen's Counsel; Queensland: 1990, Barrister and Queen's Counsel; Western Australia: 1990, Barrister, 1991, Queen's Counsel; Northern Territory: 1985, Barrister and Solicitor, 1990, Queen's Counsel; Ireland: 1991, Barrister-at-Law, King's Inn and Bar of the Republic of Ireland. *Education:* University of Sydney (B.A.; LL.B., Hons., 1969; LL.M., Hons., 1975). Co-author: "Butterworths Intellectual Property in Australia, Patents Designs and Trade Marks Law," Sydney, Australia; "Intellectual Property Rights-The Australian Experience," 1986, 2 Intellectual Property Journal 303, Carswell, Ontario, Canada. Assistant Editor, "Butterworths Intellectual Property Reports," Sydney, Australia. Author of various conference and seminar papers on intellectual property subjects. *Member:* New South Wales, Victorian and Queensland Bar Associations; International Bar Association.

Independent Legal Practitioner (Barrister) and Senior Counsel (QC) practising from Barristers' Chambers as Advocate and Consultant Legal Counsel.

GILBERT & TOBIN

Established in 1988

CARRINGTON HOUSE
50 CARRINGTON STREET
SYDNEY, NEW SOUTH WALES 2000, AUSTRALIA
Telephone: 61 2 367 3000
Fax: 61 2 367 3111

Gilbert & Tobin is a corporate and commercial practice specializing in providing legal services in the communications, media, information technology and manufacturing sectors for international, Australian and government clients.

FIRM PROFILE: The firm was established in January 1988 and comprises partners drawn from major Australian commercial law firms. The firm's client base reflects Gilbert & Tobin's international orientation. The firm now has a total of 10 Partners, 34 Senior Lawyers, 4 Paralegals and 38 Support Staff.

PARTNERS

DANIEL THOMAS GILBERT, admitted, 1973, New South Wales. *Education:* University of Sydney (LL.B). Member: Australian Institute of Company Directors; Licensing Executives Society. *Member:* Law Society of New South Wales; Corporate Lawyers Association of New South Wales; New South Wales Society for Computers and the Law. *PRACTICE AREAS:* Mergers and Acquisitions; US Securities Laws; Australian Securities Laws; Stock Exchange Compliance; Commercial Litigation; Technology Licensing and Computer Contracting.

(This Listing Continued)

GILBERT & TOBIN, *Sydney, New South Wales—*
Continued

PETER GUILDFORD LEONARD, admitted, 1980, New South Wales; 1986, Australian Capital Territory. *Education:* University of Sydney (B.Ec., Hons., LL.B., 1980; LL.M., 1991). Contributing Editor, Communications Law and Policy in Australia. Privacy Law and Policy Reporter. Senior Contributor, Australian Communications; Visiting Lecturer, Macquarie University Graduate School of Management. Member: Australian Information Industry Association; Research Foundation on Information Technology; Media and Communications Sub-Committee; Law Council of Australia. Australian Telecommunications Users Group; Electronic Data Interchange Council of Australia; Copyright Society; International Institute of Communications; Australian Computer Society; Australian Communication Association. *Member:* Law Society of New South Wales; Law Council of Australia; American Bar Association; International Bar Association; Communications and Media Law Association; New South Wales Society for Computers and the Law; Intellectual and Industrial Property Society; Computer Law Association (USA). *PRACTICE AREAS:* Information Technology and Telecommunications; Intellectual Property; Corporate Advisory; International Transactions; Business Structuring.

MARK GEOFFREY O'BRIEN, admitted, 1970, New South Wales; 1972, Australian Capital Territory 1986, Victoria. *Education:* University of Sydney (B.A.; LL.B., 1969). *Member:* Law Society of New South Wales; Communications & Media Law Association. *PRACTICE AREAS:* Media Law; Commercial Litigation; Trade Practices Law.

STEPHEN PHILIP PEACH, admitted, 1982, New South Wales. *Education:* University of Sydney (B.A.; LL.B.). Associate Editor, The Communications Law Bulletin. Australian Copyright Society (Member, Management Committee). *Member:* Law Society of New South Wales. *PRACTICE AREAS:* Copyright; Recording Industry; Film Production and Distribution; Intellectual Property Licensing and Litigation; Commercial Litigation.

EDWARD NOEL PRETTY, admitted, 1981, New South Wales; 1986, Victoria; 1991, Australian Capital Territory. *Education:* Macquarie University (B.A., LL.B., Hons., 1981). Australian Information Technology Association; Licensing Executives Society. *Member:* Law Society of New South Wales; Computer Law Association (USA); New South Wales Society for Computers and the Law; Law Institute of Victoria. *PRACTICE AREAS:* Information Technology; Technology Licensing; Telecommunications; Government Tenders and Contracting.

WILLIAM ROBERT SPAIN, admitted, 1984, New South Wales. *Education:* University of New South Wales (B.Com., 1982; LL.B., 1983); University of Sydney (LL.M., 1990). Trade Practices Discussions Group; Licensing Executives Society; Institute of Company Directors. *Member:* Law Society of New South Wales; Intellectual and Industrial Property Society. *PRACTICE AREAS:* Information Technology; Communications; Corporate Law; Trade Practices; Securities.

ANTHONY JAMES TOBIN, admitted, 1972, Queensland; 1976, New South Wales. *Education:* University of Queensland (B.A., LL.B., 1971). German/Australian Chamber of Commerce. *Member:* Law Society of New South Wales; Law Council of Australia (Member, Companies Committee Business Law Section); International Bar Association; Company Law Discussion Group; AIJA-Young Lawyers International Association; International Association of Lawyers. *PRACTICE AREAS:* Corporate and Commercial Law; Mergers and Acquisitions; Insolvency and Reconstruction; Infrastructure Finance; Technology Licensing and Transfer.

PETER FRANCIS WATERS, admitted, 1983, New South Wales. *Education:* Australian National University (B.A., 1981; LL.B., 1983); Fulbright Scholar, Harvard Law School (LL.M., 1988). Australian Telecommunications Users Group. *Member:* Law Society of New South Wales; New South Wales Society for Computers and the Law; International Bar Association; Communications and Media Law Association. *PRACTICE AREAS:* Regulatory Affairs; Information Technology; Telecommunications; Intellectual Property; Computer Systems Agreements; International Transactions.

REPRESENTATIVE CLIENTS: AAP Information Services Pty Limited and AAP Group Companies; Amdahl Corporation; AusAsean Group; Alcatel Australia; Andersen Consulting; Australian Consolidated Press Limited; Australian Development Capital Fund; Australian Film Commission; Australian Industry Development Corporation; Australian Information Industry Association; Australian Mechanical Copyright Owners Society; Australian Record Industry Association; The Ball Partnership; Capital Cities/ABC Inc.; Carpenter Pacific Resources Limited; CCI Holdings Limited; China Geological Technology Development and Import and Export Corporation; Coopers & Lybrand; Clyde Industries Group; Commercial Computer Centre Pty Limited; Commercial Services Group (NSW Government); Commodore Business Machines Pty Limited; Con-

(This Listing Continued)

cord Resources Pty Limited; Continental Cablevision; Development Capital of Australia Limited; Festival Records; Film & Video Security Office; General Publishers Limited; Hannan Group; Hong Kong Telecom; IBA Healthcare Pty Ltd.; Intag International Limited; Lotus Development Corporation; Lumley General Insurance Limited; MCI Communications Corporation; Memorex Telex Pty Limited; National Rail Corporation; New South Wales Department of Health; New South Wales Department of Transport; New South Wales Water Board; Nine Network Australia Limited; Nokia Mobile Phones; Nokia Telecommunications Pty Limited; Optus Communications Pty Limited; PolyGram Pty Limited; Qantas/Q H Tours; Regional Publishers Pty Limited; Rental Bond Board of NSW; Reinforced Earth Pty Limited; Ramtron Group; Ronin Films Pty Limited; Rural Press Limited; Scitec Communication Systems Limited; Sony Music Australia; Stanilite Electronics Pty Limited; State Bank of New South Wales; St. John of God Health Care Systems, Inc.; Tetley Manufacturing Limited; Thomson Sintra Pacific Pty Limited; Turner Broadcasting International / CNN; Unisys Australia Limited; Wang Australia Pty Limited; Warner Music Australia Pty Limited; WorkCover Authority of New South Wales.

HENRY DAVIS YORK

LEVEL 25
135 KING STREET
SYDNEY, NEW SOUTH WALES 2000, AUSTRALIA
Telephone: (612) 364 6300
Fax: (612) 235 1244

MEMBERS OF FIRM

GERALD RALPH CHRISTMAS, admitted, 1961, New South Wales. *Education:* University of Sydney (B.A.; LL.B.).

PETER DAVID SCAMMELL, admitted, 1960, New South Wales. *Education:* University of Sydney (B.A.; LL.B.).

JAMES HENRY DAVIS, admitted, 1971, New South Wales. *Education:* University of Sydney (B.A.; LL.B.).

GEOFFREY ALLAN HILTON, admitted, 1974, New South Wales. *Education:* University of Sydney (LL.M. Hons.).

JOHN DAVID LLOYD, admitted, 1974, New South Wales. *Education:* University of Queensland (LL.B.).

PHILIP JAMES CRAWFORD, admitted, 1978, New South Wales. *Education:* University of Sydney (B.A.; LL.B.).

JOHN COLIN WINDEYER, admitted, 1974, New South Wales. *Education:* University of Sydney (B.A.; LL.B.).

CHARLES MARK PERCIVAL ALLEN, admitted, 1978, New South Wales. *Education:* Dip Law (S.A.B.).

IAN DAVID ELVY, admitted, 1975, New South Wales. *Education:* Dip. Law (S.A.B.).

WENDY HANNELLY BROUN, admitted, 1977, New South Wales. *Education:* Dip. Law (S.A.B.).

JOHN SYDNEY CURRIE, admitted, 1975, New South Wales; 1981, United Kingdom. *Education:* University of Sydney (B.A.; LL.B.); University of London (LL.M.).

RICHARD AUSTIN CAVANAGH, admitted, 1982, New South Wales. *Education:* University of New South Wales (B.A.; LL.B.).

ROBERT JOHN TRACY, admitted, 1986, Victoria; 1987, New South Wales. *Education:* University of Melbourne (B.Comm, LL.B.).

STEPHEN LAWRENCE PURCELL, admitted, 1983, New South Wales. *Education:* University of Sydney (BEc.; LL.B.).

HELEN PATRICIA ABRAHAMS, admitted, 1985, New South Wales. *Education:* Macquarie University (B.A., LL.B. Hons.).

ROGER WILLIAM DOBSON, admitted, 1981, South Australia; 1989, New South Wales. *Education:* University of Adelaide (LL.B. Hons.); Columbia University, New York (LL.M.).

ANTHONY JOSEPH WOODS, admitted, 1982, New South Wales. *Education:* University of New South Wales (B.A.; LL.B.); University of Sydney (LL.M.).

MARK WILLIAM HILTON, admitted, 1983, New South Wales. *Education:* University of New South Wales (B. Comm; LL.B.).

JOHN DAVID EVANS, admitted, 1984, New South Wales. *Education:* University of New South Wales (B. Juris; LL.B.).

SIMON ANTHONY MCSWEENEY, admitted, 1982, New South Wales. *Education:* University of New South Wales (B. Comm; LL.B.); London School of Economics and Political Science (LL.M.).

(This Listing Continued)

PAUL EDWARD CAPORALE, admitted, 1987, New South Wales. *Education:* University of NSW (B.A.; Hons.; LL.B.).

JOHN KENNETH MARTIN, admitted, 1985, New South Wales. *Member:* Sydney University (B.Ec.; Hons.; LL.B.; Hons.).

SENIOR ASSOCIATES

SHANE EDWARD MARTINS, admitted, 1987, New South Wales.

RODNEY JAMES BRETAG, admitted, 1985, New South Wales.

KATHRYN JANE WILLIAMS, admitted, 1987, New South Wales.

JACQUELINE MARIE DEANE, admitted, 1988, New South Wales.

MICHAEL MARTIN ROWE, admitted, 1988, New South Wales.

STEPHEN MARK GORRY, admitted, 1987, New South Wales.

JAMES DAVID LONIE, admitted, 1988, New South Wales.

SCOTT JAMES MURRAY, admitted, 1988, New South Wales.

JAMES BERNARD RILEY, admitted, 1993, New South Wales.

CONSULTANTS

Paul Hamilton Hookway
George Alfred Weaver
Professor John Wade

H.R. HODGKINSON & CO.

Patent and Trademark Attorneys

LEVEL 3, 20 ALFRED STREET, MELSONS POINT
SYDNEY, NEW SOUTH WALES 2061, AUSTRALIA
Telephone: 61-2-922 31 99
Fax: 61-2-956 64 48

Mailing Address: P.O. Box 136, Milsons Point, N.S.W., 2061, Australia

Intellectual Property, Mechanical, Chemical and Electronic Patents, Industrial Models, License Negotiation, Patent Trademark Litigation and Prosecution, Pharmaceutical Patents, Unfair Competition.

HUGH RUDYARD HODGKINSON, born Sydney, Australia, December 15, 1944; admitted, 1980, Australia as Patent Attorney. *Education:* Sydney University (B.Sc., 1966). Registered Patent Attorney. Major Cases: Patent Extension DuPont, 1988; Trademark Infringement Moo/Moove, 1986-1990. Unfair Competition, "Fun-Ships" Carnival Cruises, 1985-1995. Vice-President, Asian Patent Attorneys Association, Tokyo. Councillor, Institute of Patent Attorneys of Australia, 1990-1995. President, Australian Group of A.P.A.A. Co-Author: "Trademarks in APAA Countries,". Lecturer, School of Industrial Design, 1982-1988. *Member:* LES,ITMA, ECTA, APAA, AIPPI, FICPI, IMTA. *PRACTICE AREAS:* Patent Law; Trademark Law; Designs; Litigation.

DAVID A. SUTTON, born Wellington, New Zealand, February 14, 1948; admitted, 1974, New Zealand as Patent Attorney. *Education:* Wellington, New Zealand. Former Registered Patent Attorney, New Zealand. *PRACTICE AREAS:* Patents; Trademarks; Litigation.

PETER L. PEARSON, born Sydney, Australia, June 3, 1944; admitted, 1974, as Registered Patent Attorney. *Education:* University of New South Wales (B.Sc.). *PRACTICE AREAS:* Patent; Trademark.

JOHN R. WALSH, born Sydney, Australia, January 20, 1953; admitted, 1972, as Registered Patent Attorney, Barrister-at-Law. *Education:* University of New South Wales (B.E., Civil). *PRACTICE AREAS:* Patent; Trademark; Litigation; Licensing.

HOLMAN WEBB

Established in 1960

13TH FLOOR, MACQUARIE HOUSE
167 MACQUARIE STREET
SYDNEY, NEW SOUTH WALES 2000, AUSTRALIA
Telephone: 02-390 8000
International: 612-390-8000
Fax: (02) 390-8390

Mailing Address: Box 119 G.P.O., Sydney, 2001

Agents in all states and territories of Australia.

(This Listing Continued)

General Practice, Administrative Law, Aviation, Acquisitions and Takeovers, Banking and Finance, Business Dispute Resolution, Bloodstock Breeding and Racing, Capital Raisings, Commercial Property Planning and Construction, Construction and Engineering, Computers, Commercial Litigation, Corporate Law, Corporate Reconstructions, Dispute Resolution and Arbitration, Employment and Industrial Relations, Entertainment Law, Export Grants, Family Law, Foreign Investment, Federal and State Taxation, Formation and Reconstruction of Business Structures, Franchising, Estate Planning, General Commercial and Corporate Advice, Hotel and Liquor Licensing, Industrial Relations, Insolvency, Insurance Advising, Insurance Litigation, Intellectual Property, Local Government, Manufacturing, Media and Defamation, Mergers, Mining and Resources, Products Liability, Professional Indemnity, Planning and Environmental Law, Private Client (Wills, Probate and Conveyancing), Property Development, Occupational Health and Safety, Retailing, Real Estate, Securities, Sports Law, Superannuation, Shipping, Transport, Trade Practices and Consumer Law, Taxation and Revenue, Tourism and Leisure, Trade and Business Transactions, Trusts and Fund Management, Telecommunications and Environmental and Planning Law.

MEMBERS OF FIRM

DOUGLAS WILLIAM WEBB, admitted, 1958, New South Wales; 1962, High Court of Australia. *Education:* University of Sydney (LL.B.).

JOHN BAINES CHEADLE, admitted, 1951, New South Wales. *Education:* University of Sydney (LL.B.).

HUGH ROSTREVOR NORTON, admitted, 1949, New South Wales, High Court of Australia. *Education:* Solicitors Admission Board.

CLIVE HUNTER MANSELL, OAM, admitted, 1956, New South Wales, High Court of Australia. *Education:* Solicitors Admission Board.

MARCUS JAMES PHILIP KEOUGH, admitted, 1957, New South Wales. *Education:* University of Sydney (LL.B.).

WARWICK RICHMOND LANGBY, admitted, 1964, New South Wales; 1965, High Court of Australia; 1975, Australian Capital Territory. *Education:* Solicitors Admission Board.

BERNARD HENRY JOHN LEVY, admitted, 1957, New South Wales. *Education:* University of Sydney (LL.B.).

D'ARCY ANTHONY KELLY, admitted, 1975, New South Wales. *Education:* Solicitors Admission Board.

MICHAEL FREDERICK STAR, admitted, 1969, New South Wales. *Education:* University of Sydney (B.A.; LL.B.).

LEE JOHN JACKSON, admitted, 1975, New South Wales; 1976, High Court of Australia. *Education:* University of Sydney (B.Ec.); Solicitors Admission Board.

PETER WILLIAM MORRIS BRIGGS, admitted, 1970, High Court of Australia; 1981, New South Wales. *Education:* University of Melbourne (LL.B.).

IAN JOEL POLKINGHORNE, admitted, 1973, New South Wales. *Education:* Solicitors Admission Board.

RICHARD JOHN ALLSOP, admitted, 1974, New South Wales; 1975, High Court of Australia. *Education:* University of Sydney (B.A., LL.B.).

MARK NICHOLAS JOHNSON, admitted, 1976, New South Wales; 1978, High Court of Australia. *Education:* University of Sydney (LL.B.).

MICHAEL LANCASTER OATES, admitted, 1962, South Africa; 1965, England; 1966, New South Wales.

NORMAN LEWIS CORKILL, admitted, 1962, New South Wales. *Education:* Solicitors Admission Board.

ROGER JOHN CORNFORTH, admitted, 1980, New South Wales. *Education:* Solicitors Admission Board.

GREGORY MARK BUSH, admitted, 1978, New South Wales. *Education:* University of Sydney (B.A.; LL.B.).

DAVID BERNARD HARTSTEIN, admitted, 1980, New South Wales. *Education:* Australian National University (B.A.; LL.B.).

WALTER JONATHAN CASSON, admitted, 1979, New South Wales. *Education:* Australian National University (B.A.; LL.B.); University of Sydney (LL.M.).

STEPHEN DAVID ROGERS, admitted, 1984, New South Wales. *Education:* Solicitors Admission Board.

(This Listing Continued)

HOLMAN WEBB, Sydney, New South Wales—Continued

PAUL BRADLEY WHOLOHAN, admitted, 1982, New South Wales. *Education:* Macquarie University (B.A.; LL.B.).

ALEXANDER JOHN WAKEFIELD, admitted, 1990, New South Wales, High Court of Australia. *Education:* Macquarie University (B.A.); Solicitors Admission Board.

PAUL BRIAN DUFFY, admitted, 1972, New South Wales; 1973, High Court of Australia. *Education:* University of Sydney (LL.B.).

VAN ANGELO MOULIS, admitted, 1979, New South Wales; 1983, High Court of Australia. *Education:* Australian National University (LL.B.).

SENIOR ASSOCIATES

ANGELA MIRA BREGOVAC, admitted, 1984, New South Wales. *Education:* University of New South Wales (LL.B., B.Com. Acctg.).

DAVID JOHN GALLOP, admitted, 1990, New South Wales. *Education:* Australian National University (B.A.); University of Sydney (LL.B.).

WENDY ANNE MACDONELL, admitted, 1989, New South Wales; 1990, High Court of Australia. *Education:* University of Sydney (B.A.; LL.B.); University of New South Wales (LL.M.).

CONSULTANTS

DAVID LEE PRICE, OAM, admitted, 1951, New South Wales. *Education:* Solicitors Admission Board.

LANDERER & COMPANY

Established in 1970

LEVEL 31
133 CASTLEREAGH STREET
SYDNEY, NEW SOUTH WALES 2000, AUSTRALIA
Telephone: (612) 261 4242
Facsimile: (612) 261 8516

FIRM PROFILE: Established 1970, Landerer & Company specialises in corporate and commercial advisory work, mergers and acquisitions, commercial litigation, and finance and property transactions.

PARTNERS

JOHN LANDERER A.M., admitted, 1970, New South Wales. *Education:* Sydney University (LL.B.).

PETER VESELY, admitted, 1975, New South Wales. *Education:* Sydney University (LL.B.).

KENNETH JOHN SEARLE, admitted, 1977, New South Wales. *Education:* Sydney University (B.A.; LL.B.).

ADRIAN JOHN BOURIS, admitted, 1984, New South Wales. *Education:* University of New South Wales (B.Com.; LL.B.).

MARK WAIN HOUSTON, admitted, 1983, South Australia; 1984, New South Wales. *Education:* University of South Australia (LL.B.; BEc).

ELLIS NEVILLE VAREJES, admitted, 1977, South Africa; 1979, Lesotho; 1981, Victoria; 1982, New South Wales. *Education:* University of the Witwatersrand (B.Com.; LL.B.). Notary Public for New South Wales.

JONATHAN CAPLAN, admitted, 1985, New South Wales. *Education:* Sydney University (B.A.; LL.M). Notary Public for New Wales. Accredited Specialist Business Law.

MICHAEL JOHN GOUGH, admitted, 1984, New South Wales. *Education:* Diploma in Law (Solicitors Admission Board).

MALLESONS STEPHEN JAQUES

LEVEL 60 GOVERNOR PHILLIP TOWER
1 FARRER PLACE
SYDNEY, NEW SOUTH WALES 2000, AUSTRALIA
Telephone: (612) 250 3000
Fax: (612) 250 3133

Melbourne, Australia Office: Level 28, Rialto, 525 Collins Street, 3000. Telephone: (613) 619 0619. Fax: (613) 614 1329.
Perth, Australia Office: Ground Floor, St. Georges Square, 225 St. George's Terrace, 6000. Telephone: (619) 324 8333. Fax: (619) 321 1017.

(This Listing Continued)

Brisbane, Australia Office: Level 30, Waterfront Place, 1 Eagle Street, 4000. Telephone: (617) 231 7500. Fax: (617) 221 1211.
Canberra, Australia Office: Level 10, Advance Bank Centre, 60 Marcus Clarke Street, 2601. Telephone: (616) 268 3900. Fax: (616) 257 3100.
Hong Kong Office: Bateson Starr in association with Mallesons Stephen Jaques, Suite 801, Asia Pacific Finance Tower, Citibank Plaza, 3 Garden Road, Central Hong Kong. Telephone: (852) 848 4600. Fax: (852) 868-0124.
Beijing, The Peoples Republic of China Office: Suite 701, Scite Tower, 22 Jianguomenwai Street, 100004. Telephone: (861) 512-3565 ext. 701. Fax: (861) 523 2018.
Taipei, Taiwan Office: 14th Floor, Mallesons Stephen Jaques, 138 Min Sheng East Road, Sec 3. Telephone: (8862) 712 5808. Fax: (8862) 712 9080.
Jakarta, Indonesia Associated Office: Law Firm Kartini Muljadi S.H. & Associates in association with Mallesons Stephen Jaques, Bina Mulia I Building, J1 HR Rasuna Said Kav 10, 12950. Telephone: (6221) 5256968. Fax: (6221) 5255561.
Port Moresby, Papua, New Guinea Office: Beresford Love, agents for Mallesons Stephen Jaques, Level 3, Hunter Building, Hunter Street. Telephone: (675) 211 942. Fax: (675) 211 586.
Singapore Office: Level 36, Hong Leong Building, 16 Raffles Quay, 0104. Telephone: (65) 321 8930. Fax: (65) 225 9060.
London, England Office: 2nd Floor, Aldermary House, 10-15 Queen Street, EC4N 1TX. Telephone: (44 171) 9820982. Fax: (44 171) 9829820.
New York, New York, U.S.A. Office: 9th floor, Suite 911, 609 Fifth Avenue, 10017-1021. Telephone: (1-212) 319-9500. Fax: (1-212) 319-9506.

Banking and Finance, Mergers and Acquisitions, Issues and Underwriting, Corporate and Commercial Foreign Investment, Federal and State Government Liaison, Property Development, Mining, Resources and Energy, Technology, Trade Practices, Intellectual Property, Tourism and Leisure, Aviation, Telecommunications, Environment, Litigation and Alternative Dispute Resolution.

MEMBERS OF FIRM
SYDNEY, AUSTRALIA OFFICE

Michael Allen	Ted Kerr
Ian Angus	John King
Philip Argy	Tom Lennox
John Atkin	Greg Lewis
Tony Bancroft	Kevin Lloyd
Reg Barrett	Peter Machin
Graham Bates	Jeff Mansfield
Jim Bennett	Richard Marshall
Gary Best	Richard Mazzoch
Ashley Black	Barry McWilliams
Tim Blue	Joe Montano
Jim Boynton	David O'Donnell
Barry Casey	David Olsson
Robyn Chalmers	Susan O'Rourke
Karen Coleman	Robert Postema
Nuncio D'Angelo	Jamie Prell
Stuart Dixon-Smith	Gerald Raftesath
John Edstein	Katrina Rathie
Paul Ellis	David Rohr
David Fairlie	Karen Rooke
Roger Featherston	Thea Rosenbaum
Michael Gammans	Howard Schreiber
Belinda Gibson	Adrienne Showering
Greg Golding	Andrew Smith
Maurice Gonsalves	Peter Stockdale
Tony Gooch	David Storr
Tim Hammon	John Stumbles
Greg Hammond	David Taylor
Michael Herring	Simon Tuxen
Mike Holm	Nicola Wakefield Evans
Ian James	Julie Ward
Martin James	Michael Wiley
John Kelly	David Williams

(This Listing Continued)

Frank Zipfinger

SYDNEY CONSULTANT

Neville Allen	Judith Heap
Bill Blanshard	Stanley Howard
Peter Butt	John Menadue
Robert Eagleson	Richard Nettleton
Richard Feetham	Roy Ringrose
	Bob Willcocks

MELBOURNE, AUSTRALIA OFFICE

Bruce Akhurst	Emilios Kyrou
Ilana Atlas	Jim Lahore
Christopher Beeny	Alison Lansley
Tony Border	Davyd Lewis
Tom Bostock	Cheng Lim
David Bretherton	Elizabeth Lomas
Frank Brody	John Malon
Donald Brooker	Eric Mayne
Neil Carabine	Robert Milliner
Andrew Clements	Stephen Minns
Michael Clough	Andrew Monotti
Tony D'Aloisio	Bruce Moore
Mark Darian-Smith	Ian Murray
Graham Dent	Richard Nelson
Peter Doyle	Frank O'Brien
Ann Dufty	Rowan Russell
Andrew Erikson	Gerald Ryan
Roger Forbes	Trevor Sheehan
Randall Gerkens	Bernie Shinners
John Hambly	Graham Thomson
Jonathan Hamer	Paula Tuckfield
Stephen Harper	Julie Turner
Jim Higgins	Robin Vague
Susan Hilliard	David Walsh
Tony Holland	Matt Walsh
Peter Kelly	John Waters
Rowan Kennedy	David Wells
Michael Kingston	Peter Willis
	David Wood

CONSULTANTS

Maxwell Ham	Roy Ricker
Frank Kenna	William Shmith
The Hon. Keith Marks, Q.C.	Colin Trumble

PERTH, AUSTRALIA OFFICE

Rob Ainslie	Michael Lishman
Andrew Barclay	Ben Luscombe
Rob Cole	John Naughton
Michael Corboy	Greg Pynt
Brahma Dharmananda	Geoff Rogers
Bruce Dodd	Tim Sharp
Grant Donaldson	Chris Stevenson
John Garvey	Gary Thomas
Chris Humphry	Leigh Warnick
Laurence Iffla	Michael Wright

CANBERRA, AUSTRALIA OFFICE

David Briggs	Dick Kemp
Chris Chenoweth	Justin Stanwix
Ian Johnson	John Topfer

BRISBANE, QUEENSLAND OFFICE

Gary Bugden	Michael McCafferty
Richard Hart	Simon Milne
Jeff Mann	John Samaha

(This Listing Continued)

Hugh Scott-Mackenzie

NEW YORK OFFICE

Peter Fox

LONDON, ENGLAND OFFICE

Rick Ladbury

TAIPEI, TAIWAN OFFICE

Paul M. Hayden

ASSOCIATED OFFICE-HONG KONG

David Bateson	Peter Ickeringill
	Paul Starr

ASSOCIATED OFFICE-JAKARTA

Kartini Muljadi S.H.	Jeremy Wade

PORT MORESBY, PAPUA, NEW GUINEA OFFICE

Beresford Love, Agents for Mallesons Stephen Jaques

MIDDLETONS, MOORE & BEVINS

Established in 1970

6TH FLOOR
7 MACQUARIE PLACE
SYDNEY, NEW SOUTH WALES 2000, AUSTRALIA
Telephone: 02 390 8100
International: 61 2 390 8100
Facsimile: 02 247 2866

Melbourne, Australia Office: 29th Floor, 200 Queen Street, 3000. Telephone: 03 602 2000. International: 61 3 602 2000. Facsimile: 03 602 5564. Telex: AA 31453.

Brisbane, Australia Office: 14th Floor, 241 Adelaide Street, QLD, 4000. Telephone: 07 231 1777. International: 61 7 231 1777. Facsimile: 07 231 1782.

Aviation, Banking, Finance and Investment, Commercial and General Litigation, Commercial Property, Companies and Securities, Construction and Development, Dispute Resolution, Environmental Law, Foreign Investment, Funds Management, Industrial Relations and Labour Law, Information Technology including Telecommunications, Computers and Media, Insolvency and Receivership, Insurance, International Business and Trade, Licensing and Trade Regulation, Mergers and Acquisitions, Product Liability, Resources and Energy, Superannuation, Taxation and Revenue, Trade Practices.

FIRM PROFILE: *Through its Melbourne office, Middletons Moore & Bevins can trace its origins back to the 1800's. MMB has been formed through the merger of three prominent commercial law firms, namely the Sydney firm of Moore & Bevins (established in 1970) which merged with the Melbourne firm of Middletons in 1992 and the Brisbane firm of Holmans in 1993. MMB Sydney is recognized for its expertise in Finance and Investment with particular emphasis on Banking and Finance, Funds Management and Superannuation. Other areas of practice are listed above.*

PARTNERS

KENNETH THOMAS WATSON, admitted, 1966, New South Wales; 1988, Victoria. *Education:* University of Sydney (LL.B.); University of Virginia (LL.M.). **LANGUAGES:** English. **PRACTICE AREAS:** Life Insurance; Mining and Petroleum; Mergers and Acquisitions.

PETER JOHN BOESENBERG, admitted, 1968, New South Wales; 1988, Victoria. *Education:* University of Sydney (B.A., LL.B.). **LANGUAGES:** English. **PRACTICE AREAS:** Commercial and Business Law; Intellectual Property; Trade Practices; Real Estate Law.

PETER ALLAN CATLEY, admitted, 1960, New South Wales; 1972, England; 1978, Northern Territory; 1988, Victoria. *Education:* University of Sydney (LL.B.). **LANGUAGES:** English. **PRACTICE AREAS:** Funds Management; Securitisation; Superannuation.

RON RENE NATHANS, admitted, 1970, New South Wales; 1988, Victoria. *Education:* University of Sydney (B.A., LL.B.). **LANGUAGES:** English and Dutch. **PRACTICE AREAS:** Commercial Litigation; Industrial and Labour Law; Environmental Law.

RICHARD MACKINTOSH GRAY, admitted, 1975, New South Wales; 1990, Victoria. *Education:* University of Sydney (B.A., LL.B., LL.M.).

(This Listing Continued)

MIDDLETONS, MOORE & BEVINS, *Sydney, New South Wales—Continued*

LANGUAGES: English. *PRACTICE AREAS:* Commercial Property; Joint Ventures and Development; Foreign Investments.

JEFFERY ALAN GOSS, admitted, 1976, New South Wales; 1988, Victoria. *Education:* University of Sydney (LL.B.). *LANGUAGES:* English. *PRACTICE AREAS:* Banking and Finance; Construction; Joint Ventures.

MURRAY LANDIS, admitted, 1975, New South Wales; 1988, Victoria. *Education:* University of Sydney (B.A., LL.B., LL.M.). *LANGUAGES:* English. *PRACTICE AREAS:* Commercial and Corporate Law; Stamp Duties.

STEPHEN HARRIS ETKIND, admitted, 1979, South Africa and Lesotho; 1983, New South Wales; 1988, Victoria. *Education:* University of Witwatersrand, Johannesburg, South Africa (B.A., B.Comm., LL.B., LL.M.). *LANGUAGES:* English, Italian, Hebrew & Afrikaans. *PRACTICE AREAS:* Public Unit Trusts and Collective Investment; Company and Trust Floats; Manufacturing and Supply of Products.

GREG HILTON COUSTON, admitted, 1978, New South Wales. *Education:* University of Sydney (LL.B.). *LANGUAGES:* English. *PRACTICE AREAS:* Commercial Litigation; Maritime Law; Insurance Litigation.

RICHARD ANDREW DAVIS, admitted, 1978, New South Wales; 1988, Victoria. Solicitors Admission Board. *LANGUAGES:* English. *PRACTICE AREAS:* Commercial Litigation; Enforcement of Securities; Insolvency.

THEO CASIMATIS, admitted, 1981, New South Wales. *Education:* University of New South Wales (B.Comm., LL.B.). *LANGUAGES:* English and Greek. *PRACTICE AREAS:* Commercial Property; Building and Construction; Local Government.

LEON GEORGE SAKARIS, admitted, 1984, New South Wales. *Education:* University of New South Wales (B.Comm., LL.B.). *LANGUAGES:* English. *PRACTICE AREAS:* Commercial Property; Banking and Finance; Insolvency.

BERNARD CHARLES EVANS, admitted, 1982, New South Wales; 1991, Victoria. *Education:* University of Sydney (B.A., LL.M.). *LANGUAGES:* English. *PRACTICE AREAS:* Commercial Law; Trade Practices; Mining and Petroleum.

ARTHUR JAMES DAVIS, admitted, 1985, New South Wales. *Education:* Macquarie University (B.Ec., LL.B.). *LANGUAGES:* English. *PRACTICE AREAS:* Commercial Law; Banking and Finance; Mining and Petroleum.

MALCOLM JOHN DAVIS, admitted, 1985, New South Wales; 1990, Victoria. *Education:* Macquarie University (B.Ec., LL.B.). *LANGUAGES:* English. *PRACTICE AREAS:* Industrial Relations; Arbitration and Alternative Dispute Resolution; Employment Contracts.

GERALD CHARLES WAKEFIELD, admitted, 1983, New South Wales; 1987, Australian Capital Territory. *Education:* University of Technology (B.Sc., LL.B.). *LANGUAGES:* English. *PRACTICE AREAS:* Telecommunications, Radio and Communications Law; Intellectual Property; Trademarks.

LESLIE JAMES KOLTAI, admitted, 1986, New South Wales. *Education:* University of New South Wales (B.A., LL.B.); Sydney University (LL.M.). *LANGUAGES:* English, German and Hungarian. *PRACTICE AREAS:* Commercial and Residential Property; Foreign Investment; Liquor Licensing.

SENIOR ASSOCIATES

STUART WILLIAM PALMER, admitted, 1987, New South Wales. *Education:* Sydney University (B.A., LL.B.). *LANGUAGES:* English, German and Spanish. *PRACTICE AREAS:* Funds Management and Capital Raising; Securities and Commercial Law; Corporations Law and Securitisation.

CHRISTOPHER JAMES BEVITT, admitted, 1987, New South Wales. *Education:* University of New South Wales (B.Comm., LL.B.). *LANGUAGES:* English and Spanish. *PRACTICE AREAS:* Corporations Law; Foreign Investment.

TERESA CATHERINE NEAL, admitted, 1986, New South Wales. *Education:* Sydney University (LL.B.). *LANGUAGES:* English. *PRACTICE AREAS:* Securitization; Capital Raising; Discretionary, Public Unit and Private Unit Trusts; Funds Management.

(This Listing Continued)

PETER G. LIMBERS, admitted, 1988, New South Wales. *Education:* University of New South Wales (B.Comm., LL.B.). *LANGUAGES:* English. *PRACTICE AREAS:* Commercial Litigation; Property and Trusts Litigation; Insolvency-Recovery and Reconstruction; Alternate Dispute Resolution.

GREG SAN MIGUEL, admitted, 1982, New South Wales. *Education:* Sydney University (B.Ec., LL.B.). *LANGUAGES:* English and Spanish. *PRACTICE AREAS:* Commercial Litigation; Intellectual Property; Contract and Trade Disputes; Insolvency-Recovery and Reconstruction.

NAMOI ELIZABETH ANNE DOUGALL, admitted, 1986, New South Wales. *Education:* Sydney University (B.A. (Hons.), LL.B., LL.M.). *LANGUAGES:* English. *PRACTICE AREAS:* Commercial Litigation; Environmental Law; Trade Practices.

ROLAND DAVID BURT, admitted, 1989, Victoria; 1993, New South Wales. *Education:* University of Melbourne (B.A., LL.B.). *LANGUAGES:* English. *PRACTICE AREAS:* Insolvency; Commercial Litigation.

DAVID JOHN BEGG, admitted, 1989, New South Wales. *Education:* University of Technology, Sydney (LL.B.). *LANGUAGES:* English. *PRACTICE AREAS:* Insurance Litigation; Building and Construction Litigation; Personal Injuries.

MARK JOHN CHRISTOPHER FEETHAM, admitted, 1988, New South Wales. *Education:* Sydney University (B.Ec., LL.B.). *LANGUAGES:* English. *PRACTICE AREAS:* Telecommunications and Information Technology; Intellectual Property; Commercial Litigation.

DAN MARJANOVIC, admitted, 1987, New South Wales. *Education:* Macquarie University (B.Ec., LL.B.). *LANGUAGES:* English. *PRACTICE AREAS:* Banking and Finance; Joint Ventures; Commercial Law.

JUDITH MARI-ANNE TOMAS, admitted, 1989, New South Wales. *Education:* University of New South Wales (B.Sc., Hons., LL.B.). *LANGUAGES:* English and Hungarian. *PRACTICE AREAS:* Property Development; SaLe and Leasing of Commercial and Residential Property; Financing.

TAXATION CONSULTANT

GORDON STEWART COOPER. *Education:* New University of Ulster (B.Sc., Econ., Hons.). *LANGUAGES:* English. *PRACTICE AREAS:* Revenue Law; Capital Gains Tax; Taxation Aspects of Mergers and Acquisitions.

CONSULTANTS

BENJAMIN HILTON COUSTON, admitted, 1951, New South Wales. *Education:* Sydney University (LL.B.). *LANGUAGES:* English. *PRACTICE AREAS:* Commercial Property; Private Trusts, Wills & Probate.

GEORGE GENGOS, admitted, 1950, New South Wales. *Education:* Sydney University (LL.B., Hons.). *LANGUAGES:* English. *PRACTICE AREAS:* Conveyancing; Wills & Probate; Discretionary and Unit Trusts.

Languages: English, Greek, Spanish, Dutch, Italian, Hebrew and Afrikaans

---

MINTER ELLISON

44 MARTIN PLACE
SYDNEY, NEW SOUTH WALES 2000, AUSTRALIA
Telephone: (02) 210 4444
Fax: (02) 235 2711

Mailing Address: Box 521, G.P.O., Sydney, Australia 2001

Melbourne, Victoria, Australia Office: 40 Market Street, 3000. Telephone: 617 4617. Fax: 617 4666.

Brisbane, Queensland, Australia Office: Waterfront Place, 1 Eagle Street, 4000. Telephone: (07) 226 6333. Fax: (07) 229 1066.

Gold Coast, Queensland, Australia Office: Surfers Paradise, Level 7, 50 Cavill Avenue, 4217. Telephone: (075) 708 444. Fax: (075) 922 640.

Canberra, Australian Capital Territory, Australia Office: 8-10 Hobart Place, 2600. Telephone: (06) 248 7533. Fax: (06) 249 8208.

London, England Office: 20 Lincoln's Inn Fields, WC2A 3ED. Telephone: 0171-831 7871. Fax: 071-404 6722.

Adelaide, Australia Associated Office: Minter Ellison Baker O'Loughlin. 1 King William Street, 5000. Telephone: (08) 233 5555. Fax: (08) 212 7518.

Auckland, New Zealand Associated Office: Rudd Watts & Stone. BNZ Tower, 125 Queen Street, P.O. Box 3798. Telephone: (09) 309 4863. Fax: NZ (09) 379 3326.

(This Listing Continued)

Wellington, New Zealand Associated Office: Rudd Watts & Stone. Trust Bank Centre, 125 The Terrace, 1. Telephone: (04) 472 4899. Fax: (04) 473 8232.

Singapore Associated Office: Khattar Wong & Partners. 80 Raffles Place, #25-01 UOB Plaza, 0104. Telephone: 535 6844. Fax: 534 4892.

Jakarta, Indonesia Associated Office: Makarim & Taira S., Level 17, Summitmas Tower, Jl. Jend. Sudirman 61-62, 12069. Telephone: +62 21 252 1272. Fax: +62 21 252 2750.

Beijing, People's Republic of China Associated Office: Oxford Associates, Inc., 205 Jianguomenwai Dajie, 10020. Telephone: +86 1 501 4681. Fax: +86 1 501 4682.

Perth, Western Australia, Australia Associated Office: Minter Ellison Northmore Hale. 152-158 St. George's Tce. 6000. Telephone: (09) 429 7444. Fax: (09) 429 7666.

Hong Kong Associated Office: McKenna & Co. in association with Minter Ellison. Lippo Tower, 5th Floor, 89 Queensway. Telephone: 2846 9100. Fax: 2845 3575.

International law firm practising in all areas of commercial and corporate law. The firm is organized into specialist practice groups: Alternative Dispute Resolution, Banking and Finance, Commercial Litigation, Corporate, Insolvency, Insurance, International Business and Trade Law, Labour Law, Major Projects and Construction, Media Law, Planning and Environment, Property, Government and Public Administration, Resources, Securities, Industry, Superannuation, Taxation and Revenue, Technology and Trade Protection.

MEMBERS OF FIRM

DAVID A.K. FERGUSON, B.A., LL.B., LL.M. *PRACTICE AREAS:* Litigation; Administrative Law.

DAVID J. HILL, LL.B., LL.M. *PRACTICE AREAS:* Litigation.

JOHN R. FRIDAY, B.A., LL.B. *PRACTICE AREAS:* Banking Law; Commercial Finance Law; Property Law.

RUSSELL A.F. STEWART, B.A., LL.B., LL.M., M.H.P. Ed. *PRACTICE AREAS:* Company Law; Commercial Law; Revenue Law.

PETER W. KUNER, LL.B. (Resident Partner, Hong Kong). *PRACTICE AREAS:* Litigation.

DAVID F. KENNEDY, LL.B. *PRACTICE AREAS:* Company Law; Commercial Law; Resources Law.

JAMES H. MOMSEN, LL.B., LL.M. (Hons.). *PRACTICE AREAS:* Revenue Law.

JULIAN G. SMALL, B.A., LL.B. *PRACTICE AREAS:* Labor Law.

PAUL K. MAZOUDIER, B.A., LL.B. *PRACTICE AREAS:* Company Law; Commercial Law.

WARREN COLMAN, LL.B., LL.M. *PRACTICE AREAS:* Company Law; Commercial Law; Revenue Law.

ROBERT A. HOLTSBAUM, LL.B. *PRACTICE AREAS:* Company Law; Commercial Law; Property Law; Alternative Dispute Resolution Law.

ALAN L. LIMBURY, B.A., M.A. *PRACTICE AREAS:* Trade Practices Law; Intellectual Property Law; Alternative Dispute Resolution Law.

ALEXANDER J. HALLIDAY, LL.B. *PRACTICE AREAS:* Banking Law; Commercial Finance Law; Property Law.

A. ADRIAN HOWIE, B.A., LL.B. *PRACTICE AREAS:* Litigation.

ROBERT C. MINTER, B.A., LL.B. *PRACTICE AREAS:* Property Law.

CHARLES D.S. ALEXANDER, B.A., LL.B. *PRACTICE AREAS:* Labor Law; Trade Practices Law; Intellectual Property Law.

LEIGH R. BROWN, B.A., LL.B. *PRACTICE AREAS:* Company Law; Commercial Law; Resources Law.

GARRY F. BEATH, LL.B., LL.M. *PRACTICE AREAS:* Revenue Law.

BRUCE E. HAMBRETT, LL.B. (Managing Partner, Sydney). *PRACTICE AREAS:* Litigation; Insolvency Law; Alternative Dispute Resolution Law.

GARY S. ULMAN, LL.B., LL.M. *PRACTICE AREAS:* Litigation; Trade Practices Law; Intellectual Property Law; Alternative Dispute Resolution Law.

GRAHAME A. COOPER, LL.B. *PRACTICE AREAS:* Company Law; Commercial Law; Revenue Law.

(This Listing Continued)

CRAIG KELLY, LL.B. *PRACTICE AREAS:* Property Law; Revenue Law.

LINDSAY POWERS, B.A., LL.M. *PRACTICE AREAS:* Insolvency Law; Litigation.

JAMES M. LINTON, Dip. Law. *PRACTICE AREAS:* Property Law; Probate Law.

PAMELA A. MADAFIGLIO, B.A., LL.B. *PRACTICE AREAS:* Litigation.

DAVID J. CRANE, B.Ec., LL.B. *PRACTICE AREAS:* Company Law; Commercial Law; Property Law; Insolvency Law.

PATRICK T. GEORGE, B.A., LL.B. *PRACTICE AREAS:* Litigation; Media Law.

ODETTE M. GOURLEY, B.A., LL.B. (Hons.). *PRACTICE AREAS:* Trade Practices Law; Intellectual Property Law.

DAVID L. WATSON, B.A., LL.B. *PRACTICE AREAS:* Company Law; Commercial Law.

MARK L. STANDEN, B.A., LL.B., LL.M. *PRACTICE AREAS:* Commercial Law.

M. LOUISE S. HERRON, B.A., LL.B., LL.M. *PRACTICE AREAS:* Intellectual Property Law; Trade Practices Law.

PROF. ROBERT P. AUSTIN, B.A., LL.B., LL.M., D.Phil. *PRACTICE AREAS:* Company Law; Commercial Law.

BRUCE A. YELDHAM, B.Comm., LL.B. *PRACTICE AREAS:* Litigation.

ANTHONY J. BERRIMAN, B.Com., LL.B. *PRACTICE AREAS:* Banking Law; Finance Law.

MICHELLE D. SINDLER, B.A. (Hons.), LL.B. *PRACTICE AREAS:* Commercial Litigation; Insurance Law.

GLEN D. O'CONNOR, Dip. Law. *PRACTICE AREAS:* Construction Law; Engineering Law; Project Law.

GEOFFREY L. COHEN, B.Comm., LL.B. *PRACTICE AREAS:* Property Law.

JOHN C. MULALLY, B.A., LL.B. *PRACTICE AREAS:* Property Law.

PAUL V.H. BLANCH, LL.B., ISMP, AFAIM. *PRACTICE AREAS:* Commercial Law.

MICHAEL R. HUGHES, B.Ec., LL.B. *PRACTICE AREAS:* Commercial Litigation.

JAMES D.R. PHILIPS, B.A., LL.B. *PRACTICE AREAS:* Company Law; Commercial Law.

DAVID MCELHONE, B.Com.; LL.B. *PRACTICE AREAS:* Company and Commercial; Banking and Finance, Insolvency.

JOHN F. OAKES, B.Comm., LL.B. *PRACTICE AREAS:* Labour Law.

ANDREW CUNNINGHAM, B.Ec, LL.B. *PRACTICE AREAS:* Employment Law; Labour Law.

ROBERT J.B. HANLEY, B.A., LL.B. *PRACTICE AREAS:* Corporate Law; Commercial Law.

LEXIA A. WILSON, B.Comm., LL.B. *PRACTICE AREAS:* Property Law.

RALPH C. AYLING, B.Comm., LL.B. *PRACTICE AREAS:* Banking Law; Commercial Finance Law; Company Law; Commercial Law.

(For List of Partners in Melbourne, Brisbane, Canberra and London Offices, see Professional Biographies at those locations)

NIEMOTKO & ASSOCIATES

Established in 1992

G.P.O. BOX 708

SYDNEY, NEW SOUTH WALES 2001, AUSTRALIA

Telephone: (02) 411 1905

Fax: (61-2) 411 1905

International Commercial Law, Legal Aspects of Transition to Market Economies in Central and Eastern Europe, Joint Ventures, Intellectual Property, Copyright, Insurance, Maritime, Law of the Sea, Executive Relocation, Mediation, Conciliation, Arbitration and Legal Research.

WALDEMAR NIEMOTKO, born Garwolin, Poland, August 15, 1931; admitted, 1964, Poland. *Education:* Mickiewicz University, Poznan (Dr. Jur., 1963); Columbia University, New York (LL.M., 1974); Parker School of Foreign and Comparative Law, New York (1974). Visiting Scholar, Harvard Law School, 1974-1976. Visiting Associate Professor, International Business, Graduate School of Business, Indiana University, 1979-1980. Justice of the Peace (New South Wales). *Member:* Poland Bar Association. *LANGUAGES:* English, German, Polish, Russian and Swedish. *PRACTICE AREAS:* International Trade Law; Privatisation; Intellectual Property; Insurance and Maritime.

NORTON SMITH & CO.

Established in 1818

20 MARTIN PLACE

SYDNEY, NEW SOUTH WALES 2000, AUSTRALIA

Telephone: (02) 930-7500

International: (+612) 930-7500

Fax: (02) 930-7600

Telex: 24633

FIRM PROFILE: Company and Commercial Law, Banking, Finance, Securities, Mergers and Acquisitions, Insolvency, Insurance, Environment, Natural Resources, Property, Construction and Arbitration, Commercial and General Litigation, Maritime and Transport Law.

PARTNERS

Ronald John White	Joseph Carlo Peter David
Maxwell John Einfeld	Erhard Fick
David Padget Avonmore Wilson	Laraine Walker
Ian Phillip Parsonage	Drew Scott James
Stephen Julian Cordell	Margot Louise Waring
David Ross Richardson	Martin Joseph O'Connor
Stanley Robert Lewis	Peter David Murphy
Michael Vincent Ryan	John Wynne Fitzpatrick
William David Rose	Chris Quennell
Peter Charles Calov	Michelle Esther Harpur
Paul Maurice Dalby	George Anthony Gibara

SENIOR ASSOCIATES

Louise Lesley Flanagan	Patricia Louise Bishop
Janet Ruth Oliver	Julie Anne Soars
Miles Grant	Robert Reginald Wilson
Douglas Syme Drysdale	Timothy Martin Bee
	Dominic Gerald Emmett

CONSULTANTS

Ernest Ormund Butler Thomas	John I. Einfeld A.M.
	Andrew Stuart-Robertson

THE LAW OFFICES OF LUIGI PALOMBI

Solicitors and Intellectual Property Attorneys

LEVEL 5, IBSA HOUSE

2 BLIGH STREET

SYDNEY, NEW SOUTH WALES 2000, AUSTRALIA

Telephone: 61-2-223 9400

Facsimile: 61-2-223 9547

Domestic and Foreign Intellectual Property Law, Trademarks, Copyright, Unfair Competition, Trade Secrets, Litigation and Patent Litigation, Licensing, Arbitration, International Trade, Trade Practices, Antitrust, Bio-Technology, Information Technology and other Technology Law.

(This Listing Continued)

PARTNERS

LUIGI PALOMBI, admitted, 1982, South Australia as a Barrister and Solicitor; 1984, New South Wales as a Solicitor; 1986, Victoria as a Barrister and Solicitor. *Education:* University of Adelaide (LL.B., 1981; B.Ec., 1986); University of California, Berkeley & Davis (Certificate, US Law, 1990). With Davies Collison & Cave, 1986; Partner, 1988; Consultant, 1990. Department Head, Intellectual Property Litigation, Michell Sillar, 1990. Author: "The Patents Act 1990," Intellectual Property Society of Australia Conference, Canberra, June 1990; "The Litigation Implications of the New Product Liability Laws of Insurance Companies and Their Clients," Ernst & Young Industry Seminar, April 1991; "Maximising the Value Added of Intellectual Property," Australian Catholic University, August 1991; "What Lawyers Need to Know About the Patents Act," College of Law, April 1992; "Recent Developments in Intellectual Property Law," Seminar, Sydney, September 1993; "The Patentability of Biotechnological Innovations in the Pacific Rim," 11th Biannual Conference, Australian Biotechnology Association, Perth, September 1993. Member, Advisory Board of the Orientation in U.S.A. Law, University of California, Berkeley & Davis, 1994. *Member:* Intellectual Property Society of Australia (Vice-President; National Committee Chairman, New South Wales Division, 1990-1994); American Intellectual Property Lawyers Association; Australian Biotechnology Association; Licensing Executive Society; Copyright Law Society; International Bar Association; Australian Council of Law.

ASSOCIATES

SHARMILA AMERASINGHE, admitted, 1992, Australian Capital Territory as a Barrister and Solicitor; 1993, Victoria as a Barrister and Solicitor. *Education:* Australian National University (LL.B., 1991; B.Sc., 1991); University of Melbourne (LL.M., 1995). With Griffith Hack & Co., 1993. Joined the Law Offices of Luigi Palombi, 1995—.

ROSENBLUM & PARTNERS

Established in 1964

LEVEL 29 GOVERNOR PHILLIP TOWER

1 FARRER PLACE

SYDNEY, NEW SOUTH WALES 2000, AUSTRALIA

Telephone: (612) 258 5811

Facsimile: (612) 258 5800

International Transactions, Corporate and Commercial Law, Banking and Finance, Takeovers and Reconstruction, Revenue Law, Commercial Litigation and Alternative Dispute Resolution, Commercial Property.

FIRM PROFILE: The firm was established in 1964 and offers a full range of legal services. It is a progressive corporate and commercial firm with a significant international practice. Representative clients are public listed companies, stock brokers, trading banks, merchant banks, manufacturers, property developers and government and semi-government instrumentalities.

MEMBERS OF FIRM

RODNEY ISAAC ROSENBLUM, born 1934; admitted, 1959, New South Wales. *Education:* University of Sydney (B.A.; LL.M., Hons.). *Member:* Law Society of New South Wales; Taxation Institute of Australia. *LANGUAGES:* English. *PRACTICE AREAS:* Taxation Law.

RICHARD ARTHUR GELSKI, born 1948; admitted, 1974, as a Barrister of the Supreme Court of New South Wales. *Education:* University of Sydney (B.A.; LL.B., Hons.); University of London, England (LL.M.). Sydney Law School University Medalist, 1971. *Member:* Law Society of New South Wales; Taxation Institute of Australia; Law Institute of Australia and North America; International Fiscal Association; International Bar Association. *LANGUAGES:* English and German. *PRACTICE AREAS:* Taxation Law; Intellectual Property Law; Corporate Law.

PETER JOHN MCMAHON, born 1950; admitted, 1976, New South Wales and Australian Capital Territory. *Education:* University of New South Wales (B.Com.; LL.B.); University of Sydney (LL.M.). *Member:* Law Society of New South Wales; Banking Law Association; Taxation Institute of Australia; Law Council of Australia; International Bar Association; LAWASIA; Inter-Pacific Bar Association; Mortgage Bankers Association of Australia. *LANGUAGES:* English. *PRACTICE AREAS:* Banking Law; Corporate Finance Law; Stamp Duties Law.

PHILLIP WISEMAN, born 1946; admitted, 1970, New South Wales. *Education:* University of Sydney (B.A.; LL.M., Hons.). *Member:* Law Society of New South Wales; Taxation Institute of Australia. *LANGUAGES:* English. *PRACTICE AREAS:* Taxation Law; Commercial Law.

(This Listing Continued)

KENNETH RAPHAEL, born 1944; admitted, 1969, England; 1978, New South Wales and Australian Capital Territory; 1988, Special District Court Arbitrator, New South Wales. *Education:* University of Birmingham, England (LL.B., Hons.); Polytechnic of Central London, England (Dip. Town Planning). *Member:* Law Society of New South Wales. *LANGUAGES:* English. *PRACTICE AREAS:* Litigation; Alternative Dispute Resolution.

RICHARD MICHAEL DUKES, born 1959; admitted, 1983, New South Wales. *Education:* University of New South Wales (B.Com.; LL.B.); University of Sydney (LL.M.). *Member:* Law Society of New South Wales; Taxation Institute of Australia; International Fiscal Association. *LANGUAGES:* English. *PRACTICE AREAS:* Foreign Investments; Taxation Law.

ALLEN RODNEY COX, born 1955; admitted, 1986, New South Wales. *Education:* University of New South Wales (B.Com.; LL.B.). *Member:* Law Society of New South Wales; Taxation Institute of Australia. *LANGUAGES:* English. *PRACTICE AREAS:* Corporate Law; Employment Law; Taxation Law.

IAN GERALD BETTS, born 1941; admitted, 1965, New South Wales. *Education:* University of Sydney (B.A.; LL.B., Hons.). *Member:* International Association of the Protection of Intellectual Property (Australia Group); Intellectual Property Society; Law Council of Australia; Intellectual Property Committee Member. *LANGUAGES:* English and French. *PRACTICE AREAS:* Commercial Law; Trade Practices; Intellectual Property.

CHARLES NAOTAKA KOYAMA, born 1953; admitted, 1983, Victoria; 1984, High Court of Australia; 1985, New South Wales; 1991, Australian Capital Territory; 1992, Queensland; 1993, Registered Migration Agent. *Education:* Monash University (LL.M.); Sophia University, Tokyo (B.A.). *Member:* Law Society of New South Walea; Law Council of Australia; Law Institute of Victoria; Queensland Law Society; Inter-Pacific Bar Association; Japanese Society of Sydney. *LANGUAGES:* English and Japanese. *PRACTICE AREAS:* Foreign Investment; International Trade; Mergers and Acquisitions; International Finance; Joint Ventures; Mining and Natural Resources.

LESLIE RONALD HOUSEMAN, born 1944; admitted, 1969, New South Wales. *Education:* University of Sydney (B.A.; LL.B.). *Member:* Law Society of New South Wales. *LANGUAGES:* English. *PRACTICE AREAS:* Conveyancing; Environmental Law; Property and Real Estate Law; Rent and Lease Law; Commercial Law.

PHILIP LIPSHITZ, born 1949; admitted, 1974, South Africa; 1988, New South Wales. *Education:* University of Cape Town, South Africa (B.Com.; LL.B., Hons.); University of Sydney (LL.M.). *Member:* Law Society of New South Wales; Corporate Lawyers Association. *LANGUAGES:* English and Afrikaans. *PRACTICE AREAS:* Corporate Law; Foreign Investments; Intellectual Property Law.

IVOR LAURENCE KAPLAN, born 1951; admitted, 1976, Attorney of the Supreme Court of South Africa; 1980, Attorney of the High Court of Lesotho; 1988, New South Wales. *Education:* Rhodes University, South Africa (B.Com.; LL.B.). *Member:* Law Society of New South Wales. *LANGUAGES:* English and Afrikaans. *PRACTICE AREAS:* Commercial Property Law; Property Finance Law; Commercial Law.

GAI MARIE MCGRATH, born 1961; admitted, 1985, New South Wales. *Education:* University of Sydney (B.A.; LL.B., Hons.); London School of Economics and Political Science, University of London (LL.M Dist.). *Member:* Law Society of New South Wales; Women Lawyer's Association. *LANGUAGES:* English. *PRACTICE AREAS:* Corporate Law; Securities; Foreign Investments; Commercial Law.

CRAIG STEPHEN SIMPSON, born 1963; admitted, 1989, New South Wales. *Education:* University of Sydney (B.Ec., LL.B.,). *Member:* Law Society of New South Wales. *LANGUAGES:* English. *PRACTICE AREAS:* Corporate Law; Foreign Investments; Taxation Law.

PETER RONALD FALUDI, born 1958; admitted, 1982, New South Wales. *Education:* University of New South Wales (B.Com.; LL.B.); University of Sydney (LL.M.). *Member:* Law Society of New South Wales; Securities Institute of Australia; Corporate Lawyers Association. *LANGUAGES:* English and Hungarian. *PRACTICE AREAS:* Banking Law; Corporate Law; Stamp Duties.

SANDRA MARGARET LANIGAN, born 1964; admitted, 1988, Barrister of Supreme Court of New South Wales; 1990, Australian Capital Territory; 1991, Solicitor of Supreme Court of New South Wales. *Education:*

(This Listing Continued)

University of Canberra (B.A.); University of Sydney (LL.M.). *Member:* Law Society of New South Wales; Taxation Institute of Australia; Australian Society of Certified Practising Accountants. *LANGUAGES:* English. *PRACTICE AREAS:* Administrative Law; Corporate Law; Foreign Investments; Taxation Law.

SENIOR ASSOCIATES

CHRISTINE LYNNE ECOB, born 1962; admitted, 1985, New South Wales; 1989, High Court of Australia. *Education:* Macquarie University (B.A.; LL.B., Hons.). *Member:* Law Society of New South Wales; Copyright Society of Australia Inc.; The Intellectual and Industrial Property Society Inc.; New South Wales Society for Computers and the Law; Law Council of Australia. *LANGUAGES:* English. *PRACTICE AREAS:* Competition Law; Constitutional Law; Consumer Protection Law; Litigation; Negligence Law; Product Liability; Intellectual Property Law.

ANNE LOUISE HARGRAVE, born 1961; admitted, 1986, New South Wales. *Education:* University of Sydney (B.A., Hons.; LL.B.). *Member:* Law Society of New South Wales; Banking Law Association. *LANGUAGES:* English. *PRACTICE AREAS:* Banking Law; Corporate Law; Foreign Investments; Stamp Duties Law.

VINCENT TIAM SENG LIM, born 1964; admitted, 1989, New South Wales. *Education:* University of Sydney (B.Ec.; LL.B.). *Member:* Law Society of New South Wales; Young Lawyers. *LANGUAGES:* English, Bahasa Malaysia, Hokkien, Cantonese and Hakka. *PRACTICE AREAS:* Commercial Litigation.

ROBERT BERNARD MORAN, born 1964; admitted, 1988, New South Wales. *Education:* University of Sydney (B.Ec., LL.B. Hons.). *Member:* Law Society of New South Wales. *LANGUAGES:* English. *PRACTICE AREAS:* Constitutional Law; Corporate Law; Distributorship, Agency and Franchise Law; Foreign Investments; Taxation Law; Accounting Standards.

ANNE MAREE TAYLOR, born 1966; admitted, 1992, New South Wales. *Education:* University of Technology (LL.B.); University of Sydney (B.A.). *Member:* Law Society of New South Wales. *LANGUAGES:* English. *PRACTICE AREAS:* Property; Banking; Finance.

MATTHEW JOHN WALLACE, born 1964; admitted, 1988, New South Wales. *Education:* University of Sydney (B.Ec.; LL.B.). *Member:* Law Society of New South Wales. *LANGUAGES:* English. *PRACTICE AREAS:* Taxation; Corporate Law; Foreign Investments; International Contracts.

SKADDEN, ARPS, SLATE, MEAGHER & FLOM

LEVEL 26-STATE BANK CENTRE
52 MARTIN PLACE
SYDNEY, NEW SOUTH WALES 2000, AUSTRALIA
Telephone: 011-61-2-224-6000
Fax: 011-61-2-224-6044

New York, New York Office: 919 Third Avenue, 10022. Telephone: 212-735-3000. Fax: 212-735-2000; 212-735-2001. Telex: 645899 Skarslaw.

Boston, Massachusetts Office: One Beacon Street, 02108. Telephone: 617-573-4800. Fax: 617-573-4822.

Washington, D.C. Office: 1440 New York Avenue, N.W., 20005. Telephone: 202-371-7000. Fax: 202-393-5760.

Wilmington, Delaware Office: One Rodney Square, 19899. Telephone: 302-651-3000. Fax: 302-651-3001.

Los Angeles, California Office: 300 South Grand Avenue, 90071. Telephone: 213-687-5000. Fax: 213-687-5600.

Chicago, Illinois Office: 333 West Wacker Drive, 60606. Telephone: 312-407-0700. Fax: 312-407-0411.

San Francisco, California Office: Four Embarcadero Center, 94111. Telephone: 415-984-6400. Fax: 415-984-2698.

Houston, Texas Office: 1600 Smith Street, Suite 4460, 77002. Telephone: 713-655-5100. Fax: 713-655-5181.

Newark, New Jersey Office: One Riverfront Plaza, 07102. Telephone: 201-596-4440. Fax: 201-596-4444.

Tokyo, Japan Office: 12th Floor, The Fukoku Seimei Building, 2-2-2, Uchisaiwaicho, Chiyoda-ku, 100. Telephone: 011-81-3-3595-3850. Fax: 011-81-3-3504-2780.

London, England Office: 25 Bucklersbury EC4N 8DA. Telephone: 011-44-71-248-9929. Fax: 011-44-71-489-8533.

(This Listing Continued)

SKADDEN, ARPS, SLATE, MEAGHER & FLOM,
Sydney, New South Wales—Continued

Hong Kong Office: 30/F Peregrine Tower, Lippo Centre, 89 Queensway, Central. Telephone: 011-852-820-0700. Fax: 011-852-820-0727.

Toronto, Ontario Office: Suite 1820, North Tower, P.O. Box 189, Royal Bank Plaza, M5J 2J4. Telephone: 416-777-4700. Fax: 416-777-4747.

Paris, France Office: 105 rue du Faubourg Saint-Honoré, 75008. Telephone: 011-33-1-40-75-44-44. Fax: 011-33-1-49-53-09-99.

Brussels, Belgium Office: 523 avenue Louise, Box 30, 1050. Telephone: 011-32-2-648-7666. Fax: 011-32-2-640-3032.

Frankfurt, Germany Office: MesseTurm, 27th Floor, 60308. Telephone: 011-49-69-9757-3000. Fax: 011-49-69-9757-3050.

Beijing, China Office: 1605 Capital Mansion Tower, No. 6 Xin Yuan Nan Road, Chao Yang District, 100004. Telephone: 011-86-1-466-8800. Fax: 011-86-1-466-8822.

Budapest, Hungary Office: Mahart Building, H-1052 Apáczai Csere János u.11, Vl.em. Telephone: 011-36-1-266-2145. Fax: 011-36-1-266-4033.

Prague, Czech Republic Office: Revolucni 16, 110 00. Telephone: 011-42-2-231-75-18. Fax: 011-42-2-231-47-33.

Moscow, Russia Office: Pleteshkovsky Pereulok 1, 107005. Telephone: 011-7-501-940-2304. Fax: 011-7-501-940-2511.

Firm engaged in general American and International law practice.

ROBERT C. HINKLEY, born Sidney, N.Y., 1951; admitted, 1979, New York; 1981, Massachusetts; 1983, New Hampshire (Not admitted in Australia). *Education:* Fordham University (B.S., 1973; J.D., 1978).

(For Biographical data on other Personnel, see New York, New York Professional Biographies).

SLY & WEIGALL

In association with Deacons/Graham & James

GOLD FIELDS HOUSE
1 ALFRED STREET, CIRCULAR QUAY
SYDNEY, NEW SOUTH WALES 2000, AUSTRALIA

Telephone: (02) 330 8000 International: +61 2 330 8000
Facsimile: (02) 330 8111

Mailing Address: G.P.O. Box 3872, Sydney, 2001

Brisbane, Australia Office: Riverside Centre, 123 Eagle Street, 4000. Telephone: (07) 833 0444. International: +61 7 833 0444. Facsimile: (07) 833 0555.

Canberra City, Australia Office: GPO Box 2013, 2601. Telephone: (06) 249 7666. International: +61 6 249 7666. Facsimile: (06) 257 2560.

Melbourne, Australia Office: 385 Bourke Street, 3000. Telephone: (03) 608 0411. International: +61 3 608 0411. Facsimile: (03) 608 0505.

Perth, Australia Office: 108 St. George's Terrace, 6000. Telephone: (09) 321 9379. International: +61 9 321 9379. Facsimile: (09) 324 1334.

RESIDENT PARTNERS

Donald Gordon Mackay	Robert Duncan Hugh
Brian Henry Davidson	Sandra Katherine Di Bella
Jeremy James Bingham	Edward Lindsay Roux Houghton
John Ashton Beardow	Barry Gordon Richardson
John Frederick Warburton	Terence Brian Grace
Andrew Dymock Forsyth	Stanley Simon Kalinko
Warwick Philip O'Rourke	Richard Geoffery Lewis
Roger Andrew FitzSimons	Peter Ronald Rigg
Michael Rodney Wynter	Martin Cassimir Przybylski
Robert Gordon Haines	Paul William Robinson
Timothy George Peken	Ian Stuart Wylie
Margaret Sidis	Heather Patricia Irish
Michel Bernard Reymond	Ronald William Forster
Robert Warwick Anderson	Hugh Francis Arthur Williamson
Jennifer Helen Wily	Phillip David Crowley
Andrew John Tunmer Martin	(Not admitted in Australia)
Nino Di Bartolomeo	

CONSULTANTS

Thomas Chiu	Warren James Pengilley
Timothy James McCarthy	Antony Tunmer Martin
Albert James de Montfort	Robert Ian Grant
John King Bowen, O.B.E.	Russell Stuart Debney

(This Listing Continued)

Christopher Brian Shine

SENIOR ASSOCIATES

John Harris	Antony Corel
Neil Geoffrey Napper	Julie Anne Rasmussen
John Paul Vohralik	Nicholas Michael Lawson Afaras
Susan Ann Dixon	Victor John Hugo
John Charles Grimes	Mitchell Mathas
Catriona Mary Robertson	

WILLIAMS NIBLETT

Solicitors

LEVEL 32, ST MARTINS TOWER
31 MARKET STREET
SYDNEY, NEW SOUTH WALES 2000, AUSTRALIA

Telephone: 61-2-261.5000
Facsimile: 61-2-267.9974

Intellectual Property Litigation and Licensing.

MEMBERS OF FIRM

SIMON D. WILLIAMS, admitted, 1977, Australia. *Education:* University of Sydney (B.A., LL.B.); University of London (LL.M.). Solicitor, Supreme Court of New South Wales. *Member:* Licensing Executive Society, Australia; Intellectual Property Society of Australia; International Trademark Association; American Intellectual Property Law Association; European Community Trademark Practitioners Association; Institute of Patent Attorneys of Australia (Associate). *PRACTICE AREAS:* Patent, Trademark and Copyright Law; Technology Law; Intellectual Property Law.

JOHN G. HINDE, admitted, 1970, New South Wales; 1978, Australia. *Education:* University of New South Wales (B.Sc., Mathematics, Physics and Chemistry; Diploma of Education); Solicitors Admission Board of New South Wales (Diploma of Law). Notary Public. Fellow, Institute of Patent Attorneys of Australia. Lecturer, Sydney University Law School. *Member:* Licensing Executive Society, Australia; Association International for the Protection of Industrial Property; Asian Patent Attorneys Association; American Intellectual Property Law Association; American Bar Association. *PRACTICE AREAS:* Patent, Trademark and Copyright Law; Technology Law; Intellectual Property Law.

KATE JOHNSTON, admitted, 1979, Australia. *Education:* University of New England (B.A.); University of New South Wales (LL.M.). Solicitor, Supreme Court of New South Wales and Supreme Court of England. *Member:* Licensing Executive Society, Australia; Intellectual Property Society of Australia; Institute of Patent Attorneys of Australia (Associate). *PRACTICE AREAS:* Patent, Trademark and Copyright Law; Technology Law; Intellectual Property Law.

ASSOCIATES

JILL NEWTON, admitted, 1987, Australia. *Education:* University of New South Wales (M.Sc., Immunology); Macquarie University (B.A., LL.B.). Solicitor, Supreme Court of New South Wales. *PRACTICE AREAS:* Patent, Trademark and Copyright Law; Technology Law; Intellectual Property Law.

(This Listing Continued)

KHAJAQUE KORTIAN, admitted, 1994, Australia. *Education:* University of Technology (LL.B.). Solicitor, Supreme Court of New South Wales. *PRACTICE AREAS:* Patent; Trade Mark and Copyright Law; Technology Law; Intellectual Property Law.

NEW ZEALAND

BELL GULLY BUDDLE WEIR

THE AUCKLAND CLUB TOWER
34 SHORTLAND STREET
P.O. BOX 4199
AUCKLAND 1, NEW ZEALAND
Telephone: (09) 3090-859
Fax: (09) 3093-312

REVISERS OF THE NEW ZEALAND LAW DIGEST FOR THIS DIRECTORY.

South Auckland Office: 3rd Floor, Parkview Tower, 28 Davies Avenue, Manukau City. Telephone:(09) 262 1979. Fax: (09) 262 2045.
Wellington, New Zealand Office: 171 Featherston Street, P.O. Box 1291. Telephone: (04) 4737-777. Fax: (04) 4733-845.

General Practice, Commercial, Corporate Securities, Takeover, Merger and Acquisitions, Lending and Borrowing Instruments, Foreign Investment, Taxation. Industrial, Environmental, Energy, Mining, Oil and Gas. Commercial and General Litigation including Patent, Trademark and Copyright, Banking and Insurance Aviation and Maritime.

CHIEF EXECUTIVE

SEAN H.W. LARKAN, born 1953. *Education:* University of Stellenbosch (B.A., Law, 1974); University of Natal (LL.B., 1976); University of Dublin, Trinity College (M.B.A., 1978); University of South Africa (C. Tax, 1982).

RESIDENT PARTNERS

RAYMOND ARTHUR JOHN BOLLAND, born Auckland, New Zealand, 1940; admitted, 1966, New Zealand. *Education:* University of Auckland (LL.B., N.Z). *PRACTICE AREAS:* Property Law.

DAVID GRANT BOSWELL, born Waipukurau, New Zealand, 1948; admitted, 1977, New Zealand. *Education:* Victoria University of Wellington (B.C.A.); University of Auckland (LL.B.). *PRACTICE AREAS:* Corporate Law; Commercial Law.

ANDREW ALEXANDER MCKENZIE BROWN, born Wellington, New Zealand, August 8, 1959; admitted, 1982, Wellington, New Zealand. *Education:* Victoria University of Wellington (LL.B., 1981). *PRACTICE AREAS:* Corporate Law; Commercial Law.

NIELS RODERICK CAMPBELL, born England, 1954; admitted, 1978, New Zealand. *Education:* Auckland University (B.Comm., 1975; LL.B., 1978). *PRACTICE AREAS:* Taxation.

MATTHEW GARY COCKRAM, born Christchurch, New Zealand, 1963; admitted, 1985, New Zealand. *Education:* University of Canterbury (LL.B., 1984). *Member:* New Zealand Law Society. *PRACTICE AREAS:* Property Law.

BRUCE IAN JAMES COWPER, born 1949; admitted, 1971, New Zealand. *Education:* University of Auckland (LL.B. Hons.). *Member:* Auckland District Law Society. *PRACTICE AREAS:* Litigation.

GARRY MAURICE DOWNS, born Matamata, New Zealand, 1960; admitted, 1984, New Zealand. *Education:* University of Otago; Victoria University (LL.B., 1983). *PRACTICE AREAS:* Corporate Law; Commercial Law.

KEITH ROSS FAMILTON, born Christchurch, New Zealand, 1946; admitted, 1969, New Zealand. *Education:* University of Auckland (LL.B., Hons.). *PRACTICE AREAS:* Corporate Law; Commercial Law.

RODERICK HAROLD FEE, born Christchurch, New Zealand, 1959; admitted, 1983, New Zealand. *Education:* University of Canterbury (LL.B., Hons.). *PRACTICE AREAS:* Litigation.

JONATHAN ROBERT FLAWS, born Auckland, New Zealand, 1950; admitted, 1973, New Zealand. *Education:* University of Auckland (LL.B Hons., M.Jur.). *PRACTICE AREAS:* Banking Law; Finance Law.

(This Listing Continued)

NATHAN STANLEY GEDYE, born Invercargill, New Zealand, 1957; admitted, 1979, New Zealand. *Education:* Auckland University (LL.B.). *LANGUAGES:* German. *PRACTICE AREAS:* Litigation.

BRUCE DWIGHT GRAY, born Auckland, New Zealand, 1955; admitted, 1979, New Zealand. *Education:* University of Auckland (LL.B.); University of Virginia (LL.M.). *PRACTICE AREAS:* Litigation.

RICHARD MCRAE HANNA, born Auckland, New Zealand, 1950; admitted, 1973, New Zealand. *Education:* Auckland University (LL.B.). *PRACTICE AREAS:* Banking Law; Finance Law.

ALASTAIR CHARLES WAYNE HUDSON, born Christchurch, New Zealand, 1952; admitted, 1980, New Zealand. *Education:* Auckland University (B.A.; LL.B. Hons.). *LANGUAGES:* Japanese, French and German. *PRACTICE AREAS:* Corporate Law; Commercial Law.

MICHAEL DANTON JONAS, born Auckland, New Zealand, 1957; admitted, 1981, New Zealand. *Education:* Auckland University (LL.B.). *LANGUAGES:* French. *PRACTICE AREAS:* Banking Law; Finance Law.

GERALD FRANCIS KEMBER, born Wellington, New Zealand, 1945; admitted, 1969, New Zealand. *Education:* Victoria University of Wellington (LL.M.).

SIMON JEREMY KEMBER, born Wellington, New Zealand, 1955; admitted, 1977, New Zealand. *Education:* Victoria University of Wellington (LL.B.). *LANGUAGES:* French. *PRACTICE AREAS:* Property Law.

MARY JAYNE KIRTON, born Wellington, New Zealand, 1960; admitted, 1983, New Zealand. *Education:* Victoria University of Wellington (LL.B.). *PRACTICE AREAS:* Corporate Law; Commercial Law.

BRIAN ROGER LATIMOUR, born Auckland, New Zealand, 1950; admitted, 1972, New Zealand. *Education:* University of Auckland (B.A.; LL.B.). *LANGUAGES:* French and German. *PRACTICE AREAS:* Litigation.

GAVIN JOHN MACDONALD, born Auckland, New Zealand, 1961; admitted, 1984, New Zealand. *Education:* Auckland University (B.A.; LL.B.). *PRACTICE AREAS:* Corporate Law; Commercial Law.

DAVID MCGREGOR, O.B.E., E.D., born Rotorua, New Zealand, 1946; admitted, 1971, New Zealand. *Education:* Victoria University of Wellington; University of Auckland (LL.B.). *PRACTICE AREAS:* Property Law.

ALAN DAVID MCDOUGALL, born Napier, New Zealand, 1945; admitted, 1974, New Zealand. *Education:* University of Otago; Victoria University of Wellington (LL.B.). *PRACTICE AREAS:* Banking Law; Finance Law.

GRAHAM ANDREW MCKENZIE, born Christchurch, New Zealand, 1951; admitted, 1975, New Zealand. *Education:* Victoria University of Wellington (LL.B.); Warwick University, England (LL.M.). Notary Public. *PRACTICE AREAS:* Banking Law; Finance Law.

ROGER JOHN CHARLES PARTRIDGE, born Auckland, New Zealand, 1961; admitted, 1984, New Zealand, England and Wales. *Education:* Auckland University (B.Com., 1983; LL.B., Hons., 1984); University of Cambridge (LL.M., Hons., 1986). Author: "Ultra Vires, Directors Duties and Companies Amendment Act (No. 2) 1983," Auckland University Law Review, 1984; "Ratification and the Release of Directors from Personal Liability," Cambridge Law Journal, 1987. Tutor, Economic Department and Law School, Auckland University, 1982-1985. *Member:* New Zealand Law Society; The Law Society (England and Wales); New Zealand Legal Research Foundation (Council Member, 1984-1985). *PRACTICE AREAS:* Litigation.

ALAN LESLIE RINGWOOD, born Kent, England, 1960; admitted, 1984, New Zealand. *Education:* Auckland University (LL.B.). *PRACTICE AREAS:* Litigation.

DAVID HUGH RISHWORTH, born Auckland, New Zealand, 1941; admitted, 1965, New Zealand. *Education:* University of Auckland (LL.B.). Notary Public. *LANGUAGES:* French. *PRACTICE AREAS:* Property Law.

HAMISH GRAHAM ROSS, born Te Awamutu, New Zealand, December 6, 1960; admitted, 1984, New Zealand. *Education:* Victoria University of Wellington (B.C.A., 1982; LL.B., 1984).

BRUCE KENNETH GEORGE SANDERSON, born Auckland, New Zealand, 1944; admitted, 1967, New Zealand. *Education:* University of Auckland (LL.B.). Notary Public. *PRACTICE AREAS:* Property Law.

(This Listing Continued)

BELL GULLY BUDDLE WEIR, Auckland—Continued

DAVID KEITH SIMCOCK, born Hamilton, New Zealand, 1951; admitted, 1975, New Zealand. *Education:* University of Auckland (LL.B., Hons.; B.Com.); University of British Columbia (LL.M.). *LANGUAGES:* French. *PRACTICE AREAS:* Taxation.

RALPH GEORGE SIMPSON, born New Zealand, 1961; admitted, 1985, New Zealand. *Education:* University of Auckland (B.Com., 1984; LL.B., 1985). *Member:* New Zealand Law Society. *PRACTICE AREAS:* Litigation.

MARTIN RUSSELL SYMONDS, born London, England, 1947; admitted, 1972, England; 1978, Hong Kong; 1987, New Zealand. *Education:* University of Exeter (LL.B. Hons.). *PRACTICE AREAS:* Banking Law; Finance Law.

CLIVE BOWIE TAYLOR, born Palmerston North, New Zealand, 1956; admitted, 1981, New Zealand. *Education:* University of Auckland (B.Sc.; LL.B. Hons.). *PRACTICE AREAS:* Corporate Law; Commercial Law.

PHILLIP ROBERT THORPE TAYLOR, born Christchurch, New Zealand, 1946; admitted, 1971, New Zealand. *Education:* University of Canterbury (LL.B.). *PRACTICE AREAS:* Corporate Law; Commercial Law.

RICHARD HEYWOOD TAYLOR, born Wanganui, New Zealand, 1956; admitted, 1979, New Zealand. *Education:* University of Auckland (B.Com.; LL.B.; A.C.I.S.). *PRACTICE AREAS:* Taxation.

WILLIAM GEORGE THURSTON, born Palmerston North, New Zealand, 1941; admitted, 1963, New Zealand. *Education:* Victoria University of Wellington (LL.B). *PRACTICE AREAS:* Corporate Law; Commercial Law.

CONSULTANT

THOMAS NORMAN JOHNSTON, born Queenstown, New Zealand, 1928; admitted, 1951, New Zealand. *Education:* University of Otago (LL.B.). *PRACTICE AREAS:* Commercial Law; Corporate Law.

Barristers and Solicitors of the High Court of New Zealand and Members of Auckland or Wellington District Law Societies.

REVISERS OF THE NEW ZEALAND LAW DIGEST FOR THIS DIRECTORY.

BROOKFIELDS

LEVELS 8-12
19 VICTORIA STREET WEST
P.O. BOX 240
AUCKLAND, NEW ZEALAND
Telephone: 64 9 379 9350
Facsimile: 64 9 379 3224

Manukau, New Zealand Office: Level 2, Osterley Way, P.O. Box 76 004, Auckland. Telephone: 64 9 262 2145. Facsimile: 64 9 262 3875.

FIRM PROFILE: Brookfields emerged from the former Brandon Brookfield national practice, as a separate and significant firm servicing the Auckland market across a wide spectrum of legal services. The original practice traces it's origins to sole practitioner F M P Brookfield in 1856 and today divides it's practice into three broad Client Services Groups-Business Services, Private Clients and Public Authorities.

AUCKLAND PARTNERS

CHARLES STUART BLACKIE, born England, 1947; admitted, 1969, New Zealand. *Education:* Auckland University (LL.B.). Awarded: Volunteer Reserve Decoration (VRD). Judge Advocate, New Zealand Armed Forces. Commanding Officer, Auckland Division, Naval Reserve. *Member:* Refugee Appeal Authority; Deputy Chairman, Auckland District Legal Services Commission. *PRACTICE AREAS:* Litigation; Defamation; Civil Litigation; Admiralty Law; Family Law; Matrimonial Law.

MARTIN JOHN BROWN, born Auckland, New Zealand, 1957; admitted, 1982, New Zealand; 1989, England. *Education:* Auckland University (LL.B.). *PRACTICE AREAS:* Property Law; Developments; Contracts and Leasing.

CLIVE ROBERT CARTER, born Wellington, New Zealand, 1937; admitted, 1961, New Zealand. *Education:* Wellington College (LL.B.). Crown Counsel, Hong Kong. Past President, Newmarket Rotary Club; Member,

(This Listing Continued)

Wellington College Old Boys Association. *PRACTICE AREAS:* Asian Law; Property Law; Securities; Business Transactions.

JOHN RAYMOND FERNER, born 1955; admitted, 1978, New Zealand. *Education:* Canterbury University (LL.B., Hons., 1976; Commission of the European Econo mic Community Certificate, 1979). *Member:* New Zealand German Business Association. *LANGUAGES:* German. *PRACTICE AREAS:* Intellectual Property; Trade Practices Law; Commercial Law.

ANTONIA CHRISTINA MARIA FISHER, born Tokoroa, New Zealand, 1958; admitted, 1982, New Zealand. *Education:* LL.B. *PRACTICE AREAS:* Medical-Legal Law; Matrimonial Law.

MICHAEL JOHN FISHER, born Putaruru, New Zealand, 1961; admitted, 1988, New Zealand. *Education:* Otago University (LL.B., Hons.). *PRACTICE AREAS:* Banking Litigation; Commercial Litigation; Judicial Review; Civil Litigation; Dispute Resolution.

JEREMY JAMES MALLABY GOODWIN, born Wellington, New Zealand, 1956; admitted, 1979, New Zealand. *Education:* Victoria University of Wellington (LL.B.). (Managing Partner). *PRACTICE AREAS:* Estates and Trusts; Taxation.

ANDREW MICHAEL BASFORD GREEN, born Auckland, New Zealand, 1956; admitted, 1978, New Zealand. *Education:* LL.B.; Certificate of Environmental Law. Author: Updating, "Spratt & McKenzie Laws of Insolvency," Laws of New Zealand, Section on Liquor Law, 1993. *Member:* International Bar Association. *LANGUAGES:* French and German. *PRACTICE AREAS:* Advocacy; Environmental Law; Resource Management; Liquor Licensing; Insolvency.

HOWARD PAUL JOHNSTON, born Auckland, New Zealand, 1949; admitted, 1971, New Zealand. *Education:* Auckland University (LL.B., 1971). Board Member: New Zealand Gymnastics Association. *PRACTICE AREAS:* Commercial Law; Property Law; Contract Law.

WILLIAM ALLAN LAXON, born Auckland, New Zealand, 1936; admitted, 1959, New Zealand; Notary Public. *Education:* Auckland University (LL.B.). Author: "Steamers Down the Firth"; "Steam on the Manukau"; "The Shire Line". Director: Past President, Auckland Institute and Museum; Mount Wellington Trust Hotels Limited. Chairman, Presbyterian Support Services (Northern). *LANGUAGES:* French. *PRACTICE AREAS:* Resource Management; Insurance Law; Maritime Law; Corporate Law; Public Law; Commercial Law.

HAROLD IAN MCCOMBE, born Dunedin, New Zealand, 1951; admitted, 1975, New Zealand. *Education:* Auckland University (LL.B). Director, McDonnell Douglas Information Systems Limited. *PRACTICE AREAS:* Property; Commercial Property; Leasing.

DAVID ALBERT MACDONALD, born Rotorua, New Zealand, 1931; admitted, 1955, New Zealand. *Education:* Auckland University (B.A.; LL.B.). Chairman, Corbans Wines Limited, 1973-1983. Director, Magnum Corporation Limited, 1960-1990. Editor, "Business Investment in New Zealand," for Brandon Brookfield. *PRACTICE AREAS:* Commercial Law; Administrative Law; Company Law.

DAVID JOHN NEUTZE, born Auckland, New Zealand, 1959; admitted, 1983, New Zealand; 1989, United Kingdom and Hong Kong. *Education:* Auckland University (B.A.; LL.B.). *LANGUAGES:* French and German. *PRACTICE AREAS:* Judicial Review; Commercial Litigation; Criminal; Litigation.

LAURENCE JOHN NEWHOOK, born Auckland, New Zealand, 1950; admitted, 1972, New Zealand. *Education:* Auckland University (LL.B., Hons., 1972). *Member:* International Computer Law Association. *PRACTICE AREAS:* Intellectual Property; Civil Litigation; Commercial Litigation; Resource Management; Planning Advocacy.

MICHAEL DAVID SAGE, born Auckland, New Zealand, 1964; admitted, 1987, New Zealand. *Education:* B.A.; LL.B. *PRACTICE AREAS:* Commercial Law; Insolvency; Corporate; Mergers and Acquisitions; Financing; Joint Ventures; Energy Law; Intellectual Property; Trade; Foreign Investment.

PETER WILLIAM SARGENT, born Auckland, New Zealand, 1959; admitted, 1985, New Zealand. *Education:* Auckland University (LL.B.). *PRACTICE AREAS:* Banking; Finance and Securities.

MURRAY LAWRENCE SCHNAUER, born Auckland, New Zealand, 1940; admitted, 1967, New Zealand. *Education:* Auckland University (LL.B.). *PRACTICE AREAS:* Commercial Property; Residential Real Estate; Mortgage Finance.

(This Listing Continued)

JOHN MORRIS SHEPPARD, born Auckland, New Zealand, 1943; admitted, 1966, New Zealand. *Education:* University of Auckland (LL.B., 1966; B.A., 1977). *PRACTICE AREAS:* Local Government; Property.

MAUREEN JEANETTE SOUTHWICK, born Auckland, New Zealand, 1949; admitted, 1972, New Zealand. *Education:* (LL.B.). Member: New Zealand Law Society Family Law Committee; Child Protection Trust Advocacy Committee. *PRACTICE AREAS:* Litigation; Family Law; Matrimonial Law; Children.

RICHARD WALLIS, born Auckland, New Zealand, 1954; admitted, 1977, New Zealand. *Education:* (LL.B.). *PRACTICE AREAS:* Banking; Commercial Litigation; Intellectual Property; Administrative Law.

MANUKAU PARTNERS

JOHN ALEXANDER DELUGAR, born Te Puke, New Zealand, 1943; admitted, 1967, New Zealand. *Education:* Auckland University (LL.B.). *PRACTICE AREAS:* Commercial Property; Leasing; Security Documentation.

PETER ALBERTUS THEODORUS MARIA KEMPS, born Eindhoven, The Netherlands, 1951; admitted, 1975, New Zealand. *Education:* (LL.B.). *LANGUAGES:* Dutch. *PRACTICE AREAS:* Commercial Law; Property; Financing.

HANNAH SARGISSON, born 1950; admitted, 1977, New Zealand. *Education:* (B.A.; LL.B., Hons.). *PRACTICE AREAS:* Public Law; Local Government; Resource Management; Civil Litigation.

BUDDLE FINDLAY

Barristers, Solicitors and Notaries Public

FLOORS 13, 14, 17, 18, 19 AND 20
STOCK EXCHANGE CENTRE, 191-201 QUEEN STREET
P.O. BOX 1433

AUCKLAND, NEW ZEALAND

Telephone: 64-9-358-2555
Fax: 64-9-358-2055

Wellington, New Zealand Office: Floors 9, 15, 16 and 17, BNZ Centre, 1 Willis Street, P.O. Box 2694. Telephone: 64-4-499-4242. Fax: 64-4-499-4141.

Christchurch, New Zealand Office: Floors 12 & 13, Clarendon Tower, 78 Worcester Street, P.O. Box 322. Telephone: 64-3-379-1747. Fax: 64-3-379-5659.

Commercial Legal Advice, Transaction Documentation and Litigation in all Courts and Tribunals. Banking and Securities, General Corporate and Commercial Activity, International Joint Ventures, Mergers and Acquisitions, Overseas Investment and Trade, Transport, Telecommunications, Broadcasting, and Energy, Government and Public Law, Commercial Property, Taxation.
Barristers and Solicitors of the High Court of New Zealand.

CHAIRMAN OF AUCKLAND PARTNERS

BERNARD MATTHEW HILL, born New Zealand, 1949; admitted, 1975, New Zealand. *Education:* Victoria University (LL.B.). *PRACTICE AREAS:* Business Service and Corporate Advice; Competition Law.

RESIDENT PARTNERS

NORMAN JOHN CAHILL, born New Zealand, 1953; admitted, 1976, New Zealand. *Education:* Auckland University (B.A.; LL.B. Hons.). *PRACTICE AREAS:* Business Service and Corporate Advice; Personal Legal Services.

ROGER MICHAEL CRADDOCK, born New Zealand, 1945; admitted, 1968, New Zealand. *Education:* Otago University (B.A.; LL.B.). *PRACTICE AREAS:* Business Service and Corporate Advice.

MICHAEL JONATHAN DINEEN, born New Zealand, 1958; admitted, 1981, New Zealand. *Education:* Canterbury University (LL.B.). *PRACTICE AREAS:* Banking and Finance.

ANTHONY RICHARD DRAKE, born New Zealand, 1950; admitted, 1981, New Zealand. *Education:* Auckland University (B.A.; LL.B.). *PRACTICE AREAS:* Litigation; Arbitration; Dispute Resolution; Employment Law.

LESLIE KARIN MARIANNE FORSYTH, born 1962, New Zealand; admitted, 1987, New Zealand. *Education:* Victoria University (LL.B., 1984). *PRACTICE AREAS:* Corporate Finance; Structured Finance; General Banking; General Commercial.

(This Listing Continued)

RICHARD THOMAS FLIGHT FYERS, born New Zealand, 1951; admitted, 1983, New Zealand. *Education:* Auckland University (LL.B.). *PRACTICE AREAS:* Business Service and Corporate Advice; Environmental Law.

TIMOTHY PETER GREVILLE, born New Zealand, 1948; admitted, 1971, New Zealand. *Education:* Auckland University (LL.B.). *PRACTICE AREAS:* Business Services and Corporate Advice; Commercial Property.

GRAEME WILLIAM HALL, born New Zealand, 1963; admitted, 1986, New Zealand. *Education:* Auckland University (B.Com; LL.B., 1986). *PRACTICE AREAS:* Commercial Litigation; Banking; Insolvency; Insurance.

PETER BERNARD HASSELL, born Rhodesia, 1949; admitted, 1975, Zimbabwe; 1978, New Zealand. *Education:* University of Capetown (B.A.); University of Zimbabwe (B.L.). *PRACTICE AREAS:* Banking; Finance; Insolvency.

GRAHAM VINCENT HUBBLE, born New Zealand, 1941; admitted, 1964, New Zealand. *Education:* Auckland University (LL.B.). *PRACTICE AREAS:* Litigation; Arbitration; Dispute Resolution.

MURRAY PHILIP JEWELL, born New Zealand, 1951; admitted, 1975, New Zealand. *Education:* Auckland University (LL.B.); Victoria University (LL.M.). *PRACTICE AREAS:* Taxation.

ROBERT JOHN MOODY, born New Zealand, 1948; admitted, 1971, New Zealand. *Education:* Auckland University (LL.B. Hons.). *PRACTICE AREAS:* Litigation; Arbitration; Dispute Resolution.

LESLIE JOAN OLSEN, born Canada, 1949; admitted, 1987, New Zealand. *Education:* University of British Columbia (B.A., 1971; B.S.W., 1978); Simon Fraser University (P.D.P.); University of Auckland (LL.B., Hons, 1987). *PRACTICE AREAS:* Arbitration and Dispute Resolution.

PETER OWLES, born New Zealand, 1963; admitted, 1988, New Zealand. *Education:* University of Auckland (LL.B., 1986). *PRACTICE AREAS:* Banking; Project Finance; Corporate Finance; Commercial.

FRANCIS REGINALD PORTER, born New Zealand, 1957; admitted, 1980, New Zealand. *Education:* Auckland University (LL.B.). *PRACTICE AREAS:* Banking and Finance.

MICHAEL WILLIAM RATCLIFFE, born England, 1942; admitted, 1986, New Zealand. *Education:* Auckland University (LL.B.). *PRACTICE AREAS:* Business Service and Corporate Advice.

DERMOT MICHAEL MABYN ROSS, born Nigeria, 1959; admitted, 1979, New Zealand; 1984, England and Wales. *Education:* Victoria University (LL.M.). Solicitor of the Supreme Court of England and Wales, 1984. *PRACTICE AREAS:* Banking and Finance.

CARL EDWARD JOHN ROWLING, born New Zealand, 1961; admitted, 1985, New Zealand; 1985, California. *Education:* University of Canterbury (LL.B.). *PRACTICE AREAS:* Business Services and Corporate Advice; Communications.

NEIL A. RUSS, born New Zealand, 1961; admitted, 1986, New Zealand; 1991, England and Wales. *Education:* Victoria University (LL.B., Hons, 1985). *PRACTICE AREAS:* Structured Financing; Syndicated Lending; Dept Restructuring; Project Financing; Property Financing.

BRIAN MAXWELL STEWART, born New Zealand, 1953; admitted, 1976, New Zealand; 1983, England and Wales. *Education:* Victoria University (LL.B.). *PRACTICE AREAS:* Litigation; Arbitration and Dispute Resolution; Banking and Insolvency; Environmental Law.

JOHN WILLIAM TURNER, born New Zealand, 1954; admitted, 1978, New Zealand; 1983, Papua New Guinea; 1985, Victoria, Australia; 1985 High Court of Australia; 1986, England and Wales. *Education:* Auckland University (LL.B. Hons); M. Jur.; Dalhousie University, Canada (LL.M.). *PRACTICE AREAS:* Litigation, Arbitration and Dispute Resolution.

All Partners are Members of the Auckland District Law Society.

Languages: English, French, Japanese, German and Mandarin

(For complete biographical data on Wellington and Christchurch personnel, see Professional Biographies at Wellington and Christchurch, New Zealand).

CHAPMAN TRIPP SHEFFIELD YOUNG

LEVEL 35
23-29 ALBERT STREET
P.O. BOX 2206
AUCKLAND 1, NEW ZEALAND
Telephone: 64-9-357-9000
Fax: 64-9-357-9099

Wellington, New Zealand Office: AMP Centre, Grey Street. P.O. Box 993. Telephone: 64-4-499 5999 Fax: 64-4-472-7111.

General Practice, Aviation, Banking, Civil and Commercial Litigation, Computer, Information Technology, Commercial, Conveyancing, Corporation, Energy, Estates, Finance, Foreign Investment, Franchising, Insurance, Intellectual Property, International Financing and Trade, Joint Ventures, Licensing, Marine, Mergers, Takeovers and Acquisitions, Mining, Oil and Gas, Patents, Planning, Property Development, Real Estate Transactions, Taxation, Trademarks and Trustee Law.
Barristers and Solicitors of High Court of New Zealand.

MEMBERS OF FIRM AT AUCKLAND

DOUGLAS SEYMOUR ALDERSLADE, born 1952; admitted, 1976, New Zealand. *Education:* University of Auckland (LL.B.). *PRACTICE AREAS:* Civil Law; Commercial Litigation; Banking and Securities Enforcement; Insurance; Employment Law.

MICHAEL GERARD ANDERSON, born 1954; admitted, 1983, New Zealand. *Education:* University of Canterbury (B.A., LL.B. Hons.). *PRACTICE AREAS:* International Banking Law; Securities Offerings; Securitisation; Banking and Finance Law.

STEPHEN LAUD ANDERSON, born 1947; admitted, 1969, New Zealand. *Education:* University of Auckland (LL.B. Hons). Harvard Law School Programme of Instruction for Lawyers, 1993. Editor, University of Auckland Law Review, 1969. Lecturer in Building Law, University of Auckland, 1971-1972. Examiner in Commercial Law, NZ Society of Accountants, 1972. Tutor in Commercial Papers and Practice, University of Auckland, 19 76-1981. *PRACTICE AREAS:* Company Law; Securities Law; International Financing Law; Media Law.

RAYMOND JOHN BEECH, born 1950; admitted, 1973, New Zealand. *Education:* University of Auckland (LL.B., A.Arb.INZ). Member: New Zealand Mining and Exploration Association; The Packaging Industry Advisory Council. *PRACTICE AREAS:* Resource Management Law; Property Litigation; Mining Law.

ROBERT ANDREW BYCROFT, born 1959; admitted, 1983, New Zealand. *Education:* University of Auckland (B.Com.; LL.B.). *PRACTICE AREAS:* Intellectual Property Law; Computer and Information Technology Law; Franchise Law; Corporate Law; Mergers Law; Acquisitions Law.

CHERYL RAEWYN GWYN, born 1955; admitted, 1987, New Zealand. *Education:* University of Auckland (B.A.; LL.B., Hons.). *PRACTICE AREAS:* Commercial Litigation; Industrial Relations; Medico-Legal Issues; Human Rights Legislation.

ANDREW LEONARD HAMES, born 1958; admitted, 1982, New Zealand. *Education:* University of Auckland (B.Com. LL.B.). *PRACTICE AREAS:* Corporate Law; Commercial Law; Insurance Law.

BARNARD HUGH WYNYARD HUTCHINSON, born 1951; admitted, 1975, New Zealand. *Education:* Auckland University (B.Com; LL.B., Hons.; M.Tax.S.). *PRACTICE AREAS:* Energy Law; Taxation Law; Securities Law; Corporate Law.

ANTHONY JOHN KEENAN, born 1948; admitted, 1974, New Zealand. *Education:* University of Canterbury (LL.B.). *PRACTICE AREAS:* Real Estate Law; Representing Overseas Investors in Real Estate; Public Real Estate Law Issues; Real Estate Development and Leasing; Real Estate Joint Ventures.

ALLAN RICHARD MCRAE, born 1957; admitted, 1982, New Zealand. *Education:* Otago University (LL.B., B.Com.). *PRACTICE AREAS:* Banking Law; Commercial Law; Acquisitions and Dispositions; Superannuation Law.

STEPHEN JOHN MILLS, born 1947; admitted, 1978, New Zealand. *Education:* University of Auckland (LL.B. Hons); University of Pennsylvania (LL.M.). Instructor, University of Michigan Law School, 1972-1973; Lecturer/Senior Lecturer, University of Auckland, Faculty of Law; Associate Professor, Lewis & Clark Law School, 1978-1979, University of Western Ontario, 1978-1979 and Dalhousie University, 1980-1987. *PRACTICE*

(This Listing Continued)

AREAS: Contract Law; Construction Law; Commercial Litigation; Public Law; Media Law.

PETER JAMES MURPHY, born 1958; admitted, 1983, New Zealand. *Education:* University of Auckland (B.Com., LL.B.,). (Managing Partner). *PRACTICE AREAS:* Corporate and Commercial; Structuring; Acquisitions and Dispositions.

ROBERT IAN PARKER, born 1952; admitted, 1976, New South Wales; 1979, Federal Court of Australia; 1984, Australian Capital Territory; 1988, New Zealand. *Education:* Sydney University (Dip. Law SAB). *PRACTICE AREAS:* Commercial Property; Property Joint Ventures; Shopping Center Developments; Leasing; Property Trusts.

ALAN MURRAY PATERSON, born 1957; admitted, 1981, New Zealand. *Education:* University of Auckland (B.Com.; LL.B., Hons.). *PRACTICE AREAS:* Commercial Property Law.

WARWICK ALEXANDER SMITH, born 1951; admitted, 1974, New Zealand. *Education:* Otago University (B.A., LL.B.). Harvard Law School Programme of Instruction for Lawyers, 1993. *PRACTICE AREAS:* Civil Litigation; Intellectual Property.

ROSS WILLIAM STITT, born 1960; admitted, 1984, New Zealand. *Education:* University of Auckland (B.Com., LL.B.). *PRACTICE AREAS:* Taxation Law.

JOHN WILLIAM STROWGER, born 1962; admitted, 1987, New Zealand. *Education:* Canterbury University (LL.B., Hons.). *PRACTICE AREAS:* Corporate Law; Contract Law; Securities Law; Privatisation.

MICHAEL CARMODY WALLS, born 1945; admitted, 1968, New Zealand. *Education:* Victoria University of Wellington (B.A., LL.B.); The London School of Economics, University of London (LL.M.). Former Lecturer, The City of London Polytechnic. (Also at Wellington Office). *PRACTICE AREAS:* International Financing Law; Mergers Law; Takeovers Law; Banking Law; Securities Law.

EVAN CHRISTOPHER WILLIAMS, born 1953; admitted, 1976, New Zealand. *Education:* Victoria University of Wellington (LL.M., Hons.). Lecturer in Law, Victoria University of Wellington, 1976-1978. *PRACTICE AREAS:* Corporate and Securities Law; Corporate Acquisitions and Dispositions; Insurance Law; Energy Law.

ARTHUR WILLIAM YOUNG, born 1935; admitted, 1958, New Zealand. *Education:* University of Auckland (LL.B.). Former Tutor in Commercial Law and Moderator for Introduction to Commercial Law, Auckland University. *PRACTICE AREAS:* Commercial Property Development Law; Corporate Law; Commercial Law; Corporate Acquisitions; Trustee Law.

CONSULTANTS

DAVID HAROLD CORNWELL, born 1959; admitted, 1981, New Zealand; 1985, Victoria and New South Wales; 1992, England. *Education:* University of Canterbury (LL.B., Hons.); University of Auckland (M.Jur.). *PRACTICE AREAS:* International Law; Asian Law; Cross Border Transactions; Banking Law; Finance Transactions; Corporate Law; Commercial Law.

TREVOR CLENDON GOULD, born 1947; admitted, 1969, New Zealand. *Education:* University of Auckland (LL.B., Hons). *PRACTICE AREAS:* Town Planning; Environmental Law; Resource Management Law.

GEOFFREY PALMER, born 1943. *Education:* Victoria University of Wellington (LL.B.); University of Chicago (Doctor of Law, cum laude, 1967). Professor of Law, Victoria University of Wellington, 1991. (Also at Wellington Office). *PRACTICE AREAS:* Public Law; Maori Issues.

JOSEPH THOMAS SHEFFIELD, born 1917; admitted, 1942, New Zealand. *Education:* University of New Zealand (LL.M. 1st Class Hons.; B.Com.; ACANZ). Former Lecturer and Examiner in Contract Law at Auckland University.

All of the above are members of the Auckland District Law Society.

(This Listing Continued)

OUT: "Limited"); Mainzeal Group Ltd.; Maori Development Corporation; McConnell Dowell Corporation Ltd.; Metropolitan Lifecare Group Ltd.; National Mutual Finance Ltd.; National Provident Fund; New Zealand Dairy Board; New Zealand Forestry Corporation Ltd.; BHP New Zealand Steel Ltd.; NZ Forest Products Ltd.; Penguin Books (NZ) Ltd.; Pepsico Inc.; Petroleum Corporation of New Zealand Ltd.; Progressive Enterprises Ltd.; R.J.R. Nabisco Inc.; St. Luke's Group Ltd.; Sumitomo Chemical Company Ltd.; Telecom Corporation of New Zealand Ltd.; The Shipowners' Protection & Indemnity Association in the International Group; Transit New Zealand; Victoria University of Wellington; Wellcome Foundation Ltd.; Westpac Banking Corp.; Williams & Kettle Ltd.; Woolworths NZ Ltd.; Works Development Services NZ Corp.

(For Biographical Data of the Wellington Personnel, see Professional Biographies at Wellington).

HESKETH HENRY

A Member of the Gadens Ridgeway Group

Established in 1865

2 KITCHENER STREET
PRIVATE BAG 92093
AUCKLAND, NEW ZEALAND
Telephone: (09) 3090-552
Fax: (09) 3094-494
Certified to ISO 9001 International Service Quality Standard

General Practice. Corporate and Commercial, Securities, Banking, Tax, Foreign Investment, Construction Law, Computer and Licensing Law, Commercial and Residential Real Estate, Civil and General Litigation, Arbitration, Probate, Trusts and Maritime.
Barristers and Solicitors of the High Court of New Zealand. Notaries Public.

MEMBERS OF FIRM

RICHARD ANDREW CAUGHEY, born November 12, 1932; B.A. (New Zealand), LL.B. (Otago). Notary Public.

ROBERT SELWYN BEZAR, born August 6, 1942; LL.B. (Auckland). Member, Royal New Zealand Yacht Squadron.

JOHN WILLIAM STEWART, born October 16, 1943; LL.B. (Auckland). Member, Royal New Zealand Yacht Squadron.

MURRAY PIERCE WILLIAMS WARD, born June 23, 1945; LL.B. (Auckland).

ANTHONY CLIVE SANDLANT, born October 1, 1943; LL.B. (Auckland). Formerly with Thompson, Snell & Passmore, Tunbridge Wells, England, 1968-1971.

BALDWIN THOMAS MARCH, born February 1, 1941; LL.B. (Victoria University of Wellington). Commissioner for Oaths for Fiji. Barrister and Solicitor of Supreme Court Fiji.

MARK EVERSFIELD PERKINS, born December 27, 1947; LL.B. (Auckland); LL.M. (Victoria University of Wellington). *Member:* Maritime Law Association of Australia and New Zealand; New Zealand Law Association (Inc.).

IAN HENDRIK BODE, born December 5, 1948; LL.B. (Auckland). Formerly with Lovell, White & King, London, 1973-1974.

ANTHONY DAVID BANBROOK, born December 18, 1945; B.Sc., LL.B. (Auckland). *Member:* Maritime Law Association of Australia and New Zealand.

JOHN RICHARD AVERY, born December 21, 1950; LL.B. (Auckland). Board Member, The Royal New Zealand Ballet.

WILLIAM KEITH WILLOUGHBY, born June 30, 1948; LL.B. (Auckland). Formerly with Blatchfords, London, 1973-1975.

SIMON MIDDLETON PALMER, born October 3, 1955; LL.B. (Auckland).

JEREMY AUSTIN CARR, born September 8, 1954; LL.B. (Auckland). Notary Public. *Member:* Royal New Zealand Yacht Squadron.

RICHARD JOHN OSBORNE, born September 8, 1949; LL.B., Hons. (Auckland), M.I.L.R., J.S.D. (Cornell). Solicitor, England. With: Graham & James, San Francisco, 1975-1976; Venable, Baetjer & Howard, Baltimore, 1976-1978; MacFarlanes, London, 1979-1983. *Member:* Maryland and American Bar Associations.

CHRISTOPHER MAXWELL WALKER, born June 19, 1955; LL.B. (Auckland).

(This Listing Continued)

PETER THOMAS KIELY, born September 1, 1957; B.A., LL.B. (Auckland). Admitted to the Supreme Court of Victoria and High Court of Australia, 1985. Formerly with Lawler, Felix & Hall, Los Angeles, 1985. Member, Board of Advisors UCLA Pacific Basin Law Journal, 1986—. Director, Pacific Forum Line, Ltd.

ERICH BACHMANN, born July 20, 1956. LL.B. (Auckland). Author of the New Zealand Section of "Recht des Eigentumsvorbehalts," (Retention of Title), published by German Machinery and Plant Breeding Association. Legal Advisor to the Embassy and Consulate of the Federal Republic of Germany in New Zealand. *Member:* New Zealand-German Business Association.

BRETT WILLIAM MORLEY, born June 2, 1955. B.A., LL.B. (Auckland).

ANDREW ROBERT GILCHRIST, born September 19, 1962; B.Com., LL.B. (Otago).

DAVID MARTIN CONNOR, born July 30, 1962; LL.B. (Auckland).

KEVIN DAVID KILGOUR, born January 24, 1948; LL.B. (Wellington). Commissioner for Oaths, Supreme Courts of Queensland and Victoria. *Member:* Arbitrators Institute of New Zealand (Associate).

DEBRA DORRINGTON, born October 20, 1960; LL.B. (Wellington). Vice President, New Zealand Federation of Business & Professional Women Inc., 1994.

All Members of the Firm are Barristers and Solicitors of the High Court of New Zealand and Members of the Auckland District and New Zealand Law Societies.
Firm is a Member of American Chamber of Commerce in New Zealand and Lawlink, an association of independent legal practices throughout New Zealand.

Languages: German, Spanish, French, Italian, Chinese (Cantonese and Mandarin dialects), Dutch, Malay, Hokkien and Afrikaans.

A List of Representative Clients is available upon request.

KENSINGTON SWAN

22 FANSHAWE STREET
PRIVATE BAG 92101
AUCKLAND, NEW ZEALAND
Telephone: (9)-379-4196
DX: 57
Fax: (9) 309-4276

Wellington, New Zealand Office: 89 The Terrace, P.O. Box 10-246. Telephone: (4) 472-7877. Facsimile: (4) 472-2291.

Arbitration, Commercial, Criminal, Environmental, Estate Planning, Family Industrial and Taxation Law, Property Transactions, Receiverships and Liquidations, Town Planning, Corporate Law, Mergers and Acquisitions, Property and Real Estate Law, Commercial Property, Estate Administration, Wills and Trusts, Commercial Litigation, Conveyancing, Building Society Law, Construction Law (including Arbitrations), Transportation Law, Corporate Financing, Franchising and Distribution Law, Insolvency and Receiverships, Real Property, Private Corporations, Trusts, Personal Tax, Duties Planning, Commercial Law, Insurance Law, Civil, Commercial and Corporate Litigation, Inheritance Estate and Gift Taxation, District and New Commercial Litigation, General Legal Practice, Securities Law, Finance, General Intellectual Property Practice, Competition Law. Notary Public.

PARTNERS

DONALD FREDERICK DUGDALE, admitted, 1951, New Zealand as Solicitor; 1952, New Zealand, as Barrister. *Education:* University of New Zealand (B.A.; LL.B., 1952). *PRACTICE AREAS:* Commercial Litigation; Insurance Law; Real Property Litigation.

KENNETH ROYDEN HUBAND, admitted, 1948, New Zealand. *Education:* Auckland University (LL.B.). *PRACTICE AREAS:* Property Law; Commercial Law; Estate Administration Law; Wills Law; Trusts Law.

IAN LESLIE HAYNES, admitted, 1960, New Zealand. *Education:* University of Auckland (B.A.; LL.B., 1959). *PRACTICE AREAS:* Commercial Property; Construction Law; Energy Law; Insolvency Law.

HOWARD CARISBROOKE KEYTE, admitted, 1963, New Zealand. *Education:* University of Auckland (LL.B., 1963). *PRACTICE AREAS:* Trade Practice Law; Insolvency Law; Employment Law; Commercial Litigation.

(This Listing Continued)

KENSINGTON SWAN, Auckland—Continued

JAMES DENHAM SHALE, admitted, 1967, New Zealand. *Education:* University of Auckland (LL.B., 1967). *PRACTICE AREAS:* Corporate Law; Mergers and Acquisitions Law; Corporate Financing Law.

KEITH WILLIAM BERMAN, admitted, 1965, New Zealand. *Education:* University of Auckland (LL.B., 1965; Dip. Town Planning, 1971). *PRACTICE AREAS:* Franchising Law; Distribution Law; Insolvency Law; Receiverships Law; Commercial Litigation; Town Planning Law.

JUDITH MARJORIE POTTER, admitted, 1964, New Zealand. *Education:* Auckland University (LL.B., 1965). *PRACTICE AREAS:* Corporate Law; Insurance Law; Securities Law; Mergers and Acquisitions.

MATTHEW EUGENE CASEY, admitted, 1975, New Zealand. *Education:* Auckland University (LL.B., Hons., 1975). *PRACTICE AREAS:* Commercial Litigation; Resource Management Law; Local Government Law; Administrative Law.

ROBERT MANWARRING NOAKES, admitted, 1973, New Zealand, Notary Public. *Education:* Auckland University (LL.B., Hons.). *PRACTICE AREAS:* Corporate Law; Commercial Law; Competition Law; Commercial Property; Mergers and Acquisitions; Foreign Investment.

TIMOTHY JOHN MAC AVOY, admitted, 1973, New Zealand. *Education:* University of Auckland (LL.B., 1973). *PRACTICE AREAS:* Commercial Law; Superannuation Law; Computer Law; Insurance Law.

PETER HENRY NOLAN, admitted, 1976, New Zealand. *Education:* University of Auckland; University of Otago (B.A.; LL.B.). *PRACTICE AREAS:* Property Law; Securities Law.

NIGEL ANTHONY SEEBOLD, admitted, 1975, New Zealand. *Education:* University of Auckland (B.A.; LL.B.). *PRACTICE AREAS:* Corporate Law; Banking and Finance Law; Securities Law; Insolvency Law.

GREGORY CARL EVERARD, admitted, 1977, New Zealand; 1983, Victoria, Australia. *Education:* University of Auckland (LL.B.). *PRACTICE AREAS:* Professional Indemnity; Insurance Law; Insolvency Law.

MURRAY ASHLEY GILBERT, admitted, 1977, New Zealand. *Education:* University of Auckland (LL.B., 1977). *PRACTICE AREAS:* Commercial Litigation.

PAUL CARGILL SUMPTER, admitted, 1977, New Zealand. *Education:* Canterbury University of New Zealand (B.A.); University of Auckland (M.A., Hons.; LL.B.). (Registered, Patent Attorney). *PRACTICE AREAS:* Intellectual Property Law; Competition Law; Franchising Law.

CHRISTOPHER JOHN BOOTH, admitted, 1978, New Zealand. *Education:* Victoria University of Wellington (LL.B., Hons.). *PRACTICE AREAS:* Banking Law; Corporate and Trade Practices; Litigation; Arbitration; Construction Law.

JANE ELIZABETH LATIMER, admitted, 1979, New Zealand; 1986, Solicitor of England and Wales. *Education:* University of Auckland (LL.B., 1979). *PRACTICE AREAS:* Commercial Litigation; Employment Law.

MATTHEW PATRICK PASLEY, admitted, 1984, New Zealand; 1987, New South Wales. *Education:* University of Auckland (LL.B.). *PRACTICE AREAS:* Mergers and Acquisitions; Banking and Finance; Corporate Law.

DAVID JOHN CHISHOLM, admitted, 1984, New Zealand. *Education:* University of Auckland (LL.B.); University of London (LL.M.). *PRACTICE AREAS:* Intellectual Property; Insolvency Law; Banking and Finance.

FRANCIS W. ROSE, admitted, 1983, New Zealand. *Education:* University of Auckland (LL.B., 1983). *PRACTICE AREAS:* Insurance Law.

All Partners are members of the Auckland and New Zealand Law Societies.

Languages Spoken by Members of Kensington Swan: English, Maori, French, Italian, German, Japanese, Polish, Greek, Mandarin, Fukien, Cantonese, Malay.

MARTELLI McKEGG WELLS & CORMACK

Barristers & Solicitors

TOWER 1, NATIONAL BANK CENTRE
209 QUEEN STREET
P.O. BOX 5745

AUCKLAND, NEW ZEALAND
Telephone: (09) 379 7333
Facsimile: (09) 309 4112

Commercial Law, Corporate Law, Finance, Conveyancing and Property Law, Taxation and Tax Planning, Franchising and Licensing, Overseas Investment, Immigration, International Commerce and Trade, Intellectual Property, Insolvency, Negotiations, Arbitrations, Litigation, Town Planning, Liquor Licensing, Domestic and Matrimonial, Wills, Estates, Trusts and Estate Planning.

FIRM PROFILE: The firm was established some 70 years ago and adopted its present name and structure in 1977. The practice is business based but with a well established private client service. The firm represents foreign investors in New Zealand and has links in Australia, the Pacific Basin and in Europe. It is a member of Commercial Law Affiliates (C.L.A.).

PARTNERS

MICHAEL CAMPBELL MCINTOSH CORMACK, born 1938; admitted, 1966, United Kingdom. *Education:* University of New Zealand (LL.B., 1962). *Member:* The Law Society. *PRACTICE AREAS:* Corporate; Commercial; Business Law.

PHILIP SAMPSON WELLS, born 1944. *Education:* University of Auckland (LL.B., 1967). *PRACTICE AREAS:* Corporate; Commercial; Acquisitions; Business Law.

STEPHEN PERRY BRYERS, born 1948. *Education:* University of Auckland (LL.B., Hons., 1971). *PRACTICE AREAS:* Litigation; Environmental Law; Arbitration; Insurance.

WARREN DOUGLAS BYGRAVE, born 1948. *Education:* University of Auckland (LL.B., 1971). *PRACTICE AREAS:* Commercial; Property; Franchising.

TIMOTHY RICHARD MAFFEY, born 1953. *Education:* University of Auckland (LL.B., 1974). *PRACTICE AREAS:* Conveyancing; Property.

CATHERINE ANN ATCHISON, born 1951; admitted, 1979, United Kingdom. *Education:* University of Victoria and Auckland (LL.B., Hons., 1975). *PRACTICE AREAS:* Trusts; Wills; Estates.

JOHN KEITH KENYON, born 1954. *Education:* University of Auckland (LL.B., 1977). *PRACTICE AREAS:* Conveyancing; Leasing; Commercial Property.

ANDREW GRAEME MACDONALD, born 1959. *Education:* University of Auckland (LL.B., 1984). *PRACTICE AREAS:* Taxation; Corporate; Securities.

STEVEN DUKESON, born 1953. *Education:* University of Auckland (LL.M., Hons., 1979). Contributor, The New Zealand Law Journal on Commercial, Company & Contract Law, 1979—. *PRACTICE AREAS:* Contracts; Commercial; Distributorship; Banking; Insolvency.

DAVID ALAN TOWLE, born 1961. *Education:* University of Auckland (LL.B., 1984). *PRACTICE AREAS:* Litigation; Debt Recovery; Administrative Law.

All Partners are admitted as Barristers and Solicitors of the High Court of New Zealand and are members of the Auckland District Law Society and the New Zealand Law Society.

Languages: English, French, German, Cantonese, Malay, Mandarin, Hokkein and Korean

McELROYS

Barristers & Solicitors

LEVEL 15, SOUTHPAC TOWER
CORNER QUEEN & CUSTOMS STREETS
P.O. BOX 835
AUCKLAND, NEW ZEALAND
Telephone: 64 9 307 2003
Fax: 64 9 309 7558; 64 9 302 0615 (Library)

Litigation in Insurance, Personal Injury, Marine and Shipping, Construction, Commerce and Civil Law.

PARTNERS

MICHAEL RING, born 1955; admitted, 1978, New Zealand. *Education:* University of Auckland (LL.B.).

PATRICIA COURTNEY, born 1960; admitted, 1983, New Zealand. *Education:* University of Auckland (LL.B.).

PHILIP RZEPECKY, born 1959; admitted, 1986, New Zealand. *Education:* Victoria University of Wellington (LL.B.).

ANDREW HOOKER, born 1963; admitted, 1991, New Zealand. *Education:* University of Auckland (LL.B.).

RUDD WATTS & STONE

Established in 1880

BANK OF NEW ZEALAND TOWER
125 QUEEN STREET
P.O. BOX 3798
AUCKLAND, NEW ZEALAND
Telephone: 64-9 309 4863
Fax: 64-9-379 3326

Wellington, New Zealand Office: Trust Bank Centre, 125 The Terrace, P.O. Box 2793. Telephone: 64-4 472 4899. Fax: 64-4 473 8232.

New Plymouth, New Zealand Office: 32 Vivian Street, P.O. Box 34. Telephone: 64-6 758 5397. Fax: 64-6 758 1822.

Sydney, New South Wales, Australia Associated Office: Minter Ellison, 44 Martin Place, 2000. Telephone: 61-2 210 4444. Fax: 61-2 235 2711.

Melbourne, Victoria, Australia Associated Office: Minter Ellison, 40 Market Street, 3000. Telephone: 61-3 617 4617. Fax: 61-3 617 4666.

Brisbane, Queensland, Australia Associated Office: Minter Ellison, Waterfront Place, 1 Eagle Street, 4000. Telephone: 61-7 226 6333. Fax: 61-7 229 1066.

Canberra, Australia Capital Territory, Australia Associated Office: Minter Ellison, 8-10 Hobart Place, 2600. Telephone: 61-6 248 7533. Fax: 61-6 249 8208.

Adelaide, South Australia, Australia Associated Office: Minter Ellison Baker O'Loughlin, 1 King William Street, 5000. Telephone: 61-8 233 5555. Fax: 61-8 212 7518.

Perth, Western Australia, Australia Associated Office: Minter Ellison Northmore Hale, 152-158 St. George's Terrace, 6000. Telephone: 61-9 429 7444. Fax: 61-9 429 7666.

London, England Associated Office: Minter Ellison, 20 Lincoln's Inn Fields, WC2A 3ED. Telephone: 44-171 831 7871. Fax: 44-171 404 4610.

Hong Kong Associated Office: McKenna & Co. in association with Minter Ellison, 5th Floor, Lippo Tower, 89 Queensway. Telephone: 852-2-846 9100. Fax: 852-2-845-3575.

Beijing, People's Republic of China Associated Office: Minter Ellison, Representative Office, Oxford Associates Inc., 205 International Club, 21 Jianguomenwai Dajie, 100020. Telephone: 86-1-532 5750. Fax: 86-1-513 6179.

Singapore Associated Office: Khattar Wong & Partners, 80 Raffles Place, #25-01 UOB Building, 0104. Telephone: 65-535 6844 Fax: 65-534 4892. Telex: 24896.

Legal services including: company and commercial, banking and finance, securities, mergers and acquisitions, computer law, telecommunications, competition law, consumer law, intellectual property, product liability, international trade, corporate recovery and insolvency, energy and resources, environmental law, construction, commercial property, shipping and aviation, media and entertainment, business immigration, alternative dispute resolution, commercial litigation, taxation, trusts and superannuation, employment, government liaison, insurance.

(This Listing Continued)

AUCKLAND PARTNERS

CHRISTOPHER JOHN ALLAN, admitted, 1965, New Zealand. LL.M. *PRACTICE AREAS:* Commercial Litigation; Competition Law; Intellectual Property.

ALLAN MICHAEL BOYLE, admitted, 1982, New Zealand. B.Sc.; LL.B. *PRACTICE AREAS:* Labour and Employment Law; Commercial Litigation; Insurance; Energy; Construction.

GERARD MATTHEW BROWN, admitted, 1983, New Zealand; 1991, England. B.A.; LL.B. *PRACTICE AREAS:* Company and Commercial; Mergers and Acquisitions; Banking and Finance.

GARNET ANDREW CROWHEN, admitted, 1973, New Zealand. LL.M. *PRACTICE AREAS:* Company and Commercial; Mergers and Acquisitions; Telecommunications; Computer Law.

BRUCE NELSON DAVIDSON, admitted, 1961, New Zealand. LL.M. *PRACTICE AREAS:* Property; Corporations; Commercial; Trusts.

FRANCIS DAWSON, admitted, 1973, England; 1984, New Zealand. B.A.; BCL (Oxon). *PRACTICE AREAS:* Company and Commercial; Banking and Finance.

MICHAEL ANTHONY EWEN, admitted, 1974, New Zealand. LL.B. (Hons). *PRACTICE AREAS:* Competition Law; Intellectual Property; Consumer Protection; Licensing/Franchising; Product Liability.

ROBERT IAN FALVEY, admitted, 1982, New Zealand; 1991, Fiji. LL.B. (Hons). *PRACTICE AREAS:* Company and Commercial; Mergers and Acquisitions; Entertainment.

GILLIAN JANE GOODWIN, admitted, 1978, New Zealand. LL.B. *PRACTICE AREAS:* Banking and Finance; Securities.

GRAHAM BRAMWELL HARFORD, admitted, 1979, New Zealand; 1989, New South Wales, Australia; 1990, Victoria and Australian Capital Territory, Australia. LL.B.; M.Phil. (Commercial Law) (Hons). *PRACTICE AREAS:* Company and Commercial; Mergers and Acquisitions; New Zealand/Australian CER Issues.

SIMON EDWIN HERBERT, admitted, 1986, New Zealand. B.Com.; LL.B. *PRACTICE AREAS:* Commercial Property.

DAVID GILES HURD, admitted, 1976, New Zealand. LL.B. (Hons). *PRACTICE AREAS:* Commercial Litigation; Competition Law; Intellectual Property; Administrative Law.

LEIGH ANNETTE MCGREGOR, admitted, 1985, New Zealand. LL.B. *PRACTICE AREAS:* Resource Management; Town Planning; Local Government; Liquor Licensing; Environmental Law.

BRENDAN PHILLIP MEECH, admitted, 1984, New Zealand. B.Com.; LL.B. *PRACTICE AREAS:* Banking and Finance.

ROSS HENRY PATTERSON, admitted, 1970, New Zealand. LL.B. (Hons); LL.M. (Queen's, Ontario). *PRACTICE AREAS:* Company and Commercial; Competition Law; Intellectual Property.

WILLIAM MALCOLM PATTERSON, admitted, 1965, New Zealand. LL.M. *PRACTICE AREAS:* Company and Commercial; Taxation; Trust and Estate Planning; Superannuation.

ROSS HUGH PICKMERE, admitted, 1974, New Zealand. LL.B. *PRACTICE AREAS:* Commercial Property.

CASEY MICHAEL VAUGHAN PLUNKET, admitted, 1985, New Zealand; 1989, New York, U.S.A. BCA, LL.B. (Hons); LL.M. (Mich). *PRACTICE AREAS:* Taxation.

PETER JAMES ROWE, admitted, 1964, New Zealand. LL.M., J.D. (Chicago). *PRACTICE AREAS:* Company and Commercial; Mergers and Acquisitions; Joint Ventures; Government; Shipping; Aviation.

GEOFFREY MARK SANDELIN, admitted, 1985, New Zealand. B.A.; LL.B. *PRACTICE AREAS:* Commercial Litigation; Insolvency; Creditors Remedies; Resource Management.

WILLIAM ANTHONY SANDSTON, admitted, 1977, New Zealand. LL.B. *PRACTICE AREAS:* Commercial Property.

ANTHONY FRANCIS SEGEDIN, admitted, 1972, New Zealand. LL.B.; Notary Public. *PRACTICE AREAS:* Commercial Property; Banking and Finance.

BERNARD PETER SMITH, admitted, 1984, New Zealand. LL.B.; M.Com. Law (Hons). *PRACTICE AREAS:* Banking and Finance; Securities Law.

(This Listing Continued)

RUDD WATTS & STONE, Auckland—Continued

ALAN CHARLES STONES, admitted, 1971, New Zealand. LL.B. **PRACTICE AREAS:** Commercial; Commercial Property; Banking; Securities; Environmental Risk Management.

JOSEPH MICHAEL WINDMEYER, admitted, 1985, New Zealand. B.Com., LL.B. (Hons). **PRACTICE AREAS:** Company and Commercial; Mergers and Acquisitions.

SENIOR ASSOCIATES

CRAIG IRVING ALEXANDER, LL.B. **PRACTICE AREAS:** Banking and Finance.

WENDY KAYE BLENNERHASSETT, LL.B. **PRACTICE AREAS:** Commercial Litigation.

FUI LOONG CHAN, LL.B. **PRACTICE AREAS:** Commercial Property; Immigration; Asian Law Practice.

GLENN JAMES COOPER, LL.B. (Hons). **PRACTICE AREAS:** Commercial Litigation.

JULIET LINNELL GREENAWAY, LL.B. (Hons). **PRACTICE AREAS:** Commercial Litigation; Insolvency; Creditors Remedies; Employment; Health and Safety; Resource Management.

CAROLYN JOAN HARDING, B.A. (Hons) Law. **PRACTICE AREAS:** Consumer Protection; Intellectual Property; Competition Law.

ANTHONY ROSS HOSKING, LL.B. (Hons); M.A. (Hons); M.Jur.; M.Phil. **PRACTICE AREAS:** Intellectual Property; Commercial Litigation; Competition Law.

EWE LEONG LIM, LL.B.; M.Phil. (Commercial Law, Hons). **PRACTICE AREAS:** Company and Commercial; Joint Ventures; Mergers and Acquisitions; Securities Law.

STEPHEN ROBERT MURRAY, LL.B. **PRACTICE AREAS:** Estate Planning; Taxation; Trusts; Superannuation.

ANTONY PAUL NAGEL, LL.B. **PRACTICE AREAS:** Company and Commercial; Commercial Litigation.

KRISTIN LAURA PERCY, B.A.; LL.B. **PRACTICE AREAS:** Commercial Property.

ELIZABETH CHRISTINA SINCLAIR, B.Com.; LL.B. **PRACTICE AREAS:** Company and Commercial.

SIMON STOKES, B.A.; LL.B. (Hons). **PRACTICE AREAS:** Construction; Commercial Litigation.

JACINTHA TAN, B.A.; LL.B. (Hons). **PRACTICE AREAS:** Commercial Property.

MELANIE RUTH TOLLEMACHE, B.Com.; LL.B. **PRACTICE AREAS:** Competition Law; Telecommunications; Energy Markets.

Languages: Cantonese, French, Hakka, Hokkien, Indonesian, Malay, Mandarin, Serbo-Croatian and Spanish.

RUSSELL McVEAGH McKENZIE BARTLEET & CO.

Established in 1863

8TH FLOOR, THE SHORTLAND CENTRE
51-53, SHORTLAND STREET
P.O. BOX 8
AUCKLAND 1, NEW ZEALAND
Telephone: (64) (09) 3098-839
Cable Address: Barrister
Telex: NZ 21305
Fax: (64) (09) 377-1849

Wellington, New Zealand Office: Levels 5, 6, 7 & 8, The Todd Building, 171-177, Lambton Quay, P.O. Box 10-214. Telephone: (64) (04) 499-9555. Telex: NZ 21305. Fax: (64) (04) 499-9556

Commercial and General Practice, emphasizing Corporate, Securities, Banking, Tax, Foreign Investment, Commercial Property Development, Insurance, Labour, Mining, Construction, Energy Law, Copyrights, Patents and Trademarks, Administrative Law, Real Property, Environmental and Resource Management Law, Probate, Wills and Trusts, Economic Regula-
(This Listing Continued)

tion, Entertainment, Shipping and Admiralty, Aviation, Immigration, Communications, Legislative Drafting, Civil and General Litigation. Barristers and Solicitors of the High Court of New Zealand.

FIRM PROFILE: *The firm's practice was established in February 1863, in Auckland. Since April 1988, the firm has also had a significant office in Wellington. The firm has a complement of approximately 400 people. It is a predominantly commercial firm, although offers the full range of legal services. Among many specialties offered is overseas investment in New Zealand. The firm has a strong focus on the Asia-Pacific region, with partners and staff involved in projects in Pacific and Asian countries. Within New Zealand, the firm's practice extends nationwide.*

MEMBERS OF FIRM

JOHN COLLINGWOOD KING, born Auckland, New Zealand, January 29, 1939; admitted, 1961, New Zealand as a Solicitor; 1962, New Zealand as a Barrister. *Education:* University of New Zealand, Auckland University College (LL.B.). Vice President, The Banking Law Association Limited. **PRACTICE AREAS:** Commercial Law; Corporate Law; Takeovers and Mergers; Foreign Investments; Securities.

JOHN OLLIVER LUSK, born Tauranga, New Zealand, May 21, 1940; admitted, 1963, New Zealand. *Education:* University of New Zealand, Auckland University College (LL.B.). **PRACTICE AREAS:** Commercial Law; Corporate Law; Takeovers and Mergers; Foreign Investments; Securities.

GEOFFREY THOMAS RICKETTS, born Auckland, New Zealand, February 5, 1946; admitted, 1969, New Zealand. *Education:* University of Auckland (LL.B., Hons.). **PRACTICE AREAS:** Commercial Law; Corporate Law; Takeovers and Mergers; Competition Law; Foreign Investments; Property Law.

GERARD PAUL CURRY, born Carterton, New Zealand, May 26, 1944; admitted, 1971, New Zealand. *Education:* Victoria University of Wellington (B.A.; LL.M.); George Washington University (S.J.D.). Lecturer in Law (Contract, Tort and Criminal Law), Victoria University of Wellington, 1969-1971. Assistant Professor of Law, George Washington University and Catholic University of America, 1972-1973. **PRACTICE AREAS:** Civil Litigation; Industrial Law; Labour Law; Arbitration; Mining Law; Criminal Law.

ANDREW HAWKSWORTH BROWN, born Auckland, New Zealand, November 14, 1949; admitted, 1972, New Zealand. *Education:* University of Auckland (LL.B., Hons.); Oxford University (B.C.A.). Rhodes Scholar, Oxford University, 1973. Co-author: (with A.F. Grant), *The Law of Intellectual Property in New Zealand,* Wellington, Butterworths, 1989. *Member:* Licensing Executives Society of Australia and New Zealand. **PRACTICE AREAS:** Intellectual Property Law; Copyright Law; Patent Litigation; Trademark Litigation; Liquor Licensing; Civil Litigation.

RICHARD ARKLE GREEN, born Wayland, Norfolk, England, October 19, 1947; admitted, 1971, New Zealand. *Education:* Victoria University of Wellington (LL.B., Hons.); Queen's University, Ontario (LL.M.). Senior Lecturer in Law (Taxation and Corporate Law) Victoria University of Wellington, 1976-1980. Editor, "Estate Planning: Selected Aspects and Developments," 1978. *Member:* International Fiscal Association; Taxation Institute of Australia; Canadian Tax Foundation. **PRACTICE AREAS:** Taxation Law.

GUY BROUGHAM CHAPMAN, born Auckland, New Zealand, December 18, 1946; called to Bar, 1974, England and Wales (Lincoln's Inn); admitted, 1976, New Zealand as a Barrister; 1977, New Zealand as a Solicitor; called to Bar, 1980, New South Wales; admitted, 1984, Papua New Guinea. *Education:* University of Auckland (B.A.); Princeton University (M.A.); Oxford University (M.A.). **PRACTICE AREAS:** Civil Litigation; Contracts; Administrative Law; Arbitration; Building and Construction Law; Energy Law; Constitutional Law; Insurance Law; Local Government Law.

JOHN PAUL HASLETT OLDFIELD, born Wellington, New Zealand, April 28, 1950; admitted, 1973, New Zealand. *Education:* Victoria University of Wellington (LL.B.,Hons.); University of London (LL.M .). Editor, Anderson's Company Law Service, 1976-1982. Partner, Buddle Findlay, 1977-1984. **PRACTICE AREAS:** Banking Law; Commercial Law; Corporate Law.

CAMERON FLEMING, born Rotorua, New Zealand, March 24, 1952; admitted, 1976, New Zealand. *Education:* University of Auckland (B.Com.; LL.B.). Partner, Martelli McKegg Wells & Cormack, 1979-1984. **PRACTICE AREAS:** Commercial Law; Corporate Law; Takeovers and Mergers.
(This Listing Continued)

GREGORY JOHN SHANAHAN, born Wellington, New Zealand, July 13, 1949; admitted, 1973, New Zealand. *Education:* Victoria University of Wellington (LL.M., Hons.). Partner, Shanahan Partners, 1976-1990. *PRACTICE AREAS:* Commercial Property Development Law; Corporation Law; Commercial Law.

DEREK ARTHUR NOLAN, born Auckland, New Zealand, September 11, 1952; admitted, 1976, New Zealand. *Education:* University of Auckland (LL.B., Hons.); University of London (LL.M.). *PRACTICE AREAS:* Planning Law; Environmental Law; Resource Management Law.

JEFFREY ROBERT MORRISON, born Thames, New Zealand, October 2, 1955; admitted, 1979, New Zealand. *Education:* University of Auckland (LL.B.). *PRACTICE AREAS:* Conveyancing; Property Law.

GEOFFREY DENIS CLEWS, born Auckland, New Zealand, April 6, 1957; admitted, 1980, New Zealand. *Education:* University of Auckland (LL.B., Hons.; M.Jur., Dist.). Notary Public. *PRACTICE AREAS:* Taxation Law; Superannuation Law.

ROBERT LEONARD TOWNER, born Des Moines, Iowa, U.S.A., December 31, 1949; admitted, 1982, New Zealand. *Education:* Stanford University (B.A.); University of Auckland (LL.B., Hons.). Co-Author: (with P.G. Skelton) New Zealand Section, "International Handbook on Contracts of Employment," Boston, Kluwer Law and Taxation Publishers, 1988. *PRACTICE AREAS:* Industrial Law; Labour Law; Civil Litigation; Immigration Law.

ANTHONY FREDERICK GRANT, born Christchurch, New Zealand, May 14, 1948; called to Bar, 1971, England and Wales (Inner Temple); admitted, 1977, New Zealand as a Barrister; 1978, New Zealand as a Solicitor. *Education:* University of Bristol, England (LL.B.). Co-author: (with A.H. Brown), *The Law of Intellectual Property in New Zealand*, Wellington, Butterworths, 1989. Partner, Sheffield Young & Ellis, 1979-1984. *PRACTICE AREAS:* Intellectual Property Law; Copyright Law; Patent Litigation; Trademark Litigation; Civil Litigation.

FRANCIS XAVIER QUIN, born Palmerston North, New Zealand, January 16, 1951; admitted, 1978, New Zealand. *Education:* Victoria University of Wellington (LL.B.); University of Auckland (LL.M., Hons.). Legal Advisor, New Zealand Police Department, 1975-1982. *PRACTICE AREAS:* Competition Law; Commercial Law; Corporate Law; Intellectual Property Law.

PHILIP CHARLES CREAGH, born Auckland, New Zealand, May 16, 1956; admitted, 1981, New Zealand. *Education:* University of Auckland (B.Sc.; LL.B.). *PRACTICE AREAS:* Property Law; Property Investment; Property Development; Financing Law; Commercial Law; Building and Construction Contracts.

LAWRENCE STEPHEN MAYNE, born Whakatane, New Zealand, June 12, 1958; admitted, 1981, New Zealand. *Education:* University of Auckland (B.Com., LL.B.). *PRACTICE AREAS:* Securities Law; Commercial Law.

ANDREW WILLIAM HARMOS, born Auckland, New Zealand, April 8, 1959; admitted, 1981, New Zealand. *Education:* University of Auckland (B.Com.; LL.B., Hons.). *PRACTICE AREAS:* Commercial Law; Corporate Law; Takeovers and Mergers; Public Share Issues; Foreign Investment.

JOHN ROBERT FORTESCUE FARDELL, born Christchurch, New Zealand, December 30, 1952; admitted, 1976, New Zealand. *Education:* University of Canterbury (LL.B., Hons.). Partner, Rout Milner and Fitchett (Nelson) 1979-1980, & Meredith Connell and Co., 1984-1986. Crown Counsel, Crown Law Office, Wellington, 1980-1984. Editor, Section Headed: "Objection, Penalties and Appeals," Butterworths Taxation Library, 1986. *PRACTICE AREAS:* Civil Litigation; Administrative Law; Competition Law; Criminal Law; Tax Litigation.

JOHN MAXWELL COLLINGS, born Auckland, New Zealand, May 28, 1946; admitted, 1970, New Zealand. *Education:* University of Auckland (LL.B., Hons.). Partner, McElroy Milne (and predecessor firms), 1971-1987. *PRACTICE AREAS:* Commercial Law; Corporate Law; Foreign Investments; Financing; Acquisitions.

FREDERICK JOHN THORP, born Gisborne, New Zealand, March 18, 1956; admitted, 1979, New Zealand. *Education:* Victoria University of Wellington (LL.B., Hons.); University of Nottingham (M.Phil.). *PRACTICE AREAS:* Contracts; Arbitration; Building and Construction Law.

GREGORY WILLIAM THOMPSON, born Hamilton, New Zealand, May 19, 1957; admitted, 1981, New Zealand. *Education:* University of Auckland (LL.B., Hons). Partner, Stace Hammond Grace & Partners, 1983-1987. *PRACTICE AREAS:* Commercial Property Development Law; Commercial Law; Building and Construction Law; Property Joint Ventures.

CHRISTOPHER PATRICK BROWNE, born Auckland, New Zealand, August 30, 1954; admitted, 1980, New Zealand; 1986, Victoria. *Education:* University of Auckland (B.A.; LL.B., Hons.). Crown Counsel, Crown Law Office, Wellington, 1984-1987. *PRACTICE AREAS:* Media Law; Administrative Law; Contracts; Insurance Law; Shipping; Criminal Law.

SIMON JOHN BERRY, born Auckland, New Zealand, November 26, 1959; admitted, 1983, New Zealand. *Education:* University of Auckland (LL.B., Hons.). New Zealand Reporter, "Journal of Energy and Natural Resources Law.". *PRACTICE AREAS:* Environmental Law; Resource Management Law; Planning Law.

CHRISTOPHER PATRICK EISDELL MOORE, born Auckland, New Zealand, March 9, 1955; admitted, 1978, New Zealand. *Education:* University of Otago (LL.B.). Partner, Hamerton Chappell Dumbill & Moore, Whakatane, 1981-1987. *PRACTICE AREAS:* Property Law; Conveyancing; Commercial Property Development Law.

MATTHEW NICHOLAS DUNNING, born Paeroa, New Zealand, July 17, 1959; admitted, 1983, New Zealand. *Education:* University of Auckland (LL.B., Hons.); Oxford University (B.C.L.). *PRACTICE AREAS:* Civil Litigation; Trade Law; Contracts; Tort.

DAVID GEORGE WETHERELL, born Wellington, New Zealand, January 14, 1961; admitted, 1987, New Zealand. *Education:* University of Otago (B.A., Hons.); University of Auckland (LL.B.). *PRACTICE AREAS:* Banking and Financing Law; Commercial Law; Corporate Law.

PHILIP GEORGE SKELTON, born Auckland, New Zealand, August 1, 1960; admitted, 1983, New Zealand. *Education:* University of Auckland (B.Comm.; LL.B.); Oxford University (B.C.L.). Co-Author: (with R. L. Towner) New Zealand Section, "International Handbook on Contracts of Employment," Boston, Kluwer Law and Taxation Publishers, 1988. *PRACTICE AREAS:* Civil Litigation; Employment Law; Construction Law.

STEPHEN BRUCE LOWE, born Auckland, New Zealand, April 15, 1961; admitted, 1985, New Zealand. *Education:* University of Auckland (B.Com.; LL.B.). *PRACTICE AREAS:* Corporate Law; Commercial Law; Takeovers and Mergers; Foreign Investment; Public Share Issues.

PAUL FRANCIS MAJUREY, born Thames, New Zealand, May 3, 1962; admitted, 1985, New Zealand. *Education:* University of Auckland (LL.B., Hons.). *PRACTICE AREAS:* Energy and Mining Law; Environmental Law; Resource Management Law.

SHELLEY ANNE HODGE, born Te Awamutu, New Zealand, May 15, 1962; admitted, 1985, New Zealand. *Education:* University of Auckland (B.Com.; LL.B.). *PRACTICE AREAS:* Banking and Finance Law; Commercial Law; Property Financing.

BETSY-ANN HOWE, born Matamata, New Zealand, March 19, 1961; admitted, 1982, New Zealand. *Education:* University of Auckland (LL.B., Hons.); Victoria University of Wellington (LL.M.). *PRACTICE AREAS:* Taxation Law.

PAUL WILSON DAVID, born Vegberg, Germany, October 26, 1956; called to Bar, 1981, England and Wales (Inner Temple); admitted, 1990, New Zealand. *Education:* Cambridge University (B.A., Hons.; LL.M.); City University, London (Dip. Law). *Member:* Maritime Law Association of Australia and New Zealand; Australia and New Zealand Sports Law Association. *PRACTICE AREAS:* Civil Litigation; International Trade Law; Insurance Law; Shipping.

PRAVIR ATINDRA TESIRAM, born Suva, Fiji, June 14, 1960; admitted, 1983, New Zealand. *Education:* University of Auckland (LL.B.); University of Toronto (LL.M.). Partner, McElroy Milne, McElroy Morrison, McElroy Milne, 1987-1990. *PRACTICE AREAS:* Superannuation Law; Tax Law.

MARK JOHN GAVIN, born Auckland, New Zealand, May 27, 1963; admitted, 1986, New Zealand. *Education:* University of Auckland (LL.B., Hons.). *PRACTICE AREAS:* Civil Litigation; Intellectual Property Law; Mining Law.

SIMON MICHAEL HORNER, born Farnham, Surrey, England, January 29, 1963; admitted, 1987, England and Wales as Solicitor; 1993, New Zealand. *Education:* University of Exeter (LL.B.). *PRACTICE AREAS:* Commercial Law; Corporate Law.

GRAEME DAVID QUIGLEY, born Dunedin, New Zealand, August 6, 1960; admitted, 1988, New Zealand. *Education:* University of Auckland

(This Listing Continued)

RUSSELL McVEAGH McKENZIE BARTLEET & CO.,
Auckland—Continued

(B.A.; LL.B). *PRACTICE AREAS:* Commercial Law; Corporate Law;
Takeovers and Mergers.

MICHAEL REX CRONIN, born Auckland, New Zealand, March 23,
1963; admitted, 1986, New Zealand. *Education:* University of Auckland
(B.A.; LL.B). *PRACTICE AREAS:* Commercial Law; Corporate Law;
Intellectual Property; Media Law.

CONSULTANTS

ROBIN LANCE CONGREVE, born Blenheim, New Zealand, March
21, 1944; admitted, 1965, New Zealand. *Education:* Victoria University of
Wellington (LL.M.); University of London (Ph.D.). Co-Author: "Law of
Estate and Gift Duties in New Zealand", 1969; "Tax Free Fringe Benefits",
1975. Senior Lecturer in Law, Victoria University of Wellington, 1973-
1975. *Member:* International Fiscal Association (Council Member). *PRAC-
TICE AREAS:* Taxation Law.

CELIA MARY CAUGHEY, born Auckland, New Zealand, September
7, 1957; admitted, 1985, New Zealand. *Education:* University of Auckland
(B.A.; LL.B., Hons.); Oxford University (B.C.L.). *PRACTICE AREAS:*
Banking Litigation; Civil Litigation; Criminal Law.

All Partners are Members of the Auckland District Law Society.

Languages: English, Chinese languages and dialects, French, German,
Italian and Japanese

(For complete biographical data on personnel at Wellington office, see
professional biographies at Wellington)

SIMPSON GRIERSON

92-96 ALBERT STREET
PRIVATE BAG 92518, WELLESLEY STREET
AUCKLAND 1, NEW ZEALAND
Telephone: (09) 358-2222
Facsimile: (09) 307 0331

Wellington, New Zealand Office: Unisys House, 44-52 The Terrace.
Telephone: (04) 499-4599 Facsimile: (04) 472-6986.

*LAW: Administrative Law, Aviation Law, Antitrust Law, Arbitration
Banking Law, Bankruptcy, Company Law, Constitutional Law, Construc-
tion Law, Conveyancing, Corporate Law, Electricity Law, Employer's Lia-
bility, Entertainment Law, Family Law, Foreign Investments, Immigration
Law, Industrial Relations and Labour Law, Insurance Law, International
Contracts, International Private Law, Litigation, Maritime and Admiralty
Law, Oil and Mining Law, Property and Real Estate Law, Rent and
Lease, Trade Regulations, General Legal Practice, Local Government.*
*INTELLECTUAL PROPERTY: Chemical Patents, Copyright Law, Indus-
trial Models, Patent Litigation, Patent Prosecution, Trademark Litigation,
Trademark Prosecution, General Intellectual Property Practice.*
*TAXATION: Capital Taxation, Corporate Taxation, Deferred Taxation,
Indirect Taxation, Inheritance, Estate and Gift Taxation, Personal Income
Taxation, Sales, Turnover, Value added Taxes, General Tax Practice.*

MEMBERS OF FIRM

WILLIAM AKEL, born 1948; admitted, 1971, New Zealand. *Education:*
University of Auckland (LL.B., Hons; M.Jur.); Oxford University (B.C.L.);
Winter Williams Scholar Oxford (1973). Tutor in Law Auckland Univer-
sity, 1977-1981. *PRACTICE AREAS:* Defamation Law; Media Law; Com-
mercial Litigation; Property Litigation; Real Estate Law; Insurance Law;
Air Law.

CLIVE RICHARD BRADBURY, born 1954; admitted, 1980, New
Zealand. *Education:* University of Auckland (LL.B). *PRACTICE AREAS:*
Banking Law; Finance Law; Corporate Law; Commercial Law; Insolvency
Law.

NEIL RODNEY CAMERON, born 1946; admitted, 1969, New
Zealand. *Education:* University of Auckland (LL.B. Hons.); University of
Toronto (LL.M.). Assistant Professor of Law, University of Saskatchewan,
Canada, 1972-1975. *PRACTICE AREAS:* Corporate Law; Commercial
Law; Mergers and Acquisitions; Foreign Investment; Superannuation.

GRAEME JOHN CHRISTIE, born 1956; admitted, 1980, New
Zealand; 1986, England and Wales. *Education:* Victoria University of Wellington (LL.B., Hons.). With Linklaters and Paines, London, 1984-1986.

(This Listing Continued)

AU64B

PRACTICE AREAS: Arbitration Law; Construction Law; Commercial
Litigation; Insurance Law.

MICHAEL SECUNDUS COLE, born 1941; admitted, 1965, New
Zealand. *Education:* University of Auckland (LL.B.). *PRACTICE AREAS:*
Commercial Litigation.

MARK LESLIE SMITH COOPER, born 1954; admitted, 1979, New
Zealand. *Education:* University of Auckland (LL.B., Hons.; M.Jur.).
PRACTICE AREAS: Local Government Law.

CAROLE BEATRICE DURBIN, born 1955; admitted, 1977, New
Zealand. *Education:* University of Auckland (LL.B. Hons.; B.Com.). Fellow, Arbitrators' Institute of New Zealand. Associate, Chartered Institute
of Arbitrators, London. *PRACTICE AREAS:* Construction Law; Contract
Law; Energy Law; Insurance Law.

PETER JOCK FERGUSON, born 1947; admitted, 1972, New Zealand.
Education: University of Auckland (LL.B.). *PRACTICE AREAS:* Banking
Law; Finance Law.

DEREK SINCLAIR FIRTH, born 1942; admitted, 1965, New Zealand.
Education: University of Auckland (LL.B.). Fellow, Chartered Institute of
Arbitrators. President, Auckland Medico-Legal Society, 1983-1984.
PRACTICE AREAS: Construction Law; Energy Law; Product Liability
Law.

ROBERT ANTHONY FISHER, born 1944; admitted, 1968, New
Zealand. *Education:* University of Auckland (LL.B.; Dip. T.P.). *Member:*
International Bar Association (Vice Chairman, Committee F, Environmen-
tal Law, 1990-1994). *PRACTICE AREAS:* Energy Law; Environmental
Law; Planning Law; Mining Law.

ROBERT MALCOLM GAPES, born 1957; admitted, 1982, New
Zealand. *Education:* University of Auckland (LL.B. Hons.; B.Com.). Lecturer, University of Auckland, 1986-1987. Associate, Chartered Institute of
Arbitrators. Member, Auckland Law Practitioners Disciplinary Tribunal,
1987-13 ; Tribunal Chairman, 1990 and 1994. ADLS Council Member,
1983-1985. *PRACTICE AREAS:* Commercial Litigation; Product Liability
Law; Arbitration; Environmental Litigation.

SUSAN GWYNFA MARY GLAZEBROOK, born 1956; admitted,
1984, New Zealand. *Education:* Auckland University (M.A.; LL.B. Hons.);
Oxford University (D.Phil.). *LANGUAGES:* French. *PRACTICE
AREAS:* Tax Law.

JOHN REYNELL GRESSON, born 1957; admitted, 1983, New
Zealand. *Education:* University of Auckland; University of London (LL.B.
Hons.). *Member:* Maritime Law Association of Australia and New
Zealand. *PRACTICE AREAS:* Admiralty Law; Shipping Law; Insurance
Law; Products Liability Law.

ROYDEN DOUGLAS CLIFFORD HINDLE, born 1959; admitted,
1983, New Zealand. *Education:* Canterbury University (LL.B. Hons.);
Cambridge University (LL.M.). Tutor in Law, Auckland University,
1983—. *PRACTICE AREAS:* Commercial Litigation; Trade Practices
Law; Arbitration.

ANNE ELIZABETH HINTON, born 1955; admitted, 1977, New
Zealand. *Education:* University of Auckland (LL.B. Hons.). *Member:* Bank-
ing Law Association of Australia and New Zealand. *PRACTICE AREAS:*
Banking Law; Finance Law; Commercial Litigation; Insolvency Law.

PETER BRUCE HINTON, born 1954; admitted, 1976, New Zealand.
Education: University of Auckland (LL.B., Hons.; B.Com.); Harvard Uni-
versity (LL.M.). With Covington & Burling, Washington, 1979-1980.
PRACTICE AREAS: Corporate Law; Trade Practices Law; Commercial
Law; Banking Law; Finance Law.

STUART GRANT HUTCHINSON, born 1957; admitted, 1982, New
Zealand. *Education:* University of Auckland (LL.B.; B.Com.). *PRACTICE
AREAS:* Tax Law.

RONALD MACGREGOR IRVINE, born 1937; admitted, 1963, New
Zealand. *Education:* University of Auckland (LL.B.). Notary Public.
PRACTICE AREAS: Corporate Law; Property Law; Casino Licensing
Law; Immigration Law.

KEVIN JAFFE, born 1963; admitted, 1987, New Zealand. *Education:*
University of Auckland (LL.B., Hons.; B.Com.); Oxford University
(B.C.L.). With Parker & Parker, Perth, 1989. *PRACTICE AREAS:* Corpo-
rate Law; Commercial Law; Trade Practices Law; Health Industry.

DONALD RODNEY JAINE, born 1954; admitted, 1982, New Zealand.
Education: University of Auckland (LL.B.), Registered Patent Attorney.
PRACTICE AREAS: Corporate Law; Commercial Law; Computer Law;

(This Listing Continued)

Franchising Law; Intellectual Property Law; International Trade; Sponsorship Law; Technology Transfer; Trade Practices Law.

DAVID ALASTAIR KIRKPATRICK, born 1960; admitted, 1984, New Zealand. *Education:* University of Auckland (LL.B., Hons.). *PRACTICE AREAS:* Intellectual Property; Local Government Law; Natural Resources Law; Planning Law.

RICHARD BARRY LANGE, born 1960; admitted, 1982, New Zealand. *Education:* University of Auckland (LL.B.). *PRACTICE AREAS:* Banking Law; Finance Law; Commercial Litigation; Insolvency Law.

LIAM MCENTEGART, born 1959; admitted, 1982, New Zealand. *Education:* University of Auckland (LL.B., Hons.). *PRACTICE AREAS:* Commercial Litigation.

ROBERT FITZROY MCLEAN, born 1959; admitted, 1984, New Zealand. *Education:* University of Auckland (B.Com., LL.B.). *PRACTICE AREAS:* Corporate Law; Commercial Law; Trade Practices Law.

DENIS MICHAEL MCNAMARA, born 1948; admitted, 1970, New Zealand. *Education:* University of Auckland (LL.B., Hons.). *PRACTICE AREAS:* Corporate Law; Commercial Law; Foreign Investment.

PHILLIP JAMES MERFIELD, born 1950; admitted, 1975, New Zealand. *Education:* University of Auckland (B.A.; LL.M., Hons.). Author: "Brooker's Building Law.". *PRACTICE AREAS:* Local Government Law; Commercial Property Law.

GARRY ALBERT MUIR, born 1954; admitted, 1981, New Zealand; 1985, Australian Capital Territory. *Education:* Auckland University (LL.B. Hons., Dr.Jur.); Oxford University (B.C.L.). Co-editor, Auckland University Law Review, 1980, New Zealand Matrimonial Property Cases, 1981. Lecturer in Law, Australian National University, 1983-1987. Visiting Lecturer, University of Leeds, 1986-1987. *PRACTICE AREAS:* Tax Law.

PHILLIPA MARGARET MUIR, born 1959; admitted, 1983, New Zealand. *Education:* University of Otago (B.A.; LL.B.). *PRACTICE AREAS:* Commercial Litigation; Industrial Relations Law; Employment Law.

RICHARD BAILLIE NELSON, born 1955; admitted, 1980, New Zealand. *Education:* University of Auckland (B.Com.; LL.B.). *Member:* New Zealand Society of Accountants (Provisional Member). *PRACTICE AREAS:* Corporate Law; Commercial Law.

COLIN FRANCIS PARKER, born 1953; admitted, 1976, New Zealand. *Education:* University of Auckland (LL.B.). *PRACTICE AREAS:* Commercial Property Law.

RABIN SOCKALINGAM RABINDRAN, born 1949; admitted, 1980, England (Middle Temple); 1982, Singapore; 1988, New Zealand. *Education:* Inns of Court School of Law (Barrister-in-Law); City of London Polytechnic (MA Business Law). *LANGUAGES:* Indonesian, Malay. *PRACTICE AREAS:* Construction Law; Energy Law; International Project Negotiation and Documentation; Immigration Law.

SUSAN GRIFFITHS RHODES, born 1951; admitted, 1974, New Zealand. *Education:* University of Auckland (LL.B.). *PRACTICE AREAS:* Environmental Law; Planning Law.

PETER GEOFFREY STUBBS, born 1962; admitted, 1985, New Zealand. *Education:* University of Auckland (LL.B., Hons.). *Member:* ADLS (Insolvency Practitioners Division); New Zealand Society of Accountants. *PRACTICE AREAS:* Corporate Law; Commercial Law; Corporate Insolvency Law; Forestry and Wood Products; Events Marketing and Sponsorship.

GREGORY BRETT TOWERS, born 1961; admitted, 1985, New Zealand. *Education:* University of Auckland (LL.B., Hons.; B.Com.). *PRACTICE AREAS:* Corporate Law; Commercial Law; Commerical Property Law.

MARIETTE MARIA BERNADETTE VAN RYN, born 1958; admitted, 1983, New Zealand. *Education:* University of Auckland (B.A., LL.B.). *LANGUAGES:* Dutch, German. *PRACTICE AREAS:* Banking Law; Finance Law; Commercial Litigation; Insolvency Law.

RODNEY GEORGE WILLIS, born 1943; admitted, 1967, New Zealand. *Education:* University of Auckland (LL.B.). *PRACTICE AREAS:* Commercial Property Law.

RICHARD WESTWOOD WORTH OBE, born 1948; admitted, 1970, New Zealand. *Education:* University of Auckland (LL.B. Hons.; M.Jur.). Co-editor, Auckland University Law Review, 1969. Fellow, International Comparative Law Centre, Dallas, 1975. Lecturer, Court Practice, Univer-

(This Listing Continued)

sity of Auckland, 1976-1981. Consul to Government of Colombia, 1994. *Member:* New Zealand Law Society (Governing Board, 1993—). *PRACTICE AREAS:* Insurance Law; Commercial Litigation.

CONSULTANTS

EWEN DUNCAN CAMERON, born 1924; admitted, 1989, New Zealand. *Education:* University of Auckland.

PETER FRANCIS CLAPSHAW, born 1931; admitted, 1954, New Zealand. *Education:* Auckland University College (LL.B.). ADLS Council Member, 1973-1982; President, 1982. *Member:* New Zealand Law Society (Vice President, 1983; President, 1985-1988). *PRACTICE AREAS:* Corporate Law; Commercial Law.

GEORGE PHILIP HANNA, born 1916; admitted, 1937, New Zealand. *Education:* Auckland University College (LL.M.). Lecturer, University of Auckland, 1947-1951.

BERNARD LEO MACEDO, born 1918; admitted, 1948, New Zealand. *Education:* University of Canterbury (LL.B.). *Member:* Auckland District Law Society.

All partners are members of the Auckland District Law Society.

(For complete biographical data on personnel at Wellington, see Wellington listing).

BUDDLE FINDLAY

Barristers, Solicitors and Notaries Public

FLOORS 12 & 13
CLARENDON TOWER, 78 WORCESTER STREET
P.O. BOX 322
CHRISTCHURCH, NEW ZEALAND
Telephone: 64-3-379-1747
Fax: 64-3-379-5659

Wellington, New Zealand Office: Floors 9, 15, 16 and 17, BNZ Centre, 1 Willis Street, P.O. Box 2694. Telephone: 64-4-499-4242. Fax: 64-4-499-4141.

Auckland, New Zealand Office: Floors 14, 17, 18, 19 and 20, Stock Exchange Centre, 191-201 Queen Street, P.O. Box 1433. Telephone: 64-9-358-2555. Fax: 64-9-358-2055.

Commercial Legal Advice, Transaction Documentation and Litigation in all Courts and Tribunals. Banking and Securities, General Corporate and Commercial Activity, International Joint Ventures, Mergers and Acquisitions, Overseas Investment and Trade, Transport, Telecommunications, Broadcasting, and Energy, Government and Public Law, Commercial Property, Taxation.
Barristers and Solicitors of the High Court of New Zealand.

NATIONAL CHAIRMAN OF PARTNERS

DAVID JOHN STOCK, born New Zealand, 1942; admitted, 1965, New Zealand. *Education:* Canterbury University (LL.B.). *PRACTICE AREAS:* Business Services and Corporate Advice.

PARTNERS

JOHN HOLLAND, born 1962, New Zealand; admitted, 1986, New Zealand. *Education:* Canterbury University (B.Comm., 1985; LL.B., 1985). *PRACTICE AREAS:* General Corporate; Commercial Law; Electricity; Industry; Banking.

CHARLES HORT LEVIN, born New Zealand, 1958; admitted, 1982, New Zealand. *Education:* Canterbury University (LL.B. Hons.). *PRACTICE AREAS:* Taxation; Commercial.

MARK WILLIAM RUSSELL, born New Zealand, 1956; admitted, 1978, New Zealand. *Education:* Canterbury University (LL.B. Hons.); Cambridge University (LL.M.). *PRACTICE AREAS:* Banking; Finance; Business Services and Corporate Advice.

DENIS MATTHEW SHEARD, born New Zealand, 1948; admitted, 1971, New Zealand. *Education:* Canterbury University (LL.B. Hons.). *PRACTICE AREAS:* Personal Legal Services and Corporate Advice.

KERRY GRAEME SMITH, born New Zealand, 1959; admitted, 1983, New Zealand. *Education:* Canterbury University (LL.B.). *PRACTICE AREAS:* Litigation; Arbitration and Dispute Resolution.

THOMAS CROWLEY WESTON, born New Zealand, 1958; admitted, 1982, New Zealand. *Education:* Canterbury University (LL.B., Hons). *PRACTICE AREAS:* Litigation; Arbitration and Dispute Resolution.

(This Listing Continued)

BUDDLE FINDLAY, Christchurch—Continued

All Partners are Members of the Canterbury District Law Society.

(For Complete Biographical Data on Wellington and Auckland Personnel, see Professional Biographies at Wellington and Auckland, New Zealand).

BALDWIN SON & CAREY

Established in 1896

LEVEL 14, AT&T BUILDING
342 LAMBTON QUAY
P.O. BOX 852
WELLINGTON, NEW ZEALAND
Telephone: 04 472-1094 (Internal)
64-4-472-1094 (International)
Telex: NZ 3918
Facsimile: 04 473-6712 (Internal)
64-4-473-6712; 64-4-494-0299 (Gp 4) (International)

Auckland, New Zealand Office: Chamber of Commerce Bldg., 100 Mayoral Drive, P.O. Box 5999, Wellesley Street. Telephone: 64-9-373-3137. Telex: NZ 3918. Facsimile: 64-9-373-2123.

Christchurch, New Zealand Office: Level 12, Forsyth Barr House, 764 Colombo St., P.O. Box 1617. Telephone: 64-3-366-3929. Facsimile: 64-3-366-4743.

Intellectual Property Law, Patents, Trade Marks, Designs, Copyright; Licensing, Exploitation and Enforcement of Intellectual Property Rights. Barristers and Solicitors, Registered Patent Attorneys.

FIRM PROFILE: Baldwin, Son & Carey has practised in the area of Intellectual Property law since 1896. One of the largest and leading specialist Intellectual Property law firms, Baldwins maintains offices in Auckland, Wellington and Christchurch. The firm has a staff of over 100 with 10 Partners and 33 professional staff members qualified in the areas of law, chemistry, biological sciences, electronics, physical sciences, the arts and engineering.

The firm's clients include some of the world's major research firms in a wide spectrum of disciplines including pharmaceuticals, genetic engineering, agricultural, electronics and food related areas.

MEMBERS OF FIRM

RICHARD JONATHAN TRAVERS ELLIS, born Wellington, New Zealand, June 22, 1941. *Member:* Fellow, New Zealand Institute of Patent Attorneys (Past President); AIPPI New Zealand Group; Licensing Executives Society; Asian Patent Attorneys Association. *PRACTICE AREAS:* Trade Marks; Branding; Passing Off; Licensing.

DENIS ENG TUFFERY, born New Plymouth, New Zealand, November 9, 1945. *Education:* Victoria University of Wellington (B.Sc., 1966; M.Sc., Hons., 1968). *Member:* Fellow, New Zealand Institute of Patent Attorneys; AIPPI New Zealand Group; Licensing Executives Society; Asian Patent Attorneys Association. *PRACTICE AREAS:* Patents; Trade Marks; Copyright; Licensing; Designs.

MICHAEL HOWARD HAWKINS, born Pontypridd, Wales, November 20, 1946. *Education:* University of Wales (B.Eng., Hons., 1968). *Member:* Fellow, New Zealand Institute of Patent Attorneys (Past President); FICPI (Current President, New Zealand Group); Asian Patent Attorneys Association; Licensing Executives Society; AIPPI New Zealand Group. *PRACTICE AREAS:* Patents; Trade Marks; Designs; Licensing; Copyright.

PHILIP AUBYN BERTRAM THOREAU, born Auckland, New Zealand, February 2, 1950. *Member:* Fellow, New Zealand Institute of Patent Attorneys; FICPI; Licensing Executives Society; AIPPI New Zealand Group; Asian Patent Attorneys Association (President, New Zealand Group; Vice-President, International Group). *PRACTICE AREAS:* Patents; Trade Marks; Copyright; Designs.

PETER CHARLES DENGATE THRUSH, born Hamilton, New Zealand, August 24, 1955; admitted, 1982, New Zealand. *Education:* Victoria University of Wellington (B.Sc., 1977; LL.B., 1981). *Member:* Fellow, New Zealand Institute of Patent Attorneys; New Zealand and Wellington District Law Societies; AIPPI (New Zealand Executive); American Intellectual Property Law Association; Licensing Executives Society; International Bar Association; American Bar Association. *PRACTICE AREAS:* Intellectual Property Litigation; Patents; Designs; Trade Marks; Copyright.

(This Listing Continued)

JOHN BRUNO HACKETT, born Lower Hutt, New Zealand, April 16, 1954; admitted, 1980, New Zealand. *Education:* Victoria University of Wellington (LL.B., 1979). *Member:* Fellow, New Zealand Institute of Patent Attorneys; Pharmaceutical Trade Mark Group; AIPPI New Zealand Group; Asian Patent Attorneys Association; Asian-Pacific Lawyers Association (New Zealand President); Auckland District Law Society. *LANGUAGES:* French and Italian. *PRACTICE AREAS:* Trade Marks; Copyright; Branding; Licensing.

COLIN LYELL HADLEY, born Wellington, New Zealand, October 27, 1945; admitted, 1969, New Zealand Notary Public. *Education:* Victoria University of Wellington (LL.B., 1970). *Member:* Fellow, New Zealand Institute of Patent Attorneys; New Zealand and Wellington District Law Societies; Licensing Executives Society; Corporate Lawyers Association; AIPPI New Zealand Group; Wellington Society of Notaries. *PRACTICE AREAS:* Trade Marks; Licensing; Copyright; Litigation.

RICHARD JOHN LYTH, born Harrow, U.K., September 18, 1947. *Member:* Fellow, New Zealand Institute of Patent Attorneys; Asian Patent Attorneys Association. *PRACTICE AREAS:* Patents; Trade Marks; Copyright; Designs; Licensing.

CLIVE LINCOLN ELLIOTT, born Durban, South Africa, July 4, 1956; admitted, 1985, South Africa and New Zealand. *Education:* University of Natal (B.A., 1978; LL.B., 1981); Victoria University of Wellington (LL.M., 1991). *Member:* Fellow, New Zealand Institute of Patent Attorneys; New Zealand Law Society; Licensing Executives Society; Corporate Lawyers Association; Intellectual and Industrial Property Association. *PRACTICE AREAS:* Intellectual Property Litigation; Patents; Copyright; Designs; Licensing.

JULIE ANNE BALLANCE, born Taihape, New Zealand, June 12, 1961; admitted, 1991, New Zealand. *Education:* Victoria University of Wellington (B.Sc., Hons., 1984; LL.B., 1990). *Member:* Fellow, New Zealand Institute of Patent Attorneys; New Zealand and Wellington District Law Societies. *PRACTICE AREAS:* Patents; Trade Marks; Copyright; Designs; Litigation.

ASSOCIATE

JOHN KINNEAR TERRY, born Lower Hutt, New Zealand, August 11, 1963; admitted, 1991, New Zealand. *Education:* University of Canterbury (B.E., (Elec), 1986); Victoria University of Wellington (LL.B., 1990). *Member:* Fellow, New Zealand Institute of Patent Attorneys; New Zealand and Wellington District Law Societies; Vice-President, New Zealand Society for Computers and Law. *PRACTICE AREAS:* Patents; Trade Marks; Designs; Copyright; Electronics; Licensing.

JANE ELIZABETH PAIRMAN, born Sutton Coldfield, U.K., June 11, 1962. *Education:* Imperial College of London University (B.Sc., Hons., 1983); Oxford University (D. Phil., 1986). *Member:* Biochemical Society, London; New Zealand Biotechnology Association; New Zealand Biochemical and Molecular Biology Society; New Zealand Microbiological Society. *Member:* Fellow, New Zealand Institute of Patent Attorneys. *PRACTICE AREAS:* Patents; Trade Marks; Designs; Biotechnology.

BELL GULLY BUDDLE WEIR

171 FEATHERSTON STREET
P.O. BOX 1291
WELLINGTON 1, NEW ZEALAND
Telephone: (04) 4737-777
Fax: (04) 4733-845

REVISERS OF THE NEW ZEALAND LAW DIGEST FOR THIS DIRECTORY.

Auckland, New Zealand Office: The Auckland Club Tower, 34 Shortland Street, P.O. Box 4199. Telephone: (09) 3090-859. Fax: (09) 3093-312.

South Auckland, New Zealand Office: 3rd Floor, Parkview Tower, 28 Davies Avenue, Manukau City. Telephone: (09) 262 1979 Fax: (09) 262 2045.

General Practice, Commercial, Corporate Securities, Takeover, Merger and Acquisitions, Lending and Borrowing Instruments, Foreign Investment, Taxation, Industrial, Environmental, Energy, Mining, Oil and Gas. Commercial and General Litigation including Patent, Trademark and Copyright, Banking and Insurance, Aviation and Maritime.

(This Listing Continued)

CHIEF EXECUTIVE

SEAN H.W. LARKAN, born 1953. *Education:* University of Stellenbosch (B.A., Law, 1974); University of Natal (LL.B., 1976); University of Dublin, Trinity College (M.B.A., 1978); University of South Africa (C. Tax, 1982).

RESIDENT PARTNERS

EUAN HAMILTON ABERNETHY, born Hamilton, New Zealand, 1936; admitted, 1960, New Zealand. *Education:* Victoria University College (LL.B.). *PRACTICE AREAS:* Corporate Law; Commercial Law.

WILLIAM BRENT ARMSTRONG, born New Plymouth, New Zealand, 1955; admitted, 1978, New Zealand. *Education:* Otago University (LL.B., 1978). Member, Council District Law Society, 1982-1987. *PRACTICE AREAS:* Property Law.

PETER BARKER, born Wellington, New Zealand, 1948; admitted, 1972, New Zealand. *Education:* Victoria University of Wellington (B.A. Hons., LL.M.). *PRACTICE AREAS:* Banking Law; Finance Law.

PETER RICHARD CASTLE, born Wellington, New Zealand, 1954; admitted, 1980, New Zealand. *Education:* Victoria University of Wellington (LL.B.). *PRACTICE AREAS:* Corporate Law; Commercial Law.

NICHOLAS DAVID DAVIDSON, born London, England, 1944; admitted, 1970, England; 1984, New Zealand. *Education:* University of London, College of Law. *LANGUAGES:* French, German and Maori. *PRACTICE AREAS:* Corporate Law; Commercial Law.

ROGER BRUCE DOUGLAS DRUMMOND, born Dunedin, New Zealand, 1953; admitted, 1977, New Zealand. *Education:* Victoria University of Wellington (LL.B., B.C.A., Dip. Acc.). *PRACTICE AREAS:* Banking Law; Finance Law.

CHRISTOPHER FRANCIS FINLAYSON, born Wellington, New Zealand, December 4, 1956; admitted, 1981, Wellington, New Zealand. *Education:* Victoria University, Wellington (B.A., 1979); Victoria University, Wellington (LL.B., 1980; LL.M., 1984). *LANGUAGES:* French, Portuguese and Latin. *PRACTICE AREAS:* Litigation.

TIMOTHY FABER FOOKES, born New Plymouth, New Zealand, 1940; admitted, 1963, New Zealand. *Education:* Victoria University of Wellington (LL.B.). *PRACTICE AREAS:* Litigation.

ANTHONY DAVID FORD, born Hokitika, New Zealand, 1942; admitted, 1970, New Zealand. *Education:* University of Auckland (LL.B.). *PRACTICE AREAS:* Litigation.

MARK WILLIAM FREEMAN, born Palmerston North, New Zealand, 1960; admitted, 1983, New Zealand. *Education:* Victoria University of Wellington (LL.B. Hons). *PRACTICE AREAS:* Commercial and Corporate Law.

QUENTIN MORRIS HAY, born Wellington, New Zealand, 1953; admitted, 1977, New Zealand; 1982, England and Wales. *Education:* Victoria University of Wellington (LL.B. Hons); Oxon (B.C.L.). *LANGUAGES:* French (written only). *PRACTICE AREAS:* Banking Law; Finance Law.

JANE KATHARINE MEARES, born Leicester, England, July 16, 1959; admitted, 1986, London, England; 1990, Wellington, New Zealand. *Education:* Birmington University (LL.B., Hons.); Limoges University (Diploma on French Studies); Lancaster Gate College of Law (Hons.). *LANGUAGES:* French, Spanish. *PRACTICE AREAS:* Corporate Law; Commercial Law.

DAVID EDWIN MCLAY, born Hastings, New Zealand, 1957; admitted, 1981, New Zealand. *Education:* Victoria University of Wellington (LL.B., Hons.; M.C.A.); University of Michigan (LL.M.). *PRACTICE AREAS:* Taxation.

TERENCE STANLEY NOWLAND, born Huntly, New Zealand, 1945; admitted, 1968, New Zealand. *Education:* Victoria University of Wellington (LL.B.). *PRACTICE AREAS:* Property Law.

MARK DAVID O'BRIEN, born Auckland, New Zealand, 1957; admitted, 1980, New Zealand. *Education:* Victoria University of Wellington (LL.B.). *PRACTICE AREAS:* Litigation.

PAUL JAMES RADICH, born Hawera, New Zealand, 1964; admitted, 1986, New Zealand. *Education:* Victoria University of Wellington (LL.B. Hons). *PRACTICE AREAS:* Litigation.

STEPHEN LINDSAY REVILL, born Sydney, Australia, 1956; admitted, 1980, Australia; 1980, New South Wales; 1984, England & Wales (Not admitted in New Zealand). *Education:* Georgetown University; Australia

(This Listing Continued)

National University (B.A.; LL.B.); (A.N.U.). *PRACTICE AREAS:* Banking Law; Finance Law.

CHRISTOPHER JONATHAN ROSS, born Warri, Nigeria, 1954; admitted, 1980, New Zealand; 1982, New York. *Education:* Victoria University of Wellington (LL.B. Hons.); Oxon (B.A.; B.C.L.). *PRACTICE AREAS:* Banking Law; Finance Law.

GEOFFREY JOHN HATTON SHARP, admitted, 1982, Australia and New Zealand. *Education:* Victoria University of Wellington (LL.B., 1982). *PRACTICE AREAS:* Litigation.

GRAEME ALBERT SMAILL, born Dunedin, New Zealand, 1956; admitted, 1980, New Zealand. *Education:* University of Otago (LL.B. Hons., B.Com.). *PRACTICE AREAS:* Taxation.

JEREMY BRODRICK BOWES STEEL, born Christchurch, New Zealand, 1956; admitted, 1980, New Zealand. *Education:* University of Auckland (LL.B. Hons.); Oxon (B.C.L.). Notary Public. *PRACTICE AREAS:* Banking Law; Finance Law.

LESLIE JOHN TAYLOR, born Palmerston North, New Zealand, 1954; admitted, 1982, New Zealand. *Education:* University of Canterbury (LL.B. Hons.). *PRACTICE AREAS:* Litigation.

DONALD JAMES TURLEY, born Invercargill, New Zealand, 1949; admitted, 1973, New Zealand; 1976, Victoria, Australia. *Education:* Victoria University of Wellington (LL.B.). *LANGUAGES:* Italian, French. *PRACTICE AREAS:* Litigation.

JAMES MAX DUDDINGSTON WILLIS, born Wanganui, New Zealand, 1952; admitted, 1976, New Zealand. *Education:* Victoria University of Wellington (LL.M. Hons., Dip. Acc.). *PRACTICE AREAS:* Corporate Law; Commercial Law.

WILLIAM MCLEOD WILSON, born Auckland, New Zealand, 1946; admitted, 1968, New Zealand. *Education:* Victoria University of Wellington (LL.M. Hons.). *PRACTICE AREAS:* Litigation.

CONSULTANT

ROBERT DRUMMOND BURNARD, born Wellington, New Zealand, 1939; admitted, 1961, New Zealand. *Education:* University of Otago; Victoria University College (LL.M., N.Z.); Harvard Law School, Cambridge, Massachusetts. *PRACTICE AREAS:* Litigation.

Barristers and Solicitors of the High Court of New Zealand and Members of Auckland or Wellington District Law Societies.

REVISERS OF THE NEW ZEALAND LAW DIGEST FOR THIS DIRECTORY.

BUDDLE FINDLAY

Barristers, Solicitors and Notaries Public

FLOORS 9, 15, 16 AND 17
BNZ CENTRE, 1 WILLIS STREET
P.O. BOX 2694
WELLINGTON, NEW ZEALAND
Telephone: 64-4-499-4242
Fax: 64-4-499-4141

Auckland, New Zealand Office: Floors 13, 14, 17, 18, 19 and 20, Stock Exchange Centre, 191-201 Queen Street, P.O. Box 1433. Telephone: 64-9-358-2555. Fax: 64-9-358-2055.

Christchurch, New Zealand Office: Floors 12 & 13, Clarendon Tower, 78 Worcester Street, P.O. Box 322. Telephone 64-3-379-1747. Fax: 64-3-379-5659.

Commercial Legal Advice, Transaction Documentation and Litigation in all Courts and Tribunals in the fields of: Banking and Securities, General Corporate and Commercial Activity, International Joint Ventures, Mergers and Acquisitions, Overseas Investment and Trade, Transport, Telecommunications, Broadcasting, and Energy, Government and Public Law, Commercial Property, Taxation.
Barristers and Solicitors of the High Court of New Zealand.

CHAIRMAN OF WELLINGTON PARTNERS

JAMES DAVID LYNCH, born New Zealand, 1947; admitted, 1970, New Zealand. *Education:* Victoria University (LL.B.). *PRACTICE AREAS:* Business Service and Corporate Advice; Environmental and Resource Management Law; Litigation.

(This Listing Continued)

BUDDLE FINDLAY, Wellington—Continued

PARTNERS

CHRISTOPHER SCOTT CHAPMAN, born England, 1954; called to Bar 1980 England, admitted 1983, New Zealand. *Education:* Victoria University (B.Sc., LL.M.). *PRACTICE AREAS:* Litigation; Arbitration; Dispute Resolution.

DAVID JOHN CHAPMAN, born New Zealand, 1953; admitted, 1977, New Zealand. *Education:* Victoria University (LL.B., Hons.). *PRACTICE AREAS:* Business Services and Corporate Advice.

WAYNE SEYMOUR CHAPMAN, born New Zealand, 1944; admitted, 1974, New Zealand; 1982, Notary Public. *Education:* Victoria University (LL.B.). *PRACTICE AREAS:* Personal Legal Service.

PETER CRAIG CHEMIS, born New Zealand, 1959; admitted, 1985, New Zealand. *Education:* Victoria University (LL.B.). *PRACTICE AREAS:* Litigation; Arbitration; Dispute Resolution; Employment Law.

DENIS KIERAN CLIFFORD, born New Zealand, 1952; admitted, 1979, New Zealand. *Education:* Otago University (B.A.); Victoria University (LL.B. Hons.). *PRACTICE AREAS:* Banking and Finance.

ALASTAIR C. HERCUS, born New Zealand, 1960; admitted, 1991, New Zealand. *Education:* Otago University (B.A. (Hons) First Class, 1982); Victoria University (LL.B., 1985). *PRACTICE AREAS:* Public Law; Corporate Law; Commercial Law; Fisheries Law.

HILARY JANE HUNT, born New Zealand, 1962; admitted, 1985, New Zealand; 1992, London. *Education:* Canterbury University (LL.B., 1984). *PRACTICE AREAS:* Structured Financing; Project Financing; General Lending and Advice.

DAVID JOHN MACKENZIE, born United Kingdom, 1948; admitted, 1973, New Zealand. *Education:* Otago University (LL.B.). *PRACTICE AREAS:* Business Services and Corporate Advice.

RICHARD RONALDSON MCLEAN, born New Zealand, 1940; admitted, 1963, New Zealand. *Education:* Victoria University (LL.M. Hons.). *PRACTICE AREAS:* Banking and Finance.

JOHN LIVINGSTON MARSHALL, born New Zealand, 1946; admitted, 1969, New Zealand; 1991, Supreme Court of Western Australia and High Court of Australia. *Education:* Victoria University (LL.B.). *PRACTICE AREAS:* Litigation; Arbitration and Dispute Resolution; Environmental and Resource Management Law; Commercial Law.

JOHN MARSDEN NANKERVIS, born New Zealand, 1946; admitted, 1969, New Zealand. *Education:* Victoria University (B.C.A., LL.B.). *PRACTICE AREAS:* Banking and Finance.

CHRISTOPHER MURRAY RICKIT, born New Zealand, 1949; admitted, 1972, New Zealand. *Education:* Victoria University (LL.B.). Notary Public. *PRACTICE AREAS:* Business Services and Corporate Advice; Commercial Property.

SARAH MARY ROBERTS, born New Zealand, 1963; admitted, 1986, New Zealand. *Education:* Victoria University (LL.B., Hons.). *PRACTICE AREAS:* Business Services and Corporate Advice; Commercial Property.

TREVOR PHILIP ROBINSON, born New Zealand, 1959; admitted, 1983, New Zealand. *Education:* Otago University (B.A., LL.B., Hons.). *PRACTICE AREAS:* Litigation; Arbitration and Dispute Resolution; Environmental and Resource Management Law.

ALASTAIR GEORGE SHERRIFF, born New Zealand, 1952; admitted, 1975, New Zealand. *Education:* Victoria University (LL.B.). *PRACTICE AREAS:* Litigation; Arbitration and Dispute Resolution; Employment Law.

JAMES RICHARD ALAN STEVENSON, born New Zealand, 1947; admitted, 1976, New Zealand. *Education:* Auckland University (B.A., LL.B.). *PRACTICE AREAS:* Competition; Communications; Public Law.

IAN GORDON STEWART, born Canada, 1955; admitted, 1980, New Zealand. *Education:* Victoria University (B.A., LL.M.). *PRACTICE AREAS:* Banking and Finance; Commercial Law.

GERARD JUSTIN TOEBES, born New Zealand, 1954; admitted, 1978, New Zealand. *Education:* Victoria University (LL.B.). *PRACTICE AREAS:* Litigation; Arbitration and Dispute Resolution; Insolvency.

CAROLYN MARY WAINWRIGHT, born New Zealand, 1958; admitted, 1982, New Zealand. *Education:* Victoria University (B.A., LL.M., Hons). *PRACTICE AREAS:* Constitutional and Administrative Law.

(This Listing Continued)

STEPHEN CHARLES WHITTINGTON, born New Zealand, 1954; admitted, 1978, New Zealand. *Education:* Victoria University (LL.B.). *PRACTICE AREAS:* Business Services and Corporate Advice; Commercial Property.

All Partners are Members of the Wellington District Law Society.

Languages: English, French and Spanish

(For Biographical Data on Auckland and Christchurch Personnel, see Professional Biographies at Auckland and Christchurch, New Zealand).

CHAPMAN TRIPP SHEFFIELD YOUNG

Established in 1875

AMP CENTRE
GREY STREET
P.O. BOX 993
WELLINGTON, NEW ZEALAND
Telephone: 64-4-499 5999
Fax: 64-4-472 7111

Auckland, New Zealand Office: Level 35, 23-29 Albert Street, Auckland 1. Telephone: 64-9-357-9000. Fax: 64-9-357-9099.

General Practice. Aviation, Banking, Civil and Commercial Litigation, Computer, Information Technology, Commercial, Conveyancing, Corporation, Energy, Estates, Finance, Foreign Investment, Franchising, Insurance, Intellectual Property, International Financing and Trade, Joint Ventures, Licensing, Marine, Mergers, Takeovers and Acquisitions, Mining, Oil and Gas, Patents, Planning, Property Development, Real Estate Transactions, Taxation, Trademarks and Trustee Law.
Barristers and Solicitors of High Court of New Zealand.

MEMBERS OF FIRM AT WELLINGTON

JOAN EDRA STERLING ALLIN, born 1951; admitted, 1987, New Zealand. *Education:* University of Western Ontario (B.A. Hons); University of Windsor (LL.B.); York University (LL.M.). Senior Lecturer in Law, Victoria University of Wellington, 1984-1987. *PRACTICE AREAS:* Environmental Law; Planning Law.

PAUL ARTHUR BARNETT, born 1950; admitted, 1973, New Zealand. *Education:* Victoria University of Wellington (LL.M.). Notary Public. *PRACTICE AREAS:* Financing Law; Trusts Law; Acquisition of Information Technology.

PETER WILLIAM BENNETT, born 1953; admitted, 1976, New Zealand. *Education:* Victoria University of Wellington (LL.B., Hons.). *PRACTICE AREAS:* International Financing Law; Banking Law; Securities Law; Mergers Law; Takeovers Law.

HELEN MARGARET BOWIE, born 1960; admitted, 1982, New Zealand. *Education:* Victoria University of Wellington (LL.B. Hons.). *PRACTICE AREAS:* Commercial Law; Telecommunications Law; Broadcasting Law; Superannuation Law.

THOMAS JOHN BROADMORE, born 1944; admitted, 1968, New Zealand; 1969, Western Australia. *Education:* Victoria University of Wellington (B.A.; LL.B.). Examiner in Law of Sea Transport, Chartered Institute of Transport, New Zealand. *PRACTICE AREAS:* Maritime Law; Insurance Litigation.

BARRY JOHN BROWN, born 1950; admitted, 1974, New Zealand. *Education:* Victoria University of Wellington (LL.B., Hons). *PRACTICE AREAS:* International Financing Law; Mergers Law; Takeovers Law; Banking Law; Securities Law.

RICHARD SPENCER CLARKE, born 1946; admitted, 1971, New Zealand. *Education:* Victoria University of Wellington (B.A.; LL.M.). Co-Author: "Securities Law in New Zealand". Member, New Zealand Contracts and Commercial Law Reform Committee. *PRACTICE AREAS:* Statutory Drafting Law; Securities Law; Banking Law; Government Law.

DAVID JAMES COCHRANE, born 1952; admitted, 1975, New Zealand. *Education:* Victoria University of Wellington (LL.M. Distinction). *PRACTICE AREAS:* Commercial Law; Superannuation Law; Legislative Drafting Law.

ROSS MITCHELL CROTTY, born 1945; admitted, 1968, New Zealand. *Education:* Victoria University of Wellington (LL.M.); University of Virginia (LL.M.). *PRACTICE AREAS:* Employment Law.

(This Listing Continued)

GRANT WALTER DAVID, born 1951; admitted, 1979, New Zealand. *Education:* University of Auckland (LL.B.). *PRACTICE AREAS:* Commercial Law; Trade Practices Law; International Finance Law; Public Law.

STEPHEN LESLIE FRANKS, born 1950; admitted, 1975, New Zealand. *Education:* Victoria University of Wellington (B.A.; LL.B., Hons.). *PRACTICE AREAS:* Securities Law; Mergers Law; Flotations Law.

MALCOLM ROSS GILLESPIE, born 1956; admitted, 1987, New Zealand. *Education:* Victoria University of Wellington (LL.B.); Otago University (B.A.). *PRACTICE AREAS:* Commercial Law; Mergers and Acquisitions Law; Energy Law.

DAVID JOHN GODDARD, born 1963; admitted, 1989, New Zealand. *Education:* Victoria University of Wellington (B.A., Hons.; B.A. (Oxon)). *PRACTICE AREAS:* Civil Litigation; Commercial Law.

ANTHONY MICHAEL GRACE, born 1961; admitted, 1985, New Zealand. *Education:* University of Otago (B.Com.; LL.B., Hons.); Cambridge University (LL.M.). *PRACTICE AREAS:* Taxation.

NEIL EDWARD GRAY, born 1934; admitted, 1956, New Zealand. *Education:* Victoria University College, Wellington (LL.B.). *PRACTICE AREAS:* Energy Law; Insurance Law; Corporate Law; State Owned Enterprises; Estate and Superannuation Law.

JOHN PAUL GREENWOOD, born 1950; admitted, 1974, New Zealand; 1985, State of Victoria, Australia. *Education:* Victoria University of Wellington (LL.B.). *PRACTICE AREAS:* Commercial Property Law; Securities Law.

ELEONORE CATHERINE ANNE HARRISON, born 1951; admitted, 1982, New Zealand. *Education:* University of Auckland (M.A., LL.B., Dip. NZLS). Harvard Law School Programme of Instruction for Lawyers, 1992. *PRACTICE AREAS:* Commercial Law; Corporate Financing Law.

LAWRENCE IRWIN HINTON, born 1949; admitted, 1976, New Zealand. *Education:* University of Canterbury (M.A., LL.B. Hons). *PRACTICE AREAS:* Commercial Law; Insolvency Law; Banking Law.

JACK EDWARD HODDER, born 1952; admitted, 1978, New Zealand. *Education:* Victoria University of Wellington (B.A., LL.B., Hons.); London University (LL.M.). Harvard Law School Programme of Instruction for Lawyers, 1991. *PRACTICE AREAS:* Intellectual Property Law; Commercial Litigation.

LINDA MARGARET HOWES, born 1953; admitted, 1978, New Zealand. *Education:* London University (LL.B., Hons.). *PRACTICE AREAS:* International Banking Law; Finance Law.

ROBERT KENNETH MACDONALD, born 1953; admitted, 1978, New Zealand. *Education:* Victoria University of Wellington (LL.B., B.C.A.). *PRACTICE AREAS:* International Finance Law; Banking Law.

PETER ALEXANDER MCLEOD, born 1956; admitted, 1980, New Zealand. *Education:* University of Otago (LL.B.). *PRACTICE AREAS:* Taxation.

DAVID ERNEST MARRIOTT, born 1958; admitted, 1982, New Zealand. *Education:* Canterbury University (LL.B. Hons.). *PRACTICE AREAS:* Company Flotations Law.

FORREST MILLER, born 1956; admitted, 1980, New Zealand. *Education:* University of Otago (B.A., LL.B. Hons.). *PRACTICE AREAS:* Civil Litigation; Banking Law.

KIMBALL IAN MURRAY, born 1952; admitted, 1977, New Zealand. *Education:* University of Auckland (LL.B.); London School of Economics (LL.M.). *PRACTICE AREAS:* Civil Litigation; Administrative Law.

MARK ANDREW O'REGAN, born 1953; admitted, 1977, New Zealand. *Education:* Victoria University of Wellington (B.A.; LL.M.). Lecturer in Law, Victoria University of Wellington, 1977-1978. *PRACTICE AREAS:* Mergers Law; Takeovers Law; Trade Practices Law; Securities Law.

PAUL WARREN O'REGAN, born 1948; admitted, 1972, New Zealand. *Education:* Victoria University of Wellington (LL.M.). *PRACTICE AREAS:* Energy Law; Mining Law; Joint Ventures Law; Securities Law.

PETER MARK REESE, born 1960; admitted, 1984, New Zealand. *Education:* University of Canterbury (LL.B., Hons). *PRACTICE AREAS:* Banking Law; Finance Law.

(This Listing Continued)

BRUCE ALEXANDER SCOTT, born 1961; admitted, 1985, New Zealand. *Education:* Victoria University of Wellington (LL.B.). *PRACTICE AREAS:* Commercial Litigation; Fisheries Law.

JOHN GILBERT SPROAT, born 1958; admitted, 1985, New Zealand. *Education:* University of Canterbury (B.A.; LL.B., Hons.). *PRACTICE AREAS:* Banking Law; Finance Law.

MICHAEL CARMODY WALLS, born 1945; admitted, 1968, New Zealand. *Education:* Victoria University of Wellington (B.A.; LL.B.); The London School of Economics, University of London (LL.M.). Former Lecturer, The City of London Polytechnic. (Also at Auckland Office). *PRACTICE AREAS:* International Financing Law; Mergers Law; Takeovers Law; Banking Law; Securities Law.

RUPERT JOHN WILSON, born 1951; admitted, 1975, New Zealand. *Education:* Victoria University of Wellington (LL.B., Hons.). *PRACTICE AREAS:* Commercial Property Law; Receivership Law.

CONSULTANTS

THOMAS WILLIAM BLENNERHASSETT, born 1924; admitted, 1948, New Zealand. *Education:* Victoria University College, Wellington (LL.B.). *Member:* New Zealand Law Society (Former Member and Chairman, Joint Audit Committee). Chairman, New Zealand Government Higher Salaries Commission. *PRACTICE AREAS:* Commercial Property Law; Energy Law; Trust Law.

BARRY RONALD BOON, born 1933; admitted, 1956, New Zealand. *Education:* Victoria University College, Wellington (LL.B.). Former Lecturer in Civil Procedure, Victoria University of Wellington. *PRACTICE AREAS:* Civil Litigation; Local Government Law; Planning Law; Insurance Law.

GEOFFREY PALMER, born 1943. *Education:* Victoria University of Wellington (LL.B.); University of Chicago (Doctor of Law, cum laude, 1967). Professor of Law, Victoria University of Wellington, 1991. (Also at Auckland Office). *PRACTICE AREAS:* Public Law; Maori Issues.

VICTORIA HELEN STACE, born 1960; admitted, 1984, New Zealand. *Education:* Victoria University of Wellington (LL.B., Hons.); Cambridge University (LL.M., Cantab.). *PRACTICE AREAS:* Taxation Law; Superannuation Law; Life Insurance.

All of the above are members of the Wellington District Law Society.

REPRESENTATIVE CLIENTS: Air New Zealand Ltd.; Airways Corporation of New Zealand; American Home Assurance Co. (a member company of American International Group); American Steamship Owners Mutual Protection and Indemnity Assn.; Australasian Performing Rights Association Ltd.; Australian Mutual Provident Society; Backer Spielvogel Bates New Zealand Ltd.; Blueport A.C.T. Ltd.; Carter Holt Harvey Ltd.; Chubb New Zealand Ltd.; Comalco Ltd.; Dart & Kraft Inc.; Electricity Corporation of New Zealand Ltd.; Fisher & Paykel Industries Ltd.; Fletcher Challenge Limited; G.E.C. Ltd.; Government Property Services Ltd.; H.J. Heinz Co. Ltd.; Hong Kong and Shanghai Banking Corp.; I.B.M.; International Paper Co.; Kentucky Fried Chicken ; Mainzeal Group Ltd.; McConnell Dowell Corporation Ltd.; National Mutual Finance Ltd.; National Provident Fund; New Zealand Dairy Board; New Zealand Forestry Corporation Ltd.; BHP New Zealand Steel Ltd.; NZ Forest Products Ltd.; Penguin Books (NZ) Ltd.; PepsiCo Inc.; Petroleum Corporation of New Zealand Ltd.; Progressive Enterprises Ltd.; R.J.R. Nabisco Inc.; Sumitomo Chemical Company Ltd.; Telecom Corporation of New Zealand Ltd.; The Shipowners' Protection & Indemnity Association in the International Group; Transit New Zealand; Victoria University of Wellington; Westpac Banking Corp.; Williams & Kettle Ltd.; Works and Development Services Corp. (NZ) Ltd.

(For Biographical Data of the Auckland Personnel, see Professional Biographies at Auckland).

HENRY HUGHES

Patent and Trade Mark Attorneys

Established in 1882

138 THE TERRACE

P.O. BOX 356

WELLINGTON, NEW ZEALAND

Telephone: 64-4-473-5038

Fax: 64-4-472-3634

Other Wellington, New Zealand Office: Henry Hughes & Co., 138 The Terrace, P.O. Box 356. Telephone: 64-4-473-5038. Fax: 64-4-472-3634.

Patents, Trade Marks, Designs, Copyright, Licensing, Fair Trading.

MARGARET DOUCAS, born Wellington, New Zealand; admitted, Barrister and Solicitor of High Court, Registered Patent Attorney. *Education:* Victoria University of Wellington (B.Sc.; LL.B.). *Member:* Fellow,

(This Listing Continued)

HENRY HUGHES, Wellington—Continued

New Zealand Institute of Patent Attorneys (current Vice-President); AIPPI New Zealand Group; Asian Patent Attorneys Association; Licensing Executives Society; Wellington District Law Society; American Bar Association; American Intellectual Property Law Association. *PRACTICE AREAS:* Patents (especially biotechnology, chemistry); Trademarks; Copyright.

BRIAN KENNETH BURTON, born Gisborne, New Zealand; admitted, Registered Patent Attorney. *Education:* Victoria University of Wellington (LL.B.). *Member:* Fellow, New Zealand Institute of Patent Attorneys; FICPI New Zealand Group. *PRACTICE AREAS:* Trademarks; Fair Trading; Passing Off; Copyright.

MARK CHRISTOPHER EFTIMOV, born Wellington, New Zealand; admitted, Registered Patent Attorney. *Education:* Wellington Polytechnic (N.Z.C.E.). *Member:* Fellow, New Zealand Institute of Patent Attorneys; AIPPI New Zealand Group; Asian Patent Attorneys Association. *PRACTICE AREAS:* Patents; Registered Designs; Trademarks.

FRANCIS GEORGE CALLUS, born Hythe, England; admitted, Registered Patent Attorney; Chartered Patent Attorney (U.K.). *Education:* N.E. London Polytechnic (B.Sc., Hons). Passed European Patent Office qualifying examination. *Member:* Fellow, New Zealand Institute of Patent Attorneys; AIPPI New Zealand Group; Asian Patent Attorneys Association. *PRACTICE AREAS:* Patents; Trademarks.

BARBARA MARY SULLIVAN, born Wellington, New Zealand; admitted, Barrister and Solicitor of High Court; Registered Trade Mark Agent (U.K.); Barrister and Solicitor, Victoria, Australia; Solicitor, New South Wales, Australia. *Education:* Victoria University of Wellington (B.A.; LL.B.). *Member:* Associate, New Zealand Institute of Patent Attorneys; Licensing Executives Society; Wellington District Law Society; AIPPI New Zealand Group; Australian Institute of Patent Attorneys (Overseas Member). *PRACTICE AREAS:* Trademarks; Copyright; Fair Trading; Licensing; Passing Off.

HENRY HUGHES & CO.

Intellectual Property Attorneys, Barristers and Solicitors

Associated with Henry Hughes, Patent and Trade Mark Attorneys

Established in 1991

138 THE TERRACE

P.O. BOX 356

WELLINGTON, NEW ZEALAND

Telephone: 64-4-473-5038

Fax: 64-4-472-3634

Other Wellington, New Zealand Office: Henry Hughes, 138 The Terrace, P.O. Box 356. Telephone: 64-4-473-5038. Fax: 64-4-472-3634.

Patents, Trade Marks, Designs, Copyright, Licensing, Fair Trading.

MEMBERS OF FIRM

MARGARET DOUCAS, born Wellington, New Zealand; admitted, Barrister and Solicitor of High Court, Registered Patent Attorney. *Education:* Victoria University of Wellington (B.Sc.; LL.B.). *Member:* Fellow, New Zealand Institute of Patent Attorneys (current Vice-President); AIPPI New Zealand Group; Asian Patent Attorneys Association; Licensing Executives Society; Wellington District Law Society; American Bar Association; American Intellectual Property Law Association. *PRACTICE AREAS:* Patent Litigation; Copyright.

BARBARA MARY SULLIVAN, born Wellington, New Zealand; admitted, Barrister and Solicitor of High Court; Registered Trade Mark Agent (U.K.); Barrister and Solicitor, Victoria, Australia; Solicitor, New South Wales, Australia. *Education:* Victoria University of Wellington (B.A.; LL.B.). *Member:* Associate, New Zealand Institute of Patent Attorneys; Licensing Executives Society; Wellington District Law Society; AIPPI New Zealand Group; Australian Institute of Patent Attorneys (Overseas Member). *PRACTICE AREAS:* Trademarks; Copyright; Licensing; Fair Trading; Passing Off.

KENSINGTON SWAN

89 THE TERRACE

P.O. BOX 10-246

WELLINGTON 1, NEW ZEALAND

Telephone: (4)472 7877

Facsimile: (4)472 2291

Auckland, New Zealand Office: 22 Fanshawe Street, Private Bag 92101. Telephone: (9) 379-4196. DX: 57. Fax: (9) 309-4276.

Commercial and Civil Litigation, Building and Civil Engineering Contracts, Industrial, Insurance, Negligence, Compensation, Town Planning, Taxation, Corporation and Business Law, Real Property, Probate, Trust and Family Law. Technology Licensing and Transfer, Energy and Mining Law, Mergers and Acquisitions. Off-shore Loan Transactions. Superannuation. Notary Public.

PARTNERS

WARREN LANCELOT ALLEN, admitted, 1960, New Zealand. *Education:* Victoria University of Wellington (B.A.; LL.B.). Notary Public, 1975. (National Managing Partner).

JOHN TERENCE INGERSON, admitted, 1966, New Zealand. *Education:* Victoria University of Wellington (LL.B.). *PRACTICE AREAS:* Corporate Law; Capital Market Transactions; Trusts Law; Superannuation.

RICHARD HAROLD CATHIE, admitted, 1967, New Zealand. *Education:* Victoria University of Wellington (LL.B.). *PRACTICE AREAS:* Corporate Law; Construction Law; Commercial Property Law; Partnerships.

ROBERT JAMES BACON, admitted, 1968, New Zealand, as Solicitor; 1969, New Zealand, as Barrister. *Education:* Victoria University of Wellington (LL.B.). *PRACTICE AREAS:* Insolvency Law; Construction Law; Commercial Property Law.

SHERWYN STANLEY WILLIAMS, admitted, 1969, New Zealand, as Solicitor; 1970, New Zealand, as Barrister. *Education:* Victoria University of Wellington (LL.B.). *PRACTICE AREAS:* Construction Law; Civil Litigation; Arbitration.

BRYAN NORMAN GUNDERSEN, admitted, 1972, New Zealand. *Education:* Victoria University (LL.B., Hons.). *PRACTICE AREAS:* Corporate Law; Competition Law; Mergers and Acquisitions; Health Reform Law.

JOHN WILLIAM MEADS, admitted, 1973, New Zealand. *Education:* Victoria University of Wellington (LL.B.). *PRACTICE AREAS:* Property Law; Real Estate Law; Corporate Law.

DONALD FRANCIS CAMPBELL FULLER, admitted, 1974, New Zealand. *Education:* Victoria University of Wellington (LL.B.). *PRACTICE AREAS:* Matrimonial Property Law; Family Law; Sports Law; Entertainment Law.

DONALD VICTOR BREADEN, admitted, 1972, Tasmania; 1975, New Zealand. *Education:* University of Tasmania (LL.B.). *PRACTICE AREAS:* Trustee Law; Estate Law; Commercial and Property Law; Inheritance Law; Estate and Gift Taxation Law.

MICHAEL FRANCIS QUIGG, admitted, 1976, New Zealand. *Education:* Victoria University (LL.B.; LL.M.). *PRACTICE AREAS:* Employment Law; Environmental Law; Insurance Law.

SIMON PHILLIP MARK, admitted, 1977, New Zealand. *Education:* Victoria University of Wellington (LL.B., Hons.). *PRACTICE AREAS:* Superannuation Law; Commercial Property Law; Education Law.

PHILIP HUNTER COOK, admitted, 1975, New Zealand. *Education:* University of Otago, Dunedin (LL.B.). *PRACTICE AREAS:* Insurance Law; Medical Law; General Litigation.

DAVID JAMES QUIGG, admitted, 1981, New Zealand. *Education:* Victoria University of Wellington (LL.B., Hons; LL.M.). *PRACTICE AREAS:* Corporate Law; Mergers and Acquisitions Law; Energy and Natural Resources Law.

ANTHONY JAMES LINES, admitted, 1980, New Zealand. *Education:* Victoria University of Wellington (LL.B.; LL.M.). *PRACTICE AREAS:* Domestic and International Taxation Law; Capital Markets Law.

MICHAEL RONALD BURROWES, admitted, 1983, New Zealand. *Education:* Victoria University of Wellington (LL.B., Hons). *PRACTICE AREAS:* Antitrust Law; Insolvency Law; Corporate Law; Insurance Law.

DAVID WILLIAM MALCOLM BENNETT, admitted, 1980, New Zealand. *Education:* University of Canterbury (LL.B.). *PRACTICE*

(This Listing Continued)

AREAS: Property Law; Commercial Law; Finance Law; Estates and Trusts.

ROSS STUART JOHNSTON, admitted, 1982, New Zealand; Enrolled Solicitor of the Supreme Court of England and Wales, 1986. *Education:* University of Auckland (B.Com., 1977; LL.B., Hons., 1979); McGill University (LL.M., 1980). *PRACTICE AREAS:* Intellectual Property Law; Information Technology Law; Commercial Law.

MARTIN HUGH DALGLEISH, admitted, 1982, New Zealand. *Education:* Victoria University of Wellington (LL.B.). *PRACTICE AREAS:* Corporate Law; Commercial Law; Securities Law.

PAMELA JEAN ANDREWS, admitted, 1984, New Zealand. *Education:* Victoria University of Wellington (B.A., 1967; LL.B., 1982). *PRACTICE AREAS:* Civil Litigation; Commercial Litigation; Insolvency Law; Banking Law.

GERALD FRASER FITZGERALD, admitted, 1984, New Zealand. *Education:* University of Otago (B.A., Hons., 1979; LL.B, 1982). *PRACTICE AREAS:* Corporate Law; Banking Law; International Financial Contracts Law.

MATTHEW FAIRFAX MCCLELLAND, admitted, 1976, New Zealand. *Education:* University of Canterbury (LL.B., Hons.). *PRACTICE AREAS:* Medical Law; Arbitration and Litigation; Environmental Law.

GRAHAM GEORGE TUBB, admitted, 1980, New Zealand. *Education:* University of Canterbury (LL.B.). *PRACTICE AREAS:* Taxation Law; Estate Planning; Corporate Law.

DEBORAH ANNE EDMUNDS, admitted, 1979, New Zealand. *Education:* Victoria University of Wellington (B.A., 1978; LL.B., 1978). *PRACTICE AREAS:* Corporate Law; Resource and Energy Law; Administrative Law.

JOHN LEGARD LAND, admitted, 1986, New Zealand. *Education:* Victoria University of Wellington (LL.B., Hons.). *PRACTICE AREAS:* Trade Practices Law; Company Law; Insurance Law.

SIMON JOHN MCARLEY, admitted, 1985, New Zealand; 1990 United Kingdom. *Education:* Victoria University of Wellington (LL.B., Hons.). *PRACTICE AREAS:* Banking Law; Securities Law; Insolvency Law; Corporate Law.

All Partners are members of the Wellington and New Zealand Law Societies.

Languages Spoken by Members of Kensington Swan: English, Maori, French, Italian, German, Japanese, Polish, Greek, Mandarin, Fukien, Cantonese, Malay.

A J PARK & SON

Established in 1891

HUDDART PARKER BUILDING
POST OFFICE SQUARE
P.O. BOX 949
WELLINGTON 1, NEW ZEALAND
Telephone: 644-473-8278
Telex: NZ 3947
Telecopier: 644 472-3358; 644 472-3351

Auckland, New Zealand Office: 12 Kent Street, Newmarket, P.O. Box 565. Telephone: 64-9-520-6029.

Patents, Trademarks, Designs and Copyright, Intellectual Property Litigation, Plant Variety Rights, Unfair Competition, Licensing, Foreign Investment, Corporation, Commercial and General Law.
Barristers, Solicitors and Registered Patent Attorneys.

MEMBERS OF FIRM

WILLIAM DAVID HOWIE, born Kaitangata, New Zealand, November 9, 1936; admitted, 1967, New Zealand. *Education:* Victoria University of Wellington (LL.B., 1967). *Member:* Wellington District Law Society; Institute of Patent Attorneys of Australia (Overseas Member); American Intellectual Property Law Association (Foreign Member); AIPPI New Zealand Group; Asian Patent Attorney's Association (New Zealand Group); FICPI (New Zealand National Section). Fellow, New Zealand Institute of Patent Attorneys.

THOMAS HAROLD SYDDALL, born Auckland, New Zealand, December 23, 1938; admitted, 1966, New Zealand. *Education:* Victoria University College (B.Sc., 1960); Victoria University of Wellington (LL.B., 1966). *Member:* Wellington District Law Society; New Zealand Institute of

(This Listing Continued)

Chemistry; AIPPI New Zealand Group; Asian Patent Attorney's Association (New Zealand Group); FICPI (New Zealand National Section); Chartered Institute of Patent Agents (British Overseas Member). Fellow, New Zealand Institute of Patent Attorneys.

PETER MICHAEL LUXFORD, born Wanganui, New Zealand, October 14, 1946; admitted, 1969, New Zealand. *Education:* Victoria University of Wellington (LL.B., 1969). *Member:* Wellington District Law Society; AIPPI New Zealand Group; Asian Patent Attorneys Association (New Zealand Group); International Trademark Association. Fellow, New Zealand Institute of Patent Attorneys.

DAVID JOHN JONES, born Christchurch, New Zealand, June 20, 1947; admitted, 1977, New Zealand. *Education:* Victoria University of Wellington (B.Sc., 1972; LL.B., 1977). *Member:* Auckland District Law Society; American Intellectual Property Law Association (Foreign Member); AIPPI New Zealand Group; Asian Patent Attorneys Association (New Zealand Group); FICPI (New Zealand National Section). Fellow, New Zealand Institute of Patent Attorneys.

BRYAN LINDSAY THOMPSON, born Wellington, New Zealand, January 25, 1950; admitted, 1974, New Zealand. *Education:* Auckland University (LL.B., 1973). *Member:* Auckland District Law Society; AIPPI New Zealand Group; Asian Patent Attorneys Association (New Zealand Group). Fellow, New Zealand Institute of Patent Attorneys.

ANDREW JOHN COLLINS, born Christchurch, New Zealand, May 29, 1949; admitted, 1973, New Zealand. *Education:* Victoria University of Wellington (B.A., 1970; LL.B., 1972). *Member:* Wellington District Law Society; AIPPI New Zealand Group; Asian Patent Attorney's Association (New Zealand Group); FICPI (New Zealand National Section), Pharmaceutical Trade Mark Group. Fellow, New Zealand Institute of Patent Attorneys.

KENNETH REGINALD MOON, born Te Awamutu, New Zealand, May 31, 1946; admitted, 1979, New Zealand. *Education:* University of Auckland (B.E., Elec., 1970); Victoria University of Wellington (LL.B., with honors, 1978). *Member:* Auckland District Law Society; Institution of Electrical Engineers, London (Associate Member); Institute of Professional Engineers, N.Z. (Graduate Member); Computer Law Association; International Bar Association (Computer Law Committee); Institute of Patent Attorneys of Australia (Overseas Member); American Intellectual Property Law Association (Foreign Member); AIPPI New Zealand Group; FICPI (New Zealand National Section). Fellow, New Zealand Institute of Patent Attorneys.

DOUGLAS CHARLES CALHOUN, born Montreal, Canada, May 5, 1944; admitted, 1980, New Zealand. *Education:* Bishop's University, Quebec, Canada (B.Sc., 1965); Queen's University, Ontario, Canada (M.Sc., 1968); Victoria University of Wellington (LL.B., 1980). *Member:* Wellington District Law Society; Patent and Trademark Institute of Canada (Associate); American Intellectual Property Law Association (Foreign Member); AIPPI New Zealand Group; Asian Patent Attorneys Association (New Zealand Group); FICPI (New Zealand National Section). Fellow, New Zealand Institute of Patent Attorneys.

KEITH CHARLES THOMSON, born Stratford, New Zealand, September 11, 1948; admitted, 1986, New Zealand. *Education:* University of Auckland (B.E. Chem., 1972); Victoria University of Wellington (LL.B., 1985). *Member:* Wellington District Law Society; Asian Patent Attorney's Association (New Zealand Group). Fellow, New Zealand Institute of Patent Attorneys.

MICHAEL ROY BENNETT, born Hamilton, New Zealand, October 5, 1960; admitted, 1986, New Zealand. *Education:* Victoria University of Wellington (B.Sc., 1982; LL.B., 1986). *Member:* Wellington District Law Society. Fellow, New Zealand Institute of Patent Attorneys.

COLLEEN MARGARET ISABEL CAVANAGH, born Stratford, New Zealand, November 17, 1959; admitted, 1983, New Zealand. *Education:* Victoria University of Wellington (LL.B., 1982). *Member:* Auckland District Law Society; Asian Patent Attorneys Association (New Zealand Group). Fellow, New Zealand Institute of Patent Attorneys.

GREGORY FRANCIS ARTHUR, born Stratford, New Zealand, May 9, 1963; admitted, 1986, New Zealand. *Education:* Victoria University of Wellington (B.Sc., 1985; LL.B., 1986); University of London (LL.M., with Merit, 1990). *Member:* Wellington District Law Society. Fellow, New Zealand Institute of Patent Attorneys.

(This Listing Continued)

A J PARK & SON, *Wellington—Continued*

CONSULTANTS

THOMAS EWART ENNIS, born Wellington, New Zealand, July 1, 1909; admitted, 1931, New Zealand. *Education:* Victoria University College (LL.B., 1930). *Member:* Wellington District Law Society; Institute of Patent Attorneys of Australia (Overseas Member); AIPPI New Zealand Group. Fellow, New Zealand Institute of Patent Attorneys.

ARCHIBALD CARLYLE CALLANDER, born Hawera, New Zealand, April 27, 1918; admitted, 1963, New Zealand. *Education:* Victoria University of Wellington. *Member:* Auckland District Law Society; Institution of Electrical Engineers, London (Chartered Engineer); American Intellectual Property Law Association (Foreign Member); AIPPI New Zealand Group; Asian Patent Attorney's Association (New Zealand Group). Fellow, New Zealand Institute of Patent Attorneys.

RUDD WATTS & STONE

Established in 1880

TRUST BANK CENTRE
125 THE TERRACE
P.O. BOX 2793
WELLINGTON, NEW ZEALAND
Telephone: 64-4 472 4899
Fax: 64-4 473 8232

Auckland, New Zealand Office: Bank of New Zealand Tower, 125 Queen Street, P.O. Box 3798. Telephone: 64-9-309 4863. Fax: 64-9-379 3326.

New Plymouth, New Zealand Office: 32 Vivian Street, P.O. Box 34. Telephone: 64-6 758 5397. Fax: 64-6 758 1822.

Sydney, New South Wales, Australia Associated Office: Minter Ellison, 44 Martin Place, 2000. Telephone: 61-2 210 4444. Fax: 61-2 235 2711.

Melbourne, Victoria, Australia Associated Office: Minter Ellison, 40 Market Street, 3000. Telephone: 61-3 617 4617. Fax: 61-3 617 4666.

Brisbane, Queensland, Australia Associated Office: Minter Ellison, Waterfront Place, 1 Eagle Street, 4000. Telephone: 61-7 226 6333. Fax: 61-7 229 1066.

Canberra, Australia Capital Territory, Australia Associated Office: Minter Ellison, 8-10 Hobart Place, 2600. Telephone: 61-6 248 7533. Fax: 61-6 249 8208.

Adelaide, South Australia, Australia Associated Office: Minter Ellison Baker O'Loughlin, 1 King William Street, 5000. Telephone: 61-8 233 5555. Fax: 61-8 212 7518.

Perth, Western Australia, Australia Associated Office: Minter Ellison Northmore Hale, 152-158 St. George's Terrace, 6000. Telephone: 61-9 429 7444. Fax: 61-9 429 7666.

London, England Associated Office: Minter Ellison, 20 Lincoln's Inn Fields, WC2A 3ED. Telephone: 44-171 831 7871. Fax: 44-171 404 4610.

Hong Kong Associated Office: McKenna & Co. in association with Minter Ellison, 5th Floor, Lippo Tower, 89 Queensway. Telephone: 852-2-846 9100. Fax: 852-2-845 3575.

Beijing, People's Republic of China Associated Office: Minter Ellison, Representative Office, Oxford Associates Inc., 205 International Club, 21 Jianguomenwai Dajie, 100020. Telephone: 86-1-532 5750. Fax: 86-1-513 6179.

Singapore Associated Office: Khattar Wong & Partners, 80 Raffles Place, #25-01 UOB Building, 0104. Telephone: 65-535 6844 Fax: 65-534 4892. Telex: 24896.

Legal services including: company and commercial, banking and finance, securities, mergers and acquisitions, computer law, telecommunications, competition law, consumer law, intellectual property, product liability, international trade, corporate recovery and insolvency, energy and resources, environmental law, construction, commercial property, shipping and aviation, media and entertainment, business immigration, alternative dispute resolution, commercial litigation, taxation, trusts and superannuation, employment, government liaison, insurance.

WELLINGTON AND NEW PLYMOUTH PARTNERS

JOHN GAVIN ADLAM, admitted, 1974, New Zealand. LL.B.; BCA. *PRACTICE AREAS:* Energy; Construction; Information Technology; Joint Ventures; Company and Commercial; Government Enterprises; Superannuation.

JOHN RICHARD ALLEN, admitted, 1984, New Zealand. LL.B. *PRACTICE AREAS:* Commercial Litigation; Competition Law; Government.

JAMES ROBERT ARMOUR, admitted, 1965, New Zealand. LL.B. *PRACTICE AREAS:* Company and Commercial; Restrictive Trade Practices; Superannuation; Electricity.

JOHN SUTHERLAND AULD, admitted, 1973, New Zealand. LL.B. *PRACTICE AREAS:* Energy; Company and Commercial; Property; Resource Management.

MARK HAMILTON BLAIR, admitted, 1979, New Zealand; 1992, England. LL.B. (Hons). *PRACTICE AREAS:* Intellectual Property; Company and Commercial; Commercial Property.

DAVID RENDEL KINGSTON GASCOIGNE, CBE, admitted, 1962, New Zealand. LL.M. *PRACTICE AREAS:* Commercial; Government; Media; Competition Law.

FRANCIS JOSHUA HANDY, admitted, 1967, New Zealand. M.A.; LL.B. *PRACTICE AREAS:* Energy; Construction; Commercial Litigation.

KENNETH BARRY JOHNSTON, admitted, 1979, New Zealand. LL.B. (Middle Temple). National Managing Partner. *PRACTICE AREAS:* Commercial Litigation.

MICHAEL JOHN LEGGAT, admitted, 1982, New Zealand. LL.B. *PRACTICE AREAS:* Commercial Litigation; Insurance; Employment Law.

ALAN DONALD MACKENZIE, admitted, 1968, New Zealand. B.A.; LL.M. *PRACTICE AREAS:* Insurance; Commercial Litigation; Shipping; Banking and Finance.

MURRAY FRANCIS MCEWEN, admitted, 1976, New Zealand. LL.B. *PRACTICE AREAS:* Company and Commercial; Energy; Property.

ROBERT DOUGLAS MCINNES, admitted, 1978, New Zealand. LL.M. *PRACTICE AREAS:* Banking and Finance; Insolvency; Company and Commercial.

GRAHAM SELWYN JOHN MOUAT, admitted, 1983, South Africa and Zimbabwe; 1990, New Zealand. LL.B.; B.A. *PRACTICE AREAS:* Banking and Finance.

DAVID JOHN PATTERSON, admitted, 1983, New Zealand; 1986, New York State, U.S.A. BCA; LL.B. (Hons); LL.M. (Harv). *PRACTICE AREAS:* Taxation; Company and Commercial.

CATHERINE AGNES QUINN, admitted, 1986, New Zealand. LL.B. *PRACTICE AREAS:* Company and Commercial; Mergers and Acquisitions.

PETER EDWARD RATNER, admitted, 1973, California, U.S.A.; 1977, Connecticut, U.S.A.; 1978, New York State, U.S.A.; 1983, New Zealand. B.A.; J.D. (Columbia). *PRACTICE AREAS:* Company and Commercial; Telecommunications; Commerce and Securities Acts; Mergers and Acquisitions.

JENNIFER EVES SUTTON, admitted, 1988, New Zealand. LL.B. (Hons). *PRACTICE AREAS:* Commercial Litigation; Corporate Recovery; Insolvency; Maritime Law.

CONSULTANTS

JOHN SANDISON BEECH BROWN, LL.B.

ALISTAIR JOHN NICOLSON, LL.B.

TREVOR ATHOL ROBERTS, LL.B.

CHARLES KEMPTHORNE STONE, LL.B.

SENIOR ASSOCIATES

LOUISE ANNE AFFLECK, LL.B. *PRACTICE AREAS:* Insolvency; Employment; Commercial Litigation.

JOHN PETER BLOOMFIELD, B.A.; LL.B. *PRACTICE AREAS:* Estate Planning; Probate; Trust and Estate Administration; Wills and Property.

GILLIAN ANNE CLARKE, B.A.; LL.B. (Hons). *PRACTICE AREAS:* Commercial Litigation.

KARA MARIE DALY, LL.B. (Hons). *PRACTICE AREAS:* Company and Commercial; Banking and Finance; Corporate Trusts; Computer Law.

SCOTT DAVID GALLOWAY, B.A.; LL.B. *PRACTICE AREAS:* Commercial Litigation.

(This Listing Continued)

ANN-LOUISE MARGARET GOWER, B.A.; LL.B. *PRACTICE AREAS:* Company and Commercial; Securities Law.

WARREN JOHN HOARE, LL.B. *PRACTICE AREAS:* Commercial Property.

DAVID HAMPDEN JENKINS, LL.B. (Hons). *PRACTICE AREAS:* Commercial Litigation; Banking; Insurance; Employment Law.

REGINA MARY RUDLAND, B.A.; LL.B. (Hons). *PRACTICE AREAS:* Company and Commercial; Maori Business.

RICHARD STUART SCOULAR, B.A., LL.B. (Hons.). *PRACTICE AREAS:* Taxation.

JEANETTE MARGARET WATSON, B.Sc.; LL.B. *PRACTICE AREAS:* Energy; Company and Commercial; Information Technology; Joint Ventures; Resource Management.

Languages: Cantonese, French, Hakka, Hokkien, Indonesian, Malay, Mandarin, Serbo-Croatian and Spanish.

(For biographical data of the Auckland Partners and Associates, see Professional Biographies at Auckland, New Zealand)

RUSSELL McVEAGH McKENZIE
BARTLEET & CO.

Established in 1863

LEVELS 5, 6, 7 & 8
THE TODD BUILDING
171-177, LAMBTON QUAY
P.O. BOX 10-214
WELLINGTON 1, NEW ZEALAND
Telephone: (64) (04) 499-9555
Telex: NZ 21305
Fax: (64) (04) 499-9556

Auckland, New Zealand Office: 8th Floor, The Shortland Centre, 51-53, Shortland Street, P.O. Box 8. Telephone: (64) (09) 309-8839. Cable Address: Barrister. Telex: NZ 21305. Fax: (64) (09) 377-1849.

Commercial and General Practice, emphasizing Corporate, Securities, Banking, Tax, Foreign Investment, Commercial Property Development, Insurance, Labour, Mining, Construction, Energy Law, Copyrights, Patents and Trademarks, Administrative Law, Real Property, Environmental and Resource Management Law, Probate, Wills and Trusts, Economic Regulation, Entertainment, Shipping and Admiralty, Aviation, Immigration, Communications, Legislative Drafting, Civil and General Litigation. Barristers and Solicitors of the High Court of New Zealand.

FIRM PROFILE: *The firm's practice was established in February 1863, in Auckland. Since April 1988, the firm has also had a significant office in Wellington. The firm has a complement of approximately 400 people. It is a predominantly commercial firm, although offers the full range of legal services. Among many specialties offered is overseas investment in New Zealand. The firm has a strong focus on the Asia-Pacific region, with partners and staff involved in projects in Pacific and Asian countries. Within New Zealand, the firm's practice extends nationwide.*

MEMBERS OF FIRM

FOSS MICHAEL SHANAHAN, born Wellington, New Zealand, February 11, 1940; admitted, 1967, New Zealand. *Education:* Victoria University of Wellington (LL.B.). Partner: Rainey Collins Armour & Boock (and predecessor firms), 1967-1976; Shanahan Partners, 1976-1990. *PRACTICE AREAS:* Community Property Development Law; Corporate Law; Commercial Law.

PATRICK CALLAGHAN BOWLER, born Wellington, New Zealand, September 6, 1948; admitted, 1972, New Zealand. *Education:* Victoria University of Wellington (LL.B.). General Counsel, Mobil Oil New Zealand Limited, 1980-1983. *PRACTICE AREAS:* Energy Law; Commercial Law; Merchant Banking Law.

DEREK SAMUEL JOHNSTON, born Whangarei, New Zealand, May 2, 1957; admitted, 1979, New Zealand. *Education:* University of Auckland (LL.B., Hons.); M.Jur., Dist.); University of Toronto (S.J.D.). *Member:* Licensing Executives Society of Australia and New Zealand; Energy and Natural Resources Law Association of New Zealand. *PRACTICE AREAS:* Commercial Law; Corporate Law; Oil and Gas Law; Intellectual Property; Trade Practices.

(This Listing Continued)

JOHN STEPHEN KOS, born Mosgiel, New Zealand, January 23, 1959; admitted, 1982, New Zealand. *Education:* Victoria University of Wellington (LL.B., Hons); Cambridge University (LL.M.). Partner, Perry Castle, 1986-1988. *Member:* Licensing Executives Society of Australia and New Zealand; Arbitrator's Institute of New Zealand Inc. *PRACTICE AREAS:* Civil Litigation; Commercial Law; Corporate Law; Contracts; Energy Law; Media Law.

PETER JOHN ESLICK TREGEAR, born Christchurch, New Zealand, January 5, 1961; admitted, 1983, New Zealand. *Education:* University of Canterbury (LL.B., Hons). *PRACTICE AREAS:* Commercial Property Development Law; Property Development and Financing Law; Commercial Law.

ALAN STANLEY JAMES A'COURT, born Wellington, New Zealand, August 25, 1949; admitted, 1973, New Zealand. *Education:* Victoria University of Wellington (LL.B.). Partner, Buddle Findlay, (and predecessor firms) 1975-1988. *PRACTICE AREAS:* Banking and Financing Law; Commercial Law.

PRUDENCE MARY FLACKS, born Gisborne, New Zealand, February 23, 1957; admitted, 1979, New Zealand. *Education:* Victoria University of Wellington (LL.B.); University of London (LL.M.). Partner, Buddle Findlay, 1986-1988. *PRACTICE AREAS:* Banking; Merchant Banking Law; Commercial Law.

GEOFFREY JOHN HARLEY, born Nelson, New Zealand, April 3, 1953; admitted, 1976, New Zealand. *Education:* Victoria University of Wellington (LL.M.); University of Michigan (LL.M., S.J.D.). Partner, Rudd Watts & Stone, 1983-1989. *Member:* International Fiscal Association; Tax Education Office. *PRACTICE AREAS:* Taxation Law; Commercial Law.

JOHN RENWICK HARKNESS, born Hastings, New Zealand, March 10, 1950; admitted, 1973, New Zealand. *Education:* Victoria University of Wellington (LL.B.). Partner: Scott Morison Dunphy (and predecessor firms), 1975-1987; Shanahan Partners, 1987-1990. *PRACTICE AREAS:* Commercial Property Development Law; Commercial Law; Corporate Law.

LANCE HAMILTON HEENAN, born Auckland, New Zealand, April 20, 1962; admitted, 1985, New Zealand. *Education:* University of Auckland (B.Com.; LL.B). *PRACTICE AREAS:* Taxation Law.

PAUL GERARD FOLEY, born Napier, New Zealand, April 2, 1962; admitted, 1985, New Zealand. *Education:* Victoria University of Wellington (LL.B.). *PRACTICE AREAS:* Commercial and Corporate Law; Trade Practices; Takeovers and Mergers; Insolvency.

RICHARD BRUCE GOLDING MEHRTENS, born Christchurch, New Zealand, November 29, 1960; admitted, 1985, New Zealand. *Education:* University of Otago (B.Com.; LL.B.). Partner, Anderson Lloyd, 1989. *PRACTICE AREAS:* Commercial and Corporate Law; Aviation Law; Acquisitions, Takeovers and Mergers.

JUSTIN BAIN MACRAE SMITH, born Palmerston North, New Zealand, June 13, 1957; admitted, 1981, New Zealand. *Education:* University of Canterbury (LL.B.). Partner, Kensington Swan, 1988-1994. *PRACTICE AREAS:* Civil Litigation; Building and Construction Law; Arbitration; Resource Management Law; Intellectual Property Law.

LLOYD ANTHONY JAMES KAVANAGH, born Waiuku, New Zealand, August 28, 1961; admitted, 1984, New Zealand. *Education:* University of Otago (LL.B.). *PRACTICE AREAS:* Banking Law; Commercial Law.

KERRY WAYNE FULTON, born Hamilton, New Zealand, July 3, 1963; admitted, 1987, New Zealand. *Education:* Victoria University of Wellington (LL.B., Hons.); Cambridge University (LL.M.). Junior Lecturer in Law, Victoria University of Wellington, 1987. *PRACTICE AREAS:* Commercial Litigation; Banking and Insolvency Law; Restrictive Trade Practices; Administrative Law.

CONSULTANT

CELIA MARY CAUGHEY, born Auckland, New Zealand, September 7, 1957; admitted, 1985, New Zealand. *Education:* University of Auckland (B.A.; LL.B., Hons.); Oxford University (B.C.L.). *PRACTICE AREAS:* Banking Litigation; Civil Litigation; Criminal Law.

All Partners are Members of the Wellington District Law Society.

Languages: English, Chinese languages and dialects, French, German, Italian and Japanese

(For complete biographical data on personnel at Auckland, see professional biographies at Auckland).

SIMPSON GRIERSON

UNISYS HOUSE
44-52 THE TERRACE
P.O. BOX 2402
WELLINGTON, NEW ZEALAND
Telephone: (04) 499-4599
Facsimile: (04) 472-6986

Auckland, New Zealand Office: 92-96 Albert Street, Private Bag 92518, Wellesley Street. Telephone: (09) 358-2222. Facsimile (09) 307-0331.

General Corporate and Commercial, Local Government, Mining, Oil and Gas, Foreign Investment and International Trade, Construction Law Arbitration, Patent and Trademarks, Environmental and Planning Law, Copyright, Insurance, Litigation, Taxation, Securities, Shipping, Real Property, General Practice, Media, Sports and Entertainment.

MEMBERS OF FIRM

CONSTANTINE ANASTASIOU, born 1949; admitted, 1973, New Zealand. *Education:* Victoria University of Wellington (B.A.; LL.B., Hons). Associate Member, New Zealand Institute of Management. *PRACTICE AREAS:* Admiralty Law; Shipping Law; Commercial Litigation; Environmental Law; Planning Law.

COLIN ANDREW NIELSEN BEYER, born 1938; admitted, 1962, New Zealand. *Education:* Victoria University of Wellington (LL.B.). *PRACTICE AREAS:* Corporate Law; Mining Law.

STEPHEN BARRIE FLYNN, born 1959; admitted, 1983, New Zealand. *Education:* Victoria University of Wellington (LL.B. Hons.). *Member:* New Zealand Society (Committee on Insolvency Law Reform). *PRACTICE AREAS:* Banking Law; Finance Law; International Financing Law; Corporate Insolvency Law.

HAMISH FORRESTER GORDON, born 1951; admitted, 1975, New Zealand. *Education:* Victoria University of Wellington (LL.B.). *PRACTICE AREAS:* Banking Law; Finance Law; Corporate Law; Insolvency Law; Insurance Law; Mining Law.

ALAN JOSEPH HENWOOD, born 1950; admitted, 1976, New Zealand. *Education:* Victoria University of Wellington (B.A., LL.B.). *PRACTICE AREAS:* Commercial Property Law; Leasing Law; Public Sector Law; Commercial Law.

JOHN DAVID HOWMAN, born 1948; admitted, 1972, New Zealand. *Education:* Victoria University of Wellington (B.A., LL.B. Hons.); University of Pennsylvania (LL.C.M. Penn.). *PRACTICE AREAS:* Custody Law; Matrimonial Property Law; Medico-Legal; Sports Law.

MARK ATKINSON JEFFRIES, born 1961; admitted, 1984, New Zealand. *Education:* University of Auckland (LL.B.; M. Tax S., Hons.). *PRACTICE AREAS:* Corporate and International Taxation Law; Taxation Law; Commercial Law; Corporate Structuring; Law and Technology; Maori Legal Issues.

JAN MARIE KELLY, born 1961; admitted, 1984, New Zealand. *Education:* Canterbury University (LL.B., Hons.). *PRACTICE AREAS:* Banking and Finance Litigation; Insurance Law; Competition Law; Product Liability; Commercial Litigation.

DUNCAN JAMES SIMPSON LAING, born 1952; admitted, 1976, New Zealand. *Education:* Otago University of Dunedin (B.A.); Victoria University of Wellington (LL.B. Hons., LL.M.). Co-editor: "Brooker's Resource Management Law.". *PRACTICE AREAS:* Environmental Law; Local Government Law; Insurance Law.

JONATHAN MARK TRAVERS SALTER, born 1955; admitted, 1984, New Zealand. *Education:* Otago University (B.A. Hons., LL.B.). *PRACTICE AREAS:* Local Government; Employment Law.

MICHAEL FRANCIS SCANNELL, born 1956; admitted, 1979, New Zealand. *Education:* Victoria University of Wellington (LL.B.). Notary Public. *Member:* WDLS (Property Law Committee). *PRACTICE AREAS:* Property Law; Commercial Property Law; Banking Law; Finance Law; Leasing Law.

TERRY SISSONS, born 1949; admitted, 1972, New Zealand. *Education:* Canterbury University (LL.B., Hons.); Fellow Arbitrators Institute of New Zealand. *PRACTICE AREAS:* Commercial Litigation; Insurance; Professional Indemnity; Securities; Insolvency; Arbitration; Mediation.

(This Listing Continued)

CHRISTINE BETTY SOUTHEY, born 1960; admitted, 1984, New Zealand; 1989, New South Wales, Australia. *Education:* University of Otago (B.A., Hons.; LL.B.). *PRACTICE AREAS:* Business Law; Foreign Investment; Securities issuance; Public Offerings and Takeovers; Trade Practices.

MICHAEL GEORGE CANTRICK STEPHENS, born 1956; admitted, 1981, New Zealand. *Education:* University of Canterbury (B.A.); Victoria University of Wellington (LL.B.). *PRACTICE AREAS:* Banking Law; Finance Law; Commercial Property Law; Property Law.

MARK JOHN VERBIEST, born 1958; admitted, 1982, New Zealand. *Education:* Victoria University of Wellington (LL.B.). *PRACTICE AREAS:* Antitrust Law; Competition Law; Corporate Law; Foreign Investment Law; Energy and Mining Law; Mergers and Acquisitions Law; Securities Offerings Law.

STEPHEN PATRICK WARD, born 1959; admitted, 1983, New Zealand; 1987, Solicitor, England and Wales. *Education:* Canterbury University of Christchurch (LL.B.). *PRACTICE AREAS:* Banking Law; Finance Law; Corporate Law; Insolvency Law; Superannuation Law; Pension Law; Insurance Law.

MICHAEL RICHARD HOLDEN WEBB, born 1953; admitted, 1976, New Zealand. *Education:* Victoria University of Wellington (LL.B.). Convenor New Zealand Law Society Commercial and Business Law Committee, New Zealand. Co-commentator - Journal of International Banking Law, Banking Law Associates and LawAsia. *PRACTICE AREAS:* Banking Law; Finance Law; Capital Markets Law; Insolvency Law; Banking Regulation Law; Superannuation and Pension Law.

JAMES JOHN MAURICE WILTSHIRE, born 1932; admitted, 1958, New Zealand. *Education:* Victoria University of Wellington (LL.B.). Co-author: Wiltshire, Laing & McVeagh on "Public Works" and "Land Sub-Division and Development and Roads." Advisor to Local Authorities and Public Bodies, Investors and Developers particularly relating to Resource Management and Development issues. *PRACTICE AREAS:* Resource Management Law including Planning and Development and Water and Soil.

GORDON BRENT WONG, born 1958; admitted, 1983, New Zealand. *Education:* Victoria University of Wellington (LL.B. Hons.). *PRACTICE AREAS:* Corporate Law; Commercial Law; Energy Law; Treaty of Waitangi; Forestry.

All partners are members of the Wellington District Law Society.

(For complete biographical data on personnel at Auckland, see Auckland listing)

WEST-WALKER McCABE

Established in 1958
160-162 WILLIS STREET
P.O. BOX 215
WELLINGTON, NEW ZEALAND
Telephone: 644 382 9085
Fax: 644 473 0466

Intellectual Property Law, Corporate and Commercial.

FIRM PROFILE: The firm was established in 1958 and offers a full range of services in intellectual property law and advises on corporate and commercial matters for clients setting up in business in New Zealand or doing business with New Zealand parties. The client base is international. This three partner firm has a legal support staff of 11.

MEMBERS OF FIRM

PHILIP THOMAS MCCABE. *LANGUAGES:* English and French. *PRACTICE AREAS:* Copyright; Trademarks; Litigation; Licensing; General Legal Practice.

GREGORY JAMES WEST-WALKER. *LANGUAGES:* English. *PRACTICE AREAS:* Patents (Engineering, Electrical and General); Copyright; Licensing; General Practice.

FRANCIS NIGEL WEST-WALKER (Consultant). *LANGUAGES:* English. *PRACTICE AREAS:* Patents (Engineering and Mechanical); Copyright; Licensing.

ASSOCIATES

TIMOTHY GRAHAM JACKSON. *LANGUAGES:* English. *PRACTICE AREAS:* Patents (Chemical).

(This Listing Continued)

KARL MALCOLM ROGERS. *LANGUAGES:* English. *PRACTICE AREAS:* Patents (Biochemistry).

PETER UERBOEKET. *LANGUAGES:* English. *PRACTICE AREAS:* Patents (Engineering); Trademarks; General Practice.

KATIE MARY HUNT. *LANGUAGES:* English. *PRACTICE AREAS:* Patents (Biochemistry); Trademarks; General Practice.

REPRESENTATIVE CLIENTS: USA: AT&T; Elf Atochem Corporation; Buckman Laboratories Inc.; Campbell Soup Company; Colgate Palmolive Company; Eveready Battery Co.; Johnson & Johnson; McNeil Laboratories; Nashua Corp.; Ralston Purina Company; Texas Instruments Inc.

NIUE

MOSSACK FONSECA & CO. NIUE

NO. 5 COMMERCIAL CENTRE SQUARE
P.O. BOX 71
ALOFI, NIUE
Telephone: (683) 4228, ext. 86 or 87
Fax: (683) 4357

Panama, Republic of Panama Office: Mossack Fonseca & Co. Arango-Orillac Bldg., 54th Street, P.O. Box 8320. Telephones: (507) 63-889; 64-2322. Fax: (507) 63-9218; 63-7327.

Road Town, Tortola, British Virgin Islands Office: Mossack Fonseca & Co. (BUI) Ltd., Skelton Bldg., Main Street, P.O. Box 3136. Telephones: (809) 494-4840; 494-4976. Fax: (809) 494-4841; 494-5884.

Nassau, Bahamas Office: Mossack Fonseca & Co. (Bahamas) Ltd., Bitco Bldg., 3rd Floor, P.O. Box N-8188. Telephone: (809) 322-7601. Fax: (809) 322-5807; 325-3583.

LAW: Corporate Law, Shipping and Admiralty, Banking Law, Aviation, Patent and Trade Marks, Foreign Investments, International Law, Trusts, Investment Management.
TAXATION: Corporate Taxation, International Taxation, Formation and Management of International Business Companies, Trusts, and related offshore services.

PAPUA NEW GUINEA

ALLENS ARTHUR ROBINSON

LEVEL 11
PACIFIC PLACE
CNR MUSGRAVE STREET & CHAMPION PARADE
PORT MORESBY, PAPUA NEW GUINEA
Telephone: (675) 202 000
Rapifax: (675) 200 588

Mailing Address: P.O. Box 1178, Port Moresby, Papau New Guinea

Allens Arthur Robinson is an international network of group and associated offices representing the Allens Arthur Robinson group in Australia.
Group and Associated Offices:
London, England: Allens Arthur Robinson, Level 5, Bucklersbury House, 3 Queen Victoria Street, EC4N 8EL. Telephone: (44 171) 248 6130. Rapifax: (44 171) 248 6334.
New York, NY: Allens Arthur Robinson, 280 Park Avenue, 10017. Telephone: (1 212) 867 1555. Rapifax: (1 212) 867 7979.
Singapore: Allens Arthur Robinson, 65 Chulia Street #42-05, OCBC Centre, 0104. Telephone: (65) 535 6622. Rapifax: (65) 535 4855.
Hong Kong: Dunstan Styles & Co, Suite 1504, One Exchange Square, 8 Connaught Place, Central. Telephone: (852) 2840 1202. Rapifax: (852) 2840 0686.
Jakarta, Indonesia: Wiriadinata & Widyawan, Niaga Tower, 26th Floor, Jl. Jend. Sudirman, Kav 58, 12190. Telephone: (62 21) 250 5175. Rapifax: (62 21) 250 5185.
Shanghai, People's Republic of China: AAR China Limited, Fuxing Xi Lu 37 Long 6 Hao. 200031. Telephone: (86 21) 437 7582. Rapifax: (86 21) 473 7819.

(This Listing Continued)

Allens Arthur Robinson's international network of offices represents:
Sydney, New South Wales, Australia: Allen Allen & Hemsley, The Chifley Tower, 2 Chifley Square, 2000. Telephone: (61 2) 230 4000. Rapifax: (61 2) 233 7022.
Canberra, Australian Capital Territory, Australia: Allen Allen & Hemsley, 3rd Floor, 16 Moore Street, 2601. Telephone: (61 6) 247 5800. Rapifax: (61 6) 257 1369.
Melbourne, Victoria, Australia: Arthur Robinson & Hedderwicks, Levels 27-34, 530 Collins Street, 3000. Telephone: (61 3) 614 1011. Rapifax: (61 3) 614 4661.
Brisbane, Queensland, Australia: Feez Ruthning, Riverside Centre, 123 Eagle Street, 4000. Telephone: (61 7) 833 3333. Rapifax: (61 7) 832 4233.
Surfers Paradise, Queensland, Australia: Feez Ruthning, Level 14, 50 Cavill Avenue, 4217. Telephone: (61 75) 70 0200. Rapifax: (61 75) 92 2285.
Perth, Western Australia, Australia: Parker & Parker, AMP Building, 140 St George's Terrace, 6000. Telephone: (61 9) 322 0321. Rapifax: (61 9) 322 2243.
Adelaide, South Australia, Australia: Finlaysons, 81 Flinders Street, 5000. Telephone: (61 8) 235 7400. Rapifax: (61 8) 232 2944.

FIRM PROFILE: Allens Arthur Robinson is engaged in local and international law practice and the practice of law in Papua New Guinea. Admitted to practice in Papua New Guinea.

RESIDENT PARTNER

BEN PASSINGAN, admitted, Papua New Guinea. *LANGUAGES:* English. *PRACTICE AREAS:* Banking; Finance; Property Law; Resources.

CONSULTANT

Peter Lowing

BLAKE DAWSON WALDRON

MOGORU MOTO BUILDING
CHAMPION PARADE
P.O. BOX 850
PORT MORESBY, PAPUA NEW GUINEA
Telephone: (675) 21 1977
Telex: NE 22223
Facsimile: (675) 21 2630

Sydney, New South Wales, Australia Office: Grosvenor Place 225 George Street 2000. Telephone: (02) 2586000. Facsimile: (02) 2586999. Telex: AA22867DWN.
Melbourne, Victoria, Australia Office: 101 Collins Street, 3000. Telephone: (03) 679-3000. Facsimile: (03) 679-3111. Telex: AA31033.
Brisbane, Queensland, Australia Office: Riverside Centre, 123 Eagle Street, 4000. Telephone: (07) 259-7000. Facsimile: (07) 259-7111. Telex: AA22867DWN.
Perth, Western Australia, Australia Office: Forrest Centre, 221 St. George's Terrace, 6000. Telephone: (09) 366-8000. Facsimile: (09) 366-8111. Telex: AA22867DWN.
Canberra, Australian Capital Territory, Australia Office: 12 Moore Street, 2601. Telephone: (06) 234 4000. Facsimile: (06) 234 4111. Telex: AA22867DWN.
London, England Office: 66 Gresham Street, EC2V 7BB. Telephone: (071) 600 3030. Facsimile: (071)600 3392.
Jakarta, Indonesia Associated Office: Soebagjo, Roosdiono, Jatim & Djarot. Chase Plaza, Jalan Jendral Sudirman Kav 21, 12910. Telephone: (6221) 570 6436. Fax: (6221) 570 6437. Telex: 62 941 SRJDIA.
Port Vila, Vanuatu Associated Office: Hudson & Co. Lo Lam House, Kumul Highway. Telephone: (678) 22166. Fax: (678) 24260.

FIRM PROFILE: One of Australia's largest national law firms providing legal services in all areas required by commerce, finance and government. The firm has offices in all the major Australian commercial centres. Our practice also has international offices in London, Port Moresby and associated offices in Jakarta and Port Vila.

PORT MORESBY PARTNERS

TIMOTHY GLENN. *PRACTICE AREAS:* Commercial Litigation; Marine and Aviation Law.

MATTHEW MAY. *PRACTICE AREAS:* Commercial Law; Resources Law.

(This Listing Continued)

BLAKE DAWSON WALDRON, Port Moresby—Continued

DAVID C. FRECKER. PRACTICE AREAS: Banking; Project Finance; Mining & Resources Law; Commercial Law.

ANTHONY SIAGURU KBE. PRACTICE AREAS: Corporate; Commercial.

PHILLIP PAYNE. PRACTICE AREAS: Commercial Litigation.

(For complete personnel and biographical data, see professional biographies at Sydney, Australia).

GADENS RIDGEWAY
PACIFIC PLACE
CNR MUSGRAVE STREET & CHAMPION PARADE
P.O. BOX 1042
PORT MORESBY, PAPUA NEW GUINEA
Telephone: (675) 21-1033
Fax: (675) 21-1885

Sydney, New South Wales, Australia Office: Levels 12-15, Skygarden
(This Listing Continued)

Building, 77 Castlereagh Street, 2000. Telephone: (612) 232-5566. Fax: (612) 931-4888.

Melbourne, Victoria, Australia Office: Levels 20-23, AMP Tower, 535 Bourke Street, 3000. Telephone: (613) 614-4844. Fax: (613) 614-3770.

Brisbane, Queensland, Australia Office: Levels 39-40, Central Plaza One, 345 Queen Street, 4000, GPO Box 129, Brisbane 4001. Telephone: (617) 231-1666. Fax: (617) 229-5850.

Cairns, Queensland, Australia Office: 95 Sheridan Street, 4870. Telephone: (6170) 31-1622. Fax: (6170) 61 7828.

RESIDENT PARTNERS

Stephen Lewin	Winifred Kamit
Julie Skinner	Campbell Hudson
Michael Sullivan	Erik Andersen

SENIOR ASSOCIATES

Leo Hopsick	Brien Leibinger
	Patricia Koiri

(For list of Personnel at Sydney, Brisbane, Melbourne and Cairns, Australia, see professional biographies at those locations).

PROFESSIONAL BIOGRAPHIES SECTION

MIDDLE EAST, AFRICA

The Professional Biographies Section presents information about lawyers and law firms that has proved to be most helpful in the selection of associate counsel or when data is desired for other reasons.

Most jurisdictions permit attorneys at law or counselors to associate in accordance with defined regulations of each Bar. The user of the International Volumes of the Directory should not necessarily infer that each firm presented is practicing as a partnership.

Algeria	Mauritius
Bahrain	Morocco
Burkina-Faso	Nigeria
Cameroon	Oman
Cote d'Ivoire	Qatar
Egypt	Saudi Arabia
Ethiopia	Sierra Leone
Ghana	South Africa
Iran	Sudan
Iraq	Syria
Israel	Tanzania
Jordan	Tunisia
Kenya	United Arab Emirates
Kuwait	Yemen
Lebanon	Zimbabwe

ALGERIA

LAW OFFICE OF MOURAD HAMDI

Established in 1982

IMMEUBLE LAFAYETTE
7 RUE LAFAYETTE
16000 ALGIERS, ALGERIA
Telephone: (213) 263.70.52
Facsimile: (213) 261.31.27

Banking Law, International Contracts (Engineering), Commercial Law, Foreign Investments, International Litigation and General Practice.

MOURAD HAMDI, born Telagh, Algeria, March 28, 1944; admitted, 1974, Algiers. Education: Faculte de Droit d'Aix-Marseille, France (Licence en Droit, 1967). Head of the Legal Department, Engineering Division, Algerian National Oil Company (Sonatrach), 1972-1981. Admitted before the Supreme Court of Algeria.

Languages: Arabic, English and French.

YAMINA KEBIR

BP 298 HYDRA
16035 ALGIERS, ALGERIA
Telephone: (213) 2-56.27.88
Telecopier: (213) 2-56.52.31

Legal Consultancy and Litigation. General Practice and International including Commercial and Business Law. Contract Law. Foreign Investments. Banking Law. Maritime. Labour Law. Family Law. Patents and Trademarks.

YAMINA KEBIR, admitted, 1982, Algeria (Authorized to appear before the Supreme Court of Algeria). Education: Faculté de Droit d'Alger (Licence en Droit, 1977); Université d'Alger (Licence en Lettres); Université de Paris II (D.E.A. de Droit des Affaires, 1979; Brevet de Traduction Juridique, 1979; D.E.A. de Droit de la Propriété Industrielle); Université de Strasbourg (Diplôme de Droit Comparé). Authorship: "Arresting Ships in Algeria," Lloyd's of London Press, 1988; "The Commercial Laws of Algeria," Oceana, New York, 1988. Head of Legal Department, National Steel Company, 1980-1981. Member: International Bar Association; Union Internationale Des Avocats. **PRACTICE AREAS:** Administrative Law; Admiralty; Civil Law; Commercial Law; Family Law (International Family Law); General Practice; Intellectual Property; International Law; Investments; Labour.

Languages: Arabic, English (Legal Translator) and French

BAHRAIN

LAW OFFICE OF SHAIKH ISA BIN MOHAMMED AL KHALIFA

In Association with Clifford Chance

P.O. BOX 20717
MANAMA, BAHRAIN
Telephone: (973) 531535; 531073
Fax: (973) 536272/530608

Amsterdam, The Netherlands Office: Apollolaan 171, 1077 AS, P.O. Box 7301, 1007 JH. Telephone: (31 20) 577 71 11. Fax: (31 20) 676 93 26.
Barcelona, Spain Office: Pau Claris 102, 08009. Telephone: (34 3) 318 68 64. Fax: (34 3) 317 73 23.
Brussels, Belgium Office: Avenue Louise 65, Box 2, 1050. Telephone: (32 2) 533 59 11. Fax: (32 2) 533 59 59.
Budapest, Hungary Office: Köves & Partners, Clifford Chance. Madách Trade Center, Madách Imre Út 14, 1075. Telephone: (36 1) 268 1600. Fax: (36 1) 268 1610.

(This Listing Continued)

Dubai, United Arab Emirates Office: 18th Floor, Dubai World Trade Centre, P.O. Box 9380. Telephone: (971 4) 314333. Fax: (971 4) 313990; 314565.
Frankfurt/Main, Germany Office: Friedrichstraße 2-6, 60323. Telephone: (49 69) 971 4090. Fax: (49 69) 971 40977.
Hanoi, Vietnam Office: 52 Nguyen Binh Khiem. Telephone: (844) 229 182/3/4/5/6. Fax: (844) 229 190.
Hong Kong Office: 30th Floor, Jardine House, One Connaught Place. Telephone: (852) 2810 0229. Fax: (852) 2810 4708; 2810 4858; 2810 4743.
London, England Office: 200 Aldersgate Street, EC1A 4JJ. Telephone: (44 171) 600 1000. Fax: (44 171) 600 5555.
Madrid, Spain Office: Paseode la Castellana 110, 28046. Telephone (34 1) 562 7674. Fax: (34 1) 562 49 93.
Milan, Italy Associated Office: Studio Legale Grimaldi e Clifford Chance. Via Gesú, 3, 20121. Telephone: (39 2) 7600 8040. Fax: (39 2) 7600 4950.
Moscow, Russia Office: Ul. Sadovaya - Samotechnaya 24/27, 2nd Floor, 103051. Telephone: (7 501) 258 50 51; Satellite: (7 502) 221 3018/9. Fax: (7 501) 258 50 51; Satellite: (7 502) 221 3020.
New York, New York Office: Swiss Bank Tower, 10 East 50th Street, 10022. Telephone: (1 212) 750 1440. Fax: (1 212) 758 6625.
Paris, France Office: 112 avenue Kléber, BP 163 Trocadéro, 75770 Paris Cedex 16. Telephone: (33 1) 44 05 52 52. Fax: (33 1) 44 05 52 00.
Riyadh, Saudi Arabia Associated Office: The Law Firm of Salah Al-Hejailan. P.O. Box 1454, 11431. Telephone: (966 1) 479 2200. Fax: (966 1) 479 1717.
Rome, Italy Associated Office: Studio Legale Grimaldi e Clifford Chance. Viale G. Rossini 7, 00198. Telephone: (39 6) 807 2251. Fax: (39 6) 807 8201.
Shanghai, People's Republic of China Office: Suite 898, Shanghai Centre, 1376 Nanjing Xi Lu, 200040. Telephone: (86 21) 279 8461. Fax: (86 21) 279 8462.
Singapore Office: 16 Collyer Quay #31-00, 0104. Telephone: (65) 535 1855. Fax: (65) 535 6855.
Tokyo, Japan Office: 6th Floor, South Hill Nagatacho Building, 11-30 Nagatacho 1-chome, Chiyoda-ku, 100. Telephone: (81 3) 3581 4311. Fax: (81 3) 3593 0651.
Warsaw, Poland Office: Warsaw Corporate Centre, ul. Emilii Plater 28, 00-688. Telephone: (48 2) 630 3344. Fax: (48 2) 630 3355.

General and International Practice including Financial, Corporate, Commercial, International Trade and Construction.

RESIDENT MANAGER

KATHLEEN CHOUAI, (Not admitted in Bahrain). University of Pittsburgh (J.D., magna cum laude); Indiana University of Pennsylvania (B.A.).

MEMBERS OF FIRM

MARK SHIPMAN, (Not admitted in Bahrain). admitted, 1990, Solicitor, University of Reading (LL.B., Hons.).

(For the names of Partners resident in other offices, see Professional Biographies for those Offices)

HAYA RASHED AL KHALIFA LAW FIRM

HAWAR BUILDING 'A'- SUITE 201/204
DIPLOMATIC AREA
P.O. BOX 1188
MANAMA, BAHRAIN
Telephone: 537771
Telefax: 537117

HAYA RASHED AL KHALIFA, admitted, 1979, Bahrain. Education: University of Kuwait (LL.B., 1974); University of Alexandria, Egypt (Diploma in Civil Private Law, 1986); University of Ain Chams, Egypt (Diploma in Comparative Law, 1988). Former Counsel at the Ministry of State for Legal Affairs, Bahrain. Member Bahrain Bar Association (Ex Vice-President). **LANGUAGES:** Arabic, English and French. **PRACTICE AREAS:** Construction; Banking; Islamic Laws; International Commercial Arbitration.

MEMBERS OF FIRM

KAMAL ELDIN OSMAN ABDALLA, admitted, 1972, Khartoum, Sudan. Education: University of Khartoum (LL.B., 1972); International Finance Corporation/World Bank, Washington, D.C. (1978). Former Legal Counsel: Attorney General's Chamber, Sudan; Sudan Development

(This Listing Continued)

HAYA RASHED AL KHALIFA LAW FIRM, Manama—Continued

Corporation and Gulf Petro-Chemical Industries Company, Bahrain. *LANGUAGES:* Arabic and English. *PRACTICE AREAS:* Investment Laws; Construction Laws; International Commercial Arbitration.

LAMIYA MOHAMED SALEH AL SHAIKH, admitted, 1991, Bahrain. *Education:* Cairo University, Egypt (LL.B., 1990). admitted before the Courts of Bahtain and Practicing Bahraini Lawyer. *LANGUAGES:* Arabic, English and French.

MARIUM ISA AL KHALIFA, admitted, 1994, Bahrain. *Education:* University of Kuwait (LL.B., 1973). admitted before the Courts of Bahrain and Practicing Bahraini Lawyer. *LANGUAGES:* Arabic, English and French.

RASHED ABDULLA EBRAHIM, admitted, 1987, Bahrain. *Education:* University of Beirut (LL.B., 1986). *LANGUAGES:* Arabic and English.

NORTON ROSE

UNITAG HOUSE
GOVERNMENT AVENUE
P.O. BOX 20437
MANAMA, BAHRAIN
Telephone: +973 232224
Cable Address: "Norbah Bahrain"
Telex: NORBAH BN 9276
Fax: +973 259810

Other Offices: London, Brussels, Hong Kong, Moscow, Paris, Piraeus, Prague and Singapore.

FIRM PROFILE: Norton Rose is a leading City and International law firm with its principal office in the City of London. The firm provides a wide range of legal services primarily to the business and financial communities as well as to a number of sovereign governments and state organizations. We are known particularly for our corporate and debt finance, banking, company and commercial law, natural resources, insurance, property development, aerospace and maritime practices and wide-ranging expertise on tax matters. Norton Rose has a major litigation department handling all forms of commercial dispute resolution.

In Bahrain the firm specialises in assets finance; banking; corporate and commercial work; insurance; litigation and arbitration; project finance; shipping.

RESIDENT LAWYERS

DAVID N. HUDSON, admitted, 1981, England and Wales.

Languages: English, French and Spanish

(For Complete Biographical Data on all Personnel, see Professional Biographies at London, England).

HASSAN RADHI & ASSOCIATES

Established in 1974

SUITE 503, DIPLOMAT TOWER
DIPLOMATIC AREA
P.O. BOX 5366
MANAMA, BAHRAIN
Telephone: (0973) 535252
Telex: 9455 CBAHAR BN
Fax: (0973) 533358

Commercial, Banking and Civil Law.

FIRM PROFILE: General Practice in all Courts, including Court of Cassation, Consultancy and Opinion on all Bahraini Laws, Domestic and International Arbitration.

SENIOR PARTNERS

HASSAN ALI RADHI, born Sitra, Bahrain, March 21, 1947; admitted, 1974, Bahrain; 1983, Kuwait. *Education:* University of Mohamed V. Rabat, Morocco (LL.B.); New York University (Workshop of Foreign Lawyers, 1981). *Member:* Bahrain Bar Society (Ex-President). *LANGUAGES:* Arabic and English. *PRACTICE AREAS:* Commercial Law; Banking Law; Civil Law; Arbitration.

(This Listing Continued)

PARTNERS

JALILA SAYED AHMED, born Bahrain, 1963; admitted, 1987, Bahrain. *Education:* Universite de Franche-Comté (Licence in Law). *Member:* Bahrain Bar Society. *LANGUAGES:* Arabic, French and English. *PRACTICE AREAS:* Commercial Law; Labour Law; Civil Law.

ASSOCIATES

RENGASAMI MUTHU KRISHNAN, born Thanjavur, India, 1943. *Education:* Delhi University (M.A.; LL.B.); Madras University (M.Com.). *Member:* Bar Council of Delhi. *LANGUAGES:* English and Hindi. *PRACTICE AREAS:* Commercial Law; Banking Law; Arbitration.

SALMAN A. HASSAN AL ORAIBI, born Bahrain, 1957. *Education:* University of Beirut (licence in Law). *LANGUAGES:* Arabic and English. *PRACTICE AREAS:* Insurance Law; Labour Law; Commercial Law.

SAEED MOHAMMED S. AL HALWANI, born Imbaba, Egypt, 1955. *Education:* University of Cairo (Licence in Law). *Member:* Bar Association of Cairo. *LANGUAGES:* Arabic. *PRACTICE AREAS:* Civil Law; Insurance Law; Labour Law.

Languages: Arabic, English, French and Hindi.

SAYADI, TAQI & MOHAMED AHMED

Attorneys at Law & Legal Consultants

OFFICE 302-304, YATEEM CENTRE 2, 2ND FLOOR
ALKHALIFA AVENUE
P.O. BOX 1414
MANAMA, BAHRAIN
Telephone: 210212/213343
Facsimile: 213633/211392

Banking and Business Law, Corporate Law, Civil Law, Commercial and Marine Law, Insurance Law, Litigation and Arbitration.

MEMBERS

SALMAN ISA SAYADI, born Muharraq, Bahrain, 1952; admitted, 1978, Bahrain. *Education:* University of Cairo (LL.B., 1977). *Member:* Bahrain Bar Society. *LANGUAGES:* Arabic and English.

HUSSAIN ALI TAQI, born Bahrain, October 9, 1953; admitted, 1979, Bahrain. *Education:* Alexandria University (LL.B., 1979). *Member:* International Bar Association; Arab Lawyer's Union; Bahrain Bar Society. *LANGUAGES:* Arabic and English.

MOHAMED AHMED ABDULLA, born Bahrain, January 1, 1956; admitted, 1981, Bahrain. *Education:* Cairo University (LL.B., 1981). *Member:* Bahrain Bar Society; Arab Lawyer's Union. *LANGUAGES:* Arabic and English.

ASSOCIATES

EBRAHIM SALEH EBRAHIM, born Bahrain, 1953; admitted, 1979, Bahrain. *Education:* Kiev University (Master of Law, LL.M., 1979). *Member:* Bahrain Bar Society; Arab Lawyer's Union. *LANGUAGES:* Arabic, English, French and Russian.

SAMI ESSA SAYADI, born Bahrain, January 1, 1961; admitted, 1990, Bahrain. *Education:* Beirut Arabian College (LL.B., 1989). *Member:* Bahrain Bar Society. *LANGUAGES:* Arabic and English.

ABDUL RAHMAN MOHAMMED GHUNAIM, born Al Fayoom, Egypt, May 14, 1961; admitted, 1988, Cairo, Egypt. *Education:* Cairo University (LL.B., 1987). *Member:* Egyptian Bar Association; Arab Association for International Arbitration (Paris). *LANGUAGES:* Arabic.

MOHAMMED JAFFAR AL TARANJA, born Bahrain, 1961; admitted, 1993, Bahrain. *Education:* Beirut Arabian College (LL.B., 1992). *Member:* Bahrain Bar Society. *LANGUAGES:* Arabic.

LAW OFFICES OF AHMED ZAKI YAMANI

Established in 1979

P.O. BOX 342
MANAMA, BAHRAIN
Telephone: (973) 211-433/622
Telefax: (973) 210-373
Telex: 8991 YAMANI

Jeddah, Saudi Arabia Office: Shaker Building, P.O. Box 1351, Jeddah 21431. Telephones: (966-2) 6429550/ 6429551. Telefax: (966-2) 6437511. Telex: 605853 GANONI SJ.

Riyadh, Saudi Arabia Office: P.O. Box 7159, Riyadh 11462. Telephone: (966-1) 464-2144. Telefax: (966-1) 464-8718.

Corporate, Banking and Finance, Taxation, Investment and Joint Ventures, Intellectual Property, Aviation, Litigation, Arbitration, Government Affairs and Relations, Energy, Environmental, Construction, Insurance, Mining, Maritime and Transportation, Copyrights and Trademarks, Labor and Trade Relations.

SENIOR MEMBERS OF FIRM

OMER O. EL MARDI, born Sudan, 1944; admitted, 1968, Sudan. *Education:* University of Khartoum (LL.B., 1968). Deputy Undersecretary of the Minister of Justice, Sudan; Prosecutor General, Counsel for Contracts and International Agreements, Secretary of the National Law Reform Commission, 1976. Fellowships: United Nations Institute for Training and Research (UNITAR); The World Peace Through Law Center; The U.S.-African Youth Leadership Programme; The Sudan Bar Association. (Partner, Bahrain Office). *LANGUAGES:* Arabic and English. *PRACTICE AREAS:* Corporate Law; Agency Law; Banking and Finance; Insurance; Trusts and Estates; Arbitration and Litigation.

AHMED ZAKI YAMANI, born Mecca, Saudi Arabia, June 30, 1930. *Education:* Cairo University, Cairo, Egypt (License en Droit, 1952); Harvard and New York Universities (Graduate studies in Law). Founder of The Law Offices of Ahmed Zaki Yamani, Saudi Arabia's First Private Law Office, 1952. Formerly, Legal Advisor to the Saudi Council of Ministers, 1957. Cabinet Member as Minister of State, 1960 and later as the Minister of Petroleum and Mineral Resources, 1962-1987. First Secretary-General of the Organization of Petroleum Exporting Countries (OPEC), and is regarded as the Architect of many of the Kingdom's Modern Laws and Regulations. Chairman of the Centre for Global Energy Studies and the Al Furqan Islamic Heritage Foundation. *LANGUAGES:* Arabic, English and French. *PRACTICE AREAS:* Islamic Law; Energy; Government Affairs and Procedures.

ZAKI MUSTAFA, born Sudan, November 17, 1934; admitted, 1963, Sudan. *Education:* University of Khartoum (LL.B., 1959); London School of Economics (LL.M., 1961); University of London, London, England (Ph.D., 1969). Author: "The Legal System of the Sudan," Cairo, Egypt (Arabic), 1969; "The Common Law in Sudan," Oxford, England, 1977. Associate Professor, Contract and Commercial Law, Khartoum, 1961-1965. Visiting Lecturer, UCLA, 1964. Professor and Dean of Law, Contracts, Commercial and Corporate Law, Khartoum, 1965-1969. Professor and Dean, Ahamadu Bello University, Nigeria, 1969-1972. Visiting Professor, Haile Selassie I University, Addis Ababa, Ethiopia, 1972-1973, and Harvard Law School, 1989-1990. National Chairman, World Peace Through Law Center, 1964-1975. Advisor to the Supreme Council of State, Sudan, 1965-1969. President, Society of Law Teachers, Africa, 1965-1972. Member: Society of Public Teachers of Law, 1969; Law Reform Commission, Nigeria, 1970-1973; National Council for Higher Education, Sudan, 1975—. Chairman; Law Reform Commission, Sudan, 1973—; University Grants Commission, Sudan, 1975-1979. Attorney General, Minister of Justice, Sudan 1973-1975. Advisor on Law Revision and Law Reform to the President of Sudan, 1975-1979. (Managing Partner at Jeddah Office). *LANGUAGES:* Arabic, English and French. *PRACTICE AREAS:* Corporate Law; Contract Law; Commercial Law; Aviation; Insurance; Mining and Environmental Law.

(For Firm Profile and Biographical Data on other Personnel, see Professional Biographies at Jeddah and Riyadh, Saudi Arabia)

HATIM S. ZU'BI

(Al Mahmood and Zu'bi)

Established in 1971
BAB EL BAHRAIN BUILDING
SUITE NO. 1, 3RD FLOOR
P.O. BOX 502
MANAMA, BAHRAIN
Telephone: (0973) 251911; 251695; 258207
Cable Address: "Hatimzubi"
Facsimile: 23264 3

Amman, Jordan Associated Office: Ali Sharif Zu'bi & Sharif Ali Zu'bi, Astra Building, First Circle, Jabal Amman, P.O. Box 35267. Telephone: (962) 6.6642908; 648908; 644743. Telex: 21186 ASZUBI JO. Facsimile: (962) 6. 6634277. Cable Address: "INTLAWPRAC" Amman.

General and International Law Practice in the Arabian Gulf States and Jordan, including the right to appear before the Local Courts and Arbitration Tribunals. Regional and International Arbitration. Commercial, Corporate, Banking, Construction, Maritime, Labour Law, Trademark and Commercial Agencies.

HATIM S. ZU'BI, HON. G.B.E., admitted, 1950, England (Barrister at Law); 1954, Jordan; 1971, licensed Legal Consultant, Abu Dhabi and Saudi Arabia; Bahrain, licensed to practice in Association with Hamid Al Mahmood, Qatar and Muscat, Oman. *Education:* University College, London University (LL.B., Hons., 1949); Kings College, London School of Economics and Political Science; Lincoln's Inn, London. Advocate and Legal Advisor to Ministry of Finance, Jeddah and Dammam, Saudi Arabia, 1951-1954. Deputy General Manager and Director, Cairo Amman Bank, Jordan, 1955-1965. Minister of National Economy of Jordan, 1965-1969. Governor for Jordan at the International Bank for Reconstruction and Development, Washington, D.C., 1965-1969. *Member:* Jordan Bar; International Bar Association; ICC Jordan National Committee; Arab Society for Protection of Industrial Property. Fellow: Chartered Institute of Arbitrators, England (F.C.I. Arb.). Editorial Advisory Board: Int. Construction Law Review, London. *LANGUAGES:* Arabic, English and French. *PRACTICE AREAS:* Corporate; Banking; Commercial; Construction; International Arbitration.

PARTNER

HAMID AL-MAHMOOD LL.B. (Advocate). *LANGUAGES:* Arabic and English. *PRACTICE AREAS:* Litigation.

ASSOCIATES

QAYS H. ZU'BI B.A. (Econ.), M.A. Law (Cantab.). *LANGUAGES:* Arabic and English. *PRACTICE AREAS:* Corporate; Labour.

E. HUGH STOKES M.A. (Oxon), Solicitor of the Supreme Court of England and Wales. *LANGUAGES:* English. *PRACTICE AREAS:* Corporate; Banking; Maritime; Construction.

MA'AWIA AL NAYAL B.A., LL.B. (Khartoum), Member of the Sudan Bar. *LANGUAGES:* Arabic and English. *PRACTICE AREAS:* Litigation; Commercial; Banking; Labour.

WAFA AL ZAYANI LL.B. *LANGUAGES:* Arabic. *PRACTICE AREAS:* Litigation.

LEGAL SUPPORT PERSONNEL

NAGI AL SHAFIE LL.B.

BURKINA-FASO

DABIRE ET SORGHO

Avocats Associés

Established in 1975

01 BP 1026
OUAGADOUGOU 01, BURKINA-FASO
Telephone: (226) 30 46 93
Fax: (226) 30 48 30

Bobo-Dioulasso Office: 01 BP 1429 Bobo-Dioulasso, Burkina Faso. Telephone: (226) 98 20 27. Fax: (226) 30 48 30.

(This Listing Continued)

DABIRE ET SORGHO, Ouagadougou—Continued

International and General Business Law, Civil and International Law, Commercial Law, Press Law, Contracts.

MEMBERS OF FIRM

BERNARDIN DABIRE, born Danane (Côte d'Ivoire), May 20, 1947; admitted, 1975, Burkina - Faso. Education: Lycée Classique d'Abidjan (B.A.C., 1966); Université de Lyon (Licence en Droit, 1971); Institut Supérieur de Droit du Travail et de Sécurité Sociale de Lyon (D.E.S.S., 1971). Member: l'Union Interafricaine des Avocats; l'Association des Barreaux Francophones.

MARIE-ANTOINETTE SORGHO, born Burkina-Fasso, May 16, 1963; admitted, 1993, Burkina-Fasso. Education: Université de Ouagadougou-Burkina-Fasso, Maítrise en doit des Affaires (1985); Faculté de Droit et de Sciences Economiques de Tours, France, DESS en droit de Commerce International (1986).

Languages: French and English

CAMEROON

HALLE CHAMBERS

Barristers & Solicitors of the Supreme Court of Cameroon

Established in 1985

8 AVENUE DOUALA MANGA BELL
B.P. 4876 DOUALA, CAMEROON
Telephone: 42, 64, 79
Fax: 43, 26, 34

Specialists in: Banking and Finance, Investment, Natural Resources, Commercial and Corporate Law, Civil and Criminal Counselling, Conveyancing, Maritime Transactions/Law, Intellectual and Industrial Property Protection, Product Liability, Real Estate Transaction, Probate Matters, Assignments and Bailments, Labour and Trade Relations, Civil Aviation Law, Arbitration, Fiscal Legislation.

FIRM PROFILE: The firm was established in 1985 and offers a full range of legal services. The firm has become renowned over the years not only because of it's mastery and command in commercial and corporate matters but also for it's expeditiousness and bilingualism. Its' client base is Africa, Europe and the U.S.A.

MEMBERS OF FIRM

NICO. HALLE, born 1953; admitted, 1985, Cameroon. **LANGUAGES:** English and French. **PRACTICE AREAS:** Corporate Law; Finance Law; Arbitration; Civil Aviation Law; Bank Finance; Natural Resources; Real Estate; Commercial Law.

FOMUKONG ISABELLE, born 1965; admitted, 1993, Nigeria; 1994, Cameroon. **LANGUAGES:** English and French. **PRACTICE AREAS:** Maritime Law; Conveyancing; Bailments; Civil and Criminal Counselling.

NGU SIMON CHE, born 1961; admitted, 1991, Cameroon. **LANGUAGES:** English and French. **PRACTICE AREAS:** Commercial Law/-Transactions; Criminal Law and Counselling; Real Estate Transactions; Commercial and Corporate Law.

ABENG ROLANG DZE, born 1970; admitted, 1994, Cameroon. **LANGUAGES:** English and French. **PRACTICE AREAS:** Intellectual and Industrial Property Protection; Labour Law and Trade Relations; Product Liability; Civil Aviation Law and Arbitration.

LEGAL SUPPORT PERSONNEL

JURISTES

DZUDIE NICOLAS. LANGUAGES: French and English. **PRACTICE AREAS:** Tortious Suits; Research; Labour Law; Civil Suit Drafting; Attachments; Banking Finance; Real Estate Transactions.

KINYANG GEORGE. LANGUAGES: French and English. **PRACTICE AREAS:** Investment Law; Probate Law; Assignments and Bailments; Fiscal Legislation.

(This Listing Continued)

AKKUM CARLTON. LANGUAGES: French and English. **PRACTICE AREAS:** Fiscal Legislation; Real Estate Transactions; Intellectual and Industrial Property Protection.

NTETMEN IRÈNE. LANGUAGES: French and English. **PRACTICE AREAS:** Maritime Law; Conveyancing; Air Transport Law; Debt Recovery.

SECRETARIAT

NDI HELEN ASUMBU, Secretariat Management and Typist, Library Science and Filing. (Senior Secretary). **LANGUAGES:** English and French.

MARY ETONDE, Computer and Photocopying Management, Software and Data Safety. **LANGUAGES:** English and French.

REPRESENTATIVE CLIENTS: The National Railway Corporation (REGIFER-CAM); Cameroon Airlines; Cameroon Shipping Lines (CAMSHIP); The National Bus Services (SOTUC); The National Electricity Corporation (SONEL); The National Water Corporation (SNEC); The International Bank for Commerce and Industry (B.I.C.I.C.); The Rubber Corporation (HEVECAM); The National Palm Oil Corporation (SOCAPALM); DEL MONTE International Cameroon.

CABINET
CELESTIN KENGOUM

AMACAM'S BUILDING, 3RD FLOOR
83 RUE BOUE DE LAPEYRERE - AKWA
P.O. BOX 12 724
DOUALA, CAMEROON
Telephone: (237) 42-05-61
Fax: (237) 42-50-22
Telex: 6058 BUDDCAM

Civil Litigation, Commercial Law, Joint Ventures, Maritime Law, Insurance Law, Labour Law, Debt recovery.

FIRM PROFILE: Cabinet Kengoum was founded in 1990 as a general practice. The firm is a member of Cameroon Bar Association. The owner of the firm is a member of the International Association of Young Lawyers and several Law Associations.

PARTNER

CÉLESTIN KENGOUM, born 1963; admitted, 1987, Cameroon. Education: University of Yaounde, Cameroon (Master Degree). Author: "Les Entreprises Publiques au Cameroun" (1986); "Comprendre le Nouveau Code du Travail ou l'autopsie de la loi no 92-007 du 10 Aout 1992" (1993); "Creer des Opportunites d'Affaires et de Joint Ventures en Arabie Saoudite" (1993). Many articles written on diverses areas. **LANGUAGES:** French and English. **PRACTICE AREAS:** Commercial Law; Debt Recovery; Civil Litigation; Maritime Law.

COUNSEL

PASCAL POUNGA, born 1959; (admission pending). Education: University of Yaounde, Cameroon (LL.B.). **LANGUAGES:** French and English. **PRACTICE AREAS:** Labour Law; Insurance Law.

CÔTE D'IVOIRE

SCPA ADJE-ASSI-METAN

Established in 1985

RESIDENCE LE TREFLE
59, RUE DES SAMBAS (INDENIE)
ABIDJAN, CÔTE D' IVOIRE
Telephone: (225) 21 53 43 / 22 82 56 / 22 72 48
Fax: (225) 21 59 45
(This Listing Continued)

Mailing Address: 01 B.P. 6568 Abidjan 01 Cote d'Ivoire (Ivory Coast)

Firm Engaged in Business and Corporate Law, Taxation and Banking Law, Transportation and Insurance Law, Real Estate and Labor Law practice. Entitled to plead before the Ivorian courts.

PARTNERS

LUC KACOU ADJE, admitted, 1982, Ivory Coast. *Education:* University of Abidjan, Faculty of Law (Maîtrise, 1980). *Member:* Ivorian Young Lawyers Association (President); West African Young Lawyers Association (President). *LANGUAGES:* French and English. *PRACTICE AREAS:* Transport; Insurance; Real Estate Law.

EMMANUEL ASSI, admitted, 1980, Ivory Coast. *Education:* University of Montpellier, France, Faculty of Law (Maîtrise, 1978; DEA in Private Law, 1979; DEA in Political Studies, 1979; SJD in Private Law, 1982. *LANGUAGES:* French and English. *PRACTICE AREAS:* Financial Law; Taxation; Banking Law.

LOUIS AMANY METAN, admitted, 1983, Ivory Coast. *Education:* University of Paris II (Panyhron-Sorbonne), France, Faculty of Law (Maîtrise, 1980; DEA in Private Law, with honors, 1981). *Member:* Ivory Coast Bar Association (Permanent Secretary); Commission for the Revision of Lawyers' Professional Regulation. *LANGUAGES:* French and English. *PRACTICE AREAS:* Corporation; Business Law; Labor Law.

ASSOCIATES

KIZITO MICHEL BRIZOUA-BI, admitted, 1992, Ivory Coast. *Education:* University of Abidjan, Faculty of Law (Maîtrise, 1988); University of Toulouse I, France (DEA in Business Law, 1989). *Member:* Ivorian Young Lawyers Association. *LANGUAGES:* French and English.

KETTY NIABA-YAPOBI, admitted, 1993, Ivory Coast. *Education:* University of Abidjan, Faculty of Law (Maîtrise, with honors, 1986). *Member:* Ivorian Young Lawyers Association. *LANGUAGES:* French and English.

ADELE M'BAIPOR, admitted, 1993, Ivory Coast. *Education:* University of Abidjan, Faculty of Law (Maîtrise, 1980); DEA in Private Law, 1992). *Member:* Ivorian Young Lawyers Association. *LANGUAGES:* French And English.

OF COUNSEL

MARIE-LYDIE MOULO, born Abengourou, Ivory Coast, August, 1966. *Education:* University of Abidjan, Faculty of Law (Maîtrise, 1989); The George Washington, National Law Center, Washington, D.C. USA (LL.M., option: International and Comparative Law, 1993). *LANGUAGES:* French, English and Spanish.

JEAN-PIERRE ELISHA

10TH FLOOR, SUITE 102
EDEN
44 AVENUE LAMBLIN 04 BP 1687
ABIDJAN, CÔTE D' IVOIRE
Telephone: (225) 21-18-80 / 33-18-70
Telecopier: (225) 21-18-70

Mailing Address: P.O. Box 04 B.P 1687, Abidjan, 04 Cote D'Ivoire

International Banking and Business Law, Transport, Corporate, Labor Law, Commercial and Civil Litigation, Intellectual Property Rights. Entitled to appear before the Courts in: Benin, Burkina Faso, Niger, Togo.

FIRM PROFILE: The firm was established in 1993 and offers a full range of legal services, known for its Commercial and Banking Practice. The client base is North American and European in scope.

JEAN-PIERRE ELISHA, born Porto-Novo, Benin, August 29, 1948; admitted, 1986, Abidjan, Côte d'Ivoire. *Education:* Poitiers Law School (Master 1975); Georgetown University Law School (LL.M., 1991). *LANGUAGES:* French and English.

ASSOCIATE

LYDIE GOLLI, born Bouaké, Côte d'Ivoire, March 25, 1969; admitted, 1994, Abidjan. *Education:* University of Abidjan (Judicial Law, 1991). *LANGUAGES:* French. *PRACTICE AREAS:* Civil Litigation; Commercial Litigation; Labor Law.

(This Listing Continued)

LEGAL SUPPORT PERSONNEL

BÉATRICE NEMIN, born Abidjan, April, 1963. *Education:* University of Reims France (Private Law, 1990). Legal Research, Drafting, Client Correspondence.

N'GOAN, DIE-KACOU & ASSOCIES

SOCIÉTÉ D'AVOCATS
Established in 1981
IMMEUBLE CCIA (WORLD TRADE CENTER)
01 BP 5797 ABIDJAN, CÔTE D' IVOIRE
Telephone: (225) 21.44.24; 21.41.08
Fax: (225) 21.63.08

Authorized to Plead in the Courts of the Côte d'Ivoire, General Ivorian and International Law, Privatization, Contract Negotiation, Public Debt Restructuring, Corporations, Legislation, Stock Exchange and Securities, International Banking, Tax, Intellectual Property and Computer Law, Maritime Law and Air Law, Employment Law.
Counsel to the Republic of Côte d'Ivoire and Counsel to the Committee on Privatization and Restructuring of the Public Sector.

GEORGES N'GOAN, born Bongouanou, Côte d'Ivoire, April 24, 1948; admitted, 1979, Côte d'Ivoire. *Education:* University of Abidjan Law School (Licence, 1974); University of Grenoble, France Law School (Maîtrise, 1975); University of Paris II Law School (Certificat d'Aptitude à la Profession d'Avocat, 1978); University of Paris I (D.E.A. in Political Science, 1978). *LANGUAGES:* French and English.

FRANCOIS DIE-KACOU, born Bamako, Mali, June 19, 1948; admitted, 1979, Côte d'Ivoire. *Education:* University of Abidjan Law School (Licence, 1972; Certificat d'Aptitude à la Profession d'Avocat, 1978); Higher Institute of Foreign Commerce of Paris (Diplôme in Finance, 1974). *LANGUAGES:* French and English.

CÉSAR ASMAN, born Bouaké, Côte d'Ivoire, September 26, 1956; admitted, 1985, Côte d'Ivoire. *Education:* University of Abidjan Law School (Licence, 1978; Maîtrise, 1979; Certificat d'Aptitude à la Profession d'Avocat, 1983); University of Aix-Marseille III Law School (D.E.S.S. in International Business Law, 1980). *LANGUAGES:* French and English.

OF COUNSEL

CHERYL PACKWOOD, born New York, New York, June 1, 1961; admitted, 1988, New York; 1990, District of Columbia (Not admitted in Côte d' Ivoire). *Education:* Yale University (B.A., cum laude, 1983); Harvard University (J.D., 1987). Associate, Shearman & Sterling, New York, 1987-1990. Co-Author: United States Chapter of *Handbook on Lawyers' Confidentiality* , Committee on Lawyers' Confidentiality, International Bar Association, 1989. Ivory Coast: Economic Revitalization, International Financial Law Review, January 1991. *LANGUAGES:* English, French and Spanish.

ASSOCIATES

MARC LEBOUATH CAYSKAND, born Bouaké, Côte d'Ivoire, July 6, 1956; admitted, 1989, Côte d'Ivoire. *Education:* University of Abidjan Law School (Licence, 1981; Maîtrise, 1982; Certificat d'Aptitude à la Profession d'Avocat, 1989).

THENA MARIE-IRENE NIAMKEY, born Abidjan, Côte d'Ivoire, September 10, 1961; admitted, 1989, Côte d'Ivoire. *Education:* University of Paris XI (Sceaux) Law School (Licence, 1984; Maîtrise, 1985; Maîtrise in Business Law, 1986); Professional Training Center for the Paris Bar (Certificat d'Aptitude à la Profession d'Avocat, 1988).

ADIARATOU KONE, born Abidjan, Côte, d'Ivoire, May 4, 1958; admitted, 1990, Côte d'Ivoire. *Education:* University of Abidjan Law School (Licence, 1982; Maîtrise, 1983; Certificat d'Aptitude à la Profession d'Avocat, 1990).

(This Listing Continued)

PAULE FOLQUET-DIALLO, born Agboville, Côte d'Ivoire, June 6, 1957; admitted, 1991, Côte d'Ivoire. *Education:* University of Paris I Law School (Licence in Business Law, 1984); University of Paris III (D.E.A. in English, Honors, 1984); University of Abidjan Law School (Maîtrise in Business Law, 1985; Certificat d'Aptitude à la Profession d'Avocat, 1990). *LANGUAGES:* English and French.

EGYPT

ELDIB & PARTNERS

Advocates

32, BOULEVARD SAAD ZAGHLOUL

P.O. BOX 152

ALEXANDRIA, EGYPT

Telephone: 03-4820111; 03-4820115; 03-4820161; 03-4820178; 03-4820216

Cable Address: "AICOSS, Alexandria"

Telex: 54046 ELDIB UN; 54696 Eldib UN

Fax: 03-4821900

Port Said, Egypt Office: Simonini Building, Abdel Moneim and Al Gomhouria Street, P.O. Box 920. Telephone: 066-239779; 066-239781. Telex: 63057 Eldib UN. Fax: 066-239760.

Suez, Egypt Office: 6, Imam El Emam El Leithy Street, Port Tewfik. Telephone: 062-221570. Telex: 66116 Eldib UN. Fax: 062-228930.

Cairo, Egypt Office: 78, Al Goumhouria Street. Telephone: 02-912983. Fax: 02-924564.

Maritime, Admiralty, Administration, Banking, Competition, Constitutional, Corporate, Customs and Excise, Foreign Investments, International Contracts, Litigation, Oil and Mining, Trade Regulations and Transportation Law. General Practice. Intellectual Property, Patents, Copyright Law. Industrial Models, Licensing, Patent Litigation, Trademark Litigation, Trademark Prosecution, Transfer of Technology, Taxation, Capital Taxation and Corporate Taxation.

SENIOR PARTNER

MOUFID EL DIB, born Cairo, Egypt, 1929; admitted, 1952, Egypt; 1965, Cassation Court. *Education:* Faculty of Law, University of Cairo (LL.B., 1952). Honorary Consul, of Chile in Alexandria and of Belgium in Alexandria. *Member:* Egyptian Bar Association; International Bar Association (IBA); International Law Association (ILA); Association Internationale Pour la Protection de la Propriete Industrielle (AIPPI); United States Trademark Association (USTA); Stanford Research Institute (SRI; Associate Member of Conference Board); Asia-Pacific Lawyers Association; Egyptian Maritime Society (Board Member); Society D'Economie Politique, de Statistique et de Legislation; Law of the Sea Institute; Egyptian-American Friendship Association; Egyptian-Japanese Friendship Association; Arab Society for the Protection of Industrial Property (ASPIP); Marques (Association of European Trade Mark Proprietors); International Law Association (Honorary Secretary, Egypt Branch). *LANGUAGES:* Arabic, English and French.

PARTNERS

SAYED ALLAM, born Alexandria, Egypt, 1926; admitted, 1949, Egypt; 1964, Cassation Court and Supreme Administrative Court. *Education:* Faculty of Law, University of Alexandria (LL.B., 1949). *Member:* Egyptian Bar Association. *LANGUAGES:* Arabic, English and French.

HISHAM EL DIB, born Alexandria, Egypt, 1959; admitted, 1983, Egypt; 1990, Court of Appeal. *Education:* Faculty of Law, University of Alexandria (LL.B., 1983). *Member:* Egyptian Bar Association; International Law Association (ILA); International Bar Association (IBA); Arab Society for the Protection of Industrial Property (ASPIP). *LANGUAGES:* Arabic and English.

AMR EL DIB, born Alexandria, Egypt, 1963; admitted, 1984, Egypt; 1990, Court of Appeal. *Education:* Faculty of Law, University of Alexandria (LL.B., 1984). *Member:* Egyptian Bar Association; International Law Association (ILA); International Bar Association (IBA); Arab Society for the Protection of Industrial Property (ASPIP). *LANGUAGES:* Arabic and English.

(This Listing Continued)

CONSULTANTS

MAHMOUD ABDEL AZIZ, born Alexandria, Egypt, 1928; admitted, 1949, Egypt; 1962, Cassation Court. *Education:* Faculty of Law, University of Alexandria (LL.B., 1948). *Member:* Egyptian Bar Association. *LANGUAGES:* Arabic and English.

ABDEL SAMIE AWAD, born El Mansoura, Egypt, 1923; admitted, 1948, Egypt; 1969, Cassation Court. *Education:* Faculty of Law, University of Alexandria (LL.B., 1948). *Member:* Egyptian Bar Association. *LANGUAGES:* Arabic, English and French.

SENIOR ASSOCIATES

ASHRAF EL SWEFY, born Alexandria, Egypt, 1952; admitted, 1982, Courts of Appeal; 1992, Court of Cassation. *Education:* Faculty of Law, University of Alexandria (LL.B., 1975). *Member:* Egyptian Bar Association; Egyptian Maritime Society. *LANGUAGES:* Arabic and English.

AHMED MAMDOUH EL TOUKHI, born Mansoura, Egypt, 1943; admitted, 1968, Courts of Appeal, Egypt; 1984, Court of Cassation. *Education:* Faculty of Law, University of Alexandria (LL.B., 1968). *Member:* Egyptian Bar Association. *LANGUAGES:* Arabic and English.

ASSOCIATES

AHDY EL SAHN, born Alexandria, Egypt, 1952; admitted, 1982, Courts of Appeal, Egypt; 1992, Court of Cassation. *Education:* Faculty of Law, University of Alexandria (LL.B., 1976). *Member:* Egyptian Bar Association. *LANGUAGES:* Arabic, English and French.

AKRAM ADHAM EL NAKEEB, born Alexandria, Egypt, 1961; admitted, 1983, Egypt; 1990, High Court of Appeal and The High Administrative Court. *Education:* Faculty of Law, University of Alexandria (LL.B., 1983). *Member:* Egyptian Bar Association. *LANGUAGES:* Arabic and English.

MADIH KAMAL, born Zagazig, Egypt, 1939; admitted, 1969, Egypt; 1979, Court of Cassation. *Education:* Faculty of Law, University of Alexandria (LL.B., 1964). *Member:* Egyptian Bar Association. *LANGUAGES:* Arabic and English.

SAID WASFY, born Alexandria, Egypt, 1954; admitted, 1977, Egypt; 1983, Court of Appeal. *Education:* Faculty of Law, University of Alexandria (LL.B., 1976). *Member:* Egyptian Bar Association; Egyptian Maritime Society. *LANGUAGES:* Arabic and English.

HAMDY MADKOUR, born Alexandria, Egypt, 1953; admitted, 1977, Courts of Appeal, Egypt; 1983, Court of Cassation. *Education:* Faculty of Law, University of Alexandria (LL.B., 1976). *Member:* Egyptian Bar Association. *LANGUAGES:* Arabic and English.

MAGDY SAAD, born Alexandria, Egypt, 1960; admitted, 1982, Egypt; 1990, High Court of Appeal. *Education:* Faculty of Law, University of Alexandria (LL.B., 1981). *Member:* Egyptian Bar Association. *LANGUAGES:* Arabic and English.

HASSAN KHASHAB, born Alexandria, Egypt, 1960; admitted, 1983, Egypt. *Education:* Faculty of Law, University of Alexandria (LL.B., 1982). *Member:* Egyptian Bar Association. *LANGUAGES:* Arabic and English.

MARIE BESTAVROS, born Alexandria, Egypt, 1962; admitted, 1984, Egypt; 1992, High Court of Appeal. *Education:* Faculty of Law, University of Alexandria (LL.B., 1984). *Member:* Egyptian Bar Association. *LANGUAGES:* Arabic, English and French.

ABDEL HAMID HEIDAR FAHMY, born Alexandria, Egypt, 1960; admitted, 1985, Egypt; 1992, High Court of Appeal. *Education:* Faculty of Law, University of Alexandria (LL.B., 1984). *Member:* Egyptian Bar Association. *LANGUAGES:* Arabic, French, English, Greek, Italian and Spanish.

BADIE SAMY GUIRGUIS, born Alexandria, Egypt, 1958; admitted, 1988, Egypt. *Education:* Faculty of Law, University of Alexandria (LL.B., 1988). *Member:* Egyptian Bar Association. *LANGUAGES:* Arabic, English and French.

MAHMOUD BELAL, born Alexandria, Egypt, 1961; admitted, 1988, Egypt. *Education:* Faculty of Law, University of Alexandria (LL.B., 1985). *Member:* Egyptian Bar Association. *LANGUAGES:* Arabic and English.

REPRESENTATIVE CLIENTS AND REFERENCES: Citibank of New York; Bank of America; Lloyds Bank; Gulfstream Resources (Canada); Consolidated Petroleum Co.; Coca Cola Company; BASF; Warner & Lambert; Colgate Palmolive; Shell International; Squibb Corporation; Amoco.

BAKER & McKENZIE

TWENTIETH FLOOR
56 GAMYAT EL DOWAL EL ARABEYA STREET
MOHANDESSIN, GIZA
CAIRO, EGYPT
Telephone: 360-0071; 360-0072; 360-9571; 360-9572
Intn'l Dialing: (20-2) 360-0071; 360-0072; 360-9571; 360-9572
Telex: 21847
Answer Back: 21847 ABOGA UN
Facsimile: (20-2) 360-0073

Associated Offices of Baker & McKenzie in: Almaty, Amsterdam, Bangkok, Barcelona, Beijing, Berlin, Bogotá, Brasília, Brussels, Budapest, Buenos Aires, Caracas, Chicago, Dallas, Frankfurt, Geneva, Hanoi, Ho Chi Minh City, Hong Kong, Juárez, Kiev, London, Madrid, Manila, Melbourne, México City, Miami, Milan, Monterrey, Moscow, New York, Palo Alto, Paris, Prague, Rio de Janeiro, Riyadh, Rome, St. Petersburg, San Diego, San Francisco, São Paulo, Singapore, Stockholm, Sydney, Taipei, Tijuana, Tokyo, Toronto, Valencia, Warsaw, Washington, D.C. and Zürich.
Correspondent Law Firm: Hadiputranto, Hadinoto & Partners, Jakarta.

PARTNERS

SAMIR M. HAMZA, born Alexandria, Egypt, November 9, 1938; admitted, 1961, Egypt. Education: Faculty of Law, Cairo University (LL.B., 1961). Member: Egyptian Bar Association; The Egyptian Society of International Law. LANGUAGES: Arabic and English.

M. TAHER HELMY, born Egypt, December 14, 1949; admitted, 1975, Illinois, U.S.A.; 1977, Egypt; 1979, U.S. Supreme Court and Saudi Arabia. Education: St. Louis University Law School (J.D., 1974). Member: Illinois State and American Bar Associations; Egyptian Bar; Saudi Arabian Bar. LANGUAGES: Arabic, English and French.

LOCAL PARTNER

MOHAMMAD B. SAMIH TALAAT, born Giza, Egypt, January 10, 1957; admitted, 1978, Egypt. Education: Faculty of Law, Cairo University (License en Droit, 1978); Chicago-Kent College of Law (LL.M., 1983). Member: Egyptian Bar; American Bar Association (Associated Member); The Egyptian Association of International Law; The Egyptian Association of Economical and Political Studies. LANGUAGES: Arabic and English.

ASSOCIATES

KARIM ALI AZMI, born Alexandria, Egypt, September 9, 1967; admitted, 1990, Egypt. Education: Alexandria University (LL.B., 1989); Cairo University/Institut fr Droit des Affaires Internationales (LL.M., 1992). Member: Egyptian Society of International Law. LANGUAGES: Arabic, English and French.

HATEM SAYED BADR, born Cairo, Egypt, October 17, 1963; admitted, 1987, Kuwait (Not admitted in Egypt). Education: Kuwait University Law School (LL.B., 1987); Fordham University Law School (LL.M., 1992). LANGUAGES: Arabic and English.

SHERIF ALI KHALIL EL ATFY, born The Hague, Netherlands, February 11, 1965; admitted, 1990, Egypt. Education: University of Cairo (LL.B., 1988); University of Hull (England) (LL.M., 1992). Member: Egyptian Bar Association; International Law Association. LANGUAGES: Arabic, English and Dutch.

MOHAMED ADEL GHANNAM, born Cairo, Egypt, March 7, 1963; admitted, 1985, Egypt. Education: Faculty of Law, Cairo University (LL.B., 1985); Harvard Law School (LL.M., 1988). Phi Alpha Delta. Assistant District Attorney, Public Prosecutor's Office, Ministry of Justice, 1987-1988. Member: Egyptian Bar Association; The Egyptian Society of International Law; The Judges Association in Cairo; The Law and Economic Institution. LANGUAGES: Arabic and English.

MOHAMED ADEL NOUR, born Cairo, Egypt, December 6, 1961; admitted, 1983, Egypt. Education: Foothill College, California (Summer Courses in Business Law, 1981); Faculty of Law, Cairo University (LL.B., 1983; LL.M., 1986). Member: Egyptian Society of International Law; Egyptian Society of Political Economy, Statistics and Legislation; Egyptian American Friendship Society. LANGUAGES: Arabic, English and French.

ELGHATIT LAW FIRM

Established in 1932
36, MANSOUR MUHAMMAD STREET, ZAMALEK
CAIRO, EGYPT
Telephone: (202) 3406015, 3407367
Telex: 21439 GHLF UN
Telefax: (202) 3410706
Cable Address: "Ghatlaw"

European Office: ElGhatit Associates, c/o Von Erlach & Partner, P.O. Box 4088, Dreikonigstrasse 7, 8022 Zurich, Switzerland. Telephone: 01-2832111. Fax: 01-2020707.

International Arbitration, Litigation and Consultation in the field of International Economic Financial Law and Transactions, Capital Market and Privatization, International negotiation of Financing and Debts, Banking and Taxation, International Development, Transfer of Technology and Construction Law.

FIRM PROFILE: First established in 1932 by the late Muhammad Aly Elghatit.

MEMBERS OF FIRM

PROF. DR. ALY H. ELGHATIT, born Cairo; admitted, 1961, Egypt. Education: Cairo University (LL.B., 1961; LL.M., 1964); University of California at Berkeley (LL.M., Juris Doctor, 1972). International Arbitrator. "Specialist of Transnational and Comparative Economic Law, adjunct Professor at Ain Shams University Law School and Solicitor/Barrister of the Egyptian Supreme Courts." 1976—. Founding Member and C0-Chairman of the Mediterranean and Middle East Institute of Arbitration (Cyprus). Vice-President, Egyptian Society of International Law (Cairo). Member, Board of Directors, International Commission of Arbitration, (Paris). Co-Editor, Arbitration Quarterly, (Milan & Cairo). Special Consultant to the Egyptian Parliament on Economic and Fiscal Legislation, 1977-1981. Rapporteur for the Companies Act of 1981; Rapporteur for the Tax Law of 1981. International and U.S. Counsel, IBM, (New York) and IBM Europe, (Paris), 1972-1977. Editor, International Contract Manual, Federal Publication, Inc., 1983 (New York). Comparative Law Specialist, University of California at Berkeley, 1969-1972. Senior Deputy Attorney General, Cairo, 1967-1968. Member: The Association of the Bar of the City of New York; British Institute of International and Comparative Law (London); The Institute of International Business Law and Practice (Paris); Egyptian Society of Economics and Legislation (Cairo); International Law Association (London); American Society of International Law; American Society for the Study of Comparative Law (Berkeley); International Academy of Trial Lawyers; International Bar Association, London; (Formerly Member, Standing Committee on Arab Comparative and Sharia Law; Regional Representative for Arab Countries to IBA Business Law Section; Arab Countries Regional Representative to IBA Committee on International Construction Law). LANGUAGES: Arabic, English and French.

MOHAMED DAWOUD, born Cairo, Egypt; admitted, 1942, Egypt. Education: Cairo University (LL.B., 1942). Former Egypt's Solicitor General. LANGUAGES: Arabic and French.

IBRAHIM M. EL KADY, born Cairo, Egypt; admitted, 1959, Egypt. Education: Faculte de Droit, Paris, France (Licencie en Droit, 1951); Cairo University (LL.M., 1958-1959) Private and Public Law. Member: Egyptian Society of International Law (Cairo); Egyptian Society of Economics and Legislation (Cairo). Legal Advisor, Civil Aviation Ministry, 1951-1975. LANGUAGES: Arabic, French and English.

AHMED SHAKER, born Cairo, Egypt; admitted, 1956, Egypt. Education: Cairo University (LL.B., 1956; LL.M., 1961). Legal Adviser, 1956-1968 and Member of the State Council, 1958-1964, The Land Bank of Egypt. LANGUAGES: Arabic and English.

MRS. SHAHINAZ ROSTOM, born Cairo, Egypt; admitted, 1964, Egypt. Education: Cairo University (LL.B., 1964). Legal Adviser, General Organization for Social Securities, 1964-1978. LANGUAGES: Arabic, English and French.

MRS. FARIDA TEWFIK, born Cairo, Egypt; admitted, 1988, Egypt. Education: Alexandria University (LL.B., 1976). LANGUAGES: Arabic, French and English.

SABER ISMAIL SOLIMAN, born Cairo, Egypt; admitted, 1986, Egypt. Education: Ein Shams University (LL.B., 1985). LANGUAGES: Arabic and English.

(This Listing Continued)

ELGHATIT LAW FIRM, Cairo—Continued

LAMYAA ALY ELGHATIT, born Cairo, Egypt; admitted, 1988, Egypt. *Education:* Cairo University (LL.B., 1988). *LANGUAGES:* Arabic, English and French.

MOHAMED ABDEL RAOUF ALI, born Giza, Egypt; admitted, 1992, Egypt. *Education:* Cairo University (LL.B., 1991). *LANGUAGES:* Arabic, English and French.

OMNIA ELHEFNY, born Cairo, Egypt; admitted, 1990, Egypt. *Education:* Ein Shams University (LL.B., 1990). *LANGUAGES:* Arabic and English.

Languages: Arabic, English and French.

REPRESENTATIVE CLIENTS: IBM World Trade Corp. (USA and Europe); General Electric Co. (USA and England); Northrop Corp. (USA); Universal Instruments (USA); British Aerospace (England); Owens Illinois (USA and Switzerland); Thompson CSF (France); Trafalgar Group (England); Higgs and Hill (England); Mitsui, Sumitomo, Mazda, NEC (Japan); Sadelmi (Italy and New York); Raymond Corporate Group (USA and England); MISROOB (Egypt); Ismailia Misr Poultry Company (Egypt).

FOX & GIBBONS

Solicitors

Established in 1964

126 MOHEI EL DIN ABUL EZZ STREET

9TH FLOOR

MOHANDISEEN, GIZA

CAIRO, EGYPT

Telephone: (202) 3485955

Fax: (202) 3492210

London, England Office: 2 Old Burlington Street, W1X 2QA. Telephone: (44-171) 439 8271. Telex: 267108. Telefax: (44-171) 734 8843.

Abu Dhabi, United Arab Emirates Office: Kudsi Fox & Gibbons Office: P.O. Box 46010. Telephone: (9712) 322858. Fax: (9712) 331586.

Dubai, United Arab Emirates Office: P.O. Box 1756. Telephone: (9714) 310220. Fax: (9714) 310201. Telex: 45614 GBLAW EM.

Fujairah, United Arab Emirates Office: P.O. Box 701. Telephone: (971 9) 229390. Fax: (971 9) 226470.

Kuwait Associated Office: P.O. Box 26473, Safat, 13125 Safat. Telephone: (965) 2462323/2462525/2462929. Fax: (965) 242 5830. Telex: 30844 ZINA KT.

Ruwi, Oman Office: P.O. Box 3552, Postal Code 112. Telephone: (968) 564346. Fax: (968) 564395. Telex: 5630 GIBLAW ON.

Gibraltar Office: P.O. Box 246. Telephone: (350) 77750. Fax: (350) 77800.

Yemen Associated Office: P.O. Box 148, Crater, Aden. Telephone: (9672) 255305/253824. Fax: (9672) 255305/255117.

Lebanon Associated Office: Saba K. Zreik Law Offices. Autostrade Dora, Cite Dora 3 Building, 10th Floor, P.O.Box 90-710, Beirut, Lebanon. Telephone: (961 1) 881322. Fax: (961 1) 881387. Telex: 42949 MANAL LE.

Advice and assistance on all aspects of doing business in Egypt. Advice on selection of appropriate legal structures. Handling all Administrative procedures. General legal consulting and business planning. International investment, Trade and joint ventures, Commercial contract drafting, negotiation and interpretation.

Foreign Investment, Banking, Privatisations, Shipping, Construction, Taxation, Labour and Social Insurance, Oil & Gas, Patents and Trademarks, Litigation, Arbitration, Licensing, Import and Export, Customs, Foreign Exchange and Property.

MANAGING PARTNER

Paul Gibbs (London Office)

David Drake (Resident Manager)

LEGAL SUPPORT PERSONNEL

Safaa El Din El Oteifi

(For a list of other Personnel, see Biographical Cards at London, England, Dubai, Fujairah and Abu Dhabi, United Arab Emirates, Ruwi, Sultanate of Oman, Kuwait, Gibraltar, Lebanon and Yemen)

AF8B

HASHEM, IBRAHIM & TAWFIK

Established in 1953

23, KASR EL-NIL STREET

CAIRO, EGYPT

Telephone: (202) 3933766 (4 Lines); 3933827; 3933948; 3933974

Cable Address: "Zhatt", Cairo

Telex: 92423 ZH

Fax: (202) 3933585

Arbitration, Banking Law, Business Law, Company Law, Corporate Law, Distributionship and Agency Law, Entertainment and the Arts, Finance, Foreign Investments, Franchises & Franchising, International Contracts, International Private Law, Labour & Employment, Leases, Litigation, Natural Resources, Products Liability, Property, Resorts and Leisure.

PARTNERS OF FIRM

DR. ZAKI HASHEM, born Cairo, Egypt, February 3, 1922; admitted, 1942, Egypt; 1956, Supreme Court of Egypt. *Education:* Harvard University (M.A., 1947; Ph.D., 1950); Cairo University (LL.B.). Formerly, Minister of Tourism, Government of Egypt, 1972-1973. Member, Egyptian Council of State, 1946. Deputy Legal Counsellor, Ministry of Foreign Affairs and of Commerce and Industry, 1950-1954. Member, The National Economic Council of Egypt. *Member:* The Bar Association of Egypt; American Bar Association (International Associate); Egyptian Society of International Law (President). *LANGUAGES:* Arabic, English and French.

MOHAMED MAHMOUD IBRAHIM, born Cairo, Egypt, February 22, 1923; admitted, 1946, Egypt; 1966, Supreme Court of Egypt. *Education:* Cairo University (LL.B., 1946). Head of Legal Department, Bank of Egypt, 1955. *Member:* The Bar Association of Egypt; International Law Society (Egypt). *LANGUAGES:* Arabic, English and French.

OSAMA TAWFIK HAFEZ, born Cairo, Egypt, June 21, 1935; admitted, 1956, Egypt; 1969, Supreme Court of Egypt. *Education:* Cairo University (LL.B., 1956). Lecturer, American University in Cairo, 1987—. *Member:* The Bar Association of Egypt; International Law Society (Egypt); Egyptian American Friendship Association (Secretary General, 1985—). *LANGUAGES:* Arabic, English and French.

ASSOCIATES

HEND EL BAKLY, (MRS.), born Alexandria, Egypt, 1931; admitted, 1978, Supreme Court of Egypt. *Education:* Ain Shams University (LL.B., 1956). Formerly legal advisor to the Egyptian Iron & Steel Company. *Member:* The Bar Association of Egypt. *LANGUAGES:* Arabic, English and French.

MOHAMED ABDEL HAMID, born Cairo, Egypt, 1939; admitted, 1968, Supreme Court of Egypt. *Education:* Cairo University (LL.M., 1971). Formerly Deputy Legal Advisor, Ministry of Industry and Petroleum and Ministry of Electricity. *LANGUAGES:* Arabic and English.

YOUSSEF ABOU ZEID, born Cairo, Egypt, 1953; admitted, 1978, Courts of Appeal. *Education:* Cairo University (LL.B., 1975). *LANGUAGES:* Arabic and English.

SAMEH KHODEIR, born Kafr El Zayat, Egypt, 1953; admitted, 1981, Courts of Appeal. *Education:* Cairo University (LL.B., 1975). *LANGUAGES:* Arabic and English.

HALA HASHEM, (MRS), born Cairo, Egypt, 1958; admitted, 1981, Primary Courts. *Education:* American University in Cairo (B.A. Political Science, 1979); Cairo University (LL.B., 1979); Harvard University (LL.M., 1984). *LANGUAGES:* Arabic, English and German.

HUSSEIN AMER, born Mahala Koubra, Egypt, 1954. admitted, 1980 to practice before the Courts of Appeal. *Education:* Cairo University (LL.B., 1980). *LANGUAGES:* Arabic and English.

YOUSSEF TAHER, born Cairo, Egypt, 1961. admitted to practice before the Courts of First Instance, 1985. *Education:* Cairo University (LL.B.). *LANGUAGES:* Arabic and English.

AMR GALAL, born Giza, Egypt, 1960; admitted, 1991, Courts of Appeal. *Education:* Cairo University (LL.B., 1982). *LANGUAGES:* Arabic and English.

AHMED ZAKARIA, born Cairo, Egypt, 1962. admitted, 1986, to practice before the Primary Courts. *Education:* Cairo University (LL.B.). *LANGUAGES:* Arabic and English.

(This Listing Continued)

ASSER GHAZI, born Giza, Egypt, 1962; admitted, 1990, Primary Courts. *Education:* Ain Shams University (LL.B., 1987). *LANGUAGES:* Arabic, English and French.

MOHAMED LABIB, born Cairo, Egypt, 1965. admitted, 1988, to practice before the Primary Courts. *Education:* Ain Shams University (LL.B.). *LANGUAGES:* Arabic and English.

YASSER HASHEM, born Cairo, Egypt, 1960. admitted, 1989, to practice before the Primary Courts. *Education:* American University, Cairo; Cairo University (LL.B.). *LANGUAGES:* Arabic, English, French and German.

OF COUNSEL

ATEF EL AZAB, born Dakahlia, Egypt, 1924; admitted, 1946, Egypt. *Education:* Cairo University (LL.B., 1946). Formerly, First Deputy President of the Council of State (Conceil d'Etat). *LANGUAGES:* Arabic, English, French and German.

HABIB IBRAHIM SOLIMAN, born Assiut, Egypt, 1935. *Education:* Ain Shams University (LL.B., 1955); Cairo University (LL.M., 1957; Ph.D., 1967). Formerly Professor of Civil Law and Comparative Law (Algeria and Iraq). *LANGUAGES:* Arabic, English and French.

REPRESENTATIVE CLIENTS: American Express; Alotalia; American Cyanamid; American Home Products; Arab Bank, Ltd.; Arab Otsuka; Banca Commercial Italiana; Bank of Tokyo; Boots; Bridgestone; British Gas; Club Med; Colgate-Palmolive; DHL; Export Guarantee Corporation; Fiat; Freeport McMoran Minerals; Hoescht; Hughes Aircraft; IECO (an affiliate of ENI Italy); Intercontinental Hotels; ITT Sheraton Corporation; Johnson Wax; Kajima; LaRoche; McDermott; Meridien Hotels; Merksharpe & Dohme; Mitsubishi; Mitsui; Montedison; Nissho Awai; Otis Elevators; PepsiCo; Pfizer; Phillips Petroleum; Phoenix; Raytheon; Saipem; Santa Fe International; Sperry Sun; SwissPharma; Thomas Cook.

HASSOUNA & ABOU ALI

Established in 1987

CAIRO CENTER, 5TH FLOOR
2 ABDEL KADER HAMZA STREET, GARDEN CITY
P.O. BOX 175, ATABA
CAIRO, EGYPT
Telephone: (20-2) 3557188; (20-2) 3560852
Fax: (20-2) 3556140

Corporate Law, Foreign Investment, Petroleum, Banking, Construction, Government Regulations, Resolution of Trade Disputes, Commercial Litigation and Arbitration, Intellectual Property Law, Taxation, Labor and Employment Law, Environmental Law.

FIRM PROFILE: The firm was established in 1987 and offers a full range of legal services. The client base is mainly North American and European. The firm is well known for its Commercial, Corporate and Petroleum Law.

MEMBERS OF FIRM

MOHAMMED A.K. HASSOUNA, born Alexandria, Egypt, August 11, 1933; admitted, 1959, Egypt. *Education:* Faculty of Law, Cairo University (LL.B., 1955); Cambridge University, England (M.A., 1957). National Bank of Egypt, 1957-1958. Manager and Director, Public Sector Companies, 1959-1974. Partner: ASN, 1977-1983; Sidley & Austin & Naguib, 1983-1987. *Member:* Bar Association of Egypt; Egyptian Society of Political Economy (Legislation and Statistics); Egyptian Society of International Law; International Bar Association; American Chamber of Commerce, Egypt (Vice President, Legal Affairs, 1988-1991). *LANGUAGES:* Arabic, English, French and German.

AHMED G. ABOU ALI, born Port Said, Egypt, January 30, 1959; admitted, 1981, Egypt. *Education:* Faculty of Law, Cairo University (LL.B., 1980; Diploma, 1982); Harvard Law School (LL.M., 1984). Member: Abou Ali Law Firm, Port Said, Egypt, 1981-1983; Sidley & Austin, Chicago, Illinois, 1985-1987. *Member:* Bar Association of Egypt; Egyptian Society of International Law; American Bar Association; International Bar Association. *LANGUAGES:* Arabic and English.

REPRESENTATIVE CLIENTS: Aga Khan Trust for Culture; Dow Chemical Company; Degremont S.A.; Ebasco Overseas Corporation; Exxon Chemical; General Electric Company; Gulf Canada Resources Limited; Hewlett Packard S.A.; Merlin Gerin S.A.; Mobil Petrochemicals International; Les Laboratoires Servier; Sinai Company for Touristic Development; Smithkline Beecham; The Coca-Cola Company; Turkish Petroleum International Company; U.S. Agency for International Development; Worms.

IUSFINDER

Established in 1994
NILE TOWER
21, GIZA STREET, 17TH FLOOR
CAIRO, EGYPT
Telephone: (202).571.63.40; 571.63.41
Fax: (202).571.63.42

Madrid, Spain: office: C/ Goya 48 Bajo Dcha, 28001. Telephone: (34) 91.431.37.75; 91.431.37.02. Fax: (34) 91.575.61.64.
Bilbao, Spain Office: C/ Diputación 10 - 4° dcha. dcha. - 48008-BILBAO. Teléfono: 94.415.13.91. Fax: 94.415.64.69.
Barcelona, Spain Office: C/Cardenal Reig, 19-1° 3 - 08028-BARCELONA. Teléfono: 93.440.23.49.
Zaragoza, Spain Office: C/ Fco. de Vitoria, 16- Pricipal C. 50008-ZARAGOZA. Teléfono: 976.21.21.64. Fax: 976.23.12.83.
Pamplona, Spain Office: C/San Fermín, 43-1° 31004 PAMPLONA. Teléfono: 948.23.69.50. Fax: 948.15.26.36.
Palma de Mallorca, Spain Office: C/San Miguel n° 30-Edificio Antoniet 6° H. 07002-PALMA DE MALLORCA. Teléfono: 971.71.35.85. Fax: 971.71.35.85.
Valencia, Spain Office: C/Serrano Morales n° 3 -4° 10ª 46004-VALENCIA. Teléfono: 96.373.75.61. Fax: 96.374.15.99.
Valladolid, Spain Office: C/ Santiago, 24.1 Dcha. 47001 VALLADOLID Telephone: (34) 983.35.96.99. Fax: 983.35.97.99.

General Practice, Civil, Commercial, Company, Insolvency, Banking, Finance, Securities, Taxation, International, EEC, Administrative, Real Estate, Mergers and Acquisitions, Foreign Investment, Licensing, Patent, Trademark and Copyright Law, Maritime.

RESIDENT LAWYER

LISSET DUMIT DE SARKIS, born Santo Domingo, Dominican Republic, September 13, 1969; admitted, 1994. *Education:* University Nacional Pedro Enriques Ureña (Law Degree); University of Manchester (LL.M.). Formerly Associated with Messina & Messina. Honorary Consul of the Dominican Republic. *LANGUAGES:* Arab, Spanish, English and French.

(For complete biographical data on all personnel, see Professional Biographies at Madrid, Spain)

KAMEL LAW OFFICE

(IN ASSOCIATION WITH:
KAMEL, YEHIA, ABUL ELA & SAKR ATTORNEYS AT LAW)
Established in 1981

4 EL SHAHEED AHMED YEHIA IBRAHIM STREET
MOHANDESSEEN, GIZA
CAIRO, EGYPT
Telephone: 347-4102; 347-9453; 347-3597; 347-7179
Fax: 345-2009

Alexandria, Egypt Office: 22 Avenue Horreya. Telephone: (03) 482775. Fax: (03) 482775.
Associated New York Office: Afridi, Angell & Baker, New York, N.Y.

General Practice, Banking, Investment, Trade and Joint Venture Transactions. Major Contract Drafting and Negotiation. Civil, Commercial, Corporate, Tax, Labor, Customs. Petroleum, Mining, Maritime, Patents and Trademarks, Litigation and International Arbitration.
Only Lawyers Admitted to the Egyptian Bar are Authorized to Appear Before Egyptian Courts or to Practice Law in Egypt. Other Counsel Associated with the Firm act in Consultation with Lawyers Admitted to the Egyptian Bar.

FIRM PROFILE: Founded at the outset of Egypt's open door policy initiated by President Sadat in 1970's, Kamel Law Office joined with Kamel, Yehia and Abul-Ela, the professional arm of the association in 1983. These associated firms specialize in providing a complete range of high quality legal and consulting services to banks, corporations, foundations and individuals doing or seeking to do business in Egypt and the Arab World, as well as to embassies, governments and international organizations.

To carry out this mission, the associated firms maintain a staff of 20 Egyptian lawyers having substantial background experience in corporate, commercial and international business transactions as well as litigation and international arbitration, with one permanent senior U.S. legal consultant and several paralegal experts and office administrators.

(This Listing Continued)

KAMEL LAW OFFICE (IN ASSOCIATION WITH: KAMEL, YEHIA, ABUL ELA & SAKR ATTORNEYS AT LAW), Cairo— Continued

Over the years, the associated firms have developed excellent relationships with the governmental authorities regulating business and have established public and private sector contacts which are indispensable in the effective representation and protection of their clients' interests in Egypt and the Middle East.

Our firm is well versed in all aspects of laws and procedures relating to banking, foreign investment, international trade and licensing, corporate finance, mergers and acquisitions, capital markets and public and private issues of securities including debt/equity swaps, as well as the special rules governing the establishment of investment companies and funds in Egypt. Also, we have had long experience and possess special capabilities in Egyptian corporate and commercial law and international business and financial transactions.

PRINCIPAL MEMBERS

DR. MOHAMED KAMEL, born Mit Ghamr, Dakahlia, Egypt, 1944; admitted, 1966, Egypt. *Education:* Alexandria University Faculty of Law (Bachelor of Law, 1966); Faculte de Droit et de Science Economique de l'Universite d'Orleans (Doctorat d'Etat de Science Politique, 1968). Lecturer in International Law and Political Science, Cairo University, Higher Institute of African Studies, 1970-1973. Member of the Shura Council (The Egyptian Senate), elected 1990. *Member:* Egyptian Bar Association; International Bar Association; Inter-Pacific Bar Association. *LANGUAGES:* Arabic, English and French. *PRACTICE AREAS:* Company Investment; Real Estate; Tax and Commercial Law; International Commercial Arbitration; International and Islamic Banking and Finance.

AHMED YEHIA (1932-1986).

ABDEL HALIM ABUL ELA, born Biala, Kafr El Sheikh, Egypt, 1921; admitted, 1949, Egypt. *Education:* Alexandria University Faculty of Law (Bachelor of Law, 1948). With Wallace & Tagher Law Firm, Alexandria, 1955-1984. Attorney, Cassation Court. Member Board of Directors, Caltex Petroleum Company, 1961-1964; Abu Kir Land Reclamation Company; Alexandria Engineering Company, 1959-1963. Member, Arab Oil Organization of the Arab League, 1960—. *Member:* Egyptian Bar Association. *LANGUAGES:* Arabic and English. *PRACTICE AREAS:* Corporate and Commercial Law; Sale and Transfer of Egyptian Corporate Securities; International Business, Banking and Financial Transactions.

JOHN BENTLEY, born Cheyenne, Wyoming, 1940; admitted, 1972, California (Not admitted in Egypt). *Education:* Harvard University (A.B., cum laude, 1962); University of California at Berkeley (J.D., 1968). Managing Editor, California Law Review, 1967-1968. Lecturer, Faculty of Law, University of Singapore, 1969-1971. University of California Resident Consultant to the Foreign Investment Board of Indonesia, 1971. Attorney with Latham & Watkins, Los Angeles, California, 1972-1977. Ford Foundation Legal Advisor on Companies and Tax Law Reform to the Ministry of Economy, Investment and Finance, Government of Egypt, 1978-1982. Legal Advisor to the Governments of the Republics of Yemen and Indonesia on Investment Law and Commercial Reform, 1989—. World Bank (Foreign Investment Advisory Service) Legal Advisor to the Governments of Saudi Arabia and Oman on Commercial Law Reform and Investment Regulations and Procedures, 1990-1991. Member, 1980-1990, Secretary, 1981-1982 and Chairman, 1982-1989, Board of Directors, Cairo American College. Co-Founder, 1982 and President, 1983, American Chamber of Commerce in Egypt. *Member:* California State and American (International Law Section) Bar Associations. [Lieutenant, U.S. Army, 1962-1966, Stationed in Japan]. (Currently on leave of absence to serve as Resident Legal Advisor, Ministry of Justice, Government of Vietnam under UNDP funded project). *LANGUAGES:* English. *PRACTICE AREAS:* International Financial Business Transactions; Investment; Trade; Licensing.

MOHAMED SAKR, born Doumiat, Egypt, 1945; admitted, 1970, Egypt. *Education:* Cairo University Faculty of Law (Bachelor of Law, 1969). Military Prosecutor, 1970-1974, Egyptian Army. Specialized experience in Trademark Registration in Egypt and Arabian Gulf Countries. Also, in Companies and Labour Law. *Member:* Egyptian Bar Association. *LANGUAGES:* Arabic and English. *PRACTICE AREAS:* Litigation; Corporate Law; Labour Law; Civil Law; Commercial Law; Patents and Trademarks.

MEMBERS OF FIRM

GAMIL SHEHATA (1929-1994).

(This Listing Continued)

ADEL AMIRA, born Alexandria, Egypt, 1930. *Education:* Alexandria University Faculty of Law (Bachelor of Law, 1956). International Trade and Customs Expert, Ford Motor Company (Egypt), 1956-1978. Joined Kamel Law Office, 1979. *LANGUAGES:* Arabic and English. *PRACTICE AREAS:* Taxation; Customs; Drafting Company Contracts.

KAMEL EL-WAKIL, born Cairo, Egypt, 1949; admitted, 1973, Supreme Court of Appeal. *Education:* Cairo University (LL.B., 1973). With Hashem, Ibrahim & Tawflick Law Firm (1979-1992). *Member:* Bar Association of Egypt; Egyptian Society of International Law. *LANGUAGES:* Arabic, French and English. *PRACTICE AREAS:* Corporate Law; Litigation; Banking.

MAHMOUD WAHBA, born Cairo, Egypt, 1950; admitted, 1978, Egypt. *Education:* Cairo University Faculty of Law (Bachelor of Law, 1977). *Member:* Egyptian Bar Association. *LANGUAGES:* Arabic and English. *PRACTICE AREAS:* Corporate Law; Labour Law; Patents and Trademark; Investment Law.

ABUL FADL HOSNI, born Cairo, Egypt, 1955; admitted, 1979, Egypt. *Education:* Cairo University Faculty of Law (Bachelor of Law, 1977). *Member:* Egyptian Bar Association. *LANGUAGES:* Arabic and English. *PRACTICE AREAS:* Litigation.

MOHAMED ABDEL RAOUF, born El Gharbiya, Egypt, 1956; admitted, 1980, Egypt. *Education:* Alexandria University Faculty of Law (Bachelor of Law, 1979). *Member:* Egyptian Bar Association. *LANGUAGES:* Arabic and English. *PRACTICE AREAS:* Corporate Law; Litigation.

MOSTAFA M. MOSTAFA, born El Fayoum, Egypt, 1955; admitted, 1980, Egypt. *Education:* Cairo University Faculty of Law (Bachelor of Law, 1979). Military Lawyer, Egyptian Army, 1980-1981. *Member:* Egyptian Bar Association. *LANGUAGES:* Arabic and English. *PRACTICE AREAS:* Litigation.

RADWAN M. RADWAN (1956-1987).

GAMAL EL SADAT, born Cairo, Egypt, 1953; admitted, 1982, Egypt. *Education:* Alexandria University Faculty of Law (Bachelor of Law, 1981). *Member:* Egyptian Bar Association. *LANGUAGES:* Arabic. *PRACTICE AREAS:* Customs; Work Permits; Licenses.

EL SAYED MOHAMED EL SAYED AMMAR, born Sers El Layan, Mounoufia, Egypt, 1959; admitted, 1985, Egypt. *Education:* Cairo University Faculty of Law (Bachelor of Law, 1982). *Member:* Egyptian Bar Association. *LANGUAGES:* Arabic. *PRACTICE AREAS:* Patents and Trademarks; Litigation; Labour; Civil; Commercial Law.

JAMES MACINTYRE, born Melbourne, Australia, 1959; admitted, 1987, Victoria (Not admitted in Egypt). *Education:* Monash University (B.Sc., 1984; LL.B., 1987). Solicitor, MacMillan Segal and Lenton, and Coltmans, 1987-1989. Licensing Officer, ICI Australia, 1989-1991. *Member:* Law Institute of Victoria. [Commando, Australian Army, Commando Regiment, 1989-1991]. *LANGUAGES:* English. *PRACTICE AREAS:* Company Law; Labour Law; Commercial Law; Intellectual Property; Licensing.

YEHIA IBRAHIM EL SAYED EL KASSED, born Mounoufia, Egypt, 1960; admitted, 1984, Egypt. *Education:* Cairo University Faculty of Law (Bachelor of Law, 1984). *Member:* Egyptian Bar Association. *LANGUAGES:* Arabic. *PRACTICE AREAS:* Litigation.

JOSEPH MORCOS MORCOS, born Cairo, Egypt, 1964; admitted, 1987, Egypt. *Education:* Ein Shams University Faculty of Law (Bachelor of Law, 1986). *Member:* Egyptian Bar Association. *LANGUAGES:* Arabic. *PRACTICE AREAS:* Litigation.

AMAL MOHAMED MOUSTAFA, born Giza, Egypt, 1965; admitted, 1988, Egypt. *Education:* Cairo University Faculty of Law (Bachelor of Law, 1987). *Member:* Egyptian Bar Association. *LANGUAGES:* Arabic. *PRACTICE AREAS:* Litigation.

TAREK ZAHRAN, born Mounoufia, Egypt, 1960; admitted, 1984, Egypt. *Education:* Ein Shams University Cairo, Faculty of Law (Bachelor of Law, 1984); Diploma in Criminal Law (1985). *LANGUAGES:* Arabic. *PRACTICE AREAS:* Litigation; Criminal Law.

RAWYA AMER, born Cairo, Egypt, 1966; admitted, 1988, Egypt. *Education:* Cairo University, Faculty of Law (Bachelor of Law, 1988). *Member:* International Law Society. *LANGUAGES:* French, Arabic and English. *PRACTICE AREAS:* Arbitration.

ASHRAF AHMED YEHIA, born Alexandria, Egypt, 1967; admitted, 1989, Egypt. *Education:* Alexandria University, Faculty of Law (Bachelor

(This Listing Continued)

of Law, 1989). *LANGUAGES:* Arabic, English and French. *PRACTICE AREAS:* Corporate Law; Litigation.

REPRESENTATIVE CLIENTS: American Standard; Bristol-Myers Squibb; Caltex Petroleum Group; Cable Network (CNN); Denison Mines Limited; Equator Bank; Chemical Bank; Owens Corning Fiberglas; Philip Morris; Procter & Gamble; Singer; Ford Foundation; Thomas Cook; Union Bank of Finland; Walt Disney; Xerox Corporation; YKK-Yoshida Kogyo K.K. Zipper S.A.E.; Cairo American College (CAC); Pfizer; Lebanese Embassy; Texas Instruments; CIT Leasing Corporation; Bank of Nova Acotia; Euro-Disney S.C.A.; Bank of America; Tidewater Pacific Inc.; McDonald's; Bavaria GMBH; Montgomery Harza; Stanley Consultants; Nalco Italiana; Race Brook Petroleum Lrd., Fougerolle Dragados; USAID; Tetra Pak Egypt; JMA Information Engineering; Kier International Ltd; Willbros Eng; TRANE; 3M; Voice of America; RCI Europe Ltd; Agriculture Cooperative Development International; OPSCP 92'; Commodity Specialists (CSC); Toepfer; Case Corporation; Caterpiller; China Airlines (Cairo Branch); Courtaulds Plc; D.A. Exterminating Co. Inc.; Egyptian American Sanitary Wares; Kajima International Inc.; Seti Grain; Price Waterhouse LLP; U.S.A. Department of Justice; U.S.A. Naval Medical Research Unit 3.

KOSHERI, RASHED & RIAD

16, MAAMAL EL SOKKAR STREET
GARDEN CITY - 11451
CAIRO, EGYPT
Telephone: 3547158; 3552096; 3559228
Fax: 3558521
Telex: 22913 KR UN, 92614 ETIDC UN

Paris, France Rep. Office: 44 Avenue du President Wilson, 75016.
   Telephone: 0033 1 47270028. Fax: 0033 47047724. Telex: 42 649080.

General Practice, International Law, Corporate, Licensing Contracts, Commercial and Maritime Matters, Joint Ventures, Investments, Major Drafting of Local International Business Contracts, Banking, Mining and Petroleum Concessions, Tax, Construction, Labour Law, Patents, Trademarks Applications and Litigations, Business Litigation and Construction Arbitration.

MEMBERS OF THE FIRM

PROF. DR. AHMED SADEK EL-KOSHERI, born Cairo, Egypt, April 4, 1932, Egyptian Citizen; admitted, 1952, Egypt. *Education:* Cairo University (LL.B., 1952; D.E.S., in Islamic Law, 1954; D.E.S. in Private Law, 1955; D.E.S. in Public Law, 1956); Paris University (D.E.S. in Political Science, 1957; D.E.S. in Comparative Law, 1956); Rennes University (D.E.S. in Philosophy of Law, 1960); Doctorat d'etat, France, 1962. Member of Council of State, 1952-1958. Member of Faculty Staff, Ain Shams University Law School, 1958-1973. Legal Advisor for the Ministry of Finance and Oil, Kuwait, 1969-1970. Founding General Counsellor, Arab Fund for Economic & Social Development in Kuwait, 1973-1974. Of Counsel, Baker & McKenzie, Chicago, Illinois, 1975. Secretary General, Islamic Development Bank, Jeddah, Saudi Arabia, 1977-1978. Adjunct Professor of International Economic Law, Ain Shams University Law School, 1983. Professor of Law and Vice-president of Senghor University (Alexandria) (1986—). Adhoc Judge in the International Court of Justice, Hague (1992—). *Member:* The Bar Association of Egypt; Council of Commercial International Arbitration; Council of Uro-Arab Arbitration System; Institute De Droit International Egyptian Society International Law.

PROF. DR. SAMIA SADEK RASHED, born Alexandria, Egypt, Egyptian Citizen; admitted, 1956, Egypt. *Education:* Cairo University (LL.B., 1956; D.E.S. in Private Law, 1957; D.E.S. in Public Law, 1958; Ph.D., 1966); Yale University Law School (1961); Academy of International Law, The Hague (1966). Member of Faculty Staff, Cairo University Law School, 1956—. Professor and Chairman of Private International Law Department, Cairo University Law School.

DR. WAGDI RAGEB FAHMY, admitted, 1979, Egypt. *Education:* Cairo University (LL.B., 1952; D.E.S. in Private Law, 1953; D.E.S. in Public Law, 1954); Ain Shams University (Ph.D., 1967). Member of Council of State, 1952-1953. Member of Faculty Staff, Ain Shams University Law School, 1954. Visiting Professor, Kuwait University Law School, 1977-1982. Chairman, Civil and Commercial Procedure Department, Ain Shams University Law School, 1982.

DR. TAREK FOUAD A. RIAD, born Alexandria, Egypt, 1958, Egyptian Citizen; admitted, 1980, Egypt; 1985, New York. *Education:* Cairo University (LL.B., 1980); Harvard University Law School (LL.M., 1982; S.J.D., 1985). Crocker Bank, London Branch, 1976. Wells Fargo Bank, N.A., San Francisco, 1977. Member of Council of State, 1981. Lecturer in Private International Law, Cairo University Law School, Beni Suef Branch, 1982-1988. Associate, Paul Weiss, Rifkind Wharton & Garrison, New York, 1983-1984. Special Legal Council to the Speaker of the Egyptian Peo-

(This Listing Continued)

ple's Assembly, 1994—. *Member:* The Bar Association of Egypt; American Bar Association; American Arbitration Association; American Society of International Law; Egyptian Society of International Law.

HALA RIAD, born Alexandria, Egypt, Egyptian Citizen; admitted, 1982, Egypt. *Education:* Cairo University (LL.B., 1982); Dijon University, France (D.E.A., 1983); Academy of International Law, the Hague (1983); Yale University (LL.M., 1984). Associate of Kosheri & Rashed, 1982-1988. Associate of White & Case, New York, 1988-1991. Partner since, 1991. *Member:* The Egyptian Bar; New York Bar; U.S. District, International Bar Association; Egyptian Society of Economics and Legislation; Egyptian Society of International Law.

DR. OMAYA HASSAN ELWAN. *Education:* Cairo University (LL.B., 1953; D.E.S. in Private Law, 1954; D.E.S. in Public Law, 1955); University of Heidelberg (Doctor Jura, cum laude, 1961). Director of Studies, Institut für Ausländisches und Internationales Privatund Wirtschaftsrecht der Universität Heidelberg. U.N. Legal Consultant.

DR. HATEM GABR, born Cairo, Egypt; admitted, 1953, Egypt. *Education:* Cairo University (LL.B., 1952; D.E.S. in Public Law, 1953; D.E.S. in Political Economy, 1954; Ph.D., 1968; Iiap Diplome, France, 1971). Member Council of State, 1955-1979. Head of Legal Department, Arab Organization for Industrialization, 1976-1979.

PEIDER KONZ, born Switzerland, 1927; admitted, 1956, District of Columbia. *Education:* Licence en Droit, Geneva (1948); George Washington University (LL.B./J.D., 1957). Research Associate, the Harvard Law School, 1957-1959. Senior Legal Consultant, IAEA, 1959-1961. Deputy Secretary, Brussels Conference of Maritime Law, 1961-1962. Head Legal Service and Secretary of the Council, OECD, 1961-1965. Resident Counsel in Europe, Donovan, Leisure Newton & Irvine, 1965-1968. Vice President and Director for Asia, International Legal Center, 1968-1971. Director, UNSDRI, 1971-1977. Director, Policy Coordination, Unido, 1977-1978.

NAWAL SCHOEIB, admitted, 1970, Egypt. *Education:* Ain Shams University (LL.B., 1970).

MOHAMED MAHMOUD ABDEL MEGUID, admitted, 1984, Egypt. *Education:* Cairo University (LL.B., 1982).

EZAAT ABDEL SAMIE, admitted, 1987, Egypt. *Education:* Cairo University (LL.B., 1987).

AHMED HELMY SALEM, admitted, 1985, Egypt. *Education:* Cairo University (LL.B., 1984).

MOSTAFA ABDEL LATIF, admitted, 1981, Egypt. *Education:* Cairo University (LL.B., 1980).

GAMAL EL SHERBINI, admitted, 1981, Egypt. *Education:* Cairo University (LL.B., 1980).

EMAD HANAFY SALEH, admitted, 1985, Egypt. *Education:* Cairo University (LL.B., 1984).

RAFIK KAMEL, admitted, 1982. *Education:* Cairo University (LL.B., 1982).

SHERIF SAAD

Law Offices

For Legal & International Consultation

MAADI PALACE TOWER
MAADI STATION SQUARE
5TH FLOOR, ARAB AFRICAN INTERNATIONAL BANK BUILDING
P.O. BOX 90 MAADI
CAIRO 11728, EGYPT
Telephone: (202) 3786201; (202) 3786202; (202) 3786203
Telex: 22121 SSLAW UN
Facsimile: (202) 3786204; (202) 3786205

Los Angeles, California Correspondent Office: Sidley & Austin. 2049 Century Park East, 90067. Telephone: (213) 553-8100. Telex: 18-1391 (S & A LAW LSA). Telecopier: (213) 553-9192.
New York, New York Correspondent Office: Sidley & Austin. 520 Madison Avenue, 10022. Telephone: (212) 418-2100. Telex: 97-1696 (SID AUS A NYK). Telecopier: (212) 750-9688.
Chicago, Illinois Correspondent Office: Sidley & Austin. One First National Plaza, 60603. Telephone: (312) 853-7000. Telex: 25-43654 (SIDLEY AUS CGO). Telecopier: (312) 853-7669; (312) 853-7396.

(This Listing Continued)

SHERIF SAAD, Cairo—Continued

Washington, D.C. Correspondent Office: Sidley & Austin. 1722 Eye Street, N.W., 20006. Telephone: (202) 429-4000. Telex: 89-463 (SIDLEY AUS WSH). Telecopier: (202) 331-7285.

London, England Correspondent Office: 18 King William Street, EC4N 7SA. Telephone: (441) 621-1616. Telex: 924125.

Singapore Correspondent Office: 5 Shenton Way, 20-08 UIC Building, 0106. Telephone: (65) 224-5000. Telex: 28754. Telecopier: (65) 224-0530.

General Practice, Civil Law, Commercial Law, Maritime Law, Taxes Law, Banking Law, International Law, Labour Law, Petrolium Sector Matter, Patent and Trademarks Law-Registration, Insurance Claims, Court Litigation, Local Arbitration, International Arbitration.

SHERIF SAAD, born 1956; admitted, 1980, Egypt.

SAAS ADVISORY SERVICES LTD.

5 TAHSIN FARGHALY STREET
MADENAT NASR
CAIRO, EGYPT
Telephone: 20-2-2601204
Fax: 20-2-2601204

Amman, Jordan Office: Sadi Abdin Law Firm, P.O. Box 950565, Amman 11195. Telephone: 962.6.692540. Fax: 962.6.692541.

Arab, Civil and Commercial Laws, Litigation, Arbitration, TradeMarks and Patents.

(For complete Biographical Data on all personnel, see Amman, Jordan Biographical Section.
All correspondence should be sent to Amman, Jordan Office.)

SELIM & ASSOCIATES

140 26TH OF JULY STREET, 11TH FLOOR
CAIRO, EGYPT
Telephone: (202) 3407620
Fax: (202) 3414264

Corporate Law, Investment Planning and Protection, Energy and Petroleum Law, Construction, Commercial Arbitration and Litigation, Securities and Stock Exchange Regulations and Taxation.

FIRM PROFILE: *The Firm offers a full range of legal services in the above Areas, and its clientele is mainly North American, European, Far Asian, and Middle Eastern.*

PRINCIPAL MEMBER

YEHIA M. SELIM, born Cairo, Egypt, 1959; admitted, 1981, Egypt. *Education:* Washington College of Law, American University, Wash., D.C. (LL.M., 1985); Cairo University Law School (LL.B., 1981). District Attorney, Central Cairo, 1982-1985. Assistant to the Director and Legal Advisor, Cairo Arbitration Center, 1982-1984, 1991-1993. Associate, Sidley & Austin, Wash., D.C., 1984-1985; Attorney, Amoco Corporation, London, 1985-1986; Senior Associate, Baker & McKenzie, Cairo, 1986-1988; Counsel, Kuwait Finance House and Kuwait National Petroleum Corporation, Kuwait, 1988-1990; World Bank Legal Advisor to the Government of the Sultanate of Oman for reforms of Investment and Commercial Laws, 1992-1993; Senior Attorney, Kamel Law Office, Cairo, 1990-1994; Legal Advisor to USAID for reforms of Egyptian and Palestinian Commercial Laws, 1992-1995. *Member:* National Contract Management Association, U.S.A. *LANGUAGES:* Arabic and English. **PRACTICE AREAS:** Drafting and Negotiation of Contracts; Litigation; Arbitration in International Commercial Matters; Energy Law Matters; Securities Law and Regulations.

ASSOCIATES

MOHAMED A. GOUD, born Cairo, 1959; admitted, 1986, Egypt. *Education:* Cairo University (LL.B., 1985). *Member:* Egyptian Bar Association. *LANGUAGES:* Arabic and English.

AHMED Y. MOTAA, born Cairo, 1964; admitted, 1991, Egypt. *Education:* Beirut University (LL.B., 1987). *Member:* Egyptian Bar Association. *LANGUAGES:* Arabic and English.

(This Listing Continued)

AHMED M. ABDALLA, born Giza, 1969; admitted, 1992, Egypt. *Education:* Cairo University (LL.B., 1991). *Member:* Egyptian Bar Association.

REPRESENTATIVE CLEINTS: Enron Corporation (Texas); Toshiba Corporation; Banque IndoSuez; RCI Europe Ltd.; Hermes Financial; KPMG; Saudi American Bank; World Bank; U.S. and Egyptian Governments.

SARWAT A. SHAHID LAW FIRM

20 B ADLY STREET
CAIRO, EGYPT
Telephone: (202) 3917511-3933593-3929224
Facsimile (202) 3935447

Corporate, Commercial, Pravite, International Law, Tax, Foreign Investments and International Business, Securities and Insurance Law, Real Estate, Constitutional, Administrative and Public Law, General Litigation, Company Formations, Acquisitions and Mergers, International Contracts and Commercial Arbitration.

FIRM PROFILE: *The Firm has an additional office in Heliopolis, Cairo. Member of the firm are almost 25 persons as Counsels, Lawyers, Of Counsels, Secretariat and Administrative Personnel. The office represents many Joint-Ventures and other Egyptian Companies and Individuals.*

SARWAT A. SHAHID, born Egypt, December 22, 1946; admitted, 1987, Cairo. *Education:* Ein Shams University, Faculty of Law, Cairo, (LL.B., 1967; LL.M., 1972). Judicial positions in Egypt up to Counsellor at the Egyptian Counseil d'Etat. Board Member of several Joint-Ventures Companies. *Member:* Egyptian Bar Association. *LANGUAGES:* English and Arabic.

REPRESENTATIVE CLIENTS: Banque Paribas, France; Renault Vehicles Industriels, France; Sucden Kerry International Company, France; Glaxo Group Limited, England; Abercrombie, England; General Re Europe Limited (GREL), England; Bayer Company, Germany; Eli Lilly and Company, Indiana, U.S.A.; General Re Insurance Company, U.S.A.; Sonesta Hotels Internationals, U.S.A.; Brother Company, Japan; Taichi Company Ltd., Japan; Sharp Corporation, Japan; Banque Continental de Luxembourg, Luxembourg; Tata Exports Limited Company, Bombay, India; Sunkyong Limited Company, Seoul, Korea; Middle East Cement Shipping & Handling Company, Greece; Seamed Bulk Handling, Panama; Al-Kaaki Group of Companies, Saudi Arabia.

SHALAKANY LAW OFFICE

(Founded 1912 by Abdel Fattah El-Shalakany)

12, EL MARASHLY STREET, ZAMALEK
CAIRO, EGYPT
Telephone: (202) 3403331; 3403760; 3404214
Telex: 93656 ASLO UN 21101 SHALA UN
Fax: (202) 3420661

General Practice, International Business Transaction, Major Contracts, Investment Agreements, Litigation and International Arbitration, Banking, Financing, Swaps, Mergers, Acquisitions, Capital Markets and Securities, Privatization, Labor, Tax, Maritime Commercial, Corporate, Insurance, Computer and Industrial Property Rights, Real Estate Law.

PARTNERS

ALI EL-SHALAKANY, born Cairo, Egypt, 1923; admitted, 1944, Egypt. *Education:* Cairo University (LL.B., 1943; Diploma in Public Law, 1945; Diploma in Economics, 1946); University of Paris (Diploma in Political Economics, 1950). Associate, Major Fanner's Law Office, Cairo, 1951-1956. Journalist, 1957-1962, Economic Consultant to President of Algeria, Algiers, 1962-1963. Deputy Chairman, Alakhbar Newspaper, Cairo, 1963-1964. Manager, Industrial Relations, Iron and Steel Company, Helwan, 1964-1970. Senior and Managing Partner, Shalakany Law Office, 1971—. *Member:* Egyptian Bar Association; Egyptian Society for International Law; International Bar Association; Institute of International Business Law and Practice (ICC, Paris). *LANGUAGES:* Arabic, English and French.

SALAH MORSI, born Cairo, Egypt, 1939; admitted, 1970, Egypt. *Education:* Ain Shams University, Cairo (LL.B., 1969); training in private law offices, 1969-1970. Lawyer, Egyptian Iron and Steel Company, Research, Legal Opinion and Contracts Department, 1970-1972 and Barrister, Litigation Department, 1972-1976. Technical Assistant and Office Manager, 1974-1978 and Partner, 1978—, Shalakany Law Office. *Member:* Egyptian Bar Association; International Bar Association (Member, Section on Business Law). *LANGUAGES:* Arabic and English.

SALEH HAFEZ, born Cairo, Egypt, 1942; admitted, 1969, Egypt. *Education:* Ain Shams University, Cairo (LL.B., 1968). Lawyer, Central Bank of Egypt, Litigation Department, 1969-1972. Research and Legal Counsel,

(This Listing Continued)

Talal Ghazawi's Law Firm, Dammam, Saudi Arabia, 1975-1976. Associate and Partner, Shalakany Law Office, 1976—. *Member:* Egyptian Bar Association; International Bar Association; Asia - Pacific Lawyer Association. *LANGUAGES:* Arabic and English.

MONA ZULFICAR, born Cairo, Egypt, 1948; admitted, 1980, Egypt. *Education:* Cairo University (B.Sc., Economics and Political Science, 1969); Mansoura University (LL.B., 1980). Research Specialist, National Assembly of Egypt, 1969-1970. Administrative Assistant: World Health Organization (WHO), Regional office at Alexandria and United Nations Development Program (UNDP), Educational Technology Project at Cairo, 1970-1975. Economist and Office Manager, 1976-1978 and Partner, 1978—, Shalakany Law Office. *Member:* Egyptian Bar Association; International Bar Association. *LANGUAGES:* Arabic, English and French.

KHALED EL-SHALAKANY, born Cairo, Egypt, 1956; admitted, 1987, Ontario, Canada; 1989, Egypt; 1992, as registered patent and trademark agent, Egypt. *Education:* Cairo University (B.Sc. Electronics Engineering, 1978); American University (Professional Diploma in Management, 1982); University of Toronto (LL.B., 1985); University of Cambridge (LL.M., 1992). System Engineer IBM World Trade Corporation, Cairo, Egypt, 1979-1982. Articled Law Student, Fasken & Calvin, Toronto, Canada, 1985-1986. Counsel, 1987-1989 and Partner, 1989—, Shalakany Law Office. *Member:* Canadian Bar Association; Association of Egyptian Engineers; Law Society of Upper Canada. *LANGUAGES:* Arabic, English and French.

ASSOCIATES

AHMED EL-DEEB, born Behera Governorate, Egypt, 1930; admitted, 1956, Egypt. *Education:* Alexandria University (LL.B., 1956). Lawyer: Bassouni Law Office, 1956-1962; Iron and Steel Company Helwan, 1962-1983; Shalakany Law Office, 1983—. *Member:* Egyptian Bar Association. *LANGUAGES:* Arabic and English.

MOSTAFA EL HAKIM, born Aswan, Egypt, 1938; admitted, 1961, Egypt. *Education:* Ain Shams University (LL.B., 1961). Lawyer: El-Hakim Law Firm, 1961-1985; Shalakany Law Office, 1985—. *Member:* Egyptian Bar Association. *LANGUAGES:* Arabic and English.

MAHMOUD SHEDID, born Cairo, Egypt, 1952; admitted, 1976, Egypt. *Education:* Ain Shams University (LL.B., 1974). Lawyer: Madinet Nasr Company for Housing and Reconstruction, 1977-1984; Shalakany Law Office, 1984—. *Member:* Egyptian Bar Association. *LANGUAGES:* Arabic and English.

RAMADAN M. BAYOUMI, born Gharbeya Governorate, Egypt, 1933; admitted, 1977, Egypt. *Education:* Cairo University (LL.B., 1976). Lawyer, Litigation Department, Nasr Company, Petrochemicals, 1962-1977. Independent Lawyer, 1977-1981; Shalakany Law Office, 1981—. *Member:* Egyptian Bar Association. *LANGUAGES:* Arabic and English.

AHMED MAHROUS, born Cairo, Egypt, 1946; admitted, 1987, Egypt. *Education:* Ain Shams University (LL.B., 1970). Military Prosecutor, Armed Forces, 1970-1976. Manager, Legal Department, Ministry of Social Affairs, 1976-1987. Lawyer, Shalakany Law Office, 1987—. *Member:* Egyptian Bar Association. *LANGUAGES:* Arabic and English.

MOHAMED EL BERRY, born Giza, Egypt, 1956; admitted, 1979, Egypt. *Education:* Ain Shams University (LL.B., 1978). Administrative Work: Esso Suez, Inc., 1983-1986; Shalakany Law office, 1986-1988, 1988-1989. Human Resource Manager and Company Lawyer, Bechtel, Egypt, 1988-1989. 1989. Lawyer, Shalakany Law Office. *Member:* Egyptian Bar Association. *LANGUAGES:* Arabic and English.

MOHAMED SHAKER, born Zagazig, Egypt, 1951; admitted, 1988, Egypt. *Education:* Ain Shams University (LL.B., 1974); Two Management Training Program in Bahrain (1980-1981). Manager Operator, A.T. Danjan Saudi Public Transport Company, 1979-1987. Lawyer, Shalakany Law Office, 1987—. *Member:* Egyptian Bar Association. *LANGUAGES:* Arabic and English.

ASHRAF IHAB, born Giza, Egypt, 1962; admitted, 1985, Egypt. *Education:* Cairo University (LL.B., 1985). Lawyer, Shalakany Law Office, 1985—. *Member:* Egyptian Bar Association. *LANGUAGES:* Arabic and English.

AMINA GAMAL EL DIN EL OTEIFI, born Giza, Egypt, 1964; admitted, 1988, Egypt. *Education:* American University (B.Sc., Economics and Political Science, 1987); Cairo University (LL.B., 1988); King's College, London (Master's Degree, International Law, 1990). Lawyer, Shalakany Law Office, 1987—. *Member:* Egyptian Bar Association. *LANGUAGES:* Arabic, English and French.

HUSSEIN MOHAMED HUSSEIN GHONEIM, born Cairo, Egypt, 1930; admitted, 1956, Egypt. *Education:* Cairo University (LL.B., 1955). Vice Chairman, Egyotian Contracting Company (Makhtar Ibrahim), 1964-1989. Attorney, Shalakany Law Office, 1989—. *Member:* Egyptian Bar Association. *LANGUAGES:* Arabic and English.

LAILA BAAHA EL DIN, born Cairo, Egypt, 1962; admitted, 1985, Egypt. *Education:* Cairo University (LL.B., 1984). Lawyer, Shalakany Law Office, 1985—. *Member:* Egyptian Bar Association. *LANGUAGES:* Arabic and English.

EMAD SALAH EL SHALAKANY, born Cairo, Egypt, 1952; admitted, 1992, Egypt. *Education:* Cairo University (LL.B., 1991); Diploma in Human Resources 1981. Administrative Director, Fakhry Hospital, Saudi Arabia (1977-1982). Public Relation Office ARAMCO (1982-1989). General Manager on International Egypt (1989-1992). Attorney, Shalakany Law Office, 1989—. *Member:* Egyptian Bar Association. *LANGUAGES:* Arabic, English and French.

MOHAMED MOSTAFA TAWFIK, born Cairo, Egypt 1964; admitted, 1986, Egypt. *Education:* Ain Shams University (LL.B., 1985). The Cabinet Information and Decision support Center (1986-1989). Attorney Shalakany Law Office, 1989—. *Member:* Egyptian Bar Association. *LANGUAGES:* Arabic and English.

ADEL FOUAD HANNA, born Cairo, Egypt, 1965; admitted, 1989, Egypt. *Education:* Ain Shams University (LL.B., 1986). Business Lawyer (1986-1989). Attorney, Shalakany Law Office, 1989—. *Member:* Egyptian Bar Association. *LANGUAGES:* Arabic and English.

NOHA MOHAMED SHERIF, born Cairo, Egypt, 1963; admitted, 1992, Egypt. *Education:* Ain Shams University (B.Sc., 1984; LL.B., 1992). Lawyer, Shalakany Law Office, 1992—. *Member:* Egyptian Bar Association. *LANGUAGES:* Arabic and English.

INGY BADAWY, born Cairo, Egypt, 1972; admitted, 1993, Egypt. *Education:* Cairo University (LL.B., 1992); Institute de Droit d'Affaires International (Masters Degree, 1994). Shalakany Law Office, 1992—. *Member:* Egyptian Bar Association. *LANGUAGES:* Arabic, English and French.

OF COUNSEL

MAHMOUD SAFWAT, born Cairo, Egypt, 1919; admitted, 1952, Egypt. *Education:* Cairo University (LL.B., 1940; Diploma in Economics, 1946). Tax Inspector for Government of Egypt, 1944-1947. Secretary General and Chairman, Arab Land Bank, Cairo, 1947-1970. Regional General Manager in Jordan, Arab Land Bank, 1973-1974. General Manager, United Arab Emirates Development Bank, 1975-1978. Senior Partner, Shalakany Law Office, 1978-1994 and Of Counsel, 1994—. *Member:* Egyptian Bar Association. *LANGUAGES:* Arabic and English.

ANWAR M. SHAKER, born Cairo, Egypt, 1920; admitted, 1945, Court of Cassation; 1976, Egypt. *Education:* Cairo University (LL.B., 1940; Diploma Private Law, 1947; Diploma Public Law, 1948; Diploma in Economics, 1956). Lawyer with Maitre Abdel Fattah El Shalakany, 1946-1952. Prosecutor, Judge and Vice-President, Court of First Instance, 1952-1954. Vice President, Supreme Court of Ghaza, 1964-1965. Senior Judge, Ministry of Justice, 1966-1971. Vice President, Cairo Court of Appeals, 1971-1975. Associate and Partner, 1975-1982 and Consultant, 1983—, Shalakany Law Office. *Member:* Egyptian Bar Association. *LANGUAGES:* Arabic and English.

IHAB MOSTAFA, born Cairo, Egypt, 1935; admitted, 1958, Egypt. *Education:* Cairo University (LL.B., 1957). Lawyer with, Zoheir Garrana and Kamel Thabet Law Offices, Cairo, 1958-1960. Legal Advisor, Ministry of Industry, Government of Egypt (on public sector company project in Egypt), 1960-1973. Legal Advisor in Italy to Government of Egypt for procurement and contracts on Talkha 2 project, 1973-1978. Partner, Shalakany Law Office, 1978-1994 and Of Counsel, 1994—. *Member:* Egyptian Bar Association. *LANGUAGES:* Arabic and English.

NADIA A. FAHMY, born Cairo, Egypt, 1939. admitted to plead before Courts of Appeal, 1981, Egypt. *Education:* Cairo University (LL.B., 1969; Diploma in Public Law, 1973; Diploma in Tax Legislation, 1974). Lawyer, Egyptian Central Auditing Agency, 1970-1974. Legal Advisor to Arab African International Bank, 1976-1982. Associate, 1982-1989 and Partner, 1989-1994 and of Counsel, 1994—, Shalakany Law Office. *Member:* Egyptian Bar Association. *LANGUAGES:* Arabic, English and French.

HOSNI ABDEL WAHED, born Cairo, Egypt, 1946; admitted, 1968, Egypt. *Education:* Cairo University (LL.B., 1968); Diploma in Public Law, 1973; Diploma Administrative Science, 1974; Ph.D. Public Law, 1984); University of Paris (Diploma of French Language, 1974); Legal Studies,

(This Listing Continued)

SHALAKANY LAW OFFICE, Cairo—Continued

National School of the Judiciary, Paris (1975-1976). Prosecutor, 1969-1976. Judge, 1976-1980. President of Tribunal Cairo, 1980-1984. Counsellor Ministry of Justice, 1984-1989. Of Counsel, Shalakany Law Office, 1989—. *Member:* Egyptian Bar Association. *LANGUAGES:* Arabic, English and French.

MOHAMED EZZAT, born Cairo, Egypt, 1922; admitted, 1966, Egypt High Court of Appeal. *Education:* Cairo University (LL.B., 1943; Diploma Public Law, 1967); Central Bank of Egypt (Diploma in Banking, 1972); ARAC Center (Diploma in Administration, 1974). Lawyer then Manager Legal Department Ranque Misr SAE, 1948-1969. General Manager of Administration and Commercial Affair, Banque Misr SAE, 1969-1984. Adviser, Administrative Manager and Secretary to the Board of Directors of Qatar Petrochemical Complex In Doha, Qatar, 1976-1984. Attorney, Shalakany Law Office, 1987—. *LANGUAGES:* Arabic, English and French.

DR. MOHAMED-HOSSAM LOUTFI, born Cairo, Egypt, 1957. *Education:* Cairo University (LL.B., 1978; Diploma, Private Law, 1979; Diploma, Criminal Sciences, 1980); University of Paris No. 11, Sceaux (Doctorat d'Etat, Private Law, 1983). Lawyer, 1978-1979. Public Prosecutor, 1979-1984. Lecturer, Faculty of Law of Beni Souef, Cairo University, 1984—. Associate Professor, Faculty of Law of Beni Souef, Cairo University. Of Counsel, Shalakany Law Office, 1989—. *LANGUAGES:* Arabic, French, English, Spanish and German.

BAHAA DESSOUKI, born Montreal, Canada, 1968; admitted, 1990, Egypt. *Education:* Cairo University (LL.B., 1990; Diploma in International Trade Law, 1991; LL.M., Lexmercatoria, 1993). Assistant Lecturer, Faculty of Law, Manoleya University, 1990—. Of Counsel, Shalakany Law Office, 1992. *LANGUAGES:* Arabic, English and French.

Languages: Arabic, English and French

REPRESENTATIVE CLIENTS: *Banks:* Citibank, N.A.; Bank of America; Chase Manhattan; American Express Bank; Lloyds Bank Plc.; Credit Suisse; Hong Kong Egyptian Bank; National Bank of Pakistan; Chemical Bank; Banque De Paribas; Bank of Oman, Ltd.; National Bank of Oman; The Bank of New York; Misr Iran Development Bank; Saudi Egyptian Investment and Finance Company; Commercial International Bank, SAE; Egyptian American Bank, SAE; *Industrial Companies:* General Motors Corporation; General Motors Egypt; Daimler Benz AG.; American Telephone and Telegraph International; Revlon; Ferrostaal; Warner Lamber Company; Kodac; *Construction Company:* Bechtel; SGE; Technip; Interinfra Arabco (Cairo Regional Metro Project); Cementation International; Arab Contractors; S. Saad & Co.; *Hotels and Services:* Marriott Corporation; Oberoi International; Ramada Inc.; Gulf Egypt for Hotels and Tourism; Swiss Air; C. Itoh, Ltd.; *Oil:* Shell Marketing Egypt; Deminex; Schlumberger; Tri-State, Baker Eastern.

VEIL ARMFELT JOURDE

4 GABER IBN HAYAN STREET, DOKKI
CAIRO, EGYPT
Telephone: 20.2 349 2217/2498/8678
Fax: 20.2. 349 3655

Paris, France Office: 69, avenue Victor Hugo, 75116. Telephone: 33.1. 44.17.50.50. Fax: 33.1. 45.01.77.21.

London, England Office: 4 Carlton Gardens, Pall Mall, SW1Y 5AA. Telephone: 44. 0171 930 8644. Fax: 44. 0171 321 0670.

General Commercial and Corporate Law, Joint Ventures and Project Financing, Construction Law and Arbitration, Banking Law and Transfer of Technology. Advice on Egyptian Law and Egyptian Litigation in association with the Law Office of Dr. Yehia El Gamal.

PARTNER IN CHARGE

ANDREW P. ARMFELT, admitted, 1970, Solicitor of the Supreme Court of England and Wales; 1986, Avocat à la Cour de Paris.

RESIDENT

NIGEL HARTRIDGE, admitted, 1977, Solicitor of the Supreme Court of England and Wales. (Solicitor).

(For complete biographical data on personnel and for Firm Profile, see Professional Biographies at Paris, France)

ETHIOPIA

TESHOME GABRE-MARIAM BOKAN

Established in 1982
P.O. BOX 101485
ADDIS ABABA, ETHIOPIA
Telephone: (251-1) 51 84 84; 15 80 20
Residence: 51 33 32
Telefax: (251-1) 51 35 00

General Practice with emphasis on Contract, Corporate and Natural Resource Laws.

TESHOME GABRE-MARIAM BOKAN, born Addis Ababa, Ethiopia, December 15, 1931; admitted, 1982, Ethiopia. *Education:* University of College of Addis Ababa (B.A., with distinction, 1954); Faculty of Law, McGill University, Canada (B.C.L., 1957); Institute of Air & Space Law, McGill University, Canada (1957); Faculty of Comparative Law, International University of Comparative Sciences, Luxembourg - Diplome de Droit Compare (1958); Economic Development Institute, World Bank, Washington D.C., Fellow thereof 1964. Part-time Lecturer in Law, Haile Selassie University, 1964-1967. Principal Legal Advisor, and Executive Assistant to the General Manager of Ethiopian Airlines, 1958-1961. Director General, Ministry of Public Works and Communications, Government of Ethiopia, 1961-1962. Principal Legal Advisor of and Secretary to Board of Directors, Development Bank of Ethiopia, 1962-1963. Member, Drafting Committee, OAU Charter and Principal Legal Advisor to the Constituent Assembly of the African Heads of State and Government, May 1963. Attorney-General of Ethiopia, 1965-1967. Vice Minister, and later Minister of State, Ministry of Mines and Energy, Government of Ethiopia, 1967-1974. Political detainee, 1974-1982. Principal Advisor, Ministry of Labour and Social Affairs, Government of Ethiopia, 1982-1983. *Member:* Addis Ababa Bar Association; African International Law Association (Vice President, 1986—); International Bar Association (Member, Section of Energy and Natural Resources Law with particular interest in Committee B); Constitution Drafting Commission for Ethiopia (1993-1994). *LANGUAGES:* Amharic, Oromo, Sidamo, English, French and Italian (spoken).

REPRESENTATIVE CLIENTS: AL-TAD Ethiopia Plc.; Alitalia Airline; American African Finance Corporation; Amoco Ethiopia; British Petroleum Development Limited; CONCERN (Irish Humanitarian Organization); Cooperativa Muratori & Cimmentisti (CMC); Deminex Deutsche Erdolversorgungsgesellschaft mbH, Essen, Germany; Ethiopia Amalgamated Ltd.; Hilton International; Hunt Oil Company; IBM International; International Finance Corporation (IFC); International Livestock Centre for Africa (ILCA); International Petroleum Corporation (IPC); Lonrho International; Lufthansa German Airline; Maxus Energy Corporation; Medicin Sans Frontier (MSF), Belgium; Medicin Sans Frontier (MSF), Holland; Sheraton International Inc.; Skanska International; Muslim World League; United Nations - DTCD (advised on behalf of UN/DTCD, governments of: Angola, Ethiopia, Kenya, Lesotho, Mozambique, Tanzania, Yemen).

GHANA

AKUFO-ADDO, PREMPEH & CO.

Established in 1979

67 KOJO THOMPSON ROAD
ADABRAKA
P.O. BOX 207
ACCRA, GHANA
Telephone: 233 (21) 229875
Fax: 233 (21) 220307

Firm engaged in Human Rights Law, Constitutional Law, Environmental Law, Administrative Law, Legal Aspects of Foreign Investments in Ghana, Securities, International Corporate and Business Law, Commercial Law, Company Law, Mining Law, Aviation Law, Taxation, International Economic Trademarks and Patent, Insurance, Banking and International Finance and Litigation.

FIRM PROFILE: Established in 1979. Akufo-Addo, Prempeh & Co. has grown to become one of Ghana's leading commercial law firms. The firm has a broadly based practice with a reputation for offering a full range of quality legal services. The firm has represented a number of multinational companies and has been instructed on a number of occasions by leading

(This Listing Continued)

law firms in America and Europe. The firm has 2 partners and 13 associates.

MEMBERS OF FIRM

NANA AKUFO-ADDO, born Accra, Ghana, March 29, 1944; admitted, 1971, England (Middle Temple); 1975, Ghana. *Education:* University of Ghana (B.Sc., Econ., 1967). Associate Counsel, Coudert Freres, Paris, 1971-1975. *Member:* International Bar Association; Ghana Bar Association (President, Greater Accra Regional Branch, 1992—; Member, Legal Committee). *LANGUAGES:* French and English. *PRACTICE AREAS:* Constitutional Law; Company Law; Investment Law; Mining Law; Litigation.

DR. EDMUND PREMPEH, born Kumasi, Ghana, September 6, 1945; admitted, 1968, England (Middle Temple); 1975, Ghana. *Education:* University of London (LL.M., 1972); Cambridge University (Ph.D., 1974). Lecturer, Faculty of Law, University of Ghana, 1974-1981. Fellow, International Academy of Trial Lawyers. *Member:* Ghana Bar Association; African Business Round Table. *LANGUAGES:* French and English. *PRACTICE AREAS:* Commercial Law; International Economic Law; Criminal Law; Company Law.

JUSTINA TETE-DONKOR, born Accra, Ghana, July 20, 1953; admitted, 1977, Ghana. *Education:* University of Ghana (LL.B., Hons., 1975); Ghana School of Law (B.L., 1977). *Member:* Ghana Bar Association. *LANGUAGES:* English. *PRACTICE AREAS:* Aviation Law; Company Law; Litigation.

DAVID ADU-TUTU, born Koforidua, Ghana; admitted, 1981, Ghana. *Education:* University of Ghana (LL.B., Hons., 1979); Ghana School of Law (B.L., 1981). *Member:* Ghana Bar Association. *LANGUAGES:* English. *PRACTICE AREAS:* Commercial Law; Trademarks and Patents; Administrative Law; Litigation.

KUNTUNKRUNKU AMPOFO, born Accra, Ghana; admitted, 1982, Ghana. *Education:* University of Ghana (LL.B., Hons., 1980); Ghana School of Law (B.L., 1982); Cambridge University (LL.M., 1983). Legal Officer, Taylor Woodrow, London. Lecturer, Faculty of Law, University of Ghana, 1985—. *Member:* Ghana Bar Association. *LANGUAGES:* English. *PRACTICE AREAS:* International Commercial Law; Shipping and Mercantile Law; Construction Law; Litigation.

KWAME AFARI YEBOAH, born Koforidua, Ghana, July 19, 1958; admitted, 1984, Ghana. *Education:* University of Ghana (LL.B., Hons., 1982); Ghana School of Law (B.L., 1984). Tutorial Assistant, Faculty of Law, University of Ghana, 1984-1986. Teaching Assistant, School of Business Administration, University of Ghana, 1984-1986. Lecturer, Institute of Adult Education, University of Ghana, 1984-1986. *Member:* Ghana Bar Association. *LANGUAGES:* English. *PRACTICE AREAS:* Trademarks and Patents; Shipping and Mercantile Law; Litigation.

KEN BROOKMAN-AMISSAH, admitted, 1987, Ghana. *Education:* University of Ghana (B.A., Hons., 1985); Ghana School of Law (B.L., 1987). *Member:* Ghana Bar Association. *LANGUAGES:* English. *PRACTICE AREAS:* Commercial Law; International Economic Law; Company Law; Litigation.

PHILIP ADDISON, born Accra, Ghana, November 6, 1961; admitted, 1988, Ghana. *Education:* University of Ghana (LL.B., Hons., 1986); Ghana School of Law (B.L., 1988). Research Assistant to Supreme Court Judge, 1988. Tutorial Assistant, Faculty of Law, University of Ghana, 1989-1990. *Member:* Ghana Bar Association. *LANGUAGES:* French and English. *PRACTICE AREAS:* Foreign Investment Law; Commercial Law; Mining Law.

JOE GHARTEY, born Accra, Ghana, June 15, 1961; admitted, 1988, Ghana. *Education:* University of Ghana (LL.B., Hons., 1986); Ghana School of Law (B.L., 1988). Ghana Stock Exchange Certificate in Advanced Securities. Financial and Social Secretary, Greater Accra Regional Branch, Ghana Bar Association, 1992—. *Member:* Ghana Bar Association (Secretary, Legal Committee, 1992—). *LANGUAGES:* English. *PRACTICE AREAS:* Foreign Investment Law; Banking Law; International Finance Law; Securities; Taxation Law; Human Rights Law; Litigation.

NEILS HALDANE-LUTTERODT, born Accra, Ghana, May 4, 1961; admitted, 1988, Ghana. *Education:* University of Ghana (LL.B., Hons., 1984); Ghana School of Law (B.L., 1988); University of Wales (LL.M., 1993). Author: "The Legal Position of Aliens within the Economic Community of West African States," to be published; "Tendering Procedures for Contracts Financed Under the Lomé Convention," to be published. *Member:* Ghana Bar Association. *LANGUAGES:* English. *PRACTICE AREAS:* Public Procurement Law; Public Law; European Community Law; Commercial Law; Company Law; Litigation.

(This Listing Continued)

ALEX QUAYNOR, born Accra, Ghana, February 26, 1962; admitted, 1988, Ghana. *Education:* University of Ghana (LL.B., Hons., 1986); Ghana School of Law (B.L., 1988). Research Assistant to Supreme Court Judge, 1989-1990. Assistant Solicitor, Berrymans Solicitors, London, 1992. Associate Barrister, Michael Crystals Chambers, Grays Inn, London, 1992. *Member:* Ghana Bar Association. *LANGUAGES:* English. *PRACTICE AREAS:* Commercial Law; Securities; Construction Law; Human Rights Law; Litigation.

EFUA GHARTEY, born Accra, Ghana, November 11, 1966; admitted, 1991, Ghana. *Education:* University of Ghana (B.A., Hons., 1989); Ghana School of Law (B.L., 1991). *Member:* Ghana Bar Association; International Federation of Women Lawyers (FIDA) (Executive Member, FIDA Ghana). *LANGUAGES:* English and French. *PRACTICE AREAS:* Human Rights Law; Trademarks and Patents; Commercial Law.

SIGISMUND DZEBLE, born Accra, Ghana, September 21, 1966; admitted, 1991, Ghana. *Education:* University of Ghana (LL.B., Hons., 1989); Ghana School of Law (B.L., 1991). *Member:* Ghana Bar Association. *LANGUAGES:* English. *PRACTICE AREAS:* Environmental Law; Company Law; Litigation.

AKOTO AMPAW, born Lolobi-Ashiambi, Ghana, 1950; admitted, 1993, Ghana. *Education:* University of Ghana (LL.B., Hons., 1973); Ghana School of Law (B.L., 1993). *Member:* Ghana Bar Association. *LANGUAGES:* English. *PRACTICE AREAS:* Commercial Law; Company Law; Industrial Law; Litigation.

ATTA AKYEA, born Accra, Ghana, August 20, 1962; admitted, 1993, Ghana. *Education:* University of Ghana (B.A., Hons., 1989); Ghana School of Law (B.L., 1993). *Member:* Ghana Bar Association. *LANGUAGES:* English. *PRACTICE AREAS:* Criminal Law; Human Rights Law; Foreign Investment Law; Litigation.

LEGAL SUPPORT PERSONNEL

BEN MYERS (Senior Clerk).

JOHN SEKOH (Clerk).

AMARTEIFIO AND COMPANY

Solicitors, Advocates and Notaries Public

Established in 1980

AYAWASO CHAMBERS, 11TH LANE, OSU R.E.

P.O. BOX 4916

ACCRA, GHANA

Telephone: 773145; 773125

Telex: 2340 MNJ

Fax: 773175

Corporate Law, Civil Litigation, International Business Law, Admiralty and Shipping Law, Trusts, Estates and Real Property Law, Patents and Trade Mark.

FIRM PROFILE: Ayawaso Chambers was established in 1980 by Amarkai Amarteifio, Esq., who until that date was Assistant Director of Legal Services, Ministry of Defence, Accra. The firm operated from its offices on the High Street, Accra, till February, 1990 when it moved to its present offices at Osu R.E. The firm has grown to be one of the leading civil law firms in Ghana.

Its client base is largely European and North American in scope. It enjoys association with leading firms of Schön, Nolte, Finkelnburg & Clemm based in Hamburg and Messrs. Kibedi, Solicitors of London.

The head of the firm, Amarkai Amarteifio is also the Consul General of Sweden in Ghana. He also served as Minister in the Republic of Ghana.

The firm has five Associates and provides quality service to clients, including multi-national corporations.

AMARKAI AMARTEIFIO, born Accra, Ghana, April 15, 1943; called to the Bar at the Inner Temple, London, 1970. *Education:* Lanchester College, Coventry; Holborn College, University of London (LL.B., 1968); Inner Temple (B.L., 1970). Assistant Director, Legal Services, Ministry of Defence, 1971-1979. Lecturer, Company Law and Administrative Law, University of Science and Technology, Kumasi, 1977-1980. Minister of State, Republic of Ghana, 1982-1986. Consul General of Sweden in Ghana, 1990—. *Member:* Ghana Bar Association. *LANGUAGES:* English.

GEORGE AMISSAH ESHUN, born Cape Coast, Ghana, July 20, 1956; admitted, 1986, Ghana. *Education:* University of Ghana, Legion

(This Listing Continued)

AMARTEIFIO AND COMPANY, Accra—Continued

(LL.B., 1992); Ghana School of Law (B.L., 1986). Lecturer, Ghana Institute of Journalism, 1984-1991. Senior Lecturer, Ghana Institute of Journalism, 1991-1994. Author: "Press Law in Ghana," for Students of Ghana Institute of Journalism. National Union of Ghana Students Assistant to all Africa Students Union, 1982-1984. *Member:* Ghana Bar Association. *LANGUAGES:* English. *PRACTICE AREAS:* International Trade; Investment Law; Admiralty; Intellectual Property Law; Immovable Property; General Civil; Commercial Practice.

AMA SERWAH ASANTE, born Tema, Ghana, February 17, 1962; admitted, 1987, Ghana. *Education:* University of Ghana, Legion (LL.B., 1984); Ghana Law School (B.L., 1987). *Member:* Ghana Bar Association. *LANGUAGES:* English, French and Spanish.

JENNIFER AKUA TAGOE, born Accra, Ghana, October 31, 1956; admitted, 1988, Ghana. *Education:* University of Ghana. Legion (B.A., Hons., 1985); Ghana School of Law (B.L., 1988). Investigations Unit, Ghana Customs, Exise and Preventive Service, Headquarters, Accra. *Member:* Ghana Bar Association. *LANGUAGES:* English.

PETER LANKAI LAMPTEY, born Accra, Ghana, March 1, 1957; admitted, 1993, Ghana. *Education:* University of Ghana, Legion (B.A., Political Science, 1981; M.P.A., 1987); School of Law (P.C.L., 1990; B.L., 1992). Assistant Lecturer, Public Administration, School of Administration, University of Ghana, 1988-1993. *Member:* Ghana Bar Association; Ghana Institute of Management. *LANGUAGES:* English.

OTROKU TETE, born Larteh Akwapin, Ghana, December, 1948; admitted, 1993, Ghana. *Education:* University of Ghana (B.A., Hons., 1982, Post Graduate Diploma in Communication Studies, 1986); Ghana School of Law (PCL, 1990; B.L., 1993). Lecturer, Public Relations and Press Law, Ghana Institute of Journalism, 1987—. *Member:* Ghana Bar Association. *LANGUAGES:* English.

BENTSI-ENCHILL & LETSA

Established in 1990

39 CANTONMENTS ROAD
OSU R.E. ACCRA, GHANA
Telephone: (23321) 773970/773435/772591/226129/221171
Telex: 2586 (ABSC GH)
Fax: (23321) 220629/772145/772295

Mailing Address: P.O. Box 1632, Accra, Ghana

Other Accra, Ghana Office: 1st. Floor, West Wing Teachers Hall Office Complex, Off Barnes Road

Corporate, Bank Finance, Investment, Commercial and Business, Property and Conveyancing, Natural Resources, Mining, Labour, Insurance, Immigration, Entertainment, Shipping, Aviation, Taxation, Information Technology, Intellectual Property, Environment, Litigation, Alternate Dispute Resolution, Constitutional Law.

FIRM PROFILE: The firm provides prompt practical thorough and up-to-date advice to local and international corporations and law firms on all legal aspects of commerce, industry, finance and investments in Ghana's improving economy.

Also the firm contributes publications (e.g., Euromoney special supplement on International Banking Regulation) and to fora on problems of Ghana Law (e.g., World Bank Round Table on enhancing the role of Ghan's private sector in the economy's recovery).

The firm in conjunction with the Volta River Authority, Ghana National Petroleum Corporation, Minerals Commission and Accra Business Services Centre, has completed the preparation of a full text computerized database of Ghana's laws, 1982-1992 (Solon 1) business and financial laws in force. 1951-1994 (Solon 2); law reports, law journal articles, Bank of Ghana and other regulatory notices, orders, etc. Work is proceeding on the rest of Ghana's laws.

MEMBERS OF FIRM

KOJO BENTSI-ENCHILL, born Cape Coast, Ghana, April 3, 1950; admitted, 1975, Ghana. *Education:* University of Ghana, Legon (B.A., Political Science, 1971; LL.B., 1973); Ghana Law School (QCL., 1975); Magdalene College, Cambridge, Post Graduate Research on Mining Concessions Law; J. Donaldson Bye-Fellow, 1978-1979. Assistant Programme Officer, International Human Rights, Ford Foundation, 1982-1984. Foreign Associate, Shearman & Sterling, New York, 1984-1986. *Member:*

(This Listing Continued)

Ghana Bar Association; Shepherd: Fellowship of Christian Businessmen & Professionals International. *LANGUAGES:* English, French, Fanti and Ga.

DIVINE KWAKU DUWOSE LETSA, born Kumasi, Ghana, April 19, 1950; admitted, 1975, Ghana. *Education:* University of Ghana, Legon (LL.B., 1973); Ghana Law School (QCL., 1975). Legal Officer, State Insurance Corporation of Ghana, 1975-1979. Private Legal Practice, Sekyere Chambers, Kumasi, 1979-1984. Lecturer, Faculty of Law, University of Cross River State, Nigeria, 1984-1986. Assistant Director, Civil Litigation and Legal Advice, Ministry of Justice, Cross River State, Nigeria, 1986-1988. *Member:* Ghana Bar Association; Chartered Institute of Arbitrators, London (Associate). *LANGUAGES:* English, Ewe, Twi and Ga.

KWABENA ASARE ADAIR MATE, born London, U.K., August 23, 1955; admitted, 1980, Ghana. *Education:* University of Ghana, Legon (LL.B., 1978); Ghana Law School (QCL., 1980). Law Reporter, Council for Law Reporting, 1980-1984. Junior Counsel, Private Legal Practice, 1981-1984. Legal Officer, Bank for Housing and Construction, 1984-1990. Senior Legal Officer, Minerals Commission, 1990-1993. *Member:* Ghana Bar Association. *LANGUAGES:* English, French, German, Ga and Twi.

ASSOCIATES

PHILIPPA THERESA DENNIS AMABLE, (MRS.), born Cape Coast, Ghana, October 1, 1953; admitted, 1979, Ghana. *Education:* University of Ghana, Legion (B.A., Hons., English); Ghana School of Law (QCL., 1979). Lecturer in English, Ghana Institute of Languages, 1975-1981. Junior Counsel, Private Legal Practice, Akyem Chambers, 1979-1981. Private Chambers (Bill J. Carrol), Ithaca N.Y., U.S.A., 1982-1985. Private Practice, Mawulorm Chambers, Senior Counsel, 1988-1993. Head, Legal Department, DataCenta, 1993. *Member:* Ghana Bar Association. *LANGUAGES:* English, French, German, Ga, Twi, Fanti, Ewe.

AMELIA BADZA, (MRS.), born Cape Coast, Ghana, May 26, 1965; admitted, 1989, Ghana. *Education:* University of Ghana (LL.B., 1987); Ghana School of Law (QCL., 1989). *Member:* Ghana Bar Association. *LANGUAGES:* English, French, Fanti and Ga.

SADIA ATAMI CHINERY-HESSE, (MRS.), born Freetown, Sierra Leone, August 5, 1965; admitted, 1990, U.K. *Education:* University of London, U.K. (LL.B., 1986); The Law Society (Solicitor, 1990). Article Clerk, Assistant Solicitor, Philip Ross & Co., London, 1987-1991. Senior Secretarial Assistant, Whitbread OPLC, London, 1991-1993. *Member:* The Law Society; The Sierra Leone Bar Association; The International Federation of Women Lawyers Associate; Chartered Institute of Secretaries and Administrators. *LANGUAGES:* English and Krio.

KWESI ATTA PANYIN BAIDEN, born Sekondi, Ghana, January 7, 1968; admitted, 1993, Ghana. *Education:* University of Ghana (LL.B., 1991); Ghana School of Law (QCL., 1993). *Member:* Ghana Bar Association. *LANGUAGES:* English and Akan.

LEGAL SUPPORT PERSONNEL

Albert Addo Allotey
(Secretary, Law Clerk)
Brenda Aikins, (Mrs.)
(Secretary)

Moira Gbedemah-Ewa, (Mrs.)
(Accountant)

BRUCE-LYLE, BANNERMAN & THOMPSON

Established in 1969

87 LIBERTY AVENUE
P.O. BOX 581
ACCRA, GHANA
Telephone: 221491
Cable Address: "Reggis" Accra
Fax: 233 21 773738

Commercial, Company, Trade Marks and Patents, Merchant Shipping, Real Property Law. Civil Wrongs. International Business Transactions, Maritime Law, Banking, Industrial Relations and Labor Law.

FIRM PROFILE: The firm was established in 1969 and offers the range of services listed. The client base is mainly British and North American.

(This Listing Continued)

PRINCIPAL MEMBER

REGINALD E. BANNERMAN, born Accra, Ghana, April 22, 1934; admitted, 1958, England; 1959, Ghana; 1960, Nigeria. *Education:* St. Peter's College; Oxford University (B.A., Hons., 1957; M.A., 1960); Gray's Inn, London (Barrister-at-law, 1958); Yale University, U.S.A. (LL.M., 1963). Notary Public, Ghana, 1970. Author: Negligence: "The Reasonable Man and Duty of Care In Anglo-American Jurisprudence," University of Ghana Law Review, 1966; Briefing on Ghana: "Encouraging Foreign Investors," International Financial Law Review, (IFL) October, 1983; "Foreign Investment in Ghana," IFL , March, 1986; "Digging for Gold in Ghana," IFL, July 1987. Joint Author: "Recovery of Commercial Debt in Ghana," Practical Guide for Commercial Information and Debt Collection in A.C.P. Countries, Dakar Union, May, 1988; "Ghana's Petroleum Tax Law," IFL, January, 1989; "Ghana's Bank Reform," IFL, July, 1991. Briefing on (a) Financial Institutions (Non-Banking) Law. (b) Finance Lease Law, IFL, December, 1993. Lecturer, Law of Torts and Public International Law, Faculty of Law. Ahmadu Bello University, Nigeria, 1964-1966. Mayor and Chairman, Accra-Tema City Council, 1968-1969. Moderator, Institute of Chartered Accountants, 1971-1980. Director, Capital Investments Board, 1972-1980. Member, Inter-Ministerial Committee for the Establishment of Industries, 1977-1980. *Member:* Ghana Bar Association (Assistant Secretary, 1971-1972). *LANGUAGES:* English. *PRACTICE AREAS:* Trademarks and Patents; International Business Transactions.

VIDAL L. BUCKLE & CO.

WUOWOTI CHAMBERS
10 CANTONMENTS ROAD ACCRA
ACCRA, GHANA
Telephone: 775468 Accra
Cable Address: "Wuowoti" Accra
Telex: 3033
Fax: 233-21-665960; 233-21-662680

Mailing Address: P.O. Box 362 Accra

General Counselling and General Trial Appellate and Administrative Practice. Corporate, Commercial, Revenue, Maritime, Shipping, Transportation, Aviation, Immigration and Nationality, Building and Construction, Mining, Labor, Banking, Insurance, Investment, Intellectual Property and Property and Real Estate Law. Collections. Trademark and Patent Agents.

FIRM PROFILE: Incorporated in 1970 as successors to the Law Office of Wuowoti Chambers founded in 1911 by Vernon Lushington Buckle, Barrister-at-Law of Lincoln's Inn, this Law Firm has, over the years, extended its scope of practice from that of a Sole Practitioner to that of a fully-equipped Law Firm served by a Partner, two Principal Associates, four Senior Associates and two Associates with supporting staff of two Para-Legal Assistants, two Secretaries and two Law Clerks. The Firm provides a wide range of business-related services for corporate clients requiring professional representation and service in a broad range of business activities including Trade and Commerce, Banking, Investments, Insurance, Building and Construction, Mining, Shipping and Aviation.

SOLE PARTNER

VIDAL LUSHINGTON BUCKLE, born Accra, Ghana, July 21, 1927. called to the English Bar at Lincoln's Inn, 1959; admitted to practice as Barrister and Solicitor, Ghana, 1959; Sierra Leone, 1983. *Education:* Fourah Bay College University of Durham (B.A., English, Economics, Philosophy, 1950); Lincoln's Inn, London, England (Barrister-at-Law, 1959). Assistant Solicitor, Ghana Internal Revenue Department, 1960-1961. Head of Legal Department, Bank of Ghana and Foreign Exchange Controller, 1961-1968. Corporation Counsel and Corporation Secretary, Ghana Industrial Holding Corporation, 1968-1970. Head of Chambers Vidal L. Buckle & Co. since 1970; Correspondent, International Banking and Securities Law, published by Euromoney Publications Plc.; Doing Business in Sub-Saharan Africa, published by the American Bar Association Section of International Law and Practice. Contributing Author: The Digest of Commercial Laws of the World and The Digest of Patent and Trademark Laws of the World; Commercial Agencies and Distributorships; International Guide, Edited by Adam Fremantle of Coudert Brothers and published by Prentice Hall Law and Business. Member of the Bar: England and Wales, Ghana and Sierra Leone. *Member:* International Bar Association; Commonwealth Lawyers' Association; Union Internationale des Avocats; World Association of Lawyers; World Peace Through Law Center; American Bar Association (Associate Member); Inter-American Bar Association (Associate Member); Ghana Bar Association (Disciplinary Committee Member). Notary Public. *LANGUAGES:* English and Ga. *PRACTICE AREAS:* Corporate; Com-

(This Listing Continued)

mercial; Revenue; Shipping; Aviation; Banking; Insurance; Investment and Securities Law.

PRINCIPAL ASSOCIATES

THOMAS NUAKO WARD-BREW, born Kumasi, Ghana, March 29, 1941. admitted to practice in Ghana as Barrister-at-Law and Solicitor, 1977. *Education:* University of Ghana (B.A., Economics, Political Science, Sociology, 1969). *LANGUAGES:* English and Fanti. *PRACTICE AREAS:* Corporate; Commercial; Revenue; Banking; Investment Law.

FELIX KODZO KORLEY, born Anloga, Ghana, May 18, 1942. admitted to practice in Ghana as Barrister-at-Law and Solicitor, 1981. *Education:* University of Ghana (B.A., Geography, Sociology, Political Science, 1968); Ghana Institute of Management and Public Administration (Cert. P.A., 1971). *LANGUAGES:* English and Ewe. *PRACTICE AREAS:* Commercial; Public Utilities; Investment Law.

SENIOR ASSOCIATES

DAVID ANDREAS HESSE, born Accra, Ghana, June 26, 1960. admitted to practice in Ghana as Barrister-at Law and Solicitor, 1984. *Education:* University of Ghana (LL.B. Hons., 1982). *Member:* International Bar Association; Commonwealth Lawyers' Association; American Bar Association (Associate Member). *LANGUAGES:* English and Ga. *PRACTICE AREAS:* Corporate; Commercial; Investment Nationality; Immigration Law; Commercial Investment Law.

SAMUEL MARFUL-SAU, born Assin Adubiase, Ghana, February 3, 1956. admitted to practice in Ghana as Barrister-at-Law and Solicitor, 1984. *Education:* University of Ghana (LL.B. Hons., 1982). *LANGUAGES:* English and Fanti. *PRACTICE AREAS:* Nationality; Immigration; Human Rights; Commercial Law.

MOHAMMED NABON, born Tumu, Ghana, June 6, 1956. admitted to practice in Ghana as Barrister-at-Law and Solicitor, 1988. *Education:* University of Ghana (B.A., Hons., 1985). *LANGUAGES:* English and Hausa. *PRACTICE AREAS:* Corporate; Commercial; Insurance Law.

SIMON MENSAH AKOLLOR, born Ghana, August 23, 1953. Admitted to practice as Barrister-at-Law and Solicitor in 1986. *Education:* University of Science and Technology (Economics and Geography Social Science 1976); University of Ghana and Ghana School of Administration 1987; Commissioned Ghana Military Academy 1977. Military Intelligence Service, 1978-1991, Ghana Border Guard Headquarters, 1981-1986, Investigating Counsel National Drug Abuse Task Force, 1986, United Nations Peace Keeping Medal: 1980; Vidal L. Buckle & Co. since 1992. *LANGUAGES:* English and Ewe. *PRACTICE AREAS:* International Trade and Revenue Law.

ASSOCIATES

CHRISTINE DOWUONA-HAMMOND, born Accra, December 16, 1964. admitted to practice as Barrister-at-Law and Solicitor 1990. *Education:* University of Ghana (LL.B. Hons, 1987); Ghana Law School (Awarded John Mensah Sarbah Prize for best Overall performance) 1988-1989; University of Michigan (LL.M., 1991). Lecturer, faculty of Law University of Ghana from October, 1991. Visiting Senior Research Fellow, Faculty of Law State University of Leyden in the Netherlands, Vidal L. Buckle & Co from 1992. *LANGUAGES:* English, Ga and Fanti. *PRACTICE AREAS:* Corporate; Commercial; Banking; Investment Law.

TRUEDY OKARLEY BROWN, born Accra, December 10, 1967. *Education:* University of Ghana Legon (B.A., 1992); Ghana School of Law (1994). admitted to practice in Ghana as Barrister-at-Law and Solicitor, 1994. *LANGUAGES:* English, Ga and Twi. *PRACTICE AREAS:* Investment and Banking Law.

Language: English.

FUGAR & COMPANY

Established in 1977

WESLEY HOUSE
LIBERIA ROAD
P.O. BOX 6274
ACCRA, GHANA
Telephone: 233 (021) 229675; 229699; 228988
Fax: 233 (021) 669589

Corporate, Banking, Investment, Immigration, Construction and Building, Real Estate & Property, Industrial Relations and Labour, Mining, International Business Transactions, Mercantile and Shipping, Intellectual Property Taxation Litigation, Environmental Law, Notaries Public.

MEMBERS OF FIRM

WILLIAM EDEM FUGAR, born April 25, 1942. *Education:* University of Ghana (B.A., 1967; LL.B., Hons., 1971); Ghana School of Law (B.L., 1973). Notary Public. *Members:* International Bar Association (Section on Business Law). (Managing Partner). *LANGUAGES:* English and Ewe. *PRACTICE AREAS:* Investment Law; Mining Law; Company Law; Banking; Litigation; Taxation.

ASSOCIATES

GERTRUDE ARABA ESAABA TORKORNOO, born September 11, 1962. *Education:* University of Ghana (B.A., 1984); Ghana School of Law (B.L., 1986). Associate Solicitor, Construction Law Department, Nabarro Nathanson, London, 1989-1991. Associate Consultant, Management and Development Productivity Institute. *Member:* International Federation of Women Lawyers; International Bar Association; International Constructions Contracts Committee. *LANGUAGES:* English and Fante. *PRACTICE AREAS:* Construction Law; Contract Law; Company Law; Labour Law; Intellectual Property Law; Advocacy.

LAWRENCE OTOO, born February 24, 1964. *Education:* University of Ghana (LL.B., 1987); Ghana School of Law (B.L., 1989). Research Assistant to Supreme Court Judge. Author: "Expulsion of Aliens, the African Experience." *Member:* International Bar Association. *LANGUAGES:* English, Fante and Ga. *PRACTICE AREAS:* Immigration and Advocacy; Litigation.

MARIANNE QUANSAH, born August 21, 1966. *Education:* University of Ghana (B.A., 1988); Ghana School of Law (B.L., 1991); Diploma, Language and Secretarial Skills. Research Assistant to Supreme Court Judge. *LANGUAGES:* English, Fante and Ga.

ALIKEM JOSEPHA ADADEVOH, born March 18, 1967. *Education:* University of Ghana (LL.B., 1989); Ghana School of Law (B.L., 1992). *Member:* International Federation of Women Lawyers (FIDA). *LANGUAGES:* English and Ewe. *PRACTICE AREAS:* Human Rights; Intellectual Property.

ANTHONY ASHITEI LITHUR, born January 26, 1964. *Education:* University of Ghana, Legion (LL.B., 1988); Ghana School of Law (B.L., 1990). *LANGUAGES:* English and Ewe. *PRACTICE AREAS:* Corporate Law; Litigation.

GODWIN NUNYA FUGAR, born August 26, 1964. *Education:* University of Ghana (B.A., 1990); Ghana School of Law (B.L., 1993). *LANGUAGES:* English, Ewe and Ga. *PRACTICE AREAS:* Company Law; Litigation and Insurance.

JULIANA EWURAESI AMONOO-NEIZER, born February 13, 1966. *Education:* University of Ghana (LL.B., 1990); Ghana School of Law (B.L., 1992). *Member:* International Federation of Women Lawyers (FIDA). *LANGUAGES:* English and Fante. *PRACTICE AREAS:* Environmental Law; Natural Resources Law; Family Law.

VIVIANE ZOE VAN DYCK, born December 20, 1964. *Education:* University of ghana (B.A., 1990); Ghana School of Law (B.L., 1994). *Member:* International Federation of Women Lawyers (FIDA). *LANGUAGES:* English, French, Spanish and Fante. *PRACTICE AREAS:* Company Law; Advocacy and Family Law.

All Lawyers are both Solicitors and Barristers and are Members of the Ghana Bar Association.

SAM OKUDZETO & ASSOCIATES
SENA CHAMBERS

Established in 1971

MOBIL HOUSE
LIBERIA ROAD
P.O. BOX 5520
ACCRA, GHANA
Telephone: 233-21-666377; 668114
Fax: 233-21-668115
Telex: 2017 TAKMIL GH; 2219 FARMEX GH

Mining and Mineral Law, Privatization, Corporate Law Practice, Commercial, Civil Litigation, Immigration, Industrial and Labour Law, International Trade and Investment, Human Rights, Mercantile and Shipping Law, Air and Space Law, Investment Law, Notary Public, Intellectual Property, Patents and Trademarks.

SENIOR PARTNER

SAM OKUDZETO, born September 4, 1935. called to the Bar, 1963, Inner Temple, London; 1963, Ghana. *Education:* Corporation of Secretaries (Final Certificate, 1958; Licentiate Membership, 1959); London University (Bachelor of Laws, Honours, 1961); College of Europe (Certificate of Advance European Studies, 1963; Diploma, 1963). Fellow, Chartered Institute of Secretaries and Administrators, 1972. Notary Public, 1975. Senior Advocate of Ghana, 1991. *Member:* International Bar Association; Commonwealth Law Society. *LANGUAGES:* English. *PRACTICE AREAS:* Mining and Mineral Law; Privatization Law; Corporate Law; Commercial Litigation; Immigration Law; Industrial Law; Labour Law; International Trade Law; International Investment Law; Human Rights Law; Mercantile Law; Shipping Law; Air and Space Law; Investment Law; Intellectual Property Law.

JUNIOR PARTNER

NENE ABAYATEYE OFOE AMEGATCHER, born February 3, 1953. *Education:* University of Ghana, Legon (B.A., Comb-Honours-Law and Political Science, 1977); Ghana School of Law (B.L., 1980). *Member:* International Bar Association (Member, Section on General Practice); Ghana Bar Association. *LANGUAGES:* English. *PRACTICE AREAS:* Civil Litigation; Commercial Litigation; International Trade Law; Investment Law; Human Rights Law; Corporate Law; Shipping Law; Air and Space Law; Constitutional Law; Property Law.

ASSOCIATES

BEATRICE AKUA ABREKNA DUNCAN, born July 15, 1964. *Education:* University of Ghana, Legon (LL.B., 1986); Ghana School of Law (B.L., 1988). *LANGUAGES:* English. *PRACTICE AREAS:* Commercial Law; Investment Law; Women's Rights; Public Policy; International Law; Constitutional Law.

ROBERTSON WOLANYO KPATSA, born January 27, 1964. *Education:* University of Ghana, Legon (LL.B., 1988); Ghana School of Law (B.L., 1990). Solicitor and Advocate to the Legal Aid Board, Ghana. *LANGUAGES:* English. *PRACTICE AREAS:* Commercial Law; Immigration Law; Conveyancing; Property Law.

AWURAA ABENA SAFOA AFRIYIE BOAFO, born September 13, 1966. *Education:* University of Ghana, Legon (LL.B., 1989); Ghana School

(This Listing Continued)

of Law (B.L., 1991). Teaching Assistant, Faculty of Law, University of Ghana, Legon 1991-1992. *LANGUAGES:* English. *PRACTICE AREAS:* Contract Law.

IRAN

ALEXANDER AGHAYAN & ASSOCIATES
ATTORNEYS AT LAW

Established in 1912

149 SARHANG SAKHAI AVENUE (FORMER SEVOM ESFAND)
TEHRAN 11354, IRAN
Telephone: (98-21) 675056
Telefax: (98-21) 674858
Cable Address: "Aghayan, Tehran"
Telex: 212894 AAG IR

Paris, France liaison Office: 9, Rue D'Anjou, 75008. Telephone: 42 65 13 04. Telex: 660853. Fax: 47 42 72 15.
New York, N.Y. liaison Office: 666 Fifth Avenue, 10103. Telephone: (212) 586-7272. Fax: (212) 307-7623.

International Law. General Civil Practice. Tax, Insurance, Corporate, Commercial, Banking, Trial, Foreign Investment, Maritime, Patents and Trademarks.

MEMBERS OF FIRM

ALEXANDER AGHAYAN, born May 13, 1952; admitted, 1976, District of Columbia; 1980, New York (Not admitted in Iran). *Education:* Williams College (B.A. in Economics, 1973); Harvard Law School (J.D., 1976). (Resident, New York, N.Y. Office). *LANGUAGES:* Farsi, English, French, Spanish and Portuguese.

SHAHIN AGHAYAN, born January 28, 1918; admitted, 1965, Iran; 1988, as Conseil Juridique, France. *Education:* Brussels University, Belgium (Licencie en Sciences Economiques et Financieres). (Resident, Paris France Office); (Also Of Counsel, Cabinet Mitchell-Heggs & Associes, Paris, France). *LANGUAGES:* Farsi, English, French, Spanish and Portuguese.

J. BOZORGMEHR, born Astara, Iran, 1914; admitted, 1961, Iran. *Education:* University of Tehran School of Law (LL.B., 1939). *Member:* Tehran Bar Association.

H. KHAYATZADEH, born Khorramabad, Iran, June 25, 1932; admitted, 1974, Iran. *Education:* University of Tehran (License in Law). *Member:* Tehran Bar Association.

INTERNATIONAL LAW OFFICE
DR. BEHROOZ AKHLAGHI AND
ASSOCIATES

Established in 1978

NO. 17, FOURTH LANE, AHMAD GHASSIR AVE. (BUCCAREST AVE.)
TEHRAN 15146, IRAN
Telephone: (21) 873 66 11; (21) 873 21 38
Cable Address: Dr. Akhlaghi
Telex: 222541 ILOA IR
Telefax: (21) 873 41 29

Civil and Commercial, International Trade, Foreign Investment, Transportation specially Shipping Affairs, International Contracts, Banking Affairs, Labour, Corporates, Trademark, Patent and Arbitration Law.

FIRM PROFILE: The firm offers a full range of legal services. The procedure for rendering services in this firm is based on team work through specialized groups with cooperation of a number of highly qualified lawyers as well as eminent attorneys and experts in various branches. The firm has a legal support staff of 8 consisting of paralegal personnel, CPAs and office administrators.

(This Listing Continued)

MEMBERS OF FIRM

DR. BEHROOZ AKHLAGHI, born Iran, December 1, 1937; admitted, 1964, Iran. *Education:* Tehran University, Faculty of Law (Bachelor and Doctorate Degree); Law Faculty of Aix-en-Provence (France: Doctorat d'etat-Ph.D.); Oxford University, Faculty of Law. Author: "Commercial Law: Negotiable Instruments-Commercial Contracts," "International Trade Law," "Maritime Law," "Air Law," published at the Law Faculty of Tehran University, 1989. Associate Professor at Tehran University. *Member:* Iranian and American Bar Associations. *LANGUAGES:* Farsi, French, English and Arabic. *PRACTICE AREAS:* Commercial Law; International Trade Law.

DR. PARVIZ PARVIZIAN, born Iran, February 12, 1938. *Education:* Oxford University (International Relations Course, 1972); Tehran University, Faculty of Law and Political Sciences (Ph.D., 1978). *LANGUAGES:* English and Farsi. *PRACTICE AREAS:* Foreign Investment; International Contracts.

MRS. MAHNAZ MEHRINFAR (AKHLAGHI), born Iran, 1953. *Education:* Tehran University, Faculty of Law and Political Sciences (LL.B., in International Relations); Oxford University (Airlines Affairs). *LANGUAGES:* Farsi and English. *PRACTICE AREAS:* Contracts; Airlines Affairs.

LEGAL SUPPORT PERSONNEL
PARALEGAL

DR. FATEMEH GHADIMIPOUR, born Iran, October 25, 1945. *Education:* Tehran University Faculty of Law and Political Science (B.A., 1967); Free University of Brussels (Ph.D., in Political Science and International Relations, 1973). Former Assistant Professor, Center for International Studies, Tehran University. *LANGUAGES:* Farsi, English and French. *PRACTICE AREAS:* Foreign Investment; Free Economic Zones.

MRS. SHIRIN NAYERNOURI, born Iran, May 10, 1958. *Education:* Faculty of Law of National University of Iran (1976-1978); American College in Paris (B.A. in International Affairs, 1981); Law Faculty of Université Paris II (LL.B., 1983; LL.M., 1984). *LANGUAGES:* Farsi, English and French. *PRACTICE AREAS:* International Contracts and Trade; Corporate Law; Trademark and Patent.

MRS. ZARRINTAJ SHAMSIMEYMANDI, born Iran, November 25, 1952. *Education:* Tehran University Faculty of Law (B.A., 1974); University of Dallas, Texas, U.S.A. (M.S. in Industrial Administration, 1978). *LANGUAGES:* Farsi and English. *PRACTICE AREAS:* Industrial Administration; Banking Affairs.

MRS. SOUSSAN KHATTATAN, born Tehran, 1951. *Education:* Tehran University Faculty of Law (B.A., 1973); Cambridge University (Diploma, Comparative Legal Studies, 1976). *LANGUAGES:* Farsi and English. *PRACTICE AREAS:* Foreign Investment; International Contracts.

PROFESSOR S.H. AMIN

TEHRAN, IRAN

(See Edinburgh, Scotland)

Middle East and Islamic Law.

DR. ANVARI & ASSOCIATES
LAW OFFICE

TEHRAN, IRAN

(See London, England)

Consultant on the Laws of Iran.
Iranian lawyer practicing in London, registered with the Law Society of England since 1982.

LAW OFFICES
A.A. ATAI & ASSOCIATES

Attorneys at Law

Established in 1975

NO. 8, 3RD FLOOR, 14 STREET
KHALED ISLAMBOLI AVENUE (VOZARA)
P.O. BOX 15875-1633
TEHRAN 15117, IRAN
Telephone: 021-8713850
Telefax: 021-8715252
Telex: (021) 213286 RICH IR; 214007 SETC IR

Commercial Law, International Business, Corporate, Marine and Contracts Law, Litigation.

FIRM PROFILE: *The firm was established in 1975. It offers a full range of Legal Services, its offices are situated in the Commercial and Diplomatic Area of Tehran and is well known for its International experience. Has been acting for the International and Iranian Clients including Banks, Manufactures, Foreign Investors and Commercial Companies.*

ALI AKBAR ATAI, born Tehran, Iran, 1942; admitted, 1973, Tehran. *Education:* University of Tabriz (B.A., 1966); University of Tehran (LL.B., 1970); University of Iran (M.A., Law). *Member:* Iranian Bar Association. *LANGUAGES:* English, Farsi, and German. *PRACTICE AREAS:* International Contracts; Investment and Establishment of Joint Ventures.

ASSOCIATES

HOOSHANG NEJAD TOULAMI, born 1939; admitted, 1976, Tehran. *Education:* (LL.B.). *Member:* Tehran Bar Association. *LANGUAGES:* Farsi. *PRACTICE AREAS:* Litigation.

HOSSEIN LOTFI, born 1957; admitted, 1990, Tehran. *Education:* (LL.B., M.A.). *Member:* Tehran Bar Association. *LANGUAGES:* English and Farsi. *PRACTICE AREAS:* International Business; Marine and Registration.

LEGAL SUPPORT PERSONNEL

T.A. POUR. LANGUAGES: English and Farsi. *PRACTICE AREAS:* Commercial and Technical Matters.

S.J. SALEHI

REPRESENTATIVE CLIENTS: Telefonaktiebolaget L M Ericsson; Sandvik Int. AB (Sweden); Motorenfabrik Hatz GmbH & Co.KG; Deutsche Bank AG; OSRAM GmbH (Germany); ILBAU Gesellschaft mbH (Austria); Saipem SPA (Italy); Lavalin Snc International (Canada).

LAW OFFICE OF
ALBERT BERNARDI & ASSOCIATES

Attorneys at Law

Established in 1948

262, FERDOWSSI AVENUE
TEHRAN, IRAN
Telephone: 304322; 3118984
Cable Address: Bernardi
Fax: 9821/304322

Penal and Civil Proceedings, Corporate Law, Transportation and Maritime Law, Arbitration, Trademarks and Patents.

ALBERT BERNARDI, born Tehran, Iran, May 21, 1926; admitted, 1948, Iran. *Education:* University of Tehran, Faculty of Law (LL.B., 1948); Honorary Doctorate of Law, International University Foundation of Delaware, 1989. Author: Translation from English into Persian of the book *Courtroom* by Quentin Reynolds, 450 pages. Former Counselor, Iranian Government, the Iran-United States Claims Arbitration Tribunal in the Hague, The Netherlands, 1984-1985. *Member:* Iranian Bar Association (Member of Council, 1970-1972); International Bar Association. *LANGUAGES:* Persian (Native Language), English, French and Armenian. *PRACTICE AREAS:* Penal and Civil Proceedings; Corporate Law; Transportation and Maritime Law; Trademarks and Patents.

ASSOCIATES

ALI NOURI, born 1947; admitted, 1972, Iran. *LANGUAGES:* Persian and French. *PRACTICE AREAS:* Corporate Law.

(This Listing Continued)

REPRESENTATIVE CLIENTS: Mitsubishi Corporation of Japan; Chiyoda Corporation of Japan; West of England (P & I Club).
REFERENCES: R.J. Reynolds Tobacco Co. (Patent Department) of N.C., USA; Braun Aktiengesellschaft of Germany; Italian Consulate in Tehran, Iran (Legal adviser); Beecham Pharmaceuticals (England).

LAW OFFICES
DR. DASHTARA & ASSOCIATES

16 SECOND ST., PAKISTAN AVE.
TEHRAN 15316, IRAN
Telephone: (21) 8732161
Fax: (21) 8746010

Investment, Corporation, Contract, Joint Venture, Taxation, Insurance, Banking, Financing, Construction, Transfer of Technology, Patent & Trademark, Transportation & Maritime, Litigation and Arbitration.

MEMBERS OF FIRM

REZA DASHTARA, born 1930; admitted, 1957, Iran. *Education:* Tehran University Law School (LL.B., 1955); George Washington University Law School (LL.M., 1971; S.J.D., 1973). Legal Advisor: The National Iranian Oil Company, The National Iranian Gas Company, The National Petrochemical Company of Iran, TAVANIR Co. (Iran Power Generation & Transmission) 1955-1981. Professorial Lecturer: Private International Law, Shipping Law, Insurance Law, Law of the Sea: National University of Iran, School of Law and Business Administration; ECO International School of Insurance; University of Marine Sciences 1974-1985. *Member:* Iranian Bar Association; International Bar Association; American Society of International Law. (Senior Partner).

IRADJ MIRZA MAHMOUD. *Education:* Frankfurt University (B.A.); National University of Iran (LL.B.).

MUSSA AKHAVI. *Education:* Tehran University (LL.B.); Paris University (LL.D.).

FATOLLAH NASSIRI. *Education:* Tehran University (LL.B.); Paris University (LL.D.).

KHOSROW ASSADI. *Education:* Tehran University (B.A.; M.A.); Paris University (Ph.D.).

JAMALUDDIN FARJAD. *Education:* Tehran University (LL.B.).

Languages: English, French, German

LAW OFFICES OF
DR. MOSTAFA EMAMI & ASSOCIATES

Established in 1967

358 TALEGHANI AVE.
P.O. BOX 11365-3153
TEHRAN 15636, IRAN
Telephone: 761464; 750-5959; 688643
Fax: 0098-21-761464

U.S. Mailing Address: 3366 Mt. Diablo Blvd. #20, Lafayette, CA 94549. Telephone/Fax: (510) 284-1326.

International Business Contracts, Trademarks and Patents, Settlement of Disputes, Civil and Corporate Law, Banking, Investments, Credit Financing.

MOSTAFA EMAMI, born Tehran, Iran, May 1, 1925; admitted, 1961, Tehran. *Education:* University of Tehran (LL.B., 1958; Doctorate, 1961). Lecturer: Basic Civil Law, International Relations, History of Political Thoughts, Law of Banking, University of Tehran, 1965-1974; Azad University, 1994. *Member:* Iranian Bar Association. *LANGUAGES:* English. *PRACTICE AREAS:* International Business Contracts; Trademarks; Patents; Settlement of Disputes; Civil Law; Corporate Law; Banking; Investments; Credit Financing.

ASSOCIATE

ASGHAR DILMAGHANIAN, born Oromyeh, Iran, January 14, 1925; admitted, 1971, Tehran. *Education:* University of Tehran (LL.B., 1958). *Member:* Iranian Bar Association. *LANGUAGES:* English.

(This Listing Continued)

REPRESENTATIVE CLIENTS: Bank Melli Iran; Telecommunication Company of Iran; Iran Mines Export Development Co. (IMEDCO) (Ministry of Metals & Mines); Lloyds Bank Rep. Office in Iran; ANZ Grindlays Bank Rep.; Kanematsu Iran Ltd.; Kerman White Cement Co.; Tehran Commercial Complex Co.; International Charity Foundation of Iran; Ministry of Jihad.

MAHMOUD KATIRAI

NUMBER 4 SECOND STREET, MIR-EMAD AVENUE
SUITE 3
TEHRAN, IRAN
Telephone: 857887
Fax: 843913

Washington, D.C. Office: 1300 Nineteenth Street, N.W., Suite 407, 20036. Telephone: 202-659-4245.

General Practice of law with particular attention to Corporate Law, International Law; Serving as an Expert on Iranian Law before Courts and Arbitration Tribunals; Providing Advice on Contract, Corporate and Immigration Laws; Transnational Agreements and Investment Arrangements; Negotiating and Drafting Contracts and Joint Venture Agreements; Organizing Companies and Partnerships, Preparing Corporate Legal Documents and Registering both Foreign and Domestic Legal Entities in Iran.

MAHMOUD KATIRAI, born Shiraz, Iran, 1943; admitted, 1969, Iran; 1985, District of Columbia. Education: University of Tehran (Licentiate in Law, 1965); National University of Iran (LL.M., 1972); Georgetown University Law School (M.C.L., 1983). Co-Author, "Establishing a Joint Stock Company in Iran," The Industrial & Mining Development Bank of Iran, 1971. Instructor, Commercial Law, School of Insurance, Tehran, 1971. Official English Translator, Iranian Ministry of Justice, 1971-1980. Partner, Katirai & Fathipour Law Offices, Tehran, 1980-1981. Principal and Partner: John A. Westberg & Associates, Inc. and Katirai & Associates, Tehran, 1975-1979. Law Clerk: Patton, Boggs & Blow, Washington, D.C., 1972-1973. Apprentice in Law, Law Offices of Dr. Musa Sabi, 1969. Associate: John A. Westberg & Associates, Inc., Tehren, 1969-1972, 1973-1974; Law Offices of Dr. Alexander Aghayan & Associates, Tehran, 1973-1974. Member: District of Columbia Bar; Tehran Bar Association. **LANGUAGES:** Farsi and English. **PRACTICE AREAS:** General Practice; International Law; Business Law; Iranian Law.

KORDESTANI, TOROSSIAN & ASSOCIATES

Established in 1977

NO. 17, KUYE SAAM
G. FARAHANI AVENUE
TEHRAN 15899, IRAN
Telephone: 832353; 826779; 839486
Cable Address: Kordestani Tehran
Telex: 213815 KTM IR
Fax: (021) 839487

Corporate, Commercial, Tax, Foreign Investment, Insurance, Banking, Maritime, Civil and International Law, Litigation and Arbitration, Patent and Trademarks.

FIRM PROFILE: The firm was established in 1977 and offers a full range of legal services. It is well known for its Corporate and Commercial Law with an emphases on international issues. The client base is European, Asian and North American in scope.

MEMBERS OF FIRM

DARVISH M. KORDESTANI, born Tehran, Iran, October 15, 1939; admitted, 1971, Iran. Education: University of California at Hayward (B.A., with honors, 1967); Boalt Hall School of Law, University of California (J.D., 1971). Managing Editor, University of California Law Review, 1970-1971. **LANGUAGES:** Farsi and English.

VREJ TOROSSIAN, born Tehran, Iran, October 4, 1947; admitted, 1974, Iran. Education: National University of Iran (License in Law, with honors, 1971). **LANGUAGES:** Farsi, Armenian and English.

RAANA HAGHIGHAT KASHANI, born Tehran, Iran, November 21, 1963. Education: San Jose State University (B.A. with honors, 1987); Santa Clara University Law School (J.D., 1991). President, Middle Eastern Law Student Association. **LANGUAGES:** Farsi and English.

(This Listing Continued)

REPRESENTATIVE CLIENTS: Abbott Laboratories; Bank of America; Citibank N.A.; Eastman Kodak Co.; Ford Aerospace & Communications International Inc.; Daimler-Benz AG; ABB Asea Brown Boveri Ltd.; SAE SADELMI S.p.A.; ALITALIA; S. Dyrup & Co. A/S; Maersk Line; Nissho Iwai Corp.; Sumitomo Corp.; Mitsubishi Corp.; Schering-Plough Corp.; Mannesmann AG; Robert Bosch GmbH. Nestle S.A.; Daf N.V.; Peugeot S.A.; Metra Corporation; Eli Lilly International Corp.

PARS ASSOCIATES

12 MOGHAN STREET
4TH STREET, ZARTOSHT AVENUE
P.O. BOX 11365-6665
TEHRAN, IRAN
Telephone: 98.21.651169
Fax: 98.21.657197
Telex: 212107 MATN IR

Paris, France Office: Gérard Guillot Pars Associates. 33 Rue De La Bienfaisance, 75008. Telephone: 33.1.43 59 15 70. Fax: 33.1.42 56 14 80.

Construction law, Corporate law, Banking law, Oil and Mining law, Foreign investments, general legal and tax practice.

FIRM PROFILE: Firm established in 1979. Specialized in legal assistance to international contractors and investors in Iran. Maître Gérard Guillot, the international partner, opened the international branch in 1980 in Paris. Editor of the Iranian codes and of the weekly legal and tax bulletin "legal information service" in English.

MEMBERS OF FIRM

Zoreh Majdzadeh
Reza Matine

M. Khajeh Nouri
Gérard Guillot (Resident, Paris, France Office)

SABI & ASSOCIATES

TEHRAN, IRAN

(See London, England)

Consultants in Iranian Law, International Arbitration, Iran-U.S. Claims Tribunal, Expert Evidence on Iranian Law, International Commercial Contracts, Oil, Gas, Constructions, Banking, Finance.
Not authorized to appear before the English Courts. Founded 1939 by late Musa Sabi (translated all major Iranian codifications into English). The clientele includes major oil companies, multinational corporations; state agencies and governments.

SOTOODEH & ASSOCIATES

P.O. BOX 14155-3383
TEHRAN, IRAN

U.S. Correspondence Address: 5 Hutton Centre Drive, Suite 860, Santa Ana, CA. 92707. Telephone: (714) 662-2664. Fax: (714) 838-0585.

Consultants in Iranian Law, Joint Ventures, Foreign Investments, Patents and Trademark Registration, Incorporation of Joint Companies, Construction, Commercial, Banking and Tax Practice.

BABAK SOTOODEH, born Tehran, Iran, June 16, 1958; admitted, 1984, California; 1985, U.S. District Court, Central District of California. Education: University of Geneva, Switzerland; University of California at Los Angeles; California State University at Fullerton (B.A., Economics, 1981); University of California at Davis (J.D.,1984). Beta Gamma Sigma. Member: State Bar of California; American Bar Association. (Also Of Counsel, Law Office of James M. Donovan, Los Angeles, California and Also Member, Sotoodeh & Associates, Santa Ana, California). **LANGUAGES:** French and Persian.

TAVAKOLI & SHAHABI

Established in 1964

P.O. BOX 19395 - 3448
TEHRAN, IRAN
Telephone: (021) 26 86 65
Telex: 22 23 32
Telefax: (021) 26 86 22

Arbitration, Banking, Construction, Corporate, Distributorship and Agency, Foreign Investment, Intellectual Property, International Contracts, International Trade and Transportation, Litigation, Maritime, Oil and Mining.

MEMBERS OF FIRM

MEHRAN TAVAKOLI, born 1924; admitted, 1954.

MOSTAFA SHAHABI, born 1946; admitted, 1971.

MASSUD ESLAMI-VARZANEH, born 1949; admitted, 1976.

AHMAD EHTESHAM, born 1949. (Not admitted in Iran).

ASSOCIATES

HAMID RAFII-FARD, born 1951; admitted, 1978.

COUNSEL

CYRUS GHANI, born 1929. (Not admitted in Iran).

MOHAMMAD TEHRANI, born 1924; admitted, 1976.

Languages: English, Farsi and French.

REPRESENTATIVE CLIENTS AND REFERENCES: Aeroports de Paris; Alghanim Industries; American Express Bank Ltd; Arab Banking Corporation; Asea Brown Boveri; Banca Commerciale Italiana; Banque Nationale de Paris; BHP Minerals; British Petroleum; Buhler GmbH; Carrier; Coca Cola; Conoco; Credit Suisse; Danieli S.p.A.; Electrolux AB; Federal Express; Glaxo; Gulf Oil International; M.W. Kellogg; Lancer Boss Group; Lloyds Bank; McDermott; NEC Corporation; Nokia; L'Oreal; Otis; PepsiCo; Postipankki; Rabobank Nederland; Scott Fetzer Company; Siemens-Plessey; Skanska AB; Tecnimont S.p.A.; Tokai Bank Ltd; Tomen Corporation; Trafalgar House Construction; Vaillant GmbH; The World Bank.

IRAQ

PROFESSOR S.H. AMIN

BAGHDAD, IRAQ

(See Edinburgh, Scotland)

Middle East and Islamic Law.

ISRAEL

AVNI, HERZOG, SHUALY & GUREVICH

1 YAVNE STREET
P.O. BOX 45687
HAIFA 33501, ISRAEL
Telephone: 972-4-675488
Facsimile: 972-4-672106

General Practice, Commercial, Corporate Law, Banking, Labor Law, Real Estate, Tort, Patents, Intellectual Property, Taxation, Financing, Cooperative (Kibbutz) law.

MEMBERS OF FIRM

YAIR AVNI, born Israel, October 2, 1956; admitted, 1988, Israel. *Education:* Tel-Aviv University, Tel-Aviv (Bc.s., Math & Computers; LL.B.). *Member:* Israel Bar Association. **LANGUAGES:** Hebrew and English. **PRACTICE AREAS:** Banks and Banking Law; Business Law; Computers and Software Law; Contract Law; Finance Law; Leases and Leasing Law; Litigation; Property Law; Securities; Taxation Law.

EHUD HERZOG, born Israel, September 5, 1961; admitted, 1989, Israel. *Education:* Tel-Aviv University, Tel-Aviv (LL.B.). *Member:* Israel Bar Association. **LANGUAGES:** Hebrew, English and Arabic. **PRACTICE AREAS:** Civil Law; Debtor Creditor Law; Health Care Law; Insurance Law; Insurance Defense Law; Medical Malpractice Law; Negligence Law; Personal Injury Law; Products Liability Law; Tort Law.

(This Listing Continued)

GUREVICH ILAN, born Israel, May 23, 1960; admitted, 1987, Israel. *Education:* Ilan University, Tel Aviv (LL.B.). *Member:* Israel Bar Association. **LANGUAGES:** Hebrew and English. **PRACTICE AREAS:** Labor Relation; Labor Unions; Industrial Relations; Collective Bargaining; Social Insurance; Social Security; Management Labor and Employment; Sport Law.

YEHUDA SHUALY, born Israel, August 25, 1954; admitted, 1989, Israel. *Education:* Tel-Aviv University, Tel-Aviv (LL.B.). *Member:* Israel Bar Association. **LANGUAGES:** Hebrew and English. **PRACTICE AREAS:** Advertising and Marketing Law; Construction Law; Corporate Law; Franchise and Franchising Law; Government Contract Law; Real Estate Law; Taxation Law; Trade Regulation Law; Wills; Agricultural Law.

ASSOCIATES

BEN-ARI AVIA, born U.S.S.R., August 28, 1964; admitted, 1990, Israel. *Education:* Tel Aviv University, Tel Aviv (LL.B.). *Member:* Israel Bar Association. **LANGUAGES:** Hebrew, English, Russian and German. **PRACTICE AREAS:** Commercial Real Estate; Contracts; Construction Contracts; Establishment of Business; Joint Ventures; Sale of Goods; Company Contracts; Municipal Law; Property Litigation.

GABRIEL LURIE, born Israel, December 26, 1965; admitted, 1992, Israel. *Education:* Hebrew University, Jerusalem (LL.B.). *Member:* Israel Bar Association. **LANGUAGES:** Hebrew and English. **PRACTICE AREAS:** Commercial Law; Compulsory Purchase; Contract Law; Corporate Law; Municipal Law; Real Estate Law; Tort Law.

AVNIEL, SALOMON & CO.

1 JERUSALEM STREET
P.O. BOX 4882
31 048 HAIFA, ISRAEL
Telephone: +972 4 671520
Fax: +972 4 670564

General Practice, Corporate Law, Securities, Insolvency, International Trade, International Business, Commercial Law, Construction, Real Estate, Litigation and Arbitration.

MEMBERS OF FIRM

YOEL SALOMON, born Jerusalem, June 28, 1922; admitted, 1948, Israel. *Education:* Jerusalem Law Classes. Member, Statutory Committee for Election of Judges, 1987-1988. *Member:* The Israel Bar (Chairman, Haifa and Northern District Committee, 1983-1987). **LANGUAGES:** Hebrew, English, Arabic (spoken).

YOAV SALOMON, born Haifa, Israel, October 28, 1952; admitted, 1979, Israel. *Education:* Tel Aviv University (LL.B., 1978). Publications: The Rights of the Unpaid Seller of Sold Goods: An Israeli Perspective, The Comparative Law Yearbook of International Business, Vol. 14, 1992, Graham & Trotman; Protection of Foreign Sellers of Goods in Israel, International Business Lawyer, Vol. 15 No. 6., 1987. *Member:* The Israel Bar (Judge of the Disciplinary Court of the Bar, 1991—); International Bar Association. **LANGUAGES:** Hebrew and English.

AVRAHAM AVRAHAM, born Syria, May 16, 1959; admitted, 1988, Israel. *Education:* Hebrew University of Jerusalem (LL.B., 1987). *Member:* The Israel Bar. **LANGUAGES:** Hebrew, English and Arabic.

JONATHAN D. FRIEDLAND

Attorney at Law

12 JERUSALEM STREET
33132 HAIFA, ISRAEL
Telephone: (972) 4-670-615
Fax: (972) 4-675-757

Commercial International Agreements, Corporate, Admiralty and Maritime, Transnational Estate Law, Commercial and Maritime Litigation.

JONATHAN D. FRIEDLAND, born New York, New York, February 17, 1948; admitted, 1979, New York; 1982, Israel. *Education:* Yale University (B.A., 1970); New York University, School of Law (J.D., 1978). Consular Agent of the United States of America, 1986—. *Member:* Israel Bar Association; Maritime Law Association of the United States; Maritime Law

(This Listing Continued)

Association of Israel; Consular Corp of Israel. *LANGUAGES:* English, Hebrew and Spanish.

REPRESENTATIVE CLIENTS: U.S. Department of State; U.S. Department of Defense; Oil Refineries Ltd. (Israel); U.S.O. (Israel); The Haifa Foundation; Deutsche Nah Ost Linien, GmbH.

S. FRIEDMAN & CO., ADVOCATES

31 HAATZMAUTH ROAD
P.O. BOX 695
HAIFA 31006, ISRAEL
Telephone: 04-670701
Cable Address: "Saneygor Haifa"
Telex: 46750 ADFRI
Telecopier: (Group 2-3) 04-670754

Tel Aviv, Israel Office: 2 Weizman Street (IBM Building), P.O. Box 33056, Tel Aviv 64239. Telephone: 03-6960183. Telecopier: (Group 2-3) 03-6910228.

General Practice, Maritime, Commercial, Corporate, Banking, Construction, Real Estate, Personal Injury, Insurance.

MEMBERS OF FIRM

URI YANOVSKI, born Jerusalem, Israel, December 30, 1930; admitted, 1955, Israel. *Education:* Hebrew University, Jerusalem, M.Jr. (Magister Juris). *Member:* Israel Bar Association; Israel Maritime Law Society; Israel Maritime Research Institute. *LANGUAGES:* Hebrew and English. *PRACTICE AREAS:* Commercial; Corporation; Shipping; Real Estate; Construction; Anti-Trust; Agriculture; Marketing.

GIDEON GORDON, born Haifa, Israel, July 10, 1930; admitted, 1955, Israel. *Education:* Hebrew University, Jerusalem, M.Jr. (Magister Juris). *Member:* Israel Bar Association (Deputy Chairman, elected, National Council of Israel Chamber of Advocates, 1989); Israel Maritime Law Society. *LANGUAGES:* Hebrew, English and Arabic. *PRACTICE AREAS:* Shipping; Litigation; Personal Injury; Insurance; Criminal Law (Liability cases).

AMIRAM SAFRAN, born Haifa, Israel, February 20, 1939; admitted, 1966, Israel. *Education:* Hebrew University, Jerusalem (LL.B.). Member, National Committee for the Prevention of Pollution of the Sea by Oil. *Member:* Israel Bar Association; Israel Maritime Law Society. *LANGUAGES:* Hebrew and English. *PRACTICE AREAS:* Shipping; Banking and Finance; Commercial.

YEHUDA LIFSHITZ, born Tel-Aviv, Israel, April 24, 1936; admitted, 1964, Israel. *Education:* Tel-Aviv University (LL.B.). *Member:* Israel Bar Association. *LANGUAGES:* Hebrew and English. *PRACTICE AREAS:* Commercial; Corporation; Agriculture and General Practice.

DAVID MALKOFF, born Jerusalem, Israel, November 21, 1947; admitted, 1973, Israel. *Education:* Hebrew University, Jerusalem (LL.B.). *Member:* Israel Bar Association (Member, District Court of Discipline for Haifa and Northern District). *LANGUAGES:* Hebrew and English. *PRACTICE AREAS:* Shipping; General Corporate and Real Estate; Construction; Commercial and Civil Litigation.

ALEXANDER KESARY, born Liberec, Czechoslovakia, January 15, 1948; admitted, 1977, Israel. *Education:* Tel Aviv University (LL.B.). *Member:* Israel Bar Association. *LANGUAGES:* Hebrew and English. *PRACTICE AREAS:* Shipping; Insurance; Labour Relations; Commercial and Civil Litigation.

SARIT MOLCHO (YANOVSKI), born Haifa, Israel, June 9, 1957; admitted, 1982, Israel. *Education:* Hebrew University, Jerusalem (LL.B.). *Member:* Israel Bar Association. *LANGUAGES:* Hebrew and English. *PRACTICE AREAS:* Commercial and Corporate.

ASSOCIATES

TALMA YUVAL, born Haifa, Israel, March 27, 1945; admitted, 1971, Israel. *Education:* Hebrew University, Jerusalem (LL.B.). *Member:* Israel Bar Association. *LANGUAGES:* Hebrew and English. *PRACTICE AREAS:* Real Estate.

ISRAELA KRAY-GUERON, born Tel-Aviv, Israel, June 10, 1959; admitted, 1984, Israel. *Education:* Hebrew University, Jerusalem (LL.B.). *Member:* Israel Bar Association. *LANGUAGES:* Hebrew and English. *PRACTICE AREAS:* Litigation; Personal Injury.

(This Listing Continued)

BATYA Y. SHACHAR, born Petah Tikva, Israel, March 4, 1959; admitted, 1985, Israel. *Education:* Hebrew University, Jerusalem (LL.B.). *Member:* Israel Bar Association. *LANGUAGES:* Hebrew and English.

ORIT SIDI, born Haifa, Israel, December 4, 1960; admitted, 1986, Israel. *Education:* Hebrew University, Jerusalem (LL.B.). *Member:* Israel Bar Association. *LANGUAGES:* Hebrew and English.

LILLY DORON, born Tel-Aviv, Israel, January 19, 1962; admitted, 1987, Israel. *Education:* Bar-Ilan University (LL.B.). *Member:* Israel Bar Association. *LANGUAGES:* Hebrew and English.

TAL ENAT-BEN ARIEH, born New York, U.S.A., February 3, 1963; admitted, 1988, Israel. *Education:* Hebrew University, Jerusalem (LL.B.). *Member:* Israel Bar Association. *LANGUAGES:* Hebrew and English.

AMIR COHEN-DOR, born Haifa, Israel, April 6, 1961; admitted, 1989, Israel. *Education:* Tel Aviv University (LL.B.). *Member:* Israel Bar Association. *LANGUAGES:* Hebrew and English.

NAVA YOURVEXEL, born Tel-Aviv, Israel, April 3, 1962; admitted, 1990, Israel. *Education:* Hebrew University, Jerusalem (LL.B.). *Member:* Israel Bar Association. *LANGUAGES:* Hebrew and English.

AVIA BEN-ARI, born U.S.S.R., August 28, 1964; admitted, 1988, Israel. *Education:* Tel-Aviv University (LL.B.). *Member:* Israel Bar Association. *LANGUAGES:* Hebrew and English.

SHULAMIT BRESLAW, born Haifa, Israel, June 16, 1964; admitted, 1991, Israel. *Education:* Hebrew University, Jerusalem (LL.B.). *Member:* Israel Bar Association. *LANGUAGES:* Hebrew and English.

AVIVI PERELMAN, born Haifa, Israel, August 11, 1961; admitted, 1992, Israel. *Education:* Tel Aviv University (LL.B.). *Member:* Israel Bar Association. *LANGUAGES:* Hebrew and English.

GALIT ADIR DE-TOLEDO, born Haifa, Israel, November 11, 1964; admitted, 1992, Israel. *Education:* Tel Aviv University (LL.B.). *Member:* Israel Bar Association. *LANGUAGES:* Hebrew and English.

DORIT TAMIR, born Givataim, Israel, December 10, 1966; admitted, 1992, Israel. *Education:* Tel-Aviv University (LL.B.). *Member:* Israel Bar Association. *LANGUAGES:* Hebrew and English.

GALINA TOMPAKOV, born Irkutsk, USSR, December 27, 1952; admitted, 1993, Israel. *Education:* Odessa University, M.Jr. (Magister Juris). *Member:* Israel Bar Association. *LANGUAGES:* Hebrew, English and Russian.

LIMOR ZER, born Haifa, Israel, September 4, 1966; admitted, 1993, Israel. *Education:* Tel-Aviv University (LL.B.). *Member:* Israel Bar Association. *LANGUAGES:* Hebrew and English.

ODED REHAN, born Haifa, Israel, October 12, 1967; admitted, 1994, Israel. *Education:* Reading University (LL.B.). *Member:* Israel Bar Association. *LANGUAGES:* Hebrew and English.

IFTACH KIPPERMAN, born Safed, Israel, April 27, 1964; admitted, 1994, Israel. *Education:* Chelmsfords University (LL.B.). *Member:* Israel Bar Association. *LANGUAGES:* Hebrew and English.

CONSULTANTS

SOLLY FRIEDMAN, born Strand, Cape Province, South Africa, January 21, 1913; admitted, 1935, Cape Province, South Africa; 1939, Israel. *Education:* University of Cape Town (B.A.; LL.B.). *Member:* Israel Bar Association; Israel Maritime Law Society; Israel Maritime Research Institute. *LANGUAGES:* Hebrew and English. *PRACTICE AREAS:* Civil and Commercial.

Languages: Hebrew, English, Arabic and Russian.

HARRIS & MARWITZ

Advocates and Notaries

Established in 1977

5 DAVID PINSKY STREET
MOUNT CARMEL
HAIFA 34 351, ISRAEL
Telephone: 4-385175; 4-384625; 4-385587
Telex: 46720 MRLAW IL
Telecopier: 4-371525

Admiralty and Maritime, Corporate and Commercial.
(This Listing Continued)

HARRIS & MARWITZ, Haifa—Continued

FIRM PROFILE: The firm was established in 1977 and has a general civil practice with an emphasis on Admiralty and Maritime, Corporate and Commercial matters, both in the litigous and non-litigous fields.

The firm, by intention, is compact and integrated in order to provide an efficient, prompt and personal service.

The firm's client base is divided between Israel and foreign clients.

MEMBERS OF FIRM

JOHN HARRIS, born Johannesburg, Republic of South Africa, August 31, 1940; admitted, 1962, Rhodesia, (Zimbabwe); 1971, Israel. *Education:* University of Capetown (Bachelor of Arts); Law School of Capetown University (Bachelor of Laws). *Member:* Rhodesian (Zimbabwe) Bar; Israel Bar; Israel Maritime Association; International Bar Association. *LANGUAGES:* English and Hebrew. *PRACTICE AREAS:* Admiralty and Maritime; Corporate and Commercial.

DAN MARWITZ, born Haifa, Israel, April 4, 1944; admitted, 1971, Israel. *Education:* Hebrew University, Jerusalem (Bachelor of Laws). *Member:* Israel Bar; Israel Maritime Association. *LANGUAGES:* English and Hebrew. *PRACTICE AREAS:* Admiralty and Maritime; Corporate and Commercial.

JOCHANAN CAHN, born Cologne, Germany, June 22, 1928; admitted, 1975, Israel. *Education:* University of London (Bachelor of Laws, 1969); School of Navigation Warsash, Southampton (Extra Master). Director, Israel Shipping and Aviation Research Institute, 1970-1973 and 1982-1985. *Member:* Israel Bar; Shipping Research Society of Israel (Chairman, 1981-1982; 1988). *LANGUAGES:* Hebrew and English. *PRACTICE AREAS:* Admiralty and Maritime; Corporate and Commercial.

JOSEPH JESHURUN & CO.

Established in 1963

5 PALYAM AVENUE
P.O. BOX 2233
HAIFA 31021, ISRAEL
Telephone: 04-679707
Facsimile: 04-677032

General Practice, Commercial, Corporate, Banking, Maritime, Patents and Intellectual Property.

MEMBERS OF FIRM

JOSEPH JESHURUN, born Poland, July 17, 1933; admitted, 1960, Israel. *Education:* Hebrew University, Jerusalem (M.Jur.). Military Prosecutor, Southern Command, Israel Defense Forces, 1957-1958. *Member:* The Israel Bar; American Bar Association. *LANGUAGES:* Hebrew and English. *PRACTICE AREAS:* Corporate and Commercial Law; Banking Law; Intellectual Property Law; Maritime Law.

JEHUDA BEN-AROYA, born Israel, January 24, 1943; admitted, 1971, Israel. *Education:* Hebrew University, Jerusalem (LL.B.). *Member:* The Israel Bar. *LANGUAGES:* Hebrew. *PRACTICE AREAS:* Banking Law; Real Estate Law.

SHLOMO KROUB, born Israel, January 5, 1957; admitted, 1991, Israel. *Education:* Tel Aviv University, Tel Aviv (LL.B.). *Member:* The Israel Bar. *LANGUAGES:* Hebrew and English. *PRACTICE AREAS:* Banking Law.

SANDRA SACKSTEIN, born Belgium, July 18, 1965; admitted, 1989, Israel. *Education:* Bar Ilan University, Ramat Gan (LL.B.). *Member:* The Israel Bar. *LANGUAGES:* Hebrew, English and French. *PRACTICE AREAS:* General Practice.

NA'AMA SELA, born Israel, June 16, 1964; admitted, 1992, Israel. *Education:* Hebrew University, Jerusalem (LL.B.). *Member:* The Israel Bar. *LANGUAGES:* Hebrew and English. *PRACTICE AREAS:* General Practice.

DANIEL FISCH, born U.S.A., December 12, 1958; admitted, 1992, Israel. *Education:* Tel Aviv University, Tel Aviv (LL.B.). *LANGUAGES:* Hebrew and English. *PRACTICE AREAS:* International Transactions; General Practice.

ROSENBERG, LEVINSON, YANAY & CO.

28 HERZLIYA STREET
33 301 HAIFA, ISRAEL
Telephone: 532216
Facsimile: 529228
Cable Address: "Levros" Haifa

General Practice, Commercial, Corporate, International and Offshore Taxation, Investments, Real Estate, Probate, Immigration, Marriage and Divorce Law.

FIRM PROFILE: George A. Rosenberg, who had practised law in Montreal, Canada, prior to immigrating to Israel in 1968, founded the firm in 1969 together with Menachem Levinson, and it was then known as Rosenberg & Levinson. Raphael Yanay joined the firm and became a partner in 1981. The firm carries on an extensive international practice in financial and tax law in association with law firms in the U.S.A., Canada, and Europe.

MEMBERS OF FIRM

GEORGE A. ROSENBERG, born Vienna, Austria, June 9, 1936; admitted, 1962, Quebec, Canada; 1969, Israel. *Education:* McGill University, Montreal, Canada (B.A.; B.C.L.); University of Paris. Lecturer on Law, McGill University, 1963-1966.

MENACHEM LEVINSON, born Haifa, Israel, December 28, 1940; admitted, 1966, Israel. *Education:* Hebrew University, Jerusalem (LL.B.).

RAPHAEL YANAY, born Haifa, Israel, April 4, 1946; admitted, 1973, Israel. *Education:* Hebrew University, Jerusalem (LL.B.).

ORIT KEREN-POLAK, born Hedera, Israel, June 24, 1952; admitted, 1977, Israel. *Education:* Hebrew University, Jerusalem (LL.B., 1976).

HANA WINTER KLAUSNER, born Haifa, Israel, July 26, 1962; admitted, 1987, Israel. *Education:* Bar-Ilan University, Tel-Aviv (LL.B., 1985).

Languages: Hebrew, English, French and German.

YAACOV SALOMON, LIPSCHUTZ & CO.

Established in 1921

YOEL HOUSE
64 HAMEGINIM AVENUE
P.O. BOX 303
HAIFA, ISRAEL
Telephone: 04-535231, 2, 3, 4, 5 Int'l: 972-4-535231, 2, 3, 4, 5
Cable Address: "CLIENT" Haifa
Facsimile: (Grps 2 & 3) 04-557038
Int'l: 972-4-557038

REVISERS OF THE ISRAEL LAW DIGEST FOR THIS DIRECTORY.

Tel Aviv (Ramat-Gan), Israel Office: "Beit Silver", 7 Abba Hillel Silver Street, P.O. Box 3424, 52522. Telephone: 03-5757712. Int'l: 972-3-5757712. Cable Address: "Salipad" Tel-Aviv. Facsimile: (Grps 2 & 3) 03-5757725. Int'l: 972-3-5757725.

General Practice. Commercial, Corporation, Tax and Maritime Law, Banking, Labor Law, Insurance, Franchising & Licensing, Real Estate, Construction, Town Planning, Securities, Capital Markets, Energy Law, Patent and Trademarks.

MEMBERS OF FIRM

YAACOV SALOMON (1905-1980).

BEN-ZION SERAYA, born Haifa, Israel, June 30, 1928; admitted, 1954, Israel. *Education:* Hebrew University of Jerusalem. *Member:* Israel Bar Association. *LANGUAGES:* Hebrew, English, Arabic and French.

ALEXANDER SAMUEL, born Izmir, January 9, 1937; admitted, 1965, Israel. *Education:* Hebrew University of Jerusalem. *Member:* Israel Bar Association. *LANGUAGES:* Hebrew, English and French.

MOSHE Y. LIPSCHUTZ, born Israel, April 5, 1939; admitted, 1965, Israel. *Education:* Hebrew University of Jerusalem. *Member:* Israel Bar Association. *LANGUAGES:* Hebrew and English.

JOSEPH GILLOR, born Jerusalem, Israel, October 6, 1940; admitted, 1966, Israel. *Education:* Hebrew University of Jerusalem. *Member:* Israel Bar Association. *LANGUAGES:* Hebrew, English and Arabic.

(This Listing Continued)

DAVID GOLDENBLATT, born Montreal, Quebec, Canada, September 19, 1940; admitted, 1965, Quebec, Canada; 1978, Israel. *Education:* McGill University, Montreal, Canada (B.A.; B.C.L.). *Member:* Canadian and Israel Bar Associations. *LANGUAGES:* Hebrew, English and French.

DR. GIDEON KLUGMAN, born Tel-Aviv, Israel, 1952; admitted, 1985, New York; 1986, Israel. *Education:* Tel-Aviv University (LL.B.); Columbia University (LL.M.); Harvard University (S.J.D.). Author: "Convention between the Government of the State of Israel and the Government of the United States of America with Respect to Taxes on Income," (1993, 527 p.) (in Hebrew); "Transnational Taxation of Foreign Investments in Israel," 1992; "Income Tax Considerations related to the Free Trade Area Agreement between the United States and Israel," *The U.S. - Israel Free Trade Area Agreement*(Business Laws, Inc., Ohio, 1989); "Offsetting the Real Differential from Securities'," Vol. B2 *Taxes*A-30, (1988) (in Hebrew); "Linkage Differentials and Interest on Value Added Tax Refunds when Excess Advances are Refunded," 16 Taxes Quarterly 134, (1988) (in Hebrew); "A Commentary on the Legislature's Approach Regarding Depreciation Deductions During Periods of Inflation," 15 Taxes Quarterly 243, (1987) (in Hebrew); "Adjustment of the Tax Brackets, the Deductions and Credits in a Special Tax Year and Offsetting of Losses," 35(4) The Accountant 346, (1987) (in Hebrew); "Peering into Your Neighbor's House: A Civil Wrong?" E/2 Tel Aviv Univ. L. Rev. 425, (1976) (in Hebrew). Appointed by Income Tax Commissioner of Israel: Member and advisor of the Israel delegation for negotiation of a tax treaty with the United States, 1989—; Member of the governmental committee for examination of the corporate tax system in Israel, 1990—. Appointment by Minister of Justice as a Member of the Boards of Land Appreciation Tax Appeals, adjunct to the courts in Tel-Aviv and Haifa, 1990—; (appointment by Minister of Justice). Associate, Cohen and Uretz, Washington D.C., 1982-1984. Member of the Tax Committee of the Israeli Bar. Member of the Tax Section of the American Bar Association. *LANGUAGES:* Hebrew and English.

ELISHA BEN-SHACHAR, born Haifa, Israel, July 19, 1952; admitted, 1978, Israel. *Education:* Bar Ilan University. *Member:* Israel Bar Association. *LANGUAGES:* Hebrew and English.

JAACOV RIVANOWITCH, born Haifa, Israel, February 15, 1951; admitted, 1981, Israel. *Education:* Hebrew University of Jerusalem. *Member:* Israel Bar Association. *LANGUAGES:* Hebrew, English and Arabic.

DORON N. TISHMAN, born Israel, November 23, 1961; admitted, 1987, Israel. *Education:* Tel Aviv University. *Member:* Israel Bar Association. *LANGUAGES:* Hebrew and English.

CONSULTANT

NAPHTALI LIPSCHUTZ, born Austria, May 7, 1908; admitted, 1931, United Kingdom; 1937, Israel. *Education:* University College, London; Gray's Inn, London. *Member:* Israel Bar Association. *LANGUAGES:* Hebrew, English, Arabic and German.

ASSOCIATES

BATIA HAIMOV ROMAN, born Haifa, Israel, December 6, 1953; admitted, 1980, Israel. *Education:* Tel Aviv University. *Member:* Israel Bar Association. *LANGUAGES:* Hebrew and English.

MERAV ARAD-SALOMON, born Israel, October 13, 1958; admitted, 1984, Israel. *Education:* Hebrew University, Jerusalem. *Member:* Israel Bar Association. *LANGUAGES:* Hebrew and English.

RAMZI ABBDALAH HADIED, born Israel, March 24, 1965; admitted, 1989, Israel. *Education:* Hebrew University, Jerusalem. *Member:* Israel Bar Association. *LANGUAGES:* Hebrew, Arabic and English.

OFER SCHWEIZER, born Haifa, Israel, January 5, 1962; admitted, 1989, Israel. *Education:* Bar-Ilan University. *Member:* Israel Bar Association.

SHAI COHEN, born Haifa, Israel, April 12, 1963; admitted, 1992, Israel. *Education:* Tel Aviv University. *Member:* Israel Bar Association. *LANGUAGES:* Hebrew and English.

DIEFALLA AWWAD, born Nazareth, Israel, July 29, 1969; admitted, 1992, Israel. *Education:* Hebrew University. *Member:* Israel Bar Association. *LANGUAGES:* Arabic, Hebrew and English.

HANOCH MORGENSTERN, born Tel Aviv, Israel, March 6, 1964; admitted, 1992, Israel. *Education:* Bar Ilan University. *Member:* Israel Bar Association. *LANGUAGES:* Hebrew and English.

(This Listing Continued)

NIMROD TEPPER, born Kibbutz, Yagur, Israel, April 7, 1964; admitted, 1993, Israel. *Education:* Tel-Aviv University. *Member:* Israel Bar Association. *LANGUAGES:* Hebrew and English.

Languages: Hebrew, English, Arabic, French, Yiddish and German.

REVISERS OF THE ISRAEL LAW DIGEST FOR THIS DIRECTORY.

ALEXANSER TIROSH, ATTIAS, MAYER & FRUCHTER

2 KHUORY STREET, HAVEVIIM TOWER
P.O. BOX 4133
HAIFA, ISRAEL
Telephone: 04-622447; 04-628448; 04-628449
Telex: 46400E BXHA IL. Ext. 8209
Fax: 972 4 625508

General Practice, Commercial, Corporation, Tax, Maritime Law, Real Estate, Banking, Insurance, Town Planning, Building and Industrial Parks.

FIRM PROFILE: Firm established in 1945 by Alexander Tirosh and H.Z. Mayer as representatives of Bernard Joseph & Co., a law firm in Jerusalem and Tel Aviv.

In 1948 upon Dr. Bernard Joseph becoming a member of the government of Israel, the firm of Bernard Joseph & Co. was dissolved and the firm carried in under the name of Alexander Tirosh & Co., and later under the name of Alexander Tirosh & Mayer, Michael Mayer, the son of H.Z. Mayer, joined the firm in 1981 and Ofer Attias and Chaim Fruchter joined it in 1992.

MEMBERS OF FIRM

ALEXANDER TIROSH, born Poland, February 11, 1910; admitted, 1932, Poland; 1941, Palestine. *Education:* Faculty of Law and Economics at Warsaw University, Palestine Law examination (M.I.). *Member:* The Israel Bar. *LANGUAGES:* Hebrew, English, German, Polish and Russian.

OFER ATTIAS, born Israel, November 5, 1949; admitted, 1975, Israel. *Education:* Hebrew University, Jerusalem (LL.B.); Faculty of Law, University of Toronto, Canada. *Member:* The Israel Bar. *LANGUAGES:* Hebrew, English and Arabic.

MICHAEL MAYER, born Israel, December 24, 1952; admitted, 1977, Israel. *Education:* Bar Ilan University (LL.B.). *Member:* The Israel Bar. *LANGUAGES:* Hebrew and English.

CHAIM FRUCHTER, born Romania, February 28, 1955; admitted, 1981, Israel. *Education:* Tel Aviv Faculty of Law (LL.B.). *Member:* The Israel Bar. *LANGUAGES:* Hebrew, English and Hungarian.

ASSOCIATES

DANNY SARFATY, born Israel, February 14, 1963; admitted, 1990, Israel. *Education:* Bar Ilan University (LL.B.). *Member:* The Israel Bar. *LANGUAGES:* Hebrew and French.

NACHUM FISCHENDLER, born Israel, March 1962; admitted, 1991, Israel. *Education:* Tel Aviv Faculty of Law (LL.B.). *Member:* The Israel Bar. *LANGUAGES:* Hebrew and English.

YAEL AHILEA, born Israel, October 28, 1967; admitted, 1993, Israel. *Education:* Faculty of Law, Hebrew University of Jerusalem (LL.B). *Member:* The Israel Bar. *LANGUAGES:* Hebrew and English.

ORIT ASNIN, born Israel, December 10, 1968; admitted, 1994, Israel. *Education:* Faculty of Business Law, City of London, Polytechnic (today known as London and Guildhall university (LL.B.). *Member:* The Israel Bar. *LANGUAGES:* Hebrew and English.

ADOVCATE DAVID A. LEITMAN

20 WEIZMAN STREET
HERZILYA 46498, ISRAEL
Telephone: 972.9.560.787
Facsimile: 972.9.560.789

Commercial Transactions, Trade, Insurance and Reinsurance, Intellectual Property, Technology and Computers, Real Estate, Trusts and Estates, Matrimonial and Family, Multinational Estates, Aviation and Travel, Litigation in all Courts throughout Israel.

(This Listing Continued)

ADOVCATE DAVID A. LEITMAN, Herzilya—Continued

DAVID A. LEITMAN, born Montreal, Canada, December 24, 1954; admitted, 1982, New York; 1991, Israel. *Education:* Georgetown University, School of Foreign Service (B.S.F.S., 1977); Syracuse University Law School (J.D., 1980). Lead Articles Editor, Syracuse Journal of International Law and Commerce, 1979-1980. National Deputy Chairman, Absorption Committee of the Israel Bar, 1992—. Lecturer: Law School, College of Management, 1991—; International Trade Institute, College of Management, 1994—. *Member:* Israel Bar; American Bar Association; New York State Bar Association; International Bar Association; International Forum of Travel and Tourism Advocates; Association of Americans and Canadians in Israel; Israel-Asia Chamber of Commerce; Israel-United States Chamber of Commerce. *LANGUAGES:* English and Hebrew.

YIGAL ARNON & CO.

31 HILLEL STREET
P.O. BOX 69
JERUSALEM 91000, ISRAEL
Telephone: 972.2.239.239
Cable Address: "ARNATAN"
Telecopier: 972.2.25 7.333.

Tel Aviv, Israel Office: 3 Daniel Frisch Street, P.O. Box 33777, 64731. Telephone: 972.3.692.6868. Cable Address: "YIGAR." Telecopier: 972.3-696-4770.

(For complete biographical data on all personnel, see Professional Biographies at Tel Aviv, Israel)

S.L. BECKER & CO.

Advocates, Notaries, Solicitors

Established in 1970

10 CORESH STREET
JERUSALEM 94144, ISRAEL
Telephone: (2) 232 603
Fax: (2) 259 407

SAMUEL LAURENCE BECKER, admitted, 1962, Solicitor, England; Advocate, Israel. *Education:* LL.B. (Hons., London).

ESTHER BERK. *Education:* LL.B. (Israel).

MICHAEL SACOFSKY. *Education:* LL.B. (Hons.).

DR. HENRY GOLDBLUM. *Education:* Ph.d.; LL.M. (London).

SHRAGA F. BIRAN & CO.

CITY TOWER
34 BEN YEHUDA STREET
JERUSALEM 94583, ISRAEL
Telephone: (972) 2 258161
Facsimile: (972) 2 259284

Tel Aviv, Israel Office: Textile and Fashion Centre, 2 Kaufman Street, 68012. Telephone: (972) 3 5105767. Facsimile: (972) 3 5106108.

Real Estate: Planning, Construction, Housing, Industrial Parks, Hotels. International Transactions: Finance and Investments, Commerce and Trade.

Corporate Finance: Public Offerings, Sales and Acquisitions.

MEMBERS OF FIRM

SHRAGA F. BIRAN, born Poland, 1932; admitted, 1959, Israel. *Education:* Hebrew University, Jerusalem (M.J., 1958). Notary Public. *Member:* Israel Bar Association; International Forum of Travel and Tourism Advocates. *LANGUAGES:* Hebrew and English.

ZIDKIAHU HERMOLIN, born Tel Aviv, Israel, June 5, 1947; admitted, 1974, Israel. *Education:* Hebrew University, Jerusalem (LL.B., 1973). *Member:* Israel Bar Association. *LANGUAGES:* Hebrew and English.

(This Listing Continued)

ASSOCIATES

PAUL OLIVER LENGA, born London, England, May 22, 1953; admitted, 1977, England; 1984 Israel. *Education:* College of Law, London. Notary Public, 1989. *Member:* Israel Bar Association; The Law Society, England. *LANGUAGES:* English, Hebrew and French.

DAVID ASHER BENJAMIN, born London, England, July 25, 1948; admitted, 1986, Israel. *Education:* Hebrew University, Jerusalem (LL.B., 1983). *Member:* Israel Bar Association; Institute of Certified Public Accountants in Israel; Institute of Chartered Accountants in England and Wales. *LANGUAGES:* English and Hebrew.

JOSEPH BARZILAI, born Tel Aviv, Israel, May 16, 1960; admitted, 1987, Israel. *Education:* Hebrew University, Jerusalem (LL.B., 1985). *Member:* Israel Bar Association. *LANGUAGES:* Hebrew and English.

BOAZ JOSHUA BIRAN, born Jerusalem, Israel, May 8, 1963; admitted, 1990, Israel. *Education:* Hebrew University, Jerusalem (LL.B., 1989). *Member:* Israel Bar Association. *LANGUAGES:* Hebrew and English.

ARIELLA YONA APPELBAUM, born Beersheba, Israel, March 28, 1969; admitted, 1992, Israel. *Education:* Hebrew University, Jerusalem (LL.B., 1991). *Member:* Israel Bar Association. *LANGUAGES:* Hebrew and English.

ELI LEVINSON-SELA, born Jerusalem, Israel, December 22, 1966; admitted, 1993, Israel. *Education:* Hebrew University, Jerusalem (LL.B., 1992). *Member:* Israel Bar Association. *LANGUAGES:* Hebrew and English.

SALI BEN-ZVI, born Tel Aviv, Israel, October 9, 1962; admitted, 1992, Israel. *Education:* Tel Aviv University (B.A., Political Science, 1984; LL.B., 1990). *Member:* Israel Bar Association. *LANGUAGES:* French, Hebrew and English.

TEL AVIV OFFICE

MEMBERS OF FIRM

AVIGDOR ZIV, born Riga, Latvia, August 12, 1931; admitted, 1957, Israel. *Education:* Hebrew University, Jerusalem (LL.B., 1955). *Member:* Israel Bar Association. *LANGUAGES:* Hebrew and English.

ZACHARIA FIET, born Jambul, Russia, June 5, 1944; admitted, 1968, Israel. *Education:* Hebrew University, Jerusalem (LL.B., 1967). *Member:* The Israel Bar Association. *LANGUAGES:* Hebrew and English.

ZVIKA MARGALIT, born Israel, September 28, 1956; admitted, 1984, Israel. *Education:* Tel Aviv University (LL.B., 1983). *Member:* The Israel Bar Association. *LANGUAGES:* Hebrew and English.

GIDEON HATUKA, born Rosh Ha'ayin, Israel, April 16, 1958; admitted, 1985, Israel. *Education:* Bar Ilan University, Tel Aviv (LL.B., 1986). *Member:* The Israel Bar Association. *LANGUAGES:* Hebrew and English.

ASSOCIATES

SHMUEL LECHNER, born Tel Aviv, Israel, August 21, 1964; admitted, 1991, Israel. *Education:* Tel Aviv University (LL.B., 1989). *Member:* Israel Bar Association. *LANGUAGES:* Hebrew and English.

LOUIS GARB & CO.

14 ZERACH BARNET STREET
JERUSALEM 95404, ISRAEL
Telephone: 972-2-528093
Facsimile: 972-2-519306

Effective April '95: Telephone: 972-2-6528903. Facsimile: 972-2-6519306.

also at Tel Aviv, Israel Office: 2 Koifman Street, 63324.

Enforcement of Foreign Judgements, Commercial Litigation, International Bankruptcy, Arbitration and Deceased Estates.

MEMBERS OF FIRM

LOUIS GARB, born Darlington, England, October 29, 1934; admitted, 1957, Transvaal, South Africa; 1967, Botswana; 1974, Israel. *Education:* Witwatersrand, South Africa (B.A., 1953; LL.B., 1956). Author: Volume on Insurance in S.A. Encyclopaedia of Forms and Precedents, Butterworths, 1972. Editor: "A Practical Guide To The Enforcement Of Foreign Judgements," Kluwer Law and Taxation, 1994.

LAW OFFICES OF
JOEL H. GOLOVENSKY

Established in 1988

23 HILLEL STREET, SUITE 500
P.O. BOX 4462
JERUSALEM 91043, ISRAEL
Telephone: (972) (2) 233250
Fax: (972) (2) 233248

Mineola, New York Office: 210 Old Country Road. Telephone: 516-742-1480. Fax: 516-742-1473.

Tel Aviv, Office: 2 Kaufman Street, 68012. Telephone: 972-3-510-2666. Fax: 972-3-510-2166.

Commercial, International Investment, Business, Real Estate, Labor and Employment, Civil and Corporate Litigation.

JOEL H. GOLOVENSKY, born New York, N.Y., September 15, 1942; admitted, 1968, New York; 1969, U.S. District Court, Southern and Eastern Districts of New York; 1972, U.S. District Court, District of Connecticut and U.S. Court of Appeals, Second Circuit; 1979, U.S. Supreme Court; 1988, Israel Chamber of Advocates. *Education:* University of Pennsylvania (A.B., magna cum laude, 1964); Harvard Law School (J.D., 1967); New York University (LL.M., in Labor Law, 1973). Phi Beta Kappa. Author: Comment, "New York State Compulsory Interest Arbitration, " 52 New York University Law Review 1255, 1977. *Member:* The Association of the Bar of the City of New York; New York State and American Bar Associations; Israel Bar Association; Federal Bar Council; International Bar Association. (Also of Counsel, Balter, Guth, Aloni & Co., Tel Aviv, Israel).

Languages: Hebrew and English.

E. LANDAU LAW OFFICES

8 KEREN HAYESOD STREET
JERUSALEM 92 101, ISRAEL
Telephone: 02-618845
Fax: 02-618847
Telex: 2-6133 JURA IL

MEMBERS OF FIRM

ELCHANAN LANDAU, born Vienna, Austria, July 31, 1926; admitted, 1955, Israel. *Education:* University of Jerusalem (LL.M., 1954). *Member:* Israel Chamber of Advocates, International Bar Association (Section on Business Law).

ZVI HOWARD NIXON, born Toronto, Canada, March 6, 1954; admitted, 1981, Israel. *Education:* University of British Columbia, Vancouver, Canada (B.A., hons., 1975); University of Oxford, Magdalen College (B.A. hons., 1977; B.C.L., hons., 1978). *Member:* Israel Chamber of Advocates.

YEHUDA RAVEH & CO.

(Formerly Gideon Hausner Law Offices)

26, USSISHKIN STREET
P.O. BOX 7722
JERUSALEM 91077, ISRAEL
Telephone: 972-2-635232-5; 661231-4
Cable Address: "Hausad"
Telex: 26307 Raveh IL
Telecopier Fax: 972-2-617101

Tel Aviv, Israel Office: America House, 35 Shaul Hamelech Boulevard, P.O. Box 33804, 64927. Telephone: 972-3-6956152. Telecopier (Fax): 972-3-6919102.

General Practice. Commercial, Corporate, Real Estate, Hotels, Banking, Insurance, Hi-Tech, Industry, Foreign Investments, Free-Trade Agreements and Patents and Trademark Law.

MEMBERS OF FIRM

YEHUDA RAVEH, born Israel, September 3, 1944; admitted, 1970, Israel. *Education:* Hebrew University of Jerusalem (LL.B.); New York University. *Member:* Israel Bar Association. *LANGUAGES:* Hebrew and English.

LISA TROSS, born South Africa, January 6, 1955; admitted, 1980, Israel. *Education:* Hebrew University of Jerusalem (LL.B.). Teaching Assis-

(This Listing Continued)

tant, Hebrew University Law School, 1976-1978. *Member:* Bar Association of Israel. *LANGUAGES:* Hebrew and English.

HAIM STERN, born Tel Aviv, Israel, October 24, 1955; admitted, 1984, Israel. *Education:* Tel Aviv University (LL.B., 1983). *LANGUAGES:* Hebrew and English.

YUVAL GRAYEVSKY, born Jerusalem, Israel, May 20, 1958; admitted, 1984, Israel. *Education:* Hebrew University of Jerusalem (LL.B.). *Member:* Bar Association of Israel. *LANGUAGES:* Hebrew and English.

YEHUDA GLATT, born New York, U.S.A., January 9, 1958; admitted, 1985, Israel. *Education:* Hebrew University of Jerusalem (LL.B.). *Member:* Bar Association of Israel. *LANGUAGES:* Hebrew and English.

ASSOCIATES

SARA SHALOM, born Haifa, Israel, April 18, 1951; admitted, 1979, Israel. *Education:* Hebrew University (LL.B.). *LANGUAGES:* Hebrew and English.

URI YAMIN, born Jerusalem, Israel, May 9, 1960; admitted, 1988, Israel. *Education:* Hebrew University of Israel (LL.B.). *Member:* Bar Association of Israel. *LANGUAGES:* Hebrew, English and French.

CARMIT BAR-ON, born London, England, May 5, 1960; admitted, 1986, Israel. *Education:* Hebrew University of Jerusalem (LL.B., 1985). *Member:* Bar Association of Israel. *LANGUAGES:* Hebrew and English.

DANIEL SAVITCH, born Israel, 1961; admitted, 1988, Israel. *Education:* Hebrew University of Jerusalem (LL.B.). *Member:* Bar Association of Israel. *LANGUAGES:* Hebrew, English and German.

MYRIAM ABITBOL, born Morocco, July 9, 1956; admitted, 1980, France; 1991, Israel. *Education:* University of Grenoble (Maitrise en Droit). *Member:* Bar Association of France; Bar Association of Israel. *LANGUAGES:* Hebrew, French, English and German.

MIRIAM ILANY, born Spain, March 4, 1967; admitted, 1991, Israel. *Education:* Bar-Ilan University (LL.B.). *Member:* Bar Association of Israel. *LANGUAGES:* Hebrew, English and Spanish.

DGANIT ZAHAV, born Tel Aviv, Israel, January 22, 1961; admitted, 1993, Israel. *Education:* Tel Aviv University (LL.B., B.Sc.). *Member:* Bar Association of Israel. *LANGUAGES:* Hebrew and English.

GARY LEIBLER, born Melbourne, Australia, November 20, 1965; admitted, 1992, Israel. *Education:* Monash University of Melbourne (LL.B., B.Ec.). *Member:* Bar Association of Israel. *LANGUAGES:* Hebrew and English.

JEREMY ROSENSHINE, born Colorado, U.S.A., October 27, 1962; admitted, 1991, Israel. *Education:* Hebrew University of Jerusalem (LL.B.); University of Chicago (LL.M.). *Member:* Bar Association of Israel. *LANGUAGES:* Hebrew, English.

RON ISRAELI, born Jerusalem, Israel, October 9, 1962; admitted, 1992, Israel. *Education:* Hebrew University of Jerusalem (LL.B.; MB.A). *Member:* Bar Association of Israel. *LANGUAGES:* Hebrew and English.

OF COUNSEL

TAMAR RAVEH, born Israel, November 7, 1945; admitted, 1970, Israel. *Education:* Hebrew University of Jerusalem (LL.B.). *Member:* Bar Association of Israel. *LANGUAGES:* Hebrew, English.

REFERENCES: Mr. Milton Handler, Kaye Scholer, Fierman Hays and Handler, New York, N.Y.; Evelyn H. Lauder, Corporate V/P Estee Lauder Inc., New York, N.Y.; Roger Gerber, President, Meyers Parking Systems Inc. and Prudential Maintenance Corp., Inc., New York, N.Y.; Mr. Michael Steinhardt, Principal, Steinhardt Partners, New York, N.Y.

SILBER & SCHOTTENFELS

8 BEZALEL STREET
JERUSALEM 94591, ISRAEL
Telephone: (972-2) 247148; 257746; 257751
Telecopier: (972-2) 250461

Corporate and Commercial Law, General International Trade, Technology Transfer, Administrative Law, Civil Litigation, Coordination of Binational Litigation.

FIRM PROFILE: *The firm was established in 1985 and offers a full range of legal services. It is a member of the International Lawyers Network.*

(This Listing Continued)

SILBER & SCHOTTENFELS, Jerusalem—Continued

MEMBERS OF FIRM

JOEL S. SILBER, born New York, New York, 1953; admitted, 1979, New York; 1983, Israel. *Education:* Yeshiva College (A.B.); Harvard Law School (J.D.). Associate, Fried, Frank, Harris, Shriver & Jacobson, 1979-1982. *PRACTICE AREAS:* Civil Litigation.

DAVID SCHOTTENFELS, born Cincinnati, Ohio, 1952; admitted, 1981, Israel. *Education:* Yale University (A.B.); Hebrew University (LL.B.). Law Clerk, Justice Miriam Ben Porat, Supreme Court of Israel, 1979-1980. *PRACTICE AREAS:* Corporate Law; Commercial Law.

OF COUNSEL

NATHANIEL L. GERBER, born Boston, Massachusetts, 1948; admitted, 1973, New York; 1983, Israel. *Education:* Columbia University (A.B.); Harvard University (J.D.). Assistant U.S. Attorney, Southern District of New York, 1974-1978. Member, Reavis & McGrath (now Fulbright & Jaworski), 1981-1983. *PRACTICE AREAS:* Technology Transfer; U.S. Litigation.

Languages: English and Hebrew.

WINE, MISHEIKER & ERNSTOFF

Established in 1981

12 MOSHE HESS STREET
JERUSALEM 94185, ISRAEL
Telephone: 972-2-251522
Fax: 972-2-259262

Corporate, Property, Computer Law, Wills, Trusts and Estates, Commercial Litigation, Torts, Education Law, General Practice.

FIRM PROFILE: The firm, comprising native English speakers fully integrated into Israeli legal society, serves as an interface between Israeli society and the English-speaking world. The client base is primarily North Americans or other English speakers doing business in Israel, or Israelis dealing abroad.

MEMBERS OF FIRM

BRIAN D. WINE, born Saskatoon, Sask, September 4, 1939; admitted, 1965, Canada; 1973, Israel. *Education:* University of British Columbia (B.Comm., 1963; LL.B., 1964); Hebrew University of Jerusalem (LL.M., 1969). Teaching Assistant, Hebrew University of Jerusalem. Deputy Legal Advisor, Ministry of Finance of Israel, 1973-1980. Member Presidium, World Zionist Organization, 1989—. Member, Public Council for Protection of Privacy, 1990—. *Member:* Israel Bar Society. *LANGUAGES:* English and Hebrew. *PRACTICE AREAS:* Corporate; Computer Law; Tax.

JONATHAN EUGENE MISHEIKER, born Johannesburg, South Africa, December 14, 1944; admitted, 1972, Israel. *Education:* Hebrew University of Jerusalem (LL.B., 1966; LL.M., 1976). Assistant to Attorney General, 1971-1973. Assistant State Attorney, 1973-1974. Deputy Legal Adviser, Ministry of Education and Culture, 1974-1981. *Member:* Israel Bar Association. *LANGUAGES:* English and Hebrew. *PRACTICE AREAS:* Commercial Litigation; Torts; Education Law.

BARRY DAVID ERNSTOFF, born Brooklyn, New York, February 6, 1946; admitted, 1971, Washington; 1975, U.S. Supreme Ct.; 1986, Israel. *Education:* Columbia College (A.B., 1967); New York University (J.D., 1971). *Member:* Washington State Bar Association (1971—); Israel Bar Association (1986—). Partner, Ziontz, Pirtle, Morisset, Ernstoff & Chestnut, Seattle, WA, 1972-1986. Association of Americans & Canadians in Israel (Jerusalem Region, Chairman, 1990-1992; National Vice President, 1992—). *LANGUAGES:* English and Hebrew. *PRACTICE AREAS:* Wills; Trusts and Estates; Real Property.

ASSOCIATES

DAPHNA ROTEM, born Holon, Israel, November 2, 1964; admitted, 1992, Israel. *Education:* Hebrew University of Jerusalem (LL.B., 1990). *Member:* Israel Bar Association (1992—). *LANGUAGES:* English and Hebrew. *PRACTICE AREAS:* Litigation.

DANNY KABIR, born Jerusalem, Israel, May 5, 1966; admitted, 1994, Israel. *Education:* Tel Aviv University (LL.B., 1993). *Member:* Israel Bar Association (1994—). *LANGUAGES:* English, Hebrew and Arabic. *PRACTICE AREAS:* Litigation; Torts; Administrative Law.

WOLFF, BREGMAN & GOLLER

3 MITUDELA STREET
P.O. BOX 1352
JERUSALEM 91013, ISRAEL
Telephone: 972-2-635745
Telex: 26144 BXJM IL Ext. 7166
Telecopier: 972-2-630996

General Intellectual Property Practice, including Chemical Patents, Microbiological Patents, Pharmaceutical Patents, Electronic Patents, Optical Patents, Mechanical Patents, Plants Breeders' Rights, Trade Marks, Service Marks, Aesthetic and Industrial Designs, Patent Prosecution, Patent Litigation, Trademark Prosecution, Trademark Litigation, Design Prosecution, Design Litigation, Patent, Design and Trademark Searches.

FIRM PROFILE: Established by David Wolff in 1965, and expanded into the firm of Wolff, Bregman and Goller in 1972 when joined by Zwi Bregman and Gilbert Goller, the firm has grown to become one of the leading firms in Israel dealing exclusively with Patent, Design and Trademark matters and handling applications of well-known European, North American and Japanese clients as well as the preparation, filing and prosecution of applications in Israel and abroad for local clients.

Advantageously located in Jerusalem, site of the Israel Patent and Trademark Offices, the firm enjoys immediate and close working contact with both their personnel and Examiners.

MEMBERS OF FIRM

*ZWI BREGMAN, born Berlin, Germany, February 19, 1938; admitted to practice before Israel Patent Office, 1970. *Education:* Eastern Ontario Institute of Technology (Electronics 1963); Carleton University, Ottawa, Canada (B.Sc. Physics, 1965). Chief Examiner, Mechanical and Electronics Divisions, Israel Patent Office, 1968-1969; Superintendent of Examiners, Israel Patent Office, 1970-1972. *Member:* USTA; AIPPI Israel Group; FICPI; Association of Israel Patent Attorneys. *LANGUAGES:* Hebrew, English and German. *PRACTICE AREAS:* Patents (Circuit and network, computer, electrical, electronic, engineering, fiber optics; and physics).

*GILBERT GOLLER, born Brooklyn, New York, U.S.A., July 10, 1943. Passed New York bar 1968; admitted to practice before U.S. Patent and Trademark Office, 1969; admitted to practice before Israel Patent Office, 1972. *Education:* Yeshiva University, New York (B.A. Chemistry, with honors 1965); New York University School of Law (J.D., 1968). Author: "Competing, Complementary and Blocking Patents," Journal of the Patent Office Society, Nov. 1968. *Member:* AIPPI Israel Group; FICPI; Association of Israel Patent Attorneys. *LANGUAGES:* Hebrew, English and French. *PRACTICE AREAS:* Patents (agricultural, organic, and polymer chemistry, biological and pharmaceutical).

ASSOCIATE

HAIM SCHNEIDER, born 1921, Vienna, Austria. *Education:* TGM, Vienna, Austria, British Institute of Technology (C & G Mech. Eng. 1945). Lecturer: Theory of Instruments, Brandeis Center, Jerusalem, 1946-1977. *LANGUAGES:* Hebrew, English and German.

*Patent Attorneys qualified to practice before the Israel Patent Office, and qualified to appear before the Israel Courts when accompanied by the Advocate of the Party concerned.

YIGAL ARNON & CO.

3 DANIEL FRISCH STREET
P.O. BOX 33777
TEL AVIV 64731, ISRAEL
Telephone: 972.3.692.6868
Cable Address: "YIGAR"
Telecopier: 972-3-696-4770.

Jerusalem, Israel Office: 31 Hillel Street, P.O. Box 69, 91000. Telephone: 972.2.239.239. Cable Address: "ARNATAN." Telecopier: 972.2.257.333.

MEMBERS OF FIRM

YIGAL ARNON, born Tel-Aviv, Israel, December 9, 1929; admitted, 1954, Israel. *Education:* Hebrew University, Jerusalem (LL.M., 1953). Lecturer in Law, Hebrew University, Jerusalem, 1977-1979. Chairman, First International Bank of Israel, 1987—. *Member:* Israel Bar Association (Chairman, Jerusalem District, 1972-1979).

(This Listing Continued)

DROR VIGDOR, born Jerusalem, Israel, December 2, 1940; admitted, 1967, Israel. *Education:* Hebrew University, Jerusalem (LL.B., cum laude, 1965); New York University (LL.M., 1985). *Member:* Israel Bar Association (Member: Jerusalem District Disciplinary Court, 1972-1979; National Disciplinary Court, 1987-1993).

RAMI KOOK, born Jerusalem, Israel, August 28, 1945; admitted, 1970, Israel. *Education:* Hebrew University, Jerusalem (LL.B., 1969). *Member:* Israel Bar Association; National Disciplinary Court. (Resident, Jerusalem, Israel Office).

PAUL H. BARIS, born New York, N.Y., May 8, 1934; admitted, 1958, New York; 1972, District of Columbia; 1973, U.S. Supreme Court; 1974, Israel. *Education:* Cornell University (A.B., with honors, 1955); Harvard Law School (J.D., cum laude, 1958). Law Clerk, Judge Alexander Bicks, U.S. District Court, Southern District of New York, 1959-1960. Associate, 1960-1964 and Member, 1965-1973, Berlack, Israels & Liberman, New York, N.Y. Visiting Professor of Law, Bar Ilan University, 1971-1972. Professor of Law, Bar Ilan University, 1973—. Co-Author: "Creditors' Rights Against Business Debtors in Israel," International Loan Workouts and Bankruptcies, Butterworth Legal Publishers, 1989. Author: Chapter on Israel Securities Law in International Capital Markets and Securities Regulation, Multi-Volume Treatise, Clark Boardman Callaghan, 1994. *Member:* New York State and American Bar Associations; Israel Bar Association; International Bar Association (Reporter for Israel, Committee on Issues and Trading Securities, Section on Business Law; Country Chair, Committee J on Creditors' Rights, Insolvency, Liquidation and Reorganizations).

NIRA KURITZKY, born Tel-Aviv, Israel; admitted, 1967, Israel. *Education:* Tel-Aviv University (LL.B., 1966; LL.M., 1979). *Member:* Israel Bar Association.

AMALIA MESHI, born Worozlav, Poland; admitted, 1972, Israel. *Education:* Hebrew University, Jerusalem (LL.B., 1970). *Member:* Israel Bar Association.

AMNON LORCH, born Tel-Aviv, Israel, March 29, 1953; admitted, 1980, Israel. *Education:* Hebrew University, Jerusalem (LL.B., 1978). Author: "Lexicon of Israeli Legal Terms," Keter Publishing House, Jerusalem, 1988. Co-Author: "Creditors' Rights Against Business Debtors in Israel," International Loan Workouts and Bankruptcies, Butterworth Legal Publishers, 1989. With Shea & Gould, New York, N.Y., 1981. Chairman, Board of Directors, East Jerusalem Development Ltd., 1994—; Chairman, Board of Directors, Tahal Ltd., 1994—. *Member:* Israel Bar Association. (Resident, Jerusalem, Israel Office).

ERAN ILAN, born Tel-Aviv, Israel, June 17, 1954; admitted, 1982, Israel. *Education:* Hebrew University, Jerusalem (LL.B., 1980). *Member:* Israel Bar Association.

HAGAI SHMUELI, born Jerusalem, Israel, September 8, 1953; admitted, 1980, Israel. *Education:* Hebrew University, Jerusalem (LL.B., 1978). *Member:* Israel Bar Association. (Resident, Jerusalem, Israel Office).

BARRY LEVENFELD, born Chicago, Illinois, September 7, 1954; admitted, 1981, New York and Southern and Eastern Districts of New York; 1983, U.S. Court of Appeals, Second Circuit; 1985, Israel. *Education:* Harvard College (A.B., with honors, 1976); Fletcher School of Law and Diplomacy; Harvard Law School (J.D., with honors, 1980). Author: "Copyright Protection for Computer Software in Israel," The Computer Lawyer, Volume 4, Number 8, August 1987; "Israel Considers Comprehensive Computer Law," Computer Law Advisor, Vol. 2. No. 6, March, 1988; "Look and Feel New Law of the Land: This and Other Recent Developments in Israel," The International Computer Lawyer, Volume 1, Number 4, March 1993. *Member:* Editorial Advisory Board, The International Computer Lawyer, 1992—. Associate, Kronish, Leib, Weiner & Hellman, New York, N.Y., 1980-1983. *Member:* Israel Bar Association.

DAVID H. SCHAPIRO, born New York, November 5, 1962; admitted, 1988, New York; 1991, Israel. *Education:* Yeshiva University (B.A., cum laude, 1984); Benjamin N. Cardozo School of Law, Yeshiva University (J.D., magna cum laude, 1987). Member, Cardozo Law Review, 1985-1987. Belkin Scholar. Alexander Fellow. Law Clerk, Judge Charles P. Sifton, U.S. District Court, Eastern District of New York, 1986. Corporate Department, Fried, Frank, Harris, Shriver & Jacobson, 1987-1990. *Member:* American and Israel Bar Associations.

ASSOCIATES

DAN BEN-DROR, born Jerusalem, Israel, December 25, 1954; admitted, 1982, Israel. *Education:* Hebrew University, Jerusalem (LL.B., 1980). Member, Legal Staff, Israel Income Tax Commissioner, 1982-1985. *Member:* Israel Bar Association.

(This Listing Continued)

CHAGIT BAVLY-GLUSMAN, born Haifa, Israel, November 25, 1959; admitted, 1984, Israel. *Education:* Hebrew University (LL.B., 1982). *Member:* Israel Bar Association.

EYAL FRIEDMAN, born Haifa, Israel, December 29, 1960; admitted, 1987, Israel. *Education:* Hebrew University, Jerusalem (LL.B., 1986). *Member:* Israel Bar Association.

RUTI RONNEN, born Jerusalem, Israel, November 11, 1962; admitted, 1988, Israel; 1990, New York. *Education:* Hebrew University (B.A., cum laude, 1987). Law Clerk, Justice Shamgar, President of the Supreme Court of Israel, 1986. Foreign Intern, Corporate Department, Skadden, Arps, Slate, Meagher & Flom, 1990-1991.

ORNA SASSON, born Tel-Aviv, Israel, September 9, 1963; admitted, 1988, Israel. *Education:* Tel-Aviv University (LL.B., 1987; LL.M., 1993). *Member:* Israel Bar Association.

BETTY NULMAN, born Colombia, July 14, 1960; admitted, 1989, Israel. *Education:* Hebrew University, Jerusalem (B.A., 1981; LL.B., 1988; M.A., 1989). *Member:* Israel Bar Association. (Resident, Jerusalem, Israel Office).

ASSAF SHAHAM, born Ramat-Gan, July 15, 1959; admitted, 1988, Israel. *Education:* Hebrew University, Jerusalem (LL.B., 1988). *Member:* Israel Bar Association. (Resident, Jerusalem, Israel Office).

CHEN LIVNAT, born Tel-Aviv, Israel, July 5, 1961; admitted, 1991, Israel. *Education:* Hebrew University Jerusalem (LL.B., 1989). *Member:* Israel Bar Association. (Resident, Jerusalem, Israel Office).

MORDECHAI BAICZ, born Kfar Chabad, November 20, 1955; admitted, 1985, Israel. *Education:* Hebrew University, Jerusalem (LL.B., 1984; LL.M., 1988). *Member:* Israel Bar Association. (Resident, Jerusalem, Israel Office).

BENJAMIN HOREF, born Haifa, Israel, November 25, 1956; admitted, 1990, Israel. *Education:* Tel Aviv University (B.A., Psychology and B.A., Philosophy, 1986; LL.B., 1989). *Member:* Israel Bar Association.

SHIRI SHAHAM, born Tel Aviv, Israel, July 8, 1967; admitted, 1991, Israel. *Education:* Hebrew University (LL.B., cum laude, 1990); Cambridge University (LL.M., first class, 1992). Member, Law Review of the Hebrew University, 1988. Law Clerk, Justice Goldberg, the Supreme Court of Israel, 1990. Pegasus Scholar, 1992. Foreign Intern, Corporate and Banking Departments, Clifford Chance, 1992. *Member:* Israel Bar Association.

BARAK TAL, born Rehovot, Israel, February 17, 1963; admitted, 1992, Israel. *Education:* Tel Aviv University (LL.B., 1991). Assistant Lecturer, Tel Aviv University, 1990-1992. *Member:* Israel Bar Association.

DORON TAMIR, born Jerusalem, Israel, September 7, 1965; admitted, 1992, Israel. *Education:* Hebrew University (LL.B., 1991). *Member:* Israel Bar Association.

DANIEL ABARBANEL, born Haifa, Israel, November 5, 1961; admitted, 1992, Israel. *Education:* Hebrew University, Jerusalem (LL.B., 1990). Member, Law Review of Hebrew University, 1988-1989. *Member:* Israel Bar Association.

LEA PASSERMAN, born Rome, Italy, December 3, 1965; admitted, 1989, Israel. *Education:* Bar-Ilan University (LL.B., magna cum laude, 1989); London School of Economics (LL.M., European Law, with merit, 1991). Member, Editorial Board, Bar-Ilan Law Review, 1986-1987. *Member:* Israel Bar Association.

MICHAL FRENKIEL, born Nairobi, Kenya, November 3, 1967; admitted, 1993, Israel. *Education:* Tel-Aviv University (LL.B., 1991). *Member:* Israel Bar Association.

MERAV COHEN, born Tel Aviv, Israel, February 16, 1967; admitted, 1992, Israel. *Education:* Tel Aviv University (LL.B., 1991). *Member:* Israel Bar Association.

DONNA L. (SCHWARTZ) GERSHOWITZ, born New York, March 28, 1964; admitted, 1989, California; 1993, Israel. *Education:* Brandeis University (B.A., cum laude, 1986); Boalt Hall School of Law, University of California (J.D., 1989). Associate Editor, Ecology Law Quarterly, 1988-1989. Associate, Hosie, Wes, McLauglin & Sacks (formerly Manwell & Wes), San Francisco, CA, 1989-1991. *Member:* State Bar of California; Israel Bar Association.

NOA MAYER-HASSIN, born Jerusalem, Israel, July 26, 1967; admitted, 1993, Israel. *Education:* Hebrew University, Jerusalem (LL.B., 1992). *Member:* Israel Bar Association.

(This Listing Continued)

YIGAL ARNON & CO., Tel Aviv—Continued

DAVID T. OSBORNE, born Amersham, England, January 10, 1956; admitted, 1985, England and Wales; 1994, Israel. *Education:* St. John's College Oxford (B.A., Honours, 1978; M.A., Honours, 1985). Associate, Nabarro Nathanson, 1985-1987. Partner, Rabin Leacok Lipman, 1987-1993. *Member:* Israel Bar Association.

ERIC S. SHERBY, born Philadelphia, PA, December 29, 1961; admitted, 1988, New York; 1989, District of Columbia, U.S. Court of Appeals, Third, Seventh and Ninth Circuits and the U.S. Court of International Trade; 1994, Israel. *Education:* Jewish Theological Seminary of America (B.A., 1983); Columbia University (B.A., 1984); Benjamin N. Cardozo School of Law, Yeshiva University (J.D., cum laude, 1987). Member, Cardozo Law Review, 1985-1987. Editor, ILSA Journal of International Law, 1986-1987. Author: "The United States-Israel Free Trade Area: Is It Valid Under the GATT?" XI ILSA Journal of International Law 199, 1987. Associate: Reavis & McGrath, 1987-1988; Fried, Frank, Harris, Shriver & Jacobson, 1988-1993. *Member:* American Bar Association (Tel Aviv Correspondent, International Litigation Quarterly), New York State Bar Association (Israeli Representative, Council of Foreign Legal Consultants); Isreal Bar Association.

GIL OREN, born Haifa, Israel, October 29, 1962; admitted, 1994, Israel. *Education:* Tel Aviv University (LL.B., 1992). *Member:* Israel Bar Association.

VERED EITANI, born Tel Aviv, Israel, June 27, 1964; admitted, 1994, Israel. *Education:* Tel Aviv University (LL.B., 1992). *Member:* Israel Bar Association.

STEPHEN H. BLACK, born Watford, England, March 21, 1958; admitted, 1983, England and Wales; 1994, Israel. *Education:* Manchester University (B.A., Honours, Law, 1979). Author: "Doing Business in the United Kingdom through a Joint Venture Company," The Journal of the Israel - British Chamber of Commerce, January, 1983. Associate, Martineau Johnson, 1990-1992; Finers, 1992-1993. *Member:* Law Society of England and Wales; International Bar Association; British Israel Chamber of Commerce; Israel Bar Association.

EZRA D. BARIS, born New York, N.Y., July 16, 1966; admitted, 1994, Israel. *Education:* Hebrew University (LL.B., 1993). Member, Hebrew University Law Review, 1991-1992. Articles Editor, Israel Law Review, 1992-1993. Law Clerk, Justice Theodore Or, Supreme Court of Israel, 1993-1994. *Member:* Israel Bar Association.

YITZHAK YAARI, born The Hague, Netherlands, September 21, 1965; admitted, 1994, Israel. *Education:* Hebrew University, Jerusalem (LL.B., 1993). *Member:* Israel Bar Association.

LESLIE KIM TREIGER, born New York, N.Y., October 27, 1963; admitted, 1993, New York (Not admitted in Israel). *Education:* Yale University (B.A., cum laude, 1985); Yale Law School (J.D., 1989). Articles Editor, Yale Law Journal, 1988-1989. Law Clerk, Judge H. Lee Sarokin, U.S. District Court, District of New Jersey, 1990-1991. Author: "Protecting Satire Against Libel Claims: A New Reading of the First Amendment's Opinion Privilege," 98 Yale Law Journal 1215 (1989). Co-Author: "Revitalizing Public Interest Law in the 1990's: The Story of One Effort to Address the Problem of Homelessness," Howard Law Journal (Spring 1992). *Member:* State Bar of New York.

MARK MOSHINSKY, born Melbourne, Australia, August 12, 1965; admitted, 1992, Victoria. *Education:* University of Melbourne (B.A., 1987; LL.B., 1989); University of Oxford (B.C.L., 1991). Co-Editor, Melbourne University Law Review, 1987. Rhodes Scholar, Australia-at-Large, 1989. Solicitor, Arthur Robinson & Hedderwicks, Melbourne, 1992-1994.

ODED SALOMY, born Tel Aviv, Israel, July 17, 1967; admitted, 1993, New York and Maryland (Not admitted in Israel). *Education:* Harvard University (A.B., cum laude, 1989); University of Pennsylvania Law School (J.D., 1992). Editor and Associate Editor, University of Pennsylvania Law Review, 1990-1992. Corporate and Finance Department, Kaye, Scholer, Fierman, Hays & Handler, 1992-1993.

BACH, ARAD, SCHARF & CO.
LAW OFFICES
1, YAVNE STREET
TEL AVIV 65791, ISRAEL
Telephone: 972-3-5250120
Fax: 972-3-5250119

Corporate, Civil Litigation, Arbitration, Administrative Law.

MEMBERS OF FIRM

JONATHAN BACH, born Jerusalem, Israel, May 27, 1959; admitted, 1985, Israel. *Education:* Tel-Aviv University Law School (LL.B., 1984). Assistant Lecturer, Administrative Law, Tel Aviv University Law School, 1983-1985. Lecturer, Israel Management Center, 1994-1995, Public Tenders. *Member:* Israel Bar.

EHUD ARAD, born Jerusalem, Israel, March 22, 1960; admitted, 1987, Israel. *Education:* Hebrew University Law School (LL.B., 1986). *Member:* Israel Bar.

ZE'EV SCHARF, born Jerusalem, Israel, March 31, 1961; admitted, 1987, Israel. *Education:* Bar-Ilan University Law School (LL.B. magna cum laude, 1986). Member, Editorial Board, Bar-Ilan Law Review, 1985-1986. Assistant Lecturer, Bar-Ilan University Law School, Property Law, 1986-1987. *Member:* Israel Bar.

SHARON HALE-GILAD, born Jerusalem, Israel, September 21, 1967; admitted, 1993, Israel. *Education:* Hebrew University Law School (LL.B., 1992). *Member:* Israel Bar.

IFAT CHERPACK, born Tel-Aviv, Israel, October 1969; admitted, 1993, Israel. *Education:* Tel-Aviv University Law School (LL.B., 1991). *Member:* Israel Bar.

REBECCA HAZAN, born Jeusalem, Israel, February 25, 1966; admitted, 1993, Israel. *Education:* Hebrew University Law School (LL.B., 1992). *Member:* Israel Bar.

YAIR AHARONSON-OREN, born Jerualem, Israel, September 21, 1962; admitted, 1993, Israel. *Education:* Tel-Aviv University Law School (LL.B., 1992). *Member:* Israel Bar.

BARATZ & CO.
Established in 1982

8 SHAUL HAMELECH BOULEVARD
TEL AVIV 64733, ISRAEL
Telephone: 972-3-6963115
Facsimile: 972-3-6960986

Commercial, Corporate, International Transactions, Banking, Real Estate, Labor, Taxes, Licensing, Estates, Civil Litigation, Arbitration.

FIRM PROFILE: The firm was established in 1982 and offers a full range of civil and commercial services.

MEMBERS OF FIRM

BENJAMIN BARATZ, born Herzliya, Israel, January 22, 1952; admitted, 1979, Israel. *Education:* University of Tel Aviv (LL.B., 1977). *Member:* Israel Bar Association. **LANGUAGES:** Hebrew, English, French, Rumanian. **PRACTICE AREAS:** Business Law; Company Law; Banking Law.

YAEL BARATZ, born New York, USA, October 21, 1956; admitted, 1979, Israel. *Education:* University of Tel Aviv (LL.B., 1978). General Counsel to Eisenberg Group of Companies, 1981-1992. *Member:* Israel Bar Association. **LANGUAGES:** English, Hebrew. **PRACTICE AREAS:** Agencies and Distributorships; Cross Border Transactions; Technology Law; Science Law.

RUTH KREMERMAN, born Petach Tikva, Israel, February 13, 1954; admitted, 1980, Israel. *Education:* Tel Aviv University (LL.B., 1979). *Member:* Israel Bar Association. **LANGUAGES:** Hebrew, English, French. **PRACTICE AREAS:** Real Estate Law; Wills; Estates.

ASSOCIATES

SHLOMI BARDUGO, born Mekness, Morocco, August 28, 1962; admitted, 1989, Israel; 1992, New York. *Education:* Tel Aviv University (LL.B., 1988); New York University (LL.M. in Taxation, 1991). *Member:* Israel and New York Bar Associations. **LANGUAGES:** Hebrew, English,

(This Listing Continued)

French. *PRACTICE AREAS:* Taxation Law; Company Law; Commercial Law.

BARAK LUCHTENSTEIN, born Rhodesia, March 6, 1960; admitted, 1990, Israel. *Education:* Tel Aviv University (LL.B., 1989). *Member:* Israel Bar Association. *LANGUAGES:* Hebrew and English. *PRACTICE AREAS:* Securities; Company Law; Commercial Law.

ODED SHAHAM, born Haifa, Israel, December 17, 1963; admitted, 1991, Israel. *Education:* Hebrew University of Jerusalem (LL.B., 1990). *Member:* Israel Bar Association. *LANGUAGES:* Hebrew, English and Arabic. *PRACTICE AREAS:* Litigation; Maritime Law; Commercial Law.

ANAT S. SKLADMAN, born Ramat-Gan, Israel, September 20, 1968; admitted, 1994, Israel. *Education:* University of Tel Aviv (LL.B., 1993). *Member:* Israel Bar Association. *LANGUAGES:* Hebrew, English, Rumanian. *PRACTICE AREAS:* Securities; Company Law; Commercial Law; Labor Law.

MICHAL AMIT, born Tel Aviv, Israel, November 8, 1968; admitted, 1993, Israel. *Education:* University of Tel Aviv (LL.B., 1993). *Member:* Israel Bar Association. *LANGUAGES:* Hebrew, English, French. *PRACTICE AREAS:* Litigation; Securities; Commercial Law.

I. AMIHUD BEN-PORATH
LAW OFFICES

Established in 1982

CENTURY TOWER
124, IBN GVIROL STREET
TEL AVIV 62038, ISRAEL
Telephone: (972) 3-5222147
Cable Address: 33536 AMJUR IL
Fax: (972) 3-5222451 Group II & III
Telex: 33536 AMJUR IL

Mailing Address: P.O. Box 227, Tel-Aviv, Israel 61001

Commercial Law, Contracts Law, Company Law, International Transactions, Securities, Banking Law, Investment Law, Construction and Housing, Administrative and Constitutional Law, Real Estate, Public Law, Taxation Law, Hotel Construction and Management, Government Contracts, Antitrust Law, Litigation, Resorts and Leisure, Agency and Distributorship, Debtor & Creditor, Labor, Appellate Practice, Civil Law, Estates, Oil and Gas and Energy.

MEMBERS OF FIRM

I. AMIHUD BEN-PORATH, born Jerusalem, Israel, August 14, 1931; admitted, 1958, Israel. *Education:* Hebrew University, Jerusalem (LL.B., 1958); Harvard Law School (LL.M., 1962). *Member:* Israel Bar. *LANGUAGES:* Hebrew, English and Yiddish. *PRACTICE AREAS:* Commercial Law; Contract Law; Company Law; International Transactions; Securities; Banking Law; Investment Law; Construction and Housing; Administrative and Constitutional Law; Public Law; Taxation Law; Hotel Construction and Management; Government Contracts; Antitrust Law; Litigation; Appellate Practice; Civil Arbitration.

RACHEL BEN-PORATH, born Israel, November 11, 1942; admitted, 1977, Israel. *Education:* Hebrew University, Jerusalem (LL.B., 1977). *Member:* Israel Bar. *LANGUAGES:* Hebrew and English. *PRACTICE AREAS:* Construction and Housing Contracts; Real Estate Law; Taxation Law; Estates.

EITAN ADAR, born Haifa, Israel, October 17, 1954; admitted, 1982, Israel. *Education:* Tel Aviv University (LL.B., 1981). Assistant, Tel Aviv University, 1982-1986. *Member:* Israel Bar. *LANGUAGES:* Hebrew and English. *PRACTICE AREAS:* Contract Law; Corporate Law; Labor Law; Litigation; Commercial Law; Banking Law; Construction and Housing Contracts; Agency and Distributorship; Antitrust Law; Resorts and Leisure; Civil Law; Appellate Practice; Civil Arbitration.

SHMUEL HAMOU, born Morocco, December 6, 1960; admitted, 1988, Israel. *Education:* Tel-Aviv University (LL.B., 1987). Assistant, Tel-Aviv University, 1987-1988. *Member:* Israel Bar. *LANGUAGES:* Hebrew, French and English. *PRACTICE AREAS:* Contract Law; Corporate Law; Securities; Labor Law; Agency and Distributorship; Antitrust Law; Debtor Creditor Law; Litigation; Company Law; Civil Law.

AMIT PINES, born Tel-Aviv, Israel, July 10, 1963; admitted, 1990, Israel. *Education:* Tel-Aviv University (LL.B., 1990). *Member:* Israel Bar. *LANGUAGES:* Hebrew and English. *PRACTICE AREAS:* Litigation;

(This Listing Continued)

Contract Law; Antitrust Law; Labor Law; Corporate Law; Agency and Distributorship; Debtor Creditor Law.

OF COUNSEL

PHILIP MANDELKER, born New York, N.Y., U.S.A., October 9, 1946; admitted, 1971, New York; 1976, Israel. *Education:* Columbia College (B.A., cum laude, 1968); Columbia University Law School (J.D., cum laude, 1971). Notes Editor, Columbia Law Review. *Member:* Israel Bar; American Bar Association (Member, Sections On: International Law; National Resources; Energy and Environmment). *LANGUAGES:* Hebrew, English and French. *PRACTICE AREAS:* Commercial and Corporate Law; Contract Law; Partnership Law; Investments Law; International Law; Oil and Gas and Energy Law; Antitrust Law; Multinational Litigation; Alternate Dispute Resolution.

ASSOCIATES

ITZHAK N. EVEN-ARI, born Tel-Aviv, Israel, 1964; admitted, 1992, Israel. *Education:* Bar Ilan University (LL.B., 1991). *Member:* Israel Bar. *LANGUAGES:* Hebrew, English and Yiddish. *PRACTICE AREAS:* Contract Law; Corporate Law; Labor Law; Litigation; Real Estate Law; Civil Law.

MIRIAM SCHLER, born New York, U.S.A., July 2, 1965; admitted, 1993, Israel. *Education:* University of Michigan (B.A., 1987); Tel-Aviv University (LL.B., 1993). *Member:* Israel Bar. *LANGUAGES:* Hebrew and English. *PRACTICE AREAS:* Civil Law; Contract Law; Administrative Law; Labor Law.

SAGIT AMIT, born Beer-Sheva, Israel, 1968; admitted, 1992, Israel. *Education:* Tel-Aviv University (LL.B., 1992). *Member:* Israel Bar. *LANGUAGES:* Hebrew and English. *PRACTICE AREAS:* Company Law; Military Law; Criminal Law.

Languages: Hebrew, English, French and Yiddish.

SHRAGA F. BIRAN & CO.

TEXTILE AND FASHION CENTRE
2 KAUFMAN STREET
TEL AVIV 68012, ISRAEL
Telephone: (972) 3 5105767
Facsimile: (972) 3 5106108

Jerusalem, Israel Office: City Tower, 34 Ben Yehuda Street, 94583. Telephone: (972) 2 258161. Facsimile: (972) 2 259284.

Real Estate: Planning, Construction, Housing, Industrial Parks, Hotels. International Transactions: Finance and Investments, Commerce and Trade.
Corporate Finance: Public Offerings, Sales and Acquisitions.

MEMBERS OF FIRM

AVIGDOR ZIV, born Riga, Latvia, August 12, 1931; admitted, 1957, Israel. *Education:* Hebrew University, Jerusalem (LL.B., 1955). *Member:* Israel Bar Association. *LANGUAGES:* Hebrew and English.

ZACHARIA FIET, born Jambul, Russia, June 5, 1944; admitted, 1968, Israel. *Education:* Hebrew University, Jerusalem (LL.B., 1967). *Member:* The Israel Bar Association. *LANGUAGES:* Hebrew and English.

ZVIKA MARGALIT, born Israel, September 28, 1956; admitted, 1984, Israel. *Education:* Tel Aviv University (LL.B., 1983). *Member:* The Israel Bar Association. *LANGUAGES:* Hebrew and English.

GIDEON HATUKA, born Rosh Ha'ayin, Israel, April 16, 1958; admitted, 1985, Israel. *Education:* Bar Ilan University, Tel Aviv (LL.B., 1986). *Member:* The Israel Bar Association. *LANGUAGES:* Hebrew and English.

ASSOCIATES

SHMUEL LECHNER, born Tel Aviv, Israel, August 21, 1964; admitted, 1991, Israel. *Education:* Tel Aviv University (LL.B., 1989). *Member:* Israel Bar Association. *LANGUAGES:* Hebrew and English.

(For Complete Biographical Data on all Personnel, see Professional Biographies at Jerusalem, Israel).

CASPI & CO.

Established in 1952

33 YAVETZ STREET

TEL AVIV 65258, ISRAEL

Telephone: 972-3-5171010

Facsimile: 972-3-5172357; 5106644

Commercial Litigation, Arbitration, Corporate, International Transactions, Real Estate Transactions and Tax Implications, Cooperative Societies, Estates and Family Law.

MEMBERS OF FIRM

MICHAEL CASPI, born Israel, 1914; admitted, 1936, England; 1940, Israel. *Education:* University College, London (LL.B., with honours); Grays Inn, London (Barrister at Law, 1936). Guest Lecturer, Tel Aviv University. Deputy Mayor, Municipality of Tel Aviv, 1964-1966. Member, Israel Bar Association, Central Committee, 1956-1958. *Member:* British Bar Association; International Bar Association; Jewish Bar Association. *LANGUAGES:* Hebrew and English. *PRACTICE AREAS:* Commercial and Criminal Law; Litigation.

SHLOMO LEVRON, born Poland, 1920; admitted, 1947, Israel. *Education:* Hebrew University (LL.B.). *Member:* Israel Bar Association (President of Disciplinary Tribunals). *LANGUAGES:* Hebrew, English, German, Polish and Yiddish. *PRACTICE AREAS:* Commercial and Property Law; Litigation.

RAM CASPI, born Israel, 1939; admitted, 1964, Israel. *Education:* Hebrew University (LL.M., cum laude, 1962). Lecturer, Tel Aviv University Faculty of Law, 1965-1966. *Member:* Israel Bar Association. *LANGUAGES:* Hebrew and English. *PRACTICE AREAS:* Commercial and Property Law; International Transactions; Banking and Litigation.

ASSAPH CASPI, born Israel, 1942; admitted, 1967, Israel. *Education:* Hebrew University (LL.B., 1965). Member, Savyon City Council, 1984—. Member, Tel Aviv Central Committee, Israel Bar Association, 1987-1990. *Member:* Israel Bar Association. [Judge, Military Tribunal, Lt. Col., Reserves]. *LANGUAGES:* Hebrew and English. *PRACTICE AREAS:* Commercial and Property Law; International Transactions; Extradition; Arbitration and Litigation.

SHLOMO SHAFIR, born Israel, 1950; admitted, 1974, Israel. *Education:* Tel Aviv University (LL.B., 1973). *Member:* Israel Bar Association. *LANGUAGES:* Hebrew and English. *PRACTICE AREAS:* Commercial Law; Litigation and Arbitration.

GERSHON SHNEIDER, born Germany, 1946; admitted, 1974, Israel. *Education:* Hebrew University (B.A., 1972); Tel Aviv University (LL.B., 1973). Lecturer, Tel Aviv University, Faculty of Law, 1973-1975. *Member:* Israel Bar Association (Judge on Bar Disciplinary Committee). *LANGUAGES:* Hebrew and English. *PRACTICE AREAS:* Family Law; Estate Law and Litigation.

SHMUEL INY, born Israel, 1958; admitted, 1986, Israel. *Education:* Tel Aviv University (LL.B., 1984). *Member:* Israel Bar Association. *LANGUAGES:* Hebrew and English. *PRACTICE AREAS:* Property Law and Commercial Transactions; Litigation.

ZVI LEVRON, born Israel, 1958; admitted, 1986, Israel. *Education:* Hebrew University (LL.B., 1985); University of London, Queen Mary College (LL.M., 1988). *Member:* Israel Bar Association. *LANGUAGES:* Hebrew and English. *PRACTICE AREAS:* Property Law and Commercial Transactions.

GUY MORDECHAI CASPI, born Israel, 1962; admitted, 1990, Israel. *Education:* Tel Aviv University (LL.B., 1989). *Member:* Israel Bar Association. *LANGUAGES:* Hebrew and English. *PRACTICE AREAS:* Intellectual Property Law; Libel and Slander Law; Litigation.

ORNA KEDAR, born Israel, 1957; admitted, 1984, Israel. *Education:* Tel Aviv University (LL.B., 1983). *Member:* Israel Bar Association. *LANGUAGES:* Hebrew and English. *PRACTICE AREAS:* Transport Law and Cooperative Society Litigation.

GAD TICHO, born Israel, 1960; admitted, 1988, Israel. *Education:* Tel Aviv University (LL.B., 1987). Teaching Assistant, Tel Aviv University, 1987-1989. *Member:* Israel Bar Association. *LANGUAGES:* Hebrew and English. *PRACTICE AREAS:* Commercial and Criminal Law; Litigation.

(This Listing Continued)

ASSOCIATES

ANAT BAHARAV-KEREN, born Israel, 1962; admitted, 1988, Israel. *Education:* Tel Aviv University (LL.B., 1987). *Member:* Israel Bar Association. *LANGUAGES:* Hebrew and English. *PRACTICE AREAS:* Commercial Law and Litigation.

RAM EPHRATI, born Israel, 1961; admitted, 1989, Israel. *Education:* Tel Aviv University (LL.B., 1988). *Member:* Israel Bar Association. *LANGUAGES:* Hebrew and English. *PRACTICE AREAS:* Arbitration; Cooperative Societies; Pension Fund Law.

YOSSI RICHTER, born Israel, 1962; admitted, 1991, Israel. *Education:* Tel Aviv University (LL.B., 1990). *Member:* Israel Bar Association. *LANGUAGES:* Hebrew and English.

KENNETH E. MANN, born Los Angeles, 1947; admitted, 1978, District of Columbia; 1981, Israel. *Education:* University of California, Berkeley, California (J.D., 1975); Center for the Study of Law & Society (M.A., 1976); Post Graduate Legal Studies, Hebrew University Jerusalem 1975-1977; Yale University (Ph.D., 1980). Professor, Faculty of Law, Tel Aviv University, Evidence, Criminal Procedure, White-Collar Crime. Assistant District Attorney, Tel Aviv, 1981-1982. Author, Defending White Collar Crime, Yale University Press (1981), Punitive Civil Sanctions, 101 Yale Law Journal (1992). Member, National Commission for Revision of Police Powers. *LANGUAGES:* English, Hebrew. *PRACTICE AREAS:* Litigation; Civil & Criminal; Extradition.

ROY MILLER, born Tel Aviv, 1967; admitted, 1993, Israel. *Education:* London Guildhall University (formerly City of London Polytechnic) (LL.B., 1991). *Member:* Israel Bar Association. *LANGUAGES:* English, Hebrew.

YITZHAK NAIMI, born Israel, 1964; admitted, 1993, Israel. *Education:* Bar Ilan University (LL.B., 1992). *Member:* Israel Bar Association. *LANGUAGES:* English, Hebrew, Iranian.

COREY SILBERSTEIN SHDAIMAH, born New York, 1965; admitted, 1993, Israel. *Education:* Tel Aviv University (LL.B., 1992). *Member:* Israel Bar Association. *LANGUAGES:* English, Hebrew.

RONIT AMIR-YANIV, born 1965; admitted, 1993, Israel. *Education:* Tel Aviv University (LL.B., 1992). *Member:* Israel Bar Association. *LANGUAGES:* English, Hebrew. *PRACTICE AREAS:* Commercial Law and Litigation.

REFERENCES: Mr. Kenneth Bialkin, Skaaden Aarps, Meagher & Flom, New York, N.Y.; Mr. Arthur Brown, Altheimer Gray, Chicago, Illinois; Mr. Laurent Epstein, Baker-Makenzie, Paris, France; Mr. Derek Bluston, Malkins Solicitors, London, England.

CHAIMOVSKI, ARAD, EITANI & CO.

111 ARLOZOROV STREET

P.O. BOX 21222

TEL AVIV 61211, ISRAEL

Telephone: (972-3) 691 71 91

Facsimile: (972-3) 691 71 95

Commercial Law, Corporate Law, International Business Transactions, Taxation Law (Criminal and Civil), Maritime Law, Real Estate Law, Arbitration.

MEMBERS OF FIRM

RON CHAIMOVSKI, born Tel-Aviv, Israel, September 3, 1959; admitted, 1989, Israel. *Education:* Tel-Aviv University (LL.B., 1988); University of London (LL.M., 1990). *Member:* Israel Bar Association; Israel Maritime Law Society. *LANGUAGES:* Hebrew and English.

YORAM ARAD, born Haifa, Israel, September 23, 1959; admitted, 1986, Israel. *Education:* Hebrew University of Jerusalem (LL.B., 1985). *Member:* Israel Bar Association; Israel Maritime Law Society; International Bar Association. *LANGUAGES:* Hebrew and English.

DORON EITANI, born Nazareth, Israel, February 26, 1959; admitted, 1989, Israel. *Education:* Tel-Aviv University (LL.B., 1988); Tel-Aviv College of Administration (Tax Advisors, 1993). *Member:* Israel Bar Association. *LANGUAGES:* Hebrew, English and German.

DR. SHLOMO COHEN & CO.
LAW OFFICES

Established in 1979

CENTURY TOWER
124 IBN GVIROL
TEL AVIV 62 038, ISRAEL
Telephone: (03) 527 1919
Fax: (03) 527 2666

Patent Law, Design, Trademarks and Copyright, Commercial, Industrial and Intellectual Property, Licensing and Franchising, Air Law, Telecommunications, Litigation and International Transactions.

DR. SHLOMO COHEN, born Tel Aviv, Israel, 1947; admitted, 1973, Israel. *Education:* Tel Aviv University (LL.B., LL.M.); New York University (LL.M., Trade Regulation, J.S.D.); University of Brussels (Diploma). Author: "Compulsory Licensing of Patents," IDEA, The Journal of Law and Technology, Vol. 20, p. 153, 1979 and LES Nouvelles, Vol. 14, p 262, 1979; "Limitations of Patent Rights - The Public Interest," Tel Aviv University Law Review, Vol 7, p. 5, 1979; "National Protection of Industrial Property in the EEC," Hebrew University Law Review, Vol. 11, p. 107, 1981; "Monopoly in EEC Law," Israel Bar Law Review, Vol. 33, p. 487, 1981; "Licensing to LDC's in the 1980's," LES Nouvelles, Vol. 26, p. 159, 1981; "The Right to Legal Aid," Tel Aviv University Law Review, Vol 4, p. 145, 1974. Israel Chapter, Enforcement of U.S. Judgments Abroad, ABA Publication, 1989; Security Interests in Intellectual Property in Israel (with Ron Klagsbald), Intellectual Property Journal, Vol. 2, p. 148 (1991); " GATT-A Trip in the Right Direction," Trademark World, Jan. 1995; Israel Chapter, Worldwide Trademark Transfers, Clark-Boardman, 1992; Israel reporter: Trademark World, Copyright World, IIC--International Review of Industrial Property and Copyright Law, European Intellectual Property Review and World Intellectual Property Review. J.S.D. Thesis, "Licensing of Technology: EEC -U.S.," New York University, 1976. Adjunct Professor, Law of Technology, Patents and Trademarks, New York University School of Law, 1977-1993. Lecturer, Hebrew University School of Law, Jerusalem, 1981—. Chairman, Justice Ministry Committee to Revise the Registered Design Act, 1985—. Member, Justice Ministry Commissions to Revise Patent and Copyright Acts, 1985—. Israeli Representative to WIPO Convention to Draft Treaty for the Protection of Semiconductor Chip Design, 1989. Chairman, Public Committee for the Protection of Privacy. *Member:* Israel Bar Association (Member, Board of Directors); Israel Press Council; The Association of the Bar of the City of New York; Licensing Executive Society (President, LES Israel); International Trademark Association; American Patent Lawyers Association; AIPPI; AIPLA.

RON KLAGSBALD, born Tel Aviv, Israel, 1957; admitted, 1985, Israel. *Education:* Tel Aviv University School of Law (LL.B., 1984). Member, Editorial Board, Tel Aviv University Law Review, 1983-1984. Author: "Security Interests in Intellectual Property in Israel" (with Dr. Shlomo Cohen), Intellectual Property Journal, Vol. 2 (1991), p. 148 and Trademark World, Issue 44 (February 1992), p. 44. Teaching Assistant, Tel Aviv University, Faculty of Business Administration School of Accounting, 1984-1985. *Member:* Israel Bar Association; AIPPI; ALAI; Licensing Executive Society.

LIAD WHATSTEIN, born Tel Aviv, Israel, 1965; admitted, 1991, Israel. *Education:* Tel Aviv University, School of Law (LL.B., Cum Laude, 1990); London School of Economics and Political Science (LL.M., with Merit, 1992). Associate Editor, Tel Aviv University Law Review, 1988-1989. Author: "Securities Manipulation and Corporate Control Struggles," 28 Banking Law Quarterly 55, 1990; "Extraterritorial Application of EC Competition Law - Comments and Reflections," 26 Israel Law Review 195, 1992. Teaching Assistant, Tel Aviv University Business School, 1989-1991. *Member:* Israel Bar Association; AIPPI; International Trademark Association.

DORI KADMON, born Haifa, Israel, 1963; admitted, 1990, Israel. *Education:* Hebrew University School of Law (LL.B., cum laude, 1988); London School of Economics and Political Sciences (LL.M., 1989). *Member:* Israel Bar Association; AIPPI; International Trademark Association.

IVAN ROTHMAN, born New York, U.S.A., 1961; admitted, 1990, Israel. *Education:* Hebrew University of Jerusalem (B.A., cum laude, 1985); London University, King's College (LL.B., 1988); Hebrew University School of Law (LL.M., cum laude, 1994). Research Assistant, Hebrew University, 1991. Author and Editor: "Case Digest Surveying Israeli Supreme Court Decisions," Israel Law Review, 1990-1992. *Member:* Israel Bar Association; AIPPI; International Trademark Association.

(This Listing Continued)

NAOMI HILLEL, born London, U.K., 1958; admitted, 1991, Israel. *Education:* Brandeis University, USA, Faculty of Arts (B.A., Music, summa cum laude, 1983); Hebrew University School of Law (LL.B., 1990). Translator and Editor, Case Digest Surveying Israeli Supreme Court Decisions, published in the Israel Law Review, 1988-1990. *Member:* Israel Bar Association; AIPPI; International Trademark Association.

RONIT BARZIK-SOFFER, born Tel Aviv, Israel, 1968; admitted, 1994, Israel. *Education:* Tel Aviv University School of Law (LL.B., 1993). Research Assistant, Tel Aviv University, 1990-1991. *Member:* Israel Bar Association; AIPPI; International Trademark Association.

Languages: Hebrew, English and French.

DR. REINHOLD COHN AND PARTNERS

PATENT ATTORNEYS

9-11 YAVNE STREET
P.O. BOX 4060
TEL AVIV 65791, ISRAEL
Telephone: 972-3-566-4455
Telex: 341137 copt il
Telephone copier: 972-3-560-6405; 972-3-566-3782

Intellectual Property Protection, particularly patents in all technological fields, trademarks, designs and plant varieties.

FIRM PROFILE: The firm has continuously developed since its establishment in 1934 and today has over 80 members comprising professional and support staff. The professional members of the firm, who are qualified to practice before the Israel Patent Office and before the Israel courts when accompanied by the advocate of the party concerned, have technological qualifications and experience covering the widest fields in chemistry and biochemistry, biology and biotechnology, electrical, electronic and mechanical engineering and computer technology.

MEMBERS OF FIRM

MICHAEL COHN, born Germany, September 21, 1926, admitted to practice before Israel Patent Office, 1956. *Education:* University of Zurich (Ph.D., Chemistry, 1954). Former President, Israel Group of Association Internationale pour la Protection de la Propriété Industrielle (AIPPI). *Member:* Federation Internationale des Conseils en Propriété Industrielle (FICPI) (Israel Section); Association of Israel Patent Attorneys; International Trademark Association; Overseas Member of the Institute of Trade Mark Agents, London; Committees for the Revision of the Israel Patents and Trademark Laws. *LANGUAGES:* Hebrew, English and German.

ISRAEL SHACHTER, born England, July 14, 1926. admitted to practice before British Patent Office, 1959; Israel Patent Office, 1960; European Patent Office, 1978. *Education:* Queen's University, Belfast, Ireland (B.Sc., Physics, 1951). Fellow, Chartered Institute of Patent Agents. *Member:* Association Internationale pour la Protection de la Propriété Industrielle (AIPPI) (Israel Group); Federation Internationale des Conseils en Propriété Industrielle (FICPI) (Israel Section); Association of Israel Patent Attorneys; Licensing Executives Society; Committees for the Revision of the Israel Designs and Trademarks Laws; Committee for Considering the Introduction of a Semi-conductor Topography Protection Law. *LANGUAGES:* English, Hebrew and German.

ILAN COHN, born Israel, March 31, 1955. admitted to practice before Israel Patent Office, 1989. *Education:* Hebrew University, Jerusalem (Ph.D., Biology, 1988; B.Sc., Biology, 1980). *Member:* Association Internationale pour la Protection de la Propriété Industrielle (AIPPI) (Israel Group); Federation Internationale des Conseils en Propriété Industrielle (FICPI) (Israel Section); Association of Israel Patent Attorneys. *LANGUAGES:* Hebrew, English and German.

ZWI VROMEN, born Israel, August 3, 1938. admitted to practice before Israel Patent Office, 1987. *Education:* University of London, Imperial College (B.Sc., Chem. Eng. 1960); University of Jerusalem, Tel-Aviv Branch (Diploma of Business Administration, 1965) *Member:* Association Internationale pour la Protection de la Propriété Industrielle (AIPPI) (Israel Group); Association of Israel Patent Attorneys. *LANGUAGES:* Hebrew, English, German and French.

ASSOCIATES

NAFTALI DANIELI, born Germany, July 21, 1928. admitted to practice before Israel Patent Office, 1972. *Education:* Hebrew University, Jerusalem (Ph.D., Organic Chemistry, 1958; M.Sc., 1954). *Member:* Association Internationale pour la Protection de la Propriété Industrielle (AIPPI) (Is-

(This Listing Continued)

DR. REINHOLD COHN AND PARTNERS PATENT
ATTORNEYS, Tel Aviv—Continued

rael Group); Association of Israel Patent Attorneys. *LANGUAGES:* Hebrew, English and German.

JONATHAN TOPPER, born England, October 25, 1955. admitted to practice before Israel Patent Office. *Education:* Cambridge University, Cambridge (M.A.Engineering, 1978). *Member:* Institution of Electrical Engineers (MIEE) (U.K.); Association Internationale pour la Protection de la Propriété Industrielle (AIPPI) (Israel Group); Association of Israel Patent Attorneys. *LANGUAGES:* English, Hebrew and French.

ELENA LEVIN, born Latvia, January 12, 1955. admitted to practice before Israel Patent Office. *Education:* Leningrad Institute of Engineering (Computer Sciences) (Dipl. Eng., 1977); Central College of Patent Studies, Leningrad, 1981. *Member:* Association Internationale pour le Protection de la Propriété Industrielle (AIPPI) (Israel Group); Association of Israel Patent Attorneys. *LANGUAGES:* Russian, Latvian, Hebrew and English.

NAVA BLUMENFELD, born Israel, May 4, 1959. admitted to practice before Israel Patent Office. *Education:* Tel-Aviv University (M.Sc. Biology, 1986). *Member:* Association Internationale pour la Protection de la Propriété Industrielle (AIPPI) (Israel Group). *LANGUAGES:* Hebrew and English.

DAVID DE VRIES, born Israel, November 14, 1958. admitted to practice before Israel Patent Office. *Education:* Beer-Sheba University (B.Sc. Mechanical Engineering, 1986). *Member:* Association Internationale pour la Protection de la Propriété Industrielle (AIPPI) (Israel Group). *LANGUAGES:* Hebrew and English.

TAMAR GALLILY, born Israel, May 26, 1964. admitted to practice before Israel Patent Office. *Education:* Hebrew University, Jerusalem (B.Sc. Biology, 1988; M.Sc. Physiology, 1990). *Member:* Association Internationale pour la Protection de la Propriété Industrielle (AIPPI) (Israel Group). *LANGUAGES:* Hebrew and English.

EHUD HAUSMAN, born Israel, July 22, 1960. admitted to practice before Israel Patent Office. *Education:* BOSMAT, Haifa (qualified Instruments and Control Technician, 1979); Technion - Israel Institute of Technology, Haifa (B.A. Computer Sciences cum laude, 1986; M.Sc. Computer Sciences, 1989). *Member:* Association Internationale pour la Protection de la Propriété Industrielle (AIPPI) (Israel Group). *LANGUAGES:* Hebrew and English.

BOSSMAT GONEN, born Israel, January 25, 1959. admitted to practice before Israel Patent Office. *Education:* Tel-Aviv University (Ph.D. Biology-Immunology, 1990; B.Sc. Biology, 1981; M.Sc. Biology, 1984). *Member:* Association Internationale pour la Protection de la Propriété Industrielle (AIPPI) (Israel Group). *LANGUAGES:* Hebrew, English and French.

JONATHAN PATINKIN, born U.S.A., June 25, 1951. *Education:* Hebrew University, Jerusalem (B.Sc. Biology, 1974); The Weizmann Institute of Science, Rehovot (M.Sc. Biochemistry, 1979). *Member:* Association Internationale pour la Protection de la Propriété Industrielle (AIPPI) (Israel Group); Association of Israel Patent Attorneys. *LANGUAGES:* English, Hebrew and French.

TECHNICAL SUPPORT PERSONNEL

ENA PUGATSCH, born Russia, January 29, 1956. *Education:* Leningrad Institute of Mechanics and Optics (M.Sc. Mech. and Opt. Eng., 1979); Central Patent Courses, 1986; Central College of Patent Studies, Leningrad, 1988. *Member:* Association Internationale pour la Protection de la Propriété Industrielle (AIPPI) (Israel Group). *LANGUAGES:* Russian, Hebrew and English.

MICHAEL B. KAYE, born England, September 24, 1944. *Education:* University of London (B.Sc., Physics, 1967); The Hebrew University of Jerusalem (M.Sc. Physics, 1971); Ben-Gurion University of the Negev, Beer-Sheva (Ph.D. Physics, 1977). *Member:* Association Internationale pour la Protection de la Propriété Industrielle (AIPPI) (Israel Group); The Institute of Electrical and Electronics Engineers (IEEE). *LANGUAGES:* English and Hebrew.

GIL INGEL, born Israel, November 5, 1955. *Education:* Technion-Israel Institute of Technology, Haifa (B.Sc. Chemical Engineering, 1976); Tel-Aviv University (M.Sc. Engineering, 1981); Weizmann Institute of Science, Rehovot (Ph.D. Chemistry, 1992). *Member:* Association Internationale pour la Protection de la PropriéTé Industrielle (AIPPI) (Israel Group). *LANGUAGES:* Hebrew, English and French.

(This Listing Continued)

DOCUMENTATION AND ON-LINE DATA BASE SEARCHES

DEBRAH MARCUS, born South Africa, July 10, 1957. *Education:* University of Cape Town (B.A., Languages, 1979); Beth Berl College (Translation Diploma, 1984); Bar Ilan University (Post Graduate Diploma, Information Science, 1985). *LANGUAGES:* English, Hebrew and French.

SANFORD T. COLB & CO.

Established in 1976

BEIT AMOT MISHPAT
8 SHAUL HAMELECH BOULEVARD
P.O. BOX 23008
TEL AVIV, ISRAEL
Telephone: 972-3-6938560
Fax: 972-3-6938561

Rehovot, Israel Office: P.O.B. 2273, 4 Shaar Hagai, Marmorek, 76 122 Rehovot. Telephone: 972-8-455122. Fax: 972-8-454556, 972-8-491040.
Jerusalem, Israel Office: Lev Hagiva, 3 Beit Hadphus Street. Telephone: 972-2-519453. Fax: 972-3-519454.

Patent, Design, Trademark and Copyright Law, Industrial Property, Licensing and Litigation.

FIRM PROFILE: The firm was established in 1976 and offers a full range of legal services connected with Intellectual Property. The firm employs attorneys at law, advocates and patent attorneys qualified to practice before the Israel courts and the Israel Patent Office, and is backed up by a staff of patent agents, paralegal personnel, draftsmen and accounts and secretarial staff.

SANFORD T. COLB, born Cleveland, Ohio, U.S.A., July 18, 1948; admitted, 1975, Massachusetts; 1976, Israel, to practice before Patent Office; practice before U.S. Patent and Trademark Office. *Education:* University of Pennsylvania (B.A., magna cum laude, Physics, 1970; Ms.C., Physics, 1970); University of Cambridge (LL.B., with honors, 1972); Harvard Law School (J.D., 1974). Phi Beta Kappa. Lecturer, Intellectual Property and Patent Law, Bar Ilan University, 1983-1991. Arbitrator, American Arbitration Association. *Member:* American Patent Law Association (Member, International Law Committee, 1980—); Israel Association of Patent Attorneys; AIPPI (Member, Legal Committee, AACI, 1977—); Licensing Executives Society; U.S. Trademark Association; Pharmaceutical Trade Marks Group. *LANGUAGES:* English, Hebrew, French. *PRACTICE AREAS:* Patents; Licensing.

OF COUNSEL

BENJAMIN J. BARISH, born Detroit, Michigan, May 25, 1925; admitted, 1950, District of Columbia; 1957, Michigan; 1968, Israel; registered to practice before the U.S. Patent and Trademark Office and Israel Patent Office. *Education:* Illinois Institute of Technology, Chicago (B.S., E.E., 1946); George Washington University, Washington, D.C. (J.D., 1950 with honors; LL.M., 1951). Patent Examiner, U.S. Patent Office, 1947-1952. Patent Attorney: U.S. Air Force, Wright Air Development Center, Dayton, Ohio, 1952-1954; Burroughs Corporation, Detroit, Michigan, 1954-1963; Tel Aviv, Israel, 1963—. *Member:* State Bar of Michigan; The District of Columbia Bar; The Israel Bar; AIPPI, Israel Group (Treasurer, 1973-1988); Association of Israel Patent Attorneys. *LANGUAGES:* English and Hebrew. *PRACTICE AREAS:* Patents; Licensing.

REUVEN BORKOVSKY, born Israel, November 4, 1946; admitted, 1978, Israel. *Education:* Hebrew University of Jerusalem (B.A., Economics and Statistics, 1972; M.B.A., 1976; LL.B., 1976). Research Assistant, Falk Institute of Economical Research, 1971-1973. Researcher, Harry Sacher Legal Research Institute, 1974-1976. *Member:* Israel Bar Association. *LANGUAGES:* Hebrew and English. *PRACTICE AREAS:* Litigation.

ASSOCIATES

STANLEY J. DAVIS, born London, November 22, 1929; admitted, 1987, Israel, to practice before Patent Office. *Education:* Woolwich Polytechnic (B.Sc., Chemistry, Class 1); Imperial College, London, England (Ph.D., Organic Chemistry); University of London, London (B.A.; LL.M.); Holborn College of Law (LL.B.); London School of Economics. Fulbright Travel Fellowship, 1953-1956. Senior Examiner, U.K. Patent Office, 1958-1984. *LANGUAGES:* English, Hebrew. *PRACTICE AREAS:* Patents (Chemical and Biological).

RUTH M. SEGEL, born London, England, 1932; admitted, 1983, Israel. *Education:* University College, London University, England (LL.B., 1954). Lecturer in English, Bar Ilan University, Israel, 1974—. *Member:*

(This Listing Continued)

Solicitors' Law Society, London. *LANGUAGES:* English, Hebrew. *PRACTICE AREAS:* Trademarks.

ELLEN B. SHANKMAN, born Memphis, Tennessee, U.S.A., July 18, 1956; admitted, 1981, Massachusetts; 1982, Maryland; 1985, New York; 1988, Israel. *Education:* Barnard College, Columbia University (B.A., magna cum laude, English, 1978); Boston University (J.D., 1981). *Member:* Israel, Maryland State, Massachusetts and New York State Bar Associations. *LANGUAGES:* English, Hebrew. *PRACTICE AREAS:* Trademarks.

GAIL BEN-DAVID, born Brooklyn, New York, U.S.A., March 21, 1961; admitted, 1990, Israel, to practice before Patent Office. *Education:* Queens College of the City University of New York (Applied Mathematics/Biology B.A., 1983); New York University, Graduate School of Arts & Science (Mathematics M.Sc., 1985). *LANGUAGES:* English, Hebrew. *PRACTICE AREAS:* Patents.

AARON S. LEWIN, born Montreal, Canada, 1949; admitted, 1982, Israel. *Education:* Yeshiva University, New York (B.A., 1970); Harvard University, Cambridge (M.A., 1974); Hebrew University of Jerusalem, Israel (LL.B., 1980);. *LANGUAGES:* English, Hebrew. *PRACTICE AREAS:* Litigation; Patents; Trademarks.

ERAN SOROKER, born Jerusalem, Israel, 1963; admitted, 1990, Israel. *Education:* Hebrew University of Jerusalem, Israel (LL.B., 1989). *LANGUAGES:* Hebrew, English. *PRACTICE AREAS:* Litigation.

PAUL FENSTER, born New York, U.S.A., 1939; admitted, 1988, U.S. Patent Office; 1990, Israel. *Education:* City College of New York (B.E.E., magna cum laude, 1960); Polytechnic Institute of Brooklyn, NY (M.S., 1964; Ph.D., 1967). *LANGUAGES:* English, Hebrew. *PRACTICE AREAS:* Patents.

SUSIE R. DYM, born London, 1962; admitted, 1988, Israel Patent Office; 1994, United States Pa tent Office. *Education:* Hebrew University of Jerusalem (B.A., magna cum laude, 1985); Bar Ilan University (M.A.). *LANGUAGES:* English and Hebrew. *PRACTICE AREAS:* Patents.

DORON HANDELMAN, born Bucharest, Romania, August 10, 1955; admitted, 1944, to practice before Patent Office. *Education:* Tel Aviv University of Israel (B.Sc., Physics and Mathematics, 1979; M.Sc., Physics, 1985). *LANGUAGES:* Hebrew, English and Romanian. *PRACTICE AREAS:* Patents.

EITAN SHAULSKY, born Zfat, Israel, August 23, 1966; admitted, 1993, Israel. *Education:* Tel Aviv University, Israel (LL.B cum laude, 1991). Teaching Assistant, Ramot Mishpat Law School, Constitutional Law, 1993-1994. *LANGUAGES:* Hebrew and English. *PRACTICE AREAS:* Litigation.

GALIT WELLNER, born Tel Aviv, Israel, 1967; admitted, 1994, Israel. *Education:* Tel Aviv University, Israel (LL.B., 1992). *LANGUAGES:* Hebrew, English and French. *PRACTICE AREAS:* Litigation.

DEKEL SHILOH, born Tel Aviv, February 27, 1964; admitted, 1994, Israel, to practice before the Patent Office. *Education:* Hebrew University, Jerusalem, Israel (B.Sc., Physics, 1989; LL.B., 1993).

DANZIGER, KLAGSBALD & CO.

Law - Offices

THE DIAMOND TOWER, 30TH FLOOR

3A JABOTINSKI STREET

TEL AVIV (RAMAT GAN) 52520, ISRAEL

Telephone: 972-3-752-7333

Telecopier: 972-3-752-7373

Administrative Law, Advertising and Marketing, Agency and Distributorship, Alternative Dispute Resolution, Antitrust, Appellate Practice, Bankruptcy, Banks and Banking, International Loans, Business Law, Charitable Organizations, Civil Law, Class Actions, Commercial Law, Communications and Media, Company Law, Computers, Constitutional Law, Contracts, Corporate Law, Debtor and Creditor, Franchises, General Practice, Government, Intellectual Property, International Law, Investments, Labor Law, Libel and Defamation, Litigation, Mergers and Acquisitions, Property, Real Estate, Securities, Taxation, Trusts and Estates, White Collar Crimes, Wills, Zoning and Planning.

DR. YORAM DANZIGER, born Israel, 1953; admitted, 1980, Israel. *Education:* Tel-Aviv University (LL.B., LL.M.); University of London

(This Listing Continued)

(Ph.D.). *Member:* Israel Bar Association. *LANGUAGES:* Hebrew and English.

DR. AVIGDOR KLAGSBALD, born Israel, 1953; admitted, 1981, Israel. *Education:* Tel-Aviv University (LL.B., LL.M., Ph.D.). *Member:* Israel Bar Association. *LANGUAGES:* Hebrew and English.

ORI ROSEN, born Israel, 1963; admitted, 1986, Israel; 1991, New York. *Education:* Tel-Aviv University (LL.B., LL.M.); University of Michigan Law School (LL.M.). *Member:* Israel Bar Association; New York State Bar. *LANGUAGES:* Hebrew and English.

MICHAL BLEICH, born Israel, 1955; admitted, 1983, Israel. *Education:* Tel-Aviv University (B.Sc., LL.B.); University of London (LL.M.). *Member:* Israel Bar Association. *LANGUAGES:* Hebrew and English.

EREZ TIKOLSKER, born Israel, 1965; admitted, 1993, Israel. *Education:* Tel-Aviv University (LL.B.). *Member:* Israel Bar Association. *LANGUAGES:* Hebrew and English.

ILAN MAGAR, born Israel, 1961; admitted, 1983, Israel. *Education:* Tel-Aviv University (LL.B.). *Member:* Israel Bar Association. *LANGUAGES:* Hebrew and English.

SHARON KLAINMAN-SOFER, born Israel, 1967; admitted, 1994, Israel. *Education:* Tel-Aviv University (LL.B.). *Member:* Israel Bar Association. *LANGUAGES:* Hebrew and English.

ARYE EDELIST, PARITZKY & CO.

Established in 1992

SILVER BUILDING, 7TH FLOOR

7 ABBA HILLEL ROAD

52522 TEL AVIV (RAMAT GAN), ISRAEL

Telephone: 972-3-751-2121

Fax: 972-3-751-2233

General Practice, Corporations, Contracts, Copyright, Employment Law, Insolvency and Civil Litigation.

ARYE EDELIST, born Poland, 1924; admitted, 1965, Israel. *Education:* Ecole des Hautes Etudes Sociales, Paris (Diplome, 1952); Hebrew University, Jerusalem (LL.B., 1960). *Member:* Israel Bar Association. *LANGUAGES:* Hebrew, English, French, Polish and Yiddish.

JOSEPH I. PARITZKY, born Jerusalem, Israel, 1955; admitted, 1983, Israel; 1986, New York. *Education:* Hebrew University, Jerusalem (LL.B., 1981). *Member:* Israel, American and New York State Bar Associations. *LANGUAGES:* Hebrew and English.

PNINA PARITZKY, born Tel Aviv, Israel, 1956; admitted, 1981, Israel. *Education:* Hebrew University, Jerusalem (LL.B., 1980). *Member:* Israel Bar Association. *LANGUAGES:* Hebrew and English.

ARYE LIANY, born Ramia, Israel, 1964; admitted, 1993, Israel. *Education:* Hebrew University of Jerusalem (LL.B., 1991). *Member:* Israel Bar Association. *LANGUAGES:* Hebrew and English.

EFRATI, GALILI & CO.

6 WISSOTSKY STREET

TEL AVIV 62338, ISRAEL

Telephone: 972-3-605-1010

Fax: 972-3-604-0111

General Corporate, Securities, Financing, Mergers and Acquisitions, Taxation, International Business Transactions, Commercial Insurance, Negligence, Torts and Real Estate Law.

MEMBERS OF FIRM

DAVID EFRATI, born Jerusalem, Israel, May 2, 1943; admitted, 1972, Israel. *Education:* Hebrew University of Jerusalem (LL.B.); Tel-Aviv University (LL.M., with honors). Author: "Capital Gains Tax and Tax on Registering Shares on the Stock Exchange According to Amendment 21 of the Income Tax Ordinance," Vol. 25, p. 365, Roeh Haheshbon (The Journal of the Institute of Certified Public Accountants in Israel), 1975; "General Rules for Defining Capital Gains," p. 325. Cahiers de Droit Fiscal International, 1976; "The Canadian-Israeli Tax Convention," p. 20, Tax Management International, January, 1977; "Income Tax Law" (published in Hebrew by Schoken, 1980, 1985). *Member:* Israel Bar Association. *LANGUAGES:* Hebrew and English.

(This Listing Continued)

EFRATI, GALILI & CO., Tel Aviv—Continued

ALON GALILI, born Tel-Aviv, Israel, November 9, 1945; admitted, 1969, Israel. *Education:* Hebrew University of Jerusalem (LL.B.). With District Attorney's Office, Civil Department, 1969-1976. *Member:* Israel Bar Association. *LANGUAGES:* Hebrew and English.

ASSOCIATES

SHAULA BERG, born Tel-Aviv, Israel, November 13, 1950; admitted, 1977, Israel. *Education:* Tel-Aviv University (LL.B., with honors). *Member:* Israel Bar Association; The Society for Medicine and Law in Israel. *LANGUAGES:* Hebrew and English.

MICHAELA MIZRAHI, born Tel-Aviv, Israel, December 28, 1957; admitted, 1984, Israel. *Education:* Bar Ilan University (LL.B.). *Member:* Israel Bar Association. *LANGUAGES:* Hebrew and English.

HANAN FELDMUS, born Kiryat Ono, Israel, January 25, 1958; admitted, 1986, Israel. *Education:* Tel-Aviv University (LL.B.). *Member:* Israel Bar Association. *LANGUAGES:* Hebrew and English.

MOSHE TOBOLSKY, born Tel-Aviv, Israel, January 10, 1961; admitted, 1988, Israel. *Education:* Tel-Aviv University (LL.B., with honors, 1987). *Member:* Israeli Bar Association. *LANGUAGES:* Hebrew and English.

YUVAL HORN, born California, U.S.A., February 22, 1967; admitted, 1990, Israel. *Education:* Tel-Aviv University (LL.B., LL.M.). Law Teacher, Tel-Aviv University Leon Recanati School of Business. Legal Advisor, I.D.F. Chief of Staff Bureau, 1991-1993. Aide, Chief Military Prosecutor, Israel Defense Forces, 1988-1991. *Member:* Israel Bar Association. *LANGUAGES:* Hebrew and English.

SARI ELLENBERG, born Tel-Aviv, Israel, March 31, 1958; admitted, 1990, Israel. *Education:* Tel-Aviv University (B.A., LL.B.). *Member:* Israeli Bar Association. *LANGUAGES:* Hebrew and English.

IAN ROSTOWSKY, born Johannesburg, South Africa, August 21, 1964; admitted, 1990, Israel. *Education:* University of the Witwatersrand, Johannesburg (B.A., LL.B.). *Member:* Israeli Bar Association. *LANGUAGES:* English and Hebrew.

NOAM SHER, born Afula, Israel, March 7, 1964; admitted, 1992, Israel. *Education:* Tel-Aviv University (B.A., M.A., Economics, LL.B.). *Member:* Israel Bar Association. *LANGUAGES:* Hebrew and English.

JAY S. ZAUDERER, born Philadelphia, Pennsylvania, September 17, 1961; admitted, 1986, New York; 1993, Israel. *Education:* Yeshiva University (B.S., magna cum laude); Cornell Law School (J.D.). *Member:* New York State and Israel Bar Associations. *LANGUAGES:* English and Hebrew.

OSNAT YARDENI, born Tel-Aviv, Israel, April 29, 1968; admitted, 1993, Israel. *Education:* Tel-Aviv University (LL.B.). *Member:* Israel Bar Association. *LANGUAGES:* Hebrew and English.

OMER SEGEL, born Hadera, Israel, September 23, 1965; admitted, 1994, Israel. *Education:* University of Essex, England (LL.B.); New York University (LL.M.). *Member:* Israel Bar Association. *LANGUAGES:* Hebrew and English.

Languages: Hebrew and English

REPRESENTATIVE CLIENTS: Dead Sea Bromine Group; Israeli Telecommunications Company-Bezek; Israel Chemicals Ltd.; Israel Government Companies Authority-Ministry of Finance; Abic Ltd. Pharmaceutical & Chemical Industries; Red Sea Hotels, Ltd.; Rada Electronic Industries, Ltd.; I.I.S.-Intelligent Information Systems, Ltd.; Akerstein Zvi Group; Edusoft Ltd.; Degem Systems, Ltd.; Oxton International Capital Corporation; Orbit Semiconductors.

A. TALLY EITAN - ZEEV PEARL & CO.
LAW OFFICES

22 MASKIT STREET
TEL AVIV (HERZLIA) 46733, ISRAEL
Telephone: 972-9-565-561
Fax: 972-9-565-562

General Practice Business Law emphasizing Intellectual Property Law (patents, copyrights, trademarks, mask works, trade secrets and unfair competition) and related business transactions and litigations. Patent and Trademark Prosecution.

(This Listing Continued)

FIRM PROFILE: The firm provides a wide range of intellectual property, business law and litigation services. The intellectual property practice encompasses the procurement, enforcement and licensing of patents, trademarks, copyrights, masks work rights, technical know-how and trade secrets. The firm represents clients in negotiating and structuring licensing and technology transfer agreements, in corporate acquisitions, incorporation, various types of security transactions and international joint ventures in which the technology owned or to be developed by the participants is an important element of the transaction. The firm also represents litigants in disputes that turn on technological issues with emphasis on the intellectual property area. Dealings and negotiations with the private and government sectors in connection with investments, and/ or public grants are also within the Firm's special expertise.

TALLY EITAN, born Tel Aviv, Israel, November 6, 1953; admitted, 1981, Israel; 1987, California, USA. *Education:* Hebrew University, Jerusalem, Israel (B.S., Statistics, 1976; J.D., 1980). Partner, Skjerven, Morril, MacPherson, Franklin and Friel, San Jose, California until 1992. *Member:* Israel Bar Association; California State Bar Association; INTA; AIPPI. *LANGUAGES:* Hebrew and English.

HEIDI M. BRUN, born Wayland, Massachusetts, February 17, 1962; admitted, 1991, Israel Patent Office; U.S. Patent Agent. *Education:* Massachusetts Institute of Technology (B.S., Mechanical Engineering, 1985 and M.S., Mechanical Engineering, 1985). *Member:* AIPPI. *LANGUAGES:* Hebrew, English and Spanish. *PRACTICE AREAS:* Patent Prosecution.

ZEEV PEARL, born Tel-Aviv, Israel, September 16, 1962; admitted, 1994, Israel and Israel Patent Office. *Education:* Hebrew University, Jerusalem, Israel (B.Sc., Chemistry and Geology, 1986); Weizman Institute of Science, Rehovot, Israel (M.Sc., Chemistry, 1989); Tel-Aviv University, Tel-Aviv, Israel (LL.B., 1992). *Member:* Israel Bar Association; AIPPI. *LANGUAGES:* Hebrew and English.

HENRY M. SINAI, born Manchester, England, October 22, 1946. *Education:* Salford University (B.Sc., Civil Engineering, 1968); Manchester University (B.A., Law, 1978). Chartered Engineer. *Member:* Institution of Civil Engineers (England); AIPPI. *LANGUAGES:* Hebrew, English, German and French.

ROSLYN NEWMAN, born Sydney, Australia, March 1, 1961; admitted, 1984, Supreme Court of New South Wales and High Court of Australia. *Education:* University of New South Wales (B.Comm., LL.B). Lawyer: Clayton Utz, Solicitors, Sydney. *LANGUAGES:* English and Hebrew.

EPSTEIN, GROSS & CO.

6 WILSON STREET
TEL AVIV 65220, ISRAEL
Telephone: (972-3) 5614777
Fax: (972-3) 5614776

General Corporate, Foreign Investments, Real Estate, International Commercial Transactions, Anti Trust, Intellectual Property, Trusts and Estates, Civil and Commercial Litigation.

MEMBERS OF FIRM

EYTAN EPSTEIN, born Haifa, Israel, December 15, 1955; admitted, 1985, Israel. *Education:* Tel Aviv University (LL.B., 1984). Lecturer and Assistant Professor: Tax Law, Tel Aviv University Law School, 1984-1985; Tel Aviv Business College, 1991—. Author: "Israel and the Common Market," 1988; "Exclusive Distribution Agreements in the EC," 1992. Governmental Committee for the Preparation of Israel towards 1992. *Member:* Israel Bar Association; International Bar Association. *LANGUAGES:* English, French and Hebrew.

RONIT Y.L. GROSS, born Tel-Aviv, Israel, July 25, 1955; admitted, 1984, Israel. *Education:* Tel-Aviv University (LL.B., 1983). *Member:* Israel Bar Association; New York State Bar Association. *LANGUAGES:* English, French and Hebrew.

LISA LEVY, born London, Great Britain, March 18, 1965; admitted, 1991, Israel. *Education:* Tel Aviv University (LL.B., 1990). *Member:* Israel Bar Association. *LANGUAGES:* English and Hebrew.

VARDA LAVON-BERMAN, born Tel Aviv, Israel, June 9, 1961; admitted, 1988, Israel. *Education:* Tel Aviv University (LL.B., 1987). *Member:* Israel Bar Association. *LANGUAGES:* English and Hebrew.

(This Listing Continued)

BOAZ HADARI, born Tel-Aviv, Israel, August 11, 1963; admitted, 1994, Israel. *Education:* Tel-Aviv University (LL.B., 1990). *Member:* Israel Bar Association. *LANGUAGES:* English and Hebrew.

FEITH & ZELL, P.C.

Established in 1986

*TEXTILE CENTER
2 KAUFMAN STREET*
TEL AVIV 68012, ISRAEL
*Telephone: 03-5102666
Fax: 972-3-5102166*

Washington, D.C. Office: 2300 M Street, N.W., Suite 600. Telephone: 202-293-1600. Fax: 202-293-8965.

Administrative, Corporate, Government Contracts, International Trade and Investment, Antitrust, Agency Representation, Legislation and Civil Litigation.

L. MARC ZELL, born Washington, D.C., February 25, 1953; admitted, 1977, Maryland; 1978, District of Columbia; 1981, Virginia; 1982, Israel Chamber of Advocates. *Education:* Princeton University (A.B., 1974); University of Maryland (J.D., with honors, 1977). Order of the Coif. Notes, Comments and Research Editor, International Trade Law Journal, 1976-1977. Author (with G. Miron), Israeli Restrictive Business Practices Act of 1988, International Merger Law Journal (1992). Lecturer and Author of Course Materials, International Government Contracts, 1980-1986. Chairman, Israel Community Development Foundation, 1989-1993. Law Clerk to Hon. Irving A. Levine, Court of Appeals of Maryland, 1977-1978. (Also Member, Balter, Guth, Aloni & Co. (Zell & Co.), Tel Aviv, Israel). *LANGUAGES:* English, Hebrew, French, German, Italian, Russian, Dutch, Spanish, Yiddish. *PRACTICE AREAS:* International Business Law; International Taxation; Corporate Law; Government Contracts Law.

MEIR ROSENNE, born Iassy, Romania, February 19, 1931; admitted, 1969, Israel Chamber of Advocates; (not admitted in the U.S.). *Education:* Institute for Advanced International Studies (Post-Doctorate Diploma, 1961); University of Paris (Ph.D., International Law, with honors, 1957; LL.B., 1955); Institut D'Etudes Politiques, Sorbonne (M.A., 1953). Recipient, The Harold Weil Medal for Outstanding Contributions to International Law, New York University, 1978. Senior Lecturer; University of Jerusalem; University of Tel Aviv, University of Haifa. President and Chief Executive Officer, Development Corporation of Israel (Israel Bonds), 1989-1994. Israeli Ambassador to the United States, 1983-1987. Israeli Ambassador to France, 1979-1983. Legal Advisor: Israeli Foreign Ministry, 1971-1979; Israel's Delegations, Geneva Peace Conference, 1973; Camp David Peace Negotiations, 1978. Board of Directors: Israel Discount Development Corp.; Israel Discount Holding Corp.; Jerusalem Mortgage Bank. *Member:* Israel Bar Association; American Society for International Law; French Society of International Law; Peace Through Law Center, Washington, D.C. (Resident: Jerusalem, Israel Office). *LANGUAGES:* English, Hebrew, French, Yiddish, Romanian and German. *PRACTICE AREAS:* International Law; International Business.

BERNEL GOLDBERG, born Modesto, California, June 16, 1961; admitted, 1987, Pennsylvania; 1989, District of Columbia. *Education:* University of Colorado (B.A., 1983); Hebrew University of Jerusalem, Israel; Georgetown University Law Center (J.D., 1987); Georgetown University (Masters of Science in Foreign Service, 1987). Phi Beta Kappa. Attorney and International Trade Analyst, Office of Unfair Import Investigations, U.S. International Trade Commission, 1987-1988. (Resident). *PRACTICE AREAS:* International Trade; Investments.

(For Complete Biographical Data on all Personnel see Professional Biographies at Washington, D.C.)

LEON FINE

Advocate and Attorney At Law

105 HAHASHMONAIM STREET
TEL AVIV 61204, ISRAEL
*Telephone: 972-3-5614340
Facsimile: 972-3-5614342*

Collections, Commercial, Corporate, Estates, Litigation, Real Estate.

LEON FINE, born New York, N.Y., June 7, 1932; admitted, 1966, Israel. *Education:* University of Cincinnati (B.A., 1952); New York University Law School (J.S.D., 1955). Assistant District Attorney, Tel Aviv. Au-

(This Listing Continued)

thor: "Will the Real Israel Please Stand Up?" and "The Newcomers Guide to Israel." *Member:* Israel Bar Association; New York State Bar Association. *LANGUAGES:* English and Hebrew.

I. FISCHER & CO.

Advocates & Notary

25 IBN GVIROL STREET
TEL AVIV 64078, ISRAEL
*Telephone: 972-3-298828
Facsimile: 972-3-201041
E-mail: 6515401@mcimail.com*

Commercial and Corporate Matters, Commercial Litigation, Technology Law, Real Estate, Securities, International Transactions, Investments and Private Placements, Mergers and Acquisitions, Labor Law, EEC Law, Trusts and Estates Law.

MEMBERS OF FIRM

ISACHAR FISCHER, born Yugoslavia, 1929; admitted, 1958, Israel. *Education:* Tel Aviv School for Law and Economics (LL.B., M.JUR.). Lt. Colonel (Res.) and President, Military District Court (1968-1982). *Member:* Israel Bar Association. *LANGUAGES:* Hebrew, English, German, Hungarian, Serbo-Croatian and Yiddish.

AVI FISCHER, born Tel-Aviv, Israel, 1956; admitted, 1983, Israel. *Education:* Tel Aviv University, Faculty of Law (LL.B., 1983). Lecturer, Civil Procedure and Labor Law, Tel Aviv University. *Member:* Israel Bar Association. *LANGUAGES:* Hebrew, English, German and Arabic.

EZRA KATZEN, born Rochester, New York, 1954; admitted, 1980, Florida; 1981, New York; 1990, Israel. *Education:* University of Cincinnati (B.A., with High Honors, 1977) (Phi Beta Kappa); University of Chicago (J.D., 1980). Partner, Lacy, Katzen, Ryen & Mittleman, Rochester, New York, 1985-1989. General Counsel, Teledata Communication Ltd., 1992-1993. Lecturer, Business Law, St. John Fisher College, Pittsford, New York, 1986-1989. *Member:* American Bar Association; International Bar Association; Israel Bar Association. *LANGUAGES:* English and Hebrew.

ASSOCIATES

MOSHE TOLEDANO, born Meknes, Morocco, 1957; admitted, 1984, Israel. *Education:* Hebrew University of Jerusalem, Faculty of Law (LL.B., 1983); Universite Libre de Bruxelles (3e Cycle, European Law with Honors, Grande Distinctions, 1989). *Member:* Israel Bar Association. *LANGUAGES:* French, Hebrew and English.

REUVEN GOVRIN, born Petach Tikva, Israel, 1960; admitted, 1988, Israel. *Education:* Tel Aviv University, Faculty of Law (LL.B., 1986). *Member:* Israel Bar Association. *LANGUAGES:* Hebrew and English.

URI HEIFETZ, born Haifa, Israel, 1960; admitted, 1987, Israel. *Education:* Tel Aviv University, Faculty of Law (LL.B., 1986). *Member:* Israel Bar Association. *LANGUAGES:* Hebrew, English, French, Arabic.

ERAN LAUFMAN, born Petach Tikva, Israel, 1959; admitted, 1989, Israel. *Education:* Tel Aviv University, Faculty of Liberal Arts (B.A., with honors, 1986) and Faculty of Law (LL.B., 1987). *Member:* Israel Bar Association. *LANGUAGES:* Hebrew and English.

J. DAVID CHERTOK, born Coatesville, Pennsylvania, 1962; admitted, 1991, Israel. *Education:* Columbia College (A.B., 1983); Tel Aviv University, Faculty of Law (LL.B., 1990). *Member:* Israel Bar Association. *LANGUAGES:* English, Hebrew and Arabic.

NOÉMI SCHMAYER, born Bakau, Romania, 1967; admitted, 1991, Israel. *Education:* Tel Aviv University School of Law (LL.B., 1989). Captain, Judge Advocate General's Corps, Israel Defense Forces, 1989-1992. *Member:* Israel Bar Association. *LANGUAGES:* Romanian, Hebrew and English.

ROBERTO CHAIT, born Cordoba, Argentina, 1965; admitted, 1991, Israel. *Education:* Hebrew University of Jerusalem, Faculty of Law (B.A., cum laude, 1990); The London School of Economics and Political Science (LL.M., 1992). Clerk to Hon. Meir Shamgar, President of the Supreme Court of Israel, 1990-1991. Member, Israel Capital Markets Forum; Correspondent, European Financial Service Law Review. *Member:* Israel Bar Association. *LANGUAGES:* Spanish, Hebrew and English.

DAVID COHEN, born London, England, 1965; admitted, 1992, England and Wales (Not admitted in Israel). *Education:* Cambridge University (B.A., Law, 1988); Lancaster Gate (1989). *Member:* Law Society of

(This Listing Continued)

I. FISCHER & CO., Tel Aviv—Continued

England and Wales. *LANGUAGES:* English, Hebrew, French, Spanish, Russian, Italian.

ISRAEL FISCHER, born Jerusalem, Israel, 1960; admitted, 1988, Israel. *Education:* Hebrew University of Jerusalem, Faculty of Law (LL.B., 1987). Lecturer, Philosophy, Tel-Aviv University. *Member:* Israel Bar Association. *LANGUAGES:* Hebrew and English.

Languages: Hebrew, English, French, German, Hungarian, Arabic, Romanian, Russian, Italian, Serbo-Croatian and Yiddish.

GLUSMAN, CHOWERS & COMPANY

AMOT MISHPAT BUILDING
8 KING SHAUL HAMELECH BOULEVARD
TEL AVIV 64733, ISRAEL
Telephone: 972-3-6938686
Fax: 972-3-6938680

Washington, D.C. Office: 1412 29th Street, N.W., 20007. Telephone: 202-337-3882. Facsimile: 202-333-3031.

International Business Transactions, Industrial and High Tech Transactions, Investment Law, Free Processing Zone Law, Customs Law, Rules of Origin Matters, Intellectual Property Law, Corporate Law, Real Estate and Commercial Law, Israeli and International Tax Law, International Trade Law.

MEMBERS OF THE FIRM

OFER GLUSMAN, born Hertzelia, August 11, 1952; admitted, 1983, Israel. *Education:* Jerusalem, Hebrew University (B.A., 1979; LL.B., 1982). *Member:* Israeli Bar. *PRACTICE AREAS:* International Business Transactions; Industrial and High Tech Transactions; Corporate Law; Investment Law.

ZVI CHOWERS, born Haifa, Israel, June 25, 1954; admitted, 1984, Israel. *Education:* Jerusalem, Hebrew University (B.A., Economic and Business Administration, 1982; LL.B., 1983). *Member:* Israeli Bar. *PRACTICE AREAS:* Intellectual Property Law; Real Estate Law; Commercial Law; Contract Law.

MAGEN ALTUVIA, born Haifa, Israel, March 12, 1956; admitted, 1982, Israel. *Education:* Jerusalem, Hebrew University (LL.B., 1981). Assistant Economic Minister-Embassy of Israel, Washington, D.C., 1990-1994. Member, United States-Israel Free Trade Area Agreement (FTAA) Joint Committee, 1990-1994. Head of the Real Estate Taxation Division, Israel's Income Tax Commission, 1987-1990. *Member:* Israeli Bar. *PRACTICE AREAS:* International Trade Law; Tax Law; Customs Law.

KAREN MAROM, born Canada, November 10, 1966; admitted, 1992, Israel. *Education:* Hebrew University, Jerusalem (LL.B., 1991). *Member:* Israeli Bar. *PRACTICE AREAS:* Contract Law; Commercial Law; Corporate Law.

YEHUDIT ARIAN SELLA, born Tel Aviv, Israel, November 22, 1948; admitted, 1974, Israel. *Education:* Tel Aviv University (LL.B., 1972). Associate, Willkie Far & Gallagher, N.Y., 1983-1984. *Member:* Israeli Bar. *PRACTICE AREAS:* Real Estate; Estates Administration.

OF COUNSEL

ABRAHAM SOFER, born Tiberias, Israel, July 28, 1954; admitted, 1982, Israel; 1985, New York; 1991, District of Columbia. *Education:* Tel Aviv University (LL.B., cum laude, 1982); University of Virginia School of Law (LL.M., cum laude, 1984). *Member:* Israeli Bar; New York State Bar Association; District of Columbia Bar; International Fiscal Association. *PRACTICE AREAS:* International Tax Law; International Investment Law.

GOLAN, BEN-DROR & CO.

AVGAD BUILDING, 15TH FLOOR
5 JABOTINSKI STREET
TEL AVIV (RAMAT-GAN) 52520, ISRAEL
Telephone: 972-3-5757830
Facsimile: 972-3-5757836

International Transactions and Foreign Investments, Corporate, Commercial and Real Estate Law, Securities, Hi-Tech, Commercial Litigation and Arbitration.

(This Listing Continued)

MEMBERS OF FIRM

DANIEL GOLAN, born 1944; admitted, 1974, Israel. *Education:* Hebrew University, Jerusalem (B.A., Economics, 1969; LL.B., 1973). Counsellor for Economic and Commercial Affairs in South Africa (1984-1988). *Member:* Israel Bar Association,.

YOSSI BEN-DROR, born Jerusalem, Israel, 1956; admitted, 1985, Israel; 1990, New York. *Education:* Hebrew University, Jerusalem, (LL.B., 1984). Hale and Dorr, Corporate and International Departments, Boston, Massachusetts (1989-1991). *Member:* Israel Bar Association; New York State Bar Association.

SIMON ANSTEY, born Cape Town, South Africa, 1967; admitted, 1990, South Africa; 1992, Israel. *Education:* University of Cape Town (B. Soc. Sci., 1987; LL.B., 1989). *Member:* Israel Bar Association; South Africa Bar Association.

M. GOLDBERG & CO.

Established in 1974

124 IBN GVIROL STREET
TEL AVIV 62032, ISRAEL
Telephone: (03) 527-2801
Facsimile: 972-3-527-1835

Rehovot, Israel Office: 20 Smilanski Street, 76446. Telephone: (08) 461341. Facsimile: 972-8-461278.

General Practice, US-Israel Trade and Custom Laws and Free Trade Area Matters, Joint Ventures, Corporate and Commercial Law, Civil Litigation, Competition Law, International Trade Law, Investments, Torts and Insurance, Franchising, Banking Law and Real Estate Law.

FIRM PROFILE: The firm was established by Moshe Goldberg in 1974 and offers a wide range of legal services. It is known for its Commercial and US-Israel Trade Law. The client base is Israeli, European and North American in scope. The firm comprises a team of seven lawyers plus paralegal/administrative personnel.

MEMBERS OF FIRM

MOSHE GOLDBERG, admitted, 1974, Israel; 1987, New York. (LL.B., Jeru.). *Member:* New York State Bar Association; Israel Bar Association. *LANGUAGES:* English and Hebrew. *PRACTICE AREAS:* US-Israel Trade and Customs Law; International Trade Law; Joint Ventures; Commercial Law.

MENAHEM RAPHAEL, admitted, 1977, Israel; 1987, California. (LL.B., Jeru.). *Member:* California State Bar Association; Israel Bar Association. *LANGUAGES:* English and Hebrew. *PRACTICE AREAS:* Commercial Law and Investments; International Trade Law.

OSNAT HUTA, admitted, 1987, Israel. (LL.B., Bar Ilan). *Member:* Israel Bar Association. *LANGUAGES:* Hebrew and English. *PRACTICE AREAS:* Civil Litigation; Torts; Insurance.

ILANA EYAL, admitted, 1987, Israel. (LL.B., Bar Ilan). *Member:* Israel Bar Association. *LANGUAGES:* Hebrew and English. *PRACTICE AREAS:* Real Estate Law.

HADASSAH ASIF, admitted, 1987, Israel. (LL.B., Bar Ilan). *Member:* Israel Bar Association. *LANGUAGES:* Hebrew and English. *PRACTICE AREAS:* Civil Litigation.

MARCELLE NOCHUMSOHN, admitted, 1987, South Africa; 1991, Israel. (LL.B., Wits Johannesburg). *Member:* Israel Bar Association. *LANGUAGES:* English and Hebrew. *PRACTICE AREAS:* International Trade; Commercial Law.

TAMIR SELA, admitted, 1993, Israel. *Education:* (LL.B., Tel Aviv). *Member:* Israel Bar Association. *LANGUAGES:* Hebrew and English. *PRACTICE AREAS:* Corporate and Commercial Law.

GOLDFARB, LEVY, ERAN & CO.

ELIAHU HOUSE
2 IBN GVIROL
TEL AVIV 64077, ISRAEL
Telephone: 972-3-695-4343
Telecopier: 972-3-695-4344

Corporations, Securities, Mergers and Acquisitions, International Commercial Transactions, Investments, Taxation, Real Estate, Real Estate Development, Litigation and Licensing of Intellectual Property.

MEMBERS OF FIRM

WILLIAM B. GOLDFARB, born Cleveland, Ohio, May 24, 1928; admitted, 1956, Ohio; 1970, U.S. Supreme Court; 1972, Israel; 1987, New York. *Education:* Case Western Reserve University (B.A., summa cum laude, 1950; J.D., summa cum laude, 1956); Columbia University (M.A., 1951); Phi Beta Kappa; Order of the Coif; Society of Benchers. Member, 1954-1956 and Editor-in-Chief, 1955-1956, Case Western Reserve Law Review. Partner and Member of Executive Committee, Hahn Loeser & Parks, Cleveland, Ohio, 1956-1971. President, Bureau of Jewish Education of Cleveland, 1965-1969. Legal Advisor, Government of Israel Investment Authority, Ministry of Finance, 1962-1963. Member, Board of Directors, Committee for Economic Growth of Israel, 1987—. *Member:* Cleveland, Cuyahoga County, Ohio State and New York State Bar Associations; The Israel Bar. *LANGUAGES:* English, Hebrew, French, German and Yiddish. *PRACTICE AREAS:* Corporations; Securities; Mergers and Acquisitions; International Commercial Transactions; Investments; Licensing of Intellectual Property.

YEHUDA M. LEVY, born Haifa, Israel, June 10, 1945; admitted, 1971, Israel; 1988, New York. *Education:* Hebrew University, Jerusalem (LL.B., 1969). Co-author: "Corporate Duties of Directors and Officers-New Legislation in Corporate Law," 1991. Director, Israel Discount Bank Ltd. *Member:* New York State Bar Association; The Israel Bar. *LANGUAGES:* Hebrew, English and French. *PRACTICE AREAS:* Corporations; Securities; Mergers and Acquisitions; International Commercial Transactions; Investments; Licensing of Intellectual Property; Taxation; Real Estate; Real Estate Development.

REUVEN REIF, born Tel Aviv, Israel, May 1, 1951; admitted, 1977, Israel. *Education:* Tel Aviv University (LL.B., 1976). *Member:* The Israel Bar. *LANGUAGES:* Hebrew and English. *PRACTICE AREAS:* Litigation.

ODED ERAN, born Tel Aviv, Israel, May 28, 1955; admitted, 1981, Israel; 1984, New York. *Education:* Tel Aviv University (LL.B., cum laude, 1981; LL.M., cum laude, 1983). Associate Editor, Tel Aviv University Law Review, 1981-1982. Lecturer, Faculty of Law, Tel Aviv University, 1980-1982. Associate, Kronish, Lieb, Weiner & Hellman, New York, N.Y., 1983-1986. *Member:* New York State Bar Association; The Israel Bar. *LANGUAGES:* Hebrew and English. *PRACTICE AREAS:* Taxation; Securities; Investments; International Commercial Transactions.

MARC A. RABIN, born Cleveland, Ohio, April 18, 1955; admitted, 1980, Ohio and U.S. District Court, Northern District of Ohio; 1986, Israel; 1987, New York. *Education:* Case Western Reserve University (B.S., cum laude, 1977; J.D., 1980). Case Western Reserve Law Review. *Member:* Ohio State and New York State Bar Associations; The Israel Bar. *LANGUAGES:* English and Hebrew. *PRACTICE AREAS:* Licensing of Intellectual Property; Corporations; Mergers and Acquisitions; International Commercial Transactions; Securities; Investments.

MICHAEL M. OHAYON, born Casablanca, Morocco, May 7, 1959; admitted, 1988, Israel. *Education:* Tel Aviv University (LL.B., 1987). Co-author: "Corporate Duties of Directors and Officers-New Legislation in Corporate Law," 1991. *Member:* The Israel Bar.

YAIR SHOHAM, born Tiberias, Israel, May 21, 1953; admitted, 1985, Illinois; 1989, Israel. *Education:* Haifa University (B.A., 1982); Loyola University of Chicago School of Law (J.D., 1985). Associate, Sonnenschein Carlin Nath & Rosenthal, Chicago, Illinois, 1985-1988. *Member:* Illinois State and American Bar Associations; The Israel Bar.

ASSOCIATES

SHIRIN HALPERN-HERZOG, born Tel Aviv, Israel, November 1, 1961; admitted, 1988, Israel; 1990, New York. *Education:* Hebrew University (LL.B., 1987); New York University School of Law (LL.M., with distinction, 1990). Associate, Simpson Thacher & Bartlett, New York City, 1990-1993. Co-Author: "Liability Insurance and Latent Diseases," Insurance, Quarterly Review, 1987. Teaching Assistant, Taxation Law, 1986-

(This Listing Continued)

1987. *Member:* Israel Bar Association; American Bar Association; The Association of the Bar of the City of New York. *LANGUAGES:* Hebrew and English.

AMIR TZAFRIR, born Tel Aviv, Israel, August 28, 1962; admitted, 1990, Israel. *Education:* Tel Aviv University (LL.B., 1989). *Member:* The Israel Bar.

GALAI SHARIR, born Rehovot, Israel, October 26, 1957; admitted, 1990, Israel. *Education:* Tel Aviv University Law School (LL.B., 1989). *Member:* The Israel Bar.

RONIT LASRY-TZAFRIR, born Beer Sheva, Israel, September 27, 1965; admitted, 1991, Israel. *Education:* Tel Aviv University (LL.B., 1990). *Member:* The Israel Bar.

ASHOK J. CHANDRASEKHAR, born Pittsburgh, Pennsylvania, March 4, 1963; admitted, 1990, California (Not admitted in Israel). *Education:* Yale University (B.A., 1985); New York University (J.D., 1990). Law Clerk, J.P. Vukasin, Jr., U.S. District Judge, San Francisco, California, 1990-1991. Associate, Pillsbury Madison & Sutro, San Francisco, California, 1991-1993. *Member:* The California Bar. *LANGUAGES:* English and French.

ARIELLA D. LAHAV, born Tel Aviv, Israel, September 30, 1959; admitted, 1991, Israel. *Education:* Tel Aviv University (B.A., 1983; LL.B., 1989). *Member:* The Israel Bar. *LANGUAGES:* Hebrew, English and French.

JAY S. NEUSTADTER, born Cleveland, Ohio, March 4, 1967; admitted, 1992, New York; 1993, Israel. *Education:* Yeshiva University (B.A., magna cum laude, 1988); Columbia University (J.D., 1991). *Member:* New York State Bar Association; The Israel Bar. *LANGUAGES:* English and Hebrew.

YORAM SHIV, born Tel Aviv, Israel, February 16, 1966; admitted, 1993. *Education:* Pacific Western University (B.S., 1992); Tel Aviv University (LL.B., 1993). Assistant Lecturer, Tel Aviv University Faculty of Law. *Member:* The Israel Bar.

LIONEL KESTENBAUM, born Brooklyn, New York, November 10, 1926; admitted, 1952, New York; 1955, U.S. Supreme Court; 1962, District of Columbia; 1973, Israel. *Education:* Yale University (A.B., cum laude, 1948); Columbia University (LL.B., 1951). Member, Board of Editors, Columbia Law Review. Adjunct or Visiting Professor, Georgetown Law School, 1965-1967, 1974-1975; Faculties of Law, Tel Aviv University, 1971-1972, 1987, Hebrew University, 1978, 1984, Bar Ilan University, 1990—. Office of General Counsel, U.S. Atomic Energy Commission, 1959-1961. Antitrust Division, U.S., 1961-1969, including Chief, Evaluation Section, Director of Policy Planning. Department of Justice. Partner, Bergson, Borkland, Margolis & Adler, Washington, D.C., 1969-1986. Member, Advisory Board, Antitrust & Trade Regulation Report, 1969-1985. *Member:* American and International Bar Association.

REPRESENTATIVE CORPORATE CLIENTS: *Israel:* AVX Israel Ltd. (Parent, New York Stock Exchange); Bio-Technology General (Israel) Ltd. (Parent, Over The Counter, NASDAQ); Cargal Ltd.; Tel Aviv Stock Exchange); Dankner Investment Ltd. (Tel Aviv Stock Exchange); Discount Investment Corp. (Tel Aviv Stock Exchange); ELCO Ltd. (Tel Aviv Stock Exchange); ELCO Industries (1975) Ltd, (Tel Aviv Stock Exchange); Electra (Israel) Ltd. (Tel Aviv Stock Exchange); ECI Telecom Ltd. (Over The Counter); Elitec Industries 77 Ltd. (Tel Aviv Stock Exchange); Euro-Trade Bank, Ltd.; Formula Systems (1985) Ltd. (Tel Aviv Stock Exchange); Indigo Ltd. (Parent, Over the Counter, NASDAQ); Jerusalem Pacific Ventures Ltd.; Kitan Consolidated Ltd. (Tel Aviv Stock Exchanges); Lannet Data Communications Ltd. (Over the Counter); Liraz Systems Ltd. (Tel Aviv Stock Exchange); M-Systems Flash Disk Pioneers Ltd. (Over The Counter, NASDAQ); Maman-Cargo Terminals and Handling Ltd.; Opal Technologies Ltd.; Scitex Corporation Ltd. (Over The Counter, NASDAQ); Spectronix Ltd. (Tel Aviv Stock Exchange); Taya Investment Company Ltd. (Tel Aviv Stock Exchange); *Foreign:* ABN-AMRO Bank N.V., Netherlands; Athena Venture Partners, L.P.; Body Shop International PLC; CPC International, Inc. (New York Stock Exchange); Evergreen Canada Israel Investment Ltd. (Tel Aviv Stock Exchange); Hägen-Dazs Brands, Inc.; International Franchise Association; Pioneer Hi-Bred International, Inc. (Over the Counter, NASDAQ); Southwestern Bell Corporation (New York Stock Exchange); TRW, Inc. (New York Stock Exchange).
REFERENCES: Bank Hapoalim, Hameasfim (Eliahu House) Branch, Tel Aviv.

HERMANN SCHWARTZ PELED WINDER BEN-ISRAEL & CO.
ADVOCATES

Established in 1949

6 AHUZAT BAIT STREET
TEL AVIV 65143, ISRAEL
Telephone: (03) 517 9431
Cable Address: Attornatus
Facsimile: (Groups 2-3) 03-5171779

Administrative, Business Law, Corporation, Air Law, Labor, Real Estate, Estates, Probate and Trust, Contracts, Torts, Insurance, International, Intellectual Property.

MEMBERS OF FIRM

DR. DAVID DESIDERIU HERMANN, born Ciachi-Garbou, Hungary, April 29, 1909; admitted, 1935, Rumania; 1948, Israel. *Education:* Hochschule Fur Welthandel, Vienna, Austria (Licensed Merchant); Faculty of Law, University of Cluj (Doctorate of Law). Lecturer in Air Law, Hebrew University of Jerusalem and Tel-Aviv, 1956-1975. Member, Supreme Court of General Federation of Labour in Israel, 1957. *Member:* Israel Bar Association.

DR. WILHELM SCHWARTZ, born Cluj, Rumania, February 26, 1912; admitted, 1936, Rumania; 1949, Israel. *Education:* Faculty of Law, University of Cluj, Rumania (Doctor of Law, 1934). Member, Panel of Arbitrators, American Arbitration Association. *Member:* Israel Bar Association; AIPPI, Association Internationale pour la Protection de La Propriete Industrielle, Israel National Group.

DR. SHLOMO PELED, born Luxembourg, June 17, 1921; admitted, 1954, Israel. *Education:* University St. Joseph, Beirut, Lebanon (Doctor of Law, 1945). Member, Panel of Arbitrators, American Arbitration Association. *Member:* Israel Bar Association; AIPPI, Association Internationale pour la Protection de La Propriete Industrielle, Israel National Group; International Forum of Travel and Tourist Advocates; New York Academy of Sciences.

ISAAC WINDER, born Israel, November 1, 1941; admitted, 1970, Israel. *Education:* Faculty of Law, Hebrew University, Jerusalem. *Member:* American Arbitration Association (Panel of Arbitrators).

ELIAHU BEN-ISRAEL, born Jerusalem, Israel, October 1, 1930; admitted, 1958, Israel. *Education:* Faculty of Law, Hebrew University of Jerusalem (M.Jur.). Senior Vice-President Coordination & Corporate Secretary of El Al Israel Airlines, Ltd., 1980-1988. Chairman of Europolitical Advisory Group of I.A.T.A., 1988-1989.

THOMAS MANOR, born Berlin, Germany, November 21, 1955; admitted, 1985, Israel. *Education:* Faculty of Law, Tel-Aviv University (LL.B.).

ASSOCIATES

YAEL SHEFFER, born Israel, October 24, 1947; admitted, 1973, Israel. *Member:* International Forum of Travel and Tourist Advocates.

MICHAL MANOR, born Israel, February 23, 1959; admitted, 1985, Israel.

MOSHE HUBERMAN, born Israel, November 1, 1958; admitted, 1987, Israel.

DALIT BEN-ISRAEL, born Israel, March 8, 1965; admitted, 1990, Israel.

TAMAR MEIRAS, born Israel, June 17, 1963; admitted, 1993, Israel.

Languages: Hebrew, English, French, German, Rumanian and Hungarian.

REFERENCE: Union Bank of Israel Ltd.

HERZOG FOX & NEEMAN

ASIA HOUSE
4 WEIZMANN STREET
TEL AVIV, ISRAEL
Telephone: (972-3) 692 2020
Fax: (972-3) 696 6464; 696 0082

Jerusalem, Israel Office: 14 Tel Hai Street. Telephone: (972-2) 639 038; 639 046. Fax: (972-2) 639 292.

(This Listing Continued)

MEMBERS OF FIRM

MICHAEL FOX, born London, England, March 8, 1934. admitted as Solicitor of the Supreme Court of England, 1958; admitted, 1969, Israel. *Education:* Kings College, University of London, England (LL.B.); Law Society of England (Solicitor). *Member:* Law Society of England; Israel Bar Association; International Bar Association.

YAAKOV NEEMAN, born Tel Aviv, Israel, September 16, 1939; admitted, 1966, Israel. *Education:* Hebrew University, Jerusalem (LL.B., 1964); New York University (LL.M., 1965; J.S.D., 1968). *Member:* Israel Bar Association.

TUVIA ERLICH, born Germany, September 14, 1948; admitted, 1976, Israel. *Education:* Bar Ilan University (LL.B.).

MEIR LINZEN, born Israel, June 26, 1958; admitted, 1982, Israel. *Education:* Tel Aviv University (LL.B.).

ALAN SACKS, born London, England, March 13, 1956. admitted as Solicitor of the Supreme Court, 1981, England; admitted, 1985, Israel. *Education:* Cambridge University (M.A., Law); London University (LL.M.).

YAACOV BRANDT, born Lodz, Poland, July 25, 1950; admitted, 1985, Israel. *Education:* Hebrew University, Jerusalem (B.A., Economics and Political Science; LL.B.).

ISAAC HERZOG, born Tel Aviv, Israel, September 22, 1960; admitted, 1987, Israel. *Education:* Tel Aviv University (LL.B.).

EHUD SOL, born Tel Aviv, Israel, May 1, 1956; admitted, 1986, Israel. *Education:* Tel Aviv University (LL.B.).

MIRA GLADSTONE, born Haifa, Israel, January 25, 1958; admitted, 1984, Israel. *Education:* Hebrew University, Jerusalem (LL.B.).

ANER BERGER, born Jerusalem, Israel, March 27, 1963; admitted, 1986, Israel. *Education:* Hebrew University, Jerusalem (LL.B.).

HANOCH DAGAN, born Tel Aviv, Israel, January 16, 1964; admitted, 1990, Israel. *Education:* Tel Aviv University (LL.B.).

DANIEL CHINN, born London, England, September 18, 1965; admitted, 1990, Israel. *Education:* University College, Oxford (B.A., Jurisprudence).

GADI RUBIN, born Jerusalem, Israel, January 14, 1963; admitted, 1990, Israel. *Education:* Hebrew University, Jerusalem (LL.B.).

OSNAT LEAVE, born Ashkelon, Israel, January 22, 1965; admitted, 1991, Israel. *Education:* Tel Aviv University (LL.B.).

YAEL BAR-SHAI, born Tel Aviv, Israel, November 8, 1966; admitted, 1991, Israel. *Education:* Hebrew University, Jerusalem (LL.B.).

JANET LEVY PAHIMA, born New York, USA, December 30, 1959; admitted, 1986, New York; 1992, Israel. *Education:* Tufts University (B.A.); Georgetown University (J.D.; MSFS).

SHAI BUBER, born Jerusalem, Israel, April 18, 1964; admitted, 1992, Israel. *Education:* Hebrew University, Jerusalem (LL.B.).

AVIAD KOBRINE, born Tel Aviv, Israel, October 10, 1963; admitted, 1992, Israel. *Education:* Tel Aviv University (LL.B. and Bsc. in Economics).

AMIR SERAYA, born Haifa, Israel, January 20, 1964; admitted, 1992, Israel. *Education:* Tel Aviv University (LL.B.).

EDITH ROTH, born Hungary, May 2, 1947; admitted, 1992, Israel. *Education:* Haifa University (B.A., Languages); Tel Aviv University (LL.B.).

CLIFFORD M. J. FELIG, born New Haven, Connecticut, USA, February 8, 1961; admitted, 1987, New York; 1993, Israel. *Education:* Yale University (B.A.); Harvard Law School (J.D.).

EYAL NEIGER, born Jerusalem, Israel, November 9, 1961; admitted, 1993, Israel. *Education:* Hebrew University, Jerusalem (B.A., Accounting and Economics); Bar Ilan University, Tel Aviv (LL.B.).

YARIV MILLETT, born Jerusalem, Israel, October 10, 1963; admitted, 1994, Israel. *Education:* Tel Aviv University (LL.B.).

ITZHAK FRID, born Tel Aviv, Israel, March 5, 1964; admitted, 1994, Israel. *Education:* Tel Aviv University (LL.B.).

RAN GRODECKY, born Tel Aviv, Israel, March 20, 1965; admitted, 1994, Israel. *Education:* Tel Aviv University (LL.B.).

(This Listing Continued)

BARUCH KATZMAN, born Tel Aviv, May 16, 1963; admitted, 1994, Israel. *Education:* Tel Aviv University (B.A. Political Science); Bar Ilan University, Tel Aviv (LL.B.).

S. HOROWITZ & CO.

Advocates, Notaries and Patent Attorneys

31 AHAD HA'AM STREET
TEL AVIV 65202, ISRAEL
Telephone: 011-972-3-5663737
Telex: 341488 AGOS IL
Telecopier: 011-972-3-5601143; 011-972-3-5660974

FIRM PROFILE: *Legal and Public Capacities: Advocates, Notaries and Patent Attorneys.*

MEMBERS OF FIRM

ABRAHAM LEVIN (1901-1988).

NEHEMIA SALOMON (1903-1990).

PARTNERS

AMNON GOLDENBERG, born Tel Aviv, Israel, February 11, 1935; admitted, 1963, Israel. *Education:* Hebrew University, Jerusalem (M. Jur., with distinction, 1956); University of London (Ph.D., 1961). Senior Lecturer, Law of Property, Tel Aviv University, 1961-1984. *Member:* Israel Bar.

RUTH OREN, born Jerusalem, Israel; admitted, 1959, Israel. *Education:* Hebrew University, Jerusalem (M. Jur., 1957). *Member:* Israel Bar.

ZVI KALIR, born Tel Aviv, Israel, March 28, 1939; admitted, 1966, Israel. *Education:* Hebrew University, Jerusalem (LL.B., 1964). Notary Public. *Member:* Israel Bar.

HUGH MICHAEL KOWARSKY, born Johannesburg, South Africa, March 31, 1943; admitted, 1969, Israel. *Education:* University of Witwatersrand, Johannesburg (B.A. Hons., in Political Science, 1963); Magdalen College, Oxford University (B.A. Hons., Juris., 1966; M.A., 1978). *Member:* Israel Bar.

ASGAD STERN, born Tel Aviv, Israel, July 14, 1947; admitted, 1974, Israel. *Education:* Tel Aviv University (LL.B., 1974). *Member:* Israel Bar.

YEHOSHUA HORESH, born Afula, Israel, November 10, 1949; admitted, 1976, Israel. *Education:* Tel Aviv University (LL.B., 1976). *Member:* Israel Bar.

REUVEN BEHAR, born Jerusalem, Israel, December 13, 1953; admitted, 1981, Israel. *Education:* Hebrew University Law School (LL.B., Cum Laude, 1980). Editor and Member of the Editorial Board, Mishpatim, 1976-1980. Assistant Teacher, Hebrew University School of Law, Corporations and Criminal Law, 1979-1981. *Member:* Israel Bar.

YOAV BEN-DROR, born Jerusalem, Israel, October 1, 1952; admitted, 1978, Israel. *Education:* Hebrew University Law School (LL.B., 1977; LL.M., 1979); School of Law (Boalt Hall), University of California, Berkeley (LL.M., 1980; J.S.D., 1982). Teaching Assistant, Faculty of Law, Tel Aviv University, Private International Law, 1977-1978. Research Assistant, Tel Aviv University Peace Project, 1978-1979. Guest Lecturer: Faculty of Law, Tel Aviv University, Corporation, 1984—; Negotiable Instruments, 1985. Guest Lecturer: Tel Aviv University Business School, Business Law, 1986—; Corporation, 1986—. Lawyer-from-Abroad: Covington & Burling, Washington, D.C., U.S.A., 1982-1983; Ervin, Cohen & Jessup, Beverly Hills, California, U.S.A., 1980. *Member:* Israel Bar.

ALEX HERTMAN, born Tel Aviv, Israel, April 6, 1956; admitted, 1982, Israel. *Education:* Hebrew University Law School (LL.B., Cum Laude, 1982). Member, Editorial Board, Mishpatim, 1979-1981. Assistant Teacher, Tel Aviv University Business School, 1981-1984. *Member:* Israel Bar.

TAL BAND, born Tel Aviv, Israel, April 10, 1957; admitted, 1984, Israel. *Education:* Hebrew University Law School (LL.B., Cum Laude, 1983). Editor and Member of the Editorial Board, Mishpatim, Hebrew University Law Review, 1980-1983. Assistant Teacher, Hebrew University Law School, Torts, 1983-1985. *Member:* Israel Bar.

SHOSHANA GAVISH, born New York, USA, August 3, 1953; admitted, 1984, Israel. *Education:* Bar Ilan University (B.A., Magna Cum Laude, 1977); Faculty of Law, Tel Aviv University (LL.B., Cum Laude, 1983). Assistant Editor, Tel Aviv University Studies in Law, 1983-1984. *Member:* Israel Bar.

(This Listing Continued)

BOAZ OKON, born Tel Aviv, Israel, October 7, 1958; admitted, 1985, Israel. *Education:* Tel Aviv University Law School (LL.B., Cum Laude, 1984). Associate Editor and Member of the Editorial Board, Tel Aviv University Law Review, 1983-1984. *Member:* Israel Bar.

ASSOCIATES

JUDITH SHWEIGER, born Buenos Aires, Argentina, July 16, 1949; admitted, 1978, Israel. *Education:* Hebrew University, Jerusalem (B.A., 1972); Tel Aviv University (LL.B., 1976). *Member:* Israel Bar.

SHEILA ELLIS, born Chicago, USA, May 19, 1958; admitted, 1985, Israel. *Education:* University of Chicago (B.A., 1979); Faculty of Law, Tel Aviv University, Business School, Corporations, 1988-1987. *Member:* Israel Bar.

DINA GIL, born Afula, Israel, December 30, 1955; admitted, 1989, Israel. *Education:* Tel Aviv University Law School (LL.B., 1987). *Member:* Israel Bar.

EHUD ARZI, born Haifa, Israel, November 23, 1962; admitted, 1990, Israel. *Education:* Tel Aviv University Law School (LL.B., Cum Laude, 1989). Assistant Editor, Tel Aviv University Law Review, 1987-1988. Assistant Teacher, Constitutional Law, Faculty of Law, Tel Aviv University, 1988-1990. Research Assistant, Constitutional Law, Faculty of Law, Tel Aviv University. *Member:* Israel Bar.

AMIR KESS, born Tel Aviv, Israel, February 22, 1962; admitted, 1990, Israel. *Education:* Tel Aviv University Law School (LL.B., 1989). Assistant Teacher, Constitutional Law, Faculty of Law, Tel Aviv University, 1988-1990. *Member:* Israel Bar.

HAGAY BRENNER, born Holon, Israel, January 23, 1964; admitted, 1991, Israel. *Education:* Hebrew University Law School, Jerusalem (LL.B., Cum Laude, 1990). *Member:* Israel Bar.

HELEN HELSTON, born Bristol, England, March 15, 1960; admitted, 1991, Israel. *Education:* University of East Anglia, England (LL.B., First Class Honors, 1981); London School of Economics and Political Science, London (LL.M., 1982). Admitted Bar of England and Wales, 1984. Member of Inner Temple. Lecturer in Law, University of Buckingham, 1985-1989. Research Assistant, British Institute of International and Comparative Law, London, 1988-1989. *Member:* Israel Bar.

NIV ZECLER, born Beersheba, Israel, July 21, 1963; admitted, 1991, Israel. *Education:* Tel Aviv University Law School (LL.B., 1990; B.A., Economics, Magna Cum Laude, 1990). Member of the Editorial Board, Tel Aviv University Law Review, 1989. *Member:* Israel Bar.

ERAN BAREKET, born Petah Tikva, Israel, January 23, 1964; admitted, 1992, Israel. *Education:* Tel Aviv University Law School (LL.B., Cum Laude, 1990). Member of the Editorial Board, Tel Aviv University Law Review, 1988. Assistant Teacher, Property Law, 1989-1990. *Member:* Israel Bar.

IRIS SOROKER, born Tel Aviv, Israel, June 14, 1964; admitted, 1990, Israel. *Education:* Hebrew University (LL.B., Cum Laude, 1989). Member of the Editorial Board, Mishpatim, Hebrew University Law Review, 1987-1988. Assistant Teacher, Hebrew University Law School, Constitutional Law, Property Law, 1988-1989. *Member:* Israel Bar.

VARDIT GURFINKEL, born Ramat Gan, Israel, October 8, 1964; admitted, 1992, Israel. *Education:* Tel Aviv University Law School (LL.B., Cum Laude, 1990). Member, Editorial Board, Tel Aviv University Law Review, 1988. Assistant Teacher, Negotiable Instrument, Tel Aviv University Law School, 1991-1992. *Member:* Israel Bar.

MICHAEL P. AARON, born Detroit, USA, July 12, 1956; admitted, 1987, New York; 1992, Israel. *Education:* University of Michigan (A.B., Political Science, Phi Beta Kappa, 1978); Hofstra University School of Law (J.D., with distinction, 1986). Editor and Member, Hofstra Law Review, 1985-1986. *Member:* Israel Bar; New York Bar.

ANTHONY MICHAEL BLOCH, born Cape Town, Africa, May 4, 1962; admitted, 1988, South Africa; 1992, Israel. *Education:* University of Cape Town (Bachelor of Business Science, (Honours), 1983; LL.B., Cum Laude, 1985; LL.M., with distinction, 1991). *Member:* Israel Bar.

MOTI ARAD, born Rio de Janeiro, Brazil, August 22, 1965; admitted, 1992, Israel. *Education:* University of Tel Aviv (LL.B., 1991). *Member:* Israel Bar. **PRACTICE AREAS:** Administrative and Constitutional Law.

DAVID GILAT, born London, England, August, 1960; admitted, 1992, Israel. *Education:* Hebrew University, Jerusalem (Natural Sciences, (Chemistry) B.Sc., 1986, Cum Laude); Tel Aviv University Faculty of Law (LL.B.,

(This Listing Continued)

S. HOROWITZ & CO., Tel Aviv—Continued

1990). Research Fellow, Max Planck Institute for Foreign and International Patent Copyright and Competition Law, Munich, Germany, 1993. *Member:* Israel Bar.

ISAAC MARCIANO, born Fez, Morocco, June 7, 1961; admitted, 1993, (CPA ISR) Israel. *Education:* Hebrew University, Jerusalem, Faculty of Law (LL.B. Cum Laude, 1989); Faculty of Social Sciences (B.A.) degree in Accounting and Economics (1989); London School of Economics and Political Science (LL.M., 1991). Editor and Member of the Editorial Board, Mishpatim, Hebrew University Law Review, 1986-1988. Assistant Teacher Hebrew University Family Law and Economics, 1986-1989. *Member:* Israel Bar.

ITAY HACOHEN, born Tel Aviv, Israel, February 13, 1964; admitted, 1991, Israel. *Education:* Bar Ilan University Law School (LL.B with distinction, 1990). *Member:* Israel Bar.

HAGAI HALEVY, born Tel Aviv, Israel, January 12, 1964; admitted, 1992, Israel. *Education:* Bar Ilan University Law School (LL.B. with distinction, 1990). Member of the Editorial Board, Bar Ilan Law Studies, 1990. *Member:* Israel Bar.

HILLA BLAT, born Tel Aviv, Israel, October 17, 1967; admitted, 1992, Israel. *Education:* Tel Aviv University Law School (LL.B., Cum Laude, 1991). Assistant Teacher, Business Law, Tel Aviv University Business School, 1990-1991. *Member:* Israel Bar.

AVI ORDO, born Tel Aviv, Israel, May 17, 1965; admitted, 1993, Israel. *Education:* Tel Aviv University Faculty of Law School (LL.B., Cum Laude, 1992); Tel Aviv University Faculty of Social Sciences (Post Graduate B.A. Degree in Economics, 1992). Assistant Teacher, Civil Procedure, Tel Aviv University Law School, 1991-1992. Member of Editorial Board "Iunei Mishpat," The Student Law Review, Faculty of Law Tel Aviv University. *Member:* Israel Bar.

BOAZ BEN-AMITAI, born Tel Aviv, Israel, January 2, 1965; admitted, 1993, Israel. *Education:* Tel Aviv University Faculty of Law School (LL.B., Cum Laude, 1992). *Member:* Israel Bar.

YARON GROFMAN, born Tel Aviv, Israel. December 6, 1964; admitted, 1993, Israel. *Education:* Tel Aviv University Faculty of Law School (LL.B., Cum Laude, 1992). Assistant Teacher, Property Law, Tel Aviv University Law School, 1993-1994. *Member:* Israel Bar.

TOMAR ROSNER, born Tel Aviv, Israel, December 2, 1969; admitted, 1993, Israel. *Education:* Tel Aviv University Faculty of Law School (LL.B., Cum Laude, 1992). *Member:* Israel Bar.

ODED SHACHAM, born Haifa, Israel, October 2, 1964; admitted, 1993, Israel. *Education:* Hebrew University Law School (LL.B., Cum Laude, 1992). Assistant Teacher, Criminal Law, Hebrew University Law School, 1991-1992. Member of the Editorial Board "Mishpatim." *Member:* Israel Bar.

MICHAL SHITZER-GAL, born Haifa, Israel, December 19, 1966; admitted, 1993, Israel. *Education:* Tel Aviv University Law School (LL.B., Cum Laude, 1992). Assistant Teacher, Legal Systems, Tel Aviv University Law School, 1991. Member of the Editorial Board "Iunei Mishpat," The Student Law Review, Faculty of Law Tel Aviv University. *Member:* Israel Bar.

AVIGAIL KASTIEL, born Tel Aviv, Israel, August 7, 1966; admitted, 1994, Israel. *Education:* Tel Aviv University Law School (LL.B., Cum Laude, 1993). *Member:* Israel Bar.

Languages: Hebrew, English, French and German

JOEL & JOEL

Advocates, Barrister & Notary

Established in 1943

4 ROTHSCHILD BOULEVARD
TEL AVIV 66881, ISRAEL
Telephone: +972-3-5178317; +972-3-5171519
Facsimile: +972-3-5162302

General Practice, Commercial, Estate and Tort Matters.
(This Listing Continued)

FIRM PROFILE: *The firm was initially established by the late Georg Joel in 1943, serves as legal advisers to foreign embassies, including the Swiss, Swedish, German and Japanese embassies, foreign news media (Press & T.V.), foreign legal aid insurance companies.*

MEMBERS OF FIRM

DAN JOEL, born Tel Aviv, Israel, July 26, 1940; admitted, 1967, England and Wales; 1968, Israel. *Education:* Jerusalem (LL.B.); London L.S.E. (LL.M.; Diploma, Air and Space Law). Notary, 1983—. *Member:* Bar of England and Wales. *LANGUAGES:* Hebrew, English and German. *PRACTICE AREAS:* Agency and Distribution; Air Law; International Civil Law; International Commercial Law; Notarial Services; International Commercial Contracts; Extradition; Conflict of Laws.

ERRELA JOEL, born Tel Aviv, Israel; admitted, 1981, Israel. *Education:* Tel Aviv (LL.B., with Honors, 1981; LL.M., with Honors, 1987). Licensed Physiotherapist, Israel. M.C.S.P., England. *Member:* Israel Bar. *LANGUAGES:* Hebrew and English. *PRACTICE AREAS:* Media Law; International Family Law; Labour and Employment; Medical-Legal Law; Products Liability; International Estates and Succession.

Languages: Hebrew, English and German.

ALON KAPLAN LAW OFFICE

Established in 1975

1. DAVID HAMELECH BOULEVARD
TEL AVIV 64953, ISRAEL
Telephone: 972 3 695 4463
Fax: 972 695 5575

Commercial, Corporate, Real Estate, International Taxation, Offshore, Trusts, Estates, Tourist Trade and Airlines and Aircraft Transactions.

FIRM PROFILE: *The firm was established in 1975 and offers a full range of services in the fields of Corporations, Trusts, Real Estate, Tax, Aircraft Transactions and Business Litigation. The firm has extensive international activity in Europe, co-ordinated by its branch office in Germany, in the areas of Trust, Companies, Distributorships and International Taxation.*

MEMBERS OF FIRM

ALON KAPLAN, born Israel, October 28, 1939; admitted, 1970, Israel; 1989, Notary, Israel; 1990, New York; 1991, Rechtsbeistand, Frankfurt-am-Main. *Education:* Hebrew University of Jerusalem (LL.B., LL.M., 1974). Teaching Assistant, Common Law, Tel Aviv University Law School, 1969-1975. General Editor, Israel Law and Business (Kluwer) Publication, October 1994. *Member:* Israel Bar Association; New York State Bar Association; Frankfurt-am-Main Bar Consultant Rechtsbeistand. *LANGUAGES:* Hebrew, English and German. *PRACTICE AREAS:* Agency and Distributorships; Business Law; Corporate Law; Trusts; Real Estate Law; International Taxation.

ALAN ARONSON, born Bloemfontein, South Africa, August 28, 1962; admitted, 1989, South Africa; 1993, Israel. *Education:* University of Witwatgrand (B.A., 1984; LL.B., 1986). Author: "Proposed Israel Offshore Financial Centre," Israel Law and Business Guide, Kluwer Publisher, October 1994. *Member:* Transvaal Law Society, 1989-1990; Israel Bar Association, 1993—. *LANGUAGES:* English, Hebrew and Afrikaans. *PRACTICE AREAS:* Business Law; Corporate Law; Trusts.

OF COUNSEL

ABRAHAM SIMON, born U.S.S.R., September 8, 1945; admitted, 1974, Israel. *Education:* Tel Aviv University (LL.B., 1973). *Member:* Israel Bar Association. *LANGUAGES:* Hebrew, Yiddish and English. *PRACTICE AREAS:* Real Estate Law; Taxation Law.

MORDECHAI SUGARMAN, born Petah Tikva, Israel, December 11, 1938; admitted, 1969, Israel. *Education:* Hebrew University (LL.B., 1968). Editor: Book, Constitutional Laws, Mifal Hashichpul, 1968; Israel-South Africa Double Taxation Treaty in Israel Law and Business Guide, Kluwer, October 1994. Instructor: Labour Law, Conducting Seminars, 1969-1974. Member, Ramak Hasharon Local Authority-Municipal and Social Activities. Member, Israel-South Africa Chamber of Commerce, 1982—. *Member:* Israel Bar Association, 1969—; District Committee of Israel Bar Association (Member, Foreign Relations Committee, 1992-1994). *LANGUAGES:* Hebrew, English and Yiddish. *SPECIAL AGENCIES:* Human Rights representative of local petitioners with claims sumitted to the U.N. Human Rights Commission (Geneva) against the U.S.S.R. Government.
(This Listing Continued)

TRANSACTIONS: Involved in Commercial Transactions over the past 10 years worth 100 million dollars. *PRACTICE AREAS:* Commercial Law; Foreign Investment; Real Estate; Town Planning; Hi-Tech Projects.

KLEIN & HILL

1 DAVID HAMELECH BOULEVARD
TEL AVIV 64953, ISRAEL
Telephone: 972-3-695-4463
Fax: 972-3-695-5575

New York, New York Office: 521 Fifth Avenue. 10175. Telephone: 212-697-4455. Fax: 212-697-9570.

International Business Transactions, Transfer of Technology, Corporate, Contracts, Commercial Litigation, Trusts and Estates.

REUVEN KLEIN, born Braslaw, Poland, September 21, 1946; admitted, 1972, Israel; 1982, New York. *Education:* Tel-Aviv University School of Law (LL.B., 1971); New York University (LL.M., 1981). *Member:* New York State and American Bar Associations; The Israel Bar Association. (Also Counsel, Gerald & Lawrence Blumberg, New York, N.Y.). *LANGUAGES:* Hebrew.

GADI G. HILL, born Tel-Aviv, Israel, August 23, 1957; admitted, 1985, New York and U.S. District Court, Southern and Eastern Districts of New York. *Education:* University of Pennsylvania (B.S., B.A., cum laude, 1979); University of Minnesota (J.D., cum laude, 1984). *Member:* New York State and American Bar Associations. (Also Counsel, Gerald & Lawrence Blumberg, New York, N.Y.). *LANGUAGES:* Hebrew.

(For Complete Biographical Data on all Personnel, See Professional Biographies at New York, New York)

KLEINHENDLER AND HALEVY

Established in 1984

30 KALISHER STREET
TEL AVIV 65257, ISRAEL
Telephone: (972) (3) 5107575
Fax: (972) (3) 5107528

Corporate, Securities, Commercial, International Commercial Transactions, Investments, Taxation, Real Estate, Litigation.

MEMBERS OF FIRM

GENE KLEINHENDLER, born Haifa, Israel, March 6, 1953; admitted, 1980, New York and U.S. District Court, Southern and Eastern Districts of New York; 1984, Israel. *Education:* New York University (B.A., 1976); Brooklyn Law School (J.D., 1979). *Member:* Israel Bar Association; New York State and American Bar Associations. *LANGUAGES:* English and Hebrew.

AMIR HALEVY, born Jerusalem, Israel, May 3, 1952; admitted, 1979, Israel. *Education:* Tel-Aviv University (LL.B., 1978). *Member:* Israel Bar Association; International Association of Jewish Lawyers and Jurists (Member, Executive Committee, 1988—). *LANGUAGES:* Hebrew and English.

JOANN R. BLASBERG, born New York, N.Y., April 16, 1952; admitted, 1980, New York; 1982, U.S. District Court, Southern District of New York; 1987, Israel. *Education:* Queens College (B.A., 1974); Brooklyn Law School (J.D., summa cum laude, 1979). Editor, Brooklyn Law Review, 1978-1979. Law Clerk, Chief Judge Lawrence H. Cooke, New York State Court of Appeals, 1979-1982. *Member:* Israel Bar Association; New York State Bar Association. *LANGUAGES:* English and Hebrew.

ASSOCIATES

IDAN BEN-ARI, born Tel-Aviv, Israel, 1963; admitted, 1993, Israel. *Education:* Tel-Aviv University (LL.B., 1992). *LANGUAGES:* Hebrew and English.

BENNY STEINBERG, born Jerusalem, Israel, 1966; admitted, 1994, Israel. *Education:* Hebrew University (LL.B., 1992). *LANGUAGES:* Hebrew and English.

LESHEM-KIPPERMAN LAW OFFICES

56 IBN GVIROL STREET
TEL AVIV 64362, ISRAEL
Telephone: 972-3-6910152
Facsimile: 972-3-6958079

Aviation Law, Marine, Shipping and Transport Law, International Law, Civil and Commercial Litigation, Insurance and General Practice.

MEMBERS OF FIRM

MOSHE LESHEM, born Afula, Israel, January 21, 1944; admitted, 1980, Israel. *Education:* Tel Aviv University (LL.B., 1972); McGill University (LL.M., 1978). Author: "Powers of the Aircraft Commander under the Air Navigation (Offenses and Jurisdiction) Law 5731-1971," 3 Tel Aviv University Law Review, 320, 1973. *Member:* American Bar Association (Associate Member); American Society of International Law; International Bar Association; Israel Maritime Law Association. *LANGUAGES:* Hebrew and English. *PRACTICE AREAS:* General Practice; Aviation Law; Business Torts; Insurance Law; International Law; Litigation; Maritime Law; Tort Law.

IRIT KIPPERMAN, born Haifa, Israel, June 23, 1953; admitted, 1979, Israel. *Education:* Tel Aviv University (LL.B., 1977); University College London (LL.M., 1982). *Member:* American Bar Association (Associate Member); Israel Maritime Law Association. *LANGUAGES:* Hebrew and English. *PRACTICE AREAS:* General Practice; Aviation Law; Business Torts; Insurance Law; International Law; Litigation; Maritime Law; Tort Law.

Languages: Hebrew and English.

LEVY, TADMORE

4 KOIFMAN STREET
68012 TEL AVIV, ISRAEL
Telephone: 03-5102491
Facsimile: 03-5102493

Corporate Law, Securities, International Trade, Commercial Transactions, Government Contracts.

JOSEPH LEVY, born Israel, March 26, 1953; admitted, 1981, Israel. *Education:* Hebrew University (LL.B., 1980); Georgetown University (LL.M., 1983). Assistant Economic Minister, Embassy of Israel, Washington, D.C.. Tax Associate, Fried, Frank, Harris, Shriver & Jacobson, 1983-1985. *LANGUAGES:* English, Hebrew and Spanish.

DR. DAVID E. TADMOR, born Israel, April 6, 1960; admitted, 1987, Israel; 1989, New York. *Education:* Hebrew University (LL.B., 1986); New York University (LL.M., 1988; S.J.D., 1992). Law Clerk to Hon. Meir Shamgar, Chief Justice of the Supreme Court of Israel. Editorial Board, Mishpatim Law Review. Fulbright Scholar. Corporate Associate, Wachtell, Lipton, Rosen & Katz, 1988-1992. *Member:* New York State, Israel and American Bar Associations. *LANGUAGES:* English and Hebrew.

ASSOCIATES

KEN SHAKED, born Israel, April 23, 1962; admitted, 1991, Israel. *Education:* Tel Aviv University (LL.B., 1990). *Member:* Israel Bar Association. *LANGUAGES:* English and Hebrew.

OREN BER, born Israel, February 3, 1966; admitted, 1992, Israel. *Education:* Tel Aviv University (LL.B., 1991). *Member:* Israel Bar Association. *LANGUAGES:* English and Hebrew.

NOA MEI-DAN, born Israel, December 23, 1970; admitted, 1994, Israel. *Education:* Cardiff University (LL.B., 1992). *Member:* Israel Bar Association. *LANGUAGES:* English and Hebrew.

PROF. YUVAL LEVY & CO.

Advocates and Notary

Established in 1973

8 NESS-ZIONA STREET

P.O. BOX 26379

TEL AVIV 63904, ISRAEL

Telephone: (972-3) 5172303

Telecopier: (972-3) 5164185

General Corporate, International Commercial Transactions, International Banking and Business Law, Mergers and Acquisitions, Civil and Patent Litigation.

FIRM PROFILE: The firm was established in 1973 and offers a full range of civil and commercial services. The client base is Israeli, West European and North American in scope. The firm has a legal support staff consisting of paralegal and administrative personnel.

The firm is the Israeli member of Legal Network International, a selective network of law firms in 28 countries formed to provide their clients' international activities with specialized legal counsel.

MEMBERS OF FIRM

PROF. YUVAL LEVY, born Tel-Aviv, Israel, 1932; admitted, 1961, Israel. Education: Hebrew University (M.Jur., 1954); Yale Law School (LL.M., 1959; J.S.D., 1960). Lecturer, Bar Ilan University, 1965-1970. Senior Lecturer, Tel-Aviv University Law School, 1961-1982. Professor, Criminal Law, Tel Aviv University Law School, 1982—. Deputy Director, Institute of Criminology and Criminal Law, Tel-Aviv University, 1968-1983. Member of Board, Israel Institute of Continuing Legal Studies, 1969-1986. Member, Criminal Law Revision Committee appointed by government for revising the Criminal Code, 1965-1979. Chairman, Law Revision Committee on Directors' and Auditors' Responsibilities in Public Companies, 1975-1978. Author: "Principles of Criminal Responsibility," Ramot Edition, 1981. Member: Israel Bar Association; International Bar Association; Association of University Teachers and Professors. LANGUAGES: Hebrew, English and French. PRACTICE AREAS: Corporate Law; International Commercial Transactions; Banking Law; Business Law; Mergers and Acquisitions; Litigation.

OPHER LEVY, born 1959; admitted, 1986, Israel; 1989, New York. Education: Tel-Aviv University (LL.B., 1985); New York University (LL.M. Corp., 1989). Member: Israel and New York State Bar Associations. LANGUAGES: Hebrew and English. PRACTICE AREAS: Corporate Law; International Commercial Transactions; Banking Law; Business Law; Patent Law; Litigation.

YECHIEL KASHER, born 1961; admitted, 1987, Israel. Education: Tel-Aviv University (LL.B., cum laude, 1986). Teaching Assistant, Negotiable Instruments Law, Tel-Aviv University Law School, 1986-1987 and Corporate Law, 1987-1988. Member: Israel Bar Association. LANGUAGES: Hebrew and English. PRACTICE AREAS: Corporate Law; Civil Litigation.

DANIELLA YARON, born 1966; admitted, 1992, Israel. Education: Tel-Aviv University (LL.B., 1991). Editor, Tel Aviv University Law Review. Clerk, Justice Dr. Shlomo Levin, Israel Supreme Court. Teaching Assistant, Faculty of Business Management Tel Aviv University. LANGUAGES: Hebrew and English. PRACTICE AREAS: Corporate Law; Business Law; Civil Litigation.

ISRAEL HUSHANI, born 1962; admitted, 1993, Israel. Education: Tel-Aviv University (LL.B., 1991). LANGUAGES: Hebrew and English. PRACTICE AREAS: Corporate Law; Business Law; Civil Litigation.

MICAH A. MENES, born U.S.A., 1964; admitted, 1993, Israel. Education: Tel-Aviv University (LL.B., 1992). Member: Israel Bar Association. LANGUAGES: Hebrew and English. PRACTICE AREAS: Corporate Law; Business Law; Civil Litigation.

LUTHI & CO.

AMERICA HOUSE

35, SHAUL HAMELECH BOULEVARD

P.O. BOX 33113

TEL AVIV 64927, ISRAEL

Telephone: (3) 6952268

Fax: (3) 6951120

Telex: 371704 (GOLDNET IL.) Att: GLD5: AGE910

Patents, Trademarks, Designs, Copyright, Trade Secrets, Restrictive Practices, Industrial and Intellectual Property Litigation and Commercial Litigation.

RICHARD LUTHI, born Lausanne, Switzerland, December 25, 1952; admitted, 1983, Israel. Education: University of Southampton, England (LL.B., Hons., 1980). Recipient, Winston Churchill Memorial Prize for Best Academic Performance. Member: Israel Bar Association; AIPPI; U.S.-T.A.; Israel Copyright Association; ALAI. LANGUAGES: Hebrew and English.

ASSOCIATES

MOSHE GOLDBERG, born Israel, October 20, 1961; admitted, 1989, Israel. Education: Tel Aviv University Law School (LL.B., with distinction, 1988); Columbia University (LL.M., 1993). Law Instructor, Assistant Teacher, Contract Law, Tel Aviv University Law School. Member: Israel Bar Association; AIPPI; Israel Copyright Association; ALAI.

MOSHE MAOZ, born Israel, February 4, 1962; admitted, 1990, Israel. Education: Tel Aviv University Law School (LL.B., with distinction, 1989). Member: Israel Bar Association.

MATY BARZAM, born Israel, November 10, 1956; admitted, 1992, Israel. Education: Fairleigh Dickinson University, U.S.A. (B.Sc. Mech. Eng., 1983); New York Institute of Technology, U.S.A. (M.B.A., 1985); Tel Aviv University Law School (LL.B., 1991). Member: Israel Bar Association. LANGUAGES: Hebrew and English.

TAMAR GOREN, born Israel, May 20, 1961; admitted, 1994, Israel. Education: Hebrew University (B.Sc., 1985); Tel Aviv University (LL.B., 1993). Clinical Dietitian (1986). Member: Israel Bar Association.

LIPA MEIR & CO.

Established in 1987

3 DANIEL FRISCH STREET

TEL AVIV 64731, ISRAEL

Telephone: 972-3-691-7291

Facsimile: 972-3-691-8855

Commercial, Corporate, Liquidations and Reorganizations, Commercial Litigation, Investments, Insurance, Real Estate, Securities, International Transactions, Administrative Law.

MEMBERS OF FIRM

DR. LIPA MEIR, born October 16, 1947; admitted, 1974, Israel. Education: Tel-Aviv University (LL.B., 1973; LL.M., 1980); Toronto University (S.J.D., 1984). Guest Lecturer: "Company Liquidation and Reorganization," Bar Ilan University, 1988—. Member: Israel Bar Association. LANGUAGES: Hebrew and English. PRACTICE AREAS: Corporations; Liquidation and Reorganization; Insurance; Securities.

ZURIEL LAVIE, born April 28, 1959; admitted, 1986, Israel. Education: Hebrew University, Jerusalem (LL.B., 1985). Lecturer, Bar Ilan University Law School. Member: Israel Bar Association. LANGUAGES: Hebrew and English. PRACTICE AREAS: Corporations; Banking; Receivership and Liquidation; Agricultural Law.

JACOB SPIGELMAN, born November 19, 1961; admitted, 1989, Israel. Education: Bar Ilan University (LL.B., 1988). Member: Israel Bar Association. PRACTICE AREAS: Corporations; Commercial Litigation; Real Estate Transactions.

ASSOCIATES

DR. YEHUDA BEN MEIR, born July 27, 1939; admitted, 1993, Israel. Education: Columbia University (Ph.D., 1962); Bar Ilan University (LL.B., 1991). Deputy Minister of Foreign Affairs, 1981-1984. Member of Knesset, 1971-1984. Member: Israel Bar Association. LANGUAGES: Hebrew and English. PRACTICE AREAS: Contracts; Administrative Law; International Transactions.

(This Listing Continued)

ISRAEL AZIEL, born September 27, 1962; admitted, 1990, Israel. *Education:* Tel Aviv University (LL.B., 1989). *Member:* Israel Bar Association. *PRACTICE AREAS:* Commercial Litigation; Corporations; Real Estate.

GIL RON, born July 31, 1965; admitted, 1991, Israel. *Education:* Tel Aviv University (LL.B., 1990). *Member:* Israel Bar Association. *PRACTICE AREAS:* Securities; Corporations.

CHAYIM HIRSCHFELD, born June, 11, 1963; admitted, 1991, Israel. *Education:* Tel Aviv University (LL.B., 1990). *Member:* Israel Bar Association. *LANGUAGES:* Hebrew and English. *PRACTICE AREAS:* Real Estate; Corporations; Insurance.

MEITAR, LITTMAN, NECHMAD & CO.

Law Offices

Established in 1962

16 ABBA HILLEL STREET
TEL AVIV (RAMAT GAN) 52506, ISRAEL
Telephone: 972-3-5756155
Telecopier: 972-3-5756154

Corporate and Commercial Law (emphasis on acquisitions), Real Estate, Cable T.V., Computers and Information Systems, Arbitration.

ZVI MEITAR, born Tel Aviv, Israel, October 12, 1933; admitted, 1959, Israel. *Education:* Hebrew University, Jerusalem (M.Jur., 1957). *Member:* The Israel Bar (President, Tel Aviv District, 1983—). *LANGUAGES:* Hebrew and English. *PRACTICE AREAS:* Corporate and Commercial Law; Real Estate; Arbitration.

PAZ LITTMAN, born Haifa, Israel, June 13, 1956; admitted, 1985, Israel; 1987, New York. *Education:* Hebrew University, Jerusalem (LL.B., 1983; LL.M., with Honors, 1985). Associate, Skadden Arps Slate Meagher & Flom, New York, 1987-1990. *Member:* The Israel Bar; American Bar Association. *LANGUAGES:* Hebrew and English. *PRACTICE AREAS:* Corporate; Mergers and Acquisitions.

AMIR NECHMAD, born Israel, July 27, 1958; admitted, 1988, Israel. *Education:* Tel-Aviv University (LL.B., 1988). *Member:* The Israel Bar. *LANGUAGES:* Hebrew, English and French. *PRACTICE AREAS:* Telecommunications; Commercial Law; Real Estate.

MAYA LIQUORNIK, born Haifa, Israel, December 29, 1956; admitted, 1987, Israel. *Education:* Tel-Aviv University (B.A., 1981; LL.B., 1985, with Honors). Associate, Weil, Gotshal & Manges, New York, 1992-1994. *Member:* The Israel Bar. *LANGUAGES:* Hebrew and English. *PRACTICE AREAS:* Corporate; Securities.

ASSOCIATES

ISRAEL PFEFFER, born Israel, July 27, 1958; admitted, 1986, Israel. *Education:* Tel-Aviv University (LL.B., 1985). *Member:* The Israel Bar. *LANGUAGES:* Hebrew and English.

DAFNA MEITAR-NECHMAD, born Tel-Aviv, Israel, November 26, 1961; admitted, 1989, Israel. *Education:* Tel Aviv University (B.A., Social Sciences, 1986; LL.B., 1989). *Member:* The Israel Bar. *LANGUAGES:* Hebrew and English.

SHARON HALUTS, born Israel, September 8, 1958; admitted, 1990, Israel. *Education:* Tel Aviv University (B.A. in Social Work, 1983; LL.B., 1990). *Member:* The Israel Bar. *LANGUAGES:* Hebrew and English.

MINNA FERZIGER FELIG, born New York, N.Y., July 26, 1962; admitted, 1990, New York and U.S. District Court, Southern and Eastern Districts of New York; 1994, Israel. *Education:* Barnard College (B.A., 1984); Georgetown University Law Center (J.D., 1988). Associate, Gold Farrell and Marks, New York, 1992; Articles Clerk S. Horowitz, Tel Aviv, 1994. *Member:* The Israel Bar, New York Bar, American Bar Association. *LANGUAGES:* English and Hebrew. *PRACTICE AREAS:* Corporate; Intellectual Property Entertainment Law.

RONEN BEZALEL, born Israel, November 10, 1966; admitted, 1994, Israel. *Education:* Essex University, England (LL.B., 1992). *Member:* The Israel Bar. *LANGUAGES:* Hebrew and English. *PRACTICE AREAS:* Corporate.

DAVID BROG, born Atlantic City, New Jersey, August 18, 1966; admitted, 1992, Pennsylvania and New Jersey (Not admitted in Israel). *Education:* Princeton University (B.A., with Honors, 1988); Harvard Law

(This Listing Continued)

School (J.D., with Honors, 1991). Associate, Duane, Morris & Heckscher, Philadelphia, 1991-1993. *Member:* Amercian Bar Association. *LANGUAGES:* Hebrew and English. *PRACTICE AREAS:* Corporate.

MELCER & CO.
LAW OFFICES

Established in 1978

2 KAPLAN STREET
TEL AVIV, ISRAEL
Telephone: 972-3-6951160
Telecopier: 972-3-6951104

Administrative, Civil Litigation, Computer, Corporate, Air, Communications, European Community, Securities, Bankruptcy, Real Estate, Banking, Probate, Labor and Commercial Contract Law, International Transactions.

HANAN MELCER, born Tel Aviv, Israel, April 12, 1951; admitted, 1977, Israel. *Education:* Tel Aviv University, Faculty of Law (LL.B., with honors, 1974). Author: "Application to Ombudsman as a Prerequisite to High Court Proceedings," Volume 2, No. 2, Tel Aviv University Law Review, 1972. Legal Teaching Assistant, Administrative and Constitutional Law, Tel Aviv University, Faculty of Law, 1973-1982. *Member:* Israel Bar Association.

DANIEL FEDER, born Israel, May 19, 1959; admitted, 1986, Israel. *Education:* Tel Aviv University (B.A. in Philosophy with honors, 1985); Tel Aviv University, Faculty of Law (LL.B., 1985). *Member:* Israel Bar Association.

RONA ORLICKY, born Tel Aviv, Israel, December 20, 1962; admitted, 1988, Israel. *Education:* Tel Aviv University, Faculty of Law (LL.B., 1987). *Member:* Israel Bar Association.

DR. YIZHAR TAL, born Jerusalem, Israel, June 21, 1954; admitted, 1982, Israel. *Education:* Tel Aviv University, Faculty of Law (LL.B., 1981); Oxford University, Faculty of Law (D.Phil). Lecturer, European Community Law, Faculty of Law, Tel Aviv University, 1992—. *Member:* Solicitors' European Group, London; University Association for Contemporary European Studies, London; Israel Bar Association.

ASSOCIATES

ODED KARIV, born Tel Aviv, Israel, November 11, 1944; admitted, 1989, Israel. *Education:* Weizmann Institute of Science (Ph.D., 1976); Tel Aviv University (LL.B., 1988). Assistant Professor in Computer Science Technion, Israel Institute of Technology, Haifa, 1978-1982. *Member:* Israel Bar Association.

NAVA ILAN, born Nahariya, Israel, November 1, 1965; admitted, 1991, Israel. *Education:* Hebrew University, Faculty of Law (LL.B., 1990). *Member:* Israel Bar Association.

CRAIG D. KUGLER, born Brooklyn, New York, June 5, 1958; admitted, 1988, Israel; 1990, New York. *Education:* Suny Stony Brook (1976-1978); Bar-Ilan University (B.A., 1982; M.A., 1988); Tel Aviv University (LL.B., 1987). Lecturer, Political Studies, Bar-Ilan University, 1985-1989. *Member:* American Bar Association; Israel Bar Association; New York Bar Association.

YORAM MOKADY, born Zambia, February 21, 1966; admitted, 1992, Israel. *Education:* Hebrew University (LL.B., 1991). *Member:* Israel Bar Association.

YISGAV NAKDIMON, born Tel-Aviv, Israel, July 11, 1969; admitted, 1994, Israel. *Education:* Tel-Aviv University, Faculty of Law (LL.B., 1993). *Member:* Israel Bar Association.

AYELET SIMON-WEXLER, born Eilat, Israel, November 25, 1968; admitted, 1994, Israel. *Education:* Hebrew University (LL.B., 1993). *Member:* Israel Bar Association. *LANGUAGES:* Hebrew, English.

Languages: Hebrew, English, Yiddish, Polish, Romanian and French.

D. MIRKIN & CO.

Advocates

Established in 1983

1, KING DAVID AVENUE
P.O. BOX 16138 TEL AVIV 61 160
TEL AVIV 64 953, ISRAEL
Telephone: 6962126
Telex: 342392 MIRKN IL
Facsimile: (972-3) 6969737

General Practice, Commercial, Maritime Law, Copyright and Trademarks.

FIRM PROFILE: *The firm offers a full range of legal services as described above. Recently, in view of the events in the former Soviet Union, the firm commenced handling various transactions with the CIS Republics since three of the firm's members are fluent in Russian. The firm also has a branch office in Jerusalem.*

DANIEL MIRKIN, born Paris, France, November 17, 1937; admitted, 1972, Israel. *Education:* Hebrew University of Jerusalem; Tel-Aviv University. Guest Lecturer, Trial Advocacy, Law Faculty, Tel Aviv University (1989-1991). *Member:* AIPPI Israel Group; United States Trademark Association. *LANGUAGES:* Hebrew, English, French and Russian. *PRACTICE AREAS:* Intellectual Property; Corporate Law; International Transactions; Hotel Business.

EFRAIM BARAK, born Argentina, November 6, 1957; admitted, 1987, Israel. *Education:* Tel-Aviv University (LL.B., 1987). Teaching Assistant, Labour Law, Tel Aviv University Law Faculty and Social Sciences Faculty, 1986-1988. *LANGUAGES:* Hebrew, English and Spanish. *PRACTICE AREAS:* Labour Law; General Practice.

GALIT BONÉ-YONA, born Israel, February 28, 1964; admitted, 1990, Israel. *Education:* Tel-Aviv University (LL.B). *LANGUAGES:* Hebrew and English. *PRACTICE AREAS:* General Practice.

YOHAI HURVITZ, born Israel, September 13, 1964; admitted, 1992, Israel. *Education:* Tel-Aviv University (LL.B.; B.A., Economics). *LANGUAGES:* Hebrew and English. *PRACTICE AREAS:* General Practice.

MARINA TSEFANSKY, born U.S.S.R., October 8, 1963; admitted, 1985, U.S.S.R.; 1992, Israel. *Education:* Government University, Tashkent (former U.S.S.R.). *LANGUAGES:* Russian and Hebrew. *PRACTICE AREAS:* General Practice.

OF COUNSEL

URIEL GORNEY, born Riga, Latvia, June 6, 1921; admitted, 1945, (Palestine) Israel; 1948, United Kingdom, Middle Temple, London. Lecturer on Government Corporations, Faculty of Law, Tel-Aviv University, 1983—. District Attorney, Tel-Aviv, 1951-1956. General Counsel, Ministry of Defense, 1974-1981. President, Disciplinary Tribunal, Bar Association of Tel-Aviv, 1960-1965. *LANGUAGES:* Hebrew, English, German, French and Russian. *PRACTICE AREAS:* Corporations (including Government Corporations); Administrative Law and Town Planning; Estates, Wills and Trusts.

YAACOV MUSEL

Established in 1992

12 KAPLAN STREET
P.O. BOX 7205-61071
64734 TEL AVIV, ISRAEL
Telephone: 972-3-6961112
Fax: 972-3-6968153

Commercial Transactions, Copyrights, Joint Ventures (Israel-Former U.S.S.R. Countries), Investments in Israel.

YAACOV MUSEL, born Israel, 1958; admitted, 1987, Israel. *Education:* Tel-Aviv University (LL.B., 1986); Monash University, Melbourne, Australia (LL.M., 1991). Main Research: U.S.A. Federal Law: "Computer Programs Copyright in the United States - the correct test regarding infringement.". *LANGUAGES:* Hebrew and English.

NASCHITZ, BRANDES & CO.
ADVOCATES AND NOTARIES

136 ROTHSCHILD BOULEVARD
TEL AVIV 65272, ISRAEL
Telephone: 972-3-6857766
Facsimile: 972-3-6857535 or 972-3-6850069

Haifa, Israel Office: 5 Jerusalem Street, 33132. Telephone: 972-4-670413, 670760, 640769. Facsimile: 972-4-670764.

Jerusalem, Israel Office: 3 Schatz Street, 94267. Telephone: 972-2-243236, 231275. Facsimile: 972-2-248522.

Commercial, Corporate, Maritime, Taxation, Insurance, Securities, Banking, Labor, Patent and Trademarks, Private and Public International Law.

MEMBERS OF FIRM

PETER GAD NASCHITZ, born July 16, 1932; admitted, 1957, Israel. *Education:* Tel-Aviv University (LL.B., cum laude, LL.M.). *Member:* Israel Bar; International Bar Association; AIDA (Association Internationale de Droit d'Assurance); Israel Maritime Law Association; AIPPI (International Association for the Protection of Industrial Property); United States Trademark Association; American Bar Association (Associate Member). *LANGUAGES:* English, French, German and Hungarian.

HANINA BRANDES, born May 2, 1937; admitted, 1965, Israel. *Education:* Hebrew University of Jerusalem - Tel Aviv (LL.B.). *Member:* Israel Bar; International Bar Association. *LANGUAGES:* English.

AZRIEL ROTHMAN, born 1955; admitted, 1981, Israel. *Education:* Tel Aviv University (LL.B.). *Member:* Israel Bar. *LANGUAGES:* English.

AARON M. LAMPERT, born 1957; admitted, 1982, New York; 1985, U.S. Supreme Court; 1987, Israel. *Education:* Touro College (B.A., 1978); Columbia University School of Law (J.D., 1981). *Member:* Israel Bar; Association of the Bar of the City of New York; New York State and American Bar Associations. *LANGUAGES:* English.

EITAN A. NASCHITZ, admitted, 1989, Israel; New York. *Education:* Tel Aviv University (LL.B.); New York University (LL.M.). *Member:* Israel Bar; New York State Bar Association.

GIL BRANDES, admitted, 1990, Israel. *Education:* University of Buckingham, England (LL.B.). *Member:* Israel Bar.

SHIMON D. CHERTOW, admitted, 1984, Israel. *Education:* Columbia University, New York City (B.A.); Tel Aviv University (LL.B.). *Member:* Israel Bar.

JOSEPH DOLAN, admitted, 1981, Israel. *Education:* Hebrew University, Jerusalem (LL.B.). Legal Adviser, Income Tax Division of the Ministry of Finance, 1981-1986. *Member:* Israel Bar.

AVNER COHEN, admitted, 1986, Israel. *Education:* Hebrew University, Jerusalem (LL.B.). *Member:* Israel Bar.

ILAN ORLY, admitted, 1988, Israel. *Education:* Tel Aviv University. *Member:* Israel Bar.

BETTINA TAUBER, admitted, 1988, Israel. *Education:* Tel Aviv University. *Member:* Israel Bar.

SHMUEL IRONI, admitted, 1980, Israel. *Education:* Tel-Aviv University (LL.B.).

OFER MOTOLA, admitted, 1990, Israel. *Education:* Tel-Aviv University (LL.B.). *Member:* Israel Bar.

YARON HOROVITZ, admitted, 1988, Israel. *Education:* Hebrew University, Jerusalem (LL.B.). *Member:* Israel Bar.

YOAV RAZIN, admitted, 1991, Israel. *Education:* Tel-Aviv University (LL.B.). *Member:* Israel Bar.

RUSSELL D. MAYER, admitted, 1982, New York and U.S. District Courts for the Southern and Eastern Districts of New York; 1986, New Jersey and U.S. District Court for the District of New Jersey; 1991, Israel. *Education:* Queens College (B.A., 1978); Benjamin N. Cardozo School of Law of Yeshiva University (J.D., 1981). Member, Banking Law Committee, New York County Lawyers' Association, 1982-1991. *Member:* Israel Bar; American Bar Association (Business Law Committee; Ad Hoc Committee on New Payment Systems).

PNINA BRODER MANOR, admitted, 1990, Israel. *Education:* Tel-Aviv University (LL.B.). *Member:* Israel Bar.

(This Listing Continued)

ANAT NASCHITZ, admitted, 1992, Israel. *Education:* Tel Aviv University (LL.B.). *Member:* Israel Bar.

SHIRLY BRANDES-BALLAN, admitted, 1993, Israel. *Education:* London Guildhall University (LL.B.). *Member:* Israel Bar.

IRIS LEVY, admitted, 1993, Israel. *Education:* Tel-Aviv University (LL.B). *Member:* Israel Bar.

GIL KARSEBOOM, admitted, 1994, Israel. *Education:* University of Essex (LL.B.); Kings College, London (LL.M.). *Member:* Israel Bar.

GIL ATAR, admitted, 1994, Israel. *Education:* Tel-Aviv University (LL.B.). *Member:* Israel Bar.

AYELLET (MIMI) YAVIN, admitted, 1994, Israel. *Education:* Tel-Aviv University (LL.B.). *Member:* Israel Bar.

SHARON STERN, admitted, 1994, Israel. *Education:* Tel-Aviv University (LL.B.). *Member:* Israel Bar.

DAN MANOR, admitted, 1994, Israel. *Education:* Tel-Aviv University (LL.B.). *Member:* Israel Bar.

SIGAL MULLA-COHEN, admitted, 1994, Israel. *Education:* Tel-Aviv University (LL.B.). *Member:* Israel Bar.

Languages: Hebrew, English, French, German, Russian and Hungarian.

M. PORATH & CO.

Advocates & Notaries

Established in 1952

10 CARLEBACH STREET
4TH FLOOR
P.O. BOX 20045
TEL AVIV 67132, ISRAEL
Telephone: (972) (3) 561 0111
Fax: (972) (3) 561 0934

FIRM PROFILE: *The Firm was established in 1952 and offers a full range of civil and commercial services, including the following fields of practice: Commercial and Corporate Law, Insurance, Securities, Banking, Labor, Real Estate, Computer Law, Bankruptcy/Insolvency, Trusts and Estates, Civil Litigation.*

MEMBERS OF FIRM

MOSHE PORATH, born Bialystock, Poland, May 7, 1920; admitted, 1945, Israel. *Education:* University of Warsaw, Poland; University of Liverpool, England; Jerusalem Law School (Advocate, 1944). General Counsel, Agricultural Center, General Federation of Labour in Israel, 1945-1948. Ministry of Finance, Government of Israel, 1948-1952. Custodial of Absentee Property, Government of Israel, 1950-1952. *Member:* Israel Bar Association. *LANGUAGES:* Hebrew, English and German.

JOSEPH HALEVY, born Sofia, Bulgaria, June 17, 1946; admitted, 1973, Israel. *Education:* Hebrew University, Jerusalem (LL.B., 1970). *Member:* Israel Bar Association. *LANGUAGES:* Hebrew and English.

ISRAEL PORATH, born Tel-Aviv, Israel, December 5, 1954; admitted, 1985, Israel. *Education:* University of Tel-Aviv (LL.B., 1985); University of Jerusalem (B.A., Economics and International Affairs, 1979). *Member:* Israel Bar Association. *LANGUAGES:* Hebrew and English.

MOSHE M. KAHN, born London, England, September 14, 1957; admitted, 1984, Israel; 1987, New York. *Education:* Bar Ilan University, Israel (LL.B., 1983). Associate, Rosenman and Colin, New York, 1985-1987. *Member:* Israel Bar Association. *LANGUAGES:* Hebrew and English.

ITZHAK LEVY, born Tel-Aviv, Israel, March 14, 1960; admitted, 1984, Israel. *Education:* Tel-Aviv University (LL.B., 1982). *Member:* Israel Bar Association. [Served with Military Advocate General, 1982-1987]. *LANGUAGES:* Hebrew and English.

ASSOCIATES

SHMUEL NIR, admitted, 1958, Israel. Advocate and Notary.

ANAT BAR-HAI, admitted, 1991, Israel. Advocate.

RAVIT ARBEL, admitted, 1993, Israel. Advocate.

SHABY DAVID, admitted, 1991, Israel.

JONNA STEINBOCK, admitted, 1989, California. (Not admitted in Israel).

(This Listing Continued)

REUVEN HELLER, born Czernowitz, Bucovina, Romania, April 6, 1929; admitted, 1962, Israel. *Education:* University of Tel Aviv (LL.B., 1959). *Member:* Israel Bar Association. [Defense Counsel with Military Advocate General, 1960-1962]. *LANGUAGES:* Hebrew, English and German.

EYAL PRICE LAW OFFICES

AMOT MISHPAT BUILDING
8 SHAUL HAMELECH BOULEVARD
TEL AVIV 64733, ISRAEL
Telephone: (972) 3 693 8415
Facsimile: (972) 3 693 8414

Copyright, Trademarks, Patents, Designs, Licensing, Intellectual Property Litigation, Commercial Law.

EYAL PRICE, born Tel-Aviv, Israel, 1962; admitted, 1990, Israel. *Education:* Tel Aviv University, School of Law (LL.B. 1990); University of Georgia Law School, U.S.A. (LL.M., 1991). Lecturer, Copyright and Designs Law, Bezalel Academy of Arts and Designs, Jerusalem. Research Assistant, Tel Aviv University School of Law, 1989-1990. *Member:* Israel Bar Association; AIPPI; ALAI; LES.

RAFAEL, RABINOWITZ, MEHULAL & CO.

27 HAMERED STREET
P.O. BOX 50119
TEL AVIV 61500, ISRAEL
Telephone: 972-3-5103366
Fax: 972-3-5103368

Tax Law, Securities Law, Corporate and Commercial Law, Real Estate, Probate and Complex Litigation.

AMNON RAFAEL, born Haifa, Israel, 1941; admitted, 1968, Israel; 1987, New York. *Education:* Hebrew University of Jerusalem (LL.B.); New York University (LL.M. in Taxation; J.S.D.). Author: "Income Tax Law" (published in Hebrew by Schoken, 1980, 1985, 1991 Vol. 3). Member, Special Taxation Committee of Experts for the Reform of Individual Taxation, 1987. Chairman - Special Committee of Experts on International Taxation, 1991. *Member:* Israel Bar Association; International Fiscal Association. *LANGUAGES:* Hebrew, English and French.

ASHER RABINOWITZ, born Haifa, Israel, 1945; admitted, 1973, Israel. *Education:* Hebrew University (LL.B.). *Member:* Israel Bar Association. *LANGUAGES:* Hebrew and English.

YARON MEHULAL, born Tel Aviv, Israel, 1955; admitted, 1983, Israel. *Education:* Tel Aviv University Law School (LL.B.). Co-author: with Amnon Rafael, "Income Tax," Volume 3. *Member:* Israel Bar Association. *LANGUAGES:* Hebrew, English and Arabic.

DAVID A. DEUEL, born Israel, 1951; admitted, 1979, Israel. *Education:* Tel Aviv University Law School (LL.B.); Hebrew University of Jerusalem, Advanced Business Administration Studies. *Member:* Israel Bar Association. *LANGUAGES:* Hebrew and English.

YEHUDA MORITZ, born Austria, 1924; admitted, 1955, Israel. *Education:* London University (LL.B.). *Member:* Israel Bar Association. *LANGUAGES:* Hebrew, English and German.

OMRY YAKIR, born Tel Aviv, Israel, 1957; admitted, 1991, Israel. *Education:* Tel Aviv University (M.A., Political Science); Tel Aviv University Law School (LL.B.). *Member:* Israel Bar Association. *LANGUAGES:* Hebrew and English.

URI SUDRI, born Rehovot, Israel, 1963; admitted, 1991, Israel. *Education:* Tel Aviv University Law School (LL.B.). *Member:* Israel Bar Association. *LANGUAGES:* Hebrew and English.

IRIT LANGSAN, born Tel Aviv, Israel, 1965; admitted, 1992, Israel. *Education:* Hebrew University of Jerusalem (LL.B.). *Member:* Israel Bar Association. *LANGUAGES:* Hebrew and English.

NISSAN CASPI, born Jerusalem, Israel, 1963; admitted, 1993, Israel. *Education:* Tel Aviv University Law School (LL.B.). *Member:* Israel Bar Association. *LANGUAGES:* Hebrew and English.

(This Listing Continued)

RAFAEL, RABINOWITZ, MEHULAL & CO., Tel Aviv—
Continued

IRIT KESSELMAN-MILLET, born Moscow, Russia, 1966; admitted, 1993, Israel. *Education:* Tel Aviv University Law School (LL.B.). *Member:* Israel Bar Association. *LANGUAGES:* Hebrew, English and Russian.

YARON TIKOTZKY, born Haifa, Israel, 1965; admitted, 1994, Israel. *Education:* Tel Aviv University Law School (LL.B.); Tel Aviv University Business School (B.A., Accountancy). *Member:* Israel Bar Association. *LANGUAGES:* Hebrew and English.

YEHUDA RAVEH & CO.

(Formerly Gideon Hausner Law Offices)

AMERICA HOUSE
35 SHAUL HAMELECH BOULEVARD
P.O. BOX 33804
TEL AVIV 64927, ISRAEL
Telephone: 972-3-6956152
Telecopier (Fax): 972-3-6919102

Jerusalem, Israel Office: 26, Ussishkin Street, 91077, P.O. Box 7722. Telephone: 972-2-635232-5; 661231-4. Cable Address: "Hausad". Telex: 26307 Raveh IL. Telecopier Fax: 972-2-617101.

General Practice. Commercial, Corporate, Real Estate, Hotels, Banking, Insurance, Hi-Tech, Industry, Foreign Investments, Free-Trade Agreements and Patents and Trademark Law.

MEMBERS OF FIRM

YEHUDA RAVEH, born Israel, September 3, 1944; admitted, 1970, Israel. *Education:* Hebrew University of Jerusalem (LL.B.); New York University. *Member:* Israel Bar Association. *LANGUAGES:* Hebrew and English.

LISA TROSS, born South Africa, January 6, 1955; admitted, 1980, Israel. *Education:* Hebrew University of Jerusalem (LL.B.). Teaching Assistant, Hebrew University Law School, 1976-1978. *Member:* Bar Association of Israel. *LANGUAGES:* Hebrew and English.

HAIM STERN, born Tel Aviv, Israel, October 24, 1955; admitted, 1984, Israel. *Education:* Tel Aviv University (LL.B., 1983). *LANGUAGES:* Hebrew and English.

YUVAL GRAYEVSKY, born Jerusalem, Israel, May 20, 1958; admitted, 1984, Israel. *Education:* Hebrew University of Jerusalem (LL.B.). *Member:* Bar Association of Israel. *LANGUAGES:* Hebrew and English.

YEHUDA GLATT, born New York, U.S.A., January 9, 1958; admitted, 1985, Israel. *Education:* Hebrew University of Jerusalem (LL.B.). *Member:* Bar Association of Israel. *LANGUAGES:* Hebrew and English.

ASSOCIATES

SARA SHALOM, born Haifa, Israel, April 18, 1951; admitted, 1979, Israel. *Education:* Hebrew University (LL.B.). *LANGUAGES:* Hebrew and English.

URI YAMIN, born Jerusalem, Israel, May 9, 1960; admitted, 1988, Israel. *Education:* Hebrew University of Israel (LL.B.). *Member:* Bar Association of Israel. *LANGUAGES:* Hebrew, English and French.

CARMIT BAR-ON, born London, England, May 5, 1960; admitted, 1986, Israel. *Education:* Hebrew University of Jerusalem (LL.B., 1985). *Member:* Bar Association of Israel. *LANGUAGES:* Hebrew and English.

DANIEL SAVITCH, born Israel, 1961; admitted, 1988, Israel. *Education:* Hebrew University of Jerusalem (LL.B.). *Member:* Bar Association of Israel. *LANGUAGES:* Hebrew, English and German.

MYRIAM ABITBOL, born Morocco, July 9, 1956; admitted, 1980, France; 1991, Israel. *Education:* University of Grenoble (Maitrise en Droit). *Member:* Bar Association of France; Bar Association of Israel. *LANGUAGES:* Hebrew, French, English and German.

MIRIAM ILANY, born Spain, March 4, 1967; admitted, 1991, Israel. *Education:* Bar-Ilan University (LL.B.). *Member:* Bar Association of Israel. *LANGUAGES:* Hebrew, English and Spanish.

DGANIT ZAHAV, born Tel Aviv, Israel, January 22, 1961; admitted, 1993, Israel. *Education:* Tel Aviv University (LL.B., B.Sc.). *Member:* Bar Association of Israel. *LANGUAGES:* Hebrew and English.

(This Listing Continued)

GARY LEIBLER, born Melbourne, Australia, November 20, 1965; admitted, 1992, Israel. *Education:* Monash University of Melbourne (LL.B., B.Ec.). *Member:* Bar Association of Israel. *LANGUAGES:* Hebrew and English.

JEREMY ROSENSHINE, born Colorado, U.S.A., October 27, 1962; admitted, 1991, Israel. *Education:* Hebrew University of Jerusalem (LL.B.); University of Chicago (LL.M.). *Member:* Bar Association of Israel. *LANGUAGES:* Hebrew, English.

RON ISRAELI, born Jerusalem, Israel, October 9, 1962; admitted, 1992, Israel. *Education:* Hebrew University of Jerusalem (LL.B.; MB.A). *Member:* Bar Association of Israel. *LANGUAGES:* Hebrew and English.

OF COUNSEL

TAMAR RAVEH, born Israel, November 7, 1945; admitted, 1970, Israel. *Education:* Hebrew University of Jerusalem (LL.B.). *Member:* Bar Association of Israel. *LANGUAGES:* Hebrew, English.

REFERENCES: Mr. Milton Handler, Kaye Scholer, Fierman Hays and Handler, New York, N.Y.; Evelyn H. Lauder, Corporate V/P Estee Lauder Inc., New York, N.Y.; Roger Gerber, President, Meyers Parking Systems Inc. and Prudential Maintenance Corp., Inc., New York, N.Y.; Mr. Michael Steinhardt, Principal, Steinhardt Partners, New York, N.Y.

YAACOV SALOMON, LIPSCHUTZ & CO

Established in 1921

"BEIT SILVER"
7 ABBA HILLEL SILVER STREET
P.O. BOX 3424
TEL AVIV (RAMAT GAN) 52522, ISRAEL
Telephone: 03-5757712 Int'l: 972-3-5757712
Cable Address: "Salipad" Tel Aviv
Facsimile: (Grps 2 & 3) 03-5757725
Int'l: 972-3-5757725

REVISERS OF THE ISRAEL LAW DIGEST FOR THIS DIRECTORY.

Haifa, Israel Office: Yoel House, 64 Hameginim Avenue. Telephone: 04-535231, 2, 3, 4, 5. Int'l: 972-4-535231, 2, 3, 4, 5. Cable Address: "Client" Haifa. Facsimile: (Grps 2 & 3) 04-557038. Int'l: 972-4-557038.

General Practice. Commercial, Corporation, Tax and Maritime Law, Banking, Labor Law, Insurance, Franchising and Licensing, Real Estate, Construction, Town Planning, Securities, Capital Markets, Energy Law, Patent and Trademarks.

MEMBERS OF FIRM

YAACOV SALOMON (1905-1980).

BEN-ZION SERAYA, born Haifa, Israel, June 30, 1928; admitted, 1954, Israel. *Education:* Hebrew University of Jerusalem. *Member:* Israel Bar Association. *LANGUAGES:* Hebrew, English, Arabic and French.

ALEXANDER SAMUEL, born Izmir, January 9, 1937; admitted, 1965, Israel. *Education:* Hebrew University of Jerusalem. *Member:* Israel Bar Association. *LANGUAGES:* Hebrew, English and French.

MOSHE Y. LIPSCHUTZ, born Israel, April 5, 1939; admitted, 1965, Israel. *Education:* Hebrew University of Jerusalem. *Member:* Israel Bar Association. *LANGUAGES:* Hebrew and English.

JOSEPH GILLOR, born Jerusalem, Israel, October 6, 1940; admitted, 1966, Israel. *Education:* Hebrew University of Jerusalem. *Member:* Israel Bar Association. *LANGUAGES:* Hebrew, English and Arabic.

DAVID GOLDENBLATT, born Montreal, Quebec, Canada, September 19, 1940; admitted, 1965, Quebec, Canada; 1978, Israel. *Education:* McGill University, Montreal, Canada (B.A.; B.C.L.). *Member:* Canadian and Israel Bar Associations. *LANGUAGES:* Hebrew, English and French.

DR. GIDEON KLUGMAN, born Tel-Aviv, Israel, 1952; admitted, 1985, New York, U.S.A.; 1986, Israel. *Education:* Tel-Aviv University (LL.B.); Columbia University (LL.M.); Harvard University (S.J.D.). Author: "Convention between the Government of the State of Israel and the Government of the United States of America with Respect to Taxes on Income," (1993, 527 p.) (in Hebrew); "Transnational Taxation of Foreign Investments in Israel," 1992; "Income Tax Considerations related to the Free Trade Area Agreement between the United States and Israel," *The U.S. - Israel Free Trade Area Agreement*(Business Laws, Inc., Ohio, 1989); "Offsetting the Real Differential from Securities'," Vol. B2 *Taxes*A-30, (1988) (in Hebrew); "Linkage Differentials and Interest on Value Added Tax Refunds when Excess Advances are Refunded," 16 Taxes Quarterly 134, (1988) (in

(This Listing Continued)

Hebrew); "A Commentary on the Legislature's Approach Regarding Depreciation Deductions During Periods of Inflation," 15 Taxes Quarterly 243, (1987) (in Hebrew); "Adjustment of the Tax Brackets, the Deductions and Credits in a Special Tax Year and Offsetting of Losses," 35(4) The Accountant 346, (1987) (in Hebrew); "Peering into Your Neighbor's House: A Civil Wrong?" E/2 Tel Aviv Univ. L. Rev. 425, (1976) (in Hebrew). Appointed by Income Tax Commissioner of Israel: Member and advisor of the Israel delegation for negotiation of a tax treaty with the United States, 1989—; Member of the governmental committee for examination of the corporate tax system in Israel, 1990—. Appointment by Minister of Justice as a Member of the Boards of Land Appreciation Tax Appeals, adjunct to the courts in Tel-Aviv and Haifa, 1990—; (appointment by Minister of Justice). Associate, Cohen and Uretz, Washington D.C., 1982-1984. Member of the Tax Committee of the Israeli Bar. Member of the Tax Section of the American Bar Association. *LANGUAGES:* Hebrew and English.

ELISHA BEN-SHACHAR, born Haifa, Israel, July 19, 1952; admitted, 1978, Israel. *Education:* Bar Ilan University. *Member:* Israel Bar Association. *LANGUAGES:* Hebrew and English.

JAACOV RIVANOWITCH, born Haifa, Israel, February 15, 1951; admitted, 1981, Israel. *Education:* Hebrew University of Jerusalem. *Member:* Israel Bar Association. *LANGUAGES:* Hebrew, English and Arabic.

DORON N. TISHMAN, born Israel, November 23, 1961; admitted, 1987, Israel. *Education:* Tel Aviv University. *Member:* Israel Bar Association. *LANGUAGES:* Hebrew and English.

CONSULTANT

NAPHTALI LIPSCHUTZ, born Austria, May 7, 1908; admitted, 1931, United Kingdom; 1937, Israel. *Education:* University College, London; Gray's Inn, London. *Member:* Israel Bar Association. *LANGUAGES:* Hebrew, English, Arabic and German.

ASSOCIATES

BATIA HAIMOV ROMAN, born Haifa, Israel, December 6, 1953; admitted, 1980, Israel. *Education:* Tel-Aviv University. *Member:* Israel Bar Association. *LANGUAGES:* Hebrew and English.

MERAV ARAD-SALOMON, born Israel, October 13, 1958; admitted, 1984, Israel. *Education:* Hebrew University, Jerusalem. *Member:* Israel Bar Association. *LANGUAGES:* Hebrew and English.

RAMZI ABBDALAH HADIED, born Israel, March 24, 1965; admitted, 1989, Israel. *Education:* Hebrew University, Jerusalem. *Member:* Israel Bar Association. *LANGUAGES:* Hebrew, Arabic and English.

OFER SCHWEIZER, born Haifa, Israel, January 5, 1962; admitted, 1989, Israel. *Education:* Bar-Ilan University. *Member:* Israel Bar Association.

SHAI COHEN, born Haifa, Israel, April 12, 1963; admitted, 1992, Israel. *Education:* Tel Aviv University. *Member:* Israel Bar Association. *LANGUAGES:* Hebrew and English.

DIEFALLA AWWAD, born Nazareth, Israel, July 29, 1969; admitted, 1992, Israel. *Education:* Hebrew University. *Member:* Israel Bar Association. *LANGUAGES:* Arabic, Hebrew and English.

HANOCH MORGENSTERN, born Tel Aviv, Israel, March 6, 1964; admitted, 1992, Israel. *Education:* Bar Ilan University. *Member:* Israel Bar Association. *LANGUAGES:* Hebrew and English.

NIMROD TEPPER, born Kibbutz, Yagur, Israel, April 7, 1964; admitted, 1993, Israel. *Education:* Tel-Aviv University. *Member:* Israel Bar Association. *LANGUAGES:* Hebrew and English.

Languages: Hebrew, English, Arabic, French, Yiddish and German.

REVISERS OF THE ISRAEL LAW DIGEST FOR THIS DIRECTORY.

JOSEPH SAMUEL & CO.

Law Offices & Notaries

2, LEVONTIN STREET
TEL AVIV 65111, ISRAEL
Telephone: 972-3-5608566; 972-3-5662586
Fax: 972-3-5606981

Corporate and Commercial Law, Real Estate, Tax Laws, Estates and Probation, Building Constructions, Arbitration, Succession, Civil Litigation and General Practice.

(This Listing Continued)

MEMBERS OF FIRM

JOSEPH SAMUEL (1909-1993).

SAMY SAMUEL, born Bulgaria, 1923; admitted, 1950, Israel. *Education:* Law School, Jerusalem, 1950. Vice President of the Israel Bar.

ISRAEL COHEN, born Bulgaria, 1947; admitted, 1975, Israel. *Education:* Tel-Aviv University (LL.B., 1974). *Member:* The Israel Bar.

ALON SAMUEL, born Israel, 1961; admitted, 1988, Israel. *Education:* Tel-Avic University (LL.B., 1986). *Member:* The Israel Bar.

ASSOCIATES

YOSSI YOSSEFI, born Israel, 1962; admitted, 1991, Israel. *Education:* Tel-Aviv University (LL.B., 1990). *Member:* The Israel Bar.

ODEYA COHEN, born 1967; admitted, 1992, Israel. *Education:* Hebrew University of Jerusalem (LL.B., 1991). *Member:* The Israel Bar.

Languages: Hebrew, English, French, Bulgarian, Persian and Spanish.

M. SELIGMAN & CO.

Established in 1930

24 RAMBAM STREET
P.O. BOX 4090
TEL AVIV 61040, ISRAEL
Telephone: 972-3- 662661
Cable Address: "MAXSEL"
Telex: 35770 COIN IL EXT. RLV
FAX: 972-3-662668

Commercial and Corporate Law, Accident and General Insurance, International Banking, International Trade, Succession, Real Estate, Computer Law, Medical-Legal Practice, Communications Law, Securities Law.

FIRM PROFILE: *M. Seilgman & Co. was founded in 1930. One of the Chief Justices of the Israeli Supreme Court and another Justice of that court started their careers with the firm. The firm offers a full range of legal services meeting virtually every client needs. The firm represents clients on both a national and international level. The firm is comprised of a full staff of legal support and personnel. All of the staff are fluent in English and many of them in other foreign languages.*

MEMBERS OF FIRM

MAX SELIGMAN (1902-1987).

ELI ZOHAR, born Tel Aviv, Israel, October 15, 1940; admitted, 1965, Israel. *Education:* Hebrew University, Jerusalem (LL.B.). Author: "The Rights of the Unborn," Medico-Legal Society in Israel, 1978; "Legal and Social Aspects of Artificial Insemination," Medico-Legal Society in Israel, 1985. Tutor in Torts, Hebrew University, 1965-1967. Lecturer, Insurance Institute, 1970-1973. Lecturer, Law of Evidence and Legal Practice, Faculty of Medicine, Tel Aviv University, 1988—. *Member:* Israel Bar Association; Tel Aviv Bar Association (Secretary, 1970-1976); Medico-Legal Society of Israel (Chairman, Research Committee, 1988—; Member, Management Committee). *LANGUAGES:* Hebrew and English. *PRACTICE AREAS:* Commercial Law; Banking Law; Securities; Communications Law; Medico-Legal Law; General Practice; Litigation.

CHAIM ZELICHOV, born Israel, April 22, 1949; admitted, 1975, Israel. *Education:* Hebrew University, Jerusalem (LL.B.). *Member:* Israel Bar Association. *LANGUAGES:* Hebrew and English. *PRACTICE AREAS:* Commercial Law; Tort Law; Insurance Law; Medical Malpractice Law.

GABRIEL HAKE, born Tel Aviv, Israel, February 10, 1954; admitted, 1982, Israel. *Education:* University of Kent, Canterbury, U.K. (B.A.; LL.B.); Tel Aviv University. *Member:* Israel Bar Association. *LANGUAGES:* Hebrew and English. *PRACTICE AREAS:* Corporate Law; Securities Law; Secured Transactions Law; Banking Law; Computer Law; International Business Law.

ASSOCIATES

ORNA LIN, born Haifa, Israel, March 27, 1956; admitted, 1981, Israel. *Education:* Hebrew University, Jerusalem (LL.B.). *Member:* Israel Bar Association. *LANGUAGES:* Hebrew and English. *PRACTICE AREAS:* Labor Law; Commercial Law; Maritime Law; Tort Law.

NILI ZOHAR, born Israel, October 28, 1946; admitted, 1991, Israel. *Education:* University of Bar Ilan (LL.B.). *Member:* Israel Bar Association. *LANGUAGES:* English and Hebrew. *PRACTICE AREAS:* Litigation; Medical Malpractice Law; Commercial Law.

(This Listing Continued)

M. SELIGMAN & CO., Tel Aviv—Continued

MIRI NISSANI-YITZCHAK, born Afula, Israel, February 5, 1958; admitted, 1984, Israel. *Education:* Hebrew University of Jerusalem (LL.B.). *Member:* Israel Bar Association. *LANGUAGES:* Hebrew and English. *PRACTICE AREAS:* Tort Law; Insurance Law; Medical Malpractice Law.

EINAT RAVID, born Israel, September 18, 1961; admitted, 1987, Israel. *Education:* Hebrew University, Jerusalem (LL.B.). *Member:* Israel Bar Association. *LANGUAGES:* Hebrew, English and French. *PRACTICE AREAS:* Litigation; Commercial Law; Corporate Law.

IRIS RABINOVICH, born Tel Aviv, Israel, August 1965; admitted, 1990, Israel. *Education:* Hebrew University of Jerusalem (LL.B.); Oxford, England (B.C.L.). *Member:* Israel Bar Association. *LANGUAGES:* Hebrew, English and French. *PRACTICE AREAS:* Commercial Law; Import and Export Law.

YARON SOBOL, born Jerusalem, Israel, October 23, 1959; admitted, 1988, Israel. *Education:* Tel Aviv University (LL.B.); American University, Washington, D.C. (LL .M., International Legal Studies). *Member:* Israel Bar Association. *LANGUAGES:* Hebrew and English. *PRACTICE AREAS:* Corporate Law; Commercial Law; Securities Law; Secured Transactions Law; International Business Law; Arbitration.

MICHAL AMITAI-TAHORI, born Tel Aviv, Israel, July 7, 1962; admitted, 1987, Israel. *Education:* Hebrew University of Jerusalem (LL.B.). *Member:* Israel Bar Association. *LANGUAGES:* English and Hebrew. *PRACTICE AREAS:* Tort Law; Insurance Law; Medical Malpractice Law.

GALIA ROSENBAUM-TIRAN, born Ein-Hashofet, Israel, June 22, 1961; admitted, 1991, Israel. *Education:* Tel Aviv University (LL.B.). *Member:* Israel Bar Association. *LANGUAGES:* Hebrew and English. *PRACTICE AREAS:* Commercial Law; Tort Law; Insurance Law; Medical Malpractice Law; Real Estate Transactions and Land Registration.

YAGEL ADORAM, born Tel Aviv, Israel, May 14, 1965; admitted, 1993, Israel. *Education:* University of Bar Ilan (LL.B.). *Member:* Israel Bar Association. *LANGUAGES:* English and Hebrew. *PRACTICE AREAS:* Corporate Law; Contract and Commercial Law; Real Estate Transactions and Land Registration.

GAL CHET, born Rehovot, Israel, September 19, 1966; admitted, 1994, Israel. *Education:* Hebrew University of Jerusalem (LL.B.). *Member:* Israel Bar Association. *LANGUAGES:* English and Hebrew. *PRACTICE AREAS:* Corporate Law; Commercial Law; Securities Law.

OFER DORON, born Tel Aviv, Israel, August 23, 1966; admitted, 1994, Israel. *Education:* Tel Aviv University (LL.B.). *Member:* Israel Bar Association. *LANGUAGES:* English and Hebrew. *PRACTICE AREAS:* Corporate Law; Contract and Commercial Law; Litigation; Tort Law; Insurance Law; Medical Malpractice Law.

RACHEL BAR-EL, born Tel Aviv, Israel, November 1946; admitted, 1970, Israel. *Education:* Hebrew University of Jerusalem (LL.B.). *Member:* Israel Bar Association. *LANGUAGES:* Hebrew and English. *PRACTICE AREAS:* Real Estate Transactions and Land Registration.

CONSULTANTS

MAX KRITZMAN, born Chicago, Illinois, October 6, 1914; admitted, 1941, Israel. *Education:* University College, University of London (LL.B.). *Member:* Israel Bar Association (Deputy Chairman, Disciplinary Court, 1970-1977). (Retired). *LANGUAGES:* Hebrew and English.

HAGGAI CARMON, born Israel, November 5, 1944; admitted, 1983, Israel. *Education:* St. John's University (M.A. Hons.; Cert. International Law, Hons., 1986); Tel-Aviv University Law School (LL.B. cum laude, 1981). Lecturer, Contract Law, The Technion Israel Institute of Technology, Extension Division, 1982. Vice President, Israel American Chamber of Commerce, 1983. Chief Delegate (Hon.) of the Israeli Labor Party to the U.S., 1985-1987. *Member:* Association of the Bar of the City of New York; American and International Bar Associations. *LANGUAGES:* Hebrew, English and French.

Languages: Hebrew, English, French, Arabic and Yiddish.

SELIGSOHN & GABRIELI

60 ROTHSCHILD BOULEVARD
P.O. BOX 1426
TEL AVIV 61 013, ISRAEL
Telephone: (03) 566-1446
Cable Address: SELPATENT
Facsimile: 972-3- 560-8458; 972-3-560-8398

Industrial and Intellectual Property Law.

ARNAN GABRIELI, born Haifa, Israel, January 15, 1934; admitted, 1960, Israel. *Education:* Faculty of Law, Hebrew University, Jerusalem (M.J.). Editor, Hapraklit, (The Attorney), Israel Bar's Quarterly Review, 1980—. Contributor, "Pinner's World Unfair Competition Law," 1978. Lecturer, Industrial Property, Tel Aviv University, Faculty of Law, 1972—. *LANGUAGES:* Hebrew, English, German and French.

ASSOCIATES

DAVID BLUM, born Roumania, April 14, 1947; admitted, 1983, Israel. *Education:* University of Connecticut, School of Engineering, Stors, Connecticut (E.E. Computers Option); University of Tel Aviv (LL.B.). *LANGUAGES:* Hebrew, English and German.

ALFRED THEE, born Germany, February 2, 1932. registered as Patent Attorney, 1979, Israel. *Education:* Yeshiva University, USA (B.A. Chemistry, 1954); Rabbinical Ordination (1956); Brooklyn College (M.S. Chemistry, 1964). Consultant for Patent Matters, Ben-Gurion University of the Negev, 1974-1984. *Member:* American Chemical Society (Member, Division of Chemistry and Law, 1987). *LANGUAGES:* English, Hebrew and German. *PRACTICE AREAS:* Chemicals and Chemistry.

ADI LEVIT, born Israel, August 22, 1958; admitted, 1988, Israel. *Education:* Tel Aviv University (B.Sc. Biology, 1983; LL.B., 1987). *Member:* Israel Bar Association. *LANGUAGES:* Hebrew, English and French.

YIRMIYAHU M. BEN-DAVID, born London, England, July 1, 1961. *Education:* South Bank Polytechnic (B.Sc., Hons., Civil Engineering, 1984). registered as Patent Attorney, 1987, Israel. *LANGUAGES:* Hebrew, English and French.

ELIAV KORAKH, born Israel, June 11, 1964. registered as Patent Attorney, 1993, Israel. *Education:* Tel Aviv University (B.Sc. Physics, 1990). *LANGUAGES:* Hebrew, English and French.

Languages: Hebrew, English, German and French.

SHIBOLETH, YISRAELI, ROBERTS, YERUSHALMI, ZISMAN & HOLENDER

Established in 1973

46 MONTEFIORE STREET
TEL AVIV 65201, ISRAEL
Telephone: 972 (3) 5663311
Fax: 972 (3) 5663326

New York, New York Office: Yerushalmi, Shiboleth, Yisraeli & Roberts. Empire State Building, 60th Floor, 350 Fifth Avenue, 10118. Telephone: (212) 244-2400. Fax: (212) 563-7108.

Amsterdam, Netherlands Office: Yerushalmi Shiboleth, Yisraeli, Roberts & Kuttner, Brada Advocaten, Koningslaan 14, 1075 AC Amsterdam, The Netherlands. Telephone: (0)20 676 6323. Fax (0)20 673 9777.

MEMBERS OF FIRM

AMNON SHIBOLETH, born Haifa, Israel, 1943; admitted, 1968, Israel; 1983, New York. *Education:* Hebrew University of Jerusalem (LL.B., 1967). *Member:* New York State and Israel Bar Associations; National Tribunal of Code of Ethics. *LANGUAGES:* Hebrew, English, German and Portuguese.

YAACOV YISRAELI, born Lithuania, 1939; admitted, 1968, Israel; 1980, New York. *Education:* Hebrew University of Jerusalem (1968). Vice President, Israel-American Chamber of Commerce. *Member:* New York State and Israel Bar Associations. *LANGUAGES:* Hebrew and English.

RICHARD M. ROBERTS, born Kew Gardens, New York, 1941; admitted, 1968, Israel. *Education:* Hebrew University, Jerusalem (LL.B., 1967). Member of the Board, Israel-Japan, Chamber of Commerce. *Member:* Israel Bar Association. *LANGUAGES:* Hebrew and English.

JOSEPH YERUSHALMI, born Jerusalem, 1940; admitted, 1969, Israel; 1976, New York. *Education:* Hebrew University of Jerusalem (1968).

(This Listing Continued)

Member: New York State and Israel Bar Associations. (Resident, New York Office). *LANGUAGES:* Hebrew and English.

ITZHAK ZISMAN, born Poland, 1937; admitted, 1965, Israel; 1992, New York. *Education:* Hebrew University of Jerusalem (LL.B., 1964). *Member:* Israel Bar Association. *LANGUAGES:* Hebrew, English and Polish.

DR. ZEEV HOLENDER, born Russia, 1957; admitted, 1983, Israel; 1986, New York. *Education:* Tel Aviv University Law School (LL.B., cum laude, 1982); Harvard Law School (S.J.D., 1986). Lecturer: Taxation and Corporate Taxation, Tel Aviv University, Faculty of Law; Commercial Law, Tel Aviv University Faculty of Business Administration; Taxation, Department of External Studies, Haifa University. *Member:* New York State and Israel Bar Associations. *LANGUAGES:* Hebrew and English.

SHAI KUTTNER, born Tel Aviv, Israel, 1960; admitted, 1986, Israel; 1988, New York. *Education:* Hebrew University Law School (LL.B., 1985); Amsterdam Law School (European Community Law, 1991). *Member:* Israel and New York State Bar Associations. (Resident, Amsterdam Office). *LANGUAGES:* Hebrew, English and French.

LIOR AVIRAM, born Israel, 1962; admitted, 1989, Israel. *Education:* Tel Aviv University Law School (LL.B., 1988). Member of Board, Israel - Italy Chamber of Commerce. *Member:* Israel Bar Association. *LANGUAGES:* Hebrew, English and French.

HELENA BEILIN, born Germany; admitted, 1974, Israel. *Education:* Tel Aviv University Law School (LL.B., 1973). *Member:* Israel Bar Association. *LANGUAGES:* Hebrew, English and Polish.

HILLEL ISH-SHALOM, born Jerusalem, 1958; admitted, 1985, Israel. *Education:* Hebrew University of Jerusalem (LL.B. cum laude, 1984). Editor, "Mishpatim" - Law Review. Lecturer, Corporations and Taxation, Hebrew University, Jerusalem, Tel Aviv University, Faculty of Law. *Member:* Israel Bar Association. *LANGUAGES:* Hebrew and English.

ASSOCIATES

ORIT STERNHELL, born Israel, 1965; admitted, 1990, Israel. *Education:* Tel Aviv University Law School (LL.B., 1989). *Member:* Israel Bar Association. *LANGUAGES:* Hebrew and English.

DINA FRANKENTHAL, born Boston, Massachusetts, June 2, 1960; admitted, 1986, Israel; 1988, New York. *Education:* Hebrew University, Jerusalem (LL.B., with distinction, 1984); Harvard University Law School (1985-1986). Editorial Board Member, Hebrew University Law Journal "Mishpatim," 1982-1983. Associate, Davis Polk & Wardwell, New York, N.Y., 1987-1990. *Member:* American Bar Association; Israel Bar Association. *LANGUAGES:* Hebrew and English.

GIL ARIE, born Israel, 1964; admitted, 1992, Israel. *Education:* Tel Aviv University Law School (LL.B., 1991). *Member:* Israel Bar Association. *LANGUAGES:* Hebrew and English.

RONEN ADINI, born Israel, 1963; admitted, 1992, Israel. *Education:* Hebrew University Law School, Jerusalem (LL.B., 1991); Hebrew University, Jerusalem (M.A., International Relations, cum laude, 1991). *Member:* Israel Bar Association. *LANGUAGES:* Hebrew, English and French.

MARC D. LEVE, born Buffalo, New York, 1957; admitted, 1984, Israel; 1993, New York. *Education:* Bar Ilan University, Ramat Gan, Israel (LL.B., 1984). Military Prosecutor, Lieutenant, Israel Defense Forces (1982-1985); Prosecutor, Israel Bar Association Disciplinary Tribunal, Tel Aviv (1988-1990). *Member:* Israel Bar Association; Association of Civil Rights in Israel; American and New York Bar Associations; Association of the Bar of the City of New York. [Prosecutor, Lieutenant, Israel Defense Forces (1982-1985)]. (Resident, New York Office). *LANGUAGES:* English, Hebrew and German.

OFER SHAPIRA, born Israel, 1967; admitted, 1991, Israel. *Education:* Bar Ilan University, Ramat Gan, Israel (LL.B., 1989; LL.M., 1993). Military Prosecutor, Captain, Israel Defense Forces (1989-1994). *Member:* Israel Bar Association. *LANGUAGES:* Hebrew and English.

HEATHER ADRIENNE STONE, born Washington, D.C., U.S.A., 1964; admitted, 1988, New Jersey and U.S. District Court of New Jersey; 1993, Israel. *Education:* Wellesley College, Wellesley, MA (B.A., 1985); Rutgers University School of Law, Camden, N.J. (Juris Doctor Degree, 1988); The Tecnion, Israel Institute of Technology, Haifa, Israel (Candidate for Philosophy Doctorate Degree). *Member:* Israel Bar Association; New Jersey State Bar Association. *LANGUAGES:* Hebrew, English and French.

CHAIM (JACK) CYMBERKNOPF, born Caracas, Venezuela, 1958; admitted, 1983, Venezuela; 1988, Israel. *Education:* Universidad Católica

(This Listing Continued)

Andrés Bello, Caracas, Venezuela (J.D. Degree, 1982); New York University School of Law (LL.M., 1985); Queen Mary & Westfield College, University of London. *Member:* Venezuelan Bar and Israel Bar Associations. (Resident, Amsterdam Office). *LANGUAGES:* English, Hebrew, Spanish and Italian.

MEIR OREN, born Israel, 1963; admitted, 1994, Israel. *Education:* Bar Ilan University, Ramat Gan, Israel (B.A., in Economics and Political Science, 1989; LL.B., 1993). *Member:* Israel Bar Association. *LANGUAGES:* Hebrew and English.

AVIV HILLO, born Israel, 1964; admitted, 1994, Israel. *Education:* Tel Aviv University Law School (LL.B., 1993). *Member:* Israel Bar Association. *LANGUAGES:* Hebrew, English and Arabic.

ITAI BRAFMAN, born Israel, 1985; admitted, 1995, Israel. *Education:* Tel Aviv University Law School (LL.B., 1994). *Member:* Israel Bar Association. *LANGUAGES:* Hebrew and English.

SHINE, HUNTER, MARTIN & CO.

119 ROTHSCHILD BLVD.
TEL AVIV 65271, ISRAEL
Telephone: (972) 3-562-0022
Fax: (972) 3-562-0031

General Civil Practice, Corporate Law, Securities, Tax, Finance, International Investments, Real Estate, Estates/Trusts, International Trade, Family Law, Litigation, Extradition.

FIRM PROFILE: The firm consists of 3 partners, 8 associates, 5 articled clerks (law graduates awaiting admission), and a financial manager. The firm specializes in matters involving multi-national interests or having multi-national ramifications. Lawyers at the firm are admitted to practice in Israel, Europe, the U.S., England, South America, South Africa, and the Ukraine. Correspondence can be carried out in Hebrew, English, German, Dutch, Spanish, Portuguese, French, Russian, Ukrainian, Hungarian and other languages.

MEMBERS OF FIRM

MICHAEL SHINE, born London, England, 1946; admitted, 1967, England; 1970, Israel. *Education:* University of London. Former Member, Ministry of Justice Committee for Revision of the Israeli Corporation Law. *LANGUAGES:* English, Hebrew, French.

MICHAEL HUNTER, born London, England, 1943; admitted, 1964, England; 1981, Israel. *Education:* London School of Economics. Former Partner, Teacher, Stern, Hunter & Selby, London, England. *LANGUAGES:* English, Hebrew.

DAVID MARTIN, born New York, N.Y., 1951; admitted, 1976, New York; 1977, District of Columbia; 1981, Israel. *Education:* Columbia University Law School. Adjunct Professor, International Business, Boston University Masters Program at Ben Gurion University, Israel. Editor, Columbia Law Review. Former Law Clerk to the Hon. Lee Gagliardi, US District Court, Southern District of New York. Former Adjunct Professor of Law, Georgetown University, Washington, D.C. Former Associate, Fried, Frank, Harris, Shriver & Kampelman, NYC and Washington, D.C. *LANGUAGES:* English, Hebrew, French, Yiddish.

ASSOCIATES

JITZCHAK ALSTER, born Amsterdam, The Netherlands, 1953; admitted, 1981, Israel; 1992, New York. *Education:* Hebrew University Law School, Jerusalem. Formerly: Director of the General Law Division, Ministry of Foreign Affairs; Legal Advisor to the Israeli Negotiating Team on the US-Israel Free Trade Area Agreement. Adjunct Professor, International Business, Boston University Masters Program at Ben Gurion University, Israel. Former Teacher, Public International Law, Hebrew University. *Member:* International Law Association (Secretary, Israeli Branch). *LANGUAGES:* Hebrew, English, Dutch. *PRACTICE AREAS:* International Trade Law.

LESLIE HENAN, born Bethal, South Africa, 1956; admitted, 1985, Israel. *Education:* Tel Aviv University Law School. *LANGUAGES:* Hebrew, English. *PRACTICE AREAS:* Real Estate Transactions.

BEN HALPERN, born Manchester, England, 1945; admitted, 1967, England; 1985, Israel. *Education:* University of Manchester. Former Partner, Howarth, Goodman & Co., Manchester, England. *LANGUAGES:* English, Hebrew. *PRACTICE AREAS:* Estates; Trusts; Intellectual Property.

(This Listing Continued)

SHINE, HUNTER, MARTIN & CO., Tel Aviv—Continued

LEON LEWIS, born Durban, South Africa, 1926; admitted, 1951, South Africa; 1986, Israel. *Education:* Natal University, South Africa. Former Partner, Marcus, Lewis Robinson & Goulding, Durban, South Africa. *LANGUAGES:* English, Hebrew. *PRACTICE AREAS:* International Investment Law.

REUBEN TOBELEM, born Rio de Janeiro, Brazil, 1922; admitted, 1973, Brazil; 1983, Israel. *Education:* University of Rio de Janeiro, Brazil. *LANGUAGES:* Portuguese, Spanish, English, Hebrew.

ISRAEL SHIMONI, born Ashkelon, Israel, 1962; admitted, 1989, Israel. *Education:* Hebrew University Law School, Jerusalem. *LANGUAGES:* Hebrew, English. *PRACTICE AREAS:* Litigation.

GIORA LANDAU, born Haifa, Israel, 1959; admitted, 1988, Israel. *Education:* Tel Aviv University Law School. Member, Executive Committee, Association for Civil Rights in Israel (Tel Aviv Branch). *LANGUAGES:* Hebrew, English. *PRACTICE AREAS:* Litigation.

EFRAT MANOACH, born Israel, 1968; admitted, 1994, Israel. *Education:* Brunel University. *LANGUAGES:* Hebrew, English and French.

FINANCIAL MANAGER

HAROLD RABKIN, born Capetown, South Africa, 1930. Certified Public Accountant, 1954, South Africa; 1956, England. *Education:* University of Cape Town.

RONIT SCHWARTZ, born Israel, 1968; (Not admitted in Israel). *Education:* Tel Aviv University. (Articled Clerk). *LANGUAGES:* Hebrew and English.

RAPHAEL LANTSMAN, born Soviet Union, 1945; admitted, 1975, Ukraine (Not admitted in Israel). *Education:* University of Lvov. *LANGUAGES:* Hebrew, Ukrainian, Russian and German.

RAFI NEZER, born Israel, 1962; (Not admitted in Israel). *Education:* Tel Aviv University. (Articled Clerk). *LANGUAGES:* Hebrew and English.

ALON NOKRAI, born Israel, 1967; (Not admitted in Israel). *Education:* Brunel University. (Articled Clerk). *LANGUAGES:* Hebrew and English.

YUVAL BAR-DOV, born Israel, 1961; (Not admitted in Israel). *Education:* Tel Aviv University (Articled Clerk). *LANGUAGES:* Hebrew, English and Hungarian.

ZVI TAMIR & CO.

70 HEY IYAR STREET
TEL AVIV 62198, ISRAEL
Telephone: 972-3-454186; 454187/8/9
Facsimile: 972-3-5468519
Telex: 361411 TARON IL

General Civil Practice, International Trade, Intellectual Property, Licensing and Know-how Agreements, Transnational Joint-Ventures, Distributorship, Agency and Franchise, Banking and Finance, Corporate.

MEMBERS OF FIRM

ZVI N. TAMIR, born Tel-Aviv, Israel, October 26, 1935; admitted, 1959, Israel. *Education:* Tel-Aviv University (LL.B., 1957; M. Jur., 1959); Hebrew University of Jerusalem (D. Jur., 1972). Senior Lecturer: Faculty of Law, Bar Ilan University; Israeli Export Institute; Israeli Chamber of Commerce. Author: "Retention of Title," IBA conference 169 (New York, 1986); "Conflict of Sellers and Buyers General Terms and Conditions," IBA conference 155 (New York, 1986); "Israeli Law on Protection of Intellectual Property Transfers: An Overview, Licensing Agreements: Patents, Know-How, Trade Secrets and Software," (K. Yelpala, D.R. Worley, D. Campbell (Ed.) Salzburg, 1988); "Developments in Israel's Regulations of Trade," (Tel Aviv, 1988); "Practical Legal Aspects of Franchising in Israel," (Matthew Bender New York); "Immigration and Nationality-The Israeli View," (Nijhoff, Amsterdam, 1992); "Recent Trends in Israeli Adjudication Regarding Retention of Title," (Kluwer, the Netherlands, 1992). *Member:* Israel Bar Association; The International Bar Association Society for Medicine and Law; International Advisory Board, The Transnational Lawyer; FOI, Fellow of The Offshore Institute; AIPPI, Association Internationale pour la Protection de la Propriete Industrielle; Parker School of Foreign and Com-

(This Listing Continued)

parative Law, Columbia University, New York City (Member, Arbitration Panel); The Israeli Institute for Business Arbitration (Member, Arbitration Panel). *LANGUAGES:* Hebrew and English.

EREL J. TAMIR, born Tel-Aviv, Israel, August 30, 1962; admitted, 1989, Israel. *Education:* Bar-Ilan University (LL.B., 1988). *Member:* Israel Bar Association. *LANGUAGES:* Hebrew and English.

ASSOCIATES

MICHAL ILANI, born Beer Sheba, Israel, January 3, 1964; admitted, 1990, Israel. *Education:* Tel-Aviv University (LL.B., 1989). *Member:* Israel Bar Association. *LANGUAGES:* Hebrew, English and French.

MICHAEL TAMIR, born Oklahoma City, Oklahoma, U.S.A., May 2, 1962; admitted, 1990, Israel. *Education:* Tel-Aviv University (LL.B., 1989). *Member:* Israel Bar Association. *LANGUAGES:* Hebrew and English.

TAMAR TAMIR, born Tel-Aviv, Israel, July 21, 1967; admitted, 1992, Israel. *Education:* Bar-Ilan University (LL.B., 1992). *Member:* Israel Bar Association. *LANGUAGES:* Hebrew and English.

GIDEON FISHER, born 1965; admitted, 1994, Israel. *Education:* Leeds University, U.K. (LL.B., Honours); Cambridge University, U.K. (LL.M.). Author: "Israeli Supreme Court - Documentary Credit," European Transport Law; Journal of Law &b Economics (Vol. XXVIII No. 4 - 1993) (Nov. '93); "Israeli Bank's Liability Under Documentary Credit," Lloyd's Maritime & Commercial Law Quarterly, Lloyd's of London Press (1-144, Part 1) (Feb. '93); "Bank's Liability in Negligence," Journal of International Banking Law, Sweet & Maxwell/ESC Publishing (Vol. 7 Issue 11) (Nov. '93). Associate Lecturer, in International Law, Faculty of Law, Tel-Aviv University. *Member:* Israel Bar Association. *LANGUAGES:* Hebrew and English.

OF COUNSEL

DAVID M. SASSOON, born Tel-Aviv, Israel, February 2, 1934; admitted, 1983, Israel. *Education:* Hebrew University of Jerusalem (M. Jur., 1956); Oxford University, U.K. (D. Phil., 1958). Author: interalia, "FOB Contracts," Stevens publication, 1960; "CIF & FOB Contracts, Vol. 5, British Shipping Law (Three Editions)," Stevens publication; "Documentary Credits," Schocken publication, 1986; "Insurance Law," Schocken publication, 1988; "International Contracting & Procurement for Development Projects," ILI publication, Georgetown University, 1982. Editor, "Judicial Enforcement of International Debt Obligations," ILI publication, Georgetown University, 1987. Member, Editorial Boards: Journal of Business Law; Israel Banking Quarterly. Previously Editor in Chief, Journal of Maritime Law & Commerce. Former Procurement Advisor to the World Bank. *Member:* American Arbitration Association (A.A.A.) (Member, of the Panel of Arbitrators). *LANGUAGES:* Hebrew and English.

MICHAEL I. TEPLOW LAW OFFICES

100 ALLENBY STREET
TEL AVIV 65815, ISRAEL
Telephone: 972-3-560-7780/5554
Facsimile: 972-3-566-0471

Corporate, Commercial, International, Tax, Securities, Estates, Litigation.

MICHAEL I. TEPLOW, born Boston, Massachusetts, June 28, 1961; admitted, 1987, New York; 1989, U.S. Tax Court; 1991, Israel. *Education:* Columbia College (B.A., cum laude, 1983); Columbia University School of Law (J.D., 1986); Honors-Parker Program in Int'l and Foreign Law. *Member:* Israel Bar Association; American Bar Association. *LANGUAGES:* English and Hebrew.

ZEEV WEISS & CO.

94 HAYARKON STREET
63903 TEL AVIV ISRAEL
Telephone: 972-3-527 0373
Facsimile: 972-3-524 1902

Offices also in Brussels and Tokyo.

Commercial, International Transactions, Corporate, Real Estate, Intellectual Property, Securities, Banking, Investments, Administrative Law, Litigation.

MEMBERS OF FIRM

ZEEV WEISS. *Education:* Tel Aviv (LL.B.). *Member:* Israel Bar Association.

(This Listing Continued)

ELLEN PORAT. *Education:* Tel Aviv (LL.B.). *Member:* Israel Bar Association.

ALAN PHILIP HITTER. *Education:* Tel Aviv (LL.B.); University of Brussels Law School. *Member:* Israel and Belgium Bar Associations. (Resident in Brussels).

DINA (COHEN) MASS. *Education:* Tel Aviv (LL.B.). *Member:* Israel Bar Association.

DAVID HELLER. *Education:* Tel Aviv (LL.B.). *Member:* Israel Bar Association. (Resident in Tokyo).

WILLIAM R. COHEN. *Education:* Rutgers University (B.A.); Yale Law School (J.D.). *Member:* Israel and New Jersey State Bar Associations.

Hebrew, English, French, German, Japanese, Flemish and Yiddish.

WEKSLER, BREGMAN & CO.

Established in 1936

13 ACHAD HA'AM STREET
TEL AVIV 65151, ISRAEL
Telephone: 972-3-5103870
Facsimile: 972-3-5103873

Mailing Address: P.O. Box 29621, Tel Aviv 61028

Commercial and Trade Law, Corporate Law, Banking Law, Securities, Real Estate, Planning and Construction Law, Finance and Investments, Foreign Currency Control Law, Commercial and International Transactions, General Litigation and Arbitration.

MEMBERS OF FIRM

JACOB WEKSLER, born Israel, 1936; admitted, 1962, Israel. *Education:* Hebrew University, Jerusalem (M.J., 1958). *Member:* Israel Bar Association. *LANGUAGES:* Hebrew, English.

URI BREGMAN, born Israel, 1953; admitted, 1980, Israel. *Education:* Tel Aviv University, Tel Aviv (LL.B., 1979). *LANGUAGES:* Hebrew, English.

ORA DVIR, born Israel, 1949; admitted, 1973, Israel. *Education:* Hebrew University, Jerusalem (LL.B., 1972). *Member:* Israel Bar Association. *LANGUAGES:* Hebrew, English.

ZVI CAFTORY, born Israel, 1942; admitted, 1986, Israel. *Education:* Tel Aviv University, Tel Aviv (LL.B., 1985). *Member:* Israel Bar Association. *LANGUAGES:* Hebrew, English.

AMIR CHEN, born Israel, 1958; admitted, 1987, Israel. *Education:* Hebrew University, Jerusalem (LL.B., 1986). *Member:* Israel Bar Association. *LANGUAGES:* Hebrew, English.

DORON DAN, born Israel, 1956; admitted, 1987, Israel. *Education:* Tel Aviv University, Tel Aviv (LL.B., 1986). *LANGUAGES:* Hebrew, English.

EREZ NACHTOMY, born Israel, 1961; admitted, 1989, Israel. *Education:* Tel Aviv University, Tel Aviv (LL.B., 1988). *Member:* Israel Bar Association. *LANGUAGES:* Hebrew, English.

ASSOCIATES

DOROTHY L. ROBBINS-FATTAL, born United States, 1952; admitted, 1977, Canada; 1981, Israel. *Education:* University of Alberta, Edmonton, Alberta, Canada (B.A., 1973); Osgoode Hall Law School, Toronto, Ontario, Canada (LL.B., 1976). *Member:* Barrister and Solicitor, Law Society of British Columbia; Canadian Bar Association; Israel Bar Association. *LANGUAGES:* English, Hebrew.

IRIT BIRAN, born Israel, 1965; admitted, 1990, Israel. *Education:* Hebrew University, Jerusalem (LL.B., 1989). *Member:* Israel Bar Association. *LANGUAGES:* Hebrew, English.

RONEN MATRY, born Israel, 1963; admitted, 1990, Israel. *Education:* Hebrew University, Jerusalem (LL.B., 1989). *Member:* Israel Bar Association. *LANGUAGES:* Hebrew, English.

SHARON GALLER-AHARONI, born Israel, 1967; admitted, 1994, Israel. *Education:* Tel Aviv University, Tel Aviv (LL.B., 1992). *Member:* Israel Bar Association. *LANGUAGES:* Hebrew, English.

OFER YANCOVICH, born Israel, 1964; admitted, 1994, Israel. *Education:* Tel Aviv University, Tel Aviv (LL.B., 1993). *Member:* Israel Bar Association. *LANGUAGES:* Hebrew, English.

(This Listing Continued)

TALY SALTON-YESHUA, born Israel, 1968; admitted, 1994, Israel. *Education:* Hebrew University, Jerusalem (LL.B., 1993). *Member:* Israel Bar Association. *LANGUAGES:* Hebrew, English.

OF COUNSEL

RON N. SALPETER, born Israel, 1961; admitted, 1989, Israel. *Education:* Tel Aviv University, Tel Aviv (LL.B., 1988); Osaka University, Japan (LL.M., 1993). *Member:* Israel Bar Association. *LANGUAGES:* Hebrew, English, French and Japanese.

YEMIN, KAN-TOR, SCHWARTZ & CO.

Established in 1983

8 SHAUL HAMELECH BOULEVARD
TEL AVIV 64733, ISRAEL
Telephone: (972) 3 693 8425
Telefax: (972) 3 693 8427

Netanya Office: 14 Shtamper Street, 42402. Telephone: 972-9-617336. Fax: 972-9-619266.

U.S. Israeli and International Immigration Law, Real Property and Construction, International Commercial Law, Torts Law, Notary.

MEMBERS OF FIRM

MOSHE YEMIN, born Israel, 1955; admitted, 1983, Israel. *Education:* Tel Aviv University (LL.B., 1982). *LANGUAGES:* Hebrew and English. *PRACTICE AREAS:* Commercial Real Estate; Taxation and Investment; Planning and Land Use.

TSVI KAN-TOR, born Israel, 1953; admitted, 1984, Israel. *Education:* Tel Aviv University (LL.B., 1982). *LANGUAGES:* Hebrew and English. *PRACTICE AREAS:* Commercial Law; Real Estate Finance.

LIAM SCHWARTZ, born Boston, Massachusetts, 1957; admitted, 1984, New York and New Jersey; 1987, Israel. *Education:* John Hopkins University (B.A., 1979); Benjamin N. Cardozo Law School (LL.B., 1983). Author: *United States Immigration Law* (Hebrew language). *Member:* American Immigration Lawyers Association. *LANGUAGES:* English and Hebrew. *PRACTICE AREAS:* U.S. Israeli and International Business Immigration; Consular Law; Residency Permits; Employment Contracts.

REVA AMIR, born Chicago, Illinois, 1963; admitted, 1988, Israel. *Education:* Tel Aviv University (LL.B., 1987). *LANGUAGES:* Hebrew and English. *PRACTICE AREAS:* Torts Law; Medical Malpractice.

SHRAGA F. JACOBS, born Johannesburg, South Africa, 1933; admitted, 1958, South Africa; 1987, Israel. *Education:* University of Witwatersrand (Dip. Law, 1957). Authorized Notary before U.S. and other English-speaking Embassies in Israel. *LANGUAGES:* English and Hebrew.

YOSSIFOFF, AMIR, COHEN & CO. LAW OFFICES

Established in 1991

6 WISSOTSKY STREET
TEL AVIV 62338, ISRAEL
Telephone: 972-3-6042323
Fax: 972-3-6044222

Mailing Address: P.O. Box 33026, Tel-Aviv, Israel 61330

London, England Office: 26 Hendon Avenue, M3 1UE. Telephone: 0044-81-3430424. Fax: 0044-81-3430792.

Firm engaged in Israeli Law Practice. Entitled to plead before the Israeli Courts.
Tax Law, Real Estate Law, Computer and Technology Law, Securities and Finance Law, Corporate Law, General International Trade Law, Labor Law, Inheritance Law, Litigation and Arbitration.

FIRM PROFILE: Established in 1991 by merging the law practices of Y. Yossifoff (established in 1984) and Arie Amir (established in 1983). The firm has a broadly based practice with a reputation for offering a wide range of legal services. The client base consists primarily of corporate clients from Israel that receive services from the Firm in all of the legal matters on a regular and current basis. The firm has three partners, 12 assistants and a large office staff. The firm recently opened a branch in London, England.

(This Listing Continued)

AF53B

YOSSIFOFF, AMIR, COHEN & CO. LAW OFFICES, Tel Aviv—Continued

PARTNERS

YORAM YOSSIFOFF, born Tel-Aviv, Israel, September 27, 1953; admitted, 1979, Israel. *Education:* Tel-Aviv University (LL.B., 1978). *Member:* Israel Bar Association (Judge, District Disciplinary Tribunal, 1992—); International Bar Association. (Resident Partner London Office). *LANGUAGES:* Hebrew, English, French, Bulgarian. *PRACTICE AREAS:* Tax Law; Real Estate Law; Computer and Technology Law; Corporate and Securities Law; Tax and Commercial Litigation.

AYALA AMIR, born Tel-Aviv, Israel, August 14, 1959; admitted, 1987, Israel. *Education:* Tel-Aviv University (LL.B., 1986). *Member:* Israel Bar Association. *LANGUAGES:* Hebrew and English. *PRACTICE AREAS:* Real Estate Law; Corporate Law; Commercial Law.

AVI COHEN, born Tel Aviv, Israel, October 25, 1950; admitted, 1986, Israel. *Education:* Tel-Aviv University (LL.B., 1984); The Hebrew University (B.A. Oriental Studies, 1972). *Member:* Israel Bar Association. *LANGUAGES:* Hebrew, English, Arabic, Italian and French. *PRACTICE AREAS:* Commercial Law; Intellectual Property Law; Real Estate Law; Litigation.

ASSOCIATES

AVIGAIL GOLDSTEIN, born Bombay, India, January 6, 1955; admitted, 1987, Israel. *Education:* Tel-Aviv University (LL.B., 1986); Bar-Ilan University (B.A., English Literature and Linguistics, 1978). *Member:* Israel Bar Association. *LANGUAGES:* Hebrew and English. *PRACTICE AREAS:* Commercial Law; Corporate Law; Computer Law; Labor Law; Litigation.

GADI OPPENHEIMER, born Tel-Aviv, Israel, January 26, 1949; admitted, 1988, Israel. *Education:* Tel-Aviv University (LL.B., 1975). Public Representative in Police Disciplinary Court. *Member:* Israel Bar Association; IPA-Information Processing Association of Israel; Public Council for the Protection of Privacy. *LANGUAGES:* Hebrew and English. *PRACTICE AREAS:* Computer Law; Corporate Law.

RAKEFET HAHAM-SHEFFER, born Bat-Yam, Israel, October 17, 1962; admitted, 1991, Israel. *Education:* The Hebrew University (LL.B., 1990); The Hebrew University (B.A., Economics and Business Administration, 1989). *Member:* Israel Bar Association. *LANGUAGES:* Hebrew and English. *PRACTICE AREAS:* Commercial Law; Corporate Law; Securities Law.

ETTI KOREN, born Petach-Tikva, Israel, March 1, 1966; admitted, 1993, Israel. *Education:* Tel-Aviv University (LL.B., 1991). *Member:* Israel Bar Association. *LANGUAGES:* Hebrew and English. *PRACTICE AREAS:* Commercial Law; Real Estate Law; Computer Law; Litigation.

NITZAN SHAHAM, born Tel-Aviv, Israel, November 27, 1963; admitted, 1993, Israel. *Education:* The Hebrew University (LL.B. honors, 1991). *Member:* Israel Bar Association. *LANGUAGES:* Hebrew and English. *PRACTICE AREAS:* Corporate Law; Contract Law; Real Estate Law; Intellectual Property Law; Litigation.

AVI GRODBERG, born Givataim, Israel, September 28, 1967; admitted, 1993, Israel. *Education:* Tel-Aviv University (LL.B., 1992). *Member:* Israel Bar Association. *LANGUAGES:* Hebrew and English. *PRACTICE AREAS:* Commercial Law; Real Estate; Land Tax Law; Corporate Law; Litigation.

EREZ YAKUEL, born Tel-Aviv, Israel, September 10, 1965; admitted, 1993. *Education:* Sheffield University, England (LL.B., 1991). *Member:* Israel Bar Association. *LANGUAGES:* Hebrew and English. *PRACTICE AREAS:* Commercial Law; Corporate Law; Intellectual Property Law; Contract Law and Litigation.

OF COUNSEL

ARIE AMIR, born Jerusalem, December 16, 1951; admitted, 1981, Israel. *Education:* The Hebrew University (LL.B., 1980). General Manager of the Ministry of Economics and Planning, 1994. *Member:* Israel Bar Association. *LANGUAGES:* Hebrew and English. *PRACTICE AREAS:* Real Estate and Commercial Projects.

ZADOK, STRIKS, SELLA & CO.

Established in 1956

38 ROTHSCHILD BLVD.
TEL AVIV 66 883, ISRAEL
Telephone: 3-5103232
Cable Address: "Zadokco, Tel Aviv"
Fax: 3-5606791

Mailing Address: P.O. Box 1234, TEL AVIV 61012, ISRAEL

Commercial, Corporate, Tax, Investments, International Business, Constitutional, Administrative and Securities Law.

HAIM J. ZADOK, born 1913; admitted, 1945, Israel. *Education:* Jerusalem Law School. *Member:* The Israel Bar.

HAIM STRIKS, born 1927; admitted, 1953, Israel; admitted as Legal Consultant, 1981, New York. *Education:* School of Law and Economics, Tel Aviv (LL.B., 1952). *Member:* The Israel Bar.

MENACHEM SELLA, born 1940; admitted, 1968, Israel. *Education:* Hebrew University, Jerusalem (LL.B., 1967). *Member:* The Israel Bar; The Association of the Bar of the City of New York.

ILAN SHAVIT-STRIKS, born 1951; admitted, 1981, Israel. *Education:* Tel Aviv University (LL.B., 1979). *Member:* The Israel Bar.

TZACHI FELDMAN, born 1958; admitted, 1986, Israel. *Education:* Tel Aviv University (LL.B., 1984). *Member:* The Israel Bar.

EYAL ROSOVSKY, born 1959; admitted, 1987, Israel. *Education:* Hebrew University, Jerusalem (LL.M., 1986). *Member:* The Israel Bar.

EHOOD SCHNEIDER, born 1956; admitted, 1987, Israel. *Education:* Hebrew University, Jerusalem (LL.B., 1986). *Member:* The Israel Bar.

TAGAR AMIEL, born 1960; admitted, 1987, Israel. *Education:* Hebrew University, Jerusalem (LL.B., 1986). *Member:* The Israel Bar.

GIDEON TOLEDANO, born 1959; admitted, 1988, Israel; 1991, Michigan. *Education:* Hebrew University (LL.B., 1987); University of Michigan (LL.M., 1990). *Member:* The Israel Bar; The State Bar of Michigan.

YIZHAK BLAU, born 1963; admitted, 1991, Israel. *Education:* Bar-Ilan University (LL.B., 1990). *Member:* The Israel Bar.

DROR STRUM, born 1963; admitted, 1992, Israel. *Education:* Tel Aviv University (LL.B., 1990). *Member:* The Israel Bar.

DR. HILLEL SOMMER, born 1961; admitted, 1992, New York; 1994, Israel. *Education:* Tel Aviv University (LL.B., 1988); Yale Law School (LL.M., 1989; J.S.D., 1993). *Member:* The Israel Bar; The New York Bar.

Languages: Hebrew, English, French, German, Yiddish and Polish.

ZELLERMAYER & PELOSSOF, ADVOCATES

EUROPE HOUSE
37 SHAUL HAMELECH BOULEVARD
TEL AVIV 64928, ISRAEL
Telephone: 972-3-695-4222
Telecopier: 972-3-695-2884

London, England Office: Zellermayer, Pelossof & Schiffer, 46 Mount Street, W1Y 5RD. Telephone: 44-71-629-1920. Telecopier: 44-71-408-0202.

Corporate Finance, Acquisitions, Divestitures and Mergers, Public and Private Offerings, Transfer of Technology, R & D Transactions, International Business, Trade and Finance, Contract, Personal Property Leasing and Lease Financing, Secured Transactions, Tax Law.

PARTNERS

MICHAEL ZELLERMAYER, born Israel, September 22, 1942; admitted, 1968, Israel; 1977, New York. *Education:* Hebrew University, Jerusalem (LL.B., 1967). *Member:* New York State (Member, Corporation, Banking and Business Law Sections), American and Israel Bar Associations. *LANGUAGES:* Hebrew, English and German.

AVI D. PELOSSOF, born Tel-Aviv, Israel, September 1, 1948; admitted, 1974, Israel. *Education:* Tel-Aviv University (LL.B., 1974). Managing Director, Elite Ltd., 1980-1986. Member of the Board: Israel Aircraft Industries Ltd., 1987; Tel-Aviv Stock Exchange, 1987. *LANGUAGES:* Hebrew, English, French and Spanish.

(This Listing Continued)

ELI MEI-TAL, born Israel, December 16, 1943; admitted, 1973, Israel. *Education:* Tel-Aviv University (LL.B., 1972). Assistant Lecturer, Law of Tort, Tel-Aviv University, 1973-1976. Lecturer, Labor Law, Haifa University, Faculty of Law. *LANGUAGES:* Hebrew and English.

MICHAEL BARNEA, born Tel-Aviv, Israel, March 14, 1956; admitted, 1985, Israel. *Education:* Tel-Aviv University, Faculty of Law (LL.B., 1984). Assistant Lecturer, Taxation, Departments of Accounting and Business Administration, Tel-Aviv University, 1985-1986. *Member:* Israel Bar Association. *LANGUAGES:* Hebrew, English and French.

REVITAL KEREM, born Tel-Aviv, Israel, June 17, 1962; admitted, 1987, Israel. *Education:* Tel-Aviv University (LL.B., Cum Laude, 1986). Associate Editor, Tel-Aviv University Law Review, 1984-1985. *Member:* Israel Bar Association. *LANGUAGES:* Hebrew and English.

ACHU FRANK, born Israel, September 9, 1958; admitted, 1989, Israel. *Education:* Tel-Aviv University (B.A., 1979; LL.B., 1988). Member, Institute of Certified Public Accountants, Israel. *Member:* Israel Bar Association. *LANGUAGES:* Hebrew and English.

GUY TSAFRIR, born Israel, March 18, 1962; admitted, 1991, Israel. *Education:* Tel-Aviv University (B.A., 1991; LL.B., 1991). *Member:* Israel Bar Association. *LANGUAGES:* Hebrew and English.

GIL MOORE, born Tel-Aviv, Israel, September 19, 1963; admitted, 1989, Israel. *Education:* Tel-Aviv University (LL.B., 1988); Oxford University (B.C.L., 1991). *Member:* Israel Bar Association. *LANGUAGES:* Hebrew and English.

RONIT INBAR, born Israel, June 17, 1962; admitted, 1992, New York; 1993, Israel. *Education:* Boston University (J.D., Cum Laude, 1992). *Member:* New York State, American and Israel Bar Association. *LANGUAGES:* Hebrew, English and German.

ARIE GOTAL, born Haifa, Israel, April 16, 1963; admitted, 1993, Israel. *Education:* Tel-Aviv University (LL.B., 1992). *Member:* Israel Bar Association. *LANGUAGES:* Hebrew, English, Portuguese and Spanish.

NURIT AMODAY, born Tel-Aviv, Israel, April 13, 1964; admitted, 1994, Israel. *Education:* Tel-Aviv University (LL.B., 1993). *Member:* Israel Bar Association. *LANGUAGES:* Hebrew and English.

ZUR & FRIEDMAN

AVGAD TOWER
5 JABOTINSKY STREET
TEL AVIV (RAMAT-GAN) 52520, ISRAEL
Telephone: 972-3-7526170
Telecopier: 972-3-7526169

Commercial Law, Foreign Investments, Securities Law, Real Estate, Franchise Law, General Litigation.

MEMBERS OF FIRM

ISRAEL ZUR, born February 14, 1944; admitted, 1970, Israel. *Education:* Hebrew University School of Law (LL.B., 1968). President, Israel Jaycees, 1973-1974. Member: Board of Governors, Hapoel Holon Sports Association, 1986—; Board of Management, Israel Franchise Association, 1988—. *Member:* Israel Bar Association. *LANGUAGES:* Hebrew and English.

ROBERT FRIEDMAN, born December 30, 1957; admitted, 1982, New York; 1985, Israel. *Education:* Brooklyn College of the City University of New York (B.A., magna cum laude, 1978); New York University School of Law (J.D., 1981). Associate, Stroock & Stroock & Lavan, New York, N.Y., 1981-1983. Author: "Franchising in Israel," 2 Franchise Legal Digest 11, 1990. General Counsel, Israel-Asia Chamber of Commerce, 1988-1991. Lecturer: International Commercial Transactions, School of Law, Israel College of Administration, 1991-1992; Bar-Ilan University, School of Law, 1993—. *Member:* New York and Israel Bar Associations. *LANGUAGES:* English and Hebrew.

ASSOCIATES

MORDECHAI SOFFER, born October 22, 1949; admitted, 1974, Israel. *Education:* Tel Aviv University School of Law (LL.B., 1975). *Member:* Israel Bar Association. *LANGUAGES:* Hebrew and English.

GLENN SHALOM-WINTER, born July 11, 1957; admitted, 1983, New York; 1987, Israel. *Education:* Yeshiva University (B.A., 1979); Boston University School of Law (J.D., cum laude, 1982). Case and Note Editor, Boston University International Law Journal, 1981-1982. Associate, Cole

(This Listing Continued)

& Deitz, New York, N.Y., 1982-1985. Author: "National Labor Relations Board Jurisdiction Over International Secondary Boycotts," 1 Boston University International Law Journal 11, 1982. *Member:* New York and Israel Bar Associations. *LANGUAGES:* English and Hebrew.

ERAN MARIENBERG, born December 7, 1966; admitted, 1994, Israel. *Education:* Essex University School of Law (LL.B., 1992). *Member:* Israel Bar Association. *LANGUAGES:* Hebrew and English.

JORDAN

SADI ABDIN LAW FIRM

Established in 1976

P.O. BOX 950565
AMMAN 11195, JORDAN
Telephone: 962.6.692540
Fax: 962.6.692541

Cairo, Egypt Office: Saas Advisory Services Ltd., 5 Tahsin Farghaly Street, Madenat Nasr, Cairo, Egypt. Telephone: 20-2-2601204. Fax: 20-2-2601204.

Trademarks, Patents, Arab Civil and Commercial Laws, Litigation, Arbitration, Contracts, Insurance, Tort and Intellectual Property.

FIRM PROFILE: It was established by lawyer Sadi Abdin and other associates in Amman. In 1985 the firm extended all over Jordan, and other Arab Countries through a national law offices net work. As a member of "IGL" (International Grouping of Lawyers) it takes on it's response all kinds of legal services through a net work of about 60 non Arabic Countries Worldwide. The firm is the exclusive representative for PKF (Panell Kerr Foster) in Jordan and Egypt. The firm owns "SAAS Advisory Services Ltd" Cyprus, Jordan Law On-line Data Bank and also Publisher of Jordan Law Pocket Encyclopedia.

MEMBERS OF FIRM

SADI ABDIN, (FOUNDER), born Hebron, April 17, 1945; admitted, 1970, Jordan. *Education:* Cairo (LL.B.). Chief Editor, Jordan Law Pocket Encyclopedia. *Member:* Jordan Bar Association (JBA); ICC; International Bar Association (IBA); International Grouping of Lawyers (IGL); Union Internationale Des Avocats (UIA). *LANGUAGES:* Arabic and English. *PRACTICE AREAS:* Civil Law; Commercial Law; Computer Contracts; Copyright Law; Construction Law; Banking; Contract Law; Patents; Designs; Arbitration; Alternative Dispute Resolution.

NADA ABDIN, born Hebron, January 1, 1962; admitted, 1983, Jordan. *Education:* Amman (LL.B.). *Member:* Jordan Bar Association (JBA). *LANGUAGES:* Arabic and English. *PRACTICE AREAS:* Civil Law; Commercial Law; Company Law; Trademarks; Intellectual Property; Patents; Contracts Law; Taxation Law.

ASSOCIATES

EMAN MOQBEL, born Amman, September 1, 1962; admitted, 1984, Jordan. *Education:* Amman (LL.B.). *Member:* Jordan Bar Association (JBA). *LANGUAGES:* Arabic and English. *PRACTICE AREAS:* Administrative Law; Environmental Law; Health Law; Civil Law; Commercial Law; Contracts.

HUSAM MOUASHER, born Amman, May 30, 1969; admitted, 1991, Jordan. *Education:* Amman (LL.B.; LL.M.). *Member:* Jordan Bar Association (JBA). *LANGUAGES:* Arabic, English and French. *PRACTICE AREAS:* Banking; International Business Law; Contract Law; Foreign Investments; Franchising; Commercial Law; Civil Law.

RUBA QALYOUBI, born Baghdad, July 8, 1971; admitted, 1992, Jordan. *Education:* Amman (LL.B.). *LANGUAGES:* Arabic, English and French. *PRACTICE AREAS:* General Practice; Trademarks.

RAWAND KARAMAN, born Nablus, January 1, 1972; admitted, 1993, Jordan. *Education:* Amman (LL.B.). *LANGUAGES:* Arabic and English. *PRACTICE AREAS:* General Practice.

HANADA HADADDIEN, born Amman, September 12, 1972; admitted, 1994, Jordan. *Education:* Amman (LL.B.). *LANGUAGES:* Arabic and English. *PRACTICE AREAS:* General Practice.

REPRESENTATIVE CLIENTS: Mebco Bank (Geneve); Ma'aref School and College (Jordan); Jordan National Contracting Co. (Mining) (Jordan); World Plastics for Instruction Industries (Jordan); Shmaisani Hospital (Jordan); Al Alamiah Electronics (Saudi Arabia); General Computers & Electronics Co.

(This Listing Continued)

SADI ABDIN LAW FIRM, Amman—Continued

(GCE) (Jordan); Computer & Engineering Bureau (C.E.B.) (Jordan); United Arab Shipping Co. (Kuwait); N.C.M. (Holland); International Systems & Electronic Development Co. (SEDCO) (Jordan); Eurodrip (Greece); Jordan Computer Society (JCS) (Jordan); Arab European Co. for Irrigation and Agriculture (Egypt); Rainbow Travel & Tourism Co. (Jordan); Dae Ryuk International, Inc. (D.R.I.) (N.J., USA); Grains Fodders & Meat Production Company (Grameco) (Jordan); Getratex (Geneva); Rida Jardaneh Drag Stores (Jordan); Scientific & Medical Company (Jordan).

ABU-GHAZALEH LEGAL SERVICES
(ABLE)

Established in 1987

P.O. BOX 921100
AMMAN, JORDAN
Telephone: 962-6-687944; 687910
Fax: 962-6-696284

Cairo, Egypt Office: P.O. Box 96, Imbaba, 12411. Telephone: 20-2-347-9952. Fax: 20-2-344-5729.

Muscat, Oman Office: P.O. Box 2366, Ruwi 112. Telephone: 968-562-274. Fax: 968-563-249.

Abu Dhabi, United Arab Emirates Office: P.O. Box 4295, Abu Dhabi. Telephone: 971-2-781-495. Fax: 971-2-722945.

Dubai, United Arab Emirates Headquarters Office: P.O. Box 1991, Deira, Dubai. Telephone: 971-4-682194. Fax: 971-4-665-132.

Ramallah, West Bank Office: P.O. Box 3800, Ramallah al Birah. Telephone: 972-2-954-850. Fax: 972-2-954-849.

Intellectual Property Law, Arbitration, Banking and Finance, Commercial and Corporate Law, International Transactions and Investment, Labor Law, Conflict of Laws and Bankruptcy.

FIRM PROFILE: ABLE grew out of the legal department of Talal Abu Ghazaleh International, which for three decades has offered the Middle East the highest degree of professional services in the areas of accounting, management consulting and intellectual property. ABLE's strengths complement the services rendered by TAGI.

MEMBERS OF FIRM

FOUAD BOUSTANI, Legal Counsel. Professor, Law, Sorbonne University. (Resident in Paris & Beirut).

HABIB BOURGHIBA, JR., Legal Counsel. Former Minister, Foreign Affairs, Tunisia. (Resident in Tunis).

SUFYAN OBEIDAT, Managing Director, Dubai Headquarters Office. Former Director, TMP Agents Regional Office, Amman.

SALAH-EDDIN AL BASHIR. *Education:* University of Jordan (LL.B.); Harvard University (LL.M.); McGill University (Ph.D., Comparative Law). Manager, Regional Office, Amman. Legal Counsel.

ANNA MARIA F. ADAMO, General Counsel, Regional Office, Amman. Former U.S. Dept of Interior Public Affairs Officer, U.S. Dept of State Foreign Service Officer.

AHMED AL-SANHOURI, Former Head, Egyptian Patent Office, Cairo. Cairo Branch Office.

OMAR LOTFY ABDEL FATTEH, Legal Counsel. Former Vice President, Arab Land Bank, Cairo. Cairo Branch Office.

HAMDY ZAGLOUL AHMED ZAGLOUL, Legal Counsel. Former Director General, Department of Industrial Property Office, Egypt. Cairo Branch Office.

MOHAMMAD EL-FATEH FAWZI, Legal Counsel, Former Vice President, Arab Land Bank, Cairo. Cairo Branch Office.

TARIK AL-BAKRI, Legal Counsel, Dubai Headquarters Office.

YOUSRIAH ABU-AL-EZZ EL SHERBINI, Legal Counsel, Abu Dhabi, Branch Office.

MONA T. AMER, Legal Counsel, Muscat, Branch Office.

ALAA MOHAMMAD, Legal Counsel, Muscat, Branch Office.

RA'ED ABU RUMMAN, Legal Counsel, Amman Regional Office.

IBRAMEEM S. SHAQERAT, Legal Counsel, Amman Regional Office.

(This Listing Continued)

TAWFIQ A. ZWAYYED, Legal Counsel, Amman Regional Office.

MOHAMMAD NIDAL S. DAJANI, Legal Counsel, Amman Regional Office.

Languages: English and Arabic.

ARAB AND FOREIGN LEGAL RESEARCH CENTRE

P.O. BOX 815303
AMMAN, JORDAN
Telephone: 629823
Fax: 629823

FIRM PROFILE: *The office offers a full range of legal services. The office specializes in all Civil Law branches Arbitration, International Contracts, Litigation, General Legal Practice and Intellectual Property.*

NAJI ASSAF, born Jordan, 1937. *Education:* University of London (LL.B., with Second Class Honours, 1966). **LANGUAGES:** Arabic. **PRACTICE AREAS:** Intellectual Property Law; Arbitration; Litigation.

LEGAL SUPPORT PERSONNEL

NAZMI DAKKA, born Jordan, 1956. *Education:* University of Baghdad (Bachelor of Law, 1982). **PRACTICE AREAS:** Civil Law.

NAYEL JAFFAL, born Jordon, 1957. *Education:* University of Rabat, Morocco (Bachelor of Law, 1981). **PRACTICE AREAS:** General Legal Practice.

REFERENCES: The Clorox Company, Oakland, California.

MICHAEL T. DABIT & ASSOCIATES

SHEMEISANI
AL-HINDI COMMERCIAL CENTER
P.O. BOX 20502
AMMAN, JORDAN
Telephone: 962-6-682622; 682633
Fax: 962-6-682644

FIRM PROFILE: *Michael T. Dabit & Associates is a Jordanian law firm with six associates specializing in International Law, International Commercial Contracts, International Trade, Admiralty Law, Banking Law, Financial Services, Securities, Economic Regulation, Collections, Foreign Investment, Commercial and Government Contracts, Natural Resources, Communication Law, Construction, Tax, Commercial and Civil Litigation, and Mining Law.*

MICHAEL T. DABIT, admitted, 1984, Jordan. *Education:* College De La Salle, Amman (1984); University of Jordan (Bachelor of Science, Civil and International Law); Oxford University, London, U.K. (Internship, British Law, July-August, 1988); Training Workshops (U.S. Legal System and International Law, July-August, 1991); International Law Institute, Washington, D.C. (Seminar, Orientation in the U.S. Legal System, Public Enterprise and Privatization, July 1993). Certified Translator, English-/Arabic and Arabic/English. Publications: "Arbitration," a study in Jordanian arbitration law, comparative arbitration laws and the I.C.C. arbitration law. *Member:* Jordanian Bar Association. **LANGUAGES:** Arabic, English and French.

OFFICE OF ANIS F. KASSIM

P.O. BOX 961919
11196 AMMAN, JORDAN
Telephone: (962-6) 696-326
Fax: (962-6) 680-076

Agency and Franchise, Aviation, Construction and Engineering, Corporate, Foreign Investment and Joint Ventures, Government Contracts, International and Local Arbitration and Disputes Resolution, Palestinian Territory Law (West Bank and Gaza Strip).

ANIS FAWZI KASSIM, born December 25, 1939, Jordan. *Education:* Damascus University Law School, Syria (LL.B., 1965); University of Miami School of Law, Florida (M.C.L., 1968); George Washington University Law School, Washington, D.C. (LL.M., 1970; S.J.D., 1973). Publications in English: "Conflicting Claims in the Persian Gulf," A Study in the Law of the Sea, 4 Journal of Law & Economic Development 282, 1969; "The Palestine

(This Listing Continued)

Liberation Organization's Claims to Status: A Juridical Analysis under International Law," 9 Denver Journal of International Law and Policy, 1, 1980; "Dialogue: The Legal Status of the PLO," 10 Denver Journal of International Law and Policy 221, 1981; "The New Civil Code of Kuwait: The Contracting Dimension," Middle East Executive Reports, Feb. 1982; "The Development of the Kuwait Capital Market and the Role of Legislation-I," Middle East Executive Reports, May 1982; "The Development of the Kuwait Capital Market and the Role of Legislation-II," Middle East Executive Reports, July 1982; "Legal Practice in Kuwait," in II-Transnational Legal Practice, ed. Dennis Campbell, 239, 1982; "Legal Systems and Developments in Palestine," 1 Palestine Yearbook of International Law, 1984; "The New York Convention on the Recognition and Enforcement of Foreign Arbitral Awards in certain Arab Countries," ICC Institute of International Business and Practice, Paris, 1989. Publications in Arabic: "Israel's Law of Return and Nationality Law: A Juridical Study in Municipal and International Law," Research Center, Beirut, 1972; "The Right to Nationality in Liberia and Israel: The Case of the Black Hebrews," Palestine Affairs, 35, March 1973; "The Industrial Bank of Kuwait Bonds: A Kuwaiti Experiment in Law and Development," 3 Journal of Gulf and Arabian Peninsula Studies, 129, April 1977, University of Kuwait; "The Gulf Crisis: The Palestinian between the Hammer and the Anvil," Journal of Palestine Studies 3, Jan. 1991. Editor-in-Chief, The Palestine Yearbook of International Law. Professional Experience: Attorney, Legal Department, International, Sun Oil International, Inc., Philadelphia, USA, 1973-1975; Legal Counsel, The Industrial Bank of Kuwait, Kuwait, 1975-1977; Senior Partner: Al-Saleh and Graham & James Partners, Kuwait, 1977-1992; Al-Saleh and Partner, Kuwait, 1992—. Judge, The Administrative Tribunal of the Arab League, 1981-1984. Member: Jordan Bar Association; Al-Shaybani Society of International Law (President); American Society of International Law.

LAW & ARBITRATION CENTRE

Established in 1985

ZEYAD SALAH BUILDING, 3RD FLOOR
50 ABDUL HAMID SHARAF STREET
P.O. BOX 926544
AMMAN 11110, JORDAN
Telephone: 672222; 672333
Telex: 24277 LAC JO
Fax: 699222

Corporations, Insurance, Contracts, Banking, Patent, Arbitration, Civil and Commercial Law in General, Litigation, Foreign Investment.

MEMBERS OF FIRM

AHMAD OBEIDAT, born Jordan, 1938. *Education:* Baghdad University, Faculty of Law (J.D., 1961). Director, Jordan Intelligence Department, 1982. Minister of Interior, 1982-1984. Prime Minister of Jordan, January 1984-April 1985. Senator, Jordan's Upper House of Parliament, 1985—. Chairman, Royal Committee for Jordan's National Charter. Chairman, Jordan Environment Society. *Member:* Jordan Bar Association. *LANGUAGES:* Arabic and English. *PRACTICE AREAS:* Constitutional and Environmental Law; Mediation; Legislative Consultancy.

HAMZEH HADDAD, born Jordan, 1950. *Education:* Damascus University, Syria (LL.B., 1971); Cairo University, Egypt (LL.M. and Doctor of Laws, 1976); University of Bristol, England (Ph.D. in International Commercial Contracts, 1985). Author: "The Hamburg Rules for the Carriage of Goods by Sea," (Dirasat Journal, University of Jordan, 1978); "The Meaning of Goods According to the 1978 Hamburg Rules for the International Carriage of Goods by Sea," (BAJ, 1979); "International Commercial Law," (Al-Dar Al-Muttahida, Beirut, 1980); "Remedies of the Unpaid Seller in International Sale of Goods (LAC-Amman, 1985); "Avoidance of a Contract under ULIS 1964 and the U.N. Convention of 1980," (Amman, 1986); "Enforcement and Recognition of Foreign Judgments and Arbitral Awards under Jordanian and Iraqi Laws," (for IBA, Bahrain, 1988); "Agency and Distribution Agreements in Jordan," "International Agency and Distribution Agreements," (Butterworth, London, 1991); "Inter-Arab Conventions on Commercial Arbitration," (for Euro-Arab Chamber of Commerce, 1989); "The Amman Convention of 1987 on Commercial Arbitration," (the American Journal of International Arbitration, Columbia University, Vol.1/No.1, 1990). "UNCITRAL Model Law on International Commercial Arbitration: Scope of Applicability," (1st Conference of Arab Association for International Arbitration, Cairo, 1992). *Member:* Jordan Bar Association; The Arbitration Board of the Arab-Swiss Chamber of Commerce; International Center for Settlement of Investment Disputes; International Bar Association. *LANGUAGES:* Arabic and English. *PRACTICE*

(This Listing Continued)

AREAS: Arbitration; Banking; International Contracts; Corporate Law; Insurance; Construction; Agencies and Distributorships.

THAMER OBEIDAT, born Jordan, 1965; admitted, 1991, New York. *Education:* University of Jordan (LL.B. Hons., 1987); Harvard Law School (LL.M., 1988). Associate, White & Case, New York, 1988-1991. *Member:* Jordan Bar Association; American Bar Association. *LANGUAGES:* Arabic and English. *PRACTICE AREAS:* Agency and Distributorship Contracts; Banking; General Corporate Practice; International Business Transactions; Foreign Investment; Intellectual Property.

ASSOCIATES

ABDUL-GHAFAR FREIHAT, born Jordan, 1955; admitted, 1982, Jordan. *Education:* Damascus University (LL.B., 1979). Judge, 1985-1992. Investigating Public Attorney regarding irregular banking practices, 1990-1992. *Member:* Jordan Bar Association. *LANGUAGES:* Arabic. *PRACTICE AREAS:* Banking; Maritime; Shipping; White-Collar Crime; Civil; Commercial and Criminal Litigation.

RAMI M. AL-HADIDI, born Jordan, 1964; admitted, 1990, Jordan. *Education:* University of Jordan (LL.B., 1988). *Member:* Jordan Bar Association. *LANGUAGES:* Arabic, English and Conversational French. *PRACTICE AREAS:* Corporate Law; Contracts; Foreign Investment; Intellectual Property; Patents; Trademarks; Litigation.

SANAA OBEIDAT, born Jordan, 1971. *Education:* University of Jordan (LL.B., 1992); McGill University (LL.M., 1994). *Member:* Jordan Bar Association. *LANGUAGES:* Arabic, English and French. *PRACTICE AREAS:* Arbitration; Banking; Trademarks; Foreign Investment.

NABULSI AND ASSOCIATES

Counsellors & Attorneys at Law

Established in 1977

RIYADH CENTER
3RD CIRCLE
P.O. BOX 35116
AMMAN 11180, JORDAN
Telephone: (962 6) 654411; 654422
Fax: (962 6) 657555

New York Associated Office: Afridi, Angell & Baker, New York, N.Y.

Civil, Commercial, Company, Banking, Insurance, Telecommunications, Carriage of Goods by Sea Land, Investment and Construction Laws. International Business Transactions. Litigation before all Courts and Arbitral Tribunals.

OMAR N. NABULSI, born 1936; admitted, 1959, Jordan. *Education:* Victoria College, Alexandria, Egypt; Cairo University (LL.B.; LL.M.). Held Cabinet Posts of: National Economy, 1970-1972; Agriculture, 1973-1974; Labor and Reconstruction and Development, 1979-1980. Former Ambassador to the United Kingdom and to the Netherlands, 1972-1973. Former Legal Advisor to the Arab Fund for Economic and Social Development in Kuwait, 1975-1977. Conciliator and Arbitrator on the Panel of the World Bank International Center for Settlement of Investment Disputes. Member of the Board of the Arbitration System of the Euro Arab Chambers of Commerce. Member of Jordan National Committee of the International Chamber of Commerce. Former Member of Jordan National Consultative Assembly. Member of the Jordanian Senate, Upper House of Parliament (member of the Senate's Legal Committee) 1989-1993. *LANGUAGES:* Arabic and English.

ASSOCIATES

Ousama Melkawi, LL.B.
Bassam Abu Rassa'a, LL.B.
Zina Nabulsi, LL.B. (Hons.); LL.M. (Lond.)
Radi O. Nabulsi, LL.B. (Hons.); LL.M. (Lond.)
Zaid O. Nabulsi, LL.B. (Hons.); LL.M. (Lond.)
Luma M. Saqqaf, LL.M. (Bristol)

Languages: Arabic, English and French.

REPRESENTATIVE CLIENTS: Alia, Royal Jordanian Airlines; Jordan Phosphate Mines Co.; Amman Investment Bank; ANZ Grindlays Bank (Jordan); Cairo-Amman Bank; Jordon Industrial Estates Corporation; Ministry of Education; Arab Company For Drug Industries and Medical Appliances; Manufacturers Hanover Trust Co. (Chemical Banking Corporation U.S.A.); United States Leasing; Overseas Bechtel Corporation; Amoco Production Co.; Philips International B.V.; Lockheed Corporation; Banque Societe Generale (France);

(This Listing Continued)

NABULSI AND ASSOCIATES, Amman—Continued

OMV Aktiengesellschaft (Austria); Kenzo Tange Associates (Japan); Estee Lauder (U.S.A.); Benetton Group (Italy); International Finance Corporation (IFC) of the World Bank, Washington D.C.; Berndorf F.A.S. (Austria); Ferruzzi Trading (U.S.A.); Motorola Inc. (U.S.A.).

ATIYEH SALEM & ASSOCIATES

101 TERRASANCTA SALAM BUILDINGS
AL-WEYBDEH
P.O. BOX 244/11118
AMMAN, JORDAN
Telephone: (962) 6 623827; 622489
Fax: (962) 6 621000
Telex: 21450

Insurance, Commercial and Corporate Practice, Intellectual Property, Civil Litigation and Arbitration, Construction Law, Environmental Law, Administrative and Public Law, Matrimonial Matters.

FIRM PROFILE: *The firm was established in 1954 and offers a full range of legal services. The two member firm has a number of associates along with legal support staff.*

MEMBERS

ATIYEH SALEM, born 1925; admitted, 1954, Jordan. *Education:* Jerusalem Law School. *Member:* The Jordan Bar Association.

SAMER A. SALEM, born 1961; admitted, 1986, Jordan. *Education:* University of Kent at Canterbury (B.A. Hons, 1983). *Member:* Jordan Bar Association; Gray's Inn.

Languages: English, Arabic and French.

ALI SHARIF ZU'BI & SHARIF ALI ZU'BI

Advocates and Legal Consultants
Established in 1921
ASTRA BUILDING
FIRST CIRCLE, JABAL AMMAN
P.O. BOX 35267
AMMAN, JORDAN
Telephone: (962.6) 642908; 647908; 648908
Cable Address: "INTLAWPRAC" AMMAN
Telex: 21186 ASZUBI JO
Fax: (962.6) 634277

Manama, Bahrain Associated Office: Hatim S. Zu'bi Law Office. Bab-El-Bahrain Building, Suite No. 1, 2nd Floor, P.O. Box 502. Telephone: (973) 251911; 251695; 258207. Telex: 8365 HSZUBI BN. Fax: (973) 232643.

FIRM PROFILE: *The firm was established in Nazareth, Palestine in 1921 by the late Sharif Ali Zu'bi. In 1953, the firm opened its Amman Office and later, in the 1970's, established offices in Bahrain and Abu Dhabi. The firm specializes in General Civil and Commercial Practice, Corporate, Government Contracts, International Trade, Construction, Foreign Investment, Taxation, Banking, Insurance, Franchise and Distributorship, Litigation before all Courts and Arbitration.*

PARTNERS

ALI SHARIF ZU'BI, born Nazareth, Palestine, April 1917; admitted, 1943, Palestine. *Education:* The Jerusalem Law School. *Member:* Jordanian Bar Association; International Bar Association; ICC Arbitrator/Jordan Regional Committee. *LANGUAGES:* Arabic and English.

SHARIF ALI ZU'BI, born Amman, Jordan, May 1963; admitted, 1986, Jordan. *Education:* University of Bristol (LL.B., LL.M. in Commercial Laws). *Member:* Jordanian Bar Association; International Bar Association. *LANGUAGES:* Arabic and English.

ASSOCIATES

THAER Y. AMRO, admitted, 1992, Jordan. *Education:* Jordan University (LL.B.); University of Bristol (LL.M.). *Member:* Jordanian Bar Association. *LANGUAGES:* Arabic and English.

KHALED U. ASFOUR, admitted, 1992, Minnesota. *Education:* University of Minnesota (J.D., 1991); University of Wisconsin (M.B.A., 1988). *Member:* Jordanian Bar Association. *LANGUAGES:* Arabic and English.

(This Listing Continued)

MOHAMMAD Z. ZU'BI, admitted, 1993, Jordan. *Education:* Jordan University (LL.B.); University of Aberdeen (LL.M.). *Member:* Jordanian Bar Association. *LANGUAGES:* Arabic and English.

NADINE F. KHAMIS. *Education:* University of Buckingham (LL.B., honours, 1990). *Member:* Jordanian Bar Association. *LANGUAGES:* Arabic, English and French.

SALEH M. ABD EL-ATI. *Education:* Jordan University (B.A.); Exeter University (LL.M.). *Member:* Jordanian Bar Association. *LANGUAGES:* Arabic and English.

LOCAL COUNSEL FOR: Citibank N.A.; The First National Bank of Chicago; Visa International; Arab Banking Corporation; Credit Lyonnais; IBM World Trade Corporation; British Petroleum; General Electric Company (USA); Westinghouse Electric Corporation; Siemens AG; Philip Morris; Bechtel International Inc.; George Wimpey International Limited; Tarmac International Limited; Jordan Phosphate Mines Company Limited; Marubeini Corporation; Nissho Iwai Corporation; Fujitsu Limited; Furukawa Electric Co.; Saudi Arabian Airlines; Middle East Airlines/Airliban; Indo-Jordan Chemicals Company; Nippon-Jordan Fertilizer Company.

KENYA

HAMILTON HARRISON & MATHEWS

Established in 1902
I.C.E.A. BUILDING
KENYATTA AVENUE
P.O. BOX 30333
NAIROBI, KENYA
Telephone: (+254 2) 330870
Cable Address: "Equity", Nairobi
Telex: 22564 EQUITY
Telecopier (Fax): +254 2 222318

General Practice, Arbitration, Antitrust and Trade Regulation, Appellate Practice, Aviation, Bankruptcy, Banks and Banking, International Loans, Business Law, Charitable Organisations, Civil Law, Commercial Law, Company Law, Construction Law, Contracts, Conveyancing, Copyrights, Corporate Law, Finance, Franchises, Government Contracts, Insurance, Intellectual Property, Investments, Leases and Leasing, Libel and Defamation, Mergers, Acquisitions and Divestments, Mortgages, Negligence, Patents, Personal Injury, Probate, Products Liability, Professional Liability, Property, Real Estate, Securities, Torts, Trademarks, Transportation, Trusts and Estates, Wills.

FIRM PROFILE: *The firm was established in 1902 and offers a full range of legal services. It is well known for its corporate, commercial, banking, conveyancing and litigation. Its clients are both local and international. The firm has 9 partners, 8 assistant advocates and a legal support staff of 6.*

J.D.M. SILVESTER, born Kenya, 1935; B.A. (Oxon.), ACIARB; admitted, 1958, England (Barrister-at-Law); 1959, Kenya (Advocate); 1966, Uganda and Tanzania; 1979, Seychelles. Notary Public. Commissioner for Oaths. Editor, *East Africa Law Reports,* 1967-1975. Member, Board of Investment Promotion Centre. *Member:* Law Society of Kenya; Institute of Trademark Agents, London. *LANGUAGES:* English. *PRACTICE AREAS:* Corporate Law; Commercial Law; Banking Law.

M.L. SOMEN, born Kenya, 1937; M.A. (Oxon.); admitted, 1961, England (Barrister-at-Law); 1962, Kenya. Commissioner for Oaths. Notary Public. *Member:* Law Society of Kenya. *LANGUAGES:* English. *PRACTICE AREAS:* Corporate Law; Commercial Law; Banking Law.

P. LE PELLEY, born Kenya, 1931; M.A. (Oxon.) FCIArb; admitted, 1957, England (Barrister-at-Law); 1958, Kenya. Editor, *East Africa Law Reports,* Butterworths, London, 1970-1975. *Member:* Law Society of Kenya (President, 1969-1970). *LANGUAGES:* English. *PRACTICE AREAS:* Civil Law; Commercial Law; Banking law.

K.A. FRASER, born England, 1948; admitted, 1969, England (Barrister-at-Law); 1970, Kenya. *Member:* Law Society of Kenya. *LANGUAGES:* English. *PRACTICE AREAS:* Civil & Commercial Litigation.

R. OMWELA, born Kenya, 1956; LL.B. (Nbi.); admitted, 1980, Kenya. Commissioner for Oaths. Notary Public. *Member:* Law Society of Kenya. *LANGUAGES:* English. *PRACTICE AREAS:* Civil & Commercial Litigation.

(This Listing Continued)

J.G. NYAMU, born Kenya, 1948; LL.B. (Lond.); admitted, 1972, Kenya. Commissioner for Oaths. Notary Public. *Member:* Law Society of Kenya. *LANGUAGES:* English. *PRACTICE AREAS:* Civil & Commercial Litigation.

A.K. SOAR, born Kenya, 1957; LL.B. (Nbi.); admitted, 1983, Kenya. Commissioner for Oaths. Notary Public. *Member:* Law Society of Kenya. *LANGUAGES:* English. *PRACTICE AREAS:* Conveyancing Law; Real Property Law.

K. KIMANI, born Kenya, 1964; admitted, 1988, Kenya. *Education:* (NBI) LL.B. *Member:* Law Society of Kenya. *LANGUAGES:* English. *PRACTICE AREAS:* Civil & Commercial Litigation.

C.A. AGIMBA, born Kenya, 1963; admitted, 1986, Kenya. *Education:* NBI (LL.B.); Warwick (LL.M.). *Member:* Law Society of Kenya. *LANGUAGES:* English. *PRACTICE AREAS:* Conveyancing; Real Property Law; Intellectual Property Law.

ASSOCIATES

R.M. Githaiga (Mrs)	W.I. Maema
W. Asiko	G.G. Murugara
J.C. Kinyua	P. Waiyaki

Foreign Associate Member: U.S. Trade Mark Association.

KAPLAN & STRATTON

Advocates and Notaries Public

Established in 1934

QUEENSWAY HOUSE
KAUNDA STREET
P.O. BOX 40111
NAIROBI, KENYA
Telephone: 335333
Cable Address: "ADJUDICATE"
Telex: 22309 ADJUDICAT
Facsimile: 254-2-340827
International Law Firm Network - Lex Africa

International Finance, Commercial and Corporate Law. Tax Planning, Civil and Criminal Litigation, Trusts, Succession, Property, Conveyancing, Trademarks and Patents.

MEMBERS OF FIRM

W.S. DEVERELL, born England, 1938. B.A. (Oxon); Barrister-at-Law (Gray's Inn), England, 1961; Advocate, 1963, Kenya. *Member:* Law Society of Kenya; International Bar Association; Chartered Institute of Arbitrators (Associated Member). *PRACTICE AREAS:* Commercial; Banking; Construction Litigation.

E.A. BRISTOW, born England, 1930. LL.B. (Newcastle-upon-Tyne); Solicitor, 1953, England; Advocate, 1954, Kenya. Commissioner for Oaths. *Member:* Law Society (England and Wales); Law Society of Kenya; International Bar Association; Institute of Trademark Agents, London (Overseas Member); Fellow, Institute of Directors (U.K.). *PRACTICE AREAS:* Trusts; Tax Planning; Successions.

P.J. HIME, born Kenya, 1944. B.Com. (Leeds); Advocate, 1971, Kenya. *Member:* Law Society of Kenya; United States Trademark Association; Institute of Trademark Agents, London (Overseas Member). *LANGUAGES:* English, French and Kiswahili. *PRACTICE AREAS:* Intellectual Property; Commercial Law.

K.H.W. KEITH, born Kenya, 1948. Solicitor, 1973, England; Advocate, 1974, Kenya. *Member:* Law Society (England and Wales); Law Society of Kenya; International Bar Association. *LANGUAGES:* English and Kiswahili. *PRACTICE AREAS:* Commercial and Corporate Banking; Project Financing; International Finance.

F.O.O.N. OJIAMBO, born Kenya, 1950. LL.B. (Nairobi); Advocate, 1975, Kenya. Commissioner of Oaths. Notary Public. *Member:* Law Society of Kenya (Chairman, 1989-1990); International Bar Association. *LANGUAGES:* English and Kiswahili. *PRACTICE AREAS:* Civil Litigation.

O.M. FOWLER, born Kenya, 1952. LL.B. (Bristol); Solicitor, 1977, England; Advocate, 1979, Kenya. *Member:* Law Society of Kenya. *LANGUAGES:* English and Kiswahili. *PRACTICE AREAS:* Commercial and Corporate Banking; Project Financing.

C.J.B. LARBY, born Kenya, 1937. M.A., LLB (Cantab); Barrister at Law (Middle Temple), 1962, England; Advocate, 1965, Kenya. *Member:*
(This Listing Continued)

Law Society of Kenya; International Bar Association. *LANGUAGES:* English and Kiswahili. *PRACTICE AREAS:* Property; Commercial Law.

S.N. WAINAINA, born Kenya, 1952. LL.B. (Nairobi); Advocate, 1978, Kenya. Commissioner for Oaths, Notary Public. *Member:* Law Society of Kenya; Institute of Trademark Agents, London (Overseas Member). *LANGUAGES:* English and Kiswahili. *PRACTICE AREAS:* Commercial; Intellectual Property.

F.A. OCHIENG, born Kenya, 1956. LL.B. (Nairobi); Advocate, 1983, Kenya. Commissioner for Oaths, Notary Public. *Member:* Law Society of Kenya. *LANGUAGES:* English and Kiswahili. *PRACTICE AREAS:* Civil Litigation.

J.B. HAVELOCK, born Kenya, 1944. Advocate, 1972, Kenya. *Member:* Law Society of Kenya. *LANGUAGES:* English and Kiswahili. *PRACTICE AREAS:* Civil Litigation.

N.H. SHAW, born Kenya, 1961. LL.B. (Leicester); Barrister at Law (Grays Inn), 1989, England; Advocate, 1991, Kenya. *Member:* Law Society of Kenya. *LANGUAGES:* English and Kiswahili. *PRACTICE AREAS:* Commercial Law; Conveyancing.

B.M. MUSAU, born Kenya, 1963. LL.B. (Nairobi); Advocate, 1989, Kenya. *Member:* Law Society of Kenya. *LANGUAGES:* English and Kiswahili. *PRACTICE AREAS:* Commercial and Corporate Banking; Project Financing; International Finance.

P.M. GACHUHI, born Kenya, 1961. LL.B. (Bombay); Advocate, 1990, Kenya. Commissioner for Oaths. *Member:* Law Society of Kenya; International Commission of Jurists (Kenya Section). *LANGUAGES:* English and Kiswahili. *PRACTICE AREAS:* Civil Litigation.

R.G. GOTA, born Kenya, 1965. LL.B. (Nairobi); Advocate, 1991, Kenya. Commissioner of Oaths. *Member:* Law Society of Kenya; International Commission of Jurists. *LANGUAGES:* English and Kiswahili. *PRACTICE AREAS:* Commercial Law; Conveyancing.

NDUNGU NJOROGE & KWACH

Advocates, Commissioners for Oaths and Notaries Public

Established in 1986

12TH FLOOR, BRUCE HOUSE
STANDARD STREET
P.O. BOX 41546
NAIROBI, KENYA
Telephone: 229281
(Int. + 254 - 2)
Telex: 25227 NEWLAW
Fax: 254-2-215544

International Finance, Commercial and Corporate Law. Tax Planning, Civil and Criminal Litigation, Trusts, Succession, Property, Conveyancing, Trademarks and Patents.

MEMBERS OF FIRM

PAUL N. NDUNGU, born Nyeri, Kenya, July 24, 1943; admitted, 1969, Kenya. *Education:* Kenya School of Law. Notary Public. Commissioner for Oaths. Chairman, Rotary Club of Nairobi North, 1980-1981. *Member:* Law Society of Kenya (Member, Governing Council of Law Society), 1981-1982; Member, Property and Conveyancing Sub-Committee, 1981—. Chairman, Budget and Finance Subcommittee, 1981—. *Member:* Commonwealth Lawyers' Association. *LANGUAGES:* English, Kiswahili and Kikuyu. *PRACTICE AREAS:* Trust Law; Successions; Property Law; Conveyancing.

ELIUD N. NJOROGE, born Nairobi, Kenya, July 24, 1944; admitted, 1971, Kenya. *Education:* Kenya School of Law. Commissioner for Oaths. Notary Public. Member, Council of Legal Education Kenya. Member, 1980-1984, Member, Governing Council of Law Society, 1977 and Member, Commercial Law Sub-Committee, Law Society of Kenya. *LANGUAGES:* English, Kiswahili and Kikuyu. *PRACTICE AREAS:* International Finance Law; Commercial Law; Corporate Law; Trademark Law; Patent Law; Tax Planning.

RAPHAEL K. NG'ETHE, born Kiambu, Kenya, February 4, 1947; admitted, 1972, Kenya. *Education:* University of Dar-es-Salaam. Notary Public. Commissioner for Oaths. Member, Council of Legal Education. *Member:* Law Society of Kenya; International Bar Association. *LANGUAGES:* English, Kiswahili and French. *PRACTICE AREAS:* Trust Law; Successions; Property Law; Conveyancing.
(This Listing Continued)

NDUNGU NJOROGE & KWACH, Nairobi—Continued

P. KIHARA KARIUKI, born Kiambu, Kenya, May 11, 1954; admitted, 1978, Kenya. *Education:* University of Nairobi (LL.B. with honors). Commissioner for Oaths. Notary Public. Provincial Chancellor, Church of the Province of Kenya and Chancellor, Diocese of Nairobi, 1981—. Commissioner, The Nairobi City Commission, 1985-1986. Correspondent Attorney, Lawyers' International Agency. *Member:* Law Society of Kenya. *LANGUAGES:* English, Kikuyu and Kiswahili. *PRACTICE AREAS:* Civil Litigation; Arbitration; Trust Law; Successions; Property Law; Conveyancing.

KUWAIT

AL-AYOUB & PARTNERS

Middle Eastern Counselors and Attorneys at Law

Established in 1982

AL-KHATRASH & AL-MISHARY BUILDING
10TH FLOOR, FAHD AL-SALEM STREET
P.O. BOX 1714 SAFAT
13018 KUWAIT, KUWAIT
Telephone: 011 965 246-4321/2/3; 246-9943/4/5
Fax: 011 965 246-6591; 243-4711

Cairo, Egypt Office: Alaa Eldin Abdul Monim, Al-Oroba Road, Al-Obor Buildings No. 9 Flat No. 1. Telephone: (202) 261-6175. Fax: (202) 618-740.

Washington, D.C., U.S.A. Office: 700 13th Street, N.W., Suite 950, 20005-3960. Telephone: (202) 347-2400. Fax: (202) 347-2229.

Affiliated Offices:

Bahrain, Oman, Saudi, Dubai, Yemen, Morocco, Jordan, Iran.

General Civil, Commercial, Corporate Oil and Gas, Banking, Finance, Taxation, Intellectual Property, Labour Law and Insurance Law Practice, Commercial Arbitration and Litigation.

FIRM PROFILE: The firm was established in 1982 and offers a full range of legal services. It is well known for its Commercial and Corporate Law Practice. It has a diversified client base including European, North American and Far Eastern Corporations. The firm is the only Middle-Eastern firm with offices in the U.S. The firm also serves as experts on Middle-Eastern laws to numerous U.S. and English law firms in both transactional and litigation matters.

PARTNERS

ABDULLAH K. AL-AYOUB, born Kuwait, July 17, 1947; admitted, 1978, Kuwait; 1984, United Arab Emirates (Dubai). *Education:* Kuwait University (LL.B., 1975); University College of London (1976-1977). Assistant, Kuwait Faculty of Law, 1976. District Attorney of Kuwait, 1975-1978. Editor, "Lawyer," a magazine for lawyers and legal scholars in the Gulf Cooperation Council ("GCC") countries. *Member:* Kuwait Bar Association (President, 1994—and Chairman Legal Ethics Committee); Arab Lawyers Union and Martyrs' Committee (Board Member); Arab Association for International Arbitration (AAIA); American Bar Association (Associate Member). *LANGUAGES:* Arabic and English. *PRACTICE AREAS:* Commercial Transactions; Corporate Transactions; Litigation.

REEMA I. ALI, born Denver, Colorado, USA, September 13, 1958; admitted, 1989, District of Columbia. *Education:* Southern Methodist University, Dallas, Texas (J.D., 1983); Leeds Polytechnic University, Leeds, England (LL.B., hons., 1981). Associate, Al-Saleh Graham and James, 1984-1990. Co-Managing Partner, International Practice of the firm, 1991—. Member and Vice President, Legal Affairs, American Business Council, Kuwait, 1985-1990. *LANGUAGES:* Arabic and English. *PRACTICE AREAS:* General Corporate; Commercial Transactions.

ASSOCIATES & SENIOR COUNSEL

SAMI AYISH, born Elyria, Ohio, U.S.A., April 1, 1964; admitted, 1992, Virginia. *Education:* Ohio State University (B.A., 1986; J.D., 1990). Intern: U.S. District Court, 1988; Commonwealth Attorney's Office, Alexandria, Virginia, 1993. *LANGUAGES:* English. *PRACTICE AREAS:* General Corporate; Commercial Transactions.

JAWAD I. ALI, born Jerusalem, October 4, 1969; admitted, 1994, New York. *Education:* University of Liverpool School of Law (LL.B., hons,

(This Listing Continued)

1993); Boston University School of Law, Boston (LL.M., 1994; International Banking and Finance Law). *LANGUAGES:* Arabic and English. *PRACTICE AREAS:* General Commercial; Corporate Transactions; Banking Law; Financial Law.

MOHAMMED A. AMMAR, born Cairo, Egypt, July 20, 1929; admitted, 1954, Egypt; admitted to practice before all Egyptian Courts. *Education:* University of Helippolis (LL.B., 1954; Diploma in Public Law, 1956; Diploma in Private Law, Ph.D., 1958; Ain Shams, Ph.D. Law of Contracts, 1961). Lecturer, University of Cairo, Khartoum Branch, 1961-1962. Legal Advisor and Attorney for the Egyptian Government, 1962-1980. Attorney before the Egyptian Courts and before the Supreme Court in Libya 1973-1977 (Secondment). Member, National Assembly Drafting Committee, Egypt, 1977-1980. Member, Constitutional Committee, Egypt, 1971. *LANGUAGES:* Arabic. *PRACTICE AREAS:* Civil Litigation; Commercial Litigation; Oil and Gas Insurance; Taxation.

MOHAMMED H. OMAR ALI, born Mansoura, Egypt, March 27, 1959; admitted, 1982, Egypt; 1990, Court of Appeals, Egypt. *Education:* Mansoura University (LL.B., 1981). Associate, Arbitration Committee of Corporate Future Credit Shares, Law Offices of Moheb Habib. *Member:* Lawyers' Union of Egypt. *LANGUAGES:* Arabic. *PRACTICE AREAS:* Civil Law; Commercial Law; Insurance; Maritime; Corporate Transactions; Litigation.

JAMAL A. ABDULLAH, born Kuwait, May 19, 1958; admitted, 1986, Kuwait. *Education:* Kuwait University (LL.B., 1985). With, Kuwait National Petroleum Company, 1977-1985. *Member:* Kuwait Law Society; International Bar Association; American Bar Association (Associate Member). *LANGUAGES:* Arabic. *PRACTICE AREAS:* Civil Law; Commercial Law; Criminal Law; Litigation.

SAMIH G. SERWIY, born Mansoura, Egypt, January 1, 1953; admitted, 1985, Egypt (Not admitted in Kuwait). *Education:* University of Cairo (LL.B., 1975). Ministry of Defense, Egypt, 1975-1979. Attorney of the Ministry of Social Affaires, Iraq, 1979-1981. Legal Researcher, Ministry of Justice, Kuwait, 1982-1986. *Member:* Lawyers' Union of Egypt; Military Courts. *LANGUAGES:* Arabic. *PRACTICE AREAS:* Labour Law; Family Law; Estate Planning.

SHERIF L. ELSEBAEY SHEHATA, born Mansoura, Egypt, September 22, 1964; admitted, 1988, Egypt (Not admitted in Kuwait). *Education:* Mansoura University (LL.B., 1986). *Member:* Lawyers' Union of Egypt. *LANGUAGES:* Arabic. *PRACTICE AREAS:* Civil Law; Corporate and Commercial Transactions; Intellectual Property.

AYYAD ADWANI, born Kuwait, April 15, 1967; admitted, 1991, Kuwait. *Education:* Kuwait University (LL.B., 1990). *LANGUAGES:* Arabic. *PRACTICE AREAS:* Civil, Commercial and Criminal Litigation.

ZAKARYA GALAL METWALLY NAKRISH, born Mansoura, Egypt, October 20, 1959; admitted, 1983, Egypt. *Education:* Mansoura University (LL.B., 1981); Ain Shams University (Diploma in Private/Special Law, 1984; Diploma in General Law, 1985; M.A. Civil Law, 1993). Ministry of Defense, Egypt, 1982-1984. Lawyer, Egyptian Real Estate Bank, 1986-1993. *Member:* Lawyer's Union of Egypt; Egyptian Society for International Law. *LANGUAGES:* Arabic. *PRACTICE AREAS:* Civil Law; Commercial Transactions; Litigation.

ABDUL AZIZ AL-SOUNSI, admitted, 1972, Kuwait. *Education:* Kuwait University, Faculty of Law (LL.B., 1972). Legal Counsel, Kuwait Ministry of Justice, 1972-1976. Kuwait Airway V.P. Personnel, 1976-1988. *LANGUAGES:* Arabic and English. *PRACTICE AREAS:* Civil Law; Commercial Law; Corporate Transaction; Litigation.

REHAM AL-FOZAN, born Kuwait; admitted, 1993, Kuwait. *Education:* Kuwait Faculty of Law (1993). Worked with firm, preparation of claims for damages resulting from the Iraqi invasion for the Kuwaiti Government. *LANGUAGES:* Arabic and English.

OF COUNSEL

MOHAMMAD T. AL-MADANY, born Banha, Egypt, October 14, 1917; admitted, 1941, Egypt; admitted to practice before all Egyptian Courts (Not admitted in Kuwait). *Education:* University of King Fuad, now Cairo University (LL.B., 1941); Institute of Criminal Science (Diploma, 1943). Attorney General of Fazzan and Ben Gazi, Libya, 1958-1963. Public Attorney, Egyptian Supreme Court, 1963-1969. Lecturer of Law, Al Alzhar University, 1965-1969. Legal Counsellor to Government Holding Company, Egypt, 1970-1972. Judge, Supreme Court of Egypt, 1973-1974.

(This Listing Continued)

Judge, Cassation Court of Kuwait, 1974-1983. *Member:* Lawyers' Union of Egypt. *LANGUAGES:* Arabic. *PRACTICE AREAS:* General Corporate; Commercial Law.

Languages: Arabic and English.

LAW OFFICES OF
MISHARE M. AL-GHAZALI & PARTNERS

(In Affiliation with Graham & James)

Established in 1992

P.O. BOX 4970 SAFAT

13050 KUWAIT, KUWAIT

Telephone: (965) 2439690/1; 2439790/1

Fax: (965) 242 2895

Telex: 6505517949 MCI UW

US/Intl. Electronic Mail Addresses: MCI Mail Id: 551 7949
X.400. Address: S=kuwaitlaw: DDA:ID=5517949; A=mci; C=us

Affiliated Graham & James Offices: One World Trade Center, Long Beach, California.

725 South Figueroa Street, Los Angeles, California.

885 Third Avenue, New York, New York.

4675 MacArthur Court, Newport Beach, California.

525 University Avenue, Palo Alto, California.

Station Square, 224 South Dawson, Raleigh, North Carolina.

400 Capitol Mall, Sacramento, California.

One Maritime Plaza, Third Floor, San Francisco, California.

2000 M Street., Washington, D.C.

Deacons and Graham & James, CITIC Building., Jianguomenwai Dajie, No. 19, Beijing, China.

Via Visconti di Modrone, 2, Milano, Italy.

Livdahl Gaikokuhu Jimu, Bengoshi Jimusho, Graham & James, Toranomon Chome, Tokyo, Japan.

Taylor Joynson Garrett, 180 Fleet Street, London, United Kingdom.

Law Offices of Ahmed Zaki Yamani, Manama Center, P. O. Box 342, Manama, Bahrain.

Taylor Johnson Garret, 14 Rue Montoyer, 1040 Brussels, Belgium.

Haarmann, Hemmelrath & Partner, Budapester Strasse 40a, D-1000 Berlin, Germany.

Haarmann, Hemmelrath & Partner, Am Wehrhahn 70, D-4000, Dusseldorf, Germany.

Haarmann, Hemmelrath & Partner, Effnerstrasse 38, D-8000 Munchen, Munich, Germany.

Hanafish Soeharto Ponggawa, BNI Building, Suite 2702, Jalan Jenderal, Sudirman I, Jakarta, Indonesia.

Law Offices of Ahmed Zaki Yamani, P.O. Box 1381, Jeddah, Saudi Arabia.

Law Offices of Ahmed Zaki Yamani, P.O. Box 7159, Riyadh, Saudi Arabia.

Deacons and Graham & James, Vithayu Place, 89/17 Wireless Road, Bangkok, Thailand.

Sly & Weigal, Riverside Centre, 123 Eagle Street, Brisbane, Australia.

Sly & Weigal, 54 Marcus Clarke Street, Canberra City, Australia.

Sly & Weigal, 385 Bourke Street, Melborne, Australia.

Sly & Weigal, R & I Tower, 108 St. Georges Terrace, Perth, Australia.

Sly & Weigal, Goldfields House, Circular Quay, Sydney, Australia.

Deacons, Solicitors and Notaries, In Association with Graham & James, Alexandra House, Hong Kong.

Corporate, Banking and Finance, Taxation, Investment and Joint Ventures, Intellectual Property, Aviation, Litigation, Arbitration, Government Affairs and Relations, Energy, Environment, Construction, Insurance, Mining, Maritime and Transportation, Copyrights and Trademarks, Labor and Trade Relations.

FIRM PROFILE: The firm concentrates in domestic and international commercial transactions, banking and finance. The firm works closely with its affiliated attorney network through the international law firm of Graham & James. The firm utilizes the specialized areas of expertise of over 900 attorneys with its affiliated offices in the U.S., Europe, Asia and Australia.

(This Listing Continued)

SENIOR MEMBERS OF FIRM

MISHARE M. AL-GHAZALI, born Kuwait, 1962; admitted, 1985, Kuwait. *Education:* Kuwait University (Civil Law and Sharia, 1985). In House Counsel for the Ministry of Housing, the Kuwait Security Forces, and the Gulf Bank. Formerly a partner with the law offices of Mohammad Musaed Al-Saleh. *LANGUAGES:* English and Arabic. *PRACTICE AREAS:* Arbitration and Dispute Resolution; Agency and Partnership; Banking and Finance; Corporate; Commercial; Criminal; Patent and Trademark.

FAHID S. FARRAJ, born February 7, 1961; admitted, 1991, Michigan (Not admitted in Kuwait). *Education:* University of Michigan (B.G.S.); Detroit College of Law (J.D., with honors). *Member:* American Bar Association. *LANGUAGES:* English and Arabic. *PRACTICE AREAS:* International Commercial Law and Transactions; Agency and Distributorships; Banking; Taxation; Patents and Trademark; Arbitration; Litigation.

M. SAMI AL-BADAWI, born Egypt, 1930; admitted, 1953, Egyptian Court of Cassation. *Education:* Cairo University (LL.B., 1953). *LANGUAGES:* Arabic and English. *PRACTICE AREAS:* Civil and Criminal Law.

MAHMOUD A. MUSTAFA, born Egypt, 1959; admitted, 1982, Cairo. *Education:* Ein Shams University (LL.B., 1981). *LANGUAGES:* Arabic. *PRACTICE AREAS:* Litigation; Corporate; Securities; Civil; Criminal; Labour.

IMAD BU-RASHID, born Kuwait, 1963; admitted, 1991, Kuwait. *Education:* University of Kuwait Law School (LL.B., 1991). *LANGUAGES:* Arabic and English. *PRACTICE AREAS:* Banking; Commercial; Real Estate; Commodities; Administrative; Civil Litigation.

AL-SARRAF, AL-RUWAYEH &
STEPHENSON HARWOOD

Established in 1991

SALHIYA COMPLEX, GATE 1

3RD FLOOR

P.O. BOX 1448 SAFAT

KUWAIT 13015, KUWAIT

Telephone: 011 965 240-0061/2/3

Telefax: 011 965 240-0064

Telex: 23502 Lawyer KT

Associated Offices: London, England Office: Stephenson Harwood, One, St. Paul's Churchyard, EC4M 8SH. Telephone: 071 329 4422. Fax: 071 606 0822. Telex: 886789 SHSPC G.

Brussels, Belgium Office: Stephenson Harwood, Avenue du Diamant 139, 1040. Telephone: 2-735 91 90. Fax: 2-7322237.

Guangzhou, The People's of Republic of China Office: Stephenson Harwood & Lo, Room 516, China Hotel, Liu Hua Lu, 510015. Telephone: 010 86-20 6666 888 ext 516. Telex: 44888 CHLGZ CN. Fax: 010 86-20 667 7014/7288.

Hong Kong, Hong Kong Office: Stephenson Harwood & Lo, 18th Floor, Edinburgh Tower, The Landmark, 15 Queen's Road Central. Telephone: 852 8680789. Fax: 852-8681504. Telex: 66278 SHL HX.

Madrid, Spain Office: Stephenson Harwood, Fernando El Santo 15-3°, 28014. Telephone: 010 341 319 1212. Fax: 010 341 319 1940.

International Banking and Commercial Law, Government Contracts, Foreign Investment, International Arbitration, Litigation and Advocacy, Real Estate, Insurance, Corporate, Intellectual Property Law, Shipping, International Financing, Construction Law and General International Trade Law.

FIRM PROFILE: Al Sarraf Al Ruwayeh & Stephenson Harwood is a Joint Venture Law Firm established in July 1991 between Al Sarraf & Al Ruwayeh Law Bureau in Kuwait and Stephenson Harwood in London.

Al Sarraf & Al Ruwayeh Law Bureau is the largest law firm in Kuwait and has strong connections throughout the Gulf. Stephenson Harwood is an international law firm with 75 partners, 230 lawyers and over 500 staff worldwide. The core of its business is banking, construction, corporate and commercial, litigation and arbitration, property and shipping work, which more often than not has an international element.

The Joint Venture is staffed by lawyers from Al Sarraf & Al Ruwayeh Law Bureau and by English solicitors from Stephenson Harwood who are permanently resident in Kuwait and who between them are able to advise on both Kuwaiti and English law.

(This Listing Continued)

AL-SARRAF, AL-RUWAYEH & STEPHENSON HARWOOD, Kuwait—Continued

MEMBERS OF FIRM

HAMEED AL-SARRAF, born April 30, 1947. *Education:* Kuwait University (LL.B.). *LANGUAGES:* English and Arabic. *PRACTICE AREAS:* Finance Law; Commercial Law; Litigation.

AHMED AL-RUWAYEH, born April 29, 1950. *Education:* Kuwait University (LL.B.). *LANGUAGES:* English and Arabic. *PRACTICE AREAS:* Civil Litigation; Commercial Litigation.

ISAM HABBAS, born August 30, 1958. *Education:* University of Santa Clara (B.A., with honors); Boston College Law School (J.D.). *LANGUAGES:* English and Arabic. *PRACTICE AREAS:* Banking Law; International Business Transactions; International Arbitration; Construction Law.

PAUL GODWIN, born April 6, 1949. *Education:* Cambridge University, England (LL.B.). *LANGUAGES:* English. *PRACTICE AREAS:* Corporate Law; Commercial Law; International Banking Law; Mergers and Acquisitions; Joint Ventures.

ASSOCIATES

SIMON BIANCARDI, born September 25, 1969. *Education:* University of Wales, Cardiff (LL.B., with honors). *LANGUAGES:* English and French. *PRACTICE AREAS:* Commercial Law; Litigation.

ALEXANDER N. SALEH, born July 3, 1966. *Education:* Wayne State University (B.A., magna cum laude, 1988) Georgetown University (J.D., 1991). *LANGUAGES:* English. *PRACTICE AREAS:* Commercial Law; International Transactions; Real Estate; Corporate Law; Litigation.

RESIDENT PARTNERS - LONDON

TONY SCALES, born January 3, 1942; admitted, 1968. *LANGUAGES:* English. *PRACTICE AREAS:* International Transactions; Corporate Law; Corporate Finance.

CHRISTOPHER TITE, born December 22, 1959; admitted, 1985. *LANGUAGES:* English and French. *PRACTICE AREAS:* Corporate Law; Commercial Law; International Transactions; Joint Ventures; Privatizations; Mergers and Acquisitions.

DIXON & DIXON, LTD., L.L.P.

A Registered Limited Liability Partnership Including Professional Corporations

AL-HILALI STREET, MURGAB
AL-BURRAK BUILDING 2
P.O. BOX 22833 SAFAT
KUWAIT 13089, KUWAIT
Telephone: 011-965-241-5617
FAX: 011-965-240-7030

Omaha, Nebraska Office: Suite 1800, One First National Center, Sixteenth & Dodge Streets, 68102. Telephone: 402-345-3900. Fax: 402-345-0965 or 402-345-3341.

Washington, D.C. Office: 1850 M Street, N.W., Suite 450, 20036. Telephone: 202-452-1034. Fax: 202-452-1822.

Dallas, Texas Office: Suite 2500, Fountain Place, 1445 Ross Avenue, 75202. Telephone: 214-754-0155. Fax: 214-754-0704.

Los Angeles, California Office: Suite 2000, Wells Fargo Center, 333 South Grand Avenue, 90071. Telephone: 213-346-8310. Fax: 213-620-1811.

Geneva, Switzerland Office: Avenue Giuseppe-Motta 52, CH-1211 Geneva 16. Telephone 022-734-2343. Fax: 022-734-0322.

International Claims, Banking, Securities, Corporate, Bankruptcy, Real Estate, Insurance, Legislation, Regulation, Environmental, Insurance and Litigation.

RAYMOND J. TERMINI, (P.C.), born Galveston, Texas, November 12, 1942; admitted, 1967, Texas; 1969, U.S. District Court, Northern District of Texas; 1990, Nebraska. *Education:* University of Edinburgh; Tulane University (B.A., cum laude, 1964); University of Texas (LL.B., 1967); Southern Methodist University (M.C.L., 1968). Phi Beta Kappa; Delta Theta Phi; Phi Eta Sigma. Recipient, American Jurisprudence Awards for Achievement in Comparative Law I, January, 1969, Comparative Civil Procedure, January, 1969 and Comparative Private International Law, January, *(This Listing Continued)*

ary, 1969. Co-Reporter: "Gulf War Claims Reporter," International Law Institute, 1992. Author: "Covenants Against Competition in Franchise Agreements-Arkansas," Forum on Franchising, American Bar Association, 1992. *Member:* Dallas, Nebraska State and American (Member, Section on Real Property, Probate and Trust Law) Bar Associations; State Bar of Texas. Life Fellow, Texas Bar Foundation; Fellow, Dallas Bar Foundation. (Also at Dallas, Texas Office). *PRACTICE AREAS:* Real Estate Law; Banking Law; Savings Institutions Law; Environmental Law; International Law.

(For Biographical Data on Personnel at Los Angeles, California, Washington, D.C., Omaha, Nebraska, Dallas Texas and Geneva, Switzerland, see Professional Biographies at those locations)

AL-SALEH & PARTNERS

AL-ANJARI BUILDING, SECOND FLOOR
ALI AL-SALEM STREET
P.O. BOX 3246
13033 SAFAT, KUWAIT
Telephone: 2467670/1/2/3
Telefax: 2431039

Agency and Franchise, Aviation, Construction and Engineering, Corporate and Joint Ventures, Financial Services, Foreign Investment and Joint Ventures, Government Contracts, Intellectual Property, International and Local Arbitration and Disputes Resolution, International Investment, Tax Planning, Labour, Maritime and Transportation and General Matters.

FIRM PROFILE: The firm was established in 1975 under the name of Al-Saleh and Graham & James (now Al-Saleh & Partners). The senior partner of the firm, Muhammad Musaed Al-Saleh, is the holder of Kuwait Bar License No. 1 and is the first registered lawyer in Kuwait. Since its early establishment and until now, the firm participates in major domestic, regional and international dispute resolutions. The firm also arranged and participated in seminars and workshops relating to inter alia certain selected debatable legal topics in Kuwait and/or the region. The firm prepared the legal documents and/or negotiated contracts and constituent instruments relating to most existing business concerns and industrial projects.

SENIOR PARTNERS

MUHAMMAD MUSAED AL-SALEH, born Kuwait, December 29, 1935; admitted, 1961, Kuwait. *Education:* Cairo University (LL.B., 1958). *Member:* Kuwait Lawyers Association; Arab Lawyers Union.

NADER ABDUL GHAFAR AL-AWADHI, born Kuwait, December 3, 1953; admitted, 1977, Kuwait. *Education:* Kuwait University (LL.B., 1977). *Member:* Kuwait Lawyers Association.

SENIOR CONSULTANT

EL-FAITH EL-SHAZALY OSMAN, born Sudan, January 1, 1945; admitted, 1969, Sudan (Not admitted in Kuwait). *Education:* University of Khartoum (LL.B., 1969); Indiana University (LL.M., 1980). *Member:* Sudan Bar.

PARTNERS

ISSAM BADER YOUSEF AL-ESSA, born Kuwait, January 18, 1948; admitted, 1972, Kuwait. *Education:* Kuwait University (LL.B., 1972). *Member:* Kuwait Lawyers Association.

HASSAN HUSSEIN EL-BASSIOUNI, born Egypt, October 21, 1928; admitted, 1949, Egypt (Not admitted in Kuwait). *Education:* Cairo University (LL.B.). Retired Chief, Court of Appeals, Cairo. *Member:* Egyptian Bar.

ABDUL RAHMANN AL-ESSA, born Egypt, June 28, 1945; admitted, 1973, Egypt (Not admitted in Kuwait). *Education:* Cairo University (LL.B., 1967). *Member:* Egyptian Bar.

AYYAD HAMMAD AL-ADWANI, born Kuwait, April 15, 1967; admitted, 1990, Algeria (Not admitted in Kuwait). *Education:* Algeria University (LL.B., 1990). *Member:* Kuwait Bar Association; Kuwait Lawyers Association; International Bar Association.

FOX & GIBBONS

Solicitors

Established in 1991

In Association with Al-Baghli & Al-Molah

P.O. BOX 26473 SAFAT

13125 SAFAT, KUWAIT

Telephone: (965) 2462323/2462525/2462929

Fax: (965) 2425830

Telex: 30844 ZINA KT

London, England Office: 2 Old Burlington Street, W1X 2QA. Telephone: (44-171) 439 8271. Telex: 267108. Telefax: (44-171) 734 8843. Abu Dhabi, United Arab Emirates Kudsi Fox & Gibbons Office: P.O. Box 46010. Telephone: (9712) 322858. Fax: (9712) 331586.

Dubai, United Arab Emirates Office: P.O. Box 1756. Telephone: (9714) 310220. Fax: (9714) 310201. Telex: 45614 GBLAW EM.

Fujairah, United Arab Emirates Office: P.O. Box 701. Telephone: (971 9) 229390. Fax: (971 9) 226470.

Cairo, Egypt Office: 126 Mohei El Din Abul Ezz Street, 9th Floor, Mohandiseen, Giza, Cairo, Egypt. Telephone: (202) 3485955. Fax: (202) 3492210.

Ruwi, Oman Office: P.O. Box 3552, Postal Code 112. Telephone: (968) 564346; Fax: (968) 564395. Telex: 5630 GIBLAW ON.

Gibraltar Office: P.O. Box 246. Telephone: (350) 77750. Fax: (350) 77800. Telex: 2336.

Yemen Associated Office: P.O. Box 148, Crater, Aden. Telephone: (9672) 255305/253824. Fax: (9672) 255305/255117.

Lebanon Associated Office: Saba K. Zreik Law Offices. Autostrade Dora, Cite Dora 3 Building, 10th Floor, P.O. Box 90-710, Beirut, Lebanon. Telephone (961 1) 881322. Fax: (961 1) 881387. Telex: 42949 MANAL LE.

Corporate and Company work; registration of companies; Agencies Distributorships and Joint Ventures; Banking Law; Contracts; Legal Opinions; Arbitration; Litigation; Marine & Insurance Law; Taxation and Legal Translations.

MANAGING PARTNERS

Ali Al-Molah

(For a list of other Personnel, see Biographical Cards at London, England, Dubai, Fujairah and Abu Dhabi, United Arab Emirates, Cairo, Egypt, Ruwi, Sultanate of Oman, Gibraltar, Lebanon and Yemen)

LEBANON

LAW OFFICES OF
A. ABBOUD & ASSOCIATES

MAKDESSI BUILDING

BLISS STREET

P.O. BOX 113-6100

BEIRUT, LEBANON

Telephone: (01) 860391; (01) 603166 - MCI; 001 (212) 478-1017 cellular; (01) 804341; (01) 804342

Telex: 23039 (LE) JURIST; 44859 (LE) AXIOM

General Practice, Commercial, including Arbitration and Agency Agreements, Banking, Business Law, Corporate, Financial, Labor, Social Security, Land, Property, Insurance, Maritime and Civil Law, Income Tax Matters and International Contracts, Governmental and Private Tenders.

ANTOÍNE G. ABBOUD, born Cairo, Egypt, June 2, 1933; admitted, 1956, Lebanon. *Education:* Cairo University (Licence en Droit; LL.M.; LL.D.); Faculte de Droit, Universite St. Joseph, Beirut (Licence en Droit); Blackstone School of Law, Chicago, U.S.A. (J.D.). Author: "Analysis of the Social Security Law in Lebanon," 1967; Synopsis on "Commercial Representation in Lebanon," 1972; Pamphlet, "Legal Aspect of Foreign Investment in Lebanon," 1972. Co-author: "Analysis re Amendments of the Lebanese Labor Law," 1973; "The Annotated Lebanese Labor and Social Security Codes (With Comparative Studies of the Egyptian and French Laws)", 1973. Lecturer, Lebanese Management Association, 1970—. Assistant to the Head of the Litigation Department-Credit Foncier Egyptian, 1955-1961. Legal Adviser, American Life Insurance Company, Beirut, 1962-

(This Listing Continued)

1964. Associate Counsel, Law Firm of Simon Siksek and Edouard Hanna, 1964-1968. Partner: Law Offices of S. Siksek, E. Hanna and A. Abboud, 1968-1976; Middle East Industrial Relations Counselors, Inc., 1968-1976; Associated Middle East Consultants, 1977—. Founder, Law Offices of A. Abboud & Associates. Secretary, Ad-Hoc Lebanese American Business Committee, 1977. Board and Executive Member, Y.M.C.A., 1977-1986. Board Member, University Christian Center, 1977-1984. President, Beirut Business Forum, 1980—. *Member:* Alumni Association of the Academy of American and International Law (Vice-President, 1968-1969); International Bar Association; World Peace Through Law Center; American Society of International Law. **LANGUAGES:** Arabic, English and French.

CHARLES SACRE, born Lebanon, August 24, 1945; admitted, 1971, Lebanon. *Education:* College St. Sauveur, Beirut (Baccalaureat IIe. Part); Lebanese University (Licence en Droit). *Member:* Beirut Bar Association. **LANGUAGES:** Arabic, French and English.

ANTOINE WAKIM, born Lebanon, February 17, 1944; admitted, 1968, Lebanon. *Education:* College Sacre-Coeur des Freres (Baccalaureat IIe Part); Faculte de Droit, Universite St. Joseph (Licence en Droit, Licence Sciences Politiques, Diplome d'Etudes Superieures). **LANGUAGES:** Arabic, English and French.

RAGI ABOU HAIDAR, born Beirut, Lebanon, January 22, 1948; admitted, 1970, Lebanon. *Education:* Southwestern Legal Foundation International Comparative Law Center (Business English and Management, 1971); St. Joseph University (Licence en Droit Francais; Licence en Droit Libanais). *Member:* American and International Law Center; Beirut Bar Association. **LANGUAGES:** Arabic, French and English.

SABA H. SABA, born Lebanon, 1924. Retired Judge, High Court, Cour de Cassation. Lawyer, 1948-1960. Magistrate, 1992-retirement. **LANGUAGES:** Arabic, French and English.

NADIM A. ABBOUD, born Lebanon, July 12, 1969; admitted, 1994, Lebanon. *Education:* Notre Dame-Jamhour, Jesuit Institution (Lebanese Baccalayreat lle Part and French Baccalaureat, Ter. D. 1988); St. Joseph University (Licence en Droit Libanais).

KAISAR C. FEGHALI, born Lebanon, September 9, 1965; admitted, 1994, Lebanon. *Education:* Notre Dame-Jamhour, Jesuit Institution (Lebanese Baccalaureat lle Part); St. Joseph University (Licence en Droit Libanais).

Languages: Arabic, English and French.

REPRESENTATIVE CLIENTS: The American University of Beirut; The American Community School; Bankers Trust; British American Insurance Co.; Cheseborough Pond's (Geneve) S.A.; C.B.S. News; Freeman, Mathews & Milne; G.D. Searle & Co.; International College; 3M Inc.; Marine Midland Bank; Midland Bank; Norwich Union Fire Insurance Society Ltd.; Pratt & Whitney; Rolls Royce Ltd.; Siemens; Stelrad Group Ltd.; Sumitomo Marine & Fire Insurance; Trane S.A.; Toplis & Harding International, Ltd.; The Plessey Co.

ABOUHAMAD, MERHEB, NOHRA,
NASSIF & HENNAOUI

22, SHEBARO STREET

P.O. BOX 8000

BEIRUT, LEBANON

Telephone: (01) 331737; (01) 321166; (1) 200177; (1) 200178; (1) 602629

Cable Address: "Kabomad Beirut"

Telex: 20241 LE KAB; 43648 LE KAB

Telefax: (01) 200179; (1) 602629

General Practice.

MEMBERS OF FIRM

KHALYL MICHEL ABOUHAMAD (1936-1992).

ANTOINE J. MERHEB, born Beirut, 1939; admitted, 1964, Beirut. *Education:* St. Joseph University (Licences Libanaise et Française en droit, 1964). *Member:* Beirut Bar Associations.

FOUAD S. NOHRA, born Beirut, December, 1931; admitted, 1960, Beirut. *Education:* St. Joseph University (Licences Libanaise et Française en droit, 1960). Author of several articles on banking law. *Member:* Beirut Bar Association.

ISKANDAR N. NASSIF, born Jezzine, September 10, 1943; admitted, 1966, Beirut. *Education:* St. Joseph University (Licences Libanaise et Française en droit, 1966). *Member:* Beirut Bar Association.

(This Listing Continued)

ABOUHAMAD, MERHEB, NOHRA, NASSIF & HENNAOUI, Beirut—Continued

IBRAHIM G. HENNAOUI, born Beirut, 1943; admitted, 1965, Beirut. *Education:* St. Joseph University (Licences Libanaise et Française en droit, 1965). *Member:* Beirut Bar Association.

ELIE E. CHAMOUN, born Deir-El-Kamar, May 29, 1954; admitted, 1980, Beirut. *Education:* St. Joseph University (Licences Française, 1976; et Libanaise, 1979, en droit privé et public); D.E.A. in Private Law (1978). Author: "Les problèmes posés par le choix et le cumul de la responsabilité contractuelle et de la responsabilité délictuelle," 1978. Professor, Business Law, Business Administration Department, St. Joseph University, 1979—. *Member:* Beirut Bar Association.

NASSIB J. CHEDID, born Beirut, October 9, 1956; admitted, 1980, Beirut. *Education:* St. Joseph University (Licences Libanaise et Française en droit, 1980). *Member:* Beirut Bar Association; Union Internationale des Avocats.

NADA ABOUHAMAD, born Beirut, February 6, 1967; admitted, 1989, Beirut. *Education:* Saint Joseph University (licence en Droit Prive, 1989; Diplôme d' Etudes Supérieures Spécialises en Droit Bancaire et Financier-D.E.S.S. Sorbonne, Paris, 1990). *Member:* Paris and Beirut Bar Associations.

ASSOCIATES

NASRI ANTOINE DIAB, born Beirut, 1962; admitted, 1984, Beirut. *Education:* Saint Joseph University (License en droit privé, 1984; License en droit Public, 1984); Georgetown University Law School (Master's of Law, 1985); St. Joseph University (Diplôme d'Etudes Supérieures en droit Privé, 1987); Université de Paris - Panthéon - Assas (Doctorat en droit, 1991). *Member:* Beirut Bar Association.

RACHID A. FARAH, born Saida, November 9, 1955; admitted, 1981, Beirut. *Education:* St. Joseph University (Licences Libanaise et Francaise en droit, 1977; D.E.A. en droit privé, 1979). *Member:* Beirut Bar Association.

NICOLAS E. GEAHCHAN, born Beirut, March 14, 1943; admitted, 1966, Beirut. *Education:* St. Joseph University (Licences Libanaise et Française en droit, 1966). *Member:* Beirut Bar Association.

GABRIEL MAALOULY, born Beirut, January 30, 1964; admitted, 1988, Beirut. *Education:* Saint Joseph University (licence en Droit Privé, 1988. *Member:* Beirut Bar Association.

SAID E. MEOUCHI, born Jezzine, 1932; admitted, 1968, Beirut. *Education:* St. Joseph University (Licences Française, 1966; et Libanaise, 1968, en droit). *Member:* Beirut Bar Association.

BASSAM J. ONAISSI, born Accra, March 31, 1956; admitted, 1980, Beirut. *Education:* St. Joseph University (Licences Libanaise et Française en droit, 1978; University of Paris (D.E.A., en droit privé général, 1979). Assistant Lecturer, Civil Law, 1980— and International Private Law, 1981—, St. Joseph University. *Member:* Brussels and Beirut Bar Associations.

HADY N. RACHED, born Beirut, 1966; admitted, 1990, Beirut. *Education:* Saint Joseph University (licence en Droit Privé, 1990) Paris (Assas) D E A in International Private Law and International Trade Law, 1991. Author: "L'ordre Public en tant que moyen de Protection du for," 1991. Professor, International Trade Law, 1992—. *Member:* Beirut Bar Association.

MARWAN S. SAKR, born Bejjah, 1967; admitted, 1988, Beirut. *Education:* St. Joseph University (Licence en D Privé, 1988). *Member:* Beirut Bar Association; Association Internationale des Jeunes Avocats.

NADIM SOUHAID, born Beirut, 1968; admitted, 1993, Beirut. *Education:* Saint Joseph University (licence en Droit Privé, 1992). *Member:* Beirut Bar Association.

FAYÇAL TARABAY, born Beirut, 1968. *Education:* Lebanese University (licence en droit, 1992).

Languages: Arabic, French and English

ALEM & ASSOCIATES

Established in 1955

CORNISHE MAZRAA, GONDOLE BUILDING
5TH FLOOR, SUITE 10
BEIRUT, LEBANON
Telephone: (961) (1) 818191; (961) (1) 318615
Fax: (961) (1) 818191

Firm engaged in Lebanese, Middle Eastern and International Law practice Entitled to plead before Lebanese courts.
International Arbitration, Banking, Commercial Real Estate, Competition Corporate, Environment, Financial, Financial Institutions, Intellectual & Commercial Property, International Trade, Joint-Ventures, Litigation, Lobbying, Mergers & Acquisitions, Securities and Taxation.

FIRM PROFILE: *Established in 1955 by Me Youssef Alem, Alem Law Firm has evolved to become one of Lebanon's youngest and leading law firms.*

The firm has a reputation of being committed to international legal services for business and finance the firm has three partners and six associates based in Beirut and has a close association with the law practice of Me Khaldoun Naja in Tripoli. The firm has several correspondents around the globe and maintains close contacts with international law firms in Canada, USA, and Europe.

MEMBERS OF FIRM

MOHAMED Y. ALEM, born Beirut, Lebanon, 1965; admitted, 1989, Beirut. *Education:* Lebanese University (LL.B., 1988); Universite de Caen, France (D.E.A., 1990); Mc Gill University, Institute of Comparative Law, Montreal, Canada (LL.M., 1991). Chief Editor, Classeur Législatif du Liban, General Encyclopedia of Lebanese Laws. *Member:* Beirut Bar Association; International Association of Young Lawyers. **LANGUAGES:** French, English, Arabic and Italian. **PRACTICE AREAS:** International Business; General Commercial; Corporate; Financial Institutions; International Arbitration.

LEILA Y. ALEM, born Beirut, Lebanon, 1967; admitted, 1989, Lebanon. *Education:* Lebanese University (LL.B., 1989). Editorial Committee, Classeur Législatif Libanais, General Encyclopedia of Lebanese Laws. **LANGUAGES:** Arabic, French and English. **PRACTICE AREAS:** Competition Law; Litigation; Environmental Law.

AMIRA H. JAANA, born Beirut, Lebanon, 1967; admitted, 1991, Lebanon. *Education:* Arab University (LL.B., 1991). Editorial Committee, Classeur Législatif Libanais, General Encyclopedia of Lebanese Laws. Member, Aija, 1993. **LANGUAGES:** Arabic, English and French.

NADER N. OBEID, born Lebanon, 1963; admitted, 1988, Lebanon. *Education:* Lebanese University (LL.B., 1987). Editorial Committee, Classeur Législatif Libanais, General Encyclopedia of Lebanese Laws. **LANGUAGES:** Arabic and English. **PRACTICE AREAS:** Civil Law; General; General Commercial; Real Estate; Taxation.

MARWAN A. SINNO, born Beirut, Lebanon, 1968; admitted, 1993, Lebanon. *Education:* Lebanese University (LL.B., 1992). Editorial Committee, Classeur Législatif Libanais, General Encyclopedia of Lebanese Laws. **LANGUAGES:** Arabic, French and English.

FARID E. EL KHOURY
LAW OFFICE

Established in 1968

261 MONOT STREET
P.O. BOX 116-2051
BEIRUT, LEBANON
Telephone: (961-1) 202005
Facsimile: (961-1) 219535; (34-5) 282 9729

Business and Corporate Law. Agency, Distributorship and Franchising. Hotel Investment, Development and Management.

FIRM PROFILE: *Since its establishment in 1968, this firm has specialized in representing multinational corporations in Lebanon and the Middle East.*

(This Listing Continued)

MEMBERS OF FIRM

FARID E. EL KHOURY, born Lebanon, October 13, 1937; admitted, 1959, Beirut. *Education:* Beirut Law Faculty (Licence en Droit); University of Lyon (Licence en Droit); University College, London (A. P.D.L.); Trinity College, Cambridge (LL.M.). *Member:* Beirut Bar Association; International Law Association.

ANTOINE K. HALAL, born Lebanon, January 17, 1950; admitted, 1972, Beirut. *Education:* Beirut Law Faculty (Licence en Droit); University of Lyon (Licence en Droit). Lecturer in Law, School of Business Administration, University St. Joseph. *Member:* Beirut Bar Association.

KHAIRALLAH & CHAIBAN

MAKTABI BUILDING, SUITE 16
CLEMENCEAU STREET
BOITE POSTALE 118336
BEIRUT, LEBANON
Telephone: 369758
Cable Address: "Khairban, Beirut"

REVISERS OF THE LEBANON LAW DIGEST FOR THIS DIRECTORY.

Private International Law, Estates, Personal Status, Commercial Law, Corporations. Marine Insurance. Maritime Law. Patent Law. Banking, Civil Law.

IBRAHIM A. KHAIRALLAH (1889-1970).

CHAKER CHAIBAN (1901-1992).

CLAUDE CHAIBAN, born Beirut, April 23, 1935; admitted, 1957, Lebanon; 1982, Paris, France. *Education:* Université St. Joseph (Baccalaureat Francais); Faculte de Droit, Beirut, Université de Lyon (Docteur en droit); Diplômes d'Etudes Supérieures de Droit Public, Droit Privé and Economy. *Author:* "Persons Physical and Moral in the Lebanese Law"; "Legal Immunities of Carriers by Sea under the Lebanese, French, American and English Laws"; "Errors of Navigation and Management of Ships." Lecturer at the Lebanese Faculty of Law, 1966-1975. The French Faculty of Law (Beirut), 1960-1972; The American University of Beirut, 1963-1973. *Member:* Beirut and Paris Bar Associations. (Also Member, Chaiban & Klopp, 22 rue des Vignes, Paris, France). *LANGUAGES:* English, French and Arabic.

KHALIL CHAIBAN, born Zahleh, March 23, 1923; admitted, 1947, Lebanon. *Education:* International College, American University (Baccalaureat Francais); Faculté de Droit, Beirut University de Lyon (Licence en Droit). *Member:* Beirut Bar Association. *LANGUAGES:* Spanish, French, English and Arabic.

Languages: English, French, Spanish and Arabic

REPRESENTATIVE CLIENTS: United Centrifugal Pumps; Federal Mogul Corp.; Kimberly-Clark Corp.; Parsons & Whittemore Inc.; The Black Clawson Company; Beirut Riyad Bank; Manufacturer Hanover Trust.

REVISERS OF THE LEBANON LAW DIGEST FOR THIS DIRECTORY.

KHATTAR & ASSOCIÉS

CORNICHE DU FLEUVE, PLACE DU MUSEE
P.O. BOX 116-2211
BEIRUT, LEBANON
Telephone: (961-1) 393195/424898/390638
Facsimile: (961-1) 424898/393195/390638

Litigation, Corporate Law, Corporate Finance, Contract and Civil Law, Construction Law, Banking Law, Patent and Trademark, Private Council, Real Estate, Arbitration.

FIRM PROFILE: The office has almost 16 Junior and Senior Associates with different legal expertise.

MEMBERS OF FIRM

MICHEL N. KHATTAR, born Lebanon, 1926; admitted, 1949, Lebanon. *Education:* St. Joseph University (Master, 1948); University of Lyon, Paris (1949). *Member:* Beirut Bar Association (President, 1993—). *LANGUAGES:* French, English and Arabic. *PRACTICE AREAS:* Litigation; Banking Law; Maritime Law; Real Estate Law; Arbitration.

NAOUM M. KHATTAR, born January 22, 1962; admitted, 1985, Beirut, Lebanon; 1989, Paris as Conseil Juridique; 1991, Paris as Advocate. *Education:* Saint Joseph University Law School (Maîtrise, 1985); University

(This Listing Continued)

of Paris II, Sorbonne (D.E.A., 1986); Harvard Law School, Boston, Massachusetts (LL.M., 1987). Professor, Environmental Law, Institut D' urbanisme De L'alba, Beirut, Lebanon 1993—. Member, Harvard Law School Alumni, 1987. *Member:* Beirut Bar Association; Paris Bar Association; American Trial Lawyers Association (ATLA). *LANGUAGES:* Arabic, French English and Spanish. *PRACTICE AREAS:* Banking Law; Corporate Law; Construction Law; Taxation; International Law.

LAW OFFICES OF ALBERT LAHAM

Established in 1956
701 HAMRA STREET
P.O. BOX 4361
BEIRUT, LEBANON
Telephone: 345907, 341390
Fax: (1-212) 4781963

European Mailing Address: 62 Route de Florissant, 1206 Geneva, Switzerland. Telephone: (4122) 7894506. Fax: (4122) 7894507.

General Practice, Corporation, International, Aviation, Administrative and Tax Law, Patents, Real Estate and Arbitration.

FIRM PROFILE: The firm represented, before the Lebanese war of 1975-1991, a number of major American corporations operating in Lebanon and the Middle East in petroleum, aviation, industrial and commercial fields. It has established a solid reputation for offering a full range of quality legal services and has cooperated, in a number of cases, with prominent European and American law firms.

MEMBERS OF FIRM

Albert Laham	Antoine Traboulsi
Fuad S. Kawar	Marwan Atallah
Amine Sinno	Toufic Nehmé
	Mohammad Saab

Languages: Arabic, English and French.

THE LAW OFFICES OF LYAN & ASSOCIÉS

Established in 1959
ACHRAFIEH
HABIB BACHA EL-SAAD STREET
THE LYAN BUILDING
P.O. BOX 116-2116
BEIRUT, LEBANON
Telephone: +961-1-202-616
Telefax: +961-1-602-616

Panama City, Panama Associated Office: 123 Via Esoaña, Citibank Building Suite 604. Telephone: +507-64-6266. Telefax: +507-64-6296.
London, England Associated Office: 14 Theobalds Road, WCIX 8PF. Telephone: +44-71-831-6969. Telefax: +44-71-831-7817.

General Practice counseling particularly in International transactions, Investments, Banking, Taxation, Company Law, Commercial Law, Bankruptcy, Mergers and Acquisitions, Trusts and Estates, Real Estate Law, Social law, Intellectual Property, Insurance and Admiralty.
Litigation Department handling Commercial Law, Civil Law and Business Crime Cases, as well as national and ICC arbitration.

PARTNERS

NICOLAS N. LYAN, born Beirut, Lebanon, April 30, 1931; admitted, 1957, Beirut, Lebanon. *Education:* Académie Libanaise de Droit, Beirut, Lebanon (Master of Law, 1957). Member, Universal Bank S.A.L., Board of Directors. *Member:* Beirut Bar Association (Board Member, 1974-1981); Lebanese International Law Association. *LANGUAGES:* English, French and Arabic.

MICHEL F. LYAN, born Zahleh, Lebanon, July 23, 1944; admitted, 1966, Beirut, Lebanon. *Education:* Académie de Lyon, Lyon, France (Bachelor of French Law, 1965); Saint Joseph University, Beirut, Lebanon (Master of Lebanese Law, 1966). *Member:* Beirut Bar Association (Board Member, 1981-1987; Retirement Fund, 1987-1991, and 1994—); Union Internationale des Avocats (U.I.A.); Lebanese International Law Association. *LANGUAGES:* French and Arabic.

(This Listing Continued)

THE LAW OFFICES OF LYAN & ASSOCIÉS, Beirut— Continued

MONA A. OFEICH, born Beirut, Lebanon, December 24, 1942; admitted, 1966, Beirut, Lebanon. *Education:* Saint Joseph University, Beirut, Lebanon (Bachelor of French Law; Master of Lebanese Law). *Member:* Beirut Bar Association; Universities Association of Lebanon. *LANGUAGES:* English, French and Arabic.

NAJIB N. LYAN, born Beirut, Lebanon, June 7, 1959; admitted, 1981, Beirut, Lebanon. *Education:* New York University School of Law, New York, U.S.A. (Master of Comparative Jurisprudence, 1985); Saint Joseph University, Beirut, Lebanon (Bachelor of French Law, 1980; Master of Lebanese Law, 1981; D.E.S. of Private Law, 1983). Author: "Le régime juridique du droit á la prorogation légale du contrat de bail"; "Piercing the Corporate Veil under United States Law"; "The Perils of the Sea under COGSA"; "The European Lawyer in the EEC." *Member:* Beirut Bar Association; Association Internationale des Jeunes Avocats (A.I.J.A.); Lebanese International Law Association; Lebanese Egyptian Businessman Association. *LANGUAGES:* English, French and Arabic.

NAYLA N. HATEM, born Beirut, Lebanon, September 29, 1945; admitted, 1969, Beirut, Lebanon. *Education:* Saint Joseph University, Beirut, Lebanon (Bachelor of French Law, 1968; Bachelor of Political Science, 1969; Master of Lebanese Law, 1969). *Member:* Beirut Bar Association. *LANGUAGES:* English, French and Arabic.

GEORGE A. ALOUF, born Baalbeck, Lebanon, June 18, 1946; admitted, 1971, Beirut, Lebanon. *Education:* Saint Joseph University, Beirut, Lebanon (Bachelor of French Law, 1970; Master of Lebanese Law, 1971). *Member:* Beirut Bar Association. *LANGUAGES:* French and Arabic.

ASSOCIATES

Jade Y. Khalil   Dany M. Lattouf
Pierre I. Chidiac   Carla L. Abousleiman
            Mireille F. Geagea

CONSULTANTS

MANUEL JOSÉ BERROCAL, born Panama, Republic of Panama, February 27, 1961; admitted, 1984, Republic of Panama. *Education:* University of Barcelona School of Law, Barcelona, Spain (Doctorate in Commercial Law); New York University School of Law, New York, U.S.A. (Master of Comparative Jurisprudence); Santa Maria La Antigua University School of Law, Panama, Republic of Panama (Law Degree). Author: "Disolución y Liquidación de Sociedades Anónimas"; "Investment In Panama"; "Reorganization as a Shield Against Massive Tort Liability: a misuse." *Member:* Panamanian Bar Association; Association Internationale des Jeunes Avocats (A.I.J.A.); American Bar Association; Inter-American Bar Association; The Panama Chamber of Commerce; Association for the Protection of Industrial Property. *LANGUAGES:* English and Spanish.

Languages: English, French and Arabic

REPRESENTATIVE CLIENTS: Banque Arabe et Internationale d'Investissement (B.A.I.I.); Saudi American Bank; Gulf International Bank B.S.C.; Universal Bank S.A.L.; Hyundai Engineering & Construction Co., Ltd.; Hochtlef Aoktiengesellshaft; Arthur Andersen & Co.; Monroe Europe; Sodexho International; American Telephone & Telecommunications (AT&T); Telecel International; The Pritchard Corporation; Dumez-GTM; Trans World Television; Natural Law Party; The American Missionary Association of America; The Lebanese International Association; National Ammunition Company (Winchester) S.A.L.; The Diab Group of Companies; E&C Group of Companies; Unigroup Real Estate Company S.A.L.; Orièvrerie Habis S.A.L.; Centre d'études et de publications S.A.L.; Mediterranean Snack Industries S.A.L.; Ghantous & Abou Raad; Assurex S.A.L.; CHAL, Bekapress; Radioscope; Watermaster.

MOGHAIZEL LAW OFFICES

Established in 1953

145 TABARIS SQUARE
P.O. BOX 166742
BEIRUT, LEBANON
Telephone: (961-1) 333753/218580/336458
Fax: (961-1) 201354/602693
Telex: 43124 JLM LE

Arbitration, business law, corporate law, banking and insurance law, administrative law, civil and commercial litigation, real estate and construction law, intellectual property law, labor and social security law, criminal law.

(This Listing Continued)

MEMBERS OF FIRM

JOSEPH MOGHAIZEL, born Tebnine, Lebanon, 1924; admitted, 1950, Beirut. *Education:* Saint Joseph University, Beirut (lícence en droit francais, 1949; licence en droit libanais, 1950). *Member:* Lebanese Parliament; Beirut Bar Association (Former Board Member); Lebanese High Court of Justice. *LANGUAGES:* Arabic, French and English. *PRACTICE AREAS:* Litigation; Business Law; Civil Law; Intellectual Property Law; Criminal Law; Administrative Law.

LAURE MOGHAIZEL, born Sabah, Lebanon, 1929; admitted, 1952, Beirut. *Education:* Saint Joseph University, Beirut (licence en droit francais, 1950; licence en droit libanais, 1952). Former Vice President, International Council for Women. *LANGUAGES:* Arabic, French and English. *PRACTICE AREAS:* Civil Law; Labor Law; Social Security Law.

SAMI WARDE, born Beirut, Lebanon, 1929; admitted, 1952, Beirut. *Education:* Saint Joseph University, Beirut (licence en droit francais; licence en droit libanais, 1952; Diplome d'Etudes Superieures en Droit Prive, 1962). *LANGUAGES:* Arabic, French and English. *PRACTICE AREAS:* Banking Law; Bankruptcy Law; General Commercial Law; Contracts Law.

MOUNIR DAOU, born Ballouneh, Lebanon, 1953; admitted, 1983, Beirut. *Education:* Saint Joseph University, Beirut (licence en droit, 1981). *LANGUAGES:* Arabic and French. *PRACTICE AREAS:* General Commercial Law; Taxation; Litigation; Real Estate Law; Administrative Law.

FADI MOGHAIZEL, born Beirut, Lebanon, 1963; admitted, 1985, Lebanon; 1993, Paris. *Education:* St. Joseph University, Beirut (Licence en droit, 1985); University of London (LL.M., 1986; Ph.D., 1990). *LANGUAGES:* Arabic, French and English. *PRACTICE AREAS:* Business Law; Corporate Law; Arbitration; Commercial Law.

FADI NADER, born Beirut, Lebanon, 1963; admitted, 1985, Beirut. *Education:* Saint Joseph University, Beirut (licence en droit, 1985); University of London (LL.M., 1986). *LANGUAGES:* Arabic, French, Spanish and English. *PRACTICE AREAS:* Banking Law; Corporate Law; International Business Transactions Law; Transactions Law; Contracts Law.

CHAFIC NEHME, born Chekka, Lebanon, 1963; admitted, 1986, Beirut. *Education:* Saint Joseph University, Beirut (licence en droit, 1985; Diplome d'Etudes Superieures en Droit Prive, 1986); Paris II University (candidate to the Doctorate). *LANGUAGES:* Arabic, French and English. *PRACTICE AREAS:* Commercial Law; Banking Law; Agency Law; Litigation.

AMINE BARSA, born Beirut, Lebanon, 1966; admitted, 1988, Beirut. *Education:* Saint Joseph University, Beirut (licence en droit, 1988; Diplome d'Etudes Superieures en Droit Prive, 1989); Paris II University (candidate to the Doctorate). Lecture, Tutorial Classes, Faculty of Law, Saint Joseph University, Beirut. *LANGUAGES:* Arabic, French and English. *PRACTICE AREAS:* Litigation; Commercial law; Civil Law; Private International Law.

KATIA BOU ASSI, born Abadia, Lebanon, 1968; admitted, 1991, Beirut. *Education:* Saint Joseph University, Beirut (licence en droit, 1990). *LANGUAGES:* Arabic, French and English. *PRACTICE AREAS:* Corporate Law; Litigation; General Commercial Law.

MIRNA SAKR, born Ain Ibl, Lebanon, 1966; admitted, 1991, Beirut. *Education:* Lebanese University (licence en droit, 1990). *LANGUAGES:* Arabic and French. *PRACTICE AREAS:* Litigation; Civil Law; General Commercial Law.

RICHARD RIACHI, born Khenchara, Lebanon, 1967; admitted, 1992, Beirut. *Education:* Lebanese University (licence en droit, 1991). *LANGUAGES:* Arabic and French. *PRACTICE AREAS:* General Commercial Law; Civil Law; Litigation.

LAW OFFICES OF
DR. MUHAMAD MUGRABY

Established in 1966

202 LIONS BUILDING
SORATI STREET, HAMRA
P.O. BOX 113-6310
BEIRUT, LEBANON
Telephone: (01) 341060; (01) 348120
Telex: 20455 PETROS LE
Fax: (01) 348121; (01) 341061

General Corporate and Commercial Practice. Investments, Banking, Conflicts, International Transactions, Patents and Trademarks.

FIRM PROFILE: The firm has a solid reputation for counselling on Middle Eastern legal matters, particularly for transactions and disputes in, or concerning, member countries of the Gulf Cooperation Council. It also offers a full range of services within the legal system of Lebanon. The client base is Middle Eastern, European and North American. The firm works closely with several American law firms, and has many associations, formal and informal, with local practitioners throughout the region. Dr. Mugraby has five associates and the office employs several paralegals and other assistants.

DR. MUHAMAD MUGRABY, born Beirut, Lebanon, December 5, 1938; admitted, 1960, Lebanon; 1968, Saudi Arabia; 1970, Dubai; 1977, Abu Dhabi. *Education:* International College (A.B., 1956); American University of Beirut (M.B.A., 1962); Lebanese University Law School (LL.B., 1960); Columbia University Law School (M.C.L., 1963; LL.M., 1964; J.S.D., 1966). Columbia University Fellow, 1962-1963. International Law Fellow, Columbia University, 1963-1965. Author: "Permanent Sovereignty Over Oil Resources, A Study of Middle East Oil Concessions and Legal Change," 1966 (Arabic Edition, 1968). Lecturer in Law: Lebanese University Law School, 1965-1970; American University of Beirut, 1966. Director, Islamic Wakf Council, Beirut, 1966-1968. Legal Advisor: Organization of Petroleum Exporting Countries, 1967; Minister of Petroleum of the Kingdom of Libya, 1967-1969. *Member:* Beirut Bar Association. *LANGUAGES:* Arabic, English and French. *PRACTICE AREAS:* Complex litigation/arbitration; transaction and business structuring; international business law; Sharia (Islamic) law; natural resources; construction; entertainment.

NASSER & NASSER & ASSOCIATES

Established in 1981

P.O. BOX 11-4668
BEIRUT, LEBANON
Telephone: (961-1) 867 422
Fax: Thru New York (212) 478-2293
Telex: 20610; 22335

U.S. Mailing Address: 84 N. Sabra Ave., Agoura, California, USA 91301. Telephone: (818) 597-8004. Fax: (818) 879-9338.

General Practice, Corporate, Commercial and Contracts Laws, Banking Law, Anti-Trust, Public Tenders, Copyright, Trademarks and Patents, Taxation, and Arbitration.

ABDALLAH H. NASSER, born Houssain, 1924. *Education:* St. Joseph University, Beirut (Licenses Libanaise and Francaise en Droit, 1949). Author: "La Chambre des Mises en Accusation en Droit Libanais." Member, Committee of Experts Charged with the Reviews and Amendment of all Lebanese Laws. President, La Cour Des Comptes, 1990-1992. President, Court of Cassation, 1988-1990. President, Court for Banks under Liquidation, 1980-1988. President, Court of Appeals of Beirut, 1967-1980. Member, Superior Council of Judges, 1984-1987. Legal Advisor, Supreme Banking Commission, 1967-1992. Lecturer, School of Judges, 1962-1967. President, Court of Appeals, Mount Lebanon, 1961-1967. President, Court of First Instance, Zahle, 1953-1959. President, Expropriation Committee, 1964-1992. Founding Member, The International Arbitration Center, Lebanon. *LANGUAGES:* French and Arabic. *PRACTICE AREAS:* Banking Law; Corporate Law; Commercial Law; Contract Law; Taxation Law; Arbitration.

WALID A. NASSER, born Jbeil, 1951; admitted, 1975, Beirut. *Education:* Saint Joseph University, Beirut (Licenses Libanaise and Francaise en Droit, 1975); Universite Jean Moulin, Lyon, France (DEA Droit des Affaires, 1977); Harvard Law School (LL.M., 1984). Author: "Effectiveness of

(This Listing Continued)

the Arab Boycott Office". Drafter, New Lebanese Copyright Bill. Associate with a major New York law firm, 1984-1985. *Member:* American Bar Association; International Bar Association; Beirut Bar Association. *LANGUAGES:* English, French and Arabic. *PRACTICE AREAS:* Patent, Trademark and Copyright Law; Corporate Law; Commercial Law; Contract Law; Anti-Trust; Public Tenders.

RAPHAËL, ZIADÉ, ABIRACHED ET
ASSOCIÉS

IMMEUBLE KASSIS-ANTELIAS
P.O. BOX BOITE POSTALE 70-868
BEIRUT, LEBANON
Telephone: 405 401
FAX: 601908

Jeddah, Saudi Arabia Office: Almabani, Hael Street, P.O. Box 2781. Telephone: (9662) 651.34.12.
Paris, France Associated Office: Thieffry & Associes, 23, Avenue Hoche, 75008. Telephone: (331) 40.75.02.57.
Cairo, Egypt Associated Office: Sami Borael, Kasr el Nil Street. Telephone: (202) 391.72.82.

General Practice, Corporate Commercial and Contracts Law, Banking Law, Arbitration, Litigation, Agency and Distribution, Construction, Admiralty and Aviation Law, Private International Law, Patent Trademark and Copyright, Franchise, Leasing and Public Law.

MOUSSA RAPHAËL, born Dlebta, 1932; admitted, 1957, Beirut. *Education:* St. Joseph University (French and Lebanese Master of Laws, 1957).

CAMILLE ZIADÉ, born Beirut, 1943; admitted, 1967, Beirut. *Education:* St Joseph University (French and Lebanese Masters of Laws, 1967). Member of the Lebanese Parliament, 1992—.

RENÉ ABIRACHED, born Beirut, 1944; admitted, 1965, Beirut. *Education:* St. Joseph University (French and Lebanese Masters of Laws, 1965); Diplome d 'Etudes Suptrieures (Private Laws), Paris University, France 1966—, Diplome d'Etudes Suptrieures (Criminal Sciences), Paris University 1967—. Assistant Professor, Paris University, 1967-1970. Professor of Criminal Law and International Private Law, St. Josephs University. Beirut from 1972 to present.

LILAINNE CHAMI RAPHAËL, born Beirut, 1942; admitted, Beirut, 1965. *Education:* St. Joseph University (French and Lebanese Master of Laws, 1965).

SOUHAIL HADDAD, born Haifa, 1934; admitted, Beirut, 1959. *Education:* St. Joseph University (French and Labanese Master of Laws, 1959).

HALA MURR HADDAD, born Bteghrine, 1943; admitted, 1966, Beirut. *Education:* St. Joseph University (French and Lebanese Master of Laws, 1966).

ISSA SACRE, born Beirut, 1945; admitted, Beirut, 1971. *Education:* St. Joseph University (French and Lebanese Master of Laws); Master of Political Sciences, St. Joseph University, 1972. Master of History and Geography, St. Joseph University, 1973.

ELIE RAPHEËL, born Dlebta, 1944; admitted, 1969, Beirut. *Education:* Sagesse University (French and Labanese Master of Laws, 1969).

ROBERT SALAMOUNI, born Beirut, 1953; admitted, Beirut, 1980. *Education:* St. Joseph University (French and Lebanese Master of Laws, 1980).

MARC DE CHADAREVIAN, born Beirut, 1954; admitted, 1980, Beirut. *Education:* St. Joseph University (French and Lebanese Master of Laws, 1980). (Resident, Jeddah, Saudi Arabia Office).

ADEL NASSAR, born Bikfaya, 1964; admitted, 1987, Beirut, Lebanon; 1993, Paris, France. *Education:* St. Joseph University (Maîtrise du Droit Privé; Maîtrise de Droit Public, 1987); Paris II University (Diplôme d'Etudes Approfondies de Droit Privé General, 1988); Harvard Law School (LL.M., 1991). Publications: International Arbitration in Lebanon, International Arbitration, 1994. Arbitrage et Ordre Public Transnational, Bull. Suisse de l' Arbitrage 1994. L'offset dans les pays du Golf, Revue du Droit et Pratiques du Commerce International 1993.

HALA RAPHAEL, born Dlebta, 1966; admitted, 1989, Beirut. *Education:* St. Joseph University (Master of Laws); Georgetown University (Master of Laws, 1991).

(This Listing Continued)

RAPHAËL, ZIADÉ, ABIRACHED ET ASSOCIÉS,
Beirut—Continued

ELIANE GHANNAGÉ, born Beirut, 1971; admitted, 1992, Beirut. *Education:* St Joseph University (Master of Laws, 1992).

IBRAHIM SATTOUT, born Beirut, 1967; admitted, 1994, Beirut. *Education:* St. Joseph University (Master of Private Laws, 1990); Paris II University (Master of Private Laws, 1991), Diplome d'Eudes Approfondies, International Law, Paris II University France, 1992. Author: "Joint-Venture in the Gulf Countries: Saoudi-Arabia, Kuwait and Oman".

Arabic, French, English, Portuguese and Italian.

NAWAF A. SALAM

Avocat à la Cour

SABBAGH CENTER - HAMRA ST.
BEIRUT, LEBANON
Telephone: (961-1) 342633/4
Telefax: (961-1) 347031 (Satellite); (1-212) 478 12 52
Telex: 42058 Le

General Lebanese and International Law Practice. Agency and Franchise, Commercial, Corporate, Construction, Industrial and Intellectual Property, International Contracts, Litigation, Real Estate.

NAWAF A. SALAM, born Beirut, Lebanon, 1953; admitted, 1985, Beirut. *Education:* Institut d'etudes politiques de Paris (Doctorat d'Etat, Summa Cum Laude); Harvard Law School (LL.M.); Sorbonne University (Doctorat de 3ème cycle, Summa Cum Laude); Lebanese University (Licence en Droit). Former Foreign Legal Consultant, Edwards & Angell, Boston. Author: "The Institution of the presidency in Lebanon"; "The question of citizenship in Islamdom," - with Philip O'Neill Jr. "Is the Exceptio non adimpleti contractus part of Lex Mearcatoria." *Member:* Beirut Bar Association; American Bar Association (Associate); International Law Association. *LANGUAGES:* Arabic, French and English.

TYAN & ASSOCIES

22, LA SAGESSE STREET
BEIRUT, LEBANON
Telephone: 337968
Fax: 200969
Telex: 43928 LEX

Paris, France Office: Law Offices of Nady Tyan, 12, Avenue Pierre ler de Serbie, 75116 Paris. Telephone: 4.720.18.50. Fax: 47200628.
Associated with Whitman Breed Abbott & Morgan, 200 Park Avenue, New York, N.Y. Telephone: 212-351-3000. 212-351-3022. Fax: 212-351-3131. 212-351-3003.

Private International Law particularly related to Middle Eastern Countries, Litigation, Admiralty, Patent and Trademark, Taxation, Banking, Corporate and Contracts, Arbitration, Aviation, Bankruptcy, Agency & Distribution, Labor Law, Insurance Trade Law, Real Estate, Partnership, Wills and Probate.

MEMBERS OF FIRM

NADY TYAN, born Beirut, Lebanon, 1938; admitted, 1962, Lebanon; 1979, France. *Education:* Université de Lyon, France (Docteur en Droit, 1970); Université Saint Joseph, Beirut, Lebanon; Université de Lyon, France (Diplôme d'Etudes Supérieures de Doctorat en Droit, 1963; Licence en Droit Français et Libanais, 1962; Licence en Sciences Politiques, 1963). Member, National Committee of the International Chamber of Commerce-Paris. Author: "The Executive Power in Lebanon." Professor, Law School of the Lebanese University. President, National Association of Political Sciences, Beirut. Arbitrator, I.C.C. *Member:* Beirut Bar Association; Paris Bar Association; American Bar Association (Associate). *LANGUAGES:* Arabic, English and French.

BECHARA TARABAY, born Chatine, Lebanon, 1952; admitted, 1979, Lebanon; 1992, France. *Education:* Lebanese University (License en Droit Français et Libanais, 1978). *Member:* Beirut Bar Association. (Resident, Paris, France Office). *LANGUAGES:* Arabic and French.

CHAMEL BASSIL, born Smar-Jbeil, Lebanon, 1943; admitted, 1975, Lebanon. *Education:* Université Saint-Joseph, Beirut, Lebanon (Licence en Droit Français et Libanais, 1973; Diplôme d'Etudes Supérieures de Doc-
(This Listing Continued)

torat en Droit, 1980). *Member:* Beirut Bar Association. *LANGUAGES:* Arabic, French and English.

MAURICE ABSI, born Beirut, Lebanon, 1924; admitted, 1947, Lebanon. *Education:* Université Saint-Joseph (Licence en Droit Francais et Libanais); Legal Consultant. *LANGUAGES:* Arabic, English and French.

SOUHEIL ELIAS, born Beirut, Lebanon, 1924; admitted, 1964, Lebanon. *Education:* Université Saint-Joseph (Licence en Droit Francais et Libanais); Legal Consultant. *LANGUAGES:* Arabic, English and French.

MIREILLE RICHA, born Beirut, Lebanon, 1963; admitted, 1985, Lebanon. *Education:* Université Saint-Joseph (Licence en droit, 1985; Diplome d'Etudes Supérieures de Doctorat en Droit, 1987). *Member:* Beirut Bar Association. *LANGUAGES:* Arabic, English and French.

GRAZIELLA SALIBA, born Beirut, Lebanon, 1963; admitted, 1986, Lebanon. *Education:* Université Saint-Joseph (Licence en Droit, 1986). *Member:* Beirut Bar Association. *LANGUAGES:* Arabic, English and French.

GHADA YAZBECK, born Beirut, Lebanon, 1967; admitted, 1993, Lebanon. *Education:* Université Saint-Joseph (Licence en Droit, 1989); The American University, Washington, D.C. (LL.M., 1991). *Member:* Beirut Bar Association. *LANGUAGES:* Arabic, English and French.

OF COUNSEL

ANTOINE BASILE, born Beirut, Lebanon, 1938; admitted, 1962, Lebanon; 1982, France. *Education:* Université de Paris, Panthéon - Sorbonne, France (Docteur d'Etat ès Sciences Economiques, summa cum laude, 1969, Docteur d'Etat en Droit, summa cum laude, 1986); France (Diplôme d'Etudes Supérieures de Doctorat ès Sciences Economiques, Major, 1962; Licences en Droit Français et en Droit Libanais, Laureate of the Faculty, 1961). Author or Co-Author of several books on international trade and finance, holdings, joint ventures and offshore companies, multinational enterprises, free economic zones, debt equity conversions and privatization. Author of numerous articles in leading international specialized journals. Professor, Université de Paris, France and Saint Joseph University, Beirut. Fulbright Scholar, Columbia University, New York. Former Member, Council of Development and Reconstruction, Lebanon. Member: National Committee of the International Chamber of Commerce, Paris, UN Task Force on New Independent States, New York. Adviser to multinational enterprises, Governments, Central Banks OECD and other multilateral organizations; Interregional Adviser, UN Legal Advisory Services for Development - DESD - New York. Arbitrator, I.C.C., A.A.A., Euro-Arab system, Vice-President American Foreign Law Association. *Member:* Beirut Bar Association; Paris Bar Association; American Bar Association (Associate); International Law Association, Rotary International. *LANGUAGES:* Arabic, English, French and German.

BERGE SETRAKIAN, born Beirut, Lebanon, 1949; admitted, 1972, Lebanon; 1982, New York; Licensed as Legal Consultant in New York, 1978. *Education:* Université Saint-Joseph, Beirut, Lebanon; Université de Lyon, France (Diplôme d'Etudes Supérieures de Doctorat en Droit, 1974; Licence en Droit Français, 1972); F.I.E.D.C., Strasbourg, France (Diplôme d'Etudes Supérieures de Droit Comparé, 1974); Lebanese University, Beirut, Lebanon (Licence en Droit Libanais, 1972). Author: "Arbitration under the Legal System of the Middle Eastern Countries," MEED, 1978. *Member:* Beirut Bar Association; New York State Bar Association; American Bar Association (International Associate); International Association for Comparative Law; Middle East Institute; American Foreign Law Association. (Also Member, Whitman Breed Abbott & Morgan, New York, N.Y.). *LANGUAGES:* Arabic, English and French.

SABA K. ZREIK LAW OFFICES

Solicitors

P.O. BOX 90-710
BEIRUT, LEBANON
Telephone: (961 1) 881322
Fax: (961 1) 881387
Telex: 42949 MANAL LE

Tripoli, Lebanon Office: P.O. Box 139. Telephone: c/o Beirut Office (961 1) 881322. Fax: c/o Beirut Office (961 1) 881387. Telex: 42949 MANAL LE.

London England Office: 2 Old Burlington Street, W1X 2QA. Telephone: (44-171) 439 8271. Telex: 267108. Fax: (44-171) 734 8843.

Dubai, United Arab Emirates Office: P.O. Box 1756. Telephone: (9714) 310220. Fax: (9714) 310201. Telex: 45614 GBLAW EM.

Abu Dhabi, United Arab Emirates Office: Kudsi Fox & Gibbons Office: P.O. Box 46010. Telephone: (9712) 322858. Fax: (9712) 331586.

Cairo, Egypt Office: 126 Mohei El Din Abul Ezz Street, 9th Floor, Mohandiseen, Giza, Cairo, Egypt. Telephone: (202) 3485955. Fax: (202) 3492210.

Ruwi, Oman Office: P.O. Box 3552, Postal Code 112. Telephone: (968) 564346. Fax: (968) 564395. Telex: 5630 GIBLAW ON.

Gibraltar Office: P.O. Box 246. Telephone: (350) 77750. Fax: (350) 77800.

Fujairah, United Arab Emirates Office: P.O. Box 701. Telephone: (971 9) 229390. Fax: (971 9) 226470.

Kuwait Associated Office: P.O. Box 26473, Safat, 13125 Safat. Telephone: (965) 2462323/2462525/2462929. Fax: (965) 242 5830. Telex: 30844 ZINA KT.

Yemen Associated Office: P.O.Box 148, Crater, Aden. Telephone: (9672) 255305/253824. FAX: (9672) 255305/255117.

Corporate, Contract, Commercial, Taxation, Intellectual Property Protection.

MANAGING PARTNER

Saba Kaissar Zreik

LEGAL SUPPORT STAFF AT BEIRUT OFFICE

Jihad George Karam
Amale Bahige Abi Saab
Rafic Abdel Adel Ouweidat

LEGAL SUPPORT STAFF AT TRIPOLI OFFICE

Toni Jean Tajer
Lama Mouaffa Alam Eldine

(For a list of other Personnel, see Biographical Cards at London, England, Dubai, Abu Dhabi and Fujairah, United Arab Emirates, Cairo, Egypt, Ruwi, Sultanate of Oman, Gibraltar, Kuwait and Yemen)

MAURITIUS

BENOIT & GLOVER

Barristers and Legal Advisers

CHAMBERS
6TH FLOOR, CERNÉ HOUSE
CHAUSSÉE
PORT LOUIS, MAURITIUS
Telephone: (230) 212 5011
Telefax: (230) 208 8037

Arbitration, Business Law, Commercial Property, Company Law, Consultancy, Foreign Investment, Investment and Financial Service, Offshore Business, Partnerships, Real Estate, Shipping, Tax (Company, Offshore, Personal), Trusts.

MEMBERS OF CHAMBERS

CLAREL BENOIT, M.A. (Cantab), Barrister-at-Law, Middle Temple, England. Lecturer, Council of Legal Education, Supreme Court of Mauritius. Ex-Lecturer, University of Mauritius. Ex-State Counsel and Magistrate.

BRIAN GLOVER, LL.B. (Hons), (Exxon), Barrister-at-Law, Middle Temple, England.

(This Listing Continued)

CONSULTANT

SIR MAURICE RAULT, Q.C., Retired Chief Justice of the Supreme Court of Mauritius. Ex-Vice Chancellor of the University of Mauritius. Advises in Banking, Commercial Law and Taxation.

English and French

CHAMBERS OF MARC HEIN

(Incorporating MARC HEIN & ASSOCIATES)

CATHEDRAL SQUARE
PORT LOUIS, MAURITIUS
Telephone: (230) 2085526; 2126976
Fax: (230) 2085586; 2126030

Business Law, Offshore Business, Trusts, Registration of Offshore Companies, Corporate Investment, Maritime, Air Law, Tax, Banking, Insurance, Immigration, Labour, Trade Marks and Constitutional. Consultancy and Litigation.

FIRM PROFILE: *All members practice at the Bar of Mauritius. The chambers has a large variety of international and local clients and has developed a extensive expertise in offshore activities. The Chambers acts for several international banks, financial institutions and fund managers in the offshore sector.*

CONSULTANTS

L. ROBERT AHNEE, *Education:* Barrister at Law, Middle Temple, London. Former Puisne Judge of the Supreme Court. Judge of the Preferential Trade Agreement for East Africa.

J. PAUL HEIN, CMG, *Education:* M.A. (Oxon), Barrister at Law, Middle Temple, London. Former Attorney-General of Mauritius.

MEMBERS OF CHAMBERS

MARC HEIN, *Education:* Wales (LL.B., Honors); Aix en Provence, France (License-en-Droit). Barrister at Law, Gray's Inn, London. Past Chairman, Mauritius Bar Association. Mauritius representative to the International Bar Association.

URMILA BOOLELLE, *Education:* Reading (LL.B. Honors), Barrister at Law, Lincoln's Inn, London. Author of the Compendium of Mauritius Case Law.

M. JANE NG WONG HING, *Education:* (LL.B. Honors), London, Barrister at Law, Middle Temple, London.

AASHA Y.D. JUDDOO, *Education:* (LL.B. Honors). Barrister at Law, Mauritius.

JOHAN MOUTOU, *Education:* (LL.B. Honors), Mauritius, Barrister at Law, Mauritius.

Languages: English, French and Hindi

ME RASHARD KHADAROO

Attorney at Law, Solicitor, Patent & Trademark Agent

Established in 1959

4 SIR VIRGIL NAZ STREET
P.O. BOX 1099
PORT LOUIS, MAURITIUS
Telephone: 230-2080349
Fax: 230-2080349; 230-6966289

Bankruptcy, Insolvency, Civil Litigation, Commercial, Commercial Property, Company, Debt Recovery, Defamation, Family, House Purchase, Conveyancing, Insolvency, Insurance, Matrimonial, Mortgages, Notaries, Partnerships, Personal Injury, Real Estate Purchase, Wills and Probate, Patent and Trademark Law.

Me Rashard Khadaroo, Attorney-at-Law
Mr. Rohit Ramdenee, Barrister-at-Law
Mr. Boorgesh Ramsewack, Q.C., Barrister-at-Law

(This Listing Continued)

ME RASHARD KHADAROO, Port Louis—Continued

CONSULTANT

Sir Ramesh Jeewoolall, Barrister-at-Law

In collaboration with Sir Ramesh Jeewoolall, Barrister-at-Law.

Languages: English, French, Hindu and Urdu

CHAMBERS OF SIR HAMID MOOLLAN, Q.C.

43, SIR WILLIAM NEWTON STREET
PORT LOUIS, MAURITIUS
Telephone: (230) 212-6913/18; (230) 208-3881
Fax: (230) 208-8351

General Practice, Civil, Constitutional, Public or Private, Banking and Finance, Taxation, Insurance, Maritime, Labour, International Trade, Criminal, Administrative, Company, International Practice including both Litigation and Advisory work, Offshore, Banking, Trust.

FIRM PROFILE: Head of Chambers: Sir Hamid Moollan, Q.C.

Counsel in Chambers: 11.

MEMBERS OF CHAMBERS

Sir. Hamid Moollan, Q.C.	Mr. Shaukat Oozeer
Sir. Cassam Moollan, Q.C.	Mr. Ravindra Chetty
Mr. Dabee Seesaram	Mr. Moorari Gujadhur
Mr. Yusuf Aboobaker	Mr. Nandkishore Ramburn
Mr. Eric Ribot	Miss. Fahmida Jeerooburkhan
Miss. Feerdaus Bundhun	

The firm is the adviser to the Central Bank, Several Commercial Banks, The Stock Exchange of Mauritius, Insurance Companies and Major Commercial Firms and Industries based in Mauritius.

Languages: English, French and Hindi

MOROCCO

MOHAMED MEHDI IBN ABDELJALIL

129, RUE PRINCE MOULAY ABDELLAH
CASABLANCA, MOROCCO
Telephone: (212.2) 22.15.92; (212.2) 20.07.94
Cable Address: Law Adviser
Facsimile: (212.2) 22.19.81

Commercial and Civil Law and Arab Countries.
Patente and Trademark

MOHAMED MEHDI IBN ABDELJALIL, born Casablanca, Morocco, January 12, 1930; admitted, 1965, Morocco; High Court. Education: Institute de Science Politic de Paris (1950-1953); Faculté de Droit de Paris (B.A., D.E.S., Droit Public and D.E.S., Droit Priveé, 1950-1954); Institute des Hauts Etudes International, Faculté de Paris (1954-1956). Author: "Reform for the Mining Laws of 1958"; "Petroleum Code". Under-Secretary of the State for Industrial Production and Mining, 1957. General Secretary of the Ministry of Economy and Finances, 1957. Director General of the Bureau d'Etudes et de Participations Industrielles (BEPI), 1960. Ambassador in Bonn, 1962-1965. Ambassador in Tehran, also Accredited to Turkey and Afghanistan, 1968-1973. Ambassador to the Court of St. James, 1981-1987. LANGUAGES: Arabic, French and English.

MOHAMED MEHDI SALMOUNI-ZERHOUNI

Law Offices
RÉSIDENCE IBN BATOUTA - TOUR D
PLACE PRINCE SIDI MOHAMED (EX P. SÉMARD)
20300 CASABLANCA, MOROCCO
Telephone: (212.2) 24.24.48; 24.96.42
Fax: (212.2) 24.20.83; 40.06.34
Telex: 28018 M (BUSSER)

Industrial Property Law, Patent, Trademark and Models Law, Filing in Morocco, Arab Countries and Africans, Copyright Law, Infringement Actions, International Private Law, Commercial Law, Negotiation and Writing International Contracts, Foreign Investments in Morocco, International Arbitration.

MOHAMED MEHDI SALMOUNI-ZERHOUNI, born Morocco, February 20, 1949; admitted, 1981, Strasbourg, France; 1986, Casablanca. Education: Oujda Morocco (General Certificate of Education); University Law of Strasbourg, France (Bachelor's Degree and Mastery, Private Law); Arts University, Strasbourg, France (Graduated in Arab Studies); D.E.S.S. (Doctorate). Patent Attorney. Judicial Expert in Industrial Property. Ex-Translator, sworn before the courts of Strasbourg, France. Author: "Arbitration in matter of the industrial property," 1981; "Contribution to the study of patent of invention in Moroccan Law," 1989; "Industrial Models and designs in Moroccan Law," 1989; "Franchising," 1990. Member: FICPI; IDEF; IREF for Morocco (franchising); Commission of the industrial and intellectual property of CNM of the CCI, Paris, France.

SEDDIK ZAARI LAW OFFICES

Established in 1970
121 AVENUE HASSAN II
CASABLANCA, MOROCCO
Telephone: (212-2) 27-77-56; (212-2) 27-92-80; (212-2) 20-47-13
Fax: (212-2) 26-47-12; (212-2) 20-46-01;
Telex: 22011 (ZARLAW)

General Practice, International Litigation and Arbitration, Commercial and Trademarks Law, Corporate, Banking, Foreign Investments, Oil, Mining, Real Estate and Maritime Law.

SEDDIK ZAARI, born Rabat, Morocco, August 29, 1940; admitted, 1965, Paris, France; 1970, Casablanca. Education: Lycée Gouraud, Rabat; Yale University, Connecticut; Claremont Men's College, California; Diplôme de l'Institut d'Etudes Politiques (Licence en Droit; Diplôme d'Etudes Supérieures de Droit, Doctorat). Faculté de Droit et des Sciences Economiques de Paris. Former President, Association Marocaine de Droit Maritime. Member: International Bar Association; International Lawyers Network.

Languages: Arabic, French, English and Spanish

NIGERIA

J.B. MAJIYAGBE & CO.

4 HUMAN RIGHTS AVENUE
P.O. BOX 726
KANO, NIGERIA
Telephone: 234-64-621261; 234-64-644171
Telefax: 234-64-647146
Cable: JAYBEE; KANO

Barristers, Solicitors, Notaries Public, General Commercial Practice, Banking and Insurance, Aviation, Air Law, Patents & Trade Marks, Civil Litigation & Arbitration, Real Property.

MEMBERS OF FIRM

J.B. MAJIYAGBE, LL.B. (London); B.L. (Middle Temple, London); S.A.N. (Senior Advocate of Nigeria).

M.A.O. OKULAJA, LL.B. (Hons.); B.L.

MOHAMMED BELLO, LL.B. (Hons.); B.L.

(This Listing Continued)

ISSAC AMBULE, LL.B. (Hons.); B.L.

(MRS.) NOWA I. OKPO, LL.B. (Hons.); B.L.

O.A. DADA, LL.B. (Hons.); B.L.

T.T. ABE, LL.B. (Hons.); B.L.

D.C.U. OKORO, LL.B. (Hons.); B.L.

M.S. SHUAIB, LL.B. (Hons.); B.L.

E.C. OKPE, LL.B. (Hons.); B.L.

V.I. ASIKA, LL.B. (Hons.); B.L.

M.A. SMITH, LL.B. (Hons.); B.L.

(MRS.) L.S. BUHARI, LL.B. (Hons.); B.L.

ABDULAI, TAIWO & CO.

Established in 1975

Notaries Public and Solicitors of the Supreme Court of Nigeria

GOODWILL HOUSE
278 IKORODU ROAD
P.O. BOX 536, YABA
LAGOS, NIGERIA
Telephone: (234-1) 960838; 967982; 4970562; 960076; 4937140
Telex: 20117 (atten. TDS 038)
Fax: (234-1) 685759; 4970562

Abuja, Nigeria Office: 8 Abeokuta Street, Area 8, Garki, Abuja.
Telephone: (234-9) 2341735.

Banking Law, Commercial Law, Company Law, Company Acquisitions and Mergers, Company Formation, Corporate Finance, Cross-Border Transactions, Finance Project and Asset, Investment Foreign and Local, Joint Venture Capital, Mediation, Conciliation and Arbitration, Notary Public, Privatization, Secured Lending, Stock Exchange Regulations, Syndicated Loans, Tax, Trademarks and Patents.

FIRM PROFILE: *Abdulai, Taiwo & Co. has a broadly based corporate practice and is often consulted to render advice as local counsel to foreign lawyers and organisations. The clientele ranges from the largest multinational companies to the small companies, and includes Government bodies and individuals alike. Our firm is the author of a book titled "Establishing a Business in Nigeria," now in its 4th Edition, which is frequently commended in business circles as the leading authority on the establishment and regulation of businesses in Nigeria. The firm is also the author of a book titled "Law Office Etiquette-Essential Habits of Successful Firms," as well as being the contributing author on the Nigerian section of the book titled "Legal Aspects of Doing Business in Africa," published by Kluwer Law and Tax Publishers of the Netherlands.*

In 1991, the firm became the first Nigerian law firm to be registered as consultants to the African Development Bank. One of the Partners, A. Abdulai, is current Chairman of the Body of Tax Appeal Commissioners, which is a statutory body of tax jurists, and another Partner, L. Taiwo is the country representative and current zonal Vice-President (Africa Region) of the International Association of Practising Lawyers. The firm is comprised of 5 Resident Partners, 21 Resident Lawyers and Paralegals and 1 Resident Consultant.

PROF. CORNELIUS TAIWO, OBE, OON, MA (Cantab); MA, MSc, PhD, D.Litt. (London). (Consultant).

DR. AHMED ABDULAI, LL.B. LL.M. PhD. (Partner).

LADI TAIWO, LL.B. AMNIM. (Partner).

FUNLAYO DAVID, LL.B. FNIT. (Partner).

AKIN OSINBAJO, LL.B. LL.M. (Partner).

OLADELE JEGEDE, LL.B. LL.M. (Partner).

MATTHEW KARIEREN, LL.B.

RACHEL OLENLOA, LL.B.

AJIBIKE OSHODI, LL.B.

ALAYO OGUNBIYI, LL.B.

OLAMIDE BEN-AJAYI, LL.B.

UGOCHUKWU EJIKE, LL.B.

PATRICK UWADIA, A.C.I.S.

(This Listing Continued)

SOPHIA INNIH, LL.B.

TEJU AWOBENO, LL.B.

CLAUDIUS ALLEN, HND, ACA.

All Attorneys are Members of Association of Business Law Firms; International Association of Practising Lawyers; Nigerian Bar Association.

Languages: English, French, Yoruba, Igbo, Edo and Urhobo

ABUKA, AJEGBO, ILOGU & NWAOGU

10TH FLOOR, WESTERN HOUSE
8-10 BROAD STREET
P.O. BOX 7022
LAGOS, NIGERIA
Telephone: (234) 1-263 3024; 1-263 4656; 1-263 1708
Telex: 21893 AAIN
Cable: LAWHOUSE, LAGOS
Telefax: 01-263 1687

Port Harcourt, Nigeria Office: 13 Ohaeto Street, D'Line Diobu, P.O. Box 1916. Telephone: (234) 84-331492; 84-332435.

Abuja, Federal Capital Territory, Nigeria Office: Suite No. 8, Nicon-Noga Hilton Hotel, P.O. Box 1702. Telephone: (234) 9-523 1596. Telefax: (234) 9-523 1388.

Corporate, Commercial, International Trade and Finance, Banking and Security Documentation, Patent and Trademark, Air Law, Aviation Insurance Claims, Merchant Shipping, Admiralty, Marine Insurance and Claims, Petroleum Law and Arbitration

FIRM PROFILE: *The firm was founded on March 28, 1979 by the four name-partners who had practised individually and separately until that date.*

They immediately won the recognition and confidence of the Nigerian and International business community. This brought increased work load. More lawyers and paralegal staff were hired. The present bigger and better appointed premises were acquired. Computer assisted legal research was introduced.

The firm expanded to Port Harcourt on October 1, 1980, following the increasing needs of clients in commerce and industry in Eastern Nigeria.

The Abuja office was set up in 1987, initially with a view to effectively providing the complex and sophisticated legal services required by a major international corporate client, with businesses in over 90 countries.

As the seat of government has gradually moved to Abuja, the firm is in the best position to conduct dealings with government on behalf of its clients from its own offices in the new capital. The firm has won the respect of the Nigerian government and of foreign embassies in Nigeria.

The firm represents a large number of international clients and collaborates with correspondent and associate law firms around the world.

MEMBERS OF FIRM

PATRICK C. ABUKA, born February 17, 1942; admitted, 1974, Nigeria. Solicitor and Advocate of the Supreme Court of Nigeria. *Education:* Universities of Ife and Lagos and the Nigerian Law School (LL.B. Hons., 1973; B.L., 1974; M.B.A., 1975). Visiting Lecturer, University of Lagos, Graduate School of Business, MBA Class, 1976-1978. Member: The Lagos Chamber of Commerce; Nigerian-American Chamber of Commerce; Nigerian-British Chamber of Commerce; International Maritime Bureau of the International Chamber of Commerce. *Member:* International Bar Association; American Bar Association (International Associate Member). *LANGUAGES:* English, Igbo and Yoruba. *PRACTICE AREAS:* Joint Ventures; Banking and Finance; Corporate and Commercial; Intellectual and Real Property.

MICHAEL I. AJEGBO, born March 23, 1949; admitted, 1975, Nigeria. Solicitor and Advocate of the Supreme Court of Nigeria. Notary Public. *Education:* University of Ife and the Nigerian Law School (LL.B. Hons., 1974; B.L., 1975). *Member:* Nigerian Bar Association; International Bar Association; Lagos Chamber of Commerce; Franco-Nigerian Chamber of Commerce; American Bar Association (International Associate Member). *LANGUAGES:* English and Igbo. *PRACTICE AREAS:* Corporate and Commercial.

LUKE C. ILOGU, born October, 1949; admitted, 1975, Nigeria. Solicitor and Advocate of the Supreme Court of Nigeria. *Education:* University of Ife and the Nigerian Law School (LL.B. Hons., 1974; B.L., 1975; LL.M., 1992). *Member:* Nigerian Bar Association; International Bar Association;

(This Listing Continued)

ABUKA, AJEGBO, ILOGU & NWAOGU, Lagos—Continued

American Bar Association (International Associate Member). *LANGUAGES:* English, Igbo and Yoruba. *PRACTICE AREAS:* Intellectual and Real Property; Maritime and Aviation Law.

BENEDICT O. NWAOGU, born January 11, 1948; admitted, 1975, Nigeria. Solicitor and Advocate of the Supreme Court of Nigeria. *Education:* Universities of Ife and Lagos and the Nigerian Law School (LL.B. Hons., 1974; B.L., 1975; MBA, 1978). *Member:* Nigerian Bar Association; International Bar Association; American Bar Association (International Associate Member). *LANGUAGES:* English and Igbo. *PRACTICE AREAS:* Intellectual and Real Property; Litigation.

PATRICK OKECHUKWU EKEANYANWU, born December 16, 1958; admitted, 1985, Nigeria. Solicitor and Advocate of the Supreme Court of Nigeria. *Education:* University of Calabar and the Nigerian Law School (LL.B. Hons., 1984; B.L., 1985). *Member:* Nigerian Bar Association. (Resident in Port Harcourt). *LANGUAGES:* English and Igbo. *PRACTICE AREAS:* Litigation.

ASSOCIATES

ANTHONY UGOCHUKWU OGAKWU, born August 4, 1964; admitted, 1985, Nigeria. Solicitor and Advocate of the Supreme Court of Nigeria. *Education:* University of Nigeria and the Nigerian Law School (LL.B., Hons., 1984; B.L.,1985). *Member:* Nigerian Bar Association. *LANGUAGES:* English and Igbo.

MARY MAWE ALEXANDRA ORITSEJOLOMISAN TEDEYE, (MISS.), born February 17, 1965; admitted, 1986, Nigeria. Solicitor and Advocate of the Supreme Court of Nigeria. *Education:* University of Benin and the Nigerian Law School (LL.B., Hons., 1985; B.L., 1986). *Member:* Nigerian Bar Association. *LANGUAGES:* English.

JOSEPH CHIDI ONUOHA, born October 12, 1958; admitted, 1989, Nigeria. Solicitor and Advocate of the Supreme Court of Nigeria. *Education:* Universities of Calabar and Benin and the Nigerian Law School (B.A., Hons., English/Literary Studies, 1983; LL.B., Hons, 1983; B.L., 1989). *Member:* Nigerian Bar Association. (Resident in Abuja). *LANGUAGES:* English and Igbo. *PRACTICE AREAS:* Litigation.

ANDREW IFEANYICHUKWU OKEKEIFERE, born August 12, 1962; admitted, 1989, Nigeria. Solicitor and Advocate of the Supreme Court of Nigeria. *Education:* University of Maidugiri, and the Nigerian Law School (LL.B., Hons., 1988; B.L., 1989). *Member:* Nigerian Bar Association. (Resident in Port Harcourt). *LANGUAGES:* English and Igbo. *PRACTICE AREAS:* Litigation.

HARRY ETINI ADOLPHUS, born March 4, 1967; admitted, 1990, Nigeria. Solicitor and Advocate of the Supreme Court of Nigeria. *Education:* University of Benin, and the Nigerian Law School (LL.B., Hons., 1989; B.L., 1990). *Member:* Nigerian Bar Association. *LANGUAGES:* English.

NELLY CHIDINMA UKADIKE, (MISS.), born November 12, 1966; admitted, 1993, Nigeria. Solicitor and Advocate of the Supreme Court of Nigeria. *Education:* University of Benin, Edo State University, and the Nigerian Law School (B.A., Hons., English/Literature, 1987; LL.B., Hons., 1992; B.L., 1993). *Member:* Nigerian Bar Association. *LANGUAGES:* English and Igbo.

BEATRICE TUSHA OTUKA, (MRS.), born March 2, 1957; admitted, 1993, Nigeria. Solicitor and Advocate of the Supreme Court of Nigeria. *Education:* Wusakihi School of Nursing, Zambia, University of Uyo and the Nigerian Law School (RSN, 1978; LL.B., Hons., 1992; B.L., 1993). *Member:* Nigerian Bar Association. *LANGUAGES:* English.

REPRESENTATIVE CLIENTS: Nicon-Noga-Hilton Hotel; International Merchant Bank Ltd.; Nigerian Merchant Bank Ltd.; United Bank for Africa Ltd.; Union Bank Ltd.; African Continental Bank Ltd.; National Fertilizer Company of Nigeria Ltd.; British-American Insurance Company (Nigeria) Ltd.; Lion of Africa Insurance Company Ltd.; Sentinel Assurance Company Ltd.; Atlantic Mediterranean Oilfield Services Company Ltd.; Best & Crompton Engineering Company (Nigeria) Ltd.

ADEPETUN, CAXTON-MARTINS & AGBOR

Established in 1991

38/40, STRACHAN STREET, LAGOS (5TH FLOOR)
P.O. BOX 55285, IKOYI
LAGOS, NIGERIA
Telephone: (01) 2633258/2631960/2637178
Fax: 2647374
Telex: 21670 ADCAX NG.

Intellectual Property, Shipping and International Trade, Marine Insurance, Aviation, Oil and Gas, Insurance, Taxation, Entertainment, Foreign Investment, Banking, Company/Commercial Law, Property, General and Commercial Litigation.

MEMBERS OF FIRM
PARTNERS

ADESOLA O. ADEPETUN, born Lagos, Nigeria, July 16, 1960; admitted, 1982, Nigeria. *Education:* Lagos University (LL.B., Honours, 1981); London School of Economics; University of London (LL.M., 1984). Assistant Lecturer, Department of Commercial and Industrial Law, University of Ibadan, 1982. Senior Counsel, O.O. Koleoso & Co., 1985. Principal Counsel, Sola Adepetun & Co. Solicitors, 1988. Author: Legal Controls Regulating Oil Pollution Hazards in Nigeria. *Member:* Nigerian Bar Association, The LSE Club. *LANGUAGES:* Yoruba and English. *PRACTICE AREAS:* Petroleum, Energy and Natural Resources Law; Banking and Securities Law; Company and Commercial Law; Foreign Investments.

AFOLABI O. CAXTON-MARTINS, born Lagos, Nigeria, June 18, 1961; admitted, 1984, Nigeria. *Education:* University of London (LL.B., Honours, 1983). State Counsel, Ministry of Justice, Lagos State, 1985. Senior Associate, Ajumogobia, Okeke, Oyebode & Aluko, 1986. *Member:* Nigerian Bar Association; Institute of Trade Mark Agents (ITMA). *LANGUAGES:* Yoruba and English. *PRACTICE AREAS:* Company/Commercial Law; Joint Venture Packaging; Patent and Trade Marks Registration; Oppositions; Litigation; Foreign Investments.

OLUFUNKE A. AGBOR, born Lagos, Nigeria, November 3, 1959; admitted, 1982, Nigeria. *Education:* University of Lagos (LL.B. Honours, 1981); University College, University of London (LL.M., 1984). Lecturer, Criminal Law and Evidence, Police College Kaduna, 1982. Counsel, Fola Sasegbon Law Office, Lagos, 1985-1993. *Member:* Nigerian Bar Association; Nigerian Maritime Law Association; Petroleum Energy and Mining Law Association of Nigeria (Assistant Secretary); The Bentham Club of the University College, London. *LANGUAGES:* Yoruba and English. *PRACTICE AREAS:* Maritime Law and Litigation; Energy; Marine Insurance; Entertainment Law.

SENIOR ASSOCIATES

OLUYOMI O. AUDIFFEREN, born Kano, Nigeria, August 30, 1967; admitted, 1989, Nigeria. *Education:* University of Warwick, England (LL.B., Honours, 1987). Company Secretary and Legal Adviser, Audy's Mart Limited, 1988. Legal Associate, Alpha Nominees, Aye Ayeni & Co., Company Secretaries and Chartered Accountants, 1988. *Member:* Nigerian Bar Association. *LANGUAGES:* Yoruba and English. *PRACTICE AREAS:* Company/Commercial Law; Oil and Gas Law; Foreign Investments.

ASSOCIATES

OMOYINKA O. DINA, born Lagos, Nigeria, May 3, 1969; admitted, 1990, Nigeria. *Education:* University of Ife (LL.B., Honours, 1989, International Public Law Award). Legal Officer, United Bank of Africa, 1990. Associate, Giwa & Co, 1991. Associate, Burke & Co., 1992. *Member:* Nigerian Bar Association. *LANGUAGES:* Yoruba and English. *PRACTICE AREAS:* Commercial Litigation/Arbitration; International Law; Aviation Law; Banking and Securities Law and Maritime Law.

F. OLUKEMI SEGUN, born United Kingdom, June 10, 1966; admitted, 1991, Nigeria. *Education:* University of Ife (B.A., Honours, History, 1986); University of Lagos (LL.B., Honours, 1991, Commercial Law Award). Associate, Burke & Co., 1992. *Member:* Nigerian Bar Association. *LANGUAGES:* Yoruba and English. *PRACTICE AREAS:* Company/Commercial Law; Petroleum, Energy and Natural Resources Law; Revenue Law; Foreign Investments.

BABATUNDE O. AWODIRAN, born Lagos, Nigeria, November 24, 1968; admitted, 1993, Nigeria. *Education:* University of Ibadan (LL.B., Honours, 1992). *Member:* Nigerian Bar Association. *LANGUAGES:* Yor-

(This Listing Continued)

uba and English. *PRACTICE AREAS:* Company/Commercial Law; Oil and Gas; Intellectual Property Law.

FOLASADE FALASE, born Kampala, Uganda, November 29, 1971; admitted, 1993, Nigeria. *Education:* Obafemi Awolowo University, Ile-Ife (LL.B., Honours, 1992). *Member:* Nigerian Bar Association. *LANGUAGES:* Yoruba, English and French. *PRACTICE AREAS:* Company/-Commercial Law; Intellectual Property Law; Litigation; Foreign Investments.

OLISA AGBAKOBA & ASSOCIATES

Established in 1983

MARITIME COMPLEX
34 CREEK ROAD
P.O. BOX 3169, APAPA
LAGOS, NIGERIA
Telephone: 234-1-5876876; 234-1-5876706
Fax: 234-1-5876876

General Business, Trade and Ancillary Litigation, Corporate and Commercial Law Maritime Law (including International Carriage of Goods), Intellectual Properties, Human Rights, General Legal Advisory Services, Opinions, Research and Counseling, Credit Operations Support Facilities, Legislative Advocacy.

FIRM PROFILE: *The firm was established in 1983 and offers full range of legal services. It is especially recognized for its innovative approach to debt recoveries and capital market and credit operations support facilities. Its client base spans the European and American business communities with a special concentration on Nigeria and Africa. It consists of 2 Consultants, a Principal Partner and 10 Lawyers excluding Para-legal Staff and Office Administrators.*

MEMBERS OF FIRM

THE HONOURABLE G.C.U. AGBAKOBA, (CONSULTANT), admitted, 1950, England; 1951, Nigeria. Former Acting Chief Justice, East Central State of Nigeria. *Member:* Grays Inn, London. *LANGUAGES:* English. *PRACTICE AREAS:* General Legal Advisory Services.

OLISA AGBAKOBA, born Jos, Plateau State, Nigeria, May 29, 1953; admitted, 1978, Nigeria. *Education:* University of Nigeria, Enugu Campus (LL.B., Hons, 1977); London School of Economics and Political Science (1980). Research Fellow, Nigerian Institute of International Affairs, 1981. Visiting Lecturer, Military and Command School, Jaji, 1981. President, Civil Liberties Organization (CLO), Lagos, Nigeria. Author: *"Behind the Wall"*, an expose on Nigeria Prisons by the Civil Liberties Organization (CLO); *"Incursions into the Legal Profession:* The Way Out"; "The Statute of Limitations in Admiralty Proceedings"; "A Case for Fresh Initiatives in Maritime Laws"; "Reforms in Marine Insurance Law"; "Debt Recoveries: New Techniques for the Banks"; "The Role of Lawyers in the Observance of Human Rights"; "Problems of Credit and Security Administration in Nigeria"; "Bankruptcy and Winding-up Proceedings"; "Potential Mechanism for Speedier Debt Recoveries"; "Protection of Copyright under Nigerian Law with special emphasis on Computer Literature"; "Repossessory Rights under Equipment Leases - New Vistas for the Aggrieved Lessor"; "A Proposal for the Establishment of Commercial Courts in Nigeria"; "The Problems of Broadcast, Consent & Transmission under the New Regime of Private Broadcasting"; "A Review of the National Shipping Policy Act." *Member:* Nigerian Bar Association (NBA); International Bar Association (IBA) (Member, Section on Business Law). *LANGUAGES:* English. *PRACTICE AREAS:* Maritime Law; Human Rights; International Trade Law; Oil and Gas Pollution; Banking and Corporate Finance.

JEAN CHIAZOR, born Lagos, Lagos State, Nigeria, July 14, 1961; admitted, 1985, Nigeria. *Education:* University of Ife, Ile-Ife (now Obafemi Awolowo University; LL.B. Hons); University of Lagos (LL.M.). Solicitor, Chambers of Jane Afolabi & Co., Lagos, 1988-1989; Head of Chambers, Bayo Kehinde & Co., Lagos, 1989-1994. Author: "Unification of Laws in Conflict," University of Lagos, Post Graduate Class. *Member:* Nigerian Bar Association; International Bar Association (Notary Public). *LANGUAGES:* English, French, German and Ibo. *PRACTICE AREAS:* Criminal Law; Personal Injuries; General Commercial Law; Matrimonial; Appeals; Tribunals; Landlord and Tenant; Contract and Judicial Review; Employment Law; Libel; Slander; Building Disputes.

ABIOLA ALUKO, born Moscow, Russia, December, 1964; admitted, 1986, Nigeria. *Education:* Obafemi Awolowo University, Ile-Ife, Nigeria (LL.B. Hons, 1986); University of Lagos (LL.M.). *Member:* Nigeria Association of Law Teachers; Nigerian Bar Association; Nigeria Society of Inter-

(This Listing Continued)

national Law; Nigeria Maritime Lawyers Association. *LANGUAGES:* English, French and Yoruba. *PRACTICE AREAS:* Maritime Law.

STEPHEN ONYEJOSE, born Agbor, Delta State, Nigeria, September 2, 1968; admitted, 1990, Nigeria. *Education:* Bendel State University, Ekpoma (LL.B. Hons, 1989). *Member:* Nigerian Bar Association (NBA). *LANGUAGES:* English and Ido. *PRACTICE AREAS:* International Commerce; Banking and Financial Service Law; Foreign Investment and Securities Law.

IFEANYI D. EME, born Port Harcourt, River State, Nigeria, May 24, 1964; admitted, 1991, Nigeria. *Education:* University of Nigeria (LL.B. Hons, 1990). *Member:* Nigerian Bar Association (NBA); Civil Liberties Organization (CLO); Nigerian Institute of Management (NIM). *LANGUAGES:* English, French and Ibo. *PRACTICE AREAS:* Constitutional and Administrative Law; Consumer Protection; Product Liability and International Trade Law.

PRISCILLA OHIARE, born Iiorin, Kwara State, June 2, 1969; admitted, 1991, Nigeria. *Education:* Ahmadu Bello University, Zaria (LL.B. Hons, 1990). *Member:* Nigerian Bar Association (NBA); Civil Liberties Organization (CLO). *LANGUAGES:* English, Hausa and Igbira. *PRACTICE AREAS:* Corporate Finance; General Legal Advisory Services and Foreign Investments Laws.

CHINONYE OBIAGWU, born Umuahia, Abia State, December, 1964; admitted, 1992, Nigeria. *Education:* University of Nigeria (B.A. Hons, 1986); University of Ibadan, Ibadan (LL.B. Hons, 1991). *Member:* Nigerian Bar Association (NBA). *LANGUAGES:* English and Ibo. *PRACTICE AREAS:* Appellate Litigation; Research; Business Litigation; Credit Operations Support Services.

LEGAL SUPPORT PERSONNEL

PARALEGAL

SUNDAY OKOJIE, born Agbor, Delta State, Nigeria, July 1, 1962. *Education:* Trans Continental Micro-Tech Computer Institute, Lagos. *Member:* Institute of Chartered Accountant of Nigeria. Legal Research, Drafting, Client Services and File Investigation. *LANGUAGES:* English and Esan.

REPRESENTATIVE CLIENTS: Savannah Bank of Nigeria Plc (Nigeria); Newcastle P & I Insurance (U.K.); Total Partnership International Limited (U.K.); Rhein Mass Und See Gmbh (Germany); Yugoslavia Air Transport (JAT).

B.A. AGUSTO & CO.

Established in 1948

1ST FLOOR, 15 BIADUO STREET
S.W. IKOYI
P.O. BOX 75190, VICTORIA ISLAND
LAGOS, NIGERIA
Telephone: 269-3814
Fax: 269-3815

Barristers, Solicitors, Legal Consultants, Corporate and Commercial Law, Foreign Investment and Joint Ventures, International Banking and Finance Law, Insurance and Taxation Law, Real Property and Conveyancing Law, Immigration, Arbitration, Civil and Criminal Investigation and Litigation, Family Law and Administration of Estates Law.

FIRM PROFILE: *B.A. Agusto & Company is a Lagos based Law Firm. Agusto is a well known family name in the history of Lagos-based legal offices in Nigeria. The present principal partner, Mrs. O.K. Aderinokun falls in a third generation of lawyers in the famous family name. The first in the generation of lawyers, being the late M.L.B. Agusto, Q.C., born in Lagos, Nigeria in 1886, sworn in on February 26, 1924 and died in 1971. His son B.A. Agusto, was born in Lagos, Nigeria in 1919, admitted into the Middle Temple in 1945, obtained B.L. (Hons.) University of London, enrolled in Nigeria in 1948 and died in 1989. Both M.L.B. Agusto, Q.C. and B.A. Agusto, during their lifetime, each had long career in legal practice at the Nigerian Bar, During which time they jointly and severally maintained enviable records of honesty, sound advocacy and good leadership with vast experience in Civil and Criminal Litigation, diverse aspects of Corporate and Commercial Law and Land Matters generally. The said experience and training has been passed down to Mrs. O.K. Aderinokun, the daughter of B.A. Agusto, who in maintaining the established practicing attribute and etiquette of the family and profession, can modestly be attributed with the above stated virtues.*

B.A. Agusto & Co. has highly diversified clients base in Nigeria providing

(This Listing Continued)

B.A. AGUSTO & CO., Lagos—Continued

legal services to large and medium-sized organisations in respect of the above stated areas of Law.

PARTNERS OF FIRM

ADEBUSOLA TITILAYO OLOTU, born Lagos, Nigeria, October 23, 1957; admitted, 1979, Nigeria. *Education:* University of Ife (LL.B., Honours, 1978). Senior State Counsel, Ministry of Justice, Ilorin, Kwara State, Nigeria 1980-1988. *Member:* Nigerian Bar Association.

OLUFUNLOLA KAFAYAT ADERINOKUN, born Lagos, Nigeria, February 14, 1957; admitted, 1981, Nigeria. *Education:* University of Ife (LL.B., Honours, 1980). Assistant Registrar of Companies, Federal Ministry of Commerce, Companies Registry in Lagos, January, 1982 - August, 1982. Counsel, Chief Rotimi Williams' Chambers Lagos, Nigeria, Setember, 1982-1987. *Member:* Nigerian Bar Association.

Languages: English and Yoruba

AJUMOGOBIA, OKEKE, OYEBODE & ALUKO

LAGOS, NIGERIA

(See Aluko & Oyebode)

F. O. AKINRELE & CO.

188, AWOLOWO ROAD
S.W. IKOYI
LAGOS, NIGERIA
Telephone: 01 2693998-9; 01 686212-13
Telex: 22851 FOAC NG
Facsimile: 01-2692889; 01-2694088

Other Lagos, Nigeria Office: 130, Broad Street, P.O. Box 1296.
Telephone: 663165. Cable: FOACLEX.

General Litigation, Taxation, Banking, International Trade and Finance, Construction, Aviation, Shipping, Foreign Investment, Patent and Trademark, Insurance, Corporate and Petroleum/Mining Law.

FIRM PROFILE: F.O. Akinrele & Co. established in 1959 by its Senior Partner, Chief F.O. Akinrele S.A.N. (Senior Advocate of Nigeria) is a Lagos-based law firm engaged in general corporate and commercial law practice with thirteen full time lawyers consisting of three partners, ten associates and twelve paralegal staff.

The client base is versatile. The firm acts for a number of large manufacturing, construction, trading, shipping, banking and oil/mining concerns most of which are foreign, or their Nigerian affiliates. Furthermore, it acts for international law firms largely based in the cities of London, Paris and Brussels.

MEMBERS OF FIRM

F. O. AKINRELE, born Ondo State, Nigeria, March 8, 1932; admitted, 1955, Middle Temple, England and Nigeria. *Education:* University of Hull England (LL.B., Hons., 1954), Andrew Marvell Prize for the best law student; University of Hull (LL.M., 1955). Senior Advocate of Nigeria. Council Member, Nigerian Institute of Advanced Legal Studies. Former President and now Patron of the Nigerian-American Chamber of Commerce, 1990. Recipient, Distinguished Service Award by the Nigerian-American Chamber of Commerce for outstanding leadership performance in promoting friendship and economic development between Nigeria and the U.S. *Member:* Nigerian Bar Association; Nigerian Body of Benchers; Legal Privileges Committee. *LANGUAGES:* English and Yoruba. *PRACTICE AREAS:* Commercial Law; Arbitration; Shipping; Corporate Law.

E.K. OGUNLEYE, born Ondo State, Nigeria, May 6, 1934; admitted, 1965, England and Nigeria. *Education:* University of London (LL.B., Hons., 1964). Served on the Council of Legal Association. Ex-Senator in the National Assembly, Federal Republic of Nigeria, 1979-1983. *Member:* Nigerian Body of Benchers; Drafting Committee on Human Rights at the I.P.U. Manila, Philippines. *LANGUAGES:* English and Yoruba. *PRACTICE AREAS:* Commercial Law; Arbitration; Admiralty and Maritime Law; Natural Resources; Trade Marks/Patents.

(This Listing Continued)

ADEMOLA AKINRELE, born Lagos State, Nigeria, June 3, 1961; admitted, 1983, Nigeria. *Education:* University College, London (LL.B., Hons., 1982); Fitzwilliam College, University of Cambridge (LL.M., 1984). Rotimi Williams' Chambers, 1984-1987. Co-Editor, Nigerian Legal Practitioners Review. Country Correspondent, Euromoney International Financial Practice Law files. Recipient, Grand Merit Award for distinction in Law Practice by the Law Society, Faculty of Law, University of Lagos, Nigeria, 1991. *Member:* Nigerian Bar Association. *LANGUAGES:* English, Yoruba and French. *PRACTICE AREAS:* Litigation; Commercial Law; Arbitration; Corporate Law; Banks and Banking.

MAKANJUOLA ALABI, born Lagos State, Nigeria, April 27, 1961; admitted, 1987, Nigeria. *Education:* University of Kent, Canterbury, England (B.A., Hons., International Relations and Politics, 1984; B.A., Hons., Law, 1986). *Member:* Nigerian Bar Association; World Trade Center, Nigeria. *LANGUAGES:* English, Yoruba and French. *PRACTICE AREAS:* International Law; Construction Law; Insurance.

ADEDOLAPO AKINRELE, born Lagos State, Nigeria, November 23, 1964; admitted, 1987, Nigeria. *Education:* University of East Anglia, Norwich, England (LL.B., Hons., 1985); University College, London (LL.M., 1986). Co-Editor, Memorandum on Investment in Nigeria. *Member:* Nigerian Bar Association; Nigerian Maritime Law Association; Nigerian Petroleum Association; International Bar Association. *LANGUAGES:* English and Yoruba. *PRACTICE AREAS:* Admiralty and Maritime Law; Aviation and Aerospace; Natural Resources; Investments.

MISS. ODUNEWU EBUN B., born Lagos State, Nigeria, March 8, 1966; admitted, 1987, Nigeria. *Education:* University of Ife, Nigeria (LL.B., Hons., 1986); University of Cambridge, England (LL.M., 1988). Phoebe Chiadikobi Ajayi-Obe Prize for best female student in the LL.B. Degree Examinations, 1986. Counsel, Burke & Co., 1988-1989. Investment Banker with Center Point Merchant Bank, 1989-1992. *Member:* Nigerian Bar Association; International Law Association (British Branch). *LANGUAGES:* English and Yoruba. *PRACTICE AREAS:* Investments; Taxation; Corporate Law; Natural Resources; Banks and Banking; Trademark and Patents.

ADAMU M. USMAN, born Lagos State, Nigeria, July 7, 1965; admitted, 1988, Nigeria. *Education:* Ahmadu Bello University (LL.B. Hons., 1987). Co-Editor, Memorandum on Investment in Nigeria. *Member:* Nigerian Bar Association; Association of Nigerian Business Lawyers. *LANGUAGES:* English, Hausa and French. *PRACTICE AREAS:* Banks and Banking; Investments; Natural Resources; Corporate Law; Taxation.

EMMANUEL ACHUKWU, born Anambra State, Nigeria, June 13, 1965; admitted, 1988, Nigeria. *Education:* University of Maiduguri, Nigeria (LL.B., Hons., 1987). Recipient, University Faculty Prize for the Best Law Student. Counsel in David Garrick and Co., (Patent and Trademark Agents, 1988-1989). Counsel in Mbanefo & Mbanefo, 1989-1992. *Member:* Nigerian Maritime Law Association; Nigerian Bar Association. *LANGUAGES:* English and Igbo. *PRACTICE AREAS:* Commercial Law; Admiralty and Maritime Law; Aviation and Aerospace; Arbitration; Trade Marks/Patents.

MISS. OLUWATOYIN A. OLASHOJU, born Lagos State, Nigeria, March 11, 1967; admitted, 1990, Nigeria. *Education:* University of Keele England (B.A., Joint Honors, Law and Economics, 1988); University of Bristol England (LL.M., 1989). Recipient: FIDA Prize for the best female student, Nigerian Bar Examination, 1989-1990; Fatai Williams' Prize for the best student of the year (2nd Place), Nigerian Bar Examination, 1989-1990. *Member:* Nigerian Bar Association. *LANGUAGES:* English, French and Yoruba. *PRACTICE AREAS:* Investments; Corporate Law; Admiralty and Maritime Law; Arbitration; Taxation.

CHIAGOZIE HILARY-NWOKONKO, born Imo State, Nigeria, June 23, 1965; admitted, 1991, Nigeria. *Education:* Fitzwilliam College, University of Cambridge (B.A., Hons., Cantab, 1986). Formerly Assistant Brand Manager Unilever Plc U.K., 1986-1988. Burke & Co. (Patent and Trademark Agents, 1988-1990. *Member:* Nigerian Bar Association; International Association for the Protection of Industrial Property (AIPPI). *LANGUAGES:* English and Igbo. *PRACTICE AREAS:* Investments; Natural Resources; Trade Marks/Patents; Taxation.

OGHOGHO AKPATA, born Edo State, Nigeria, March 19, 1968; admitted, 1991, Nigeria. *Education:* University of Benin, Nigeria (LL.B., Hons., 1990). *Member:* Nigerian Bar Association. *LANGUAGES:* English. *PRACTICE AREAS:* Litigation; Commercial Law; Trade Marks/Patents; Construction Law; International Law; Insurance.

OLUMIDE BRAITHWAITE, born Lagos State, Nigeria, November 12, 1969; admitted, 1992, Nigeria. *Education:* University of East Anglia, Norwich, England (LL.B., Hons., 1991). *Member:* Nigerian Bar Association.

(This Listing Continued)

LANGUAGES: English, Yorubo and French. *PRACTICE AREAS:* Commercial Law; Investments; International Law; Admiralty and Maritime Law; Corporate Law.

OLUFUNKE AKINDOJU, born Lagos State, Nigeria, September 24, 1970; admitted, 1992, Nigeria. *Education:* Lagos State University, Lagos, Nigeria (LL.B., Hons., 1991). Recipient: Prof. Olawoyin Prize for Best Student in Commercial Law; Chief Ernest Shonekan Prize for Best Student in Commercial Law. Co-Ordinator, Quarterly Law Digest. *Member:* Nigerian Bar Association. *LANGUAGES:* English, French and Yoruba. *PRACTICE AREAS:* Investments; Natural Resources; Patents; Trademarks; Corporate Law.

Languages: English, French, Yoruba, Igbo and Hausa.

ALUKO & OYEBODE

(Barristers, Solicitors & Trademark Agents)

Established in 1993

35 MOLONEY STREET
P.O. BOX 2293 (MARINA)
LAGOS, NIGERIA
Telephone: 260-0080-4
Fax: 263-2249; 264-7505

Port Harcourt, Nigeria Office: 8 Nnamdi Azikiwe Road. Telephone: 084-235579.

General Commercial Practice, Company and Commercial Law, Banking and Insurance, Trademarks and Patents, Taxation, Shipping and Admiralty, Civil Litigation, Joint Ventures, Mergers and Acquisitions, Oil and Gas Law and Taxation.

FIRM PROFILE: ALUKO & OYEBODE is a Lagos based law firm providing a comprehensive range of specialist legal services for Nigeria's changing business needs. Established in January 1993, the firm, recently evolved from the nucleus of a previously existing Lagos law firm, is among the ranks of the largest integrated law firms in Nigeria with sixteen full time lawyers and a support staff strength of twenty to ensure efficient and effective service to clients. Occupying 550 square metres, the firm's offices are situated principally on the 2nd, and 3rd floors of No. 35 Moloney Street, Lagos, Lagos State, and in addition, with other offices at No. 8, Nnamdi Azikiwe Road, Port Harcourt, Rivers State.

The firm is structured on a general partnership basis, the current partners having brought several years of experience from one prominent Kano law firm, three prominent Lagos law firms, a large New York firm, and a multi-national corporation in the oil industry to this young and dynamic establishment.

The firm's activities are enhanced by its modern suite of offices and a comprehensive law library, facilitating the performance of needed research in the most efficient manner.

The office is equipped with modern data processing equipment to increase its efficiency and to assist in the accounting and management controls necessary for the operations of a full service law firm. It also has adequate communications equipment to facilitate excellent communication with domestic and international clients.

CLIENTS: ALUKO & OYEBODE'S client base is highly diversified. It has relationships with a number of large and medium-sized manufacturing, building and construction, trading and service companies nationwide, in addition to some reputable financial institutions including insurance companies and banks. Furthermore, the firm represents several foreign companies and their Nigerian affiliates.

PARTNERS OF FIRM

GBENGA OYEBODE, born London, England, March 30, 1959; admitted, 1980, Nigeria; 1983, New York. *Education:* University of Ife (LL.B. Honours, 1979); University of Pennsylvania, Philadelphia (LL.M., 1982). Work: Associated with White and Case, 14 Wall Street, New York, 1982-1983 and Gulf Oil Company, Lagos and Houston, 1983-1985. Partner in Ajumogobia, Okeke, Oyebode & Aluko (Barristers, Solicitors and Notaries), 1985-1992. Author: "Governmental Regulatory Approval Process in Nigeria on Acquisition and Disposals of Oil Producing Properties" (paper delivered at the International Bar Association, Section on Energy and Natural Resources Law Seminar, The Netherlands, April 22-27, 1990); "Project Financing in the Nigerian Petroleum Industry-The Oso Condensate Project" (paper delivered at the International Bar Association 23rd Biannual Conference, September 19-23, 1990). *Member:* Nigerian Bar Association;

(This Listing Continued)

American Bar Association; American Society of International Law; International Bar Association (Committee Member, Oil Law and Electricity Law, Section on Energy and Natural Resources Law). *LANGUAGES:* Yoruba and English. *PRACTICE AREAS:* Corporate and Commercial Law; Natural Resources; General Practice.

BANKOLE OLUMIDE ALUKO, born Lagos, Nigeria, August 2, 1956; admitted, 1978, Nigeria; 1990, Notary Public. *Education:* University of Lagos (LL.B. Honours, 1977); L.S.E. University of London (LL.M., 1981). Recipient, Federal Government of Nigeria Merit Award for overall performance at the University of Lagos, 1974-1975; Chief Rotimi Williams Award for Best Performance in Conveyancing and Legal Drafting, Nigerian Law School, 1978. Final Rounds of Phillip C. Jessup International Law Moot Court Competition, San Francisco, California, U.S.A., 1977. Work: J.B. Majiyagbe & Co. Barristers and Solicitors, 1978-1979; Kehinde Sofola & Co. Barristers and Solicitors, 1981-1983. Leading Counsel, Chief Rotimi Williams Chambers, Barristers & Solicitors, 1983-1990. Partner, Ajumogobia, Okeke, Oyebode & Aluko (Barristers, Solicitors and Notaries), 1990-1992. *Member:* Nigerian Bar Association. *LANGUAGES:* Yoruba, English and French. *PRACTICE AREAS:* Litigation; Corporate and Commercial Law; General Practice.

SENIOR ASSOCIATES

ADEBIMPE ELEBUTE, born Ibadan, Oyo State, Nigeria, November 30, 1965; admitted, 1987, Nigeria. *Education:* University of Ife, Ile-lfe (LL.B., Hons., 1986); University College London (LL.M., 1990). Work: Senior Associate, Bentley, Edu & Co., 1987-Jan 1993. *Member:* Nigerian Bar Association; Asia-Pacific Lawyers Association; United States Trademark Association (International Committee, 1994-1995); International Bar Association; Institute of Trademark Agents. *LANGUAGES:* Yoruba, English and French. *PRACTICE AREAS:* Intellectual Property; Trademarks; Corporate and Commercial Law; General Practice.

ASSOCIATES

MORENIKE RANSOME-KUTI, born Lagos, Lagos State, September 14, 1965; admitted, 1988, Nigeria. *Education:* University of Lagos (LL.B., 1987). Work: Abegunde, Omotayo & Co., Kaduna 1988-1989. Associate, Ajumogobia, Okeke, Oyebode & Aluko (Barristers, Solicitors and Notaries), 1990-1992. *Member:* Nigerian Bar Association. *LANGUAGES:* English and Yoruba. *PRACTICE AREAS:* Corporate and Commercial Law; General Practice; Litigation.

HARVEY A. IDEOZU, born Ahoada, Rivers State, March 17, 1964; admitted, 1989, Nigeria. *Education:* Rivers State University of Science and Technology, Port Harcourt (LL.B., 1988). Work: Chief Sam Adegoke & Co., 1989-1990; C.V. Georgewill & Co., 1990-1991. Associate, Ajumogobia, Okeke, Oyebode & Aluko (Barristers, Solicitors and Notaries), 1991-1992. *Member:* Nigerian Bar Association. *LANGUAGES:* Ekpeye and English. *PRACTICE AREAS:* Corporate and Commercial Law; General Practice; Litigation.

ADENIYI A. ADEGBONMIRE, born Ibadan, Oyo State, March 27, 1968; admitted, 1988, Nigeria. *Education:* University of lfe, Ile-lfe (LL.B. Hons., 1987). Work: A.O. Openiyi & Co., Lagos, 1989-1990; Jide Aladejana & Co., July-December, 1990; Lanre Ogunlesi & Co., January 1991-February 1993. *Member:* Nigerian Bar Association. *LANGUAGES:* Yoruba and English. *PRACTICE AREAS:* Corporate and Commercial Law; Litigation.

OLAJIDE O. BELLO, born Kano, Kano State, March 13, 1963; admitted, 1992, Nigeria. *Education:* Ahmadu Bello University (B.A. Hons., 1981); University of Jos (LL.B. Hons., 1991). Work: Adewale Bello Construction Co., Ltd., Kaduna, 1977; Ogun State Broadcasting Corporation, 1981-1982; Ikeji Investments Ltd., Ilorin, 1986; Kwara State Broadcasting Corporation, 1986-1987; Service Masters (Nig) Ltd., 1987-1991. *Member:* Nigerian Bar Association. *LANGUAGES:* Yoruba, Hausa, Yagba and English. *PRACTICE AREAS:* Corporate and Commercial Law; Litigation.

TUNDE J. FAGBOHUNLU, born London, United Kingdom, May 4, 1967; admitted, 1988, Nigeria. *Education:* University of lfe, Ile-Ife (LL.B. Hons., 1987); University of Lagos (LL.M., 1991). Work: Festus Oguntoye & Co., Kaduna, 1988-1989; Olisa Agbakoba & Associated, 1989-1993. *Member:* Nigerian Bar Association; Civil Liberties Organization. *LANGUAGES:* Yoruba and English. *PRACTICE AREAS:* Corporate and Commercial Law; Litigation.

RONKE IDOWU, born Ibadan, Oyo State, December 7, 1968; admitted, 1988, Nigeria. *Education:* Ogun State University (LL.B. Hons., 1987). Work: Atilade Ojo & Co., Oyo State, 1989; Chief M.P. Ohwovoriole & Co., 1990; Ighodalo & Associates, October 1990 March 1993. *Member:* Nigerian

(This Listing Continued)

ALUKO & OYEBODE, Lagos—Continued

Bar Association. *LANGUAGES:* English, Yoruba and French. *PRACTICE AREAS:* Company Law; General Practice.

CHIEDU J. EBIE, born Ibadan, Oyo State, January 2, 1971; admitted, 1992, Nigeria. *Education:* University of Benin, Benin-City (LL.B. Hons., 1991). Work: Broad Bank of Nigeria Limited, Lagos, December 1992 October 1993. *Member:* Nigerian Bar Association. *LANGUAGES:* Ibo, Ika and English. *PRACTICE AREAS:* Corporate and Commercial Law; General Practice.

OMONIKE A. OLADAPO, born Lagos, Lagos State, February 22, 1969; admitted, 1992, Nigeria. *Education:* Lagos State University (LL.B. Hons., 1991). Work: Nigerian Agip Oil Company, 1992-1993. *Member:* Nigerian Bar Association; International Federation of Female Lawyers. *LANGUAGES:* English and Yoruba. *PRACTICE AREAS:* Corporate and Commercial Law; Trademarks.

OLUSOLA A. OGUNDIMU, born London, England, August 5, 1965; admitted, 1992, Nigeria. *Education:* University of Ife (B.A., Hons., 1986); Obafemi Awolowo University (LL.B., Hons., 1991). Work: Atlantic Textile Millls Nigeria Limited, Lagos, 1986-1987; Oceanic Bank International Nigeria Limited, Port Harcourt, 1993-1994. *Member:* Nigerian Bar Association. *LANGUAGES:* English and Yoruba. *PRACTICE AREAS:* Corporate and Commercial Law; Litigation.

ROTIMI M. ODUSOLA, born Lagos, Nigeria, February 28, 1971; admitted, 1993, Nigeria. *Education:* Ogun State University (LL.B., Hons., 1992). *Member:* Nigerian Bar Association. *LANGUAGES:* English and Yoruba. *PRACTICE AREAS:* Corporate and Commercial Law; Litigation.

BOMA D. GRAHAM-DOUGLAS, born Port Harcourt, Nigeria, August 4, 1972; admitted, 1993, Nigeria. *Education:* University of Benin (LL.B., Hons., 1992). *Member:* Nigerian Bar Association. *LANGUAGES:* English. *PRACTICE AREAS:* Corporate and Commercial Law; Litigation.

WINIFRED ODIKPO, born Enugu, Nigeria, November 18, 1971; admitted, 1993, Nigeria. *Education:* University of Nigeria (LL.B., Hons., 1992). *Member:* Nigerian Bar Association. *LANGUAGES:* English and Ibo. *PRACTICE AREAS:* Corporate and Commercial Law; Litigation.

ANGA & EMUWA

Barristers, Solicitors & Notaries Public

Established in 1990

14, ALHAJI KANIKE CLOSE
P.O. BOX 52901, IKOYI
LAGOS, NIGERIA
Telephone: (01) 681773; 2692072; 684042
23199 CMG-NG; Fax: (01) 2692072; 684042

Port Harcourt, Nigeria Office: 8, Kaiama Street, P.O. Box 12636. Telephone: (234-84) 239873. Fax: (234-84) 239592.

Admiralty and Maritime Law, Arbitration and Alternative Dispute Resolution, Aviation, Banking and Finance, Business Organization, Civil Litigation, Construction and Engineering, Commercial Law, Company Law, Copyright, Trademarks and Patent Infringement, Energy, Oil & Gas, Environmental Law and Pollution, Fraud, Insurance, Intellectual Property, Taxation.

FIRM PROFILE: *Anga & Emuwa is a young but dynamic international law firm that was formed in 1990 as a result of the merger of two commercial law practices. The firm offers specialist services in many areas and represents a wide range of clients including Governments, multinational companies and their local affiliates, banks and other financial institutions, international airlines and shipping companies as well as high net worth individuals.*

The firm has offices in the two main port cities of Nigeria. These are Lagos, which is the gateway to the western and northern parts of Nigeria, and Port Harcourt, the gateway to the Eastern part of Nigeria.

The firm is a member of Commercial Law Affiliates (CLA), an international network of independent law firms.

MEMBERS OF FIRM

LAWRENCE FUBARA ANGA, born London, England, December 30, 1957; admitted, 1984, Nigeria. *Education:* Yale College, Yale University (B.A., 1980); Churchill College, Cambridge, University of Cambridge, England (B.A., 1983; M.A., 1988); Nigerian Law School (B.L., 1984). Notary

(This Listing Continued)

Public of the Supreme Court of Nigeria. Trustee, King's College Old Boys Association 697375 set, 1987—. Secretary, Yale University Alumni Association of Nigeria. *Member:* Nigerian Bar Association; American Bar Association (International Associate); International Bar Association; Nigerian Maritime Law Association; Nigerian Insurance Law Association; Nigerian Institute of Management; Institute of Intellectual Property Agents; Institute of Trade Mark Agents, London (Overseas Member). *LANGUAGES:* English, Ijaw and Yoruba. *PRACTICE AREAS:* Admiralty and Maritime; Arbitration; Alternative Dispute Resolution; Aviation; Commercial Law; Copyright Infringement; Environmental Law; Oil and Gas Law; Trademark Prosecution; Trademark Registration.

THEOPHILUS IFEANYICHUKWU EMUWA, born Nigeria, May 17, 1959; admitted, 1983, England & Wales; 1984, Nigeria. *Education:* Imperial College of Science and Technology, University of London, London, England (B.Sc., (Eng) Mechanical Engineering, ACGI, 1979; M.Sc., (Eng), DIC, 1980); Polytechnic of Central London, London, England (Dip. Law, 1982); Nigerian Law School (B.L., 1984). Formerly, State Counsel, Ministry of Justice, Imo State, Nigeria. Honorary Secretary, Imperial College Alumni Association of Nigeria, 1987—. Member, Council of Chartered Institute of Taxation. Chairman, Sub-committee on Law of the Examinations & Students' Affairs Committee of the Chartered Institute of Taxation of Nigeria. *Member:* Gray's Inn, London; Nigerian Bar Association; International Bar Association; American Bar Association (International Associate); Nigerian Insurance Law Association; Chartered Institute of Taxation of Nigeria; Nigerian Maritime Law Association; Institute of Intellectual Property Agents; International Trade Mark Association; Nigerian Society of Engineers; The Institution of Mechanical Engineers. *LANGUAGES:* English and Igbo. *PRACTICE AREAS:* Arbitration; Environmental Law; Maritime Law; Patents and Trademarks; Taxation.

ASSOCIATES

SUZANNE MANA WANIKO, born Nigeria, 1965; admitted, 1988, Nigeria. *Education:* University of Wales Institute of Science & Technology, Wales (LL.B., 1987). *Member:* Nigerian Bar Association. *LANGUAGES:* English, Hausa, French and Bassange. *PRACTICE AREAS:* Corporate Law; Banking and Finance Law; Insurance.

JULIUS DEINMA ANGA, born Nigeria, April 16, 1967; admitted, 1989, Nigeria. *Education:* University of Nigeria, Nsukka, Nigeria (LL.B., 1988). Assistant Registrar, Corporate Affairs Commission, Abuja, Nigeria. *Member:* Nigerian Bar Association; International Bar Association; Nigerian Insurance Law Association. *LANGUAGES:* English, Ijaw and Yoruba. *PRACTICE AREAS:* Corporate Law; Oil and Gas; Commercial Law; Business Organization.

IFEANYI ANTHONY OKOLI, born Enugu, Nigeria, March 7, 1966; admitted, 1992, Nigeria. *Education:* Institute of Management & Technology, Enugu, Nigeria (H.N.D., 1987); Anambra State University of Technology (LL.B., 1991); Nigerian Law School, Lagos (B .L., 1992). *Member:* Nigerian Bar Association. *LANGUAGES:* English and Igbo. *PRACTICE AREAS:* Commercial Law; Taxation and Conveyancing; Civil Litigation.

HENRY HAMILTON TOBIN-WEST, born Lagos, Nigeria, June 12, 1967; admitted, 1992, Nigeria. *Education:* Rivers State University of Science & Technology, Port Harcourt (LL.B., 1991); Nigerian Law School, Lagos (B.L., 1992). *Member:* Nigeria Bar Association. *LANGUAGES:* English, Kalabari and Igbo. *PRACTICE AREAS:* Commercial Law; Company Law; Intellectual Property; Civil Litigation; Conveyancing.

CHIKE KANAYO EKWUEME, born Enugu, Nigeria, December 5, 1970; admitted, 1991, Nigeria. *Education:* University of Benin, Benin City, Nigeria (LL.B., 1990); Nigerian Law School, Lagos (B.L., 1991). *Member:* Nigerian Bar Association. *LANGUAGES:* English and Igbo. *PRACTICE AREAS:* Land Law; Company Law; Employment Law; Business Law.

REFERENCES: Chevron International Oil Comp., Inc.; International Capital Markets Group Ltd.; Equity Indemnity Insurance Company Ltd.

AYO-KASUMU & COMPANY

21 AJASA STREET, ONIKAN
P.O. BOX 70256 (VICTORIA ISLAND)
LAGOS, NIGERIA
Telephone: (01) 2631446; 2631106
Facsimile: 234-1-2635405
Telex: 20117 Box 110 MARINA

Property & Conveyancing Law, Corporate & Commercial Law, Litigation & Alternative Dispute Resolution, New Areas of Professional Endeavour, African Trade & Projects, Intellectual Property Law, Oil & Gas Law, Maritime & Admiralty.

MEMBERS

KEHINDE AYO-KASUMU, born Lagos, Nigeria, May 20, 1963; admitted, 1986, Nigeria. *Education:* University of Keele, Staffordshire, England (B. Soc.Sc., 1985); Nigerian La w School (B.L., 1986). Member: World Trade Center, Nigeria; Institute of Directors; Nigerian Institute of International Affairs; Lagos Chamber of Commerce & Industry; Nigerian-Asean Chamber of Commerce. *Member:* Nigerian Bar Association; International Bar Association. *LANGUAGES:* Yoruba and English. *PRACTICE AREAS:* Property and Conveyancing Law; Corporate Law; Commercial Law; Litigation; Alternative Dispute Resolution; African Trade and Projects; Intellectual Property Law; Oil and Gas; Maritime and Admiralty Law.

ASSOCIATES

NNAJI IGWE, born Ibadan, Nigeria, December 19, 1964; admitted, 1989, Nigeria. *Education:* University of Nigeria (LL.B., Hons., 1988); Nigerian Law School (B.L., 1989). Author: "Legal Aspects of Environmental Protection," Published in, African Petroleum Monitor, Vol 2. No. 4 July/August, 1993. *Member:* Nigerian Bar Association. *LANGUAGES:* Igbo and English. *PRACTICE AREAS:* Corporate Law; Commercial Law; Property and Conveyancing Law; Intellectual Property; Foreign Investment Law; Commercial Litigation; General Litigation.

OLUYOMI TAIWO ADEJUMO, born Lagos, Nigeria, May 20, 1963; admitted, 1990, Nigeria. *Education:* University of Ife (B.A., Hons., 1985); University of Lagos (LL.B., Hons., 1989) Nigerian Law School (B.L., 1990). *Member:* Nigerian Bar Association. *LANGUAGES:* Yoruba and English. *PRACTICE AREAS:* Property and Conveyancing Law; Commercial Litigation; General Litigation; Corporate Law; Commercial Law; Foreign Investment Law; Admiralty & Maritime Law.

MICHAEL OLADIPO AGBEDARE, born Lagos, Nigeria, January 21, 1966; admitted, 1990, Nigeria. *Education:* Obafemi Awolowo University (LL.B., Hons., 1989); Nigerian Law School (B.L., 1990). *Member:* Nigerian Bar Association. *LANGUAGES:* Yoruba and English. *PRACTICE AREAS:* Property and Conveyancing Law; Commercial Litigation; General Litigation; Company Incorporation; Foreign Investment Law; Maritime and Shipping Law.

BABALAKIN & CO.

Established in 1988

THE ROOFTOP, 8TH-10TH FLOORS
24A CAMPBELL STREET, LAGOS
P.O. BOX 80320, LAFIAJI
LAGOS, NIGERIA
Telephone: (01) 2632559; 2635644; 2633207; 2632162; 2635179; 2632185; 2600930-9 (10 lines)
Telex: 28158 babco NG
Fax: (01) 2630594; 2637136

London Office: 78 New Oxford Street, (5th Floor), London, WCIA 1HB. Telephone: 071-580-9677. Fax: 071-637-2251.

General Commercial Practice. Company Law, Banking and Insurance, Administrative Law, Agency and Franchise Law, Exchange Control and Trade Regulations, Administration of Estates, Mergers and Acquisitions, Oil and Gas Law, Consumer Protection Law, Arbitration, Industrial Relations and Labour Law, Real Property and Conveyancing Law, Copyrights, Trademarks and Patents, Shipping and Admiralty Law. Civil Litigation, Aviation Law, International Finance and Economic Law, Joint Ventures and Taxation Law.

FIRM PROFILE: Babalakin & Co. was established in 1988 by Dr. B. Olawale Babalakin. With a total staff strength of 50, the firm offers a very wide range of legal services and prides itself with its ability to provide top quality services to its various clients, within the shortest possible time. Thus, the firm has a well-developed practice of assisting its individual and corporate clients in many areas. The firm operates from three floors of a modern office block in central Lagos, which is the commercial capital of Nigeria. This location, apart from affording the firm easy access to the law courts, also makes it readily accessible to most of its corporate and other clients. The firm has a representative office in central London in England. Members of the firm have had vast experience negotiating on behalf of corporate and individual clients, in relation to matters involving their operations both within and outside Nigeria and have actively participated in various local and international legal seminars.

BOLANLE OLAWALE BABALAKIN, born Ibadan, Nigeria, July 1, 1960; admitted, 1982, Nigeria. *Education:* University of Lagos, Lagos State, Nigeria (LL.B., Hons., 1981); Nigerian Law School (B.L., 1982); University of Cambridge (LL.M., 1983; Ph.D., 1986). Author: "Buyers Right of Rejection: Whither Nigerian Courts," 1980, "The Supreme Court and Constitutional Developments in Nigeria, 1960-1985," 1986. Commonwealth Scholar, University of Cambridge, 1984-1986. *Member:* Nigerian Bar Association; International Bar Association. *LANGUAGES:* English. *PRACTICE AREAS:* Corporate Law; General Commercial Practice; Civil Litigation; Taxation Law; Constitutional Law; Mergers and Acquisitions; International Finance and Economic Law; Oil and Gas Law; Aviation Law; Administrative Law.

SENIOR ASSOCIATES

OLAWALE ADEOLA AKONI, born Lagos, Nigeria, March 27, 1962; admitted, 1987, Nigeria. *Education:* University of Ibadan, Oyo State (B.Sc. Hons. Political Science, 1982; LL.B. Hons, 1986); Nigerian Law School (B.L., 1987). Recipient: Prince Bola Ajibola Prize for best performance in Civil Procedure at the Nigerian Law School, 1987; Chief T O S Prize for best performance at the Nigerian Law School, 1987; Sir Adetokunbo Ademola Prize for best student of the year at the Nigerian Law School, 1987. Author: "Effectiveness of International Law: A Study of U.N. Resolutions on African Liberation," 1982; "Contractual Element in Illegal Contracts: A Review of Judicial Attitude to the Enforcement of Illegal Contracts," 1986. *Member:* Nigerian Bar Association; International Bar Association. *LANGUAGES:* English. *PRACTICE AREAS:* General Commercial Practice; Company Law; Civil Litigation; Taxation Law; Patent Law; Copyrights Law; Shipping and Admiralty Law; Administration of Estates; Oil and Gas Law; Aviation Law.

ADENIKE OLUFUNKE THOMAS, born Lagos, Nigeria, April 6, 1964; admitted, 1985, Nigeria. *Education:* Obafemi Awolowo University, Ile-Ife, Osun State, Nigeria (LL.B., Hons, 1984); Nigerian Law School (B.L., 1985). Recipient: Faculty Prize for best overall performance in the LL B final year examinations (Obafemi Awolowo University, 1984); Prince Bola Ajibola Prize awarded for best performance in Commercial Law in the LL B final year examinations (Obafemi Awolowo University, 1984). *Member:* Nigerian Bar Association; International Bar Association. *LANGUAGES:* English and French. *PRACTICE AREAS:* General Commercial Practice; Company Law; Banking Law; Insurance Law; Real Property and Conveyancing Law; Joint Ventures; Exchange Control and Trade Regulations; Arbitration.

AYODELE OLATOKUNBO MARTINS, born London, England, March 17, 1961; admitted, 1986, London and Wales; 1992, Nigeria. *Education:* North East London Polytechnic, London, England (B.A. Hons. Law, 1984); University of Cambridge, London (LL.M., 1985); Nigerian Law School (B.L., 1992). Recipient: Sweet and Maxwell Law Prize Winner for best overall law student, North East London Polytechnic (1984); Lizzett Bartwick Prize Winner for best overall performance in the Master of Laws programme, University of Cambridge (1985); Hardwicke Scholar of the Council of Legal Education of England and Wales (1986). *Member:* Nigerian Bar Association; International Bar Association. *LANGUAGES:* English. *PRACTICE AREAS:* General Commercial Practice; Company Law; Exchange Control and Trade Regulations; Mergers and Acquisitions; Copyrights, Trademark, and Patents; Shipping and Admiralty Law; Oil and Gas Law; Taxation Law.

AKINOLA ORIBOLAWA OLADEJI, born Sekondi, Ghana, October 2, 1960; admitted, 1983, Nigeria. *Education:* Obafemi Awolowo University, Ile-Ife, Osun State (LL.B., Hons, 1982); Nigerian Law School (B.L., 1983). State Counsel, Ministry of Justice, Ibadan, Oyo State, Nigeria, 1985-1988. Ag. Senior Legal Officer, Ministry of Justice, Ibadan, Oyo State, Nigeria, 1988-1989. *Member:* Nigerian Bar Association; International Bar Association. *LANGUAGES:* English. *PRACTICE AREAS:* Civil Litigation; Criminal Law and Practice; Legal Drafting and Ministerial Counselling; General Commercial Practice; Banking Law; Insurance Law.

(This Listing Continued)

BABALAKIN & CO., Lagos—Continued

ADEBAYO GBENGA ADARALEGBE, born Ibadan, Nigeria, November 1, 1965; admitted, 1988, Nigeria. *Education:* Obafemi Awolowo University, Ile-Ife, Osun State, Nigeria (LL.B., Hons., 1987); Nigerian Law School (B.L., 1988). *Member:* Nigerian Bar Association. *LANGUAGES:* English. *PRACTICE AREAS:* General Commercial Practice; Civil Litigation; Arbitration; Industrial Relations and Labour Law; Shipping and Admiralty Law.

MOBOLAJI ADETUNJI OLUSEGUN KUTI, born Ibadan, Nigeria, April 14, 1969; admitted, 1989, Nigeria. *Education:* Obafemi Awolowo University, Ile-Ife, Osun State, Nigeria (LL.B., Hons., 1988); Nigerian Law School (B.L., 1989). *Member:* Nigerian Bar Association. *LANGUAGES:* English. *PRACTICE AREAS:* General Commercial Practice; Civil Litigation; Arbitration.

ASSOCIATES

ONOCHIE MARTINS OGBOLU, born Kaduna, Nigeria, August 24, 1966; admitted, 1989, Nigeria. *Education:* Ahmadu Bello University, Zaria; Kaduna State, Nigeria (LL.B., Hons., 1988); Nigerian Law School, Lagos (B.L., 1989). *Member:* Nigerian Bar Association. *LANGUAGES:* English. *PRACTICE AREAS:* General Commercial Practice; Company Law; Real Property and Conveyancing Law.

BABAJIDE CHRISTOPHER OMOWORARE, born Ile-Ife, Nigeria, October 31, 1968; admitted, 1990, Nigeria. *Education:* Obafemi Awolowo University, Ile-Ife, Osun State, Nigeria (LL.B., Hons., 1989); Nigerian Law School (B.L., 1990). *Member:* Nigerian Bar Association. *LANGUAGES:* English. *PRACTICE AREAS:* General Commercial Practice; Real Property and Conveyancing Law; Civil Litigation.

AYOTUNDE OKESANYA, JR., born Lagos, Nigeria, September 21, 1965; admitted, 1990, Nigeria. *Education:* University of Keele, Staffordshire, England (LL.B., Hons., 1988); Kings College, University of London, England (LL.M., 1989); Nigerian Law School (B.L., 1990). *Member:* Nigerian Bar Association. *LANGUAGES:* English. *PRACTICE AREAS:* General Commercial Practice; Company Law; International Finance and Economic Law; Exchange Control and Trade Regulations; Civil Litigation; Administration of Estates.

TEMITOPE OLUWAYOMI ELUSOGBON, born Abeokuta, Nigeria, January 3, 1968; admitted, 1990, Nigeria. *Education:* Obafemi Awolowo University, Ile-Ife, Osun State, Nigeria (LL.B. Hons. 1989) ; Nigerian Law School (B.L., 1990). *Member:* Nigerian Bar Association. *LANGUAGES:* English. *PRACTICE AREAS:* General Commercial Practice; Civil Litigation.

OGOCHUKWU ANTHONIA KACHIKWU, born Issele-Uku, Nigeria, February 10, 1968; admitted, 1991, Nigeria. *Education:* University of Benin, Benin City, Edo State, Nigeria (LL.B. Hons 1990); Nigerian Law School (B.L., 1991). *Member:* Nigerian Bar Association. *LANGUAGES:* English. *PRACTICE AREAS:* General Commercial Practice; Company Law; Civil Litigation.

CHIBOGWU IRENE ONYIUKE, born Bida, Nigeria, April 24, 1965; admitted, 1991, Nigeria. *Education:* University of Nigeria, Nsukka, Enugu State, Nigeria (B.A. Hons. History, 1985); University of Lagos, Lagos State, Nigeria (LL.B. Hons. 1990); Nigerian Law School (B.L., 1991). *Member:* Nigerian Bar Association. *LANGUAGES:* English. *PRACTICE AREAS:* General Commercial Practice; Company Law; Real Property and Conveyancing Law; Banking and Insurance Law; Civil Litigation.

TEMITAYO OLUWATOYIN FAWEHINMI, born London, England, May 21, 1966; admitted, 1991, Nigeria. *Education:* Ogun State University, Ago-Iwoye, Ogun State, Nigeria (LL.B. Hons. 1990); Nigerian Law School (B.L., 1991). *Member:* Nigerian Bar Association. *LANGUAGES:* English. *PRACTICE AREAS:* General Commercial Practice; Civil Litigation; Banking Law.

ENITAN OMAWUNMI REWANE, born Lagos, Nigeria, March 16, 1968; admitted, 1991, Nigeria. *Education:* University of Hull, Hull, North Humberside, England (B.A. Hons. Law, 1990); Nigerian Law School (B.L., 1991). *Member:* Nigerian Bar Association. *LANGUAGES:* English. *PRACTICE AREAS:* General Commercial Practice; Civil Litigation; Exchange Control and Trade Regulations.

FOLAKE OKUSANYA, born London, England, May 9, 1964; admitted, 1991, Nigeria. *Education:* Lagos State University, Lagos State, Nigeria (LL.B., Hons., 1990); Nigerian Law School (B.L., 1991). *Member:* Nigerian Bar Association. *LANGUAGES:* English. *PRACTICE AREAS:* General Commercial Practice; Civil Litigation.

(This Listing Continued)

TARE CHARLES BRISIBE, born Benin, Nigeria, August 13, 1968; admitted, 1991, Nigeria. *Education:* University of Jos, Jos, Plateau State, Nigeria (LL.B., Hons., 1990); Nigerian Law School (B.L., 1991). *Member:* Nigerian Bar Association. *LANGUAGES:* English. *PRACTICE AREAS:* Mergers and Acquisitions; General Commercial Practice; Civil Litigation.

AGNES AJIBIKE FERNANDEZ, born London, England, March 20, 1963; admitted, 1992, Nigeria. *Education:* Lagos State University, Lagos State, Nigeria (LL.B., Hons., 1990); Nigerian Law School (B.L., 1992). *Member:* Nigerian Bar Association. *LANGUAGES:* English. *PRACTICE AREAS:* General Commercial Practice; Civil Litigation.

AKINWUNMI DAVID OMISADE, born Ibadan, Nigeria, October 3, 1970; admitted, 1992, Nigeria. *Education:* Obafemi Awolowo University, Ile-Ife, Osun State, Nigeria (LL.B., Hons., 1991); Nigerian Law School (B.L., 1992). *Member:* Nigerian Bar Association. *LANGUAGES:* English. *PRACTICE AREAS:* General Commercial Practice; Civil Litigation.

BANWO & IGHODALO

Barristers and Solicitors

Established in 1991

98 AWOLOWO ROAD
SOUTH WEST IKOYI
P.O. BOX 53756, FALOMO, IKOYI
LAGOS, NIGERIA
Telephone: (234-1) 2694576; 2694724; 686003
Fax: (234-1) 2694576; 2690294
Voicemail: (234-1) 2030310

Corporate and Commercial Law, Investment Laws of Nigeria, Oil and Gas Law, Banking and Corporate Finance Transactions, Securities and Stock Issues, Shipping and Admiralty, Intellectual Property, Real Estate, International Trade, Commercial Arbitration and Litigation.

FIRM PROFILE: Our firm, which is engaged in the traditional and emerging disciplines of law, is structured as a partnership and provides its clients with legal advice on all aspects of financial and commercial activities. Counsel in Chambers have considerable experience in the various aspects of the practice in which the firm is engaged.

The firm is regularly consulted by overseas law firms, corporations and other professionals on the laws and practices in Nigeria, particularly in the areas of Investment and Divestment, Oil and Gas, Corporate practice, Shipping, and Intellectual Property.

Its client base includes many local and international finance institutions, shipping companies and agents, individual and corporate investors, joint venturers and venture capitalists.

The partners are members of several professional and bilateral trade organizations while the firm itself is a member of the Nigerian-American Chamber of Commerce, the Nigerian-British Chamber of Commerce, the Nigerian-Asian Chamber of Commerce, the Lagos Chamber of Commerce and the Association of Business Law Firms.

The firm has invested substantially in up to date telecommunications and data processing equipment to facilitate information retrieval and legal research, to the benefit of its clients.

Our offices are situated in the prime commercial district of South West Ikoyi and enjoys proximity to the principal offices of all major financial institutions and multinational corporations in Lagos, Nigeria.

MEMBERS OF FIRM

FEMI BANWO, born Lagos, Nigeria, March 28, 1958; admitted, 1982, Nigeria. *Education:* University of Lagos (LL.B., 1981). Associate: Segun O. Idowu & Associates, 1982. State Counsel, Ministry of Justice, Lagos State, 1983. Associate: Chris O. Okunowo & Co., 1983-1988. *Member:* International Trademark Association (INTA); Institute of Trade Mark Agents (ITMA); World Trade Centre of Nigeria. *LANGUAGES:* English and Yoruba. *PRACTICE AREAS:* Company and Commercial Law; Foreign Investments and Divestments; Oil and Gas Law; Intellectual Property; Real Estate; Banking and Corporate Finance; Commercial Arbitration.

ASUERINME A. IGHODALO, born Annua-Oyo, Nigeria, July 19, 1959; admitted, 1985, Nigeria. *Education:* University of Ibadan (B.Sc., Economics, 1981); London School of Economics, University of London (LL.B., 1984). Associate, Chris Ogunbanjo & Co., 1985-1990. *Member:* International Bar Association; Maritime Law Association; Lagos Chamber of Commerce and Industry (Commercial Law and Taxation Group); World

(This Listing Continued)

Trade Centre of Nigeria. *LANGUAGES:* English, Yoruba and Ishan. *PRACTICE AREAS:* Corporate and Commercial Law; Oil and Gas Law; Investment Laws; Securities and Stock Issues; Taxation; Shipping and Admiralty; Commercial Litigation.

TEMITOPE O. SOLOLA, born Lagos, Nigeria, August 12, 1966; admitted, 1988, Nigeria. *Education:* University of Lagos (LL.B., 1987). Associate, C. Kunle Oyero & Co., 1988-1989. Assistant, Company Secretary and Legal officer, Municomp Limited, 1991-1993. *LANGUAGES:* English and Yoruba.

HABEEB ADEKUNLE FASINRO, born Lagos, Nigeria, November 14, 1963; admitted, 1990, Nigeria. *Education:* University of Buckingham (B.A., (Hons.) Politics, Economics and Law, 1987; LL.B., 1989). Credit Analyst, Guarantee Trust Bank Ltd., 1990-1991. *LANGUAGES:* English, French and Yoruba.

IMOH KENNETH ETIM, born Lagos, Nigeria, November 30, 1967; admitted, 1991, Nigeria. *Education:* University of Cross Rivers State, Uyo (LL.B., 1990). Legal officer, Ondo State House of Assembly, 1991-1992. *LANGUAGES:* English, Annang and Yoruba.

TINUADE TOLULOPE AWE, (MISS), born Ibadan, Nigeria, January 30, 1971; admitted, 1992, Nigeria. *Education:* Obafemi Awolowo University, Ile-Ife (LL.B., 1991). Best graduating student, First class, Bar Finals, 1992. *LANGUAGES:* English and Yoruba.

IBOROMA T. AKPANA, born Lagos, Nigeria, August 9, 1964; admitted, 1993, Nigeria. *Education:* University of Jos (LL.B., 1992). *LANGUAGES:* English, kalabari and Ibo.

HELEN ONYESIANYA, (MISS), born Lagos, Nigeria, November 1, 1969; admitted, 1993, Nigeria. *Education:* Abla State University (LL.B., 1992). *LANGUAGES:* English and Ibo.

All lawyers are both Solicitors and Barristers and are Members of the Nigerian Bar Association.

BENTLEY, EDU & COMPANY

SLEE CHAMBERS
AKURO HOUSE
24/26 CAMPBELL STREET, 7TH FLOOR
LAGOS, NIGERIA
Telephone: 601830-4; 637555; 631130
Cable Address: "Benlico" Lagos
Telex: 21911 NIFRAC; 21054 PATCOD
Fax: 2635319

Banking, Insurance, Commercial, Company and Conveyancing Law, Trademarks and Patents, General Intellectual Property Practice, International Finance and Economic Law, Civil Litigations, Admiralty and Merchant Shipping, Oil and Gas Law and Taxation, General Practice.

FIRM PROFILE: *Bentley, Edu & Company is the present result of the 1980 merger (itself a rarity in the Nigerian Legal Industry) of two fairly large; highly successful and comparatively specialized law firms.*

The composite law firms were: Bentley & Company and Edu, Adelakun and Company.

The older of the two fully merged and integrated firms was: Bentley and Company: established in 1963 and until the merger referred to above managed by John Graham Bentley.

The firm has a present complement of five partners and sixteen other fee-earners, who have individually and collectively brought to the firm as wide and varied a background as could be desired in any number of professionals and legal practitioners.

The firm which is presently in an associateship relationship with Irving & Bonnar (Solicitors) (the oldest law firm in Nigeria) is structured into five major, distinct but complementary divisions: with each supervised by a partner namely: Intellectual Property; Banking and Finance including Securities and Taxation; Corporate and Commercial including Real-Estate, Energy and Petroleum Law; General Civil Litigations including Admiralty Practice; General Practice and Legal Consultancy.

The firm is the only Nigerian member of the International Lawyers Network.

(This Listing Continued)

MEMBERS OF FIRM

SAIFUDEEN ADEMOLA EDU, born Lagos, Nigeria, October 21, 1945; admitted, 1973, Nigeria. *Education:* University of Lagos (LL.B.); Nigeria Law School. Senior Partner, Messrs. Irving & Bonnar, Solicitors, 1917. *Member:* Nigeria Bar Association; International Bar Association; International Lawyers Network. *LANGUAGES:* English and Yoruba. *PRACTICE AREAS:* Intellectual Property; Banking and Finance; General Practice; Legal Consultancy.

ENIOLA AJOKE FADAYOMI, (MRS.), born Lagos, Nigeria, March 12, 1951; admitted, 1973, Nigeria. *Education:* University of Lagos (LL.B.); Nigeria Law School. Senior State Counsel, Lagos State Ministry of Justice, 1980. Deputy Legal Adviser, First Bank of Nigeria Limited, 1986. Attorney-General and Commissioner for Justice, Lagos State, 1986-1990. Chairman, Afribank Nigeria Limited. Member, Steering Committee for Establishment of Eko Bank of Nigeria Limited, 1987. Chairman, Development of Lagos State Estates Committee, Lagos, 1988. Member: Council of Legal Education; Body of Benchers; Judicial Service Committee; General Council of the Bar. *Member:* International Bar Association; International Federation of Women Lawyers; Atlantic Educational Trust Council. *LANGUAGES:* Yoruba, French and English. *PRACTICE AREAS:* Banking and Finance; General Practice; Legal Consultancy.

ANTHONY GEORGE-IKOLI, born Brass, Nigeria, December 18, 1956; admitted, 1981, Nigeria. *Education:* University of Ife (LL.B.); Nigeria Law School. Founding Member and Regional Coordinator, International Lawyers Network. *Member:* Nigerian Bar Association; International Bar Association. *LANGUAGES:* English, Yoruba and Ijaw. *PRACTICE AREAS:* Intellectual Property; Litigation; Corporate and Commercial Law; General Civil Litigations; General Practice; Legal Consultancy.

SAM N. OKAGBUE, born Umuahia, Nigeria, November 22, 1958; admitted, 1981, Nigeria. *Education:* University of Ife (LL.B.); Nigerian Law School; London School of Economics; University of London (LL.M.). *Member:* Nigerian Bar Association. *LANGUAGES:* English, French, Igbo and Yoruba. *PRACTICE AREAS:* Banking and Finance; Corporate and Commercial Law; General Practice; Legal Consultancy.

LOOKMAN DUROSINMI-ETTI, born Otta, Nigeria, November 3, 1958; admitted, 1982, Nigeria. *Education:* University of Lagos (LL.B); Nigeria Law School); University of London (LL.M.). *Member:* Nigerian Bar Association; Institute of Trade Mark Agents; International Lawyers Network. *LANGUAGES:* English and Yoruba. *PRACTICE AREAS:* Intellectual Property; Banking and Finance; Corporate and Commercial Law; General Practice; Legal Consultancy.

ASSOCIATES

OLUFUNMILAYO AKIYODE, (MRS.), born Lagos, Nigeria, December 1, 1961; admitted, 1986, Nigeria. *Education:* University of Lagos (B.Sc. Hons., 1982); University of Kent at Canterbury (B.A. Hons., 1985); Nigeria Law School. *Member:* Nigeria Bar Association; Asia-Pacific Lawyers Association. *LANGUAGES:* English, Yoruba and Igbo. *PRACTICE AREAS:* Intellectual Property; Corporate and Commercial Law; General Litigation.

HABEEB ADEWALE OLUMUYIWA ABIRU, born Lagos, Nigeria, October 17, 1964; admitted, 1985, Nigeria. *Education:* University of Ife (LL.B. and LL.M.); Nigerian Law School. *Member:* Nigerian Bar Association; Asia-Pacific Lawyers Association. *LANGUAGES:* English and Yoruba. *PRACTICE AREAS:* Corporate and Commercial Law; General Litigations; Banking and Finance.

KEHINDE SIMISOLA AFE, (MRS.), born Lagos, Nigeria, September 28, 1963; admitted, 1986, Nigeria. *Education:* University of Lagos (LL.B.); Nigerian Law School. *Member:* Nigerian Bar Association; International Lawyers Network. *LANGUAGES:* English, French and Yoruba. *PRACTICE AREAS:* Banking and Finance; Corporate and Commercial Law; General Litigations.

MUSTAPHA ADEKOYEJO EDU, born Lagos, Nigeria, November 5, 1963; admitted, 1986, Nigeria. *Education:* University of Bristol, England (LL.B.); Nigerian Law School; King's College; University of London (LL.M.). *Member:* Nigerian Bar Association; Asia-Pacific Lawyers Association. *LANGUAGES:* English, Yoruba and French. *PRACTICE AREAS:* Intellectual Property; Litigation; Banking and Finance; Corporate and Commercial Law; General Civil Litigations.

REGINALD OPUNABO GEORGE, born Lagos, Nigeria, December 22, 1960; admitted, 1988, Nigeria. *Education:* University of Lagos (B.A. Hons., 1983; LL.B., 1987); Nigerian Law School. *Member:* Nigerian Bar Association. *LANGUAGES:* English, Kalabari and Igbo. *PRACTICE*

(This Listing Continued)

BENTLEY, EDU & COMPANY, Lagos—Continued

AREAS: Intellectual Property; Litigation; Banking and Finance; Corporate and Commercial Law; General Civil Litigation.

UWA ABIOLA OHIKU, (MRS.), born Port-Harcourt, Nigeria, March 31, 1962; admitted, 1986, Nigeria. *Education:* University of Benin, Nigeria (LL.B.). *Member:* Nigerian Bar Association; International Trade Mark Association (INTA); Asia-Pacific Lawyers Association. *LANGUAGES:* English, Yoruba and Edo. *PRACTICE AREAS:* Intellectual Property; Corporate and Commercial Law; General Practice.

OMODELE OLATOKUNBOH IBRAHIM, born Montreal, Canada, June 17, 1960; admitted, 1988, Nigeria. *Education:* University of London (LL.B.); Nigerian Law School. *Member:* Nigerian Bar Association; Asia-Pacific Lawyers Association (Nigerian Chapter). *LANGUAGES:* English and Yoruba. *PRACTICE AREAS:* General Practice; Corporate and Commercial Law; Banking and Finance.

FOLASHADE FEYISARA LANIYAN, (MRS.), born London, England, March 2, 1966; admitted, 1988, Nigeria. *Education:* University of Ife, Ile-Ife (LL.B.); Nigerian Law School. *Member:* Nigerian Bar Association; International Federation of Women Lawyers (FIDA); International Trade Mark Association, (INTA); Asia-Pacific Lawyers Association. *LANGUAGES:* English and Yoruba. *PRACTICE AREAS:* Intellectual Property; Corporate and Commercial Law; General Practice.

ANITA OLUREMI SIMKAIYE, born Kaduna, Nigeria, April 10, 1967; admitted, 1989, Nigeria. *Education:* University Ife, Nigeria (LL.B.); Nigeria Law School. *Member:* Nigerian Bar Association; Asia-Pacific Lawyers Association (Nigerian Chapter); International Federation of Women Lawyers (FIDA); International Trade Mark Association (INTA). *LANGUAGES:* English, Yoruba and Efik. *PRACTICE AREAS:* Intellectual Property; Corporate and Commercial Law and General Practice.

NKEMAMAKA CHRISTOBEL OBIOHA, born Uyo, Nigeria, August 29, 1965; admitted, 1989, Nigeria. *Education:* University of Jos, Nigeria (LL.B.); Nigeria Law School. *Member:* Nigerian Bar Association; International Federation of Women Lawyers (FIDA); Asia-Pacific Lawyers Association (Nigerian Chapter). *LANGUAGES:* English and Igbo. *PRACTICE AREAS:* Intellectual Property; Banking and Finance; Corporate and Commercial Law; General Practice.

BOLANLE OLUSINA OGUNLEYE, born Akure, Nigeria, February 17, 1965; admitted, 1986, Nigeria. *Education:* University of Ife, Nigeria (LL.B.); Nigeria Law School. *Member:* Nigerian Bar Association; Asia-Pacific Lawyers Association (Nigerian Chapter). *LANGUAGES:* English and Yoruba. *PRACTICE AREAS:* Litigation; Corporate and Commercial Law; Banking and Finance; General Practice.

CHINYERE ANAYOCHUKWU ALIGWEKWE, born London, England, October 24, 1967; admitted, 1991, Nigeria. *Education:* Imo State University Okigwe, Imo State, Nigeria (LL.B.); Nigeria Law School. *Member:* Nigerian Bar Association; International Federation of Women Lawyers (FIDA); International Trade Mark Association (INTA); Asia-Pacific Lawyers Association. *LANGUAGES:* English and Ibo. *PRACTICE AREAS:* Intellectual Property; Corporate and Commercial Law; General Practice.

FOLASADE EDITH LAWRENCE, born Lagos, Nigeria, September 7, 1964; admitted, 1991, Nigeria. *Education:* University of Ibadan, Nigeria (B.A., Russian, 1986; LL.B., 1990); Nigeria Law School. *Member:* Nigerian Bar Association; International Trade Marks Association; Asia-Pacific Lawyers Association. *LANGUAGES:* English, Russian, Togolese and Yoruba. *PRACTICE AREAS:* Intellectual Property; Corporate and Commercial Law and General Practice.

EZE-OZIMS MADUFOR, born Owerri, Nigeria, March 20, 1964; admitted, 1992, Nigeria. *Education:* University of Calabar, Nigeria (B.A., 1985); University of Benin, Nigeria (LL.B., 1991); Nigerian Law School. *Member:* Nigerian Bar Association. *LANGUAGES:* English, Yoruba and Igbo. *PRACTICE AREAS:* Intellectual Property Litigation; Corporate and Commercial Law; Banking and Finance; General Litigation and Practice.

CONSULTANT

JOHN GRAHAM BENTLEY, born London, England, June 9, 1929; admitted, 1953, England; 1955, Malaya; 1957, Nigeria; 1961, Cameroons. *Education:* Wadham College, Oxford University (B.A., M.A.); Lincoln's Inn, London (Barrister-at-Law). Notary Public. *Member:* English Bar Association; Nigeria Bar Association; Institute of Trade Mark Agents (Overseas Member). Sundowners, Picaterre, Alderney, Channel Islands, U.K.; Telephone: 048-182-1698. *LANGUAGES:* English and French. *PRAC-*

(This Listing Continued)

TICE AREAS: Intellectual Property; Banking and Finance; Corporate and Commercial Law; General Practice; Legal Consultancy.

REPRESENTATIVE CLIENTS: First Bank of Nigeria Ltd.; Bristow Helicopters (Nigeria) Ltd.; Nidat Ltd.; Knight, Frank & Rutley (Nigeria); African Alliance Insurance Ltd.; African Insurance Co. Ltd.; Aluminium Manufacturing Company of Nigeria Ltd.; Blackwood Hodge Ltd.; Elder Dempter Agencies Ltd.; Hademec Ltd.; H. Clarkson Edu and Partners; Holman Brothers (Nigeria) Ltd.; Technical Constructions (Nigeria) Ltd.; The Nigerian Chamber of Mines.

GEORGE ETOMI & PARTNERS

Established in 1984

Barristers, Solicitors, Notaries Public, Energy, Aviation and Investment Consultants

16 ALHAJI KANIKE CLOSE, S.W. IKOYI
LAGOS, NIGERIA
Telephone: 01-2693644; 2693645; 2693646; 2693647; 2693648; 2693649; 2693650; 2693651
Fax: 01-2691188

Abuja Office: Abuja Sofitel Hotel, Garki Abuja. Telephone: 09-2340906. Fax: 09-230907.

Port Harcourt Office: Pan African Bank Limited, Head Office Building, 4th Floor, 3 Azikiwe Road, Port Harcourt. Telephone: 084-334592.

Commercial and Corporate Law, Aviation Law, Insurance Law, Energy Law, Taxation Law, Conveyancing Law, Maritime Law, Banking and Securities Law, International Business Transactions, Company Law and Company Secretarial Matters, Environmental Law, Litigation and Arbitration.

FIRM PROFILE: Established in 1984, the firm of George Etomi & Partners, a member of the International Network, has grown in ten years to become one of the largest and most reputable commercial law firms in Nigeria. It is located in Lagos and has offices in Abuia (the new Federal Capital) and Port Harcourt (the nation's oil and gas center). The firm has 3 partners and over 14 fee-earners and is continually expanding in line with the growing commercial environment in Nigeria. It has witnessed an appreciable increase in its banking and aviation practice. Presently the firm is providing legal consultancy and general secretarial back-up for th JVA between Nigerian Telecommunications and a multi-national company for the installation and operation of Mobile Telecommunications nationwide.

PROPRIETOR AND PRINCIPAL PARTNER

GEORGE ETOMI, born Ilesha Osun State Nigeria, February 6, 1954; admitted, 1977, Nigeria. *Education:* University of Ife (OAU) (ll.B., Hons, 1976); Nigeria Law School (B.L., 1976; London School of Economics and Political Science, University of London (LL.M., 1976). Committee of the United Nations General Assembly, 1990. Director, Daily Times of Nigeria PLC. Author: "Energy Law in Nigeria," in a special supplement of Global Energy Law published by Euromoney Publication Inc., London 1991; "The Fidic Contract Under the Nigerian Jurisdiction; Selected Issues" paper presented at the Fidic Works Programme at the 1991 Hong Kong Conference of the IBA. *Member:* Nigerian and International Bar Associations. *LANGUAGES:* English, French, Ishan, Yoruba. *PRACTICE AREAS:* Petroleum Law; Maritime Law; Aviation Law; Tax Law; Banking and Arbitration.

ABIMBOLA T. ADEFOPE (MRS.), born Lagos, Nigeria, January 16, 1954; admitted, 1980, Nigeria. *Education:* School of Oriental and African studies, University of London (LL.B., 1978); London School of Economics, University of London (LL.M., 1979); Nigerian Law School (B.L., 1980). FIDA, Institute of Directors, Nigerian Insurance Association. Directorship in several companies including Grand Union Assurances Limited; Lawson Corporation; Acorn Petroleum. *Member:* Nigerian and International Bar Associations,. *LANGUAGES:* English, French, German and Yoruba. *PRACTICE AREAS:* Insurance; Corporate Law.

SOTONYE INYEINENGI ETOMI, born Port Harcourt, Nigeria, December 25, 1957; admitted, 1988, Nigeria. *Education:* University of Lagos (B.A., Hons, 1984); University of Lagos (LL.B., Hons, 1987); Nigerian Law School (B.L., 1988). *Member:* Nigerian and International Bar Associations. *LANGUAGES:* English, Ijaw, Yoruba. *PRACTICE AREAS:* Commercial Law; Energy Law; Arbitration; Banking and Insurance Law; Revenue Law; Litigation and Secretarial Practice.

TAMARAKARE A.C. YEKWE (MS.), born Nigeria; admitted, 1981, Nigeria. *Education:* University of Lagos (LL.B., 1980); Nigerian Law School (B.L., 1981). Directorship in several companies including, International Merchant Bank Plc. *Member:* Nigerian and International Bar Associ-

(This Listing Continued)

ations; FIDA; Society of International Lawyers; Nigerian Institute of International Affairs (Member, Governing Council). *LANGUAGES:* English and Ijaw. *PRACTICE AREAS:* Banking; Petroleum Law; Maritime Law; Corporate Law.

JOY NDIDIAMAKA OJEHOMON (MRS.), born Nigeria, March 20, 1957; admitted, 1981, Nigeria. *Education:* University of Lagos (LL.B., 1980); Nigerian Law School (B.L., 1981). *Member:* Nigerian Bar Association. *LANGUAGES:* English, Spanish and Ibo. *PRACTICE AREAS:* Commercial Law and Practice; Commercial Litigation.

ELECHI CHINEDUM CHARLES, born Owo-Asa, Nigeria, January 4, 1963; admitted, 1988, Nigeria. *Education:* University of Calabar (LL.B., Hons, 1987); Nigeria Law School (B.L., 1988). *Member:* Nigerian Bar Association. *LANGUAGES:* English and Ibo. *PRACTICE AREAS:* Corporate Law Practice; Civil and Criminal Litigation; Environmental Law.

ISRAEL ABAM, born Okrika, Nigeria, June 2, 1959; admitted, 1988, Nigeria. *Education:* University of Science and Technology Port Harcourt (LL.B., Hons, 1989); Nigerian Law School (B.L., 1988). *Member:* Nigerian and International Bar Associations. *LANGUAGES:* English and Ijaw. *PRACTICE AREAS:* General Litigation; Commercial Practice; Mortgages and Securitizations.

KUNLE OKESANYA, born Lagos, Nigeria, May 4, 1967; admitted, 1988, Nigeria. *Education:* Liverpool Polytechnic (LL.B., Hons, 1987); Kings College London, University of London (LL.M., 1989); Nigerial Law School (B.L., 1988). *Member:* Nigerian Bar Association. *LANGUAGES:* English and Yoruba. *PRACTICE AREAS:* Corporate and Commercial Law; Litigation.

BEN OWUMI, born Lagos, Nigeria, February 13, 1965; admitted, 1991, Nigeria. *Education:* Bendel State University (B.A., Hons., 1986); University of Lagos (LL.B., Hons., 1990; LL.M., 1992); Nigerian Law School (B.L., 1991). *Member:* Nigerian Bar Association. *LANGUAGES:* Urhobo, English and Yoruba. *PRACTICE AREAS:* Company Law; Commercial Law; Land Law.

OBOSA U. AKPATA (MRS.), born Benin City, Nigeria, July 6, 1969; admitted, 1991, Nigeria. *Education:* Edo State University Ekpoma (LL.B., Hons., 1990); Nigerian Law School (B.L., 1991). *Member:* Nigerian Bar Association. *LANGUAGES:* English and Edo. *PRACTICE AREAS:* Aviation Law; Commercial Law; Secretarial Practice.

UCHENNA ANTHONY UWECHIA, born Onitsha, Nigeria, November 24, 1967; admitted, 1991, Nigeria. *Education:* University of Science and Technology, Port Harcourt, (LL.B., Hons., 1990); Nigerian Law School (B.L., 1991; LL.M. 1994). *Member:* Nigerian Bar Association. *LANGUAGES:* English and Ibo. *PRACTICE AREAS:* Security and Property Law; Industrial and Labour Law; Civil and Commercial Litigation.

OSAYANDE AIWERIOGHENE, born Benin City, Nigeria, December 24, 1964; admitted, 1992, Nigeria. *Education:* University of Benin (B.A., 1987; LL.B., 1991); Nigerian Law School (B.L., 1992). *Member:* Nigerian Bar Association. *LANGUAGES:* English and Edo. *PRACTICE AREAS:* Petroleum Law; Conveyancing; Commercial Law.

EKUA ABUDU TITILOLA (MRS.), born Lagos, Nigeria, September 8, 1965; admitted, 1988, Nigeria. *Education:* University of East Anglia, Norwich, England (LL.B., Hons., 1987); Nigerian Law School (B.L., 1988). Author: Chapter on Intellectual Property, Comparative Law Yearbook, International Business; "Energy Law in Nigeria," Energy Law Supplement, Financial Law Review, 1992. *Member:* Nigerian Bar Association; Institute of Chartered Secretary and Administrators. *LANGUAGES:* English and Yoruba. *PRACTICE AREAS:* Commercial Law; Conveyancing; Banking and Company Secretarial Practice.

EYIMOFE ATAKE & COMPANY

7TH FLOOR, GREAT NIGERIA HOUSE
47/57 MARTINS STREET
LAGOS, NIGERIA
Telephone: 2665282; 2668023; 2660395
Telex: 21995 WHIPCO NG
Fax: 2668071; 2664799

Commercial Law, Banking Law, Maritime Law, Oil and Gas, Trademarks and Patents, Taxation, Property and International Law.

(This Listing Continued)

MEMBERS OF FIRM

HON. JUSTICE FRANKLIN ATAKE, born Sapele, Nigeria, May 6, 1928; admitted, 1954, Nigeria, England and Wales. *Education:* Council of Legal Education, England (Barrister-at-Law, 1954). Private Practice, 1954-1959. Magistrate, Lagos, 1959-1960. Senior Magistrate, Lagos, 1960-1963. Chief Magistrate, Mid-Western Region, 1963-1968. Judge, High Court, Mid-Western State, 1968-1975; Bendel State, 1976-1977; Senator, Federal House of Senate, 1978-1982. (Consultant). *LANGUAGES:* English, Itsekiri and Yoruba.

DR. EYIMOFE DOYLE ATAKE, born Nigeria, February 20, 1958; admitted, 1983, Nigeria. *Education:* London School of Economics and Political Science, University of London; University of Cambridge; Darwin College (B.A.; LL.M.; Ph.D.). Member, Sub-committee for the Privatisation of Nigerian National Fish Company Limited. Delivered Public lecture on the Legal Aspects of Privatization and Commercialization at International Conference on Privatization. Legal Adviser and Member of the Executive Council Nigeria/Nordic Chamber of Commerce, Industry and Agriculture. Author: "Contempt In The Face Of The Court," (1992). *Member:* Nigerian and International Bar Associations. *LANGUAGES:* English and Itsekiri. *PRACTICE AREAS:* Litigation; Commercial :aw Practice; Maritime Law and Oil and Gas.

ASSOCIATES

EBELE EGBARIN, born Lagos, Nigeria, March 2, 1966; admitted, 1989, Nigeria. *Education:* University of East Anglia, Norwich, England (LL.B., Hons., 1988); Nigerian Law School (1989). *Member:* Nigerian Bar Association. *LANGUAGES:* English and Yoruba.

UGOJI CHIJIOKE ABAGWE, born Enugu, Nigeria, July 25, 1962; admitted, 1986, Nigeria. *Education:* University of Ife (LL.B., 1985); Nigerian Law School (1986). *Member:* Nigerian Bar Association. *LANGUAGES:* English and Igbo. *PRACTICE AREAS:* Corporate Law; Commercial Law; Criminal Law; Patent Law; Copyright Law; Banking Law; Insurance Law.

FATUTUDE RICHARD ADEINIUMI, born Makurdi Benue State, March 9, 1963; admitted, 1987, Nigeria. *Education:* Federal Government College Ogbomosho, University of Benin, Benin City (LL.B., 1986); Nigerian Law School (B.L., 1987). *Member:* Nigerian Bar Association. *LANGUAGES:* English, Yoruba and Hausa. *PRACTICE AREAS:* Litigation; Trademarks; Patents; Company Law; Banking; Insurance; Copyrights.

ATAKE ADEWALE EYITEMI, born Lagos, Nigeria, January 18, 1962; admitted, 1991, Nigeria. *Education:* University of Jos, Jos, Plateal State, Nigeria (LL.B., 1990); Nigerian Law School, Victoria-Island, Lagos, Nigeria (B.L., 1991). *Member:* Nigerian Bar Association. *LANGUAGES:* English and Itsekiri. *PRACTICE AREAS:* Company Law; Contract Law; Commercial Law.

DOROTHY ATAKE, born New Castle Upon Tyme, June 25, 1965; admitted, 1992, Nigeria. *Education:* University of Lagos (B.A., Hons., 1985; LL.B., 1991; B.L., 1992). *Member:* Nigerian Bar Association. *LANGUAGES:* English and Yoruba. *PRACTICE AREAS:* Commercial Law; Oil and Gas; Maritime Law.

LEGAL SUPPORT PERSONNEL

JOSEPHINE HARRIMAN, born December 7, 1968. *Education:* University of Buckingham, Buckinghire (LL.B., 1989; LL.M., 1991). *LANGUAGES:* English. *PRACTICE AREAS:* Commercial Law; Maritime Law; Oil and Gas.

REPRESENTATIVE CLIENTS: Nigerian National Shipping Line Limited; Mobil Producing Nigeria; Whipstock (United Kingdom) Limited; Zapata Marine Service (Nigeria) Limited; Nigerian-Nordic Chamber of Commerce; Industry and Agriculture; Centre-Point Merchant Bank Limited; Commercial Bank (Credit Lyonnais Nigeria) Limited; Solus Schall (Nigeria) Limited.

F.O. FAGBOHUNGBE & CO.

Barristers, Solicitors, Notaries Public

Established in 1985

CO-OP BUILDING
30 MARINA (5TH FLOOR)
P.O. BOX 9881

LAGOS, NIGERIA
Telephone: (01)-2669514; 2667982
Fax: (01)-2660403

Civil and Criminal Litigation, Company and Commercial Law, Debt Collection, Company Formation and Acquisitions, Copyright, Trade Marks, Patents and Designs, Wills, Probate and Trusts, Passing off, International Practice including Shipping and Insurance.

FELIX OLUSEGUN FAGBOHUNGBE LL.B. (Hons.) BL.

ASSOCIATES

Osamudiame Oluwole Iyamu
Iyamu, LL.B. (Hons.) BL.
V.O.M. Alonge, (Mrs.),
LL.B. (Hons.) BL.

Ayoola Olufemi Ajayi,
LL.B. (Hons.) BL.
Felix Agbuake Masagbor

Members: Nigerian Bar Association.

Language: English

DAVID GARRICK & CO.

25 OLANREWAJU STREET
OREGUN INDUSTRIAL ESTATE
OREGUN IKEJA
P.O. BOX 2471

LAGOS, NIGERIA
Telephone: 960753; 2660160; 2661804
Fax: 234-1-2662375; 2611134; 2635595 & 2615661
Telex: 23173 GARIK NG.
Cable Address: "Patents, Lagos"

Barristers, Solicitors, Notaries Public, Copyright, Patent, Design, Trademark and Tax Attorneys.

DAVID L. GARRICK, BCL, M.A. (Oxon) of Lincoln's Inn and The Supreme Court of Nigeria, Barrister.

OLUGBOYEGA KAYODE, LL.M. (Lond.) of the Supreme Court of Nigeria, Barrister-at-Law.

GIWA-OSAGIE & COMPANY

Established in 1989

Barristers & Solicitors & Notaries Public

37A, RAYMOND-NJOKU STREET
P.O. BOX 51057

IKOYI-LAGOS, NIGERIA
Telephone: (234-1) 2694725; 688822; 680944
Fax: (234-1) 685881

General Commercial Practice, Admiralty and Maritime Law, Securities and Exchange Laws, Stock Issues: Oil and Gas, Banking and Foreign Investment Laws, Taxation Law, Civil Litigation, International Trade and Investment Law, Takeovers and Mergers, Corporate Recovery and Insolvency.

FIRM PROFILE: Giwa-Osagie & Co. is a medium sized commercial law based practice. The firm offers a wide range of professional services. The firm offers professional services to international institutions and organizations, Oil and Gas Companies, Engineering and Construction Companies.

Giwa-Osagie & Company is renowned for the excellent services it provides to both local and international banks (Commercial and Merchant), and financial institutions. It pays particular attention to details, and regularly handles and concludes complex transactions within the shortest time possible. The client base is Africa, Europe and North America in scope.

(This Listing Continued)

AF82B

MEMBERS OF FIRM

OSAYABA GIWA-OSAGIE, born Port-Harcourt, Nigeria, June 7, 1957; admitted, 1986, Nigeria; 1993, Notary Public. *Education:* University of Warwick, Coventry, England (LL.B. Hons 1985). attached to the chambers of Chief G.O.K. Ajayi, S.A.N., 1986. Associate Counsel in chambers of Abayomi Sogbesan S.A.N., 1987. Author: (i) "Credit Risk, Securitization and Loan Guarantees in Nigeria"-Seminar by the United Nations Centre on Transnational Conference Corporations; "Contract Modification" delivered at a National Conference on operating guidelines for effective contract administration. *Member:* International Bar Association; Nigerian Bar Association; Nigerian Maritime Law Association; Nigerian Institute of International Affairs; Association of Business Law Firms. *LANGUAGES:* English and Edo. *PRACTICE AREAS:* International Business Transactions; Oil and Gas; Admiralty Law; Securities and Exchange Laws; Foreign Trade; Investments Laws; Legal Consultancy; Contract Law.

KOFOWOROLA COKER, born Lagos, Nigeria, June 30, 1965; admitted, 1987, Nigeria. *Education:* University of Keele, Staffordshire, England (B.Soc. Sci., 1985); Kings College, London, England (LL.M. Tax Law 1989). *Member:* Nigeria Bar Association; Nigeria Institute of International Affairs; Association of Business Law Firms; Institute of Advanced Legal Studies. *LANGUAGES:* English, French, Yoruba and Edo. *PRACTICE AREAS:* Taxation Law; International Trade; Finance; Banking Law; Documentation; Environmental Law; Joint Ventures; Trademarks and Patents.

ASSOCIATES

ABISOLA THOMAS, born Lagos, Nigeria, May 6, 1960; admitted, 1985, Nigeria. *Education:* University of Warwick, Coventry, England (LL.B. Hons., 1984); University of Lagos (M.I.L.D., 1986). *Member:* Nigerian Bar Association. *LANGUAGES:* English and Yoruba. *PRACTICE AREAS:* Company Law; Company Secretarial Matters; Insurance Law; Stock Issues; Banking Law.

BOSEDE EFUNYEMI GIWA-OSAGIE, born Lagos, Nigeria, November 5, 1967; admitted, 1988, Nigeria. *Education:* Obafemi Awolowo University, Ile-Ife, (LL.B Hons, 1987); University of Lagos (M.I.L.D., 1990). *Member:* Nigerian Bar Association; Nigerian Institute of International Affairs. *LANGUAGES:* French, English and Yoruba. *PRACTICE AREAS:* International Business Laws; Environmental Law; Bank Security Documentation; Foreign Laws; Investment.

EVBUSOGIE AMADASUN, born Benin-city, Nigeria, September 30, 1968; admitted, 1991, Nigeria. *Education:* University of Benin, Benin-city, Nigeria (LL.B. Hons, 1990). *Member:* Nigerian Bar Association. *LANGUAGES:* English and Edo. *PRACTICE AREAS:* Intellectual Property Rights; Trademarks; Copyrights; Patents.

DONATUS OKORO, born Owerri, Nigeria, August 9, 1966; admitted, 1993, Nigeria. *Education:* University of Uyo, Uyo, Nigeria (LL.B. Hons, 1992). *Member:* Nigerian Bar Association. *LANGUAGES:* English and Ibo. *PRACTICE AREAS:* Estate and Probate Laws; Commercial Litigation; Corporate Law; Securities Law.

EMEKA NGIGE & CO.

Established in 1987

ANAMBRA HOUSE 27/29 MARTINS STREET, 4TH FLOOR
P.O. BOX 662

LAGOS, NIGERIA
Telephone: (234-1) 264-0103; 264-1947
Telefax: (234-1) 264-0104

U.S.A. Contact Office: Zalco Building, 8701 Georgia Avenue Suite 600, Silver Spring, M.D., 20910. Telephone: (301) 565-2424. Telefax: (301) 565-2426.

Banking, Commercial and Company Law, Divorce, Civil and Criminal Litigation, Intellectual Property, Real Estate, Practitioners in Natural Resources, Energy and Environmental Law including Immigration Practice and Arbitration.

FIRM PROFILE: The firm was established in August 1987 and offers a wide ranging legal services listed above.

MEMBERS OF FIRM

EMEKA NGIGE, ESQ, born Alor, Nigeria, July 11, 1961; admitted, 1985, Nigeria. *Education:* University of Nigeria (LL.B.); Nigeria Law School. Notary Public. Principal Partner, Emeka Ngige & Co. *Member:* Nigerian Bar Association; International Bar Association; American Bar Association (Associate Member, 1991—). *LANGUAGES:* English, Igbo

(This Listing Continued)

and Hausa. **PRACTICE AREAS:** Civil Litigation; Criminal Litigation; Constitutional Matters; Intellectual Property; Natural Resources; Energy; Environmental Law.

MRS. NJIDEKA NWACHUKWU, born Enugu, Nigeria, July 4, 1948; admitted, 1987, Nigeria. *Education:* University of Nigeria (LL.B.); Nigerian Law School (LL.M.); University of London. Associate in Chambers. *Member:* Nigerian Bar Association. **LANGUAGES:** English and Igbo. **PRACTICE AREAS:** Company Law; Commercial Law; Arbitration; Insurance Law.

INTERNATIONAL CONSULTANT

MRS. UZOEMENA NWADIKE, born Enugu, Nigeria, 1959; admitted, 1982, Nigeria; 1990, New York; 1991, Maryland. *Education:* University of Ife, Ile-Ife, Nigeria (LL.B.); Nigerian Law School (B.L.); University of Lagos (LL.M.). *Member:* Nigerian Bar Association; American Bar Association. **LANGUAGES:** English, Igbo and Yoruba. **PRACTICE AREAS:** Personal Injury; Immigration; Domestic Relations; Business Law.

TUNDE ODANYE & COMPANY

Established in 1985

15, MAJARO STREET
ONIKE-YABA
P.O. BOX 50102, FALOMO
LAGOS, NIGERIA
Telephone: 862365, 863846, 860913, 868666
Fax: 01-860913

Commercial Law, Maritime/Admiralty, Banking, Insurance, Copyrights, Trademarks and Patents, General Corporate/Company Law Practice, Company Secretarial Practice, Civil and Criminal Litigation.

FIRM PROFILE: *The firm was established in 1985 and offers a full range of legal services. There are 2 consultants, 12 lawyers and several Paralegal and administrative staff including a Chartered Accountant and other Accounts and Administrative Staff.*

CONSULTANTS

CHIEF S.P.A. AJIBADE, called Middle Temple England, 1960. enrolled Nigerian Bar 1960. Crown Counsel later private practice. One time Attorney General of Western State of Nigeria. **LANGUAGES:** English and Yoruba. **PRACTICE AREAS:** Commercial Law; Civil Litigation.

MR. M. OLAPADE ODANYE, called Lincolns Inn England 1961. enrolled Nigerian Bar 1961. Crown Counsel later Legal Adviser/Company Secretary Union Trading Company Limited (now U.T.C. (Nigeria) Limited. Now in private Practice. **LANGUAGES:** English and Yoruba. **PRACTICE AREAS:** Commercial Law; Company Secretarial Practice; Civil Litigation.

MEMBERS OF THE FIRM

TUNDE ODANYE, called Nigerian Bar (B.L.) 1978. *Education:* University of Ife, Nigeria (now Obafemi Awolowo University, Ile-Ife) (LL.B., 1977). *Member:* I.B.A. **LANGUAGES:** English and Yoruba. **PRACTICE AREAS:** Foreign Investments and Trade; Maritime; Trademarks and Patents; Company/Corporate/Commercial Law; Civil; Litigation.

JOHN ABILI, BL (1989) LL.B. (1988). **LANGUAGES:** English and Igbo. **PRACTICE AREAS:** Copyrights; Intellectual Property; International Franchising Rights; Civil Litigation; Maritime Law.

MR. ALEXANDER NDUKA MUOKA, BL (1991) LL.B. (1990). **LANGUAGES:** English and Igbo. **PRACTICE AREAS:** Foreign Investments and Policies; Banking Law; Company Law; Issues and Trading in Securities; Real Estate; Property Law.

MR. ALEXANDER MOLOKWU, BL (1989) LL.B. (1988). **PRACTICE AREAS:** Torts; Criminal Law; Civil Litigation.

MR. ABIMBOLA AWOSOLA, BL (1990) LL.B. (1989). **PRACTICE AREAS:** Insurance Law; Company/Commercial Law; Company Secretarial Practice; Maritime Law.

MR. ADEKUNLE OYENUSI, BL (1990) LL.B. (1989). **PRACTICE AREAS:** Banking Law; Savings and Mortgage Lending Institutions; Environmental Law; Civil Litigation.

MR. OLUFEMI OKUNOWO, BL (1990) LL.B. (1989). **PRACTICE AREAS:** Transport and Aviation Law; Banking Law; Wills Trusts and Succession; Civil and Criminal Litigation.

(This Listing Continued)

MR. UWAKWE ABALOGU, BL (1990) LL.B. (1989). **PRACTICE AREAS:** Labour Law; Administrative Law; Family Law; Human Rights; Civil Litigation.

MR. OLAYINKA DIVOEYE, BL (1991) LL.B. (1990). **PRACTICE AREAS:** Procedures for Settling Disputes; Environmental Law; Real Estate; Property Law; Insurance Law; Civil Litigation.

MR. FELIX ADESANWO, BL (1991) LL.B. (1990). **PRACTICE AREAS:** Company/Commercial Law; Banking Law; Insurance Law; Civil Litigation.

MR. KEHINDE DAWODU, BL (1992) LL.B. (1991). **PRACTICE AREAS:** Banking Law; Company Law; Commercial Law; Company Secretarial Practice.

MISS. ADEDAYO FADEYI, BL (1990) LL.B. (1989). **PRACTICE AREAS:** Issues and Trading in Securities; Banking Law; Insurance Law; Company/Commercial Law.

L. OGUNSHILE AND ASSOCIATES

15 MAJARO STREET (NY QUEEN'S COLLEGE)
ONIKE - YABA
P.O. BOX 50102 FALOMO
LAGOS, NIGERIA
Telephone: 234-1-863846; 860913; 862365
Evening: 234-1-867959 Facsimilie: 860913

Oil and Gas Transactions, International Finance Arbitration, Corporate and Commercial Law Expatriate Quota, Business Permits, Probate and Family Law Real Estate, Intellectual Property Law, Immigration, Trusts and Wills and Tax Law.

FIRM PROFILE: *L. Ogunshile and Associates is a Lagos based firm established in 1987. Its members belong to various national and international organizations, such as the International Bar Association, British Institute of Comparative Law, and the Nigeria Bar Association.*

The firm is closely associated with the Nigerian National Petroleum Corporation (NAPIMS) and the Legal Department of the Ministry of Petroleum and Mineral Resources. Additionally, the firm maintains connections with several multi-national oil producing corporations in Nigeria.

LOLA OGUNSHILE, born Kaduna, Nigeria, February 7, 1964; admitted, 1987, Nigeria. *Education:* University of Ibadan (LL.B., Hons., 1986) Nigerian Law School (B.L., 1987); University of Lagos (Diploma in Management, 1992). *Member:* Nigerian Bar Association; International Bar Association; British Institute of Comparative Law, London; Nigerian Petroleum and Mining Law Association, Lagos.

ASSOCIATES

ABIOLA OLAWUYI, *Education:* LL.B. (Honors); B.L.; B.A. (Hons.).

GLORIA AKIODE, *Education:* LL.B. (Honors); B.L.

GBOLAHAN IDOWU, *Education:* LL.B. (Honors); B.L.

Languages: French and English

OYAGBOLA CHAMBERS

Established in 1987

PRINCES PLAZA, 2, ARAROMI STREET, MOLONEY LAGOS
P.O. BOX 50828, FALOMO, IKOYI
LAGOS, NIGERIA
Telephone: (234) 1 2646456-8
Fax: (234) 2646455
Telex: 22940 OYALAW NG

Banking, Commercial, Corporate, Immigration, Insurance, Intellectual Property, International Finance, International Trade, Marine Insurance, Merchant Shipping, Property and Conveyancing and Taxation Law.

MEMBERS OF FIRM

ADEBAYO ADEKUNLE OYAGBOLA, born Lagos, Nigeria, August 8, 1958; admitted, 1983, Nigeria. *Education:* University College, London University (LL.B., LL.M.); Nigeria Law School. Co-Editor, "Legal Practitioner's Review." Author of "Anton Pillar Orders: A viable Procedure in Nigeria?"; "Is a foreign Company a juristic person in Nigeria?"; "Exchange Control and recovery in Nigeria of debts owed to foreign creditors"; "Duress, negligence, breach of Fiduciary duty and bad faith in Bank Lending." *Member:* Nigerian Bar Association; The English Honourable Society of the

(This Listing Continued)

OYAGBOLA CHAMBERS, Lagos—Continued

Middle Temple. *LANGUAGES:* English and Yoruba. *PRACTICE AREAS:* Intellectual Property; Banking; International Finance; Marine Insurance; Taxation; Corporate Law; Merchant Shipping.

HAMZA ABDULLAHI ATTA, born Lagos, Nigeria, June 13, 1964; admitted, 1991, Nigeria. *Education:* University of Hull, England (LL.B.); Nigeria Law School. *Member:* Nigerian Bar Association. *LANGUAGES:* English, Spanish and Ebira. *PRACTICE AREAS:* Immigration; Property and Conveyancing.

JIMOH FESTUS ADENIYI, born Arigidi, Ondo State, Nigeria, June 15, 1964; admitted, 1990, Nigeria. *Education:* University of Ibadan (LL.B.); Nigeria Law School. *Member:* Nigerian Bar Association. *LANGUAGES:* English and Yoruba. *PRACTICE AREAS:* Commercial; Property and Conveyancing; Probate; Immigration; General Insurance.

TITILAYO RASHIDAT OGUNLOLA, born Lagos, Nigeria, June 2, 1968; admitted, 1990, Nigeria. *Education:* Ogun State University (LL.B.); Nigeria Law School. *Member:* Nigerian Bar Association. *LANGUAGES:* English and Yoruba. *PRACTICE AREAS:* Banking; Commercial; Corporate; Property and Conveyancing.

CONSULTANTS

CHIEF THOMAS ADEDOKUN OYAGBOLA, born Aiyetoro, Ogun State, Nigeria, March 25, 1930; admitted, 1962, England; 1964, Nigeria. Member of the Nigerian Constituent Assembly, 1978-1979. Notary Public. *Member:* The English Honourable Society of the Middle Temple; Nigerian Bar Association; International Bar Association. *LANGUAGES:* English and Yoruba. *PRACTICE AREAS:* Property and Conveyancing; International Trade.

AMINATU ADEBAYO OYAGBOLA, born Lagos, Nigeria, April 26, 1961; admitted, 1983, Nigeria. *Education:* Ahmadu Bello University (LL.B.); Trinity College, Cambridge University (LL.M.); Nigeria Law School. Senior Banker with a Nigerian Commercial Bank. *Member:* Nigerian Bar Association. *LANGUAGES:* English, Ebira, Yoruba and French. *PRACTICE AREAS:* Banking; International Trade; Merchant Shipping.

STRACHAN PARTNERS

Formerly J.B. Majiyagbe & Co.

Established in 1991

4TH FLOOR H.O. DAVIES BUILDING
38/40 STRACHAN STREET
P.O. BOX 52177, IKOYI
LAGOS, NIGERIA
Telephone: (234-1) 2634919; 2647102; 2645022; 24 Hours Telephone (234) 90400538; (234-1) 680225
Fax: (234-1) 2637277; 2645022

Commercial Litigation, Maritime Law and International Trade, Banking and Finance Law, Company Commercial Law.

FIRM PROFILE: This major Nigerian law firm was established in Lagos as the autonomous satellite of J.B. Majiyagbe & Co., a thirty year old commercial practice in Kano. Northern Nigeria. That practice is extant but J.B. Majiyagbe & Co. (Lagos) became independent in 1994 under the new name of STRACHAN PARTNERS.

This practice stands on the substantial experience, and local and international connections and correspondents assiduously nurtured by its partners.

Its substantial resources in manpower and technology ensures service of the highest efficiency, quality and integrity.

There are seven lawyers and twelve para-legals in this office.

MEMBERS OF FIRM

ADEYEMI CANDIDE-JOHNSON, ESQ., LL.B. (Hons) (Reading); LL.M. (London). Notary Public. called to the Nigerian Bar, 1984. Former Social Secretary Nigeria Bar, Kano. Author: Oil and other Pollution Liability in Nigerian Navigable Waters, 1992; "Hamburg from Lagos" - How Nigerian Courts will apply the Hamburg Rules 1992; "Dealing With Nigerians New Admiralty Jurisdiction," 1993. Associate, Chartered Institute of Arbitrators, London. *Member:* International Bar Association; Nigerian Maritime Law Association; Rotary Club of Ikoyi (Secretary); Deputy General Editor, Legal Practitions Review, Institute of Maritime Law. University of Southampton Shipping Law Course, 1992. *LANGUAGES:* English.

(This Listing Continued)

PRACTICE AREAS: Commercial and Banking Litigation; Maritime and Admiralty Law.

EMMANUEL MAJEBI, called, 1987. Former Counsel, Kwara State Government. Former Secretary and Legal Adviser, Ivy Bull Society Limited, political commentator. *LANGUAGES:* English and Egbira. *PRACTICE AREAS:* Company and Commercial Law; Litigation.

OMOLARA COKER, called 1988. *LANGUAGES:* English. *PRACTICE AREAS:* International Trade; Banking & Finance; Commercial Litigation.

C. ABIYE ATORUDIBO, ESQ., called 1990. Former Associate, Burke & Co. Solicitors & Trade Mark & Patent Agents. *LANGUAGES:* English. *PRACTICE AREAS:* Intellectual Property; Company Commercial Law.

MUYIWA MARTINS, called, 1990. Former Associate, Ayanlaja & Adesanya, Legal Practitioner.

RAKIYA IBRAHIM, called 1991. *LANGUAGES:* English and Hausa. *PRACTICE AREAS:* Company Commercial Law.

TITILOLA OMISORE, called 1995.

UDO UDOMA & BELO-OSAGIE

Established in 1983

NO. 9 MILITARY STREET, ONIKAN
P.O. BOX 53123, IKOYI
LAGOS, NIGERIA
Telephone: 234-1-2633745; 2630986; 2636957; 2636880; 2634831
Telex: 23750 PETCTI-NG
Facsimile: 234-1-2634541; 2691769; 2692043

Accra, Ghana, Associated Office: Bentsi-Enchill & Letsa. 39 Cantonment Road. Osu R.E., P.O. Box 1632. Telephone: (23321) 772591/773970/773435. Telex: 2586 (ABSC GH). Fax: (23321) 772295/2202629.

Petroleum, Energy and Natural Resources, Foreign Investment, Banking and Finance, Environmental Law, Intellectual Property, Property, and Company and Commercial Law.

FIRM PROFILE: From its inception as a one-lawyer office in 1983, Udo Udoma & Belo Osagie has developed a broad-based corporate and institutional commercial practice. The firm has developed a reputation for providing its clients with sophisticated legal advice. It has developed particular specialities in areas such as banking, exchange control, Foreign investment, complex financing, public and private offerings of securities, corporate taxation, bankruptcy, petroleum and energy matters and natural resources law, mergers and acquisitions, construction and engineering contracts, the negotiation of complex commercial property transactions and intellectual property law (patents, trademarks and copyrights). The firm has experience in the structuring of up stream and down stream oil and gas as well as petro chemical projects.

The firm's corporate clients are in the main, joint venture companies, comprising of Nigerian and foreign entities, but also include a number of foreign based companies with business interests in Nigeria, as well as wholly owned Nigerian enterprises. The firm represents various governments, most of the major commercial and merchant banks and financial institutions, consulting and engineering companies and some international organizations. In addition, the firm represents oil trading, exploration and service companies, breweries, pharmaceutical companies, and acts as legal advisor to certain state governments as well as the Government of the Federal Republic of Nigeria; and provides legal advisory services to professional colleagues in Nigeria and abroad.

The firm has an active commercial civil litigation practice and a small criminal defense practice, and also provides trusteeship services to clients.

MEMBERS

UDOMA UDO UDOMA, born Aba, Abia State, Nigeria, February 26, 1954; admitted, 1978, Lagos. *Education:* Oxford University, England (B.A. Jurisprudence, 1976; B.C.L., 1977; M.A., Honoris Causa, 1981). Law Lecturer, University of Lagos, 1979-1980. Investment Analyst, Chase Merchant Bank, Lagos, 1980. Associate, Chris Ogunbanjo & Co. (Solicitors), 1980-1981. Partner, David Garrick & Co. (Solicitors), 1981-1983. Consultant, Nigerian Liquified Natural Gas (LNG), 1981-1983. Member of Team, Nigerian Government to implement the LNG project in joint venture with 3 international oil companies, 1984-1989. Consultant on current privatisation of Government owned companies and Solicitor for the sale of Government shares in African Petroleum Limited, 1988-1989; Consultant to New

(This Listing Continued)

York law firm of Shearman and Sterling, 1989-1991, appointed as first Chairman of the Corporate Affairs Commission, February, 1991, and Member of the Study Group on the Legal Aspects of Privatisation and Commercialisation Programme set up by the Federal Government. Special Adviser, Honorable Minister for Petroleum & Natural Resources, September 1993 - March 1994. *Member:* Nigerian Bar Association; International Bar Association. *LANGUAGES:* English and Ibibio. *PRACTICE AREAS:* General Corporate; Joint Ventures; Mergers and Acquisitions; Trusteeship Services; Notary Public.

DR. MYMA BELO-OSAGIE, born Accra, Ghana, February 22, 1954; admitted, 1977, Ghana; 1983, New York; 1984, Nigeria. *Education:* University of Ghana (LL.B., 1975); Harvard Law School, Cambridge, Massachusetts (LL.M., 1978; S.J.D., 1985). *Member:* Ghana Bar Association; New York State Bar Association; Nigerian Bar Association; International Bar Association. *LANGUAGES:* English, Ga and Akan. *PRACTICE AREAS:* Petroleum, Energy and Natural Resources Law; Probate Matters; Money Market Instruments.

OLUFEMI DOMINIC LIJADU, born London, England, February 21, 1959; admitted, 1981, Nigeria. *Education:* University of Durham (B.A., Law, 1980); University College London (LL.M., 1983). Associated with Fani-Kayode & Sowemimo, 1981 and 1983-1987. Attached to the Ikeja Division of the High Court of Lagos State, 1981. State Counsel, Ministry of Justice, Ilorin, 1981-1982. *Member:* Nigerian Bar Association; International Tax and Planning Association. *LANGUAGES:* English, French and Yoruba. *PRACTICE AREAS:* Commercial Law; Investment Law; Exchange Control; Construction and Engineering Contracts.

ASSOCIATES

DANIEL O. AGBOR, born Lagos, Lagos State, Nigeria, January 7, 1960; admitted, 1986, Nigeria. *Education:* University of Calabar (B.Sc., Political Science, 1980; M.P.A., 1982); Benin University, Nigeria (LL.B., 1985). Lecturer in Political Science, Rivers State College, 1980-1981. Associated with Ajumogobia, Okeke, Oyebode & Aluko, 1986-1987. Legal Officer, Nigerian International Bank, 1987-1988. Product Manager, Corporate Finance Unit, Nigerian International Bank, 1988-1990. *Member:* Nigerian Bar Association. *LANGUAGES:* English and Efik. *PRACTICE AREAS:* Banking and Finance; Taxation.

UZOMA H. AZIKIWE, born Igbodo, Delta State, Nigeria, December 11, 1959; admitted, 1986, Nigeria. *Education:* University of Ife, Nigeria (LL.B., 1985). State Counsel, Oyo State Ministry of Justice, 1986-1987. With R. A. Salami & Co., 1987; With G. S. Ebeagwu & Co., 1988-1990. *Member:* Nigerian Bar Association. *LANGUAGES:* English and Igbo. *PRACTICE AREAS:* Commercial Litigation.

ANIEKAN ENOBONG UKPANAH, born Nsekhe, Akwa Ibom State, Nigeria, December 27, 1963; admitted, 1988, Nigeria. *Education:* Dorset College, England (B.A., Joint Honours Law and Economics, 1987). Research Analyst with Hubert James (Solicitors), England, 1986. With Obong A. J. Ukpanah & Co., 1987. With Chief Mike J. Akpabio & Co., 1988. Attached to the Lagos State High Court, 1988. *Member:* Nigerian Bar Association. *LANGUAGES:* English and Ibibio. *PRACTICE AREAS:* Industrial Property; Patents Designs, Trademark and Copyright.

KAFAYAT OLAJUMOKE LAMBO, born Ibadan, Oyo State, Nigeria, May 16, 1966; admitted, 1989, Nigeria. *Education:* University of Bristol, England (LL.B., 1988). With David Agnew & Co., Solicitors, England, 1984. With H. T. O. Coker (SAN), 1989. Attached to the Lagos State Magistrates Court, 1989. *Member:* Nigerian Bar Association. *LANGUAGES:* English and Yoruba. *PRACTICE AREAS:* Investment Law; Exchange Control; Construction and Engineering Contracts.

JULIET MFON CHUNU, born Lagos, Lagos State, Nigeria, July 30, 1963; admitted, 1984, Nigeria. *Education:* University of Nigeria, Nsukka (LL.B., hons., 1983). Administrative Officer, Petroleum Training Institute, Warri, Nigeria, 1984-1985. Associated with: Chief A. O. Akpedye (Legal Practitioners), 1985-1986; Oki & Oki (Legal Practitioners), 1986-1987; E. L. Akpofure & Co., (Legal Practitioners), 1988-1989; M. O. Awoyemi & Co., (Legal Practitioners), 1990-1991. *Member:* Nigerian Bar Association. *LANGUAGES:* English, Ibo and Ibibio. *PRACTICE AREAS:* Commercial Litigation.

GREGORY CHUKWUDI DIOKA, born Lagos, Lagos State, Nigeria, March 6, 1968; admitted, 1990, Nigeria. *Education:* Anambra State University of Technology, Enugu (LL.B., hons., 1989). Alliance Francaise au Nigeria (Certificate D'Etudes Francaises-ler Degre de l'Alliance Francaise 1990; 2eme degre de l'Alliance Francaise 1991). With Udo Udoma & Belo-Osagie, 1990. Attached to the Lagos Division of the High Court of Lagos State, 1990. *Member:* Nigerian Bar Association. *LANGUAGES:* English,

(This Listing Continued)

French and Ibo. *PRACTICE AREAS:* Industrial Property; Patents Designs, Trademark and Copyright.

ANIRE KANYI, born Lagos, Lagos State, Nigeria, October 25, 1965; admitted, 1990, Nigeria. *Education:* University of Benin (LL.B., hons., 1989). With Amachree & Ogbemi, 1990. Attached to the Ikeja Division of the High Court of Lagos State, 1990. *Member:* Nigerian Bar Association. *LANGUAGES:* English, Yoruba and Itsekiri. *PRACTICE AREAS:* Trusteeship Services and Foreign Investment.

SOLOMON MMEH ETUK, born Ekparakwa, Akwa Ibom State, Nigeria, July 21, 1956; admitted, 1991, Nigeria. *Education:* University of Calabar (B.Sc., 1984); University of Uyo (LL.B., 1990); The Nigerian Law School (B.L., 1991). Member, Shola Martin & Co., 1991. Attached to the High Court of Akwa Ibom State, 1991. *Member:* Nigerian Bar Association; Association of Microbiologists. *LANGUAGES:* English and Ibibio. *PRACTICE AREAS:* Commercial Litigation; Industrial Property Law; Company and Commerical Law.

DORA AIMIEDE OMOLE, born Lagos, Lagos State, Nigeria, July 19, 1958; admitted, 1990, Nigeria. *Education:* University of Lagos (LL.B., 1989); The Nigerian Law School (B.L., 1990). Attached to E. Omoboye-Leyimu's Chambers (Legal Practitioners) 1990. Attached to the Ikeja Division, Lagos State High Court. *Member:* Nigerian Bar Association. *LANGUAGES:* English, Ishan and Yoruba. *PRACTICE AREAS:* Company Secretarial Practice.

OLUKEMI OGUTUGA, born Lagos, Lagos State, Nigeria, June 29, 1966; admitted, 1992. *Education:* University of Warwick (LL.B. Hons., 1989); University of Nottingham (LL.M., 1990). Attached to Chris Ogunbanjo & Co., Solicitors, 1991. Attached to the Ikeja Division, Lagos State High Court. *Member:* Nigerian Bar Association. *LANGUAGES:* English and Yoruba. *PRACTICE AREAS:* Foreign Investment and Environmental Law.

CONSULTANTS

ANIOLA DUROSINMI-ETTI, born Port-Harcourt, Rivers State, Nigeria, January 2, 1961; admitted, 1982, Lagos. *Education:* University of Lagos, Nigeria (LL.B., 1981); Cambridge University, England (LL.M., 1984). Research Officer, Nigerian Law Reform Commission, 1982-1983. Associated with Sun Laboratories (Nigeria) Limited, 1989—. Legal Officer, Credit Transactions & Investments Company Limited, 1987—. *Member:* Nigerian Bar Association. *LANGUAGES:* English. *PRACTICE AREAS:* Insurance; Debt Recovery; Product Liability Law.

FUNMILAYO ADE-AJAYI, born Ibadan, Oyo State, Nigeria, January 22, 1961; admitted, 1986, Lagos. *Education:* Leicester University, England (B.A., History, 1980); Cambridge University, England (B.A. Laws, 1985). Administration Assistant, Products Marketing Department, NNPC, 1980-1981. Research Assistant/Administrator, LNG Project Office, 1981-1982. Associate, Peter Elliot & Co., Solicitors Firm, England, 1976 and 1986. London Representative, Credit Transactions and Investments Company Limited, 1986-1987. Legal Officer, Credit Transactions and Investments Company Limited, 1987-1988. Associated with Sun Laboratories Limited. Associated with Kenneth Michael and Co. *Member:* Nigerian Bar Association. *LANGUAGES:* English. *PRACTICE AREAS:* Company Law; Financial and Trust Documentation.

Member ICC Group of International Lawyers.

Languages: English and French.

UKIRI & SHASORE

4TH FLOOR 35, MOLONEY STREET
P.O. BOX 9945 (MARINA)
LAGOS, NIGERIA
Telephone: 2634286; 2637725; 2632359
Facsmile: (234 1) 2637107

FIRM PROFILE: The firm specializes primarily in corporate commercial legal work particularly in the area relating to taxation; shipping and admiralty law; the law relating to Foreign Investment, with special reference to investment by joint venture partners in natural resources, construction, manufacturing and agricultural projects; energy law (especially in the areas of oil and gas law); immigration law and the law of intellectual property (patents, trademarks and copyrights). The firm also has experience in banking and exchange control law; receivership; engineering, construction and other major contracts; undertakes negotiations on behalf of various clients who have contacts with governmental institutions and other

(This Listing Continued)

UKIRI & SHASORE, Lagos—Continued

large organizations and companies. The firm undertakes commercial litigation and arbitration.

MEMBERS

OVIE EDWARD UKIRI, born Lagos, Nigeria, August 15, 1963; admitted, 1987, Nigeria. *Education:* Keele University, England (B.Soc. Sci. Law and Economics, 1986); Kings College London, England (LL.M., Tax Law, 1988). With Kehinde Sofola & Co., 1987. Attached to the Lagos Division of the High Court of Lagos, 1987. Associated with: Burke and Co., 1988-1990; Udo Udoma & Belo-Osagie, 1991-1993. *Member:* Nigerian and International Bar Associations; Nigerian Institute of Taxation. *LANGUAGES:* English and Yoruba. *PRACTICE AREAS:* Taxation; Investment Law; Petroleum Law; Energy Law; Banking; Finance.

OLASUPO A. SHASORE, born Lagos, Nigeria, January 22, 1964; admitted, 1987, Nigeria. *Education:* University of Ife (LL.B., 1986); University of Lagos (LL.M. International Law, 1990). Attached to the Lagos Division of the High Court of Lagos State, 1987. With: Olisa Chukura (SAN), 1987; Burke and Company, 1988-1990; Ajumogobia, Okeke, Oyebode & Aluko, 1991-1992; Ajumogobia & Okeke, 1993. Managing Associate, R.O. Akinjide and Co., 1990. *Member:* Nigerian Bar Association; Business Association of Nigeria and the Southern African Region; Nigerian Society of International Law. *LANGUAGES:* English and Yoruba. *PRACTICE AREAS:* Shipping; Admiralty Law; Intellectual Property Law; Insolvency Law; Commercial Litigation; Arbitration.

OLADIPUPO O. BELLO, born Akure, Nigeria, April 5, 1969; admitted, 1992, Nigeria. *Education:* Lagos State University (LL.B., 1991). With: Tayo Oyetibo & Co., 1991; M.O. Bello & Co., 1993. Attached to the Akure Judicial Division of the High Court of Ondo State, 1992. *Member:* Nigerian Bar Association. *LANGUAGES:* English and Yoruba. *PRACTICE AREAS:* Immigration Law; Property Law; Commercial Litigation.

VICTORIA E. AKAN, born Calabar, Nigeria, August 12, 1971; admitted, 1993, Nigeria. *Education:* University of Calabar (LL.B., 1992). With, Puul Erokoro & Associates, 1993. Attached to the High Court of Calabar, 1992. *Member:* Nigerian Bar Association. *LANGUAGES:* English and Ibibio. *PRACTICE AREAS:* Intellectual Property; Banking Law; Insurance Law; Company Law.

N. NWANODI & CO.

Engaged in Nigerian and International Law Practice. Entitled to Plead Before Nigerian Courts

PLOT "D" GOLF COURSE LAYOUT

P.O. BOX 140

PORT HARCOURT, NIGERIA

Telephone: 234-(0)84-330729; 234-(0)84-236613

Fax: 234-(0)84-234138

FIRM PROFILE: *Established as a Firm in 1963. N. Nwanodi & Co. is a well known Firm of Legal Practitioners with a strong base in Port Harcourt. The practice of the firm is broadly based and has a good reputation for offering a wide range of excellent quality legal services, Commercial, Investment, Property, Intellectual Property and Labour Relations, Litigation work in all of the fields mentioned including Appellate Court work. Clientele in International in scope. The firm is small in number, but has a good working relationship with other Legal Firms in Lagos, Nigeria.*

NWOBIDIKE NWANODI, born Port Harcourt (Diobu), Nigeria, February 2, 1933; admitted, 1959, England and Nigeria. *Education:* McGill University (B.A., with Honors, 1955), University of Oxford, England (M.Litt., 1958); Lincoln College; Nuffield College; Council of Legal Education (Grays Inn), London (B.L., 1959). (Principal). *LANGUAGES:* English. *PRACTICE AREAS:* Commercial Law; Property Law; Constitutional Law; Administrative Law; Admiralty Law.

ASSOCIATES

ELSIE NWANURI THOMPSON, born Port Harcourt, Nigeria, September 17, 1960; admitted, 1985, Nigeria. *Education:* Queen Mary College, University of London (LL.B., 1983); Inns of Court School of Law, Grays Inn (B.L., 1984); Nigerian Law School, Lagos, Nigeria (B.L., 1985). *LANGUAGES:* English. *PRACTICE AREAS:* Company Law; Oil and Gas Law; Intellectual Property Law; Real Property Law.

(This Listing Continued)

AMONI PETERSIDE, born Lagos, Nigeria, July 7, 1957; admitted, 1992, Nigeria. *Education:* Rivers State University of Science and Technology (LL.B., 1991); Nigerian Law School (B.L., 1991). *PRACTICE AREAS:* Company Law; Commercial Law; Civil Law; Real Property Law.

OMAN

ADHAM & ASSOCIATES

P.O. BOX 2301 POSTAL CODE 112

MUSCAT, SULTANATE OF OMAN

Telephone: 796146; 799956 (Muscat)

Fax: 796170

Telex: 3712 "Adreco" On

Khartoum, Sudan Office: Adham & Associates. P.O. Box 2272. Telephone: 81489; 80469; 79279 (Khartoum). Telex: 22223 "Adjco" SD.

General Practice and Litigation, Insurance, Shipping, Investment, International Finance, Banking, Taxation, Civil Engineering, Labour Law, Company Law, Mining and Petroleum, Trademarks and Patents, Legal Transportation, Advocates and Commissioners for Oaths.

ANWAR ADHAM, born 1934; admitted to bar, 1960. *Education:* Cairo University (LL.B., 1959).

Languages: Corresponds in Arabic and English.

AL SAFA LEGAL CONSULTANTS

(Legal Consultants and Advocates)

Established in 1982

AL SAFA HOUSE BUILDING

MUSCAT, OMAN

Telephone: 793375-793376

Telefax: 700033

Mailing Address: P.O. Box 3746, Ruwi, 112, Oman

General Legal Practice, Corporate and Commercial Litigation, Representation before all Courts in Oman, Foreign Investment, Joint Venture Companies, Taxation, Agencies, Maritime Law, Environmental, Banking, Insurance, Trademark Registration and Patent Protection.

MEMBERS OF FIRM

ALI KHAMIS AL ALAWI, born Sultanate of Oman, 1956. *Education:* LL.B., 1981, Cairo. Directors, Oman Chamber of Commerce & Industry. Associate Member, Gulf Consultants for the Protection of Intellectual Property. *LANGUAGES:* Arabic and English. *PRACTICE AREAS:* Property Transactions; Contracts; Agencies; Trademarks and Patents.

MOHAMMED AL MURTADA HAMID, born Sudan, 1957. *Education:* LL.B., 1983, Alexandria. Practicing Advocate, 1884. *LANGUAGES:* Arabic and English. *PRACTICE AREAS:* Banking; Agency; Labour; Criminal.

ABDULLATIF GASMALLA, born Sudan, 1957. *Education:* LL.B., 1982, Khartoum. Practicing Advocate, 1983;. *LANGUAGES:* Arabic and English. *PRACTICE AREAS:* Company; Insurance; Banking.

ABDULAZIZ A. BABIKER, born Sudan, 1953. *Education:* LL.B., 1979, Khartoum. Practicing Advocate, 1982. *LANGUAGES:* Arabic and English. *PRACTICE AREAS:* Foreign Investments; Maritime; Engineering Construction; Energy Law.

ABDUL WAHAB A. AL HASSAN, born Sudan, 1942. *Education:* LL.B., 1970, Cairo. Practicing Advocate, 1990. *LANGUAGES:* Arabic and English. *PRACTICE AREAS:* Taxation; Labour; Criminal Litigation.

FOX & GIBBONS

Solicitors

Established in 1981

P.O. BOX 3552 POSTAL CODE 112
RUWI, SULTANATE OF OMAN
Telephone: (968) 564346
Fax: (968) 564395
Telex: 5630 GIBLAW ON

London, England Office: 2 Old Burlington Street, W1X 2QA. Telephone: (44-171) 439 8271. Telex: 267108. Telefax: (44-171) 734 8843.

Dubai, United ArabEmirates Office: P.O. Box 1756. Telephone: (9714) 310220. Fax: (9714) 310201. Telex: 45614 GBLAW EM.

Abu Dhabi, United Arab Emirates Kudsi Fox & Gibbons Office: P.O. Box 46010. Telephone: (9712) 322858. Fax: (9712) 331586.

Cairo, Egypt Office: 126 Mohei El Din Abul Ezz Street, 9th Floor, Mohandiseen, Giza, Cairo, Egypt. Telephone: (202) 3485955. Fax: (202) 3492210.

Gibraltar Office: P.O. Box 246. Telephone: (350) 77750. Fax: (350) 77800.

Fujairah, United Arab Emirates Office: P.O. Box 701. Telephone: (971 9) 229390. Fax: (971 9) 226470.

Kuwait Associated Office: P.O. Box 26473, Safat, 13125 Safat. Telephone: (965) 2462323/2462525/2462929. Fax: (965) 242 5830. Telex: 30844 ZINA KT.

Yemen Associated Office: P.O. Box 148, Crater, Aden. Telephone: (9672) 255305/253824. Fax: (9672) 255305/255117.

Lebanon Associated Office: Saba K. Zreik Law Offices. Autostrade Dora, Cite Dora 3 Building, 10th Floor, P.O. Box 90-710, Beirut, Lebanon. Telephone (961 1) 881322. Fax: (961 1) 881387. Telex: 42949 MANAL LE.

Corporate and Company work; registration of companies; Agencies distributorships and Joint Ventures; Banking Law; Contracts; Local Securities Law; Project Finance and Construction; Gas and Oil; Copyright and Trademark Law; Legal Opinions; Arbitration; Litigation; Marine & Insurance Law; Taxation and Legal Translations.

MANAGING PARTNER

Alan N. Rodgers

LEGAL SUPPORT STAFF

J. Alasdair Jeffrey
Abdul Rahman Mohamed Elnafie (Arab Lawyer)
Bridget McKinney (American Lawyer)
Nouraddin Alkheir Ahmed (Arab Lawyer)
Alastair Hirst (Arabist Lawyer)
Louise Howard (Solicitor)

(For a list of other Personnel, see Biographical Cards at London, England, Dubai, Fujairah and Abu Dhabi, United Arab Emirates, Cairo, Egypt, Kuwait, Gibraltar, Lebanon and Yemen)

QATAR

LAW OFFICES OF GEBRAN MAJDALANY

Established in 1967

P.O. BOX 4004
DOHA, QATAR
Telephone: 974-428899
Telex: 4527 LEGAL DH
Fax: 974-417817

Beirut, Lebanon Office: Hamra Street, Saroulla Building. Telephone: 353422; 344134/5-342700. Fax: 351422.

FIRM PROFILE: Established in 1967, the Law Office of Gebran Majdalany has expertise in the laws of Qatar, United Arab Emirates, Lebanon, and Egypt. The firm specialises in banking, company law, civil law, including construction law and real estate law, insurance and matters relating to international commerce. The firm has 7 lawyers and English, Arabic and French is spoken. In addition, the firm is a member of the association of law firms established in Dubai, United Arab Emirates, in 1992 which carries on business there under the name of "Nabarro Nathanson".

(This Listing Continued)

The firm also acts as honorary legal adviser to the Embassies of most Arab Embassies, France, Italy and the United Kingdom.

GEBRAN N. MAJDALANY. *Education:* Lyon (LL.L, 1949); St. Joseph, Beirut (1950). (Senior Partner). *LANGUAGES:* English, Arabic and French. *PRACTICE AREAS:* Business and Commercial Law; Banking Law; Company Law.

ELIAS M. KHOURY. *Education:* Beirut (LL.L., 1970). (Assoc.). *LANGUAGES:* English and Arabic. *PRACTICE AREAS:* Patents and Trademarks.

ADRIENNE S. MACARTNEY, Solicitor of the Supreme Court of Judicature of Northern Ireland, 1979. (Assoc.). *LANGUAGES:* English. *PRACTICE AREAS:* Business and Commercial Law; Company Law; Banking; Commercial Agency and Distributorship.

HUSSAIN ALI NAJM, President, Court of Appeal of Mansoura (Egypt), 1984-1990. (Legal Consultant). *LANGUAGES:* Arabic and English. *PRACTICE AREAS:* Litigation; Contracts; Construction Law.

ABDUL WAHAB SAYED. *Education:* Cario (LL.L., 1980). (Assoc.). *LANGUAGES:* Arabic and English.

MOHAMMED SHAFIC EL-MELIJI. *Education:* Cairo University (Egypt) 1955. President of Court of Appeal of Cairo, 1992-1993 (Legal Consultant). *LANGUAGES:* Arabic and English. *PRACTICE AREAS:* Contracts and Litigation.

OMAR MIRGAHANI AL-MANNA. *Education:* University of Khartoom, 1967. Member, Federal Supreme Court, 1988-1994 (Legal Consultant). Head of Judiciary Whiltenile State - Sudan 1994 (Legal Consultant). *LANGUAGES:* Arabic and English. *PRACTICE AREAS:* Company Law; Banking Law; Contracts.

Principal Office: Beirut, Lebanon.
Overseas Offices: Dubai in association with Nabarro Nathanson.

SAUDI ARABIA

DR. AUDHALI LAW FIRM

Established in 1972

P.O. BOX 1158
AL-KHOBAR 31952, SAUDI ARABIA
Telephone: 03-864-3011; 864-3793; 899-1655
Telefax: 03-894-5837
Cable Address: Audhali

General Practice in all areas of Saudi Law.

FIRM PROFILE: Dr. Audhali is assisted by large number of highly qualified and experience lawyers and Translators.

DR. AHMED A. AUDHALI, Barrister-at-Law (English Bar), 1970; 1972, Saudi Arabia. *Education:* LL.B. (London), Ph.D., Business Law, Islamic Law (various Degrees).

REPRESENTATIVE CLIENTS: McDonald Douglas; G.E.; Bechtel; AT&T; McDermott; British Air Corp.; Saudi Hollandi Bank; Korean Corp.; Babcock; Sumitomo; Mitsubishi; G.I.E.; Belleli; Zamil Group; Siemens; Sabic; Dresser; Baker Hughes; Petromin-Shell.

AL-GHAZZAWI PROFESSIONAL ASSOCIATION

GHAZZAWI BUILDING
AL HAMRA, ANDALOUS STREET
P.O. BOX 7346
JEDDAH 21462, SAUDI ARABIA
Telephone: (2) 6531576
Fax: (2) 6532612

Dammam, Saudi Arabia Office: ABC Building, 8th Floor, King Abdulaziz Street, P.O. Box 381, 31411. Telephone: (3) 8331611. Fax: (3) 8331981.

Riyadh, Saudi Arabia Office: Al Balla Building, Old Airport Road, P.O. Box 9029, 11413. Telephone: (1) 4783635. Fax: (1) 4783712.

(This Listing Continued)

AL-GHAZZAWI PROFESSIONAL ASSOCIATION,
Jeddah—Continued

Administrative, Agency & Distribution, Arbitration, Banking and Finance, Bankruptcy/Insolvency, Civil Litigation, Commercial Disputes, Commercial Property, Company, Contracts, Debt Recovery, Franchising, Customs, Insurance, Intellectual Property, International Investment & Financial Services, Labour Relations, Mergers & Acquisition, Partnerships & Joint Ventures, Real Estate, Shipping/Admiralty, Taxation, Trademarks, Trade Names & Patents.

PARTNERS

DR. TALAL AMIN AL GHAZZAWI. *Education:* SJD (LL.D., 1969). (Senior Partner).

BELAL TALAL AL GHAZZAWI. *Education:* (LL.B., 1984). (Managing Partner).

HUSSAM TALAL AL GHAZZAWI. *Education:* (LL.B., 1992). (Executive Partner).

ASSOCIATES

KAMIL MOHD FARAH. *Education:* (LL.B., 1971).

GAAFAR ALSIR ALI. *Education:* (LL.B., 1975).

SOBAHI MOHD. SOBAHI. *Education:* (LL.B., 1977).

OSMAN GEALAB. *Education:* (LL.B., 1973).

MOHAMMED EL-SOBKY. *Education:* (LL.B., 1984).

TAJELDIN HASSAN. *Education:* (LL.B., 1986).

TALAL AL AHMEDI. *Education:* (LL.B., 1988).

MAMOUN M. AL-HASSON. *Education:* (LL.B., 1983).

ABDULLAH M. AL-WAZZAN. *Education:* (1979).

Languages: Arabic and English

THE LAW FIRM OF SALAH AL-HEJAILAN

Established in 1967

ALIREZA TOWER, 11TH FLOOR, MEDINA ROAD
P.O. BOX 15141
JEDDAH 21444, SAUDI ARABIA
Telephone: (02) 653 4422
Telex: 606766
Fax: (02) 651 7241

Riyadh, Saudi Arabia Office: Al Dahna Center, Al Ahsa Street, P.O. Box 1454, Riyadh 11431. Telephone: (1) 479 2200. Telex: 401109. Fax: (1) 479 1717.

In Association with CLIFFORD CHANCE, London, England.
Also in Association with GRAHAM & JAMES, San Francisco, California.

General and International Practice including Corporate, Financial, Banking, Tax, Real Estate, Commercial, Civil, Maritime, Criminal and Administrative Law, Litigation and Arbitration.

MEMBERS OF FIRM

SALAH AL-HEJAILAN, born Saudi Arabia, 1941; admitted, 1962, Saudi Arabia. *Education:* University of Cairo (Degree in Law, 1962); University of Southern California, Los Angeles (Masters Degree in International Public Administration, 1968). Legal Advisor, Council of Ministers, Kingdom of Saudi Arabia, 1962-1973. Counsel, Bribery and Forgery Committees of the Board of Grievances, Kingdom of Saudi Arabia, 1963-1972. Legal Consultant, Royal Commission for Jubail and Yanbu, 1963-1986. Member, Government Committees for Promulgation of Regulations, Resolutions and Decrees, 1963-1973. Member, Board of Directors, Ports Authority, Kingdom of Saudi Arabia, 1976-1987. Chairman, The Higher Board of the Euro-Arab Arbitration System, London, 1985—. Member, Arbitration Council, Arab-Swiss Chamber of Commerce, 1985—. Founding Shareholder, Saudi American Bank, Saudi Arabia, 1977—. Partner and Member of the Board of Directors, Arabian International Maritime Company (an affiliate of Mobil Oil Corporation), 1977—. Partner and Chairman of the Board of Directors, Thyssen Saudi Arabia Limited (an affiliate of Thyssen Handelsunion), Germany, 1977—. Director, ABC International Bank, London (an affiliate of Arab Banking Corporation), 1991—. Council

(This Listing Continued)

AF88B

Member, Centre for Islamic & Middle Eastern Law (CIMEL), School of Oriental and African Studies, London University, 1989—. Member, Nominating Committee, Eisenhower Exchange Fellowship Program, 1989—. Member, Arab Arbitration Group of ICC International Court of Arbitration, Paris, 1992—. Director, Cairo Regional Centre for Commercial Arbitration, 1994—. Member, World Intellectual Property Arbitration Consultative Commission, 1994—. *LANGUAGES:* Arabic and English.

REMSEN M. KINNE, IV, admitted, 1991, California (Not admitted in Saudi Arabia). *Education:* Yale University (B.A., 1981); Boston College Law School (J.D., cum laude, 1989). (Also Associate, Graham & James). *LANGUAGES:* English and French.

MAJED MOHAMED GAROUB, born Jeddah, Saudi Arabia, 1966. *Education:* King Abdul Aziz University (B.A., Law, 1990). *LANGUAGES:* Arabic and English.

DR. MOHAMED MOHAMED BADRAN, born Al-Dakahlia, Egypt, 1941; admitted, 1994, Court of Cassation, Supreme Administrative Court and Supreme Constitutional Court, Egypt (Not admitted in Saudi Arabia). *Education:* Cairo University (License in Law, 1967; Post-Graduate Diplomas, 1968, 1969); Birmingham University, England (MSC, 1975 and Ph.D., 1979). Professor of Public Law, Cairo University, 1993—. Faculty Member, Cairo University, 1967—. Legal Advisor of the People's Assembly (Egyptian Parliament), 1987-1990, and Cairo University, 1990-1994. *LANGUAGES:* Arabic and English.

KHALID ABDULAZIZ ALNOWAISER, born Mecca, Saudi Arabia, 1961; admitted, 1986, Saudi Arabia. *Education:* King Abdulaziz University (B.A., Political Science, 1986); Edinburgh University, Scotland (LL.B. courses & LL.M., 1991); Bristol University, England (cur rent Ph.D. candidate, Commercial Law). *LANGUAGES:* Arabic and English.

OF COUNSEL

DR. MOHAMED SABER EL-KALIOUBI, born Egypt, 1946; admitted, 1973, Egypt (Not admitted in Saudi Arabia). *Education:* Paris II University (Ph.D., 1990; Postgraduate Diploma in Private Law, 1977); Cairo University (Postgraduate Diploma in Sharia Law (Hons), 1975; Postgraduate Diploma in Private Law (Hons), 1974; B.A., Law (Hons), 1973). Assistant Professor and Seminar Lecturer, Maritime and Commercial Law, Faculty of Law, Cairo University, 1976-1993. *LANGUAGES:* Arabic, French and English.

LAW OFFICES OF DR. MUJAHID M. AL-SAWWAF

Established in 1978

P.O. BOX 5840
JEDDAH 21432, SAUDI ARABIA
Telephone: 966-2-669-0751
Telefax: 966-2-665-5052
Telex: 602262 FURAT SJ

Riyadh Office: P.O. Box 86581, Riyadh 11632, Saudi Arabia. Telephone: 966-1-454-9200. Telefax: 966-1-454-5856. Telex: 406724 LEGAL SJ.

Foreign Investment, Corporate, Commercial, Banking, Joint Venture, Civil Litigation, Arbitration and Shipping and Insurance Law.

MEMBERS OF FIRM

DR. MUJAHID M. AL-SAWWAF, born Baghdad, Iraq, September 12, 1942. Citizen of the Kingdom of Saudi Arabia; admitted, 1980, Saudi Arabia. *Education:* Baghdad University, College of Sharia Law (B.A., 1963); Oxford University (Doctor of Philosophy in Koranic Law, 1969); Harvard University (Visiting Scholar, 1976-1977). Associate Professor of Law, 1970-1978 and Professor of Islamic Law, 1978-1984, Shari'a Law College of Umm Al Qura University, Makkah, Saudi Arabia. *LANGUAGES:* Arabic and English.

DAVID M. WELLS, born Decatur, Illinois, January 30, 1943; admitted, 1972, California (Not admitted in Saudi Arabia). *Education:* Northwestern University (B.A., 1965); Georgetown University Law Center (J.D., 1971). *LANGUAGES:* English.

RICHARD J. TYNER, born Shenandoah, Iowa, November 21, 1947; admitted, 1979, California (Not admitted in Saudi Arabia). *Education:* University of Iowa (B.A., summa cum laude, 1970); University of Manchester, England (M.A., 1971); London School of Economics (Ph.D., 1975); Yale Law School (J.D., 1979). Phi Beta Kappa. Marshall Scholar. Editor, Yale

(This Listing Continued)

Studies in World Public Order, 1978-1979. *LANGUAGES:* English and French.

JOHN F. PIERCE, born Seattle, Washington, July 2, 1962; admitted, 1993, Washington (Not admitted in Saudi Arabia). *Education:* San Francisco State University (B.A., highest honors, department valedictorian, 1990); University of Washington School of Law (J.D., 1993). Editor-in-Chief, Pacific Rim Law & Policy Journal, 1992-1993. Author: "Philippine Foreign Investment Efforts: The Foreign Investments Act and the Local Governments Code," 1 Pac. Rim L. & Pol'y. J. 169, 1992. *LANGUAGES:* English, Mandarin and Tagalog/Illongo.

REPRESENTATIVE CLIENTS: American Express Bank; American Home Products; Armstrong World Industries, Inc.; Avon Products; The Bank of America NT & SA; Bank of Tokyo; Bayerische Motoren Werke AG; The Boeing Co.; Bristol-Myers Squibb & Co.; Caterpillar Overseas S.A.; Cathay Pacific Airways Limited; Chevron Corporation; Chiyoda Corp.; Compagnie de Saint Gobain; Compagnie Francaise d' Assurance pour le Commerce Exterieur (CO-FACE); Conoco Inc.; CPC International, Inc.; Dow Jones & Company; Electrolux AB; Federal Express; First National Bank of Chicago; The Foxboro Company; General Electric Co.; General Motors Corp.; Hoechst A.G.; Japan Airlines; Lloyds Bank p.l.c.; The Lubrizol Corp.; McDonalds Corporation; Molnlycke AB; Nalco Chemical Co.; National Westminster Bank; Pfizer Corp.; Phillip Morris Inc.; Pont-a-Mousson S.A.; Philips B.V.; Royal Insurance; Societe Gererale d'Entreprises; Sony Corp.; Standard Chartered Bank; Tate & Lyle Plc.; Toshiba Corp.; Upjohn Company.

LAW OFFICE OF ABDULAZIZ H. FAHAD

In Cooperation with Gibson, Dunn & Crutcher

HAJI HUSSEIN ALIREZA BUILDING, SIXTH FLOOR
BAB MAKKAH
P.O. BOX 16206
JEDDAH 21464, SAUDI ARABIA
Telephone: 011-966-2-644-2663
Telecopier: 011-966-2-643-5401

Los Angeles, California Office: Gibson, Dunn & Crutcher, 333 South Grand Avenue, 90071-3197. Telephone: 213-229-7000. Telex: 188171 GIBTRASK LSA (TRT), 674930 GIBTRASK LSA (WUT). Cable Address: GIBTRASK LOS ANGELES. Telecopier: 213-229-7520.

General and International Law Practice.
Associated Firm of Gibson, Dunn & Crutcher is engaged in American and International Law Practice.

FIRM PROFILE: The Law Office of Abdulaziz H. Fahad is staffed by Saudi Arabian and American lawyers and provides expertise to our clients on a wide range of legal matters, including banking and finance, commercial transactions, companies law matters, Saudi Arabian government contracts, joint ventures, licensing, agencies, taxation, trademarks and litigation. They also provide "on-the spot" representation of foreign clients seeking to do business in the Middle East and clients resident in the Middle East who invest abroad, particularly in the United States, Europe and Asia. The clients of the office include major international and local companies in the banking, manufacturing and trading sectors.

The associated firm of Gibson, Dunn & Crutcher, originating in Los Angeles, California, has been providing legal services to clients since 1890. Today, the firm has grown to one of the largest law firms in the world with approximately 650 attorneys in 17 offices situated in most of the world's important business centers. The firm has experts in virtually every area of the law, particularly those which relate to commercial transactions and disputes, and has more effective geographical coverage in the United States than any other major firm. The firm's lawyers and staff are dedicated to providing quality service on a timely and cost effective basis.

ABDULAZIZ H. FAHAD, born September 10, 1953; admitted, 1985, Saudi Arabia. *Education:* Michigan State University (B.A., 1979); Johns Hopkins University (M.A., 1980); Yale Law School (J.D., 1984). Post-Doctoral Fellow (Center for Middle Eastern Studies) and Research Fellow (Law School), Harvard University, 1984-1985. *LANGUAGES:* Arabic and English.

ASSOCIATE

DAVID W. JACKSON, born February 24, 1955; admitted, 1988, New York and District of Columbia (Not admitted in Saudi Arabia). *Education:* Pennsylvania State University (B.A., 1976); Georgetown University (M.A., Arab Studies, with distinction, 1983; J.D., magna cum laude, 1987). Order of the Coif. Notes and Comments/Articles Editor, Georgetown Law Journal, 1985-1987. *LANGUAGES:* English, Arabic and French. *PRACTICE AREAS:* International; Corporate Finance.

(This Listing Continued)

(For information on firm personnel, address and telephone information regarding the firm's offices located in Century City, Irvine, San Diego, Menlo Park and San Francisco, California; Denver, Colorado; Washington, D.C.; New York, N.Y.; Dallas, Texas; Seattle, Washington; Paris, France; London, England; Hong Kong; Tokyo, Japan and Riyadh, Saudi Arabia (Affiliated Office), see professional biographies at Los Angeles, California)

LAW OFFICES OF HIS ROYAL HIGHNESS PRINCE SAAD AL FAISAL BIN ABDUL AZIZ

(In Association with Arent Fox Kintner Plotkin & Kahn)

P.O. BOX 15836
JEDDAH 21454, SAUDI ARABIA
Telephone: (966-2) 651-9373
Facsimile: (966-2) 651-9465

Associated Firm: Arent Fox Kintner Plotkin & Kahn, 1050 Connecticut Avenue, N.W., Washington, D.C. 20036. Telephone: 202-857-6000. Facsimile: 202-857-6395, with regional offices in Vienna, Virginia and Bethesda, Maryland.
In Budapest, Hungary: NAGYMEZO utca 44, H-1065 Budapest, Hungary. Telephone: (36-1) 269 0596. Facsimile: (36-1) 269 0599.
New York: 1675 Broadway, 25th Floor, New York, N.Y. 10019. Telephone: (212) 484-3900. Fax: (212) 484-3990.

MEMBERS OF FIRM

STEVEN R. MILES, born Heidelberg, Germany, March 24, 1958; admitted, 1984, Virginia; 1985, Massachusetts and District of Columbia (Not admitted in Saudi Arabia). *Education:* Union College (B.A., summa cum laude, 1980); Cornell University (M.B.A., 1984; J.D., 1984). Phi Beta Kappa; Omicron Delta Epsilon. Editor, Cornell Law Review, 1984. Staff Member, Energy and Commerce Committee, U.S. House of Representatives, 1983. Resident, Kingdom of Saudi Arabia Office, 1992-1993. *PRACTICE AREAS:* International Business Law; International Practice; Energy Law; Middle East Law; Telecommunications Law.

LAW OFFICE OF HASSAN MAHASSNI

(In Association with White and Case)

AL HADA BUILDING
2013 WALI AL-AHD STREET
P.O. BOX 2256
JEDDAH 21451, SAUDI ARABIA
Telephone: (966-2) 651-3535
Facsimile: (966-2) 651-3636
Telex: 604750 LIBRA SJ

New York, New York: Telephone: 212-819-8200. Facsimile: 212-354-8113.
Washington, D.C.: Telephone: 202-872-0013. Facsimile: 202-872-0210.
Los Angeles, California: Telephone: 213-620-7700. Facsimile: 213-687-0758; 213-617-2205.
Miami, Florida: Telephone: 305-371-2700. Facsimile: 305-358-5744.
Mexico City, Mexico: Telephone: (52-5) 207-9717. Facsimile: (52-5) 208-3628.
Tokyo, Japan: Telephone: (81-3) 3239-4300. Facsimile: (81-3) 3239-4330.
Hong Kong: Telephone: (852) 2822-8700. Facsimile: (852) 2845-9070; Grice & Co., Solicitors, Telephone: (852) 2826-0333. Facsimile: (852) 2526-7166.
Singapore, Republic of Singapore: Telephone: (65) 225-6000. Facsimile: (65) 225-6009.
Bangkok, Thailand: Pacific Legal Group Ltd., In Association With White & Case, Telephone: (662) 236-6154/7. Facsimile: (662) 237-6771.
Hanoi, Viet Nam: Representative Office, Telephone: (84-4) 227-575/6/7. Facsimile: (84-4) 227-297.
Bombay, India: Telephone: (91-22) 282-6300. Facsimile: (91-22) 282-6305.
London, England: Telephone: (44-171) 726-6361. Facsimile: (44-171) 726-4314; (44-171) 726-8558.

(This Listing Continued)

LAW OFFICE OF HASSAN MAHASSNI, Jeddah—Continued

Paris, France: Telephone: (33-1) 42-60-34-05. Facsimile: (33-1) 42-60-82-46.

Brussels, Belgium: Telephone: (32-2) 647-05-89. Facsimile: (32-2) 647-16-75.

Stockholm, Sweden: Telephone: (46-8) 679-80-30. Facsimile: (46-8) 611-21-22.

Helsinki, Finland: Telephone: (358-0) 631-100. Facsimile: (358-0) 179-477.

Moscow, Russia: Telephone: (7-095) 201-9292/3/4/5. Facsimile: (7-095) 201-9284.

Budapest, Hungary: Telephone: (36-1) 269-0550; (36-1) 131-0933. Facsimile: (36-1) 269-1199.

Prague, Czech Republic: Telephone: (42-2) 2481-1796. Facsimile: (42-2) 232-5522.

Warsaw, Poland: Telephone/Facsimile: (48-22) 26-80-53; (48-22) 27-84-86. International Telephone/Facsimile: (48-39) 12-19-06.

Istanbul, Turkey: Telephone: (90-212) 275-68-98; (90-212) 275-75-33. Facsimile: (90-212) 275-75-43.

Ankara, Turkey: Telephone: (90-312) 446-2180. Facsimile: (90-312) 437-9677.

Riyadh, Saudi Arabia: Law Office of Hassan Mahassni, Telephone: (966-1) 476-7099. Facsimile: (966-1) 479-0110.

Almaty, Kazakhstan: Telephone: (7-3272) 50-7491/2. Facsimile: (7-3272) 61-0842.

General International Practice.
Firm engaged in Saudi Arabian, American and International Law Practice.

HASSAN MAHASSNI, born Damascus, Syria, February 18, 1934. Admitted to practice, 1966 in Saudi Arabia. Citizen, Saudi Arabia. *Education:* Damascus College, Damascus, Syria (Baccalaureate, 1953); Syrian University, Faculty of Law, Damascus, Syria (LL.B., 1957). Legal Advisor to Ministry of Foreign Affairs, Kingdom of Saudi Arabia, 1965-1970. *Member:* International Bar Association. (Partner, White & Case, New York, New York).

ALEXANDER S. KRITZALIS, born New York, New York, March 19, 1945; admitted, 1970, New York (Not admitted in Saudi Arabia). *Education:* Brown University (A.B., 1966); University of Virginia (LL.B., 1969). *Member:* Association of the Bar of the City of New York; New York State, American and International Bar Associations; Federal Bar Council; Maritime Law Association of the United States. (Partner, White & Case, New York, New York).

RESIDENT ASSOCIATES

E. WILLIAM CATTAN, JR., born New York, N.Y., May 14, 1961; admitted, 1990, New York; 1992, District of Columbia (Not admitted in Saudi Arabia). *Education:* Dartmouth College (B.A., 1983); Georgetown University (J.D., 1989).

IMAD AI-DINE GHAZI, born Damascus, Syria, July 11, 1946; admitted, 1972, Syria (Not admitted in Saudi Arabia). *Education:* Syrian University, Faculty of Law, Damascus, Syria (LL.B., 1971).

ANAS KAILANI, born Hammah, Syria, May 9, 1935; (Not admitted in Saudi Arabia). *Education:* Syrian University, Faculty of Law, Damascus, Syria (LL.B., 1961). Judge, Syria, 1961-1988. (Legal Consultant).

FAROUK KOUATLI, born Damascus, Syria, December 21, 1933; (Not admitted in Saudi Arabia). *Education:* Damascus College, Damascus, Syria (Baccalaureate, 1953); Syrian University, Faculty of Law, Damascus, Syria (LL.B., 1957). (Legal Consultant).

WALID LABADI, born Chicago, Illinois, July 19, 1961; admitted, 1987, Illinois; 1991, New York (Not admitted in Saudi Arabia). *Education:* University of Illinois (B.A., 1982); University of Michigan (J.D., 1986).

AMIN MUNAJED, born Aleppo, Syria, October 28, 1947; admitted, 1977, Syria (Not admitted in Saudi Arabia). *Education:* Syrian University, Faculty of Law, Damascus, Syria (LL.B., 1976).

GASSIM ZANOON, born El-Obied, Sudan, September 14, 1942; admitted, 1967, Sudan (Not admitted in Saudi Arabia). *Education:* University of Khartoum (LL.B., 1966); University of London (LL.M., 1973).

(This Listing Continued)

(For biographical data as to other locations, see Professional Biographies at New York, New York; Washington, D.C.; Los Angeles, California; Miami, Florida; Mexico City, Mexico; Tokyo, Japan; Hong Kong; Singapore, Republic of Singapore; Bangkok, Thailand; Hanoi, Viet Nam; Bombay, India; London, England; Paris, France; Brussels, Belgium; Stockholm, Sweden; Helsinki, Finland; Moscow, Russia; Budapest, Hungary; Prague, Czech Republic; Warsaw, Poland; Istanbul and Ankara, Turkey; Riyadh, Saudi Arabia; Almaty, Kazakhstan).

NADER LAW OFFICES

Established in 1977

19 ABO ZINADAH STREET
P.O. BOX 3595
JEDDAH 21481, SAUDI ARABIA
Telephone: (02) 6652067
Telefax: 6608709

Riyadh, Saudi Arabia Office: Villa No. 481, Farazdak Street, Al-Dhobbat Quarters, Al-Malaz District, P.O. Box 89704, Riyadh 11692. Telephone: 01-4793733. Fax: 01-4792311.

London, England Office: Nader Mideast Law Ltd., 41 Redcliffe Close, 276, Old Brompton Road, SW5 9YR. Telephone: 071 373 0975. Fax: 071 835 2251.

Company, Commercial, Maritime, Foreign Investment, Insurance, Aviation, Labor, Contracts, Sharia (Islamic Law), Civil, Litigation and Arbitration.

FIRM PROFILE: *Nader Law Offices, among the largest in number of lawyers and paralegals, is a leader in its field. The firm offers legal advice in all lines of law and Sharia in Saudi Arabia. The firm can also facilitate business contacts and promotions through associate firms in Saudi Arabia. Complete staff for management, accounting and paralegals.*

MEMBERS OF FIRM

DR. MOHAMED M. JABER NADER, born Madina, February 4, 1930; admitted, 1977, Jeddah. *Education:* Faculty of Law, Cairo University (1953); International University, New York (Doctor of Philosophy in Management [Life Accomplishment Evaluation], 1984); American Pacific University, Irvine, California (M.B.A., 1986). Author: "Conciliation and Arbitration in Saudi Arabia under the Chambers of Commerce and Industry," Saudi Arabia, June 1985. "Legal Practical Guide for the Businessman in Saudi Arabia," 1994. *Member:* American Bar Association (Associate); International Bar Association; Saudi Arabian Bar Association (Lawyers Committee); Chartered Institute of Arbitrators and Institute of Directors, London (Former Fellow); Euro-Arab Forum for Arbitration and Business Law, Paris (Founding Member); Association Arabe de l'Arbitrage Internationale, Paris (Founding Member and Board Director). *LANGUAGES:* Arabic and English. *PRACTICE AREAS:* Shariah (Islamic Law); Arbitration Law; Civil Litigation.

AKRAM M. J. NADER, born 1953. Licensed by Ministry of Commerce for debt collection. Licensed to Practice Law by Saudi Sharia Court in 1991. Founder Member of Saudi Computer Society. *LANGUAGES:* Arabic and English. *PRACTICE AREAS:* Litigation.

RASIKLAL K. SHAH, born India, September 25, 1925; admitted, 1951, Ahmedabad, Gujarat, India; 1953 High Court of Judicature at Bombay; 1954, Supreme Court of the Colony of Aden; 1967, High Court of Judicature at Gujarat; 1976, New York (Not admitted in Saudi Arabia). *Education:* Bombay University (B.A., 1948; LL.B., 1951). *LANGUAGES:* English, Gujarati, Urdu and Hindi. *PRACTICE AREAS:* Labor Law; Contracts Law; Agency and Maritime Law.

MUSTAFA A. MALLASI, born Port Sudan, February 3, 1939; (Not admitted in Saudi Arabia). *Education:* University of Cairo, Khartoum Branch (1971). *Member:* Sudan Bar Association and International Bar Association. (Resident, London, England Office). *LANGUAGES:* Arabic, English and Russian. *PRACTICE AREAS:* Commercial Law; Company Law; Maritime Law.

DR. MOHIELDIN ISMAIL ALAMELDIN, born Egypt, 1933; admitted, 1967, Cairo, Egypt (Not admitted in Saudi Arabia). *Education:* Cairo University (Doctor in Commercial Law, 1967). Professor, Faculty of Law, Rabat University, 1975-1982. Avocat a'la Cour, Egyptian Court of Cassation. *Member:* Court of Arbitrator of the ICC, Paris. (Resident, London, England Office). *LANGUAGES:* Arabic, English and French. *PRACTICE AREAS:* Arbitration; Banking Law; Commercial Law; Contracts; Investment Law.

(This Listing Continued)

SIDDIG MOHAMED ALI, born 1949; admitted, 1977, Republic of Sudan (Not admitted in Saudi Arabia). *Education:* Cairo University, Khartoum Branch (LL.B., 1974). *Member:* Sudanese Bar Association. *LANGUAGES:* Arabic and English. *PRACTICE AREAS:* Labor Law; Foreign Investment Law; Trademarks; Commercial Law.

ATTIA ZAKI EL-GERBEED, born Kafir Al-Sheik, Egypt, December 17, 1941; admitted, 1964, Cairo, Egypt; 1965, Alexandria, Egypt (Not admitted in Saudi Arabia). *Education:* Alexandria University (Licence of Land and M.A. in Islamic Law); Marine Transport Academy in Alexandria (M.A. in Marine Law). Author: "Lawyer at Marine Cargo in Alexandria," 1965, Cases Manager. *Member:* Lawyers Union, Cairo and Alexandria; International Bar Association. *LANGUAGES:* Arabic and English. *PRACTICE AREAS:* Commercial Law; Aviation Law; Shariah (Islamic Law).

KAMAL MOHAMED AHMED UWAIDAH, born Gaza, Palestine, 1944; (Not admitted in Saudi Arabia). *Education:* Alexandria University, Egypt (Graduate of Law, 1969); Diploma in Islamic Law, Cairo, Egypt (1977). *LANGUAGES:* Arabic and English. *PRACTICE AREAS:* Labor Law; Social Insurance Law; Company Law; Arbitration Law; Commercial Law.

ABUBAKER O. KEKIA, born Asmara, 1952; admitted, 1991. *Education:* Kiev State University (LL.M., 1977); University of London (Postgraduate Diploma, International Law, 1982). *Member:* London's Institute of Advanced Legal Studies. *LANGUAGES:* Arabic, English, Russian and Italian. *PRACTICE AREAS:* International Law (Institutions and Sea); General Legal Practice.

SALEH MAHMOUD EL MARAKBY, born 1954; (Not admitted in Saudi Arabia). *Education:* Faculty of Law, Mansoura University (1980). *Member:* Egyptian Bar Association. *LANGUAGES:* Arabic, English and Italian. *PRACTICE AREAS:* Criminal Law; Public Law; Commercial Law; Litigation.

Languages: Arabic, English and French.

LAW OFFICES OF AHMED ZAKI YAMANI

Established in 1952

P.O. BOX 1351

JEDDAH 21431, SAUDI ARABIA
Telephone: (966-2) 6429550/6429551
Telefax: (966-2) 6437511
Telex: 605853 GANONI SJ.

Riyadh, Saudi Arabia Office: P.O. Box 7159, Riyadh 11462. Telephone: (966- 1) 464-2144. Telefax: (966-1) 464-8718.

Manama, Bahrain Office: Manama Centre, Entrance 4, 4th Floor, Suites 406 & 407, P.O. Box 342, Manama, Bahrain. Telephones: (973) 211-433; 211-662. Telefax: (973) 219-373. Telex: 8991 YAMANI BN.

Corporate, Banking and Finance, Taxation, Investment and Joint Ventures, Intellectual Property, Aviation, Litigation, Arbitration, Government Affairs and Relations, Energy, Environmental, Construction, Insurance, Mining, Maritime and Transportation, Copyrights and Trademarks, Labor and Trade Relations.

SENIOR MEMBERS OF FIRM

AHMED ZAKI YAMANI, born Mecca, Saudi Arabia, June 30, 1930. *Education:* Cairo University, Cairo, Egypt (License en Droit, 1952); Harvard and New York Universities (Graduate studies in Law). Founder of The Law Offices of Ahmed Zaki Yamani, Saudi Arabia's First Private Law Office, 1952. Formerly, Legal Advisor to the Saudi Council of Ministers, 1957. Cabinet Member as Minister of State, 1960 and later as the Minister of Petroleum and Mineral Resources, 1962-1987. First Secretary-General of the Organization of Petroleum Exporting Countries (OPEC), and is regarded as the Architect of many of the Kingdom's modern laws and regulations. Chairman of the Centre for Global Energy Studies and the Al Furqan Islamic Heritage Foundation. *LANGUAGES:* Arabic, English and French. *PRACTICE AREAS:* Islamic Law; Energy; Government Affairs and Procedures.

ZAKI MUSTAFA, born Sudan, November 17, 1934; admitted, 1963, Sudan. *Education:* University of Khartoum (LL.B., 1959); London School of Economics (LL.M., 1961); University of London, London, England (Ph.D., 1969). Author: "The Legal System of the Sudan," Cairo, Egypt (Arabic), 1969; "The Common Law in Sudan," Oxford, England, 1977. Associate Professor, Contract and Commercial Law, Khartoum, 1961-1965. Visiting Lecturer, UCLA, 1964. Professor and Dean of Law, Contracts, Com-

(This Listing Continued)

mercial and Corporate Law, Khartoum, 1965-1969. Professor and Dean, Ahamadu Bello University, Nigeria, 1969-1972. Visiting Professor, Haile Selassie I University, Addis Ababa, Ethiopia, 1972-1973, and Harvard Law School, 1989-1990. National Chairman, World Peace Through Law Center, 1964-1975. Advisor to the Supreme Council of State, Sudan, 1965-1969. President, Society of Law Teachers, Africa, 1965-1972. Member: Society of Public Teachers of Law, 1969; Law Reform Commission, Nigeria, 1970-1973; National Council for Higher Education, Sudan, 1975—. Chairman; Law Reform Commission, Sudan, 1973—; University Grants Commission, Sudan, 1975-1979. Attorney General, Minister of Justice, Sudan 1973-1975. Advisor on Law Revision and Law Reform to the President of Sudan, 1975-1979. (Managing Partner, Law Offices of Ahmed Zaki Yamani). *LANGUAGES:* Arabic, English and French. *PRACTICE AREAS:* Corporate Law; Contract Law; Commercial Law; Aviation; Insurance; Mining and Environmental Law.

AHMED FATHI HUSSEIN, born Assyout, Egypt, March 4, 1931; admitted, 1952, Egypt; admitted to practice in Saudi Arabia under Special Licence, 1963. *Education:* Cairo University, Cairo, Egypt (License en Droit, 1952; Higher Diploma in Private and Public Law, 1957; M.A., 1959). Legal Advisor, Ministry of Communication, Saudi Arabia, 1960-1962. Special Counsel to Saudi Arabian Airlines (SAUDIA); Vice-President and Special Counsel, Al Watany Bank, Cairo, Egypt. Member: Society of Economy and Legislation, Egypt, 1964—; International Bar Association, London. *LANGUAGES:* Arabic, English and French. *PRACTICE AREAS:* Contract Law; Corporate Law; Commercial Law; Civil Aviation; Litigation; Banking and Joint Ventures.

ISMAIL HUSSEIN HUSSEIN, born 1930, Egypt; admitted, 1952, Egypt; admitted to practice in Saudi Arabia under Special License, 1956. *Education:* University of Cairo (License en Droit, 1952). Legal Adviser to Binladin Organization (Saudi Arabia). *LANGUAGES:* Arabic, English and French. *PRACTICE AREAS:* Corporate Law; Commercial Law; Licensing; Trade and Labor Law; Liquidation; Government Relations.

REPRESENTATIVE CLIENTS: Alfa Laval, Sweden; Computer Sciences Corporation; Caltex; Union Carbide; Ethyl Corporation; TRW; Procter & Gamble AG; Detergent Products, S.A.; Hewlett-Packard; Pasco Corp. (Japan); Lloyds Underwriters; Lossinger, S.A.; Philip Holzman; Philip Morris; Holophane, Inc.; ITT Standard; Cementation; Fidelity Bank; Habib Bank; Saudi American Bank; Arab Asian Bank; Arab African Bank; Finnmap (Finland); Meteorological and Environmental Protection Agency (MEPA); Credit and Commerce Insurance Co. Ltd., S.A.; Islamic Arab Insurance; Danish Export Council; Continental Grain; Modern Industries; ABU Dawood Group of Companies; Juffali Brothers; Saudi Arabian Airlines; Binladin Brothers, S.A.; Binzacr, S.A.; Olayan Finance Company; Algosaibi Brothers; Al Baida Est., S.A.; Hanyang Corporation, South Korea; Samho Corporation, South Korea; Agricultural Dev. Corp., Hiller Brewing Co.; Mitsubishi; Johnson Controls; Ralston Purina; Saudi Bechtel Co.; Electrolux.

(For Biographical Data on other Personnel, see Professional Biographies at Riyadh, Saudi Arabia and Manama, Bahrain)

LEGAL ADVISORS
DR. MOSAAD M. AL-AIBAN

License No. 188

(In Association with Baker & McKenzie)

KING FAISAL FOUNDATION BUILDING
KING FAHAD ROAD
P.O. BOX 4288

RIYADH 11491, SAUDI ARABIA
Telephone: (01) 462-9886
Intn'l. Dialing: (966-1) 462-9886
Facsimile: (966-1) 463-2657

In Association with Baker & McKenzie with offices in:
Chicago, Illinois: One Prudential Plaza, 130 East Randolph Drive, 60601.
Dallas, Texas: 4500 Trammell Crow Center, 2001 Ross Avenue, 75201.
Miami, Florida: Barnett Tower, 701 Brickell Avenue, Suite 1600, 33131-2827.
New York, New York: 805 Third Avenue, 10022.
Palo Alto, California: 660 Hansen Way, P.O. Box 60309, 94304-0309.
San Diego, California: The Wells Fargo Plaza, Twelfth Floor, 101 West Broadway, 92101.
San Francisco, California: Two Embarcadero Center, 24th Floor, 94111-3909.
Washington, D.C.: 815 Connecticut Avenue, N.W., 20006-4078.

General International Practice.

(This Listing Continued)

LEGAL ADVISORS DR. MOSAAD M. AL-AIBAN,
Riyadh—Continued

SECONDED PERSONNEL

JOHN E. XEFOS, born New York, N.Y., April 8, 1954; admitted, 1980, Illinois, U.S.A. (Not admitted in Saudi Arabia). *Education:* Cornell University (B.A., with distinction, 1977); University of Pennsylvania (J.D., 1980). *Member:* Chicago, Illinois State and American Bar Associations. *PRACTICE AREAS:* Banking and Finance; Corporate and Partnership Law; Mergers and Acquisitions; Public Contracts and Utilities; Trade (Saudi Arabia).

BRIAN D. EARP, born Regina, Canada, September 25, 1955; admitted, 1985, New York, U.S.A. (Not admitted in Saudi Arabia). *Education:* University of Winnipeg (B.A., 1978); University of Manitoba (LL.B., 1981). *LANGUAGES:* English, French and Arabic. *PRACTICE AREAS:* Banking and Finance; Securities and Financial Products; Trade; Regulatory Law; Corporate and Partnership Law.

NADIM KYRIAKOS-SAAD, born Beirut, Lebanon, August 27, 1964; admitted, 1988, Lebanon (Not admitted in Saudi Arabia). *Education:* Saint Joseph University, Beirut, Lebanon (M.Pv. & Pub. Law, 1988; B.A., Pol. Sc., 1989); Columbia University, New York, N.Y. (LL.M., 1992). *Member:* Beirut Bar Association. *LANGUAGES:* English, French, Arabic. *PRACTICE AREAS:* Corporate and Partnership Law; Regulatory Law; Trade (Gulf Cooperation Council); Franchise Law; Intellectual Property Law.

HAZIM ABD EL-GHAFAR RIZKANA, born Kuwait, December 13, 1960; admitted, 1982, Egypt (Not admitted in Saudi Arabia). *Education:* McGeorge School of Law, Sacramento, California (LL.M. in Business and Taxation, Transnational Practice); Zagazig University, Egypt (B.A., Law). *Member:* Egyptian Bar Association; International Bar Association; American Society of International Law. *LANGUAGES:* Arabic and English. *PRACTICE AREAS:* Corporate and Partnership Law; Labor and Employment Law; Banking and Finance; Commercial Litigation.

GEORGE SAYEN, born Philadelphia, Pennsylvania, July 30, 1958; admitted, 1987, New York, U.S.A. (Not admitted in Saudi Arabia). *Education:* Dartmouth College (A.B., magna cum laude, 1980); University of Pennsylvania (J.D., cum laude, 1986; Certificate in Islamic Studies and Islamic Law, 1986). *Member:* American Bar Association. *LANGUAGES:* English, Arabic and French. *PRACTICE AREAS:* Trade (Saudi Arabia; GCC); Corporate and Partnership Law; Public Contracts and Utilities; Labor and Employment Law; Banking and Finance.

AL HASAN & AL AKEEL

Established in 1982

SUITE 423, 4TH FLOOR
AL AKARIA SHOPPING CENTER
P.O. BOX 8650
RIYADH 11492, SAUDI ARABIA
Telephone: 463 4156; 463 4160
Facsimile: (966 1) 463 4160

FIRM PROFILE: The firm was established in 1982 and offers a full range of legal services. The firm handles a wide general practice of law which covers all areas, like Agency and Distributorship Agreements, Corporate and Commercial Law, Litigation and Debt Collections, License and Trademarks Registration, Management and Technical Assistance Agreements.

MEMBERS OF FIRM

DR. ABDULATIF AL HASAN, born Iraq, July 7, 1937; admitted, 1961, Basra, Iraq; 1979, Riyadh. *Education:* Baghdad University (LL.B., 1961); Cairo University (LL.M., Islamic Law, 1962; LL.M., Public Law, 1963); Manchester University (Ph.D., 1974). Author: "Islamic Law," Basra Press, 1965; "Marriage and Divorce", Basra Press, 1967. Teaching Faculty, University of Basra, Iraq, 1964-1978. General Counsel, Saudi Arabia Basic Industries Corporation, 1979-1984. *Member:* American Bar Association; The United States Trademarks Association. *LANGUAGES:* Arabic, English and French. *PRACTICE AREAS:* Commercial, Sharia and Corporation Law.

KHALED A. AL AKEEL, born Iraq, October 10, 1949; admitted, 1972, Zobair, Iraq; 1974, Riyadh. *Education:* Baghdad University (LL.B., 1972); University of Miami (M.C.L., 1980). Counsel, Organization of Social Insur-

(This Listing Continued)

ance, 1974-1976. Deputy General Counsel, Saudi Arabia Basic Industries Corporation, 1980-1982. *Member:* American Bar Association; United States Trademarks Association. *LANGUAGES:* Arabic and English. *PRACTICE AREAS:* Sharia Law and Commercial Law.

LEGAL SUPPORT PERSONNEL

THAYEB TAGELDEEN OMAR, born Sudan, 1953; admitted, 1977, Sudan. *Education:* University of Khartoum, Sudan (LL.B.). Former: Legal Advisor-Ministry of Interior Sudan; General Secretariat Council of Ministers; General Manager Assistant for Legal Affairs, Islamic Bank for Western Sudan. Lecturer in Law of Banking and Business Law. *LANGUAGES:* Arabic and English.

Languages: Arabic and English.

THE LAW FIRM OF SALAH AL-HEJAILAN

Established in 1967

AL DAHNA CENTER, AL AHSA STREET
P.O. BOX 1454
RIYADH 11431, SAUDI ARABIA
Telephone: (1) 479 2200
Telex: 401109
Fax: (1) 479 1717

Jeddah, Saudi Arabia Office: Alireza Tower, 11th Floor, Medina Rd., P.O. Box 15141, Jeddah 21444. Telephone: (2) 653 4422. Telex: 606766. Fax: (2) 651 7241.

In Association with CLIFFORD CHANCE in:
Amsterdam, Bahrain, Barcelona, Brussels, Budapest, Dubai, Frankfurt/Main, Hanoi, Hong Kong, London, Madrid, Moscow, New York, Paris, Rome, Shanghai, Singapore, Tokyo, and Warsaw.

Also in Association with GRAHAM & JAMES in:
Bangkok, Beijing, Berlin, Brisbane, Brussels, Canberra, Dusseldorf, Frankfurt, Hanoi, Hong Kong, Jakarta, Kuwait, Leipzig, London, Los Angeles, Melbourne, Mexico City, Milan, Munich, Newport Beach, New York, Palo Alto, Perth, Raleigh, Sacramento, San Francisco, Sydney, Taipei, Tokyo, and Washington, D.C.

General and International Practice including Corporate, Financial, Banking, Tax, Real Estate, Commercial, Civil, Maritime, Criminal and Administrative Law, Litigation and Arbitration.

MEMBERS OF FIRM

SALAH AL-HEJAILAN, born Saudi Arabia, 1941; admitted, 1962, Saudi Arabia. *Education:* University of Cairo (Degree in Law, 1962); University of Southern California, Los Angeles (Masters Degree in International Public Administration, 1968). Legal Advisor, Council of Ministers, Kingdom of Saudi Arabia, 1962-1973. Counsel, Bribery and Forgery Committees of the Board of Grievances, Kingdom of Saudi Arabia, 1963-1972. Legal Consultant, Royal Commission for Jubail and Yanbu, 1963-1986. Member, Government Committees for Promulgation of Regulations, Resolutions and Decrees, 1963-1973. Member, Board of Directors, Ports Authority, Kingdom of Saudi Arabia, 1976-1987. Chairman, The Higher Board of the Euro-Arab Arbitration System, London, 1985—. Member, Arbitration Council, Arab-Swiss Chamber of Commerce, 1985—. Founding Shareholder, Saudi American Bank, Saudi Arabia, 1977—. Partner and Member of the Board of Directors, Arabian International Maritime Company (an affiliate of Mobil Oil Corporation), 1977—. Partner and Chairman of the Board of Directors, Thyssen Saudi Arabia Limited (an affiliate of Thyssen Handelsunion), Germany, 1977—. Director, ABC International Bank, London (an affiliate of Arab Banking Corporation), 1991—. Council Member, Centre for Islamic & Middle Eastern Law (CIMEL), School of Oriental and African Studies, London University, 1989—. Member, Nominating Committee, Eisenhower Exchange Fellowship Program, 1989—. Member, Arab Arbitration Group of ICC International Court of Arbitration, Paris, 1992—. Director, Cairo Regional Centre for Commercial Arbitration, 1994—. Member, World Intellectual Property Organization Arbitration Consultative Commission, 1994—. *LANGUAGES:* Arabic and English.

ANTHONY M. ABRAHAMS, admitted, 1969, Australia (New South Wales) as Solicitor; 1973, France as Advocat at French Bar (Not admitted in Saudi Arabia). *Education:* University of Sydney (B.A., LL.B., 1968). Lecturer on Construction Law, University of Tours, France, 1983-1993. *Member:* International Bar Association. (Also Partner, Clifford Chance, Paris). *LANGUAGES:* English and French.

(This Listing Continued)

JOSEPH E. PARENTEAU, born U.S.A., 1950; admitted, 1985, New York; 1986, New Jersey, U.S. District Court, Southern District of New York and U.S. District Court, District of New Jersey (Not admitted in Saudi Arabia). *Education:* Duke University, North Carolina (B.A., 1974); City College of the City University of New York (B.S., Architecture); Fordham University School of Law, New York (J.D., 1984). *Member:* American and International Bar Associations; American Institute of Architects; The American Society of International Law. (Also Associate, Graham & James).

MICHAEL DARK, born Huddersfield, Yorkshire, England, 1945; admitted, 1971, England as Barrister; 1980, England as Solicitor (Not admitted in Saudi Arabia). *Education:* University of Oxford (M.A. Jurisprudence, 1966). (Also Associate, Clifford Chance, London).

ROBERT THOMS, born Nutley, New Jersey, 1948; admitted, 1977, New York (Not admitted in Saudi Arabia). *Education:* Georgetown University, Washington, D.C. (A.B., Philosophy, 1970); Harvard Law School (J.D., 1976). *Member:* American Bar Association (Sections on International and Business Law); City of New York and New York State Bar Associations.

CHARLES MAGEE, born Dallas, Texas, 1952; admitted, 1977, Texas; 1985, U.S. District Court, Northern District of Texas (Not admitted in Saudi Arabia). *Education:* Southern Methodist University (B.B.A., 1974; J.D., 1977). *Member:* State Bar of Texas; Dallas Bar Association.

YOUSEF AL-JADAAN, born Mecca, Saudi Arabia, 1965; admitted, 1988, Saudi Arabia. *Education:* King Saud University (LL.B., 1988). *LANGUAGES:* Arabic and English.

IBRAHIM AL-FEHAID, born Saudi Arabia, 1966; admitted, 1989, Saudi Arabia. *Education:* King Saud University (LL.B., 1989). *LANGUAGES:* Arabic and English.

ABDULLAH J. ASSABHAN, admitted, 1983, Saudi Arabia. *Education:* Imam Mohammed Bin Saud Islamic University (B.A., Sharia Law, 1982; Diploma in Law, 1983). *LANGUAGES:* Arabic and English.

KHALED NOUH AL BASEET, admitted, 1988, Saudi Arabia. *Education:* King Saud University (B.A., Law, 1988). *LANGUAGES:* Arabic and English.

PROF. DR. ABDUL FATTAH KHEDR, born Al-Ghorbia, Egypt, 1941; admitted, 1967, Egypt (Not admitted in Saudi Arabia). *Education:* University of Cairo (Ph.D. in Criminal Law, 1975). Professor of Criminal Law, Institute of Public Administration, Riyadh, 1975-1986. *LANGUAGES:* Arabic, English and French.

DR. MOTAMED MOHARRAM ABDELGANI, born Minia, Egypt, 1939; admitted, 1982, High Courts of Appeal and State Council, Egypt (Not admitted in Saudi Arabia). *Education:* Faculty of Law, Cairo University (LL.B., 1960; Postgraduate Diploma in Islamic Law, 1962); Paris II University (Postgraduate Diploma in Private Law, 1968; State Doctorate in Private Law (Commercial, Maritime and Air Law) 1973 Hons.). Professor of Commercial and Maritime Law: Cairo University, Egypt, 1973-1982; King Saud University, Saudi Arabia, 1983-1990. *Member:* State Council, Egypt, 1960-1966. *LANGUAGES:* Arabic, French and English.

PROF. DR. ABDUL FATTAH EL SAIFY, born West District, Egypt, 1924; admitted, 1949, Egypt (Not admitted in Saudi Arabia). *Education:* Cairo University (Bachelor of Law, 1948); Alexandria University (Doctorate in Criminal Law, 1958). Legal Adviser, Alexandria University, 1967-1985. Full Professor of Criminal law, Alexandria University, 1970—. Head of Law Departments, Imam Mohammed Bin Saud Islamic University, 1976-1981; King Saud University, 1986-1992. *LANGUAGES:* Arabic, Italian, English and French.

EBAISH ZEBAR, born Aleppo, Syria, 1938; admitted, 1965, Syria (Not admitted in Saudi Arabia). *Education:* Damascus University (LL.B., 1964). *Member:* Aleppo Bar Association. *LANGUAGES:* Arabic and English.

AMIN BALLA AL AMIN, born Medani, Sudan, 1940; admitted, 1969, Sudan (Not admitted in Saudi Arabia). *Education:* Khartoum University (LL.B., Honours, 1969). Former Senior Legal Counsel, Attorney General's Chamber, Sudan. *Member:* Sudanese Bar Association. *LANGUAGES:* Arabic and English.

IDRIS GAMIL, born Gedarif, Sudan, 1959; admitted, 1983, Sudan (Not admitted in Saudi Arabia). *Education:* Khartoum University (LL.B., Honours, 1983). Former Senior Legal Counsel, T. Lord's Law Firm, Sudan. Legal Consultant for Saudi P.T.T and Al-Jeraisy Group, Saudi Arabia. *Member:* Sudanese Bar Association. *LANGUAGES:* Arabic and English.

(This Listing Continued)

JEDDAH OFFICE
MEMBERS OF FIRM

REMSEN M. KINNE, IV, admitted, 1991, California (Not admitted in Saudi Arabia). *Education:* Yale University (B.A., 1981); Boston College Law School (J.D., cum laude, 1989). (Also Associate, Graham & James). *LANGUAGES:* English and French.

MAJED MOHAMED GAROUB, born Jeddah, Saudi Arabia, 1966. *Education:* King Abdul Aziz University (B.A., Law, 1990). *LANGUAGES:* Arabic and English.

DR. MOHAMED MOHAMED BADRAN, born Al-Dakahlia, Egypt, 1941; admitted, 1994, Court of Cassation, Supreme Administrative Court and Supreme Constitutional Court, Egypt (Not admitted in Saudi Arabia). *Education:* Cairo University (License in Law, 1967; Post-Graduate Diplomas, 1968, 1969); Birmingham University, England (MSC, 1975 and Ph.D., 1979). Professor of Public Law, Cairo University, 1993—. Faculty Member, Cairo University, 1967—. Legal Advisor of the People's Assembly (Egyptian Parliament), 1987-1990, and Cairo University, 1990-1994. *LANGUAGES:* Arabic and English.

KHALID ABDULAZIZ ALNOWAISER, born Mecca, Saudi Arabia, 1961; admitted, 1986, Saudi Arabia. *Education:* King Abdulaziz University (B.A., Political Science, 1986); Edinburgh University, Scotland (LL.B. courses & LL.M., 1991); Bristol University, England (cur rent Ph.D. candidate, Commercial Law). *LANGUAGES:* Arabic and English.

OF COUNSEL

AMBASSADOR ABBAS GHAZZAWI, admitted, 1979, Saudi Arabia. *Education:* School of Law, Cairo University (1957). Former Deputy Minister of Information, 1963-1968. Saudi Arabian Ambassador in Germany, 1988—.

DR. AHMED KESMET AL-GEDDAWY, admitted, 1957, Jurist, State Council of Egypt; 1977, Egyptian Supreme Court Bar (Not admitted in Saudi Arabia). Chairman of Private International Law Department, Law Faculty of Ain Shams University, Cairo. *LANGUAGES:* Arabic, English and French.

DR. AKSAM AL KHOLI, admitted, Egypt (Not admitted in Saudi Arabia). Professor of Commercial and Maritime Law, Cairo University. *LANGUAGES:* Arabic, English and French.

G. WILLIAM MILLER, (Not admitted in Saudi Arabia). Former U.S. Secretary of the Treasury. Former Chairman of the Board of Governors of the U.S. Federal Reserve System.

ABDULAZIZ A. AL-MOHAIMEED LAW FIRM

Established in 1978

SUITES 601-607 YAMAMA CEMENT CO. BLDG.
AL-BATHA STREET
P.O. BOX 16545
RIYADH 11474, SAUDI ARABIA
Telephone: 405-3274 (5 Lines)
Facsimile: 966-1-4029549

Jeddah, Saudi Arabia Office: Al-Faleh Center Building, Al-Medina Road. P.O. Box 17945, 21494. Telephone: (02) 643-3301. Facsimile: 966-2-6428622.

Dammam, Saudi Arabia Office: 6th Floor Al-Maajil Commercial Center, Al-Dhahran St., P.O. Box 9305, 31413. Telephone: (03) 834-2118. Facsimile: 834-2118.

U.S.A. Associate Office: U.S. Arab International Law Firm, P.O. Box 1855, Woodbridge, VA, 22193. Telephone: (703) 680-5969. Facsimile: (703) 680-5969.

Commercial, Corporate, Agencies, Administrative, Patent and Trade Marks, Arbitration, Negotiable Instruments, Maritime, Banking, Insurance, Labor, Collection Cases and Shariah Law.

MEMBERS OF FIRM

ABDULAZIZ ABDULRAHMAN AL-MOHAIMEED, born Gizan, Saudi Arabia, 1939; admitted, 1971, Saudi Arabia. *Education:* Damascus University (LL.B., 1969). Post Graduate, Legal Administration, London (1971). Director, Legal Department, General Organization For Social Insurance, Saudi Arabia, 1971. Member, Supreme Commission For Settlement of Disputes, Saudi Arabia, 1973. Board Member: Mediterranean and Middle East Institute of Arbitration; Panel of Arbitrators: Regional Centre

(This Listing Continued)

ABDULAZIZ A. AL-MOHAIMEED LAW FIRM,
Riyadh—Continued

For International Commercial Arbitration. Regional Arbitrator, Middle East: American Arbitration Association. Co-Founder, Arabian Association For The Protection of Industry Property. *Member:* International Bar Association; International Law Association; Euro-Arab Forum For Arbitration and International Commercial Law. *LANGUAGES:* English and Arabic. *PRACTICE AREAS:* Arbitration; Commercial Law; Corporate Law; Administrative Law; Insurance Law; Patent and Trademark Law; Labor and Sharia Law.

SYED Z. TAUHID, born Patna, India, 1943; (Not admitted in Saudi Arabia). *Education:* India (M.A., Labor & Social Welfare, 1963); Karachi University, Pakistan (LL.B., 1967); New York University (LL.M., Labor Law, 1973); Clemson University, U.S.A. (M. In. Ed., Human Resources Management, 1989). Legal Advisor, Ministry of Labor & Social Affairs, Saudi Arabia, 1976. *Member:* International Bar Association; International Law Association; American Arbitration Association; Law & Society Association U.S.A.; Panel of American Arbitration Association. *LANGUAGES:* English, Arabic, Urdu and Hindi. *PRACTICE AREAS:* Arbitration; Mediation; Commercial Law; Labor Law; International Law.

ASSOCIATES

ABDULLAH ABDULAZIZ AL FALLAJ, admitted, 1990, Saudi Arabia. *Education:* LL.B., Riyadh. *LANGUAGES:* English and Arabic.

ALI AL AHMARY, admitted, 1992, Saudi Arabia. *Education:* LL.B., Riyadh. Public Administrative Institute, Higher Diploma in Systems, Riyadh. *LANGUAGES:* English and Arabic.

ABDULLAH A. AL-ATEEQ, admitted, 1992, Saudi Arabia. *Education:* LL.M., Riyadh. *LANGUAGES:* Arabic.

JAMAL ELDIN M. HAMAM, (Not admitted in Saudi Arabia). *Education:* LL.B., Cairo, 1975. *LANGUAGES:* English and Arabic. *PRACTICE AREAS:* Patent and Trade Marks Law; Administrative Law; Corporate Law; Sharia Law.

ABDULLAH AL FAISAL ALI, (Not admitted in Saudi Arabia). *Education:* LL.B., Cairo, 1979. *LANGUAGES:* English and Arabic. *PRACTICE AREAS:* Negotiable Instrument; Banking Law; Labor and Sharia Law.

ABDULFATTAH FATHI AMIN, (Not admitted in Saudi Arabia). *Education:* LL.B., Ainshams, 1979. *LANGUAGES:* English and Arabic. *PRACTICE AREAS:* Administrative Law; Labor and Sharia Law.

KHALED AFIFI EL SAYED AFIFI, (Not admitted in Saudi Arabia). *Education:* LL.B., El-Mansoura, 1984. *LANGUAGES:* English and Arabic. *PRACTICE AREAS:* Collection Law; Insurance Law; Maritime Law; Labor and Sharia Law.

ABU OBAIDAH AHMAD ALIKARAR, (Not admitted in Saudi Arabia). *Education:* LL.B., Khartoum, 1985. *LANGUAGES:* English and Arabic.

YOSRI MOHAMMAD ALI MAHMOUD, (Not admitted in Saudi Arabia). *Education:* LL.B., El-Mansoura, 1979. *LANGUAGES:* Arabic. *PRACTICE AREAS:* Administrative Law; Sharia Law.

FATHI DHAHABI, (Not admitted in Saudi Arabia). *Education:* LL.B., Ainshams, 1966. *LANGUAGES:* English and Arabic.

HATEM ISMAIL, (Not admitted in Saudi Arabia). *Education:* LL.B., Benisueif, 1990. *LANGUAGES:* Arabic.

MAMDOUH M. TAUFIK, (Not admitted in Saudi Arabia). *Education:* LL.B., Al-Azhar, 1988. *LANGUAGES:* Arabic.

MOHAMMAD ABDULAZIM, (Not admitted in Saudi Arabia). *Education:* LL.B., Cairo, 1969. *LANGUAGES:* Arabic.

SAEED GUM'A, (Not admitted in Saudi Arabia). *Education:* LL.B., Cairo, 1985. *LANGUAGES:* Arabic.

TARIQ M. HAMAM, (Not admitted in Saudi Arabia). *Education:* (LL.B., Ainshams, 1993). *LANGUAGES:* Arabic.

MOHAMMAD A. JENDY, (Not admitted in Saudi Arabia). *Education:* (LL.B., Tanta, 1990). *LANGUAGES:* English and Arabic.

(This Listing Continued)

AF94B

ABDEL MONEIM OSMAN, (Not admitted in Saudi Arabia). *Education:* (LL.B., Khartoum, 1988). *LANGUAGES:* English and Arabic.

LEGAL EXPEDITERS

Mohammad Ahmad Al-Masrahi   **Khalid Mohammad Abdulaziz**
Abdu Arar Kamkumh   **AL-Fahd**

Member: American Arbitration Association.

REPRESENTATIVE CLIENTS: Blue Cross & Blue Shield Association; American Tobacco Corporation; California Garden Products, Inc.; Western American Foods, Inc. (Chef West); Redi Electric; Cimi Saudi Ltd.; Baggermaatschappy Boskalis; Decaux; Yves Saint Laurent; Chanel S.A.; Procter & Gamble SA; Cartier International BV; Vimpex Handells Geselschaft MBH; Hanshin Construction Co. Ltd.; Life Construction Co. Ltd.; Dong Ah Construction & Industrial Co. Ltd.; Bombay Suburban Electric Supply Ltd.; Khashoggi Group of Companies; Otis Elevators; Shamel Group of Companies; Advanced Saudi Electronic Co. Ltd.; B.A.I.I.; Saudi Hollandi Bank; Saudi Petrochemical Co. (SADAF); Saudi Methanol Co.; Al Quarar Est.; Al Ouda Trading Co.; Prince Huzlool bin Abdulaziz Al Saud; Prince Abdulrahman bin Saud bin Abdulaziz; Prince Saiful Islam bin Saud bin Abdulaziz; Prince Salman bin Saud bin Abdulaziz; Prince Turki bin Mohammad bin Abdullah Al Saud; Prince Faisal bin Turki Al Saud; Prince Abdullah bin Turki Al Saud.

LAW OFFICES OF
DR. MUJAHID M. AL-SAWWAF

Established in 1978

P.O. BOX 86581
RIYADH 11632, SAUDI ARABIA
Telephone: 966-1-454-9200
Telefax: 966-1-454-5856
Telex: 406724 LEGAL SJ

Jeddah Office: P.O. Box 5840, Jeddah 21432, Saudi Arabia. Telephone: 966-2-669-0751. Telefax: 966-2-665-5052. Telex: 602262 FURAT SJ.

Foreign Investment, Corporate, Commercial, Banking, Joint Venture, Civil Litigation, Arbitration and Shipping and Insurance Law.

DAVID M. WELLS, born Decatur, Illinois, January 30, 1943; admitted, 1972, California (Not admitted in Saudi Arabia). *Education:* Northwestern University (B.A., 1965); Georgetown University Law Center (J.D., 1971). *LANGUAGES:* English.

RICHARD J. TYNER, born Shenandoah, Iowa, November 21, 1947; admitted, 1979, California (Not admitted in Saudi Arabia). *Education:* University of Iowa (B.A., summa cum laude, 1970); University of Manchester, England (M.A., 1971); London School of Economics (Ph.D., 1975); Yale Law School (J.D., 1979). Phi Beta Kappa. Marshall Scholar. Editor, Yale Studies in World Public Order, 1978-1979. *LANGUAGES:* English and French.

(For Complete Biographical Data on all Firm Personnel, see Professional Biographies at Jeddah, Saudi Arabia).

LAW OFFICE OF ABDULAZIZ H. FAHAD

In Cooperation with Gibson, Dunn & Crutcher

JARIR PLAZA
4TH FLOOR, OLAYA STREET
POST OFFICE BOX 15870
RIYADH 11454, SAUDI ARABIA
Telephone: 011-966-1-464-8081
Telex: 406176 LAWS SJ
Telecopier: 011-966-1-462-4968

Los Angeles, California Office: Gibson, Dunn & Crutcher, 333 South Grand Avenue, 90071-3197. Telephone: 213-229-7000. Telex: 188171 GIBTRASK LSA (TRT), 674930 GIBTRASK LSA (WUT). Cable Address: GIBTRASK LOS ANGELES. Telecopier: 213-229-7520.

General and International Law Practice.
Associated Firm of Gibson, Dunn & Crutcher is engaged in American and International Law Practice.

FIRM PROFILE: The Law Office of Abdulaziz H. Fahad is staffed by Saudi Arabian and American lawyers and provides expertise to our clients on a wide range of legal matters, including banking and finance, commercial transactions, companies law matters, Saudi Arabian government contracts, joint ventures, licensing, agencies, taxation, trademarks and litigation. They also provide "on-the spot" representation of foreign clients seeking to do business in the Middle East and clients resident in the Middle

(This Listing Continued)

East who invest abroad, particularly in the United States, Europe and Asia. The clients of the office include major international and local companies in the banking, manufacturing and trading sectors.

The associated firm of Gibson, Dunn & Crutcher, originating in Los Angeles, California, has been providing legal services to clients since 1890. Today, the firm has grown to one of the largest law firms in the world with approximately 650 attorneys in 17 offices situated in most of the world's important business centers. The firm has experts in virtually every area of the law, particularly those which relate to commercial transactions and disputes, and has more effective geographical coverage in the United States than any other major firm. The firm's lawyers and staff are dedicated to providing quality service on a timely and cost effective basis.

ABDULAZIZ H. FAHAD, born September 10, 1953; admitted, 1985, Saudi Arabia. *Education:* Michigan State University (B.A., 1979); Johns Hopkins University (M.A., 1980); Yale Law School (J.D., 1984). Post-Doctoral Fellow (Center for Middle Eastern Studies) and Research Fellow (Law School), Harvard University, 1984-1985. *LANGUAGES:* Arabic and English.

OF COUNSEL

RICHARD C. HEGGER, born 1956; admitted, 1982, New York; 1984, Missouri (Not admitted in Saudi Arabia). *Education:* Vanderbilt University (B.A., 1978); Columbia University (J.D., 1981). Phi Beta Kappa. Author of "Investments in Saudi Arabia; a Legal Minefield" (International Financial Law Review, June 1992), "Selling Investments to Saudi Nationals" (Middle East Executive Reports, September 1992), "New Trends in Saudi Financings" (Middle East Executive Reports, August 1989), "Freezing of Assets of Debtors" (Middle East Executive Reports, July 1989), "Partner Disputes in Saudi Arabia: Risks, Recourse, Safeguards" (Middle East Executive Reports, May 1989), and "Renegotiating Contracts and Terminating Employees: An Easing of Policy?" (Middle East Executive Reports, February 1987). *Member:* American Bar Association (Member, International Law and Practice Section). *PRACTICE AREAS:* International Business Transactions; Banking and Finance; General Corporate.

ASSOCIATES

ABDUL AZIZ I. AL-AJLAN, born Medina, Saudi Arabia, 1956; (Not admitted in Saudi Arabia). *Education:* Sharia College - The Islamic University in Al-Medina (1979) and Northeastern University (graduate studies). *LANGUAGES:* Arabic; English.

ABDULLAH A. AL HABARDI, born Riyadh, Saudi Arabia, 1963; (Not admitted in Saudi Arabia). *Education:* King Saud University (B.A., 1986) and Law Program of the Institute of Public Administration, Riyadh.

(For information on firm personnel, address and telephone information regarding the firm's offices located in Century City, Irvine, San Diego, Menlo Park and San Francisco, California; Denver, Colorado; Washington, D.C.; New York, N.Y.; Dallas, Texas; Seattle, Washington; Paris, France; London, England; Hong Kong; Tokyo, Japan and Jeddah, Saudi Arabia (Affiliated Office), see professional biographies at Los Angeles, California)

GIDE LOYRETTE NOUEL

P.O. BOX 4615
RIYADH 11412, SAUDI ARABIA
Telephone: (966.1) 476.60.39
Telex: 401677 NASHWA
Telecopier: (966.1) 476.18.96

Paris, France Office: 26 Cours Albert 1er, 75008. Telephone: (1) 40.75.60.00. Cable Address: "3 Avocagidva Paris 86." Telex: 651261F GILOY. Telecopier: (1) 43.59.37.79.

New York, New York Office: Swiss Bank Tower, 10 East 50th Street, 10022. Telephone: (1-212) 644-1201. Telex: 424353 GIDE. Telecopier: (1-212) 644-1205.

Brussels, Belgium Office: Rue de la Loi 99.101, B-1040. Telephone: (32.2) 231.11.40. Telecopier: (32.2) 231.11.77.

Warsaw, Poland Office: Ul. Kopernika 17, 00-359. Telephone: (48.22) 26.22.21. Telecopier: (48.22) 26.03.02.

Tokyo, Japan Office: Homei Building 3F, 3-19 Akasaka 1-Chome, Minato-Ku, 107. Telephone: (81.3) 55.62.03.01. Telecopier: (81.3) 55.62.03.06.

Beijing, People's Republic of China Office: Suite 3309 A, Jing Guang Centre, Hu Jia Lou, Chaoyang District, 100020. Telephone: (86.1) 501 4511. Telecopier: (86.1) 501 4551.

(This Listing Continued)

Prague, Czech Republic Office: 34 Jindrisska, 11207. Telephone: (42.2) 24.21.34.65;24.21.36.50. Telecopier: (42.2) 24.21.09.12;24.22.58.53.

St. Petersburg, Russia Office: 34 Souvorovsky Prospect, App 45, P.O. Box 172, 193015. Telephone by satellite: (7.812) 850.16.85. Telecopier by satellite: (7.812) 850.16.86.

Moscow, Russia Office: 9, Ulitsa Tverskaya - App 66, 103009. Telephone by satellite: (7.501) 940.45.00. Telecopier by satellite: (7.501) 940.45.01.

Budapest VII, Hungary Office: EMKE Building, Rákóczi út 42, BP 409, 1072. Telephone: (36.1) 268.1236; 268.1237; 268.1238. Telecopier: (36.1) 268.1239.

Madrid, Spain Office: Antonio Maura 7, 6°, 28014. Telephone: (34.1) 531.25.01. Telecopier: (34.1) 531.35.30.

Hanoi, Vietnam Office: Hanoi Business Centre, 51 Ly Thai To. Telephone: (84.42) 66.122.3. Telecopier: (84.42) 66.030.1.

French and International Law.

RESIDENT ASSOCIATES

Hugues Scalbert
Bruno Gloaguen

(For Biographical Data on Personnel, see Professional Biographies at Paris, France).

LAW OFFICES OF
DR. MOHAMED H. HOSHAN

Established in 1969

OLAYA BUILDING
OLAYA ROAD
P.O. BOX 2626
RIYADH 11461, SAUDI ARABIA
Telephone: 464-8353; 464-8363; 464-9166
Fax: 463-2083 Cables: Jurist

International Law, Business and Commercial Law, Agency/Distributorship and Franchising Law, International Arbitration, Intellectual Property Law, Oil, Gas and Energy Law, Corporate and Company Law, Computers and High Tech Law, Administrative Law, Banking Law.

FIRM PROFILE: *Established twenty five years ago, Law Offices Mohamed H. Hoshan is one of the oldest law offices in Saudi Arabia providing broad based general legal services. Clients include major U.S., European and multi-national corporations. The firm is a founding member of Gulf Consultants for the Protection of Intellectual Property.*

MEMBERS OF FIRM

DR. MOHAMED H. HOSHAN, born Medina, Saudi Arabia, April 14, 1929; admitted to practice, 1969, Saudi Arabia. *Education:* Faculty of Law, Cairo University (License en Droit, 1954); University of Poitiers, France (Diplome D'Etude Superieures de Droit Public, 1965); University of Paris (Doctorat D'Etat en Droit, 1966). Director General of Pensions Department, 1957-1961 and Legal Advisor, 1961-1970, Ministry of Finance. Senior Officer for Specialized Studies, Legal Department, Organization of Petroleum Exporting Countries (OPEC), 1966-1968. Associate Professor of Law, 1970-1973 and Acting Chairman of the Law Department, 1970-1973, King Saud University. President, Committee of Saudi Arabian Legal Advisors and Vice President of I.C.C. National Committee, Council of Saudi Chambers Commerce & Industry. Vice President of Arab Association for International Arbitration, Paris. Member of the International Court of Arbitration of the I.C.C., Paris. Enrolled in the roster of the Chambre Arbitrale Maritime de Monaco. Board Member of the Arab Society for the Protection of Industrial Property (ASPIP), Munich. Author: Text Book, "Introduction to the Study of Law, A Comparative Approach," King Saud University, 1975. Co-Author: Section of Kingdom of Saudi Arabia in Jordan's International Corporate Procedures, 1992. Editor, Saudi Arabian Legal Encyclopedia. *Member:* International Bar Association. *LANGUAGES:* Arabic, English and French. *PRACTICE AREAS:* International Arbitration; Maritime Law; Saudi and Middle East Business and Commercial Law; Litigation; Islamic Law; Transportation Law; International Contract Law; Energy and Oil Law; Administrative Law.

MAREN LOUISE HANSON, born Milwaukee, Wisconsin, June 3, 1943; admitted, 1976, California, U.S.A. *Education:* University of Oklahoma (B.A., 1965; M.A., 1971); University of San Diego School of Law (J.D., 1976); Faculty of Law, University of Tours, France (Diplome d'Etudes Approfondies, Public Law, 1982); University of San Diego School of

(This Listing Continued)

LAW OFFICES OF DR. MOHAMED H. HOSHAN, Riyadh—Continued

Law, Institute on International and Comparative Law (Diploma, Islamic and Middle Eastern Law, 1983). Attorney, Riyadh, Saudi Arabia, 1978-1980. Attorney, Paris, France, 1987-1988. Author: "Silt Deposits in Westlake Lake - A Legal Study," 1981; News updates on Saudi Arabian Legal Developments for World Law and West International Law Bulletin, 1982-1983; "The Influence of French Law on the Legal Development of Saudi Arabia," Arab Law Quarterly, August, 1987. Contributor to Trademark World, Patent World, Middle East Executive Reports, Managing Intellectual Property. Co-author: Section on Kingdom of Saudi Arabia in Jordan's International Corporate Procedures, 1992. Member, Advisory Board, International Lawyers' Newsletter. Corporate Secretary of Gulf Consultants for the Protection of Intellectual Property. Observer of the Arab Society for the Protection of Industrial Property (ASPIP) to the World Intellectual Property Organization (WIPO). *Member:* American Bar Association (Member, Section of International Law and Practice; Section on Patent, Trademark and Copyright Law); International Trademark Association (INTA) (Member, International Committee); International Bar Association. *LANGUAGES:* English and French. *PRACTICE AREAS:* Saudi & Middle East Business and Commercial Law; Computer Software; Technology Transfer; Intellectual Property Law; Islamic Law; International Contract Law; Hospital Law.

MOHAMED AHMED MOHAMED ELFAKI ABDALLA, born Merowe, Sudan, January 1, 1957; admitted, 1985, Sudan. *Education:* Faculty of Law, Khartoum University, Khartoum, Sudan (LL.B., 1984). Advocate and Legal Advisor, Khartoum, Sudan, 1985-1986. Legal Advisor, Attorney General Chambers, Khartoum, Sudan, 1986-1989. General Introductory Course on Industrial Property, (WIPO-ARIPO), Lilongwe, Malawi, July, 1988. *LANGUAGES:* Arabic and English. *PRACTICE AREAS:* Company Law; Trademark and Patent Law.

OF COUNSEL

Sheikh Saleh Al-Hoshan (For Sharia Law Cases)

REPRESENTATIVE CLIENTS: General Organization of Social Insurance (GOSI); Exxon Saudi Arabia Inc.; Oil Transport Co. Ltd.; Oil Field Chemicals; The Arabian Oil Company Ltd. (Japanese); Mecan-Arbed; The Farnsworth Co. Ltd.; General Electric Co. (U.K.); Yamamah Bricks Factory; Brown Daltas & Associates Ltd.; J.E. Sirene Corp.; Jones-Lang Wootton; Dunlop (U.K.); Kone Corp. (Finland); The Partek Group (Finland); Held & Francke (Germany); Dyckerhoff & Widmann; Prichard Services Group; GKN International; Thomas Cook; Stork (Netherlands); Al Bank Al Saudi Al Hollandi; Al Jazirah Bank; Royal-Orion Bank Ltd. (U.K.); General Foods Corporation (U.S.A.); Glaxo Holdings; O.J. Perrin; Produits Rouges; Smith & Wesson; Export Development Corporation of Canada; Saudi Chemical Co. Ltd.; United Plastic Company; Misubishi; Yamamah Insurance Co.; SSangyong Group (Korea); Samsonite Corp. (USA); Arabian Secured Transport Co., Ltd.; Arabian Security & Safety Services Co. Ltd.; European Vinyls Corp. (USA-Belgium); Link 51 (UK); Bausch & Lomb; L'Oreal (France); Outokumpu Oy (Finland); Ascinter Otis (France); Reckitt & Colman plc (UK); Hawker-Siddeley Power Engineering Ltd. (UK).

KADASAH LAW FIRM

In Cooperation with Bryan Cave, A Partnership including A

Professional Corporation

P.O. BOX 20883

RIYADH 11465 SAUDI ARABIA

Telephone: 465-1371; 465-1165

Facsimile: 966-1-464-3789

St. Louis, Missouri Office: Bryan Cave, One Metropolitan Square, 211 North Broadway, Suite 3600, 63102-2750. Telephone: (314) 259-2000. Facsimile: (314) 259-2020.

Washington, D.C. Office: Bryan Cave, 700 Thirteenth Street, N.W., 20005-3960. Telephone: (202) 508-6000. Facsimile: (202) 508-6200.

New York, N.Y. Office: Bryan Cave, 245 Park Avenue, 10167-0034. Telephone: (212) 692-1800. Facsimile: (212) 692-1900 and Other New York, N.Y. Office: 575 Lexington Avenue, 10022. Telephone: (212) 371-1660. Facsimile: (212) 593-0243.

Kansas City, Missouri Office: Bryan Cave, 3300 One Kansas City Place, 1200 Main Street, 64141-6914. Telephone: (816) 374-3200. Facsimile: (816) 374-3300.

Overland Park, Kansas Office: Bryan Cave, 7500 College Boulevard, Suite 1100, 66210-4035. Telephone: (913) 338-7700. Facsimile: (913) 338-7777.

(This Listing Continued)

Phoenix, Arizona Office: Bryan Cave, 2800 North Central Avenue, Twenty-First Floor, 85004-1098. Telephone: (602) 230-7000. Facsimile: (602) 266-5938.

Los Angeles, California Office: Bryan Cave, 777 South Figueroa, 27th Floor, 90017. Telephone: (213) 243-4300. Facsimile: (213) 243-4343.

Santa Monica, California Office: Bryan Cave, 120 Broadway, Suite 500, 90401-2305. Telephone: (310) 576-2100. Facsimile: (310) 576-2200.

Irvine, California Office: Bryan Cave, 18881 Von Karman, Suite 250, 92715-1500. Telephone: (714) 757-8100. Facsimile: (714) 757-8106.

London SW1H 9BU, England Office: Bryan Cave, 29 Queen's Gate. Telephone: 011-44-71-222-0511. Facsimile: 011-44-71-222-1240.

Frankfurt, Federal Republic of Germany Office: In Cooperation with Rossbach & Partner, Stresemannallee 33, D-60596 Frankfurt am Main. Telephone: 011-49-69-631 50 24. Facsimile: 011-49-69-631 31 64.

Dubai, U.A.E. Office: Al-Mehairi-Bryan Cave, Holiday Centre, Commercial Tower, Suite 1103, P.O. Box 13677, UAE. Telephone: 0110971-4-314-123. Facsimile: 011-971-4-318-287.

Hong Kong Office: Bryan Cave, Suite 2106- Lippo Tower, 21/F, Lippo Centre, 89 Queensway. Telephone: 011-852-2522-2821. Facsimile: 011-852-2522-3830.

General International and Business Law.

PARTNERS

CLYDE E. ELLIS, JR., born Virginia, 1952; admitted, 1984, Missouri (Not admitted in Saudi Arabia). *Education:* University of Virginia (B.A., with distinction, 1975); Institute of Islamic Studies; McGill University; Washington College of Law (J.D., 1984).

SAM E. EVERSMAN, born Indiana, 1963; admitted, 1987, Missouri (Not admitted in Saudi Arabia). *Education:* Indiana University (B.S., in Accounting with high distinction; J.D., magna cum laude, 1987). Order of the Coif. Certified Public Accountant, Illinois, 1985. (Also at Dubai Office).

NASSIR A. KADASAH, born Saudi Arabia, 1945. *Education:* Damascus University, Faculte du Droit (B.A., 1972). General Organization of Social Insurance, Legal Advisor, 1972-1979.

JOHN V. LONSBERG, born Michigan, 1955; admitted, 1979, Missouri (Not admitted in Saudi Arabia). *Education:* University of Notre Dame (B.A., summa cum laude, 1976); University of Michigan (J.D., cum laude, 1979). Phi Beta Kappa; Pi Sigma Alpha. *Member:* American Bar Association (Chairman, Middle East Law Section, 1988-1991). (Also at St. Louis, Missouri Office).

WILLIAM J. SHANNON, born Massachusetts, 1939; admitted, 1971, Hawaii, U.S. District Court, District of Hawaii and U.S. Court of Appeals, Ninth Circuit; 1987, New York; 1988, Japan (Gaikokuho-Jimu-Bengoshi). *Education:* United States Merchant Marine Academy (B.S., cum laude, 1961); Cornell University (Doctor of Law with Specialization in International Affairs, 1971). Associate Note Editor, Cornell International Law Journal, 1970-1971. Foreign Legal Consultant and Gaikokuho-Jimu-Bengoshi, Braun Moriya Hoashi & Kubota, Tokyo, 1985-1990. Partner, Kelley, Drye & Warren, Tokyo, 1990-1992. *LANGUAGES:* Japanese, German and French. *PRACTICE AREAS:* Transnational Business Transactions.

REPRESENTATIVE CLIENTS: Chrysler Technologies Corporation; De Smet Engineerings & Contractors, S.A.; El Seif Development Establishment; ESCO Electronics Corp.; Guardian Industries; Hellmuth, Obata & Kassabaum, Inc.; McDonnell Douglas Middle East Ltd.; Mitsui & Co. Ltd.; Price Waterhouse & Co.; Reynolds International, Inc.; Samsung Construction Co.; Saudi Investment Bank; Sikorsky Aircraft; Sunkyong Engineering and Construction Co.; Syscon Corp.; Tetra Pak International; Westinghouse Electric Corp.

LAW OFFICE OF HASSAN MAHASSNI

(In Association with White and Case)

AL MA'ATHER STREET

P.O. BOX 17411

RIYADH 11484, SAUDI ARABIA

Telephone: (966-1) 476-7099

Facsimile: (966-1) 479-0110

New York, New York: Telephone: 212-819-8200. Facsimile: 212-354-8113.

Washington, D.C.: Telephone: 202-872-0013. Facsimile: 202-872-0210.

Los Angeles, California: Telephone: 213-620-7700. Facsimile: 213-687-0758; 213-617-2205.

(This Listing Continued)

Miami, Florida: Telephone: 305-371-2700. Facsimile: 305-358-5744.

Mexico City, Mexico: Telephone: (52-5) 207-9717. Facsimile: (52-5) 208-3628.

Tokyo, Japan: Telephone: (81-3) 3239-4300. Facsimile: (81-3) 3239-4330.

Hong Kong: Telephone: (852) 2822-8700. Facsimile: (852) 2845-9070; Grice & Co., Solicitors, Telephone: (852) 2826-0333. Facsimile: (852) 2526-7166.

Singapore, Republic of Singapore: Telephone: (65) 225-6000. Facsimile: (65) 225-6009.

Bangkok, Thailand: Pacific Legal Group Ltd., In Association With White & Case, Telephone: (662) 236-6154/7. Facsimile: (662) 237-6771.

Hanoi, Viet Nam: Representative Office, Telephone: (84-4) 227-575/6/7. Facsimile: (84-4) 227-297.

Bombay, India: Telephone: (91-22) 282-6300. Facsimile: (91-22) 282-6305.

London, England: Telephone: (44-171) 726-6361. Facsimile: (44-171) 726-4314; (44-171) 726-8558.

Paris, France: Telephone: (33-1) 42-60-34-05. Facsimile: (33-1) 42-60-82-46.

Brussels, Belgium: Telephone: (32-2) 647-05-89. Facsimile: (32-2) 647-16-75.

Stockholm, Sweden: Telephone: (46-8) 679-80-30. Facsimile: (46-8) 611-21-22.

Helsinki, Finland: Telephone: (358-0) 631-100. Facsimile: (358-0) 179-477.

Moscow, Russia: Telephone: (7-095) 201-9292/3/4/5. Facsimile: (7-095) 201-9284.

Budapest, Hungary: Telephone: (36-1) 269-0550; (36-1) 131-0933. Facsimile: (36-1) 269-1199.

Prague, Czech Republic: Telephone: (42-2) 2481-1796. Facsimile: (42-2) 232-5522.

Warsaw, Poland: Telephone/Facsimile: (48-22) 26-80-53; (48-22) 27-84-86. International Telephone/Facsimile: (48-39) 12-19-06.

Istanbul, Turkey: Telephone: (90-212) 275-68-98; (90-212) 275-75-33. Facsimile: (90-212) 275-75-43.

Ankara, Turkey: Telephone: (90-312) 446-2180. Facsimile: (90-312) 437-9677.

Jeddah, Saudi Arabia: Law Office of Hassan Mahassni, Telephone: (966-2) 651-3535. Facsimile: (966-2) 651-3636.

Almaty, Kazakhstan: Telephone: (7-3272) 50-7491/2. Facsimile: (7-3272) 61-0842.

General International Practice.
Firm engaged in Saudi Arabian, American and International Law Practice.

HASSAN MAHASSNI, born Damascus, Syria, February 18, 1934. Admitted to practice, 1966 in Saudi Arabia. Citizen, Saudi Arabia. *Education:* Damascus College, Damascus, Syria (Baccalaureate, 1953); Syrian University, Faculty of Law, Damascus, Syria (LL.B., 1957). Legal Advisor to Ministry of Foreign Affairs, Kingdom of Saudi Arabia, 1965-1970. *Member:* International Bar Association. (Partner, White & Case, New York, New York).

RESIDENT ASSOCIATE

JAMES R. BILLINGSLEY, JR., born New York, N.Y., July 25, 1962; admitted, 1988, New York (Not admitted in Saudi Arabia). *Education:* Bowdoin College (B.A., 1984); University of Virginia (J.D., 1987).

(For biographical data as to other locations, see Professional Biographies at New York, New York; Washington, D.C.; Los Angeles, California; Miami, Florida; Mexico City, Mexico; Tokyo, Japan; Hong Kong; Singapore, Republic of Singapore; Bangkok, Thailand; Hanoi, Viet Nam; Bombay, India; London, England; Paris, France; Brussels, Belgium; Stockholm, Sweden; Helsinki, Finland; Moscow, Russia; Budapest, Hungary; Prague, Czech Republic; Warsaw, Poland; Istanbul and Ankara, Turkey; Jeddah, Saudi Arabia; Almaty, Kazakhstan).

NADER LAW OFFICES
481 FARAZDAK STREET, AL-DHOBBAT, AL-MALAZ DISTRICT
P.O. BOX 89704
RIYADH 11692, SAUDI ARABIA
Telephone: (01) 4793733
Fax: (01) 4792311

Jeddah, Saudi Arabia, Head Office: 19 Abo Zinadah Street, Off. Madina Road, Mushrefa Dist., P.O. Box 3595, Jeddah 21481. Telephone: 02-6652067. Telex: 603285 Jaber SJ. Telefax: 6608709.

London, England Office: Nader Mideast Law Ltd., 41, Redcliffe Close, 276, Old Brompton Road, SW5 9HY. Telephone: 071 373 0975. Fax: 071 835 2251.

Company, Commercial, Maritime, Foreign Investment, Insurance, Aviation, Labor, Contracts, Sharia (Islamic Law), Civil, Litigation and Arbitration.

FIRM PROFILE: Nader Law Offices, among the largest in number of lawyers and paralegals, is a leader in its field. The firm offers legal advice in all lines of law and Sharia in Saudi Arabia. The firm can also facilitate business contacts and promotions through associate firms in Saudi Arabia.

HASAN AWAD ABDEL LATIF, born Khartoum, Sudan, 1958; (Not admitted in Saudi Arabia). *Education:* University of Cairo, Khartoum Branch (1986). *Member:* Sudanese Bar Association. *LANGUAGES:* Arabic and English. *PRACTICE AREAS:* Commercial; Contract; Labour Law; Litigation.

LAW OFFICES OF
SAUDI CONSULTING CENTER
Established in 1976

SAUDI BRITISH BANK BUILDING
KING ABDUL AZIZ ROAD AT
AL-SHARKIYA STREET
P.O. BOX 57270
RIYADH 11574, SAUDI ARABIA
Telephone: 966-1-456-0481
Telefax: 966-1-454-5209

Foreign Investment, International Commercial Transactions, Intellectual Property, Franchising, Joint Ventures, Defense Contracting, Banking and Finance, Corporate, Arbitration, Shipping and Insurance.

FIRM PROFILE: The Law Offices of Saudi Consulting Center are staffed by American, Saudi and other Arab lawyers dedicated to providing the highest quality work in a timely, efficient and cost-effective manner. The firm's attorneys are experienced in a wide range of issues affecting foreign companies doing business in the Kingdom and the Mideast, including agency, joint ventures, commercial transactions, dispute resolution, intellectual property, franchising, licensing, contracts and technology transfer. The firm provides American-style quality legal service to clients involved in in-bound and out-bound investment, trade and contracting.

MEMBERS OF FIRM

DR. EID M. AL-JHANI, born Saudi Arabia, 1951; admitted, 1976, Saudi Arabia. *Education:* Cairo University (Bachelor of Law, 1976; Master of Law, 1979; Doctor of Law, 1983). Recommended Arbitrator, Euro-Arab Chamber of Commerce. Member, Arab-Belgian Arbitration Board. Founder, Saudi Consulting Center, 1976. Author: "Saudi Regulations Governing the Use of Cheques"; "An Explanation of Saudi Arbitration"; "Saudi Regulations Governing the Use of Promissory Notes"; "Share Investments in the Saudi Market"; "The Theory of Successful Investment"; "The Theory of Administrative Control Between Administrative Law and Public Management"; "The Grievance Board in the Kingdom of Saudia Arabia"; "Council of Ministers in the Kingdom of Saudi Arabia-Between Islamic Sharia and Contemporary Constitutional Trends"; "Shura and the Art of Government in the Kingdom of Saudi Arabia"; "Gulf Earthquake-A Mediative View"; "Contemporary International Issues"; "Contemplations in the Contemporary Economy"; "Politics Between the Possible and Impossible"; "Economy and Development in Kingdom of Saudi Arabia"; "Administrative Jurisdiction and its Application in the Kingdom of Saudi Arabia"; "Talk of Eighties-Saudi Yemeni Border and Relations.". *LANGUAGES:* English and Arabic. *PRACTICE AREAS:* Corporate; Commercial; Banking; Construction; Arbitration; Maritime; Insurance; Contract; Litigation.

(This Listing Continued)

LAW OFFICES OF SAUDI CONSULTING CENTER,
Riyadh—Continued

CHRISTOPHER H. JOHNSON, born Munich, Germany, February 24, 1951; admitted, 1979, New York, U.S. District Court, Southern and Eastern Districts of New York and U.S. Court of Appeals, Second Circuit (Not admitted in Saudi Arabia). *Education:* Princeton University (B.A., 1974); New York University (J.D., 1978). Associated with Burlingham Underwood & Lord, New York, 1978-1984. Editorial Assistant, American Maritime Cases, 1979-1984. Author: "Investing, Licensing and Trading Conditions in Saudi Arabia," Business International, 1989; "Legal Aspects of Doing Business in Saudi Arabia," Kluwers, 1993. Franchising in the International Marketplace, Saudi Arabia, International Franchising, 1993. Secretary, Committee on Admiralty, The Association of the Bar of the City of New York, 1981-1984. American Business Council of the Gulf Countries, Principal Member and Riyadh Representative, 1992—. Member, Steering Committee, American Businessmen's Group of Riyadh, 1990—. Chairman, Doorknock Committee, 1992—. Recommended Arbitrator, Euro-Arab Arbitration System. *Member:* American and International Bar Associations. *LANGUAGES:* English and French. *PRACTICE AREAS:* Corporate; Contracts; Commercial; Defense; Banking; Litigation; Arbitration; Construction; Maritime.

DAVID M. PFEIFFER, born Barron, Wisconsin, 1962; admitted, 1989, Illinois and Wisconsin; 1991, New York and Connecticut; 1992, Minnesota and the Federated States of Micronesia; 1993, California (Not admitted in Saudi Arabia). *Education:* University of St. Andrews, Scotland (Master of Arts (Hons), 1986); University of Wisconsin Law School (Juris Doctor, 1989); Georgetown University Law Center (Master of Laws, 1993). Associated, Vedder Price, Kaufman, Kammholz & Day, New York, 1989-1992. Staff Counsel, Congress of the Federated States of Micronesia, 1992-1993. General Counsel, The Accountants Coalition, Washington, D.C., 1993-1994. Managing Attorney, Saudi Consulting Center, Riyadh, Saudi Arabia, 1994—. *LANGUAGES:* English. *PRACTICE AREAS:* Banking; Corporate; Contracts; Commercial; Litigation; Arbitration; Intellectual Property; Labor; Administrative.

ALLAUDDIN Z. OSMAN, born Sudan, 1948; admitted, 1978, Sudan (Not admitted in Saudi Arabia). *Education:* Khartoum University (LL.B., Honors, 1977). Sudan Judiciary, 1978-1983. *LANGUAGES:* Arabic and English. *PRACTICE AREAS:* Labor; Administrative; Corporate; Commercial; Litigation; Trademarks.

HUSSEIN MOHAMMED, born Egypt, 1936; admitted, 1956, Egypt (Not admitted in Saudi Arabia). *Education:* (Bachelor of Laws, 1956; Master of Laws, 1964). Director, Legal Department, Egyptian Exports and Imports Authority, Saudi Consulting Center, 1981—. *LANGUAGES:* English and Arabic. *PRACTICE AREAS:* Contracts; Arbitration; Government Tender Regulations; Administrative; Maritime.

LABIB MOHAMMED AL-ASSALI, born Jordan, 1937; admitted, 1964, Jordan (Not admitted in Saudi Arabia). *Education:* Damascus University (Bachelor of Laws, 1964); Cairo University (Master of Laws, 1972). Lawyer and Saudi Ministry of Information, 1976-1986; Saudi Consulting Center, 1986—. *LANGUAGES:* English and Arabic. *PRACTICE AREAS:* Contracts; Corporate; Administrative; Liquidation and Trademarks.

REPRESENTATIVE CLIENTS: Johnson Controls International, Inc.; Martin Marietta Corp.; Vinnell Corp.; Saudi American Bank; Harris Corp.; Lear Siegler Management Services Corp.; A.I. Alkhorayef Sons' Co.

LAW OFFICE OF SAUD M.A. SHAWWAF

(In Association with Jones, Day, Reavis & Pogue)

P.O. BOX 2700
RIYADH 11461, SAUDI ARABIA
Telephone: (966-1) 465-6543, (966-1) 464-8534 or (966-1) 464-8540
Telex: 401831 SAUCON SJ
Telecopier: (966-1) 464-8480

In Atlanta, Georgia: 3500 One Peachtree Center. 303 Peachtree Street, N.E. Telephone: 404-521-3939. Cable Address: "Attorneys Atlanta". Telex: 54-2711. Telecopier: 404-581-8330.

In Brussels, Belgium: Avenue Louise 480, 7th Floor. B-1050 Brussels. Telephone: 32-2-645-14-11. Telecopier: 32-2-645-14-45.

In Chicago, Illinois: 77 West Wacker. Telephone: 312-782-3939. Telecopier: 312-782-8585.

(This Listing Continued)

AF98B

In Cleveland, Ohio: North Point, 901 Lakeside Avenue. Telephone: 216-586-3939. Cable Address: "Attorneys Cleveland." Telex: 980389. Telecopier: 216-579-0212.

In Columbus, Ohio: 1900 Huntington Center. Telephone: 614-469-3939. Cable Address: "Attorneys Columbus." Telecopier: 614-461-4198.

In Dallas, Texas: 2300 Trammell Crow Center, 2001 Ross Avenue. Telephone: 214-220-3939. Cable Address: "Attorneys Dallas." Telex: 730852. Telecopier: 214-969-5100.

In Frankfurt, Germany: Triton Haus, Bockenheimer Landstrasse 42, 60323 Frankfurt am Main. Telephone: 49-69-9726-3939. Telecopier: 49-69-9726-3993.

In Geneva, Switzerland: 20, rue de Candolle. Telephone: 41-22-320-2339. Telecopier: 41-22-320-1232.

In Hong Kong: 1501 One Exchange Square, 8 Connaught Place. Telephone: 852-2526-6895. Telecopier: 852-2810-5787.

In Irvine, California: 2603 Main Street, Suite 900. Telephone: 714-851-3939. Telex: 194911 Lawyers LSA. Telecopier: 714-553-7539.

In London, England: One Mount Street. Telephone: 44-71-493-9361. Cable Address: "Surgoe London WI." Telecopier: 44-71-493-9666.

In Los Angeles, California: 555 West Fifth Street, Suite 4600. Telephone: 213-489-3939. Telex: 181439 UD. Telecopier: 213-243-2539.

In New York, New York: 599 Lexington Avenue. Telephone: 212-326-3939. Cable Address: "JONESDAY NEWYORK." Telex: 237013 JDRP UR. Telecopier: 212-755-7306.

In Paris, France: 62, rue du Faubourg Saint-Honore. Telephone: 33-1-44-71-3939. Cable Address: "Surgoe Paris." Telex: 290156 Surgoe. Telecopier: 33-1-49-24-0471.

In Pittsburgh, Pennsylvania: 500 Grant Street, 31st Floor. Telephone: 412-391-3939. Cable Address: "Attorneys Pittsburgh". Telecopier: 412-394-7959.

In Taipei, Taiwan: 8th Floor, 2 Tun Hwa South Road, Section 2. Telephone: (886-2) 704-6808. Telecopier: (886-2) 704-6791.

In Tokyo, Japan: Toranomon MT Building, 4th Floor, 10-3, Toranomon 3-chome, Minato-Ku. Telephone: 81-3-3433-3939. Telecopier: 81-3-5401-2725.

In Washington, D.C.: Metropolitan Square, 1450 G Street, N.W. Telephone: 202-879-3939. Cable Address: "Attorneys Washington." Telex: 89-2410 ATTORNEYS WASH. Telecopier: 202-737-2832.

General Practice. Firm engaged in International and Saudi Arabian Law Practice.

RESIDENT LAWYERS

SAUD M.A. SHAWWAF, SAUDI NATIONAL, born Hama, Syria, February 17, 1939; admitted to bar, 1968, Saudi Arabia. *Education:* American University of Beirut and Amherst College (B.A., 1960); University of Cincinnati College of Law (J.D., 1965); Academy of American and International Law, International and Comparative Law Center, Southwestern Legal Foundation, 1967. Special Legal Assistant to Minister of Petroleum and Mineral Resources, 1965-1968. Head of Legal Department, Organization of Arab Petroleum Exporting Countries (OAPEC), 1969-1971. Member, Supreme Labor Commission of Saudi Arabia, 1965-1968. Member of the IBA. (Member of Firm).

VERNON CASSIN, JR., born Amman, Jordan, September 28, 1952; admitted, 1978, New York (Not admitted in Saudi Arabia). *Education:* Princeton University (A.B., 1974); Harvard University (J.D., 1977). (Partner, Associated Office).

MARTIN L. CAMP, born Oklahoma City, Oklahoma, June 2, 1954; admitted, 1979, Texas (Not admitted in Saudi Arabia). *Education:* Centenary College (B.A., 1976); Southern Methodist University (J.D., 1979). Order of the Coif. (Partner, Associated Office).

HASSAN M. HAMMAD, SUDANESE NATIONAL, (Not admitted in Saudi Arabia). born Babanoosa, 1954; admitted to bar, 1981, Sudan. *Education:* University of Khartoum, Sudan (LL.B., 1979). *Member:* Sudanese Bar.

SALEH SALMAN AL AMIN, born Khartoum, Sudan, January, 1956; admitted, 1980, Sudan (Not admitted in Saudi Arabia). *Education:* University of Khartoum (LL.B., 1979).

WALID M. AYACHE, AMERICAN NATIONAL, born Lebanon, 1960; admitted, 1990, California (Not admitted in Saudi Arabia). *Education:* California State University, Long Beach (B.S., 1985); Western State University (J.D., 1990).

Languages: Arabic, English, French

LAW OFFICE OF MOHAMED A.H. TOUBAN

OLAYA THAMANIN STREET
P.O. BOX 7606
RIYADH 11472, SAUDI ARABIA
Telephone: 001-966-1-4651460
Facsimile: 001-966-1-4632238

Jeddah, Saudi Arabia Office: Ali Reza Tower-9th Floor, Medina Road, P.O. Box 22393, Jeddah 21495. Telephone: 001-966-2-6521073. Facsimile: 001-966-2-6520845.

General and International Practice, Corporate, Financial Banking, Tax, Real Estate, Trade Marks, Agency's, Joint Venture, Commercial, Civil, Maritime, Criminal, Labour and Administrative Law Litigation and Arbitration.

MOHAMED A.H. TOUBAN, born Saudi Arabia, March 16, 1928; admitted, 1971, Egypt; 1980, Saudi Arabia. *Education:* University of Cairo, Egypt (License en Droit, 1949). Chief Deputy Attorney General, Cairo, 1950-1962. Judge, Civil, Leasing and Shari'ah Matters, Cairo, 1962-1968. President, Court of Labor Appeals, 1968-1969. Judge, Court of Appeals, Cairo, 1969-1971. Legal Advisor: Investigation and Disciplinary Board, Riyadh, 1972-1980; National Commercial Bank, Riyadh, 1980-1982.

SAMEH M. TOUBAN, born Saudi Arabia, December 14, 1965; admitted, 1990, Saudi Arabia. *Education:* University of Cairo, Egypt (License en Droit, 1987). *Member:* International Bar Association.

TARIQ DEMERDASH, born Egypt, August 27, 1962; admitted, 1989, Egypt (Not admitted in Saudi Arabia). *Education:* University of Cairo, Egypt (Licence en Droit, 1986).

JHON A. GRAY, born Lima, Peru, May 30, 1930; admitted, 1955, Washington, D.C. (Not admitted in Saudi Arabia). *Education:* Dartmouth College (A.B., 1951); George Washington University Law School (LL.B., 1954). (Taxation Section).

Languages: Arabic, English, French and Spanish.

WOHABE LAW OFFICES

HWEIRINY BUILDING
AL-AHSA STREET
P.O. BOX 15512
RIYADH 11454, SAUDI ARABIA
Telephone: 477-6962
Telecopier: 478-7506

New York, N.Y. Office: 375 Park Avenue, 10152. Telephone: 212-838-7380. Telecopier: 212-838-7463.

Corporate, Commercial, Foreign and Comparative Law, International Transactions, Litigation and Administrative Law.

DR. ABDUL W. WOHABE, born Riyadh, Saudi Arabia, 1935; admitted to bar, 1966, New York; 1967, U.S. District Court, Southern District of New York; 1981, Saudi Arabia; 1982, U.S. District Court, Eastern District of New York; 1986, U.S. Court of Appeals, Third Circuit and U.S. Court of International Trade. *Education:* Williams College, Williamstown, Massachusetts (B.A., 1959); Cornell Law School, Ithaca, New York (J.D., International Legal Affairs, 1963). Commissioned by the Government of Saudi Arabia to review Code of Business Corporations, Consumer Protection Code and a Proposed Code to Regulate the Marketing of Financial Securities in the Kingdom. Associate, White & Case, 1963-1969. Founder and Member, Board of Directors, 1973-1980, UBAF Arab American Bank. Speaker, GulfAmerica Conference, 1988. *Member:* Association of the Bar of the City of New York; New York State, American (Member, Committees on: Middle Eastern Law; Foreign Investments in the United States) and International Bar Associations; American Society of International Law; American Mideast Business Association (Director, 1985-1988); World Trade Club of Westchester. *LANGUAGES:* Arabic and English.

DAVID P. WOHABE, born Ithaca, New York, 1960; admitted to bar, 1986, New York; 1987, U.S. District Court, Southern and Eastern Districts of New York; 1991, Saudi Arabia. *Education:* Williams College, Williamstown, Massachusetts (B.A., 1982); Cornell Law School, Ithaca, New York (J.D., cum laude, 1985). Member, Cornell Law Review, 1983-1985. Author: Note, "Chemical Bank v. Washington Public Power Supply System: The Questionable Use of the Ultra Vires Doctrine to Invalidate Governmental Take-or-Pay Obligations", 69 Cornell Law Review 1094, 1984. Associate,

(This Listing Continued)

Milbank, Tweed, Hadley & McCloy, 1985-1988. *Member:* Association of the Bar of the City of New York; New York State and American Bar Associations.

OMAR S. WOHABE, born New York, New York, 1963; admitted to bar, 1988, Connecticut; 1989, New York; 1989, U.S. District Court, Southern and Eastern Districts of New York (Not admitted in Saudi Arabia). *Education:* Williams College, Williamstown, Massachusetts (B.A., 1985); Cornell Law School, Ithaca, New York (J.D., 1988). Associate, Shearman & Sterling, 1988-1992. *Member:* Association of the Bar of the City of New York; New York State and American Bar Associations.

LAW OFFICES OF AHMED ZAKI YAMANI

#11 WADI AL AKHDAR STREET
P.O. BOX 7159
RIYADH 11462, SAUDI ARABIA
Telephone: (966-1) 464-2144
Telefax: (966-1) 464-8718

Jeddah, Saudi Arabia: Shaker Building, P.O. Box 1351, Jeddah 21431. Telephones: (966-2) 6429550; 6429551. Telefax: (966-2) 6437511. Telex: 605853 GANONI SJ.

Manama, Bahrain: Manama Centre, Entrance 4, 4th Floor, Suites 406 & 407, P.O. Box 342. Telephones: (973) 211-433; 211-662. Telefax: (973) 219-373. Telex: 8991 YAMANI BN.

SENIOR MEMBERS OF FIRM

AHMED ZAKI YAMANI, born Mecca, Saudi Arabia, June 30, 1930. *Education:* Cairo University, Cairo, Egypt (License en Droit, 1952); Harvard and New York Universities (Graduate studies in Law). Founder of The Law Offices of Ahmed Zaki Yamani, Saudi Arabia's First Private Law Office, 1952. Formerly, Legal Advisor to the Saudi Council of Ministers, 1957. Cabinet Member as Minister of State, 1960 and later as the Minister of Petroleum and Mineral Resources, 1962-1987. First Secretary-General of the Organization of Petroleum Exporting Countries (OPEC), and is regarded as the Architect of many of the Kingdom's Modern Laws and Regulations. Chairman of the Centre for Global Energy Studies and the Al Furqan Islamic Heritage Foundation. *LANGUAGES:* Arabic, English and French. *PRACTICE AREAS:* Islamic Law; Energy; Government Affairs and Procedures.

ZAKI MUSTAFA, born Sudan, November 17, 1934; admitted, 1963, Sudan. *Education:* University of Khartoum (LL.B., 1959); London School of Economics (LL.M., 1961); University of London, London, England (Ph.D., 1969). Author: "The Legal System of the Sudan," Cairo, Egypt (Arabic), 1969; "The Common Law in Sudan," Oxford, England, 1977. Associate Professor, Contract and Commercial Law, Khartoum, 1961-1965. Visiting Lecturer, UCLA, 1964. Professor and Dean of Law, Contracts, Commercial and Corporate Law, Khartoum, 1965-1969. Professor and Dean, Ahamadu Bello University, Nigeria, 1969-1972. Visiting Professor, Haile Selassie I University, Addis Ababa, Ethiopia, 1972-1973, and Harvard Law School, 1989-1990. National Chairman, World Peace Through Law Center, 1964-1975. Advisor to the Supreme Council of State, Sudan, 1965-1969. President, Society of Law Teachers, Africa, 1965-1972. Member: Society of Public Teachers of Law, 1969; Law Reform Commission, Nigeria, 1970-1973; National Council for Higher Education, Sudan, 1975—. Chairman; Law Reform Commission, Sudan, 1973—; University Grants Commission, Sudan, 1975-1979. Attorney General, Minister of Justice, Sudan 1973-1975. Advisor on Law Revision and Law Reform to the President of Sudan, 1975-1979. (Managing Partner at Jeddah Office). *LANGUAGES:* Arabic, English and French. *PRACTICE AREAS:* Corporate Law; Contract Law; Commercial Law; Aviation; Insurance; Mining and Environmental Law.

MOHAMMED SALIH EL-ZUBEIR, born Sudan, 1948; admitted, 1972, Sudan. *Education:* University of Khartoum, Sudan (LL.B.-LL.M., 1972-1974). Legal Advisor to the Ministry of Health, Public Service and Administrative Reform, Sudan, 1974-1979. Legal Advisor to the Sudanese Red Sea Joint Commission, 1979-1982, Jeddah, Saudi Arabia. Joined the Firm as Legal Consultant in 1979. (Managing Attorney Riyadh Office). *LANGUAGES:* Arabic and English. *PRACTICE AREAS:* Corporate Law; Commercial Law; Contract Law; Banking and Finance; Taxation Law; Litigation; Construction.

LOTFI M. O. MADANI, born Jeddah, Saudi Arabia, 1952; admitted, 1982, Saudi Arabia. *Education:* Cairo University. Of Counsel to the Law Office of Ahmed Zaki Yamani and Surrey and Morse, 1982; Jones Day Reavis and Pogue, 1984-1987. *LANGUAGES:* Arabic, English and French.

(This Listing Continued)

LAW OFFICES OF AHMED ZAKI YAMANI, Riyadh—Continued

PRACTICE AREAS: Civil Litigation; Arbitration Law; Commercial Law; Partnership and Joint Ventures; Construction and Government Affairs.

MOHAMMED GAAFAR MOHAMMED, born Sudan, 1950; admitted, 1972, Sudan. *Education:* University of Khartoum (LL.B.-LL.M., with honors, 1976). Magistrate, Sudan Judiciary, 1973-1979. Member, The Human Rights Protection Society. *LANGUAGES:* Arabic, English and French. *PRACTICE AREAS:* Construction; Corporate Law; Commercial Law; Contract Law; Taxation; Insurance; Intellectual Property; Litigation.

(For Biographical data on other Personnel, see Professional Biographies at Jeddah, Saudi Arabia and Manama, Bahrain)

ABDUL RAHMAN ZAHRANI LAW OFFICE

In association with Meyer-Reumann Legal Consultancy

Established in 1989

KING FAYSAL FOUNDATION BLDG.

P.O. BOX 55409

RIYADH 11534, SAUDI ARABIA

Telephone: 966-1-462-7808/462-9847

Facsimile: 966-1-462-9519

Administrative, Arbitration, Corporate, Commercial, Company, Insurance, International Business Transactions, Joint Ventures, Litigation, Shariah Law, Trademarks and Patent Law.

FIRM PROFILE: Established in the year 1989, the firm represents and renders legal services to a vast spectrum of Arab and western companies involved in government construction contracts, good computer programs and pharmaceutical products distributorships.

MEMBERS OF FIRM

ABDUL RAHMAN ZAHRANI, born Makkah, Saudi Arabia, January 11, 1959; admitted, 1985, Saudi Arabia. *Education:* Mohammed Bin Saud Islamic University, Riyadh, Saudi Arabia (1981); Academy of American and International Law, Dallas, Texas, U.S.A. (1989). Junior Counsel, Shariah High Court of Riyadh, 1981-1985. Attorney, Saud Shawwaf Law Office, 1985-1989. *LANGUAGES:* Arabic and English. *PRACTICE AREAS:* Sharl'a Law; Arbitration.

MICHAEL M. FARAG, born Alexandria, Egypt, 1956; admitted, 1989, Berlin, Germany (Not admitted in Saudi Arabia). *Education:* University of Passau, Germany (1985). *LANGUAGES:* German, English, French and Arabic. *PRACTICE AREAS:* Commercial Law; Agencies.

EDUARDO MOANE DRAGO, born Lima, Peru, December 27, 1960; admitted, 1987, Peru (Not admitted in Saudi Arabia). *Education:* Pontifical Catholic University of Peru (J.D., 1984); Southwestern Legal Foundation, Dallas, Texas, U.S.A. (1989); International Development Law Institute, Rome, Italy (1990); Southern Methodist University, Dallas, Texas, U.S.A. (LL.M., 1991). *LANGUAGES:* Spanish and English. *PRACTICE AREAS:* International Law; Franchise Law.

OSAMA AHMED AL REFAIE, born Taif, Saudi Arabia, 1966; admitted, 1991, Saudi Arabia. *Education:* King Saud University, Riyadh, Saudi

(This Listing Continued)

Arabia (1989). Attorney, Rabi Al-Saadoun Law Office, 1990-1992. *LANGUAGES:* Arabic and English. *PRACTICE AREAS:* Negotiable Instruments; Company Law.

Languages: Arabic, English, German, French and Spanish.

SIERRA LEONE

BASMA & MACAULAY

Barristers and Solicitors

Established in 1981

21 CHARLOTTE STREET

P.O. BOX 83

FREETOWN, SIERRA LEONE

Telephone: (22) 222798; 223561; 228114

Fax: (22) 224248

General Civil Practice, Admiralty Matters, Shipping, Corporate Work, Trade Marks and Patents.

PARTNERS

Shakib Najib Kalil Basma, LL.B., Commissioner for Oaths, Notary Public

Berthan Macaulay, (Jnr), LL.B., Notary Public

ASSOCIATES

E. Bunton Cole, LL.B.; B.A.

Jamesina E.L. Johnson, LL.B.

Languages: English.

SOUTH AFRICA

ADAMS & ADAMS

Patent Attorneys

Established in 1917

2817 TRUST BANK CENTRE

HEERENGRACHT

CAPE TOWN 8001, SOUTH AFRICA

Telephone: National (021) 25 3607, International +27 21 25 3607

Facsimile: 27 21 4195729

Mailing Address: P.O. Box 1513, Cape Town, 8000

Pretoria, South Africa Office: 429 Church Street, 0002. P.O. Box 1014, 0001. Telephone: National (012) 320 8500, International +27 12 320 8500. Telex: 3 22157 ADAMS SA. Facsimile: 27 12 320 8550.

Johannesburg, South Africa Office: 3rd floor, North Park, 20 Girton Rd, Parktown 2193. P.O. Box 10155, 2000. Telephone: National (011) 642 5057, International +27 11 6425057. Facsimile: 27 11 6421914.

Durban, South Africa Office: 6th floor, 136 Victoria Embankment, 4001. P.O. Box 1538, 4000. Telephone: National (031) 304 3773, International +27 31 304 3773. Facsimile: 27 31 304 3799.

Patent and Trademark.

RESIDENT PARTNERS

B. BACON. *PRACTICE AREAS:* Patent Drafting; Prosecution and Litigation.

S. G. VAN DER SCHANS. *PRACTICE AREAS:* Patent Drafting; Prosecution and Filing.

(For Complete List of Personnel, see Professional Biographies at Pretoria).

FINDLAY & TAIT INCORPORATED

Attorneys

Established in 1885

S.A. RESERVE BANK BUILDING, 10TH FLOOR
30 HOUT STREET
P.O. BOX 248
CAPE TOWN 8001, SOUTH AFRICA
Telephone: National: 021-247015
International: + 27 21 247015
Telex: 57-27962 SA
Cable Address: "Fintait"
Telecopier: International (+ 27 21) 24 1688 (24 hrs.)

In Association with Webber Wentzel, Johannesburg, & Shepstone & Wylie, Durban

Admiralty, Aviation, Corporate, Commercial, International Joint Ventures, Copyright, Building and Construction Law, Real Estate, Prospecting and Mineral Rights, Commercial Litigation and Arbitration, General Practice, Labour Law, Industrial Relations.

FIRM PROFILE: *The firm was established in 1885 and provides a full range of legal services. It is well known internationally for the admiralty, bankruptcy and commercial law services which it offers.*

NOEL GEORGE TUNBRIDGE, born 1927; admitted, 1956, Cape Province, Notary and Conveyancer. *Education:* St. Andrew's College; Rhodes University Grahamstown (1942-1950). Served, on the Council of the Law Society of the Cape of Good Hope. Vice-President, on the Council of the Law Society of the Cape of Good Hope, 1980. Founder, Maritime Law Association of the Republic of South Africa, 1974. Secretary and Treasurer, Executive Committee, Maritime Law Association of the Republic of South Africa, 1974—. *Member:* International Bar Association; Asia Pacific Lawyers Association. (Senior Partner). *LANGUAGES:* English and Afrikaans. *PRACTICE AREAS:* Arbitration Law; International Contract Law; Admiralty Law; Commercial Law; Estate Planning; Trusts; Litigation.

ROY ASHCRAFT ANDERSON, born Windhoek, Namibia, October 15, 1942; admitted, 1966, Cape Province, Notary and Conveyancer; 1976, Lesotho. *Education:* University of Cape Town (Diploma in Law; Diploma in Advanced Company Law). *Member:* Law Society of The Cape of Good Hope; Attorneys Association of Cape Town; International Bar Association. *LANGUAGES:* English and Afrikaans. *PRACTICE AREAS:* General Practice; Corporate Law; Commercial Law; Liquor Law; Estate Planning; Trust Law; Bankruptcy Law; Litigation; Alternative Dispute Resolution.

TIMOTHY BRIAN MCINTOSH, born Grahamstown, South Africa, December 31, 1942; admitted, 1966, Cape Province; 1975, Lesotho. *Education:* University of Cape Town (Diploma in Law). Notary, South Africa and Lesotho. Chairman, Board of Control, school for legal practice, University of Cape Town. *Member:* Law Society of The Cape of Good Hope; Association of Law Societies (Member, Standing Committee on Legal Education). *LANGUAGES:* English and Afrikaans. *PRACTICE AREAS:* Corporate Law; Construction Law; International Contract Law; Bankruptcy Law.

MALCOLM FOSTER BLACK, born Cape Town, South Africa, December 23, 1946; admitted, 1970, Cape Province. *Education:* University of Cape Town (Diploma in Law). *LANGUAGES:* English and Afrikaans. *PRACTICE AREAS:* Conveyancing; Notarial Law; Property Law; Real Estate Law.

JOHN DYASON, born Johannesburg, South Africa, January 13, 1945; admitted, 1971, Cape of Good Hope. *Education:* University of Stellenbosch (B.A.); University of Cape Town (Dipl. Law; Post Graduate Diploma in Maritime Law). Author: "The New South African Admiralty Court Rules," Cargo Claims Analysis, May, 1987; "Security Arrests in South Africa," 1 LMCLQ 9, 1990. *Member:* Law Society of The Cape of Good Hope; International Bar Association; Maritime Law Association of South Africa. *LANGUAGES:* English, Afrikaans and French (correspondence). *PRACTICE AREAS:* International Contract Law; Admiralty Law; Litigation; Insurance Law; Aviation Law.

EDWARD ROBERT VON WITT, born Bulawayo, Zimbabwe, June 6, 1947; admitted, 1974, South Africa. *Education:* University of Stellenbosch (B.A.; LL.B.). *Member:* Cape Town Attorneys Association; Law Society of The Cape of Good Hope; International Bar Association. *LANGUAGES:* English, Afrikaans and German. *PRACTICE AREAS:* Family Law; Industrial Law; Litigation; Alternate Dispute Resolution.

(This Listing Continued)

RICHARD GRANT SHERRY, born Port Elizabeth, South Africa, January 25, 1949; admitted, 1975, Cape Province; 1976, Lesotho. *Education:* University of Cape Town (Diploma in Law). *LANGUAGES:* English and Afrikaans. *PRACTICE AREAS:* Property Law; Real Estate Law; General Legal Practice.

GRAHAM NIVEN CHARNOCK, born Cape Town, South Africa, November 5, 1946; admitted, 1976, South Africa, Lesotho and Namibia. *Education:* University of Cape Town (B.Comm.; LL.B.; Diploma in Business Management). *Member:* Maritime Law Association of South Africa; Cape Town Attorneys Association; Law Society of The Cape of Good Hope; International Bar Association. *LANGUAGES:* English and Dutch. *PRACTICE AREAS:* General Legal Practice; Litigation; Negligence Law; Admiralty Law; Insurance Law; Personal Injury Law; Environmental Law; Bankruptcy Law; Client Recoveries; Construction Contract Law; Alternative Dispute Resolution.

ALBERT ROBERT LOUIS BERTRAND, born Cape Town, South Africa, March 14, 1951; admitted, 1979, South Africa. *Education:* St. Stithians College; University of Stellenbosch (B.Comm.; LL.B.). Notary and Conveyancer. Lecturer, Candidate Conveyancers. Member, "Pro-Life," Church of England, South Africa. *Member:* Law Society of The Cape of Good Hope; Cape Town Attorneys Association; International Property Lawyers Association; Property Owners' Association. *LANGUAGES:* English and Afrikaans. *PRACTICE AREAS:* Property Law; Real Estate Law; Section Titles; Conveyancing; Township Law; Notarial Law.

PETER EUGENE WHELAN, born Johannesburg, South Africa, September 21, 1954; admitted, 1982, South Africa. *Education:* University of Cape Town (B.A.; LL.B.). *LANGUAGES:* English and Afrikaans. *PRACTICE AREAS:* Insurance Law; Personal Injury Law; Litigation; Bankruptcy Law; Aviation Law; Client Recoveries; Construction Contract Law; Alternative Dispute Resolution.

PAUL WOLTER STELLING, born Durban, South Africa, August 2, 1957; admitted, 1983, Supreme Court of South Africa. *Education:* University of Cape Town (B.Proc., 1980). *LANGUAGES:* English and Afrikaans. *PRACTICE AREAS:* Real Estate Law; Conveyancing; Property Law.

GORDON IAN RUSHTON, born January 29, 1958; admitted, 1985, South Africa. *Education:* University of Cape Town (B.A.; LL.B.). *LANGUAGES:* English and Afrikaans. *PRACTICE AREAS:* Litigation; Client Recoveries; Compulsory Motor Vehicle Insurance Law; Criminal Law; Bankruptcy Law; Media Law; Personal Law; Family Law; Insurance Law.

LOUIS NEIL VAN ZYL, born Griquatown, South Africa, May 11, 1957; admitted, 1985, Cape Province; 1987, Transvaal. *Education:* University of Stellenbosch (B.A., 1978; LL.B., 1980). *LANGUAGES:* English and Afrikaans. *PRACTICE AREAS:* Labour Law; Industrial Relations.

MICHAEL JOHN DOIDGE, born East London, South Africa, February 24, 1938; admitted, 1988, Cape Province. *Education:* University of South Africa (B.A., 1967; B.Comm, 1969; B.Proc., 1986). *Member:* Law Society of The Cape of Good Hope. *LANGUAGES:* English and Afrikaans. *PRACTICE AREAS:* Estate Law; Trustee Law; Client Investment Law; Deceased Estate Law; Estate Planning; Trust Law; Wills; Taxation Law.

CONSULTANTS

LOUIS STEYN VAN ZYL, admitted, 1952, South Africa.

DENIS MORTIMORE TATHAM, admitted, 1946, South Africa.

JEAN-MARY BRECHIN, admitted, 1972, South Africa.

CRAIG NEIL CUNNINGHAM, admitted, 1991, South Africa.

GAVIN FITZMAURICE, admitted, 1994, South Africa.

ANTHONY EDWARD SAUERMAN, admitted, 1993, South Africa.

ANDREW MCCALMAN SIDDLE, admitted, 1989, South Africa.

MADGE JEAN TORRINGTON, admitted, 1967, South Africa.

RICHARD EDWARD MARCUS, admitted, 1989, South Africa.

AMANDA CATTO, admitted, 1995, South Africa.

JAMES MCKINNELL, admitted, 1995, South Africa.

TEMBA KALI, admitted, 1995, South Africa.

Languages: English, Afrikaans, Dutch, German, Xhosa.

MALLINICK, RESS, RICHMAN & CLOSENBERG

Attorneys, Notaries & Conveyancers

2 LONG STREET
CAPE TOWN 8001, SOUTH AFRICA
Telephone: + 27-21-419-4411
Telefax: + 27-21-217-207

European Office: 4 Carlton Gardens, Pall Mall, London, SW1Y 5AA. Telephone: + 44-171-930-8702. Telefax: + 44-171-930-8737.

General Practice, Corporate, Commercial, Taxation, Telecommunications, Entertainment, Arbitration, Banking, Foreign Investment, Property, Mortgages, Conveyancing, Labour, Litigation, Deceased Estates, Estate Planning, Trusts, Wills, Intellectual Property, Insolvency, Unfair Competition, Passing Off, Franchising, Licensing.

SOUTH AFRICAN RESIDENT PARTNERS

GERALD MALLINICK, Dip. Law (UCT); Admitted, 1960. *PRACTICE AREAS:* Commercial Law; Litigation.

JEFFREY CLOSENBERG, B.A., LL.B. (Rhodes); Admitted, 1963. *PRACTICE AREAS:* Commercial Law.

JOHN ADRIAN LEVIN, B.A. (Stell); Dip. Law (UCT); Admitted, 1967. *PRACTICE AREAS:* Commercial Law; Contract Law.

HILTON GISCHEN, B. Proc. (Wits); Admitted, 1979. *PRACTICE AREAS:* Commercial Litigation; Insolvency Law.

MICHAEL RADOMSKY, B. Proc. (UCT); Admitted, 1980. *PRACTICE AREAS:* Property Law; Conveyancing Law.

ALAN JAMES JEFTHA, B.A., LL.B. (UWC); Admitted, 1982. *PRACTICE AREAS:* Intellectual Property; Advertising Law; Marketing Law; Trade Law.

JILL HILARY SINGER, B.A., LL.B. (UCT); Admitted, 1986. *PRACTICE AREAS:* Commercial Law; Family Law.

STEPHEN CHARLES HARDING, B. Proc. (Wits); Admitted, 1978. *PRACTICE AREAS:* Property Law; Conveyancing Law.

FREDERICK STIGLINGH HUMAN, B. Comm., LL.B. (Stell); Admitted, 1983. *PRACTICE AREAS:* Commercial Law.

SIMEON GERALD KORBER, B.A., LL.B. (UCT); Admitted, 1988. *PRACTICE AREAS:* Commercial Litigation; Insolvency Law.

ALAN CHRISTOPHER DODSON, B. Comm., LL.B. (Natal); LL.M. (Cantab); Higher Diploma in Tax Law (UCT); Admitted, 1987. *PRACTICE AREAS:* Commercial Law; Litigation; Administrative Law; Labour Law.

MICHAEL JOHN READ EVANS, B.A. (Hons.), LL.B. Higher Diploma in Tax Law (UCT); Admitted, 1989. *PRACTICE AREAS:* Commercial Litigation; Administrative Law; Public Interest Law.

CONSULTANTS

ARNOLD SIMON RUCH, Dip. Law; Admitted, 1956. *PRACTICE AREAS:* Property Law; Conveyancing Law.

PIERRE ANDRÉ DU PREEZ, B. Comm., LL.B. (Stell); LL.M. (London); Admitted, 1980. *PRACTICE AREAS:* Commercial Law; Labour Law.

LONDON RESIDENT PARTNERS

MICHAEL JOSEPH RICHMAN, Dip. Law (UNISA); Admitted, 1962. *PRACTICE AREAS:* Commercial Law; International Trade.

ABRAHAM ANDRE COETZEE, B.A., LL.B. (Stell); Ph.D. (Edinburgh); Higher Diploma in Company Law (Wits); Admitted, 1982. *PRACTICE AREAS:* Commercial Law; Entertainment; Telecommunications Law.

JUSTIN FRANK HARDCASTLE, B. Proc. LL.B. (UCT); LL.M. (London); Admitted, 1990. *PRACTICE AREAS:* Commercial Law; Telecommunication Law; International Trade Law; Immigration Law.

ROBERT SCHEINER, B.A., LL.B. (Cape Town); Admitted, 1987. *PRACTICE AREAS:* Commercial and Company Law; Telecommunications Law; Fishing and Food Distribution; Shipping Law.

(This Listing Continued)

MELLISSA PALMER, B.A., LL.B. (Cape Town); LL.M. (Cantab); Admitted, 1989. *PRACTICE AREAS:* Litigation; Commercial Law; Telecommunications Law; International Trade Law.

NON-RESIDENT LONDON CONSULTANT

PROF. JOHN R.P. MORRIS, B. Comm. (Wits); C.A. (S.A.) A.C.M.A.; (Not Admitted). *PRACTICE AREAS:* Tax Law.

SILBERBAUERS

Established in 1885

1ST FLOOR, SOUTHERN LIFE CENTRE
8 RIEBEEK STREET
P.O. BOX 921, CAPE TOWN 8000
CAPE TOWN 8001, SOUTH AFRICA
Telephone: (2721) 4199040
Telex: 57-20349 SA
Telefax: (2721) 214348
Cable Address: "Silberbauer"

Commercial, Marine, Marine Insurance, Salvage, Administrative, Taxation, Arbitration, Litigation, Insurance, Administration of Estates and Conveyancing Law.

MEMBERS OF FIRM

JOHN FREDERICK VAN NIEKERK, admitted, 1960, South Africa.

LUCIEN JOHANN LE ROUX, admitted, 1970, South Africa.

GRAHAM LARRY HESTER, admitted, 1971, South Africa.

ANTHONIE TROSKIE, admitted, 1973, South Africa.

MATTHYS ANDRIES JOHANNES SEYFFERT, admitted, 1975, South Africa.

MARTHINUS THEUNIS STEYN, admitted, 1977, South Africa.

MARTINE COLLETTE NEWMAN, admitted, 1983, South Africa.

GERHARD JOZUA BRITS, admitted, 1984, South Africa.

FRANCIS TURNER NEWHAM, admitted, 1982, South Africa.

ANTON MORLAND MUSGRAVE, admitted, 1981, South Africa.

HENDRIK JOHANNES MOUTON, admitted, 1987, South Africa.

LEON BLIGNAUT, admitted, 1984, South Africa.

ANTONY PETER STILES, admitted, 1990, South Africa.

DAWID JOHANNES MALAN, admitted, 1988, South Africa.

JOHN BRUCE KIRKPATRICK, admitted, 1989, South Africa.

CHRISTOPHER JOHN MCCALLUM, admitted, 1990, South Africa.

EDUARD DEREK WILLE, admitted, 1990, South Africa.

MATHEW SYDNEY ASH, admitted, 1991, South Africa.

ASSOCIATES

Arlene Hearshaw   Nicola Caine
Carol Jean Wiggett   Lizette Frank
     Andrew Heiberg

SONNENBERG, HOFFMANN & GALOMBIK

Established in 1936

NORWICH ON ST. GEORGES
9 ST. GEORGES MALL
8001 CAPE TOWN, SOUTH AFRICA
Telephone: (021) 419 2360
Fax: (021) 419 8928 International +2721
Telex: (021) 52 1057 Telegrams: "Enact" DX 14

London, England Office: 45 Crawford Place, W1H 1HX. Telephone: 0944-171-7241241. Telefax: 0944-171-7242260.

FIRM PROFILE: Established in 1936, Sonnenberg Hoffmann & Galombiks growth to its present size of over 40 qualified lawyers has led to its becoming one of Cape Town's leading law firms. The firm's practice is broadly-based and members offer a high level of competence and experience in all areas of legal practice, having regard to the highest professional

(This Listing Continued)

standards and ethics. All our members speak English and Afrikaans and a number speak French, German and Hebrew.

MEMBERS OF FIRM

DAVID MORRIS NUREK, admitted, 1973, Cape Town. (Chairman). *PRACTICE AREAS:* Commercial Law; Corporate Law; Securities Regulation; Liquor Licensing.

MICHAEL GRAHAM BELLAIRS, admitted, 1983, Cape Town. *PRACTICE AREAS:* Debt Collection.

BRIAN STUART BIEBUYCK, admitted, 1985, Cape Town. *PRACTICE AREAS:* Commercial Litigation; Building Law; Construction Law; Engineering Litigation.

PETRUS COENRAAD FABER, admitted, 1986, Cape Town. (Managing Director). *PRACTICE AREAS:* Labour Law; Industrial Relations; Employment Contracts.

JEFFREY RODNEY FLAX, admitted, 1972, Cape Town. *PRACTICE AREAS:* Personal Planning; Estates; Trust Administration; Exchange Control.

ROBERT MENDEL GAD, admitted, 1988, Cape Town. *PRACTICE AREAS:* Taxation.

CECIL GELBART, admitted, 1972, Cape Town. Notary Public. *PRACTICE AREAS:* Commercial Litigation; Maritime Law; International Trade.

LAWRENCE HELMAN, admitted, 1987, Cape Town. *PRACTICE AREAS:* Commercial Law; Corporate Law.

LEONARD MALCOLM HERSCH, admitted, 1975, Cape Town. *PRACTICE AREAS:* Property Law.

LEONARD CHARLES KATZ, admitted, 1987, Cape Town. *PRACTICE AREAS:* Insolvency Law; Corporate Reconstruction.

STEPHEN BARRY LEVETAN, admitted, 1980, Cape Town. *PRACTICE AREAS:* Insurance Litigation; Professional Indemnity; Public Liability; Fidelity Insurance; Medical Malpractice.

GRAHAM BAREND LIEBENBERG, admitted, 1969, Cape Town. *PRACTICE AREAS:* Property Law.

ANTON MICHIEL JACOBUS MELCK, admitted, 1989, Cape Town. Notary Public. *PRACTICE AREAS:* Property Law.

MICHAEL LEONARD SAREMBOCK, admitted, 1961, Cape Town. Notary Public. *PRACTICE AREAS:* Commercial Law; Corporate Law; Securities Regulation; Personal Planning.

BRIAN SCHEINER, admitted, 1989, Cape Town. *PRACTICE AREAS:* Commercial Law; Corporate Law; Environmental Law.

CHARLES ADAMSON SMITH, admitted, 1965, Pretoria. Notary Public. *PRACTICE AREAS:* Property Law; Environmental Law.

ALAN SOLOMONS, admitted, 1978, Cape Town. *PRACTICE AREAS:* Matrimonial Law; Family Law; Commercial Litigation; Insurance Law; Medical Malpractice.

SUSAN STELZNER, admitted, 1989, Cape Town. *PRACTICE AREAS:* Labour Law; Industrial Relations; Employment Contracts.

JOHN MICHAEL ZIEFF, admitted, 1989, Cape Town. *PRACTICE AREAS:* Constitutional Law; Commercial Litigation.

ARNOLD GALOMBIK, admitted, 1945, Cape Town. (Executive Consultant). *PRACTICE AREAS:* Commercial Law; Corporate Law; Securities Regulation.

DAVID ZACKON, admitted, 1955, Grahamstown. (Executive Consultant). *PRACTICE AREAS:* Property Law.

CULLEN PENNY, C.A., S.A. (General Manager).

SYFRET GODLONTON-FULLER MOORE INC.

Attorneys, Notaries & Conveyancers
Established in 1853
10TH & 11TH FLOORS, WALDORF, ST. GEORGE'S MALL
P.O. BOX 695
CAPE TOWN 8000, SOUTH AFRICA
Telephone: 247030
International: 27 21 247030
Cable Address: "Sygolo"
Telex: 527881
Telefax: 245801

General Practice, Litigation, Corporate, Commercial, Tax, Trust and Real Estate Law.

FIRM PROFILE: OUR MISSION IS TO DELIVER A COMPREHENSIVE AND QUALITY LEGAL SERVICE TO THOSE DOING BUSINESS IN SOUTH AFRICA.

MAX HENRY HALES, admitted, 1954. *LANGUAGES:* English. *PRACTICE AREAS:* Commercial and Trust Law; Ecclesiastical Law.

PATRICK ARTHUR MULLINER, admitted, 1957. *LANGUAGES:* English. *PRACTICE AREAS:* Commercial and Property Law.

ANDREW CLIVE FULLER, admitted, 1961. *LANGUAGES:* English. *PRACTICE AREAS:* Property; Mortgages.

ANDREW DENNIS DALLING, admitted, 1969. *LANGUAGES:* English. *PRACTICE AREAS:* Litigation and Labour Law.

JOHN JARDIM GOMES, admitted, 1970. *LANGUAGES:* English. *PRACTICE AREAS:* Zoning; Planning; Land Use; Condominium Law.

ANTHONY JOHN NOYES PLUMMER, admitted, 1964. *LANGUAGES:* English. *PRACTICE AREAS:* Zoning; Planning; Mortgages.

JOHN LESLIE ROBERTSON, admitted, 1960. *LANGUAGES:* English. *PRACTICE AREAS:* Property Law.

ALEXANDER GORDON DOSE, admitted, 1964. *LANGUAGES:* English. *PRACTICE AREAS:* Trusts, Estates and Wills.

PETER GIDEON JOUBERT, admitted, 1961. *LANGUAGES:* English. *PRACTICE AREAS:* Property Law.

WILLIAM HENRY PEGRUM, admitted, 1969. *LANGUAGES:* English. *PRACTICE AREAS:* Property Law.

JOHAN NESER, admitted, 1982. *LANGUAGES:* English. *PRACTICE AREAS:* Commercial; Copyright; Trademark; Taxation.

NICHOLAS WILLIAM MULLER, admitted, 1981. *LANGUAGES:* English. *PRACTICE AREAS:* Litigation; Medical Malpractice; Personal Injury.

INGRID BROODRYK, admitted, 1985. *LANGUAGES:* English. *PRACTICE AREAS:* Litigation.

MICHAEL RHODES COLLINS, admitted, 1987. *LANGUAGES:* English. *PRACTICE AREAS:* Property; Environmental Law.

FRANCES GLYNN ANDERSON, admitted, 1989. *LANGUAGES:* English. *PRACTICE AREAS:* Labour Law.

DAVID MICHAEL THOMPSON, admitted, 1990. *LANGUAGES:* English. *PRACTICE AREAS:* Commercial; Taxation.

ASSOCIATES

BASIL JOHN COWDRY, admitted, 1992. *LANGUAGES:* English. *PRACTICE AREAS:* Property; Mortgages.

DAVID JOHN DARLEY WADDILOVE, admitted, 1992. *LANGUAGES:* English. *PRACTICE AREAS:* Litigation; Environmental Law.

GABRIEL CORDIER LE ROUX, admitted, 1988. *LANGUAGES:* English.

VICTOR SOUTHWELL, admitted, 1993. *LANGUAGES:* English. *PRACTICE AREAS:* Constitutional Law.

ELMARIE DE BRUIN, admitted, 1991. *LANGUAGES:* English. *PRACTICE AREAS:* Trademark Law.

(This Listing Continued)

SYFRET GODLONTON-FULLER MOORE INC., Cape Town—Continued

RICHARD MARCUS, admitted, 1989. *LANGUAGES:* English. *PRACTICE AREAS:* Litigation; Environmental Law.

CONSULTANTS

B. K. Corder
J. Bellamy
B.J. Van Heerden

ADAMS & ADAMS

Patent Attorneys, Trademark Agents, Attorneys, Conveyancers and
Maritime Lawyers

Established in 1917

6TH FLOOR, 136 VICTORIA EMBANKMENT
DURBAN 4001, SOUTH AFRICA

Telephone: National (031) 304 3773, International +27 31 304 3773
Facsimile: 27 31 3043799

Mailing Address: P.O. Box 1538, Durban, 4000

Pretoria, South Africa Office: 429 Church Street, 0002. P.O. Box 1014, Pretoria, 0001. Telephone: National (012) 320 8500, International +27 12 320 8500. Telex: 3 22157 ADAMS SA. Facsimile: 27 12 320 8550.

Johannesburg, South Africa Office: 3rd floor, North Park, 20 Girton Rd, Parktown 2193. P.O. Box 10155, 2000. Telephone: National (011) 6425057 International +27 11 6425057. Facsimile: 27 11 6421914.

Cape Town, South Africa Office: 2817 Trust Bank Centre, Heerengracht, 8001. P.O. Box 1513, 8000. Telephone: National (021) 25 3607, International +27 21 25 3607. Facsimile: 27 21 4195729.

Patent and Trademark.

RESIDENT PARTNERS

M.W.H. POSEMANN. *PRACTICE AREAS:* Maritime Law; Labour Law.

M. ROTTEVEEL. *PRACTICE AREAS:* Patent Drafting; Prosecution and Filing.

(For Complete List of Personnel, see Professional Biographies at Pretoria).

COX YEATS

Established in 1964

12TH FLOOR, VICTORIA MAINE
71 VICTORIA EMBANKMENT
DURBAN 4001, SOUTH AFRICA
Telephone: 27-31-3042851
Fax: 27-31-3013540

Business and Banking Law, Mergers and Acquisitions, Tax Law, Arbitration and Civil Litigation, Labour Law, Maritime and Admiralty Law, Property Law, Trusts and Estates.

FIRM PROFILE: The activities of our corporate clients include banking, property development, mining, engineering, building, manufacturing, local government, merchandising, property development, sugar milling, farming and shipping. For individual clients we do financial planning, trusts, wills, conveyancing including sectional title and share block transactions and the administration of estates.

MEMBERS OF FIRM

GRAHAM COX, born Bloemfontein, South Africa, 1932; admitted, 1960, Pietermaritzburg. *Education:* University of Cape Town (B.Com.; LL.B.). *Member:* Natal Law Society (President, 1981-1983); Law Society of Swaziland; International Bar Association; Fellow of the Association of Arbitrators. *LANGUAGES:* English. *PRACTICE AREAS:* Corporate Law; Banking Law; Taxation Law; Arbitration; Alternative Dispute Resolution.

JEREMY YEATS, born England, 1941; admitted, 1965, Pietermaritzburg. *Education:* University of Natal (B.A.; LL.B.). Notary Public. *Member:* Natal Law Society. *LANGUAGES:* English. *PRACTICE AREAS:* Corporate Law; Property and Real Estate Law; Mining Law.

(This Listing Continued)

ROGER GREEN, born Durban, South Africa, 1947; admitted, 1973, Pietermaritzburg. *Education:* University of Natal (B.Com.; LL.B.). *Member:* Natal Law Society. *LANGUAGES:* English. *PRACTICE AREAS:* Property and Real Estate Law.

ALASTAIR HAY, born Vereeniging, South Africa, 1952; admitted, 1978, Pietermaritzburg. *Education:* University of Natal (B.Com.; LL.B.; Diploma in Shipping Law). Notary Public. *Member:* Natal Law Society. *LANGUAGES:* English. *PRACTICE AREAS:* Construction Law; Maritime Law; Admiralty Law; Labour Law; Trusts and Estates.

CAMPBELL ALEXANDER, born Durban, South Africa, 1954; admitted, 1983, Pietermaritzburg. *Education:* University of Natal (B.Com.; LL.B.). *Member:* Natal Law Society. *LANGUAGES:* English. *PRACTICE AREAS:* Civil Litigation; Aviation Law; Bankruptcy Law.

PETER NEL, born Cape Town, South Africa, 1956; admitted, 1984, Cape Town. *Education:* University of Cape Town (B.A.; LL.B.); University of Natal (Diploma in Tax Law). *Member:* Natal Law Society. *LANGUAGES:* English. *PRACTICE AREAS:* Corporate Law; Taxation Law.

MICHAEL VAN ZYL, born Durban, South Africa, 1957; admitted, 1985, Pietermaritzburg. *Education:* University of Natal (B.A.; LL.B.). Notary Public. *Member:* Natal Law Society. *LANGUAGES:* English. *PRACTICE AREAS:* Property and Real Estate Law.

THABANI JALI, born Durban, South Africa, 1959; admitted, 1987, Pietermaritzburg. *Education:* University of Fort Hare (B.A.); University of Natal (LL.B.); Tulane University (LL.M.). *Member:* Natal Law Society. *LANGUAGES:* English, Zulu and Xhosa. *PRACTICE AREAS:* Civil Litigation; Mediation Law; Alternative Dispute Resolution; Labour Law.

IAN COX, born Durban, South Africa, 1960; admitted, 1987, Johannesburg. *Education:* University of Natal (B.A.; LL.B., Diploma in Tax Law). *Member:* Natal Law Society. *LANGUAGES:* English. *PRACTICE AREAS:* Civil Litigation; Transport Law; Arbitration; Local Government; Administrative Law.

MICHAEL JACKSON, born East London, South Africa, 1960; admitted, 1990, Pietermaritzburg. *Education:* University of Natal (B.Com.; LL.B.); University of Cambridge (LL.M.). *Member:* Natal Law Society. *LANGUAGES:* English. *PRACTICE AREAS:* Civil Litigation.

RICHARD DONACHIE, born Zimbabwe, 1963; admitted, 1991. *Education:* University of Natal (B.A.; LL.B.). *Member:* Natal Law Society. *LANGUAGES:* English. *PRACTICE AREAS:* Civil Litigation; Property and Real Estate Law; Estates.

CRAIG BRENNAN, born Durban, South Africa, 1963; admitted, 1992. *Education:* University of Natal (B.A.; LL.B.), Notary Public. *Member:* Natal Law Society. *LANGUAGES:* English. *PRACTICE AREAS:* Civil Litigation; Administration of Estates.

PETER FEUILHERADE, born Durban, 1964; admitted, 1993. *Education:* University of Natal (B.A., Hons; LL.B.). *Member:* Natal Law Society. *LANGUAGES:* English. *PRACTICE AREAS:* Civil Litigation; Bankruptcy Law.

DENEYS REITZ

4TH FLOOR, SALISBURY HOUSE
332 SMITH STREET
P.O. BOX 2010
DURBAN, SOUTH AFRICA
Telephone: (International): (27) (031) 301-7345 or (031) 301-8361
Teletex: (9) 650049
Fax: (27) (031) 301-3346

Johannesburg Office: 10 Anderson Street, Johannesburg, 2001. P.O. Box 61334, Marshalltown 2107. Telephone: (27) (011) 833-5600. Telex: 4-85432 SA. Teletex: (9) 450607. Fax: (27) (011) 838-7444. Docex 215.

Sandton Office: Ground Floor, Kohler House, 4 Pybus Road, (Sandton 2199). P.O. Box 784903, Sandton 2146. Telephone: (27) (011) 783-8875 and (011) 884-4900. Fax: (27) (011) 884-5489. Telex: 4-26324 SA.

(For Complete Biographical Data on all Personnel see Professional Biographies at Johannesburg)

GARLICKE & BOUSFIELD INC.

Established in 1867

23RD FLOOR, DURBAN BAY HOUSE
333 SMITH STREET
DURBAN 4001, SOUTH AFRICA
Telephone: 27-31-3057595
Fax: 27-31-3042784 (Grps 2 & 3)
Telex: 620151 SA (BGBDBN)
Teletex: 959-650032
Dx: DOCEX 2, Durban

GARLICKE & BOUSFIELD INC is a member of LAWLINK in association with
BOWMAN GILFILLAN HAYMAN GODFREY INC.- Johannesburg and London
FAIRBRIDGE ARDERNE & LAWTON INC.- Cape Town
MacROBERT DeVILLIERS LUNNON & TINDALL INC.- Pretoria
Also in association with- VENN NEMETH & HART- Pietermaritzburg

Corporate and Commercial, Taxation, Sugar, Stock Exchange, Intellectual Property (patents, trademarks, copyright), Property and Conveyancing, Building, Construction and Engineering, Estates and Trust, Estate Planning, Environmental Law, Aviation, Insurance, Mining, General Litigation, Insolvency, Banking, Family Mediation, Industrial Relations, Arbitration, Collections, Shipping and International Trade, Customs, Excise and Water.

FIRM PROFILE: Garlicke & Bousfield was established in 1867 and is one of Durban's largest law firms offering clients a comprehensive range of legal services. The firm is structured so as to ensure that clients are served by practitioners whose training and experience relate to the specific legal problems with which they deal.

DAVID R D WHITE. PRACTICE AREAS: Commercial; Corporate; Stock Exchange; Taxation.

NOEL R PISTORIUS. PRACTICE AREAS: Commercial; Corporate; Sugar; Estate Planning; Property.

PETER SLACK. PRACTICE AREAS: Corporate; Commercial; Sugar; Property; Intellectual Property.

RICHARD C W PEMBERTON. PRACTICE AREAS: Litigation; Labour Law; Arbitration.

ROBERT REID. PRACTICE AREAS: Conveyancing; Property; Township Development.

CRAIG JONES. PRACTICE AREAS: Litigation; Water; Banking Law; Insolvency.

BRIAN S JENNINGS. PRACTICE AREAS: Corporate; Commercial; Mining; Sport and Recreation.

DAVID H RAMSAY. PRACTICE AREAS: Conveyancing; Property; Shareblock/Sectional Title Developments.

DON B ALLAWAY. PRACTICE AREAS: Corporate; Commercial; Building; Construction; Engineering; Arbitration.

ASHWIN TRIKAMJEE. PRACTICE AREAS: Litigation; Criminal Law.

GARY M RADEMEYER. PRACTICE AREAS: Litigation; Insolvency; Taxation; Building; Engineering.

JOSEPH G WHITTLE. PRACTICE AREAS: Collections; Litigation.

DAVID J VINNICOMBE. PRACTICE AREAS: Labour; Litigation.

LAURON F BUYS. PRACTICE AREAS: Estates; Trusts; Family Mediation; Estate Planning.

ANTHONY J. L. NORTON. PRACTICE AREAS: Shipping; International Trade and Finance.

JENNY MCINTOSH. PRACTICE AREAS: Shipping; International Trade and Finance; Customs and Excise.

CHRISTOPHER N MORTIMER. PRACTICE AREAS: Environmental; Insolvency; Labour; General Litigation.

YVONNE L BODEN. PRACTICE AREAS: Estates; Estate Planning; Trusts.

STEVEN I WALLACE. PRACTICE AREAS: Shipping; International Trade and Finance.

(This Listing Continued)

JEREMY MILES. PRACTICE AREAS: Shipping; International Trade; Immigration.

MICHAEL D GAMMIE. PRACTICE AREAS: Commercial; Property.

MICHAEL A C MURPHY. PRACTICE AREAS: Insolvency; Labour; General Litigation.

HAYDN T HILLESTAD. PRACTICE AREAS: Corporate; Commercial; Tax.

CONSULTANTS

David Geerdts
Michael E Emanuel

David Pistorius
Ishwarbhai Amin

SHEPSTONE & WYLIE

Established in 1892

SCOTSWOOD
35 ALIWAL STREET
DURBAN 4001, SOUTH AFRICA
Telephone: 27-31-3020111
Fax: 27-31-3042862

Corporate and Commercial Law, Maritime, International and Insurance Law, Industrial Relations and Labour Law, Litigation, Financial Recoveries and Matrimonial Law, Property Services and Conveyancing, Municipal and Media Law, Planning and Environmental Law, Intellectual Property Law, Sports and Recreation Law, Trusts, Estates and Family Law.

FIRM PROFILE: Established in 1892, Shepstone & Wylie is a leading South African legal firm offering a full range of personal, corporate and commercial legal services. With 28 partners, and a number of local and international affiliations, the practice provides representation throughout Southern Africa and in Europe. To ensure focused representation, the firm has developed specialist departments to deal with each legal discipline.

MEMBERS OF FIRM

DAVID ASHERSON, born Durban, South Africa, May 29, 1949. *Education:* UNISA (Attorneys Admission). *Member:* Association of Law Societies of RSA (President); Durban Regional Chamber of Business (Member, Trade and Info Committee). *LANGUAGES:* English and Afrikaans. *PRACTICE AREAS:* Corporate and Commercial; Mergers and Acquisitions; Joint Ventures.

NORMAN BRAUTESETH, born Salisbury, Rhodesia, February 7, 1954. *Education:* Natal University. *Member:* Association of Law Societies (Chairman, Environmental Committee); Environmental Law Association of South Africa (Chairman). *LANGUAGES:* English and Afrikaans. *PRACTICE AREAS:* Municipal Law; Media Law; Environmental Law.

DICK BREYTENBACH, born Bethlehem, South Africa, May 11, 1950. *Education:* University of The Orange Free State (B.A., Proc.). *LANGUAGES:* English and Afrikaans. *PRACTICE AREAS:* Property Law.

LIONEL BURGER, born Johannesburg, South Africa, April 29, 1959. *Education:* Natal University (B.A.; LL.B.). *LANGUAGES:* English and Afrikaans. *PRACTICE AREAS:* Litigation; Criminal Law; Financial Recoveries.

PAUL CANTER, born Durban, South Africa, May 1, 1946. *Education:* Natal University, Durban (B.A.); UNISA (B.I.U.E.I.S.). *Member:* S.A. Institute of International Affairs; Durban Childrens Home (President); Operation Upgrade (Adult Literacy). *LANGUAGES:* English and Afrikaans. *PRACTICE AREAS:* Trusts; Estates; Family Law.

SIMON CHETWYND-PALMER, born Lusaka, Zambia. *Education:* Natal University (B.A.; LL.B.); University of Victoria (Accreditation Certificate); University of British Columbia (Real Estate and Sub Mortgage Brokers Course). *Member:* Law Society of British Columbia; Natal Law Society. *LANGUAGES:* English. *PRACTICE AREAS:* Litigation; Financial Recoveries; Canadian Immigration Law.

WILLIE COETZEE, born Germiston, South Africa, December 6, 1951. *Education:* Stellenbosch University (B.Com.; LL.B.). Arbitrator; I.M.S.S.A.; A.D.R.A.S.A. *Member:* Durban Regional Chamber of Business (Member, Human Resource Committee). *LANGUAGES:* English and Afrikaans. *PRACTICE AREAS:* Industrial Relations Law; Labour Law.

ESTELLE DE WET, born Pietermaritzburg, South Africa, February 22, 1958. *Education:* University of Natal, Durban (B.A.; LL.B.). *LANGUAGES:* English and Afrikaans. *PRACTICE AREAS:* Litigation; Matrimonial and Family Law.

(This Listing Continued)

SHEPSTONE & WYLIE, Durban—Continued

ANDREW DONNELLY, born Durban, South Africa, April 24, 1960. *Education:* University of Natal, Durban (B.A.; LL.B.). *LANGUAGES:* English and Afrikaans. *PRACTICE AREAS:* Litigation; Commercial and Insolvency.

SHANE DWYER, born Pietermaritzburg, Natal, April 5, 1946. *Education:* Stellenbosch University (B.A.); Natal University (LL.B.). *Member:* Maritime Law Association; Institute of Shipbrokers; S.A. Institute of International Affairs. *LANGUAGES:* English, Afrikaans and Zulu. *PRACTICE AREAS:* Maritime; Air; Commodity and International Law.

DUNSTAN FARRELL, born Durban, South Africa, August 18, 1959. *Education:* University of Natal, Pietermaritzburg (B.A.; LL.B.); Edinburgh University (Dip. I.R.; LL.M.). *LANGUAGES:* English, Afrikaans and Zulu. *PRACTICE AREAS:* Industrial Relations; Labour Law.

ROGER GIFFORD, born Simla, India, August 13, 1933. *Education:* Natal University (Attorneys Admission). *LANGUAGES:* English and Afrikaans. *PRACTICE AREAS:* Maritime Law; Liquidations.

MICHAEL HANDS, born Durban, South Africa, April 5, 1941. *Education:* University of Natal (B.A.; LL.B.). *Member:* Association of Arbitrators (S.A.); Natal Municipal Association (Legal Sub-Committee). *LANGUAGES:* English and Afrikaans. *PRACTICE AREAS:* Administrative; Regulatory; Constitutional Law; Media Law.

KEVIN HOJEM, born Durban, South Africa, July 25, 1944. *Education:* UNISA (Attorneys Admission). *Member:* Durban Regional Chamber of Business (Council Member and Central Business Division); Goldstone Commission. *LANGUAGES:* English and Afrikaans. *PRACTICE AREAS:* Commercial Litigation; Arbitration; Foreclosures and Financial Recoveries.

BRIAN LEISEGANG, born Nkandla, Zululand, January 24, 1931. *Education:* UNISA (B.A.); Natal University (LL.B.). Member, Operation Upgrade (Adult Literacy). *LANGUAGES:* English and Afrikaans. *PRACTICE AREAS:* Property Law.

MURRAY LEYDEN, born Durban, South Africa, March 23, 1953. *Education:* University of Natal (B.Com.; LL.B.). *Member:* Insurance Institute of South Africa. *LANGUAGES:* English and Afrikaans. *PRACTICE AREAS:* Insurance Law; Personal Injury Claims.

MIKE MAESO, born Chingola, Zambia, March 23, 1960. *Education:* University of Natal (B.A., LL.B.). *LANGUAGES:* English and Afrikaans. *PRACTICE AREAS:* Industrial Relations; Labour Law.

BEVERLEY NELSON, born Johannesburg, South Africa, December 13, 1956. *Education:* University of Witwatersrand (B.A.; LL.B.). Trustee, Thembalabantu Community Creche, Bambayi. *Member:* Natal Law Society Council. *LANGUAGES:* English. *PRACTICE AREAS:* Property Law.

MARTIN OOSTHUIZEN, born Port Elizabeth, Eastern Cape, January 15, 1948. *Education:* University of Stellenbosch (B.A.: LL.B.). *LANGUAGES:* English. *PRACTICE AREAS:* Industrial Relations; Labour Law.

ANDY PIKE, born Johannesburg, South Africa, October 5, 1958. *Education:* University of Witwatersrand (B.A.; LL.B.). *Member:* Maritime Law Association; Society of Risk Managers, South Africa; S.A. Institute of Ship Brokers; Durban for the Olympics Legal Working Group. *LANGUAGES:* English and Afrikaans. *PRACTICE AREAS:* Maritime; Insurance; Sports Law.

KRISH REDDY, born Durban, South Africa, January 7, 1949. *Education:* UNISA (B.Proc.). *Member:* Maritime Law Association; Institute of Shipbrokers; S.A. Institute of International Affairs. *LANGUAGES:* English. *PRACTICE AREAS:* Maritime Law.

NICK THEUNISSEN, born Durban, South Africa, August 3, 1943. *Education:* University of Natal (B.Econ.; LL.B.); UNISA (Dip in Law of Taxation). Member, Council, University of Natal. *LANGUAGES:* English and Afrikaans. *PRACTICE AREAS:* Corporate and Commercial Law; Mergers and Acquisitions; Joint Ventures.

DAVID WARMBACK, born Durban, South Africa, October 4, 1961. *Education:* University of Natal (B.A., LL.B.). *PRACTICE AREAS:* Property Law.

(This Listing Continued)

NIGEL WOODROFFE, born February 8, 1957. *Education:* Natal University (B.A., LL.B). *LANGUAGES:* English and Afrikaans. *PRACTICE AREAS:* Industrial Relations; Labour Law.

ADAMS & ADAMS

Patent Attorneys

Established in 1917

3RD FLOOR, NORTH PARK, 20 GIRTON ROAD, PARKTOWN 2193
JOHANNESBURG 2001, SOUTH AFRICA
Telephone: National (011) 6425057, International +27 11 642 5057
Facsimile: 27 11 6421914

Mailing Address: P.O. Box 10155, Johannesburg, 2000

Pretoria, South Africa Office: 429 Church Street, 0002. P.O. Box 1014, Pretoria, 0001. Telephone: National (012) 320 8500, International +27 12 320 8500. Telex: 3 22157 ADAMS SA. Facsimile: 27 12 320 8550.

Cape Town, South Africa Office: 2817 Trust Bank Centre, Heerengracht, 8001. P.O. Box 1513, 8000. Telephone: National (021) 25 3607, International +27 21 25 3607. Facsimile: 2721 4195729.

Durban, South Africa Office: 6th floor, 136 Victoria Embankment, 4001. P.O. Box 1538, 4000. Telephone: National (031) 304 3773, International +27 31 304 3773. Facsimile: 27 31 304 3799.

Patent and Trademark.

RESIDENT PARTNERS

A. LEWIS. PRACTICE AREAS: Patent Drafting; Prosecution and Litigation.

C.H. BERMAN. PRACTICE AREAS: Patent Drafting; Prosecution and Filing.

(For Complete List of Personnel, see Professional Biographies at Pretoria).

BELL, DEWAR & HALL

Attorneys, Notaries Public & Conveyancers

Established in 1889

20TH FLOOR, 78 FOX STREET
JOHANNESBURG 2001, SOUTH AFRICA
Telephone: 011-838-8830
International: + (2711) 838-8830
Cable Address: "Justinian"
Telex: 4-88122
Telefax: 011-838-5088
Docex: 71 Johannesburg

Mailing Address: P.O. Box 4284, Johannesburg 2000, South Africa

Law: Administrative Law, Advertising Law, Arbitration, Bankruptcy, Competition Law, Conveyancing, Corporate Law, Criminal Law, Distributorship, Agency and Franchise Law, Employer's Liability, Entertainment Law, Family Law, Food and Drug Regulations, Foreign Investments, Industrial Relations and Labour Law, Insurance Law, International Contracts, International Private Law, Public Interest Law, Litigation, Negligence Law, Pension Law, Personal Injury Law, Product Liability Law, Property and Real Estate Law, Rent and Lease, Transport Law, General Legal Practice.
Intellectual Property: Copyright Law, License Negotiation, Trade Mark Litigation, Transfer of Technology, General Intellectual Property Practice.
Taxation: Corporation Taxation, Indirect Taxation, Inheritance, Estate and Gift Taxation, Personal Income Taxation, Exchange Control, General Tax Practice.
Management: Corporate Strategy, Data Processing, Distribution, Mergers and Acquisitions.

PARTNERS

DUNCAN KERR SINCLAIR, admitted, 1972, South Africa. *Education:* (B.A.; LL.B.). (Senior Partner).

PAUL CHRISTOPHER BOTHA, admitted, 1988, South Africa. *Education:* (B.A.; LL.B.; H.Dip., Co. Law; H.Dip., Tax).

NIGEL DEAN CARMAN, admitted, 1976, South Africa. *Education:* (B.A.; LL.B.).

(This Listing Continued)

RUPERT OWEN GUSH, admitted, 1959, South Africa; 1961, Swaziland. *Education:* (B.Com.; LL.B.).

CLIFFORD LINDSAY GREEN, admitted, 1975, South Africa. *Education:* (B.A.; LL.B.).

DAVID REGINALD HOFFE, admitted, 1980, South Africa. *Education:* (B.A.; LL.B.; H.Dip., Tax).

BARRY DANE JACOBY, admitted, 1970, South Africa; 1974, Lesotho as Notary and Conveyancer; 1980, Victoria, Australia as Barrister and Solicitor. *Education:* (B.A.; Dip., Law).

STEPHEN FRANK LANGBRIDGE, admitted, 1987, South Africa. *Education:* (B.A.; LL.B.).

ANDREW NICHOLAS LEONTSINIS, admitted, 1977, South Africa and Lesotho. *Education:* (B.Com.; LL.B.).

ANDREW MITCHELL, admitted, 1978, South Africa. *Education:* (B.Sc., Eng.; LL.B.).

GREGORY ANTHONY NOTT, admitted, 1988, South Africa. *Education:* (B.A.; LL.B.).

OLEBOGANG MPUELENG ELIAS POOE, admitted, 1987, South Africa. *Education:* (B.Proc.).

CONSTANTINE RAKITZIS, admitted, 1988, South Africa. *Education:* (B.Juris, Econ; LL.B.).

NICOLAAS JACOBUS ROODT, admitted, 1981, South Africa. *Education:* (B.Com.; LL.B.).

MICHAEL JAMES SIMPSON, admitted, 1965, South Africa. *Education:* (B.A.; LL.B.; H.Dip., Tax).

ASSOCIATES

SUSAN CAROLINE ALBERTYN, admitted, 1990, South Africa. *Education:* (B.A.; LL.B.).

ROBERT RITCHIE CHARLTON, admitted, 1991, South Africa. *Education:* (B.A.; LL.B.).

SIBONGILE BEATRICE NCALA, admitted, 1987, South Africa. *Education:* (B.Proc.).

RICHARD GEORGE ROBINSON, admitted, 1989, South Africa. *Education:* (B.A., Hons.; LL.B.).

MICHAEL CRAIG VAN VUREN, admitted, 1991, South Africa. *Education:* (B.Com.; LL.B.; H.Dip., Tax).

MELINDA JANE WILSON, admitted, 1991, South Africa. *Education:* (B.A.; LL.B.).

CONSULTANTS

JAMES ANGUS SUTHERLAND, admitted, 1985, South Africa. *Education:* (B.Proc.).

PROFESSIONAL ASSISTANTS

Michael David Edmunds; Eric Van Den Berg; Beverley Wrighton-Clark.

Languages: English, Afrikaans and Black Languages.

BOWMAN GILFILLAN HAYMAN GODFREY INC.

Attorneys, Notaries and Conveyancers

Established in 1902

JCI HOUSE, 12TH FLOOR
28 HARRISON STREET
P.O. BOX 2439
JOHANNESBURG 2000, SOUTH AFRICA
Telephone: 27-11-836-2811
Fax: 27-11-836-6909

London England Office: Bowman Gilfillan Hayman Godfrey Limited. 36 John Street, London WC1N 2AT. Telephone: (071) 430-0888. Fax: (071) 430-2030.

General Practice, Corporate and Commercial Law, Income Tax, Property Law, Mining Law, Litigation, Labour Law, Estate Planning and Administration, Insolvency Law and Environmental Law.

MICHAEL WILFRED ADCOCK, admitted, 1970, South Africa.

(This Listing Continued)

CHARLES LEONARD VALKIN, admitted, 1963, South Africa.

CHRISTOPHER PETER BRIGGS, admitted, 1967, South Africa.

DENNIS EDWARD JOOSTE, admitted, 1968, South Africa; 1975, Lesotho.

MICHAEL FRANCIS DOHERTY, admitted, 1969, South Africa; 1980 California.

HYLTON WILSON COCHRANE, admitted, 1971, South Africa.

NEIL DAVID RISSIK, admitted, 1973, South Africa.

WALTER JULIUS TASMER, admitted, 1968, South Africa.

ANDREW DUNCAN, admitted, 1972, South Africa; 1977, Lesotho.

DAVID JOHN ADAMS, admitted, 1976, South Africa.

JONATHAN H. SCHLOSBERG, admitted, 1979, South Africa.

RAYMOND SAMUEL HALLATT, admitted, 1970, South Africa.

ROGER EDGAR WESTLEY BURMAN, admitted, 1981, South Africa.

PATRICK MILES CARTER, admitted, 1984, South Africa.

TIMOTHY JAMES GORDON-GRANT, admitted, 1984, South Africa.

ERNST PHILIPPUS ACKERMANN, admitted, 1984, South Africa.

GRAHAM HUGH DAMANT, admitted, 1983, South Africa.

VALERIE MOGG, admitted, 1981, South Africa.

JAN HUGO FYFER, admitted, 1975, South Africa.

IAN RONALD ELIAS JACOBSBERG, admitted, 1984, South Africa.

ROBERT ANDREW LEGH, admitted, 1988, South Africa.

PAULUS PETRUS JOHANNES COETSER, admitted, 1990, South Africa.

ERIC RUDYARD ARCHIBALD TRUEBODY, admitted, 1984, South Africa.

KAREN ANNE FULTON, admitted, 1991, South Africa.

COLLEEN ELVENA CURRIN, admitted, 1986, South Africa.

BRINK COHEN LE ROUX & ROODT INC.

SOUTH WING PPS HOUSE
6 ANERLEY ROAD
PARKTOWN 2193
JOHANNESBURG, SOUTH AFRICA
Telephone: +(11) 486 1555
Facsimile: +(11) 486 0303

Mailing Address: P.O. Box 2404, Houghton 2041, Johannesburg, South Africa

Administrative Law, Alternative Dispute Resolution, Banking and Finance, Competition, Computer Law, Constitutional Law, Construction and Engineering, Corporate and Commercial Law, Energy and Resources Law, Environmental Law, Estate Planning and Trusts, Exchange Control, Financial Markets & Securities Laws, Foreign Investment & Joint Ventures, Human Rights, Intellectual Property, Labour Law, Licensing, Franchising and Sponsorships, Litigation, Management Buy-Outs, Mining Law, Occupational Safety Law, Project and Structured Finance, Property: Commercial Planning and Development, Securities Regulation Panel, Share-blocks & Timeshare, Stock Exchange, Taxation, Takeovers, Mergers and Acquisitions.

JOHAN LOUW BRINK, born Pretoria, South Africa, March 16, 1953; admitted, 1979, South Africa. *Education:* University of Pretoria (B.Com., 1974); University of South Africa (LL.B., 1978); London School of Economics, LSE, (LL.M., 1980); University of the Witwatersrand (H. Dip. Tax, 1982). Lecturer, Dept. of Mercantile Law, University of South Africa, 1978-1979. Guest Lecturer: University of South Africa; Rand Afrikaans University; University of the Orange Free State. Co-Author: "Companies," Butterworths' The Law of South Africa, Joubert. *Member:* International Bar Association (Capital Markets Forum & Committees); Transvaal Law Society; Johannesburg Attorneys' Association. *LANGUAGES:* English and Afrikaans. *PRACTICE AREAS:* Takeovers, Mergers and Acquisitions; Foreign Investment and Joint Ventures; Stock Exchange Law; Flota-

(This Listing Continued)

BRINK COHEN LE ROUX & ROODT INC.,
Johannesburg—Continued

tions; Issues and Rights Offers; Financial Law; Capital Markets and Securities Law; Commercial Law.

JOHAN ANTON ROODT, born Pretoria, South Africa, May 8, 1953; admitted, 1980, South Africa. *Education:* University of Pretoria (B.Com., 1974); University of South Africa (B.Proc., 1977). *Member:* The Standing Advisory Committee on Company Law (Member, Share Blocks Sub Committee); International Bar Association (Sections on: Energy & Resources Law; Business Law); Law Society of Transvaal; Association of Corporate Treasurers of South Africa. *LANGUAGES:* Afrikaans and English. *PRACTICE AREAS:* Corporate Law; Commercial Law; Mergers and Acquisitions; Mining & Natural Resources Law; Banking; Finance and Financial Markets; Property Planning & Development Law.

WILLEM PETRUS LE ROUX, born Lichtenburg, South Africa, June 14, 1952; admitted, 1981, South Africa. *Education:* University of Pretoria (B. Jur., 1973; LL.B., 1975). Associate Professor, Labour Law, Rand Afrikaans University, 1994. Arbitrator in Labour Law, Independent Mediation Service of South Africa, 1991—. *Member:* National Manpower Commission (Member, 1993—); Johannesburg Attorneys Association; Transvaal Law Society. *LANGUAGES:* English and Afrikaans. *PRACTICE AREAS:* Labour Law; Occupational Health and Safety Law; Environmental Law; Commercial Arbitration.

JOHN RAYMOND COHEN, born Johannesburg, South Africa, May 22, 1957; admitted, 1983, South Africa. *Education:* University of the Witwatersrand (B.A., 1979; LL.B., 1991). *Member:* Johannesburg Attorneys Association; Law Society of the Transvaal. *LANGUAGES:* English and Afrikaans. *PRACTICE AREAS:* Mergers and Acquisitions; Licensing; Franchising; Competition Law; Corporate.

JOHAN OLIVIER, born Pretoria, South Africa, April 5, 1961; admitted, 1989, South Africa. *Education:* University of Stellenbosch (B.A., 1984; LL.B., 1986); Rand Afrikaans University (LL.M., 1991). Guest Lecturer, Labour Law Department, Rand Afrikaans University, 1994. Arbitrator, Independent Mediation Services of South Africa (IMMSA). *Member:* Johannesburg Law Society; Transvaal Law Society; Lawyers for Human Rights. *LANGUAGES:* Afrikaans, English and Dutch. *PRACTICE AREAS:* Labour Law; Litigation; Health and Safety Law.

DEBRA DANIELLE CHALMERS, born Johannesburg, South Africa, September 5, 1963; admitted, 1990, South Africa as Attorney and Conveyancer; 1991, Notary Public. *Education:* University of the Witwatersrand (B.A., 1986; LL.B., cum laude, 1988; H. Dip. Tax, cum laude, 1992). Tutor, Legal Theory 1, University of the Witwatersrand, 1987. *Member:* Transvaal Law Society; Johannesburg Attorneys Association. *LANGUAGES:* English. *PRACTICE AREAS:* Takeovers, Mergers and Acquisitions; Commercial Law; Contracts; Financial Markets and Securities Law; Mining Law; Banking Law.

ASSOCIATES

DAN ABRAHAM ROSENGARTEN, born Tel-Aviv, Israel, March 4, 1959; admitted, 1991, South Africa. *Education:* University of the Witwatersrand (B.A., cum laude, 1981; LL.B., cum laude, 1988); Rand Afrikaans University (H.Dip. Lab Law, cum laude, 1993). Author: "Workers Compensation-South Africa a Case Study," DSG/Critical Health No. 3, 1983; "HIV and Aids-Critical Problems in Employment Law," in South African Journal on Human Rights, Vol. 1, Part 9, 1993, JTA and Co. *Member:* Law Society of South Africa; Johannesburg Attorneys Association; Lawyers for Human Rights; National Association of Democratic Lawyers. *LANGUAGES:* English. *PRACTICE AREAS:* Commercial Litigation; Constitutional Law; Administrative Law; Employment Law.

REPRESENTATIVE CLIENTS: Nippon Denko; The Fuji Bank Limited; Ericsson; Mobil Saudi Arabia; Compaq Computer; Madge; Digital Equipment Corporation; Carson Products Company; GEC Alsthom N.V.; Cegelec and Pivovar Ostravar; Franco-Nevada Mining Corporation (International); Genbel; Genmin; RMP Properties; Yabeng; Investec; Standard Bank, PG Bison; Trans-Caledon Tunnel Authority; Iscor; Persetel Holdings; Fraser Alexander; Reunert; The Chamber of Mines of SA; Gengold; Impala Platinum; Palabora Mining; Rio Tinto; Vaal Reefs and Western Deep Levels; Rand Merchant Bank; UAL Merchant Bank; Nedcor Bank; Mathieson & Ashley Holdings, Seefin Bank, Blue Circle (National).
REFERENCES: Mr. K. Asamidori (Fuji Bank); Mr. D. Gould (Yabeng); Mr. D. Henwood (Persetel Limited); Mr. C. Hohental (Ericsson); Mr. D. McIntosh (Rand Merchant Bank).

CLIFFE DEKKER & TODD INC.

Attorneys Notaries Public and Conveyancers

Established in 1895

23RD FLOOR, 78 FOX STREET
JOHANNESBURG 2001, SOUTH AFRICA
Telephone: 011-832-2911
International Code + (2711) 832-2911
Cable Address: "Surety"
Telex: 4-88320
Telefax: 832-2940

Mailing Address: P.O. Box 61089, Marshalltown, Johannesburg 2107, South Africa

REVISERS OF THE SOUTH AFRICA LAW DIGEST FOR THIS DIRECTORY.

Randburg, South Africa Office: 10th Floor, Sanlam Centre, Pretoria Street, Ranburg. P.O. Box 1887, Randburg 2125. Telephone: (011) 787 1008. International Code + (2711) 787 1008. Cable Address: "Surety". Telex: 4-88320. Telefax: 886-4422.

General Practice. Corporate, Company, Commercial, Taxation, Investments, Mortgages, Conveyancing, Probate, Deceased Estates, Trusts and Wills, Litigation and Debt Collections. Notaries Public.

FIRM PROFILE: *Established in 1895, Cliffe Dekker & Todd Inc has built a reputation for quality service and added value. The firm offers a broad range of legal services the emphasis however being on corporate, banking and property law. The client base is primarily industrial, banking industrialists and property based organizations. The firm has 16 directors and 5 associates and 6 assistants practising in Johannesburg and Randburg. The firm is a member of the International Lawyers Network and has a close association with the Norton 5 Group in the United Kingdom and in particular Boodle Hatfield in London.*

DIRECTORS

D.R. CLARKE, LL.B. (Witwatersrand). Admitted: 1956. *LANGUAGES:* Afrikaans and English. *PRACTICE AREAS:* Banking; Corporate; Litigation; Estate Planning.

H.P. BILBROUGH, Admitted: 1960. *LANGUAGES:* Afrikaans and English. *PRACTICE AREAS:* Corporate; Taxation; Mining; Estate Planning.

N.G. JOOSTE, LL.B. (Stell). Admitted: 1971. *LANGUAGES:* Afrikaans and English. *PRACTICE AREAS:* Corporate; Taxation; Banking.

G.A.C. PRETORIUS, LL.B. (Stell). Admitted: 1969. *LANGUAGES:* Afrikaans and English. *PRACTICE AREAS:* Construction; Arbitration; Litigation; Corporate; Computer Law.

M.B. JACKSON, LL.B. (Witwatersrand). Admitted: 1973. *LANGUAGES:* Afrikaans and English. *PRACTICE AREAS:* Estate Planning; Wills; Trusts; Estates.

H.S. JACKSON, LL.M. (Witwatersrand). Admitted: 1975. *LANGUAGES:* Afrikaans and English. *PRACTICE AREAS:* Property; Mortgage Finance Schemes; Conveyancing.

C.H. EWING, LL.B. (Witwatersrand). Admitted: 1976. *LANGUAGES:* Afrikaans and English. *PRACTICE AREAS:* Corporate; Mining; Liquidation.

R.S.K. JARVIS, LL.B. (Witwatersrand). Admitted: 1976. *LANGUAGES:* Afrikaans and English. *PRACTICE AREAS:* Property; Conveyancing.

S.J. OOSTHUIZEN, B.Proc. (R.A.U.). Admitted: 1985. *LANGUAGES:* Afrikaans and English. *PRACTICE AREAS:* Banking; Litigation.

J.M. WITTS-HEWINSON, LL.B. (Stell.). Admitted: 1985. *LANGUAGES:* Afrikaans and English. *PRACTICE AREAS:* Litigation; Insolvency.

T.E. MILLS, LL.B. (Rhodes). H.Dip. Labour Law. Admitted: 1986. *LANGUAGES:* Afrikaans and English. *PRACTICE AREAS:* Litigation; Industrial Relations.

L. ERASMUS, LL.B. (R.A.U.). Admitted: 1984. *LANGUAGES:* Afrikaans and English. *PRACTICE AREAS:* Property; Conveyancing.

K.L. KLEIN, B.Proc (Unisa). Admitted: 1983. *LANGUAGES:* Afrikaans and English. *PRACTICE AREAS:* Corporate; Engineering.

(This Listing Continued)

J.L. MACKENZIE, LL.B. (Witwatersrand). Admitted: 1992. *LANGUAGES:* English and Afrikaans. *PRACTICE AREAS:* Litigation.

K. CURLEWIS, LL.B. (Shell.). Admitted: 1992. *LANGUAGES:* English and Afrikaans. *PRACTICE AREAS:* Property; Conveyancing.

I.K. HAYES, LL.B. (Witwatersrand). Admitted: 1993. *LANGUAGES:* English and Afrikaans. *PRACTICE AREAS:* Corporate Law.

ASSOCIATES

P. MARCHAND, Admitted: 1994. *PRACTICE AREAS:* Corporate Law.

C. KRIPOTOS, Admitted: 1992. *PRACTICE AREAS:* Conveyancing.

T.S. FLETCHER, LL.B. (Witwatersrand) Admitted: 1991. *LANGUAGES:* Afrikaans and English. *PRACTICE AREAS:* Civil and Criminal Litigation.

LEGAL SUPPORT PERSONNEL

A.C.M. ANDERSON, (ACIS) (General Manager). *LANGUAGES:* English.

GARY FULTON, (CA SA) (Financial Manager). *LANGUAGES:* English.

ANN VAN WEZEL, (BA) (Information and Computer Manager). *LANGUAGES:* Afrikaans and English.

REVISERS OF THE SOUTH AFRICA LAW DIGEST FOR THIS DIRECTORY.

DENEYS REITZ

10 ANDERSON STREET
JOHANNESBURG 2001, SOUTH AFRICA
Telephone: (International): (27) 11-833-5600
Fax: (27) 11 838-7444
Telex: 4-85432 SA
Teletex: (9) 450607

Mailing Address: P.O. Box 61334, Marshalltown, 2107

Sandton, South Africa Office: Ground Floor, Kohler House, 4 Pybus Road, P.O. Box 784903, 2146. Telephone: (27) 11 884-4900 or 783-8875. Telex: 4-26324 SA. Fax: (27) 11 884-5489.

Durban, South Africa Office: 4th Floor, Salisbury House, 332 Smith Street, P.O. Box 2010, 4000. Telephone: (27) 31 301-8361 or 301-7345. Teletex: (9) 650049. Fax: (27) 31 301-3346.

PARTNERS

M. KAPELUS (Senior Partner). *PRACTICE AREAS:* Insurance Law; General Practice; Insurance Litigation.

M.J. HART. *PRACTICE AREAS:* Insurance Law; General Practice; Insurance Litigation; Dispute Resolution.

P. NAUDE. *PRACTICE AREAS:* Aviation Law; Insurance Law; General Practice; Insurance Litigation; Dispute Resolution; Statutory Enquiries.

M.O. DALE. *PRACTICE AREAS:* Mining Law; Mining Litigation; Environmental Law.

M. JACOBS. *PRACTICE AREAS:* Personal Injury Claims; General Practice; Insurance Litigation; Criminal Law.

J.M. KRON. *PRACTICE AREAS:* Insurance Law; General Practice; Insurance Litigation; Dispute Resolution.

J.N.R. CALDOW (Resident, Durban Office). *PRACTICE AREAS:* Insurance Law; General Practice; Insurance Litigation; Statutory Enquiries; Admiralty Law; Shipping Law.

M. TABACK. *PRACTICE AREAS:* Banking Law; International Finance Law; Commercial Law; Corporate Law; Taxation Law.

P.C. VILJOEN. *PRACTICE AREAS:* Intellectual Property Law; Banking Law; International Finance Law; Commercial Law; Corporate Law; Taxation Law.

J.M. NEAVES. *PRACTICE AREAS:* Insurance Law; General Practice; Insurance Litigation; Dispute Resolution; Environmental Law.

L. VAN STADEN. *PRACTICE AREAS:* Fraud Recovery; Interdicts; Commercial Law; Property Litigation; Dispute Resolution; Insolvency Law.

K.R. CRON. *PRACTICE AREAS:* Commercial Law; Corporate Law; Banking Law; International Finance Law; Taxation Law; Wills; Estate Planning; Trusts.

P.A. BRACHER. *PRACTICE AREAS:* Insurance Law; General Practice; Insurance Litigation; Mining Litigation; Environmental Law; Human Rights Law; Constitutional Law.

G.G. BOUWER. *PRACTICE AREAS:* Personal Injury Claims; Insurance Law; General Practice; Insurance Litigation; Dispute Resolution; Family Law.

R. GREENHALGH (Resident, Durban Office). *PRACTICE AREAS:* Admiralty Law; Shipping Law; Insurance Law; Insurance Litigation; Dispute Resolution.

A.F. BEMBRIDGE. *PRACTICE AREAS:* Property Law; Conveyancing Law; Wills; Estate Planning; Trusts.

P.M. CHRONIS. *PRACTICE AREAS:* Insurance Law; General Practice; Insurance Litigation; Dispute Resolution; Admiralty Law; Shipping Law.

R.R. PERROTT (Resident, Sandton Office). *PRACTICE AREAS:* Employment Law; Labour Litigation; Dispute Resolution.

F.C. BAM. *PRACTICE AREAS:* Constitutional Law; Public Interest Law; Industrial and Labour Relations; Arbitration; Mediation.

A.J. CHAPPEL. *PRACTICE AREAS:* Environmental Law; Insurance Law; Insurance Litigation; General Practice; Dispute Resolution.

R. SMITH. *PRACTICE AREAS:* Fraud Recovery; Interdicts; Commercial Law; Litigation; Insolvency Law; Statutory Enquiries.

B.G. PATTERSON (Resident, Sandton Office). *PRACTICE AREAS:* Employment Law; Labour Litigation; Statutory Enquiries.

ST. E. WILKEN (Resident, Sandton Office). *PRACTICE AREAS:* Employment Law; Labour Litigation; Statutory Enquiries.

L.A. MORPHET. *PRACTICE AREAS:* Insurance Law; General Practice; Litigation; Dispute Resolution.

F.E. LEPPAN (Resident, Sandton Office). *PRACTICE AREAS:* Employment Law; Labour Litigation; Statutory Enquiries.

C. WOOLLEY (Resident, Durban Office). *PRACTICE AREAS:* Insurance Law; General Practice; Litigation; Dispute Resolution; Liquidations.

M.H. ALEXANDER (Resident, Durban Office). *PRACTICE AREAS:* Employment Law; Labour Litigation; Statutory Enquiries; Dispute Resolution.

C.J. STEVENS. *PRACTICE AREAS:* Mining Law; Environmental Law.

P.J. JACKSON. *PRACTICE AREAS:* Commercial Law; Corporate Law; Banking Law; International Finance Law; Taxation Law; International Trade Law; International Business Law.

S. RANEY. *PRACTICE AREAS:* Commercial Law; Environmental Law.

A.B. HARDIE. *PRACTICE AREAS:* Insurance Law; General Practice; Litigation; Dispute Resolution.

D. WOODHOUSE (Resident, Sandton Office). *PRACTICE AREAS:* Employment Law; Labour Litigation; Statutory Enquiries; Dispute Resolution.

J. BEZUIDENHOUT. *PRACTICE AREAS:* Commercial Law; Corporate Law; Banking Law; International Finance Law; Taxation Law.

A.G.S. DIXON. *PRACTICE AREAS:* Commercial Law; Corporate Law; Stock Exchange Law; Taxation Law; Estate Planning.

A.K. STRACHAN. *PRACTICE AREAS:* Insurance Law; Litigation.

C.F. OWEN. *PRACTICE AREAS:* Human Rights Law; Constitutional Law.

D.D. HAYWARD (Resident, Sandton Office). *PRACTICE AREAS:* Industrial and Labour Relations.

A.P.M. ROBINSON (Resident, Durban Office). *PRACTICE AREAS:* Admiralty Law; Shipping Law; Environmental Law.

(This Listing Continued)

(This Listing Continued)

DENEYS REITZ, Johannesburg—Continued

K. GAWITH. PRACTICE AREAS: Insurance Law; General Practice; Insurance Litigation.

R. SCOTT. PRACTICE AREAS: Insurance Law; General Practice; Insurance Litigation.

EDWARD NATHAN & FRIEDLAND INC.

Attorneys, Notaries and Conveyancers

Established in 1905

23RD FLOOR, SANLAMSENTRUM
206/214 JEPPE STREET
P.O. BOX 3370
JOHANNESBURG 2000, SOUTH AFRICA
Telephone: National: (011) 337-2100
International: + 27-11 337-2100
Telefax: 333-6942
Teletex: 450 059 ENF

Mailing Address: P.O. Box 3370, Johannesburg, 2000

General Practice, Building, Commercial, Competition, Corporate, Deceased Estates, Environmental Law, Estate Planning, Exchange Control, Insolvency, Insurance, Labour Law, Litigation and Arbitration, Non-Governmental Organisations, Charitable Organisations, Public Interest, Real Estate, Stock Exchange, Taxation and Trusts.

FIRM PROFILE: One of South Africa's largest law firms involved primarily in Commercial Practice (including taxation) and Commercial Litigation, and also Real Estate, Labour, Public Interest and Trusts.

MICHAEL MERVYN KATZ, (SENIOR PARTNER). LANGUAGES: Hebrew. **PRACTICE AREAS:** Commercial; Corporate; Stock Exchange; Competition; International Trade; Taxation.

PHILIP PENCHARZ. PRACTICE AREAS: General Practice; Commercial; Corporate; Estate Planning; Litigation & Arbitration; Real Estate; Stock Exchange; Taxation.

BASIL WUNSH. PRACTICE AREAS: Commercial; Corporate; Estate Planning; Stock Exchange; Taxation; Trusts; Exchange Control; Banking.

BARRY MICHAEL JAMMY. PRACTICE AREAS: Labour Law & Industrial Relations; Human Rights; Public Interest; Sports Law; Entertainment Law.

GENÉ SIMON. PRACTICE AREAS: Real Estate; Conveyancing; Deceased Estates.

STEPHEN ANTHONY LEWIS. PRACTICE AREAS: Commercial; Competition; Corporate; Insolvency; Stock Exchange; Taxation.

PATRICK HENRY CRONIN. PRACTICE AREAS: Commercial; Corporate; Stock Exchange; Mining; Transportation Law; Real Estate.

MICHAEL SOSNOVIK. PRACTICE AREAS: Commercial; Corporate; Estate Planning; Stock Exchange; Taxation; Trusts; Financial Accounting.

RICHARD CODRON. PRACTICE AREAS: Real Estate; Conveyancing.

CECIL IVOR STEINHAUER. LANGUAGES: Hebrew. **PRACTICE AREAS:** Commercial; Litigation & Arbitration; International Trade.

MIRANDA JANET FEINSTEIN. PRACTICE AREAS: Commercial; Corporate; Environmental; Stock Exchange; Property.

ERROL NEWTON KNOWLES. PRACTICE AREAS: Litigation & Arbitration.

ALAN CECIL FEINSTEIN. PRACTICE AREAS: Commercial; Corporate; Stock Exchange.

PETRA ANNE VISSER. PRACTICE AREAS: Litigation & Arbitration; Family Law.

CECIL LEON WULFSOHN. PRACTICE AREAS: Commercial; Corporate; Insolvency; Litigation & Arbitration.

PIERRE LOUIS FERREIRA. PRACTICE AREAS: Litigation & Arbitration; Insurance.

IAN VARGA LINDSAY. PRACTICE AREAS: Litigation & Arbitration; Insolvency.

(This Listing Continued)

MOHAMED JUNAID HUSAIN. LANGUAGES: Urdu. **PRACTICE AREAS:** Litigation & Arbitration; Public Interest; Building; Constitutional Law; Human Rights.

JOHANNES SCHOEMAN. PRACTICE AREAS: Commercial; Corporate; Environmental Law; Financial Services; Health Services.

ARLENE LYRICE SMUKLER. LANGUAGES: French. **PRACTICE AREAS:** Litigation & Arbitration.

HILGARD BELL. PRACTICE AREAS: Labour Law & Industrial Relations; Health Services.

JACQUES TREDOUX. PRACTICE AREAS: Litigation & Arbitration; Insolvency.

WILLIAM JAMES MIDGLEY. PRACTICE AREAS: Real Estate; Conveyancing; Value Added Tax.

JENNYLIND MARGARET LOUIS. PRACTICE AREAS: Real Estate; Conveyancing; Mining.

SEAN CRAIG LEDERMAN. PRACTICE AREAS: Commercial.

ANDREW CRAIG BROOKING. PRACTICE AREAS: Labour Law & Industrial Relations.

KEVIN WAYNE JOSELOWITZ. PRACTICE AREAS: Commercial; Stock Exchange.

VICTOR GEORGE MANSELL (Practising Consultant). **PRACTICE AREAS:** General Practice; Commercial; Estate Planning.

GOLDMAN JUDIN AND WERNER

Established in 1936

1ST FLOOR, VILLAGE WALK
MAUDE STREET
JOHANNESBURG 2146 (SANDTON), SOUTH AFRICA
Telephone: (21711) 883 5667/8
Fax: (21711) 883 5669

Corporate and Commercial Law, Mergers and Acquisitions, Joint Ventures, Litigation, Property, Employment and Labour Law, Criminal Law.

FIRM PROFILE: The firm was established in 1936 and offers a full range of legal services. It is well known in the Republic of South Africa and enjoys an excellent reputation. The client base is South African and International. This two partner firm has a legal support staff of nine consisting of a professional assistant, para-legal personnel, bookkeeper and office administrator.

MEMBERS OF FIRM

JOHN MICHAEL JUDIN, born Johannesburg, South Africa, August 5, 1946; admitted, 1969, South Africa, Botswana, Lesotho and Swaziland. Education: University of the Witwatersrand, South Africa (Dip. Law). Author, "Lawful Piracy of American Trademarks," and "Trade Law in South Africa," both published in "International Business Lawyer". Member: International Bar Association; American Bar Association (Associate Member); American Chamber of Commerce in Southern Africa (a director). LANGUAGES: English. PRACTICE AREAS: Corporate and Commercial Law; Mergers and Acquisitions; Joint Ventures and Commercial Litigation.

MICHAEL ANDREW WERNER, born Johannesburg, South Africa, June 3, 1951; admitted, 1976, South Africa. Education: University of the Witwatersrand, South Africa (Dip. Law). Commissioner, Small Claims Court, 1988. LANGUAGES: English and Afrikaans. PRACTICE AREAS: Criminal Law and Litigation..

ASSOCIATES

PATRICIA VIVIENNE TERNENT, born Durban, South Africa, November 28, 1964; admitted, 1992, South Africa. Education: University of Witwatersrand, South Africa (B.A., LL.B.). LANGUAGES: English. PRACTICE AREAS: Litigation; Commercial and Labour Law.

D.M. KISCH INC.

Patent Attorneys, Trademark Agents, Attorneys, Notaries &
Conveyancers

Established in 1874

SYFRETS PARK
23 GIRTON ROAD
PARKTOWN
P.O. BOX 668

JOHANNESBURG 2000, SOUTH AFRICA
Telephone: (National) 011-484-4122/9
(International) +27-11-484-4122/9
Telex: 4-85739 SA
Facsimile: +27-11-484-2653/4 (24hrs)

Pretoria, South Africa Office: 8th Floor, Mutual & Federal Centre, 220 Vermeulen Street, P.O. Box 3668, 0001. Telephone: +27-12-325-1581. Telex: 3-20534 SA. Facsimile: +27-12-325-1582 (24 hrs).

Patent, Trademark, Industrial Design and Copyright Law, Advertising Law, Advertising Standards Authority Procedures, Business Names, Commercial Law, Companies and Close Corporations, Conveyancing, Franchising, Licensing, Merchandise Marks, Passing-off, Plant Breeders Rights, Product Liability, Environmental Law, Supreme Court Litigation, Trade Secrets and Unlawful Competition.

J. T. TRUTER Pr. Eng., B.Sc. (Elec.) Eng., Dip. Law.

J. LAMPRECHT B.Sc. (Hons.) (Chem.), B.Iuris.

R. LE ROUX B.Sc. (Mech.) Eng., LL.B.

D. B. MOMBERG B.A., LL.B.

N. J. VERMAAK B.Sc. (Chem. Phys.), LL.B.

M. LE ROUX B.Sc. (Mech.) Eng., B.Proc.

A. K. VAN DER MERWE B.Sc. (Chem. Maths.), LL.B.

P. A. STERN B.A. (Hons.), B.A. (Comm.), LL.B.

A. KRÜGER (Hons.) B.Eng. (Elec.), LL.B.

H.R. MOUBRAY Pr.Eng., B.Sc. (Mech.) Eng., B.Proc.

F.J.J. POTGIETER B.Iuris., LL.B.

B.A. WIMPEY B.Proc., LL.B.

C.P. VAN BILJON M.Sc. (Chem.); LL.B.

H. VORSTER B.Com.; LL.B.

J.D.M. MCLEISH B.A., LL.B.

T.H. DOUBELL B.Eng. (Chem., Met.), B.Proc.

M.S. MANN B.Journ., LL.B.

CONSULTING DIRECTOR

A.C. COUZYN B.Sc. (Chem.), Eng., Dip. Law..

LINDSAY, KELLER & PARTNERS

Established in 1942

6TH FLOOR, JHI HOUSE
11 CRADOCK AVENUE, ROSEBANK
JOHANNESBURG 2196, SOUTH AFRICA
Telephone: 880-8980
Fax: 880-9182

Mailing Address: P.O. Box 195, Saxonwold 2132

Commercial, Corporate Law, Banking, Foreign Loans, Investments, Project Finance, Real Estate, Taxation, General Insurance Law including Product Liability, Estate Planning, Trusts, Deceased Estates, Trademark and Copyright, Labor and Industrial Law, General and Commercial Litigation, Constitutional Law, German, English and European Law.

(This Listing Continued)

MEMBERS OF FIRM

Friedrich W. Keller,
B.Com., LL.B. (Rand)

Terrence Davis, B.Com., LL.B.,
H. Dip. Tax, H. Dip. Co. Law
(Rand). Qualified as Solicitor
in England

Carl M. Witepski,
B.Com., LL.B. (UCT)

Daniel F. Weideman,
B.Com., LL.B. (RAU)

Victor De Bruyn, B.Proc.

Leicester Adams, B.Proc.

ASSOCIATES

Karl H. (Kay) Schröder,
Rechtsanwalt, Admitted at the
Regional Appeal Court
(Oberlandesgericht),
**Düsseldorf, Consultant in
E.E.C. Law**

Michael J. Tucker,
B.Com., LL.B.

Claudia Privato, B.A., LL.B.

D. Judelsohn

Languages: English, German, French and Afrikaans

MALCOLM LYONS & MUNRO

Established in 1965

INNER COURT
74/86 KERK STREET
P.O. BOX 1513

JOHANNESBURG 2000, SOUTH AFRICA
Telephone: 11 29-8341
Fax: 11 337-2894

Cape Town, South Africa Office: Malcolm Lyons, Munro and Sohn, 9th Floor, ISM Building, 27 Wale Street, 8000. Telephone: 21 24-2638/54. Fax: 21 24-0474.

FIRM PROFILE: Founded in 1965, Malcolm Lyons and Munro is the first and probably the only specialist firm in South Africa dealing exclusively in personal injury claims on behalf of injured persons or dependents of persons killed. The firm is acknowledged as expert in the field and handles cases involving motor vehicle accidents, medical negligence and injuries or death from any other cause. It has acted in numerous reported cases relating to these fields in South African law.

The client base is drawn from personal recommendation and reputation. The partners lecture at courses for candidate attorneys on behalf of the Association of Law Societies of South Africa, address various groups and offer legal advice on radio on medico-legal topics. There are five partners and two assistants in the Johannesburg office. A sixth partner is based in the associated Cape Town office.

MEMBERS OF FIRM

MALCOLM LYONS, born Leeds, England, 1935; admitted, 1961, South Africa. Co-Author: "Insurance," volume 12, of the encyclopaedic work the "Law of South Africa." Author: "Preparation and Presentation of MVA Claims," for the Association of Law Societies of South Africa. *Member:* International Medical Society of Paraplegia; South African Clinical Neurological Association; Association of Personal Injury Lawyers in the United Kingdom. **PRACTICE AREAS:** Personal Injury Law.

HILTON ROSS-MUNRO, born Johannesburg, South Africa, 1947; admitted, 1976, South Africa. Lecturer, Medico-Legal Matters. *Member:* International Medical Society of Paraplegia; South African Clinical Neurological Association; Association of Personal Injury Lawyers in the United Kingdom. **PRACTICE AREAS:** Personal Injury Law.

Languages: English and Afrikaans.

MOSS-MORRIS INC.

Established in 1903

20TH FLOOR, OFFICE TOWER
SANDTON CITY, FIFTH STREET
SANDTON
P.O. BOX 7066
JOHANNESBURG 2000, SOUTH AFRICA
Telephone: (27) 11-884-9367
Telefax: (27) 11-884-7949

Alternative Dispute Resolution, Banking, Corporate, Commercial and Tax, Entertainment, Environment, Estates and Trusts, Exchange Control, Insolvency and Liquidation, Insurance, International Business, Labour and Employment, Litigation, Oil Industry, Parliamentary Liaison and Public Interest, Pharmaceutical Industry, Property and Conveyancing.

FIRM PROFILE: The firm traces its beginnings to the days when Johannesburg was a bustling if rough and dusty mining town. As the city has grown over the decades into the financial and industrial centre that it is now, so the firm has grown, adapted and kept pace and today takes its place among the foremost law firms in Johannesburg. The firm believes that its commitment to achieving excellence and integrity in professionalism and in service to clients will enable it to serve the commercial community as effectively in the New South Africa as it has in the past.

PARTNERS

M J Fluxman	K G E Mulligan
C Greenfield	G I Wolff
S Cohen	S Wapnick
J M Hall	M T Sacks
A Tugendhaft	E G Migdal
D H M Gibson	L P Cowan
I G Shapiro	R L Appelbaum
D N Polovin	M G Black
A P M de Villiers	

WEBBER WENTZEL BOWENS

Attorneys, Notaries & Conveyancers

Patent Attorneys & Trademark Agents

Established in 1868

60 MAIN STREET
JOHANNESBURG 2001, SOUTH AFRICA
Telephone: National (011) 832-2636
International: +27 11 832-2636
Telex: 48-5230 SA
Telegrams: Solon
Telefax: (011) 834-670 1; 832-1623/4

Mailing Address: P.O. Box 61771, Marshalltown, South Africa 2107

Offices in Sandton and Pretoria.

Overseas Offices: Maitland & Co., London, Luxembourg, Geneva and the Isle of Man.

Corporate: General Commercial, Companies, Stock Exchange (Listings, Takeovers and Mergers), Managed and Leveraged Buy-Outs, Taxation (Local & International), International Trade and Business, Mining and Minerals, Banking Exchange Control, Publishing and Newspaper Law, Media Law, Competition Law. Litigation: General and Commercial Litigation, Overseas and Foreign Claims, Insurance, Shipping, Banking, Engineering and Construction Disputes, Professional and Product Liability, Arbitrations, Mining and Industrial Enquiries, Property, Environmental Law. Estates and Trusts: Asset Management. Employment and Industrial Relations: Employment related Litigation, Unfair Labour Practice Determinations, Dispute Resolving, Collective Bargaining, Industrial Relations Training and Workshops, Public Interest Law. Intellectual Property: Registration of Patents, Trademarks, Designs and Copyrights locally and internationally, Related Searches, Assignments, Opinions and Litigation, Drafting and Negotiation of Licence and Franchise Agreements, Advice on Related Tax, Exchange Control, Corporate Structures, Valuations of Intellectual Property.

FIRM PROFILE: Webber Wentzel Bowens, Africa's largest law firm, and one of South Africa's oldest, has a network of lawyers, nationally and internationally, representing some of the country's major mining, commercial, financial and industrial institutions. Webber Wentzel Bowens specialises in corporate law, as well as mining, patents, trademarks, copyright,

commercial litigation, banking, insurance, property, industrial relations and media law. There are over 100 fee earners in the practice.

PARTNERS

Peter Edward Blaine Reynolds
Ronald Stuart Napier
Pieter Daniel De Wet
Harold Edwin Till
Norman Ewart Clegg Barlow
Edward Montagu Southey
Eric Peter Pfaff
John Arnold Kuys Jarvis
Lawrence Pinkney Reyburn
Kenneth John Douglas
Louis Auret Kernick
John Angus Louw
David Roelof Scholtz
Peter Robert Newton Arthur
Ashley Factor
Peter John Wentzel
Gabrielle Elizabeth Norton
Alden Michael John Pinnock
Arnold Cigler
Rory Charles Kerr
Johannes Rudolph Marais Louw
Roderick Anthony Lawrence Harper
Graham Edwards
Dairmuid Harcourt Short
Michael Edward Solomon
Anthony Henry Markham
Rupert Lawrence Worsdale
St John Alan Bruce-Brand
Peter Samuel Guy Leon
Steven Geprgala
Stephen Irwin Meltzer
Stuart McCafferty
Jacobus Gideon Louw Nel
Paul Michael Jenkins
David Malcolm Lancaster
Nicolaas Mechiel van Niekerk
Lionel Unterhalter
Daniel Benjamin Le Roux
Gustav Arthur Fichardt
Jorge Pereira Araujo
Leora Blumberg
Sara Caroline Gon
Judith Magdalena Scheepers
Nicholas John Arundel Robb
Desmond John Mitchell Barry
John Meredith Bellew
Bernard Anthony Matheson
Andrew Pearce
Bruce Alan Cleaver
Peter Damien Grealy
Lutricia Martha Roos
Johann Willem Scholtz
Adelé Linda Tulley
Wend Borwin Wendland
Ronald Brandon Richard Wheeldon
Christiaan Lambert Giliomee
Peter Graylin
Stuart Gardiner

ASSOCIATES

Anthony Addison
Vanessa Angela Dennett
Clive Edward Hertog
Warren Anthony Hiepner
Anne Hamilton Larter
Sharon Scarrott
Nicole Frances Newton King
Jose Dana Verster

CONSULTANTS

Harold John Barker
Michael John Matterson Bennett

(This Listing Continued)

(This Listing Continued)

Carveth Harcourt Geach
Lionel Cyril Konson
Derric Bottomley Reid
Gavin Quentin Routledge
Kenneth Cyril Simon

PATENT AGENTS

Hans Helmut Hahn
Alan James Strickland Dunlop

LEGAL SUPPORT PERSONNEL

Brian Bernard King (Chief Executive Officer)

WERKSMANS

Established in 1917

22 GIRTON ROAD
PARKTOWN 2193

P.O. BOX 927

JOHANNESBURG 2000, SOUTH AFRICA

Telephone: 27-11-488-0000
Telex: 4-24259SA; 4-24645SA
Answer Back Code: WKSMN SA
Telefax: 484-3100; 484-3200
Docex: 2 Jhb

Corporate, Litigation, Property and Real Estate, Taxation (all aspects), Conveyancing, Personal Injury, Insurance, Industrial and Labor, Foreign Investments, Entertainment and Construction Law.

MEMBERS OF FIRM

A.J. Behrmann (Senior Partner)
A.J. Aaron
B.R. Bleazard
J.M. Bortz
C.F. Butler (Executive Director)
R.M. Carr
L.J. Civin
A.M. Costa
I.S. Epstein
A.R. Gorley
V.W. Harrison
D. Hertz
J.S. Janks
L.R. Johannes
B.M. Kew
J.A. Lapin
M. Levenberg
S.M. Levenberg
B.S. Levene
E. Levenstein
H. Pelkowitz
D.H. Rabin
D.L. Rod
F. Rodrigues
M.B. Simon
C.D. Stein
M. van den Berg
D.G. Williams
P.A. Winer
M. Yachad

ASSOCIATES

W.F. Berry
S.L. Chemaly
A. Da Costa
R.N. Wakefield

ADAMS & ADAMS

Patent Attorneys, Trademark Agents, Attorneys, Notaries and Conveyancers.

Established in 1917

429 CHURCH STREET
PRETORIA 0002, SOUTH AFRICA
Telephone: National (012) 320 8500, International +27 12 320 8500
Telex: 3 22157 ADAMS SA
Facsimile: 27 12 320 8550

Mailing Address: P.O. Box 1014, Pretoria, 0001

Johannesburg, South Africa Office: 3rd floor, North Park, 20 Girton Rd, Parktown 2193. P.O. Box 10155, 2000. Telephone: National (011) 6425057, International +27 11 6425057. Facsimile: 2711 6421914.

Cape Town, South Africa Office: 2817 Trust Bank Centre, Heerengracht, 8001. P.O. Box 1513, 8000. Telephone: National (021) 25-3607, International +27 21 25 3607. Facsimile: 2721-419-5729.

Durban, South Africa Office: 6th floor, 136 Victoria Embankment, 4001. P.O. Box 1538, 4000. Telephone: National (031) 304 3773, International +27 31 304 3773. Facsimile: 27 31 304 3799.

FIRM PROFILE: The firm offers a full range of legal services including intellectual property and has an international client base. The firm has 35 partners and a comprehensive support staff.

PARTNERS

C. SLABBERT, B.Sc. (Civil Engineering), LL.B., Ph.D., (Registered Patent Attorney). **PRACTICE AREAS:** Patent Litigation and Filings; Construction Engineering.

B.R. SOMMERVILLE, B.A., LL.B. **PRACTICE AREAS:** Trademark Filings; Searches and Prosecution.

C.A. STEWART, Dip. Proc. **PRACTICE AREAS:** Trademark Assignments and Registered Users.

J.F. HOME, Dip. Proc. **PRACTICE AREAS:** Property Law; Real Estate.

B.E. OLDRIDGE, Dip Proc. **PRACTICE AREAS:** Trademark Filing, Searches and Prosecution.

A.V. VAN R. SCHWEIZER, B.Sc. (Chemical Engineering), B.Iuris., (Registered Patent Attorney). **PRACTICE AREAS:** Patent Drafting and Prosecution-Chemistry and Pharmaceutical.

D.M. DOLD, Dip. Proc. (Registered Patent Attorney). **PRACTICE AREAS:** Patent Drafting and Prosecution-Electrical and Electronic.

A.J.G. HOBBS, B.Iuris. **PRACTICE AREAS:** Probate Law.

D.F. SHEPPARD, B.Sc. (Honours Chemistry) CPA Dip. Proc., (Registered Patent Attorney). **PRACTICE AREAS:** Patent Litigation and Filings.

B. BACON, B.Proc., CPA, (Registered Patent Attorney). (Resident, Cape Town Office). **PRACTICE AREAS:** Patent Litigation-Mechanical Engineering.

A. LEWIS, B.Sc. (Physics & Maths); B.Sc. (Electrical Engineering); B.Proc., (Registered Patent Attorney). (Resident, Johannesburg Office). **PRACTICE AREAS:** Patent Litigation-Electrical and Electronic.

T.M. MAHON, B.Iuris. **PRACTICE AREAS:** Banking Law; Construction Law; Engineering Law.

J.F. WILLIAMS, B.Iuris. **PRACTICE AREAS:** Property Law; Commercial Law.

A.J. SMITH, B.Proc., (Registered Patent Attorney). **PRACTICE AREAS:** Trademark and Copyright Litigation; Exchange Control.

S. G. VAN DER SCHANS, B.Sc. (Electrical Engineering), B.Proc., (Registered Patent Attorney). (Resident, Cape Town Office). **PRACTICE AREAS:** Patent Drafting and Prosecution-Electrical and Electronic.

M. ROTTEVEEL, B.Sc. (Mechanical Engineering); LL.B., (Registered Patent Attorney). (Resident, Durban Office). **PRACTICE AREAS:** Patent Drafting and Prosecution-Mechanical Engineering.

S.C. FERREIRA, B.Sc. (Mechanical Engineering), LL.B., (Registered Patent Attorney). **PRACTICE AREAS:** Patent Assignments, Amendments and Restorations.

(This Listing Continued)

ADAMS & ADAMS, Pretoria—Continued

C.K. JOB, B.Sc., B.Proc. (Registered Patent Attorney). **PRACTICE AREAS:** Trademark; Passing off Litigation; Unlawful Competition Litigation; Copyright Litigation.

E.M. EYBERS, B.Proc. **PRACTICE AREAS:** Litigation.

G.S. KOTZE, B.Sc. (Chemical Engineering), B.Proc., (Registered Patent Attorney). **PRACTICE AREAS:** Patent Assignments, Amendments and Restorations.

E.D. DU PLESSIS, B.Sc. (Chemistry) LL.B., (Registered Patent Attorney). **PRACTICE AREAS:** Patent Drafting and Prosecution-Chemistry and Pharmaceutical.

A.M. SEYMOUR, B.A., LL.B. **PRACTICE AREAS:** Trademark Agreements; Licensing; Franchising.

J.C. VON WIELLIGH, B.Proc. **PRACTICE AREAS:** Property Law; Real Estate.

M.W.H. POSEMANN, B.A., LL.B. (Resident, Durban Office). **PRACTICE AREAS:** Maritime Law.

C.B. YEO, B.A., LL.B. **PRACTICE AREAS:** Family Law; Litigation.

D.M. TAYLOR, B.Sc. (Honours Chemistry); B.Proc., (Registered Patent Attorney). **PRACTICE AREAS:** Patent Drafting and Prosecution-Plastics/Polymer Technology.

G.L. ERLANK, B.Sc. (Chemistry), LL.B., (Registered Patent Attorney). **PRACTICE AREAS:** Patent Renewals.

J.F. STANDER, B.A., LL.B. **PRACTICE AREAS:** Trademark and Copyright Litigation.

H.S. ROGERS, B.A., B.Proc. **PRACTICE AREAS:** Trademark Renewals.

A. PAPAGEORGE, B.A. (Hons.), B.Admin., B.Proc. **PRACTICE AREAS:** Labour Law; Litigation.

C.H. BERMAN, B.Sc. (Electrical Engineering); B.Proc., (Registered Patent Attorney). (Resident, Johannesburg Office). **PRACTICE AREAS:** Patent Drafting and Prosecution-Electrical and Electronic.

D.F. TANZIANI, B.Sc. (Chemistry), B.Proc., (Registered Patent Attorney). **PRACTICE AREAS:** Patent Drafting and Prosecution-Biotechnology.

J.L. DU PREEZ, B.A., LL.B. **PRACTICE AREAS:** Trademark Filings and Prosecution.

C. MACKENZIE, B.Sc. (Mechanical Engineering) B.Proc., (Registered Patent Attorney). **PRACTICE AREAS:** Patent Drafting and Prosecution-Mechanical Engineering.

N.I. HICKMAN, B.A. (Hons.), LL.B. **PRACTICE AREAS:** Trademark and Copyright Litigation.

Languages: English, Afrikaans, Dutch, French, German, Greek, Italian and Portuguese.

DENEYS REITZ

GROUND FLOOR, KOHLER HOUSE
4 PYBUS ROAD
P.O. BOX 784903
SANDTON, SOUTH AFRICA
Telephone: (International): (27) (011) 783-8875; (011) 884-4900
Fax: (27) (011) 884-5489;
Telex: 4-26324

Johannesburg Office: 10 Anderson Street, Johannesburg, 2001. P.O. Box 61334, Marshalltown 2107. Telephone: (27) (011) 833-5600. Telex: 4-85432 SA. Teletex: (9) 450607. Fax: (27) (011) 838-7444. Docex 215.
Durban Office: 4th Floor, Salisbury House 332 Smith Street, P.O. Box 2010, Durban 4000.

(For Complete Biographical Data on all Personnel see Professional Biographies at Johannesburg)

SUDAN

ADHAM & ASSOCIATES

P.O. BOX 2272
KHARTOUM, SUDAN
Telephone: 81489; 80469; 79279 (Khartoum)
Telex: 22223 "Adjco" SD

Sultanate of Oman, Muscat Office: Adham & Associates, P.O. Box 2301 - Postal Code 112, Sultanate of Oman. Telephone: 796146; 799956 (Muscat). Fax: 796170. Telex: 3712 "Adreco" On.

General Practice and Litigation, Insurance, Shipping, Investment, International Finance, Banking, Taxation, Civil Engineering, Labour Law, Company Law, Mining and Petroleum, Trademarks and Patents, Legal Transportation, Advocates and Commissioners for Oaths.

ANWAR ADHAM, born 1934; admitted to bar, 1960. Education: Cairo University (LL.B., 1959).

Languages: Corresponds in Arabic and English.

SYRIA

LAW OFFICES OF DR. MOUSTAFA AL-SAYED

Established in 1974

23, BAHSA STR.
P.O. BOX 11317
DAMASCUS, SYRIA
Telephone: (011) 221 9177; 221 2220
Telex: 412819 Sydlaw
Fax: (011) 224 1251

General Practice, Commercial and Corporate, Banking and Finance, Tax, Patent Litigation, Contracts, International Transactions.

FIRM PROFILE: Family Professional Partnership.

DR. MOUSTAFA AL-SAYED, born Aleppo, Syria, September, 1928; admitted, 1974, Syria. Education: University of Damascus; University of Geneva (Dr. of Law Degree). Former Professor, Public and Private International Law, University of Damascus School of Law. Former Minister: Foreign Affairs and Higher Education. Judge, Court of Organization, Arab Petroleum Exporting Countries. Member: Syrian Bar Association; American Society of International Law. LANGUAGES: Arabic, French and English. PRACTICE AREAS: International Arbitrations; Company Law; Construction Law; International Contracts; Corporate Law.

FALAH KATEB, born Aleppo, Syria, October, 1939; admitted, 1984, Syria. Education: University of Damascus. Former Chief of the Legal Section at the Commercial Bank of Syria. LANGUAGES: Arabic and English. PRACTICE AREAS: Agency and Distributorships; Bank and Banking; Commercial Law; Family Law.

ABDULHAY SAYED, born Damascus, Syria, July 1969; admitted, 1993, Syria. Education: Damascus University (Bachelor's Degree in Law); Harvard Law School (LL.M.); The Graduate Institute of International Studies, Geneva University (DES Certificate of International Studies). LANGUAGES: Arabic, English and French. PRACTICE AREAS: International Arbitration; Business Law; Company Law; Contracts; Corporate Law; International Law.

LAW OFFICES OF ARAB CONSULTANTS

Legal, Economic, Financial and Administrative Services

PORT SAID STREET-NAHHAS BUILDING

5TH FLOOR

P.O. BOX 254

DAMASCUS, SYRIA

Telephone: 2217577-2233444

Telex: 441876 OUSSI Sy.

Fax: 00963-11-33 12 581

Affiliated U.S.A. Office: N. Peter Antone, P.C., 16445 West Twelve Mile Road, Suite 100, Southfield, Michigan 48076. Telephone: 1-810-559-0707. Fax: 1-810-559-0790.

Legal, Economic, Administrative and Financial Consultations. General Practice, Business, Insurance, Contracts, Taxation, International Transactions, Arbitration, Feasibility Studies, Market Survey, Financial Studies, Trademarks, Patents, Corporations, Foreign Investments and Administrative Consultations in Syria and other Arab Countries.

HANI BITAR, born Lattakia, 1921; admitted, 1944. *Education:* University of St. Joseph, Beirut; (University of Leon France (Licensed). *Member:* Syrian Bar Association. *LANGUAGES:* Arabic, French and English.

ANTOUN JOUBRAN, born Damascus, 1933; admitted, 1957, Syria. *Education:* University of Damascus. Former: State Minister for Cabinet Affairs; Minister of Social Affairs and Labor; Minister of Parliament Affairs; Minister for Industry. *Member:* Syrian Bar (Former Secretary). *LANGUAGES:* Arabic and English.

DR. MATANIOS HABIB, born Adideh-Safita, 1939. *Education:* University of Damascus (Accountancy, 1965; M.A. Ph.D., in Economics, 1971). Professor of Economics. Former: Minister of Petroleum; Dean of School of Economics, Damascus University; Deputy Dean for the Administration Affairs; Head of Economics Department; Professor of Economics (Const. University of Algeria). *LANGUAGES:* Arabic, French, English and Russian.

GABRIEL OUSSI, born Damascus, 1935; admitted, 1968. *Education:* University of Damascus School of Law. *Member:* Syrian Bar Association; International Association of Lawyers. *LANGUAGES:* Arabic and English.

RESIDENT
AFFILIATED OFFICE

NAHIL PETER ANTONE, born Baghdad, January 17, 1952; admitted, 1985, Michigan. *Education:* Engineering School, American Jesuit University, Baghdad (B.Sc. in Civil Engineering, with highest distinction, 1971); University of Surrey, Surrey, England (M.Sc., 1974); Detroit College of Law (J.D., summa cum laude, 1985). Listed in the Marquis Who's Who in American Law and Who's Who in the World. Registered Professional Engineer, Michigan, 1979. Instructor, Legal Research, Detroit College of Law, 1986-1987. Vice-President, Hennessey Engineers, Inc., Trenton, Michigan, 1979-1985. *Member:* State Bar of Michigan. *LANGUAGES:* English, Arabic and Chaldean.

GHAZI S. GHAZZI

BUREAU OF LEGAL SERVICES

TIBI & SILO BUILDING

69 SALHIE STREET

P.O. BOX 4238

DAMASCUS, SYRIA

Telephone: 2 229798; 2 224036

Cable Address: "Avoghaz"

Telex: 411275 SY

Fax: 2 229798

General Practice. Government, Administrative, Business, Corporation, Merchant, Commercial, Joint Ventures, International, Foreign Investments, Taxation, Aviation, Civil, Labor and Arbitration Law.

GHAZI S. GHAZZI, born Damascus, Syria, November, 1937; admitted, 1960, Syria. *Education:* Syrian University, Damascus (General Law Degree). *Member:* Bar Association of Lawyers in Syria. *LANGUAGES:* Arabic, English and French.

REPRESENTATIVE CLIENTS: Barks Williams International United Refining, Ltd.; Entrepose; Centrimex; OTA; International Bechtel Inc.; American Arab Trading Co., Inc. (U.S.A.); Solar Electronics (Lebanon); Nissho-IWAI (Japan); Scandinavian Airlines; Austrian Airlines; Scorfico Ltd. (Syria); LOR, Inc. (U.S.A.); Amerco (U.S.A.); Aminoil (U.S.A.); Kone Westinghouse (Finland);

(This Listing Continued)

Volvo International (Sweden); Davy-McKee Inc. (U.S.A.); American Express (England); Kenzo Tange & Ortek (Japan); Texas Instrument (U.S.A); Carrier Corp. (U.S.A.); Westinghouse Electric Corp. (U.S.A.); Solar International Corp. (U.S.A.); Stahl Eisen Maschinnen (W. Germany); Stroj Export (Czechoslovakia); Warner-Lmbert (U.S.A.); Monsanto StL. (U.S.A.); Pectin Petroleum Co. (U.S.A.); Crysen-Montenay (U.S.A.); Union Carbide (U.S.A.); Arab Investment Co. (Dubai); DHL (U.K.); Xerox Corp. (U.S.A.); Koch Carbon Inc. (U.S.A.); Abbott Laboratories (U.S.A.); Syntex (France); Alfa-Laval (Sweden); Ensco (U.S.A.); Baxter (U.S.A.); Marathon (U.S.A.); Procter & Gamble; Exxon; Benetton (Italy); Ferrestool (Germany/U.S.A.).

TANZANIA

MAAJAR & RWECHUNGURA LAW OFFICE

Established in 1991

9TH FLOOR IPS BUILDING

MAKTABA STREET

P.O. BOX 7495

DAR ES SALAAM, TANZANIA

Telephone: 255 51 35356/34743

Telefax: 255 51 46191/38784/75105

General Practice, Commercial and Corporate, Mergers and Acquisitions, Banking, Investments and Financial Services, International Business Transactions, Arbitration and Litigation.

PARTNERS

MWANAIDI SINARE MAAJAR, admitted, 1986, Tanzania. *Education:* University of Dar es Salaam (LL.B., Hons., LL.M.). Member, Governing Council of the Tanganyika Law Society. Member, Tanzania Women Lawyers Association. Legal Officer, Central Bank of Tanzania, 1978-1983. Legal Advisor and Head of Legal and Business Development Department, Coopers and Lybrand (Tanzania), 1983-1991.

CHARLES R.B. RWECHUNGURA, admitted, 1987, Tanzania. *Education:* University of Dar es Salaam (LL.B., Hons.). Deputy Corporate Counsel, National Textile Corporation (TEXCO), 1980-1986. Chief Legal Counsel and Secretary, Tanzania Investment Bank, 1986-1993. *Member:* Tanganyika Law Society; International Bar Association.

LEGAL OFFICERS

LAU KEGO MASHA. *Education:* University of Dar es Salaam (LL.B., Hons.); Georgetown University (LL.M.). *Member:* The Association of the Bar of the City of New York; Tanganyika Law Society.

VICTORIA E.A. LYIMO. *Education:* University of Dar es Salaam (LL.B., Hons.). *Member:* Tanganyika Law Society; Tanzania Women Lawyers Association.

FATIMA IDDRISSU. *Education:* St. Olaf College USA (B.A., Hons.); Warwick (LL.B., Hons.). *Member:* Tanganyika Law Society; Tanzania Women Lawyers Association.

MKONO & COMPANY (ADVOCATES)

Established in 1977

2ND FLOOR, TDFL BUILDING

OHIO STREET/UPANGA ROAD

P.O. BOX 4369

DAR ES SALAAM, TANZANIA

Telephone: (Ë051) 44125, 37986, 31344, 38190 & 35935

FAX: (Ë051) 46690 & 44928

Arbitration, Admiralty, Advocacy, Banking, Corporate Mergers and Acquisitions, Tax, Commercial Contracts, Conveyancing, Debt Swaps and Recoveries, Foreign Investments, Intellectual Property, International Trade, Insolvencies, Joint Ventures, Landlord and Tenant, Labour, Litigation, Military, Mining, Mineral, Oil and Gas, Privatization and Divestures, Probate and Administration, Succession, Secured Lending.

PARTNERS

NIMROD ELIREHEEMAH MKONO, born Musoma, Tanzania, 1943; admitted, 1977, Tanzania. *Education:* University of East Africa (Dar, LL.B., 1970); South West London College (A.C.I.S., Diploma, 1975; M.A., Business Law, CNAA, UK, 1976. Founder, 1977, Dar es Salaam. *Member:* F.C.L.S., London, 1986. Advocate, Tanzania, 1977; Advocate, Zanzibar,

(This Listing Continued)

MKONO & COMPANY (ADVOCATES), Dar Es Salaam—Continued

1993. Honours: Honorary Legal Counsel to: The British High Commissioner, The Royal Danish Ambassador, and the Royal Swedish Ambassador.

CAPT. AUDAX KIJANA KAMEJA, born Bukoba, Tanzania, 1950; admitted, 1984, Dar es Salaam. *Education:* University of Dar es Salaam (LL.B., Hons), 1975; University of Glasgow (LL.M., 1983). Advocate, Tanzania, 1987.

ASSOCIATES

PROF. ZEBRON STEVE GONDWE, born Lindi, Tanzania, 1953; admitted, 1984, Dar es Salaam. *Education:* University of Dar es Salaam (LL.M., 1983); University of Wisconsin-Madison (LL.M., 1986; S.I.D., 1989). Advocate, Tanzania, 1989.

PAULINE H. KASONDA, born Tukuyu, Tanzania, 1958; admitted, 1991, Dar es Salaam. *Education:* University of Dar es Salaam (LL.B., Hons., 1983). Advocate, Tanzania, 1993.

ALOYSIUS KIBUUKA SSERUNKUMA MUJULIZI, born Muleba, Tanzania, 1963; admitted, 1994, Dar es Salaam. *Education:* Makerere University (LL.B., Hons., 1987); Law Development Centre (Diploma, 1988).

Members of the Tanganyika Law Society

Languages: English and Kiswahili

TUNISIA

SAMIR EL ANNABI

Established in 1969

11, RUE AZZOUZ REBAÏ, IMPASSE 7
2092 EL MANAR 2
TUNIS, TUNISIA
Telephone: (216-1) 88.61.81
Fax: (216-1) 88.61.82

International Contracts, Commercial, Investment, Arbitration, Energy and Patent Law.

SAMIR EL ANNABI, born Tunis, Tunisia, September 22, 1944; admitted, 1969, Tunisia; admitted to practice before the Supreme Court and the Council of State. *Education:* University of Tunis (B.A., 1967; LL.B., 1967); University of Paris-Sorbonne (M.S., 1969; LL.M., 1968); Maxwell School, Syracuse University, New York (M.P.A., 1971). Co-author: "Tunisian Administrative Law," 1975. Assistant Professor of Public Law, School of Public Administration, 1973-1982. Assistant Professor, Faculty of Law, Tunis, 1983—. *Member:* Tunisian Bar Association (Member, Executive Board, 1981-1983); International Bar Association; International Union of Lawyers; UN Fellows Association; Tunisian Arbitration Association (Treasurer); American Bar Association (International Associate); American Arbitration Association. *LANGUAGES:* Arabic, English and French.

Languages: Arabic, English and French.

ADLY BELLAGHA AND ASSOCIATES

126 RUE DE YOUGOSLAVIE
1000 TUNIS, TUNISIA
Telephone: (2161) 347.117/349.117
Telecopier: (2161) 343.746
Telex: 13.633 LAMAD

General Practice, Commercial, Civil, Investment, Oil and Gas, Business Contracts, International Transactions, Banking, Tax.

PARTNERS

ADLY BELLAGHA, born Tunis, Tunisia, March, 1954; admitted, 1977; 1987, Lawyer at Supreme Court. *Education:* Paris University; London International School of English. *Member:* Tunis Bar Association and International Bar Association. *LANGUAGES:* Arabic, French, English and Italian.

LAMINE BELLAGHA, born 1922; admitted, 1949, Lawyer at Supreme Court. *Education:* Paris University (Docteur en droit). Directeur au Plan,

(This Listing Continued)

1956. Professor, Tunis University. *Member:* Tunis Bar Association and Bar Law Association. *LANGUAGES:* Arabic, French and English.

ASSOCIATES

Faycal Triki
Mouloud Yahia Bacha
Abdettaziz Kamel

SALAHEDDINE CAID ESSEBSI AND ASSOCIATES

Established in 1961

14 AVENUE ALAIN SAVARY
1002 TUNIS, TUNISIA
Telephone: (216 1) 785.611
Telecopier: (216 1) 783.913

General Practice, Corporation, Tax and Administrative Law, Business Contracts, International Business Transactions, Banking, Oil and Gas, Trades, Arbitration.

PARTNERS

SALAHEDDINE CAID ESSEBSI, born 1933; admitted, 1961, Tunisia. Lawyer at the Supreme Court. *Education:* Université of Paris (Licence en Droit et Sciences Economiques); Certificat d'Etudes Supérieures Commerciales of Ecole des Hautes Etudes Commerciales de Paris. *Member:* Bar Association of Tunisia; American Society of International Law. *LANGUAGES:* French, English and Arabic.

BEJI CAID ESSEBSI, born 1926; admitted, 1952, Tunisia. *Education:* Université of Paris (Licence en Droit). Ministre of the Government, Interior and Defense Nationale, 1965-1970. Ambassadeur of Tunisia in Paris, 1971. Ministre of the Government, Foreign Affairs, 1980-1986. Ambassadeur of Tunisia in Bonn, 1987. Member of the Tunisian Parliament: Chairman, Parliament's Committee for Politics and Foreign Affairs, 1989; Chairman, Parliament, 1991. *Member:* Bar Association of Tunisia. *LANGUAGES:* French, Arabic and English.

NOUREDDINE FERCHIOU ET ASSOCIES

Established in 1984

34, PLACE DU 7 NOVEMBRE 1987
1001 TUNIS, TUNISIA
Telephone: (216-1) 345 373, 255 798
Telex: 15579 FERLO TN
Facsimile: (216-1) 350 028

Commercial Law, International Contracts, Investment, Real Estate, Taxation, Administrative and Banking Law, Business and Corporate Law, General Practice.

FIRM PROFILE: The firm's general corporate practice encompasses all aspects of business and commercial law. Clients of the firm are predominantly international corporations doing business in Tunisia. The firm also represents many national and multi-national corporations in such business sectors as banking, mining, oil and gas, manufacturing and services. The firm has played an important part in the founding and growth of several major Tunisian companies and has also played an active role in assisting foreign investors in their ventures with Tunisian partners. As a result, the firm has developed distinctive expertise in these sectors and is one of the leading commercial law firms in Tunisia.

MEMBERS OF FIRM

NOUREDDINE FERCHIOU, born Tunis, Tunisia, October 30, 1954; admitted, 1981, Tunisia. *Education:* Université de Tunis (M.A., Law, 1978); Université de Paris (D.E.A., en droit des affaires; D.E.A. en droit privé). Professor of Commercial Law, Institut des Hautes Etudes Commerciales Tunis (I.H.E.C.), 1981-1986. Member: Tunisian Administrative Reform Committee; Tunisian Investment Code Reform Committee. *Member:* International Lawyers Club. *LANGUAGES:* Arabic, French, English and Italian.

FOUAD MEBAZAA, born Tunis, Tunisia, June 15, 1933; admitted, 1960, Tunisia. *Education:* University of Paris (Law Degree). Member of Parliament, 1960-1964 and 1974-1981. Director, National Security, 1965-1967. Mayor of Tunis, 1969-1973. Minister of: Youth and Sports, 1987-1988; Public Health; Cultural Affairs; Information. Tunisian Ambassador to the United Nations in Geneva, 1981-1986. Tunisian Ambassador in Mo-

(This Listing Continued)

rocco, 1986-1987. President, Refugees Executive Committee, 1985-1986. *LANGUAGES:* Arabic and French.

ASSOCIATES

Abdelfattah Benhaji

Slim Ben Salah

Maher Snoussi

Languages: Arabic, French, English and Italian

MALOUCHE LAW FIRM

Associated Lawyers

Established in 1924

3 RUE HÉDI NOUIRA

1001 TUNIS, TUNISIA
Telephone: (216-1) 350 172
Fax: (216-1) 350 485

*Firm engaged in Tunisian and International Law practice. Entitled to plead before Tunisian Courts.
Business Law, Commercial Law, Corporate Finance, Investment Law, Litigation and International Arbitration.*

FIRM PROFILE: Established in 1924, Malouche Law Firm has been created by the deceased Mahmoud Malouche and has now reached its third generation of lawyers. The firm has a broadly based practice with a reputation for offering a full range of quality legal services.

MEMBERS OF FIRM

HABIB MALOUCHE, born Kairouan, Tunisia, August 24, 1927; admitted, 1957, Tunisia. *Education:* University of Paris (Post Graduate Diploma, 1953); ENA Paris (1956). Lecturer, Tunisian Law, Economics and Administration Centers, 1956-1975. Author: "Arbitration in Economic Relations with Arabic Countries," 1978; "Les Entreprises Publiques et l'Arbitrage en Droit Tunisien," Revue de l'Arbitrage, p. 374, 1989; "Recent Developments in Arbitration Law in Tunisia," 8 Journal of International Arbitration, pp. 23-31, 1991.*Member:* Arab Association of International Arbitration; ICC International Arbitration Commission; ICC Adaption Contracts Committee; ICC Institute of International Business Law and Practice; International Chamber of Commerce of Milan, Mediterranean and Middle East Arbitration Institute; Union Internationale des Avocats; French Arbitration Committee; Swiss Arbitration Association. *LANGUAGES:* Arabic, English, French and Italian. *PRACTICE AREAS:* Arbitration; Real Estate Law; Banking Law.

ELYES MALOUCHE, born Tunis, Tunisia, August 2, 1960; admitted, 1988, Tunisia. *Education:* University of Paris (1985). Author: "The Incorporation of a Company Submitted to Tunisian Law," 1992; "The Arbitration Clause," 1990. International Practice in Paris, 1986-1987. *Member:* Tunisian Bar Association; Economic Law Association. *LANGUAGES:* Arabic, English, French and Italian. *PRACTICE AREAS:* Litigation; Commercial and Business Law.

SLIM MALOUCHE, born Tunis, Tunisia, December 26, 1963; admitted, 1992, Tunisia. *Education:* University of Paris (Post Graduate Diploma, with honors, 1989). Author: "International Trading Companies," 1992; "Economical Customs-Free Zone," 1993. International Practice in Paris and
(This Listing Continued)

London, 1988-1991. *Member:* Tunisian Bar Association; TUNIASIA Association. *LANGUAGES:* Arabic, English, French and Italian. *PRACTICE AREAS:* Investment Law; Corporate Finance; Corporation Law.

UGANDA

KABUGO & COMPANY, ADVOCATES

Solicitors, Trademark & Patent Attorneys
Notaries Public, Commissioners for Oaths

Established in 1984

1ST FLOOR INSURANCE HOUSE (EAGEN)
14 KAMPALA ROAD
P.O. BOX 6538
KAMPALA, UGANDA
Telephone: 256-41-256718; 235740
Fax: 256-41-234252
Telex: 61186

Intellectual Property, Investment Law, International Business Law, General International Trade Law, Trademark and Patent Law.

MEMBERS OF FIRM

CHARLES ROBERT KABUGO MUSOKE, admitted, 1979, Uganda. *Education:* Makerere Univ. (LL.B., 1977); Law Centre (Dip. in Legal Practice, 1978). Commissioner for Oaths and Notary Public. Member, Uganda Law Society. *Member:* Uganda Arbitration Asso. *LANGUAGES:* English and Swahili. *PRACTICE AREAS:* Insurance; Aviation; Property Conveyancing; Foreign Investment; Corporate.

JOHN MAGEZI, admitted, 1991, Uganda. *Education:* Makerere Univ. (LL.B., 1984); Law Centre (Dip., L.P., 1985); Univ. of London (LL.M., 1989). Member, Uganda Law Society. *Member:* International Bar Asso. ; Uganda Arbitration Asso.; Chartered Institute of Arbitrators. *LANGUAGES:* English and Swahili. *PRACTICE AREAS:* Patents and Trademarks; Intellectual Property Law; Foreign Investment; Corporate; Commercial; Arbitration.

UNITED ARAB EMIRATES

AFRIDI & ANGELL

BIN HAMOODAH BUILDING
P.O. BOX 3961
ABU DHABI, UNITED ARAB EMIRATES
Telephone: 9712-329-134
Fax: 9712-326-905
Telex: 23632 Ordig Em
Cable Address: "Dignior Abu Dhabi"

Dubai, United Arab Emirates Office: City Tower, Level 8, Dubai-Abu Dhabi Road, P.O. Box 9371. Telephone: 9714-310-900. Fax: 9714-310-800. Telex: 46145 Ordig Em. Cable Address: "Dignior Dubai.
Sharjah, United Arab Emirates Office: Al-Boorj Avenue, P.O. Box 5925. Telephone: 9716-544-062. Fax: 9716-547-336. Telex: 68331 Ordig Em. Cable Address: "Dignior Sharjah.
Jebel Ali, United Arab Emirates Office: Jebel Ali Free Trade Zone, P.O. Box 16894. Telephone: 9714-816-010. Fax: 9714-816-774. Telex: 46145 Ordig Em.
Other Offices: New York, N.Y. Office: 230 Park Avenue. 10169. Telephone: 212-697-0300. Fax: 212-697-0385. Pakistan Office: 8. Street 31, 8th Avenue F-7/1, Islamabad 44000. Telephone: 92-51-217.031. Fax: 92-51-217-032.

General International, Regional and United Arab Emirates practice including representation of Clients in Administrative, Corporate, Banking, Maritime, Commercial, Financial, Real Estate, Petroleum, Arbitration and Litigation Matters; also Commercial Agency, Governmental Licensing and Registration, Employment, Islamic Law, Construction and Project Development.
(This Listing Continued)

AFRIDI & ANGELL, Abu Dhabi—Continued

FIRM PROFILE: The United Arab Emirates based firm of Afridi & Angell is a partnership among M.A.K. Afridi, Nicholas B. Angell, C. Chakradaran, Amjad Ali Khan, Charles S. Laubach, Hassen A. Ferris and Bashir Ahmed, who have several years of experience practicing law in the United Arab Emirates ("U.A.E."). The legal staff of Afridi & Angell currently consist of those seven partners and four associates with translation and paralegal support and fluency in English, Arabic, Urdu, Pushtu, Tamil and French. Afridi & Angell are licensed as Legal Consultants in the United Arab Emirates, but are not licensed to appear in Court.

Afridi & Angell conducts a diversified regional and international practice and provides legal services in all aspects of commercial matters, including banking and financial services, corporate, maritime and transport, governmental licensing, commercial agency, project development and intellectual property laws. The Firm also handles military procurement, anti-boycott and F.C.P.A. matters.

PARTNERS

CHARLES S. LAUBACH, born Syracuse, New York, February 7, 1957. Admitted to bar, 1985, Pennsylvania; 1986, District of Columbia (not admitted in United Arab Emirates). Education: Dartmouth College (B.A., 1979); University of Pennsylvania (J.D., 1984; M.A., 1985). Author: "U.A.E. Armed Forces Tenders," " Middle East Executive Reports, 1989; "Fraud and Related Offenses under U.A.E. Law," Middle East Executive Reports, 1988. Co-Author: with John O. Gerald, "Conversion of Partnerships to Limited Liability Companies under the U.A.E. Companies Law," Middle East Executive Reports, 1989. Chairman, American Business Group in Abu Dhabi. Member: Pennsylvania Bar Association; The District of Columbia Bar. LANGUAGES: English, Arabic, Urdu and French.

ASSOCIATES

HERBERT S. WOLFSON, born New York, N.Y., February 17, 1964; admitted, 1990, Pennsylvania (not admitted in the United Arab Emirates). Education: University of Pennsylvania (B.A., magna cum laude, 1985; J.D., magna cum laude, 1988; M.A., 1991). Order of the Coif. Author: "Saudi Arabia: New Regulation Governing Professional Partnerships," Middle East Executive Reports, 1991. Co-Author: with Charles S. Laubach, "U.A.E. Draft Federal Trademark Law," Middle East Executive Reports, 1992; with Philip J. Azar, "U.A.E. Draft Federal Copyright Law," Middle East Executive Reports, 1992; with Charles S. Laubach, "U.A.E. Draft Patents Law," Middle East Executive Reports, 1992; with Philip J. Azar, United Arab Emirates chapter in Ideas in the Making: A Guide to the Consolidation of Intellectual Property Protection (1992 Supplement, International Financial Law Review). Member, American Business Group in Abu Dhabi. Member: Pennsylvania and American Bar Associations. LANGUAGES: English and Arabic.

(For Biographical data on other firm personnel, see Professional Biographies at Dubai and Sharjah, United Arab Emirates, Islamabad, Pakistan and New York, N.Y.)

AL-SAYEGH RICHARDS BUTLER

SAIF BIN GHOBASH BUILDING
ZAYED THE SECOND STREET
P.O. BOX 46904
ABU DHABI, UNITED ARAB EMIRATES
Telephone: 2-725561
Telex: 22261 RBLAW EM
Fax: 2-778630

London, England Office: Richards Butler. Beaufort House, 15 St Botolph Street, EC3A 7EE. Telephone: 0171-247 6555. Telex: 949494 RBLAW G. Fax: 0171-247 5091.
Hong Kong Office: Richards Butler. Alexandra House, Twentieth Floor, 16-20 Chater Road. Telephone: 810 8008. Telex: 62554 RBLAW HX. Fax: 810 0664.
Brussels, Belgium Office: Richards Butler. Avenue de la Renaissance 1, Bte 11, 1040. Telephone: 2-732 20 55. Fax: 2-735 46 91.
Paris, France Office: Richards Butler. 134 rue du Faubourg Saint Honoré, 75008. Telephone: 1-44 13 63 53. Fax: 1-42 89 20 60.

(This Listing Continued)

RESIDENT PARTNERS

MOHAMMED AL-SAYEGH, born Muharaq, Bahrain, 1952; admitted, 1981, Abu Dhabi, United Arab Emirates. Education: Damascus University, Syria (Licence in Islamic Jurisprudence and Law, 1981). With Legal Affairs and Research Department, Ministry of Foreign Affairs, United Arab Emirates, 1974. LANGUAGES: Arabic, English and French.

ANTHONY L.G. TREW, born Bournemouth, England, March 20, 1942; admitted, as Solicitor of the Supreme Court of England and Wales, 1968 (Not admitted in United Arab Emirates). Education: London College of Law, England. Part-time Lecturer in Law, City of London Polytechnic, 1971-1973. LANGUAGES: English. PRACTICE AREAS: Aviation Law; Banking Law; Corporate Law; International Law; Commercial Litigation; Maritime Law; Transportation Law.

(For Complete List of Partners, see Professional Biographies at London, England).

AL TAMIMI & COMPANY

DALMA CENTRE BUILDING 13TH FLOOR
HAMDAN STREET
P.O. BOX 44046
ABU DHABI, UNITED ARAB EMIRATES
Telephone: (9712) 339904
Fax: (9712) 318993

Dubai, United Arab Emirates Office: Dubai World Trade Centre, 18th Floor, P.O. Box 9275. Telephone: (9714) 317090. Fax: (9714) 313177.
Sharjah, United Arab Emirates Office: ADCB Building, Port Road, 7th Floor, P.O. Box 5099. Telephone: (9716) 356122. Fax: (9716) 377740.

Local, Regional and International Practice including Corporate, Commercial, Financial, Banking, Foreign Investment, Intellectual Property, Maritime, Insurance, Litigation and Arbitration. Licensed to appear before U.A.E. Courts.

MANAGING ATTORNEYS

ESSAM AL TAMINI, born Sharjah, United Arab Emirates, June 1, 1961; admitted, 1985, United Arab Emirates. Education: Al Ain University, Al Ain (License en Droit, 1983); Harvard University (LL.M., 1984). Author: "Arrests of Ships in the U.A.E." Editor, Law Update Newsletter. Member: IBA Middle East Forum Committee. LANGUAGES: Arabic and English.

(For Complete Biographical data on all personnel, see Professional Biographies at Dubai, United Arab Emirates)

ALI H. GHOSHEH & PARTNERS

Established in 1971
SUITE 1001, 10TH FLOOR, THE BLUE TOWER
KHALIFA STREET
P.O. BOX 767
ABU DHABI, UNITED ARAB EMIRATES
Telephone: 02/322323 (5 lines)
Telefax: 02/332996
Cable: "Mohamoun"

Manama, Bahrain Associated Office: Hatim S. Zu'bi Law Offices. Bab-El-Bahrain Building, Suite No. 1, 2nd Floor, P.O. Box 502. Telephone: (0973) 251911. Fax: 232643.

Commercial, Corporate, Banking, Industrial, Protection of Intellectual Property Rights, Trademarks and Patents, Private International Law, Arbitration and Labour Law.

MEMBERS OF FIRM

ALI H. GHOSHEH. Education: Damascus (Graduated in Law). Licensed Advocate: Abu Dhabi, Dubai and Jordan. Ex-Judge, Jordan, 1963-1968. LANGUAGES: Arabic and English. PRACTICE AREAS: Consultancy; Litigation.

HUSSAIN A. JAGHOUB. Education: Alexandria (Graduated in Law, 1954). Ex-Judge, Jordan Court of Appeal, 1965. Ex-Member, Legislative Committee, Jordan, 1974. Ex-Judge, Abu Dhabi Civil Court, 1976. LANGUAGES: Arabic and English. PRACTICE AREAS: Consultancy.

VIQUAR I. CHOUDHURY. Education: B.A. (Hons.); Barrister-at-Law (1961) of Lincoln's Inn, London. LANGUAGES: English. PRACTICE AREAS: Consultancy.

(This Listing Continued)

TURKI A. RAHMAN ABDULLA. *Education:* U.A.E. University (LL.B.). Practicing as Licensed Advocate before Courts in the U.A.E. at all Levels. *LANGUAGES:* Arabic and English. *PRACTICE AREAS:* Litigation.

AHMED ABDULGHANI. *Education:* University of Alexandria (LL.B., 1945). Practiced as Licensed Advocate in Egypt, 1947-1985 and presently practicing before Courts in the U.A.E. at all levels. *LANGUAGES:* Arabic and English. *PRACTICE AREAS:* Litigation.

KUDSI FOX & GIBBONS

Solicitors

Established in 1981

P.O. BOX 46010

ABU DHABI, UNITED ARAB EMIRATES

Telephone: (9712) 322858

Fax: (9712) 331586

London, England Office: 2 Old Burlington Street, W1X 2QA. Telephone: (44-171) 439 8271. Telex: 267108. Telefax: (44-171) 734 8843.

Dubai, United ArabEmirates Office: P.O. Box 1756. Telephone: (9714) 310220. Fax: (9714) 310201. Telex: 45614 GBLAW EM.

Cairo, Egypt Office: 126 Mohei El Din Abul Ezz Street, 9th Floor, Mohandiseen, Giza, Cairo, Egypt. Telephone: (202) 3485955. Fax: (202) 3492210.

Fujairah, United Arab Emirates Office: P.O. Box 701. Telephone (971 9) 229390. Fax: (971 9) 226470.

Kuwait Associated Office: P.O. Box 26473, Safat, 13125 Safat. Telephone: (965) 2462323/2462525/2462929. Fax: (965) 242 5830. Telex: 30844 ZINA KT.

Ruwi, Oman Office: P.O. Box 3552, Postal Code 112. Telephone: (968) 564346; Fax: (968) 564395. Telex: 5630 GIBLAW ON.

Gibraltar Office: P.O. Box 246. Telephone: (350) 77750. Fax: (350) 77800.

Yemen Associated Office: P.O. Box 148, Crater, Aden. Telephone: (9672) 255305/253824. Fax: (9672) 255305/255117.

Lebanon Associated Office: Saba K. Zreik Law Offices. Autostrade Dora, Cite Dora 3 Building, 10th Floor, P.O. Box 90-710, Beirut Lebanon. Telephone: (961 1) 881322. Fax: (961 1) 881387. Telex 42949 MANAL LE.

MANAGING PARTNER

Rhys Lewis

LEGAL SUPPORT PERSONNEL

Marguerite Danaher (Senior Solicitor)

(For a list of other Personnel, see Biographical Cards at London, England, Dubai and Fujairah, United Arab Emirates, Cairo, Egypt, Kuwait, Ruwi, Sultanate of Oman, Gibraltar, Lebanon and Yemen)

SHEARMAN & STERLING

P.O. BOX 2948

ABU DHABI, UNITED ARAB EMIRATES

Telephone: (971-2) 324477

Fax: (971-2) 774533

New York, N.Y. Office: 599 Lexington Avenue, New York, New York 10022-6069 and Citicorp Center, 153 East 53rd Street, New York, New York 10022-4676. Telephone: (212) 848-4000. Telex: 667290 Num Lau. Fax: 599 Lexington Avenue: (212) 848-7179. Citicorp Center: (212) 848-5252.

Beijing, People's Republic of China Office: Suite #2205, Capital Mansion, No. 6, Xin Yuan Nan Road. Chao Yang District Beijing, 100004. Telephone: (861) 465-4574. Fax: (861) 465-4578.

Budapest, Hungary Office: Szerb utca 17-19, 1056 Budapest. Telephone: (36-1) 266-3522. Fax: (36-1) 266-3523.

Düsseldorf, Federal Republic of Germany Office: Königsallee 46, D-40212 Düsseldorf. Telephone: (49-211) 13 62 80. Telex: 8 588 294 NYLO. Fax: (49-211) 13 33 09.

Frankfurt, Federal Republic of Germany Office: Bockenheimer Landstrasse 55, D-60325 Frankfurt am Main. Telephone: (49-69) 97-10-70. Fax: (49-69) 97-10-71-00.

Hong Kong, Hong Kong Office: Standard Chartered Bank Building, 4 Des Voeux Road Central, Hong Kong. Telephone: (852) 2978-8000. Fax: (852) 2978-8099.

(This Listing Continued)

London, England Office: 199 Bishopsgate, London EC2M 3TY. Telephone: (44-71) 920-9000. Fax: (44-71) 920-9020.

Los Angeles, California Office: 725 South Figueroa Street, 21st Floor, 90017-5421. Telephone: (213) 239-0300. Fax: (213) 239-0381, 614-0936.

Paris, France Office: 12 rue d'Astorg, 75008. Telephone: (33-1) 44-71-17-17. Telex: 282964 Royale. Fax: (33-1) 44-71-01-01.

San Francisco, California Office: 555 California Street, 94104-1522. Telephone: (415) 616-1100. Fax: (415) 616-1199.

Taipei, Taiwan Office: 7th Floor, Hung Kuo Building, 167 Tun Hwa North Road. Telephone: (886-2) 545-3300. Fax: (866-2) 545-3322.

Tokyo, Japan Office: Shearman & Sterling (Thomas Wilner Gaikokuho-Jimu-Bengoshi Jimusho), Fukoku Seimei Building, 5th Fl. 2-2-2, Uchisaiwaicho, Chiyoda-ku, Tokyo 100, Japan. Telephone: (81 3) 5251-1601. Fax: (81 3) 5251-1602.

Toronto, Ontario, Canada Office: Commerce Court West, Suite 4405, P.O. Box 247, M5L 1E8. Telephone: (416) 360-8484. Fax: (416) 360-2958.

Washington, D.C. Office: 801 Pennsylvania Avenue, N.W., Suite 900, 20004-2604. Telephone: (202) 508-8000. Fax: (202) 508-8100.

General Practice.

Firm engaged in American and General International Law Practice, but not authorized to appear before the Courts of the United Arab Emirates.

FIRM PROFILE: Shearman & Sterling, founded in 1873, has more than 500 lawyers in 15 offices throughout the world. The firm's practice encompasses most major areas of business law, including: Antitrust and Trade Regulation; Banking; Bankruptcy and Corporate Reorganization; Compensation and Benefits; Environmental; Finance (including Corporate Finance, Domestic Private Finance, Financial Institutions, International Private Finance and Project Finance); Individual Clients, Trusts and Estates; Insurance; International Trade and Government Relations; Litigation and Arbitration; Mergers and Acquisitions; Oil and Gas; Privatizations; Real Estate; and Tax. The Firm is also engaged in the practice of French, German and Hungarian law through its offices in France, Germany and Hungary.

MANAGING PARTNER

PHILIP B. DUNDAS, JR., born Middletown, Connecticut, 1948; admitted, 1974, New York (Not admitted in United Arab Emirates). *Education:* Wesleyan University (B.A., 1970); Washington and Lee University (J.D., 1973).

RESIDENT ASSOCIATE

WILLIAM F. RANIERI, born 1969; admitted, 1991, New Jersey and New York (Not admitted in United Arab Emirates). *Education:* University of South Florida (B.A., 1983); New York Law School (J.D., 1991).

OF COUNSEL

MICHAEL W. SMITH, born Davenport, Iowa, 1956; admitted, 1981, New York. *Education:* University of Iowa (B.B.A., with distinction, 1977); Duke University (J.D., 1980).

(For Biographical data of all partners, see Professional Biographies at New York, N.Y.).

AFRIDI & ANGELL

CITY TOWER, LEVEL 8

DUBAI-ABU DHABI ROAD

DUBAI, UNITED ARAB EMIRATES

Telephone: 9714-310-900

Fax: 9714-310-800

Telex: 46145 Ordig em

Cable Address: "Dignior Dubai"

Abu Dhabi, United Arab Emirates Office: Bin Hamoodah Building, P.O. Box 3961. Telephone: 9712-329-134. Fax: 9712-326-905. Telex: 23632 Ordig Em. Cable Address: "Dignior Abu Dhabi".

Sharjah, United Arab Emirates Office: Al-Boorj Avenue, P.O. Box 5925. Telephone: 9716-544-062. Fax: 9716-547-336. Telex: 68331 Ordig Em. Cable Address: "Dignior Sharjah".

Jebel Ali, United Arab Emirates Office: Jebel Ali Free Trade Zone, P.O. Box 16894. Telephone: 9714-816-010. Fax: 9714-816-774. Telex: 46145 Ordig Em.

Other Offices: New York, N.Y. Office: 230 Park Avenue. 10169. Telephone: 212-697-0300. Fax: 212-697-0385.

(This Listing Continued)

AFRIDI & ANGELL, Dubai—Continued

Pakistan Office: 8. Street 31, 8th Avenue F-7/1, Islamabad 44000.
Telephone: 92-51-217-031. Fax: 92-51-217-032.

General International, Regional and United Arab Emirates practice including representation of Clients in Administrative, Corporate, Banking, Maritime, Commercial, Financial, Real Estate, Petroleum, Arbitration and Litigation Matters; also Commercial Agency, Governmental Licensing and Registration, Employment, Islamic Law, Construction, and Project Development.

FIRM PROFILE: The United Arab Emirates based firm of Afridi & Angell is a partnership among M.A.K. Afidi, Nicholas B. Angell, C. Chakradaran, Amjad Ali Khan, Charles S. Laubach, Hassen A. Ferris and Bashir Ahmed, who have several years of experience practicing law in the United Arab Emirates ("U.A.E."). The legal staff of Afridi & Angell currently consist of those seven partners and four associates with translation and paralegal support and fluency in English, Arabic, Urdu, Pushtu, Tamil and French. Afridi & Angell are licensed as Legal Consultants in the United Arab Emirates, but are not licensed to appear in Court.

Afridi & Angell conducts a diversified regional and international practice and provides legal services in all aspects of commercial matters, including banking and financial services, corporate, maritime and transport, governmental licensing, commercial agency, project development and intellectual property laws. The Firm also handles military procurement, anti-boycott and F.C.P.A. matters.

PARTNERS

M.A.K. AFRIDI, born Karachi, Pakistan, February 2, 1936; admitted, 1958, Pakistan; 1974 admitted as a legal consultant (Not admitted as Advocate in the United Arab Emirates). *Education:* Peshawar University (LL.B., 1958). Author: "The Emirates Lay Down the Law on Interest-Free Banking," International Financial Law Review, 1985; "Construction Contracting in the United Arab Emirates," International Construction Law Review, 1985. Co-Author: with Amjad Ali Khan, "The Effect of Islamic Principles on the Conduct of Business in the Gulf," paper presented at Gulf America conference Houston, Texas, 1988; with Nicholas B. Angell, "Recent Developments in the United Arab Emirates," paper delivered at International Bar Association Conference, Singapore, 1985. Correspondent: International Construction Law Review. Partner, Orr Dignam & Co., Pakistan, 1964-1974. Resident Partner, Orr Dignam & Co., Middle East Office, Sharjah, United Arab Emirates, 1974-1980. Partner, Chadbourne, Parke & Afridi, Middle East Offices, United Arab Emirates, 1980-1991. *Member:* The ICC International Court of Arbitration (Pakistan Representative); International Bar Association. *LANGUAGES:* English, Urdu and Pushtu.

NICHOLAS B. ANGELL, born New York, N.Y., June 30, 1932; admitted, 1961, New York; admitted as a legal consultant in the United Arab Emirates (not admitted as an Advocate in the United Arab Emirates). (Resident in the New York Office).

C. CHAKRADARAN, born Trincomalee, Sri Lanka, February 6, 1941; admitted, as Advocate, 1966, Sri Lanka; 1991, admitted as a legal consultant in the United Arab Emirates (Not admitted as an Advocate in the United Arab Emirates). *Education:* Ceylon Law College, Colombo, Sri Lanka. Author: "Arrest of Ships in the United Arab Emirates," Chapter in Lloyd's of London Press, Arrest of Ships, 1987; "An Overview of the New U.A.E. Federal Maritime Law," Middle East Executive Reports, 1982. Co-author: with M.K. Afridi, "Arrest of Vessels in the United Arab Emirates," Chapter in Maritime Law Handbook published by the International Bar Association, 1987; with Bashir Ahmed, "Marine Cargo Claims under the Laws of the United Arab Emirates," published in Lloyd's Maritime and Commercial Law Quarterly, November, 1992; with Bashir Ahmed and Haider K. Afridi, "Ship Finance in the United Emirates," published by Euromoney in their "Shipping Finance Annual," 1993/1994; with Bashir Ahmed, "Regulation of Banking and Financial Services in the United Arab Emirates," published by International Financial Law Review in the "International Banking Yearbook," 1993/1994 edition; with Bashir Ahmed, "Banking and the Law," published in the Telerate Bank Register, August, 1993 - an International Financial Law Review publication. Visiting Lecturer and Examiner, Incorporated Council of Legal Education in Sri Lanka. Partner, Chadbourne, Park & Afridi, Middle East Offices, Sharjah, 1987-1991. Correspondent: Lloyd's Maritime and Commercial Law Quarterly. *Member:* Sri Lankan and International Bar Associations. *LANGUAGES:* English and Tamil.

AMJAD ALI KHAN, born Peshawar, Pakistan, August 27, 1955. Admitted to bar, 1980, Punjab; 1983, New York; 1991, admitted as a legal

(This Listing Continued)

consultant in the United Arab Emirates (Not admitted as an advocate in the United Arab Emirates). *Education:* Government College Lahore (B.A., 1976); Punjab University (LL.B., 1979); University of California, Berkeley (LL.M., 1981). Author: "The Courts and the Legal System in the U.A.E.," - Middle East Executive Reports, August 1983; "Agency and Distributorship in the U.A.E.," - Middle East Executive Reports, August 1985; "U.A.E. Draft Regulations for Financial Institutions," Middle East Executive Reports, December 1988; "Establishing a Business Presence in the United Arab Emirates," - Outlook, February 1991; "United Arab Emirates, - General Questions on Banking and Securities Law," - International Financial Law Practice Files, 1991; "Commercial Agencies and Distributorships: An International Guide," - Prentice Hall, 1992. Co-Author: with Gary R. Feulner, "Dispute Resolution in the Emirates," - Middle East Executive Reports, July 1985; with M.A.K. Afridi, "The Effect of Islamic Legal Principles on the Conduct of Business in the Gulf," paper presented at the Gulf America conference, Houston, Texas, 1988; with Gary R. Feulner, "U.A.E. Brokerage Regulations," - Middle East Executive Reports, April 1988; with Charles Laubach, "Recent Legal and Business Developments in the U.A.E.," - Middle East Executive Reports, August 1988; A Special Report on Arbitration," published as a special supplement of the International Financial Law Review, May 1993. *Member:* New York State Bar Association. *LANGUAGES:* English and Urdu.

HASSEN A. FERRIS, born Kherbit Rouha, Lebanon, June 25, 1955. Admitted to bar: 1983, New York; 1984, U.S. District Court, Southern District of New York; 1990, Illinois (Not admitted in the United Arab Emirates). *Education:* North Dakota State University (B.S., 1978; B. Architecture, 1979); Cornell University (J.D., 1982, magna cum laude, Order of the Coif). Author: "Taxation of Foreign Companies in Saudi Arabia," Middle East Executive Digest, 1986; Co-Author with Joe M. Hawbaker, "100% Foreign Ownership Allowed in Jebel Ali," Middle East Executive Reports, November 1992; "Jebel Ali Free Zone Establishments,' Middle East Executive Reports, December 1992. *Member:* American Bar Association; Arab-American Bar Association of Illinois. Associate Member: American Business Council of Dubai and the Northern Emirates. *LANGUAGES:* English and Arabic.

ASSOCIATES

JOE M. HAWBAKER, born Mount Pleasant, Iowa, February 22, 1959. Admitted to bar, 1990, Illinois (Not admitted in United Arab Emirates). *Education:* Grinnell College (B.A., 1980); University of Chicago (M.A., 1984); University of Michigan (J.D., 1989). Author: "Marketing Investment Products in the United Arab Emirates," Middle East Executive Reports, May 1993. Co-Author with Hassen A. Ferris, "100% Foreign Ownership Allowed in Jebel Ali," Middle East Executive Reports, November 1992. *Member:* Illinois State and American Bar Associations. Associate Member: American Business Council of Dubai and the Northern Emirates. *LANGUAGES:* English and Arabic.

MICHAEL M. MCDANIEL, born Little Rock, Arkansas, August 14, 1956; (admission pending). *Education:* Fordham University (B.A., Middle East studies, 1988; J.D., 1994).

HAIDER K. AFRIDI, born Kohat, Pakistan, November 2, 1964. Admitted to bar, 1990, Pakistan. (not admitted in United Arab Emirates). *Education:* University of Bristol (B.A., Jurisprudence, 1988); Fordham University (LL.M., International Business and Trade Law, 1991). Author: "Islamic Leasing and Tax Issues," - a special supplement to the World Leasing Yearbook 1993 published by Euromoney. Co-author: with C. Chakradaran and Basher Ahmed, "Ship Financing in the United Arab Emirates," published by Euromoney in their "Shipping Finance Annual," 1993-1994. *LANGUAGES:* English and Urdu.

(For Biographical data on other firm personnel, see Professional Biographies at Abu Dhabi and Sharjah, United Arab Emirates, Islamabad, Pakistan and New York, N.Y.)

AL-ARAIMI & AL-KABBAN

Advocates & Legal Consultants
DUBAI TOWER, OFF. NO. 202
BENIYAS SQUIRE, DEIRA
P.O. BOX 4790
DUBAI, UNITED ARAB EMIRATES
Telephone: 212900/211283
Fax: 215112

General Practice in all courts including court of cassation & Federal High Court, consultancy and advise in all U.A.E. Laws, Public International Law, Private International Law, International Business Law, International Arbitration and International Maritime Law.

FIRM PROFILE: Al-Araimi Al- Kabban has grown to become a reputed law firm in U.A.E. having branches in Al-Ain & Dubai. The firm is offering a wide range of quality legal service inside and outside the region.

DR. RIYADH AL KABBAN, born Iraq, 1950; admitted, 1971. *Education:* Basra University, Iraq (Honours Degree in Law, LL.B.); Cairo University (LL .M., Public Law); Glasgow University (Diploma in Forensic Medicine, Ph.D. in Maritime Law). Judge, Court of First Instance Basra. Practise in all U.A.E. courts including Dubai Court of Cassation. *Member:* Iraqi Bar Association; U.A.E. Bar Association (Ministry Justice); London Court of International Arbitration; Abu Dhabi Commercial Conciliation and Arbitration Centre. *LANGUAGES:* Arabic and English. *PRACTICE AREAS:* Commercial Law; Banking Law; Civil Law; Criminal Law; Copyright and Trademark Laws.

FAYEZ AL ARAIMI, born Al-Ain, 1948; admitted, 1983. *Education:* Baghdad University (Degree in Law). Practice in U.A.E. courts including Federal High Court of U.A.E. and Dubai Court of Cassation. *Member:* U.A.E. Bar Association (Ministry of Justice). *LANGUAGES:* Arabic and English. *PRACTICE AREAS:* Commercial law; Banking Law; Civil Law; Criminal Law; Copyright and Trademark Laws.

J.V. AARON, born Secunderabad, India, 1954; admitted, 1983. *Education:* Kanpur University, India (Degree in Law, LL.B.). *Member:* Andhra Pradesh (Bar Council). *LANGUAGES:* English and Hindi. *PRACTICE AREAS:* Commercial law; Banking Law; Civil Law; Criminal Law; Copyright and Trademark Laws.

ISSA MUSTAFA ADAM, born Sudan, 1947; admitted, 1970. *Education:* Khartoum University, Sudan (Degree in Law). Practice in all U.A.E. Courts. *Member:* U.A.E. Bar Association (Ministry of Justice). *LANGUAGES:* English and Arabic. *PRACTICE AREAS:* Commercial Law; Banking Law; Civil Law; Criminal Law; Copyright and Trademark Laws.

AL-MEHAIRI-BRYAN CAVE

Bryan Cave is a Partnership including a Professional Corporation
HOLIDAY CENTRE
COMMERCIAL TOWER
SUITE 1103
P.O. BOX 13677
DUBAI, UNITED ARAB EMIRATES
Telephone: 971-4-314-123
Facsimile: 971-4-318-287

St. Louis, Missouri Office: Bryan Cave, One Metropolitan Square, 211 North Broadway, Suite 3600, 63102-2750. Telephone: (314) 259-2000. Facsimile: (314) 259-2020.

Washington, D.C. Office: Bryan Cave, 700 Thirteenth Street, N.W., 20005-3960. Telephone: (202) 508-6000. Facsimile: (202) 508-6200.

New York, N.Y. Office: Bryan Cave, 245 Park Avenue, 10167-0034. Telephone: (212) 692-1800. Facsimile: (212) 692-1900 and Other New York, N.Y. Office: 575 Lexington Avenue, 10022. Telephone: (212) 371-1660. Facsimile: (212) 593-0243.

Kansas City, Missouri Office: Bryan Cave, 3300 One Kansas City Place, 1200 Main Street, 64141-6914. Telephone: (816) 374-3200. Facsimile: (816) 374-3300.

Overland Park, Kansas Office: Bryan Cave, 7500 College Boulevard, Suite 1100, 66210-4035. Telephone: (913) 338-7700. Facsimile: (913) 338-7777.

Phoenix, Arizona Office: Bryan Cave, 2800 North Central Avenue, Twenty-First Floor, 85004-1098. Telephone: (602) 230-7000. Facsimile: (602) 266-5938.

(This Listing Continued)

Los Angeles, California Office: Bryan Cave, 777 South Figueroa Street, Suite 2700. 90017-5418. Telephone: (213) 243-4300. Facsimile: (213) 243-4343.

Santa Monica, California Office: Bryan Cave, 120 Broadway, Suite 500, 90401-2305. Telephone: (310) 576-2100. Facsimile: (310) 576-2200.

Irvine, California Office: Bryan Cave, 18881 Von Karman, Suite 250, 92715-1500. Telephone: (714) 757-8100. Facsimile: (714) 757-8106.

London SW1H 9BU England Office: Bryan Cave, 29 Queen Anne's Gate. Telephone: 011-44-71-222-0511. Facsimile: 011-44-71-222-1240.

Frankfurt, Federal Republic of Germany Office: Bryan Cave, In Cooperation with Rossbach & Partner, Stresemannallee 33, D-60596 Frankfurt am Main. Telephone: 011-49-69-631 50 24. Facsimile: 011-49-69-631 31 64.

Riyadh 11465 Saudi Arabia Office: In Cooperation with Kadasah Law Firm, P.O. Box 20883. Telephones: 011-966-1-465-1371 and 1165. Facsimile: 011-966-1-464-3789.

Hong Kong Office: Bryan Cave, Suite 2106, Lippo Tower 21/F, Lippo Centre, 89 Queensway. Telephone: 011-852-2522-2821. Facsimile: 011-852-2522-2330.

General Civil Practice. Administrative, Antitrust, Aviation, Banking, Bankruptcy, Coal, Communications, Computer, Corporate Financing, Corporation, Environmental, Estate Planning, Government Contract, Health Care, Immigration, Intellectual Property, International, Labor, Legislative, Mining, Patent and Trademark, Probate, Products Liability, Real Estate, Securities, Tax Exempt Financing, Taxation, Technology, Transportation, Trust and University Law. General Civil Trial and Appellate Practice.

PARTNERS

KHALID M. KADFOOR AL-MEHAIRI, born U.A.E., 1962. *Education:* Arab University of Beirut Faculty of Law (B.A. Law, 1987); The American University (LL.M., 1994); Ministry of Justice of Egypt (D.P.L. in Private Law and Military Prosecution, 1991). Legal Advisor and Deputy Director of Military Justice, United Arab Emirates' Federal Armed Forces. Author: "Criminal Law: An Interpretation of the Emirates' Criminal Law," (1992). *PRACTICE AREAS:* International Transactions; Criminal and Military Law.

SAM E. EVERSMAN, born Indiana, 1963; admitted, 1987, Missouri (Not admitted in United Arab Emirates). *Education:* Indiana University (B.S., in Accounting with high distinction; J.D., magna cum laude, 1987). Order of the Coif. Certified Public Accountant, Illinois, 1985. (Also at Riyadh, Saudi Arabia Office).

ASSOCIATES

WILLIAM E. PYRON, JR., born Georgia, 1963; admitted, 1988, Georgia (Not admitted in United Arab Emirates). *Education:* University of Georgia (B.A., cum laude, 1985): School of Law, University of Georgia (J.D., 1988). *LANGUAGES:* French, Japanese. *PRACTICE AREAS:* Immigration; International.

HASSAN MOSTAFA EL-SAYED, born Egypt, 1962; (Not admitted in United Arab Emirates). *Education:* Ain Shams University (B.A. Law, 1985). *PRACTICE AREAS:* Corporate and Commercial Law; Licensing and Trademark Matters; International Arbitration.

AL TAMIMI & COMPANY

DUBAI WORLD TRADE CENTRE 18TH LEVEL
P.O. BOX 9275
DUBAI, UNITED ARAB EMIRATES
Telephone: (9714) 317090
Fax: (9714) 313177

Abu Dhabi, United Arab Emirates Office: Dalma Centre Building, Hamdan Street, 13th Floor, P.O. Box 44046. Telephone (9712) 339904. Fax: (9712) 318993.

Sharjah, United Arab Emirates Office: ADCB Building, Port Road, 7th Floor, P.O. Box 5099. Telephone: (9716) 356122. Fax: (9716) 377740.

Local, Regional and International Practice including Corporate, Commercial, Financial, Banking, Foreign Investment, Intellectual Property, Maritime, Insurance, Litigation and Arbitration. Licensed to appear before U.A.E. Courts.

MANAGING ATTORNEYS

ESSAM AL TAMINI, born Sharjah, United Arab Emirates, June 1, 1961; admitted, 1985, United Arab Emirates. *Education:* Al Ain University, Al Ain (License en Droit, 1983); Harvard University (LL.M., 1984). Author: "Arrests of Ships in the U.A.E." Editor, Law Update Newsletter.

(This Listing Continued)

AL TAMIMI & COMPANY, Dubai—Continued

Member: IBA Middle East Forum Committee. *LANGUAGES:* Arabic and English.

DAVID J. KARL, born Detroit, Michigan, October 4, 1960; admitted, 1992, Virginia; 1993, District of Columbia (Not admitted in United Arab Emirates). *Education:* Sonoma State University (B.A., 1984); George Washington University (J.D., 1992). Member, George Washington Journal of International Law and Economics. Author: Note, "Islamic Law in Saudi Arabia: What Foreign Attorneys Should Know," George Washington Journal of International Law and Economics, Vol. 25, No. 1, 1991. *LANGUAGES:* Arabic and Norwegian.

SAID EL SHARIF, born Nablus, Jordan May 13, 1944; admitted, 1971, Egypt (Not admitted in United Arab Emirates). *Education:* Cairo University (License of Law, 1969). *Member:* Jordanian Bar Association. *LANGUAGES:* English and Arabic.

ASSOCIATES

OMAR EL SHAIKH SID AHMED, born Khartoum, Sudan, January 1, 1949; admitted, 1979, Sudan; 1990, United Arab Emirates. *Education:* Cairo University, Khartoum (License of Law, 1978). Judgeships: Magistrate Judge, Province Judge, Sudan. *Member:* Sudan Legal Profession Board; Sudanese Bar Association. *LANGUAGES:* Arabic and English.

BASIL HASAN SIDDIQI, born Saharanpur, India, April 2, 1958; admitted, 1983, Bombay (Not admitted in United Arab Emirates). *Education:* Government Law College, Bombay (B.Sc., Hons, LL.B., 1985). Part time Professor of Law, K.C. Law college, Bombay, India, 1987-1992. *Member:* Bombay Bar Association. *LANGUAGES:* English, Hindi and Urdu.

ANDREW ANTHONY DAVID SHANTHA KUMAR, born Madras, India, December 3, 1961; admitted, 1992, Bangalore, India (Not admitted in United Arab Emirates). *Education:* Loyola College, Madras (Bachelor of Science, 1982); XLRI, Jamshedpur (Post Graduate Honours Diploma in Industrial Relations and Personnel Management, 1985); College of Law, Bangalore (LL.B., B.M.S., 1992). *Member:* Karnataka Bar Association (an affiliate of the Indian Council). *LANGUAGES:* English, French, German, Hindi, Tamil, Malayalam and Kannada.

CHRISTOPHER ROBSON KERRY, born Easington, England, May 29, 1968. admitted to the Roll of Solicitors, England, 1993 (Not admitted in United Arab Emirates). *Education:* Essex Institute of Higher Education, Chelmsford, Essex (LL.B., Hons, 1989) Solicitors Final Examination, Guildford, Surrey, 1990. *Member:* The Law Society of England.

AYOUB GAZI, born Sharjah, United Arab Emirates, January 2, 1962; admitted, 1988, United Arab Emirates. *Education:* Al Ain University, United Arab Emirates (License of Law, 1987). *LANGUAGES:* Arabic and English.

RUTA SHEKHAR GOTHOSKAR, born Sawantwadi, India, October 24, 1963; admitted, 1987, Bombay (Not admitted in United Arab Emirates). *Education:* Rani Parvati Devi College, Belgaum (B.A., 1984); Raja Lakhangauda Law College Belgaum (LL.B., 1987); Karnataka University, India. Appointed Assistant Government Pleader, State of Maharashtra, Bombay, 1992. *Member:* Bombay Bar Association. *LANGUAGES:* English, Hindi, Marathi and Kannada.

JAMAL ALI SAYED MOHAMMED AL SHAINQITI, born Dubai, United Arab Emirates, September 3, 1958; admitted, 1994, Dubai, United Arab Emirates. *Education:* Beirut University, Egypt (License of Law, 1993). *LANGUAGES:* Arabic and English.

JASSIM MOHAMMED ABDULLAH, born Dubai, United Arab Emirates, December 11, 1961; admitted, 1994, United Arab Emirates. *Education:* Al Ain University, United Arab Emirates (License of Law, 1987). *LANGUAGES:* Arabic, Hindi and English.

SAYED WASEL, born Cairo, Egypt, July 24, 1959; admitted, 1984, Egypt (Not admitted in United Arab Emirates). *Education:* Cairo University (Bachelor of Law, 1984). *Member:* Cairo Bar Association; Egypt Society for Criminal Science and Human Rights. *LANGUAGES:* Arabic.

ALLEN & OVERY

501 AL FUTTAIM TOWER
P.O. BOX 3251
DEIRA, DUBAI, UNITED ARAB EMIRATES
Telephone: (971 4) 282296
Facsimile: (971 4) 212860

London, England Office: One New Change, EC4M 9QQ. Telephone: 0171 330 3000. Facsimile: 0171 330 9999.

Beijing, China Office: Suite 3204, Jing Guang Centre, Hu Jia Lou, Chaoyang District, 100020. Telephone: (86 1) 501 4681. Facsimile: (86 1) 501 4682.

Brussels, Belgium Office: Rue de la Loi 99, Box 8, 1040. Telephone: (32 2) 230 27 91. Facsimile: (32 2) 230 66 13.

Budapest, Hungary Office: Mádach Trade Center, Mádach Imre utca 13-14, H-1075. Telephone: (361) 268 1511. Facsimile: (361) 268 1515.

Frankfurt, Germany Office: Taunusanlage 11, 11th Floor, 60329. Telephone: (49 69) 242 6120. Facsimile: (49 69) 242 61220.

Hong Kong Office: 9th Floor, Three Exchange Square, 8 Connaught Place. Telephone: (852) 2840 1282. Telex: 68757. Facsimile: (852) 2840 0515.

Madrid, Spain Office: Antonio Maura 7, 6°, 28014. Telephone: (34 1) 521 2654. Facsimile: (34 1) 523 0458.

Moscow, Russia Office: 9 ul Tverskaya, Entrance No 5, 8th Floor, 103009. Telephone: (7 501) 940 4500. Facsimile: (7 501) 940 4501.

New York Office: Swiss Bank Tower, 10 East 50th Street, 10022. Telephone (1-212) 754 3340. Facsimile: (1-212) 754 7903.

Paris, France Office: 1 Avenue Franklin D. Roosevelt, 75008. Telephone (33-1) 49 53 06 37. Telex: 651079. Facsimile: (33-1) 49 53 91 52.

Prague, Czech Republic Office: Jindřišská 34, 110 00 Prague 1. Telephone: (42 2) 2410 3317. Facsimile: (42 2) 2410 3235.

Singapore Office: 20 Raffles Place #08-03, Ocean Towers, 0104. Telephone: (65) 533 0988. Facsimile: (65) 533 1322.

Tokyo, Japan Office: NSE Building, 5th Floor, 1-7-1 Kanda Jinbo-cho, Chiyoda-ku Tokyo 101. Telephone (81 3) 3259 9898. Facsimile (81 3) 3259 9888.

Warsaw, Poland Office: ul. Kopernika 17, IV Floor, 00-359. Telephone: (48 22) 262 226. Facsimile: (48 22) 262 360.

Firm engaged in Dubai, English and General International Practice. Licensed as Dubai Legal Consultants. Dubai Court work undertaken through Local Advocates.

RESIDENT PARTNERS

Richard Horsfall Turner

(For Complete List of Firm Personnel, see Professional Biographies at London, England).

CLIFFORD CHANCE

Established in 1975

18TH FLOOR, DUBAI WORLD TRADE CENTRE
P.O. BOX 9380
DUBAI, UNITED ARAB EMIRATES
Telephone: (971 4) 314333
Fax: (971 4) 313990; 314565

Amsterdam, The Netherlands Office: Apollolaan 171, 1077 AS, P.O. Box 7301, 1007 JH. Telephone: (31 20) 577 71 11. Fax: (31 20) 676 93 26.

Bahrain, Manama Associated Office: Law Office of Shaikh Isa bin Mohammed Al Khalifa. P.O. Box 20717. Telephone: (973) 531535; 531073. Fax: (973) 536272; 530608.

Barcelona, Spain Office: Pau Claris 102, 08009. Telephone: (34 3) 318 68 64. Fax: (34 3) 317 73 23.

Brussels, Belgium Office: Avenue Louise 65, Box 2, 1050. Telephone: (32 2) 533 59 11. Fax: (32 2) 533 59 59.

Budapest, Hungary Office: Köves & Partners, Clifford Chance. Madách Trade Center, Madách Imre Út 14, 1075. Telephone: (36 1) 268 1600. Fax: (36 1) 268 1610.

Frankfurt/Main, Germany Office: Friedrichstraße 2-6, 60323. Telephone: (49 69) 971 4090. Fax: (49 69) 971 40977.

Hanoi, Vietnam Office: 52 Nguyen Binh Khiem. Telephone: (844) 229 182/3/4/5/6. Fax: (844) 229 190.

Hong Kong Office: 30th Floor, Jardine House, One Connaught Place. Telephone: (852) 2810 0229. Fax: (852) 2810 4708; 2810 4858; 2810 4743.

(This Listing Continued)

London, England Office: 200 Aldersgate Street, EC1A 4JJ. Telephone: (44 171) 600 1000. Fax: (44 171) 600 5555.

Madrid, Spain Office: Paseode la Castellana 110, 28046. Telephone (34 1) 562 7674. Fax: (34 1) 562 49 93.

Milan, Italy Associated Office: Studio Legale Grimaldi e Clifford Chance. Via Gesú, 3, 20121. Telephone: (39 2) 7600 8040. Fax: (39 2) 7600 4950.

Moscow, Russia Office: Ul. Sadovaya - Samotechnaya 24/27, 2nd Floor, 103051. Telephone: (7 501) 258 50 51; Satellite: (7 502) 221 3018/9. Fax: (7 501) 258 50 51; Satellite: (7 502) 221 3020.

New York, New York Office: Swiss Bank Tower, 10 East 50th Street, 10022. Telephone: (1 212) 750 1440. Fax: (1 212) 758 6625.

Paris, France Office: 112 avenue Kléber, BP 163 Trocadéro, 75770 Paris Cedex 16. Telephone: (33 1) 44 05 52 52. Fax: (33 1) 44 05 52 00.

Riyadh, Saudi Arabia Associated Office: The Law Firm of Salah Al-Hejailan. P.O. Box 1454, 11431. Telephone: (966 1) 479 2200. Fax: (966 1) 479 1717.

Rome, Italy Associated Office: Studio Legale Grimaldi e Clifford Chance. Viale G. Rossini 7, 00198. Telephone: (39 6) 807 2251. Fax: (39 6) 807 8201.

Shanghai, People's Republic of China Office: Suite 898, Shanghai Centre, 1376 Nanjing Xi Lu, 200040. Telephone: (86 21) 279 8461. Fax: (86 21) 279 8462.

Singapore Office: 16 Collyer Quay #31-00, 0104. Telephone: (65) 535 1855. Fax: (65) 535 6855.

Tokyo, Japan Office: 6th Floor, South Hill Nagatacho Building, 11-30 Nagatacho 1-chome, Chiyoda-ku, 100. Telephone: (81 3) 3581 4311. Fax: (81 3) 3593 0651.

Warsaw, Poland Office: Warsaw Corporate Centre, ul. Emilii Plater 28, 00-688. Telephone: (48 2) 630 3344. Fax: (48 2) 630 3355.

Domestic and International Banking and Financial Transactions: Projects including Joint Ventures, Construction, Leasing, Operation, Supply/Offtake, Finance and Security; Privatisations; International Trade and Commercial Advice; Company Law and Inward Investment; Natural Resources and Utilities; Shipping, Aviation and Insurance; Services to Governments; Dispute Settlement and Arbitration.

Firm engaged in UAE, English and General International Practice.

RESIDENT PARTNER

RICHARD PRICE, admitted, 1976, Solicitor. **PRACTICE AREAS:** Arbitration; Admiralty; Litigation; Maritime.

ASSOCIATES

SCHEHEREZADE ALIM, Barrister, called, 1969.

RICHARD BRIGGS, admitted, 1992, Solicitor.

EWAN CAMERON, admitted, 1990, Solicitor.

JAMES GUBBINS, admitted, 1991, Solicitor.

CHRISTOPHER HARRISON, admitted, 1992, Solicitor.

PAUL LARKMAN, admitted, 1983, Solicitor, New Zealand.

WALID EL-SOLH, Lawyer.

JOHN MURKETT, Solicitor, admitted, 1987.

BABUL PARIKH, Solicitor, admitted, 1990.

AUDLEY SHEPPARD, admitted, 1985, Solicitor, New Zealand; 1990, England and Wales.

Languages: English, French, German and Arabic

(For the names of Partners resident in other offices, see Professional Biographies for those offices).

CLYDE & CO.

Middle East Regional Office

CITY TOWER 2
3RD FLOOR
SHEIKH ZAYED ROAD
DUBAI, UNITED ARAB EMIRATES
Telephone: (971) 4-311102
Telex: 46644 Clyde EM
Fax: (971) 4-319920

London, England Office: 51 Eastcheap, EC3M 1JP. Telephone: (44) 171-623 1244. Telex: 884886 Clyde G. Fax: (44) 171-623 5427.

(This Listing Continued)

Also offices in Guildford (England), Cardiff (Wales), Hong Kong, Singapore, Sao Paulo (Brazil), Caracas (Venezuela). Associate Offices: Paris and St. Petersburg. For full details of these offices, see entry under London, England.

International Commercial Practice, covering Trade, Shipping, Banking, Project Finance, Company/Commercial, Marine and non-Marine Insurance, Reinsurance, Oil and Gas, Construction, Licensing and Intellectual Property and Litigation Matters.

RESIDENT PARTNERS

Jonathan Silver
Julian Gray
Simon Adams

ASSISTED BY

Michael Pilkington
Andrew Hayward
Christopher Jobson
Christopher Burdett
Mary Jabbour

Languages: English, French, German, Arabic

FOX & GIBBONS

Solicitors

Established in 1969

P.O. BOX 1756

DUBAI, UNITED ARAB EMIRATES
Telephone: (9714) 310220
Fax: (9714) 310201
Telex: 45614 GBLAW EM

London, England Office: 2 Old Burlington Street, W1X 2QA. Telephone: (44-171) 439 8271. Telex: 267108. Telefax: (44-171) 734 8843.

Abu Dhabi, UnitedArab Emirates Kudsi Fox & Gibbons Office: P.O. Box 46010. Telephone: (9712) 322858. Fax: (9712) 331586.

Cairo, Egypt Office: 126 Mohei El Din Abul Ezz Street, 9th Floor, Mohandiseen, Giza, Cairo, Egypt. Telephone: (202) 3485955. Fax: (202) 3492210.

Ruwi, Oman Office: P.O. Box 3552, Postal Code 112. Telephone: (968) 564346. Fax: (968) 564395. Telex: 5630 GIBLAW ON.

Gibraltar Office: P.O. Box 246. Telephone: (350) 77750. Fax: (350) 77800.

Fujairah, United Arab Emirates Office: P.O. Box 701. Telephone: (971 9) 229390. Fax: (971 9) 226470.

Kuwait Associated Office: P.O. Box 26473 Safat, 13125 Safat. Telephone: (965) 2462323/2462525/2462929. Fax: (965) 242 5830. Telex: 30844 ZINA KT.

Yemen Associated Office: P.O. Box 148, Crater, Aden. Telephone (9672) 255305/253824. Fax: (9672) 255305/255117.

Lebanon Associated Office: Saba K. Zreik Law Offices. Autostrade Dora, Cite Dora 3 Building, 10th Floor, P.O. Box 90-710, Beirut, Lebanon. Telephone: (961 1) 881322. Fax: (961 1) 881387. Telex: 42949 MANAL LE.

FIRM PROFILE: The Dubai office of Fox & Gibbons has been in existence for over 25 years, and employs lawyers who advise with a multilingual capability on all matters of commercial law including corporate and company structuring, banking, construction, maritime, insurance and litigation services.

The Firm provides modern and efficient legal services for companies and businessmen, both local and international, who seek to do business in Dubai and the Gulf region. The Firm has offices in Abu Dhabi and Fujairah and elsewhere throughout the Middle East, with its head office in London, and can draw on the experience and expertise of its lawyers in those jurisdictions.

MANAGING PARTNER

JEREMY KEY (Managing Partner). **LANGUAGES:** English. **PRACTICE AREAS:** Construction.

LEGAL SUPPORT STAFF

ANDREW PHILIP ROBERTS (Partner).

JANE PITTAWAY (Solicitor).

PAUL HOLLAND (Solicitor).

(This Listing Continued)

FOX & GIBBONS, Dubai—Continued

MIRIAM ELLIS (Solicitor).

ALI OMRAN (Syrian Lawyer).

OSAMA AHMED HASSAN (Sudanese Lawyer).

(For a list of other Personnel, see Biographical Cards at London, England, Fujairah and Abu Dhabi, United Arab Emirates, Cairo, Egypt, Ruwi, Sultante of Oman, Gibraltar, Kuwait, Lebanon and Yemen)

ZIAD GALADARI & ASSOCIATES

Advocates & Legal Consultants

2ND FLOOR
HABIB BANK AG ZURICH BUILDING
AL NASR SQUARE
P.O. BOX 7992
DUBAI, UNITED ARAB EMIRATES
Telephone: 04-214487; 04-214490
Fax: 04-238126
Telex: 46480 ZAG EM

Civil, Criminal, Industrial, Commercial Building, Finances, Insurance, Maritime, Immigration and Labour Laws.

FIRM PROFILE: The firm negotiates and reaches an amicable settlement of claims if so authorized by the clients. Drafts documents for incorporation of sale Proprietorship and Partnership Firms, and Public as well as Private Limited Liabilities Companies and Draft any or all other legal documents related to or connected with such firms and companies incorporated or to be incorporated in the whole of United Arab Emirates (U.A.E.).

Provide authentic Translation of Documents Service from English to Arabic and vice-virsa.

Represent Clients as Plaintiff or Defendant as the case may be, in Courts at all levels in U.A.E. as well as Rent Committee and other Local Authorities throughout the Emirates of U.A.E.

The Firm presently consists of Thirteen (13) highly qualified and well experienced Lawyers and Legal Consultants. This number is likely to grow soon with the potential growth in the Professional activities of the Firm.

This Law Firm is very well equipped with experienced Para-legal staff members. On account of such experienced staff this firm is in a position to provide very efficient para-legal services to its clients, in Commercial, Labour, Civil and Criminal matters in all the Courts in U.A.E.

Ziad Abdulla Galadari
Ahmed Abdulla Galadari
Ihsan Al Moukayed
Marwan Al Sherka
Sayed Siddiq Al Husain
Omer Siddiq Omer
Khidir Ibrahim Khidir
Shiekhuddin M. Al Mahdi
Mohamed Izzat Shourbaji
Moizuddin Sayyed
K. K. Sarachandra Bose
Ashok S. Angadi
Ashraf Mohammed Kamal El Bakri

GREENWALD & van de KRAATS

CITY TOWER, SUITE 211
P.O. BOX 23927
DUBAI, UNITED ARAB EMIRATES
Telephone: (9714) 316-123
Fax: (9714) 310-844

FIRM PROFILE: Greenwald & van de Kraats is specialized international legal consultancy practice working closely with select clients on a world-wide basis establishing new business; structing transactions, joint ventures, projects and investments; developing and implementing businesses plans and strategies, and solving problems. In this practice, Greenwald & van de Kraats works with leading law firms in the countires of the Gulf region, Europe, Asia and the United States.

(This Listing Continued)

MANAGING PARTNER

DANIEL J. GREENWALD, III, born Minneapolis, Minnesota, 1949; admitted, 1977, New York; 1980, Washington, D.C.; 1990, as licensed Legal Consultant, Dubai. *Education:* University of Minnesota (J.D., 1976; B.A., 1971). President, American Business Council, Dubai, 1989-1992. Chairman, American Business Council, Gulf Countries, 1991-1993.

A.R. HILAL & ASSOCIATES

Advocates & Legal Consultants

P.O. BOX 7372
DUBAI, UNITED ARAB EMIRATES
Telephone: (9714) 284196 / 232546
Fax: (9714) 231435

Abu Dhabi, United Arab Emirates Office: P.O. Box 46033. Telephone: 9712-327617. Fax: 9712-336279.

Sharjah, United Arab Emirates Office: P.O. Box 5520. Telephone: 9716-354602/352262. Fax: 9716-374902.

Umm Al Qaiwain, United Arab Emirates Office: P.O. Box 773. Telephone: 9716-665666. Fax: 9716-667112.

Ras Al Khaimah, United Arab Emirates Office: P.O. Box 1942. Telephone: 9717-333800. Fax: 9717-333949.

Litigation and consultation concerning the following areas of law: Banking, Corporate, Maritime, Commercial, Civil, Air, Insurance, Labour, Trademark, Patent and Copyright, Arbitration.

FIRM PROFILE: The firm has nine lawyers, including advocates and legal consultants. There are eighteen other members of the staff, including para-legal assistants and secretaries.

PARTNERS

ABDULLA RASHID AHMED HILAL, born Emirate of Umm Al Qaiwain, United Arab Emirates, 1950; admitted, 1978, Advocate and Legal Consultant, United Arab Emirates. *Education:* Law College, University of Cairo (LL.B., 1976). Editor, Digest of eight volumes containing the judgements of the Appeal Courts and the Supreme Court of the United Arab Emirates, 1970 and 1980. Member, Federal National Council of the United Arab Emirates, 1977 and 1983. *Member:* U.A.E. Jurists' Association; International Bar Association; Arab Lawyers' Union (co-operating). *LANGUAGES:* Arabic and English. *PRACTICE AREAS:* Commercial Law; Maritime Law; Air Law.

JAAFAR MOHAMED MOHAMED SALEH, born Khartoum, Republic of Sudan, February 9, 1939; admitted, 1978, Advocate, Republic of Sudan; 1979, Advocate, United Arab Emirates. *Education:* Faculty of Law, University of Khartoum, Sudan (LL.B., 1964). Legal Assistant, 1964 (in judiciary - Republic of Sudan) and promoted to Province Judge. Resigned 1978. Advocate, U.A.E., 1979—. Visiting Lecturer, Emirates Bankers' Institute Sharjah, United Arab Emirates, 1991-1992. *Member:* Bar Association, Republic of Sudan; Middle East Arbitration Society. *LANGUAGES:* Arabic and English. *PRACTICE AREAS:* Banking Law; Insurance; Tort.

ABDUL KARIM HAMMAD, born Al Oja, Palestine, 1942; admitted, 1970, Advocate, Jordan; 1979, Advocate, United Arab Emirates. *Education:* Faculty of Law, University of Alexandria, Egypt (LL.B., 1969). *Member:* Jordanian Bar Association. *LANGUAGES:* Arabic and English. *PRACTICE AREAS:* Civil Law.

EISSA ADBUL LATHEEF, born Emirate of Umm Al Qaiwain, United Arab Emirates, July 1, 1962; admitted, 1984, Advocate, United Arab Emirates. *Education:* Al Ain University, United Arab Emirates (LL.B., 1983). *LANGUAGES:* Arabic and English. *PRACTICE AREAS:* Corporate Law; Banking Law; Civil Law.

SULTAN RASHID AHMED HILAL, born Emirate of Umm Al Qaiwain, United Arab Emirates, November 28, 1963; admitted, 1987, Advocate, United Arab Emirates. *Education:* Al Ain University, United Arab Emirates (LL.B., 1987). *LANGUAGES:* Arabic and English. *PRACTICE AREAS:* Civil Law; Commercial Law; Trademark; Patent Law; Copyright Law.

JAMAL HASSAN ABDO AL NAJJAR, born Gaza, Palestine, June 3, 1957; admitted, 1983, Advocate, Umm Al Qaiwain, United Arab Emirates; 1990, Advocate, Ras Al Khaimah, United Arab Emirates. *Education:* University of Baghdad, Iraq (LL.B., 1980); Supreme Institute of Islamic Studies, Cairo, Egypt (Diploma in Islamic Studies, 1985) Islamic, Shari'a, Cairo, Egypt (Intermediate Master's Studies, 1988). *Member:* U.A.E. Jurists' As-

(This Listing Continued)

sociation. *LANGUAGES:* Arabic and English. *PRACTICE AREAS:* Civil Law; Commercial Law; Criminal Law; Maritime Law; Personal Law.

ASSOCIATES

RAMNI TANEJA, born Delhi, India, December 4, 1955; admitted, 1980, Advocate, Bar Council of Maharashtra, India (Not admitted in United Arab Emirates). *Education:* University of Bombay, India (B.A. (Honours), English Literature (Major), French Literature (Subsidiary), 1977; LL.B., 1980); Diplôme Supérieur de l'Alliance Francaise de Paris (1975). Advocate: High Court Bombay and with Little & Co., Bombay, India, 1980-1982; Delhi High Court and Supreme Court of India, 1989-1990. Legal Consultant, A.R. Hilal & Associates, 1983-1989 and 1990—. Author: Legal Articles, "Pressures on the Judiciary," "Shah Report ban," "The Transfer of Judges," "The Air-Hostesses Case," Himmat, 1980-1982. *LANGUAGES:* English, Hindi and French.

K.V. PRAKASH, born Cochin, Kerala, India, February 11, 1949; admitted, 1976, Advocate, Bar Council of Kerala, India (Not admitted in United Arab Emirates). *Education:* University of Kerala, India (B.A. (Economics), 1970); University of Jabalpur, India (M.A. (Economics), 1974; LL.B., 1975). Advocate, India, 1976-1989. Legal Consultant, A.R. Hilal & Associates, 1989—. *Member:* Kerala High Court Advocates' Association, India (Life Member and Ex-Honorary Secretary). *LANGUAGES:* English, Hindi, Tamil and Malayalam.

LEGAL CONSULTANT

MUZZAMMIL BAKHIT OSMAN, born Khartoum, Republic of Sudan, September 1, 1958. *Education:* University of Morocco (LL.B., 1982). Legal Consultant, A.R. Hilal & Associates, 1985—. *LANGUAGES:* Arabic and English.

McNEILL & ASSOCIATES

English Solicitors & Legal Consultants

(A Member of Frere Cholmeley Bischoff Partnership)

P.O. BOX 2510

DUBAI, UNITED ARAB EMIRATES
Telephone: (4) 267085/268336/268722
Telex: 45493 LAWMC EM
Fax: (4) 260206 Cables: Lawmac Dubai

Other Offices:
London, England Office: 4 John Carpenter Street. Telephone: 071 615 8000. Fax: 071 615 8080. Telex: 27623 Freres G.
Paris, France Office: 42 Avenue du Président Wilson. Telephone: (33) (1) 44 34 71 00. Fax: (33) (1) 44 34 71 ll. Telex: 645944 FRERCHO.
Rome, Italy Office: Studio Legale Associato, 47 Viale Bruno Buozzi. Telephone: (39) (6) 807 6076 Fax: (39) (6) 807 6077.
Milan, Italy Office: Via San Clemente 1, . Telephone: (39) (2) 7200 2363. Fax: (39) (2) 7200 1907.
Brussels, Belgium Office: Rue Guimard 15. Telephone: (32) (2) 513 86 04. Fax: (32) (2) 512 04 26.
Monaco Office: Est-Quest, 24 Boulevard Princesse Charlotte. Telephone: (33) 93 50 85 70. Fax: (33) 93 50 22 10.
Berlin, Germany Office: Internationales Handelszentrum. Telephone (49) 30 231 53 95. Fax: (49) 30 2643 30 26.
Moscow, Russia Office: Malaya Semenovskaya, 1, 105023. Telephone: (7) 095 963 8948. Fax: (7) 095 963 6190. Telex: 412348 ALMSU.

Arbitration (Commercial, Shipping & Construction), Aviation & Aerospace, Banking Law, Commercial Law, Company Law, Construction Law & Disputes, Corporate Finance, Cross-Border Transactions, Debt Recovery, Distribution Agency, Employment, Foreign Investment, Foreign National Laws (Arab Law & Islamic Sharia), Franchise Agreements, Freight Forwarding, Insurance (Marine & Aviation), Intellectual Property, Litigation, Multi-Jurisdictional Transactions, Oil & Gas, Partnerships, Shipping Litigation & Arbitration, International Tax, Trademarks, Patents & Copyright & Anti-Counterfeiting.

NEIL G. MCNEILL, admitted, Solicitor, England and Wales, Scotland & India; 1961, United Arab Emirates. *Education:* M.A.; LL.B.; Dip. Crim. (Resident Partner).

(This Listing Continued)

ASSOCIATES

PAUL W. DAVIES, admitted, Solicitor in England and Wales.

JANE E. TOWNSEND, admitted, Solicitor in England and Wales.

LAYLA O. MUKHTAR, admitted, Solicitor in England and Wales.

NABARRO NATHANSON

P.O. BOX 13779
DEIRA, DUBAI, UNITED ARAB EMIRATES
Telephone: (9714) 287157
Fax: (0974) 287086

London, England Office: 50 Stratton Street, London W1X 5FL, England. Telephone: 0171-493-9933. Telex: 8813144 NABARO G. Fax: 0171-629-7900.
Doncaster, England Office: The Lodge, South Parade, Doncaster DN1 2DQ, England. Telephone: 01302-344455. Fax: 01302-738408.
Hull, England Office: 12Marina Court, Castle Street, Hull HU1 1TJ, England. Telephone: 01482-219111. Fax: 01482-218444.
Budapest, Hungary Office: Istanhegyi ut 9/b, Budapest 1126, Hungary.
Warsaw, Poland Office: Ul. Senatorska 12, 00-082 Warsaw, Poland. Telephone: 48-2-227 6144/7901/9227. Fax: 48-2-227 4838.

General Practice.

PARTNER

A. PENNINGTON. *PRACTICE AREAS:* Commercial Law.

(For Personnel and Biographical Data, see Professional Biographies at London, England).

STOCKWELL & ASSOCIATES

SUITE 1301 PEARL BUILDING
P.O. BOX 6750
DUBAI, UNITED ARAB EMIRATES
Telephone: 971-4-283194
Telefax: 971-4-227250

International Commercial Practice. Firm engaged in American and General International Law Practice in Commercial and Corporate Matters.

FIRM PROFILE: The Lawyers in the Dubai office have 39 years resident experience in the Middle East. Their practice is divided almost equally between advising U.A.E. and multinational companies with respect to contracts and licensing operations, local labor law issues, bankruptcy and work-outs, franchising, arbitration, maritime law, local litigation, alternative dispute resolution, construction claims, boycott law, trademark protection and the regulation of investment, as well as issues affecting corporate and commercial operations in the Middle East.

DAVID M. STOCKWELL, born Saudi Arabia, August 10, 1951; admitted, 1976, Texas; 1989, as Licensed Legal Consultant (Solicitor), Dubai. *Education:* University of Pennsylvania (B.A., International Relations with a Specialization, Middle East, 1973); Villanova University (J.D., 1976). Foreign Service Officer, 1977-1985. Economic/Commercial Officer and Commercial Attache, United States Embassy, Kuwait, 1977-1979; Country Officer, Bahrain, Qatar and U.A.E., U.S. State Department, Washington, D.C., 1979-1980. United States Embassy, Tunisia, 1981-1982. United States Consul and Officer in Charge, United States Embassy, Dubai, U.A.E., 1982-1985. Associate, Sidley & Austin, 1985-1987. Of Counsel, Bryan, Cave, McPheeters & McRoberts, 1987-1990. American Business Council Dubai (Former Vice President, Legal Affairs and Secretary of the Board). National Council on U.S.-Arab Relations. *Member:* State Bar of Texas; American Bar Association; International Bar Association; Houston Bar Association. *LANGUAGES:* English and Arabic. *PRACTICE AREAS:* Commercial Arbitration; Construction Arbitration; Commercial Law; Corporate Law; Agency and Licensing Contracts; Administrative Law.

ASSOCIATES

CHARLOTTE KRUCKOW VELLING, born Herning, Denmark, January 1969. *Education:* University of Aarhus, Denmark (Law Degree, 1992); University of Exeter, England (LL.M., 1993). *LANGUAGES:* English and Danish. *PRACTICE AREAS:* Company Law; Company Formation; Trademark; Labor Law.

REPRESENTATIVE CLIENTS: PepsiCo; General Motors; Eastman Kodak; SAAB Automobiles AB; Philippine Airlines; Dow Export S.A.; Halliburton Limited; FMC International S.A.

FOX & GIBBONS

Solicitors

Established in 1991

P.O. BOX 701

FUJAIRAH, UNITED ARAB EMIRATES

Telephone: (971 9) 229390

FAX: (971 9) 226470

London, England Office: 2 Old Burlington Street, W1X 2QA. Telephone: (44-171) 439 8271. Telex: 267108. Telefax: (44-171) 734 8843.

Dubai, United Arab Emirates Office: P.O. Box 1756. Telephone: (9714) 310220. Fax: (9714) 310201. Telex: 45614 GBLAW EM.

Abu Dhabi, United Arab Emirates Kudsi Fox & Gibbons Office: P.O. Box 46010. Telephone: (9712) 322858. Fax: (9712) 331586.

Cairo, Egypt Office: 126 Mohei El Din Abul Ezz Street, 9th Floor, Mohandiseen, Giza, Cairo, Egypt. Telephone: (202) 3485955. Fax: (202) 3492210.

Ruwi, Oman Office: P.O. Box 3552, Postal Code 112, Telephone: (968) 564346. Fax: (968) 564395. Telex: 5630 GIBLAW ON.

Kuwait Associated Office: P.O. Box 26473 Safat, 13125 Safat. Telephone: (965) 2462323/2462525/2462929. Fax: (965) 242 5830. Telex: 30844 ZINA KT.

Gibraltar Office: P.O. Box 246. Telephone: (350) 77750. Fax: (350) 77800.

Yemen Associated Office: P.O. Box 148, Crater, Aden. Telephone: (9672) 255305/253824. Fax: (9672) 255305/255117.

Lebanon Associated Office: Saba K. Zreik Law Offices. Autostrade Dora, Cite Dora 3 Building, 10th Floor, P.O. Box 90-710, Beirut, Lebanon. Telephone: (961 1) 881322. Fax: (961 1) 881387. Telex: 42949 MANAL LE.

MANAGING PARTNERS

Jeremy Key (Managing Partner)

LEGAL SUPPORT STAFF

Andrew Philip Roberts (Partner)
Jane Pittaway (Solicitor)
Paul Holland (Solicitor)
Miriam Ellis (Solicitor)
Ali Omran (Syrian Lawyer)
Osama Ahmed Hassan (Sudanese Lawyer)

(For a list of other Personnel, see Biographical Cards at London, England, Dubai and Abu Dhabi, United Arab Emirates, Cairo, Egypt, Ruwi, Sultanate of Oman, Kuwait, Gibraltar, Lebanon and Yemen)

AFRIDI & ANGELL

AL-BOORJ AVENUE

P.O. BOX 5925

SHARJAH, UNITED ARAB EMIRATES

Telephone: 9716-544-062

Fax: 9716-547-336

Telex: 68331 Ordig Em

Cable Address: "Dignior Sharjah"

Abu Dhabi, United Arab Emirates Office: Bin Hamoodah Building, P.O. Box 3961. Telephone: 9712-329-134. Fax: 9712-326-905. Telex: 23632 Ordig Em. Cable Address: "Dignior Abu Dhabi".

Dubai, United Arab Emirates Office: City Tower, Level 8, Dubai-Abu Dhabi Road, P.O. Box 9371. Telephone: 9714-310-900. Fax: 9714-310-800. Telex: 46145 Ordig Em. Cable Address: "Dignior Dubai".

Jebel Ali, United Arab Emirates Office: Jebel Ali Free Trade Zone, P.O. Box 16894. Telephone: 9714-816-010. Fax: 9714-816-774. Telex: 46145 Ordig Em.

Other Offices: New York, N.Y. Office: 230 Park Avenue. 10169. Telephone: 212-697-0300. Fax: 212-697-0385.

Pakistan Office: 8. Street 31, 8th Avenue F-7/1, Islamabad 44000. Telephone: 92-51-217-031. Fax: 92-51-217-032.

General International, Regional and United Arab Emirates practice including representation of Clients in Administrative, Corporate, Banking, Maritime, Commercial, Financial, Real Estate, Petroleum, Arbitration and Litigation Matters; also Commercial Agency, Governmental Licensing and

(This Listing Continued)

Registration, Employment, Islamic Law, Construction, and Project Development.

FIRM PROFILE: *The United Arab Emirates based firm of Afridi & Angell is a partnership among M.A.K. Afridi, Nicholas B. Angell, C. Chakradaran, Amjad Ali Khan, Charles S. Laubach, Hassen A. Ferris and Bashir Ahmed, who have several years of experience practicing law in the United Arab Emirates ("U.A.E."). The legal staff of Afridi & Angell currently consist of those seven partners and four associates with translation and paralegal support and fluency in English, Arabic, Urdu, Pushtu, Tamil and French. Afridi & Angell are licensed as Legal Consultants in the United Arab Emirates, but are not licensed to appear in Court.*

Afridi & Angell conducts a diversified regional and international practice and provides legal services in all aspects of commercial matters, including banking and financial services, corporate, maritime and transport, governmental licensing, commercial agency, project development and intellectual property laws. The Firm also handles military procurement, anti-boycott and F.C.P.A. matters.

PARTNERS

M.A.K. AFRIDI, born Karachi, Pakistan, February 2, 1936; admitted, 1958, Pakistan; 1974 admitted as a legal consultant (not admitted as Advocate in the United Arab Emirates). *Education:* Peshawar University (LL.B., 1958). Author: "The Emirates Lay Down the Law on Interest-Free Banking," International Financial Law Review, 1985; "Construction Contracting in the United Arab Emirates," International Construction Law Review, 1985. Co-Author: with Amjad Ali Khan, "The Effect of Islamic Principles on the Conduct of Business in the Gulf," paper presented at Gulf America conference Houston, Texas, 1988; with Nicholas B. Angell, "Recent Developments in the United Arab Emirates," paper delivered at International Bar Association Conference, Singapore, 1985. Correspondent: International Construction Law Review. Partner, Orr Dignam & Co., Pakistan, 1964-1974. Resident Partner, Orr Dignam & Co., Middle East Office, Sharjah, United Arab Emirates, 1974-1980. Partner, Chadbourne, Parke & Afridi, Middle East Offices, United Arab Emirates, 1980-1991. *Member:* The ICC International Court of Arbitration (Pakistan Representative); International Bar Association. **LANGUAGES:** English, Urdu and Pushtu.

C. CHAKRADARAN, born Trincomalee, Sri Lanka, February 6, 1941; admitted, as Advocate, 1966, Sri Lanka; 1991, admitted as a legal consultant in the United Arab Emirates (not admitted as an Advocate in the United Arab Emirates). *Education:* Ceylon Law College, Colombo, Sri Lanka. Author: "Arrest of Ships in the United Arab Emirates," Chapter in Lloyd's of London Press, Arrest of Ships, 1987; "An Overview of the New U.A.E. Federal Maritime Law," Middle East Executive Reports, 1982. Co-author: with M.K. Afridi, "Arrest of Vessels in the United Arab Emirates," Chapter in Maritime Law Handbook published by the International Bar Association, 1987; with Bashir Ahmed, "Marine Cargo Claims under the Laws of the United Arab Emirates," published in Lloyd's Maritime and Commercial Law Quarterly, November, 1992; with Bashir Ahmed and Haider K. Afridi, "Ship Finance in the United Emirates," published by Euromoney in their "Shipping Finance Annual," 1993/1994; with Bashir Ahmed, "Regulation of Banking and Financial Services in the United Arab Emirates," published by International Financial Law Review in the "International Banking Yearbook," 1993/1994 edition; with Bashir Ahmed, "Banking and the Law," published in the Telerate Bank Register, August, 1993 - an International Financial Law Review publication. Visiting Lecturer and Examiner, Incorporated Council of Legal Education in Sri Lanka. Partner, Chadbourne, Park & Afridi, Middle East Offices, Sharjah, 1987-1991. Correspondent: Lloyd's Maritime and Commercial Law Quarterly. *Member:* Sri Lankan and International Bar Associations. **LANGUAGES:** English and Tamil.

BASHIR AHMED, born Gujrat, Pakistan, 1961. Admitted as an advocate, 1989, Lahore High Court (not admitted in United Arab Emirates); 1994, New York. *Education:* Oxford University (B.A. Jurisprudence, 1983); Punjab University (LL.M., 1986). Co-Author: with Sami Zafar, "Foreign Investment Laws of Pakistan," Punjab University Law Journal, 1987; with Sami Zafar, "International Contracts: The Judicial Treatment of Ouster of Jurisdiction Clause of Pakistan," Punjab University Law Journal, 1986; with C. Chakradaran, "Marine Cargo Claims under the Laws of the United Arab Emirates," published in the Lloyd's Maritime and Commercial Law Quarterly, November 1992; with C. Chakradaran and Haider K. Afridi, "Ship Finance in the United Arab Emirates," published by Euromoney in their "Shipping Finance Annual," 1993-1994; with C. Chakradaran, "Regulation of Banking and Financial Services in the United Arab Emirates," published by International Financial Law Review in the "International Banking Yearbook," 1993-1994 edition; with C. Chakradaran, "Banking and

(This Listing Continued)

the Law," published in the Telerate Bank Register, August 1993 - an International Financial Law Review publication. *Member:* Lahore High Court Bar; Punjab Bar.

ASSOCIATES

AHMED IBRAHIM NOFAL, born Cairo, Egypt, November 18, 1955; admitted, 1980, Egypt. *Education:* University of Cairo (LL.B., 1980). *Member:* Egyptian Bar Association. *LANGUAGES:* Arabic and English.

(For Biographical data on other firm personnel, see Professional Biographies at Abu Dhabi and Dubai, United Arab Emirates, Islamabad, Pakistan and New York, N.Y.)

YEMEN

FOX & GIBBONS

Solicitors

Established in 1991

P.O. BOX 148
CRATER
ADEN, YEMEN
Telephone: (967 2) 255305/253824
FAX: (967 2) 255117

London, England Office: 2 Old Burlington Street, W1X 2QA. Telephone: (44-171) 439 8271. Telex: 267108. Telefax: (44-171) 734 8843.

Dubai, United Arab Emirates Office: P.O. Box 1756. Telephone: (9714) 310220. Fax: (9714) 310201. Telex: 45614 GBLAW EM.

Abu Dhabi, United Arab Emirates Kudsi Fox & Gibbons Office: P.O. Box 46010. Telephone: (9712) 322858. Fax: (9712) 331586.

Cairo, Egypt Office: 126 Mohei El Din Abul Ezz Street, 9th Floor, Mohandiseen, Giza, Cairo, Egypt. Telephone: (202) 3485955. Fax: (202) 3492210.

Fujairah, United Arab Emirates Office: P.O. Box 701. Telephone: (971 9) 229390. Fax: (971 9) 226470.

Ruwi, Oman Office: P.O. Box 3552, Postal Code 112, Telephone: (968) 564346. Fax: (968) 564395. Telex: 5630 GIBLAW ON.

Kuwait Associated Office: P.O. Box 26473 Safat, 13125 Safat. Telephone: (965) 2462323/2462525/2462929. Fax: (965) 242 5830. Telex: 30844 ZINA KT.

Gibraltar Office: P.O. Box 246. Telephone: (350) 77750. Fax: (350) 77800.

Lebanon Associated Office: Saba K. Zreik Law Offices. Autostrade Dora, Cite Dora 3 Building, 10th Floor, P.O. Box 90-710, Beirut, Lebanon. Telephone: (961 1) 881322. Fax: (961 1) 881387. Telex: 42949 MANAL LE.

MANAGING PARTNER

Sheikh Tariq Abdullah (Solicitor)

(For a list of other Personnel, see Biographical Cards at London, England, Dubai, Abu Dhabi and Fujairah, United Arab Emirates, Cairo, Egypt, Ruwi, Sultanate of Oman, Kuwait, Gibraltar and Lebanon)

ADVOCACY & LEGAL CONSULTATIONS OFFICE

P.O. BOX 2536
SANA'A, YEMEN
Telephone: 206814
Fax: 206814

Commercial Law, Contracts, and Registration of Trademarks and Commercial Companies.

(This Listing Continued)

FIRM PROFILE: *The firm is equipped with a well qualified Staff experienced in legal affairs, translation services and computer systems.*

ALI ABDEL KADIR AL-HEBSHI, born 1949. Attorney at the Supreme Court of Republic. *Education:* Damascus University (License of Law, 1974); Ecole Nationale de la Maigestrade, France (Diploma ENM, 1977). Member, Chairman of Yemeni Bar Association, Sana'a Capital Branch, 1993—.*Member:* Arab Bar Association; International Bar Association.

ZIMBABWE

COGHLAN, WELSH & GUEST

Established in 1907

EXECUTIVE CHAMBERS
GEORGE SILUNDIKA AVENUE
P.O. BOX 53 OR 2093
HARARE, ZIMBABWE
Telephone: 758472 - 9
International: 263-4
Telegrams: "CODEX", HARARE
Telex: 22071, CODEX ZW
Telefax: 756268

MEMBERS OF FIRM

DAVID J. LEWIS, born Bulawayo, Zimbabwe, July 27, 1927; admitted, 1953, Zimbabwe. *Education:* Cape Town University (B.A., Law, 1948); Oxford University (M.A., Jurisp., 1951).

DAVID L. MORGAN, born Harare, Zimbabwe, April 21, 1935; admitted, 1964, Zimbabwe. *Education:* Cape Town University (B.Commerce, 1957; B. Laws, 1957); Oxford University (B.Arts, 1960).

CHARLES R. HARTLEY, born Harare, Zimbabwe, January 12, 1937; admitted, 1959, Zimbabwe.

ALEXANDER N. MASTERSON, born Gwanda, Zimbabwe, April 6, 1936; admitted, 1960, Zimbabwe. *Education:* University of Cape Town (B.A., 1956; LL.B., 1958).

LESLIE ALEXANDER DONNELLY, born United Kingdom, June 20, 1945; admitted, 1982, Harare, Zimbabwe. *Education:* University of Rhodesia (B.L., 1979).

IAN S. COX, born Bloemfontein, R.S.A., November 12, 1933; admitted, 1960, Zimbabwe. *Education:* University of Cape Town (B.A., 1954; LL.B., 1956).

CHRISTOPHER CHARLES SEDDON, born Port Said, Egypt, February 3, 1936; admitted, 1958, Zimbabwe; 1987, England. *Education:* College of Law, Christleton Hall, Chesire.

FRASER A. EDKINS, born Harare, Zimbabwe, November 18, 1954; admitted, 1980, Zimbabwe. *Education:* University of Rhodesia (B.L., 1978; LL.B., 1979).

THEMBIWE C. MAZINGI, born Harare, Zimbabwe, March 11, 1959; admitted, 1982, Zimbabwe. *Education:* University of Zimbabwe (B.L., 1980; LL.B., 1981).

KEVIN J. ARNOTT, born Harare, Zimbabwe, March 8, 1961; admitted, 1984, South Africa; 1989, Zimbabwe. *Education:* University of Cape Town (B.Proc., 1984).

COLLEN KUHUNI, born Inyanga, Zimbabwe, July 12, 1961; admitted, 1987, Zimbabwe. *Education:* University of Zimbabwe (B.L., 1985; LL.B., 1987).

WILLIAM R.S. RUSSELL, born Bulawayo, Zimbabwe, January 20, 1957; admitted, 1985, Zimbabwe. *Education:* University of Zimbabwe (B.L., 1985; LL.B., 1984).

SERVICES, SUPPLIERS, CONSULTANTS SECTION

EUROPE, ASIA
AUSTRALASIA
MIDDLE EAST, AFRICA

The Services, Suppliers, Consultants Section presents information on categories of businesses and professionals serving the legal community. Each volume is indexed by region, by category and listed alphabetically by service name for each country and province/city. Whether you are looking for a court reporter in your own jurisdiction or an expert witness in another country, the Services, Suppliers, Consultants Section is your direct link to legal support services.

EUROPE	ASIA	AUSTRALASIA	MIDDLE EAST, AFRICA
Albania	Bangladesh	Australia	Algeria
Austria	Brunei Darussalam	New Zealand	Bahrain
Republic of Belarus	Cambodia	Niue	Burkina-Faso
Belgium	People's Republic of China	Papua New Guinea	Cameroon
Bulgaria	Guam		Cote d'Ivoire
Channel Islands	Hong Kong		Egypt
Croatia	India		Ethiopia
Cyprus	Indonesia		Ghana
Czech Republic	Japan		Iran
Denmark	Kazakhstan		Iraq
England	Korea		Israel
Estonia	Laos		Jordan
Finland	Malaysia		Kenya
France	Mongolia		Kuwait
Germany	Myanmar		Lebanon
Gibraltar	Nepal		Mauritius
Greece	Pakistan		Morocco
Hungary	Republic of the Philippines		Nigeria
Iceland	Singapore		Oman
Ireland	Sri Lanka		Qatar
Isle of Man	Taiwan		Saudi Arabia
Italy	Thailand		Sierra Leone
Republic of Latvia	U.S. Pacific Territories		South Africa
Liechtenstein	Vietnam		Sudan
Lithuania			Syria
Luxembourg			Tanzania
Madeira			Tunisia
Malta			United Arab Emirates
Monaco			Yemen
The Netherlands			Zimbabwe
Northern Ireland			
Norway			
Poland			
Portugal			
Romania			
Russia			
Scotland			
Slovakia			
Slovenia			
Spain			
Sweden			
Switzerland			
Turkey			
Ukraine			
Yugoslavia			

"These days, law firms are watching the bottom line very closely. I have to find the best candidates, and not spend a lot of time doing it. The Martindale-Hubbell® & LEXIS® Student Directory helps me do just that."

Ann Ogburn has a big responsibility. Finding the right candidates for Baker & McKenzie. To do the job right, she chose the Martindale-Hubbell & LEXIS Student Directory. "Our focus is mostly tax law," states Ann. "It's hard to find people with that particular specialty. People who are really interested. This online service efficiently searches for candidates with specific experience or background. It's frustrating to think you've found the perfect resume in your files, only to find out they have already been hired. This service eliminates that problem because you receive only current resumes." Call your LEXIS representative or check the career library online and enter "RESUME." See how the Martindale-Hubbell & LEXIS Student Directory service can help bring you the best candidates, while protecting your bottom line.

**Ann Ogburn,
Director of Recruiting & Client
Services, Baker & McKenzie
Washington, D.C.**

LEXIS·NEXIS

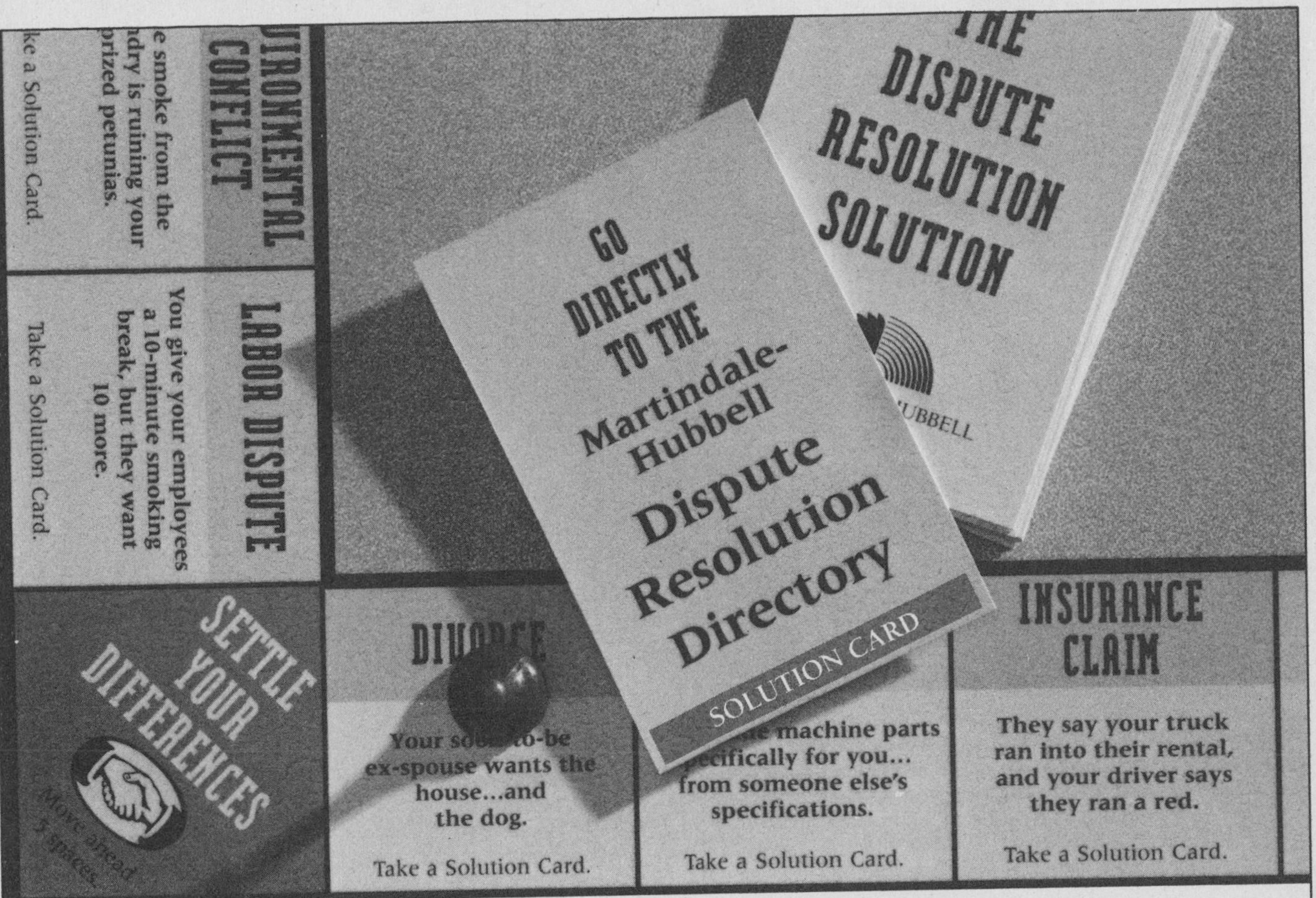

SERVICES, SUPPLIERS, CONSULTANTS
List of Categories

Abstractors
Accident Investigation & Reconstruction Services
Accountants
Actuaries
Admiralty & Maritime Litigation Support
Advertising & Public Relations Firms
Agricultural Economist Consultant
Alternate Dispute Resolution
  (See Arbitration & Mediation)
Apellate Printing Service
Appraisal Services
Appraisal Services - Coin & Bullion
Appraisal Services - Jewelry & Gems
Appraisal Services - Machinery & Equipment
Appraisal Services - Personal Property
Appraisal Services/Automotive
Arbitration & Mediation Services
Asset Locators
Attorney Referral Services
Attorney Services
Auctioneers & Appraisers of Autographs, Rare Books
Audio/Video Services
Autographs, Rare Books
  (See Auctioneers & Appraisers of)
Automotive Safety Design & Analysis

Banking Consultants
Banking/Law Books and Bank Databases
Banks & Trust Companies
Bicycle Litigation
Binding Services
Biomechanics
Blue Sky Bk. Deal/Invst. Adv. Reg. & Maint. Svcs.
Bonds - Bail
Bonds - Surety & Fidelity
Brief Preparation
Briefs
  (See Legal Brief Printers)
Building Evaluation - Due Diligence
Business & Financial Information Providers
Business Valuations

Captioning
Career Services
Case Consultants
Case Management Systems
CD-ROM Products
CD-ROM/Federal Contracting Regulations
Chemical & Environmental Consultant
Child Custody - School Evaluation
Class Settlement Administration
CLE
  (See Continuing Legal Education Services)
Coins and Currency
Collection Agencies
Collection/Commercial Attorneys
Computer Conversion & Migration
Computer - Data Entry Services
Computer - Programming & Consulting
Computer Animation, Graphics & Simulation
Construction Accidents, Safety
Construction Consultants
Consultant - Aerospace/Defense
Consulting Services
Consulting Services - Computer Security/Fax Automation
Continuing Legal Education Services
Contract Attorneys
Contract Management Systems
Copyright Search Services
Corporate Kits, Certificates and Seals
Corporation Companies
Corrections/Police Consultants
Cost Recovery
Courier & Document Delivery Services
Court Recording Systems
Court Reporters

Court Research
Court Services
Criminal Records Research

Damages - Economic Analysis
Demonstrative Evidence
Deposition Summary Services
Disabilities
  (See Accessibility Consulting/ADA Compliance)
Discovery and Document Reproduction Services
DMV Record Checks
DNA Forensic Testing
Document Delivery Systems
  (See Process Servers)
Document Filing/Retrieval
Document Management Services
Document Scanning
Document/Communication - Threat Analysis

Economic and Statistic Consulting Services
Economic Expert Witness
Educational Consultant
Employment Agencies - Permanent/Temporary
Engineering - Metallurgy/Reconstruction/Forensic/Consulting
Engineering & Scientific Consulting Services
Engineers
Environmental Consultants
Environmental Engineering & Remediation Services
Environmental Investigations
Environmental Project Cost Control
Environmental Valuation
Environmental & Ecological Services
Equine - Appraisers & Consultants
Escrow Services
Evidential Photographers
Examiners of Questioned Documents (Handwriting Experts)
Executive Protection Services
Executive Search Consultants
Exhibit Preparation
Expert Witness - Accidents/Fires/Product Liability
Expert Witness - Accounting Malpractice
Expert Witness - Accounting & Auditing
Expert Witness - Acoustics - Sound, Noise & Vibration
Expert Witness - Agri-Horticultural/Trees/Pesticides
Expert Witness - Alcohol & Drug Abuse
Expert Witness - Aquatic Injuries & Drownings
Expert Witness - Architects
Expert Witness - Audio Analysis/Tape Enhancement
Expert Witness - Auto Dealership/Economics
Expert Witness - Automotive Engineering
Expert Witness - Auto, Truck, Bus and Agricultural Equipment
Expert Witness - Aviation
Expert Witness - Bacteriology
Expert Witness - Ballistics
Expert Witness - Banking & Finance
Expert Witness - Bicycles
Expert Witness - Boating/Waterskiing
Expert Witness - Breast/Abdominal Surgery
Expert Witness - Cardiology/Internal Medicine
Expert Witness - Cardiovascular Thoracic Surgery
Expert Witness - Ceramics and Glass
Expert Witness - Civil/Mechanical/Structural Engineers
Expert Witness - Computer Programming & Consulting
Expert Witness - Construction
Expert Witness - Construction Equipment
Expert Witness - Construction/Architecture/Landscape
Expert Witness - Cooling Towers
Expert Witness - Criminalistic
Expert Witness - Damages/Lost Profits
Expert Witness - Dental
Expert Witness - Drug Issues/Sexual Issues
Expert Witness - Economic and Financial Valuation
Expert Witness - Economic Damages
Expert Witness - Economics & Statistics
Expert Witness - Economics, Vocational & Medical
Expert Witness - Economist

Expert Witness - Escrow/Closings
Expert Witness - Elevators & Escalators
Expert Witness - Employability/Wage Earning Capacity
Expert Witness - Employee/Employer Standards of Conduct
Expert Witness - Employment Discrimination
Expert Witness - Employment Practices
Expert Witness - Engineering
Expert Witness - Environmental Engineering
Expert Witness - Fine Arts & Furniture
Expert Witness - Fire Protection Equipment
Expert Witness - Fire Protection, Investigation
Expert Witness - Fire Reconstruction
Expert Witness - Fire & Explosion
Expert Witness - Flooring/Carpet
Expert Witness - Forensic Civil Engineers
Expert Witness - Forensic Engineers/Architects/Scientists
Expert Witness - Forklift Trucks
Expert Witness - Franchising
Expert Witness - Garage Doors
Expert Witness - Gasoline Station: Accid; Bus Prac; UG Leaks
Expert Witness - Geologists
Expert Witness - Glass
Expert Witness - Highway Safety/Accident Reconstruction
Expert Witness - Homicide Events, Reconstruction
Expert Witness - Horses (Equine)
Expert Witness - Hospitality & Hotel Management
Expert Witness - Human Factors & Safety
Expert Witness - Industrial Hygiene
Expert Witness - Insurance
Expert Witness - Insurance Bad Faith
Expert Witness - Insurance, Property/Casualty
Expert Witness - Intellectual Property/Infringement Damages
Expert Witness - Legal Fees
Expert Witness - Legal Malpractice/Professional Ethics
Expert Witness - Lender Liability
Expert Witness - Libel/Linguistic Analysis
Expert Witness - Magazine Publishing
Expert Witness - Marine Equipment
Expert Witness - Materials Engineering
Expert Witness - Mechanical Failure/Auto & Industrial
Expert Witness - Medical
  (See Medical Expert Witness)
Expert Witness - Medical Device Failure
Expert Witness - Metallurgy/Failure Analysis
Expert Witness - Meteorology/Climatology
Expert Witness - Mining
Expert Witness - Mortality/Longevity Analysis
Expert Witness - Mortgage Banking
Expert Witness - Motorcycle-Accident Reconstruction
Expert Witness - Natural Gas Business Issues
Expert Witness - Negligence Hiring/Retention
Expert Witness - Nephrology
Expert Witness - Neurology/Neurosurgery
Expert Witness - Neurology/Psychiatry
Expert Witness - Neuropsychiatry & Psychiatry
Expert Witness - Neuropsychology
Expert Witness - Oncology/Hematology
Expert Witness - Ophthalmology
Expert Witness - Optics: Devices, Instruments, Systems
Expert Witness - Packaging
Expert Witness - Paints and Protective Coatings
Expert Witness - Patent Law
Expert Witness - Pediatric Cardiology
Expert Witness - Pediatrics
Expert Witness - Personal Defense Sprays
Expert Witness - Plastic Reconstructive Surgery/Burns
Expert Witness - Playground/Recreation Accidents
Expert Witness - Plumbing and Piping
Expert Witness - Police Dogs
Expert Witness - Police, Security Malpractice
Expert Witness - Premises Security & Liability
Expert Witness - Product Liability; OSHA Regs/Procedures
Expert Witness - Psychiatry/Psychopharmacology
Expert Witness - Psychological Trauma
Expert Witness - Psychology
Expert Witness - Psychology/Social/Mitigation
Expert Witness - Radiology
Expert Witness - Radiology/MRI/Musculoskeletal Imaging
Expert Witness - Railroads
Expert Witness - Real Estate
Expert Witness - Real Estate Appraisal & Valuation Services

Expert Witness - Real Estate Licensee/Standard of Conduct
Expert Witness - Recreational Hazards
Expert Witness - Roofing & WaterProofing
Expert Witness - Safety Engineering
Expert Witness - Scaffolding
Expert Witness - Scientific Engineering
Expert Witness - Security/Law Enforcement/Forensics
Expert Witness - Security Negligence
  (See Also Security; Expert Witness)
Expert Witness - Sexual Harassment/Sexual Assault
Expert Witness - Slip, Trip and Fall
Expert Witness - Sports, Leisure, Recreation
Expert Witness - Statistical Analysis
Expert Witness - Surgical Pathology
Expert Witness - Technical Literature
Expert Witness - Tire & Wheel
Expert Witness - Toxic Exposure
Expert Witness - Toxicology
Expert Witness - Traffic Engineering & Safety
Expert Witness - Truck/Bus/Railroad
Expert Witness - Trucking Industry
Expert Witness - Trusts & Investments
Expert Witness - Underground Tanks
Expert Witness - Unlawful Restraint
Expert Witness - Urology
Expert Witness - Vascular Surgery
Expert Witness - Venture Capital
Expert Witness - Vocational/Medical Rehabilitation
Expert Witness - Warehousing & Distribution
Expert Witness - Wetlands
Expert Witness - Woodscience & Technology
Expert Witnesses
Expert Witness Referral Services

Fax - Automation
Fax Filing of Court Documents
Fax Server Software
Fax, Broadcast and Enhanced
Fiduciary Accountants
Fiduciary Services
File/File Room Management Systems
Filing & Searching Services
Financing Legal Fees & Claims Advance Funding
Fine Art and Furniture
  (See Auctioneers & Appraisers of)
Fire Investigators
Fire Loss Experts
Firearms Consultants
Foreclosure Services
Foreign Embassy Services
Forensic Accounting
Forensic Documentation - Demonstrative Evidence
Forensic Engineers
Forensic Financial Analysis
Forensic Psychiatry
Forensic Services
Foresters - Consulting
Forms - Legal
  (See Legal Forms)

Genealogical Services
Government Regulatory Research Specialists
Graphic Artists

Handwriting Experts
Heir Tracers
Heir/Probate Research
Horses
  (See Equine)
Hotel/Restaurant Consultants & Experts
Hotels and Conference Centers
Hydrologist

Incorporation Services
Information Brokers
Injury Analysis - Highway, Industrial
Insurance
Insurance - Claims Management
Insurance - Professional Liability
Insurance - Property/Casualty

Interpreters
  (See Also Interpreters & Translators; Translation Services)
Interpreters & Translators
  (See Also Translation Services)
Investigative Consultants
Investigators

Judgment Satisfaction
Jury Consultants

Kidnapping
  (See Parental Abductions)

Labor Relations, Products & Services
Laboratories - Parentage Testing
Laboratories - Testing & Analytical
Law Books - New/Used
Law Library Furniture
Law Office Automation Services
Law Office Furniture
Lawyer Search & Placement Consultants
Legal Advertising
Legal Auditors
Legal Brief Printers
Legal Forms - Computerized
Legal Information Brokers
Legal Marketing & Business Development Consultants
Legal Office Supplies
Legal Publications
Legal Research
Legal Rersearch/Appellate Practice
Legal Software
Legal Software - Bankruptcy
Legal Support Personnel - Temporary & Permanent
Legislative History Research
Library Cataloging
Library Management Services
Lie Detectors
  (See Polygraph)
Life Care Planning
  (See Vocational Evaluations)
Litigation Consulting
Litigation Support Services
Locator Service - People

Management Consultants
Maritime Litigation
  (See Admiralty)
Marketing
Media Research
Mediation Services
Medical Case Review & Preparation/Trial Consulting
Medical Devices
Medical Expert Witness
Medical Expert Witness - Emergency Medicine/Malpractice
Medical Expert Witness - Forensic Psychiatry
Medical Expert Witness - Neonatal/Perinatal
Medical Expert Witness - Referral Service
Medical Expert Witness - Sleep Disorders/Fatigue
Medical Illustrators
Medical Malpractice Consulting/Personal Injury
Medical Record Retrieval
Medical Services
Medical/Legal Research and Writing
Mergers & Acquisitions
Meteorology
Microfilming Services
Mining/Design Engineering
Mutual Fund/Reg. & Maint. Svcs.

Nursing Consultants
Nursing/Medical Costs
Neurorehabilitation

Oil & Gas Engineers

Paralegal Services
Paramedical Malpractice Support
Parental Abductions
Patent Copyright & Trademark Agents

Patent Illustrator
Patent Searching Services
Periodicals/Subscription Services
Personal Injury
  (See Medical Malpractice)
Personnel Consultants
Photographs, Video & Map Analysis
Photography
Polygraph Examination Services
Printers & Stationers
Private Case Management
Process Server Directory - Nationwide
Process Servers & Document Delivery Services
Process Service - International
Product Defect Libary - Searches/Analysis/Research
Product Safety
Psychiatric & Psychological Research Services
Purchases & Buying of Judgements

QDRO - Computer Software

Real Estate - Auctioneer/Appraise
Real Estate Appraisal/Valuation Services
Real Estate Consultants
Record Services
Repossession Services
Reorganization & Insolvency Services
Resume & Cover Letter Services
Research & Support Services
Risk/Decision Tree Analysis

Secretarial Services
Security Consultants
Security; Expert Witness
  (See Also Expert Witness - Security Negligence)
Security Guards & Services
Skip Tracers
Software Escrow
Source Code Escrow
Storage/Record Services
Strategic Planning
Structural Engineers
Structured Settlements
Subpoena Preparation Services
Surveys & Opinion Research

Technical Services Company
Teleconferencing
Television
  (See Video)
Time Billing Software/Systems
Title Abstract Companies
Title Insurance
Total Quality Management
Trademark & Copyright Search & Filing Services
Trademark Investigation
Trademark Management Systems
Trademark Search Services
Transcription Services
Translation Services
  (See Also Interpreters; Interpreters & Translators)
Transportation Engineering - Consulting & Forensic Services
Trial Consultants
Trust Companies

UCC Search Services

Valuation Services
Video Production, Editing & Graphics
Video Tape Services
Video Teleconferencing
Vocational Evaluations/Life Care Planning
Vocational Expert - Psychologist

White Collar Criminal/Fraud Investigation
Wine - Appraisal/Valuation/Consultant
Word Processing
Writ Services

Your case has you traveling? Call Jurist. We'll meet you there.

We do everything except try the case.™

Litigation and Legal Services. (partial listing)

- Court Reporters; Certified Shorthand Reporters, Registered Professional Reporters, Federally approved reporters, Merit, realtime, speed-contest writers, and a Senate-approved reporter.
- Worldwide, 24 hours a day, seven days a week.
- Centralized noticing and coordination of scheduled depositions.
- Interpreters, paralegals and computer programmers.
- Jurist Business Centers.
- Instant, daily, realtime.
- Direct-transcript modeming.
- ASCII disks, Discovery ᶻˣ™, CAT-Links™, Summation.
- Compressed-format transcripts with keyword indexing.
- Video: taping, synchronization, teleconferencing.
- Deposition suites.
- National and international service of process.

- Service of subpoenas, complaints and summonses.
- Court filing.
- Scanning, OCR, optical disk and CD Rom.
- Microfilming and microfiching.
- Records reproduction.
- X-Ray copying.
- Exhibit mounting.
- Computer animation.
- Investigative services: skip tracing, witness statements, photography.
- Storage archiving in high-security database.
- On-line document depository.
- Forensic Accounting.
- Alternative Dispute Resolution with a national panel of expert neutrals.

And last, but not least,
- Mac Wise is here.

Total Litigation Support™

800.345.4940   FAX: 800.600.3768
Corporate Headquarters
1701 Locust Street, Suite 1920, Philadelphia, PA. 19103

Philadelphia • Princeton • New York • Wilmington

NATIONAL NETWORK REPORTING COMPANY

Services, Suppliers, Consultants
In This Volume

EUROPE
ASSET LOCATORS

ENGLAND
LONDON .... WIND ASSOCIATES, INC.

BANKS & TRUST COMPANIES

CHANNEL ISLANDS
ST. HELIER, JERSEY .... CENTRETRUST LIMITED
STRACHANS

ST. PETER PORT, GUERNSEY .... THE LEGIS GROUP

LIECHTENSTEIN
VADUZ .... ALLGEMEINES TREUUNTERNEHMEN GENERAL
TRUST COMPANY

BUSINESS & FINANCIAL INFORMATION PROVIDERS

ENGLAND
LONDON .... MOODY'S INVESTORS SERVICE

COURT REPORTERS

ENGLAND
LONDON .... ANGLO-AMERICAN COURT REPORTERS
MARTEN WALSH CHERER LIMITED
NEWGATE REPORTERS LIMITED

FRANCE
PARIS .... ASSOCIATED EUROPEAN REPORTERS

THE NETHERLANDS
THE HAGUE .... ASSOCIATED EUROPEAN REPORTERS

GENEALOGICAL SERVICES

ENGLAND
LONDON .... INTERNATIONAL GENEALOGICAL SEARCH, INC.
TITLE RESEARCH

GERMANY
BERLIN .... INTERNATIONAL GENEALOGICAL SEARCH, INC.

HEIR TRACERS

ENGLAND
LONDON .... FRASER & FRASER
TITLE RESEARCH

FRANCE
PARIS .... FRASER & FRASER

LEGAL PUBLICATIONS

THE NETHERLANDS
AMSTERDAM .... INTERNATIONAL BUREAU OF FISCAL
DOCUMENTATION

LITIGATION SUPPORT SERVICES

ENGLAND
LONDON .... ANGLO-AMERICAN COURT REPORTERS
MARTEN WALSH CHERER LIMITED
QUORUM LITIGATION SERVICE, INC.

EUROPE (Continued)
TRUST COMPANIES

LIECHTENSTEIN
VADUZ .... JURICON TREUHAND ANSTALT

AUSTRALASIA
COURT REPORTERS

AUSTRALIA
SYDNEY, NEW SOUTH WALES .... AUSTRALIAN LEGAL REPORTING GROUP

HEIR TRACERS

AUSTRALIA
SYDNEY, NEW SOUTH WALES .... FRASER & FRASER

CHANNEL ISLANDS

ST. HELIER, JERSEY, 76,050

Banks & Trust Companies

CentreTrust Limited

(associated with Union Bancaire Privée, Geneva)

Company & Trust Administration

P.O. Box 301, Queens House, Don Road, St. Helier, Jersey.

Tel. UK 0534-33334
Tel. International 44-534-33334
Fax. UK 0534-36206
Fax. International 44-534-36206

A professionally-based organisation specialising in the formation and administration of companies and trusts in all of the principal tax haven jurisdictions.

The directors and senior staff of CentreTrust comprise qualified lawyers, chartered accountants and other personnel experienced in banking and trust matters.

Using a flexible and innovative approach CentreTrust devotes its resources and expertise to tailoring a set of legal structures which satisfy the needs of the client and his professional advisers.

CentreTrust is associated with Union Bancaire Privée of Geneva, one of the largest Swiss banks, with paid-up capital and reserves of nearly 700 million Swiss francs.

Explanatory brochures which provide further details of CentreTrust's services and the advantages of operating out of Jersey are available upon request.

CBI-TDB

Strachans

(The registered business name of STRACHAN
MANAGEMENT SERVICES LIMITED)

Sommerville House,
Phillips Street,
St. Helier, Jersey,
Channel Islands,
Great Britain.

Telephone: UK (01534) 888999
(International: 44-1534-888999)
Telecopier: U.K. (01534) 23902
(International: 44-1534-23902)

R.J. EGGLISHAW, Bachelor of Science, Fellow of the Institute of Chartered Accountants in England and Wales.

T.A. JEHAN, Fellow of the Institute of Chartered Accountants in England and Wales.

P.J. EGGLISHAW, Bachelor of Arts, Fellow of the Institute of Chartered Accountants in England and Wales.

P.E. DE FIGUEIREDO, Bachelor of Arts, Associate of the Institute of Chartered Accountants in England And Wales.

D. McNutt, Associate of the Chartered Institute of Secretaries.

Senior Personnel

W. McDermott, Member of the Institute of Chartered Accountants in Scotland

M. Murray

A Mixed-discipline professional corporation formed by Strachan & Co., Chartered Accountants (Established 1947) to provide specialist company and trust administration services together with international tax and financial consultancy.

A full range of company formation and administration services are provided around the globe, including the provision of directors, secretaries, registered office, shareholders, accounting services, invoicing etc.

Trust formations and the provision of Corporate trustees are similarly undertaken around the globe.

Financial consultancy is provided to individuals and corporations living, working or investing outside their home countries, especially the structuring of international loans and international joint ventures. Specialist services for international sportsmen and women and those involved in the entertainment industry.

References: Names furnished upon request.

ASSOCIATED OFFICES WORLDWIDE

ST. PETER PORT, GUERNSEY, 53,268

Banks & Trust Companies

THE LEGIS GROUP
P.O. Box 186
1 Le Marchant Street
St. Peter Port
Guernsey
CHANNEL ISLANDS

Tel: +44 (0)1481 726034
Fax: +44 (0)1481 726029

The Legis Group are a group of companies incorporated in Guernsey, Channel Islands which provide offshore company formation and trust creation services and thereafter act in their administration.

The Legis Group is wholly-owned and controlled by Partners of Ozanne van Leuvan Perrot & Evans. Guernsey advocates and notaries public. Partners of the law firm are directors of every Legis Group company, thus ensuring that essential legal input on clients' affairs is readily available.

The services of The Legis Group include:

● COMPANY FORMATION - in Guernsey and other jurisdictions

● COMPANY ADMINISTRATION - ranging from basic secretarial administration maintaining "good standing", to the preparation of full accounts and the overseeing of such matters as the production of invoices, the maintenance of bank accounts, the management of assets such as properties, investment portfolios and vessels and liaising with investment advisers and other professionals.

● NOMINEE SHAREHOLDERS AND DIRECTORS - may be supplied on request, although the provision of nominee directors will only be considered for non-trading situations.

● TRUST CREATION - a partner in the law firm Ozanne van Leuven Perrot & Evans will advise on the drafting of a Guernsey trust deed to suit individual circumstances.

● TRUST ADMINISTRATION - the trustees will manage and safeguard trust assets, liaising with investment advisers and other professionals as appropriate.

● ACCOUNTING SERVICES - for companies and trusts under our administration clients may wish to determine the complexity or otherwise of the financial reporting required over and above that specified by relevant legislation.

If you would like further details of any of the services offered by The Legis Group, please request a brochure pack.

ENGLAND

LONDON, * 8,203,900

Asset Locators

WIND ASSOCIATES, INC.
INFORMATION SERVICES
450 SEVENTH AVENUE
SUITE 2009
NEW YORK, NY 10123
TEL 800-444-6782
FAX 212-290-0029

Wind Associates, Inc. is a leader in asset information retrieval and provides a wide variety of thorough and concise asset location reports. For matters ranging from collection to divorce and child support to corporate white collar crime, our ability to provide asset and background information rivals that of the best investigative firms in the nation. We are able to provide this data most cost effectively. Many of our searches can be ordered on a "no locate no charge basis."

More than ten years of collection and information retrieval experience makes Wind Associates a primary resource for asset information nationwide. Our investigations make use of the latest datbases and skiptracing techniques available.

The data we provide will enable the attorney to collect judgements more cost effectively then ever. Our reports are extremely helpful prior to litigation as well, especially in determining the identity and location of defendants. We expedite criminal records checks, nationwide driver license and vehicle abstracts, UCC/Lien/Judgement abstracts, and telephone and address verifications. Our mastery of the art "skiptracing" makes your task of locating an individual across the country much easier.

Judgments needn't gather dust, matters needn't be inordinarly delayed. Wind Associates will meet the formidable challenge of locating assets and people for you. Call 800-444-6782 today for our descriptive report and price list. Inquire about our in house computer bulletin board accessible from your personal computer. Internet e-mail: windasso@panix.com.

Business & Financial Information Providers

Moody's Investors Service
99 Church Street, New York, NY 10007
212-553-0546

Moody's Manuals
Moody's Industrial Manual
Moody's OTC Industrial Manual
Moody's OTC Unlisted Manual
Moody's Transportation Manual
Moody's Public Utility Manual
Moody's Bank & Finance Manual
Moody's Municipal & Government Manual
Moody's International Manual
Moody's Manuals on Microfiche

Moody's CD-ROMS
Moody's Company Data™ with EDGAR
Moody's International Company Data™
Moody's International Company Data™ with Source
  Documents on CD-ROM
Moody's Manuals and Discs

(This Listing Continued)

MOODY'S INVESTORS SERVICE (Continued)

Moody's Investment Guides
Moody's Handbook of Common Stocks
Moody's Handbook of Nasdaq Stocks
Moody's Handbook of Dividend Achievers
Moody's Dividend Record & Annual Dividend Record
Moody's Unit Investment Trusts Service
Moody's Bond Record & Annual Bond Record Service
Moody's Bond Survey
Moody's Industry Review
Latin American Companies Handbook
Japan Company Handbooks I & II
Asian Company Handbook

Additional Services
Moody's also provides electronically delivered information services, including Moody's Dividend Record, Unit Investment Trusts Service, and informational support for Moody's on Dialog Files 555, 556 and 557.

Financial Information Services (FIS) has sustained a tradition of excellence that dates to 1900, when John Moody published the world's first comprehensive guide to public companies. Throughout the years, we have made a commitment to producing the highest quality products and services, and supporting product development with ongoing customer dialogue.

FIS competes in the marketplace for business and financial information on publicly held companies. This market is characterized by a need for detailed, in-depth, quality information used by equity and fixed-income analysts, portfolio managers, investment bankers, reference professionals, stock and bond traders, attorneys, and other professionals to support a variety of business applications such as investment decision making, merger and acquisition activity, strategic planning, and competitive analysis.

Moody's editors, researchers and publisher meticulously match information needs with highly useful formats to bring to the marketplace an extraordinary array of products - from Moody's Manuals, the foremost resource of authoritative descriptions of business operations and detailed financial statements; to Moody's Investment Guides, covering the world of finance with invaluable statistics, business descriptions, payment information and unique charts; to CD-ROMs, combining the vital business and financial information in Moody's Manuals with the industry's most sophisticated software system, MoodEASE™

**1-800-342-5647 EXT. 0546
CALL TODAY FOR FREE DEMONSTRATION DISKS and INFORMATION ON OUR CD-ROMS, MANUALS AND INVESTMENT GUIDES.**

To update your listing
in the **Martindale-Hubbell Law Directory**
call **1-800-MARTIND(ALE).**

Court Reporters

ANGLO-AMERICAN COURT REPORTERS
Incorporating EUROPAMERICAN COURT REPORTERS
TENNYSON & COMPANY
(Established 1962)
EUROPEAN and LONDON SERVICE

150 Minories, 1st Floor London EC3N 1LS, England	27 Woodger Close Merrow Park, Guildford GU47XR, Nr. London

Telephones: 01144-48368358 &01144-712424164.
Fax: 01144-483306087.

Deposition Room.   24-hour Answering.

Computer Assisted Transcription; Daily and Expedited transcripts. Litigation support. Disks supplied. Video-conferencing. American Videotape Service (NTSC) by U.S. Certified Video-Technician. Legally experienced interpreters in all languages. Notaries Public supplied.

Members: National Court Reporters Association, U.S.A. (21 years); Fellow, British Institute of Verbatim Reporters, London.

References: McKenna's (London); Clifford Chance (London & Paris); Debevoise & Plimpton (Paris & London); U.S. Embassy (London); Fulbright & Jaworski (London & Texas); Willkie Farr & Gallagher (London); Gibson Dunn & Crutcher (London & California); Wilmer Cutler & Pickering (London & U.S.A.); Dewey-Ballentine (New York & Moscow).

MARTEN WALSH CHERER

MARTEN WALSH CHERER LTD.

For Depositions in England and Europe

-100 years experience of court reporting-

Combined withexpert staff and the latest computer technology

Computer aided transcription
Litigation Support Services:
ASCII and WP disks, compressed format and Keyword Index
Agents for Discovery ZX (DOS and Windows version)
Specialists in Patent, Insurance and Reinsurance, Marine, Technical and Medical Depositions
Specialists in Daily and Expedited Transcription Work
Technical Arbitrations

Marten Walsh Cherer Ltd., Midway House
27-29 Cursitor Street, London EC4A 1LT, United Kingdom.
Tel. No.: 011 44171 405 5010. Fax: 01144171 405 5026.

LONDON (Continued)
Court Reporters (Continued)

Marten Walsh Cherer Limited

Midway House, 27/29 Cursitor Street
London, EC4A 1LT
Telephone: 01144-171-405 5010
Fax: 01144-171-405 5026

Contact Marten Walsh Cherer, Europe's most established and forward-looking firm of verbatim reporters to dicuss new ways to facilitate the management of any of your proceedings.

Specialists in daily transcription work; computer aided transcription (disks supplied), litigation management and support; Discovery ZX.

Conference room facilities and access to videotape service; qualified interpreters in 26 languages; national or international facilities are also available.

Member:
Institute of Shorthand Writers
National Shorthand Reporters Association

References: Harry E. Barlow, U.S. Dept. of Justice, Washington; Baker Mills & Glast; Morgan Lewis & Bockius; Engel & Mullholland; Kenyon & Kenyon; Bristows Cooke & Carpmael, U.K.; Simmons & Simmons, U.K.; Bird & Bird, U.K.; McKennas, U.K.

SEE OUR AD ON PAGE EU3S

NEWGATE REPORTERS LIMITED

Ludgate House 107-111 Fleet Street
LONDON EC4A 2AB

Telephone: 011 4471 353 4414
Facsimile: 011 4471 353 3435

MEMBERS:

National Court Reporters Association
Institute of British Verbatim Reporters
Institute of Directors

******

Qualified and Experienced British and American Reporters
for

Computer Aided Transcription
Litigation Support/Discovery ZX
ASCII and WORDPERFECT
DAILY DELIVERY/REAL-TIME FACILITIES

******

Depositions
Arbitrations
Disciplinary Hearings
Conferences
Criminal and Civil Proceedings

*****

Conference Room Facilities
Video Tape Service
Qualified Interpreters

*****

REFERENCES AVAILABLE UPON REQUEST

****

Genealogical Services

International Genealogical Search, Inc.

P.O. Box 34000
Seattle, Washington 98124-1000
Telephone: 604/294-1811
Fax: 604/294-1780
Contact: C. Tim Rodenbush, President

Reasonable Fees Non-Percentage Based

Results Guaranteed...Or No Charge

At IGS we believe the cost of locating missing heirs should be reasonable and based upon data available. NOT THE SIZE OF THE ESTATE. You wouldn't choose to give a search firm up to one-half of your inheritance just to be found. The missing heirs you represent in a fiduciary capacity wouldn't want to either.

When you need to locate missing heirs or beneficiaries, or to satisfy the court that all heirs have been accounted for, we suggest the following guideline to selecting an heir search firm.

1:   Before hiring anyone, obtain a written proposal and quotation of their fees.

2:   Determine how the search firm bases their fees and then decide which method would be most preferred by the missing heir. Remember, you're spending their money.

3:   Insist on several letters of reference being provided and then check the references diligently. Be assured that the firm has the experience to locate heirs on a world-wide scale.

4:   Be perfectly clear, when discussing the case with the prospective search firm, to advise them that they should not proceed with the search unless authorized, by you, in writing.

5:   Enter into an agreement for a specific period of time only. Don't leave the contract open-ended. Expect results in a reasonable period of time.

6:   If applicable, seek court approval of the search firm's proposal and their fee quotation before proceeding.

7:   Be sure that the company you select has adequate Errors and Omissions insurance coverage to protect all parties.

Call or Write today
For A No-Obligation Fee Quotation
and a Free Laminated Consanguinity Chart

Need an extra copy of the **Martindale-Hubbell Law Directory?** Or of a specific volume? Call Martindale-Hubbell Customer Service at
1-800-526-4902

TITLE RESEARCH
Genealogists and International Researchers

HEIRS MISSING OVERSEAS?

Title Research is a leading British firm of International Genealogists specializing in locating missing heirs.

We provide a complete service to Lawyers from any jurisdiction and draw on over 50 years experience to maintain the highest standards. Complimentary assessments are submitted on all cases and we work to an agreed estimate or on a "no success: no fee" basis.

If you are seeking heirs outside the USA we can demonstrate an outstanding success rate around the world:

- Britain and all Europe - including the former Eastern Bloc and Baltic States
- Canada
- Australia and New Zealand
- Southern Africa

If our expertise interests you please telephone, fax, or write for a copy of our free brochure.

TITLE RESEARCH
Africa House
64-78 Kingsway
LONDON
WC2B 6AH
ENGLAND

Telephone: 011 44 171 242 5446
Facsimile: 011 44 171 831 7816

Now you can find the lawyer even if you don't know where he or she practices - with the **Martindale-Hubbell Law Directory Alphabetical Index.**

The **Martindale-Hubbell Law Directory** is now available online...exclusively through the LEXIS®/NEXIS® services.

LONDON (Continued)
Litigation Support Services (Continued)

Marten Walsh Cherer Limited

Midway House, 27/29 Cursitor Street
London, EC4A 1LT
Telephone: 01144-171-405 5010
Fax: 01144-171-405 5026

Contact Marten Walsh Cherer, Europe's most established and forward-looking firm of verbatim reporters to dicuss new ways to facilitate the management of any of your proceedings.

Specialists in daily transcription work; computer aided transcription (disks supplied), litigation management and support; Discovery ZX.

Conference room facilities and access to videotape service; qualified interpreters in 26 languages; national or international facilities are also available.

Member:
Institute of Shorthand Writers
National Shorthand Reporters Association

References: Harry E. Barlow, U.S. Dept. of Justice, Washington; Baker Mills & Glast; Morgan Lewis & Bockius; Engel & Mullholland; Kenyon & Kenyon; Bristows Cooke & Carpmael, U.K.; Simmons & Simmons, U.K.; Bird & Bird, U.K.; McKennas, U.K.

QUORUM LITIGATION SERVICES, INC.

No. 1 Northumberland Avenue
Suite 231
Trafalgar Square
London WC2N 5BW
United Kingdom
071 872 5586
FAX: 071 753 2759

Since 1966, Quorum Litigation Services has been the world leader in computerized case document management for the U.S., Canada, and the United Kingdom. Quorum has an international reputation for setting the standard by which litigation support is measured in terms of technical expertise and operational excellence. Litigation support services include:

- Case Automation and Database Design
- Discovery Management
- Document Scanning and Coding
- Optical Character Recognition
- Knowledge*Link Image Retrieval and Review
- Repository Management
- Full-text Database Conversion
- Electronic Trial Support

Quorum Information Services (QIS), a newly acquired imaging company, combines Quorum's twenty-eight years of litigation management experience with the resources and skilled technical staff of an established U.K. scanning company. QIS provides both paper and microfilm scanning, image base indexing, and OCR.

Quorum's Knowledge*Link is a complete system image management software that includes image retrieval and review capability integrated with database searching. This non-proprietary program integrates its open architecture system with law firm or corporate legal department hardware and software. Knowledge*Link is a Windows-based system which can operate as a stand-alone, as part of a project-specific network, or as part of an organisation-wide network.

Quorum's world headquarters and central processing facility is located in Minneapolis, Minnesota with an East coast facility in Wilmington, Delaware. U.S. branch offices are located in New York, Branford, CT, Philadelphia, Pittsburgh, Washington, D.C., Chicago, Dallas, Los Angeles, and San Francisco. International offices are located in London and Manila. Kelvin McGregor-Alcorn is the United Kingdom Director of Quorum Litigation Services. David Lewis is the Principal Consultant.

FRANCE

PARIS, * 2,850,189

Court Reporters

ASSOCIATED EUROPEAN REPORTERS

EXPERIENCED AMERICAN AND EUROPEAN REPORTERS
AVAILABLE FOR ARBITRATIONS, DEPOSITIONS, MEETINGS,
CONFERENCES AND HEARINGS.

ACCESS TO AMERICAN COMPATIBLE VIDEO EQUIPMENT,
QUALIFIED AND EXPERIENCED OPERATORS.

INTERPRETERS PROVIDED UPON REQUEST.

FLUENT FRENCH; FRENCH STENOGRAPHERS AVAILABLE.

COMPUTER-AIDED TRANSCRIPTION, ASCII DISCS SUPPLIED, OZ
PC, PREMIER POWER, CONDENSED FORMAT, EXPEDITED
TRANSCRIPTS.

SERVING ALL OF EUROPE

CONTACT: FRANCE: 15 rue de CADIX,
                           75015 - PARIS.
                           Tel: 33-1-48-56-68-22
                           Fax: 33-1.48.56.68.25

             The NETHERLANDS: Groot HOEFIJZERLAAN 67,
                              2244 GG WASSENAAR,
                              The Netherlands.
                              Tel: 31-1751-40052
                              Fax: 31-1751-77581

Now you can find the lawyer even if you don't
know where he or she practices -
with the **Martindale-Hubbell Law
Directory Alphabetical Index.**

The **Martindale-Hubbell Law Directory** is now
available online...exclusively
through the LEXIS®/NEXIS® services.

Heir Tracers

FRASER & FRASER

GENEALOGISTS
AND INTERNATIONAL PROBATE RESEARCHERS

Lost Kin?

Take the easy step towards finding them

When no Will exists, we prepare a family tree to discover all possible
claimants. When people named in a Will or Trust have disappeared, we are
expert in tracing them.

We have behind us over 50 years' experience and a full-time staff of
specialist researchers. We have at our fingertips the latest computer systems
which enable us to access some of the world's largest databases. With our
network of international offices we are able to carry out research
throughout Europe, Scandinavia and Commonwealth countries.

The partners, Simon and Nathan Fraser, together with their own staff,
travel extensively to carry out research worldwide, with offices in London,
Rome, Paris and Warsaw.

If you would like more information please write for explanatory
brochure.

**Messrs. Fraser & Fraser
Manfield House
376 Strand
London WC2R 0LR England
Telephone: 44 171 240 0788
Fax: 44 171 836 9975**

Member
The Association of Genealogist and Record Agents

Now it's easy to find lawyers practicing a specific
area of law! Simply consult the
**Martindale-Hubbell Law Directory
Areas of Practice Index.**

Fast ... Easy ... Flexible...
**The Martindale-Hubbell Law Directory on
CD-ROM** gives you instant access through
multiple search criteria to information on over
800,000 lawyers. For more details and a FREE
demonstration disc, call **1-800-323-3288.**

GERMANY

BERLIN, 1,860,084

Genealogical Services

International Genealogical Search, Inc.

P.O. Box 34000
Seattle, Washington 98124-1000
Telephone: 604/294-1811
Fax: 604/294-1780
Contact: C. Tim Rodenbush, President

Reasonable Fees Non-Percentage Based

Results Guaranteed...Or No Charge

At IGS we believe the cost of locating missing heirs should be reasonable and based upon data available. NOT THE SIZE OF THE ESTATE. You wouldn't choose to give a search firm up to one-half of your inheritance just to be found. The missing heirs you represent in a fiduciary capacity wouldn't want to either.

When you need to locate missing heirs or beneficiaries, or to satisfy the court that all heirs have been accounted for, we suggest the following guideline to selecting an heir search firm.

1: Before hiring anyone, obtain a written proposal and quotation of their fees.

2: Determine how the search firm bases their fees and then decide which method would be most preferred by the missing heir. Remember, you're spending their money.

3: Insist on several letters of reference being provided and then check the references diligently. Be assured that the firm has the experience to locate heirs on a world-wide scale.

4: Be perfectly clear, when discussing the case with the prospective search firm, to advise them that they should not proceed with the search unless authorized, by you, in writing.

5: Enter into an agreement for a specific period of time only. Don't leave the contract open-ended. Expect results in a reasonable period of time.

6: If applicable, seek court approval of the search firm's proposal and their fee quotation before proceeding.

7: Be sure that the company you select has adequate Errors and Omissions insurance coverage to protect all parties.

**Call or Write today
For A No-Obligation Fee Quotation
and a Free Laminated Consanguinity Chart**

To update your listing
in the **Martindale-Hubbell Law Directory**
call 1-800-MARTIND(ALE).

LIECHTENSTEIN

VADUZ, * 4,704

Banks & Trust Companies

Allgemeines Treuunternehmen
General Trust Company

Aeulestrasse 5
P.O. Box 83
FL-9490 Vaduz, Liechtenstein
Telephone: (41 75) 237 34 34
Telefax: (41 75) 237 34 60
Telex: 889355 tuv fl
Cable Address: TREUHAND AG, VADUZ

The General Trust Company (Allgemeines Treuunternehmen) was founded in 1929 and is one of Liechtenstein's largest fiduciary enterprises. Among others, the company is specialized in services such as: Legal advice, Financial advice, Tax consultancy, Formation of companies, Administration, Fiduciary activities, Trusteeships, Accountancy/Auditing, Capital management, Patents, Trade marks and Licences. Today, the General Trust Company has a staff of approximately 90 people.

Languages: English, French, Italian, Spanish, German, Czech and Russian.

Publications: List of specialised literature available on request.

Reference: Private Trust Bank Corporation, Vaduz.

Members of the Board:

BRAXATOR KAMIL, Doctor of Commercial Law, HSG, born 1950, Nitra. Education: St. Gallen, Switzerland, Graduate School (HSG) Doctor of Economics (Commercial Law); University of Zürich, Switzerland (Public and Private Law); District Court of Zürich (Court practice).

FRICK EDMUND, Auditor and Trustee, born 1938, Balzers. Member: President of Liechtenstein Trustee Association.

KEICHER WERNER, Doctor of Law, born 1944, Biel. Education: University of Zürich; Doctor of Law (Public and Private Law), 1975.

MEIER GUIDO W., Attorney at Law, born 1948, Vaduz. Admitted to the Liechtenstein Bar 1979. Education: University of Tampa, Florida 1968-1969 (Economics); University of Basel, Switzerland, Doctor of Law (Public and Private Law), 1977. Member: Liechtenstein Bar Association.

WALSER OLAF, born 1923, Vaduz. Vice-President of the Private Trust Bank Corporation, Vaduz. Member: Liechtenstein Trustee Association.

Need an extra copy of the **Martindale-Hubbell Law Directory**? Or of a specific volume?
Call Martindale-Hubbell Customer Service at
1-800-526-4902

Trust Companies

Juricon Treuhand Anstalt
Juricon Trust Company Establishment
Meierhofstrasse 2
P.O. Box 184
FL-9490 VADUZ, LIECHTENSTEIN
Telephone: 075/2355151
Telex: 889 383
Telefax: 075/2355161

The Juricon Trust Company Establishment was founded in 1976 and has a staff of approximately 25, all of them highly qualified. The company renders services such as:

Advice on international legal, tax, financial and commercial matters. Formation and administration of Liechtenstein and foreign companies. Provision of registered offices and of local representative for inland and foreign companies. Book-keeping and auditing services. Availability of office and conference rooms. Secretarial and other services. Execution and completion of international commercial and financial business. Investment advice and administration of assets. Patents, licenses, trademarks. Trust matters. Legal opinions.

Languages: English, French, Italian, Spanish, German.

Publications: The Foundation according to the law of the Principality of Liechtenstein

Management

DR.IUR ALFRED STEINBRUGGER, born Austria, September 2, 1944; *Education:* University of Graz, Austria, Faculty of Law (Dr. iur. 1970); *Member:* Foundation member of the International Advisory Group (IAG), an international organisation with 35 member firms of lawyers, accountants, tax counsel and trustees, Advisory Council of Allgemeine Kreditbank, Zürich, 100% subsidiary of Bayerische Hypotheken- u. Wechsel-Bank AG (1987—); **LANGUAGES:** German and English

LIC.IUR. WILFRIED HOOP, born Liechtenstein, February 16, 1961; admitted, 1992, Liechtenstein; *Education:* University of Fribourg, Switzerland, Faculty of Law and Economics (lic. iur.1988); *Member:* Liechtenstein Bar Association, Association International des Jeunes Avocats, DACH Deutsch-Oesterreichisch-Schweizerisch-Liechtensteinische Anwaltsvereinigung e.V.; **LANGUAGES:** German, English and French

DIPL.-KFM. KLAUS STARK, born Austria, June 18, 1938; *Education:* graduated from Vienna School of Economics, 1960, Swiss accounting diploma, 1982; *Member:* Liechtenstein Association of Accountants and Tax Advisers, Transnational Taxation Network (TTN), **LANGUAGES:** German, English and Italian

DR.IUR. RENATE WOHLWEND, born Vienna, Austria, February 20, 1952; 1978, Liechtenstein; *Education:* University of Vienna and University of Linz, Austria, Faculty of Law (Dr. iur. 1978), Member of Parliament 1993—; *Member:* International Advisory Group (IAG); **LANGUAGES:** German, English and French

---

THE NETHERLANDS

AMSTERDAM, * 835,835

Legal Publications

INTERNATIONAL BUREAU OF FISCAL DOCUMENTATION
Sarphatistraat 600
1018 AV Amsterdam
The Netherlands
Tel.: +31 20 6267726
Fax: +31 20 6228658

Looking for information on international taxation?

The International Bureau of Fiscal Documentation (IBFD) can meet your needs with accurate, objective and up-to-date taxation information. IBFD is one of the most respected organizations studying and documenting international taxation systems and investment legislation. Services include:

Publications
IBFD's wholly owned publishing house, IBFD Publications BV, publishes expertly written journals, loose-leafs, books and data bases on international taxation and investment.

Library
IBFD maintains the largest library in the world on international tax law and investment legislation, based at IBFD's head office in Amsterdam. Materials include 25,000 books on taxation and related topics, journals, newsletters, official gazettes and related journals from almost every country in the world.

Education and Conferences
IBFD's International Tax Academy offers training and education in international and comparative taxation and organizes seminars and conferences worldwide.

At IBFD's head office in Amsterdam, the Netherlands, a multilingual staff writes and edits publications, while a network of tax specialists relays information from all over the world.

The organization operates internationally with clients including attorneys, accountancy practices, international corporations, banks and Ministries of Finance.

US Service Office:
IBFD Publications USA, Inc.,
24 Hudson Street
Kinderhook NY 12106
Tel.: (518) 758-2245   Fax: (518) 758-2246

THE HAGUE, * 701,844

Court Reporters

The **Martindale-Hubbell Law Directory** is now available online...exclusively through the LEXIS®/NEXIS® services.

Now it's easy to find lawyers practicing a specific area of law! Simply consult the **Martindale-Hubbell Law Directory Areas of Practice Index.**

AUSTRALIA

SYDNEY, NEW SOUTH WALES, 2,444,735

Court Reporters

Australian Legal Reporting Group

SYDNEY: Tel: (61-2) 221-6660
              Fax: (61-2) 221-6707

Registered Professional Reporters (USA)
Video Depositions
ASCII & WordPerfect
Real-time reporting
Compressed transcripts
Word and Master Word Indexes
Deposition Rooms

Offices throughout Australia

MELBOURNE: Tel: (61-3) 642-0104
                 Fax: (61-3) 600-1350

BRISBANE: Tel: (61-7) 221-4445
               Fax: (61-7) 221-2029

ADELAIDE: Tel: (61-8) 373-0630
               Fax: (61-8) 271-9200

Court Reporters with International experience
offering full litigation services.

Heir Tracers

FRASER & FRASER

GENEALOGISTS
AND INTERNATIONAL PROBATE RESEARCHERS

Lost Kin?

Take the easy step towards finding them

When no Will exists, we prepare a family tree to discover all possible claimants. When people named in a Will or Trust have disappeared, we are expert in tracing them.

We have behind us over 50 years' experience and a full-time staff of specialist researchers. We have at our fingertips the latest computer systems which enable us to access some of the world's largest databases. With our network of international offices we are able to carry out research throughout Europe, Scandinavia and Commonwealth countries.

The partners, Simon and Nathan Fraser, together with their own staff, travel extensively to carry out research worldwide, with offices in London, Rome, Paris and Warsaw.

If you would like more information please write for explanatory brochure.

Messrs. Fraser & Fraser
Manfield House
376 Strand
London WC2R 0LR England
Telephone: 44 171 240 0788
Fax: 44 171 836 9975

Member
The Association of Genealogist and Record Agents